Hospital, Address, Telephone, Administrator, Approval, Facility, and Physician Codes, Health Care System, Network	Classi-fication Codes		Utilization Data					Expense (thousands) of dollars		
★ American Hospital Association (AHA) membership □ Joint Commission on Accreditation of Healthcare Organizations (JCAHO) accreditation + American Osteopathic Healthcare Association (AOHA) membership ○ American Osteopathic Association (AOA) accreditation △ Commission on Accreditation of Rehabilitation Facilities (CARF) accreditation Control codes 61, 63, 64, 71, 72 and 73 indicate hospitals listed by AOHA, but not registered by AHA. For definition of numerical codes, see page A4	Control	Service	Staffed Beds	Admissions	Census	Outpatient Visits	Births	Total	Payroll	Personnel

ANYTOWN—Universal County
★ COMMUNITY HOSPITAL, First Street and Main Avenue Zip 62835; tel 204/391–2345; Jane Doe, Administrator **A**1 2 3 4 6 9 10 **F**1 2 3 4 5 6 8 9 10 23 24 34; **P**1 2 3 4; **S** Acme HCS

| | 23 | 10 | 346 | 10778 | 248 | 75953 | 1693 | 20695 | 9973 | 796 |

1   2   3

1 Approval Codes

Reported by the approving bodies specified, as of the dates noted.

1 Accreditation under the hospital program of the Joint Commission on Accreditation of Healthcare Organizations (April 1999).

2 Cancer program approved by American College of Surgeons (January 1999).

†3 Approval to participate in residency training, by the Accreditation Council for Graduate Medical Education (January 1999). As of June 30, 1975, internship (formerly code 4) was included under residency, code 3.

†5 Medical school affiliation, reported to the American Medical Association (January 1999).

6 Hospital–controlled professional nursing school, reported by National League for Nursing.

7 Accreditation by Commission on Accreditation of Rehabilitation Facilities (January 1999).

8 Member of Council of Teaching Hospitals of the Association of American Medical Colleges (January 1999).

9 Hospitals contracting or participating in Blue Cross Plan, reported by the Blue Cross and Blue Shield Association (January 1999).

10 Certified for participation in the Health Insurance for the Aged (Medicare) Program

by the U.S. Department of Health and Human Services (January 1999).

11 Accreditation by American Osteopathic Association (January 1999).

12 Internship approved by American Osteopathic Association (January 1999).

13 Residency approved by American Osteopathic Association (January 1999).

Nonreporting indicates that the hospital was registered **after** the mailing of the 1998 Annual Survey, or, that the 1998 Annual Survey questionnaire for the hospital had not been received prior to publication.

2 Facility Codes

Provided directly by the hospital, its health care system, or network, or through a formal arrangement with another provider; for definitions, see page A6.

(Alphabetical/Numerical Order)

1 Adult day care program
2 Alcoholism–drug abuse or dependency inpatient unit
3 Alcoholism–drug abuse or dependency outpatient services
4 Angioplasty
5 Arthritis treatment center
6 Assisted living
7 Birthing room–LDR room–LDRP room
8 Breast cancer screening/mammograms
9 Burn care services
10 Cardiac catheterization laboratory
11 Cardiac intensive care services
12 Case management
13 Children wellness program
14 Community health reporting
15 Community health status assessment
16 Community health status based service planning
17 Community outreach
18 Crisis prevention
19 CT scanner
20 Dental services
21 Diagnostic radioisotope facility

22 Emergency department
23 Extracorporeal shock wave lithotripter (ESWL)
24 Fitness center
25 Freestanding outpatient care center
26 Geriatric services
27 Health facility transportation (to/from)
28 Health fair
29 Health information center
30 Health screenings
31 HIV–AIDS services
32 Home health services
33 Hospice
34 Hospital–based outpatient care center–services
35 Magnetic resonance imaging (MRI)
36 Meals on wheels
37 Medical surgical intensive care services
38 Neonatal intensive care services
39 Nutrition programs
40 Obstetrics services
41 Occupational health services
42 Oncology services
43 Open heart surgery
44 Outpatient surgery
45 Patient education center
46 Patient representative services
47 Pediatric intensive care services
48 Physical rehabilitation inpatient services
49 Physical rehabilitation outpatient services

50 Positron emission tomography scanner (PET)
51 Primary care department
52 Psychiatric acute inpatient services
53 Psychiatric child adolescent services
54 Psychiatric consultation–liaison services
55 Psychiatric education services
56 Psychiatric emergency services
57 Psychiatric geriatric services
58 Psychiatric outpatient services
59 Psychiatric partial hospitalization program
60 Radiation therapy
61 Reproductive health services
62 Retirement housing
63 Single photon emission computerized tomography (SPECT)
64 Skilled nursing or other long–term care services
65 Social work services
66 Sports medicine
67 Support groups
68 Teen outreach services
69 Transplant services
70 Trauma center (certified)
71 Ultrasound
72 Urgent care center
73 Volunteer services department
74 Women's health center/services

3 Physician Codes

Actually available within, and reported by the institution; for definitions, see page A9.

(Alphabetical/Numerical Order)

1 Closed physician–hospital organization (PHO)

2 Equity model
3 Foundation
4 Group practice without walls
5 Independent practice association (IPA)

6 Integrated salary model
7 Management service organization (MSO)
8 Open physician–hospital organization (PHO)

†Data from the Graduate Medical Education Database, Copyright 1998, American Medical Association, Chicago, Illinois.

Hospital, Address, Telephone, Administrator, Approval, Facility, and Physician Codes, Health Care System, Network	Classi- fication Codes		Utilization Data					Expense (thousands) of dollars		
	Control	Service	Staffed Beds	Admissions	Census	Outpatient Visits	Births	Total	Payroll	Personnel

★ American Hospital Association (AHA) membership
☐ Joint Commission on Accreditation of Healthcare Organizations (JCAHO) accreditation
+ American Osteopathic Healthcare Association (AOHA) membership
○ American Osteopathic Association (AOA) accreditation
△ Commission on Accreditation of Rehabilitation Facilities (CARF) accreditation
Control codes 61, 63, 64, 71, 72 and 73 indicate hospitals listed by AOHA, but not registered by AHA. For definition of numerical codes, see page A4

ANYTOWN—Universal County

★ COMMUNITY HOSPITAL, First Street and Main Avenue Zip 62835; tel 204/391–2345; Jane Doe, Administrator **A**1 2 3 4 6 9 10 **F**1 2 3 4 5 6 8 9 10 23 24 34; **P**1 2 3 4; **S** Acme HCS **N** ABC

23	10	346	10778	248	75953	1693	20695	9973	796

4	**6**	**7**

4 Health Care System Code and Name

A code number has been assigned to each health care system headquarters. The inclusion *of one of these codes (1) indicates that the hospital belongs to a health care system and* *(2) identifies the specific system to which the hospital belongs.*

6 Classification Codes

Control

Government, nonfederal
12 State
13 County
14 City
15 City–county
16 Hospital district or authority

Nongovernment not–for–profit
21 Church operated
23 Other

Investor–owned (for–profit)
31 Individual
32 Partnership
33 Corporation

Government, federal
41 Air Force
42 Army
43 Navy

44 Public Health Service other than 47
45 Veterans Affairs
46 Federal other than 41–45, 47–48
47 Public Health Service Indian Service
48 Department of Justice

Osteopathic
61 Church operated
63 Other not–for–profit
64 Other
71 Individual for–profit
72 Partnership for–profit
73 Corporation for–profit

Service
10 General medical and surgical
11 Hospital unit of an institution (prison hospital, college infirmary, etc.)
12 Hospital unit within an institution for the mentally retarded
22 Psychiatric

33 Tuberculosis and other respiratory diseases
44 Obstetrics and gynecology
45 Eye, ear, nose, and throat
46 Rehabilitation
47 Orthopedic
48 Chronic disease
49 Other specialty
50 Children's general
51 Children's hospital unit of an institution
52 Children's psychiatric
53 Children's tuberculosis and other respiratory diseases
55 Children's eye, ear, nose, and throat
56 Children's rehabilitation
57 Children's orthopedic
58 Children's chronic disease
59 Children's other specialty
62 Institution for mental retardation
82 Alcoholism and other chemical dependency

* Control codes 61, 63, 64, 71, 72 and 73 indicate hospitals listed by the AOHA but not registered by AHA.

When a hospital restricts its service to a specialty not defined by a specific code, it is coded 49 (59 if a children's hospital) and the specialty is indicated in parentheses following the name of the hospital.

7 Headings

Definitions are based on the American Hospital Association's Hospital Administration Terminology. Where a 12–month period is specified, hospitals were requested to report on the Annual Survey of Hospitals for the 12 months ending September 30, 1998. Hospitals reporting for less than a 12–month period are so designated.

Utilization Data:

Beds–Number of beds, cribs, and pediatric bassinets regularly maintained (set up and staffed for use) for inpatients as of the close of the reporting period.

Admissions–Number of patients accepted for inpatient service during a 12–month period; does not include newborn.

Census–Average number of inpatients receiving care each day during the 12–month reporting period; does not include newborn.

Outpatient Visits–A visit by a patient who is not lodged in the hospital while receiving medical, dental, or other services. Each appearance of an outpatient in each unit constitutes one visit regardless of the number of diagnostic and/or therapeutic treatments that a patient receives.

Births–Number of infants born in the hospital and accepted for service in a newborn infant bassinet during a 12–month period; excludes stillbirths.

Expense: Expense for a 12–month period; both total expense and payroll components are shown. Payroll expenses include all salaries and wages.

Personnel: Includes persons on payroll on September 30, 1998; includes full–time equivalents of part–time personnel. Full–time equivalents were calculated on the basis that two part–time persons equal one full–time person.

AHA Guide™ to the Health Care Field

1999–2000 Edition

AHA Institutional Members $175
Nonmembers $315
AHA catalog NUMBER C–010099
Telephone ORDERS 1–800–AHA–2626

ISSN 0094–8969
ISBN 0–87258–749–5

Contents

Lists of Health
Organizations,
Agencies and
Providers

Indexes

† List supplied by the Joint Commission on
Accreditation of Healthcare Organizations

Acknowledgements and Advisements

Acknowledgements

The AHA Guide™ to the Health Care Field is published annually by Health Forum LLC, an affiliate of the American Hospital Association. Contributions made by Computer Application Services, Member Relations, Office of the President, Office of the Secretary, Printing Services Group and Resource Center.

Health Forum LLC acknowledges the cooperation given by many professional groups and government agencies in the health care field, particularly the following: American College of Surgeons; American Medical Association; American Osteopathic Healthcare Association; Blue Cross and Blue Shield Association; Council of Teaching Hospitals of the Association of American Medical Colleges; Joint Commission on Accreditation of Healthcare Organizations; Commission on Accreditation of Rehabilitation Facilities; American Osteopathic Association; Health Care Financing Administration; and various offices within the U.S. Department of Health and Human Services.

Advisements

The data published here should be used with the following advisements: The data are based on replies to an annual survey that seeks a variety of information, not all of which is published in this book. The information gathered by the survey includes specific services, but not all of each hospital's services. Therefore, the data do not reflect an exhaustive list of all services offered by all hospitals. For information on the availability of additional data, please contact Health Forum LLC at 800/821–2039.

Health Forum LLC does not assume responsibility for the accuracy of information voluntarily reported by the individual institutions surveyed. **The purpose of this publication is to provide basic data reflecting the delivery of health care in the United States and associated areas, and is not to serve as an official and all inclusive list of services offered by individual hospitals. The information reflected is based on data collected as of April 16, 1999.**

Each of the three major sections of the AHA Guide begins with its own table of contents and pertinent definitions or explanatory information. Sections B, C and indices have bleed bar tabs for easy identification. The three major sections are:

- Hospitals
- Networks, Health Care Systems and Alliances
- Health Organizations, Agencies and other Health Care Providers

Please note that many area codes may have changed, check before you call.

Hospitals

This section lists:

- AHA–registered and osteopathic hospitals in the U.S. and associated areas, by state within city.
- U.S. government hospitals outside the United States.
- Index of hospitals alphabetically.
- Index of health care professionals.
- AHA Associate members.

AHA member hospitals are identified by a star (★). Hospitals accredited under one of the programs of the Joint Commission on Accreditation of Healthcare Organizations are identified by a hollow box (□). Preceding the list of hospitals is a statement of the formal requirements for registration by the AHA.

The lists provide a variety of information about each hospital, including the administrator's name; various approvals; selected facilities and services; relationship to a health care system; classification by control, service; physician arrangement relationships, and other selected statistical data from the 1998 AHA Annual Survey.

Also the *AHA Guide* includes state population data from the U.S. Bureau of the Census, *Statistical Abstract of the United States: 1998 (118th edition.) Washington, DC, 1998. They include the following:*

- Total resident population (in thousands)
- Percent of resident population in metro areas
- Birth rate per 1,000 population
- Percent of population 65 years and over
- Percent of persons without health insurance

Some of this information is coded. These include approval, facility and classification codes.

Approval codes refer to approvals held by a hospital; they represent information supplied by various national approving and reporting bodies. For example, code A–1 indicates accreditation under one of the programs of the Joint Commission on

Accreditation of Healthcare Organizations – formal evidence that a hospital meets established standards for quality of patient care.

Physician codes refer to the different types of physician arrangements in which the hospital participates.

Health Care system names reference specific health care system headquarters. The presence of the system name indicates the hospital belongs to a health care system. Absence of a system name indicates that the hospital does not belong to a health care system.

Classification codes indicate the type of organization that controls or operates the hospital and type of service. Code numbers in the 10s denote nonfederal (states and local) government hospitals; in the 20s, nongovernment not–for–profit hospitals; in the 40s, federal government hospitals; and in the 60s and 70s, nonregistered osteopathic hospitals. Among **service codes,** the most common code is 10, indicating a general hospital. Other numbers designate various special services. For example, code 22 indicates psychiatric hospitals and codes in the 50s indicate different types of children's hospitals.

Facility codes refer to facilities and services provided directly by the hospital, its health care system or network or through a formal arrangement with another provider.

(For easy reference, there is an alphabetical/numerical list for all of the codes on page A4).

Names of osteopathic hospitals, supplied by the American Osteopathic Healthcare Association are provided in the list of hospitals. Codes and symbols identifying these institutions are explained on page A4 and in the headnote at the top of each page of the list of hospitals. Also included in this section is an **index of hospitals** in alphabetical order by hospital name, followed by the city and state and the page reference to the hospital's listing in Section A. This section is designated by tabs along the side of the pages. Immediately following this section is an **index of health care professionals** in alphabetical order by name, followed by the hospital and/or health care system, the city and state and the page reference to the health care professional's listing in section A or B. This section is also designated by tabs along the side of the pages.

This section also lists **other AHA institutional members** not listed elsewhere

in the AHA Guide and **AHA associate members.** The list of AHA institutional members includes Canadian hospitals, associated university programs in health administration, hospital schools of nursing, and nonhospital preacute and postacute care facilities. The list of associate members includes ambulatory centers and home care agencies, Blue Cross plans, health maintenance organizations/health care corporations, health system agencies, other inpatient care institutions, shared services organizations and other associate members.

Networks, Health Care Systems and Alliances

Networks

The *AHA Guide* lists the names and addresses of networks including network partners by state, alphabetically by name. **Please see page B2 for more information**.

Health Care Systems

This is an alphabetical listing of health care systems and their hospitals. Data on bed size for each hospital in the system is provided along with an indication of whether the hospital is owned, leased, sponsored, or contract–managed.

Following this listing is an index for health care system headquarters listed geographically by state. **Please see page B2 for more information**.

Alliances

Alliances provide information on multistate alliances and their members. Alliances are listed alphabetically by name. Members are listed alphabetically by state, city and then by name. **Please see page B2 for more information**.

Health Organizations, Agencies and Other Health Care Providers

There are four major categories in this section.

First is an alphabetical listing of national, international, and regional organizations. Many voluntary organizations that are interested in, or of interest to, the health care field are included. Also included is the Healthfinder® listing.

The second category lists United States government agencies.

The third category presents a list of state and local organizations and government agencies. The list for states and provinces include Blue Cross and Blue Shield plans, health systems agencies, hospital associations and councils, hospital licensure agencies, medical and nursing licensure agencies, peer review organizations, state health planning and development agencies, and state and provincial government agencies.

The fourth category consists of lists of various health care providers including JCAHO accredited freestanding long–term care organizations, JCAHO accredited freestanding substance abuse organizations, and JCAHO accredited freestanding mental health care organizations, freestanding hospices, freestanding ambulatory surgery centers and health maintenance organizations (HMOs). **Please see page C2 for more information**.

These lists are provided for your information and are not exhaustive. Inclusion or omission of any organization's name indicates neither approval nor disapproval by Health Forum LLC.

We hope you find the *AHA Guide* a valuable resource. If you have any questions or comments, please call Health Forum LLC, at 800/821–2039.

AHA Offices, Officers, and Historical Data

Chicago: One North Franklin, Chicago, IL 60606–3401; tel. 312/422–3000

Washington: 325 Seventh Street, N.W., Suite 700, Washington, DC 20004; tel. 202/638–1100

Speaker of the House of Delegates: Reginald M. Ballantyne III, PMH Health Resources, Inc., 1201 S. Seventh Avenue, Box 21207, Phoenix, AZ 85036
Chairman of the Board of Trustees: Fred L. Brown, FACHE, BJC Health System, 120 S. Central, Suite 1200, St. Louis, MO 63105

Chairman–Elect of the Board of Trustees: Carolyn B. Lewis, Greater Southeast Community Hospital, 2920 W Street, S.E., Washington, D.C. 20020
President: Richard J. Davidson, 325 Seventh Street, N.W., Suite 700, Washington, DC 20004; tel. 202/638–1100

Senior Vice President and Secretary: Michael P. Guerin, One North Franklin, Chicago, IL 60606–3401
Treasurer: Dallas Carroll, One North Franklin, Chicago, IL 60606–3401

Past Presidents/Chairs†

1899	★James S. Knowles	1932	★Paul H. Fesler	1966	Philip D. Bonnet, M.D.
1900	★James S. Knowles	1933	★George F. Stephens, M.D.	1967	George E. Cartmill
1901	★Charles S. Howell	1934	★Nathaniel W. Faxon, M.D.	1968	★David B. Wilson, M.D.
1902	★J. T. Duryea	1935	★Robert Jolly	1969	George William Graham, M.D.
1903	★John Fehrenbatch	1936	★Robin C. Buerki, M.D.	1970	★Mark Berke
1904	★Daniel D. Test	1937	★Claude W. Munger, M.D.	1971	★Jack A. L. Hahn
1905	★George H. M. Rowe, M.D.	1938	★Robert E. Neff	1972	Stephen M. Morris
1906	★George P. Ludlam	1939	★G. Harvey Agnew, M.D.	1973	★John W. Kauffman
1907	★Renwick R. Ross, M.D.	1940	★Fred G. Carter, M.D.	1974	★Horace M. Cardwell
1908	★Sigismund S. Goldwater, M.D.	1941	★B. W. Black, M.D.	1975	Wade Mountz
1909	★John M. Peters, M.D.	1942	★Basil C. MacLean, M.D.	1976	H. Robert Cathcart
1910	★H. B. Howard, M.D.	1943	★James A. Hamilton	1977	John M. Stagl
1911	★W. L. Babcock, M.D.	1944	★Frank J. Walter	1978	★Samuel J. Tibbitts
1912	★Henry M. Hurd, M.D.	1945	★Donald C. Smelzer, M.D.	1979	W. Daniel Barker
1913	★F. A. Washburn, M.D.	1946	★Peter D. Ward, M.D.	1980	★Sister Irene Kraus
1914	★Thomas Howell, M.D.	1947	★John H. Hayes	1981	Bernard J. Lachner
1915	★William O. Mann, M.D.	1948	★Graham L. Davis	1982	Stanley R. Nelson
1916	★Winford H. Smith, M.D.	1949	★Joseph G. Norby	1983	Elbert E. Gilbertson
1917	★Robert J. Wilson, M.D.	1950	★John H. Hatfield	1984	Thomas R. Matherlee
1918	★A. B. Ancker, M.D.	1951	★Charles F. Wilinsky, M.D.	1985	Jack A. Skarupa
1919	★A. R. Warner, M.D.	1952	★Anthony J. J. Rourke, M.D.	1986	Scott S. Parker
1920	★Joseph B. Howland, M.D.	1953	★Edwin L. Crosby, M.D.	1987	Donald C. Wegmiller
1921	★Louis B. Baldwin, M.D.	1954	★Ritz E. Heerman	1988	Eugene W. Arnett
1922	★George O'Hanlon, M.D.	1955	★Frank R. Bradley	1989	Edward J. Connors
1923	★Asa S. Bacon	1956	★Ray E. Brown	1990	David A. Reed
1924	★Malcolm T. MacEachern, M.D.	1957	★Albert W. Snoke, M.D.	1991	C. Thomas Smith
1925	★E. S. Gilmore	1958	★Tol Terrell	1992	D. Kirk Oglesby, Jr.
1926	★Arthur C. Bachmeyer, M.D.	1959	★Ray Amberg	1993	Larry L. Mathis
1927	★R. G. Brodrick, M.D.	1960	Russell A. Nelson, M.D.	1994	Carolyn C. Roberts
1928	★Joseph C. Doane, M.D.	1961	★Frank S. Groner	1995	Gail L. Warden
1929	★Louis H. Burlingham, M.D.	1962	★Jack Masur, M.D.	1996	Gordon M. Sprenger
1930	★Christopher G. Parnall, M.D.	1963	T. Stewart Hamilton, M.D.	1997	Reginald M. Ballantyne III
1931	★Lewis A. Sexton, M.D.	1964	Stanley A. Ferguson	1998	John G. King
		1965	Clarence E. Wonnacott		

Chief Executive Officers

1917–18	★William H. Walsh, M.D.	1943–54	★George Bugbee	1986–91	Carol M. McCarthy, Ph.D., J.D.
1919–24	★Andrew Robert Warner, M.D.	1954–72	★Edwin L. Crosby, M.D.	1991	Jack W. Owen (acting)
1925–27	★William H. Walsh, M.D.	1972	Madison B. Brown, M.D. (acting)	1991	Richard J. Davidson (current)
1928–42	★Bert W. Caldwell, M.D.	1972–86	J. Alexander McMahon		

Distinguished Service Award

1934	★Matthew O. Foley	1958	★John N. Hatfield	1979	★Horace M. Cardwell
1939	★Malcolm T. MacEachern, M.D.	1959	★Edwin L. Crosby, M.D.	1980	Donald W. Cordes
1940	★Sigismund S. Goldwater, M.D.	1960	★Oliver G. Pratt	1981	★Sister Mary Brigh Cassidy
1941	★Frederic A. Washburn, M.D.	1961	★E. M. Bluestone, M.D.	1982	R. Zach Thomas, Jr.
1942	★Winford H. Smith, M.D.	1962	Mother Loretto Bernard, S.C., R.N.	1983	H. Robert Cathcart
1943	★Arthur C. Bachmeyer, M.D.	1963	★Ray E. Brown	1984	Matthew F. McNulty, Jr., Sc.D.
1944	★Rt. Rev. Msgr. Maurice F. Griffin, LL.D.	1964	Russell A. Nelson, M.D.	1985	J. Alexander McMahon
1945	★Asa S. Bacon	1965	★Albert W. Snoke, M.D.	1986	★Sister Irene Kraus
1946	★George F. Stephens, M.D.	1966	★Frank S. Groner	1987	W. Daniel Barker
1947	★Robin C. Buerki, M.D.	1967	★Rev. John J. Flanagan, S.J.	1988	Elbert E. Gilbertson
1948	★James A. Hamilton	1968	Stanley W. Martin	1989	Donald G. Shropshire
1949	★Claude W. Munger, M.D.	1969	T. Stewart Hamilton, M.D.	1990	John W. Colloton
1950	★Nathaniel W. Faxon, M.D.	1970	★Charles Patteson Cladwell, Jr.	1991	Carol M. McCarthy, Ph.D., J.D.
1951	★Bert W. Caldwell, M.D.	1971	★Mark Berke	1992	David H. Hitt
1952	★Fred G. Carter, M.D.	1972	Stanley A. Ferguson	1993	Edward J. Connors
1953	★asil C. MacLean, M.D.	1973	★Jack A. L. Hahn		Jack W. Owen
1954	★George Bugbee	1974	George William Graham, M.D.	1994	George Adams
1955	★Joseph G. Norby	1975	George E. Cartmill	1995	Scott S. Parker
1956	★Charles F. Wilinsky, M.D.	1976	D. O. McClusky, Jr.	1996	John A. Russell
1957	★John H. Hayes	1977	★Boone Powell	1997	D. Kirk Oglesby, Jr.
		1978	★Richard J. Stull	1998	Henry B. Betts, M.D.
				1999	Mitchell T. Rabkin, M.D.

★Deceased

†On June 3, 1972, the House of Delegates changed the title of the chief elected officer to chairman of the Board of Trustees, and the title of president was conferred on the chief executive officer of the Association.

© 1999 AHA Guide

Award of Honor

1966	★Senator Lister Hill	**1992**	Donald W. Dunn
1967	★Emory W. Morris, D.D.S.		Ira M. Lane, Jr.
1971	Special Committee on Provision of Health	**1993**	Elliott C. Roberts, Sr.
	Services (staff also)		William A. Spencer, M.D.
1982	Walter J. McNemey	**1994**	Robert A. Derzon
1989	Ruth M. Rothstein	**1995**	Russell G. Mawby, Ph.D.
1990	Joyce C. Clifford, R.N.		John K. Springer
1991	★Haynes Rice	**1996**	★Stephen J. Hegarty

	Mothers Against Drunk Driving (MADD)
1997	Paul B. Batalden, M.D.
	Habitat for Humanity International
1998	John E. Curley, Jr.
	National Civic League
1999	★Joseph Cardinal Bernardin, Literacy
	Volunteers of America

Justin Ford Kimball Innovators Award

1958	★E. A. van Steenwyk	**1972**	★John R. Mannix	**1988**	★Ernest W. Saward, M.D.
1959	George A. Newbury	**1973**	Herman M. Somers	**1990**	James A. Vohs
1960	★C. Rufus Rorem, Ph.D.	**1974**	William H. Ford, Ph.D.	**1993**	John C. Lewin, M.D.
1961	★James E. Stuart	**1975**	Earl H. Kammer	**1994**	Donald A. Brennan
1962	Frank Van Dyk	**1976**	J. Ed McConnell	**1995**	E. George Middleton, Jr.
1963	★William S. McNary	**1978**	Edwin R. Werner		Glenn R. Mitchell
1964	★Frank S. Groner	**1979**	★Robert M. Cunningham, Jr.	**1997**	Harvey Pettry
1965	★J. Douglas Colman	**1981**	★Maurice J. Norby		D. David Sniff
1967	Walter J. McNemey	**1982**	Robert E. Rinehimer	**1998**	Montana Health Research and Education
1968	★John W. Paynter	**1983**	John B. Morgan, Jr.		Foundation
1970	★Edwin L. Crosby, M.D.	**1984**	★Joseph F. Duplinsky	**1999**	Kenneth W. Kizer, M.D.
1971	★H. Charles Abbott	**1985**	David W. Stewart		

Trustees Award

1959	★Joseph V. Friel	**1974**	★James E. Hague	**1987**	Michael Lesparre
	★John H. Hayes		★Sister Marybelle	**1988**	Barbara A. Donaho, R.N.
1960	Duncan D. Sutphen, Jr.	**1975**	Helen T. Yast	**1989**	Walter H. MacDonald
1963	Eleanor C. Lambertsen, R.N., Ed.D.	**1976**	Boynton P. Livingston		Donald R. Newkirk
1964	★John R. Mannix		James Ludlam	**1990**	William T. Robinson
1965	Albert G. Hahn		★Helen McGuire	**1992**	Jack C. Bills
	★Maurice J. Norby	**1979**	★Newton J. Jacobson		Anne Hall Davis
1966	Madison B. Brown, M.D.		Edward W. Weimer	**1993**	Theodore C. Eickhoff, M.D.
	Kenneth Williamson	**1980**	★Robert B. Hunter, M.D.		Stephen W. Gamble
1967	★Alanson W. Wilcox		★Samuel J. Tibbitts		Yoshi Honkawa
1968	★E. Dwight Barnett, M.D.	**1981**	Vernon A. Knutson	**1994**	Roger M. Busfield, Jr., Ph.D.
1969	★Vane M. Hoge, M.D.		John E. Sullivan	**1995**	Stephen E. Dorn
	Joseph H. McNinch, M.D.	**1982**	John Bigelow		William L. Yates
1972	David F. Drake, Ph.D.		Robert W. O'Leary	**1996**	Leigh E. Morris
	Paul W. Earle		Jack W. Owen		John Quigley
	Michael Lesparre	**1984**	Howard J. Berman	**1998**	John D. Leech
	Andrew Pattullo		O. Ray Hurst	**1999**	Sister Carol Keehan
1973	Tilden Cummings		James R. Neely		C. Edward McCawley
	Edmond J. Lanigan	**1985**	★James E. Ferguson		Stephen Rogness
			Cleveland Rodgers		
		1986	Rex N. Olsen		

Citation for Meritorious Service

1968	★F. R. Knautz		Gordon McLachlan	**1983**	★David M. Kinzer
	Sister Conrad Mary, R.N.	**1977**	Theodore Cooper, M.D.	**1984**	Donald L. Custis, M.D.
1971	Hospital Council of Southern California	**1979**	Norman D. Burkett	**1985**	John A. D. Cooper, M.D.
1972	College of Misericordia, Dallas, PA		John L. Quigley		Imperial Council of the Ancient Arabic
1973	Madison B. Brown, M.D.		★William M. Whelan		Order of the Nobles of the Mystic Shrine
	★Samuel J. Tibbitts	**1980**	★Sister Grace Marie Hiltz		for North America
1975	★Kenneth B. Babcock, M.D.		Leo J. Gehrig, M.D.	**1986**	Howard F. Cook
	Sister Mary Maurita Sengelaube	**1981**	Richard Davi	**1987**	David H. Hitt
1976	Chaiker Abbis		Pearl S. Fryar		★Lucile Packard
	★Susan Jenkins	**1982**	Jorge Brull Nater		

This citation is no longer awarded

* AHA–registered hospitals in the United States and associated areas are
approved for registration by the Executive Committee of the Board of
Trustees of the American Hospital Association. This list of registered
hospitals is complete as of April 1999. The list of osteopathic hospitals,
integrated in this section is supplied by the American Osteopathic Healthcare
Association.

Registration Requirements for Hospitals

This directory includes hospitals registered by the American Hospital Association and osteopathic hospitals listed by the American Osteopathic Association. Identification codes for both types of hospitals are explained fully on pages A4–5. For the reader's convenience, the codes for osteopathic hospitals are also summarized in the notes at the top of each page of this section. Beginning in November 1970, osteopathic hospitals became eligible to apply for registration with the American Hospital Association. Registered osteopathic hospitals carry the same codes as all other hospitals registered by the American Hospital Association.

The following requirements were approved by the Executive Committee of the Board of Trustees, May 13, 1986.

AHA–Registered Hospitals

Any institution that can be classified as a hospital according to the requirements may be registered if it so desires. Membership in the American Hospital Association is not a prerequisite.

The American Hospital Association may, at the sole discretion of the Executive Committee of the Board of Trustees, grant, deny, or withdraw the registration of an institution.

An institution may be registered by the American Hospital Association as a hospital if it is accredited as a hospital by the Joint Commission on Accreditation of Healthcare Organizations or is certified as a provider of acute services under Title 18 of the Social Security Act and has provided the Association with documents verifying the accreditation or certification.

In lieu of the preceding accreditation or certification, an institution licensed as a hospital by the appropriate state agency may be registered by AHA as a hospital by meeting the following alternative requirements:

Function: The primary function of the institution is to provide patient services, diagnostic and therapeutic, for particular or general medical conditions.

1. The institution shall maintain at least six inpatient beds, which shall be continuously available for the care of patients who are nonrelated and who stay on the average in excess of 24 hours per admission.
2. The institution shall be constructed, equipped, and maintained to ensure the health and safety of patients and to provide uncrowded, sanitary facilities for the treatment of patients.
3. There shall be an identifiable governing authority legally and morally responsible for the conduct of the hospital.
4. There shall be a chief executive to whom the governing authority delegates the continuous responsibility for the operation of the hospital in accordance with established policy.
5. There shall be an organized medical staff of fully licensed physicians* that may include other licensed individuals permitted by law and by the hospital to provide patient care services independently in the hospital. The medical staff shall be accountable to the governing authority for maintaining proper standards of medical care, and it shall be governed by bylaws adopted by said staff and approved by the governing authority.
6. Each patient shall be admitted on the authority of a member of the medical staff who has been granted the privilege to admit patients to inpatient services in accordance with state law and criteria for standards of medical care established by the individual medical staff. Each patient's general medical condition is the responsibility of a qualified physician member of the medical staff. When nonphysician members of the medical staff are granted privileges to admit patients, provision is made for prompt medical evaluation of these patients by a qualified physician. Any graduate of a foreign medical school who is permitted to assume responsibilities for patient care shall possess a valid license to practice medicine, or shall be certified by the Educational Commission for Foreign Medical Graduates, or shall have qualified for and have successfully completed an academic year of supervised clinical training under the direction of a medical school approved by the Liaison Committee onGAT Medical Education.
7. Registered nurse supervision and other nursing services are continuous.
8. A current and complete+ medical record shall be maintained by the institution for each patient and shall be available for reference.
9. Pharmacy service shall be maintained in the institution and shall be supervised by a registered pharmacist.
10. The institution shall provide patients with food service that meets their nutritional and therapeutic requirements; special diets shall also be available.

*Physician–Term used to describe an individual with an M.D. or D.O. degree who is fully licensed to practice medicine in all its phases.

‡The completed records in general shall contain at least the following: the patient's identifying data and consent forms, medical history, record of physical examination, physicians' progress notes, operative notes, nurses' notes, routine x–ray and laboratory reports, doctors' orders, and final diagnosis.

Types of Hospitals

In addition to meeting these 10 general registration requirements, hospitals are registered as one of four types of hospitals: general, special, rehabilitation and chronic disease, or psychiatric. The following definitions of function by type of hospital and special requirements for registration are employed:

General

The primary function of the institution is to provide patient services, diagnostic and therapeutic, for a variety of medical conditions. A general hospital also shall provide:

- diagnostic x–ray services with facilities and staff for a variety of procedures
- clinical laboratory service with facilities and staff for a variety of procedures and with anatomical pathology services regularly and conveniently available
- operating room service with facilities and staff.

Special

The primary function of the institution is to provide diagnostic and treatment services for patients who have specified medical conditions, both surgical and nonsurgical. A special hospital also shall provide:

- such diagnostic and treatment services as may be determined by the Executive Committee of the Board of Trustees of the American Hospital Association to be appropriate for the specified medical conditions for which medical services

are provided shall be maintained in the institution with suitable facilities and staff. If such conditions do not normally require diagnostic x–ray service, laboratory service, or operating room service, and if any such services are therefore not maintained in the institution, there shall be written arrangements to make them available to patients requiring them.
- clinical laboratory services capable of providing tissue diagnosis when offering pregancy termination services.

Rehabilitation and Chronic Disease

The primary function of the institution is to provide diagnostic and treatment services to handicapped or disabled individuals requiring restorative and adjustive services. A rehabilitation and chronic disease hospital also shall provide:

- arrangements for diagnostic x–ray services, as required, on a regular and conveniently available basis
- arrangements for clinical laboratory service, as required on a regular and conveniently available basis
- arrangements for operating room service, as required, on a regular and conveniently available basis
- a physical therapy service with suitable facilities and staff in the institution
- an occupational therapy service with suitable facilities and staff in the institution
- arrangements for psychological and social work services on a regular and conveniently available basis
- arrangements for educational and vocational services on a regular and conveniently available basis

- written arrangements with a general hospital for the transfer of patients who require medical, obstetrical, or surgical services not available in the institution.

Psychiatric

The primary function of the institution is to provide diagnostic and treatment services for patients who have psychiatric–related illnesses. A psychiatric hospital also shall provide:

- arrangements for clinical laboratory service, as required, on a regular and conveniently available basis
- arrangements for diagnostic x–ray services, as required on a regular and conveniently available basis
- psychiatric, psychological, and social work service with facilities and staff in the institution
- arrangements for electroencephalograph services, as required, on a regular and conveniently available basis.
- written arrangements with a general hospital for the transfer of patients who require medical, obstetrical, or surgical services not available in the institution.

The American Hospital Association may, at the sole discretion of the Executive Committee of the Board of Trustees, grant, deny, or withdraw the registration of an institution.

AOHA–Listed Hospitals

The list of osteopathic hospitals includes both members and nonmembers of the American Osteopathic Healthcare Association.

---

*Physician–Term used to describe an individual with an M.D. or D.O. degree who is fully licensed to practice medicine in all its phases.

‡The completed records in general shall contain at least the following: the patient's identifying data and consent forms, medical history, record of physical examination, physicians' progress notes, operative notes, nurses' notes, routine x–ray and laboratory reports, doctors' orders, and final diagnosis.

Explanation of Hospital Listings

Hospital, Address, Telephone, Administrator, Approval, Facility, and Physician Codes, Health Care System, Network	Classi-fication Codes		Utilization Data						Expense (thousands) of dollars		
	Control	Service	Staffed Beds	Admissions	Census	Outpatient Visits	Births	Total	Payroll	Personnel

★ American Hospital Association (AHA) membership
□ Joint Commission on Accreditation of Healthcare Organizations (JCAHO) accreditation
+ American Osteopathic Healthcare Association (AOHA) membership
○ American Osteopathic Association (AOA) accreditation
△ Commission on Accreditation of Rehabilitation Facilities (CARF) accreditation
Control codes 61, 63, 64, 71, 72 and 73 indicate hospitals listed by AOHA, but not registered by AHA. For definition of numerical codes, see page A4

ANYTOWN—Universal County
★ COMMUNITY HOSPITAL, First Street and Main Avenue Zip 62835; tel 204/391-2345; Jane Doe, Administrator **A**1 2 3 4 6 9 10 **F**1 2 3 4 5 6 8 9 10 23 24 34; **P**1 2 3 4; **S** Acme HCS

| | | 23 | 10 | 346 | 10778 | 248 | 75953 | 1693 | 20695 | 9973 | 796 |

(bracketed groups: 1, 2, 3)

1 Approval Codes

Reported by the approving bodies specified, as of the dates noted.

1 Accreditation under the hospital program of the Joint Commission on Accreditation of Healthcare Organizations (April 1999).
2 Cancer program approved by American College of Surgeons (January 1999).
†3 Approval to participate in residency training, by the Accreditation Council for Graduate Medical Education (January 1999). As of June 30, 1975, internship (formerly code 4) was included under residency, code 3.
†5 Medical school affiliation, reported to the American Medical Association (January 1999).

6 Hospital–controlled professional nursing school, reported by National League for Nursing.
7 Accreditation by Commission on Accreditation of Rehabilitation Facilities (January 1999).
8 Member of Council of Teaching Hospitals of the Association of American Medical Colleges (January 1999).
9 Hospitals contracting or participating in Blue Cross Plan, reported by the Blue Cross and Blue Shield Association (January 1999).
10 Certified for participation in the Health Insurance for the Aged (Medicare) Program

by the U.S. Department of Health and Human Services (January 1999).
11 Accreditation by American Osteopathic Association (January 1999).
12 Internship approved by American Osteopathic Association (January 1999).
13 Residency approved by American Osteopathic Association (January 1999).

Nonreporting indicates that the hospital was registered **after** the mailing of the 1998 Annual Survey, or, that the 1998 Annual Survey questionnaire for the hospital had not been received prior to publication.

2 Facility Codes

Provided directly by the hospital, its health care system, or network, or through a formal arrangement with another provider; for definitions, see page A6.

(Alphabetical/Numerical Order)
1 Adult day care program
2 Alcoholism–drug abuse or dependency inpatient unit
3 Alcoholism–drug abuse or dependency outpatient services
4 Angioplasty
5 Arthritis treatment center
6 Assisted living
7 Birthing room–LDR room–LDRP room
8 Breast cancer screening/mammograms
9 Burn care services
10 Cardiac catheterization laboratory
11 Cardiac intensive care services
12 Case management
13 Children wellness program
14 Community health reporting
15 Community health status assessment
16 Community health status based service planning
17 Community outreach
18 Crisis prevention
19 CT scanner
20 Dental services
21 Diagnostic radioisotope facility

22 Emergency department
23 Extracorporeal shock wave lithotripter (ESWL)
24 Fitness center
25 Freestanding outpatient care center
26 Geriatric services
27 Health facility transportation (to/from)
28 Health fair
29 Health information center
30 Health screenings
31 HIV–AIDS services
32 Home health services
33 Hospice
34 Hospital–based outpatient care center–services
35 Magnetic resonance imaging (MRI)
36 Meals on wheels
37 Medical surgical intensive care services
38 Neonatal intensive care services
39 Nutrition programs
40 Obstetrics services
41 Occupational health services
42 Oncology services
43 Open heart surgery
44 Outpatient surgery
45 Patient education center
46 Patient representative services
47 Pediatric intensive care services
48 Physical rehabilitation inpatient services
49 Physical rehabilitation outpatient services

50 Positron emission tomography scanner (PET)
51 Primary care department
52 Psychiatric acute inpatient services
53 Psychiatric child adolescent services
54 Psychiatric consultation–liaison services
55 Psychiatric education services
56 Psychiatric emergency services
57 Psychiatric geriatric services
58 Psychiatric outpatient services
59 Psychiatric partial hospitalization program
60 Radiation therapy
61 Reproductive health services
62 Retirement housing
63 Single photon emission computerized tomography (SPECT)
64 Skilled nursing or other long–term care services
65 Social work services
66 Sports medicine
67 Support groups
68 Teen outreach services
69 Transplant services
70 Trauma center (certified)
71 Ultrasound
72 Urgent care center
73 Volunteer services department
74 Women's health center/services

3 Physician Codes

Actually available within, and reported by the institution; for definitions, see page A9.

(Alphabetical/Numerical Order)
1 Closed physician–hospital organization (PHO)
2 Equity model
3 Foundation
4 Group practice without walls
5 Independent practice association (IPA)
6 Integrated salary model
7 Management service organization (MSO)
8 Open physician–hospital organization (PHO)

---

†Data from the Graduate Medical Education Database, Copyright 1998, American Medical Association, Chicago, Illinois.

Hospital, Address, Telephone, Administrator, Approval, Facility, and Physician Codes, Health Care System, Network	Classi-fication Codes		Utilization Data					Expense (thousands) of dollars		
★ American Hospital Association (AHA) membership ☐ Joint Commission on Accreditation of Healthcare Organizations (JCAHO) accreditation + American Osteopathic Healthcare Association (AOHA) membership ○ American Osteopathic Association (AOA) accreditation △ Commission on Accreditation of Rehabilitation Facilities (CARF) accreditation Control codes 61, 63, 64, 71, 72 and 73 indicate hospitals listed by AOHA, but not registered by AHA. For definition of numerical codes, see page A4	Control	Service	Staffed Beds	Admissions	Census	Outpatient Visits	Births	Total	Payroll	Personnel
ANYTOWN—Universal County										
★ COMMUNITY HOSPITAL, First Street and Main Avenue Zip 62835; tel 204/391–2345; Jane Doe, Administrator **A**1 2 3 4 6 9 10 **F**1 2 3 4 5 6 8 9 10 23 24 34; **P**1 2 3 4; **S** Acme HCS **N** ABC	23	10	346	10778	248	75953	1693	20695	9973	796

(4 — beneath Control/Service) (6 — beneath Control/Service classification) (7 — beneath Utilization Data through Expense)

4 Health Care System Code and Name

A code number has been assigned to each health care system headquarters. The inclusion of one of these codes (1) indicates that the hospital belongs to a health care system and (2) identifies the specific system to which the hospital belongs.

6 Classification Codes

Control

Government, nonfederal
12 State
13 County
14 City
15 City–county
16 Hospital district or authority

Nongovernment not–for–profit
21 Church operated
23 Other

Investor–owned (for–profit)
31 Individual
32 Partnership
33 Corporation

Government, federal
41 Air Force
42 Army
43 Navy

44 Public Health Service other than 47
45 Veterans Affairs
46 Federal other than 41–45, 47–48
47 Public Health Service Indian Service
48 Department of Justice

Osteopathic
61 Church operated
63 Other not–for–profit
64 Other
71 Individual for–profit
72 Partnership for–profit
73 Corporation for–profit

Service
10 General medical and surgical
11 Hospital unit of an institution (prison hospital, college infirmary, etc.)
12 Hospital unit within an institution for the mentally retarded
22 Psychiatric

33 Tuberculosis and other respiratory diseases
44 Obstetrics and gynecology
45 Eye, ear, nose, and throat
46 Rehabilitation
47 Orthopedic
48 Chronic disease
49 Other specialty
50 Children's general
51 Children's hospital unit of an institution
52 Children's psychiatric
53 Children's tuberculosis and other respiratory diseases
55 Children's eye, ear, nose, and throat
56 Children's rehabilitation
57 Children's orthopedic
58 Children's chronic disease
59 Children's other specialty
62 Institution for mental retardation
82 Alcoholism and other chemical dependency

* Control codes 61, 63, 64, 71, 72 and 73 indicate hospitals listed by the AOHA but not registered by AHA.

When a hospital restricts its service to a specialty not defined by a specific code, it is coded 49 (59 if a children's hospital) and the specialty is indicated in parentheses following the name of the hospital.

7 Headings

Definitions are based on the American Hospital Association's Hospital Administration Terminology. Where a 12–month period is specified, hospitals were requested to report on the Annual Survey of Hospitals for the 12 months ending September 30, 1998. Hospitals reporting for less than a 12–month period are so designated.

Utilization Data:

Beds–Number of beds, cribs, and pediatric bassinets regularly maintained (set up and staffed for use) for inpatients as of the close of the reporting period.

Admissions–Number of patients accepted for inpatient service during a 12–month period; does not include newborn.

Census–Average number of inpatients receiving care each day during the 12–month reporting period; does not include newborn.

Outpatient Visits–A visit by a patient who is not lodged in the hospital while receiving medical, dental, or other services. Each appearance of an outpatient in each unit constitutes one visit regardless of the number of diagnostic and/or therapeutic treatments that a patient receives.

Births–Number of infants born in the hospital and accepted for service in a newborn infant bassinet during a 12–month period; excludes stillbirths.

Expense: Expense for a 12–month period; both total expense and payroll components are shown. Payroll expenses include all salaries and wages.

Personnel: Includes persons on payroll on September 30, 1998; includes full–time equivalents of part–time personnel. Full–time equivalents were calculated on the basis that two part–time persons equal one full–time person.

Annual Survey

Each year, an annual survey of hospitals is conducted by the American Hospital Association through its Health Forum affiliate.

The facilities and services found below are either provided by the hospital, its health care system, or network or through a formal arrangement with another provider.

The AHA Guide to the Health Care Field does not include all data collected from the 1998 Annual Survey. Requests for purchasing other Annual Survey data should be directed to Health Forum LLC, an affiliate of the American Hospital Association, One North Franklin, Chicago, IL 60606–3401, 800/821–2039.

Definitions of Facility Codes

1. **Adult day care program** Program providing supervision, medical and psychological care, and social activities for older adults who live at home or in another family setting, but cannot be alone or prefer to be with others during the day. May include intake assessment, health monitoring, occupational therapy, personal care, noon meal, and transportation services.

2. **Alcoholism–drug abuse or dependency inpatient services** Provides, diagnosis and therapeutic services to patients with alcoholism or other drug dependencies. Includes care for inpatient/residential treatment for patients whose course of treatment involves more intensive care than provided in an outpatient setting or where patient requires supervised withdrawal.

3. **Alcoholism–drug abuse or dependency outpatient services** Organized hospital services that provide medical care and/or rehabilitative treatment services to outpatients for whom the primary diagnosis is alcoholism or other chemical dependency.

4. **Angioplasty** The reconstruction or restructuring of a blood vessel by operative means or by nonsurgical techniques such as balloon dilation or laser.

5. **Arthritis treatment center** Specifically equipped and staffed center for the diagnosis and treatment of arthritis and other joint disorders.

6. **Assisted living** A special combination of housing, supportive services, personalized assistance and health care designed to respond to the individual needs of those who need help in activities of daily living and instrumental activities of daily living. Supportive services are available, 24 hours a day, to meet scheduled and unscheduled needs, in a way that promotes maximum independence and dignity for each resident and encourages the involvement of a resident's family, neighbor and friends.

7. **Birthing room–LDR room–LDRP room** A single room–type of maternity care with a more homelike setting for families than the traditional three–room unit (labor/delivery/recovery) with a separate postpartum area. A birthing room combines labor and delivery in one room. An LDR room accommodates three stages in the birthing process—labor, delivery, and recovery. An LDRP room accommodates all four stages of the birth process—labor, delivery, recovery and postpartum.

8. **Breast cancer screening/mammograms** Mammography screening–the use of breast x–ray to detect unsuspected breast cancer in asymptomatic women. Diagnostic mammography–the x–ray imaging of breast tissue in symptomatic women who are considered to have a substantial likelihood of having breast cancer already.

9. **Burn care services** Provides care to severely burned patients. Severely burned patients are those with any of the following: 1. Second–degree burns of more than 25% total body surface area for adults or 20% total body surface area for children; 2. Third–degree burns of more than 10% total body surface area; 3. Any severe burns of the hands, face, eyes, ears or feet or; 4. All inhalation injuries, electrical burns, complicated burn injuries involving fractures and other major traumas, and all other poor risk factors.

10. **Cardiac catheterization laboratory** Facilities offering special diagnostic procedures for cardiac patients. Available procedures must include, but need not be limited to, introduction of a catheter into the interior of the heart by way of a vein or artery or by direct needle puncture. Procedures must be performed in a laboratory or a special procedure room.

11. **Cardiac intensive care services** Provides patient care of a more specialized nature than the usual medical and surgical care, on the basis of physicians' orders and approved nursing care plans. The unit is staffed with specially trained nursing personnel and contains monitoring and specialized support or treatment equipment for patients who, because of heart seizure, open–heart surgery, or other life–threatening conditions, require intensified, comprehensive observation and care. May include myocardial infarction, pulmonary care, and heart transplant units.

12. **Case management** A system of assessment, treatment planning, referral and follow–up that ensures the provision of comprehensive and continuous services and the coordination of payment and reimbursement for care.

13. **Children wellness program** A program that encourages improved health status and a healthful lifestyle of children through health education, exercise, nutrition and health promotion.

14. **Community health reporting** Does your hospital either by itself or in conjunction with others disseminate reports to the community on the quality and costs of health care services?

15. **Community health status assessment** Does your hospital work with other providers, public agencies, or community representatives to conduct a health status assessment of the community?

16. **Community health status based service planning** Does your hospital use health status indicators (such as

rates of health problems or surveys of self–reported health) for defined populations to design new services or modify existing services?

17. **Community outreach** A program that systematically interacts with the community to identify those in need of services, alerting persons and their families to the availability of services, locating needed services, and enabling persons to enter the service delivery system.

18. **Crisis prevention** Services provided in order to promote physical and mental well being and the early identification of disease and ill health prior to the onset and recognition of symptoms so as to permit early treatment.

19. **CT scanner** Computed tomographic scanner for head or whole body scans.

20. **Dental services** An organized dental service, not necessarily involving special facilities, that provides dental or oral services to inpatients or outpatients.

21. **Diagnostic radioisotope facility** The use of radioactive isotopes (Radiopharmaceutical) as tracers or indicators to detect an abnormal condition or disease.

22. **Emergency department** Hospital facilities for the provision of unscheduled outpatient services to patients whose conditions require immediate care. Must be staffed 24 hours a day.

23. **Extracorporeal shock wave lithotripter (ESWL)** A medical device used for treating stones in the kidney or ureter. The device disintegrates kidney stones noninvasively through the transmission of acoustic shock waves directed at the stones.

24. **Fitness center** Provides exercise, testing, or evaluation programs and fitness activities to the community and hospital employees.

25. **Freestanding outpatient care center** A facility owned and operated by the hospital, but physically separate from the hospital, that provides various medical treatments on an outpatient basis only. In addition to treating minor illnesses or injuries, the center will stabilize seriously ill or injured patients before transporting them to a hospital. Laboratory and radiology services are usually available.

26. **Geriatric services** The branch of medicine dealing with the physiology of aging and the diagnosis and treatment of disease affecting the aged. Services could include: Adult day care program; Alzheimer's diagnostic–assessment services; Comprehensive geriatric assessment; Emergency response system; Geriatric acute care unit; and/or Geriatric clinics.

27. **Health facility transportation (to/from)** A long–term care support service designed to assist the mobility of the elderly. Some programs offer improved financial access by offering reduced rates and barrier–free buses or vans with ramps and lifts to assist the elderly or handicapped; others offer subsidies for public transport systems or operate mini–bus services exclusively for use by senior citizens.

28. **Health fair** Community health education events that focus on the prevention of disease and promotion of health through such activities as audiovisual exhibits and free diagnostic services.

29. **Health information center** Education which is directed at increasing the information of individuals and populations. It is intended to increase the ability to make informed personal, family and community health decisions by providing consumers with informed choices about health matters with the objective of improving health status.

30. **Health screenings** A preliminary procedure, such as a test or examination to detect the most characteristic sign or signs of a disorder that may require further investigation.

31. **HIV–AIDS services** Services may include one or more of the following: HIV–AIDS unit (special unit or team designated and equipped specifically for diagnosis, treatment, continuing care planning, and counseling services for HIV–AIDS patients and their families.) General inpatient care for HIV–AIDS (inpatient diagnosis and treatment for human immunodeficiency virus and acquired immunodeficiency syndrome patients, but dedicated unit is not available.) Specialized outpatient program for HIV–AIDS (special outpatient program providing diagnostic, treatment, continuing care planning, and counseling for HIV–AIDS patients and their families.)

32. **Home health services** Service providing nursing, therapy, and health–related homemaker or social services in the patient's home.

33. **Hospice** A program providing palliative care, chiefly medical relief of pain and supportive services, addressing the emotional, social, financial, and legal needs of terminally ill patients and their families. Care can be provided in a variety of settings, both inpatient and at home.

34. **Hospital–based outpatient care center–services** Organized hospital health care services offered by appointment on an ambulatory basis. Services may include outpatient surgery, examination, diagnosis, and treatment of a variety of medical conditions on a nonemergency basis, and laboratory and other diagnostic testing as ordered by staff or outside physician referral.

35. **Magnetic resonance imaging (MRI)** The use of a uniform magnetic field and radio frequencies to study tissue and structure of the body. This procedure enables the visualization of biochemical activity of the cell in vivo without the use of ionizing radiation, radioisotopic substances, or high–frequency sound.

36. **Meals on wheels** A hospital sponsored program which delivers meals to people, usually the elderly, who are unable to prepare their own meals. Low cost, nutritional meals are delivered to individuals' homes on a regular basis.

37. **Medical surgical intensive care services** Provides patient care of a more intensive nature than the usual medical and surgical care, on the basis of physicians' orders and approved nursing care plans. These units are staffed with specially trained nursing personnel and contain monitoring and specialized support equipment of patients who, because of shock, trauma, or other life–threatening conditions, require intensified, comprehensive observation and care. Includes mixed intensive care units.

38. **Neonatal intensive care services** A unit that must be separate from the newborn nursery providing intensive care to all sick infants including those with the very lowest birth weights (less that 1500 grams). NICU has potential for providing mechanical ventilation, neonatal surgery, and special care for the sickest infants born in the hospital or transferred from another institution.

A full-time neonatologist serves as director of the NICU.

39. **Nutrition programs** Those services within a health care facility which are designed to provide inexpensive, nutritionally sound meals to patients.

40. **Obstetrics services** Levels should be designated: (1) unit provides services for uncomplicated maternity and newborn cases; (2) unit provides services for uncomplicated cases, the majority of complicated problems, and special neonatal services; and (3) unit provides services for all serious illnesses and abnormalities and is supervised by a full-time maternal/fetal specialist.

41. **Occupational health services** Includes services designed to protect the safety of employees from hazards in the work environment.

42. **Oncology services** An organized program for the treatment of cancer by the use of drugs or chemicals.

43. **Open heart surgery** Heart surgery where the chest has been opened and the blood recirculated and oxygenated with the proper equipment and the necessary staff to perform the surgery.

44. **Outpatient surgery** Scheduled surgical services provided to patients who do not remain in the hospital overnight. The surgery may be performed in operating suites also used for inpatient surgery, specially designated surgical suites for outpatient surgery, or procedure rooms within an outpatient care facility.

45. **Patient education center** Written goals and objectives for the patient and/or family related to therapeutic regimens, medical procedures, and self care.

46. **Patient representative services** Organized hospital services providing personnel through whom patients and staff can seek solutions to institutional problems affecting the delivery of high-quality care and services.

47. **Pediatric intensive care services** Provides care to pediatric patients that is of a more intensive nature than that usually provided to pediatric patients. The unit is staffed with specially trained personnel and contains monitoring and specialized support equipment for treatment of patients who, because of shock, trauma, or other life-threatening conditions, require intensified, comprehensive observation and care.

48. **Physical rehabilitation inpatient services** Provides care encompassing a comprehensive array of restoration services for the disabled and all support services necessary to help patients attain their maximum functional capacity.

49. **Physical rehabilitation outpatient services** Outpatient program providing medical, health-related, therapy, social, and/or vocational services to help disabled persons attain or retain their maximum functional capacity.

50. **Positron emission tomography scanner (PET)** is a nuclear medicine imaging technology which uses radioactive (positron emitting) isotopes created in a cyclotron or generator and computers to produce composite pictures of the brain and heart at work. PET scanning produces sectional images depicting metabolic activity or blood flow rather than anatomy.

51. **Primary care department** A unit or clinic within the hospital that provides primary care services (e.g. general pediatric care, general internal medicine, family practice and gynecology) through hospital-salaried medical and or nursing staff, focusing on evaluating and diagnosing medical problems and providing medical treatment on an outpatient basis.

52. **Psychiatric acute inpatient services** Provides acute or long-term care to emotionally disturbed patients, including patients admitted for diagnosis and those admitted for treatment of psychiatric problems, on the basis of physicians' orders and approved nursing care plans. Long-term care may include intensive supervision to the chronically mentally ill, mentally disordered, or other mentally incompetent persons.

53. **Psychiatric child adolescent services** Provides care to emotionally disturbed children and adolescents, including those admitted for diagnosis and those admitted for treatment.

54. **Psychiatric consultation-liaison services** Provides organized psychiatric consultation/liaison services to nonpsychiatric hospital staff and/or department on psychological aspects of medical care that may be generic or specific to individual patients.

55. **Psychiatric education services** Provides psychiatric educational services to community agencies and workers such as schools, police, courts, public health nurses, welfare agencies, clergy and so forth. The purpose is to expand the mental health knowledge and competence of personnel not working in the mental health field and to promote good mental health through improved understanding, attitudes, and behavioral patterns.

56. **Psychiatric emergency services** Services or facilities available on a 24-hour basis to provide immediate unscheduled outpatient care, diagnosis, evaluation, crisis intervention, and assistance to persons suffering acute emotional or mental distress.

57. **Psychiatric geriatric services** Provides care to emotionally disturbed elderly patients, including those admitted for diagnosis and those admitted for treatment.

58. **Psychiatric outpatient services** Provides medical care, including diagnosis and treatment of psychiatric outpatients.

59. **Psychiatric partial hospitalization program** Organized hospital services of intensive day/evening outpatient services of three hours or more duration, distinguished from other outpatient visits of one hour.

60. **Radiation therapy** The branch of medicine concerned with radioactive substances and using various techniques of visualization, with the diagnosis and treatment of disease using any of the various sources of radiant energy. Services could include: megavoltage radiation therapy; radioactive implants; stereotactic radiosurgery; therapeutic radioisotope facility; X-ray radiation therapy.

61. **Reproductive health services** Services that include any or all of the following:

Fertility counseling A service that counsels and educates on infertility problems and includes laboratory and surgical workup and management for individuals having problems conceiving children.

In vitro fertilization Program providing for the induction of fertilization of a surgically removed ovum by donated sperm in a culture medium followed by a short incubation period. The embryo is then reimplanted in the womb.

62. **Retirement housing** A facility which provides social activities to senior citizens, usually retired persons, who do not require health care but some short–term skilled nursing care may be provided. A retirement center may furnish housing and may also have acute hospital and long–term care facilities, or it may arrange for acute and long term care through affiliated institutions.

63. **Single photon emission computerized tomography (SPECT)** is a nuclear medicine imaging technology that combines existing technology of gamma camera imaging with computed tomographic imaging technology to provide a more precise and clear image.

64. **Skilled nursing or other long–term care services** Provides non–acute medical and skilled nursing care services, therapy, and social services under the supervision of a licensed registered nurse on a 24–hour basis.

65. **Social work services** Services may include one or more of the following: Organized social work services (services that are properly directed and sufficiently staffed by qualified individuals who provide assistance and counseling to patients and their families in dealing with social, emotional, and environmental problems associated with illness or disability, often in the context of financial or discharge planning coordination.) Outpatient social work services (social work services provided in ambulatory care areas.) Emergency department social work services (social work services provided to emergency department patients by social workers dedicated to the emergency department or on call.)

66. **Sports medicine** Provision of diagnostic screening and assessment and clinical and rehabilitation services for the prevention and treatment of sports–related injuries.

67. **Support groups** A hospital sponsored program which allows a group of individuals with the same or similar problems who meet periodically to share experiences, problems, and solutions, in order to support each other.

68. **Teen outreach services** A program focusing on the teenager which encourages an improved health status and a healthful lifestyle including physical, emotional, mental, social, spiritual and economic health through education, exercise, nutrition and health promotion.

69. **Transplant services** The branch of medicine that transfers an organ or tissue from one person to another or from one body part to another to replace a diseased structure or to restore function or to change appearance. Services could includes: Bone marrow transplant program; kidney transplant; organ transplant (other than kidney); tissue transplant.

70. **Trauma center (certified)** A facility certified to provide emergency and specialized intensive care to critically ill and injured patients.

71. **Ultrasound** The use of acoustic waves above the range of 20,000 cycles per second to visualize internal body structures.

72. **Urgent care center** A facility that provides care and treatment for problems that are not life–threatening but require attention over the short term. These units function like emergency rooms but are separate from hospitals with which they may have backup affiliation arrangements.

73. **Volunteer services department** An organized hospital department responsible for coordinating the services of volunteers working within the institution.

74. **Women's health center/services** An area set aside for coordinated education and treatment services specifically for and promoted by women as provided by this special unit. Services may or may not include obstetrics but include a range of services other than OB.

Definitions of Physician Codes

1. **Closed physician–hospital organization (PHO)** A PHO that restricts physician membership to those practitioners who meet criteria for cost effectiveness and/or high quality.

2. **Equity model** Allows established practitioners to become shareholders in a professional corporation in exchange for tangible and intangible assets of their existing practices.

3. **Foundation** A corporation, organized either as a hospital affiliate or subsidiary, which purchases both the tangible and intangible assets of one or more medical group practices. Physicians remain in a separate corporate entity but sign a professional services agreement with the foundation.

4. **Group practice without walls** Hospital sponsors the formation of, or provides capital to physicians to establish, a 'quasi' group to share administrative expenses while remaining independent practitioners.

5. **Independent practice association (IPA)** An IPA is a legal entity that hold managed care contracts. The IPA then contracts with physicians, usually in solo practice, to provide care either on a fee–for–services or capitated basis. The purpose of an IPA is to assist solo physicians in obtaining managed care contracts.

6. **Integrated salary model** Physicians are salaried by the hospital or another entity of a health system to provide medical services for primary care and specialty care.

7. **Management services organization (MSO)** A corporation, owned by the hospital or a physician/hospital joint venture, that provides management services to one or more medical group practices. The MSO purchases the tangible assets of the practices and leases them back as part of a full–service management agreement, under which the MSO employs all non–physician staff and provides all supplies/administrative systems for a fee.

8. **Open physician–hospital organization (PHO)** A joint venture between the hospital and all members of the medical staff who wish to participate. The PHO can act as a unified agent in managed care contracting, own a managed care plan, own and operate ambulatory care centers or ancillary services projects, or provide administrative services to physician members.

Hospitals in the United States, by State

ALABAMA

Resident population 4,352 (in thousands)
Resident population in metro areas 66.5%
Birth rate per 1,000 population 14.2
65 years and over 13.0%
Percent of persons without health insurance 12.9%

Hospital, Address, Telephone, Administrator, Approval, Facility, and Physician Codes, Health Care System, Network	Classi-fication Codes		Utilization Data					Expense (thousands) of dollars		
★ American Hospital Association (AHA) membership □ Joint Commission on Accreditation of Healthcare Organizations (JCAHO) accreditation + American Osteopathic Healthcare Association (AOHA) membership ○ American Osteopathic Association (AOA) accreditation △ Commission on Accreditation of Rehabilitation Facilities (CARF) accreditation Control codes 61, 63, 64, 71, 72 and 73 indicate hospitals listed by AOHA, but not registered by AHA. For definition of numerical codes, see page A4	Control	Service	Staffed Beds	Admissions	Census	Outpatient Visits	Births	Total	Payroll	Personnel

ALABASTER—Shelby County

☒ SHELBY BAPTIST MEDICAL CENTER, 1000 First Street North, Zip 35007–0488, Mailing Address: Box 488, Zip 35007–0488; tel. 205/620–8100; Charles C. Colvert, President (Total facility includes 18 beds in nursing home–type unit) (Nonreporting) **A**1 2 9 10 **S** Baptist Health System, Birmingham, AL — 13 10 228 — — — — — — —

ALEXANDER CITY—Tallapoosa County

☒ RUSSELL MEDICAL CENTER, (Formerly Russell Hospital), U.S. 280 By–Pass, Zip 35010, Mailing Address: P.O. Box 939, Zip 35011–0939; tel. 256/329–7100; Frank W. Harris, President and Chief Executive Officer **A**1 9 10 **F**7 8 10 14 15 16 19 21 22 28 29 30 32 33 34 35 36 37 38 39 40 42 44 45 46 48 49 51 63 65 67 71 73 74 **P**7 — 23 10 81 3891 35 61996 374 27103 10948 420

ANDALUSIA—Covington County

☒ ANDALUSIA REGIONAL HOSPITAL, (Formerly Columbia Andalusia Regional Hospital), 849 South Three Notch Street, Zip 36420–5325, Mailing Address: P.O. Box 760, Zip 36420–0760; tel. 334/222–8466; Barry L. Keel, Chief Executive Officer **A**1 9 10 **F**7 8 12 14 19 21 22 35 37 40 44 49 71 **S** LifePoint Hospitals, Inc., Nashville, TN — 33 10 87 3408 31 30815 370 — — 230

ANNISTON—Calhoun County

☒ NORTHEAST ALABAMA REGIONAL MEDICAL CENTER, 400 East Tenth Street, Zip 36207–4716, Mailing Address: P.O. Box 2208, Zip 36202–2208; tel. 256/235–5121; Allen P. Fletcher, President and Chief Executive Officer **A**1 2 9 10 **F**7 8 10 14 15 16 17 19 21 22 28 30 31 32 34 35 37 40 41 42 44 45 46 49 52 54 55 56 57 58 60 65 66 67 70 71 73
Web address: www.rmccares.org — 16 10 259 15016 183 119030 1652 86011 37042 1272

□ STRINGFELLOW MEMORIAL HOSPITAL, 301 East 18th Street, Zip 36207–3999; tel. 205/235–8900; Vincent T. Cherry, Jr., Administrator (Nonreporting) **A**1 9 10 **S** Health Management Associates, Naples, FL — 33 10 66 — — — — — — —

ASHLAND—Clay County

★ CLAY COUNTY HOSPITAL, 83825 Highway 9, Zip 36251, Mailing Address: P.O. Box 1270, Zip 36251–1277; tel. 256/354–2131; Linda U. Jordan, Administrator (Total facility includes 63 beds in nursing home–type unit) (Nonreporting) **A**9 10 — 13 10 116 — — — — — — —

ATHENS—Limestone County

☒ ATHENS–LIMESTONE HOSPITAL, 700 West Market Street, Zip 35611–2457, Mailing Address: P.O. Box 999, Zip 35612–0999; tel. 256/233–9292; Philip E. Dotson, Administrator and Chief Executive Officer **A**1 9 10 **F**7 8 12 15 16 19 21 22 28 29 30 32 37 39 40 44 45 49 65 71 **P**6
Web address: www.alhosp.com — 16 10 101 4639 51 48082 417 33990 15098 546

ATMORE—Escambia County

□ ATMORE COMMUNITY HOSPITAL, 401 Medical Park Drive, Zip 36502–3091; tel. 334/368–2500; Robert E. Gowing, Interim Administrator (Nonreporting) **A**1 9 10 **S** Escambia County Health Care Authority, Brewton, AL — 13 10 51 — — — — — — —

BAY MINETTE—Baldwin County

□ NORTH BALDWIN HOSPITAL, 1815 Hand Avenue, Zip 36507, Mailing Address: P.O. Box 1409, Zip 36507–1409; tel. 334/937–5521; Wilma D. Powell, Administrator (Total facility includes 60 beds in nursing home–type unit) **A**1 9 10 **F**7 15 16 17 19 21 22 32 33 34 35 37 40 41 44 49 64 65 71 73 — 13 10 103 1833 81 36770 193 8477 — 159

BESSEMER—Jefferson County

☒ BESSEMER CARRAWAY MEDICAL CENTER, 995 Ninth Avenue S.W., Zip 35022, Mailing Address: P.O. Box 847, Zip 35021–0847; tel. 205/481–7000; Dan M. Eagar, Jr., Administrator **A**1 2 9 10 **F**2 3 7 8 10 11 12 14 19 20 21 26 27 28 30 33 37 39 40 41 44 48 49 52 54 55 56 57 65 67 70 71 73 74 **P**4 7 — 23 10 210 6869 100 62536 369 64167 24691 883

BIRMINGHAM—Jefferson County

BIRMINGHAM BAPTIST MEDICAL CENTER–MONTCLAIR CAMPUS See Montclair Baptist Medical Center
BIRMINGHAM BAPTIST MEDICAL CENTER–PRINCETON See Princeton Baptist Medical Center
BRADFORD HEALTH SERVICES AT BIRMINGHAM, 1221 Alton Drive, Zip 35210–4308, Mailing Address: P.O. Box 129, Warrior, Zip 35180–0129; tel. 205/833–4000; W. Clay Simmons, Executive Vice President **F**2 14 64 **S** Bradford Health Services, Birmingham, AL — 33 82 90 1727 47 5458 0 — — 98

☒ BROOKWOOD MEDICAL CENTER, 2010 Brookwood Medical Center Drive, Zip 35209; tel. 205/877–1000; Gregory H. Burfitt, President and Chief Executive Officer **A**1 2 9 10 **F**1 2 4 5 7 8 10 11 12 14 16 17 18 19 21 22 23 24 25 26 28 29 30 31 32 33 34 35 37 38 39 40 41 42 43 44 45 48 49 51 52 53 56 57 58 59 60 61 64 65 66 67 71 73 74 **P**6 **S** TENET Healthcare Corporation, Santa Barbara, CA
Web address: www.brookwood–medical.com — 33 10 468 20814 290 103776 3671 — — 2661

Hospital, Address, Telephone, Administrator, Approval, Facility, and Physician Codes, Health Care System, Network	Classi-fication Codes		Utilization Data					Expense (thousands) of dollars		
	Control	Service	Staffed Beds	Admissions	Census	Outpatient Visits	Births	Total	Payroll	Personnel

★ American Hospital Association (AHA) membership
□ Joint Commission on Accreditation of Healthcare Organizations (JCAHO) accreditation
+ American Osteopathic Healthcare Association (AOHA) membership
○ American Osteopathic Association (AOA) accreditation
△ Commission on Accreditation of Rehabilitation Facilities (CARF) accreditation
Control codes 61, 63, 64, 71, 72 and 73 indicate hospitals listed by AOHA, but not registered by AHA. For definition of numerical codes, see page A4

Hospital	Control	Service	Staffed Beds	Admissions	Census	Outpatient Visits	Births	Total	Payroll	Personnel
✠ CARRAWAY METHODIST MEDICAL CENTER, 1600 Carraway Boulevard, Zip 35234–1990; tel. 205/502–6000; Cindy Williams, FACHE, Administrator **A**1 2 3 5 8 9 10 **F**2 4 7 8 10 11 12 14 15 16 17 19 20 21 22 23 24 25 26 28 30 31 32 33 34 35 37 39 40 41 42 43 44 45 46 48 49 51 52 53 54 55 56 57 58 60 65 67 70 71 73 **P**3 8 **S** Carraway Methodist Health System, Birmingham, AL **Web address:** www.carraway.org	23	10	383	14807	222	114556	478	153971	58714	1644
✠ CHILDREN'S HOSPITAL OF ALABAMA, 1600 Seventh Avenue South, Zip 35233–1785; tel. 205/939–9100; Jim Dearth, M.D., Chief Executive Officer **A**1 3 5 9 10 **F**9 12 13 14 15 16 17 19 20 21 22 28 29 30 31 34 35 38 39 41 42 44 45 46 47 48 49 51 52 53 54 55 56 58 65 66 67 68 70 71 72 73 **P**7 **Web address:** www.chsys.org	23	50	195	10690	145	221036	0	155780	73885	1975
✠ COOPER GREEN HOSPITAL, 1515 Sixth Avenue South, Zip 35233–1688; tel. 205/930–3200; Max Michael, M.D., Chief Executive Officer and Medical Director **A**1 3 5 9 10 **F**4 7 8 10 12 14 15 16 17 19 22 31 34 35 37 40 42 43 44 49 51 56 60 65 71 **P**5	13	10	131	5759	72	68638	1449	64237	25435	669
✠ EYE FOUNDATION HOSPITAL, 1720 University Boulevard, Zip 35233–1816; tel. 205/325–8100; Steve C. Schultz, Administrator (Nonreporting) **A**1 3 5 9 10 **Web address:** www.health.uab.edu/eyes	23	45	81	—		—		—	—	
□ △ HEALTHSOUTH LAKESHORE REHABILITATION HOSPITAL, 3800 Ridgeway Drive, Zip 35209–5599; tel. 205/868–2000; Terry Brown, Administrator and Chief Executive Officer **A**1 7 9 10 **F**6 14 15 16 19 20 21 22 25 27 30 34 35 37 41 42 44 46 48 49 51 65 66 67 71 **P**8 **S** HEALTHSOUTH Corporation, Birmingham, AL	33	46	100	2239	94	10333	0	—	—	270
✠ HEALTHSOUTH MEDICAL CENTER, 1201 11th Avenue South, Zip 35205–5299; tel. 205/930–7000; Luke Standeffer, Chief Operating Officer **A**1 9 10 **F**1 8 10 12 14 19 21 22 34 35 37 44 48 49 63 65 66 67 71 73 **S** HEALTHSOUTH Corporation, Birmingham, AL	33	10	181	6091	64	41474	0	71783	22616	621
□ HILL CREST BEHAVIORAL HEALTH SERVICES, 6869 Fifth Avenue South, Zip 35212–1866; tel. 205/833–9000; Steve McCabe, Chief Executive Officer **A**1 9 10 **F**3 12 17 18 26 27 39 41 45 46 48 52 53 54 55 56 57 58 64 65 67 68 **P**5 **S** Ramsay Health Care, Inc., Coral Gables, FL	33	22	119	1291	100	0	0	10150	5090	193
✠ △ MEDICAL CENTER EAST, 50 Medical Park East Drive, Zip 35235–9987; tel. 205/838–3000; David E. Crawford, FACHE, Executive Vice President and Chief Operating Officer **A**1 2 3 5 7 9 10 **F**1 2 3 4 6 7 8 9 10 11 12 14 15 16 17 19 21 22 23 24 25 27 28 29 30 31 32 33 34 35 37 38 39 40 41 42 43 44 45 46 47 48 49 51 52 53 54 55 56 57 58 59 60 61 62 64 65 67 69 70 71 72 73 74 **P**5 6 7 **S** Eastern Health System, Inc., Birmingham, AL	23	10	257	12448	148	86369	909	94842	33351	980
✠ MONTCLAIR BAPTIST MEDICAL CENTER, (Formerly Birmingham Baptist Medical Center–Montclair Campus), 800 Montclair Road, Zip 35213–1984; tel. 205/592–1000; John Shelton, President (Total facility includes 112 beds in nursing home–type unit) (Nonreporting) **A**1 2 3 5 8 9 10 **S** Baptist Health System, Birmingham, AL	21	10	1023	—		—		—	—	
✠ PRINCETON BAPTIST MEDICAL CENTER, (Formerly Birmingham Baptist Medical Center–Princeton), 701 Princeton Avenue S.W., Zip 35211–1305; tel. 205/783–3000; Charlie Faulkner, President (Nonreporting) **A**1 2 3 5 8 9 10 **S** Baptist Health System, Birmingham, AL	21	10	1033	—		—		—	—	
✠ ST. VINCENT'S HOSPITAL, 810 St. Vincent's Drive, Zip 35205–1695, Mailing Address: P.O. Box 12407, Zip 35202–2407; tel. 205/939–7000; Curtis James, Acting President and Chief Executive Officer (Nonreporting) **A**1 2 3 5 9 10 **S** Daughters of Charity National Health System, Saint Louis, MO **Web address:** www.stv.org	23	10	338	—		—		—	—	
✠ UNIVERSITY OF ALABAMA HOSPITAL, 619 South 19th Street, Zip 35233–6505; tel. 205/934–4011; Martin Nowak, Interim Executive Director (Total facility includes 39 beds in nursing home–type unit) **A**1 2 3 5 8 9 10 12 **F**2 3 4 5 7 8 9 10 11 12 14 15 16 17 19 20 21 22 23 24 25 26 27 28 29 30 31 32 33 34 35 37 38 39 40 41 42 43 44 46 48 49 50 51 52 53 54 55 56 57 58 59 60 61 63 64 65 66 67 68 70 71 72 73 74 **P**3 7 **Web address:** www.uab.edu	12	10	854	38837	679	389496	3187	485425	182826	4427
✠ VETERANS AFFAIRS MEDICAL CENTER, 700 South 19th Street, Zip 35233–1927; tel. 205/933–8101; Y. C. Parris, Director (Nonreporting) **A**1 2 3 5 8 **S** Department of Veterans Affairs, Washington, DC **Web address:** www.va.gov	45	10	317	—		—		—	—	

BOAZ—Marshall County

Hospital	Control	Service	Staffed Beds	Admissions	Census	Outpatient Visits	Births	Total	Payroll	Personnel
✠ MARSHALL MEDICAL CENTER SOUTH, U.S. Highway 431 North, Zip 35957–0999, Mailing Address: P.O. Box 758, Zip 35957–0758; tel. 256/593–8310; J. Marlin Hanson, Administrator **A**1 9 10 **F**4 7 8 9 12 14 15 16 17 19 21 22 24 28 30 32 35 37 39 40 41 42 44 46 47 49 54 55 56 57 60 63 65 66 67 71 73 74 **S** Marshall County Health Care Authority, Guntersville, AL	13	10	102	4751	59	178611	614	42405	17108	599

BREWTON—Escambia County

Hospital	Control	Service	Staffed Beds	Admissions	Census	Outpatient Visits	Births	Total	Payroll	Personnel
□ D. W. MCMILLAN MEMORIAL HOSPITAL, 1301 Belleville Avenue, Zip 36426–1306, Mailing Address: P.O. Box 908, Zip 36427–0908; tel. 334/867–8061; Phillip L. Parker, Administrator **A**1 9 10 **F**7 8 14 15 16 19 21 22 27 28 30 32 34 35 37 39 40 42 44 45 49 65 67 71 73 **P**4 7 **S** Escambia County Health Care Authority, Brewton, AL **Web address:** www.bhcpns.org	23	10	67	2889	31	34252	283	15506	6965	264

Hospital, Address, Telephone, Administrator, Approval, Facility, and Physician Codes, Health Care System, Network	Classi-fication Codes		Utilization Data					Expense (thousands) of dollars		
	Control	Service	Staffed Beds	Admissions	Census	Outpatient Visits	Births	Total	Payroll	Personnel

Approval Key (left legend):

★ American Hospital Association (AHA) membership
☐ Joint Commission on Accreditation of Healthcare Organizations (JCAHO) accreditation
+ American Osteopathic Healthcare Association (AOHA) membership
○ American Osteopathic Association (AOA) accreditation
△ Commission on Accreditation of Rehabilitation Facilities (CARF) accreditation
Control codes 61, 63, 64, 71, 72 and 73 indicate hospitals listed by AOHA, but not registered by AHA. For definition of numerical codes, see page A4

Hospital	Control	Service	Staffed Beds	Admissions	Census	Outpatient Visits	Births	Total	Payroll	Personnel
BRIDGEPORT—Jackson County ☐ NORTH JACKSON HOSPITAL, Mailing Address: 47005 U.S. Highway 72, Zip 35740; tel. 256/437–2101; Thomas O. Lackey, Administrator (Total facility includes 60 beds in nursing home–type unit) (Nonreporting) **A**1 9 10	16	10	109	—	—	—	—	—	—	—
CAMDEN—Wilcox County J. PAUL JONES HOSPITAL, 317 McWilliams Avenue, Zip 36726–1610; tel. 205/682–4131; Arden Chesnut, Administrator (Nonreporting) **A**9 10	15	10	20	—	—	—	—	—	—	—
CARROLLTON—Pickens County ☐ PICKENS COUNTY MEDICAL CENTER, Route 2, Zip 35447, Mailing Address: P.O. Box 478, Zip 35447–0478; tel. 205/367–8111; Tunisia Lavender, R.N., Chief Operating Officer **A**1 9 10 **F**7 8 14 19 20 22 24 25 28 30 32 34 35 37 40 42 44 45 65 67 71 73	23	10	50	2185	26	94356	182	—	—	250
CENTRE—Cherokee County ✠ CHEROKEE BAPTIST MEDICAL CENTER, 400 Northwood Drive, Zip 35960–1023; tel. 256/927–5531; Barry S. Cochran, President **A**1 9 10 **F**8 11 12 14 15 16 17 19 21 22 24 28 30 32 33 44 49 54 66 71 73 74 **S** Baptist Health System, Birmingham, AL	23	10	45	1295	14	18800	0	10763	4240	137
CENTREVILLE—Bibb County BIBB MEDICAL CENTER, 164 Pierson Avenue, Zip 35042–1199; tel. 205/926–4881; Terry J. Smith, Administrator (Total facility includes 113 beds in nursing home–type unit) (Nonreporting) **A**9 10	13	10	138	—	—	—	—	—	—	—
CHATOM—Washington County WASHINGTON COUNTY INFIRMARY AND NURSING HOME, St. Stephens Avenue, Zip 36518, Mailing Address: P.O. Box 597, Zip 36518–0597; tel. 334/847–2223; John S. Eads, Administrator (Total facility includes 73 beds in nursing home–type unit) (Nonreporting) **A**9 10 **S** Infirmary Health System, Inc., Mobile, AL	13	10	88	—	—	—	—	—	—	—
CLANTON—Chilton County ☐ CHILTON MEDICAL CENTER, (Formerly Vaughan Chilton Medical Center), 1010 Lay Dam Road, Zip 35045; tel. 205/755–2500; Randy Smith, Chief Executive Officer (Nonreporting) **A**1 9 10 **S** NetCare Health Systems, Inc., Nashville, TN	33	10	45	—	—	—	—	—	—	—
CULLMAN—Cullman County ✠ CULLMAN REGIONAL MEDICAL CENTER, 1912 Alabama Highway 157, Zip 35055, Mailing Address: P.O. Box 1108, Zip 35056–1108; tel. 256/737–2000; Jesse O. Weatherly, President **A**1 2 9 10 **F**4 7 8 10 12 14 15 16 17 19 21 22 24 28 29 30 32 33 34 35 37 40 41 42 44 45 46 49 60 65 66 67 71 73 74 **S** Baptist Health System, Birmingham, AL	23	10	115	6522	66	200189	603	49036	19017	728
✠ WOODLAND MEDICAL CENTER, 1910 Cherokee Avenue S.E., Zip 35055–5599; tel. 256/739–3500; Lowell S. Benton, Executive Director **A**1 9 10 **F**7 8 11 12 13 15 17 19 22 28 29 30 32 35 37 39 40 41 42 44 45 46 48 49 52 55 56 57 58 66 71 **S** Community Health Systems, Inc., Brentwood, TN	33	10	100	2736	27	28667	176	15013	6019	212
DADEVILLE—Tallapoosa County ★ LAKESHORE COMMUNITY HOSPITAL, 201 Mariarden Road, Zip 36853, Mailing Address: P.O. Box 248, Zip 36853–0248; tel. 256/825–7821; Mavis B. Halko, Administrator **A**9 10 **F**19 22 32 34 44 71 **S** Healthcorp of Tennessee, Inc., Chattanooga, TN	23	10	28	1296	9	13573	0	6242	3905	165
DAPHNE—Baldwin County ✠ MERCY MEDICAL, 101 Villa Drive, Zip 36526–4653, Mailing Address: P.O. Box 1090, Zip 36526–1090; tel. 334/626–2694; Sister Mary Eileen Wilhelm, President and Chief Executive Officer (Total facility includes 137 beds in nursing home–type unit) **A**1 10 **F**1 6 12 15 16 17 20 26 31 32 33 34 39 42 49 62 64 65 67 73 **P**7 **S** Catholic Health East, Newtown Square, PA **Web address:** www.mercymedical.com	21	46	162	1641	140	6902	0	29447	15111	619
DECATUR—Morgan County ✠ DECATUR GENERAL HOSPITAL, 1201 Seventh Street S.E., Zip 35601, Mailing Address: P.O. Box 2239, Zip 35609–2239; tel. 256/341–2000; Robert L. Smith, President and Chief Executive Officer (Nonreporting) **A**1 2 9 10	16	10	273	—	—	—	—	—	—	—
DECATUR GENERAL HOSPITAL–WEST, 2205 Beltline Road S.W., Zip 35601–3687, Mailing Address: P.O. Box 2240, Zip 35609–2240; tel. 205/350–1450; Dennis Griffith, Vice President (Nonreporting)	33	22	64	—	—	—	—	—	—	—
☐ NORTH ALABAMA REGIONAL HOSPITAL, Highway 31 South, Zip 35609, Mailing Address: P.O. Box 2221, Zip 35609–2221; tel. 205/353–9433; Kay Greenwood, R.N., MS, Facility Director **A**1 10 **F**14 16 19 20 21 22 35 50 52 60 63 65 71 73 **P**6	12	22	74	461	74	0	0	7194	4444	153
✠ PARKWAY MEDICAL CENTER HOSPITAL, 1874 Beltline Road S.W., Zip 35601–5509, Mailing Address: P.O. Box 2211, Zip 35609–2211; tel. 256/350–2211; Phillip J. Mazzuca, Chief Executive Officer (Nonreporting) **A**1 9 10 **S** Community Health Systems, Inc., Brentwood, TN	33	10	94	—	—	—	—	—	—	—
DEMOPOLIS—Marengo County ✠ BRYAN W. WHITFIELD MEMORIAL HOSPITAL, Highway 80 West, Zip 36732, Mailing Address: P.O. Box 890, Zip 36732–0890; tel. 334/289–4000; Charles E. Nabors, FACHE, Administrator and Chief Executive Officer **A**1 9 10 **F**1 8 12 13 14 15 16 17 19 21 22 24 25 28 30 32 33 34 37 39 40 42 44 45 46 51 63 65 67 68 71 73 **P**5	16	10	99	3582	46	20106	483	19559	8786	351
DOTHAN—Houston County ✠ FLOWERS HOSPITAL, 4370 West Main Street, Zip 36305, Mailing Address: P.O. Box 6907, Zip 36302–6907; tel. 334/793–5000; Keith Granger, President and Chief Executive Officer (Nonreporting) **A**1 2 9 10 **S** Quorum Health Group/Quorum Health Resources, Inc., Brentwood, TN	33	10	215	—	—	—	—	—	—	—

Hospital, Address, Telephone, Administrator, Approval, Facility, and Physician Codes, Health Care System, Network	Classi-fication Codes		Utilization Data					Expense (thousands) of dollars		
★ American Hospital Association (AHA) membership □ Joint Commission on Accreditation of Healthcare Organizations (JCAHO) accreditation + American Osteopathic Healthcare Association (AOHA) membership ○ American Osteopathic Association (AOA) accreditation △ Commission on Accreditation of Rehabilitation Facilities (CARF) accreditation Control codes 61, 63, 64, 71, 72 and 73 indicate hospitals listed by AOHA, but not registered by AHA. For definition of numerical codes, see page A4	Control	Service	Staffed Beds	Admissions	Census	Outpatient Visits	Births	Total	Payroll	Personnel

	Control	Service	Staffed Beds	Admissions	Census	Outpatient Visits	Births	Total	Payroll	Personnel
□ SOUTHEAST ALABAMA MEDICAL CENTER, 1108 Ross Clark Circle, Zip 36301–3024, Mailing Address: P.O. Box 6987, Zip 36302–6987; tel. 334/793–8111; Ronald S. Owen, Chief Executive Officer **A**1 2 9 10 **F**4 7 8 10 11 12 16 17 19 21 23 28 29 30 32 34 35 37 39 40 41 42 43 44 45 46 49 52 60 63 65 67 70 71 73 **P**6 7 **Web address:** www.samc.org	16	10	353	16798	207	218562	1080	132166	56724	1805
ELBA—Coffee County										
ELBA GENERAL HOSPITAL, 987 Drayton Street, Zip 36323–1494; tel. 334/897–2257; Ellen Briley, Administrator and Chief Executive Officer (Total facility includes 101 beds in nursing home–type unit) **A**9 10 **F**22 26 64 **P**5	16	10	121	1272	108	11840	0	3328	1760	174
ENTERPRISE—Coffee County										
✠ MEDICAL CENTER ENTERPRISE, 400 North Edwards Street, Zip 36330–9981; tel. 334/347–0584; Earl S. Whiteley, CHE, Chief Executive Officer **A**1 9 10 **F**7 8 12 16 19 21 22 35 41 44 49 65 66 71 **S** Quorum Health Group/Quorum Health Resources, Inc., Brentwood, TN	33	10	117	4443	44	—	918	22176	8067	327
EUFAULA—Barbour County										
□ LAKEVIEW COMMUNITY HOSPITAL, 820 West Washington Street, Zip 36027–1899; tel. 205/687–5761; Carl D. Brown, Administrator (Nonreporting) **A**1 9 10 **S** Healthcorp of Tennessee, Inc., Chattanooga, TN	33	10	74	—	—	—	—	—	—	—
EUTAW—Greene County										
GREENE COUNTY HOSPITAL, 509 Wilson Avenue, Zip 35462–1099; tel. 205/372–3388; Robert J. Coker, Jr., Administrator (Nonreporting) **A**9 10	13	10	72	—	—	—	—	—	—	—
FAIRFIELD—Jefferson County										
✠ LLOYD NOLAND HOSPITAL AND HEALTH SYSTEM, 701 Lloyd Noland Parkway, Zip 35064–2699; tel. 205/783–5106; Garry L. Gause, Chief Executive Officer (Nonreporting) **A**1 2 3 5 9 10 **S** TENET Healthcare Corporation, Santa Barbara, CA **Web address:** www.tenethealth.com	33	10	222	—	—	—	—	—	—	—
FAIRHOPE—Baldwin County										
✠ THOMAS HOSPITAL, 750 Morphy Avenue, Zip 36532–1812, Mailing Address: Drawer 929, Zip 36533–0929; tel. 334/928–2375; G. Owen Bailey, Administrator (Nonreporting) **A**1 9 10 **Web address:** www.thomashosp.com	16	10	150	—	—	—	—	—	—	—
FAYETTE—Fayette County										
✠ FAYETTE MEDICAL CENTER, 1653 Temple Avenue North, Zip 35555–1314, Mailing Address: P.O. Drawer 878, Zip 35555–0878; tel. 205/932–5966; Harold Reed, Administrator (Total facility includes 122 beds in nursing home–type unit) **A**1 9 10 **F**8 15 19 22 28 30 32 33 34 35 37 41 42 44 64 65 71 73 **P**5 **S** DCH Health System, Tuscaloosa, AL	13	10	183	1839	145	44135	0	19184	8742	283
FLORALA—Covington County										
FLORALA MEMORIAL HOSPITAL, 515 East Fifth Avenue, Zip 36442–0189, Mailing Address: P.O. Box 189, Zip 36442–0189; tel. 334/858–3287; Blair W. Henson, Administrator (Nonreporting) **A**9 10 **S** United Hospital Corporation, Memphis, TN	33	10	23	—	—	—	—	—	—	—
FLORENCE—Lauderdale County										
✠ ELIZA COFFEE MEMORIAL HOSPITAL, (Includes Mitchell–Hollingsworth Annex), 205 Marengo Street, Zip 35630–6033, Mailing Address: P.O. Box 818, Zip 35631–0818; tel. 256/768–9191; Richard H. Peck, President and Chief Executive Officer (Total facility includes 202 beds in nursing home–type unit) **A**1 9 10 **F**4 7 8 10 11 15 19 21 22 28 34 35 37 40 42 43 44 45 46 49 52 53 54 55 56 57 64 65 67 71 73 **S** Coffee Health Group, Florence, AL	16	10	455	12270	371	57515	1285	74831	36396	1549
✠ FLORENCE HOSPITAL, 2111 Cloyd Boulevard, Zip 35630–1595, Mailing Address: P.O. Box 2010, Zip 35631–2010; tel. 256/767–8700; Carl W. Bailey, Chief Executive Officer (Nonreporting) **A**1 9 10 **S** Coffee Health Group, Florence, AL	16	10	155	—	—	—	—	—	—	—
FOLEY—Baldwin County										
✠ SOUTH BALDWIN REGIONAL MEDICAL CENTER, 1613 North McKenzie Street, Zip 36535–2299; tel. 334/952–3400; Robert F. Jernigan, Jr., Administrator **A**1 9 10 **F**7 8 10 14 15 16 17 19 21 22 25 28 30 32 34 35 36 37 39 40 41 42 44 45 46 49 51 65 67 70 71 73 74 **Web address:** www.southbaldwinrmc.com	16	10	82	4447	48	61208	404	27089	12705	455
FORT PAYNE—DeKalb County										
✠ DEKALB BAPTIST MEDICAL CENTER, 200 Medical Center Drive, Zip 35968–3415, Mailing Address: P.O. Box 680778, Zip 35968–1608; tel. 256/845–3150; Barry S. Cochran, President **A**1 9 10 **F**7 8 12 14 15 16 19 21 22 24 26 27 28 30 31 32 33 35 37 40 41 44 46 49 65 66 67 68 70 71 74 **P**5 7 **S** Baptist Health System, Birmingham, AL **Web address:** www.bhsala.com	23	10	91	3560	37	49293	727	27781	10607	299
FORT RUCKER—Coffee County										
✠ LYSTER U. S. ARMY COMMUNITY HOSPITAL, U.S. Army Aeromedical Center, Zip 36362–5333; tel. 334/255–7360; Lieutenant Colonel Donald Henderson, Jr., Deputy Commander for Administration **A**1 **F**3 8 12 13 14 15 16 17 18 19 27 28 29 30 31 34 39 41 44 46 49 51 54 58 65 67 71 73 74 **P**1 **S** Department of the Army, Office of the Surgeon General, Falls Church, VA	42	10	35	242	2	154149	0	25986	17136	476
GADSDEN—Etowah County										
✠ GADSDEN REGIONAL MEDICAL CENTER, 1007 Goodyear Avenue, Zip 35903–1195; tel. 256/494–4000; James F. O'Loughlin, Chief Executive Officer **A**1 2 9 10 **F**4 7 8 10 12 14 16 19 21 22 23 28 30 32 33 34 35 37 40 41 42 43 44 46 49 52 56 57 58 59 60 65 66 70 71 74 **P**5 **S** Quorum Health Group/Quorum Health Resources, Inc., Brentwood, TN	33	10	233	11032	138	125851	1121	85510	30504	963

Hospital, Address, Telephone, Administrator, Approval, Facility, and Physician Codes, Health Care System, Network	Classi-fication Codes		Utilization Data					Expense (thousands) of dollars		
★ American Hospital Association (AHA) membership □ Joint Commission on Accreditation of Healthcare Organizations (JCAHO) accreditation + American Osteopathic Healthcare Association (AOHA) membership ○ American Osteopathic Association (AOA) accreditation △ Commission on Accreditation of Rehabilitation Facilities (CARF) accreditation Control codes 61, 63, 64, 71, 72 and 73 indicate hospitals listed by AOHA, but not registered by AHA. For definition of numerical codes, see page A4	Control	Service	Staffed Beds	Admissions	Census	Outpatient Visits	Births	Total	Payroll	Personnel
□ MOUNTAIN VIEW HOSPITAL, 3001 Scenic Highway, Zip 35901–9956, Mailing Address: P.O. Box 8406, Zip 35902–8406; tel. 205/546–9265; Jon Orr, Administrator (Nonreporting) **A**1 9 10	33	22	68	—	—	—	—	—	—	—
□ RIVERVIEW REGIONAL MEDICAL CENTER, 600 South Third Street, Zip 35901–5399, Mailing Address: P.O. Box 268, Zip 35999–0268; tel. 205/543–5200; J. David McCormack, Executive Director (Nonreporting) **A**1 9 10 **S** Health Management Associates, Naples, FL	33	10	281	—	—	—	—	—	—	—
GENEVA—Geneva County										
★ WIREGRASS MEDICAL CENTER, (Formerly Wiregrass Hospital), 1200 West Maple Avenue, Zip 36340–1694; tel. 334/684–3655; John L. Robertson, Chief Executive Officer (Total facility includes 86 beds in nursing home–type unit) **A**9 10 **F**8 19 22 28 34 37 44 49 64 65 71	13	10	151	2606	116	21906	0	13255	5893	205
GEORGIANA—Butler County										
GEORGIANA HOSPITAL, 515 Miranda Street, Zip 36033, Mailing Address: P.O. Box 548, Zip 36033–0548; tel. 334/376–2205; Harry Cole, Interim Administrator (Nonreporting) **A**9 10	33	10	22	—	—	—	—	—	—	—
GREENSBORO—Hale County										
HALE COUNTY HOSPITAL, 508 Green Street, Zip 36744–2316; tel. 334/624–3024; Richard M. McGill, Administrator (Nonreporting) **A**9 10	13	10	30	—	—	—	—	—	—	—
GREENVILLE—Butler County										
▣ L. V. STABLER MEMORIAL HOSPITAL, Highway 10 West, Zip 36037–0915, Mailing Address: Box 1000, Zip 36037–0915; tel. 334/382–2676; Tom R. McDougal, Jr., Chief Executive Officer **A**1 9 10 **F**7 8 11 12 17 19 20 21 22 24 26 28 30 32 34 35 40 41 44 45 46 49 52 57 63 71 73 **S** Community Health Systems, Inc., Brentwood, TN	33	10	67	1972	23	18183	40	—	—	—
GROVE HILL—Clarke County										
GROVE HILL MEMORIAL HOSPITAL, 295 South Jackson Street, Zip 36451, Mailing Address: P.O. Box 935, Zip 36451; tel. 334/275–3191; Floyd N. Price, Administrator **A**9 10 **F**7 8 12 15 16 19 22 28 32 40 44 71 73 **P**5 **S** Infirmary Health System, Inc., Mobile, AL	16	10	41	1198	10	17307	192	5147	2115	74
GUNTERSVILLE—Marshall County										
▣ MARSHALL MEDICAL CENTER NORTH, 8000 Alabama Highway 69, Zip 35976; tel. 256/753–8000; Gary R. Gore, Chief Executive Officer **A**1 9 10 **F**4 7 8 11 12 14 15 16 17 19 21 22 24 28 30 32 35 37 39 40 41 42 44 46 48 49 52 54 55 56 57 60 63 65 66 67 71 73 74 **P**8 **S** Marshall County Health Care Authority, Guntersville, AL **Web address:** www.mmcnorth.com	16	10	90	4500	56	—	569	31756	11320	411
HALEYVILLE—Winston County										
▣ CARRAWAY BURDICK WEST MEDICAL CENTER, Highway 195 East, Zip 35565–9536, Mailing Address: P.O. Box 780, Zip 35565–0780; tel. 205/486–5213; Donald J. Jones, Administrator **A**1 9 10 **F**2 4 7 8 10 11 12 14 16 17 19 20 21 22 23 24 25 26 27 28 29 30 31 32 34 35 37 40 42 43 44 45 46 48 49 51 52 59 60 61 65 66 70 71 73 74 **P**3 5 **S** Carraway Methodist Health System, Birmingham, AL	23	10	43	2372	25	22147	0	12286	5616	233
HAMILTON—Marion County										
▣ MARION BAPTIST MEDICAL CENTER, 1256 Military Street South, Zip 35570–5001; tel. 205/921–6200; Evan S. Dillard, President (Total facility includes 69 beds in nursing home–type unit) **A**1 9 10 **F**8 12 14 15 16 19 21 22 24 26 28 32 34 35 37 42 44 46 49 51 63 64 65 66 71 73 74 **P**4 7 **S** Baptist Health System, Birmingham, AL	33	10	112	1474	83	21864	—	13027	5877	134
HARTSELLE—Morgan County										
▣ HARTSELLE MEDICAL CENTER, 201 Pine Street N.W., Zip 35640–2309, Mailing Address: P.O. Box 969, Zip 35640–0969; tel. 256/773–6511; Mike H. McNair, Chief Executive Officer (Nonreporting) **A**1 9 10 **S** Community Health Systems, Inc., Brentwood, TN	33	10	150	—	—	—	—	—	—	—
HUNTSVILLE—Madison County										
▣ CRESTWOOD MEDICAL CENTER, (Formerly Columbia Medical Center of Huntsville), One Hospital Drive, Zip 35801–3403; tel. 256/882–3100; Thomas M. Weiss, Chief Executive Officer **A**1 9 10 **F**2 3 7 8 10 12 16 17 19 21 22 28 30 35 37 39 42 44 52 54 55 58 59 65 66 71 72 73 **S** Triad Hospitals, Inc., Dallas, TX	32	10	92	4282	49	66174	0	42677	14350	460
□ △ HEALTHSOUTH REHABILITATION HOSPITAL OF NORTH ALABAMA, 107 Governors Drive S.W., Zip 35801–4329; tel. 205/535–2300; Rod Moss, Chief Executive Officer **A**1 7 10 **F**5 11 19 22 27 35 48 49 65 71 **S** HEALTHSOUTH Corporation, Birmingham, AL	33	46	59	1103	50	15125	0	9836	5050	140
▣ HUNTSVILLE HOSPITAL, (Includes Huntsville Hospital East, 911 Big Cove Road S.E., Zip 35801–3784; tel. 205/517–8020), 101 Sivley Road, Zip 35801–4470; tel. 256/517–8020; L. Joe Austin, Chief Executive Officer **A**1 2 3 5 9 10 **F**4 7 8 10 11 12 14 15 16 17 19 21 22 23 24 25 28 32 34 35 37 38 39 40 41 42 43 44 45 46 47 49 52 55 56 57 58 59 60 65 71 72 73 74 **P**7	16	10	558	35164	413	297216	4744	293868	121804	3161
JACKSON—Clarke County										
JACKSON MEDICAL CENTER, (Formerly Vaughn Jackson Medical Center), 220 Hospital Drive, Zip 36545–2459, Mailing Address: P.O. Box 428, Zip 36545–0428; tel. 334/246–9021; Teresa F. Grimes, Administrator (Nonreporting) **A**9 10	33	10	35	—	—	—	—	—	—	—

Hospital, Address, Telephone, Administrator, Approval, Facility, and Physician Codes, Health Care System, Network	Classi-fication Codes		Utilization Data					Expense (thousands) of dollars		
★ American Hospital Association (AHA) membership □ Joint Commission on Accreditation of Healthcare Organizations (JCAHO) accreditation + American Osteopathic Healthcare Association (AOHA) membership ○ American Osteopathic Association (AOA) accreditation △ Commission on Accreditation of Rehabilitation Facilities (CARF) accreditation Control codes 61, 63, 64, 71, 72 and 73 indicate hospitals listed by AOHA, but not registered by AHA. For definition of numerical codes, see page A4	Control	Service	Staffed Beds	Admissions	Census	Outpatient Visits	Births	Total	Payroll	Personnel

JACKSONVILLE—Calhoun County

✖ JACKSONVILLE HOSPITAL, 1701 Pelham Road South, Zip 36265–3399, Mailing Address: P.O. Box 999, Zip 36265–0999; tel. 256/435–4970; Charles Mitchener, Jr., Chief Executive Officer **A**1 9 10 **F**7 8 12 14 17 19 21 22 25 26 28 29 30 31 35 36 37 40 41 44 49 61 71 73 **P**1 7 **S** Quorum Health Group/Quorum Health Resources, Inc., Brentwood, TN **Web address:** www.jaxhosp.com	33	10	56	1969	16	31755	243	12935	5531	173

JASPER—Walker County

✖ WALKER BAPTIST MEDICAL CENTER, 3400 Highway 78 East, Zip 35501–8956, Mailing Address: P.O. Box 3547, Zip 35502–3547; tel. 205/387–4000; Jeff Brewer, President **A**1 9 10 **F**1 7 8 10 12 14 15 16 17 19 21 22 28 30 32 33 35 37 40 41 42 44 45 49 52 54 56 57 65 70 71 73 **S** Baptist Health System, Birmingham, AL	23	10	245	7399	72	59337	768	44357	17107	584

LUVERNE—Crenshaw County

CRENSHAW BAPTIST HOSPITAL, 1625 South Forrest Avenue, Zip 36049; tel. 334/335–3374; L. Wayne Sasser, Vice President and Administrator **A**9 10 **F**2 7 14 15 16 17 19 22 25 28 32 34 41 44 45 49 52 56 57 65 66 71 73 **S** Baptist Health, Montgomery, AL	23	10	52	1166	18	2639	171	6283	3468	109

MADISON—Madison County

BRADFORD HEALTH SERVICES AT HUNTSVILLE, 1600 Browns Ferry Road, Zip 35758–9769, Mailing Address: P.O. Box 176, Zip 35758–0176; tel. 205/461–7272; Bob Hinds, Executive Director (Nonreporting) **A**9 **S** Bradford Health Services, Birmingham, AL	33	82	84	—	—	—	—	—	—	—

MARION—Perry County

VAUGHAN PERRY HOSPITAL, 505 East Lafayette Street, Zip 36756–0149, Mailing Address: P.O. Box 149, Zip 36756–0149; tel. 334/683–9696; Rene W. Sumlin, Chief Executive Officer and Administrator (Total facility includes 61 beds in nursing home–type unit) (Nonreporting) **A**10	23	10	76	—	—	—	—	—	—	—

MOBILE—Mobile County

□ CHARTER BEHAVIORAL HEALTH SYSTEM, 5800 Southland Drive, Zip 36693–3396, Mailing Address: P.O. Box 991800, Zip 36691–1800; tel. 334/661–3001; Keith Cox, CHE, Chief Executive Officer (Nonreporting) **A**1 5 9 10 **S** Magellan Health Services, Atlanta, GA	33	22	94	—	—	—	—	—	—	—
✖ MOBILE INFIRMARY MEDICAL CENTER, (Includes Rotary Rehabilitation Hospital), 5 Mobile Infirmary Drive North, Zip 36601, Mailing Address: P.O. Box 2144, Zip 36652–2144; tel. 334/435–2400; E. Chandler Bramlett, Jr., President and Chief Executive Officer **A**1 2 9 10 **F**4 5 6 7 8 10 11 12 13 14 15 17 19 21 22 24 25 26 27 28 29 31 32 33 34 35 37 39 40 41 42 43 44 45 46 47 48 49 51 52 53 54 55 57 58 59 60 61 62 63 64 65 66 67 71 72 73 74 **S** Infirmary Health System, Inc., Mobile, AL **Web address:** www.mimc.com	23	10	489	24129	366	233135	1000	164492	64836	2485
✖ PROVIDENCE HOSPITAL, 6801 Airport Boulevard, Zip 36608–3785, Mailing Address: P.O. Box 850429, Zip 36685–0429; tel. 334/633–1000; John R. Roeder, President and Chief Executive Officer **A**1 2 9 10 **F**4 7 8 10 11 12 15 16 17 19 21 22 23 24 30 31 32 33 34 35 36 37 40 42 43 44 45 46 49 60 65 66 67 71 73 **P**5 6 7 **S** Daughters of Charity National Health System, Saint Louis, MO **Web address:** www.providencehospital.org	21	10	349	16382	225	182658	1066	124677	47352	1637
ROTARY REHABILITATION HOSPITAL See Mobile Infirmary Medical Center										
□ SPRINGHILL MEMORIAL HOSPITAL, 3719 Dauphin Street, Zip 36608–1798, Mailing Address: P.O. Box 8246, Zip 36608–8246; tel. 334/344–9630; Bill A. Mason, President **A**1 9 10 **F**40 **Web address:** www.springhill.org	31	10	198	9363	108	55419	1491	—	—	1032
□ UNIVERSITY OF SOUTH ALABAMA KNOLLWOOD PARK HOSPITAL, 5600 Girby Road, Zip 36693–3398; tel. 334/660–5120; Thomas J. Gibson, Administrator (Nonreporting) **A**1 3 5 9 10 **S** University of South Alabama Hospitals, Mobile, AL	12	10	150	—	—	—	—	—	—	—
□ UNIVERSITY OF SOUTH ALABAMA MEDICAL CENTER, 2451 Fillingim Street, Zip 36617–2293; tel. 334/471–7000; Stephen H. Simmons, Administrator (Nonreporting) **A**1 2 3 5 8 9 10 **S** University of South Alabama Hospitals, Mobile, AL	12	10	316	—	—	—	—	—	—	—
□ USA CHILDREN'S AND WOMEN'S HOSPITAL, 1700 Center Street, Zip 36604–3391; tel. 334/415–1000; Stanley K. Hammack, Administrator (Nonreporting) **A**1 3 5 9 10 **S** University of South Alabama Hospitals, Mobile, AL	12	10	131	—	—	—	—	—	—	—

MONROEVILLE—Monroe County

✖ MONROE COUNTY HOSPITAL, 1901 South Alabama Avenue, Zip 36460, Mailing Address: P.O. Box 886, Zip 36461–0886; tel. 334/575–3111; Joe Zager, Chief Executive Officer (Nonreporting) **A**1 9 10 **S** Quorum Health Group/Quorum Health Resources, Inc., Brentwood, TN	13	10	59	—	—	—	—	—	—	—

MONTGOMERY—Montgomery County

✖ BAPTIST MEDICAL CENTER, 2105 East South Boulevard, Zip 36116–2498, Mailing Address: Box 11010, Zip 36111–0010; tel. 334/288–2100; Michael D. DeBoer, President and Chief Executive Officer **A**1 3 5 9 10 **F**2 3 4 7 8 10 11 12 13 14 15 16 17 18 19 21 22 23 24 25 26 27 28 29 30 31 32 33 34 35 37 38 39 40 41 42 43 44 45 49 51 52 55 56 58 61 62 65 67 71 72 73 74 **P**6 7 **S** Baptist Health, Montgomery, AL	23	10	329	19171	237	68466	2510	138850	49263	2745
✖ BAPTIST MEDICAL CENTER DOWNTOWN, (Formerly Columbia Regional Medical Center), 301 South Ripley Street, Zip 36104–4495; tel. 334/269–8000; Alfred E. Hargrave, Administrator (Nonreporting) **A**1 9 10 **S** Baptist Health, Montgomery, AL	33	10	250	—	—	—	—	—	—	—

Hospital, Address, Telephone, Administrator, Approval, Facility, and Physician Codes, Health Care System, Network	Classi-fication Codes		Utilization Data					Expense (thousands) of dollars		
	Control	Service	Staffed Beds	Admissions	Census	Outpatient Visits	Births	Total	Payroll	Personnel

★ American Hospital Association (AHA) membership
□ Joint Commission on Accreditation of Healthcare Organizations (JCAHO) accreditation
+ American Osteopathic Healthcare Association (AOHA) membership
○ American Osteopathic Association (AOA) accreditation
△ Commission on Accreditation of Rehabilitation Facilities (CARF) accreditation
Control codes 61, 63, 64, 71, 72 and 73 indicate hospitals listed by AOHA, but not registered by AHA. For definition of numerical codes, see page A4

Hospital	Control	Service	Staffed Beds	Admissions	Census	Outpatient Visits	Births	Total	Payroll	Personnel
⊠ BAPTIST MEDICAL CENTER EAST, 400 Taylor Road, Zip 36117–3512, Mailing Address: P.O. Box 241267, Zip 36124–1267; tel. 334/277–8330; John W. Melton, Administrator (Nonreporting) **A**1 9 10 **S** Baptist Health, Montgomery, AL	33	10	150	—	—	—	—	—	—	—
⊠ CENTRAL ALABAMA VETERAN AFFAIRS HEALTH CARE SYSTEM, (Includes Montgomery Division, 215 Perry Hill Road, tel. 334/272–4670; Veterans Affairs Health Care System–Tuskegee Division, 2400 Hospital Road, Tuskegee, Zip 36083–5001; tel. 334/727–0550), 215 Perry Hill Road, Zip 36109–3798; tel. 334/272–4670; Kenneth Rugle, Interim Director (Total facility includes 160 beds in nursing home–type unit) **A**1 5 **F**1 3 4 10 12 15 16 17 18 19 20 21 22 25 26 27 28 29 30 33 34 35 37 39 41 42 44 45 46 48 49 51 52 54 55 56 57 58 59 61 64 65 67 71 72 73 74 **S** Department of Veterans Affairs, Washington, DC	45	10	443	4417	441	—	0	120860	80418	1614
COLUMBIA REGIONAL MEDICAL CENTER See Baptist Medical Center Downtown										
□ HEALTHSOUTH REHABILITATION HOSPITAL OF MONTGOMERY, 4465 Narrow Lane Road, Zip 36116–2900; tel. 334/284–7700; Linda Wade, Administrator and Director of Operations **A**1 9 10 **F**5 12 14 15 16 24 25 26 27 28 30 34 39 41 45 48 49 65 66 67 73 **S** HEALTHSOUTH Corporation, Birmingham, AL	33	46	87	1410	78	6215	0	14127	7273	265
⊠ JACKSON HOSPITAL AND CLINIC, 1725 Pine Street, Zip 36106; tel. 334/293–8000; Donald M. Ball, President (Nonreporting) **A**1 2 9 10 **Web address:** www.jackson.org	23	10	379	—	—	—	—	—	—	—
★ LONG TERM CARE HOSPITAL AT JACKSON, 1235 Forest Avenue, 5 North, Zip 36106, Mailing Address: P.O. Box 11649, Zip 36111; tel. 334/264–1884; Barbara Estep, Administrator (Nonreporting) **A**10	23	49	30	—	—	—	—	—	—	—
MOULTON—Lawrence County										
⊠ LAWRENCE BAPTIST MEDICAL CENTER, 202 Hospital Street, Zip 35650–0039, Mailing Address: P.O. Box 39, Zip 35650–0039; tel. 256/974–2200; Cheryl Hays, Administrator (Nonreporting) **A**1 9 10 **S** Baptist Health System, Birmingham, AL	13	10	30	—	—	—	—	—	—	—
MOUNT VERNON—Mobile County										
□ SEARCY HOSPITAL, Mailing Address: P.O. Box 1001, Zip 36560–1001; tel. 334/829–9411; John T. Bartlett, Director (Nonreporting) **A**1 3 5 9 10	12	52	530	—	—	—	—	—	—	—
MUSCLE SHOALS—Colbert County										
⊠ MEDICAL CENTER SHOALS, 201 Avalon Avenue, Zip 35661–2805, Mailing Address: P.O. Box 3359, Zip 35662–3359; tel. 256/386–1600; Connie Hawthorne, Chief Executive Officer (Nonreporting) **A**1 9 10 **S** Coffee Health Group, Florence, AL	16	10	128	—	—	—	—	—	—	—
NORTHPORT—Tuscaloosa County										
NORTHPORT HOSPITAL–DCH See Northport Medical Center										
⊠ NORTHPORT MEDICAL CENTER, (Formerly Northport Hospital–DCH), 2700 Hospital Drive, Zip 35476–3380; tel. 205/333–4500; Charles L. Stewart, Administrator **A**1 9 10 **F**2 4 7 8 10 12 14 15 16 17 18 19 21 22 23 24 25 26 28 29 30 31 32 34 35 37 38 39 40 41 42 43 44 45 46 47 48 49 51 52 54 55 56 57 60 65 66 67 70 71 73 74 **P**7 8 **S** DCH Health System, Tuscaloosa, AL	16	10	156	5749	104	58864	882	43107	18189	590
ONEONTA—Blount County										
★ MEDICAL CENTER BLOUNT, (Formerly Blount Memorial Hospital), 150 Gilbreath, Zip 35121–2534, Mailing Address: P.O. Box 1000, Zip 35121–1000; tel. 205/625–3511; George McGowan, FACHE, Chief Executive Officer **A**9 10 **F**8 13 14 15 16 19 21 22 28 29 30 32 33 34 37 39 42 44 46 49 65 71 73 **S** Eastern Health System, Inc., Birmingham, AL	23	10	56	1876	23	34080	0	12952	5055	141
OPELIKA—Lee County										
⊠ EAST ALABAMA MEDICAL CENTER, 2000 Pepperell Parkway, Zip 36802–3201; tel. 334/749–3411; Terry W. Andrus, President (Total facility includes 28 beds in nursing home–type unit) **A**1 2 9 10 **F**1 2 3 4 7 8 10 11 12 14 15 16 17 18 19 21 22 24 26 27 28 29 30 31 32 33 34 35 37 40 41 42 43 44 45 52 53 54 55 56 57 58 59 60 61 63 64 65 66 67 71 73 74 **P**2 **Web address:** www.eamc.org	16	10	280	14436	197	78322	1510	85446	40831	1430
OPP—Covington County										
★ MIZELL MEMORIAL HOSPITAL, 702 Main Street, Zip 36467–1626, Mailing Address: P.O. Box 1010, Zip 36467–1010; tel. 334/493–3541; Allen Foster, Administrator **A**9 10 **F**7 8 11 12 15 16 17 19 21 28 31 32 33 35 40 44 49 65 66 70 71 73 74 **S** Baptist Health Care Corporation, Pensacola, FL	23	10	57	1734	21	20246	135	7328	4279	213
OZARK—Dale County										
□ DALE MEDICAL CENTER, 100 Hospital Avenue, Zip 36360–2080; tel. 334/774–2601; Robert F. Bigley, Administrator **A**1 9 10 **F**7 8 10 12 14 15 16 17 19 21 22 24 25 28 29 30 32 33 34 35 37 39 40 41 43 44 45 49 56 58 59 63 65 66 67 71 72 74 **P**3 5 7	15	10	85	2983	30	29731	307	17479	7440	301
PELHAM—Shelby County										
BRADFORD HEALTH SERVICES AT OAK MOUNTAIN, 2280 Highway 35, Zip 35124–6120; tel. 205/664–3460; William Weaver, Administrator (Nonreporting) **A**9 **S** Bradford Health Services, Birmingham, AL	33	52	84	—	—	—	—	—	—	—
PELL CITY—St. Clair County										
★ ST. CLAIR REGIONAL HOSPITAL, 2805 Hospital Drive, Zip 35125–1499; tel. 205/338–3301; Douglas H. Beverly, CHE, Chief Operating Officer (Nonreporting) **A**9 10 **S** Eastern Health System, Inc., Birmingham, AL	13	10	51	—	—	—	—	—	—	—
PHENIX CITY—Russell County										
⊠ PHENIX REGIONAL HOSPITAL, 1707 21st Avenue, Zip 36867–3753, Mailing Address: P.O. Box 190, Zip 36868–0190; tel. 334/291–8502; Lance B. Duke, FACHE, President and Chief Executive Officer **A**1 9 10 **F**2 3 7 8 10 12 15 16 17 18 19 21 22 24 26 28 29 30 31 32 34 35 37 38 40 41 42 44 45 46 47 48 49 51 52 54 55 56 60 63 64 65 67 70 71 72 73 74 **P**6 8 **S** Columbus Regional Health System, Columbus, GA	23	10	114	3723	45	38891	464	20656	8635	312

Hospital, Address, Telephone, Administrator, Approval, Facility, and Physician Codes, Health Care System, Network	Classi-fication Codes		Utilization Data					Expense (thousands) of dollars		
	Control	Service	Staffed Beds	Admissions	Census	Outpatient Visits	Births	Total	Payroll	Personnel

★ American Hospital Association (AHA) membership
□ Joint Commission on Accreditation of Healthcare Organizations (JCAHO) accreditation
+ American Osteopathic Healthcare Association (AOHA) membership
○ American Osteopathic Association (AOA) accreditation
△ Commission on Accreditation of Rehabilitation Facilities (CARF) accreditation
Control codes 61, 63, 64, 71, 72 and 73 indicate hospitals listed by AOHA, but not registered by AHA. For definition of numerical codes, see page A4

PRATTVILLE—Autauga County

| ✖ PRATTVILLE BAPTIST HOSPITAL, 124 South Memorial Drive, Zip 36067–3619, Mailing Address: P.O. Box 681630, Zip 36067–1638; tel. 334/365–0651; William E. Hines, Administrator **A**1 9 10 **F**4 6 7 8 10 12 13 14 15 16 17 19 21 22 23 24 25 26 27 28 29 30 31 34 35 37 41 42 43 44 45 46 49 51 53 54 55 56 57 58 59 60 61 65 66 67 70 71 72 73 74 **P**5 **S** Baptist Health, Montgomery, AL | 23 | 10 | 51 | 1383 | 13 | 27794 | 0 | 9763 | 4193 | — |

RED BAY—Franklin County

| RED BAY HOSPITAL, 211 Hospital Road, Zip 35582, Mailing Address: Box 490, Zip 35582; tel. 205/356–9532; Ralph J. Wilson, Administrator **A**9 10 **F**8 14 19 32 44 71 **P**5 | 13 | 10 | 33 | 1075 | 12 | 25126 | 0 | 5388 | 2665 | 124 |

ROANOKE—Randolph County

| ★ RANDOLPH COUNTY HOSPITAL, 59928 Highway 22, Zip 36274, Mailing Address: P.O. Box 670, Zip 36274–0670; tel. 334/863–4111; Moultrie D. Plowden, CHE, President **A**9 10 **F**2 15 19 22 34 35 37 40 44 49 59 65 67 71 73 **S** Baptist Health System, Birmingham, AL | 13 | 10 | 71 | 2326 | 18 | 12091 | 97 | 12132 | 4888 | 189 |

RUSSELLVILLE—Franklin County

| ✖ RUSSELLVILLE HOSPITAL, (Formerly Russellville Medical Center), 15155 Highway 43, Zip 35653, Mailing Address: P.O. Box 1089, Zip 35653–1089; tel. 256/332–1611; Christine R. Stewart, President and Chief Executive Officer **A**1 9 10 **F**7 8 10 11 12 14 15 16 19 21 22 24 28 29 30 32 33 34 35 37 39 40 41 42 44 49 65 66 68 71 73 74 **S** Coffee Health Group, Florence, AL | 15 | 10 | 100 | 3708 | 41 | 22516 | 216 | — | — | 327 |
| RUSSELLVILLE MEDICAL CENTER See Russellville Hospital | | | | | | | | | | |

SCOTTSBORO—Jackson County

| □ JACKSON COUNTY HOSPITAL, 380 Woods Cove Road, Zip 35768–2428, Mailing Address: P.O. Box 1050, Zip 35768–1050; tel. 256/259–4444; Ronald L. Sparkman, Administrator (Total facility includes 50 beds in nursing home–type unit) (Nonreporting) **A**1 9 10 | 13 | 10 | 142 | — | — | — | — | — | — | — |

SELMA—Dallas County

| ✖ SELMA BAPTIST HOSPITAL, (Formerly Columbia Four Rivers Medical Center), 1015 Medical Center Parkway, Zip 36701–6352; tel. 334/418–4100; John Anderson, Administrator **A**1 2 3 5 9 10 **F**7 8 10 12 15 16 17 19 20 22 28 30 37 40 41 42 44 45 49 52 57 60 71 73 **S** Baptist Health, Montgomery, AL | 23 | 10 | 192 | 4710 | 59 | 53717 | 565 | — | — | 333 |
| ✖ VAUGHAN REGIONAL MEDICAL CENTER, 1050 West Dallas Avenue, Zip 36701–6515, Mailing Address: P.O. Box 328, Zip 36702–0328; tel. 334/418–6000; Jerome H. Horn, President and Chief Executive Officer **A**1 3 5 9 10 **F**6 7 8 10 11 12 16 17 19 21 22 24 28 30 32 35 37 40 44 46 63 65 71 **P**3 | 23 | 10 | 112 | 4829 | 54 | — | 658 | 23711 | 9883 | 398 |

SHEFFIELD—Colbert County

| ✖ HELEN KELLER HOSPITAL, 1300 South Montgomery Avenue, Zip 35660–6334, Mailing Address: P.O. Box 610, Zip 35660–0610; tel. 256/386–4556; Ralph H. Clark, Jr., President **A**1 9 10 **F**2 3 7 8 10 11 12 15 16 17 19 21 22 24 27 28 29 30 34 35 37 39 40 41 42 44 46 49 52 57 58 59 60 63 65 66 71 73 74 **Web address:** www.helenkeller.com | 16 | 10 | 152 | 6451 | 86 | 54267 | 804 | 41641 | 17008 | 681 |

SYLACAUGA—Talladega County

| ✖ COOSA VALLEY BAPTIST MEDICAL CENTER, 315 West Hickory Street, Zip 35150–2996; tel. 256/249–5000; Steven M. Johnson, President (Total facility includes 75 beds in nursing home–type unit) (Nonreporting) **A**1 9 10 **S** Baptist Health System, Birmingham, AL | 21 | 10 | 176 | — | — | — | — | — | — | — |

TALLADEGA—Talladega County

| ✖ CITIZENS BAPTIST MEDICAL CENTER, 604 Stone Avenue, Zip 35160–2217, Mailing Address: P.O. Box 978, Zip 35161–0978; tel. 256/362–8111; Steven M. Johnson, President (Nonreporting) **A**1 9 10 **S** Baptist Health System, Birmingham, AL **Web address:** www.bhsala.com | 23 | 10 | 97 | — | — | — | — | — | — | — |

TALLASSEE—Elmore County

| ✖ COMMUNITY HOSPITAL, 805 Friendship Road, Zip 36078–1234, Mailing Address: P.O. Box 780700, Zip 36078–0700; tel. 334/283–6541; Jennie R. Rhinehart, Administrator and Chief Executive Officer (Nonreporting) **A**1 9 10 | 23 | 10 | 69 | — | — | — | — | — | — | — |

THOMASVILLE—Clarke County

| THOMASVILLE INFIRMARY, 1440 Highway 43 North, Zip 36784–3302; tel. 334/636–4431; Albert Ban, Jr., Administrator **A**9 10 **F**16 19 22 28 30 32 33 44 49 65 71 **P**5 **S** Infirmary Health System, Inc., Mobile, AL | 23 | 10 | 27 | 570 | 7 | 9927 | 0 | 3166 | 1222 | 68 |

TROY—Pike County

| ✖ EDGE REGIONAL MEDICAL CENTER, 1330 Highway 231 South, Zip 36081–1224; tel. 334/670–5000; David E. Loving, Chief Executive Officer (Nonreporting) **A**1 9 10 **S** Community Health Systems, Inc., Brentwood, TN | 33 | 10 | 87 | — | — | — | — | — | — | — |

TUSCALOOSA—Tuscaloosa County

| □ BRYCE HOSPITAL, 200 University Boulevard, Zip 35401–1294; tel. 205/759–0799; James F. Reddoch, Jr., Director (Total facility includes 354 beds in nursing home–type unit) (Nonreporting) **A**1 9 10 | 12 | 22 | 870 | — | — | — | — | — | — | — |
| ✖ DCH REGIONAL MEDICAL CENTER, 809 University Boulevard East, Zip 35401–9961; tel. 205/759–7111; William H. Cassels, Administrator **A**1 2 3 5 9 10 **F**2 4 7 8 10 11 12 17 18 19 21 22 23 24 25 28 30 32 34 35 37 38 40 41 42 43 44 45 46 47 48 49 52 54 55 56 57 60 64 65 66 67 70 71 73 74 **S** DCH Health System, Tuscaloosa, AL **Web address:** www.chhhealthcare.com | 23 | 10 | 485 | 23513 | 402 | 233317 | 1961 | 183629 | 82787 | 2499 |

Hospital, Address, Telephone, Administrator, Approval, Facility, and Physician Codes, Health Care System, Network	Classi-fication Codes		Utilization Data					Expense (thousands) of dollars		
★ American Hospital Association (AHA) membership □ Joint Commission on Accreditation of Healthcare Organizations (JCAHO) accreditation + American Osteopathic Healthcare Association (AOHA) membership ○ American Osteopathic Association (AOA) accreditation △ Commission on Accreditation of Rehabilitation Facilities (CARF) accreditation Control codes 61, 63, 64, 71, 72 and 73 indicate hospitals listed by AOHA, but not registered by AHA. For definition of numerical codes, see page A4	Control	Service	Staffed Beds	Admissions	Census	Outpatient Visits	Births	Total	Payroll	Personnel
⊠ VETERANS AFFAIRS MEDICAL CENTER, 3701 Loop Road, Zip 35404–5015; tel. 205/554–2000; W. Kenneth Ruyle, Director (Total facility includes 178 beds in nursing home–type unit) **A**1 3 **F**1 2 3 4 6 8 12 15 16 17 18 19 20 21 22 24 26 27 28 29 30 31 32 33 34 35 37 39 41 42 43 44 45 46 48 49 51 52 54 55 56 57 58 59 60 64 65 67 71 73 74 **P**6 **S** Department of Veterans Affairs, Washington, DC	45	22	352	1985	321	111359	0	—	35108	890
TUSKEGEE—Macon County VETERANS AFFAIRS HEALTH CARE SYSTEM–TUSKEGEE DIVISION See Central Alabama Veteran Affairs Health Care System, Montgomery										
UNION SPRINGS—Bullock County BULLOCK COUNTY HOSPITAL, 102 West Conecuh Avenue, Zip 36089–1303; tel. 334/738–2140; Jacques Jarry, Administrator **A**9 10 **F**15 16 17 19 21 22 32 44 51 71	33	10	30	951	8	10141	0	1571	—	76
VALLEY—Chambers County □ LANIER HEALTH SERVICES, (Formerly George H Lanier Memorial Hospital and Health Services), 4800 48th Street, Zip 36854–3666; tel. 334/756–3111; Robert J. Humphrey, Administrator (Total facility includes 93 beds in nursing home–type unit) (Nonreporting) **A**1 9 10 **Web address:** www.lanierhospital.com	23	10	175	—	—	—	—	—	—	—
WEDOWEE—Randolph County ★ WEDOWEE HOSPITAL, 209 North Main Street, Zip 36278–5138, Mailing Address: P.O. Box 307, Zip 36278–0307; tel. 256/357–2111; Moultrie D. Plowden, CHE, President (Nonreporting) **A**9 10 **S** Baptist Health System, Birmingham, AL	23	10	34	—	—	—	—	—	—	—
WETUMPKA—Elmore County ELMORE COMMUNITY HOSPITAL, 500 Hospital Drive, Zip 36092–1625, Mailing Address: P.O. Box 120, Zip 36092–0120; tel. 334/567–4311; Marshall L. Nero, Chief Executive Officer **A**9 10 **F**2 8 19 22 28 32 33 34 44 46 49 65 71 73	16	10	45	1029	15	18038	0	7059	3006	145
WINFIELD—Marion County ⊠ CARRAWAY NORTHWEST MEDICAL CENTER, Highway 78 West, Zip 35594, Mailing Address: P.O. Box 130, Zip 35594–0130; tel. 205/487–7000; Robert E. Henger, Administrator **A**1 9 10 **F**7 8 12 14 15 16 17 19 21 22 24 28 29 30 32 34 37 39 40 41 42 44 45 46 49 51 59 61 63 65 66 71 73 74 **P**1 5 **S** Carraway Methodist Health System, Birmingham, AL **Web address:** www.carraway.org	21	10	63	2804	30	63844	399	18278	7531	333

ALASKA

Resident population 614 (in thousands)
Resident population in metro areas 40.9%
Birth rate per 1,000 population 17
65 years and over 5.3%
Percent of persons without health insurance 13.5%

★ American Hospital Association (AHA) membership
□ Joint Commission on Accreditation of Healthcare Organizations (JCAHO) accreditation
+ American Osteopathic Healthcare Association (AOHA) membership
○ American Osteopathic Association (AOA) accreditation
△ Commission on Accreditation of Rehabilitation Facilities (CARF) accreditation
Control codes 61, 63, 64, 71, 72 and 73 indicate hospitals listed by AOHA, but not registered by AHA. For definition of numerical codes, see page A4

Hospital, Address, Telephone, Administrator, Approval, Facility, and Physician Codes, Health Care System, Network	Classification Codes		Utilization Data					Expense (thousands) of dollars		
	Control	Service	Staffed Beds	Admissions	Census	Outpatient Visits	Births	Total	Payroll	Personnel

ANCHORAGE—2nd Judicial Division

ⓧ ALASKA NATIVE MEDICAL CENTER, (Formerly U.S. Public Health Service Alaska Native Medical Center), 4315 Diplomacy Drive, Zip 99508; tel. 907/563–2662; Richard Mandsager, M.D., Administrator (Nonreporting) **A**1 10 **S** U. S. Public Health Service Indian Health Service, Rockville, MD — 47 10 140 — — — — — — —

□ ALASKA PSYCHIATRIC INSTITUTE, (Formerly Alaska Psychiatric Hospital), 2900 Providence Drive, Zip 99508–4677; tel. 907/269–7100; Randall P. Burns, Director and Chief Executive Officer (Nonreporting) **A**1 10 — 12 22 79 — — — — — — —

ⓧ ALASKA REGIONAL HOSPITAL, 2801 Debarr Road, Zip 99508, Mailing Address: P.O. Box 143889, Zip 99514–3889; tel. 907/276–1131; Ernie Meier, President and Chief Executive Officer (Nonreporting) **A**1 9 10 **S** Columbia/HCA Healthcare Corporation, Nashville, TN — 33 10 189 — — — — — — —

ⓧ CHARTER NORTH STAR BEHAVIORAL HEALTH SYSTEM, 1650 South Bragaw, Zip 99508–3467; tel. 907/258–7575; Kathleen Cronen, Chief Executive Officer (Nonreporting) **A**1 **S** Magellan Health Services, Atlanta, GA — 33 22 34 — — — — — — —

ⓧ CHARTER NORTH STAR BEHAVIORAL HEALTH SYSTEM, 2530 DeBarr Road, Zip 99508; tel. 907/258–7575; Kathleen Cronen, Chief Executive Officer (Nonreporting) **A**1 10 **S** Magellan Health Services, Atlanta, GA — 33 22 80 — — — — — — —

ⓧ PROVIDENCE ALASKA MEDICAL CENTER, 3200 Providence Drive, Zip 99508, Mailing Address: P.O. Box 196604, Zip 99519–6604; tel. 907/562–2211; Gene L. O'Hara, Administrator **A**1 3 5 9 10 **F**3 4 6 7 8 10 11 12 15 16 17 19 21 22 23 28 30 32 34 35 37 38 39 40 42 43 44 45 46 47 48 49 50 52 53 54 56 57 58 59 60 63 64 65 67 71 73 **P**4 7 8 **S** Sisters of Providence Health System, Seattle, WA — 21 10 341 14563 503 352169 2651 220683 97785 2180

U.S. PUBLIC HEALTH SERVICE ALASKA NATIVE MEDICAL CENTER See Alaska Native Medical Center

BARROW—4th Judicial Division

ⓧ SAMUEL SIMMONDS MEMORIAL HOSPITAL, (Formerly U. S. Public Health Service Alaska Native Hospital), 1296 Agvik Street, Zip 99723, Mailing Address: P.O. Box 29, Zip 99723; tel. 907/852–4611; Michael S. Herring, Administrator (Nonreporting) **A**1 10 **S** U. S. Public Health Service Indian Health Service, Rockville, MD — 47 10 15 — — — — — — —

BETHEL—1st Judicial Division

ⓧ YUKON–KUSKOKWIM DELTA REGIONAL HOSPITAL, Mailing Address: P.O. Box 528, Zip 99559–3000; tel. 907/543–6300; Edwin L. Hansen, Vice President (Nonreporting) **A**1 10 **S** U. S. Public Health Service Indian Health Service, Rockville, MD — 47 10 50 — — — — — — —

CORDOVA—2nd Judicial Division

★ CORDOVA COMMUNITY MEDICAL CENTER, 602 Chase Avenue, Zip 99574, Mailing Address: Box 160, Zip 99574; tel. 907/424–8000; Peter Birkholz, Administrator and Chief Executive Officer (Total facility includes 13 beds in nursing home–type unit) (Nonreporting) **A**10 — 14 10 23 — — — — — — —

DILLINGHAM—1st Judicial Division

ⓧ KANAKANAK HOSPITAL, Mailing Address: P.O. Box 130, Zip 99576; tel. 907/842–5201; Darrel C. Richardson, Chief Operating Officer (Nonreporting) **A**1 10 **S** U. S. Public Health Service Indian Health Service, Rockville, MD — 47 10 16 — — — — — — —

ELMENDORF AFB—2nd Judicial Division

ⓧ U. S. AIR FORCE REGIONAL HOSPITAL, 24800 Hospital Drive, Zip 99506–3700; tel. 907/552–4033; Colonel Larry J. Sutterer, MSC, USAF, Administrator **A**1 **F**2 3 4 6 7 8 10 11 12 13 16 17 18 19 20 21 22 23 28 29 30 32 33 34 35 37 38 39 40 41 42 43 44 46 47 48 49 52 53 54 55 56 57 58 60 61 64 65 70 71 73 74 **S** Department of the Air Force, Bowling AFB, DC — 41 10 35 2166 17 239876 696 43739 — 866

FAIRBANKS—1st Judicial Division

ⓧ FAIRBANKS MEMORIAL HOSPITAL, 1650 Cowles Street, Zip 99701; tel. 907/452–8181; Michael K. Powers, Administrator (Total facility includes 90 beds in nursing home–type unit) **A**1 2 9 10 **F**3 4 7 8 9 12 14 15 16 17 19 20 21 22 23 26 28 30 32 34 35 37 38 39 40 41 42 44 45 46 49 52 56 59 63 64 65 66 67 70 71 73 74 **S** Lutheran Health Systems, Fargo, ND — 23 10 198 5929 143 215612 969 73093 29740 1037

FORT WAINWRIGHT—1st Judicial Division

ⓧ BASSETT ARMY COMMUNITY HOSPITAL, 1060 Gaffney Road, Box 7400, Zip 99703–7400; tel. 907/353–5108; Lieutenant Colonel Gordon Lewis, Deputy Commander for Administration (Nonreporting) **A**1 **S** Department of the Army, Office of the Surgeon General, Falls Church, VA — 42 10 43 — — — — — — —

HOMER—3rd Judicial Division

★ SOUTH PENINSULA HOSPITAL, 4300 Bartlett Street, Zip 99603; tel. 907/235–8101; Charles C. Franz, Chief Executive Officer (Total facility includes 20 beds in nursing home–type unit) **A**10 **F**7 8 11 12 15 16 19 21 22 28 32 37 40 44 49 64 65 71
Web address: www.sphosp.com — 16 10 40 885 29 13891 140 13151 6496 200

Hospital, Address, Telephone, Administrator, Approval, Facility, and Physician Codes, Health Care System, Network	Classi-fication Codes		Utilization Data						Expense (thousands) of dollars		
	Control	Service	Staffed Beds	Admissions	Census	Outpatient Visits	Births	Total	Payroll	Personnel

Classification Codes key:

★ American Hospital Association (AHA) membership
□ Joint Commission on Accreditation of Healthcare Organizations (JCAHO) accreditation
+ American Osteopathic Healthcare Association (AOHA) membership
○ American Osteopathic Association (AOA) accreditation
△ Commission on Accreditation of Rehabilitation Facilities (CARF) accreditation
Control codes 61, 63, 64, 71, 72 and 73 indicate hospitals listed by AOHA, but not registered by AHA. For definition of numerical codes, see page A4

Hospital	Control	Service	Staffed Beds	Admissions	Census	Outpatient Visits	Births	Total	Payroll	Personnel
JUNEAU—3rd Judicial Division										
⊞ BARTLETT REGIONAL HOSPITAL, 3260 Hospital Drive, Zip 99801; tel. 907/586–2611; Robert F. Valliant, Administrator (Nonreporting) **A**1 10 **S** Quorum Health Group/Quorum Health Resources, Inc., Brentwood, TN Web address: www.bartletthospital.org	15	10	64	—	—	—	—	—	—	—
KETCHIKAN—3rd Judicial Division										
⊞ KETCHIKAN GENERAL HOSPITAL, 3100 Tongass Avenue, Zip 99901–5746; tel. 907/225–5171; Edward F. Mahn, Chief Executive Officer (Total facility includes 28 beds in nursing home–type unit) **A**1 2 9 10 **F**8 14 15 16 19 22 29 32 40 41 42 44 49 53 58 64 71 73 **S** PeaceHealth, Bellevue, WA	23	10	64	2262	37	79241	238	26542	13760	322
KODIAK—2nd Judicial Division										
★ PROVIDENCE KODIAK ISLAND MEDICAL CENTER, 1915 East Rezanof Drive, Zip 99615; tel. 907/486–3281; Phillip E. Cline, Administrator (Total facility includes 19 beds in nursing home–type unit) **A**9 10 **F**7 8 15 19 22 28 30 31 32 37 39 40 41 44 48 52 54 55 56 58 64 65 71 73 **S** Sisters of Providence Health System, Seattle, WA	21	10	44	868	21	11116	239	12873	6413	—
KOTZEBUE—2nd Judicial Division										
⊞ MANIILAQ HEALTH CENTER, Zip 99752–0043; tel. 907/442–3321; Clinton Gray, Jr., Administrator (Nonreporting) **A**1 10 **S** U. S. Public Health Service Indian Health Service, Rockville, MD	47	10	17	—	—	—	—	—	—	—
NOME—2nd Judicial Division										
⊞ NORTON SOUND REGIONAL HOSPITAL, Bering Straits, Zip 99762, Mailing Address: P.O. Box 966, Zip 99762–0966; tel. 907/443–3311; Charles Fagerstrom, Vice President (Total facility includes 15 beds in nursing home–type unit) (Nonreporting) **A**1 10 **S** U. S. Public Health Service Indian Health Service, Rockville, MD Web address: www.nshcorp.org	23	10	34	—	—	—	—	—	—	—
PALMER—2nd Judicial Division										
⊞ VALLEY HOSPITAL, 515 East Dahlia Street, Zip 99645, Mailing Address: P.O. Box 1687, Zip 99645; tel. 907/352–2860; Dave Pfeifer, Chief Executive Officer **A**1 10 **F**8 12 14 15 16 17 19 21 22 23 24 25 27 28 29 30 32 33 34 35 37 39 40 41 42 44 45 46 49 51 64 65 67 70 71 72 73	23	10	36	2481	22	82123	369	35107	15887	375
PETERSBURG—3rd Judicial Division										
PETERSBURG MEDICAL CENTER, 103 Fram Street, Zip 99833, Mailing Address: Box 589, Zip 99833–0589; tel. 907/772–4291; John F. Bringhurst, Administrator (Total facility includes 14 beds in nursing home–type unit) **A**10 **F**2 7 8 11 14 15 16 22 28 30 31 32 34 40 44 52 56 61 64 71 **P**6	14	10	25	148	14	13913	23	4036	2284	58
SEWARD—2nd Judicial Division										
★ PROVIDENCE SEWARD MEDICAL CENTER, 417 First Avenue, Zip 99664, Mailing Address: P.O. Box 365, Zip 99664–0365; tel. 907/224–5205; J. C. Rathje, Administrator (Nonreporting) **A**9 10 **S** Sisters of Providence Health System, Seattle, WA	14	10	20	—	—	—	—	—	—	—
SITKA—3rd Judicial Division										
⊞ SEARHC MT. EDGECUMBE HOSPITAL, 222 Tongass Drive, Zip 99835–9416; tel. 907/966–2411; Frank Sutton, Vice President Hospital Services **A**1 10 **F**7 8 12 15 16 19 20 22 24 27 28 34 39 40 44 52 53 54 56 57 58 65 67 68 71 74 **S** U. S. Public Health Service Indian Health Service, Rockville, MD	23	10	60	1590	24	40719	67	—	—	280
★ SITKA COMMUNITY HOSPITAL, 209 Moller Avenue, Zip 99835–7145; tel. 907/747–3241; Grant Asay, Chief Executive Officer (Total facility includes 5 beds in nursing home–type unit) (Nonreporting) **A**10	15	10	22	—	—	—	—	—	—	—
SOLDOTNA—3rd Judicial Division										
⊞ CENTRAL PENINSULA GENERAL HOSPITAL, 250 Hospital Place, Zip 99669; tel. 907/262–4404; Roy C. Vinson, Interim Chief Executive Officer **A**1 9 10 **F**7 8 12 14 15 16 17 19 22 26 28 31 37 40 41 42 44 46 49 56 65 71 73 **P**5 **S** Quorum Health Group/Quorum Health Resources, Inc., Brentwood, TN	23	10	43	2262	18	35993	399	21923	10069	—
VALDEZ—3rd Judicial Division										
★ VALDEZ COMMUNITY HOSPITAL, 911 Meals Avenue, Zip 99686–0550, Mailing Address: P.O. Box 550, Zip 99686–0550; tel. 907/835–2249; James R. Culley, Administrator **A**9 10 **F**3 7 8 14 15 18 22 28 32 40 44 58 64 65 67 71 **P**4 7	14	10	15	131	4	4902	36	2882	1680	37
WRANGELL—3rd Judicial Division										
★ WRANGELL MEDICAL CENTER, First Avenue & Bennett Street, Zip 99929, Mailing Address: P.O. Box 1081, Zip 99929; tel. 907/874–7000; Brian D. Gilbert, Chief Executive Officer (Total facility includes 14 beds in nursing home–type unit) **A**10 **F**14 22 28 32 34 44 51 64 65 71 **P**6	14	10	22	167	14	14547	16	4592	2208	49

ARIZONA

Resident population 4,669 (in thousands)
Resident population in metro areas 83.1%
Birth rate per 1,000 population 17.2
65 years and over 13.2%
Percent of persons without health insurance 24.1%

Hospital, Address, Telephone, Administrator, Approval, Facility, and Physician Codes, Health Care System, Network	Classi-fication Codes		Utilization Data					Expense (thousands) of dollars		
★ American Hospital Association (AHA) membership □ Joint Commission on Accreditation of Healthcare Organizations (JCAHO) accreditation + American Osteopathic Healthcare Association (AOHA) membership ○ American Osteopathic Association (AOA) accreditation △ Commission on Accreditation of Rehabilitation Facilities (CARF) accreditation Control codes 61, 63, 64, 71, 72 and 73 indicate hospitals listed by AOHA, but not registered by AHA. For definition of numerical codes, see page A4	Control	Service	Staffed Beds	Admissions	Census	Outpatient Visits	Births	Total	Payroll	Personnel

BENSON—Cochise County
□ BENSON HOSPITAL, 450 South Ocotillo Street, Zip 85602, Mailing Address: P.O. Box 2290, Zip 85602; tel. 520/586–2261; Ronald A. McKinnon, Administrator **A**1 9 10 **F**8 14 15 16 22 28 34 44 49 64 71
Web address: www.bensonhospital.theriver.com
— Row: 16 10 22 399 7 8789 0 3789 1967 94

BISBEE—Cochise County
□ COPPER QUEEN COMMUNITY HOSPITAL, 101 Cole Avenue, Zip 85603–1399; tel. 520/432–5383; Marty Schaller, Interim Chief Executive Officer (Total facility includes 21 beds in nursing home–type unit) (Nonreporting) **A**1 9 10
— Row: 23 10 49 — — — — — — —

BULLHEAD CITY—Mohave County
★ MOHAVE VALLEY HOSPITAL AND MEDICAL CENTER, 1225 East Hancock Road, Zip 86442–5941; tel. 520/758–3931; John L. Hoopes, Administrator (Nonreporting) **A**9 10
— Row: 33 10 12 — — — — — — —

⊞ WESTERN ARIZONA REGIONAL MEDICAL CENTER, 2735 Silver Creek Road, Zip 86442–8303; tel. 520/763–2273; James Sato, Senior Vice President and Chief Executive Officer (Total facility includes 120 beds in nursing home–type unit) **A**1 9 10 **F**3 7 8 10 11 12 15 16 17 19 21 22 23 28 30 32 33 35 39 40 41 44 49 58 63 64 65 67 71 **S** Baptist Hospitals and Health Systems, Inc., Phoenix, AZ
— Row: 23 10 203 3500 120 39913 431 30142 13417 515

CASA GRANDE—Pinal County
⊞ CASA GRANDE REGIONAL MEDICAL CENTER, 1800 East Florence Boulevard, Zip 85222–5399; tel. 520/426–6300; J. Marty Dernier, President and Chief Executive Officer (Total facility includes 128 beds in nursing home–type unit) **A**1 9 10 **F**7 8 10 12 19 22 24 28 35 37 40 44 49 64 65 71 73 **P**8 **S** Quorum Health Group/Quorum Health Resources, Inc., Brentwood, TN
— Row: 23 10 244 6200 173 51054 845 42991 17227 369

CHANDLER—Maricopa County
⊞ CHANDLER REGIONAL HOSPITAL, 475 South Dobson Road, Zip 85224–4230; tel. 602/963–4561; Larry D. Shoemaker, M.D., Executive Vice President and Chief Operating Officer (Nonreporting) **A**1 9 10
Web address: www.evrhs.org
— Row: 23 10 120 — — — — — — —

□ CHARTER BEHAVIORAL HEALTH SYSTEM–EAST VALLEY, 2190 North Grace Boulevard, Zip 85224–7903; tel. 602/899–8989; Sal A. Edwards, Chief Executive Officer (Nonreporting) **A**1 9 10 **S** Magellan Health Services, Atlanta, GA
— Row: 33 22 80 — — — — — — —

CHINLE—Apache County
⊞ CHINLE COMPREHENSIVE HEALTH CARE FACILITY, Highway 191, Zip 86503, Mailing Address: P.O. Drawer PH, Zip 86503; tel. 520/674–7011; Ronald Tso, Chief Executive Officer **A**1 10 **F**1 3 7 12 13 14 15 16 17 20 22 25 27 30 34 37 39 40 44 46 49 54 56 58 61 65 68 71 74 **P**6 **S** U. S. Public Health Service Indian Health Service, Rockville, MD
— Row: 47 10 60 2954 34 144213 621 25025 13791 360

CLAYPOOL—Gila County
⊞ COBRE VALLEY COMMUNITY HOSPITAL, One Hospital Drive, Zip 85532, Mailing Address: P.O. Box 3261, Zip 85532–3261; tel. 520/425–3261; Charles E. Bill, CHE, Chief Executive Officer **A**1 9 10 **F**7 8 12 14 15 16 17 19 21 22 26 27 28 30 31 34 35 37 39 40 42 44 46 49 65 66 67 68 71 73 74 **S** Brim Healthcare, Inc., Brentwood, TN
— Row: 23 10 41 1900 40 — 386 17677 6206 183

COTTONWOOD—Yavapai County
⊞ VERDE VALLEY MEDICAL CENTER, (Formerly Marcus J. Lawrence Medical Center), 269 South Candy Lane, Zip 86326; tel. 520/634–2251; Craig A. Owens, President and Chief Operating Officer **A**1 9 10 **F**7 8 12 14 15 16 17 19 21 22 23 28 29 30 32 33 34 35 37 39 40 41 42 44 45 46 49 51 60 63 65 67 71 73 **P**1 4 5 7
— Row: 23 10 75 3903 36 53859 505 30749 12325 381

DAVIS–MONTHAN AFB—Pima County
★ U. S. AIR FORCE HOSPITAL, 4175 South Alamo Avenue, Zip 85707–4405; tel. 520/228–2930; Lieutenant Colonel Nancy A. Waite, Administrator and Deputy Commander (Nonreporting) **S** Department of the Air Force, Bowling AFB, DC
— Row: 41 10 20 — — — — — — —

DOUGLAS—Cochise County
□ SOUTHEAST ARIZONA MEDICAL CENTER, Route 1, Box 30, Zip 85607; tel. 520/364–7931; Thomas L. Haywood, Chief Executive Officer (Total facility includes 43 beds in nursing home–type unit) (Nonreporting) **A**1 9 10
— Row: 23 10 75 — — — — — — —

FLAGSTAFF—Coconino County
ASPEN HILL BEHAVIORAL HEALTH SYSTEM See Flagstaff Medical Center
⊞ △ FLAGSTAFF MEDICAL CENTER, (Includes Aspen Hill Behavioral Health System, 305 West Forest Avenue, Zip 86001–1464; tel. 520/773–1060; Thor Kolle, Chief Executive Officer), 1200 North Beaver Street, Zip 86001–3198; tel. 520/779–3366 (Nonreporting) **A**1 7 9 10
— Row: 23 10 137 — — — — — — —

FLORENCE—Pinal County
⊞ CENTRAL ARIZONA MEDICAL CENTER, Adamsville Road, Zip 85232, Mailing Address: P.O. Box 2080, Zip 85232–2080; tel. 520/868–2003; Carmen G. Perea, R.N., Interim Administrator (Total facility includes 27 beds in nursing home–type unit) (Nonreporting) **A**1 9 10 **S** Quorum Health Group/Quorum Health Resources, Inc., Brentwood, TN
— Row: 23 10 77 — — — — — — —

Hospital, Address, Telephone, Administrator, Approval, Facility, and Physician Codes, Health Care System, Network	Classi-fication Codes		Utilization Data					Expense (thousands) of dollars		
★ American Hospital Association (AHA) membership □ Joint Commission on Accreditation of Healthcare Organizations (JCAHO) accreditation + American Osteopathic Healthcare Association (AOHA) membership ○ American Osteopathic Association (AOA) accreditation △ Commission on Accreditation of Rehabilitation Facilities (CARF) accreditation Control codes 61, 63, 64, 71, 72 and 73 indicate hospitals listed by AOHA, but not registered by AHA. For definition of numerical codes, see page A4	Control	Service	Staffed Beds	Admissions	Census	Outpatient Visits	Births	Total	Payroll	Personnel

FORT DEFIANCE—Apache County

✠ FORT DEFIANCE INDIAN HEALTH SERVICE HOSPITAL, Mailing Address: P.O. Box 649, Zip 86504–0649; tel. 520/729–5741; Franklin Freeland, Ed.D., Chief Executive Officer **A**1 10 **F**1 3 7 12 13 14 15 20 24 30 40 44 58 65 71 72 **S** U. S. Public Health Service Indian Health Service, Rockville, MD	47	10	49	1860	16	—	0	16137	9914	—

GANADO—Apache County

□ SAGE MEMORIAL HOSPITAL, Highway 264, Zip 86505, Mailing Address: P.O. Box 457, Zip 86505–0457; tel. 520/755–3411; Elizabeth Johnson, Chief Executive Officer **A**1 9 10 **F**7 12 16 17 20 22 24 25 27 28 30 39 40 46 49 51 65 68 71 **P**6	23	10	20	663	6	56509	70	12608	6314	239

GLENDALE—Maricopa County

✠ ARROWHEAD COMMUNITY HOSPITAL AND MEDICAL CENTER, 18701 North 67th Avenue, Zip 85308–5722; tel. 602/561–1000; Richard S. Alley, Executive Vice President and Chief Executive Officer **A**1 9 10 **F**1 4 7 8 10 11 12 14 15 17 19 22 28 29 30 32 33 34 35 37 39 40 41 42 43 44 49 62 64 65 67 71 73 **P**8 **S** Baptist Hospitals and Health Systems, Inc., Phoenix, AZ **Web address:** www.baptisthealth.com	23	10	104	6266	53	57079	1822	47849	16325	533
□ CHARTER BEHAVIORAL HEALTH SYSTEM–GLENDALE, 6015 West Peoria Avenue, Zip 85302–1201; tel. 602/878–7878; Marsha Olender, Chief Executive Officer (Nonreporting) **A**1 9 10 **S** Magellan Health Services, Atlanta, GA	33	22	90	—	—	—	—	—	—	—
□ HEALTHSOUTH VALLEY OF THE SUN REHABILITATION HOSPITAL, 13460 North 67th Avenue, Zip 85304–1042; tel. 602/878–8800 (Total facility includes 18 beds in nursing home–type unit) (Nonreporting) **A**1 10 **S** HEALTHSOUTH Corporation, Birmingham, AL	33	46	42	—	—	—	—	—	—	—
✠ THUNDERBIRD SAMARITAN MEDICAL CENTER, (Includes Samaritan Behavioral Health Center–Thunderbird Samaritan Campus), 5555 West Thunderbird Road, Zip 85306–4696; tel. 602/588–5555; Robert H. Curry, Senior Vice President and Chief Executive Officer **A**1 9 10 **F**1 2 3 4 7 8 10 12 14 15 16 17 18 19 21 22 23 25 26 27 28 30 31 32 33 34 35 39 40 41 42 43 44 46 49 50 51 52 53 54 55 56 57 58 59 60 61 63 65 67 68 71 72 73 74 **P**3 5 7 **S** Samaritan Health System, Phoenix, AZ	23	10	266	17573	175	94047	3814	91178	40926	1239
✠ U. S. AIR FORCE HOSPITAL LUKE, Luke AFB, 7219 Litchfield Road, Zip 85309–1525; tel. 602/856–7501; Colonel Talbot N. Vivian, MSC, USAF, Administrator **A**1 **F**3 4 5 7 8 10 12 13 14 15 16 19 20 21 22 23 24 25 26 28 29 30 31 32 33 34 35 37 39 40 41 42 44 46 49 50 51 53 54 55 56 57 58 59 60 61 63 65 66 70 71 72 73 74 **P**1 3 5 7 8 **S** Department of the Air Force, Bowling AFB, DC	41	10	38	1812	11	190503	494	—	—	—

KEAMS CANYON—Navajo County

✠ U. S. PUBLIC HEALTH SERVICES INDIAN HOSPITAL, Mailing Address: P.O. Box 98, Zip 86034–0098; tel. 520/738–2211; Taylor Satala, Service Unit Director (Nonreporting) **A**1 10 **S** U. S. Public Health Service Indian Health Service, Rockville, MD	47	10	17	—	—	—	—	—	—	—

KINGMAN—Mohave County

✠ KINGMAN REGIONAL MEDICAL CENTER, 3269 Stockton Hill Road, Zip 86401–3691; tel. 520/757–2101; Brian Turney, Chief Executive Officer (Total facility includes 14 beds in nursing home–type unit) **A**1 9 10 **F**4 7 8 10 12 14 19 21 22 23 29 32 34 35 37 39 40 41 42 44 45 46 49 51 60 63 64 65 67 70 71 73 **P**2 5 8 **Web address:** www.azkrmc.com	23	10	124	6672	81	57817	555	33107	15051	539

LAKE HAVASU CITY—Mohave County

✠ HAVASU REGIONAL MEDICAL CENTER, 101 Civic Center Lane, Zip 86403–5683; tel. 520/855–8185; Kevin P. Poorten, Chief Executive Officer (Total facility includes 20 beds in nursing home–type unit) (Nonreporting) **A**1 9 10 **S** Province Healthcare Corporation, Brentwood, TN	23	10	118	—	—	—	—	—	—	—

MESA—Maricopa County

□ CHARTER BEHAVIORAL HEALTH SYSTEM OF ARIZONA/DESERT VISTA, (Formerly Desert Vista Behavioral Health Services), 570 West Brown Road, Zip 85201–3227; tel. 602/962–3900; Kimbrough Hall, Chief Executive Officer (Total facility includes 19 beds in nursing home–type unit) (Nonreporting) **A**1 9 10 **S** Magellan Health Services, Atlanta, GA	33	22	119	—	—	—	—	—	—	—
✠ DESERT SAMARITAN MEDICAL CENTER, (Includes Samaritan Behavioral Health Center–Desert Samaritan Medical Center, 2225 West Southern Avenue, Zip 85202; tel. 602/464–4000), 1400 South Dobson Road, Zip 85202–9879; tel. 602/835–3000; Bruce E. Pearson, Senior Vice President and Chief Executive Officer (Total facility includes 166 beds in nursing home–type unit) **A**1 9 10 **F**3 4 7 8 10 11 12 14 15 16 18 19 21 22 27 28 29 30 31 34 35 37 39 40 41 42 43 44 46 47 49 50 52 53 54 55 56 58 59 60 61 63 64 65 66 67 68 70 71 72 73 74 **P**5 **S** Samaritan Health System, Phoenix, AZ **Web address:** www.samariran.edu DESERT VISTA BEHAVIORAL HEALTH SERVICES See Charter Behavioral Health System of Arizona/Desert Vista	23	10	536	26652	413	94602	6645	169871	63106	2099
✠ ○ MESA GENERAL HOSPITAL MEDICAL CENTER, 515 North Mesa Drive, Zip 85201–5989; tel. 602/969–9111; Patrick T. Walz, Chief Executive Officer (Total facility includes 13 beds in nursing home–type unit) **A**1 9 10 11 12 13 **F**1 3 4 7 8 10 12 19 21 22 25 26 28 30 31 32 34 35 37 38 39 40 41 42 43 44 45 46 48 49 50 53 54 55 56 57 58 59 63 64 65 71 73 74 **P**5 7 8 **S** TENET Healthcare Corporation, Santa Barbara, CA	33	10	143	5315	59	41870	909	34227	14300	357

Hospital, Address, Telephone, Administrator, Approval, Facility, and Physician Codes, Health Care System, Network	Classi-fication Codes		Utilization Data					Expense (thousands) of dollars		
	Control	Service	Staffed Beds	Admissions	Census	Outpatient Visits	Births	Total	Payroll	Personnel

★ American Hospital Association (AHA) membership
□ Joint Commission on Accreditation of Healthcare Organizations (JCAHO) accreditation
+ American Osteopathic Healthcare Association (AOHA) membership
○ American Osteopathic Association (AOA) accreditation
△ Commission on Accreditation of Rehabilitation Facilities (CARF) accreditation
Control codes 61, 63, 64, 71, 72 and 73 indicate hospitals listed by AOHA, but not registered by AHA. For definition of numerical codes, see page A4

Hospital	Control	Service	Staffed Beds	Admissions	Census	Outpatient Visits	Births	Total	Payroll	Personnel
✚ △ MESA LUTHERAN HOSPITAL, 525 West Brown Road, Zip 85201–3299; tel. 602/834–1211; Robert A. Rundio, Executive Director of Hospital Operations (Total facility includes 60 beds in nursing home–type unit) A1 2 7 9 10 F4 7 8 10 12 13 14 15 16 17 18 19 20 21 22 23 25 26 27 28 29 30 32 33 34 35 36 37 39 40 41 42 43 44 45 46 48 49 51 52 57 58 59 60 64 65 67 70 71 72 73 74 P1 3 5 S Lutheran Health Systems, Fargo, ND	23	10	272	12793	173	—	2325	100090	40535	1338
✚ VALLEY LUTHERAN HOSPITAL, 6644 Baywood Avenue, Zip 85206–1797; tel. 602/981–2000; Robert A. Rundio, Executive Director of Hospital Operations A1 9 10 F4 7 8 10 12 13 14 15 16 17 19 20 21 22 23 25 26 27 28 29 30 32 33 34 35 36 37 39 40 41 42 43 44 45 46 49 51 57 58 59 60 65 67 70 71 72 73 74 P1 3 5 S Lutheran Health Systems, Fargo, ND	23	10	232	12336	145	92970	971	86834	36226	862
NOGALES—Santa Cruz County										
✚ CARONDELET HOLY CROSS HOSPITAL, 1171 West Target Range Road, Zip 85621–2496; tel. 520/287–2771; Carol Field, Senior Corporate Director and Administrator (Total facility includes 49 beds in nursing home–type unit) (Nonreporting) A1 9 10 S Carondelet Health System, Saint Louis, MO	21	10	80							
PAGE—Coconino County										
✚ PAGE HOSPITAL, 501 North Navajo Drive, Zip 86040, Mailing Address: P.O. Box 1447, Zip 86040–1447; tel. 520/645–2424; Richard Polheber, Chief Executive Officer A1 9 10 F1 7 8 12 14 15 16 19 22 28 30 31 32 34 35 40 41 42 44 46 48 49 65 71 73 P3 5 7 S Samaritan Health System, Phoenix, AZ	23	10	25	555	4	11331	203	6902	3137	78
PARKER—La Paz County										
★ ○ LA PAZ REGIONAL HOSPITAL, 1200 Mohave Road, Zip 85344–6349; tel. 520/669–9201; William G. Coe, Executive Vice President and Chief Executive Officer (Nonreporting) A9 10 11 S Baptist Hospitals and Health Systems, Inc., Phoenix, AZ	23	10	39	—	—	—	—	—	—	—
✚ U. S. PUBLIC HEALTH SERVICE INDIAN HOSPITAL, Mailing Address: Route 1, Box 12, Zip 85344; tel. 520/669–2137; Gary Davis, Service Unit Director (Nonreporting) A1 10 S U. S. Public Health Service Indian Health Service, Rockville, MD	47	10	18							
PAYSON—Gila County										
✚ PAYSON REGIONAL MEDICAL CENTER, 807 South Ponderosa Street, Zip 85541–5599; tel. 520/474–3222; Russell V. Judd, Chief Executive Officer (Nonreporting) A1 9 10 S Community Health Systems, Inc., Brentwood, TN	33	10	34	—	—	—	—	—	—	—
PHOENIX—Maricopa County										
□ ARIZONA STATE HOSPITAL, 2500 East Van Buren Street, Zip 85008–6079; tel. 602/244–1331; Jack B. Silver, M.P.H., Chief Executive Officer (Nonreporting) A1	12	22	372							
✚ CARL T. HAYDEN VETERANS AFFAIRS MEDICAL CENTER, 650 East Indian School Road, Zip 85012–1892; tel. 602/277–5551; John R. Fears, Director (Total facility includes 104 beds in nursing home–type unit) A1 2 3 5 F1 2 3 4 8 10 11 12 14 16 17 18 19 20 21 22 23 24 25 26 27 28 29 30 31 32 33 34 35 37 39 41 42 43 44 45 46 49 50 51 52 54 56 57 58 60 63 64 65 67 68 69 71 72 73 74 P6 S Department of Veterans Affairs, Washington, DC Web address: www.va.gov	45	10	331	9602	223	352832	0	138643	62169	1862
COLUMBIA MEDICAL CENTER See Phoenix Regional Medical Center										
✚ ○ COMMUNITY HOSPITAL MEDICAL CENTER, 6501 North 19th Avenue, Zip 85015–1690; tel. 602/249–3434; Patrick T. Walz, Chief Executive Officer (Nonreporting) A1 10 11 13 S TENET Healthcare Corporation, Santa Barbara, CA Web address: www.tenethealth.com/communityhospital	33	10	59	—	—	—	—	—	—	—
✚ △ GOOD SAMARITAN REGIONAL MEDICAL CENTER, 1111 East McDowell Road, Zip 85006–2666, Mailing Address: P.O. Box 2989, Zip 85062–2989; tel. 602/239–2000; Steven L. Seiler, Senior Vice President and Chief Executive Officer (Total facility includes 158 beds in nursing home–type unit) A1 2 3 5 7 8 9 10 F3 4 5 7 8 10 14 15 16 19 21 22 23 26 29 31 32 35 37 39 40 41 42 43 44 48 49 50 52 53 54 57 58 59 60 61 63 64 65 68 70 71 72 73 74 S Samaritan Health System, Phoenix, AZ Web address: www.samaritan.edu	23	10	697	29532	482	202115	7644	278109	105035	3305
✚ ○ JOHN C LINCOLN HOSPITAL–DEER VALLEY, 19829 North 27th Avenue, Zip 85027–4002; tel. 602/879–6100; Tim Tracy, Senior Vice President and Chief Operating Officer A1 9 10 11 13 F1 4 7 8 10 11 12 13 15 16 17 18 19 20 22 26 27 28 29 30 32 33 34 35 36 37 40 41 42 43 44 45 49 51 54 60 64 65 66 69 70 71 72 73 74 P8	23	10	69	2708	33	23966	203	30103	12091	377
✚ JOHN C. LINCOLN HEALTH NETWORK, 250 East Dunlap Avenue, Zip 85020–2446; tel. 602/943–2381; Dan C. Coleman, President and Chief Executive Officer A1 9 10 F1 4 7 8 10 11 12 13 14 15 16 17 19 20 21 22 24 25 27 28 29 30 32 33 34 35 36 37 39 40 41 42 43 44 45 49 54 60 62 63 65 66 67 70 71 73 74 P4 5 6 8 Web address: www.jcl.com	23	10	243	1378	128	66091	1134	95576	44352	1024
✚ MARICOPA MEDICAL CENTER, 2601 East Roosevelt Street, Zip 85008–4956; tel. 602/334–5111; Mark Hillard, Chief Executive Officer A1 2 3 5 8 9 10 12 F4 7 8 9 10 11 12 13 15 16 17 19 20 21 22 23 25 26 27 28 30 31 32 33 34 35 37 38 39 40 41 42 43 44 45 46 47 49 51 52 57 60 64 65 70 71 73 74 P1 S Quorum Health Group/Quorum Health Resources, Inc., Brentwood, TN Web address: www.maricopa.gov/medcentwer/mmc.htmc	13	10	491	17699	262	373193	3028	189020	70887	2454
✚ MARYVALE HOSPITAL MEDICAL CENTER, (Formerly Maryvale Samaritan Medical Center), 5102 West Campbell Avenue, Zip 85031–1799; tel. 602/848–5000; Art Layne, Chief Executive Officer (Total facility includes 26 beds in nursing home–type unit) (Nonreporting) A1 2 9 10	23	10	213							

Hospital, Address, Telephone, Administrator, Approval, Facility, and Physician Codes, Health Care System, Network	Classification Codes		Utilization Data					Expense (thousands) of dollars		Personnel
	Control	Service	Staffed Beds	Admissions	Census	Outpatient Visits	Births	Total	Payroll	

★ American Hospital Association (AHA) membership
□ Joint Commission on Accreditation of Healthcare Organizations (JCAHO) accreditation
+ American Osteopathic Healthcare Association (AOHA) membership
○ American Osteopathic Association (AOA) accreditation
△ Commission on Accreditation of Rehabilitation Facilities (CARF) accreditation
Control codes 61, 63, 64, 71, 72 and 73 indicate hospitals listed by AOHA, but not registered by AHA. For definition of numerical codes, see page A4

Hospital	Control	Service	Staffed Beds	Admissions	Census	Outpatient Visits	Births	Total	Payroll	Personnel
★ MAYO CLINIC HOSPITAL, 5777 East Mayo Boulevard, Zip 85024; tel. 480/515–6296; Thomas C. Bour, Administrator **A**10 **F**4 8 10 11 12 19 21 22 23 34 35 37 41 42 43 44 46 48 49 64 65 67 68 71 72 73 **P**3 **S** Mayo Foundation, Rochester, MN	23	10	178	1200	74	1200	0	—	—	—
✚ PARADISE VALLEY HOSPITAL, 3929 East Bell Road, Zip 85032–2196; tel. 602/867–1881; Rebecca C. Kuhn, President and Chief Executive Officer (Nonreporting) **A**1 2 9 10 **S** Triad Hospitals, Inc., Dallas, TX	33	10	140	—	—	—	—	—	—	—
✚ PHOENIX BAPTIST HOSPITAL AND MEDICAL CENTER, 2000 West Bethany Home Road, Zip 85015–2110; tel. 602/249–0212; Michael Purvis, Executive Vice President and Chief Executive Officer (Nonreporting) **A**1 2 3 5 9 10 **S** Baptist Hospitals and Health Systems, Inc., Phoenix, AZ **Web address:** www.baptisthealth.com	23	10	222	—	—	—	—	—	—	—
✚ PHOENIX CHILDREN'S HOSPITAL, (PEDIATRIC TERTIARY CARE), 1111 East McDowell Road, Zip 85006–2666, Mailing Address: 1300 North 12th Street, Suite 404, Zip 85006–2896; tel. 602/239–5960; Burl E. Stamp, Chief Executive Officer **A**1 3 5 9 **F**10 12 13 15 16 17 19 20 21 22 25 27 28 29 30 31 32 34 35 38 39 41 42 43 44 45 46 47 49 50 52 53 54 55 56 58 59 60 63 65 67 69 70 71 72 73 **Web address:** www.phxchildrens.com	23	50	127	9492	167	35210	—	101503	37258	687
✚ PHOENIX MEMORIAL HEALTH SYSTEM, (Formerly PMH Health Services Network), 1201 South Seventh Avenue, Zip 85007–3995; tel. 602/258–5111; Jeffrey K. Norman, Chief Executive Officer (Total facility includes 28 beds in nursing home–type unit) **A**1 2 9 10 12 13 **F**1 2 3 4 5 6 7 8 9 10 11 12 13 14 15 16 17 18 19 20 21 22 23 24 25 26 27 28 29 30 31 32 33 34 35 36 37 39 40 41 42 43 44 45 46 47 48 49 51 52 53 54 55 56 57 58 59 60 61 62 63 64 65 66 67 68 70 71 72 73 74 **P**4 5 6 8 **S** PMH Health Resources, Inc., Phoenix, AZ **Web address:** www.phzmemorialhospital.com	23	10	195	12263	119	185090	1731	151363	33869	895
✚ △ PHOENIX REGIONAL MEDICAL CENTER, (Formerly Columbia Medical Center), 1947 East Thomas Road, Zip 85016–7795; tel. 602/650–7600; Denny W. Powell, Chief Executive Officer (Total facility includes 13 beds in nursing home–type unit) **A**1 7 9 10 **F**4 5 10 12 14 15 16 17 19 20 21 22 26 28 29 30 33 35 37 39 41 42 43 44 45 46 48 49 51 52 57 60 63 64 65 67 68 70 71 73 **P**7 **S** Triad Hospitals, Inc., Dallas, TX	33	10	174	5790	82	23081	0	71812	20794	527
PMH HEALTH SERVICES NETWORK See Phoenix Memorial Health System										
★ SAMARITAN–WENDY PAINE O'BRIEN TREATMENT CENTER, 5055 North 34th Street, Zip 85018–1498; tel. 602/955–6200; Robert F. Meyer, M.D., Chief Executive Officer **A**9 10 **F**1 2 3 4 7 8 9 10 11 12 13 15 16 18 19 21 22 25 26 29 30 31 32 33 34 35 37 38 40 41 42 43 44 45 46 47 48 49 50 51 52 53 54 55 56 57 58 59 60 61 63 64 65 67 68 70 71 73 **P**5 **S** Samaritan Health System, Phoenix, AZ	23	52	89	613	84	1819	0	8124	4689	140
✚ △ ST. JOSEPH'S HOSPITAL AND MEDICAL CENTER, 350 West Thomas Road, Zip 85013–4496, Mailing Address: P.O. Box 2071, Zip 85001–2071; tel. 602/406–3100; Mary G. Yarbrough, President and Chief Executive Officer (Nonreporting) **A**1 2 3 5 7 8 9 10 **S** Catholic Healthcare West, San Francisco, CA **Web address:** www.chw.edu	21	10	514	—	—	—	—	—	—	—
□ ST. LUKE'S BEHAVIORAL HEALTH CENTER, 1800 East Van Buren, Zip 85006–3742; tel. 602/251–8484; Patrick D. Waugh, Chief Executive Officer **A**1 9 10 **F**2 3 12 18 22 52 53 55 56 57 58 59 **S** TENET Healthcare Corporation, Santa Barbara, CA	33	22	70	2699	46	—	0	—	—	134
✚ ST. LUKE'S MEDICAL CENTER, 1800 East Van Buren Street, Zip 85006–3742; tel. 602/251–8100; Mary Jo Gregory, Chief Executive Officer (Total facility includes 55 beds in nursing home–type unit) (Nonreporting) **A**1 9 10 **S** TENET Healthcare Corporation, Santa Barbara, CA	33	10	296	—	—	—	—	—	—	—
✚ U. S. PUBLIC HEALTH SERVICE PHOENIX INDIAN MEDICAL CENTER, 4212 North 16th Street, Zip 85016–5389; tel. 602/263–1200; Anna Albert, Chief Executive Officer **A**1 10 **F**4 7 8 12 14 16 17 19 20 22 23 25 26 28 30 31 35 37 39 40 42 44 45 46 49 51 53 54 58 61 65 67 71 73 74 **S** U. S. Public Health Service Indian Health Service, Rockville, MD	47	10	127	5244	67	207510	780	54276	27656	766
□ VENCOR HOSPITAL–PHOENIX, 40 East Indianola Avenue, Zip 85012–2059; tel. 602/280–7000; John L. Harrington, Jr., FACHE, Administrator **A**1 **F**4 6 10 14 19 20 21 22 27 31 32 33 35 37 39 41 42 44 45 46 49 50 54 60 63 65 67 71 **S** Vencor, Incorporated, Louisville, KY	33	10	58	464	42	—	0	15559	6046	147
WESTBRIDGE TREATMENT CENTER, 1830 East Roosevelt Street, Zip 85006–3641; tel. 602/254–0884; Mike Perry, Chief Executive Officer (Nonreporting) **A**9 **S** Century Healthcare Corporation, Tulsa, OK	33	52	78	—	—	—	—	—	—	—
PRESCOTT—Yavapai County										
✚ VETERANS AFFAIRS MEDICAL CENTER, 500 Highway 89 North, Zip 86313–5000; tel. 520/445–4860; Patricia A. McKlem, Medical Center Director (Total facility includes 80 beds in nursing home–type unit) **A**1 **F**1 3 6 15 16 17 18 19 20 21 22 25 26 27 28 29 30 31 32 33 34 35 39 41 42 44 45 46 48 49 51 54 56 57 58 60 63 64 65 67 71 73 74 **P**6 **S** Department of Veterans Affairs, Washington, DC	45	10	225	1905	224	90607	0	40977	27839	582
✚ YAVAPAI REGIONAL MEDICAL CENTER, 1003 Willow Creek Road, Zip 86301–1668; tel. 520/445–2700; Timothy Barnett, Chief Executive Officer **A**1 9 10 **F**7 8 11 15 16 17 19 21 22 24 25 28 30 32 33 34 35 37 39 40 41 42 44 46 49 63 65 67 71 73 **P**8	23	10	84	6292	58	58027	758	43407	19115	541

Hospital, Address, Telephone, Administrator, Approval, Facility, and Physician Codes, Health Care System, Network	Classi-fication Codes		Utilization Data					Expense (thousands) of dollars		
	Control	Service	Staffed Beds	Admissions	Census	Outpatient Visits	Births	Total	Payroll	Personnel

★ American Hospital Association (AHA) membership
□ Joint Commission on Accreditation of Healthcare Organizations (JCAHO) accreditation
+ American Osteopathic Healthcare Association (AOHA) membership
○ American Osteopathic Association (AOA) accreditation
△ Commission on Accreditation of Rehabilitation Facilities (CARF) accreditation
Control codes 61, 63, 64, 71, 72 and 73 indicate hospitals listed by AOHA, but not registered by AHA. For definition of numerical codes, see page A4

SACATON—Pinal County

Hospital	Control	Service	Staffed Beds	Admissions	Census	Outpatient Visits	Births	Total	Payroll	Personnel
★ HUHUKAM MEMORIAL HOSPITAL, Seed Farm & Skill Center Road, Zip 85247–0038, Mailing Address: P.O. Box 38, Zip 85247–0038; tel. 602/528–1200; Viola L. Johnson, Chief Executive Officer (Nonreporting) **A**1 10 **S** U. S. Public Health Service Indian Health Service, Rockville, MD	47	10	10	—	—	—	—	—	—	—

SAFFORD—Graham County

Hospital	Control	Service	Staffed Beds	Admissions	Census	Outpatient Visits	Births	Total	Payroll	Personnel
★ MOUNT GRAHAM COMMUNITY HOSPITAL, 1600 20th Avenue, Zip 85546–4097; tel. 520/348–4000; Karl E. Johnson, Chief Executive Officer **A**1 9 10 **F**7 8 11 14 15 16 19 21 22 24 28 30 32 33 34 35 37 40 41 42 44 46 49 68 71 73 **P**8	16	10	44	3207	23	59212	571	15277	6207	244

SAN CARLOS—Gila County

Hospital	Control	Service	Staffed Beds	Admissions	Census	Outpatient Visits	Births	Total	Payroll	Personnel
★ U. S. PUBLIC HEALTH SERVICE INDIAN HOSPITAL, Mailing Address: P.O. Box 208, Zip 85550–0208; tel. 520/475–2371; Nella Ben, Chief Executive Officer (Nonreporting) **A**1 10 **S** U. S. Public Health Service Indian Health Service, Rockville, MD	47	10	28	—	—	—	—	—	—	—

SCOTTSDALE—Maricopa County

Hospital	Control	Service	Staffed Beds	Admissions	Census	Outpatient Visits	Births	Total	Payroll	Personnel
□ HEALTHSOUTH MERIDIAN POINT REHABILITATION HOSPITAL, 11250 North 92nd Street, Zip 85260–6148; tel. 602/860–0671; Denise Kann, Administrator and Chief Operating Officer (Nonreporting) **A**1 10 **S** HEALTHSOUTH Corporation, Birmingham, AL	33	46	43	—	—	—	—	—	—	—
★ SAMARITAN BEHAVIORAL HEALTH CENTER–SCOTTSDALE, 7575 East Earll Drive, Zip 85251–6998; tel. 602/941–7500; Robert F. Meyer, M.D., Chief Executive Officer (Nonreporting) **A**1 9 10 **S** Samaritan Health System, Phoenix, AZ	23	22	60	—	—	—	—	—	—	—
★ △ SCOTTSDALE HEALTHCARE–OSBORN, 7400 East Osborn Road, Zip 85251–6403; tel. 480/675–4000; Peggy Reiley, Senior Vice President and Chief Clinical Officer (Total facility includes 60 beds in nursing home–type unit) (Nonreporting) **A**1 2 3 5 7 9 10 **S** Scottsdale Healthcare, Scottsdale, AZ Web address: www.smhsi.com	23	10	258	—	—	—	—	—	—	—
★ SCOTTSDALE HEALTHCARE–SHEA, 9003 East Shea Boulevard, Zip 85260–6771; tel. 602/860–3000; Thomas J. Sadvary, FACHE, Senior Vice President and Chief Operating Officer **A**1 2 3 5 9 10 **F**1 2 3 4 5 6 7 8 9 10 11 12 13 14 15 16 17 18 19 20 21 22 23 24 25 26 27 28 29 30 31 32 33 34 35 36 37 38 39 40 41 42 43 44 45 46 47 48 49 51 52 56 60 61 63 64 65 67 68 70 71 72 73 74 **P**6 8 **S** Scottsdale Healthcare, Scottsdale, AZ Web address: www.shc.org	23	10	251	17800	192	83329	2559	142045	52999	1056

SELLS—Pima County

Hospital	Control	Service	Staffed Beds	Admissions	Census	Outpatient Visits	Births	Total	Payroll	Personnel
★ U. S. PUBLIC HEALTH SERVICE INDIAN HOSPITAL, Mailing Address: P.O. Box 548, Zip 85634–0548; tel. 520/383–7251; Darrell Rumley, Service Unit Director and Chief Executive Officer (Nonreporting) **A**1 10 **S** U. S. Public Health Service Indian Health Service, Rockville, MD	47	10	34	—	—	—	—	—	—	—

SHOW LOW—Navajo County

Hospital	Control	Service	Staffed Beds	Admissions	Census	Outpatient Visits	Births	Total	Payroll	Personnel
★ NAVAPACHE REGIONAL MEDICAL CENTER, 2200 Show Low Lake Road, Zip 85901–7800; tel. 520/537–4375; Leigh Cox, Chief Executive Officer **A**1 9 10 **F**4 7 8 10 12 14 17 19 22 23 25 29 30 32 34 35 37 40 41 44 49 63 65 71 73 **S** Brim Healthcare, Inc., Brentwood, TN Web address: www.nrmc.org	23	10	54	4088	35	41657	803	28066	12011	350

SIERRA VISTA—Cochise County

Hospital	Control	Service	Staffed Beds	Admissions	Census	Outpatient Visits	Births	Total	Payroll	Personnel
★ SIERRA VISTA REGIONAL HEALTH CENTER, (Formerly Sierra Vista Community Hospital), 300 El Camino Real, Zip 85635–2899; tel. 520/458–4641; Dale A. Decker, President and Chief Executive Officer **A**1 9 10 **F**7 8 12 15 16 19 20 21 22 28 32 33 34 35 37 39 40 41 44 46 48 49 63 65 71 73 **P**6 Web address: www.svch.com	23	10	81	4210	30	154399	1032	30185	14105	427

SPRINGERVILLE—Apache County

Hospital	Control	Service	Staffed Beds	Admissions	Census	Outpatient Visits	Births	Total	Payroll	Personnel
★ WHITE MOUNTAIN REGIONAL MEDICAL CENTER, 118 South Mountain Avenue, Zip 85938, Mailing Address: P.O. Box 880, Zip 85938–0880; tel. 520/333–4368; Jerry Campeau, Interim Chief Executive Officer (Total facility includes 64 beds in nursing home–type unit) (Nonreporting) **A**1 9 10	23	10	89	—	—	—	—	—	—	—

SUN CITY—Maricopa County

Hospital	Control	Service	Staffed Beds	Admissions	Census	Outpatient Visits	Births	Total	Payroll	Personnel
★ WALTER O. BOSWELL MEMORIAL HOSPITAL, 10401 West Thunderbird Boulevard, Zip 85351–3092, Mailing Address: P.O. Box 1690, Zip 85372–1690; tel. 623/977–7211; George Perez, Executive Vice President and Chief Operating Officer (Total facility includes 47 beds in nursing home–type unit) **A**1 2 9 10 **F**3 4 6 8 10 11 12 15 16 17 19 21 22 27 28 29 30 32 33 34 35 36 37 39 41 42 43 44 45 48 49 52 54 55 56 57 58 59 60 62 64 65 67 71 72 73 **P**1 5 **S** Sun Health Corporation, Sun City, AZ	23	10	267	15185	204	85292	0	112317	41570	1153

SUN CITY WEST—Maricopa County

Hospital	Control	Service	Staffed Beds	Admissions	Census	Outpatient Visits	Births	Total	Payroll	Personnel
★ DEL E. WEBB MEMORIAL HOSPITAL, 14502 West Meeker Boulevard, Zip 85375–5299, Mailing Address: P.O. Box 5169, Sun City, Zip 85375–5169; tel. 623/214–4000; Thomas C. Dickson, Executive Vice President and Chief Operating Officer (Total facility includes 36 beds in nursing home–type unit) **A**1 9 10 **F**1 3 6 8 10 11 12 15 16 17 19 21 23 26 27 28 29 30 31 32 33 34 35 36 39 41 42 43 44 45 46 48 49 52 54 55 56 57 58 59 60 62 64 65 67 70 71 73 **P**1 5 **S** Sun Health Corporation, Sun City, AZ Web address: www.sunhealth.org	23	10	170	6548	105	67516	0	45464	18723	478

TEMPE—Maricopa County

Hospital	Control	Service	Staffed Beds	Admissions	Census	Outpatient Visits	Births	Total	Payroll	Personnel
★ TEMPE ST. LUKE'S HOSPITAL, 1500 South Mill Avenue, Zip 85281–6699; tel. 602/784–5510; Mary Jo Gregory, Chief Executive Officer (Nonreporting) **A**1 9 10 12 13 **S** TENET Healthcare Corporation, Santa Barbara, CA	33	10	110	—	—	—	—	—	—	—

Hospital, Address, Telephone, Administrator, Approval, Facility, and Physician Codes, Health Care System, Network	Classi-fication Codes		Utilization Data					Expense (thousands) of dollars		
	Control	Service	Staffed Beds	Admissions	Census	Outpatient Visits	Births	Total	Payroll	Personnel

Approval codes legend:

★ American Hospital Association (AHA) membership
☐ Joint Commission on Accreditation of Healthcare Organizations (JCAHO) accreditation
+ American Osteopathic Healthcare Association (AOHA) membership
○ American Osteopathic Association (AOA) accreditation
△ Commission on Accreditation of Rehabilitation Facilities (CARF) accreditation
Control codes 61, 63, 64, 71, 72 and 73 indicate hospitals listed by AOHA, but not registered by AHA. For definition of numerical codes, see page A4

TUBA CITY—Coconino County

Hospital	Control	Service	Staffed Beds	Admissions	Census	Outpatient Visits	Births	Total	Payroll	Personnel
✸ TUBA CITY INDIAN MEDICAL CENTER, Main Street, Zip 86045–6211, Mailing Address: P.O. Box 600, Zip 86045–6211; tel. 520/283–2501; Susie John, M.D., Chief Executive Officer (Nonreporting) **A**1 10 **S** U. S. Public Health Service Indian Health Service, Rockville, MD	47	10	69	—	—	—	—	—	—	—

TUCSON—Pima County

Hospital	Control	Service	Staffed Beds	Admissions	Census	Outpatient Visits	Births	Total	Payroll	Personnel
✸ △ CARONDELET ST. JOSEPH'S HOSPITAL, 350 North Wilmot Road, Zip 85711–2678; tel. 520/296–3211; Sister St. Joan Willert, President and Chief Executive Officer **A**1 7 9 10 **F**3 4 7 8 9 10 11 12 14 15 16 17 18 19 21 22 25 28 29 30 31 32 33 34 35 37 39 40 41 42 43 44 46 48 49 53 54 55 56 57 58 59 63 64 65 67 71 72 73 74 **P**1 2 6 7 **S** Carondelet Health System, Saint Louis, MO	21	10	300	13484	160	126565	2210	94901	39875	1367
✸ △ CARONDELET ST. MARY'S HOSPITAL, 1601 West St. Mary's Road, Zip 85745–2682; tel. 520/622–5833; Sister St. Joan Willert, President and Chief Executive Officer **A**1 7 9 10 **F**4 7 8 9 10 11 12 14 15 16 17 19 21 22 26 28 29 30 31 32 33 34 35 36 37 40 41 42 43 44 46 48 49 52 53 54 55 56 57 58 59 63 64 65 67 71 72 73 74 **P**1 6 7 8 **S** Carondelet Health System, Saint Louis, MO	21	10	354	18648	235	147428	884	140573	60154	1979
DESERT HILLS CENTER FOR YOUTH AND FAMILIES, 2797 North Introspect Drive, Zip 85745–9491; tel. 520/622–5437; Joe W. King, M.D., President, Chief Executive Officer and Medical Director (Nonreporting) **A**3	33	52	140	—	—	—	—	—	—	—
✸ EL DORADO HOSPITAL, 1400 North Wilmot Road, Zip 85712–4498, Mailing Address: P.O. Box 13070, Zip 85732–3070; tel. 520/886–6361; Rhonda Dean, Chief Executive Officer (Total facility includes 31 beds in nursing home–type unit) **A**1 9 10 **F**4 8 10 11 12 14 15 16 19 22 26 28 30 32 33 34 35 36 37 39 41 43 44 48 49 52 57 64 65 71 73 **P**5 6 **S** Triad Hospitals, Inc., Dallas, TX **Web address:** www.eldoradohospital.com	33	10	166	4922	77	32778	0	32712	14917	441
☐ HEALTHSOUTH REHABILITATION INSTITUTE OF TUCSON, 2650 North Wyatt Drive, Zip 85712–6108; tel. 520/325–1300; Jason Roeback, Chief Executive Officer (Total facility includes 17 beds in nursing home–type unit) **A**1 10 **F**12 14 41 48 49 64 73 **S** HEALTHSOUTH Corporation, Birmingham, AL	33	46	80	907	41	9216	0	—	—	192
☐ KINO COMMUNITY HOSPITAL, 2800 East Ajo Way, Zip 85713–6289; tel. 520/294–4471; Karen Shields, Chief Operating Officer (Total facility includes 20 beds in nursing home–type unit) **A**1 3 5 9 10 **F**7 8 12 15 16 17 19 20 22 25 28 32 33 34 36 37 40 41 44 46 49 52 55 56 64 65 70 71 72 73 **P**8	13	10	155	5223	88	130914	649	57082	24474	782
✸ NORTHWEST MEDICAL CENTER, 6200 North La Cholla Boulevard, Zip 85741–3599; tel. 520/742–9000; W. Jefferson Comer, FACHE, Chief Executive Officer (Total facility includes 16 beds in nursing home–type unit) (Nonreporting) **A**1 9 10 **S** Triad Hospitals, Inc., Dallas, TX	33	10	152	—	—	—	—	—	—	—
PALO VERDE MENTAL HEALTH SERVICES See Tucson Medical Center										
SIERRA TUCSON, 16500 North Lago Del Oro Parkway, Zip 85739–9637; tel. 520/624–4000; Terry A. Stephens, Executive Director (Nonreporting) **A**9	33	49	70	—	—	—	—	—	—	—
✸ ○ TUCSON GENERAL HOSPITAL, 3838 North Campbell Avenue, Zip 85719–1497; tel. 520/318–6300; Allan Harrington, Jr., Chief Executive Officer **A**1 9 10 11 12 13 **F**7 8 11 12 14 15 16 17 19 21 22 26 28 29 30 34 35 36 37 40 42 44 46 49 50 52 57 65 71 73 **P**5 7 8 **S** TENET Healthcare Corporation, Santa Barbara, CA	33	10	80	3230	38	23391	782	23201	9022	338
✸ TUCSON MEDICAL CENTER, (Includes Palo Verde Mental Health Services, 2695 North Craycroft, Zip 85712–2244; tel. 520/324–4340), 5301 East Grant Road, Zip 85712–2874; tel. 520/327–5461; Frank D. Alvarez, President and Chief Executive Officer (Nonreporting) **A**1 2 3 5 9 10	23	10	523	—	—	—	—	—	—	—
✸ UNIVERSITY MEDICAL CENTER, 1501 North Campbell Avenue, Zip 85724–0002; tel. 520/694–0111; Gregory A. Pivirotto, President and Chief Executive Officer (Nonreporting) **A**1 3 5 8 9 10	23	10	322	—	—	—	—	—	—	—
☐ VENCOR HOSPITAL – TUCSON, 355 North Wilmot Road, Zip 85711–2635; tel. 520/747–8200; Kevin Christiansen, Administrator (Nonreporting) **A**1 10 **S** Vencor, Incorporated, Louisville, KY	33	49	51	—	—	—	—	—	—	—
✸ △ VETERANS AFFAIRS MEDICAL CENTER, 3601 South 6th Avenue, Zip 85723–0002; tel. 520/792–1450; Jonathan H. Gardner, Chief Executive Officer (Total facility includes 84 beds in nursing home–type unit) **A**1 3 5 7 8 **F**1 2 3 4 5 6 8 10 12 14 15 16 17 19 20 21 22 23 25 26 27 28 29 30 31 32 33 34 35 37 39 41 42 43 44 45 46 48 49 51 52 54 55 56 57 58 59 60 63 64 65 67 71 72 73 74 **P**6 **S** Department of Veterans Affairs, Washington, DC	45	10	268	6003	194	275203	0	104074	53985	1311

WHITERIVER—Navajo County

Hospital	Control	Service	Staffed Beds	Admissions	Census	Outpatient Visits	Births	Total	Payroll	Personnel
✸ U. S. PUBLIC HEALTH SERVICE INDIAN HOSPITAL, State Route 73, Box 860, Zip 85941–0860; tel. 520/338–4911; Carla Alchesay-Nachu, Service Unit Director **A**1 **F**7 15 16 19 20 22 25 28 34 40 44 49 54 56 65 68 71 74 **P**6 **S** U. S. Public Health Service Indian Health Service, Rockville, MD	47	10	36	2015	19	107308	209	14077	9144	306

WICKENBURG—Maricopa County

Hospital	Control	Service	Staffed Beds	Admissions	Census	Outpatient Visits	Births	Total	Payroll	Personnel
✸ WICKENBURG REGIONAL HOSPITAL, 520 Rose Lane, Zip 85390–1447; tel. 520/684–5421; David Garnas, Administrator (Total facility includes 55 beds in nursing home–type unit) **A**1 9 10 **F**16 19 22 28 37 44 64 65 71 **S** Lutheran Health Systems, Fargo, ND	23	10	73	829	12	3566	0	5385	1959	108

WILLCOX—Cochise County

Hospital	Control	Service	Staffed Beds	Admissions	Census	Outpatient Visits	Births	Total	Payroll	Personnel
✸ NORTHERN COCHISE COMMUNITY HOSPITAL, 901 West Rex Allen Drive, Zip 85643–1009; tel. 520/384–3541; Chris Cronberg, Chief Executive Officer (Total facility includes 24 beds in nursing home–type unit) **A**1 9 10 **F**8 12 14 15 16 19 22 25 28 29 34 39 44 45 46 51 64 65 71 73 **S** Brim Healthcare, Inc., Brentwood, TN	16	10	48	624	34	—	0	5484	2656	110

Hospital, Address, Telephone, Administrator, Approval, Facility, and Physician Codes, Health Care System, Network	Classi-fication Codes		Utilization Data					Expense (thousands) of dollars		
★ American Hospital Association (AHA) membership □ Joint Commission on Accreditation of Healthcare Organizations (JCAHO) accreditation + American Osteopathic Healthcare Association (AOHA) membership ○ American Osteopathic Association (AOA) accreditation △ Commission on Accreditation of Rehabilitation Facilities (CARF) accreditation Control codes 61, 63, 64, 71, 72 and 73 indicate hospitals listed by AOHA, but not registered by AHA. For definition of numerical codes, see page A4	Control	Service	Staffed Beds	Admissions	Census	Outpatient Visits	Births	Total	Payroll	Personnel

WINSLOW—Navajo County

★ WINSLOW MEMORIAL HOSPITAL, 1501 Williamson Avenue, Zip 86047–2797; tel. 520/289–4691; Michael King, Administrator **A**9 10 **F**7 8 14 16 19 22 26 32 33 40 44 49 65 71 73 **P**5	33	10	34	1285	9	18200	233	8964	4602	135

YUMA—Imperial County

U. S. PUBLIC HEALTH SERVICE INDIAN HOSPITAL See Winterhaven, CA										
⊠ YUMA REGIONAL MEDICAL CENTER, 2400 South Avenue A, Zip 85364–7170; tel. 520/344–2000; Robert T. Olsen, CHE, President and Chief Executive Officer (Total facility includes 20 beds in nursing home–type unit) **A**1 9 10 **F**4 7 8 10 11 12 15 16 17 18 19 20 21 22 23 24 26 28 30 31 32 34 35 37 39 40 41 42 44 51 60 64 65 67 70 71 72 73 74 **P**5 8 **Web address:** www.yumaregional.org	23	10	257	14457	160	101437	2754	104259	40122	1196

ARKANSAS

Resident population 2,538 (in thousands)
Resident population in metro areas 47.8%
Birth rate per 1,000 population 14.2
65 years and over 14.3%
Percent of persons without health insurance 21.7%

Hospital, Address, Telephone, Administrator, Approval, Facility, and Physician Codes, Health Care System, Network	Classi-fication Codes		Utilization Data					Expense (thousands) of dollars		
	Control	Service	Staffed Beds	Admissions	Census	Outpatient Visits	Births	Total	Payroll	Personnel

★ American Hospital Association (AHA) membership
□ Joint Commission on Accreditation of Healthcare Organizations (JCAHO) accreditation
+ American Osteopathic Healthcare Association (AOHA) membership
○ American Osteopathic Association (AOA) accreditation
△ Commission on Accreditation of Rehabilitation Facilities (CARF) accreditation
Control codes 61, 63, 64, 71, 72 and 73 indicate hospitals listed by AOHA, but not registered by AHA. For definition of numerical codes, see page A4

ARKADELPHIA—Clark County										
✚ BAPTIST MEDICAL CENTER ARKADELPHIA, 3050 Twin Rivers Drive, Zip 71923–4299; tel. 870/245–1100; Dan Gathright, Senior Vice President and Administrator **A**1 9 10 **F**7 8 12 15 16 19 21 22 27 30 31 32 33 35 36 37 40 41 42 44 49 65 70 71 73 **P**1 3 5 6 7 **S** Baptist Health, Little Rock, AR	23	10	57	1579	18	19733	236	14196	6178	227
ASHDOWN—Little River County										
LITTLE RIVER MEMORIAL HOSPITAL, Fifth and Locke Streets, Zip 71822–0577; Mailing Address: P.O. Box 577, Zip 71822–0577; tel. 870/898–5011; Judy Adams, Administrator and Chief Executive Officer **A**9 10 **F**11 15 16 19 22 41 44 49 63 71 **P**5	13	10	42	1015	12	6228	0	4192	2336	116
BATESVILLE—Independence County										
✚ WHITE RIVER MEDICAL CENTER, 1710 Harrison Street, Zip 72501–2197, Mailing Address: P.O. Box 2197, Zip 72503–2197; tel. 870/793–1200; Gary Bebow, Administrator and Chief Executive Officer **A**1 9 10 **F**7 8 10 11 12 14 15 16 19 21 22 28 30 31 32 34 35 37 40 41 42 44 46 48 49 50 52 57 63 64 65 66 71 73 **P**3 8 Web address: www.wrmc.com	23	10	174	8322	112	62202	540	46603	19520	625
BENTON—Saline County										
□ RIVENDELL BEHAVIORAL HEALTH SERVICES, 100 Rivendell Drive, Zip 72015–9100; tel. 501/316–1255; Mark E. Schneider, Chief Executive Officer (Nonreporting) **A**1 9 10 **S** Children's Comprehensive Services, Inc., Nashville, TN	33	52	77	—	—	—	—	—	—	—
✚ SALINE MEMORIAL HOSPITAL, 1 Medical Park Drive, Zip 72015–3354; tel. 501/776–6000; Roger D. Feldt, FACHE, President and Chief Executive Officer (Total facility includes 7 beds in nursing home–type unit) **A**1 9 10 **F**7 8 11 12 14 19 21 22 24 32 33 34 35 40 41 42 43 44 46 49 52 53 54 55 56 57 58 59 64 65 71 73 74 **P**8 **S** Quorum Health Group/Quorum Health Resources, Inc., Brentwood, TN Web address: www.scmc.com	23	10	77	4702	62	39983	441	30391	12683	586
BENTONVILLE—Benton County										
BATES MEDICAL CENTER See Northwest Medical Center, Springdale										
BERRYVILLE—Carroll County										
★ CARROLL REGIONAL MEDICAL CENTER, 214 Carter Street, Zip 72616–4303; tel. 870/423–3355; Rudy Darling, President and Chief Executive Officer **A**9 10 **F**8 12 15 16 19 20 22 24 28 29 30 31 32 33 37 39 40 41 42 44 45 46 49 51 64 65 66 67 71 73 74 **P**1 **S** Sisters of Mercy Health System–St. Louis, Saint Louis, MO Web address: www.carrollregional.com	23	10	39	1668	15	15297	208	9967	4759	220
BLYTHEVILLE—Mississippi County										
✚ BAPTIST MEMORIAL HOSPITAL–BLYTHEVILLE, 1520 North Division Street, Zip 72315, Mailing Address: P.O. Box 108, Zip 72316–0108; tel. 870/838–7300; Al Sypniewski, Administrator (Total facility includes 70 beds in nursing home–type unit) **A**1 9 10 **F**3 8 11 12 13 15 16 17 19 21 22 23 24 27 28 29 30 31 32 33 35 37 39 40 41 42 44 45 46 49 52 57 58 59 60 64 65 67 71 73 **P**7 8 **S** Baptist Memorial Health Care Corporation, Memphis, TN Web address: www.bmhcc.org	21	10	195	3631	105	70164	779	19828	6850	317
BOONEVILLE—Logan County										
★ BOONEVILLE COMMUNITY HOSPITAL, 880 West Main Street, Zip 72927–3420, Mailing Address: P.O. Box 290, Zip 72927–0290; tel. 501/675–2800; Robert R. Bash, Administrator **A**9 10 **F**8 12 19 22 26 28 30 32 34 44 49 73 **P**1	23	10	26	678	9	27886	0	3373	1838	84
CALICO ROCK—Izard County										
MEDICAL CENTER OF CALICO ROCK, 103 Grasse Street, Zip 72519, Mailing Address: P.O. Box 438, Zip 72519–0438; tel. 870/297–3726; Terry L. Amstutz, CHE, Chief Executive Officer and Administrator (Nonreporting) **A**9 10	23	10	26	—	—	—	—	—	—	—
CAMDEN—Ouachita County										
✚ OUACHITA MEDICAL CENTER, 638 California Street, Zip 71701–4699, Mailing Address: P.O. Box 797, Zip 71701–0797; tel. 870/836–1000; C. C. McAllister, President and Chief Executive Officer **A**1 9 10 **F**1 2 3 7 8 12 14 15 16 17 19 21 22 23 26 27 28 30 33 34 35 36 37 40 42 44 46 49 50 51 52 57 65 67 71 73 74 **P**1	23	10	118	3670	44	24895	387	21038	10635	553
CHEROKEE VILLAGE—Sharp County										
★ EASTERN OZARKS REGIONAL HEALTH SYSTEM, 122 South Allegheny Drive, Zip 72529–7300; tel. 870/257–4101; Cindy Hall, Administrator (Nonreporting) **A**9 10	33	10	40	—	—	—	—	—	—	—
CLARKSVILLE—Johnson County										
JOHNSON REGIONAL MEDICAL CENTER, 1100 East Poplar Street, Zip 72830–4419, Mailing Address: P.O. Box 738, Zip 72830–0738; tel. 501/754–5454; Kenneth R. Wood, Administrator **A**9 10 **F**7 8 11 12 14 15 19 20 21 22 27 28 30 32 34 35 37 39 40 41 44 45 46 49 52 54 56 57 61 65 71 73 **P**1 3	23	10	68	2502	32	28537	329	13322	6215	258

Hospital, Address, Telephone, Administrator, Approval, Facility, and Physician Codes, Health Care System, Network	Classi-fication Codes		Utilization Data					Expense (thousands) of dollars		
	Control	Service	Staffed Beds	Admissions	Census	Outpatient Visits	Births	Total	Payroll	Personnel

★ American Hospital Association (AHA) membership
□ Joint Commission on Accreditation of Healthcare Organizations (JCAHO) accreditation
+ American Osteopathic Healthcare Association (AOHA) membership
○ American Osteopathic Association (AOA) accreditation
△ Commission on Accreditation of Rehabilitation Facilities (CARF) accreditation
Control codes 61, 63, 64, 71, 72 and 73 indicate hospitals listed by AOHA, but not registered by AHA. For definition of numerical codes, see page A4

CLINTON—Van Buren County

OZARK HEALTH MEDICAL CENTER, (Formerly Van Buren County Memorial Hospital), Highway 65 South, Zip 72031, Mailing Address: P.O. Box 206, Zip 72031–0206; tel. 501/745–2401; Barry Brady, Administrator (Total facility includes 120 beds in nursing home–type unit) (Nonreporting) **A**9 10 **S** United Hospital Corporation, Memphis, TN

	Control	Service	Staffed Beds	Admissions	Census	Outpatient Visits	Births	Total	Payroll	Personnel
OZARK HEALTH MEDICAL CENTER	23	10	144	—	—	—	—	—	—	—

CONWAY—Faulkner County

✠ CONWAY REGIONAL MEDICAL CENTER, 2302 College Avenue, Zip 72032–6297; tel. 501/329–3831; James A. Summersett, III, FACHE, President and Chief Executive Officer **A**1 9 10 **F**7 8 10 11 12 14 15 16 19 21 22 23 24 25 28 32 33 34 35 37 38 40 41 42 44 46 49 52 57 60 64 65 66 71 73 **P**3 8
Web address: www.conwayregional.org

	Control	Service	Staffed Beds	Admissions	Census	Outpatient Visits	Births	Total	Payroll	Personnel
CONWAY REGIONAL MEDICAL CENTER	23	10	116	6208	73	56723	1218	54560	23515	814

CROSSETT—Ashley County

★ ASHLEY COUNTY MEDICAL CENTER, 1015 Unity Road, Zip 71635–2930, Mailing Address: P.O. Box 400, Zip 71635–0400; tel. 870/364–4111; Russ D. Sword, Interim Administrator **A**9 10 **F**7 8 19 21 22 24 28 32 34 35 37 39 42 44 49 51 57 58 63 64 65 67 71 **P**1

	Control	Service	Staffed Beds	Admissions	Census	Outpatient Visits	Births	Total	Payroll	Personnel
ASHLEY COUNTY MEDICAL CENTER	23	10	37	1207	10	30514	5	9636	4480	216

DANVILLE—Yell County

CHAMBERS MEMORIAL HOSPITAL, Highway 10 at Detroit, Zip 72833, Mailing Address: P.O. Box 639, Zip 72833–0639; tel. 501/495–2241; Scott Peek, Administrator **A**9 10 **F**7 15 17 19 22 28 32 41 44 49 65 71 **P**5

	Control	Service	Staffed Beds	Admissions	Census	Outpatient Visits	Births	Total	Payroll	Personnel
CHAMBERS MEMORIAL HOSPITAL	23	10	41	1027	11	13633	63	7233	2701	121

DARDANELLE—Yell County

DARDANELLE HOSPITAL, 200 North Third Street, Zip 72834–3802, Mailing Address: P.O. Box 578, Zip 72834–0578; tel. 501/229–4677; Shawn Cathey, Administrator (Nonreporting) **A**9 10

	Control	Service	Staffed Beds	Admissions	Census	Outpatient Visits	Births	Total	Payroll	Personnel
DARDANELLE HOSPITAL	13	10	44	—	—	—	—	—	—	—

DE QUEEN—Sevier County

★ DE QUEEN REGIONAL MEDICAL CENTER, (Formerly Columbia De Queen Regional Medical Center), 1306 Collin Raye Drive, Zip 71832–2198; tel. 870/584–4111; Charles H. Long, Chief Executive Officer **A**9 10 **F**7 8 11 12 14 15 16 19 20 21 22 23 25 28 29 30 34 35 37 39 40 44 48 49 65 71 73 74 **P**1 7 **S** Triad Hospitals, Inc., Dallas, TX
Web address: www.columbia.net

	Control	Service	Staffed Beds	Admissions	Census	Outpatient Visits	Births	Total	Payroll	Personnel
DE QUEEN REGIONAL MEDICAL CENTER	33	10	75	1952	19	9142	232	9700	4218	183

DE WITT—Arkansas County

DEWITT CITY HOSPITAL, Highway 1 and Madison Street, Zip 72042, Mailing Address: P.O. Box 32, Zip 72042–0032; tel. 870/946–3571; Joe E. Smith, Administrator and Chief Executive Officer (Total facility includes 54 beds in nursing home–type unit) (Nonreporting) **A**9 10

	Control	Service	Staffed Beds	Admissions	Census	Outpatient Visits	Births	Total	Payroll	Personnel
DEWITT CITY HOSPITAL	14	10	88	—	—	—	—	—	—	—

DUMAS—Desha County

★ DELTA MEMORIAL HOSPITAL, 300 East Pickens Street, Zip 71639–2710, Mailing Address: P.O. Box 887, Zip 71639–0887; tel. 870/382–4303; Kurt Meyer, Administrator **A**9 10 **F**8 17 19 22 26 28 30 32 34 44 49 52 57 65 71 **P**6 8 **S** Quorum Health Group/Quorum Health Resources, Inc., Brentwood, TN

	Control	Service	Staffed Beds	Admissions	Census	Outpatient Visits	Births	Total	Payroll	Personnel
DELTA MEMORIAL HOSPITAL	23	10	35	961	8	14267	131	7437	3528	125

EL DORADO—Union County

✠ △ MEDICAL CENTER OF SOUTH ARKANSAS, (Includes Union Medical Center, 700 West Grove Street, Zip 71730; Warner Brown Hospital, 460 West Oak Street, Zip 71730; tel. 501/863–2000), 700 West Grove Street, Zip 71730–4416, Mailing Address: P.O. Box 1998, Zip 71731–1998; tel. 870/864–3200; Luther J. Lewis, Chief Executive Officer **A**1 3 5 7 9 10 **F**7 8 10 12 14 15 16 17 19 21 22 23 26 28 29 30 31 32 33 34 35 37 38 39 40 41 42 44 45 46 48 49 51 56 60 63 65 66 67 71 73 74 **P**7 8 **S** Triad Hospitals, Inc., Dallas, TX
Web address: www.mesaeldo.com

	Control	Service	Staffed Beds	Admissions	Census	Outpatient Visits	Births	Total	Payroll	Personnel
MEDICAL CENTER OF SOUTH ARKANSAS	32	10	167	5033	57	38213	800	43174	18019	656

EUREKA SPRINGS—Carroll County

★ EUREKA SPRINGS HOSPITAL, 24 Norris Street, Zip 72632–3541; tel. 501/253–7400; Joe Hammond, Administrator (Nonreporting) **A**9 10

	Control	Service	Staffed Beds	Admissions	Census	Outpatient Visits	Births	Total	Payroll	Personnel
EUREKA SPRINGS HOSPITAL	23	10	16	—	—	—	—	—	—	—

FAYETTEVILLE—Washington County

□ CHARTER BEHAVIORAL HEALTH SYSTEM OF NORTHWEST ARKANSAS, 4253 North Crossover Road, Zip 72703–4596; tel. 501/521–5731; Patrick Kelly, Chief Executive Officer (Nonreporting) **A**1 9 10 **S** Magellan Health Services, Atlanta, GA

	Control	Service	Staffed Beds	Admissions	Census	Outpatient Visits	Births	Total	Payroll	Personnel
CHARTER BEHAVIORAL HEALTH SYSTEM OF NORTHWEST ARKANSAS	33	22	49	—	—	—	—	—	—	—

□ HEALTHSOUTH REHABILITATION HOSPITAL, 153 East Monte Painter Drive, Zip 72703–4002; tel. 501/444–2200; Dennis R. Shelby, Chief Executive Officer (Nonreporting) **A**1 9 10 **S** HEALTHSOUTH Corporation, Birmingham, AL

	Control	Service	Staffed Beds	Admissions	Census	Outpatient Visits	Births	Total	Payroll	Personnel
HEALTHSOUTH REHABILITATION HOSPITAL	33	46	60	—	—	—	—	—	—	—

✠ VETERANS AFFAIRS MEDICAL CENTER, 1100 North College Avenue, Zip 72703–6995; tel. 501/443–4301; Richard F. Robinson, Director **A**1 5 9 **F**3 8 19 20 25 27 29 30 31 33 34 37 39 41 42 44 45 46 49 51 52 58 61 65 67 71 72 73 74 **S** Department of Veterans Affairs, Washington, DC

	Control	Service	Staffed Beds	Admissions	Census	Outpatient Visits	Births	Total	Payroll	Personnel
VETERANS AFFAIRS MEDICAL CENTER	45	10	51	2545	45	126440	0	42137	21420	482

✠ WASHINGTON REGIONAL MEDICAL CENTER, 1125 North College Avenue, Zip 72703–1994; tel. 501/713–1000; Patrick D. Flynn, President and Chief Executive Officer (Total facility includes 12 beds in nursing home–type unit) (Nonreporting) **A**1 2 3 5 9 10

	Control	Service	Staffed Beds	Admissions	Census	Outpatient Visits	Births	Total	Payroll	Personnel
WASHINGTON REGIONAL MEDICAL CENTER	23	10	203	—	—	—	—	—	—	—

FORDYCE—Dallas County

DALLAS COUNTY HOSPITAL, 201 Clifton Street, Zip 71742–3099; tel. 501/352–3155; Greg R. McNeil, Administrator **A**9 10 **F**8 19 22 27 32 49 52 57 59 65 **S** Healthcorp of Tennessee, Inc., Chattanooga, TN

	Control	Service	Staffed Beds	Admissions	Census	Outpatient Visits	Births	Total	Payroll	Personnel
DALLAS COUNTY HOSPITAL	33	10	26	681	10	12323	0	8666	4122	201

FORREST CITY—St. Francis County

✠ BAPTIST MEMORIAL HOSPITAL–FORREST CITY, 1601 Newcastle Road, Zip 72335, Mailing Address: P.O. Box 667, Zip 72336–0667; tel. 870/261–0000; Charles R. Daugherty, Administrator **A**1 9 10 **F**3 7 8 11 19 21 22 26 28 30 32 33 35 37 39 40 41 44 46 49 52 55 57 64 65 67 69 71 73 **S** Baptist Memorial Health Care Corporation, Memphis, TN

	Control	Service	Staffed Beds	Admissions	Census	Outpatient Visits	Births	Total	Payroll	Personnel
BAPTIST MEMORIAL HOSPITAL–FORREST CITY	23	10	86	2217	27	17331	570	—	—	218

Hospital, Address, Telephone, Administrator, Approval, Facility, and Physician Codes, Health Care System, Network	Classi-fication Codes		Utilization Data					Expense (thousands) of dollars		
	Control	Service	Staffed Beds	Admissions	Census	Outpatient Visits	Births	Total	Payroll	Personnel

★ American Hospital Association (AHA) membership
☐ Joint Commission on Accreditation of Healthcare Organizations (JCAHO) accreditation
- American Osteopathic Healthcare Association (AOHA) membership
○ American Osteopathic Association (AOA) accreditation
△ Commission on Accreditation of Rehabilitation Facilities (CARF) accreditation
Control codes 61, 63, 64, 71, 72 and 73 indicate hospitals listed by AOHA, but not registered by AHA. For definition of numerical codes, see page A4

FORT SMITH—Sebastian County										
HARBOR VIEW MERCY HOSPITAL, 10301 Mayo Road, Zip 72903–1631, Mailing Address: P.O. Box 17000, Zip 72917–7000; tel. 501/484–5550; Richard Cameron, M.D., Administrator (Nonreporting) **A**9 10 **S** Sisters of Mercy Health System–St. Louis, Saint Louis, MO	21	22	80	—	—	—	—	—	—	—
☐ HEALTHSOUTH REHABILITATION HOSPITAL OF FORT SMITH, 1401 South J Street, Zip 72901–5155; tel. 501/785–3300; Claudia A. Eisenmann, Director Operations (Nonreporting) **A**1 9 10 **S** HEALTHSOUTH Corporation, Birmingham, AL	33	46	80	—	—	—	—	—	—	—
★ SPARKS REGIONAL MEDICAL CENTER, 1311 South I Street, Zip 72901–4995, Mailing Address: P.O. Box 17006, Zip 72917–7006; tel. 501/441–4000; Michael D. Helm, President (Nonreporting) **A**1 2 3 5 9 10 Web address: www.sparks.org	23	10	439	—	—	—	—	—	—	—
★ ST. EDWARD MERCY MEDICAL CENTER, 7301 Rogers Avenue, Zip 72903–4189, Mailing Address: P.O. Box 17000, Zip 72917–7000; tel. 501/484–6000; Michael L. Morgan, President and Chief Executive Officer **A**1 2 5 9 10 **F**1 3 4 7 8 10 14 15 16 19 20 21 22 24 25 26 29 31 32 33 34 35 37 40 41 42 43 44 49 52 53 54 55 56 57 58 59 63 64 65 67 68 71 72 73 **P**6 8 **S** Sisters of Mercy Health System–St. Louis, Saint Louis, MO	21	10	260	15063	219	105655	1805	114167	38633	1421
GRAVETTE—Benton County										
GRAVETTE MEDICAL CENTER HOSPITAL, 1101 Jackson Street S.W., Zip 72736–0470, Mailing Address: P.O. Box 470, Zip 72736–0470; tel. 501/787–5291; John F. Phillips, Administrator (Nonreporting) **A**9 10	23	10	58	—	—	—	—	—	—	—
HARRISON—Boone County										
★ NORTH ARKANSAS REGIONAL MEDICAL CENTER, 620 North Willow Street, Zip 72601–2994; tel. 870/365–2000; Timothy E. Hill, Chief Executive Officer (Total facility includes 14 beds in nursing home–type unit) **A**9 10 **F**7 8 10 12 14 15 16 17 19 21 22 23 28 30 32 33 35 37 40 41 42 44 45 46 49 60 64 65 67 71 73 74 **P**8	23	10	125	5349	59	270724	503	33934	15925	597
HEBER SPRINGS—Cleburne County										
★ BAPTIST MEDICAL CENTER HEBER SPRINGS, 2319 Highway 110 West, Zip 72543; tel. 501/206–3000; Edward L. Lacy, Administrator **A**1 10 **F**8 14 15 16 19 22 28 30 32 34 44 71 **P**3 7 **S** Baptist Health, Little Rock, AR	23	10	24	510	5	14293	0	5371	2624	106
HELENA—Phillips County										
★ HELENA REGIONAL MEDICAL CENTER, 1801 Martin Luther King Drive, Zip 72342, Mailing Address: P.O. Box 788, Zip 72342–0788; tel. 870/338–5800; Steve Reeder, Chief Executive Officer (Nonreporting) **A**1 9 10 **S** Quorum Health Group/Quorum Health Resources, Inc., Brentwood, TN	23	10	125	—	—	—	—	—	—	—
HOPE—Hempstead County										
★ MEDICAL PARK HOSPITAL, (Formerly Columbia Medical Park Hospital), 2001 South Main Street, Zip 71801–8194; tel. 870/777–2323; Jimmy Leopard, Chief Executive Officer **A**1 9 10 **F**8 12 14 15 16 19 21 22 28 30 34 35 37 38 39 41 44 45 46 49 57 65 71 73 74 **P**7 8 **S** Triad Hospitals, Inc., Dallas, TX	33	10	79	2988	37	31487	328	15304	6513	234
HOT SPRINGS—Garland County										
★ NATIONAL PARK MEDICAL CENTER, 1910 Malvern Avenue, Zip 71901–7799; tel. 501/321–1000; Jerry D. Mabry, Executive Director **A**1 9 10 **F**4 7 8 10 12 16 19 21 22 23 27 28 29 32 34 35 37 39 40 41 42 43 44 45 46 48 49 52 55 56 57 63 64 65 67 71 73 74 **P**4 5 7 8 **S** TENET Healthcare Corporation, Santa Barbara, CA	33	10	166	6879	127	112448	703	48977	17236	583
★ ST. JOSEPH'S REGIONAL HEALTH CENTER, 300 Werner Street, Zip 71913–6448, Mailing Address: P.O. Box 29001, Zip 71913–9001; tel. 501/622–1000; Randall J. Fale, FACHE, President and Chief Executive Officer (Total facility includes 57 beds in nursing home–type unit) **A**1 2 9 10 **F**4 7 8 10 11 12 15 16 17 19 21 22 26 27 28 29 30 32 34 35 36 37 39 40 41 42 43 44 46 48 49 52 57 60 64 65 66 67 71 72 73 74 **S** Sisters of Mercy Health System–St. Louis, Saint Louis, MO Web address: www.saintjosephs.com	21	10	266	11691	193	288829	851	103769	40562	1353
HOT SPRINGS NATIONAL PARK—Garland County										
★ LEVI HOSPITAL, 300 Prospect Avenue, Zip 71901–4097; tel. 501/624–1281; Patrick McCabe, Jr., Executive Director **A**1 9 10 **F**5 15 16 19 21 26 27 28 29 32 33 34 35 49 52 53 54 56 57 58 59 65 66 67 71 Web address: www.levihospital.com	23	22	15	246	5	—	0	6534	4081	159
JACKSONVILLE—Pulaski County										
★ △ REBSAMEN MEDICAL CENTER, (Formerly Rebsamen Regional Medical Center), 1400 West Braden Street, Zip 72076–3788; tel. 501/985–7000; Thomas R. Siemers, Chief Executive Officer **A**1 7 9 10 **F**7 8 10 12 19 21 22 23 26 28 29 30 32 34 37 39 40 41 42 44 46 48 49 52 57 65 66 67 71 73 74 **P**1 7 **S** Quorum Health Group/Quorum Health Resources, Inc., Brentwood, TN	23	10	113	4430	65	73780	442	35353	15432	486
★ U. S. AIR FORCE HOSPITAL LITTLE ROCK, Little Rock AFB, Zip 72099–5057; tel. 501/987–7411; Colonel Norman L. Sims, MSC, USAF, Commander (Nonreporting) **A**9 **S** Department of the Air Force, Bowling AFB, DC	41	10	12	—	—	—	—	—	—	—
JONESBORO—Craighead County										
☐ △ HEALTHSOUTH REHABILITATION HOSPITAL OF JONESBORO, 1201 Fleming Avenue, Zip 72401–4311, Mailing Address: P.O. Box 1680, Zip 72403–1680; tel. 870/932–0440; Brenda Antwine, Administrator **A**1 7 9 10 **F**12 15 16 25 27 28 30 34 48 49 65 66 67 **S** HEALTHSOUTH Corporation, Birmingham, AL	33	46	60	1079	50	23422	0	10141	5285	158

	Classi-fication Codes		Utilization Data					Expense (thousands) of dollars		

Hospital, Address, Telephone, Administrator, Approval, Facility, and Physician Codes, Health Care System, Network

★ American Hospital Association (AHA) membership
□ Joint Commission on Accreditation of Healthcare Organizations (JCAHO) accreditation
+ American Osteopathic Healthcare Association (AOHA) membership
○ American Osteopathic Association (AOA) accreditation
△ Commission on Accreditation of Rehabilitation Facilities (CARF) accreditation
Control codes 61, 63, 64, 71, 72 and 73 indicate hospitals listed by AOHA, but not registered by AHA. For definition of numerical codes, see page A4

Column headers: Control | Service | Staffed Beds | Admissions | Census | Outpatient Visits | Births | Total | Payroll | Personnel

☒ **REGIONAL MEDICAL CENTER OF NORTHEAST ARKANSAS,** (Formerly Methodist Hospital of Jonesboro), 3024 Stadium Boulevard, Zip 72401–7493; tel. 870/972–7000; Philip H. Walkley, Jr., Chief Executive Officer **A**1 5 9 10 **F**4 7 8 10 11 12 14 16 17 19 20 21 22 26 28 29 30 31 32 33 34 35 37 38 39 40 41 42 43 44 45 46 47 48 49 63 65 66 67 69 71 72 73 74 **P**8 **S** TENET Healthcare Corporation, Santa Barbara, CA
Web address: www.tenethealth.com/jonesboro
— Control 33, Service 10, Staffed Beds 104, Admissions 4114, Census 51, Outpatient Visits 66165, Births 656, Total 31010, Payroll 10184, Personnel 342

□ **ST. BERNARD'S BEHAVIORAL HEALTH,** 2712 East Johnson Avenue, Zip 72401–1874; tel. 870/932–2800; Andrew DeYoung, Administrator **A**1 10 **F**2 3 4 6 7 8 10 11 12 13 14 15 16 17 18 19 20 21 22 23 24 25 26 27 28 29 30 32 33 34 35 37 39 40 41 42 43 44 45 46 48 49 52 53 54 55 56 57 58 59 60 61 62 64 65 66 67 70 71 73 74 **P**3 8
— Control 21, Service 22, Staffed Beds 60, Admissions 1124, Census 33, Outpatient Visits 5677, Births 0, Total 6709, Payroll 3371, Personnel 75

☒ **ST. BERNARDS REGIONAL MEDICAL CENTER,** 224 East Matthews Street, Zip 72401–3156, Mailing Address: P.O. Box 9320, Zip 72403–9320; tel. 870/972–4100; Ben E. Owens, President (Total facility includes 27 beds in nursing home–type unit) **A**1 2 3 5 9 10 **F**2 3 4 6 7 8 10 11 12 13 14 15 16 17 18 19 20 21 22 23 24 25 26 27 28 29 30 31 32 33 34 35 36 37 39 40 41 42 43 44 45 49 52 53 54 55 56 57 58 60 61 62 64 65 66 67 68 71 73 74 **P**3 8
Web address: www.sbrmc.com
— Control 21, Service 10, Staffed Beds 306, Admissions 17616, Census 259, Outpatient Visits 127732, Births 1591, Total 109538, Payroll 36633, Personnel 1462

LAKE VILLAGE—Chicot County

★ **CHICOT MEMORIAL HOSPITAL,** 2729 Highway 65 and 82 South, Zip 71653, Mailing Address: P.O. Box 512, Zip 71653–0512; tel. 870/265–5351; Robert R. Reddish, Administrator and Chief Executive Officer (Nonreporting) **A**9 10 **S** Quorum Health Group/Quorum Health Resources, Inc., Brentwood, TN
— Control 13, Service 10, Staffed Beds 35, Admissions —, Census —, Outpatient Visits —, Births —, Total —, Payroll —, Personnel —

LITTLE ROCK—Pulaski County

☒ △ **ARKANSAS CHILDREN'S HOSPITAL,** 800 Marshall Street, Zip 72202–3591; tel. 501/320–1100; Jonathan R. Bates, M.D., President and Chief Executive Officer **A**1 3 5 7 8 9 10 **F**3 4 5 9 10 11 12 13 14 17 19 20 21 22 27 28 30 31 34 35 38 39 42 43 44 46 47 48 49 51 54 56 58 63 65 66 67 68 71 73 **P**7 8
Web address: www.ach.uams.ed
— Control 23, Service 50, Staffed Beds 237, Admissions 10499, Census 179, Outpatient Visits 232655, Births 0, Total 164400, Payroll 74369, Personnel 2403

☒ **ARKANSAS STATE HOSPITAL,** 4313 West Markham Street, Zip 72205–4096; tel. 501/686–9000; Glenn R. Sago, Administrator **A**1 3 5 9 10 **F**3 12 16 52 53 55 65
Web address: www.state.ar.us/dhs/dmhs
— Control 12, Service 22, Staffed Beds 182, Admissions 1306, Census 153, Outpatient Visits —, Births 0, Total —, Payroll —, Personnel —

☒ **BAPTIST MEDICAL CENTER,** 9601 Interstate 630, Exit 7, Zip 72205–7299; tel. 501/202–2000; Steven Douglas Weeks, Senior Vice President and Administrator **A**1 3 5 6 9 10 **F**2 3 4 6 7 8 10 11 12 13 14 15 16 17 18 19 20 21 22 23 24 25 26 27 28 29 30 31 32 33 34 35 37 38 39 40 41 42 43 44 45 46 48 49 52 53 54 55 56 57 58 59 60 61 62 63 64 65 66 67 68 70 71 72 73 74 **P**1 3 5 6 7 **S** Baptist Health, Little Rock, AR
— Control 23, Service 10, Staffed Beds 519, Admissions 25601, Census 389, Outpatient Visits 187099, Births 2314, Total 244061, Payroll 94162, Personnel 2855

☒ △ **BAPTIST REHABILITATION INSTITUTE,** 9601 Interstate 630, Exit 7, Zip 72205–7249; tel. 501/202–7000; Steven Douglas Weeks, Senior Vice President and Administrator **A**1 3 5 7 9 10 **F**2 3 4 6 7 8 10 11 12 13 14 15 16 17 18 19 20 21 22 23 24 25 26 27 28 29 30 31 32 33 34 35 36 37 38 39 40 41 42 43 44 45 46 48 49 50 52 63 64 65 66 67 68 70 71 72 73 74 **P**1 3 5 6 7 **S** Baptist Health, Little Rock, AR
— Control 23, Service 46, Staffed Beds 100, Admissions 1583, Census 65, Outpatient Visits 51320, Births 0, Total 18417, Payroll 8709, Personnel 261

□ **BHC PINNACLE POINTE HOSPITAL,** 11501 Financial Center Parkway, Zip 72211–3715; tel. 501/223–3322; Jerry Hooper, Chief Executive Officer (Nonreporting) **A**1 9 10 **S** Behavioral Healthcare Corporation, Nashville, TN
— Control 33, Service 22, Staffed Beds 98, Admissions —, Census —, Outpatient Visits —, Births —, Total —, Payroll —, Personnel —

☒ **CENTRAL ARKANSAS VETERANS AFFAIRS HEALTHCARE SYSTEM,** (Includes North Little Rock Division, North Little Rock), 4300 West Seventh Street, Zip 72205–5484; tel. 501/257–1000; George H. Gray, Jr., Director (Total facility includes 152 beds in nursing home–type unit) **A**1 2 3 5 8 9 **F**1 3 4 5 8 10 11 12 16 17 18 19 20 21 22 24 26 28 30 31 32 34 35 37 39 41 42 44 45 46 48 49 51 52 54 55 56 57 58 59 61 63 64 65 67 71 73 74 **P**6 **S** Department of Veterans Affairs, Washington, DC
— Control 45, Service 10, Staffed Beds 502, Admissions 9872, Census 607, Outpatient Visits 422665, Births 0, Total 221436, Payroll 111002, Personnel 2983

COLUMBIA DOCTORS HOSPITAL See St. Vincent Doctors Hospital

□ **SOUTHWEST REGIONAL MEDICAL CENTER,** (Formerly Southwest Hospital), 11401 Interstate 30; Zip 72209–7056; tel. 501/455–7100; R. Mark Cain, Executive Director (Nonreporting) **A**1 9 10 **S** Health Management Associates, Naples, FL
— Control 23, Service 10, Staffed Beds 125, Admissions —, Census —, Outpatient Visits —, Births —, Total —, Payroll —, Personnel —

★ **ST. VINCENT DOCTORS HOSPITAL,** (Formerly Columbia Doctors Hospital), 6101 West Capitol, Zip 72205–5331; tel. 501/661–4000 (Nonreporting) **A**9 10 **S** Columbia/HCA Healthcare Corporation, Nashville, TN
— Control 33, Service 10, Staffed Beds 308, Admissions —, Census —, Outpatient Visits —, Births —, Total —, Payroll —, Personnel —

☒ **ST. VINCENT INFIRMARY MEDICAL CENTER,** Two St. Vincent Circle, Zip 72205–5499; tel. 501/660–3000; Diana T. Hueter, President and Chief Executive Officer (Total facility includes 57 beds in nursing home–type unit) **A**1 2 3 5 9 10 **F**4 5 6 7 8 10 11 12 14 15 16 17 18 19 20 21 22 23 24 25 26 27 29 30 31 32 33 34 35 36 37 38 39 40 41 42 43 44 46 48 49 50 51 52 53 54 55 57 58 59 60 63 64 65 67 71 73 74 **P**7 8 **S** Catholic Health Initiatives, Denver, CO
Web address: www.stvincenthealth.org
— Control 21, Service 10, Staffed Beds 657, Admissions 20848, Census 292, Outpatient Visits 299699, Births 1226, Total 196998, Payroll 79904, Personnel 3364

☒ **UNIVERSITY HOSPITAL OF ARKANSAS,** 4301 West Markham Street, Zip 72205–7102; tel. 501/686–7000; Richard Pierson, Executive Director, Clinical Programs **A**1 2 3 5 8 9 10 **F**4 5 7 8 10 11 12 14 15 16 19 20 21 22 26 28 29 30 31 32 34 35 37 38 39 40 41 42 43 44 45 46 49 50 51 54 55 56 57 58 60 61 63 64 66 67 68 71 72 73 74 **P**3
Web address: www.uams.edu/medcenter
— Control 12, Service 10, Staffed Beds 283, Admissions 13954, Census 251, Outpatient Visits 277153, Births 2054, Total 190317, Payroll 78506, Personnel 2544

Hospital, Address, Telephone, Administrator, Approval, Facility, and Physician Codes, Health Care System, Network	Classi-fication Codes		Utilization Data					Expense (thousands) of dollars		
	Control	Service	Staffed Beds	Admissions	Census	Outpatient Visits	Births	Total	Payroll	Personnel

MAGNOLIA—Columbia County

✛ MAGNOLIA HOSPITAL, 101 Hospital Drive, Zip 71753–2416, Mailing Address: Box 629, Zip 71753–0629; tel. 870/235–3000; Kirk Reamey, Chief Executive Officer **A**1 9 10 **F**7 8 11 17 19 21 22 28 30 32 34 39 40 41 44 45 46 48 49 65 67 71 73 **S** Christus Health, Houston, TX — 14 10 62 2109 29 31204 220 13123 6561 289

MALVERN—Hot Spring County

★ H.S.C. MEDICAL CENTER, 1001 Schneider Drive, Zip 72104–4828; tel. 501/337–4911; Jeff Curtis, President and Chief Executive Officer (Nonreporting) **A**9 10 **S** Sisters of Mercy Health System–St. Louis, Saint Louis, MO — 23 10 77 — — — — — — —

MAUMELLE—Pulaski County

☐ CHARTER BEHAVIORAL HEALTH SYSTEM OF LITTLE ROCK, 1601 Murphy Drive, Zip 72113; tel. 501/851–8700; Lucinda DeBruce, Chief Executive Officer **A**1 9 10 **F**2 3 14 34 52 53 54 55 56 57 58 59 **S** Magellan Health Services, Atlanta, GA — 33 22 60 1065 34 198 0 — — 82

MCGEHEE—Desha County

MCGEHEE–DESHA COUNTY HOSPITAL, 900 South Third, Zip 71654–0351, Mailing Address: Box 351, Zip 71654–0351; tel. 501/222–5600 (Nonreporting) **A**9 10
Web address: www.menamedical.com — 13 10 26 — — — — — — —

MENA—Polk County

MENA MEDICAL CENTER, 311 North Morrow Street, Zip 71953–2516; tel. 501/394–6100; Albert Pilkington, III, Administrator and Chief Executive Officer (Nonreporting) **A**9 10 **S** Quorum Health Group/Quorum Health Resources, Inc., Brentwood, TN — 14 10 42 — — — — — — —

MONTICELLO—Drew County

★ DREW MEMORIAL HOSPITAL, 778 Scogin Drive, Zip 71655–5728; tel. 870/367–2411; Darren Caldwell, Chief Executive Officer **A**9 10 **F**7 8 12 14 15 16 19 21 22 28 29 30 32 34 35 36 37 39 40 41 42 44 45 46 49 65 71 **P**8
Web address: www.drewmemorial.org — 13 10 50 2546 29 18226 322 10983 4717 216

MORRILTON—Conway County

★ ST. ANTHONY'S HEALTHCARE CENTER, 4 Hospital Drive, Zip 72110–4510; tel. 501/354–3512; Johnson L. Smith, Chief Executive Officer and Administrator **A**9 10 **F**1 7 8 11 12 16 17 19 21 22 26 27 32 33 35 37 40 41 44 46 49 52 56 57 64 65 66 67 71 73 **P**8 — 21 10 73 1711 29 18493 82 11336 5481 256

MOUNTAIN HOME—Baxter County

★ BAXTER COUNTY REGIONAL HOSPITAL, 624 Hospital Drive, Zip 72653–2954; tel. 870/424–1000; H. William Anderson, Administrator (Total facility includes 35 beds in nursing home–type unit) (Nonreporting) **A**2 9 10
Web address: www.baxterregional.org — 23 10 194 — — — — — — —

MOUNTAIN VIEW—Stone County

STONE COUNTY MEDICAL CENTER, Highway 14 East, Zip 72560, Mailing Address: P.O. Box 510, Zip 72560–0510; tel. 870/269–4361; Stanley Townsend, Administrator **A**9 10 **F**8 19 20 22 32 33 44 49 65 71 — 33 10 30 729 8 15562 4 5328 2521 115

MURFREESBORO—Pike County

PIKE COUNTY MEMORIAL HOSPITAL, 315 East 13th Street, Zip 71958–9541; tel. 870/285–3182; Rosemary Fritts, Administrator **A**9 10 **F**19 22 32 34 71 **P**5 — 13 10 32 780 7 4877 0 1595 924 54

NASHVILLE—Howard County

★ HOWARD MEMORIAL HOSPITAL, 800 West Leslie Street, Zip 71852–0381, Mailing Address: Box 381, Zip 71852–0381; tel. 870/845–4400; Rex Jones, Chief Executive Officer **A**9 10 **F**8 12 16 19 21 22 26 28 29 30 32 35 37 44 46 49 52 57 65 67 71 73 **P**3 8 **S** Quorum Health Group/Quorum Health Resources, Inc., Brentwood, TN — 23 10 50 957 13 19632 0 8642 3856 196

NEWPORT—Jackson County

✛ HARRIS HOSPITAL, 1205 McLain Street, Zip 72112–3533; tel. 870/523–8911; Robin E. Lake, Chief Executive Officer (Nonreporting) **A**1 9 10 **S** Community Health Systems, Inc., Brentwood, TN — 33 10 88 — — — — — — —

★ NEWPORT HOSPITAL AND CLINIC, 2000 McLain Street, Zip 72112–3697; tel. 870/523–6721; Eugene Zuber, Administrator **A**9 10 **F**7 8 10 11 17 19 21 22 28 30 31 32 34 35 40 42 44 71 73
Web address: www.biz.ipa.net/newporthospital — 33 10 86 2566 33 11405 88 10141 4418 171

NORTH LITTLE ROCK—Pulaski County

✛ BAPTIST MEMORIAL MEDICAL CENTER, One Pershing Circle, Zip 72114–1899; tel. 501/202–3000; Harrison M. Dean, Senior Vice President and Administrator **A**1 9 10 **F**3 4 6 7 8 10 11 12 13 14 16 17 19 21 22 23 24 26 27 28 29 30 31 32 33 34 35 37 39 40 41 42 43 44 45 46 48 49 51 52 53 54 55 56 57 58 59 60 62 63 64 65 66 67 68 70 71 72 73 74 **P**1 3 5 7 **S** Baptist Health, Little Rock, AR
Web address: www.baptist–health.org — 23 10 200 7685 86 66397 572 61232 27401 889

☐ BRIDGEWAY, 21 Bridgeway Road, Zip 72113; tel. 501/771–1500; Barry Pipkin, Chief Executive Officer and Managing Director (Nonreporting) **A**1 9 10 **S** Universal Health Services, Inc., King of Prussia, PA
NORTH LITTLE ROCK DIVISION See Central Arkansas Veterans Affairs Healthcare System, Little Rock — 33 22 70 — — — — — — —

OSCEOLA—Mississippi County

✛ BAPTIST MEMORIAL HOSPITAL–OSCEOLA, 611 West Lee Avenue, Zip 72370–3001, Mailing Address: P.O. Box 607, Zip 72370–0607; tel. 870/563–7000; Joel E. North, Administrator **A**1 9 10 **F**12 14 15 16 19 22 28 30 32 33 37 44 46 53 65 71 **P**3 7 **S** Baptist Memorial Health Care Corporation, Memphis, TN — 21 10 59 2214 24 17210 0 7783 3263 133

Hospital, Address, Telephone, Administrator, Approval, Facility, and Physician Codes, Health Care System, Network	Classi-fication Codes		Utilization Data					Expense (thousands) of dollars		
★ American Hospital Association (AHA) membership □ Joint Commission on Accreditation of Healthcare Organizations (JCAHO) accreditation + American Osteopathic Healthcare Association (AOHA) membership ○ American Osteopathic Association (AOA) accreditation △ Commission on Accreditation of Rehabilitation Facilities (CARF) accreditation Control codes 61, 63, 64, 71, 72 and 73 indicate hospitals listed by AOHA, but not registered by AHA. For definition of numerical codes, see page A4	Control	Service	Staffed Beds	Admissions	Census	Outpatient Visits	Births	Total	Payroll	Personnel

OZARK—Franklin County

★ MERCY HOSPITAL–TURNER MEMORIAL, 801 West River Street, Zip 72949–3000; tel. 501/667–4138; John C. Neal, Regional Administrator and Chief Administrative Officer (Nonreporting) **A**9 10 **S** Sisters of Mercy Health System–St. Louis, Saint Louis, MO

| | 21 | 10 | 39 | — | — | — | — | — | — | — |

PARAGOULD—Greene County

⊠ △ ARKANSAS METHODIST HOSPITAL, 900 West Kingshighway, Zip 72450–5942, Mailing Address: P.O. Box 339, Zip 72451–0339; tel. 870/239–7000; Ronald K. Rooney, President **A**1 7 9 10 **F**7 8 10 12 15 16 17 19 21 22 23 24 26 27 28 30 32 34 35 37 40 41 42 44 45 48 49 51 61 65 71 74 **P**8
Web address: www.amhparagould.com

| | 23 | 10 | 129 | 4202 | 58 | 41119 | 329 | 25945 | 10096 | 466 |

PARIS—Logan County

★ NORTH LOGAN MERCY HOSPITAL, 500 East Academy, Zip 72855–4099; tel. 501/963–6101; Jim L. Maddox, Chief Administrative Officer **A**9 10 **F**1 2 3 4 5 6 7 8 9 10 11 12 13 14 15 16 17 18 19 20 21 22 23 24 25 26 27 28 29 30 31 32 33 34 35 36 37 38 39 40 41 42 43 44 45 46 47 48 49 50 51 52 53 54 55 56 57 58 59 60 61 62 63 64 65 66 67 68 70 71 72 73 74 **P**5 8 **S** Sisters of Mercy Health System–St. Louis, Saint Louis, MO

| | 21 | 10 | 16 | 233 | 3 | 8146 | 0 | 3083 | 1317 | 54 |

PIGGOTT—Clay County

★ PIGGOTT COMMUNITY HOSPITAL, 1206 Gordon Duckworth Drive, Zip 72454–1911; tel. 870/598–3881; James L. Magee, Executive Director **A**9 10 **F**8 19 22 27 32 35 44 49 65 71

| | 14 | 10 | 35 | 1096 | 14 | 23112 | 0 | 5785 | 3311 | 142 |

PINE BLUFF—Jefferson County

⊠ JEFFERSON REGIONAL MEDICAL CENTER, 1515 West 42nd Avenue, Zip 71603–7089; tel. 870/541–7100; Robert P. Atkinson, President and Chief Executive Officer (Total facility includes 160 beds in nursing home–type unit) **A**1 2 3 5 6 9 10 **F**3 4 7 8 10 11 12 14 15 16 17 18 19 21 22 23 24 25 27 28 29 30 31 32 33 34 35 37 39 40 41 42 43 44 45 46 48 49 51 52 54 55 56 57 58 59 60 63 64 65 66 67 70 71 72 73 74

| | 23 | 10 | 535 | 13083 | 350 | 74023 | 1487 | 113310 | 45169 | 1484 |

POCAHONTAS—Randolph County

★ RANDOLPH COUNTY MEDICAL CENTER, 2801 Medical Center Drive, Zip 72455–9497; tel. 870/892–6000; Michael G. Layfield, Chief Executive Officer (Nonreporting) **A**9 10 **S** Community Health Systems, Inc., Brentwood, TN

| | 33 | 10 | 50 | — | — | — | — | — | — | — |

ROGERS—Benton County

⊠ ST. MARY–ROGERS MEMORIAL HOSPITAL, 1200 West Walnut Street, Zip 72756–3599; tel. 501/636–0200; Susan Barrett, President and Chief Executive Officer **A**1 2 9 10 **F**1 7 8 10 11 12 14 15 16 19 21 22 28 32 33 34 35 38 39 40 41 42 44 49 63 64 65 67 71 73 **P**6 **S** Sisters of Mercy Health System–St. Louis, Saint Louis, MO
Web address: www.mercyhealthnwa.smhs.com

| | 21 | 10 | 102 | 5971 | 58 | 49075 | 1156 | 38559 | 18442 | 636 |

RUSSELLVILLE—Pope County

⊠ △ SAINT MARY'S REGIONAL MEDICAL CENTER, 1808 West Main Street, Zip 72801–2724; tel. 501/968–2841; Mike McCoy, Chief Executive Officer **A**1 7 9 10 **F**7 8 10 11 12 15 16 17 19 21 22 23 24 25 26 28 29 30 32 34 35 37 40 41 42 44 46 48 49 59 60 63 64 65 66 67 71 73 74 **P**7 8 **S** TENET Healthcare Corporation, Santa Barbara, CA

| | 33 | 10 | 157 | 5827 | 82 | 97764 | 1032 | 33451 | 12961 | 452 |

SALEM—Fulton County

FULTON COUNTY HOSPITAL, Highway 9, Zip 72576, Mailing Address: P.O. Box 517, Zip 72576–0517; tel. 501/895–2691; Franklin E. Wise, Administrator (Nonreporting) **A**9 10

| | 13 | 10 | 30 | — | — | — | — | — | — | — |

SEARCY—White County

⊠ △ CENTRAL ARKANSAS HOSPITAL, 1200 South Main Street, Zip 72143–7397; tel. 501/278–3131; David C. Laffoon, CHE, Chief Executive Officer **A**1 2 7 9 10 **F**7 10 11 14 15 16 19 21 22 24 27 32 34 35 37 38 40 42 44 48 52 56 63 65 67 71 73 74 **P**6 7 8 **S** TENET Healthcare Corporation, Santa Barbara, CA

| | 33 | 10 | 120 | 5138 | 73 | 83458 | 499 | 9283 | 13098 | — |

⊠ WHITE COUNTY MEDICAL CENTER, 3214 East Race, Zip 72143–4847; tel. 501/268–6121; Raymond W. Montgomery, II, President and Chief Executive Officer **A**1 2 9 10 **F**7 10 11 12 13 15 16 19 20 21 22 23 24 25 28 30 31 32 33 34 35 37 38 40 41 42 44 45 46 48 49 62 65 66 67 68 71 73 74

| | 23 | 10 | 154 | 6811 | 71 | 35890 | 643 | 30821 | 13384 | 563 |

SHERWOOD—Pulaski County

□ △ ST. VINCENT REHABILITATION HOSPITAL, (Formerly St Vincent–North Rehabilitation Hospital), 2201 Wildwood Avenue, Zip 72120–5074, Mailing Address: P.O. Box 6930, Zip 72124–6930; tel. 501/834–1800; Ronnie Sairls, Administrator (Total facility includes 10 beds in nursing home–type unit) **A**1 7 9 10 **F**14 15 16 48 49 64 **S** HEALTHSOUTH Corporation, Birmingham, AL

| | 32 | 46 | 60 | 823 | 39 | 10417 | 0 | 10822 | 5249 | 147 |

SILOAM SPRINGS—Benton County

★ SILOAM SPRINGS MEMORIAL HOSPITAL, 205 East Jefferson Street, Zip 72761–3697; tel. 501/524–4141; Donald E. Patterson, Administrator **A**9 10 **F**7 8 12 16 17 19 21 22 28 30 32 34 37 39 40 44 45 46 64 65 67 71 73 **S** Quorum Health Group/Quorum Health Resources, Inc., Brentwood, TN

| | 14 | 10 | 52 | 2682 | 31 | 17813 | 208 | 12388 | 6095 | 257 |

SPRINGDALE—Washington County

⊠ NORTHWEST MEDICAL CENTER, (Includes Bates Medical Center, 602 North Walton Boulevard, Bentonville, Zip 72712; tel. 501/273–2481), 609 West Maple Avenue, Zip 72764–5394, Mailing Address: P.O. Box 47, Zip 72765–0047; tel. 501/751–5711; Greg K. Stock, Chief Executive Officer (Total facility includes 22 beds in nursing home–type unit) (Nonreporting) **A**1 2 9 10 **S** Quorum Health Group/Quorum Health Resources, Inc., Brentwood, TN

| | 23 | 10 | 222 | — | — | — | — | — | — | — |

Hospital, Address, Telephone, Administrator, Approval, Facility, and Physician Codes, Health Care System, Network	Classi-fication Codes		Utilization Data					Expense (thousands) of dollars		
★ American Hospital Association (AHA) membership ▢ Joint Commission on Accreditation of Healthcare Organizations (JCAHO) accreditation ✦ American Osteopathic Healthcare Association (AOHA) membership ◯ American Osteopathic Association (AOA) accreditation △ Commission on Accreditation of Rehabilitation Facilities (CARF) accreditation Control codes 61, 63, 64, 71, 72 and 73 indicate hospitals listed by AOHA, but not registered by AHA. For definition of numerical codes, see page A4	Control	Service	Staffed Beds	Admissions	Census	Outpatient Visits	Births	Total	Payroll	Personnel

STUTTGART—Arkansas County

★ STUTTGART REGIONAL MEDICAL CENTER, North Buerkle Road, Zip 72160, Mailing Address: P.O. Box 1905, Zip 72160–1905; tel. 870/673–3511; Jim E. Bushmaier, Administrator and Chief Executive Officer **A**9 10 **F**7 15 19 21 22 30 34 35 37 40 41 44 48 49 65 71 **P**3	23	10	60	2284	28	—	201	15120	6644	235

VAN BUREN—Crawford County

▢ CRAWFORD MEMORIAL HOSPITAL, East Main & South 20th Streets, Zip 72956, Mailing Address: P.O. Box 409, Zip 72957–0409; tel. 501/474–3401; Richard Boone, Executive Director **A**1 9 10 **F**7 8 11 12 15 16 17 19 21 22 23 24 26 27 28 29 30 32 34 35 37 39 40 41 44 46 49 65 66 67 71 73 74 **P**6 **S** Health Management Associates, Naples, FL **Web address:** www.noonanrusso.com	33	10	103	2799	32	22827	43	17699	7120	220

WALDRON—Scott County

★ MERCY HOSPITAL OF SCOTT COUNTY, Highways 71 and 80, Zip 72958–9984, Mailing Address: Box 2230, Zip 72958–2230; tel. 501/637–4135; Sister Mary Alvera Simon, Administrator (Total facility includes 105 beds in nursing home–type unit) **A**9 10 **F**8 11 19 22 28 30 32 34 37 44 49 64 71 **P**5 8 **S** Sisters of Mercy Health System–St. Louis, Saint Louis, MO	21	10	129	505	103	12604	0	—	—	121

WALNUT RIDGE—Lawrence County

LAWRENCE MEMORIAL HOSPITAL, (Includes Lawrence Hall Nursing Home), 1309 West Main, Zip 72476–1430, Mailing Address: P.O. Box 839, Zip 72476–0839; tel. 501/886–1200; Lee Gentry, President (Total facility includes 181 beds in nursing home–type unit) **A**9 10 **F**8 12 16 17 19 21 22 28 29 30 32 36 39 41 44 49 64 65 67 71 73 **P**3 6	13	10	205	742	187	16288	0	11512	5123	178

WARREN—Bradley County

★ BRADLEY COUNTY MEDICAL CENTER, 404 South Bradley Street, Zip 71671; tel. 870/226–3731; Edward L. Nilles, President and Chief Executive Officer **A**9 10 **F**1 6 7 8 11 12 13 16 17 18 19 20 21 22 26 27 28 29 30 31 32 33 34 36 39 41 44 45 46 49 51 53 54 55 56 57 58 59 63 65 67 68 71 73 **P**1 3	23	10	56	1795	25	17780	172	11624	5341	189

WEST MEMPHIS—Crittenden County

▣ △ CRITTENDEN MEMORIAL HOSPITAL, 200 Tyler Avenue, Zip 72301–4223, Mailing Address: P.O. Box 2248, Zip 72303–2248; tel. 870/735–1500; Ross Hooper, Chief Executive Officer (Nonreporting) **A**1 7 9 10	23	10	95	—	—	—	—	—	—	—

WYNNE—Cross County

★ CROSS COUNTY HOSPITAL, 310 South Falls Boulevard, Zip 72396–3013, Mailing Address: P.O. Box 590, Zip 72396–0590; tel. 870/238–3300; Harry M. Baker, Chief Executive Officer **A**9 10 **F**11 15 19 22 32 35 40 44 64 65 71	13	10	53	1330	16	14632	77	6336	3002	143

CALIFORNIA

Resident population 32,667 (in thousands)
Resident population in metro areas 94.3%
Birth rate per 1,000 population 17.5
65 years and over 11.1%
Percent of persons without health insurance 20.1%

Hospital, Address, Telephone, Administrator, Approval, Facility, and Physician Codes, Health Care System, Network	Classi-fication Codes		Utilization Data					Expense (thousands) of dollars		
★ American Hospital Association (AHA) membership □ Joint Commission on Accreditation of Healthcare Organizations (JCAHO) accreditation + American Osteopathic Healthcare Association (AOHA) membership ○ American Osteopathic Association (AOA) accreditation △ Commission on Accreditation of Rehabilitation Facilities (CARF) accreditation Control codes 61, 63, 64, 71, 72 and 73 indicate hospitals listed by AOHA, but not registered by AHA. For definition of numerical codes, see page A4	Control	Service	Staffed Beds	Admissions	Census	Outpatient Visits	Births	Total	Payroll	Personnel

ALAMEDA—Alameda County

★ ALAMEDA HOSPITAL, 2070 Clinton Avenue, Zip 94501; tel. 510/522–3700; William J. Dal Cielo, Chief Executive Officer (Total facility includes 23 beds in nursing home–type unit) **A**1 9 10 **F**7 8 11 15 16 19 21 22 26 28 29 32 33 34 37 39 40 41 42 44 45 49 52 57 63 64 71 73 **P**1 4 5 6
Web address: www.alamedahospital.org

| | 23 | 10 | 135 | 4118 | 55 | 35873 | 414 | 34587 | 20635 | 338 |

ALHAMBRA—Los Angeles County

□ △ ALHAMBRA HOSPITAL, 100 South Raymond Avenue, Zip 91801, Mailing Address: Box 510, Zip 91802–0510; tel. 626/570–1606; Lee Suyenaga, Chief Executive Officer (Total facility includes 42 beds in nursing home–type unit) (Nonreporting) **A**1 2 7 9 10

| | 32 | 10 | 144 | — | — | — | — | — | — | — |

ALTURAS—Modoc County

MODOC MEDICAL CENTER, 228 McDowell Street, Zip 96101; tel. 916/233–5131; Woody J. Laughlin, Chief Executive Officer (Total facility includes 71 beds in nursing home–type unit) (Nonreporting) **A**9 10

| | 13 | 10 | 87 | — | — | — | — | — | — | — |

ANAHEIM—Orange County

□ ANAHEIM GENERAL HOSPITAL, 3350 West Ball Road, Zip 92804–9998; tel. 714/827–6700; Michael F. Hunn, Chief Executive Officer (Nonreporting) **A**1 10
Web address: www.anaheimgeneral.com

| | 33 | 10 | 146 | — | — | — | — | — | — | — |

□ ANAHEIM MEMORIAL MEDICAL CENTER, 1111 West La Palma Avenue, Zip 92801; tel. 714/774–1450; Michael C. Carter, Chief Executive Officer (Nonreporting) **A**1 2 9 10 **S** Memorial Health Services, Long Beach, CA

| | 23 | 10 | 192 | — | — | — | — | — | — | — |

★ KAISER FOUNDATION HOSPITAL, 441 North Lakeview Avenue, Zip 92807; tel. 714/279–4100; Major Janice Head, Vice President and Service Area Manager **A**1 2 3 10 **F**2 3 4 7 8 10 11 12 13 14 15 16 17 18 19 20 21 22 23 28 29 30 31 32 33 35 37 38 39 40 41 42 43 44 45 46 47 48 49 51 52 53 54 55 57 58 59 60 61 63 64 65 66 67 68 71 72 73 **S** Kaiser Foundation Hospitals, Oakland, CA
Web address: www.kaiserpermanenteca.org

| | 23 | 10 | 150 | 9999 | 101 | 53880 | 3617 | — | — | 964 |

★ MARTIN LUTHER HOSPITAL, 1830 West Romneya Drive, Zip 92801–1854; tel. 714/491–5200; Stephen E. Dixon, President and Chief Executive Officer (Total facility includes 22 beds in nursing home–type unit) **A**1 2 9 10 **F**7 8 9 10 11 12 14 15 16 17 19 21 22 26 28 29 30 32 33 35 37 38 39 40 41 42 44 46 48 49 52 54 56 60 61 64 65 67 71 73 74 **P**5 **S** Catholic Healthcare West, San Francisco, CA
Web address: www.mdselect.com

| | 23 | 10 | 205 | 5926 | 76 | 45244 | 1696 | 40614 | 20976 | 479 |

★ WEST ANAHEIM MEDICAL CENTER, 3033 West Orange Avenue, Zip 92804–3184; tel. 714/827–3000; David Culberson, Chief Executive Officer (Total facility includes 22 beds in nursing home–type unit) (Nonreporting) **A**1 2 9 10 **S** Columbia/HCA Healthcare Corporation, Nashville, TN

| | 33 | 10 | 219 | — | — | — | — | — | — | — |

★ WESTERN MEDICAL CENTER HOSPITAL ANAHEIM, 1025 South Anaheim Boulevard, Zip 92805; tel. 714/533–6220; Mark A. Meyers, President and Chief Executive Officer (Nonreporting) **A**1 9 10 **S** TENET Healthcare Corporation, Santa Barbara, CA

| | 33 | 10 | 171 | — | — | — | — | — | — | — |

ANTIOCH—Contra Costa County

★ SUTTER DELTA MEDICAL CENTER, 3901 Lone Tree Way, Zip 94509; tel. 925/779–7200; Linda Horn, Administrator **A**1 9 10 **F**7 10 12 14 15 16 19 21 22 23 35 37 41 44 49 64 65 71 73 **P**5 **S** Sutter Health, Sacramento, CA

| | 23 | 10 | 100 | 5641 | 59 | 61387 | 971 | 52788 | 21897 | 484 |

APPLE VALLEY—San Bernardino County

★ ST. MARY REGIONAL MEDICAL CENTER, 18300 Highway 18, Zip 92307–0725, Mailing Address: Box 7025, Zip 92307–0725; tel. 760/242–2311; Catherine M. Pelley, President and Chief Executive Officer (Total facility includes 20 beds in nursing home–type unit) **A**1 2 9 10 **F**4 7 8 10 12 13 15 17 19 22 26 28 32 33 34 35 37 38 40 42 43 44 45 57 64 65 68 71 73 **P**5 7 **S** St. Joseph Health System, Orange, CA

| | 21 | 10 | 195 | 8130 | 86 | 63817 | 1300 | 65159 | 21261 | 670 |

ARCADIA—Los Angeles County

★ METHODIST HOSPITAL OF SOUTHERN CALIFORNIA, 300 West Huntington Drive, Zip 91007, Mailing Address: P.O. Box 60016, Zip 91066–6016; tel. 626/445–4441; Dennis M. Lee, President **A**1 2 9 10 **F**4 7 8 10 11 12 15 16 17 19 21 22 28 30 32 33 34 36 37 38 39 40 41 42 43 44 45 48 49 52 54 55 56 57 58 59 60 64 65 66 67 68 70 71 73 **P**1 3 5 7 **S** Southern California Healthcare Systems, Pasadena, CA

| | 23 | 10 | 409 | 14928 | 191 | 64797 | 2385 | 104873 | 44341 | 1109 |

ARCATA—Humboldt County

□ MAD RIVER COMMUNITY HOSPITAL, 3800 Janes Road, Zip 95521, Mailing Address: P.O. Box 1115, Zip 95521–1115; tel. 707/822–3621; Doug Shaw, Administrator (Nonreporting) **A**1 9 10

| | 33 | 10 | 78 | — | — | — | — | — | — | — |

ARROYO GRANDE—San Luis Obispo County

□ ARROYO GRANDE COMMUNITY HOSPITAL, 345 South Halcyon Road, Zip 93420; tel. 805/489–4261; Gale E. Gascho, Chief Executive Officer **A**1 9 10 **F**4 8 15 16 19 21 22 23 26 28 31 32 34 35 37 41 42 44 49 64 66 71 72 **P**5

| | 23 | 10 | 30 | 2389 | 30 | 68384 | 0 | 19375 | 7094 | 239 |

ospital, Address, Telephone, Administrator, Approval, Facility, and Physician Codes, ealth Care System, Network	Classi-fication Codes		Utilization Data					Expense (thousands) of dollars		
American Hospital Association (AHA) membership Joint Commission on Accreditation of Healthcare Organizations (JCAHO) accreditation American Osteopathic Healthcare Association (AOHA) membership American Osteopathic Association (AOA) accreditation Commission on Accreditation of Rehabilitation Facilities (CARF) accreditation Control codes 61, 63, 64, 71, 72 and 73 indicate hospitals listed by AOHA, but not registered by AHA. For definition of numerical codes, see page A4	Control	Service	Staffed Beds	Admissions	Census	Outpatient Visits	Births	Total	Payroll	Personnel

ATASCADERO—San Luis Obispo County

☐ ATASCADERO STATE HOSPITAL, 10333 El Camino Real, Zip 93422–7001, Mailing Address: P.O. Box 7001, Zip 93423–7001; tel. 805/461–2000; Jon Demorales, Executive Director (Nonreporting) **A**1 3 5

| | 12 | 22 | 981 | — | — | — | — | — | — | — |

AUBURN—Placer County

✚ SUTTER AUBURN FAITH COMMUNITY HOSPITAL, 11815 Education Street, Zip 95604, Mailing Address: Box 8992, Zip 95604–8992; tel. 530/888–4518; Joel E. Grey, Administrator (Total facility includes 12 beds in nursing home–type unit) (Nonreporting) **A**1 9 10 **S** Sutter Health, Sacramento, CA

| | 23 | 10 | 105 | — | — | — | — | — | — | — |

AVALON—Los Angeles County

AVALON MUNICIPAL HOSPITAL AND CLINIC, 100 Falls Canyon Road, Zip 90704, Mailing Address: Box 1563, Zip 90704–1563; tel. 310/510–0700; Leah Tang, Administrator (Total facility includes 4 beds in nursing home–type unit) (Nonreporting) **A**10

| | 23 | 10 | 12 | — | — | — | — | — | — | — |

BAKERSFIELD—Kern County

✚ BAKERSFIELD MEMORIAL HOSPITAL, (Includes Memorial Center, 5201 White Lane, Zip 93309; tel. 805/398–1800), 420 34th Street, Zip 93301, Mailing Address: P.O. Box 1888, Zip 93303–1888; tel. 805/327–1792; C. Larry Carr, Regional Executive Vice President and President (Total facility includes 24 beds in nursing home–type unit) **A**1 2 9 10 **F**2 3 4 7 8 10 11 12 15 16 17 19 21 22 23 27 28 30 32 33 35 37 38 40 41 42 43 44 49 52 53 54 55 58 59 60 64 65 71 72 73 74 **P**1 3 4 5 7 **S** Catholic Healthcare West, San Francisco, CA

| | 23 | 10 | 345 | 11173 | 172 | 65112 | 1690 | 86536 | 33635 | 817 |

✚ GOOD SAMARITAN HOSPITAL, 901 Olive Drive, Zip 93308–4137; tel. 805/399–4461; Robert W. Orr, Administrator (Nonreporting) **A**1 9 10 **S** Columbia/HCA Healthcare Corporation, Nashville, TN

| | 33 | 10 | 64 | — | — | — | — | — | — | — |

☐ HEALTHSOUTH BAKERSFIELD REHABILITATION HOSPITAL, 5001 Commerce Drive, Zip 93309; tel. 661/323–5500; Robyn Field, Ph.D., Chief Operating Officer (Nonreporting) **A**1 9 10 **S** HEALTHSOUTH Corporation, Birmingham, AL

| | 33 | 46 | 60 | — | — | — | — | — | — | — |

☐ KERN MEDICAL CENTER, 1830 Flower Street, Zip 93305–4197; tel. 805/326–2000; Peter K. Bryan, Chief Executive Officer **A**1 2 3 5 8 9 10 **F**1 3 4 7 8 10 11 12 14 15 16 17 18 19 21 22 25 26 28 29 30 31 32 34 35 36 37 38 39 40 41 42 43 44 45 46 49 51 52 53 54 56 60 61 65 71 72 73 **P**6

| | 13 | 10 | 173 | 11602 | 123 | 171993 | 3001 | 105847 | 47746 | 1158 |

MEMORIAL CENTER See Bakersfield Memorial Hospital

✚ MERCY HOSPITAL, (Formerly Mercy Healthcare–Bakersfield), 2215 Truxtun Avenue, Zip 93301, Mailing Address: Box 119, Zip 93302; tel. 661/632–5000; Bernard J. Herman, President and Chief Executive Officer (Total facility includes 50 beds in nursing home–type unit) **A**1 2 9 10 **F**7 8 10 14 15 16 17 22 23 28 30 32 34 35 37 38 39 40 41 42 44 45 46 49 60 64 65 67 71 72 73 74 **P**5 7 **S** Catholic Healthcare West, San Francisco, CA
Web address: www.chw.edu

| | 21 | 10 | 261 | 12166 | 159 | 150632 | 2351 | 94491 | 36893 | — |

★ MERCY SOUTHWEST HOSPITAL, 400 Old River Road, Zip 93311; tel. 805/663–6000 (Nonreporting) **S** Catholic Healthcare West, San Francisco, CA

| | 23 | 10 | 67 | — | — | — | — | — | — | — |

✚ SAN JOAQUIN COMMUNITY HOSPITAL, 2615 Eye Street, Zip 93301, Mailing Address: Box 2615, Zip 93303–2615; tel. 661/395–3000; Douglas L. Lafferty, President and Chief Executive Officer (Nonreporting) **A**1 9 10 **S** Adventist Health, Roseville, CA

| | 23 | 10 | 178 | — | — | — | — | — | — | — |

BANNING—Riverside County

✚ SAN GORGONIO MEMORIAL HOSPITAL, 600 North Highland Springs Avenue, Zip 92220; tel. 909/845–1121; Donald N. Larkin, Chief Executive Officer (Total facility includes 16 beds in nursing home–type unit) **A**1 9 10 **F**7 8 12 15 16 17 18 19 21 22 28 30 34 37 40 41 44 49 57 58 63 64 65 67 71 72 73 74 **S** Brim Healthcare, Inc., Brentwood, TN

| | 23 | 10 | 68 | 2693 | 35 | 34675 | 295 | — | — | — |

BARSTOW—San Bernardino County

✚ BARSTOW COMMUNITY HOSPITAL, 555 South Seventh Street, Zip 92311; tel. 760/256–1761; George F. Naylor, III, Chief Executive Officer (Nonreporting) **A**1 2 9 10 **S** Community Health Systems, Inc., Brentwood, TN

| | 33 | 10 | 56 | — | — | — | — | — | — | — |

BEALE AFB—Yuba County

★ U. S. AIR FORCE HOSPITAL, 15301 Warren Shingle Road, Zip 95903–1907; tel. 530/634–4838; Lieutenant Colonel Robert G. Quinn, MSC, USAF, FACHE, Administrator (Nonreporting) **S** Department of the Air Force, Bowling AFB, DC

| | 41 | 10 | 6 | — | — | — | — | — | — | — |

BELLFLOWER—Los Angeles County

☐ BELLFLOWER MEDICAL CENTER, 9542 East Artesia Boulevard, Zip 90706; tel. 562/925–8355; Stanley Otake, Chief Executive Officer (Nonreporting) **A**1 9 10 **S** Pacific Health Corporation, Long Beach, CA

| | 33 | 10 | 145 | — | — | — | — | — | — | — |

☐ BELLWOOD GENERAL HOSPITAL, 10250 East Artesia Boulevard, Zip 90706; tel. 562/866–9028; Michael Kerr, Administrator **A**1 9 **F**7 11 15 16 17 19 22 28 30 34 35 37 40 44 49 65 67 71 73 74 **P**5

| | 33 | 10 | 60 | 3391 | 43 | 20818 | 902 | 27639 | 10672 | 331 |

✚ KAISER FOUNDATION HOSPITAL–BELLFLOWER, 9400 East Rosecrans Avenue, Zip 90706–2246; tel. 562/461–3000; Margaret Silebi, Director Operations **A**1 2 3 10 **F**2 3 4 7 8 9 10 12 13 14 15 16 17 18 19 20 21 22 23 25 26 28 29 30 31 32 33 34 35 37 38 39 40 41 42 43 44 45 46 47 48 49 50 51 52 53 54 55 56 57 58 59 60 61 63 64 65 67 68 71 72 73 74 **P**6 **S** Kaiser Foundation Hospitals, Oakland, CA
Web address: www.ca.kaiserpermanente.org

| | 23 | 10 | 306 | 19868 | 175 | 1629059 | 5143 | — | — | 1584 |

Hospital, Address, Telephone, Administrator, Approval, Facility, and Physician Codes, Health Care System, Network	Classi-fication Codes		Utilization Data					Expense (thousands) of dollars		
★ American Hospital Association (AHA) membership □ Joint Commission on Accreditation of Healthcare Organizations (JCAHO) accreditation + American Osteopathic Healthcare Association (AOHA) membership ○ American Osteopathic Association (AOA) accreditation △ Commission on Accreditation of Rehabilitation Facilities (CARF) accreditation Control codes 61, 63, 64, 71, 72 and 73 indicate hospitals listed by AOHA, but not registered by AHA. For definition of numerical codes, see page A4	Control	Service	Staffed Beds	Admissions	Census	Outpatient Visits	Births	Total	Payroll	Personnel

BERKELEY—Alameda County

✚ △ ALTA BATES MEDICAL CENTER–ASHBY CAMPUS, (Includes Alta Bates Medical Center–Herrick Campus, 2001 Dwight Way, Zip 94704; tel. 510/204–4444), 2450 Ashby Avenue, Zip 94705; tel. 510/204–4444; Warren J. Kirk, President and Chief Administrative Officer (Total facility includes 81 beds in nursing home–type unit) (Nonreporting) **A**1 2 7 9 10 **S** Sutter Health, Sacramento, CA
Web address: www.ahabates.com

	23	10	468	—	—	—	—	—	—	—

BIG BEAR LAKE—San Bernardino County

✚ BEAR VALLEY COMMUNITY HOSPITAL, 41870 Garstin Road, Zip 92315, Mailing Address: P.O. Box 1649, Zip 92315–1649; tel. 909/866–6501; Mary Norman, Chief Executive Officer (Total facility includes 21 beds in nursing home–type unit) **A**1 9 10 **F**12 14 15 17 19 21 22 26 28 29 30 32 36 44 46 49 64 65 71 73 **P**5

	16	10	30	564	20	18266	1	7462	3309	112

BISHOP—Inyo County

✚ NORTHERN INYO HOSPITAL, 150 Pioneer Lane, Zip 93514–2599; tel. 760/873–5811; Herman J. Spencer, Administrator **A**1 9 10 **F**7 8 19 22 33 34 37 40 44 49 65 71

	16	10	30	1267	10	23600	299	19523	9839	235

BLYTHE—Riverside County

□ PALO VERDE HOSPITAL, 250 North First Street, Zip 92225; tel. 760/922–4115; M. Victoria Clark, Chief Executive Officer **A**1 9 10 **F**8 12 15 16 19 22 28 29 32 35 37 40 44 49 56 65 71 73 **S** Province Healthcare Corporation, Brentwood, TN

	33	10	35	1916	15	19086	300	8784	3934	109

BRAWLEY—Imperial County

✚ PIONEERS MEMORIAL HEALTHCARE DISTRICT, 207 West Legion Road, Zip 92227–9699; tel. 760/351–3333; Claire Kuczkowski, Administrator **A**1 9 10 **F**7 8 14 15 16 17 19 21 22 28 30 31 34 35 37 38 40 41 44 46 49 63 65 68 71 73 74 **P**5 6 **S** Brim Healthcare, Inc., Brentwood, TN

	16	10	80	3978	38	43478	952	31923	12670	399

BREA—Orange County

□ BREA COMMUNITY HOSPITAL, 380 West Central Avenue, Zip 92821; tel. 714/529–0211; Gaetano Zanfini, Chief Executive Officer (Nonreporting) **A**1 9 10 **S** Doctors Community Healthcare Corporation, Scottsdale, AZ

	33	10	60	—	—	—	—	—	—	—

□ VENCOR HOSPITAL–BREA, 875 North Brea Boulevard, Zip 92821; tel. 714/529–6842; Mindy S. Moore, Administrator (Nonreporting) **A**1 10 **S** Vencor, Incorporated, Louisville, KY

	33	10	48	—	—	—	—	—	—	—

BUENA PARK—Orange County

ORANGE COUNTY COMMUNITY HOSPITAL OF BUENA PARK, 6850 Lincoln Avenue, Zip 90620–5703; tel. 714/827–1161; Michael Kerr, Chief Executive Officer (Nonreporting) **A**10

	33	22	55	—	—	—	—	—	—	—

BURBANK—Los Angeles County

✚ PROVIDENCE SAINT JOSEPH MEDICAL CENTER, 501 South Buena Vista Street, Zip 91505–4866; tel. 818/843–5111; Michael J. Madden, Chief Executive Officer (Total facility includes 121 beds in nursing home–type unit) **A**1 2 9 10 **F**4 7 8 10 11 12 13 14 15 16 17 19 21 22 23 24 26 27 28 29 30 31 32 33 34 35 37 38 39 40 41 42 43 44 45 46 48 49 60 64 65 67 68 71 72 73 74 **P**5 **S** Sisters of Providence Health System, Seattle, WA
Web address: www.providence.org

	21	10	423	20963	329	257203	2416	176724	80545	1966

BURLINGAME—San Mateo County

✚ MILLS–PENINSULA HEALTH SERVICES, (Includes Mills Hospital, 100 South San Mateo Drive, San Mateo, Zip 94401; tel. 415/696–4400; Peninsula Hospital, 1783 El Camino Real, tel. 415/696–5400), 1783 El Camino Real, Zip 94010–3205; tel. 650/696–5400; Robert W. Merwin, Chief Executive Officer (Total facility includes 75 beds in nursing home–type unit) **A**1 2 9 10 **F**1 2 3 4 5 7 8 10 11 12 14 15 16 17 18 19 20 21 22 23 24 26 27 28 29 30 31 32 34 35 37 40 41 42 43 44 45 46 48 49 52 53 54 55 56 57 58 59 60 63 64 65 67 71 72 73 74 **P**5 7 **S** Sutter Health, Sacramento, CA

	23	10	395	15817	242	399215	2291	182938	87722	1266

CAMARILLO—Ventura County

✚ ST. JOHN'S PLEASANT VALLEY HOSPITAL, 2309 Antonio Avenue, Zip 93010–1459; tel. 805/389–5800; William J. Clearwater, Vice President and Site Administrator (Total facility includes 99 beds in nursing home–type unit) **A**1 9 10 **F**7 8 11 15 16 17 19 21 22 23 28 29 30 31 35 37 40 44 45 46 49 63 64 65 67 71 73 **P**3 5 7 **S** Catholic Healthcare West, San Francisco, CA

	23	10	180	3999	109	38664	609	28707	14676	358

CAMP PENDLETON—San Diego County

✚ NAVAL HOSPITAL, Mailing Address: Box 555191, Zip 92055–5191; tel. 760/725–1288; Captain Thomas Burkhard, Commanding Officer (Nonreporting) **A**1 3 5 **S** Department of Navy, Washington, DC

	43	10	209	—	—	—	—	—	—	—

CANOGA PARK—Los Angeles County, See Los Angeles

CARMICHAEL—Sacramento County

✚ MERCY AMERICAN RIVER/MERCY SAN JUAN HOSPITAL, (Includes Mercy American River Hospital; Mercy San Juan Hospital, 6501 Coyle Avenue), 6501 Coyle Avenue, Zip 95608, Mailing Address: P.O. Box 479, Zip 95608; tel. 916/537–5000; Michael H. Erne, President (Nonreporting) **A**1 2 9 10 **S** Catholic Healthcare West, San Francisco, CA

	21	10	352	—	—	—	—	—	—	—

CASTRO VALLEY—Alameda County

✚ EDEN MEDICAL CENTER, 20103 Lake Chabot Road, Zip 94546; tel. 510/537–1234; George Bischalaney, President and Chief Executive Officer (Total facility includes 67 beds in nursing home–type unit) **A**1 9 10 **F**6 7 8 10 11 12 14 15 17 19 21 22 26 27 28 29 30 35 37 38 39 40 41 42 44 46 48 49 52 57 58 59 62 64 65 67 70 71 73 74 **P**5 **S** Sutter Health, Sacramento, CA
Web address: www.edenmedcenter.org

	23	10	258	9295	138	123598	1196	74466	—	626

Hospital, Address, Telephone, Administrator, Approval, Facility, and Physician Codes, Health Care System, Network	Classi- fication Codes		Utilization Data					Expense (thousands) of dollars		
American Hospital Association (AHA) membership Joint Commission on Accreditation of Healthcare Organizations (JCAHO) accreditation American Osteopathic Healthcare Association (AOHA) membership American Osteopathic Association (AOA) accreditation Commission on Accreditation of Rehabilitation Facilities (CARF) accreditation Control codes 61, 63, 64, 71, 72 and 73 indicate hospitals listed by AOHA, but not registered by AHA. For definition of numerical codes, see page A4	Control	Service	Staffed Beds	Admissions	Census	Outpatient Visits	Births	Total	Payroll	Personnel

ATHEDRAL CITY—Riverside County

☐ CHARTER BEHAVIORAL HEALTH SYSTEM–PALM SPRINGS, 69–696 Ramon Road, Zip 92234; tel. 760/321–2000; Diane W. Sharpe, Chief Executive Officer (Nonreporting) **A**1 10 **S** Magellan Health Services, Atlanta, GA

| | 33 | 22 | 80 | — | — | — | — | — | — | — |

EDARVILLE—Modoc County

SURPRISE VALLEY COMMUNITY HOSPITAL, Main and Washington Streets, Zip 96104, Mailing Address: P.O. Box 246, Zip 96104–0246; tel. 530/279–6111; Joyce Gysin, Administrator (Total facility includes 4 beds in nursing home–type unit) **A**9 10 **F**14 15 20 22 26 28 30 32 34 36 39 64 71 73 **P**6

| | 16 | 10 | 26 | 89 | 22 | 2119 | 6 | 2482 | 1666 | 66 |

ERRITOS—Los Angeles County

☐ COLLEGE HOSPITAL, 10802 College Place, Zip 90703–1579; tel. 562/924–9581; Stephen Witt, Chief Executive Officer (Nonreporting) **A**1 3 10 **S** College Health Enterprises, Costa Mesa, CA

| | 33 | 22 | 125 | — | — | — | — | — | — | — |

HESTER—Plumas County

☐ SENECA DISTRICT HOSPITAL, 130 Brentwood Drive, Zip 96020, Mailing Address: Box 737, Zip 96020; tel. 530/258–2151; Bernard G. Hietpas, Administrator (Total facility includes 16 beds in nursing home–type unit) **A**9 10 **F**7 8 14 22 28 31 33 34 40 44 64 65 71 72 73

| | 16 | 10 | 26 | 432 | 20 | 28182 | 39 | 7785 | 3583 | 113 |

CHICO—Butte County

☐ CHICO COMMUNITY HOSPITAL, 560 Cohasset Road, Zip 95926; tel. 916/896–5000; John E. Fidler, FACHE, Chief Executive Officer (Total facility includes 21 beds in nursing home–type unit) **A**1 9

| | 33 | 10 | 105 | — | — | — | — | — | — | — |

✪ ENLOE MEDICAL CENTER, (Formerly N T Enloe Memorial Hospital), 1531 Esplanade, Zip 95926–3386; tel. 530/891–7300; Philip R. Wolfe, Chief Executive Officer **A**1 2 9 10 **F**4 8 10 11 12 13 14 15 17 19 21 22 25 28 30 31 32 33 34 35 36 37 38 39 40 41 42 43 44 45 46 51 60 65 67 70 71 72 73 **P**7

| | 23 | 10 | 208 | 10670 | 123 | 197821 | 1600 | 112676 | 49957 | 2153 |

CHINO—San Bernardino County

☐ BHC CANYON RIDGE HOSPITAL, 5353 G Street, Zip 91710; tel. 909/590–3700; Cynthia K. Brown, R.N., Chief Executive Officer (Nonreporting) **A**1 10 **S** Behavioral Healthcare Corporation, Nashville, TN

| | 33 | 22 | 59 | — | — | — | — | — | — | — |

✪ CHINO VALLEY MEDICAL CENTER, (Formerly Chino Valley Hospital), 5451 Walnut Avenue, Zip 91710; tel. 909/464–8600; Gary Maier, Chief Executive Officer **A**1 9 10 **F**7 8 12 14 15 16 17 19 21 22 27 28 29 30 34 36 37 39 40 41 42 44 45 49 64 65 67 70 71 73 74 **P**4 5 7 **S** Columbia/HCA Healthcare Corporation, Nashville, TN
Web address: www.cvmc.com

| | 33 | 10 | 114 | 6123 | 68 | 42729 | 1065 | 37141 | 17371 | 352 |

HOSPITAL OF THE CALIFORNIA INSTITUTION FOR MEN, 14901 Central Avenue, Zip 91710, Mailing Address: Box 128, Zip 91710; tel. 909/597–1821; Pat Garleb, Administrator **F**1 3 4 5 6 9 10 11 12 18 19 20 21 22 25 27 29 30 31 33 34 35 37 39 41 42 43 44 45 46 48 49 50 51 52 54 55 56 57 58 59 60 63 64 65 67 69 70 71 72

| | 12 | 11 | 80 | 1211 | 59 | — | 0 | — | — | 261 |

CHOWCHILLA—Madera County

CHOWCHILLA DISTRICT MEMORIAL HOSPITAL, 1104 Ventura Avenue, Zip 93610, Mailing Address: Box 1027, Zip 93610; tel. 559/665–3781; Barbara Faller, Administrator (Nonreporting) **A**9 10

| | 16 | 10 | 23 | — | — | — | — | — | — | — |

CHULA VISTA—San Diego County

☐ BAYVIEW HOSPITAL AND MENTAL HEALTH SYSTEM, 330 Moss Street, Zip 91911–2005; tel. 619/426–6310; Roy Rodriguez, M.D., Chief Executive Officer **A**1 9 10 **F**14 15 16 17 18 27 34 46 52 53 54 55 56 57 58 59 65 67 68

| | 32 | 22 | 64 | 1305 | 37 | 20095 | 0 | 11955 | 4979 | 176 |

✪ SCRIPPS HOSPITAL–CHULA VISTA, 435 H Street, Zip 91912–1537, Mailing Address: P.O. Box 1537, Zip 91910–1537; tel. 619/691–7000; John Grah, Administrator **A**1 3 9 10 **F**1 2 3 4 6 7 8 10 11 12 14 15 16 17 19 21 22 23 24 25 26 27 28 29 30 31 32 34 35 36 37 39 40 41 42 43 44 45 46 48 49 52 53 54 55 56 57 58 59 60 63 64 65 67 70 71 73 74 **P**3 5 7 **S** Scripps Health, San Diego, CA

| | 23 | 10 | 159 | 7466 | 98 | 58123 | 1699 | 45663 | 26772 | 481 |

✪ SHARP CHULA VISTA MEDICAL CENTER, 751 Medical Center Court, Zip 91911, Mailing Address: Box 1297, Zip 91912; tel. 619/482–5800; Britt Berrett, Chief Executive Officer (Total facility includes 133 beds in nursing home–type unit) **A**1 2 3 9 10 **F**4 7 8 10 12 14 15 16 17 19 21 22 27 28 29 30 32 33 34 35 37 38 39 40 41 42 43 44 45 46 49 51 60 64 65 67 71 73 74 **P**7 **S** Sharp Healthcare, San Diego, CA

| | 23 | 10 | 306 | 10249 | 238 | 49546 | 2005 | 67153 | 29431 | 674 |

CLEARLAKE—Lake County

✪ REDBUD COMMUNITY HOSPITAL, 18th Avenue and Highway 53, Zip 95422, Mailing Address: P.O. Box 6720, Zip 95422; tel. 707/994–6486; Richard D. Hathaway, Chief Operating Officer (Nonreporting) **A**1 9 10 **S** Adventist Health, Roseville, CA

| | 16 | 10 | 34 | — | — | — | — | — | — | — |

CLOVIS—Fresno County

✪ CLOVIS COMMUNITY MEDICAL CENTER, 2755 Herndon Avenue, Zip 93611; tel. 209/323–4000; Mike Barber, Facility Service Integrator (Nonreporting) **A**1 9 10 **S** Community Health System of Northern California, Fresno, CA

| | 23 | 10 | 143 | — | — | — | — | — | — | — |

COALINGA—Fresno County

COALINGA REGIONAL MEDICAL CENTER, 1191 Phelps Avenue, Zip 93210; tel. 209/935–6562; Marjorie Vander Aarde, Administrator and Chief Executive Officer (Total facility includes 54 beds in nursing home–type unit) **A**9 10 **F**8 19 22 28 35 44 49 64 66 71 72 73 74

| | 16 | 10 | 78 | 1033 | 48 | 21762 | 123 | 8796 | 4016 | 142 |

Hospital, Address, Telephone, Administrator, Approval, Facility, and Physician Codes, Health Care System, Network	Classi-fication Codes		Utilization Data					Expense (thousands) of dollars		
★ American Hospital Association (AHA) membership □ Joint Commission on Accreditation of Healthcare Organizations (JCAHO) accreditation + American Osteopathic Healthcare Association (AOHA) membership ○ American Osteopathic Association (AOA) accreditation △ Commission on Accreditation of Rehabilitation Facilities (CARF) accreditation Control codes 61, 63, 64, 71, 72 and 73 indicate hospitals listed by AOHA, but not registered by AHA. For definition of numerical codes, see page A4	Control	Service	Staffed Beds	Admissions	Census	Outpatient Visits	Births	Total	Payroll	Personnel

COLTON—San Bernardino County

★ ○ ARROWHEAD REGIONAL MEDICAL CENTER, (Formerly San Bernardino County Medical Center), 400 North Pepper Avenue, Zip 92324; tel. 909/580–1000; Mark H. Uffer, Chief Executive Officer **A**2 3 5 10 11 12 13 **F**3 4 7 9 10 12 15 16 17 18 19 20 21 22 25 26 27 28 29 30 31 32 34 35 37 38 40 41 42 44 45 49 51 52 53 55 56 57 58 59 60 61 63 65 67 68 70 71 72 73 74 **P**5	13	10	293	14190	201	225168	1448	157244	67922	1726

COLUSA—Colusa County

□ COLUSA COMMUNITY HOSPITAL, 199 East Webster Street, Zip 95932, Mailing Address: P.O. Box 331, Zip 95932–0331; tel. 530/458–5821; Woody J. Laughnan, Interim Chief Executive Officer **A**1 9 10 **F**7 8 19 22 26 28 32 37 39 40 41 44 49 64 65 67 71 73	23	10	38	914	11	27844	214	10011	4105	119

CORCORAN—Kings County

CORCORAN DISTRICT HOSPITAL, 1310 Hanna Avenue, Zip 93212, Mailing Address: Box 758, Zip 93212; tel. 209/992–5051; David R. Green, Administrator **A**9 10 **F**8 12 14 19 20 21 22 25 27 30 31 32 34 42 44 46 49 61 64 65 71 74 **P**5 **S** Brim Healthcare, Inc., Brentwood, TN	16	10	32	630	11	24122	2	5618	2067	93

CORONA—Riverside County

□ CHARTER BEHAVIORAL HEALTH SYSTEM OF SOUTHERN CALIFORNIA–CORONA, 2055 Kellogg Avenue, Zip 91719; tel. 909/735–2910; Diana C. Hanyak, Chief Executive Officer **A**1 10 **F**2 3 12 26 52 53 54 55 56 57 58 59 **S** Magellan Health Services, Atlanta, GA	33	22	92	2346	38	6032	0	7960	3271	65
□ CORONA REGIONAL MEDICAL CENTER, (Includes Corona Regional Medical Center–Rehabilitation, 730 Magnolia Avenue, Zip 91719; tel. 909/736–7200), 800 South Main Street, Zip 91720; tel. 909/737–4343; John Calderone, Ph.D., Chief Executive Officer (Total facility includes 30 beds in nursing home–type unit) **A**1 2 9 10 **F**7 8 11 12 13 14 15 16 17 19 22 26 27 28 29 30 32 33 34 35 37 39 40 41 42 44 45 46 48 49 52 55 57 58 59 64 65 71 72 73 74 **P**5 7	23	10	195	10231	127	111139	1804	69950	23951	597

CORONADO—San Diego County

⊠ SHARP CORONADO HOSPITAL, 250 Prospect Place, Zip 92118; tel. 619/522–3600; Marcia K. Hall, Chief Executive Officer (Total facility includes 149 beds in nursing home–type unit) (Nonreporting) **A**1 10 **S** Sharp Healthcare, San Diego, CA	23	10	195	—	—	—	—	—	—	—

COSTA MESA—Orange County

□ COLLEGE HOSPITAL COSTA MESA, 301 Victoria Street, Zip 92627; tel. 949/574–3322; Dale A. Kirby, Chief Executive Officer (Nonreporting) **A**1 10 **S** College Health Enterprises, Costa Mesa, CA	33	22	119	—	—	—	—	—	—	—

COVINA—Los Angeles County

⊠ CHARTER BEHAVIORAL HEALTH SYSTEM OF SOUTHERN CALIFORNIA–CHARTER OAK, 1161 East Covina Boulevard, Zip 91724–1161; tel. 626/966–1632; Todd A. Smith, Chief Executive Officer **A**1 10 **F**3 15 16 52 53 55 56 57 58 59 **P**5 7 8 **S** Magellan Health Services, Atlanta, GA	33	22	95	2800	43	5980	0	—	—	69
CITRUS VALLEY MEDICAL CENTER INTER–COMMUNITY CAMPUS, 210 West San Bernardino Road, Zip 91723–1901; tel. 626/331–7331; Peter E. Makowski, President and Chief Executive Officer (Nonreporting) **A**2 9 10 **S** Citrus Valley Health Partners, Covina, CA	23	10	252	—	—	—	—	—	—	—

CRESCENT CITY—Del Norte County

⊠ SUTTER COAST HOSPITAL, 800 East Washington Boulevard, Zip 95531; tel. 707/464–8511; John E. Menaugh, Chief Executive Officer (Nonreporting) **A**1 9 10 **S** Sutter Health, Sacramento, CA	23	10	47	—	—	—	—	—	—	—

CULVER CITY—Los Angeles County

⊠ BROTMAN MEDICAL CENTER, 3828 Delmas Terrace, Zip 90231–2459, Mailing Address: Box 2459, Zip 90231–2459; tel. 310/836–7000; Sonja Hagel, Chief Executive Officer (Total facility includes 21 beds in nursing home–type unit) (Nonreporting) **A**1 9 10 **S** TENET Healthcare Corporation, Santa Barbara, CA	33	10	240	—	—	—	—	—	—	—
□ WASHINGTON MEDICAL CENTER, 12101 West Washington Boulevard, Zip 90231, Mailing Address: Box 2787, Zip 90231; tel. 310/391–0601; Harry F. Adams, Administrator **A**1 9 10 **F**2 11 16 19 22 27 35 37 44 49 52 59 64 65 71 73	33	10	98	2033	52	9244	0	—	—	221

DALY CITY—San Mateo County

⊠ SETON MEDICAL CENTER, 1900 Sullivan Avenue, Zip 94015; tel. 650/992–4000; Bernadette Smith, Chief Operating Officer (Total facility includes 65 beds in nursing home–type unit) **A**1 2 3 5 9 10 **F**1 2 3 4 7 8 9 10 11 12 13 14 15 16 17 19 21 22 23 26 28 29 30 31 32 33 34 35 37 38 39 40 41 42 43 44 46 47 48 49 52 58 59 60 64 65 66 68 71 72 73 74 **S** Catholic Healthcare West, San Francisco, CA **Web address:** www.chwwestbay.org	23	10	283	11264	222	295363	1110	134103	59819	1055

DAVIS—Yolo County

⊠ SUTTER DAVIS HOSPITAL, 2000 Sutter Place, Zip 95616, Mailing Address: P.O. Box 1617, Zip 95617; tel. 530/756–6440; Lawrence A. Maas, Administrator (Nonreporting) **A**1 3 9 10 **S** Sutter Health, Sacramento, CA	23	10	48	—	—	—	—	—	—	—

DEER PARK—Napa County

⊠ ST. HELENA HOSPITAL, 650 Sanitarium Road, Zip 94576, Mailing Address: P.O. Box 250, Zip 94576; tel. 707/963–3611; JoAline Olson, R.N., President and Chief Executive Officer (Total facility includes 23 beds in nursing home–type unit) (Nonreporting) **A**1 9 10 **S** Adventist Health, Roseville, CA	21	10	168	—	—	—	—	—	—	—

Hospital, Address, Telephone, Administrator, Approval, Facility, and Physician Codes, Health Care System, Network	Classification Codes		Utilization Data					Expense (thousands) of dollars		
	Control	Service	Staffed Beds	Admissions	Census	Outpatient Visits	Births	Total	Payroll	Personnel

Key:
★ American Hospital Association (AHA) membership
☐ Joint Commission on Accreditation of Healthcare Organizations (JCAHO) accreditation
✚ American Osteopathic Healthcare Association (AOHA) membership
◯ American Osteopathic Association (AOA) accreditation
△ Commission on Accreditation of Rehabilitation Facilities (CARF) accreditation
Control codes 61, 63, 64, 71, 72 and 73 indicate hospitals listed by AOHA, but not registered by AHA. For definition of numerical codes, see page A4

DELANO—Kern County

☐ DELANO REGIONAL MEDICAL CENTER, 1401 Garces Highway, Zip 93215, Mailing Address: Box 460, Zip 93216; tel. 661/725–4800; Gerald A. Starr, Executive Officer (Total facility includes 45 beds in nursing home–type unit) (Nonreporting) **A**1 9 10 — Control 23, Service 10, Staffed Beds 156

DINUBA—Tulare County

ALTA DISTRICT HOSPITAL, 500 Adelaide Way, Zip 93618–1698; tel. 209/591–4171; Joseph A. DeStefano, Chief Executive Officer (Total facility includes 18 beds in nursing home–type unit) (Nonreporting) **A**9 10 — Control 16, Service 10, Staffed Beds 50

DOS PALOS—Merced County

DOS PALOS MEMORIAL HOSPITAL, 2118 Marguerite Street, Zip 93620; tel. 209/392–6106; Darryl E. Henley, Administrator (Nonreporting) **A**9 10 — Control 23, Service 10, Staffed Beds 15

DOWNEY—Los Angeles County

☐ DOWNEY COMMUNITY HOSPITAL FOUNDATION, (Includes Downey Community Hospital), 11500 Brookshire Avenue, Zip 90241–4990; tel. 562/904–5000; Allen R. Korneff, President and Chief Executive Officer (Total facility includes 20 beds in nursing home–type unit) (Nonreporting) **A**1 9 10 12 13 — Control 23, Service 10, Staffed Beds 222

★ △ LAC–RANCHO LOS AMIGOS NATIONAL REHABILITATION CENTER, (Formerly LAC–Rancho Los Amigos Medical Center), 7601 East Imperial Highway, Zip 90242; tel. 562/401–7022; Consuelo C. Diaz, Chief Executive Officer **A**1 3 5 7 9 10 **F**1 4 5 6 7 8 10 12 13 14 15 17 19 20 21 22 23 25 26 27 28 29 30 31 32 33 34 35 37 39 41 42 43 44 45 46 48 49 50 51 53 54 55 56 57 58 59 60 61 63 65 66 68 70 71 72 73 74 **P**6 **S** Los Angeles County–Department of Health Services, Los Angeles, CA
Web address: www.rancho.org

	Control	Service	Staffed Beds	Admissions	Census	Outpatient Visits	Births	Total	Payroll	Personnel
LAC–Rancho Los Amigos	13	10	190	3252	187	55385	—	210669	54696	1412

DUARTE—Los Angeles County

★ CITY OF HOPE NATIONAL MEDICAL CENTER, (CANCER ONCOLOGY), 1500 East Duarte Road, Zip 91010–3000; tel. 626/359–8111; Gil Schwartzberg, President and Chief Executive Officer **A**1 2 3 5 9 10 **F**8 12 15 17 19 21 28 29 30 31 32 34 35 37 42 44 45 46 47 49 60 63 65 67 68 71 72 73 **P**4 7 — Control 23, Service 49, Staffed Beds 137, Admissions 4105, Census 108, Outpatient Visits 109406, Births 0, Total 187108, Payroll 61312, Personnel 2111

☐ SANTA TERESITA HOSPITAL, 819 Buena Vista Street, Zip 91010–1703; tel. 626/359–3243; Robert G. Shell, Chief Executive Officer (Total facility includes 133 beds in nursing home–type unit) (Nonreporting) **A**1 2 10 — Control 21, Service 10, Staffed Beds 283

EDWARDS AFB—Kern County

★ △ U. S. AIR FORCE HOSPITAL, 30 Hospital Road, Building 5500, Zip 93524–1730; tel. 661/277–2010; Lieutenant Colonel Thomas E. Yingst, USAF, MSC, Administrator (Nonreporting) **A**1 7 **S** Department of the Air Force, Bowling AFB, DC — Control 41, Service 10, Staffed Beds 10

EL CAJON—San Diego County

KAISER FOUNDATION HOSPITAL See Kaiser Foundation Hospital, San Diego
SCRIPPS HOSPITAL–EAST COUNTY See Scripps Memorial Hospital East County

★ SCRIPPS MEMORIAL HOSPITAL EAST COUNTY, (Formerly Scripps Hospital–East County), 1688 East Main Street, Zip 92021; tel. 619/440–1122; Deborah Dunne, Administrator (Total facility includes 35 beds in nursing home–type unit) **A**1 9 10 **F**4 7 8 10 12 13 17 19 22 27 28 31 32 33 34 35 37 40 41 42 43 44 45 46 48 49 56 57 59 64 65 67 68 70 71 72 73 74 **S** Scripps Health, San Diego, CA
Web address: www.scrippshealth.org — Control 23, Service 10, Staffed Beds 105, Admissions 3958, Census 53, Outpatient Visits 31559, Births 0, Total 29225, Payroll 14358, Personnel 328

EL CENTRO—Imperial County

★ EL CENTRO REGIONAL MEDICAL CENTER, 1415 Ross Avenue, Zip 92243; tel. 760/339–7100; Ted Fox, Administrator and Chief Executive Officer **A**1 9 10 **F**7 8 15 17 19 21 22 23 27 28 29 30 34 35 37 39 40 44 45 46 51 63 65 67 69 71 72 73 74 **P**4 5 7 — Control 14, Service 10, Staffed Beds 107, Admissions 6588, Census 68, Outpatient Visits 100895, Births 1368, Total 43784, Payroll 17021, Personnel 483

ELDRIDGE—Sonoma County

SONOMA DEVELOPMENTAL CENTER, 15000 Arnold Drive, Zip 95431; tel. 707/938–6000; Timothy L. Meeker, Executive Director (Nonreporting) **A**10 — Control 12, Service 62, Staffed Beds 996

ENCINITAS—San Diego County

☐ BHC SAN LUIS REY HOSPITAL, 335 Saxony Road, Zip 92024–2723; tel. 619/753–1245; William T. Sparrow, Chief Executive Officer (Nonreporting) **A**1 9 **S** Behavioral Healthcare Corporation, Nashville, TN — Control 33, Service 22, Staffed Beds 122

★ △ SCRIPPS MEMORIAL HOSPITAL–ENCINITAS, 354 Santa Fe Drive, Zip 92024, Mailing Address: P.O. Box 230817, Zip 92023; tel. 760/753–6501; Rebecca Ropchan, Administrator (Nonreporting) **A**1 2 7 9 10 **S** Scripps Health, San Diego, CA — Control 23, Service 10, Staffed Beds 145

ENCINO—Los Angeles County, See Los Angeles

ESCONDIDO—San Diego County

★ PALOMAR MEDICAL CENTER, 555 East Valley Parkway, Zip 92025–3084; tel. 760/739–3000; Victoria M. Penland, Administrator and Chief Operating Officer (Total facility includes 125 beds in nursing home–type unit) **A**1 2 9 10 **F**3 4 7 8 10 17 19 21 22 23 25 27 28 29 30 31 32 33 34 35 36 37 38 39 40 41 42 43 44 45 46 48 49 51 52 54 55 56 57 58 59 60 63 64 65 66 70 71 73 **P**7 **S** Palomar Pomerado Health System, San Diego, CA — Control 16, Service 10, Staffed Beds 424, Admissions 15339, Census 253, Outpatient Visits 208141, Births 2656, Total 140860, Payroll 52491, Personnel 1494

EUREKA—Humboldt County

☐ △ GENERAL HOSPITAL, 2200 Harrison Avenue, Zip 95501; tel. 707/445–5111; Martin Love, Chief Executive Officer **A**1 7 9 10 **F**7 8 12 16 19 20 21 22 23 25 28 30 31 32 33 34 35 37 38 40 41 42 44 46 48 49 51 61 63 65 71 72 73 74 **S** Province Healthcare Corporation, Brentwood, TN — Control 33, Service 10, Staffed Beds 66, Admissions 2424, Census 36, Outpatient Visits 44381, Births 339, Total 28300, Payroll 12843, Personnel 399

Hospital, Address, Telephone, Administrator, Approval, Facility, and Physician Codes, Health Care System, Network	Classi-fication Codes		Utilization Data					Expense (thousands) of dollars		

★ American Hospital Association (AHA) membership
□ Joint Commission on Accreditation of Healthcare Organizations (JCAHO) accreditation
+ American Osteopathic Healthcare Association (AOHA) membership
○ American Osteopathic Association (AOA) accreditation
△ Commission on Accreditation of Rehabilitation Facilities (CARF) accreditation
Control codes 61, 63, 64, 71, 72 and 73 indicate hospitals listed by AOHA, but not registered by AHA. For definition of numerical codes, see page A4

Hospital	Control	Service	Staffed Beds	Admissions	Census	Outpatient Visits	Births	Total	Payroll	Personnel
✠ SAINT JOSEPH HOSPITAL, 2700 Dolbeer Street, Zip 95501; tel. 707/445–8121; Gary G. Fybel, President and Chief Executive Officer **A**1 2 9 10 **F**2 3 4 7 8 10 11 14 15 16 17 19 20 21 22 27 28 29 30 31 33 34 35 37 40 41 42 43 44 45 46 49 51 52 60 65 67 71 73 74 **P**3 6 **S** St. Joseph Health System, Orange, CA	21	10	96	4647	58	199823	399	57286	18360	586
EXETER—Tulare County										
□ MEMORIAL HOSPITAL AT EXETER, 215 Crespi Avenue, Zip 93221–1399; tel. 559/592–2151; Sally Brewer, Vice President and Administrator (Total facility includes 62 beds in nursing home–type unit) (Nonreporting) **A**1 10	23	10	80	—	—	—	—	—	—	—
FAIRFIELD—Solano County										
✠ NORTHBAY MEDICAL CENTER, 1200 B. Gale Wilson Boulevard, Zip 94533–3587; tel. 707/429–3600; Deborah Sugiyama, President (Total facility includes 11 beds in nursing home–type unit) **A**1 2 9 10 **F**1 6 7 8 10 12 13 14 15 16 17 19 21 22 23 28 30 32 33 35 36 37 39 40 41 42 44 49 60 64 65 67 71 73 **P**3 **S** NorthBay Healthcare System, Fairfield, CA **Web address:** www.northbay.org	23	10	121	5397	56	72661	1499	60587	24085	358
FALL RIVER MILLS—Shasta County										
MAYERS MEMORIAL HOSPITAL DISTRICT, Highway 299 East, Zip 96028, Mailing Address: Box 459, Zip 96028; tel. 530/336–5511; Judi Beck, Administrator and Chief Executive Officer (Total facility includes 99 beds in nursing home–type unit) **A**9 10 **F**7 8 16 17 19 20 22 27 28 32 33 35 44 64 71 **P**5 **Web address:** www.burneyfalls.com/mayers	16	10	121	712	92	13214	98	—	—	198
FALLBROOK—San Diego County										
✠ FALLBROOK HOSPITAL DISTRICT, 624 East Elder Street, Zip 92028; tel. 760/728–1191; Corey A. Seale, Chief Executive Officer (Total facility includes 95 beds in nursing home–type unit) (Nonreporting) **A**1 9 10	16	10	142	—	—	—	—	—	—	—
FOLSOM—Sacramento County										
✠ MERCY HOSPITAL OF FOLSOM, 1650 Creekside Drive, Zip 95630; tel. 916/983–7400; Donald C. Hudson, Vice President and Chief Operating Officer **A**1 9 10 **F**4 7 8 9 10 11 12 14 15 16 17 19 22 25 26 28 29 30 31 32 33 35 37 38 40 41 42 43 44 46 47 48 49 50 60 62 64 65 66 67 71 72 73 74 **P**3 5 **S** Catholic Healthcare West, San Francisco, CA	21	10	95	3187	28	32155	722	22368	10548	336
□ VENCOR HOSPITAL–SACRAMENTO, 223 Fargo Way, Zip 95630; tel. 916/351–9151; Meredith Taylor, Administrator (Nonreporting) **A**1 10 **S** Vencor, Incorporated, Louisville, KY	33	10	32	—	—	—	—	—	—	—
FONTANA—San Bernardino County										
✠ KAISER FOUNDATION HOSPITAL, 9961 Sierra Avenue, Zip 92335–6794; tel. 909/427–5000; Gerald A. McCall, Senior Vice President and Service Area Manager **A**1 2 3 5 10 **F**2 3 4 7 8 9 10 11 12 14 15 16 19 21 22 23 25 28 29 30 32 33 35 37 38 40 41 42 43 44 45 46 48 49 51 52 53 54 55 56 58 59 60 61 64 65 66 67 69 71 72 73 **S** Kaiser Foundation Hospitals, Oakland, CA	23	10	317	21630	211	79582	4210	—	—	3869
FORT BRAGG—Mendocino County										
□ MENDOCINO COAST DISTRICT HOSPITAL, 700 River Drive, Zip 95437; tel. 707/961–1234; Bryan M. Ballard, Chief Executive Officer **A**1 9 10 **F**7 8 11 12 14 19 21 22 25 30 31 32 33 34 35 36 37 39 40 41 42 44 45 46 49 63 65 67 71 73	16	10	51	1625	23	46805	227	20349	9111	213
FORT IRWIN—San Bernardino County										
✠ WEED ARMY COMMUNITY HOSPITAL, Zip 92310–5065; tel. 760/380–3108; Colonel Michael McCaffrey, Commander (Nonreporting) **A**1 **S** Department of the Army, Office of the Surgeon General, Falls Church, VA	42	10	27	—	—	—	—	—	—	—
FORTUNA—Humboldt County										
✠ REDWOOD MEMORIAL HOSPITAL, 3300 Renner Drive, Zip 95540; tel. 707/725–3361; Neil Martin, President and Chief Executive Officer (Nonreporting) **A**1 2 9 10 **S** St. Joseph Health System, Orange, CA	21	10	35	—	—	—	—	—	—	—
FOUNTAIN VALLEY—Orange County										
✠ FOUNTAIN VALLEY REGIONAL HOSPITAL AND MEDICAL CENTER, 17100 Euclid at Warner, Zip 92708; tel. 714/966–7200; Tim Smith, President and Chief Executive Officer **A**1 2 5 9 10 **F**1 4 7 8 10 11 12 14 15 16 17 19 21 22 27 28 29 31 32 34 35 37 38 39 40 42 43 44 45 46 47 49 52 57 59 63 64 65 66 67 71 73 74 **P**5 **S** TENET Healthcare Corporation, Santa Barbara, CA	33	10	384	15814	201	76270	4205	105713	44369	1217
□ ORANGE COAST MEMORIAL MEDICAL CENTER, 9920 Talbert Avenue, Zip 92708; tel. 714/378–7000; Barry S. Arbuckle, Ph.D., Chief Executive Officer **A**1 3 10 **F**2 3 4 7 8 9 10 12 13 14 16 17 19 21 22 23 25 26 28 29 30 32 33 34 35 36 37 39 40 41 42 43 44 45 47 48 49 50 52 53 54 55 56 57 58 59 60 61 63 64 65 67 69 70 71 72 73 74 **P**5 7 **S** Memorial Health Services, Long Beach, CA **Web address:** www.memorialcare.org	23	10	170	6569	65	32052	525	63801	18720	526
FREMONT—Alameda County										
□ BHC FREMONT HOSPITAL, 39001 Sundale Drive, Zip 94538; tel. 510/796–1100; Ed Owen, Chief Executive Officer **A**1 9 10 **F**2 3 12 15 16 52 53 55 56 57 59 65 67 **S** Behavioral Healthcare Corporation, Nashville, TN **Web address:** www.fremonthospital.com	33	22	78	2003	41	6141	0	—	—	61
✠ WASHINGTON TOWNSHIP HEALTH CARE DISTRICT, 2000 Mowry Avenue, Zip 94538–1716; tel. 510/797–1111; Nancy D. Farber, Chief Executive Officer (Nonreporting) **A**1 2 9 10	16	10	202	—	—	—	—	—	—	—
FRENCH CAMP—San Joaquin County										
□ △ SAN JOAQUIN GENERAL HOSPITAL, 500 West Hospital Road, Zip 95231, Mailing Address: P.O. Box 1020, Stockton, Zip 95201; tel. 209/468–6600; Michael N. Smith, Director Healthcare Services **A**1 3 5 7 10 **F**2 3 4 7 8 10 11 12 13 14 15 16 17 18 19 20 21 22 23 25 26 27 28 29 30 31 32 33 34 35 37 38 39 40 41 42 43 44 45 46 48 49 51 52 53 54 55 56 57 58 60 63 65 66 67 69 71 72 73 **P**5 6	13	10	181	8655	116	260359	1816	105560	39714	1172

Hospital, Address, Telephone, Administrator, Approval, Facility, and Physician Codes, Health Care System, Network	Classi-fication Codes		Utilization Data					Expense (thousands) of dollars		
	Control	Service	Staffed Beds	Admissions	Census	Outpatient Visits	Births	Total	Payroll	Personnel

★ American Hospital Association (AHA) membership
☐ Joint Commission on Accreditation of Healthcare Organizations (JCAHO) accreditation
+ American Osteopathic Healthcare Association (AOHA) membership
○ American Osteopathic Association (AOA) accreditation
△ Commission on Accreditation of Rehabilitation Facilities (CARF) accreditation
Control codes 61, 63, 64, 71, 72 and 73 indicate hospitals listed by AOHA, but not registered by AHA. For definition of numerical codes, see page A4

FRESNO—Fresno County

	Control	Service	Staffed Beds	Admissions	Census	Outpatient Visits	Births	Total	Payroll	Personnel
☐ BHC CEDAR VISTA HOSPITAL, 7171 North Cedar Avenue, Zip 93720; tel. 209/449–8000; Richard Adams, Ph.D., Administrator (Nonreporting) **A**1 9 10 **S** Behavioral Healthcare Corporation, Nashville, TN	33	22	61	—	—	—	—	—	—	—
✚ △ FRESNO COMMUNITY HOSPITAL AND MEDICAL CENTER, Fresno and R Streets, Zip 93721, Mailing Address: Box 1232, Zip 93715; tel. 209/442–6000; J. Philip Hinton, M.D., President and Chief Executive Officer (Nonreporting) **A**1 2 7 9 10 **S** Community Health System of Northern California, Fresno, CA	23	10	375	—	—	—	—	—	—	—
FRESNO SURGERY CENTER–THE HOSPITAL FOR SURGERY, (SURGERY CENTER), 6125 North Fresno Street, Zip 93710; tel. 559/431–8000; Alan H. Pierrot, M.D., Chief Executive Officer **A**10 **F**6 15 16 19 23 28 34 44	32	49	20	2019	11	4150	0	18591	7257	173
✚ KAISER FOUNDATION HOSPITAL, 7300 North Fresno Street, Zip 93720; tel. 559/448–4555; Edward S. Glavis, Administrator **A**1 10 **F**2 3 4 7 8 9 10 11 12 15 16 17 19 21 22 23 24 26 29 30 31 32 33 35 37 38 40 42 43 44 46 47 48 49 52 60 64 65 70 71 73 **S** Kaiser Foundation Hospitals, Oakland, CA	23	10	121	8028	72	33616	1493	—	—	316
✚ SAINT AGNES MEDICAL CENTER, 1303 East Herndon Avenue, Zip 93720–3397; tel. 559/449–3000; Sister Ruth Marie Nickerson, President and Chief Executive Officer **A**1 2 9 10 **F**1 2 3 4 7 8 10 11 12 14 15 16 17 18 19 21 22 25 26 27 28 29 30 31 32 33 34 35 37 38 39 40 41 42 43 44 48 49 50 52 53 54 55 56 57 58 59 60 63 65 66 67 68 71 72 73 74 **P**5 **S** Holy Cross Health System Corporation, South Bend, IN **Web address:** www.samc.org	21	10	326	20431	215	401765	2796	177389	78000	1931
☐ △ SAN JOAQUIN VALLEY REHABILITATION HOSPITAL, 7173 North Sharon Avenue, Zip 93720; tel. 559/436–3600; W. David Smiley, Chief Executive Officer (Nonreporting) **A**1 7 9 10	33	46	62	—	—	—	—	—	—	—
✚ UNIVERSITY MEDICAL CENTER, 445 South Cedar Avenue, Zip 93702–2907; tel. 209/459–4000; Andres Fernandez, Facility Services Integrator and Administrator (Nonreporting) **A**1 8 10 **S** Community Health System of Northern California, Fresno, CA	13	10	334	—	—	—	—	—	—	—
✚ VETERANS AFFAIRS MEDICAL CENTER, 2615 East Clinton Avenue, Zip 93703; tel. 559/225–6100; Alan S. Perry, Director (Total facility includes 60 beds in nursing home–type unit) **A**1 2 3 5 **F**2 3 14 15 16 19 20 21 22 26 27 28 29 30 31 32 33 34 37 39 41 42 44 45 46 49 51 52 54 56 57 58 65 67 71 73 74 **S** Department of Veterans Affairs, Washington, DC **Web address:** www.fresno.med.va.gov	45	10	205	3700	115	163171	—	66524	34518	801

FULLERTON—Orange County

	Control	Service	Staffed Beds	Admissions	Census	Outpatient Visits	Births	Total	Payroll	Personnel
✚ △ ST. JUDE MEDICAL CENTER, 101 East Valencia Mesa Drive, Zip 92635; tel. 714/992–3000; Robert J. Fraschetti, President and Chief Executive Officer (Nonreporting) **A**1 2 7 9 10 **S** St. Joseph Health System, Orange, CA	21	10	347	—	—	—	—	—	—	—

GARBERVILLE—Humboldt County

	Control	Service	Staffed Beds	Admissions	Census	Outpatient Visits	Births	Total	Payroll	Personnel
SOUTHERN HUMBOLDT COMMUNITY HEALTHCARE DISTRICT, 733 Cedar Street, Zip 95542–3292; tel. 707/923–3921; George Koortbojian, Interim Administrator (Total facility includes 8 beds in nursing home–type unit) (Nonreporting) **A**9 10 **Web address:** www.shchd.org	16	10	18	—	—	—	—	—	—	—

GARDEN GROVE—Orange County

	Control	Service	Staffed Beds	Admissions	Census	Outpatient Visits	Births	Total	Payroll	Personnel
✚ GARDEN GROVE HOSPITAL AND MEDICAL CENTER, 12601 Garden Grove Boulevard, Zip 92843–1959; tel. 714/741–2700; Mark A. Meyers, President and Chief Executive Officer (Total facility includes 12 beds in nursing home–type unit) **A**1 9 10 **F**7 12 13 14 16 19 21 22 23 26 27 28 30 31 32 35 37 38 40 41 42 44 49 63 64 71 73 **S** TENET Healthcare Corporation, Santa Barbara, CA	33	10	167	9263	85	77939	2341	41743	20625	572

GARDENA—Los Angeles County

	Control	Service	Staffed Beds	Admissions	Census	Outpatient Visits	Births	Total	Payroll	Personnel
☐ COMMUNITY HOSPITAL OF GARDENA, 1246 West 155th Street, Zip 90247–4062; tel. 310/323–5330; Raymond N. Smith, Chief Executive Officer (Total facility includes 15 beds in nursing home–type unit) **A**1 9 10 **F**16 19 27 28 35 37 41 44 49 60 64 65 71 72 **P**5	33	10	35	792	12	6541	0	6961	3365	106
☐ MEMORIAL HOSPITAL OF GARDENA, 1145 West Redondo Beach Boulevard, Zip 90247; tel. 310/532–4200; Frank Katsuda, Administrator (Nonreporting) **A**1 10	33	10	107	—	—	—	—	—	—	—

GILROY—Santa Clara County

	Control	Service	Staffed Beds	Admissions	Census	Outpatient Visits	Births	Total	Payroll	Personnel
✚ SOUTH VALLEY HOSPITAL, (Formerly Columbia South Valley Hospital), 9400 No Name Uno, Zip 95020–2368; tel. 408/848–2000; Beverly Gilmore, Chief Executive Officer (Total facility includes 21 beds in nursing home–type unit) (Nonreporting) **A**1 9 10 **S** Columbia/HCA Healthcare Corporation, Nashville, TN	33	10	93	—	—	—	—	—	—	—

GLENDALE—Los Angeles County

	Control	Service	Staffed Beds	Admissions	Census	Outpatient Visits	Births	Total	Payroll	Personnel
✚ △ GLENDALE ADVENTIST MEDICAL CENTER, 1509 Wilson Terrace, Zip 91206–4007; tel. 818/409–8000; Fred Manchur, President and Chief Executive Officer (Nonreporting) **A**1 2 3 5 7 9 10 **S** Adventist Health, Roseville, CA **Web address:** www.glendaleadventist.com	21	10	396	—	—	—	—	—	—	—
✚ GLENDALE MEMORIAL HOSPITAL AND HEALTH CENTER, 1420 South Central Avenue, Zip 91204–2594; tel. 818/502–2201; Arnold R. Schaffer, President and Chief Executive Officer **A**1 2 10 **F**3 4 7 8 10 11 12 13 14 15 16 17 19 21 22 26 27 28 29 30 31 32 33 34 35 37 38 39 40 41 42 43 44 45 48 49 52 54 55 56 57 58 59 60 63 64 65 67 69 71 72 73 74 **P**4 5 7 **S** Catholic Healthcare West, San Francisco, CA **Web address:** www.glendalememorial.com	23	10	275	14837	225	105450	1678	110038	51392	1307

Hospital, Address, Telephone, Administrator, Approval, Facility, and Physician Codes, Health Care System, Network	Classification Codes		Utilization Data					Expense (thousands) of dollars		
	Control	Service	Staffed Beds	Admissions	Census	Outpatient Visits	Births	Total	Payroll	Personnel

★ American Hospital Association (AHA) membership
□ Joint Commission on Accreditation of Healthcare Organizations (JCAHO) accreditation
+ American Osteopathic Healthcare Association (AOHA) membership
○ American Osteopathic Association (AOA) accreditation
△ Commission on Accreditation of Rehabilitation Facilities (CARF) accreditation
Control codes 61, 63, 64, 71, 72 and 73 indicate hospitals listed by AOHA, but not registered by AHA. For definition of numerical codes, see page A4

Hospital	Control	Service	Staffed Beds	Admissions	Census	Outpatient Visits	Births	Total	Payroll	Personnel
✠ VERDUGO HILLS HOSPITAL, 1812 Verdugo Boulevard, Zip 91208; tel. 818/790–7100; Bernard Glossy, President and Chief Executive Officer (Total facility includes 18 beds in nursing home–type unit) A1 9 10 F7 8 11 12 13 14 15 16 19 20 21 22 24 26 28 29 30 32 35 37 40 43 44 45 49 52 57 58 59 63 64 65 66 67 71 73 P5 6	23	10	134	6117	68	20056	1093	43789	17885	365
GLENDORA—Los Angeles County										
✠ FOOTHILL PRESBYTERIAN HOSPITAL–MORRIS L. JOHNSTON MEMORIAL, 250 South Grand Avenue, Zip 91741; tel. 626/963–8411; Larry S. Fetters, Administrator and Chief Operating Officer A1 2 9 10 F4 7 8 9 10 11 12 14 15 16 17 19 21 22 28 30 32 33 34 35 36 37 38 39 40 41 43 44 45 46 48 49 52 53 60 63 64 65 66 67 71 72 73 74 P1 3 5 7 S Citrus Valley Health Partners, Covina, CA	23	10	106	5153	51	126408	1107	34499	14028	483
✠ HUNTINGTON EAST VALLEY HOSPITAL, 150 West Alosta Avenue, Zip 91740–4398; tel. 626/335–0231; James W. Maki, Chief Executive Officer (Nonreporting) A1 10 S Southern California Healthcare Systems, Pasadena, CA	23	10	128	—	—	—	—	—	—	—
GRANADA HILLS—Los Angeles County, See Los Angeles										
GRASS VALLEY—Nevada County										
✠ SIERRA NEVADA MEMORIAL HOSPITAL, 155 Glasson Way, Zip 95945, Mailing Address: P.O. Box 1029, Zip 95945–1029; tel. 530/274–6000; C. Thomas Collier, President and Chief Executive Officer (Total facility includes 13 beds in nursing home–type unit) A1 2 9 10 F7 8 10 11 12 14 15 16 19 22 23 27 32 33 34 35 37 40 42 44 45 49 60 64 65 71 72 P3 5 S Catholic Healthcare West, San Francisco, CA	23	10	58	5717	58	113033	515	56145	24362	567
GREENBRAE—Marin County										
✠ MARIN GENERAL HOSPITAL, 250 Bon Air Road, Zip 94904, Mailing Address: Box 8010, San Rafael, Zip 94912–8010; tel. 415/925–7000; Henry J. Buhrmann, President and Chief Executive Officer A1 2 9 10 F4 7 8 10 11 12 14 15 16 17 18 19 21 22 23 27 28 29 30 31 32 34 35 37 38 40 41 42 43 44 45 46 52 53 54 55 56 57 58 59 60 64 65 67 71 73 74 P1 3 7 S Sutter Health, Sacramento, CA	23	10	165	10238	106	97838	1695	107614	43770	848
GREENVILLE—Plumas County										
INDIAN VALLEY HOSPITAL DISTRICT, 184 Hot Springs Road, Zip 95947; tel. 530/284–7191; Lynn Seaberg, Administrator and Chief Executive Officer (Total facility includes 19 beds in nursing home–type unit) (Nonreporting) A9 10	16	10	26	—	—	—	—	—	—	—
GRIDLEY—Butte County										
BIGGS–GRIDLEY MEMORIAL HOSPITAL, 240 Spruce Street, Zip 95948, Mailing Address: Box 97, Zip 95948; tel. 530/846–5671; Charles R. Norton, Administrator (Nonreporting) A9 10	23	10	55	—	—	—	—	—	—	—
HANFORD—Kings County										
✠ CENTRAL VALLEY GENERAL HOSPITAL, 1025 North Douty Street, Zip 93230, Mailing Address: Box 480, Zip 93232; tel. 559/583–2100; Kendall R. Fults, Chief Operating Officer (Nonreporting) A1 9 10 S Adventist Health, Roseville, CA **Web address:** www.hanfordhealth.com	33	10	40	—	—	—	—	—	—	—
✠ HANFORD COMMUNITY MEDICAL CENTER, 450 Greenfield Avenue, Zip 93230–0240, Mailing Address: Box 240, Zip 93232–0240; tel. 209/582–9000; Darwin R. Remboldt, President and Chief Executive Officer A1 9 10 F7 8 10 12 14 15 16 19 22 25 28 30 32 33 34 35 37 39 40 41 42 44 45 46 51 60 70 71 72 73 P3 S Adventist Health, Roseville, CA **Web address:** www.adventisthealth.org	21	10	59	4849	46	264394	1067	52222	19036	692
HARBOR CITY—Los Angeles County, See Los Angeles										
HAWTHORNE—Los Angeles County										
HAWTHORNE HOSPITAL See Los Angeles Metropolitan Medical Center, Los Angeles										
✠ ROBERT F. KENNEDY MEDICAL CENTER, 4500 West 116th Street, Zip 90250; tel. 310/973–1711; Peter P. Aprato, Administrator and Chief Operating Officer (Total facility includes 34 beds in nursing home–type unit) (Nonreporting) A1 9 10 S Catholic Healthcare West, San Francisco, CA	23	10	195	—	—	—	—	—	—	—
HAYWARD—Alameda County										
✠ KAISER FOUNDATION HOSPITAL, 27400 Hesperian Boulevard, Zip 94545–4297; tel. 510/784–4313; Richard D. Cordova, Senior Vice President A1 10 F3 4 7 8 10 11 12 14 15 16 19 21 22 23 24 25 27 29 30 31 32 33 35 37 38 39 40 41 42 43 44 45 46 49 51 53 54 55 56 57 58 59 60 61 65 66 67 68 69 70 71 72 73 74 P3 S Kaiser Foundation Hospitals, Oakland, CA	23	10	198	13488	132	618469	3261	—	—	—
□ ST. ROSE HOSPITAL, 27200 Calaroga Avenue, Zip 94545–4383; tel. 510/264–4000; Michael P. Mahoney, President and Chief Executive Officer (Total facility includes 46 beds in nursing home–type unit) (Nonreporting) A1 2 9 10 S Via Christi Health System, Wichita, KS	21	10	175	—	—	—	—	—	—	—
HEALDSBURG—Sonoma County										
✠ HEALDSBURG GENERAL HOSPITAL, 1375 University Avenue, Zip 95448; tel. 707/431–6500; Edward C. Bland, President and Chief Executive Officer (Nonreporting) A1 9 10 **Web address:** www.healdsburghospital.com	33	10	49	—	—	—	—	—	—	—
HEMET—Riverside County										
✠ HEMET VALLEY MEDICAL CENTER, 1117 East Devonshire Avenue, Zip 92543; tel. 909/652–2811; Barbara Taylor, R.N., Interim Administrator (Nonreporting) A1 9 10 S Valley Health System, Hemet, CA	16	10	285	—	—	—	—	—	—	—

Hospital, Address, Telephone, Administrator, Approval, Facility, and Physician Codes, Health Care System, Network	Classi-fication Codes		Utilization Data					Expense (thousands) of dollars		
	Control	Service	Staffed Beds	Admissions	Census	Outpatient Visits	Births	Total	Payroll	Personnel

★ American Hospital Association (AHA) membership
☐ Joint Commission on Accreditation of Healthcare Organizations (JCAHO) accreditation
+ American Osteopathic Healthcare Association (AOHA) membership
○ American Osteopathic Association (AOA) accreditation
△ Commission on Accreditation of Rehabilitation Facilities (CARF) accreditation
Control codes 61, 63, 64, 71, 72 and 73 indicate hospitals listed by AOHA, but not registered by AHA. For definition of numerical codes, see page A4

Hospital info	Control	Service	Staffed Beds	Admissions	Census	Outpatient Visits	Births	Total	Payroll	Personnel
HOLLISTER—San Benito County										
★ HAZEL HAWKINS MEMORIAL HOSPITAL, (Includes Hazel Hawkins Convalescent Hospital–Southside, 3110 Southside Road, Zip 95023; tel. 408/637–5711), 911 Sunset Drive, Zip 95023–5695; tel. 831/637–5711; Keith Mesmer, Chief Executive Officer (Total facility includes 52 beds in nursing home–type unit) **A**1 9 10 **F**7 8 11 14 15 16 17 19 20 22 25 26 28 29 30 31 32 34 35 37 40 41 42 44 45 46 49 51 57 58 64 65 66 67 71 73 **P**1 5 7 **S** Brim Healthcare, Inc., Brentwood, TN	16	10	71	2278	67	84781	527	23371	9953	232
HOLLYWOOD—Los Angeles County, See Los Angeles										
HUNTINGTON BEACH—Orange County										
★ HUNTINGTON BEACH HOSPITAL, (Formerly Huntington Beach Medical Center), 17772 Beach Boulevard, Zip 92647–9932; tel. 714/842–1473; Carol B. Freeman, Chief Executive Officer (Total facility includes 12 beds in nursing home–type unit) **A**1 9 10 **F**4 8 10 12 14 16 19 21 22 27 28 30 34 35 37 44 46 52 54 55 56 57 58 59 64 65 71 73 **P**5 **S** Columbia/HCA Healthcare Corporation, Nashville, TN	33	10	114	3966	63	54477	0	31565	14646	305
HUNTINGTON PARK—Los Angeles County										
★ COMMUNITY HOSPITAL OF HUNTINGTON PARK, (Includes Mission Hospital of Huntington Park, 3111 East Florence Avenue, tel. 213/582–8261), 2623 East Slauson Avenue, Zip 90255; tel. 323/583–1931; Charles Martinez, Ph.D., Chief Executive Officer (Nonreporting) **A**1 9 10 **S** TENET Healthcare Corporation, Santa Barbara, CA	33	10	226	—	—	—	—	—	—	—
INDIO—Riverside County										
★ JOHN F. KENNEDY MEMORIAL HOSPITAL, 47–111 Monroe Street, Zip 92201, Mailing Address: P.O. Drawer LLLL, Zip 92202–2558; tel. 760/347–6191; Larry W. Payton, Chief Operating Officer **A**1 9 10 **F**1 4 7 8 10 11 12 13 14 15 16 17 19 21 22 23 25 28 29 30 31 32 33 34 35 36 37 38 39 40 41 42 43 44 46 47 49 51 52 54 55 56 57 58 59 60 64 65 67 70 71 72 73 74 **P**5 **S** TENET Healthcare Corporation, Santa Barbara, CA	33	10	130	8139	77	61863	2109	45503	18940	488
INGLEWOOD—Los Angeles County										
★ △ CENTINELA HOSPITAL MEDICAL CENTER, 555 East Hardy Street, Zip 90301–4073, Mailing Address: Box 720, Zip 90307–0720; tel. 310/673–4660; Michael A. Rembis, FACHE, Chief Executive Officer **A**1 2 3 7 9 10 **F**4 8 10 11 12 15 17 19 21 22 23 26 32 34 35 37 38 40 41 42 43 44 48 49 51 52 55 56 57 58 60 61 64 65 66 67 71 72 **P**5 **S** TENET Healthcare Corporation, Santa Barbara, CA	33	10	377	12682	188	156086	2278	108608	44783	1125
★ △ DANIEL FREEMAN MEMORIAL HOSPITAL, 333 North Prairie Avenue, Zip 90301–4514; tel. 310/674–7050; Joseph W. Dunn, Ph.D., Chief Executive Officer (Total facility includes 29 beds in nursing home–type unit) **A**1 2 5 7 9 10 **F**1 2 3 4 7 8 10 11 12 15 16 18 19 21 22 23 24 25 27 30 32 34 35 36 37 38 39 40 42 43 44 45 46 48 49 52 53 55 56 57 58 59 60 63 64 65 71 73 74 **P**7 **S** Carondelet Health System, Saint Louis, MO	21	10	360	13097	220	110226	3080	142676	55926	1674
IRVINE—Orange County										
★ IRVINE MEDICAL CENTER, 16200 Sand Canyon Avenue, Zip 92618–3714; tel. 949/753–2000; Dan F. Ausman, Chief Executive Officer **A**1 9 10 **F**4 7 8 10 12 14 15 16 17 19 21 22 23 27 28 29 30 32 34 35 37 38 40 41 42 43 44 46 49 52 56 57 60 64 65 67 71 73 74 **P**5 7 **S** TENET Healthcare Corporation, Santa Barbara, CA	33	10	176	6036	70	93154	1699	—	—	399
JACKSON—Amador County										
★ SUTTER AMADOR HOSPITAL, 810 Court Street, Zip 95642–2379; tel. 209/223–7500; Scott Stenberg, Chief Executive Officer (Total facility includes 44 beds in nursing home–type unit) (Nonreporting) **A**1 9 10 **S** Sutter Health, Sacramento, CA	23	10	85	—	—	—	—	—	—	—
JOSHUA TREE—San Bernardino County										
★ HI–DESERT MEDICAL CENTER, 6601 White Feather Road, Zip 92252–6601; tel. 760/366–3711; James R. Larson, President and Chief Executive Officer (Total facility includes 75 beds in nursing home–type unit) **A**1 9 10 **F**8 15 16 17 19 20 21 22 25 26 27 28 30 31 32 33 34 35 37 39 41 44 45 46 49 59 64 65 67 71 73 **P**1	16	10	103	2608	100	54885	0	31161	11184	434
KENTFIELD—Marin County										
☐ BHC ROSS HOSPITAL, 1111 Sir Francis Drake Boulevard, Zip 94904; tel. 415/258–6900; Judy G. House, Chief Executive Officer (Nonreporting) **A**1 10 **S** Behavioral Healthcare Corporation, Nashville, TN	33	22	56	—	—	—	—	—	—	—
☐ KENTFIELD REHABILITATION HOSPITAL, 1125 Sir Francis Drake Boulevard, Zip 94904, Mailing Address: P.O. Box 338, Zip 94914–0338; tel. 415/456–9680; John Behrmann, Administrator and Chief Executive Officer (Total facility includes 12 beds in nursing home–type unit) (Nonreporting) **A**1 9 10	33	46	60	—	—	—	—	—	—	—
KING CITY—Monterey County										
☐ GEORGE L. MEE MEMORIAL HOSPITAL, 300 Canal Street, Zip 93930–3410; tel. 831/385–6000; Walter Beck, Chief Executive Officer **A**1 9 10 **F**7 8 11 12 14 15 16 17 19 22 30 32 35 39 40 44 45 46 64 65 71 73 74	23	10	42	760	22	19351	391	15192	8550	231
KINGSBURG—Fresno County										
KINGSBURG DISTRICT HOSPITAL, 1200 Smith Street, Zip 93631; tel. 559/897–5841; William J. Casey, Administrator (Total facility includes 20 beds in nursing home–type unit) (Nonreporting) **A**9 10	16	10	35	—	—	—	—	—	—	—
LA JOLLA—San Diego County										
★ GREEN HOSPITAL OF SCRIPPS CLINIC, 10666 North Torrey Pines Road, Zip 92037–1093; tel. 619/455–9100; Thomas C. Gagen, Senior Vice President (Nonreporting) **A**1 2 5 8 9 10 **S** Scripps Health, San Diego, CA	23	10	165	—	—	—	—	—	—	—

Hospital, Address, Telephone, Administrator, Approval, Facility, and Physician Codes, Health Care System, Network	Classi-fication Codes		Utilization Data					Expense (thousands) of dollars		
★ American Hospital Association (AHA) membership □ Joint Commission on Accreditation of Healthcare Organizations (JCAHO) accreditation + American Osteopathic Healthcare Association (AOHA) membership ○ American Osteopathic Association (AOA) accreditation △ Commission on Accreditation of Rehabilitation Facilities (CARF) accreditation Control codes 61, 63, 64, 71, 72 and 73 indicate hospitals listed by AOHA, but not registered by AHA. For definition of numerical codes, see page A4	Control	Service	Staffed Beds	Admissions	Census	Outpatient Visits	Births	Total	Payroll	Personnel
⊠ △ SCRIPPS MEMORIAL HOSPITAL–LA JOLLA, 9888 Genesee Avenue, Zip 92037–1276, Mailing Address: P.O. Box 28, Zip 92038–0028; tel. 619/626–4123; Thomas C. Gagen, Senior Vice President and Regional Administrator (Total facility includes 29 beds in nursing home–type unit) (Nonreporting) **A**1 2 3 7 9 10 **S** Scripps Health, San Diego, CA	23	10	431	—	—	—	—	—	—	—
LA MESA—San Diego County										
⊠ △ GROSSMONT HOSPITAL, 5555 Grossmont Center Drive, Zip 91942, Mailing Address: Box 158, Zip 91944–0158; tel. 619/465–0711; Michele T. Tarbet, R.N., Chief Executive Officer (Total facility includes 30 beds in nursing home–type unit) **A**1 2 3 7 9 10 12 **F**4 7 8 10 11 12 15 16 17 19 20 21 22 23 25 26 27 30 31 32 33 34 35 36 37 38 39 40 41 42 43 44 46 48 49 51 52 53 54 55 56 57 58 59 60 61 63 64 65 66 67 68 70 71 72 73 74 **P**5 7 **S** Sharp Healthcare, San Diego, CA **Web address:** www.sharp.com	23	10	384	18154	217	132987	2490	141037	61668	1602
LA PALMA—Orange County										
⊠ △ LA PALMA INTERCOMMUNITY HOSPITAL, 7901 Walker Street, Zip 90623–5850, Mailing Address: P.O. Box 5850, Buena Park, Zip 90622; tel. 714/670–7400; Stephen E. Dixon, President and Chief Executive Officer (Nonreporting) **A**1 2 7 9 10 **S** Catholic Healthcare West, San Francisco, CA **Web address:** www.unihealth.org	23	10	139	—	—	—	—	—	—	—
LAGUNA HILLS—Orange County										
□ SADDLEBACK MEMORIAL MEDICAL CENTER, 24451 Health Center Drive, Zip 92653; tel. 949/837–4500; Barry S. Arbuckle, Ph.D., Chief Executive Officer (Total facility includes 15 beds in nursing home–type unit) **A**1 2 9 10 **F**4 7 8 10 12 14 15 16 17 18 19 21 22 24 25 26 28 29 30 31 32 33 34 35 36 37 38 39 40 41 42 43 44 45 46 48 49 59 60 64 65 71 72 73 74 **P**5 7 **S** Memorial Health Services, Long Beach, CA	23	10	148	11112	135	247472	2433	103374	41841	1425
LAKE ARROWHEAD—San Bernardino County										
□ SAN BERNARDINO MOUNTAINS COMMUNITY HOSPITAL DISTRICT, 29101 Hospital Road, Zip 92352, Mailing Address: Box 70, Zip 92352; tel. 909/336–3651; John J. McCormick, Chief Executive Officer (Total facility includes 18 beds in nursing home–type unit) (Nonreporting) **A**1 9 10	16	10	36	—	—	—	—	—	—	—
LAKE ISABELLA—Kern County										
KERN VALLEY HOSPITAL DISTRICT, 6412 Laurel Avenue, Zip 93240, Mailing Address: P.O. Box 1628, Zip 93240; tel. 760/379–2681; Robert Knight, Chief Executive Officer (Total facility includes 74 beds in nursing home–type unit) **A**9 10 **F**8 12 13 14 17 19 22 24 25 28 29 30 32 34 36 37 39 41 44 45 49 51 64 65 71 72 73 **P**3	16	10	101	1463	85	19326	0	13548	6377	250
LAKEPORT—Lake County										
⊠ SUTTER LAKESIDE HOSPITAL, 5176 Hill Road East, Zip 95453–6111; tel. 707/262–5001; Gilbert Silbernagel, Chief Executive Officer (Nonreporting) **A**1 9 10 **S** Sutter Health, Sacramento, CA **Web address:** www.sutterlake.org	23	10	54	—	—	—	—	—	—	—
LAKEWOOD—Los Angeles County										
⊠ LAKEWOOD REGIONAL MEDICAL CENTER, 3700 East South Street, Zip 90712; tel. 562/531–2550; Gustavo A. Valdespino, Chief Executive Officer **A**1 2 9 10 **F**3 4 7 8 9 10 11 12 15 16 17 19 20 22 23 26 27 28 30 32 33 34 35 37 38 40 41 42 43 44 45 46 47 48 49 52 57 59 60 64 65 68 71 73 74 **P**5 7 **S** TENET Healthcare Corporation, Santa Barbara, CA	33	10	148	8400	101	51160	1135	50904	21917	640
LANCASTER—Los Angeles County										
⊠ ANTELOPE VALLEY HOSPITAL, 1600 West Avenue J, Zip 93534–2894; tel. 805/949–5000; Mathew Abraham, Chief Executive Officer **A**1 9 10 **F**2 4 7 8 9 10 11 12 13 15 16 17 19 21 22 23 26 32 34 35 37 38 40 42 43 44 47 48 49 52 61 63 64 67 71 73 74 **P**7 **Web address:** www.avhospital.org	16	10	332	18964	236	134858	4760	133257	58034	2016
⊠ LAC–HIGH DESERT HOSPITAL, 44900 North 60th Street West, Zip 93536; tel. 661/945–8461; Mel Grussing, Administrator (Total facility includes 50 beds in nursing home–type unit) **A**1 10 **F**4 8 12 13 17 19 20 28 31 32 34 35 37 42 43 44 46 49 51 53 54 55 56 59 60 64 65 71 73 **P**6 **S** Los Angeles County–Department of Health Services, Los Angeles, CA	13	10	75	1625	77	48139	—	64268	18483	579
□ LANCASTER COMMUNITY HOSPITAL, 43830 North Tenth Street West, Zip 93534; tel. 661/948–4781; John E. Fidler, FACHE, Chief Executive Officer **A**1 9 10 **F**4 10 11 16 19 22 32 34 35 41 43 44 48 65 67 71 72 73 **S** Paracelsus Healthcare Corporation, Houston, TX	33	10	117	5387	75	39451	0	38231	14933	419
LEMOORE—Kings County										
⊠ NAVAL HOSPITAL, 930 Franklin Avenue, Zip 93246–5000; tel. 209/998–4201; Captain Steven Hart, Commanding Officer (Nonreporting) **A**1 **S** Department of Navy, Washington, DC **Web address:** www.lenhfsa.med.navy.mil	43	10	25	—	—	—	—	—	—	—
LINDSAY—Tulare County										
★ LINDSAY DISTRICT HOSPITAL, 740 North Sequoia Avenue, Zip 93247, Mailing Address: Box 40, Zip 93247; tel. 559/562–4955; Edwin L. Ermshar, President and Chief Executive Officer (Total facility includes 53 beds in nursing home–type unit) (Nonreporting) **A**9 10	16	10	106	—	—	—	—	—	—	—
LIVERMORE—Alameda County										
VALLEYCARE MEMORIAL HOSPITAL, (Formerly Valley Memorial Hospital), 1111 East Stanley Boulevard, Zip 94550; tel. 925/447–7000; Marcelina Feit, President and Chief Executive Officer (Total facility includes 14 beds in nursing home–type unit) (Nonreporting) **A**2 9 10 **S** ValleyCare Health System, Pleasanton, CA	23	10	110	—	—	—	—	—	—	—
VETERANS AFFAIRS PALO ALTO HEALTH CARE SYSTEM, LIVERMORE DIVISION See Veterans Affairs Palo Alto Health Care System, Palo Alto										

Hospital, Address, Telephone, Administrator, Approval, Facility, and Physician Codes, Health Care System, Network	Classi-fication Codes		Utilization Data					Expense (thousands) of dollars		

	Control	Service	Staffed Beds	Admissions	Census	Outpatient Visits	Births	Total	Payroll	Personnel
LODI—San Joaquin County										
⊞ LODI MEMORIAL HOSPITAL, (Includes Lodi Memorial Hospital West, 800 South Lower Sacramento Road, Zip 95242; tel. 209/333–0211), 975 South Fairmont Avenue, Zip 95240–5179, Mailing Address: P.O. Box 3004, Zip 95241–1908; tel. 209/334–3411; Joseph P. Harrington, Chief Executive Officer **A**1 9 10 **F**1 2 3 4 5 7 8 9 10 11 12 13 14 15 16 17 19 20 21 22 23 24 25 27 28 29 30 32 34 35 37 38 39 40 41 42 43 44 45 46 47 48 49 51 52 53 54 55 56 57 58 59 60 61 63 64 65 66 67 69 71 72 73 **P**5 7 **Web address:** www.lodihealth.org	23	10	181	6744	104	149790	1281	65922	29414	824
LOMA LINDA—San Bernardino County										
⊞ JERRY L. PETTIS MEMORIAL VETERANS MEDICAL CENTER, 11201 Benton Street, Zip 92357; tel. 909/825–7084; Dean R. Stordahl, Chief Executive Officer (Total facility includes 106 beds in nursing home–type unit) **A**1 3 5 8 **F**3 4 5 8 10 11 12 14 18 19 20 21 22 23 24 25 26 27 28 30 31 32 33 34 35 37 39 41 42 43 44 45 46 49 51 52 54 55 56 57 58 59 60 61 63 64 65 67 68 71 72 73 74 **P**1 **S** Department of Veterans Affairs, Washington, DC **Web address:** www.desertpacific.med.va.gov	45	10	231	5191	186	—	0	131350	—	1255
□ △ LOMA LINDA UNIVERSITY MEDICAL CENTER, (Includes Loma Linda University Community Medical Center, 25333 Barton Road, Zip 92354–3053; tel. 909/796–0167), 11234 Anderson Street, Zip 92354–2870, Mailing Address: P.O. Box 2000, Zip 92354–0200; tel. 909/824–0800; B. Lyn Behrens, President (Nonreporting) **A**1 2 3 5 7 8 9 10 **S** Loma Linda University Health Sciences Center, Loma Linda, CA **Web address:** www.llumc.edu	21	10	653	—	—	—	—	—	—	—
LOMPOC—Santa Barbara County										
□ LOMPOC HEALTHCARE DISTRICT, (Formerly Lompoc District Hospital), 508 East Hickory Street, Zip 93436, Mailing Address: Box 1058, Zip 93438; tel. 805/737–3300; James Raggio, Administrator (Total facility includes 110 beds in nursing home–type unit) (Nonreporting) **A**1 9 10 **S** Quorum Health Group/Quorum Health Resources, Inc., Brentwood, TN	16	10	170	—	—	—	—	—	—	—
LONE PINE—Inyo County										
SOUTHERN INYO COUNTY LOCAL HEALTH CARE DISTRICT, 501 East Locust Street, Zip 93545, Mailing Address: Box 1009, Zip 93545; tel. 760/876–5501; Ashvin Pandya, M.D., Interim Administrator (Nonreporting) **A**9 10	16	10	37	—	—	—	—	—	—	—
LONG BEACH—Los Angeles County										
⊞ LONG BEACH COMMUNITY MEDICAL CENTER, 1720 Termino Avenue, Zip 90804; tel. 562/498–1000; Makoto Nakayama, President **A**1 2 9 10 **F**1 4 7 8 10 11 12 14 15 16 17 19 21 22 26 27 28 29 30 31 33 34 35 37 38 39 40 41 42 43 44 45 46 47 49 51 52 54 55 56 57 58 59 60 63 64 65 67 68 71 72 73 74 **S** Catholic Healthcare West, San Francisco, CA **Web address:** www.lbcommunity.com	23	10	278	9990	115	47368	2042	85045	31585	692
□ LONG BEACH DOCTORS HOSPITAL, 1725 Pacific Avenue, Zip 90813–1798; tel. 310/599–3551; Manuel Anel, M.D., Administrator and Chief Executive Officer (Nonreporting) **A**1	32	10	43	—	—	—	—	—	—	—
□ LONG BEACH MEMORIAL MEDICAL CENTER, 2801 Atlantic Avenue, Zip 90806, Mailing Address: Box 1428, Zip 90801–1428; tel. 562/933–2000; Chris D. Van Gorder, Chief Executive Officer (Total facility includes 62 beds in nursing home–type unit) (Nonreporting) **A**1 2 3 5 8 9 10 **S** Memorial Health Services, Long Beach, CA **Web address:** www.memorialcare.org	23	10	726	—	—	—	—	—	—	—
□ ○ PACIFIC HOSPITAL OF LONG BEACH, 2776 Pacific Avenue, Zip 90806–2699, Mailing Address: P.O. Box 1268, Zip 90801; tel. 562/595–1911; Michael D. Drobot, President and Chief Executive Officer (Total facility includes 27 beds in nursing home–type unit) **A**1 5 9 10 11 12 13 **F**8 11 12 15 16 17 19 20 21 22 26 30 31 32 33 34 35 37 40 41 42 44 49 51 52 55 56 57 61 64 65 71 73 **P**5	33	10	119	3867	66	55562	450	33961	17798	512
REDGATE MEMORIAL HOSPITAL, 1775 Chestnut Avenue, Zip 90813; tel. 310/599–8444; Larry Gentile, Chief Executive Officer (Nonreporting)	23	82	63	—	—	—	—	—	—	—
⊞ ST. MARY MEDICAL CENTER, 1050 Linden Avenue, Zip 90801, Mailing Address: P.O. Box 887, Zip 90813–0887; tel. 562/491–9000; Tammie McMann Brailsford, Administrator and Chief Operating Officer **A**1 2 3 5 9 10 **F**4 6 7 8 10 11 12 13 14 15 16 17 19 21 22 24 25 26 27 28 30 31 32 33 34 35 37 38 39 40 41 42 43 44 46 47 48 49 50 51 52 57 58 59 60 63 64 65 68 70 71 72 73 74 **P**5 7 **S** Catholic Healthcare West, San Francisco, CA **Web address:** www.sc.chw.edu	23	10	402	11700	199	253966	2144	114001	42255	1379
⊞ VETERANS AFFAIRS MEDICAL CENTER, 5901 East Seventh Street, Zip 90822–5201; tel. 562/494–5400; Lawrence C. Stewart, Director (Total facility includes 110 beds in nursing home–type unit) **A**1 2 3 5 8 **F**2 3 4 8 10 11 12 15 16 17 18 19 20 21 22 23 24 25 26 27 28 29 30 31 32 33 34 35 37 39 41 42 44 45 46 49 50 51 52 54 55 56 57 58 60 65 67 70 71 72 73 74 **S** Department of Veterans Affairs, Washington, DC **Web address:** www.long–beach.va.gov	45	10	448	6477	311	317312	0	182266	—	2134
LOS ALAMITOS—Orange County										
⊞ LOS ALAMITOS MEDICAL CENTER, 3751 Katella Avenue, Zip 90720; tel. 562/598–1311; Gustavo A. Valdespino, Chief Executive Officer (Total facility includes 20 beds in nursing home–type unit) **A**1 2 9 10 **F**2 3 4 7 8 9 10 11 12 13 15 16 17 19 20 21 22 23 26 28 29 30 31 32 33 35 36 37 38 39 40 42 43 44 46 47 48 52 57 58 60 63 64 65 67 68 70 71 73 74 **P**4 5 7 **S** TENET Healthcare Corporation, Santa Barbara, CA	33	10	173	8680	96	36701	1991	48818	23284	658

Hospital, Address, Telephone, Administrator, Approval, Facility, and Physician Codes, Health Care System, Network	Classi-fication Codes		Utilization Data					Expense (thousands) of dollars		
	Control	Service	Staffed Beds	Admissions	Census	Outpatient Visits	Births	Total	Payroll	Personnel

★ American Hospital Association (AHA) membership
□ Joint Commission on Accreditation of Healthcare Organizations (JCAHO) accreditation
+ American Osteopathic Healthcare Association (AOHA) membership
○ American Osteopathic Association (AOA) accreditation
△ Commission on Accreditation of Rehabilitation Facilities (CARF) accreditation
Control codes 61, 63, 64, 71, 72 and 73 indicate hospitals listed by AOHA, but not registered by AHA. For definition of numerical codes, see page A4

LOS ANGELES—Los Angeles County
(Mailing Addresses - Canoga Park, Encino, Granada Hills, Harbor City, Hollywood, Mission Hills, North Hollywood, Northridge, Panorama City, San Pedro, Sepulveda, Sherman Oaks, Sun Valley, Sylmar, Tarzana, Van Nuys, West Hills, West Los Angeles, Woodland Hills)

Hospital	Control	Service	Staffed Beds	Admissions	Census	Outpatient Visits	Births	Total	Payroll	Personnel
⊞ BARLOW RESPIRATORY HOSPITAL, 2000 Stadium Way, Zip 90026–2696; tel. 213/250–4200; Margaret W. Crane, Chief Executive Officer **A**1 3 5 10 **F**15 16 19 34 35 37 65 67 71 **P**8	23	10	61	409	39	619	0	18112	8321	275
□ BAY HARBOR HOSPITAL, 1437 West Lomita Boulevard, Harbor City, Zip 90710–2097; tel. 310/325–1221; John M. Wilson, President (Total facility includes 212 beds in nursing home–type unit) (Nonreporting) **A**1 2 9 10 **S** Little Company of Mary Sisters Healthcare System, Evergreen Park, IL	23	10	346	—	—	—	—	—	—	—
⊞ CALIFORNIA HOSPITAL MEDICAL CENTER, 1401 South Grand Avenue, Zip 90015–3063; tel. 213/748–2411; Melinda D. Beswick, President **A**1 2 3 5 9 10 **F**7 8 11 12 15 16 17 19 21 22 27 28 30 37 38 40 41 42 44 47 49 51 52 57 60 61 63 64 65 67 68 71 72 73 74 **P**5 **S** Catholic Healthcare West, San Francisco, CA **Web address:** www.chmcla.com	23	10	303	12856	155	129674	4276	107594	41716	981
⊞ CEDARS–SINAI MEDICAL CENTER, 8700 Beverly Boulevard, Zip 90048–1865, Mailing Address: Box 48750, Zip 90048–0750; tel. 310/855–5000; Thomas M. Priselac, President and Chief Executive Officer **A**1 2 3 5 8 9 10 **F**3 4 5 7 8 10 11 12 13 14 15 16 17 18 19 20 21 22 23 26 28 29 30 31 32 33 34 35 36 37 38 39 40 41 42 43 44 45 46 47 48 49 50 51 52 53 54 55 56 57 58 59 60 61 63 64 65 66 67 68 70 71 73 74 **P**3 5 8	23	10	846	41861	636	161245	6758	645114	260911	5965
⊞ CENTURY CITY HOSPITAL, 2070 Century Park East, Zip 90067; tel. 310/553–6211; John R. Nickens, III, Chief Executive Officer (Nonreporting) **A**1 9 10 **S** TENET Healthcare Corporation, Santa Barbara, CA	33	10	156	—	—	—	—	—	—	—
⊞ CHILDRENS HOSPITAL OF LOS ANGELES, (TERTIARY), 4650 Sunset Boulevard, Zip 90027–6089, Mailing Address: Box 54700, Zip 90054–0700; tel. 323/660–2450; Walter W. Noce, Jr., President and Chief Executive Officer **A**1 2 3 5 9 10 **F**10 11 12 14 15 16 17 19 20 22 27 34 35 38 39 42 43 44 47 48 49 53 60 68 70 72 73 **P**5 7	23	59	279	10942	222	198344	0	239218	91562	2256
□ EAST LOS ANGELES DOCTORS HOSPITAL, 4060 Whittier Boulevard, Zip 90023–2596; tel. 323/268–5514; Frank Kutsuda, Administrator and Chief Executive Officer (Total facility includes 25 beds in nursing home–type unit) (Nonreporting) **A**1 9 10	33	10	127	—	—	—	—	—	—	—
□ EDGEMONT HOSPITAL, 4841 Hollywood Boulevard, Zip 90027–5388; tel. 213/913–9000; Cynthia L. Kern, Administrator (Nonreporting) **A**1 9 10	33	22	61	—	—	—	—	—	—	—
⊞ ENCINO–TARZANA REGIONAL MEDICAL CENTER ENCINO CAMPUS, 16237 Ventura Boulevard, Encino, Zip 91436–2201; tel. 818/995–5000 **A**1 3 9 10 **F**1 3 4 7 8 10 11 12 15 16 19 21 22 23 26 32 35 37 42 43 44 45 48 49 52 57 60 61 64 65 71 73 74 **P**2 3 4 5 7 8 **S** TENET Healthcare Corporation, Santa Barbara, CA	33	10	138	3700	75	32557	0	40822	—	325
★ ENCINO–TARZANA REGIONAL MEDICAL CENTER TARZANA CAMPUS, 18321 Clark Street, Tarzana, Zip 91356; tel. 818/881–0800; Dale Surowitz, President and Chief Executive Officer **A**9 10 **F**2 4 7 8 9 10 11 12 15 19 21 22 23 27 28 29 30 32 34 35 37 38 39 40 42 43 44 45 46 47 48 49 50 52 57 60 61 62 63 64 65 66 67 69 71 72 73 74 **P**5 7 **S** TENET Healthcare Corporation, Santa Barbara, CA	33	10	232	11188	127	37133	3006	—	—	665
□ GATEWAYS HOSPITAL AND MENTAL HEALTH CENTER, 1891 Effie Street, Zip 90026–1711; tel. 323/644–2000; Saul Goldfarb, President and Chief Executive Officer **A**1 10 **F**2 3 52 53 54 55 57 58 59	23	22	35	618	29	5576	0	12513	7488	200
□ △ GOOD SAMARITAN HOSPITAL, 1225 Wilshire Boulevard, Zip 90017–2395; tel. 213/977–2121; Andrew B. Leeka, President and Chief Executive Officer **A**1 2 7 9 10 **F**4 7 8 10 11 12 15 17 19 21 22 23 24 27 28 29 30 32 34 35 37 38 40 41 42 43 44 45 46 47 48 60 61 63 64 65 66 67 70 71 73	23	10	377	14965	235	104076	2766	168603	69488	1514
□ GRANADA HILLS COMMUNITY HOSPITAL, 10445 Balboa Boulevard, Granada Hills, Zip 91394–9400; tel. 818/360–1021; Thomas M. Wallace, President and Chief Executive Officer (Total facility includes 23 beds in nursing home–type unit) (Nonreporting) **A**1 9 10 **Web address:** www.ghch.com	23	10	139	—	—	—	—	—	—	—
□ HOLLYWOOD COMMUNITY HOSPITAL OF HOLLYWOOD, (Includes Hollywood Community Hospital of Van Nuys, 14433 Emelita Street, Zip 91401; tel. 818/787–1511), 6245 De Longpre Avenue, Zip 90028–9001; tel. 213/462–2271; Robert A. Schapper, Chief Executive Officer (Nonreporting) **A**1 10	33	10	160	—	—	—	—	—	—	—
HOLLYWOOD COMMUNITY HOSPITAL OF VAN NUYS See Hollywood Community Hospital of Hollywood										
★ KAISER FOUNDATION HOSPITAL, (Includes Kaiser Foundation Mental Health Center, 765 West College Street, Zip 90012; tel. 213/580–7200), 4747 Sunset Boulevard, Zip 90027–6072; tel. 323/783–4011; Joseph W. Hummel, Senior Vice President **A**2 3 5 10 **F**3 4 7 8 9 10 11 13 14 15 16 19 21 22 23 25 26 28 29 30 31 32 33 34 35 37 38 39 40 41 42 43 44 45 46 47 49 50 51 52 53 54 55 56 57 58 59 60 63 64 65 67 69 71 72 73 **S** Kaiser Foundation Hospitals, Oakland, CA **Web address:** www.lac.usc.org	23	10	384	21802	278	—	3145	—	—	1672

Hospital, Address, Telephone, Administrator, Approval, Facility, and Physician Codes, Health Care System, Network	Classi-fication Codes		Utilization Data					Expense (thousands) of dollars		
	Control	Service	Staffed Beds	Admissions	Census	Outpatient Visits	Births	Total	Payroll	Personnel

★ American Hospital Association (AHA) membership
□ Joint Commission on Accreditation of Healthcare Organizations (JCAHO) accreditation
+ American Osteopathic Healthcare Association (AOHA) membership
○ American Osteopathic Association (AOA) accreditation
△ Commission on Accreditation of Rehabilitation Facilities (CARF) accreditation
Control codes 61, 63, 64, 71, 72 and 73 indicate hospitals listed by AOHA, but not registered by AHA. For definition of numerical codes, see page A4

Hospital	Control	Service	Staffed Beds	Admissions	Census	Outpatient Visits	Births	Total	Payroll	Personnel
⊞ KAISER FOUNDATION HOSPITAL, 25825 South Vermont Avenue, Harbor City, Zip 90710; tel. 310/325–5111; Judith Ann North, Administrator **A**1 2 10 **F**2 3 4 7 8 10 11 12 17 18 19 21 22 23 25 26 28 29 30 31 32 33 34 35 37 38 39 40 41 42 43 44 45 46 47 49 51 53 54 55 56 57 58 59 60 61 65 66 67 68 71 72 73 **S** Kaiser Foundation Hospitals, Oakland, CA	23	10	189	10497	99	80271	2019	—	—	970
⊞ KAISER FOUNDATION HOSPITAL, 13652 Cantara Street, Panorama City, Zip 91402; tel. 818/375–2000; Dev Mahadevan, Administrator **A**1 5 10 **F**3 4 7 8 10 12 13 14 15 16 17 18 19 21 22 26 27 28 29 30 31 32 33 34 35 37 38 40 41 43 44 45 46 49 50 51 53 54 55 56 57 58 59 60 61 63 65 66 67 68 69 71 72 73 **S** Kaiser Foundation Hospitals, Oakland, CA	23	10	166	11559	104	1661557	2279	—	—	779
⊞ KAISER FOUNDATION HOSPITAL, 5601 DeSoto Avenue, Woodland Hills, Zip 91365–4084; tel. 818/719–3808; Deborah M. Lee–Eddie, Senior Vice President and Area Manager **A**1 3 5 10 **F**2 3 4 7 8 10 11 12 14 15 16 17 18 19 21 22 23 26 28 29 30 31 32 33 34 35 37 38 40 41 42 43 44 45 48 49 50 51 52 53 54 55 56 58 59 60 61 64 65 66 67 68 70 71 72 73 74 **S** Kaiser Foundation Hospitals, Oakland, CA	23	10	188	9934	103	—	2133	—	—	320
⊞ KAISER FOUNDATION HOSPITAL–WEST LOS ANGELES, 6041 Cadillac Avenue, Zip 90034; tel. 323/857–2201; Joseph W. Hummel, Administrator **A**1 2 3 5 10 **F**4 7 8 10 12 13 19 20 21 22 23 25 26 27 28 29 30 31 32 33 34 35 37 38 39 40 41 42 44 45 46 49 50 51 53 54 55 56 57 58 59 60 61 63 65 67 69 71 72 73 74 **S** Kaiser Foundation Hospitals, Oakland, CA	23	10	160	11619	111	77611	1962	—	—	320
KAISER FOUNDATION MENTAL HEALTH CENTER See Kaiser Foundation Hospital										
⊞ LAC–KING–DREW MEDICAL CENTER, 12021 South Wilmington Avenue, Zip 90059; tel. 310/668–4321; Randall S. Foster, Administrator and Chief Executive Officer **A**1 2 3 5 8 9 10 **F**1 4 7 8 10 11 12 13 14 15 16 17 18 19 20 21 22 25 26 27 28 29 30 31 32 34 35 37 38 40 41 42 43 44 47 49 50 51 52 53 54 55 56 57 58 59 60 61 63 65 68 70 71 72 73 74 **P**8 **S** Los Angeles County–Department of Health Services, Los Angeles, CA	13	10	249	18226	207	236006	1865	298254	147016	3000
⊞ LAC–OLIVE VIEW–UCLA MEDICAL CENTER, 14445 Olive View Drive, Sylmar, Zip 91342–1495; tel. 818/364–1555; Melinda Anderson, Administrator **A**1 3 5 10 **F**3 4 7 8 10 12 13 17 19 20 21 22 25 26 27 28 29 30 31 34 35 37 38 39 40 41 42 43 44 45 46 49 50 51 52 53 54 56 57 58 59 60 61 63 65 67 68 70 71 72 73 74 **P**6 **S** Los Angeles County–Department of Health Services, Los Angeles, CA	13	10	220	13417	189	165097	1879	287064	70243	1590
⊞ LAC/UNIVERSITY OF SOUTHERN CALIFORNIA MEDICAL CENTER, (Includes General Hospital, 1200 North State Street, Zip 90033; Women's and Children's Hospital, 1240 North Mission Road, Zip 90033), 1200 North State Street, Zip 90033–1084; tel. 323/226–2622; Roberto Rodriguez, Executive Director **A**1 2 3 5 8 9 10 **F**1 3 4 5 6 7 8 9 10 11 12 13 14 15 16 17 18 19 20 21 22 23 25 26 27 28 29 30 31 32 34 35 37 38 39 40 41 42 43 44 45 46 47 49 51 52 53 54 55 56 57 58 59 60 61 63 65 66 67 68 70 71 72 73 74 **P**1 3 6 8 **S** Los Angeles County–Department of Health Services, Los Angeles, CA	13	10	1328	47007	771	751192	3464	1085216	232314	6561
□ LINCOLN HOSPITAL MEDICAL CENTER, 443 South Soto Street, Zip 90033–4398; tel. 213/261–1181; Tim Kollars, Administrator and Chief Executive Officer (Nonreporting) **A**1 10	33	10	61	—	—	—	—	—	—	—
□ LOS ANGELES COMMUNITY HOSPITAL, (Includes Los Angeles Community Hospital of Norwalk, 13222 Bloomfield Avenue, Zip 90650; tel. 562/863–4763), 4081 East Olympic Boulevard, Zip 90023–3300; tel. 323/267–0477; Remy Hart, Chief Executive Officer (Nonreporting) **A**1 9 10	33	10	186	—	—	—	—	—	—	—
LOS ANGELES COUNTY CENTRAL JAIL HOSPITAL, 441 Bauchet Street, Zip 90012–2994; tel. 213/974–5045; Tom Flaherty, Assistant Administrator (Nonreporting)	13	11	190	—	—	—	—	—	—	—
□ LOS ANGELES METROPOLITAN MEDICAL CENTER, (Includes Hawthorne Hospital, 13300 South Hawthorne Boulevard, Zip 90250; tel. 310/679–3321; Marvin Herschberg, Chief Executive Officer), 2231 South Western Avenue, Zip 90018–1399; tel. 323/730–7342; Marc A. Furstman, Chief Executive Officer (Nonreporting) **A**1 10 **S** Pacific Health Corporation, Long Beach, CA	32	10	173	—	—	—	—	—	—	—
⊞ MIDWAY HOSPITAL MEDICAL CENTER, 5925 San Vicente Boulevard, Zip 90019–6696; tel. 323/938–3161; John R. Nickens, III, Chief Executive Officer (Total facility includes 21 beds in nursing home–type unit) (Nonreporting) **A**1 9 10 **S** TENET Healthcare Corporation, Santa Barbara, CA	33	10	150	—	—	—	—	—	—	—
MISSION COMMUNITY HOSPITAL–PANORAMA CITY CAMPUS See Mission Community Hospital–San Fernando Campus, San Fernando										
⊞ MOTION PICTURE AND TELEVISION FUND HOSPITAL AND RESIDENTIAL SERVICES, 23388 Mulholland Drive, Woodland Hills, Zip 91364–2792; tel. 818/876–1888; William F. Haug, FACHE, President and Chief Executive Officer (Total facility includes 165 beds in nursing home–type unit) (Nonreporting) **A**1 10 **Web address:** www.mptvfund.org	23	10	218	—	—	—	—	—	—	—
⊞ NORTHRIDGE HOSPITAL AND MEDICAL CENTER, SHERMAN WAY CAMPUS, 14500 Sherman Circle, Van Nuys, Zip 91405; tel. 818/997–0101; Richard D. Lyons, President and Chief Executive Officer (Total facility includes 38 beds in nursing home–type unit) **A**1 9 10 **F**1 2 3 4 7 8 9 10 11 12 15 16 17 18 19 21 22 23 26 27 28 30 31 32 33 34 35 37 38 39 40 41 42 43 44 45 47 48 49 51 52 53 54 55 56 57 58 59 60 61 63 64 65 66 67 68 70 71 73 74 **S** Catholic Healthcare West, San Francisco, CA	23	10	211	3040	94	39867	1763	42693	17607	478

Hospital, Address, Telephone, Administrator, Approval, Facility, and Physician Codes, Health Care System, Network	Classi-fication Codes		Utilization Data					Expense (thousands) of dollars		
	Control	Service	Staffed Beds	Admissions	Census	Outpatient Visits	Births	Total	Payroll	Personnel

★ American Hospital Association (AHA) membership
□ Joint Commission on Accreditation of Healthcare Organizations (JCAHO) accreditation
+ American Osteopathic Healthcare Association (AOHA) membership
○ American Osteopathic Association (AOA) accreditation
△ Commission on Accreditation of Rehabilitation Facilities (CARF) accreditation
Control codes 61, 63, 64, 71, 72 and 73 indicate hospitals listed by AOHA, but not registered by AHA. For definition of numerical codes, see page A4

Hospital	Control	Service	Staffed Beds	Admissions	Census	Outpatient Visits	Births	Total	Payroll	Personnel
⊠ △ NORTHRIDGE HOSPITAL MEDICAL CENTER–ROSCOE BOULEVARD CAMPUS, 18300 Roscoe Boulevard, Northridge, Zip 91328; tel. 818/885–8500; Roger E. Seaver, President and Chief Executive Officer (Total facility includes 31 beds in nursing home–type unit) **A**1 2 3 5 7 9 10 **F**1 3 4 7 8 10 11 12 15 16 17 18 19 20 21 22 24 26 30 31 32 33 34 35 37 38 39 40 41 42 43 44 45 46 47 48 49 51 52 53 54 55 56 57 58 59 60 63 64 65 67 68 70 71 72 73 74 **P**3 5 **S** Catholic Healthcare West, San Francisco, CA	23	10	415	15493	256	94876	2425	165983	58261	1552
□ ORTHOPAEDIC HOSPITAL, 2400 South Flower Street, Zip 90007–2697, Mailing Address: Box 60132, Terminal Annex, Zip 90060; tel. 213/742–1000; James V. Luck, Jr., M.D., Chief Executive Officer and Medical Director **A**1 2 3 5 10 **F**12 14 15 19 20 22 34 35 37 41 42 44 49 63 65 66 67 73 **P**4 7	23	47	73	1576	17	70407	0	33911	10048	292
□ PACIFIC ALLIANCE MEDICAL CENTER, 531 West College Street, Zip 90012–2385; tel. 213/624–8411; John R. Edwards, Administrator and Chief Executive Officer (Nonreporting) **A**1 9 10	32	10	89	—	—	—	—	—	—	—
□ PACIFICA HOSPITAL OF THE VALLEY, 9449 San Fernando Road, Sun Valley, Zip 91352; tel. 818/252–2380; Trude Williams, R.N., Administrator **A**1 9 10 **F**4 8 10 11 12 14 15 16 19 20 21 22 29 34 35 37 38 40 41 42 43 44 45 47 49 52 54 56 59 64 65 71 **P**5 **S** Doctors Community Healthcare Corporation, Scottsdale, AZ	33	10	197	4796	120	43158	665	46372	20073	472
□ PINE GROVE HOSPITAL, (Formerly ValueMark Pine Grove Behavioral Healthcare System), 7011 Shoup Avenue, Canoga Park, Zip 91307; tel. 818/348–0500; Stacey Gentry–Young, Chief Executive Officer (Nonreporting) **A**1 10 **S** ValueMark Healthcare Systems, Inc., Atlanta, GA	33	22	62	—	—	—	—	—	—	—
⊠ PROVIDENCE HOLY CROSS MEDICAL CENTER, 15031 Rinaldi Street, Mission Hills, Zip 91345–1285; tel. 818/365–8051; Michael J. Madden, Chief Executive Officer (Total facility includes 48 beds in nursing home–type unit) **A**1 9 10 **F**4 7 8 10 11 12 14 15 16 17 19 21 22 25 28 29 30 32 33 34 35 37 40 41 42 43 44 45 46 48 49 60 64 65 67 70 71 73 74 **P**5 **S** Sisters of Providence Health System, Seattle, WA **Web address:** www.providence.org	21	10	255	10338	168	70984	1489	86791	37114	911
□ QUEEN OF ANGELS–HOLLYWOOD PRESBYTERIAN MEDICAL CENTER, 1300 North Vermont Avenue, Zip 90027–0069; tel. 213/413–3000; John V. Fenton, Chief Executive Officer (Total facility includes 89 beds in nursing home–type unit) (Nonreporting) **A**1 2 9 10 **S** TENET Healthcare Corporation, Santa Barbara, CA	23	10	409	—	—	—	—	—	—	—
□ △ SAN PEDRO PENINSULA HOSPITAL, 1300 West Seventh Street, San Pedro, Zip 90732; tel. 310/832–3311; John M. Wilson, President and Chief Executive Officer (Total facility includes 128 beds in nursing home–type unit) (Nonreporting) **A**1 2 7 9 **S** Little Company of Mary Sisters Healthcare System, Evergreen Park, IL	23	10	309	—	—	—	—	—	—	—
□ SAN VICENTE HOSPITAL, 6000 San Vicente Boulevard, Zip 90036; tel. 213/937–2504; R. Wayne Ives, Administrator **A**1 9 10 **F**14 15 16 44 65 71	33	10	17	110	1	—	0	—	—	52
⊠ SANTA MARTA HOSPITAL, 319 North Humphreys Avenue, Zip 90022–1499; tel. 323/266–6500; Harry E. Whitney, President and Chief Executive Officer **A**1 9 10 **F**4 8 11 12 15 16 17 19 22 27 28 30 32 34 35 37 38 40 44 47 49 52 64 65 71 72 73 74 **P**1 5 **S** Carondelet Health System, Saint Louis, MO	21	10	83	3289	45	—	876	30973	11682	299
□ SHERMAN OAKS HOSPITAL AND HEALTH CENTER, 4929 Van Nuys Boulevard, Sherman Oaks, Zip 91403; tel. 818/981–7111; David Levinsonn, Chief Executive Officer **A**1 9 10 **F**8 9 11 12 15 19 21 22 26 27 28 30 31 32 34 37 39 41 42 44 45 46 52 54 57 59 63 64 65 66 67 71 73 **P**3 5 7 8	23	10	153	3111	54	16399	0	37558	16478	357
⊠ SHRINERS HOSPITALS FOR CHILDREN, LOS ANGELES, 3160 Geneva Street, Zip 90020–1199; tel. 213/388–3151; Frank LaBonte, FACHE, Administrator **A**1 3 5 **F**15 17 19 21 22 27 34 35 41 44 47 49 51 56 65 67 68 70 71 73 **P**6 **S** Shriners Hospitals for Children, Tampa, FL	23	57	60	1557	37	14449	0	18741	10151	246
⊠ ST. VINCENT MEDICAL CENTER, 2131 West Third Street, Zip 90057–0992, Mailing Address: P.O. Box 57992, Zip 90057; tel. 213/484–7111; William D. Parente, President (Total facility includes 27 beds in nursing home–type unit) **A**1 3 5 9 10 **F**4 8 10 11 12 15 19 21 24 27 28 29 30 34 35 36 37 41 42 43 44 49 50 60 63 64 65 68 71 72 73 **P**3 5 7 **S** Catholic Healthcare West, San Francisco, CA **Web address:** www.stvincentmedicalcenter.com	21	10	317	9359	159	41255	0	117026	39505	1054
□ TEMPLE COMMUNITY HOSPITAL, 235 North Hoover Street, Zip 90004–3672; tel. 213/382–7252; Herbert G. Needman, Administrator and Chief Executive Officer (Total facility includes 11 beds in nursing home–type unit) **A**1 10 **F**8 11 19 20 21 31 35 37 44 45 60 63 64 71 73 **P**5	33	10	130	3127	60	7092	0	27862	9347	294
⊠ UNIVERSITY OF CALIFORNIA LOS ANGELES MEDICAL CENTER, 10833 Le Conte Avenue, Zip 90095–1730; tel. 310/825–9111; Michael Karpf, M.D., Vice Provost Hospital System and Director Medical Center **A**1 2 3 5 8 9 10 **F**4 5 7 8 10 11 12 13 15 17 19 20 21 22 23 25 26 27 28 29 30 31 32 34 35 36 37 38 39 40 41 42 43 44 45 46 47 48 49 50 51 60 61 65 66 67 68 70 71 72 73 74 **P**5 6 **S** University of California–Systemwide Administration, Oakland, CA **Web address:** www.medctr.ucla.edu	23	10	650	25911	427	636037	1529	532768	225277	6292
⊠ UNIVERSITY OF CALIFORNIA LOS ANGELES NEUROPSYCHIATRIC HOSPITAL, 760 Westwood Plaza, Zip 90095; tel. 310/825–0511; Fawzy I. Fawzy, M.D., Medical Director (Nonreporting) **A**1 3 5 9 10 **S** University of California–Systemwide Administration, Oakland, CA **Web address:** www.npi.ucla.edu	12	22	117	—	—	—	—	—	—	—

Hospital, Address, Telephone, Administrator, Approval, Facility, and Physician Codes, Health Care System, Network	Classi-fication Codes		Utilization Data					Expense (thousands) of dollars		
	Control	Service	Staffed Beds	Admissions	Census	Outpatient Visits	Births	Total	Payroll	Personnel

★ American Hospital Association (AHA) membership
☐ Joint Commission on Accreditation of Healthcare Organizations (JCAHO) accreditation
+ American Osteopathic Healthcare Association (AOHA) membership
○ American Osteopathic Association (AOA) accreditation
△ Commission on Accreditation of Rehabilitation Facilities (CARF) accreditation
Control codes 61, 63, 64, 71, 72 and 73 indicate hospitals listed by AOHA, but not registered by AHA. For definition of numerical codes, see page A4

	Control	Service	Staffed Beds	Admissions	Census	Outpatient Visits	Births	Total	Payroll	Personnel
✪ UNIVERSITY OF SOUTHERN CALIFORNIA–KENNETH NORRIS JR. CANCER HOSPITAL, 1441 Eastlake Avenue, Zip 90033–1085, Mailing Address: P.O. Box 33804, Zip 90033–3804; tel. 323/865–3000; Adrianne Black Bass, Administrator **A**1 2 3 5 9 10 **F**8 12 14 15 16 17 19 21 28 31 32 33 34 35 37 39 41 42 44 45 46 49 50 54 60 65 67 68 71 73 **P**5 6 **S** TENET Healthcare Corporation, Santa Barbara, CA **Web address:** www.uscnorris.com	23	10	60	2016	37	84113	0	54771	13095	354
✪ USC UNIVERSITY HOSPITAL, 1500 San Pablo Street, Zip 90033–4585; tel. 323/442–8500; Edward Schreck, Chief Executive Officer **A**1 3 5 8 9 10 **F**3 4 5 7 8 10 11 12 13 17 18 19 21 22 23 25 26 28 30 31 32 34 35 37 41 42 43 44 46 48 49 50 51 52 53 54 55 57 58 59 60 61 64 65 66 67 68 71 72 73 74 **P**4 5 7 8 **S** TENET Healthcare Corporation, Santa Barbara, CA **Web address:** www.uscuh.com	33	10	285	6264	150	53930	0	126393	51875	1102
✪ VALLEY PRESBYTERIAN HOSPITAL, 15107 Vanowen Street, Van Nuys, Zip 91405; tel. 818/782–6600; Robert C. Bills, President and Vice Chairman (Total facility includes 32 beds in nursing home–type unit) **A**1 2 9 10 **F**4 7 8 10 11 12 13 14 15 16 17 18 19 21 22 24 26 27 28 29 30 32 33 34 35 36 37 38 39 40 41 42 43 44 45 46 47 48 49 60 64 65 66 67 69 71 73 74 **P**5 7 **Web address:** www.valleypres.org	23	10	347	11419	154	68357	2796	85115	34264	904
VALUEMARK PINE GROVE BEHAVIORAL HEALTHCARE SYSTEM See Pine Grove Hospital										
☐ VAN NUYS HOSPITAL, 15220 Vanowen Street, Van Nuys, Zip 91405; tel. 818/787–0123; Brent Lamb, Administrator (Nonreporting) **A**1 9 10	33	22	41	—	—	—	—	—	—	—
☐ VENCOR HOSPITAL–LOS ANGELES, 5525 West Slauson Avenue, Zip 90056; tel. 310/642–0325; Theresa Hamilton, Chief Executive Officer (Nonreporting) **A**1 10 **S** Vencor, Incorporated, Louisville, KY	33	49	81	—	—	—	—	—	—	—
✪ △ VETERANS AFFAIRS MEDICAL CENTER–WEST LOS ANGELES, 11301 Wilshire Boulevard, Zip 90073–0275; tel. 310/268–3132; Smith Jenkins, Jr., Acting Chief Executive Officer (Total facility includes 240 beds in nursing home–type unit) (Nonreporting) **A**1 5 7 8 **S** Department of Veterans Affairs, Washington, DC	45	10	1327	—	—	—	—	—	—	—
✪ WEST HILLS HOSPITAL AND MEDICAL CENTER, (Formerly West Hills Medical Center), 7300 Medical Center Drive, West Hills, Zip 91307–9937, Mailing Address: P.O. Box 7937, Zip 91309–9937; tel. 818/676–4000; James F. Sherman, President and Chief Executive Officer **A**1 9 10 **F**4 8 10 11 12 14 15 16 17 19 21 22 24 25 26 28 30 34 35 37 38 39 42 43 44 45 46 49 51 54 60 61 64 65 66 67 71 73 74 **P**7 **S** Columbia/HCA Healthcare Corporation, Nashville, TN **Web address:** www.whrmc.com	33	10	236	8214	109	—	1453	66148	30953	795
WEST HILLS MEDICAL CENTER See West Hills Hospital and Medical Center										
✪ △ WHITE MEMORIAL MEDICAL CENTER, 1720 Cesar E Chavez Avenue, Zip 90033–2481; tel. 323/268–5000; Fred Manchur, President and Chief Executive Officer **A**1 2 3 5 7 9 10 **F**4 7 8 10 11 12 15 16 17 19 22 26 27 28 29 30 31 32 34 35 37 38 40 41 42 43 44 47 48 49 51 52 56 59 60 63 64 65 67 68 70 71 73 74 **P**3 5 **S** Adventist Health, Roseville, CA	21	10	344	13920	218	110451	0	125648	50779	1669
LOS GATOS—Santa Clara County										
✪ △ COMMUNITY HOSPITAL OF LOS GATOS, 815 Pollard Road, Zip 95030; tel. 408/378–6131; Daniel P. Doore, Chief Executive Officer (Nonreporting) **A**1 7 9 10 **S** TENET Healthcare Corporation, Santa Barbara, CA	33	10	153	—	—	—	—	—	—	—
LOYALTON—Sierra County										
SIERRA VALLEY DISTRICT HOSPITAL, 700 Third Street, Zip 96118, Mailing Address: Box 178, Zip 96118; tel. 530/993–1225; Chase Mearian, Administrator (Total facility includes 34 beds in nursing home–type unit) (Nonreporting) **A**9 10	16	10	40	—	—	—	—	—	—	—
LYNWOOD—Los Angeles County										
✪ ST. FRANCIS MEDICAL CENTER, 3630 East Imperial Highway, Zip 90262; tel. 310/603–6000; Gerald T. Kozai, President (Total facility includes 30 beds in nursing home–type unit) (Nonreporting) **A**1 6 9 10 **S** Catholic Healthcare West, San Francisco, CA	21	10	414	—	—	—	—	—	—	—
MADERA—Madera County										
☐ MADERA COMMUNITY HOSPITAL, 1250 East Almond Avenue, Zip 93637–5606, Mailing Address: Box 1328, Zip 93639–1328; tel. 559/675–5501; Robert C. Kelley, President and Chief Executive Officer **A**1 9 10 **F**7 8 11 12 15 19 21 22 23 25 28 30 32 34 35 37 39 40 41 42 44 46 47 49 65 67 71 72 73 **P**8	23	10	100	4926	53	97983	1482	32069	14895	557
☐ △ VALLEY CHILDREN'S HOSPITAL, 9300 Valley Children's Place, Zip 93638–8763; tel. 559/225–3000; James D. Northway, M.D., President and Chief Executive Officer **A**1 3 5 7 10 **F**10 13 14 15 16 17 19 21 22 25 28 30 32 34 35 38 41 42 43 44 45 46 47 48 49 51 58 60 65 67 71 72 73 **P**1 5	23	50	230	9011	146	140942	0	143881	60082	1795
MAMMOTH LAKES—Mono County										
☐ MAMMOTH HOSPITAL, 85 Sierra Park Road, Zip 93546, Mailing Address: P.O. Box 660, Zip 93546; tel. 760/934–3311; Gary Myers, Administrator **A**1 9 10 **F**7 8 14 15 16 19 20 22 28 30 34 37 40 44 46 61 65 66 71 72 73 74	16	10	15	415	3	25449	0	—	—	—
MANTECA—San Joaquin County										
✪ DOCTORS HOSPITAL OF MANTECA, 1205 East North Street, Zip 95336; tel. 209/823–3111; Patrick W. Rafferty, Administrator (Nonreporting) **A**1 9 10 **S** TENET Healthcare Corporation, Santa Barbara, CA	33	10	73	—	—	—	—	—	—	—
✪ ST. DOMINIC'S HOSPITAL, 1777 West Yosemite Avenue, Zip 95337; tel. 209/825–3500; Richard Aldred, Chief Administrative Officer **A**1 9 10 **F**3 4 6 7 8 10 11 12 13 14 15 16 17 19 21 22 28 29 30 32 33 37 38 40 41 42 43 44 45 46 49 51 54 55 56 57 58 59 60 62 63 65 67 71 72 73 74 **P**7 **S** Catholic Healthcare West, San Francisco, CA	21	10	65	1940	46	23029	389	19500	7552	218

Hospital, Address, Telephone, Administrator, Approval, Facility, and Physician Codes, Health Care System, Network	Classification Codes		Utilization Data					Expense (thousands) of dollars		
	Control	Service	Staffed Beds	Admissions	Census	Outpatient Visits	Births	Total	Payroll	Personnel

★ American Hospital Association (AHA) membership
□ Joint Commission on Accreditation of Healthcare Organizations (JCAHO) accreditation
+ American Osteopathic Healthcare Association (AOHA) membership
○ American Osteopathic Association (AOA) accreditation
△ Commission on Accreditation of Rehabilitation Facilities (CARF) accreditation
Control codes 61, 63, 64, 71, 72 and 73 indicate hospitals listed by AOHA, but not registered by AHA. For definition of numerical codes, see page A4

MARIPOSA—Mariposa County

JOHN C. FREMONT HEALTHCARE DISTRICT, 5189 Hospital Road, Zip 95338, Mailing Address: Box 216, Zip 95338; tel. 209/966–3631 (Total facility includes 10 beds in nursing home–type unit) (Nonreporting) **A**9 10 — 16, 10, 34, —

MARTINEZ—Contra Costa County

□ CONTRA COSTA REGIONAL MEDICAL CENTER, 2500 Alhambra Avenue, Zip 94553; tel. 925/370–5000; Frank J. Puglisi, Jr., Executive Director **A**1 2 3 5 10 **F**1 3 4 7 8 12 13 15 16 17 19 23 26 27 28 29 30 31 32 34 35 36 37 39 40 41 42 43 44 45 46 49 51 52 53 54 55 56 57 58 59 60 61 65 67 69 70 71 72 73 74 **P**6 — 13, 10, 101, 7775, 111, 326909, 1298, 151711, 78255, 1088

KAISER FOUNDATION HOSPITAL See Kaiser Foundation Hospital, Walnut Creek

MARYSVILLE—Yuba County

RIDEOUT MEMORIAL HOSPITAL, 726 Fourth Street, Zip 95901–2128, Mailing Address: 989 Plumas Street, Yuba City, Zip 95991; tel. 530/749–4300; Thomas P. Hayes, Chief Executive Officer (Total facility includes 11 beds in nursing home–type unit) **A**9 10 **F**7 8 10 14 15 16 17 19 22 25 26 28 32 33 34 35 37 38 40 41 42 44 49 53 57 58 60 64 71 72 **P**5 **S** Fremont–Rideout Health Group, Yuba City, CA — 23, 10, 97, 5668, 84, 26420, 0, 51968, 20013, 566

MENLO PARK—San Mateo County

□ RECOVERY INN OF MENLO PARK, 570 Willow Road, Zip 94025; tel. 415/324–8500; Carole Wilson, Administrator (Nonreporting) **A**1 9 10 **S** Vencor, Incorporated, Louisville, KY — 33, 10, 16, —

MERCED—Merced County

⊠ MERCY HOSPITAL AND HEALTH SERVICES, 2740 M Street, Zip 95340–2880; tel. 209/384–6444; John Headding, Chief Administrative Officer **A**1 9 10 **F**8 11 12 14 15 16 17 19 22 23 25 26 29 32 34 35 39 40 41 42 44 46 49 65 67 71 73 **P**3 5 **S** Catholic Healthcare West, San Francisco, CA — 21, 10, 101, 5412, 63, 50179, 1056, 37190, 16716, 527

⊠ SUTTER MERCED MEDICAL CENTER, 301 East 13th Street, Zip 95340–6211; tel. 209/385–7000; Brian S. Bentley, Administrator (Nonreporting) **A**1 3 5 9 10 **S** Sutter Health, Sacramento, CA — 23, 10, 158, —
Web address: www.sutterhealth.org

MISSION HILLS—Los Angeles County, See Los Angeles

MISSION VIEJO—Orange County

□ CHARTER BEHAVIORAL HEALTH SYSTEM OF SOUTHERN CALIFORNIA/MISSION VIEJO, 23228 Madero, Zip 92691; tel. 714/830–4800; Timothy Allen, Chief Executive Officer **A**1 10 **F**1 3 17 26 34 52 53 54 56 57 58 59 67 **S** Magellan Health Services, Atlanta, GA — 33, 22, 80, 1543, 30, 6237, 0, 6301, 3301, —

⊠ △ MISSION HOSPITAL REGIONAL MEDICAL CENTER, 27700 Medical Center Road, Zip 92691; tel. 949/364–1400; Peter F. Bastone, President and Chief Executive Officer **A**1 2 5 7 9 10 **F**4 7 8 10 11 15 16 17 19 21 22 24 25 26 27 28 32 35 37 39 40 41 42 43 44 45 48 49 60 63 64 65 66 70 71 73 **P**3 4 7 **S** St. Joseph Health System, Orange, CA — 23, 10, 252, 15424, 181, —, 3243, 121304, 47638, 1289
Web address: www.mhrmc.com

MODESTO—Stanislaus County

⊠ △ DOCTORS MEDICAL CENTER, 1441 Florida Avenue, Zip 95350–4418, Mailing Address: P.O. Box 4138, Zip 95352–4138; tel. 209/578–1211; Tim A. Joslin, Chief Executive Officer **A**1 2 3 5 7 9 10 **F**1 2 4 7 8 10 11 12 13 14 15 16 17 19 21 22 23 25 27 32 33 34 35 37 38 39 40 41 42 43 44 45 52 53 54 55 57 58 59 61 63 65 67 68 70 71 73 74 **P**5 7 **S** TENET Healthcare Corporation, Santa Barbara, CA — 33, 10, 392, 19031, 241, 79188, 3774, 135252, 66502, 1750

⊠ MEMORIAL HOSPITALS ASSOCIATION, (Includes Memorial Hospital Los Banos, 520 West I Street, Los Banos, Zip 93635; tel. 209/826–0591; Memorial Medical Center, 1700 Coffee Road, Zip 95355), Mailing Address: P.O. Box 942, Zip 95353; tel. 209/526–4500; David P. Benn, President and Chief Executive Officer **A**1 2 9 10 **F**4 7 8 10 12 15 19 21 22 32 35 37 38 39 40 41 42 43 44 60 64 65 70 71 73 **P**3 5 **S** Sutter Health, Sacramento, CA — 23, 10, 273, 15383, 212, 81912, 2107, 150796, 55702, —

MONROVIA—Los Angeles County

□ MONROVIA COMMUNITY HOSPITAL, 323 South Heliotrope Avenue, Zip 91016, Mailing Address: Box 707, Zip 91017–0707; tel. 626/359–8341; John Javier, Administrator (Nonreporting) **A**1 10 — 32, 10, 49, —

MONTCLAIR—San Bernardino County

□ U.S. FAMILYCARE MEDICAL CENTER, 5000 San Bernardino Street, Zip 91763; tel. 909/625–5411; Ronald W. Porter, Chief Executive Officer (Nonreporting) **A**1 9 10 13 — 33, 10, 102, —

MONTEBELLO—Los Angeles County

⊠ BEVERLY HOSPITAL, 309 West Beverly Boulevard, Zip 90640; tel. 323/726–1222; Matthew S. Gerlach, Chief Executive Officer and President **A**1 2 9 10 **F**4 7 8 10 11 12 14 15 16 17 19 21 22 23 27 28 30 32 35 37 38 39 40 41 42 43 44 46 49 67 68 71 73 74 **P**4 5 7 — 23, 10, 170, 10656, 123, 73719, 2435, 71619, 28665, 628
Web address: www.beverly.org

MONTEREY—Monterey County

⊠ COMMUNITY HOSPITAL OF THE MONTEREY PENINSULA, 23625 Holman Highway, Zip 93940, Mailing Address: Box 'HH', Zip 93942–1085; tel. 831/624–5311; Steven J. Packer, M.D., Chief Executive Officer **A**1 2 9 10 **F**1 3 7 8 12 14 15 16 17 19 21 22 23 25 28 30 31 32 33 34 35 37 40 41 42 44 46 49 52 53 54 55 56 57 58 59 60 63 64 65 67 71 73 **P**7 — 23, 10, 197, 11127, 124, 249562, 1872, 156861, 64974, 1272
Web address: www.chomp.org

Hospital, Address, Telephone, Administrator, Approval, Facility, and Physician Codes, Health Care System, Network	Classi-fication Codes		Utilization Data					Expense (thousands) of dollars		
	Control	Service	Staffed Beds	Admissions	Census	Outpatient Visits	Births	Total	Payroll	Personnel

★ American Hospital Association (AHA) membership
□ Joint Commission on Accreditation of Healthcare Organizations (JCAHO) accreditation
+ American Osteopathic Healthcare Association (AOHA) membership
○ American Osteopathic Association (AOA) accreditation
△ Commission on Accreditation of Rehabilitation Facilities (CARF) accreditation
Control codes 61, 63, 64, 71, 72 and 73 indicate hospitals listed by AOHA, but not registered by AHA. For definition of numerical codes, see page A4

MONTEREY PARK—Los Angeles County

✖ △ GARFIELD MEDICAL CENTER, 525 North Garfield Avenue, Zip 91754; tel. 626/573–2222; Philip A. Cohen, Chief Executive Officer (Nonreporting) **A**1 2 7 9 10 **S** TENET Healthcare Corporation, Santa Barbara, CA — 33 10 207 — — — — — — —

✖ MONTEREY PARK HOSPITAL, 900 South Atlantic Boulevard, Zip 91754; tel. 626/570–9000; Philip A. Cohen, Interim Chief Executive Officer (Nonreporting) **A**1 2 9 10 **S** TENET Healthcare Corporation, Santa Barbara, CA — 33 10 95 — — — — — — —

MORENO VALLEY—Riverside County

✖ MORENO VALLEY COMMUNITY HOSPITAL, 27300 Iris Avenue, Zip 92555; tel. 909/243–0811; Janice Ziomek, Administrator **A**1 9 10 **F**2 7 8 12 13 14 16 19 20 21 22 23 27 28 29 30 32 33 34 35 37 39 40 42 44 46 49 54 56 60 61 63 65 67 68 69 71 73 **P**5 7 **S** Valley Health System, Hemet, CA — 16 10 71 5379 48 30486 1374 27006 10120 310

□ RIVERSIDE COUNTY REGIONAL MEDICAL CENTER, 26520 Cactus Avenue, Zip 92555; tel. 909/486–4000; Kenneth B. Cohen, Director and Administrator **A**1 3 5 10 **F**7 8 12 13 14 15 16 17 19 20 22 26 27 28 30 31 32 33 34 35 37 38 39 40 41 42 44 45 46 47 49 51 54 61 65 67 70 71 72 73 74 **P**5 6 — 13 10 282 9422 124 151751 1132 134450 48732 1461

MORGAN HILL—Santa Clara County

✖ SAINT LOUISE HOSPITAL, 18500 Saint Louise Drive, Zip 95037; tel. 408/779–1500; Terrence Curley, Administrator (Total facility includes 19 beds in nursing home–type unit) **A**1 9 10 **F**4 7 8 10 12 13 14 15 16 17 19 21 22 28 30 32 33 34 35 37 40 41 42 43 44 45 46 49 57 60 63 64 65 67 68 71 73 **P**2 5 6 7 **S** Catholic Healthcare West, San Francisco, CA — 21 10 55 2150 27 40896 477 20173 9302 155

MOSS BEACH—San Mateo County

✖ SETON MEDICAL CENTER COASTSIDE, (LONG TERM ACUTE CARE), Marine Boulevard and Etheldore Street, Zip 94038; tel. 650/728–5521; Bernadette Smith, Chief Operating Officer (Total facility includes 112 beds in nursing home–type unit) **A**1 9 10 **F**2 3 4 5 6 7 8 9 10 11 12 13 14 15 16 17 18 19 21 22 23 24 25 26 27 28 29 30 31 32 33 34 35 36 37 38 39 40 41 42 43 44 45 46 47 48 49 51 52 53 54 55 56 57 58 59 60 61 63 64 65 66 67 71 72 73 74 **P**5 7 **S** Catholic Healthcare West, San Francisco, CA — 21 49 121 136 113 3417 0 9128 4823 108

MOUNT SHASTA—Siskiyou County

✖ MERCY MEDICAL CENTER MOUNT SHASTA, 914 Pine Street, Zip 96067, Mailing Address: P.O. Box 239, Zip 96067–0239; tel. 530/926–6111; Rick J. Barnett, Executive Vice President and Chief Operating Officer (Total facility includes 47 beds in nursing home–type unit) **A**1 9 10 **F**7 8 15 17 19 22 24 25 26 28 31 33 35 37 39 40 41 44 56 64 65 66 70 71 73 **P**5 **S** Catholic Healthcare West, San Francisco, CA — 23 10 80 1694 47 39454 175 19924 8470 260
Web address: www.mercy.org

MOUNTAIN VIEW—Santa Clara County

✖ EL CAMINO HOSPITAL, (Formerly Camino Healthcare), 2500 Grant Road, Zip 94040, Mailing Address: P.O. Box 7025, Zip 94039; tel. 650/940–7000; Richard M. Warren, Chief Executive Officer (Total facility includes 22 beds in nursing home–type unit) **A**1 9 10 **F**3 4 7 8 10 12 15 16 17 18 19 22 25 27 28 29 32 33 34 35 37 38 40 41 42 43 44 49 52 54 55 56 57 58 59 60 64 65 67 68 71 73 74 **S** Sutter Health, Sacramento, CA — 16 10 242 16524 170 168132 4089 157387 70427 1394

MURRIETA—Riverside County

□ RANCHO SPRINGS MEDICAL CENTER, (Formerly Sharp Healthcare Murrieta), 25500 Medical Center Drive, Zip 92562–5966; tel. 909/696–6000; Juanice Lovett, Chief Executive Officer (Total facility includes 42 beds in nursing home–type unit) (Nonreporting) **A**1 9 10 **S** TENET Healthcare Corporation, Santa Barbara, CA — 23 10 91 — — — — — — —

NAPA—Napa County

□ NAPA STATE HOSPITAL, 2100 Napa–Vallejo Highway, Zip 94558; tel. 707/253–5454; Frank Turley, Ph.D., Executive Director **A**1 3 10 **F**19 20 22 26 31 35 41 45 52 57 58 59 64 65 71 73 — 12 22 932 428 792 — 0 108108 65318 1680

✖ QUEEN OF THE VALLEY HOSPITAL, 1000 Trancas Street, Zip 94558, Mailing Address: Box 2340, Zip 94558; tel. 707/252–4411; Dennis Sisto, President and Chief Executive Officer **A**1 9 10 **F**4 7 8 10 12 15 16 17 19 21 22 23 26 27 28 29 30 31 32 33 34 35 39 41 42 43 44 46 60 64 65 67 70 71 72 73 74 **P**5 **S** St. Joseph Health System, Orange, CA — 21 10 163 7507 107 158805 783 84461 32021 869

NATIONAL CITY—San Diego County

✖ △ PARADISE VALLEY HOSPITAL, 2400 East Fourth Street, Zip 91950; tel. 619/470–4321; Eric Martinsen, President **A**1 7 9 10 **F**3 7 8 11 12 14 15 16 17 19 21 22 25 28 29 30 32 33 34 35 37 38 39 40 41 42 44 45 46 48 49 51 52 58 59 63 64 65 71 73 **P**5 **S** Adventist Health, Roseville, CA — 21 10 236 9128 140 146163 1557 76348 31855 810

NEEDLES—San Bernardino County

✖ COLORADO RIVER MEDICAL CENTER, 1401 Bailey Avenue, Zip 92363; tel. 760/326–4531; James Arp, Chief Executive Officer **A**1 9 10 **F**7 8 12 14 15 16 19 22 28 32 34 36 37 40 44 48 49 64 65 71 **P**5 **S** Province Healthcare Corporation, Brentwood, TN — 33 10 49 2280 23 8583 233 11545 5739 225

NEWHALL—Los Angeles County

NEWHALL COMMUNITY HOSPITAL, 22607 6th Street, Zip 91322–1328, Mailing Address: Box 221328, Zip 91321–1328; tel. 805/259–4555; Bienvenido Tan, M.D., Chief Executive Officer (Nonreporting) — 12 10 13 — — — — — — —

Hospital, Address, Telephone, Administrator, Approval, Facility, and Physician Codes, Health Care System, Network	Classi-fication Codes		Utilization Data					Expense (thousands) of dollars		
★ American Hospital Association (AHA) membership □ Joint Commission on Accreditation of Healthcare Organizations (JCAHO) accreditation + American Osteopathic Healthcare Association (AOHA) membership ○ American Osteopathic Association (AOA) accreditation △ Commission on Accreditation of Rehabilitation Facilities (CARF) accreditation Control codes 61, 63, 64, 71, 72 and 73 indicate hospitals listed by AOHA, but not registered by AHA. For definition of numerical codes, see page A4	Control	Service	Staffed Beds	Admissions	Census	Outpatient Visits	Births	Total	Payroll	Personnel

NEWPORT BEACH—Orange County

☒ HOAG MEMORIAL HOSPITAL PRESBYTERIAN, One Hoag Drive, Zip 92663–4120, Mailing Address: Box 6100, Zip 92658–6100; tel. 949/645–8600; Michael D. Stephens, President and Chief Executive Officer **A**1 2 5 9 10 **F**2 3 4 7 8 10 11 12 15 16 17 19 22 23 25 27 28 30 31 32 34 35 36 37 38 39 40 41 42 43 44 46 49 60 64 65 67 69 71 72 73 74 **P**5 7
Web address: www.hoag.org

| | | | | | | | | | | |
| 23 | 10 | 356 | 21722 | 256 | 187792 | 4563 | 263568 | 87717 | 2837 |

NORTH HOLLYWOOD—Los Angeles County, See Los Angeles
NORTHRIDGE—Los Angeles County, See Los Angeles
NORWALK—Los Angeles County

□ COAST PLAZA DOCTORS HOSPITAL, 13100 Studebaker Road, Zip 90650; tel. 562/868–3751; Gerald J. Garner, Chairman of the Board (Total facility includes 12 beds in nursing home–type unit) **A**1 10 **F**11 14 15 16 19 21 22 26 30 35 41 44 63 64 65 71

| 32 | 10 | 111 | 3886 | 43 | — | 0 | — | — | — |

LOS ANGELES COMMUNITY HOSPITAL OF NORWALK See Los Angeles Community Hospital, Los Angeles

□ METROPOLITAN STATE HOSPITAL, 11400 Norwalk Boulevard, Zip 90650; tel. 562/863–7011; William G. Silva, Executive Director (Total facility includes 136 beds in nursing home–type unit) **A**1 5 10 **F**19 20 22 24 26 27 30 31 35 41 45 46 52 53 55 57 59 64 65 67 71 73

| 12 | 22 | 1096 | 900 | 851 | — | — | 92085 | — | 1678 |

NOVATO—Marin County

☒ NOVATO COMMUNITY HOSPITAL, 1625 Hill Road, Zip 94947, Mailing Address: P.O. Box 1108, Zip 94948; tel. 415/897–3111; Anne Hosfeld, Chief Administrative Officer (Total facility includes 11 beds in nursing home–type unit) **A**1 9 10 **F**4 7 8 11 12 14 15 16 17 18 19 21 22 23 27 28 29 30 31 32 34 35 37 38 40 41 42 44 45 46 49 52 53 54 55 56 57 58 59 60 64 65 71 73 74 **P**1 **S** Sutter Health, Sacramento, CA

| 23 | 10 | 33 | 1880 | 22 | 32590 | 0 | 23962 | 9252 | 191 |

OAKDALE—Stanislaus County

☒ OAK VALLEY DISTRICT HOSPITAL, 350 South Oak Street, Zip 95361; tel. 209/847–3011; Norman J. Andrews, Chief Executive Officer (Total facility includes 108 beds in nursing home–type unit) (Nonreporting) **A**1 9 10 **S** Catholic Healthcare West, San Francisco, CA

| 16 | 10 | 141 | — | — | — | — | — | — | — |

OAKLAND—Alameda County

□ ALAMEDA COUNTY MEDICAL CENTER–HIGHLAND CAMPUS, 1411 East 31st Street, Zip 94602; tel. 510/437–5081; Michael Smart, Chief Executive Officer (Nonreporting) **A**1 3 5 10 **S** Alameda County Health Care Services Agency, San Leandro, CA

| 13 | 10 | 247 | — | — | — | — | — | — | — |

□ CHILDREN'S HOSPITAL OAKLAND, 747 52nd Street, Zip 94609; tel. 510/428–3000; Antonie H. Paap, President and Chief Executive Officer **A**1 3 5 9 10 **F**4 9 10 12 13 14 15 16 17 19 20 21 22 25 27 28 29 30 31 34 35 38 39 41 42 43 44 45 47 48 49 51 53 54 55 56 58 65 67 68 70 71 72 73 **P**5 8
Web address: www.kidsfirst.org

| 23 | 50 | 205 | 9846 | 152 | 158591 | 0 | 162705 | 78244 | 1428 |

☒ KAISER FOUNDATION HOSPITAL, 280 West MacArthur Boulevard, Zip 94611; tel. 510/987–1000; Bettie L. Coles, R.N., Senior Vice President (Nonreporting) **A**1 3 5 10 **S** Kaiser Foundation Hospitals, Oakland, CA

| 23 | 10 | 264 | — | — | — | — | — | — | — |

□ SUMMIT MEDICAL CENTER, 350 Hawthorne Avenue, Zip 94609; tel. 510/655–4000; Irwin C. Hansen, President and Chief Executive Officer (Total facility includes 48 beds in nursing home–type unit) (Nonreporting) **A**1 2 9 10

| 23 | 10 | 420 | — | — | — | — | — | — | — |

OCEANSIDE—San Diego County

☒ TRI-CITY MEDICAL CENTER, 4002 Vista Way, Zip 92056–4593; tel. 760/724–8411; Arthur A. Gonzalez, Dr.PH, President and Chief Executive Officer **A**1 2 9 10 **F**1 4 5 7 8 10 11 12 14 15 16 17 18 19 20 21 22 26 28 29 30 32 33 34 35 37 38 39 40 41 42 43 44 45 46 50 52 54 55 56 57 58 59 60 63 64 65 71 72 73 74
Web address: www.tri–citymed.com

| 16 | 10 | 397 | 16727 | 197 | 263703 | 3029 | 136652 | 51527 | — |

OJAI—Ventura County

□ OJAI VALLEY COMMUNITY HOSPITAL, 1306 Maricopa Highway, Zip 93023–3180; tel. 805/646–1401; Mark Turner, Chief Executive Officer (Total facility includes 45 beds in nursing home–type unit) (Nonreporting) **A**9 10 **S** Province Healthcare Corporation, Brentwood, TN

| 33 | 10 | 116 | — | — | — | — | — | — | — |

ONTARIO—San Bernardino County

□ VENCOR HOSPITAL–ONTARIO, 550 North Monterey, Zip 91764; tel. 909/391–0333; Virgis Narbutas, Administrator (Nonreporting) **A**1 5 10 **S** Vencor, Incorporated, Louisville, KY

| 33 | 10 | 100 | — | — | — | — | — | — | — |

ORANGE—Orange County

☒ CHAPMAN MEDICAL CENTER, 2601 East Chapman Avenue, Zip 92869; tel. 714/633–0011; Maxine T. Cooper, Chief Executive Officer **A**1 9 10 **F**1 2 3 4 7 8 10 11 12 16 17 18 19 21 22 25 26 27 28 29 30 31 32 34 35 37 38 40 41 42 43 44 45 46 47 48 49 52 57 60 64 65 66 67 68 70 71 72 73 74 **P**5 7 **S** TENET Healthcare Corporation, Santa Barbara, CA

| 33 | 10 | 40 | 2832 | 38 | 18402 | 513 | — | — | 304 |

□ CHILDREN'S HOSPITAL OF ORANGE COUNTY, 455 South Main Street, Zip 92868–3874; tel. 714/997–3000; Kimberly C. Cripe, Chief Executive Officer **A**1 2 3 5 9 10 **F**11 12 13 14 15 16 17 19 21 22 30 31 32 34 35 38 42 43 44 47 49 50 51 53 54 55 63 65 67 68 71 72 73 **P**4 5 7

| 23 | 50 | 192 | 5405 | 75 | 95625 | 0 | 97501 | 33305 | 1020 |

Hospital, Address, Telephone, Administrator, Approval, Facility, and Physician Codes, Health Care System, Network	Classi-fication Codes		Utilization Data					Expense (thousands) of dollars		
	Control	Service	Staffed Beds	Admissions	Census	Outpatient Visits	Births	Total	Payroll	Personnel

★ American Hospital Association (AHA) membership
□ Joint Commission on Accreditation of Healthcare Organizations (JCAHO) accreditation
+ American Osteopathic Healthcare Association (AOHA) membership
○ American Osteopathic Association (AOA) accreditation
△ Commission on Accreditation of Rehabilitation Facilities (CARF) accreditation
Control codes 61, 63, 64, 71, 72 and 73 indicate hospitals listed by AOHA, but not registered by AHA. For definition of numerical codes, see page A4

Hospital	Control	Service	Staffed Beds	Admissions	Census	Outpatient Visits	Births	Total	Payroll	Personnel
✠ ST. JOSEPH HOSPITAL, 1100 West Stewart Drive, Zip 92668, Mailing Address: P.O. Box 5600, Zip 92613–5600; tel. 714/633–9111; Larry K. Ainsworth, President and Chief Executive Officer (Total facility includes 34 beds in nursing home–type unit) **A**1 2 3 5 9 10 **F**2 3 4 7 8 10 11 12 14 15 16 17 18 19 20 21 22 23 24 25 26 27 28 30 32 33 34 36 37 38 39 40 41 42 43 44 45 46 47 49 52 54 56 58 59 60 64 65 66 67 68 71 72 73 74 **P**3 5 8 **S** St. Joseph Health System, Orange, CA	21	10	395	20960	273	185421	5515	232235	73663	2483
✠ UNIVERSITY OF CALIFORNIA, IRVINE MEDICAL CENTER, 101 The City Drive, Zip 92668–3298; tel. 714/456–6011; Mark R. Laret, Director **A**1 2 3 5 8 9 10 **F**4 5 8 9 10 11 12 13 15 16 17 18 19 21 22 25 26 28 29 30 31 34 35 37 38 39 40 41 42 43 44 45 46 47 48 49 51 52 53 54 55 56 57 58 59 60 65 66 67 68 70 71 72 73 74 **P**6 **S** University of California–Systemwide Administration, Oakland, CA **Web address:** www.ucihealth.com	23	10	383	13430	218	416690	1617	203259	88238	2161
OROVILLE—Butte County										
□ OROVILLE HOSPITAL, 2767 Olive Highway, Zip 95966–6185; tel. 530/533–8500; Robert J. Wentz, President and Chief Executive Officer (Total facility includes 20 beds in nursing home–type unit) **A**1 9 10 **F**7 8 12 13 15 16 17 18 19 20 21 22 23 24 25 26 28 29 30 31 32 34 35 37 40 41 42 44 45 46 49 51 61 63 64 65 67 70 71 72 73 74 **P**8 **Web address:** www.orohealth.com	23	10	100	6004	77	232838	571	58578	23512	796
OXNARD—Ventura County										
✠ ST. JOHN'S REGIONAL MEDICAL CENTER, 1600 North Rose Avenue, Zip 93030; tel. 805/988–2500; James R. Hoss, Administrator and Chief Operating Officer **A**1 9 10 **F**4 7 8 10 11 15 16 17 19 21 22 28 29 30 34 35 37 38 40 41 42 43 44 45 46 48 49 52 57 63 71 73 **P**3 5 7 **S** Catholic Healthcare West, San Francisco, CA	23	10	230	12189	172	92936	2183	100670	41154	1057
PALM SPRINGS—Riverside County										
✠ DESERT REGIONAL MEDICAL CENTER, 1150 North Indian Canyon Drive, Zip 92262, Mailing Address: Box 2739, Zip 92263; tel. 760/323–6511; Truman L. Gates, President and Chief Executive Officer (Nonreporting) **A**1 2 9 10 **S** TENET Healthcare Corporation, Santa Barbara, CA	33	10	348	—	—	—	—	—	—	—
PALO ALTO—Santa Clara County										
✠ LUCILE SALTER PACKARD CHILDREN'S HOSPITAL AT STANFORD, 725 Welch Road, Zip 94304; tel. 650/497–8000; Christopher G. Dawes, President (Nonreporting) **A**1 3 5 9 10 **S** UCSF Stanford Health Care, San Francisco, CA	23	50	162	—	—	—	—	—	—	—
✠ △ VETERANS AFFAIRS PALO ALTO HEALTH CARE SYSTEM, (Includes Palo Alto Division, 3801 Miranda Avenue, tel. 415/493–5000; Veterans Affairs Palo Alto Health Care System, Livermore Division, 4951 Arroyo Road, Livermore, Zip 94550; tel. 510/447–2560; Clarence H. Nixon, Director), 3801 Miranda Avenue, Zip 94304–1207; tel. 650/493–5000; James A. Goff, FACHE, Director (Total facility includes 379 beds in nursing home–type unit) **A**1 2 3 5 7 8 **F**1 2 3 4 5 6 8 10 11 12 14 15 16 17 18 19 20 21 22 23 24 25 26 27 28 29 30 31 32 33 34 35 37 39 41 42 43 44 45 46 48 49 50 51 52 54 55 56 57 58 59 60 61 63 64 65 67 68 71 72 73 74 **S** Department of Veterans Affairs, Washington, DC **Web address:** www.icon.palo–alto.med.va.gov	45	10	949	10280	821	404947	0	324616	199206	3508
PANORAMA CITY—Los Angeles County, See Los Angeles										
PARADISE—Butte County										
✠ FEATHER RIVER HOSPITAL, 5974 Pentz Road, Zip 95969–5593; tel. 530/877–9361; Michael Schultz, Chief Executive Officer (Total facility includes 21 beds in nursing home–type unit) (Nonreporting) **A**1 9 10 **S** Adventist Health, Roseville, CA	21	10	122	—	—	—	—	—	—	—
PARAMOUNT—Los Angeles County										
✠ SUBURBAN MEDICAL CENTER, 16453 South Colorado Avenue, Zip 90723; tel. 562/531–3110; Gustavo Valdespino, Chief Executive Officer (Total facility includes 34 beds in nursing home–type unit) **A**1 10 **F**2 3 4 7 8 10 11 12 15 16 17 19 21 22 28 29 30 32 33 35 37 38 39 40 41 42 44 46 48 52 57 58 60 64 65 71 73 74 **P**5 **S** TENET Healthcare Corporation, Santa Barbara, CA **Web address:** www.tenethealth.com/suburban	33	10	132	5215	72	36045	2427	—	15124	477
PASADENA—Los Angeles County										
✠ HUNTINGTON MEMORIAL HOSPITAL, 100 West California Boulevard, Zip 91105, Mailing Address: P.O. Box 7013, Zip 91109–7013; tel. 626/397–5000; Stephen A. Ralph, President and Chief Executive Officer (Total facility includes 75 beds in nursing home–type unit) **A**1 2 3 5 8 9 10 **F**4 7 8 10 11 12 15 16 17 19 21 22 23 26 28 29 30 31 32 34 35 37 38 40 41 42 43 44 47 48 49 51 52 54 55 56 57 58 59 60 61 64 65 70 71 72 73 **P**3 5 **S** Southern California Healthcare Systems, Pasadena, CA	23	10	557	22988	337	214885	3995	198725	85439	2346
IMPACT DRUG AND ALCOHOL TREATMENT CENTER, 1680 North Fair Oaks Avenue, Zip 91103; tel. 818/681–2575; James M. Stillwell, Director (Nonreporting)	23	82	130	—	—	—	—	—	—	—
✠ LAS ENCINAS HOSPITAL, 2900 East Del Mar Boulevard, Zip 91107–4375; tel. 626/795–9901; Roland Metivier, Chief Executive Officer (Nonreporting) **A**1 9 10 **S** Columbia/HCA Healthcare Corporation, Nashville, TN	33	22	138	—	—	—	—	—	—	—
✠ ST. LUKE MEDICAL CENTER, 2632 East Washington Boulevard, Zip 91107–1994; tel. 626/797–1141; Kenneth I. Rivers, Chief Executive Officer (Total facility includes 18 beds in nursing home–type unit) (Nonreporting) **A**1 2 9 10 **S** TENET Healthcare Corporation, Santa Barbara, CA	33	10	120	—	—	—	—	—	—	—

Hospital, Address, Telephone, Administrator, Approval, Facility, and Physician Codes, Health Care System, Network	Classi-fication Codes		Utilization Data					Expense (thousands) of dollars		
★ American Hospital Association (AHA) membership □ Joint Commission on Accreditation of Healthcare Organizations (JCAHO) accreditation + American Osteopathic Healthcare Association (AOHA) membership ○ American Osteopathic Association (AOA) accreditation △ Commission on Accreditation of Rehabilitation Facilities (CARF) accreditation Control codes 61, 63, 64, 71, 72 and 73 indicate hospitals listed by AOHA, but not registered by AHA. For definition of numerical codes, see page A4	Control	Service	Staffed Beds	Admissions	Census	Outpatient Visits	Births	Total	Payroll	Personnel

PATTON—San Bernardino County

□ PATTON STATE HOSPITAL, 3102 East Highland Avenue, Zip 92369; tel. 909/425–7000; William L. Summers, Executive Director **A**1 **F**1 4 5 7 8 10 12 18 19 20 21 22 26 28 29 30 31 35 39 41 42 43 44 45 46 49 50 52 53 54 57 60 61 63 65 69 70 71 72 73 **P**6

12	22	1121	1153	1204	0	0	113671	73945	1823

PETALUMA—Sonoma County

★ PETALUMA VALLEY HOSPITAL, 400 North McDowell Boulevard, Zip 94954–2339; tel. 707/778–1111; Alanna Brogan, Chief Operating Officer (Total facility includes 14 beds in nursing home–type unit) (Nonreporting) **A**1 2 9 10 **S** St. Joseph Health System, Orange, CA

16	10	84	—	—	—	—	—	—	—

PINOLE—Contra Costa County

★ DOCTORS MEDICAL CENTER–PINOLE CAMPUS, 2151 Appian Way, Zip 94564; tel. 510/970–5000; Gary Sloan, Chief Executive Officer (Total facility includes 40 beds in nursing home–type unit) (Nonreporting) **A**1 9 10 **S** TENET Healthcare Corporation, Santa Barbara, CA
Web address: www.tenethealth.com

33	10	137	—	—	—	—	—	—	—

PLACENTIA—Orange County

★ PLACENTIA LINDA HOSPITAL, 1301 Rose Drive, Zip 92870; tel. 714/993–2000; Maxine T. Cooper, Chief Executive Officer **A**1 9 10 **F**7 8 11 12 14 15 16 17 18 19 21 22 27 28 29 30 31 32 34 35 36 37 39 40 41 42 44 46 49 54 56 61 63 65 66 67 71 73 **P**5 7 8 **S** TENET Healthcare Corporation, Santa Barbara, CA
Web address: www.tenethealth.com/placentialinda

33	10	114	2770	24	21785	641	20315	8040	296

PLACERVILLE—El Dorado County

★ MARSHALL HOSPITAL, 1100 Marshall Way, Zip 95667; tel. 530/622–1441; Frank Nachtman, Administrator (Nonreporting) **A**1 9 10

23	10	107	—	—	—	—	—	—	—

PLEASANTON—Alameda County

VALLEYCARE MEDICAL CENTER, 5555 West Positas Boulevard, Zip 94588, Mailing Address: 555 West Los Positas Boulevard, Zip 94588; tel. 925/847–3000; Marcy Feit, Chief Executive Officer (Nonreporting) **A**9 **S** ValleyCare Health System, Pleasanton, CA

23	10	68	—	—	—	—	—	—	—

POMONA—Los Angeles County

★ △ CASA COLINA HOSPITAL FOR REHABILITATIVE MEDICINE, 255 East Bonita Avenue, Zip 91767–9966, Mailing Address: P.O. Box 6001, Zip 91769–6001; tel. 909/593–7521; Dale E. Eazell, Ph.D., President and Chief Executive Officer (Total facility includes 13 beds in nursing home–type unit) **A**1 7 9 10 **F**1 12 14 15 16 17 24 25 26 34 41 45 48 49 64 65 67 73

23	46	20	532	29	12331	0	8160	3611	195

LANTERMAN DEVELOPMENTAL CENTER, 3530 Pomona Boulevard, Zip 91768, Mailing Address: P.O. Box 100, Zip 91769; tel. 909/595–1221; Ruth Maples, Executive Director (Nonreporting) **A**10

12	62	771	—	—	—	—	—	—	—

★ POMONA VALLEY HOSPITAL MEDICAL CENTER, 1798 North Garey Avenue, Zip 91767–2918; tel. 909/865–9500; Richard E. Yochum, President (Total facility includes 38 beds in nursing home–type unit) **A**1 2 3 9 10 **F**4 7 8 10 11 12 13 14 15 16 17 19 20 21 22 23 24 25 28 29 30 31 34 35 36 37 38 39 40 41 42 43 44 45 46 47 49 51 60 63 64 65 66 67 71 72 73 74 **P**5
Web address: www.pvhmc.org

23	10	381	20238	245	—	4742	194355	87280	1891

PORT HUENEME—Ventura County

□ ANACAPA HOSPITAL, 307 East Clara Street, Zip 93041; tel. 805/488–3661; John J. Megara, Chief Executive Officer **A**1 9 10 **F**1 3 12 17 18 19 21 26 27 35 45 46 52 53 54 55 56 57 58 59 65 67 68 71 **P**7 8

33	22	44	804	33	—	0	6322	2533	106

PORTERVILLE—Tulare County

PORTERVILLE DEVELOPMENTAL CENTER, 26501 Avenue 140, Zip 93257–9430, Mailing Address: Box 2000, Zip 93258–2000; tel. 559/782–2222; Harold Pitchford, Executive Director **A**10 **F**4 7 12 16 17 18 19 20 21 24 26 28 29 30 31 32 35 41 44 46 50 53 54 57 60 64 65 67 73 **P**6

12	62	817	64	826	—	0	84134	50861	1491

SIERRA VIEW DISTRICT HOSPITAL, 465 West Putnam Avenue, Zip 93257–3320; tel. 559/784–1110; Kelly C. Morgan, President and Chief Executive Officer **A**9 10 **F**7 8 14 15 16 19 21 24 28 29 30 32 35 37 39 40 42 44 45 46 60 65 67 70 71 72 73 74 **P**7

16	10	119	5778	59	40059	1168	43849	15079	518

PORTOLA—Plumas County

EASTERN PLUMAS DISTRICT HOSPITAL, 500 First Avenue, Zip 96122; tel. 530/832–4277; Charles Guenther, Administrator (Total facility includes 14 beds in nursing home–type unit) **A**9 10 **F**7 8 13 14 15 16 17 19 20 22 32 33 40 41 44 45 46 64 71 72 73 74 **P**6

16	10	24	506	20	24697	0	7247	3104	—

POWAY—San Diego County

★ POMERADO HOSPITAL, 15615 Pomerado Road, Zip 92064; tel. 619/485–6511; Marvin W. Levenson, M.D., Administrator and Chief Operating Officer (Total facility includes 129 beds in nursing home–type unit) **A**1 2 9 10 **F**3 4 7 8 10 11 12 14 15 16 17 19 22 23 27 29 30 31 32 33 34 35 36 37 38 39 40 41 42 43 44 45 46 49 52 54 55 56 57 58 59 60 61 64 65 67 68 69 70 71 72 73 74 **P**7 **S** Palomar Pomerado Health System, San Diego, CA
Web address: www.pphs.org

16	10	238	6244	172	95810	1282	54183	20915	504

QUINCY—Plumas County

□ PLUMAS DISTRICT HOSPITAL, 1065 Bucks Lake Road, Zip 95971–9599; tel. 530/283–2121; R. Michael Barry, Administrator (Nonreporting) **A**1 9 10
Web address: www.pdh.org

16	10	32	—	—	—	—	—	—	—

RANCHO MIRAGE—Riverside County

★ EISENHOWER MEMORIAL HOSPITAL AND BETTY FORD CENTER AT EISENHOWER, 39000 Bob Hope Drive, Zip 92270; tel. 760/340–3911; Andrew W. Deems, President and Chief Executive Officer **A**1 2 5 9 10 **F**1 4 5 7 8 10 11 12 15 16 19 21 22 23 24 25 29 30 32 33 34 35 37 38 39 40 41 42 43 44 45 46 49 59 65 66 67 71 72 73 74 **P**5

23	10	261	14185	157	273817	1574	146074	53015	1239

Hospital, Address, Telephone, Administrator, Approval, Facility, and Physician Codes, Health Care System, Network	Classi-fication Codes		Utilization Data					Expense (thousands) of dollars		

★ American Hospital Association (AHA) membership
□ Joint Commission on Accreditation of Healthcare Organizations (JCAHO) accreditation
+ American Osteopathic Healthcare Association (AOHA) membership
○ American Osteopathic Association (AOA) accreditation
△ Commission on Accreditation of Rehabilitation Facilities (CARF) accreditation
Control codes 61, 63, 64, 71, 72 and 73 indicate hospitals listed by AOHA, but not registered by AHA. For definition of numerical codes, see page A4

	Control	Service	Staffed Beds	Admissions	Census	Outpatient Visits	Births	Total	Payroll	Personnel
RED BLUFF—Tehama County										
✠ ST. ELIZABETH COMMUNITY HOSPITAL, 2550 Sister Mary Columba Drive, Zip 96080–4397; tel. 530/529–8000; Thomas F. Grimes, III, Executive Vice President and Chief Operating Officer **A**1 9 10 **F**7 11 12 14 15 16 17 19 22 28 32 33 34 35 40 44 49 65 71 73 **P**3 **S** Catholic Healthcare West, San Francisco, CA **Web address:** www.mercy.org	21	10	53	3416	30	42421	579	29781	12509	375
REDDING—Shasta County										
✠ MERCY MEDICAL CENTER REDDING, (Formerly Mercy Medical Center), 2175 Rosaline Avenue, Zip 96001, Mailing Address: P.O. Box 496009, Zip 96049–6009; tel. 530/225–6000; John Di Perry, Jr., Executive Vice President and Chief Operating Officer (Total facility includes 17 beds in nursing home–type unit) **A**1 2 3 5 9 10 **F**1 4 7 8 10 11 12 15 16 19 21 22 23 24 25 27 29 30 31 32 33 34 35 36 37 38 39 40 41 42 43 44 49 51 60 63 64 65 67 68 70 71 72 73 74 **P**3 **S** Catholic Healthcare West, San Francisco, CA **Web address:** www.mercy.org	21	10	202	9965	117	183125	1471	114885	42352	1223
✠ REDDING MEDICAL CENTER, 1100 Butte Street, Zip 96001–0853, Mailing Address: Box 496072, Zip 96049–6072; tel. 530/244–5454; Steve Schmidt, Chief Executive Officer (Nonreporting) **A**1 9 10 **S** TENET Healthcare Corporation, Santa Barbara, CA	33	10	162	—	—	—	—	—	—	—
REDLANDS—San Bernardino County										
□ LOMA LINDA UNIVERSITY BEHAVIORAL MEDICINE CENTER, 1710 Barton Road, Zip 92373; tel. 909/793–9333; Alan Soderblom, Administrator (Nonreporting) **A**1 5 9 10 **S** Loma Linda University Health Sciences Center, Loma Linda, CA	21	22	89	—	—	—	—	—	—	—
□ REDLANDS COMMUNITY HOSPITAL, 350 Terracina Boulevard, Zip 92373, Mailing Address: Box 3391, Zip 92373–0742; tel. 909/335–5500; James R. Holmes, President (Nonreporting) **A**1 9 10 **Web address:** www.redlandshospital.com	23	10	194	—	—	—	—	—	—	—
REDWOOD CITY—San Mateo County										
✠ KAISER FOUNDATION HOSPITAL, 1150 Veterans Boulevard, Zip 94063–2087; tel. 650/299–2000; Helen Wilmot, Administrator (Nonreporting) **A**1 3 5 10 **S** Kaiser Foundation Hospitals, Oakland, CA	23	10	144	—	—	—	—	—	—	—
✠ SEQUOIA HOSPITAL, 170 Alameda De Las Pulgas, Zip 94062; tel. 650/369–5811; Glenna L. Vaskelis, Administrator (Total facility includes 44 beds in nursing home–type unit) **A**1 9 10 **F**4 7 8 10 12 14 15 16 17 19 21 22 23 27 28 29 30 31 32 33 34 35 36 37 40 41 42 43 44 45 46 48 49 52 53 56 58 59 60 63 64 65 66 67 71 72 73 74 **P**3 5 **S** Catholic Healthcare West, San Francisco, CA **Web address:** www.chwbay.org	23	10	231	10518	145	99862	1318	116843	57829	797
REEDLEY—Fresno County										
✠ SIERRA–KINGS DISTRICT HOSPITAL, 372 West Cypress Avenue, Zip 93654; tel. 559/638–8155; Daniel DeSantis, Administrator (Total facility includes 9 beds in nursing home–type unit) **A**1 9 10 **F**7 8 12 14 15 16 17 19 22 24 28 30 34 39 40 44 45 49 64 65 71 73 74	16	10	36	2345	12	30896	810	10356	4532	187
RIDGECREST—Kern County										
✠ RIDGECREST REGIONAL HOSPITAL, 1081 North China Lake Boulevard, Zip 93555; tel. 760/446–3551; David A. Mechtenberg, Chief Executive Officer **A**1 9 10 **F**7 11 15 16 19 22 28 32 33 35 36 37 40 41 44 45 46 49 65 71 73 **Web address:** www.rrh.org	23	10	80	2564	24	48473	454	22744	9631	290
RIVERSIDE—Riverside County										
✠ KAISER FOUNDATION HOSPITAL–RIVERSIDE, 10800 Magnolia Avenue, Zip 92505–3000; tel. 909/353–4600; Robert S. Lund, Administrator **A**1 2 3 10 **F**3 4 7 8 10 12 14 15 16 21 22 31 32 33 35 37 38 40 41 42 43 44 45 46 53 54 55 56 58 63 65 69 71 72 73 74 **S** Kaiser Foundation Hospitals, Oakland, CA	23	10	166	10991	99	—	2891	—	—	1983
□ PARKVIEW COMMUNITY HOSPITAL MEDICAL CENTER, 3865 Jackson Street, Zip 92503; tel. 909/688–2211; Norm Martin, President and Chief Executive Officer **A**1 2 9 10 **F**7 8 10 11 12 14 15 16 17 19 21 22 26 28 30 32 33 35 36 37 38 40 41 42 44 46 49 60 65 67 68 71 72 73	23	10	193	10740	107	163744	3227	73255	27992	800
□ RIVERSIDE COMMUNITY HOSPITAL, 4445 Magnolia Avenue, Zip 92501–1669, Mailing Address: Box 1669, Zip 92502–1669; tel. 909/788–3000; Jeffrey P. Winter, Chief Executive Officer **A**1 9 10 **F**4 7 8 10 11 12 13 14 19 21 22 23 25 31 32 33 35 38 39 40 41 42 43 44 48 49 60 63 64 65 68 70 71 72 73 74 **P**5 7 **Web address:** www.pchmc.org	33	10	329	13259	170	63330	1960	95416	34698	839
ROSEMEAD—Los Angeles County										
□ BHC ALHAMBRA HOSPITAL, 4619 North Rosemead Boulevard, Zip 91770–1498, Mailing Address: P.O. Box 369, Zip 91770; tel. 626/286–1191; Peggy Minnick, Administrator (Nonreporting) **A**1 9 10 **S** Behavioral Healthcare Corporation, Nashville, TN	33	22	98	—	—	—	—	—	—	—
ROSEVILLE—Placer County										
✠ SUTTER ROSEVILLE MEDICAL CENTER, One Medical Plaza, Zip 95661–3477; tel. 916/781–1000; Patrick R. Brady, Chief Executive Officer (Total facility includes 14 beds in nursing home–type unit) (Nonreporting) **A**1 2 9 10 **S** Sutter Health, Sacramento, CA	23	10	183	—	—	—	—	—	—	—
SACRAMENTO—Sacramento County										
✠ BHC HERITAGE OAKS HOSPITAL, 4250 Auburn Boulevard, Zip 95841; tel. 916/489–3336; Ingrid L. Whipple, Chief Executive Officer (Nonreporting) **A**1 9 10 **S** Behavioral Healthcare Corporation, Nashville, TN	33	22	76	—	—	—	—	—	—	—

Hospital, Address, Telephone, Administrator, Approval, Facility, and Physician Codes, Health Care System, Network	Classification Codes		Utilization Data					Expense (thousands) of dollars		
	Control	Service	Staffed Beds	Admissions	Census	Outpatient Visits	Births	Total	Payroll	Personnel

Key (legend):

★ American Hospital Association (AHA) membership
□ Joint Commission on Accreditation of Healthcare Organizations (JCAHO) accreditation
+ American Osteopathic Healthcare Association (AOHA) membership
○ American Osteopathic Association (AOA) accreditation
△ Commission on Accreditation of Rehabilitation Facilities (CARF) accreditation
Control codes 61, 63, 64, 71, 72 and 73 indicate hospitals listed by AOHA, but not registered by AHA. For definition of numerical codes, see page A4

Hospital	Control	Service	Staffed Beds	Admissions	Census	Outpatient Visits	Births	Total	Payroll	Personnel
□ BHC SIERRA VISTA HOSPITAL, 8001 Bruceville Road, Zip 95823; tel. 916/423–2000; Ingrid L. Whipple, Chief Executive Officer **A**1 9 10 **F**2 15 52 53 54 55 56 57 58 59 60 **S** Behavioral Healthcare Corporation, Nashville, TN	33	22	72	1364	43	5007	0	6015	2765	87
✦ KAISER FOUNDATION HOSPITAL, 2025 Morse Avenue, Zip 95825–2115; tel. 916/973–5000; Sarah Krevans, Administrator (Nonreporting) **A**1 3 5 10 **S** Kaiser Foundation Hospitals, Oakland, CA	23	10	304	—	—	—	—	—	—	—
✦ KAISER FOUNDATION HOSPITAL, 6600 Bruceville Road, Zip 95823; tel. 916/688–2430; Sarah Krevans, Senior Vice President (Nonreporting) **A**1 3 10 **S** Kaiser Foundation Hospitals, Oakland, CA	23	10	221	—	—	—	—	—	—	—
✦ MERCY GENERAL HOSPITAL, 4001 J Street, Zip 95819; tel. 916/453–4950; Thomas A. Petersen, Vice President and Chief Operating Officer (Total facility includes 95 beds in nursing home–type unit) **A**1 2 9 10 **F**4 7 8 10 11 12 15 17 18 19 21 22 23 25 26 28 29 30 31 32 33 34 35 37 39 40 41 42 43 46 48 49 50 53 54 55 56 57 58 59 60 61 64 65 66 67 71 72 73 74 **P**3 5 **S** Catholic Healthcare West, San Francisco, CA	21	10	402	17644	241	113355	1956	157064	62186	1360
✦ METHODIST HOSPITAL OF SACRAMENTO, (Formerly Methodist Hospital), 7500 Hospital Drive, Zip 95823; tel. 916/423–3000; Stanley C. Oppegard, Vice President and Chief Operating Officer (Total facility includes 158 beds in nursing home–type unit) **A**1 3 9 10 **F**4 7 8 10 11 14 15 16 17 19 20 21 22 23 24 25 26 27 28 29 30 31 34 35 37 38 39 40 41 42 43 44 45 46 49 50 51 53 54 55 56 57 58 59 60 63 64 65 66 67 68 71 72 73 74 **P**3 5 **S** Catholic Healthcare West, San Francisco, CA	23	10	258	7867	145	28332	1748	56456	29290	592
✦ SHRINERS HOSPITALS FOR CHILDREN, NORTHERN CALIFORNIA, 2425 Stockton Boulevard, Zip 95817–2215; tel. 916/453–2000; Margaret Bryan, Administrator (Nonreporting) **A**1 5 **S** Shriners Hospitals for Children, Tampa, FL Web address: www.shrinershq.org	23	57	48	—	—	—	—	—	—	—
★ SUTTER CENTER FOR PSYCHIATRY, 7700 Folsom Boulevard, Zip 95826–2608; tel. 916/386–3000; Diane Gail Stewart, Administrator **A**9 10 **F**3 4 7 8 10 11 13 14 15 16 17 19 21 22 26 27 28 29 30 31 32 33 34 35 37 38 39 40 41 42 43 44 45 46 47 48 49 50 51 52 54 55 56 57 58 59 60 61 62 63 65 66 67 68 71 72 73 74 **P**3 5 **S** Sutter Health, Sacramento, CA Web address: www.sutterhealth.org	23	22	69	2125	43	7781	0	9596	5380	187
SUTTER GENERAL HOSPITAL See Sutter Medical Center										
✦ SUTTER MEDICAL CENTER, (Formerly Sutter Community Hospitals), (Includes Sutter General Hospital, 2801 L Street, Zip 95816; tel. 916/454–2222; Sutter Memorial Hospital, 5151 F Street), 5151 F Street, Zip 95819–3295; tel. 916/454–3333; Lou Lazatin, Chief Executive Officer (Total facility includes 198 beds in nursing home–type unit) **A**1 2 3 5 9 10 **F**1 2 3 4 5 6 7 8 10 11 12 14 15 16 17 18 19 20 21 22 23 25 26 27 28 29 30 31 32 33 34 35 36 37 38 39 40 41 42 43 44 45 46 47 49 50 52 53 54 55 56 57 58 59 60 61 63 64 65 67 68 70 71 72 73 74 **P**3 5 **S** Sutter Health, Sacramento, CA Web address: www.sutterhealth.org	23	10	497	28919	483	249675	4656	311887	130900	3048
✦ UNIVERSITY OF CALIFORNIA, DAVIS MEDICAL CENTER, 2315 Stockton Boulevard, Zip 95817–2282; tel. 916/734–2011; Robert E. Chason, Interim Director (Nonreporting) **A**1 2 3 5 8 9 10 **S** University of California–Systemwide Administration, Oakland, CA	12	10	448	—	—	—	—	—	—	—

SALINAS—Monterey County

Hospital	Control	Service	Staffed Beds	Admissions	Census	Outpatient Visits	Births	Total	Payroll	Personnel
✦ NATIVIDAD MEDICAL CENTER, 1441 Constitution Boulevard, Zip 93906, Mailing Address: P.O. Box 81611, Zip 93912–1611; tel. 831/755–4111; Howard H. Classen, Chief Executive Officer (Total facility includes 52 beds in nursing home–type unit) (Nonreporting) **A**1 3 5 9 10 Web address: www.natividad.com	13	10	181	6720	109	119064	1481	67573	27714	596
✦ SALINAS VALLEY MEMORIAL HEALTHCARE SYSTEM, (Formerly Salinas Valley Memorial Hospital), 450 East Romie Lane, Zip 93901–4098; tel. 831/757–4333; Samuel W. Downing, Chief Executive Officer (Total facility includes 21 beds in nursing home–type unit) **A**1 2 9 10 **F**1 4 6 7 8 10 11 12 13 14 15 16 17 19 20 21 22 24 25 26 28 29 30 32 33 34 35 36 37 39 40 41 42 43 44 45 46 48 49 60 62 63 64 65 67 69 71 72 73 74 **P**5 Web address: www.svmh.com	16	10	193	13490	146	110124	2618	173879	72816	1217

SAN ANDREAS—Calaveras County

Hospital	Control	Service	Staffed Beds	Admissions	Census	Outpatient Visits	Births	Total	Payroll	Personnel
✦ MARK TWAIN ST. JOSEPH'S HOSPITAL, 768 Mountain Ranch Road, Zip 95249–9710; tel. 209/754–2515; Michael P. Lawson, Administrator **A**1 9 10 **F**7 8 14 15 16 17 19 21 22 28 29 30 31 34 37 40 41 42 44 46 49 65 67 71 72 73 74 **P**5 7 **S** Catholic Healthcare West, San Francisco, CA	23	10	30	1514	16	56299	65	17456	7136	207

SAN BERNARDINO—San Bernardino County

Hospital	Control	Service	Staffed Beds	Admissions	Census	Outpatient Visits	Births	Total	Payroll	Personnel
✦ COMMMUNITY HOSPITAL OF SAN BERNARDINO, 1805 Medical Center Drive, Zip 92411; tel. 909/887–6333; Bruce G. Satzger, Administrator (Total facility includes 99 beds in nursing home–type unit) (Nonreporting) **A**1 10 **S** Catholic Healthcare West, San Francisco, CA Web address: www.chsb.org	23	10	380	—	—	—	—	—	—	—
SAN BERNARDINO COUNTY MEDICAL CENTER See Arrowhead Regional Medical Center										
✦ ST. BERNARDINE MEDICAL CENTER, 2101 North Waterman Avenue, Zip 92404; tel. 909/883–8711; Bruce G. Satzger, Administrator (Total facility includes 44 beds in nursing home–type unit) **A**1 2 9 10 **F**4 7 8 10 12 14 15 16 19 21 22 23 24 28 30 32 33 34 35 37 38 40 41 42 43 44 46 49 54 58 59 60 64 65 68 71 72 73 **P**5 7 **S** Catholic Healthcare West, San Francisco, CA	23	10	268	14692	170	66891	1742	104001	42917	997

SAN CLEMENTE—Orange County

Hospital	Control	Service	Staffed Beds	Admissions	Census	Outpatient Visits	Births	Total	Payroll	Personnel
✦ SAN CLEMENTE HOSPITAL AND MEDICAL CENTER, 654 Camino De Los Mares, Zip 92673; tel. 949/496–1122; Patricia L. Wolfram, R.N., Chief Executive Officer **A**1 9 10 **F**7 8 12 14 15 16 17 19 21 22 23 28 29 30 33 34 35 36 37 39 40 41 44 45 46 49 63 64 65 67 71 73 **P**5 **S** NetCare Health Systems, Inc., Nashville, TN	33	10	71	2640	29	18329	386	20273	9661	248

Hospital, Address, Telephone, Administrator, Approval, Facility, and Physician Codes, Health Care System, Network	Classi-fication Codes		Utilization Data					Expense (thousands) of dollars		
★ American Hospital Association (AHA) membership □ Joint Commission on Accreditation of Healthcare Organizations (JCAHO) accreditation + American Osteopathic Healthcare Association (AOHA) membership ○ American Osteopathic Association (AOA) accreditation △ Commission on Accreditation of Rehabilitation Facilities (CARF) accreditation Control codes 61, 63, 64, 71, 72 and 73 indicate hospitals listed by AOHA, but not registered by AHA. For definition of numerical codes, see page A4	Control	Service	Staffed Beds	Admissions	Census	Outpatient Visits	Births	Total	Payroll	Personnel

SAN DIEGO—San Diego County

Hospital	Control	Service	Staffed Beds	Admissions	Census	Outpatient Visits	Births	Total	Payroll	Personnel
⊞ ALVARADO HOSPITAL MEDICAL CENTER, 6655 Alvarado Road, Zip 92120–5298; tel. 619/287–3270; Barry G. Weinbaum, Chief Executive Officer **A**1 2 3 10 **F**4 7 8 10 11 12 15 16 17 19 22 23 26 27 30 32 34 35 37 38 39 40 42 43 44 45 46 48 49 61 63 64 65 67 71 73 **S** TENET Healthcare Corporation, Santa Barbara, CA	33	10	199	8968	112	34564	912	—	—	960
□ CHARTER BEHAVIORAL HEALTH SYSTEM OF SAN DIEGO, 11878 Avenue of Industry, Zip 92128; tel. 619/487–3200; Robert A. Deney, Chief Executive Officer (Nonreporting) **A**1 10 **S** Magellan Health Services, Atlanta, GA	33	22	80	—	—	—	—	—	—	—
□ △ CHILDREN'S HOSPITAL AND HEALTH CENTER, (PEDIATRIC), 3020 Children's Way, Zip 92123–4282; tel. 619/576–1700; Blair L. Sadler, President (Total facility includes 59 beds in nursing home–type unit) **A**1 3 5 7 9 10 **F**5 10 13 15 16 17 19 20 21 22 28 31 32 33 34 35 38 41 42 43 44 46 47 49 53 54 58 64 65 68 70 71 72 73 **P**5 **Web address:** www.chsd.org	23	59	271	10962	182	221377	0	177384	67236	1630
⊞ KAISER FOUNDATION HOSPITAL, (Includes Kaiser Foundation Hospital, 203 Travelodge Drive, El Cajon, Zip 92020; tel. 619/528–5000), 4647 Zion Avenue, Zip 92120; tel. 619/528–5000; Kenneth F. Colling, Senior Vice President and Area Manager **A**1 2 3 5 10 **F**2 3 4 7 8 10 12 13 14 15 16 17 18 19 21 22 23 25 26 28 29 30 31 32 33 35 37 38 39 40 41 42 43 44 45 46 51 52 53 56 58 59 60 61 63 64 65 67 69 71 72 73 74 **S** Kaiser Foundation Hospitals, Oakland, CA	23	10	343	24775	240	15199	6020	—	—	—
⊞ MISSION BAY HOSPITAL, (Formerly Mission Bay Memorial Hospital), 3030 Bunker Hill Street, Zip 92109–5780; tel. 619/274–7721; Deborah Brehe, Chief Executive Officer (Total facility includes 26 beds in nursing home–type unit) **A**1 9 10 **F**8 11 12 14 16 17 19 22 26 27 28 30 34 35 37 41 44 46 49 52 57 64 65 71 73 **S** Triad Hospitals, Inc., Dallas, TX **Web address:** www.mbhosp.com	33	10	91	2334	30	16256	0	20048	9610	216
⊞ NAVAL MEDICAL CENTER, 34800 Bob Wilson Drive, Zip 92134–5000; tel. 619/532–6400; Rear Admiral Alberto Diaz, Jr., MC, USN, Commander **A**1 2 3 5 **F**3 4 5 7 8 10 11 12 13 16 18 19 20 21 22 23 24 25 28 29 30 31 34 35 37 38 39 40 41 42 43 44 45 46 47 49 51 52 53 54 56 58 60 61 63 65 66 67 68 71 73 **S** Department of Navy, Washington, DC	43	10	288	18311	171	1055365	3674	—	—	5054
□ SAN DIEGO COUNTY PSYCHIATRIC HOSPITAL, 3851 Rosecrans Street, Zip 92110, Mailing Address: P.O. Box 85524, Zip 92138–5524; tel. 619/692–8211; Karen C. Hogan, Administrator and Chief Executive Officer (Nonreporting) **A**1 10	13	22	109	—	—	—	—	—	—	—
★ SAN DIEGO HOSPICE, 4311 Third Avenue, Zip 92103; tel. 619/688–1600; Janet E. Cetti, President and Chief Executive Officer (Nonreporting) **A**10	23	49	24	—	—	—	—	—	—	—
⊞ SCRIPPS MERCY HOSPITAL, 4077 Fifth Avenue, Zip 92103–2180; tel. 619/294–8111; Thomas A. Gammiere, Senior Vice President and Regional Administrator (Nonreporting) **A**1 2 3 5 9 10 **S** Scripps Health, San Diego, CA	30	10	417	—	—	—	—	—	—	—
★ SHARP CABRILLO HOSPITAL, 3475 Kenyon Street, Zip 92110–5067; tel. 619/221–3400; Randi Larsson, Chief Operating Officer and Administrator (Total facility includes 79 beds in nursing home–type unit) (Nonreporting) **A**9 **S** Sharp Healthcare, San Diego, CA	23	10	227	—	—	—	—	—	—	—
⊞ △ SHARP MEMORIAL HOSPITAL, 7901 Frost Street, Zip 92123–2788; tel. 619/541–3400; Dan Gross, Chief Executive Officer (Nonreporting) **A**1 2 3 7 9 10 **S** Sharp Healthcare, San Diego, CA	23	10	488	—	—	—	—	—	—	—
⊞ UNIVERSITY OF CALIFORNIA SAN DIEGO MEDICAL CENTER, 200 West Arbor Drive, Zip 92103–8970; tel. 619/543–6222; Sumiyo E. Kastelic, Director **A**1 2 3 5 8 9 10 **F**4 7 8 9 10 11 12 15 19 21 22 23 25 26 28 29 30 31 32 34 35 37 38 39 40 41 42 43 44 45 46 47 49 51 52 53 54 56 57 58 60 61 65 68 70 71 72 73 74 **P**1 **S** University of California–Systemwide Administration, Oakland, CA	12	10	439	18364	270	482073	1734	266389	103271	3180
□ VENCOR HOSPITAL–SAN DIEGO, 1940 El Cajon Boulevard, Zip 92104; tel. 619/543–4500; Michael D. Cress, Administrator (Nonreporting) **A**1 10 **S** Vencor, Incorporated, Louisville, KY	33	10	70	—	—	—	—	—	—	—
⊞ VETERANS AFFAIRS MEDICAL CENTER, 3350 LaJolla Village Drive, Zip 92161; tel. 619/552–8585; Gary J. Rossio, Director and Chief Executive Officer (Total facility includes 69 beds in nursing home–type unit) **A**1 2 3 5 8 **F**1 2 3 4 5 6 8 10 11 12 14 15 16 17 18 19 20 21 22 23 24 25 26 27 28 29 30 31 32 33 34 35 37 39 41 42 43 44 45 46 48 49 50 51 52 54 55 56 57 58 59 60 64 65 67 68 71 72 73 74 **P**6 **S** Department of Veterans Affairs, Washington, DC	45	10	232	5807	143	311696	0	170153	94671	1836
□ VILLAVIEW COMMUNITY HOSPITAL, 5550 University Avenue, Zip 92105, Mailing Address: P.O. Box 5587, Zip 92105; tel. 619/582–3516; Reggie Panis, President (Nonreporting) **A**1 10	23	10	100	—	—	—	—	—	—	—

SAN DIMAS—Los Angeles County

Hospital	Control	Service	Staffed Beds	Admissions	Census	Outpatient Visits	Births	Total	Payroll	Personnel
⊞ SAN DIMAS COMMUNITY HOSPITAL, 1350 West Covina Boulevard, Zip 91773–0308; tel. 909/599–6811; Patrick A. Petre, Chief Executive Officer **A**1 2 9 10 **F**7 8 12 15 17 19 21 22 25 26 28 30 35 37 40 41 44 46 49 64 65 71 73 74 **S** TENET Healthcare Corporation, Santa Barbara, CA **Web address:** www.tenethealth.com	33	10	93	2692	50	21978	616	—	—	289

SAN FERNANDO—Los Angeles County

Hospital	Control	Service	Staffed Beds	Admissions	Census	Outpatient Visits	Births	Total	Payroll	Personnel
□ MISSION COMMUNITY HOSPITAL–SAN FERNANDO CAMPUS, (Includes Mission Community Hospital–Panorama City Campus, 14850 Roscoe Boulevard, Panorama City, Zip 91402–4618; tel. 818/787–2222), 700 Chatsworth Drive, Zip 91340–4299; tel. 818/361–7331; Cathy Fickes, R.N., Chief Executive Officer (Nonreporting) **A**1 9	23	10	152	—	—	—	—	—	—	—

Hospital, Address, Telephone, Administrator, Approval, Facility, and Physician Codes, Health Care System, Network	Classi-fication Codes		Utilization Data					Expense (thousands) of dollars		
★ American Hospital Association (AHA) membership □ Joint Commission on Accreditation of Healthcare Organizations (JCAHO) accreditation + American Osteopathic Healthcare Association (AOHA) membership ○ American Osteopathic Association (AOA) accreditation △ Commission on Accreditation of Rehabilitation Facilities (CARF) accreditation Control codes 61, 63, 64, 71, 72 and 73 indicate hospitals listed by AOHA, but not registered by AHA. For definition of numerical codes, see page A4	Control	Service	Staffed Beds	Admissions	Census	Outpatient Visits	Births	Total	Payroll	Personnel

SAN FRANCISCO—San Francisco County

⊠ △ CALIFORNIA PACIFIC MEDICAL CENTER, (Includes California Pacific Medical Center–Davies Campus, Castro and Duboce Streets, Zip 94114; tel. 415/565–6000; Greg Monardo, President and Chief Executive Officer), 2333 Buchanan Street, Zip 94115, Mailing Address: P.O. Box 7999, Zip 94120; tel. 415/563–4321; Martin Brotman, M.D., President and Chief Executive Officer (Total facility includes 205 beds in nursing home–type unit) **A**1 2 3 5 7 8 9 10 **F**1 3 7 8 10 11 12 14 15 16 17 19 20 21 22 23 26 28 29 30 31 32 33 34 35 37 38 40 41 42 43 44 46 47 48 49 51 52 54 55 56 57 58 60 61 64 65 67 69 71 73 74 **P**3 5 7 **S** Sutter Health, Sacramento, CA **Web address:** www.cpmc.org	23	10	613	24551	407	200079	4642	294980	147163	3271
⊠ CHINESE HOSPITAL, 845 Jackson Street, Zip 94133–4899; tel. 415/982–2400; Thomas M. Harlan, Chief Executive Officer **A**1 9 10 **F**4 7 8 9 10 12 14 15 16 17 19 21 22 25 27 28 29 30 32 33 35 37 38 40 41 42 43 44 45 46 47 48 50 52 60 63 64 65 67 69 70 71 73 **P**5 7	23	10	54	2008	31	42326	16	28418	9032	126
⊠ KAISER FOUNDATION HOSPITAL, 2425 Geary Boulevard, Zip 94115; tel. 415/202–2000; Julie A. Petrini, Senior Vice President and Area Manager **A**1 3 5 10 **F**3 4 7 8 10 11 12 13 14 15 16 17 18 19 20 21 22 23 24 26 27 28 29 30 31 32 33 34 35 37 38 39 40 41 42 43 44 45 46 49 50 51 53 54 56 57 58 59 60 61 63 65 66 67 69 70 71 72 73 **P**1 **S** Kaiser Foundation Hospitals, Oakland, CA	23	10	236	12261	140	819426	2504	—	—	1032
★ LAGUNA HONDA HOSPITAL AND REHABILITATION CENTER, 375 Laguna Honda Boulevard, Zip 94116–1499; tel. 415/664–1580; Lawrence J. Funk, Executive Administrator (Total facility includes 1214 beds in nursing home–type unit) (Nonreporting) **A**10	15	48	1249	—	—	—	—	—	—	—
□ PACIFIC COAST HOSPITAL, (PODIATRIC), 1210 Scott Street, Zip 94115–4000; tel. 415/292–0554; Robert D. Roberts, Interim President and Chief Executive Officer **A**1 9 10 **F**14 15 16 17 28 30 34 44 49 51 65 71 **P**4 5 7 **Web address:** www.ccpm.edu	23	49	17	52	0	10000	0	12547	6381	142
⊠ △ SAINT FRANCIS MEMORIAL HOSPITAL, 900 Hyde Street, Zip 94109, Mailing Address: Box 7726, Zip 94120–7726; tel. 415/353–6000; Cheryl A. Fama, Administrator, Vice President and Chief Operating Officer **A**1 2 3 7 9 10 **F**1 4 7 8 9 10 11 12 15 16 17 18 19 21 22 23 24 25 27 28 29 30 31 32 33 34 35 37 38 40 41 42 43 44 45 46 47 48 49 51 52 53 54 55 56 57 58 59 60 61 62 64 65 66 67 69 71 72 73 74 **P**1 3 4 5 8 **S** Catholic Healthcare West, San Francisco, CA	21	10	190	6154	111	157250	0	75968	37580	612
⊠ SAN FRANCISCO GENERAL HOSPITAL MEDICAL CENTER, 1001 Potrero Avenue, Zip 94110; tel. 415/206–8000; Gene O'Connell, Executive Administrator and Director Patient Care Services Community Health Network (Nonreporting) **A**1 2 3 5 8 10 **Web address:** www.sfgh.org	15	10	357	—	—	—	—	—	—	—
□ ST. LUKE'S HOSPITAL, 3555 Cesar Chavez Street, Zip 94110; tel. 415/647–8600; Jack Fries, President (Total facility includes 39 beds in nursing home–type unit) **A**1 9 10 **F**7 8 12 13 15 16 17 19 20 21 22 23 26 28 30 31 34 35 37 39 40 41 42 44 45 46 49 52 54 56 58 59 61 64 65 66 71 72 73 74 **P**5	23	10	225	7321	141	176119	899	80115	—	773
⊠ ST. MARY'S MEDICAL CENTER, 450 Stanyan Street, Zip 94117–1079; tel. 415/668–1000; Rosemary Fox, Vice President and Chief Operating Officer (Total facility includes 48 beds in nursing home–type unit) (Nonreporting) **A**1 2 3 5 8 9 10 **S** Catholic Healthcare West, San Francisco, CA	21	10	256	—	—	—	—	—	—	—
⊠ UNIVERSITY OF CALIFORNIA SAN FRANCISCO MEDICAL CENTER, (Includes University of California–San Francisco Mount Zion Medical Center, 1600 Divisadero Street, Zip 94143–1601; tel. 415/567–6600), 500 Parnassus, Zip 94143–0296; tel. 415/476–1000; Bruce Schroffel, Chief Operating Officer (Total facility includes 31 beds in nursing home–type unit) (Nonreporting) **A**1 2 3 5 8 9 10 **S** UCSF Stanford Health Care, San Francisco, CA **Web address:** www.ucsfstanford.org	23	10	663	—	—	—	—	—	—	—
⊠ VETERANS AFFAIRS MEDICAL CENTER, 4150 Clement Street, Zip 94121–1598; tel. 415/221–4810; Sheila M. Cullen, Director (Total facility includes 120 beds in nursing home–type unit) **A**1 2 3 5 8 **F**1 3 4 10 11 16 17 19 20 21 22 25 26 27 28 29 30 31 32 33 34 35 37 39 41 42 43 44 45 46 49 51 52 54 56 57 58 59 63 64 65 67 68 69 71 73 74 **P**6 **S** Department of Veterans Affairs, Washington, DC	45	10	244	5097	212	309201	0	176893	110094	1783

SAN GABRIEL—Los Angeles County

⊠ SAN GABRIEL VALLEY MEDICAL CENTER, 438 West Las Tunas Drive, Zip 91776, Mailing Address: P.O. Box 1507, Zip 91778–1507; tel. 626/289–5454; Thomas D. Mone, President and Chief Executive Officer **A**1 9 10 **F**3 7 8 10 12 15 16 17 19 21 22 25 26 27 28 30 32 34 35 37 38 40 41 42 44 46 48 49 52 55 57 58 59 60 63 64 65 67 68 71 73 74 **S** Catholic Healthcare West, San Francisco, CA **Web address:** www.unihealth.org/sgvmc	23	10	274	9435	157	50965	1534	64700	34592	766

SAN JOSE—Santa Clara County

□ ALEXIAN BROTHERS HOSPITAL, 225 North Jackson Avenue, Zip 95116–1691; tel. 408/259–5000; Steven R. Barron, President and Chief Executive Officer (Nonreporting) **A**1 9 10	21	10	192	—	—	—	—	—	—	—
⊠ GOOD SAMARITAN HOSPITAL, 2425 Samaritan Drive, Zip 95124, Mailing Address: P.O. Box 240002, Zip 95154–2402; tel. 408/559–2011; William K. Piche, Chief Executive Officer (Total facility includes 27 beds in nursing home–type unit) **A**1 9 10 **F**1 3 4 7 8 10 11 12 15 16 19 21 22 24 34 35 37 38 40 42 43 44 47 49 52 58 59 60 64 65 70 71 73 74 **S** Columbia/HCA Healthcare Corporation, Nashville, TN	33	10	333	17532	218	—	4352	164629	72874	1483

Hospital, Address, Telephone, Administrator, Approval, Facility, and Physician Codes, Health Care System, Network	Classi-fication Codes		Utilization Data					Expense (thousands) of dollars		
	Control	Service	Staffed Beds	Admissions	Census	Outpatient Visits	Births	Total	Payroll	Personnel

★ American Hospital Association (AHA) membership
☐ Joint Commission on Accreditation of Healthcare Organizations (JCAHO) accreditation
+ American Osteopathic Healthcare Association (AOHA) membership
○ American Osteopathic Association (AOA) accreditation
△ Commission on Accreditation of Rehabilitation Facilities (CARF) accreditation
Control codes 61, 63, 64, 71, 72 and 73 indicate hospitals listed by AOHA, but not registered by AHA. For definition of numerical codes, see page A4.

Hospital	Control	Service	Staffed Beds	Admissions	Census	Outpatient Visits	Births	Total	Payroll	Personnel
⊠ O'CONNOR HOSPITAL, 2105 Forest Avenue, Zip 95128; tel. 408/947–2500; Joan A. Bero, Regional Vice President and Chief Operating Officer (Total facility includes 24 beds in nursing home–type unit) **A**1 2 9 10 **F**4 7 8 10 11 12 13 14 15 16 17 19 21 22 24 28 30 32 33 34 35 36 37 40 41 42 43 44 45 46 49 52 57 60 63 64 65 67 68 71 73 **P**2 3 5 6 7 **S** Catholic Healthcare West, San Francisco, CA	21	10	257	11828	136	96712	2424	111591	45371	829
⊠ SAN JOSE MEDICAL CENTER, 675 East Santa Clara Street, Zip 95112, Mailing Address: P.O. Box 240003, Zip 95154–2403; tel. 408/998–3212; William L. Gilbert, Chief Executive Officer (Total facility includes 26 beds in nursing home–type unit) (Nonreporting) **A**1 2 3 5 9 10 **S** Columbia/HCA Healthcare Corporation, Nashville, TN	33	10	327	—	—	—	—	—	—	—
☐ SANTA CLARA VALLEY HEALTH AND HOSPITAL SYSTEM, (Formerly Santa Clara Valley Medical Center), 751 South Bascom Avenue, Zip 95128; tel. 408/885–5000; Robert Sillen, Executive Director (Nonreporting) **A**1 2 3 5 10	13	10	377	—	—	—	—	—	—	—
⊠ SANTA TERESA COMMUNITY HOSPITAL, 250 Hospital Parkway, Zip 95119; tel. 408/972–7000; Joann Zimmerman, Administrator **A**1 3 10 **F**2 3 4 6 7 8 9 10 11 12 13 14 15 16 17 18 19 20 21 22 23 24 25 26 27 28 29 30 31 32 33 34 35 37 38 39 40 41 42 43 44 45 46 47 48 49 51 52 53 54 55 56 57 58 59 60 61 63 64 65 66 67 68 69 70 71 72 73 74 **S** Kaiser Foundation Hospitals, Oakland, CA	23	10	218	13768	116	—	2619	—	—	220
SAN LEANDRO—Alameda County										
ALAMEDA COUNTY MEDICAL CENTER, 15400 Foothill Boulevard, Zip 94578–1091; tel. 510/667–7920; Michael G. Smart, Administrator (Total facility includes 119 beds in nursing home–type unit) (Nonreporting) **S** Alameda County Health Care Services Agency, San Leandro, CA	13	49	193	—	—	—	—	—	—	—
⊠ SAN LEANDRO HOSPITAL, 13855 East 14th Street, Zip 94578–0398; tel. 510/357–6500; Kelly Mather, Chief Executive Officer (Nonreporting) **A**1 10 **S** Triad Hospitals, Inc., Dallas, TX	33	10	136	—	—	—	—	—	—	—
☐ VENCOR HOSPITAL–SAN LEANDRO, 2800 Benedict Drive, Zip 94577; tel. 510/357–8300; Wayne M. Lingenfelter, Ed.D., Administrator and Chief Executive Officer **A**1 10 **F**12 15 16 19 35 39 44 45 46 51 54 65 71 **S** Vencor, Incorporated, Louisville, KY	33	10	58	357	38	0	0	14161	6479	190
SAN LUIS OBISPO—San Luis Obispo County										
CALIFORNIA MENS COLONY HOSPITAL, Highway 1, Zip 93409–8101, Mailing Address: P.O. Box 8101, Zip 93409–8101; tel. 805/547–7913; Galen Kirn, Administrator (Nonreporting)	12	11	39	—	—	—	—	—	—	—
☐ FRENCH HOSPITAL MEDICAL CENTER, 1911 Johnson Avenue, Zip 93401; tel. 805/543–5353; Gale E. Gascho, Chief Executive Officer (Nonreporting) **A**1 9 10	33	10	124	—	—	—	—	—	—	—
☐ SAN LUIS OBISPO GENERAL HOSPITAL, 2180 Johnson Avenue, Zip 93401, Mailing Address: Box 8113, Zip 93403–8113; tel. 805/781–4800; Paul L. Stormoen, Interim Chief Executive Officer (Nonreporting) **A**1 9 10	13	10	46	—	—	—	—	—	—	—
⊠ △ SIERRA VISTA REGIONAL MEDICAL CENTER, 1010 Murray Street, Zip 93405, Mailing Address: Box 1367, Zip 93406–1367; tel. 805/546–7600; Sean O'Neal, Administrator (Total facility includes 15 beds in nursing home–type unit) **A**1 7 9 10 **F**4 7 8 10 11 12 15 16 19 21 22 30 32 34 35 38 40 42 44 46 48 49 56 60 63 64 65 67 71 **P**5 **S** TENET Healthcare Corporation, Santa Barbara, CA	33	10	175	6653	92	142640	1089	53378	23684	657
SAN MATEO—San Mateo County										
MILLS HOSPITAL See Mills–Peninsula Health Services, Burlingame										
☐ SAN MATEO COUNTY GENERAL HOSPITAL AND CLINICS, 222 West 39th Avenue, Zip 94403–4398; tel. 650/573–2222; Timothy B. McMurdo, Chief Executive Officer (Total facility includes 124 beds in nursing home–type unit) (Nonreporting) **A**1 3 5 10	13	10	240	—	—	—	—	—	—	—
SAN PABLO—Contra Costa County										
⊠ DOCTORS MEDICAL CENTER–SAN PABLO CAMPUS, 2000 Vale Road, Zip 94806; tel. 510/970–5102; Gary Sloan, Chief Executive Officer (Total facility includes 106 beds in nursing home–type unit) (Nonreporting) **A**1 2 9 10 **S** TENET Healthcare Corporation, Santa Barbara, CA	33	10	286	—	—	—	—	—	—	—
SAN PEDRO—Los Angeles County, See Los Angeles										
SAN RAFAEL—Marin County										
⊠ KAISER FOUNDATION HOSPITAL, 99 Montecillo Road, Zip 94903–3397; tel. 415/444–2000; Mary Ann Thode, Administrator (Nonreporting) **A**1 10 **S** Kaiser Foundation Hospitals, Oakland, CA	23	10	119	—	—	—	—	—	—	—
SAN RAMON—Contra Costa County										
⊠ △ SAN RAMON REGIONAL MEDICAL CENTER, 6001 Norris Canyon Road, Zip 94583; tel. 925/275–9200; Philip P. Gustafson, Administrator **A**1 7 9 10 **F**1 3 4 7 8 10 11 12 15 16 17 19 21 22 27 28 30 31 34 35 37 38 39 40 41 42 44 46 48 49 52 60 61 65 66 67 68 71 73 74 **P**4 5 7 **S** TENET Healthcare Corporation, Santa Barbara, CA Web address: www.sanramonmedctr.com	33	10	95	4319	44	46097	953	35806	17176	383
SANGER—Fresno County										
☐ SANGER GENERAL HOSPITAL, 2558 Jensen Avenue, Zip 93657–2296; tel. 209/875–6571; William J. Casey, Chief Executive Officer (Nonreporting) **A**1 9 10	32	10	25	—	—	—	—	—	—	—
SANTA ANA—Orange County										
⊠ COASTAL COMMUNITIES HOSPITAL, 2701 South Bristol Street, Zip 92704–9911; tel. 714/754–5454; Kent G. Clayton, Chief Executive Officer (Total facility includes 46 beds in nursing home–type unit) **A**1 9 10 **F**8 12 15 16 19 20 21 22 27 34 35 37 39 40 41 44 46 51 52 57 60 63 64 65 71 73 74 **P**7 **S** TENET Healthcare Corporation, Santa Barbara, CA	33	10	177	3959	83	20470	1715	—	—	406

Hospital, Address, Telephone, Administrator, Approval, Facility, and Physician Codes, Health Care System, Network	Classi-fication Codes		Utilization Data					Expense (thousands) of dollars		
★ American Hospital Association (AHA) membership □ Joint Commission on Accreditation of Healthcare Organizations (JCAHO) accreditation + American Osteopathic Healthcare Association (AOHA) membership ○ American Osteopathic Association (AOA) accreditation △ Commission on Accreditation of Rehabilitation Facilities (CARF) accreditation Control codes 61, 63, 64, 71, 72 and 73 indicate hospitals listed by AOHA, but not registered by AHA. For definition of numerical codes, see page A4	Control	Service	Staffed Beds	Admissions	Census	Outpatient Visits	Births	Total	Payroll	Personnel

	Control	Service	Staffed Beds	Admissions	Census	Outpatient Visits	Births	Total	Payroll	Personnel
✠ SANTA ANA HOSPITAL MEDICAL CENTER, 1901 North Fairview Street, Zip 92706; tel. 714/554–1653; Kent G. Clayton, Chief Executive Officer **A**1 9 10 **F**3 4 7 8 9 10 11 12 15 16 17 19 21 22 23 25 26 27 28 29 30 31 32 33 34 35 37 38 39 40 41 42 43 44 45 46 47 48 49 50 53 54 56 57 58 59 60 61 63 65 66 67 68 71 72 73 74 **P**5 8 **S** TENET Healthcare Corporation, Santa Barbara, CA	33	10	76	2991	17	10266	2019	15109	7103	167
SPECIALTY HOSPITAL OF SANTA ANA, 1901 North College Avenue, Zip 92706; tel. 714/564–7800; Richard Luna, Chief Executive Officer (Nonreporting)	33	10	54	—	—	—	—	—	—	—
✠ WESTERN MEDICAL CENTER–SANTA ANA, 1001 North Tustin Avenue, Zip 92705–3502; tel. 714/835–3555; Daniel Brothman, Chief Executive Officer **A**1 2 3 5 9 10 **F**1 4 7 8 10 11 12 15 16 17 19 21 22 23 27 28 30 32 35 36 37 38 40 41 42 43 44 46 47 48 49 52 53 54 56 57 59 60 64 65 67 68 70 71 72 73 **P**5 **S** TENET Healthcare Corporation, Santa Barbara, CA **Web address:** www.tenethealth.com/westermedical	33	10	288	12777	154	80226	2930	103549	44097	1008
SANTA BARBARA—Santa Barbara County										
□ GOLETA VALLEY COTTAGE HOSPITAL, 351 South Patterson Avenue, Zip 93111, Mailing Address: Box 6306, Zip 93160; tel. 805/967–3411; Diane Wisby, President and Chief Executive Officer (Nonreporting) **A**1 9 10 **S** Cottage Health System, Santa Barbara, CA	23	10	79	—	—	—	—	—	—	—
□ REHABILITATION INSTITUTE AT SANTA BARBARA, 427 Camino Del Remedio, Zip 93110; tel. 805/683–3788; Rusty Pollock, President and Chief Executive Officer (Nonreporting) **A**1 9 10	23	46	40	—	—	—	—	—	—	—
□ SANTA BARBARA COTTAGE HOSPITAL, (Includes Santa Barbara Cottage Care Center), Pueblo at Bath Streets, Zip 93105, Mailing Address: Box 689, Zip 93102; tel. 805/682–7111; James L. Ash, President and Chief Executive Officer **A**1 2 3 5 9 10 **F**2 3 4 8 10 11 12 14 15 16 17 18 19 21 22 23 24 25 26 27 28 29 30 34 35 37 38 39 40 41 42 43 44 46 47 49 52 56 58 60 64 65 67 71 73 74 **S** Cottage Health System, Santa Barbara, CA	23	10	336	16912	203	92083	2249	128388	51347	1789
✠ ST. FRANCIS MEDICAL CENTER OF SANTA BARBARA, 601 East Micheltorena Street, Zip 93103; tel. 805/568–5705; Ron Biscaro, Administrator and Chief Operating Officer (Total facility includes 15 beds in nursing home–type unit) **A**1 9 10 **F**6 7 8 10 11 12 14 15 16 17 19 22 26 27 28 30 35 37 39 40 41 44 46 49 52 57 64 65 67 71 73 **S** Catholic Healthcare West, San Francisco, CA	21	10	20	2930	38	19925	343	26124	11374	254
SANTA CLARA—Santa Clara County										
✠ KAISER FOUNDATION HOSPITAL, 900 Kiely Boulevard, Zip 95051–5386; tel. 408/236–6400; Helen Wilmot, Administrator (Nonreporting) **A**1 3 5 10 **S** Kaiser Foundation Hospitals, Oakland, CA	23	10	249	—	—	—	—	—	—	—
SANTA CRUZ—Santa Cruz County										
✠ DOMINICAN HOSPITAL, (Formerly Dominican Santa Cruz Hospital), 1555 Soquel Drive, Zip 95065; tel. 831/462–7700; Sister Julie Hyer, President and Chief Executive Officer (Total facility includes 41 beds in nursing home–type unit) **A**1 9 10 **F**4 6 7 8 10 12 13 14 15 19 22 25 30 34 35 37 38 40 41 42 43 44 45 46 48 49 52 54 56 59 62 64 65 66 67 68 69 71 72 73 74 **P**3 5 7 **S** Catholic Healthcare West, San Francisco, CA **Web address:** www.dominicanhospital.org	21	10	275	11652	167	120298	1275	109437	49188	983
✠ SUTTER MATERNITY AND SURGERY CENTER OF SANTA CRUZ, 2900 Chanticleer Avenue, Zip 95065–1816; tel. 831/477–2200; Iris C. Frank, Administrator (Nonreporting) **A**1 10 **S** Sutter Health, Sacramento, CA	23	10	30	—	—	—	—	—	—	—
SANTA MARIA—Santa Barbara County										
✠ MARIAN MEDICAL CENTER, 1400 East Church Street, Zip 93454, Mailing Address: Box 1238, Zip 93456; tel. 805/739–3000; Charles J. Cova, Executive Vice President and Chief Operating Officer (Total facility includes 95 beds in nursing home–type unit) **A**1 2 9 10 **F**4 7 8 10 11 12 14 15 16 17 19 20 21 22 26 27 28 29 30 31 32 33 34 35 39 40 41 42 43 44 45 46 49 54 56 60 64 65 67 68 70 71 73 74 **P**7 **S** Catholic Healthcare West, San Francisco, CA	21	10	225	8070	159	98792	1624	61054	22490	748
SANTA MONICA—Los Angeles County										
✠ SAINT JOHN'S HOSPITAL AND HEALTH CENTER, 1328 22nd Street, Zip 90404–2032; tel. 310/829–5511; Bruce Lamoureux, Chief Executive Officer (Total facility includes 22 beds in nursing home–type unit) **A**1 2 9 10 **F**2 3 4 7 8 10 11 12 14 15 16 17 19 21 22 23 28 29 30 32 34 35 36 37 38 39 40 41 42 43 44 49 52 54 55 56 57 58 59 60 64 65 71 73 74 **P**1 5 7 **S** Sisters of Charity of Leavenworth Health Services Corporation, Leavenworth, KS	21	10	271	14759	222	271978	1381	144956	66473	1380
✠ SANTA MONICA–UCLA MEDICAL CENTER, 1250 16th Street, Zip 90404–1200; tel. 310/319–4000 (Nonreporting) **A**1 2 3 5 9 10 **S** University of California–Systemwide Administration, Oakland, CA	12	10	221	—	—	—	—	—	—	—
SANTA PAULA—Ventura County										
□ SANTA PAULA MEMORIAL HOSPITAL, 825 North Tenth Street, Zip 93060–0270, Mailing Address: P.O. Box 270, Zip 93061–0270; tel. 805/525–7171; William M. Greene, FACHE, President **A**1 9 10 **F**7 8 14 15 16 17 19 21 22 25 30 34 35 37 39 40 42 44 49 65 71 73 **P**5 **S** Quorum Health Group/Quorum Health Resources, Inc., Brentwood, TN	23	10	54	1853	19	40672	282	13379	5697	209
SANTA ROSA—Sonoma County										
✠ KAISER FOUNDATION HOSPITAL, 401 Bicentennial Way, Zip 95403; tel. 707/571–4000; Susan Janvrin, R.N., Site Leader and Nurse Executive **A**1 10 **F**7 8 12 13 14 15 16 17 19 22 24 25 27 28 29 30 31 32 33 34 35 37 39 40 41 42 44 45 46 49 53 54 55 56 58 61 65 67 68 71 72 73 **P**6 **S** Kaiser Foundation Hospitals, Oakland, CA **Web address:** www.ca.kaiserpermanente.org	23	10	103	6546	59	579512	1382	—	—	1005

Hospital, Address, Telephone, Administrator, Approval, Facility, and Physician Codes, Health Care System, Network	Classification Codes		Utilization Data					Expense (thousands) of dollars		
	Control	Service	Staffed Beds	Admissions	Census	Outpatient Visits	Births	Total	Payroll	Personnel

★ American Hospital Association (AHA) membership
□ Joint Commission on Accreditation of Healthcare Organizations (JCAHO) accreditation
+ American Osteopathic Healthcare Association (AOHA) membership
○ American Osteopathic Association (AOA) accreditation
△ Commission on Accreditation of Rehabilitation Facilities (CARF) accreditation
Control codes 61, 63, 64, 71, 72 and 73 indicate hospitals listed by AOHA, but not registered by AHA. For definition of numerical codes, see page A4

	Control	Service	Staffed Beds	Admissions	Census	Outpatient Visits	Births	Total	Payroll	Personnel
☒ NORTH COAST HEALTH CARE CENTERS, 1287 Fulton Road, Zip 95401; tel. 707/543–2400; Robert H. Fish, President and Chief Executive Officer (Nonreporting) **A**1 9 10 **S** St. Joseph Health System, Orange, CA	33	10	119	—	—	—	—	—	—	—
☒ SANTA ROSA MEMORIAL HOSPITAL, 1165 Montgomery Drive, Zip 95405, Mailing Address: Box 522, Zip 95402; tel. 707/546–3210; Robert H. Fish, President and Chief Executive Officer (Nonreporting) **A**1 2 9 10 **S** St. Joseph Health System, Orange, CA	21	10	225	—	—	—	—	—	—	—
☒ SUTTER MEDICAL CENTER, SANTA ROSA, 3325 Chanate Road, Zip 95404; tel. 707/576–4000; Cliff Coates, Chief Executive Officer **A**1 3 5 10 **F**7 8 10 12 13 14 16 19 20 21 22 26 28 29 30 31 32 33 34 35 37 38 39 40 41 44 47 49 51 52 54 56 64 65 67 71 72 73 74 **P**3 **S** Sutter Health, Sacramento, CA	23	10	114	5156	54	—	1467	71456	25195	575
□ WARRACK MEDICAL CENTER HOSPITAL, 2449 Summerfield Road, Zip 95405; tel. 707/542–9030; Dale E. Iversen, President and Chief Executive Officer (Nonreporting) **A**1 10 Web address: www.warrack.com	33	10	79	—	—	—	—	—	—	—
SEBASTOPOL—Sonoma County										
☒ PALM DRIVE HOSPITAL, 501 Petaluma Avenue, Zip 95472; tel. 707/823–8511 (Total facility includes 10 beds in nursing home–type unit) (Nonreporting) **A**1	23	10	48							
SELMA—Fresno County										
□ SELMA DISTRICT HOSPITAL, 1141 Rose Avenue, Zip 93662–3293; tel. 559/891–2201; Edward C. Palacios, R.N., Acting Chief Executive Officer (Total facility includes 14 beds in nursing home–type unit) **A**1 9 10 **F**7 12 15 16 17 19 22 28 30 32 34 35 40 41 44 64 65 67 71 73 **S** Adventist Health, Roseville, CA	16	10	47	2144	21	39623	490	13458	5182	205
SEPULVEDA—Los Angeles County, See Los Angeles										
SHERMAN OAKS—Los Angeles County, See Los Angeles										
SIMI VALLEY—Ventura County										
☒ SIMI VALLEY HOSPITAL AND HEALTH CARE SERVICES, (Includes Simi Valley Hospital and Health Care Services–South Campus, 1850 Heywood Street, Zip 93065; tel. 805/582–5050), 2975 North Sycamore Drive, Zip 93065–1277; tel. 805/527–2462; Alan J. Rice, President (Total facility includes 74 beds in nursing home–type unit) (Nonreporting) **A**1 2 9 10 **S** Adventist Health, Roseville, CA	21	10	225	—	—	—	—	—	—	—
SOLVANG—Santa Barbara County										
□ SANTA YNEZ VALLEY COTTAGE HOSPITAL, 700 Alamo Pintado Road, Zip 93463; tel. 805/688–6431; James L. Ash, President and Chief Executive Officer (Nonreporting) **A**1 9 10 **S** Cottage Health System, Santa Barbara, CA	23	10	20							
SONOMA—Sonoma County										
□ SONOMA VALLEY HOSPITAL, 347 Andrieux Street, Zip 95476–6811, Mailing Address: Box 600, Zip 95476–0600; tel. 707/935–5000; Dennis R. Burns, Administrator and Chief Executive Officer **A**1 9 10 **F**7 8 12 14 15 16 17 19 21 22 23 30 32 34 35 37 39 40 41 44 49 63 64 65 67 71 **P**5	16	10	77	2471	37	74042	166	28727	13350	310
SONORA—Tuolumne County										
☒ SONORA COMMUNITY HOSPITAL, 1 South Forest Road, Zip 95370; tel. 209/532–3161; Lary Davis, President (Total facility includes 68 beds in nursing home–type unit) **A**1 9 10 **F**7 8 11 12 15 16 17 19 21 22 25 26 27 28 30 32 34 35 37 39 40 41 42 44 45 46 49 51 64 65 66 67 71 72 73 **P**5 **S** Adventist Health, Roseville, CA Web address: www.sonoracom.com	21	10	118	3644	97	149151	464	47201	19249	589
□ TUOLUMNE GENERAL HOSPITAL, 101 Hospital Road, Zip 95370; tel. 209/533–7100; Joseph K. Mitchell, Administrator (Total facility includes 32 beds in nursing home–type unit) (Nonreporting) **A**1 10	13	10	77	—	—	—	—	—	—	—
SOUTH EL MONTE—Los Angeles County										
☒ GREATER EL MONTE COMMUNITY HOSPITAL, 1701 South Santa Anita Avenue, Zip 91733–9918; tel. 626/579–7777; Elizabeth A. Primeaux, Chief Executive Officer (Total facility includes 13 beds in nursing home–type unit) **A**1 9 10 **F**1 2 3 4 5 6 8 9 10 11 12 13 15 16 17 18 19 20 21 22 23 24 25 26 27 28 29 30 31 32 33 34 35 36 37 38 39 40 41 42 43 44 45 46 47 49 50 52 53 54 55 56 57 58 59 60 63 64 65 66 67 68 70 71 72 73 74 **P**5 **S** TENET Healthcare Corporation, Santa Barbara, CA	33	10	115	3910	48	22911	1073	22047	10237	277
SOUTH LAGUNA—Orange County										
☒ SOUTH COAST MEDICAL CENTER, 31872 Coast Highway, Zip 92677; tel. 949/499–1311; T. Michael Murray, President (Total facility includes 29 beds in nursing home–type unit) **A**1 9 10 **F**2 3 7 8 11 12 14 15 16 17 19 21 22 25 27 28 29 30 31 32 34 35 36 37 39 40 41 42 44 45 46 49 52 56 57 58 59 60 64 65 67 71 73 74 **P**5 7 **S** Adventist Health, Roseville, CA	21	10	155	4643	61	44055	431	41266	17758	377
SOUTH LAKE TAHOE—El Dorado County										
□ BARTON MEMORIAL HOSPITAL, 2170 South Avenue, Zip 96158, Mailing Address: Box 9578, Zip 96158; tel. 916/541–3420; William G. Gordon, Chief Executive Officer (Nonreporting) **A**1 9 10	23	10	81	—	—	—	—	—	—	—
SOUTH SAN FRANCISCO—San Mateo County										
☒ KAISER FOUNDATION HOSPITAL, 1200 El Camino Real, Zip 94080–3299; tel. 650/742–2401; Gail Wuotila, Director Hospital Operations (Nonreporting) **A**1 10 **S** Kaiser Foundation Hospitals, Oakland, CA	23	10	79	—	—	—	—	—	—	—

	Classi-fication Codes		Utilization Data					Expense (thousands) of dollars		
Hospital, Address, Telephone, Administrator, Approval, Facility, and Physician Codes, Health Care System, Network	Control	Service	Staffed Beds	Admissions	Census	Outpatient Visits	Births	Total	Payroll	Personnel

★ American Hospital Association (AHA) membership
□ Joint Commission on Accreditation of Healthcare Organizations (JCAHO) accreditation
+ American Osteopathic Healthcare Association (AOHA) membership
○ American Osteopathic Association (AOA) accreditation
△ Commission on Accreditation of Rehabilitation Facilities (CARF) accreditation
Control codes 61, 63, 64, 71, 72 and 73 indicate hospitals listed by AOHA, but not registered by AHA. For definition of numerical codes, see page A4

STANFORD—Santa Clara County

⊞ STANFORD HOSPITAL AND CLINICS, 300 Pasteur Drive, Zip 94305–5584; tel. 650/723–4000; William B. Kerr, Executive Vice President and Chief Operating Officer **A**1 3 5 8 9 10 **F**3 4 5 8 10 11 12 14 15 16 17 19 21 22 29 30 31 32 34 35 37 41 42 43 44 45 46 48 49 51 52 54 55 56 57 58 59 60 61 63 64 65 66 67 68 70 71 72 73 **P**4 5 7 **S** UCSF Stanford Health Care, San Francisco, CA **Web address:** www.ucsfstanford.org	23	10	440	17788	262	649025	0	480748	181554	4899

STOCKTON—San Joaquin County

□ DAMERON HOSPITAL, 525 West Acacia Street, Zip 95203; tel. 209/944–5550; Luis Arismendi, M.D., Administrator (Nonreporting) **A**1 9 10 **S** Sutter Health, Sacramento, CA	23	10	211	—	—	—	—	—	—	—
⊞ ST. JOSEPH'S BEHAVIORAL HEALTH CENTER, 2510 North California Street, Zip 95204–5568; tel. 209/948–2100; James Sondecker, Director **A**1 9 10 **F**2 3 4 5 6 7 8 9 10 11 12 13 14 15 16 17 18 19 20 22 23 24 25 26 27 28 29 30 31 32 34 35 37 38 39 40 41 42 43 44 45 46 47 48 49 51 52 53 54 55 56 57 58 59 60 61 62 64 65 67 69 70 71 72 73 74 **P**3 5 6 7 **S** Catholic Healthcare West, San Francisco, CA **Web address:** www.sjrhs.org	23	22	24	1309	25	4084	0	4353	2265	—
⊞ ST. JOSEPH'S MEDICAL CENTER, 1800 North California Street, Zip 95204, Mailing Address: P.O. Box 213008, Zip 95213–3008; tel. 209/943–2000; Donald J. Wiley, Senior Vice President and Chief Operating Officer **A**1 2 9 10 **F**2 3 4 6 7 8 10 11 12 13 14 15 16 17 18 19 20 21 22 23 25 26 27 28 29 30 31 32 33 35 37 38 40 41 43 44 45 46 49 52 53 54 55 56 57 58 59 60 62 64 65 66 67 68 71 72 73 74 **S** Catholic Healthcare West, San Francisco, CA **Web address:** www.sjrhs.org	21	10	294	16164	212	346178	1896	160463	65811	1697

SUN CITY—Riverside County

⊞ MENIFEE VALLEY MEDICAL CENTER, 28400 McCall Boulevard, Zip 92585–9537; tel. 909/679–8888; Susan Ballard, Administrator (Nonreporting) **A**1 9 10 **S** Valley Health System, Hemet, CA	16	10	84	—	—	—	—	—	—	—

SUN VALLEY—Los Angeles County, See Los Angeles

SUSANVILLE—Lassen County

⊞ LASSEN COMMUNITY HOSPITAL, 560 Hospital Lane, Zip 96130–4809; tel. 530/257–5325; David S. Anderson, FACHE, Administrator (Total facility includes 30 beds in nursing home–type unit) **A**1 9 10 **F**7 8 12 15 16 19 22 28 30 32 33 34 35 37 40 44 64 65 71 73 **S** Lutheran Health Systems, Fargo, ND	23	10	58	1179	29	23460	256	11344	5398	141

SYLMAR—Los Angeles County, See Los Angeles

TAFT—Kern County

★ MERCY WESTSIDE HOSPITAL, (Formerly Westside District Hospital), 110 East North Street, Zip 93268; tel. 661/763–4211; Margo Arnold, Administrator (Total facility includes 63 beds in nursing home–type unit) (Nonreporting) **A**9 10 **S** Catholic Healthcare West, San Francisco, CA	12	10	73							

TARZANA—Los Angeles County, See Los Angeles

TEHACHAPI—Kern County

★ TEHACHAPI HOSPITAL, 115 West E Street, Zip 93561, Mailing Address: P.O. Box 1900, Zip 93581; tel. 661/822–3241; Raymond T. Hino, Chief Executive Officer (Total facility includes 16 beds in nursing home–type unit) **A**9 10 **F**22 28 44 71 **S** Brim Healthcare, Inc., Brentwood, TN	16	10	28	84	15		0	6408	2605	82

TEMPLETON—San Luis Obispo County

⊞ TWIN CITIES COMMUNITY HOSPITAL, 1100 Las Tablas Road, Zip 93465; tel. 805/434–3500; Harold E. Chilton, Chief Executive Officer **A**1 9 10 **F**8 10 11 12 19 22 28 32 35 37 38 40 41 42 44 48 49 64 65 71 72 73 **P**5 **S** TENET Healthcare Corporation, Santa Barbara, CA	33	10	84	4403	49	64669	489	30723	13170	337

THOUSAND OAKS—Los Angeles County

⊞ LOS ROBLES REGIONAL MEDICAL CENTER, 215 West Janss Road, Zip 91360–1899; tel. 805/497–2727; Robert C. Shaw, President and Chief Executive Officer (Total facility includes 42 beds in nursing home–type unit) **A**1 2 9 10 **F**4 7 10 11 12 14 15 16 17 19 21 22 26 28 29 30 31 34 35 36 37 38 39 40 41 42 43 44 45 46 48 49 52 54 57 60 63 64 65 67 71 72 73 74 **S** Columbia/HCA Healthcare Corporation, Nashville, TN **Web address:** www.losrobleshospital.com	33	10	255	11168	167	72320	2083	104528	43306	1012

TORRANCE—Los Angeles County

□ DEL AMO HOSPITAL, 23700 Camino Del Sol, Zip 90505; tel. 310/530–1151; Lisa K. Montes, Administrator and Chief Executive Officer (Nonreporting) **A**1 10 **S** Universal Health Services, Inc., King of Prussia, PA	33	22	166	—	—	—	—	—	—	—
⊞ LAC–HARBOR–UNIVERSITY OF CALIFORNIA AT LOS ANGELES MEDICAL CENTER, 1000 West Carson Street, Zip 90509; tel. 310/222–2101; Tecla A. Mickoseff, Administrator **A**1 2 3 5 10 **F**4 8 10 11 16 19 21 22 23 29 31 34 35 37 38 40 41 42 43 44 47 52 54 56 58 60 61 63 65 66 68 70 71 72 73 74 **P**6 **S** Los Angeles County–Department of Health Services, Los Angeles, CA	13	10	336	23289	324	330515	1779	455845	129566	2735
□ LITTLE COMPANY OF MARY HOSPITAL, 4101 Torrance Boulevard, Zip 90503–4698; tel. 310/540–7676; Mark Costa, President (Total facility includes 121 beds in nursing home–type unit) **A**1 2 9 10 **F**3 4 5 7 8 10 12 14 15 16 17 19 21 22 23 25 27 29 30 32 33 34 35 37 38 40 41 42 43 44 46 49 51 54 57 60 63 64 65 67 71 72 73 74 **P**3 5 **S** Little Company of Mary Sisters Healthcare System, Evergreen Park, IL **Web address:** www.lcmhs.org	23	10	348	16602	259	125676	2483	108234	47948	1451

Hospital, Address, Telephone, Administrator, Approval, Facility, and Physician Codes, Health Care System, Network	Classi-fication Codes		Utilization Data					Expense (thousands) of dollars		
	Control	Service	Staffed Beds	Admissions	Census	Outpatient Visits	Births	Total	Payroll	Personnel

★ American Hospital Association (AHA) membership
□ Joint Commission on Accreditation of Healthcare Organizations (JCAHO) accreditation
+ American Osteopathic Healthcare Association (AOHA) membership
○ American Osteopathic Association (AOA) accreditation
△ Commission on Accreditation of Rehabilitation Facilities (CARF) accreditation
Control codes 61, 63, 64, 71, 72 and 73 indicate hospitals listed by AOHA, but not registered by AHA. For definition of numerical codes, see page A4

	Control	Service	Staffed Beds	Admissions	Census	Outpatient Visits	Births	Total	Payroll	Personnel
✠ TORRANCE MEMORIAL MEDICAL CENTER, 3330 Lomita Boulevard, Zip 90505–5073; tel. 310/325–9110; George W. Graham, President **A**1 2 9 10 **F**3 4 7 8 9 10 12 15 17 19 21 22 23 25 26 27 28 29 30 31 32 33 34 35 37 38 40 41 42 43 44 45 46 49 51 52 54 55 56 57 58 59 60 64 65 67 71 72 73 74 **P**5 Web address: www.tmmc.com	23	10	360	22161	253	141041	4542	152033	60286	1564
TRACY—San Joaquin County										
✠ SUTTER TRACY COMMUNITY HOSPITAL, 1420 North Tracy Boulevard, Zip 95376–3497; tel. 209/835–1500; Gary D. Rapaport, Chief Executive Officer **A**1 9 10 **F**7 8 12 15 16 17 19 21 22 28 29 32 33 35 37 40 41 44 49 64 65 67 71 72 73 **P**3 5 **S** Sutter Health, Sacramento, CA Web address: www.suttertracy.org	23	10	61	3192	34	32377	481	24485	8875	300
TRAVIS AFB—Solano County										
✠ DAVID GRANT MEDICAL CENTER, 101 Bodin Circle, Zip 94535–1800; tel. 707/423–7300; Lieutenant Colonel John Hill, MSC, USAF, FACHE, Administrator (Nonreporting) **A**1 2 3 5 **S** Department of the Air Force, Bowling AFB, DC	41	10	185	—	—	—	—	—	—	—
TRUCKEE—Nevada County										
□ TAHOE FOREST HOSPITAL DISTRICT, 10121 Pine Avenue, Zip 96161, Mailing Address: Box 759, Zip 96160; tel. 530/587–6011; Lawrence C. Long, Chief Executive Officer (Total facility includes 37 beds in nursing home–type unit) **A**1 9 10 **F**3 7 8 12 15 16 17 19 22 23 28 29 30 32 33 34 35 37 40 41 42 44 46 49 64 65 66 67 71 73 **P**5 Web address: www.tfhd.com	16	10	72	2130	52	50426	399	33787	12368	344
TULARE—Tulare County										
✠ TULARE DISTRICT HOSPITAL, 869 Cherry Street, Zip 93274–2287; tel. 209/688–0821; Robert M. Montion, Chief Executive Officer **A**1 9 10 **F**7 8 12 14 15 16 17 19 22 28 29 31 34 35 37 39 40 41 42 44 45 67 69 71 73	16	10	88	4952	48	97631	958	34361	13183	512
TURLOCK—Stanislaus County										
✠ EMANUEL MEDICAL CENTER, 825 Delbon Avenue, Zip 95382, Mailing Address: P.O. Box 819005, Zip 95381–9005; tel. 209/667–4200; Robert A. Moen, President and Chief Executive Officer (Total facility includes 145 beds in nursing home–type unit) **A**1 9 10 **F**6 7 8 11 12 14 15 16 17 19 20 21 22 23 25 26 27 28 29 30 32 33 34 35 36 37 39 40 41 42 44 49 62 64 65 67 71 72 74 **P**1 5 Web address: www.emanuelmed.org	21	10	270	7078	194	37340	1473	57339	22339	776
TUSTIN—Orange County										
□ TUSTIN HOSPITAL AND MEDICAL CENTER, (Formerly Tustin Hospital), 14662 Newport Avenue, Zip 92680; tel. 714/838–9600; Timothy L. Carda, Chief Executive Officer (Total facility includes 24 beds in nursing home–type unit) (Nonreporting) **A**1	33	10	117	—	—	—	—	—	—	—
□ TUSTIN REHABILITATION HOSPITAL, 14851 Yorba Street, Zip 92680; tel. 714/832–9200; Beverly S. Quaye, Administrator **A**1 9 10 **F**12 49 64 66	32	46	117	799	43	3637	0	14584	4603	—
TWENTYNINE PALMS—San Bernardino County										
✠ NAVAL HOSPITAL, Mailing Address: Box 788250, MCAGCC, Zip 92278–8250; tel. 760/830–2492; Captain R. S. Kayler, MSC, USN, Commanding Officer **A**1 **F**1 2 3 4 5 7 8 9 10 11 12 13 14 15 16 19 20 21 22 23 24 26 27 28 29 30 31 34 35 37 38 39 40 41 42 43 44 45 46 47 48 49 50 51 52 53 56 57 58 59 60 61 63 64 65 66 68 69 70 71 72 73 **P**7 **S** Department of Navy, Washington, DC Web address: http://nh29palms.med.navy.mil/nhtp/	43	10	30	1290	8	112363	479	36044	24947	496
UKIAH—Mendocino County										
✠ UKIAH VALLEY MEDICAL CENTER, (Includes Ukiah Valley Medical Center–Dora Street, 1120 South Dora Street; Ukiah Valley Medical Center–Hospital Drive), 275 Hospital Drive, Zip 95482; tel. 707/462–3111; ValGene Devitt, President and Chief Executive Officer **A**1 9 10 **F**7 8 10 12 15 16 19 21 22 23 30 32 35 37 38 40 41 42 44 45 46 49 64 65 71 72 73 74 **P**3 5 **S** Adventist Health, Roseville, CA	21	10	85	5506	40	29162	751	2784	1251	407
UPLAND—San Bernardino County										
✠ SAN ANTONIO COMMUNITY HOSPITAL, 999 San Bernardino Road, Zip 91786–4920, Mailing Address: Box 5001, Zip 91785; tel. 909/985–2811; George A. Kuykendall, President and Chief Executive Officer **A**1 2 9 10 **F**2 3 4 7 8 10 11 12 14 15 16 18 19 21 22 25 32 34 35 37 38 40 41 42 43 44 46 49 52 58 59 60 61 63 65 67 71 72 73 **P**7 Web address: www.sach.org	23	10	308	17546	182	251381	3816	137871	57981	1701
VACAVILLE—Solano County										
CALIFORNIA MEDICAL FACILITY, 1600 California Drive, Zip 95696–2000; tel. 707/448–6841; Shelby Farrow, Administrator **F**1 3 4 10 11 19 20 21 22 27 30 31 33 35 41 42 43 44 49 50 52 54 56 58 60 65 67 69 70 71 **P**6	12	11	215	1217	246	3937	0	—	—	443
✠ VACAVALLEY HOSPITAL, 1000 Nut Tree Road, Zip 95687; tel. 707/446–4000; Deborah Sugiyama, President **A**1 9 10 **F**1 6 7 8 10 12 13 14 15 16 17 19 21 22 23 28 30 32 33 35 36 37 39 40 41 42 44 49 60 64 65 71 73 **P**3 **S** NorthBay Healthcare System, Fairfield, CA Web address: www.northbay.org	23	10	43	1936	17	20704	0	22352	8094	106
VALENCIA—Los Angeles County										
□ △ HENRY MAYO NEWHALL MEMORIAL HOSPITAL, 23845 McBean Parkway, Zip 91355; tel. 805/253–8000; Duffy Watson, President and Chief Executive Officer (Total facility includes 54 beds in nursing home–type unit) **A**1 2 7 9 10 **F**1 7 8 11 12 14 15 16 17 18 19 20 21 22 25 26 27 28 29 30 31 32 33 34 35 37 39 40 41 42 44 45 46 48 49 52 56 57 58 59 60 63 64 65 67 70 71 73	23	10	217	8945	147	116577	1348	78404	27620	757

Hospital, Address, Telephone, Administrator, Approval, Facility, and Physician Codes, Health Care System, Network	Classification Codes		Utilization Data					Expense (thousands) of dollars		
★ American Hospital Association (AHA) membership □ Joint Commission on Accreditation of Healthcare Organizations (JCAHO) accreditation + American Osteopathic Healthcare Association (AOHA) membership ○ American Osteopathic Association (AOA) accreditation △ Commission on Accreditation of Rehabilitation Facilities (CARF) accreditation Control codes 61, 63, 64, 71, 72 and 73 indicate hospitals listed by AOHA, but not registered by AHA. For definition of numerical codes, see page A4	Control	Service	Staffed Beds	Admissions	Census	Outpatient Visits	Births	Total	Payroll	Personnel

VALLEJO—Solano County

□ FIRST HOSPITAL VALLEJO, 525 Oregon Street, Zip 94590; tel. 707/648–2200; Joe H. McWaters, Jr., Administrator and Chief Executive Officer (Nonreporting) **A**1 9 10	33	22	61	—	—	—	—	—	—	—
✠ KAISER FOUNDATION HOSPITAL AND REHABILITATION CENTER, 975 Sereno Drive, Zip 94589; tel. 707/651–1000; Sandra Small, Senior Vice President and Area Manager **A**1 10 **F**2 3 7 8 9 11 12 13 14 15 16 17 19 22 25 29 30 32 33 35 37 40 41 42 44 45 46 48 49 51 52 54 58 60 64 65 67 71 72 73 **P**1 **S** Kaiser Foundation Hospitals, Oakland, CA	23	10	287	15086	146	—	2421	—	—	1028
✠ SUTTER SOLANO MEDICAL CENTER, 300 Hospital Drive, Zip 94589–2517, Mailing Address: P.O. Box 3189, Zip 94589; tel. 707/554–4444; Polly J. Walker, R.N., Interim Chief Executive Officer (Total facility includes 6 beds in nursing home–type unit) **A**1 9 10 **F**7 8 10 11 12 14 15 16 19 21 22 28 29 30 34 35 36 39 40 41 42 44 49 63 64 65 71 73 74 **S** Sutter Health, Sacramento, CA **Web address:** www.sutterhealth.org	23	10	60	5486	57	62900	745	42458	19032	451

VAN NUYS—Los Angeles County, See Los Angeles

VANDENBERG AFB—Santa Barbara County

✠ U. S. AIR FORCE HOSPITAL, 338 South Dakota, Zip 93437–6307; tel. 805/734–8232; Colonel Donald T. Davies, Commander (Nonreporting) **A**1 **S** Department of the Air Force, Bowling AFB, DC	41	10	8	—	—	—	—	—	—	—

VENICE—Los Angeles County

✠ DANIEL FREEMAN MARINA HOSPITAL, 4650 Lincoln Boulevard, Zip 90291–6360; tel. 310/823–8911; Joseph W. Dunn, Ph.D., Chief Executive Officer (Nonreporting) **A**1 9 10 **S** Carondelet Health System, Saint Louis, MO	21	10	179	—	—	—	—	—	—	—

VENTURA—Ventura County

□ BHC VISTA DEL MAR HOSPITAL, 801 Seneca Street, Zip 93001; tel. 805/653–6434; Jerry Conway, Chief Executive Officer **A**1 9 10 **F**1 2 3 18 19 26 35 52 53 54 55 56 57 58 59 65 67 **S** Behavioral Healthcare Corporation, Nashville, TN	33	22	89	2098	46	4542	0	7835	4402	145
✠ COMMUNITY MEMORIAL HOSPITAL OF SAN BUENAVENTURA, 147 North Brent Street, Zip 93003–2854; tel. 805/652–5011; Michael D. Bakst, Ph.D., Executive Director (Nonreporting) **A**1 9 10	23	10	217	—	—	—	—	—	—	—
□ VENTURA COUNTY MEDICAL CENTER, 3291 Loma Vista Road, Zip 93003; tel. 805/652–6058; Samuel Edwards, Associate Administrator Hospital Services (Nonreporting) **A**1 3 5 9 10	13	10	162	—	—	—	—	—	—	—

VICTORVILLE—San Bernardino County

□ DESERT VALLEY HOSPITAL, 16850 Bear Valley Road, Zip 92392; tel. 760/241–8000; David DeValk, Administrator **A**1 9 10 **F**1 3 4 5 6 7 8 10 11 12 13 14 15 16 17 18 19 20 21 22 23 24 25 26 27 28 29 30 31 32 33 34 35 36 37 39 40 41 42 43 44 45 46 49 50 51 53 54 55 56 57 58 59 60 61 62 63 65 66 67 69 70 71 72 73 74 **P**5 7	33	10	83	6037	46	27751	919	32950	11662	327
□ VICTOR VALLEY COMMUNITY HOSPITAL, 15248 11th Street, Zip 92392; tel. 760/245–8691; Joan Phillips, Interim Administrator (Nonreporting) **A**1 2 9 10	23	10	119	—	—	—	—	—	—	—

VISALIA—Tulare County

✠ KAWEAH DELTA HEALTH CARE DISTRICT, (Includes Community Health Center, 1633 South Court Street, Zip 93277, Mailing Address: Box 911, Zip 93277; tel. 209/625–7221; Lindsay K. Mann, Senior Vice President), 400 West Mineral King Avenue, Zip 93291; tel. 209/625–2211; Thomas M. Johnson, Chief Executive Officer (Total facility includes 51 beds in nursing home–type unit) **A**1 2 9 10 **F**4 7 8 10 12 14 16 17 19 21 22 23 24 25 26 27 28 29 30 31 32 33 34 35 37 39 40 41 42 43 44 45 46 48 49 51 52 57 58 59 60 64 65 67 71 72 73 74 **Web address:** www.kdhcd.org	16	10	252	15049	234	251718	3431	133657	60932	1928

WALNUT CREEK—Contra Costa County

□ BHC WALNUT CREEK HOSPITAL, 175 La Casa Via, Zip 94598; tel. 925/933–7990; Jay R. Kellison, Chief Executive Officer (Nonreporting) **A**1 9 10 **S** Behavioral Healthcare Corporation, Nashville, TN	33	22	108	—	—	—	—	—	—	—
✠ JM/MD HEALTH SYSTEM, (Includes John Muir Medical Center, 1601 Ygnacio Valley Road, Zip 94598–3194; tel. 925/939–3000; Martin H. Diamond, President and Chief Administrative Officer; Mount Diablo Medical Center, 2540 East Street, Concord, Zip 94520, Mailing Address: P.O. Box 4110, Zip 94524–4110; tel. 925/682–8200), 1400 Treat Boulevard, Zip 94556; tel. 925/941–2100; J. Kendall Anderson, President and Chief Executive Officer (Total facility includes 501 beds in nursing home–type unit) (Nonreporting) **A**1 2 9 10	23	10	946	—	—	—	—	—	—	—
✠ KAISER FOUNDATION HOSPITAL, (Includes Kaiser Foundation Hospital, 200 Muir Road, Martinez, Zip 94553–4696; tel. 510/372–1000), 1425 South Main Street, Zip 94596; tel. 925/295–4000; Sandra Small, Administrator **A**1 10 **F**2 3 4 7 8 9 10 11 12 13 14 15 16 17 19 21 22 25 26 28 29 30 31 32 33 34 35 37 38 40 41 42 43 44 45 46 47 48 49 50 51 52 53 54 55 56 57 58 59 60 61 62 63 64 65 67 68 71 72 73 74 **P**1 **S** Kaiser Foundation Hospitals, Oakland, CA	23	10	210	18462	156	131073	3684	—	—	—

WATSONVILLE—Santa Cruz County

□ WATSONVILLE COMMUNITY HOSPITAL, 75 Nielson Street, Zip 95076; tel. 831/724–4741; Barry S. Schneider, Chief Executive Officer (Total facility includes 13 beds in nursing home–type unit) (Nonreporting) **A**1 9 10 **S** Community Health Systems, Inc., Brentwood, TN **Web address:** www.watsonville.com\hospital	33	10	130	—	—	—	—	—	—	—

Hospital, Address, Telephone, Administrator, Approval, Facility, and Physician Codes, Health Care System, Network	Classi-fication Codes		Utilization Data					Expense (thousands) of dollars		
★ American Hospital Association (AHA) membership □ Joint Commission on Accreditation of Healthcare Organizations (JCAHO) accreditation + American Osteopathic Healthcare Association (AOHA) membership ○ American Osteopathic Association (AOA) accreditation △ Commission on Accreditation of Rehabilitation Facilities (CARF) accreditation Control codes 61, 63, 64, 71, 72 and 73 indicate hospitals listed by AOHA, but not registered by AHA. For definition of numerical codes, see page A4	Control	Service	Staffed Beds	Admissions	Census	Outpatient Visits	Births	Total	Payroll	Personnel
WEAVERVILLE—Trinity County										
TRINITY HOSPITAL, 410 North Taylor Street, Zip 96093, Mailing Address: P.O. Box 1229, Zip 96093–1229; tel. 916/623–5541; David L. Yarbrough, R.N., JD, Administrator, Chief Financial Officer and Director Patient Service (Total facility includes 26 beds in nursing home–type unit) **A**9 10 **F**7 8 12 14 15 16 17 19 22 26 27 28 29 30 31 32 39 40 44 45 64 65 67 68 71 73 74	13	10	65	1105	31	14442	74	7599	3270	134
WEST COVINA—Los Angeles County										
□ CITRUS VALLEY MEDICAL CENTER–QUEEN OF THE VALLEY CAMPUS, 1115 South Sunset Avenue, Zip 91790, Mailing Address: Box 1980, Zip 91793; tel. 626/962–4011; Peter E. Makowski, President and Chief Executive Officer (Nonreporting) **A**1 9 10 **S** Citrus Valley Health Partners, Covina, CA	23	10	263	—	—	—	—	—	—	—
COVINA VALLEY COMMUNITY HOSPITAL, 845 North Lark Ellen Avenue, Zip 91791; tel. 818/339–5451; John Hogue, Administrator (Nonreporting) **A**9	32	10	76	—	—	—	—	—	—	—
□ DOCTORS HOSPITAL OF WEST COVINA, 725 South Orange Avenue, Zip 91790–2614; tel. 626/338–8481; Gerald H. Wallman, Administrator (Total facility includes 24 beds in nursing home–type unit) (Nonreporting) **A**1 10	33	10	51	—	—	—	—	—	—	—
WEST HILLS—Los Angeles County, See Los Angeles										
WEST LOS ANGELES—Los Angeles County, See Los Angeles										
WHITTIER—Los Angeles County										
□ PRESBYTERIAN INTERCOMMUNITY HOSPITAL, 12401 Washington Boulevard, Zip 90602–1099; tel. 562/698–0811; Daniel F. Adams, President and Chief Executive Officer (Nonreporting) **A**1 2 3 5 9 10	23	10	312	—	—	—	—	—	—	—
✠ WHITTIER HOSPITAL MEDICAL CENTER, 9080 Colima Road, Zip 90605; tel. 562/907–1541; Sandra M. Chester, Chief Executive Officer (Total facility includes 39 beds in nursing home–type unit) (Nonreporting) **A**1 9 10 **S** TENET Healthcare Corporation, Santa Barbara, CA	33	10	172	—	—	—	—	—	—	—
WILDOMAR—Riverside County										
□ INLAND VALLEY REGIONAL MEDICAL CENTER, 36485 Inland Valley Drive, Zip 92595; tel. 909/677–1111; Christopher L. Boyd, Chief Executive Officer and Managing Director **A**1 9 10 **F**7 8 10 12 14 15 16 19 21 22 27 28 29 30 37 39 40 41 44 46 49 67 70 71 73 74 **S** Universal Health Services, Inc., King of Prussia, PA	33	10	80	6101	49	39434	1043	29181	15340	607
WILLITS—Mendocino County										
✠ FRANK R. HOWARD MEMORIAL HOSPITAL, 1 Madrone Street, Zip 95490; tel. 707/459–6801; Kevin R. Erich, President **A**1 9 10 **F**8 12 16 17 19 22 28 32 33 35 37 39 41 44 45 49 65 71 73 **P**3 **S** Adventist Health, Roseville, CA	23	10	28	952	9	22535	2	9997	4171	102
WILLOWS—Glenn County										
GLENN MEDICAL CENTER, 1133 West Sycamore Street, Zip 95988; tel. 530/934–1800; Bernard G. Hietpas, Chief Executive Officer (Nonreporting) **A**9 10	23	10	27	—	—	—	—	—	—	—
WINTERHAVEN—Imperial County										
✠ U. S. PUBLIC HEALTH SERVICE INDIAN HOSPITAL, Mailing Address: P.O. Box 1368, Yuma, AZ, Zip 85366–1368; tel. 760/572–0217; Hortense Miguel, R.N., Service Unit Director (Nonreporting) **A**1 10 **S** U. S. Public Health Service Indian Health Service, Rockville, MD	47	10	34	—	—	—	—	—	—	—
WOODLAND—Yolo County										
✠ WOODLAND HEALTHCARE, (Formerly Woodland Memorial Hospital), 1325 Cottonwood Street, Zip 95695–5199; tel. 530/662–3961; William Hunt, Chief Operating Officer (Nonreporting) **A**1 9 10 **S** Catholic Healthcare West, San Francisco, CA	23	10	103	—	—	—	—	—	—	—
WOODLAND HILLS—Los Angeles County, See Los Angeles										
YOUNTVILLE—Napa County										
VETERANS HOME OF CALIFORNIA, 100 California Drive, Zip 94599–1413; tel. 707/944–4500; James D. Helzer, Administrator (Total facility includes 514 beds in nursing home–type unit) (Nonreporting) **A**10	12	10	540	—	—	—	—	—	—	—
YREKA—Siskiyou County										
□ FAIRCHILD MEDICAL CENTER, 444 Bruce Street, Zip 96097; tel. 530/842–4121; Dwayne Jones, Chief Executive Officer **A**1 9 10 **F**7 8 14 15 16 17 19 22 30 32 35 37 40 44 46 48 49 63 71 73	23	10	20	1653	13	47349	175	16119	6825	227
YUBA CITY—Sutter County										
□ FREMONT MEDICAL CENTER, 970 Plumas Street, Zip 95991; tel. 530/751–4000; Thomas P. Hayes, Chief Executive Officer **A**1 9 10 **F**7 8 10 14 15 16 17 19 22 25 26 28 30 32 33 35 37 38 39 40 44 49 52 60 71 72 **S** Fremont-Rideout Health Group, Yuba City, CA	23	10	78	7449	71	41089	2147	41080	16490	405

COLORADO

Resident population 3,971 (in thousands)
Resident population in metro areas 80.9%
Birth rate per 1,000 population 14.5
65 years and over 10.1%
Percent of persons without health insurance 16.6%

Hospital, Address, Telephone, Administrator, Approval, Facility, and Physician Codes, Health Care System, Network	Classi-fication Codes		Utilization Data					Expense (thousands) of dollars		
★ American Hospital Association (AHA) membership ☐ Joint Commission on Accreditation of Healthcare Organizations (JCAHO) accreditation + American Osteopathic Healthcare Association (AOHA) membership ○ American Osteopathic Association (AOA) accreditation △ Commission on Accreditation of Rehabilitation Facilities (CARF) accreditation Control codes 61, 63, 64, 71, 72 and 73 indicate hospitals listed by AOHA, but not registered by AHA. For definition of numerical codes, see page A4	Control	Service	Staffed Beds	Admissions	Census	Outpatient Visits	Births	Total	Payroll	Personnel

ALAMOSA—Alamosa County

☒ SAN LUIS VALLEY REGIONAL MEDICAL CENTER, 106 Blanca Avenue, Zip 81101–2393; tel. 719/589–2511; Paul Herman, Chief Executive Officer **A**1 9 10 **F**6 7 8 12 14 15 16 17 18 19 20 21 22 23 25 26 27 28 29 30 31 32 33 34 35 37 39 40 41 42 44 45 46 49 51 53 54 55 56 57 58 59 61 62 65 66 67 69 70 71 72 73 74 **P**3
| | 21 | 10 | 85 | 2993 | 24 | 29401 | 603 | 15186 | 7018 | 196 |

ASPEN—Pitkin County

☒ ASPEN VALLEY HOSPITAL DISTRICT, 401 Castle Creek Road, Zip 81611–1159; tel. 970/925–1120; Randy Middlebrook, Chief Executive Officer and Administrator (Nonreporting) **A**1 9 10
Web address: www.avhaspen.org
| | 16 | 10 | 41 | — | — | — | — | — | — | — |

AURORA—Adams County

☒ AURORA REGIONAL MEDICAL CENTER, (Formerly Columbia Medical Center of Aurora), (Includes Columbia Regional Medical Center–South Campus, 1501 South Potomac, Zip 80012; North Campus and Columbia Aurora Presbyterian Transitional Care Center, 700 Potomac Street, Zip 80011–6792; tel. 303/363–7200), 1501 South Potomac Street, Zip 80012–5499; tel. 303/695–2600; Louis O. Garcia, President and Chief Executive Officer (Nonreporting) **A**1 2 9 10 **S** Columbia/HCA Healthcare Corporation, Nashville, TN
| | 33 | 10 | 334 | — | — | — | — | — | — | — |

☒ △ SPALDING REHABILITATION HOSPITAL, 900 Potomac Street, Zip 80011–6716; tel. 303/367–1166; Lynn Dawson, Chief Executive Officer **A**1 5 7 10 **F**14 16 45 46 48 49 64 66 67 **S** Columbia/HCA Healthcare Corporation, Nashville, TN
| | 33 | 46 | 138 | 2919 | 92 | 9479 | 0 | 28534 | 12891 | 360 |

BOULDER—Boulder County

☒ △ BOULDER COMMUNITY HOSPITAL, 1100 Balsam, Zip 80304–3496, Mailing Address: P.O. Box 9019, Zip 80301–9019; tel. 303/440–2273; David P. Gehant, President and Chief Executive Officer **A**1 2 7 9 10 **F**3 4 5 7 8 10 11 12 14 15 19 21 22 24 25 26 29 30 31 32 33 34 35 37 40 41 42 43 44 45 46 48 49 51 52 53 54 55 56 57 58 59 60 63 65 66 67 68 70 71 72 73 74 **P**6 7
Web address: www.bch.org
| | 23 | 10 | 197 | 9416 | 120 | 174625 | 1672 | 113537 | 51522 | 2093 |

BRIGHTON—Adams County

☒ PLATTE VALLEY MEDICAL CENTER, 1850 Egbert Street, Zip 80601–2404, Mailing Address: P.O. Box 98, Zip 80601–0098; tel. 303/659–1531; John R. Hicks, President and Chief Executive Officer **A**1 9 10 **F**7 8 11 12 14 15 16 17 19 21 22 24 27 28 30 32 34 35 37 39 40 41 42 44 46 49 51 64 65 66 67 71 73 **P**8
| | 23 | 10 | 49 | 2026 | 17 | 27227 | 678 | 18162 | 8084 | 251 |

BRUSH—Morgan County

★ EAST MORGAN COUNTY HOSPITAL, 2400 West Edison Street, Zip 80723–1640; tel. 970/842–5151; Anne Platt, Administrator **A**9 10 **F**3 8 15 16 17 19 22 24 26 28 29 30 32 33 34 35 39 41 42 44 45 46 49 51 58 64 66 70 71 72 73 **P**5 8 **S** Lutheran Health Systems, Fargo, ND
| | 23 | 10 | 24 | 465 | 5 | — | 0 | — | — | 77 |

BURLINGTON—Kit Carson County

★ KIT CARSON COUNTY MEMORIAL HOSPITAL, 286 16th Street, Zip 80807–1697; tel. 719/346–5311; James Jordan, Chief Executive Officer **A**9 10 **F**7 8 10 12 14 15 16 17 19 21 22 28 29 30 32 33 34 35 40 42 44 45 49 51 64 67 70 71
| | 16 | 10 | 24 | 538 | 7 | 9778 | 85 | 4231 | 2021 | 94 |

CANON CITY—Fremont County

☒ ST. THOMAS MORE HOSPITAL AND PROGRESSIVE CARE CENTER, 1338 Phay Avenue, Zip 81212–2221; tel. 719/269–2000; C. Ray Honaker, Chief Executive Officer (Total facility includes 163 beds in nursing home–type unit) (Nonreporting) **A**1 9 10 **S** Catholic Health Initiatives, Denver, CO
Web address: www.centura.org
| | 21 | 10 | 218 | — | — | — | — | — | — | — |

CHEYENNE WELLS—Cheyenne County

★ KEEFE MEMORIAL HOSPITAL, 602 North Sixth Street West, Zip 80810, Mailing Address: P.O. Box 578, Zip 80810–0578; tel. 719/767–5661; Curtis Hawkinson, Chief Executive Officer **A**9 10 **F**8 12 14 15 16 17 19 22 26 27 28 30 32 34 35 36 39 42 44 45 46 49 53 54 58 64 65 71 73 74 **P**6
Web address: www.yampa.com/npo/hprhn/keefe/keefe.htm
| | 13 | 10 | 12 | 185 | 2 | 9298 | 0 | 2698 | 1494 | 58 |

COLORADO SPRINGS—El Paso County

☐ CEDAR SPRINGS PSYCHIATRIC HOSPITAL, 2135 Southgate Road, Zip 80906–2693; tel. 719/633–4114; Connie Mull, Chief Executive Officer **A**1 9 10 **F**1 2 3 12 15 20 26 46 52 53 54 55 56 57 58 59 65 67 **S** Healthcare America, Inc., Austin, TX
Web address: www.brownschools.com
| | 33 | 22 | 100 | 1075 | 77 | 9305 | 0 | — | — | 118 |

☒ MEMORIAL HOSPITAL, 1400 East Boulder Street, Zip 80909–5599, Mailing Address: Box 1326, Zip 80901–1326; tel. 719/365–5000; J. Robert Peters, Executive Director **A**1 2 9 10 **F**4 7 8 10 11 12 14 15 16 17 19 21 22 26 28 29 30 31 32 34 35 37 38 39 40 41 42 43 44 45 46 47 48 49 51 60 61 63 65 67 70 71 73 74 **P**5
Web address: www.memorialhospital.com
| | 14 | 10 | 334 | 18343 | 255 | 237023 | 2643 | 191395 | 89375 | 2629 |

Hospital, Address, Telephone, Administrator, Approval, Facility, and Physician Codes, Health Care System, Network	Classi-fication Codes		Utilization Data					Expense (thousands) of dollars		
★ American Hospital Association (AHA) membership □ Joint Commission on Accreditation of Healthcare Organizations (JCAHO) accreditation + American Osteopathic Healthcare Association (AOHA) membership ○ American Osteopathic Association (AOA) accreditation △ Commission on Accreditation of Rehabilitation Facilities (CARF) accreditation Control codes 61, 63, 64, 71, 72 and 73 indicate hospitals listed by AOHA, but not registered by AHA. For definition of numerical codes, see page A4	Control	Service	Staffed Beds	Admissions	Census	Outpatient Visits	Births	Total	Payroll	Personnel

Hospital	Control	Service	Staffed Beds	Admissions	Census	Outpatient Visits	Births	Total	Payroll	Personnel
✠ △ PENROSE–ST. FRANCIS HEALTH SERVICES, (Includes Penrose Community Hospital, 3205 North Academy Boulevard, Zip 80917; tel. 719/776–3000; Penrose Hospital, 2215 North Cascade Avenue, Zip 80907; tel. 719/776–5000; St Francis Health Center, 825 East Pikes Peak Avenue, Zip 80903; tel. 719/776–8800), Donna L. Bertram, R.N., Administrator **A**1 2 3 5 7 9 10 **F**1 3 4 5 6 7 8 10 11 12 13 14 15 16 17 18 19 20 21 22 23 24 26 27 28 29 30 31 32 33 34 35 37 38 39 40 41 42 43 44 45 46 48 49 51 52 53 54 55 56 57 58 60 61 62 63 64 65 66 67 68 70 71 72 73 74 **P**5 7 **S** Catholic Health Initiatives, Denver, CO	21	10	423	20335	274	232851	3053	168466	72969	2354
CORTEZ—Montezuma County										
✠ SOUTHWEST MEMORIAL HOSPITAL, 1311 North Mildred Road, Zip 81321–2299; tel. 970/565–6666; Bob Peterson, Chief Executive Officer **A**1 9 10 **F**7 8 12 14 15 16 17 19 20 22 27 30 31 32 35 36 37 39 40 41 44 45 46 49 65 67 70 71 73 **P**3 7 8 **S** Quorum Health Group/Quorum Health Resources, Inc., Brentwood, TN	23	10	42	2464	20	27926	279	20211	8752	268
CRAIG—Moffat County										
✠ MEMORIAL HOSPITAL, 785 Russell Street, Zip 81625–9906; tel. 970/824–9411; M. Randell Phelps, Administrator **A**1 9 10 **F**7 8 14 15 16 17 19 21 22 28 30 31 35 37 39 40 41 42 44 49 56 64 65 67 70 71 73 **P**8 **S** Quorum Health Group/Quorum Health Resources, Inc., Brentwood, TN	13	10	29	1011	9	15978	121	10122	4178	108
DELTA—Delta County										
✠ DELTA COUNTY MEMORIAL HOSPITAL, 100 Stafford Lane, Zip 81416–2297, Mailing Address: P.O. Box 10100, Zip 81416–5003; tel. 970/874–7681; Jerry Cantwell, Administrator **A**1 9 10 **F**7 8 14 19 21 22 28 33 35 37 40 41 44 46 49 65 70 71 **P**5 8 **S** Presbyterian Healthcare Services, Albuquerque, NM	16	10	44	2090	19	33629	214	14326	6531	263
DENVER—Denver, Adams and Arapahoe Counties										
□ CENTURA SPECIAL CARE HOSPITAL, 1601 North Lowell Boulevard, Zip 80204–1597; tel. 303/899–5170; Silas M. Weir, Chief Executive Officer (Nonreporting) **A**1	23	10	24	—	—	—	—	—	—	—
✠ CHILDREN'S HOSPITAL, 1056 East 19th Avenue, Zip 80218–1088; tel. 303/861–8888; Doris J. Biester, R.N., President and Chief Executive Officer **A**1 3 5 9 10 **F**4 5 9 10 12 13 14 15 16 17 18 19 20 21 22 25 28 29 31 32 34 35 38 39 41 42 43 44 45 46 47 49 51 52 53 54 55 56 58 59 60 65 67 68 70 71 72 73 **P**4 7 **Web address:** www.tchden.org	23	50	198	7969	141	246562	0	167292	75347	1934
□ COLORADO MENTAL HEALTH INSTITUTE AT FORT LOGAN, 3520 West Oxford Avenue, Zip 80236–3197; tel. 303/761–0220; Allan Brock Willett, M.D., Director (Nonreporting) **A**1 9 10	12	22	315	—	—	—	—	—	—	—
COLUMBIA PRESBYTERIAN–ST LUKE'S MEDICAL CENTER See Presbyterian–St. Luke's Medical Center										
□ DENVER HEALTH MEDICAL CENTER, 777 Bannock Street, Zip 80204–4507; tel. 303/436–6000; Patricia A. Gabow, M.D., Chief Executive Officer and Medical Director **A**1 3 5 9 10 **F**2 3 4 7 8 10 11 12 13 14 15 16 17 19 20 21 22 25 26 27 29 30 31 32 34 35 37 38 39 40 41 42 43 44 46 47 48 49 51 52 53 54 56 58 59 60 61 63 65 66 67 68 69 70 71 72 73 74 **P**6	16	10	303	15568	199	518746	2774	257626	128222	2822
✠ EXEMPLA SAINT JOSEPH HOSPITAL, 1835 Franklin Street, Zip 80218–1191; tel. 303/837–7111; Jeffrey D. Selberg, President and Chief Executive Officer **A**1 2 3 9 10 **F**3 4 7 8 10 11 12 15 17 19 21 22 23 24 25 26 29 32 33 34 35 37 38 40 41 42 43 44 45 46 49 51 52 53 54 56 57 58 59 60 64 65 67 70 71 73 74 **P**5 6 **S** Exempla Healthcare, Inc., Denver, CO	21	10	404	24657	260	328871	5503	174242	83836	1519
✠ NATIONAL JEWISH MEDICAL AND RESEARCH CENTER, 1400 Jackson Street, Zip 80206–2762; tel. 303/388–4461; Lynn M. Taussig, M.D., President and Chief Executive Officer (Nonreporting) **A**1 3 5 9 10 **Web address:** www.nationaljewish.org	23	49	58	—	—	—	—	—	—	—
✠ PORTER ADVENTIST HOSPITAL, 2525 South Downing Street, Zip 80210–5876; tel. 303/778–1955; Ruthita J. Fike, Administrator (Total facility includes 34 beds in nursing home–type unit) (Nonreporting) **A**1 2 9 10 **Web address:** www.centura.org	21	10	339	—	—	—	—	—	—	—
✠ PRECEDENT HEALTH CENTER, 1650 Fillmore Street, Zip 80206; tel. 303/226–2000; Jeffrey Mishell, M.D., Chief Executive Officer **A**1 10 **F**7 8 12 17 19 21 22 26 28 29 30 32 33 35 37 39 40 44 45 46 49 56 61 65 71 72 73 74 **P**7	33	10	39	387	7	4866	205	—	4585	—
PRESBYTERIAN–DENVER HOSPITAL See Presbyterian–St. Luke's Medical Center										
✠ △ PRESBYTERIAN–ST. LUKE'S MEDICAL CENTER, (Formerly Columbia Presbyterian–St Luke's Medical Center), (Includes Presbyterian–Denver Hospital, 1719 East 19th Avenue, Zip 80218–1124; tel. 303/839–6565), 1719 East 19th Avenue, Zip 80218–1281; tel. 303/839–6000; Kevin Gross, Chief Executive Officer **A**1 2 3 5 7 9 10 13 **F**1 2 3 4 5 6 7 8 10 12 13 14 15 16 17 18 19 21 22 23 24 25 26 27 28 29 30 33 34 35 36 37 38 39 40 41 42 43 44 45 46 47 48 49 51 52 53 56 58 59 60 61 63 64 65 66 67 68 70 71 72 73 74 **P**7 **S** Columbia/HCA Healthcare Corporation, Nashville, TN	32	10	442	14365	246	88977	1726	161179	62536	1192
✠ △ ROSE MEDICAL CENTER, 4567 East Ninth Avenue, Zip 80220–3941; tel. 303/320–2121; Kenneth H. Feiler, President and Chief Executive Officer (Nonreporting) **A**1 2 3 5 7 9 10 **S** Columbia/HCA Healthcare Corporation, Nashville, TN **Web address:** www.rosebabies.com	33	10	250	—	—	—	—	—	—	—

Hospital, Address, Telephone, Administrator, Approval, Facility, and Physician Codes, Health Care System, Network	Classification Codes		Utilization Data					Expense (thousands) of dollars		
	Control	Service	Staffed Beds	Admissions	Census	Outpatient Visits	Births	Total	Payroll	Personnel

★ American Hospital Association (AHA) membership
□ Joint Commission on Accreditation of Healthcare Organizations (JCAHO) accreditation
+ American Osteopathic Healthcare Association (AOHA) membership
○ American Osteopathic Association (AOA) accreditation
△ Commission on Accreditation of Rehabilitation Facilities (CARF) accreditation
Control codes 61, 63, 64, 71, 72 and 73 indicate hospitals listed by AOHA, but not registered by AHA. For definition of numerical codes, see page A4

Hospital	Control	Service	Staffed Beds	Admissions	Census	Outpatient Visits	Births	Total	Payroll	Personnel
✠ ST. ANTHONY CENTRAL HOSPITAL, 4231 West 16th Avenue, Zip 80204–4098; tel. 303/629–3511; Matthew S. Fulton, Senior Vice President and Administrator **A**1 2 3 5 9 10 **F**1 2 4 6 7 8 9 10 11 12 14 15 17 19 21 22 24 26 28 32 33 35 37 38 40 42 43 44 46 47 48 49 51 52 57 60 62 64 65 70 71 73 74 **P**7 **S** Catholic Health Initiatives, Denver, CO	21	10	302	16885	191	68966	1459	137386	55225	—
✠ UNIVERSITY OF COLORADO HOSPITAL, 4200 East Ninth Avenue, Zip 80262; tel. 303/372–0000; Dennis C. Brimhall, President **A**1 2 3 5 8 9 10 **F**3 4 5 7 8 9 10 12 14 15 16 17 18 19 20 21 25 26 28 29 30 31 34 35 37 38 39 40 41 42 43 44 45 46 48 49 51 53 54 55 56 58 59 60 61 63 64 65 66 67 68 70 71 72 73 74 **P**4 7 Web address: www.uchsc.edu/uh/	16	10	327	13684	190	320415	1706	222039	83249	2362
✠ △ VETERANS AFFAIRS MEDICAL CENTER, 1055 Clermont Street, Zip 80220–3877; tel. 303/399–8020; Edgar Thorsland, Jr., Director **A**1 2 3 5 7 8 **F**4 8 10 12 14 16 17 19 20 21 22 24 25 26 27 31 32 33 34 35 37 41 42 43 44 46 48 49 51 52 54 56 57 58 59 60 64 65 67 69 71 72 73 74 **S** Department of Veterans Affairs, Washington, DC	45	10	228	5382	133	269782	0	140957	62657	1675

DURANGO—La Plata County

Hospital	Control	Service	Staffed Beds	Admissions	Census	Outpatient Visits	Births	Total	Payroll	Personnel
✠ MERCY MEDICAL CENTER, 375 East Park Avenue, Zip 81301; tel. 970/247–4311; Kirk Dignum, Administrator (Total facility includes 10 beds in nursing home–type unit) **A**1 2 9 10 **F**4 7 8 10 11 12 14 15 16 17 19 20 21 22 24 28 29 30 32 33 34 35 36 37 38 39 40 41 44 46 47 48 49 51 52 53 56 58 60 64 65 66 67 70 71 72 73 74 **P**1 4 5 6 7 8 **S** Catholic Health Initiatives, Denver, CO Web address: www.mercydurango.org	21	10	81	3986	42	88416	591	52292	26716	635

EADS—Kiowa County

Hospital	Control	Service	Staffed Beds	Admissions	Census	Outpatient Visits	Births	Total	Payroll	Personnel
★ WEISBROD MEMORIAL COUNTY HOSPITAL, (Formerly Weisbrod Memorial Hospital), 1208 Luther Street, Zip 81036, Mailing Address: P.O. Box 817, Zip 81036–0817; tel. 719/438–5401; Marvin O. Bishop, Administrator (Total facility includes 34 beds in nursing home–type unit) **A**9 10 **F**14 22 27 32 34 36 48 49 51 64 65 **P**6	16	10	42	116	26	11650	0	2387	1625	67

ENGLEWOOD—Arapahoe County

Hospital	Control	Service	Staffed Beds	Admissions	Census	Outpatient Visits	Births	Total	Payroll	Personnel
✠ △ CRAIG HOSPITAL, 3425 South Clarkson Street, Zip 80110–2899; tel. 303/789–8000; Dennis O'Malley, President **A**1 7 9 10 **F**12 14 15 16 17 19 20 21 22 23 24 34 35 39 41 44 45 46 48 49 50 60 63 65 67 70 71 73 Web address: www.craighospital.org	23	46	76	491	68	5968	0	33531	14581	426
✠ SWEDISH MEDICAL CENTER, 501 East Hampden Avenue, Zip 80110–0101; tel. 303/788–5000; Mary M. White, President and Chief Executive Officer **A**1 2 3 5 9 10 **F**1 3 4 5 6 10 12 13 14 15 16 17 18 19 20 21 22 23 24 25 26 27 28 29 30 31 33 34 35 37 38 39 40 41 42 43 44 45 46 48 49 53 54 55 56 57 58 59 60 61 62 63 64 65 66 67 68 70 71 72 73 74 **P**6 **S** Columbia/HCA Healthcare Corporation, Nashville, TN Web address: www.swedishhospital.com	32	10	349	18327	233	136637	2630	147813	57467	1415

ESTES PARK—Larimer County

Hospital	Control	Service	Staffed Beds	Admissions	Census	Outpatient Visits	Births	Total	Payroll	Personnel
★ ESTES PARK MEDICAL CENTER, 555 Prospect Avenue, Zip 80517, Mailing Address: P.O. Box 2740, Zip 80517; tel. 970/586–2317; Andrew Wills, Chief Executive Officer (Total facility includes 60 beds in nursing home–type unit) **A**9 10 **F**7 8 20 26 28 29 40 44 49 62 64 71 **P**7	16	10	76	556	49	25078	52	9685	4669	188

FORT CARSON—El Paso County

Hospital	Control	Service	Staffed Beds	Admissions	Census	Outpatient Visits	Births	Total	Payroll	Personnel
✠ EVANS U. S. ARMY COMMUNITY HOSPITAL, Zip 80913–5101; tel. 719/526–7200; Lieutenant Colonel Michael D. Wheeler, MSC, Deputy Commander, Administration **A**1 2 **F**3 4 7 8 9 10 11 12 13 15 16 17 19 20 22 24 25 26 28 29 30 31 34 37 38 39 40 41 42 43 44 45 46 47 49 51 52 53 54 55 56 57 58 59 60 61 65 66 67 68 70 71 72 73 74 **P**4 5 6 7 **S** Department of the Army, Office of the Surgeon General, Falls Church, VA	42	10	117	3076	23	363674	1185	57393	21598	1133

FORT COLLINS—Larimer County

MOUNTAIN CREST HOSPITAL See Poudre Valley Hospital

Hospital	Control	Service	Staffed Beds	Admissions	Census	Outpatient Visits	Births	Total	Payroll	Personnel
✠ POUDRE VALLEY HOSPITAL, (Includes Mountain Crest Hospital, 4601 Corbett Drive, Zip 80525; tel. 970/225–9191), 1024 South Lemay Avenue, Zip 80524; tel. 970/495–7000; Rulon F. Stacey, President and Chief Executive Officer (Nonreporting) **A**1 2 3 9 10	23	10	266	—	—	—	—	—	—	—

FORT MORGAN—Morgan County

Hospital	Control	Service	Staffed Beds	Admissions	Census	Outpatient Visits	Births	Total	Payroll	Personnel
✠ COLORADO PLAINS MEDICAL CENTER, 1000 Lincoln Street, Zip 80701–3298; tel. 970/867–3391; Thomas Thomson, Chief Executive Officer (Nonreporting) **A**1 9 10 **S** Province Healthcare Corporation, Brentwood, TN	33	10	40	—	—	—	—	—	—	—

FRUITA—Mesa County

Hospital	Control	Service	Staffed Beds	Admissions	Census	Outpatient Visits	Births	Total	Payroll	Personnel
FAMILY HEALTH WEST, 228 North Cherry Street, Zip 81521–2101, Mailing Address: P.O. Box 130, Zip 81521–0130; tel. 303/858–9871; Dennis E. Ficklin, Chief Executive Officer (Total facility includes 352 beds in nursing home–type unit) (Nonreporting) **A**9 10	23	10	358	—	—	—	—	—	—	—

GLENWOOD SPRINGS—Garfield County

Hospital	Control	Service	Staffed Beds	Admissions	Census	Outpatient Visits	Births	Total	Payroll	Personnel
✠ VALLEY VIEW HOSPITAL, 1906 Blake Avenue, Zip 81601–4259, Mailing Address: P.O. Box 1970, Zip 81602–1970; tel. 970/945–6535; Gary L. Brewer, Chief Executive Officer **A**1 9 10 **F**2 7 8 12 15 16 19 21 22 32 33 34 35 36 37 38 39 40 41 42 44 46 48 49 63 65 66 70 71 73 **P**5 **S** Quorum Health Group/Quorum Health Resources, Inc., Brentwood, TN Web address: www.vvh.com	23	10	54	2591	27	24884	515	31703	13486	364

Hospital, Address, Telephone, Administrator, Approval, Facility, and Physician Codes, Health Care System, Network	Classi-fication Codes		Utilization Data					Expense (thousands) of dollars		
	Control	Service	Staffed Beds	Admissions	Census	Outpatient Visits	Births	Total	Payroll	Personnel

★ American Hospital Association (AHA) membership
□ Joint Commission on Accreditation of Healthcare Organizations (JCAHO) accreditation
+ American Osteopathic Healthcare Association (AOHA) membership
○ American Osteopathic Association (AOA) accreditation
△ Commission on Accreditation of Rehabilitation Facilities (CARF) accreditation
Control codes 61, 63, 64, 71, 72 and 73 indicate hospitals listed by AOHA, but not registered by AHA. For definition of numerical codes, see page A4

Hospital	Control	Service	Staffed Beds	Admissions	Census	Outpatient Visits	Births	Total	Payroll	Personnel
GRAND JUNCTION—Mesa County										
□ + ○ COMMUNITY HOSPITAL, 2021 North 12th Street, Zip 81501–2999; tel. 970/242–0920; Randy Phillips, Chief Executive Officer (Nonreporting) **A**1 9 10 11 Web address: www.gjhosp.org	23	10	51	—	—	—	—	—	—	—
✠ ST. MARY'S HOSPITAL AND MEDICAL CENTER, 2635 North 7th Street, Zip 81501–8204, Mailing Address: P.O. Box 1628, Zip 81502–1628; tel. 970/244–2273; Kenneth Tomlon, Interim Chief Executive Officer (Total facility includes 30 beds in nursing home–type unit) **A**1 2 3 9 10 **F**1 2 3 4 5 7 8 9 10 11 12 13 14 15 16 17 18 19 20 21 22 23 24 25 26 27 28 29 30 31 32 33 34 35 36 37 38 39 40 41 42 43 44 45 46 48 49 51 52 53 54 55 56 57 58 59 60 61 64 65 66 67 68 70 71 72 73 74 **P**3 6 **S** Sisters of Charity of Leavenworth Health Services Corporation, Leavenworth, KS	33	10	281	13337	175	325323	1354	127253	56939	1681
✠ VETERANS AFFAIRS MEDICAL CENTER, 2121 North Avenue, Zip 81501–6499; tel. 970/242–0731; Kurt W. Schlegelmilch, M.D., Director (Total facility includes 30 beds in nursing home–type unit) **A**1 **F**3 4 8 10 12 14 15 16 17 19 20 21 22 26 28 29 30 31 32 33 34 35 37 39 41 42 43 44 45 46 49 51 52 54 56 57 58 59 60 64 65 67 71 73 74 **P**6 **S** Department of Veterans Affairs, Washington, DC	45	10	53	1267	48	66187	0	28542	13443	325
GREELEY—Weld County										
✠ NORTH COLORADO MEDICAL CENTER, 1801 16th Street, Zip 80631–5199; tel. 970/352–4121; Karl B. Gills, Administrator **A**1 2 3 9 10 **F**2 3 4 7 8 9 10 12 14 15 16 17 19 21 22 23 25 26 27 28 29 30 31 32 33 34 35 37 39 40 41 42 43 44 45 46 48 49 51 52 53 54 55 56 57 58 59 60 63 64 65 66 67 70 71 73 74 **P**5 7 **S** Lutheran Health Systems, Fargo, ND	23	10	262	12806	149	241945	1912	129630	54421	1463
GUNNISON—Gunnison County										
GUNNISON VALLEY HOSPITAL, 214 East Denver Avenue, Zip 81230–2296; tel. 970/641–1456; Robert S. Austin, President **A**9 10 **F**7 8 9 12 14 15 16 17 19 20 22 28 29 32 34 35 37 40 41 44 46 49 66 70 71 Web address: www.montrose.net/gvh/	13	10	22	580	4	24499	134	5113	2864	86
HAXTUN—Phillips County										
★ HAXTUN HOSPITAL DISTRICT, 235 West Fletcher Street, Zip 80731–0308, Mailing Address: Box 308, Zip 80731–0308; tel. 970/774–6123; James E. Brundige, Administrator (Total facility includes 32 beds in nursing home–type unit) (Nonreporting) **A**9 10	16	10	48	—	—	—	—	—	—	—
HOLYOKE—Phillips County										
★ MELISSA MEMORIAL HOSPITAL, 505 South Baxter Avenue, Zip 80734–1496; tel. 970/854–2241; George V. Larson, II, Chief Executive Officer **A**9 10 **F**7 8 14 15 17 19 20 22 24 27 28 30 32 34 40 41 44 45 49 51 64 70 71 **P**3 6	16	10	18	317	5	10878	39	3998	1909	85
HUGO—Lincoln County										
★ LINCOLN COMMUNITY HOSPITAL AND NURSING HOME, 111 Sixth Street, Zip 80821, Mailing Address: P.O. Box 248, Zip 80821–0248; tel. 719/743–2421; Herman Schreivogel, Administrator and Chief Executive Officer (Total facility includes 35 beds in nursing home–type unit) **A**9 10 **F**7 19 32 35 41 44 49 52 64 70 71	13	10	56	490	31	12767	38	4743	2186	113
JULESBURG—Sedgwick County										
SEDGWICK COUNTY HEALTH CENTER, 900 Cedar Street, Zip 80737–1199; tel. 970/474–3323; Bill Patten, Administrator (Total facility includes 32 beds in nursing home–type unit) **A**9 10 **F**1 6 7 8 11 14 15 16 19 20 22 24 28 29 30 32 33 34 35 37 39 40 42 44 45 46 49 51 53 54 55 56 57 58 59 60 64 65 71 **P**1	13	10	66	245	33	6363	27	3892	1862	102
KREMMLING—Grand County										
KREMMLING MEMORIAL HOSPITAL, Fourth and Grand Avenue, Zip 80459, Mailing Address: P.O. Box 399, Zip 80459–0399; tel. 970/724–3442; Thomas Andron, Chief Executive Officer **A**9 10 **F**8 14 15 16 24 28 34 39 42 44 51 70 71 73 **P**6	16	10	19	146	10	19860	0	3302	1873	61
LA JARA—Conejos County										
□ CONEJOS COUNTY HOSPITAL, Mailing Address: P.O. Box 639, Zip 81140–0639; tel. 719/274–5121; Richard Cormier, Ph.D., Chief Executive Officer (Total facility includes 34 beds in nursing home–type unit) **A**1 9 10 **F**7 13 14 15 16 19 22 28 30 32 33 40 42 44 46 49 51 64 65 70 71 73 **P**1	16	10	49	964	39	1821	36	6121	3473	133
LA JUNTA—Otero County										
✠ ARKANSAS VALLEY REGIONAL MEDICAL CENTER, 1100 Carson Avenue, Zip 81050–2799; tel. 719/383–6000; Lynn Crowell, Chief Executive Officer (Total facility includes 115 beds in nursing home–type unit) **A**1 9 10 **F**7 8 10 12 15 17 19 22 23 25 28 30 32 33 34 35 37 39 40 41 42 44 46 49 64 65 67 70 71 **S** Quorum Health Group/Quorum Health Resources, Inc., Brentwood, TN	23	10	182	3001	148	75549	317	23275	11316	443
LAMAR—Prowers County										
✠ PROWERS MEDICAL CENTER, 401 Kendall Drive, Zip 81052–3993; tel. 719/336–4343; Earl J. Steinhoff, Chief Executive Officer **A**1 9 10 **F**1 2 3 4 5 7 8 9 10 11 14 15 16 17 19 20 21 22 23 25 26 27 28 29 30 32 33 34 35 36 37 38 39 40 41 42 43 44 45 46 47 48 49 50 51 52 53 54 55 56 57 58 59 60 61 63 64 65 66 67 69 70 71 73 74 **S** Quorum Health Group/Quorum Health Resources, Inc., Brentwood, TN	16	10	40	1664	13	25292	268	13435	6656	214
LEADVILLE—Lake County										
ST. VINCENT GENERAL HOSPITAL, 822 West Fourth Street, Zip 80461–3897; tel. 719/486–0230; Phillip Lowe, Chief Executive Officer (Nonreporting) **A**9 10	16	10	31	—	—	—	—	—	—	—

Hospital, Address, Telephone, Administrator, Approval, Facility, and Physician Codes, Health Care System, Network	Classi-fication Codes		Utilization Data					Expense (thousands) of dollars		
	Control	Service	Staffed Beds	Admissions	Census	Outpatient Visits	Births	Total	Payroll	Personnel

★ American Hospital Association (AHA) membership
☐ Joint Commission on Accreditation of Healthcare Organizations (JCAHO) accreditation
+ American Osteopathic Healthcare Association (AOHA) membership
◯ American Osteopathic Association (AOA) accreditation
△ Commission on Accreditation of Rehabilitation Facilities (CARF) accreditation
Control codes 61, 63, 64, 71, 72 and 73 indicate hospitals listed by AOHA, but not registered by AHA. For definition of numerical codes, see page A4

LITTLETON—Arapahoe County

	Control	Service	Staffed Beds	Admissions	Census	Outpatient Visits	Births	Total	Payroll	Personnel
★ LITTLETON ADVENTIST HOSPITAL, 7700 South Broadway Street, Zip 80122–2628; tel. 303/730–8900; Ruthita J. Fike, Administrator (Nonreporting) **A**9	21	10	106	—	—	—	—	—	—	—

LONGMONT—Boulder County

✠ △ LONGMONT UNITED HOSPITAL, 1950 West Mountain View Avenue, Zip 80501–3162, Mailing Address: Box 1659, Zip 80502–1659; tel. 303/651–5111; Kenneth R. Huey, President and Chief Executive Officer (Total facility includes 15 beds in nursing home–type unit) **A**1 2 7 9 10 **F**1 3 7 8 10 12 14 15 16 17 19 20 21 22 24 25 26 27 28 29 30 31 32 33 34 35 37 39 40 41 42 44 45 46 48 49 52 53 54 55 56 57 58 59 60 64 65 66 67 68 70 71 73 **P**8 **Web address:** www.luhonline.org	23	10	122	5878	64	220766	955	52332	22933	725

LOUISVILLE—Boulder County

✠ AVISTA ADVENTIST HOSPITAL, 100 Health Park Drive, Zip 80027–9583; tel. 303/673–1000; John Sackett, Administrator (Nonreporting) **A**1 3 9 10	21	10	58	—	—	—	—	—	—	—
☐ CHARTER CENTENNIAL PEAKS BEHAVIORAL HEALTH SYSTEM, 2255 South 88th Street, Zip 80027–9716; tel. 303/673–9990; Sharon Worsham, Administrator (Nonreporting) **A**1 9 10 **S** Magellan Health Services, Atlanta, GA	33	22	72	—	—	—	—	—	—	—

LOVELAND—Larimer County

✠ MCKEE MEDICAL CENTER, 2000 Boise Avenue, Zip 80538–4281; tel. 970/669–4640; Charles F. Harms, Administrator (Total facility includes 16 beds in nursing home–type unit) **A**1 9 10 **F**1 7 8 12 14 15 16 17 18 19 21 22 23 28 29 30 32 34 35 37 39 40 41 42 44 45 46 48 49 55 64 65 66 67 70 71 73 74 **P**7 8 **S** Lutheran Health Systems, Fargo, ND	23	10	108	5401	57	56634	685	41941	19915	700

MEEKER—Rio Blanco County

★ PIONEERS HOSPITAL OF RIO BLANCO COUNTY, (Includes Walbridge Memorial Convalescent Wing), 345 Cleveland Street, Zip 81641–0000; tel. 970/878–5047; Thomas E. Lake, Chief Executive Officer (Total facility includes 29 beds in nursing home–type unit) **A**9 10 **F**1 22 24 27 36 44 49 64 70 71 **P**8 **S** Quorum Health Group/Quorum Health Resources, Inc., Brentwood, TN	13	10	46	265	31	6400	2	5026	2259	85

MONTROSE—Montrose County

✠ MONTROSE MEMORIAL HOSPITAL, 800 South Third Street, Zip 81401–4291; tel. 970/249–2211; Jan V. Carrell, Chief Executive Officer and Administrator **A**1 9 10 **F**2 3 7 8 11 12 14 15 16 17 18 19 20 21 22 23 24 26 28 29 30 33 34 35 37 39 40 41 42 44 45 46 47 48 49 52 53 54 55 56 57 58 59 63 65 66 67 68 70 71 72 73 74 **P**5 8 **S** Quorum Health Group/Quorum Health Resources, Inc., Brentwood, TN	13	10	63	2724	28	70461	442	25453	11670	363

PUEBLO—Pueblo County

☐ COLORADO MENTAL HEALTH INSTITUTE AT PUEBLO, 1600 West 24th Street, Zip 81003–1499; tel. 719/546–4000; Robert L. Hawkins, Superintendent (Nonreporting) **A**1 9 10	12	22	605	—	—	—	—	—	—	—
✠ △ PARKVIEW MEDICAL CENTER, 400 West 16th Street, Zip 81003–2781; tel. 719/584–4000; C. W. Smith, President and Chief Executive Officer (Total facility includes 9 beds in nursing home–type unit) **A**1 7 9 10 **F**1 2 3 4 7 8 10 12 14 15 16 17 18 19 21 22 23 26 28 30 31 32 35 37 39 40 41 42 43 44 45 46 48 49 52 53 54 55 56 57 58 59 64 65 66 70 71 73 **P**7 8 **S** Quorum Health Group/Quorum Health Resources, Inc., Brentwood, TN **Web address:** www.parkviewmc.com	23	10	260	10536	146	93681	1165	85954	38714	1319
✠ ST. MARY–CORWIN MEDICAL CENTER, 1008 Minnequa Avenue, Zip 81004–3798; tel. 719/560–4000; John D. Julius, Interim Administrator (Total facility includes 16 beds in nursing home–type unit) (Nonreporting) **A**1 2 3 9 10 **S** Catholic Health Initiatives, Denver, CO	21	10	261	—	—	—	—	—	—	—

RANGELY—Rio Blanco County

★ RANGELY DISTRICT HOSPITAL, 511 South White Avenue, Zip 81648–2104; tel. 970/675–5011; Merrill A. Frank, Chief Executive Officer (Total facility includes 16 beds in nursing home–type unit) **A**9 10 **F**8 13 15 22 28 30 32 34 36 39 44 46 49 51 70 71 **P**6	16	10	25	71	14	15902	0	3352	1828	57

RIFLE—Garfield County

★ GRAND RIVER HOSPITAL DISTRICT, 701 East Fifth Street, Zip 81650–2970, Mailing Address: P.O. Box 912, Zip 81650–0912; tel. 970/625–1510; Robert Peterson, Interim Administrator (Total facility includes 57 beds in nursing home–type unit) **A**9 10 **F**7 8 16 19 22 32 33 36 40 44 49 51 64 65 70 71 **P**6 **S** Quorum Health Group/Quorum Health Resources, Inc., Brentwood, TN	16	10	75	533	53	14088	80	8915	4808	212

SALIDA—Chaffee County

★ HEART OF THE ROCKIES REGIONAL MEDICAL CENTER, 448 East First Street, Zip 81201–0429, Mailing Address: P.O. Box 429, Zip 81201–0429; tel. 719/539–6661; Howard D. Turner, Chief Executive Officer **A**9 10 **F**7 8 11 12 17 19 22 28 32 33 35 36 37 40 41 42 44 49 70 71 73 **P**5 **S** Quorum Health Group/Quorum Health Resources, Inc., Brentwood, TN **Web address:** www.hrrmc.com	16	10	33	1196	12	27351	134	11138	4793	168

SPRINGFIELD—Baca County

★ SOUTHEAST COLORADO HOSPITAL AND LONG TERM CARE, 373 East Tenth Avenue, Zip 81073–1699; tel. 719/523–4501; Al Campbell, Chief Executive Officer (Total facility includes 56 beds in nursing home–type unit) (Nonreporting) **A**9 10	23	10	81	—	—	—	—	—	—	—

Hospital, Address, Telephone, Administrator, Approval, Facility, and Physician Codes, Health Care System, Network	Classi-fication Codes		Utilization Data					Expense (thousands) of dollars		
	Control	Service	Staffed Beds	Admissions	Census	Outpatient Visits	Births	Total	Payroll	Personnel

American Hospital Association (AHA) membership
□ Joint Commission on Accreditation of Healthcare Organizations (JCAHO) accreditation
+ American Osteopathic Healthcare Association (AOHA) membership
○ American Osteopathic Association (AOA) accreditation
△ Commission on Accreditation of Rehabilitation Facilities (CARF) accreditation
Control codes 61, 63, 64, 71, 72 and 73 indicate hospitals listed by AOHA, but not registered by AHA. For definition of numerical codes, see page A4

STEAMBOAT SPRINGS—Routt County

Hospital	Control	Service	Staffed Beds	Admissions	Census	Outpatient Visits	Births	Total	Payroll	Personnel
ROUTT MEMORIAL HOSPITAL, 80 Park Avenue, Zip 80487–5010; tel. 970/879–1322; Margaret D. Sabin, Chief Executive Officer (Total facility includes 50 beds in nursing home–type unit) (Nonreporting) A1 9 10	23	10	74	—	—	—	—	—	—	—

STERLING—Logan County

| STERLING REGIONAL MEDCENTER, 615 Fairhurst Street, Zip 80751–0500, Mailing Address: P.O. Box 3500, Zip 80751–0500; tel. 970/522–0122; Michael J. Gillen, Administrator A1 9 10 F7 8 11 12 13 14 16 17 19 21 22 23 24 26 28 29 30 32 33 34 35 36 37 39 40 41 42 44 45 46 47 48 49 51 64 65 66 67 68 70 71 73 P2 4 5 6 8 S Lutheran Health Systems, Fargo, ND | 23 | 10 | 36 | 1906 | 19 | 10369 | 250 | 20317 | 8426 | 299 |

THORNTON—Adams County

| NORTH SUBURBAN MEDICAL CENTER, (Formerly Columbia North Suburban Medical Center), 9191 Grant Street, Zip 80229–4341; tel. 303/451–7800; Margaret C. Cain, Chief Executive Officer (Total facility includes 15 beds in nursing home–type unit) (Nonreporting) A1 9 10 S Columbia/HCA Healthcare Corporation, Nashville, TN | 33 | 10 | 125 | — | — | — | — | — | — | — |
| □ SUNHEALTH SPECIALTY HOSPITAL FOR DENVER, (Formerly Mediplex Rehabilitation–Denver), 8451 Pearl Street, Zip 80229–4804; tel. 303/288–3000; Walter Sackett, Chief Executive Officer (Total facility includes 50 beds in nursing home–type unit) (Nonreporting) A1 5 9 10 **Web address:** www.sunh.com | 33 | 46 | 117 | — | — | — | — | — | — | — |

TRINIDAD—Las Animas County

| MOUNT SAN RAFAEL HOSPITAL, 410 Benedicta Avenue, Zip 81082–2093; tel. 719/846–9213; Paul Herman, Chief Executive Officer A1 9 10 F7 8 15 16 19 21 22 32 35 40 44 51 71 P8 S Quorum Health Group/Quorum Health Resources, Inc., Brentwood, TN | 23 | 10 | 31 | 1093 | 14 | 43784 | 140 | 9003 | 4239 | 158 |

USAF ACADEMY—El Paso County

| U. S. AIR FORCE ACADEMY HOSPITAL, 4102 Pinion Drive, Zip 80840–4000; tel. 719/333–5102; Colonel Jay D. Sprenger, MSC, USAF, Commander (Nonreporting) A1 S Department of the Air Force, Bowling AFB, DC | 41 | 10 | 46 | — | — | — | — | — | — | — |

VAIL—Eagle County

| VAIL VALLEY MEDICAL CENTER, 181 West Meadow Drive, Zip 81657–5059; tel. 970/476–2451; Clifford M. Eldredge, President and Chief Executive Officer A1 3 9 10 F1 7 8 10 12 13 15 16 17 19 20 21 22 24 25 26 27 28 29 30 31 32 33 34 35 37 39 40 41 42 44 45 46 49 65 66 67 68 70 71 72 73 74 P5 | 23 | 10 | 49 | 2160 | 17 | 40579 | 503 | 39358 | 12299 | 425 |

WALSENBURG—Huerfano County

| ★ HUERFANO MEDICAL CENTER, 23500 U.S. Highway 160, Zip 81089–9524; tel. 719/738–5100; Vonnie Maier, President and Chief Executive Officer A9 10 F3 5 8 15 16 17 19 20 22 26 27 28 29 30 31 32 33 34 35 39 42 44 45 46 49 64 65 66 71 73 74 | 16 | 10 | 24 | 670 | 10 | 20085 | 0 | 6599 | 2141 | 191 |

WESTMINSTER—Jefferson County

| CLEO WALLACE CENTERS HOSPITAL, 8405 Church Ranch Boulevard, Zip 80021; tel. 303/639–1700; James M. Cole, President and Chief Executive Officer A1 10 F2 12 16 20 22 24 27 39 45 46 52 53 54 55 56 59 P8 | 23 | 52 | 207 | 4181 | 276 | 0 | 0 | 23836 | 14298 | 413 |
| ★ ST. ANTHONY NORTH HOSPITAL, 2551 West 84th Avenue, Zip 80030–3887; tel. 303/426–2151; Matthew S. Fulton, Chief Executive Officer A9 10 F1 2 4 6 8 9 10 11 12 13 15 17 19 21 22 24 26 28 32 33 34 35 37 38 40 42 43 44 45 46 47 48 49 51 52 57 62 64 65 70 71 73 74 P7 S Catholic Health Initiatives, Denver, CO | 21 | 10 | 118 | 7874 | 74 | 68113 | 1236 | 45830 | 19899 | — |

WHEAT RIDGE—Jefferson County

| EXEMPLA LUTHERAN MEDICAL CENTER, (Includes Exempla West Pines, 3400 Lutheran Parkway, Zip 80033; tel. 303/467–4000), 8300 West 38th Avenue, Zip 80033–6005; tel. 303/425–4500; Jeffrey D. Selberg, President and Chief Executive Officer (Total facility includes 120 beds in nursing home–type unit) A1 2 9 10 F7 8 10 11 12 14 15 16 17 19 22 30 32 33 34 35 37 38 39 40 41 42 43 44 45 46 49 51 52 53 54 56 58 59 60 62 64 67 70 71 73 74 P5 6 S Exempla Healthcare, Inc., Denver, CO | 23 | 10 | 489 | 16576 | 201 | 167303 | 2387 | 156764 | 78854 | 2936 |

WRAY—Yuma County

| ★ WRAY COMMUNITY DISTRICT HOSPITAL, 1017 West 7th Street, Zip 80758–1420; tel. 970/332–4811; Daniel Dennis, Administrator (Nonreporting) A3 9 10 | 16 | 10 | 25 | — | — | — | — | — | — | — |

YUMA—Yuma County

| ★ YUMA DISTRICT HOSPITAL, 910 South Main Street, Zip 80759–3098, Mailing Address: P.O. Box 306, Zip 80759–0306; tel. 970/848–5405; Timothy F. Reardon, FACHE, Chief Executive Officer A9 10 F7 8 14 15 17 19 22 28 35 40 44 48 49 58 64 70 71 P6 | 16 | 10 | 11 | 261 | 2 | 21748 | 35 | 4567 | 2281 | 85 |

CONNECTICUT

Resident population 3,274 (in thousands)
Resident population in metro areas 95.6%
Birth rate per 1,000 population 13.5
65 years and over 14.4%
Percent of persons without health insurance 11%

Hospital, Address, Telephone, Administrator, Approval, Facility, and Physician Codes, Health Care System, Network	Classi-fication Codes		Utilization Data					Expense (thousands) of dollars		
	Control	Service	Staffed Beds	Admissions	Census	Outpatient Visits	Births	Total	Payroll	Personnel

American Hospital Association (AHA) membership
□ Joint Commission on Accreditation of Healthcare Organizations (JCAHO) accreditation
+ American Osteopathic Healthcare Association (AOHA) membership
○ American Osteopathic Association (AOA) accreditation
△ Commission on Accreditation of Rehabilitation Facilities (CARF) accreditation
Control codes 61, 63, 64, 71, 72 and 73 indicate hospitals listed by AOHA, but not registered by AHA. For definition of numerical codes, see page A4

BETHLEHEM—Litchfield County

★ WELLSPRING FOUNDATION, 21 Arch Bridge Road, Zip 06751–0370, Mailing Address: P.O. Box 370, Zip 06751–0370; tel. 203/266–7235; Herbert L. Hall, Chief Executive Officer **F**52 53 54 55 58 59 **Web address:** www.wellspring.com	23	22	35	73	18	994	0	—	2417	56

BRANFORD—New Haven County

□ THE CONNECTICUT HOSPICE, (HOSPICE CARE HOSPITAL), 61 Burban Drive, Zip 06405–4003; tel. 203/481–6231; Rosemary Johnson Hurzeler, President and Chief Executive Officer **A**1 10 **F**12 14 15 16 31 32 33 65 73 **P**6 **Web address:** www.hospice.com	23	49	52	1315	40	0	0	8034	2838	110

BRIDGEPORT—Fairfield County

✉ BRIDGEPORT HOSPITAL, 267 Grant Street, Zip 06610–2875, Mailing Address: P.O. Box 5000, Zip 06610–0120; tel. 203/384–3000; Robert J. Trefry, President and Chief Executive Officer **A**1 2 3 5 6 8 9 10 **F**3 4 7 8 9 10 11 12 13 15 16 17 18 19 20 21 22 27 28 29 30 31 32 33 34 35 36 37 38 39 40 41 42 43 44 45 46 47 48 49 51 52 53 54 55 56 57 59 60 61 65 66 67 68 69 70 71 72 73 74 **P**1 5 7 **S** Yale New Haven Health System, New Haven, CT	23	10	346	16797	242	146688	2474	182084	70878	1711
GREATER BRIDGEPORT COMMUNITY MENTAL HEALTH CENTER See Southwest Connecticut Mental Health System										
SOUTHWEST CONNECTICUT MENTAL HEALTH SYSTEM, (Formerly Greater Bridgeport Community Mental Health Center), 1635 Central Avenue, Zip 06610–2700, Mailing Address: P.O. Box 5117, Zip 06610–5117; tel. 203/551–7444; James M. Pisciotta, Chief Executive Officer **A**10 **F**2 12 52 56 58 **S** Connecticut Department of Mental Health and Addiction Services, Hartford, CT	12	22	62	1880	54	174644	0	20882	—	346
✉ ST. VINCENT'S MEDICAL CENTER, 2800 Main Street, Zip 06606–4292; tel. 203/576–6000; William J. Riordan, President and Chief Executive Officer **A**1 2 3 5 8 9 10 **F**1 4 7 8 10 11 12 14 15 16 17 19 21 22 25 26 27 28 29 30 31 32 33 34 35 37 39 40 41 42 43 44 46 48 49 51 53 54 56 58 59 60 65 67 68 70 71 72 73 74 **P**7 **S** Daughters of Charity National Health System, Saint Louis, MO **Web address:** www.stvincents.org	21	10	259	14592	217	142513	1830	137670	66742	1377

BRISTOL—Hartford County

✉ BRISTOL HOSPITAL, P.O. Box 977, Brewster Road, Zip 06011–0977; tel. 860/585–3000; Thomas D. Kennedy, III, President and Chief Executive Officer **A**1 2 9 10 **F**1 3 4 7 8 12 13 14 15 17 18 19 21 22 24 26 27 28 29 30 31 32 33 34 35 36 37 38 39 40 41 42 43 44 46 49 50 51 52 53 54 55 56 57 58 59 60 61 65 66 67 68 70 71 72 73 74 **P**5 7 8 **Web address:** www.bristolhospital.org	23	10	79	6501	76	116829	889	72155	34555	746

DANBURY—Fairfield County

✉ DANBURY HOSPITAL, 24 Hospital Avenue, Zip 06810; tel. 203/797–7000; Frank J. Kelly, President and Chief Executive Officer **A**1 2 3 5 8 9 10 **F**3 5 7 8 10 11 12 13 17 18 20 22 23 24 26 28 29 30 31 32 33 34 37 38 39 40 41 42 44 45 46 48 49 51 52 54 55 56 58 59 70 **Web address:** www.danhosp.org	23	10	284	13502	169	205884	2382	184791	81332	1727

DERBY—New Haven County

✉ GRIFFIN HOSPITAL, 130 Division Street, Zip 06418–1377; tel. 203/735–7421; Patrick Charmel, President and Chief Executive Officer **A**1 2 3 5 9 10 **F**1 3 7 8 14 15 16 19 21 22 28 29 30 35 37 38 41 42 44 45 46 49 51 52 53 56 58 59 61 71 72 73 74 **Web address:** www.lnvalley.org/griffin	23	10	160	5349	76	98387	585	64406	30144	619

FARMINGTON—Hartford County

✉ UNIVERSITY OF CONNECTICUT HEALTH CENTER, JOHN DEMPSEY HOSPITAL, 263 Farmington Avenue, Zip 06030–1956; tel. 860/679–2000; Andria Martin, R.N., MS, Director and Vice President Operations **A**1 2 3 5 8 9 10 **F**3 4 5 7 8 10 12 14 15 16 17 18 19 20 21 22 23 26 28 30 31 32 33 34 35 36 37 38 39 40 41 42 43 44 46 49 51 52 54 55 56 57 58 59 60 61 62 63 65 66 67 68 71 72 73 74 **P**6 **Web address:** www.uconnhealth.org	12	10	131	6228	121	524809	581	125896	47842	1007

GREENWICH—Fairfield County

✉ GREENWICH HOSPITAL, 5 Perryridge Road, Zip 06830–4697; tel. 203/863–3000; Frank A. Corvino, President and Chief Executive Officer **A**1 2 3 5 9 10 **F**2 3 7 8 10 11 12 13 14 15 16 17 18 19 20 21 22 24 26 28 29 30 31 32 33 34 35 37 38 39 40 41 42 44 45 46 49 51 53 54 55 56 57 58 60 61 63 64 65 66 67 68 70 71 73 74 **P**5 **S** Yale New Haven Health System, New Haven, CT **Web address:** www.greenhosp.chime.org	23	10	160	6828	101	276351	1375	104890	51277	1155

HARTFORD—Hartford County

✉ CONNECTICUT CHILDREN'S MEDICAL CENTER, 282 Washington Street, Zip 06106–3316; tel. 860/545–9000; Larry M. Gold, President and Chief Executive Officer **A**1 3 9 10 **F**10 14 15 16 17 19 20 21 22 32 34 35 38 39 41 42 43 44 47 49 51 54 56 65 67 69 70 71 73 **P**3 **Web address:** www.ccmckids.org	23	50	123	4076	69	99110	0	68677	25831	778

Hospital, Address, Telephone, Administrator, Approval, Facility, and Physician Codes, Health Care System, Network	Classi-fication Codes		Utilization Data					Expense (thousands) of dollars		
★ American Hospital Association (AHA) membership □ Joint Commission on Accreditation of Healthcare Organizations (JCAHO) accreditation + American Osteopathic Healthcare Association (AOHA) membership ○ American Osteopathic Association (AOA) accreditation △ Commission on Accreditation of Rehabilitation Facilities (CARF) accreditation Control codes 61, 63, 64, 71, 72 and 73 indicate hospitals listed by AOHA, but not registered by AHA. For definition of numerical codes, see page A4	Control	Service	Staffed Beds	Admissions	Census	Outpatient Visits	Births	Total	Payroll	Personnel

Hospital	Control	Service	Staffed Beds	Admissions	Census	Outpatient Visits	Births	Total	Payroll	Personnel
✠ △ HARTFORD HOSPITAL, (Includes Institute of Living, 400 Washington Street, Zip 06106–3392; tel. 860/545–7000), 80 Seymour Street, Zip 06102–5037, Mailing Address: P.O. Box 5037, Zip 06102–5037; tel. 860/545–5000; John J. Meehan, President and Chief Executive Officer (Total facility includes 104 beds in nursing home–type unit) **A**1 2 3 5 7 8 9 10 **F**1 3 4 7 8 10 11 14 15 16 17 19 20 21 22 24 25 26 29 30 31 32 33 34 35 36 37 38 39 40 41 42 43 44 45 46 47 48 49 50 51 52 53 54 55 56 57 58 59 60 61 64 65 66 67 68 70 71 72 73 74 **P**5 6 8 **Web address:** www.harthosp.org	23	10	822	32138	576	188767	4314	417965	212836	4970
✠ SAINT FRANCIS HOSPITAL AND MEDICAL CENTER, 114 Woodland Street, Zip 06105–1299; tel. 860/714–4000; David D'Eramo, President and Chief Executive Officer **A**1 2 3 5 8 9 10 **F**3 4 7 8 10 11 12 13 14 15 16 17 19 20 21 22 24 25 26 28 29 30 31 32 33 34 35 36 37 38 40 41 42 43 44 45 46 48 49 50 51 52 53 54 55 56 57 58 59 60 61 63 65 66 67 68 70 71 72 73 74 **P**4 7 8 **Web address:** www.stfranciscare.org	21	10	510	25966	365	297090	3273	326407	138080	2963
MANCHESTER—Hartford County										
✠ MANCHESTER MEMORIAL HOSPITAL, 71 Haynes Street, Zip 06040–4188; tel. 860/646–1222; Marc H. Lory, President and Chief Executive Officer **A**1 9 10 **F**3 7 8 11 12 13 15 16 17 18 19 21 22 26 28 29 30 31 32 33 34 35 36 37 39 40 41 42 44 45 46 48 49 52 53 54 55 56 57 58 59 63 64 65 66 67 68 71 72 73 74 **P**4 5 6 7 8	23	10	182	7294	92	175144	895	94515	46918	1170
MANSFIELD CENTER—Tolland County										
□ NATCHAUG HOSPITAL, 189 Storrs Road, Zip 06250–1638; tel. 860/456–1311; Stephen W. Larcen, Ph.D., Chief Executive Officer (Nonreporting) **A**1 9 10	23	22	58	—	—	—	—	—	—	—
MERIDEN—New Haven County										
✠ MIDSTATE MEDICAL CENTER, (Formerly Veterans Memorial Medical Center), (Includes East Campus, 883 Paddock Avenue, Zip 06450–7094), 435 Lewis Avenue, Zip 06451; tel. 203/694–8200; Theodore H. Horwitz, FACHE, President and Chief Executive Officer **A**1 2 10 **F**3 7 8 12 15 16 17 18 19 21 22 24 25 26 29 30 31 32 33 34 35 37 40 42 44 46 52 53 54 55 56 57 58 59 60 63 65 67 68 71 72 73 **P**1 5 8 **Web address:** www.midstate.org	23	10	103	7298	83	93751	1081	112061	47099	838
MIDDLETOWN—Middlesex County										
□ CONNECTICUT VALLEY HOSPITAL, (Includes Whiting Forensic Division of Connecticut Valley Hospital, O'Brien Drive, Zip 06457, Mailing Address: Box 70, Zip 06457–3942; tel. 203/344–2541), Silver Street, Zip 06457–7023, Mailing Address: P.O. Box 351, Zip 06457–0351; tel. 860/262–5000; Garrell S. Mullaney, Chief Executive Officer (Nonreporting) **A**1 5 10 **S** Connecticut Department of Mental Health and Addiction Services, Hartford, CT	12	22	418	—	—	—	—	—	—	—
✠ MIDDLESEX HOSPITAL, 28 Crescent Street, Zip 06457–3650; tel. 860/344–6000; Robert Gerard Kiely, President and Chief Executive Officer **A**1 2 3 5 9 10 **F**1 2 3 6 7 8 11 12 13 14 15 16 17 18 19 21 22 25 26 28 29 30 31 32 33 34 35 37 38 40 41 42 44 45 46 48 49 51 52 53 54 55 56 57 58 59 60 61 62 65 66 67 70 71 72 73 74 **P**5 8 **Web address:** www.midhosp.chime.org	23	10	119	9298	99	809000	1184	126275	65602	1299
RIVERVIEW HOSPITAL FOR CHILDREN, River Road, Zip 06457–3918, Mailing Address: P.O. Box 621, Zip 06457–0621; tel. 203/344–2700; Richard J. Wiseman, Ph.D., Superintendent (Nonreporting) **A**3	12	52	55	—	—	—	—	—	—	—
WHITING FORENSIC DIVISION OF CONNECTICUT VALLEY HOSPITAL See Connecticut Valley Hospital										
MILFORD—New Haven County										
✠ MILFORD HOSPITAL, 300 Seaside Avenue, Zip 06460–4603; tel. 203/876–4000; Paul E. Moss, President **A**1 2 9 10 **F**7 8 12 14 17 19 21 22 28 30 32 34 35 36 37 39 40 42 44 46 56 63 65 67 71 72 73 **P**5 7	23	10	59	3812	49	49177	465	39649	19661	430
NEW BRITAIN—Hartford County										
✠ △ HOSPITAL FOR SPECIAL CARE, (CHRONIC DISEASE & REHAB), 2150 Corbin Avenue, Zip 06053–2263; tel. 860/827–4758; David Crandall, President and Chief Executive Officer **A**1 7 9 10 **F**12 15 16 20 24 26 34 39 41 48 49 54 65 66 67 73 **P**6 **Web address:** www.hfsc.org	23	49	199	579	175	19051	0	56450	31989	682
✠ NEW BRITAIN GENERAL HOSPITAL, 100 Grand Street, Zip 06052–2000, Mailing Address: P.O. Box 100, Zip 06050–0100; tel. 860/224–5011; Laurence A. Tanner, President and Chief Executive Officer **A**1 2 3 5 8 9 10 **F**1 2 3 4 6 7 8 10 11 12 14 15 16 17 18 19 21 22 23 24 25 26 27 29 30 31 32 33 34 35 36 37 38 39 40 41 42 43 44 45 46 49 51 52 53 54 55 56 57 58 59 60 61 62 63 65 66 67 69 71 73 74 **P**5 8 **Web address:** www.nbgh.org	23	10	258	13515	177	256320	2080	164335	94670	1989
NEW CANAAN—Fairfield County										
✠ SILVER HILL HOSPITAL, 208 Valley Road, Zip 06840–3899; tel. 203/966–3561; Richard J. Frances, M.D., President and Medical Director (Nonreporting) **A**1 9 10 **Web address:** www.silverhillhospital.com	23	22	61	—	—	—	—	—	—	—
NEW HAVEN—New Haven County										
□ CONNECTICUT MENTAL HEALTH CENTER, 34 Park Street, Zip 06519–1187, Mailing Address: P.O. Box 1842, Zip 06508–1842; tel. 203/974–7144; Selby Jacobs, M.D., Director **A**1 3 5 10 **F**3 12 17 19 20 21 22 35 39 46 52 53 54 55 56 58 59 65 67 70 71 **S** Connecticut Department of Mental Health and Addiction Services, Hartford, CT	12	22	39	852	25	—	0	—	—	506

Hospital, Address, Telephone, Administrator, Approval, Facility, and Physician Codes, Health Care System, Network	Classi-fication Codes		Utilization Data					Expense (thousands) of dollars		
	Control	Service	Staffed Beds	Admissions	Census	Outpatient Visits	Births	Total	Payroll	Personnel

Hospital	Control	Service	Staffed Beds	Admissions	Census	Outpatient Visits	Births	Total	Payroll	Personnel
✪ HOSPITAL OF SAINT RAPHAEL, 1450 Chapel Street, Zip 06511–1450; tel. 203/789–3000; David W. Benfer, President and Chief Executive Officer (Total facility includes 125 beds in nursing home–type unit) **A**1 2 3 5 8 9 10 **F**1 3 4 7 8 10 11 12 13 14 15 16 17 18 19 20 21 22 26 27 28 29 30 31 32 34 35 37 39 40 41 42 43 44 45 46 48 49 51 52 53 54 55 56 57 58 59 60 61 63 64 65 67 68 70 71 72 73 74 **P**2 5 7 8 Web address: www.srhs.org	21	10	589	22333	474	198620	1143	264924	126535	2873
□ YALE PSYCHIATRIC INSTITUTE, 184 Liberty Street, Zip 06520, Mailing Address: P.O. Box 208038, Zip 06520; tel. 203/785–7200; Thomas H. McGlashan, M.D., Director and Psychiatrist–in–Chief (Nonreporting) **A**1 3 5 9 10	23	22	55	—	—	—	—	—	—	—
✪ YALE–NEW HAVEN HOSPITAL, 20 York Street, Zip 06504–3202; tel. 203/688–4242; Joseph A. Zaccagnino, President and Chief Executive Officer **A**1 2 3 5 8 9 10 **F**3 4 7 8 10 11 12 13 14 15 16 17 18 19 20 21 22 23 25 26 27 28 29 30 31 32 33 34 35 37 38 39 40 41 42 43 44 45 46 47 48 49 50 51 52 53 54 55 56 57 58 59 60 61 63 65 66 67 68 70 71 72 73 74 **P**5 7 8 **S** Yale New Haven Health System, New Haven, CT Web address: www.ynhh.org	23	10	735	35269	557	377493	4923	442093	201666	4575
NEW LONDON—New London County										
✪ LAWRENCE & MEMORIAL HOSPITAL, 365 Montauk Avenue, Zip 06320–4769; tel. 860/442–0711; William T. Christopher, President and Chief Executive Officer **A**1 9 10 **F**3 7 8 10 11 13 14 15 16 17 19 21 22 25 30 31 34 35 37 38 39 40 41 42 44 45 46 48 49 52 53 54 55 56 57 58 59 60 61 65 67 71 72 73 74	23	10	228	12016	173	101247	1711	136305	66097	1464
NEW MILFORD—Litchfield County										
✪ NEW MILFORD HOSPITAL, 21 Elm Street, Zip 06776–2993; tel. 860/355–2611; Richard E. Pugh, President and Chief Executive Officer **A**1 9 10 **F**7 8 11 12 14 15 16 17 18 19 20 21 22 24 28 31 33 35 37 39 40 41 42 44 49 56 61 63 65 66 67 71 72 73 74 Web address: www.nmh.chime.org	23	10	62	2805	36	68382	383	40708	18991	424
NEWINGTON—Hartford County										
□ CEDARCREST HOSPITAL, 525 Russell Road, Zip 06111–1595; tel. 860/666–4613; John H. Simsarian, Superintendent (Nonreporting) **A**1 10 **S** Connecticut Department of Mental Health and Addiction Services, Hartford, CT	12	22	146	—	—	—	—	—	—	—
NORWALK—Fairfield County										
✪ △ NORWALK HOSPITAL, 34 Maple Street, Zip 06856–5050; tel. 203/852–2000; David W. Osborne, President and Chief Executive Officer **A**1 2 3 5 7 9 10 **F**2 3 7 8 10 11 12 13 15 16 17 18 19 20 21 22 23 24 25 26 28 29 30 31 34 35 37 38 39 40 41 42 44 45 46 48 49 51 52 53 54 55 56 57 58 59 60 61 65 67 68 71 73 74 **P**5 7 Web address: www.norwalkhealth.org	23	10	285	11960	186	145461	2221	152740	73236	1401
NORWICH—New London County										
✪ WILLIAM W. BACKUS HOSPITAL, 326 Washington Street, Zip 06360–2742; tel. 860/889–8331; Thomas P. Pipicelli, President and Chief Executive Officer **A**1 9 10 **F**4 7 8 10 12 14 15 16 17 19 21 22 26 28 29 30 31 32 33 34 35 37 38 39 40 41 42 44 45 49 51 52 54 55 56 57 58 59 60 63 65 67 68 70 71 72 73	23	10	164	9964	125	792462	1101	95857	43985	1017
PORTLAND—Middlesex County										
□ ELMCREST BEHAVIORAL HEALTH NETWORK, (Formerly Elmcrest Psychiatric Institute), 25 Marlborough Street, Zip 06480–1829; tel. 860/342–0480; Anthony A. Ferrante, M.D., President and Chief Executive Officer (Nonreporting) **A**1 9 10 **S** Magellan Health Services, Atlanta, GA	32	22	92	—	—	—	—	—	—	—
PUTNAM—Windham County										
✪ DAY KIMBALL HOSPITAL, 320 Pomfret Street, Zip 06260–1869, Mailing Address: P.O. Box 6001, Zip 06260–6001; tel. 860/928–6541; Charles F. Schneider, President **A**1 10 **F**3 7 8 12 13 14 15 16 17 18 19 21 22 25 26 27 28 29 30 32 33 34 35 37 40 44 46 49 52 54 55 56 57 58 59 61 63 65 66 67 68 71 72 73 74 **P**8 Web address: www.hnne.org	23	10	101	4755	48	302917	582	55128	28521	535
ROCKY HILL—Hartford County										
□ VETERANS HOME AND HOSPITAL, 287 West Street, Zip 06067–3501; tel. 860/529–2571; Joanne M. Blum, Administrator **A**1 10 **F**2 3 8 15 16 18 19 20 21 22 26 27 31 33 35 39 42 43 44 45 46 50 54 56 57 58 59 60 63 64 65 67 71 73 74	12	48	253	8204	199	0	0	—	—	438
SHARON—Litchfield County										
✪ SHARON HOSPITAL, 50 Hospital Hill Road, Zip 06069–0789, Mailing Address: P.O. Box 789, Zip 06069–0789; tel. 860/364–4141; Michael R. Gallacher, President and Chief Executive Officer **A**1 2 9 10 **F**7 8 14 16 17 19 21 22 29 30 33 34 35 37 39 40 41 42 44 45 46 49 51 57 65 67 70 71 72 73 **P**5 7 Web address: www.sharon.org	23	10	57	2644	33	—	331	31020	13055	369
SOMERS—Tolland County										
CONNECTICUT DEPARTMENT OF CORRECTION'S HOSPITAL, 100 Bilton Road, Zip 06071, Mailing Address: P.O. Box 100, Zip 06071–0100; tel. 860/749–8391; Edward A. Blanchette, M.D., Director (Nonreporting)	12	11	29	—	—	—	—	—	—	—
SOUTHINGTON—Hartford County										
✪ BRADLEY MEMORIAL HOSPITAL AND HEALTH CENTER, 81 Meriden Avenue, Zip 06489–3297; tel. 860/276–5000; Clarence J. Silvia, President and Chief Executive Officer **A**1 9 10 **F**8 11 12 15 16 17 19 21 22 23 26 28 29 30 33 34 35 37 39 41 42 44 45 49 54 55 56 58 63 65 67 71 73 74 **P**5	16	10	74	2481	35	76007	0	25253	12941	272

Hospital, Address, Telephone, Administrator, Approval, Facility, and Physician Codes, Health Care System, Network	Classi-fication Codes		Utilization Data					Expense (thousands) of dollars		
★ American Hospital Association (AHA) membership □ Joint Commission on Accreditation of Healthcare Organizations (JCAHO) accreditation + American Osteopathic Healthcare Association (AOHA) membership ○ American Osteopathic Association (AOA) accreditation △ Commission on Accreditation of Rehabilitation Facilities (CARF) accreditation Control codes 61, 63, 64, 71, 72 and 73 indicate hospitals listed by AOHA, but not registered by AHA. For definition of numerical codes, see page A4	Control	Service	Staffed Beds	Admissions	Census	Outpatient Visits	Births	Total	Payroll	Personnel

STAFFORD SPRINGS—Tolland County

□ JOHNSON MEMORIAL HOSPITAL, 201 Chestnut Hill Road, Zip 06076–0860, Mailing Address: P.O. Box 860, Zip 06076–0860; tel. 860/684–4251; Alfred A. Lerz, President and Chief Executive Officer **A**1 9 10 **F**3 7 8 12 13 14 15 16 17 18 19 21 22 24 25 26 28 29 30 31 32 33 34 35 37 39 40 41 42 44 45 46 49 51 52 53 54 55 56 57 58 59 63 65 67 68 71 73 74 **P**5
Web address: www.jmhosp.org | 23 | 10 | 89 | 3954 | 47 | 70200 | 287 | 35703 | 18016 | 395 |

STAMFORD—Fairfield County

✠ STAMFORD HOSPITAL, 6 Shelburne Road, Zip 06902–3696; tel. 203/325–7000; Philip D. Cusano, President and Chief Executive Officer **A**1 2 3 5 8 9 10 **F**1 6 7 8 10 11 12 14 15 16 17 19 20 21 22 24 25 26 27 28 29 30 31 32 33 34 35 37 38 39 40 41 42 44 45 46 48 49 51 52 53 54 55 56 57 58 59 60 61 63 64 65 67 68 70 71 72 73 74 **P**7 | 23 | 10 | 256 | 11880 | 163 | 144674 | 2442 | 117515 | 54524 | 1114 |

TORRINGTON—Litchfield County

□ CHARLOTTE HUNGERFORD HOSPITAL, 540 Litchfield Street, Zip 06790, Mailing Address: P.O. Box 988, Zip 06790–0988; tel. 860/496–6666; Rosanne U. Griswold, President and Chief Executive Officer **A**1 2 9 10 **F**7 8 11 12 13 14 15 16 17 18 19 20 21 22 25 28 29 30 31 32 33 34 35 36 37 39 40 41 42 44 45 46 49 52 53 54 56 58 59 60 63 65 66 67 70 71 72 73 74 **P**6 8 | 23 | 10 | 90 | 5653 | 76 | 196043 | 626 | 65413 | 31146 | 768 |

VERNON ROCKVILLE—Hartford County

✠ ROCKVILLE GENERAL HOSPITAL, 31 Union Street, Zip 06066–3160; tel. 860/872–0501; Marc H. Lory, President and Chief Executive Officer **A**1 9 10 **F**3 7 8 12 13 15 16 17 19 21 22 23 28 29 30 31 32 33 34 35 36 37 39 40 41 42 44 46 48 49 52 53 54 55 56 57 58 59 63 64 65 67 68 71 72 73 74 **P**4 5 6 7 8 | 23 | 10 | 102 | 3859 | 41 | 58287 | 582 | 42143 | 20270 | 710 |

WALLINGFORD—New Haven County

✠ △ GAYLORD HOSPITAL, Gaylord Farm Road, Zip 06492, Mailing Address: P.O. Box 400, Zip 06492; tel. 203/284–2800; Paul H. Johnson, President and Chief Executive Officer **A**1 5 7 9 10 **F**12 39 48 49 65 66 67 73 **P**6 | 23 | 46 | 78 | 992 | 74 | 46971 | 0 | 33000 | 18600 | 434 |

✠ MASONIC GERIATRIC HEALTHCARE CENTER, (LONG TERM CARE), 22 Masonic Avenue, Zip 06492–3048, Mailing Address: P.O. Box 70, Zip 06492–7002; tel. 203/284–3924; Ronald L. Waack, President (Total facility includes 468 beds in nursing home–type unit) **A**1 10 **F**1 3 4 6 8 10 11 12 14 15 16 17 18 19 20 21 22 26 27 28 30 32 33 34 35 36 37 39 41 42 44 49 51 52 54 56 57 58 59 60 62 64 65 67 70 71 73 **P**4 7
Web address: www.masonicare.org | 23 | 49 | 503 | 1084 | 504 | 13947 | 0 | 38310 | 19710 | 578 |

WATERBURY—New Haven County

✠ ST. MARY'S HOSPITAL, 56 Franklin Street, Zip 06706–1200; tel. 203/574–6000; Sister Marguerite Waite, President and Chief Executive Officer **A**1 2 3 5 9 10 **F**3 5 7 8 10 11 12 13 14 15 16 17 18 19 20 21 22 25 26 28 29 30 31 33 34 35 36 37 39 40 41 42 44 45 46 49 51 52 54 55 56 58 59 60 63 65 67 70 71 72 73 **P**7 8 | 21 | 10 | 193 | 9450 | 117 | 168465 | 1293 | 124273 | 60849 | 1359 |

✠ WATERBURY HOSPITAL, 64 Robbins Street, Zip 06721, Mailing Address: P.O. Box 1589, Zip 06721–1589; tel. 203/573–6000; John H. Tobin, President and Chief Executive Officer **A**1 2 3 5 9 10 **F**3 5 7 8 10 11 12 14 15 16 17 18 19 20 21 22 24 27 28 29 30 31 32 33 34 35 37 38 39 40 41 42 44 45 46 49 51 52 53 54 55 57 58 59 60 64 65 66 67 69 70 71 72 73 74 **P**1 6 7
Web address: www.waterburyhospital.org | 23 | 10 | 246 | 11520 | 151 | 146652 | 1362 | 133184 | 68025 | 1405 |

WEST HARTFORD—Hartford County

★ HEBREW HOME AND HOSPITAL, (CHRONIC DISEASE), 1 Abrahms Boulevard, Zip 06117–1525; tel. 860/523–3800; Bonnie B. Gauthier, Chief Executive Officer (Total facility includes 293 beds in nursing home–type unit) **A**10 **F**1 6 12 16 17 26 27 32 34 36 39 49 57 62 64 65 67 73 **P**6
Web address: www.hebrew.home.hosp.org | 23 | 49 | 334 | 227 | 289 | — | 0 | 27931 | 15606 | 442 |

WEST HAVEN—New Haven County

✠ VETERANS AFFAIRS CONNECTICUT HEALTHCARE SYSTEM–WEST HAVEN DIVISION, (Includes West Haven Division, 950 Campbell Avenue, Zip 06516–2700; tel. 203/932–5711), 950 Campbell Avenue, Zip 06516; tel. 203/932–5711; Paul J. McCool, Acting Director (Total facility includes 74 beds in nursing home–type unit) (Nonreporting) **A**1 2 3 5 8 9 **S** Department of Veterans Affairs, Washington, DC | 45 | 10 | 343 | — | — | — | — | — | — | — |

WESTPORT—Fairfield County

✠ HALL–BROOKE HOSPITAL, A DIVISION OF HALL–BROOKE FOUNDATION, 47 Long Lots Road, Zip 06880–3800; tel. 203/227–1251; Seth Berman, President and Chief Executive Officer **A**1 9 10 **F**2 14 15 16 52 53 56 57 58 59 65 67 73 **P**1 | 23 | 22 | 60 | 1306 | 46 | 21209 | 0 | 13650 | 7374 | 205 |

WILLIMANTIC—Windham County

□ WINDHAM COMMUNITY MEMORIAL HOSPITAL, 112 Mansfield Avenue, Zip 06226–2082; tel. 860/456–9116; Jeanette Weldon, Acting President and Chief Executive Officer **A**1 9 10 **F**7 8 14 16 17 19 22 23 26 30 35 36 37 40 42 44 49 54 56 65 67 71 73 74 **P**8
Web address: www.windhamhospital.org | 23 | 10 | 78 | 4155 | 46 | 101938 | 520 | 43228 | 19350 | 469 |

DELAWARE

Resident population 744 (in thousands)
Resident population in metro areas 79.8%
Birth rate per 1,000 population 14.3
65 years and over 12.9%
Percent of persons without health insurance 13.4%

Hospital, Address, Telephone, Administrator, Approval, Facility, and Physician Codes, Health Care System, Network	Classi-fication Codes		Utilization Data					Expense (thousands) of dollars		
★ American Hospital Association (AHA) membership □ Joint Commission on Accreditation of Healthcare Organizations (JCAHO) accreditation + American Osteopathic Healthcare Association (AOHA) membership ○ American Osteopathic Association (AOA) accreditation △ Commission on Accreditation of Rehabilitation Facilities (CARF) accreditation Control codes 61, 63, 64, 71, 72 and 73 indicate hospitals listed by AOHA, but not registered by AHA. For definition of numerical codes, see page A4	Control	Service	Staffed Beds	Admissions	Census	Outpatient Visits	Births	Total	Payroll	Personnel

DOVER—Kent County

★ BAYHEALTH MEDICAL CENTER, (Includes Bayhealth Medical Center at Kent General, 640 South State Street; Bayhealth Medical Center, Milford Memorial Hospital, 21 West Clarke Avenue, Milford, Zip 19963–1840; tel. 302/424–5613), 640 South State Street, Zip 19901–3597; tel. 302/674–4700; Dennis E. Klima, President and Chief Executive Officer **A**1 2 9 10 **F**3 7 8 10 11 12 13 15 16 17 19 21 22 23 24 25 27 28 29 30 31 32 34 35 37 38 39 40 41 42 44 45 46 48 49 50 51 52 53 54 55 56 57 59 60 61 63 64 65 66 67 70 71 72 73 74 **P**6 8
| | 23 | 10 | 345 | 16166 | 212 | 304436 | 1850 | 133363 | 62063 | 1678 |

★ U. S. AIR FORCE HOSPITAL DOVER, 260 Chad Street, Zip 19902–7260; tel. 302/677–2525; Lieutenant Colonel Frederick L. Woods, MSC, USAF, Administrator (Nonreporting) **A**1 **S** Department of the Air Force, Bowling AFB, DC
| | 41 | 10 | 16 | — | — | — | — | — | — | — |

LEWES—Sussex County

★ BEEBE MEDICAL CENTER, 424 Savannah Road, Zip 19958–0226; tel. 302/645–3300; Jeffrey M. Fried, FACHE, President and Chief Executive Officer (Total facility includes 89 beds in nursing home–type unit) **A**1 2 6 9 10 **F**1 3 7 8 10 12 13 14 15 16 17 19 21 22 23 25 26 27 28 29 30 31 32 34 35 37 39 40 41 42 44 45 46 49 51 63 64 65 67 71 72 73 74 **P**8
Web address: www.beebemed.org
| | 23 | 10 | 212 | 7532 | 163 | 137153 | 583 | 75022 | 32890 | 1040 |

MILFORD—Sussex County

BAYHEALTH MEDICAL CENTER, MILFORD MEMORIAL HOSPITAL See Bayhealth Medical Center, Dover

NEW CASTLE—New Castle County

□ DELAWARE PSYCHIATRIC CENTER, 1901 North Dupont Highway, Zip 19720–1199; tel. 302/577–4381; Jiro R. Shimono, Director (Total facility includes 83 beds in nursing home–type unit) **A**1 3 9 10 **F**12 14 17 18 19 20 21 26 29 35 39 41 45 46 49 50 52 56 57 58 63 65 67 71 73 **P**6
| | 12 | 22 | 334 | 1067 | 319 | 0 | 0 | 31136 | 16392 | 749 |

□ MEADOW WOOD BEHAVIORAL HEALTH SYSTEM, 575 South Dupont Highway, Zip 19720–4600; tel. 302/328–3330; Joseph Pyle, Administrator **A**1 9 10 **F**14 15 16 52 53 57 58 59 **P**6 **S** Hospital Group of America, Wayne, PA
| | 33 | 62 | 50 | 1680 | 42 | 7000 | 0 | — | — | 113 |

NEWARK—New Castle County

★ CHRISTIANA CARE, (Includes Christiana Hospital; Wilmington Hospital; Eugene DuPont Preventive Medicine and Rehabilitation Institute; Riverside Long Term and Transitional Care), Mailing Address: 501 West 14th Street, P.O. Box 1668, Wilmington, Zip 19899; tel. 302/733–1000; Charles M. Smith, M.D., President and Chief Executive Officer (Total facility includes 99 beds in nursing home–type unit) **A**1 2 3 5 8 9 10 **F**1 4 7 8 10 11 13 15 16 17 19 20 21 23 24 25 29 30 31 32 34 35 37 38 39 40 41 42 43 44 45 46 47 48 49 51 52 53 54 56 58 60 61 63 64 65 67 68 70 71 73 74 **S** Christiana Care Corporation, Wilmington, DE
Web address: www.christianacare.org
| | 23 | 10 | 872 | 38897 | 663 | 480460 | 6353 | 523837 | 253721 | 5761 |

★ ROCKFORD CENTER, 100 Rockford Drive, Zip 19713–2121; tel. 302/996–5480; Barbara Neuse, Chief Executive Officer (Nonreporting) **A**1 9 10 **S** Columbia/HCA Healthcare Corporation, Nashville, TN
| | 33 | 22 | 70 | — | — | — | — | — | — | — |

SEAFORD—Sussex County

★ NANTICOKE MEMORIAL HOSPITAL, 801 Middleford Road, Zip 19973–3698; tel. 302/629–6611; Edward H. Hancock, President (Total facility includes 90 beds in nursing home–type unit) **A**1 9 10 **F**2 3 4 7 8 10 12 14 15 16 17 19 22 24 28 30 32 35 37 39 40 41 42 44 45 46 49 52 56 57 58 59 64 65 66 67 71 73 74 **P**1 5 6
| | 23 | 10 | 200 | 5360 | 145 | 47451 | 801 | 46108 | 29946 | 643 |

WILMINGTON—New Castle County

★ △ ALFRED I.DUPONT HOSPITAL FOR CHILDREN, (Formerly duPont Hospital for Children), 1600 Rockland Road, Zip 19803–3616, Mailing Address: Box 269, Zip 19899–0269; tel. 302/651–4000; Thomas P. Ferry, Administrator and Chief Executive **A**1 3 5 7 9 10 **F**10 11 12 13 14 15 16 19 20 21 22 34 35 38 39 42 43 44 46 47 48 49 51 53 54 58 65 66 67 68 71 72 73 **P**3
Web address: www.kidshealth.org
| | 23 | 50 | 108 | 6922 | 79 | 109591 | 0 | 82264 | 37411 | — |

★ ST. FRANCIS HOSPITAL, Seventh and Clayton Streets, Zip 19805–0500, Mailing Address: P.O. Box 2500, Zip 19805–0500; tel. 302/421–4100; Daniel J. Sinnott, President and Chief Executive Officer **A**1 2 3 5 9 10 **F**2 4 5 7 8 10 12 13 14 15 16 17 18 19 20 21 22 23 25 26 28 29 30 31 32 33 34 35 37 38 39 40 41 42 44 45 46 47 48 49 51 52 63 64 65 66 67 68 71 72 73 74 **S** Catholic Health Initiatives, Denver, CO
| | 21 | 10 | 240 | 9442 | 132 | 216759 | 1188 | 101512 | 45296 | 961 |

★ VETERANS AFFAIRS MEDICAL CENTER, 1601 Kirkwood Highway, Zip 19805–4989; tel. 302/633–5201; Dexter D. Dix, Director (Total facility includes 60 beds in nursing home–type unit) **A**1 2 3 5 8 **F**3 15 16 17 19 20 21 22 24 25 26 27 28 29 30 31 32 33 34 37 39 41 42 44 45 46 49 51 58 63 64 65 67 68 71 73 74 **P**6 **S** Department of Veterans Affairs, Washington, DC
Web address: www.va.gov/station
| | 45 | 10 | 138 | 2521 | 126 | 130000 | 0 | 57621 | 26185 | 586 |

WILMINGTON HOSPITAL See Christiana Care, Newark
CHRISTIANA CARE, See Newark

DISTRICT OF COLUMBIA

Resident population 523 (in thousands)
Resident population in metro areas 100%
Birth rate per 1,000 population 16.3
65 years and over 13.9%
Percent of persons without health insurance 14.8%

Hospital, Address, Telephone, Administrator, Approval, Facility, and Physician Codes, Health Care System, Network	Classi-fication Codes		Utilization Data					Expense (thousands) of dollars		
★ American Hospital Association (AHA) membership ☐ Joint Commission on Accreditation of Healthcare Organizations (JCAHO) accreditation + American Osteopathic Healthcare Association (AOHA) membership ○ American Osteopathic Association (AOA) accreditation △ Commission on Accreditation of Rehabilitation Facilities (CARF) accreditation Control codes 61, 63, 64, 71, 72 and 73 indicate hospitals listed by AOHA, but not registered by AHA. For definition of numerical codes, see page A4	Control	Service	Staffed Beds	Admissions	Census	Outpatient Visits	Births	Total	Payroll	Personnel

WASHINGTON—District of Columbia County

	Control	Service	Staffed Beds	Admissions	Census	Outpatient Visits	Births	Total	Payroll	Personnel
✚ CHILDREN'S NATIONAL MEDICAL CENTER, 111 Michigan Avenue N.W., Zip 20010–2970; tel. 202/884–5000; Edwin K. Zechman, Jr., President and Chief Executive Officer **A**1 3 5 8 9 10 **F**4 5 10 12 14 15 16 17 19 20 21 22 25 27 28 29 30 31 32 33 34 35 38 39 41 42 43 44 45 46 47 49 51 52 53 54 55 56 58 59 63 65 67 68 70 71 72 73 **P**6 **Web address:** www.cnmc.org	23	50	188	9796	158	216177	0	173822	85990	2224
✚ COLUMBIA HOSPITAL FOR WOMEN MEDICAL CENTER, 2425 L Street N.W., Zip 20037–1433; tel. 202/293–6500; Gerald Beaulieu, Acting President and Chief Executive Officer **A**1 9 10 **F**7 8 12 14 15 16 21 29 34 37 38 39 40 42 44 45 46 51 60 61 63 65 67 71 73 74 **P**4 6 7 **Web address:** www.chwmc.org	23	44	76	5819	46	14816	3766	60405	26130	533
✚ DISTRICT OF COLUMBIA GENERAL HOSPITAL, 19th Street and Massachusetts Avenue S.E., Zip 20003; tel. 202/675–5000; John A. Fairman, Executive Director **A**1 3 5 9 10 **F**2 7 10 11 13 14 15 16 17 19 20 21 25 27 28 30 31 34 35 37 38 40 44 46 49 51 60 63 65 70 71 73 **P**6	14	10	250	9458	155	224943	736	150963	93588	1897
✚ GEORGE WASHINGTON UNIVERSITY HOSPITAL, 901 23rd Street N.W., Zip 20037–2377; tel. 202/994–1000; Phillip S. Schaengold, JD, Chief Executive Officer **A**1 2 3 5 8 9 10 **F**1 4 7 8 10 11 12 14 15 16 17 19 21 22 23 25 27 28 29 30 31 34 35 37 38 39 40 41 42 43 44 45 46 48 49 51 52 54 55 56 57 59 60 61 63 65 66 67 68 70 71 72 73 74 **S** Universal Health Services, Inc., King of Prussia, PA **Web address:** www.gwumc.edu	32	10	285	12230	162	156311	902	120953	54015	1257
✚ GEORGETOWN UNIVERSITY HOSPITAL, 3800 Reservoir Road N.W., Zip 20007–2197; tel. 202/784–3000; Sharon Flynn Hollander, Chief Executive Officer **A**1 2 3 5 8 9 10 **F**3 4 5 7 8 10 12 13 17 18 19 21 22 23 25 26 27 28 29 30 31 34 35 37 38 39 40 41 42 43 44 45 46 47 49 51 52 53 54 55 56 57 58 59 60 61 63 65 66 67 68 70 71 72 73 74 **P**6 **Web address:** www.dml.georgetown.edu	23	10	359	14704	257	183320	1427	215157	81889	2175
✚ △ GREATER SOUTHEAST COMMUNITY HOSPITAL, 1310 Southern Avenue S.E., Zip 20032–4699; tel. 202/574–6000; Stephen C. Rupp, Chief Operating Officer **A**1 2 3 5 7 9 10 **F**1 3 7 8 10 11 12 15 16 17 19 21 22 24 26 28 29 30 32 34 36 37 38 39 40 41 42 44 45 46 48 49 51 52 54 55 56 58 59 60 64 65 67 71 73 **S** Greater Southeast Healthcare System, Washington, DC	23	10	262	11576	210	79740	977	117544	56327	1485
☐ HADLEY MEMORIAL HOSPITAL, 4601 Martin Luther King Jr. Avenue S.W., Zip 20032–1199; tel. 202/574–5700; Ana Raley, Administrator (Total facility includes 77 beds in nursing home–type unit) **A**1 9 10 **F**8 19 21 22 28 37 44 49 64 65 71 73 **S** Doctors Community Healthcare Corporation, Scottsdale, AZ	33	10	148	2044	111	9829	0	30269	12465	318
✚ △ HOSPITAL FOR SICK CHILDREN, 1731 Bunker Hill Road N.E., Zip 20017–3096; tel. 202/832–4400; Thomas W. Chapman, President and Chief Executive Officer **A**1 7 9 **F**12 13 14 15 16 17 19 20 21 22 27 33 34 35 44 45 46 49 51 53 54 55 56 58 59 61 65 67 70 71 73 **P**3 6	23	56	115	317	63	4715	0	29779	14415	267
✚ HOWARD UNIVERSITY HOSPITAL, 2041 Georgia Avenue N.W., Zip 20060–0002; tel. 202/865–6100; Sherman P. McCoy, Executive Director and Chief Executive Officer **A**1 2 3 5 8 9 10 **F**7 8 10 11 12 14 15 16 17 19 20 21 22 28 29 30 31 34 35 37 38 40 41 42 44 45 46 49 50 52 53 54 56 57 58 60 61 63 64 65 66 68 70 71 73 74 **P**8	23	10	317	11642	233	105331	577	169872	88677	2099
★ MEDLINK HOSPITAL AND NURSING CENTER, 700 Constitution Avenue N.E., Zip 20002; tel. 202/546–5700; Peter Shin, DPM, President and Chief Executive Officer (Total facility includes 114 beds in nursing home–type unit) **A**10 **F**8 12 27 34 49 51 64 65 67 71 73 **Web address:** www.medlink–dc.com	23	10	174	345	159	—	0	—	—	—
✚ △ NATIONAL REHABILITATION HOSPITAL, 102 Irving Street N.W., Zip 20010–2949; tel. 202/877–1000; Edward A. Eckenhoff, President and Chief Executive Officer (Total facility includes 19 beds in nursing home–type unit) **A**1 3 5 7 9 10 **F**3 4 5 7 8 9 10 11 12 14 17 18 19 20 21 22 23 25 26 27 28 29 30 31 32 33 34 35 37 38 39 40 41 42 43 44 45 46 48 49 51 52 54 56 57 58 59 60 61 63 64 65 66 67 68 70 71 73 74 **P**1 6 7 **S** MedStar Health, Columbia, MD	23	46	160	1754	104	54931	0	49935	25642	494
✚ PROVIDENCE HOSPITAL, 1150 Varnum Street N.E., Zip 20017–2180; tel. 202/269–7000; Sister Carol Keehan, President (Total facility includes 240 beds in nursing home–type unit) **A**1 2 3 5 9 10 **F**2 3 7 8 9 10 11 14 15 16 17 18 19 22 24 25 26 27 28 30 33 34 35 36 37 38 39 40 41 42 44 45 47 48 49 51 52 54 55 56 57 58 59 61 64 65 67 71 72 73 74 **P**5 **S** Daughters of Charity National Health System, Saint Louis, MO **Web address:** www.provhosp.org	21	10	556	12860	464	71198	1547	127069	67412	1957
☐ PSYCHIATRIC INSTITUTE OF WASHINGTON, 4228 Wisconsin Avenue N.W., Zip 20016–2138; tel. 202/965–8550; Kenneth F. Courage, Jr., Chief Executive Officer **A**1 5 9 10 **F**3 16 52 53 54 55 56 57 58 59 **P**4 5 6 7	33	22	104	1356	63	—	0	—	—	161

Hospital, Address, Telephone, Administrator, Approval, Facility, and Physician Codes, Health Care System, Network	Classi-fication Codes		Utilization Data					Expense (thousands) of dollars		
★ American Hospital Association (AHA) membership □ Joint Commission on Accreditation of Healthcare Organizations (JCAHO) accreditation + American Osteopathic Healthcare Association (AOHA) membership ○ American Osteopathic Association (AOA) accreditation △ Commission on Accreditation of Rehabilitation Facilities (CARF) accreditation Control codes 61, 63, 64, 71, 72 and 73 indicate hospitals listed by AOHA, but not registered by AHA. For definition of numerical codes, see page A4	Control	Service	Staffed Beds	Admissions	Census	Outpatient Visits	Births	Total	Payroll	Personnel
⊠ SIBLEY MEMORIAL HOSPITAL, 5255 Loughboro Road N.W., Zip 20016–2695; tel. 202/537–4000; Robert L. Sloan, Chief Executive Officer (Total facility includes 17 beds in nursing home–type unit) **A**1 2 3 5 9 10 **F**7 8 10 11 12 16 19 21 22 26 28 30 31 32 34 35 37 39 40 41 42 44 45 46 49 52 53 55 56 57 58 60 61 64 65 66 67 71 73 74 **P**5 **Web address:** www.sibley.org	23	10	237	11136	168	63835	1402	100864	48259	1067
★ ST. ELIZABETHS HOSPITAL, 2700 Martin Luther King Jr. Avenue S.E., Zip 20032–2698; tel. 202/373–7166; Saverio C. Fantasia, Chief Financial Officer (Nonreporting) **A**10	14	22	817	—	—	—	—	—	—	—
⊠ VETERANS AFFAIRS MEDICAL CENTER, 50 Irving Street N.W., Zip 20422–0002; tel. 202/745–8100; Sanford M. Garfunkel, Director (Total facility includes 120 beds in nursing home–type unit) **A**1 2 3 5 8 **F**1 3 4 10 11 12 14 15 16 17 18 19 20 21 22 26 28 29 30 31 32 33 35 37 39 41 42 43 44 45 46 48 49 51 52 54 55 56 57 58 59 60 64 65 67 71 73 74 **S** Department of Veterans Affairs, Washington, DC **Web address:** www.va.gov/station	45	10	278	6301	254	339778	0	173394	110172	1770
⊠ WALTER REED ARMY MEDICAL CENTER, 6825 16th Street N.W., Zip 20307–5001; tel. 202/782–6393; Colonel Robert James Heckert, Jr., MSC, Chief of Staff **A**1 2 3 5 **F**3 4 5 8 10 11 12 13 14 15 16 17 18 19 21 22 23 24 27 28 29 30 31 35 37 39 41 42 43 44 45 46 47 48 49 51 52 53 54 55 56 57 58 59 60 61 63 65 66 67 68 70 71 73 74 **S** Department of the Army, Office of the Surgeon General, Falls Church, VA	42	10	439	12849	209	524176	0	—	—	4430
⊠ WASHINGTON HOSPITAL CENTER, 110 Irving Street N.W., Zip 20010–2975; tel. 202/877–7000; Kenneth A. Samet, President **A**1 2 3 5 8 9 10 **F**3 4 5 7 8 9 10 11 12 14 15 16 17 19 20 21 22 26 27 28 29 30 31 32 33 34 35 37 38 39 40 41 42 43 44 45 46 48 49 51 52 54 56 57 58 59 60 63 64 65 66 67 68 70 71 73 **P**1 6 7 **S** MedStar Health, Columbia, MD **Web address:** www.whc.mhg.edu	23	10	714	37274	609	275329	3877	503123	241276	4721

FLORIDA

Resident population 14,916 (in thousands)
Resident population in metro areas 89.7%
Birth rate per 1,000 population 13.3
65 years and over 18.5%
Percent of persons without health insurance 18.9%

Hospital, Address, Telephone, Administrator, Approval, Facility, and Physician Codes, Health Care System, Network	Classi-fication Codes		Utilization Data					Expense (thousands) of dollars		
★ American Hospital Association (AHA) membership □ Joint Commission on Accreditation of Healthcare Organizations (JCAHO) accreditation + American Osteopathic Healthcare Association (AOHA) membership ○ American Osteopathic Association (AOA) accreditation △ Commission on Accreditation of Rehabilitation Facilities (CARF) accreditation Control codes 61, 63, 64, 71, 72 and 73 indicate hospitals listed by AOHA, but not registered by AHA. For definition of numerical codes, see page A4	Control	Service	Staffed Beds	Admissions	Census	Outpatient Visits	Births	Total	Payroll	Personnel

ALTAMONTE SPRINGS—Seminole County
FLORIDA HOSPITAL–ALTAMONTE See Florida Hospital, Orlando

APALACHICOLA—Franklin County

GEORGE E. WEEMS MEMORIAL HOSPITAL, 135 Avenue G., Zip 32320, Mailing Address: P.O. Box 580, Zip 32329–0580; tel. 850/653–8853; Susan Ficklen, Administrator (Nonreporting) **A**9 10	33	10	29	—						

APOPKA—Orange County
FLORIDA HOSPITAL–APOPKA See Florida Hospital, Orlando

ARCADIA—De Soto County

⊞ DESOTO MEMORIAL HOSPITAL, 900 North Robert Avenue, Zip 34266–8765, Mailing Address: P.O. Box 2180, Zip 34265–2180; tel. 941/494–3535; Vincent B. DiFranco, Interim Chief Executive Officer (Nonreporting) **A**1 9 10 **S** Quorum Health Group/Quorum Health Resources, Inc., Brentwood, TN	23	10	62	—						
G. PIERCE WOOD MEMORIAL HOSPITAL, 5847 S.E. Highway 31, Zip 34266–9627; tel. 941/494–3323; Myers R. Kurtz, Administrator (Nonreporting) **A**5 10	12	22	450	—						

ATLANTIS—Palm Beach County

⊞ J. F. K. MEDICAL CENTER, 5301 South Congress Avenue, Zip 33462–1197; tel. 561/965–7300; Phillip D. Robinson, Chief Executive Officer (Total facility includes 20 beds in nursing home–type unit) (Nonreporting) **A**1 2 9 10 **S** Columbia/HCA Healthcare Corporation, Nashville, TN	33	10	363	—						

AVON PARK—Highlands County

FLORIDA CENTER FOR ADDICTIONS AND DUAL DISORDERS, 100 West College Drive, Zip 33825–9341; tel. 941/452–3858; Arthur J. Cox, Sr., Director (Nonreporting)	23	82	50	—	—	—	—	—	—	—

BARTOW—Polk County

⊞ BARTOW MEMORIAL HOSPITAL, 1239 East Main Street, Zip 33830–5005, Mailing Address: Box 1050, Zip 33830–1050; tel. 941/533–8111; Brian P. Baumgardner, Administrator **A**1 9 10 **F**1 3 4 7 8 10 12 14 16 17 19 20 21 22 23 27 28 29 30 31 32 33 34 35 36 37 39 40 41 42 43 44 45 46 48 49 50 51 53 54 55 56 57 58 59 60 61 63 64 65 67 69 70 71 72 73 74 **P**5 **S** LifePoint Hospitals, Inc., Nashville, TN **Web address:** www.koala.columbia.net	32	10	56	2279	19	33534	377	18141	6699	305

BAY PINES—Pinellas County

⊞ △ VETERANS AFFAIRS MEDICAL CENTER, Bay Pines & 100 Way, Zip 33744, Mailing Address: P.O. Box 5005, Zip 33744–5005; tel. 727/398–6661; Thomas H. Weaver, FACHE, Director (Total facility includes 184 beds in nursing home–type unit) **A**1 2 3 5 7 **F**2 3 8 10 12 14 15 16 17 19 20 21 22 25 26 30 31 32 33 34 35 37 39 41 42 44 45 46 48 49 51 52 54 55 56 57 58 59 63 64 65 67 71 73 74 **P**6 **S** Department of Veterans Affairs, Washington, DC	45	10	533	9010	475	405140	0	162947	92762	2107

BELLE GLADE—Palm Beach County

⊞ GLADES GENERAL HOSPITAL, 1201 South Main Street, Zip 33430–4911; tel. 561/996–6571; Gene Faile, Chief Executive Officer (Nonreporting) **A**1 9 10	16	10	47	—	—	—	—	—	—	—

BLOUNTSTOWN—Calhoun County

★ CALHOUN–LIBERTY HOSPITAL, 424 Burns Avenue, Zip 32424–1097; tel. 850/674–5411; David Paris, Administrator (Nonreporting) **A**9 10	23	10	30	—						

BOCA RATON—Palm Beach County

⊞ BOCA RATON COMMUNITY HOSPITAL, 800 Meadows Road, Zip 33486–2368; tel. 561/393–4002; Randolph J. Pierce, President and Chief Executive Officer **A**1 2 9 10 **F**7 8 10 11 14 15 16 17 18 19 21 22 24 27 28 30 31 32 34 35 37 39 40 41 42 44 45 46 49 60 61 63 65 67 71 73 74 **Web address:** www.brch.com	23	10	355	17407	235	170358	1426	145148	58870	1648
⊞ WEST BOCA MEDICAL CENTER, 21644 State Road 7, Zip 33428–1899; tel. 561/488–8000; Richard Gold, Chief Executive Officer (Nonreporting) **A**1 9 10 **S** TENET Healthcare Corporation, Santa Barbara, CA	33	10	150	—						

BONIFAY—Holmes County

⊞ DOCTORS MEMORIAL HOSPITAL, 401 East Byrd Avenue, Zip 32425–3007, Mailing Address: P.O. Box 188, Zip 32425–0188; tel. 850/547–1120; Dale Larson, Chief Executive Officer (Nonreporting) **A**1 9 10 **S** Community Health Systems, Inc., Brentwood, TN	33	10	34	—	—	—	—	—	—	—

BOYNTON BEACH—Palm Beach County

⊞ BETHESDA MEMORIAL HOSPITAL, 2815 South Seacrest Boulevard, Zip 33435–7995; tel. 561/737–7733; Robert B. Hill, President and Chief Executive Officer (Total facility includes 27 beds in nursing home–type unit) **A**1 2 9 10 **F**7 8 10 11 12 14 15 16 19 22 23 24 27 32 35 37 38 40 41 42 44 45 46 49 52 56 59 60 61 64 65 66 67 71 73 74 **P**5 7 **Web address:** www.bethesdaweb.com	23	10	335	14110	182	130346	2217	116831	44854	1863

Hospital, Address, Telephone, Administrator, Approval, Facility, and Physician Codes, Health Care System, Network	Classification Codes		Utilization Data					Expense (thousands) of dollars		
	Control	Service	Staffed Beds	Admissions	Census	Outpatient Visits	Births	Total	Payroll	Personnel

★ American Hospital Association (AHA) membership
□ Joint Commission on Accreditation of Healthcare Organizations (JCAHO) accreditation
+ American Osteopathic Healthcare Association (AOHA) membership
○ American Osteopathic Association (AOA) accreditation
△ Commission on Accreditation of Rehabilitation Facilities (CARF) accreditation
Control codes 61, 63, 64, 71, 72 and 73 indicate hospitals listed by AOHA, but not registered by AHA. For definition of numerical codes, see page A4

BRADENTON—Manatee County

✠ △ BLAKE MEDICAL CENTER, 2020 59th Street West, Zip 34209–4669, Mailing Address: P.O. Box 25004, Zip 34206–5004; tel. 941/792–6611; Lindell W. Orr, Chief Executive Officer (Total facility includes 28 beds in nursing home–type unit) **A**1 2 7 9 10 **F**4 7 10 11 12 13 14 15 16 17 19 21 22 23 25 26 28 30 33 34 35 37 39 40 41 42 43 44 45 48 49 60 63 64 65 67 71 72 73 74 **S** Columbia/HCA Healthcare Corporation, Nashville, TN

□ MANATEE MEMORIAL HOSPITAL, 206 Second Street East, Zip 34208–1000; tel. 941/746–5111; Michael Marquez, Chief Executive Officer (Total facility includes 10 beds in nursing home–type unit) **A**1 2 9 10 **F**2 3 4 7 8 10 11 12 14 15 16 17 19 21 22 24 25 28 30 32 34 37 38 40 41 42 43 44 45 46 52 53 58 59 64 65 67 71 72 73 74 **P**8 **S** Universal Health Services, Inc., King of Prussia, PA

BRANDON—Hillsborough County

✠ BRANDON REGIONAL HOSPITAL, 119 Oakfield Drive, Zip 33511–5799; tel. 813/681–5551; Michael M. Fencel, Chief Executive Officer **A**1 9 10 **F**7 8 10 11 12 14 16 19 21 22 27 28 30 32 35 37 38 40 44 45 47 49 59 60 63 64 65 67 71 73 **P**5 **S** Columbia/HCA Healthcare Corporation, Nashville, TN
Web address: www.brandonhospital.com

BROOKSVILLE—Hernando County

✠ BROOKSVILLE REGIONAL HOSPITAL, 55 Ponce De Leon Boulevard, Zip 34601–0037, Mailing Address: P.O. Box 37, Zip 34605–0037; tel. 352/796–5111; Robert Foreman, Associate Administrator (Nonreporting) **A**1 9 10 **S** Health Management Associates, Naples, FL

□ GREENBRIER HOSPITAL, 7007 Grove Road, Zip 34609–8610; tel. 352/596–4306; Susan L. Wright, Administrator (Nonreporting) **A**1 9 10

BUNNELL—Flagler County

★ MEMORIAL HOSPITAL–FLAGLER, Moody Boulevard, Zip 32110, Mailing Address: HCR1, Box 2, Zip 32110; tel. 904/437–2211; Clark P. Christianson, Senior Vice President and Administrator (Total facility includes 8 beds in nursing home–type unit) **A**9 10 **F**4 7 8 10 12 14 15 16 17 19 20 21 22 24 25 26 28 29 30 31 32 33 34 35 37 39 41 42 43 44 45 46 49 60 64 65 66 67 71 72 73 74 **P**8 **S** Memorial Health Systems, Ormond Beach, FL

CAPE CORAL—Lee County

CAPE CORAL HOSPITAL, 636 Del Prado Boulevard, Zip 33990–2695; tel. 941/574–2323; Earl Tamar, Chief Operating Officer (Nonreporting) **A**9 10

CHATTAHOOCHEE—Gadsden County

FLORIDA STATE HOSPITAL, U.S. Highway 90 East, Zip 32324–1000, Mailing Address: P.O. Box 1000, Zip 32324–1000; tel. 850/663–7536; Robert B. Williams, Administrator **A**10 **F**4 8 10 11 12 17 19 20 21 22 23 26 28 29 30 31 35 37 39 40 41 42 43 45 46 50 52 54 55 57 60 63 64 65 67 70 71 73 74 **P**6

CHIPLEY—Washington County

✠ NORTHWEST FLORIDA COMMUNITY HOSPITAL, 1360 Brickyard Road, Zip 32428–6303, Mailing Address: P.O. Box 889, Zip 32428–0889; tel. 850/638–1610; Stephen D. Mason, Administrator **A**1 9 10 **F**8 14 19 22 24 28 30 32 34 37 41 44 49 64 65 66 71 73

CLEARWATER—Pinellas County

MORTON PLANT HOSPITAL, 323 Jeffords Street, Zip 33756, Mailing Address: P.O. Box 210, Zip 34657–0210; tel. 727/462–7000; Philip K. Beauchamp, FACHE, President and Chief Executive Officer (Total facility includes 126 beds in nursing home–type unit) (Nonreporting) **A**2 3 5 9 10 **S** Morton Plant Mease Health Care, Dunedin, FL

□ WINDMOOR HEALTHCARE OF CLEARWATER, 11300 U.S. 19 North, Zip 33764; tel. 727/541–2646; C. William Brett, Ph.D., President and Chief Executive Officer (Nonreporting) **A**1 10

CLERMONT—Lake County

□ SOUTH LAKE HOSPITAL, 847 Eighth Street, Zip 34711–2196; tel. 352/394–4071; Leslie Longacre, Executive Director and Chief Executive Officer **A**1 9 10 **F**1 3 4 5 6 7 8 10 12 13 14 15 16 17 18 19 20 21 22 23 24 25 26 27 28 29 30 31 32 33 34 35 36 37 39 41 42 43 44 45 46 49 50 51 53 54 55 56 58 59 60 61 62 63 64 65 66 67 69 70 71 72 73 74 **S** Orlando Regional Healthcare System, Orlando, FL

CLEWISTON—Hendry County

✠ HENDRY REGIONAL MEDICAL CENTER, 500 West Sugarland Highway, Zip 33440–3094; tel. 941/983–9121; J. Rudy Reinhardt, Administrator **A**1 9 10 **F**8 12 13 14 15 16 17 19 20 21 22 25 26 28 29 30 31 32 33 34 35 37 39 41 42 44 45 49 51 53 54 55 56 57 58 65 69 71 73 **P**6 **S** Quorum Health Group/Quorum Health Resources, Inc., Brentwood, TN

COCOA BEACH—Brevard County

✠ HEALTH FIRST/CAPE CANAVERAL HOSPITAL, 701 West Cocoa Beach Causeway, Zip 32931–5595, Mailing Address: P.O. Box 320069, Zip 32932–0069; tel. 407/799–7111; Christopher S. Kennedy, President and Chief Operating Officer **A**1 2 9 10 **F**7 8 10 12 14 17 19 21 22 24 25 28 30 32 33 35 37 40 41 44 45 48 49 51 65 67 71 72 73 **P**5 7

CORAL GABLES—Dade County

✠ CORAL GABLES HOSPITAL, 3100 Douglas Road, Zip 33134–6990; tel. 305/445–8461; Martha Garcia, Chief Executive Officer (Nonreporting) **A**1 9 10 **S** TENET Healthcare Corporation, Santa Barbara, CA

Hospital	Control	Service	Staffed Beds	Admissions	Census	Outpatient Visits	Births	Total	Payroll	Personnel
BLAKE MEDICAL CENTER	33	10	284	12836	193	82745	477	74535	33547	746
MANATEE MEMORIAL HOSPITAL	33	10	512	15790	200	139441	1866	113137	39507	1120
BRANDON REGIONAL HOSPITAL	33	10	255	11915	154	—	3093	81939	39207	984
BROOKSVILLE REGIONAL HOSPITAL	23	10	91	—	—	—	—	—	—	—
GREENBRIER HOSPITAL	33	22	36	—	—	—	—	—	—	—
MEMORIAL HOSPITAL–FLAGLER	23	10	81	2111	28	27256	0	19193	7653	242
CAPE CORAL HOSPITAL	23	10	201	—	—	—	—	—	—	—
FLORIDA STATE HOSPITAL	12	22	930	599	927	0	0	94679	56259	2317
NORTHWEST FLORIDA COMMUNITY HOSPITAL	13	10	71	1462	49	25672	0	13957	6150	235
MORTON PLANT HOSPITAL	23	10	742	—	—	—	—	—	—	—
WINDMOOR HEALTHCARE OF CLEARWATER	33	22	50	—	—	—	—	—	—	—
SOUTH LAKE HOSPITAL	16	10	64	2248	29	30888	0	16859	8560	200
HENDRY REGIONAL MEDICAL CENTER	16	10	45	947	15	27112	0	13376	6019	200
HEALTH FIRST/CAPE CANAVERAL HOSPITAL	23	10	125	6505	69	22708	813	60019	18064	643
CORAL GABLES HOSPITAL	33	10	205	—	—	—	—	—	—	—

Hospital, Address, Telephone, Administrator, Approval, Facility, and Physician Codes, Health Care System, Network	Classi-fication Codes		Utilization Data					Expense (thousands) of dollars		
★ American Hospital Association (AHA) membership □ Joint Commission on Accreditation of Healthcare Organizations (JCAHO) accreditation + American Osteopathic Healthcare Association (AOHA) membership ○ American Osteopathic Association (AOA) accreditation △ Commission on Accreditation of Rehabilitation Facilities (CARF) accreditation Control codes 61, 63, 64, 71, 72 and 73 indicate hospitals listed by AOHA, but not registered by AHA. For definition of numerical codes, see page A4	Control	Service	Staffed Beds	Admissions	Census	Outpatient Visits	Births	Total	Payroll	Personnel

□ HEALTHSOUTH DOCTORS' HOSPITAL, 5000 University Drive, Zip 33146–2094; tel. 305/666–2111; Lincoln S. Mendez, Chief Executive Officer (Total facility includes 29 beds in nursing home–type unit) (Nonreporting) **A**1 3 9 10 **S** HEALTHSOUTH Corporation, Birmingham, AL **Web address:** www.healthsouth.com	33	10	157	—	—	—	—	—	—	—
VENCOR HOSPITAL–CORAL GABLES, 5190 S.W. Eighth Street, Zip 33134–2495; tel. 305/445–1364; Theodore Welding, Chief Executive Officer (Nonreporting) **S** Vencor, Incorporated, Louisville, KY	33	10	53	—	—	—	—	—	—	—
CORAL SPRINGS—Broward County										
⊞ CORAL SPRINGS MEDICAL CENTER, 3000 Coral Hills Drive, Zip 33065; tel. 954/344–3000; Debbie Mulvihill, Interim Administrator (Nonreporting) **A**1 3 5 9 10 **S** North Broward Hospital District, Fort Lauderdale, FL	16	10	167	—	—	—	—	—	—	—
CRESTVIEW—Okaloosa County										
⊞ NORTH OKALOOSA MEDICAL CENTER, 151 Redstone Avenue S.E., Zip 32539–6026; tel. 850/689–8100; Roger L. Hall, Chief Executive Officer (Total facility includes 10 beds in nursing home–type unit) **A**1 9 10 **F**7 8 10 12 14 15 16 17 19 22 24 25 28 29 30 32 34 35 37 40 41 44 45 46 49 51 63 64 65 67 72 73 74 **P**7 **S** Community Health Systems, Inc., Brentwood, TN	33	10	83	4804	53	71111	582	25388	11401	436
CRYSTAL RIVER—Citrus County										
⊞ SEVEN RIVERS COMMUNITY HOSPITAL, 6201 North Suncoast Boulevard, Zip 34428–6712; tel. 352/795–6560; Michael L. Collins, Chief Executive Officer (Nonreporting) **A**1 9 10 **S** TENET Healthcare Corporation, Santa Barbara, CA	33	10	128	—	—	—	—	—	—	—
DADE CITY—Pasco County										
⊞ PASCO COMMUNITY HOSPITAL, 13100 Fort King Road, Zip 33525–5294; tel. 352/521–1100; William G. Buck, President and Chief Executive Officer **A**1 9 10 **F**3 4 7 8 10 12 14 15 16 17 19 21 22 26 28 29 30 34 35 37 39 40 41 44 45 46 49 63 64 65 67 70 71 73 74 **S** Columbia/HCA Healthcare Corporation, Nashville, TN	33	10	120	3729	45	31299	191	—	—	167
DAVENPORT—Polk County										
□ HEART OF FLORIDA REGIONAL MEDICAL CENTER, 1615 U.S. Highway 27N, Zip 33837, Mailing Address: P.O. Box 67, Haines City, Zip 33844–0067; tel. 941/422–4971; Robert Mahaffey, Administrator (Nonreporting) **A**1 9 10 **S** Health Management Associates, Naples, FL	33	10	51	—	—	—	—	—	—	—
DAYTONA BEACH—Volusia County										
⊞ ATLANTIC MEDICAL CENTER–DAYTONA, 400 North Clyde Morris Boulevard, Zip 32114–2770, Mailing Address: P.O. Box 9000, Zip 32120–9000; tel. 904/239–5000; Pam Corliss, Chief Executive Officer **A**1 9 10 **F**2 3 8 10 12 16 17 18 19 22 26 27 28 29 30 34 35 37 41 42 44 45 46 48 49 52 54 55 56 57 58 63 65 71 73 **P**7 **S** Columbia/HCA Healthcare Corporation, Nashville, TN	33	10	214	3428	41	53567	0	22524	9657	240
⊞ HALIFAX COMMUNITY HEALTH SYSTEM, (Includes Halifax Behavioral Services, 841 Jimmy Ann Drive, Zip 32117–4599; tel. 904/274–5333), 303 North Clyde Morris Boulevard, Zip 32114–2700; tel. 904/322–4785; Ron R. Rees, President and Chief Executive Officer **A**1 2 3 5 9 10 **F**1 2 3 4 7 8 9 10 11 12 13 15 16 17 18 19 20 21 22 23 24 25 26 27 28 29 30 31 32 33 34 35 37 38 39 40 41 42 43 44 45 46 47 49 51 52 53 54 55 56 57 58 59 60 61 63 64 65 66 67 68 70 71 72 73 74 **P**6 **Web address:** www.halifax.org	16	10	478	21776	284	352929	2096	214228	73828	2189
DE FUNIAK SPRINGS—Walton County										
WALTON REGIONAL HOSPITAL, 336 College Avenue, Zip 32433; tel. 904/892–5171; Jim Thompson, Chief Executive Officer (Nonreporting) **A**9 10	33	10	34	—	—	—	—	—	—	—
DE LAND—Union County										
⊞ MEMORIAL HOSPITAL–WEST VOLUSIA, 701 West Plymouth Avenue, Zip 32720–3291, Mailing Address: P.O. Box 6509, DeLand, Zip 32721–0509; tel. 904/943–3320; Johnette L. Vodenicker, Administrator **A**1 9 10 **F**4 7 8 10 12 14 15 17 19 22 23 28 29 30 32 33 35 37 40 42 43 44 45 49 52 56 60 65 67 71 73 74 **P**6 **S** Memorial Health Systems, Ormond Beach, FL	23	10	130	6857	88	97649	1040	50826	16944	604
DELRAY BEACH—Palm Beach County										
⊞ DELRAY MEDICAL CENTER, 5352 Linton Boulevard, Zip 33484–6580; tel. 561/498–4440; Mitchell S. Feldman, Chief Executive Officer (Nonreporting) **A**1 9 10 **S** TENET Healthcare Corporation, Santa Barbara, CA **Web address:** www.tenethealth.com	33	10	211	—	—	—	—	—	—	—
□ FAIR OAKS HOSPITAL, 5440 Linton Boulevard, Zip 33484–6578; tel. 561/495–1000; Bill Russell, Chief Operating Officer and Administrator (Nonreporting) **A**1 10 **S** TENET Healthcare Corporation, Santa Barbara, CA	33	22	102	—	—	—	—	—	—	—
□ △ PINECREST REHABILITATION HOSPITAL, 5360 Linton Boulevard, Zip 33484–6538; tel. 561/495–0400; Paul D. Echelard, Administrator (Nonreporting) **A**1 7 10 **S** TENET Healthcare Corporation, Santa Barbara, CA	33	46	90	—	—	—	—	—	—	—
DUNEDIN—Pinellas County										
□ MEASE HOSPITAL DUNEDIN, 601 Main Street, Zip 34698–5891, Mailing Address: P.O. Box 760, Zip 34697–0760; tel. 727/733–1111; James A. Pfeiffer, Chief Operating Officer (Total facility includes 20 beds in nursing home–type unit) (Nonreporting) **A**1 9 10 **S** Morton Plant Mease Health Care, Dunedin, FL	23	10	258	—	—	—	—	—	—	—
EGLIN AFB—Okaloosa County										
⊞ U. S. AIR FORCE REGIONAL HOSPITAL, 307 Boatner Road, Suite 114, Zip 32542–1282; tel. 850/883–8221; Colonel William C. Head, MSC, USAF, Administrator (Nonreporting) **A**1 3 5 **S** Department of the Air Force, Bowling AFB, DC	41	10	85	—	—	—	—	—	—	—

Hospital, Address, Telephone, Administrator, Approval, Facility, and Physician Codes, Health Care System, Network	Classi-fication Codes		Utilization Data					Expense (thousands) of dollars		
★ American Hospital Association (AHA) membership □ Joint Commission on Accreditation of Healthcare Organizations (JCAHO) accreditation + American Osteopathic Healthcare Association (AOHA) membership ○ American Osteopathic Association (AOA) accreditation △ Commission on Accreditation of Rehabilitation Facilities (CARF) accreditation Control codes 61, 63, 64, 71, 72 and 73 indicate hospitals listed by AOHA, but not registered by AHA. For definition of numerical codes, see page A4	Control	Service	Staffed Beds	Admissions	Census	Outpatient Visits	Births	Total	Payroll	Personnel

ENGLEWOOD—Sarasota County

✠ ENGLEWOOD COMMUNITY HOSPITAL, 700 Medical Boulevard, Zip 34223–3978; tel. 941/475–6571; Robert C. Meade, Chief Executive Officer **A**1 9 10 **F**8 10 12 17 19 21 22 27 30 35 37 44 49 51 64 66 71 73 **P**6 8 **S** Columbia/HCA Healthcare Corporation, Nashville, TN
| | | 33 | 10 | 100 | 4589 | 60 | 58963 | 0 | 29704 | 11319 | 283 |

EUSTIS—Lake County

✠ FLORIDA HOSPITAL WATERMAN, 201 North Eustis Street, Zip 32726–3488; Mailing Address: P.O. Box B, Zip 32727–0377; tel. 352/589–3333; Kenneth R. Mattison, President and Chief Executive Officer **A**1 2 9 10 **F**7 8 10 12 14 15 16 17 19 21 22 23 24 25 27 28 30 31 32 33 35 37 39 40 42 44 45 46 49 57 58 59 63 64 65 66 67 68 71 73 74 **P**1 5 6 7 **S** Adventist Health System Sunbelt Health Care Corporation, Winter Park, FL
Web address: www.fhwat.org
| | | 21 | 10 | 181 | 8501 | 131 | 108552 | 694 | 81332 | 37083 | 1024 |

FERNANDINA BEACH—Nassau County

✠ BAPTIST MEDICAL CENTER–NASSAU, 1250 South 18th Street, Zip 32034–3098; tel. 904/321–3501; Jim L. Mayo, Administrator **A**1 9 10 **F**7 8 11 12 17 19 21 22 30 32 33 35 37 40 44 48 49 51 66 71 73 **P**6 8 **S** Daughters of Charity National Health System, Saint Louis, MO
Web address: www.baptist–stvincents.com
| | | 23 | 10 | 24 | 1743 | 18 | 39455 | 325 | 16721 | 6826 | 238 |

FORT LAUDERDALE—Broward County

□ ATLANTIC SHORES HOSPITAL, 4545 North Federal Highway, Zip 33308–5274; tel. 954/771–2711; Edward J. Whitehouse, Chief Executive Office (Nonreporting) **A**1 10
| | | 31 | 22 | 86 | — | — | — | — | — | — | — |

BHC FORT LAUDERDALE HOSPITAL, 1601 East Las Olas Boulevard, Zip 33301–2393; tel. 954/463–4321; Andrew Fuhrman, Chief Executive Officer (Nonreporting) **A**9 10 **S** Behavioral Healthcare Corporation, Nashville, TN
| | | 33 | 22 | 100 | — | — | — | — | — | — | — |

✠ BROWARD GENERAL MEDICAL CENTER, 1600 South Andrews Avenue, Zip 33316–2510; tel. 954/355–4400; Timothy P. Menton, Interim Administrator (Total facility includes 20 beds in nursing home–type unit) (Nonreporting) **A**1 2 3 9 10 12 **S** North Broward Hospital District, Fort Lauderdale, FL
| | | 16 | 10 | 548 | — | — | — | — | — | — | — |

□ CLEVELAND CLINIC HOSPITAL, 2835 North Ocean Boulevard, Zip 33308–7599; tel. 954/568–1000; Chantal Leconte, Administrator (Nonreporting) **A**1 3 9 10
| | | 23 | 10 | 120 | — | — | — | — | — | — | — |

✠ FLORIDA MEDICAL CENTER HOSPITAL, 5000 West Oakland Park Boulevard, Zip 33313–1585; tel. 954/735–6000; Joel Bergenfeld, Chief Executive Officer (Nonreporting) **A**1 9 10 **S** TENET Healthcare Corporation, Santa Barbara, CA
| | | 32 | 10 | 459 | — | — | — | — | — | — | — |

□ HEALTHSOUTH SUNRISE REHABILITATION HOSPITAL, 4399 Nob Hill Road, Zip 33351–5899; tel. 954/749–0300; Kevin R. Conn, Administrator **A**1 10 **F**1 3 5 12 14 15 16 17 19 24 25 26 27 28 34 35 39 41 42 46 48 49 65 66 67 71 73 **S** HEALTHSOUTH Corporation, Birmingham, AL
| | | 33 | 46 | 108 | 1902 | 105 | 41873 | 0 | 23993 | 12686 | 319 |

□ △ HOLY CROSS HOSPITAL, 4725 North Federal Highway, Zip 33308–4668, Mailing Address: P.O. Box 23460, Zip 33307–3460; tel. 954/771–8000; John C. Johnson, Chief Executive Officer (Nonreporting) **A**1 2 7 9 10 **S** Catholic Health East, Newtown Square, PA
Web address: www.holy–cross.com
| | | 21 | 10 | 437 | — | — | — | — | — | — | — |

✠ IMPERIAL POINT MEDICAL CENTER, 6401 North Federal Highway, Zip 33308–1495; tel. 954/776–8500; Dorothy J. Mancini, R.N., Regional Vice President Administration **A**1 9 10 **F**4 5 7 8 10 12 14 15 16 17 19 22 23 24 26 28 30 31 32 33 34 35 37 39 41 42 43 44 49 51 52 56 57 58 59 60 65 66 70 71 73 **P**6 7 **S** North Broward Hospital District, Fort Lauderdale, FL
| | | 16 | 10 | 160 | 5231 | 97 | 63688 | 0 | 39738 | 20065 | 467 |

✠ NORTH RIDGE MEDICAL CENTER, 5757 North Dixie Highway, Zip 33334–4182, Mailing Address: P.O. Box 23160, Zip 33307; tel. 954/776–6000; Emil P. Miller, Chief Executive Officer (Nonreporting) **A**1 9 10 **S** TENET Healthcare Corporation, Santa Barbara, CA
Web address: www.tenethealth/northridge.com
| | | 33 | 10 | 391 | — | — | — | — | — | — | — |

□ VENCOR HOSPITAL–FORT LAUDERDALE, 1516 East Las Olas Boulevard, Zip 33301–2399; tel. 954/764–8900; Lewis A. Ransdell, Administrator **A**1 10 **F**12 14 15 16 19 20 22 27 35 37 41 44 49 60 65 67 71 73 **S** Vencor, Incorporated, Louisville, KY
Web address: www.vencor.com
| | | 33 | 10 | 64 | 385 | 56 | 0 | 0 | — | — | 260 |

FORT MYERS—Lee County

□ CHARTER GLADE BEHAVIORAL HEALTH SYSTEM, 3550 Colonial Boulevard, Zip 33912–1065; tel. 941/939–0403; Vickie Lewis, Chief Executive Officer (Nonreporting) **A**1 9 10 **S** Magellan Health Services, Atlanta, GA
Web address: www.charterbehavioral.com
| | | 33 | 22 | 104 | — | — | — | — | — | — | — |

✠ ○ GULF COAST HOSPITAL, 13681 Doctors Way, Zip 33912–4309; tel. 941/768–5000; Valerie A. Jackson, Chief Executive Officer **A**1 9 10 11 **F**4 7 8 10 12 14 15 16 19 21 22 25 26 29 30 34 35 37 39 40 41 42 43 44 47 49 57 60 61 64 65 66 68 71 73 **S** Columbia/HCA Healthcare Corporation, Nashville, TN
| | | 33 | 10 | 120 | 4461 | 43 | 29638 | 1006 | 24103 | 9827 | 192 |

✠ △ LEE MEMORIAL HEALTH SYSTEM, 2776 Cleveland Avenue, Zip 33901–5855, Mailing Address: P.O. Box 2218, Zip 33902–2218; tel. 941/332–1111; William D. Johnson, President (Total facility includes 90 beds in nursing home–type unit) **A**1 2 7 9 10 **F**4 7 8 10 11 12 13 14 15 16 19 21 22 23 24 25 26 28 29 30 31 32 33 34 35 36 37 38 39 40 41 42 43 44 45 46 47 48 49 51 53 54 55 56 57 58 59 60 61 64 65 66 67 70 71 72 73 74 **P**1
| | | 16 | 10 | 949 | 35065 | 537 | 235025 | 3973 | 324465 | 148026 | 3779 |

✠ SOUTHWEST FLORIDA REGIONAL MEDICAL CENTER, 2727 Winkler Avenue, Zip 33901–9396; tel. 941/939–1147; Stephen L. Royal, President and Chief Executive Officer (Total facility includes 20 beds in nursing home–type unit) **A**1 9 10 **F**4 8 10 11 12 14 15 19 21 22 26 27 30 31 32 34 35 37 39 41 42 43 44 45 49 50 51 63 64 65 67 68 71 72 73 74 **P**8 **S** Columbia/HCA Healthcare Corporation, Nashville, TN
| | | 33 | 10 | 400 | 12546 | 158 | 98553 | 0 | 108811 | 36271 | 1509 |

Hospital, Address, Telephone, Administrator, Approval, Facility, and Physician Codes, Health Care System, Network	Classi-fication Codes		Utilization Data					Expense (thousands) of dollars		

★ American Hospital Association (AHA) membership
□ Joint Commission on Accreditation of Healthcare Organizations (JCAHO) accreditation
+ American Osteopathic Healthcare Association (AOHA) membership
○ American Osteopathic Association (AOA) accreditation
△ Commission on Accreditation of Rehabilitation Facilities (CARF) accreditation
Control codes 61, 63, 64, 71, 72 and 73 indicate hospitals listed by AOHA, but not registered by AHA. For definition of numerical codes, see page A4

	Control	Service	Staffed Beds	Admissions	Census	Outpatient Visits	Births	Total	Payroll	Personnel

FORT PIERCE—St. Lucie County

☒ LAWNWOOD REGIONAL MEDICAL CENTER, (Includes Lawnwood Pavilion, 1860 North Lawnwood Circle, Zip 34950; tel. 361/466–1500), 1700 South 23rd Street, Zip 34950–0188; tel. 561/461–4000; Thomas R. Pentz, President and Executive Officer (Total facility includes 33 beds in nursing home–type unit) **A**1 9 10 **F**3 4 7 8 10 12 13 14 15 16 17 19 20 22 23 24 25 28 29 30 31 32 33 34 35 36 37 38 39 40 41 42 44 45 48 49 52 53 55 58 59 60 64 65 66 71 73 74 **S** Columbia/HCA Healthcare Corporation, Nashville, TN | 33 | 10 | 363 | 13163 | 226 | 101258 | 1336 | — | | |

FORT WALTON BEACH—Okaloosa County

☒ FORT WALTON BEACH MEDICAL CENTER, 1000 Mar–Walt Drive, Zip 32547–6795; tel. 850/862–1111; Wayne Campbell, Chief Executive Officer **A**1 9 10 **F**7 8 10 11 12 14 15 16 17 19 20 21 22 23 28 29 33 35 37 40 41 42 44 46 48 49 52 56 59 64 71 73 74 **S** Columbia/HCA Healthcare Corporation, Nashville, TN | 33 | 10 | 247 | 9963 | 152 | 80263 | 932 | 52906 | 24573 | 757 |

GULF COAST TREATMENT CENTER, 1015 Mar–Walt Drive, Zip 32547–6612; tel. 850/863–4160; Raul D. Ruelas, M.D., Administrator (Nonreporting) **A**10 **S** Ramsay Health Care, Inc., Coral Gables, FL | 33 | 52 | 79 | — | — | — | — | — | — | — |

GAINESVILLE—Alachua County

☒ MALCOM RANDALL VETERANS AFFAIRS MEDICAL CENTER, (Formerly Veterans Affairs Med Center), 1601 S.W. Archer Road, Zip 32608–1197; tel. 352/376–1611; Elwood J. Headley, M.D., System Director (Total facility includes 53 beds in nursing home–type unit) **A**1 3 5 8 9 **F**1 2 3 4 8 10 12 15 16 17 18 19 20 21 25 26 27 28 29 30 31 32 34 35 37 39 41 42 43 44 46 49 51 52 54 55 56 57 58 59 60 63 64 65 67 71 73 74 **P**1 **S** Department of Veterans Affairs, Washington, DC
Web address: www.va.gov | 45 | 10 | 256 | 6150 | 144 | 270158 | 0 | 144924 | 69696 | 1655 |

☒ NORTH FLORIDA REGIONAL MEDICAL CENTER, 6500 Newberry Road, Zip 32605–4392, Mailing Address: P.O. Box 147006, Zip 32614–7006; tel. 352/333–4000; Brian C. Robinson, Chief Executive Officer (Total facility includes 24 beds in nursing home–type unit) (Nonreporting) **A**1 2 9 10 **S** Columbia/HCA Healthcare Corporation, Nashville, TN | 33 | 10 | 278 | — | — | — | — | — | — | — |

☒ SHANDS AT AGH, (Includes Shands at Vista, 8900 N.E. 39th Avenue, Zip 32606; tel. 904/338–0097), 801 S.W. Second Avenue, Zip 32601–6289; tel. 352/372–4321; Robert B. Williams, Administrator **A**1 2 3 5 9 10 **F**2 3 7 8 9 10 11 12 14 15 16 19 21 22 30 32 33 35 36 37 38 40 41 42 43 44 46 47 48 49 50 51 52 53 54 55 56 57 58 59 60 63 64 65 66 67 68 71 73 **P**6 7 8 **S** Shands HealthCare, Gainesville, FL | 23 | 10 | 269 | 9769 | 129 | 274362 | 1026 | 73956 | 33589 | 996 |

☒ SHANDS AT THE UNIVERSITY OF FLORIDA, 1600 S.W. Archer Road, Zip 32610–0326, Mailing Address: P.O. Box 100326, Zip 32610–0326; tel. 352/395–0111; Jodi J. Mansfield, Executive Vice President and Chief Operating Officer **A**1 2 3 5 8 9 10 **F**1 2 3 4 7 8 9 10 11 12 13 15 16 17 18 19 20 21 22 23 25 26 28 30 31 32 34 35 36 37 38 39 40 41 42 43 44 46 47 48 49 51 52 53 54 55 56 57 58 59 60 61 63 64 65 66 67 68 71 73 74 **P**6 8 **S** Shands HealthCare, Gainesville, FL | 23 | 10 | 564 | 24423 | 416 | 315649 | 2344 | 335069 | 129302 | 4195 |

★ △ SHANDS REHAB HOSPITAL, 8900 N.W. 39th Avenue, Zip 32606–5625; tel. 352/338–0091; Cynthia M. Toth, Administrator **A**7 10 **F**2 3 4 7 8 9 10 11 12 14 15 16 17 18 19 21 22 23 25 28 29 30 31 32 34 35 36 37 38 39 40 41 42 43 44 45 46 47 48 49 50 52 53 54 55 56 57 58 59 60 63 64 65 66 67 68 71 73 74 **P**6 **S** Shands HealthCare, Gainesville, FL | 23 | 46 | 40 | 641 | 29 | 6322 | 0 | 7376 | 3439 | 132 |

VETERANS AFFAIRS MED CENTER See Malcom Randall Veterans Affairs Medical Center

GRACEVILLE—Jackson County

CAMPBELLTON GRACEVILLE HOSPITAL, 5429 College Drive, Zip 32440; tel. 850/263–4431; Judy Schiros, Administrator **A**9 10 **F**14 15 16 19 22 28 30 33 34 64 65 71 **P**5 8 | 16 | 10 | 35 | 509 | 6 | 6242 | 0 | 3537 | 1830 | 75 |

GREEN COVE SPRINGS—Clay County

□ VENCOR–NORTH FLORIDA, (LONG TERM ACUTE CARE), 801 Oak Street, Zip 32043–4317; tel. 904/284–9230; Tim Simpson, Administrator **A**1 10 **F**14 15 16 19 22 37 65 71 **S** Vencor, Incorporated, Louisville, KY | 33 | 49 | 60 | 434 | 50 | 0 | 0 | — | — | 193 |

GULF BREEZE—Santa Rosa County

GULF BREEZE HOSPITAL, 1110 Gulf Breeze Parkway, Zip 32561, Mailing Address: P.O. Box 159, Zip 32562; tel. 850/934–2000; Richard C. Fulford, Administrator **A**9 10 **F**1 2 3 4 6 7 8 9 10 11 12 13 14 15 16 18 19 21 22 23 26 27 28 29 30 31 32 33 35 37 39 40 41 42 43 44 45 46 48 49 51 52 53 54 55 56 57 58 59 60 61 62 63 64 65 66 67 70 71 72 73 74 **P**5 6 7 **S** Baptist Health Care Corporation, Pensacola, FL | 23 | 10 | 60 | 2152 | 25 | 42324 | 0 | 18018 | 6547 | 193 |

THE FRIARY OF BAPTIST HEALTH CENTER, 4400 Hickory Shores Boulevard, Zip 32561–9113; tel. 904/932–9375; Leo J. Donnelly, Executive Director (Nonreporting) **A**9 **S** Baptist Health Care Corporation, Pensacola, FL | 23 | 82 | 30 | — | — | — | — | — | — | — |

HIALEAH—Dade County

☒ HIALEAH HOSPITAL, 651 East 25th Street, Zip 33013–3878; tel. 305/693–6100; Clifford J. Bauer, Chief Executive Officer (Nonreporting) **A**1 9 10 **S** TENET Healthcare Corporation, Santa Barbara, CA | 33 | 10 | 411 | — | — | — | — | — | — | — |

□ PALM SPRINGS GENERAL HOSPITAL, 1475 West 49th Street, Zip 33012–3275, Mailing Address: Box 2804, Zip 33012–2804; tel. 305/558–2500; Carlos Milanes, Executive Vice President and Administrator **A**1 9 10 **F**8 17 19 22 26 27 30 34 35 37 44 45 49 65 67 71 73 | 33 | 10 | 190 | 8922 | 145 | 24808 | 0 | — | — | 600 |

Hospital, Address, Telephone, Administrator, Approval, Facility, and Physician Codes, Health Care System, Network	Classi-fication Codes		Utilization Data					Expense (thousands) of dollars		
	Control	Service	Staffed Beds	Admissions	Census	Outpatient Visits	Births	Total	Payroll	Personnel

★ American Hospital Association (AHA) membership
□ Joint Commission on Accreditation of Healthcare Organizations (JCAHO) accreditation
+ American Osteopathic Healthcare Association (AOHA) membership
○ American Osteopathic Association (AOA) accreditation
△ Commission on Accreditation of Rehabilitation Facilities (CARF) accreditation
Control codes 61, 63, 64, 71, 72 and 73 indicate hospitals listed by AOHA, but not registered by AHA. For definition of numerical codes, see page A4

⊠ PALMETTO GENERAL HOSPITAL, 2001 West 68th Street, Zip 33016–1898; tel. 305/823–5000; Ron Stern, Chief Executive Officer (Nonreporting) **A**1 9 10 12 13 **S** TENET Healthcare Corporation, Santa Barbara, CA	33	10	360	—	—	—	—	—	—	—
□ ○ SOUTHERN WINDS HOSPITAL, 4225 West 20th Street, Zip 33012–5835; tel. 305/558–9700; Gilda Baldwin, Chief Executive Officer (Nonreporting) **A**1 10 11 13	33	22	60	—	—	—	—	—	—	—
HOLLYWOOD—Broward County										
⊠ △ HOLLYWOOD MEDICAL CENTER, 3600 Washington Street, Zip 33021–8216; tel. 954/966–4500; Holly Lerner, Chief Executive Officer (Nonreporting) **A**1 7 9 10 **S** TENET Healthcare Corporation, Santa Barbara, CA	33	10	238	—	—	—	—	—	—	—
□ HOLLYWOOD PAVILION, 1201 North 37th Avenue, Zip 33021–5498; tel. 954/962–1355; Karen Kallen–Zury, Chief Executive Officer (Nonreporting) **A**1 10	33	22	46	—	—	—	—	—	—	—
⊠ △ MEMORIAL REGIONAL HOSPITAL, (Includes Joe DiMaggio Children's Hospital), 3501 Johnson Street, Zip 33021–5421; tel. 954/987–2000; C. Kennon Hetlage, Administrator (Total facility includes 120 beds in nursing home–type unit) **A**1 2 3 7 9 10 **F**1 2 3 4 5 7 8 10 11 12 13 14 15 16 17 18 19 20 21 22 23 24 25 26 27 28 29 30 31 32 33 34 35 37 38 39 40 42 43 44 45 46 47 48 49 51 52 53 54 55 56 57 58 59 60 61 63 64 65 67 68 69 70 71 72 73 74 **P**5 8 **S** Memorial Healthcare System, Hollywood, FL Web address: www.mhs–net.com	16	10	674	28180	443	304249	2777	237877	109694	3694
HOMESTEAD—Dade County										
⊠ HOMESTEAD HOSPITAL, 160 N.W. 13th Street, Zip 33030–4299; tel. 305/248–3232; Bo Boulenger, Chief Executive Officer (Nonreporting) **A**1 9 10 **S** Baptist Health System of South Florida, Coral Gables, FL	23	10	100	—	—	—	—	—	—	—
HUDSON—Pasco County										
★ REGIONAL MEDICAL CENTER–BAYONET POINT, 14000 Fivay Road, Zip 34667–7199; tel. 727/863–2411; Don Griffin, Ph.D., President and Chief Executive Officer (Nonreporting) **A**9 10 **S** Columbia/HCA Healthcare Corporation, Nashville, TN	33	10	256	—	—	—	—	—	—	—
INVERNESS—Citrus County										
⊠ CITRUS MEMORIAL HOSPITAL, 502 West Highland Boulevard, Zip 34452–4754; tel. 352/344–6582; Charles A. Blasband, Chief Executive Officer **A**1 9 10 **F**7 8 10 12 15 19 21 22 25 28 30 32 34 35 36 37 39 40 44 49 51 65 67 71 72	23	10	171	8474	111	203257	453	65366	24204	797
JACKSONVILLE—Duval County										
⊠ BAPTIST MEDICAL CENTER, 800 Prudential Drive, Zip 32207–8203; tel. 904/202–2000; John F. Wilbanks, Senior Vice President and Administrator **A**1 2 3 5 9 10 **F**2 3 4 7 8 10 11 12 14 16 17 18 19 20 21 22 23 24 25 26 27 28 29 30 31 32 34 35 37 38 39 40 41 42 43 44 45 46 49 51 52 53 54 55 56 57 58 59 60 61 63 64 65 66 67 68 70 71 72 73 74 **P**5 7 **S** Daughters of Charity National Health System, Saint Louis, MO BHC ST. JOHNS RIVER HOSPITAL See St. Johns River Hospital	23	10	506	23229	316	486360	3221	239260	86930	2152
⊠ △ BROOKS REHABILITATION HOSPITAL, (Formerly Genesis Rehabilitation Hospital), 3599 University Boulevard South, Zip 32216–4211, Mailing Address: P.O. Box 16406, Zip 32245–6406; tel. 904/858–7600; Donald H. Hutton, FACHE, President and Chief Executive Officer **A**1 7 10 **F**12 14 15 16 17 19 20 21 22 24 25 27 28 30 34 35 41 45 46 48 49 50 53 54 63 65 66 67 71 73 **P**4 7 Web address: www.brookshealth.org	23	46	110	1626	94	—	0	22119	12601	322
⊠ MEMORIAL HOSPITAL OF JACKSONVILLE, 3625 University Boulevard South, Zip 32216–4240, Mailing Address: P.O. Box 16325, Zip 32216–6325; tel. 904/399–6111; H. Rex Etheredge, President and Chief Executive Officer (Nonreporting) **A**1 2 9 10 **S** Columbia/HCA Healthcare Corporation, Nashville, TN	33	10	310	—	—	—	—	—	—	—
⊠ METHODIST MEDICAL CENTER, 580 West Eighth Street, Zip 32209–6553; tel. 904/798–8000; Marcus E. Drewa, President and Chief Executive Officer (Total facility includes 27 beds in nursing home–type unit) **A**1 5 9 10 **F**3 4 7 8 10 12 14 15 16 17 19 21 22 27 28 29 30 31 32 33 34 35 37 39 41 42 43 44 45 46 49 51 53 54 55 56 57 58 59 60 64 65 67 68 70 71 73 74 **P**7	23	10	191	7226	124	30079	0	73299	26115	816
⊠ NAVAL HOSPITAL, 2080 Child Street, Zip 32214–5000; tel. 904/777–7300; Captain M. J. Benson, MSC, USN, Commanding Officer **A**1 3 5 **F**2 3 4 5 6 7 8 9 10 11 12 13 14 15 16 17 18 19 20 21 22 23 24 25 26 27 28 29 30 31 32 33 34 35 37 38 39 40 41 42 43 44 45 46 47 48 49 50 51 52 53 54 55 56 57 58 59 60 61 63 64 65 67 68 71 72 73 74 **P**6 **S** Department of Navy, Washington, DC	43	10	69	4878	37	708536	1085	—	—	—
⊠ SPECIALTY HOSPITAL JACKSONVILLE, (LONG TERM ACUTE CARE), 4901 Richard Street, Zip 32207; tel. 904/737–3120; W. Raymond C. Ford, Chief Executive Officer **A**1 9 10 **F**3 4 7 8 9 10 11 12 17 19 21 22 23 24 25 26 28 29 30 31 32 34 35 37 39 40 41 42 43 44 45 46 48 49 50 51 54 55 56 57 58 59 61 65 66 67 71 73 74 **P**7 8 **S** Columbia/HCA Healthcare Corporation, Nashville, TN Web address: www.heartofhealthcare.com	33	49	61	641	51	0	0	17179	8356	223
□ ST. JOHNS RIVER HOSPITAL, (Formerly BHC St. Johns River Hospital), 6300 Beach Boulevard, Zip 32216–2782; tel. 904/724–9202; Paul Pruitt, Administrator **A**1 9 10 **F**1 2 3 4 5 6 7 8 9 10 11 12 13 14 16 17 18 19 20 21 22 23 24 25 26 27 28 29 30 31 32 33 34 35 36 37 38 39 40 41 42 43 44 45 46 47 48 49 50 51 52 53 54 55 56 57 58 59 60 61 62 63 64 65 66 67 68 69 70 71 72 73 74 **P**1 2 3 4 5 6 8 **S** Behavioral Healthcare Corporation, Nashville, TN	33	22	66	1890	34	5705	0	6423	3117	116

Hospital, Address, Telephone, Administrator, Approval, Facility, and Physician Codes, Health Care System, Network	Classi-fication Codes		Utilization Data					Expense (thousands) of dollars		
	Control	Service	Staffed Beds	Admissions	Census	Outpatient Visits	Births	Total	Payroll	Personnel

★ American Hospital Association (AHA) membership
□ Joint Commission on Accreditation of Healthcare Organizations (JCAHO) accreditation
+ American Osteopathic Healthcare Association (AOHA) membership
○ American Osteopathic Association (AOA) accreditation
△ Commission on Accreditation of Rehabilitation Facilities (CARF) accreditation
Control codes 61, 63, 64, 71, 72 and 73 indicate hospitals listed by AOHA, but not registered by AHA. For definition of numerical codes, see page A4

	Control	Service	Staffed Beds	Admissions	Census	Outpatient Visits	Births	Total	Payroll	Personnel
✦ ST. LUKE'S HOSPITAL, 4201 Belfort Road, Zip 32216–5898; tel. 904/296–3700; Robert M. Walters, Administrator (Total facility includes 17 beds in nursing home–type unit) **A**1 2 3 5 8 9 10 **F**4 7 8 10 12 19 21 22 23 25 28 30 32 34 35 37 39 40 41 42 43 44 49 51 60 63 64 65 66 67 68 71 73 **P**3 6 **S** Mayo Foundation, Rochester, MN	23	10	239	9833	146	64504	659	122937	43184	1442
✦ ST. VINCENT'S MEDICAL CENTER, 1800 Barrs Street, Zip 32204–2982, Mailing Address: P.O. Box 2982, Zip 32203–2982; tel. 904/308–7300; John W. Logue, Executive Vice President and Chief Operating Officer (Total facility includes 223 beds in nursing home–type unit) **A**1 2 3 5 9 10 **F**2 3 4 7 8 10 11 12 14 15 16 17 18 19 21 22 23 25 26 27 28 29 30 31 32 33 34 35 36 37 38 39 40 41 42 43 44 45 47 49 51 52 53 54 55 56 57 58 59 60 61 63 64 65 66 67 68 70 71 73 74 **P**1 **S** Daughters of Charity National Health System, Saint Louis, MO **Web address:** www.baptist–stvincents.com	21	10	722	21944	510	121266	1969	201480	69793	2516
□ UNIVERSITY MEDICAL CENTER, 655 West Eighth Street, Zip 32209–6595; tel. 904/549–5000; Robert G. Norton, President and Chief Executive Officer **A**1 2 3 5 8 9 10 **F**4 7 8 10 11 12 13 14 15 16 17 18 19 20 21 22 25 26 28 30 31 34 35 37 38 40 41 42 43 44 45 46 47 49 51 52 54 55 56 57 58 59 60 61 63 65 66 67 68 70 71 72 73 74 **P**7	23	10	332	20546	261	304583	3234	194468	67478	2457
JACKSONVILLE BEACH—Duval County										
✦ BAPTIST MEDICAL CENTER–BEACHES, 1350 13th Avenue South, Zip 32250–3205; tel. 904/247–2900; Joseph Mitrick, Administrator **A**1 9 10 **F**4 7 8 10 11 12 17 19 21 22 23 24 27 28 30 32 35 37 38 40 41 42 43 44 45 46 47 49 50 51 52 53 54 55 56 57 59 60 63 64 65 66 70 71 72 73 74 **P**5 6 **S** Daughters of Charity National Health System, Saint Louis, MO	23	10	82	4347	54	70990	600	33852	14012	442
JASPER—Hamilton County										
★ HAMILTON MEDICAL CENTER, 506 N.W. Fourth Street, Zip 32052; tel. 904/792–7200; Amelia Tompkins, Administrator **A**9 10 **F**7 19 22 44 71 **S** Columbia/HCA Healthcare Corporation, Nashville, TN	33	10	20	514	7	7019	0	—	—	50
JAY—Santa Rosa County										
JAY HOSPITAL, 221 South Alabama Street, Zip 32565–1070, Mailing Address: P.O. Box 397, Zip 32565–0397; tel. 850/675–8000; Robert E. Gowing, Administrator (Nonreporting) **A**9 10 **S** Baptist Health Care Corporation, Pensacola, FL	23	10	47	—	—	—	—	—	—	—
JUPITER—Palm Beach County										
✦ JUPITER MEDICAL CENTER, 1210 South Old Dixie Highway, Zip 33458–7299; tel. 561/747–2234; Hart Ransdell, Chief Executive Officer (Total facility includes 120 beds in nursing home–type unit) **A**1 2 9 10 **F**8 12 13 17 19 21 22 24 25 27 28 30 32 34 35 37 39 42 44 49 60 63 64 65 67 71 74 **P**7 **Web address:** www.jupitermed.com/	23	10	276	7624	200	74833	0	67611	26202	821
KEY WEST—Monroe County										
✦ LOWER FLORIDA KEYS HEALTH SYSTEM, (Includes De Poo Hospital, 1200 Kennedy Drive, Zip 33041; tel. 305/294–4692; Florida Keys Memorial Hospital), 5900 College Road, Zip 33040–4396, Mailing Address: P.O. Box 9107, Zip 33041–9107; tel. 305/294–5531; Roberto Sanchez, Administrator (Nonreporting) **A**1 9 10 **S** Health Management Associates, Naples, FL	23	10	169	—	—	—	—	—	—	—
KISSIMMEE—Osceola County										
□ CHARTER BEHAVIORAL HEALTH SYSTEM–ORLANDO, 206 Park Place Drive, Zip 34741–2356; tel. 407/846–0444; Daniel Kearney, Chief Executive Officer (Nonreporting) **A**1 9 10 **S** Magellan Health Services, Atlanta, GA	33	22	60	—	—	—	—	—	—	—
FLORIDA HOSPITAL KISSIMMEE See Florida Hospital, Orlando										
✦ OSCEOLA REGIONAL MEDICAL CENTER, 700 West Oak Street, Zip 34741–4996, Mailing Address: P.O. Box 422589, Zip 34742–2589; tel. 407/846–2266; E. Tim Cook, Chief Executive Officer (Nonreporting) **A**1 9 10 **S** Columbia/HCA Healthcare Corporation, Nashville, TN	33	10	156	—	—	—	—	—	—	—
LAKE BUTLER—Union County										
NORTH FLORIDA RECEPTION CENTER HOSPITAL, State Road 231 South, Zip 32054, Mailing Address: P.O. Box 628, Zip 32054–0628; tel. 904/496–6111; Bob Torrescano, Administrator **F**3 16 18 19 20 21 22 30 31 35 41 42 44 49 50 51 52 54 56 57 58 59 60 63 64 65 67 71	12	11	100	1919	96	—	0	—	—	285
LAKE CITY—Columbia County										
✦ LAKE CITY MEDICAL CENTER, 1050 Commerce Boulevard North, Zip 32055–3718; tel. 904/719–9000; Todd Gallati, Chief Executive Officer (Total facility includes 5 beds in nursing home–type unit) **A**1 9 10 **F**8 10 12 14 15 16 17 19 21 22 23 26 28 30 31 33 34 35 37 39 42 44 45 49 52 54 55 56 57 58 59 64 65 71 73 **P**7 **S** Columbia/HCA Healthcare Corporation, Nashville, TN	33	10	75	3825	54	44434	0	19622	9693	300
✦ SHANDS AT LAKE SHORE, 560 East Franklin Street, Zip 32055–3047, Mailing Address: P.O. Box 1989, Zip 32056–1989; tel. 904/754–8000; Neil Whipkey, Administrator (Nonreporting) **A**1 9 10 **S** Shands HealthCare, Gainesville, FL **Web address:** www.shands.org	23	10	128	—	—	—	—	—	—	—
✦ VETERANS AFFAIRS MEDICAL CENTER, 801 South Marion Street, Zip 32025–5898; tel. 904/755–3016; Marlis Meyer, Division Director (Total facility includes 200 beds in nursing home–type unit) **A**1 3 5 **F**3 15 16 19 20 21 22 25 26 28 32 33 37 39 41 44 45 46 49 51 52 54 55 56 57 58 64 65 67 71 73 74 **S** Department of Veterans Affairs, Washington, DC	45	10	313	3825	289	103600	0	72569	45268	984
LAKE WALES—Polk County										
LAKE WALES MEDICAL CENTERS See Winter Haven Hospital, Winter Haven										

Hospital, Address, Telephone, Administrator, Approval, Facility, and Physician Codes, Health Care System, Network	Classi-fication Codes		Utilization Data					Expense (thousands) of dollars		
★ American Hospital Association (AHA) membership □ Joint Commission on Accreditation of Healthcare Organizations (JCAHO) accreditation + American Osteopathic Healthcare Association (AOHA) membership ○ American Osteopathic Association (AOA) accreditation △ Commission on Accreditation of Rehabilitation Facilities (CARF) accreditation Control codes 61, 63, 64, 71, 72 and 73 indicate hospitals listed by AOHA, but not registered by AHA. For definition of numerical codes, see page A4	Control	Service	Staffed Beds	Admissions	Census	Outpatient Visits	Births	Total	Payroll	Personnel

LAKELAND—Polk County

□ HEART OF FLORIDA BEHAVIORAL CENTER, 2510 North Florida Avenue, Zip 33805–2298; tel. 941/682–6105; David M. Polunas, Administrator and Chief Executive Officer (Nonreporting) **A**1 **S** Health Management Associates, Naples, FL	33	22	40	—	—	—	—	—	—	—
★ LAKELAND REGIONAL MEDICAL CENTER, 1324 Lakeland Hills Boulevard, Zip 33805–4543, Mailing Address: P.O. Box 95448, Zip 33804–5448; tel. 941/687–1100; Jack T. Stephens, Jr., President and Chief Executive Officer **A**1 2 5 9 10 **F**2 3 4 7 10 11 14 15 16 17 19 21 22 23 26 27 28 29 30 34 37 38 39 40 42 43 44 45 47 52 53 54 55 56 57 58 59 60 65 67 70 71 72 73 74 **Web address:** www.lrmc.com	23	10	574	28515	364	131115	2745	233558	92706	2479

LANTANA—Palm Beach County

A. G. HOLLEY STATE HOSPITAL, 1199 West Lantana Road, Zip 33462–1514, Mailing Address: P.O. Box 3084, Zip 33465–3084; tel. 561/540–3783; David Ashkin, M.D., Medical Executive Director (Nonreporting) **A**10	12	33	50	—	—	—	—	—	—	—

LARGO—Pinellas County

□ CHARTER BEHAVIORAL HEALTH SYSTEM OF TAMPA BAY AT LARGO, 12891 Seminole Boulevard, Zip 33778; tel. 727/587–6000; Jim Hill, Chief Executive Officer (Nonreporting) **A**1 9 **S** Magellan Health Services, Atlanta, GA	33	22	64	—	—	—	—	—	—	—
□ △ HEALTHSOUTH REHABILITATION HOSPITAL, 901 North Clearwater–Largo Road, Zip 33770; tel. 727/586–2999; Elaine O. Ebaugh, Chief Executive Officer (Nonreporting) **A**1 7 10 **S** HEALTHSOUTH Corporation, Birmingham, AL	33	46	60	—	—	—	—	—	—	—
★ LARGO MEDICAL CENTER, 201 14th Street S.W., Zip 33770–3133, Mailing Address: P.O. Box 2905, Zip 33779–2905; tel. 727/588–5200; Thomas L. Herron, FACHE, President and Chief Executive Officer (Total facility includes 13 beds in nursing home–type unit) **A**1 2 9 10 **F**4 7 8 10 11 12 14 15 16 19 20 21 22 23 24 28 29 30 31 32 33 34 35 37 38 39 40 41 42 43 46 49 51 60 61 64 65 67 71 73 74 **P**1 7 **S** Columbia/HCA Healthcare Corporation, Nashville, TN **Web address:** www.largomedicalcenter.com	33	10	243	11127	127	54927	699	—	—	721
□ + ○ SUN COAST HOSPITAL, 2025 Indian Rocks Road, Zip 34644, Mailing Address: P.O. Box 2025, Zip 34649–2025; tel. 813/581–9474; Jeffrey A. Collins, Chief Executive Officer (Total facility includes 14 beds in nursing home–type unit) (Nonreporting) **A**1 9 10 11 12 13	23	10	241	—	—	—	—	—	—	—

LEESBURG—Lake County

★ △ LEESBURG REGIONAL MEDICAL CENTER, 600 East Dixie Avenue, Zip 34748–5999; tel. 352/323–5000; Richard L. Wooten, President and Chief Executive Officer (Total facility includes 120 beds in nursing home–type unit) **A**1 7 9 10 **F**4 7 8 10 12 14 15 16 19 21 22 23 24 25 26 28 30 31 32 34 35 37 39 40 41 42 44 45 46 48 49 60 64 65 67 71 72 **Web address:** www.Leesburgregional.com	23	10	414	13726	260	92805	1086	97060	39616	1276

LEHIGH ACRES—Lee County

★ EAST POINTE HOSPITAL, 1500 Lee Boulevard, Zip 33936–4897; tel. 941/369–2101; Valerie A. Jackson, Chief Executive Officer (Total facility includes 13 beds in nursing home–type unit) **A**1 9 10 **F**4 7 8 10 12 13 14 15 16 17 19 21 22 23 24 26 27 28 29 30 31 34 35 36 37 39 40 41 42 43 44 45 46 47 49 52 55 58 59 61 63 64 65 66 67 68 71 72 73 74 **P**8 **S** Columbia/HCA Healthcare Corporation, Nashville, TN	33	10	88	2320	31	35472	218	20579	9032	206

LIVE OAK—Suwannee County

★ SHANDS AT LIVE OAK, 1100 S.W. 11th Street, Zip 32060–3608, Mailing Address: P.O. Drawer X, Zip 32060; tel. 904/362–1413; Rhonda Sherrod, Administrator **A**1 9 10 **F**8 12 16 19 22 26 28 30 34 39 44 51 65 71 **P**6 **S** Shands HealthCare, Gainesville, FL	23	10	17	434	4	64610	0	7361	3260	92

LONGWOOD—Seminole County

□ SOUTH SEMINOLE HOSPITAL, 555 West State Road 434, Zip 32750–4999; tel. 407/767–1200; Sue Whelan–Williams, Site Administrator (Nonreporting) **A**1 9 **S** Orlando Regional Healthcare System, Orlando, FL	32	10	206	—	—	—	—	—	—	—

LOXAHATCHEE—Palm Beach County

★ PALMS WEST HOSPITAL, 13001 Southern Boulevard, Zip 33470–1150; tel. 561/798–3300; Alex M. Marceline, Chief Executive Officer (Nonreporting) **A**1 9 10 **S** Columbia/HCA Healthcare Corporation, Nashville, TN **Web address:** www.web–xpress.com/palmswest	33	10	117	—	—	—	—	—	—	—

LUTZ—Hillsborough County

□ CHARTER HOSPITAL OF PASCO, 21808 State Road 54, Zip 33549–6938; tel. 813/948–2441; Miriam K. Williams, Administrator (Nonreporting) **A**1 10 **S** Magellan Health Services, Atlanta, GA	33	22	72	—	—	—	—	—	—	—

MACCLENNY—Baker County

ED FRASER MEMORIAL HOSPITAL, 159 North Third Street, Zip 32063–0484; tel. 904/259–3151; Dennis R. Markos, Chief Executive Officer (Total facility includes 62 beds in nursing home–type unit) (Nonreporting) **A**9 10	23	10	68	—	—	—	—	—	—	—

MACDILL AFB—Hillsborough County

★ U. S. AIR FORCE HOSPITAL, 8415 Bayshore Boulevard, Zip 33621–1607; tel. 813/828–3258; Colonel Gregory C. Baggerly, MC, USAF, Commander (Nonreporting) **A**1 **S** Department of the Air Force, Bowling AFB, DC	41	10	50	—	—	—	—	—	—	—

MADISON—Madison County

MADISON COUNTY MEMORIAL HOSPITAL, 201 East Marion Street, Zip 32340–2561; tel. 850/973–2271; Jeffrey S. Howell, Administrator **A**9 10 **F**15 22 32 34 37 71	23	10	26	384	6	7562	0	4473	2471	106

Hospital, Address, Telephone, Administrator, Approval, Facility, and Physician Codes, Health Care System, Network	Classification Codes		Utilization Data					Expense (thousands) of dollars		
	Control	Service	Staffed Beds	Admissions	Census	Outpatient Visits	Births	Total	Payroll	Personnel

★ American Hospital Association (AHA) membership
☐ Joint Commission on Accreditation of Healthcare Organizations (JCAHO) accreditation
+ American Osteopathic Healthcare Association (AOHA) membership
○ American Osteopathic Association (AOA) accreditation
△ Commission on Accreditation of Rehabilitation Facilities (CARF) accreditation
Control codes 61, 63, 64, 71, 72 and 73 indicate hospitals listed by AOHA, but not registered by AHA. For definition of numerical codes, see page A4

MARATHON—Monroe County

☐ FISHERMEN'S HOSPITAL, 3301 Overseas Highway, Zip 33050–0068; tel. 305/743–5533; Patrice L. Tavernier, Administrator (Nonreporting) **A**1 9 10 **S** Health Management Associates, Naples, FL | 33 | 10 | 58 | — | — | — | — | — | — | —

MARIANNA—Jackson County

⊞ JACKSON HOSPITAL, 4250 Hospital Drive, Zip 32446–1939, Mailing Address: P.O. Box 1608, Zip 32447–1608; tel. 850/526–2200 **A**1 9 10 **F**7 8 12 14 15 16 19 21 22 23 30 31 35 44 46 49 65 71 73 **S** Quorum Health Group/Quorum Health Resources, Inc., Brentwood, TN | 16 | 10 | 85 | 4131 | 48 | 49963 | 620 | 26585 | 10891 | 428

MELBOURNE—Brevard County

☐ CIRCLES OF CARE, 400 East Sheridan Road, Zip 32901–3184; tel. 407/722–5200; James B. Whitaker, President **A**1 9 10 **F**2 3 6 12 14 15 16 17 18 22 25 26 34 52 53 54 55 56 57 58 59 65 67 **P**1 6 | 23 | 22 | 86 | 5376 | 58 | — | 0 | 17530 | 10400 | 378

DEVEREUX HOSPITAL AND CHILDREN'S CENTER OF FLORIDA, 8000 Devereux Drive, Zip 32940–7907; tel. 407/242–9100; Michael Becker, Executive Director **F**14 52 53 **S** Devereux Foundation, Villanova, PA | 23 | 52 | 100 | 107 | 99 | 0 | 0 | 11249 | 5546 | 355

☐ △ HEALTHSOUTH SEA PINES REHABILITATION HOSPITAL, 101 East Florida Avenue, Zip 32901–9966; tel. 407/984–4600; Henry J. Cranston, Chief Executive Officer (Nonreporting) **A**1 7 10 **S** HEALTHSOUTH Corporation, Birmingham, AL | 33 | 46 | 80 | — | — | — | — | — | — | —

⊞ HOLMES REGIONAL MEDICAL CENTER, 1350 South Hickory Street, Zip 32901–3276; tel. 407/727–7000; Stephen P. Bunker, President and Chief Operating Officer **A**1 2 9 10 **F**4 6 7 8 10 11 12 13 14 15 16 17 19 21 22 23 24 25 27 28 30 31 32 33 35 37 38 39 40 41 42 43 44 45 46 49 60 64 65 67 70 71 74 **P**5 6 7 | 23 | 10 | 528 | 21876 | 280 | 169816 | 2106 | 206789 | 85406 | 1900

MIAMI—Dade County

★ AVENTURA HOSPITAL AND MEDICAL CENTER, 20900 Biscayne Boulevard, Zip 33180–1407; tel. 305/682–7100; Davide M. Carbone, Chief Executive Officer **A**9 10 **F**1 2 3 4 5 7 8 9 10 11 12 13 14 15 16 17 18 19 20 21 22 23 25 26 27 28 30 31 32 33 34 35 37 38 39 40 42 43 44 45 46 47 48 49 51 52 54 55 56 57 58 59 60 61 63 64 65 67 71 72 73 74 **P**5 7 **S** Columbia/HCA Healthcare Corporation, Nashville, TN
Web address: www.aventurahospital.com | 33 | 10 | 316 | 12977 | 179 | 104842 | 891 | 77923 | 35975 | 781

⊞ △ BAPTIST HOSPITAL OF MIAMI, 8900 North Kendall Drive, Zip 33176–2197; tel. 305/596–1960; Lee S. Huntley, Chief Executive Officer **A**1 2 3 7 9 10 **F**2 3 4 5 7 8 10 12 14 15 16 17 19 21 22 24 25 26 27 28 29 30 31 32 33 34 35 37 38 40 41 42 43 44 45 46 47 48 49 50 60 61 63 64 65 66 67 71 72 73 74 **P**5 6 7 **S** Baptist Health System of South Florida, Coral Gables, FL
Web address: www.baptisthealth.net | 23 | 10 | 457 | 26652 | 385 | 209154 | 3416 | 247843 | 102768 | 2923

⊞ BASCOM PALMER EYE INSTITUTE–ANNE BATES LEACH EYE HOSPITAL, 900 N.W. 17th Street, Zip 33136–1199, Mailing Address: Box 016880, Zip 33101–6880; tel. 305/326–6000; Richard C. Thomas, Administrator **A**1 3 5 9 10 **F**14 16 22 44 49 65 68 71 **P**4 7 **S** Quorum Health Group/Quorum Health Resources, Inc., Brentwood, TN
Web address: www.bpei.med.miami.edu | 23 | 45 | 35 | 682 | 4 | 136344 | 0 | 31987 | 13047 | 439

⊞ CEDARS MEDICAL CENTER, 1400 N.W. 12th Avenue, Zip 33136–1003; tel. 305/325–5511; Steven Sonenreich, Chief Executive Officer **A**1 2 3 5 9 10 **F**4 5 8 10 11 12 15 16 19 21 22 23 26 28 29 30 31 34 35 37 39 41 42 43 44 45 46 49 52 54 55 56 57 60 63 64 65 67 71 72 73 **S** Columbia/HCA Healthcare Corporation, Nashville, TN | 32 | 10 | 493 | 18945 | 328 | — | — | 128675 | 50309 | 1453

COLUMBIA BEHAVIORAL HEALTH CENTER See Doral Palms Hospital

⊞ DEERING HOSPITAL, 9333 S.W. 152nd Street, Zip 33157–1780; tel. 305/256–5100; Jude Torchia, Chief Executive Officer (Nonreporting) **A**1 9 10 **S** Columbia/HCA Healthcare Corporation, Nashville, TN | 33 | 10 | 233 | — | — | — | — | — | — | —

⊞ DORAL PALMS HOSPITAL, (Formerly Columbia Behavioral Health Center), 11100 N.W. 27th Street, Zip 33172–5000; tel. 305/591–3230; Cheryl Siegwald–Mays, Administrator (Nonreporting) **A**1 9 10 **S** Columbia/HCA Healthcare Corporation, Nashville, TN | 33 | 22 | 88 | — | — | — | — | — | — | —

☐ △ HEALTHSOUTH REHABILITATION HOSPITAL, 20601 Old Cutler Road, Zip 33189–2400; tel. 305/251–3800; Nelson Lazo, Chief Executive Officer (Nonreporting) **A**1 7 10 **S** HEALTHSOUTH Corporation, Birmingham, AL | 33 | 46 | 45 | — | — | — | — | — | — | —

⊞ JACKSON MEMORIAL HOSPITAL, (Includes Highland Park Hospital, 1660 N.W. Seventh Court, Zip 33136; tel. 305/324–8111; Stuart Podolnick, Administrator), 1611 N.W. 12th Avenue, Zip 33136–1094; tel. 305/585–6754; Ira C. Clark, President **A**1 2 3 5 8 9 10 **F**1 2 3 4 5 7 8 9 10 11 12 13 14 15 16 17 18 19 20 21 22 23 24 25 26 27 28 29 30 31 32 34 35 37 38 39 40 41 42 43 44 45 46 47 48 49 51 52 53 54 55 56 57 58 59 60 61 63 65 66 67 68 70 71 72 73 74 **P**6 | 13 | 10 | 1320 | 50075 | 958 | 495498 | 5068 | 697799 | 318736 | 8344

⊞ KENDALL MEDICAL CENTER, 11750 Bird Road, Zip 33175–3530; tel. 305/223–3000; Victor Maya, Chief Executive Officer **A**1 9 10 **F**1 2 3 4 5 7 8 10 11 12 14 15 16 19 20 21 22 23 26 27 28 30 31 32 33 34 35 37 39 40 41 42 43 44 45 46 48 49 52 53 54 55 56 57 58 59 60 63 65 67 68 71 72 73 74 **P**2 3 4 5 **S** Columbia/HCA Healthcare Corporation, Nashville, TN | 32 | 10 | 235 | 12638 | 174 | — | 1417 | 91945 | 33347 | 968

⊞ △ MERCY HOSPITAL, 3663 South Miami Avenue, Zip 33133–4237; tel. 305/854–4400; Edward J. Rosasco, Jr., President and Chief Executive Officer **A**1 2 6 7 9 10 **F**4 8 10 11 12 14 15 16 17 19 21 22 23 25 27 28 31 32 33 34 37 39 40 41 42 43 44 45 46 48 49 51 52 55 57 58 59 60 65 71 73 **P**4 5 7 **S** Catholic Health East, Newtown Square, PA | 21 | 10 | 339 | 14991 | 245 | 85598 | 1737 | 137707 | 61416 | 1852

Hospital, Address, Telephone, Administrator, Approval, Facility, and Physician Codes, Health Care System, Network	Classi-fication Codes		Utilization Data					Expense (thousands) of dollars		
	Control	Service	Staffed Beds	Admissions	Census	Outpatient Visits	Births	Total	Payroll	Personnel

★ American Hospital Association (AHA) membership
□ Joint Commission on Accreditation of Healthcare Organizations (JCAHO) accreditation
+ American Osteopathic Healthcare Association (AOHA) membership
○ American Osteopathic Association (AOA) accreditation
△ Commission on Accreditation of Rehabilitation Facilities (CARF) accreditation
Control codes 61, 63, 64, 71, 72 and 73 indicate hospitals listed by AOHA, but not registered by AHA. For definition of numerical codes, see page A4

Hospital	Control	Service	Staffed Beds	Admissions	Census	Outpatient Visits	Births	Total	Payroll	Personnel
⊞ MIAMI CHILDREN'S HOSPITAL, 3100 S.W. 62nd Avenue, Zip 33155–3009; tel. 305/666–6511; Thomas M. Rozek, President and Chief Executive Officer **A**1 3 5 9 10 12 13 **F**2 3 4 5 6 7 8 10 12 13 14 15 16 17 18 19 20 21 22 23 24 25 26 27 28 31 32 33 34 35 38 39 40 41 42 43 44 45 46 47 49 51 52 53 54 55 56 57 58 59 60 62 64 65 67 68 70 71 72 73 74 **P**1 7 Web address: www.mch.com	23	50	268	7993	132	180270	0	178065	83619	1984
⊞ MIAMI HEART INSTITUTE AND MEDICAL CENTER, 4701 Meridian Avenue, Zip 33140–2910; tel. 305/674–3114; Ralph A. Aleman, Chief Executive Officer (Total facility includes 10 beds in nursing home–type unit) (Nonreporting) **A**1 9 10 **S** Columbia/HCA Healthcare Corporation, Nashville, TN	32	10	278	—	—	—	—	—	—	—
★ MIAMI JEWISH HOME AND HOSPITAL FOR AGED, 5200 N.E. Second Avenue, Zip 33137–2706; tel. 305/751–8626; Terry Goodman, Executive Director (Nonreporting) **A**3 10 Web address: www.douglasgardens.com	23	10	32	—	—	—	—	—	—	—
⊞ NORTH SHORE MEDICAL CENTER, 1100 N.W. 95th Street, Zip 33150–2098; tel. 305/835–6000; Steven M. Klein, President and Chief Executive Officer **A**1 2 9 10 **F**4 7 8 11 12 14 15 16 17 19 21 22 28 29 30 31 32 34 35 37 38 39 40 41 42 43 44 45 46 49 52 58 59 60 63 65 67 68 70 71 73 74 **P**1 **S** TENET Healthcare Corporation, Santa Barbara, CA Web address: www.nsmc.com	33	10	197	11228	182	129328	1500	79925	34641	1007
⊞ PAN AMERICAN HOSPITAL, 5959 N.W. Seventh Street, Zip 33126–3198; tel. 305/264–1000; Carolina Calderin, Chief Executive Officer **A**1 9 10 **F**1 4 7 8 10 11 12 14 15 17 19 21 22 26 27 30 32 33 34 35 37 40 42 43 44 45 48 49 51 61 63 64 65 67 69 71 73 74 **P**1 8	23	10	146	7536	120	73766	0	63343	27799	993
□ SOUTH FLORIDA EVALUATION AND TREATMENT CENTER, 2200 N.W. 7th Avenue, Zip 33127–4291; tel. 305/637–2500; Cheryl Y. Brantley, Administrator **A**1 **F**14 15 16 20 52 65	12	22	200	184	196	0	0	—	—	436
⊞ △ SOUTH MIAMI HOSPITAL, 6200 S.W. 73rd Street, Zip 33143–9990; tel. 305/661–4611; D. Wayne Brackin, Chief Executive Officer (Nonreporting) **A**1 7 9 10 **S** Baptist Health System of South Florida, Coral Gables, FL Web address: www.baptisthealth.net	23	10	397	—	—	—	—	—	—	—
⊞ UNIVERSITY OF MIAMI HOSPITAL AND CLINICS, 1475 N.W. 12th Avenue, Zip 33136–1002; tel. 305/243–6418; Admiral John Rossfeld, Administrator **A**1 2 3 5 9 10 **F**8 12 14 15 16 19 20 21 27 28 29 30 33 35 42 44 45 46 49 51 54 58 60 63 65 71 73 **P**1 **S** Quorum Health Group/Quorum Health Resources, Inc., Brentwood, TN	23	10	40	785	15	146193	0	53436	17857	402
⊞ VETERANS AFFAIRS MEDICAL CENTER, 1201 N.W. 16th Street, Zip 33125–1624; tel. 305/324–4455; Thomas C. Doherty, Medical Director (Total facility includes 172 beds in nursing home–type unit) **A**1 3 5 8 **F**1 3 4 5 8 10 11 12 14 15 16 17 18 19 20 21 22 23 25 26 27 28 29 30 31 32 33 34 35 37 39 41 42 43 44 45 46 48 49 51 52 54 55 56 57 58 59 60 63 64 65 67 69 71 73 74 **S** Department of Veterans Affairs, Washington, DC	45	10	504	7431	439	421890	0	198566	100716	2615
+ ○ WESTCHESTER GENERAL HOSPITAL, 2500 S.W. 75th Avenue, Zip 33155–9947; tel. 305/264–5252; Gilda Baldwin, Chief Executive Officer (Nonreporting) **A**5 9 10 11 12 13	33	10	110	—	—	—	—	—	—	—
□ WINDMOOR HEALTHCARE OF MIAMI, 1861 N.W. South River Drive, Zip 33125–2787; tel. 305/642–3555; Lee Ghezzi, Administrator (Nonreporting) **A**1 10	33	22	94	—	—	—	—	—	—	—
MIAMI BEACH—Dade County										
□ △ MOUNT SINAI MEDICAL CENTER, 4300 Alton Road, Zip 33140–2800; tel. 305/674–2121; Bruce M. Perry, Chief Executive Officer (Total facility includes 150 beds in nursing home–type unit) **A**1 2 3 5 7 8 9 10 **F**2 3 4 5 7 8 10 11 12 14 15 16 17 19 20 21 22 25 26 27 28 29 30 31 32 33 34 35 37 38 39 40 41 42 43 44 45 46 48 49 51 52 54 55 56 57 58 59 60 61 63 64 65 66 67 71 73 74 **P**1 6 7	23	10	563	21571	527	172000	1874	223670	107314	3503
⊞ SOUTH SHORE HOSPITAL AND MEDICAL CENTER, 630 Alton Road, Zip 33139–5502; tel. 305/672–2100; William Zubkoff, Ph.D., Chief Executive Officer (Nonreporting) **A**1 9 10	23	49	178	—	—	—	—	—	—	—
MILTON—Santa Rosa County										
□ SANTA ROSA MEDICAL CENTER, 1450 Berryhill Road, Zip 32570–4028, Mailing Address: P.O. Box 648, Zip 32572–0648; tel. 850/626–7762; M. P. Gandy, Jr., Chief Executive Officer (Total facility includes 10 beds in nursing home–type unit) **A**1 9 10 **F**1 3 4 7 8 10 11 12 14 15 16 17 19 21 22 26 28 29 30 33 35 36 39 40 41 42 44 45 49 51 54 56 64 65 67 71 73 74 **P**8 **S** Paracelsus Healthcare Corporation, Houston, TX	33	10	96	3477	40	45621	401	21991	9669	292
NAPLES—Collier County										
⊞ △ NAPLES COMMUNITY HOSPITAL, 350 Seventh Street North, Zip 34102–4746, Mailing Address: P.O. Box 413029, Zip 34101–3029; tel. 941/436–5000; William G. Crone, President and Chief Executive Officer (Total facility includes 24 beds in nursing home–type unit) **A**1 2 7 9 10 **F**2 3 4 7 8 9 10 11 12 13 14 15 16 17 19 21 22 23 24 25 26 27 28 29 30 31 32 33 34 35 37 38 39 40 41 42 43 44 45 46 47 48 49 51 52 56 57 58 59 60 64 65 66 67 70 71 72 73 74 **P**8	23	10	458	24513	319	171325	2359	198126	78451	2132
□ WILLOUGH AT NAPLES, 9001 Tamiami Trail East, Zip 34113–3316; tel. 941/775–4500; Patricia Perfetto, MSN, Executive Director **A**1 10 **F**2 3 52 59 67 **P**1	33	22	70	489	16	2117	0	6440	2973	75

Hospital, Address, Telephone, Administrator, Approval, Facility, and Physician Codes, Health Care System, Network	Classi-fication Codes		Utilization Data					Expense (thousands) of dollars		
★ American Hospital Association (AHA) membership □ Joint Commission on Accreditation of Healthcare Organizations (JCAHO) accreditation + American Osteopathic Healthcare Association (AOHA) membership ○ American Osteopathic Association (AOA) accreditation △ Commission on Accreditation of Rehabilitation Facilities (CARF) accreditation Control codes 61, 63, 64, 71, 72 and 73 indicate hospitals listed by AOHA, but not registered by AHA. For definition of numerical codes, see page A4	Control	Service	Staffed Beds	Admissions	Census	Outpatient Visits	Births	Total	Payroll	Personnel

NEW PORT RICHEY—Pasco County

✠ COMMUNITY HOSPITAL OF NEW PORT RICHEY, 5637 Marine Parkway, Zip 34652–4331, Mailing Address: P.O. Box 996, Zip 34656–0996; tel. 727/848–1733; Andrew Oravec, Jr., Administrator (Nonreporting) **A**1 9 10 **S** Columbia/HCA Healthcare Corporation, Nashville, TN — 33 10 414 — — — — — — —

✠ △ NORTH BAY HOSPITAL, (Formerly North Bay Medical Center), 6600 Madison Street, Zip 34652–1900; tel. 727/842–8468; William A. Jennings, Chief Operating Officer and Administrator (Nonreporting) **A**1 7 9 10 **S** TENET Healthcare Corporation, Santa Barbara, CA — 33 10 122 — — — — — — —

NORTH BAY MEDICAL CENTER See North Bay Hospital

NEW SMYRNA BEACH—Volusia County

✠ BERT FISH MEDICAL CENTER, 401 Palmetto Street, Zip 32168–7399; tel. 904/424–5000; Kathy Leonard, Vice President and Administrator **A**1 9 10 **F**3 4 7 8 10 12 14 15 16 17 19 21 22 25 26 28 29 30 32 33 34 35 37 39 40 41 42 43 44 45 46 49 51 52 54 56 60 61 65 67 68 70 71 72 73 74 **P**1 6 **S** Quorum Health Group/Quorum Health Resources, Inc., Brentwood, TN **Web address:** www.bertfish.com — 23 10 116 4020 57 158452 0 46503 15729 592

NICEVILLE—Okaloosa County

✠ TWIN CITIES HOSPITAL, 2190 Highway 85 North, Zip 32578–1045; tel. 850/678–4131; David Whalen, Chief Executive Officer **A**1 9 10 **F**8 12 14 15 16 17 19 21 22 25 28 29 30 33 37 44 45 49 51 63 64 71 **S** Columbia/HCA Healthcare Corporation, Nashville, TN — 33 10 75 2347 26 27399 0 18619 6720 234

NORTH MIAMI—Dade County

□ △ VILLA MARIA HOSPITAL, 1050 N.E. 125th Street, Zip 33161–5881; tel. 305/891–8850; Jack Rutenberg, Administrator (Total facility includes 212 beds in nursing home–type unit) **A**1 7 10 **F**1 6 12 16 17 20 26 27 31 32 33 34 39 41 45 46 48 49 54 55 62 64 65 67 73 — 21 46 252 1092 218 1734 0 17220 6122 248

NORTH MIAMI BEACH—Dade County

✠ △ PARKWAY REGIONAL MEDICAL CENTER, 160 N.W. 170th Street, Zip 33169–5576; tel. 305/654–5050; Peter A. Marmerstein, Chief Executive Officer (Nonreporting) **A**1 7 9 **S** TENET Healthcare Corporation, Santa Barbara, CA — 33 10 392 — — — — — — —

OCALA—Marion County

□ CHARTER SPRINGS HOSPITAL, 3130 S.W. 27th Avenue, Zip 34474–4485, Mailing Address: P.O. Box 3338, Zip 34478–3338; tel. 352/237–7293; David C. Nissen, Chief Executive Officer **A**1 9 10 **F**1 2 3 12 14 15 17 18 26 45 52 53 54 55 56 57 58 59 65 67 **S** Magellan Health Services, Atlanta, GA — 33 22 92 1237 30 2742 0 7894 2182 144

✠ MUNROE REGIONAL MEDICAL CENTER, 131 S.W. 15th Street, Zip 34474–4059, Mailing Address: P.O. Box 6000, Zip 34478–6000; tel. 352/351–7200; Dyer T. Michell, President **A**1 5 9 10 **F**4 7 8 10 11 12 13 14 15 16 19 21 22 23 24 26 28 29 30 31 32 34 35 37 39 40 41 43 44 45 46 49 51 65 66 71 72 73 74 **P**6 8 — 23 10 318 18833 244 100981 1531 142873 58701 1684

✠ OCALA REGIONAL MEDICAL CENTER, 1431 S.W. First Avenue, Zip 34474–4058, Mailing Address: P.O. Box 2200, Zip 34478–2200; tel. 352/401–1000; Stephen Mahan, Chief Executive Officer **A**1 2 9 10 **F**4 7 8 10 11 12 14 19 21 22 37 39 40 41 42 43 44 49 60 63 65 66 71 73 **P**8 **S** Columbia/HCA Healthcare Corporation, Nashville, TN — 33 10 210 13156 172 88070 733 78553 32518 975

OCOEE—Orange County

✠ HEALTH CENTRAL, 10000 West Colonial Drive, Zip 34761–3499; tel. 407/296–1000; Richard M. Irwin, Jr., President and Chief Executive Officer (Total facility includes 228 beds in nursing home–type unit) **A**1 9 10 **F**1 4 7 8 10 11 12 15 17 19 20 21 22 23 26 27 28 30 31 32 33 34 35 37 39 40 41 42 44 45 46 49 64 65 67 70 71 72 73 74 **Web address:** www.health–central.org — 16 10 338 5920 273 59777 848 49781 19490 577

OKEECHOBEE—Okeechobee County

✠ RAULERSON HOSPITAL, 1796 Highway 441 North, Zip 34972, Mailing Address: P.O. Box 1307, Zip 34973–1307; tel. 941/763–2151; Frank Irby, Chief Executive Officer **A**1 9 10 **F**8 10 11 12 15 16 17 19 22 23 25 28 30 33 34 35 37 42 44 46 49 64 71 73 **P**4 **S** Columbia/HCA Healthcare Corporation, Nashville, TN — 33 10 101 4270 63 49463 3 26132 12246 356

ORANGE PARK—Clay County

✠ ORANGE PARK MEDICAL CENTER, 2001 Kingsley Avenue, Zip 32073–5156; tel. 904/276–8500; Robert M. Krieger, Chief Executive Officer (Nonreporting) **A**1 9 10 **S** Columbia/HCA Healthcare Corporation, Nashville, TN — 33 10 196 — — — — — — —

ORLANDO—Orange County

COLUMBIA PARK MEDICAL CENTER See Lucerne Medical Center

✠ ○ △ FLORIDA HOSPITAL, (Includes Florida Hospital East Orlando, 7727 Lake Underhill Drive, Zip 32822; tel. 407/277–8110; Florida Hospital Kissimmee, 200 Hilda Street, Kissimmee, Zip 34741–2301; tel. 407/846–4343; Florida Hospital–Altamonte, 601 East Altamonte Drive, Altamonte Springs, Zip 32701; tel. 407/830–4321; Florida Hospital–Apopka, 201 North Park Avenue, Apopka, Zip 32703; tel. 407/889–2566), 601 East Rollins Street, Zip 32803–1489; tel. 407/896–6611; Thomas L. Werner, President (Total facility includes 52 beds in nursing home–type unit) **A**1 2 3 5 7 9 10 11 12 13 **F**3 4 6 7 8 9 10 11 12 13 14 15 16 17 18 19 20 21 22 23 24 25 26 28 29 30 31 32 33 34 35 36 37 38 39 40 41 42 43 44 45 46 47 48 49 51 52 53 54 55 56 57 58 59 60 61 62 63 64 65 66 67 68 70 71 72 73 74 **P**1 8 **S** Adventist Health System Sunbelt Health Care Corporation, Winter Park, FL **Web address:** www.flhosp.org — 23 10 1382 63655 894 521438 7685 680105 288245 9203

Hospital, Address, Telephone, Administrator, Approval, Facility, and Physician Codes, Health Care System, Network	Classi-fication Codes		Utilization Data					Expense (thousands) of dollars		
★ American Hospital Association (AHA) membership □ Joint Commission on Accreditation of Healthcare Organizations (JCAHO) accreditation + American Osteopathic Healthcare Association (AOHA) membership ○ American Osteopathic Association (AOA) accreditation △ Commission on Accreditation of Rehabilitation Facilities (CARF) accreditation Control codes 61, 63, 64, 71, 72 and 73 indicate hospitals listed by AOHA, but not registered by AHA. For definition of numerical codes, see page A4	Control	Service	Staffed Beds	Admissions	Census	Outpatient Visits	Births	Total	Payroll	Personnel
✠ △ LUCERNE MEDICAL CENTER, (Formerly Columbia Park Medical Center), 818 Main Lane, Zip 32801; tel. 407/649–6111 (Total facility includes 20 beds in nursing home–type unit) **A**1 7 9 10 **F**1 3 4 7 8 10 11 12 15 16 17 19 20 21 22 23 24 25 26 27 28 29 30 31 32 33 34 35 36 37 39 40 41 42 43 44 45 46 48 49 51 53 54 55 56 57 58 59 60 61 63 64 65 66 67 71 72 73 74 **P**1 **S** Columbia/HCA Healthcare Corporation, Nashville, TN **Web address:** www.columbia.net	33	10	267	8539	122	34247	817	70686	28466	678
✠ ORLANDO REGIONAL MEDICAL CENTER, (Includes Arnold Palmer Hospital for Children and Women; M. D. Anderson Cancer Center and Sand Lake Hospital), 1414 Kuhl Avenue, Zip 32806–2093; tel. 407/841–5111; Abe Lopman, Executive Director (Total facility includes 29 beds in nursing home–type unit) **A**1 2 3 5 8 9 10 **F**2 3 4 6 7 8 9 10 11 12 13 14 15 16 17 18 19 20 21 22 23 24 25 26 28 29 30 31 32 34 35 37 38 39 40 41 42 43 44 45 46 47 48 49 51 52 53 54 55 56 57 58 59 60 61 63 64 65 66 67 70 71 73 74 **P**4 5 6 7 **S** Orlando Regional Healthcare System, Orlando, FL **Web address:** www.orhs.org	23	10	1049	53281	695	495463	6761	524724	219200	7165
□ PRINCETON HOSPITAL, 1800 Mercy Drive, Zip 32808–5694; tel. 407/295–5151; Kenneth W. Lukhard, Chief Executive Officer (Nonreporting) **A**1 9 10	23	10	150	—	—	—	—	—	—	—
UNIVERSITY BEHAVIORAL CENTER, 2500 Discovery Drive, Zip 32826–3711; tel. 407/281–7000; David L. Beardsley, Administrator (Nonreporting) **A**10 **S** Health Management Associates, Naples, FL	33	22	100	—	—	—	—	—	—	—
VALUEMARK BEHAVIORAL HEALTHCARE SYSTEM OF FLORIDA, (Formerly ValueMark–Laurel Oaks Health), 6601 Central Florida Parkway, Zip 32821–8091; tel. 407/345–5000; Robert Berteau, Chief Executive Officer (Nonreporting) **S** ValueMark Healthcare Systems, Inc., Atlanta, GA	31	52	52	—	—	—	—	—	—	—
ORMOND BEACH—Volusia County										
✠ ○ △ ATLANTIC MEDICAL CENTER–ORMOND, 264 South Atlantic Avenue, Zip 32176–8192; tel. 904/672–4161; Pam Corliss, Chief Executive Officer **A**1 7 9 10 11 12 13 **F**2 3 8 10 11 12 16 19 22 26 27 28 29 30 34 35 37 41 44 45 46 48 49 52 54 55 56 57 58 59 64 65 71 73 **P**7 **S** Columbia/HCA Healthcare Corporation, Nashville, TN	33	10	119	2816	50	25395	0	19959	9622	327
✠ MEMORIAL HOSPITAL–ORMOND BEACH, 875 Sterthaus Avenue, Zip 32174–5197; tel. 904/676–6000; Clark P. Christianson, Senior Vice President and Administrator (Total facility includes 17 beds in nursing home–type unit) **A**1 9 10 **F**4 7 8 10 11 12 14 15 16 17 19 20 21 22 24 25 26 28 29 30 31 32 33 34 35 37 39 40 41 42 43 44 45 46 49 60 61 64 65 66 67 71 72 73 74 **P**8 **S** Memorial Health Systems, Ormond Beach, FL	23	10	205	8826	130	59315	581	79247	29767	917
PALATKA—Putnam County										
✠ PUTNAM COMMUNITY MEDICAL CENTER, Highway 20 West, Zip 32177, Mailing Address: P.O. Box 778, Zip 32178–0778; tel. 904/328–5711; Rodney R. Smith, Chief Executive Officer **A**1 9 10 **F**7 8 12 14 15 16 17 19 21 22 27 28 29 30 31 34 35 37 39 40 41 42 44 45 46 49 51 60 63 64 65 66 67 71 73 **P**8 **S** Columbia/HCA Healthcare Corporation, Nashville, TN	33	10	141	6092	84	74616	497	—	—	503
PALM BEACH GARDENS—Palm Beach County										
✠ PALM BEACH GARDENS MEDICAL CENTER, 3360 Burns Road, Zip 33410–4304; tel. 561/622–1411; Clint Matthews, Chief Executive Officer (Nonreporting) **A**1 9 10 **S** TENET Healthcare Corporation, Santa Barbara, CA **Web address:** www.TENETHEALTH.COM/PALMBEACHGARDENS	33	10	204	—	—	—	—	—	—	—
PANAMA CITY—Bay County										
✠ BAY MEDICAL CENTER, 615 North Bonita Avenue, Zip 32401–3600, Mailing Address: P.O. Box 59515, Zip 32402–2515; tel. 850/769–1511; Ronald V. Wolff, President and Chief Executive Officer **A**1 2 9 10 **F**4 7 8 10 11 12 14 15 16 17 19 21 22 24 25 27 28 30 31 32 33 34 35 37 39 40 41 42 43 44 46 48 49 52 56 59 60 63 65 66 71 72 73 74 **P**7 **Web address:** www.baymedical.org	16	10	315	13235	189	94060	728	121538	49206	1687
✠ GULF COAST MEDICAL CENTER, 449 West 23rd Street, Zip 32405–4593, Mailing Address: P.O. Box 15309, Zip 32406–5309; tel. 850/769–8341; Brent A. Marsteller, Chief Executive Officer (Total facility includes 11 beds in nursing home–type unit) **A**1 2 9 10 **F**7 8 10 12 14 15 16 19 21 22 25 26 34 35 37 38 40 42 44 49 51 60 64 67 71 **S** Columbia/HCA Healthcare Corporation, Nashville, TN	33	10	176	8006	98	106816	1442	45189	19225	575
✠ U. S. AIR FORCE HOSPITAL, Tyndall AFB, Zip 32403–5300; tel. 850/283–7515; Admiral James H. Foster, Commander (Nonreporting) **A**1 **S** Department of the Air Force, Bowling AFB, DC	41	10	25	—	—	—	—	—	—	—
PEMBROKE PINES—Broward County										
✠ MEMORIAL HOSPITAL PEMBROKE, 7800 Sheridan Street, Zip 33024; tel. 954/962–9650; J. E. Piriz, Administrator **A**1 9 10 **F**1 2 3 4 5 6 7 8 9 10 11 12 13 14 15 16 17 18 19 20 21 22 23 24 25 26 27 28 29 30 31 32 33 34 35 36 37 38 39 40 41 42 43 44 45 46 47 48 49 50 51 52 53 54 55 56 57 58 59 60 61 62 63 64 65 66 67 68 70 71 72 73 74 **P**5 8 **S** Memorial Healthcare System, Hollywood, FL	16	10	190	4733	67	51744	0	34184	13818	294
✠ MEMORIAL HOSPITAL WEST, 703 North Flamingo Road, Zip 33028; tel. 954/436–5000; Zeff Ross, Administrator **A**1 9 10 **F**1 2 3 4 7 8 10 11 12 13 14 15 16 17 18 19 20 21 22 23 24 25 26 27 28 29 30 31 32 33 34 35 37 38 39 40 42 43 44 46 47 48 49 51 52 53 54 55 56 57 58 59 60 61 63 64 65 66 67 70 71 72 73 74 **P**1 3 5 7 **S** Memorial Healthcare System, Hollywood, FL	16	10	110	11458	117	162333	3441	70308	30536	747

Hospital, Address, Telephone, Administrator, Approval, Facility, and Physician Codes, Health Care System, Network	Classi-fication Codes		Utilization Data					Expense (thousands) of dollars		
	Control	Service	Staffed Beds	Admissions	Census	Outpatient Visits	Births	Total	Payroll	Personnel

★ American Hospital Association (AHA) membership
□ Joint Commission on Accreditation of Healthcare Organizations (JCAHO) accreditation
+ American Osteopathic Healthcare Association (AOHA) membership
○ American Osteopathic Association (AOA) accreditation
△ Commission on Accreditation of Rehabilitation Facilities (CARF) accreditation
Control codes 61, 63, 64, 71, 72 and 73 indicate hospitals listed by AOHA, but not registered by AHA. For definition of numerical codes, see page A4

Hospital	Control	Service	Staffed Beds	Admissions	Census	Outpatient Visits	Births	Total	Payroll	Personnel
SOUTH FLORIDA STATE HOSPITAL, 1000 S.W. 84th Avenue, Zip 33025; tel. 954/967–7000; Sal A. Barbera, FACHE, Administrator (Nonreporting) A10	12	22	355	—	—	—	—	—	—	—

PENSACOLA—Escambia County

Hospital	Control	Service	Staffed Beds	Admissions	Census	Outpatient Visits	Births	Total	Payroll	Personnel
⊞ BAPTIST HOSPITAL, 1000 West Moreno, Zip 32501–2393, Mailing Address: P.O. Box 17500, Zip 32522–7500; tel. 850/469–2313; Quinton Studer, President (Total facility includes 57 beds in nursing home–type unit) A1 2 9 10 F2 3 4 6 7 8 10 11 12 14 15 16 17 18 19 21 22 23 24 25 26 27 28 29 30 31 32 33 34 35 37 39 40 41 42 43 44 45 46 49 51 52 53 54 55 56 57 58 59 60 61 62 63 64 65 66 67 68 70 71 72 73 74 P4 5 6 7 S Baptist Health Care Corporation, Pensacola, FL **Web address:** www.bhcpns.org	23	10	492	14058	245	150024	1145	117828	45209	1546
⊞ NAVAL HOSPITAL, 6000 West Highway 98, Zip 32512–0003; tel. 850/505–6413; Commander Patrick J. Kelly, Director, Administration (Nonreporting) A1 3 5 S Department of Navy, Washington, DC	43	10	113							
REHABILITATION INSTITUTE OF WEST FLORIDA See West Florida Regional Medical Center										
⊞ SACRED HEART HOSPITAL OF PENSACOLA, 5151 North Ninth Avenue, Zip 32504–8795, Mailing Address: P.O. Box 2700, Zip 32513–2700; tel. 850/416–7000; Patrick J. Madden, President and Chief Executive Officer (Total facility includes 89 beds in nursing home–type unit) A1 2 3 5 9 10 F4 7 8 10 11 12 13 14 15 16 17 19 20 21 22 23 24 25 28 30 31 32 33 34 35 37 38 39 40 41 42 43 44 45 47 49 56 60 63 64 65 66 67 71 72 73 74 P6 S Daughters of Charity National Health System, Saint Louis, MO **Web address:** www.sacred–heart.org	21	10	520	17137	319	252042	2782	142721	59130	2206
⊞ △ WEST FLORIDA REGIONAL MEDICAL CENTER, (Includes Rehabilitation Institute of West Florida, tel. 850/494–6000; The Pavilion, tel. 904/494–5000), 8383 North Davis Highway, Zip 32514–6088, Mailing Address: P.O. Box 18900, Zip 32523–8900; tel. 850/494–4000; Stephen Brandt, President and Chief Executive Officer A1 7 9 10 F2 3 4 7 8 10 11 12 14 15 16 17 19 21 23 24 26 27 28 29 30 35 37 39 40 41 42 43 44 45 48 49 52 53 54 56 57 58 59 60 63 64 65 66 67 70 71 73 74 S Columbia/HCA Healthcare Corporation, Nashville, TN	33	10	531	14318	245	121756	724	96843	43520	1509

PERRY—Taylor County

Hospital	Control	Service	Staffed Beds	Admissions	Census	Outpatient Visits	Births	Total	Payroll	Personnel
DOCTOR'S MEMORIAL HOSPITAL, 407 East Ash Street, Zip 32347–2104, Mailing Address: P.O. Box 1847, Zip 32348–1847; tel. 850/584–0800; Alan Levine, Chief Executive Officer A9 10 F3 8 13 14 15 16 17 19 22 24 27 28 29 30 32 34 35 37 39, 41 42 44 45 46 49 51 64 65 66 67 68 71 73 74 P8	23	10	48	2200	25	99000	0			

PLANT CITY—Hillsborough County

Hospital	Control	Service	Staffed Beds	Admissions	Census	Outpatient Visits	Births	Total	Payroll	Personnel
⊞ SOUTH FLORIDA BAPTIST HOSPITAL, 301 North Alexander Street, Zip 33566–9058, Mailing Address: Drawer H, Zip 33564–9058; tel. 813/757–1200; William G. Ulbricht, Chief Operating Officer (Total facility includes 15 beds in nursing home–type unit) (Nonreporting) A1 9 10	23	10	100	—	—	—	—	—	—	—

PLANTATION—Broward County

Hospital	Control	Service	Staffed Beds	Admissions	Census	Outpatient Visits	Births	Total	Payroll	Personnel
⊞ PLANTATION GENERAL HOSPITAL, 401 N.W. 42nd Avenue, Zip 33317–2882; tel. 954/587–5010; Anthony M. Degina, Jr., Chief Executive Officer (Nonreporting) A1 9 10 S Columbia/HCA Healthcare Corporation, Nashville, TN	33	10	264	—	—	—	—	—	—	—
⊞ WESTSIDE REGIONAL MEDICAL CENTER, 8201 West Broward Boulevard, Zip 33324–9937; tel. 954/473–6600; Michael G. Joseph, Chief Executive Officer (Nonreporting) A1 9 10 S Columbia/HCA Healthcare Corporation, Nashville, TN	33	10	204	—	—	—	—	—	—	—

POMPANO BEACH—Broward County

Hospital	Control	Service	Staffed Beds	Admissions	Census	Outpatient Visits	Births	Total	Payroll	Personnel
COLUMBIA NORTHWEST MEDICAL CENTER See Northwest Medical Center										
⊞ △ NORTH BROWARD MEDICAL CENTER, 201 Sample Road, Zip 33064–3502; tel. 954/941–8300; James R. Chromik, Regional Vice President, Administration (Total facility includes 18 beds in nursing home–type unit) A1 2 7 9 10 F2 3 4 7 8 10 11 12 13 14 15 16 17 18 19 21 22 23 24 26 27 28 29 30 31 32 33 34 35 37 38 39 40 41 42 43 44 45 46 47 48 49 50 51 52 53 54 55 56 57 58 59 60 61 63 64 65 66 67 68 70 71 72 73 P6 S North Broward Hospital District, Fort Lauderdale, FL	16	10	334	13250	203	232455	0	107688	45483	1103
⊞ NORTHWEST MEDICAL CENTER, (Formerly Columbia Northwest Medical Center), 2801 North State Road 7, Zip 33063–5727, Mailing Address: P.O. Box 639002, Margate, Zip 33063–9002; tel. 954/978–4000; Gina Melby, Chief Executive Officer (Nonreporting) A1 9 10 S Columbia/HCA Healthcare Corporation, Nashville, TN	33	10	150	—	—	—	—	—	—	—

PORT CHARLOTTE—Charlotte County

Hospital	Control	Service	Staffed Beds	Admissions	Census	Outpatient Visits	Births	Total	Payroll	Personnel
⊞ BON SECOURS–ST. JOSEPH HEALTHCARE GROUP, 2500 Harbor Boulevard, Zip 33952–5396; tel. 941/766–4122; Michael L. Harrington, Chief Executive Officer (Total facility includes 101 beds in nursing home–type unit) (Nonreporting) A1 5 9 10 S Bon Secours Health System, Inc., Marriottsville, MD	21	10	313	—	—	—	—	—	—	—
⊞ △ FAWCETT MEMORIAL HOSPITAL, 21298 Olean Boulevard, Zip 33952–6765, Mailing Address: P.O. Box 4028, Punta Gorda, Zip 33949–4028; tel. 941/629–1181; Terry Chaffin, President and Chief Executive Officer (Total facility includes 15 beds in nursing home–type unit) (Nonreporting) A1 7 9 10 S Columbia/HCA Healthcare Corporation, Nashville, TN	33	10	249	—	—	—	—	—	—	—

PORT SAINT JOE—Gulf County

Hospital	Control	Service	Staffed Beds	Admissions	Census	Outpatient Visits	Births	Total	Payroll	Personnel
GULF PINES HOSPITAL, 102 20th Street, Zip 32456–2356, Mailing Address: P.O. Box 70, Zip 32456–0070; tel. 850/227–1121; Kenneth E. Dykes, Sr., Administrator and Chief Executive Officer (Nonreporting) A9 10	33	10	45	—	—	—	—	—	—	—

Hospital, Address, Telephone, Administrator, Approval, Facility, and Physician Codes, Health Care System, Network	Classi-fication Codes		Utilization Data					Expense (thousands) of dollars		
	Control	Service	Staffed Beds	Admissions	Census	Outpatient Visits	Births	Total	Payroll	Personnel

★ American Hospital Association (AHA) membership
□ Joint Commission on Accreditation of Healthcare Organizations (JCAHO) accreditation
+ American Osteopathic Healthcare Association (AOHA) membership
○ American Osteopathic Association (AOA) accreditation
△ Commission on Accreditation of Rehabilitation Facilities (CARF) accreditation
Control codes 61, 63, 64, 71, 72 and 73 indicate hospitals listed by AOHA, but not registered by AHA. For definition of numerical codes, see page A4

PORT ST. LUCIE—St. Lucie County

□ SAVANNAS HOSPITAL, 2550 S.E. Walton Road, Zip 34952–7197; tel. 561/335–0400; Patricia W. Brown, Executive Director (Nonreporting) **A**1 10	33	22	70	—	—	—	—	—	—	—
⊠ ST. LUCIE MEDICAL CENTER, (Formerly Columbia Medical Center–Port St Lucie), 1800 S.E. Tiffany Avenue, Zip 34952–7580; tel. 561/335–4000; Gary Cantrell, President and Chief Executive Officer (Total facility includes 24 beds in nursing home–type unit) (Nonreporting) **A**1 9 10 **S** Columbia/HCA Healthcare Corporation, Nashville, TN	33	10	150	—	—	—	—	—	—	—

PUNTA GORDA—Charlotte County

□ CHARLOTTE REGIONAL MEDICAL CENTER, 809 East Marion Avenue, Zip 33950–3898, Mailing Address: P.O. Box 51–1328, Zip 33951–1328; tel. 941/639–3131; Joshua S. Putter, Executive Director (Nonreporting) **A**1 9 10 **S** Health Management Associates, Naples, FL	33	10	148	—	—	—	—	—	—	—

QUINCY—Gadsden County

GADSDEN COMMUNITY HOSPITAL, U.S. Highway 90 East, Zip 32353, Mailing Address: P.O. Box 1979, Zip 32353–1979; tel. 850/875–1100; Donald L. Bradford, Chief Executive Officer (Nonreporting) **A**9 10	23	10	51	—	—	—	—	—	—	—

ROCKLEDGE—Brevard County

□ WUESTHOFF HOSPITAL, 110 Longwood Avenue, Zip 32955–2887, Mailing Address: P.O. Box 565002, Mail Stop 1, Zip 32956–5002; tel. 407/636–2211; Titus Hall, Chief Executive Officer **A**1 2 9 10 **F**3 4 6 7 8 10 11 12 13 14 15 16 17 19 21 22 23 24 26 28 29 30 31 32 33 34 35 37 38 39 40 41 42 43 44 45 46 49 52 54 55 57 58 59 63 64 65 66 67 71 73 74 **P**7	23	10	215	10889	133	154977	967	92827	38965	1677

SAFETY HARBOR—Pinellas County

MEASE COUNTRYSIDE HOSPITAL, 3231 McMullen–Booth Road, Zip 34695–1098, Mailing Address: P.O. 1098, Zip 34695–1098; tel. 813/725–6111; James A. Pfeiffer, Chief Operating Officer (Nonreporting) **A**9 10 **S** Morton Plant Mease Health Care, Dunedin, FL	23	10	100	—	—	—	—	—	—	—

SAINT AUGUSTINE—St. Johns County

⊠ FLAGLER HOSPITAL, (Includes Flagler Hospital–West, 1955 U.S. 1 South, Zip 32086; tel. 904/826–4700), 400 Health Park Boulevard, Zip 32086–5779; tel. 904/829–5155; James D. Conzemius, President (Total facility includes 14 beds in nursing home–type unit) **A**1 9 10 **F**7 8 10 15 16 19 21 22 23 28 32 35 37 40 41 44 49 52 64 65 73	23	10	260	9022	157	100896	756	74079	31709	1077

SAINT CLOUD—Lowndes County

ST. CLOUD HOSPITAL, A DIVISION OF ORLANDO REGIONAL HEALTHCARE SYSTEM, 2906 17th Street, Zip 34769–6099; tel. 407/892–2135; Jim Norris, Executive Director (Nonreporting) **A**9 **S** Orlando Regional Healthcare System, Orlando, FL	23	10	68	—	—	—	—	—	—	—

SAINT PETERSBURG—Pinellas County

□ ALL CHILDREN'S HOSPITAL, (PEDIATRIC SPECIALTY), 801 Sixth Street South, Zip 33701–4899; tel. 813/898–7451; J. Dennis Sexton, President **A**1 3 5 8 9 10 **F**4 10 12 13 14 16 17 19 20 21 22 24 25 27 28 29 30 31 32 34 35 37 38 39 41 42 43 44 45 49 51 53 65 66 67 68 70 71 73 **P**1 5 Web address: www.allkids.org	23	59	216	7039	139	94519	0	133748	57250	1611
⊠ △ BAYFRONT MEDICAL CENTER, 701 Sixth Street South, Zip 33701–4891; tel. 727/823–1234; Sue G. Brody, President and Chief Executive Officer **A**1 2 3 5 7 9 10 **F**1 3 4 5 7 8 10 11 12 13 15 16 17 18 19 21 22 24 25 26 28 29 30 31 32 34 35 37 38 39 40 41 42 44 45 46 48 49 51 53 54 55 56 57 58 59 60 63 64 65 66 67 70 71 72 73 74 **P**1	23	10	300	17000	208	—	—	—	—	1700
⊠ EDWARD WHITE HOSPITAL, 2323 Ninth Avenue North, Zip 33713–6898, Mailing Address: P.O. Box 12018, Zip 33733–2018; tel. 727/323–1111; Barry S. Stokes, President and Chief Executive Officer (Total facility includes 10 beds in nursing home–type unit) **A**1 9 10 **F**4 7 8 10 12 14 17 19 20 21 22 23 24 25 26 28 29 30 31 33 34 35 37 41 42 43 44 46 49 51 59 63 64 65 66 67 71 73 74 **P**1 **S** Columbia/HCA Healthcare Corporation, Nashville, TN Web address: www.columbia.net	33	10	134	3194	48	39156	0	24846	9962	241
⊠ ○ NORTHSIDE HOSPITAL AND HEART INSTITUTE, 6000 49th Street North, Zip 33709–2145; tel. 727/521–4411; Bradley K. Grover, Sr., Ph.D., FACHE, President and Chief Executive Officer (Total facility includes 13 beds in nursing home–type unit) (Nonreporting) **A**1 9 10 11 12 13 **S** Columbia/HCA Healthcare Corporation, Nashville, TN Web address: www.northsidehospital.com	33	10	301	—	—	—	—	—	—	—
⊠ PALMS OF PASADENA HOSPITAL, 1501 Pasadena Avenue South, Zip 33707–3798; tel. 727/381–1000; John D. Bartlett, Chief Executive Officer (Total facility includes 13 beds in nursing home–type unit) **A**1 2 9 10 **F**10 11 12 19 22 28 30 32 34 37 39 41 44 46 49 60 64 65 71 **P**5 **S** TENET Healthcare Corporation, Santa Barbara, CA	33	10	213	6382	99	115261	0	56114	20587	616
⊠ ST. ANTHONY'S HOSPITAL, 1200 Seventh Avenue North, Zip 33705–1388, Mailing Address: P.O. Box 12588, Zip 33733–2588; tel. 727/825–1100; Sue G. Brody, President and Chief Executive Officer (Total facility includes 30 beds in nursing home–type unit) **A**1 2 9 10 **F**1 4 7 8 9 10 11 12 14 15 16 17 19 21 22 24 25 26 27 28 29 30 31 32 34 35 37 38 39 40 41 42 43 44 46 47 48 49 52 54 55 56 57 58 59 60 61 64 65 66 67 70 71 73 74 **P**1 7 **S** Catholic Health East, Newtown Square, PA Web address: www.stanthonys.org	23	10	370	11885	189	146650	236	83583	32770	1237

Hospital, Address, Telephone, Administrator, Approval, Facility, and Physician Codes, Health Care System, Network	Classi-fication Codes		Utilization Data					Expense (thousands) of dollars		

★ American Hospital Association (AHA) membership
□ Joint Commission on Accreditation of Healthcare Organizations (JCAHO) accreditation
+ American Osteopathic Healthcare Association (AOHA) membership
○ American Osteopathic Association (AOA) accreditation
△ Commission on Accreditation of Rehabilitation Facilities (CARF) accreditation
Control codes 61, 63, 64, 71, 72 and 73 indicate hospitals listed by AOHA, but not registered by AHA. For definition of numerical codes, see page A4

	Control	Service	Staffed Beds	Admissions	Census	Outpatient Visits	Births	Total	Payroll	Personnel
★ ST. PETERSBURG GENERAL HOSPITAL, 6500 38th Avenue North, Zip 33710–1629; tel. 727/384–1414; Daniel J. Friedrich, III, President and Chief Executive Officer (Total facility includes 20 beds in nursing home–type unit) **A**1 9 10 **F**4 7 8 10 11 12 16 18 19 21 22 26 27 30 33 35 37 39 40 41 42 43 44 45 48 49 56 57 58 59 60 61 64 65 67 70 71 73 74 **S** Columbia/HCA Healthcare Corporation, Nashville, TN	33	10	160	5438	55	53200	915	37886	15822	477
VENCOR HOSPITAL–ST PETERSBURG, 3030 Sixth Street South, Zip 33705–3720; tel. 727/894–8719; Pamela M. Riter, R.N., Administrator (Nonreporting) **S** Vencor, Incorporated, Louisville, KY	33	49	60	—	—	—	—	—	—	—
SANFORD—Seminole County										
★ CENTRAL FLORIDA REGIONAL HOSPITAL, (Formerly Columbia Medical Center Sanford), 1401 West Seminole Boulevard, Zip 32771–6764; tel. 407/321–4500; Doug Sills, President and Chief Executive Officer (Nonreporting) **A**1 9 10 **S** Columbia/HCA Healthcare Corporation, Nashville, TN	33	10	226	—	—	—	—	—	—	—
SARASOTA—Sarasota County										
★ DOCTORS HOSPITAL OF SARASOTA, 5731 Bee Ridge Road, Zip 34233–5056; tel. 941/342–1100; William C. Lievense, President and Chief Executive Officer **A**1 2 9 10 **F**7 8 10 12 14 15 16 19 21 22 25 27 32 33 34 35 37 40 41 42 44 45 48 51 54 55 57 58 63 64 65 67 71 73 **P**8 **S** Columbia/HCA Healthcare Corporation, Nashville, TN	33	10	168	8812	106	77294	692	66383	24127	734
□ △ HEALTHSOUTH REHABILITATION HOSPITAL OF SARASOTA, 3251 Proctor Road, Zip 34231–8538; tel. 941/921–8600; Jeff Garber, Administrator and Chief Executive Officer (Nonreporting) **A**1 7 10 **S** HEALTHSOUTH Corporation, Birmingham, AL	33	46	60	—	—	—	—	—	—	—
★ △ SARASOTA MEMORIAL HOSPITAL, 1700 South Tamiami Trail, Zip 34239–3555; tel. 941/917–9000; Michael H. Covert, FACHE, President and Chief Executive Officer **A**1 2 5 7 9 10 **F**2 3 4 7 8 10 11 12 14 15 16 17 19 21 22 23 25 26 28 29 30 32 33 34 35 37 38 39 40 42 43 44 45 46 48 49 51 52 53 54 55 56 58 59 60 63 64 65 66 67 71 72 73 74 **P**4 7 8 Web address: www.smh.com	16	10	529	27015	371	298797	2210	254897	90164	2406
SEBASTIAN—Indian River County										
□ SEBASTIAN RIVER MEDICAL CENTER, 13695 North U.S. Highway 1, Zip 32958–3230, Mailing Address: Box 780838, Zip 32978–0838; tel. 561/589–3186; Diane D. Torres, R.N., Executive Director (Nonreporting) **A**1 9 10 **S** Health Management Associates, Naples, FL	33	10	133	—	—	—	—	—	—	—
SEBRING—Highlands County										
★ FLORIDA HOSPITAL HEARTLAND DIVISION, 4200 Sun'n Lake Boulevard, Zip 33872, Mailing Address: P.O. Box 9400, Zip 33872; tel. 941/314–4466; John R. Harding, President and Chief Executive Officer (Total facility includes 20 beds in nursing home–type unit) **A**1 9 10 **F**3 7 8 12 14 15 16 17 19 21 22 23 24 28 30 32 33 35 37 40 41 44 45 46 49 52 56 57 58 64 67 71 73 **P**8 **S** Adventist Health System Sunbelt Health Care Corporation, Winter Park, FL Web address: www.flhosp–heartland.org	21	10	195	7857	108	93236	578	70343	25643	878
□ HIGHLANDS REGIONAL MEDICAL CENTER, 3600 South Highlands Avenue, Zip 33870–5495, Mailing Address: Drawer 2066, Zip 33871–2066; tel. 941/385–6101; Micheal Terry, Executive Director (Nonreporting) **A**1 9 10 **S** Health Management Associates, Naples, FL	33	10	126	—	—	—	—	—	—	—
SOUTH MIAMI—Dade County										
□ LARKIN COMMUNITY HOSPITAL, 7031 S.W. 62nd Avenue, Zip 33143–4781; tel. 305/284–7500; Jack Michel, M.D., Chief Executive Officer (Nonreporting) **A**1 9 10	33	10	112	—	—	—	—	—	—	—
SPRING HILL—Hernando County										
★ OAK HILL HOSPITAL, 11375 Cortez Boulevard, Zip 34611, Mailing Address: P.O. Box 5300, Zip 34611–5300; tel. 352/596–6632; Jaime A. Wesolowski, Chief Executive Officer (Nonreporting) **A**1 2 9 10 **S** Columbia/HCA Healthcare Corporation, Nashville, TN	16	10	204	—	—	—	—	—	—	—
★ SPRING HILL REGIONAL HOSPITAL, 10461 Quality Drive, Zip 34609; tel. 352/688–8200; Thomas Bard, Chief Executive Officer (Nonreporting) **A**1 9 10 **S** Health Management Associates, Naples, FL	23	10	75	—	—	—	—	—	—	—
STARKE—Bradford County										
★ SHANDS AT STARKE, 922 East Call Street, Zip 32091–3699; tel. 904/368–2300; Jeannie Baker, Administrator (Nonreporting) **A**1 9 10 **S** Shands HealthCare, Gainesville, FL	23	10	23	—	—	—	—	—	—	—
STUART—Martin County										
★ MARTIN MEMORIAL HEALTH SYSTEMS, (Includes Martin Memorial Hospital South, 2100 S.E. Salerno Road, Zip 34997; tel. 561/223–5945), 300 S.E. Hospital Drive, Zip 34995–9014, Mailing Address: P.O. Box 9010, Zip 34995–9010; tel. 561/223–5945; Richmond M. Harman, President and Chief Executive Officer **A**1 2 9 10 **F**5 7 8 10 12 14 15 16 17 19 21 22 23 24 25 26 27 28 29 30 31 32 33 34 35 36 37 39 40 41 42 44 45 46 49 51 54 57 58 59 60 63 65 67 71 72 73 74 **P**5 6 8 Web address: www.mmhs.fla.org	23	10	310	16212	213	201804	1233	146566	66383	1876
SUN CITY CENTER—Hillsborough County										
★ SOUTH BAY HOSPITAL, 4016 State Road 674, Zip 33573–5298; tel. 813/634–3301; Hal Muetzel, Chief Executive Officer (Nonreporting) **A**1 9 10 **S** Columbia/HCA Healthcare Corporation, Nashville, TN	33	10	112	—	—	—	—	—	—	—

Hospital, Address, Telephone, Administrator, Approval, Facility, and Physician Codes, Health Care System, Network	Classi-fication Codes		Utilization Data					Expense (thousands) of dollars		
	Control	Service	Staffed Beds	Admissions	Census	Outpatient Visits	Births	Total	Payroll	Personnel

★ American Hospital Association (AHA) membership
□ Joint Commission on Accreditation of Healthcare Organizations (JCAHO) accreditation
+ American Osteopathic Healthcare Association (AOHA) membership
○ American Osteopathic Association (AOA) accreditation
△ Commission on Accreditation of Rehabilitation Facilities (CARF) accreditation
Control codes 61, 63, 64, 71, 72 and 73 indicate hospitals listed by AOHA, but not registered by AHA. For definition of numerical codes, see page A4

SUNRISE—Broward County

□ △ SUNRISE REGIONAL MEDICAL CENTER, (Formerly The Retreat), 555 S.W. 148th Avenue, Zip 33325–3072; tel. 954/370–0200; Humberto J. Munoz, Chief Executive Officer (Nonreporting) **A**1 7 10 **Web address:** www.sunriseregional.com THE RETREAT See Sunrise Regional Medical Center	33	22	100	—	—	—	—	—	—	—

TALLAHASSEE—Leon County

□ △ HEALTHSOUTH REHABILITATION HOSPITAL OF TALLAHASSEE, 1675 Riggins Road, Zip 32308–5315; tel. 850/656–4800; Armando Colombo, Chief Executive Officer (Nonreporting) **A**1 7 10 **S** HEALTHSOUTH Corporation, Birmingham, AL	33	46	70	—	—	—	—	—	—	—
☒ TALLAHASSEE COMMUNITY HOSPITAL, 2626 Capital Medical Boulevard, Zip 32308–4499; tel. 850/656–5000; Thomas Paul Pemberton, Chief Executive Officer (Nonreporting) **A**1 9 10 **S** Columbia/HCA Healthcare Corporation, Nashville, TN	33	10	180	—	—	—	—	—	—	—
☒ TALLAHASSEE MEMORIAL HEALTHCARE, (Formerly Tallahassee Memorial Regional Medical Center), 1300 Miccosukee Road, Zip 32308–5093; tel. 850/681–1155; Duncan Moore, President and Chief Executive Officer (Total facility includes 102 beds in nursing home–type unit) **A**1 2 3 5 9 10 **F**3 4 7 8 10 11 14 15 16 17 19 21 22 23 24 25 26 27 28 29 30 31 32 34 35 37 38 39 40 41 42 43 44 45 46 47 49 51 52 53 54 55 56 57 58 59 60 61 63 64 65 66 67 68 71 73 74 **P**6 **Web address:** www.TMH.COM	23	10	614	24977	425	251665	3824	206423	102977	3011

TAMARAC—Broward County

☒ UNIVERSITY HOSPITAL AND MEDICAL CENTER, (Includes University Pavilion, 7425 North University Drive, Zip 33328; tel. 305/722–9933), 7201 North University Drive, Zip 33321–2996; tel. 954/721–2200; James A. Cruickshank, Chief Executive Officer (Nonreporting) **A**1 9 10 **S** Columbia/HCA Healthcare Corporation, Nashville, TN	33	10	211	—	—	—	—	—	—	—

TAMPA—Hillsborough County

□ CHARTER BEHAVIORAL HEALTH SYSTEM OF TAMPA BAY, 4004 North Riverside Drive, Zip 33603–3212; tel. 813/238–8671; James C. Hill, Chief Executive Officer (Nonreporting) **A**1 **S** Magellan Health Services, Atlanta, GA	33	22	146	—	—	—	—	—	—	—
☒ H. LEE MOFFITT CANCER CENTER AND RESEARCH INSTITUTE, (CANCER), 12902 Magnolia Drive, Zip 33612–9497; tel. 813/972–4673; John C. Ruckdeschel, M.D., Director and Chief Executive Officer **A**1 2 3 5 8 9 10 **F**8 12 14 16 17 19 20 21 26 30 31 33 34 37 39 42 44 45 46 49 54 55 58 60 63 65 68 71 73 74 **S** Quorum Health Group/Quorum Health Resources, Inc., Brentwood, TN **Web address:** www.moffitt.usf.edu	23	49	117	5055	80	95937	0	118869	45947	1254
☒ △ JAMES A. HALEY VETERANS HOSPITAL, 13000 Bruce B. Downs Boulevard, Zip 33612–4798; tel. 813/972–2000; Richard A. Silver, Director (Total facility includes 209 beds in nursing home–type unit) (Nonreporting) **A**1 3 5 7 8 **S** Department of Veterans Affairs, Washington, DC	45	10	640	—	—	—	—	—	—	—
☒ MEMORIAL HOSPITAL OF TAMPA, 2901 Swann Avenue, Zip 33609–4057; tel. 813/873–6400; Charles F. Scott, President and Chief Executive Officer (Nonreporting) **A**1 5 9 10 **S** TENET Healthcare Corporation, Santa Barbara, CA **Web address:** www.tenethealth.com/tampa	32	10	174	—	—	—	—	—	—	—
☒ SHRINERS HOSPITALS FOR CHILDREN, TAMPA, 12502 North Pine Drive, Zip 33612–9499; tel. 813/972–2250; John Holtz, Administrator **A**1 3 5 **F**14 15 17 19 21 27 30 34 35 44 49 63 65 71 73 **S** Shriners Hospitals for Children, Tampa, FL	23	57	60	1172	32	10465	0	—	—	244
☒ ST. JOSEPH'S HOSPITAL, (Includes Tampa Children's Hospital at St. Joseph's, St. Joseph's Women's Hospital – Tampa, 3030 West Dr. Martin L. King Boulevard, Zip 33607–6394; tel. 813/879–4730), 3001 West Martin Luther King Jr. Boulevard, Zip 33607–6387, Mailing Address: P.O. Box 4227, Zip 33677–4227; tel. 813/870–4000; Isaac Mallah, President and Chief Executive Officer (Total facility includes 19 beds in nursing home–type unit) (Nonreporting) **A**1 2 5 9 10 **S** Catholic Health East, Newtown Square, PA	21	10	883	—	—	—	—	—	—	—
★ △ TAMPA GENERAL HEALTHCARE, Davis Islands, Zip 33606, Mailing Address: P.O. Box 1289, Zip 33601–1289; tel. 813/251–7000; Bruce Siegel, M.D., M.P.H., President and Chief Executive Officer (Total facility includes 24 beds in nursing home–type unit) **A**3 5 7 8 9 10 **F**3 4 5 7 8 9 10 11 12 13 14 15 16 17 18 19 21 22 23 24 25 26 28 29 30 31 32 34 35 37 38 40 41 42 43 44 45 46 47 48 49 51 52 53 54 55 56 57 58 59 60 61 64 65 66 67 68 70 71 72 73 74 **P**4 **Web address:** www.tgh.org	23	10	734	22458	405	259577	3079	296460	103400	2888
☒ TOWN AND COUNTRY HOSPITAL, 6001 Webb Road, Zip 33615–3291; tel. 813/885–6666; Charles F. Scott, President and Chief Executive Officer (Total facility includes 15 beds in nursing home–type unit) **A**1 5 9 10 **F**2 3 8 10 12 14 16 19 21 22 30 31 32 34 35 41 42 44 45 49 54 55 56 57 58 59 63 64 65 66 67 71 73 **P**7 8 **S** TENET Healthcare Corporation, Santa Barbara, CA **Web address:** www.tenethealth.com/town&country	32	10	155	4214	63	35320	0	—	—	—
□ UNIVERSITY COMMUNITY HOSPITAL, 3100 East Fletcher Avenue, Zip 33613–4688; tel. 813/971–6000; Norman V. Stein, President (Total facility includes 27 beds in nursing home–type unit) **A**1 2 9 10 **F**4 7 8 10 11 12 14 15 16 17 19 20 21 22 23 24 26 27 28 29 30 32 34 35 37 38 39 40 41 42 43 44 45 46 47 48 49 60 61 63 64 65 67 71 72 73 74 **Web address:** www.uch.org	23	10	384	18349	259	102613	2224	154419	68464	2181

Hospital, Address, Telephone, Administrator, Approval, Facility, and Physician Codes, Health Care System, Network	Classi-fication Codes		Utilization Data					Expense (thousands) of dollars		
★ American Hospital Association (AHA) membership ◻ Joint Commission on Accreditation of Healthcare Organizations (JCAHO) accreditation • American Osteopathic Healthcare Association (AOHA) membership ○ American Osteopathic Association (AOA) accreditation △ Commission on Accreditation of Rehabilitation Facilities (CARF) accreditation Control codes 61, 63, 64, 71, 72 and 73 indicate hospitals listed by AOHA, but not registered by AHA. For definition of numerical codes, see page A4	Control	Service	Staffed Beds	Admissions	Census	Outpatient Visits	Births	Total	Payroll	Personnel

○ UNIVERSITY COMMUNITY HOSPITAL–CARROLLWOOD, 7171 North Dale Mabry Highway, Zip 33614–2699; tel. 813/558–8001; Larry J. Archbell, Vice President Operations (Nonreporting) **A**9 10 11 12 13 **Web address:** www.uch.org	23	10	120	—	—	—	—	—	—	—
◻ VENCOR HOSPITAL – CENTRAL TAMPA, 4801 North Howard Avenue, Zip 33603–1484; tel. 813/874–7575; Ken Stone, Administrator (Nonreporting) **A**1 5 10 **S** Vencor, Incorporated, Louisville, KY	33	49	102	—	—	—	—	—	—	—
◻ VENCOR HOSPITAL–TAMPA, 4555 South Manhattan Avenue, Zip 33611–2397; tel. 813/839–6341; Theresa Hunkins, Administrator (Nonreporting) **A**1 3 5 10 **S** Vencor, Incorporated, Louisville, KY	33	49	73	—	—	—	—	—	—	—
TARPON SPRINGS—Pinellas County										
★ HELEN ELLIS MEMORIAL HOSPITAL, 1395 South Pinellas Avenue, Zip 34689–3721, Mailing Address: P.O. Box 1487, Zip 34688–1487; tel. 727/942–5000; Joseph N. Kiefer, Administrator (Total facility includes 18 beds in nursing home–type unit) **A**1 9 10 **F**7 8 10 11 12 15 16 17 19 21 22 23 25 28 29 30 32 34 35 37 39 40 41 42 44 45 46 49 64 67 71 72 73 **P**8	23	10	168	7954	115	77458	567	64160	25529	770
TAVERNIER—Monroe County										
★ MARINERS HOSPITAL, 91500 Overseas Highway, Zip 33070; tel. 305/852–4418; Robert H. Luse, Chief Executive Officer **A**1 9 10 **F**8 15 16 17 19 21 22 28 29 30 32 33 34 35 37 44 45 46 49 63 65 67 71 73 74 **P**1 3 **S** Baptist Health System of South Florida, Coral Gables, FL **Web address:** www.bhssf.org	23	10	31	1094	12	16602	1	12362	5071	146
TEQUESTA—Martin County										
◻ SANDYPINES, 11301 S.E. Tequesta Terrace, Zip 33469–8146; tel. 561/744–0211; Mary S. Bohne', Administrator **A**1 9 **F**14 15 16 52 53 **S** Health Management Associates, Naples, FL	33	52	60	136	57	0	0	—	—	75
TITUSVILLE—Brevard County										
◻ PARRISH MEDICAL CENTER, 951 North Washington Avenue, Zip 32796–2194; tel. 407/268–6111; Rod L. Baker, President and Chief Executive Officer **A**1 2 9 10 **F**1 3 5 7 8 10 12 14 15 16 17 19 20 21 22 23 24 25 27 28 29 30 31 32 33 34 35 37 39 40 42 44 45 46 49 56 60 63 65 66 67 69 71 72 73 74	16	10	210	8661	107	93400	569	59202	25888	730
VENICE—Sarasota County										
★ BON SECOURS–VENICE HOSPITAL, 540 The Rialto, Zip 34285–2900; tel. 941/485–7711; Michael G. Guley, Chief Executive Officer (Total facility includes 36 beds in nursing home–type unit) **A**1 2 9 10 **F**8 10 12 15 16 17 19 21 22 23 25 26 27 28 29 30 31 32 34 35 37 41 42 44 45 46 49 52 56 57 64 65 67 71 72 73 **P**8 **S** Bon Secours Health System, Inc., Marriottsville, MD **Web address:** www.bshsi.fl.com	21	10	254	9656	141	165677	0	70910	25525	1238
VERO BEACH—Indian River County										
◻ △ HEALTHSOUTH TREASURE COAST REHABILITATION HOSPITAL, 1600 37th Street, Zip 32960–6549; tel. 561/778–2100; Denise B. McGrath, Chief Executive Officer (Nonreporting) **A**1 7 10 **S** HEALTHSOUTH Corporation, Birmingham, AL	33	46	70	—	—	—	—	—	—	—
★ INDIAN RIVER MEMORIAL HOSPITAL, 1000 36th Street, Zip 32960–6592; tel. 561/567–4311; Jeffrey L. Susi, President and Chief Executive Officer (Total facility includes 28 beds in nursing home–type unit) **A**1 2 9 10 **F**3 7 8 10 12 15 17 19 21 22 23 25 26 28 29 30 31 34 35 37 40 41 42 44 45 46 49 52 53 54 55 56 57 58 59 60 63 64 65 67 71 73 74 **P**8 **Web address:** www.irmh.com	23	10	280	11248	171	67537	949	96363	41024	1234
WEST PALM BEACH—Palm Beach County										
45TH STREET MENTAL HEALTH CENTER, 1041 45th Street, Zip 33407–2494; tel. 561/844–9741; Terry H. Allen, Executive Director (Nonreporting) **A**10	23	22	44	—	—	—	—	—	—	—
◻ ○ COLUMBIA HOSPITAL, 2201 45th Street, Zip 33407–2069; tel. 561/842–6141; Sharon L. Roush, Chief Executive Officer **A**1 9 10 11 12 **F**3 4 5 7 8 10 11 12 13 14 15 16 17 19 20 21 22 23 25 26 27 28 29 30 31 34 35 37 39 40 41 42 43 44 45 46 47 49 51 52 53 54 55 56 57 58 59 60 61 63 64 65 66 67 68 71 73 74 **P**5 7 **S** Columbia/HCA Healthcare Corporation, Nashville, TN	32	10	250	8017	115	38169	499	—	—	777
★ GOOD SAMARITAN MEDICAL CENTER, Flagler Drive at Palm Beach Lakes Boulevard, Zip 33401–3499; tel. 561/655–5511; Phillip C. Dutcher, President and Chief Executive Officer **A**1 2 9 10 **F**2 3 4 7 8 10 11 12 13 14 15 16 17 18 19 21 22 23 24 25 26 28 29 30 31 32 33 34 35 36 37 38 39 40 41 42 43 44 45 46 47 48 49 51 52 53 54 56 57 58 59 60 61 63 65 66 67 68 70 71 73 74 **P**1 5 6 7 **S** Catholic Health East, Newtown Square, PA	23	10	341	12367	178	—	2278	109903	30972	3574
HOSPICE OF PALM BEACH COUNTY, 5300 East Avenue, Zip 33407–2352; tel. 561/848–5200 (Nonreporting)	23	49	24	—	—	—	—	—	—	—
★ △ ST. MARY'S HOSPITAL, 901 45th Street, Zip 33407–2495, Mailing Address: P.O. Box 24620, Zip 33416–4620; tel. 561/844–6300; Phillip C. Dutcher, President and Chief Executive Officer **A**7 9 10 **F**2 3 4 7 8 10 11 12 13 14 15 16 17 18 19 21 22 23 24 25 26 28 29 30 31 32 33 34 35 36 37 38 39 40 41 42 43 44 45 46 47 48 49 51 52 53 54 56 57 58 59 60 61 63 65 66 67 68 70 71 73 74 **P**1 4 5 7 **S** Catholic Health East, Newtown Square, PA	21	10	460	16938	280	131234	3021	159397	58433	2277
★ VETERANS AFFAIRS MEDICAL CENTER, 7305 North Military Trail, Zip 33410–6400; tel. 561/882–8262; Edward H. Seiler, Director (Total facility includes 98 beds in nursing home–type unit) **A**1 **F**1 3 8 12 16 17 19 20 21 22 26 28 30 31 32 34 35 37 41 42 44 45 46 49 50 51 52 56 58 60 64 65 67 71 73 74 **P**1 **S** Department of Veterans Affairs, Washington, DC **Web address:** www.vagov.com	45	10	192	3988	168	296207	0	—	—	1312

Hospital, Address, Telephone, Administrator, Approval, Facility, and Physician Codes, Health Care System, Network	Classi-fication Codes		Utilization Data					Expense (thousands) of dollars		
★ American Hospital Association (AHA) membership □ Joint Commission on Accreditation of Healthcare Organizations (JCAHO) accreditation + American Osteopathic Healthcare Association (AOHA) membership ○ American Osteopathic Association (AOA) accreditation △ Commission on Accreditation of Rehabilitation Facilities (CARF) accreditation Control codes 61, 63, 64, 71, 72 and 73 indicate hospitals listed by AOHA, but not registered by AHA. For definition of numerical codes, see page A4	Control	Service	Staffed Beds	Admissions	Census	Outpatient Visits	Births	Total	Payroll	Personnel

	Control	Service	Staffed Beds	Admissions	Census	Outpatient Visits	Births	Total	Payroll	Personnel
□ ○ WELLINGTON REGIONAL MEDICAL CENTER, 10101 Forest Hill Boulevard, Zip 33414–6199; tel. 561/798–8500; Gregory E. Boyer, Chief Executive Officer (Nonreporting) **A**1 2 9 10 11 12 13 **S** Universal Health Services, Inc., King of Prussia, PA **Web address:** www.wellingtonregmedctr.com	33	10	93	—	—	—	—	—	—	—
WILLISTON—Levy County										
□ NATURE COAST REGIONAL HEALTH NETWORK, 125 S.W. Seventh Street, Zip 32696, Mailing Address: P.O. Drawer 550, Zip 32696–0550; tel. 352/528–2801; James LeBrun, Chief Executive Officer (Nonreporting) **A**1 9 10	33	10	40	—	—	—	—	—	—	—
WINTER HAVEN—Polk County										
⊠ △ WINTER HAVEN HOSPITAL, (Includes Lake Wales Medical Centers, 410 South 11th Street, Lake Wales, Zip 33853–4256, Mailing Address: P.O. Box 3460, Zip 33859–3460; tel. 941/676–1433; Joe M. Connell, Chief Executive Officer), 200 Avenue F. N.E., Zip 33881–4193; tel. 941/297–1899; Lance W. Anastasio, President (Total facility includes 277 beds in nursing home–type unit) **A**1 7 9 10 **F**7 8 10 11 12 13 15 16 17 18 19 20 21 22 23 24 28 29 30 32 33 34 35 37 38 39 40 41 42 44 48 49 51 52 54 55 56 57 58 59 60 64 65 66 67 71 72 73 74 **P**6	23	10	611	19933	263	294592	2273	163008	83971	2725
WINTER PARK—Orange County										
⊠ WINTER PARK MEMORIAL HOSPITAL, (Includes Winter Park Psychiatric Care Center, 1600 Dodd Road, Zip 32792; tel. 407/677–6842), 200 North Lakemont Avenue, Zip 32792–3273; tel. 407/646–7000; Douglas P. DeGraaf, Chief Executive Officer (Nonreporting) **A**1 2 9 10 **S** Columbia/HCA Healthcare Corporation, Nashville, TN	33	10	339	—	—	—	—	—	—	—
ZEPHYRHILLS—Pasco County										
⊠ EAST PASCO MEDICAL CENTER, 7050 Gall Boulevard, Zip 33541–1399; tel. 813/788–0411; Paul Michael Norman, President (Total facility includes 11 beds in nursing home–type unit) **A**1 9 10 **F**7 8 10 12 14 15 16 17 19 22 24 25 29 32 34 35 37 40 41 44 46 49 51 60 64 65 67 71 73 74 **P**5 **S** Adventist Health System Sunbelt Health Care Corporation, Winter Park, FL	21	10	120	8172	92	58317	609	81521	36068	581

GEORGIA

Resident population 7,642 (in thousands)
Resident population in metro areas 65.9%
Birth rate per 1,000 population 15.6
65 years and over 9.9%
Percent of persons without health insurance 17.8%

Hospital, Address, Telephone, Administrator, Approval, Facility, and Physician Codes, Health Care System, Network	Classi-fication Codes		Utilization Data					Expense (thousands) of dollars		
★ American Hospital Association (AHA) membership □ Joint Commission on Accreditation of Healthcare Organizations (JCAHO) accreditation + American Osteopathic Healthcare Association (AOHA) membership ○ American Osteopathic Association (AOA) accreditation △ Commission on Accreditation of Rehabilitation Facilities (CARF) accreditation Control codes 61, 63, 64, 71, 72 and 73 indicate hospitals listed by AOHA, but not registered by AHA. For definition of numerical codes, see page A4	Control	Service	Staffed Beds	Admissions	Census	Outpatient Visits	Births	Total	Payroll	Personnel

ADEL—Cook County

□ MEMORIAL HOSPITAL OF ADEL, 706 North Parrish Avenue, Zip 31620–0677; Mailing Address: Box 677, Zip 31620–0677; tel. 912/896–2251; Greg Griffith, Chief Executive Officer (Total facility includes 95 beds in nursing home–type unit) **A**1 9 10 **F**7 12 19 22 28 32 37 44 64 65 71 73 **S** New American Healthcare Corporation, Brentwood, TN

	33	10	155	2458	117	18407	189	—	—	280

ALBANY—Dougherty County

✦ PALMYRA MEDICAL CENTERS, 2000 Palmyra Road, Zip 31702–1908, Mailing Address: P.O. Box 1908, Zip 31702–1908; tel. 912/434–2000; Allen Golson, Chief Executive Officer (Nonreporting) **A**1 9 10 **S** Columbia/HCA Healthcare Corporation, Nashville, TN
Web address: www.columbia.net

	33	10	156	—	—	—	—	—	—	—

✦ PHOEBE PUTNEY MEMORIAL HOSPITAL, 417 Third Avenue, Zip 31701–1828, Mailing Address: P.O. Box 1828, Zip 31703–1828; tel. 912/883–1800; Joel Wernick, President and Chief Executive Officer (Nonreporting) **A**1 2 3 5 9 10
Web address: www.ppmh.org

	23	10	418	—	—	—	—	—	—	—

ALMA—Bacon County

□ BACON COUNTY HOSPITAL, 302 South Wayne Street, Zip 31510–2997, Mailing Address: P.O. Drawer 1987, Zip 31510–1987; tel. 912/632–8961; Cindy R. Turner, Interim Chief Executive Officer (Total facility includes 88 beds in nursing home–type unit) (Nonreporting) **A**1 9 10

	16	10	126	—	—	—	—	—	—	—

AMERICUS—Sumter County

✦ SUMTER REGIONAL HOSPITAL, 100 Wheatley Drive, Zip 31709–3799; tel. 912/924–6011; Jerry W. Adams, President (Total facility includes 100 beds in nursing home–type unit) **A**1 9 10 **F**4 7 8 10 11 12 15 16 17 19 21 22 23 27 28 29 30 32 33 34 35 37 39 40 42 43 44 45 46 48 49 51 52 56 57 64 65 67 68 70 71 72 73 **P**8

	15	10	221	4966	149	42319	899	33142	14452	—

ARLINGTON—Calhoun County

CALHOUN MEMORIAL HOSPITAL, 209 Academy & Carswell Streets, Zip 31713, Mailing Address: Drawer R, Zip 31713; tel. 912/725–4272; Peggy Pierce, Administrator (Nonreporting) **A**9 10

	16	10	24	—	—	—	—	—	—	—

ATHENS—Clarke County

✦ ATHENS REGIONAL MEDICAL CENTER, 1199 Prince Avenue, Zip 30606–2793; tel. 706/549–9977; John A. Drew, President and Chief Executive Officer **A**1 9 10 **F**3 4 7 8 10 11 12 15 16 17 19 21 22 23 25 30 31 34 35 37 38 40 41 42 43 44 49 52 57 59 60 61 65 66 67 71 73
Web address: www.armc.org

	16	10	315	15342	215	71538	1446	133307	54102	1723

□ CHARTER WINDS HOSPITAL, 240 Mitchell Bridge Road, Zip 30606–2043; tel. 706/546–7277; Susan Lister, Chief Executive Officer (Nonreporting) **A**1 10 **S** Magellan Health Services, Atlanta, GA

	33	22	80	—	—	—	—	—	—	—

✦ ST. MARY'S HEALTH CARE SYSTEM, 1230 Baxter Street, Zip 30606–3791; tel. 706/548–7581; Edward J. Fechtel, Jr., President and Chief Executive Officer (Total facility includes 120 beds in nursing home–type unit) **A**1 9 10 **F**6 7 8 10 12 14 15 16 17 19 20 21 22 24 26 27 28 29 30 31 32 33 34 35 37 38 39 40 41 42 44 45 46 49 60 62 64 65 66 67 71 73 74 **P**7 **S** Catholic Health East, Newtown Square, PA
Web address: www.stmarysathens.com

	23	10	283	8958	186	95106	1210	60047	31716	1126

ATLANTA—Fulton and De Kalb Counties County

✦ ATLANTA MEDICAL CENTER, (Formerly Georgia Baptist Medical Center), 303 Parkway Drive N.E., Zip 30312–1239; tel. 404/265–4000; James E. Lathren, President and Chief Executive Officer (Total facility includes 72 beds in nursing home–type unit) (Nonreporting) **A**1 2 3 5 8 10 **S** TENET Healthcare Corporation, Santa Barbara, CA

	33	10	450	—	—	—	—	—	—	—

CHARTER ANCHOR HOSPITAL, 5454 Yorktowne Drive, Zip 30349–5305; tel. 770/991–6044; Matthew Crouch, Chief Executive Officer (Nonreporting) **A**9 10 **S** Magellan Health Services, Atlanta, GA
Web address: www.talbottcampus.com

	33	82	84	—	—	—	—	—	—	—

□ CHARTER BEHAVIORAL HEALTH SYSTEM OF ATLANTA, 811 Juniper Street N.E., Zip 30308–1398; tel. 404/881–5800; Dennis Workman, M.D., Medical Director (Nonreporting) **A**1 9 10 **S** Magellan Health Services, Atlanta, GA

	33	22	40	—	—	—	—	—	—	—

□ CHARTER BEHAVIORAL HEALTH SYSTEM OF ATLANTA AT PEACHFORD, 2151 Peachford Road, Zip 30338–6599; tel. 770/455–3200; Aleen S. Davis, Chief Executive Officer (Nonreporting) **A**1 9 10 **S** Magellan Health Services, Atlanta, GA

	33	22	224	—	—	—	—	—	—	—

✦ CRAWFORD LONG HOSPITAL OF EMORY UNIVERSITY, 550 Peachtree Street N.E., Zip 30365–2225; tel. 404/686–4411; John Dunklin Henry, Sr., FACHE, Chief Executive Officer **A**1 2 3 5 8 9 10 **F**1 2 3 4 7 8 10 11 12 13 14 17 19 21 22 23 24 25 26 30 31 32 33 34 35 37 38 39 40 41 42 43 44 46 47 48 49 50 51 52 53 54 55 56 57 58 59 60 61 63 64 65 66 67 68 70 71 74
Web address: www.emory.org

	23	10	409	19264	302	86196	2285	199391	73319	1856

Hospital, Address, Telephone, Administrator, Approval, Facility, and Physician Codes, Health Care System, Network	Classi-fication Codes		Utilization Data					Expense (thousands) of dollars		
	Control	Service	Staffed Beds	Admissions	Census	Outpatient Visits	Births	Total	Payroll	Personnel
✸ DUNWOODY MEDICAL CENTER, 4575 North Shallowford Road, Zip 30338–6499; tel. 770/454–2000; Thomas D. Gilbert, President and Chief Executive Officer **A**1 10 **F**7 8 10 12 14 15 17 19 21 22 28 29 30 34 37 38 39 40 41 44 45 46 61 63 64 65 71 73 74 **P**1 8 **S** Columbia/HCA Healthcare Corporation, Nashville, TN **Web address:** www.columbia.net	33	10	140	3710	38	26300	1375	28263	13477	305
☐ EGLESTON CHILDREN'S HOSPITAL, (Formerly Egleston Children's Health Care System), (PEDIATRIC MED/SURG), 1405 Clifton Road N.E., Zip 30322–1101; tel. 404/325–6000; James E. Tally, Ph.D., President and Chief Executive Officer **A**1 3 5 8 9 10 **F**4 10 11 12 13 15 16 17 19 20 21 22 25 27 28 29 30 31 34 35 38 39 41 42 43 44 45 46 47 48 49 51 52 53 54 55 58 59 63 65 66 67 68 70 71 72 73 **P**1 7 **S** ESR Children's Health Care System, Inc., Atlanta, GA	23	59	202	7290	142	216187	0	156842	65863	1758
✸ △ EMORY UNIVERSITY HOSPITAL, 1364 Clifton Road N.E., Zip 30322–1102; tel. 404/712–7021; John Dunklin Henry, Sr., FACHE, Chief Executive Officer **A**1 2 3 5 7 8 9 10 **F**2 3 4 7 8 10 11 12 14 16 17 19 21 22 23 25 26 28 29 30 31 34 35 37 39 41 42 43 44 45 46 48 49 50 51 52 54 55 56 57 58 59 60 61 63 65 66 67 68 71 72 73 74 **P**1 **Web address:** www.emory.org	23	10	473	19807	360	92978	0	290037	100677	2728
GEORGIA BAPTIST MEDICAL CENTER See Atlanta Medical Center										
GEORGIA MENTAL HEALTH INSTITUTE, 1256 Briarcliff Road N.E., Zip 30306–2694; tel. 404/894–5911; B. C. Robbins, Superintendent (Nonreporting) **A**3 5	12	22	222	—	—	—	—	—	—	—
✸ GRADY MEMORIAL HOSPITAL, 80 Butler Street S.E., Zip 30335–3801, Mailing Address: P.O. Box 26189, Zip 30335–3801; tel. 404/616–4252; Edward J. Renford, President and Chief Executive Officer (Total facility includes 354 beds in nursing home–type unit) (Nonreporting) **A**1 2 3 5 8 10	16	10	1200	—	—	—	—	—	—	—
★ HILLSIDE HOSPITAL, 690 Courtney Drive N.E., Zip 30306–0206, Mailing Address: P.O. Box 8247, Zip 31106–0247; tel. 404/875–4551; Teresa Stoker, Chief Executive Officer **F**12 14 15 16 20 52 53 55 56 59 65 67	23	52	61	24	61	0	0	8105	4615	174
✸ METROPOLITAN HOSPITAL, (Formerly Columbia Metropolitan Hospital), 3223 Howell Mill Road N.W., Zip 30327–4135; tel. 404/351–0500; Jean Calhoun, Administrator (Nonreporting) **A**1 10 **S** Columbia/HCA Healthcare Corporation, Nashville, TN	33	49	64	—	—	—	—	—	—	—
✸ NORTHSIDE HOSPITAL, 1000 Johnson Ferry Road N.E., Zip 30342–1611; tel. 404/851–8000; Sidney Kirschner, President and Chief Executive Officer (Nonreporting) **A**1 2 9 10	23	44	352	—	—	—	—	—	—	—
✸ △ PIEDMONT HOSPITAL, 1968 Peachtree Road N.W., Zip 30309–1231; tel. 404/605–5000; Richard B. Hubbard, III, President and Chief Executive Officer (Total facility includes 37 beds in nursing home–type unit) **A**1 2 3 5 7 9 10 **F**4 7 8 10 11 12 14 17 19 21 22 24 25 26 27 28 29 30 31 33 34 35 37 38 39 40 41 42 43 44 45 46 48 49 60 61 64 65 66 67 68 71 72 73 74 **P**1 3 6 **Web address:** www.piedmonthospital.org	23	10	442	25046	314	195788	4251	—	—	2766
✸ SAINT JOSEPH'S HOSPITAL OF ATLANTA, 5665 Peachtree Dunwoody Road N.E., Zip 30342–1764; tel. 404/851–7001; Brue Chandler, President and Chief Executive Officer (Nonreporting) **A**1 2 9 10 **S** Catholic Health East, Newtown Square, PA **Web address:** www.stjosephsatlanta.org	23	10	346	—	—	—	—	—	—	—
☐ △ SCOTTISH RITE CHILDREN'S MEDICAL CENTER, 1001 Johnson Ferry Road N.E., Zip 30342–1600; tel. 404/256–5252; James E. Tally, Ph.D., President and Chief Executive Officer **A**1 3 5 7 9 10 **F**10 11 12 13 15 16 17 19 20 21 22 28 29 30 32 34 35 38 39 41 42 43 44 45 46 47 48 49 51 52 53 54 58 65 66 67 68 70 71 72 73 **P**7 8 **S** ESR Children's Health Care System, Inc., Atlanta, GA **Web address:** www.srcmc.org	23	50	165	13480	117	166683	0	144460	65363	1545
✸ △ SHEPHERD CENTER, 2020 Peachtree Road N.W., Zip 30309–1465; tel. 404/352–2020; Gary R. Ulicny, Ph.D., President and Chief Executive Officer (Nonreporting) **A**1 7 9 10 **Web address:** www.shepherd.org	23	46	100	—	—	—	—	—	—	—
☐ SOUTHWEST HOSPITAL AND MEDICAL CENTER, 501 Fairburn Road S.W., Zip 30331–2099; tel. 404/699–1111; Marie Cameron, FACHE, President and Chief Executive Officer **A**1 3 5 9 10 **F**7 8 12 15 16 17 19 21 22 26 27 28 29 30 31 33 34 37 39 40 42 44 49 51 57 58 59 65 67 71 72 73 74	23	10	100	1991	26	20987	288	19816	9082	—
☐ VENCOR HOSPITAL–ATLANTA, (LONG TERM ACUTE CARE), 705 Juniper Street N.E., Zip 30365–2500; tel. 404/873–2871; Skip Wright, Administrator **A**1 10 **F**12 14 15 19 22 35 41 42 46 60 65 71 **S** Vencor, Incorporated, Louisville, KY	32	49	70	377	54	—	0	29827	15422	413
✸ WESLEY WOODS CENTER OF EMORY UNIVERSITY, (Formerly Wesley Woods Geriatric Hospital), 1821 Clifton Road N.E., Zip 30329–5102; tel. 404/728–6200; William L. Minnix, Jr., President and Chief Executive Officer **A**1 3 5 10 **F**3 4 6 8 10 11 12 13 15 17 19 20 21 22 24 25 26 27 28 29 30 31 32 34 35 36 37 39 41 42 43 44 45 46 48 49 50 51 52 53 54 55 56 57 58 59 60 61 62 63 64 65 66 67 68 70 71 72 73 74 **P**1 6 **Web address:** www.emory.org	23	22	92	1834	57	33486	0	27915	11077	336
✸ WEST PACES MEDICAL CENTER, 3200 Howell Mill Road N.W., Zip 30327–4101; tel. 404/350–5600; Thomas D. Gilbert, President and Chief Executive Officer (Nonreporting) **A**1 2 3 10 **S** Columbia/HCA Healthcare Corporation, Nashville, TN	33	10	294	—	—	—	—	—	—	—
AUGUSTA—Richmond County										
✸ △ COLUMBIA–AUGUSTA MEDICAL CENTER, 3651 Wheeler Road, Zip 30909–6426; tel. 706/651–3232; Michael K. Kerner, President and Chief Executive Officer (Nonreporting) **A**1 7 9 10 **S** Columbia/HCA Healthcare Corporation, Nashville, TN **Web address:** www.columbia.augusta.com	33	10	284	—	—	—	—	—	—	—

Hospital, Address, Telephone, Administrator, Approval, Facility, and Physician Codes, Health Care System, Network	Classi-fication Codes		Utilization Data					Expense (thousands) of dollars		
★ American Hospital Association (AHA) membership □ Joint Commission on Accreditation of Healthcare Organizations (JCAHO) accreditation + American Osteopathic Healthcare Association (AOHA) membership ○ American Osteopathic Association (AOA) accreditation △ Commission on Accreditation of Rehabilitation Facilities (CARF) accreditation Control codes 61, 63, 64, 71, 72 and 73 indicate hospitals listed by AOHA, but not registered by AHA. For definition of numerical codes, see page A4	Control	Service	Staffed Beds	Admissions	Census	Outpatient Visits	Births	Total	Payroll	Personnel
□ GEORGIA REGIONAL HOSPITAL AT AUGUSTA, 3405 Mike Padgett Highway, Zip 30906–3897; tel. 706/792–7019; Benjamin H. Walker, Facility Administrator **A**1 3 10 **F**1 3 4 5 6 7 8 10 12 13 14 17 18 19 20 21 22 23 24 25 26 27 28 29 30 31 32 33 34 35 36 39 41 42 43 44 45 46 49 50 51 52 53 54 55 56 57 58 59 60 61 62 63 64 65 66 67 68 70 71 72 73 74	12	22	177	2313	159	0	0	18196	11687	430
✖ MEDICAL COLLEGE OF GEORGIA HOSPITAL AND CLINICS, 1120 15th Street, Zip 30912–5000; tel. 706/721–0211; Patricia Sodomka, FACHE, Executive Director **A**1 2 3 5 8 9 10 12 **F**4 7 8 10 11 12 13 15 16 17 19 20 21 22 23 26 27 28 29 30 31 34 35 37 38 39 40 41 42 43 44 46 47 49 51 52 53 54 55 56 57 58 59 60 61 63 65 66 67 68 70 71 73 74 **P**6 **Web address:** www.mcg.edu	12	10	490	14984	288	453374	1611	240909	114995	3631
✖ ST. JOSEPH HOSPITAL, 2260 Wrightsboro Road, Zip 30904–4726; tel. 706/481–7000; J. William Paugh, President and Chief Executive Officer **A**1 9 10 **F**7 8 10 12 13 14 15 16 17 19 22 23 25 26 28 29 30 32 33 34 35 37 38 39 40 42 44 45 49 51 65 67 71 73 74 **P**8 **S** Carondelet Health System, Saint Louis, MO **Web address:** www.stjoshosp.org	21	10	149	6012	79	22768	1299	75853	33177	875
✖ UNIVERSITY HEALTH CARE SYSTEM, (Formerly University Hospital), 1350 Walton Way, Zip 30901–2629; tel. 706/722–9011; J. Larry Read, President and Chief Executive Officer **A**1 2 3 5 9 10 **F**1 2 3 4 6 7 8 10 11 12 14 15 16 17 18 20 21 22 23 24 25 28 29 30 31 32 34 35 37 38 39 40 41 42 43 44 45 46 47 49 51 52 54 55 56 57 58 59 60 61 63 65 66 67 68 71 72 73 74 **P**1 5 7	23	10	548	19854	293	252699	2538	222024	81124	2738
✖ VETERANS AFFAIRS MEDICAL CENTER, 1 Freedom Way, Zip 30904–6285; tel. 706/733–0188; Ellen DeGeorge–Smith, Director (Total facility includes 60 beds in nursing home–type unit) **A**1 2 3 5 8 **F**3 4 8 10 11 16 17 19 20 21 26 27 29 30 31 32 33 34 35 37 39 41 42 43 44 45 46 48 49 51 52 54 55 56 57 58 59 60 63 64 65 67 71 72 73 74 **P**6 **S** Department of Veterans Affairs, Washington, DC **Web address:** www.va.gov	45	10	444	6243	389	246516	0	165608	81713	2005
✖ △ WALTON REHABILITATION HOSPITAL, 1355 Independence Drive, Zip 30901–1037; tel. 706/724–7746; Dennis B. Skelley, President and Chief Executive Officer **A**1 7 10 **F**1 2 3 4 5 6 7 8 9 10 11 12 13 14 15 16 17 18 19 20 21 22 23 24 25 26 27 28 29 30 31 32 33 34 35 36 37 38 39 40 41 42 43 44 45 46 47 48 49 50 51 52 53 54 55 56 57 58 59 60 61 62 63 64 65 66 67 69 70 71 72 73 74 **P**7 **S** Carondelet Health System, Saint Louis, MO **Web address:** www.wrh.org	23	46	58	1060	43	20484	0	17353	8979	205
AUSTELL—Cobb County										
✖ △ WELLSTAR COBB HOSPITAL, 3950 Austell Road, Zip 30106–1121; tel. 770/732–4000; Thomas E. Hill, Chief Executive Officer (Nonreporting) **A**1 2 7 9 10 **S** WellStar Health System, Marietta, GA **Web address:** www.promina.org	23	10	311	—	—	—	—	—	—	—
BAINBRIDGE—Decatur County										
✖ MEMORIAL HOSPITAL AND MANOR, 1500 East Shotwell Street, Zip 31717–4294; tel. 912/246–3500; James G. Peak, Chief Executive Officer (Total facility includes 107 beds in nursing home–type unit) (Nonreporting) **A**1 9 10	16	10	187	—	—	—	—	—	—	—
BAXLEY—Appling County										
□ APPLING HEALTHCARE SYSTEM, 301 East Tollison Street, Zip 31513–2898; tel. 912/367–9841; Terry Stratton, Chief Executive Officer (Total facility includes 101 beds in nursing home–type unit) (Nonreporting) **A**1 10 **Web address:** www.appling–hospital.org	16	10	141	—	—	—	—	—	—	—
BLAIRSVILLE—Union County										
✖ UNION GENERAL HOSPITAL, 214 Hospital Drive, Zip 30512–6538; tel. 706/745–2111; Rebecca T. Dyer, Administrator (Total facility includes 105 beds in nursing home–type unit) (Nonreporting) **A**1 9 10	16	10	150	—	—	—	—	—	—	—
BLAKELY—Early County										
□ EARLY MEMORIAL HOSPITAL, 630 Columbia Street, Zip 31723–1798; tel. 912/723–4241; Rodney C. Watford, Administrator (Total facility includes 127 beds in nursing home–type unit) **A**1 10 **F**8 12 14 15 16 19 22 28 30 32 33 34 35 40 44 49 64 65 71 73 **P**8 **S** Archbold Medical Center, Thomasville, GA	23	10	164	692	137	4723	87	5200	3176	161
BLUE RIDGE—Fannin County										
✖ FANNIN REGIONAL HOSPITAL, 2855 Old Highway 5, Zip 30513; tel. 706/632–3711; Barry L. Mousa, Chief Executive Officer (Total facility includes 12 beds in nursing home–type unit) **A**1 9 10 **F**8 11 12 16 17 19 20 22 28 30 34 35 37 39 40 44 46 49 64 65 67 71 **P**6 **S** Community Health Systems, Inc., Brentwood, TN	33	10	46	1689	20	27604	106	12463	5761	142
BOWDON—Carroll County										
BOWDON AREA HOSPITAL, 501 Mitchell Avenue, Zip 30108–1499; tel. 770/258–7207; Yvonne Willis, Administrator **A**9 10 **F**8 15 19 22 28 33 35 39 41 44 48 49 65 67 71 **S** Bowdon Corporate Offices, Atlanta, GA	33	10	41	634	12	4111	0	4737	1636	72
BREMEN—Haralson County										
✖ HIGGINS GENERAL HOSPITAL, 200 Allen Memorial Drive, Zip 30110–2012, Mailing Address: P.O. Box 655, Zip 30110–0655; tel. 770/537–5851; Robbie Smith, Administrator **A**1 9 10 **F**8 10 14 15 16 19 21 22 28 37 42 44 46 49 71 **S** Quorum Health Group/Quorum Health Resources, Inc., Brentwood, TN	15	10	39	882	14	18417	0	7944	3412	113

Hospital, Address, Telephone, Administrator, Approval, Facility, and Physician Codes, Health Care System, Network	Classi-fication Codes		Utilization Data					Expense (thousands) of dollars		
★ American Hospital Association (AHA) membership □ Joint Commission on Accreditation of Healthcare Organizations (JCAHO) accreditation + American Osteopathic Healthcare Association (AOHA) membership ○ American Osteopathic Association (AOA) accreditation △ Commission on Accreditation of Rehabilitation Facilities (CARF) accreditation Control codes 61, 63, 64, 71, 72 and 73 indicate hospitals listed by AOHA, but not registered by AHA. For definition of numerical codes, see page A4	Control	Service	Staffed Beds	Admissions	Census	Outpatient Visits	Births	Total	Payroll	Personnel

BRUNSWICK—Glynn County

☒ SOUTHEAST GEORGIA REGIONAL MEDICAL CENTER, 3100 Kemble Avenue, Zip 31520–4252, Mailing Address: P.O. Box 1518, Zip 31521–1518; tel. 912/264–7000; E. Berton Whitaker, President and Chief Executive Officer (Total facility includes 16 beds in nursing home–type unit) **A**1 2 10 **F**7 8 10 11 14 15 16 19 21 22 23 28 29 30 31 33 34 35 37 40 41 42 44 46 49 52 56 59 60 64 65 67 71 72 73 **P**5 8 **S** Quorum Health Group/Quorum Health Resources, Inc., Brentwood, TN

| 16 | 10 | 337 | 12456 | 169 | 129997 | 1156 | 103590 | 42371 | 1275 |

CAIRO—Grady County

□ GRADY GENERAL HOSPITAL, 1155 Fifth Street S.E., Zip 31728–3142, Mailing Address: P.O. Box 360, Zip 31728–0360; tel. 912/377–1150; Glen C. Davis, Administrator (Nonreporting) **A**1 9 10 **S** Archbold Medical Center, Thomasville, GA **Web address:** www.archbold.org

| 23 | 10 | 45 | — | | | | | | |

CALHOUN—Gordon County

☒ GORDON HOSPITAL, 1035 Red Bud Road, Zip 30701–2082, Mailing Address: P.O. Box 12938, Zip 30703–7013; tel. 706/629–2895; Dennis Kiley, President **A**1 9 10 **F**7 8 10 12 15 17 19 21 22 23 26 28 30 32 34 35 37 40 44 45 49 50 57 63 65 67 71 72 74 **P**1 **S** Adventist Health System Sunbelt Health Care Corporation, Winter Park, FL

| 21 | 10 | 54 | 2780 | 28 | 109985 | 475 | 24668 | 11355 | 351 |

CAMILLA—Mitchell County

□ MITCHELL COUNTY HOSPITAL, 90 Stephens Street, Zip 31730–1899, Mailing Address: P.O. Box 639, Zip 31730–0639; tel. 912/336–5284; Ronald M. Gilliard, FACHE, Administrator **A**1 10 **F**7 12 14 15 16 17 19 22 28 30 35 39 40 44 46 49 65 71 73 **P**6 **S** Archbold Medical Center, Thomasville, GA

| 23 | 10 | 24 | 789 | 11 | 13236 | 167 | 6376 | 3203 | 106 |

CANTON—Cherokee County

☒ NORTHSIDE HOSPITAL – CHEROKEE, 201 Hospital Road, Zip 30114–2408, Mailing Address: P.O. Box 906, Zip 30114–0906; tel. 770/720–5100; Douglas M. Parker, Chief Executive Officer **A**1 9 10 **F**7 8 12 15 16 19 21 22 23 28 29 31 35 37 39 40 42 44 45 49 65 67 70 71 73 74

| 23 | 10 | 60 | 2896 | 31 | 35726 | 414 | 21697 | 8794 | 292 |

CARROLLTON—Carroll County

☒ TANNER MEDICAL CENTER, 705 Dixie Street, Zip 30117–3818; tel. 770/836–9666; Loy M. Howard, Chief Executive Officer (Total facility includes 20 beds in nursing home–type unit) **A**1 9 10 **F**3 7 8 10 12 15 16 17 18 19 21 22 23 26 30 32 33 35 36 37 39 40 41 42 44 46 49 52 59 60 62 63 64 65 67 71 73 74 **P**7 8 **S** Quorum Health Group/Quorum Health Resources, Inc., Brentwood, TN **Web address:** www.tanner.org/

| 16 | 10 | 176 | 7613 | 97 | 126537 | 1131 | 59335 | 25813 | 925 |

CARTERSVILLE—Bartow County

☒ COLUMBIA CARTERSVILLE MEDICAL CENTER, 960 Joe Frank Harris Parkway, Zip 30120, Mailing Address: P.O. Box 200008, Zip 30120–9001; tel. 770/382–1530; Keith Sandlin, Chief Executive Officer (Nonreporting) **A**1 9 10 **S** Columbia/HCA Healthcare Corporation, Nashville, TN

| 33 | 10 | 80 | — | — | — | — | — | — | — |

CEDARTOWN—Polk County

☒ POLK MEDICAL CENTER, 424 North Main Street, Zip 30125–2698; tel. 770/748–2500; Mark Nichols, Chief Executive Officer **A**1 9 10 **F**8 12 14 15 16 17 19 22 26 28 31 44 65 70 71 73 **S** Columbia/HCA Healthcare Corporation, Nashville, TN

| 33 | 10 | 35 | 805 | 8 | 25311 | 0 | 6722 | 2704 | 102 |

CHATSWORTH—Murray County

□ MURRAY MEDICAL CENTER, 707 Old Ellijay Road, Zip 30705–2060, Mailing Address: P.O. Box 1406, Zip 30705–1406; tel. 706/695–4564; Mickey Rabuka, Administrator **A**1 9 10 **F**8 15 19 20 22 30 32 33 36 37 39 41 44 46 49 53 65 67 71 73

| 23 | 10 | 33 | 869 | 9 | — | 0 | 9840 | 4138 | 139 |

CLAXTON—Evans County

□ EVANS MEMORIAL HOSPITAL, 200 North River Street, Zip 30417–1659, Mailing Address: P.O. Box 518, Zip 30417–0518; tel. 912/739–5000; Eston Price, Jr., Administrator (Nonreporting) **A**1 9 10

| 16 | 10 | 32 | — | — | — | — | — | — | — |

CLAYTON—Rabun County

★ RABUN COUNTY MEMORIAL HOSPITAL, South Main Street, Zip 30525, Mailing Address: P.O. Box 705, Zip 30525–0705; tel. 706/782–4233; Richard B. Wallace, Chief Executive Officer **A**10 **F**12 15 16 19 22 28 30 31 32 33 34 44 49 54 62 65 71 **Web address:** www.rabun.net

| 16 | 10 | 21 | 1010 | 8 | 16009 | 0 | 4182 | 1597 | 64 |

☒ RIDGECREST HOSPITAL, 393 Ridgecrest Circle, Zip 30525; tel. 706/782–4297; Maryann J. Greenwell, Chief Executive Officer **A**1 9 10 **F**8 12 14 15 16 17 19 20 22 23 28 29 30 32 34 39 41 44 46 49 64 65 67 70 71 72 73 74

| 23 | 10 | 49 | 1069 | 10 | 17332 | 0 | 11473 | 4362 | 138 |

COCHRAN—Bleckley County

BLECKLEY MEMORIAL HOSPITAL, 408 Peacock Street, Zip 31014–1559, Mailing Address: P.O. Box 536, Zip 31014–0536; tel. 912/934–6211; Scott D. Adkins, Administrator (Nonreporting) **A**10 **S** Memorial Health Services, Adel, GA

| 16 | 10 | 45 | — | — | — | — | — | — | — |

COLQUITT—Miller County

MILLER COUNTY HOSPITAL, 209 North Cuthbert Street, Zip 31737–1015, Mailing Address: P.O. Box 7, Zip 31737–0007; tel. 912/758–3385; Colleen B. Houston, Administrator (Total facility includes 97 beds in nursing home–type unit) (Nonreporting) **A**10

| 16 | 10 | 135 | | | | | | | |

COLUMBUS—Muscogee County

BRADLEY CENTER OF ST. FRANCIS See St. Francis Hospital

Hospital, Address, Telephone, Administrator, Approval, Facility, and Physician Codes, Health Care System, Network	Control	Service	Staffed Beds	Admissions	Census	Outpatient Visits	Births	Total	Payroll	Personnel
★ American Hospital Association (AHA) membership □ Joint Commission on Accreditation of Healthcare Organizations (JCAHO) accreditation + American Osteopathic Healthcare Association (AOHA) membership ○ American Osteopathic Association (AOA) accreditation △ Commission on Accreditation of Rehabilitation Facilities (CARF) accreditation Control codes 61, 63, 64, 71, 72 and 73 indicate hospitals listed by AOHA, but not registered by AHA. For definition of numerical codes, see page A4										
⊠ DOCTORS HOSPITAL, 616 19th Street, Zip 31901–1528, Mailing Address: P.O. Box 2188, Zip 31902–2188; tel. 706/571–4262; Hugh D. Wilson, Chief Executive Officer **A**1 2 9 10 **F**3 7 8 10 12 16 19 21 22 23 26 27 28 29 30 33 34 35 37 39 40 41 42 44 45 46 49 52 57 58 59 60 61 65 67 68 70 71 73 74 **P**8 **S** Columbia/HCA Healthcare Corporation, Nashville, TN	33	10	171	5001	66	54741	973	34613	15145	514
⊠ HUGHSTON SPORTS MEDICINE HOSPITAL, 100 First Court, Zip 31908–7188, Mailing Address: P.O. Box 7188, Zip 31908–7188; tel. 706/576–2101; Hugh C. Tappan, Chief Executive Officer **A**1 3 5 10 **F**2 3 4 7 8 10 11 12 15 16 17 19 21 22 26 28 29 30 34 35 37 40 42 43 44 45 46 48 49 52 60 65 66 71 73 74 **P**3 4 5 **S** Columbia/HCA Healthcare Corporation, Nashville, TN **Web address:** www.hughstonsports.com/hsmh.htm	33	47	100	3622	37	8606	0	26921	8350	268
⊠ ST. FRANCIS HOSPITAL, (Includes Bradley Center of St. Francis, 2000 16th Avenue, Zip 31906–0308; tel. 706/320–3700), 2122 Manchester Expressway, Zip 31904–6878, Mailing Address: P.O. Box 7000, Zip 31908–7000; tel. 706/596–4000; Michael E. Garrigan, FACHE, President and Chief Executive Officer **A**1 9 10 **F**2 3 4 7 8 10 11 12 14 16 17 19 22 24 26 28 29 30 32 34 35 37 40 42 43 44 45 49 52 53 54 56 57 58 59 71 73 **Web address:** www.sfhga.com	23	10	217	7534	110	63844	0	68595	29677	975
⊠ THE MEDICAL CENTER, 710 Center Street, Zip 31902, Mailing Address: P.O. Box 951, Zip 31902–0951; tel. 706/571–1000; Lance B. Duke, FACHE, President and Chief Executive Officer (Total facility includes 128 beds in nursing home–type unit) **A**1 2 3 5 9 10 12 **F**2 3 7 8 10 12 15 16 17 18 19 21 22 24 26 27 28 29 30 31 32 34 35 37 38 40 41 42 44 45 46 47 48 49 51 52 54 55 56 58 60 63 64 65 67 68 70 71 72 73 74 **P**6 8 **S** Columbus Regional Health System, Columbus, GA	23	10	537	13422	316	124009	2585	119595	46003	1449
COMMERCE—Jackson County										
⊠ BJC MEDICAL CENTER, 70 Medical Center Drive, Zip 30529–9989; tel. 706/335–1000; J. David Lawrence, Jr., Chief Executive Officer (Total facility includes 167 beds in nursing home–type unit) **A**1 9 10 **F**8 11 15 16 19 21 22 28 30 34 39 40 44 45 46 64 65 67 71 73	16	10	233	1420	179	18764	65	9016	5203	285
CONYERS—Rockdale County										
⊠ ROCKDALE HOSPITAL, 1412 Milstead Avenue N.E., Zip 30207–9990; tel. 770/918–3000; Nelson Toebbe, Chief Executive Officer **A**1 2 9 10 **F**7 8 11 12 15 16 17 19 21 22 23 28 29 30 32 34 35 37 39 40 42 44 45 46 49 60 65 66 67 71 72 73 74 **P**1 **Web address:** www.rockdale.org	23	10	107	6443	62	94179	1836	49186	19789	634
CORDELE—Crisp County										
⊠ CRISP REGIONAL HOSPITAL, 902 North Seventh Street, Zip 31015–5007; tel. 912/276–3100; D. Wayne Martin, President and Chief Executive Officer (Nonreporting) **A**1 9 10	16	10	65	—	—	—	—	—	—	—
COVINGTON—Newton County										
⊠ NEWTON GENERAL HOSPITAL, 5126 Hospital Drive, Zip 30014; tel. 770/786–7053; James F. Weadick, Administrator and Chief Executive Officer **A**1 9 10 **F**7 8 15 17 19 22 23 28 29 30 32 33 34 35 37 40 41 44 45 56 63 65 67 68 71 73 **P**8	23	10	90	3576	37	97142	296	29800	13837	421
CUMMING—Forsyth County										
⊠ BAPTIST MEDICAL CENTER, (Formerly Baptist North Hospital), 1200 Baptist Medical Center Drive, Zip 30041; tel. 770/887–2355; John M. Herron, Administrator (Nonreporting) **A**1 10 **S** Georgia Baptist Health Care System, Atlanta, GA BAPTIST NORTH HOSPITAL See Baptist Medical Center	21	10	30	—	—	—	—	—	—	—
CUTHBERT—Randolph County										
★ SOUTHWEST GEORGIA REGIONAL MEDICAL CENTER, 109 Randolph Street, Zip 31740–1338; tel. 912/732–2181; Keith J. Petersen, Chief Executive Officer (Total facility includes 80 beds in nursing home–type unit) **A**9 10 **F**8 14 15 16 22 44 46 49 58 64 73 **P**4 7	16	10	120	603	87	14297	30	5684	3182	163
DAHLONEGA—Lumpkin County										
□ CHESTATEE REGIONAL HOSPITAL, 227 Mountain Drive, Zip 30533; tel. 706/864–6136; Anne Thompson, Chief Executive Officer **A**1 10 **F**7 8 11 12 15 17 19 22 23 28 30 33 34 35 37 40 41 42 44 48 49 65 71 73 74 **P**1 **S** NetCare Health Systems, Inc., Nashville, TN	33	10	49	1359	11	—	115	11359	4145	186
DALLAS—Paulding County										
⊠ WELLSTAR PAULDING HOSPITAL, 600 West Memorial Drive, Zip 30132–1335; tel. 770/445–4411; Thomas E. Hill, Chief Executive Officer (Total facility includes 169 beds in nursing home–type unit) (Nonreporting) **A**1 9 10 **S** WellStar Health System, Marietta, GA	23	10	208	—	—	—	—	—	—	—
DALTON—Whitfield County										
⊠ HAMILTON MEDICAL CENTER, 1200 Memorial Drive, Zip 30720–2529, Mailing Address: P.O. Box 1168, Zip 30722–1168; tel. 706/272–6000; Ned B. Wilford, President and Chief Executive Officer **A**1 2 10 **F**1 3 6 7 8 10 12 13 15 16 17 18 19 21 22 23 24 25 27 28 30 31 32 33 34 35 37 39 40 41 42 44 45 46 49 52 53 54 55 56 57 58 59 60 62 65 66 67 70 71 73 74 **P**8	23	10	282	10836	126	194180	2229	99559	39071	1103
DECATUR—De Kalb County										
□ DECATUR HOSPITAL, (LONG TERM ACUTE CARE), 450 North Candler Street, Zip 30030–2671, Mailing Address: P.O. Box 40, Zip 30031–0040; tel. 404/377–0221; Richard T. Schmidt, Executive Director **A**1 9 10 **F**5 7 8 10 11 12 13 14 15 16 19 21 22 24 25 26 28 29 30 32 34 35 37 38 39 40 41 42 44 45 46 48 49 51 52 60 64 65 66 71 72 73 **P**1 **Web address:** www.dkmc.org	23	49	84	117	18	—	0	12801	4291	—

		Classification Codes		Utilization Data					Expense (thousands) of dollars		
		Control	Service	Staffed Beds	Admissions	Census	Outpatient Visits	Births	Total	Payroll	Personnel

Symbols legend:

★ American Hospital Association (AHA) membership
□ Joint Commission on Accreditation of Healthcare Organizations (JCAHO) accreditation
+ American Osteopathic Healthcare Association (AOHA) membership
○ American Osteopathic Association (AOA) accreditation
△ Commission on Accreditation of Rehabilitation Facilities (CARF) accreditation
Control codes 61, 63, 64, 71, 72 and 73 indicate hospitals listed by AOHA, but not registered by AHA. For definition of numerical codes, see page A4.

Hospital	Control	Service	Staffed Beds	Admissions	Census	Outpatient Visits	Births	Total	Payroll	Personnel
★ △ DEKALB MEDICAL CENTER, 2701 North Decatur Road, Zip 30033–5995; tel. 404/501–1000; John R. Gerlach, Chief Executive Officer and Administrator (Total facility includes 48 beds in nursing home–type unit) (Nonreporting) **A**1 2 7 9 10 **Web address:** www.drhs.org	23	10	397	—	—	—	—	—	—	—
□ GEORGIA REGIONAL HOSPITAL AT ATLANTA, 3073 Panthersville Road, Zip 30034–3828; tel. 404/243–2100; Ronald C. Hogan, Superintendent (Total facility includes 110 beds in nursing home–type unit) **A**1 3 5 10 **F**1 3 4 5 6 7 8 10 12 13 14 15 17 18 19 20 21 22 23 24 25 26 27 28 29 30 31 32 33 34 35 36 39 41 42 43 44 45 46 49 50 51 52 53 54 55 56 57 58 59 60 61 63 64 65 66 67 69 70 71 72 73 74 **P**6	12	22	366	4938	181	0	0	34830	20749	959
★ VETERANS AFFAIRS MEDICAL CENTER, 1670 Clairmont Road, Zip 30033–4004; tel. 404/321–6111; Robert A. Perreault, Director (Total facility includes 100 beds in nursing home–type unit) **A**1 3 5 8 **F**3 4 8 10 11 12 19 20 21 22 23 26 27 28 29 30 31 32 33 35 36 37 39 41 42 43 44 45 46 49 51 52 54 55 56 57 58 59 60 63 64 65 67 71 72 73 74 **S** Department of Veterans Affairs, Washington, DC	45	10	291	5877	257	337670	0	149529	73737	1566
DEMOREST—Habersham County										
★ HABERSHAM COUNTY MEDICAL CENTER, Highway 441, Zip 30535, Mailing Address: P.O. Box 37, Zip 30535–0037; tel. 706/754–2161; C. Richard Dwozan, President (Total facility includes 106 beds in nursing home–type unit) **A**1 9 10 **F**6 7 8 12 15 16 17 19 20 21 22 24 27 28 29 30 32 34 35 37 39 40 41 44 45 46 48 49 64 65 66 67 71 72 73 **P**1 7 **S** Quorum Health Group/Quorum Health Resources, Inc., Brentwood, TN	16	10	159	2666	131	48387	392	22877	8563	416
DONALSONVILLE—Seminole County										
□ DONALSONVILLE HOSPITAL, Hospital Circle, Zip 31745, Mailing Address: P.O. Box 677, Zip 31745–0677; tel. 912/524–5217; Charles H. Orrick, Administrator (Total facility includes 75 beds in nursing home–type unit) (Nonreporting) **A**1 10	23	10	140	—	—	—	—	—	—	—
DOUGLAS—Coffee County										
★ COFFEE REGIONAL MEDICAL CENTER, 1101 Ocilla Road, Zip 31533–3617, Mailing Address: P.O. Box 1248, Zip 31534–1248; tel. 912/384–1900; George L. Heck, III, President and Chief Executive Officer **A**1 10 **F**7 8 12 13 14 15 16 17 18 19 22 28 29 30 33 35 37 40 44 45 49 50 51 61 64 65 66 67 68 71 72 73 74 **P**5	16	10	88	4490	39	56794	831	40590	16993	555
DOUGLASVILLE—Douglas County										
INNER HARBOUR HOSPITALS, 4685 Dorsett Shoals Road, Zip 30135–4999; tel. 770/942–2391; Susan Hallman, Administrator **F**14 15 16 22 39 46 52 53 54 55 59 65 67 73 **P**6	23	52	165	334	168	0	0	14070	8894	315
★ WELLSTAR DOUGLAS HOSPITAL, 8954 Hospital Drive, Zip 30134–2282; tel. 770/949–1500; Thomas E. Hill, Chief Executive Officer (Nonreporting) **A**1 9 10 **S** WellStar Health System, Marietta, GA **Web address:** www.promina.org	23	10	98	—	—	—	—	—	—	—
DUBLIN—Laurens County										
★ FAIRVIEW PARK HOSPITAL, 200 Industrial Boulevard, Zip 31021–2997, Mailing Address: P.O. Box 1408, Zip 31040–1408; tel. 912/275–2000; James B. Wood, Chief Executive Officer **A**1 2 9 10 **F**7 8 11 12 14 15 16 17 19 21 22 23 24 25 28 30 32 33 34 35 37 39 40 41 42 44 45 48 49 60 63 65 66 71 73 74 **P**6 **S** Columbia/HCA Healthcare Corporation, Nashville, TN	33	10	190	7774	92	72378	1038	35591	17400	631
★ VETERANS AFFAIRS MEDICAL CENTER, 1826 Veterans Boulevard, Zip 31021–3620; tel. 912/272–1210; James F. Trusley, III, Director (Total facility includes 112 beds in nursing home–type unit) (Nonreporting) **A**1 **S** Department of Veterans Affairs, Washington, DC	45	10	253	—	—	—	—	—	—	—
DULUTH—Gwinnett County										
JOAN GLANCY MEMORIAL HOSPITAL See Promina Gwinnett Hospital System, Lawrenceville										
EAST POINT—Fulton County										
★ SOUTH FULTON MEDICAL CENTER, 1170 Cleveland Avenue, Zip 30344; tel. 404/305–3500; H. Neil Copelan, President and Chief Executive Officer (Total facility includes 36 beds in nursing home–type unit) **A**1 2 9 10 **F**7 8 10 11 12 14 15 16 17 19 20 21 22 24 26 28 29 30 32 33 34 35 37 39 40 41 42 44 45 46 48 49 51 60 63 64 65 67 71 72 73 74 **P**1 6	23	10	369	10367	141	82939	1871	90638	41031	1328
EASTMAN—Dodge County										
□ DODGE COUNTY HOSPITAL, 715 Griffin Street S.W., Zip 31023–2223, Mailing Address: P.O. Box 4309, Zip 31023–4309; tel. 912/374–4000; Meredith H. Smith, Administrator **A**1 9 10 **F**8 15 17 19 21 22 24 30 35 36 37 40 44 45 46 49 52 57 67 71 73	16	10	87	3155	42	22271	148	16194	8095	301
EATONTON—Putnam County										
□ PUTNAM GENERAL HOSPITAL, Lake Oconee Parkway, Zip 31024–4330, Mailing Address: Box 4330, Zip 31024–4330; tel. 706/485–2711; Darrell M. Oglesby, Administrator **A**1 10 **F**2 8 15 16 19 22 28 37 44 49 71 **P**2	16	10	50	901	8	13100	0	6253	3240	109
ELBERTON—Elbert County										
★ ELBERT MEMORIAL HOSPITAL, 4 Medical Drive, Zip 30635–1897; tel. 706/283–3151; Mark LeNeave, Chief Executive Officer **A**1 9 10 **F**7 8 12 15 16 17 19 21 22 23 24 28 30 34 35 37 39 40 44 45 46 49 65 66 67 71 73 74 **P**5 **S** Quorum Health Group/Quorum Health Resources, Inc., Brentwood, TN	16	10	42	1987	21	10891	164	10530	5264	178
ELLIJAY—Gilmer County										
□ NORTH GEORGIA MEDICAL CENTER, 1362 South Main Street, Zip 30540–0346, Mailing Address: P.O. Box 2239, Zip 30540–0346; tel. 706/276–4741; Randy Carson, Chief Executive Officer (Total facility includes 100 beds in nursing home–type unit) **A**1 9 10 **F**12 15 16 19 21 22 28 33 35 44 49 50 51 63 64 65 70 73 **P**8 **S** NetCare Health Systems, Inc., Nashville, TN	33	10	150	1626	116	18981	0	10389	4060	219

Hospital, Address, Telephone, Administrator, Approval, Facility, and Physician Codes, Health Care System, Network	Classi-fication Codes		Utilization Data					Expense (thousands) of dollars		
★ American Hospital Association (AHA) membership ☐ Joint Commission on Accreditation of Healthcare Organizations (JCAHO) accreditation + American Osteopathic Healthcare Association (AOHA) membership ○ American Osteopathic Association (AOA) accreditation △ Commission on Accreditation of Rehabilitation Facilities (CARF) accreditation Control codes 61, 63, 64, 71, 72 and 73 indicate hospitals listed by AOHA, but not registered by AHA. For definition of numerical codes, see page A4	Control	Service	Staffed Beds	Admissions	Census	Outpatient Visits	Births	Total	Payroll	Personnel

FITZGERALD—Ben Hill County

☐ DORMINY MEDICAL CENTER, Perry House Road, Zip 31750, Mailing Address: Drawer 1447, Zip 31750–1447; tel. 912/424–7100; Steve Barber, Administrator **A**1 9 10 **F**7 8 14 19 21 22 28 33 34 35 37 40 44 49 50 63 65 71 73 **P**7
Web address: www.dorminy–hosp.org
| | 16 | 10 | 60 | 2000 | 26 | 23888 | 173 | 14554 | 6989 | 302 |

FOLKSTON—Charlton County

☐ CHARLTON MEMORIAL HOSPITAL, 1203 North Third Street, Zip 31537–1303, Mailing Address: P.O. Box 188, Zip 31537–0188; tel. 912/496–2531; James L. Leis, Jr., Administrator and Chief Executive Officer **A**1 9 10 **F**19 22 26 27 34 37 44 49 51 71 73
| | 16 | 10 | 36 | 267 | 3 | 10154 | 0 | 4415 | 2659 | 83 |

FORSYTH—Monroe County

☐ MONROE COUNTY HOSPITAL, 88 Martin Luther King Jr. Drive, Zip 31029, Mailing Address: P.O. Box 1068, Zip 31029–1068; tel. 912/994–2521; Gale V. Tanner, Administrator **A**1 9 10 **F**8 15 16 19 22 31 34 35 44 48 65 71 73
| | 16 | 10 | 37 | 885 | 10 | 14903 | 0 | 7228 | 2874 | 105 |

FORT BENNING—Muscogee County

✠ MARTIN ARMY COMMUNITY HOSPITAL, Mailing Address: P.O. Box 56100, Building 9200, Zip 31905–6100; tel. 706/544–2516; Lieutenant Colonel Joe W. Butler, Deputy Commander Administration (Nonreporting) **A**1 2 3 **S** Department of the Army, Office of the Surgeon General, Falls Church, VA
| | 42 | 10 | 126 | — | — | — | — | — | — | — |

FORT GORDON—Richmond County

✠ DWIGHT DAVID EISENHOWER ARMY MEDICAL CENTER, Hospital Drive, Building 300, Zip 30905–5650; tel. 706/787–3253; Lieutenant Colonel David A. Rubenstein, Chief Operating Officer (Nonreporting) **A**1 2 3 5 **S** Department of the Army, Office of the Surgeon General, Falls Church, VA
Web address: www.ddeamc.amedd.army.mil
| | 42 | 10 | 313 | — | — | — | — | — | — | — |

FORT OGLETHORPE—Catoosa County

✠ HUTCHESON MEDICAL CENTER, 100 Gross Crescent Circle, Zip 30742–3669; tel. 706/858–2000; Robert T. Jones, M.D., President and Chief Executive Officer (Total facility includes 109 beds in nursing home–type unit) **A**1 9 10 **F**1 7 8 10 11 12 14 15 16 19 21 22 25 28 29 30 32 33 35 37 38 40 41 42 44 45 46 49 53 54 55 56 57 58 59 64 65 66 67 70 71 72 73 74
Web address: www.hutchesonmed.org
| | 16 | 10 | 288 | 7075 | 207 | 105333 | 1097 | 63899 | 25972 | 1119 |

FORT VALLEY—Peach County

☐ PEACH REGIONAL MEDICAL CENTER, 601 North Camellia Boulevard, Zip 31030–4599; tel. 912/825–8691; Nancy Peed, Administrator **A**1 9 10 **F**8 12 13 14 15 16 17 19 20 22 25 28 29 30 37 41 44 45 46 48 51 65 67 71 73 74 **P**6
| | 16 | 10 | 36 | 780 | 7 | 23186 | 0 | 7859 | 3546 | 127 |

GAINESVILLE—Hall County

✠ LANIER PARK HOSPITAL, 675 White Sulphur Road, Zip 30505, Mailing Address: P.O. Box 1354, Zip 30503–1354; tel. 770/503–3000; Jerry Fulks, Chief Executive Officer (Total facility includes 10 beds in nursing home–type unit) **A**1 10 **F**4 8 10 12 14 15 16 17 19 21 22 23 28 29 30 32 34 35 37 39 41 42 44 45 46 49 51 63 64 65 66 67 71 73 74 **P**8 **S** Columbia/HCA Healthcare Corporation, Nashville, TN
Web address: www.lanierpark.com
| | 33 | 10 | 119 | 3320 | 42 | 39617 | 0 | 33057 | 11709 | 345 |

✠ △ NORTHEAST GEORGIA MEDICAL CENTER, 743 Spring Street N.E., Zip 30501–3899; tel. 770/535–3553; Henry Rigdon, Executive Vice President (Total facility includes 15 beds in nursing home–type unit) (Nonreporting) **A**1 2 7 9 10
Web address: www.nghs.com
| | 23 | 10 | 338 | — | — | — | — | — | — | — |

GLENWOOD—Wheeler County

WHEELER COUNTY HOSPITAL, 111 Third Street, Zip 30428, Mailing Address: P.O. Box 398, Zip 30428–0398; tel. 912/523–5113; Brenda Josey, Administrator (Nonreporting) **A**10 **S** Accord Health Care Corporation, Clearwater, FL
| | 33 | 10 | 30 | — | — | — | — | — | — | — |

GRACEWOOD—Richmond County

GRACEWOOD STATE SCHOOL AND HOSPITAL, 100 Myrtle Boulevard, Zip 30812–1500; tel. 706/790–2030; Joanne P. Miklas, Ph.D., Superintendent (Total facility includes 56 beds in nursing home–type unit) (Nonreporting) **A**10
| | 12 | 12 | 71 | — | — | — | — | — | — | — |

GREENSBORO—Greene County

✠ MINNIE G. BOSWELL MEMORIAL HOSPITAL, 1201 Siloam Highway, Zip 30642–2811; tel. 706/453–7331; Earnest E. Benton, Chief Executive Officer (Total facility includes 29 beds in nursing home–type unit) (Nonreporting) **A**1 9 10
| | 16 | 10 | 58 | — | — | — | — | — | — | — |

GRIFFIN—Spalding County

✠ SPALDING REGIONAL HOSPITAL, 601 South Eighth Street, Zip 30224–4294, Mailing Address: P.O. Drawer V, Zip 30224–1168; tel. 770/228–2721; Jim Litchford, Executive Director **A**1 2 9 10 **F**3 4 6 7 8 9 10 12 14 15 16 17 19 20 21 22 23 27 28 29 30 32 33 34 35 36 37 38 39 40 41 42 43 44 46 47 48 52 53 54 55 56 57 58 59 60 64 65 67 71 72 73 **P**8 **S** TENET Healthcare Corporation, Santa Barbara, CA
| | 33 | 10 | 158 | 7474 | 85 | 92899 | 927 | 37594 | 16686 | 652 |

HAHIRA—Lowndes County

SMITH HOSPITAL, 117 East Main Street, Zip 31632–1156, Mailing Address: P.O. Box 337, Zip 31632–0337; tel. 912/794–2502; Amanda M. Hall, Administrator (Nonreporting) **A**9 10 **S** Memorial Health Services, Adel, GA
| | 33 | 10 | 71 | — | — | — | — | — | — | — |

HARTWELL—Hart County

✠ HART COUNTY HOSPITAL, Gibson and Cade Streets, Zip 30643–0280, Mailing Address: P.O. Box 280, Zip 30643–0280; tel. 706/856–6100; Matt McRee, Administrator (Total facility includes 92 beds in nursing home–type unit) **A**1 9 10 **F**6 7 12 15 16 17 19 22 28 37 40 41 42 44 46 49 54 58 65 66 71 73 74 **P**5
| | 23 | 10 | 175 | 1363 | 52 | 15000 | 0 | — | 5591 | 277 |

Hospital, Address, Telephone, Administrator, Approval, Facility, and Physician Codes, Health Care System, Network	Classi-fication Codes		Utilization Data					Expense (thousands) of dollars		
★ American Hospital Association (AHA) membership □ Joint Commission on Accreditation of Healthcare Organizations (JCAHO) accreditation + American Osteopathic Healthcare Association (AOHA) membership ○ American Osteopathic Association (AOA) accreditation △ Commission on Accreditation of Rehabilitation Facilities (CARF) accreditation Control codes 61, 63, 64, 71, 72 and 73 indicate hospitals listed by AOHA, but not registered by AHA. For definition of numerical codes, see page A4	Control	Service	Staffed Beds	Admissions	Census	Outpatient Visits	Births	Total	Payroll	Personnel

HAWKINSVILLE—Pulaski County

⊠ TAYLOR REGIONAL HOSPITAL, Macon Highway, Zip 31036, Mailing Address: P.O. Box 1297, Zip 31036–1297; tel. 912/783–0200; Dan S. Maddock, President **A**1 9 10 **F**7 8 10 12 14 15 16 19 22 23 27 28 33 35 37 42 44 46 49 63 66 71 73 **P**6 | 23 | 10 | 55 | 2051 | 22 | 36399 | 417 | 22385 | 9056 | 412

HAZLEHURST—Jeff Davis County

□ JEFF DAVIS HOSPITAL, 1215 South Tallahassee Street, Zip 31539–2921, Mailing Address: P.O. Box 1200, Zip 31539–1200; tel. 912/375–7781; Oreta Williams, Administrator (Nonreporting) **A**1 10 | 16 | 10 | 50 | — | — | — | — | — | — | —

HIAWASSEE—Towns County

□ CHATUGE REGIONAL HOSPITAL AND NURSING HOME, 110 Main Street, Zip 30546, Mailing Address: P.O. Box 509, Zip 30546–0509; tel. 706/896–2222; Charles T. Adams, President and Chief Executive Officer (Total facility includes 112 beds in nursing home–type unit) **A**1 9 10 **F**8 11 12 15 19 22 28 30 32 33 44 49 65 67 70 71 73 **S** NetCare Health Systems, Inc., Nashville, TN | 33 | 10 | 142 | 635 | 118 | — | 0 | 5970 | 2599 | 146

HINESVILLE—Liberty County

□ LIBERTY REGIONAL MEDICAL CENTER, 462 East G. Parkway, Zip 31313, Mailing Address: P.O. Box 919, Zip 31313; tel. 912/369–9400; H. Scott Kroell, Jr., Chief Executive Officer **A**1 9 10 **F**7 8 14 15 16 18 19 22 30 35 40 41 44 45 48 49 64 66 71 73 | 16 | 10 | 32 | 1309 | 11 | 27438 | 327 | 10811 | 4599 | 201

⊠ WINN ARMY COMMUNITY HOSPITAL, 1061 Harmon Avenue, Zip 31314–5611; tel. 912/370–6965; Colonel Donald J. Kasperik, Commander **A**1 **F**3 4 5 8 10 11 12 13 14 15 16 18 19 20 22 24 25 26 27 28 29 30 31 34 35 37 39 40 41 42 43 44 45 46 49 51 52 53 54 55 58 59 60 61 65 67 68 71 72 73 74 **P**6 **S** Department of the Army, Office of the Surgeon General, Falls Church, VA | 42 | 10 | 83 | 7709 | 37 | 235731 | 1400 | 39000 | 16400 | 813

HOMERVILLE—Clinch County

★ CLINCH MEMORIAL HOSPITAL, 524 North Carswell Street, Zip 31634–1507, Mailing Address: P.O. Box 516, Zip 31634–0516; tel. 912/487–5211; Bruce Shephard, Administrator (Nonreporting) **A**10 | 13 | 10 | 36 | — | — | — | — | — | — | —

JACKSON—Butts County

★ SYLVAN GROVE HOSPITAL, 1050 McDonough Road, Zip 30233–1599; tel. 770/775–7861; Mike Patterson, Administrator (Nonreporting) **A**9 10 **S** TENET Healthcare Corporation, Santa Barbara, CA Web address: www.tenethealth.com | 33 | 10 | 28 | — | — | — | — | — | — | —

JESUP—Wayne County

⊠ WAYNE MEMORIAL HOSPITAL, 865 South First Street, Zip 31598, Mailing Address: P.O. Box 408, Zip 31598–0408; tel. 912/427–6811; Charles R. Morgan, Administrator **A**1 9 10 **F**7 8 12 14 15 19 22 28 29 30 34 35 37 39 40 41 44 45 46 49 65 71 73 **S** Quorum Health Group/Quorum Health Resources, Inc., Brentwood, TN | 16 | 10 | 110 | 3851 | 50 | 38147 | 406 | 24358 | 10822 | 355

KENNESAW—Cobb County

DEVEREUX GEORGIA TREATMENT NETWORK, 1291 Stanley Road N.W., Zip 30152–4359; tel. 770/427–0147; Elizabeth M. Chadwick, JD, Executive Director **F**14 15 16 22 52 53 55 **P**6 **S** Devereux Foundation, Villanova, PA Web address: www.devereux.org | 23 | 52 | 115 | 77 | 82 | — | 0 | 11261 | 6108 | 218

LA GRANGE—Troup County

⊠ WEST GEORGIA HEALTH SYSTEM, 1514 Vernon Road, Zip 30240–4199; tel. 706/882–1411; Charles L. Foster, Jr., FACHE, President and Chief Executive Officer (Total facility includes 266 beds in nursing home–type unit) **A**1 2 9 10 **F**1 3 6 7 8 10 11 12 13 14 15 16 17 18 19 21 22 23 26 27 28 29 30 32 33 34 35 37 39 40 41 42 44 45 46 49 50 51 52 53 54 55 57 58 59 60 63 64 65 67 68 70 71 73 74 **P**7 Web address: www.wghs.org | 23 | 10 | 460 | 9103 | 254 | 142638 | 1052 | 76817 | 32493 | 1319

LAKELAND—Lanier County

⊠ LOUIS SMITH MEMORIAL HOSPITAL, 852 West Thigpen Avenue, Zip 31635–1099; tel. 912/482–3110; Randy Sauls, Administrator (Total facility includes 62 beds in nursing home–type unit) **A**1 10 **F**7 14 15 16 17 19 22 28 30 31 34 35 40 41 44 46 49 56 64 65 71 72 73 | 23 | 10 | 102 | 608 | 85 | 7989 | 33 | 6232 | 3006 | 143

LAWRENCEVILLE—Gwinnett County

⊠ PROMINA GWINNETT HOSPITAL SYSTEM, (Includes Gwinnett Medical Center, 1000 Medical Center Boulevard, Zip 30245; Joan Glancy Memorial Hospital, McClure Bridge Road, Duluth, Zip 30136; tel. 770/497–4800), Mailing Address: P.O. Box 348, Zip 30246–0348; tel. 770/995–4321; Franklin M. Rinker, President and Chief Executive Officer (Nonreporting) **A**1 2 9 10 Web address: www.promina.org | 16 | 10 | 390 | — | — | — | — | — | — | —

LITHIA SPRINGS—Douglas County

⊠ PARKWAY MEDICAL CENTER, (Formerly Columbia Parkway Medical Center), 1000 Thornton Road, Zip 30122, Mailing Address: P.O. Box 570, Zip 30122–0570; tel. 770/732–7777; Deborah S. Guthrie, Chief Executive Officer (Nonreporting) **A**1 2 10 **S** Columbia/HCA Healthcare Corporation, Nashville, TN Web address: www.columbia–parkway.com | 33 | 10 | 233 | — | — | — | — | — | — | —

LOUISVILLE—Jefferson County

□ JEFFERSON HOSPITAL, 1067 Peachtree Street, Zip 30434–1599; tel. 912/625–7000; Rita Culvern, Administrator **A**1 9 10 **F**8 14 15 16 19 22 24 28 30 34 44 65 71 | 16 | 10 | 37 | 837 | 10 | 49842 | 3 | 6380 | 3323 | 104

Hospital, Address, Telephone, Administrator, Approval, Facility, and Physician Codes, Health Care System, Network	Classi-fication Codes		Utilization Data					Expense (thousands) of dollars		
	Control	Service	Staffed Beds	Admissions	Census	Outpatient Visits	Births	Total	Payroll	Personnel

★ American Hospital Association (AHA) membership
□ Joint Commission on Accreditation of Healthcare Organizations (JCAHO) accreditation
+ American Osteopathic Healthcare Association (AOHA) membership
○ American Osteopathic Association (AOA) accreditation
△ Commission on Accreditation of Rehabilitation Facilities (CARF) accreditation
Control codes 61, 63, 64, 71, 72 and 73 indicate hospitals listed by AOHA, but not registered by AHA. For definition of numerical codes, see page A4

MACON—Bibb County

	Control	Service	Staffed Beds	Admissions	Census	Outpatient Visits	Births	Total	Payroll	Personnel
□ CHARTER BEHAVIORAL HEALTH SYSTEM/CENTRAL GEORGIA, 3500 Riverside Drive, Zip 31210–2509; tel. 912/474–6200; Blair R. Johanson, Administrator (Nonreporting) **A**1 10 **S** Magellan Health Services, Atlanta, GA	33	22	118	—	—	—	—	—	—	—
⊞ COLISEUM MEDICAL CENTERS, 350 Hospital Drive, Zip 31213; tel. 912/765–7000; Timothy C. Tobin, Chief Executive Officer **A**1 9 10 **F**3 7 8 10 12 13 16 19 21 22 23 25 27 28 29 30 33 34 35 37 38 40 41 42 44 48 49 51 52 53 54 55 56 58 59 60 61 65 67 71 72 73 74 **P**7 **S** Columbia/HCA Healthcare Corporation, Nashville, TN	33	10	194	8372	120	93536	1345	—	—	886
⊞ COLISEUM PSYCHIATRIC HOSPITAL, (Formerly Columbia Coliseun Psychiatric Hospital), 340 Hospital Drive, Zip 31217–8002; tel. 912/741–1355; Edward W. Ruffin, Administrator (Nonreporting) **A**1 9 10 **S** Columbia/HCA Healthcare Corporation, Nashville, TN	33	22	92	—	—	—	—	—	—	—
□ HEALTHSOUTH CENTRAL GEORGIA REHABILITATION HOSPITAL, 3351 Northside Drive, Zip 31210–2591; tel. 912/471–3536; Elbert T. McQueen, Chief Executive Officer **A**1 9 10 **F**1 2 3 4 5 6 7 8 9 10 11 12 13 14 15 16 17 18 19 20 21 22 23 24 25 26 27 28 29 30 31 32 33 34 35 36 37 38 39 40 41 42 43 44 45 46 47 48 49 50 51 52 53 54 55 56 57 58 59 60 61 62 63 64 65 66 67 68 70 71 72 73 74 **P**1 **S** HEALTHSOUTH Corporation, Birmingham, AL	33	46	50	901	45	13614	0	10061	4851	155
★ MACON NORTHSIDE HOSPITAL, 400 Charter Boulevard, Zip 31210–4853, Mailing Address: P.O. Box 4627, Zip 31208–4627; tel. 912/757–8200; Bud Costello, Administrator and Chief Executive Officer (Nonreporting) **A**9 10 **S** Columbia/HCA Healthcare Corporation, Nashville, TN	33	10	103	—	—	—	—	—	—	—
⊞ MEDICAL CENTER OF CENTRAL GEORGIA, 777 Hemlock Street, Zip 31201–2155, Mailing Address: P.O. Box 6000, Zip 31208–6000; tel. 912/633–1000; A. Donald Faulk, FACHE, President **A**1 2 3 5 8 9 10 **F**4 7 8 10 11 12 13 14 15 16 17 18 19 20 21 22 24 25 26 27 28 29 30 31 32 33 34 35 37 38 39 40 41 42 43 44 45 46 47 49 51 52 53 54 55 56 57 60 61 65 66 67 68 70 71 72 73 74 **P**1 7 **Web address:** www.mccg.org	23	10	495	23439	309	365892	2751	267500	115422	3413
⊞ MIDDLE GEORGIA HOSPITAL, 888 Pine Street, Zip 31201–2186, Mailing Address: P.O. Box 6278, Zip 31208–6278; tel. 912/751–1111; Richard L. McConahy, Chief Executive Officer (Nonreporting) **A**1 10 **S** Columbia/HCA Healthcare Corporation, Nashville, TN	33	10	119	—	—	—	—	—	—	—

MADISON—Morgan County

	Control	Service	Staffed Beds	Admissions	Census	Outpatient Visits	Births	Total	Payroll	Personnel
□ MORGAN MEMORIAL HOSPITAL, Canterbury Park, Zip 30650, Mailing Address: P.O. Box 860, Zip 30650–0860; tel. 706/342–1667; Patrick Green, Administrator **A**1 9 10 **F**12 14 16 17 19 22 28 34 44 49 71 **Web address:** www.mmh.org	16	10	20	435	5	10494	0	3934	1532	104

MARIETTA—Cobb County

	Control	Service	Staffed Beds	Admissions	Census	Outpatient Visits	Births	Total	Payroll	Personnel
⊞ △ WELLSTAR KENNESTONE HOSPITAL, 677 Church Street, Zip 30060–1148; tel. 770/793–5000; Thomas E. Hill, Chief Executive Officer (Nonreporting) **A**1 2 7 9 10 **S** WellStar Health System, Marietta, GA	23	10	439	—	—	—	—	—	—	—
⊞ WELLSTAR WINDY HILL HOSPITAL, 2540 Windy Hill Road, Zip 30067–8632; tel. 770/644–1000; Thomas E. Hill, Chief Executive Officer (Nonreporting) **A**1 9 10 **S** WellStar Health System, Marietta, GA	23	10	100	—	—	—	—	—	—	—

MCRAE—Telfair County

	Control	Service	Staffed Beds	Admissions	Census	Outpatient Visits	Births	Total	Payroll	Personnel
TELFAIR COUNTY HOSPITAL, U.S. 341 South, Zip 31055, Mailing Address: P.O. Box 150, Zip 31055–0150; tel. 912/868–5621; Gail B. Norris, Administrator **A**9 10 **F**7 8 10 11 12 14 15 16 19 21 22 28 30 32 34 35 37 40 42 44 48 49 51 65 71 **P**5 **S** Memorial Health Services, Adel, GA	23	10	52	665	9	7563	0	3923	1927	86

METTER—Candler County

	Control	Service	Staffed Beds	Admissions	Census	Outpatient Visits	Births	Total	Payroll	Personnel
⊞ CANDLER COUNTY HOSPITAL, Cedar Road, Zip 30439, Mailing Address: P.O. Box 597, Zip 30439–0597; tel. 912/685–5741; Michael Alexander, President and Chief Executive Officer **A**1 9 10 **F**8 19 22 37 44 71	16	10	42	1484	22	22835	0	9087	3967	165

MILLEDGEVILLE—Baldwin County

	Control	Service	Staffed Beds	Admissions	Census	Outpatient Visits	Births	Total	Payroll	Personnel
□ CENTRAL STATE HOSPITAL, Broad Street, Zip 31062; tel. 912/445–4128; Joseph T. Hodge, Jr., Facility Administrator (Total facility includes 861 beds in nursing home–type unit) **A**1 3 10 **F**1 2 3 6 8 12 17 18 19 20 21 22 26 28 30 34 35 37 39 41 42 44 45 46 49 51 52 53 54 55 56 57 58 59 60 64 65 67 71 73 **P**6	12	22	1258	3159	1165	43305	0	118216	70622	2517
⊞ OCONEE REGIONAL MEDICAL CENTER, 821 North Cobb Street, Zip 31061–2351, Mailing Address: P.O. Box 690, Zip 31061–0690; tel. 912/454–3500; Brian L. Riddle, President and Chief Executive Officer **A**1 9 10 **F**4 7 8 12 14 15 16 17 19 21 22 23 24 27 28 30 33 35 36 37 39 40 42 44 45 46 49 60 64 65 66 67 70 71 72 73 74 **S** Quorum Health Group/Quorum Health Resources, Inc., Brentwood, TN	16	10	143	4521	55	64821	646	42121	17853	476

MILLEN—Jenkins County

	Control	Service	Staffed Beds	Admissions	Census	Outpatient Visits	Births	Total	Payroll	Personnel
★ JENKINS COUNTY HOSPITAL, 515 East Winthrope Avenue, Zip 30442–1600; tel. 912/982–4221; Pete Mills, Chief Executive Officer **A**9 10 **F**7 14 15 19 21 22 31 44 71 **P**5	16	10	33	687	6	9376	27	3786	1761	72

MONROE—Walton County

	Control	Service	Staffed Beds	Admissions	Census	Outpatient Visits	Births	Total	Payroll	Personnel
⊞ WALTON MEDICAL CENTER, 330 Alcovy Street, Zip 30655–2140, Mailing Address: P.O. Box 1346, Zip 30655–1346; tel. 770/267–8461; Ronald L. Campbell, Chief Executive Officer (Total facility includes 58 beds in nursing home–type unit) **A**1 9 10 **F**7 8 16 19 20 21 22 24 28 30 34 35 37 40 42 44 49 64 65 70 71 73 74 **S** Quorum Health Group/Quorum Health Resources, Inc., Brentwood, TN	16	10	113	2137	75	48926	223	21155	9463	321

Hospital, Address, Telephone, Administrator, Approval, Facility, and Physician Codes, Health Care System, Network	Classification Codes		Utilization Data					Expense (thousands) of dollars		
	Control	Service	Staffed Beds	Admissions	Census	Outpatient Visits	Births	Total	Payroll	Personnel

★ American Hospital Association (AHA) membership
☐ Joint Commission on Accreditation of Healthcare Organizations (JCAHO) accreditation
+ American Osteopathic Healthcare Association (AOHA) membership
○ American Osteopathic Association (AOA) accreditation
△ Commission on Accreditation of Rehabilitation Facilities (CARF) accreditation
Control codes 61, 63, 64, 71, 72 and 73 indicate hospitals listed by AOHA, but not registered by AHA. For definition of numerical codes, see page A4

MONTEZUMA—Macon County

Hospital	Control	Service	Staffed Beds	Admissions	Census	Outpatient Visits	Births	Total	Payroll	Personnel
⊠ FLINT RIVER COMMUNITY HOSPITAL, 509 Sumter Street, Zip 31063–0770; Mailing Address: P.O. Box 770, Zip 31063–0770; tel. 912/472–3100; James D. Tesar, Chief Executive Officer **A**1 9 10 **F**8 15 16 19 22 23 32 34 35 39 44 45 46 49 65 71 **S** Paracelsus Healthcare Corporation, Houston, TX	33	10	49	957	11	19356	0	10828	5669	173

MONTICELLO—Jasper County

Hospital	Control	Service	Staffed Beds	Admissions	Census	Outpatient Visits	Births	Total	Payroll	Personnel
JASPER MEMORIAL HOSPITAL, 898 College Street, Zip 31064–1298; tel. 706/468–6411; Donna Holman, Administrator (Total facility includes 44 beds in nursing home–type unit) (Nonreporting) **A**9 10	16	10	72	—	—	—	—	—	—	—

MOODY AFB—Lowndes County

Hospital	Control	Service	Staffed Beds	Admissions	Census	Outpatient Visits	Births	Total	Payroll	Personnel
★ U. S. AIR FORCE HOSPITAL MOODY, 3278 Mitchell Boulevard, Zip 31699–1500; tel. 912/257–3772; Colonel Stephan A. Giesecke, USAF, MSC, Commander (Nonreporting) **S** Department of the Air Force, Bowling AFB, DC	41	10	16	—	—	—	—	—	—	—

MOULTRIE—Colquitt County

Hospital	Control	Service	Staffed Beds	Admissions	Census	Outpatient Visits	Births	Total	Payroll	Personnel
⊠ COLQUITT REGIONAL MEDICAL CENTER, 3131 South Main Street, Zip 31768–6701, Mailing Address: P.O. Box 40, Zip 31776–0040; tel. 912/985–3420; James R. Lowry, FACHE, Chief Executive Officer **A**1 10 **F**1 3 7 8 10 11 12 14 15 16 17 19 20 21 22 23 26 27 28 29 30 31 32 33 34 35 37 39 40 41 42 44 45 46 49 51 58 59 61 63 65 66 67 70 71 72 73 74 **P**2 5 8	16	10	101	3708	40	89246	549	35719	15366	628
TURNING POINT HOSPITAL, 3015 East By–Pass, Zip 31776, Mailing Address: P.O. Box 1177, Zip 31768–1177; tel. 912/985–4815; Ben Marion, Chief Executive Officer **A**10 **F**2 3 14 15 16 27 59 65 **S** Universal Health Services, Inc., King of Prussia, PA	33	82	59	582	7	26693	0	3526	1856	—

NASHVILLE—Berrien County

Hospital	Control	Service	Staffed Beds	Admissions	Census	Outpatient Visits	Births	Total	Payroll	Personnel
⊠ BERRIEN COUNTY HOSPITAL, 1221 East McPherson Street, Zip 31639–2326, Mailing Address: P.O. Box 665, Zip 31639–0665; tel. 912/686–7471; James L. Jarrett, Chief Executive Officer (Total facility includes 108 beds in nursing home–type unit) (Nonreporting) **A**1 10 **S** Community Health Systems, Inc., Brentwood, TN	33	10	155	—	—	—	—	—	—	—

NEWNAN—Coweta County

Hospital	Control	Service	Staffed Beds	Admissions	Census	Outpatient Visits	Births	Total	Payroll	Personnel
⊠ NEWNAN HOSPITAL, 80 Jackson Street, Zip 30263–1941, Mailing Address: Box 997, Zip 30264–0997; tel. 770/253–2330; Glenn M. Flake, Executive Director (Total facility includes 153 beds in nursing home–type unit) **A**1 9 10 **F**8 10 12 15 16 19 21 22 23 24 30 35 37 39 41 42 44 46 64 65 71 73 **Web address:** www.newnanhospital.com	23	10	253	4199	197	49232	0	41983	17370	589
⊠ PEACHTREE REGIONAL HOSPITAL, (Formerly Columbia Peachtree Regional Hospital), 60 Hospital Road, Zip 30264, Mailing Address: P.O. Box 2228, Zip 30264–2228; tel. 770/253–1912; Linda Jubinsky, Chief Executive Officer (Nonreporting) **A**1 10 **S** Columbia/HCA Healthcare Corporation, Nashville, TN	33	10	144	—	—	—	—	—	—	—

OCILLA—Irwin County

Hospital	Control	Service	Staffed Beds	Admissions	Census	Outpatient Visits	Births	Total	Payroll	Personnel
☐ IRWIN COUNTY HOSPITAL, 710 North Irwin Avenue, Zip 31774–1098; tel. 912/468–3845; Sue Spivey, Administrator (Total facility includes 30 beds in nursing home–type unit) (Nonreporting) **A**1 10	16	10	64	—	—	—	—	—	—	—

PERRY—Houston County

Hospital	Control	Service	Staffed Beds	Admissions	Census	Outpatient Visits	Births	Total	Payroll	Personnel
⊠ PERRY HOSPITAL, 1120 Morningside Drive, Zip 31069–2906, Mailing Address: Drawer 1004, Zip 31069–1004; tel. 912/987–3600; Lora Davis, Administrator **A**1 9 10 **F**2 3 7 8 10 12 13 14 15 16 17 18 19 20 22 26 27 28 29 30 31 32 33 34 35 36 37 39 40 42 44 45 46 49 51 52 54 56 60 65 66 67 68 71 72 73 74 **P**7	16	10	45	1936	20	33891	252	12664	6450	223

QUITMAN—Brooks County

Hospital	Control	Service	Staffed Beds	Admissions	Census	Outpatient Visits	Births	Total	Payroll	Personnel
☐ BROOKS COUNTY HOSPITAL, 903 North Court Street, Zip 31643–1315, Mailing Address: P.O. Box 5000, Zip 31643–5000; tel. 912/263–4171; Andrew J. Finnegan, CHE, Administrator (Nonreporting) **A**1 9 10 **S** Archbold Medical Center, Thomasville, GA	23	10	35	—	—	—	—	—	—	—

REIDSVILLE—Tattnall County

Hospital	Control	Service	Staffed Beds	Admissions	Census	Outpatient Visits	Births	Total	Payroll	Personnel
TATTNALL MEMORIAL HOSPITAL, Highway 121 South, Zip 30453, Mailing Address: Route 1, Box 261, Zip 30453; tel. 912/557–4731; Don E. Tomberlin, Interim Administrator (Nonreporting) **A**10	16	10	40	—	—	—	—	—	—	—

RICHLAND—Stewart County

Hospital	Control	Service	Staffed Beds	Admissions	Census	Outpatient Visits	Births	Total	Payroll	Personnel
STEWART–WEBSTER HOSPITAL, 300 Alston Street, Zip 31825–1406, Mailing Address: P.O. Box 190, Zip 31825–0190; tel. 912/887–3366; Stephen H. Noble, President (Nonreporting) **A**9 10 **S** Accord Health Care Corporation, Clearwater, FL	33	10	25	—	—	—	—	—	—	—

RIVERDALE—Clayton County

Hospital	Control	Service	Staffed Beds	Admissions	Census	Outpatient Visits	Births	Total	Payroll	Personnel
⊠ SOUTHERN REGIONAL MEDICAL CENTER, 11 Upper Riverdale Road S.W., Zip 30274–2600; tel. 770/991–8000; Eugene A. Leblond, FACHE, President and Chief Executive Officer **A**1 2 9 10 **F**2 3 7 8 10 11 12 14 16 17 18 19 21 22 23 25 26 28 29 30 31 32 33 34 35 37 38 39 40 41 42 44 45 46 49 51 52 53 54 55 56 57 58 59 60 61 65 67 71 72 73 74 **P**1	23	10	324	14478	179	128538	2575	121838	54437	1601

ROBINS AFB—Houston County

Hospital	Control	Service	Staffed Beds	Admissions	Census	Outpatient Visits	Births	Total	Payroll	Personnel
★ U. S. AIR FORCE HOSPITAL ROBINS, 655 Seventh Street, Zip 31098–2227; tel. 912/327–7996; Colonel John A. Lee, USAF, MSC, Commander (Nonreporting) **S** Department of the Air Force, Bowling AFB, DC **Web address:** www.robins.af.mil/orgs/abw/78MEDGP/INEX/HTM	41	10	32	—	—	—	—	—	—	—

Hospital, Address, Telephone, Administrator, Approval, Facility, and Physician Codes, Health Care System, Network	Classification Codes		Utilization Data					Expense (thousands) of dollars		
	Control	Service	Staffed Beds	Admissions	Census	Outpatient Visits	Births	Total	Payroll	Personnel

★ American Hospital Association (AHA) membership
☐ Joint Commission on Accreditation of Healthcare Organizations (JCAHO) accreditation
+ American Osteopathic Healthcare Association (AOHA) membership
○ American Osteopathic Association (AOA) accreditation
△ Commission on Accreditation of Rehabilitation Facilities (CARF) accreditation
Control codes 61, 63, 64, 71, 72 and 73 indicate hospitals listed by AOHA, but not registered by AHA. For definition of numerical codes, see page A4.

ROME—Floyd County

	Control	Service	Staffed Beds	Admissions	Census	Outpatient Visits	Births	Total	Payroll	Personnel
⊞ △ FLOYD MEDICAL CENTER, 304 Turner McCall Boulevard, Zip 30165–2734, Mailing Address: P.O. Box 233, Zip 30162–0233; tel. 706/802–2000; Kurt Stuenkel, FACHE, President and Chief Executive Officer **A**1 2 3 5 7 9 10 **F**3 4 5 7 8 10 11 12 13 15 16 17 18 19 20 21 22 23 24 25 26 27 28 29 30 31 32 33 34 35 37 38 39 40 41 42 44 45 46 47 48 49 51 54 55 56 57 58 59 61 63 65 66 67 70 71 72 73 74 **P**1 5 Web address: www.floydmed.org	23	10	216	10835	128	163948	2168	89731	36285	1459
☐ NORTHWEST GEORGIA REGIONAL HOSPITAL, 1305 Redmond Circle, Zip 30165–1393; tel. 706/295–6246; Thomas W. Muller, M.D., Superintendent (Total facility includes 128 beds in nursing home–type unit) **A**1 10 **F**14 15 16 20 52 53 55 57 64 65 73	12	22	265	2762	255	0	0	28137	17503	632
⊞ REDMOND REGIONAL MEDICAL CENTER, 501 Redmond Road, Zip 30165–7001, Mailing Address: Box 107001, Zip 30164–7001; tel. 706/291–0291; James R. Thomas, Chief Executive Officer **A**1 2 9 10 **F**4 8 10 11 12 19 21 22 23 25 28 30 32 34 35 37 41 42 43 44 45 49 50 51 63 65 66 67 71 72 73 74 **P**4 7 **S** Columbia/HCA Healthcare Corporation, Nashville, TN Web address: www.columbia.hca.com	33	10	199	10051	124	80132	0	82150	24918	789

ROSWELL—Fulton County

	Control	Service	Staffed Beds	Admissions	Census	Outpatient Visits	Births	Total	Payroll	Personnel
⊞ NORTH FULTON REGIONAL HOSPITAL, 3000 Hospital Boulevard, Zip 30076–9930; tel. 770/751–2500; John F. Holland, President **A**1 9 10 **F**7 11 19 21 22 25 28 29 30 34 35 36 37 38 39 40 41 42 44 46 48 49 50 51 65 66 67 70 71 73 74 **P**1 **S** TENET Healthcare Corporation, Santa Barbara, CA Web address: www.tenethealth.com/northfulton	33	10	167	6337	83	57750	559	42700	17794	562

ROYSTON—Franklin County

	Control	Service	Staffed Beds	Admissions	Census	Outpatient Visits	Births	Total	Payroll	Personnel
⊞ COBB MEMORIAL HOSPITAL, (Includes Brown Memorial Convalescent Center, Cobb Health Care Center and Cobb Terrace Personal Care Center), 577 Franklin Springs Street, Zip 30662–3909, Mailing Address: P.O. Box 589, Zip 30662–0589; tel. 706/245–5071; H. Thomas Brown, Administrator (Total facility includes 260 beds in nursing home–type unit) **A**1 9 10 **F**6 7 8 12 13 14 15 16 17 19 21 22 28 33 36 37 39 40 41 44 46 49 62 64 65 71 73 74 Web address: www.tycobbhealthcare.org	23	10	331	2403	300	36000	127	22033	11443	513

SAINT MARYS—Camden County

	Control	Service	Staffed Beds	Admissions	Census	Outpatient Visits	Births	Total	Payroll	Personnel
★ CAMDEN MEDICAL CENTER, 2000 Dan Proctor Drive, Zip 31558; tel. 912/576–4200; Alan E. George, Administrator (Nonreporting) **A**9 10 **S** Quorum Health Group/Quorum Health Resources, Inc., Brentwood, TN	23	10	40	—	—	—	—	—	—	—

SAINT SIMONS ISLAND—Glynn County

	Control	Service	Staffed Beds	Admissions	Census	Outpatient Visits	Births	Total	Payroll	Personnel
☐ CHARTER BY–THE–SEA BEHAVIORAL HEALTH SYSTEM, 2927 Demere Road, Zip 31522–1620; tel. 912/638–1999; Wes Robbins, Chief Executive Officer (Nonreporting) **A**1 9 10 **S** Magellan Health Services, Atlanta, GA	33	22	101	—	—	—	—	—	—	—

SANDERSVILLE—Washington County

	Control	Service	Staffed Beds	Admissions	Census	Outpatient Visits	Births	Total	Payroll	Personnel
⊞ WASHINGTON COUNTY REGIONAL HOSPITAL, 610 Sparta Highway, Zip 31082–1362, Mailing Address: P.O. Box 636, Zip 31082–0636; tel. 912/552–3901; Shirley R. Roberts, Administrator (Total facility includes 60 beds in nursing home–type unit) (Nonreporting) **A**1 9 10	16	10	116	—	—	—	—	—	—	—

SAVANNAH—Chatham County

	Control	Service	Staffed Beds	Admissions	Census	Outpatient Visits	Births	Total	Payroll	Personnel
⊞ CANDLER HOSPITAL, 5353 Reynolds Street, Zip 31405–6013, Mailing Address: P.O. Box 9787, Zip 31412–9787; tel. 912/692–6000; Paul P. Hinchey, President and Chief Executive Officer (Nonreporting) **A**1 9 10	23	10	335	—	—	—	—	—	—	—
☐ CHARTER SAVANNAH BEHAVIORAL HEALTH SYSTEM, 1150 Cornell Avenue, Zip 31406–2797; tel. 912/354–3911; Thomas L. Ryba, Chief Executive Officer (Nonreporting) **A**1 9 10 **S** Magellan Health Services, Atlanta, GA	33	22	112	—	—	—	—	—	—	—
☐ GEORGIA REGIONAL HOSPITAL AT SAVANNAH, Eisenhower Drive at Varnedoe, Zip 31406, Mailing Address: P.O. Box 13607, Zip 31416–0607; tel. 912/356–2011; Doug Osborne, Facility Administrator **A**1 10 **F**15 20 26 52 53 54 55 56 57 65 73 **P**1	12	22	178	975	124	—	0	—	—	374
⊞ △ MEMORIAL HEALTH SYSTEM, 4700 Waters Avenue, Zip 31404–6283, Mailing Address: P.O. Box 23089, Zip 31403–3089; tel. 912/350–8000; Robert A. Colvin, President and Chief Executive Officer (Nonreporting) **A**1 2 3 5 7 8 10 **S** Quorum Health Group/Quorum Health Resources, Inc., Brentwood, TN Web address: www.memorialmed.com	16	10	373	—	—	—	—	—	—	—
☐ △ ST. JOSEPH'S HOSPITAL, 11705 Mercy Boulevard, Zip 31419–1791; tel. 912/927–5404; Paul P. Hinchey, President and Chief Executive Officer (Nonreporting) **A**1 2 7 9 10 **S** Sisters of Mercy of the Americas–Regional Community of Baltimore, Baltimore, MD	21	10	305	—	—	—	—	—	—	—

SMYRNA—Cobb County

	Control	Service	Staffed Beds	Admissions	Census	Outpatient Visits	Births	Total	Payroll	Personnel
⊞ EMORY–ADVENTIST HOSPITAL, 3949 South Cobb Drive S.E., Zip 30080–6300; tel. 770/434–0710; Terry Owen, Chief Executive Officer (Total facility includes 12 beds in nursing home–type unit) **A**1 10 **F**8 10 19 21 22 23 26 28 30 32 34 35 37 42 44 45 46 49 57 64 65 71 73 **S** Adventist Health System Sunbelt Health Care Corporation, Winter Park, FL	23	10	54	1698	26	29692	0	20330	7238	247
⊞ RIDGEVIEW INSTITUTE, 3995 South Cobb Drive S.E., Zip 30080–6397; tel. 770/434–4567; John E. Gronewald, Chief Operating Officer **A**1 3 5 9 10 **F**2 3 12 14 15 16 17 26 34 52 53 54 55 56 57 58 59 65 67 74	23	22	56	2373	36	23567	0	18088	6567	192
☐ VALUEMARK–BRAWNER BEHAVIORAL HEALTHACARE SYSTEM–NORTH, 3180 Atlanta Street S.E., Zip 30080–8256; tel. 404/436–0081; Edward J. Osborne, Chief Executive Officer (Nonreporting) **A**1 3 10 **S** ValueMark Healthcare Systems, Inc., Atlanta, GA	33	22	108	—	—	—	—	—	—	—

Hospital, Address, Telephone, Administrator, Approval, Facility, and Physician Codes, Health Care System, Network	Classi-fication Codes		Utilization Data					Expense (thousands) of dollars		
★ American Hospital Association (AHA) membership □ Joint Commission on Accreditation of Healthcare Organizations (JCAHO) accreditation + American Osteopathic Healthcare Association (AOHA) membership ○ American Osteopathic Association (AOA) accreditation △ Commission on Accreditation of Rehabilitation Facilities (CARF) accreditation Control codes 61, 63, 64, 71, 72 and 73 indicate hospitals listed by AOHA, but not registered by AHA. For definition of numerical codes, see page A4	Control	Service	Staffed Beds	Admissions	Census	Outpatient Visits	Births	Total	Payroll	Personnel

SNELLVILLE—Gwinnett County

☒ EASTSIDE MEDICAL CENTER, (Formerly Columbia Eastside Medical Center), 1700 Medical Way, Zip 30078, Mailing Address: P.O. Box 587, Zip 30078–0587; tel. 770/979–0200; Les Beard, Chief Executive Officer (Nonreporting) **A**1 9 10 **S** Columbia/HCA Healthcare Corporation, Nashville, TN | 33 | 10 | 114 | — | — | — | — | — | — | —

SPARTA—Hancock County

★ HANCOCK MEMORIAL HOSPITAL, 453 Boland Street, Zip 31087–1105, Mailing Address: P.O. Box 490, Zip 31087–0490; tel. 706/444–7006; Henry T. Gibbs, Administrator and Chief Executive Officer (Nonreporting) **A**9 10 | 23 | 10 | 35 | — | — | — | — | — | — | —

SPRINGFIELD—Effingham County

☒ EFFINGHAM HOSPITAL, 459 Highway 119 South, Zip 31329–3021, Mailing Address: P.O. Box 386, Zip 31329–0386; tel. 912/754–6451; Terrance R. Frech, Chief Executive Officer (Total facility includes 105 beds in nursing home–type unit) (Nonreporting) **A**1 10 | 16 | 10 | 146 | — | — | — | — | — | — | —

STATESBORO—Bulloch County

□ BULLOCH MEMORIAL HOSPITAL, 500 East Grady Street, Zip 30458–5105, Mailing Address: P.O. Box 1048, Zip 30459–1048; tel. 912/486–1000; C. Scott Campbell, Executive Director **A**1 2 9 10 **F**4 7 8 11 12 17 19 20 21 22 23 26 28 29 30 32 33 35 37 39 40 44 45 49 63 65 66 67 70 71 73 **S** Health Management Associates, Naples, FL | 33 | 10 | 158 | 6361 | 76 | 68348 | 1178 | 32523 | 16171 | 525

WILLINGWAY HOSPITAL, 311 Jones Mill Road, Zip 30458–4765; tel. 912/764–6236; Jimmy Mooney, Chief Executive Officer (Nonreporting)
Web address: www.willingway.com | 33 | 82 | 40 | — | — | — | — | — | — | —

STOCKBRIDGE—Henry County

☒ HENRY MEDICAL CENTER, 1133 Eagle's Landing Parkway, Zip 30281–5099; tel. 770/389–2200; Joseph G. Brum, President and Chief Executive Officer **A**1 9 10 **F**7 8 10 14 15 16 17 19 22 28 29 30 34 35 37 38 39 40 44 45 60 65 67 68 70 71 72 73 74 **P**1 5 | 23 | 10 | 118 | 6467 | 73 | 54999 | 1507 | 59584 | 23461 | 697

SWAINSBORO—Emanuel County

☒ EMANUEL COUNTY HOSPITAL, 117 Kite Road, Zip 30401–3231, Mailing Address: P.O. Box 879, Zip 30401–0879; tel. 912/237–9911; Richard W. Clarke, Chief Executive Officer (Total facility includes 49 beds in nursing home–type unit) **A**1 10 **F**7 8 15 19 21 22 28 29 30 34 35 37 39 40 44 46 64 65 67 71 73 **P**6 | 16 | 10 | 91 | 2158 | 69 | 12252 | 211 | 13857 | 6395 | 254

SYLVANIA—Screven County

★ SCREVEN COUNTY HOSPITAL, 215 Mims Road, Zip 30467–2097; tel. 912/564–7426; George H. St. George, Chief Executive Officer **A**9 10 **F**8 15 16 17 19 22 30 34 41 44 49 64 65 71 | 16 | 10 | 40 | 1096 | 14 | 13970 | 0 | 4710 | 1967 | 76

SYLVESTER—Worth County

☒ BAPTIST HOSPITAL, WORTH COUNTY, (Formerly Worth County Hospital), 807 South Isabella Street, Zip 31791–0545, Mailing Address: Box 545, Zip 31791–0545; tel. 912/776–6961; Billy Hayes, Administrator **A**1 9 10 **F**7 8 15 16 17 19 22 28 37 40 44 46 49 71 73 **P**5 **S** Georgia Baptist Health Care System, Atlanta, GA | 33 | 10 | 49 | 1078 | 13 | 24197 | 66 | 7368 | 2818 | 142

THOMASTON—Upson County

☒ UPSON REGIONAL MEDICAL CENTER, 801 West Gordon Street, Zip 30286–2831, Mailing Address: P.O. Box 1059, Zip 30286–1059; tel. 706/647–8111; Samuel S. Gregory, Administrator **A**1 9 10 **F**7 8 14 15 16 19 21 22 23 28 30 33 35 37 40 44 49 50 65 71 72 73 **S** Quorum Health Group/Quorum Health Resources, Inc., Brentwood, TN | 23 | 10 | 115 | 4558 | 45 | 82712 | 778 | 35343 | 16219 | 547

THOMASVILLE—Thomas County

☒ JOHN D. ARCHBOLD MEMORIAL HOSPITAL, Gordon Avenue at Mimosa Drive, Zip 31792–6113, Mailing Address: P.O. Box 1018, Zip 31799–1018; tel. 912/228–2000; Jason H. Moore, President and Chief Executive Officer (Total facility includes 64 beds in nursing home–type unit) **A**1 2 9 10 **F**1 2 3 4 7 8 10 11 12 14 15 16 17 18 19 20 21 22 23 25 26 27 28 29 30 31 32 33 34 35 37 39 40 41 42 43 44 45 46 48 49 50 51 52 53 54 55 56 57 58 59 60 61 63 64 65 66 67 68 70 71 72 73 **P**8 **S** Archbold Medical Center, Thomasville, GA
Web address: www.archbold.org | 23 | 10 | 264 | 9875 | 220 | 164442 | 927 | 90010 | 38354 | 1484

THOMSON—McDuffie County

☒ MCDUFFIE COUNTY HOSPITAL, 521 Hill Street S.W., Zip 30824–2199; tel. 706/595–1411; Douglas C. Keir, Chief Executive Officer **A**1 9 10 **F**1 2 3 4 5 6 7 8 9 10 11 12 13 15 16 17 18 19 20 21 22 23 24 25 26 27 28 29 30 31 32 33 34 35 36 37 38 39 40 41 42 43 44 45 46 47 48 49 50 51 52 53 54 55 56 57 58 59 60 61 62 63 64 65 66 67 68 70 71 72 73 74 **S** Quorum Health Group/Quorum Health Resources, Inc., Brentwood, TN
Web address: www.mch.com | 16 | 10 | 33 | 1637 | 18 | 27596 | 0 | 11724 | 5379 | 212

TIFTON—Tift County

☒ TIFT GENERAL HOSPITAL, 901 East 18th Street, Zip 31794–3648, Mailing Address: Drawer 747, Zip 31793–0747; tel. 912/382–7120; William T. Richardson, President and Chief Executive Officer **A**1 10 **F**7 8 10 12 14 15 16 17 19 21 22 23 27 28 33 35 37 39 40 42 44 45 46 48 49 60 65 71 72 73 74 **P**8
Web address: www.tiftgeneral.com | 16 | 10 | 181 | 7538 | 84 | 79159 | 1098 | 57845 | 19215 | 723

TOCCOA—Stephens County

☒ STEPHENS COUNTY HOSPITAL, 2003 Falls Road, Zip 30577–9700; tel. 706/282–4200; Edward C. Gambrell, Jr., Administrator (Total facility includes 82 beds in nursing home–type unit) **A**1 9 10 **F**6 7 8 14 15 16 17 19 22 23 30 33 35 37 40 41 44 45 49 62 63 64 65 68 71 73
Web address: www.stephenscountyhospital.com | 16 | 10 | 178 | 3552 | 111 | 33021 | 392 | 26058 | 12558 | 464

Hospital, Address, Telephone, Administrator, Approval, Facility, and Physician Codes, Health Care System, Network	Classi-fication Codes		Utilization Data					Expense (thousands) of dollars		
★ American Hospital Association (AHA) membership ☐ Joint Commission on Accreditation of Healthcare Organizations (JCAHO) accreditation + American Osteopathic Healthcare Association (AOHA) membership ○ American Osteopathic Association (AOA) accreditation △ Commission on Accreditation of Rehabilitation Facilities (CARF) accreditation Control codes 61, 63, 64, 71, 72 and 73 indicate hospitals listed by AOHA, but not registered by AHA. For definition of numerical codes, see page A4	Control	Service	Staffed Beds	Admissions	Census	Outpatient Visits	Births	Total	Payroll	Personnel

TUCKER—De Kalb County

⊠ NORTHLAKE REGIONAL MEDICAL CENTER, 1455 Montreal Road, Zip 30084; tel. 770/270–3000; Thomas D. Gilbert, Chief Executive Officer **A**1 2 10 **F**7 8 12 14 17 19 20 21 22 28 31 35 37 38 39 40 41 42 44 48 49 65 71 73 **P**5 **S** Columbia/HCA Healthcare Corporation, Nashville, TN

| | 33 | 10 | 112 | 2461 | 37 | 23052 | 287 | — | — | 283 |

VALDOSTA—Lowndes County

GREENLEAF CENTER, 2209 Pineview Drive, Zip 31602–7316; tel. 912/247–4357; Michael Lane, Administrator and Chief Executive Officer (Nonreporting) **A**9 10

| | 33 | 22 | 70 | — | — | — | — | — | — | — |

⊠ △ SOUTH GEORGIA MEDICAL CENTER, 2501 North Patterson Street, Zip 31602–1735, Mailing Address: P.O. Box 1727, Zip 31603–1727; tel. 912/333–1000; John S. Bowling, President and Chief Executive Officer **A**1 2 7 10 **F**1 4 6 7 8 10 11 12 13 14 15 16 17 19 20 21 22 23 25 26 27 28 29 30 31 32 33 34 35 37 38 39 40 41 42 43 44 45 46 48 49 51 52 53 54 55 56 57 60 62 63 65 66 67 69 71 72 73 74 **P**8 **Web address:** www.sgmc.org

| | 16 | 10 | 288 | 13002 | 168 | 129044 | 1968 | 99653 | 38051 | 1531 |

VIDALIA—Toombs County

☐ MEADOWS REGIONAL MEDICAL CENTER, 1703 Meadows Lane, Zip 30474–8915, Mailing Address: P.O. Box 1048, Zip 30474–1048; tel. 912/537–8921; Barry Michael, Chief Executive Officer (Total facility includes 35 beds in nursing home–type unit) **A**1 10 **F**7 8 14 15 16 19 21 22 23 25 28 30 31 33 34 35 37 39 40 41 44 45 46 49 63 64 65 66 67 71 72 73

| | 23 | 10 | 108 | 3620 | 66 | 47965 | 509 | 23165 | 11142 | 361 |

VIENNA—Dooly County

⊠ DOOLY MEDICAL CENTER, 1300 Union Street, Zip 31092–7541, Mailing Address: P.O. Box 278, Zip 31092–0278; tel. 912/268–4141; Kent W. McMackin, Administrator **A**1 9 10 **F**14 15 16 19 22 28 34 35 37 44 46 49 65 71 **S** Georgia Baptist Health Care System, Atlanta, GA

| | 16 | 10 | 32 | 587 | 9 | 8204 | 0 | 4782 | 2286 | 81 |

VILLA RICA—Carroll County

⊠ TANNER MEDICAL CENTER–VILLA RICA, 601 Dallas Road, Zip 30180–1202, Mailing Address: P.O. Box 638, Zip 30180–0638; tel. 770/456–3100; Larry N. Steed, Administrator **A**1 9 10 **F**8 11 15 16 19 21 22 23 28 30 33 35 37 40 44 49 63 65 71 73 74 **P**8 **S** Quorum Health Group/Quorum Health Resources, Inc., Brentwood, TN **Web address:** www.tanner.org

| | 16 | 10 | 45 | 1281 | 11 | 17238 | 171 | 10356 | 4633 | 139 |

WARM SPRINGS—Meriwether County

★ BAPTIST MERIWETHER HOSPITAL, 5995 Spring Street, Zip 31830, Mailing Address: P.O. Box 8, Zip 31830–0008; tel. 706/655–3331; Lynn Jackson, Administrator (Total facility includes 79 beds in nursing home–type unit) (Nonreporting) **A**10 **S** Georgia Baptist Health Care System, Atlanta, GA

| | 21 | 10 | 105 | — | — | — | — | — | — | — |

☐ ROOSEVELT WARM SPRINGS INSTITUTE FOR REHABILITATION, Highway 27, Zip 31830, Mailing Address: P.O. Box 1000, Zip 31830–0268; tel. 706/655–5001; Frank C. Ruzycki, Executive Director **A**1 10 **F**16 48 **Web address:** www.roosevelt.rehab.org

| | 12 | 46 | 71 | 634 | 44 | 7180 | 0 | 15385 | — | 429 |

WARNER ROBINS—Houston County

⊠ HOUSTON MEDICAL CENTER, 1601 Watson Boulevard, Zip 31093–3431, Mailing Address: Box 2886, Zip 31099–2886; tel. 912/922–4281; Arthur P. Christie, Administrator **A**1 9 10 **F**2 7 8 10 12 14 15 16 17 19 20 22 23 25 28 29 30 34 35 37 39 40 42 44 45 46 48 49 52 54 55 56 57 58 59 65 66 67 71 72 73 74 **P**7 **Web address:** www.hhc.org

| | 16 | 10 | 186 | 11886 | 118 | 82669 | 1143 | 60677 | 26249 | 860 |

WASHINGTON—Wilkes County

★ WILLS MEMORIAL HOSPITAL, 120 Gordon Street, Zip 30673–1602, Mailing Address: P.O. Box 370, Zip 30673–0370; tel. 706/678–2151; Tim E. Merritt, Chief Executive Officer **A**9 10 **F**7 8 15 17 19 22 28 30 33 35 37 40 41 44 45 49 54 65 71 73 **S** Quorum Health Group/Quorum Health Resources, Inc., Brentwood, TN

| | 15 | 10 | 38 | 1309 | 17 | 9115 | 62 | 8489 | 3909 | 167 |

WAYCROSS—Ware County

⊠ SATILLA REGIONAL MEDICAL CENTER, 410 Darling Avenue, Zip 31501–5246, Mailing Address: P.O. Box 139, Zip 31502–0139; tel. 912/283–3030; Robert M. Trimm, President and Chief Executive Officer (Nonreporting) **A**1 9 10

| | 23 | 10 | 116 | — | — | — | — | — | — | — |

WAYNESBORO—Burke County

☐ BURKE COUNTY HOSPITAL, 351 Liberty Street, Zip 30830–9686; tel. 706/554–4435; Michael A. Haddle, Chief Executive Officer and Chief Financial Officer **A**1 9 10 **F**7 8 14 15 16 17 19 22 28 30 33 34 41 44 49 65 71 73

| | 13 | 10 | 40 | 1583 | 16 | 10676 | 183 | 7368 | 2828 | 142 |

WILDWOOD—Dade County

WILDWOOD LIFESTYLE CENTER AND HOSPITAL, Lifestyle Lane, Zip 30757, Mailing Address: P.O. Box 129, Zip 30757–0129; tel. 706/820–1493; Larry E. Clements, Administrator (Nonreporting)

| | 23 | 10 | 13 | — | — | — | — | — | — | — |

WINDER—Barrow County

⊠ BARROW MEDICAL CENTER, (Formerly Columbia Barrow Medical Center), 316 North Broad Street, Zip 30680–2150, Mailing Address: P.O. Box 768, Zip 30680–0768; tel. 770/867–3400; Randy Mills, Chief Executive Officer (Total facility includes 4 beds in nursing home–type unit) (Nonreporting) **A**1 9 10 **S** LifePoint Hospitals, Inc., Nashville, TN

| | 33 | 10 | 60 | — | — | — | — | — | — | — |

HAWAII

Resident population 1,193 (in thousands)
Resident population in metro areas 73.1%
Birth rate per 1,000 population 15.7
65 years and over 13.2%
Percent of persons without health insurance 8.6%

Hospital, Address, Telephone, Administrator, Approval, Facility, and Physician Codes, Health Care System, Network	Classi-fication Codes		Utilization Data					Expense (thousands) of dollars		
	Control	Service	Staffed Beds	Admissions	Census	Outpatient Visits	Births	Total	Payroll	Personnel

★ American Hospital Association (AHA) membership
□ Joint Commission on Accreditation of Healthcare Organizations (JCAHO) accreditation
+ American Osteopathic Healthcare Association (AOHA) membership
○ American Osteopathic Association (AOA) accreditation
△ Commission on Accreditation of Rehabilitation Facilities (CARF) accreditation
Control codes 61, 63, 64, 71, 72 and 73 indicate hospitals listed by AOHA, but not registered by AHA. For definition of numerical codes, see page A4

EWA BEACH—Honolulu County

Hospital	Control	Service	Staffed Beds	Admissions	Census	Outpatient Visits	Births	Total	Payroll	Personnel
⌷ KAHI MOHALA, 91–2301 Fort Weaver Road, Zip 96706; tel. 808/671–8511; Margi Drue, Administrator (Nonreporting) **A**1 3 10 **S** Sutter Health, Sacramento, CA	33	22	88	—	—	—	—	—	—	—
⌷ ST. FRANCIS MEDICAL CENTER–WEST, 91–2141 Fort Weaver Road, Zip 96706; tel. 808/678–7000; Sister Gretchen Gilroy, President and Chief Executive Officer **A**1 10 **F**2 3 4 7 8 10 11 12 14 15 16 17 19 20 21 22 23 28 32 33 34 35 37 39 40 41 42 43 44 46 49 60 64 65 67 68 71 73 **P**8 **S** Sisters of the 3rd Franciscan Order, Syracuse, NY	21	10	100	4033	80	107764	480	46555	17676	517

HILO—Hawaii County

Hospital	Control	Service	Staffed Beds	Admissions	Census	Outpatient Visits	Births	Total	Payroll	Personnel
⌷ HILO MEDICAL CENTER, 1190 Waianuenue Avenue, Zip 96720–2095; tel. 808/974–4743; Robert Morris, M.D., Administrator (Total facility includes 108 beds in nursing home–type unit) (Nonreporting) **A**1 5 9 10 **S** Hawaii Health Systems Corporation, Honolulu, HI	12	10	274	—	—	—	—	—	—	—

HONOKAA—Hawaii County

Hospital	Control	Service	Staffed Beds	Admissions	Census	Outpatient Visits	Births	Total	Payroll	Personnel
★ HALE HO'OLA HAMAKUA, (Formerly Honokaa Hospital), Mailing Address: P.O. Box 237, Zip 96727–0237; tel. 808/775–7211; Romel Dela Cruz, Administrator (Nonreporting) **A**9 10 **S** Hawaii Health Systems Corporation, Honolulu, HI	12	10	50	—	—	—	—	—	—	—

HONOLULU—Honolulu County

Hospital	Control	Service	Staffed Beds	Admissions	Census	Outpatient Visits	Births	Total	Payroll	Personnel
⌷ KAISER FOUNDATION HOSPITAL, 3288 Moanalua Road, Zip 96819; tel. 808/834–5333; Bruce Behnke, Administrator (Total facility includes 55 beds in nursing home–type unit) **A**1 2 3 5 9 10 **F**3 4 7 8 10 11 12 13 14 16 17 19 21 22 23 25 26 27 28 30 31 32 33 34 35 37 38 40 41 42 43 44 46 49 51 53 54 55 58 59 60 61 63 64 65 67 68 69 70 71 72 73 74 **P**3 **S** Kaiser Foundation Hospitals, Oakland, CA Web address: www.kaiserhawaii.com	23	10	196	10170	158	1156024	2026	—	—	950
⌷ KAPIOLANI MEDICAL CENTER FOR WOMEN AND CHILDREN, 1319 Punahou Street, Zip 96826–1032; tel. 808/983–6000; Frances A. Hallonquist, Chief Executive Officer (Nonreporting) **A**1 3 5 9 10	23	44	276	—	—	—	—	—	—	—
⌷ KUAKINI MEDICAL CENTER, 347 North Kuakini Street, Zip 96817–2381; tel. 808/536–2236; Gary K. Kajiwara, President and Chief Executive Officer **A**1 2 3 5 9 10 **F**1 4 8 10 11 12 14 15 16 19 21 22 23 25 26 28 29 30 32 33 34 35 37 39 41 42 43 44 45 46 49 60 63 64 65 66 67 71 73 74 **P**8 Web address: www.kuakini.org	23	10	154	5794	126	38174	0	88580	44318	1142
★ LEAHI HOSPITAL, 3675 Kilauea Avenue, Zip 96816; tel. 808/733–8000; Jerry Walker, Administrator (Total facility includes 179 beds in nursing home–type unit) **A**3 5 9 10 **F**1 16 19 20 21 35 41 50 57 63 64 65 71 **S** Hawaii Health Systems Corporation, Honolulu, HI	12	33	192	136	161	—	0	16789	9366	303
⌷ QUEEN'S MEDICAL CENTER, 1301 Punchbowl Street, Zip 96813; tel. 808/538–9011; Arthur A. Ushijima, President and Chief Executive Officer (Total facility includes 28 beds in nursing home–type unit) **A**1 2 3 5 8 9 10 **F**3 4 7 8 10 11 12 13 14 15 16 18 19 20 21 22 23 25 26 28 29 30 31 32 33 34 35 36 37 39 40 41 42 43 44 45 46 49 50 51 52 53 54 55 56 57 58 59 60 63 64 65 68 70 71 72 73 **P**5 **S** Queen's Health Systems, Honolulu, HI Web address: www.quens.org	23	10	430	17946	347	198287	1582	308185	131213	3556
⌷ REHABILITATION HOSPITAL OF THE PACIFIC, 226 North Kuakini Street, Zip 96817–9881; tel. 808/531–3511; William D. O'Connor, President and Chief Executive Officer **A**1 9 10 **F**12 14 15 16 19 21 25 27 32 34 35 36 39 41 46 48 49 65 66 67 71 73 **P**2	23	46	86	1486	68	66700	0	26866	14169	310
⌷ SHRINERS HOSPITALS FOR CHILDREN, HONOLULU, 1310 Punahou Street, Zip 96826–1099; tel. 808/941–4466; Thomas J. Brotherton, Administrator **A**1 3 5 **F**5 15 20 34 39 48 49 65 71 73 **P**6 **S** Shriners Hospitals for Children, Tampa, FL Web address: www.shrinershq.org	23	57	40	398	27	6790	0	—	—	136
□ ST. FRANCIS MEDICAL CENTER, 2230 Liliha Street, Zip 96817–9979, Mailing Address: P.O. Box 30100, Zip 96820–0100; tel. 808/547–6484; Cynthia Okinaka, Administrator (Total facility includes 46 beds in nursing home–type unit) (Nonreporting) **A**1 2 3 5 9 10 **S** Sisters of the 3rd Franciscan Order, Syracuse, NY Web address: www.sfhs–hi.org	21	10	221	—	—	—	—	—	—	—
□ STRAUB CLINIC AND HOSPITAL, 888 South King Street, Zip 96813; tel. 808/522–4000; Jonathan D. Grimes, Chief Executive Officer (Nonreporting) **A**1 2 3 5 9 10	33	10	139	—	—	—	—	—	—	—
⌷ TRIPLER ARMY MEDICAL CENTER, Zip 96859–5000; tel. 808/433–6661; Major Nancy R. Adams, Commander **A**1 2 3 5 9 **F**3 4 8 10 12 13 14 15 16 17 18 19 20 21 22 23 24 25 26 28 29 30 31 34 35 37 38 39 40 41 42 43 44 45 46 47 49 50 51 52 53 54 55 56 57 58 59 60 61 63 65 66 67 68 69 70 71 72 73 74 **P**5 6 **S** Department of the Army, Office of the Surgeon General, Falls Church, VA Web address: www.tamc.amedd.army.mil	42	10	254	11765	156	553389	2824	56728	—	—

Hospital, Address, Telephone, Administrator, Approval, Facility, and Physician Codes, Health Care System, Network	Classi-fication Codes		Utilization Data					Expense (thousands) of dollars		
★ American Hospital Association (AHA) membership □ Joint Commission on Accreditation of Healthcare Organizations (JCAHO) accreditation + American Osteopathic Healthcare Association (AOHA) membership ○ American Osteopathic Association (AOA) accreditation △ Commission on Accreditation of Rehabilitation Facilities (CARF) accreditation Control codes 61, 63, 64, 71, 72 and 73 indicate hospitals listed by AOHA, but not registered by AHA. For definition of numerical codes, see page A4	Control	Service	Staffed Beds	Admissions	Census	Outpatient Visits	Births	Total	Payroll	Personnel

KAHUKU—Honolulu County

⊠ KAHUKU HOSPITAL, 56–117 Pualalea Street, Zip 96731–2052; tel. 808/293–9221; Wayne Fairchild, Chief Executive Officer (Nonreporting) **A**1 9 10

| | 23 | 10 | 24 | — | — | — | — | — | — | — |

KAILUA—Honolulu County

⊠ CASTLE MEDICAL CENTER, 640 Ulukahiki Street, Zip 96734–4498; tel. 808/263–5500; Robert J. Walker, President (Total facility includes 10 beds in nursing home–type unit) **A**1 9 10 **F**2 3 7 8 10 12 14 15 16 17 19 21 28 29 30 32 37 40 41 42 44 46 49 52 58 59 64 65 67 70 71 73 74 **P**8 **S** Adventist Health, Roseville, CA
Web address: www.cmc.ah.org

| | 21 | 10 | 150 | 5780 | 85 | 117295 | 498 | 59878 | 28191 | 677 |

KANEOHE—Honolulu County

□ HAWAII STATE HOSPITAL, 45–710 Keaahala Road, Zip 96744–3597; tel. 808/236–8237; Wayne P. Law, Acting Administrator (Nonreporting) **A**1 3 5

| | 12 | 22 | 167 | — | — | — | — | — | — | — |

KAPAA—Kauai County

★ SAMUEL MAHELONA MEMORIAL HOSPITAL, 4800 Kawaihau Road, Zip 96746–1998; tel. 808/822–4961; Neva M. Olson, Chief Executive Officer (Total facility includes 61 beds in nursing home–type unit) (Nonreporting) **A**9 10 **S** Hawaii Health Systems Corporation, Honolulu, HI

| | 12 | 49 | 82 | — | — | — | — | — | — | — |

KAUNAKAKAI—Maui County

⊠ MOLOKAI GENERAL HOSPITAL, Mailing Address: P.O. Box 408, Zip 96748–0408; tel. 808/553–5331; Calvin M. Ichinose, Administrator (Total facility includes 16 beds in nursing home–type unit) (Nonreporting) **A**1 9 10 **S** Queen's Health Systems, Honolulu, HI

| | 23 | 10 | 30 | — | — | — | — | — | — | — |

KEALAKEKUA—Hawaii County

⊠ KONA COMMUNITY HOSPITAL, Mailing Address: P.O. Box 69, Zip 96750–0069; tel. 808/322–4429; Joseph C. Wall, Administrator (Total facility includes 22 beds in nursing home–type unit) (Nonreporting) **A**1 9 10 **S** Hawaii Health Systems Corporation, Honolulu, HI

| | 12 | 10 | 75 | — | — | — | — | — | — | — |

KOHALA—Hawaii County

★ KOHALA HOSPITAL, Mailing Address: P.O. Box 10, Kapaau, Zip 96755–0010; tel. 808/889–6211; Herbert K. Yim, Administrator (Nonreporting) **A**9 10 **S** Hawaii Health Systems Corporation, Honolulu, HI

| | 12 | 10 | 26 | — | — | — | — | — | — | — |

KULA—Maui County

★ KULA HOSPITAL, 204 Kula Highway, Zip 96790–9499; tel. 808/878–1221; Alan G. Lee, Administrator (Total facility includes 103 beds in nursing home–type unit) (Nonreporting) **A**9 10 **S** Hawaii Health Systems Corporation, Honolulu, HI

| | 12 | 49 | 105 | — | — | — | — | — | — | — |

LANAI CITY—Maui County

★ LANAI COMMUNITY HOSPITAL, 628 Seventh Street, Zip 96763–0797, Mailing Address: P.O. Box 797, Zip 96763–0797; tel. 808/565–6411; John Schaumburg, Administrator (Nonreporting) **A**9 10 **S** Hawaii Health Systems Corporation, Honolulu, HI

| | 12 | 10 | 14 | — | — | — | — | — | — | — |

LIHUE—Kauai County

⊠ WILCOX MEMORIAL HOSPITAL, 3420 Kuhio Highway, Zip 96766; tel. 808/245–1100; David W. Patton, Ph.D., President and Chief Executive Officer (Total facility includes 110 beds in nursing home–type unit) **A**1 2 9 10 **F**1 3 7 8 12 15 16 17 19 20 21 22 25 26 27 28 29 30 31 32 33 34 35 37 39 40 41 42 43 44 45 46 49 51 53 54 56 58 61 63 64 65 67 68 70 71 72 73 **P**5 6

| | 23 | 10 | 177 | 4865 | 155 | 59515 | 683 | 43467 | 21436 | 647 |

PAHALA—Hawaii County

★ KAU HOSPITAL, Mailing Address: P.O. Box 40, Zip 96777–0040; tel. 808/928–8331; Dawn S. Pung, Administrator (Total facility includes 19 beds in nursing home–type unit) (Nonreporting) **A**9 10 **S** Hawaii Health Systems Corporation, Honolulu, HI

| | 12 | 10 | 21 | — | — | — | — | — | — | — |

WAHIAWA—Honolulu County

⊠ WAHIAWA GENERAL HOSPITAL, 128 Lehua Street, Zip 96786, Mailing Address: P.O. Box 580, Zip 96786–0580; tel. 808/621–8411; Tyler A. Erickson, Chief Executive Officer (Total facility includes 93 beds in nursing home–type unit) **A**1 3 5 9 10 **F**7 8 11 17 19 20 21 22 26 30 32 33 34 37 40 41 42 44 46 49 64 65 66 67 68 71 73 **P**5 8 **S** Quorum Health Group/Quorum Health Resources, Inc., Brentwood, TN

| | 23 | 10 | 162 | 2376 | 126 | 33226 | 287 | 25470 | 12292 | 354 |

WAILUKU—Maui County

⊠ MAUI MEDICAL MEMORIAL CENTER, (Formerly Maui Memorial Hospital), 221 Mahalani Street, Zip 96793–2581; tel. 808/244–9056; William B. Kleefisch, Chief Executive Officer (Nonreporting) **A**1 2 9 10 **S** Hawaii Health Systems Corporation, Honolulu, HI

| | 12 | 10 | 203 | — | — | — | — | — | — | — |

WAIMEA—Kauai County

⊠ KAUAI VETERANS MEMORIAL HOSPITAL, Waimea Canyon Road, Zip 96796, Mailing Address: P.O. Box 337, Zip 96796–0337; tel. 808/338–9431; Orianna A. Skomoroch, Chief Executive Officer (Total facility includes 20 beds in nursing home–type unit) (Nonreporting) **A**1 9 10 **S** Hawaii Health Systems Corporation, Honolulu, HI

| | 12 | 10 | 49 | — | — | — | — | — | — | — |

IDAHO

Resident population 1,229 (in thousands)
Resident population in metro areas 36.3%
Birth rate per 1,000 population 15.5
65 years and over 11.3%
Percent of persons without health insurance 16.5%

Hospital, Address, Telephone, Administrator, Approval, Facility, and Physician Codes, Health Care System, Network	Classi-fication Codes		Utilization Data						Expense (thousands) of dollars		
★ American Hospital Association (AHA) membership □ Joint Commission on Accreditation of Healthcare Organizations (JCAHO) accreditation + American Osteopathic Healthcare Association (AOHA) membership ○ American Osteopathic Association (AOA) accreditation △ Commission on Accreditation of Rehabilitation Facilities (CARF) accreditation Control codes 61, 63, 64, 71, 72 and 73 indicate hospitals listed by AOHA, but not registered by AHA. For definition of numerical codes, see page A4	Control	Service	Staffed Beds	Admissions	Census	Outpatient Visits	Births	Total	Payroll	Personnel

AMERICAN FALLS—Power County

★ HARMS MEMORIAL HOSPITAL DISTRICT, 510 Roosevelt Road, Zip 83211–0420, Mailing Address: P.O. Box 420, Zip 83211–0420; tel. 208/226–3200; Katharine Ann Campbell, Administrator (Total facility includes 31 beds in nursing home–type unit) **A**9 10 **F**2 3 8 17 22 26 28 30 32 40 46 51 64 65 70 71 73 **P**6

| | 16 | 10 | 41 | 145 | 28 | 8053 | 6 | 3858 | 2026 | 69 |

ARCO—Butte County

★ LOST RIVERS DISTRICT HOSPITAL, 551 Highland Drive, Zip 83213–9771, Mailing Address: P.O. Box 145, Zip 83213–0145; tel. 208/527–8206; Harry Aubert, Chief Executive Officer (Total facility includes 33 beds in nursing home–type unit) **A**9 10 **F**1 7 8 22 25 28 32 40 44 49 64 65 71 **P**6 8

| | 16 | 10 | 43 | 284 | 26 | — | 40 | — | 1969 | 107 |

BLACKFOOT—Bingham County

⊠ BINGHAM MEMORIAL HOSPITAL, 98 Poplar Street, Zip 83221–1799; tel. 208/785–4100; Louis Kraml, Chief Executive Officer (Total facility includes 60 beds in nursing home–type unit) **A**1 9 10 **F**11 14 15 16 17 19 21 22 28 29 30 35 37 39 40 41 44 45 46 49 64 65 67 68 71 73 **P**8 **S** Quorum Health Group/Quorum Health Resources, Inc., Brentwood, TN

| | 13 | 10 | 100 | 1633 | 70 | | 320 | 13909 | 5975 | 198 |

□ STATE HOSPITAL SOUTH, 700 East Alice Street, Zip 83221–0400, Mailing Address: Box 400, Zip 83221–0400; tel. 208/785–1200; Ray Laible, Administrative Director (Total facility includes 30 beds in nursing home–type unit) **A**1 9 10 **F**16 52 53 54 55 56 57 64 **P**6

| | 12 | 22 | 136 | 366 | 109 | 0 | 0 | 15472 | 8884 | 285 |

BOISE—Ada County

□ BHC INTERMOUNTAIN HOSPITAL, 303 North Allumbaugh Street, Zip 83704–9266; tel. 208/377–8400; Vernon G. Garrett, Chief Executive Officer (Nonreporting) **A**1 9 10 **S** Behavioral Healthcare Corporation, Nashville, TN

| | 33 | 22 | 75 | — | — | — | — | — | — | — |

★ △ IDAHO ELKS REHABILITATION HOSPITAL, 204 Fort Place, Zip 83702–4597, Mailing Address: Box 1100, Zip 83701–1100; tel. 208/343–2583; Joseph P. Caroselli, Administrator (Total facility includes 16 beds in nursing home–type unit) **A**7 9 10 **F**12 16 24 27 28 41 48 49 64 65 66 67 73

| | 23 | 46 | 64 | 1219 | 42 | 16900 | 0 | 14598 | 7005 | 284 |

⊠ △ SAINT ALPHONSUS REGIONAL MEDICAL CENTER, 1055 North Curtis Road, Zip 83706–1370; tel. 208/378–2121; Sandra B. Bruce, President and Chief Executive Officer (Total facility includes 11 beds in nursing home–type unit) (Nonreporting) **A**1 2 3 5 7 9 10 **S** Holy Cross Health System Corporation, South Bend, IN

| | 21 | 10 | 287 | — | — | — | — | — | — | — |

⊠ ST. LUKE'S REGIONAL MEDICAL CENTER, 190 East Bannock Street, Zip 83712–6298; tel. 208/381–2222; Edwin E. Dahlberg, President (Total facility includes 31 beds in nursing home–type unit) **A**1 2 3 5 9 10 **F**4 7 8 10 11 12 13 14 15 16 17 19 20 21 22 25 26 28 29 30 31 32 33 34 35 37 38 39 40 41 42 43 44 45 46 47 49 51 53 54 56 57 60 61 63 64 65 67 68 71 72 73 74 **P**6

Web address: www.slrmc.org

| | 23 | 10 | 326 | 18208 | 188 | 459481 | 4705 | 200519 | 81706 | 2335 |

⊠ VETERANS AFFAIRS MEDICAL CENTER, 500 West Fort Street, Zip 83702–4598; tel. 208/422–1100; Wayne C. Tippets, Director (Total facility includes 40 beds in nursing home–type unit) (Nonreporting) **A**1 3 5 9 **S** Department of Veterans Affairs, Washington, DC

| | 45 | 10 | 176 | — | — | — | — | — | — | — |

BONNERS FERRY—Boundary County

★ BOUNDARY COMMUNITY HOSPITAL, (Includes Boundary County Nursing Home), 6640 Kaniksu Street, Zip 83805–7532, Mailing Address: HCR 61, Box 61A, Zip 83805–9500; tel. 208/267–3141; William T. McClintock, FACHE, Chief Executive Officer (Total facility includes 52 beds in nursing home–type unit) **A**9 10 **F**1 8 12 14 15 16 17 22 26 27 28 30 32 34 39 41 44 49 51 56 57 64 65 67 68 72 73 74 **P**8

Web address: www.boundarycommhosp.com

| | 13 | 10 | 62 | 362 | 46 | 12872 | 0 | 6107 | 3358 | 138 |

BURLEY—Cassia County

⊠ CASSIA REGIONAL MEDICAL CENTER, 1501 Hiland Avenue, Zip 83318–2675; tel. 208/678–4444; Richard Packer, Administrator (Total facility includes 34 beds in nursing home–type unit) (Nonreporting) **A**1 2 9 10 **S** Intermountain Health Care, Inc., Salt Lake City, UT

| | 23 | 10 | 87 | — | — | — | — | — | — | — |

CALDWELL—Canyon County

⊠ WEST VALLEY MEDICAL CENTER, 1717 Arlington, Zip 83605–4864; tel. 208/459–4641; Mark Adams, Chief Executive Officer **A**1 9 10 **F**7 8 10 11 12 15 18 19 20 21 22 23 26 28 30 32 33 34 35 36 40 41 44 45 46 49 52 53 54 55 56 57 58 64 65 66 67 71 73 74 **P**5 **S** Columbia/HCA Healthcare Corporation, Nashville, TN

Web address: www.columbia.net

| | 33 | 10 | 122 | 4535 | 47 | 27902 | 687 | 26751 | 13089 | 432 |

CASCADE—Valley County

★ CASCADE MEDICAL CENTER, 402 Old State Highway, Zip 83611, Mailing Address: P.O. Box 151, Zip 83611–0151; tel. 208/382–4242; Vicki Shelly, R.N., Interim Administrator (Nonreporting) **A**9 10 **S** Holy Cross Health System Corporation, South Bend, IN

| | 13 | 10 | 10 | — | — | — | — | — | — | — |

Hospital, Address, Telephone, Administrator, Approval, Facility, and Physician Codes, Health Care System, Network	Classi-fication Codes		Utilization Data					Expense (thousands) of dollars		
★ American Hospital Association (AHA) membership □ Joint Commission on Accreditation of Healthcare Organizations (JCAHO) accreditation + American Osteopathic Healthcare Association (AOHA) membership ○ American Osteopathic Association (AOA) accreditation △ Commission on Accreditation of Rehabilitation Facilities (CARF) accreditation Control codes 61, 63, 64, 71, 72 and 73 indicate hospitals listed by AOHA, but not registered by AHA. For definition of numerical codes, see page A4	Control	Service	Staffed Beds	Admissions	Census	Outpatient Visits	Births	Total	Payroll	Personnel

COEUR D'ALENE—Kootenai County

★□ KOOTENAI MEDICAL CENTER, (Includes North Idaho Behavioral Health, Division of Kootenai Medical Center, 2301 North Ironwood Place, Zip 83814–2650; tel. 208/765–4800), 2003 Lincoln Way, Zip 83814–2677; tel. 208/666–2000; Joseph E. Morris, III, Chief Executive Officer (Total facility includes 26 beds in nursing home–type unit) **A**1 2 9 10 **F**1 3 4 7 8 10 11 12 14 15 16 17 19 21 22 23 25 27 29 34 35 37 39 40 41 42 44 45 46 48 49 52 53 54 55 56 57 58 59 60 64 65 67 70 71 72 73 **P**8	16	10	225	11116	134	86635	1290	73532	33420	1009

COTTONWOOD—Idaho County

★ ST. MARY'S HOSPITAL, Lewiston and North Streets, Zip 83522, Mailing Address: P.O. Box 137, Zip 83522–0137; tel. 208/962–3251; Casey Uhling, Chief Executive Officer (Total facility includes 10 beds in nursing home–type unit) (Nonreporting) **A**9 10 **S** Benedictine Health System, Duluth, MN	21	10	28	—	—	—	—	—	—	—

COUNCIL—Adams County

COUNCIL COMMUNITY HOSPITAL AND NURSING HOME, 205 North Berkley Street, Zip 83612; tel. 208/253–4242; Sandy Niehm, Administrator (Total facility includes 20 beds in nursing home–type unit) **A**9 10 **F**22 32 64 65	16	10	26	79	19	3143	0	1354	732	51

DRIGGS—Teton County

★ TETON VALLEY HOSPITAL, 283 North First East, Zip 83422–0728, Mailing Address: P.O. Box 728, Zip 83422–0728; tel. 208/354–2383; Susan Kunz, Administrator **A**9 10 **F**7 8 12 14 15 16 17 19 22 28 30 32 33 34 36 40 41 44 46 49 65 66 67 68 71 73 **P**8	13	10	13	520	5	19095	58	4007	1988	94

EMMETT—Gem County

WALTER KNOX MEMORIAL HOSPITAL, 1202 East Locust Street, Zip 83617–2715; tel. 208/365–3561; Max Long, Chief Executive Officer **A**9 10 **F**7 8 14 17 19 22 28 32 34 35 40 44 71 **P**6	13	10	24	561	4	14096	66	3929	1967	62

GOODING—Gooding County

GOODING COUNTY MEMORIAL HOSPITAL, 1120 Montana Street, Zip 83330–1858; tel. 208/934–4433; Jim Henshaw, President and Chief Executive Officer **A**9 10 **F**14 15 16 17 22 25 28 30 32 34 44 51 71 72 73	16	10	14	408	4	15847	0	3916	1967	67

GRANGEVILLE—Idaho County

SYRINGA GENERAL HOSPITAL, 607 West Main Street, Zip 83530–1396; tel. 208/983–1700; Jess Hawley, Administrator (Nonreporting) **A**9 10	16	10	16	—	—	—	—	—	—	—

HAILEY—Blaine County

BLAINE COUNTY MEDICAL CENTER See Wood River Medical Center, Sun Valley

IDAHO FALLS—Bonneville County

★□ EASTERN IDAHO REGIONAL MEDICAL CENTER, (Formerly Columbia Eastern Idaho Regional Medical Center), 3100 Channing Way, Zip 83404–7533, Mailing Address: P.O. Box 2077, Zip 83403–2077; tel. 208/529–6111; Douglas Crabtree, Chief Executive Officer (Total facility includes 16 beds in nursing home–type unit) **A**1 9 10 **F**4 5 7 8 10 12 14 15 16 17 19 21 22 24 25 28 30 35 37 38 39 40 41 42 43 44 45 48 49 52 53 54 56 58 63 64 65 66 67 70 71 72 73 74 **P**8 **S** Columbia/HCA Healthcare Corporation, Nashville, TN **Web address:** www.eirmc.org	33	10	294	11829	171	149523	1741	81531	34624	1065
★ IDAHO FALLS RECOVERY CENTER, 1957 East 17th Street, Zip 83404–6429; tel. 208/529–5285; Jackie Street, President **A**9 10 **Web address:** www.ifrc.ida.net	23	10	10	636	3	681	0	1758	560	22

JEROME—Jerome County

★ ST. BENEDICTS FAMILY MEDICAL CENTER, 709 North Lincoln Avenue, Zip 83338–1851, Mailing Address: P.O. Box 586, Zip 83338–0586; tel. 208/324–4301; Lynne M. Mattison, FACHE, Interim Administrator (Total facility includes 40 beds in nursing home–type unit) (Nonreporting) **A**9 10 **S** Holy Cross Health System Corporation, South Bend, IN	21	10	65	—	—	—	—	—	—	—

KELLOGG—Shoshone County

★□ SHOSHONE MEDICAL CENTER, 3 Jacobs Gulch, Zip 83837–2096; tel. 208/784–1221 (Total facility includes 14 beds in nursing home–type unit) **A**1 9 10 **F**2 3 7 8 11 14 15 19 22 24 26 28 30 31 32 34 35 37 40 41 44 49 64 65 71 72 **P**3 5 8	16	10	44	834	20	22640	131	8609	3711	162

LEWISTON—Nez Perce County

★□ ST. JOSEPH REGIONAL MEDICAL CENTER, 415 Sixth Street, Zip 83501–0816; tel. 208/743–2511; Howard A. Hayes, President and Chief Executive Officer (Total facility includes 16 beds in nursing home–type unit) **A**1 2 9 10 **F**7 8 11 13 14 15 16 17 18 19 20 21 22 23 24 26 27 28 29 30 31 32 33 34 35 36 37 39 40 41 42 44 45 46 49 52 54 55 56 57 58 60 63 64 65 66 67 68 70 71 72 73 74 **P**5 **S** Carondelet Health System, Saint Louis, MO	21	10	156	6566	83	94624	745	54386	23932	657

MALAD CITY—Oneida County

ONEIDA COUNTY HOSPITAL, 150 North 200 West, Zip 83252–0126, Mailing Address: Box 126, Zip 83252–0126; tel. 208/766–2231; Todd Winder, Administrator (Total facility includes 41 beds in nursing home–type unit) **A**9 10 **F**1 7 8 12 15 16 17 22 26 28 29 32 33 34 37 40 44 46 64 65 66 71 72	13	10	52	190	37	1126	15	3095	1476	79

MCCALL—Valley County

★ MCCALL MEMORIAL HOSPITAL, 1000 State Street, Zip 83638, Mailing Address: P.O. Box 906, Mc Call, Zip 83638–0906; tel. 208/634–2221; Karen J. Kellie, President **A**9 10 **F**7 8 14 15 19 22 28 35 37 39 40 41 44 45 49 65 71 73 **S** Holy Cross Health System Corporation, South Bend, IN	16	10	15	564	4	14688	85	5513	1937	66

MONTPELIER—Bear Lake County

★ BEAR LAKE MEMORIAL HOSPITAL, 164 South Fifth Street, Zip 83254–1597; tel. 208/847–1630; Rod Jacobson, Administrator (Total facility includes 37 beds in nursing home–type unit) **A**9 10 **F**7 12 14 15 19 22 28 30 32 33 34 35 37 39 44 46 49 64 65 71 73	13	10	58	455	38	—	75	5686	2841	158

Hospital, Address, Telephone, Administrator, Approval, Facility, and Physician Codes, Health Care System, Network	Classi-fication Codes		Utilization Data					Expense (thousands) of dollars		
★ American Hospital Association (AHA) membership □ Joint Commission on Accreditation of Healthcare Organizations (JCAHO) accreditation + American Osteopathic Healthcare Association (AOHA) membership ○ American Osteopathic Association (AOA) accreditation △ Commission on Accreditation of Rehabilitation Facilities (CARF) accreditation Control codes 61, 63, 64, 71, 72 and 73 indicate hospitals listed by AOHA, but not registered by AHA. For definition of numerical codes, see page A4	Control	Service	Staffed Beds	Admissions	Census	Outpatient Visits	Births	Total	Payroll	Personnel

MOSCOW—Latah County

⊠ GRITMAN MEDICAL CENTER, 700 South Washington Street, Zip 83843–3047; tel. 208/882–4511; Thomas Stegbauer, Chief Executive Officer **A**1 9 10 **F**7 8 11 12 15 16 17 19 21 22 27 28 29 30 32 33 34 35 37 39 40 41 42 44 45 46 49 65 66 67 70 71 73 **P**5 8 **S** Quorum Health Group/Quorum Health Resources, Inc., Brentwood, TN	23	10	35	1851	16	49276	444	17513	8048	193

MOUNTAIN HOME—Elmore County

★ ELMORE MEDICAL CENTER, 895 North Sixth East Street, Zip 83647–2207, Mailing Address: P.O. Box 1270, Zip 83647–1270; tel. 208/587–8401; Gregory L. Maurer, Administrator (Total facility includes 53 beds in nursing home–type unit) **A**9 10 **F**7 8 14 15 19 22 34 39 40 44 49 64 71 73 **S** Holy Cross Health System Corporation, South Bend, IN	16	10	80	1088	48	21997	83	8351	3867	139

MOUNTAIN HOME AFB—Elmore County

⊠ U. S. AIR FORCE HOSPITAL MOUNTAIN HOME, 90 Hope Drive, Zip 83648–5300; tel. 208/828–7600; Colonel Cynthia Terriberry, USAF, Commanding Officer **A**1 **F**7 8 12 16 20 22 28 34 44 58 65 71 **S** Department of the Air Force, Bowling AFB, DC	41	10	10	892	5	92735	275	20578	14339	377

NAMPA—Canyon County

⊠ MERCY MEDICAL CENTER, 1512 12th Avenue Road, Zip 83686–6008; tel. 208/467–1171; Joseph Messmer, President and Chief Executive Officer **A**1 9 10 **F**2 3 4 7 8 10 14 15 16 19 22 25 27 32 33 35 36 37 40 41 44 49 64 65 71 73 **S** Catholic Health Initiatives, Denver, CO	21	10	149	6043	77	117311	1129	44613	18213	605

OROFINO—Clearwater County

★ CLEARWATER VALLEY HOSPITAL AND CLINICS, 301 Cedar, Zip 83544–9029; tel. 208/476–4555; Richard L. Wheat, Chief Financial Officer **A**9 10 **F**7 8 13 15 16 17 19 22 28 30 32 33 44 49 65 71 73 **P**6 **S** Benedictine Health System, Duluth, MN **Web address:** www.cvh–clrwater.com	23	10	18	975	9	50909	58	7416	4016	117
STATE HOSPITAL NORTH, 300 Hospital Drive, Zip 83544–9034; tel. 208/476–4511; A. Jay Kessinger, Administrative Director **A**9 **F**2 14 16 39 52 54 65 **P**6	12	22	60	327	54	0	0	5622	3359	110

POCATELLO—Bannock County

⊠ BANNOCK REGIONAL MEDICAL CENTER, 651 Memorial Drive, Zip 83201–4004; tel. 208/239–1000; Fred R. Eaton, Administrator (Total facility includes 118 beds in nursing home–type unit) **A**1 2 3 9 10 **F**4 7 8 10 11 12 13 14 15 16 17 19 20 21 22 23 25 26 28 29 30 31 32 34 35 37 38 39 40 41 42 43 44 45 46 47 49 51 60 61 63 64 65 66 67 68 70 71 72 73 74 **P**1 5 8 **Web address:** www.brmc.org	13	10	237	5906	153	123398	1279	52860	20271	642
⊠ △ POCATELLO REGIONAL MEDICAL CENTER, 777 Hospital Way, Zip 83201–2797; tel. 208/234–0777; Earl L. Christison, Administrator **A**1 3 7 9 10 **F**7 8 10 11 12 14 15 16 17 19 21 22 23 24 28 29 30 32 34 35 39 40 41 44 46 48 49 63 64 65 67 71 73 74 **P**8 **S** Intermountain Health Care, Inc., Salt Lake City, UT **Web address:** www.ihc.com	23	10	87	2451	29	71282	284	29280	13433	419

PRESTON—Franklin County

★ FRANKLIN COUNTY MEDICAL CENTER, 44 North First East Street, Zip 83263–1399; tel. 208/852–0137; Michael G. Andrus, Administrator and Chief Executive Officer (Total facility includes 45 beds in nursing home–type unit) **A**9 10 **F**1 7 8 12 17 20 22 28 30 32 33 39 41 44 49 64 65 71 73 **P**1 **Web address:** www.fcmc.org	13	10	65	430	41	—	109	5548	2956	112

REXBURG—Madison County

★ MADISON MEMORIAL HOSPITAL, 450 East Main Street, Zip 83440–2048, Mailing Address: P.O. Box 310, Zip 83440–0310; tel. 208/356–3691; Keith M. Steiner, Chief Executive Officer **A**9 10 **F**8 11 12 13 16 19 20 21 22 28 29 30 32 35 37 39 40 41 44 45 46 49 65 66 67 71 73 **P**8 **Web address:** www.rexburg.com/hospital	13	10	42	2938	19	30845	873	17033	7033	274

RUPERT—Minidoka County

★ MINIDOKA MEMORIAL HOSPITAL AND EXTENDED CARE FACILITY, 1224 Eighth Street, Zip 83350–1599; tel. 208/436–0481; Carl Hanson, Administrator (Total facility includes 78 beds in nursing home–type unit) (Nonreporting) **A**9 10	13	10	101	—						

SAINT MARIES—Benewah County

★ BENEWAH COMMUNITY HOSPITAL, 229 South Seventh Street, Zip 83861–1894; tel. 208/245–5551; Camille Scott, Administrator **A**9 10 **F**7 8 12 14 15 16 17 19 22 28 30 34 37 39 40 41 42 44 49 51 61 64 65 66 67 71 73 74 **P**4 6 7	13	10	25	526	4	16362	62	7398	2947	104

SALMON—Lemhi County

★ STEELE MEMORIAL HOSPITAL, Main and Daisy Streets, Zip 83467, Mailing Address: P.O. Box 700, Zip 83467–0700; tel. 208/756–4291; Kay H. Springer, Administrator **A**9 10 **F**8 14 17 22 28 34 37 40 41 44 46 56 65 71 **P**6	13	10	28	587	5	10370	47	3095	1758	63

SANDPOINT—Bonner County

⊠ BONNER GENERAL HOSPITAL, 520 North Third Avenue, Zip 83864–0877, Mailing Address: Box 1448, Zip 83864–0877; tel. 208/263–1441; Gene Tomt, FACHE, Chief Executive Officer **A**1 9 10 **F**7 8 11 17 19 22 28 30 31 32 33 34 39 40 41 44 45 46 48 56 65 71 73 **P**3 8	23	10	48	2241	16	37441	385	15643	7916	239

SODA SPRINGS—Caribou County

★ CARIBOU MEMORIAL HOSPITAL AND NURSING HOME, 300 South Third West Street, Zip 83276–1598; tel. 208/547–3341; Arthur J. Phillips, Administrator (Total facility includes 43 beds in nursing home–type unit) (Nonreporting) **A**9 10	13	10	65	—		—	—	—	—	—

Hospital, Address, Telephone, Administrator, Approval, Facility, and Physician Codes, Health Care System, Network	Classi-fication Codes		Utilization Data					Expense (thousands) of dollars		
	Control	Service	Staffed Beds	Admissions	Census	Outpatient Visits	Births	Total	Payroll	Personnel

SUN VALLEY—Blaine County

★ WOOD RIVER MEDICAL CENTER, (Includes Blaine County Medical Center, 706 South Main Street, Hailey, Zip 83333, Mailing Address: Box 927, Zip 83333; tel. 208/788–2222; Moritz Community Hospital, Mailing Address: P.O. Box 86, Zip 83353; tel. 208/622–3333), Sun Valley Road, Zip 83353, Mailing Address: P.O. Box 86, Zip 83353–0086; tel. 208/622–3333; Jon Moses, Administrator (Total facility includes 25 beds in nursing home–type unit) (Nonreporting) **A**9 10 — 15 10 64 — — — — — — —

TWIN FALLS—Twin Falls County

⊞ MAGIC VALLEY REGIONAL MEDICAL CENTER, 650 Addison Avenue West, Zip 83301–5444, Mailing Address: P.O. Box 409, Zip 83303–0409; tel. 208/737–2000; Gerald L. Hart, Chief Executive Officer (Total facility includes 20 beds in nursing home–type unit) **A**1 2 9 10 **F**3 4 7 8 10 12 15 16 19 21 22 26 28 30 32 33 35 37 38 39 40 41 42 44 45 46 47 49 52 53 54 55 56 57 58 60 64 65 70 71 73 — 13 10 177 6457 76 92718 1127 51441 20768 723

TWIN FALLS CLINIC HOSPITAL, 666 Shoshone Street East, Zip 83301–6168, Mailing Address: P.O. Box 1233, Zip 83301–1233; tel. 208/733–3700; Michael Arehart, Chief Executive Officer (Nonreporting) **A**9 10 — 33 10 40 — — — — — — —

WEISER—Washington County

★ MEMORIAL HOSPITAL, 645 East Fifth Street, Zip 83672–2202, Mailing Address: P.O. Box 550, Zip 83672–0550; tel. 208/549–0370; Susan McGough, Administrator **A**9 10 **F**7 11 14 16 17 19 22 32 37 40 44 64 65 70 71 72 73 — 16 10 27 395 2 13566 84 3588 1883 70

ILLINOIS

Resident population 12,045 (in thousands)
Resident population in metro areas 82.7%
Birth rate per 1,000 population 15.7
65 years and over 12.5%
Percent of persons without health insurance 11.3%

Hospital, Address, Telephone, Administrator, Approval, Facility, and Physician Codes, Health Care System, Network	Classi-fication Codes		Utilization Data					Expense (thousands) of dollars		
★ American Hospital Association (AHA) membership □ Joint Commission on Accreditation of Healthcare Organizations (JCAHO) accreditation + American Osteopathic Healthcare Association (AOHA) membership ○ American Osteopathic Association (AOA) accreditation △ Commission on Accreditation of Rehabilitation Facilities (CARF) accreditation Control codes 61, 63, 64, 71, 72 and 73 indicate hospitals listed by AOHA, but not registered by AHA. For definition of numerical codes, see page A4	Control	Service	Staffed Beds	Admissions	Census	Outpatient Visits	Births	Total	Payroll	Personnel

ALEDO—Mercer County

★ MERCER COUNTY HOSPITAL, 409 N.W. Ninth Avenue, Zip 61231–1296; tel. 309/582–5301; Bruce D. Peterson, Administrator (Total facility includes 18 beds in nursing home–type unit) **A**9 10 **F**8 15 16 17 19 22 30 32 33 34 36 37 39 40 44 49 51 61 64 65 66 67 71 73 **P**6

| | 13 | 10 | 45 | 741 | 28 | 21511 | 51 | 8454 | 4263 | 219 |

ALTON—Madison County

✠ ALTON MEMORIAL HOSPITAL, One Memorial Drive, Zip 62002–6722; tel. 618/463–7311; Ronald B. McMullen, President (Total facility includes 64 beds in nursing home–type unit) **A**1 2 9 10 **F**7 8 10 12 15 16 17 19 20 21 22 28 30 31 33 34 35 36 37 40 42 44 46 49 60 63 64 65 67 71 73 **P**1 5 6 7 **S** BJC Health System, Saint Louis, MO
Web address: www.bjc.org

| | 23 | 10 | 202 | 5777 | 136 | 76627 | 629 | 54495 | 24642 | 719 |

□ ALTON MENTAL HEALTH CENTER, 4500 College Avenue, Zip 62002–5099; tel. 618/465–5593; Karl Kruckeberg, Director (Nonreporting) **A**1 10

| | 12 | 22 | 194 | — | — | — | — | — | — | — |

✠ △ SAINT ANTHONY'S HEALTH CENTER, (Includes Saint Clare's Hospital, 915 East Fifth Street, Zip 62002–6434; tel. 618/463–5151), 1 Saint Anthony's Way, Zip 62002–4579, Mailing Address: P.O. Box 340, Zip 62002–0340; tel. 618/465–2571; William E. Kessler, President (Total facility includes 38 beds in nursing home–type unit) **A**1 2 7 9 10 **F**1 2 3 4 7 8 10 12 13 14 15 16 17 18 19 20 21 22 23 26 28 29 30 31 32 33 34 35 36 37 39 40 41 42 44 45 48 49 51 52 54 55 56 57 58 59 60 61 63 64 65 67 71 72 73 74
Web address: www.sahc.org

| | 23 | 10 | 292 | 7117 | 103 | 131620 | 693 | 65583 | 26767 | 810 |

ANNA—Union County

□ CHOATE MENTAL HEALTH AND DEVELOPMENTAL CENTER, 1000 North Main Street, Zip 62906–1699; tel. 618/833–5161; LeAn Taylor, Acting Facility Director **A**1 **F**1 3 14 18 19 20 21 31 35 50 52 53 54 55 56 57 58 59 63 71

| | 12 | 22 | 488 | 527 | 361 | 0 | 0 | — | — | 577 |

✠ UNION COUNTY HOSPITAL DISTRICT, 517 North Main Street, Zip 62906–1696; tel. 618/833–4511; Carol L. Goodman, Administrator and Chief Executive Officer (Total facility includes 22 beds in nursing home–type unit) **A**1 9 10 **F**8 14 15 16 17 19 21 22 24 26 28 30 32 33 34 39 44 45 46 49 51 64 65 71 72 73

| | 16 | 10 | 58 | 1139 | 32 | 61359 | 0 | 9417 | 5263 | 234 |

ARLINGTON HEIGHTS—Cook County

✠ NORTHWEST COMMUNITY HEALTHCARE, 800 West Central Road, Zip 60005–2392; tel. 847/618–1000; Bruce K. Crowther, President and Chief Executive Officer **A**1 2 9 10 **F**1 3 4 7 8 10 11 12 14 15 16 17 18 19 21 22 23 24 25 26 27 28 29 30 32 33 34 35 37 39 40 41 42 43 45 46 49 52 53 54 55 56 57 58 59 60 63 64 65 66 67 70 71 72 73 74 **P**8
Web address: www.nch.org

| | 23 | 10 | 342 | 18051 | 207 | 330469 | 2533 | 174738 | 83259 | 2282 |

AURORA—Du Page and Kane Counties County

✠ PROVENA MERCY CENTER, 1325 North Highland Avenue, Zip 60506; tel. 630/859–2222; Mary R. Sheahen, President and Chief Executive Officer **A**1 2 9 10 **F**1 2 3 4 6 7 8 10 12 13 14 15 16 17 18 19 20 21 22 23 26 27 28 29 30 31 32 33 34 35 36 37 39 40 41 42 43 44 45 46 49 50 51 52 53 54 55 56 57 58 59 60 61 62 63 64 65 66 67 68 69 70 71 72 73 74 **P**5 7 **S** Provena Health, Frankfort, IL
Web address: www.provenamercy.com

| | 23 | 10 | 241 | 9812 | 119 | 140557 | 1149 | 69002 | 29374 | 697 |

✠ △ RUSH–COPLEY MEDICAL CENTER, 2000 Ogden Avenue, Zip 60504–4206; tel. 630/978–6200; Martin Losoff, President and Chief Operating Officer **A**1 2 3 5 7 10 **F**1 3 4 5 6 7 8 10 11 12 13 14 15 16 17 18 19 20 21 22 23 24 25 26 27 28 29 30 31 32 33 34 35 36 37 38 39 40 41 42 43 44 45 46 48 49 50 51 53 54 55 56 57 58 59 60 61 62 63 64 65 66 67 68 70 71 72 73 74 **P**5 6 7 8 **S** Rush–Presbyterian–St. Luke's Medical Center, Chicago, IL

| | 23 | 10 | 140 | 7818 | 88 | 96805 | 1845 | 67509 | 26792 | 793 |

BARRINGTON—Lake County

✠ GOOD SHEPHERD HOSPITAL, 450 West Highway 22, Zip 60010–1901; tel. 847/381–9600; Russell E. Feurer, Chief Executive **A**1 2 9 10 **F**7 8 12 15 16 17 18 19 21 22 23 32 34 35 36 37 40 41 42 44 46 49 52 60 63 65 66 67 70 71 73 **P**5 7 8 **S** Advocate Health Care, Oak Brook, IL
Web address: www.advocatehealth.com

| | 21 | 10 | 154 | 7692 | 79 | 90858 | 2003 | 70690 | 28517 | 813 |

BELLEVILLE—St. Clair County

✠ MEMORIAL HOSPITAL, 4500 Memorial Drive, Zip 62226–5399; tel. 618/233–7750; Harry R. Maier, President (Total facility includes 108 beds in nursing home–type unit) **A**1 2 9 10 **F**3 4 7 8 10 16 19 21 22 23 24 28 30 32 33 34 35 36 37 40 41 43 44 45 46 49 52 54 58 63 64 65 66 67 71 73 **P**8

| | 23 | 10 | 449 | 14714 | 262 | 213878 | 1530 | 112988 | 49829 | 1685 |

✠ △ ST. ELIZABETH'S HOSPITAL, 211 South Third Street, Zip 62222–0694; tel. 618/234–2120; Gerald M. Harman, Executive Vice President and Administrator **A**1 2 3 7 9 10 **F**1 2 3 4 5 7 8 10 12 13 14 15 16 17 18 19 20 21 22 24 25 26 28 29 30 31 32 33 34 35 36 37 38 39 40 41 42 43 44 45 46 48 49 52 54 55 56 57 58 59 60 65 66 67 68 71 72 73 **P**8 **S** Hospital Sisters Health System, Springfield, IL
Web address: www.apci.net/~ste

| | 21 | 10 | 319 | 13362 | 215 | 126750 | 588 | 106370 | 39058 | 1282 |

Hospital, Address, Telephone, Administrator, Approval, Facility, and Physician Codes, Health Care System, Network	Classi-fication Codes		Utilization Data					Expense (thousands) of dollars		
American Hospital Association (AHA) membership Joint Commission on Accreditation of Healthcare Organizations (JCAHO) accreditation American Osteopathic Healthcare Association (AOHA) membership American Osteopathic Association (AOA) accreditation Commission on Accreditation of Rehabilitation Facilities (CARF) accreditation Control codes 61, 63, 64, 71, 72 and 73 indicate hospitals listed by AOHA, but not registered by AHA. For definition of numerical codes, see page A4	Control	Service	Staffed Beds	Admissions	Census	Outpatient Visits	Births	Total	Payroll	Personnel

BELVIDERE—Boone County

NORTHWEST SUBURBAN COMMUNITY HOSPITAL, (Formerly Highland Community Hospital), 1625 South State Street, Zip 61008–5900; tel. 815/547–5441; Trevor J. Dyksterhouse, President and Chief Executive Officer (Nonreporting) **A**1 9 10 — 23 10 69 — — — — — — —

SAINT JOSEPH HOSPITAL, 1005 Julien Street, Zip 61008–9932; tel. 815/544–3411; David A. Schertz, Administrator (Total facility includes 34 beds in nursing home–type unit) (Nonreporting) **A**1 9 10 **S** OSF Healthcare System, Peoria, IL — 21 10 58 — — — — — — —

BENTON—Franklin County

FRANKLIN HOSPITAL AND SKILLED NURSING CARE UNIT, 201 Bailey Lane, Zip 62812–1999; tel. 618/439–3161; Virgil Hannig, Senior Vice President and Administrator (Total facility includes 83 beds in nursing home–type unit) **A**1 9 10 **F**3 6 7 8 12 14 15 16 17 18 19 20 21 22 24 26 28 29 30 32 33 35 36 37 38 39 41 42 44 45 47 49 51 60 61 63 64 65 66 67 71 72 74 **P**7 **S** Southern Illinois Hospital Services, Carbondale, IL — 16 10 117 1090 91 16128 0 9510 4232 200

BERWYN—Cook County

MACNEAL HOSPITAL, 3249 South Oak Park Avenue, Zip 60402–0715; tel. 708/795–9100; Brian J. Lemon, President (Total facility includes 40 beds in nursing home–type unit) **A**1 2 3 5 8 9 10 **F**2 3 4 7 8 10 12 14 15 16 17 18 19 20 21 22 25 26 27 28 29 30 31 32 33 34 35 36 37 39 40 41 42 44 45 46 49 50 51 52 53 54 55 56 57 58 59 60 61 63 64 65 66 67 68 70 71 73 74 **P**6 7
Web address: www.macneal.com — 23 10 333 17704 234 70524 2050 150405 66203 3072

BLOOMINGTON—McLean County

BROMENN LIFECARE CENTER See BroMenn Healthcare, Normal

ST. JOSEPH MEDICAL CENTER, 2200 East Washington Street, Zip 61701–4323; tel. 309/662–3311; Kenneth J. Natzke, Administrator (Total facility includes 13 beds in nursing home–type unit) (Nonreporting) **A**1 2 9 10 **S** OSF Healthcare System, Peoria, IL
Web address: www.osfhealthcare.org — 21 10 154 — — — — — — —

BLUE ISLAND—Cook County

SAINT FRANCIS HOSPITAL AND HEALTH CENTER, 12935 South Gregory Street, Zip 60406–2470; tel. 708/597–2000; Jay E. Kreuzer, FACHE, President **A**1 2 9 10 **F**4 7 8 10 12 14 16 17 18 19 21 22 24 25 28 29 30 31 32 33 34 35 36 37 39 40 41 42 43 44 49 54 60 63 65 67 71 72 73 74 **P**6 8 **S** SSM Health Care, Saint Louis, MO — 21 10 254 11872 140 84456 1158 111691 47498 1093

BREESE—Clinton County

ST. JOSEPH'S HOSPITAL, 9515 Holy Cross Lane, Zip 62230–0099; tel. 618/526–4511; Jacolyn M. Schlautman, Executive Vice President and Administrator **A**1 9 10 **F**7 8 14 15 16 19 21 22 28 30 32 33 35 37 40 42 44 49 65 71 73 **S** Hospital Sisters Health System, Springfield, IL — 21 10 57 1936 18 41794 468 15540 6963 224

CANTON—Fulton County

GRAHAM HOSPITAL, 210 West Walnut Street, Zip 61520–2497; tel. 309/647–5240; D. Ray Slaubaugh, President (Total facility includes 54 beds in nursing home–type unit) **A**1 6 9 10 **F**1 7 8 12 14 15 16 17 19 21 22 28 30 32 33 35 37 40 42 44 46 64 65 67 71 73 — 23 10 124 2754 75 45868 294 27273 12480 408

CARBONDALE—Jackson County

MEMORIAL HOSPITAL OF CARBONDALE, 405 West Jackson Street, Zip 62901–1467, Mailing Address: P.O. Box 10000, Zip 62902–9000; tel. 618/549–0721; George Maroney, Senior Vice President and Administrator **A**1 2 3 5 9 10 **F**7 8 10 14 16 17 19 21 22 23 28 30 32 33 35 37 38 40 42 44 45 49 60 63 65 66 67 69 71 73 **P**7 **S** Southern Illinois Hospital Services, Carbondale, IL — 23 10 133 7713 83 134450 2041 65532 24506 806

CARLINVILLE—Macoupin County

CARLINVILLE AREA HOSPITAL, 1001 East Morgan Street, Zip 62626–1499; tel. 217/854–3141; Robert W. Porteus, President and Chief Executive Officer **A**1 9 10 **F**8 16 19 22 24 26 32 33 34 35 41 44 49 71
Web address: www.cahcare.com — 23 10 33 1217 14 22288 — 9767 4378 139

CARMI—White County

WHITE COUNTY MEDICAL CENTER, 400 Plum Street, Zip 62821–1799; tel. 618/382–4171; Phillip C. Blair, Interim Administrator (Total facility includes 98 beds in nursing home–type unit) **A**1 9 10 **F**8 12 19 21 22 32 34 41 49 64 65 71 — 16 10 112 324 80 15600 0 7643 3326 148

CARROLLTON—Greene County

THOMAS H. BOYD MEMORIAL HOSPITAL, (Includes Reisch Memorial Nursing Home), 800 School Street, Zip 62016–1498; tel. 217/942–6946; Deborah Campbell, Administrator (Total facility includes 38 beds in nursing home–type unit) (Nonreporting) **A**9 10 **S** Quorum Health Group/Quorum Health Resources, Inc., Brentwood, TN — 23 10 60 — — — — — — —

CARTHAGE—Hancock County

MEMORIAL HOSPITAL, South Adams Street, Zip 62321, Mailing Address: P.O. Box 160, Zip 62321–0160; tel. 217/357–3131; Keith E. Heuser, Chief Executive Officer **A**1 9 10 **F**7 8 12 15 19 21 22 28 29 33 34 35 36 40 42 44 49 65 67 71 73 74 **P**5 **S** Quorum Health Group/Quorum Health Resources, Inc., Brentwood, TN — 23 10 59 1101 11 15880 75 8212 3743 141

CENTRALIA—Marion County

ST. MARY'S HOSPITAL, 400 North Pleasant Avenue, Zip 62801–3091; tel. 618/532–6731; James W. McDowell, President and Chief Executive Officer **A**1 2 9 10 **F**1 2 3 7 8 10 12 14 15 16 17 18 19 20 22 26 27 30 31 32 33 34 35 37 39 40 41 42 44 45 46 49 51 52 53 54 55 56 57 58 59 60 63 65 66 67 68 71 73 74 **P**6 **S** SSM Health Care, Saint Louis, MO — 21 10 276 7997 109 86722 557 62987 22699 800

Hospital, Address, Telephone, Administrator, Approval, Facility, and Physician Codes, Health Care System, Network	Classi-fication Codes		Utilization Data					Expense (thousands) of dollars		
★ American Hospital Association (AHA) membership □ Joint Commission on Accreditation of Healthcare Organizations (JCAHO) accreditation + American Osteopathic Healthcare Association (AOHA) membership ○ American Osteopathic Association (AOA) accreditation △ Commission on Accreditation of Rehabilitation Facilities (CARF) accreditation Control codes 61, 63, 64, 71, 72 and 73 indicate hospitals listed by AOHA, but not registered by AHA. For definition of numerical codes, see page A4	Control	Service	Staffed Beds	Admissions	Census	Outpatient Visits	Births	Total	Payroll	Personnel

CENTREVILLE—St. Clair County

⊠ TOUCHETTE REGIONAL HOSPITAL, 5900 Bond Avenue, Zip 62207; tel. 618/332–3060; Robert Klutts, Chief Executive Officer (Nonreporting) A1 9 10	23	10	104	—	—	—	—	—	—	—

CHAMPAIGN—Champaign County

BURNHAM HOSPITAL See Provena Covenant Medical Center, Urbana

□ THE PAVILION, 809 West Church Street, Zip 61820; tel. 217/373–1700; Nina W. Eisner, Chief Executive Officer (Nonreporting) A1 9 10 S Universal Health Services, Inc., King of Prussia, PA	33	22	46	—	—	—	—	—	—	—

CHESTER—Randolph County

□ CHESTER MENTAL HEALTH CENTER, Chester Road, Zip 62233–0031, Mailing Address: Box 31, Zip 62233–0031; tel. 618/826–4571; Stephen L. Hardy, Ph.D., Facility Director (Nonreporting) A1	12	22	314	—	—	—	—	—	—	—
⊠ MEMORIAL HOSPITAL, 1900 State Street, Zip 62233–0609, Mailing Address: P.O. Box 609, Zip 62233–0609; tel. 618/826–4581; Eric Freeburg, Administrator A1 9 10 F3 7 8 11 12 15 16 17 19 20 21 22 23 27 28 30 33 35 36 39 40 41 42 44 49 54 56 58 65 67 71 S Quorum Health Group/Quorum Health Resources, Inc., Brentwood, TN	16	10	40	1152	18	40388	98	11306	5056	19

CHICAGO—Cook County

BERNARD MITCHELL HOSPITAL See University of Chicago Hospitals

⊠ BETHANY HOSPITAL, 3435 West Van Buren Street, Zip 60624–3399; tel. 773/265–7700; Lena Dobbs–Johnson, Chief Executive A1 9 10 F7 8 12 13 14 15 16 17 19 21 22 27 28 30 32 34 35 37 39 40 41 42 44 49 50 51 52 56 57 59 60 61 63 65 67 68 71 73 74 P6 7 8 S Advocate Health Care, Oak Brook, IL **Web address:** www.advocatehealth.com	23	10	102	5750	63	37142	959	40311	16717	390
⊠ CHICAGO LAKESHORE HOSPITAL, 4840 North Marine Drive, Zip 60640–4296; tel. 773/878–9700; Marcia S. Shapiro, Chief Executive Officer A1 3 5 10 F2 3 14 15 17 18 19 21 27 32 34 35 52 53 54 55 56 57 58 59 67 S Columbia/HCA Healthcare Corporation, Nashville, TN	33	22	102	2640	77	—	0	—	—	16

CHICAGO LYING–IN HOSPITAL See University of Chicago Hospitals

□ CHICAGO–READ MENTAL HEALTH CENTER, 4200 North Oak Park Avenue, Zip 60634–1457; tel. 773/794–4000; Thomas Simpatico, M.D., Facility Director and Network System Manager A1 10 F1 2 3 6 11 12 14 15 16 19 20 21 22 26 27 31 35 37 39 41 42 44 46 49 50 52 53 54 55 56 57 58 63 64 65 67 70 71 73	12	22	200	1405	182	0	0	—	25736	518

CHILDREN'S HOSPITAL See University of Chicago Hospitals

⊠ CHILDREN'S MEMORIAL HOSPITAL, 2300 Children's Plaza, Zip 60614–3394; tel. 773/880–4000; Patrick M. Magoon, President and Chief Executive Officer A1 2 3 5 8 9 10 F4 5 10 12 13 15 16 17 18 19 20 21 22 23 25 28 29 30 31 32 34 35 38 39 42 43 44 45 46 47 49 51 52 53 54 55 56 58 59 60 63 65 67 69 70 71 72 73 **Web address:** www.childrensmemorial.org	23	50	218	8356	140	239217	0	207255	83528	—

COLUMBIA GRANT HOSPITAL See Grant Hospital
COLUMBIA MICHAEL REESE HOSPITAL AND MEDICAL CENTER See Michael Reese Hospital and Medical Center

⊠ COLUMBUS HOSPITAL, 2520 North Lakeview Avenue, Zip 60614–1895; tel. 773/388–7300; Sister Theresa Peck, President and Chief Executive Officer A1 3 5 9 10 F2 3 4 5 6 7 8 10 11 12 13 15 16 17 19 21 22 25 26 27 28 29 30 31 32 33 34 35 37 38 39 40 41 42 43 44 45 46 48 49 51 52 54 55 56 57 58 59 60 61 62 63 64 65 66 67 71 72 73 74 P6 8 S Catholic Health Partners, Chicago, IL **Web address:** www.cath–health.org	21	10	227	4914	98	47476	0	81183	29577	592
⊠ COOK COUNTY HOSPITAL, 1835 West Harrison, Zip 60612–3785; tel. 312/633–6000; Lacy Thomas, Director A1 2 3 5 8 9 10 12 F3 4 5 8 9 10 11 12 13 14 15 17 18 19 20 21 22 25 27 28 29 30 31 33 34 35 37 38 39 40 41 42 43 44 45 46 47 49 51 53 54 55 56 57 58 60 61 67 68 70 71 72 73 74 P6 S Cook County Bureau of Health Services, Chicago, IL	13	10	591	25509	393	729019	2019	—	—	4732
□ DOCTORS HOSPITAL OF HYDE PARK, 5800 South Stony Island Avenue, Zip 60637–2099; tel. 773/643–9200; Henry A. Brown, Chief Executive Officer (Nonreporting) A1 10	31	10	200	—	—	—	—	—	—	—
⊠ EDGEWATER MEDICAL CENTER, 5700 North Ashland Avenue, Zip 60660–4086; tel. 773/878–6000; Joann A. Skvarek, Executive Vice President A1 2 10 F4 8 10 14 15 17 19 21 22 26 27 28 30 31 32 33 34 37 39 42 43 44 49 54 56 60 65 67 71	23	10	213	7533	142	26646	0	64364	24011	621
⊠ △ GRANT HOSPITAL, (Formerly Columbia Grant Hospital), 550 Webster Avenue, Zip 60614–9980; tel. 773/883–2000; Richard L. West, President and Chief Executive Officer (Total facility includes 20 beds in nursing home–type unit) A1 7 9 10 F2 3 4 8 10 12 16 17 19 20 21 22 26 27 28 29 30 31 34 35 37 39 41 42 43 44 46 48 49 51 52 54 55 56 57 58 59 64 65 66 71 73 P5	33	10	116	4654	82	31839	0	38435	17389	437
□ HARTGROVE HOSPITAL, 520 North Ridgeway Avenue, Zip 60624–1299; tel. 773/722–3113; Suzanne Barry, Administrator and Chief Operating Officer A1 10 F3 52 53 54 55 56 57 58 59 65 S Hospital Group of America, Wayne, PA	33	22	119	2706	92	10140	0	—	—	201
⊠ △ HOLY CROSS HOSPITAL, 2701 West 68th Street, Zip 60629–1882; tel. 773/471–8000; Mark C. Clement, President and Chief Executive Officer (Total facility includes 37 beds in nursing home–type unit) A1 2 7 9 10 F7 8 10 11 12 13 14 15 16 17 19 21 22 27 28 29 30 32 33 34 35 37 38 39 40 41 42 44 45 46 48 49 56 64 65 67 71 73 74 P6 8	23	10	282	12822	193	145886	1153	103355	58341	1450

spital, Address, Telephone, Administrator, Approval, Facility, and Physician Codes, alth Care System, Network	Classi-fication Codes		Utilization Data						Expense (thousands) of dollars		

American Hospital Association (AHA) membership Joint Commission on Accreditation of Healthcare Organizations (JCAHO) accreditation American Osteopathic Healthcare Association (AOHA) membership American Osteopathic Association (AOA) accreditation Commission on Accreditation of Rehabilitation Facilities (CARF) accreditation Control codes 61, 63, 64, 71, 72 and 73 indicate hospitals listed by AOHA, but not registered by AHA. For definition of numerical codes, see page A4	Control	Service	Staffed Beds	Admissions	Census	Outpatient Visits	Births	Total	Payroll	Personnel
ILLINOIS MASONIC MEDICAL CENTER, 836 West Wellington Avenue, Zip 60657–5193; tel. 773/975–1600; Bruce C. Campbell, President and Chief Executive Officer (Total facility includes 216 beds in nursing home–type unit) **A**1 2 3 5 8 9 10 12 **F**1 3 4 5 6 7 8 10 11 12 13 14 15 16 17 18 19 20 21 22 25 26 27 28 29 30 31 32 33 34 35 38 39 40 41 42 43 44 45 46 47 49 51 52 53 54 55 56 57 58 59 60 61 63 64 65 66 67 68 70 71 72 73 74 **P**5 6 **Web address:** www.immc.org	23	10	544	19189	421	358826	3805	250440	130154	3036
JACKSON PARK HOSPITAL AND MEDICAL CENTER, 7531 Stony Island Avenue, Zip 60649–3993; tel. 773/947–7500; Peter E. Friedell, M.D., President (Nonreporting) **A**1 2 3 9 10	23	10	254	—	—	—	—	—	—	—
JOHNSTON R. BOWMAN HEALTH CENTER See Rush–Presbyterian–St. Luke's Medical Center										
LARABIDA CHILDREN'S HOSPITAL AND RESEARCH CENTER, East 65th Street at Lake Michigan, Zip 60649–1395; tel. 773/363–6700; Paula Kienberger Jaudes, M.D., President and Chief Executive Officer **A**1 5 9 10 **F**5 9 12 13 17 19 20 21 22 25 27 28 29 30 31 34 35 37 38 39 44 45 47 48 49 50 51 52 53 54 58 59 63 65 66 67 71 72 73 **P**6	23	59	62	1353	34	28957	0	24420	11770	369
LORETTO HOSPITAL, 645 South Central Avenue, Zip 60644–9987; tel. 773/626–4300; Steven C. Drucker, President and Chief Executive Officer **A**1 10 **F**2 3 8 15 16 17 18 19 21 22 25 26 27 28 30 33 34 37 41 44 45 46 49 51 52 54 55 57 58 60 65 67 71 **P**5	23	10	183	4753	100	30058	0	29895	15044	467
LOUIS A. WEISS MEMORIAL HOSPITAL, 4646 North Marine Drive, Zip 60640–1501; tel. 773/878–8700; Gregory A. Cierlik, President and Chief Executive Officer (Nonreporting) **A**1 2 3 5 9 10 **S** University of Chicago Health System, Chicago, IL **Web address:** www.weisshospital.org	23	10	200	—	—	—	—	—	—	—
MERCY HOSPITAL AND MEDICAL CENTER, 2525 South Michigan Avenue, Zip 60616–2477; tel. 312/567–2000; Charles B. Van Vorst, President and Chief Executive Officer (Total facility includes 28 beds in nursing home–type unit) **A**1 2 3 5 8 9 10 **F**2 3 4 5 7 8 10 11 12 13 16 17 18 19 20 21 22 25 26 27 28 29 30 31 32 33 34 35 37 38 39 40 41 42 43 44 45 46 47 48 49 51 52 53 54 56 58 59 60 61 63 64 65 66 67 68 71 72 73 **P**5 6 7 **Web address:** www.mercychicago.org	21	10	414	16786	238	—	2864	162219	84085	1797
METHODIST HOSPITAL OF CHICAGO, 5025 North Paulina Street, Zip 60640–2797; tel. 773/271–9040; Steven H. Friedman, Ph.D., Executive Vice President (Total facility includes 17 beds in nursing home–type unit) (Nonreporting) **A**1 2 10	23	10	189	—	—	—	—	—	—	—
METROPOLITAN CHILDREN AND ADOLESCENT INSTITUTE, 1601 Taylor Street, Zip 60612–4397; tel. 312/433–8300; James T. Barter, M.D., Director (Nonreporting)	12	22	83	—	—	—	—	—	—	—
△ MICHAEL REESE HOSPITAL AND MEDICAL CENTER, (Formerly Columbia Michael Reese Hospital and Medical Center), 2929 South Ellis Avenue, Zip 60616–3376; tel. 312/791–2000; Ken Bauer, Chief Executive Officer (Nonreporting) **A**1 2 3 5 7 8 9 10 **S** Doctors Community Healthcare Corporation, Scottsdale, AZ	33	10	523	—	—	—	—	—	—	—
△ MOUNT SINAI HOSPITAL MEDICAL CENTER OF CHICAGO, California Avenue and 15th Street, Zip 60608–1610; tel. 773/542–2000; Benn Greenspan, President and Chief Executive Officer (Nonreporting) **A**1 2 3 5 7 8 9 10 **Web address:** www.sinai.org	23	10	315	—	—	—	—	—	—	—
NORTHWESTERN MEMORIAL HOSPITAL, (Includes Norman and Ida Stone Institute of Psychiatry, 320 East Huron Street; Prentice Women's Hospital, 333 East Superior Street), Superior Street and Fairbanks Court, Zip 60611; tel. 312/926–2000; Gary A. Mecklenburg, President and Chief Executive Officer **A**1 2 3 5 8 9 10 **F**2 3 4 5 7 8 10 12 13 14 15 16 17 18 19 20 21 22 23 24 26 27 28 29 30 31 32 33 35 37 38 39 40 41 42 43 44 45 46 47 49 51 52 53 54 55 56 57 58 59 60 61 63 64 65 66 67 68 70 71 73 74 **P**3 5 6 8 **Web address:** www.nmh.org	23	10	683	38209	448	247316	6213	411836	188978	4871
NORWEGIAN–AMERICAN HOSPITAL, 1044 North Francisco Avenue, Zip 60622–2794; tel. 773/292–8200; Clarence A. Nagelvoort, President and Chief Executive Officer (Nonreporting) **A**1 10	23	10	230	—	—	—	—	—	—	—
OUR LADY OF THE RESURRECTION MEDICAL CENTER, 5645 West Addison Street, Zip 60634–4455; tel. 773/282–7000; Ronald E. Struxness, Executive Vice President and Chief Executive Officer (Total facility includes 66 beds in nursing home–type unit) **A**1 2 9 10 **F**1 2 3 4 6 7 8 9 10 11 12 15 16 17 18 19 20 21 22 24 25 26 27 28 29 30 31 32 33 34 35 36 37 38 39 40 41 42 43 44 45 46 47 48 49 51 52 53 54 55 56 57 58 59 60 61 62 63 64 65 67 68 71 73 74 **P**5 6 7 **S** Resurrection Health Care Corporation, Chicago, IL **Web address:** www.reshealthcare.org	21	10	282	11121	207	115175	0	80040	34254	979
PRENTICE WOMEN'S HOSPITAL See Northwestern Memorial Hospital										
PROVIDENT HOSPITAL OF COOK COUNTY, 500 East 51st Street, Zip 60615–2494; tel. 312/572–2000; Stephanie Wright–Griggs, Chief Operating Officer **A**1 3 10 **F**2 3 4 5 7 8 9 10 11 12 13 14 15 16 17 18 19 20 21 22 23 25 26 28 29 30 31 34 35 38 39 40 41 42 43 44 45 46 47 49 52 60 63 64 65 66 67 68 70 71 72 73 74 **P**6 **S** Cook County Bureau of Health Services, Chicago, IL	13	10	113	5243	70	101386	912	74411	37357	807
△ RAVENSWOOD HOSPITAL MEDICAL CENTER, 4550 North Winchester Avenue, Zip 60640–5205; tel. 773/878–4300; John E. Blair, Chief Executive (Nonreporting) **A**1 2 3 5 6 7 9 10 **S** Advocate Health Care, Oak Brook, IL	23	10	301	—	—	—	—	—	—	—

Hospital, Address, Telephone, Administrator, Approval, Facility, and Physician Codes, Health Care System, Network	Classi-fication Codes		Utilization Data					Expense (thousands) of dollars		
★ American Hospital Association (AHA) membership □ Joint Commission on Accreditation of Healthcare Organizations (JCAHO) accreditation + American Osteopathic Healthcare Association (AOHA) membership ○ American Osteopathic Association (AOA) accreditation △ Commission on Accreditation of Rehabilitation Facilities (CARF) accreditation Control codes 61, 63, 64, 71, 72 and 73 indicate hospitals listed by AOHA, but not registered by AHA. For definition of numerical codes, see page A4	Control	Service	Staffed Beds	Admissions	Census	Outpatient Visits	Births	Total	Payroll	Personnel

Hospital	Control	Service	Staffed Beds	Admissions	Census	Outpatient Visits	Births	Total	Payroll	Personnel
★ △ REHABILITATION INSTITUTE OF CHICAGO, 345 East Superior Street, Zip 60611–4496; tel. 312/908–6000; Wayne M. Lerner, DPH, President and Chief Executive Officer (Total facility includes 40 beds in nursing home–type unit) A1 3 5 7 8 10 F14 15 16 19 21 24 32 34 35 41 45 46 48 49 50 63 64 65 66 67 71 73 74 P3 6 **Web address:** www.rehabchicago.org	23	46	155	1937	111	61664	0	67749	35362	752
★ △ RESURRECTION MEDICAL CENTER, 7435 West Talcott Avenue, Zip 60631–3746; tel. 773/774–8000; Sister Donna Marie, Executive Vice President and Chief Executive Officer (Total facility includes 298 beds in nursing home–type unit) A1 2 3 5 7 9 10 F3 4 7 8 10 15 16 17 19 21 22 24 29 31 32 34 35 37 38 40 41 42 43 44 45 46 48 49 53 54 55 56 57 58 59 60 61 64 65 66 67 71 73 74 P1 5 6 7 S Resurrection Health Care Corporation, Chicago, IL **Web address:** www.reshealthcare.org	21	10	667	16893	502	172661	1230	183664	74872	2252
★ ROSELAND COMMUNITY HOSPITAL, 45 West 111th Street, Zip 60628–4294; tel. 773/995–3000; Oliver D. Krage, President and Chief Executive Officer A1 9 10 F8 11 12 14 16 17 19 21 22 25 26 27 28 30 31 33 34 39 40 42 44 45 46 48 49 51 56 65 67 71 72 73 P1	23	10	128	6394	73	55564	704	32227	14747	465
★ △ RUSH–PRESBYTERIAN–ST. LUKE'S MEDICAL CENTER, (Includes Johnston R. Bowman Health Center, 700 South Paulina, Zip 60612; tel. 312/942–7000; James T. Frankenbach, President), 1653 West Congress Parkway, Zip 60612–3833; tel. 312/942–5000; Leo M. Henikoff, President and Chief Executive Officer (Total facility includes 44 beds in nursing home–type unit) A1 2 3 5 7 8 10 F1 3 4 5 6 7 8 10 11 12 13 14 17 18 19 20 21 22 23 25 26 28 29 30 31 32 33 34 35 37 38 39 40 41 42 43 44 45 46 47 48 49 50 51 52 53 54 55 56 57 58 59 60 61 63 64 65 66 67 68 71 73 74 P6 8 S Rush–Presbyterian–St. Luke's Medical Center, Chicago, IL	23	10	719	25323	501	50359	2189	690468	333265	6727
□ SACRED HEART HOSPITAL, 3240 West Franklin Boulevard, Zip 60624–1599; tel. 773/722–3020; Edward Novak, President and Chief Executive Officer (Nonreporting) A1 10 S Quorum Health Group/Quorum Health Resources, Inc., Brentwood, TN	33	10	96	—	—	—	—	—	—	—
★ SAINT ANTHONY HOSPITAL, 2875 West 19th Street, Zip 60623–3596; tel. 773/521–1710; Sister Theresa Peck, President and Chief Executive Officer A1 3 10 F2 3 7 8 11 12 13 15 16 17 19 21 22 25 26 27 28 30 31 32 33 34 37 38 39 40 41 42 43 44 45 46 48 49 51 52 54 55 56 57 58 59 60 63 64 65 67 68 71 72 73 74 P6 8 S Catholic Health Partners, Chicago, IL **Web address:** www.cath–health.org	21	10	165	7979	111	53471	1962	52467	25198	639
★ SAINT MARY OF NAZARETH HOSPITAL CENTER, 2233 West Division Street, Zip 60622–3086; tel. 312/770–2000; Sister Stella Louise, President and Chief Executive Officer (Total facility includes 20 beds in nursing home–type unit) A1 2 3 9 10 F1 4 7 8 10 11 12 15 16 17 19 21 22 26 27 28 30 31 32 33 34 35 37 39 40 41 42 43 44 45 48 49 52 53 54 55 56 57 58 59 60 63 64 65 67 71 72 73 74 P5 6 8 S Sisters of the Holy Family of Nazareth–Sacred Heart Province, Des Plaines, IL	23	10	325	13791	209	173133	1616	111514	54018	1410
★ △ SCHWAB REHABILITATION HOSPITAL AND CARE NETWORK, 1401 South California Boulevard, Zip 60608–1612; tel. 773/522–2010; Judith C. Waterston, President and Chief Executive Officer (Nonreporting) A1 3 7 8 10	23	46	85	—	—	—	—	—	—	—
★ SHRINERS HOSPITALS FOR CHILDREN–CHICAGO, 2211 North Oak Park Avenue, Zip 60707; tel. 773/622–5400; A. James Spang, Administrator A1 3 5 F5 12 13 15 16 17 19 20 21 27 34 35 39 41 44 45 47 48 49 54 65 66 67 68 71 73 P6 S Shriners Hospitals for Children, Tampa, FL	23	57	60	1684	26	16633	0	—	—	234
★ SOUTH SHORE HOSPITAL, 8012 South Crandon Avenue, Zip 60617–1199; tel. 773/768–0810; Jesus M. Ong, President (Nonreporting) A1 10	23	10	125	—	—	—	—	—	—	—
□ ST. BERNARD HOSPITAL AND HEALTH CARE CENTER, 326 West 64th Street, Zip 60621; tel. 773/962–3900; Sister Elizabeth Van Straten, President and Chief Executive Officer (Nonreporting) A1 10	21	10	194	—	—	—	—	—	—	—
★ ST. ELIZABETH'S HOSPITAL, 1431 North Claremont Avenue, Zip 60622–1791; tel. 773/278–2000; JoAnn Birdzell, President and Chief Executive Officer (Total facility includes 27 beds in nursing home–type unit) A1 2 3 9 10 F2 3 4 5 7 8 10 12 13 14 15 16 17 18 19 22 23 25 26 27 28 29 30 31 32 33 34 35 36 37 39 40 41 42 44 45 46 49 51 52 53 54 55 56 57 58 59 60 64 65 67 70 71 73 P3 5 6 7 8 S Ancilla Systems Inc., Hobart, IN	21	10	224	10734	161	107977	485	74166	34894	979
★ ST. JOSEPH HOSPITAL, 2900 North Lake Shore Drive, Zip 60657–6274; tel. 773/665–3000; Sister Theresa Peck, President and Chief Executive Officer A1 2 3 5 9 10 F2 3 4 5 6 7 8 10 11 12 13 15 16 17 19 21 22 25 26 27 28 29 30 31 32 33 34 35 37 38 39 40 41 42 43 44 45 46 48 49 51 52 54 55 56 57 58 59 60 61 62 63 64 65 66 67 71 72 73 74 P6 8 S Catholic Health Partners, Chicago, IL	21	10	324	13711	228	56883	2411	123566	54251	1495
★ SWEDISH COVENANT HOSPITAL, 5145 North California Avenue, Zip 60625–3688; tel. 773/878–8200; Edward A. Cucci, President and Chief Executive Officer A1 2 3 5 9 10 F4 7 8 10 12 13 15 16 17 18 19 21 22 23 24 26 27 28 29 30 31 32 33 34 35 36 37 39 40 41 42 43 44 46 48 49 51 52 55 56 57 58 60 62 63 64 65 66 67 69 70 71 72 73 P1 5 7 8	21	10	265	11321	209	100910	1359	106251	50434	1556
★ THOREK HOSPITAL AND MEDICAL CENTER, 850 West Irving Park Road, Zip 60613–3099; tel. 773/525–6780; Frank A. Solare, President and Chief Executive Officer A1 10 F8 14 15 17 19 21 22 23 27 28 30 31 33 34 35 36 37 39 41 42 44 49 51 60 65 67 71 73 P8	23	10	140	4763	81	137240	0	47859	20707	487

Hospital, Address, Telephone, Administrator, Approval, Facility, and Physician Codes, Health Care System, Network	Classification Codes		Utilization Data					Expense (thousands) of dollars		
	Control	Service	Staffed Beds	Admissions	Census	Outpatient Visits	Births	Total	Payroll	Personnel

★ American Hospital Association (AHA) membership
☐ Joint Commission on Accreditation of Healthcare Organizations (JCAHO) accreditation
✦ American Osteopathic Healthcare Association (AOHA) membership
◯ American Osteopathic Association (AOA) accreditation
△ Commission on Accreditation of Rehabilitation Facilities (CARF) accreditation
Control codes 61, 63, 64, 71, 72 and 73 indicate hospitals listed by AOHA, but not registered by AHA. For definition of numerical codes, see page A4

Hospital	Control	Service	Staffed Beds	Admissions	Census	Outpatient Visits	Births	Total	Payroll	Personnel
✚ TRINITY HOSPITAL, 2320 East 93rd Street, Zip 60617–9984; tel. 773/978–2000; John N. Schwartz, Chief Executive Officer **A**1 10 **F**2 3 4 7 8 10 11 12 13 15 16 17 19 20 21 22 24 27 28 29 30 32 34 35 37 39 40 41 42 44 45 46 49 51 54 58 59 61 62 65 67 68 71 72 73 74 **P**8 **S** Advocate Health Care, Oak Brook, IL	21	10	217	10058	129	84229	1701	75116	32120	767
✚ UNIVERSITY OF CHICAGO HOSPITALS, (Includes Bernard Mitchell Hospital; Chicago Lying–in Hospital; Children's Hospital), 5841 South Maryland Avenue, Zip 60637–1470; tel. 773/702–1000; Steven Lipstein, President and Chief Operating Officer **A**1 2 3 5 8 9 10 **F**4 5 7 8 9 10 11 12 13 15 16 17 19 20 21 22 23 25 26 27 28 30 31 32 33 34 35 36 37 38 39 40 42 43 44 45 46 47 49 50 51 52 53 54 55 56 57 58 59 60 61 63 65 66 67 68 70 71 73 74 **P**4 5 6 8 **S** University of Chicago Health System, Chicago, IL	23	10	517	24331	406	435275	3269	456272	209072	4781
✚ △ UNIVERSITY OF ILLINOIS AT CHICAGO MEDICAL CENTER, 1740 West Taylor Street, Zip 60612–7236; tel. 312/996–7000; Sidney E. Mitchell, Executive Director **A**1 2 3 5 7 8 10 **F**3 4 5 7 8 10 11 12 14 15 16 17 18 19 20 21 22 23 25 26 27 28 29 30 31 34 35 37 38 39 40 41 42 43 44 45 46 47 48 49 51 52 53 54 55 56 57 58 59 60 61 65 66 67 68 70 71 73 74 **P**4 7 Web address: www.hospital.uic.edu	12	10	437	17066	294	404097	2728	296335	150161	2883
VENCOR HOSPITAL–CHICAGO CENTRAL, (LONG TERM ACUTE CARE), 4058 West Melrose Street, Zip 60641–4797; tel. 773/736–7000; Richard Cerceo, Administrator **A**10 **F**12 16 19 22 26 27 46 65 67 71 **S** Vencor, Incorporated, Louisville, KY Web address: www.vencor.com	33	48	76	348	56	24	0	15647	6300	170
VENCOR HOSPITAL–CHICAGO NORTH, 2544 West Montrose Avenue, Zip 60618–1589; tel. 773/267–2622; Susan Legg, Administrator (Nonreporting) **S** Vencor, Incorporated, Louisville, KY	33	49	111	—	—	—	—	—	—	—
✚ VETERANS AFFAIRS CHICAGO HEALTH CARE SYSTEM–LAKESIDE DIVISION, 333 East Huron Street, Zip 60611–3004; tel. 312/640–2100; Joseph L. Moore, Director (Nonreporting) **A**1 3 5 8 **S** Department of Veterans Affairs, Washington, DC	45	10	252	—	—	—	—	—	—	—
✚ VETERANS AFFAIRS CHICAGO HEALTH CARE SYSTEM–WEST SIDE DIVISION, 820 South Damen Avenue, Zip 60612–3776, Mailing Address: P.O. Box 8195, Zip 60680–8195; tel. 312/666–6500; Joseph L. Moore, Director (Nonreporting) **A**1 2 3 5 **S** Department of Veterans Affairs, Washington, DC	45	10	323	—	—	—	—	—	—	—

CHICAGO HEIGHTS—Cook County

Hospital	Control	Service	Staffed Beds	Admissions	Census	Outpatient Visits	Births	Total	Payroll	Personnel
✚ ST. JAMES HOSPITAL AND HEALTH CENTERS, 1423 Chicago Road, Zip 60411–3483; tel. 708/756–1000; Peter J. Murphy, President and Chief Executive Officer (Total facility includes 101 beds in nursing home–type unit) **A**1 2 10 **F**7 8 10 11 12 14 15 16 17 19 21 22 24 26 27 28 29 30 32 33 34 35 36 37 40 41 42 44 45 46 51 60 64 65 66 67 68 71 73 74 **P**5 6 8 **S** Sisters of St. Francis Health Services, Inc., Mishawaka, IN Web address: www.st jameshhc.org	21	10	332	11433	221	78220	1075	100234	45505	1152

CLINTON—Dewitt County

Hospital	Control	Service	Staffed Beds	Admissions	Census	Outpatient Visits	Births	Total	Payroll	Personnel
★ DR. JOHN WARNER HOSPITAL, 422 West White Street, Zip 61727–2199; tel. 217/935–9571; Hervey Davis, Administrator (Total facility includes 9 beds in nursing home–type unit) **A**9 10 **F**8 11 15 16 19 20 22 32 34 35 44 45 49 54 64 65 66 71	14	10	33	956	13	16213	0	8686	3755	140

DANVILLE—Vermilion County

Hospital	Control	Service	Staffed Beds	Admissions	Census	Outpatient Visits	Births	Total	Payroll	Personnel
✚ PROVENA UNITED SAMARITANS MEDICAL CENTER, (Includes United Samaritans Medical Center, 600 Sager Avenue, Zip 61832; tel. 217/442–6300), 812 North Logan, Zip 61832–3788; tel. 217/443–5000; Dennis J. Doran, President and Chief Executive Officer **A**1 2 9 10 **F**3 7 8 12 14 15 16 17 19 21 22 23 26 28 29 32 33 35 36 37 39 40 41 42 44 45 46 49 52 54 56 57 58 59 60 64 65 67 70 71 72 73 **P**6 7 8 **S** Provena Health, Frankfort, IL Web address: www.provenausmc.org	21	10	308	10406	150	228207	1014	85872	35894	1214
✚ VETERANS AFFAIRS MEDICAL CENTER, 1900 East Main Street, Zip 61832–5198; tel. 217/442–8000; James S. Jones, Director (Total facility includes 175 beds in nursing home–type unit) **A**1 3 5 **F**1 3 6 8 12 14 15 16 17 18 19 20 21 22 24 25 26 27 28 29 30 31 32 34 37 39 41 44 45 46 48 49 51 52 54 55 57 58 59 63 64 65 67 71 73 74 **P**6 **S** Department of Veterans Affairs, Washington, DC	45	10	484	4650	443	183319	0	83059	46573	1201

DE KALB—De Kalb County

Hospital	Control	Service	Staffed Beds	Admissions	Census	Outpatient Visits	Births	Total	Payroll	Personnel
✚ KISHWAUKEE COMMUNITY HOSPITAL, 626 Bethany Road, Zip 60115–4939, Mailing Address: P.O. Box 707, Zip 60115–0707; tel. 815/756–1521; Robert S. Thebeau, President and Chief Executive Officer **A**1 2 9 10 **F**3 7 8 14 15 16 19 21 22 26 28 29 30 31 33 35 36 37 39 40 41 42 44 46 49 52 53 54 55 56 57 58 59 60 65 66 67 71 73 74 **P**3 5 **S** Kishwaukee Health System, De Kalb, IL	23	10	114	4081	37	92236	834	37863	15070	519

DECATUR—Macon County

Hospital	Control	Service	Staffed Beds	Admissions	Census	Outpatient Visits	Births	Total	Payroll	Personnel
✚ DECATUR MEMORIAL HOSPITAL, 2300 North Edward Street, Zip 62526–4192; tel. 217/876–8121; Kenneth L. Smithmier, President and Chief Executive Officer (Total facility includes 69 beds in nursing home–type unit) **A**1 2 3 5 9 10 **F**1 3 7 8 10 12 13 15 16 17 18 19 20 21 22 26 27 28 29 30 32 33 34 35 36 37 39 40 41 42 44 45 49 60 64 65 66 67 70 71 72 73 74 **P**6 8	23	10	237	10008	147	190039	1024	96261	41556	1489
✚ ST. MARY'S HOSPITAL, 1800 East Lake Shore Drive, Zip 62521–3883; tel. 217/464–2966; Keith L. Callahan, Executive Vice President and Administrator (Total facility includes 45 beds in nursing home–type unit) **A**1 3 5 9 10 **F**1 3 7 8 14 15 16 17 18 19 21 22 26 27 28 29 30 32 33 34 35 37 39 40 41 42 44 45 47 49 52 53 54 55 56 57 58 59 60 64 65 67 71 73 **S** Hospital Sisters Health System, Springfield, IL	21	10	176	8053	125	178661	759	59870	27385	985

Hospital, Address, Telephone, Administrator, Approval, Facility, and Physician Codes, Health Care System, Network	Classification Codes		Utilization Data					Expense (thousands) of dollars		
	Control	Service	Staffed Beds	Admissions	Census	Outpatient Visits	Births	Total	Payroll	Personnel

★ American Hospital Association (AHA) membership
□ Joint Commission on Accreditation of Healthcare Organizations (JCAHO) accreditation
+ American Osteopathic Healthcare Association (AOHA) membership
○ American Osteopathic Association (AOA) accreditation
△ Commission on Accreditation of Rehabilitation Facilities (CARF) accreditation
Control codes 61, 63, 64, 71, 72 and 73 indicate hospitals listed by AOHA, but not registered by AHA. For definition of numerical codes, see page A4

DES PLAINES—Cook County

□ FOREST HOSPITAL, 555 Wilson Lane, Zip 60016–4794; tel. 847/635–4100; Richard Michael Ackley, Administrator and Chief Executive Officer (Nonreporting) **A**1 10	31	22	80	—	—	—	—	—	—	—
□ HOLY FAMILY MEDICAL CENTER, 100 North River Road, Zip 60016–1255; tel. 847/297–1800; Sister Patricia Ann Koschalke, President and Chief Executive Officer (Nonreporting) **A**1 2 9 10 **S** Sisters of the Holy Family of Nazareth–Sacred Heart Province, Des Plaines, IL	23	10	183	—	—	—	—	—	—	—

DIXON—Lee County

★ KATHERINE SHAW BETHEA HOSPITAL, 403 East First Street, Zip 61021–3187; tel. 815/288–5531; Darryl L. Vandervort, President and Chief Executive Officer (Total facility includes 15 beds in nursing home–type unit) **A**9 10 **F**1 3 7 8 11 12 14 15 16 17 19 20 21 22 24 26 27 28 29 30 32 33 34 35 36 37 39 40 41 42 44 45 46 49 51 52 53 54 55 56 57 58 59 60 62 63 64 65 66 67 71 73 **P**6 Web address: www.ksbhospital.com	23	10	100	3674	43	79808	366	39605	18701	537

DOWNERS GROVE—Du Page County

⊞ GOOD SAMARITAN HOSPITAL, 3815 Highland Avenue, Zip 60515–1590; tel. 630/275–5900; David M. McConkey, Chief Executive (Total facility includes 30 beds in nursing home–type unit) **A**1 2 9 10 **F**1 4 7 8 10 11 12 13 15 16 17 19 21 22 23 24 25 26 27 28 29 30 31 32 33 34 35 37 38 39 40 41 42 43 44 49 51 52 53 54 55 56 57 58 59 62 63 64 65 66 67 70 71 72 73 74 **P**8 **S** Advocate Health Care, Oak Brook, IL Web address: www.advocatehealth.com	21	10	267	14497	199	147281	2260	144191	56643	1737

DU QUOIN—Perry County

⊞ MARSHALL BROWNING HOSPITAL, 900 North Washington Street, Zip 62832–1230, Mailing Address: P.O. Box 192, Zip 62832–0192; tel. 618/542–2146; William J. Huff, Chief Executive Officer **A**1 9 10 **F**6 7 8 14 15 16 17 19 21 22 33 34 35 36 39 40 44 49 63 64 65 66 71	23	10	33	910	13	23783	36	7923	3388	153

EAST ST. LOUIS—St. Clair County

⊞ ST. MARY'S HOSPITAL, 129 North Eighth Street, Zip 62201–2999; tel. 618/274–1900; Richard J. Mark, President and Chief Executive Officer **A**1 9 10 **F**3 8 12 13 14 15 16 17 18 19 20 22 27 28 29 30 31 32 33 34 37 39 44 45 46 48 49 52 53 54 55 56 58 59 65 67 70 71 73 74 **P**5 **S** Ancilla Systems Inc., Hobart, IN	23	10	119	3866	57	43994	0	30493	15176	514

EFFINGHAM—Effingham County

⊞ ST. ANTHONY'S MEMORIAL HOSPITAL, 503 North Maple Street, Zip 62401–2099; tel. 217/347–1495; Anthony D. Pfitzer, Executive Vice President and Administrator (Total facility includes 13 beds in nursing home–type unit) **A**1 2 9 10 **F**7 8 14 15 16 19 21 22 23 28 32 33 34 35 36 37 40 42 44 49 60 63 64 65 67 71 73 **S** Hospital Sisters Health System, Springfield, IL Web address: www.effingham.net	21	10	146	6487	80	171514	680	43926	16941	528

ELDORADO—Saline County

★ FERRELL HOSPITAL, 1201 Pine Street, Zip 62930–1634; tel. 618/273–3361; E. T. Seely, Administrator (Nonreporting) **A**9 10 **S** Southern Illinois Hospital Services, Carbondale, IL	33	10	51	—	—	—	—	—	—	—

ELGIN—Kane County

□ ELGIN MENTAL HEALTH CENTER, 750 South State Street, Zip 60123–7692; tel. 847/742–1040; Nancy Staples, Administrator **A**1 10 **F**14 15 16 52 65 73	12	22	501	1287	501	0	0	—	45827	1162
⊞ PROVENA SAINT JOSEPH HOSPITAL, 77 North Airlite Street, Zip 60123–4912; tel. 847/695–3200; Larry Narum, President **A**1 2 10 **F**3 7 8 10 12 15 16 17 18 19 21 22 25 26 27 28 29 30 31 32 33 34 35 36 37 39 40 41 42 44 45 46 48 49 52 53 54 55 56 57 58 59 60 64 65 66 67 70 71 72 73 74 **P**5 **S** Provena Health, Frankfort, IL	23	10	186	7215	102	234897	1210	75363	29920	807
⊞ SHERMAN HOSPITAL, 934 Center Street, Zip 60120–2198; tel. 847/742–9800; John A. Graham, President and Chief Executive Officer **A**1 2 9 10 **F**4 7 8 10 11 12 13 15 16 17 18 19 20 21 22 23 25 26 27 28 29 30 31 32 33 34 35 36 37 39 40 41 42 43 44 45 49 55 56 63 64 65 67 68 70 71 72 73 74 **P**5 7 8 Web address: www.shermanhealth.com	23	10	234	10734	119	107882	1905	101750	38092	1240

ELK GROVE VILLAGE—Cook County

⊞ △ ALEXIAN BROTHERS MEDICAL CENTER, 800 Biesterfield Road, Zip 60007–3397; tel. 847/437–5500; Michael J. Schwartz, President and Chief Executive Officer **A**1 2 7 10 **F**3 4 7 8 10 11 12 14 15 16 17 18 19 20 21 22 26 27 28 29 30 31 32 33 34 35 37 39 40 41 42 43 44 45 46 48 49 51 52 53 54 55 56 57 58 59 60 61 64 65·67 70 71 73 **P**2 5 6 **S** Alexian Brothers Health System, Inc., Elk Grove Village, IL Web address: www.alexian.org	21	10	395	18474	275	168662	3119	158999	76418	2143

ELMHURST—Du Page County

⊞ ELMHURST MEMORIAL HOSPITAL, 200 Berteau Avenue, Zip 60126–2989; tel. 630/833–1400; Leo F. Fronza, Jr., President and Chief Executive Officer (Total facility includes 36 beds in nursing home–type unit) **A**1 2 9 10 **F**3 4 7 8 10 11 12 13 15 16 17 18 19 21 22 23 25 27 28 29 30 32 33 34 35 36 37 39 40 41 42 43 44 45 49 51 52 53 54 55 56 57 58 59 60 61 63 64 65 66 67 68 70 71 72 73 **P**3 5 8 Web address: www.emhs.com	23	10	321	16111	225	—	1905	152738	72463	2133

EUREKA—Woodford County

EUREKA COMMUNITY HOSPITAL See BroMenn Healthcare, Normal

Hospital, Address, Telephone, Administrator, Approval, Facility, and Physician Codes, Health Care System, Network	Classi-fication Codes		Utilization Data					Expense (thousands) of dollars		
	Control	Service	Staffed Beds	Admissions	Census	Outpatient Visits	Births	Total	Payroll	Personnel

Key:
* American Hospital Association (AHA) membership
☐ Joint Commission on Accreditation of Healthcare Organizations (JCAHO) accreditation
 American Osteopathic Healthcare Association (AOHA) membership
○ American Osteopathic Association (AOA) accreditation
△ Commission on Accreditation of Rehabilitation Facilities (CARF) accreditation
Control codes 61, 63, 64, 71, 72 and 73 indicate hospitals listed by AOHA, but not registered by AHA. For definition of numerical codes, see page A4

EVANSTON—Cook County

△ EVANSTON NORTHWESTERN HEALTHCARE, (Formerly Evanston Hospital), (Includes Glenbrook Hospital, 2100 Pfingsten Road, Glenview, Zip 60025; tel. 847/657–5800), 2650 Ridge Avenue, Zip 60201–1797; tel. 847/570–2000; Mark R. Neaman, President and Chief Executive Officer (Total facility includes 32 beds in nursing home–type unit) **A**1 2 3 5 7 8 9 10 **F**1 2 3 4 5 7 8 9 10 11 12 14 15 16 17 18 19 20 21 22 23 24 25 26 27 28 29 30 31 32 33 34 35 36 37 38 39 40 41 42 43 44 45 46 48 49 51 52 53 54 55 56 57 58 59 60 61 63 64 65 66 67 68 70 71 72 73 74 **P**1 5 6 7 Web address: www.enh.org	23	10	484	30159	395	888256	4023	291767	124094	3721
ST. FRANCIS HOSPITAL, 355 Ridge Avenue, Zip 60202–3399; tel. 847/316–4000; Kenneth W. Wood, President and Chief Executive Officer (Total facility includes 105 beds in nursing home–type unit) (Nonreporting) **A**1 2 3 5 9 10 **S** Resurrection Health Care Corporation, Chicago, IL	21	10	440	—	—	—	—	—	—	—

EVERGREEN PARK—Cook County

LITTLE COMPANY OF MARY HOSPITAL AND HEALTH CARE CENTERS, 2800 West 95th Street, Zip 60805–2795; tel. 708/422–6200; Sister Kathleen McIntyre, President **A**1 2 9 10 **F**1 2 3 7 8 10 11 12 13 15 16 17 18 19 21 22 25 26 28 29 30 31 32 33 34 35 37 38 39 40 41 42 44 45 46 47 49 51 52 53 54 55 56 57 58 59 60 63 65 67 71 72 73 74 **P**1 7 **S** Little Company of Mary Sisters Healthcare System, Evergreen Park, IL	21	10	323	15780	198	153612	1685	110642	56251	1612

FAIRFIELD—Wayne County

FAIRFIELD MEMORIAL HOSPITAL, 303 N.W. 11th Street, Zip 62837–1203; tel. 618/842–2611; Terry Thompson, Chief Executive Officer (Total facility includes 104 beds in nursing home–type unit) **A**1 9 10 **F**7 8 14 15 16 19 22 26 28 33 34 35 36 37 40 42 44 49 64 65 71 73 **S** Norton Healthcare, Louisville, KY	23	10	185	1393	125	17912	132	11589	4901	259

FLORA—Clay County

CLAY COUNTY HOSPITAL, 700 North Mill Street, Zip 62839–1823, Mailing Address: P.O. Box 280, Zip 62839–0280; tel. 618/662–2131; Tony Schwarm, President (Nonreporting) **A**1 9 10 **S** BJC Health System, Saint Louis, MO Web address: www.wabash.net	13	10	31	—	—	—	—	—	—	—

FOREST PARK—Cook County

RIVEREDGE HOSPITAL, 8311 West Roosevelt Road, Zip 60130–2500; tel. 708/771–7000; Thomas J. Dattalo, Chief Executive Officer **A**1 9 10 **F**1 2 3 12 14 15 16 26 34 46 52 53 54 55 56 57 58 59 **S** Columbia/HCA Healthcare Corporation, Nashville, TN	33	22	96	953	49	6560	0	—	—	—

FREEPORT—Stephenson County

FREEPORT MEMORIAL HOSPITAL, 1045 West Stephenson Street, Zip 61032–4899; tel. 815/235–4131; Dennis L. Hamilton, Chief Executive Officer (Total facility includes 43 beds in nursing home–type unit) **A**1 2 9 10 **F**7 8 10 11 12 14 15 16 17 19 21 22 23 24 28 30 32 33 35 36 37 40 41 42 44 45 49 60 64 65 66 70 71 72 73 **P**3 Web address: www.freeporthealthnet.com	23	10	174	6331	95	128929	614	46334	17718	946

GALENA—Jo Daviess County

★ GALENA–STAUSS HOSPITAL, 215 Summit Street, Zip 61036–1697; tel. 815/777–1340; Roger D. Hervey, Administrator (Total facility includes 60 beds in nursing home–type unit) **A**9 10 **F**1 15 22 28 49 64 65 71	16	10	85	418	62	18619	0	4495	2056	100

GALESBURG—Knox County

GALESBURG COTTAGE HOSPITAL, 695 North Kellogg Street, Zip 61401–2885; tel. 309/343–8131; Dennis J. Renander, President and Chief Executive Officer **A**1 10 **F**2 3 7 8 11 15 17 19 21 22 26 30 32 34 35 36 37 39 40 44 49 52 54 55 56 58 63 64 65 70 71 73 **P**6 8 Web address: www.cottagehospital.com	23	10	182	5075	79	57815	478	42517	18128	639
ST. MARY MEDICAL CENTER, 3333 North Seminary Street, Zip 61401–1299; tel. 309/344–3161; Richard S. Kowalski, Administrator and Chief Executive Officer (Total facility includes 14 beds in nursing home–type unit) **A**1 2 9 10 **F**7 8 11 12 14 15 16 17 19 22 23 25 28 32 33 35 37 40 41 42 44 49 51 64 65 67 70 71 73 74 **P**6 **S** OSF Healthcare System, Peoria, IL	21	10	141	3964	46	48851	400	31812	14622	504

GENESEO—Henry County

HAMMOND–HENRY HOSPITAL, 210 West Elk Street, Zip 61254–1099; tel. 309/944–6431; Nathan C. Olson, President and Chief Executive Officer (Total facility includes 57 beds in nursing home–type unit) (Nonreporting) **A**1 9 10 **S** Brim Healthcare, Inc., Brentwood, TN	16	10	105	—	—	—	—	—	—	—

GENEVA—Kane County

DELNOR–COMMUNITY HOSPITAL, 300 Randall Road, Zip 60134–4200; tel. 630/208–3000; Craig A. Livermore, President and Chief Executive Officer **A**1 2 9 10 **F**6 7 8 10 12 14 15 16 17 19 20 21 22 24 26 28 29 30 32 33 35 37 39 40 41 42 44 45 46 49 53 63 65 66 67 70 71 **P**5 Web address: www.delnor.com	23	10	118	6773	69	80793	1473	58808	24195	751

GIBSON CITY—Ford County

GIBSON AREA HOSPITAL AND HEALTH SERVICES, (Formerly Gibson Community Hospital), (Includes Gibson Community Hospital Nursing Home), 1120 North Melvin Street, Zip 60936–1066, Mailing Address: P.O. Box 429, Zip 60936–0429; tel. 217/784–4251; Craig A. Jesiolowski, Chief Executive Officer (Total facility includes 42 beds in nursing home–type unit) (Nonreporting) **A**1 9 10 **S** Quorum Health Group/Quorum Health Resources, Inc., Brentwood, TN	23	10	82	—	—	—	—	—	—	—

Hospital, Address, Telephone, Administrator, Approval, Facility, and Physician Codes, Health Care System, Network	Classi-fication Codes		Utilization Data					Expense (thousands) of dollars		
★ American Hospital Association (AHA) membership □ Joint Commission on Accreditation of Healthcare Organizations (JCAHO) accreditation + American Osteopathic Healthcare Association (AOHA) membership ○ American Osteopathic Association (AOA) accreditation △ Commission on Accreditation of Rehabilitation Facilities (CARF) accreditation Control codes 61, 63, 64, 71, 72 and 73 indicate hospitals listed by AOHA, but not registered by AHA. For definition of numerical codes, see page A4	Control	Service	Staffed Beds	Admissions	Census	Outpatient Visits	Births	Total	Payroll	Personnel

GLENDALE HEIGHTS—Du Page County

✱ GLENOAKS HOSPITAL, 701 Winthrop Avenue, Zip 60139–1403; tel. 630/545–8000; Brinsley Lewis, Senior Executive Officer **A**1 9 10 **F**3 7 8 11 12 13 14 15 16 17 18 19 21 22 27 28 30 31 32 33 34 35 37 38 39 40 41 42 44 49 51 52 53 54 55 56 57 58 59 65 66 67 68 70 71 73 **P**5 7 **S** Adventist Health System Sunbelt Health Care Corporation, Winter Park, FL **Web address:** www.glenoaks.org — 21 10 116 3349 53 47154 529 32790 11909 420

	21	10	116	3349	53	47154	529	32790	11909	420

GLENVIEW—Cook County

GLENBROOK HOSPITAL See Evanston Northwestern Healthcare, Evanston

GRANITE CITY—Madison County

✱ ST. ELIZABETH MEDICAL CENTER, 2100 Madison Avenue, Zip 62040–4799; tel. 618/798–3000; Ted Eilerman, President (Total facility includes 40 beds in nursing home–type unit) **A**1 9 10 **F**2 3 7 8 10 12 13 14 15 16 17 19 21 22 24 26 28 29 30 32 33 34 35 36 37 39 40 41 42 44 45 46 49 51 52 53 54 55 56 57 58 59 63 64 65 66 67 68 71 73 74 **P**4 7 **Web address:** www.sehs.com

	21	10	185	7062	110	274409	346	61526	25887	936

GREAT LAKES—Lake County

✱ NAVAL HOSPITAL, 3001A Sixth Street, Zip 60088–5230; tel. 847/688–4560; Captain Elaine C. Holmes, MC, USN, Commanding Officer **A**1 2 **F**2 3 8 12 13 14 15 16 17 18 19 20 21 22 24 25 27 28 29 30 34 35 37 39 41 44 45 46 49 51 52 55 56 58 63 65 66 67 68 71 73 74 **P**1 5 8 **S** Department of Navy, Washington, DC

	43	10	75	1651	24	461109	0	84513	57634	1247

GREENVILLE—Bond County

✱ EDWARD A. UTLAUT MEMORIAL HOSPITAL, (Includes Fair Oaks), 200 Health Care Drive, Zip 62246–1156; tel. 618/664–1230; Charles Bouis, President and Chief Executive Officer (Total facility includes 160 beds in nursing home–type unit) (Nonreporting) **A**1 9 10 **Web address:** www.utlaut.com

	23	10	192	—	—	—	—	—	—	—

HARVARD—McHenry County

✱ HARVARD MEMORIAL HOSPITAL, 901 Grant Street, Zip 60033–1898, Mailing Address: P.O. Box 850, Zip 60033–0850; tel. 815/943–5431; Dan Colby, President and Chief Executive Officer (Total facility includes 45 beds in nursing home–type unit) **A**1 10 **F**1 3 4 5 6 7 8 10 13 15 17 18 19 20 21 22 23 24 25 26 27 28 29 30 31 32 33 34 35 36 37 39 40 41 42 43 44 45 46 49 50 51 53 54 55 56 57 58 59 60 61 62 63 64 65 66 67 68 70 71 72 73 74

	23	10	81	815	40	51724	198	9352	4185	136

HARVEY—Cook County

✱ △ INGALLS HOSPITAL, One Ingalls Drive, Zip 60426–3591; tel. 708/333–2300; Robert L. Harris, President and Chief Executive Officer (Total facility includes 39 beds in nursing home–type unit) (Nonreporting) **A**1 2 7 9 10 **Web address:** www.ingalls.org

	23	10	424	—	—	—	—	—	—	—

HAVANA—Mason County

✱ MASON DISTRICT HOSPITAL, 615 North Promenade Street, Zip 62644–0530, Mailing Address: P.O. Box 530, Zip 62644–0530; tel. 309/543–4431; Harry Wolin, Administrator and Chief Executive Officer **A**1 9 10 **F**8 14 15 16 17 19 22 28 32 35 36 37 39 41 44 71 72 73

	16	10	36	580	7	36394	0	7974	3794	154

HAZEL CREST—Cook County

✱ SOUTH SUBURBAN HOSPITAL, 17800 South Kedzie Avenue, Zip 60429–0989; tel. 708/799–8000; Robert Rutkowski, Chief Executive (Total facility includes 41 beds in nursing home–type unit) **A**1 2 9 10 **F**7 8 10 12 14 15 16 17 19 21 22 25 27 28 30 32 33 34 35 37 40 41 42 44 49 60 63 64 67 71 73 **P**1 7 **S** Advocate Health Care, Oak Brook, IL **Web address:** www.advocatehealth.com

	23	10	185	11227	129	92776	1436	86739	38949	932

HERRIN—Williamson County

✱ HERRIN HOSPITAL, 201 South 14th Street, Zip 62948–3631; tel. 618/942–2171; Virgil Hannig, Senior Vice President and Administrator (Total facility includes 13 beds in nursing home–type unit) **A**1 9 10 **F**3 4 5 6 7 8 10 12 13 14 15 16 17 18 19 20 21 22 23 24 25 26 27 28 30 31 32 33 35 36 37 39 41 42 44 45 46 47 48 49 51 60 61 63 64 65 66 67 70 71 72 73 74 **P**7 **S** Southern Illinois Hospital Services, Carbondale, IL **Web address:** www.sih.net

	23	10	92	3208	50	49429	0	32680	15866	369

HIGHLAND—Madison County

✱ ST. JOSEPH'S HOSPITAL, 1515 Main Street, Zip 62249–1656; tel. 618/654–7421; Anthony G. Mastrangelo, Executive Vice President and Administrator (Total facility includes 30 beds in nursing home–type unit) **A**1 9 10 **F**8 12 17 19 21 22 27 28 29 30 31 32 33 34 35 36 37 39 41 42 44 46 49 54 63 64 65 66 67 71 73 74 **P**1 **S** Hospital Sisters Health System, Springfield, IL **Web address:** www.stjosephs–highland.org

	21	10	76	1306	32	39155	0	13033	5827	227

HIGHLAND PARK—Lake County

✱ HIGHLAND PARK HOSPITAL, 718 Glenview Avenue, Zip 60035–2497; tel. 847/432–8000; Ronald G. Spaeth, President and Chief Executive Officer (Total facility includes 28 beds in nursing home–type unit) **A**1 2 9 10 **F**1 3 4 7 8 10 11 12 14 15 16 17 19 20 21 22 23 24 26 28 29 30 32 33 34 35 36 39 40 41 42 43 44 45 46 49 52 53 54 55 56 57 58 59 60 61 63 64 65 67 70 71 73 74 **P**5 7 8 **Web address:** www.hphosp.org

	23	10	191	7327	81	221397	1830	102251	38872	988

Hospital, Address, Telephone, Administrator, Approval, Facility, and Physician Codes, Health Care System, Network	Classification Codes		Utilization Data					Expense (thousands) of dollars		
American Hospital Association (AHA) membership; Joint Commission on Accreditation of Healthcare Organizations (JCAHO) accreditation; American Osteopathic Healthcare Association (AOHA) membership; American Osteopathic Association (AOA) accreditation; Commission on Accreditation of Rehabilitation Facilities (CARF) accreditation; Control codes 61, 63, 64, 71, 72 and 73 indicate hospitals listed by AOHA, but not registered by AHA. For definition of numerical codes, see page A4	Control	Service	Staffed Beds	Admissions	Census	Outpatient Visits	Births	Total	Payroll	Personnel

HILLSBORO—Montgomery County
HILLSBORO AREA HOSPITAL, 1200 East Tremont Street, Zip 62049–1900; tel. 217/532–6111; Rex H. Brown, President (Total facility includes 40 beds in nursing home–type unit) A1 9 10 F7 8 12 14 15 16 17 19 20 21 22 26 28 30 32 33 34 35 37 39 40 42 44 45 49 64 65 66 67 70 71 73 P8 S Brim Healthcare, Inc., Brentwood, TN — 23 10 95 1583 66 32606 97 9410 4500 182

HINES—Cook County
JOHN J. MADDEN MENTAL HEALTH CENTER, 1200 South First Avenue, Zip 60141; tel. 708/338–7202; Ugo Formigoni, Metro–West Network Manager A1 10 F14 15 52 — 12 22 163 2162 167 0 0 — 18214 390

△ VETERANS AFFAIRS EDWARD HINES, JR. HOSPITAL, Fifth Avenue & Roosevelt Road, Zip 60141–5000, Mailing Address: P.O. Box 5000, Zip 60141–5000; tel. 708/202–8387; John J. DeNardo, Director (Total facility includes 240 beds in nursing home–type unit) (Nonreporting) A1 3 5 7 8 S Department of Veterans Affairs, Washington, DC — 45 10 957 — — — —

HINSDALE—Du Page County
△ HINSDALE HOSPITAL, 120 North Oak Street, Zip 60521–3890; tel. 630/856–9000; Ernie W. Sadau, President and Chief Executive Officer A1 2 3 5 7 9 10 F2 3 4 5 6 7 8 10 11 12 13 15 16 17 18 19 20 21 22 25 26 28 29 30 31 32 33 34 35 37 38 39 40 41 42 43 44 45 46 47 48 49 51 52 53 55 56 57 58 59 60 61 63 64 65 66 67 68 70 71 72 73 74 P5 6 7 S Adventist Health System Sunbelt Health Care Corporation, Winter Park, FL
Web address: www.hinsdalehospital.org — 21 10 339 13965 166 — 2860 169299 63668 1778

R. M. L. SPECIALTY HOSPITAL, 5601 South County Line Road, Zip 60521–8900; tel. 708/783–5800; James Richard Prister, President A1 10 F12 14 16 19 22 27 65 71 73 — 23 10 45 293 31 20 0 13845 5670 182

HOFFMAN ESTATES—Cook County
ALEXIAN BROTHERS BEHAVIORAL HEALTH HOSPITAL, (Formerly Columbia Woodland Hospital), 1650 Moon Lake Boulevard, Zip 60194–5000; tel. 847/882–1600; Mark A. Frey, President and Chief Executive Officer (Nonreporting) A1 10 S Alexian Brothers Health System, Inc., Elk Grove Village, IL — 21 22 94 — — — — — — —

ST. ALEXIUS MEDICAL CENTER, (Formerly Hoffman Estates Medical Center), 1555 Barrington Road, Zip 60194; tel. 847/843–2000; Edward M. Goldberg, President and Chief Executive Officer (Total facility includes 23 beds in nursing home–type unit) A1 2 9 10 F1 2 3 4 7 8 10 11 12 14 15 16 17 19 21 22 27 30 34 35 37 39 40 41 42 44 45 46 49 51 52 53 54 55 56 57 58 61 63 64 65 67 70 71 73 74 P1 2 5 7 8 S Alexian Brothers Health System, Inc., Elk Grove Village, IL — 33 10 195 10917 120 80944 2491 — — 794

HOOPESTON—Vermilion County
HOOPESTON COMMUNITY MEMORIAL HOSPITAL, 701 East Orange Street, Zip 60942–1871; tel. 217/283–5531; Frank T. Caruso, Chief Executive Officer (Total facility includes 75 beds in nursing home–type unit) (Nonreporting) A1 9 10 — 23 10 97 — — — — — — —

HOPEDALE—Tazewell County
HOPEDALE MEDICAL COMPLEX, 107 Tremont Street, Zip 61747; tel. 309/449–3321; L. J. Rossi, M.D., Chief Executive Officer (Total facility includes 95 beds in nursing home–type unit) (Nonreporting) A9 10 — 23 10 119 — — — — — — —

JACKSONVILLE—Morgan County
PASSAVANT AREA HOSPITAL, 1600 West Walnut Street, Zip 62650–1136; tel. 217/245–9541; Chester A. Wynn, President and Chief Executive Officer (Total facility includes 15 beds in nursing home–type unit) A1 2 9 10 F4 7 8 15 16 17 19 21 22 28 29 30 33 35 36 37 39 40 41 42 44 45 46 49 51 53 57 59 60 63 65 66 67 70 71 72 73 P8
Web address: www.passavanthospital.com — 23 10 116 4129 57 64468 391 39627 16961 536

JERSEYVILLE—Jersey County
JERSEY COMMUNITY HOSPITAL, 400 Maple Summit Road, Zip 62052–2028, Mailing Address: P.O. Box 426, Zip 62052–0426; tel. 618/498–6402; Lawrence P. Bear, Administrator A1 9 10 F3 7 8 15 16 17 19 21 22 24 27 28 30 31 33 34 35 36 37 39 40 41 42 44 46 49 65 66 67 71 73 74 — 16 10 67 2104 17 26299 223 13082 5468 198

JOLIET—Will County
△ PROVENA SAINT JOSEPH MEDICAL CENTER, 333 North Madison Street, Zip 60435–6595; tel. 815/725–7133 A1 2 7 9 10 F3 4 7 8 10 11 12 13 14 15 16 17 18 19 20 21 22 24 25 26 27 28 29 30 31 32 33 34 35 37 39 40 41 42 43 44 45 46 47 48 49 51 52 53 54 55 56 57 58 59 60 63 64 65 66 67 68 70 71 73 74 P1 4 6 7 S Provena Health, Frankfort, IL — 21 10 412 17922 267 440292 2080 175601 74016 1818

SILVER CROSS HOSPITAL, 1200 Maple Road, Zip 60432–1497; tel. 815/740–1100; Paul Pawlak, President and Chief Executive Officer A1 2 9 10 F1 2 3 4 5 6 7 8 9 10 11 12 13 14 15 16 17 18 19 20 21 22 23 24 25 26 27 28 29 30 32 33 34 35 36 37 38 39 40 41 42 43 44 45 46 47 48 49 50 51 52 53 54 55 56 57 58 59 60 61 62 63 64 65 66 67 68 69 70 71 73 74 P5 6 7 8
Web address: www.silvercross.org — 23 10 227 9684 110 136921 1286 86498 34364 825

KANKAKEE—Kankakee County
PROVENA ST. MARY'S HOSPITAL, 500 West Court Street, Zip 60901–3661; tel. 815/937–2400; Paula Jacobi, President and Chief Executive Officer (Total facility includes 24 beds in nursing home–type unit) A1 2 10 F1 3 4 5 7 8 10 12 15 16 17 19 21 22 23 24 26 27 28 29 30 31 32 33 35 37 39 40 41 42 43 44 45 46 49 50 51 52 53 54 55 56 57 58 59 60 61 63 64 65 69 70 71 73 74 P8 S Provena Health, Frankfort, IL
Web address: www.provena–stmarys.com — 21 10 197 6907 95 186236 589 64060 23663 957

Hospital, Address, Telephone, Administrator, Approval, Facility, and Physician Codes, Health Care System, Network	Classi-fication Codes		Utilization Data					Expense (thousands) of dollars		
★ American Hospital Association (AHA) membership □ Joint Commission on Accreditation of Healthcare Organizations (JCAHO) accreditation + American Osteopathic Healthcare Association (AOHA) membership ○ American Osteopathic Association (AOA) accreditation △ Commission on Accreditation of Rehabilitation Facilities (CARF) accreditation Control codes 61, 63, 64, 71, 72 and 73 indicate hospitals listed by AOHA, but not registered by AHA. For definition of numerical codes, see page A4	Control	Service	Staffed Beds	Admissions	Census	Outpatient Visits	Births	Total	Payroll	Personnel
✠ △ RIVERSIDE MEDICAL CENTER, 350 North Wall Street, Zip 60901–0749; tel. 815/933–1671; Dennis C. Millirons, President and Chief Executive Officer (Total facility includes 100 beds in nursing home–type unit) **A**1 2 7 9 10 **F**2 3 6 7 8 10 11 12 13 14 15 16 17 18 19 20 21 23 24 26 27 28 29 30 31 32 33 34 35 36 37 39 40 41 42 44 45 46 48 49 50 52 53 54 55 56 57 58 59 60 61 62 63 64 65 66 67 68 70 71 73 74 **P**5 8	23	10	365	9207	240	240301	1029	108494	46482	1388
KEWANEE—Henry County										
✠ KEWANEE HOSPITAL, 719 Elliott Street, Zip 61443–2711, Mailing Address: P.O. Box 747, Zip 61443–0747; tel. 309/853–3361; William H. Thieben, Chief Executive Officer (Total facility includes 14 beds in nursing home–type unit) **A**1 9 10 **F**7 8 11 12 15 16 19 22 24 27 30 32 33 34 35 36 37 39 40 42 44 46 49 64 65 66 67 71 73 74 **P**6 8 **Web address:** www.kewaneehospital.com	23	10	63	2056	26	47938	168	25605	11481	385
LA GRANGE—Cook County										
✠ LA GRANGE MEMORIAL HOSPITAL, 5101 South Willow Spring Road, Zip 60525–2680; tel. 708/352–1200; Todd S. Werner, Senior Executive Officer (Total facility includes 51 beds in nursing home–type unit) **A**1 2 3 5 9 10 **F**4 5 7 8 10 11 12 13 15 16 17 19 20 21 22 26 27 28 29 30 31 34 35 37 39 40 41 42 43 44 45 46 49 53 54 55 56 57 58 59 60 61 63 64 65 66 67 70 71 73 74 **P**1 **S** Adventist Health System Sunbelt Health Care Corporation, Winter Park, FL	33	10	175	10015	141	70006	900	82183	39978	1090
LAKE FOREST—Lake County										
✠ △ LAKE FOREST HOSPITAL, 660 North Westmoreland Road, Zip 60045–1696; tel. 847/234–5600; William G. Ries, President (Total facility includes 88 beds in nursing home–type unit) **A**1 2 7 10 **F**1 3 5 7 8 12 15 17 19 21 22 24 25 26 28 29 30 31 32 33 34 35 36 37 39 40 41 42 43 44 45 46 49 51 54 56 58 60 61 63 64 65 66 67 70 71 73 74 **P**1 6 7 **Web address:** www.lakeforesthospital.com	23	10	204	7394	155	203628	2366	101549	48516	965
LAWRENCEVILLE—Lawrence County										
★ LAWRENCE COUNTY MEMORIAL HOSPITAL, 2200 West State Street, Zip 62439–1853; tel. 618/943–1000; Gerald E. Waldroup, Administrator **A**9 10 **F**8 11 14 15 17 18 19 22 28 29 30 33 34 35 37 39 40 44 46 49 52 53 54 55 56 57 59 63 65 67 71 73	13	10	58	1332	18	29837	44	7920	3449	157
LEMONT—Cook County										
□ ROCK CREEK CENTER, 40 Timberline Drive, Zip 60439; tel. 630/257–3636; Wendy Mamoon, Chief Executive Officer (Nonreporting) **A**1 10 **Web address:** www.rockcreek–hosp.com	32	22	60	—	—	—	—	—	—	—
LIBERTYVILLE—Lake County										
✠ CONDELL MEDICAL CENTER, 801 South Milwaukee Avenue on Condell Drive, Zip 60048–3199; tel. 847/362–2900; Eugene Pritchard, President **A**1 2 10 **F**1 3 7 8 10 12 13 14 15 16 17 18 19 20 21 22 24 25 28 29 32 33 34 35 37 39 40 41 42 44 45 46 49 52 54 55 56 57 59 65 66 67 70 71 72 73 74 **P**1 5 7 **Web address:** www.condell.org	23	10	175	11565	108	281814	1619	90031	40208	1246
LINCOLN—Logan County										
✠ ABRAHAM LINCOLN MEMORIAL HOSPITAL, 315 8th Street, Zip 62656–2698; tel. 217/732–2161; Forrest G. Hester, President and Chief Executive Officer **A**1 9 10 **F**2 8 11 12 15 16 17 18 19 21 22 27 33 34 35 37 39 40 41 42 44 46 49 52 53 54 56 58 65 66 71 72 73 **P**3 5 **S** Memorial Health System, Springfield, IL **Web address:** www.almh.com	23	10	60	1877	20	45081	245	17063	7612	265
LINCOLN DEVELOPMENTAL CENTER, 861 South State Street, Zip 62656–2599; tel. 217/735–2361; Martin Downs, Facility Director (Nonreporting)	12	62	450	—	—	—	—	—	—	—
LITCHFIELD—Montgomery County										
✠ ST. FRANCIS HOSPITAL, 1215 Franciscan Drive, Zip 62056, Mailing Address: P.O. Box 1215, Zip 62056–1215; tel. 217/324–2191; Michael Sipkoski, Executive Vice President and Administrator (Total facility includes 35 beds in nursing home–type unit) **A**1 9 10 **F**7 8 11 14 15 16 19 22 30 32 33 35 37 39 40 41 44 45 63 64 65 67 71 **S** Hospital Sisters Health System, Springfield, IL	21	10	97	2927	40	58058	307	19807	8774	313
MACOMB—McDonough County										
✠ MCDONOUGH DISTRICT HOSPITAL, 525 East Grant Street, Zip 61455–3318; tel. 309/833–4101; Stephen R. Hopper, President and Chief Executive Officer (Total facility includes 16 beds in nursing home–type unit) **A**1 2 9 10 **F**1 3 7 8 14 15 16 19 21 22 23 24 26 28 29 30 32 33 35 37 39 40 41 42 44 45 53 56 57 58 64 65 67 71 73 74 **P**7 8 **Web address:** www.mdh.org	16	10	120	3955	51	42630	308	33056	15766	523
MARION—Williamson County										
✠ MARION MEMORIAL HOSPITAL, 917 West Main Street, Zip 62959–1836; tel. 618/997–5341; Ronald Seal, President and Chief Executive Officer **A**1 9 10 **F**7 8 11 12 14 15 16 19 21 22 28 36 40 41 42 44 45 48 49 63 71 **P**8 **S** Community Health Systems, Inc., Brentwood, TN	33	10	84	3443	38	69723	392	21563	10359	318
✠ △ VETERANS AFFAIRS MEDICAL CENTER, 2401 West Main Street, Zip 62959–1194; tel. 618/997–5311; Earl F. Falast, Medical Center Director (Total facility includes 60 beds in nursing home–type unit) **A**1 7 **F**3 8 12 16 17 19 21 22 25 26 27 28 30 31 32 33 34 35 37 39 41 42 44 46 49 51 52 54 56 57 58 63 64 65 67 71 73 74 **S** Department of Veterans Affairs, Washington, DC **Web address:** www.za.va.gov	45	10	99	2674	95	182700	0	50850	32166	679

Hospital, Address, Telephone, Administrator, Approval, Facility, and Physician Codes, Health Care System, Network	Classi-fication Codes		Utilization Data					Expense (thousands) of dollars		
★ American Hospital Association (AHA) membership ☐ Joint Commission on Accreditation of Healthcare Organizations (JCAHO) accreditation + American Osteopathic Healthcare Association (AOHA) membership ○ American Osteopathic Association (AOA) accreditation △ Commission on Accreditation of Rehabilitation Facilities (CARF) accreditation Control codes 61, 63, 64, 71, 72 and 73 indicate hospitals listed by AOHA, but not registered by AHA. For definition of numerical codes, see page A4	Control	Service	Staffed Beds	Admissions	Census	Outpatient Visits	Births	Total	Payroll	Personnel

MARYVILLE—Madison County

| ✖ ANDERSON HOSPITAL, 6800 State Route 162, Zip 62062–8500, Mailing Address: P.O. Box 1000, Zip 62062–1000; tel. 618/288–5711; R. Coert Shepard, President **A**1 9 10 **F**4 7 8 10 12 14 15 16 17 19 21 22 24 26 28 29 30 31 32 33 34 35 36 37 39 40 42 44 45 46 49 56 63 64 65 66 67 70 71 73 74 **P**5 | 23 | 10 | 115 | 5045 | 50 | 71213 | 903 | 37694 | 17040 | 477 |

MATTOON—Coles County

| ✖ SARAH BUSH LINCOLN HEALTH CENTER, 1000 Health Center Drive, Zip 61938–0372, Mailing Address: P.O. Box 372, Zip 61938–0372; tel. 217/258–2525; Gary L. Barnett, President and Chief Executive Officer (Total facility includes 23 beds in nursing home–type unit) **A**1 2 9 10 **F**7 8 11 12 14 15 16 19 20 21 22 23 24 26 28 30 31 32 33 35 37 40 41 42 44 45 46 49 52 53 54 55 56 57 58 59 60 63 64 65 66 67 70 71 73 74 **P**4 5 6 7
Web address: www.sarahbush.org | 23 | 10 | 174 | 6821 | 74 | 201633 | 891 | 77454 | 35760 | 973 |

MAYWOOD—Cook County

| ☐ LOYOLA UNIVERSITY MEDICAL CENTER, 2160 South First Avenue, Zip 60153–5585; tel. 708/216–9000; Anthony L. Barbato, M.D., President and Chief Executive Officer **A**1 2 3 5 8 9 10 **F**3 4 5 7 8 9 10 11 12 13 15 16 17 19 20 21 22 23 24 25 26 28 30 31 32 33 34 35 37 38 39 40 41 42 43 44 45 46 47 48 49 50 51 52 53 54 55 56 57 58 59 60 61 63 65 66 67 68 70 71 73 74 **P**3
Web address: www.lumc.edu | 23 | 10 | 541 | 19220 | 323 | 481115 | 1687 | 391958 | 168600 | 4109 |

MCHENRY—McHenry County

| ☐ △ NORTHERN ILLINOIS MEDICAL CENTER, 4201 Medical Center Drive, Zip 60050–9506; tel. 815/344–5000; Paul E. Laudick, President and Chief Executive Officer (Total facility includes 18 beds in nursing home–type unit) **A**1 2 7 9 10 **F**4 7 8 10 12 14 15 16 17 19 20 22 24 25 26 27 28 29 30 32 33 34 35 36 37 39 40 41 42 44 45 46 48 49 52 53 54 55 56 57 58 59 60 64 65 67 70 71 73 74 **P**5 7 | 23 | 10 | 148 | 7622 | 96 | 130623 | 934 | 82137 | 33507 | 848 |

MCLEANSBORO—Hamilton County

| ✖ HAMILTON MEMORIAL HOSPITAL DISTRICT, 611 South Marshall Avenue, Zip 62859–1297; tel. 618/643–2361; Randall W. Dauby, Interim Administrator (Total facility includes 60 beds in nursing home–type unit) **A**1 9 10 **F**15 16 19 21 22 28 30 32 34 35 44 45 46 49 64 65 71 **P**6
Web address: www.mcleansboro.com | 16 | 10 | 91 | 1094 | 85 | 20493 | — | 7340 | 3914 | 104 |

MELROSE PARK—Cook County

| ✖ GOTTLIEB MEMORIAL HOSPITAL, 701 West North Avenue, Zip 60160–1692; tel. 708/681–3200; John Morgan, President (Total facility includes 32 beds in nursing home–type unit) **A**1 5 9 10 **F**4 5 7 8 10 11 12 14 15 16 17 18 19 21 22 26 27 28 29 30 31 32 33 34 35 37 39 40 41 42 43 44 45 49 63 64 65 66 67 70 71 73 74 **P**6 8 | 23 | 10 | 206 | 9297 | 125 | 165961 | 1306 | 80477 | — | 1103 |
| ☐ △ WESTLAKE COMMUNITY HOSPITAL, 1225 Lake Street, Zip 60160–4000; tel. 708/681–3000; Kenneth W. Wood, Chief Executive Officer (Total facility includes 17 beds in nursing home–type unit) (Nonreporting) **A**1 2 3 7 10 **S** Resurrection Health Care Corporation, Chicago, IL | 23 | 10 | 239 | — | — | — | — | — | — | — |

MENDOTA—La Salle County

| ✖ MENDOTA COMMUNITY HOSPITAL, 1315 Memorial Drive, Zip 61342–1496; tel. 815/539–7461; Susan Urso, Administrator (Total facility includes 14 beds in nursing home–type unit) **A**1 9 10 **F**3 7 8 12 14 15 16 17 19 21 22 28 29 30 32 36 37 39 40 41 42 44 45 49 51 64 65 67 71 73
Web address: www.mendotahospital.com | 23 | 10 | 57 | 1639 | 17 | 63393 | 111 | 12567 | 6369 | 214 |

METROPOLIS—Massac County

| ✖ MASSAC MEMORIAL HOSPITAL, 28 Chick Street, Zip 62960–2481, Mailing Address: P.O. Box 850, Zip 62960–0850; tel. 618/524–2176; Mark Edwards, Chief Executive Officer **A**1 9 10 **F**12 19 21 22 32 33 37 44 71 **S** Norton Healthcare, Louisville, KY | 16 | 10 | 38 | 1353 | 15 | 22457 | 0 | 9271 | 3947 | 169 |

MOLINE—Rock Island County

TRINITY MEDICAL CENTER–SEVENTH STREET CAMPUS See Trinity Medical Center–West Campus, Rock Island

MONMOUTH—Warren County

| COMMUNITY MEMORIAL HOSPITAL, 1000 West Harlem Avenue, Zip 61462–1099; tel. 309/734–3141; Donald G. Brown, Chief Executive Officer (Total facility includes 35 beds in nursing home–type unit) **A**9 10 **F**8 12 14 15 16 17 18 19 20 21 25 26 28 30 32 33 39 41 44 45 46 49 51 63 64 65 67 70 71 73 | 23 | 10 | 58 | 1341 | 38 | 20403 | — | 8438 | 3784 | 156 |

MONTICELLO—Piatt County

| ✖ JOHN AND MARY KIRBY HOSPITAL, 1111 North State Street, Zip 61856–1116; tel. 217/762–2115; Thomas D. Dixon, Administrator **A**1 9 10 **F**2 3 8 9 14 15 16 22 28 30 32 33 41 44 45 46 51 52 53 54 55 56 57 58 59 64 65 67 69 70 71 72 73 | 23 | 10 | 16 | 408 | 6 | 24566 | 0 | 5171 | 2677 | 83 |

MORRIS—Grundy County

| ✖ MORRIS HOSPITAL, 150 West High Street, Zip 60450–1497; tel. 815/942–2932; Clifford L. Corbett, President and Chief Executive Officer **A**1 2 9 10 **F**7 8 15 16 19 21 22 27 30 34 35 36 37 39 40 41 44 65 70 71 73
Web address: www.morrishospital.org | 23 | 10 | 82 | 3220 | 34 | 58254 | 322 | 38396 | 16665 | 404 |

MORRISON—Whiteside County

| ★ MORRISON COMMUNITY HOSPITAL, 303 North Jackson Street, Zip 61270–3042; tel. 815/772–4003; Mark F. Fedyk, Administrator (Total facility includes 38 beds in nursing home–type unit) (Nonreporting) **A**9 10 **S** Mercy Health Services, Farmington Hills, MI | 16 | 10 | 60 | — | — | — | — | — | — | — |

Hospital, Address, Telephone, Administrator, Approval, Facility, and Physician Codes, Health Care System, Network	Classification Codes		Utilization Data					Expense (thousands) of dollars		
	Control	Service	Staffed Beds	Admissions	Census	Outpatient Visits	Births	Total	Payroll	Personnel

★ American Hospital Association (AHA) membership
□ Joint Commission on Accreditation of Healthcare Organizations (JCAHO) accreditation
+ American Osteopathic Healthcare Association (AOHA) membership
○ American Osteopathic Association (AOA) accreditation
△ Commission on Accreditation of Rehabilitation Facilities (CARF) accreditation
Control codes 61, 63, 64, 71, 72 and 73 indicate hospitals listed by AOHA, but not registered by AHA. For definition of numerical codes, see page A4

MOUNT CARMEL—Wabash County

⊞ WABASH GENERAL HOSPITAL DISTRICT, 1418 College Drive, Zip 62863–2638; tel. 618/262–8621; James R. Farris, CHE, Chief Executive Officer **A**1 9 10 **F**12 15 16 19 22 30 32 33 34 35 39 41 42 44 45 46 49 65 67 71 73 **S** Norton Healthcare, Louisville, KY

| | 16 | 10 | 56 | 1270 | 16 | 24167 | 0 | 10127 | 4433 | 158 |

MOUNT VERNON—Jefferson County

★ CROSSROADS COMMUNITY HOSPITAL, 8 Doctors Park Road, Zip 62864–6224; tel. 618/244–5500; Donald J. Frederic, Chief Executive Officer (Nonreporting) **A**9 10 **S** Community Health Systems, Inc., Brentwood, TN

| | 33 | 10 | 37 | — | — | — | — | — | — | — |

⊞ GOOD SAMARITAN REGIONAL HEALTH CENTER, 605 North 12th Street, Zip 62864–2899; tel. 618/242–4600; Leo F. Childers, Jr., FACHE, President (Total facility includes 14 beds in nursing home–type unit) **A**1 2 9 10 **F**4 7 8 10 12 14 15 16 17 18 19 20 21 22 23 24 25 28 29 30 31 32 33 34 35 37 39 40 41 42 44 45 46 49 51 57 58 60 64 65 67 71 73 74 **P**2 3 4 5 6 7 8 **S** SSM Health Care, Saint Louis, MO
Web address: www.stmarys–goodsamaritan.com

| | 21 | 10 | 127 | 5142 | 66 | 80824 | 588 | 59250 | 26252 | 864 |

MURPHYSBORO—Jackson County

⊞ ST. JOSEPH MEMORIAL HOSPITAL, 2 South Hospital Drive, Zip 62966–3333; tel. 618/687–3157; Betty Gaffney, Senior Vice President and Administrator **A**1 9 10 **F**7 8 15 16 17 19 22 26 29 31 32 33 34 40 44 46 49 56 65 67 68 71 73 74 **P**7 **S** Southern Illinois Hospital Services, Carbondale, IL
Web address: www.sih.net

| | 23 | 10 | 59 | 1945 | 24 | 21348 | 207 | 13730 | 5797 | 239 |

NAPERVILLE—Du Page County

⊞ EDWARD HOSPITAL, 801 South Washington Street, Zip 60566–7060; tel. 630/355–0450; Pamela Meyer Davis, President and Chief Executive Officer (Total facility includes 14 beds in nursing home–type unit) **A**1 2 10 **F**2 3 4 7 8 10 12 13 14 15 16 17 18 19 22 24 25 26 28 29 30 31 32 33 34 35 37 39 40 41 42 43 44 45 46 49 51 52 53 54 55 56 57 58 59 60 61 64 65 66 67 70 71 72 73 74 **P**1 5 6 8
Web address: www.edward.org

| | 23 | 10 | 155 | 10790 | 121 | 176417 | 2759 | 114528 | 44626 | 1464 |

NASHVILLE—Washington County

⊞ WASHINGTON COUNTY HOSPITAL, 705 South Grand Street, Zip 62263; tel. 618/327–8236; Michael P. Ellermann, Administrator (Total facility includes 27 beds in nursing home–type unit) **A**1 9 10 **F**3 4 5 7 8 9 10 11 12 13 14 17 18 19 21 22 25 27 28 29 30 31 32 33 34 35 37 38 39 40 41 42 43 44 45 47 48 49 51 52 53 54 55 56 57 58 59 60 61 63 64 65 66 67 68 70 71 72 73 74 **P**1 6 7 **S** SSM Health Care, Saint Louis, MO

| | 16 | 10 | 53 | 564 | 28 | 41358 | 45 | 6995 | 3124 | 135 |

NORMAL—McLean County

⊞ BROMENN HEALTHCARE, (Includes Bromenn Lifecare Center, 807 North Main Street, Bloomington, Zip 61701; tel. 309/454–1400; Bromenn Regional Medical Center, tel. 309/454–1400; Eureka Community Hospital, 101 South Major Street, Eureka, Zip 61530, Mailing Address: P.O. Box 203, Zip 61530; tel. 309/467–2371), Virginia and Franklin Streets, Zip 61761, Mailing Address: P.O. Box 2850, Bloomington, Zip 61702–2850; tel. 309/454–0700; Dale S. Strassheim, President **A**1 2 9 10 **F**1 2 3 7 8 10 12 13 15 16 17 19 21 22 24 25 26 27 28 29 30 32 33 35 37 39 40 41 42 44 45 46 49 51 52 53 54 55 56 57 58 59 64 65 67 68 70 71 72 73 **P**6 7 8

| | 21 | 10 | 292 | 7993 | 99 | 98889 | 1312 | 94911 | 40109 | 1534 |

NORTH CHICAGO—Lake County

⊞ VETERANS AFFAIRS MEDICAL CENTER, 3001 Green Bay Road, Zip 60064–3049; tel. 847/688–1900; Alfred S. Pate, Director (Total facility includes 373 beds in nursing home–type unit) (Nonreporting) **A**1 3 5 **S** Department of Veterans Affairs, Washington, DC

| | 45 | 49 | 836 | — | — | — | — | — | — | — |

OAK FOREST—Cook County

⊞ △ OAK FOREST HOSPITAL OF COOK COUNTY, (LONG TERM CARE), 15900 South Cicero Avenue, Zip 60452; tel. 708/687–7200; Cynthia T. Henderson, M.D., M.P.H., Director and Chief Operating Officer (Total facility includes 531 beds in nursing home–type unit) **A**1 3 5 7 10 **F**3 8 10 12 13 14 15 16 17 18 20 22 25 26 27 28 29 30 31 33 34 36 37 39 41 42 44 45 46 48 49 51 54 57 58 64 65 67 71 73 **P**6 **S** Cook County Bureau of Health Services, Chicago, IL

| | 15 | 49 | 687 | 3146 | 570 | 55583 | 0 | 103631 | 62695 | 1563 |

OAK LAWN—Cook County

⊞ △ CHRIST HOSPITAL AND MEDICAL CENTER, (Includes Hope Children's Hospital), 4440 West 95th Street, Zip 60453–2699; tel. 708/425–8000; Carol Schneider, Chief Executive Officer **A**1 2 3 5 7 9 10 **F**1 2 3 4 7 8 10 11 12 13 15 16 17 18 19 21 22 24 25 26 27 28 30 31 32 33 34 35 36 37 38 39 40 41 42 43 44 46 47 48 49 51 52 53 54 55 57 58 59 60 61 62 64 65 66 67 68 70 71 73 74 **P**1 **S** Advocate Health Care, Oak Brook, IL
Web address: www.advocatehealth.com

| | 21 | 10 | 607 | 33142 | 503 | 259310 | 3861 | 344170 | 153788 | 4030 |

OAK PARK—Cook County

⊞ △ OAK PARK HOSPITAL, 520 South Maple Avenue, Zip 60304–1097; tel. 708/383–9300; Bruce M. Elegant, President and Chief Executive Officer (Total facility includes 47 beds in nursing home–type unit) **A**1 2 5 7 9 10 **F**1 3 4 5 6 8 9 10 11 12 15 16 17 18 19 20 21 22 25 26 27 30 31 32 33 34 35 37 38 39 40 41 42 43 44 46 47 48 49 50 51 52 53 54 55 56 57 58 59 60 61 63 64 65 66 67 68 71 73 74 **P**1 7 **S** Wheaton Franciscan Services, Inc., Wheaton, IL

| | 21 | 10 | 176 | 4384 | 103 | 63713 | 0 | 42885 | 20328 | 549 |

Hospital, Address, Telephone, Administrator, Approval, Facility, and Physician Codes, Health Care System, Network	Classi-fication Codes		Utilization Data					Expense (thousands) of dollars		
	Control	Service	Staffed Beds	Admissions	Census	Outpatient Visits	Births	Total	Payroll	Personnel

Approval legend:
★ American Hospital Association (AHA) membership
□ Joint Commission on Accreditation of Healthcare Organizations (JCAHO) accreditation
╪ American Osteopathic Healthcare Association (AOHA) membership
○ American Osteopathic Association (AOA) accreditation
△ Commission on Accreditation of Rehabilitation Facilities (CARF) accreditation
Control codes 61, 63, 64, 71, 72 and 73 indicate hospitals listed by AOHA, but not registered by AHA. For definition of numerical codes, see page A4

	Control	Service	Staffed Beds	Admissions	Census	Outpatient Visits	Births	Total	Payroll	Personnel
□ WEST SUBURBAN HOSPITAL MEDICAL CENTER, Erie at Austin Boulevard, Zip 60302–2599; tel. 708/383–6200; David M. Cecero, President and Chief Executive Officer (Total facility includes 79 beds in nursing home–type unit) **A**1 2 3 5 9 10 **F**4 5 7 8 9 10 11 12 13 14 16 17 18 19 20 21 22 24 25 26 27 28 29 30 31 32 33 34 35 37 38 39 40 41 42 43 44 45 46 47 49 51 52 53 54 56 57 58 60 61 63 64 65 66 67 68 70 71 72 73 74 **P**8	23	10	273	13139	175	133265	2122	150099	68204	1889
OLNEY—Richland County										
★ RICHLAND MEMORIAL HOSPITAL, 800 East Locust Street, Zip 62450–2598; tel. 618/395–2131; Harvey H. Pettry, President and Chief Executive Officer (Total facility includes 28 beds in nursing home–type unit) **A**1 2 9 10 **F**7 8 12 14 15 16 19 20 21 22 27 28 29 30 31 32 33 34 35 36 37 39 40 41 42 44 45 46 49 51 52 54 56 58 63 64 65 66 67 71 73	23	10	90	2858	49	71322	359	20380	9267	356
OLYMPIA FIELDS—Cook County										
★ ○ OLYMPIA FIELDS OSTEOPATHIC HOSPITAL AND MEDICAL CENTER, 20201 South Crawford Avenue, Zip 60461–1080; tel. 708/747–4000; David Scott Koenig, Chief Executive Officer **A**9 10 11 12 13 **F**3 4 5 7 8 10 11 12 13 14 16 17 18 19 21 22 23 25 26 27 28 29 30 32 33 34 35 37 39 40 41 42 43 44 45 46 48 49 50 52 53 54 55 56 57 59 60 61 63 65 66 67 68 70 71 72 73 74 **P**5 7 **S** Columbia/HCA Healthcare Corporation, Nashville, TN	33	10	181	6468	80	180720	605	76011	28051	583
OTTAWA—La Salle County										
★ COMMUNITY HOSPITAL OF OTTAWA, 1100 East Norris Drive, Zip 61350–1687; tel. 815/433–3100; Robert Schmelter, President **A**1 9 10 **F**1 2 3 6 7 8 15 19 20 21 22 26 27 28 29 30 32 33 36 37 39 40 41 42 44 45 46 49 52 53 54 56 57 58 59 65 67 70 71 73 **P**3 8 Web address: www.community-hospital.org	23	10	113	3512	36	80304	397	32231	13828	430
PALOS HEIGHTS—Cook County										
★ PALOS COMMUNITY HOSPITAL, 12251 South 80th Avenue, Zip 60463–0930; tel. 708/923–4000; Sister Margaret Wright, President **A**1 2 9 10 **F**2 3 7 8 10 11 16 19 21 22 24 25 30 31 32 33 34 35 36 37 39 40 41 42 44 45 49 52 53 54 56 57 58 59 63 65 66 67 71 72 73	23	10	339	18774	230	200619	2267	171538	87081	1780
PANA—Christian County										
★ PANA COMMUNITY HOSPITAL, 101 East Ninth Street, Zip 62557–1785; tel. 217/562–2131; Michael J. Laird, Chief Executive Officer **A**1 9 10 **F**8 12 14 15 16 17 19 21 22 29 30 31 32 33 34 36 37 39 42 44 45 46 49 51 63 65 66 71	23	10	30	725	6	16915	0	6353	2955	93
PARIS—Edgar County										
★ PARIS COMMUNITY HOSPITAL, 721 East Court Street, Zip 61944–2420; tel. 217/465–4141; J. Jay Purvis, Interim Administrator (Nonreporting) **A**1 9 10 **S** Norton Healthcare, Louisville, KY	23	10	49	—	—	—	—	—	—	—
PARK RIDGE—Cook County										
★ △ LUTHERAN GENERAL HOSPITAL, 1775 Dempster Street, Zip 60068–1174; tel. 847/723–2210; Kenneth J. Rojek, Chief Executive **A**1 2 3 5 7 8 9 10 **F**1 2 3 4 5 6 7 8 10 11 12 13 14 15 16 17 19 21 22 23 24 25 26 27 28 29 30 31 32 33 34 35 36 37 38 39 40 41 42 43 44 45 46 47 48 49 50 51 52 53 54 55 56 57 58 59 60 61 62 63 65 66 67 68 70 71 72 73 74 **P**8 **S** Advocate Health Care, Oak Brook, IL Web address: www.advocatehealth.com	23	10	555	26582	373	221279	4213	319408	121524	3268
PEKIN—Tazewell County										
★ PEKIN HOSPITAL, 600 South 13th Street, Zip 61554–5098; tel. 309/347–1151; Robert J. Moore, CHE, Chief Executive Officer (Total facility includes 20 beds in nursing home–type unit) **A**1 9 10 **F**2 3 4 7 8 10 12 14 15 16 17 18 19 20 21 22 23 24 26 28 29 30 31 32 33 34 35 36 37 38 39 40 41 42 43 44 45 46 47 49 51 52 53 54 55 56 57 58 59 60 61 63 64 65 66 67 68 69 70 71 72 73 74 **P**1 Web address: www.pekin.net/hospital	23	10	126	4290	60	73837	452	36733	14736	533
PEORIA—Peoria County										
□ GEORGE A. ZELLER MENTAL HEALTH CENTER, 5407 North University Street, Zip 61614–4785; tel. 309/693–5228; Robert W. Vyverberg, Ed.D., Director **A**1 10 **F**14 15 20 22 40 44 52 53 65	12	22	106	408	93	0	0	—	—	292
★ △ METHODIST MEDICAL CENTER OF ILLINOIS, 221 N.E. Glen Oak Avenue, Zip 61636–4310; tel. 309/672–5522; James K. Knoble, President (Total facility includes 37 beds in nursing home–type unit) **A**1 2 3 5 6 7 10 **F**4 5 7 8 10 11 12 14 15 16 17 18 19 21 22 23 24 25 26 28 29 30 31 32 33 34 35 37 39 40 41 42 43 44 45 46 48 49 50 51 52 53 54 55 56 57 58 59 60 61 63 64 65 67 68 70 71 72 73 74 **P**1 7 Web address: www.mmci.org	23	10	282	13695	204	270939	1756	170423	74386	1906
★ PROCTOR HOSPITAL, 5409 North Knoxville Avenue, Zip 61614–5094; tel. 309/691–1000; Norman H. LaConte, President and Chief Executive Officer (Total facility includes 40 beds in nursing home–type unit) **A**1 10 **F**2 3 4 7 8 10 12 13 14 15 16 19 21 22 24 25 28 29 30 32 34 35 36 37 39 40 41 43 44 45 46 49 51 63 64 65 70 71 72 73 **P**1 3 Web address: www.proctor.org	23	10	174	6236	109	176554	613	63087	24625	911
★ △ SAINT FRANCIS MEDICAL CENTER, 530 N.E. Glen Oak Avenue, Zip 61637; tel. 309/655–2000; Keith E. Steffen, Administrator **A**1 2 3 5 7 9 10 **F**1 3 4 5 6 7 8 10 11 12 13 14 15 16 17 18 19 20 21 22 23 24 25 26 27 28 29 30 31 32 33 34 35 36 37 38 39 40 41 42 43 44 45 46 47 48 49 50 51 52 53 54 55 56 57 58 59 60 61 62 64 65 67 68 70 71 72 73 74 **P**1 4 5 **S** OSF Healthcare System, Peoria, IL	21	10	536	22599	364	598989	2331	303344	135050	3454

Hospital, Address, Telephone, Administrator, Approval, Facility, and Physician Codes, Health Care System, Network	Classi-fication Codes		Utilization Data					Expense (thousands) of dollars		
★ American Hospital Association (AHA) membership □ Joint Commission on Accreditation of Healthcare Organizations (JCAHO) accreditation + American Osteopathic Healthcare Association (AOHA) membership ○ American Osteopathic Association (AOA) accreditation △ Commission on Accreditation of Rehabilitation Facilities (CARF) accreditation Control codes 61, 63, 64, 71, 72 and 73 indicate hospitals listed by AOHA, but not registered by AHA. For definition of numerical codes, see page A4	Control	Service	Staffed Beds	Admissions	Census	Outpatient Visits	Births	Total	Payroll	Personnel

PERU—La Salle County

⊞ ILLINOIS VALLEY COMMUNITY HOSPITAL, 925 West Street, Zip 61354–2799; tel. 815/223–3300; Willis F. Fry, Administrator (Total facility includes 12 beds in nursing home–type unit) **A**1 9 10 **F**1 7 8 14 15 16 19 21 22 23 26 28 29 30 31 32 33 35 36 37 39 40 41 42 44 45 46 49 52 53 54 55 56 57 58 59 64 65 66 67 71 73 74 **P**8	23	10	100	3831	51	86116	533	32246	12649	447

PINCKNEYVILLE—Perry County

★ PINCKNEYVILLE COMMUNITY HOSPITAL, 101 North Walnut Street, Zip 62274–1099; tel. 618/357–2187; John D. Schubert, Administrator and Chief Executive Officer (Total facility includes 50 beds in nursing home–type unit) **A**9 10 **F**15 16 19 21 22 24 32 33 35 36 42 44 64 65 66 71	16	10	62	995	85	56386	0	9396	4781	176

PITTSFIELD—Pike County

⊞ ILLINI COMMUNITY HOSPITAL, 640 West Washington Street, Zip 62363–1397; tel. 217/285–2113; Jete Edmisson, President and Chief Executive Officer **A**1 9 10 **F**8 11 15 16 19 22 24 26 27 28 29 30 32 33 36 37 39 40 41 44 46 49 51 65 71 73 **P**6 **S** Quorum Health Group/Quorum Health Resources, Inc., Brentwood, TN	23	10	45	1381	14	31428	108	10951	5280	189

PONTIAC—Livingston County

⊞ SAINT JAMES HOSPITAL, 610 East Water Street, Zip 61764–2194; tel. 815/842–2828; David Ochs, Administrator (Total facility includes 16 beds in nursing home–type unit) **A**1 9 10 **F**7 8 12 14 15 16 17 18 19 21 22 24 26 27 28 29 30 32 33 34 35 36 37 39 40 41 42 44 45 46 49 54 58 62 63 64 65 71 72 74 **P**6 7 **S** OSF Healthcare System, Peoria, IL	21	10	81	2329	26	73862	332	19736	8836	285

PRINCETON—Bureau County

⊞ PERRY MEMORIAL HOSPITAL, 530 Park Avenue East, Zip 61356–2598; tel. 815/875–2811; Harold S. Geller, President (Total facility includes 15 beds in nursing home–type unit) **A**1 9 10 **F**7 8 15 16 19 22 24 25 26 28 29 30 34 35 36 37 40 41 44 45 49 64 65 67 71 73 **P**8 Web address: www.perry–memorial.org	14	10	87	2470	32	44310	167	21379	9133	305

QUINCY—Adams County

⊞ △ BLESSING HOSPITAL, (Includes Blessing Hospital, Broadway & 14th Street), Broadway at 11th Street, Zip 62301, Mailing Address: P.O. Box 7005, Zip 62305–7005; tel. 217/223–1200; Lawrence L. Swearingen, President and Chief Executive Officer (Total facility includes 40 beds in nursing home–type unit) **A**1 2 3 5 7 9 10 **F**1 2 7 8 10 12 13 14 15 16 17 19 20 21 22 23 24 26 28 29 30 31 32 33 34 35 36 37 39 40 41 42 44 45 46 48 49 52 53 54 56 57 60 63 64 65 67 70 71 72 73 74 **P**1	23	10	240	11904	230	259039	1178	91430	42693	1341

RED BUD—Randolph County

⊞ ST. CLEMENT HEALTH SERVICES, (Formerly St Clement Hospital), One St. Clement Boulevard, Zip 62278–1194; tel. 618/282–3831; Michael Thomas McManus, President (Total facility includes 40 beds in nursing home–type unit) **A**1 9 10 **F**7 8 14 15 16 17 19 21 22 26 27 29 30 32 33 34 35 37 40 41 42 44 49 61 63 64 65 71 **P**5 6 7 8 **S** Sisters of Mercy Health System–St. Louis, Saint Louis, MO	21	10	115	1294	42	44393	114	13577	6398	335

ROBINSON—Crawford County

⊞ CRAWFORD MEMORIAL HOSPITAL, 1000 North Allen Street, Zip 62454; tel. 618/546–1234; Wallace R. Simmons, Chief Executive Officer (Total facility includes 48 beds in nursing home–type unit) **A**1 9 10 **F**7 8 13 14 15 16 18 19 22 24 26 27 28 30 32 33 34 35 36 37 39 40 41 42 44 46 49 51 64 65 66 67 71 73 **P**6 **S** Quorum Health Group/Quorum Health Resources, Inc., Brentwood, TN	16	10	93	1769	52	32442	299	15951	6703	223

ROCHELLE—Ogle County

⊞ ROCHELLE COMMUNITY HOSPITAL, 900 North Second Street, Zip 61068–0330; tel. 815/562–2181; Thomas R. Lemon, Chief Executive Officer **A**1 9 10 **F**7 8 12 14 15 16 19 21 22 24 30 31 33 37 39 40 41 44 46 49 51 56 64 65 66 67 71 73 **P**5 6 8	23	10	42	1043	12	97515	79	9712	4633	127

ROCK ISLAND—Rock Island County

⊞ △ TRINITY MEDICAL CENTER–WEST CAMPUS, (Includes Trinity Medical Center–Seventh Street Campus, 500 John Deere Road, Moline, Zip 61265; tel. 309/757–3131), 2701 17th Street, Zip 61201–5393; tel. 309/779–5000; Eric Crowell, President and Chief Executive Officer (Total facility includes 29 beds in nursing home–type unit) **A**1 2 7 9 10 **F**2 3 4 7 8 10 11 12 14 15 16 17 19 21 22 23 24 25 26 27 28 29 30 31 32 33 34 35 37 38 39 40 41 42 43 44 45 46 48 49 51 52 53 54 55 56 57 58 59 60 61 64 65 66 67 70 71 72 73 74 **P**1 6 Web address: www.trinityqc.com	23	10	355	13671	195	268041	1537	122124	56124	1475

ROCKFORD—Winnebago County

□ H. DOUGLAS SINGER MENTAL HEALTH AND DEVELOPMENTAL CENTER, 4402 North Main Street, Zip 61103–1278; tel. 815/987–7096; Gail Tennant, Director (Nonreporting) **A**1 10	12	22	162	—	—	—	—	—	—	—
⊞ △ ROCKFORD MEMORIAL HOSPITAL, 2400 North Rockton Avenue, Zip 61103–3692; tel. 815/971–5000; Thomas David DeFauw, President and Chief Executive Officer **A**1 2 5 7 9 10 **F**2 3 4 5 7 8 10 11 12 14 15 16 17 19 21 22 26 27 28 29 30 31 32 33 34 35 36 37 38 39 40 41 42 43 44 45 46 47 48 49 51 52 53 54 55 56 57 58 59 60 61 65 66 67 70 71 72 73 74 Web address: www.rhsnet.org	23	10	337	14494	234	295693	2324	175060	70460	2091

Hospital, Address, Telephone, Administrator, Approval, Facility, and Physician Codes, Health Care System, Network	Classi-fication Codes		Utilization Data					Expense (thousands) of dollars		
★ American Hospital Association (AHA) membership □ Joint Commission on Accreditation of Healthcare Organizations (JCAHO) accreditation + American Osteopathic Healthcare Association (AOHA) membership ○ American Osteopathic Association (AOA) accreditation △ Commission on Accreditation of Rehabilitation Facilities (CARF) accreditation Control codes 61, 63, 64, 71, 72 and 73 indicate hospitals listed by AOHA, but not registered by AHA. For definition of numerical codes, see page A4	Control	Service	Staffed Beds	Admissions	Census	Outpatient Visits	Births	Total	Payroll	Personnel

☒ SAINT ANTHONY MEDICAL CENTER, 5666 East State Street, Zip 61108–2472; tel. 815/226–2000; David A. Schertz, Administrator **A**1 2 5 9 10 **F**4 7 8 9 10 11 12 14 15 17 19 21 22 23 24 28 30 32 34 35 37 39 40 41 42 43 44 45 46 49 60 63 65 66 70 71 72 73 **P**6 **S** OSF Healthcare System, Peoria, IL **Web address:** www.osfhealth.com	21	10	184	8809	116	126395	789	120891	53907	1532
☒ SWEDISHAMERICAN HEALTH SYSTEM, 1313 East State Street, Zip 61104; tel. 815/968–4400; Robert B. Klint, M.D., President and Chief Executive Officer **A**1 2 3 5 9 10 **F**2 3 4 7 8 10 11 12 14 15 16 17 18 19 20 21 22 24 26 28 29 30 31 32 33 34 35 37 38 39 40 41 42 43 44 45 46 47 48 49 51 52 53 54 55 56 57 58 59 60 63 64 65 67 70 71 72 73 74 **P**6 7	23	10	291	11595	144	148195	1767	112407	50083	1493
ROSICLARE—Hardin County										
☒ HARDIN COUNTY GENERAL HOSPITAL, Ferrell Road, Zip 62982; tel. 618/285–6634; Roby D. Williams, Administrator (Nonreporting) **A**1 9 10	23	10	48	—	—	—	—	—	—	—
RUSHVILLE—Schuyler County										
★ SARAH D. CULBERTSON MEMORIAL HOSPITAL, 238 South Congress Street, Zip 62681–1472, Mailing Address: P.O. Box 440, Zip 62681–0440; tel. 217/322–4321; Michael C. O'Brien, Administrator (Total facility includes 30 beds in nursing home–type unit) **A**9 10 **F**7 8 14 17 19 22 30 36 40 44 62 63 64 71 73 **P**6	16	10	58	833	34	21476	128	6246	2301	108
SALEM—Marion County										
☒ PUBLIC HOSPITAL OF THE TOWN OF SALEM, 1201 Ricker Drive, Zip 62881–6250, Mailing Address: P.O. Box 1250, Zip 62881–1250; tel. 618/548–3194; James E. Robertson, Jr., President **A**1 9 10 **F**8 12 14 15 16 17 19 20 22 25 28 30 32 33 34 37 39 41 44 45 65 66 70 71 73 **S** BJC Health System, Saint Louis, MO	14	10	31	1289	17	39416	0	12087	5340	197
SANDWICH—De Kalb County										
★ VALLEY WEST COMMUNITY HOSPITAL, (Formerly Sandwich Community Hospital), 11 East Pleasant Avenue, Zip 60548–0901; tel. 815/786–8484; Roland R. Carlson, Chief Executive Officer **A**9 10 **F**15 19 21 22 28 30 34 35 37 39 40 41 44 45 49 65 71 73 **S** Kishwaukee Health System, De Kalb, IL **Web address:** www.snd.softfarm.com/sandhosp	23	10	35	339	9	5061	30	3059	1208	133
SCOTT AFB—St. Clair County										
☒ SCOTT MEDICAL CENTER, 310 West Losey Street, Zip 62225–5252; tel. 618/256–7456; Colonel Stephen J. Pribyl, MSC, USAF, Administrator **A**1 3 5 **F**3 4 5 7 8 10 12 13 15 16 17 18 19 20 21 22 23 24 25 26 27 28 29 30 31 32 33 34 35 37 39 40 42 43 44 45 46 49 50 51 53 54 55 56 57 58 59 60 61 63 65 67 68 70 71 72 73 74 **S** Department of the Air Force, Bowling AFB, DC	41	10	45	2897	21	264112	503	—	—	1110
SHELBYVILLE—Shelby County										
☒ SHELBY MEMORIAL HOSPITAL, 200 South Cedar Street, Zip 62565–1899; tel. 217/774–3961; John Bennett, President and Chief Executive Officer (Total facility includes 15 beds in nursing home–type unit) **A**1 9 10 **F**8 11 14 15 16 19 21 22 31 32 35 37 41 42 44 49 63 64 71 **P**5 **Web address:** www.bmnet.smhadm.org	23	10	52	2468	34	30258	0	8788	4148	168
SILVIS—Rock Island County										
☒ ILLINI HOSPITAL, 801 Hospital Road, Zip 61282–1893; tel. 309/792–9363; Gary E. Larson, Chief Executive Officer **A**1 10 **F**2 3 4 6 7 8 10 11 12 14 15 16 17 18 19 21 22 23 24 26 27 28 29 30 31 32 33 35 37 40 41 42 43 44 45 48 49 50 52 53 54 55 56 57 58 59 60 61 62 63 64 65 66 67 70 71 72 73 **P**3 8 **Web address:** www.genesishealth.com	23	10	100	5297	51	99893	625	—	—	693
SKOKIE—Cook County										
☒ RUSH NORTH SHORE MEDICAL CENTER, 9600 Gross Point Road, Zip 60076–1257; tel. 847/677–9600; John S. Frigo, President **A**1 2 3 5 10 **F**4 7 8 10 14 15 16 17 19 20 21 22 27 28 29 30 34 35 36 37 39 40 41 42 43 44 46 49 52 54 55 56 57 58 59 60 61 63 64 65 67 70 71 73 74 **P**8 **S** Rush–Presbyterian–St. Luke's Medical Center, Chicago, IL	23	10	237	10221	163	145277	633	100998	45703	946
SPARTA—Randolph County										
★ SPARTA COMMUNITY HOSPITAL, 818 East Broadway Street, Zip 62286–0297, Mailing Address: P.O. Box 297, Zip 62286–0297; tel. 618/443–2177; Joann Emge, Chief Executive Officer **A**9 10 **F**7 8 12 14 15 19 21 22 24 27 30 32 33 35 40 41 42 44 49 65 71 73 **P**5 **S** Brim Healthcare, Inc., Brentwood, TN	16	10	35	1304	14	30590	134	10729	4793	178
SPRING VALLEY—Bureau County										
☒ ST. MARGARET'S HOSPITAL, 600 East First Street, Zip 61362–2034; tel. 815/664–5311; Timothy Muntz, President (Total facility includes 33 beds in nursing home–type unit) **A**1 2 9 10 **F**7 8 14 15 16 19 21 22 24 27 28 30 31 32 33 35 37 39 40 41 42 44 45 46 48 49 62 64 65 66 67 71 73 74 **P**6 8 **S** Sisters of Mary of the Presentation Health Corporation, Fargo, ND **Web address:** www.st.margarets.com	21	10	123	3261	56	141395	237	33716	14476	368
SPRINGFIELD—Sangamon County										
□ ANDREW MCFARLAND MENTAL HEALTH CENTER, 901 Southwind Road, Zip 62703–5195; tel. 217/786–6994; Nieves Tan–Lachica, M.D., Superintendent (Nonreporting) **A**1	12	22	146	—	—	—	—	—	—	—
□ DOCTORS HOSPITAL, 5230 South Sixth Street, Zip 62703–5194, Mailing Address: P.O. Box 19254, Zip 62794–9254; tel. 217/529–7151; Jim Bohl, President and Chief Executive Officer (Nonreporting) **A**1 10	33	10	150	—	—	—	—	—	—	—

Hospital, Address, Telephone, Administrator, Approval, Facility, and Physician Codes, Health Care System, Network	Classi-fication Codes		Utilization Data					Expense (thousands) of dollars		
★ American Hospital Association (AHA) membership □ Joint Commission on Accreditation of Healthcare Organizations (JCAHO) accreditation + American Osteopathic Healthcare Association (AOHA) membership ○ American Osteopathic Association (AOA) accreditation △ Commission on Accreditation of Rehabilitation Facilities (CARF) accreditation Control codes 61, 63, 64, 71, 72 and 73 indicate hospitals listed by AOHA, but not registered by AHA. For definition of numerical codes, see page A4	Control	Service	Staffed Beds	Admissions	Census	Outpatient Visits	Births	Total	Payroll	Personnel
✠ △ MEMORIAL MEDICAL CENTER, 701 North First Street, Zip 62781–0001; tel. 217/788–3000; Robert T. Clarke, President and Chief Executive Officer **A**1 2 3 5 7 8 9 10 **F**3 4 7 8 9 10 11 12 14 15 16 17 18 19 20 21 22 23 25 26 27 28 29 30 31 32 33 34 35 36 37 39 40 41 42 43 44 45 46 48 49 51 52 53 54 55 57 58 59 60 61 65 66 67 68 70 71 72 73 74 **P**3 5 **S** Memorial Health System, Springfield, IL Web address: www.mhsil.com	23	10	431	18504	300	365996	1675	207816	87442	2655
✠ ST. JOHN'S HOSPITAL, 800 East Carpenter Street, Zip 62769–0002; tel. 217/544–6464; Allison C. Laabs, Executive Vice President and Administrator (Total facility includes 53 beds in nursing home–type unit) **A**1 3 5 8 10 **F**1 3 4 7 8 10 12 13 15 16 19 21 22 26 28 30 32 33 35 37 38 39 40 42 43 44 46 47 49 52 57 58 59 60 64 65 66 67 68 70 71 72 73 74 **P**7 **S** Hospital Sisters Health System, Springfield, IL	21	10	579	23780	374	138495	1964	252724	103653	3217
STAUNTON—Macoupin County										
✠ COMMUNITY MEMORIAL HOSPITAL, 400 Caldwell Street, Zip 62088–1499; tel. 618/635–2200; Patrick B. Heise, Chief Executive Officer **A**1 9 10 **F**8 19 22 32 36 44 65 71 73 **P**3 **S** Quorum Health Group/Quorum Health Resources, Inc., Brentwood, TN	23	10	44	807	9	18052	0	8331	4018	142
STERLING—Whiteside County										
✠ CGH MEDICAL CENTER, 100 East LeFevre Road, Zip 61081–1279; tel. 815/625–0400; Edward Andersen, President and Chief Executive Officer **A**1 2 9 10 **F**7 8 12 14 15 16 17 19 20 21 22 23 27 28 29 32 33 35 37 39 40 42 44 46 49 60 63 64 65 67 71 73 **P**1 Web address: www.cghmc.com	14	10	143	6149	62	63046	720	45548	18993	642
STREAMWOOD—Cook County										
□ BHC STREAMWOOD HOSPITAL, 1400 East Irving Park Road, Zip 60107–3203; tel. 630/837–9000; Jeff Bergren, Chief Executive Officer and Administrator **A**1 10 **F**2 9 11 37 38 40 41 47 52 53 54 55 56 57 58 59 65 **S** Behavioral Healthcare Corporation, Nashville, TN	33	52	100	415	50	15400	0	—	—	—
STREATOR—La Salle County										
✠ ST. MARY'S HOSPITAL, 111 East Spring Street, Zip 61364–3399; tel. 815/673–2311; James F. Dover, Executive Vice President and Administrator (Total facility includes 30 beds in nursing home–type unit) **A**1 2 9 10 **F**1 3 7 8 12 14 15 16 17 19 20 21 22 24 26 27 28 30 32 33 35 37 39 40 41 42 44 45 49 60 63 64 65 67 69 71 73 **P**8 **S** Hospital Sisters Health System, Springfield, IL Web address: www.ortelco.com/~stmaryl	21	10	170	4134	71	38195	273	26364	12649	422
SYCAMORE—De Kalb County										
□ VENCOR HOSPITAL–SYCAMORE, 225 Edward Street, Zip 60178–2197; tel. 815/895–2144; Betty Walker, Administrator (Nonreporting) **A**1 9 10 **S** Vencor, Incorporated, Louisville, KY	33	10	50	—	—	—	—	—	—	—
TAYLORVILLE—Christian County										
✠ ST. VINCENT MEMORIAL HOSPITAL, 201 East Pleasant Street, Zip 62568–1597; tel. 217/824–3331; Daniel J. Raab, President and Chief Executive Officer (Total facility includes 50 beds in nursing home–type unit) (Nonreporting) **A**1 9 10 **S** Memorial Health System, Springfield, IL	21	10	149	—	—	—	—	—	—	—
TINLEY PARK—Cook County										
□ TINLEY PARK MENTAL HEALTH CENTER, 7400 West 183rd Street, Zip 60477–3695; tel. 708/614–4000; Delores Newman, MS, Network Manager, Metro South Network **A**1 5 10 **F**52 54 56 58 59 65 73 **P**6	12	22	150	1649	143	0	0	—	17149	371
URBANA—Champaign County										
✠ △ CARLE FOUNDATION HOSPITAL, 611 West Park Street, Zip 61801–2595; tel. 217/383–3311; Michael H. Fritz, President (Total facility includes 240 beds in nursing home–type unit) **A**1 2 3 5 7 10 **F**4 6 7 8 10 12 13 14 15 16 17 19 22 23 25 26 27 28 29 30 31 32 33 34 35 37 38 39 40 41 42 43 44 45 46 48 49 51 60 61 62 64 65 66 67 70 71 72 73 74 **P**5	23	10	490	12935	299	42437	1725	112545	40916	1588
✠ △ PROVENA COVENANT MEDICAL CENTER, (Includes Burnham Hospital, 407 South Fourth Street, Champaign, Zip 61820; tel. 217/337–2500; Mercy Hospital, 1400 West Park Street, Zip 61801), 1400 West Park Street, Zip 61801–2396; tel. 217/337–2000; Diane Friedman, R.N., President and Chief Executive Officer **A**1 2 3 5 7 9 10 **F**4 7 10 12 15 16 17 19 21 22 23 26 30 32 33 34 35 37 38 39 40 42 43 44 45 46 48 49 52 54 55 56 58 60 63 64 65 67 71 73 **P**1 4 7 8 **S** Provena Health, Frankfort, IL Web address: www.covenant–cu.com	21	10	258	9732	122	179201	1263	92812	36640	1125
VANDALIA—Fayette County										
✠ FAYETTE COUNTY HOSPITAL, Seventh and Taylor Streets, Zip 62471–1296; tel. 618/283–1231; Daniel L. Gantz, President (Total facility includes 101 beds in nursing home–type unit) **A**1 9 10 **F**8 12 14 15 16 17 19 21 22 26 27 28 30 32 33 35 36 37 41 44 49 57 58 64 65 67 71 **P**7 **S** BJC Health System, Saint Louis, MO	16	10	142	1444	98	27107	1	12016	5392	232
WATSEKA—Iroquois County										
✠ IROQUOIS MEMORIAL HOSPITAL AND RESIDENT HOME, 200 Fairman Avenue, Zip 60970–1644; tel. 815/432–5841; Rex D. Conger, President and Chief Executive Officer (Total facility includes 46 beds in nursing home–type unit) (Nonreporting) **A**1 9 10 Web address: www.iroquoismemorial.com	23	10	112	—	—	—	—	—	—	—

Hospital, Address, Telephone, Administrator, Approval, Facility, and Physician Codes, Health Care System, Network	Classi-fication Codes		Utilization Data					Expense (thousands) of dollars		
★ American Hospital Association (AHA) membership □ Joint Commission on Accreditation of Healthcare Organizations (JCAHO) accreditation + American Osteopathic Healthcare Association (AOHA) membership ○ American Osteopathic Association (AOA) accreditation △ Commission on Accreditation of Rehabilitation Facilities (CARF) accreditation Control codes 61, 63, 64, 71, 72 and 73 indicate hospitals listed by AOHA, but not registered by AHA. For definition of numerical codes, see page A4	Control	Service	Staffed Beds	Admissions	Census	Outpatient Visits	Births	Total	Payroll	Personnel

WAUKEGAN—Lake County

☒ △ PROVENA SAINT THERESE MEDICAL CENTER, 2615 Washington Street, Zip 60085–4988; tel. 847/249–3900; Timothy P. Selz, President and Chief Executive Officer (Total facility includes 25 beds in nursing home–type unit) **A**1 7 9 10 **F**7 8 10 11 12 14 15 16 17 18 19 20 22 24 25 27 28 29 30 32 33 35 39 40 41 42 44 46 48 49 52 53 56 58 59 64 65 70 71 72 73 **P**3 5 7 **S** Provena Health, Frankfort, IL
| | 21 | 10 | 254 | 8336 | 115 | 190586 | 1189 | 67107 | 28845 | 724 |

☒ VICTORY MEMORIAL HOSPITAL, 1324 North Sheridan Road, Zip 60085–2181; tel. 847/360–3000; Timothy Harrington, President **A**1 2 10 **F**1 2 3 4 7 8 10 12 14 15 16 18 19 21 22 24 25 26 28 29 30 32 33 34 36 37 39 40 41 42 44 45 46 49 52 54 55 56 57 58 59 60 62 63 64 65 67 71 73 **P**1 7
| | 23 | 10 | 116 | 7308 | 84 | 70832 | 1188 | 61644 | 27871 | 751 |

WEST FRANKFORT—Franklin County

★ UNITED MINE WORKERS OF AMERICA UNION HOSPITAL, 507 West St. Louis Street, Zip 62896–1999; tel. 618/932–2155; Virgil Hannig, Senior Vice President and Administrator **A**9 10 **F**14 15 16 19 22 32 33 44 71 73 **S** Southern Illinois Hospital Services, Carbondale, IL
| | 23 | 10 | 20 | 299 | 3 | 5438 | 0 | 4269 | 1988 | 74 |

WHEATON—Du Page County

☒ △ MARIANJOY REHABILITATION HOSPITAL AND CLINICS, 26 West 171 Roosevelt Road, Zip 60187–0795, Mailing Address: P.O. Box 795, Zip 60189–0795; tel. 630/462–4000; Kathleen C. Yosko, President and Chief Executive Officer **A**1 3 5 7 10 **F**5 12 25 27 29 34 41 45 46 48 49 65 66 67 73 **P**1 **S** Wheaton Franciscan Services, Inc., Wheaton, IL
| | 21 | 46 | 110 | 1596 | 84 | 19772 | 0 | 46632 | 23742 | 417 |

WINFIELD—Du Page County

☒ CENTRAL DUPAGE HOSPITAL, (Includes Behavioral Health Center, 27 West 350 High Lake Road, tel. 630/653–4000), 25 North Winfield Road, Zip 60190; tel. 630/682–1600; David S. Fox, President **A**1 2 9 10 **F**2 3 4 6 7 8 10 11 12 14 15 16 17 19 20 21 22 23 24 25 28 29 30 32 33 34 35 37 38 40 41 42 43 44 45 46 47 49 51 52 53 54 56 57 58 59 62 64 65 67 70 71 72 73 **P**6
| | 23 | 10 | 321 | 14208 | 160 | 240089 | 3220 | 158739 | 60597 | 1493 |

WOOD RIVER—Madison County

☒ WOOD RIVER TOWNSHIP HOSPITAL, 101 East Edwardsville Road, Zip 62095–1332; tel. 618/251–7103; David G. Triebes, Chief Executive Officer **A**1 9 10 **F**3 7 8 13 14 15 16 17 19 21 22 26 33 34 35 36 37 40 41 44 48 49 52 54 55 56 65 71 73 **S** Brim Healthcare, Inc., Brentwood, TN
| | 16 | 10 | 55 | 1230 | 20 | 17479 | 205 | 15060 | 5365 | 196 |

WOODSTOCK—McHenry County

☒ MEMORIAL MEDICAL CENTER, Highway 14 and Doty Road, Zip 60098–3797, Mailing Address: P.O. Box 1990, Zip 60098–1990; tel. 815/338–2500; Paul E. Laudick, President and Chief Executive Officer (Total facility includes 24 beds in nursing home–type unit) **A**1 2 9 10 **F**3 7 8 12 14 15 16 17 18 19 20 22 24 26 27 28 29 30 32 33 34 35 36 37 39 40 41 42 44 45 46 48 49 52 53 54 55 56 57 58 59 64 65 66 67 70 71 73 74 **P**5 7
Web address: www.centegra.org
| | 23 | 10 | 123 | 5287 | 70 | 104667 | 586 | 53519 | 20764 | 607 |

ZION—Lake County

□ MIDWESTERN REGIONAL MEDICAL CENTER, (ONCOLOGY), 2520 Elisha Avenue, Zip 60099–2587; tel. 847/872–4561; Roger C. Cary, President and Chief Executive Officer **A**1 2 10 **F**8 12 14 15 16 17 19 20 21 22 27 28 29 30 31 32 33 34 35 37 39 41 42 44 45 46 49 51 60 65 66 68 71 73 **S** Cancer Treatment Centers of America, Arlington Heights, IL
Web address: www.pulbiconline.com/=mrmc
| | 33 | 49 | 70 | 1979 | 31 | 22763 | 0 | 45415 | 16156 | 367 |

INDIANA

Resident population 5,899 (in thousands)
Resident population in metro areas 71.0%
Birth rate per 1,000 population 14.3
65 years and over 12.5%
Percent of persons without health insurance 10.6%

Hospital, Address, Telephone, Administrator, Approval, Facility, and Physician Codes, Health Care System, Network	Classi-fication Codes		Utilization Data					Expense (thousands) of dollars		
★ American Hospital Association (AHA) membership □ Joint Commission on Accreditation of Healthcare Organizations (JCAHO) accreditation + American Osteopathic Healthcare Association (AOHA) membership ○ American Osteopathic Association (AOA) accreditation △ Commission on Accreditation of Rehabilitation Facilities (CARF) accreditation Control codes 61, 63, 64, 71, 72 and 73 indicate hospitals listed by AOHA, but not registered by AHA. For definition of numerical codes, see page A4	Control	Service	Staffed Beds	Admissions	Census	Outpatient Visits	Births	Total	Payroll	Personnel

ANDERSON—Madison County
COMMUNITY HOSPITAL OF ANDERSON AND MADISON COUNTY See Community Hospitals Indianapolis, Indianapolis

⊠ SAINT JOHN'S HEALTH SYSTEM, 2015 Jackson Street, Zip 46016–4339; tel. 765/649–2511; Jerry D. Brumitt, President and Chief Executive Officer (Total facility includes 27 beds in nursing home–type unit) **A**1 2 9 10 **F**2 3 7 8 10 11 12 13 14 15 16 17 18 19 20 21 22 23 25 26 27 28 29 30 31 32 33 34 35 37 39 40 41 42 44 45 46 48 49 52 53 54 55 56 57 58 59 60 63 64 65 66 67 68 71 72 73 74 **P**7 8 **S** Holy Cross Health System Corporation, South Bend, IN
Web address: www.stjohnshealthsystem.org
| | | 21 | 10 | 267 | 7452 | 103 | 334686 | 586 | 95920 | 41707 | 1153 |

ANGOLA—Steuben County
★ CAMERON MEMORIAL COMMUNITY HOSPITAL, 416 East Maumee Street, Zip 46703–2015; tel. 219/665–2141; Dennis L. Knapp, President **A**9 10 **F**3 7 8 14 15 19 22 29 30 32 33 34 35 36 37 39 40 44 46 49 58 65 71 73
Web address: www.cameronhosp.com
| | | 23 | 10 | 30 | 1131 | 9 | 75869 | 354 | 15671 | 7413 | 235 |

AUBURN—De Kalb County
⊠ DEKALB MEMORIAL HOSPITAL, 1316 East Seventh Street, Zip 46706–2515, Mailing Address: P.O. Box 542, Zip 46706–0542; tel. 219/925–4600; Jack M. Corey, President **A**1 9 10 **F**7 8 12 14 15 16 19 21 22 24 31 32 33 34 35 37 39 40 41 44 46 49 51 63 65 71 73 **P**4 6 7 8
| | | 23 | 10 | 45 | 1914 | 15 | 57887 | 463 | 23269 | 10456 | 303 |

BATESVILLE—Franklin County
⊠ MARGARET MARY COMMUNITY HOSPITAL, 321 Mitchell Avenue, Zip 47006–8953, Mailing Address: P.O. Box 226, Zip 47006–0226; tel. 812/934–6624; James L. Amos, President (Total facility includes 35 beds in nursing home–type unit) (Nonreporting) **A**1 9 10
Web address: www.mmch.org
| | | 23 | 10 | 94 | — | — | — | — | — | — | — |

BEDFORD—Lawrence County
⊠ BEDFORD REGIONAL MEDICAL CENTER, 2900 West 16th Street, Zip 47421–3583; tel. 812/275–1200; John R. Birdzell, FACHE, Chief Executive Officer **A**1 2 9 10 **F**7 8 14 15 16 17 19 20 21 22 27 28 30 32 33 34 35 37 39 40 41 42 44 45 46 49 51 63 65 67 71 72 73 **P**1 6
| | | 23 | 10 | 60 | 2495 | 23 | 177729 | 627 | 31713 | 14448 | 415 |

⊠ DUNN MEMORIAL HOSPITAL, 1600 23rd Street, Zip 47421–4704; tel. 812/275–3331; William W. Wissman, Interim Executive Director **A**1 9 10 **F**1 7 8 10 11 14 17 19 21 22 23 27 28 29 30 31 32 33 34 35 37 39 40 41 42 44 45 46 49 51 65 71 72 73 74
Web address: www.dunnmemorial.org
| | | 13 | 10 | 104 | 2783 | 28 | 67628 | 233 | 26753 | 12410 | 428 |

BEECH GROVE—Marion County
⊠ ST. FRANCIS HOSPITAL AND HEALTH CENTERS, 1600 Albany Street, Zip 46107–1593; tel. 317/787–3311; Robert J. Brody, President and Chief Executive Officer (Nonreporting) **A**1 2 3 5 9 10 **S** Sisters of St. Francis Health Services, Inc., Mishawaka, IN
Web address: www.stfrancis–indy.org
| | | 21 | 10 | 409 | — | — | — | — | — | — | — |

BLOOMINGTON—Monroe County
⊠ BLOOMINGTON HOSPITAL, 601 West Second Street, Zip 47403–2317, Mailing Address: P.O. Box 1149, Zip 47402–1149; tel. 812/336–6821; Nancy S. Carlstedt, President (Total facility includes 644 beds in nursing home–type unit) **A**1 9 10 **F**1 3 4 6 7 8 10 11 12 14 15 16 17 18 19 21 22 23 24 25 26 27 28 29 30 31 32 33 34 35 36 37 39 40 41 42 43 44 45 46 49 52 53 54 55 56 57 58 59 60 62 64 65 66 67 70 71 72 73 74 **P**1
Web address: www.bloomhealth.org
| | | 23 | 10 | 856 | 15601 | 693 | 317681 | 1790 | 148451 | 69211 | 2547 |

BLUFFTON—Wells County
⊠ CAYLOR–NICKEL MEDICAL CENTER, One Caylor–Nickel Square, Zip 46714–2529; tel. 219/824–3500; William F. Brockmann, President and Chief Executive Officer (Total facility includes 19 beds in nursing home–type unit) **A**1 2 9 10 **F**3 5 7 8 10 11 12 14 15 16 17 19 20 21 22 24 25 26 30 32 37 39 40 41 42 44 45 46 49 51 52 53 54 56 57 58 60 64 65 67 71 73 **P**8
Web address: www.caylornickel.com
| | | 23 | 10 | 95 | 3087 | 37 | 87738 | 297 | 28335 | 12282 | 427 |

⊠ WELLS COMMUNITY HOSPITAL, 1100 South Main Street, Zip 46714–3697; tel. 219/824–3210; Thomas A. Clark, Chief Executive Officer **A**1 9 10 **F**7 8 15 16 17 19 22 24 28 29 30 32 33 39 40 41 42 44 45 46 49 60 65 70 73 74
| | | 13 | 10 | 30 | 1012 | 8 | 32188 | 174 | 11704 | 5305 | 165 |

BOONVILLE—Warrick County
⊠ ST. MARY'S HOSPITAL WARRICK, 1116 Millis Avenue, Zip 47601–0629, Mailing Address: Box 629, Zip 47601–0629; tel. 812/897–4800; Jim M. Hayes, Executive Vice President and Aministrator **A**1 9 10 **F**8 14 15 16 17 19 20 22 28 30 31 32 37 41 44 48 49 65 71 73 **S** Daughters of Charity National Health System, Saint Louis, MO
| | | 23 | 10 | 28 | 994 | 11 | 20833 | 0 | 10838 | 5874 | 236 |

BRAZIL—Clay County
⊠ CLAY COUNTY HOSPITAL, 1206 East National Avenue, Zip 47834–2797; tel. 812/448–2675; Jay P. Jolly, Administrator and Chief Executive Officer **A**1 9 10 **F**7 8 14 19 21 22 30 34 35 37 40 42 44 45 51 65 71 73 **P**8
| | | 13 | 10 | 33 | 934 | 10 | 27175 | 81 | 7957 | 3407 | 129 |

Hospital, Address, Telephone, Administrator, Approval, Facility, and Physician Codes, Health Care System, Network	Classi-fication Codes		Utilization Data					Expense (thousands) of dollars		
★ American Hospital Association (AHA) membership □ Joint Commission on Accreditation of Healthcare Organizations (JCAHO) accreditation + American Osteopathic Healthcare Association (AOHA) membership ○ American Osteopathic Association (AOA) accreditation △ Commission on Accreditation of Rehabilitation Facilities (CARF) accreditation Control codes 61, 63, 64, 71, 72 and 73 indicate hospitals listed by AOHA, but not registered by AHA. For definition of numerical codes, see page A4	Control	Service	Staffed Beds	Admissions	Census	Outpatient Visits	Births	Total	Payroll	Personnel

BREMEN—Marshall County

★ COMMUNITY HOSPITAL OF BREMEN, 411 South Whitlock Street, Zip 46506–1699, Mailing Address: P.O. Box 8, Zip 46506–0008; tel. 219/546–2211; Scott R. Graybill, Chief Executive Officer and Administrator **A**9 10 **F**8 12 15 17 19 22 26 27 30 32 33 34 40 41 44 49 51 53 54 55 56 57 58 59 64 65 66 71 73 **P**1 **S** Ancilla Systems Inc., Hobart, IN

| | 23 | 10 | 28 | 391 | 4 | 36896 | 70 | 5657 | 2395 | 90 |

CARMEL—Hamilton County

ST. VINCENT CARMEL HOSPITAL See St. Vincent Hospitals and Health Services, Indianapolis

CHARLESTOWN—Clark County

□ MEDICAL CENTER OF SOUTHERN INDIANA, 2200 Market Street, Zip 47111–0069, Mailing Address: P.O. Box 69, Zip 47111–0069; tel. 812/256–3301; Kevin J. Miller, FACHE, Chief Executive Officer **A**1 9 10 **F**4 7 9 13 14 15 16 19 21 22 23 25 26 28 29 30 32 33 34 35 37 38 39 40 41 43 44 45 46 47 48 49 51 52 57 58 59 60 63 64 65 67 71 73 **P**5 7

| | 23 | 10 | 80 | 2016 | 44 | 17905 | 0 | 20373 | 9883 | 275 |

CLINTON—Vermillion County

□ WEST CENTRAL COMMUNITY HOSPITAL, 801 South Main Street, Zip 47842–0349; tel. 765/832–2451; Marilyn J. Custer–Mitchell, Administrator **A**1 9 10 **F**7 8 14 15 16 19 21 22 24 25 28 34 37 39 40 42 44 46 49 65 71 73 **P**1

| | 23 | 10 | 27 | 1329 | 14 | 41079 | 88 | 11075 | 4778 | 168 |

COLUMBIA CITY—Whitley County

□ WHITLEY MEMORIAL HOSPITAL, 353 North Oak Street, Zip 46725–1623; tel. 219/244–6191; John M. Hatcher, President (Total facility includes 81 beds in nursing home–type unit) **A**1 9 10 **F**7 8 11 14 15 16 19 22 24 28 30 32 33 35 36 37 39 40 41 44 48 49 51 64 67 71 73 **P**8 **S** Parkview Health System, Fort Wayne, IN

| | 33 | 10 | 131 | 1786 | 104 | 37079 | 348 | 20722 | 9551 | 278 |

COLUMBUS—Bartholomew County

□ BEHAVIORAL HEALTHCARE–COLUMBUS, 2223 Poshard Drive, Zip 47203–1844, Mailing Address: P.O. Box 1549, Zip 47203–1844; tel. 812/376–1711; John M. Hart, Chief Executive Officer (Nonreporting) **A**1 9 10 **S** Behavioral Healthcare Corporation, Nashville, TN

| | 33 | 22 | 60 | — | — | — | — | — | — | — |

⊞ COLUMBUS REGIONAL HOSPITAL, 2400 East 17th Street, Zip 47201–5360; tel. 812/379–4441; Douglas J. Leonard, Chief Executive Officer (Total facility includes 21 beds in nursing home–type unit) **A**1 2 9 10 **F**7 8 10 12 14 15 16 17 19 21 22 23 28 29 30 32 33 35 36 37 39 40 41 42 44 45 46 48 49 52 54 55 56 60 63 64 65 66 67 70 71 72 73 **P**3 5 8
Web address: www.crh.org

| | 13 | 10 | 239 | 10060 | 115 | 179550 | 1340 | 105427 | 44511 | 1407 |

CONNERSVILLE—Fayette County

⊞ FAYETTE MEMORIAL HOSPITAL, 1941 Virginia Avenue, Zip 47331–9990; tel. 765/825–5131; David Brandon, Chief Executive Officer (Nonreporting) **A**1 9 10

| | 23 | 10 | 111 | — | — | — | — | — | — | — |

CORYDON—Harrison County

⊞ HARRISON COUNTY HOSPITAL, 245 Atwood Street, Zip 47112–1774; tel. 812/738–4251; Steven L. Taylor, Chief Executive Officer **A**1 9 10 **F**7 8 11 14 15 17 19 21 22 30 32 34 35 40 41 42 44 45 46 49 63 65 66 67 71 **P**2 7 **S** Norton Healthcare, Louisville, KY

| | 13 | 10 | 47 | 1426 | 16 | 33364 | 111 | 15324 | 6601 | 275 |

CRAWFORDSVILLE—Montgomery County

⊞ CULVER UNION HOSPITAL, 1710 Lafayette Road, Zip 47933–1099; tel. 765/362–2800; Gregory D. Starnes, Chief Executive Officer (Total facility includes 17 beds in nursing home–type unit) (Nonreporting) **A**1 9 10 **S** TENET Healthcare Corporation, Santa Barbara, CA

| | 33 | 10 | 98 | — | — | — | — | — | — | — |

CROWN POINT—Lake County

⊞ ST. ANTHONY MEDICAL CENTER, 1201 South Main Street, Zip 46307–8483; tel. 219/738–2100; Stephen O. Leurck, President and Chief Executive Officer **A**1 2 6 9 10 **F**1 4 6 7 8 10 11 12 13 14 15 16 17 18 19 21 22 25 26 28 29 30 32 33 34 35 39 40 41 42 43 44 45 46 48 49 50 51 60 63 64 65 66 67 71 72 73 **P**6 7 8 **S** Sisters of St. Francis Health Services, Inc., Mishawaka, IN

| | 21 | 10 | 248 | 7794 | 96 | 86723 | 943 | 86578 | 35920 | 787 |

DANVILLE—Hendricks County

⊞ HENDRICKS COMMUNITY HOSPITAL, 1000 East Main Street, Zip 46122–0409, Mailing Address: P.O. Box 409, Zip 46122–0409; tel. 317/745–4451; Dennis W. Dawes, President **A**1 9 10 **F**2 7 8 12 14 15 16 19 20 21 22 24 28 29 30 31 32 34 35 36 37 39 40 41 42 44 45 49 51 52 54 55 56 57 58 60 65 66 67 71 72 73 74 **P**1 6 7
Web address: www.hendricks.org

| | 13 | 10 | 127 | 5487 | 61 | 176822 | 923 | 48622 | 22054 | 673 |

DECATUR—Adams County

⊞ ADAMS COUNTY MEMORIAL HOSPITAL, 805 High Street, Zip 46733–2311, Mailing Address: P.O. Box 151, Zip 46733–0151; tel. 219/724–2145; Marvin L. Baird, Executive Director (Total facility includes 22 beds in nursing home–type unit) **A**1 9 10 **F**1 6 7 8 14 15 16 19 22 25 26 27 28 30 32 34 35 37 39 40 41 42 44 45 46 49 51 52 54 55 56 57 58 59 61 62 64 65 67 71 72 73 74

| | 13 | 10 | 87 | 2022 | 40 | 52677 | 240 | 18792 | 7784 | 324 |

DYER—Lake County

SAINT MARGARET MERCY HEALTHCARE CENTERS–SOUTH CAMPUS See Saint Margaret Mercy Healthcare Centers, Hammond

EAST CHICAGO—Lake County

⊞ ST. CATHERINE HOSPITAL, 4321 Fir Street, Zip 46312–3097; tel. 219/392–7000; JoAnn Birdzell, President and Chief Executive Officer **A**1 9 10 **F**4 7 8 10 11 12 14 15 16 17 19 21 22 23 24 25 28 29 30 32 34 35 37 39 40 41 42 43 44 45 46 49 50 52 54 55 56 60 63 64 65 67 70 71 73 74 **P**1 **S** Ancilla Systems Inc., Hobart, IN

| | 21 | 10 | 188 | 8070 | 126 | 45942 | 510 | 70588 | 26473 | 710 |

Hospital, Address, Telephone, Administrator, Approval, Facility, and Physician Codes, Health Care System, Network	Classi-fication Codes		Utilization Data					Expense (thousands) of dollars		
★ American Hospital Association (AHA) membership □ Joint Commission on Accreditation of Healthcare Organizations (JCAHO) accreditation + American Osteopathic Healthcare Association (AOHA) membership ○ American Osteopathic Association (AOA) accreditation △ Commission on Accreditation of Rehabilitation Facilities (CARF) accreditation Control codes 61, 63, 64, 71, 72 and 73 indicate hospitals listed by AOHA, but not registered by AHA. For definition of numerical codes, see page A4	Control	Service	Staffed Beds	Admissions	Census	Outpatient Visits	Births	Total	Payroll	Personnel

ELKHART—Elkhart County

★ △ ELKHART GENERAL HOSPITAL, 600 East Boulevard, Zip 46514–2499, Mailing Address: P.O. Box 1329, Zip 46515–1329; tel. 219/294–2621; Gregory W. Lintjer, President (Total facility includes 42 beds in nursing home–type unit) **A**1 7 9 10 **F**3 4 7 8 10 11 12 14 15 16 17 18 19 21 22 23 29 30 31 32 33 35 36 37 38 39 40 41 42 43 44 46 49 52 53 54 55 56 58 59 60 64 65 67 71 72 73 **P**5 8	23	10	321	12680	164	112501	1789	113952	48086	1270

ELWOOD—Madison County

★ ST. VINCENT MERCY HOSPITAL, 1331 South A Street, Zip 46036–1942; tel. 765/552–4600; David Masterson, Administrator **A**1 9 10 **F**7 8 12 14 19 22 28 30 32 35 37 39 40 41 42 44 49 63 65 67 71 73 **P**8 **S** Daughters of Charity National Health System, Saint Louis, MO **Web address:** www.stvincent.org	21	10	32	1356	15	29191	95	9716	4653	196

EVANSVILLE—Vanderburgh County

★ DEACONESS HOSPITAL, 600 Mary Street, Zip 47747–0001; tel. 812/450–5000; Thomas H. Kramer, President (Total facility includes 48 beds in nursing home–type unit) **A**1 2 3 5 9 10 **F**4 7 8 10 11 12 14 15 16 17 19 21 22 23 24 25 26 27 28 29 30 31 32 33 34 35 36 37 39 40 41 42 43 44 46 47 49 51 54 56 60 61 62 63 64 65 67 70 71 72 73 74 **P**1 6 7 8 **Web address:** www.deaconess.com	23	10	335	15562	214	163378	1470	139863	62100	2051
□ EVANSVILLE STATE HOSPITAL, 3400 Lincoln Avenue, Zip 47714–0146; tel. 812/473–2100; Ralph Nichols, Superintendent **A**1 13 **F**14 20 41 49 52 57 64 65 73	12	22	292	127	266	0	0	21992	12265	495
□ △ HEALTHSOUTH TRI–STATE REHABILITATION HOSPITAL, 4100 Covert Avenue, Zip 47714–5567, Mailing Address: P.O. Box 5349, Zip 47716–5349; tel. 812/476–9983; Gerald F. Vozel, Administrator and Chief Executive Officer (Nonreporting) **A**1 7 9 10 **S** HEALTHSOUTH Corporation, Birmingham, AL	33	46	80	—	—	—	—	—	—	—
★ ST. MARY'S MEDICAL CENTER OF EVANSVILLE, 3700 Washington Avenue, Zip 47750; tel. 812/485–4000; Jay D. Kasey, President (Total facility includes 128 beds in nursing home–type unit) **A**1 2 3 5 9 10 **F**3 4 6 7 8 10 11 12 14 15 16 17 19 21 22 23 24 25 26 28 30 32 33 34 35 37 38 40 41 42 43 44 47 49 52 54 55 56 57 58 59 60 61 64 65 66 67 68 71 72 73 74 **P**6 7 **S** Daughters of Charity National Health System, Saint Louis, MO	21	10	487	13973	321	206124	1922	134356	59619	2051
★ △ WELBORN MEMORIAL BAPTIST HOSPITAL, 401 Southeast Sixth Street, Zip 47713–1299; tel. 812/426–8000; Marjorie Z. Soyugenc, President and Chief Executive Officer (Total facility includes 27 beds in nursing home–type unit) **A**1 2 7 9 10 **F**2 3 4 7 8 10 11 12 14 15 16 19 21 22 23 24 26 28 29 30 31 32 33 35 36 37 38 39 40 41 44 45 46 48 49 51 52 53 54 55 56 58 59 60 61 63 64 65 67 69 71 73 **P**1 5 6 **Web address:** www.welborn.com	23	10	279	9840	138	50890	767	88674	43081	1323

FORT WAYNE—Allen County

□ CHARTER BEACON, 1720 Beacon Street, Zip 46805–4700; tel. 219/423–3651; Robert Hails, Chief Executive Officer (Nonreporting) **A**1 10 **S** Magellan Health Services, Atlanta, GA	33	22	97	—	—	—	—	—	—	—
★ LUTHERAN HOSPITAL OF INDIANA, 7950 West Jefferson Boulevard, Zip 46804–1677; tel. 219/435–7001; Thomas D. Miller, President and Chief Executive Officer **A**1 3 5 9 10 **F**2 3 4 7 8 10 11 12 14 15 16 17 19 21 22 23 25 26 27 28 29 30 31 34 35 36 37 38 39 40 41 42 43 44 45 47 48 49 52 54 55 56 57 58 59 60 64 65 67 68 71 72 73 74 **P**5 7 **S** Quorum Health Group/Quorum Health Resources, Inc., Brentwood, TN	33	10	449	15915	214	194559	1847	—	—	1598
★ △ PARKVIEW HOSPITAL, 2200 Randallia Drive, Zip 46805–4699; tel. 219/484–6636; Frank D. Byrne, M.D., President (Total facility includes 28 beds in nursing home–type unit) **A**1 3 5 7 9 10 **F**2 3 4 7 8 10 11 12 14 15 16 17 19 21 22 24 25 27 28 30 33 34 36 37 38 39 40 41 42 43 44 45 46 47 48 49 51 52 53 54 55 56 57 58 59 60 63 64 65 67 68 70 71 72 73 74 **P**6 7 8 **S** Parkview Health System, Fort Wayne, IN	23	10	509	27853	343	151107	3996	234552	109060	2722
★ △ ST. JOSEPH HOSPITAL, (Formerly St. Joseph Health System), 700 Broadway, Zip 46802–1493; tel. 219/425–3000; Michael H. Schatzlein, M.D., President and Chief Executive Officer **A**1 3 5 7 9 10 **F**2 3 4 7 8 9 10 11 12 14 15 16 17 19 21 22 23 24 25 26 28 30 36 37 38 40 41 43 44 46 47 48 49 52 54 55 56 57 58 59 64 65 68 71 72 73 74 **P**5 6 8 **S** Quorum Health Group/Quorum Health Resources, Inc., Brentwood, TN **Web address:** www.stjoehealthguides.com	33	10	191	2815	84	46761	176	35810	16251	838
★ VETERANS AFFAIRS NORTHERN INDIANA HEALTH CARE SYSTEM, (Includes Veterans Affairs Northern Indiana Health Care System–Marion Campus, 1700 East 38th Street, Marion, Zip 46953–4589; tel. 765/674–3321), 2121 Lake Avenue, Zip 46805–5347; tel. 219/460–1310; Michael W. Murphy, Ph.D., Director (Total facility includes 123 beds in nursing home–type unit) **A**1 **F**1 3 12 15 17 19 20 21 22 26 27 28 29 30 31 32 33 34 35 37 41 42 44 45 46 48 49 51 52 54 55 56 57 58 59 60 64 65 67 71 73 74 **P**1 **S** Department of Veterans Affairs, Washington, DC	45	10	469	2896	432	123198	0	88454	45173	1078

FRANKFORT—Clinton County

★ CLINTON COUNTY HOSPITAL, 1300 South Jackson Street, Zip 46041–3394, Mailing Address: P.O. Box 669, Zip 46041–0669; tel. 765/659–4731; Brian R. Zeh, Chief Executive Officer **A**1 9 10 **F**3 7 8 12 14 19 20 21 22 24 26 28 29 30 34 35 37 39 40 41 42 44 45 54 55 58 63 65 67 71 73 74 **P**1 6 **S** Quorum Health Group/Quorum Health Resources, Inc., Brentwood, TN **Web address:** www.cchosp/accs.net	33	10	53	1600	14	41670	319	14946	7295	219

Hospital, Address, Telephone, Administrator, Approval, Facility, and Physician Codes, Health Care System, Network	Classi-fication Codes		Utilization Data					Expense (thousands) of dollars		

★ American Hospital Association (AHA) membership
◻ Joint Commission on Accreditation of Healthcare Organizations (JCAHO) accreditation
+ American Osteopathic Healthcare Association (AOHA) membership
◯ American Osteopathic Association (AOA) accreditation
△ Commission on Accreditation of Rehabilitation Facilities (CARF) accreditation
Control codes 61, 63, 64, 71, 72 and 73 indicate hospitals listed by AOHA, but not registered by AHA. For definition of numerical codes, see page A4

	Control	Service	Staffed Beds	Admissions	Census	Outpatient Visits	Births	Total	Payroll	Personnel
FRANKLIN—Johnson County										
✶ JOHNSON MEMORIAL HOSPITAL, 1125 West Jefferson Street, Zip 46131–2140, Mailing Address: P.O. Box 549, Zip 46131–0549; tel. 317/736–3300; Gregg A. Bechtold, President and Chief Executive Officer (Total facility includes 87 beds in nursing home–type unit) **A**1 9 10 **F**1 7 8 14 15 16 17 19 21 22 27 28 30 32 35 36 37 39 40 41 42 44 46 49 64 65 67 71 72 73 **P**6 8	13	10	160	4297	111	99598	559	41024	16613	515
GARY—Lake County										
✶ △ METHODIST HOSPITALS, (Includes Northlake Campus; Southlake Campus, 8701 Broadway, Merrillville, Zip 46410; tel. 219/738–5500), 600 Grant Street, Zip 46402–6099; tel. 219/886–4000; John H. Betjemann, President **A**1 2 3 5 7 9 10 **F**2 3 4 7 8 10 12 13 14 15 16 17 18 19 21 22 23 25 28 29 30 31 34 35 37 38 39 40 41 42 43 44 45 46 48 49 51 52 53 54 58 60 61 63 64 65 66 67 68 70 71 72 73 74 **P**5	23	10	568	23334	369	238514	2302	216044	97383	2533
GOSHEN—Elkhart County										
✶ GOSHEN GENERAL HOSPITAL, 200 High Park Avenue, Zip 46526–4899, Mailing Address: P.O. Box 139, Zip 46527–0139; tel. 219/533–2141; James O. Dague, President **A**1 9 10 **F**1 2 3 4 6 7 8 10 12 13 14 15 16 17 19 21 22 23 26 27 28 29 30 32 33 34 35 36 37 39 40 41 42 44 49 52 53 54 55 56 57 58 59 62 64 65 66 67 71 72 73 **P**7	23	10	113	5392	61	—	1247	45852	20256	593
OAKLAWN PSYCHIATRIC CENTER, INC., 330 Lakeview Drive, Zip 46528–9365, Mailing Address: P.O. Box 809, Zip 46527–0809; tel. 219/533–1234; Harold C. Loewen, President (Nonreporting) **A**10	23	22	40	—	—	—	—	—	—	—
GREENCASTLE—Putnam County										
✶ PUTNAM COUNTY HOSPITAL, 1542 Bloomington Street, Zip 46135–2297; tel. 765/653–5121; John D. Fajt, Executive Director **A**1 2 9 10 **F**7 8 14 15 16 17 19 20 21 22 26 28 30 32 35 37 39 40 41 42 44 46 49 56 63 65 67 71 **P**8	13	10	85	1754	22	46028	220	14106	6396	239
GREENFIELD—Hancock County										
✶ HANCOCK MEMORIAL HOSPITAL AND HEALTH SERVICES, 801 North State Street, Zip 46140–1270, Mailing Address: P.O. Box 827, Zip 46140–0827; tel. 317/462–5544; Robert C. Keen, Ph.D., CHE, President and Chief Executive Officer (Total facility includes 21 beds in nursing home–type unit) **A**1 9 10 **F**1 3 7 8 10 12 14 15 16 17 19 21 22 24 26 28 30 31 32 33 34 35 37 39 40 41 42 44 45 46 49 52 57 58 59 61 64 65 66 67 68 71 72 73 74 **P**1 7 Web address: www.hmhhs.org	13	10	102	3993	54	155819	557	46099	20365	566
GREENSBURG—Decatur County										
✶ DECATUR COUNTY MEMORIAL HOSPITAL, 720 North Lincoln Street, Zip 47240–1398; tel. 812/663–4331; Charles Duffy, President **A**1 9 10 **F**1 7 8 13 16 19 21 22 26 27 28 30 32 33 34 35 36 37 39 40 41 42 44 45 46 49 60 63 65 67 71 72 73 **S** Norton Healthcare, Louisville, KY	13	10	70	2289	32	70123	412	18612	8682	356
GREENWOOD—Johnson County										
◻ BHC VALLE VISTA HOSPITAL, 898 East Main Street, Zip 46143–1400; tel. 317/887–1348; Gordon L. Steinhauer, Chief Executive Officer **A**1 9 10 **F**2 3 12 15 16 17 18 26 28 30 45 52 53 54 55 56 57 58 59 65 67 **P**6 **S** Behavioral Healthcare Corporation, Nashville, TN	33	22	88	755	42	15100	0	8107	4523	107
HAMMOND—Lake County										
✶ SAINT MARGARET MERCY HEALTHCARE CENTERS, (Includes Saint Margaret Mercy Healthcare Centers–North Campus, 5454 Hohman Avenue, Zip 46320; tel. 219/932–2300; Saint Margaret Mercy Healthcare Centers–South Campus, 24 Joliet Street, Dyer, Zip 46311–1799; tel. 219/865–2141), 5454 Hohman Avenue, Zip 46320–1999; tel. 219/933–2074; Eugene C. Diamond, President and Chief Executive Officer (Total facility includes 67 beds in nursing home–type unit) (Nonreporting) **A**1 2 9 10 **S** Sisters of St. Francis Health Services, Inc., Mishawaka, IN Web address: www.clarian.com	21	10	624	—	—	—	—	—	—	—
HARTFORD CITY—Blackford County										
✶ BLACKFORD COUNTY HOSPITAL, 503 East Van Cleve Street, Zip 47348–1897; tel. 765/348–0300; Steven J. West, Chief Executive Officer **A**1 9 10 **F**7 12 14 15 16 17 19 22 28 32 35 39 40 44 45 49 63 65 67 71 73 **S** Norton Healthcare, Louisville, KY	13	10	36	819	10	20200	54	7709	2930	122
HOBART—Lake County										
◻ CHARTER BEHAVIORAL HEALTH SYSTEM OF NORTHWEST INDIANA, 101 West 61st Avenue and State Road 51, Zip 46342–6489; tel. 219/947–4464; Michael J. Perry, Chief Executive Officer (Nonreporting) **A**1 10 **S** Magellan Health Services, Atlanta, GA	33	22	60	—	—	—	—	—	—	—
✶ ST. MARY MEDICAL CENTER, 1500 South Lake Park Avenue, Zip 46342–6699; tel. 219/942–0551; Milton Triana, President and Chief Executive Officer (Nonreporting) **A**1 10 **S** Ancilla Systems Inc., Hobart, IN Web address: www.stmary–hobart.com	21	10	102	—	—	—	—	—	—	—
HUNTINGBURG—Dubois County										
◻ ST. JOSEPH'S HOSPITAL, 1900 Medical Arts Drive, Zip 47542–9521; tel. 812/683–2121; John T. Graves, President and Chief Executive Officer **A**1 10 **F**7 8 12 13 14 15 16 17 18 19 21 22 28 30 32 33 34 37 39 40 41 44 45 46 48 49 52 54 55 56 58 65 67 70 71 73	23	10	60	1898	23	55904	277	15945	7018	264
HUNTINGTON—Huntington County										
✶ HUNTINGTON MEMORIAL HOSPITAL, 1215 Etna Avenue, Zip 46750–3696; tel. 219/356–3000; L. Kent McCoy, President **A**1 9 10 **F**3 4 5 6 7 8 10 12 13 14 15 16 17 18 19 21 22 24 25 26 27 28 29 30 31 32 33 34 35 36 39 40 41 42 43 44 45 46 49 50 51 53 54 55 56 57 58 59 60 61 62 63 65 66 67 68 70 71 72 73 74 **P**5 **S** Parkview Health System, Fort Wayne, IN	23	10	37	1739	13	37728	246	17199	7935	256

Hospital, Address, Telephone, Administrator, Approval, Facility, and Physician Codes, Health Care System, Network	Classi-fication Codes		Utilization Data					Expense (thousands) of dollars		
	Control	Service	Staffed Beds	Admissions	Census	Outpatient Visits	Births	Total	Payroll	Personnel

★ American Hospital Association (AHA) membership
□ Joint Commission on Accreditation of Healthcare Organizations (JCAHO) accreditation
+ American Osteopathic Healthcare Association (AOHA) membership
○ American Osteopathic Association (AOA) accreditation
△ Commission on Accreditation of Rehabilitation Facilities (CARF) accreditation
Control codes 61, 63, 64, 71, 72 and 73 indicate hospitals listed by AOHA, but not registered by AHA. For definition of numerical codes, see page A4

INDIANAPOLIS—Marion County

Hospital	Control	Service	Staffed Beds	Admissions	Census	Outpatient Visits	Births	Total	Payroll	Personnel
□ CHARTER INDIANAPOLIS BEHAVIORAL HEALTH SYSTEM, 5602 Caito Drive, Zip 46226–1356; tel. 317/545–2111; Marina Cecchini, Chief Executive Officer **A**1 10 **F**1 2 3 4 5 6 7 8 9 10 11 12 13 14 15 17 18 19 20 21 22 23 24 25 26 27 28 29 30 31 32 33 34 35 36 37 38 39 40 41 42 43 44 45 46 47 48 49 50 51 52 53 54 55 56 57 58 59 60 61 62 63 64 65 66 67 69 70 71 72 73 74 **P**8 **S** Magellan Health Services, Atlanta, GA	33	22	80	1697	51	—	0	—	—	113
☒ CLARIAN HEALTH PARTNERS, (Includes Indiana University Medical Center, 550 North University Boulevard, Zip 46202–5262; tel. 317/274–5000; Methodist Hospital of Indiana, 1701 North Senate Boulevard, Zip 46202, Mailing Address: I. 65 at 21st Street, P.O. Box 1367, Zip 46206–1367; tel. 317/929–2000; Riley Hospital for Childrern, 702 Barnhill Drive, Zip 46202–5225), I–65 at 21st Street, Zip 46202–5250, Mailing Address: P.O. Box 1367, Zip 46206–1367; tel. 317/274–5000; William J. Loveday, President and Chief Executive Officer (Total facility includes 60 beds in nursing home–type unit) **A**1 2 3 5 8 9 10 **F**2 3 4 5 7 8 9 10 11 12 13 14 15 16 17 18 19 20 21 22 23 25 26 28 29 30 31 32 33 34 35 36 37 38 39 40 41 42 43 44 45 46 47 48 49 50 51 52 53 54 55 56 57 58 59 60 61 63 64 65 66 67 68 70 71 72 73 74 **P**6 7 COLUMBIA WOMEN'S HOSPITAL–INDIANAPOLIS See Women's Hospital–Indianapolis	23	10	1322	62985	969	948085	4853	811297	339830	8526
□ △ COMMUNITY HOSPITALS INDIANAPOLIS, (Includes Community Hospital East; Community Hospital North, 7150 Clearvista Drive, Zip 46256; tel. 317/849–6262; Community Hospital South, 1402 East County Line Road South, Zip 46227; tel. 317/887–7000; Community Hospital of Anderson and Madison County, 1515 North Madison Avenue, Anderson, Zip 46011–3453; tel. 765/642–8011), 1500 North Ritter Avenue, Zip 46219–3095; tel. 317/355–1411; William E. Corley, President (Total facility includes 30 beds in nursing home–type unit) (Nonreporting) **A**1 2 3 5 7 9 10 **Web address:** www.commhospindy.org	23	10	999	—	—	—	—	—	—	—
FAIRBANKS HOSPITAL, 8102 Clearvista Parkway, Zip 46256–4698; tel. 317/849–8222; Timothy J. Kelly, M.D., President (Nonreporting) **A**9 10 INDIANA UNIVERSITY MEDICAL CENTER See Clarian Health Partners	23	82	96	—	—	—	—	—	—	—
□ LARUE D. CARTER MEMORIAL HOSPITAL, 2601 Cold Spring Road, Zip 46222–2273; tel. 317/941–4000; Diana Haugh, MS, Superintendent (Nonreporting) **A**1 3 5 10 METHODIST HOSPITAL OF INDIANA See Clarian Health Partners	12	22	146	—	—	—	—	—	—	—
□ △ REHABILITATION HOSPITAL OF INDIANA, 4141 Shore Drive, Zip 46254–2607; tel. 317/329–2000; Kim D. Eicher, President and Chief Executive Officer (Nonreporting) **A**1 7 9 10	23	46	80	—	—	—	—	—	—	—
☒ RICHARD L. ROUDEBUSH VETERANS AFFAIRS MEDICAL CENTER, 1481 West Tenth Street, Zip 46202–2884; tel. 317/554–0000; Robert H. Sabin, Acting Director (Total facility includes 21 beds in nursing home–type unit) **A**1 2 3 5 8 **F**1 3 4 8 10 11 12 14 15 16 17 19 20 21 22 23 26 27 28 29 30 31 32 34 35 37 39 41 42 43 44 45 46 48 49 50 51 52 54 55 56 57 58 59 60 61 64 65 67 71 73 74 **P**6 **S** Department of Veterans Affairs, Washington, DC RILEY HOSPITAL FOR CHILDRERN See Clarian Health Partners	45	10	158	7873	101	308589	0	138000	70000	1512
☒ ST. VINCENT HOSPITALS AND HEALTH SERVICES, (Includes St. Vincent Carmel Hospital, 13500 North Meridian Street, Carmel, Zip 46032; tel. 317/582–7000; St. Vincent Stress Center, 8401 Harcourt Road, Zip 46260, Mailing Address: P.O. Box 80160, Zip 46280; tel. 317/338–4600; Paul Lefkovitz, Ph.D., Administrator), 2001 West 86th Street, Zip 46260–1991, Mailing Address: P.O. Box 40970, Zip 46240–0970; tel. 317/338–2345; Marsha N. Casey, President **A**1 2 3 5 8 9 10 **F**2 3 4 6 7 8 10 11 12 13 14 15 16 17 18 19 20 21 22 23 24 25 26 27 28 29 30 31 32 33 34 35 37 38 39 40 41 42 43 44 45 46 47 49 51 52 53 54 55 56 57 58 59 60 63 64 65 66 67 68 70 71 72 73 74 **P**6 7 8 **S** Daughters of Charity National Health System, Saint Louis, MO **Web address:** www.stvincent.com	21	10	802	32769	480	960803	4311	429509	172121	4972
+ ○ WESTVIEW HOSPITAL, 3630 Guion Road, Zip 46222–1699; tel. 317/924–6661; David C. Dyar, President and Administrator (Total facility includes 18 beds in nursing home–type unit) (Nonreporting) **A**9 10 11 13	23	10	67	—	—	—	—	—	—	—
☒ WINONA MEMORIAL HOSPITAL, 3232 North Meridian Street, Zip 46208–4693; tel. 317/924–3392; Clifford A. Yeager, Chief Executive Officer **A**1 9 10 **F**2 3 4 8 10 11 12 14 15 16 17 19 21 22 26 27 28 29 30 32 34 35 37 39 41 42 44 45 46 48 49 52 54 55 56 57 58 65 67 71 73 74 **P**5 7 **S** TENET Healthcare Corporation, Santa Barbara, CA **Web address:** www.tenethealth.com	33	10	169	3356	60	55532	0	—	—	494
☒ WISHARD HEALTH SERVICES, 1001 West 10th Street, Zip 46202–2879; tel. 317/630–7356; Randall L. Braddom, M.D., Chief Executive Officer and Medical Director (Total facility includes 240 beds in nursing home–type unit) (Nonreporting) **A**1 3 5 8 9 10	16	10	531	—	—	—	—	—	—	—
☒ WOMEN'S HOSPITAL–INDIANAPOLIS, (Formerly Columbia Women's Hospital–Indianapolis), 8111 Township Line Road, Zip 46260–8043; tel. 317/875–5994; Steven B. Reed, President and Chief Executive Officer (Nonreporting) **A**1 9 10 **S** Columbia/HCA Healthcare Corporation, Nashville, TN	33	10	132	—	—	—	—	—	—	—

JASPER—Dubois County

Hospital	Control	Service	Staffed Beds	Admissions	Census	Outpatient Visits	Births	Total	Payroll	Personnel
☒ MEMORIAL HOSPITAL AND HEALTH CARE CENTER, 800 West Ninth Street, Zip 47546–2516; tel. 812/482–2345; Raymond W. Snowden, President and Chief Executive Officer (Total facility includes 24 beds in nursing home–type unit) **A**1 2 9 10 **F**7 8 10 14 15 16 19 21 22 26 27 28 30 32 33 34 35 37 39 40 41 42 44 45 49 52 53 54 55 56 57 58 63 64 65 66 67 71 73 74 **S** Little Company of Mary Sisters Healthcare System, Evergreen Park, IL **Web address:** www.mhhcc.org	21	10	124	4784	66	93072	603	42819	21800	617

Hospital, Address, Telephone, Administrator, Approval, Facility, and Physician Codes, Health Care System, Network	Classi-fication Codes		Utilization Data					Expense (thousands) of dollars		
★ American Hospital Association (AHA) membership □ Joint Commission on Accreditation of Healthcare Organizations (JCAHO) accreditation + American Osteopathic Healthcare Association (AOHA) membership ○ American Osteopathic Association (AOA) accreditation △ Commission on Accreditation of Rehabilitation Facilities (CARF) accreditation Control codes 61, 63, 64, 71, 72 and 73 indicate hospitals listed by AOHA, but not registered by AHA. For definition of numerical codes, see page A4	Control	Service	Staffed Beds	Admissions	Census	Outpatient Visits	Births	Total	Payroll	Personnel

JEFFERSONVILLE—Clark County

□ CHARTER BEHAVIORAL HEALTH SYSTEM OF INDIANA AT JEFFERSON, 2700 Vissing Park Road, Zip 47130–5943; tel. 812/284–3400; James E. Ledbetter, Ph.D., Chief Executive Officer (Nonreporting) **A**1 10 **S** Magellan Health Services, Atlanta, GA — 33 22 100 — — — — — — —

☒ CLARK MEMORIAL HOSPITAL, 1220 Missouri Avenue, Zip 47130–3743, Mailing Address: Box 69, Zip 47131–0069; tel. 812/282–6631; Merle E. Stepp, President and Chief Executive Officer (Total facility includes 66 beds in nursing home–type unit) **A**1 9 10 **F**3 7 8 10 11 12 14 15 16 17 19 21 22 23 28 29 30 32 33 34 35 39 40 41 42 44 45 46 49 52 53 54 55 56 57 59 60 63 64 65 67 71 73 74 **P**6 **S** Jewish Hospital HealthCare Services, Louisville, KY **Web address:** www.cmhl.com — 13 10 243 9761 165 112551 1346 76114 35022 1165

KENDALLVILLE—Noble County

☒ MCCRAY MEMORIAL HOSPITAL, 951 East Hospital Drive, Zip 46755–2293, Mailing Address: P.O. Box 249, Zip 46755–0249; tel. 219/347–1100; John H. Matthews, Interim Chief Executive Officer **A**1 9 10 **F**7 8 15 16 19 21 22 27 30 32 33 35 37 40 41 42 44 46 49 52 54 55 56 57 63 65 71 73 — 15 10 43 1511 21 102259 233 20338 8018 250

KNOX—Starke County

□ STARKE MEMORIAL HOSPITAL, 102 East Culver Road, Zip 46534–2299; tel. 219/772–6231; Kathryn J. Norem, Executive Director (Nonreporting) **A**1 9 10 **S** Province Healthcare Corporation, Brentwood, TN — 13 10 35 — — — — — — —

KOKOMO—Howard County

□ △ HEALTHSOUTH REHABILITATION HOSPITAL OF KOKOMO, (Formerly Kokomo Rehabilitation Hospital), 829 North Dixon Road, Zip 46901–7709; tel. 765/452–6700; David Bailey, Chief Executive Officer (Nonreporting) **A**1 7 9 10 **S** HEALTHSOUTH Corporation, Birmingham, AL — 33 46 60 — — — — — — —

☒ HOWARD COMMUNITY HOSPITAL, 3500 South Lafountain Street, Zip 46904–9011; tel. 765/453–0702; James Alender, Acting President and Chief Executive Officer (Total facility includes 18 beds in nursing home–type unit) **A**1 9 10 **F**3 4 7 8 10 11 12 14 15 16 18 19 21 22 23 24 26 28 29 30 32 35 37 38 39 40 41 42 44 45 49 52 53 54 55 56 57 58 59 60 64 65 67 70 71 73 **P**2 8 — 13 10 127 5289 75 145664 391 50472 21575 690

KOKOMO REHABILITATION HOSPITAL See Healthsouth Rehabilitation Hospital of Kokomo

☒ SCCI HOSPITAL OF KOKOMO, 1907 West Sycamore Street, Zip 46901; tel. 765/452–6730; Michael T. Moore, Chief Executive Officer (Nonreporting) **A**1 10 — 33 49 19 — — — — — — —

☒ ST. JOSEPH HOSPITAL & HEALTH CENTER, 1907 West Sycamore Street, Zip 46904–9010, Mailing Address: P.O. Box 9010, Zip 46904–9010; tel. 765/452–5611; Kathleen M. Korbelak, President and Chief Executive Officer **A**1 9 10 **F**2 3 7 8 10 12 14 15 16 17 19 20 21 22 23 24 26 27 28 30 31 32 33 34 35 36 37 40 41 42 44 46 49 52 53 54 55 56 57 58 59 60 63 64 65 67 68 71 72 73 **P**8 **S** Daughters of Charity National Health System, Saint Louis, MO **Web address:** www.stjhhc.org — 21 10 145 6031 79 93972 1069 55398 24074 762

LA PORTE—La Porte County

LA PORTE HOSPITAL AND HEALTH SERVICES See La Porte Regional Health System

☒ LA PORTE REGIONAL HEALTH SYSTEM, (Formerly La Porte Hospital and Health Services), 1007 Lincolnway, Zip 46352–0250, Mailing Address: P.O. Box 250, Zip 46352–0250; tel. 219/326–1234; Leigh E. Morris, President and Chief Executive Officer (Total facility includes 55 beds in nursing home–type unit) **A**1 2 9 10 **F**3 6 7 8 10 11 12 14 15 16 17 18 19 20 21 22 23 24 25 27 28 29 30 31 32 33 34 35 36 37 39 40 41 42 44 49 51 52 53 54 55 56 57 58 60 61 63 64 65 66 67 71 72 73 **P**7 — 23 10 227 6023 119 64097 689 67631 30674 801

LAFAYETTE—Tippecanoe County

□ CHARTER BEHAVIORAL HEALTH SYSTEMS, 3700 Rome Drive, Zip 47905–4465, Mailing Address: P.O. Box 5969, Zip 47903–5969; tel. 765/448–6999; Sheila Mishler, Chief Executive Officer **A**1 9 10 **F**1 2 3 14 15 16 29 30 34 52 53 54 55 56 57 58 59 65 **P**6 **S** Magellan Health Services, Atlanta, GA — 33 22 64 1246 23 706 0 1626 — 76

☒ △ LAFAYETTE HOME HOSPITAL, 2400 South Street, Zip 47904–3052, Mailing Address: P.O. Box 7518, Zip 47903–7518; tel. 765/447–6811; John R. Walling, President and Chief Executive Officer (Total facility includes 21 beds in nursing home–type unit) (Nonreporting) **A**1 7 9 10 **Web address:** www.homehospital.com — 23 10 276 — — — — — — —

☒ ST. ELIZABETH MEDICAL CENTER, 1501 Hartford Street, Zip 47904–2126, Mailing Address: Box 7501, Zip 47903–7501; tel. 765/423–6011; John R. Walling, President and Chief Executive Officer (Total facility includes 24 beds in nursing home–type unit) **A**1 2 6 9 10 **F**4 7 8 10 11 14 15 16 17 19 21 22 23 25 26 27 28 29 30 31 32 33 34 35 37 39 40 41 42 43 44 45 49 60 63 64 65 66 67 71 72 73 74 **Web address:** www.ste.org — 21 10 186 6422 99 145900 375 82851 33339 1032

LAGRANGE—LaGrange County

□ VENCOR HOSPITAL–LAGRANGE, 207 North Townline Road, Zip 46761–1325; tel. 219/463–2143; Joe Murrell, Administrator **A**1 9 10 **F**7 8 12 14 15 16 19 20 21 22 28 29 30 31 32 33 34 35 37 39 40 41 42 44 48 49 52 53 54 55 56 57 58 65 66 71 73 **P**8 **S** Vencor, Incorporated, Louisville, KY — 33 10 53 1232 18 23271 298 11236 4908 165

Hospital, Address, Telephone, Administrator, Approval, Facility, and Physician Codes, Health Care System, Network	Classi-fication Codes		Utilization Data					Expense (thousands) of dollars		
★ American Hospital Association (AHA) membership □ Joint Commission on Accreditation of Healthcare Organizations (JCAHO) accreditation + American Osteopathic Healthcare Association (AOHA) membership ○ American Osteopathic Association (AOA) accreditation △ Commission on Accreditation of Rehabilitation Facilities (CARF) accreditation Control codes 61, 63, 64, 71, 72 and 73 indicate hospitals listed by AOHA, but not registered by AHA. For definition of numerical codes, see page A4	Control	Service	Staffed Beds	Admissions	Census	Outpatient Visits	Births	Total	Payroll	Personnel

LAWRENCEBURG—Dearborn County

✣ DEARBORN COUNTY HOSPITAL, 600 Wilson Creek Road, Zip 47025–1199; tel. 812/537–1010; Peter V. Resnick, Executive Director (Total facility includes 13 beds in nursing home–type unit) **A**1 9 10 **F**7 8 10 12 13 14 15 16 17 19 21 22 23 28 30 32 33 34 35 37 40 41 42 44 46 49 60 63 64 65 66 67 71 73 **P**6	13	10	87	3223	36	99572	455	32972	14311	444

LEBANON—Boone County

□ WITHAM MEMORIAL HOSPITAL, 1124 North Lebanon Street, Zip 46052–1776, Mailing Address: P.O. Box 1200, Zip 46052–3005; tel. 765/482–2700; Ray Ingham, President and Chief Executive Officer (Nonreporting) **A**1 9 10	13	10	60	—	—	—	—	—	—	—

LINTON—Greene County

✣ GREENE COUNTY GENERAL HOSPITAL, Rural Route 1, Box 1000, Zip 47441–9457; tel. 812/847–2281; Jonas S. Uland, Executive Director **A**1 9 10 **F**8 14 15 16 19 20 22 28 29 30 32 34 37 40 42 44 49 54 56 71 73 **P**3 **Web address:** www.greenet.net/hospital	13	10	56	1562	20	—	63	13917	6340	233

LOGANSPORT—Cass County

□ LOGANSPORT STATE HOSPITAL, 1098 South State Road 25, Zip 46947–9699; tel. 219/722–4141; Jeffrey H. Smith, Ph.D., Superintendent **A**1 **F**12 20 26 39 45 52 57 73	12	22	396	203	373	1136	0	31845	13131	723
✣ MEMORIAL HOSPITAL, 1101 Michigan Avenue, Zip 46947–7013, Mailing Address: P.O. Box 7013, Zip 46947–7013; tel. 219/753–7541; Brian T. Shockney, President and Chief Executive Officer (Total facility includes 21 beds in nursing home–type unit) **A**1 9 10 **F**7 8 14 15 16 17 19 21 22 28 29 30 32 33 35 36 37 39 40 41 42 44 46 49 63 64 65 67 71 73 **P**8 **Web address:** www.mhlogan.org	13	10	104	3085	37	51916	485	28305	12313	392

MADISON—Jefferson County

✣ KING'S DAUGHTERS' HOSPITAL, One King's Daughters' Drive, Zip 47250–3357, Mailing Address: P.O. Box 447, Zip 47250–0447; tel. 812/265–5211; Roger J. Allman, Chief Executive Officer (Total facility includes 29 beds in nursing home–type unit) **A**1 2 9 10 **F**7 8 10 11 14 15 16 19 21 22 23 25 27 28 30 32 33 34 35 37 39 40 41 42 44 49 60 64 65 66 67 71 73 **P**6	23	10	115	4815	70	113491	420	51617	25751	740
□ MADISON STATE HOSPITAL, 711 Green Road, Zip 47250–2199; tel. 812/265–2611; Steven Covington, Superintendent **A**1 10 **F**2 15 16 20 52 53 57 65 73 **P**6	12	22	316	256	291	0	0	23738	13567	518

MARION—Grant County

✣ MARION GENERAL HOSPITAL, 441 North Wabash Avenue, Zip 46952–2690; tel. 765/662–1441; Albert C. Knauss, President and Chief Executive Officer (Total facility includes 21 beds in nursing home–type unit) **A**1 9 10 **F**7 8 10 11 14 15 16 19 21 22 28 30 32 33 34 35 36 37 39 40 41 42 44 46 49 63 64 65 66 67 68 71 73 74 **P**6 **Web address:** www.mgh.net	23	10	212	8466	105	139734	783	70476	31670	1025
VETERANS AFFAIRS NORTHERN INDIANA HEALTH CARE SYSTEM–MARION CAMPUS See Veterans Affairs Northern Indiana Health Care System, Fort Wayne										

MARTINSVILLE—Morgan County

✣ MORGAN COUNTY MEMORIAL HOSPITAL, 2209 John R. Wooden Drive, Zip 46151–1840, Mailing Address: P.O. Box 1717, Zip 46151–1717; tel. 765/342–8441; S. Dean Melton, President and Chief Executive Officer **A**1 9 10 **F**7 8 12 14 15 16 19 21 22 28 29 30 32 34 35 36 37 39 40 41 42 44 45 51 64 65 71 73 **P**7 8 **Web address:** www.scican.net\hospital\mcmh.html	13	10	86	2323	27	80357	279	23765	10260	301

MERRILLVILLE—Lake County

SOUTHLAKE CAMPUS See Methodist Hospitals, Gary										

MICHIGAN CITY—La Porte County

✣ △ SAINT ANTHONY MEMORIAL HEALTH CENTERS, (Includes Memorial Hospital of Michigan City, 515 Pine Street, Zip 46360–3370; tel. 219/879–0202; Norman D. Steider, President), 301 West Homer Street, Zip 46360–4358; tel. 219/879–8511; Bruce E. Rampage, President and Chief Executive Officer **A**1 7 9 10 **F**1 3 7 8 10 12 17 19 21 22 32 33 34 35 36 39 40 41 42 44 45 48 49 52 53 54 56 57 59 61 63 64 65 71 73 **S** Sisters of St. Francis Health Services, Inc., Mishawaka, IN	21	10	162	8280	117	200617	702	66000	25560	858

MISHAWAKA—St. Joseph County

✣ + ○ △ ST. JOSEPH COMMUNITY HOSPITAL, 215 West Fourth Street, Zip 46544–1999; tel. 219/259–2431; Mary Roos, President and Chief Executive Officer **A**1 7 9 10 11 12 13 **F**3 4 7 8 10 12 13 14 15 16 17 18 19 21 22 23 25 26 28 30 32 34 35 37 39 40 41 42 44 45 46 49 53 62 63 65 66 67 71 72 73 **P**4 6 7 8 **S** Ancilla Systems Inc., Hobart, IN **Web address:** www.ancillahealthcare.org	21	10	100	4789	58	87984	1097	62611	25909	807

MONTICELLO—White County

□ WHITE COUNTY MEMORIAL HOSPITAL, 1101 O'Connor Boulevard, Zip 47960–1698; tel. 219/583–7111; John M. Avers, Chief Executive Officer **A**1 9 10 **F**7 8 14 15 16 17 19 21 22 26 27 29 30 32 34 35 37 39 40 41 42 44 45 46 48 49 51 63 65 66 67 68 71 72 73	13	10	59	1352	14	30068	151	13406	5751	195

MOORESVILLE—Morgan County

□ KENDRICK MEMORIAL HOSPITAL, 1201 Hadley Road N.W., Zip 46158–1789; tel. 317/831–1160; Charles D. Swisher, President and Chief Executive Officer (Nonreporting) **A**1 2 9 10	23	10	60	—	—	—	—	—	—	—

Hospital, Address, Telephone, Administrator, Approval, Facility, and Physician Codes, Health Care System, Network	Classi-fication Codes		Utilization Data					Expense (thousands) of dollars		
★ American Hospital Association (AHA) membership □ Joint Commission on Accreditation of Healthcare Organizations (JCAHO) accreditation + American Osteopathic Healthcare Association (AOHA) membership ○ American Osteopathic Association (AOA) accreditation △ Commission on Accreditation of Rehabilitation Facilities (CARF) accreditation Control codes 61, 63, 64, 71, 72 and 73 indicate hospitals listed by AOHA, but not registered by AHA. For definition of numerical codes, see page A4	Control	Service	Staffed Beds	Admissions	Census	Outpatient Visits	Births	Total	Payroll	Personnel

MUNCIE—Delaware County

☒ △ BALL MEMORIAL HOSPITAL, 2401 University Avenue, Zip 47303–3499; tel. 765/747–3111; Mitchell C. Carson, President (Total facility includes 39 beds in nursing home–type unit) **A**1 2 3 5 7 8 9 10 **F**2 3 4 7 8 10 11 13 14 15 16 17 19 20 21 22 23 24 25 26 28 29 30 31 32 33 34 35 36 37 38 39 40 41 42 43 44 45 46 48 49 51 52 56 57 60 61 63 64 65 66 67 71 72 73 74
Web address: www.iquest.net/bmh/

	23	10	400	17927	254	99370	1781	166583	67765	1902

MUNSTER—Lake County

□ COMMUNITY HOSPITAL, 901 MacArthur Boulevard, Zip 46321–2959; tel. 219/836–1600; Edward P. Robinson, Administrator (Nonreporting) **A**1 2 9 10

	23	10	292	—	—	—	—	—	—	—

NEW ALBANY—Floyd County

☒ FLOYD MEMORIAL HOSPITAL AND HEALTH SERVICES, 1850 State Street, Zip 47150–4997; tel. 812/949–5500; Bryant R. Hanson, President and Chief Executive Officer **A**1 2 9 10 **F**7 8 10 11 14 15 16 17 19 21 22 28 29 30 32 35 37 40 41 42 44 46 49 60 63 64 65 67 70 71 72 73 74 **P**1 6
Web address: www.floydmemorial.org

	13	10	178	8578	101	169590	804	74663	32780	974

☒ △ SOUTHERN INDIANA REHABILITATION HOSPITAL, 3104 Blackiston Boulevard, Zip 47150–9579; tel. 812/941–8300; Randy L. Napier, President and Chief Executive Officer **A**1 7 10 **F**4 7 8 9 10 11 12 15 16 17 19 21 22 25 27 28 29 30 32 34 35 37 39 40 41 43 44 45 46 48 49 51 60 64 65 66 67 68 71 73 74 **S** Jewish Hospital HealthCare Services, Louisville, KY

	23	46	60	744	54	9585	0	11737	5094	174

NEW CASTLE—Henry County

☒ HENRY COUNTY MEMORIAL HOSPITAL, 1000 North 16th Street, Zip 47362–4319, Mailing Address: P.O. Box 490, Zip 47362–0490; tel. 765/521–0890; Jack Basler, President **A**1 9 10 **F**7 8 14 15 16 17 19 21 22 32 33 34 35 37 40 41 42 44 46 49 51 65 66 67 71 73 74 **P**8
Web address: www.hcmhcares.org

	13	10	107	3202	33	45497	515	32428	14228	548

NOBLESVILLE—Hamilton County

☒ RIVERVIEW HOSPITAL, 395 Westfield Road, Zip 46060–1425, Mailing Address: P.O. Box 220, Zip 46061–0220; tel. 317/773–0760; Seward Horner, President **A**1 9 10 **F**4 7 8 10 11 14 15 16 18 19 22 25 28 30 32 33 34 35 36 37 39 40 41 42 44 46 48 49 60 63 65 66 67 71 72 73 74 **P**5 6 7 8

	13	10	111	4192	53	157272	725	56465	24535	757

NORTH VERNON—Jennings County

★ JENNINGS COMMUNITY HOSPITAL, 301 Henry Street, Zip 47265–1097; tel. 812/346–6200; Dalton L. Smart, Administrator (Nonreporting) **A**9 10

	23	10	34	—	—	—	—	—	—	—

OAKLAND CITY—Gibson County

★ WIRTH REGIONAL HOSPITAL, Highway 64 West, Zip 47660–9379, Mailing Address: Rural Route 3, Box 14A, Zip 47660–9379; tel. 812/749–6111; Frank G. Fougerousse, President and Chief Executive Officer **A**9 10 **F**8 14 16 17 22 26 34 44 46 52 54 55 56 57 65 71 73 **S** Brim Healthcare, Inc., Brentwood, TN

	23	10	11	248	3	10129	0	4107	1463	45

PAOLI—Orange County

☒ ORANGE COUNTY HOSPITAL, 642 West Hospital Road, Zip 47454–0499, Mailing Address: P.O. Box 499, Zip 47454–0499; tel. 812/723–2811; Candace Isom, Interim Administrator **A**1 9 10 **F**7 8 11 12 15 17 19 22 28 29 30 32 33 34 35 37 40 41 42 44 49 57 64 67 71 72 73 **P**6

	13	10	37	961	9	27478	181	11522	5853	175

PERU—Miami County

☒ DUKES MEMORIAL HOSPITAL, 275 West 12th Street, Zip 46970–1698; tel. 765/473–6621; R. Joe Johnston, President and Chief Executive Officer (Total facility includes 35 beds in nursing home–type unit) **A**1 9 10 **F**7 8 11 12 14 16 17 19 22 23 27 30 32 33 34 35 36 39 40 41 44 45 49 63 64 65 67 71 73 **P**7
Web address: www.dukeshospital.org

	13	10	74	3193	46	89480	382	24164	10755	370

PLYMOUTH—Marshall County

□ BEHAVIORAL HEALTHCARE OF NORTHERN INDIANA, 1800 North Oak Road, Zip 46563–3492; tel. 219/936–3784; Wayne T. Miller, Administrator (Nonreporting) **A**1 10 **S** Behavioral Healthcare Corporation, Nashville, TN

	33	22	80	—	—	—	—	—	—	—

☒ SAINT JOSEPH'S REGIONAL MEDICAL CENTER–PLYMOUTH CAMPUS, 1915 Lake Avenue, Zip 46563–9905, Mailing Address: P.O. Box 670, Zip 46563–9905; tel. 219/936–3181; Brian E. Dietz, FACHE, Executive Vice President **A**1 9 10 **F**1 4 6 7 8 10 12 14 15 16 19 21 22 23 24 26 27 28 31 33 35 36 37 40 41 42 43 44 47 48 49 60 64 65 67 70 71 73 74 **P**8 **S** Holy Cross Health System Corporation, South Bend, IN
Web address: www.sjrmc.com

	21	10	36	2175	21	51532	335	18144	7987	263

PORTLAND—Jay County

☒ JAY COUNTY HOSPITAL, 500 West Votaw Street, Zip 47371–1322; tel. 219/726–7131; Sheri Frankenfield, Chief Executive Officer (Nonreporting) **A**1 9 10

	13	10	55	—	—	—	—	—	—	—

PRINCETON—Gibson County

☒ GIBSON GENERAL HOSPITAL, 1808 Sherman Drive, Zip 47670–1043; tel. 812/385–3401; Michael J. Budnick, Administrator and Chief Executive Officer (Total facility includes 45 beds in nursing home–type unit) **A**1 9 10 **F**3 6 7 8 12 14 15 16 17 18 19 20 22 25 26 28 29 30 32 33 34 35 36 37 39 40 41 42 44 49 51 52 53 54 55 56 57 58 60 64 65 66 67 71 73 74 **S** Norton Healthcare, Louisville, KY

	23	10	109	1330	61	24895	166	12917	6407	248

RENSSELAER—Jasper County

★ JASPER COUNTY HOSPITAL, 1104 East Grace Street, Zip 47978–3296; tel. 219/866–5141; Timothy M. Schreeg, President and Chief Executive Officer (Total facility includes 21 beds in nursing home–type unit) **A**9 10 **F**7 8 11 15 17 19 22 23 24 28 30 32 33 34 35 36 37 40 41 42 44 49 64 65 66 67 70 71 73 **P**6

	13	10	69	1536	36	43038	155	15737	7843	279

Hospital, Address, Telephone, Administrator, Approval, Facility, and Physician Codes, Health Care System, Network	Classi- fication Codes		Utilization Data					Expense (thousands) of dollars		
★ American Hospital Association (AHA) membership □ Joint Commission on Accreditation of Healthcare Organizations (JCAHO) accreditation + American Osteopathic Healthcare Association (AOHA) membership ○ American Osteopathic Association (AOA) accreditation △ Commission on Accreditation of Rehabilitation Facilities (CARF) accreditation Control codes 61, 63, 64, 71, 72 and 73 indicate hospitals listed by AOHA, but not registered by AHA. For definition of numerical codes, see page A4	Control	Service	Staffed Beds	Admissions	Census	Outpatient Visits	Births	Total	Payroll	Personnel

RICHMOND—Wayne County

✉ REID HOSPITAL AND HEALTH CARE SERVICES, 1401 Chester Boulevard, Zip 47374–1986; tel. 765/983–3000; Barry S. MacDowell, President (Total facility includes 17 beds in nursing home–type unit) **A**1 2 9 10 **F**3 7 8 10 11 12 14 15 16 17 19 21 22 23 28 30 32 33 34 35 37 40 41 42 44 45 46 49 50 52 54 56 60 63 64 65 67 70 71 72 **P**8 **Web address:** www.reidhosp.com	23	10	212	12433	156	117544	927	86033	38176	1099
□ RICHMOND STATE HOSPITAL, 498 N.W. 18th Street, Zip 47374–2898; tel. 765/966–0511; James McCormick, Superintendent (Nonreporting) **A**1 10	12	22	339	—	—	—	—	—	—	—

ROCHESTER—Fulton County

WOODLAWN HOSPITAL, 1400 East Ninth Street, Zip 46975–8937; tel. 219/224–1173; James M. O'Keefe, President and Chief Executive Officer **A**9 10 **F**6 7 8 11 12 14 15 17 19 21 22 26 28 30 31 32 34 35 36 37 40 41 42 44 49 67 71 73 **P**6	13	10	35	1455	13	—	236	18602	8869	209

RUSHVILLE—Rush County

★ RUSH MEMORIAL HOSPITAL, 1300 North Main Street, Zip 46173–1198; tel. 765/932–4111; H. William Hartley, Chief Executive Officer **A**9 10 **F**8 15 16 17 19 22 26 29 30 32 34 35 37 39 42 44 45 46 49 51 65 66 71 73 **S** Norton Healthcare, Louisville, KY	13	10	52	837	18		0	9189	3855	158

SALEM—Washington County

✉ WASHINGTON COUNTY MEMORIAL HOSPITAL, 911 North Shelby Street, Zip 47167; tel. 812/883–5881; Rodney M. Coats, President and Chief Executive Officer **A**1 9 10 **F**2 3 7 8 11 14 15 16 17 19 22 29 30 32 35 37 40 41 42 44 49 52 56 57 58 59 64 66 67 71 73 **P**6 **S** Jewish Hospital HealthCare Services, Louisville, KY	13	10	58	1275	20	29354	112	13221	5457	194

SCOTTSBURG—Scott County

✉ SCOTT MEMORIAL HOSPITAL, 1415 North Gardner Street, Zip 47170–0430, Mailing Address: Box 430, Zip 47170–0430; tel. 812/752–8500; Clifford D. Nay, Executive Director **A**1 9 10 **F**7 11 12 14 15 16 17 19 22 28 30 32 34 35 39 40 41 42 44 46 49 65 67 71 73 74 **S** Jewish Hospital HealthCare Services, Louisville, KY **Web address:** www.scottcounty.hsonline.com	13	10	45	1176	11	16988	149	10071	—	169

SEYMOUR—Jackson County

✉ MEMORIAL HOSPITAL, 411 West Tipton Street, Zip 47274–5000, Mailing Address: P.O. Box 2349, Zip 47274–2349; tel. 812/522–2349; George H. James, Jr., President and Chief Executive Officer **A**1 2 9 10 **F**7 8 11 12 14 15 16 17 19 20 21 23 26 28 30 32 33 34 35 36 37 39 40 41 42 44 45 46 49 51 63 65 67 70 71 73 74	13	10	107	4046	41	95141	631	33613	15392	481

SHELBYVILLE—Shelby County

✉ MAJOR HOSPITAL, 150 West Washington Street, Zip 46176–1236; tel. 317/392–3211; Anthony B. Lennen, President and Chief Executive Officer **A**1 9 10 **F**7 8 12 14 15 16 17 19 21 22 28 29 30 32 34 35 36 37 39 40 41 42 44 45 46 49 51 54 56 58 63 65 66 67 71 73 74 **P**7 8 **Web address:** www.majorhospital.com	15	10	49	2449	25	96222	295	24156	10605	340

SOUTH BEND—St. Joseph County

✉ △ MEMORIAL HOSPITAL OF SOUTH BEND, 615 North Michigan Street, Zip 46601–9986; tel. 219/234–9041; Philip A. Newbold, President and Chief Executive Officer **A**1 2 3 5 7 9 10 **F**2 3 4 5 7 8 10 11 12 13 14 15 16 17 18 19 20 21 22 23 24 25 26 27 28 29 30 31 32 34 35 37 38 39 40 41 42 43 44 46 47 48 49 50 51 52 53 54 55 56 57 58 59 60 61 63 64 65 66 67 68 70 71 72 73 74 **P**1 6 **Web address:** www.qualityoflife.org	23	10	352	15249	214	117441	2659	165132	64707	1746
✉ △ SAINT JOSEPH'S REGIONAL MEDICAL CENTER–SOUTH BEND CAMPUS, (Formerly St Joseph's Medical Center), 801 East LaSalle, Zip 46617–2800; tel. 219/237–7111; Robert L. Beyer, President and Chief Executive Officer **A**1 2 3 5 7 9 10 **F**1 4 6 7 8 10 11 12 13 14 15 16 17 19 21 22 23 24 26 27 28 29 30 32 33 34 35 36 37 38 39 40 41 42 44 45 47 48 49 51 56 60 61 62 64 65 66 67 68 71 73 74 **P**6 8 **S** Holy Cross Health System Corporation, South Bend, IN **Web address:** www.sjmed.com	21	10	310	13701	168	85903	1151	131263	48595	2009

SULLIVAN—Sullivan County

MARY SHERMAN HOSPITAL See Sullivan County Community Hospital										
✉ SULLIVAN COUNTY COMMUNITY HOSPITAL, (Formerly Mary Sherman Hospital), 2200 North Section Street, Zip 47882, Mailing Address: P.O. Box 10, Zip 47882–0010; tel. 812/268–4311; Thomas J. Hudgins, Administrator **A**1 9 10 **F**7 8 12 13 14 15 16 19 20 22 26 28 29 30 31 32 35 37 39 40 41 42 44 45 49 53 54 55 56 57 58 63 65 66 67 71 73 74 **S** Quorum Health Group/Quorum Health Resources, Inc., Brentwood, TN	13	10	46	1757	20	40904	155	10356	4436	181

TELL CITY—Perry County

✉ PERRY COUNTY MEMORIAL HOSPITAL, 1 Hospital Road, Zip 47586–0362; tel. 812/547–7011; Bradford W. Dykes, Chief Executive Officer **A**1 9 10 **F**7 8 12 15 16 17 18 19 20 21 22 26 28 29 30 32 33 34 35 37 39 40 41 42 44 45 46 49 55 56 58 63 64 65 67 71 73 **S** Norton Healthcare, Louisville, KY **Web address:** www.pchospital.org	13	10	38	1137	11	50822	54	11148	4630	169

TERRE HAUTE—Vigo County

HAMILTON CENTER, 620 Eighth Avenue, Zip 47804–0323; tel. 812/231–8323; Galen Goode, Chief Executive Officer (Nonreporting) **A**9 10 **Web address:** www.hamiltoncenter.com	23	22	45	—	—	—	—	—	—	—

Hospital, Address, Telephone, Administrator, Approval, Facility, and Physician Codes, Health Care System, Network	Classi-fication Codes		Utilization Data					Expense (thousands) of dollars		
	Control	Service	Staffed Beds	Admissions	Census	Outpatient Visits	Births	Total	Payroll	Personnel

★ American Hospital Association (AHA) membership
□ Joint Commission on Accreditation of Healthcare Organizations (JCAHO) accreditation
+ American Osteopathic Healthcare Association (AOHA) membership
○ American Osteopathic Association (AOA) accreditation
△ Commission on Accreditation of Rehabilitation Facilities (CARF) accreditation
Control codes 61, 63, 64, 71, 72 and 73 indicate hospitals listed by AOHA, but not registered by AHA. For definition of numerical codes, see page A4

✠ TERRE HAUTE REGIONAL HOSPITAL, 3901 South Seventh Street, Zip 47802–4299; tel. 812/232–0021; Jerry Dooley, Chief Executive Officer (Total facility includes 34 beds in nursing home–type unit) **A**1 9 10 **F**3 4 7 8 10 11 12 14 16 17 19 21 22 26 28 30 34 36 37 39 40 41 42 43 44 46 50 52 54 55 56 57 58 59 60 61 64 65 66 67 71 72 73 74 **P**5 8 **S** Columbia/HCA Healthcare Corporation, Nashville, TN	33	10	236	8224	119	97206	727	41423	19291	850
✠ △ UNION HOSPITAL, 1606 North Seventh Street, Zip 47804–2780; tel. 812/238–7000; Frank Shelton, President **A**1 2 3 5 7 9 10 **F**3 4 5 7 8 10 11 12 14 15 16 17 19 20 21 22 23 24 25 27 28 29 30 31 32 33 34 35 37 38 39 40 41 42 43 44 45 46 49 51 53 56 58 59 60 61 64 65 66 67 71 72 73 74 **P**1 5 6 **Web address:** www.uhhg.org	23	10	279	13062	188	344181	1633	148172	61357	1906
TIPTON—Tipton County										
✠ TIPTON COUNTY MEMORIAL HOSPITAL, 1000 South Main Street, Zip 46072–9799; tel. 765/675–8500; Alfonso W. Gatmaitan, Chief Executive Officer (Total facility includes 50 beds in nursing home–type unit) **A**1 2 9 10 **F**6 7 8 12 17 19 21 22 28 29 30 32 35 36 37 39 40 41 42 44 45 46 49 50 63 64 65 66 71 73 74 **P**6 8 **Web address:** www.tiptonhospital.org	13	10	100	1898	56	48568	148	20091	9211	319
VALPARAISO—Porter County										
✠ △ PORTER MEMORIAL HOSPITAL, 814 La Porte Avenue, Zip 46383–5898; tel. 219/465–4600; Wiley N. Carr, President and Chief Executive Officer (Total facility includes 25 beds in nursing home–type unit) **A**1 7 9 10 **F**3 4 7 8 10 14 15 16 17 18 19 21 22 23 25 27 28 30 32 33 34 35 36 37 38 39 40 41 42 43 44 45 49 52 53 54 55 56 57 58 59 60 61 63 64 65 66 68 70 71 72 73 74 **P**3 7 8 **Web address:** www.portermemorial.org	13	10	352	13325	185	316017	1350	113541	49021	1510
VINCENNES—Knox County										
✠ GOOD SAMARITAN HOSPITAL, 520 South Seventh Street, Zip 47591–1098; tel. 812/882–5220; A. John Hidde, President and Chief Executive Officer (Total facility includes 49 beds in nursing home–type unit) **A**1 2 9 10 **F**3 4 7 8 10 11 12 13 14 15 16 18 19 20 21 22 23 24 28 29 30 32 33 34 35 37 39 40 41 42 43 44 45 46 49 52 53 54 55 56 57 58 59 60 63 64 65 67 71 72 73 74 **P**8 **Web address:** www.gshvin.org	13	10	289	10059	166	235335	525	89643	42142	1460
WABASH—Wabash County										
✠ WABASH COUNTY HOSPITAL, 710 North East Street, Zip 46992–1924, Mailing Address: P.O. Box 548, Zip 46992–0548; tel. 219/563–3131; David C. Hunter, Chief Executive Officer (Total facility includes 25 beds in nursing home–type unit) **A**1 2 9 10 **F**7 8 12 13 14 16 17 19 21 22 24 28 29 30 32 33 34 35 36 37 39 40 41 42 44 45 46 49 64 65 66 67 71 73 **Web address:** www.wchospital.com	13	10	75	1731	32	59551	198	21823	9239	274
WARSAW—Kosciusko County										
✠ KOSCIUSKO COMMUNITY HOSPITAL, 2101 East Dubois Drive, Zip 46580–3288; tel. 219/267–3200; Wayne Hendrix, President (Total facility includes 89 beds in nursing home–type unit) **A**1 9 10 **F**3 7 8 12 13 14 15 16 17 19 21 22 24 26 28 30 32 33 34 35 36 37 39 40 41 42 44 49 51 54 56 58 59 64 65 66 67 71 72 74 **P**8 **S** Quorum Health Group/Quorum Health Resources, Inc., Brentwood, TN **Web address:** www.kch.org	23	10	161	3446	101	185199	689	41938	19101	677
WASHINGTON—Daviess County										
✠ DAVIESS COUNTY HOSPITAL, 1314 East Walnut Street, Zip 47501–2198, Mailing Address: P.O. Box 760, Zip 47501–0760; tel. 812/254–2760; Marc Chircop, Chief Executive Officer (Total facility includes 29 beds in nursing home–type unit) **A**1 9 10 **F**7 8 15 16 17 19 21 22 32 33 34 35 36 37 39 40 41 42 44 45 49 53 55 56 58 59 63 64 65 66 67 71 73 **P**3 7 8 **S** Quorum Health Group/Quorum Health Resources, Inc., Brentwood, TN **Web address:** www.dchosp.com	13	10	85	2426	42	76448	329	21504	10322	331
WEST LAFAYETTE—Tippecanoe County										
△ WABASH VALLEY HOSPITAL, 2900 North River Road, Zip 47906–3766; tel. 765/463–2555; R. Craig Lysinger, Administrator (Nonreporting) **A**7 9 10	23	22	70	—	—	—	—	—	—	—
WILLIAMSPORT—Warren County										
★ ST. VINCENT WILLIAMSPORT HOSPITAL, 412 North Monroe Street, Zip 47993–0215; tel. 765/762–4000; Jane Craigin, Chief Executive Officer **A**9 10 **F**8 15 17 19 22 28 30 34 35 41 42 44 49 71 72 **P**6 **S** Daughters of Charity National Health System, Saint Louis, MO **Web address:** www.stvincent.org	23	10	16	697	7	59710	0	6147	3527	159
WINAMAC—Pulaski County										
✠ PULASKI MEMORIAL HOSPITAL, 616 East 13th Street, Zip 46996–1117; tel. 219/946–6131; Richard H. Mynark, Administrator **A**1 9 10 **F**7 8 14 15 16 17 19 20 22 28 29 30 32 33 34 35 37 39 40 41 42 44 45 49 54 58 65 67 71 73 **P**8	13	10	19	1071	10	43588	130	10064	5142	175
WINCHESTER—Randolph County										
✠ RANDOLPH COUNTY HOSPITAL AND HEALTH SERVICES, 325 South Oak Street, Zip 47394–2235, Mailing Address: P.O. Box 407, Zip 47394–0407; tel. 765/584–9001; James M. Full, Chief Executive Officer **A**1 9 10 **F**7 8 10 13 14 15 16 17 19 21 22 23 25 26 28 30 32 33 34 35 40 41 42 44 46 49 51 61 65 66 68 71 73 74 **P**6 **S** Norton Healthcare, Louisville, KY	13	10	27	753	7	28832	138	11417	4335	180

IOWA

Resident population 2,862 (in thousands)
Resident population in metro areas 44.2%
Birth rate per 1,000 population 13
65 years and over 15.0%
Percent of persons without health insurance 11.6%

Approval and codes key:

★ American Hospital Association (AHA) membership
□ Joint Commission on Accreditation of Healthcare Organizations (JCAHO) accreditation
+ American Osteopathic Healthcare Association (AOHA) membership
○ American Osteopathic Association (AOA) accreditation
△ Commission on Accreditation of Rehabilitation Facilities (CARF) accreditation
Control codes 61, 63, 64, 71, 72 and 73 indicate hospitals listed by AOHA, but not registered by AHA. For definition of numerical codes, see page A4

Hospital, Address, Telephone, Administrator, Approval, Facility, and Physician Codes, Health Care System, Network	Control	Service	Staffed Beds	Admissions	Census	Outpatient Visits	Births	Total	Payroll	Personnel
ALBIA—Monroe County										
MONROE COUNTY HOSPITAL, RR 3, Box 314–11, Zip 52531; tel. 515/932–2134; Gregory A. Paris, Administrator **A**9 10 **F**8 12 15 16 19 22 28 30 32 33 35 36 41 44 49 65 71	13	10	38	506	21	31204	0	6034	2180	118
ALGONA—Kossuth County										
★ KOSSUTH REGIONAL HEALTH CENTER, 1515 South Phillips Street, Zip 50511–3649; tel. 515/295–2451; James G. Fitzpatrick, Administrator and Chief Executive Officer **A**9 10 **F**7 8 12 13 14 15 16 17 19 22 26 28 30 31 32 33 34 35 36 37 39 40 41 42 44 45 48 49 58 64 65 66 67 71 73 **P**1 **S** Mercy Health Services, Farmington Hills, MI	13	10	29	739	8	16830	91	8512	2847	117
AMES—Story County										
⊠ MARY GREELEY MEDICAL CENTER, 1111 Duff Avenue, Zip 50010–5792; tel. 515/239–2011; Kimberly A. Russel, President and Chief Executive Officer (Total facility includes 19 beds in nursing home–type unit) **A**1 2 9 10 **F**7 8 10 12 14 15 16 17 18 19 21 22 24 26 27 28 29 30 31 32 33 34 35 36 37 38 39 40 41 42 44 45 48 49 52 53 54 55 56 57 58 59 60 61 63 64 65 66 67 71 73	14	10	194	9633	123	117980	1150	69780	31550	1047
Web address: www.mgmc.org										
ANAMOSA—Jones County										
⊠ ANAMOSA COMMUNITY HOSPITAL, 104 Broadway Place, Zip 52205–1100; tel. 319/462–6131; Vickie Asbe, Administrator **A**1 9 10 **F**1 7 8 13 15 16 17 19 22 30 32 34 40 44 49 64 65 70 71 73 **P**1 **S** Iowa Health System, Des Moines, IA	23	10	17	387	6	23469	6	4232	1748	91
ATLANTIC—Cass County										
★ CASS COUNTY MEMORIAL HOSPITAL, 1501 East Tenth Street, Zip 50022–1997; tel. 712/243–3250; Patricia Markham, Administrator **A**9 10 **F**1 7 8 12 15 16 19 21 22 28 30 32 33 34 35 36 37 39 40 41 42 44 49 52 53 55 56 57 58 59 63 65 67 71 **P**8	13	10	72	1848	29	39182	157	16478	7787	296
AUDUBON—Audubon County										
AUDUBON COUNTY MEMORIAL HOSPITAL, 515 Pacific Street, Zip 50025–1099; tel. 712/563–2611; David G. Couser, FAAMA, FACHE, Administrator **A**9 10 **F**7 8 15 19 21 22 30 33 34 35 40 42 44 49 58 63 64 70 71 **P**1	13	10	29	445	5	14187	33	3855	1627	64
BELMOND—Wright County										
★ BELMOND COMMUNITY HOSPITAL, 403 First Street S.E., Zip 50421–1201, Mailing Address: P.O. Box 326, Zip 50421–0326; tel. 515/444–3223; Kim Price, Administrator **A**9 10 **F**14 15 16 19 20 22 24 28 29 30 32 33 34 36 39 41 42 44 48 49 51 64 71 73 74 **P**3 8 **S** Mercy Health Services, Farmington Hills, MI	14	10	22	209	5	6958	0	2613	908	14
BLOOMFIELD—Davis County										
★ DAVIS COUNTY HOSPITAL, 507 North Madison Street, Zip 52537–1299; tel. 515/664–2145; Randy Simmons, Administrator (Total facility includes 32 beds in nursing home–type unit) **A**9 10 **F**7 8 13 14 15 16 19 22 30 31 32 33 34 35 36 37 39 40 42 44 45 49 64 71 73 **P**6	13	10	67	829	41	14435	65	8915	4012	174
BOONE—Boone County										
⊠ BOONE COUNTY HOSPITAL, 1015 Union Street, Zip 50036–4898; tel. 515/432–3140; Joseph S. Smith, Chief Executive Officer **A**1 9 10 **F**7 8 15 19 22 24 27 28 30 32 34 35 36 37 39 40 41 44 48 49 64 70 71 73 **S** Quorum Health Group/Quorum Health Resources, Inc., Brentwood, TN	13	10	57	1666	24	35282	129	13550	5985	247
Web address: www.boonehospital.com										
BRITT—Hancock County										
★ HANCOCK COUNTY MEMORIAL HOSPITAL, 532 First Street N.W., Zip 50423–0068, Mailing Address: P.O. Box 68, Zip 50423–0068; tel. 515/843–3801; Harriet Thompson, Administrator **A**9 10 **F**1 7 8 14 15 16 17 19 22 27 30 33 34 35 36 40 41 44 46 65 67 71 **P**1 **S** Mercy Health Services, Farmington Hills, MI	13	10	26	538	9	15106	2	4449	1544	62
BURLINGTON—Des Moines County										
⊠ BURLINGTON MEDICAL CENTER, 602 North Third Street, Zip 52601–5088; tel. 319/753–3011; Mark D. Richardson, President and Chief Executive Officer (Total facility includes 167 beds in nursing home–type unit) **A**1 9 10 **F**3 4 8 10 12 13 14 15 16 17 18 19 21 22 23 24 28 29 30 32 34 35 36 37 38 39 40 41 42 44 45 46 48 49 52 53 54 55 56 57 58 60 63 64 65 66 67 70 71 73	23	10	366	7905	238	185963	758	60528	26099	849
CARROLL—Carroll County										
⊠ ST. ANTHONY REGIONAL HOSPITAL, 311 South Clark Street, Zip 51401, Mailing Address: P.O. Box 628, Zip 51401–0628; tel. 712/792–8231; Gary P. Riedmann, President and Chief Executive Officer (Total facility includes 79 beds in nursing home–type unit) **A**1 9 10 **F**1 7 8 12 14 15 16 17 19 20 21 22 26 28 29 30 31 32 33 34 35 36 39 40 41 42 44 45 46 49 51 52 53 54 55 56 57 58 59 60 62 63 64 65 66 67 68 71 73 **P**6	21	10	142	2431	106	61205	247	20708	9185	344
CEDAR FALLS—Black Hawk County										
⊠ SARTORI MEMORIAL HOSPITAL, 515 College Street, Zip 50613–2599; tel. 319/268–3000; Daniel J. Woods, Chief Executive Officer (Total facility includes 16 beds in nursing home–type unit) **A**1 9 10 **F**3 8 12 17 19 20 22 24 25 30 32 33 34 35 36 37 39 41 42 44 49 51 64 65 66 67 71 73 **S** Wheaton Franciscan Services, Inc., Wheaton, IL	21	10	87	1528	18	51853	0	15551	6981	186

Hospital, Address, Telephone, Administrator, Approval, Facility, and Physician Codes, Health Care System, Network	Classi- fication Codes		Utilization Data					Expense (thousands) of dollars		
	Control	Service	Staffed Beds	Admissions	Census	Outpatient Visits	Births	Total	Payroll	Personnel

★ American Hospital Association (AHA) membership
☐ Joint Commission on Accreditation of Healthcare Organizations (JCAHO) accreditation
+ American Osteopathic Healthcare Association (AOHA) membership
○ American Osteopathic Association (AOA) accreditation
△ Commission on Accreditation of Rehabilitation Facilities (CARF) accreditation
Control codes 61, 63, 64, 71, 72 and 73 indicate hospitals listed by AOHA, but not registered by AHA. For definition of numerical codes, see page A4

CEDAR RAPIDS—Linn County

✠ MERCY MEDICAL CENTER, 701 Tenth Street S.E., Zip 52403–1292; tel. 319/398–6011; A. James Tinker, President and Chief Executive Officer (Total facility includes 87 beds in nursing home–type unit) **A**1 2 3 9 10 **F**2 3 4 7 8 10 12 14 15 16 19 21 22 24 26 28 29 30 31 32 33 34 35 37 38 40 41 42 44 45 46 47 49 52 54 55 56 57 58 59 60 63 64 65 67 68 71 73 74 **P**1 5 Web address: www.mercycare.org	21	10	377	10459	202	127351	1157	92933	41612	1440
✠ △ ST. LUKE'S HOSPITAL, 1026 A Avenue N.E., Zip 52402–3026, Mailing Address: P.O. Box 3026, Zip 52406–3026; tel. 319/369–7211; Stephen E. Vanourny, M.D., President and Chief Executive Officer (Total facility includes 28 beds in nursing home–type unit) **A**1 3 7 9 10 **F**2 3 4 7 8 10 11 12 14 15 16 17 19 20 21 22 24 25 26 27 28 29 30 31 32 33 34 35 36 37 38 39 40 41 42 43 44 45 46 47 49 50 51 52 53 54 55 56 57 58 59 61 63 64 65 66 67 68 70 71 72 73 74 **P**3 5 7 8 **S** Iowa Health System, Des Moines, IA	23	10	421	14098	204	262503	2198	127483	51118	1759

CENTERVILLE—Appanoose County

✠ ST. JOSEPH'S MERCY HOSPITAL, 1 St. Joseph's Drive, Zip 52544; tel. 515/437–4111; William C. Assell, President and Chief Executive Officer (Total facility includes 20 beds in nursing home–type unit) **A**1 9 10 **F**7 8 14 15 16 19 22 24 26 28 29 30 32 33 34 35 36 37 39 40 44 45 49 53 54 58 64 65 66 67 71 **S** Catholic Health Initiatives, Denver, CO	21	10	54	1249	44	49075	17	9282	4397	191

CHARITON—Lucas County

★ LUCAS COUNTY HEALTH CENTER, 1200 North Seventh Street, Zip 50049–1258; tel. 515/774–3000; Michael S. Wallace, Chief Executive Officer **A**9 10 **F**1 3 6 7 8 11 12 14 15 16 17 18 19 22 27 28 30 32 33 34 35 37 40 41 42 44 46 49 53 54 55 56 57 58 59 67 68 70 71 73	13	10	22	679	7	13683	76	8437	3656	139

CHARLES CITY—Floyd County

FLOYD COUNTY MEMORIAL HOSPITAL, 800 Eleventh Street, Zip 50616–3499; tel. 515/228–6830; Bill D. Faust, Administrator **A**9 10 **F**7 8 11 12 14 15 16 19 22 28 29 30 32 33 34 35 36 37 39 40 41 44 49 51 53 57 58 65 66 67 71 73 **S** Mayo Foundation, Rochester, MN	13	10	31	1324	15	45528	83	9819	4055	148

CHEROKEE—Cherokee County

☐ MENTAL HEALTH INSTITUTE, 1200 West Cedar Street, Zip 51012–1599; tel. 712/225–2594; Tom Deiker, Ph.D., Superintendent **A**1 10 **F**1 12 14 16 45 52 53 54 55 56 58 59 65	12	22	110	1004	73	1008	0	13799	8118	233
★ SIOUX VALLEY MEMORIAL HOSPITAL, 300 Sioux Valley Drive, Zip 51012–1205; tel. 712/225–5101; John M. Comstock, Chief Executive Officer **A**9 10 **F**7 8 11 12 14 15 16 17 19 22 24 26 28 29 30 31 32 33 34 35 36 39 40 41 42 44 45 46 49 51 53 54 55 56 57 58 64 65 66 67 71 73 **P**4 6 7	23	10	40	1173	12	20702	131	8309	3847	165

CLARINDA—Page County

★ CLARINDA REGIONAL HEALTH CENTER, 17th and Wells Streets, Zip 51632, Mailing Address: P.O. Box 217, Zip 51632–0217; tel. 712/542–2176; Rudy Snedigar, Chief Executive Officer **A**9 10 **F**8 12 15 16 17 19 22 24 26 27 28 30 32 34 35 36 37 39 40 41 42 44 49 58 65 66 67 70 71 73 **P**3	14	10	27	690	8	38763	76	7284	3335	153
MENTAL HEALTH INSTITUTE, Mailing Address: P.O. Box 338, Zip 51632–0338; tel. 712/542–2161; Mark Lund, Superintendent (Total facility includes 63 beds in nursing home–type unit) **F**14 15 16 19 20 21 25 26 35 39 41 50 52 54 55 56 57 58 60 63 64 65 71 73	12	22	83	172	65	0	0	—	—	127

CLARION—Wright County

★ COMMUNITY MEMORIAL HOSPITAL, 1316 South Main Street, Zip 50525; tel. 515/532–2811; Steve J. Simonin, Chief Executive Officer **A**9 10 **F**7 8 19 20 22 24 30 32 33 34 35 36 37 39 40 41 42 44 49 62 64 65 71 73 **S** Iowa Health System, Des Moines, IA	14	10	33	602	17	24613	76	6558	2271	90

CLINTON—Clinton County

✠ SAMARITAN HEALTH SYSTEM, (Includes Samaritan Services for Aging, 600 14th Avenue North, Zip 52732; tel. 319/244–3888), 1410 North Fourth Street, Zip 52732–2999; tel. 319/244–5555; Thomas J. Hesselmann, President and Chief Executive Officer (Total facility includes 212 beds in nursing home–type unit) **A**1 9 10 **F**1 3 7 8 10 11 12 15 16 17 18 19 20 21 22 23 24 26 28 29 30 32 33 34 35 36 40 41 42 44 46 49 52 53 54 55 56 57 58 59 60 62 64 65 67 70 71 73 74 **P**8 **S** Mercy Health Services, Farmington Hills, MI Web address: www.samhealth.com	21	10	375	7048	251	51195	593	47712	20603	745

CORNING—Adams County

★ MERCY HOSPITAL, (Formerly Alegent Health Mercy Hospital), 703 Rosary Drive, Zip 50841, Mailing Address: P.O. Box 368, Zip 50841–0368; tel. 515/322–3121; James C. Ruppert, Administrator **A**9 10 **F**7 8 12 14 15 16 17 19 22 28 29 30 32 33 34 35 36 39 40 41 42 44 49 53 55 58 65 67 71 73 **P**6 **S** Catholic Health Initiatives, Denver, CO	21	10	22	492	8	46603	47	5285	2330	114

CORYDON—Wayne County

★ WAYNE COUNTY HOSPITAL, 417 South East Street, Zip 50060–1860, Mailing Address: P.O. Box 305, Zip 50060–0305; tel. 515/872–2260; Bill D. Wilson, Administrator **A**9 10 **F**7 8 12 13 14 15 17 18 19 20 22 28 30 32 33 34 36 37 39 40 42 44 45 49 51 64 65 70 71 73	13	10	28	812	12	20202	93	5125	2334	90

COUNCIL BLUFFS—Pottawattamie County

✠ ALEGENT HEALTH MERCY HOSPITAL, (Formerly Mercy Hospital), 800 Mercy Drive, Zip 51503–3128, Mailing Address: P.O. Box 1C, Zip 51502–3001; tel. 712/328–5000; Charles J. Marr, Chief Executive Officer (Total facility includes 24 beds in nursing home–type unit) **A**1 9 10 **F**1 2 3 4 6 7 8 10 11 12 14 15 16 17 18 19 20 21 22 23 24 25 26 27 28 29 30 31 32 33 34 35 37 38 39 40 41 42 43 44 45 46 48 49 50 51 52 53 54 55 56 57 58 59 60 63 64 65 66 67 68 71 72 73 74 **P**6 8 **S** Catholic Health Initiatives, Denver, CO	21	10	209	5502	84	32080	517	43721	18233	685

Hospital, Address, Telephone, Administrator, Approval, Facility, and Physician Codes, Health Care System, Network	Classi-fication Codes		Utilization Data					Expense (thousands) of dollars		
★ American Hospital Association (AHA) membership □ Joint Commission on Accreditation of Healthcare Organizations (JCAHO) accreditation + American Osteopathic Healthcare Association (AOHA) membership ○ American Osteopathic Association (AOA) accreditation △ Commission on Accreditation of Rehabilitation Facilities (CARF) accreditation Control codes 61, 63, 64, 71, 72 and 73 indicate hospitals listed by AOHA, but not registered by AHA. For definition of numerical codes, see page A4	Control	Service	Staffed Beds	Admissions	Census	Outpatient Visits	Births	Total	Payroll	Personnel

⊠ JENNIE EDMUNDSON MEMORIAL HOSPITAL, 933 East Pierce Street, Zip 51503–4652, Mailing Address: P.O. Box 2C, Zip 51502–3002; tel. 712/328–6000; David M. Holcomb, President and Chief Executive Officer (Total facility includes 16 beds in nursing home–type unit) **A**1 2 5 9 10 **F**3 4 7 8 10 12 15 16 17 18 19 20 21 22 23 26 27 28 29 30 31 32 33 35 36 37 39 40 41 42 43 44 45 46 49 52 53 54 55 56 57 58 59 60 62 63 64 65 66 67 71 72 73 **P**6 8	23	10	103	5943	97	69451	588	49550	24902	698
CRESCO—Howard County										
★ REGIONAL HEALTH SERVICES OF HOWARD COUNTY, 235 Eighth Avenue West, Zip 52136–1098; tel. 319/547–2101; Elizabeth A. Doty, President and Chief Executive Officer **A**9 10 **F**7 8 15 19 22 30 33 35 39 40 44 49 65 71 73 **P**3 4 5 8 **S** Mercy Health Services, Farmington Hills, MI **Web address:** www.rhshc.com	13	10	32	465	5	15795	95	5579	2743	86
CRESTON—Union County										
★ GREATER COMMUNITY HOSPITAL, 1700 West Townline, Zip 50801–1099; tel. 515/782–7091; Marlys Scherlin, Chief Executive Officer **A**9 10 **F**7 8 12 15 16 19 20 22 24 27 28 30 32 33 34 35 36 37 40 41 42 44 49 50 54 56 57 58 59 60 63 65 71 73 **P**6	13	10	49	1467	18	22891	179	11752	5364	190
DAVENPORT—Scott County										
□ ○ DAVENPORT MEDICAL CENTER, 1111 West Kimberly Road, Zip 52806–5913; tel. 319/445–4020; James Fraser, Chief Executive Officer **A**1 9 10 11 12 13 **F**7 8 12 14 15 16 19 20 22 26 30 32 34 37 39 40 41 44 46 61 63 64 65 67 71 72 73 74 **P**1 2 **S** New American Healthcare Corporation, Brentwood, TN	33	10	105	1370	19	54806	148	14146	6224	220
⊠ △ GENESIS MEDICAL CENTER, (Includes Genesis Medical Center–East Campus, 1227 East Rusholme Street, Zip 52803; tel. 319/421–1000; Genesis Medical Center–West Campus, 1401 West Central Park, Zip 52804–1769; tel. 319/421–1000), 1227 East Rusholme Street, Zip 52803–2498; tel. 319/421–1000; Leo A. Bressanelli, President and Chief Executive Officer (Total facility includes 45 beds in nursing home–type unit) **A**1 2 3 5 7 9 10 **F**2 3 4 6 7 8 10 12 14 15 16 17 18 19 20 21 22 23 27 28 29 30 31 32 33 34 35 37 38 39 40 41 42 43 44 45 46 48 49 51 52 53 54 55 56 57 58 60 61 64 65 67 70 71 72 73 **P**6 7 8 **Web address:** www.genesishealth.com	23	10	461	19616	337	170001	2817	191917	73035	2216
DE WITT—Clinton County										
⊠ DEWITT COMMUNITY HOSPITAL, 1118 11th Street, Zip 52742–1296; tel. 319/659–4200; Robert G. Senneff, Chief Executive Officer (Total facility includes 77 beds in nursing home–type unit) **A**1 9 10 **F**15 19 22 36 44 49 64 65 71 **P**5	23	10	90	442	81	21444	0	6138	2715	126
DECORAH—Winneshiek County										
⊠ WINNESHIEK COUNTY MEMORIAL HOSPITAL, 901 Montgomery Street, Zip 52101–2325; tel. 319/382–2911; Allan Atkinson, Chief Executive Officer **A**1 9 10 **F**7 8 11 12 14 15 17 19 21 22 28 30 31 32 33 34 35 36 37 39 40 41 42 44 45 46 49 65 66 67 71 73 **Web address:** www.winnhosp.org	13	10	83	1140	9	38042	269	10989	5364	194
DENISON—Crawford County										
CRAWFORD COUNTY MEMORIAL HOSPITAL, 2020 First Avenue South, Zip 51442–2299; tel. 712/263–5021; Gary L. Petersen, Administrator **A**9 10 **F**3 7 8 14 15 16 17 18 19 20 21 22 24 26 27 28 29 30 31 32 33 34 35 37 39 40 41 42 44 45 46 49 51 53 54 55 56 57 58 59 62 65 66 67 71 72 73 74	13	10	72	890	11	23327	140	5379	3717	124
DES MOINES—Polk County										
⊠ BROADLAWNS MEDICAL CENTER, 1801 Hickman Road, Zip 50314–1597; tel. 515/282–2200; Richard R. Reiter, Interim Executive Director **A**1 3 5 9 10 **F**1 2 3 7 8 12 14 15 16 17 18 19 20 26 27 31 33 34 35 37 39 40 41 42 44 46 49 51 52 53 54 55 56 58 59 65 67 71 72 73 **P**6 **Web address:** www.broadlawns.org	13	10	107	5114	55	198321	500	61353	29109	831
DES MOINES DIVISION See Veterans Affairs Central Iowa Health Care System										
⊠ + ○ △ DES MOINES GENERAL HOSPITAL, 603 East 12th Street, Zip 50309–5515; tel. 515/263–4200; Roy W. Wright, President and Chief Executive Officer (Total facility includes 15 beds in nursing home–type unit) **A**1 7 9 10 11 12 13 **F**2 3 4 7 8 9 10 11 12 14 16 17 19 21 22 24 25 26 28 29 31 33 34 35 37 38 39 40 41 42 43 44 45 46 47 48 49 51 52 54 55 56 57 58 59 63 64 65 67 70 71 73 74 **S** Quorum Health Group/Quorum Health Resources, Inc., Brentwood, TN	23	10	155	3940	76	28998	199	43591	17400	453
⊠ IOWA LUTHERAN HOSPITAL, 700 East University Avenue, Zip 50316–2392; tel. 515/263–5612; James H. Skogsbergh, President (Total facility includes 16 beds in nursing home–type unit) **A**1 3 5 9 10 **F**1 2 3 4 7 8 9 10 11 12 14 15 16 17 18 19 21 22 24 25 26 27 28 29 30 31 32 33 34 35 37 38 39 40 41 42 43 44 45 46 47 48 49 51 52 53 54 55 56 57 58 59 60 61 64 65 66 67 68 70 71 72 73 74 **P**1 2 3 6 7 **S** Iowa Health System, Des Moines, IA **Web address:** www.ilsdesmoines.org	23	10	222	10057	155	268584	1330	—	—	—
⊠ IOWA METHODIST MEDICAL CENTER, (Includes Powell Convalescent Center; Raymond Blank Memorial Hospital for Children; Younker Memorial Rehabilitation Center), 1200 Pleasant Street, Zip 50309–9976; tel. 515/241–6212; James H. Skogsbergh, President **A**1 2 3 5 6 9 10 **F**1 2 3 4 7 8 9 10 11 12 14 16 17 18 19 21 22 24 25 26 27 28 29 30 31 32 33 34 35 37 38 39 40 41 42 43 44 45 46 47 48 49 51 52 53 54 55 56 57 58 59 60 61 64 65 66 67 68 70 71 72 73 74 **P**1 2 3 6 7 8 **S** Iowa Health System, Des Moines, IA **Web address:** www.ihsdesmoines.org	23	10	489	20558	299	241836	1897	—	—	—

Hospital, Address, Telephone, Administrator, Approval, Facility, and Physician Codes, Health Care System, Network	Classi-fication Codes		Utilization Data					Expense (thousands) of dollars		
★ American Hospital Association (AHA) membership □ Joint Commission on Accreditation of Healthcare Organizations (JCAHO) accreditation + American Osteopathic Healthcare Association (AOHA) membership ○ American Osteopathic Association (AOA) accreditation △ Commission on Accreditation of Rehabilitation Facilities (CARF) accreditation Control codes 61, 63, 64, 71, 72 and 73 indicate hospitals listed by AOHA, but not registered by AHA. For definition of numerical codes, see page A4	Control	Service	Staffed Beds	Admissions	Census	Outpatient Visits	Births	Total	Payroll	Personnel

Hospital	Control	Service	Staffed Beds	Admissions	Census	Outpatient Visits	Births	Total	Payroll	Personnel
⊠ MERCY HOSPITAL MEDICAL CENTER, (Includes Mercy Franklin Center, 1818 48th Street, Zip 50310; tel. 515/271–6000), 400 University Avenue, Zip 50314–3190; tel. 515/247–3121; David H. Vellinga, President and Chief Executive Officer (Total facility includes 35 beds in nursing home–type unit) **A**1 2 3 6 9 10 **F**1 3 4 5 6 7 8 10 11 12 14 15 16 17 19 20 21 22 23 24 25 26 28 29 30 31 32 33 34 35 37 38 39 40 41 42 43 44 46 47 48 49 51 52 53 54 55 56 57 58 59 60 62 63 64 65 66 67 68 70 71 72 73 74 **P**1 **S** Catholic Health Initiatives, Denver, CO **Web address:** www.mercydesmoines.org	21	10	556	27636	389	208500	3767	248486	104967	4129
⊠ VETERANS AFFAIRS CENTRAL IOWA HEALTH CARE SYSTEM, (Includes Des Moines Division, 3600 30th Street; Knoxville Division, 1515 West Pleasant, Knoxville, Zip 50138–3399; tel. 515/842–3101), 3600 30th Street, Zip 50310–5774; tel. 515/699–5999; Donald C. Cooper, Director (Total facility includes 226 beds in nursing home–type unit) **A**1 2 3 5 **F**1 2 3 4 5 8 10 12 14 16 17 18 19 20 21 22 23 25 26 27 28 29 30 31 32 33 34 35 37 39 41 42 43 44 45 46 48 49 51 52 54 55 56 57 58 60 63 64 65 67 69 70 71 73 74 **S** Department of Veterans Affairs, Washington, DC	45	10	359	3882	331	179392	0	84078	53729	1366
DUBUQUE—Dubuque County										
⊠ FINLEY HOSPITAL, 350 North Grandview Avenue, Zip 52001–6392; tel. 319/582–1881; Kevin L. Rogols, President and Chief Executive Officer (Total facility includes 32 beds in nursing home–type unit) **A**1 2 9 10 **F**4 7 8 12 13 14 15 16 17 19 20 21 22 23 24 26 27 28 29 30 31 32 33 34 35 36 37 39 40 41 42 44 45 46 49 52 57 60 61 63 64 65 66 67 70 71 72 73 74 **P**1 5 7 **S** Iowa Health System, Des Moines, IA	23	10	139	5408	63	84156	556	49524	21101	728
⊠ △ MERCY HEALTH CENTER, (Includes Mercy Health Center–St. Mary's Unit, 1111 Third Street S.W., Dyersville, Zip 52040; tel. 319/875–7101), 250 Mercy Drive, Zip 52001–7360; tel. 319/589–8000; Russell M. Knight, President and Chief Executive Officer (Total facility includes 69 beds in nursing home–type unit) **A**1 7 9 10 **F**1 2 3 4 7 8 10 11 12 13 15 16 17 19 20 21 22 23 24 26 27 28 29 30 31 32 33 34 37 38 39 40 41 42 43 44 45 48 49 51 52 53 54 55 56 57 58 59 60 64 65 66 67 68 70 71 72 73 74 **P**8 **S** Mercy Health Services, Farmington Hills, MI **Web address:** www.mercyhealth.com	21	10	385	9492	128	44892	1010	85591	34882	1164
DYERSVILLE—Dubuque County										
MERCY HEALTH CENTER–ST. MARY'S UNIT See Mercy Health Center, Dubuque										
ELDORA—Hardin County										
★ ELDORA REGIONAL MEDICAL CENTER, 2413 Edgington Avenue, Zip 50627–1541; tel. 515/939–5416; Richard C. Hamilton, Administrator **A**9 10 **F**8 12 15 16 17 19 21 22 26 28 30 32 33 34 39 41 42 44 49 51 56 58 64 66 70 71 72 73 **P**6 **S** Mercy Health Services, Farmington Hills, MI	14	10	18	220	2	11629	0	3234	1597	87
ELKADER—Clayton County										
★ CENTRAL COMMUNITY HOSPITAL, 901 Davidson Street N.W., Zip 52043–9799; tel. 319/245–2250; Fran Zichal, Chief Executive Officer **A**9 10 **F**8 11 12 15 16 17 19 22 24 26 28 29 30 32 33 35 37 39 44 45 49 51 64 65 66 67 71 **S** Mercy Health Services, Farmington Hills, MI	23	10	16	331	5	7908	0	2691	1116	57
EMMETSBURG—Palo Alto County										
★ PALO ALTO HEALTH SYSTEM, 3201 First Street, Zip 50536–2599; tel. 712/852–2434; Darrell E. Vondrak, Administrator (Total facility includes 22 beds in nursing home–type unit) **A**9 10 **F**7 8 12 14 15 16 19 21 22 26 27 29 30 32 33 34 35 36 37 39 40 41 42 44 49 62 64 65 67 71 **P**8 **S** Mercy Health Services, Farmington Hills, MI **Web address:** www.northiowamercy.com	13	10	54	929	29	19635	88	6732	3052	124
ESTHERVILLE—Emmet County										
⊠ AVERA HOLY FAMILY HEALTH, (Formerly Holy Family Health Services), 826 North Eighth Street, Zip 51334–1598; tel. 712/362–2631; Thomas Nordwick, President and Chief Executive Officer **A**1 9 10 **F**1 7 8 12 13 15 17 19 22 26 27 30 31 32 33 34 35 36 37 39 40 41 42 44 46 49 51 58 65 67 71 72 73 **P**3 **S** Avera Health, Yankton, SD	21	10	36	1075	13	32464	76	8265	3957	176
FAIRFIELD—Jefferson County										
★ JEFFERSON COUNTY HOSPITAL, 400 Highland Avenue, Zip 52556–3713, Mailing Address: P.O. Box 588, Zip 52556–0588; tel. 515/472–4111; Walter W. Brownlee, President and Chief Executive Officer (Total facility includes 36 beds in nursing home–type unit) **A**9 10 **F**3 7 8 11 14 15 16 19 22 28 30 32 34 35 37 39 40 41 42 44 49 52 56 58 64 65 67 71	13	10	83	1792	52	25116	86	11721	4889	175
FORT DODGE—Webster County										
⊠ TRINITY REGIONAL HOSPITAL, 802 Kenyon Road, Zip 50501–5795; tel. 515/573–3101; Tom Tibbitts, President **A**1 9 10 **F**2 3 7 8 12 14 15 16 17 19 21 22 23 28 29 30 32 33 34 35 37 39 40 41 44 45 46 48 49 52 53 54 55 56 57 58 59 63 64 65 66 67 71 73 **P**7	23	10	175	6502	78	109736	572	51037	21530	695
FORT MADISON—Lee County										
⊠ FORT MADISON COMMUNITY HOSPITAL, Highway 61 West, Zip 52627–0174, Mailing Address: 5445 Avenue O, Box 174, Zip 52627–0174; tel. 319/372–6530; C. James Platt, Chief Executive Officer **A**1 9 10 **F**7 8 12 14 15 16 19 22 23 24 27 28 30 32 34 35 37 40 41 42 44 45 46 48 49 60 64 65 67 71 73 74 **P**6 **S** Quorum Health Group/Quorum Health Resources, Inc., Brentwood, TN **Web address:** www.fmchcares.com	23	10	50	2232	25	35825	193	18437	7838	231

Hospital, Address, Telephone, Administrator, Approval, Facility, and Physician Codes, Health Care System, Network	Classification Codes		Utilization Data					Expense (thousands) of dollars		
★ American Hospital Association (AHA) membership □ Joint Commission on Accreditation of Healthcare Organizations (JCAHO) accreditation + American Osteopathic Healthcare Association (AOHA) membership ○ American Osteopathic Association (AOA) accreditation △ Commission on Accreditation of Rehabilitation Facilities (CARF) accreditation Control codes 61, 63, 64, 71, 72 and 73 indicate hospitals listed by AOHA, but not registered by AHA. For definition of numerical codes, see page A4	Control	Service	Staffed Beds	Admissions	Census	Outpatient Visits	Births	Total	Payroll	Personnel

GLENWOOD—Mills County

| GLENWOOD STATE HOSPITAL SCHOOL, 711 South Vine, Zip 51534–1927; tel. 712/527–4811; William E. Campbell, Ph.D., Superintendent F15 16 53 58 65 P6 | 12 | 62 | 392 | 34 | 389 | — | 0 | 38807 | 25531 | 826 |

GREENFIELD—Adair County

| ADAIR COUNTY MEMORIAL HOSPITAL, 609 S.E. Kent Street, Zip 50849–9454; tel. 515/743–2123; Myrna Erb-Gundel, Administrator A9 10 F7 8 12 14 15 17 19 22 30 32 33 34 36 37 39 40 41 42 44 49 64 71 | 13 | 10 | 22 | 428 | 5 | 6160 | 13 | 4024 | 1800 | 88 |

GRINNELL—Poweshiek County

| ⊠ GRINNELL REGIONAL MEDICAL CENTER, 210 Fourth Avenue, Zip 50112–1833; tel. 515/236–7511; Todd C. Linden, President and Chief Executive Officer A1 9 10 F1 8 12 13 14 15 16 17 19 22 23 24 27 28 29 30 31 32 33 35 37 39 40 41 42 44 45 46 49 50 51 53 54 55 56 57 58 59 63 65 67 70 71 73 P7 | 23 | 10 | 46 | 2339 | 22 | 49887 | 201 | 21722 | 10312 | 329 |

GRUNDY CENTER—Grundy County

| GRUNDY COUNTY MEMORIAL HOSPITAL, 201 East J Avenue, Zip 50638–2096; tel. 319/824–5421; James A. Faulwell, Administrator (Total facility includes 55 beds in nursing home–type unit) A9 10 F8 12 13 15 16 17 19 22 26 30 32 33 34 36 39 41 44 49 51 54 57 58 64 65 71 72 P5 S Iowa Health System, Des Moines, IA | 13 | 10 | 75 | 252 | 61 | 12588 | 0 | 3527 | 1482 | 85 |

GUTHRIE CENTER—Guthrie County

| ★ GUTHRIE COUNTY HOSPITAL, 710 North 12th Street, Zip 50115–1544; tel. 515/747–2201; Todd Hudspeth, Administrator and Chief Executive Officer A9 10 F8 11 15 16 17 19 20 21 22 28 30 33 34 35 36 39 41 42 44 49 58 65 70 71
Web address: www.pionet.net | 13 | 10 | 26 | 508 | 6 | 9789 | 0 | 3211 | 1284 | 52 |

GUTTENBERG—Clayton County

| ★ GUTTENBERG MUNICIPAL HOSPITAL, Second and Main Street, Zip 52052–0550, Mailing Address: Box 550, Zip 52052–0550; tel. 319/252–1121; Roland D. Gee, Chief Executive Officer A9 10 F7 8 16 19 22 28 30 32 33 34 35 36 37 39 40 42 44 71 S Iowa Health System, Des Moines, IA | 14 | 10 | 20 | 520 | 6 | 13889 | 48 | 4035 | 1588 | 79 |

HAMBURG—Fremont County

| GRAPE COMMUNITY HOSPITAL, 2959 U.S. Highway 275, Zip 51640; tel. 712/382–1515; Carolyn K. Hess, Administrator A9 10 F7 8 15 19 22 28 32 33 34 35 36 37 39 40 41 42 44 45 49 64 71 73 | 23 | 10 | 49 | 722 | 17 | 21308 | 3 | 5385 | 2564 | 90 |

HAMPTON—Franklin County

| ★ FRANKLIN GENERAL HOSPITAL, 1720 Central Avenue East, Zip 50441–1859; tel. 515/456–5000; Scott Wells, Chief Executive Officer (Total facility includes 52 beds in nursing home–type unit) A9 10 F3 4 5 7 8 10 11 12 14 15 16 18 19 20 22 26 27 29 30 31 32 33 34 35 37 39 40 41 42 43 44 45 49 56 58 60 62 64 65 66 67 71 73 74 P2 6 8 S Mercy Health Services, Farmington Hills, MI | 13 | 10 | 82 | 450 | 58 | 12940 | 0 | 5201 | 2430 | 115 |

HARLAN—Shelby County

| ★ SHELBY COUNTY MYRTUE MEMORIAL HOSPITAL, 1213 Garfield Avenue, Zip 51537–2057; tel. 712/755–5161; Stephen L. Goeser, Administrator A9 10 F7 8 12 13 15 16 17 18 19 21 22 24 28 30 32 33 34 35 36 37 39 40 41 42 44 49 51 53 54 56 58 66 67 68 71 73 P6 8 | 13 | 10 | 52 | 1458 | 22 | 22333 | 91 | 9972 | 3960 | 177 |

HAWARDEN—Sioux County

| ★ HAWARDEN COMMUNITY HOSPITAL, 1111 11th Street, Zip 51023–1999; tel. 712/551–3100; Stuart A. Katz, FACHE, Administrator A9 10 F8 12 15 17 19 21 22 26 27 30 32 34 41 44 46 49 65 66 67 68 71 S Mercy Health Services, Farmington Hills, MI | 14 | 10 | 17 | 201 | 6 | 13295 | 0 | 2253 | 931 | 50 |

HUMBOLDT—Humboldt County

| HUMBOLDT COUNTY MEMORIAL HOSPITAL, 1000 North 15th Street, Zip 50548–1008; tel. 515/332–4200 A9 10 F7 8 15 17 19 22 30 32 33 34 35 36 39 40 41 42 44 49 64 65 71 S Iowa Health System, Des Moines, IA | 13 | 10 | 49 | 425 | 29 | 47072 | 51 | 6011 | 3102 | 134 |

IDA GROVE—Ida County

| ★ HORN MEMORIAL HOSPITAL, 701 East Second Street, Zip 51445–1699; tel. 712/364–3311; Dan Ellis, Administrator A9 10 F7 8 14 15 16 19 22 32 33 34 35 36 37 40 41 42 44 51 54 64 65 68 71 73 | 23 | 10 | 36 | 683 | 10 | 22106 | 66 | 4778 | 2350 | 68 |

INDEPENDENCE—Buchanan County

| □ MENTAL HEALTH INSTITUTE, 2277 Iowa Avenue, Zip 50644, Mailing Address: P.O. Box 111, Zip 50644; tel. 319/334–2583; Bhasker J. Dave, M.D., Superintendent A1 10 F14 15 16 20 22 27 52 53 54 55 56 65 67 73 P6 | 12 | 22 | 181 | 895 | 113 | 8 | 0 | — | 12618 | 344 |
| ★ PEOPLE'S MEMORIAL HOSPITAL OF BUCHANAN COUNTY, 1600 First Street East, Zip 50644–3155; tel. 319/334–6071; Robert J. Richard, Administrator (Total facility includes 59 beds in nursing home–type unit) A9 10 F8 12 14 15 16 17 19 20 21 22 26 27 28 30 31 32 33 34 35 36 39 40 44 45 46 62 64 65 67 71 | 13 | 10 | 109 | 554 | 64 | 26747 | 28 | 6729 | 3418 | 157 |

IOWA CITY—Johnson County

| ⊠ MERCY HOSPITAL, 500 East Market Street, Zip 52245–2689; tel. 319/339–0300; Ronald R. Reed, President and Chief Executive Officer (Total facility includes 12 beds in nursing home–type unit) A1 2 3 5 9 10 F3 4 5 7 8 10 12 14 15 16 17 18 19 20 21 22 23 26 28 29 30 31 32 33 34 35 37 38 39 40 41 42 43 44 45 49 51 52 54 55 56 57 58 59 60 61 63 64 65 66 67 69 71 72 73 74 P1
Web address: www.mercyic.com | 21 | 10 | 240 | 8959 | 126 | 212395 | 1185 | 69380 | 30823 | 871 |

STATE PSYCHIATRIC HOSPITAL See University of Iowa Hospitals and Clinics

Hospital, Address, Telephone, Administrator, Approval, Facility, and Physician Codes, Health Care System, Network	Classi-fication Codes		Utilization Data					Expense (thousands) of dollars		
	Control	Service	Staffed Beds	Admissions	Census	Outpatient Visits	Births	Total	Payroll	Personnel

★ American Hospital Association (AHA) membership
□ Joint Commission on Accreditation of Healthcare Organizations (JCAHO) accreditation
+ American Osteopathic Healthcare Association (AOHA) membership
○ American Osteopathic Association (AOA) accreditation
△ Commission on Accreditation of Rehabilitation Facilities (CARF) accreditation
Control codes 61, 63, 64, 71, 72 and 73 indicate hospitals listed by AOHA, but not registered by AHA. For definition of numerical codes, see page A4

⊠ UNIVERSITY OF IOWA HOSPITALS AND CLINICS, (Includes Chemical Dependency Center, tel. 319/384–8765; State Psychiatric Hospital, tel. 319/356–4658; University Hospital School, tel. 319/353–6456), 200 Hawkins Drive, Zip 52242–1009; tel. 319/356–1616; R. Edward Howell, Director and Chief Executive Officer (Total facility includes 103 beds in nursing home–type unit) **A**1 2 3 5 8 9 10 **F**2 3 4 5 7 8 9 10 11 12 13 14 15 16 17 19 20 21 22 23 25 26 27 28 29 30 31 32 33 34 35 37 38 39 40 41 42 43 44 45 46 47 48 49 50 51 52 53 54 55 56 57 58 59 60 61 63 65 66 67 68 70 71 72 73 74 **P**1 7 **Web address:** www.uihc.uiowa.edu	12	10	820	40892	585	715441	1190	414945	170893	5227
⊠ VETERANS AFFAIRS MEDICAL CENTER, 601 Highway 6 West, Zip 52246–2208; tel. 319/338–0581; Gary L. Wilkinson, Director **A**1 3 5 8 **F**1 3 4 8 10 12 16 19 20 21 22 23 25 26 27 28 30 31 32 33 35 37 39 41 42 43 44 45 46 49 50 51 52 54 56 58 60 63 65 67 68 71 72 73 74 **S** Department of Veterans Affairs, Washington, DC **Web address:** www.icva.gov	45	10	113	3829	75	155960	0	76750	43647	1089
IOWA FALLS—Hardin County										
⊠ ELLSWORTH MUNICIPAL HOSPITAL, 110 Rocksylvania Avenue, Zip 50126–2431; tel. 515/648–4631; John O'Brien, Administrator **A**1 2 9 10 **F**3 7 8 12 17 19 21 22 24 28 29 30 32 33 35 37 39 40 41 44 45 46 49 52 53 54 55 56 58 59 63 65 67 71 73 **P**1 6 **S** Mercy Health Services, Farmington Hills, MI	14	10	40	1491	17	25337	174	8761	4060	166
JEFFERSON—Greene County										
⊠ GREENE COUNTY MEDICAL CENTER, 1000 West Lincolnway, Zip 50129–1697; tel. 515/386–2114; Karen L. Bossard, Administrator (Total facility includes 62 beds in nursing home–type unit) **A**1 9 10 **F**7 8 11 12 13 14 15 16 17 18 19 21 22 26 28 29 30 31 32 33 34 35 37 39 40 41 42 44 45 49 62 64 65 67 68 71 73 **P**5 **Web address:** www.gcmc.netins.net	13	10	115	976	91	24203	135	10546	5438	212
KEOKUK—Lee County										
⊠ KEOKUK AREA HOSPITAL, 1600 Morgan Street, Zip 52632–3456; tel. 319/524–7150; Allan Zastrow, FACHE, Chief Executive Officer (Total facility includes 20 beds in nursing home–type unit) **A**1 9 10 **F**3 7 8 11 14 15 16 17 19 21 22 23 28 29 30 32 33 34 35 40 44 45 46 49 52 53 54 55 56 61 64 65 66 67 71 73 **P**7	23	10	113	3957	56	46029	252	22439	10499	412
KEOSAUQUA—Van Buren County										
★ VAN BUREN COUNTY HOSPITAL, Highway 1 North, Zip 52565, Mailing Address: P.O. Box 70, Zip 52565–0070; tel. 319/293–3171; Lisa Schnedler, Administrator **A**9 10 **F**1 7 8 11 12 13 15 16 17 22 28 30 32 34 37 39 40 41 42 44 49 54 61 64 71 73 **S** Sisters of Mary of the Presentation Health Corporation, Fargo, ND **Web address:** www.netins.net/showcase/forhealth/	13	10	40	691	18	8576	36	6144	3235	147
KNOXVILLE—Marion County										
⊠ KNOXVILLE AREA COMMUNITY HOSPITAL, 1002 South Lincoln Street, Zip 50138–3121; tel. 515/842–2151; Jim Murphy, Chief Executive Officer (Total facility includes 14 beds in nursing home–type unit) **A**1 9 10 **F**7 8 11 15 16 19 21 22 28 30 33 34 35 37 40 41 44 45 49 56 63 64 65 67 71 73 **P**8 **S** Quorum Health Group/Quorum Health Resources, Inc., Brentwood, TN KNOXVILLE DIVISION See Veterans Affairs Central Iowa Health Care System, Des Moines	23	10	52	1341	28	15471	109	8602	3276	141
LAKE CITY—Calhoun County										
★ STEWART MEMORIAL COMMUNITY HOSPITAL, 1301 West Main, Zip 51449–1585; tel. 712/464–3171; Kris Baumgart, Chief Executive Officer **A**9 10 **F**7 8 14 19 22 29 30 32 33 34 35 36 37 40 41 44 49 56 65 71 **P**5 6 **Web address:** www.smhospital.org	23	10	53	1746	27	39240	128	10195	5466	178
LE MARS—Plymouth County										
FLOYD VALLEY HOSPITAL, Highway 3 East, Zip 51031, Mailing Address: P.O. Box 10, Zip 51031–0010; tel. 712/546–7871; Michael Donlin, Administrator **A**9 10 **F**6 7 8 13 15 16 17 19 22 24 28 29 30 32 33 34 35 36 40 41 42 44 45 46 49 56 64 67 71 73 **P**3 **S** Avera Health, Yankton, SD **Web address:** www.floydvalleyhospital.org	14	10	44	1368	19	33997	127	9502	3823	123
LEON—Decatur County										
⊠ DECATUR COUNTY HOSPITAL, 1405 N.W. Church Street, Zip 50144–1299; tel. 515/446–4871; Milford Grotnes, Interim Administrator **A**1 9 10 **F**7 8 14 15 16 19 22 32 34 37 40 41 42 44 46 49 53 54 55 56 57 58 59 65 67 71	13	10	49	733	11	10304	62	5184	2402	119
MANCHESTER—Delaware County										
REGIONAL MEDICAL CENTER OF NORTHEAST IOWA AND DELAWARE COUNTY, (Formerly Delaware County Memorial Hospital), 709 West Main Street, Zip 52057–0359; tel. 319/927–3232; Lon D. Butikofer, R.N., Ph.D., Administrator and Chief Executive Officer **A**9 10 **F**7 8 12 13 14 15 16 17 18 19 22 24 26 27 28 29 30 31 32 33 34 35 37 39 40 41 44 45 46 49 51 53 54 55 56 58 65 66 67 70 71 73 **P**5	13	10	35	824	9	50636	187	10128	4946	157
MANNING—Carroll County										
MANNING REGIONAL HEALTHCARE CENTER, 410 Main Street, Zip 51455–1093; tel. 712/653–2072; Michael S. Ketcham, Administrator (Total facility includes 58 beds in nursing home–type unit) **A**9 10 **F**1 2 3 7 8 14 18 19 21 22 26 29 30 31 32 34 35 40 41 44 45 46 51 54 56 64 65 67 71 73 **P**5	23	10	87	419	49	8141	28	3367	1644	105
MAQUOKETA—Jackson County										
⊠ JACKSON COUNTY PUBLIC HOSPITAL, 700 West Grove Street, Zip 52060–0910; tel. 319/652–2474; Curt Coleman, Chief Executive Officer (Total facility includes 18 beds in nursing home–type unit) **A**1 9 10 **F**7 8 15 16 19 21 22 24 30 32 34 36 37 39 40 44 45 46 49 63 64 65 71 73	13	10	61	876	26	14037	102	8366	4106	171

Hospital, Address, Telephone, Administrator, Approval, Facility, and Physician Codes, Health Care System, Network	Classi-fication Codes		Utilization Data					Expense (thousands) of dollars		
	Control	Service	Staffed Beds	Admissions	Census	Outpatient Visits	Births	Total	Payroll	Personnel

★ American Hospital Association (AHA) membership
□ Joint Commission on Accreditation of Healthcare Organizations (JCAHO) accreditation
+ American Osteopathic Healthcare Association (AOHA) membership
○ American Osteopathic Association (AOA) accreditation
△ Commission on Accreditation of Rehabilitation Facilities (CARF) accreditation
Control codes 61, 63, 64, 71, 72 and 73 indicate hospitals listed by AOHA, but not registered by AHA. For definition of numerical codes, see page A4

MARENGO—Iowa County

MARENGO MEMORIAL HOSPITAL, 300 West May Street, Zip 52301–1261, Mailing Address: P.O. Box 228, Zip 52301–0228; tel. 319/642–5543; Genny Maroc, Interim Administrator **A**9 10 **F**8 12 14 15 16 19 22 33 36 39 41 49 64 65 73	14	10	44	371	31	4661	0	4232	1974	81

MARSHALLTOWN—Marshall County

⊞ MARSHALLTOWN MEDICAL AND SURGICAL CENTER, 3 South Fourth Avenue, Zip 50158–2998; tel. 515/754–5151; Robert Cooper, Chief Executive Officer (Total facility includes 26 beds in nursing home–type unit) **A**1 9 10 **F**7 8 12 13 14 15 16 17 19 21 22 25 26 27 28 29 30 32 33 34 35 37 39 40 41 42 44 45 46 49 51 63 64 65 66 67 68 70 71 73 74 **P**7	23	10	111	3831	49	115778	547	34760	16284	434

MASON CITY—Cerro Gordo County

⊞ NORTH IOWA MERCY HEALTH CENTER, 1000 Fourth Street S.W., Zip 50401–2800; tel. 515/422–7000; James J. Sexton, President and Chief Executive Officer (Total facility includes 30 beds in nursing home–type unit) **A**1 2 3 5 9 10 **F**1 3 4 7 8 10 12 13 14 15 16 17 18 19 20 21 22 23 26 27 28 29 30 31 32 33 34 35 36 37 38 39 40 41 42 43 44 45 46 49 51 52 53 54 55 56 57 58 59 60 62 64 65 66 67 68 70 71 73 74 **P**1 6 **S** Mercy Health Services, Farmington Hills, MI Web address: www.northiowamercy.com	21	10	255	12112	137	653175	1191	138397	62031	2140

MISSOURI VALLEY—Harrison County

⊞ ALEGENT HEALTH COMMUNITY MEMORIAL HOSPITAL, 631 North Eighth Street, Zip 51555–1199; tel. 712/642–2784; James A. Seymour, Regional Administrator **A**1 9 10 **F**8 12 15 16 19 22 25 28 29 30 32 33 34 39 41 42 44 49 51 53 54 56 58 65 66 67 71 **P**8	23	10	39	634	7	15722	0	5503	2544	128

MOUNT AYR—Ringgold County

RINGGOLD COUNTY HOSPITAL, 211 Shellway Drive, Zip 50854–1299; tel. 515/464–3226; Gordon W. Winkler, Administrator **A**9 10 **F**2 3 8 19 22 30 33 34 40 41 44 49 71 **P**6	13	10	36	540	9	16592	0	5687	2507	92

MOUNT PLEASANT—Henry County

★ HENRY COUNTY HEALTH CENTER, 407 South White Street, Zip 52641–2299; tel. 319/385–3141; Robert Miller, Chief Executive Officer (Total facility includes 49 beds in nursing home–type unit) **A**9 10 **F**8 12 13 15 16 17 19 21 22 26 28 29 30 32 33 34 35 37 40 41 42 44 45 49 51 56 64 65 66 67 71 73 **P**7 8 Web address: www.webtex.net/hchc	13	10	99	1370	67	—	170	13889	6300	254
MENTAL HEALTH INSTITUTE, 1200 East Washington Street, Zip 52641–1898; tel. 319/385–7231; David J. Scurr, Superintendent **A**10 **F**2 3 12 20 45 52 65 73	12	82	80	924	61	120	0	4983	3445	76

MUSCATINE—Muscatine County

⊞ MUSCATINE GENERAL HOSPITAL, 1518 Mulberry Avenue, Zip 52761–3499; tel. 319/264–9100; Karmon Bjella, Chief Executive Officer (Total facility includes 8 beds in nursing home–type unit) **A**1 9 10 **F**3 7 8 15 16 17 19 21 22 26 28 30 35 36 37 39 40 42 44 49 64 65 71 Web address: www.mgh.edu	13	10	66	2606	29	35378	435	22143	9277	324

NEVADA—Story County

★ STORY COUNTY HOSPITAL AND LONG TERM CARE FACILITY, 630 Sixth Street, Zip 50201–2266; tel. 515/382–2111; Todd Willert, Administrator (Total facility includes 80 beds in nursing home–type unit) **A**9 10 **F**19 20 22 24 26 27 30 32 33 34 36 37 39 41 42 44 48 49 59 64 65 66 67 71 73 **P**6	13	10	122	298	85	19972	0	7054	2812	131

NEW HAMPTON—Chickasaw County

⊞ SAINT JOSEPH COMMUNITY HOSPITAL, 308 North Maple Avenue, Zip 50659–1142; tel. 515/394–4121; Carolyn Martin-Shaw, President (Total facility includes 35 beds in nursing home–type unit) **A**1 9 10 **F**7 8 12 14 15 16 18 19 21 22 26 27 28 29 30 32 33 34 39 40 41 44 45 49 63 64 65 66 67 71 73 **P**1 **S** Mercy Health Services, Farmington Hills, MI	21	10	55	825	42	21211	69	6538	3041	110

NEWTON—Jasper County

⊞ SKIFF MEDICAL CENTER, 204 North Fourth Avenue East, Zip 50208–3100; tel. 515/792–1273; Eric L. Lothe, President and Chief Executive Officer **A**1 9 10 **F**7 8 13 15 16 19 22 32 33 34 35 37 39 40 41 49 63 65 66 67 71 Web address: www.skiffmed.com	14	10	52	2331	24	57895	205	17263	8574	285

OAKDALE—Johnson County

IOWA MEDICAL AND CLASSIFICATION CENTER, Highway 965, Zip 52319, Mailing Address: IMCC, Box A, Zip 52319; tel. 319/626–2391; Russell E. Rogerson, Warden **F**2 3 5 9 10 11 12 19 20 21 22 23 25 26 29 30 31 35 37 39 40 42 43 44 45 46 48 49 50 51 52 54 55 56 57 58 60 61 63 64 65 69 70 71 72 74	12	22	23	149	19	0	0	—	—	26

OELWEIN—Fayette County

⊞ MERCY HOSPITAL OF FRANCISCAN SISTERS, 201 Eighth Avenue S.E., Zip 50662–2447; tel. 319/283–6000; Richard Schrupp, President and Chief Executive Officer (Total facility includes 39 beds in nursing home–type unit) **A**1 9 10 **F**3 7 8 15 19 21 22 26 27 28 29 30 32 33 34 35 36 37 39 40 41 44 45 46 51 63 64 65 66 67 71 73 **P**6 **S** Wheaton Franciscan Services, Inc., Wheaton, IL	21	10	64	1034	48	28753	45	9721	4498	167

ONAWA—Monona County

⊞ BURGESS HEALTH CENTER, (Formerly Burgess Memorial Hospital), 1600 Diamond Street, Zip 51040–1548; tel. 712/423–2311; Francis Tramp, President **A**1 9 10 **F**7 8 14 15 16 17 19 22 24 28 30 32 33 34 40 42 44 49 51 58 64 65 66 71 73 **P**6	23	10	48	1413	17	42303	90	10951	4980	173

Hospital, Address, Telephone, Administrator, Approval, Facility, and Physician Codes, Health Care System, Network	Classi-fication Codes		Utilization Data					Expense (thousands) of dollars		
★ American Hospital Association (AHA) membership □ Joint Commission on Accreditation of Healthcare Organizations (JCAHO) accreditation + American Osteopathic Healthcare Association (AOHA) membership ○ American Osteopathic Association (AOA) accreditation △ Commission on Accreditation of Rehabilitation Facilities (CARF) accreditation Control codes 61, 63, 64, 71, 72 and 73 indicate hospitals listed by AOHA, but not registered by AHA. For definition of numerical codes, see page A4	Control	Service	Staffed Beds	Admissions	Census	Outpatient Visits	Births	Total	Payroll	Personnel

ORANGE CITY—Sioux County

★ ORANGE CITY HOSPITAL AND CLINIC, (Formerly Orange City Municipal Hospital), 400 Central Avenue N.W., Zip 51041–1398; tel. 712/737–4984; Martin W. Guthmiller, Administrator (Total facility includes 83 beds in nursing home–type unit) **A**9 10 **F**7 8 13 14 15 16 17 18 19 20 21 22 29 30 32 33 34 35 36 37 39 40 41 42 44 45 46 58 64 65 66 67 71 73 74 **P**4 6 **S** Sioux Valley Hospitals and Health System, Sioux Falls, SD ... 14 10 113 1209 97 44688 175 12038 5565 234

OSAGE—Mitchell County

★ MITCHELL COUNTY REGIONAL HEALTH CENTER, 616 North Eighth Street, Zip 50461–1498; tel. 515/732–6005; Kimberly J. Miller, CHE, Administrator **A**9 10 **F**7 8 11 14 15 16 19 22 30 33 34 35 39 40 42 44 49 65 70 71 73 **P**1 **S** Mercy Health Services, Farmington Hills, MI ... 13 10 28 779 7 52974 66 7551 2404 107

OSCEOLA—Clarke County

★ CLARKE COUNTY HOSPITAL, 800 South Fillmore Street, Zip 50213; tel. 515/342–2184; Jack A. Burrows, Administrator **A**9 10 **F**8 15 16 19 21 22 24 30 33 36 37 41 42 44 46 49 51 71 **S** Iowa Health System, Des Moines, IA ... 13 10 48 674 37 14253 0 4775 2031 105

OSKALOOSA—Mahaska County

⊞ MAHASKA COUNTY HOSPITAL, 1229 C Avenue East, Zip 52577–4298; tel. 515/672–3100; David E. Rutter, Administrator **A**1 9 10 **F**3 7 8 11 12 13 14 15 16 17 18 19 20 21 22 25 26 27 28 29 30 31 32 33 34 35 36 37 39 40 41 42 44 45 46 49 51 53 54 55 56 57 58 59 64 65 66 67 68 71 72 73 74 **P**1 ... 13 10 53 1419 12 65477 187 13143 5985 204

OTTUMWA—Wapello County

⊞ OTTUMWA REGIONAL HEALTH CENTER, 1001 Pennsylvania Avenue, Zip 52501–2186; tel. 515/684–2300; Clarence Cory, President (Total facility includes 12 beds in nursing home–type unit) **A**1 2 9 10 **F**1 2 3 6 7 8 12 14 15 16 17 19 21 22 23 24 26 27 28 29 30 32 33 34 35 36 37 38 39 40 41 42 44 45 46 49 52 53 54 55 56 57 58 59 60 62 63 64 65 66 67 71 73 74 **P**6 8 ... 23 10 82 5578 74 119144 734 46607 20156 737

PELLA—Marion County

⊞ PELLA REGIONAL HEALTH CENTER, 404 Jefferson Street, Zip 50219–1257; tel. 515/628–3150; Robert D. Kroese, Chief Executive Officer (Total facility includes 109 beds in nursing home–type unit) **A**1 9 10 **F**1 7 8 11 14 15 16 17 19 22 23 29 30 32 33 34 35 37 39 40 41 42 44 45 46 49 63 64 65 66 67 71 73 **P**1 5 6 ... 23 10 156 1748 138 78851 271 18322 8478 419

PERRY—Dallas County

★ DALLAS COUNTY HOSPITAL, 610 10th Street, Zip 50220–2221, Mailing Address: P.O. Box 608, Zip 50220–0608; tel. 515/465–3547; Kari L. Engholm, Administrator and Chief Executive Officer **A**9 10 **F**1 8 14 15 16 17 19 22 26 28 29 30 33 34 39 41 42 44 45 49 67 70 71 72 73 **P**4 7 **S** Iowa Health System, Des Moines, IA ... 13 10 49 614 9 23908 0 7959 3072 123

POCAHONTAS—Pocahontas County

★ POCAHONTAS COMMUNITY HOSPITAL, 606 N.W. Seventh, Zip 50574–1099; tel. 712/335–3501; Jay Christensen, Administrator **A**9 10 **F**8 19 22 28 30 32 33 34 35 37 41 42 44 49 64 65 67 71 **P**6 ... 14 10 25 364 7 26085 0 3326 1452 69

PRIMGHAR—Obrien County

★ BAUM HARMON MEMORIAL HOSPITAL, 255 North Welch Avenue, Zip 51245–1034, Mailing Address: P.O. Box 528, Zip 51245–0528; tel. 712/757–2300; Trudy Pfeiffer, Interim Administrator **A**9 10 **F**8 12 15 19 22 24 28 30 32 33 34 35 36 37 41 42 44 49 64 65 66 67 71 **P**6 8 **S** Mercy Health Services, Farmington Hills, MI ... 14 10 16 172 2 7749 12 2459 850 37

RED OAK—Montgomery County

★ MONTGOMERY COUNTY MEMORIAL HOSPITAL, 2301 Eastern Avenue, Zip 51566–1300, Mailing Address: P.O. Box 489, Zip 51566; tel. 712/623–7000; Allen E. Pohren, Administrator **A**9 10 **F**7 8 12 14 15 16 17 19 22 24 28 30 32 33 34 35 36 37 40 41 42 44 49 63 65 67 71 73 74 **Web address:** www.mcmh.org ... 13 10 40 1723 28 42953 29 14463 6320 228

ROCK RAPIDS—Lyon County

★ MERRILL PIONEER COMMUNITY HOSPITAL, 801 South Greene Street, Zip 51246–1998; tel. 712/472–2591; Gordon Smith, Administrator **A**9 10 **F**7 8 15 19 22 24 28 30 32 33 35 40 41 44 49 71 **P**6 **S** Sioux Valley Hospitals and Health System, Sioux Falls, SD ... 23 10 16 396 5 7343 40 2547 1165 45

ROCK VALLEY—Sioux County

★ HEGG MEMORIAL HEALTH CENTER, 1202 21st Avenue, Zip 51247–1497; tel. 712/476–5305; Chris Thomas, Administrator and Chief Executive Officer (Total facility includes 95 beds in nursing home–type unit) **A**9 10 **F**7 8 15 16 17 19 22 24 28 29 30 32 33 34 35 36 37 39 40 41 42 44 45 49 59 62 64 65 66 67 71 73 **P**5 **S** Avera Health, Yankton, SD ... 23 10 123 340 81 20691 41 4858 2504 141

SAC CITY—Sac County

★ LORING HOSPITAL, 211 Highland Avenue, Zip 50583–0217, Mailing Address: P.O. Box 217, Zip 50583–0217; tel. 712/662–7105; Greg Miner, Administrator (Total facility includes 21 beds in nursing home–type unit) **A**9 10 **F**3 4 5 7 8 10 11 13 14 15 16 17 19 22 23 26 28 29 30 31 32 33 34 35 39 40 42 43 44 45 46 49 51 53 54 55 56 57 58 59 60 62 64 65 66 67 69 71 73 **S** Iowa Health System, Des Moines, IA ... 23 10 54 901 29 10069 29 4716 2452 101

SHELDON—Obrien County

★ NORTHWEST IOWA HEALTH CENTER, 118 North Seventh Avenue, Zip 51201–1235; tel. 712/324–5041; Charles R. Miller, Chief Executive Officer (Total facility includes 115 beds in nursing home–type unit) **A**9 10 **F**1 3 8 14 15 16 17 18 19 20 22 24 26 28 30 32 33 34 35 36 39 41 42 44 45 46 49 53 54 55 56 57 58 59 64 65 66 67 71 73 **P**6 **S** Sioux Valley Hospitals and Health System, Sioux Falls, SD ... 23 10 139 923 97 22614 126 10719 5291 209

Hospital, Address, Telephone, Administrator, Approval, Facility, and Physician Codes, Health Care System, Network	Classi-fication Codes		Utilization Data					Expense (thousands) of dollars		
★ American Hospital Association (AHA) membership □ Joint Commission on Accreditation of Healthcare Organizations (JCAHO) accreditation + American Osteopathic Healthcare Association (AOHA) membership ○ American Osteopathic Association (AOA) accreditation △ Commission on Accreditation of Rehabilitation Facilities (CARF) accreditation Control codes 61, 63, 64, 71, 72 and 73 indicate hospitals listed by AOHA, but not registered by AHA. For definition of numerical codes, see page A4	Control	Service	Staffed Beds	Admissions	Census	Outpatient Visits	Births	Total	Payroll	Personnel

SHENANDOAH—Page County
★ SHENANDOAH MEMORIAL HOSPITAL, 300 Pershing Avenue, Zip 51601–2397; tel. 712/246–1230; Charles L. Millburg, CHE, Chief Executive Officer (Total facility includes 62 beds in nursing home–type unit) **A**9 10 **F**7 8 14 15 16 19 21 22 24 27 28 30 32 34 35 36 37 39 41 42 44 46 49 60 64 67 71 73 **P**1 7	23	10	87	1021	64	17180	93	11291	4941	210

SIBLEY—Osceola County
★ OSCEOLA COMMUNITY HOSPITAL, Ninth Avenue North, Zip 51249–0258, Mailing Address: P.O. Box 258, Zip 51249–0258; tel. 712/754–2574; Janet Dykstra, Chief Executive Officer **A**9 10 **F**7 8 11 13 14 15 16 17 19 20 22 26 27 28 29 30 31 32 33 34 35 36 39 40 41 42 44 45 46 49 51 53 54 55 56 57 58 59 62 64 65 66 67 68 69 71 73 74 **P**5 **S** Avera Health, Yankton, SD	23	10	32	538	7	17217	82	3972	1710	75

SIGOURNEY—Keokuk County
KEOKUK COUNTY HEALTH CENTER, 1312 South Stuart Street, Zip 52591–0286, Mailing Address: P.O. Box 286, Zip 52591–0286; tel. 515/622–2720; Douglas A. Sheetz, Chief Executive Officer **A**9 10 **F**14 19 21 22 35 50 63 65 71	13	10	26	157	12	8097	0	2043	1289	—

SIOUX CENTER—Sioux County
SIOUX CENTER COMMUNITY HOSPITAL AND HEALTH CENTER, 605 South Main Avenue, Zip 51250–1398; tel. 712/722–1271; Marla Toering, Administrator (Total facility includes 69 beds in nursing home–type unit) **A**9 10 **F**7 8 11 14 15 16 19 21 22 28 30 32 33 34 35 39 40 41 44 49 64 65 67 71 73 74 **S** Avera Health, Yankton, SD	23	10	90	505	75	31241	190	8616	3481	177

SIOUX CITY—Woodbury County
⊞ △ MARIAN HEALTH CENTER, (Includes Marian Behavioral Health Center, 4301 Sergeant Road, Zip 51106; tel. 712/279–2446), 801 Fifth Street, Zip 51102, Mailing Address: P.O. Box 3168, Zip 51102–3168; tel. 712/279–2010; Deborah VandenBroek, President and Chief Executive Officer (Total facility includes 20 beds in nursing home–type unit) **A**1 2 3 5 7 9 10 **F**3 4 6 7 8 10 11 12 13 14 15 16 17 19 21 22 23 26 27 28 29 30 31 32 33 34 35 36 37 39 40 41 42 43 44 45 46 48 49 51 52 53 54 55 56 57 58 59 60 63 64 65 67 70 71 72 73 **P**5 6 8 **S** Mercy Health Services, Farmington Hills, MI **Web address:** www.mercyhealth.com/marian	21	10	284	10933	159	334045	869	131104	54044	1727
⊞ ST. LUKE'S REGIONAL MEDICAL CENTER, 2720 Stone Park Boulevard, Zip 51104–2000; tel. 712/279–3500; John D. Daniels, President and Chief Executive Officer **A**1 2 3 5 6 9 10 **F**4 6 7 8 9 10 11 12 13 14 15 16 17 19 20 21 22 23 27 28 29 30 32 35 36 37 38 39 40 41 42 44 45 47 49 51 52 56 59 61 62 64 65 67 68 71 72 73 74 **P**1 6 **S** Iowa Health System, Des Moines, IA **Web address:** www.siouxlan.com/stlukes	23	10	196	10930	132	101160	1679	82035	33228	1151

SPENCER—Clay County
★ SPENCER MUNICIPAL HOSPITAL, 1200 First Avenue East, Zip 51301–4321; tel. 712/264–6198; John Allen, President and Chief Executive Officer (Total facility includes 14 beds in nursing home–type unit) **A**9 10 **F**3 7 8 12 14 15 16 17 19 20 21 22 26 27 28 30 32 33 34 35 36 37 39 40 41 42 44 45 46 49 52 54 55 56 57 58 59 60 63 64 65 66 67 70 71 73 **S** Sioux Valley Hospitals and Health System, Sioux Falls, SD	14	10	86	2927	35	31767	262	24114	10798	369

SPIRIT LAKE—Dickinson County
□ DICKINSON COUNTY MEMORIAL HOSPITAL, Highway 71 South, Zip 51360, Mailing Address: Box AB, Zip 51360; tel. 712/336–1230; Richard C. Kielman, President and Chief Executive Officer **A**1 9 10 **F**3 7 8 15 16 19 22 27 30 32 34 35 36 37 39 40 42 44 65 66 67 71 73	13	10	49	1625	19	32139	176	12943	5427	205

STORM LAKE—Buena Vista County
⊞ BUENA VISTA COUNTY HOSPITAL, 1525 West Fifth Street, Zip 50588–0309; tel. 712/732–4030; James O. Nelson, Administrator **A**1 9 10 **F**1 3 7 8 11 12 14 15 16 19 21 22 24 27 30 32 33 34 35 36 39 40 41 42 44 49 64 65 67 71 73 **S** Iowa Health System, Des Moines, IA	13	10	30	1755	18	66840	295	15048	6428	246

SUMNER—Bremer County
COMMUNITY MEMORIAL HOSPITAL, 909 West First Street, Zip 50674–1203, Mailing Address: P.O. Box 148, Zip 50674–0148; tel. 319/578–3275; Scott Knode, Co–Administrator **A**9 10 **F**3 7 8 14 19 22 30 32 33 34 35 36 39 41 44 49 65 71 73	23	10	23	482	5	14579	25	3894	1657	59

VINTON—Benton County
★ VIRGINIA GAY HOSPITAL, 502 North Ninth Avenue, Zip 52349–2299; tel. 319/472–6200; Michael J. Riege, Chief Executive Officer (Total facility includes 58 beds in nursing home–type unit) **A**9 10 **F**14 15 16 19 22 27 32 34 44 49 62 64 65 70 71 **P**6	23	10	89	380	62	59194	0	7543	3971	140

WASHINGTON—Washington County
★ WASHINGTON COUNTY HOSPITAL, 400 East Polk Street, Zip 52353, Mailing Address: P.O. Box 909, Zip 52353; tel. 319/653–5481; Ronald D. Davis, Chief Executive Officer (Total facility includes 43 beds in nursing home–type unit) **A**9 10 **F**7 8 11 15 19 22 28 30 32 33 35 36 40 44 45 49 64 65 71 73 **S** Quorum Health Group/Quorum Health Resources, Inc., Brentwood, TN	13	10	83	1799	56	39126	111	9923	4459	181

WATERLOO—Black Hawk County
⊞ ALLEN MEMORIAL HOSPITAL, 1825 Logan Avenue, Zip 50703–1916; tel. 319/235–3987; Richard A. Seidler, FACHE, Chief Executive Officer (Total facility includes 30 beds in nursing home–type unit) **A**1 3 5 6 9 10 **F**1 3 4 7 8 10 12 14 15 16 17 19 20 21 22 23 24 25 28 29 30 31 32 33 34 35 37 38 39 40 41 42 43 44 45 46 49 51 52 53 54 55 56 57 58 59 60 61 62 64 65 67 68 70 71 73 74 **P**1 3 6 **S** Iowa Health System, Des Moines, IA	23	10	201	8658	113	210007	860	73432	31392	1003

Hospital, Address, Telephone, Administrator, Approval, Facility, and Physician Codes, Health Care System, Network	Classi-fication Codes		Utilization Data					Expense (thousands) of dollars		
★ American Hospital Association (AHA) membership □ Joint Commission on Accreditation of Healthcare Organizations (JCAHO) accreditation + American Osteopathic Healthcare Association (AOHA) membership ○ American Osteopathic Association (AOA) accreditation △ Commission on Accreditation of Rehabilitation Facilities (CARF) accreditation Control codes 61, 63, 64, 71, 72 and 73 indicate hospitals listed by AOHA, but not registered by AHA. For definition of numerical codes, see page A4	Control	Service	Staffed Beds	Admissions	Census	Outpatient Visits	Births	Total	Payroll	Personnel
✠ △ COVENANT MEDICAL CENTER, (Includes Kimball–Ridge Center, 2101 Kimball Avenue, Zip 50702), 3421 West Ninth Street, Zip 50702–5499; tel. 319/272–8000; Raymond F. Burfeind, President (Total facility includes 44 beds in nursing home–type unit) **A**1 2 3 5 7 9 10 **F**2 3 4 6 7 8 12 15 16 17 18 19 20 21 22 23 24 27 28 29 30 31 32 33 34 35 37 38 39 40 41 42 44 45 48 49 51 52 53 54 55 56 57 58 59 60 63 64 65 66 67 68 70 71 73 74 **P**6 **S** Wheaton Franciscan Services, Inc., Wheaton, IL KIMBALL–RIDGE CENTER See Covenant Medical Center	21	10	293	11140	158	498376	1539	118926	56696	1747
WAUKON—Allamakee County VETERANS MEMORIAL HOSPITAL, 40 First Street S.E., Zip 52172–2099; tel. 319/568–3411; Michael D. Myers, Administrator **A**9 10 **F**3 7 8 14 15 16 17 19 22 24 28 29 30 32 33 34 35 39 40 41 42 44 49 58 64 65 66 67 68 71 72	14	10	25	754	8	38644	53	5118	2357	152
WAVERLY—Bremer County ✠ WAVERLY MUNICIPAL HOSPITAL, 312 Ninth Street S.W., Zip 50677–2999; tel. 319/352–4120; Arnold Flessner, Administrator **A**1 9 10 **F**7 8 14 15 16 19 22 24 26 28 29 30 32 33 34 35 37 39 40 41 44 47 49 64 65 71 73 **P**6	14	10	38	1094	12	21734	93	9503	4036	138
WEBSTER CITY—Hamilton County □ HAMILTON COUNTY PUBLIC HOSPITAL, 800 Ohio Street, Zip 50595–2824, Mailing Address: P.O. Box 430, Zip 50595–0430; tel. 515/832–9400; Roger W. Lenz, Administrator **A**1 9 10 **F**7 8 12 15 16 19 22 28 30 32 35 36 39 40 41 44 49 63 64 65 67 70 71 73 **P**8	13	10	40	1999	23	14366	200	11472	5553	231
WEST UNION—Fayette County ★ PALMER LUTHERAN HEALTH CENTER, 112 Jefferson Street, Zip 52175–1022; tel. 319/422–3811; Debrah Chensvold, President **A**9 10 **F**7 8 16 19 22 26 29 30 31 32 33 34 35 41 42 44 49 52 57 58 65 66 67 71 73	23	10	30	767	11	52986	79	8185	3796	136
WINTERSET—Madison County MADISON COUNTY MEMORIAL HOSPITAL, 300 Hutchings Street, Zip 50273–2199; tel. 515/462–2373; Jill Kordick, Administrator **A**9 10 **F**3 8 12 15 16 17 19 22 26 30 31 32 33 34 35 37 39 41 42 44 45 49 51 53 54 55 56 57 58 59 64 65 66 67 68 71 73	13	10	31	723	11	32269	0	7818	3088	116
WOODWARD—Boone County WOODWARD STATE HOSPITAL–SCHOOL, Zip 50276–9999; tel. 515/438–2600 **F**4 5 8 9 10 11 19 20 21 22 23 31 35 37 42 43 44 47 50 52 53 54 55 56 57 58 60 63 70 71	12	62	283	15	278	0	0	28492	19827	634

KANSAS

Resident population 2,629 (in thousands)
Resident population in metro areas 54.2%
Birth rate per 1,000 population 14.5
65 years and over 13.5%
Percent of persons without health insurance 11.4%

Hospital, Address, Telephone, Administrator, Approval, Facility, and Physician Codes, Health Care System, Network	Classi-fication Codes		Utilization Data					Expense (thousands) of dollars		
★ American Hospital Association (AHA) membership □ Joint Commission on Accreditation of Healthcare Organizations (JCAHO) accreditation + American Osteopathic Healthcare Association (AOHA) membership ○ American Osteopathic Association (AOA) accreditation △ Commission on Accreditation of Rehabilitation Facilities (CARF) accreditation Control codes 61, 63, 64, 71, 72 and 73 indicate hospitals listed by AOHA, but not registered by AHA. For definition of numerical codes, see page A4	Control	Service	Staffed Beds	Admissions	Census	Outpatient Visits	Births	Total	Payroll	Personnel

ABILENE—Dickinson County
★ MEMORIAL HOSPITAL, 511 N.E. Tenth Street, Zip 67410–2100, Mailing Address: P.O. Box 69, Zip 67410–0069; tel. 785/263–2100; Leon J. Boor, Chief Executive Officer and Administrator **A**9 10 **F**7 8 15 19 22 24 30 32 33 34 36 39 40 42 44 49 52 57 64 65 67 71 73 **P**8

| | | 16 | 10 | 47 | 1013 | 13 | 16273 | 71 | 6688 | 2960 | 147 |

ANTHONY—Harper County
HOSPITAL DISTRICT NUMBER SIX OF HARPER COUNTY, 1101 East Spring Street, Zip 67003–2199; tel. 316/842–5111; Cindy M. McCray, Administrator and Chief Executive Officer **A**9 10 **F**8 15 19 22 42 44 51 61 64 65 71 **P**6

| | | 16 | 10 | 30 | 216 | 21 | 18678 | 0 | 3414 | 1736 | 62 |

ARKANSAS CITY—Cowley County
★ SOUTH CENTRAL KANSAS REGIONAL MEDICAL CENTER, 216 West Birch Avenue, Zip 67005–1598, Mailing Address: P.O. Box 1107, Zip 67005–1107; tel. 316/442–2500; Webster T. Russell, Chief Executive Officer (Total facility includes 10 beds in nursing home–type unit) **A**9 10 **F**7 8 12 14 15 16 17 19 22 29 30 32 34 35 36 37 39 40 41 42 44 46 49 51 63 64 65 71 73 **P**8
Web address: www.sckrmc.com

| | | 14 | 10 | 85 | 1314 | 17 | 66843 | 137 | 9046 | 3903 | 139 |

ASHLAND—Clark County
★ ASHLAND HEALTH CENTER, 709 Oak Street, Zip 67831, Mailing Address: P.O. Box 188, Zip 67831; tel. 316/635–2241; Bryan Stacey, Administrator (Total facility includes 36 beds in nursing home–type unit) **A**9 10 **F**1 8 14 16 22 24 27 32 33 34 44 46 48 49 54 56 58 64 65 71 **S** Great Plains Health Alliance, Inc., Phillipsburg, KS

| | | 16 | 10 | 48 | 92 | 28 | 4235 | 0 | 2393 | 1255 | 49 |

ATCHISON—Atchison County
⊠ ATCHISON HOSPITAL, 1301 North Second Street, Zip 66002–1297; tel. 913/367–2131; W. David Drew, President and Chief Executive Officer (Total facility includes 38 beds in nursing home–type unit) **A**1 9 10 **F**7 8 14 15 17 19 21 22 23 27 28 30 32 33 34 35 37 40 44 48 49 51 52 54 57 64 65 66 67 71 73 **P**6

| | | 23 | 10 | 121 | 2475 | 57 | 33356 | 217 | 17088 | 9390 | 329 |

ATWOOD—Rawlins County
RAWLINS COUNTY HEALTH CENTER, 707 Grant Street, Zip 67730–4700, Mailing Address: Box 47, Zip 67730–4700; tel. 785/626–3211; Donald J. Kessen, Administrator and Chief Executive Officer **A**9 10 **F**3 8 14 15 16 17 18 19 22 26 27 30 31 32 34 35 39 42 44 49 62 63 64 65 70 71 73 **S** Great Plains Health Alliance, Inc., Phillipsburg, KS

| | | 13 | 10 | 24 | 243 | 2 | 7184 | 0 | 2866 | 1480 | 48 |

AUGUSTA—Butler County
AUGUSTA MEDICAL COMPLEX, 2101 Dearborn Street, Zip 67010–0430, Mailing Address: Box 430, Zip 67010–0430; tel. 316/775–5421; Larry D. Wilkerson, Chief Executive Officer (Total facility includes 100 beds in nursing home–type unit) **A**9 10 **F**2 3 8 16 19 21 22 32 44 49 62 64 71

| | | 23 | 10 | 160 | 453 | 82 | — | 0 | — | — | — |

BELLEVILLE—Republic County
★ REPUBLIC COUNTY HOSPITAL, 2420 G Street, Zip 66935–2499; tel. 785/527–2255; Charles A. Westin, FACHE, Administrator (Total facility includes 38 beds in nursing home–type unit) **A**9 10 **F**7 8 12 14 15 17 19 20 21 22 26 28 33 34 39 41 42 44 45 46 49 64 65 66 71 **S** Great Plains Health Alliance, Inc., Phillipsburg, KS

| | | 23 | 10 | 86 | 1199 | 51 | 6051 | 83 | 6487 | 2933 | 135 |

BELOIT—Mitchell County
★ MITCHELL COUNTY HOSPITAL, 400 West Eighth, Zip 67420–1605, Mailing Address: P.O. Box 399, Zip 67420–0399; tel. 785/738–2266; John M. Osse, Administrator (Total facility includes 40 beds in nursing home–type unit) **A**9 10 **F**7 8 12 17 19 20 22 26 32 33 34 35 36 41 42 44 45 49 64 65 67 71 **S** Great Plains Health Alliance, Inc., Phillipsburg, KS

| | | 23 | 10 | 89 | 1516 | 59 | 14161 | 88 | 9769 | 4800 | 177 |

BURLINGTON—Coffey County
★ COFFEY COUNTY HOSPITAL, 801 North Fourth Street, Zip 66839–2602, Mailing Address: P.O. Box 189, Zip 66839–0189; tel. 316/364–2121; Dennis L. George, Chief Executive Officer (Total facility includes 40 beds in nursing home–type unit) **A**9 10 **F**7 8 11 15 19 22 25 28 30 32 34 37 39 40 41 44 49 64 65 71 73 **P**6

| | | 13 | 10 | 62 | 868 | 45 | 10814 | 65 | 10687 | 5453 | 204 |

CALDWELL—Sumner County
SUMNER COUNTY HOSPITAL DISTRICT ONE, 601 South Osage Street, Zip 67022–1698; tel. 316/845–6492; Virgil Watson, Administrator (Nonreporting) **A**9 10

| | | 16 | 10 | 27 | — | — | — | — | — | — | — |

CEDAR VALE—Chautauqua County
CEDAR VALE COMMUNITY HOSPITAL, 501 Cedar Street, Zip 67024, Mailing Address: P.O. Box 398, Zip 67024–0398; tel. 316/758–2266; William A. Lybarger, Administrator **A**9 10 **F**15 21 22 51 68 71 **P**5

| | | 23 | 10 | 25 | 244 | 19 | 6200 | 0 | 1177 | 949 | 46 |

CHANUTE—Neosho County
⊠ NEOSHO MEMORIAL REGIONAL MEDICAL CENTER, 629 South Plummer, Zip 66720–1928; tel. 316/431–4000; Murray L. Brown, Administrator **A**1 9 10 **F**7 8 12 15 19 20 22 23 27 28 32 33 35 37 40 41 44 49 64 65 71 73 **P**8 **S** Quorum Health Group/Quorum Health Resources, Inc., Brentwood, TN

| | | 13 | 10 | 60 | 2620 | 30 | 16696 | 314 | 14928 | 5977 | 235 |

Hospital, Address, Telephone, Administrator, Approval, Facility, and Physician Codes, Health Care System, Network	Classi-fication Codes		Utilization Data					Expense (thousands) of dollars		
★ American Hospital Association (AHA) membership □ Joint Commission on Accreditation of Healthcare Organizations (JCAHO) accreditation + American Osteopathic Healthcare Association (AOHA) membership ○ American Osteopathic Association (AOA) accreditation △ Commission on Accreditation of Rehabilitation Facilities (CARF) accreditation Control codes 61, 63, 64, 71, 72 and 73 indicate hospitals listed by AOHA, but not registered by AHA. For definition of numerical codes, see page A4	Control	Service	Staffed Beds	Admissions	Census	Outpatient Visits	Births	Total	Payroll	Personnel

CLAY CENTER—Clay County

★ CLAY COUNTY HOSPITAL, 617 Liberty Street, Zip 67432–1599; tel. 785/632–2144; John F. Wiebe, Chief Executive Officer **A**9 10 **F**7 8 15 16 19 22 28 33 39 44 45 49 65 67 71 **P**3 8

| | 13 | 10 | 35 | 836 | 12 | 21430 | 59 | 6169 | 2774 | 129 |

COFFEYVILLE—Montgomery County

✚ COFFEYVILLE REGIONAL MEDICAL CENTER, 1400 West Fourth, Zip 67337–3306; tel. 316/251–1200; Gerald Joseph Marquette, Jr., Chief Executive Officer (Total facility includes 33 beds in nursing home–type unit) **A**1 2 9 10 **F**7 8 14 15 16 19 21 22 27 28 30 31 32 33 35 37 40 42 44 49 52 53 57 58 60 64 65 66 71 73 74 **P**8 **S** Quorum Health Group/Quorum Health Resources, Inc., Brentwood, TN

| | 14 | 10 | 123 | 3957 | 68 | 19164 | 222 | 21510 | 9966 | 417 |

COLBY—Thomas County

CITIZENS MEDICAL CENTER, 100 East College Drive, Zip 67701–3799; tel. 785/462–7511; Richard B. Gamel, Chief Executive Officer (Total facility includes 80 beds in nursing home–type unit) **A**9 10 **F**7 8 11 14 15 19 21 22 29 32 34 35 36 37 40 41 42 44 45 46 49 51 64 65 67 71 73

| | 23 | 10 | 120 | 1229 | 85 | 10647 | 168 | 10344 | 4231 | 178 |

COLDWATER—Comanche County

COMANCHE COUNTY HOSPITAL, Second and Frisco Streets, Zip 67029, Mailing Address: HC 65, Box 8A, Zip 67029; tel. 316/582–2144; Nancy Zimmerman, Administrator **A**9 10 **F**8 15 19 20 22 24 30 31 32 33 36 39 41 42 44 49 56 64 66 71 **P**6 **S** Great Plains Health Alliance, Inc., Phillipsburg, KS

| | 13 | 10 | 14 | 166 | 2 | — | 0 | 1802 | — | 37 |

COLUMBUS—Cherokee County

MAUDE NORTON MEMORIAL CITY HOSPITAL, 220 North Pennsylvania Street, Zip 66725–1197; tel. 316/429–2545; Cindy Neely, Administrator **A**9 10 **F**8 15 16 19 22 28 29 30 32 36 41 44 49 64 71 73

| | 14 | 10 | 30 | 175 | 4 | 8064 | 0 | 1783 | 954 | 39 |

CONCORDIA—Cloud County

CLOUD COUNTY HEALTH CENTER, 1100 Highland Drive, Zip 66901–3997; tel. 785/243–1234; Daniel R. Bartz, Chief Executive Officer (Total facility includes 9 beds in nursing home–type unit) **A**9 10 **F**7 8 15 16 17 19 21 22 23 26 27 28 30 33 34 35 36 37 39 40 41 44 45 46 49 50 51 53 54 55 56 57 58 64 65 67 70 71 73 **P**7 8

| | 23 | 10 | 40 | 1324 | 16 | 19662 | 17 | 8136 | 3461 | 137 |

COUNCIL GROVE—Morris County

MORRIS COUNTY HOSPITAL, 600 North Washington Street, Zip 66846–1499, Mailing Address: P.O. Box 275, Zip 66846–0275; tel. 316/767–6811; Jim Reagan, M.D., Chief Executive Officer **A**9 10 **F**7 8 14 15 16 17 19 22 25 28 30 32 33 34 37 39 40 41 42 44 46 49 65 67 71 73

| | 13 | 10 | 28 | 849 | 11 | 13564 | 85 | 4246 | 2017 | 93 |

DIGHTON—Lane County

★ LANE COUNTY HOSPITAL, 243 South Second, Zip 67839, Mailing Address: P.O. Box 969, Zip 67839–0969; tel. 316/397–5321; Donna McGowan, R.N., Administrator (Total facility includes 21 beds in nursing home–type unit) **A**9 10 **F**19 22 26 28 32 35 49 51 64 65 66 71 **P**6 **S** Great Plains Health Alliance, Inc., Phillipsburg, KS

| | 13 | 10 | 31 | 226 | 26 | 5483 | 0 | 2321 | 1263 | 54 |

DODGE CITY—Ford County

✚ WESTERN PLAINS REGIONAL HOSPITAL, 3001 Avenue A, Zip 67801–6508, Mailing Address: P.O. Box 1478, Zip 67801–1478; tel. 316/225–8400; Ken Hutchenrider, President and Chief Executive Officer (Total facility includes 9 beds in nursing home–type unit) **A**1 9 10 **F**7 8 11 12 14 15 16 17 19 20 21 22 23 28 29 30 32 33 35 37 39 40 41 44 45 46 48 49 60 63 64 65 66 67 71 73 74 **S** LifePoint Hospitals, Inc., Nashville, TN

| | 33 | 10 | 101 | 3639 | 41 | 27957 | 798 | — | — | 293 |

EL DORADO—Butler County

✚ SUSAN B. ALLEN MEMORIAL HOSPITAL, 720 West Central Avenue, Zip 67042–2144; tel. 316/321–3300; Jim Wilson, President and Chief Executive Officer (Total facility includes 21 beds in nursing home–type unit) **A**1 9 10 **F**7 19 21 22 28 30 32 35 36 37 40 44 52 57 64 65 71 73 **P**8

| | 23 | 10 | 82 | 1796 | 30 | 48194 | 174 | 17497 | 8975 | 272 |

ELKHART—Morton County

★ MORTON COUNTY HEALTH SYSTEM, 445 Hilltop Street, Zip 67950–0937, Mailing Address: Box 937, Zip 67950–0937; tel. 316/697–2141; Bruce K. Birchell, Chief Executive Officer (Total facility includes 60 beds in nursing home–type unit) **A**9 10 **F**7 8 15 19 22 26 28 29 30 32 33 37 39 40 41 44 45 46 48 49 51 52 53 54 55 56 57 58 64 65 66 67 71 73 74 **P**5 6
Web address: www.mch.elkhart.com

| | 13 | 10 | 100 | 1059 | 74 | 11171 | 29 | 10619 | 6168 | 212 |

ELLINWOOD—Barton County

★ ELLINWOOD DISTRICT HOSPITAL, 605 North Main Street, Zip 67526–1440; tel. 316/564–2548; Marge Conell, R.N., Administrator **A**9 **F**8 19 20 22 34 35 36 49 64 65 69 71 **S** Great Plains Health Alliance, Inc., Phillipsburg, KS

| | 23 | 10 | 12 | 240 | 6 | 3753 | 0 | 1661 | 750 | 32 |

ELLSWORTH—Ellsworth County

ELLSWORTH COUNTY MEDICAL CENTER, (Formerly Ellsworth County Hospital), 1604 Aylward, Zip 67439–0087, Mailing Address: P.O. Drawer 87, Zip 67439–0087; tel. 785/472–3111; Roger W. Pearson, Administrator **A**9 10 **F**12 19 21 28 41 45 46 49 64 65 71 **P**8

| | 13 | 10 | 25 | 554 | 5 | 7463 | 0 | 3341 | 1370 | 67 |

EMPORIA—Lyon County

✚ NEWMAN MEMORIAL COUNTY HOSPITAL, 1201 West 12th Avenue, Zip 66801–2597; tel. 316/343–6800; Terry R. Lambert, Chief Executive Officer (Total facility includes 18 beds in nursing home–type unit) **A**1 9 10 **F**3 7 8 12 15 16 19 21 22 23 24 28 30 31 32 33 34 35 37 40 41 42 44 45 46 49 64 65 67 71 **S** Quorum Health Group/Quorum Health Resources, Inc., Brentwood, TN

| | 13 | 10 | 110 | 3498 | 41 | 32991 | 504 | 27309 | 11885 | 404 |

Hospital, Address, Telephone, Administrator, Approval, Facility, and Physician Codes, Health Care System, Network	Classi-fication Codes		Utilization Data					Expense (thousands) of dollars		
★ American Hospital Association (AHA) membership □ Joint Commission on Accreditation of Healthcare Organizations (JCAHO) accreditation + American Osteopathic Healthcare Association (AOHA) membership ○ American Osteopathic Association (AOA) accreditation △ Commission on Accreditation of Rehabilitation Facilities (CARF) accreditation Control codes 61, 63, 64, 71, 72 and 73 indicate hospitals listed by AOHA, but not registered by AHA. For definition of numerical codes, see page A4	Control	Service	Staffed Beds	Admissions	Census	Outpatient Visits	Births	Total	Payroll	Personnel

EUREKA—Greenwood County

★ GREENWOOD COUNTY HOSPITAL, 100 West 16th Street, Zip 67045–1096; tel. 316/583–7451; Emmett Schuster, Administrator and Chief Executive Officer **A**9 10 **F**8 15 16 19 20 21 22 28 30 31 32 34 39 44 46 49 65 71 73

| | 13 | 10 | 46 | 1005 | 16 | 8386 | 4 | 5379 | 2522 | 99 |

FORT LEAVENWORTH—Leavenworth County

★ MUNSON ARMY HEALTH CENTER, 550 Pope Avenue, Zip 66027–2332; tel. 913/684–6420; Colonel James Dunn, Commander (Nonreporting) **S** Department of the Army, Office of the Surgeon General, Falls Church, VA

| | 42 | 10 | 20 | — | — | — | — | — | — | — |

FORT RILEY—Geary County

⌧ IRWIN ARMY COMMUNITY HOSPITAL, 600 Caisson Hill Road, Zip 66442; tel. 785/239–7555; Lieutenant Colonel Scott D. Hendrickson, Deputy Commander for Administration **A**1 2 **F**3 8 11 12 13 15 16 19 20 22 31 35 37 40 41 44 46 51 56 58 61 65 67 71 73 **P**1 **S** Department of the Army, Office of the Surgeon General, Falls Church, VA

| | 42 | 10 | 44 | 3259 | 19 | 229747 | 847 | 47932 | 31465 | 788 |

FORT SCOTT—Bourbon County

⌧ MERCY HOSPITAL, (Formerly Mercy Health System of Kansas), 821 Burke Street, Zip 66701–2497; tel. 316/223–2200; Jerry L. Stevenson, President and Chief Executive Officer (Total facility includes 23 beds in nursing home–type unit) **A**1 9 10 **F**7 8 12 14 15 16 17 19 21 22 23 24 27 28 30 32 33 35 37 38 39 40 41 44 48 49 51 63 64 65 66 67 71 73 **P**6 **S** Sisters of Mercy Health System–St. Louis, Saint Louis, MO

| | 21 | 10 | 108 | 3268 | 45 | 63553 | 246 | 20621 | 10583 | 413 |

FREDONIA—Wilson County

★ FREDONIA REGIONAL HOSPITAL, 1527 Madison Street, Zip 66736–1751, Mailing Address: P.O. Box 579, Zip 66736–0579; tel. 316/378–2121; Terry Deschaine, Chief Executive Officer (Total facility includes 9 beds in nursing home–type unit) **A**9 10 **F**14 15 19 22 32 44 49 52 57 62 64 65 71 **S** Great Plains Health Alliance, Inc., Phillipsburg, KS

| | 14 | 10 | 51 | 820 | 12 | 14802 | 0 | 4771 | 1834 | 77 |

GARDEN CITY—Finney County

⌧ ST. CATHERINE HOSPITAL, 410 East Walnut, Zip 67846–5672; tel. 316/272–2222; Mark B. Steadham, President and Chief Executive Officer **A**1 9 10 **F**7 8 14 15 16 17 19 20 21 22 23 26 28 30 31 32 33 35 36 37 38 39 40 41 42 44 46 49 50 52 54 55 56 57 58 60 63 65 68 71 73 **S** Catholic Health Initiatives, Denver, CO

| | 21 | 10 | 100 | 5138 | 62 | 71262 | 1088 | 38825 | 16138 | 479 |

GARDNER—Johnson County

△ MEADOWBROOK HOSPITAL, 427 West Main Street, Zip 66030–1197; tel. 913/856–8747; Daniel Wilson, M.D., Administrator (Nonreporting) **A**7 10

| | 33 | 46 | 32 | — | — | — | — | — | — | — |

GARNETT—Anderson County

ANDERSON COUNTY HOSPITAL, 421 South Maple, Zip 66032–1334, Mailing Address: P.O. Box 309, Zip 66032–0309; tel. 785/448–3131; Dennis A. Hachenberg, Senior Executive Officer (Total facility includes 32 beds in nursing home–type unit) **A**9 10 **F**8 15 19 22 26 28 30 32 33 34 35 42 44 49 52 57 58 64 65 71 72 **P**8 **S** Saint Luke's Shawnee Mission Health System, Kansas City, MO

| | 23 | 10 | 56 | 547 | 38 | 24120 | 0 | 5007 | 2577 | 128 |

GIRARD—Crawford County

★ CRAWFORD COUNTY HOSPITAL DISTRICT ONE, 302 North Hospital Drive, Zip 66743–2000; tel. 316/724–8291; Gene Sailsbury, Administrator and Chief Executive Officer **A**9 10 **F**3 6 7 8 11 19 20 21 22 32 33 35 36 37 39 40 41 42 44 54 56 58 63 64 71 73

| | 16 | 10 | 38 | 1205 | 11 | 25568 | 144 | — | — | 56 |

GOODLAND—Sherman County

GOODLAND REGIONAL MEDICAL CENTER, 220 West Second Street, Zip 67735–1602; tel. 785/899–3625; Jim Chaddic, Chief Executive Officer **A**9 10 **F**3 8 11 14 15 16 19 21 22 26 28 31 34 35 36 37 39 40 42 44 45 46 48 49 58 63 64 65 67 70 71 73

| | 13 | 10 | 49 | 1114 | 15 | 29872 | 84 | 7099 | 3133 | 120 |

GREAT BEND—Barton County

⌧ CENTRAL KANSAS MEDICAL CENTER, (Includes Central Kansas Medical Center–St. Joseph Campus, 923 Carroll Avenue, Larned, Zip 67550; tel. 316/285–3161), 3515 Broadway Street, Zip 67530–3691; tel. 316/792–2511; Thomas W. Sommers, President and Chief Executive Officer (Total facility includes 79 beds in nursing home–type unit) **A**1 9 10 **F**7 8 12 15 19 21 22 23 26 28 30 32 33 34 35 36 37 39 40 41 42 44 45 46 49 51 60 64 65 66 67 71 73 **P**8 **S** Catholic Health Initiatives, Denver, CO

| | 21 | 10 | 175 | 2992 | 84 | 154979 | 467 | 31459 | 14445 | 492 |

GREENSBURG—Kiowa County

KIOWA COUNTY MEMORIAL HOSPITAL, 501 South Walnut Street, Zip 67054–1951; tel. 316/723–3341; CeCe Noll, Administrator (Total facility includes 8 beds in nursing home–type unit) **A**9 10 **F**8 15 22 24 28 30 32 34 36 39 44 49 52 64 65 71 **P**6 **S** Great Plains Health Alliance, Inc., Phillipsburg, KS

| | 13 | 10 | 46 | 409 | 18 | 7316 | 0 | 4360 | — | 72 |

HALSTEAD—Harvey County

⌧ HALSTEAD HOSPITAL, 328 Poplar Street, Zip 67056–2099; tel. 316/835–2651; David Nevill, President and Chief Executive Officer (Total facility includes 17 beds in nursing home–type unit) **A**1 9 10 **F**3 4 8 10 11 12 14 15 16 17 19 20 21 22 23 24 26 27 28 29 30 32 33 34 35 36 37 39 41 42 43 44 45 46 49 51 52 53 54 55 56 57 58 60 63 64 65 67 71 72 73 **P**7 **S** LifePoint Hospitals, Inc., Nashville, TN

| | 33 | 10 | 137 | 2534 | 48 | 22162 | 0 | 20046 | 8729 | 254 |

HANOVER—Washington County

HANOVER HOSPITAL, 205 South Hanover, Zip 66945–8857, Mailing Address: P.O. Box 38, Zip 66945–0038; tel. 785/337–2214; Roger D. Warren, M.D., Administrator (Total facility includes 27 beds in nursing home–type unit) **A**9 10 **F**11 14 19 22 32 34 35 36 37 40 44 49 64 71 **P**5

| | 16 | 10 | 45 | 444 | 26 | 1019 | 13 | 2359 | 1224 | 59 |

Hospital, Address, Telephone, Administrator, Approval, Facility, and Physician Codes, Health Care System, Network	Classi-fication Codes		Utilization Data					Expense (thousands) of dollars		
★ American Hospital Association (AHA) membership □ Joint Commission on Accreditation of Healthcare Organizations (JCAHO) accreditation + American Osteopathic Healthcare Association (AOHA) membership ○ American Osteopathic Association (AOA) accreditation △ Commission on Accreditation of Rehabilitation Facilities (CARF) accreditation Control codes 61, 63, 64, 71, 72 and 73 indicate hospitals listed by AOHA, but not registered by AHA. For definition of numerical codes, see page A4	Control	Service	Staffed Beds	Admissions	Census	Outpatient Visits	Births	Total	Payroll	Personnel

HARPER—Harper County

★ HOSPITAL DISTRICT NUMBER FIVE OF HARPER COUNTY, 1204 Maple, Zip 67058–1438; tel. 316/896–7324; Vernon Minnis, Chief Executive Officer **A**9 10 **F**1 8 12 14 17 19 22 24 30 32 33 35 36 41 44 49 51 65 69 71 73

| | 16 | 10 | 38 | 328 | 21 | 4290 | 0 | 3854 | 1866 | 86 |

HAYS—Ellis County

⌖ △ HAYS MEDICAL CENTER, (Includes Hadley Campus, 201 East Seventh Street, Zip 67601–4198; St. Anthony Campus, 2220 Canterbury Drive), 2220 Canterbury Drive, Zip 67601–2342, Mailing Address: P.O. Box 8100, Zip 67601–8100; tel. 785/623–5000; John H. Jeter, M.D., President and Chief Executive Officer (Total facility includes 20 beds in nursing home–type unit) **A**1 2 3 5 7 9 10 **F**4 7 8 10 11 12 13 15 16 17 18 19 21 22 23 26 27 28 29 30 32 33 34 35 36 37 38 39 40 41 42 44 45 48 49 51 52 54 55 56 57 58 59 60 63 64 65 67 71 73 74 **P**6 7
Web address: www.haysmed.com

| | 23 | 10 | 168 | 6198 | 97 | — | 521 | 67554 | 29941 | 945 |

HERINGTON—Dickinson County

HERINGTON MUNICIPAL HOSPITAL, 100 East Helen Street, Zip 67449–1697; tel. 785/258–2207; William D. Peterson, Administrator (Total facility includes 18 beds in nursing home–type unit) **A**9 **F**7 8 14 15 16 19 20 22 26 28 32 33 40 41 44 64 71

| | 14 | 10 | 38 | 538 | 18 | 18288 | 31 | 3764 | 1708 | 94 |

HIAWATHA—Brown County

□ HIAWATHA COMMUNITY HOSPITAL, 300 Utah Street, Zip 66434–2399; tel. 785/742–2131; John Moore, Administrator **A**1 9 10 **F**7 11 19 21 22 28 32 33 35 36 37 40 41 44 48 49 64 65 71 73 **P**6

| | 23 | 10 | 43 | 811 | 10 | 24342 | 86 | 7066 | 3170 | 121 |

HILL CITY—Graham County

★ GRAHAM COUNTY HOSPITAL, 304 West Prout Street, Zip 67642–1435, Mailing Address: P.O. Box 339, Zip 67642–0339; tel. 785/421–2121; Fred J. Meis, Administrator and Chief Executive Officer **A**9 10 **F**1 8 15 16 19 22 24 28 32 33 34 36 39 44 71

| | 13 | 10 | 26 | 748 | 9 | 13474 | 8 | 4201 | 2048 | 78 |

HILLSBORO—Marion County

HILLSBORO COMMUNITY MEDICAL CENTER, (Formerly Salem Hospital), 701 South Main Street, Zip 67063–9981; tel. 316/947–3114; Tom Faulkner, Chief Executive Officer (Total facility includes 52 beds in nursing home–type unit) **A**9 10 **F**1 7 8 12 14 15 16 17 19 22 28 30 32 33 34 35 44 49 52 57 64 65 67 71 **P**5

| | 23 | 10 | 78 | 592 | 53 | 8961 | 24 | 4541 | 2365 | 117 |

HOISINGTON—Barton County

CLARA BARTON HOSPITAL, 250 West Ninth Street, Zip 67544–1799; tel. 316/653–2114; James Turnbull, Administrator and Chief Executive Officer (Total facility includes 12 beds in nursing home–type unit) **A**9 10 **F**7 15 19 22 24 34 35 36 37 40 41 44 49 64 71 73

| | 23 | 10 | 40 | 394 | 11 | 13969 | 66 | 4411 | 2257 | 87 |

HOLTON—Jackson County

HOLTON COMMUNITY HOSPITAL, 510 Kansas Avenue, Zip 66436–1545; tel. 785/364–2116; Leonard Hernandez, Administrator and Chief Executive Officer **A**9 10 **F**1 7 8 12 15 16 17 19 22 27 29 30 32 33 34 36 39 40 41 44 46 49 64 65 67 68 71 73 74 **P**8
Web address: www.aih.org

| | 14 | 10 | 13 | 392 | 5 | 23584 | 18 | 3178 | 1747 | 67 |

HORTON—Brown County

HORTON HEALTH FOUNDATION, 240 West 18th Street, Zip 66439–1245; tel. 785/486–2642; Dale A. White, Chief Executive Officer **A**9 10 **F**8 12 14 15 16 19 30 32 34 35 36 39 42 44 64 65 71 **P**8

| | 23 | 10 | 35 | 395 | 5 | 1788 | 0 | 4354 | 2305 | 96 |

HOXIE—Sheridan County

SHERIDAN COUNTY HOSPITAL, 826 18th Street, Zip 67740–0167, Mailing Address: P.O. Box 167, Zip 67740–0167; tel. 785/675–3281; Brian Kirk, Chief Executive Officer (Total facility includes 48 beds in nursing home–type unit) **A**9 10 **F**1 6 8 14 15 16 19 22 28 30 32 33 36 39 40 44 58 63 64 65 67 71

| | 13 | 10 | 66 | 211 | 48 | 7056 | 6 | 3557 | 1866 | 122 |

HUGOTON—Stevens County

STEVENS COUNTY HOSPITAL, 1006 South Jackson Street, Zip 67951–2842, Mailing Address: P.O. Box 10, Zip 67951–0010; tel. 316/544–8511; Ted Strote, Administrator **A**9 10 **F**8 12 15 19 20 22 24 28 30 32 34 41 44 45 49 64 65 67 71 73

| | 13 | 10 | 17 | 268 | 4 | 9120 | 0 | 4396 | 2213 | 86 |

HUTCHINSON—Reno County

★ HUTCHINSON HOSPITAL CORPORATION, 1701 East 23rd Street, Zip 67502–1191; tel. 316/665–2000; Gene E. Schmidt, President (Total facility includes 19 beds in nursing home–type unit) **A**9 10 **F**3 4 6 7 10 15 16 18 19 21 22 23 32 33 34 35 37 39 40 42 43 44 48 49 52 53 54 55 56 57 58 62 64 65 67 71

| | 23 | 10 | 163 | 7627 | 123 | 91285 | 699 | 52110 | 21385 | 775 |

INDEPENDENCE—Montgomery County

⌖ MERCY HOSPITAL, 800 West Myrtle Street, Zip 67301–3240, Mailing Address: P.O. Box 388, Zip 67301–0388; tel. 316/331–2200; Jerry L. Stevenson, President and Chief Executive Officer (Total facility includes 18 beds in nursing home–type unit) **A**1 9 10 **F**7 8 12 13 14 15 16 17 18 19 21 22 24 26 28 30 32 37 40 41 44 49 51 64 65 68 71 73 **P**6 **S** Sisters of Mercy Health System–St. Louis, Saint Louis, MO

| | 21 | 10 | 58 | 1974 | 23 | 57679 | 203 | 13836 | 6252 | 221 |

IOLA—Allen County

★ ALLEN COUNTY HOSPITAL, 101 South First Street, Zip 66749–3505, Mailing Address: P.O. Box 540, Zip 66749–0540; tel. 316/365–1000; Bill May, Chief Executive Officer **A**9 10 **F**7 8 15 16 17 19 21 22 23 27 28 30 31 32 33 35 37 39 40 42 44 48 49 64 65 67 71 72 73 **S** Health Midwest, Kansas City, MO

| | 23 | 10 | 41 | 1437 | 18 | 21019 | 105 | 9946 | 3984 | 156 |

Hospital, Address, Telephone, Administrator, Approval, Facility, and Physician Codes, Health Care System, Network	Classi-fication Codes		Utilization Data					Expense (thousands) of dollars		
★ American Hospital Association (AHA) membership □ Joint Commission on Accreditation of Healthcare Organizations (JCAHO) accreditation + American Osteopathic Healthcare Association (AOHA) membership ○ American Osteopathic Association (AOA) accreditation △ Commission on Accreditation of Rehabilitation Facilities (CARF) accreditation Control codes 61, 63, 64, 71, 72 and 73 indicate hospitals listed by AOHA, but not registered by AHA. For definition of numerical codes, see page A4	Control	Service	Staffed Beds	Admissions	Census	Outpatient Visits	Births	Total	Payroll	Personnel

JETMORE—Hodgeman County

★ HODGEMAN COUNTY HEALTH CENTER, 809 Bramley Street, Zip 67854–9320, Mailing Address: P.O. Box 310, Zip 67854–0310; tel. 316/357–8361; Roger Salisbury, Administrator (Total facility includes 36 beds in nursing home–type unit) **A**9 10 **F**7 8 12 15 19 20 22 26 27 32 33 35 40 41 44 49 51 64 65 71

| 13 | 10 | 52 | 344 | 34 | 3217 | 20 | 2726 | 1515 | 66 |

JOHNSON—Stanton County

★ STANTON COUNTY HEALTH CARE FACILITY, 404 North Chestnut Street, Zip 67855–0779, Mailing Address: Box 779, Zip 67855–0779; tel. 316/492–6250; Paula Picken, Administrator (Total facility includes 25 beds in nursing home–type unit) **A**9 10 **F**8 14 15 17 22 26 27 28 30 33 40 49 64 **P**5
Web address: www.phn.org

| 13 | 10 | 43 | 142 | 22 | 2569 | 52 | 2202 | 1223 | 62 |

JUNCTION CITY—Geary County

⌖ GEARY COMMUNITY HOSPITAL, Ash and St. Mary's Road, Zip 66441, Mailing Address: P.O. Box 490, Zip 66441–0490; tel. 785/238–4131; David K. Bradley, Chief Executive Officer **A**1 3 9 10 **F**3 7 8 12 15 16 19 20 21 22 23 26 31 32 33 34 35 37 39 40 42 44 45 46 48 49 51 52 57 65 67 71 74
Web address: www.jc.net/GCH

| 13 | 10 | 49 | 1783 | 22 | 132277 | 182 | 16688 | 7957 | 297 |

KANSAS CITY—Wyandotte County

⌖ △ BETHANY MEDICAL CENTER, 51 North 12th Street, Zip 66102–9990; tel. 913/281–8400; Keith R. Poisson, President and Chief Executive Officer (Total facility includes 51 beds in nursing home–type unit) (Nonreporting) **A**1 2 3 5 7 9 10 **S** Sisters of Charity of Leavenworth Health Services Corporation, Leavenworth, KS

| 23 | 10 | 251 | — | — | — | — | — | — | — |

⌖ PROVIDENCE MEDICAL CENTER, 8929 Parallel Parkway, Zip 66112–1636; tel. 913/596–4000; Francis V. Creeden, Jr., President and Chief Executive Officer (Total facility includes 40 beds in nursing home–type unit) **A**1 2 9 10 **F**4 7 8 10 12 15 16 17 18 19 20 21 22 26 27 28 29 30 31 32 33 34 35 37 39 40 41 42 43 44 45 46 49 52 53 54 55 56 57 58 59 60 63 64 65 66 67 71 73 74 **P**5 6 7 8 **S** Sisters of Charity of Leavenworth Health Services Corporation, Leavenworth, KS
Web address: www.pmc–sjh.org

| 21 | 10 | 219 | 9066 | 128 | 48187 | 1053 | 66374 | 29020 | 872 |

⌖ UNIVERSITY OF KANSAS MEDICAL CENTER, 3901 Rainbow Boulevard, Zip 66160–7200; tel. 913/588–5000; Irene M. Cumming, Chief Executive Officer **A**1 2 3 5 8 9 10 **F**4 7 8 9 10 12 13 15 16 17 18 19 20 21 22 23 24 25 26 28 29 30 31 34 35 37 38 39 40 41 42 43 44 46 47 48 49 50 51 52 53 54 56 57 58 59 60 61 63 65 66 67 68 71 72 73 74 **P**1 3
Web address: www.kumc.edu

| 16 | 10 | 433 | 12158 | 220 | 381257 | 935 | 169038 | 65870 | 2228 |

KINGMAN—Kingman County

★ NINNESCAH VALLEY HEALTH SYSTEM, (Formerly Kingman Community Hospital), 750 Avenue D West, Zip 67068; tel. 316/532–3147; Gary L. Tiller, Chief Executive Officer **A**9 10 **F**7 8 14 15 16 19 21 22 29 30 32 34 35 36 37 40 41 42 44 45 46 48 49 51 58 64 65 67 71 73 **P**3 6 7

| 23 | 10 | 40 | 608 | 8 | 15854 | 53 | 5261 | 2642 | 99 |

KIOWA—Barber County

★ KIOWA DISTRICT HOSPITAL, 810 Drumm Street, Zip 67070–1699; tel. 316/825–4131; Buck McKinney, Jr., Chief Executive Officer **A**9 10 **F**8 12 14 15 16 19 22 28 33 44 51 64 65 71 **P**6

| 16 | 10 | 24 | 323 | 3 | 3357 | 1 | 1694 | 1012 | 42 |

LA CROSSE—Rush County

★ RUSH COUNTY MEMORIAL HOSPITAL, 801 Locust Street, Zip 67548–9673, Mailing Address: P.O. Box 520, Zip 67548–0520; tel. 785/222–2545; Teresa L. Deuel, Chief Executive Officer (Total facility includes 26 beds in nursing home–type unit) **A**9 10 **F**14 15 19 22 24 28 32 33 34 35 44 49 64 71 **P**5

| 13 | 10 | 50 | 384 | 30 | — | 9 | 2308 | 1335 | 58 |

LAKIN—Kearny County

KEARNY COUNTY HOSPITAL, 500 North Thorpe Street, Zip 67860–9604; tel. 316/355–7111; Steven S. Reiner, Administrator **A**9 10 **F**1 6 7 8 14 15 16 19 20 21 22 26 28 30 32 34 36 37 40 44 49 51 62 64 65 67 71 74 **P**5 6

| 13 | 10 | 25 | 272 | 8 | 9374 | 1 | 2911 | 1439 | 57 |

LARNED—Pawnee County

CENTRAL KANSAS MEDICAL CENTER–ST. JOSEPH CAMPUS See Central Kansas Medical Center, Great Bend

□ LARNED STATE HOSPITAL, Mailing Address: Rural Route 3, P.O. Box 89, Zip 67550–9365; tel. 316/285–2131; Mani Lee, Ph.D., Superintendent **A**1 10 **F**2 7 8 11 19 20 21 23 31 35 37 39 40 41 42 44 46 52 53 56 57 60 65 67 71 72 73

| 12 | 22 | 342 | 1327 | 285 | 0 | 0 | 28731 | 19226 | 771 |

LAWRENCE—Douglas County

□ LAWRENCE MEMORIAL HOSPITAL, 325 Maine, Zip 66044–1393; tel. 785/749–6100; Eugene W. Meyer, President and Chief Executive Officer (Total facility includes 18 beds in nursing home–type unit) **A**1 5 9 10 **F**7 8 10 14 15 16 19 21 22 28 31 32 33 35 36 37 39 40 41 44 46 49 52 59 64 65 71 73 **P**6

| 14 | 10 | 105 | 6589 | 87 | — | 956 | 53086 | 24158 | 823 |

LEAVENWORTH—Leavenworth County

□ CUSHING MEMORIAL HOSPITAL, 711 Marshall Street, Zip 66048–3235; tel. 913/684–1100; Charles L. Rogers, President (Nonreporting) **A**1 9 10

| 23 | 10 | 77 | — | — | — | — | — | — | — |

DWIGHT D. EISENHOWER VETERANS AFFAIRS MEDICAL CENTER See Veterans Affairs Eastern Kansas Health Care System, Topeka

⌖ SAINT JOHN HOSPITAL, 3500 South Fourth Street, Zip 66048–5092; tel. 913/680–6000; Mark J. Jaeger, CHE, Administrator (Total facility includes 6 beds in nursing home–type unit) **A**1 9 10 **F**7 8 15 16 17 19 22 23 26 28 30 31 32 33 34 37 40 41 42 44 49 63 64 65 67 71 73 74 **P**6 7 **S** Sisters of Charity of Leavenworth Health Services Corporation, Leavenworth, KS

| 21 | 10 | 36 | 1807 | 21 | 49862 | 237 | 14699 | 6789 | 221 |

Hospital, Address, Telephone, Administrator, Approval, Facility, and Physician Codes, Health Care System, Network	Classi-fication Codes		Utilization Data					Expense (thousands) of dollars		
★ American Hospital Association (AHA) membership □ Joint Commission on Accreditation of Healthcare Organizations (JCAHO) accreditation + American Osteopathic Healthcare Association (AOHA) membership ○ American Osteopathic Association (AOA) accreditation △ Commission on Accreditation of Rehabilitation Facilities (CARF) accreditation Control codes 61, 63, 64, 71, 72 and 73 indicate hospitals listed by AOHA, but not registered by AHA. For definition of numerical codes, see page A4	Control	Service	Staffed Beds	Admissions	Census	Outpatient Visits	Births	Total	Payroll	Personnel

LENEXA—Johnson County

□ BHC COLLEGE MEADOWS HOSPITAL, 14425 College Boulevard, Zip 66215; tel. 913/469–1100; Jerome R. Kearney, Chief Executive Officer **A**1 10 **F**2 3 12 17 48 52 53 54 55 56 58 59 65 67 **S** Behavioral Healthcare Corporation, Nashville, TN — 33 22 | 90 | 669 | 58 | 1500 | 0 | 6606 | 3884 | 128

LEOTI—Wichita County

★ WICHITA COUNTY HOSPITAL, (Includes Wichita County Hospital Long Term Care, Mailing Address: P.O. Box 968, Zip 67861), 211 East Earl, Zip 67861–0968, Mailing Address: Rural Route 2, Box 38, Zip 67861–0968; tel. 316/375–2233; Ed Finley, Administrator (Total facility includes 28 beds in nursing home–type unit) **A**9 10 **F**5 7 11 12 15 17 19 21 22 23 26 27 28 30 32 33 34 35 36 37 38 39 40 41 42 44 46 47 49 52 53 54 55 56 57 58 59 60 62 64 65 66 67 69 70 71 72 73 **P**6 — 13 10 | 38 | 246 | 22 | 5691 | 21 | 2392 | 1304 | 65

LIBERAL—Seward County

⊞ SOUTHWEST MEDICAL CENTER, 315 West 15th Street, Zip 67901–1340, Mailing Address: Box 1340, Zip 67905–1340; tel. 316/624–1651; Bill Porter, President and Chief Executive Officer (Total facility includes 18 beds in nursing home–type unit) **A**1 9 10 **F**7 8 12 15 16 17 19 21 22 23 24 25 26 28 29 32 33 34 35 37 39 40 41 42 44 45 46 49 52 57 58 60 63 64 65 67 71 73 **P**5 — 13 10 | 87 | 3226 | 47 | 34655 | 774 | 34498 | 12600 | 423

LINCOLN—Lincoln County

LINCOLN COUNTY HOSPITAL, 624 North Second Street, Zip 67455–1738, Mailing Address: P.O. Box 406, Zip 67455–0406; tel. 913/524–4403; Jolene Yager, R.N., Administrator (Total facility includes 20 beds in nursing home–type unit) **A**9 10 **F**15 19 22 32 33 34 36 41 44 49 64 65 71 **P**6 **S** Great Plains Health Alliance, Inc., Phillipsburg, KS — 13 10 | 34 | 738 | 25 | 6650 | 0 | 3694 | 2035 | 76

LINDSBORG—McPherson County

★ LINDSBORG COMMUNITY HOSPITAL, 605 West Lincoln Street, Zip 67456–2399; tel. 785/227–3308; Greg Lundstrom, Administrator and Chief Executive Officer **A**9 10 **F**8 15 22 24 30 32 34 36 44 64 65 71 **P**6 — 23 10 | 12 | 651 | 6 | 34008 | 0 | 3276 | 1652 | 68

LYONS—Rice County

★ RICE COUNTY HOSPITAL DISTRICT NUMBER ONE, 619 South Clark Street, Zip 67554–3003, Mailing Address: P.O. Box 828, Zip 67554–0828; tel. 316/257–5173; Robert L. Mullen, Administrator **A**9 10 **F**6 8 14 15 16 17 19 20 26 28 30 32 36 39 40 49 62 65 71 — 16 10 | 44 | 653 | 22 | 4855 | — | 4138 | 1917 | 77

MANHATTAN—Riley County

⊞ MERCY HEALTH CENTER OF MANHATTAN, (Includes Memorial Hospital, 1105 Sunset Avenue, Zip 66502; tel. 913/776–3300; Saint Mary Hospital, 1823 College Avenue, Zip 66502), 1823 College Avenue, Zip 66502–3381; tel. 785/776–3322; Richard L. Allen, President and Chief Executive Officer **A**1 9 10 **F**7 8 10 11 12 14 15 16 19 21 22 23 24 28 29 30 31 32 33 35 36 37 39 40 41 44 45 46 48 49 52 53 54 55 56 58 59 65 66 67 71 73 74 **S** Via Christi Health System, Wichita, KS — 23 10 | 99 | 4215 | 47 | 91859 | 727 | 33004 | 16009 | 489

MANKATO—Jewell County

JEWELL COUNTY HOSPITAL, 100 Crestvue Avenue, Zip 66956–2407, Mailing Address: P.O. Box 327, Zip 66956–0327; tel. 785/378–3137; Aloha Kier, Administrator (Total facility includes 45 beds in nursing home–type unit) **A**9 10 **F**1 8 20 22 27 28 32 33 34 49 62 64 — 13 10 | 51 | 118 | 38 | 884 | 0 | 1686 | 1028 | 89

MARION—Marion County

★ ST. LUKE HOSPITAL, 1014 East Melvin, Zip 66861–1299; tel. 316/382–2179; Craig Hanson, Administrator (Total facility includes 32 beds in nursing home–type unit) **A**9 10 **F**7 8 11 12 14 15 19 21 22 26 29 30 32 33 34 36 37 39 40 41 42 44 45 46 49 51 64 65 71 73 74 **S** Lutheran Health Systems, Fargo, ND — 23 10 | 54 | 580 | 37 | 16845 | 49 | 4567 | 2398 | 92

MARYSVILLE—Marshall County

★ COMMUNITY MEMORIAL HEALTHCARE, (Formerly Community Memorial Hospital), 708 North 18th Street, Zip 66508–1399; tel. 785/562–2311; Edward E. Riley, Chief Executive Officer (Total facility includes 60 beds in nursing home–type unit) **A**9 10 **F**1 3 7 8 12 14 15 16 19 21 22 24 26 28 32 33 34 35 36 39 40 41 42 44 46 52 53 54 55 56 57 58 63 64 65 67 71 73 **P**6 — 23 10 | 109 | 1272 | 57 | 24510 | 85 | 8259 | 3508 | 157

MCPHERSON—McPherson County

★ MEMORIAL HOSPITAL, 1000 Hospital Drive, Zip 67460–2321; tel. 316/241–2250; Stan Regehr, President and Chief Executive Officer **A**9 10 **F**7 8 14 15 16 17 19 21 22 24 28 31 32 33 35 36 37 39 40 41 42 44 45 46 49 65 71 73 — 23 10 | 41 | 1659 | 20 | 94479 | 214 | 12454 | 5586 | 189

MEADE—Meade County

MEADE DISTRICT HOSPITAL, 510 East Carthage Street, Zip 67864–0680, Mailing Address: P.O. Box 680, Zip 67864–0680; tel. 316/873–2141; Michael P. Thomas, Administrator **A**9 10 **F**7 15 19 22 24 28 32 44 48 49 64 71 — 16 10 | 20 | 486 | 7 | 16631 | 3 | 3830 | 1789 | —

MEDICINE LODGE—Barber County

★ MEDICINE LODGE MEMORIAL HOSPITAL, 710 North Walnut Street, Zip 67104–1019, Mailing Address: P.O. Drawer C, Zip 67104; tel. 316/886–3771; Kevin A. White, Administrator **A**9 10 **F**8 15 16 22 26 34 44 49 71 **P**6 **S** Great Plains Health Alliance, Inc., Phillipsburg, KS — 16 10 | 42 | 623 | 18 | 6871 | 0 | 4490 | 2306 | 96

MINNEAPOLIS—Ottawa County

★ OTTAWA COUNTY HEALTH CENTER, 215 East Eighth, Zip 67467–1999, Mailing Address: P.O. Box 209, Zip 67467–0209; tel. 785/392–2122; Joy Reed, R.N., Administrator (Total facility includes 23 beds in nursing home–type unit) **A**9 10 **F**6 14 15 16 17 20 21 22 24 26 27 32 34 36 45 49 58 64 65 71 **S** Great Plains Health Alliance, Inc., Phillipsburg, KS — 23 10 | 53 | 505 | 47 | 4664 | 0 | 3263 | 1777 | 88

Hospital, Address, Telephone, Administrator, Approval, Facility, and Physician Codes, Health Care System, Network	Classi-fication Codes		Utilization Data					Expense (thousands) of dollars		
	Control	Service	Staffed Beds	Admissions	Census	Outpatient Visits	Births	Total	Payroll	Personnel

★ American Hospital Association (AHA) membership
□ Joint Commission on Accreditation of Healthcare Organizations (JCAHO) accreditation
+ American Osteopathic Healthcare Association (AOHA) membership
○ American Osteopathic Association (AOA) accreditation
△ Commission on Accreditation of Rehabilitation Facilities (CARF) accreditation
Control codes 61, 63, 64, 71, 72 and 73 indicate hospitals listed by AOHA, but not registered by AHA. For definition of numerical codes, see page A4

MINNEOLA—Clark County

★ MINNEOLA DISTRICT HOSPITAL, 212 Main Street, Zip 67865–8511; tel. 316/885–4264; Blaine K. Miller, Administrator **A**9 10 **F**8 16 22 28 33 34 44 49 56 62 64 65 71 **S** Great Plains Health Alliance, Inc., Phillipsburg, KS

16	10	15	444	6	4703	34	2455	918	39

MOUNDRIDGE—McPherson County

★ MERCY HOSPITAL, 218 East Pack Street, Zip 67107, Mailing Address: P.O. Box 180, Zip 67107–0180; tel. 316/345–6391; Doyle K. Johnson, Administrator **A**9 10 **F**15 22 26 40 44 49

21	10	24	397	6	5761	32	1311	663	30

NEODESHA—Wilson County

★ WILSON COUNTY HOSPITAL, 205 Mill Street, Zip 66757–1817, Mailing Address: P.O. Box 360, Zip 66757–0360; tel. 316/325–2611; Deanna Pittman, Administrator **A**9 10 **F**7 8 15 16 17 19 22 26 28 30 32 33 39 40 41 44 49 52 57 65 67 71 73 **S** Quorum Health Group/Quorum Health Resources, Inc., Brentwood, TN

13	10	38	542	9	5868	46	4092	2124	—

NESS CITY—Ness County

★ NESS COUNTY HOSPITAL NUMBER TWO, 312 East Custer Street, Zip 67560–1654; tel. 785/798–2291; Clyde T. McCracken, Administrator (Total facility includes 45 beds in nursing home–type unit) **A**9 10 **F**8 15 19 22 32 48 62 64 65 71 **P**6

16	10	65	307	28	4449	0	3578	1945	116

NEWTON—Harvey County

⊠ NEWTON MEDICAL CENTER, Mailing Address: P.O. Box 308, Zip 67114–0308; tel. 316/283–2700; W. Charles Waters, President and Chief Executive Officer (Total facility includes 11 beds in nursing home–type unit) **A**1 9 10 **F**7 14 15 19 21 22 23 26 28 29 30 31 32 33 34 35 37 40 41 44 49 56 64 65 71
Web address: www.newtonmedicalcenter.com

23	10	66	2812	36	28555	443	22812	8879	300

□ PRAIRIE VIEW, 1901 East First Street, Zip 67114–5010, Mailing Address: P.O. Box 467, Zip 67114–0467; tel. 316/283–2400; Melvin Goering, Chief Executive Officer **A**1 9 10 **F**3 12 14 15 16 17 18 27 28 30 32 52 53 54 55 56 57 58 59 65 67 73 **P**6

23	22	30	860	23	—	0	14408	9152	287

NORTON—Norton County

★ NORTON COUNTY HOSPITAL, 102 East Holme, Zip 67654–0250, Mailing Address: P.O. Box 250, Zip 67654–0250; tel. 785/877–3351; Richard Miller, Administrator and Chief Executive Officer **A**9 10 **F**7 8 15 16 19 20 21 22 26 28 30 32 33 34 36 39 40 42 44 45 46 48 49 51 53 54 55 56 57 58 65 71 73 **P**4 7

13	10	24	579	14	20627	27	4382	2456	89

OAKLEY—Logan County

LOGAN COUNTY HOSPITAL, 211 Cherry Street, Zip 67748–1201; tel. 913/672–3211; Rodney Bates, Administrator (Total facility includes 30 beds in nursing home–type unit) **A**9 10 **F**6 7 8 15 19 21 22 27 34 36 37 40 44 49 62 64 65 71

13	10	51	398	13	10576	12	2861	1602	65

OBERLIN—Decatur County

★ DECATUR COUNTY HOSPITAL, 810 West Columbia Street, Zip 67749–2450, Mailing Address: P.O. Box 268, Zip 67749–0268; tel. 785/475–2208; Lynn Doeden, R.N., Interim Administrator (Total facility includes 50 beds in nursing home–type unit) **A**9 10 **F**7 8 12 14 15 16 19 22 26 32 33 34 35 36 37 42 44 49 63 64 65 71 **S** Lutheran Health Systems, Fargo, ND

23	10	74	636	48	11739	37	4052	2032	85

OLATHE—Johnson County

⊠ OLATHE MEDICAL CENTER, 20333 West 151st Street, Zip 66061–7211; tel. 913/791–4200; Frank H. Devocelle, President and Chief Executive Officer **A**1 2 9 10 **F**4 7 8 10 11 12 14 15 16 17 19 21 22 28 30 31 32 33 34 35 37 40 41 42 43 44 46 49 65 66 67 71 72 73 74 **P**3 8
Web address: www.ohsi.com

23	10	163	8329	90	113858	1157	58695	26866	782

ONAGA—Pottawatomie County

COMMUNITY HOSPITAL ONAGA, 120 West Eighth Street, Zip 66521–0120; tel. 785/889–4272; Joseph T. Engelken, Chief Executive Officer (Total facility includes 177 beds in nursing home–type unit) **A**9 10 **F**1 2 3 6 7 8 11 12 13 14 15 16 17 19 20 22 24 26 27 28 29 30 31 32 33 34 35 36 37 39 40 41 42 44 45 46 48 49 51 52 53 54 55 56 57 58 61 62 64 65 66 67 68 70 71 72 73 74 **P**6

23	10	216	1236	157	37042	91	13994	6740	327

OSAWATOMIE—Miami County

□ OSAWATOMIE STATE HOSPITAL, 500 State Hospital Drive, Zip 66064–9757, Mailing Address: P.O. Box 500, Zip 66064–9757; tel. 913/755–3151; Randy Proctor, Superintendent (Nonreporting) **A**1 10

12	22	275	—	—	—	—	—	—	—

OSBORNE—Osborne County

★ OSBORNE COUNTY MEMORIAL HOSPITAL, 424 West New Hampshire Street, Zip 67473–0070, Mailing Address: P.O. Box 70, Zip 67473–0070; tel. 785/346–2121; Patricia Bernard, R.N., Administrator **A**9 10 **F**7 8 19 20 22 33 34 36 44 64 71 **P**6 **S** Great Plains Health Alliance, Inc., Phillipsburg, KS

13	10	29	443	5	6103	26	2474	1185	63

OTTAWA—Franklin County

⊠ RANSOM MEMORIAL HOSPITAL, 1301 South Main Street, Zip 66067–3598; tel. 785/229–8200; Robert E. Bregant, Jr., Administrator **A**1 9 10 **F**7 8 15 17 19 21 22 26 27 28 30 32 33 34 35 37 39 40 41 42 44 46 49 56 63 64 65 66 67 68 71 73 **P**8
Web address: www.ransom.org

13	10	48	2006	27	40170	167	15278	6991	234

Hospital, Address, Telephone, Administrator, Approval, Facility, and Physician Codes, Health Care System, Network	Classi-fication Codes		Utilization Data					Expense (thousands) of dollars		
	Control	Service	Staffed Beds	Admissions	Census	Outpatient Visits	Births	Total	Payroll	Personnel

★ American Hospital Association (AHA) membership
□ Joint Commission on Accreditation of Healthcare Organizations (JCAHO) accreditation
+ American Osteopathic Healthcare Association (AOHA) membership
○ American Osteopathic Association (AOA) accreditation
△ Commission on Accreditation of Rehabilitation Facilities (CARF) accreditation
Control codes 61, 63, 64, 71, 72 and 73 indicate hospitals listed by AOHA, but not registered by AHA. For definition of numerical codes, see page A4

OVERLAND PARK—Johnson County

✚ MENORAH MEDICAL CENTER, 5721 West 119th Street, Zip 66209; tel. 913/498–6000; Steven D. Wilkinson, President and Chief Executive Officer **A**1 2 10 **F**1 2 3 4 5 7 8 10 11 12 14 15 16 17 18 19 21 22 23 24 25 26 27 28 29 30 31 32 33 34 35 36 37 38 39 40 41 42 43 44 45 46 48 49 51 52 53 54 55 56 57 58 59 60 61 63 64 65 66 67 68 70 71 72 73 74 **P**1 5 6 **S** Health Midwest, Kansas City, MO
Web address: www.healthmidwest.org/hospitals/mmp.shtml | 23 | 10 | 129 | 5506 | 76 | 51219 | 1122 | 62004 | 25306 | 724

✚ △ MID–AMERICA REHABILITATION HOSPITAL, 5701 West 110th Street, Zip 66211; tel. 913/491–2400; Mark J. Stepanik, Interim Chief Executive Officer (Total facility includes 15 beds in nursing home–type unit) (Nonreporting) **A**1 7 9 10 **S** HEALTHSOUTH Corporation, Birmingham, AL | 33 | 46 | 80 | — | — | — | — | — | — | —

✚ OVERLAND PARK REGIONAL MEDICAL CENTER, 10500 Quivira Road, Zip 66215–2373, Mailing Address: P.O. Box 15959, Shawnee Mission, Zip 66215–5959; tel. 913/541–5000; Kevin J. Hicks, President and Chief Executive Officer (Total facility includes 17 beds in nursing home–type unit) **A**1 9 10 **F**1 3 4 8 10 11 12 13 15 16 17 18 19 20 21 22 24 25 26 27 28 29 30 31 32 33 34 35 37 38 39 40 41 42 43 44 45 46 48 49 50 51 52 57 60 61 64 65 67 68 69 70 71 72 73 74 **S** Health Midwest, Kansas City, MO
Web address: www.overlandparkregional.com | 23 | 10 | 269 | 9136 | 134 | 97989 | 2089 | 75347 | 33569 | 797

★ SAINT LUKE'S SOUTH, 12300 Metcalf Avenue, Zip 66213; tel. 913/317–7000; George E. Hays, Senior Executive Officer (Data Not Available) **S** Saint Luke's Shawnee Mission Health System, Kansas City, MO | 23 | 10 | 75 | — | — | — | — | — | — | —

PAOLA—Miami County

★ MIAMI COUNTY MEDICAL CENTER, 2100 Baptiste, Zip 66071–0365, Mailing Address: P.O. Box 365, Zip 66071–0365; tel. 913/294–2327; Gerald Wiesner, Vice President and Chief Operating Officer **A**9 10 **F**8 13 16 19 20 21 22 24 30 31 32 34 39 41 42 44 46 49 51 56 65 66 71 73 **P**3 8 | 23 | 10 | 18 | 671 | 7 | 26866 | 0 | 9423 | 3710 | 122

PARSONS—Labette County

✚ LABETTE COUNTY MEDICAL CENTER, 1902 South U.S. Highway 59, Zip 67357–7404, Mailing Address: P.O. Box 956, Zip 67357–0956; tel. 316/421–4880; Robert E. Mac Devitt, Chief Executive Officer **A**1 9 10 **F**7 8 10 14 15 16 19 20 21 22 23 28 30 32 33 35 36 37 39 40 41 42 44 45 46 49 63 64 65 66 67 71 73 **P**4 7 | 13 | 10 | 76 | 2968 | 36 | 33691 | 271 | 28288 | 11207 | 406

PARSONS STATE HOSPITAL AND TRAINING CENTER, 2601 Gabriel Street, Zip 67357–0738, Mailing Address: Box 738, Zip 67357–0738; tel. 316/421–6550; Gary J. Daniels, Ph.D., Superintendent **F**8 17 19 20 21 22 28 35 37 42 44 48 52 64 65 71 73 | 12 | 62 | 240 | 26 | 207 | 0 | 0 | 18640 | 12910 | 257

PHILLIPSBURG—Phillips County

★ PHILLIPS COUNTY HOSPITAL, 1150 State Street, Zip 67661–1799, Mailing Address: P.O. Box 607, Zip 67661–0607; tel. 785/543–5226; James Wahlmeier, Administrator (Total facility includes 33 beds in nursing home–type unit) **A**9 10 **F**1 7 15 19 20 22 33 34 35 42 44 46 49 64 65 71 73 **S** Great Plains Health Alliance, Inc., Phillipsburg, KS | 23 | 10 | 62 | 1037 | 43 | 9351 | 34 | 6094 | 2776 | 112

PITTSBURG—Crawford County

✚ MOUNT CARMEL MEDICAL CENTER, 1102 East Centennial, Zip 66762–6686; tel. 316/231–6100; John Daniel Lingor, President and Chief Executive Officer **A**1 2 9 10 **F**1 7 8 12 13 15 16 17 19 21 22 23 27 28 30 32 33 35 37 40 41 42 44 46 49 52 54 55 56 58 59 63 64 65 66 67 71 73 **P**2 3 4 5 6 7 8 **S** Via Christi Health System, Wichita, KS | 21 | 10 | 126 | 4508 | 62 | 57311 | 313 | 34312 | 16054 | 525

PLAINVILLE—Rooks County

PLAINVILLE RURAL HOSPITAL DISTRICT NUMBER ONE, 304 South Colorado Avenue, Zip 67663–2505; tel. 785/434–4553; Richard Q. Bergling, Administrator and Chief Executive Officer **A**9 10 **F**8 14 15 16 19 21 27 28 30 32 33 36 39 44 71 73 | 16 | 10 | 25 | 287 | 4 | 2394 | 10 | 2598 | 1184 | 58

PRATT—Pratt County

★ PRATT REGIONAL MEDICAL CENTER, 200 Commodore Street, Zip 67124–3099; tel. 316/672–7451; Susan M. Page, President and Chief Executive Officer (Total facility includes 70 beds in nursing home–type unit) **A**9 10 **F**7 8 13 15 16 19 21 22 23 24 25 26 28 29 30 31 32 33 34 35 36 37 39 40 42 44 45 46 49 61 63 64 65 66 67 71 73 **P**6 7
Web address: www.prmc.org | 23 | 10 | 132 | 2102 | 74 | 74721 | 171 | 19695 | 8740 | 296

QUINTER—Gove County

GOVE COUNTY MEDICAL CENTER, 520 West Fifth Street, Zip 67752, Mailing Address: P.O. Box 129, Zip 67752; tel. 785/754–3341; Paul Davis, Administrator (Total facility includes 59 beds in nursing home–type unit) **A**9 10 **F**6 7 8 19 22 28 32 33 34 44 49 64 65 71 **P**5 | 13 | 10 | 80 | 873 | 62 | 30103 | 74 | 5341 | 2820 | 135

RANSOM—Ness County

★ GRISELL MEMORIAL HOSPITAL DISTRICT ONE, 210 South Vermont, Zip 67572–0268, Mailing Address: P.O. Box 268, Zip 67572–0268; tel. 785/731–2231; Kristine Ochs, R.N., Administrator (Total facility includes 34 beds in nursing home–type unit) **A**9 10 **F**8 19 20 22 26 32 33 36 41 44 49 51 56 64 65 71 **P**6 **S** Great Plains Health Alliance, Inc., Phillipsburg, KS | 16 | 10 | 46 | 149 | 34 | 3284 | 0 | 2584 | 1479 | 75

RUSSELL—Russell County

✚ RUSSELL REGIONAL HOSPITAL, 200 South Main Street, Zip 67665–2997; tel. 785/483–3131; Bruce Garrett, Administrator and Chief Executive Officer (Total facility includes 25 beds in nursing home–type unit) **A**1 9 10 **F**7 8 14 15 16 19 21 22 27 28 29 30 32 34 36 37 41 42 44 45 49 51 64 65 71 73 | 23 | 10 | 57 | 720 | 27 | 15063 | 5 | 7118 | 3718 | 235

Hospital, Address, Telephone, Administrator, Approval, Facility, and Physician Codes, Health Care System, Network	Classi-fication Codes		Utilization Data					Expense (thousands) of dollars		
★ American Hospital Association (AHA) membership ☐ Joint Commission on Accreditation of Healthcare Organizations (JCAHO) accreditation + American Osteopathic Healthcare Association (AOHA) membership ○ American Osteopathic Association (AOA) accreditation △ Commission on Accreditation of Rehabilitation Facilities (CARF) accreditation Control codes 61, 63, 64, 71, 72 and 73 indicate hospitals listed by AOHA, but not registered by AHA. For definition of numerical codes, see page A4	Control	Service	Staffed Beds	Admissions	Census	Outpatient Visits	Births	Total	Payroll	Personnel

SABETHA—Nemaha County

★ SABETHA COMMUNITY HOSPITAL, 14th and Oregon Streets, Zip 66534, Mailing Address: P.O. Box 229, Zip 66534; tel. 785/284–2121; Rita K. Buurman, Chief Executive Officer **A**9 10 **F**1 7 8 15 16 17 19 20 21 22 26 28 30 32 34 35 41 42 44 45 49 54 56 58 64 65 71 **P**6 **S** Great Plains Health Alliance, Inc., Phillipsburg, KS

	23	10	27	550	8	17080	59	4653	2479	76

SAINT FRANCIS—Cheyenne County

★ CHEYENNE COUNTY HOSPITAL, 210 West First Street, Zip 67756, Mailing Address: P.O. Box 547, Zip 67756–0547; tel. 785/332–2104; Leslie Lacy, Administrator **A**9 10 **F**7 8 15 16 19 22 30 42 44 49 51 64 65 71 **P**6 **S** Great Plains Health Alliance, Inc., Phillipsburg, KS

	23	10	16	253	3	12713	0	2541	1233	51

SALINA—Saline County

✠ △ SALINA REGIONAL HEALTH CENTER, (Includes Salina Regional Health Center–Penn Campus, 139 North Penn Street, Zip 67401; Salina Regional Health Center–Santa Fe Campus, 400 South Santa Fe Avenue, Zip 67401), 400 South Santa Fe Avenue, Zip 67401–4198, Mailing Address: P.O. Box 5080, Zip 67401–5080; tel. 785/452–7000; Randy Peterson, President and Chief Executive Officer (Total facility includes 26 beds in nursing home–type unit) **A**1 2 3 7 9 10 **F**7 8 10 11 12 15 16 17 19 20 21 22 23 24 26 28 29 30 31 32 33 34 35 36 37 38 39 40 41 42 43 44 45 46 48 49 52 54 55 56 57 58 59 60 63 64 65 66 67 68 71 73 74 **P**8
Web address: www.srhc.com

	23	10	257	9525	143	137628	1154	76791	33475	1127

★ ST. FRANCIS AT SALINA, 5097 West Cloud Street, Zip 67401–2348; tel. 785/825–0541; Father Phillip J. Rapp, President and Chief Executive Officer (Nonreporting) **A**9
Web address: www.st–francis.org

	23	22	26	—	—	—	—	—	—	—

SATANTA—Haskell County

★ SATANTA DISTRICT HOSPITAL, 401 South Cheyenne Street, Zip 67870, Mailing Address: P.O. Box 159, Zip 67870–0159; tel. 316/649–2761; T. G. Lee, Administrator (Total facility includes 32 beds in nursing home–type unit) **A**9 10 **F**7 8 15 17 19 22 32 34 35 39 41 44 46 64 65 71 **P**4 7 **S** Great Plains Health Alliance, Inc., Phillipsburg, KS

	16	10	45	246	28	3852	0	4520	2026	83

SCOTT CITY—Scott County

★ SCOTT COUNTY HOSPITAL, 310 East Third Street, Zip 67871–1299; tel. 316/872–5811; Greg Unruh, Chief Executive Officer **A**9 10 **F**7 8 10 16 17 19 22 28 34 35 36 39 42 44 65 67 71 73

	13	10	27	862	10	8746	65	4487	2128	115

SEDAN—Chautauqua County

SEDAN CITY HOSPITAL, 300 West North Street, Zip 67361–1051, Mailing Address: P.O. Box C, Zip 67361–1051; tel. 316/725–3115; Sheila Nettles, Administrator **A**9 10 **F**8 14 15 16 22 34 51 57 64 71

	14	10	38	118	1	4111	0	—	1154	60

SENECA—Nemaha County

NEMAHA VALLEY COMMUNITY HOSPITAL, 1600 Community Drive, Zip 66538–9758; tel. 785/336–6181; Michael J. Ryan, Administrator **A**9 10 **F**7 8 15 16 19 21 22 26 28 30 32 34 35 39 40 41 44 49 65 67 70 71

	23	10	24	513	7	10955	50	4268	1852	81

SHAWNEE MISSION—Johnson County

MENORAH MEDICAL CENTER See Overland Park

✠ SHAWNEE MISSION MEDICAL CENTER, 9100 West 74th Street, Zip 66204–4019, Mailing Address: Box 2923, Zip 66201–1323; tel. 913/676–2000; William G. Robertson, Senior Executive Officer **A**1 2 9 10 **F**2 3 4 7 8 10 11 12 13 15 16 17 19 21 22 23 24 25 29 30 31 32 34 35 37 38 39 40 41 42 43 44 45 46 49 52 53 54 55 56 57 58 59 61 64 65 66 67 71 72 73 74 **P**4 5 6 7 8 **S** Saint Luke's Shawnee Mission Health System, Kansas City, MO

	21	10	341	17065	197	225698	3274	143005	61736	1784

SMITH CENTER—Smith County

★ SMITH COUNTY MEMORIAL HOSPITAL, 614 South Main Street, Zip 66967–0349, Mailing Address: P.O. Box 349, Zip 66967–0349; tel. 785/282–6845; John Terrill, Administrator (Total facility includes 28 beds in nursing home–type unit) **A**9 10 **F**1 7 8 19 22 34 35 44 49 64 65 71 **S** Great Plains Health Alliance, Inc., Phillipsburg, KS

	23	10	54	610	31	9493	30	3571	1756	90

STAFFORD—Stafford County

★ STAFFORD DISTRICT HOSPITAL, 502 South Buckeye Street, Zip 67578–2035, Mailing Address: P.O. Box 190, Zip 67578–0190; tel. 316/234–5221; Douglas A. Newman, Administrator and Chief Executive Officer (Nonreporting) **A**9 10

	16	10	25	—	—	—	—	—	—	—

SYRACUSE—Hamilton County

HAMILTON COUNTY HOSPITAL, East Avenue G and Huser Street, Zip 67878–0909, Mailing Address: Box 909, Zip 67878–0909; tel. 316/384–7461; Cynthia O. Akers, R.N., Administrator **A**9 10 **F**19 22 40 44 64 71 **P**4 7

	13	10	26	172	3	6919	0	3396	—	90

TOPEKA—Shawnee County

✠ C. F. MENNINGER MEMORIAL HOSPITAL, (Includes Child and Adolescent Services of the Menninger Clinic), 5800 West Sixth Avenue, Zip 66606–9699, Mailing Address: P.O. Box 829, Zip 66601–0829; tel. 785/350–5000; Efrain Bleiberg, M.D., President and Chief of Staff (Nonreporting) **A**1 3 9 10
Web address: www.menninger.edu

COLMERY–O'NEIL VETERANS AFFAIRS MEDICAL CENTER See Veterans Affairs Eastern Kansas Health Care System

	23	22	143	—	—	—	—	—	—	—

Hospital, Address, Telephone, Administrator, Approval, Facility, and Physician Codes, Health Care System, Network	Classi-fication Codes		Utilization Data					Expense (thousands) of dollars		
	Control	Service	Staffed Beds	Admissions	Census	Outpatient Visits	Births	Total	Payroll	Personnel

★ American Hospital Association (AHA) membership
□ Joint Commission on Accreditation of Healthcare Organizations (JCAHO) accreditation
+ American Osteopathic Healthcare Association (AOHA) membership
○ American Osteopathic Association (AOA) accreditation
△ Commission on Accreditation of Rehabilitation Facilities (CARF) accreditation
Control codes 61, 63, 64, 71, 72 and 73 indicate hospitals listed by AOHA, but not registered by AHA. For definition of numerical codes, see page A4

KANSAS NEUROLOGICAL INSTITUTE, 3107 West 21st Street, Zip 66604–3298; tel. 785/296–5301; Leon Owens, Superintendent **F**20 64 **P**1	12	62	225	0	222	0	0	24632	16050	675
□ △ KANSAS REHABILITATION HOSPITAL, 1504 S.W. Eighth, Zip 66606–2714; tel. 785/235–6600; Julie De Jean, Administrator and Chief Executive Officer **A**1 7 10 **F**15 16 24 34 41 46 48 49 65 67 73 74	33	46	69	762	38	16216	0	9535	4675	123
✈ △ ST. FRANCIS HOSPITAL AND MEDICAL CENTER, 1700 West Seventh Street, Zip 66606–1690; tel. 785/295–8000; Sister Loretto Marie Colwell, President and Chief Executive Officer **A**1 2 3 5 7 9 10 **F**3 4 7 8 10 12 15 16 17 19 20 21 22 24 27 28 30 31 32 34 37 39 40 41 42 43 44 45 46 48 49 51 56 60 63 65 67 71 73 **P**8 **S** Sisters of Charity of Leavenworth Health Services Corporation, Leavenworth, KS **Web address:** www.stfrancistopeka.org	21	10	266	9792	133	256591	894	103718	47905	1470
✈ STORMONT–VAIL HEALTHCARE, 1500 S.W. Tenth Street, Zip 66604–1353; tel. 785/354–6000; Maynard F. Oliverius, President and Chief Executive Officer **A**1 3 5 9 10 **F**4 7 8 10 11 12 14 15 16 17 19 21 22 23 24 26 27 28 29 30 31 32 33 34 35 36 37 38 39 40 41 42 43 44 45 46 47 49 52 55 56 57 58 60 65 66 67 71 73 74 **P**6 **Web address:** www.stormontvail.org	23	10	313	11277	157	104421	2057	169019	84531	2127
✈ VETERANS AFFAIRS EASTERN KANSAS HEALTH CARE SYSTEM, (Includes Colmery–O'Neil Veterans Affairs Medical Center, 2200 Gage Boulevard, tel. 785/350–3111; Dwight D. Eisenhower Veterans Affairs Medical Center, 4101 South Fourth Street Trafficway, Leavenworth, Zip 66048–5055; tel. 913/682–2000), 2200 Gage Boulevard, Zip 66622–0002; tel. 785/350–3111; Edgar L. Tucker, Director (Total facility includes 219 beds in nursing home–type unit) **A**1 3 5 **F**3 4 5 6 8 10 12 14 15 16 17 18 19 20 21 22 23 25 26 27 28 29 30 31 32 33 34 35 37 39 41 42 43 44 45 46 48 49 51 52 54 55 56 57 58 59 60 61 63 64 65 66 67 70 71 72 73 74 **S** Department of Veterans Affairs, Washington, DC	45	10	423	3271	344	283370	0	130380	75995	1789
TRIBUNE—Greeley County										
★ GREELEY COUNTY HOSPITAL, 506 Third Street, Zip 67879, Mailing Address: P.O. Box 338, Zip 67879–0338; tel. 316/376–4221; Jerrell J. Horton, Chief Executive Officer (Total facility includes 30 beds in nursing home–type unit) **A**9 10 **F**7 8 15 16 19 20 22 27 32 33 36 39 44 46 49 56 57 64 65 66 67 71 **P**6 **S** Great Plains Health Alliance, Inc., Phillipsburg, KS	23	10	48	384	28	5721	40	3643	1769	81
ULYSSES—Grant County										
★ BOB WILSON MEMORIAL GRANT COUNTY HOSPITAL, 415 North Main Street, Zip 67880–2196; tel. 316/356–1266; Steven G. Daniel, Administrator (Nonreporting) **A**9 10 **S** Quorum Health Group/Quorum Health Resources, Inc., Brentwood, TN	13	10	39	—	—	—	—	—	—	—
WAKEENEY—Trego County										
★ TREGO COUNTY–LEMKE MEMORIAL HOSPITAL, 320 North 13th Street, Zip 67672–2099; tel. 785/743–2182; Lisa J. Freeborn, R.N., Administrator (Total facility includes 45 beds in nursing home–type unit) **A**9 10 **F**15 16 19 20 22 27 28 32 35 45 49 64 65 71 **S** Great Plains Health Alliance, Inc., Phillipsburg, KS	13	10	73	717	53	4876	0	4621	2170	101
WAMEGO—Pottawatomie County										
WAMEGO CITY HOSPITAL, 711 Genn Drive, Zip 66547–1199; tel. 785/456–2295; William K. Mahoney, Chief Executive Officer **A**9 10 **F**15 16 19 22 24 35 41 44 49 65 71 **P**6	14	10	26	567	6	14327	0	4003	2311	79
WASHINGTON—Washington County										
WASHINGTON COUNTY HOSPITAL, 304 East Third Street, Zip 66968–2098; tel. 913/325–2211; Everett Lutjemeier, Administrator **A**9 10 **F**1 7 8 9 14 15 16 19 22 24 28 30 33 35 36 37 40 44 49 51 64 65 71 **P**5	13	10	27	271	7	4065	7	1577	749	35
WELLINGTON—Sumner County										
★ SUMNER REGIONAL MEDICAL CENTER, 1323 North A Street, Zip 67152–1323; tel. 316/326–7453; Raymond Williams, III, President and Chief Executive Officer (Total facility includes 11 beds in nursing home–type unit) **A**9 10 **F**7 8 14 15 16 19 21 22 30 32 34 35 36 40 41 42 44 46 49 52 57 64 71 **P**8	15	10	80	1389	23	30376	155	9034	3839	143
WICHITA—Sedgwick County										
+ ○ RIVERSIDE HEALTH SYSTEM, 2622 West Central Street, Zip 67203–4999; tel. 316/946–5000; Robert Dixon, President and Chief Executive Officer (Total facility includes 22 beds in nursing home–type unit) **A**9 10 11 12 13 **F**7 8 11 12 13 14 15 16 17 19 20 21 22 26 28 29 30 31 32 34 35 37 39 40 41 42 44 45 46 49 54 56 63 64 65 66 67 71 73 **P**3 6	23	10	95	3610	51	31488	252	40039	19579	487
ST. JOSEPH CAMPUS See Via Christi Regional Medical Center										
✈ VETERANS AFFAIRS MEDICAL AND REGIONAL OFFICE CENTER, 5500 East Kellogg, Zip 67218; tel. 316/685–2221; Kent D. Hill, Director **A**1 3 5 **F**1 2 3 4 8 10 11 12 14 15 16 17 18 19 20 21 22 26 27 28 30 31 32 33 35 39 41 42 43 44 45 46 48 49 51 52 54 55 56 57 58 59 60 64 65 67 71 72 73 74 **P**6 **S** Department of Veterans Affairs, Washington, DC	45	10	47	1910	35	107780	0	43045	27759	561
✈ △ VIA CHRISTI REGIONAL MEDICAL CENTER, (Includes St. Francis Campus, 929 North St. Francis Street, tel. 316/268–5000; St. Joseph Campus, 3600 East Harry Street, Zip 67218–3713; tel. 316/685–1111), 929 North St. Francis Street, Zip 67214–3882; tel. 316/268–5000; Randall G. Nyp, President and Chief Executive Officer **A**1 3 5 7 10 **F**2 4 5 6 7 8 9 10 11 12 13 15 17 18 19 21 22 23 24 25 26 27 28 29 30 31 32 34 35 37 38 39 40 41 42 43 44 45 46 47 49 50 51 52 53 54 55 56 57 58 59 60 61 63 64 65 66 67 68 70 71 72 73 74 **P**3 6 7 8 **S** Via Christi Health System, Wichita, KS **Web address:** www.via–christi.org	21	10	913	33041	573	324084	3767	355648	146882	5991

Hospital, Address, Telephone, Administrator, Approval, Facility, and Physician Codes, Health Care System, Network	Classi-fication Codes		Utilization Data					Expense (thousands) of dollars		
★ American Hospital Association (AHA) membership □ Joint Commission on Accreditation of Healthcare Organizations (JCAHO) accreditation + American Osteopathic Healthcare Association (AOHA) membership ○ American Osteopathic Association (AOA) accreditation △ Commission on Accreditation of Rehabilitation Facilities (CARF) accreditation Control codes 61, 63, 64, 71, 72 and 73 indicate hospitals listed by AOHA, but not registered by AHA. For definition of numerical codes, see page A4	Control	Service	Staffed Beds	Admissions	Census	Outpatient Visits	Births	Total	Payroll	Personnel
□ VIA CHRISTI REHABILITATION CENTER, 1151 North Rock Road, Zip 67206–1262; tel. 316/634–3400; Laurie Labarca, Chief Operating Officer (Total facility includes 20 beds in nursing home–type unit) **A**1 10 **F**1 2 3 4 6 7 8 9 10 11 12 13 14 15 16 17 18 19 20 21 22 23 24 25 26 27 28 29 30 31 32 33 34 35 37 38 39 40 41 42 43 44 45 46 47 48 49 50 51 52 53 54 55 56 57 58 59 60 62 63 64 65 66 67 68 70 71 72 73 74 **P**1 3 4 5 6 **Web address:** www.via–christi.org	21	46	60	709	36	16009	0	9310	4489	210
⊠ WESLEY MEDICAL CENTER, 550 North Hillside Avenue, Zip 67214–4976; tel. 316/688–2000; Carl W. Fitch, Sr., President and Chief Executive Officer **A**1 2 3 5 9 10 **F**4 7 8 10 11 12 15 16 19 21 22 23 24 34 35 37 38 40 41 42 43 44 45 46 47 49 52 57 60 63 64 65 70 71 73 74 **P**6 **S** Columbia/HCA Healthcare Corporation, Nashville, TN **Web address:** www.wesleymc.com	33	10	506	24748	349	193935	4899	217125	94726	2232
□ △ WESLEY REHABILITATION HOSPITAL, 8338 West 13th Street North, Zip 67212–2984; tel. 316/729–9999; Lisa James, Chief Operating Officer **A**1 7 10 **F**12 14 15 16 25 27 34 46 48 49 **S** HEALTHSOUTH Corporation, Birmingham, AL	33	46	50	566	31	12321	0	8465	3842	115
WINCHESTER—Jefferson County										
JEFFERSON COUNTY MEMORIAL HOSPITAL, 408 Delaware Street, Zip 66097–4002, Mailing Address: Rural Route 1, Box 1, Zip 66097–0001; tel. 913/774–4340; Dwaine Klingman, Administrator (Total facility includes 70 beds in nursing home–type unit) **A**9 **F**14 15 16 19 22 26 28 64 65 71 72	23	10	95	102	62	4349	0	—	—	76
WINFIELD—Cowley County										
⊠ WILLIAM NEWTON MEMORIAL HOSPITAL, 1300 East Fifth Street, Zip 67156–2495; tel. 316/221–2300; Richard H. Vaught, Administrator (Total facility includes 14 beds in nursing home–type unit) **A**1 9 10 **F**7 8 13 15 16 19 21 22 27 28 30 32 36 37 39 40 41 42 44 45 46 49 52 58 64 65 66 67 71 73	14	10	41	1533	22	39766	257	14064	7747	221

KENTUCKY

Resident population 3,936 (in thousands)
Resident population in metro areas 47.6%
Birth rate per 1,000 population 13.6
65 years and over 12.5%
Percent of persons without health insurance 15.4%

Hospital, Address, Telephone, Administrator, Approval, Facility, and Physician Codes, Health Care System, Network	Classi-fication Codes		Utilization Data					Expense (thousands) of dollars		
	Control	Service	Staffed Beds	Admissions	Census	Outpatient Visits	Births	Total	Payroll	Personnel

American Hospital Association (AHA) membership
☐ Joint Commission on Accreditation of Healthcare Organizations (JCAHO) accreditation
American Osteopathic Healthcare Association (AOHA) membership
○ American Osteopathic Association (AOA) accreditation
△ Commission on Accreditation of Rehabilitation Facilities (CARF) accreditation
Control codes 61, 63, 64, 71, 72 and 73 indicate hospitals listed by AOHA, but not registered by AHA. For definition of numerical codes, see page A4

Hospital	Control	Service	Staffed Beds	Admissions	Census	Outpatient Visits	Births	Total	Payroll	Personnel
ALBANY—Clinton County										
CLINTON COUNTY HOSPITAL, 723 Burkesville Road, Zip 42602–1654; tel. 606/387–6421; Randel Flowers, Ph.D., Administrator **A**9 10 **F**11 19 22 71	23	10	42	1925	23	14999	0	6493	2984	124
ASHLAND—Boyd County										
△ KING'S DAUGHTERS' MEDICAL CENTER, 2201 Lexington Avenue, Zip 41101–2874, Mailing Address: P.O. Box 151, Zip 41105–0151; tel. 606/327–4000; Fred L. Jackson, Chief Executive Officer (Total facility includes 10 beds in nursing home–type unit) **A**1 2 7 9 10 **F**1 4 7 8 10 12 15 16 17 19 21 22 23 25 27 28 30 31 32 33 34 35 36 37 38 39 40 41 42 43 44 45 46 48 49 52 53 54 55 56 57 58 60 63 64 65 66 67 71 72 73 74 **P**8 Web address: www.kdmc.com	23	10	341	17079	239	144308	1059	135765	53401	1592
OUR LADY OF BELLEFONTE HOSPITAL, St. Christopher Drive, Zip 41101, Mailing Address: P.O. Box 789, Zip 41105–0789; tel. 606/833–3333; Robert J. Maher, President **A**1 2 9 10 **F**2 3 7 8 10 12 13 15 16 17 18 19 20 21 22 23 24 26 27 28 30 32 34 35 36 37 39 40 41 42 43 44 45 46 49 52 56 58 59 60 61 63 65 66 67 70 71 72 73 74 **P**8 **S** Franciscan Health Partnership, Inc., Latham, NY	21	10	194	8422	106	148949	191	71128	30036	962
BARBOURVILLE—Knox County										
KNOX COUNTY HOSPITAL, 321 High Street, Zip 40906–1317, Mailing Address: P.O. Box 160, Zip 40906–0160; tel. 606/546–4175; Craig Morgan, Administrator (Total facility includes 16 beds in nursing home–type unit) **A**1 9 10 **F**7 19 21 22 37 40 44 64 65 71 73 Web address: www.Barbourville.com	13	10	58	1678	36	25889	51	8905	3953	169
BARDSTOWN—Nelson County										
FLAGET MEMORIAL HOSPITAL, 201 Cathedral Manor, Zip 40004–1299; tel. 502/348–3923; Suzanne Reasbeck, President and Chief Executive Officer (Nonreporting) **A**1 9 10 **S** Catholic Health Initiatives, Denver, CO Web address: www.flaget.com	21	10	36	—	—	—	—	—	—	—
BENTON—Marshall County										
MARSHALL COUNTY HOSPITAL, 503 George McClain Drive, Zip 42025–1399, Mailing Address: P.O. Box 630, Zip 42025–0630; tel. 502/527–4800; David G. Fuqua, R.N., Chief Executive Officer (Total facility includes 34 beds in nursing home–type unit) **A**1 9 10 **F**8 12 15 16 19 22 26 27 32 34 35 37 39 41 44 45 49 51 57 63 64 65 67 71 73 **P**8 **S** Quorum Health Group/Quorum Health Resources, Inc., Brentwood, TN	16	10	80	887	47	17149	0	8786	3996	186
BEREA—Madison County										
BEREA HOSPITAL, 305 Estill Street, Zip 40403–1909; tel. 606/986–3151; David E. Burgio, FACHE, President and Chief Executive Officer (Total facility includes 102 beds in nursing home–type unit) **A**1 9 10 **F**8 12 14 15 16 17 19 20 21 22 26 27 28 30 31 34 37 39 41 44 46 49 64 65 67 71 72 73 74 **P**6	23	10	150	1798	82	38911	0	19567	8031	363
BOWLING GREEN—Warren County										
GREENVIEW REGIONAL HOSPITAL, 1801 Ashley Circle, Zip 42104–3384, Mailing Address: P.O. Box 90024, Zip 42102–9024; tel. 502/793–1000; Phillip A. Clendenin, Chief Executive Officer **A**1 9 10 **F**7 8 10 11 12 14 15 16 17 19 20 21 22 23 28 29 30 34 35 37 40 41 42 44 45 46 49 58 60 65 66 67 68 70 71 73 74 **P**5 7 **S** Columbia/HCA Healthcare Corporation, Nashville, TN Web address: www.columbia–hca.com	33	10	211	5578	81	52709	833	—	—	489
△ MEDIPLEX REHABILITATION HOSPITAL, 1300 Campbell Lane, Zip 42104–4162; tel. 502/782–6900; Jeffrey L. Durham, Chief Executive Officer (Total facility includes 10 beds in nursing home–type unit) **A**1 7 9 10 **F**12 48 64 65 67 Web address: www.sunh.com	33	46	55	986	54	0	0	25232	3954	139
THE MEDICAL CENTER AT BOWLING GREEN, (Includes Medical Center at Scottsville, 456 Burnley Road, Scottsville, Zip 42164–6355; tel. 502/622–2800; Sarah Moore, Vice President), 250 Park Street, Zip 42101–1795, Mailing Address: P.O. Box 90010, Zip 42102–9010; tel. 270/745–1000; Connie Smith, Chief Executive Officer (Total facility includes 105 beds in nursing home–type unit) **A**1 9 10 **F**3 4 7 8 10 11 12 17 18 19 20 21 22 24 25 26 27 28 29 30 31 32 34 35 37 38 39 40 41 42 43 44 45 46 49 51 52 54 55 56 57 58 59 60 64 65 67 70 71 72 73 74 **P**1	23	10	487	12406	232	50789	1217	—	—	1499
BURKESVILLE—Cumberland County										
★ CUMBERLAND COUNTY HOSPITAL, Highway 90 West, Zip 42717–0280, Mailing Address: P.O. Box 280, Zip 42717–0280; tel. 502/864–2511; Howard C. Andersen, Interim Chief Executive Officer **A**9 10 **F**8 15 17 19 21 22 28 29 34 45 49 65 71 **S** Quorum Health Group/Quorum Health Resources, Inc., Brentwood, TN	23	10	31	1682	18	19031	0	5354	2251	116
CADIZ—Trigg County										
★ TRIGG COUNTY HOSPITAL, Highway 68 East, Zip 42211, Mailing Address: P.O. Box 312, Zip 42211–0312; tel. 502/522–3215; Richard Chapman, Administrator **A**9 10 **F**8 19 21 22 28 30 32 34 39 44 46 51 64 65 71 73	15	10	29	505	8	—	0	4070	1891	104

Hospital, Address, Telephone, Administrator, Approval, Facility, and Physician Codes, Health Care System, Network	Classification Codes		Utilization Data					Expense (thousands) of dollars		
★ American Hospital Association (AHA) membership □ Joint Commission on Accreditation of Healthcare Organizations (JCAHO) accreditation + American Osteopathic Healthcare Association (AOHA) membership ○ American Osteopathic Association (AOA) accreditation △ Commission on Accreditation of Rehabilitation Facilities (CARF) accreditation Control codes 61, 63, 64, 71, 72 and 73 indicate hospitals listed by AOHA, but not registered by AHA. For definition of numerical codes, see page A4	Control	Service	Staffed Beds	Admissions	Census	Outpatient Visits	Births	Total	Payroll	Personnel

CALHOUN—McLean County

MCLEAN COUNTY HEALTH CENTER, 200 Highway 81 North, Zip 42327–2104; tel. 502/273–5252; Brenda Wright, Acting Administrator (Nonreporting) **A**9

| | 13 | 10 | 26 | — | — | — | — | — | — | — |

CAMPBELLSVILLE—Taylor County

✖ TAYLOR COUNTY HOSPITAL, 1700 Old Lebanon Road, Zip 42718–9600; tel. 502/465–3561; David R. Hayes, President **A**1 2 9 10 **F**7 8 10 14 15 19 21 22 23 24 27 28 29 30 32 33 35 37 39 40 42 44 45 46 49 50 63 70 71 73 **S** Jewish Hospital HealthCare Services, Louisville, KY

| | 16 | 10 | 90 | 3081 | 37 | 42355 | 331 | 26579 | 9549 | 403 |

CARLISLE—Nicholas County

✖ NICHOLAS COUNTY HOSPITAL, (Includes Johnson–Mathers Nursing Home), 2323 Concrete Road, Zip 40311–9721, Mailing Address: P.O. Box 232, Zip 40311–0232; tel. 606/289–7181; Doris Ecton, Administrator and Chief Executive Officer (Total facility includes 55 beds in nursing home–type unit) (Nonreporting) **A**1 9 10

| | 23 | 10 | 83 | — | — | — | — | — | — | — |

CARROLLTON—Carroll County

★ CARROLL COUNTY HOSPITAL, 309 11th Street, Zip 41008–1400; tel. 502/732–4321; Roger Williams, Chief Executive Officer (Nonreporting) **A**9 10 **S** Norton Healthcare, Louisville, KY

| | 13 | 10 | 39 | — | — | — | — | — | — | — |

COLUMBIA—Adair County

□ WESTLAKE REGIONAL HOSPITAL, Westlake Drive, Zip 42728–1149, Mailing Address: P.O. Box 468, Zip 42728–0468; tel. 502/384–4753; Rex A. Tungate, Administrator (Nonreporting) **A**1 9 10

| | 16 | 10 | 80 | — | — | — | — | — | — | — |

CORBIN—Whitley County

✖ BAPTIST REGIONAL MEDICAL CENTER, 1 Trillium Way, Zip 40701–8420; tel. 606/528–1212; John S. Henson, President (Total facility includes 23 beds in nursing home–type unit) **A**1 9 10 **F**2 3 7 8 10 11 12 15 16 17 18 19 21 22 24 28 30 34 35 37 39 40 44 45 48 49 52 53 54 55 56 57 58 59 63 64 65 67 71 73 74 **P**8 **S** Baptist Healthcare System, Louisville, KY

| | 23 | 10 | 240 | 10316 | 165 | 57536 | 960 | 60393 | 25182 | 992 |

COVINGTON—Kenton County

CHILDREN'S PSYCHIATRIC HOSPITAL OF NORTHERN KENTUCKY See NorthKey Community Care

□ HEALTHSOUTH NORTHERN KENTUCKY REHABILITATION HOSPITAL, 201 Medical Village Drive, Zip 41017–3407; tel. 606/341–2044; Timothy W. Mitchell, Chief Executive Officer (Nonreporting) **A**1 9 10 **S** HEALTHSOUTH Corporation, Birmingham, AL

| | 33 | 46 | 40 | — | — | — | — | — | — | — |

NORTHKEY COMMUNITY CARE, (Formerly Children's Psychiatric Hospital of Northern Kentucky), 502 Farrell Drive, Zip 41011–3799, Mailing Address: P.O. Box 2680, Zip 41012–2680; tel. 606/578–3200; Edward G. Muntel, Ph.D., President and Chief Executive Officer **A**9 10 **F**15 16 18 19 21 22 25 34 35 50 52 53 54 55 56 58 59 63 65 67 71 **P**5

| | 23 | 52 | 28 | 359 | 17 | — | 0 | 2967 | 1322 | 54 |

□ ST. ELIZABETH MEDICAL CENTER–NORTH, (Includes St. Elizabeth Medical Center–South, 1 Medical Village Drive, Edgewood, Zip 41017; tel. 606/344–2000), 401 East 20th Street, Zip 41014–1585; tel. 606/292–4000; Joseph W. Gross, President and Chief Executive Officer (Total facility includes 66 beds in nursing home–type unit) (Nonreporting) **A**1 2 3 9 10 **S** Catholic Healthcare Partners, Cincinnati, OH

| | 21 | 10 | 466 | — | — | — | — | — | — | — |

CYNTHIANA—Harrison County

✖ HARRISON MEMORIAL HOSPITAL, Millersburg Road, Zip 41031–0250, Mailing Address: P.O. Box 250, Zip 41031–0250; tel. 606/234–2300; Darwin E. Root, Administrator (Total facility includes 38 beds in nursing home–type unit) **A**1 9 10 **F**7 8 14 19 21 22 24 26 28 32 33 34 37 39 40 42 44 49 64 65 67 71 73

| | 23 | 10 | 77 | 2068 | 56 | 43492 | 183 | 15128 | 5964 | 267 |

DANVILLE—Boyle County

✖ EPHRAIM MCDOWELL REGIONAL MEDICAL CENTER, 217 South Third Street, Zip 40422–9983; tel. 606/239–1000; Thomas W. Smith, President and Chief Executive Officer (Total facility includes 25 beds in nursing home–type unit) **A**1 9 10 **F**1 7 8 10 12 14 15 16 17 18 19 21 22 24 25 26 27 28 29 30 31 34 35 37 38 39 40 41 42 44 45 46 49 51 52 53 54 55 56 57 58 59 63 64 65 66 67 71 73 74 **P**2 5 8
Web address: www.emrmc.com

| | 23 | 10 | 177 | 7306 | 116 | 75732 | 902 | 49366 | 22966 | 956 |

EDGEWOOD—Kenton County

ST. ELIZABETH MEDICAL CENTER–SOUTH See St. Elizabeth Medical Center–North, Covington

ELIZABETHTOWN—Hardin County

✖ HARDIN MEMORIAL HOSPITAL, 913 North Dixie Avenue, Zip 42701–2599; tel. 502/737–1212; David L. Gray, President (Total facility includes 15 beds in nursing home–type unit) **A**1 9 10 **F**4 5 7 8 10 11 12 16 17 19 21 22 23 28 30 32 34 35 37 40 42 43 44 45 46 48 49 52 56 60 63 64 65 67 71 72 73 **S** Baptist Healthcare System, Louisville, KY
Web address: www.hmh.net

| | 13 | 10 | 270 | 11200 | 168 | 118785 | 1358 | 86520 | 37413 | 1131 |

□ △ HEALTHSOUTH REHABILITATION HOSPITAL OF CENTRAL KENTUCKY, (Formerly Lakeview Rehabilitation Hospital), 134 Heartland Drive, Zip 42701–2778; tel. 502/769–3100; Teresa K. Stranko, Chief Executive Officer (Nonreporting) **A**1 7 9 10 **S** HEALTHSOUTH Corporation, Birmingham, AL
LAKEVIEW REHABILITATION HOSPITAL See HEALTHSOUTH Rehabilitation Hospital of Central Kentucky

| | 32 | 46 | 40 | — | — | — | — | — | — | — |

FLEMINGSBURG—Fleming County

✖ FLEMING COUNTY HOSPITAL, 920 Elizaville Avenue, Zip 41041, Mailing Address: P.O. Box 388, Zip 41041–0388; tel. 606/849–5000; Luther E. Reeves, Chief Executive Officer **A**1 9 10 **F**8 12 19 21 22 28 37 41 44 49 71 **P**3 **S** Quorum Health Group/Quorum Health Resources, Inc., Brentwood, TN

| | 16 | 10 | 52 | 1441 | 17 | 28209 | 0 | 9176 | 4172 | 121 |

Hospital, Address, Telephone, Administrator, Approval, Facility, and Physician Codes, Health Care System, Network	Classi-fication Codes		Utilization Data					Expense (thousands) of dollars		
American Hospital Association (AHA) membership Joint Commission on Accreditation of Healthcare Organizations (JCAHO) accreditation American Osteopathic Healthcare Association (AOHA) membership American Osteopathic Association (AOA) accreditation Commission on Accreditation of Rehabilitation Facilities (CARF) accreditation Control codes 61, 63, 64, 71, 72 and 73 indicate hospitals listed by AOHA, but not registered by AHA. For definition of numerical codes, see page A4	Control	Service	Staffed Beds	Admissions	Census	Outpatient Visits	Births	Total	Payroll	Personnel

FLORENCE—Boone County

ST. LUKE HOSPITAL WEST, 7380 Turfway Road, Zip 41042–1337; tel. 606/525–5200; Daniel M. Vinson, CPA, Senior Vice President (Total facility includes 24 beds in nursing home–type unit) **A**9 10 **F**2 3 4 5 7 8 9 10 11 12 13 14 15 16 17 18 19 20 21 22 24 25 26 27 28 29 30 31 32 33 34 35 36 37 38 39 40 41 42 43 44 45 46 48 49 50 51 52 53 54 55 56 57 58 59 60 61 63 64 65 66 67 68 70 71 72 73 74 **P**6 8 **S** Health Alliance of Greater Cincinnati, Cincinnati, OH — 23 | 10 | 136 | 6616 | 69 | 106704 | 935 | 51218 | 20552 | 554

FORT CAMPBELL—Christian County

COLONEL FLORENCE A. BLANCHFIELD ARMY COMMUNITY HOSPITAL, 650 Joel Drive, Zip 42223–5349; tel. 502/798–8040; Colonel Lester Martinez–Lopez, Director Health Services **A**1 2 **F**7 8 12 13 14 15 16 17 18 19 20 22 24 25 28 29 30 31 34 35 37 38 39 40 44 45 46 49 51 53 54 56 58 61 65 66 67 71 72 73 74 **P**6 **S** Department of the Army, Office of the Surgeon General, Falls Church, VA — 42 | 10 | 81 | 3728 | 27 | 593795 | 1849 | — | — | 1175

FORT KNOX—Hardin County

IRELAND ARMY COMMUNITY HOSPITAL, 851 Ireland Loop, Zip 40121–5520; tel. 502/624–9020; Lieutenant Colonel Robert T. Foster, Deputy Commander for Administration **A**1 5 **F**1 2 3 4 7 8 10 11 12 14 15 16 17 19 20 21 22 23 28 29 30 31 32 33 34 35 37 38 39 40 41 42 43 44 45 46 47 49 51 52 53 55 56 57 58 60 61 63 65 67 68 71 72 73 74 **P**5 8 **S** Department of the Army, Office of the Surgeon General, Falls Church, VA — 42 | 10 | 56 | 1671 | 13 | 337571 | 563 | 44204 | 13226 | 464

FORT THOMAS—Campbell County

ST. LUKE HOSPITAL EAST, 85 North Grand Avenue, Zip 41075–1796; tel. 606/572–3100; Daniel M. Vinson, CPA, Senior Vice President (Total facility includes 30 beds in nursing home–type unit) **A**1 2 10 **F**2 3 4 5 7 8 9 10 11 12 13 14 15 16 17 18 19 20 21 22 24 25 26 27 28 29 30 31 32 33 34 35 36 37 38 39 40 41 42 43 44 45 46 48 49 50 51 52 53 54 55 56 57 58 59 60 61 63 64 65 66 67 68 70 71 72 73 74 **P**6 8 **S** Health Alliance of Greater Cincinnati, Cincinnati, OH — 23 | 10 | 167 | 7348 | 83 | 81548 | 872 | 62611 | 23882 | 932

FRANKFORT—Franklin County

FRANKFORT REGIONAL MEDICAL CENTER, 299 King's Daughters Drive, Zip 40601–4186; tel. 502/875–5240; David P. Steitz, Chief Executive Officer **A**1 9 10 **F**2 3 7 8 10 11 12 14 15 16 19 20 21 22 28 29 32 33 34 35 37 39 40 41 42 44 45 46 49 51 52 54 58 60 63 65 66 67 71 73 **S** Columbia/HCA Healthcare Corporation, Nashville, TN — 33 | 10 | 147 | 4936 | 59 | 56291 | 578 | 31703 | 11826 | 468

FRANKLIN—Simpson County

FRANKLIN–SIMPSON MEMORIAL HOSPITAL, Brookhaven Road, Zip 42135–2929; Mailing Address: P.O. Box 2929, Zip 42135–2929; tel. 502/586–3253; William P. Macri, Chief Executive Officer (Total facility includes 6 beds in nursing home–type unit) **A**9 10 **F**8 14 15 16 19 26 30 34 37 39 44 49 57 64 70 71 73 **P**8 **S** Quorum Health Group/Quorum Health Resources, Inc., Brentwood, TN — 13 | 10 | 28 | 753 | 10 | 11532 | 0 | 6350 | 2453 | 90

FULTON—Fulton County

PARKWAY REGIONAL HOSPITAL, 2000 Holiday Lane, Zip 42041; tel. 502/472–2522; Mary Jo Lewis, Chief Executive Officer (Nonreporting) **A**1 9 10 **S** Community Health Systems, Inc., Brentwood, TN — 33 | 10 | 70 | — | — | — | — | — | — | —

GEORGETOWN—Scott County

GEORGETOWN COMMUNITY HOSPITAL, 1140 Lexington Road, Zip 40324–9362; tel. 502/868–1100; Jeffrey G. Seraphine, President and Chief Executive Officer (Total facility includes 10 beds in nursing home–type unit) (Nonreporting) **A**1 9 10 **S** LifePoint Hospitals, Inc., Nashville, TN — 33 | 10 | 61 | — | — | — | — | — | — | —

GLASGOW—Barren County

T. J. SAMSON COMMUNITY HOSPITAL, 1301 North Race Street, Zip 42141–3483; tel. 502/651–4444; Dwayne Moss, Chief Executive Officer (Total facility includes 16 beds in nursing home–type unit) **A**1 3 9 10 **F**1 7 8 11 12 14 15 16 17 19 21 22 23 26 27 28 29 30 32 34 35 37 38 40 44 45 46 49 51 53 54 55 56 57 58 59 60 64 65 66 67 71 73 **P**8 Web address: www.glasgow.ky.com — 23 | 10 | 196 | 7246 | 93 | 58271 | 883 | 47542 | 22589 | 884

GREENSBURG—Green County

JANE TODD CRAWFORD HOSPITAL, 202–206 Milby Street, Zip 42743–1100, Mailing Address: P.O. Box 220, Zip 42743–0220; tel. 502/932–4211; Larry Craig, Chief Executive Officer (Total facility includes 18 beds in nursing home–type unit) **A**9 10 **F**2 3 8 18 19 22 26 28 32 33 34 35 37 42 44 45 49 51 52 53 54 55 56 57 58 63 64 67 71 **P**6 — 13 | 10 | 64 | 1501 | 39 | 24738 | 0 | 6514 | 3306 | 139

GREENVILLE—Muhlenberg County

MUHLENBERG COMMUNITY HOSPITAL, 440 Hopkinsville Street, Zip 42345–1172, Mailing Address: P.O. Box 387, Zip 42345–0387; tel. 502/338–8000; Charles D. Lovell, Jr., Chief Executive Officer (Total facility includes 45 beds in nursing home–type unit) (Nonreporting) **A**1 9 10 **S** Quorum Health Group/Quorum Health Resources, Inc., Brentwood, TN — 23 | 10 | 135 | — | — | — | — | — | — | —

HARDINSBURG—Breckinridge County

BRECKINRIDGE MEMORIAL HOSPITAL, 1011 Old Highway 60, Zip 40143–2597; tel. 502/756–7000; George Walz, CHE, Chief Executive Officer (Total facility includes 18 beds in nursing home–type unit) **A**9 10 **F**8 12 14 19 20 22 32 33 35 44 46 64 71 73 **P**5 **S** Norton Healthcare, Louisville, KY Web address: www.multiplan.com — 23 | 10 | 45 | 1014 | 27 | 39783 | 0 | 6336 | 2830 | 151

Hospital, Address, Telephone, Administrator, Approval, Facility, and Physician Codes, Health Care System, Network	Control	Service	Staffed Beds	Admissions	Census	Outpatient Visits	Births	Total	Payroll	Personnel
HARLAN—Harlan County										
□ HARLAN ARH HOSPITAL, 81 Ball Park Road, Zip 40831–1792; tel. 606/573–8100; Daniel Fitzpatrick, Chief Executive Officer (Nonreporting) A1 9 10 S Appalachian Regional Healthcare, Lexington, KY	23	10	125	—	—	—	—	—	—	—
HARRODSBURG—Mercer County										
★ THE JAMES B. HAGGIN MEMORIAL HOSPITAL, 464 Linden Avenue, Zip 40330–1862; tel. 606/734–5441; Earl James Motzer, Ph.D., FACHE, Chief Executive Officer (Total facility includes 25 beds in nursing home–type unit) A9 10 F8 11 13 14 15 16 17 19 22 28 29 30 32 33 34 37 39 42 44 49 58 64 65 67 68 71 P8 S Norton Healthcare, Louisville, KY	23	10	64	994	38	26914	0	8388	3681	157
HARTFORD—Ohio County										
⊠ OHIO COUNTY HOSPITAL, 1211 Main Street, Zip 42347–1619; tel. 502/298–7411; Blaine Pieper, Administrator A1 9 10 F7 8 11 12 15 17 18 19 20 22 24 28 30 33 34 35 37 40 41 42 44 45 46 49 64 65 71 P8 S Quorum Health Group/Quorum Health Resources, Inc., Brentwood, TN	23	10	54	1268	15	38602	138	13552	4930	200
HAZARD—Perry County										
□ ARH REGIONAL MEDICAL CENTER, 100 Medical Center Drive, Zip 41701–1000; tel. 606/439–6610; Charles E. Housley, FACHE, Administrator A1 2 3 5 9 10 F7 8 10 12 19 21 22 25 28 32 33 34 35 37 40 41 42 44 49 51 52 53 54 55 58 60 65 67 71 72 73 74 S Appalachian Regional Healthcare, Lexington, KY Web address: www.arh.org	23	10	288	8334	114	249684	522	51789	20529	902
HENDERSON—Henderson County										
⊠ METHODIST HOSPITAL, (Formerly Community Methodist Hospital), 1305 North Elm Street, Zip 42420–2775, Mailing Address: P.O. Box 48, Zip 42420–0048; tel. 502/827–7700; Bruce D. Begley, Executive Director (Nonreporting) A1 9 10 Web address: www.methodisthospital.net	21	10	213	—	—	—	—	—	—	—
HOPKINSVILLE—Christian County										
□ CUMBERLAND HALL HOSPITAL, 210 West 17th Street, Zip 42240–1999; tel. 502/886–1919; William C. Heard, Administrator and Chief Executive Officer A1 9 10 F52 53 57 58 P5	33	52	48	838	33	557	0	4626	2371	64
⊠ JENNIE STUART MEDICAL CENTER, 320 West 18th Street, Zip 42241–2400, Mailing Address: P.O. Box 2400, Zip 42241–2400; tel. 502/887–0100; Lewis T. Peeples, Chief Executive Officer A1 2 9 10 F7 8 10 11 12 15 16 17 19 21 22 23 30 32 34 35 37 40 41 42 44 45 49 60 63 65 66 71 73 P7 S Quorum Health Group/Quorum Health Resources, Inc., Brentwood, TN Web address: www.jsmc.org	23	10	139	5747	69	59680	495	45187	16204	589
□ WESTERN STATE HOSPITAL, Russellville Road, Zip 42241, Mailing Address: P.O. Box 2200, Zip 42241–2200; tel. 502/886–4431; Stephen P. Wiggins, Director (Total facility includes 144 beds in nursing home–type unit) A1 10 F20 27 39 41 45 46 52 55 56 57 64 65 67 73 P6	12	22	355	1282	285	0	0	25000	—	569
HORSE CAVE—Hart County										
★ CAVERNA MEMORIAL HOSPITAL, 1501 South Dixie Street, Zip 42749–1477; tel. 502/786–2191; James J. Kerins, Sr., Administrator A9 10 F8 14 15 16 19 22 28 30 32 37 44 64 71 S Norton Healthcare, Louisville, KY	23	10	28	684	9	11226	65	3593	1512	67
HYDEN—Leslie County										
MARY BRECKINRIDGE HOSPITAL, 130 Kate Ireland Drive, Zip 41749–0000; tel. 606/672–2901; A. Ray Branaman, Administrator A9 10 F7 8 19 22 28 32 40 44 49 65 71 74	23	10	40	1302	14	37654	132	13761	7449	297
IRVINE—Estill County										
MARCUM AND WALLACE MEMORIAL HOSPITAL, 60 Mercy Court, Zip 40336–1331, Mailing Address: P.O. Box 928, Zip 40336–0928; tel. 606/723–2115; James F. Heitzenrater, Administrator A9 10 F8 15 16 19 21 22 28 41 49 64 65 71 S Catholic Healthcare Partners, Cincinnati, OH	23	10	26	577	6	39090	0	4643	2273	100
JACKSON—Breathitt County										
⊠ KENTUCKY RIVER MEDICAL CENTER, 540 Jett Drive, Zip 41339–9620; tel. 606/666–6305; O. David Bevins, Chief Executive Officer A1 9 10 F8 11 14 15 16 19 21 22 25 26 34 35 37 39 42 44 46 49 51 65 66 71 73 74 P7 S Community Health Systems, Inc., Brentwood, TN	33	10	55	3796	26	35316	2	20477	6686	171
JENKINS—Letcher County										
□ JENKINS COMMUNITY HOSPITAL, Main Street, Zip 41537–9614, Mailing Address: P.O. Box 472, Zip 41537–0472; tel. 606/832–2171; Sherrie Newcomb, Administrator A1 9 10 F15 19 22 28 32 34 37 44 65 71	31	10	60	858	6	72577	0	5604	3149	122
LA GRANGE—Oldham County										
⊠ TRI COUNTY BAPTIST HOSPITAL, 1025 New Moody Lane, Zip 40031–0559; tel. 502/222–5388; Dennis B. Johnson, Administrator (Total facility includes 30 beds in nursing home–type unit) A1 9 10 F7 8 12 15 19 21 22 34 37 40 41 42 44 49 64 71 73 74 S Baptist Healthcare System, Louisville, KY	23	10	105	2734	53	33976	364	19639	9251	276
LANCASTER—Garrard County										
GARRARD COUNTY MEMORIAL HOSPITAL, 308 West Maple Avenue, Zip 40444–1098; tel. 606/792–6844; John P. Rigsby, Administrator (Total facility includes 112 beds in nursing home–type unit) A9 10 F8 19 22 27 34 35 41 44 64 65 70 71 73	13	10	131	802	112	12289	0	—	—	158
LEBANON—Marion County										
⊠ NORTON SPRING VIEW HOSPITAL, (Formerly Spring View Hospital), 320 Loretto Road, Zip 40033–0320; tel. 502/692–3161; Patricia Ekdahl, Chief Executive Officer (Total facility includes 38 beds in nursing home–type unit) (Nonreporting) A1 9 10 S Norton Healthcare, Louisville, KY	33	10	113	—	—	—	—	—	—	—

Hospital, Address, Telephone, Administrator, Approval, Facility, and Physician Codes, Health Care System, Network	Classification Codes		Utilization Data					Expense (thousands) of dollars		
	Control	Service	Staffed Beds	Admissions	Census	Outpatient Visits	Births	Total	Payroll	Personnel

LEITCHFIELD—Grayson County

☒ TWIN LAKES REGIONAL MEDICAL CENTER, 910 Wallace Avenue, Zip 42754–1499; tel. 502/259–9400; Stephen L. Meredith, Chief Executive Officer **A**1 9 10 **F**8 12 16 19 22 24 32 37 40 44 45 46 49 62 65 66 71 73 **P**6 **S** Norton Healthcare, Louisville, KY — 23 10 75 2057 28 43245 286 15718 7022 309

LEXINGTON—Fayette County

★ △ CARDINAL HILL REHABILITATION HOSPITAL, 2050 Versailles Road, Zip 40504–1499; tel. 606/254–5701; Kerry G. Gillihan, President and Chief Executive Officer **A**3 5 7 9 10 **F**1 12 16 17 26 28 32 41 45 46 48 49 65 67 71 72 73 **P**6 — 23 46 100 1478 66 34612 0 23414 12551 470
Web address: www.cardinalhill.org

☒ CENTRAL BAPTIST HOSPITAL, 1740 Nicholasville Road, Zip 40503; tel. 606/260–6100; William G. Sisson, President (Total facility includes 12 beds in nursing home–type unit) **A**1 2 3 5 9 10 **F**4 7 8 10 11 12 15 16 17 19 21 22 28 29 30 32 35 37 38 40 41 42 43 44 46 49 60 61 67 71 73 74 **P**6 7 **S** Baptist Healthcare System, Louisville, KY — 21 10 355 18477 258 141014 3796 185523 70601 1926
Web address: www.centralbap.com

□ CHARTER RIDGE BEHAVIORAL HEALTH SYSTEM, (Formerly Charter Ridge Hospital), 3050 Rio Dosa Drive, Zip 40509–9990; tel. 606/269–2325; Barbara Kitchen, Chief Executive Officer **A**1 3 5 9 10 **F**2 3 15 19 20 22 35 52 53 55 58 59 65 67 **P**8 **S** Magellan Health Services, Atlanta, GA — 33 22 110 2296 62 15013 0 — — 106

□ EASTERN STATE HOSPITAL, 627 West Fourth Street, Zip 40508–1294; tel. 606/246–7000; Joseph A. Toy, President and Chief Executive Officer (Nonreporting) **A**1 5 10 — 12 22 197 — — — — — — —

FEDERAL MEDICAL CENTER, 3301 Leestown Road, Zip 40511–8799; tel. 606/255–6812; J. T. Holland, Warden (Nonreporting) — 33 22 56 — — — — — — —

JEWISH HOSPITAL LEXINGTON See Saint Joseph Hospital East

☒ SAINT JOSEPH HOSPITAL, One St. Joseph Drive, Zip 40504–3754; tel. 606/278–3436; Thomas J. Murray, President (Total facility includes 22 beds in nursing home–type unit) **A**1 2 3 5 9 10 **F**2 3 4 8 10 11 12 13 15 16 17 19 21 22 25 26 29 30 31 32 33 34 35 36 37 39 40 41 42 43 44 45 46 49 50 52 56 57 58 59 63 64 65 66 67 71 73 **P**3 **S** Catholic Health Initiatives, Denver, CO — 21 10 357 14076 226 78166 — 144217 55166 1573
Web address: www.sjhlex.org

☒ SAINT JOSEPH HOSPITAL EAST, (Formerly Jewish Hospital Lexington), 150 North Eagle Creek Drive, Zip 40509–1807; tel. 606/268–4800; Melinda Washburn, Chief Operating Officer (Nonreporting) **A**1 5 9 10 — 23 10 174 — — — — — — —

☒ SAMARITAN HOSPITAL, 310 South Limestone Street, Zip 40508–3008; tel. 606/226–7151; Frank Beirne, Chief Executive Officer (Total facility includes 35 beds in nursing home–type unit) **A**1 9 10 **F**7 8 10 11 12 14 15 16 17 19 20 21 22 26 28 29 30 33 34 35 36 37 39 40 41 42 44 46 48 49 52 53 54 55 56 57 58 59 64 65 71 73 **P**6 **S** Columbia/HCA Healthcare Corporation, Nashville, TN — 33 10 193 4593 73 42411 86 — — 502

☒ SHRINERS HOSPITALS FOR CHILDREN–LEXINGTON, 1900 Richmond Road, Zip 40502–1298; tel. 606/266–2101; Tony Lewgood, Administrator (Nonreporting) **A**1 3 5 **S** Shriners Hospitals for Children, Tampa, FL — 23 57 50 — — — — — — —

☒ UNIVERSITY OF KENTUCKY HOSPITAL, 800 Rose Street, Zip 40536–0084; tel. 606/323–5000; Frank Butler, Director **A**1 2 3 5 8 9 10 **F**3 4 7 8 9 10 11 12 13 14 15 16 17 18 19 20 21 22 23 24 25 26 28 29 30 31 32 33 35 37 38 39 40 41 42 43 44 45 46 47 49 50 51 52 53 54 55 56 57 58 60 61 63 65 66 67 68 70 71 73 74 **P**1 — 12 10 409 20413 323 411809 2113 276200 98080 2728
Web address: www.ukhealthcare.uky.edu

☒ VETERANS AFFAIRS MEDICAL CENTER–LEXINGTON, 2250 Leestown Pike, Zip 40511–1093; tel. 606/233–4511; Helen K. Cornish, Director (Total facility includes 198 beds in nursing home–type unit) **A**1 2 3 5 8 9 **F**1 3 4 8 10 11 12 16 17 19 20 21 22 24 26 27 28 29 30 31 32 33 34 35 37 39 41 42 43 44 45 46 48 49 51 52 54 56 57 58 60 63 64 65 67 71 73 74 **P**6 **S** Department of Veterans Affairs, Washington, DC — 45 10 407 5996 333 196178 0 110887 64642 1637

LONDON—Laurel County

☒ MARYMOUNT MEDICAL CENTER, 310 East Ninth Street, Zip 40741–1299; tel. 606/877–3705; Lowell Jones, Chief Executive Officer (Total facility includes 24 beds in nursing home–type unit) **A**1 9 10 **F**7 10 11 12 15 16 19 20 21 22 28 30 32 33 35 39 40 42 43 44 45 46 64 65 67 71 72 73 74 **P**6 **S** Catholic Health Initiatives, Denver, CO — 21 10 70 4024 50 150882 432 34554 15972 446

LOUISA—Lawrence County

☒ THREE RIVERS MEDICAL CENTER, Highway 644, Zip 41230, Mailing Address: P.O. Box 769, Zip 41230–0769; tel. 606/638–9451; Greg Kiser, Chief Executive Officer **A**1 9 10 **F**7 8 11 12 15 16 19 22 23 26 28 29 30 32 35 37 40 44 46 52 55 56 57 58 63 65 71 73 **S** Community Health Systems, Inc., Brentwood, TN — 33 10 90 2746 32 24719 92 — — 192

LOUISVILLE—Jefferson County

ALLIANT HOSPITALS See Norton Healthcare
AUDUBON HOSPITAL See Norton Audubon Hospital

☒ △ BAPTIST HOSPITAL EAST, 4000 Kresge Way, Zip 40207–4676; tel. 502/897–8100; Susan Stout Tamme, President (Total facility includes 23 beds in nursing home–type unit) **A**1 2 7 9 10 **F**2 3 4 7 8 10 11 12 13 14 15 16 17 18 19 21 22 26 28 29 30 32 34 35 37 38 40 41 42 43 44 45 46 48 49 52 53 54 55 56 57 58 59 60 63 64 65 67 68 71 72 73 74 **S** Baptist Healthcare System, Louisville, KY — 23 10 407 20239 257 159392 2927 169471 74116 2597
Web address: www.baptisteast.com

Hospital, Address, Telephone, Administrator, Approval, Facility, and Physician Codes, Health Care System, Network	Classi-fication Codes		Utilization Data					Expense (thousands) of dollars		
	Control	Service	Staffed Beds	Admissions	Census	Outpatient Visits	Births	Total	Payroll	Personnel

★ American Hospital Association (AHA) membership
□ Joint Commission on Accreditation of Healthcare Organizations (JCAHO) accreditation
+ American Osteopathic Healthcare Association (AOHA) membership
○ American Osteopathic Association (AOA) accreditation
△ Commission on Accreditation of Rehabilitation Facilities (CARF) accreditation
Control codes 61, 63, 64, 71, 72 and 73 indicate hospitals listed by AOHA, but not registered by AHA. For definition of numerical codes, see page A4

⊞ CARITAS MEDICAL CENTER, 1850 Bluegrass Avenue, Zip 40215–1199; tel. 502/361–6000; Peter J. Bernard, President and Chief Executive Officer (Total facility includes 33 beds in nursing home–type unit) **A**1 9 10 **F**1 2 3 6 8 10 11 12 14 15 16 19 21 22 24 26 28 32 34 35 36 37 39 41 44 46 49 51 52 53 54 55 56 57 58 59 60 64 65 66 67 71 73 **P**7 **S** Catholic Health Initiatives, Denver, CO	21	10	213	10375	152	99130	0	79173	33683	1009
⊞ CARITAS PEACE CENTER, 2020 Newburg Road, Zip 40205–1879; tel. 502/451–3330; Peter J. Bernard, President and Chief Executive Officer (Nonreporting) **A**1 9 10 **S** Catholic Health Initiatives, Denver, CO	23	22	156	—	—	—	—	—	—	—
□ CENTRAL STATE HOSPITAL, 10510 LaGrange Road, Zip 40223–1228; tel. 502/253–7000; Paula Tamme Cooke, Chief Executive Officer (Nonreporting) **A**1 10	12	22	175	—	—	—	—	—	—	—
□ CHARTER LOUISVILLE BEHAVIORAL HEALTH SYSTEM, 1405 Browns Lane, Zip 40207–4672; tel. 502/896–0495; Charles L. Webb, Jr., Administrator (Nonreporting) **A**1 9 10 **S** Magellan Health Services, Atlanta, GA	33	22	66	—	—	—	—	—	—	—
★ △ FRAZIER REHABILITATION CENTER, 220 Abraham Flexner Way, Zip 40202–1887; tel. 502/582–7400; Barth A. Weinberg, Vice President, Inpatient Rehabilitation **A**3 5 7 9 **F**1 2 3 4 5 7 8 9 10 11 12 13 14 15 16 17 18 19 20 21 22 23 24 25 26 27 28 29 30 31 32 33 34 35 36 37 38 39 40 41 42 43 44 45 46 47 48 49 50 51 52 53 54 55 56 57 58 59 60 61 63 64 65 66 67 68 70 71 72 73 74 **P**6 **S** Jewish Hospital HealthCare Services, Louisville, KY	23	46	95	1817	83	49009	0	26722	12417	349
⊞ JEWISH HOSPITAL, 217 East Chestnut Street, Zip 40202–1886; tel. 502/587–4011; Douglas E. Shaw, President (Total facility includes 97 beds in nursing home–type unit) **A**1 2 3 5 8 9 10 **F**1 2 3 4 5 6 7 8 9 10 11 12 13 14 15 16 17 18 19 20 21 22 23 24 25 26 27 28 29 30 31 32 33 34 35 36 37 38 39 40 41 42 43 44 45 46 47 48 49 50 51 52 53 54 55 56 57 58 59 60 61 63 64 65 66 67 68 70 71 72 73 74 **P**6 **S** Jewish Hospital HealthCare Services, Louisville, KY **Web address:** www.jhhs.org	23	10	539	21354	447	310547	0	281804	95599	2606
KOSAIR CHILDREN'S HOSPITAL See Norton Healthcare										
⊞ NORTON AUDUBON HOSPITAL, (Formerly Audubon Hospital), One Audubon Plaza Drive, Zip 40217–1397, Mailing Address: P.O. Box 17550, Zip 40217–0550; tel. 502/636–7111; Thomas D. Kmetz, Chief Administrative Officer (Nonreporting) **A**1 2 5 9 10 **S** Norton Healthcare, Louisville, KY	33	10	420	—	—	—	—	—	—	—
⊞ NORTON HEALTHCARE, (Formerly Alliant Hospitals), (Includes Kosair Children's Hospital, 231 East Chestnut Street, Zip 40202, Mailing Address: P.O. Box 35070, Zip 40232–5070; tel. 502/629–6000; Douglas J. Eighmey, Chief Administrative Officer), 200 East Chestnut Street, Zip 40202–1800, Mailing Address: P.O. Box 35070, Zip 40232–5070; tel. 502/629–8000; Stephen M. Tullman, Chief Administrative Officer (Total facility includes 17 beds in nursing home–type unit) **A**1 2 3 5 9 10 **F**3 4 5 7 8 9 10 11 12 13 14 15 16 17 19 20 21 22 23 24 26 28 29 30 31 32 34 35 37 38 40 41 42 43 44 45 46 47 49 52 53 54 55 56 57 58 59 61 64 65 67 68 70 71 72 73 74 **P**3 **S** Norton Healthcare, Louisville, KY **Web address:** www.northonhealthcare.org	23	10	646	28845	407	184005	5418	297590	97797	3693
⊞ NORTON HEALTHCARE PAVILION, (Formerly Alliant Medical Pavilion), 315 East Broadway, Zip 40202; tel. 502/629–2000; Stephen A. Williams, President and Chief Executive Officer (Nonreporting) **A**1 2 3 9 10 **S** Norton Healthcare, Louisville, KY	23	10	178	—	—	—	—	—	—	—
⊞ NORTON SOUTHWEST HOSPITAL, (Formerly Southwest Hospital), 9820 Third Street Road, Zip 40272–9984; tel. 502/933–8100; James W. Pope, Chief Administrative Officer (Total facility includes 23 beds in nursing home–type unit) **A**1 9 10 **F**4 7 8 9 10 11 12 13 17 19 21 22 23 24 25 28 30 32 33 35 37 38 40 41 42 43 44 45 46 47 49 50 53 54 55 56 57 58 59 61 63 64 65 66 67 70 71 72 73 74 **P**6 8 **S** Norton Healthcare, Louisville, KY	23	10	108	3293	48	31341	0	26713	11059	291
⊞ NORTON SUBURBAN HOSPITAL, (Formerly Suburban Hospital), 4001 Dutchmans Lane, Zip 40207–4799; tel. 502/893–1000; John A. Marshall, President and Chief Executive Officer **A**1 9 10 **F**2 3 4 7 8 9 10 11 12 13 14 15 16 17 18 19 21 22 23 24 25 26 28 29 32 33 34 35 37 38 39 40 41 42 43 44 45 46 47 49 50 52 53 54 55 56 57 58 59 60 61 63 64 65 66 67 68 70 71 72 73 74 **P**6 **S** Norton Healthcare, Louisville, KY	23	10	250	12228	164	90841	2572	73040	—	913
SOUTHWEST HOSPITAL See Norton Southwest Hospital										
SUBURBAN HOSPITAL See Norton Suburban Hospital										
□ TEN BROECK HOSPITAL, 8521 Old LaGrange Road, Zip 40242–3800; tel. 502/426–6380; Pat Hammer, Chief Executive Officer (Nonreporting) **A**1 9 10 **S** United Medical Corporation, Windermere, FL	33	22	94	—	—	—	—	—	—	—
⊞ UNIVERSITY OF LOUISVILLE HOSPITAL, 530 South Jackson Street, Zip 40202–3611; tel. 502/562–3000; James H. Taylor, President and Chief Executive Officer **A**1 2 3 5 8 9 10 **F**4 8 9 10 11 12 14 15 16 17 19 20 21 22 23 27 28 30 31 33 34 35 37 38 40 41 42 43 44 45 46 49 50 51 52 54 56 58 60 63 64 65 67 68 70 71 72 73 **P**4 7 **S** Jewish Hospital HealthCare Services, Louisville, KY **Web address:** www.ulh.org	23	10	272	12601	201	127604	1726	163191	52758	1837
□ VENCOR HOSPITAL–LOUISVILLE, 1313 St. Anthony Place, Zip 40204–1765; tel. 502/587–7001; James H. Wesp, Administrator (Total facility includes 37 beds in nursing home–type unit) **A**1 9 10 **F**8 16 19 21 34 35 42 44 60 64 65 71 **S** Vencor, Incorporated, Louisville, KY	33	10	156	480	90	9338	0	—	1219	650

Hospital, Address, Telephone, Administrator, Approval, Facility, and Physician Codes, Health Care System, Network	Classi-fication Codes		Utilization Data					Expense (thousands) of dollars		
★ American Hospital Association (AHA) membership ☐ Joint Commission on Accreditation of Healthcare Organizations (JCAHO) accreditation + American Osteopathic Healthcare Association (AOHA) membership ○ American Osteopathic Association (AOA) accreditation △ Commission on Accreditation of Rehabilitation Facilities (CARF) accreditation Control codes 61, 63, 64, 71, 72 and 73 indicate hospitals listed by AOHA, but not registered by AHA. For definition of numerical codes, see page A4	Control	Service	Staffed Beds	Admissions	Census	Outpatient Visits	Births	Total	Payroll	Personnel
✠ VETERANS AFFAIRS MEDICAL CENTER–LOUISVILLE, 800 Zorn Avenue, Zip 40206–1499; tel. 502/895–3401; Larry J. Sander, FACHE, Director **A**1 2 3 5 8 9 **F**3 4 8 10 11 16 19 20 24 25 27 28 30 31 32 33 35 37 39 42 44 45 46 49 51 52 54 55 58 60 64 65 67 70 71 73 74 **P**6 **S** Department of Veterans Affairs, Washington, DC **Web address:** www.va.gov/603louisville	45	10	104	4801	97	223591	0	103226	51657	1114
MADISONVILLE—Hopkins County										
✠ REGIONAL MEDICAL CENTER OF HOPKINS COUNTY, 900 Hospital Drive, Zip 42431–1694; tel. 502/825–5100; Bobby H. Dampier, Chief Executive Officer **A**1 2 3 5 9 10 **F**3 4 7 8 10 11 12 15 17 19 20 21 22 23 24 28 30 31 32 33 34 35 37 38 39 40 41 42 43 44 45 46 47 48 49 52 53 56 57 58 60 63 64 65 66 67 71 73 **P**6 **Web address:** www.regmedctr.com	23	10	327	10832	147	43435	838	75878	35197	1225
MANCHESTER—Clay County										
✠ MEMORIAL HOSPITAL, 401 Memorial Drive, Zip 40962–9156; tel. 606/598–5104; Jimm Bunch, Chief Executive Officer (Total facility includes 16 beds in nursing home–type unit) **A**1 9 10 **F**12 15 16 17 19 22 24 26 28 29 30 31 32 34 35 37 40 41 44 45 46 49 61 62 64 65 71 73 74 **P**6 **S** Adventist Health System Sunbelt Health Care Corporation, Winter Park, FL	21	10	61	2870	37	42827	308	18875	8260	325
MARION—Crittenden County										
✠ CRITTENDEN COUNTY HOSPITAL, Highway 60 South, Zip 42064, Mailing Address: P.O. Box 386, Zip 42064–0386; tel. 502/965–1018; Rick Napper, Chief Executive Officer **A**1 9 10 **F**7 8 12 15 19 22 28 30 32 33 34 35 37 39 40 41 42 44 45 46 49 51 54 56 57 64 65 67 71 **P**8 **S** Quorum Health Group/Quorum Health Resources, Inc., Brentwood, TN	23	10	50	2407	22	—	144	14643	5120	212
MARTIN—Floyd County										
✠ OUR LADY OF THE WAY HOSPITAL, 11022 Main Street, Zip 41649–0910; tel. 606/285–5181; Lowell Jones, Chief Executive Officer (Total facility includes 13 beds in nursing home–type unit) (Nonreporting) **A**1 9 10 **S** Catholic Health Initiatives, Denver, CO	21	10	39	—						
MAYFIELD—Graves County										
✠ PINELAKE REGIONAL HOSPITAL, 1099 Medical Center Circle, Zip 42066–1179, Mailing Address: P.O. Box 1099, Zip 42066–1099; tel. 502/251–4100; Mary Jo Lewis, Chief Executive Officer (Total facility includes 14 beds in nursing home–type unit) **A**1 9 10 **F**7 8 10 14 15 16 19 21 22 28 29 30 34 35 37 39 40 41 42 44 45 54 59 63 64 65 66 67 70 71 73 74 **P**1 2 3 5 6 7 8 **S** LifePoint Hospitals, Inc., Nashville, TN **Web address:** www.columbia.net	33	10	106	4027	53	74388	408	—	—	426
MAYSVILLE—Mason County										
✠ MEADOWVIEW REGIONAL MEDICAL CENTER, 989 Medical Park Drive, Zip 41056–8750; tel. 606/759–5311; Curtis B. Courtney, Chief Executive Officer (Total facility includes 10 beds in nursing home–type unit) **A**1 9 10 **F**7 8 10 11 12 15 16 18 19 21 22 28 30 33 35 37 38 39 40 42 44 46 49 52 53 54 55 56 58 60 64 65 70 71 73 74 **S** LifePoint Hospitals, Inc., Nashville, TN	33	10	65	3463	34	31533	489	21795	8545	352
MCDOWELL—Floyd County										
☐ MCDOWELL ARH HOSPITAL, Route 122, Zip 41647, Mailing Address: P.O. Box 247, Mc Dowell, Zip 41647–0247; tel. 606/377–3400; Dena C. Sparkman, Administrator (Nonreporting) **A**1 9 10 **S** Appalachian Regional Healthcare, Lexington, KY	23	10	74	—	—	—	—	—	—	—
MIDDLESBORO—Bell County										
☐ MIDDLESBORO APPALACHIAN REGIONAL HOSPITAL, 3600 West Cumberland Avenue, Zip 40965–2614, Mailing Address: P.O. Box 340, Zip 40965–0340; tel. 606/242–1101; Paul V. Miles, Administrator (Nonreporting) **A**1 9 10 **S** Appalachian Regional Healthcare, Lexington, KY	23	10	96							
MONTICELLO—Wayne County										
☐ WAYNE COUNTY HOSPITAL, 166 Hospital Street, Zip 42633–2416; tel. 606/348–9343; Eddy R. Stockton, Administrator **A**1 9 10 **F**8 12 14 15 16 19 22 26 33 44 46 49 58 65 71 73	23	10	30	742	11	35270	0	7344	2550	105
MOREHEAD—Rowan County										
✠ ST. CLAIRE MEDICAL CENTER, 222 Medical Circle, Zip 40351–1180; tel. 606/783–6500; Mark J. Neff, President and Chief Executive Officer **A**1 2 9 10 **F**3 7 8 10 14 15 16 17 18 19 20 21 22 25 26 28 29 30 31 32 33 34 35 37 39 40 41 42 44 46 49 51 52 53 54 55 56 57 58 59 60 63 65 67 71 73 74 **P**6	21	10	133	5199	61	342402	482	54685	26978	902
MORGANFIELD—Union County										
☐ METHODIST HOSPITAL UNION COUNTY, (Formerly Union County Methodist Hospital), 4604 Highway 60 West, Zip 42437–9570; tel. 502/389–3030; Patrick Donahue, Administrator (Total facility includes 16 beds in nursing home–type unit) **A**1 9 10 **F**8 12 15 16 19 20 26 28 30 32 33 35 37 39 44 49 53 56 57 58 64 65 71 73	21	10	53	557	19	17922	0	5426	2413	99
MOUNT STERLING—Montgomery County										
✠ GATEWAY REGIONAL HEALTH SYSTEM, Sterling Avenue, Zip 40353–1158, Mailing Address: P.O. Box 7, Zip 40353–0007; tel. 606/497–6000; Jeffrey L. Buckley, President and Chief Executive Officer (Total facility includes 40 beds in nursing home–type unit) **A**1 9 10 **F**7 8 11 12 14 15 16 17 19 20 21 22 28 30 35 37 39 40 41 42 44 46 49 51 56 63 64 65 71 73 74 **P**6 7	23	10	103	1962	63	50632	646	18995	7872	378

	Classification Codes		Utilization Data					Expense (thousands) of dollars		
Hospital, Address, Telephone, Administrator, Approval, Facility, and Physician Codes, Health Care System, Network	Control	Service	Staffed Beds	Admissions	Census	Outpatient Visits	Births	Total	Payroll	Personnel

Approval / accreditation key:

★ American Hospital Association (AHA) membership
□ Joint Commission on Accreditation of Healthcare Organizations (JCAHO) accreditation
+ American Osteopathic Healthcare Association (AOHA) membership
○ American Osteopathic Association (AOA) accreditation
△ Commission on Accreditation of Rehabilitation Facilities (CARF) accreditation
Control codes 61, 63, 64, 71, 72 and 73 indicate hospitals listed by AOHA, but not registered by AHA. For definition of numerical codes, see page A4

MOUNT VERNON—Rockcastle County

★ ROCKCASTLE HOSPITAL AND RESPIRATORY CARE CENTER, 145 Newcomb Avenue, Zip 40456–2733, Mailing Address: P.O. Box 1310, Zip 40456–1310; tel. 606/256–2195; Lee D. Keene, President and Chief Executive Officer (Total facility includes 60 beds in nursing home–type unit) **A**9 10 **F**8 14 15 16 19 21 22 34 49 64 65 71 **P**4 7

	23	10	86	1035	70	21261	0	—	—	308

MURRAY—Calloway County

⊞ MURRAY–CALLOWAY COUNTY HOSPITAL, 803 Poplar Street, Zip 42071–2432; tel. 502/762–1100; Stuart Poston, President (Total facility includes 226 beds in nursing home–type unit) **A**1 9 10 **F**1 7 8 10 12 15 16 17 19 20 21 22 26 28 29 30 32 33 34 35 37 39 40 41 42 44 46 49 54 55 56 57 58 60 63 64 65 67 70 71 73 74

	15	10	333	5364	287	153537	633	48774	21576	854

OWENSBORO—Daviess County

⊞ △ OWENSBORO MERCY HEALTH SYSTEM, (Includes HealthPark, 1006 Ford Avenue, Zip 42301; tel. 502/686–6100), 811 East Parrish Avenue, Zip 42303–3268, Mailing Address: P.O. Box 20007, Zip 42303–0007; tel. 502/688–2000; Greg L. Carlson, President and Chief Executive Officer (Total facility includes 30 beds in nursing home–type unit) **A**1 2 7 9 10 **F**2 3 4 7 8 10 11 12 14 15 16 17 19 21 22 23 24 25 26 27 28 29 30 31 32 33 34 35 37 39 40 41 42 43 44 45 46 48 49 52 54 55 56 57 58 60 63 64 65 66 67 71 72 73 74 **P**7

	23	10	377	17039	198	218166	1747	126387	51663	1936

RIVERVALLEY BEHAVIORAL HEALTH HOSPITAL, 1000 Industrial Drive, Zip 42301–8715; tel. 502/686–8477; Gayle DiCesare, President and Chief Officer **A**9 10 **F**3 16 25 52 53 54 55 56 57 58 59 **P**1
Web address: www.rvbh.com

	23	52	80	578	68	0	0	9134	4641	276

OWENTON—Owen County

OWEN COUNTY MEMORIAL HOSPITAL, 330 Roland Avenue, Zip 40359–1502; tel. 502/484–3441; Richard D. McLeod, Administrator (Total facility includes 20 beds in nursing home–type unit) (Nonreporting) **A**9 10

	33	10	50	—	—	—	—	—	—	—

PADUCAH—McCracken County

□ CHARTER BEHAVIORAL HEALTH SYSTEM OF PADUCAH, 435 Berger Road, Zip 42003–4579, Mailing Address: P.O. Box 7609, Zip 42002–7609; tel. 502/444–0444; Pat Harrod, Chief Executive Officer (Nonreporting) **A**1 9 10 **S** Magellan Health Services, Atlanta, GA

	33	22	56	—	—	—	—	—	—	—

□ LOURDES HOSPITAL, 1530 Lone Oak Road, Zip 42003, Mailing Address: P.O. Box 7100, Zip 42002–7100; tel. 502/444–2444; Robert P. Goodwin, President and Chief Executive Officer (Total facility includes 30 beds in nursing home–type unit) **A**1 9 10 **F**1 4 7 8 10 11 12 14 15 16 17 19 21 22 23 24 25 26 27 28 29 30 32 33 34 35 37 39 41 42 43 44 45 46 48 49 52 55 56 60 64 65 66 67 71 72 73 **P**5 7 8 **S** Catholic Healthcare Partners, Cincinnati, OH
Web address: www.lourdes–pad.org

	21	10	389	10953	168	202555	524	90343	38981	1349

⊞ WESTERN BAPTIST HOSPITAL, 2501 Kentucky Avenue, Zip 42003–3200; tel. 502/575–2100; Larry O. Barton, President **A**1 9 10 **F**2 3 4 7 8 10 11 12 15 16 17 19 21 22 24 27 28 29 30 32 34 35 37 38 39 40 41 42 43 44 45 48 49 51 52 53 54 55 56 57 58 59 60 64 65 67 71 72 73 74 **P**5 7 8 **S** Baptist Healthcare System, Louisville, KY

	21	10	267	12641	180	104928	1063	98930	38576	1232

PAINTSVILLE—Johnson County

□ PAUL B. HALL REGIONAL MEDICAL CENTER, 625 James S Trimble Boulevard, Zip 41240–1055, Mailing Address: P.O. Box 1487, Zip 41240–1487; tel. 606/789–3511; Deborah C. Trimble, Administrator (Nonreporting) **A**1 9 10 **S** Health Management Associates, Naples, FL

	33	10	72	—	—	—	—	—	—	—

PARIS—Bourbon County

⊞ BOURBON COMMUNITY HOSPITAL, 9 Linville Drive, Zip 40361–2196; tel. 606/987–1000; Rob Smart, Chief Executive Officer **A**1 9 10 **F**3 8 10 11 14 15 16 19 22 28 35 37 41 44 46 49 52 53 65 71 73 **P**7 **S** LifePoint Hospitals, Inc., Nashville, TN

	33	10	58	1570	20	27531	0	12817	4898	187

PIKEVILLE—Pike County

⊞ PIKEVILLE UNITED METHODIST HOSPITAL OF KENTUCKY, 911 South Bypass, Zip 41501–1595; tel. 606/437–3500; kathy Shaughnessy, Chief Operating Officer **A**1 2 9 10 **F**7 8 10 11 12 13 14 15 16 17 19 20 21 22 23 25 26 27 28 29 30 31 35 36 37 38 39 40 41 42 44 45 46 49 52 56 57 58 59 60 65 67 70 71 72 73 74

	23	10	181	8458	109	145108	936	—	—	—

PINEVILLE—Bell County

⊞ PINEVILLE COMMUNITY HOSPITAL ASSOCIATION, 850 Riverview Avenue, Zip 40977–0850; tel. 606/337–3051; J. Milton Brooks, III, Administrator (Total facility includes 30 beds in nursing home–type unit) **A**1 9 10 **F**7 8 12 16 19 20 21 22 28 30 32 34 37 39 40 44 46 49 64 65 71 73

	23	10	150	4102	55	24294	248	17682	8256	317

PRESTONSBURG—Floyd County

⊞ HIGHLANDS REGIONAL MEDICAL CENTER, 5000 Kentucky Route 321, Zip 41653, Mailing Address: P.O. Box 668, Zip 41653–0668; tel. 606/886–8511; Harold C. Warman, Jr., President and Chief Executive Officer (Nonreporting) **A**1 2 9 10

	23	10	184	—	—	—	—	—	—	—

PRINCETON—Caldwell County

⊞ CALDWELL COUNTY HOSPITAL, 101 Hospital Drive, Zip 42445–0410, Mailing Address: Box 410, Zip 42445–0410; tel. 502/365–0300; Robert R. Stanley, Interim Chief Executive Officer (Nonreporting) **A**1 9 10 **S** Quorum Health Group/Quorum Health Resources, Inc., Brentwood, TN

	23	10	15	—	—	—	—	—	—	—

Hospital, Address, Telephone, Administrator, Approval, Facility, and Physician Codes, Health Care System, Network	Classi-fication Codes		Utilization Data					Expense (thousands) of dollars		
	Control	Service	Staffed Beds	Admissions	Census	Outpatient Visits	Births	Total	Payroll	Personnel

★ American Hospital Association (AHA) membership
□ Joint Commission on Accreditation of Healthcare Organizations (JCAHO) accreditation
+ American Osteopathic Healthcare Association (AOHA) membership
○ American Osteopathic Association (AOA) accreditation
△ Commission on Accreditation of Rehabilitation Facilities (CARF) accreditation
Control codes 61, 63, 64, 71, 72 and 73 indicate hospitals listed by AOHA, but not registered by AHA. For definition of numerical codes, see page A4

	Control	Service	Staffed Beds	Admissions	Census	Outpatient Visits	Births	Total	Payroll	Personnel
RADCLIFF—Hardin County										
⊠ LINCOLN TRAIL BEHAVIORAL HEALTH SYSTEM, 3909 South Wilson Road, Zip 40160–9714, Mailing Address: P.O. Box 369, Zip 40159–0369; tel. 502/351–9444; Melvin E. Modderman, Administrator **A**1 9 10 **F**2 3 14 15 16 17 22 25 34 52 53 54 55 56 57 58 59 65 73	33	22	67	782	33	10426	0	5846	3162	101
RICHMOND—Madison County										
⊠ PATTIE A. CLAY HOSPITAL, EKU By–Pass, Zip 40475, Mailing Address: P.O. Box 1600, Zip 40476–2603; tel. 606/625–3131; Richard M. Thomas, President **A**1 9 10 **F**7 8 10 12 15 16 17 19 21 22 26 28 30 34 37 39 40 41 44 45 46 49 61 63 65 67 71 72 73 74 **S** Jewish Hospital HealthCare Services, Louisville, KY	23	10	80	4057	42	76041	911	29682	13368	475
RUSSELL SPRINGS—Russell County										
RUSSELL COUNTY HOSPITAL, Dowell Road, Zip 42642, Mailing Address: P.O. Box 1610, Zip 42642–1610; tel. 502/866–4141; Richard Hacker, Interim Administrator **A**9 10 **F**8 11 12 14 15 16 19 20 21 22 28 32 33 39 44 45 49 64 65 71 73 **S** Norton Healthcare, Louisville, KY	13	10	45	816	9	24528	0	8142	3403	155
RUSSELLVILLE—Logan County										
⊠ LOGAN MEMORIAL HOSPITAL, 1625 South Nashville Road, Zip 42276–8834, Mailing Address: P.O. Box 10, Zip 42276–0010; tel. 502/726–4011; Michael Clark, Chief Executive Officer (Total facility includes 8 beds in nursing home–type unit) **A**1 9 10 **F**2 4 6 7 8 9 10 11 15 16 18 19 20 21 22 23 26 27 28 29 30 31 32 33 35 36 37 38 39 40 41 42 43 44 47 48 49 52 60 64 65 67 69 70 71 72 73 74 **S** LifePoint Hospitals, Inc., Nashville, TN	33	10	63	1707	20	24748	156	13925	4874	184
SALEM—Livingston County										
★ LIVINGSTON HOSPITAL AND HEALTHCARE SERVICES, 131 Hospital Drive, Zip 42078; tel. 502/988–2299; Lennis Thompson, Chief Executive Officer **A**9 10 **F**8 14 15 16 17 19 22 28 30 32 33 35 42 44 46 48 49 71	23	10	26	1055	11	13457	0	8478	3302	132
SCOTTSVILLE—Allen County										
MEDICAL CENTER AT SCOTTSVILLE See The Medical Center at Bowling Green, Bowling Green										
SHELBYVILLE—Shelby County										
⊠ JEWISH HOSPITAL–SHELBYVILLE, 727 Hospital Drive, Zip 40065–1699; tel. 502/647–4000; Timothy L. Jarm, President (Total facility includes 8 beds in nursing home–type unit) **A**1 9 10 **F**2 4 7 8 9 10 11 12 13 14 15 16 17 18 19 21 22 23 24 25 26 27 28 29 30 31 32 33 34 35 37 39 40 41 42 43 44 45 46 48 49 50 52 53 54 55 56 57 58 59 60 62 63 64 65 66 67 68 70 71 73 74 **S** Jewish Hospital HealthCare Services, Louisville, KY **Web address:** www.jhhs.org	23	10	58	2645	36	32734	244	20222	9730	279
SOMERSET—Pulaski County										
⊠ △ LAKE CUMBERLAND REGIONAL HOSPITAL, 305 Langdon Street, Zip 42501, Mailing Address: P.O. Box 620, Zip 42502–2750; tel. 606/679–7441; Jon C. O'Shaughnessy, President and Chief Executive Officer (Nonreporting) **A**1 2 7 9 10 **S** LifePoint Hospitals, Inc., Nashville, TN	33	10	227	—	—	—	—	—	—	—
SOUTH WILLIAMSON—Pike County										
□ WILLIAMSON ARH HOSPITAL, 260 Hospital Drive, Zip 41503–4072; tel. 606/237–1700; Louis G. Roe, Jr., Administrator (Total facility includes 50 beds in nursing home–type unit) **A**1 9 10 **F**4 7 8 12 13 15 16 17 19 22 25 28 30 32 34 35 37 39 40 42 44 49 52 54 56 57 58 60 63 64 65 73 **P**2 3 5 6 **S** Appalachian Regional Healthcare, Lexington, KY **Web address:** www.arh.org	23	10	148	4170	101	54114	113	29393	10092	277
STANFORD—Lincoln County										
⊠ FORT LOGAN HOSPITAL, 124 Portman Avenue, Zip 40484–1200; tel. 606/365–2187; Terry C. Powers, Administrator (Total facility includes 30 beds in nursing home–type unit) **A**1 9 10 **F**7 8 14 19 20 22 26 30 31 40 44 45 49 64 65 71 73	23	10	73	1268	41	12643	138	7633	3496	166
TOMPKINSVILLE—Monroe County										
⊠ MONROE COUNTY MEDICAL CENTER, 529 Capp Harlan Road, Zip 42167–1840; tel. 502/487–9231; Mark E. Thompson, Chief Executive Officer (Nonreporting) **A**1 9 10 **S** Quorum Health Group/Quorum Health Resources, Inc., Brentwood, TN	23	10	49	—	—	—	—	—	—	—
VERSAILLES—Woodford County										
★ WOODFORD HOSPITAL, 360 Amsden Avenue, Zip 40383–1286; tel. 606/873–3111; Nancy Littrell, Chief Executive Officer (Total facility includes 23 beds in nursing home–type unit) (Nonreporting) **A**9 10	23	10	73	—	—	—	—	—	—	—
WEST LIBERTY—Morgan County										
□ MORGAN COUNTY APPALACHIAN REGIONAL HOSPITAL, 476 Liberty Road, Zip 41472–2049, Mailing Address: P.O. Box 579, Zip 41472–0579; tel. 606/743–3186; Dennis R. Chaney, Administrator (Total facility includes 25 beds in nursing home–type unit) **A**1 9 10 **F**8 12 15 16 17 19 22 25 28 29 30 32 33 34 40 44 45 46 49 51 64 65 67 71 73 **S** Appalachian Regional Healthcare, Lexington, KY **Web address:** www.2.arh.org	23	10	45	901	33	42096	0	9421	4767	133
WHITESBURG—Letcher County										
□ WHITESBURG APPALACHIAN REGIONAL HOSPITAL, 240 Hospital Road, Zip 41858–1254; tel. 606/633–3600; Donnie Fields, Administrator (Nonreporting) **A**1 9 10 **S** Appalachian Regional Healthcare, Lexington, KY	23	10	71	—	—	—	—	—	—	—
WILLIAMSTOWN—Grant County										
ST. ELIZABETH MEDICAL CENTER–GRANT COUNTY, 238 Barnes Road, Zip 41097–9460; tel. 606/824–2400; Chris Carle, Administrator **A**9 10 **F**14 15 16 19 22 33 65 71 **S** Catholic Healthcare Partners, Cincinnati, OH	21	10	20	320	3	34474	0	5088	1908	—

Hospital, Address, Telephone, Administrator, Approval, Facility, and Physician Codes, Health Care System, Network	Classi- fication Codes		Utilization Data					Expense (thousands) of dollars		
★ American Hospital Association (AHA) membership □ Joint Commission on Accreditation of Healthcare Organizations (JCAHO) accreditation + American Osteopathic Healthcare Association (AOHA) membership ○ American Osteopathic Association (AOA) accreditation △ Commission on Accreditation of Rehabilitation Facilities (CARF) accreditation Control codes 61, 63, 64, 71, 72 and 73 indicate hospitals listed by AOHA, but not registered by AHA. For definition of numerical codes, see page A4	Control	Service	Staffed Beds	Admissions	Census	Outpatient Visits	Births	Total	Payroll	Personnel

WINCHESTER—Clark County

☒ CLARK REGIONAL MEDICAL CENTER, West Lexington Avenue, Zip 40391, Mailing Address: P.O. Box 630, Zip 40392–0630; tel. 606/745–3500; Robert D. Fraraccio, Chief Executive Officer (Nonreporting) **A**1 9 10

	Control	Service	Staffed Beds	Admissions	Census	Outpatient Visits	Births	Total	Payroll	Personnel
	23	10	75	—	—	—	—	—	—	—

LOUISIANA

Resident population 4,369 (in thousands)
Resident population in metro areas 74.9%
Birth rate per 1,000 population 15.1
65 years and over 11.4%
Percent of persons without health insurance 20.9%

Hospital, Address, Telephone, Administrator, Approval, Facility, and Physician Codes, Health Care System, Network	Classification Codes		Utilization Data					Expense (thousands) of dollars		
	Control	Service	Staffed Beds	Admissions	Census	Outpatient Visits	Births	Total	Payroll	Personnel

★ American Hospital Association (AHA) membership
□ Joint Commission on Accreditation of Healthcare Organizations (JCAHO) accreditation
+ American Osteopathic Healthcare Association (AOHA) membership
○ American Osteopathic Association (AOA) accreditation
△ Commission on Accreditation of Rehabilitation Facilities (CARF) accreditation
   Control codes 61, 63, 64, 71, 72 and 73 indicate hospitals listed by AOHA, but not registered by AHA. For definition of numerical codes, see page A4

Hospital	Control	Service	Staffed Beds	Admissions	Census	Outpatient Visits	Births	Total	Payroll	Personnel
ABBEVILLE—Vermilion Parish										
□ ABBEVILLE GENERAL HOSPITAL, 118 North Hospital Drive, Zip 70510–4077, Mailing Address: P.O. Box 580, Zip 70511–0580; tel. 318/893–5466; Ray A. Landry, Administrator **A**1 9 10 **F**7 8 14 15 16 19 21 22 27 32 33 34 35 37 39 40 42 44 48 51 52 57 58 59 65 71 73	16	10	81	3701	57	49890	196	20354	10014	321
ALEXANDRIA—Rapides Parish										
⊞ △ CHRISTUS ST. FRANCES CABRINI HOSPITAL, (Formerly St. Frances Cabrini Hospital), 3330 Masonic Drive, Zip 71301–3899; tel. 318/487–1122; Daniel J. Rissing, Acting Chief Executive Officer (Total facility includes 19 beds in nursing home–type unit) (Nonreporting) **A**1 2 7 10 **S** Christus Health, Houston, TX	23	10	227	—	—	—	—	—	—	—
⊞ RAPIDES REGIONAL MEDICAL CENTER, 211 Fourth Street, Zip 71301–8421, Mailing Address: Box 30101, Zip 71301–8421; tel. 318/473–3000; A. C. Buchanan, President and Chief Executive Officer **A**1 2 3 5 9 10 **F**1 3 4 5 6 7 8 10 12 13 14 15 17 18 19 20 21 22 23 24 25 26 27 28 29 30 31 32 33 34 35 36 37 39 40 41 42 43 44 45 46 47 49 50 51 52 53 54 55 56 57 58 59 60 61 62 63 64 65 66 67 69 70 71 72 73 74 **S** Columbia/HCA Healthcare Corporation, Nashville, TN Web address: www.rapidesregional.com	32	10	359	13449	187	111644	1655	100537	44375	1402
⊞ VETERANS AFFAIRS MEDICAL CENTER, Shreveport Highway, Zip 71306–6002; tel. 318/473–0010; Allan S. Goss, Director (Total facility includes 149 beds in nursing home–type unit) **A**1 2 3 5 **F**3 8 12 15 17 19 20 21 22 25 26 27 28 30 31 32 33 34 35 37 39 41 42 44 46 49 51 52 54 56 57 58 60 61 64 65 67 71 73 74 **P**6 **S** Department of Veterans Affairs, Washington, DC	45	10	257	2483	250	123240	0	73181	45946	938
AMITE—Tangipahoa Parish										
★ HOOD MEMORIAL HOSPITAL, 301 West Walnut Street, Zip 70422–2098; tel. 504/748–9485; A. D. Richardson, Administrator (Nonreporting) **A**9 10	16	10	40	—	—	—	—	—	—	—
BASTROP—Morehouse Parish										
⊞ MOREHOUSE GENERAL HOSPITAL, 323 West Walnut Street, Zip 71220–4521, Mailing Address: P.O. Box 1060, Zip 71221–1060; tel. 318/283–3600; William W. Bing, Administrator (Total facility includes 24 beds in nursing home–type unit) **A**1 9 10 **F**1 7 8 9 11 14 15 16 19 20 21 22 26 28 29 30 32 33 34 35 37 39 40 41 42 44 45 46 49 51 52 55 57 63 64 65 67 68 71 73 **P**6 7 Web address: www.mghospital.com	16	10	106	3740	55	39685	429	29481	11939	425
BATON ROUGE—East Baton Rouge Parish										
★ △ BATON ROUGE GENERAL HEALTH CENTER, 8585 Picardy Avenue, Zip 70809–3679, Mailing Address: P.O. Box 84330, Zip 70884–4330; tel. 225/763–4500; Margare Peterson, Ph.D., Administrator **A**7 9 **F**1 3 4 6 7 8 9 10 11 12 14 15 16 17 19 21 22 23 24 26 32 34 35 37 38 40 41 42 43 44 47 48 49 52 53 56 57 58 60 61 65 67 71 72 73 74 **P**3 4 6 7 **S** General Health System, Baton Rouge, LA Web address: www.generalhealth.org	23	10	72	2793	29	26591	733	27148	9528	125
⊞ BATON ROUGE GENERAL MEDICAL CENTER, 3600 Florida Street, Zip 70806–3889, Mailing Address: P.O. Box 2511, Zip 70821–2511; tel. 225/387–7770; Milton R. Siepman, Ph.D., President and Chief Executive Officer **A**1 2 3 5 6 8 9 10 **F**1 2 3 4 6 7 8 9 10 11 12 13 14 15 16 17 19 21 22 23 24 26 30 32 33 34 35 37 38 40 41 42 43 44 47 48 49 51 52 53 54 55 56 57 58 59 60 61 65 66 71 72 73 **P**3 4 6 7 **S** General Health System, Baton Rouge, LA Web address: www.generalhealth.org	23	10	371	11157	214	109529	0	110111	47496	1676
□ BHC MEADOW WOOD HOSPITAL, 9032 Perkins Road, Zip 70810–1507; tel. 225/766–8553; Ralph J. Waite, III, Chief Executive Officer (Nonreporting) **A**1 10 **S** Behavioral Healthcare Corporation, Nashville, TN	33	22	55	—	—	—	—	—	—	—
COLUMBIA MEDICAL CENTER See Summit Hospital										
□ CONCORD HOSPITAL, 2414 Bunker Hill Drive, Zip 70808–3394; tel. 504/925–1290; Joseph Rodriguez, Chief Executive Officer (Nonreporting) **A**1 10	33	22	170	—	—	—	—	—	—	—
⊞ EARL K. LONG MEDICAL CENTER, 5825 Airline Highway, Zip 70805–2498; tel. 225/358–1000; Jonathan Roberts, Dr.PH, Chief Executive Officer **A**1 3 5 10 **F**7 8 14 15 16 19 22 31 34 37 38 40 42 44 46 47 49 52 61 65 71 73 **P**1 **S** LSU Medical Center Health Care Services Division, Baton Rouge, LA	12	10	204	10174	152	196392	1648	79311	26648	—
□ △ HEALTHSOUTH REHABILITATION HOSPITAL OF BATON ROUGE, (Formerly Rehabilitation Hospital of Baton Rouge), 8595 United Plaza Boulevard, Zip 70809–2251; tel. 225/927–0567; Michael D. Marshall, Chief Executive Officer (Nonreporting) **A**1 7 10 **S** HEALTHSOUTH Corporation, Birmingham, AL	33	46	80	—	—	—	—	—	—	—
HEALTHSOUTH REHABILITATION HOSPITAL OF SOUTH LOUISIANA, 4040 North Boulevard, Zip 70806–3829; tel. 504/383–5055; Michael D. Marshall, Chief Executive Officer (Nonreporting) **A**10 **S** HEALTHSOUTH Corporation, Birmingham, AL	33	46	40	—	—	—	—	—	—	—

Hospital, Address, Telephone, Administrator, Approval, Facility, and Physician Codes, Health Care System, Network	Classi-fication Codes		Utilization Data					Expense (thousands) of dollars		
★ American Hospital Association (AHA) membership □ Joint Commission on Accreditation of Healthcare Organizations (JCAHO) accreditation + American Osteopathic Healthcare Association (AOHA) membership ○ American Osteopathic Association (AOA) accreditation △ Commission on Accreditation of Rehabilitation Facilities (CARF) accreditation Control codes 61, 63, 64, 71, 72 and 73 indicate hospitals listed by AOHA, but not registered by AHA. For definition of numerical codes, see page A4	Control	Service	Staffed Beds	Admissions	Census	Outpatient Visits	Births	Total	Payroll	Personnel
✠ △ OUR LADY OF THE LAKE REGIONAL MEDICAL CENTER, (Includes Our Lady of the Lake–Assumption, 135 Highway 402, Napoleonville, Zip 70390; tel. 504/369–3600), 5000 Hennessy Boulevard, Zip 70808–4350; tel. 225/765–6565; Robert C. Davidge, Chief Executive Officer (Total facility includes 48 beds in nursing home–type unit) **A**1 2 7 9 10 **F**1 2 3 4 6 7 8 10 11 14 15 16 17 18 19 21 22 23 24 26 27 28 29 30 31 32 33 34 35 37 39 41 42 43 44 45 46 47 48 49 50 51 52 53 54 55 56 57 58 59 60 62 63 64 65 66 67 68 71 73 74 **P**1 **S** Franciscan Missionaries of Our Lady Health System, Inc., Baton Rouge, LA	21	10	660	23343	430	256603	0	—	—	3028
REHABILITATION HOSPITAL OF BATON ROUGE See HEALTHSOUTH Rehabilitation Hospital of Baton Rouge										
✠ SUMMIT HOSPITAL, (Formerly Columbia Medical Center), 17000 Medical Center Drive, Zip 70816–3224; tel. 225/755–4800; Steve Grimm, CHE, Chief Executive Officer **A**1 10 **F**11 12 14 15 16 19 21 22 37 44 48 49 52 57 64 71 73 **S** Quorum Health Group/Quorum Health Resources, Inc., Brentwood, TN	33	10	143	1663	26	35826	0	19471	8431	272
✠ WOMAN'S HOSPITAL, 9050 Airline Highway, Zip 70815–4192, Mailing Address: P.O. Box 95009, Zip 70895–9009; tel. 225/927–1300; Teri G. Fontenot, President and Chief Executive Officer **A**1 2 9 10 **F**7 8 12 14 15 16 17 18 19 24 25 28 29 30 32 34 37 38 39 40 41 42 44 45 46 49 61 65 67 68 71 73 74 **Web address:** www.womans.com	23	44	222	11389	110	107690	7008	85576	41382	1151
BERNICE—Union Parish										
TRI–WARD GENERAL HOSPITAL, 409 First Street, Zip 71222–9709, Mailing Address: P.O. Box 697, Zip 71222–0697; tel. 318/285–9066; Charolette Thompson, Administrator (Nonreporting) **A**9 10	16	10	11	—	—	—	—	—	—	—
BOGALUSA—Washington Parish										
✠ BOGALUSA COMMUNITY MEDICAL CENTER, 433 Plaza Street, Zip 70427–3793; tel. 504/732–7122; Terry G. Whittington, Chief Executive Officer and Administrator **A**1 9 10 **F**7 11 15 19 21 22 26 32 35 40 41 44 45 49 64 65 71 73 **S** Quorum Health Group/Quorum Health Resources, Inc., Brentwood, TN	23	10	101	3112	54	40163	20	17003	7756	312
✠ WASHINGTON–ST. TAMMANY REGIONAL MEDICAL CENTER, 400 Memphis Street, Zip 70427–0040, Mailing Address: Box 40, Zip 70429–0040; tel. 504/735–1322; Larry R. King, Administrator (Nonreporting) **A**1 10 **S** LSU Medical Center Health Care Services Division, Baton Rouge, LA	12	10	55	—	—	—	—	—	—	—
BOSSIER CITY—Bossier Parish										
✠ BOSSIER MEDICAL CENTER, 2105 Airline Drive, Zip 71111–3190; tel. 318/741–6000; Jack F. Houghton, Chief Executive Officer (Total facility includes 20 beds in nursing home–type unit) **A**1 9 10 **F**4 7 8 10 12 15 16 17 19 22 23 25 26 27 28 29 30 32 33 34 35 37 39 40 41 43 44 46 48 49 51 52 57 63 64 65 66 71 72 73 74 **P**5 8	14	10	152	4077	59	124600	234	46442	20903	734
□ SUMMIT HOSPITAL OF NORTHWEST LOUISIANA, 4900 Medical Drive, Zip 71112–4596; tel. 318/747–9500; Louise Wiggins, Chief Executive Officer and Administrator (Nonreporting) **A**1 10 **S** Summit Hospital Corporation, Atlanta, GA	33	22	54	—	—	—	—	—	—	—
BREAUX BRIDGE—St. Martin Parish										
GARY MEMORIAL HOSPITAL, 210 Champagne Boulevard, Zip 70517–3852, Mailing Address: Box 357, Zip 70517–0357; tel. 318/332–2178; Burton Dupuis, Administrator (Nonreporting) **A**9 10	16	10	12	—	—	—	—	—	—	—
BUNKIE—Avoyelles Parish										
★ BUNKIE GENERAL HOSPITAL, Evergreen Highway, Zip 71322, Mailing Address: P.O. Box 380, Zip 71322–0380; tel. 318/346–6681; Donald L. Kannady, Administrator **A**9 10 **F**1 8 12 15 16 19 22 24 26 28 30 32 35 44 52 57 59 65 70 71 **P**1	16	10	41	620	8	17343	0	6868	2554	101
CAMERON—Cameron Parish										
SOUTH CAMERON MEMORIAL HOSPITAL, 5360 West Creole Highway, Zip 70631–5127; tel. 318/542–4111; Joseph L. Soileau, Chief Executive Officer (Nonreporting) **A**9 10	16	10	33	—	—	—	—	—	—	—
CHALMETTE—St. Bernard Parish										
□ CHALMETTE MEDICAL CENTER, (Includes Virtue Street Medical Pavilion, 801 Virtue Street, Zip 70043), 9001 Patricia Street, Zip 70043–1799; tel. 504/277–8011; Larry M. Graham, Chief Executive Officer **A**1 9 10 **F**8 10 12 15 16 17 19 21 22 25 26 27 28 29 30 35 37 41 43 44 45 46 49 60 65 67 70 71 73 **P**8 **S** Universal Health Services, Inc., King of Prussia, PA	33	10	106	4867	73	36586	0	—	—	379
CHURCH POINT—Acadia Parish										
ACADIA–ST. LANDRY HOSPITAL, 810 South Broadway Street, Zip 70525–4497; tel. 318/684–5435; Alcus Trahan, Administrator (Nonreporting) **A**9 10	23	10	39	—	—	—	—	—	—	—
COLUMBIA—Caldwell Parish										
CALDWELL MEMORIAL HOSPITAL, 411 Main Street, Zip 71418, Mailing Address: P.O. Box 899, Zip 71418–0899; tel. 318/649–6111; Faye Long, Administrator (Nonreporting) **A**10	33	10	31	—	—	—	—	—	—	—
COUSHATTA—Red River Parish										
CHRISTUS COUSHATTA HEALTH CARE CENTER, (Formerly Sisters of Charity Coushatta Health Care Center), 1635 Marvel Street, Zip 71019–9022, Mailing Address: P.O. Box 589, Zip 71019–0369; tel. 318/932–2000; Sister Laureen Painter, Chief Executive Officer (Nonreporting) **A**9 10 **S** Christus Health, Houston, TX	23	10	74	—	—	—	—	—	—	—
COVINGTON—St. Tammany Parish										
COLUMBIA LAKEVIEW REGIONAL MEDICAL CENTER See Lakeview Regional Medical Center										

Hospital, Address, Telephone, Administrator, Approval, Facility, and Physician Codes, Health Care System, Network	Classi-fication Codes		Utilization Data					Expense (thousands) of dollars		
	Control	Service	Staffed Beds	Admissions	Census	Outpatient Visits	Births	Total	Payroll	Personnel

★ American Hospital Association (AHA) membership
☐ Joint Commission on Accreditation of Healthcare Organizations (JCAHO) accreditation
+ American Osteopathic Healthcare Association (AOHA) membership
○ American Osteopathic Association (AOA) accreditation
△ Commission on Accreditation of Rehabilitation Facilities (CARF) accreditation
Control codes 61, 63, 64, 71, 72 and 73 indicate hospitals listed by AOHA, but not registered by AHA. For definition of numerical codes, see page A4

Hospital	Control	Service	Staffed Beds	Admissions	Census	Outpatient Visits	Births	Total	Payroll	Personnel
☐ GREENBRIER BEHAVIORAL HEALTH SYSTEM, 201 Greenbrier Boulevard, Zip 70433–9126; tel. 504/893–2970; Cheryl M. Schleuss, Chief Executive Officer (Nonreporting) **A**1 10 **S** Ramsay Health Care, Inc., Coral Gables, FL	33	22	66	—	—	—	—	—	—	—
⊞ LAKEVIEW REGIONAL MEDICAL CENTER, (Formerly Columbia Lakeview Regional Medical Center), 95 East Fairway Drive, Zip 70433–7507; tel. 504/867–3800; Darrell Blaylock, Chief Executive Officer (Nonreporting) **A**1 10 **S** Columbia/HCA Healthcare Corporation, Nashville, TN	33	10	163	—	—	—	—	—	—	—
⊞ ST. TAMMANY PARISH HOSPITAL, 1202 South Tyler Street, Zip 70433–2394; tel. 504/898–4000; Thomas J. Stone, Administrator (Nonreporting) **A**1 2 9 10 **Web address:** www.tamnet.com/dc/stphosp	16	10	131	—	—	—	—	—	—	—
CROWLEY—Acadia Parish										
★ AMERICAN LEGION HOSPITAL, 1305 Crowley Rayne Highway, Zip 70526–9410; tel. 318/783–3222; Terry W. Osborne, Chief Executive Officer **A**9 10 **F**15 16 19 22 32 37 40 44 52 65 71 **P**2 **Web address:** www.alh.org	23	10	178	3509	35	31230	475	21199	8902	423
CUT OFF—Lafourche Parish										
⊞ LADY OF THE SEA GENERAL HOSPITAL, 200 West 134th Place, Zip 70345–4145; tel. 504/632–6401; Lane M. Cheramie, Chief Executive Officer (Nonreporting) **A**1 9 10 **S** Brim Healthcare, Inc., Brentwood, TN	16	10	55	—	—	—	—	—	—	—
DE RIDDER—Beauregard Parish										
⊞ BEAUREGARD MEMORIAL HOSPITAL, 600 South Pine Street, Zip 70634–4998, Mailing Address: P.O. Box 730, Zip 70634–0730; tel. 318/462–7100; Theodore J. Badger, Jr., Chief Executive Officer **A**1 9 10 **F**8 10 15 16 19 20 21 22 23 24 28 30 32 33 34 37 42 44 49 63 64 65 71 73 **P**1 8 **Web address:** www.beauregard.org	16	10	93	4647	53	29329	645	21333	9825	362
DELHI—Richland Parish										
RICHLAND PARISH HOSPITAL–DELHI, 407 Cincinnati Street, Zip 71232–3009; tel. 318/878–5171; Michael W. Carroll, Administrator (Nonreporting) **A**9 10	16	10	42	—	—	—	—	—	—	—
DEQUINCY—Calcasieu Parish										
DEQUINCY MEMORIAL HOSPITAL, 110 West Fourth Street, Zip 70633–3508, Mailing Address: P.O. Box 1166, Zip 70633–1166; tel. 318/786–1200; Michael E. Daiken, Administrator (Nonreporting) **A**9 10	14	10	41	—	—	—	—	—	—	—
DONALDSONVILLE—Ascension Parish										
⊞ PREVOST MEMORIAL HOSPITAL, 301 Memorial Drive, Zip 70346–4376, Mailing Address: P.O. Box 186, Zip 70346–0186; tel. 225/473–7931; Vince A. Cataldo, Administrator **A**1 9 10 **F**8 22 28 44 62 63 64 73 **P**4 7	16	10	35	260	4	12431	0	3390	1435	55
EUNICE—St. Landry Parish										
⊞ EUNICE COMMUNITY MEDICAL CENTER, (Formerly Moosa Memorial Hospital), 400 Moosa Boulevard, Zip 70535; tel. 318/457–5244; Mark L. Manuel, Administrator (Nonreporting) **A**1 9 10 **S** Province Healthcare Corporation, Brentwood, TN	16	10	67	—	—	—	—	—	—	—
FARMERVILLE—Union Parish										
UNION GENERAL HOSPITAL, 901 James Avenue, Zip 71241–2234, Mailing Address: P.O. Box 398, Zip 71241–0398; tel. 318/368–9751; Evalyn Ormond, Administrator **A**9 10 **F**12 19 21 22 28 32 35 44 49 52 57 65 71	23	10	27	670	8	25502	0	5196	2110	74
FERRIDAY—Concordia Parish										
PROFESSIONAL REHABILITATION HOSPITAL, 6818–A Highway 84, Zip 71334; tel. 318/757–7575; Bobby E. Ewell, Executive Director (Nonreporting) **A**10	33	46	40	—	—	—	—	—	—	—
RIVERLAND MEDICAL CENTER, 1700 North E 'E' Wallace Boulevard, Zip 71334, Mailing Address: P.O. Box 111, Zip 71334–0111; tel. 318/757–6551; Vernon R. Stevens, Jr., Administrator (Nonreporting) **A**9 10	16	10	49	—	—	—	—	—	—	—
FORT POLK—Vernon Parish										
⊞ BAYNE–JONES ARMY COMMUNITY HOSPITAL, 1585 Third Street, Zip 71459–5110; tel. 318/531–3928; Lieutenant Colonel Mark D. Moore, Deputy Commander and Administrator **A** **F**2 3 4 8 9 10 11 12 15 16 19 20 21 22 26 27 28 29 30 31 32 33 34 35 36 37 38 40 41 42 43 44 45 46 47 48 49 51 52 53 56 57 58 60 61 64 65 67 68 70 71 73 74 **P**5 6 **S** Department of the Army, Office of the Surgeon General, Falls Church, VA	42	10	52	1672	12	36106	542	—	—	795
FRANKLIN—St. Mary Parish										
⊞ FRANKLIN FOUNDATION HOSPITAL, 1501 Hospital Avenue, Zip 70538–3724; tel. 318/828–0760; Patricia Luker, Chief Executive Officer (Nonreporting) **A**1 9 10 **S** Quorum Health Group/Quorum Health Resources, Inc., Brentwood, TN **Web address:** www.franklinfoundation.org	16	10	60	—	—	—	—	—	—	—
FRANKLINTON—Washington Parish										
⊞ RIVERSIDE MEDICAL CENTER, 1900 Main Street, Zip 70438–3688; tel. 504/839–4431; John E. Walker, Chief Executive Officer **A**1 9 10 **F**8 12 19 21 22 28 30 32 34 35 37 41 44 64 65 71 73	16	10	48	1768	20	17580	0	10479	4528	162
GONZALES—Ascension Parish										
☐ ASCENSION HOSPITAL AND BEHAVIORAL HEALTH SERVICES, 615 East Worthy Road, Zip 70737–4240; tel. 225/647–2891; Michael J. Nolan, Chief Executive Officer **A**1 9 10 **F**12 14 15 16 17 19 22 37 39 44 52 65 71 72	16	10	74	281	28	29478	0	13602	5402	—
⊞ RIVERVIEW MEDICAL CENTER, (Formerly Columbia Riverview Medical Center), 1125 West Louisiana Highway 30, Zip 70737; tel. 504/647–5000; Kathy Bobbs, Chief Executive Officer **A**1 9 10 **F**8 12 15 16 19 22 26 30 35 37 44 45 46 49 52 57 59 64 65 71 73 **S** LifePoint Hospitals, Inc., Nashville, TN	33	10	75	2237	34	28774	0	—	—	—
GREENSBURG—St. Helena Parish										
ST. HELENA PARISH HOSPITAL, Highway 43 North, Zip 70441, Mailing Address: P.O. Box 337, Zip 70441–0337; tel. 225/222–6111; Louis Cenac, M.D., Administrator (Total facility includes 72 beds in nursing home–type unit) (Nonreporting) **A**9 10	16	10	99	—	—	—	—	—	—	—

Hospital, Address, Telephone, Administrator, Approval, Facility, and Physician Codes, Health Care System, Network	Classi-fication Codes		Utilization Data					Expense (thousands) of dollars		
	Control	Service	Staffed Beds	Admissions	Census	Outpatient Visits	Births	Total	Payroll	Personnel

★ American Hospital Association (AHA) membership
□ Joint Commission on Accreditation of Healthcare Organizations (JCAHO) accreditation
+ American Osteopathic Healthcare Association (AOHA) membership
○ American Osteopathic Association (AOA) accreditation
△ Commission on Accreditation of Rehabilitation Facilities (CARF) accreditation
Control codes 61, 63, 64, 71, 72 and 73 indicate hospitals listed by AOHA, but not registered by AHA. For definition of numerical codes, see page A4

GREENWELL SPRINGS—East Baton Rouge Parish

EASTERN LOUISIANA MENTAL HEALTH SYSTEM/GREENWELL SPRING CAMPUS, (Formerly Greenwell Springs Hospital), 23260 Greenwell Springs Road, Zip 70739-0999; Mailing Address: P.O. Box 549, Zip 70739-0549; tel. 504/261-2730; Warren T. Price, Jr., Chief Executive Officer (Nonreporting) **S** Louisiana State Hospitals, New Orleans, LA	12	22	104	—	—	—	—	—	—	—

GRETNA—Jefferson Parish

✠ MEADOWCREST HOSPITAL, 2500 Belle Chase Highway, Zip 70056-7196; tel. 504/392-3131; Gerald L. Parton, Chief Executive Officer (Total facility includes 24 beds in nursing home-type unit) **A**1 3 10 **F**2 3 4 7 8 10 11 12 14 16 19 21 22 23 24 30 31 32 35 37 38 40 41 42 43 44 45 46 48 49 52 53 54 55 56 57 58 59 60 61 63 64 65 66 68 71 73 74 **P**1 5 7 **S** TENET Healthcare Corporation, Santa Barbara, CA **Web address:** www.tenethealth.com	33	10	187	7321	98	45309	1690	47309	—	685

HAMMOND—Tangipahoa Parish

✠ NORTH OAKS MEDICAL CENTER, 15790 Medical Center Drive, Zip 70403-1436, Mailing Address: P.O. Box 2668, Zip 70404-2668; tel. 504/345-2700; James E. Cathey, Jr., Chief Executive Officer **A**1 9 10 **F**1 4 7 8 10 12 15 16 19 22 26 28 32 33 35 37 38 39 41 42 43 44 45 46 48 49 52 56 57 58 64 65 66 67 71 73 74 **P**6 **S** Quorum Health Group/Quorum Health Resources, Inc., Brentwood, TN **Web address:** www.northoaks.org	16	10	254	9961	140	147939	1631	99357	50802	1451

HOMER—Claiborne Parish

HOMER MEMORIAL HOSPITAL, 620 East College Street, Zip 71040-3202; tel. 318/927-2024; J. Larry Jordan, Administrator **A**3 5 9 10 **F**7 8 15 16 19 22 26 28 30 32 34 37 40 41 44 46 52 57 58 65 67 71 73	14	10	50	2165	26	14974	117	12081	5549	245

HOUMA—Terrebonne Parish

□ BAYOU OAKS BEHAVIORAL HEALTH SYSTEM, 8134 Main Street, Zip 70360-3404, Mailing Address: P.O. Box 4374, Zip 70361-4374; tel. 504/876-2020; Alan Hodges, Interim Chief Executive Officer (Nonreporting) **A**1 10 **S** Magellan Health Services, Atlanta, GA	33	22	70	—	—	—	—	—	—	—
✠ LEONARD J. CHABERT MEDICAL CENTER, 1978 Industrial Boulevard, Zip 70363-7094; tel. 504/873-2200; Daniel Trahan, Acting Administrator **A**1 3 10 **F**8 19 21 22 25 31 37 38 40 41 42 44 49 51 52 54 55 56 65 70 71 73 74 **S** LSU Medical Center Health Care Services Division, Baton Rouge, LA	12	10	123	5915	71	181843	1177	54769	23587	887
✠ △ TERREBONNE GENERAL MEDICAL CENTER, 8166 Main Street, Zip 70360, Mailing Address: P.O. Box 6037, Zip 70361-6037; tel. 504/873-4664; Alex B. Smith, Ph.D., Executive Director (Total facility includes 16 beds in nursing home-type unit) **A**1 7 9 10 **F**4 7 8 10 11 12 13 15 17 18 19 21 22 26 29 30 32 33 34 35 37 39 40 41 42 43 44 45 46 48 49 51 63 64 65 67 68 71 72 73 74 **P**6 7 **Web address:** www.tgmc.com	16	10	261	11667	171	86757	1040	100886	45615	1408

INDEPENDENCE—Tagipahoa Parish

✠ LALLIE KEMP MEDICAL CENTER, 52579 Highway 51 South, Zip 70443-2231; tel. 504/878-9421; LeVern Meades, Administrator **A**1 10 **F**2 3 8 11 12 15 16 19 20 22 27 28 31 32 34 37 39 41 42 44 45 48 51 60 63 64 65 67 70 71 72 73 **P**6 **S** LSU Medical Center Health Care Services Division, Baton Rouge, LA	12	10	68	2498	35	133537	0	—	—	476

JACKSON—East Feliciana Parish

□ EAST LOUISIANA STATE HOSPITAL, Mailing Address: P.O. Box 498, Zip 70748-0498; tel. 504/634-0100; Warren T. Price, Jr., Chief Executive Officer (Nonreporting) **A**1 10 **S** Louisiana State Hospitals, New Orleans, LA	12	22	452	—	—	—	—	—	—	—
★ VILLA FELICIANA MEDICAL COMPLEX, 5002 Highway 10, Zip 70748-3627, Mailing Address: P.O. Box 438, Zip 70748-0438; tel. 225/634-4000; Hayden Ellis, Administrator (Total facility includes 264 beds in nursing home-type unit) (Nonreporting) **A**10	12	48	275	—	—	—	—	—	—	—

JENA—La Salle Parish

★ LASALLE GENERAL HOSPITAL, Highway 84, Zip 71342-2780, Mailing Address: P.O. Box 2780, Zip 71342-2780; tel. 318/992-9200; Mary M. Denton, Administrator **A**9 10 **F**8 10 19 22 28 30 32 44 49 57 71	16	10	60	1650	32	11221	0	9117	4253	176

JENNINGS—Jefferson Davis Parish

✠ JENNINGS AMERICAN LEGION HOSPITAL, 1634 Elton Road, Zip 70546-3614; tel. 318/824-2490; Terry J. Terrebonne, Administrator **A**1 9 10 **F**7 8 12 13 15 16 17 19 21 22 28 30 34 35 37 39 40 41 44 46 63 65 67 71 73 **P**1 **Web address:** www.jalh.com	23	10	49	2945	26	20314	356	13086	4671	210

JONESBORO—Jackson Parish

JACKSON PARISH HOSPITAL, 165 Beech Springs Road, Zip 71251-2059; tel. 318/259-4435; L. J. Pecot, Chief Executive Officer (Nonreporting) **A**9 10	13	10	59	—	—	—	—	—	—	—

KAPLAN—Vermilion Parish

ABROM KAPLAN MEMORIAL HOSPITAL, 1310 West Seventh Street, Zip 70548-2998; tel. 318/643-8300; Lyman Trahan, Administrator **A**9 10 **F**8 17 19 21 22 28 30 32 33 41 44 52 57 64 71 73	16	10	20	662	8	—	0	5298	1939	83

KENNER—Jefferson Parish

✠ KENNER REGIONAL MEDICAL CENTER, 180 West Esplanade Avenue, Zip 70065-6001; tel. 504/468-8600; Deborah C. Keel, Chief Executive Officer (Nonreporting) **A**1 3 8 10 **S** TENET Healthcare Corporation, Santa Barbara, CA	33	10	213	—	—	—	—	—	—	—

KINDER—Allen Parish

★ ALLEN PARISH HOSPITAL, (ACUTE CARE WITH A PSYCH UNIT), 108 North Sixth Avenue, Zip 70648-3519, Mailing Address: P.O. Box 1670, Zip 70648-1670; tel. 318/738-2527; William C. Jeanmard, Chief Executive Officer **A**9 10 **F**14 19 32 52 59 65 71 **P**5	16	49	49	837	15	4930	0	5179	1629	81

Hospital, Address, Telephone, Administrator, Approval, Facility, and Physician Codes, Health Care System, Network	Control	Service	Staffed Beds	Admissions	Census	Outpatient Visits	Births	Total	Payroll	Personnel

Classification Codes — **Utilization Data** — **Expense (thousands) of dollars**

★ American Hospital Association (AHA) membership
☐ Joint Commission on Accreditation of Healthcare Organizations (JCAHO) accreditation
+ American Osteopathic Healthcare Association (AOHA) membership
○ American Osteopathic Association (AOA) accreditation
△ Commission on Accreditation of Rehabilitation Facilities (CARF) accreditation
Control codes 61, 63, 64, 71, 72 and 73 indicate hospitals listed by AOHA, but not registered by AHA. For definition of numerical codes, see page A4

LA PLACE—St. John the Baptist Parish

☐ RIVER PARISHES HOSPITAL, 500 Rue De Sante, Zip 70068–5418; tel. 504/652–7000; B. Ann Kuss, Chief Executive Officer and Managing Director **A**1 9 10 **F**7 8 12 19 21 22 26 27 34 35 36 37 40 41 42 44 49 51 65 71 73 **P**8 **S** Universal Health Services, Inc., King of Prussia, PA	33	10	79	2629	27	35591	440	25878	11317	319

LAFAYETTE—Lafayette Parish

☐ CHARTER CYPRESS BEHAVIORAL HEALTH SYSTEM, 302 Dulles Drive, Zip 70506–3099; tel. 318/233–9024; Brooks Cagle, Chief Executive Officer (Nonreporting) **A**1 9 10 **S** Magellan Health Services, Atlanta, GA	33	22	70	—	—	—	—	—	—	—
⊠ LAFAYETTE GENERAL MEDICAL CENTER, 1214 Coolidge Avenue, Zip 70503, Mailing Address: P.O. Box 52009 OCS, Zip 70505–2009; tel. 318/289–7991; John J. Burdin, Jr., President and Chief Executive Officer (Total facility includes 30 beds in nursing home–type unit) **A**1 2 6 9 10 **F**4 7 8 10 11 12 13 14 15 16 17 19 20 21 22 23 24 25 26 27 28 29 30 31 32 33 34 35 36 37 38 39 40 41 42 43 44 45 46 47 48 49 50 51 52 53 54 55 56 57 58 60 61 63 64 65 66 67 68 71 72 73 74 **P**7 8 Web address: www.lafayettegeneral.org	23	10	314	13967	187	85173	1303	125508	50748	1708
⊠ MEDICAL CENTER OF SOUTHWEST LOUISIANA, 2810 Ambassador Caffery Parkway, Zip 70506–5900; tel. 318/981–2949; Madeleine L. Roberson, Chief Executive Officer (Nonreporting) **A**1 10 **S** Columbia/HCA Healthcare Corporation, Nashville, TN Web address: www.medicalcentersw.com	33	10	107	—	—	—	—	—	—	—
⊠ OUR LADY OF LOURDES REGIONAL MEDICAL CENTER, 611 St. Landry Street, Zip 70506–4697, Mailing Address: Box 4027, Zip 70502–4027; tel. 318/289–2000; Dudley Romero, President and Chief Executive Officer (Total facility includes 28 beds in nursing home–type unit) **A**1 2 9 10 **F**4 7 8 10 11 12 14 15 16 17 19 21 22 23 24 25 29 30 31 32 33 34 35 37 39 40 41 42 43 44 45 46 47 48 49 60 63 64 65 66 67 71 72 73 **P**8 **S** Franciscan Missionaries of Our Lady Health System, Inc., Baton Rouge, LA Web address: www.lourdes.net	21	10	246	10147	155	78097	340	100497	40296	1314
⊠ UNIVERSITY MEDICAL CENTER, 2390 West Congress Street, Zip 70506–4298, Mailing Address: P.O. Box 69300, Zip 70596–9300; tel. 318/261–6001; Lawrence T. Dorsey, Administrator **A**1 2 3 5 10 **F**2 8 10 13 18 19 21 22 25 31 34 35 37 38 39 40 41 42 44 45 46 51 52 56 57 59 60 61 65 67 70 71 73 74 **P**1 **S** LSU Medical Center Health Care Services Division, Baton Rouge, LA	12	10	146	7739	102	199365	1025	59302	35177	855
★ VERMILION HOSPITAL, 2520 North University Avenue, Zip 70507–5306, Mailing Address: P.O. Box 91526, Zip 70509–1526; tel. 318/234–5614; William A. Ferry, Administrator (Nonreporting) **A**10 **S** General Health System, Baton Rouge, LA	23	22	54	—	—	—	—	—	—	—
⊠ WOMEN'S AND CHILDREN'S HOSPITAL, 4600 Ambassador Caffery Parkway, Zip 70508–6923, Mailing Address: P.O. Box 88030, Zip 70598–8030; tel. 318/981–9100; Madeleine L. Roberson, Chief Executive Officer (Nonreporting) **A**1 9 10 **S** Columbia/HCA Healthcare Corporation, Nashville, TN	33	44	96	—	—	—	—	—	—	—

LAKE CHARLES—Calcasieu Parish

⊠ △ CHRISTUS ST. PATRICK HOSPITAL, (Formerly St. Patrick Hospital), 524 South Ryan Street, Zip 70601–5799, Mailing Address: P.O. Box 3401, Zip 70602–3401; tel. 318/436–2511; James E. Gardner, Jr., Chief Executive Officer (Total facility includes 22 beds in nursing home–type unit) (Nonreporting) **A**1 2 7 9 10 **S** Christus Health, Houston, TX	21	10	298	—	—	—	—	—	—	—
⊠ DUBUIS HOSPITAL FOR CONTINUING CARE, 524 South Ryan, 5th Floor, Zip 70601; tel. 318/491–7752; Tracey Richard, Administrator (Nonreporting) **A**1	21	48	20	—	—	—	—	—	—	—
☐ △ LAKE CHARLES MEMORIAL HOSPITAL, 1701 Oak Park Boulevard, Zip 70601–8911, Mailing Address: P.O. Drawer M, Zip 70602; tel. 318/494–3000; Elton L. Williams, Jr., CPA, President (Total facility includes 20 beds in nursing home–type unit) (Nonreporting) **A**1 2 3 7 9 10 Web address: www.lcmh.com	16	10	303	—	—	—	—	—	—	—
ST. PATRICK HOSPITAL See Christus St. Patrick Hospital										
★ WALTER OLIN MOSS REGIONAL MEDICAL CENTER, 1000 Walters Street, Zip 70605; tel. 318/475–8100; Clay Dunaway, Administrator **A**5 10 **F**3 8 10 12 13 18 19 22 28 29 30 31 34 35 37 39 40 42 44 45 46 49 51 52 53 54 56 58 59 60 65 71 73 **P**4 7 **S** LSU Medical Center Health Care Services Division, Baton Rouge, LA	12	10	74	2487	35	105379	0	26390	16674	410
⊠ WOMEN AND CHILDREN'S HOSPITAL–LAKE CHARLES, 4200 Nelson Road, Zip 70605–4118; tel. 318/474–6370; Alan E. McMillin, Chief Executive Officer **A**1 9 10 **F**7 8 12 19 22 37 38 40 44 61 65 71 73 74 **S** Triad Hospitals, Inc., Dallas, TX	33	10	72	2201	20	10948	1207	14165	6760	185

LAKE PROVIDENCE—East Carroll Parish

EAST CARROLL PARISH HOSPITAL, 226 North Hood Street, Zip 71254–2194; tel. 318/559–2441; Ladonna Englerth, Administrator (Nonreporting) **A**9 10	16	10	29	—	—	—	—	—	—	—

LEESVILLE—Vernon Parish

⊠ BYRD REGIONAL HOSPITAL, 1020 West Fertitta Boulevard, Zip 71446–4697; tel. 318/239–9041; Donald Henderson, Chief Executive Officer **A**1 9 10 **F**3 8 10 12 14 15 16 19 22 26 30 32 33 35 37 39 41 44 52 57 63 71 **P**7 8 **S** Community Health Systems, Inc., Brentwood, TN	33	10	59	2286	26	16080	0	—	—	201

LULING—St. Charles Parish

☐ ST. CHARLES PARISH HOSPITAL, 1057 Paul Maillard Road, Zip 70070, Mailing Address: P.O. Box 87, Zip 70070–0087; tel. 504/785–6242; Fred Martinez, Jr., Chief Executive Officer **A**1 9 10 **F**8 11 12 14 15 17 19 22 26 28 29 30 32 34 35 37 41 42 44 45 49 52 54 55 56 57 65 66 67 71 73 **P**1	16	10	56	2119	32	19683	0	17220	8422	298

Hospital, Address, Telephone, Administrator, Approval, Facility, and Physician Codes, Health Care System, Network	Classi-fication Codes		Utilization Data					Expense (thousands) of dollars		
★ American Hospital Association (AHA) membership □ Joint Commission on Accreditation of Healthcare Organizations (JCAHO) accreditation + American Osteopathic Healthcare Association (AOHA) membership ○ American Osteopathic Association (AOA) accreditation △ Commission on Accreditation of Rehabilitation Facilities (CARF) accreditation Control codes 61, 63, 64, 71, 72 and 73 indicate hospitals listed by AOHA, but not registered by AHA. For definition of numerical codes, see page A4	Control	Service	Staffed Beds	Admissions	Census	Outpatient Visits	Births	Total	Payroll	Personnel

LUTCHER—St. James Parish

⊠ ST. JAMES PARISH HOSPITAL, 2471 Louisiana Avenue, Zip 70071–5413; tel. 225/869–5512; Joan Murray, R.N., Administrator **A**1 9 10 **F**8 15 16 17 19 22 26 27 28 29 30 32 34 36 39 41 44 45 46 49 52 55 57 58 63 64 65 66 68 71 **P**8 | 16 | 10 | 26 | 477 | 5 | 14661 | 0 | 6003 | 2680 | 93

MAMOU—Evangeline Parish

⊠ SAVOY MEDICAL CENTER, 801 Poinciana Avenue, Zip 70554–2298; tel. 318/468–5261; J. E. Richardson, Chief Executive Officer (Total facility includes 125 beds in nursing home–type unit) **A**1 9 10 **F**1 2 3 7 8 10 12 13 15 16 19 21 22 26 28 29 30 32 33 34 35 37 40 44 45 46 48 50 52 53 55 57 59 61 64 65 68 71 73 **P**1 **S** Columbia/HCA Healthcare Corporation, Nashville, TN | 33 | 10 | 330 | 5617 | 201 | 83370 | 580 | 34276 | 15865 | 665

MANDEVILLE—St. Tammany Parish

□ SOUTHEAST LOUISIANA HOSPITAL, Mailing Address: P.O. Box 3850, Zip 70470–3850; tel. 504/626–6300; Joseph C. Vinturella, Chief Executive Officer **A**1 10 **F**15 16 52 53 54 56 57 58 59 65 73 **S** Louisiana State Hospitals, New Orleans, LA | 12 | 22 | 231 | 615 | 198 | 0 | 0 | 29167 | 18227 | 644

MANSFIELD—De Soto Parish

★ DE SOTO REGIONAL HEALTH SYSTEM, 207 Jefferson Street, Zip 71052–2603, Mailing Address: P.O. Box 1636, Zip 71052–0672; tel. 318/871–3101; William F. Barrow, President and Chief Executive Officer **A**9 10 **F**8 12 14 15 17 19 22 24 28 30 32 35 39 41 42 44 49 52 54 57 58 59 65 67 71 74 **P**6 | 23 | 10 | 49 | 1402 | 21 | 15349 | 0 | 8927 | 2927 | 140

MANY—Sabine Parish

⊠ SABINE MEDICAL CENTER, 240 Highland Drive, Zip 71449–3718; tel. 318/256–5691; Patrick W. Gandy, Chief Executive Officer **A**1 9 10 **F**12 15 16 19 20 21 22 28 29 30 32 35 37 44 46 63 71 73 **S** Community Health Systems, Inc., Brentwood, TN | 33 | 10 | 48 | 1170 | 10 | 11330 | 0 | 6794 | 3173 | 88

MARKSVILLE—Avoyelles Parish

⊠ AVOYELLES HOSPITAL, 4231 Highway 1192, Zip 71351, Mailing Address: P.O. Box 255, Zip 71351; tel. 318/253–8611; David M. Mitchel, Chief Executive Officer (Nonreporting) **A**1 9 10 **S** Columbia/HCA Healthcare Corporation, Nashville, TN | 33 | 10 | 55 | — | — | — | — | — | — | —

MARRERO—Jefferson Parish

⊠ △ WEST JEFFERSON MEDICAL CENTER, 1101 Medical Center Boulevard, Zip 70072–3191; tel. 504/347–5511; A. Gary Muller, FACHE, President and Chief Executive Officer (Total facility includes 30 beds in nursing home–type unit) (Nonreporting) **A**1 7 9 10 | 16 | 10 | 382 | — | — | — | — | — | — | —

METAIRIE—Jefferson Parish

⊠ DOCTORS HOSPITAL OF JEFFERSON, 4320 Houma Boulevard, Zip 70006–2973; tel. 504/849–4000; L. Rene' Goux, Chief Executive Officer (Total facility includes 12 beds in nursing home–type unit) **A**1 10 **F**1 2 3 4 5 6 7 8 9 10 12 13 14 15 16 17 18 19 20 21 22 23 24 25 26 27 28 29 30 31 32 33 34 35 36 37 38 39 40 41 42 43 44 45 46 47 48 49 51 52 53 54 55 56 57 58 59 60 61 62 63 64 65 66 67 68 70 71 72 73 74 **P**1 5 7 **S** TENET Healthcare Corporation, Santa Barbara, CA
Web address: www.tenethealth.com | 33 | 10 | 144 | 2778 | 42 | 18181 | 0 | 34523 | 9594 | 203

⊠ △ EAST JEFFERSON GENERAL HOSPITAL, 4200 Houma Boulevard, Zip 70006–2996; tel. 504/454–4000; Peter J. Betts, President and Chief Executive Officer (Total facility includes 71 beds in nursing home–type unit) **A**1 2 3 5 7 9 10 **F**1 4 7 8 10 11 12 14 17 19 21 22 23 25 27 28 29 30 32 33 34 35 37 38 39 40 41 42 43 44 45 46 48 49 51 52 54 55 56 57 58 59 60 64 65 67 71 73 74 **P**1 6 8 | 16 | 10 | 500 | 20058 | 340 | 147623 | 1952 | 223200 | 94000 | 3003

⊠ LAKESIDE HOSPITAL, 4700 I–10 Service Road, Zip 70001–1269; tel. 504/885–3342; Gerald A. Fornoff, Chief Executive Officer **A**1 10 **F**7 8 12 15 16 19 24 34 38 40 44 45 46 48 49 59 61 65 66 71 73 74 **P**5 7 8 **S** Columbia/HCA Healthcare Corporation, Nashville, TN | 33 | 44 | 75 | 2644 | 26 | 21734 | 2642 | 20651 | 8907 | 244

MINDEN—Webster Parish

⊠ MINDEN MEDICAL CENTER, 1 Medical Plaza, Zip 71055–3330; tel. 318/377–2321; George E. French, III, Chief Executive Officer **A**1 9 10 **F**1 7 8 12 14 15 16 17 19 22 28 29 30 32 35 37 40 41 42 44 46 49 52 57 65 71 73 74 **S** TENET Healthcare Corporation, Santa Barbara, CA
Web address: www.tenethealth.com/minden | 33 | 10 | 101 | 3355 | 41 | 82294 | 722 | 19050 | 8966 | 328

MONROE—Ouachita Parish

⊠ E. A. CONWAY MEDICAL CENTER, 4864 Jackson Street, Zip 71202–6497, Mailing Address: P.O. Box 1881, Zip 71210–1881; tel. 318/330–7000; Roy D. Bostick, Director **A**1 3 5 10 **F**8 15 19 22 28 31 35 37 38 39 40 42 44 46 52 56 60 65 71 73 **P**1 **S** LSU Medical Center Health Care Services Division, Baton Rouge, LA | 12 | 10 | 174 | 7618 | 125 | 164344 | 1708 | 55421 | 23426 | 909

⊠ △ NORTH MONROE HOSPITAL, 3421 Medical Park Drive, Zip 71203–2399; tel. 318/388–1946; George E. Miller, Chief Executive Officer **A**1 7 9 10 **F**4 7 8 10 11 12 14 19 21 22 23 26 27 28 34 35 37 39 40 41 42 44 45 48 49 50 52 57 58 59 63 64 65 66 71 73 **P**8 **S** Columbia/HCA Healthcare Corporation, Nashville, TN | 33 | 10 | 186 | 7259 | 125 | 34151 | 468 | — | — | 613

⊠ ST. FRANCIS MEDICAL CENTER, 309 Jackson Street, Zip 71201–7498, Mailing Address: P.O. Box 1901, Zip 71210–1901; tel. 318/327–4000; H. Gerald Smith, President and Chief Executive Officer **A**1 2 9 10 **F**1 4 7 8 10 11 12 13 14 15 16 17 19 20 21 22 24 25 26 29 30 31 32 33 34 35 36 37 38 39 40 41 42 43 44 47 48 49 50 51 52 57 59 60 64 65 67 71 72 73 74 **P**2 6 8 **S** Franciscan Missionaries of Our Lady Health System, Inc., Baton Rouge, LA
Web address: www.stfran.com | 23 | 10 | 257 | 14192 | 228 | 91800 | 1123 | 148777 | 52763 | 1630

Hospital, Address, Telephone, Administrator, Approval, Facility, and Physician Codes, Health Care System, Network	Classi-fication Codes		Utilization Data					Expense (thousands) of dollars		
	Control	Service	Staffed Beds	Admissions	Census	Outpatient Visits	Births	Total	Payroll	Personnel

Approval codes legend:

★ American Hospital Association (AHA) membership
□ Joint Commission on Accreditation of Healthcare Organizations (JCAHO) accreditation
+ American Osteopathic Healthcare Association (AOHA) membership
○ American Osteopathic Association (AOA) accreditation
△ Commission on Accreditation of Rehabilitation Facilities (CARF) accreditation
Control codes 61, 63, 64, 71, 72 and 73 indicate hospitals listed by AOHA, but not registered by AHA. For definition of numerical codes, see page A4

Hospital	Control	Service	Staffed Beds	Admissions	Census	Outpatient Visits	Births	Total	Payroll	Personnel
□ ST. FRANCIS SPECIALTY HOSPITAL, Mailing Address: P.O. Box 71210, Zip 71210; tel. 318/327–4267; Michael G. Ryan, President and Chief Executive Officer **A**1 10 **F**15 16 48	23	46	50	365	28	—	0	—	—	133
MORGAN CITY—St. Mary Parish										
✠ LAKEWOOD MEDICAL CENTER, 1125 Marguerite Street, Zip 70380–1855, Mailing Address: Drawer 2308, Zip 70381–2308; tel. 504/384–2200; Joyce Grove Hein, Chief Executive Officer **A**1 9 10 **F**7 8 10 11 12 14 15 16 17 19 22 23 26 28 30 32 34 37 39 40 41 42 44 45 46 49 52 56 57 59 64 65 71 73 74 **S** Quorum Health Group/Quorum Health Resources, Inc., Brentwood, TN	16	10	122	2882	30	41721	511	23300	10248	342
NAPOLEONVILLE—Assumption Parish										
OUR LADY OF THE LAKE–ASSUMPTION See Our Lady of the Lake Regional Medical Center, Baton Rouge										
NATCHITOCHES—Natchitoches Parish										
□ NATCHITOCHES PARISH HOSPITAL, 501 Keyser Avenue, Zip 71457–6036, Mailing Address: P.O. Box 2009, Zip 71457–2009; tel. 318/352–1200; Mark E. Marley, Executive Director (Total facility includes 112 beds in nursing home–type unit) **A**1 9 10 **F**1 7 8 19 20 22 26 28 30 32 36 37 40 44 46 49 52 57 59 64 65 71 73 **P**5 **S** Christus Health, Houston, TX	16	10	175	3904	140	56176	632	17018	6816	346
NEW IBERIA—Iberia Parish										
✠ DAUTERIVE HOSPITAL, 600 North Lewis Street, Zip 70560, Mailing Address: P.O. Box 11210, Zip 70562–1210; tel. 318/365–7311; Kyle J. Viator, Chief Executive Officer (Nonreporting) **A**1 9 10 **S** Columbia/HCA Healthcare Corporation, Nashville, TN	33	10	92	—	—	—	—	—	—	—
✠ IBERIA GENERAL HOSPITAL AND MEDICAL CENTER, 2315 East Main Street, Zip 70560–4031, Mailing Address: P.O. Box 13338, Zip 70562–3338; tel. 318/364–0441; Isaac S. Coe, Interim Administrator (Total facility includes 12 beds in nursing home–type unit) **A**1 9 10 **F**7 8 10 12 13 14 19 20 21 22 23 27 28 30 32 34 35 37 39 40 41 44 45 49 64 65 67 71 73 **S** Brim Healthcare, Inc., Brentwood, TN	16	10	75	3447	38	51582	351	30244	14024	383
NEW ORLEANS—Orleans Parish										
□ BHC EAST LAKE HOSPITAL, 5650 Read Boulevard, Zip 70127–3145; tel. 504/241–0888; Darlene Brennan, Chief Executive Officer (Nonreporting) **A**1 10 **S** Behavioral Healthcare Corporation, Nashville, TN	33	22	52	—	—	—	—	—	—	—
CHARITY CAMPUS See Medical Center of Louisiana at New Orleans										
□ △ CHILDREN'S HOSPITAL, 200 Henry Clay Avenue, Zip 70118–5799; tel. 504/899–9511; Steve Worley, President and Chief Executive Officer **A**1 2 3 5 7 9 10 **F**4 5 10 12 13 16 17 19 20 21 22 25 28 31 34 35 38 39 42 43 44 45 46 47 48 49 51 53 54 56 58 65 66 67 68 71 72 73 **P**8	23	50	175	7060	105	124515	0	—	—	1144
DEPAUL/TULANE BEHAVIORAL HEALTH CENTER See Tulane University Hospital and Clinic										
✠ △ LAKELAND MEDICAL CENTER, 6000 Bullard Avenue, Zip 70128; tel. 504/241–6335; Tracy A. Rogers, Chief Executive Officer **A**1 7 9 10 **F**2 3 4 7 8 10 11 12 13 15 16 17 18 19 20 21 22 23 24 25 26 28 30 31 32 33 34 35 37 38 40 41 42 43 44 45 46 47 48 49 51 52 53 54 55 56 57 58 59 60 61 63 64 65 66 67 68 70 71 72 73 74 **P**7 8 **S** Columbia/HCA Healthcare Corporation, Nashville, TN **Web address:** www.columbia.net	33	10	140	5007	76	33495	804	36559	15478	592
✠ MEDICAL CENTER OF LOUISIANA AT NEW ORLEANS, (Includes Charity Campus, 1532 Tulane Avenue, Zip 70140; tel. 504/568–3201; University Campus, 2021 Perdido Street), 2021 Perdido Street, Zip 70112–1396; tel. 504/588–3000; John S. Berault, Chief Executive Officer **A**1 2 3 5 8 10 **F**4 7 8 10 12 15 16 17 18 19 20 21 22 23 28 30 31 32 33 34 35 37 38 39 40 41 42 43 44 46 47 48 49 51 52 54 58 59 60 63 65 66 67 68 70 71 73 74 **S** LSU Medical Center Health Care Services Division, Baton Rouge, LA	12	10	681	32458	520	552935	3881	376696	144420	4799
✠ MEMORIAL MEDICAL CENTER, (Includes Memorial Medical Center–Baptist Campus, 2700 Napoleon Avenue, Zip 70115–6996; tel. 504/899–9311; Memorial Medical Center–Mercy Campus, 301 North Jefferson Davis Parkway, Zip 70119–5397; tel. 504/483–5000), Randall L. Hoover, Chief Executive Officer **A**1 2 3 5 8 9 10 **F**4 7 8 10 12 15 16 17 19 20 21 22 24 26 27 28 29 30 31 32 33 35 37 38 39 40 41 42 43 44 45 46 48 49 51 53 54 55 56 59 60 61 63 64 65 66 67 68 71 73 74 **P**5 **S** TENET Healthcare Corporation, Santa Barbara, CA	33	10	717	17400	302	89941	1772	158862	68138	2127
□ METHODIST BEHAVIORAL RESOURCES, 5610 Read Boulevard, Zip 70127–3155; tel. 504/244–5661; John A. Baker, Chief Executive Officer **A**1 10 **F**1 2 3 14 18 22 25 26 34 41 52 53 54 55 56 57 58 59 65 **P**5	32	22	36	1246	38	—	0	6971	3242	119
□ NEW ORLEANS ADOLESCENT HOSPITAL, 210 State Street, Zip 70118–5797; tel. 504/897–3400; Walter W. Shervington, M.D., Chief Executive Officer (Nonreporting) **A**1 3 10 **S** Louisiana State Hospitals, New Orleans, LA	12	52	95	—	—	—	—	—	—	—
✠ △ OCHSNER FOUNDATION HOSPITAL, 1516 Jefferson Highway, Zip 70121–2484; tel. 504/842–3000; Eileen Skinner, Interim Director (Total facility includes 52 beds in nursing home–type unit) (Nonreporting) **A**1 2 3 5 7 8 9 10	23	10	392	—	—	—	—	—	—	—
✠ PENDLETON MEMORIAL METHODIST HOSPITAL, 5620 Read Boulevard, Zip 70127–3154; tel. 504/244–5100; Frederick C. Young, Jr., President (Total facility includes 35 beds in nursing home–type unit) **A**1 9 10 **F**4 8 10 11 15 17 19 21 22 23 27 32 35 37 38 39 40 41 42 43 44 46 49 52 60 64 65 67 71 73 74 **P**1 7 **Web address:** www.pmmh.org	23	10	251	8332	137	88572	970	104695	41112	1196

Hospital, Address, Telephone, Administrator, Approval, Facility, and Physician Codes, Health Care System, Network	Classification Codes		Utilization Data					Expense (thousands) of dollars		
★ American Hospital Association (AHA) membership □ Joint Commission on Accreditation of Healthcare Organizations (JCAHO) accreditation + American Osteopathic Healthcare Association (AOHA) membership ○ American Osteopathic Association (AOA) accreditation △ Commission on Accreditation of Rehabilitation Facilities (CARF) accreditation Control codes 61, 63, 64, 71, 72 and 73 indicate hospitals listed by AOHA, but not registered by AHA. For definition of numerical codes, see page A4	Control	Service	Staffed Beds	Admissions	Census	Outpatient Visits	Births	Total	Payroll	Personnel

Hospital	Control	Service	Staffed Beds	Admissions	Census	Outpatient Visits	Births	Total	Payroll	Personnel
□ PHYSICIANS HOSPITAL, (Formerly University Rehab Hospital), 3125 Canal Street, Zip 70119–6285; tel. 504/822–8222; Robert A. Leonhard, Jr., Administrator (Nonreporting) **A**1 10	33	10	40	—	—	—	—	—	—	—
□ RIVER OAKS HOSPITAL, 1525 River Oaks Road West, Zip 70123–2199; tel. 504/734–1740; Daryl Sue White, Chief Executive Officer and Managing Director (Nonreporting) **A**1 10 **S** Universal Health Services, Inc., King of Prussia, PA **Web address:** www.riveroakshospital.com	33	22	94	—	—	—	—	—	—	—
☒ ST. CHARLES GENERAL HOSPITAL, 3700 St. Charles Avenue, Zip 70115–4680; tel. 504/899–7441; Rene Goux, Chief Executive Officer **A**1 10 **F**1 3 4 7 8 10 11 12 14 15 16 17 19 21 22 23 24 25 26 28 29 30 32 34 35 37 38 41 42 43 44 46 47 48 49 52 53 56 57 58 59 60 63 64 65 68 70 71 73 74 **P**1 5 7 **S** TENET Healthcare Corporation, Santa Barbara, CA **Web address:** www.tenethealth.com	33	10	163	3221	53	9110	0	—	—	—
□ ST. CLAUDE MEDICAL CENTER, 3419 St. Claude Avenue, Zip 70117–6198; tel. 504/948–8200; Joseph R. Tucker, President (Nonreporting) **A**1 10 **S** United Medical Corporation, Windermere, FL	33	10	136	—	—	—	—	—	—	—
□ △ TOURO INFIRMARY, 1401 Foucher Street, Zip 70115–3593; tel. 504/897–7011; Gary M. Stein, President and Chief Executive Officer **A**1 2 3 5 7 8 9 10 **F**1 4 7 8 10 12 16 17 18 19 21 22 23 24 25 26 28 29 30 32 34 35 37 38 39 40 41 42 43 44 45 46 48 49 51 52 54 55 56 57 58 59 60 61 62 63 64 65 66 67 70 71 72 73 74 **P**1	23	10	330	9930	202	118500	1026	111358	53071	1404
☒ TULANE UNIVERSITY HOSPITAL AND CLINIC, (Includes DePaul/Tulane Behavioral Health Center, 1040 Calhoun Street, Zip 70118–5999; tel. 504/899–8282; David Hoidel, Chief Executive Officer), 1415 Tulane Avenue, Zip 70112–2632; tel. 504/588–5263; Shirley A. Stewart, President and Chief Executive Officer **A**1 2 3 5 8 9 10 **F**2 3 4 7 8 10 11 12 13 14 16 17 18 19 21 22 23 25 26 27 28 29 30 31 34 35 37 38 39 40 41 42 43 44 46 47 48 49 51 52 53 54 55 56 57 58 59 60 61 63 65 66 67 68 71 73 74 **P**1 **S** Columbia/HCA Healthcare Corporation, Nashville, TN **Web address:** www.tuhc.com UNIVERSITY CAMPUS See Medical Center of Louisiana at New Orleans UNIVERSITY REHAB HOSPITAL See Physicians Hospital	32	10	326	11463	221	317321	642	200069	60907	1568
□ VENCOR HOSPITAL – NEW ORLEANS, 3601 Coliseum Street, Zip 70115–3606; tel. 504/899–1555; John R. Watkins, Chief Executive Officer (Nonreporting) **A**1 10 **S** Vencor, Incorporated, Louisville, KY	33	10	78	—	—	—	—	—	—	—
☒ VETERANS AFFAIRS MEDICAL CENTER, 1601 Perdido Street, Zip 70112–1262; tel. 504/568–0811; John D. Church, Jr., Director (Total facility includes 60 beds in nursing home–type unit) **A**1 2 3 5 8 **F**1 2 3 4 5 8 10 11 12 14 15 16 17 18 19 20 21 22 25 26 27 28 29 30 31 32 33 34 35 37 39 41 42 43 44 45 46 49 51 52 54 55 56 57 58 59 60 63 64 65 67 69 71 72 73 74 **S** Department of Veterans Affairs, Washington, DC	45	10	197	4952	172	293196	0	139282	70990	1843
NEW ROADS—Pointe Coupee Parish										
★ POINTE COUPEE GENERAL HOSPITAL, 2202 False River Drive, Zip 70760–2698; tel. 225/638–6331; Larry J. Ayres, Administrator and Chief Executive Officer (Nonreporting) **A**9 10	16	10	29	—	—	—	—	—	—	—
OAK GROVE—West Carroll Parish										
WEST CARROLL MEMORIAL HOSPITAL, 706 Ross Street, Zip 71263, Mailing Address: P.O. Box 748, Zip 71263–0748; tel. 318/428–3237; Randall R. Morris, Administrator (Nonreporting) **A**9 10	23	10	21	—	—	—	—	—	—	—
OAKDALE—Allen Parish										
☒ OAKDALE COMMUNITY HOSPITAL, 130 North Hospital Drive, Zip 71463–4004, Mailing Address: P.O. Box 629, Zip 71463–0629; tel. 318/335–3700; LaQuita Johnson, Chief Executive Officer **A**1 9 10 **F**12 15 16 19 21 22 28 30 37 44 49 52 59 64 65 71 73 **P**8 **S** Columbia/HCA Healthcare Corporation, Nashville, TN	32	10	54	2785	34	25401	0	12426	4962	186
OLLA—La Salle Parish										
HARDTNER MEDICAL CENTER, Highway 165 South, Zip 71465, Mailing Address: P.O. Box 1218, Zip 71465–1218; tel. 318/495–3131; David Hamner, Administrator **A**9 10 **F**12 19 22 23 26 28 44 49 52 57 65 71 73	16	10	41	1071	15	11449	70	5339	1886	101
OPELOUSAS—St. Landry Parish										
☒ DOCTORS' HOSPITAL OF OPELOUSAS, 5101 Highway 167 South, Zip 70570–8975; tel. 318/948–2100; Bethy W. Walker, Administrator (Nonreporting) **A**1 9 10 **S** Columbia/HCA Healthcare Corporation, Nashville, TN	32	10	105	—	—	—	—	—	—	—
☒ OPELOUSAS GENERAL HOSPITAL, 520 Prudhomme Lane, Zip 70570–6454, Mailing Address: P.O. Box 1208, Zip 70571–1208; tel. 318/948–3011; Daryl J. Doise, Administrator (Total facility includes 13 beds in nursing home–type unit) **A**1 2 9 10 **F**7 10 15 16 17 19 21 22 24 28 31 32 35 37 40 42 44 45 46 49 51 59 60 63 64 65 71 73 74 **P**7 8 **S** Quorum Health Group/Quorum Health Resources, Inc., Brentwood, TN **Web address:** www.opelousasgeneral.com	16	10	140	5698	72	71989	716	39253	15494	585
PINEVILLE—Rapides Parish										
□ CENTRAL LOUISIANA STATE HOSPITAL, 242 West Shamrock Avenue, Zip 71361–5031, Mailing Address: P.O. Box 5031, Zip 71361–5031; tel. 318/484–6200; Gary S. Grand, Chief Executive Officer **A**1 10 **F**15 20 52 53 59 65 73 **S** Louisiana State Hospitals, New Orleans, LA	12	22	216	358	187	0	0	21107	12287	459
☒ HUEY P. LONG MEDICAL CENTER, 352 Hospital Boulevard, Zip 71360, Mailing Address: P.O. Box 5352, Zip 71361–5352; tel. 318/448–0811; James E. Morgan, Director (Nonreporting) **A**1 3 5 10 **S** LSU Medical Center Health Care Services Division, Baton Rouge, LA	12	10	123	—	—	—	—	—	—	—

Hospital, Address, Telephone, Administrator, Approval, Facility, and Physician Codes, Health Care System, Network	Classi-fication Codes		Utilization Data					Expense (thousands) of dollars		
★ American Hospital Association (AHA) membership □ Joint Commission on Accreditation of Healthcare Organizations (JCAHO) accreditation + American Osteopathic Healthcare Association (AOHA) membership ○ American Osteopathic Association (AOA) accreditation △ Commission on Accreditation of Rehabilitation Facilities (CARF) accreditation Control codes 61, 63, 64, 71, 72 and 73 indicate hospitals listed by AOHA, but not registered by AHA. For definition of numerical codes, see page A4	Control	Service	Staffed Beds	Admissions	Census	Outpatient Visits	Births	Total	Payroll	Personnel

PLAQUEMINE—Iberville Parish

☒ RIVER WEST MEDICAL CENTER, 59355 River West Drive, Zip 70764–9543; tel. 225/687–9222; Mark Nosacka, Chief Executive Officer **A**1 9 10 **F**7 8 12 14 15 16 19 22 26 28 30 35 37 39 40 41 42 44 48 49 65 71 73 **P**7 8 **S** Community Health Systems, Inc., Brentwood, TN	33	10	80	2405	24	23321	495	14231	5181	202

RACELAND—Lafourche Parish

□ ST. ANNE GENERAL HOSPITAL, 4608 Highway 1, Zip 70394; tel. 504/537–6841; Milton D. Bourgeois, Jr., Administrator (Total facility includes 12 beds in nursing home–type unit) **A**1 9 10 **F**8 10 12 16 19 21 22 23 32 35 37 40 44 52 56 57 58 64 65 71	16	10	78	1841	17	17997	307	16330	7241	366

RAYVILLE—Richland Parish

RICHARDSON MEDICAL CENTER, Christian Drive at Greer Road, Zip 71269–9985, Mailing Address: P.O. Box 388, Zip 71269–9985; tel. 318/728–4181; David D. Kervin, Administrator (Nonreporting) **A**9 10	16	10	60	—	—	—	—	—	—	—

RUSTON—Lincoln Parish

□ HEALTHSOUTH NORTH LOUISIANA REHABILITATION HOSPITAL, (Formerly North Louisiana Rehabilitation Hospital), 1401 Ezell Street, Zip 71270–7221, Mailing Address: P.O. Box 490, Zip 71273–0490; tel. 318/251–5354; Mark Rice, Chief Executive Officer (Nonreporting) **A**1 10 **S** HEALTHSOUTH Corporation, Birmingham, AL	33	46	90	—	—	—	—	—	—	—
☒ LINCOLN GENERAL HOSPITAL, 401 East Vaughn Street, Zip 71270–5950, Mailing Address: P.O. Drawer 1368, Zip 71273–1368; tel. 318/254–2100; E. Allen Tuten, Administrator (Total facility includes 13 beds in nursing home–type unit) **A**1 9 10 **F**4 8 10 12 17 19 21 22 23 28 30 32 33 34 35 37 40 41 42 44 49 50 64 65 71 74	23	10	124	6334	81	26850	573	35965	15028	565

SAINT FRANCISVILLE—West Feliciana Parish

☒ WEST FELICIANA PARISH HOSPITAL, Mailing Address: Box 368, Zip 70775–0368; tel. 225/635–3811; John H. Green, Administrator (Nonreporting) **A**1 9 10	16	10	23	—	—	—	—	—	—	—

SHREVEPORT—Caddo Parish

□ CHARTER BRENTWOOD BEHAVIORAL HEALTH SYSTEM, 1006 Highland Avenue, Zip 71101–4103; tel. 318/227–2221; Scott F. Blakley, Chief Executive Officer (Nonreporting) **A**1 3 9 10 **S** Magellan Health Services, Atlanta, GA	33	22	200	—	—	—	—	—	—	—
☒ CHRISTUS SCHUMPERT MEDICAL CENTER, (Formerly Schumpert Medical Center), One St. Mary Place, Zip 71101–4399, Mailing Address: P.O. Box 21976, Zip 71120–1076; tel. 318/681–4500; Daniel J. Rissing, Acting Chief Executive Officer (Nonreporting) **A**1 2 3 5 9 10 **S** Christus Health, Houston, TX	21	10	486	—	—	—	—	—	—	—
□ △ DOCTORS' HOSPITAL OF SHREVEPORT, 1130 Louisiana Avenue, Zip 71101–3998, Mailing Address: P.O. Box 1526, Zip 71165–1526; tel. 318/227–1211; Charles E. Boyd, Administrator **A**1 7 9 10 **F**2 3 8 9 12 16 17 19 22 27 28 30 35 37 38 40 41 44 46 47 48 49 65 66 67 71 74 **S** Universal Health Services, Inc., King of Prussia, PA	33	10	99	2292	44	6291	0	30946	14104	343
☒ HIGHLAND HOSPITAL, 1453 East Bert Kouns Industrial Loop, Zip 71105–6050; tel. 318/798–4300; Anthony S. Sala, Jr., Chief Executive Officer **A**1 9 10 **F**4 7 8 10 11 12 14 15 16 17 19 22 23 24 28 29 30 34 35 37 39 40 41 42 43 44 45 46 48 49 50 63 64 65 66 67 71 72 73 **P**1 7 **S** Columbia/HCA Healthcare Corporation, Nashville, TN	33	10	160	4856	70	60889	275	42199	17788	457
☒ LIFECARE HOSPITALS, (LONG TERM ACUTE CARE), 1128 Louisiana Avenue, Suite A, Zip 71101–3976, Mailing Address: P.O. Box 1680, Zip 71165–1680; tel. 318/222–2273; Robert A. Loepp, Jr., Administrator **A**1 10 **F**12 26 41	33	49	40	424	35	0	0	14188	—	98
☒ LSU MEDICAL CENTER–UNIVERSITY HOSPITAL, 1541 Kings Highway, Zip 71130–4299, Mailing Address: P.O. Box 33932, Zip 71130–3932; tel. 318/675–5000; Ingo Angermeier, FACHE, Administrator and Chief Executive Officer **A**1 2 3 5 8 10 **F**4 5 7 8 9 10 12 19 21 22 23 25 26 31 34 35 37 38 39 40 41 42 43 44 45 46 47 49 50 51 52 56 58 60 61 63 65 66 68 70 71 73 74 **P**6 **S** LSU Medical Center Health Care Services Division, Baton Rouge, LA **Web address:** www.shrinershq.org	12	10	414	18947	304	407050	2299	193557	101964	5611
☒ OVERTON BROOKS VETERANS AFFAIRS MEDICAL CENTER, 510 East Stoner Avenue, Zip 71101–4295; tel. 318/221–8411; Billy M. Valentine, Director **A**1 2 3 5 8 **F**3 4 8 10 14 15 16 17 19 20 21 22 23 25 26 27 28 30 31 32 33 34 35 37 39 41 42 43 44 46 49 50 51 52 54 56 57 58 60 63 64 65 67 69 71 73 74 **P**6 **S** Department of Veterans Affairs, Washington, DC	45	10	100	4251	87	214817	0	87685	41704	973
SCHUMPERT MEDICAL CENTER See Christus Schumpert Medical Center										
☒ SHRINERS HOSPITALS FOR CHILDREN, SHREVEPORT, 3100 Samford Avenue, Zip 71103–4289; tel. 318/222–5704; Thomas R. Schneider, Administrator (Nonreporting) **A**1 3 5 **S** Shriners Hospitals for Children, Tampa, FL	23	57	45	—	—	—	—	—	—	—
★ U. S. AIR FORCE HOSPITAL, Barksdale AFB, Zip 71110–5300; tel. 318/456–6004; Colonel Dennis Marquardt, USAF, Commander (Nonreporting) **S** Department of the Air Force, Bowling AFB, DC	41	10	25	—	—	—	—	—	—	—
☒ △ WILLIS–KNIGHTON MEDICAL CENTER, 2600 Greenwood Road, Zip 71103–2600, Mailing Address: P.O. Box 32600, Zip 71130–2600; tel. 318/632–4600; James K. Elrod, President and Chief Executive Officer (Nonreporting) **A**1 3 5 7 9 10 **Web address:** www.wkmc.com	23	10	426	—	—	—	—	—	—	—

SLIDELL—St. Tammany Parish

□ NORTHSHORE PSYCHIATRIC HOSPITAL, 104 Medical Center Drive, Zip 70461–7838; tel. 504/646–5500; George H. Perry, Ph.D., Chief Executive Officer **A**1 9 10 **F**3 16 18 26 34 52 53 54 55 56 57 58 59 **S** TENET Healthcare Corporation, Santa Barbara, CA	33	22	58	836	26	6628	0	6485	2920	110

Hospital, Address, Telephone, Administrator, Approval, Facility, and Physician Codes, Health Care System, Network	Classi-fication Codes		Utilization Data					Expense (thousands) of dollars		
★ American Hospital Association (AHA) membership □ Joint Commission on Accreditation of Healthcare Organizations (JCAHO) accreditation + American Osteopathic Healthcare Association (AOHA) membership ○ American Osteopathic Association (AOA) accreditation △ Commission on Accreditation of Rehabilitation Facilities (CARF) accreditation Control codes 61, 63, 64, 71, 72 and 73 indicate hospitals listed by AOHA, but not registered by AHA. For definition of numerical codes, see page A4	Control	Service	Staffed Beds	Admissions	Census	Outpatient Visits	Births	Total	Payroll	Personnel
★ NORTHSHORE REGIONAL MEDICAL CENTER, 100 Medical Center Drive, Zip 70461–8572; tel. 504/649–7070; Lynn C. Orfgen, Chief Executive Officer A1 10 F3 4 7 8 10 11 12 16 17 18 19 21 22 23 24 26 27 30 32 33 34 35 37 38 39 40 41 42 43 44 46 47 49 52 53 55 56 57 58 59 63 64 65 67 71 73 74 P1 5 7 S TENET Healthcare Corporation, Santa Barbara, CA	33	10	147	6337	89	42911	496	—	—	611
★ △ SLIDELL MEMORIAL HOSPITAL AND MEDICAL CENTER, 1001 Gause Boulevard, Zip 70458–2987; tel. 504/643–2200; Monica P. Gates, FACHE, Chief Executive Officer (Nonreporting) A1 2 7 9 10 Web address: www.smhplus.org	16	10	173	—	—		—			
SPRINGHILL—Webster Parish										
★ SPRINGHILL MEDICAL CENTER, 2001 Doctors Drive, Zip 71075, Mailing Address: P.O. Box 920, Zip 71075–0920; tel. 318/539–1000 A1 9 10 F7 12 15 16 19 21 22 28 30 33 35 37 40 44 49 52 57 65 71 73 S LifePoint Hospitals, Inc., Nashville, TN	33	10	63	1733	21	24587	70	18233	7331	
STERLINGTON—Ouachita Parish										
STERLINGTON HOSPITAL, Highway 2, Zip 71280, Mailing Address: P.O. Box 567, Zip 71280–0567; tel. 318/665–2526; Evalyn Ormond, Administrator (Nonreporting) A10	23	10	32	—	—					
SULPHUR—Calcasieu Parish										
★ WEST CALCASIEU CAMERON HOSPITAL, 701 East Cypress Street, Zip 70663–5000, Mailing Address: P.O. Box 2509, Zip 70664–2509; tel. 318/527–4240; Wayne A. Swiniarski, FACHE, Chief Executive Officer (Total facility includes 11 beds in nursing home–type unit) A1 9 10 F7 8 12 15 16 17 19 21 22 24 28 29 30 32 34 35 37 39 40 41 44 49 63 64 65 71 73 74 P5	16	10	85	3837	37	66619	343	31794	14851	528
TALLULAH—Madison Parish										
MADISON PARISH HOSPITAL, 900 Johnson Street, Zip 71282–4537, Mailing Address: P.O. Box 1559, Zip 71284–1559; tel. 318/574–2374; Wendell Alford, Administrator (Nonreporting) A9 10	23	10	47	—	—					
THIBODAUX—Lafourche Parish										
★ △ THIBODAUX REGIONAL MEDICAL CENTER, 602 North Acadia Road, Zip 70301–4847, Mailing Address: P.O. Box 1118, Zip 70302–1118; tel. 504/447–5500; David M. Snyder, Chief Executive Officer A1 7 9 10 F4 7 8 10 12 13 14 15 16 19 21 22 23 28 29 30 32 34 35 37 39 40 41 42 43 44 45 46 48 49 59 60 64 65 66 67 71 73 74 S Quorum Health Group/Quorum Health Resources, Inc., Brentwood, TN Web address: www.thibodaux.com	16	10	150	7103	79	85182	765	51626	21466	680
VILLE PLATTE—Evangeline Parish										
★ VILLE PLATTE MEDICAL CENTER, 800 East Main Street, Zip 70586–4618, Mailing Address: P.O. Box 349, Zip 70586–0349; tel. 318/363–5684; Linda Deville, Chief Executive Officer A1 9 10 F7 8 12 15 16 17 19 22 24 26 28 29 30 32 34 35 37 40 41 42 44 49 52 57 65 66 71 73 P8	23	10	80	3570	47	31462	246	17211	7758	290
VIVIAN—Caddo Parish										
NORTH CADDO MEDICAL CENTER, 1000 South Spruce Street, Zip 71082–3232, Mailing Address: P.O. Box 792, Zip 71082–0792; tel. 318/375–3235; Patricia S. Wilkins, Administrator A9 10 F13 15 16 19 20 22 27 29 32 33 34 36 39 44 45 49 51 64 65 71	16	10	25	692	7	4857	0	4269	2150	82
WEST MONROE—Ouachita Parish										
★ GLENWOOD REGIONAL MEDICAL CENTER, 503 McMillan Road, Zip 71291–5327, Mailing Address: P.O. Box 35805, Zip 71294–5805; tel. 318/329–4200; Raymond L. Ford, President and Chief Executive Officer (Total facility includes 12 beds in nursing home–type unit) A1 2 9 10 F7 8 10 12 13 15 16 17 19 21 22 23 24 25 28 29 30 32 33 34 35 36 37 39 40 41 42 44 45 46 47 48 49 60 63 64 65 66 67 70 71 73 74 P6	23	10	176	9480	121	113534	405	64380	23624	751
WINNFIELD—Winn Parish										
★ WINN PARISH MEDICAL CENTER, 301 West Boundary Street, Zip 71483–3427, Mailing Address: P.O. Box 152, Zip 71483–0152; tel. 318/628–2721; Bobby Jordan, Chief Executive Officer (Nonreporting) A1 9 10 S Columbia/HCA Healthcare Corporation, Nashville, TN	33	10	103	—	—		—			
WINNSBORO—Franklin Parish										
FRANKLIN MEDICAL CENTER, 2106 Loop Road, Zip 71295–3398; tel. 318/435–9411; Ann Netherland, Chief Executive Officer A9 10 F12 14 15 16 17 19 21 23 26 27 28 32 37 42 44 52 57 59 65 70 71 73	16	10	53	2503	29	33895	0	11726	4251	196
ZACHARY—East Baton Rouge Parish										
★ LANE MEMORIAL HOSPITAL, 6300 Main Street, Zip 70791–9990; tel. 225/658–4000; David W. Fuller, Chief Executive Officer (Total facility includes 50 beds in nursing home–type unit) A1 9 10 F7 8 12 17 19 20 21 22 26 28 29 30 31 32 34 35 37 39 41 44 46 49 64 65 71 73 P6 7 S Quorum Health Group/Quorum Health Resources, Inc., Brentwood, TN Web address: www.lanehospital.org	16	10	137	4337	94	109096	413	30904	15367	514

MAINE

Resident population 1,244 (in thousands)
Resident population in metro areas 35.8%
Birth rate per 1,000 population 11.2
65 years and over 13.9%
Percent of persons without health insurance 12.1%

★ American Hospital Association (AHA) membership
□ Joint Commission on Accreditation of Healthcare Organizations (JCAHO) accreditation
+ American Osteopathic Healthcare Association (AOHA) membership
○ American Osteopathic Association (AOA) accreditation
△ Commission on Accreditation of Rehabilitation Facilities (CARF) accreditation
Control codes 61, 63, 64, 71, 72 and 73 indicate hospitals listed by AOHA, but not registered by AHA. For definition of numerical codes, see page A4

Hospital, Address, Telephone, Administrator, Approval, Facility, and Physician Codes, Health Care System, Network	Control	Service	Staffed Beds	Admissions	Census	Outpatient Visits	Births	Total	Payroll	Personnel
AUGUSTA—Kennebec County										
□ AUGUSTA MENTAL HEALTH INSTITUTE, Arsenal Street, Zip 04330, Mailing Address: P.O. Box 724, Zip 04330-0724; tel. 207/287-7200; Rodney Bouffard, Superintendent (Nonreporting) **A**1 9 10	12	22	133	—	—	—	—	—	—	—
MAINEGENERAL MEDICAL CENTER–AUGUSTA CAMPUS See MaineGeneral Medical Center–Waterville Campus, Waterville										
BANGOR—Penobscot County										
✖ ACADIA HOSPITAL, 268 Stillwater Avenue, Zip 04401-3945, Mailing Address: P.O. Box 422, Zip 04402-0422; tel. 207/973-6100; Ali A. Elhaj, President and Chief Executive Officer **A**1 9 10 **F**1 2 3 4 7 8 10 11 12 13 16 17 18 19 21 22 24 26 28 29 30 31 32 33 34 37 38 39 40 41 42 43 44 45 46 47 48 49 51 52 53 54 55 56 57 58 59 60 61 63 64 65 66 67 70 71 72 73 74 **P**5 6 **S** Eastern Maine Healthcare, Bangor, ME **Web address:** www.emh.org	23	22	72	1895	85	7822	0	19433	10474	333
□ BANGOR MENTAL HEALTH INSTITUTE, 656 State Street, Zip 04402-0926, Mailing Address: P.O. Box 926, Zip 04402-0926; tel. 207/941-4000; N. Lawrence Ventura, Superintendent (Nonreporting) **A**1 9 10	12	22	188	—	—	—	—	—	—	—
✖ EASTERN MAINE MEDICAL CENTER, (Includes Ross Skilled Nursing Facility), 489 State Street, Zip 04401-6674, Mailing Address: P.O. Box 404, Zip 04402-0404; tel. 207/973-7000; Norman A. Ledwin, President and Chief Executive Officer (Total facility includes 15 beds in nursing home–type unit) **A**1 2 3 5 9 10 **F**2 3 4 6 7 8 10 11 12 13 14 15 16 17 18 19 21 22 24 26 28 29 30 31 32 33 34 37 38 39 40 41 42 44 45 46 47 48 49 51 53 54 55 56 57 58 59 60 61 63 64 65 66 67 68 70 71 72 73 74 **P**4 7 8 **S** Eastern Maine Healthcare, Bangor, ME	23	10	347	17048	262	261777	1665	205379	88761	2389
✖ ST. JOSEPH HOSPITAL, 360 Broadway, Zip 04401-3897, Mailing Address: P.O. Box 403, Zip 04402-0403; tel. 207/262-1000; Sister Mary Norberta Malinowski, President **A**1 9 10 **F**8 15 16 17 19 21 22 23 26 32 33 35 37 39 42 44 45 46 49 65 66 67 71 73 74	21	10	70	3216	46	96827	0	43973	16351	534
BAR HARBOR—Hancock County										
✖ MOUNT DESERT ISLAND HOSPITAL, Wayman Lane, Zip 04609-0008, Mailing Address: P.O. Box 8, Zip 04609-0008; tel. 207/288-5081; Leslie A. Hawkins, President **A**1 9 10 **F**3 7 8 15 16 17 19 21 22 25 28 30 34 37 39 40 41 42 44 49 51 63 65 67 71 74 **P**6 **Web address:** www.mdihospital.org	23	10	39	1532	18	24702	88	13394	6538	223
BATH—Sagadahoc County										
✖ MID COAST HOSPITAL, (Includes Bath Health Care Center, Mailing Address: 1356 Washington Street, Zip 04530-2897; Mid Coast Hospital, 58 Baribeau Drive, Brunswick, Zip 04011-3286; tel. 207/729-0181), 1356 Washington Street, Zip 04530-2897; tel. 207/443-5524; Herbert Paris, President (Total facility includes 16 beds in nursing home–type unit) **A**1 9 10 **F**3 6 7 8 12 14 15 16 17 18 19 21 22 25 26 27 28 29 30 31 32 33 34 35 36 37 39 40 41 42 44 45 46 49 52 53 54 55 56 57 58 59 60 62 63 64 65 67 69 71 72 73 74 **P**6	23	10	88	4084	56	89717	404	31754	13724	411
BELFAST—Waldo County										
□ WALDO COUNTY GENERAL HOSPITAL, Northport Avenue, Zip 04915, Mailing Address: P.O. Box 287, Zip 04915-0287; tel. 207/338-2500; Mark A. Biscone, Executive Director **A**1 9 10 **F**1 3 6 7 8 11 14 15 16 18 19 22 24 28 30 32 33 34 35 37 39 40 41 42 44 46 49 53 54 55 56 57 58 62 63 65 66 67 71 73	23	10	45	2052	26	49758	181	17806	8643	324
BIDDEFORD—York County										
✖ SOUTHERN MAINE MEDICAL CENTER, One Medical Center Drive, Zip 04005-9496, Mailing Address: P.O. Box 626, Zip 04005-0626; tel. 207/283-7000; Edward J. McGeachey, President and Chief Executive Officer **A**1 2 9 10 13 **F**7 8 10 14 15 16 19 21 22 26 28 29 30 31 32 33 34 35 37 39 40 41 42 44 45 49 52 53 54 55 56 57 58 59 60 61 63 65 67 71 73 74 **P**5 8 **Web address:** www.smmctr.org	23	10	121	5422	72	117760	598	51764	24488	776
BLUE HILL—Hancock County										
✖ BLUE HILL MEMORIAL HOSPITAL, Water Street, Zip 04614-0823, Mailing Address: P.O. Box 823, Zip 04614-0823; tel. 207/374-2836; Bruce D. Cummings, Chief Executive Officer **A**1 9 10 **F**3 6 7 8 12 13 14 15 16 17 19 22 26 28 29 30 32 33 34 35 37 39 40 42 44 45 49 51 58 61 62 65 67 71 72 73 74 **P**6	23	10	26	983	12	—	152	18073	8575	291
BOOTHBAY HARBOR—Lincoln County										
✖ ST. ANDREWS HOSPITAL AND HEALTHCARE CENTER, 3 St. Andrews Lane, Zip 04538-1732, Mailing Address: P.O. Box 417, Zip 04538-0417; tel. 207/633-2121; Margaret G. Pinkham, President and Chief Executive Officer (Total facility includes 30 beds in nursing home–type unit) **A**1 9 10 **F**8 13 15 16 17 22 26 30 32 34 39 41 44 49 51 61 64 65 66 67 71 73 74 **P**6	23	10	50	380	34	15009	0	6990	3210	142

Hospital, Address, Telephone, Administrator, Approval, Facility, and Physician Codes, Health Care System, Network	Classi-fication Codes		Utilization Data					Expense (thousands) of dollars		
★ American Hospital Association (AHA) membership □ Joint Commission on Accreditation of Healthcare Organizations (JCAHO) accreditation + American Osteopathic Healthcare Association (AOHA) membership ○ American Osteopathic Association (AOA) accreditation △ Commission on Accreditation of Rehabilitation Facilities (CARF) accreditation Control codes 61, 63, 64, 71, 72 and 73 indicate hospitals listed by AOHA, but not registered by AHA. For definition of numerical codes, see page A4	Control	Service	Staffed Beds	Admissions	Census	Outpatient Visits	Births	Total	Payroll	Personnel

BRIDGTON—Cumberland County

⊞ NORTHERN CUMBERLAND MEMORIAL HOSPITAL, South High Street, Zip 04009, Mailing Address: P.O. Box 230, Zip 04009–0230; tel. 207/647–8841; Laird Covey, Chief Executive Officer **A**1 9 10 **F**7 8 11 12 15 17 19 21 22 39 40 41 42 44 45 63 65 71 73 **P**4 7 8 Web address: www.ncmh.com	23	10	40	1611	15	24276	93	12565	6038	214

BRUNSWICK—Cumberland County

⊞ PARKVIEW HOSPITAL, 329 Maine Street, Zip 04011–3398; tel. 207/373–2000; Jon W. Gepford, President and Chief Executive Officer **A**1 9 10 **F**7 8 15 16 17 19 22 26 27 28 29 30 31 32 33 34 37 39 40 42 44 45 46 49 54 65 67 71 73 74 **P**8 Web address: www.parkviewhospital.com	21	10	45	1968	19	58944	466	17256	8686	255

CALAIS—Washington County

⊞ CALAIS REGIONAL HOSPITAL, 50 Franklin Street, Zip 04619–1398; tel. 207/454–7521; Ray H. Davis, Jr., Chief Executive Officer (Total facility includes 8 beds in nursing home–type unit) **A**1 9 10 **F**3 7 8 14 16 17 19 20 22 28 30 32 33 34 35 37 39 40 44 46 58 64 67 71 73 **S** Quorum Health Group/Quorum Health Resources, Inc., Brentwood, TN	23	10	57	1376	19	26188	128	11426	5051	186

CARIBOU—Aroostook County

⊞ CARY MEDICAL CENTER, 163 Van Buren Road, Suite 1, Zip 04736–2599; tel. 207/498–3111; Kris Doody–Chabre, Chief Executive Officer (Total facility includes 9 beds in nursing home–type unit) **A**1 9 10 **F**4 7 8 10 11 12 13 14 15 16 17 18 19 20 21 22 24 25 26 27 28 29 30 31 32 33 34 35 36 37 39 40 41 42 44 45 46 48 49 50 51 53 54 55 56 57 58 59 60 63 65 66 67 69 70 71 72 73 74 **P**8 **S** Quorum Health Group/Quorum Health Resources, Inc., Brentwood, TN Web address: www.carymed.org	14	10	74	2353	39	64892	134	25355	11205	410

DAMARISCOTTA—Lincoln County

⊞ MILES MEMORIAL HOSPITAL, Bristol Road, Zip 04543, Mailing Address: Rural Route 2, Box 4500, Zip 04543–9767; tel. 207/563–1234; Judith Tarr, Chief Executive Officer **A**1 9 10 **F**1 7 12 19 22 30 32 33 37 40 41 44 49 62 64 65 71 72 73 74 **P**2 Web address: www.mileshealthcare.org	23	10	36	1865	19	47728	188	18560	8058	407

DOVER–FOXCROFT—Piscataquis County

⊞ MAYO REGIONAL HOSPITAL, 75 West Main Street, Zip 04426–1099; tel. 207/564–8401; Ralph Gabarro, Chief Executive Officer **A**1 9 10 **F**1 7 8 14 15 16 17 19 22 28 30 37 40 41 42 44 51 54 56 65 71 73 **P**7 **S** Quorum Health Group/Quorum Health Resources, Inc., Brentwood, TN Web address: www.mayohospital.com	16	10	46	1678	16	41691	152	14189	6244	209

ELLSWORTH—Hancock County

⊞ MAINE COAST MEMORIAL HOSPITAL, 50 Union Street, Zip 04605–1599; tel. 207/667–5311 **A**1 9 10 **F**7 8 12 15 16 17 18 19 21 22 24 25 26 28 29 30 31 33 34 35 37 39 40 41 42 44 45 46 49 51 53 56 57 58 60 63 65 66 71 72 74 **P**6 **S** Quorum Health Group/Quorum Health Resources, Inc., Brentwood, TN	23	10	48	2751	29	34448	180	31947	16937	458

FARMINGTON—Franklin County

⊞ FRANKLIN MEMORIAL HOSPITAL, One Hospital Drive, Zip 04938–9990; tel. 207/778–6031; Richard A. Batt, President and Chief Executive Officer **A**1 9 10 **F**7 8 14 15 16 17 19 22 28 30 34 35 37 41 42 44 49 51 58 60 71 73 **P**1 Web address: www.fchn.org	23	10	60	2743	26	98126	413	27006	11837	550

FORT FAIRFIELD—Aroostook County

COMMUNITY GENERAL HEALTH CENTER See Aroostook Medical Center, Presque Isle										

FORT KENT—Aroostook County

⊞ NORTHERN MAINE MEDICAL CENTER, 143 East Main Street, Zip 04743–1497; tel. 207/834–3155; Martin B. Bernstein, Chief Executive Officer (Total facility includes 45 beds in nursing home–type unit) **A**1 9 10 **F**7 8 12 14 15 16 19 21 22 25 28 32 33 34 35 36 37 39 40 41 42 44 45 46 49 52 53 54 55 56 57 58 63 64 65 71 **P**6	23	10	97	1354	56	35145	92	17043	7965	214

GREENVILLE—Piscataquis County

★ CHARLES A. DEAN MEMORIAL HOSPITAL, Pritham Avenue, Zip 04441–1395, Mailing Address: P.O. Box 1129, Zip 04441–1129; tel. 207/695–2223; Philomena A. Marshall, R.N., President and Chief Executive Officer (Total facility includes 36 beds in nursing home–type unit) **A**9 10 **F**8 14 15 16 17 22 24 28 30 34 39 44 49 51 64 65 71 **S** Eastern Maine Healthcare, Bangor, ME	23	10	50	358	31	8473	6	3752	1906	96

HOULTON—Aroostook County

⊞ HOULTON REGIONAL HOSPITAL, 20 Hartford Street, Zip 04730–9998; tel. 207/532–9471; Thomas J. Moakler, Chief Executive Officer (Total facility includes 26 beds in nursing home–type unit) **A**1 9 10 **F**3 7 8 12 14 15 16 17 19 20 21 22 24 28 29 30 32 33 34 35 36 37 39 40 41 42 44 45 46 49 54 56 57 64 65 68 71 73 **P**8 **S** Quorum Health Group/Quorum Health Resources, Inc., Brentwood, TN	23	10	73	1904	40	44685	180	19970	8575	247

LEWISTON—Androscoggin County

⊞ CENTRAL MAINE MEDICAL CENTER, 300 Main Street, Zip 04240–0305; tel. 207/795–0111; William W. Young, Jr., President **A**1 2 3 5 9 10 **F**7 8 10 11 12 13 14 15 16 17 19 21 22 24 27 28 29 30 31 32 33 34 35 37 39 40 41 42 44 45 46 48 49 51 60 61 63 65 66 67 68 70 71 72 73 74 **P**5 6 8 Web address: www.cmmc.org	23	10	106	7547	100	162034	793	78219	33538	1008

Hospital, Address, Telephone, Administrator, Approval, Facility, and Physician Codes, Health Care System, Network	Classi-fication Codes		Utilization Data					Expense (thousands) of dollars		
★ American Hospital Association (AHA) membership □ Joint Commission on Accreditation of Healthcare Organizations (JCAHO) accreditation + American Osteopathic Healthcare Association (AOHA) membership ○ American Osteopathic Association (AOA) accreditation △ Commission on Accreditation of Rehabilitation Facilities (CARF) accreditation Control codes 61, 63, 64, 71, 72 and 73 indicate hospitals listed by AOHA, but not registered by AHA. For definition of numerical codes, see page A4	Control	Service	Staffed Beds	Admissions	Census	Outpatient Visits	Births	Total	Payroll	Personnel

⊞ ST. MARY'S REGIONAL MEDICAL CENTER, 45 Golder Street, Zip 04240–6033, Mailing Address: P.O. Box 291, Zip 04243–0291; tel. 207/777–8100; James E. Cassidy, President and Chief Executive Officer **A**1 2 9 10 **F**2 3 7 8 10 12 14 15 16 17 19 20 21 22 23 24 26 28 29 30 34 35 37 39 40 41 42 44 45 46 49 51 52 53 54 55 56 57 58 59 60 63 64 65 67 71 73 74 **P**6 **S** Covenant Health Systems, Inc., Lexington, MA **Web address:** www.stmarysmaine.com	23	10	187	5781	102	88403	384	51667	17445	677
LINCOLN—Penobscot County										
⊞ PENOBSCOT VALLEY HOSPITAL, Transalpine Road, Zip 04457–0368, Mailing Address: P.O. Box 368, Zip 04457–0368; tel. 207/794–3321; Ronald D. Victory, Administrator (Total facility includes 9 beds in nursing home–type unit) **A**1 9 10 **F**7 8 15 16 22 26 27 28 30 31 34 36 37 39 40 41 42 44 49 64 65 72 **P**6 8 **S** Quorum Health Group/Quorum Health Resources, Inc., Brentwood, TN	16	10	41	1112	21	35963	109	9818	4749	180
MACHIAS—Washington County										
⊞ DOWN EAST COMMUNITY HOSPITAL, Upper Court Street, Zip 04654, Mailing Address: Rural Route 1, Box 11, Zip 04654–9702; tel. 207/255–3356; Philo D. Hall, Interim Chief Executive Officer **A**1 9 10 **F**3 7 8 14 15 16 17 19 21 22 28 30 34 35 37 40 42 44 49 63 65 67 71 73 **P**8 **S** Quorum Health Group/Quorum Health Resources, Inc., Brentwood, TN **Web address:** www.nemaine.com	23	10	38	1597	17	34432	111	15398	6343	206
MARS HILL—Aroostook County										
AROOSTOOK HEALTH CENTER See Aroostook Medical Center, Presque Isle										
MILLINOCKET—Penobscot County										
⊞ MILLINOCKET REGIONAL HOSPITAL, 200 Somerset Street, Zip 04462–1298; tel. 207/723–5161; Marie E. Arant, Interim Chief Executive Officer **A**1 9 10 **F**1 7 8 12 17 19 22 24 30 35 37 39 40 41 42 44 46 49 65 71 73 **S** Quorum Health Group/Quorum Health Resources, Inc., Brentwood, TN	23	10	16	1055	13	23075	9	10816	4751	157
NORWAY—Oxford County										
⊞ STEPHENS MEMORIAL HOSPITAL, 181 Main Street, Zip 04268–1297; tel. 207/743–5933; Timothy A. Churchill, President **A**1 9 10 **F**3 6 7 8 11 12 15 16 17 19 22 28 30 32 33 34 35 40 41 44 49 51 61 62 64 65 66 67 70 71 73 **P**8 **Web address:** www.wmhcc.com	23	10	50	1820	21	96869	219	—	—	272
PITTSFIELD—Somerset County										
★ SEBASTICOOK VALLEY HOSPITAL, 99 Grove Street, Zip 04967–1199; tel. 207/487–5141; Ann Morrison, R.N., Chief Executive Officer **A**9 10 **F**2 3 8 11 12 14 17 19 22 28 30 32 33 34 39 41 42 44 46 49 56 58 65 67 71 73 74	23	10	26	1450	12	35845	0	10102	4461	138
PORTLAND—Cumberland County										
⊞ △ MAINE MEDICAL CENTER, (Includes Maine Medical Center, Brighton Campus, 335 Brighton Avenue, Zip 04102–9735; tel. 207/879–8000), 22 Bramhall Street, Zip 04102–3175; tel. 207/871–0111; Vincent S. Conti, President and Chief Executive Officer **A**1 2 3 5 7 8 9 10 **F**3 4 8 10 11 12 13 14 15 16 17 18 19 20 21 22 23 25 26 27 28 29 30 31 32 33 34 35 37 38 39 40 41 42 43 44 45 46 48 49 51 52 53 54 55 56 57 58 59 60 61 63 65 66 67 68 70 71 72 73 74 **P**4 6 7 8 **Web address:** www.mmc.org	23	10	606	27380	406	189452	2189	340884	142168	3670
⊞ MERCY HOSPITAL PORTLAND, 144 State Street, Zip 04101–3795; tel. 207/879–3000; Howard R. Buckley, President **A**1 9 10 **F**2 3 7 8 13 15 16 17 19 21 25 26 27 28 29 30 31 32 33 34 35 37 39 40 42 43 44 51 54 58 65 67 71 72 73 74 **P**6 **S** Catholic Health East, Newtown Square, PA **Web address:** www.mercyhospital.com	21	10	159	9373	115	117132	1333	65695	29085	830
□ △ NEW ENGLAND REHABILITATION HOSPITAL OF PORTLAND, 335 Brighton Avenue, Zip 04102; tel. 207/775–4000; Amy Morse, Chief Executive Officer (Nonreporting) **A**1 7 9 10 **S** HEALTHSOUTH Corporation, Birmingham, AL	33	46	76	—	—	—	—	—	—	—
PRESQUE ISLE—Aroostook County										
⊞ AROOSTOOK MEDICAL CENTER, (Includes Aroostook Health Center, 15 Highland Avenue, Mars Hill, Zip 04758; tel. 207/768–4900; Arthur R. Gould Memorial Hospital, 140 Academy Street, Zip 04769; tel. 207/768–4000; Community General Health Center, 3 Green Street, Fort Fairfield, Zip 04742; tel. 207/768–4700; Washburn Regional Health Center, Washburn, Zip 04786), 140 Academy Street, Zip 04769–3171, Mailing Address: P.O. Box 151, Zip 04769–0151; tel. 207/768–4000; David A. Peterson, President and Chief Executive Officer (Total facility includes 71 beds in nursing home–type unit) **A**1 9 10 **F**7 8 15 16 19 21 22 25 26 28 30 33 34 35 36 37 39 40 41 42 44 48 49 51 52 53 55 56 58 59 60 64 65 67 71 73 74 **P**2 6 **Web address:** www.mainerec.com/tamchome.html	23	10	154	3156	92	71469	347	36122	14922	537
ROCKPORT—Knox County										
⊞ PENOBSCOT BAY MEDICAL CENTER, 6 Glen Cove Drive, Zip 04856–4241; tel. 207/596–8000; Roy A. Hitchings, Jr., FACHE, President (Total facility includes 62 beds in nursing home–type unit) **A**1 2 9 10 **F**2 3 7 8 11 15 16 19 21 22 27 28 32 33 35 37 40 41 42 44 46 48 49 52 54 56 57 63 64 65 67 71 73 74 **P**4 6 **Web address:** www.nehealth.org	23	10	145	4314	114	82769	398	41215	21534	651
RUMFORD—Oxford County										
⊞ RUMFORD COMMUNITY HOSPITAL, 420 Franklin Street, Zip 04276–2145, Mailing Address: P.O. Box 619, Zip 04276–0619; tel. 207/364–4581; John H. Welsh, Chief Executive Officer **A**1 9 10 **F**3 7 8 11 12 14 16 17 19 20 21 22 24 28 30 40 44 49 65 67 71 73 **P**1	23	10	27	1192	14	27755	82	12473	4824	150

Hospital, Address, Telephone, Administrator, Approval, Facility, and Physician Codes, Health Care System, Network	Classi-fication Codes		Utilization Data					Expense (thousands) of dollars		
★ American Hospital Association (AHA) membership □ Joint Commission on Accreditation of Healthcare Organizations (JCAHO) accreditation + American Osteopathic Healthcare Association (AOHA) membership ○ American Osteopathic Association (AOA) accreditation △ Commission on Accreditation of Rehabilitation Facilities (CARF) accreditation Control codes 61, 63, 64, 71, 72 and 73 indicate hospitals listed by AOHA, but not registered by AHA. For definition of numerical codes, see page A4	Control	Service	Staffed Beds	Admissions	Census	Outpatient Visits	Births	Total	Payroll	Personnel

SANFORD—York County

⊠ HENRIETTA D. GOODALL HOSPITAL, 25 June Street, Zip 04073–2645; tel. 207/324–4310; Peter G. Booth, President (Total facility includes 112 beds in nursing home–type unit) **A**1 9 10 **F**6 7 8 11 13 15 16 17 19 22 28 30 34 35 40 41 44 49 64 65 71 73
Web address: www.goodallhosp.org

| | 23 | 10 | 161 | 2206 | 115 | 48400 | 264 | 26661 | 11349 | 296 |

SKOWHEGAN—Somerset County

⊠ REDINGTON–FAIRVIEW GENERAL HOSPITAL, Fairview Avenue, Zip 04976, Mailing Address: P.O. Box 468, Zip 04976–0468; tel. 207/474–5121; Richard Willett, Chief Executive Officer **A**1 2 9 10 **F**7 8 11 12 15 16 17 19 21 22 28 30 32 33 35 40 41 42 44 49 54 56 58 63 65 66 67 71 73

| | 23 | 10 | 65 | 2386 | 27 | 65214 | 252 | 21658 | 10513 | 338 |

SOUTH PORTLAND—Cumberland County

□ SPRING HARBOR HOSPITAL, (Formerly Jackson Brook Institute), 175 Running Hill Road, Zip 04106; tel. 207/761–2200; Dennis King, President (Nonreporting) **A**1 9 10 **S** Community Care Systems, Inc., Wellesley, MA

| | 33 | 22 | 106 | — | — | — | — | — | — | — |

TOGUS—Kennebec County

⊠ VETERANS AFFAIRS MEDICAL CENTER, 1 VA Center, Zip 04330; tel. 207/623–8411; John H. Sims, Jr., Director (Total facility includes 100 beds in nursing home–type unit) **A**1 2 3 5 **F**1 3 8 12 17 18 19 20 21 22 25 26 27 30 31 32 33 34 35 37 39 42 44 46 49 51 52 54 56 57 58 59 60 63 64 65 67 71 72 73 74 **P**6 **S** Department of Veterans Affairs, Washington, DC
Web address: www.togus,med.va.gov

| | 45 | 10 | 200 | 2957 | 175 | 161236 | 0 | 63910 | 34848 | 948 |

WASHBURN—Aroostook County

WASHBURN REGIONAL HEALTH CENTER See Aroostook Medical Center, Presque Isle

WATERVILLE—Kennebec County

★ + ○ INLAND HOSPITAL, 200 Kennedy Memorial Drive, Zip 04901–4595; tel. 207/861–3000; Wilfred J. Addison, President and Chief Executive Officer **A**9 10 11 **F**7 8 15 19 21 32 34 35 37 40 41 42 44 49 63 70 71 73 **S** Eastern Maine Healthcare, Bangor, ME

| | 23 | 10 | 44 | 1540 | 17 | 39656 | 166 | 16534 | 7459 | 214 |

⊠ MAINEGENERAL MEDICAL CENTER–WATERVILLE CAMPUS, (Includes MaineGeneral Medical Center–Augusta Campus, 6 East Chestnut Street, Augusta, Zip 04330–9988; tel. 207/626–1000), 149 North Street, Zip 04901–4974; tel. 207/872–1000; Scott B. Bullock, President (Total facility includes 29 beds in nursing home–type unit) **A**1 2 3 5 9 10 **F**1 2 3 7 8 11 12 13 15 16 17 19 21 22 23 26 30 31 32 33 34 35 37 39 40 41 42 44 46 48 49 51 52 53 54 56 58 59 60 63 64 65 66 67 70 71 72 73 74 **P**7 8
Web address: www.mainegeneral.org

| | 23 | 10 | 346 | 13305 | 186 | 307634 | 1178 | 136393 | 59160 | 1804 |

WESTBROOK—Cumberland County

□ WESTBROOK COMMUNITY HOSPITAL, 40 Park Road, Zip 04092–3158; tel. 207/854–8464; Charlene Wallace, Interim President **A**1 9 10 **F**22 44 67

| | 23 | 10 | 30 | 131 | 3 | 29408 | 0 | 4798 | 2250 | 67 |

YORK—York County

□ YORK HOSPITAL, 15 Hospital Drive, Zip 03909–1099; tel. 207/351–2395; Jud Knox, President (Total facility includes 13 beds in nursing home–type unit) **A**1 9 10 **F**3 4 7 8 10 11 13 15 16 17 19 20 21 22 23 24 26 27 29 30 31 32 33 34 35 36 39 40 42 44 45 46 49 54 64 65 67 68 71 73 74 **P**8

| | 23 | 10 | 79 | 3312 | 48 | 43897 | 298 | 24536 | 14450 | 439 |

MARYLAND

Resident population 5,135 (in thousands)
Resident population in metro areas 91.6%
Birth rate per 1,000 population 14.4
65 years and over 11.5%
Percent of persons without health insurance 11.4%

Hospital, Address, Telephone, Administrator, Approval, Facility, and Physician Codes, Health Care System, Network	Classi-fication Codes		Utilization Data					Expense (thousands) of dollars		
	Control	Service	Staffed Beds	Admissions	Census	Outpatient Visits	Births	Total	Payroll	Personnel

★ American Hospital Association (AHA) membership
□ Joint Commission on Accreditation of Healthcare Organizations (JCAHO) accreditation
+ American Osteopathic Healthcare Association (AOHA) membership
○ American Osteopathic Association (AOA) accreditation
△ Commission on Accreditation of Rehabilitation Facilities (CARF) accreditation
Control codes 61, 63, 64, 71, 72 and 73 indicate hospitals listed by AOHA, but not registered by AHA. For definition of numerical codes, see page A4

ANDREWS AFB—Prince George's County

⊞ MALCOLM GROW MEDICAL CENTER, 1050 West Perimeter, Zip 20762–6600, Mailing Address: 1050 West Perimeter, Suite A1–19, Zip 20762–6600; tel. 240/857–3000; Colonel Jeffrey L. Butler, Administrator **A**1 2 3 5 **F**2 3 4 5 7 8 9 10 11 12 14 15 16 19 20 21 22 28 30 34 35 36 37 38 39 40 41 42 43 44 45 46 47 49 50 51 52 54 55 56 58 59 60 61 63 65 66 67 68 70 71 72 73 74 **S** Department of the Air Force, Bowling AFB, DC	41	10	93	4978	53	394408	908	124000	—	1170

ANNAPOLIS—Anne Arundel County

⊞ ANNE ARUNDEL MEDICAL CENTER, 64 Franklin Street, Zip 21401–2777; tel. 410/267–1000; Martin L. Doordan, President **A**1 2 9 10 **F**2 3 7 8 10 11 14 15 16 17 19 20 21 22 24 25 27 28 29 30 32 33 34 35 37 38 39 40 41 42 44 46 49 60 65 67 68 70 71 72 73 74 **P**4 7 Web address: www.aahcs.org	23	10	291	15554	150	164574	3475	121500	53800	1904

BALTIMORE—Baltimore City County

⊞ BON SECOURS BALTIMORE HEALTH SYSTEM, 2000 West Baltimore Street, Zip 21223–1597; tel. 410/362–3000; Henry DeVries, Acting Chief Executive Officer (Total facility includes 22 beds in nursing home–type unit) **A**1 9 10 **F**3 8 10 11 12 14 15 16 17 18 19 20 21 22 24 25 26 27 28 30 31 32 33 34 35 37 39 41 42 44 46 49 51 53 54 55 56 58 59 62 63 64 65 67 71 73 **P**5 6 7 8 **S** Bon Secours Health System, Inc., Marriottsville, MD Web address: www.bonsecours.org	21	10	106	5867	105	52749	0	64937	24599	727
⊞ CHURCH HOSPITAL CORPORATION, 100 North Broadway, Zip 21231–1593; tel. 410/522–8000; Ann C. Failing, President (Total facility includes 31 beds in nursing home–type unit) **A**1 9 10 **F**1 2 3 4 5 6 7 8 10 11 12 13 14 16 17 18 19 21 22 23 25 26 27 28 29 30 31 32 33 34 35 37 38 39 41 42 43 44 45 46 48 49 51 52 53 54 55 56 59 60 61 62 63 64 65 66 67 71 72 73 74 **P**5 7 **S** MedStar Health, Columbia, MD Web address: www.helixhealth.org	23	10	167	4966	82	31001	0	43870	17937	570
⊞ △ DEATON SPECIALTY HOSPITAL AND HOME, (NURSING HOME CHRONIC), 611 South Charles Street, Zip 21230–3898; tel. 410/547–8500; James E. Ross, FACHE, Chief Executive Officer (Total facility includes 190 beds in nursing home–type unit) **A**1 7 10 **F**2 3 4 5 7 8 10 11 12 15 17 19 20 22 24 25 26 27 28 29 30 31 32 34 35 37 38 39 40 42 43 44 47 48 49 51 52 53 54 55 56 57 58 59 60 61 64 65 66 67 68 73 74 **P**3	23	49	316	950	272	—	0	28471	11750	314
⊞ FRANKLIN SQUARE HOSPITAL CENTER, 9000 Franklin Square Drive, Zip 21237–3998; tel. 410/682–7000; Charles D. Mross, President **A**1 2 3 5 8 9 10 **F**3 4 5 7 8 10 11 12 14 16 17 18 19 21 22 23 24 25 26 27 28 29 30 31 32 33 34 35 37 38 39 40 41 42 43 44 45 46 49 51 52 53 54 55 56 57 58 59 60 61 62 64 65 66 67 68 70 71 72 73 74 **P**2 4 5 6 7 **S** MedStar Health, Columbia, MD Web address: www.helix.org	23	10	243	19656	248	118194	2675	151162	80459	1922
⊞ △ GOOD SAMARITAN HOSPITAL OF MARYLAND, 5601 Loch Raven Boulevard, Zip 21239–2995; tel. 410/532–8000; Lawrence M. Beck, President (Total facility includes 23 beds in nursing home–type unit) **A**1 2 3 5 7 9 10 **F**1 2 3 4 5 6 7 8 10 11 12 14 15 16 17 18 19 20 21 22 23 24 25 26 27 28 29 30 31 32 33 34 35 37 38 39 40 41 42 43 44 45 46 48 49 51 52 53 54 55 56 57 58 59 60 61 62 63 64 65 66 67 71 72 73 74 **P**2 3 4 5 6 7 8 **S** MedStar Health, Columbia, MD Web address: www.helixhealth.com	23	10	272	10939	187	43130	0	100194	47755	1348
⊞ GREATER BALTIMORE MEDICAL CENTER, 6701 North Charles Street, Zip 21204–6892; tel. 410/828–2000; Robert P. Kowal, President and Chief Executive Officer (Nonreporting) **A**1 2 3 5 8 9 10 Web address: www.gbmc.org	23	10	304	—	—	—	—	—	—	—
⊞ HARBOR HOSPITAL CENTER, 3001 South Hanover Street, Zip 21225–1290; tel. 410/347–3200; L. Barney Johnson, President and Chief Executive Officer (Total facility includes 26 beds in nursing home–type unit) (Nonreporting) **A**1 2 3 5 9 10 **S** MedStar Health, Columbia, MD	23	10	176	—	—	—	—	—	—	—
⊞ △ JAMES LAWRENCE KERNAN HOSPITAL, (ORTHO REHAB HOSP), 2200 Kernan Drive, Zip 21207–6697; tel. 410/448–2500; James E. Ross, FACHE, Chief Executive Officer (Total facility includes 30 beds in nursing home–type unit) **A**1 3 5 7 9 10 **F**1 2 3 4 5 6 7 8 10 11 12 17 18 19 20 21 22 24 25 26 28 29 30 31 32 34 35 37 38 39 40 42 43 44 46 47 48 49 51 52 53 54 55 56 57 58 59 60 61 64 65 66 67 68 70 71 73 74	23	49	152	2692	96	31322	0	37599	15671	488
⊞ JOHNS HOPKINS BAYVIEW MEDICAL CENTER, 4940 Eastern Avenue, Zip 21224–2780; tel. 410/550–0100; Gregory F. Schaffer, Senior Vice President Operations (Total facility includes 295 beds in nursing home–type unit) **A**1 3 5 8 9 10 **F**1 2 3 4 5 7 8 9 10 11 12 13 14 15 16 17 18 19 20 21 22 23 24 25 26 27 28 29 30 31 34 35 37 38 39 40 41 42 43 44 45 46 47 48 49 50 51 52 53 54 55 56 57 58 59 60 61 63 64 65 66 67 68 70 71 72 73 74 **P**5 6 **S** Johns Hopkins Health System, Baltimore, MD Web address: www.jhbmc.jhu.edu	23	10	655	19125	496	254013	—	195772	69878	2443

Hospital, Address, Telephone, Administrator, Approval, Facility, and Physician Codes, Health Care System, Network	Classi-fication Codes		Utilization Data					Expense (thousands) of dollars		

★ American Hospital Association (AHA) membership
□ Joint Commission on Accreditation of Healthcare Organizations (JCAHO) accreditation
+ American Osteopathic Healthcare Association (AOHA) membership
○ American Osteopathic Association (AOA) accreditation
△ Commission on Accreditation of Rehabilitation Facilities (CARF) accreditation
Control codes 61, 63, 64, 71, 72 and 73 indicate hospitals listed by AOHA, but not registered by AHA. For definition of numerical codes, see page A4

Hospital	Control	Service	Staffed Beds	Admissions	Census	Outpatient Visits	Births	Total	Payroll	Personnel
⊠ △ JOHNS HOPKINS HOSPITAL, 600 North Wolfe Street, Zip 21287–0002; tel. 410/955–5000; Ronald R. Peterson, President **A**1 2 3 5 7 8 9 10 **F**1 2 3 4 5 6 7 8 9 10 11 12 13 14 15 16 17 18 19 20 21 22 23 24 25 26 27 28 29 30 31 32 33 34 35 37 38 39 40 41 42 43 44 45 46 47 48 49 50 51 52 53 54 55 56 57 58 59 60 61 63 64 65 66 67 68 70 71 72 73 74 **P**1 2 3 5 6 7 8 **S** Johns Hopkins Health System, Baltimore, MD **Web address:** www.med.jhu.edu	23	10	840	40119	688	266443	1851	556768	208505	6191
⊠ △ KENNEDY KRIEGER CHILDREN'S HOSPITAL, (CHILDREN'S SPECIALTY), 707 North Broadway, Zip 21205–1890; tel. 410/502–9000; Gary W. Goldstein, M.D., President **A**1 7 9 10 **F**12 14 15 16 17 19 20 21 34 35 39 45 46 48 49 50 53 54 55 58 63 65 67 71 73 **P**6 **Web address:** www.kennedykrieger.org	23	59	63	377	38	86808	0	45840	25883	1126
★ △ LEVINDALE HEBREW GERIATRIC CENTER AND HOSPITAL, 2434 West Belvedere Avenue, Zip 21215–5299; tel. 410/466–8700; Ronald Rothstein, Chief Executive Officer (Nonreporting) **A**7 9 10 **S** LifeBridge Health, Baltimore, MD **Web address:** www.sinai–balt.com	23	49	288	—	—	—	—	—	—	—
⊠ △ LIBERTY MEDICAL CENTER, 2600 Liberty Heights Avenue, Zip 21215–7892; tel. 410/383–4000; Henry DeVries, Acting Chief Executive Officer **A**1 9 10 **F**3 8 11 12 14 15 16 17 18 19 20 21 22 24 25 27 28 30 31 32 33 34 35 37 39 41 42 44 46 49 51 52 53 54 55 56 58 59 62 63 65 67 71 73 **P**5 6 7 8 **S** Bon Secours Health System, Inc., Marriottsville, MD	21	10	95	5965	89	68496	0	50178	22812	662
⊠ △ MARYLAND GENERAL HOSPITAL, 827 Linden Avenue, Zip 21201–4606; tel. 410/225–8000; James R. Wood, Chairman and Chief Executive Officer **A**1 2 3 5 7 9 10 **F**3 5 7 8 10 11 12 14 15 16 17 18 19 21 22 25 26 27 28 29 30 31 32 34 35 37 39 40 41 42 44 45 46 48 49 51 52 54 55 56 57 58 59 60 61 63 64 65 67 68 70 71 72 73 74 **P**8	23	10	223	8372	151	88486	632	88511	46496	1066
⊠ MERCY MEDICAL CENTER, 301 St. Paul Place, Zip 21202–2165; tel. 410/332–9000; Sister Helen Amos, President and Chief Executive Officer (Total facility includes 28 beds in nursing home–type unit) **A**1 3 5 9 10 **F**2 3 7 8 11 12 13 14 15 16 17 19 20 21 22 25 29 30 32 33 34 35 37 38 39 40 41 42 44 45 46 49 56 60 62 64 65 67 68 71 73 74 **P**5 6 7 **S** Sisters of Mercy of the Americas–Regional Community of Baltimore, Baltimore, MD **Web address:** www.mercymed.com	21	10	246	14280	219	129218	2884	130641	49683	1536
⊠ △ MT. WASHINGTON PEDIATRIC HOSPITAL, (PEDIATRIC SPECIALTY), 1708 West Rogers Avenue, Zip 21209–4596; tel. 410/578–8600; Sheldon J. Stein, Chief Operating Officer **A**1 7 9 10 **F**12 15 27 32 34 41 48 49 65 67 **P**5 **Web address:** www.mwph.org	23	59	102	565	47	11100	0	20079	9925	287
⊠ SHEPPARD AND ENOCH PRATT HOSPITAL, 6501 North Charles Street, Zip 21285–6815, Mailing Address: P.O. Box 6815, Zip 21285–6815; tel. 410/938–3000; Steven S. Sharfstein, M.D., President, Medical Director and Chief Executive Officer **A**1 3 5 9 10 **F**1 3 6 12 14 15 16 17 18 25 26 27 28 30 32 34 45 46 52 53 54 55 57 58 59 65 67 68 72 73 **P**4 **Web address:** www.sheppardpratt.org	23	22	188	5071	143	45907	0	58341	31529	1137
⊠ △ SINAI HOSPITAL OF BALTIMORE, 2401 West Belvedere Avenue, Zip 21215–5271; tel. 410/601–9000; Neil M. Meltzer, President and Chief Operating Officer (Nonreporting) **A**1 2 3 5 7 8 9 10 **S** LifeBridge Health, Baltimore, MD **Web address:** www.sinai–balt.com	23	10	436	—	—	—	—	—	—	—
□ SPRING GROVE HOSPITAL CENTER, 60 Wade Avenue, Zip 21228–4689; tel. 410/402–6000; Mark Pecevich, M.D., Superintendent **A**1 3 5 9 10 **F**20 26 52 57 64 65 73 **P**6	12	22	295	700	280	0	0	42000	—	811
⊠ ST. AGNES HEALTHCARE, 900 Caton Avenue, Zip 21229–5299; tel. 410/368–6000; Robert W. Adams, President and Chief Executive Officer (Total facility includes 187 beds in nursing home–type unit) **A**1 2 3 5 9 10 **F**1 3 6 7 8 10 11 12 13 14 15 16 17 19 21 22 25 26 27 28 29 30 31 32 33 34 35 37 38 39 40 41 42 44 45 46 47 49 51 53 54 56 58 60 63 64 65 67 71 73 74 **P**6 8 **S** Daughters of Charity National Health System, Saint Louis, MO **Web address:** www.stagnes.org	21	10	565	18490	359	224139	2228	190546	92688	2154
⊠ △ THE NEW CHILDREN'S HOSPITAL, 3825 Greenspring Avenue, Zip 21211–1398; tel. 410/462–6800; Robert A. Chrzan, President and Chief Executive Officer **A**1 3 5 7 9 10 **F**12 15 19 20 21 24 28 30 32 34 35 37 39 41 44 45 46 48 49 51 65 66 73	23	47	76	353	9	22527	0	11777	5331	164
⊠ △ UNION MEMORIAL HOSPITAL, 201 East University Parkway, Zip 21218–2391; tel. 410/554–2000; Harry Ryder, President and Chief Executive Officer (Total facility includes 31 beds in nursing home–type unit) (Nonreporting) **A**1 2 3 5 7 9 10 **S** MedStar Health, Columbia, MD **Web address:** www.helix.org	23	10	378	—	—	—	—	—	—	—
⊠ UNIVERSITY OF MARYLAND MEDICAL SYSTEM, 22 South Greene Street, Zip 21201–1595; tel. 410/328–8667; Morton I. Rapoport, M.D., President and Chief Executive Officer (Nonreporting) **A**1 2 3 5 8 9 10 **Web address:** www.umm.edu	23	10	768	—	—	—	—	—	—	—
⊠ VETERANS AFFAIRS MARYLAND HEALTH CARE SYSTEM–BALTIMORE DIVISION, 10 North Greene Street, Zip 21201–1524; tel. 410/605–7001; Dennis H. Smith, Director (Total facility includes 140 beds in nursing home–type unit) (Nonreporting) **A**1 2 3 5 8 **S** Department of Veterans Affairs, Washington, DC	45	10	897	—	—	—	—	—	—	—

Hospital, Address, Telephone, Administrator, Approval, Facility, and Physician Codes, Health Care System, Network	Classi-fication Codes		Utilization Data					Expense (thousands) of dollars		
	Control	Service	Staffed Beds	Admissions	Census	Outpatient Visits	Births	Total	Payroll	Personnel

★ American Hospital Association (AHA) membership
☐ Joint Commission on Accreditation of Healthcare Organizations (JCAHO) accreditation
+ American Osteopathic Healthcare Association (AOHA) membership
◯ American Osteopathic Association (AOA) accreditation
△ Commission on Accreditation of Rehabilitation Facilities (CARF) accreditation
Control codes 61, 63, 64, 71, 72 and 73 indicate hospitals listed by AOHA, but not registered by AHA. For definition of numerical codes, see page A4

BERLIN—Worcester County

✠ ATLANTIC GENERAL HOSPITAL, 9733 Healthway Drive, Zip 21811–1151; tel. 410/641–1100; Barry G. Beeman, President and Chief Executive Officer (Total facility includes 24 beds in nursing home–type unit) **A**1 9 10 **F**8 12 14 15 16 17 18 19 20 21 22 23 25 26 27 28 29 30 31 32 33 34 35 36 37 39 41 42 43 44 45 46 49 51 53 54 55 56 58 59 60 64 65 66 67 70 71 72 73 74 **P**6	23	10	62	2226	29	24208	0	15792	5955	236

BETHESDA—Montgomery County

✠ NATIONAL NAVAL MEDICAL CENTER, 8901 Wisconsin Avenue, Zip 20889–5600; tel. 301/295–5800; Rear Admiral Bonnie B. Potter, Commander (Nonreporting) **A**1 2 3 5 **S** Department of Navy, Washington, DC	43	10	217	—	—	—	—	—	—	—
✠ SUBURBAN HOSPITAL, 8600 Old Georgetown Road, Zip 20814–1497; tel. 301/896–3100; Brian G. Grissler, President and Chief Executive Officer (Total facility includes 31 beds in nursing home–type unit) **A**1 2 3 5 9 10 **F**2 3 4 6 8 10 11 12 14 15 16 17 18 19 21 22 24 26 27 28 29 30 31 32 35 37 41 42 44 45 46 49 52 53 54 55 56 57 58 59 60 61 63 64 65 67 69 70 71 72 73 74 **P**7 8 Web address: www.suburbanhospital.org	23	10	191	10325	148	81489	0	105746	46967	1249
✠ WARREN G. MAGNUSON CLINICAL CENTER, NATIONAL INSTITUTES OF HEALTH, (BIOMEDICAL RESEARCH), 9000 Rockville Pike, Zip 20892–1504; tel. 301/496–4114; John I. Gallin, M.D., Director **A**1 3 5 8 **F**3 4 8 10 19 20 21 24 26 27 31 34 35 37 39 42 44 46 49 50 52 53 54 55 57 58 59 60 63 65 67 71 73 **S** U. S. Public Health Service Indian Health Service, Rockville, MD Web address: www.cc.nih.gov	44	49	314	6250	136	70044	0	204902	94290	1833

CAMBRIDGE—Dorchester County

✠ DORCHESTER GENERAL HOSPITAL, 300 Byrn Street, Zip 21613–1908; tel. 410/228–5511; Joseph P. Ross, President and Chief Executive Officer **A**1 2 9 10 **F**2 8 12 15 16 17 19 21 22 28 29 30 31 32 33 34 35 37 39 41 42 44 46 49 51 53 54 56 57 58 59 65 71 73 74 **P**3 6	23	10	60	3278	45	71415	0	22726	10018	314
☐ EASTERN SHORE HOSPITAL CENTER, Route 50, State Route 479, Zip 21613, Mailing Address: P.O. Box 800, Zip 21613–0800; tel. 410/221–2300; Mary K. Noren, Superintendent **A**1 9 10 **F**14 15 16 37 45 46 48 52 54 55 57 58 65 73 **P**6	12	22	89	107	50	—	0	12910	7849	208

CHESTERTOWN—Kent County

✠ KENT & QUEEN ANNE'S HOSPITAL, 100 Brown Street, Zip 21620–1499; tel. 410/778–3300; William R. Kirk, Jr., President and Chief Executive Officer (Nonreporting) **A**1 9 10	23	10	64	—	—	—	—	—	—	—
☐ UPPER SHORE COMMUNITY MENTAL HEALTH CENTER, Scheeler Road, Zip 21620, Mailing Address: P.O. Box 229, Zip 21620–0229; tel. 410/778–6800; Mary K. Noren, Chief Executive Officer **A**1 10 **F**14 15 20 52 54 55 56 65 67 73	12	22	64	203	36	0	0	—	—	105

CHEVERLY—Prince George's County

GLADYS SPELLMAN SPECIALTY HOSPITAL AND NURSING CENTER, 2900 Mercy Lane, Zip 20785–1157; tel. 301/618–2010; Stewart R. Seitz, Chief Executive Officer (Nonreporting)	33	48	30	—	—	—	—	—	—	—
✠ PRINCE GEORGE'S HOSPITAL CENTER, 3001 Hospital Drive, Zip 20785–1189; tel. 301/618–2000; Phyllis Wingate–Jones, President **A**1 3 5 9 10 **F**3 4 7 8 10 11 12 14 15 16 17 18 19 20 21 22 23 24 25 26 27 28 29 30 31 34 35 36 37 38 39 40 41 42 43 44 45 46 49 51 52 53 54 56 58 59 60 62 63 64 65 67 68 70 71 72 73 74 **P**7 8 **S** Dimensions Health Corporation, Largo, MD Web address: www.princegeorgeshospital.org	23	10	370	14797	231	117052	2852	137427	65133	1316

CLINTON—Prince George's County

✠ SOUTHERN MARYLAND HOSPITAL, 7503 Surratts Road, Zip 20735–3395; tel. 301/868–8000; Francis P. Chiaramonte, M.D., President and Chief Executive Officer (Total facility includes 20 beds in nursing home–type unit) **A**1 2 9 10 **F**4 7 8 10 11 12 13 14 15 16 17 19 21 22 23 24 25 28 30 32 34 35 37 38 40 41 42 44 46 49 52 53 54 55 56 57 60 63 64 65 67 71 72 73 74 **P**6 8	33	10	370	11834	161	65660	1456	88198	37109	958

COLUMBIA—Howard County

✠ HOWARD COUNTY GENERAL HOSPITAL, 5755 Cedar Lane, Zip 21044–2912; tel. 410/740–7710; Victor A. Broccolino, President and Chief Executive Officer **A**1 2 5 9 10 **F**7 8 10 11 12 13 15 16 17 18 19 20 21 22 23 24 25 28 29 30 32 33 34 35 38 39 40 42 44 45 49 52 54 56 57 58 59 65 66 67 71 72 73 **P**1 3 8 **S** Johns Hopkins Health System, Baltimore, MD Web address: www.hcgh.org	23	10	160	11250	116	40084	2821	75865	31510	835

CRISFIELD—Somerset County

☐ EDWARD W. MCCREADY MEMORIAL HOSPITAL, 201 Hall Highway, Zip 21817–1299; tel. 410/968–1200; J. Allan Bickling, Chief Executive Officer **A**1 9 10 **F**8 13 14 15 17 18 19 21 22 23 24 25 26 27 28 29 30 31 32 34 35 39 41 42 44 45 49 52 53 54 55 57 58 65 71 **P**5 6	23	10	45	1088	35	16696	0	10223	4924	254

CROWNSVILLE—Anne Arundel County

☐ CROWNSVILLE HOSPITAL CENTER, 1520 Crownsville Road, Zip 21032–2306; tel. 410/729–6000; Ronald Hendler, Chief Executive Officer (Nonreporting) **A**1 9 10	12	22	248	—	—	—	—	—	—	—

CUMBERLAND—Allegany County

✠ △ MEMORIAL HOSPITAL AND MEDICAL CENTER OF CUMBERLAND, 600 Memorial Avenue, Zip 21502–3797; tel. 301/723–4000; Thomas C. Dowdell, Executive Director **A**1 2 7 9 10 **F**1 5 7 8 10 12 14 15 16 17 19 21 22 23 25 27 28 30 32 33 34 35 36 37 40 41 42 44 45 48 49 56 60 63 65 66 67 70 71 72 73 **P**6 **S** Daughters of Charity National Health System, Saint Louis, MO Web address: www.wmhs.com	23	10	187	7947	108	70688	613	68393	30563	864

Hospital, Address, Telephone, Administrator, Approval, Facility, and Physician Codes, Health Care System, Network	Classification Codes		Utilization Data					Expense (thousands) of dollars		
	Control	Service	Staffed Beds	Admissions	Census	Outpatient Visits	Births	Total	Payroll	Personnel

★ American Hospital Association (AHA) membership
□ Joint Commission on Accreditation of Healthcare Organizations (JCAHO) accreditation
+ American Osteopathic Healthcare Association (AOHA) membership
○ American Osteopathic Association (AOA) accreditation
△ Commission on Accreditation of Rehabilitation Facilities (CARF) accreditation
Control codes 61, 63, 64, 71, 72 and 73 indicate hospitals listed by AOHA, but not registered by AHA. For definition of numerical codes, see page A4

✠ SACRED HEART HOSPITAL, 900 Seton Drive, Zip 21502–1874; tel. 301/759–4200; William T. Bradel, Executive Director (Total facility includes 32 beds in nursing home–type unit) **A**1 2 9 10 **F**1 3 7 8 10 12 14 15 16 17 18 19 21 22 24 25 26 28 30 31 32 33 34 36 37 39 40 41 42 44 45 46 49 51 52 53 55 56 57 58 59 60 61 64 65 66 67 70 71 73 74 **P**6 **S** Daughters of Charity National Health System, Saint Louis, MO	23	10	304	8251	159	67296	554	63467	29986	862
□ THOMAS B. FINAN CENTER, 10102 Country Club Road S.E., Zip 21501, Mailing Address: P.O. Box 1722, Zip 21501–1722; tel. 301/777–2240; Archie T. Wallace, Chief Executive Officer **A**1 9 10 **F**14 15 20 41 52 53 54 55 57 58 65 73 **Web address:** www.gcnet.net	12	22	114	423	84	—	0	12197	6725	231
EAST NEW MARKET—Dorchester County										
CHARTER BEHAVIORAL HEALTH SYSTEM AT WARWICK MANOR, 3680 Warwick Road, Zip 21631–1420; tel. 410/943–8108; Marie McBee, Chief Executive Officer (Nonreporting)	33	82	42	—	—	—	—	—	—	—
EASTON—Talbot County										
✠ MEMORIAL HOSPITAL AT EASTON MARYLAND, 219 South Washington Street, Zip 21601–2996; tel. 410/822–1000; Joseph P. Ross, President and Chief Executive Officer (Total facility includes 31 beds in nursing home–type unit) **A**1 2 6 9 10 **F**3 7 8 10 14 15 16 17 19 20 21 22 25 26 28 29 30 31 32 33 34 35 37 39 40 41 42 44 45 46 49 54 56 58 59 60 63 64 65 67 71 72 73 74 **P**3 5 7 **Web address:** www.shorehealth.org	23	10	164	8645	114	88417	991	70536	27139	1067
ELKTON—Cecil County										
✠ UNION HOSPITAL, 106 Bow Street, Zip 21921–5596; tel. 410/398–4000; Michael V. Sack, President and Chief Executive Officer **A**1 9 10 **F**1 7 8 12 14 15 16 17 19 21 22 25 28 29 30 31 34 35 37 39 40 41 42 44 45 49 52 54 56 65 66 71 73 74 **P**5 7 **Web address:** www.uhcc.com	23	10	104	6426	63	110476	642	42942	17641	515
ELLICOTT CITY—Howard County										
□ TAYLOR MANOR HOSPITAL, 4100 College Avenue, Zip 21043–5506, Mailing Address: P.O. Box 396, Zip 21041–0396; tel. 410/465–3322; Morris L. Scherr, Executive Vice President **A**1 9 10 **F**14 15 16 19 21 35 46 50 52 53 55 57 58 59 63 65 71 **P**6	33	22	146	1746	93	4673	0	12383	7771	274
EMMITSBURG—Frederick County										
MOUNTAIN MANOR TREATMENT CENTER, Route 15, Zip 21727, Mailing Address: Box E, Zip 21727; tel. 301/447–2361; William J. Roby, Executive Vice President (Nonreporting)	33	82	140	—	—	—	—	—	—	—
FALLSTON—Harford County										
✠ FALLSTON GENERAL HOSPITAL, 200 Milton Avenue, Zip 21047–2777; tel. 410/877–3700; Lyle Ernest Sheldon, President and Chief Executive Officer **A**1 9 10 **F**7 8 10 12 15 16 17 19 21 22 28 30 32 33 34 35 37 41 42 44 46 49 56 65 67 71 73 **S** Upper Chesapeake Health System, Fallston, MD	23	10	113	6643	72	43334	0	40527	17419	545
FORT HOWARD—Baltimore County										
✠ VA MARYLAND HEALTH CARE SYSTEM–FORT HOWARD DIVISION, 9600 North Point Road, Zip 21052–9989; tel. 410/477–1800; Dennis H. Smith, Director (Total facility includes 47 beds in nursing home–type unit) (Nonreporting) **A**1 5 **S** Department of Veterans Affairs, Washington, DC	45	49	245	—	—	—	—	—	—	—
FORT WASHINGTON—Prince George's County										
✠ FORT WASHINGTON HOSPITAL, 11711 Livingston Road, Zip 20744–5164; tel. 301/292–7000; Paul Porter, Chief Operating Officer **A**1 9 10 **F**1 2 3 7 8 10 11 14 15 16 17 19 21 22 28 29 30 32 33 35 37 38 39 40 41 42 44 46 48 49 52 58 59 60 63 64 65 67 71 73 **P**6 **S** Greater Southeast Healthcare System, Washington, DC	23	50	37	2014	26	29471	0	20654	9019	225
FREDERICK—Frederick County										
✠ FREDERICK MEMORIAL HOSPITAL, 400 West Seventh Street, Zip 21701–4593; tel. 301/698–3300; James K. Kluttz, President and Chief Executive Officer (Total facility includes 20 beds in nursing home–type unit) **A**1 2 9 10 **F**7 8 10 11 12 13 14 15 16 17 18 19 20 21 22 25 28 29 30 31 32 33 34 35 37 39 40 41 42 44 45 46 48 49 52 53 54 55 56 58 59 60 63 64 65 66 67 71 72 73 74 **P**1 **Web address:** www.fmh.org	23	10	166	13492	166	302750	1972	110287	52387	1509
GLEN BURNIE—Anne Arundel County										
✠ NORTH ARUNDEL HOSPITAL, 301 Hospital Drive, Zip 21061–5899; tel. 410/787–4000; James R. Walker, FACHE, President and Chief Executive Officer (Nonreporting) **A**1 9 10	23	10	230	—	—	—	—	—	—	—
HAGERSTOWN—Washington County										
□ BROOK LANE PSYCHIATRIC CENTER, 13218 Brook Lane Drive, Zip 21742–1945, Mailing Address: P.O. Box 1945, Zip 21742–1945; tel. 301/733–0330; R. Lynn Rushing, Chief Executive Officer **A**1 9 10 **F**3 14 15 19 21 26 34 35 52 53 54 55 56 57 58 59 65 **P**1 **Web address:** www.brooklane.org	23	22	39	1188	24	17930	0	7793	4823	172
✠ △ WASHINGTON COUNTY HEALTH SYSTEM, (Formerly Washington County Hospital Association), 251 East Antietam Street, Zip 21740–5771; tel. 301/790–8000; Horace W. Murphy, President and Chief Executive Officer (Total facility includes 47 beds in nursing home–type unit) **A**1 2 7 9 10 **F**3 4 7 8 10 11 12 14 15 16 17 18 19 21 22 23 25 26 28 29 30 31 32 33 34 35 36 37 39 40 41 42 44 45 46 48 49 51 52 54 55 56 58 59 60 61 63 64 65 66 67 70 71 73 74 **P**6 8 **Web address:** www.wchsys.org	23	10	333	14822	195	167030	1646	119977	59850	1445

Hospital, Address, Telephone, Administrator, Approval, Facility, and Physician Codes, Health Care System, Network	Classi-fication Codes		Utilization Data					Expense (thousands) of dollars		
★ American Hospital Association (AHA) membership ☐ Joint Commission on Accreditation of Healthcare Organizations (JCAHO) accreditation + American Osteopathic Healthcare Association (AOHA) membership ○ American Osteopathic Association (AOA) accreditation △ Commission on Accreditation of Rehabilitation Facilities (CARF) accreditation Control codes 61, 63, 64, 71, 72 and 73 indicate hospitals listed by AOHA, but not registered by AHA. For definition of numerical codes, see page A4	Control	Service	Staffed Beds	Admissions	Census	Outpatient Visits	Births	Total	Payroll	Personnel

☐ WESTERN MARYLAND CENTER, 1500 Pennsylvania Avenue, Zip 21742–3194; tel. 301/791–4400; Cynthia Miller Pellegrino, Director and Chief Executive Officer (Total facility includes 60 beds in nursing home–type unit) **A**1 9 10 **F**15 16 17 20 26 27 30 31 36 39 41 45 46 48 54 57 64 65 67 73	12	48	115	130	98	—	0	13712	8154	279
HAVRE DE GRACE—Harford County										
✠ HARFORD MEMORIAL HOSPITAL, 501 South Union Avenue, Zip 21078–3493; tel. 410/939–2400; Lyle Ernest Sheldon, President and Chief Executive Officer (Total facility includes 17 beds in nursing home–type unit) **A**1 9 10 **F**6 7 10 12 15 16 17 19 21 22 23 28 30 32 33 34 35 37 40 41 42 44 46 49 52 56 64 65 67 71 73 **S** Upper Chesapeake Health System, Fallston, MD	23	10	157	6713	76	52482	765	41703	18276	597
JESSUP—Anne Arundel County										
☐ CLIFTON T. PERKINS HOSPITAL CENTER, 8450 Dorsey Run Road, Zip 20794–9486, Mailing Address: P.O. Box 1000, Zip 20794–1000; tel. 410/724–3000; M. Richard Fragala, M.D., Superintendent **A**1 3 9 **F**3 12 22 46 52 53 57 65 67 73	12	22	215	109	185	0	0	24822	15921	537
LA PLATA—Charles County										
✠ CIVISTA HEALTH, (Formerly Physicians Memorial Hospital), 701 East Charles Street, Zip 20646, Mailing Address: P.O. Box 1070, Zip 20646–1070; tel. 301/609–4000; Christine M. Stefanides, R.N., CHE, Interim President and Chief Executive Officer **A**1 2 9 10 **F**3 7 8 12 14 15 16 17 19 21 22 24 27 28 29 30 31 32 33 34 35 37 39 40 41 42 44 45 49 54 56 65 67 68 70 71 73 74 **Web address:** www.physmem.org	23	10	104	5619	68	47207	747	47731	19305	518
LANHAM—Prince George's County										
✠ DOCTORS COMMUNITY HOSPITAL, 8118 Good Luck Road, Zip 20706–3596; tel. 301/552–8118; Philip Down, President (Total facility includes 17 beds in nursing home–type unit) **A**1 9 10 **F**4 8 10 11 12 14 16 17 19 21 22 28 29 30 32 34 37 39 41 42 44 45 49 60 63 64 65 67 71 73	23	10	210	8440	136	47189	0	75858	32583	798
LAUREL—Prince George's County										
✠ △ LAUREL REGIONAL HOSPITAL, 7300 Van Dusen Road, Zip 20707–9266; tel. 301/725–4300; Patrick F. Mutch, President **A**1 7 9 10 **F**2 3 4 5 6 7 8 10 11 12 15 17 18 19 20 21 22 23 25 26 28 29 30 31 32 33 34 35 36 37 38 39 40 41 42 43 44 45 46 47 48 49 51 52 53 54 55 56 57 58 59 64 65 67 69 70 71 72 73 **P**1 6 7 **S** Dimensions Health Corporation, Largo, MD **Web address:** www.laurelregionalhospital.org	23	10	185	6514	100	48696	746	54855	26028	574
LEONARDTOWN—St. Marys County										
✠ ST. MARY'S HOSPITAL, 25500 Point Lookout Road, Zip 20650, Mailing Address: P.O. Box 527, Zip 20650; tel. 301/475–6001; Christine R. Wray, Chief Executive Officer **A**1 2 9 10 **F**7 8 12 13 15 16 17 18 19 20 21 22 23 26 28 29 30 31 33 34 35 37 39 40 41 42 44 45 46 49 52 53 54 55 56 57 58 59 63 65 67 71 73 74 **P**1 5 **Web address:** www.smhwecare.com	23	10	100	5440	61	91176	763	36464	17180	525
OAKLAND—Garrett County										
✠ GARRETT COUNTY MEMORIAL HOSPITAL, 251 North Fourth Street, Zip 21550–1334; tel. 301/334–2155; Walter P. Donalson, III, President and Chief Executive Officer **A**1 9 10 **F**7 8 11 14 15 16 17 18 19 20 21 22 27 28 30 32 33 34 39 40 41 44 45 46 49 51 54 56 63 65 66 67 71 73	23	10	76	2803	27	61227	293	19845	9093	264
OLNEY—Montgomery County										
✠ MONTGOMERY GENERAL HOSPITAL, 18101 Prince Philip Drive, Zip 20832–1512; tel. 301/774–8882; Peter W. Monge, President and Chief Executive Officer (Total facility includes 15 beds in nursing home–type unit) **A**1 2 9 10 **F**1 2 3 7 8 10 11 12 15 17 18 19 21 22 26 28 29 32 35 37 39 40 41 42 44 49 52 53 56 57 58 59 60 63 64 65 67 68 71 73 **P**1 **Web address:** www.montgomerygeneral.com	23	10	179	7976	111	31336	—	64457	31230	837
PERRY POINT—Cecil County										
✠ VETERANS AFFAIRS MARYLAND HEALTH CARE SYSTEM–PERRY POINT DIVISION, Circle Drive, Zip 21902; tel. 410/642–2411; Dennis H. Smith, Director (Total facility includes 200 beds in nursing home–type unit) **A**1 5 **F**1 2 3 4 6 8 10 11 12 16 17 19 20 21 22 25 26 27 28 29 30 31 32 33 34 35 37 39 41 42 43 44 45 46 48 49 51 52 54 55 56 57 58 60 61 63 64 65 67 69 71 72 73 74 **P**6 **S** Department of Veterans Affairs, Washington, DC	45	10	697	8437	589	476076	—	220000	121502	3725
PRINCE FREDERICK—Calvert County										
✠ CALVERT MEMORIAL HOSPITAL, 100 Hospital Road, Zip 20678–9675; tel. 410/535–4000; James J. Xinis, President and Chief Executive Officer **A**1 2 9 10 **F**8 12 13 14 15 16 17 19 22 24 25 28 29 30 32 33 34 35 36 37 39 40 41 42 44 45 46 49 52 53 54 56 58 59 60 65 66 67 68 71 72 73 74 **P**7 8	23	10	125	5921	58	—	833	34898	16537	446
RANDALLSTOWN—Baltimore County										
✠ NORTHWEST HOSPITAL CENTER, 5401 Old Court Road, Zip 21133–5185; tel. 410/521–2200; Robert W. Fischer, President **A**1 2 9 10 **F**1 3 4 5 6 7 8 10 11 12 13 15 17 18 19 20 21 23 24 25 26 27 28 29 30 31 32 33 34 35 36 37 39 41 42 43 44 45 46 49 51 53 54 55 56 57 58 59 60 61 62 63 65 66 67 68 70 71 72 73 74 **P**1 7 8 **S** LifeBridge Health, Baltimore, MD	23	10	160	9560	124	70834	0	80683	36370	1007
ROCKVILLE—Montgomery County										
☐ CHARTER BEHAVIORAL HEALTH SYSTEM OF MARYLAND AT POTOMAC RIDGE, 14901 Broschart Road, Zip 20850–3321; tel. 301/251–4500; Craig S. Juengling, Chief Executive Officer (Nonreporting) **A**1 9 10 **S** Magellan Health Services, Atlanta, GA	33	22	140	—	—	—	—	—	—	—

Hospital, Address, Telephone, Administrator, Approval, Facility, and Physician Codes, Health Care System, Network	Classi-fication Codes		Utilization Data					Expense (thousands) of dollars		
	Control	Service	Staffed Beds	Admissions	Census	Outpatient Visits	Births	Total	Payroll	Personnel

Approval codes legend:
- ★ American Hospital Association (AHA) membership
- □ Joint Commission on Accreditation of Healthcare Organizations (JCAHO) accreditation
- + American Osteopathic Healthcare Association (AOHA) membership
- ○ American Osteopathic Association (AOA) accreditation
- △ Commission on Accreditation of Rehabilitation Facilities (CARF) accreditation
  Control codes 61, 63, 64, 71, 72 and 73 indicate hospitals listed by AOHA, but not registered by AHA. For definition of numerical codes, see page A4

Hospital	Control	Service	Staffed Beds	Admissions	Census	Outpatient Visits	Births	Total	Payroll	Personnel
✠ CHESTNUT LODGE HOSPITAL, 500 West Montgomery Avenue, Zip 20850–3892; tel. 301/424–8300; Steven Goldstein, Ph.D., President and Chief Executive Officer (Total facility includes 88 beds in nursing home–type unit) **A**1 9 10 **F**2 3 6 11 12 14 15 16 17 18 37 52 53 54 55 56 57 58 59 64 65 67 68 **P**6	23	22	132	335	118	138900	0	18664	12084	388
□ SHADY GROVE ADVENTIST HOSPITAL, 9901 Medical Center Drive, Zip 20850–3395; tel. 301/279–6000; Cory Chambers, President and Chief Executive Officer **A**1 2 9 10 **F**1 3 4 6 7 8 10 12 13 14 15 16 17 19 21 22 23 24 27 28 29 30 31 32 33 35 36 37 38 39 40 41 42 44 45 46 47 49 51 53 54 55 56 57 58 59 60 63 64 65 67 71 73 74 **P**1	21	10	253	16507	201	117594	4793	131245	47235	1380
SALISBURY—Wicomico County										
□ DEER'S HEAD CENTER, (LONG TERM CARE), 351 Deer's Head Hospital Road, Zip 21802, Mailing Address: P.O. Box 2018, Zip 21802–2018; tel. 410/543–4000; Dorothy A. Bradshaw, Director (Total facility includes 60 beds in nursing home–type unit) **A**1 10 **F**4 8 10 11 14 15 16 19 20 21 22 26 28 29 30 31 33 35 37 39 42 44 45 46 48 49 52 53 54 55 56 57 58 60 64 65 67 69 71 73 **P**6	12	49	70	79	69	22166	0	14933	9453	251
□ △ HEALTHSOUTH CHESAPEAKE REHABILITATION HOSPITAL, 220 Tilghman Road, Zip 21804–1921; tel. 410/546–4600; William Roth, Chief Executive Officer (Nonreporting) **A**1 7 9 10 **S** HEALTHSOUTH Corporation, Birmingham, AL	33	46	42	—	—	—	—	—	—	—
✠ PENINSULA REGIONAL MEDICAL CENTER, 100 East Carroll Street, Zip 21801–5422; tel. 410/546–6400; R. Alan Newberry, President and Chief Executive Officer **A**1 2 9 10 **F**4 7 8 10 11 12 13 14 15 16 17 19 20 21 22 23 24 25 26 28 29 30 31 32 34 35 37 39 40 41 42 43 44 45 49 51 52 54 56 57 58 60 64 65 67 70 71 72 73 **P**5 6 Web address: www.peninsula.org	23	10	338	16475	203	422707	1949	138869	62192	—
SILVER SPRING—Montgomery County										
✠ HOLY CROSS HOSPITAL OF SILVER SPRING, 1500 Forest Glen Road, Zip 20910–1484; tel. 301/754–7000; Kevin J. Sexton, President and Chief Executive Officer (Total facility includes 100 beds in nursing home–type unit) **A**1 3 5 8 9 10 **F**1 4 7 8 10 11 12 15 16 17 18 19 21 22 25 26 27 28 29 30 31 32 33 34 35 36 37 38 39 40 41 42 44 45 46 49 51 52 54 56 60 64 65 66 67 68 71 73 74 **P**1 5 6 7 **S** Holy Cross Health System Corporation, South Bend, IN	21	10	454	22225	272	203426	5823	169263	73440	1957
★ SAINT LUKE INSTITUTE, 8901 New Hampshire Avenue, Zip 20903–3611; tel. 301/445–7970; Father Stephen J. Rossetti, Ph.D., President and Chief Executive Officer (Nonreporting)	23	22	24							
SYKESVILLE—Carroll County										
□ SPRINGFIELD HOSPITAL CENTER, 6655 Sykesville Road, Zip 21784–7966; tel. 410/795–2100; Paula A. Langmead, Chief Executive Officer **A**1 9 10 **F**14 16 41 45 52 55 57 65 67	12	22	326	798	331	0	0	—	—	843
TAKOMA PARK—Montgomery County										
✠ WASHINGTON ADVENTIST HOSPITAL, 7600 Carroll Avenue, Zip 20912–6392; tel. 301/891–7600; Kiltie Leach, Chief Operating Officer (Nonreporting) **A**1 9 10	21	10	300	—	—	—	—	—	—	—
TOWSON—Baltimore County										
✠ ST. JOSEPH MEDICAL CENTER, 7620 York Road, Zip 21204–7582; tel. 410/337–1000; James J. Cullen, President and Chief Executive Officer (Total facility includes 26 beds in nursing home–type unit) **A**1 9 10 **F**4 7 8 10 11 14 15 16 17 19 22 25 26 28 30 32 35 37 38 39 40 41 42 43 44 45 46 48 49 52 53 54 55 56 58 59 61 64 65 67 68 70 71 72 73 74 **P**2 5 7 **S** Catholic Health Initiatives, Denver, CO Web address: www.sjmcmd.org	21	10	414	20024	270	93558	2228	169277	70655	1774
WESTMINSTER—Carroll County										
✠ CARROLL COUNTY GENERAL HOSPITAL, 200 Memorial Avenue, Zip 21157–5799; tel. 410/871–6900; John M. Sernulka, President and Chief Executive Officer **A**1 9 10 **F**7 8 10 12 15 16 17 18 19 22 23 25 26 28 30 32 33 35 37 39 40 41 42 44 46 49 52 53 54 55 56 57 59 65 67 71 73 **P**3 7 Web address: www.ccgh.com	23	10	158	9360	108	105502	1140	60804	28642	915

MASSACHUSETTS

Resident population 6,157 (in thousands)
Resident population in metro areas 95.2%
Birth rate per 1,000 population 13.4
65 years and over 14.1%
Percent of persons without health insurance 12.4%

Hospital, Address, Telephone, Administrator, Approval, Facility, and Physician Codes, Health Care System, Network	Classi-fication Codes		Utilization Data					Expense (thousands) of dollars		
★ American Hospital Association (AHA) membership □ Joint Commission on Accreditation of Healthcare Organizations (JCAHO) accreditation + American Osteopathic Healthcare Association (AOHA) membership ○ American Osteopathic Association (AOA) accreditation △ Commission on Accreditation of Rehabilitation Facilities (CARF) accreditation Control codes 61, 63, 64, 71, 72 and 73 indicate hospitals listed by AOHA, but not registered by AHA. For definition of numerical codes, see page A4	Control	Service	Staffed Beds	Admissions	Census	Outpatient Visits	Births	Total	Payroll	Personnel

AMHERST—Hampshire County

UNIVERSITY HEALTH SERVICES, University of Massachusetts, Box 34310, Zip 01003–4310; tel. 413/577–5000; Bernette A. Melby, Executive Director (Nonreporting) **A**3 10	12	11	6	—	—	—	—	—	—	—

ANDOVER—Essex County

ISHAM HEALTH CENTER, 180 Main Street, Zip 01810–4161; tel. 978/749–4455; Nneka Anaebonam, Administrator (Nonreporting)	23	59	20	—	—	—	—	—	—	—

ARLINGTON—Middlesex County

□ SYMMES HOSPITAL AND MEDICAL CENTER, (Formerly Medical Center at Symmes), Hospital Road, Zip 02474–2199; tel. 781/646–1500; Timothy McCarron, Chief Operating Officer (Nonreporting) **A**1 9 10	23	10	88	—	—	—	—	—	—	—

ATHOL—Worcester County

□ ATHOL MEMORIAL HOSPITAL, 2033 Main Street, Zip 01331–3598; tel. 978/249–3511; William DiFederico, President **A**1 9 10 **F**8 12 13 14 15 16 17 19 20 22 27 28 29 30 31 32 33 34 35 37 39 41 42 44 45 49 53 54 56 58 65 67 71 73 **P**5 **Web address:** www.atholhosp.org	23	10	33	1336	17	38498	0	14720	7334	211

ATTLEBORO—Bristol County

✠ STURDY MEMORIAL HOSPITAL, 211 Park Street, Zip 02703–3137, Mailing Address: P.O. Box 2963, Zip 02703–2963; tel. 508/222–5200; Linda Shyavitz, President and Chief Executive Officer **A**1 2 9 10 **F**7 8 12 13 14 15 16 17 18 19 20 21 22 23 25 26 28 29 30 31 33 34 35 37 39 40 41 42 44 45 46 49 51 54 61 63 65 67 68 71 72 73 74 **P**6	23	10	110	5143	58	99632	869	52657	29275	760

AYER—Middlesex County

✠ DEACONESS–NASHOBA HOSPITAL, 200 Groton Road, Zip 01432–3300; tel. 978/784–9000; Jeffrey R. Kelly, President and Chief Executive Officer **A**1 9 10 **F**1 8 11 12 15 16 17 19 22 25 26 28 29 30 32 35 39 41 42 44 45 46 49 51 65 67 71 73 **P**5 8 **S** CareGroup, Boston, MA	23	10	49	1935	21	90821	0	23409	11057	273

BEDFORD—Middlesex County

✠ EDITH NOURSE ROGERS MEMORIAL VETERANS HOSPITAL, 200 Springs Road, Zip 01730–1198; tel. 781/687–2000; William A. Conte, Director (Total facility includes 232 beds in nursing home–type unit) **A**1 3 5 **F**1 3 12 20 26 27 28 30 33 34 39 46 49 51 52 54 56 57 58 59 64 65 71 73 74 **P**6 **S** Department of Veterans Affairs, Washington, DC	45	22	493	1792	519	172884	0	70225	46823	1053

BELMONT—Middlesex County

✠ MCLEAN HOSPITAL, 115 Mill Street, Zip 02478–9106; tel. 617/855–2000; Bruce M. Cohen, M.D., President and Psychiatrist–in–Chief **A**1 3 5 10 **F**1 2 3 4 5 6 7 8 9 10 11 12 13 17 18 19 20 21 22 23 24 26 28 29 30 31 32 33 34 35 36 37 38 39 40 41 42 43 44 45 46 47 48 50 51 52 53 54 55 56 57 58 59 60 61 63 64 65 66 67 68 70 71 73 74 **P**1 3 4 5 6 7 8 **S** Partners HealthCare System, Inc., Boston, MA **Web address:** www.mcleanhospital.org	23	22	135	2971	123	38170	0	69195	27122	785

BEVERLY—Essex County

✠ BEVERLY HOSPITAL, (Includes Addison Gilbert Hospital, 298 Washington Street, Gloucester, Zip 01930–4887; tel. 978/283–4000; Kathleen Allen Bliss, President), 85 Herrrick Street, Zip 01915–1777; tel. 978/922–3000; Robert R. Fanning, Jr., Chief Executive Officer **A**1 2 3 9 10 **F**1 2 3 5 6 7 8 10 12 14 15 16 17 18 19 22 23 26 28 29 30 31 32 33 34 35 36 37 39 40 41 42 44 45 46 49 51 52 53 54 55 56 57 58 59 60 61 62 64 66 67 69 71 73 74 **P**1 6 **Web address:** www.nhs–healthlink.org	23	10	339	17028	208	97705	2677	126275	53093	1609

BOSTON—Suffolk County

□ ARBOUR HOSPITAL, 49 Robinwood Avenue, Zip 02130–2156, Mailing Address: P.O. Box 9, Zip 02130; tel. 617/522–4400; Roy A. Ettlinger, Chief Executive Officer (Nonreporting) **A**1 10 **S** Universal Health Services, Inc., King of Prussia, PA	33	22	118	—	—	—	—	—	—	—
✠ BETH ISRAEL DEACONESS MEDICAL CENTER, 330 Brookline Avenue, Zip 02215–5491; tel. 617/667–7000; Herbert Yehude Kressel, M.D., President (Total facility includes 48 beds in nursing home–type unit) (Nonreporting) **A**1 2 5 8 9 10 **S** CareGroup, Boston, MA	23	10	671	—	—	—	—	—	—	—
✠ BOSTON MEDICAL CENTER, One Boston Medical Center Place, Zip 02118–2393; tel. 617/638–8000; Elaine S. Ullian, President and Chief Executive Officer (Total facility includes 20 beds in nursing home–type unit) **A**1 2 3 5 8 9 10 **F**1 3 4 5 6 7 8 10 11 12 13 14 15 16 17 18 19 20 21 22 23 24 25 26 27 28 29 30 31 32 33 34 35 36 37 38 39 40 41 42 43 44 45 46 47 48 49 51 52 53 54 55 56 57 58 60 61 62 63 64 65 67 68 70 71 72 73 74 **P**3 4 5 7 **Web address:** www.bmc.org	23	10	432	19347	311	473292	1605	543087	151314	3904
✠ BRIGHAM AND WOMEN'S HOSPITAL, 75 Francis Street, Zip 02115–6195; tel. 617/732–5500; Jeffrey Otten, President **A**1 2 3 5 8 9 10 **F**3 4 5 7 8 9 10 11 12 13 14 15 16 17 18 19 20 21 22 23 24 25 26 27 28 29 30 31 32 33 34 35 37 38 39 40 41 42 43 44 45 46 49 50 51 53 54 55 56 57 58 59 60 61 63 65 66 67 68 70 71 72 73 74 **P**3 8 **S** Partners HealthCare System, Inc., Boston, MA **Web address:** www.partners.org	23	10	650	41042	547	707958	9261	890617	274522	7708

Hospital, Address, Telephone, Administrator, Approval, Facility, and Physician Codes, Health Care System, Network	Classi-fication Codes		Utilization Data					Expense (thousands) of dollars		
	Control	Service	Staffed Beds	Admissions	Census	Outpatient Visits	Births	Total	Payroll	Personnel

★ American Hospital Association (AHA) membership
□ Joint Commission on Accreditation of Healthcare Organizations (JCAHO) accreditation
+ American Osteopathic Healthcare Association (AOHA) membership
○ American Osteopathic Association (AOA) accreditation
△ Commission on Accreditation of Rehabilitation Facilities (CARF) accreditation
Control codes 61, 63, 64, 71, 72 and 73 indicate hospitals listed by AOHA, but not registered by AHA. For definition of numerical codes, see page A4

Hospital	Control	Service	Staffed Beds	Admissions	Census	Outpatient Visits	Births	Total	Payroll	Personnel
⊠ CHILDREN'S HOSPITAL, 300 Longwood Avenue, Zip 02115–5737; tel. 617/355–6000; Stephen R. Laverty, President and Chief Operating Officer **A**1 3 5 8 9 10 **F**11 15 16 19 21 35 38 44 45 46 47 49 50 51 52 53 54 55 56 58 60 61 63 65 66 67 68 72 73 **P**3 5	23	50	324	19143	245	298870	0	405312	141133	4071
⊠ DANA–FARBER CANCER INSTITUTE, (COMPREHENSIVE CANCER CENTER), 44 Binney Street, Zip 02115–6084; tel. 617/632–3000; David G. Nathan, M.D., President **A**1 3 9 10 **F**8 12 15 16 17 19 21 22 25 28 29 30 31 32 33 34 35 37 39 41 42 44 45 46 47 49 53 54 55 56 57 58 60 63 65 67 68 70 71 73 74 **Web address:** www.dfci.harvard.edu	23	49	30	866	20	85797	0	209549	75191	1749
⊠ FAULKNER HOSPITAL, Mailing Address: 1153 Centre Sreet, Zip 02130–3400; tel. 617/983–7000; David J. Trull, President and Chief Executive Officer **A**1 2 3 5 8 9 10 **F**1 3 4 8 10 11 12 14 15 16 17 18 19 21 22 25 30 31 34 35 37 39 41 42 44 45 46 49 51 52 54 55 56 57 58 59 61 65 67 71 72 73 74 **P**2 5 **S** Partners HealthCare System, Inc., Boston, MA **Web address:** www.faulknerhospital.org	23	10	127	6218	87	138699	0	64077	33031	796
□ △ FRANCISCAN CHILDREN'S HOSPITAL AND REHABILITATION CENTER, Mailing Address: 30 Warren Street, Zip 02135–3680; tel. 617/254–3800; Paul J. Dellarocco, President and Chief Executive Officer **A**1 5 7 10 **F**1 12 15 16 17 20 30 32 33 34 39 44 48 49 52 53 58 59 65 67 71 72 73 **P**6	23	56	60	654	51	26615	0	30102	16846	463
★ HEBREW REHABILITATION CENTER FOR AGED, (CHRONIC DISEASE HOSP), Mailing Address: 1200 Centre Street, Zip 02131–1097; tel. 617/325–8000; Maurice I. May, President and Chief Executive Officer **A**10 **F**1 6 15 16 17 20 21 24 26 27 28 30 32 33 34 36 39 41 46 49 51 54 57 58 62 64 65 67 73 **P**6 **Web address:** www.hebrewrehab.org	23	49	725	200	703	488	0	54951	30847	798
⊠ JEWISH MEMORIAL HOSPITAL AND REHABILITATION CENTER, 59 Townsend Street, Zip 02119–9918; tel. 617/442–8760; Paul J. Dellarocco, President and Chief Executive Officer (Nonreporting) **A**1 3 5 10 **Web address:** www.jmhrc.org	23	49	110	—	—	—	—	—	—	—
⊠ LEMUEL SHATTUCK HOSPITAL, 170 Morton Street, Jamaica Plain, Zip 02130–3787; tel. 617/522–8110; Robert D. Wakefield, Jr., Chief Executive Officer (Nonreporting) **A**1 3 5 6 10	12	10	230	—	—	—	—	—	—	—
□ MASSACHUSETTS EYE AND EAR INFIRMARY, 243 Charles Street, Zip 02114–3096; tel. 617/523–7900; F. Curtis Smith, President **A**1 3 5 9 10 **F**12 14 15 16 17 19 21 22 25 27 28 30 32 34 35 39 41 42 44 45 46 49 50 60 65 67 70 71 72 73 **P**5 8 **Web address:** www.meei.harvard.edu	23	45	42	1964	18	208368	0	85206	24403	1144
⊠ MASSACHUSETTS GENERAL HOSPITAL, 55 Fruit Street, Zip 02114–2696; tel. 617/726–2000; James J. Mongan, M.D., President **A**1 2 3 5 8 9 10 **F**1 2 3 4 5 6 7 8 9 10 11 12 13 14 15 16 17 18 19 20 21 22 23 25 26 27 28 29 30 31 32 33 34 35 37 38 39 40 41 42 43 44 45 46 47 48 49 50 51 52 53 54 55 56 57 58 59 60 61 62 63 64 65 66 67 68 70 71 72 73 74 **P**4 8 **S** Partners HealthCare System, Inc., Boston, MA	23	10	848	35909	636	679012	2413	895395	324634	11470
⊠ NEW ENGLAND BAPTIST HOSPITAL, 125 Parker Hill Avenue, Zip 02120–3297; tel. 617/754–5800; Alan H. Robbins, M.D., President (Total facility includes 20 beds in nursing home–type unit) (Nonreporting) **A**1 3 5 6 9 10 **S** CareGroup, Boston, MA **Web address:** www.nebh.org	23	10	141	—	—	—	—	—	—	—
⊠ NEW ENGLAND MEDICAL CENTER, 750 Washington Street, Zip 02111–1845; tel. 617/636–5000; Thomas F. O'Donnell, Jr., M.D., FACS, Chief Executive Officer (Total facility includes 21 beds in nursing home–type unit) **A**1 2 3 5 8 9 10 **F**3 4 5 7 8 10 11 12 13 15 16 17 18 19 20 21 22 23 25 26 28 29 30 31 34 35 37 38 39 40 41 42 43 44 45 47 49 51 52 53 54 55 56 57 58 59 60 61 63 64 65 66 67 68 70 71 73 74 **P**5 6 **S** Lifespan Corporation, Providence, RI	23	10	314	14875	269	349544	1502	361364	148562	2798
⊠ SHRINERS HOSPITALS FOR CHILDREN, SHRINERS BURNS HOSPITAL–BOSTON, (PEDIATRIC BURNS), 51 Blossom Street, Zip 02114–2699; tel. 617/722–3000; Robert F. Bories, Jr., FACHE, Administrator **A**1 3 **F**16 19 21 22 35 45 49 53 65 67 71 73 **S** Shriners Hospitals for Children, Tampa, FL **Web address:** www.shrinershq.org	23	59	30	828	19	3458	0	—	—	231
⊠ △ SPAULDING REHABILITATION HOSPITAL, 125 Nashua Street, Zip 02114–1198; tel. 617/573–7000; John E. Cupples, Chief Executive Officer (Total facility includes 37 beds in nursing home–type unit) **A**1 3 7 10 **F**2 3 12 19 20 21 22 25 26 27 28 29 30 32 34 35 39 41 42 45 46 48 49 50 52 53 54 55 56 57 58 60 63 64 65 66 67 71 73 **S** Partners HealthCare System, Inc., Boston, MA **Web address:** www.spauldingrehab.org	23	46	296	3969	271	79434	0	83202	46755	1233
□ VENCOR HOSPITAL–BOSTON, (ACUTE LONG TERM), 1515 Commonwealth Avenue, Zip 02135–3696; tel. 617/254–1100; Donald E. Schwarz, Administrator **A**1 10 **F**12 14 15 16 19 31 41 65 71 **P**4 7 **S** Vencor, Incorporated, Louisville, KY	33	49	52	515	43	0	0	12356	5192	82
⊠ VETERANS AFFAIRS MEDICAL CENTER, Mailing Address: 150 South Huntington Avenue, Jamaica Plain Station, Zip 02130–4820; tel. 617/232–9500; Roland E. Moore, Acting Medical Center Director **A**1 2 3 5 8 **F**1 3 4 5 8 10 11 12 15 17 18 19 20 21 22 23 24 25 26 27 28 29 30 31 33 34 35 37 39 41 42 43 44 45 46 48 49 50 51 52 54 55 56 57 58 59 60 61 63 64 65 66 67 68 70 71 72 73 74 **S** Department of Veterans Affairs, Washington, DC	45	10	202	7810	212	387635	0	108709	—	1739

Hospital, Address, Telephone, Administrator, Approval, Facility, and Physician Codes, Health Care System, Network	Classi-fication Codes		Utilization Data					Expense (thousands) of dollars		
★ American Hospital Association (AHA) membership □ Joint Commission on Accreditation of Healthcare Organizations (JCAHO) accreditation + American Osteopathic Healthcare Association (AOHA) membership ○ American Osteopathic Association (AOA) accreditation △ Commission on Accreditation of Rehabilitation Facilities (CARF) accreditation Control codes 61, 63, 64, 71, 72 and 73 indicate hospitals listed by AOHA, but not registered by AHA. For definition of numerical codes, see page A4	Control	Service	Staffed Beds	Admissions	Census	Outpatient Visits	Births	Total	Payroll	Personnel

BRAINTREE—Norfolk County

⊠ HEALTHSOUTH BRAINTREE REHABILITATION HOSPITAL, 250 Pond Street, Zip 02185–5391; tel. 781/848–5353; Anne M. MacRitchie, President and Chief Executive Officer (Nonreporting) **A**1 3 10 **S** HEALTHSOUTH Corporation, Birmingham, AL
| | | 33 | 46 | 187 | — | — | — | — | — | — | — |

□ MASSACHUSETTS RESPIRATORY HOSPITAL, 2001 Washington Street, Zip 02184–8664; tel. 781/848–2600; Jay Mitchell, Chief Executive Officer (Nonreporting) **A**1 10
| | | 13 | 48 | 110 | — | — | — | — | — | — | — |

BRIDGEWATER—Plymouth County

BRIDGEWATER STATE HOSPITAL, 20 Administration Road, Zip 02324–3201; tel. 617/697–8161; Kenneth W. Nelson, Superintendent (Nonreporting)
| | | 12 | 22 | 350 | — | — | — | — | — | — | — |

BRIGHTON—Suffolk County

⊠ ST. ELIZABETH'S MEDICAL CENTER OF BOSTON, 736 Cambridge Street, Zip 02135–2997; tel. 617/789–3000; Michael F. Collins, M.D., President (Total facility includes 21 beds in nursing home–type unit) **A**1 2 3 5 6 8 9 10 **F**1 2 3 4 7 8 10 11 12 14 15 16 17 18 19 20 21 22 23 25 26 28 29 30 31 32 33 34 35 37 38 39 40 41 42 43 44 45 46 49 51 52 54 55 56 57 58 59 60 61 63 64 65 66 67 70 71 72 73 74 **P**3 5 **S** Caritas Christi Health Care, Boston, MA
Web address: www.semc.org
| | | 21 | 10 | 232 | 14345 | 244 | 124708 | 1690 | 207152 | 85581 | 2512 |

⊠ ST. JOHN OF GOD HOSPITAL, 296 Allston Street, Zip 02146–1659; tel. 617/277–5750; William K. Brinkert, President (Nonreporting) **A**1 10 **S** Caritas Christi Health Care, Boston, MA
| | | 21 | 48 | 31 | — | — | — | — | — | — | — |

BROCKTON—Plymouth County

⊠ BROCKTON HOSPITAL, 680 Centre Street, Zip 02302–3395; tel. 508/941–7000; Norman B. Goodman, President and Chief Executive Officer (Total facility includes 26 beds in nursing home–type unit) **A**1 2 3 5 6 9 10 **F**3 4 7 8 10 11 12 13 14 15 16 17 18 19 20 21 22 23 26 27 28 29 30 31 34 35 37 39 40 41 42 44 46 49 51 52 53 54 55 56 57 58 59 60 63 64 65 66 67 68 71 72 73 74 **P**6 8
Web address: www.brocktonhospital.com
| | | 23 | 10 | 247 | 10469 | 146 | 175357 | 1047 | 93408 | 55060 | 1040 |

⊠ BROCKTON VETERANS AFFAIRS MEDICAL CENTER, (Formerly Brockton–West Roxbury Veterans Affairs Medical Center), 940 Belmont Street, Zip 02401–5596; tel. 508/583–4500; Roland E. Moore, Acting Director (Total facility includes 120 beds in nursing home–type unit) **A**1 3 5 8 **F**1 2 3 4 8 10 12 17 18 19 20 21 22 25 26 27 28 30 31 32 34 37 39 41 42 43 44 46 48 49 51 52 54 55 56 57 58 59 64 65 67 71 72 73 74 **S** Department of Veterans Affairs, Washington, DC
| | | 45 | 10 | 483 | 6655 | 484 | 294094 | 0 | — | — | — |

⊠ GOOD SAMARITAN MEDICAL CENTER, (Includes Good Samaritan Medical Center – Cushing Campus), 235 North Pearl Street, Zip 02401–1794; tel. 508/427–3000; Frank J. Larkin, President and Chief Executive Officer **A**1 2 3 5 9 10 **F**7 8 11 12 14 15 16 17 19 20 21 22 23 26 28 30 33 35 37 39 40 41 42 44 46 49 54 56 65 67 71 72 73 74 **P**5 **S** Caritas Christi Health Care, Boston, MA
| | | 23 | 10 | 222 | 11727 | 155 | 145456 | 1259 | 87316 | 40746 | 979 |

BROOKLINE—Norfolk County

□ ARBOUR H. R. I. HOSPITAL, (Formerly H. R. I. Hospital), 227 Babcock Street, Zip 02146; tel. 617/731–3200; Roy A. Ettlinger, Chief Executive Officer **A**1 5 10 **F**2 3 12 16 18 25 26 34 52 53 54 55 56 57 58 59 65 74 **S** Universal Health Services, Inc., King of Prussia, PA
Web address: www.arbourhealth.com
| | | 33 | 22 | 57 | 1201 | 44 | 0 | 0 | 10365 | 4686 | 94 |

□ BOURNEWOOD HOSPITAL, 300 South Street, Zip 02467–3694; tel. 617/469–0300; Nasir A. Khan, M.D., Director **A**1 10 **F**2 3 19 34 35 52 53 54 55 56 57 58 59 65 67 68 **P**1
Web address: www.bournewood.com
| | | 33 | 22 | 75 | 2630 | 63 | 3200 | 0 | 9520 | 5783 | 177 |

BURLINGTON—Middlesex County

⊠ LAHEY CLINIC HOSPITAL, 41 Mall Road, Zip 01805–0001; tel. 781/744–8330; John A. Libertino, M.D., Chief Executive Officer **A**1 2 3 5 8 9 10 **F**4 5 8 10 11 12 13 14 15 16 17 18 19 21 22 23 25 26 27 28 29 30 31 32 34 35 37 39 41 42 43 44 45 46 48 49 51 52 53 54 55 56 57 58 60 61 63 65 66 67 68 70 71 72 73 74 **P**6
Web address: www.massnet/index.htm
| | | 23 | 10 | 230 | 15426 | 190 | 653662 | 0 | 250834 | 106750 | 3218 |

CAMBRIDGE—Middlesex County

⊠ CAMBRIDGE HEALTH ALLIANCE, (Formerly Cambridge Public Health Commission), (Includes Cambridge Hospital, 1493 Cambridge Street; Somerville Hospital, 230 Highland Avenue, Somerville, Zip 02143; tel. 617/666–4400), 1493 Cambridge Street, Zip 02139–1099; tel. 617/498–1000; John G. O'Brien, Chief Executive Officer **A**1 3 5 6 9 10 **F**1 2 3 4 7 8 10 12 13 14 15 16 17 18 19 20 21 22 25 26 27 28 29 30 31 32 33 34 35 36 37 39 40 41 42 44 45 46 49 51 52 53 54 55 56 57 58 59 61 64 65 66 67 68 71 73 74 **P**6 8
Web address: www.challiance.org
| | | 16 | 10 | 269 | 8602 | 166 | 433870 | 699 | 162083 | 81234 | 2110 |

□ M. I. T. MEDICAL DEPARTMENT, 77 Massachusetts Avenue, Zip 02139–4307; tel. 617/253–4481; Arnold N. Weinberg, M.D., Director (Nonreporting) **A**1
| | | 23 | 11 | 18 | — | — | — | — | — | — | — |

⊠ MOUNT AUBURN HOSPITAL, 330 Mount Auburn Street, Zip 02138; tel. 617/499–5700; Jeanette G. Clough, President and Chief Executive Officer **A**1 2 3 5 8 9 10 **F**3 4 7 8 10 11 12 14 15 16 17 19 21 22 23 26 28 29 30 31 32 34 35 36 37 39 40 41 42 43 44 45 46 49 51 52 54 55 56 57 58 59 60 61 63 65 66 67 71 72 73 74 **P**5 6 7 **S** CareGroup, Boston, MA
| | | 23 | 10 | 164 | 9750 | 123 | 117142 | 1244 | 123397 | 62283 | 1626 |

⊠ STILLMAN INFIRMARY, HARVARD UNIVERSITY HEALTH SERVICES, 75 Mount Auburn Street, Zip 02138–4960; tel. 617/495–2010; David S. Rosenthal, M.D., Director (Nonreporting) **A**1 10
| | | 23 | 11 | 18 | — | — | — | — | — | — | — |

Hospital, Address, Telephone, Administrator, Approval, Facility, and Physician Codes, Health Care System, Network	Classi-fication Codes		Utilization Data					Expense (thousands) of dollars		
★ American Hospital Association (AHA) membership □ Joint Commission on Accreditation of Healthcare Organizations (JCAHO) accreditation + American Osteopathic Healthcare Association (AOHA) membership ○ American Osteopathic Association (AOA) accreditation △ Commission on Accreditation of Rehabilitation Facilities (CARF) accreditation Control codes 61, 63, 64, 71, 72 and 73 indicate hospitals listed by AOHA, but not registered by AHA. For definition of numerical codes, see page A4	Control	Service	Staffed Beds	Admissions	Census	Outpatient Visits	Births	Total	Payroll	Personnel

✉ △ YOUVILLE LIFECARE, 1575 Cambridge Street, Zip 02138–4398; tel. 617/876–4344; Daniel P. Leahey, President and Chief Executive Officer (Total facility includes 140 beds in nursing home–type unit) (Nonreporting) **A**1 6 7 10 **S** Covenant Health Systems, Inc., Lexington, MA	21	46	286	—	—	—	—	—	—	—
CANTON—Norfolk County										
✉ MASSACHUSETTS HOSPITAL SCHOOL, 3 Randolph Street, Zip 02021–2397; tel. 781/828–2440; John H. Britt, Executive Director (Nonreporting) **A**1 5 10	12	56	110	—	—	—	—	—	—	—
CHELSEA—Suffolk County										
✉ LAWRENCE F. QUIGLEY MEMORIAL HOSPITAL, 91 Crest Avenue, Zip 02150–2199; tel. 617/884–5660; William D. Thompson, Commandant (Total facility includes 88 beds in nursing home–type unit) (Nonreporting) **A**1 10	12	49	159	—	—	—	—	—	—	—
CLINTON—Worcester County										
□ CLINTON HOSPITAL, 201 Highland Street, Zip 01510–1096; tel. 978/368–3000; Thomas Devins, President **A**1 5 9 10 **F**8 15 16 17 19 21 22 26 28 30 34 39 41 42 44 45 46 49 52 57 65 67 71 **P**6 8	23	10	39	1377	30	14363	0	10781	5929	176
CONCORD—Middlesex County										
✉ EMERSON HOSPITAL, 133 Old Road to Nine Acre Corner, Zip 01742–9120; tel. 978/369–1400; Geoffrey F. Cole, President and Chief Executive Officer **A**1 2 5 9 10 **F**2 3 7 8 11 12 15 16 17 19 22 26 28 29 30 31 32 33 34 35 37 40 42 44 46 48 49 50 51 52 54 55 56 57 58 59 60 63 64 65 66 67 71 72 73 74 **P**1 5 7 **Web address:** www.emersonhosp.org	23	10	185	7746	101	311218	1421	85610	37138	974
DORCHESTER—Suffolk County										
✉ CARNEY HOSPITAL, 2100 Dorchester Avenue, Zip 02124–5666; tel. 617/296–4000; Joyce A. Murphy, President (Total facility includes 27 beds in nursing home–type unit) **A**1 2 5 9 10 **F**14 15 16 17 19 22 24 25 28 29 30 31 34 35 37 39 41 42 44 45 46 49 51 52 54 55 56 58 59 64 65 68 71 73 74 **P**4 5 6 7 **S** Caritas Christi Health Care, Boston, MA	21	10	201	8468	145	102638	0	90133	51325	1262
EVERETT—Middlesex County										
WHIDDEN MEMORIAL HOSPITAL See Hallmark Health System, Melrose										
FALL RIVER—Bristol County										
CHARLTON MEMORIAL HOSPITAL See Southcoast Hospitals Group										
✉ SAINT ANNE'S HOSPITAL, 795 Middle Street, Zip 02721–1798; tel. 508/674–5741; Michael W. Metzler, President **A**1 2 9 10 **F**1 3 8 12 13 14 15 16 17 19 21 22 28 30 31 32 33 34 35 37 39 41 42 44 46 49 53 54 56 57 58 59 60 63 64 65 67 71 73 **P**3 5 7 **S** Caritas Christi Health Care, Boston, MA	21	10	139	4803	79	173650	0	61913	25329	699
✉ △ SOUTHCOAST HOSPITALS GROUP, (Includes Charlton Memorial Hospital, 363 Highland Avenue, Zip 02720–3794; tel. 508/679–3131; St. Luke's Hospital of New Bedford, 101 Page Street, New Bedford, Zip 02740, Mailing Address: P.O. Box H–3000, Zip 02741–3000; tel. 508/295–0880; Tobey Hospital, 43 High Street, Wareham, Zip 02571; tel. 508/295–0880; 363 Highland Avenue, Zip 02720–3703; tel. 508/679–7555; Ronald B. Goodspeed, M.D., M.P.H., President **A**1 2 7 10 **F**2 3 4 6 7 8 10 11 12 13 15 16 17 18 19 20 21 22 23 24 25 26 28 29 30 31 32 33 34 35 37 39 40 41 42 44 45 46 49 51 52 53 54 55 56 57 58 59 60 61 63 64 65 66 67 68 71 72 73 74 **P**4 5 6 7 8	23	10	769	33450	556	841463	3791	300673	155065	3764
FALMOUTH—Barnstable County										
✉ FALMOUTH HOSPITAL, 100 Ter Heun Drive, Zip 02540–2599; tel. 508/457–3500; Gail Frieswick, President (Nonreporting) **A**1 9 10 **S** Cape Cod Healthcare, Inc., Hyannis, MA	23	10	84	—	—	—	—	—	—	—
FITCHBURG—Worcester County										
HEALTH ALLIANCE–BURBANK HOSPITAL See Health Alliance Hospitals, Leominster										
FRAMINGHAM—Middlesex County										
✉ METROWEST MEDICAL CENTER, (Includes Framingham Union Hospital, 115 Lincoln Street, tel. 508/383–1000; Leonard Morse Hospital, 67 Union Street, Natick, Zip 01760; tel. 508/650–7000), 115 Lincoln Street, Zip 01702; tel. 508/383–1000; Thomas G. Hennessy, Chief Executive Officer **A**1 2 3 5 6 9 10 **F**7 8 10 11 12 13 14 15 16 17 19 21 22 23 24 25 26 27 28 29 30 31 32 33 34 35 37 38 39 40 41 42 44 45 46 48 49 51 52 53 54 55 56 57 58 59 60 61 63 64 65 67 68 71 72 73 74 **P**6 **S** TENET Healthcare Corporation, Santa Barbara, CA **Web address:** www.mwmc.com	32	10	357	15546	211	362634	2501	136472	62185	1809
GARDNER—Worcester County										
□ HEYWOOD HOSPITAL, 242 Green Street, Zip 01440–1373; tel. 978/632–3420; Daniel P. Moen, President and Chief Executive Officer **A**1 9 10 **F**6 7 8 14 15 16 17 19 21 22 28 30 35 37 40 41 42 44 49 51 52 57 59 61 64 65 67 71 73 **P**1	23	10	128	4345	69	140485	463	37255	19241	504
GLOUCESTER—Essex County										
ADDISON GILBERT HOSPITAL See Beverly Hospital, Beverly										
GREAT BARRINGTON—Berkshire County										
✉ FAIRVIEW HOSPITAL, 29 Lewis Avenue, Zip 01230–1713; tel. 413/528–0790; Claire L. Bowen, President (Total facility includes 19 beds in nursing home–type unit) **A**1 9 10 **F**2 3 7 8 10 11 12 13 15 16 17 18 19 20 21 22 23 28 29 30 31 32 33 35 36 37 38 39 40 41 42 44 46 48 49 51 52 54 55 56 58 59 60 64 65 66 67 70 71 72 73 74 **P**6 **S** Berkshire Health Systems, Inc., Pittsfield, MA	23	10	35	1499	31	13059	173	17436	6962	140

Hospital, Address, Telephone, Administrator, Approval, Facility, and Physician Codes, Health Care System, Network	Classification Codes		Utilization Data					Expense (thousands) of dollars		
	Control	Service	Staffed Beds	Admissions	Census	Outpatient Visits	Births	Total	Payroll	Personnel

★ American Hospital Association (AHA) membership
☐ Joint Commission on Accreditation of Healthcare Organizations (JCAHO) accreditation.
+ American Osteopathic Healthcare Association (AOHA) membership
○ American Osteopathic Association (AOA) accreditation
△ Commission on Accreditation of Rehabilitation Facilities (CARF) accreditation
Control codes 61, 63, 64, 71, 72 and 73 indicate hospitals listed by AOHA, but not registered by AHA. For definition of numerical codes, see page A4

GREENFIELD—Franklin County

☒ FRANKLIN MEDICAL CENTER, 164 High Street, Zip 01301–2613; tel. 413/773–0211; Harlan J. Smith, President and Chief Executive Officer **A**1 2 9 10 **F**1 3 7 8 12 13 15 16 17 19 21 22 26 27 29 30 31 32 33 34 35 37 39 40 41 42 44 45 48 49 51 52 53 54 55 56 57 58 59 65 67 68 71 73 **P**3 5 6 7 8 **S** Baystate Health System, Inc., Springfield, MA
Web address: www.baystatehealth.com

| | 23 | 10 | 85 | 4639 | 54 | 216948 | 561 | 54183 | 26560 | 588 |

HAVERHILL—Essex County

BALDPATE HOSPITAL, 83 Baldpate Road, Zip 01833–2399; tel. 978/352–2131; Lucille M. Batal, Administrator (Nonreporting) **A**10

| | 33 | 22 | 59 | — | — | — | — | — | — | — |

☒ HALE HOSPITAL, 140 Lincoln Avenue, Zip 01830–6798; tel. 978/374–2000; Robert J. Ingala, Chief Executive Officer **A**1 9 10 **F**7 8 10 11 12 14 15 16 19 21 22 23 28 29 30 32 33 34 35 39 40 41 42 44 45 46 53 54 56 57 58 61 63 64 65 67 68 71 73 74 **S** Quorum Health Group/Quorum Health Resources, Inc., Brentwood, TN

| | 14 | 10 | 108 | 4818 | 61 | 57521 | 511 | 39951 | 19129 | 486 |

☒ △ WHITTIER REHABILITATION HOSPITAL, 76 Summer Street, Zip 01830–5896; tel. 978/372–8000; Alfred Arcidi, M.D., President (Nonreporting) **A**1 7 10

| | 33 | 46 | 60 | — | — | — | — | — | — | — |

HOLYOKE—Hampden County

☒ HOLYOKE HOSPITAL, 575 Beech Street, Zip 01040–2296; tel. 413/534–2500; Hank J. Porten, President (Total facility includes 15 beds in nursing home–type unit) **A**1 2 9 10 **F**3 7 8 11 12 14 15 16 17 18 19 21 22 25 26 27 28 29 30 31 32 33 34 35 37 39 40 41 42 44 45 46 49 51 52 53 54 55 56 57 58 59 60 61 63 64 65 67 68 71 73 74 **P**8
Web address: www.holyokehealth.com

| | 23 | 10 | 126 | 7940 | 123 | 181922 | 488 | 64126 | 32935 | 840 |

☒ SOLDIERS' HOME IN HOLYOKE, 110 Cherry Street, Zip 01040–7002; tel. 413/532–9475; Paul A. Morin, Superintendent (Total facility includes 260 beds in nursing home–type unit) **A**1 10 **F**15 16 20 28 30 49 64 73 **P**6

| | 12 | 10 | 317 | 295 | 245 | 9456 | 0 | — | — | 327 |

HYANNIS—Barnstable County

☒ CAPE COD HOSPITAL, 27 Park Street, Zip 02601–5203; tel. 508/771–1800; Gail M. Frieswick, Ed.D., President and Chief Executive Officer (Nonreporting) **A**1 2 9 10 **S** Cape Cod Healthcare, Inc., Hyannis, MA

| | 23 | 10 | 236 | — | — | — | — | — | — | — |

LAWRENCE—Essex County

☐ LAWRENCE GENERAL HOSPITAL, 1 General Street, Zip 01842–0389, Mailing Address: P.O. Box 189, Zip 01842–0389; tel. 978/683–4000; Joseph S. McManus, President and Chief Executive Officer **A**1 2 3 9 10 **F**7 8 10 11 15 16 17 19 21 22 23 25 28 29 30 31 32 33 34 35 37 39 40 41 44 46 60 61 63 65 71 72 73 74 **P**1 4 5 7
Web address: www.lawrencegeneral.org

| | 23 | 10 | 186 | 8841 | 120 | 154436 | 1440 | 81697 | 38767 | 959 |

LEEDS—Hampshire County

☒ VETERANS AFFAIRS MEDICAL CENTER, 421 North Main Street, Zip 01053–9764; tel. 413/584–4040; Robert McNamara, Director (Total facility includes 50 beds in nursing home–type unit) **A**1 **F**1 3 12 14 16 17 18 19 20 22 24 25 26 27 28 29 30 31 33 34 39 41 44 45 46 49 51 52 54 56 57 58 59 64 65 67 71 72 73 74 **S** Department of Veterans Affairs, Washington, DC

| | 45 | 22 | 215 | 2253 | 182 | 140380 | 0 | 55721 | 26958 | 661 |

LEOMINSTER—Worcester County

☒ HEALTH ALLIANCE HOSPITALS, (Includes Health Alliance–Burbank Hospital, 275 Nichols Road, Fitchburg, Zip 01420–8209; tel. 978/343–5000), 60 Hospital Road, Zip 01453–8004; tel. 978/466–2000; Jonathan H. Robbins, M.D., President and Chief Executive Officer **A**1 3 5 9 10 **F**1 3 7 8 10 12 14 15 16 17 18 19 21 22 26 28 30 31 32 33 34 35 36 37 39 40 41 42 44 46 48 49 52 53 54 55 56 57 58 59 61 64 65 66 67 68 70 71 72 73 **P**5 8
Web address: www.healthalliance.com

| | 23 | 10 | 173 | 8044 | 108 | 109455 | 1526 | 70893 | 33268 | 715 |

LOWELL—Middlesex County

☒ LOWELL GENERAL HOSPITAL, 295 Varnum Avenue, Zip 01854–2195; tel. 978/937–6000; Robert A. Donovan, President and Chief Executive Officer (Total facility includes 21 beds in nursing home–type unit) **A**1 2 9 10 **F**1 3 7 8 10 12 14 15 16 17 19 21 22 26 28 29 30 31 34 37 39 40 41 42 44 45 46 49 52 54 55 56 57 58 59 60 64 65 66 67 70 71 73 74 **P**8
Web address: www.lowellgeneral.org

| | 23 | 10 | 231 | 9773 | 121 | 169475 | 2289 | 75350 | 37124 | 1074 |

☒ SAINTS MEMORIAL MEDICAL CENTER, One Hospital Drive, Zip 01852–1389; tel. 978/458–1411; Thom Clark, President and Chief Executive Officer **A**1 2 9 10 **F**7 8 10 12 15 16 17 19 21 22 23 28 29 30 31 33 35 36 37 39 40 41 42 44 45 46 49 51 53 54 55 56 58 59 63 65 67 68 71 72 73 74 **P**5
Web address: www.saints–memorial.org

| | 23 | 10 | 168 | 6838 | 85 | 122306 | 576 | 74892 | 33473 | 952 |

LUDLOW—Hampden County

☒ HEALTHSOUTH REHABILITATION HOSPITAL OF WESTERN MASSACHUSETTS, 14 Chestnut Place, Zip 01056–3460; tel. 413/589–7581; R. David Richer, Administrator (Nonreporting) **A**1 10 **S** HEALTHSOUTH Corporation, Birmingham, AL

| | 33 | 46 | 40 | — | — | — | — | — | — | — |

LYNN—Essex County

☒ ATLANTICARE MEDICAL CENTER, 500 Lynnfield Street, Zip 01904–1487; tel. 781/581–9200; Andrew J. Riddell, President (Total facility includes 24 beds in nursing home–type unit) (Nonreporting) **A**1 2 9 10 **S** Partners HealthCare System, Inc., Boston, MA

| | 23 | 10 | 189 | — | — | — | — | — | — | — |

MALDEN—Middlesex County

MALDEN MEDICAL CENTER See Hallmark Health System, Melrose

Hospital, Address, Telephone, Administrator, Approval, Facility, and Physician Codes, Health Care System, Network	Classi-fication Codes		Utilization Data					Expense (thousands) of dollars		
★ American Hospital Association (AHA) membership □ Joint Commission on Accreditation of Healthcare Organizations (JCAHO) accreditation + American Osteopathic Healthcare Association (AOHA) membership ○ American Osteopathic Association (AOA) accreditation △ Commission on Accreditation of Rehabilitation Facilities (CARF) accreditation Control codes 61, 63, 64, 71, 72 and 73 indicate hospitals listed by AOHA, but not registered by AHA. For definition of numerical codes, see page A4	Control	Service	Staffed Beds	Admissions	Census	Outpatient Visits	Births	Total	Payroll	Personnel

MARLBOROUGH—Middlesex County

★ UMASS MARLBOROUGH HOSPITAL, (Formerly Marlborough Hospital), 57 Union Street, Zip 01752–1297; tel. 508/481–5000; Annette B. Leahy, Chief Executive Officer **A**1 5 9 10 **F**2 3 8 12 13 14 16 17 18 19 20 22 26 28 30 32 37 39 41 42 44 46 49 52 53 54 56 57 58 59 65 66 67 68 71 72 73 74 **P**5 8 | 23 | 10 | 66 | 3338 | 40 | 66336 | 0 | 29548 | 13879 | 344

MEDFIELD—Norfolk County

★ MEDFIELD STATE HOSPITAL, 45 Hospital Road, Zip 02052–1099; tel. 508/359–7312; Theodore E. Kirousis, Area Director (Nonreporting) **A**1 10 **S** Massachusetts Department of Mental Health, Boston, MA | 12 | 22 | 212 | — | — | — | — | — | — | —

MEDFORD—Middlesex County

LAWRENCE MEMORIAL HOSPITAL OF MEDFORD See Hallmark Health System, Melrose

MELROSE—Middlesex County

★ HALLMARK HEALTH SYSTEM, (Includes Lawrence Memorial Hospital of Medford, 170 Governors Avenue, Medford, Zip 02155–1643; tel. 781/306–6000; Malden Medical Center, 100 Hospital Road, Malden, Zip 02148–3591; tel. 781/322–7560; Melrose–Wakefield Hospital, 585 Lebanon Street, Zip 02176; Whidden Memorial Hospital, 103 Garland Street, Everett, Zip 02149–5095; tel. 617/389–6270), 585 Lebanon Street, Zip 02176–3298; tel. 781/979–3000; Richard S. Quinlan, President and Chief Executive Officer (Total facility includes 94 beds in nursing home–type unit) **A**1 2 6 9 10 **F**1 3 7 8 10 12 13 14 15 16 17 18 19 21 22 23 26 27 28 29 30 32 33 34 35 37 39 40 41 42 44 49 51 52 54 55 57 58 59 60 61 63 64 65 66 67 71 73 74 **P**1 5 7 8
Web address: www.hallmarkhealth.org | 23 | 10 | 521 | 24210 | 375 | 665212 | 1701 | 226421 | 105196 | 2562

MELROSE–WAKEFIELD HOSPITAL See Hallmark Health System

METHUEN—Essex County

★ HOLY FAMILY HOSPITAL AND MEDICAL CENTER, 70 East Street, Zip 01844–4597; tel. 978/687–0151; William L. Lane, President (Total facility includes 21 beds in nursing home–type unit) **A**1 2 9 10 **F**3 7 8 10 11 12 13 14 15 16 17 18 19 20 21 22 23 25 26 28 29 30 31 32 33 34 35 37 38 39 40 41 42 44 45 46 49 51 52 53 54 55 56 57 58 59 60 63 64 65 66 67 68 69 71 72 73 74 **P**3 5 7 **S** Caritas Christi Health Care, Boston, MA
Web address: www.holyfamilyhosp.org | 21 | 10 | 243 | 9277 | 152 | 76894 | 1259 | 70061 | 33923 | 901

MIDDLEBORO—Plymouth County

□ CRANBERRY SPECIALTY HOSPITAL OF PLYMOUTH COUNTY, 52 Oak Street, Zip 02346–2091; tel. 508/947–1000; William F. Duffy, Chief Executive Officer (Nonreporting) **A**1 10 | 13 | 46 | 68 | — | — | — | — | — | — | —

MILFORD—Worcester County

★ MILFORD–WHITINSVILLE REGIONAL HOSPITAL, (Includes Whitinsville Medical Center, 18 Granite Street, Whitinsville, Zip 01588; tel. 508/234–6311), 14 Prospect Street, Zip 01757–3090; tel. 508/473–1190; Francis M. Saba, President and Chief Executive Officer **A**1 2 5 9 10 **F**7 8 12 14 15 16 17 19 21 22 28 29 30 32 34 35 37 39 40 41 42 44 45 46 49 58 63 65 67 71 72 73 74 **P**4 5 7 8
Web address: www.mwrh.org | 23 | 10 | 108 | 5623 | 62 | 154982 | 623 | 57733 | 30223 | 505

MILTON—Norfolk County

★ MILTON HOSPITAL, 92 Highland Street, Zip 02186–3807; tel. 617/696–4600; George A. Geary, President (Total facility includes 32 beds in nursing home–type unit) **A**1 9 10 **F**8 11 12 14 15 16 17 19 21 22 28 29 30 34 35 36 37 39 41 42 44 46 49 63 64 65 66 71 73 **P**6
Web address: www.miltonhospital.org | 23 | 10 | 78 | 4109 | 56 | 69076 | 0 | 37789 | 17704 | 515

NANTUCKET—Nantucket County

★ NANTUCKET COTTAGE HOSPITAL, 57 Prospect Street, Zip 02554–2799; tel. 508/228–1200; Lucille C. Giddings, R.N., CHE, President and Chief Executive Officer **A**1 9 10 **F**1 3 7 8 14 15 16 17 19 22 28 30 31 32 33 36 37 40 41 42 44 49 65 67 71
Web address: www.nantuckethospital.org | 23 | 10 | 19 | 566 | 6 | 34657 | 76 | 11030 | 5564 | 116

NATICK—Middlesex County

LEONARD MORSE HOSPITAL See MetroWest Medical Center, Framingham

NEEDHAM—Norfolk County

★ DEACONESS–GLOVER HOSPITAL CORPORATION, 148 Chestnut Street, Zip 02192–2483; tel. 781/453–3000; John Dalton, President and Chief Executive Officer **A**1 2 9 10 **F**8 12 14 15 16 17 19 21 22 26 28 29 30 32 33 34 36 37 39 41 42 44 49 65 69 71 73 **P**7 8 **S** CareGroup, Boston, MA
Web address: www.caregroup.com | 23 | 10 | 47 | 2155 | 25 | 68787 | 0 | 21181 | 9153 | 233

NEW BEDFORD—Bristol County

ST. LUKE'S HOSPITAL OF NEW BEDFORD See Southcoast Hospitals Group, Fall River

NEWBURYPORT—Essex County

★ ANNA JAQUES HOSPITAL, 25 Highland Avenue, Zip 01950–3894; tel. 978/463–1000; Allan L. DesRosiers, President (Total facility includes 20 beds in nursing home–type unit) **A**1 9 10 **F**7 8 10 12 13 15 16 17 18 19 21 22 23 28 29 30 31 32 33 34 35 36 37 39 40 41 42 44 46 49 51 52 53 54 55 56 58 59 63 65 66 67 71 73 74 **P**5 7
Web address: www.ajh.org | 23 | 10 | 169 | 6704 | 101 | 100074 | 815 | 57359 | 27818 | 694

NEWTON LOWER FALLS—Middlesex County

★ NEWTON–WELLESLEY HOSPITAL, 2014 Washington Street, Zip 02462–1699; tel. 617/243–6000; John P. Bihldorff, President and Chief Executive Officer **A**1 2 3 5 9 10 **F**3 4 7 8 12 13 14 15 16 17 18 19 21 22 26 27 28 29 30 31 32 34 35 37 38 39 40 41 42 44 45 46 49 51 52 53 54 55 56 57 58 59 61 64 65 66 67 70 71 73 **P**1 5 **S** Partners HealthCare System, Inc., Boston, MA
Web address: www.nwh.org | 23 | 10 | 228 | 12130 | 140 | 74117 | 3749 | 139953 | 68746 | 1501

Hospital, Address, Telephone, Administrator, Approval, Facility, and Physician Codes, Health Care System, Network	Classification Codes		Utilization Data					Expense (thousands) of dollars		
	Control	Service	Staffed Beds	Admissions	Census	Outpatient Visits	Births	Total	Payroll	Personnel

★ American Hospital Association (AHA) membership
□ Joint Commission on Accreditation of Healthcare Organizations (JCAHO) accreditation
+ American Osteopathic Healthcare Association (AOHA) membership
○ American Osteopathic Association (AOA) accreditation
△ Commission on Accreditation of Rehabilitation Facilities (CARF) accreditation
Control codes 61, 63, 64, 71, 72 and 73 indicate hospitals listed by AOHA, but not registered by AHA. For definition of numerical codes, see page A4

NORFOLK—Norfolk County

□ CARITAS SOUTHWOOD HOSPITAL, 111 Dedham Street, Zip 02056–1664; tel. 508/668–0385; Delia O'Connor, President (Nonreporting) **A**1 2 9 10 — Control 23, Service 10, Staffed Beds 182

NORTH ADAMS—Berkshire County

✠ NORTH ADAMS REGIONAL HOSPITAL, 71 Hospital Avenue, Zip 01247–2584; tel. 413/664–5505; John C. J. Cronin, President and Chief Executive Officer **A**1 2 9 10 **F**4 7 8 10 12 14 15 16 17 19 21 22 28 30 31 32 33 35 37 39 40 42 44 45 46 49 52 54 55 57 59 64 65 67 71 73 — Control 23, Service 10, Staffed Beds 134, Admissions 4359, Census 69, Outpatient Visits 53457, Births 356, Total 33014, Payroll 15808, Personnel 335

NORTHAMPTON—Hampshire County

✠ COOLEY DICKINSON HOSPITAL, 30 Locust Street, Zip 01061–5001, Mailing Address: P.O. Box 5001, Zip 01061–5001; tel. 413/582–2000; Craig N. Melin, President and Chief Executive Officer **A**1 2 9 10 **F**3 7 8 12 14 15 16 17 18 19 20 21 22 25 26 28 30 31 32 33 34 35 37 39 40 41 42 44 45 46 49 52 54 55 56 57 58 59 60 63 65 66 67 70 71 72 73 **P**8 — Control 23, Service 10, Staffed Beds 130, Admissions 7187, Census 82, Outpatient Visits 154068, Births 918, Total 58642, Payroll 29068, Personnel 613
Web address: www.cooley–dickinson.org
VETERANS AFFAIRS MEDICAL CENTER See Leeds

NORWOOD—Norfolk County

✠ CARITAS NORWOOD HOSPITAL, 800 Washington Street, Zip 02062–3487; tel. 781/278–6001; Delia O'Connor, President (Nonreporting) **A**1 2 5 9 10 — Control 23, Service 10, Staffed Beds 150
S Caritas Christi Health Care, Boston, MA

OAK BLUFFS—Dukes County

✠ MARTHA'S VINEYARD HOSPITAL, Linton Lane, Zip 02557, Mailing Address: P.O. Box 1477, Zip 02557; tel. 508/693–0410; Charles S. Kinney, Chief Executive Officer **A**1 10 **F**1 3 6 7 8 12 15 17 18 19 22 27 29 30 31 32 33 34 36 37 39 40 41 42 44 49 51 53 54 55 56 57 58 61 62 65 71 72 73 74 — Control 23, Service 10, Staffed Beds 22, Admissions 1365, Census 10, Outpatient Visits 13474, Births 111, Total 16352, Payroll 7948, Personnel 145

PALMER—Hampden County

✠ WING MEMORIAL HOSPITAL AND MEDICAL CENTERS, 40 Wright Street, Zip 01069–1138; tel. 413/283–7651; Richard H. Scheffer, President **A**1 5 9 10 **F**3 8 12 19 22 30 32 33 34 37 42 44 49 52 53 54 57 58 65 66 67 71 73 **P**6 — Control 23, Service 10, Staffed Beds 43, Admissions 1778, Census 23, Outpatient Visits 179232, Births 0, Total 28845, Payroll 15694, Personnel 431

PEABODY—Essex County

□ VENCOR HOSPITAL NORTH SHORE, 15 King Street, Zip 01960–4268; tel. 978/531–2900; Steven E. Levitsky, Administrator **A**1 10 **F**37 **S** Vencor, Incorporated, Louisville, KY — Control 33, Service 10, Staffed Beds 50, Admissions 401, Census 43, Births 0, Personnel 116

PEMBROKE—Plymouth County

PEMBROKE HOSPITAL, 199 Oak Street, Zip 02359–1953; tel. 781/826–8161; Michael P. Krupa, Ed.D., Chief Executive Officer (Nonreporting) **S** Magellan Health Services, Atlanta, GA — Control 33, Service 22, Staffed Beds 115

PITTSFIELD—Berkshire County

✠ △ BERKSHIRE MEDICAL CENTER, (Includes Hillcrest Hospital, 165 Tor Court, Zip 01201–3099, Mailing Address: Box 1155, Zip 01202–1155; tel. 413/443–4761; Eugene A. Dellea, President and Chief Executive Officer), 725 North Street, Zip 01201–4124; tel. 413/447–2000; Ruth P. Blodgett, Chief Operating Officer **A**1 2 3 5 7 8 9 10 12 **F**2 3 4 7 8 10 11 12 15 16 17 19 20 21 22 23 25 28 29 30 31 32 34 35 37 39 40 41 42 44 45 46 48 49 51 52 53 54 56 58 59 60 61 63 64 65 67 70 71 72 73 74 **P**6 **S** Berkshire Health Systems, Inc., Pittsfield, MA — Control 23, Service 10, Staffed Beds 272, Admissions 12544, Census 217, Outpatient Visits 219973, Births 870, Total 139769, Payroll 67399, Personnel 1493

PLYMOUTH—Plymouth County

✠ JORDAN HOSPITAL, 275 Sandwich Street, Zip 02360–2196; tel. 508/746–2001; Alan D. Knight, President and Chief Executive Officer **A**1 2 9 10 **F**1 2 3 4 7 8 11 12 14 15 16 17 19 21 22 23 27 28 29 30 31 32 33 35 37 39 40 41 42 43 44 45 46 49 52 54 56 60 64 65 66 67 68 71 73 74 **P**4 5 6 7 — Control 23, Service 10, Staffed Beds 119, Admissions 7301, Census 93, Outpatient Visits 209543, Births 813, Total 73434, Payroll 33901, Personnel 626
Web address: www.jordan.org

POCASSET—Barnstable County

BARNSTABLE COUNTY HOSPITAL, 870 County Road, Zip 02559–2199; tel. 508/563–5941; Edward B. Leary, President (Nonreporting) **A**10 — Control 13, Service 46, Staffed Beds 39

QUINCY—Norfolk County

✠ QUINCY HOSPITAL, 114 Whitwell Street, Zip 02169–1899; tel. 617/773–6100; Jeffrey Doran, Chief Executive Officer (Total facility includes 38 beds in nursing home–type unit) **A**1 9 10 **F**7 8 10 12 15 16 17 19 21 22 26 27 28 30 32 33 34 35 36 37 39 40 41 42 44 45 46 49 52 54 55 56 57 58 59 60 61 64 65 67 71 72 73 74 **S** Quorum Health Group/Quorum Health Resources, Inc., Brentwood, TN — Control 14, Service 10, Staffed Beds 146, Admissions 8336, Census 129, Outpatient Visits 218930, Births 624, Total 81059, Payroll 39024, Personnel 732

SALEM—Essex County

✠ SALEM HOSPITAL, (Includes North Shore Children's Hospital, tel. 978/745–2100), 81 Highland Avenue, Zip 01970–2768; tel. 978/741–1200; Stanley Reczek, President **A**1 2 3 5 9 10 **F**2 3 7 8 10 11 12 13 14 15 16 17 18 19 20 21 22 23 24 25 26 27 28 29 30 31 32 33 34 35 36 37 39 40 41 42 44 45 46 48 49 51 52 53 54 55 56 58 59 60 61 63 64 65 66 67 68 71 72 73 74 **P**1 6 **S** Partners HealthCare System, Inc., Boston, MA — Control 23, Service 10, Staffed Beds 228, Admissions 12044, Census 147, Outpatient Visits 578076, Births 1178, Total 143543, Payroll 76643, Personnel 2068

✠ △ SHAUGHNESSY-KAPLAN REHABILITATION HOSPITAL, Dove Avenue, Zip 01970–2999; tel. 978/745–9000; Anthony Sciola, President (Total facility includes 40 beds in nursing home–type unit) **A**1 7 10 **F**3 7 8 10 11 12 14 16 19 21 22 24 25 26 27 28 29 30 31 32 33 34 37 40 41 42 44 45 46 48 49 51 52 53 54 55 56 58 59 60 61 63 65 66 67 71 72 73 74 **P**6 **S** Partners HealthCare System, Inc., Boston, MA — Control 23, Service 46, Staffed Beds 160, Admissions 2074, Census 112, Outpatient Visits 35744, Births 0, Total 23516, Payroll 11525, Personnel 291
Web address: www.nsmc.partners.org

Hospital, Address, Telephone, Administrator, Approval, Facility, and Physician Codes, Health Care System, Network	Classification Codes		Utilization Data					Expense (thousands) of dollars		
	Control	Service	Staffed Beds	Admissions	Census	Outpatient Visits	Births	Total	Payroll	Personnel

★ American Hospital Association (AHA) membership
□ Joint Commission on Accreditation of Healthcare Organizations (JCAHO) accreditation
+ American Osteopathic Healthcare Association (AOHA) membership
○ American Osteopathic Association (AOA) accreditation
△ Commission on Accreditation of Rehabilitation Facilities (CARF) accreditation
Control codes 61, 63, 64, 71, 72 and 73 indicate hospitals listed by AOHA, but not registered by AHA. For definition of numerical codes, see page A4

SOMERVILLE—Middlesex County
SOMERVILLE HOSPITAL See Cambridge Health Alliance, Cambridge

SOUTH ATTLEBORO—Bristol County

□ FULLER MEMORIAL HOSPITAL, 200 May Street, Zip 02703–5599; tel. 508/761–8500; Landon Kite, President (Nonreporting) **A**1 10 **S** Universal Health Services, Inc., King of Prussia, PA	33	22	46	—	—	—	—	—	—	—

SOUTH WEYMOUTH—Norfolk County

⊠ SOUTH SHORE HOSPITAL, 55 Fogg Road, Zip 02190–2455; tel. 781/340–8000; David T. Hannan, President and Chief Executive Officer (Total facility includes 25 beds in nursing home–type unit) **A**1 2 10 **F**7 8 10 11 12 14 15 16 17 19 21 22 23 25 27 28 29 30 32 33 34 35 37 39 40 41 42 44 45 46 49 50 60 61 63 64 65 67 70 71 72 73 74 **P**8 **Web address:** www.sshosp.org	23	10	253	16063	186	407580	3366	166788	85423	2114

SOUTHBRIDGE—Worcester County

⊠ HARRINGTON MEMORIAL HOSPITAL, 100 South Street, Zip 01550–4045; tel. 508/765–9771; Richard M. Mangion, President and Chief Executive Officer **A**1 5 9 10 **F**3 7 8 11 14 15 16 17 18 19 22 26 28 29 30 32 33 34 35 37 39 40 41 44 45 46 49 51 52 53 54 55 56 57 58 59 65 67 71 73 **P**1	23	10	113	3766	47	191957	468	38340	22016	502

SPRINGFIELD—Hampden County

⊠ BAYSTATE MEDICAL CENTER, 759 Chestnut Street, Zip 01199–0001; tel. 413/794–0000; Mark R. Tolosky, Chief Executive Officer **A**1 2 3 5 6 8 9 10 **F**2 3 4 7 8 10 11 12 13 14 15 16 17 18 19 21 22 23 24 25 26 27 28 29 30 31 32 33 34 35 37 38 39 40 41 42 43 44 45 46 47 49 51 52 53 54 56 57 58 59 60 61 63 64 65 67 68 70 71 72 73 74 **P**1 5 6 **S** Baystate Health System, Inc., Springfield, MA **Web address:** www.baystatehealth.com	23	10	579	29087	399	400848	4472	354585	150060	3728
⊠ △ MERCY HOSPITAL, 271 Carew Street, Zip 01104–2398, Mailing Address: P.O. Box 9012, Zip 01102–9012; tel. 413/748–9000; Vincent J. McCorkle, President (Total facility includes 30 beds in nursing home–type unit) **A**1 2 7 9 10 **F**1 2 3 4 7 8 10 11 12 13 14 15 16 17 18 19 21 22 23 26 27 28 29 30 32 34 35 37 40 41 42 44 45 46 48 49 51 52 53 54 55 56 57 58 59 60 62 63 64 65 66 67 68 71 73 74 **S** Catholic Health East, Newtown Square, PA	21	10	352	13185	235	118323	657	116733	48140	1414
□ OLYMPUS SPECIALTY HOSPITAL–SPRINGFIELD, 1400 State Street, Zip 01109–2589; tel. 413/787–6700; Marilyn M. Riddle, Chief Executive Officer (Total facility includes 220 beds in nursing home–type unit) (Nonreporting) **A**1 5 10	14	49	394	—	—	—	—	—	—	—
⊠ SHRINERS HOSPITALS FOR CHILDREN, SPRINGFIELD, 516 Carew Street, Zip 01104–2396; tel. 413/787–2000; Mark L. Niederpruem, Administrator **A**1 3 5 **F**34 49 65 73 **S** Shriners Hospitals for Children, Tampa, FL **Web address:** www.shrinerspfld.org	23	57	40	769	22	12413	0	—	—	233

STOCKBRIDGE—Berkshire County

⊠ AUSTEN RIGGS CENTER, 25 Main Street, Zip 01262–0962, Mailing Address: P.O. Box 962, Zip 01262–0962; tel. 413/298–5511; Edward R. Shapiro, M.D., Medical Director and Chief Executive Officer **A**1 3 **F**15 17 52 59 **P**5 **Web address:** www.austenriggs.org	23	22	47	71	8	—	0	6781	3837	90

STOUGHTON—Plymouth County
GOOD SAMARITAN MEDICAL CENTER See Brockton

⊠ △ NEW ENGLAND SINAI HOSPITAL AND REHABILITATION CENTER, (REHABILITATION/LONG TERM ACUTE), 150 York Street, Zip 02072–1881; tel. 617/364–4850; Donald H. Goldberg, President (Total facility includes 21 beds in nursing home–type unit) **A**1 3 7 10 **F**1 5 12 15 16 17 19 20 26 28 33 34 35 39 42 48 49 54 64 65 66 67 71 73 **Web address:** www.nesinai.org	23	49	212	1838	158	30019	0	43166	23603	576

TAUNTON—Bristol County

⊠ MORTON HOSPITAL AND MEDICAL CENTER, 88 Washington Street, Zip 02780–2499; tel. 508/828–7000; Thomas C. Porter, President **A**1 2 9 10 **F**3 7 8 12 14 15 16 17 19 21 22 25 28 30 32 34 35 37 39 40 41 42 44 46 49 53 54 56 61 64 65 66 72 73 **P**4 5 7	23	10	152	5883	80	163813	735	69177	33384	776
□ TAUNTON STATE HOSPITAL, 60 Hodges Avenue Extension, Zip 02780–3034, Mailing Address: P.O. Box 4007, Zip 02780–4007; tel. 508/824–7551; Katherine Chmiel, R.N., MSN, Administrator and Chief Operating Officer **A**1 10 **F**1 12 15 16 17 18 20 39 52 53 56 57 58 59 65 73 **P**1 **S** Massachusetts Department of Mental Health, Boston, MA	12	22	185	294	174	0	0	31121	14275	433

TEWKSBURY—Middlesex County

⊠ TEWKSBURY HOSPITAL, 365 East Street, Zip 01876–1998; tel. 978/851–7321; Raymond D. Sanzone, Executive Director **A**1 6 10 **F**1 2 3 15 16 19 20 23 26 27 28 30 31 33 34 35 41 42 46 49 52 53 54 55 56 57 59 60 65 67 73 **P**6	12	48	720	262	473	0	0	36823	—	702

WALTHAM—Middlesex County

⊠ DEACONESS WALTHAM HOSPITAL, Hope Avenue, Zip 02254–9116; tel. 781/647–6000; Allen Danis, Acting Administrator (Total facility includes 21 beds in nursing home–type unit) (Nonreporting) **A**1 2 5 9 10 **S** CareGroup, Boston, MA	23	10	198	—	—	—	—	—	—	—
□ OLYMPUS SPECIALTY HOSPITAL, 775 Trapelo Road, Zip 02254, Mailing Address: P.O. Box 9151, Zip 02254–9151; tel. 781/895–7000; Reva S. Tankle, Ph.D., Chief Executive Officer (Nonreporting) **A**1 10	13	48	120	—	—	—	—	—	—	—

WARE—Hampshire County

⊠ MARY LANE HOSPITAL, 85 South Street, Zip 01082–1697; tel. 413/967–6211; Christine Shirtcliff, Executive Vice President **A**1 9 10 **F**1 3 7 8 12 15 16 17 19 21 22 27 28 29 30 32 33 34 37 39 40 41 42 45 46 49 54 58 61 65 67 68 71 72 73 74 **P**1 5 8 **S** Baystate Health System, Inc., Springfield, MA **Web address:** www.baystatehealth.com	23	10	31	1247	13	80071	237	16068	8307	217

Hospital, Address, Telephone, Administrator, Approval, Facility, and Physician Codes, Health Care System, Network	Classi-fication Codes		Utilization Data					Expense (thousands) of dollars		
★ American Hospital Association (AHA) membership □ Joint Commission on Accreditation of Healthcare Organizations (JCAHO) accreditation + American Osteopathic Healthcare Association (AOHA) membership ○ American Osteopathic Association (AOA) accreditation △ Commission on Accreditation of Rehabilitation Facilities (CARF) accreditation Control codes 61, 63, 64, 71, 72 and 73 indicate hospitals listed by AOHA, but not registered by AHA. For definition of numerical codes, see page A4	Control	Service	Staffed Beds	Admissions	Census	Outpatient Visits	Births	Total	Payroll	Personnel

WAREHAM—Plymouth County
TOBEY HOSPITAL See Southcoast Hospitals Group, Fall River

WEBSTER—Worcester County

✠ HUBBARD REGIONAL HOSPITAL, 340 Thompson Road, Zip 01570–0608; tel. 508/943–2600; Gerald J. Barbini, Administrator and Chief Executive Officer **A**1 9 10 **F**8 15 16 19 21 22 27 30 34 37 39 41 44 45 46 49 57 58 65 71 72 73 74 **P**3 7 **S** Quorum Health Group/Quorum Health Resources, Inc., Brentwood, TN	23	10	26	1296	15	51101	0	16712	7072	199

WELLESLEY—Norfolk County

□ CHARLES RIVER HOSPITAL, 203 Grove Street, Zip 02181–7413; tel. 781/304–2800; Juliette Fay, President and Chief Executive Officer (Nonreporting) **A**1 10 **S** Community Care Systems, Inc., Wellesley, MA	33	22	62	—	—	—	—	—	—	—
SIMPSON INFIRMARY, WELLESLEY COLLEGE, 106 Central Street, Zip 02481–8203; tel. 781/283–2810; Charlotte K. Sanner, M.D., Director Health Service **F**25 28 29 30 31 34 39 45 53 54 55 56 58 61 65 67 74	23	11	11	121	1	7395	0	—	—	10

WESTBOROUGH—Worcester County

□ WESTBOROUGH STATE HOSPITAL, Lyman Street, Zip 01581–0288, Mailing Address: P.O. Box 288, Zip 01581–0288; tel. 508/366–4401; Theodore E. Kirousis, Area Director (Nonreporting) **A**1 10 **S** Massachusetts Department of Mental Health, Boston, MA	12	22	220	—	—	—	—	—	—	—

WESTFIELD—Hampden County

✠ NOBLE HOSPITAL, 115 West Silver Street, Zip 01086–1634; tel. 413/568–2811; George J. Koller, President and Chief Executive Officer **A**1 2 5 9 10 **F**2 6 8 12 14 15 16 17 18 19 22 25 28 29 30 32 33 35 39 40 41 42 44 45 46 48 49 51 53 54 55 56 57 58 59 62 65 66 67 71 72 73 74 **P**5 6 7 8 **Web address:** www.noblehealth.org	23	10	97	3150	59	84780	0	29224	15366	387

WESTWOOD—Norfolk County

□ WESTWOOD LODGE HOSPITAL, 45 Clapboardtree Street, Zip 02090–2930; tel. 781/762–7764; Michael P. Krupa, Ed.D., Chief Executive Officer (Nonreporting) **A**1 10 **S** Magellan Health Services, Atlanta, GA	33	22	100	—	—	—	—	—	—	—

WHITINSVILLE—Worcester County
WHITINSVILLE MEDICAL CENTER See Milford–Whitinsville Regional Hospital, Milford

WINCHESTER—Middlesex County

✠ WINCHESTER HOSPITAL, 41 Highland Avenue, Zip 01890–9920; tel. 781/729–9000; Dale M. Lodge, President and Chief Executive Officer **A**1 2 5 9 10 **F**7 8 12 14 15 16 17 19 20 21 22 25 26 27 28 29 30 32 33 34 35 36 37 38 39 40 41 42 44 45 46 49 51 60 61 63 64 65 67 68 71 72 73 74 **P**3 4 5 6 7 8 **Web address:** www.winchesterhospital.org	23	10	132	8719	106	325542	2030	94402	44301	1124

WOBURN—Middlesex County

□ △ HEALTHSOUTH NEW ENGLAND REHABILITATION HOSPITAL, Two Rehabilitation Way, Zip 01801–6098; tel. 781/935–5050; Mary Moscato, Chief Executive Officer (Nonreporting) **A**1 7 10 **S** HEALTHSOUTH Corporation, Birmingham, AL	33	46	198	—	—	—	—	—	—	—

WORCESTER—Worcester County

ADCARE HOSPITAL OF WORCESTER, 107 Lincoln Street, Zip 01605–2499; tel. 508/799–9000; David W. Hillis, President and Chief Executive Officer (Nonreporting) **A**10	33	82	88	—	—	—	—	—	—	—
□ △ FAIRLAWN REHABILITATION HOSPITAL, 189 May Street, Zip 01602–4399; tel. 508/791–6351; Peter M. Mantegazza, President and Chief Executive Officer **A**1 5 7 10 **F**5 12 15 26 27 34 39 46 48 49 65 67 73 **S** HEALTHSOUTH Corporation, Birmingham, AL	33	46	110	1572	98	13253	0	22569	12289	275
✠ SAINT VINCENT HOSPITAL, 25 Winthrop Street, Zip 01604–4593; tel. 508/798–1234; Robert E. Maher, Jr., President and Chief Executive Officer (Nonreporting) **A**1 2 3 5 8 10 12 **S** TENET Healthcare Corporation, Santa Barbara, CA **Web address:** www.svh–worc.com	33	10	369	—	—	—	—	—	—	—
✠ UMASS MEMORIAL HEALTH CARE–MEMORIAL CAMPUS, (Formerly Memorial Hospital), (Includes Medical Center Central Massachusetts–Hahnemann, 281 Lincoln Street, Zip 01605; tel. 508/792–8000; Medical Center of Central Massachusetts–Memorial Campus; University of Massachusetts Medical Center–University Campus, 55 Lake Avenue North, Zip 01655–0002; tel. 508/856–0011; Anne Bourgeois, President), 119 Belmont Street, Zip 01605–2982; tel. 508/793–6611; Peter H. Levine, M.D., President and Chief Executive Officer (Total facility includes 31 beds in nursing home–type unit) **A**1 2 3 5 8 9 10 12 **F**2 3 4 6 7 8 9 10 11 12 13 14 15 16 17 19 21 22 23 24 25 26 27 28 29 30 31 32 33 34 35 37 38 39 40 41 42 43 44 45 46 47 49 51 52 54 55 58 59 60 61 64 65 66 67 68 71 72 73 74 **P**1 6 **Web address:** www.memorialhc.org	23	10	669	35530	499	909685	4056	508128	247277	5165
□ WORCESTER STATE HOSPITAL, 305 Belmont Street, Zip 01604–1695; tel. 508/795–1197; Raymond Robinson, Chief Operating Officer (Nonreporting) **A**1 5 10 **S** Massachusetts Department of Mental Health, Boston, MA	12	22	176	—	—	—	—	—	—	—

MICHIGAN

Resident population 9,817 (in thousands)
Resident population in metro areas 80.6%
Birth rate per 1,000 population 14.1
65 years and over 12.4%
Percent of persons without health insurance 8.9%

Hospital, Address, Telephone, Administrator, Approval, Facility, and Physician Codes, Health Care System, Network	Classi-fication Codes		Utilization Data					Expense (thousands) of dollars		
★ American Hospital Association (AHA) membership □ Joint Commission on Accreditation of Healthcare Organizations (JCAHO) accreditation + American Osteopathic Healthcare Association (AOHA) membership ○ American Osteopathic Association (AOA) accreditation △ Commission on Accreditation of Rehabilitation Facilities (CARF) accreditation Control codes 61, 63, 64, 71, 72 and 73 indicate hospitals listed by AOHA, but not registered by AHA. For definition of numerical codes, see page A4	Control	Service	Staffed Beds	Admissions	Census	Outpatient Visits	Births	Total	Payroll	Personnel

ADDISON—Lenawee County

□ ADDISON COMMUNITY HOSPITAL, 421 North Steer Street, Zip 49220–9409; tel. 517/547–6151; Robert A. Brown, Senior Vice President and Chief Operating Officer (Nonreporting) **A**1 10
16 10 | 24 | — | — | — | — | — | — |

ADRIAN—Lenawee County

✠ BIXBY MEDICAL CENTER, LENAWEE HEALTH ALLIANCE, 818 Riverside Avenue, Zip 49221–1496; tel. 517/265–0900; John R. Robertstad, President and Chief Executive Officer **A**1 2 9 10 **F**3 6 7 8 11 12 14 15 16 17 18 19 21 22 24 25 26 27 30 32 33 34 35 36 37 39 40 41 42 44 45 46 49 52 54 56 57 58 59 60 62 64 65 66 67 70 71 72 73 74 **P**1 7 **S** Lenawee Health Alliance, Adrian, MI
Web address: www.lhanet.org
23 10 | 89 | 3894 | 38 | 131470 | 750 | 43295 | 20468 | 636 |

ALBION—Calhoun County

□ TRILLIUM HOSPITAL, 809 West Erie Street, Zip 49224–1556; tel. 517/629–2191; Michael G. Boff, President **A**1 9 10 **F**7 8 11 12 14 15 16 17 19 20 21 22 26 28 29 30 32 35 37 39 40 41 44 48 51 53 54 55 56 57 58 59 63 65 71 72 73 **P**5
Web address: www.trillum.org
23 10 | 60 | 1420 | 15 | 14770 | 134 | 15360 | 6699 | 197 |

ALLEGAN—Allegan County

✠ ALLEGAN GENERAL HOSPITAL, 555 Linn Street, Zip 49010–1594; tel. 616/673–8424; James A. Klun, President **A**1 9 10 **F**7 8 11 12 14 15 16 17 18 19 21 22 27 28 30 32 34 35 37 39 40 41 42 44 45 46 49 51 52 54 55 56 58 59 65 66 67 71 72 73 **S** Quorum Health Group/Quorum Health Resources, Inc., Brentwood, TN
Web address: www.accn.org/~agh
23 10 | 63 | 1768 | 18 | 41253 | 189 | 18310 | 7769 | 224 |

ALMA—Gratiot County

✠ △ GRATIOT COMMUNITY HOSPITAL, 300 East Warwick Drive, Zip 48801–1096; tel. 517/463–1101; Bob M. Baker, President and Chief Executive Officer (Nonreporting) **A**1 7 9 10
23 10 | 127 | — | — | — | — | — | — |

ALPENA—Alpena County

✠ ALPENA GENERAL HOSPITAL, 1501 West Chisholm Street, Zip 49707–1498; tel. 517/356–7390; John A. McVeety, Chief Executive Officer **A**1 2 9 10 **F**2 3 4 7 8 10 12 15 16 17 19 21 22 27 28 29 30 31 32 33 34 35 36 37 40 41 42 44 45 46 49 52 53 54 55 56 57 58 63 65 66 67 68 70 71 73 74
Web address: www.agh.org
13 10 | 121 | 5705 | 69 | 69094 | 582 | 55847 | 26950 | 733 |

ANN ARBOR—Washtenaw County

✠ △ SAINT JOSEPH MERCY HEALTH SYSTEM, (Includes St. Joseph Mercy Hospital), 5301 East Huron River Drive, Zip 48106, Mailing Address: P.O. Box 995, Zip 48106–0995; tel. 734/712–3456; Garry C. Faja, President and Chief Executive Officer **A**1 2 3 5 7 8 9 10 **F**1 2 3 4 5 7 8 10 11 12 13 14 15 16 17 18 19 20 21 22 25 26 27 28 29 30 31 32 33 34 35 37 39 40 41 42 43 44 45 46 48 49 51 52 53 54 55 56 57 58 59 60 63 65 66 67 68 70 71 72 73 74 **P**1 5 **S** Mercy Health Services, Farmington Hills, MI
Web address: www.sjmh.com
21 10 | 475 | 26066 | 354 | 473520 | 4038 | 345253 | 137841 | 3449 |

□ UNIVERSITY OF MICHIGAN HOSPITALS AND HEALTH CENTERS, 1500 East Medical Center Drive, Zip 48109; tel. 734/936–4000; Larry Warren, Executive Director **A**1 2 3 5 8 9 10 **F**2 3 4 5 7 8 9 10 11 12 13 14 15 16 17 18 19 20 21 22 23 24 25 26 28 29 30 31 32 34 35 36 37 38 39 40 41 42 43 44 45 46 47 48 49 50 51 52 53 54 55 56 57 58 59 60 61 63 65 66 67 68 70 71 72 73 74 **P**6
23 10 | 725 | 35615 | 575 | 1149473 | 2971 | 898341 | 450283 | 9547 |

✠ VETERANS AFFAIRS MEDICAL CENTER, 2215 Fuller Road, Zip 48105–2399; tel. 734/769–7100; James W. Roseborough, CHE, Director (Total facility includes 46 beds in nursing home–type unit) **A**1 2 3 5 8 **F**3 4 8 10 11 14 16 19 20 21 22 23 25 26 27 28 30 31 32 33 34 35 37 39 41 42 43 44 45 46 49 50 51 52 54 55 56 57 58 59 60 63 64 65 67 69 71 72 73 74 **S** Department of Veterans Affairs, Washington, DC
Web address: www.ann–arbor.med.va.gov
45 10 | 164 | 4914 | 137 | 285101 | 0 | 112610 | 62017 | 1378 |

AUBURN HILLS—Oakland County

□ HAVENWYCK HOSPITAL, 1525 University Drive, Zip 48326–2675; tel. 810/373–9200; Robert A. Kercorian, Chief Executive Officer (Nonreporting) **A**1 10 **S** Ramsay Health Care, Inc., Coral Gables, FL
33 22 | 120 | — | — | — | — | — | — |

BAD AXE—Huron County

✠ HURON MEMORIAL HOSPITAL, 1100 South Van Dyke Road, Zip 48413–9799; tel. 517/269–9521; James B. Gardner, President **A**1 9 10 **F**7 8 14 15 16 19 21 22 27 28 30 32 33 34 37 39 40 41 42 44 49 63 65 67 71
23 10 | 64 | 2062 | 21 | 49563 | 330 | 20317 | 9034 | 255 |

BATTLE CREEK—Calhoun County

✠ BATTLE CREEK HEALTH SYSTEM, (Includes Community Hospital, 183 West Street, Zip 49016; Fieldstone Center, 165 North Washington Avenue, Zip 49016; tel. 616/964–7121; Leila Hospital, 300 North Avenue, Zip 49016), 300 North Avenue, Zip 49016–3396; tel. 616/966–8000; Arthur Knueppel, Interim President and Chief Executive Officer (Total facility includes 122 beds in nursing home–type unit) **A**1 2 9 10 **F**3 7 8 10 12 14 15 16 17 19 21 22 25 28 29 32 33 34 35 37 40 41 42 44 46 49 50 51 52 53 57 58 59 60 64 65 67 71 73 74 **P**1 7 **S** Mercy Health Services, Farmington Hills, MI
21 10 | 378 | 11865 | 258 | 131380 | 1198 | 118955 | 49369 | 1245 |

Hospital, Address, Telephone, Administrator, Approval, Facility, and Physician Codes, Health Care System, Network	Classi-fication Codes		Utilization Data					Expense (thousands) of dollars		
★ American Hospital Association (AHA) membership □ Joint Commission on Accreditation of Healthcare Organizations (JCAHO) accreditation + American Osteopathic Healthcare Association (AOHA) membership ○ American Osteopathic Association (AOA) accreditation △ Commission on Accreditation of Rehabilitation Facilities (CARF) accreditation Control codes 61, 63, 64, 71, 72 and 73 indicate hospitals listed by AOHA, but not registered by AHA. For definition of numerical codes, see page A4	Control	Service	Staffed Beds	Admissions	Census	Outpatient Visits	Births	Total	Payroll	Personnel
✠ △ SOUTHWEST REHABILITATION HOSPITAL, 183 West Street, Zip 49017–3424; tel. 616/965–3206; Diane D. Giannunzio, President **A**1 7 10 **F**12 15 16 17 26 30 34 48 49 65	23	46	30	365	15	—	0	5391	1748	59
✠ VETERANS AFFAIRS MEDICAL CENTER, 5500 Armstrong Road, Zip 49016; tel. 616/966–5600; Michael K. Wheeler, Director (Total facility includes 127 beds in nursing home–type unit) **A**1 5 **F**2 3 6 8 12 15 16 17 19 20 25 27 28 30 31 32 33 34 41 46 48 49 51 52 54 55 57 58 64 65 67 71 73 74 **S** Department of Veterans Affairs, Washington, DC	45	22	410	4094	274	—	0	85858	50096	1213
BAY CITY—Bay County										
✠ △ BAY MEDICAL CENTER, (Includes Bay Medical Center–West Campus, 3250 East Midland Road, Zip 48706; tel. 517/667–6750; Samaritan Health Center, 713 Ninth Street, Zip 48708; tel. 517/894–3799), 1900 Columbus Avenue, Zip 48708–6880; tel. 517/894–3000; Robert N. Wright, President and Chief Operating Officer **A**1 2 7 9 10 12 13 **F**2 3 6 7 8 10 12 14 15 16 17 18 19 20 21 22 26 28 29 30 31 32 33 34 35 36 37 39 40 41 42 44 45 46 48 49 52 53 54 55 58 59 60 63 65 66 67 70 71 72 73 74 **P**6 8	23	10	341	14744	192	238939	1036	120804	54497	1664
BAY SPECIAL CARE, (LONG TERM ACUTE CARE/CVA COPD), 3250 East Midland Road, Zip 48706–2835, Mailing Address: 3250 East Midland Road, Suite 1, Zip 48706–2835; tel. 517/667–6802; Cheryl A. Burzynski, President **A**10 **F**2 3 4 7 8 10 11 12 13 14 15 17 19 21 22 26 27 28 29 30 32 33 35 36 37 39 40 41 42 44 46 48 49 51 52 53 54 56 57 58 59 60 63 65 66 67 71 72 73 74 **P**8	23	49	21	246	19	0	0	4871	2122	71
BERRIEN CENTER—Berrien County										
LAKELAND MEDICAL CENTER, BERRIEN CENTER See Lakeland Medical Center–St. Joseph, Saint Joseph										
BIG RAPIDS—Mecosta County										
✠ MECOSTA COUNTY GENERAL HOSPITAL, 405 Winter Avenue, Zip 49307–2099; tel. 616/796–8691; Thomas E. Daugherty, Administrator **A**1 9 10 **F**7 8 10 15 16 19 22 33 34 36 37 40 42 44 45 48 49 63 65 71 72 **P**7 8 **S** Quorum Health Group/Quorum Health Resources, Inc., Brentwood, TN **Web address:** www.mecoscountygeneral.com	13	10	52	2592	29	82980	702	21726	9055	281
BRIGHTON—Livingston County										
★ BRIGHTON HOSPITAL, 12851 East Grand River Avenue, Zip 48116–8596; tel. 810/227–1211; Ramon Royal, President **A**10 **F**2 3 14 15 16 39	23	82	83	1906	46	12802	0	7904	3915	138
CADILLAC—Wexford County										
✠ MERCY HEALTH SERVICES–NORTH, 400 Hobart Street, Zip 49601–9596; tel. 616/876–7200; John Sewell, Interim Chief Executive Officer **A**1 9 10 **F**3 7 8 10 12 14 15 16 17 19 20 21 22 24 27 28 29 30 31 32 33 34 35 37 39 40 41 42 44 46 49 51 52 54 55 56 58 63 65 66 67 71 73 **P**1 2 3 4 5 6 7 8 **S** Mercy Health Services, Farmington Hills, MI **Web address:** www.mercyhealth.com	21	10	78	4404	42	61867	488	40455	15843	584
CARO—Tuscola County										
□ CARO CENTER, 2000 Chambers Road, Zip 48723–9240; tel. 517/673–3191; Rose Laskowski, R.N., Hospital Director **A**1 10 **F**3 4 5 7 8 9 10 11 12 14 15 16 18 19 20 21 22 23 26 30 31 33 35 37 39 40 42 43 44 45 46 49 52 53 54 55 56 57 58 59 60 61 65 67 69 70 71 74	12	22	204	296	209	0	0	28666	18314	511
★ CARO COMMUNITY HOSPITAL, 401 North Hooper Street, Zip 48723–1476, Mailing Address: P.O. Box 71, Zip 48723–0071; tel. 517/673–3141; William P. Miller, President and Chief Executive Officer **A**9 10 **F**8 15 16 19 22 28 29 30 35 42 44 45 46 49 51 63 65 **P**6	16	10	15	726	7	—	0	6818	3154	130
CARSON CITY—Montcalm County										
+ ○ CARSON CITY HOSPITAL, 406 East Elm Street, Zip 48811–0879, Mailing Address: P.O. Box 879, Zip 48811–0879; tel. 517/584–3131; Bruce L. Traverse, President **A**9 10 11 12 13 **F**7 14 15 16 17 19 20 22 28 30 32 34 35 37 40 41 42 44 51 52 54 55 56 58 65 67 71 72 73 74 **P**6 **Web address:** www.carsoncityhospital.com	23	10	68	2155	23	43745	372	20597	10395	385
CASS CITY—Tuscola County										
✠ HILLS AND DALES GENERAL HOSPITAL, 4675 Hill Street, Zip 48726–1099; tel. 517/872–2121; Dee McKrow, Chief Executive Officer **A**1 9 10 **F**8 12 15 16 17 18 19 21 22 24 28 29 30 31 32 33 34 39 40 41 42 44 45 46 49 51 63 65 66 67 71 72 73 **P**5	23	10	47	965	10	34014	0	9760	5080	213
CHARLEVOIX—Charlevoix County										
✠ CHARLEVOIX AREA HOSPITAL, 14700 Lake Shore Drive, Zip 49720–1931; tel. 616/547–4024; William Jackson, President **A**1 9 10 **F**7 8 14 15 16 19 20 22 28 30 37 40 41 44 65 66 71 73	23	10	33	1403	14	21800	195	13115	6367	182
CHARLOTTE—Eaton County										
□ HAYES–GREEN–BEACH MEMORIAL HOSPITAL, 321 East Harris Street, Zip 48813–1697; tel. 517/543–1050; Stephen W. Mapes, Chief Executive Officer **A**1 9 10 **F**7 8 14 15 16 17 19 21 22 24 25 26 28 30 31 32 36 39 40 41 42 44 46 49 51 65 66 67 71 72 73 74 **P**6	23	10	35	1438	12	37909	234	16185	9278	297
CHEBOYGAN—Cheboygan County										
✠ COMMUNITY MEMORIAL HOSPITAL, 748 South Main Street, Zip 49721–2299, Mailing Address: P.O. Box 419, Zip 49721–0419; tel. 616/627–5601; Howard J. Purcell, Jr., President (Total facility includes 50 beds in nursing home–type unit) **A**1 9 10 **F**8 14 15 16 19 20 21 22 24 25 32 33 34 37 39 40 44 49 64 71 73 **P**8	23	10	92	2162	72	92070	239	22628	11762	357

Hospital, Address, Telephone, Administrator, Approval, Facility, and Physician Codes, Health Care System, Network	Classi-fication Codes		Utilization Data					Expense (thousands) of dollars		
★ American Hospital Association (AHA) membership □ Joint Commission on Accreditation of Healthcare Organizations (JCAHO) accreditation + American Osteopathic Healthcare Association (AOHA) membership ○ American Osteopathic Association (AOA) accreditation △ Commission on Accreditation of Rehabilitation Facilities (CARF) accreditation Control codes 61, 63, 64, 71, 72 and 73 indicate hospitals listed by AOHA, but not registered by AHA. For definition of numerical codes, see page A4	Control	Service	Staffed Beds	Admissions	Census	Outpatient Visits	Births	Total	Payroll	Personnel

CHELSEA—Washtenaw County

□ △ CHELSEA COMMUNITY HOSPITAL, 775 South Main Street, Zip 48118–1399; tel. 734/475–1311; Kathleen S. Griffiths, President and Chief Executive Officer **A**1 3 5 7 9 10 **F**3 6 8 14 15 16 17 19 21 22 24 25 26 28 29 30 32 34 37 39 41 42 44 45 46 48 49 52 53 54 55 57 58 59 61 62 65 67 71 73 74 **Web address:** www.cch.org	23	10	97	3120	62	133410	0	41410	19584	597

CLARE—Clare County

⊠ ○ MIDMICHIGAN MEDICAL CENTER–CLARE, 104 West Sixth Street, Zip 48617–1409; tel. 517/386–9951; Lawrence F. Barco, President **A**1 9 10 11 **F**7 8 15 17 19 21 22 28 30 32 33 34 35 37 40 41 42 44 45 49 63 67 71 72 73 74 **P**3 4 8 **S** MidMichigan Health, Midland, MI	23	10	64	2415	23	37440	308	16949	6719	272

CLINTON TOWNSHIP—Macomb County

⊠ ST. JOSEPH'S MERCY HOSPITALS AND HEALTH SERVICES, (Includes St. Joseph's Mercy Hospital–East, 215 North Avenue, Mount Clemens, Zip 48043; tel. 810/466–9300; St. Joseph's Mercy Hospital–West, 15855 19 Mile Road, Zip 48038; tel. 810/263–2300; St. Joseph's Mercy–North, 80650 North Van Dyke, Romeo, Zip 48065; tel. 810/798–3551), Jack Weiner, President and Chief Executive Officer **A**1 9 10 **F**3 6 7 8 10 11 12 13 15 16 17 18 19 21 22 25 26 27 28 29 30 31 32 33 34 35 36 37 39 40 41 42 44 45 46 48 49 52 53 54 55 56 57 58 59 60 61 64 65 67 68 70 71 72 73 74 **P**6 8 **S** Mercy Health Services, Farmington Hills, MI	23	10	346	15236	251	199237	1702	124106	58610	1599

COLDWATER—Branch County

⊠ + ○ COMMUNITY HEALTH CENTER OF BRANCH COUNTY, 274 East Chicago Street, Zip 49036–2088; tel. 517/279–5400; Lieutenant Douglas L. Rahn, Chief Executive Officer **A**1 9 10 11 12 13 **F**3 7 8 10 14 16 19 21 22 28 29 30 31 32 33 35 37 40 41 42 44 49 51 52 54 55 56 57 58 59 63 65 67 70 71 72 73 **P**6 8 **S** Quorum Health Group/Quorum Health Resources, Inc., Brentwood, TN **Web address:** www.chcbc.com	13	10	96	3759	39	94166	445	34142	15724	474

COMMERCE TOWNSHIP—Oakland County

⊠ HURON VALLEY–SINAI HOSPITAL, 1 William Carls Drive, Zip 48382–2201; tel. 248/360–3300; Robert J. Yellan, Senior Vice President **A**1 5 9 10 **F**7 8 10 14 15 19 21 22 27 28 30 31 33 34 37 39 40 41 42 44 45 46 49 54 61 65 67 71 73 **P**4 6 **S** Detroit Medical Center, Detroit, MI	23	10	139	8471	94	68532	1833	69257	26732	727

CRYSTAL FALLS—Iron County

CRYSTAL FALLS COMMUNITY HOSPITAL See Iron County Community Hospital, Iron River

DEARBORN—Wayne County

⊠ OAKWOOD HOSPITAL AND MEDICAL CENTER–DEARBORN, 18101 Oakwood Boulevard, Zip 48124–4093, Mailing Address: P.O. Box 2500, Zip 48123–2500; tel. 313/593–7000; Joseph Tasse, Administrator **A**1 2 3 5 8 9 10 **F**1 3 4 6 7 8 10 11 12 13 14 15 16 17 18 19 20 21 22 23 25 26 27 28 30 31 32 33 34 35 38 39 40 41 42 43 44 46 49 51 52 53 54 55 56 57 58 59 60 61 62 63 65 66 67 68 71 72 73 74 **P**1 5 **S** Oakwood Healthcarer, Inc., Dearborn, MI **Web address:** www.oakwood.org	23	10	565	27983	428	—	4749	333611	177628	4235

DECKERVILLE—Sanilac County

⊠ DECKERVILLE COMMUNITY HOSPITAL, 3559 Pine Street, Zip 48427–0126, Mailing Address: P.O. Box 126, Zip 48427–0126; tel. 810/376–2835; Edward L. Gamache, Administrator (Nonreporting) **A**1 9 10 **S** Mercy Health Services, Farmington Hills, MI	23	10	17	—						

DETROIT—Wayne County

⊠ △ CHILDREN'S HOSPITAL OF MICHIGAN, 3901 Beaubien Street, Zip 48201–9985; tel. 313/745–0073; Larry Fleischmann, M.D., Interim Senior Vice President **A**1 3 5 7 8 9 10 **F**2 3 4 5 6 7 8 9 10 11 12 13 14 15 16 17 18 19 20 21 22 24 25 26 27 28 29 30 31 32 33 34 35 36 37 38 39 40 41 42 43 44 45 46 47 48 49 50 51 52 54 55 56 57 58 59 60 61 64 65 66 67 68 70 71 72 73 74 **S** Detroit Medical Center, Detroit, MI **Web address:** www.dmc.org/chm	23	50	245	11335	142	144410	0	172915	62214	1504
⊠ DETROIT RECEIVING HOSPITAL AND UNIVERSITY HEALTH CENTER, 4201 St. Antoine Boulevard, Zip 48201–2194; tel. 313/745–3603; Leslie C. Bowman, Regional Administrator, Ancillary Services and Site Administrator (Nonreporting) **A**1 3 5 8 9 10 **S** Detroit Medical Center, Detroit, MI **Web address:** www.dmc.org	23	10	290	—	—	—	—	—	—	—
DETROIT RIVERVIEW HOSPITAL See St. John Detroit Riverview Hospital										
⊠ GRACE HOSPITAL, 6071 West Outer Drive, Zip 48235–2679; tel. 313/966–3525; Anne M. Regling, Senior Vice President (Nonreporting) **A**1 3 5 8 9 10 12 **S** Detroit Medical Center, Detroit, MI **Web address:** www.dmc.org	23	10	352	—	—	—	—	—	—	—
⊠ HARPER HOSPITAL, 3990 John R, Zip 48201–9027; tel. 313/745–8040; John R. Whitcomb, Interim Senior Vice President (Nonreporting) **A**1 2 3 5 8 9 10 **S** Detroit Medical Center, Detroit, MI	23	10	427	—	—	—	—	—	—	—
⊠ HENRY FORD HOSPITAL, 2799 West Grand Boulevard, Zip 48202–2689; tel. 313/916–2600; Stephen H. Velick, Chief Executive Officer **A**1 2 3 5 8 9 10 **F**1 3 4 5 6 7 8 10 11 12 13 14 15 16 17 18 19 20 21 22 23 24 25 26 27 28 29 30 31 32 33 34 35 36 37 38 39 40 41 42 43 44 45 46 47 49 50 51 53 54 55 56 57 58 59 60 61 63 65 66 67 68 70 71 72 73 74 **P**6 **S** Henry Ford Health System, Detroit, MI **Web address:** www.henryfordhealth.org	23	10	634	35370	522	904575	2637	359437	147780	7657
HOLY CROSS SARATOGA HOSPITAL See St. John NorthEast Community Hospital										

Hospital, Address, Telephone, Administrator, Approval, Facility, and Physician Codes, Health Care System, Network	Classi-fication Codes		Utilization Data					Expense (thousands) of dollars		
	Control	Service	Staffed Beds	Admissions	Census	Outpatient Visits	Births	Total	Payroll	Personnel

Key:
★ American Hospital Association (AHA) membership
□ Joint Commission on Accreditation of Healthcare Organizations (JCAHO) accreditation
+ American Osteopathic Healthcare Association (AOHA) membership
○ American Osteopathic Association (AOA) accreditation
△ Commission on Accreditation of Rehabilitation Facilities (CARF) accreditation
Control codes 61, 63, 64, 71, 72 and 73 indicate hospitals listed by AOHA, but not registered by AHA. For definition of numerical codes, see page A4

Hospital	Control	Service	Staffed Beds	Admissions	Census	Outpatient Visits	Births	Total	Payroll	Personnel
☒ HUTZEL HOSPITAL, 4707 St. Antoine Boulevard, Zip 48201–0154; tel. 313/745–7555; Mark McNash, Operations Officer (Nonreporting) A1 3 5 8 9 10 S Detroit Medical Center, Detroit, MI	23	10	243	—	—	—	—	—	—	—
☒ JOHN D. DINGELL VETERANS AFFAIRS MEDICAL CENTER, 4646 John R Street, Zip 48201–1932; tel. 313/576–1000; Carlos B. Lott, Jr., Director (Total facility includes 84 beds in nursing home–type unit) A1 2 5 8 F2 3 4 5 6 8 10 11 12 14 15 16 17 18 19 20 21 22 23 26 27 28 29 30 31 32 33 34 35 37 39 41 42 43 44 45 46 49 50 51 52 54 55 56 58 59 60 61 63 64 65 67 68 70 71 72 73 74 P6 S Department of Veterans Affairs, Washington, DC	45	10	218	4856	198	268217	0	131102	64806	1539
☒ MERCY HOSPITAL, 5555 Conner Avenue, Zip 48213–3499; tel. 313/579–4000; David Spivey, President and Chief Executive Officer A1 3 9 10 F1 2 3 4 5 6 7 8 9 10 11 12 13 14 15 16 17 18 19 20 22 23 24 25 26 27 28 30 31 32 33 34 35 37 38 40 41 42 43 44 45 46 47 48 49 51 52 53 54 55 56 57 58 59 60 62 64 65 66 67 69 70 71 72 73 74 P6 8 S Mercy Health Services, Farmington Hills, MI Web address: www.mercyhealth.com/detroit	23	10	268	10522	188	199283	900	117135	53608	1310
☒ △ REHABILITATION INSTITUTE OF MICHIGAN, 261 Mack Boulevard, Zip 48201–2495; tel. 313/745–1203; Bruce M. Gans, M.D., Senior Vice President A1 3 5 7 9 10 F3 4 5 7 8 9 10 11 12 14 15 16 17 19 20 21 22 23 24 25 26 27 28 29 30 31 32 33 34 35 37 38 39 40 42 43 44 45 46 47 48 49 50 51 52 53 54 55 56 57 58 59 60 61 63 64 65 66 67 68 70 71 72 73 74 P4 5 6 7 8 S Detroit Medical Center, Detroit, MI Web address: www.dmc.org	23	46	94	1664	70	99873	0	45202	23797	537
★ ○ △ SINAI HOSPITAL, 6767 West Outer Drive, Zip 48235–2899; tel. 313/493–6800; Anne M. Regling, Senior Vice President (Nonreporting) A3 5 7 8 9 10 11 12 S Detroit Medical Center, Detroit, MI	23	10	469	—	—	—	—	—	—	—
☒ ○ ST. JOHN DETROIT RIVERVIEW HOSPITAL, (Formerly Detroit Riverview Hospital), 7733 East Jefferson Avenue, Zip 48214–2598; tel. 313/499–4000; Richard T. Young, President (Nonreporting) A1 9 10 11 12 13 S Sisters of St. Joseph Health System, Ann Arbor, MI	23	10	230	—	—	—	—	—	—	—
☒ △ ST. JOHN HOSPITAL AND MEDICAL CENTER, (Includes St. John Hospital–Macomb Center, 26755 Ballard Road, Harrison Township, Zip 48045–2458; tel. 810/465–5501; David Sessions, President), 22101 Moross Road, Zip 48236–2172; tel. 313/343–4000; Timothy J. Grajewski, President and Chief Executive Officer A1 2 3 5 7 8 9 10 F2 8 10 11 12 14 15 16 17 19 21 22 23 24 25 26 27 28 29 30 31 32 33 34 35 37 38 39 40 41 42 43 44 45 46 48 49 51 52 53 56 58 59 60 61 62 64 65 66 67 68 70 71 72 73 74 P3 5 6 8 S Sisters of St. Joseph Health System, Ann Arbor, MI	21	10	737	31983	506	375404	3589	405123	193331	4774
☒ ST. JOHN NORTHEAST COMMUNITY HOSPITAL, (Formerly Holy Cross Saratoga Hospital), 4777 East Outer Drive, Zip 48234–0401; tel. 313/369–9100; Michael F. Breen, President A1 9 10 F1 8 10 14 15 16 17 19 21 22 27 28 30 33 34 37 44 48 49 52 57 58 59 63 64 65 71 73 P5 8 S Sisters of St. Joseph Health System, Ann Arbor, MI	21	10	161	5114	117	38515	0	43147	18986	551
VENCOR HOSPITAL–METRO DETROIT, 2700 Martin Luther King Boulevard, Zip 48208; tel. 313/594–6000; Deborah A. Sopo, Administrator A10 F12 16 19 22 37 65 67 71 P6 S Vencor, Incorporated, Louisville, KY Web address: www.vencor.com	33	10	114	501	63	0	0	16284	7107	257
DOWAGIAC—Cass County										
☒ LEE MEMORIAL HOSPITAL, 420 West High Street, Zip 49047–1907; tel. 616/782–8681; Fritz Fahrenbacher, President and Chief Executive Officer A1 9 10 F3 8 11 14 15 16 17 19 21 22 25 28 29 30 33 35 36 39 41 42 44 45 46 49 53 54 55 56 57 58 59 65 66 67 71 72 73 P6 8 S Sisters of St. Joseph Health System, Ann Arbor, MI	21	10	47	1968	23	35057	0	14925	6554	192
EAST CHINA—St. Clair County										
☒ ST. JOHN RIVER DISTRICT HOSPITAL, (Formerly River District Hospital), 4100 River Road, Zip 48054; tel. 810/329–7111; Frank W. Poma, President A1 9 10 F3 7 8 12 15 16 17 19 22 26 28 30 35 37 40 41 42 44 45 46 49 51 53 54 56 58 65 67 71 73 74 P6 8 S Sisters of St. Joseph Health System, Ann Arbor, MI	21	10	68	2752	26	106816	609	24868	12911	357
EATON RAPIDS—Eaton County										
□ EATON RAPIDS COMMUNITY HOSPITAL, 1500 South Main Street, Zip 48827–0130, Mailing Address: P.O. Box 130, Zip 48827–0130; tel. 517/663–2671; Jack L. Denton, President A1 9 10 F8 12 14 19 22 28 30 34 35 36 39 41 42 44 46 49 51 56 65 71 72 73	23	10	21	633	6	27502	0	6953	3660	139
ESCANABA—Delta County										
☒ ST. FRANCIS HOSPITAL, 3401 Ludington Street, Zip 49829–1377; tel. 906/786–3311; Roger M. Burgess, Administrator A1 10 F7 8 14 15 16 17 19 21 22 26 28 29 30 32 33 34 35 37 40 41 42 44 45 48 49 51 65 66 67 71 72 73 74 P6 S OSF Healthcare System, Peoria, IL Web address: www.osfhealthcare.com	21	10	66	3329	38	70581	447	30804	14042	585
FARMINGTON HILLS—Oakland County										
★ + ○ △ BOTSFORD GENERAL HOSPITAL, 28050 Grand River Avenue, Zip 48336–5933; tel. 248/471–8000; Gerson I. Cooper, President A7 9 10 11 12 13 F1 3 6 7 8 10 11 12 13 14 15 16 17 19 21 22 24 26 27 28 29 30 31 33 34 35 37 40 41 42 44 45 48 49 51 52 54 57 58 59 62 64 65 66 67 69 71 72 73 P5 6 7 Web address: www.botsfordsystem.org	23	10	325	12808	218	379974	828	165173	79737	1956

Hospital, Address, Telephone, Administrator, Approval, Facility, and Physician Codes, Health Care System, Network	Classi-fication Codes		Utilization Data					Expense (thousands) of dollars		
★ American Hospital Association (AHA) membership □ Joint Commission on Accreditation of Healthcare Organizations (JCAHO) accreditation + American Osteopathic Healthcare Association (AOHA) membership ○ American Osteopathic Association (AOA) accreditation △ Commission on Accreditation of Rehabilitation Facilities (CARF) accreditation Control codes 61, 63, 64, 71, 72 and 73 indicate hospitals listed by AOHA, but not registered by AHA. For definition of numerical codes, see page A4	Control	Service	Staffed Beds	Admissions	Census	Outpatient Visits	Births	Total	Payroll	Personnel

FERNDALE—Oakland County

★ KINGSWOOD HOSPITAL, 10300 West Eight Mile Road, Zip 48220–2198; tel. 248/398–3200; Glenn Black, Associate Vice President and Chief Operating Officer (Nonreporting) **A**3 10 **S** Henry Ford Health System, Detroit, MI — 23 22 64 — — — — — — —

FLINT—Genesee County

✠ △ HURLEY MEDICAL CENTER, One Hurley Plaza, Zip 48503–5993; tel. 810/257–9000; Glenn A. Fosdick, President and Chief Executive Officer **A**1 2 3 5 7 8 9 10 **F**7 8 9 10 11 12 13 14 15 16 17 18 19 20 21 22 24 25 26 27 28 29 30 31 32 33 34 35 37 38 39 40 41 42 44 45 46 47 48 49 51 52 53 54 55 56 57 58 59 60 61 63 64 65 66 67 68 70 71 72 73 74 **P**3 5 6 7 8
Web address: www.hurleymc.com — 14 10 476 21514 306 423306 3185 245320 106627 2632

✠ △ MCLAREN REGIONAL MEDICAL CENTER, 401 South Ballenger Highway, Zip 48532–3685; tel. 810/342–2000; Gregory L. Beckman, President and Chief Executive Officer **A**1 2 3 5 7 8 9 10 **F**2 3 4 7 8 10 11 12 13 14 15 16 17 18 19 20 21 22 24 25 26 27 28 29 30 31 32 33 34 35 37 38 39 40 41 42 43 44 45 46 47 48 49 51 52 53 54 55 56 57 58 59 60 61 63 64 65 66 67 68 70 71 72 73 74 **P**6 7
Web address: www.mclaren.org — 23 10 467 17562 260 363423 948 178472 79976 1916

FRANKFORT—Benzie County

✠ PAUL OLIVER MEMORIAL HOSPITAL, 224 Park Avenue, Zip 49635; tel. 616/352–9621; James D. Austin, CHE, Administrator (Total facility includes 40 beds in nursing home–type unit) **A**1 9 10 **F**1 3 8 14 15 16 17 18 19 20 21 22 24 26 27 28 29 32 33 34 36 39 41 42 44 45 49 51 53 54 55 56 57 58 59 61 64 65 67 71 73 74 **P**1 3 5 7 **S** Munson Healthcare, Traverse City, MI
Web address: www.benzie.com — 23 10 48 390 41 24360 0 6343 2279 87

FREMONT—Newaygo County

✠ GERBER MEMORIAL HOSPITAL, 212 South Sullivan Street, Zip 49412–1596; tel. 616/924–3300; Ned B. Hughes, Jr., President **A**1 9 10 **F**7 8 14 15 16 17 18 19 22 26 30 32 34 35 37 39 40 41 42 44 45 46 49 52 54 55 56 57 58 65 66 67 71 72 73 74 — 23 10 73 2408 28 70787 362 27688 13697 396

GARDEN CITY—Wayne County

+ ○ △ GARDEN CITY HOSPITAL, 6245 North Inkster Road, Zip 48135–4001; tel. 734/421–3300; Gary R. Ley, President and Chief Executive Officer **A**7 9 10 11 12 13 **F**2 3 7 8 10 11 12 14 15 16 17 19 22 27 28 29 32 33 34 35 37 39 40 41 42 44 46 48 49 51 58 60 65 66 67 70 71 72 73 **P**5 8 — 23 10 270 10375 175 93857 807 98740 46151 1198

GAYLORD—Otsego County

✠ OTSEGO MEMORIAL HOSPITAL, (Includes McReynolds Hall), 825 North Center Street, Zip 49735–1560; tel. 517/731–2100; John L. MacLeod, Administrator and Chief Executive Officer (Total facility includes 34 beds in nursing home–type unit) **A**1 9 10 **F**7 8 12 14 15 16 19 22 25 28 29 30 32 33 34 35 37 39 40 41 44 48 49 63 64 65 67 68 70 71 72 73 **P**6 8
Web address: www.gaylordhospital.org — 23 10 73 1903 47 43160 269 18911 8574 311

GLADWIN—Gladwin County

✠ MIDMICHIGAN MEDICAL CENTER–GLADWIN, 515 South Quarter Street, Zip 48624–1918; tel. 517/426–9286; Mark E. Bush, Executive Vice President **A**1 9 10 **F**8 15 16 17 19 22 28 30 44 45 51 65 71 74 **P**4 5 6 **S** MidMichigan Health, Midland, MI — 23 10 42 1539 16 40106 0 10218 3980 129

GRAND BLANC—Genesee County

✠ + ○ △ GENESYS REGIONAL MEDICAL CENTER, One Genesys Parkway, Zip 48439–8066; tel. 810/606–5000; Elliot T. Joseph, President and Chief Executive Officer **A**1 2 3 5 7 9 10 11 12 13 **F**1 3 4 7 8 10 11 12 14 15 16 17 18 19 21 22 23 25 26 27 28 29 30 31 32 33 34 35 37 39 40 41 42 43 44 45 46 48 49 51 53 54 56 57 58 60 63 64 65 67 70 71 72 73 74 **P**1 2 5 6 **S** Sisters of St. Joseph Health System, Ann Arbor, MI
Web address: www.genesys.org — 21 10 379 23604 312 310253 2732 275422 113540 2566

GRAND HAVEN—Ottawa County

✠ NORTH OTTAWA COMMUNITY HOSPITAL, 1309 Sheldon Road, Zip 49417–2488; tel. 616/842–3600; Michael J. Funk, Chief Executive Officer **A**1 9 10 **F**7 8 12 14 15 16 19 21 22 26 28 30 31 32 33 34 35 36 37 39 40 41 42 44 46 49 63 65 66 67 71 72 73 74 — 23 10 81 2454 25 161161 535 36529 15146 340

GRAND RAPIDS—Kent County

□ FOREST VIEW HOSPITAL, 1055 Medical Park Drive S.E., Zip 49546–3671; tel. 616/942–9610; John F. Kuhn, Chief Executive Officer (Nonreporting) **A**1 10 **S** Universal Health Services, Inc., King of Prussia, PA
Web address: www.forestview.com — 33 22 62 — — — — — — —

□ KENT COMMUNITY HOSPITAL, (CHEMICAL DEPENDENCY LONG TERM), 750 Fuller Avenue N.E., Zip 49503–1995; tel. 616/336–3360; Lori Portfleet, Chief Executive Officer (Total facility includes 314 beds in nursing home–type unit) **A**1 10 **F**2 3 14 15 16 49 64 65 73 **S** Spectrum Health, Grand Rapids, MI — 13 49 356 2521 273 — 0 22419 9615 358

✠ △ MARY FREE BED HOSPITAL AND REHABILITATION CENTER, 235 Wealthy S.E., Zip 49503–5299; tel. 616/242–0300; William H. Blessing, President **A**1 7 10 **F**14 15 19 21 25 27 32 34 35 39 41 45 48 49 65 67 71 73 — 23 46 80 921 46 22782 0 21710 13129 443

+ ○ △ METROPOLITAN HOSPITAL, 1919 Boston Street S.E., Zip 49506–4199; Mailing Address: P.O. Box 158, Zip 49501–0158; tel. 616/252–7200; Michael D. Faas, President and Chief Executive Officer **A**7 9 10 11 12 13 **F**4 7 8 10 12 14 15 16 17 19 21 23 26 28 29 30 31 34 35 37 39 40 41 44 45 46 48 49 51 53 54 55 56 57 58 59 61 65 66 70 71 73 74 **P**6 7 8 — 23 10 214 8691 116 210069 1298 90392 42467 987

Hospital, Address, Telephone, Administrator, Approval, Facility, and Physician Codes, Health Care System, Network	Classi-fication Codes		Utilization Data					Expense (thousands) of dollars		
★ American Hospital Association (AHA) membership □ Joint Commission on Accreditation of Healthcare Organizations (JCAHO) accreditation + American Osteopathic Healthcare Association (AOHA) membership ○ American Osteopathic Association (AOA) accreditation △ Commission on Accreditation of Rehabilitation Facilities (CARF) accreditation Control codes 61, 63, 64, 71, 72 and 73 indicate hospitals listed by AOHA, but not registered by AHA. For definition of numerical codes, see page A4	Control	Service	Staffed Beds	Admissions	Census	Outpatient Visits	Births	Total	Payroll	Personnel

⊞ PINE REST CHRISTIAN MENTAL HEALTH SERVICES, 300 68th Street S.E., Zip 49501–0165, Mailing Address: P.O. Box 165, Zip 49501–0165; tel. 616/455–5000; Daniel L. Holwerda, President and Chief Executive Officer **A**1 3 5 10 **F**3 4 7 8 9 10 11 12 13 14 15 16 17 19 21 22 25 26 29 30 32 35 37 38 40 42 43 44 45 46 47 50 52 53 54 55 56 57 58 59 60 61 63 64 65 67 71 72 73 74 **Web address:** www.pinerest.org	23	22	106	2777	53	88201	0	30879	17644	580
⊞ SAINT MARY'S HEALTH SERVICES, 200 Jefferson Avenue S.E., Zip 49503–4598; tel. 616/752–6090; David J. Ameen, President and Chief Executive Officer **A**1 2 3 5 9 10 **F**7 8 10 12 14 15 16 17 19 20 21 22 24 25 26 28 29 30 31 32 34 35 37 38 39 40 41 42 44 49 51 52 54 55 60 63 64 65 66 67 68 70 71 73 74 **P**6 **S** Mercy Health Services, Farmington Hills, MI **Web address:** www.mercyhealth.com\smhc	21	10	300	12575	163	439329	2019	174628	74302	2371
⊞ SPECTRUM HEALTH–DOWNTOWN CAMPUS, 100 Michigan Street N.E., Zip 49503–2551; tel. 616/391–1774; William G. Gonzalez, Pres **A**1 2 3 5 8 9 10 **F**4 5 7 8 9 10 11 12 13 14 15 16 17 19 20 21 22 23 25 26 29 30 32 33 34 35 37 38 39 40 41 42 43 44 45 46 47 49 51 60 61 63 65 66 67 68 70 71 72 73 74 **P**6 8 **S** Spectrum Health, Grand Rapids, MI **Web address:** www.spectrum–health.com	23	10	529	29396	383	660502	5701	326837	156883	4199
⊞ SPECTRUM HEALTH–EAST CAMPUS, (Includes Ferguson Campus, 72 Sheldon Boulevard S.E., Zip 49503–4294; tel. 616/356–4000), 1840 Wealthy Street S.E., Zip 49506–2921; tel. 616/774–7444; William G. Gonzalez, President **A**1 2 3 5 8 9 10 **F**4 5 7 8 9 10 11 12 13 14 15 16 17 19 20 21 22 23 25 26 29 30 32 33 34 35 37 38 39 40 41 42 43 44 45 46 47 49 51 60 61 63 65 66 67 68 70 71 72 73 74 **P**6 8 **S** Spectrum Health, Grand Rapids, MI **Web address:** www.spectrum–health.org	23	10	332	15549	196	—	2819	149436	67326	2245
GRAYLING—Crawford County										
⊞ MERCY HEALTH SERVICES NORTH–GRAYLING, 1100 Michigan Avenue, Zip 49738–1398; tel. 517/348–5461; Stephanie J. Riemer–Matuzak, Chief Executive Officer (Total facility includes 40 beds in nursing home–type unit) (Nonreporting) **A**1 9 10 **S** Mercy Health Services, Farmington Hills, MI	21	10	98	—	—	—	—	—	—	—
GREENVILLE—Montcalm County										
⊞ UNITED MEMORIAL HOSPITAL ASSOCIATION, 615 South Bower Street, Zip 48838–2628; tel. 616/754–4691; Dennis G. Zielinski, Chief Executive Officer (Total facility includes 40 beds in nursing home–type unit) **A**1 9 10 **F**7 8 13 15 16 17 19 22 24 25 28 30 34 35 37 39 40 41 44 46 49 51 64 65 67 68 71 72 73 74 **P**3 7 8 **Web address:** www.umha.org	23	10	97	2404	56	111652	304	22484	8678	337
GROSSE POINTE—Wayne County										
⊞ BON SECOURS HOSPITAL, 468 Cadieux Road, Zip 48230–1592; tel. 313/343–1000; Richard Van Lith, Chief Executive Officer **A**1 3 5 9 10 **F**7 8 10 12 14 15 16 17 18 19 21 22 24 26 27 28 29 30 32 33 34 35 36 37 39 40 42 44 45 46 49 51 63 65 67 71 73 74 **P**6 **S** Bon Secours Health System, Inc., Marriottsville, MD **Web address:** www.bonsecoursmi.com	21	10	235	10569	148	111023	1345	100018	53170	1484
GROSSE POINTE FARMS—Wayne County										
⊞ COTTAGE HOSPITAL, (Formerly Henry Ford Cottage Hospital of Grosse Pointe), 159 Kercheval Avenue, Zip 48236–3692; tel. 313/640–1000; Richard Van Lith, Chief Executive Officer **A**1 3 9 10 **F**1 2 7 8 9 14 15 16 18 19 22 25 27 28 29 30 31 32 34 35 40 44 45 46 48 49 52 54 55 56 57 58 59 63 65 66 67 71 72 73 74 **P**6 **S** Bon Secours Health System, Inc., Marriottsville, MD	23	10	148	4491	112	125513	432	57385	21335	770
HANCOCK—Houghton County										
⊞ PORTAGE HEALTH SYSTEM, 200 Michigan Avenue, Zip 49930–1427; tel. 906/487–8000; James Bogan, Chief Executive Officer (Total facility includes 30 beds in nursing home–type unit) **A**1 9 10 **F**1 7 8 12 13 14 15 16 17 19 22 24 26 28 29 30 31 32 34 35 36 37 39 40 41 44 45 49 51 54 56 57 58 61 63 64 65 66 67 71 72 73 74 **P**6 **Web address:** www.phsys.org	23	10	74	1921	51	71731	399	22964	12468	346
HARBOR BEACH—Huron County										
★ HARBOR BEACH COMMUNITY HOSPITAL, 210 South First Street, Zip 48441–1236, Mailing Address: P.O. Box 40, Zip 48441–0040; tel. 517/479–3201; Pauline Siemen–Messing, R.N., President and Chief Executive Officer (Total facility includes 40 beds in nursing home–type unit) **A**9 10 **F**8 16 19 22 26 30 34 40 44 49 51 64 65 67 71 **P**6	23	10	61	427	42	1668	0	5821	2996	112
HARRISON TOWNSHIP—Macomb County										
ST. JOHN HOSPITAL–MACOMB CENTER See St. John Hospital and Medical Center, Detroit										
HASTINGS—Barry County										
□ PENNOCK HOSPITAL, 1009 West Green Street, Zip 49058–1790; tel. 616/945–3451; Daniel Hamilton, Chief Executive Officer **A**1 9 10 **F**7 8 11 12 14 15 16 19 21 22 24 26 28 29 30 32 33 34 35 39 40 41 42 44 45 46 49 56 62 63 65 66 67 71 73 **P**5	23	10	88	3076	43	123742	347	29528	13408	429
HILLSDALE—Hillsdale County										
⊞ HILLSDALE COMMUNITY HEALTH CENTER, 168 South Howell Street, Zip 49242–2081; tel. 517/437–4451; Charles A. Bianchi, President (Total facility includes 21 beds in nursing home–type unit) **A**1 9 10 **F**7 8 12 14 15 16 17 19 22 28 30 32 34 35 36 37 39 40 41 42 44 46 49 63 64 65 66 67 70 71 72 73 **P**8	23	10	47	2736	30	91622	367	22805	8624	293

Hospital, Address, Telephone, Administrator, Approval, Facility, and Physician Codes, Health Care System, Network	Classi-fication Codes		Utilization Data					Expense (thousands) of dollars		
★ American Hospital Association (AHA) membership □ Joint Commission on Accreditation of Healthcare Organizations (JCAHO) accreditation + American Osteopathic Healthcare Association (AOHA) membership ○ American Osteopathic Association (AOA) accreditation △ Commission on Accreditation of Rehabilitation Facilities (CARF) accreditation Control codes 61, 63, 64, 71, 72 and 73 indicate hospitals listed by AOHA, but not registered by AHA. For definition of numerical codes, see page A4	Control	Service	Staffed Beds	Admissions	Census	Outpatient Visits	Births	Total	Payroll	Personnel

HOLLAND—Ottawa County

⊞ △ HOLLAND COMMUNITY HOSPITAL, 602 Michigan Avenue, Zip 49423–4999; tel. 616/392–5141; Judeth Newham, R.N., President and Chief Executive Officer **A**1 7 9 10 **F**7 12 14 15 16 17 19 20 21 22 28 29 30 32 34 35 36 37 39 40 41 42 44 45 49 52 53 54 55 56 57 58 63 65 67 70 71 72 73 **P**8 **Web address:** www.hoho.org	23	10	163	7987	68	183490	1841	60769	28065	860

HOWELL—Livingston County

⊞ MCPHERSON HOSPITAL, 620 Byron Road, Zip 48843–1093; tel. 517/545–6000; Patricia Claffey, Executive Director **A**1 9 10 **F**1 2 3 4 5 7 8 10 11 12 13 14 15 16 17 18 19 20 21 22 25 26 27 28 29 30 31 32 33 34 35 37 39 40 41 42 43 44 45 46 48 49 51 52 53 54 55 56 57 58 59 60 61 63 65 66 67 68 70 71 72 73 74 **P**1 5 **S** Mercy Health Services, Farmington Hills, MI	21	10	45	3324	32	254237	776	41561	18824	534

IONIA—Ionia County

⊞ IONIA COUNTY MEMORIAL HOSPITAL, 479 Lafayette Street, Zip 48846–1834, Mailing Address: Box 1001, Zip 48846–1899; tel. 616/527–4200; Evonne G. Ulmer, JD, Chief Executive Officer **A**1 9 10 **F**7 8 13 14 15 16 19 22 26 28 29 30 32 33 34 35 39 40 41 42 44 46 49 51 65 66 67 71 72 73 74 **P**6	23	10	77	1254	13	16769	142	11748	5124	177

IRON MOUNTAIN—Dickinson County

⊞ DICKINSON COUNTY HEALTHCARE SYSTEM, 1721 South Stephenson Avenue, Zip 49801–3637; tel. 906/774–1313; John Schon, Administrator and Chief Executive Officer **A**1 9 10 **F**1 7 8 14 19 21 22 28 29 30 32 34 35 37 39 40 41 42 44 46 49 63 65 66 67 68 71 72 73 **P**6 **Web address:** www.dchs.org	13	10	96	4190	46	122672	555	40066	18594	472
⊞ VETERANS AFFAIRS MEDICAL CENTER, 325 East H Street, Zip 49801–4792; tel. 906/774–3300; Thomas B. Arnold, Director (Total facility includes 40 beds in nursing home–type unit) **A**1 5 **F**3 12 17 19 20 21 22 26 27 30 31 33 34 37 39 42 44 45 46 49 51 54 55 56 57 58 59 64 65 71 72 73 74 **P**6 **S** Department of Veterans Affairs, Washington, DC	45	10	57	1292	53	70675	0	31421	14704	333

IRON RIVER—Iron County

⊞ IRON COUNTY COMMUNITY HOSPITAL, (Includes Crystal Falls Community Hospital, 212 South Third Street, Crystal Falls, Zip 49920; tel. 906/875–6661), 1400 West Ice Lake Road, Zip 49935–9594; tel. 906/265–6121; David L. Hoff, Chief Executive Officer (Total facility includes 62 beds in nursing home–type unit) **A**1 9 10 **F**7 8 11 12 13 14 15 16 17 19 21 22 24 26 28 30 32 34 37 39 40 41 42 44 45 46 48 49 51 61 64 65 66 67 71 73 74 **Web address:** www.org/iron/index.html	23	10	82	1543	76	42000	41	15733	7481	207

IRONWOOD—Gogebic County

⊞ GRAND VIEW HOSPITAL, N10561 Grand View Lane, Zip 49938–9359; tel. 906/932–2525; Frederick Geissler, Chief Executive Officer **A**1 9 10 **F**7 11 14 15 16 17 19 21 22 28 30 32 33 39 40 41 42 44 45 49 61 65 66 71 73 74 **P**8 **Web address:** www.gvhs.org	23	10	35	1906	22	56602	171	17810	10006	209

ISHPEMING—Marquette County

□ △ BELL MEMORIAL HOSPITAL, 101 South Fourth Street, Zip 49849–2151; tel. 906/486–4431; Kevin P. Calhoun, President and Chief Executive Officer (Nonreporting) **A**1 7 9 10 **Web address:** www.bellmemorial.org	23	10	30	—	—	—	—	—	—	—

JACKSON—Jackson County

★ + ○ DOCTORS HOSPITAL OF JACKSON, 110 North Elm Avenue, Zip 49202–3595; tel. 517/787–1440; Michael J. Falatko, President and Chief Executive Officer **A**9 10 11 **F**8 14 15 16 17 19 21 22 23 25 28 34 35 37 41 42 44 46 49 51 63 65 71 72 73 **P**1 5 7 8 **Web address:** www.doctorshospital.org	21	10	45	1734	20	39050	0	17831	7928	257
□ DUANE L. WATERS HOSPITAL, 3857 Cooper Street, Zip 49201–7521; tel. 517/780–5600; Gerald De Voss, Acting Administrator (Nonreporting) **A**1	12	11	86	—	—	—	—	—	—	—
□ W. A. FOOTE MEMORIAL HOSPITAL, 205 North East Avenue, Zip 49201–1789; tel. 517/788–4800; Georgia R. Fojtasek, President and Chief Executive Officer **A**1 9 10 **F**2 3 7 8 10 11 12 15 17 19 21 22 24 26 28 29 30 32 33 34 35 36 37 39 40 41 42 44 45 46 48 49 51 52 53 54 55 56 57 58 59 60 63 65 66 67 71 72 73 74 **P**1 5 **Web address:** www.foote.com	23	10	432	15563	197	357556	1943	129774	61059	2064

KALAMAZOO—Kalamazoo County

⊞ △ BORGESS MEDICAL CENTER, 1521 Gull Road, Zip 49001–1640; tel. 616/226–4800; Randall Stasik, President and Chief Executive Officer (Includes Borgess–Pipp Health Center, Plainwell) **A**1 2 3 5 7 9 10 **F**3 4 5 7 8 10 11 12 14 15 16 17 18 19 20 21 22 23 24 25 26 28 29 30 31 32 33 34 35 37 39 40 41 42 43 44 45 46 48 49 51 52 53 54 55 56 57 58 59 60 63 65 66 67 68 71 72 73 74 **P**3 6 7 8 **S** Sisters of St. Joseph Health System, Ann Arbor, MI **Web address:** www.borgess.com	21	10	405	17408	231	335963	1771	240085	95876	1906
⊞ △ BRONSON METHODIST HOSPITAL, 252 East Lovell Street, Zip 49007–5345; tel. 616/341–6000; Frank J. Sardone, President and Chief Executive Officer **A**1 2 3 5 7 9 10 **F**2 3 4 6 7 8 9 10 11 12 13 14 15 16 17 18 19 20 21 23 25 26 27 28 29 30 31 32 33 34 35 37 38 39 40 41 42 43 44 45 46 47 48 49 51 52 53 54 55 56 57 58 59 60 61 62 63 64 65 66 67 68 70 71 72 73 74 **P**5 6 7 **S** Bronson Healthcare Group, Inc., Kalamazoo, MI **Web address:** www.bronsonhealth.com	23	10	307	15500	208	325537	2973	179843	76545	1935

Hospital, Address, Telephone, Administrator, Approval, Facility, and Physician Codes, Health Care System, Network	Classi-fication Codes		Utilization Data					Expense (thousands) of dollars		
★ American Hospital Association (AHA) membership □ Joint Commission on Accreditation of Healthcare Organizations (JCAHO) accreditation + American Osteopathic Healthcare Association (AOHA) membership ○ American Osteopathic Association (AOA) accreditation △ Commission on Accreditation of Rehabilitation Facilities (CARF) accreditation Control codes 61, 63, 64, 71, 72 and 73 indicate hospitals listed by AOHA, but not registered by AHA. For definition of numerical codes, see page A4	Control	Service	Staffed Beds	Admissions	Census	Outpatient Visits	Births	Total	Payroll	Personnel

□ KALAMAZOO REGIONAL PSYCHIATRIC HOSPITAL, 1312 Oakland Drive, Zip 49008–1205; tel. 616/337–3000; James Coleman, Director **A**1 10 **F**4 5 8 10 14 16 19 20 21 22 24 27 29 30 31 33 35 42 43 44 45 46 51 52 54 55 56 57 60 61 65 70 71 72 73 74	12	22	163	320	135	0	0	27257	16284	377
KALKASKA—Kalkaska County										
★ KALKASKA MEMORIAL HEALTH CENTER, 419 South Coral Street, Zip 49646; tel. 616/258–7500; James D. Austin, CHE, Administrator (Total facility includes 68 beds in nursing home–type unit) **A**9 10 **F**14 15 16 19 22 28 34 49 64 65 67 71 72 73 74 **S** Munson Healthcare, Traverse City, MI	16	10	76	367	68	32540	0	8475	4102	174
L'ANSE—Baraga County										
□ BARAGA COUNTY MEMORIAL HOSPITAL, 770 North Main Street, Zip 49946–1195; tel. 906/524–6166; John P. Tembreull, Administrator (Total facility includes 28 beds in nursing home–type unit) **A**1 9 10 **F**8 15 16 19 21 22 30 32 33 44 49 63 64 65 67 71 **Web address:** www.bcmh.org	13	10	40	896	35	18304	0	8933	4461	141
LAKEVIEW—Montcalm County										
□ KELSEY MEMORIAL HOSPITAL, 418 Washington Avenue, Zip 48850; tel. 517/352–7211; James Cliborne, Chief Operating Officer (Total facility includes 42 beds in nursing home–type unit) **A**1 9 10 **F**8 17 19 22 24 25 27 30 32 33 34 41 44 48 49 51 54 64 65 66 71 72 **S** Quorum Health Group/Quorum Health Resources, Inc., Brentwood, TN	23	10	66	680	49	31374	0	10773	4986	183
LANSING—Ingham County										
⊞ ○ △ INGHAM REGIONAL MEDICAL CENTER, (Includes Ingham Regional Medical Center, Greenlawn Campus, 401 West Greenlawn Avenue; Ingham Regional Medical Center, Pennsylvania Campus, 2727 South Pennsylvania Avenue, Zip 48910; tel. 517/372–8220), 401 West Greenlawn Avenue, Zip 48910–2819; tel. 517/334–2121; Dennis M. Litos, President and Chief Executive Officer **A**1 5 7 8 9 10 11 13 **F**4 7 8 10 11 12 13 14 15 16 17 19 21 22 25 26 28 29 30 31 32 33 34 35 37 39 40 41 42 43 44 46 48 49 51 52 54 57 58 60 65 66 67 70 71 73 74 **P**1 5 6 **Web address:** www.irmc.org	23	10	364	15411	247	274867	1068	186813	88420	2437
⊞ ○ △ SPARROW HEALTH SYSTEM, (Includes St. Lawrence Hospital and Healthcare Services, 1210 West Saginaw Street, Zip 48915–1999; tel. 517/372–3610), 1215 East Michigan Avenue, Zip 48912–1811, Mailing Address: P.O. Box 30480, Zip 48909–7980; tel. 517/483–2700; Joseph F. Damore, President and Chief Executive Officer (Total facility includes 178 beds in nursing home–type unit) **A**1 2 3 5 7 9 10 11 12 **F**2 3 4 6 7 8 9 10 11 12 14 15 16 17 18 19 21 22 23 24 25 26 28 29 30 31 32 33 34 35 36 37 38 39 40 41 42 43 44 45 46 47 48 49 51 52 53 54 55 56 57 58 59 60 61 63 64 65 66 67 70 71 72 73 74 **P**1 6 7 **Web address:** www.sparrow.com ST. LAWRENCE HOSPITAL AND HEALTHCARE SERVICES See Sparrow Health System	23	10	695	25982	384	97548	4691	311553	149999	4337
LAPEER—Lapeer County										
□ LAPEER REGIONAL HOSPITAL, 1375 North Main Street, Zip 48446; tel. 810/667–5500; Donald C. Kooy, President and Chief Executive Officer (Total facility includes 19 beds in nursing home–type unit) **A**1 9 10 **F**2 3 4 7 8 9 10 11 12 13 14 15 16 17 18 19 20 21 22 24 25 26 27 28 29 30 31 32 33 34 35 37 38 39 40 41 42 43 44 45 46 47 48 49 51 52 53 54 55 56 57 58 59 60 61 63 64 65 66 67 70 71 72 73 74 **P**6 7	23	10	222	6217	88	76865	850	45780	20883	611
LAURIUM—Houghton County										
⊞ KEWEENAW MEMORIAL MEDICAL CENTER, 205 Osceola Street, Zip 49913–2199; tel. 906/337–6500; Rick Wright, FACHE, CPA, President and Chief Executive Officer **A**1 9 10 **F**7 8 11 12 16 17 19 21 22 24 28 31 32 35 37 40 44 46 49 61 65 66 71 73 74 **P**6 **Web address:** www.kmmc.org	23	10	49	1519	16	32819	69	16051	8868	268
LIVONIA—Wayne County										
⊞ ST. MARY HOSPITAL, 36475 West Five Mile Road, Zip 48154–1988; tel. 734/655–4800; Sister Mary Renetta Rumpz, FACHE, President and Chief Executive Officer **A**1 9 10 **F**2 3 4 6 7 8 10 11 12 13 14 15 16 17 19 20 21 22 23 24 26 27 28 29 30 32 33 34 35 37 39 40 41 42 43 44 45 46 49 52 54 55 56 57 58 59 60 65 67 68 70 71 72 73 74 **P**4 5 8 **Web address:** www.stmaryhospital.org	21	10	253	11852	165	125669	1381	99655	48206	1362
LUDINGTON—Mason County										
MEMORIAL MEDICAL CENTER OF WEST MICHIGAN, One Atkinson Drive, Zip 49431–1999; tel. 616/843–2591; Robert C. Marquardt, FACHE, President and Chief Executive Officer **A**10 **F**7 8 14 15 16 17 19 21 22 30 32 34 35 37 39 40 41 42 44 49 51 52 56 63 65 67 71 73 74 **P**8 **Web address:** www.mmcwm.com	23	10	85	3169	42	75918	400	28179	12943	286
MADISON HEIGHTS—Oakland County										
⊞ MADISON COMMUNITY HOSPITAL, 30671 Stephenson Highway, Zip 48071–1678; tel. 248/588–8000; Charles F. Pinkerman, Administrator (Nonreporting) **A**1 9 10	23	10	56	—	—	—	—	—	—	—
□ + ○ ST. JOHN OAKLAND HOSPITAL, 27351 Dequindre, Zip 48071–3499; tel. 248/967–7000; Robert Deputat, President **A**1 9 10 11 12 13 **F**1 2 3 4 5 6 7 8 9 10 11 12 13 14 15 16 18 19 20 21 22 24 25 26 27 28 29 30 31 32 33 34 35 36 37 38 39 40 41 42 43 44 45 46 47 48 49 50 51 52 53 54 55 56 57 58 59 60 61 62 63 64 65 66 67 68 70 71 72 73 74 **P**4 5 7 8 **S** Sisters of St. Joseph Health System, Ann Arbor, MI	21	10	196	6598	122	45208	0	63670	30861	939

Hospital, Address, Telephone, Administrator, Approval, Facility, and Physician Codes, Health Care System, Network	Classification Codes		Utilization Data					Expense (thousands) of dollars		
	Control	Service	Staffed Beds	Admissions	Census	Outpatient Visits	Births	Total	Payroll	Personnel

★ American Hospital Association (AHA) membership
□ Joint Commission on Accreditation of Healthcare Organizations (JCAHO) accreditation
+ American Osteopathic Healthcare Association (AOHA) membership
○ American Osteopathic Association (AOA) accreditation
△ Commission on Accreditation of Rehabilitation Facilities (CARF) accreditation
Control codes 61, 63, 64, 71, 72 and 73 indicate hospitals listed by AOHA, but not registered by AHA. For definition of numerical codes, see page A4

MANISTEE—Manistee County

| WEST SHORE HOSPITAL, 1465 East Parkdale Avenue, Zip 49660–9785; tel. 616/398–1000; Burton O. Parks, III, Administrator **A**9 10 **F**7 8 11 12 14 15 16 17 19 21 22 24 28 29 30 32 33 35 39 40 41 42 44 45 46 49 63 65 67 71 73 74 **P**3 8 | 13 | 10 | 54 | 1867 | 22 | 41550 | 145 | 19579 | 8407 | 259 |

MANISTIQUE—Schoolcraft County

| ✠ SCHOOLCRAFT MEMORIAL HOSPITAL, 500 Main Street, Zip 49854–0000; tel. 906/341–3200; David B. Jahn, Administrator and Chief Financial Officer **A**1 9 10 **F**2 3 4 7 8 9 10 11 14 15 16 17 18 19 20 21 22 23 24 26 27 28 29 30 31 32 33 34 35 36 37 38 39 40 41 42 43 44 45 46 47 48 49 51 52 53 54 55 56 57 58 59 60 63 64 65 66 67 70 71 72 73 74 **P**4 7 Web address: www.scmh.org | 13 | 10 | 20 | 713 | 7 | 35203 | 115 | 9122 | 5102 | 133 |

MARLETTE—Sanilac County

| ✠ MARLETTE COMMUNITY HOSPITAL, 2770 Main Street, Zip 48453–0307, Mailing Address: P.O. Box 307, Zip 48453–0307; tel. 517/635–4000; David S. McEwen, Chief Executive Officer (Total facility includes 43 beds in nursing home–type unit) **A**1 9 10 **F**8 13 14 15 16 17 18 19 20 21 22 26 28 30 33 34 35 36 39 44 46 48 49 62 64 65 66 67 68 71 73 **S** Quorum Health Group/Quorum Health Resources, Inc., Brentwood, TN | 23 | 10 | 91 | 1308 | 60 | 35839 | 0 | 17653 | 8440 | 335 |

MARQUETTE—Marquette County

| ✠ △ MARQUETTE GENERAL HEALTH SYSTEM, (Formerly Marquette General Hospital), 420 West Magnetic Street, Zip 49855–2794; tel. 906/228–9440; William Nemacheck, Chief Executive Officer **A**1 2 3 5 7 9 10 **F**2 3 4 5 6 7 8 10 11 12 13 15 16 17 18 19 20 21 22 23 26 27 29 30 32 33 34 35 37 38 39 40 41 42 43 44 45 46 48 49 51 52 53 54 55 56 57 58 60 63 64 65 66 67 70 71 72 73 74 **P**6 Web address: www.mgh.org | 23 | 10 | 320 | 10519 | 166 | 360339 | 579 | 147158 | 74791 | 1865 |

MARSHALL—Calhoun County

| ✠ OAKLAWN HOSPITAL, 200 North Madison Street, Zip 49068–1199; tel. 616/781–4271; Rob Covert, President and Chief Executive Officer **A**1 9 10 **F**3 5 7 8 12 14 15 16 17 19 21 22 24 29 30 32 33 35 36 37 39 40 41 44 45 46 49 51 52 54 55 56 57 58 59 63 65 66 67 71 73 | 23 | 10 | 94 | 2558 | 27 | 70254 | 547 | 29737 | 13922 | 381 |

MIDLAND—Midland County

| ✠ △ MIDMICHIGAN MEDICAL CENTER–MIDLAND, 4005 Orchard Drive, Zip 48670; tel. 517/839–3000; David A. Reece, President **A**1 2 3 5 7 9 10 **F**6 7 8 10 11 12 15 16 17 19 20 21 22 24 26 27 28 29 30 31 32 33 35 36 37 39 40 41 42 44 45 46 48 49 51 52 53 54 55 56 57 58 59 60 64 65 66 67 71 72 73 74 **P**6 7 8 **S** MidMichigan Health, Midland, MI Web address: www.midmichigan.org | 23 | 10 | 250 | 11106 | 139 | 226894 | 1210 | 126371 | 54911 | 1403 |

MONROE—Monroe County

| ✠ MERCY MEMORIAL HOSPITAL, 740 North Macomb Street, Zip 48161–9974, Mailing Address: P.O. Box 67, Zip 48161–0067; tel. 734/241–1700; Richard S. Hiltz, President and Chief Executive Officer (Total facility includes 70 beds in nursing home–type unit) **A**1 9 10 **F**1 2 3 4 5 6 7 8 9 10 11 12 13 14 15 16 17 18 19 20 21 22 23 24 25 26 27 28 29 30 31 32 33 34 35 36 37 38 39 40 41 42 43 44 45 46 47 48 49 50 51 52 53 54 55 56 57 58 59 60 61 62 63 64 65 66 67 68 69 70 71 72 73 74 | 23 | 10 | 143 | 9267 | 158 | 123802 | 1080 | 66876 | 34044 | 959 |

MOUNT CLEMENS—Macomb County

| ★ + ○ MOUNT CLEMENS GENERAL HOSPITAL, 1000 Harrington Boulevard, Zip 48043–2992; tel. 810/493–8000; Robert Milewski, President and Chief Executive Officer **A**9 10 11 12 13 **F**4 7 8 10 12 13 14 15 16 17 18 19 20 21 22 25 26 27 28 29 30 31 32 33 34 35 36 37 39 40 41 42 43 44 45 46 49 51 61 63 65 66 67 71 72 73 74 **P**5 Web address: www.mcgh.org | 23 | 10 | 242 | 11429 | 147 | 513122 | 1493 | 154302 | 73620 | 1710 |

MOUNT PLEASANT—Isabella County

| ✠ + ○ CENTRAL MICHIGAN COMMUNITY HOSPITAL, 1221 South Drive, Zip 48858–3234; tel. 517/772–6700; Stephen C. Lada, President and Chief Executive Officer **A**1 9 10 11 **F**7 8 14 15 16 19 22 24 25 28 29 30 31 32 34 35 37 39 40 41 42 44 45 49 52 53 54 55 57 58 59 63 65 66 67 71 72 73 74 **P**8 Web address: www.cmch.org | 23 | 10 | 118 | 3667 | 38 | 148266 | 509 | 36465 | 19131 | 492 |

MUNISING—Alger County

| □ MUNISING MEMORIAL HOSPITAL, 1500 Sand Point Road, Zip 49862–1406; tel. 906/387–4110; Carl J. Velte, Chief Executive Officer (Nonreporting) **A**1 9 10 | 23 | 10 | 40 | — | — | — | — | — | — | — |

MUSKEGON—Muskegon County

| □ HACKLEY HEALTH, 1700 Clinton Street, Zip 49443–3302, Mailing Address: P.O. Box 3302, Zip 49443–3302; tel. 616/726–3511; Gordon A. Mudler, President and Chief Executive Officer **A**1 2 9 10 **F**3 7 8 10 12 13 14 15 16 17 19 20 21 22 24 26 27 29 30 32 33 34 35 37 39 40 41 42 44 45 46 48 49 51 52 53 54 55 56 57 58 59 60 63 65 66 67 71 72 73 **P**5 6 7 | 23 | 10 | 181 | 9125 | 118 | — | 1241 | 96217 | 44832 | 1094 |
| ✠ + ○ MERCY GENERAL HEALTH PARTNERS, (Includes Mercy General Health Partners–Oak Avenue Campus, 1700 Oak Avenue, Zip 49442–2407; tel. 616/773–3311; Mercy General Health Partners–Sherman Boulevard Campus, 1500 East Sherman Boulevard), 1500 East Sherman Boulevard, Zip 49443; tel. 616/739–3901; Roger Spoelman, President and Chief Executive Officer **A**1 9 10 11 12 13 **F**4 7 8 10 11 12 14 15 16 17 19 21 22 24 26 28 29 30 32 34 35 37 39 40 41 42 43 44 45 46 48 49 51 58 61 63 64 65 66 71 72 73 74 **P**6 8 **S** Mercy Health Services, Farmington Hills, MI | 23 | 10 | 189 | 9594 | 134 | 183171 | 1105 | 141483 | 61333 | 1442 |

Hospital, Address, Telephone, Administrator, Approval, Facility, and Physician Codes, Health Care System, Network	Classi-fication Codes		Utilization Data					Expense (thousands) of dollars		
	Control	Service	Staffed Beds	Admissions	Census	Outpatient Visits	Births	Total	Payroll	Personnel

★ American Hospital Association (AHA) membership
□ Joint Commission on Accreditation of Healthcare Organizations (JCAHO) accreditation
+ American Osteopathic Healthcare Association (AOHA) membership
○ American Osteopathic Association (AOA) accreditation
△ Commission on Accreditation of Rehabilitation Facilities (CARF) accreditation
Control codes 61, 63, 64, 71, 72 and 73 indicate hospitals listed by AOHA, but not registered by AHA. For definition of numerical codes, see page A4

NEW BALTIMORE—Macomb County

□ HARBOR OAKS HOSPITAL, 35031 23 Mile Road, Zip 48047–2097; tel. 810/725–5777; Harry Hunter, Jr., Administrator and Chief Operating Officer (Nonreporting) **A**1 10 **S** Pioneer Behavioral Health, Peabody, MA

	32	22	64	—	—	—	—	—	—	—

NEWBERRY—Luce County

✠ HELEN NEWBERRY JOY HOSPITAL, (Includes Helen Newberry Joy Hospital Annex), 502 West Harrie Street, Zip 49868–0070; tel. 906/293–9200; Wayne P. Hellerstedt, Chief Executive Officer (Total facility includes 48 beds in nursing home–type unit) **A**1 9 10 **F**8 14 15 16 17 19 21 22 28 30 32 33 34 35 42 44 46 64 71 72 **P**6
Web address: www.uphcn.org/uphcn/hnjh

	13	10	86	861	55	39421	0	11683	5952	219

NILES—Berrien County

LAKELAND MEDICAL CENTER–NILES See Lakeland Medical Center–St. Joseph, Saint Joseph

NORTHPORT—Leelanau County

✠ LEELANAU MEMORIAL HEALTH CENTER, 215 South High Street, Zip 49670, Mailing Address: P.O. Box 217, Zip 49670–0217; tel. 616/386–0000; Jayne R. Bull, Administrator (Total facility includes 72 beds in nursing home–type unit) **A**1 9 10 **F**1 8 12 14 15 16 17 22 24 27 28 29 31 32 33 34 36 39 41 44 45 46 49 51 64 65 67 71 72 73 **P**5 7 **S** Munson Healthcare, Traverse City, MI

	23	10	91	223	68	14459	0	5186	2661	117

NORTHVILLE—Wayne County

□ HAWTHORN CENTER, 18471 Haggerty Road, Zip 48167–9575; tel. 248/349–3000; Neil H. Wasserman, Chief Executive Officer and Chief Financial Officer **A**1 3 5 **F**20 52 53 65

	12	52	118	194	92	0	0	21243	13547	334

□ NORTHVILLE PSYCHIATRIC HOSPITAL, 41001 West Seven Mile Road, Zip 48167–2698; tel. 810/349–1800; Ed Stovall, Administrative Officer **A**1 10 **F**6 8 9 10 11 12 14 15 16 18 19 20 21 22 35 37 39 40 41 42 43 45 46 50 52 55 57 60 65 70 71

	12	22	427	460	373	0	0	52093	35036	829

ONTONAGON—Ontonagon County

□ ONTONAGON MEMORIAL HOSPITAL, 601 Seventh Street, Zip 49953–1496; tel. 906/884–4134; Fred Nelson, Administrator (Total facility includes 46 beds in nursing home–type unit) **A**1 9 10 **F**8 15 16 19 20 21 22 25 26 28 29 30 36 39 41 44 49 51 64 65 66 71
Web address: www.uphcn.org/uphcn/omh.html

	14	10	72	659	55	15007	0	7442	3825	136

OWOSSO—Shiawassee County

✠ MEMORIAL HEALTHCARE CENTER, 826 West King Street, Zip 48867–2198; tel. 517/723–5211; Margaret S. Gulick, President and Chief Executive Officer (Total facility includes 16 beds in nursing home–type unit) **A**1 2 9 10 **F**3 7 8 12 13 14 15 16 17 18 19 21 22 25 27 28 29 30 32 33 35 36 37 39 40 41 42 44 46 48 49 52 53 54 56 57 58 59 64 65 66 67 68 71 73 74 **P**1 6
Web address: www.healthcare.org

	23	10	137	5687	77	274234	605	53774	30590	875

PAW PAW—Van Buren County

✠ LAKEVIEW COMMUNITY HOSPITAL, 408 Hazen Street, Zip 49079–1019, Mailing Address: P.O. Box 209, Zip 49079–0209; tel. 616/657–3141; Sue E. Johnson–Phillippe, Chief Executive Officer (Total facility includes 120 beds in nursing home–type unit) **A**1 9 10 **F**7 8 12 14 15 16 17 19 20 22 26 30 32 33 34 35 37 39 40 41 44 45 49 52 54 55 57 59 61 64 65 67 71 72 73 74 **S** Quorum Health Group/Quorum Health Resources, Inc., Brentwood, TN

	16	10	168	1570	143	56809	0	22679	11489	302

PETOSKEY—Emmet County

✠ NORTHERN MICHIGAN HOSPITAL, 416 Connable Avenue, Zip 49770–2297; tel. 616/487–4000; Jeffrey T. Wendling, President and Chief Executive Officer **A**1 2 9 10 **F**1 3 4 6 7 8 10 12 13 14 15 16 17 18 19 20 21 22 24 26 27 28 29 30 31 32 33 34 35 36 37 39 40 41 42 43 44 45 49 52 53 54 56 58 59 60 61 62 63 64 65 66 67 68 71 72 73 74 **P**7
Web address: www.healthshare.org

	23	10	202	8803	122	60146	869	85657	36659	1116

PIGEON—Huron County

✠ SCHEURER HOSPITAL, 170 North Caseville Road, Zip 48755–9704; tel. 517/453–3223; Dwight Gascho, President and Chief Executive Officer (Total facility includes 19 beds in nursing home–type unit) **A**1 9 10 **F**8 14 15 16 17 19 21 22 27 28 29 30 32 33 34 35 36 39 40 41 42 44 46 49 51 54 62 63 64 65 67 71 73 **P**6

	23	10	42	768	27	—	—	12272	6023	193

PLAINWELL—Allegan County

BORGESS-PIPP HEALTH CENTER See Borgess Medical Center, Kalamazoo

PONTIAC—Oakland County

✠ NORTH OAKLAND MEDICAL CENTERS, 461 West Huron Street, Zip 48341–1651; tel. 248/857–7200; Robert L. Davis, President and Chief Executive Officer (Nonreporting) **A**1 3 5 9 10

	23	10	222	—	—	—	—	—	—	—

+ ○ POH MEDICAL CENTER, 50 North Perry Street, Zip 48342–2253; tel. 810/338–5000; Patrick Lamberti, Chief Executive Officer **A**9 10 11 12 13 **F**3 8 10 12 15 16 17 19 21 24 25 28 29 30 32 33 34 35 37 39 41 44 45 46 49 51 54 65 66 67 70 71 72 73 **P**6 8
Web address: www.pohmedical.org

	23	10	149	6942	92	102154	0	76403	36560	1081

✠ △ ST. JOSEPH MERCY OAKLAND, 900 Woodward Avenue, Zip 48341–2985; tel. 248/858–3000; Thomas L. Feurig, President and Chief Executive Officer **A**1 3 5 7 9 10 **F**2 3 4 6 7 8 10 11 12 13 14 15 16 17 18 19 21 22 25 26 27 28 29 30 31 32 33 34 35 36 37 38 39 40 41 42 43 44 46 47 48 49 51 52 53 54 55 56 57 58 59 60 61 62 64 65 66 67 68 70 71 72 73 74 **P**1 6 7
S Mercy Health Services, Farmington Hills, MI
Web address: www.mercyhealth.com/oakland

	21	10	409	18823	273	309786	2578	193487	82790	2139

Hospital, Address, Telephone, Administrator, Approval, Facility, and Physician Codes, Health Care System, Network	Classification Codes		Utilization Data					Expense (thousands) of dollars		
★ American Hospital Association (AHA) membership □ Joint Commission on Accreditation of Healthcare Organizations (JCAHO) accreditation + American Osteopathic Healthcare Association (AOHA) membership ○ American Osteopathic Association (AOA) accreditation △ Commission on Accreditation of Rehabilitation Facilities (CARF) accreditation Control codes 61, 63, 64, 71, 72 and 73 indicate hospitals listed by AOHA, but not registered by AHA. For definition of numerical codes, see page A4	Control	Service	Staffed Beds	Admissions	Census	Outpatient Visits	Births	Total	Payroll	Personnel

PORT HURON—St. Clair County

★ △ MERCY HOSPITAL, 2601 Electric Avenue, Zip 48060; tel. 810/985–1510; Mary R. Trimmer, President and Chief Executive Officer **A**1 2 7 9 10 **F**4 8 10 12 14 15 16 17 19 21 22 24 28 30 31 32 33 34 35 37 39 41 42 43 44 45 46 48 49 60 63 65 66 67 70 71 73 74 **P**8 **S** Mercy Health Services, Farmington Hills, MI
Web address: www.mercyporthuron.com
| 21 | 10 | 119 | 4871 | 74 | 106223 | 0 | 49226 | 20586 | 707 |

★ PORT HURON HOSPITAL, 1221 Pine Grove Avenue, Zip 48061–5011; tel. 810/987–5000; Donald C. Fletcher, President and Chief Executive Officer **A**1 2 9 10 **F**3 4 7 8 10 11 12 14 15 16 17 19 20 21 22 26 29 30 31 34 35 37 40 42 43 44 45 46 49 52 54 55 56 57 58 59 63 65 66 67 71 73 74 **P**8 **S** Blue Water Health Services Corporation, Port Huron, MI
| 23 | 10 | 186 | 4459 | 109 | 83370 | 601 | 37586 | 16924 | 879 |

REED CITY—Osceola County

★ SPECTRUM HEALTH–REED CITY CAMPUS, (Formerly Reed City Hospital), 7665 Patterson Road, Zip 49677–1122, Mailing Address: P.O. Box 75, Zip 49677–0075; tel. 616/832–3271; David M. Coates, Ph.D., President and Chief Executive Officer (Total facility includes 54 beds in nursing home–type unit) **A**1 9 10 **F**3 8 10 15 16 19 21 22 28 30 33 34 39 41 42 44 49 51 64 65 71 72 73 **P**6 **S** Spectrum Health, Grand Rapids, MI
| 23 | 10 | 83 | 1539 | 65 | 40211 | 0 | 15329 | 10427 | 249 |

ROCHESTER—Oakland County

□ △ CRITTENTON HOSPITAL, 1101 West University Drive, Zip 48307–1831; tel. 248/652–5000; Dennis P. Markiewicz, Vice President Hospital Operations **A**1 2 7 9 10 **F**7 8 10 11 14 15 16 19 21 24 27 28 29 30 32 33 34 35 37 39 40 41 42 44 45 46 48 49 52 54 55 56 57 58 59 60 63 65 66 67 70 71 72 73 74
| 23 | 10 | 227 | 11215 | 151 | 171284 | 1629 | 99012 | 42956 | 1195 |

ROGERS CITY—Presque Isle County

□ △ ROGERS CITY REHABILITATION HOSPITAL, 555 North Bradley Highway, Zip 49779–1599; tel. 517/734–7545; Nancy Dextrom, Executive Director (Nonreporting) **A**1 7 10
| 33 | 46 | 17 | — | — | — | — | — | — | — |

ROYAL OAK—Oakland County

★ △ WILLIAM BEAUMONT HOSPITAL–ROYAL OAK, 3601 West Thirteen Mile Road, Zip 48073–6769; tel. 248/551–5000; John D. Labriola, Senior Vice President and Hospital Director **A**1 2 3 5 7 8 9 10 **F**1 4 6 7 8 10 11 12 14 15 16 17 19 20 21 22 23 24 25 26 28 29 30 31 32 33 34 35 37 38 39 40 42 43 44 45 46 47 48 49 50 51 52 54 55 56 57 59 60 61 63 65 66 67 68 70 71 73 74 **P**6 8 **S** William Beaumont Hospital Corporation, Royal Oak, MI
Web address: www.beaumont.edu
| 23 | 10 | 869 | 47717 | 729 | 782754 | 5832 | 569038 | 259183 | 7504 |

SAGINAW—Saginaw County

★ ALEDA E. LUTZ VETERANS AFFAIRS MEDICAL CENTER, 1500 Weiss Street, Zip 48602–5298; tel. 517/793–2340; Robert H. Sabin, Acting Director (Total facility includes 81 beds in nursing home–type unit) **A**1 5 **F**3 12 14 15 16 17 19 20 22 26 27 28 30 31 32 33 34 37 41 42 44 45 46 49 51 54 58 64 65 67 71 72 73 74 **S** Department of Veterans Affairs, Washington, DC
| 45 | 10 | 114 | 1623 | 100 | 72743 | 0 | 37493 | — | 458 |

★ △ COVENANT HEALTHCARE, (Includes Covenant Medical Center–Cooper, 700 Cooper Avenue, Zip 48602–5399; tel. 517/771–6000; Covenant Medical Center–Harrison, 1447 North Harrison Street, tel. 517/771–4000), 1447 North Harrison, Zip 48602–4785; tel. 517/771–4700; Spencer Maidlow, President **A**1 3 5 7 10 **F**4 7 8 10 11 12 14 15 16 17 19 21 22 26 27 28 30 31 32 33 34 35 37 38 39 40 41 42 43 44 45 46 47 48 49 50 51 52 56 58 59 61 64 65 66 67 70 71 72 73 74 **P**8
| 23 | 10 | 539 | 24539 | 360 | — | 3870 | 254661 | 108596 | 3121 |

★ △ HEALTHSOURCE SAGINAW, (LONG TERM CARE REHAB PSYC.), 3340 Hospital Road, Zip 48603–9623, Mailing Address: P.O. Box 6280, Zip 48608–6280; tel. 517/790–7700; Lester Heyboer, Jr., President and Chief Executive Officer (Total facility includes 213 beds in nursing home–type unit) **A**1 7 10 **F**2 3 20 26 39 41 45 46 48 49 52 53 54 55 57 58 64 65 67 **P**6
| 13 | 49 | 319 | 1492 | 209 | 13480 | 0 | 19764 | 10107 | 364 |

SAGINAW GENERAL HOSPITAL See Covenant Medical Center–Harrison

ST LUKE'S HOSPITAL See Covenant Medical Center–Cooper

★ ST. MARY'S MEDICAL CENTER, 830 South Jefferson Avenue, Zip 48601–2594; tel. 517/776–8000; Frederic L. Fraizer, President and Chief Executive Officer **A**1 2 3 5 9 10 **F**4 8 9 10 11 15 16 19 21 22 23 25 27 28 29 30 33 34 35 37 39 42 43 44 45 46 49 54 56 60 63 65 67 70 71 73 **P**6 8 **S** Daughters of Charity National Health System, Saint Louis, MO
Web address: www.saintmarys–saginaw.org
| 21 | 10 | 268 | 12641 | 200 | 211164 | 0 | 141073 | 59242 | 1540 |

SAINT IGNACE—Mackinac County

MACKINAC STRAITS HOSPITAL AND HEALTH CENTER, 220 Burdette Street, Zip 49781–1792; tel. 906/643–8585; Mary E. Tamlyn, Administrator (Total facility includes 99 beds in nursing home–type unit) **A**9 10 **F**6 15 16 22 28 39 41 46 49 51 56 64 67
| 16 | 10 | 107 | 131 | 99 | 14202 | 0 | 8104 | 4708 | 163 |

SAINT JOHNS—Clinton County

★ CLINTON MEMORIAL HOSPITAL, 805 South Oakland Street, Zip 48879–0260; tel. 517/224–6881; Kathryn A. Bangs, President and Chief Executive Officer **A**1 9 10 **F**7 13 14 15 16 17 19 22 26 28 29 30 32 33 34 35 36 39 40 41 42 44 49 51 65 66 67 71 72 73 **P**1
| 23 | 10 | 28 | 1035 | 9 | 31853 | 105 | 18800 | 5522 | 183 |

RIVENDELL OF MICHIGAN, 101 West Townsend Road, Zip 48879–9200; tel. 517/224–1177; Roger Rohall, Chief Executive Officer (Nonreporting) **A**10 **S** Children's Comprehensive Services, Inc., Nashville, TN
| 33 | 22 | 63 | — | — | — | — | — | — | — |

Hospital, Address, Telephone, Administrator, Approval, Facility, and Physician Codes, Health Care System, Network	Classi-fication Codes		Utilization Data					Expense (thousands) of dollars		
★ American Hospital Association (AHA) membership □ Joint Commission on Accreditation of Healthcare Organizations (JCAHO) accreditation + American Osteopathic Healthcare Association (AOHA) membership ○ American Osteopathic Association (AOA) accreditation △ Commission on Accreditation of Rehabilitation Facilities (CARF) accreditation Control codes 61, 63, 64, 71, 72 and 73 indicate hospitals listed by AOHA, but not registered by AHA. For definition of numerical codes, see page A4	Control	Service	Staffed Beds	Admissions	Census	Outpatient Visits	Births	Total	Payroll	Personnel

SAINT JOSEPH—Berrien County

□ △ LAKELAND MEDICAL CENTER–ST. JOSEPH, (Includes Lakeland Medical Center, Berrien Center, 6418 Dean's Hill Road, Berrien Center, Zip 49102–9704; tel. 616/471-7761; Lakeland Medical Center–Niles, 31 North St. Joseph Avenue, Niles, Zip 49120–2287; tel. 616/683-5510), 1234 Napier Avenue, Zip 49085–2112; tel. 616/983-8300; Joseph A. Wasserman, President and Chief Executive Officer (Total facility includes 193 beds in nursing home–type unit) **A**1 2 7 9 10 **F**4 6 7 8 10 12 13 14 15 16 17 19 21 22 28 29 30 31 32 35 37 39 40 41 42 43 44 48 49 52 56 60 64 65 66 67 71 73 **P**1 7 — 23 10 608 15499 348 284386 2166 157603 69424 2357

SALINE—Washtenaw County

⊞ SALINE COMMUNITY HOSPITAL, 400 West Russell Street, Zip 48176–1101; tel. 734/429-1500; Garry C. Faja, President and Chief Executive Officer **A**1 9 10 **F**1 2 3 4 5 7 8 10 11 12 13 14 15 16 17 18 19 20 21 22 25 26 27 28 29 30 31 32 33 34 35 37 39 40 41 42 43 44 45 46 48 49 51 52 53 54 55 56 57 58 59 60 63 65 66 67 70 71 72 73 74 **P**1 5 **S** Mercy Health Services, Farmington Hills, MI — 21 10 38 1589 19 144880 0 21271 9269 229

SANDUSKY—Sanilac County

★ MCKENZIE MEMORIAL HOSPITAL, 120 Delaware Street, Zip 48471–1087; tel. 810/648-3770; Joseph W. Weiler, President **A**9 10 **F**3 8 12 15 16 19 21 22 26 28 33 34 35 37 40 41 42 44 45 46 49 54 56 63 65 69 71 73 **P**6 — 23 10 25 1022 8 18827 86 9885 4915 148

SAULT STE. MARIE—Chippewa County

⊞ CHIPPEWA COUNTY WAR MEMORIAL HOSPITAL, 500 Osborn Boulevard, Zip 49783–4467; tel. 906/635-4460; Daniel Wakeman, Chief Executive Officer (Total facility includes 51 beds in nursing home–type unit) **A**1 9 10 **F**3 7 8 11 14 15 16 17 19 20 21 22 24 28 30 31 32 35 37 40 41 42 44 45 46 48 49 51 63 64 65 67 68 71 72 73 74 **P**5 6 8 — 23 10 86 2290 77 68414 405 27311 12476 362

SHELBY—Oceana County

□ LAKESHORE COMMUNITY HOSPITAL, 72 South State Street, Zip 49455–1299; tel. 616/861-2156; Jay Bryan, Chief Executive Officer **A**1 9 10 **F**1 2 3 4 7 8 10 11 12 14 15 16 17 19 22 30 31 32 33 35 37 38 40 41 42 43 44 47 48 49 51 52 54 56 60 63 64 67 70 71 73 **P**4 — 23 10 24 863 8 23630 145 5235 2410 87

SHERIDAN—Montcalm County

+ ○ SHERIDAN COMMUNITY HOSPITAL, 301 North Main Street, Zip 48884–9220, Mailing Address: P.O. Box 279, Zip 48884–0279; tel. 517/291-3261; Christopher Noland, Chief Executive Officer **A**9 10 11 **F**8 14 15 16 17 19 22 25 28 30 32 34 37 41 42 44 45 46 49 51 67 71 72 73 — 23 10 19 412 4 23226 0 6137 3263 113

SOUTH HAVEN—Van Buren County

⊞ SOUTH HAVEN COMMUNITY HOSPITAL, 955 South Bailey Avenue, Zip 49090; tel. 616/637-5271; Craig J. Marks, President and Chief Executive Officer (Nonreporting) **A**1 9 10 — 16 10 52 — — — — — — —

SOUTHFIELD—Oakland County

○ △ GREAT LAKES REHABILITATION HOSPITAL, 22401 Foster Winter Drive, Zip 48075–3708; tel. 248/483-5545; Pamela Govender, Chief Operating Officer (Total facility includes 18 beds in nursing home–type unit) **A**7 9 10 11 **F**14 15 16 27 46 48 49 64 65 **P**5 — 33 46 45 827 41 2781 0 — — 193

⊞ PROVIDENCE HOSPITAL AND MEDICAL CENTERS, 16001 West Nine Mile Road, Zip 48075–4854, Mailing Address: Box 2043, Zip 48037–2043; tel. 248/424-3000; Robert F. Casalou, Interim President and Chief Executive Officer **A**1 2 3 5 8 9 10 **F**1 4 7 8 10 11 12 13 14 15 16 17 19 21 22 25 26 27 28 29 30 31 32 33 34 35 37 38 39 40 41 42 43 44 45 46 48 49 51 52 54 55 56 57 58 59 60 65 66 67 70 71 72 73 74 **P**1 6 **S** Daughters of Charity National Health System, Saint Louis, MO — 21 10 369 19522 272 448148 3545 318446 143689 3279

⊞ STRAITH HOSPITAL FOR SPECIAL SURGERY, 23901 Lahser Road, Zip 48034–3296; tel. 248/357-3360; Gregory R. Hoose, Chief Executive Officer (Nonreporting) **A**1 9 10 — 23 45 23 — — — — — — —

STANDISH—Arenac County

□ STANDISH COMMUNITY HOSPITAL, 805 West Cedar Street, Zip 48658–9526, Mailing Address: P.O. Box 579, Zip 48658–0579; tel. 517/846-4521; John Stindt, Chief Executive Officer (Total facility includes 44 beds in nursing home–type unit) (Nonreporting) **A**1 9 10 — 23 10 72 — — — — — — —

STURGIS—St. Joseph County

⊞ STURGIS HOSPITAL, 916 Myrtle, Zip 49091–2001; tel. 616/651-7824; David James, Chief Executive Officer **A**1 10 **F**7 8 11 12 14 15 16 17 18 19 21 22 24 27 28 29 30 32 33 34 35 36 37 39 40 41 42 44 45 46 49 51 63 65 66 67 71 72 73 **P**5 6 **S** Quorum Health Group/Quorum Health Resources, Inc., Brentwood, TN — 14 10 67 2310 22 73894 378 24903 11707 357

TAWAS CITY—Iosco County

⊞ ST. JOSEPH HEALTH SYSTEM, (Formerly Tawas St. Joseph Hospital), 200 Hemlock Street, Zip 48763, Mailing Address: P.O. Box 659, Zip 48764–0659; tel. 517/362-3411; Paul R. Schmidt, CHE, President and Chief Executive Officer **A**1 9 10 **F**7 8 11 13 14 15 16 17 19 22 25 26 27 28 29 30 32 33 34 37 39 40 41 42 44 49 63 65 67 71 72 73 **P**8 **S** Sisters of St. Joseph Health System, Ann Arbor, MI — 21 10 49 2340 25 103412 307 29057 14432 484

TAYLOR—Wayne County

⊞ OAKWOOD HOSPITAL–HERITAGE CENTER, 10000 Telegraph Road, Zip 48180–3349; tel. 313/295-5000; Edward E. Freysinger, Administrator (Nonreporting) **A**1 9 10 **S** Oakwood Healthcarer, Inc., Dearborn, MI — 23 10 243 — — — — — — —

Hospital, Address, Telephone, Administrator, Approval, Facility, and Physician Codes, Health Care System, Network	Classi-fication Codes		Utilization Data					Expense (thousands) of dollars		
★ American Hospital Association (AHA) membership □ Joint Commission on Accreditation of Healthcare Organizations (JCAHO) accreditation + American Osteopathic Healthcare Association (AOHA) membership ○ American Osteopathic Association (AOA) accreditation △ Commission on Accreditation of Rehabilitation Facilities (CARF) accreditation Control codes 61, 63, 64, 71, 72 and 73 indicate hospitals listed by AOHA, but not registered by AHA. For definition of numerical codes, see page A4	Control	Service	Staffed Beds	Admissions	Census	Outpatient Visits	Births	Total	Payroll	Personnel

TECUMSEH—Lenawee County

□ HERRICK MEMORIAL HOSPITAL, LENAWEE HEALTH ALLIANCE, 500 East Pottawatamie Street, Zip 49286–2097; tel. 517/424–3000; John R. Robertstad, President and Chief Executive Officer (Total facility includes 25 beds in nursing home–type unit) **A**1 9 10 **F**3 7 8 11 14 15 16 17 19 21 22 23 24 28 29 30 32 33 35 40 41 42 44 45 46 48 49 52 53 58 59 60 61 64 65 66 67 71 72 73 74 **P**1 7 **S** Lenawee Health Alliance, Adrian, MI
Web address: www.lhanet.org | 23 | 10 | 88 | 2553 | 47 | 60321 | 199 | 22227 | 9427 | 249

THREE RIVERS—St. Joseph County

⊠ △ THREE RIVERS AREA HOSPITAL, 1111 West Broadway, Zip 49093–9362; tel. 616/278–1145; Matthew Chambers, Chief Executive Officer (Nonreporting) **A**1 7 9 10 **S** Quorum Health Group/Quorum Health Resources, Inc., Brentwood, TN
Web address: www.trah.org | 16 | 10 | 60 | — | — | — | — | — | — | —

TRAVERSE CITY—Grand Traverse County

⊠ △ MUNSON MEDICAL CENTER, 1105 Sixth Street, Zip 49684–2386; tel. 616/935–5000; Ralph J. Cerny, President and Chief Executive Officer **A**1 2 3 7 9 10 12 13 **F**3 4 7 8 10 11 12 13 14 15 16 17 18 19 20 21 22 23 24 25 26 27 28 29 30 31 32 33 34 35 37 38 39 40 41 42 43 44 45 46 48 49 51 52 54 55 56 57 59 60 61 65 66 67 68 71 72 73 74 **P**6 8 **S** Munson Healthcare, Traverse City, MI
Web address: www.mhc.net | 23 | 10 | 368 | 16652 | 221 | 344950 | 1846 | 165974 | 77154 | 2118

TRENTON—Wayne County

⊠ OAKWOOD HOSPITAL SEAWAY CENTER, 5450 Fort Street, Zip 48183–4625; tel. 734/671–3800; Brian Peltz, Administrator **A**1 9 10 **F**2 3 4 6 7 8 10 11 12 13 14 15 16 17 19 21 22 25 26 27 28 29 30 31 32 35 37 38 39 40 41 42 43 44 46 48 49 51 52 53 54 55 56 57 58 59 60 61 62 63 64 65 66 67 68 69 70 71 72 73 74 **P**5 7 **S** Oakwood Healthcarer, Inc., Dearborn, MI
Web address: www.oakwood.org | 23 | 10 | 89 | 3355 | 37 | 46927 | 156 | 33484 | 13692 | —

★ + ○ RIVERSIDE OSTEOPATHIC HOSPITAL, 150 Truax Street, Zip 48183–2151; tel. 734/676–4200; Dennis R. Lemanski, D.O., Vice President and Chief Executive Officer **A**9 10 11 12 13 **F**7 8 10 11 12 14 15 16 17 18 19 21 22 24 26 27 28 29 30 31 32 33 34 35 36 37 39 40 41 42 44 45 46 49 52 54 55 56 57 60 61 63 65 66 67 70 71 73 74 **S** Henry Ford Health System, Detroit, MI | 23 | 10 | 148 | 5942 | 82 | 111394 | 797 | 60684 | 27406 | 563

TROY—Oakland County

⊠ WILLIAM BEAUMONT HOSPITAL–TROY, 44201 Dequindre Road, Zip 48098–1198; tel. 248/828–5100; Eugene F. Michalski, Vice President and Director **A**1 2 3 9 10 **F**1 4 6 7 8 10 11 12 13 14 15 16 17 19 20 21 22 23 29 30 31 32 33 34 35 37 38 39 40 42 43 44 45 46 47 48 49 50 51 52 54 55 56 57 59 60 61 63 64 65 66 67 68 70 71 73 74 **P**6 8 **S** William Beaumont Hospital Corporation, Royal Oak, MI
Web address: www.beaumont.edu | 23 | 10 | 189 | 12602 | 155 | 296028 | 1827 | 132408 | 64166 | 1801

VICKSBURG—Kalamazoo County

⊠ △ BRONSON VICKSBURG HOSPITAL, 13326 North Boulevard, Zip 49097–1099; tel. 616/649–2321; Frank J. Sardone, President **A**1 7 9 10 **F**4 7 8 9 10 11 12 13 14 19 21 22 26 28 29 30 31 32 34 35 37 38 40 41 42 43 44 45 46 47 48 49 54 61 65 70 71 72 73 74 **S** Bronson Healthcare Group, Inc., Kalamazoo, MI
Web address: www.bronsonhealth.com | 23 | 46 | 41 | 460 | 15 | 33361 | 0 | 8346 | 3345 | 93

WARREN—Macomb County

□ ARBORVIEW HOSPITAL, 6902 Chicago Road, Zip 48092–4784; tel. 810/264–8875; Donald L. Warner, Chief Executive Officer (Nonreporting) **A**1 10 | 33 | 22 | 40 | — | — | — | — | — | — | —

★ + ○ △ BI–COUNTY COMMUNITY HOSPITAL, 13355 East Ten Mile Road, Zip 48089–2065; tel. 810/759–7300; Gary W. Popiel, Executive Vice President and Chief Executive Officer **A**7 9 10 11 12 13 **F**3 7 8 10 12 14 15 16 17 19 21 22 24 27 28 29 30 31 32 33 34 35 37 39 40 41 42 44 45 46 48 49 51 53 54 55 56 60 61 63 65 66 71 73 74 **P**1 6 **S** Henry Ford Health System, Detroit, MI | 23 | 10 | 149 | 5789 | 97 | 125526 | 446 | 74020 | 34763 | 852

□ KERN HOSPITAL AND MEDICAL CENTER, 21230 Dequindre, Zip 48091–2287; tel. 810/427–1000; Manoj K. Prasad, M.D., President and Chief Executive Officer (Nonreporting) **A**1 9 10 | 23 | 49 | 20 | — | — | — | — | — | — | —

⊠ △ ST. JOHN MACOMB HOSPITAL, (Formerly Macomb Hospital Center), 11800 East Twelve Mile Road, Zip 48093–3494; tel. 810/573–5000; John E. Knox, President **A**1 2 7 9 10 **F**2 3 4 7 8 10 11 13 14 15 16 17 18 19 20 21 22 23 25 27 28 29 30 31 32 33 34 35 37 38 39 40 41 42 43 44 45 46 48 49 51 52 53 54 55 56 57 58 59 60 61 63 65 66 67 68 70 71 72 73 74 **P**8 **S** Sisters of St. Joseph Health System, Ann Arbor, MI
Web address: www.dmhc.com | 21 | 10 | 273 | 12043 | 209 | 42150 | 1285 | 113099 | 58121 | 1109

WATERVLIET—Berrien County

⊠ △ COMMUNITY HOSPITAL, Medical Park Drive, Zip 49098–0158, Mailing Address: P.O. Box 158, Zip 49098–0158; tel. 616/463–3111; Dennis Turney, Chief Executive Officer **A**1 7 9 10 **F**7 8 12 15 16 19 22 26 28 29 30 32 33 34 35 37 39 40 44 45 46 48 49 54 63 65 67 71 72 73 **P**1 **S** Quorum Health Group/Quorum Health Resources, Inc., Brentwood, TN | 23 | 10 | 55 | 1856 | 28 | 39796 | 7 | 16845 | 8014 | 287

Hospital, Address, Telephone, Administrator, Approval, Facility, and Physician Codes, Health Care System, Network	Classi-fication Codes		Utilization Data					Expense (thousands) of dollars		
★ American Hospital Association (AHA) membership □ Joint Commission on Accreditation of Healthcare Organizations (JCAHO) accreditation + American Osteopathic Healthcare Association (AOHA) membership ○ American Osteopathic Association (AOA) accreditation △ Commission on Accreditation of Rehabilitation Facilities (CARF) accreditation Control codes 61, 63, 64, 71, 72 and 73 indicate hospitals listed by AOHA, but not registered by AHA. For definition of numerical codes, see page A4	Control	Service	Staffed Beds	Admissions	Census	Outpatient Visits	Births	Total	Payroll	Personnel

WAYNE—Wayne County

✠ OAKWOOD HOSPITAL ANNAPOLIS CENTER, (Includes Oakwood Hospital Merriman Center–Westland, 2345 Merriman Road, Westland, Zip 48185; tel. 313/467–2300), 33155 Annapolis Road, Zip 48184–2493; tel. 734/467–4000; Thomas Kochis, Administrator **A**1 9 10 **F**1 2 3 4 6 7 8 10 11 12 13 14 15 16 17 18 19 21 22 25 26 27 28 30 31 32 33 34 35 37 38 39 40 41 42 43 44 46 48 49 51 52 53 54 55 56 57 58 59 60 61 62 63 64 65 66 67 71 72 73 **P**5 7 **S** Oakwood Healthcarer, Inc., Dearborn, MI	23	10	167	7249	91	81604	715	62934	23943	933

WEST BRANCH—Ogemaw County

✠ WEST BRANCH REGIONAL MEDICAL CENTER, (Formerly Tolfree Memorial Hospital), 2463 South M–30, Zip 48661–1199; tel. 517/345–3660; Douglas E. Pattullo, Chief Executive Officer **A**1 9 10 **F**7 8 11 15 16 19 22 28 32 33 34 39 40 41 42 44 49 71	14	10	92	3421	40	53876	325	17999	7993	303

WESTLAND—Wayne County

OAKWOOD HOSPITAL MERRIMAN CENTER–WESTLAND See Oakwood Hospital Annapolis Center, Wayne

□ WALTER P. REUTHER PSYCHIATRIC HOSPITAL, 30901 Palmer Road, Zip 48185–5389; tel. 734/722–4500; Norma C. Josef, M.D., Director **A**1 10 **F**14 19 20 21 26 35 48 50 52 54 56 57 63 64 65 73 **P**5	12	22	210	316	207	0	0	28072	17055	403

WYANDOTTE—Wayne County

✠ △ HENRY FORD WYANDOTTE HOSPITAL, 2333 Biddle Avenue, Zip 48192–4693; tel. 734/284–2400; William R. Alvin, President **A**1 7 9 10 **F**1 2 3 4 6 7 8 10 11 12 13 14 15 16 17 18 19 20 21 22 23 24 25 26 27 28 29 30 31 32 33 34 35 36 37 38 39 40 41 42 43 44 45 46 47 48 49 50 51 52 53 54 55 56 57 58 59 60 61 62 63 64 65 66 67 68 70 71 72 73 **P**6 **S** Henry Ford Health System, Detroit, MI **Web address:** www.henryfordhealth.org	23	10	355	15580	253	—	1103	127988	67178	1774

YPSILANTI—Washtenaw County

✠ OAKWOOD HOSPITAL BEYER CENTER–YPSILANTI, 135 South Prospect Street, Zip 48198–5693; tel. 734/484–2200; Richard Hillbom, Chief Administrative Officer **A**1 9 10 **F**1 2 3 4 6 7 8 10 11 12 13 14 15 16 17 19 21 22 26 28 30 31 32 33 34 35 37 38 40 41 42 43 44 45 46 48 49 51 52 53 54 55 56 57 58 59 60 61 62 63 64 65 66 67 68 71 72 73 **P**5 7 **S** Oakwood Healthcarer, Inc., Dearborn, MI **Web address:** www.oakwood.org	23	10	71	3064	38	37046	162	25468	11163	261

ZEELAND—Ottawa County

✠ ZEELAND COMMUNITY HOSPITAL, 100 South Pine Street, Zip 49464–1619; tel. 616/772–4644; Henry A. Veenstra, President **A**1 9 10 **F**7 8 11 12 14 15 16 17 22 28 30 33 36 39 40 41 42 44 45 48 49 60 65 71 72 73 74 **P**4 7 8	23	10	57	1927	21	49658	334	18564	8582	276

MINNESOTA

Resident population 4,725 (in thousands)
Resident population in metro areas 68.7%
Birth rate per 1,000 population 13.7
65 years and over 12.3%
Percent of persons without health insurance 10.2%

Hospital, Address, Telephone, Administrator, Approval, Facility, and Physician Codes, Health Care System, Network	Classi-fication Codes		Utilization Data					Expense (thousands) of dollars		
★ American Hospital Association (AHA) membership ☐ Joint Commission on Accreditation of Healthcare Organizations (JCAHO) accreditation + American Osteopathic Healthcare Association (AOHA) membership ○ American Osteopathic Association (AOA) accreditation △ Commission on Accreditation of Rehabilitation Facilities (CARF) accreditation Control codes 61, 63, 64, 71, 72 and 73 indicate hospitals listed by AOHA, but not registered by AHA. For definition of numerical codes, see page A4	Control	Service	Staffed Beds	Admissions	Census	Outpatient Visits	Births	Total	Payroll	Personnel

ADA—Norman County
★ BRIDGES MEDICAL SERVICES, 402 East Second Avenue, Zip 56510–0233,
Mailing Address: P.O. Box 233, Zip 56510–0233; tel. 218/784–5000; Kyle
Rasmussen, Administrator **A**9 10 **F**11 15 19 21 22 27 34 44 49 64 71 **P**6

	14	10	8	490	3	8538	0	3148	1668	49

ADRIAN—Nobles County
★ ARNOLD MEMORIAL HEALTH CARE CENTER, (GENERAL MEDICINE), 601 Louisiana
Avenue, Zip 56110–0279, Mailing Address: Box 279, Zip 56110–0279;
tel. 507/483–2668; Gerald E. Carl, Administrator (Total facility includes 41 beds
in nursing home–type unit) **A**9 10 **F**1 2 3 6 8 26 28 32 33 34 49 64 71 **S** Sioux
Valley Hospitals and Health System, Sioux Falls, SD

	23	49	50	92	42	1553	0	2253	1211	52

AITKIN—Aitkin County
★ RIVERWOOD HEALTH CARECENTER, 301 Minnesota Avenue South,
Zip 56431–1626; tel. 218/927–2121; Debra Boardman, Chief Executive Officer
(Total facility includes 48 beds in nursing home–type unit) **A**9 10 **F**7 8 11 15 19
22 28 32 33 35 39 41 42 44 49 51 64 65 67 71 73 **P**8

	23	10	68	978	56	—	39	7392	—	239

ALBANY—Stearns County
★ ALBANY AREA HOSPITAL AND MEDICAL CENTER, 300 Third Avenue,
Zip 56307–9363; tel. 320/845–2121; Ben Koppelman, Administrator **A**9 10 **F**7
8 15 16 19 22 30 32 33 40 44 48 58 65 71 73 **P**6 **S** Catholic Health
Initiatives, Denver, CO

	21	10	15	352	3	8078	48	3952	1892	73

ALBERT LEA—Freeborn County
☒ △ ALBERT LEA MEDICAL CENTER, 404 West Fountain Street, Zip 56007–2473;
tel. 507/373–2384; Ronald A. Harmon, M.D., Chief Executive Officer **A**1 7 9 10
F2 7 8 10 15 16 17 19 21 22 28 30 32 33 34 35 36 37 39 40 41 42 44 46
48 49 51 54 58 65 66 67 71 **P**6 **S** Mayo Foundation, Rochester, MN

	23	10	72	2582	28	61041	439	24967	11696	457

ALEXANDRIA—Douglas County
☒ DOUGLAS COUNTY HOSPITAL, 111 17th Avenue East, Zip 56308–3798;
tel. 320/762–1511; William G. Flaig, Administrator **A**1 9 10 **F**3 7 8 14 15 19 21
22 23 28 29 31 32 33 34 35 36 37 40 41 42 44 45 49 54 55 56 58 59 63
65 66 67 71 73
Web address: www.dchospital.com

	13	10	110	4239	46	46419	544	32650	14869	338

ANOKA—Anoka County
☐ ANOKA–METROPOLITAN REGIONAL TREATMENT CENTER, 3300 Fourth Avenue
North, Zip 55303–1119; tel. 612/576–5500; Judith Krohn, Ph.D., Chief Executive
Officer (Nonreporting) **A**1 10

	12	22	247	—	—	—	—	—	—	—

APPLETON—Swift County
APPLETON MUNICIPAL HOSPITAL AND NURSING HOME, 30 South Behl Street,
Zip 56208–1699; tel. 320/289–2422; Mark E. Paulson, Administrator (Total
facility includes 84 beds in nursing home–type unit) **A**9 10 **F**7 14 17 19 22 32
33 34 36 39 41 44 45 49 58 62 63 64 65 71 73 **P**7

	14	10	104	382	85	8346	6	5780	2772	134

ARLINGTON—Sibley County
ARLINGTON MUNICIPAL HOSPITAL, 601 West Chandler Street, Zip 55307;
tel. 507/964–2271; Michael Schramm, Administrator **A**9 10 **F**1 3 8 15 19 20 22
27 31 32 33 35 42 44 45 46 49 53 62 65 66 67 71 73 **P**7 8

	14	10	17	395	5	6809	0	2739	1138	52

AURORA—St. Louis County
★ WHITE COMMUNITY HOSPITAL, 5211 Highway 110, Zip 55705–1599;
tel. 218/229–2211; Larry Ravenberg, Administrator (Total facility includes 69
beds in nursing home–type unit) (Nonreporting) **A**9 10

	23	10	85	—	—	—	—	—	—	—

AUSTIN—Mower County
☐ AUSTIN MEDICAL CENTER, 1000 First Drive N.W., Zip 55912–2904;
tel. 507/437–4551; Timothy Johnson, M.D., President (Nonreporting) **A**1

	23	10	108	—	—	—	—	—	—	—

BAGLEY—Clearwater County
★ CLEARWATER HEALTH SERVICES, 203 Fourth Street N.W., Zip 56621–8307,
Mailing Address: Rural Route 3, Box 46, Zip 56621–0046; tel. 218/694–6501;
Larry Laudon, Administrator (Total facility includes 70 beds in nursing home–type
unit) (Nonreporting) **A**9 10
Web address: www.clearwaterhs.com

	13	10	92	—	—	—	—	—	—	—

BAUDETTE—Lake of the Woods County
★ LAKEWOOD HEALTH CENTER, 600 South Main Avenue, Zip 56623;
tel. 218/634–2120; SharRay Palm, President and Chief Executive Officer (Total
facility includes 52 beds in nursing home–type unit) **A**9 10 **F**7 8 13 14 15 16 17
19 22 27 28 30 32 33 35 40 44 63 64 65 71 **S** Catholic Health Initiatives,
Denver, CO

	21	10	64	351	55	8860	36	5622	2632	106

BEMIDJI—Beltrami County
☒ NORTH COUNTRY REGIONAL HOSPITAL, 1100 West 38th Street,
Zip 56601–9972; tel. 218/751–5430; James F. Hanko, President and Chief
Executive Officer (Total facility includes 78 beds in nursing home–type unit) **A**1 9
10 **F**4 6 7 8 12 14 15 16 17 19 21 22 28 29 30 32 33 34 35 37 39 40 41
44 45 46 49 62 64 65 67 71 73 **P**6
Web address: www.nchs.com

	23	10	163	5197	128	41208	807	42334	19413	577

Hospital, Address, Telephone, Administrator, Approval, Facility, and Physician Codes, Health Care System, Network	Classi-fication Codes		Utilization Data					Expense (thousands) of dollars		
★ American Hospital Association (AHA) membership □ Joint Commission on Accreditation of Healthcare Organizations (JCAHO) accreditation + American Osteopathic Healthcare Association (AOHA) membership ○ American Osteopathic Association (AOA) accreditation △ Commission on Accreditation of Rehabilitation Facilities (CARF) accreditation Control codes 61, 63, 64, 71, 72 and 73 indicate hospitals listed by AOHA, but not registered by AHA. For definition of numerical codes, see page A4	Control	Service	Staffed Beds	Admissions	Census	Outpatient Visits	Births	Total	Payroll	Personnel

BENSON—Swift County

★ SWIFT COUNTY–BENSON HOSPITAL, 1815 Wisconsin Avenue, Zip 56215–1653; tel. 320/843–4232; Frank Lawatsch, Chief Executive Officer **A**9 10 **F**7 8 11 15 16 19 22 28 32 33 34 35 36 37 39 40 41 42 44 49 54 58 64 65 67 71 **S** Brim Healthcare, Inc., Brentwood, TN

| | 15 | 10 | 31 | 547 | 5 | 9304 | 18 | 3772 | 1700 | 57 |

BIGFORK—Itasca County

★ NORTHERN ITASCA HEALTH CARE CENTER, 258 Pine Tree Drive, Zip 56628, Mailing Address: P.O. Box 258, Zip 56628–0258; tel. 218/743–3177; Richard M. Ash, Chief Executive Officer (Total facility includes 40 beds in nursing home–type unit) (Nonreporting) **A**9 10
Web address: www.nihcc.com

| | 16 | 10 | 56 | — | — | — | — | — | — | — |

BLUE EARTH—Faribault County

⊞ UNITED HOSPITAL DISTRICT, 515 South Moore Street, Zip 56013–2158, Mailing Address: P.O. Box 160, Zip 56013–0160; tel. 507/526–3273; Brian Kief, Administrator **A**1 9 10 **F**2 7 8 11 14 15 16 17 19 22 26 28 30 31 32 33 34 35 36 37 39 40 41 42 44 45 49 53 54 55 58 65 67 71 72 **P**8 **S** Allina Health System, Minneapolis, MN

| | 16 | 10 | 24 | 817 | 8 | 28842 | 39 | 8463 | 3165 | 119 |

BRAINERD—Crow Wing County

□ BRAINERD REGIONAL HUMAN SERVICES CENTER, 1777 Highway 18 East, Zip 56401–7389; tel. 218/828–2201; Harvey G. Caldwell, Administrator and Chief Executive Officer **A**1 10 **F**2 3 14 15 16 18 20 26 48 52 53 56 64 65 73 **P**6

| | 12 | 22 | 243 | 1094 | 195 | 6449 | 0 | 26839 | 17673 | 473 |

□ ST. JOSEPH'S MEDICAL CENTER, 523 North Third Street, Zip 56401–3098; tel. 218/829–2861; Thomas K. Prusak, President **A**1 9 10 **F**2 3 7 8 11 12 15 16 19 21 22 28 29 30 31 32 33 34 35 39 40 41 42 44 46 48 49 52 53 54 55 56 58 59 60 65 66 67 71 73 **S** Benedictine Health System, Duluth, MN
Web address: www.stjosephsmedicalctr.com

| | 21 | 10 | 153 | 6150 | 76 | 102371 | 616 | 46672 | 20723 | 497 |

BRECKENRIDGE—Wilkin County

⊞ ST. FRANCIS MEDICAL CENTER, 415 Oak Street, Zip 56520–1298; tel. 218/643–3000; David A. Nelson, President and Chief Executive Officer (Total facility includes 124 beds in nursing home–type unit) **A**1 9 10 **F**1 3 6 7 8 15 16 17 19 20 21 22 26 28 29 30 32 33 35 36 37 39 40 41 44 45 46 49 51 53 54 55 56 57 58 60 64 65 66 67 71 72 73 **S** Catholic Health Initiatives, Denver, CO

| | 21 | 10 | 171 | 1909 | 137 | 26514 | 315 | 17574 | 8337 | 304 |

BUFFALO—Wright County

⊞ BUFFALO HOSPITAL, 303 Catlin Street, Zip 55313–1947; tel. 612/682–7180; Mary Ellen Wells, Administrator **A**1 9 10 **F**7 8 11 14 15 16 17 19 21 22 26 27 28 29 30 32 33 34 35 37 39 40 41 42 44 45 46 48 49 54 56 58 65 66 67 71 72 73 **P**5 6 **S** Allina Health System, Minneapolis, MN
Web address: www.allina.com

| | 23 | 10 | 30 | 2073 | 17 | 21757 | 451 | 16051 | 7949 | 178 |

BURNSVILLE—Dakota County

⊞ FAIRVIEW RIDGES HOSPITAL, 201 East Nicollet Boulevard, Zip 55337–5799; tel. 612/892–2000; Mark M. Enger, Senior Vice President and Administrator (Nonreporting) **A**1 9 10 **S** Fairview Hospital and Healthcare Services, Minneapolis, MN
Web address: www.fairview.org

| | 21 | 10 | 124 | — | — | — | — | — | — | — |

CAMBRIDGE—Isanti County

⊞ CAMBRIDGE MEDICAL CENTER, 701 South Dellwood Street, Zip 55008–1920; tel. 612/689–7700; Anne Renz, Interim Administrator **A**1 9 10 **F**2 3 7 8 11 12 15 16 17 19 20 21 22 24 26 28 29 30 31 32 33 34 35 36 39 40 41 42 44 45 46 49 51 52 54 55 56 57 58 60 62 65 66 67 70 71 72 73 **P**8 **S** Allina Health System, Minneapolis, MN

| | 23 | 10 | 81 | 3722 | 44 | 24356 | 472 | 49466 | 25758 | 581 |

CANBY—Yellow Medicine County

★ SIOUX VALLEY CANBY CAMPUS, (Formerly Canby Community Health Services), (Includes Senior Haven Convalescent Nursing Center), 112 St. Olaf Avenue South, Zip 56220–1433; tel. 507/223–7277; Robert J. Salmon, Chief Executive Officer (Total facility includes 75 beds in nursing home–type unit) **A**9 10 **F**7 8 15 17 19 20 21 22 26 27 28 29 30 32 33 34 35 36 37 39 40 41 42 44 49 53 62 64 65 66 67 71 73 **P**6 **S** Sioux Valley Hospitals and Health System, Sioux Falls, SD
Web address: www.siouxvalley.org

| | 23 | 10 | 94 | 541 | 74 | 5960 | 29 | 6671 | 3239 | 181 |

CANNON FALLS—Goodhue County

★ COMMUNITY HOSPITAL, 1116 West Mill Street, Zip 55009–1898; tel. 507/263–4221; Randy Ulseth, Administrator **A**9 10 **F**1 2 3 4 5 6 7 8 9 10 11 12 13 14 17 18 19 20 21 22 23 24 25 26 27 28 29 30 31 32 33 34 35 36 37 39 41 42 43 44 45 46 47 48 49 50 51 52 53 54 55 56 57 58 60 61 62 63 64 65 66 67 68 70 71 72 73 74 **P**8

| | 16 | 10 | 17 | 355 | 3 | 19023 | 1 | 4162 | 1662 | 66 |

CASS LAKE—Cass County

⊞ U. S. PUBLIC HEALTH SERVICE INDIAN HOSPITAL, 7th Street and Grant Utley Avenue N.W., Zip 56633, Mailing Address: Rural Route 3, Box 211, Zip 56633; tel. 218/335–2293; Luella Brown, Service Unit Director (Nonreporting) **A**1 10 **S** U. S. Public Health Service Indian Health Service, Rockville, MD

| | 47 | 10 | 13 | — | — | — | — | — | — | — |

CLOQUET—Carlton County

★ CLOQUET COMMUNITY MEMORIAL HOSPITAL, 512 Skyline Boulevard, Zip 55720–1199; tel. 218/879–4641; James J. Carroll, Administrator (Total facility includes 88 beds in nursing home–type unit) **A**9 10 **F**7 8 12 19 22 28 30 32 34 35 36 37 39 40 41 42 44 45 46 49 64 65 67 71 72 73 **P**3 8

| | 23 | 10 | 124 | 1274 | 97 | 25949 | 113 | 13637 | 7077 | 187 |

Hospital, Address, Telephone, Administrator, Approval, Facility, and Physician Codes, Health Care System, Network	Classi-fication Codes		Utilization Data					Expense (thousands) of dollars		
★ American Hospital Association (AHA) membership □ Joint Commission on Accreditation of Healthcare Organizations (JCAHO) accreditation + American Osteopathic Healthcare Association (AOHA) membership ○ American Osteopathic Association (AOA) accreditation △ Commission on Accreditation of Rehabilitation Facilities (CARF) accreditation Control codes 61, 63, 64, 71, 72 and 73 indicate hospitals listed by AOHA, but not registered by AHA. For definition of numerical codes, see page A4	Control	Service	Staffed Beds	Admissions	Census	Outpatient Visits	Births	Total	Payroll	Personnel

COOK—St. Louis County

★ COOK HOSPITAL AND CONVALESCENT NURSING CARE UNIT, 10 South Fifth Street East, Zip 55723–9745; tel. 218/666–5945; Allen J. Vogt, Administrator (Total facility includes 41 beds in nursing home–type unit) **A**9 10 **F**1 8 14 15 16 17 22 24 26 33 34 41 49 53 54 55 58 64 65 66 71 73 **P**5	16	10	55	418	46	11934	0	4354	2225	74

COON RAPIDS—Anoka County

⊞ MERCY HOSPITAL, 4050 Coon Rapids Boulevard, Zip 55433–2586; tel. 612/421–8888; Marvin L. Dehne, Lead Administrator (Nonreporting) **A**1 9 10 **S** Allina Health System, Minneapolis, MN Web address: www.allina.com	23	10	194	—	—	—	—	—	—	—

CROOKSTON—Polk County

⊞ RIVERVIEW HEALTHCARE ASSOCIATION, 323 South Minnesota Street, Zip 56716–1600; tel. 218/281–9200; Thomas C. Lenertz, President and Chief Executive Officer (Total facility includes 162 beds in nursing home–type unit) **A**1 9 10 **F**1 2 3 6 7 8 15 16 17 19 20 21 22 26 28 29 30 31 32 33 36 37 40 41 44 45 46 49 56 64 65 66 67 70 71 73 **P**5 Web address: www.riverviewhealth.org	23	10	234	1958	179	22754	133	17953	9504	353

CROSBY—Crow Wing County

★ CUYUNA REGIONAL MEDICAL CENTER, 320 East Main Street, Zip 56441–1690; tel. 218/546–7000; Thomas F. Reek, Chief Executive Officer (Total facility includes 130 beds in nursing home–type unit) **A**9 10 **F**7 8 15 16 19 22 26 28 30 31 32 33 34 35 37 40 41 42 44 49 64 65 66 71 73 **P**7 8	16	10	160	1416	140	48993	157	18846	9191	314

DAWSON—Lac Qui Parle County

JOHNSON MEMORIAL HEALTH SERVICES, 1282 Walnut Street, Zip 56232–2333; tel. 612/769–4323; Vern Silvernale, Administrator (Total facility includes 70 beds in nursing home–type unit) **A**9 10 **F**7 8 17 19 22 26 32 33 34 36 40 41 44 45 49 64 65 71 73 **P**6	16	10	93	294	71	4437	19	5442	3091	124

DEER RIVER—Itasca County

★ DEER RIVER HEALTHCARE CENTER, 1002 Comstock Drive, Zip 56636–9700; tel. 218/246–2900; Jeffry Stampohar, Chief Executive Officer **A**9 10 **F**1 6 7 8 15 16 19 26 27 28 30 32 33 39 40 44 49 62 64 65 70 71 73 **P**6	23	10	70	460	3	2278	53	—	—	146

DETROIT LAKES—Becker County

⊞ ST. MARY'S REGIONAL HEALTH CENTER, 1027 Washington Avenue, Zip 56501–3598; tel. 218/847–5611; John H. Solheim, Chief Executive Officer (Total facility includes 100 beds in nursing home–type unit) **A**1 9 10 **F**7 8 10 12 15 16 17 19 21 22 26 27 28 30 32 33 34 35 37 39 40 41 42 44 46 49 60 62 64 65 66 67 69 71 73 74 **S** Benedictine Health System, Duluth, MN Web address: www.stmaryshealthcenter.com	21	10	163	2208	116	—	362	15152	6620	233

DULUTH—St. Louis County

⊞ △ MILLER DWAN MEDICAL CENTER, 502 East Second Street, Zip 55805–1982; tel. 218/727–8762; William H. Palmer, President **A**1 2 7 9 10 **F**2 3 6 9 12 14 15 16 17 18 19 21 23 26 28 31 34 35 37 39 41 42 44 45 46 48 49 52 53 55 56 57 58 59 60 65 67 71 73 **P**5 Web address: www.miller–dwan.com	14	10	152	3592	78	81315	0	50045	24911	650
⊞ ST. LUKE'S HOSPITAL, 915 East First Street, Zip 55805–2193; tel. 218/726–5555; John Strange, President and Chief Executive Officer **A**1 2 3 5 9 10 **F**3 4 7 8 10 11 12 14 15 16 19 20 21 22 23 28 30 31 32 33 34 35 37 39 40 41 42 43 44 49 51 52 53 54 55 56 57 58 59 60 63 65 67 70 71 72 73 **P**1 Web address: www.slhduluth.com	23	10	238	7659	102	96955	783	105742	52483	1524
⊞ ST. MARY'S MEDICAL CENTER, 407 East Third Street, Zip 55805–1984; tel. 218/726–4000; Sister Kathleen Hofer, President **A**1 2 3 5 9 10 **F**2 3 4 5 6 7 8 9 10 11 14 15 16 17 18 19 20 21 22 23 24 27 29 30 31 32 33 34 35 36 37 38 39 40 41 42 43 44 47 48 49 51 52 53 54 55 56 57 58 59 60 61 62 63 64 65 66 67 70 71 72 73 **P**6 **S** Benedictine Health System, Duluth, MN Web address: www.smdc.org	21	10	287	15970	209	101250	1545	147676	63510	1935

ELBOW LAKE—Grant County

★ GRANT COUNTY HEALTH CENTER, 930 First Street N.E., Zip 56531–4699; tel. 218/685–4461; Larry Rapp, Chief Medical and Executive Officer (Nonreporting) **A**9 10	23	10	15	—	—	—	—	—	—	—

ELY—St. Louis County

★ ELY–BLOOMENSON COMMUNITY HOSPITAL, 328 West Conan Street, Zip 55731–1198; tel. 218/365–3271; John Fossum, Administrator (Total facility includes 99 beds in nursing home–type unit) **A**9 10 **F**1 7 8 11 15 17 19 21 22 32 33 34 35 39 40 44 49 64 65 67 71 72 73 **P**6	23	10	138	721	105	6834	43	9496	5215	176

FAIRMONT—Martin County

⊞ FAIRMONT COMMUNITY HOSPITAL, (Includes Lutz Wing Convalescent and Nursing Care Unit), 835 Johnson Street, Zip 56031, Mailing Address: P.O. Box 835, Zip 56031–0835; tel. 507/238–8100; Gerry Gilbertson, Administrator (Total facility includes 40 beds in nursing home–type unit) **A**1 9 10 **F**6 7 8 14 15 16 17 19 20 21 22 23 24 28 29 32 33 34 35 37 40 41 42 44 45 46 49 60 61 64 65 66 67 71 72 73	23	10	92	2134	59	40895	294	18159	8362	213

FARIBAULT—Rice County

⊞ DISTRICT ONE HOSPITAL, 631 S.E. First Street, Zip 55021–6345; tel. 507/334–6451; James N. Wolf, Chief Executive Officer **A**1 9 10 **F**7 8 10 15 16 19 20 21 22 28 30 33 35 36 37 39 40 41 44 45 49 65 66 67 71 72 73	16	10	48	2157	20	34900	401	18368	7467	208

Hospital, Address, Telephone, Administrator, Approval, Facility, and Physician Codes, Health Care System, Network	Classi-fication Codes		Utilization Data					Expense (thousands) of dollars		
★ American Hospital Association (AHA) membership □ Joint Commission on Accreditation of Healthcare Organizations (JCAHO) accreditation + American Osteopathic Healthcare Association (AOHA) membership ○ American Osteopathic Association (AOA) accreditation △ Commission on Accreditation of Rehabilitation Facilities (CARF) accreditation Control codes 61, 63, 64, 71, 72 and 73 indicate hospitals listed by AOHA, but not registered by AHA. For definition of numerical codes, see page A4	Control	Service	Staffed Beds	Admissions	Census	Outpatient Visits	Births	Total	Payroll	Personnel
FARIBAULT REGIONAL CENTER, 802 Circle Drive, Zip 55021–6399; tel. 507/332–3000; Bridget K. Stroud, Chief Executive Officer (Nonreporting)	12	62	263	—	—	—	—	—	—	—
□ WILSON CENTER PSYCHIATRIC FACILITY FOR CHILDREN AND ADOLESCENTS, 1800 14th Street N.E., Zip 55021, Mailing Address: P.O. Box 917, Zip 55021–0917; tel. 507/334–5561; Kevin J. Mahoney, President (Nonreporting) **A**1	33	22	50	—	—	—	—	—	—	—
FARMINGTON—Dakota County										
✠ TRINITY HOSPITAL, (Formerly South Suburban Medical Center), 3410–213th Street West, Zip 55024–1197; tel. 651/463–7825; Donald J. Leivermann, Chief Executive Officer (Total facility includes 65 beds in nursing home–type unit) **A**1 9 10 **F**6 7 8 15 16 17 19 21 22 26 28 29 32 33 34 35 37 40 41 42 44 45 46 49 51 62 64 65 67 71 72 73 **P**6 **S** Benedictine Health System, Duluth, MN	23	10	85	340	68	2790	17	5397	2657	119
FERGUS FALLS—Otter Tail County										
□ FERGUS FALLS REGIONAL TREATMENT CENTER, Fir and Union Avenues, Zip 56537, Mailing Address: P.O. Box 157, Zip 56537–0157; tel. 218/739–7200; Michael Ackley, Administrator **A**1 10 **F**2 3 14 16 17 20 41 46 52 56 57 58 64 65 73 **P**6	12	22	226	1386	175	—	0	—	—	424
✠ LAKE REGION HEALTHCARE CORPORATION, 712 South Cascade Street, Zip 56537–2900, Mailing Address: P.O. Box 728, Zip 56538–0728; tel. 218/736–8000; Edward J. Mehl, Chief Executive Officer (Total facility includes 44 beds in nursing home–type unit) **A**1 9 10 **F**6 7 8 11 15 16 17 19 21 22 23 26 28 32 34 35 37 40 41 42 44 46 49 52 57 58 59 64 65 66 71 73	23	10	136	3354	79	33878	366	28980	14516	485
FOSSTON—Polk County										
★ FIRST CARE MEDICAL SERVICES, 900 South Hilligoss Boulevard East, Zip 56542–1599; tel. 218/435–1133; Debra Carlson, Acting Administrator (Total facility includes 50 beds in nursing home–type unit) **A**9 10 **F**7 8 14 15 16 19 21 24 26 27 32 33 34 35 36 42 44 45 49 51 63 64 65 66 67 70 71 **P**5 **Web address:** www.firstcare.org	23	10	71	647	55	45446	47	6487	2735	147
FRIDLEY—Anoka County										
★ UNITY HOSPITAL, 550 Osborne Road N.E., Zip 55432–2799; tel. 612/421–2222 (Nonreporting) **A**2 9 **S** Allina Health System, Minneapolis, MN **Web address:** www.allina.com	23	10	190	—	—	—	—	—	—	—
GLENCOE—McLeod County										
★ GLENCOE AREA HEALTH CENTER, 705 East 18th Street, Zip 55336–1499; tel. 320/864–3121; Jon D. Braband, Chief Executive Officer (Total facility includes 110 beds in nursing home–type unit) **A**9 10 **F**1 6 7 8 11 15 16 19 22 26 27 28 30 32 34 35 37 40 41 42 44 49 58 62 63 64 65 67 71 73 **S** HealthSystem Minnesota, Saint Louis Park, MN	14	10	149	1332	120	14392	123	15885	7447	279
GLENWOOD—Pope County										
★ GLACIAL RIDGE HOSPITAL, 10 Fourth Avenue S.E., Zip 56334–1898; tel. 320/634–4521; Douglas J. Reker, Administrator and Chief Executive Officer **A**9 10 **F**7 8 14 15 17 19 21 22 24 28 29 30 32 33 34 35 37 40 41 42 44 49 53 54 65 67 70 71 73 **P**6 **Web address:** www.runestone.net/~grh	16	10	19	589	6	9289	46	4205	2280	111
GOLDEN VALLEY—Hennepin County										
✠ VENCOR HOSPITAL—MINNEAPOLIS, 4101 Golden Valley Road, Zip 55422; tel. 612/588–2750; Thomas N. Theroult, Administrator (Nonreporting) **A**1 9 10 **S** Vencor, Incorporated, Louisville, KY	33	10	111	—	—	—	—	—	—	—
GRACEVILLE—Big Stone County										
GRACEVILLE HEALTH CENTER, 115 West Second Street, Zip 56240–0157, Mailing Address: P.O. Box 157, Zip 56240–0157; tel. 320/748–7223; Helen Jorve, Chief Executive Officer (Total facility includes 60 beds in nursing home–type unit) (Nonreporting) **A**10 **S** Missionary Benedictine Sisters American Province, Norfolk, NE	23	10	92	—	—	—	—	—	—	—
GRAND MARAIS—Cook County										
COOK COUNTY NORTH SHORE HOSPITAL, Gunflint Trail, Zip 55604, Mailing Address: P.O. Box 10, Zip 55604–0010; tel. 218/387–3040; Diane Pearson, Administrator (Total facility includes 47 beds in nursing home–type unit) **A**9 10 **F**7 8 11 17 22 32 33 40 49 64 65 71 73 **P**6	16	10	63	292	46	11129	26	5083	2872	92
GRAND RAPIDS—Itasca County										
✠ ITASCA MEDICAL CENTER, 126 First Avenue S.E., Zip 55744–3698; tel. 218/326–3401; Gary Kenner, President and Chief Executive Officer (Total facility includes 35 beds in nursing home–type unit) **A**1 9 10 **F**1 7 8 11 15 17 19 21 22 26 31 32 34 35 37 39 40 41 42 44 46 49 56 64 65 66 67 71 73 74 **S** Benedictine Health System, Duluth, MN	23	10	84	2540	57	28061	370	23200	11248	263
GRANITE FALLS—Yellow Medicine County										
✠ GRANITE FALLS MUNICIPAL HOSPITAL AND MANOR, 345 Tenth Avenue, Zip 56241–1499; tel. 320/564–3111; George Gerlach, Administrator (Total facility includes 64 beds in nursing home–type unit) **A**1 9 10 **F**7 8 14 15 16 17 19 22 28 30 31 32 33 35 36 40 44 46 49 62 63 64 65 71 **S** Allina Health System, Minneapolis, MN	14	10	94	637	64	8845	2	7736	4784	119
HALLOCK—Kittson County										
KITTSON MEMORIAL HEALTHCARE CENTER, 1010 South Birch Street, Zip 56728, Mailing Address: P.O. Box 700, Zip 56728–0700; tel. 218/843–3612; Richard J. Failing, Chief Executive Officer (Total facility includes 88 beds in nursing home–type unit) **A**9 10 **F**8 11 15 16 19 22 27 32 33 35 39 40 44 49 64 65 71 **P**5	23	10	108	264	81	6488	11	5109	2605	141

Hospital, Address, Telephone, Administrator, Approval, Facility, and Physician Codes, Health Care System, Network	Classi-fication Codes		Utilization Data					Expense (thousands) of dollars		
	Control	Service	Staffed Beds	Admissions	Census	Outpatient Visits	Births	Total	Payroll	Personnel

★ American Hospital Association (AHA) membership
□ Joint Commission on Accreditation of Healthcare Organizations (JCAHO) accreditation
+ American Osteopathic Healthcare Association (AOHA) membership
○ American Osteopathic Association (AOA) accreditation
△ Commission on Accreditation of Rehabilitation Facilities (CARF) accreditation
Control codes 61, 63, 64, 71, 72 and 73 indicate hospitals listed by AOHA, but not registered by AHA. For definition of numerical codes, see page A4

HARMONY—Fillmore County

HARMONY COMMUNITY HOSPITAL, 815 South Main Avenue, Zip 55939–6625, Mailing Address: Route 1, Box 173, Zip 55939–0173; tel. 507/886–6544; Greg Braun, Administrator (Total facility includes 45 beds in nursing home–type unit) **A**9 10 **F**1 12 15 16 17 20 26 27 28 29 30 32 33 34 39 41 45 46 49 51 54 61 64 65 67 72 73 74 **P**3 6

| | 23 | 10 | 53 | 130 | 46 | 8762 | 0 | 2848 | — | 67 |

HASTINGS—Dakota County

□ REGINA MEDICAL CENTER, 1175 Nininger Road, Zip 55033–1098; tel. 615/480–4100; Lynn W. Olson, Administrator and Chief Executive Officer (Total facility includes 61 beds in nursing home–type unit) **A**1 9 10 **F**6 7 8 11 12 15 16 17 19 22 24 27 28 29 30 32 34 35 36 39 40 41 44 46 49 51 61 62 64 65 67 71 72 73 74 **P**4 7

| | 23 | 10 | 96 | 2200 | 78 | 24427 | 341 | 21983 | 12139 | 360 |

HENDRICKS—Lincoln County

★ HENDRICKS COMMUNITY HOSPITAL, 503 East Lincoln Street, Zip 56136–9598; tel. 507/275–3134; Kirk Stensrud, Administrator (Total facility includes 70 beds in nursing home–type unit) **A**9 10 **F**1 6 7 8 11 12 14 15 16 17 19 20 21 22 24 28 30 31 32 33 34 35 37 40 44 48 63 64 65 67 71 73 **P**5

| | 23 | 10 | 84 | 378 | 73 | 6034 | 30 | 4815 | 2376 | 100 |

HIBBING—St. Louis County

⊞ UNIVERSITY MEDICAL CENTER–MESABI, 750 East 34th Street, Zip 55746–4600; tel. 218/262–4881; Richard W. Dinter, M.D., Chief Operating Officer (Nonreporting) **A**1 9 10 **S** Fairview Hospital and Healthcare Services, Minneapolis, MN

| | 23 | 10 | 132 | — | — | — | — | — | — | — |

HUTCHINSON—McLeod County

⊞ HUTCHINSON AREA HEALTH CARE, 1095 Highway 15 South, Zip 55350–3182; tel. 320/234–5000; Philip G. Graves, Administrator (Total facility includes 127 beds in nursing home–type unit) **A**1 9 10 **F**1 3 7 8 11 15 16 17 18 19 22 26 28 29 32 33 34 35 36 39 40 41 42 44 46 49 52 53 54 55 56 57 58 59 64 65 66 67 71 73 74 **S** Allina Health System, Minneapolis, MN

| | 14 | 10 | 193 | 2653 | 144 | 68401 | 409 | 28992 | 13490 | — |

INTERNATIONAL FALLS—Koochiching County

⊞ FALLS MEMORIAL HOSPITAL, 1400 Highway 71, Zip 56649–2189; tel. 218/283–4481; Mary Klimp, Administrator and Chief Executive Officer **A**1 9 10 **F**7 8 11 14 15 16 17 19 20 21 22 28 30 32 33 35 37 40 42 44 46 48 49 56 64 65 70 71 73 **S** Quorum Health Group/Quorum Health Resources, Inc., Brentwood, TN

| | 23 | 10 | 35 | 1022 | 8 | 18837 | 128 | 7884 | 3210 | 90 |

IVANHOE—Lincoln County

★ DIVINE PROVIDENCE HEALTH CENTER, 312 East George Street, Zip 56142–0136, Mailing Address: P.O. Box G., Zip 56142–0136; tel. 507/694–1414; Patrick Branco, Administrator (Total facility includes 51 beds in nursing home–type unit) **A**9 10 **F**1 11 19 21 22 30 32 33 34 39 40 41 42 44 49 64 65 67 71 73 **P**5 **S** Avera Health, Yankton, SD

| | 23 | 10 | 69 | 219 | 49 | 1864 | 2 | 3078 | 1763 | 85 |

JACKSON—Jackson County

★ JACKSON MEDICAL CENTER, 1430 North Highway, Zip 56143–1098; tel. 507/847–2420; Charlotte Heitkamp, Chief Executive Officer (Total facility includes 21 beds in nursing home–type unit) **A**9 10 **F**1 19 22 28 33 44 58 64 **P**6 **S** Sioux Valley Hospitals and Health System, Sioux Falls, SD

| | 23 | 10 | 41 | 462 | 24 | 9797 | 0 | 3062 | 1629 | 74 |

LAKE CITY—Wabasha County

⊞ LAKE CITY MEDICAL CENTER, 904 South Lakeshore Drive, Zip 55041–1899; tel. 651/345–3321; Mark Rinehardt, Administrator (Total facility includes 115 beds in nursing home–type unit) **A**1 9 10 **F**3 8 10 15 17 19 22 26 32 33 40 44 46 49 64 65 71 72 73

| | 14 | 10 | 144 | 685 | 114 | 5294 | 43 | 8115 | 4272 | 165 |

LE SUEUR—Le Sueur County

MINNESOTA VALLEY HEALTH CENTER, (Includes Gardenview Nursing Home), 621 South Fourth Street, Zip 56058–2203; tel. 507/665–3375; Jennifer D. Pfeffer, Administrator and Chief Executive Officer (Total facility includes 85 beds in nursing home–type unit) **A**9 10 **F**1 7 8 11 15 16 17 19 22 29 30 33 34 36 40 41 42 44 48 49 62 64 65 67 71 73 **P**3

| | 23 | 10 | 102 | 172 | 79 | 13574 | 32 | 4739 | 2559 | 125 |

LITCHFIELD—Meeker County

★ MEEKER COUNTY MEMORIAL HOSPITAL, 612 South Sibley Avenue, Zip 55355–3398; tel. 320/693–3242; Ronald E. Johnson, Administrator **A**9 10 **F**7 8 15 16 19 21 22 26 28 29 30 34 35 37 40 42 44 45 49 63 67 71

| | 13 | 10 | 38 | 1313 | 13 | 16158 | 187 | 8235 | 3604 | 107 |

LITTLE FALLS—Morrison County

⊞ ST. GABRIEL'S HOSPITAL, 815 Second Street S.E., Zip 56345–3596; tel. 320/632–5441; Larry A. Schulz, President and Chief Executive Officer (Total facility includes 150 beds in nursing home–type unit) **A**1 9 10 **F**1 3 6 7 8 12 15 16 17 19 20 21 22 24 26 27 28 30 31 32 33 34 35 37 39 40 41 42 44 45 46 49 53 54 55 56 57 58 59 62 63 64 65 66 67 70 71 73 **S** Catholic Health Initiatives, Denver, CO
Web address: www.upstel.net/~falls/unf.html

| | 21 | 10 | 205 | 2139 | 162 | 52000 | 249 | 26022 | 11919 | 432 |

LONG PRAIRIE—Todd County

⊞ LONG PRAIRIE MEMORIAL HOSPITAL AND HOME, 20 Ninth Street S.E., Zip 56347–1404; tel. 320/732–2141; Clayton R. Peterson, President (Total facility includes 123 beds in nursing home–type unit) **A**1 9 10 **F**1 7 8 11 14 15 16 19 22 27 28 32 33 34 35 36 40 41 44 49 64 65 73 **P**3

| | 23 | 10 | 141 | 745 | 111 | — | 77 | 9532 | 4343 | 157 |

LUVERNE—Rock County

★ LUVERNE COMMUNITY HOSPITAL, 305 East Luverne Street, Zip 56156–2519, Mailing Address: P.O. Box 1019, Zip 56156–1019; tel. 507/283–2321; Gerald E. Carl, Administrator **A**9 10 **F**3 7 8 15 16 19 22 30 32 33 34 35 39 40 41 42 44 49 58 64 65 66 67 71 73 **P**3 **S** Sioux Valley Hospitals and Health System, Sioux Falls, SD

| | 14 | 10 | 28 | 875 | 12 | 12596 | 127 | 7077 | 3348 | — |

Hospital, Address, Telephone, Administrator, Approval, Facility, and Physician Codes, Health Care System, Network	Classi-fication Codes		Utilization Data					Expense (thousands) of dollars		
★ American Hospital Association (AHA) membership □ Joint Commission on Accreditation of Healthcare Organizations (JCAHO) accreditation + American Osteopathic Healthcare Association (AOHA) membership ○ American Osteopathic Association (AOA) accreditation △ Commission on Accreditation of Rehabilitation Facilities (CARF) accreditation Control codes 61, 63, 64, 71, 72 and 73 indicate hospitals listed by AOHA, but not registered by AHA. For definition of numerical codes, see page A4	Control	Service	Staffed Beds	Admissions	Census	Outpatient Visits	Births	Total	Payroll	Personnel

MADELIA—Watonwan County

✠ MADELIA COMMUNITY HOSPITAL, 121 Drew Avenue S.E., Zip 56062–1899; tel. 507/642–3255; Candace Fenske, Administrator **A**1 9 10 **F**7 14 15 16 17 19 20 21 22 28 29 32 33 34 35 36 40 41 44 45 49 64 65 71 **P**5	23	10	25	398	4	5641	32	2718	1327	50

MADISON—Lac Qui Parle County

★ MADISON HOSPITAL, 820 Third Avenue, Zip 56256–1014, Mailing Address: P.O. Box 184, Zip 56256–0184; tel. 320/598–7556; Thomas Richter, Chief Executive Officer **A**9 10 **F**7 8 19 22 28 30 32 33 34 35 36 40 44 49 65 71 **P**1	23	10	12	319	2	5129	3	2113	867	22

MAHNOMEN—Mahnomen County

MAHNOMEN HEALTH CENTER, 414 Jefferson Avenue, Zip 56557, Mailing Address: P.O. Box 396, Zip 56557–0396; tel. 218/935–2511; Charlotte Wittey, Chief Executive Officer (Total facility includes 48 beds in nursing home–type unit) (Nonreporting) **A**9 10	23	10	66	—	—	—	—	—	—	—

MANKATO—Blue Earth County

✠ IMMANUEL ST. JOSEPH'S–MAYO HEALTH SYSTEM, 1025 Marsh Street, Zip 56001–4700, Mailing Address: P.O. Box 8673, Zip 56002–8673; tel. 507/625–4031; W. Neath Folger, M.D., President and Chief Executive Officer **A**1 2 3 5 9 10 **F**2 3 7 8 10 12 15 16 17 19 20 21 22 23 28 29 30 31 32 33 34 35 37 39 40 41 42 44 45 49 52 53 54 56 57 58 59 60 63 65 67 71 73 74 **P**8 **S** Mayo Foundation, Rochester, MN	23	10	147	7517	88	69710	1122	59089	28724	714

MAPLEWOOD—Ramsey County

★ HEALTHEAST ST. JOHN'S HOSPITAL, 1575 Beam Avenue, Zip 55109; tel. 651/232–7000; Douglas P. Cropper, Vice President and Administrator (Nonreporting) **A**3 5 9 10 **S** HealthEast, Saint Paul, MN **Web address:** www.healtheast.org	23	10	150	—	—	—	—	—	—	—

MARSHALL—Lyon County

✠ WEINER MEMORIAL MEDICAL CENTER, 300 South Bruce Street, Zip 56258–1934; tel. 507/532–9661; Richard G. Slieter, Jr., Administrator (Total facility includes 76 beds in nursing home–type unit) **A**1 9 10 **F**1 6 7 8 14 15 16 17 19 20 21 22 24 26 27 28 29 30 31 32 33 34 35 37 39 40 41 42 44 45 46 49 50 56 57 58 62 64 65 67 71 73 **Web address:** www.wmmc.org	14	10	125	1894	92	16933	439	16323	8136	254

MELROSE—Stearns County

MELROSE AREA HOSPITAL, 11 North Fifth Avenue West, Zip 56352–1098; tel. 320/256–4231; Joan Jackson, Administrator (Total facility includes 75 beds in nursing home–type unit) **A**9 10 **F**1 7 8 14 15 16 17 19 20 22 26 27 32 33 34 35 36 37 39 40 41 44 49 51 52 58 62 64 65 66 67 71 73 **P**5	14	10	87	419	79	9425	60	5094	2811	111

MINNEAPOLIS—Hennepin County

✠ △ ABBOTT NORTHWESTERN HOSPITAL, (Includes Sister Kenny Institute), 800 East 28th Street, Zip 55407–3799; tel. 612/863–4201; Mark Dixon, Administrator **A**1 2 3 5 7 9 10 **F**3 4 5 7 8 9 10 11 12 15 17 19 21 22 23 24 25 26 27 28 29 30 31 32 33 34 35 36 37 38 39 40 41 42 43 44 45 46 47 48 49 51 52 53 54 55 56 57 58 59 60 61 63 64 65 67 68 71 72 73 74 **P**5 6 8 **S** Allina Health System, Minneapolis, MN **Web address:** www.allina.com	23	10	619	31765	446	292949	3293	393346	164480	3239
□ CHILDREN'S HOSPITALS AND CLINICS, MINNEAPOLIS, (PEDIATRIC), 2525 Chicago Avenue South, Zip 55404–9976; tel. 612/813–6100; Brock D. Nelson, Chief Executive Officer **A**1 2 3 9 10 **F**4 10 12 13 14 15 16 17 19 20 21 22 23 25 27 29 30 31 32 33 34 35 38 39 41 42 43 44 45 46 47 49 50 51 53 54 55 56 58 60 63 65 67 68 70 71 73 **P**1 **Web address:** www.childrenshc.org	23	59	163	7077	125	69170	0	127364	62371	1647
FAIRVIEW RIVERSIDE HOSPITAL See Fairview–University Medical Center										
✠ FAIRVIEW SOUTHDALE HOSPITAL, 6401 France Avenue South, Zip 55435–2199; tel. 612/924–5000; Mark M. Enger, Senior Vice President and Administrator (Nonreporting) **A**1 9 10 **S** Fairview Hospital and Healthcare Services, Minneapolis, MN **Web address:** www.fairview.org	23	10	355	—	—	—	—	—	—	—
✠ FAIRVIEW–UNIVERSITY MEDICAL CENTER, (Includes Fairview Riverside Hospital, 2312 South Sixth Street, Zip 55454; St. Mary's Hospital and Rehabilitation Center, 2414 South Seventh Street, Zip 55454; tel. 612/338–2229; University of Minnesota Hospital and Clinic, 420 S.E. Delaware Street, Box 502, Zip 55455–0392; tel. 612/626–3000), 2450 Riverside Avenue, Zip 55454–1400; tel. 612/672–6000; Gordon L. Alexander, M.D., Senior Vice President and Administrator (Total facility includes 115 beds in nursing home–type unit) (Nonreporting) **A**1 2 5 6 8 9 10 **S** Fairview Hospital and Healthcare Services, Minneapolis, MN	23	10	1362	—	—	—	—	—	—	—
✠ △ HENNEPIN COUNTY MEDICAL CENTER, 701 Park Avenue South, Zip 55415–1829; tel. 612/347–2121; Jeff Spartz, Administrator (Nonreporting) **A**1 2 3 5 7 8 9 10	13	10	462	—	—	—	—	—	—	—
✠ PHILLIPS EYE INSTITUTE, 2215 Park Avenue, Zip 55404–3756; tel. 612/336–6000; Shari E. Levy, Administrator (Nonreporting) **A**1 9 10 **S** Allina Health System, Minneapolis, MN **Web address:** www.allina.com	23	45	10	—	—	—	—	—	—	—
✠ SHRINERS HOSPITALS FOR CHILDREN, TWIN CITIES, 2025 East River Parkway, Zip 55414–3696; tel. 612/335–5300; Laurence E. Johnson, Administrator **A**1 3 5 **F**15 17 19 34 35 39 44 45 46 49 53 65 67 71 73 **P**6 **S** Shriners Hospitals for Children, Tampa, FL **Web address:** www.shrinershq.org	23	57	40	803	16	8889	0	—	—	153
ST. MARY'S HOSPITAL AND REHABILITATION CENTER See Fairview–University Medical Center										
UNIVERSITY OF MINNESOTA HOSPITAL AND CLINIC See Fairview–University Medical Center										

Hospital, Address, Telephone, Administrator, Approval, Facility, and Physician Codes, Health Care System, Network	Classi-fication Codes		Utilization Data					Expense (thousands) of dollars		
	Control	Service	Staffed Beds	Admissions	Census	Outpatient Visits	Births	Total	Payroll	Personnel

★ American Hospital Association (AHA) membership
□ Joint Commission on Accreditation of Healthcare Organizations (JCAHO) accreditation
+ American Osteopathic Healthcare Association (AOHA) membership
○ American Osteopathic Association (AOA) accreditation
△ Commission on Accreditation of Rehabilitation Facilities (CARF) accreditation
Control codes 61, 63, 64, 71, 72 and 73 indicate hospitals listed by AOHA, but not registered by AHA. For definition of numerical codes, see page A4

Hospital	Control	Service	Staffed Beds	Admissions	Census	Outpatient Visits	Births	Total	Payroll	Personnel
△ VETERANS AFFAIRS MEDICAL CENTER, One Veterans Drive, Zip 55417–2399; tel. 612/725–2000; Steven Kleingloss, Acting Director (Total facility includes 104 beds in nursing home–type unit) **A**1 2 3 5 7 8 **F**1 2 3 4 5 6 8 10 11 12 16 17 18 19 20 21 22 23 24 25 26 27 28 29 30 31 32 33 34 35 37 39 41 42 43 44 45 46 48 49 50 51 52 54 55 56 57 58 59 60 61 64 65 67 68 71 72 73 74 **P**6 **S** Department of Veterans Affairs, Washington, DC	45	10	361	9745	263	411612	0	227548	116590	2695
MONTEVIDEO—Chippewa County										
CHIPPEWA COUNTY MONTEVIDEO HOSPITAL, 824 North 11th Street, Zip 56265–1683; tel. 320/269–8877; Fred Knutson, Administrator (Nonreporting) **A**9 10	15	10	29	—	—	—	—	—	—	—
MONTICELLO—Wright County										
MONTICELLO BIG LAKE HOSPITAL, 1013 Hart Boulevard, Zip 55362–8230; tel. 612/295–2945; Barbara Schwientek, Executive Director (Total facility includes 91 beds in nursing home–type unit) **A**1 9 10 **F**1 3 7 8 14 15 19 22 32 33 34 35 36 37 40 42 44 58 64 65 66 71 72	16	10	103	1228	99	19865	302	15767	7924	246
MOOSE LAKE—Carlton County										
★ MERCY HOSPITAL AND HEALTH CARE CENTER, 710 South Kenwood Avenue, Zip 55767–9405; tel. 218/485–4481; Dianne Mandernach, Chief Executive Officer (Total facility includes 94 beds in nursing home–type unit) **A**9 10 **F**7 8 12 14 15 16 17 19 22 24 28 30 32 34 37 39 40 41 44 45 46 49 61 64 65 67 70 71 73 **P**5	16	10	118	839	100	15817	121	11605	6232	—
MORA—Kanabec County										
KANABEC HOSPITAL, 300 Clark Street, Zip 55051–1590; tel. 320/679–1212; Thomas D. Kaufman, Administrator **A**1 9 10 **F**7 8 14 15 16 17 19 21 22 28 30 33 35 37 40 41 42 44 45 46 49 64 65 67 71 73 **P**5	13	10	35	982	11	14481	129	9345	4183	126
MORRIS—Stevens County										
STEVENS COMMUNITY MEDICAL CENTER, 400 East First Street, Zip 56267–1407, Mailing Address: P.O. Box 660, Zip 56267–0660; tel. 320/589–1313; John Rau, Administrator (Nonreporting) **A**1 9 10 **S** Allina Health System, Minneapolis, MN	23	10	37	—	—	—	—	—	—	—
NEW PRAGUE—Le Sueur County										
QUEEN OF PEACE HOSPITAL, 301 Second Street N.E., Zip 56071–1799; tel. 612/758–4431; Sister Jean Juenemann, Chief Executive Officer **A**1 9 10 **F**6 7 8 11 13 16 17 19 20 21 22 24 28 30 32 34 35 39 40 41 42 44 45 46 49 51 60 62 64 67 71 72 73	23	10	31	1465	13	72983	163	13282	6016	179
NEW ULM—Brown County										
NEW ULM MEDICAL CENTER, 1324 Fifth Street North, Zip 56073–1553, Mailing Address: P.O. Box 577, Zip 56073–0577; tel. 507/354–2111; David A. Grundstrom, Administrator (Nonreporting) **A**1 9 10 **S** Allina Health System, Minneapolis, MN	23	10	47	—	—	—	—	—	—	—
NORTHFIELD—Rice County										
NORTHFIELD HOSPITAL, (Includes H. O. DILLEY SKILLED NURSING FACILITY), 801 West First Street, Zip 55057–1697; tel. 507/645–6661; Kendall C. Bank, Administrator (Total facility includes 40 beds in nursing home–type unit) **A**1 9 10 **F**7 8 11 15 16 19 20 22 28 30 32 33 34 35 36 39 40 41 42 44 45 46 49 51 64 65 66 67 71 73 **S** Allina Health System, Minneapolis, MN	14	10	67	1591	48	18957	339	16207	8047	184
OLIVIA—Renville County										
RENVILLE COUNTY HOSPITAL, 611 East Fairview Avenue, Zip 56277–1397; tel. 320/523–1261; Dean G. Slagter, Administrator (Nonreporting) **A**9 10	13	10	30	—	—	—	—	—	—	—
ONAMIA—Mille Lacs County										
MILLE LACS HEALTH SYSTEM, 200 North Elm Street, Zip 56359–7978; tel. 320/532–3154; Randall A. Farrow, Administrator (Total facility includes 80 beds in nursing home–type unit) **A**1 9 10 **F**1 3 7 8 12 15 16 17 19 20 21 22 26 27 28 29 30 32 33 34 35 39 40 41 42 44 45 49 51 53 54 58 64 65 66 67 71 **P**6 **S** Allina Health System, Minneapolis, MN	23	10	98	934	76	15322	89	11621	5843	196
ORTONVILLE—Big Stone County										
★ ORTONVILLE AREA HEALTH SERVICES, 750 Eastvold Avenue, Zip 56278–1133; tel. 320/839–2502; Paul J. Anderson, Administrator (Total facility includes 74 beds in nursing home–type unit) **A**9 10 **F**7 8 15 16 19 21 22 27 30 32 33 34 35 36 39 41 42 44 45 46 49 53 54 56 57 58 64 65 67 71 73 **S** Sioux Valley Hospitals and Health System, Sioux Falls, SD	14	10	105	567	76	15456	69	6348	2635	117
OWATONNA—Steele County										
OWATONNA HOSPITAL, 903 Oak Street South, Zip 55060–3234; tel. 507/451–3850; Daniel J. Werner, Administrator (Nonreporting) **A**1 9 10 **S** Allina Health System, Minneapolis, MN **Web address:** www.allina.com	23	10	66	—	—	—	—	—	—	—
PARK RAPIDS—Hubbard County										
ST. JOSEPH'S AREA HEALTH SERVICES, 600 Pleasant Avenue, Zip 56470–1432; tel. 218/732–3311; David R. Hove, President and Chief Executive Officer **A**1 9 10 **F**7 8 15 16 19 21 22 30 32 33 35 37 40 44 49 63 65 71 **S** Catholic Health Initiatives, Denver, CO	21	10	40	1764	20	24095	159	15392	7027	222
PAYNESVILLE—Stearns County										
★ PAYNESVILLE AREA HEALTH CARE SYSTEM, 200 First Street West, Zip 56362–1496; tel. 320/243–3767; William M. LaCroix, Administrator (Total facility includes 64 beds in nursing home–type unit) **A**9 10 **F**1 7 8 11 14 15 19 21 22 24 26 27 32 33 34 35 36 39 40 42 44 46 48 52 58 62 64 65 67 71 **P**8 **Web address:** www.pahcs.com	16	10	94	688	68	16950	86	11607	5047	151

Hospital, Address, Telephone, Administrator, Approval, Facility, and Physician Codes, Health Care System, Network	Classi-fication Codes		Utilization Data					Expense (thousands) of dollars		
★ American Hospital Association (AHA) membership □ Joint Commission on Accreditation of Healthcare Organizations (JCAHO) accreditation + American Osteopathic Healthcare Association (AOHA) membership ○ American Osteopathic Association (AOA) accreditation △ Commission on Accreditation of Rehabilitation Facilities (CARF) accreditation Control codes 61, 63, 64, 71, 72 and 73 indicate hospitals listed by AOHA, but not registered by AHA. For definition of numerical codes, see page A4	Control	Service	Staffed Beds	Admissions	Census	Outpatient Visits	Births	Total	Payroll	Personnel

PERHAM—Otter Tail County

✠ PERHAM MEMORIAL HOSPITAL AND HOME, 665 Third Street S.W., Zip 56573–1199; tel. 218/346–4500; Chuck Hofius, Administrator (Total facility includes 102 beds in nursing home–type unit) (Nonreporting) **A**1 9 10	16	10	123	—	—	—	—	—	—	—

PIPESTONE—Pipestone County

PIPESTONE COUNTY MEDICAL CENTER, 911 Fifth Avenue S.W., Zip 56164; tel. 507/825–6125; Carl P. Vaagenes, Administrator (Total facility includes 43 beds in nursing home–type unit) (Nonreporting) **A**9 10 **S** Avera Health, Yankton, SD	13	10	76	—	—	—	—	—	—	—

PRINCETON—Sherburne County

✠ FAIRVIEW NORTHLAND REGIONAL HEALTH CARE, 911 Northland Drive, Zip 55371–2173; tel. 612/389–6300; Jeanne Lally, Senior Vice President and Administrator **A**1 9 10 **F**3 8 10 15 16 19 20 22 25 28 29 30 32 33 34 35 36 37 39 40 41 42 44 46 49 58 65 66 67 70 71 72 73 **P**6 **S** Fairview Hospital and Healthcare Services, Minneapolis, MN	23	10	40	2124	17	52879	484	—	—	316

RED WING—Goodhue County

✠ FAIRVIEW RED WING HOSPITAL, 1407 West Fourth Street, Zip 55066–2198; tel. 651/388–6721; Scott Wordelman, President and Chief Executive Officer **A**1 9 10 **F**2 3 7 8 15 16 17 19 22 26 28 29 30 31 32 33 34 35 36 37 39 40 41 42 44 45 46 49 51 53 54 55 58 62 63 64 65 67 70 71 73 **P**6 **S** Fairview Hospital and Healthcare Services, Minneapolis, MN **Web address:** www.fairview.org	23	10	68	2287	31	13571	375	—	—	—

REDLAKE—Beltrami County

✠ U.S. PUBLIC HEALTH SERVICE INDIAN HOSPITAL, Highway 1, Zip 56671; tel. 218/679–3912; Essimae Stevens, Service Unit Director (Nonreporting) **A**1 10 **S** U. S. Public Health Service Indian Health Service, Rockville, MD	47	10	23	—	—	—	—	—	—	—

REDWOOD FALLS—Redwood County

★ REDWOOD FALLS MUNICIPAL HOSPITAL, 100 Fallwood Road, Zip 56283–1828; tel. 507/637–2907; James E. Schulte, Administrator **A**9 10 **F**1 6 7 8 11 12 14 15 16 17 19 20 21 22 24 27 28 29 30 32 33 34 35 39 40 42 44 45 46 49 63 65 67 71 73	14	10	30	968	8	10959	127	6459	3202	97

ROBBINSDALE—Hennepin County

✠ △ NORTH MEMORIAL HEALTH CARE, 3300 Oakdale Avenue North, Zip 55422–2900; tel. 612/520–5200; Scott R. Anderson, President and Chief Executive Officer (Nonreporting) **A**1 2 3 5 7 9 10 **Web address:** www.northmemorial.com	23	10	371	—	—	—	—	—	—	—

ROCHESTER—Olmsted County

✠ OLMSTED MEDICAL CENTER, 1650 Fourth Street S.E., Zip 55904, Mailing Address: 210 Ninth Street S.E., Zip 55904; tel. 507/285–8485; G. Richard Geier, M.D., Chief Executive Officer (Nonreporting) **A**1 9 10	13	10	49	—	—	—	—	—	—	—
✠ ROCHESTER METHODIST HOSPITAL, 201 West Center Street, Zip 55902–3084; tel. 507/266–7890; John M. Panicek, Administrator (Nonreporting) **A**1 3 5 9 10 **S** Mayo Foundation, Rochester, MN	23	10	335	—	—	—	—	—	—	—
✠ △ SAINT MARYS HOSPITAL, 1216 Second Street S.W., Zip 55902–1970; tel. 507/255–5123; John M. Panicek, Administrator (Nonreporting) **A**1 3 5 7 8 9 10 **S** Mayo Foundation, Rochester, MN	23	10	797	—	—	—	—	—	—	—

ROSEAU—Roseau County

✠ ROSEAU AREA HOSPITAL AND HOMES, 715 Delmore Avenue, Zip 56751–1599; tel. 218/463–2500; David F. Hagen, President and Chief Executive Officer (Total facility includes 124 beds in nursing home–type unit) **A**1 9 10 **F**7 8 10 11 12 13 14 15 16 19 21 22 28 30 32 33 34 35 39 41 42 44 45 49 58 60 63 64 65 67 71 73 **P**5	23	10	161	1157	128	21152	231	14492	7876	271

SAINT CLOUD—Stearns County

✠ ST. CLOUD HOSPITAL, 1406 Sixth Avenue North, Zip 56303–0016; tel. 320/251–2700; John Frobenius, President and Chief Executive Officer (Total facility includes 291 beds in nursing home–type unit) **A**1 2 3 9 10 **F**1 2 3 4 6 7 8 10 11 12 13 14 15 16 17 18 19 21 22 23 26 27 28 30 31 32 33 34 35 36 37 38 39 40 41 42 43 44 45 46 48 49 51 52 53 54 55 56 57 58 59 60 61 62 63 64 65 67 70 71 72 73 74 **P**6	21	10	616	17310	428	109879	2331	171742	81218	2419
✠ VETERANS AFFAIRS MEDICAL CENTER, 4801 Eighth Street North, Zip 56303–2099; tel. 320/252–1670; Barry I. Bahl, Director (Total facility includes 220 beds in nursing home–type unit) **A**1 **F**1 3 6 8 12 19 20 22 26 30 33 34 35 39 41 44 45 46 49 51 52 54 56 57 58 59 64 65 67 71 73 74 **P**6 **S** Department of Veterans Affairs, Washington, DC	45	22	411	3000	384	138072	0	—	41244	827

SAINT JAMES—Watonwan County

ST. JAMES HEALTH SERVICES, 1207 Sixth Avenue South, Zip 56081–2415; tel. 507/375–3261; Lee Holter, Chief Executive Officer **A**9 10 **F**6 7 8 15 16 17 19 21 22 28 30 32 33 35 39 40 44 45 46 49 51 65 67 71 **P**6	23	10	24	383	4	27160	41	3553	1154	60

SAINT LOUIS PARK—Hennepin County

□ △ METHODIST HOSPITAL HEALTHSYSTEM MINNESOTA, 6500 Excelsior Boulevard, Zip 55426–4702, Mailing Address: Box 650, Minneapolis, Zip 55440–0650; tel. 612/993–5000; Mark Skubic, Vice President (Total facility includes 35 beds in nursing home–type unit) **A**1 2 3 5 7 9 10 **F**3 4 5 6 7 8 10 11 12 14 15 17 18 19 20 22 23 25 26 28 29 30 31 32 33 34 35 37 39 40 41 42 43 44 45 46 48 49 51 53 54 55 56 57 58 59 60 61 64 65 66 67 68 71 72 73 **P**6 **S** HealthSystem Minnesota, Saint Louis Park, MN	23	10	367	22780	281	233759	3096	178999	85243	1831

Hospital, Address, Telephone, Administrator, Approval, Facility, and Physician Codes, Health Care System, Network	Classification Codes		Utilization Data					Expense (thousands) of dollars		
★ American Hospital Association (AHA) membership □ Joint Commission on Accreditation of Healthcare Organizations (JCAHO) accreditation + American Osteopathic Healthcare Association (AOHA) membership ○ American Osteopathic Association (AOA) accreditation △ Commission on Accreditation of Rehabilitation Facilities (CARF) accreditation Control codes 61, 63, 64, 71, 72 and 73 indicate hospitals listed by AOHA, but not registered by AHA. For definition of numerical codes, see page A4	Control	Service	Staffed Beds	Admissions	Census	Outpatient Visits	Births	Total	Payroll	Personnel

SAINT PAUL—Ramsey County

⊠ CHILDREN'S HOSPITAL AND CLINICS, (PEDIATRIC), 345 North Smith Avenue, Zip 55102–2392; tel. 651/220–6000; Brock D. Nelson, Chief Executive Officer **A**1 3 5 9 10 **F**2 3 4 7 10 13 14 15 16 17 19 20 21 22 23 24 27 31 32 33 34 35 38 39 41 42 43 44 45 46 47 48 49 51 52 53 54 55 56 58 59 60 61 65 67 68 70 71 73 **P**1	23	50	105	5102	76	68875	0	76285	38691	777
□ △ GILLETTE CHILDREN'S SPECIALTY HEALTHCARE, (PEDIATRIC SPECIALTY), 200 University Avenue East, Zip 55101–2598; tel. 651/291–2848; Margaret Perryman, Chief Executive Officer **A**1 3 5 7 9 10 **F**5 14 15 16 17 19 20 21 22 25 34 35 39 41 44 45 46 47 48 49 50 63 65 66 67 70 71 73 **P**4 7 **Web address:** www.gillettechildrens.org	23	59	43	1115	20	36227	0	33152	13673	418
⊠ △ HEALTHEAST BETHESDA REHABILITATION HOSPITAL, (Formerly HealthEast Bethesda Lutheran Hospital and Rehabilitation Center), 559 Capitol Boulevard, Zip 55103–2101; tel. 651/232–2000; Scott Batulis, Vice President and Administrator **A**1 7 9 10 **F**1 2 3 4 5 6 7 8 10 11 12 13 14 15 16 17 18 19 20 21 22 23 24 25 26 27 28 29 30 31 32 33 34 35 36 37 38 39 40 41 42 43 44 45 46 47 48 49 50 51 52 53 54 55 56 57 58 59 60 61 62 63 64 65 66 67 68 70 71 72 73 74 **P**3 5 6 8 **S** HealthEast, Saint Paul, MN **Web address:** www.healtheast.org	23	46	129	1997	129	—	0	36485	19798	461
⊠ HEALTHEAST ST. JOSEPH'S HOSPITAL, 69 West Exchange Street, Zip 55102–1053; tel. 651/232–3000; Douglas P. Cropper, Vice President and Administrator (Nonreporting) **A**1 2 3 5 9 10 **S** HealthEast, Saint Paul, MN **Web address:** www.healtheast.org	23	10	292	—	—	—	—	—	—	—
⊠ △ REGIONS HOSPITAL, 640 Jackson Street, Zip 55101–2595; tel. 651/221–3456; Terry S. Finzen, President **A**1 2 3 5 7 8 9 10 **F**2 3 4 5 7 8 9 10 11 17 18 19 20 21 22 25 26 29 31 32 33 34 35 37 38 40 41 42 43 44 46 47 48 49 51 52 53 54 56 57 58 61 65 66 70 71 72 73 74 **P**3	23	10	390	20256	287	302011	1899	223585	108846	2471
⊠ UNITED HOSPITAL, 333 North Smith Street, Zip 55102–2389; tel. 651/220–8000; M. Barbara Balik, MSN, Ed.D., Administrator (Nonreporting) **A**1 2 3 5 9 10 **S** Allina Health System, Minneapolis, MN **Web address:** www.allina.com	23	10	386	—	—	—	—	—	—	—

SAINT PETER—Nicollet County

★ COMMUNITY HOSPITAL AND HEALTH CARE CENTER, 618 West Broadway, Zip 56082–1327; tel. 507/931–2200; Colleen A. Spike, Administrator (Total facility includes 85 beds in nursing home–type unit) (Nonreporting) **A**10 **S** Allina Health System, Minneapolis, MN	14	10	118	—	—	—	—	—	—	—
MINNESOTA SECURITY HOSPITAL See St. Peter Regional Treatment Center										
□ ST. PETER REGIONAL TREATMENT CENTER, (Includes Minnesota Security Hospital, Sheppard Drive, Zip 56082; tel. 507/931–7100), 100 Freeman Drive, Zip 56082–1599; tel. 507/931–7100; William L. Pedersen, Chief Executive Officer **A**1 9 10 **F**2 3 14 15 16 20 46 52 56 57 65 73	12	22	367	732	333	0	0	—	26430	668

SANDSTONE—Pine County

PINE MEDICAL CENTER, 109 Court Avenue South, Zip 55072–5120; tel. 320/245–2212; Michael D. Hedrix, Administrator (Total facility includes 86 beds in nursing home–type unit) **A**9 10 **F**8 12 15 16 17 19 21 22 30 41 42 44 49 51 64 65 71 **P**6 **S** Benedictine Health System, Duluth, MN	23	10	106	290	84	6203	1	6548	2960	133

SAUK CENTRE—Stearns County

★ ST. MICHAEL'S HOSPITAL, 425 North Elm Street, Zip 56378–1010; tel. 320/352–2221; Delano Christianson, Administrator (Nonreporting) **A**9 10	14	10	78	—	—	—	—	—	—	—

SHAKOPEE—Scott County

⊠ ST. FRANCIS REGIONAL MEDICAL CENTER, 1455 St. Francis Avenue, Zip 55379–3380; tel. 612/403–3000; Venetia Kudrle, Administrator (Nonreporting) **A**1 2 9 10 **S** Allina Health System, Minneapolis, MN	21	10	63	—	—	—	—	—	—	—

SLAYTON—Murray County

★ MURRAY COUNTY MEMORIAL HOSPITAL, 2042 Juniper Avenue, Zip 56172–1016; tel. 507/836–6111; Jerry Bobeldyk, Administrator **A**9 10 **F**8 15 19 30 33 35 44 60 71 **S** Sioux Valley Hospitals and Health System, Sioux Falls, SD	13	10	25	505	4	9595	0	3347	1422	59

SLEEPY EYE—Brown County

★ SLEEPY EYE MUNICIPAL HOSPITAL, 400 Fourth Avenue N.W., Zip 56085–1109; tel. 507/794–3571; Chad Cooper, Administrator **A**9 10 **F**7 8 11 12 15 17 19 20 22 28 30 33 34 35 36 37 39 40 41 44 49 65 67 71	14	10	18	464	5	4248	0	2689	1212	45

SPRING GROVE—Houston County

TWEETEN LUTHERAN HEALTH CARE CENTER, 125 Fifth Avenue S.E., Zip 55974–1309; tel. 507/498–3211; Greg Braun, Administrator (Total facility includes 71 beds in nursing home–type unit) **A**9 10 **F**3 12 14 15 16 17 20 26 27 28 29 30 32 33 34 36 39 41 44 45 46 48 49 61 62 64 65 66 71 73 74 **P**6	23	10	81	134	71	4074	0	3309	1931	108

SPRINGFIELD—Brown County

□ SPRINGFIELD MEDICAL CENTER–MAYO HEALTH SYSTEM, 625 North Jackson Avenue, Zip 56087–1714, Mailing Address: P.O. Box 146, Zip 56087–0146; tel. 507/723–6201; Scott Thoreson, Administrator **A**1 9 10 **F**7 8 15 16 19 22 28 30 32 39 40 41 44 49 58 64 65 71	23	10	24	469	5	7115	36	2566	1142	32

STAPLES—Wadena County

LAKEWOOD HEALTH SYSTEM, 401 East Prairie Avenue, Zip 56479–9415; tel. 218/894–0300; Tim Rice, President (Total facility includes 100 beds in nursing home–type unit) **A**9 10 **F**7 8 14 15 16 19 22 26 27 28 30 32 33 35 40 41 45 46 49 64 65 66 67 71 **P**7 **Web address:** www.lakewoodsystem.com	23	10	140	903	105	13891	124	11129	6557	305

Hospital, Address, Telephone, Administrator, Approval, Facility, and Physician Codes, Health Care System, Network	Classi-fication Codes		Utilization Data					Expense (thousands) of dollars		
★ American Hospital Association (AHA) membership □ Joint Commission on Accreditation of Healthcare Organizations (JCAHO) accreditation + American Osteopathic Healthcare Association (AOHA) membership ○ American Osteopathic Association (AOA) accreditation △ Commission on Accreditation of Rehabilitation Facilities (CARF) accreditation Control codes 61, 63, 64, 71, 72 and 73 indicate hospitals listed by AOHA, but not registered by AHA. For definition of numerical codes, see page A4	Control	Service	Staffed Beds	Admissions	Census	Outpatient Visits	Births	Total	Payroll	Personnel

STARBUCK—Pope County

★ MINNEWASKA DISTRICT HOSPITAL, 610 West Sixth Street, Zip 56381, Mailing Address: P.O. Box 160, Zip 56381–0160; tel. 320/239–2201; Roxann A. Wellman, Chief Executive Officer **A**9 10 **F**7 8 14 15 16 17 18 19 22 26 27 28 32 33 34 35 36 37 39 40 41 42 44 62 64 65 71	16	10	19	394	5	1806	9	2213	1020	49

STILLWATER—Washington County

✠ LAKEVIEW HOSPITAL, 927 West Churchill Street, Zip 55082–5930; tel. 651/439–5330; Jeffrey J. Robertson, Chief Executive Officer **A**1 6 9 10 **F**7 8 11 15 16 17 19 21 22 28 29 30 32 33 34 35 37 39 40 41 42 44 45 46 49 65 66 67 68 71 73 74 **P**5 **Web address:** www.lakeview.org	23	10	25	3342	25	28009	657	29705	12115	374

THIEF RIVER FALLS—Pennington County

✠ NORTHWEST MEDICAL CENTER, 120 LaBree Avenue South, Zip 56701–2819; tel. 218/681–4240; Richard A. Spyhalski, Chief Executive Officer (Total facility includes 90 beds in nursing home–type unit) **A**1 9 10 **F**7 8 15 16 17 19 21 22 28 29 30 34 35 36 37 39 40 42 44 45 46 49 52 53 54 55 56 57 58 60 64 65 66 67 71 73 74 **Web address:** www.nwmc.org	23	10	130	2070	112	14493	254	18269	10144	324

TRACY—Lyon County

★ TRACY AREA MEDICAL SERVICES, 251 Fifth Street East, Zip 56175–1536; tel. 507/629–3200; Thomas J. Quinlivan, Administrator **A**9 10 **F**7 8 11 14 15 16 17 19 22 26 28 29 30 31 32 33 34 35 37 39 40 41 42 44 45 48 49 51 54 58 62 64 65 66 71 74 **P**6 **S** Sioux Valley Hospitals and Health System, Sioux Falls, SD	14	10	18	408	3	16949	12	2520	1242	61

TWO HARBORS—Lake County

LAKE VIEW MEMORIAL HOSPITAL, 325 11th Avenue, Zip 55616–1298; tel. 218/834–7300; Brian J. Carlson, President and Chief Executive Officer (Total facility includes 50 beds in nursing home–type unit) **A**9 10 **F**3 7 14 15 40 44 49 64 65 70 71 73	23	10	66	420	56	8187	28	5348	2754	99

TYLER—Lincoln County

★ TYLER HEALTHCARE CENTER, 240 Willow Street, Zip 56178–0280; tel. 507/247–5521; James G. Blum, Administrator (Total facility includes 43 beds in nursing home–type unit) (Nonreporting) **A**9 10 **S** Avera Health, Yankton, SD	23	10	63	—	—	—	—	—	—	—

VIRGINIA—St. Louis County

✠ △ VIRGINIA REGIONAL MEDICAL CENTER, 901 Ninth Street North, Zip 55792–2398; tel. 218/741–3340; Kyle Hopstad, Administrator (Total facility includes 116 beds in nursing home–type unit) **A**1 7 9 10 **F**4 7 8 14 15 16 19 21 22 23 26 28 30 32 34 35 36 37 40 42 44 48 64 65 66 67 71 73 **S** Quorum Health Group/Quorum Health Resources, Inc., Brentwood, TN	14	10	199	3387	149	29159	283	31722	13202	411

WABASHA—Wabasha County

✠ ST. ELIZABETH HOSPITAL, 1200 Fifth Grand Boulevard West, Zip 55981–1098; tel. 651/565–4531; Thomas Crowley, President (Total facility includes 150 beds in nursing home–type unit) **A**1 9 10 **F**1 2 3 4 5 6 7 8 9 10 11 12 13 14 15 16 17 18 19 20 21 22 23 24 25 26 27 28 29 30 31 32 33 34 35 36 37 38 39 40 41 42 43 44 45 46 47 48 49 50 51 52 53 54 55 56 57 58 59 60 61 62 63 64 65 66 67 69 70 71 72 73 74 **P**1 2 3 4 5 6 8 **S** Marian Health System, Tulsa, OK	21	10	175	684	133	20618	76	10423	5386	165

WACONIA—Carver County

✠ RIDGEVIEW MEDICAL CENTER, 500 South Maple Street, Zip 55387–1791; tel. 612/442–2191; Robert Stevens, President and Chief Executive Officer **A**1 9 10 **F**7 8 10 11 14 15 19 20 21 22 25 28 29 30 32 33 34 35 37 39 40 41 42 44 45 46 49 60 61 63 65 66 67 70 71 72 73 74 **Web address:** www.ridgeviewmedical.org	14	10	90	5396	45	85946	959	43064	22579	512

WADENA—Wadena County

✠ TRI-COUNTY HOSPITAL, 415 Jefferson Street North, Zip 56482–1297; tel. 218/631–3510; Dennis C. Miley, Administrator **A**1 9 10 **F**7 8 11 14 15 16 17 19 21 22 26 28 30 32 33 34 36 37 39 40 41 42 44 45 49 53 54 58 64 65 66 67 71 73	23	10	30	1625	18	12549	164	12975	6237	173

WARREN—Marshall County

★ NORTH VALLEY HEALTH CENTER, 109 South Minnesota Street, Zip 56762–1499; tel. 218/745–4211; Jon Linnell, Administrator **A**9 10 **F**8 11 13 15 16 17 19 21 22 24 28 29 30 32 33 35 37 39 41 44 45 48 49 63 66 71 73 **P**4 7	23	10	20	310	3	1834	0	2883	1715	51

WASECA—Waseca County

✠ WASECA MEDICAL CENTER, 100 Fifth Avenue N.W., Zip 56093–2422; tel. 507/835–1210; Michael Milbrath, Administrator **A**1 9 10 **F**3 7 8 11 14 15 16 17 22 24 30 32 33 39 40 41 44 46 48 49 65 66 67 71 72 73 **P**1	23	10	24	527	3	10980	84	6528	3012	93

WESTBROOK—Cottonwood County

★ WESTBROOK HEALTH CENTER, 920 Bell Avenue, Zip 56183–0188, Mailing Address: P.O. Box 188, Zip 56183–0188; tel. 507/274–6121; Thomas J. Quinlivan, Administrator **A**9 10 **F**8 15 16 17 19 22 28 30 33 35 36 37 42 44 45 49 51 54 64 66 71 **P**3 5 **S** Sioux Valley Hospitals and Health System, Sioux Falls, SD	23	10	8	142	1	729	0	1424	712	23

WHEATON—Traverse County

WHEATON COMMUNITY HOSPITAL, 401 12th Street North, Zip 56296–1099; tel. 320/563–8226; James J. Talley, Administrator **A**9 10 **F**7 11 12 14 15 16 17 19 20 21 22 24 27 28 29 30 32 33 34 35 37 39 40 41 42 44 46 48 49 52 53 54 55 57 58 63 64 67 71 73 **P**5	14	10	25	893	6	10881	21	3487	1448	57

Hospital, Address, Telephone, Administrator, Approval, Facility, and Physician Codes, Health Care System, Network	Control	Service	Staffed Beds	Admissions	Census	Outpatient Visits	Births	Total	Payroll	Personnel

WILLMAR—Kandiyohi County

RICE MEMORIAL HOSPITAL, 301 Becker Avenue S.W., Zip 56201–3395; tel. 320/235–4543; Lawrence J. Massa, Chief Executive Officer (Total facility includes 86 beds in nursing home–type unit) **A**1 2 9 10 **F**7 8 15 19 21 22 23 30 32 33 34 35 37 40 41 42 44 45 49 52 53 54 55 56 57 58 60 63 64 65 67 71 73 | 14 | 10 | 198 | 5067 | 135 | 27563 | 817 | 47017 | 23055 | 539

WILLMAR REGIONAL TREATMENT CENTER, North Highway 71, Zip 56201–1128, Mailing Address: Box 1128, Zip 56201–1128; tel. 320/231–5100; Gregory G. Spartz, Chief Executive Officer **A**1 10 **F**1 2 3 6 12 14 15 16 17 18 19 20 21 22 25 26 27 29 32 34 35 41 44 45 46 52 53 54 55 56 57 58 59 65 67 71 73 **P**6 | 12 | 22 | 182 | 1013 | 150 | — | 0 | 29383 | 20080 | 486

WINDOM—Cottonwood County

★ WINDOM AREA HOSPITAL, Highways 60 and 71 North, Zip 56101, Mailing Address: P.O. Box 339, Zip 56101–0339; tel. 507/831–2400; J. Stephen Pautler, CHE, Administrator **A**9 10 **F**7 8 16 17 19 20 22 28 30 33 34 35 40 44 49 64 65 67 71 73 **P**6 **S** Sioux Valley Hospitals and Health System, Sioux Falls, SD | 14 | 10 | 35 | 970 | 9 | 14457 | 176 | 5712 | 2282 | 80

WINONA—Winona County

WINONA COMMUNITY MEMORIAL HOSPITAL, (Formerly Community Memorial Hospital and Convalescent and Rehabilitation Unit), 855 Mankato Avenue, Zip 55987–4894, Mailing Address: P.O. Box 5600, Zip 55987–0600; tel. 507/454–3650; Patrick M. Booth, President (Total facility includes 104 beds in nursing home–type unit) **A**1 9 10 **F**1 2 6 7 8 11 15 16 17 19 21 22 23 24 26 28 30 32 33 35 37 39 40 41 44 45 46 49 51 52 53 54 55 56 57 60 63 64 65 67 71 73 **P**8 | 23 | 10 | 186 | 3161 | 127 | — | 421 | 27352 | 14643 | 455

WORTHINGTON—Nobles County

WORTHINGTON REGIONAL HOSPITAL, 1018 Sixth Avenue, Zip 56187–2202, Mailing Address: P.O. Box 997, Zip 56187–0997; tel. 507/372–2941; Melvin J. Platt, Administrator **A**1 10 **F**7 14 15 17 19 21 22 27 30 32 33 35 36 37 39 40 41 44 45 49 52 53 65 66 71 73 **S** Sioux Valley Hospitals and Health System, Sioux Falls, SD | 14 | 10 | 66 | 2360 | 27 | 29121 | 317 | 14854 | 6943 | 194

WYOMING—Chisago County

FAIRVIEW LAKES REGIONAL MEDICAL CENTER, 5200 Fairview Boulevard, Zip 55092–8013; tel. 651/982–7000; Daniel K. Anderson, Senior Vice President and Administrator (Nonreporting) **A**1 9 10 **S** Fairview Hospital and Healthcare Services, Minneapolis, MN | 23 | 10 | 38 | — | — | — | — | — | — | —

ZUMBROTA—Goodhue County

ZUMBROTA HEALTH CARE, 383 West Fifth Street, Zip 55992–1699; tel. 507/732–5131; Daniel Will, Administrator (Total facility includes 70 beds in nursing home–type unit) (Nonreporting) **A**1 9 10 | 23 | 10 | 94 | — | — | — | — | — | — | —

MISSISSIPPI

Resident population 2,752 (in thousands)
Resident population in metro areas 34.9%
Birth rate per 1,000 population 15.3
65 years and over 12.2%
Percent of persons without health insurance 18.5%

Hospital, Address, Telephone, Administrator, Approval, Facility, and Physician Codes, Health Care System, Network	Classi-fication Codes		Utilization Data					Expense (thousands) of dollars		
★ American Hospital Association (AHA) membership □ Joint Commission on Accreditation of Healthcare Organizations (JCAHO) accreditation + American Osteopathic Healthcare Association (AOHA) membership ○ American Osteopathic Association (AOA) accreditation △ Commission on Accreditation of Rehabilitation Facilities (CARF) accreditation Control codes 61, 63, 64, 71, 72 and 73 indicate hospitals listed by AOHA, but not registered by AHA. For definition of numerical codes, see page A4	Control	Service	Staffed Beds	Admissions	Census	Outpatient Visits	Births	Total	Payroll	Personnel

Hospital	Control	Service	Staffed Beds	Admissions	Census	Outpatient Visits	Births	Total	Payroll	Personnel
ABERDEEN—Monroe County ABERDEEN–MONROE COUNTY HOSPITAL, 400 South Chestnut Street, Zip 39730–3335, Mailing Address: P.O. Box 747, Zip 39730–0747; tel. 601/369–2455; Frank Harrington, Administrator **A**9 10 **F**8 15 16 17 19 22 49 57 65 71 73 **P**5 6	15	10	27	668	14	7737	0	—	—	77
ACKERMAN—Choctaw County CHOCTAW COUNTY MEDICAL CENTER, 148 West Cherry Street, Zip 39735–0417, Mailing Address: P.O. Box 417, Zip 39735–0417; tel. 601/285–6235; Ouida Loper, Administrator (Total facility includes 66 beds in nursing home–type unit) **A**9 10 **F**19 22 57 64 71 **P**8	13	10	88	457	74	3458	0	—	—	126
AMORY—Monroe County ⊞ GILMORE MEMORIAL HOSPITAL, 1105 Earl Frye Boulevard, Zip 38821–0459, Mailing Address: P.O. Box 459, Zip 38821–0459; tel. 601/256–7111; Robert F. Letson, President and Chief Executive Officer **A**1 9 10 **F**7 8 11 12 15 16 19 22 23 24 35 37 38 39 40 41 44 47 48 49 64 65 71 73 74 **P**8	23	10	95	3479	47	43905	775	—	—	439
BATESVILLE—Panola County SOUTH PANOLA COMMUNITY HOSPITAL, 155 Keating Road, Zip 38606, Mailing Address: P.O. Box 433, Zip 38606–0433; tel. 601/563–5611; Richard W. Manning, Administrator **A**9 10 **F**7 19 21 22 40 44 65 71 73 **P**3 8	13	10	70	1354	24	15055	17	5545	3435	176
BAY SAINT LOUIS—Hancock County ⊞ HANCOCK MEDICAL CENTER, 149 Drinkwater Boulevard, Zip 39521–2790, Mailing Address: P.O. Box 2790, Zip 39521–2790; tel. 228/467–8600; Hal W. Leftwich, FACHE, Administrator **A**1 9 10 **F**7 8 11 14 15 16 17 19 21 22 23 35 37 39 40 41 44 45 46 48 49 65 71 73 74 **S** Quorum Health Group/Quorum Health Resources, Inc., Brentwood, TN **Web address:** www.hmc.org	13	10	66	3691	47	37623	289	27242	10970	385
BAY SPRINGS—Jasper County JASPER GENERAL HOSPITAL, (Includes Jasper County Nursing Home), 15 A South Sixth Street, Zip 39422–9738, Mailing Address: P.O. Box 527, Zip 39422–0527; tel. 601/764–2101; M. Kenneth Posey, FACHE, Administrator (Total facility includes 104 beds in nursing home–type unit) **A**9 10 **F**8 15 32 64 65 71	13	10	124	249	108	0	0	—	—	161
BELZONI—Humphreys County ★ HUMPHREYS COUNTY MEMORIAL HOSPITAL, 500 CCC Road, Zip 39038–3806, Mailing Address: P.O. Box 510, Zip 39038–0510; tel. 601/247–3831; Debra L. Griffin, Administrator **A**9 10 **F**7 14 15 16 21 22 24 27 44 57 73	13	10	28	1024	14	4914	1	4341	2919	96
BILOXI—Harrison County □ BILOXI REGIONAL MEDICAL CENTER, 150 Reynoir Street, Zip 39530–4199, Mailing Address: P.O. Box 128, Zip 39533–0128; tel. 228/432–1571; Joseph J. Mullany, Chief Executive Officer **A**1 2 9 10 **F**1 2 7 8 9 11 12 14 15 16 17 19 20 21 22 24 26 27 31 32 33 35 36 37 38 39 40 41 42 44 45 46 47 48 49 51 52 61 63 65 66 67 68 70 71 72 73 74 **P**5 8 **S** Health Management Associates, Naples, FL	33	10	153	6411	87	56536	618	36123	13751	445
⊞ GULF COAST MEDICAL CENTER, (Includes Gulf Oaks Hospital, 180–C Debuys Road, Zip 39531; tel. 601/388–0600), 180–A Debuys Road, Zip 39531–4405; tel. 228/388–6711; Gary L. Stokes, Chief Executive Officer **A**1 9 10 **F**2 3 7 8 11 12 15 16 17 19 21 22 31 32 33 35 37 39 40 42 44 46 52 53 54 55 56 57 58 64 65 67 69 71 73 **P**1 2 4 5 6 8 **S** TENET Healthcare Corporation, Santa Barbara, CA	33	10	189	4209	74	36393	149	34627	17604	535
⊞ VETERANS AFFAIRS MEDICAL CENTER, (Includes Veterans Affairs Medical Center, Gulfport Division, East Beach, Gulfport, Zip 39501; tel. 601/863–1972), 400 Veterans Avenue, Zip 39531–2410; tel. 228/388–5541; Julie A. Catellier, Director (Total facility includes 320 beds in nursing home–type unit) (Nonreporting) **A**1 2 3 5 9 **S** Department of Veterans Affairs, Washington, DC	45	10	510	—	—	—	—	—	—	—
BOONEVILLE—Prentiss County ⊞ BAPTIST MEMORIAL HOSPITAL–BOONEVILLE, 100 Hospital Street, Zip 38829–3359; tel. 601/720–5000; Pamela W. Roberts, Administrator **A**1 9 10 **F**7 8 11 15 16 17 19 20 21 22 24 35 37 39 40 44 45 46 51 52 54 57 65 67 71 73 **P**1 3 7 **S** Baptist Memorial Health Care Corporation, Memphis, TN	21	10	99	2383	37	24226	206	15142	4922	230
BRANDON—Rankin County ⊞ RANKIN MEDICAL CENTER, 350 Crossgates Boulevard, Zip 39042–2698; tel. 601/825–2811; Robert L. Hammond, Jr., Executive Director **A**1 2 9 10 **F**8 11 15 16 19 21 22 24 32 35 37 41 42 44 46 47 49 51 57 63 65 71 73 **P**8 **S** Health Management Associates, Naples, FL	33	10	105	3992	68	61865	0	—	—	468
BROOKHAVEN—Lincoln County ⊞ KING'S DAUGHTERS MEDICAL CENTER, 427 Highway 51 North, Zip 39601–2600, Mailing Address: P.O. Box 948, Zip 39602–0948; tel. 601/833–6011; Phillip L. Grady, Chief Executive Officer **A**1 9 10 **F**2 7 8 9 10 11 12 15 16 17 19 20 21 22 23 24 27 31 32 33 35 36 37 39 40 41 42 43 44 45 47 48 49 51 52 60 61 63 64 65 66 67 68 69 70 71 72 73 74 **P**3 **S** Quorum Health Group/Quorum Health Resources, Inc., Brentwood, TN **Web address:** www.kdmc.org	23	10	109	3793	52	37644	601	26729	11425	417

Hospital, Address, Telephone, Administrator, Approval, Facility, and Physician Codes, Health Care System, Network	Classi-fication Codes		Utilization Data					Expense (thousands) of dollars		
★ American Hospital Association (AHA) membership □ Joint Commission on Accreditation of Healthcare Organizations (JCAHO) accreditation + American Osteopathic Healthcare Association (AOHA) membership ○ American Osteopathic Association (AOA) accreditation △ Commission on Accreditation of Rehabilitation Facilities (CARF) accreditation Control codes 61, 63, 64, 71, 72 and 73 indicate hospitals listed by AOHA, but not registered by AHA. For definition of numerical codes, see page A4	Control	Service	Staffed Beds	Admissions	Census	Outpatient Visits	Births	Total	Payroll	Personnel

CALHOUN CITY—Calhoun County

HILLCREST HOSPITAL, 140 Burke–Calhoun City Road, Zip 38916–9690; tel. 601/628–6611; James P. Franklin, Administrator **A**9 10 **F**15 19 22 44 46 57 65 71	14	10	30	659	11	6311	0	3301	1287	60

CANTON—Madison County

MADISON COUNTY MEDICAL CENTER, Highway 16 East, Zip 39046, Mailing Address: P.O. Box 1607, Zip 39046–1607; tel. 601/859–1331; G. Wayne Schuler, Executive Director (Total facility includes 60 beds in nursing home–type unit) **A**9 10 **F**2 3 8 16 17 19 20 22 26 31 32 33 37 40 44 49 51 52 54 56 57 58 59 64 65 71 **P**6	13	10	127	1684	97	23271	344	11615	6982	263

CARTHAGE—Leake County

LEAKE MEMORIAL HOSPITAL, 300 Ellis Street, Zip 39051–0557, Mailing Address: P.O. Box 557, Zip 39051–0557; tel. 601/267–4511; Cindy Tadlock, Interim Administrator (Total facility includes 44 beds in nursing home–type unit) **A**9 10 **F**14 15 16 19 22 26 44 46 52 56 57 64 65 71 73 **P**6	33	10	76	1048	58	15897	0	—	—	140

CENTREVILLE—Wilkinson County

⊠ FIELD MEMORIAL COMMUNITY HOSPITAL, 270 West Main Street, Zip 39631, Mailing Address: P.O. Box 639, Zip 39631–0639; tel. 601/645–5221; Brock A. Slabach, Administrator **A**1 9 10 **F**7 8 12 16 17 19 20 22 31 32 39 40 41 44 45 59 61 64 65 71 **S** Quorum Health Group/Quorum Health Resources, Inc., Brentwood, TN	13	10	66	1452	16	13107	66	7539	3005	102

CHARLESTON—Tallahatchie County

TALLAHATCHIE GENERAL HOSPITAL, 201 South Market, Zip 38921–2236, Mailing Address: P.O. Box 230, Zip 38921–0230; tel. 601/647–5535; F. W. Ergle, Jr., Administrator (Total facility includes 61 beds in nursing home–type unit) **A**9 10 **F**2 19 20 22 46 48 64 65 71 **P**8	13	10	77	534	68	2666	0	—	—	145

CLARKSDALE—Coahoma County

□ NORTHWEST MISSISSIPPI REGIONAL MEDICAL CENTER, 1970 Hospital Drive, Zip 38614–7204, Mailing Address: P.O. Box 1218, Zip 38614–1218; tel. 601/627–2329; Roger C. LeDoux, Executive Director (Total facility includes 20 beds in nursing home–type unit) **A**1 5 9 10 **F**7 8 11 15 16 17 19 21 22 31 32 35 37 38 40 41 42 44 45 64 65 66 71 73 **S** Health Management Associates, Naples, FL	33	10	195	7230	129	23967	1155	—	—	544

CLEVELAND—Bolivar County

⊠ BOLIVAR MEDICAL CENTER, Highway 8 East, Zip 38732–9722, Mailing Address: P.O. Box 1380, Zip 38732–1380; tel. 601/846–0061; Robert L. Hawley, Jr., Chief Executive Officer (Total facility includes 34 beds in nursing home–type unit) **A**1 9 10 **F**7 8 11 12 17 19 21 22 24 27 33 37 38 39 40 42 44 45 46 48 49 63 64 65 66 67 68 70 71 73 **P**2 8 **S** Quorum Health Group/Quorum Health Resources, Inc., Brentwood, TN	13	10	144	5223	109	14770	718	24570	12797	434

COLLINS—Covington County

□ COVINGTON COUNTY HOSPITAL, Sixth and Holly Streets, Zip 39428, Mailing Address: P.O. Box 1149, Zip 39428–1149; tel. 601/765–6711; Irving Hitt, Administrator **A**1 9 10 **F**7 8 11 12 14 15 16 17 19 20 22 26 32 37 40 44 45 46 48 49 52 57 64 65 71 73	13	10	82	1697	31	18187	207	8188	4216	139

COLUMBIA—Marion County

MARION GENERAL HOSPITAL, 1560 Sumrall Road, Zip 39429–2654, Mailing Address: P.O. Box 630, Zip 39429–0630; tel. 601/736–6303; Jerry M. Howell, Chief Operating Officer **A**9 10 **F**1 2 7 8 9 10 11 12 15 17 19 20 21 22 23 27 31 32 33 35 36 37 38 40 41 43 44 46 47 48 49 51 52 60 61 65 66 69 71 72 73	13	10	79	2012	36	27470	0	—	—	218

COLUMBUS—Lowndes County

⊠ BAPTIST MEMORIAL HOSPITAL–GOLDEN TRIANGLE, 2520 Fifth Street North, Zip 39703–2095, Mailing Address: P.O. Box 1307, Zip 39701–1307; tel. 601/244–1000; Douglas L. Johnson, Administrator **A**1 9 10 **F**1 2 3 7 8 9 10 11 12 15 16 17 19 20 21 22 23 24 26 27 31 32 33 35 36 37 38 39 40 41 42 44 45 46 47 48 49 51 52 53 54 55 56 57 58 59 61 65 66 67 68 71 72 73 74 **P**3 5 **S** Baptist Memorial Health Care Corporation, Memphis, TN	21	10	328	8447	119	81647	1034	68315	23213	901
★ U. S. AIR FORCE HOSPITAL, 201 Independence, Suite 235, Zip 39701–5300; tel. 601/434–2297; Lieutenant Colonel Mark L. Allen, MSC, USAF, Administrator (Nonreporting) **S** Department of the Air Force, Bowling AFB, DC	41	10	7	—	—	—	—	—	—	—

CORINTH—Alcorn County

⊠ MAGNOLIA REGIONAL HEALTH CENTER, 611 Alcorn Drive, Zip 38834–9368; tel. 601/293–1000; Douglas Garner, Chief Executive Officer **A**1 9 10 **F**7 8 10 11 12 14 15 16 17 19 20 21 22 23 24 27 32 33 35 37 39 40 41 42 44 45 46 47 48 49 52 55 56 58 59 65 66 67 71 73 **P**5 **S** Quorum Health Group/Quorum Health Resources, Inc., Brentwood, TN	15	10	163	6040	101	58232	380	55441	19328	709

DE KALB—Kemper County

KEMPER COMMUNITY HOSPITAL, Highway 39 & 16 Intersection, Zip 39328, Mailing Address: P.O. Box 246, Zip 39328–0246; tel. 601/743–5851; Kathryn Kneibert, Administrator (Total facility includes 19 beds in nursing home–type unit) (Nonreporting) **A**9 10	33	10	24	—	—	—	—	—	—	—

DURANT—Holmes County

UNIVERSITY HOSPITAL AND CLINICS–DURANT, 713 North West Avenue, Zip 39063–3007; tel. 601/653–3081; Carol Scruggs, R.N., Interim Administrator **A**10 **F**15 16 20 22 46 48 65 71 73 **P**6	12	10	29	724	13	7223	0	—	—	76

Hospital, Address, Telephone, Administrator, Approval, Facility, and Physician Codes, Health Care System, Network	Classi-fication Codes		Utilization Data					Expense (thousands) of dollars		
	Control	Service	Staffed Beds	Admissions	Census	Outpatient Visits	Births	Total	Payroll	Personnel

★ American Hospital Association (AHA) membership
□ Joint Commission on Accreditation of Healthcare Organizations (JCAHO) accreditation
+ American Osteopathic Healthcare Association (AOHA) membership
○ American Osteopathic Association (AOA) accreditation
△ Commission on Accreditation of Rehabilitation Facilities (CARF) accreditation
Control codes 61, 63, 64, 71, 72 and 73 indicate hospitals listed by AOHA, but not registered by AHA. For definition of numerical codes, see page A4

EUPORA—Webster County										
WEBSTER HEALTH SERVICES, 500 Highway 9 South, Zip 39744; tel. 601/258–6221; Harold H. Whitaker, Sr., Administrator (Total facility includes 33 beds in nursing home–type unit) **A**9 10 **F**8 15 16 17 19 21 22 24 31 32 33 44 45 46 48 60 64 65 67 71 **P**4 **S** North Mississippi Health Services, Inc., Tupelo, MS	23	10	76	1936	55	10445	0	7635	3501	159
FAYETTE—Jefferson County										
JEFFERSON COUNTY HOSPITAL, 809 South Main Street, Zip 39069, Mailing Address: P.O. Box 577, Zip 39069–0577; tel. 601/786–3401; Virginia B. Robinson, Administrator **A**9 10 **F**14 15 16 22 26 45 52 64	13	10	27	659	8	3112	0	—	—	48
FOREST—Scott County										
LACKEY MEMORIAL HOSPITAL, 330 Broad Street, Zip 39074–0428, Mailing Address: P.O. Box 428, Zip 39074–0428; tel. 601/469–4151; Donna Riser, Administrator (Total facility includes 30 beds in nursing home–type unit) **A**10 **F**8 14 15 16 17 19 21 22 26 33 44 46 57 59 64 65 71 73 **P**5	23	10	74	1039	41	7861	0	—	—	139
GREENVILLE—Washington County										
✠ DELTA REGIONAL MEDICAL CENTER, 1400 East Union Street, Zip 38703–3246, Mailing Address: P.O. Box 5247, Zip 38704–5247; tel. 601/378–3783; Barton A. Hove, Chief Executive Officer **A**1 9 10 **F**2 3 7 8 9 10 11 16 17 19 20 21 22 23 31 32 33 35 37 39 40 42 43 44 45 49 52 63 65 67 69 71 73 **P**8 **S** Quorum Health Group/Quorum Health Resources, Inc., Brentwood, TN	13	10	159	6065	108	35746	611	47245	18154	713
✠ KING'S DAUGHTERS HOSPITAL, 300 Washington Avenue, Zip 38701–3614, Mailing Address: P.O. Box 1857, Zip 38702–1857; tel. 601/378–2020; Donald Joe Fisher, Administrator **A**1 9 10 **F**7 9 10 11 12 14 15 17 19 20 21 22 27 33 37 39 40 41 44 45 46 48 49 65 67 71 73 74	23	10	103	2889	37	54720	673	22280	10571	343
GREENWOOD—Leflore County										
✠ GREENWOOD LEFLORE HOSPITAL, 1401 River Road, Zip 38930–4030, Mailing Address: Drawer 1410, Zip 38935–1410; tel. 601/459–7000; Terrell M. Cobb, Executive Director **A**1 9 10 **F**7 8 11 14 16 17 19 20 21 22 23 26 27 31 35 37 39 40 42 44 45 46 52 63 65 67 68 71 73 74 **P**6 8	15	10	207	8186	125	115454	813	59767	24052	895
GRENADA—Grenada County										
✠ GRENADA LAKE MEDICAL CENTER, 960 Avent Drive, Zip 38901–5094; tel. 601/227–7101; Linda J. Gholston, Chief Executive Officer **A**1 9 10 **F**2 3 7 8 10 11 15 16 17 19 21 22 24 31 32 33 35 36 37 38 40 41 42 44 46 47 48 49 54 56 63 65 67 71 73 **P**8	13	10	127	6514	106	33126	773	—	—	578
GULFPORT—Harrison County										
□ BHC SAND HILL BEHAVIORAL HEALTHCARE, 11150 Highway 49 North, Zip 39503–4110; tel. 601/831–1700; David C. Bell, Chief Operating Officer **A**1 9 10 **F**2 3 12 16 17 20 22 46 52 53 55 56 58 59 65 67 **S** Behavioral Healthcare Corporation, Nashville, TN	33	22	60	801	28	0	0	—	—	160
✠ GARDEN PARK COMMUNITY HOSPITAL, 1520 Broad Avenue, Zip 39501, Mailing Address: P.O. Box 1240, Zip 39502–1240; tel. 228/864–4210; William E. Peaks, Chief Executive Officer **A**1 9 10 **F**2 7 8 10 11 12 14 15 16 17 19 20 21 22 23 24 26 27 32 33 35 37 39 40 41 42 43 44 46 48 49 50 51 52 60 61 63 64 65 66 67 69 71 72 73 74 **P**5 6 7 8 **S** Columbia/HCA Healthcare Corporation, Nashville, TN	33	10	97	3315	48	19892	359	—	—	244
✠ △ MEMORIAL HOSPITAL AT GULFPORT, 4500 13th Street, Zip 39501–2569, Mailing Address: P.O. Box 1810, Zip 39502–1810; tel. 228/867–4000; W. R. Burton, Administrator **A**1 2 7 9 10 **F**1 3 7 8 10 11 12 15 16 17 19 21 22 23 26 31 33 35 37 38 40 41 42 43 44 46 47 48 49 51 52 54 55 56 57 58 59 61 63 65 66 67 71 72 73 74 **P**3 8
Web address: www.mhg.com	15	10	313	14983	246	248564	1261	140550	56573	2044
VETERANS AFFAIRS MEDICAL CENTER, GULFPORT DIVISION See Veterans Affairs Medical Center, Biloxi										
HATTIESBURG—Forrest County										
✠ FORREST GENERAL HOSPITAL, 6051 U.S. Highway 49, Zip 39401–7243, Mailing Address: P.O. Box 16389, Zip 39404–6389; tel. 601/288–7000; William C. Oliver, President **A**1 2 9 10 **F**2 3 7 8 10 11 12 14 15 16 17 19 20 21 22 23 32 33 35 37 38 39 40 41 42 43 44 45 46 48 49 52 53 54 55 56 58 59 60 63 64 65 66 67 69 71 73 74 **P**8	13	10	537	25745	369	117584	2856	168652	66400	2848
✠ WESLEY MEDICAL CENTER, 5001 Hardy Street, Zip 39402, Mailing Address: P.O. Box 16509, Zip 39404–6509; tel. 601/268–8000; William K. Ray, President and Chief Executive Officer **A**1 9 10 **F**7 8 10 11 12 14 15 16 17 19 21 22 23 24 32 33 35 37 38 39 40 41 42 44 45 46 48 49 65 66 67 71 72 73 74 **P**8 **S** Quorum Health Group/Quorum Health Resources, Inc., Brentwood, TN	32	10	211	8646	126	79551	671	—	—	814
HAZLEHURST—Copiah County										
★ HARDY WILSON MEMORIAL HOSPITAL, 233 Magnolia Street, Zip 39083–2229, Mailing Address: P.O. Box 889, Zip 39083–0889; tel. 601/894–4541; L. Pat Moreland, Administrator **A**9 10 **F**8 19 20 22 27 31 40 44 49 52 57 65 71	13	10	49	1640	29	22389	192	—	—	139
HOLLY SPRINGS—Marshall County										
MARSHALL COUNTY MEDICAL CENTER, (Formerly Holly Springs Memorial Hospital), 1430 East Salem, Zip 38635, Mailing Address: P.O. Box 6000, Zip 38634–6000; tel. 601/252–1212; Bill Renick, Administrator **A**10 **F**12 15 16 17 19 22 26 27 33 39 44 46 51 52 57 58 59 65 67 71 73 **S** NetCare Health Systems, Inc., Nashville, TN	33	10	40	921	14	18608	0	5976	3934	100
HOUSTON—Chickasaw County										
□ TRACE REGIONAL HOSPITAL, Highway 8 East, Zip 38851, Mailing Address: P.O. Box 626, Zip 38851–0626; tel. 601/456–3700; Bristol Messer, Chief Executive Officer **A**1 9 10 **F**2 8 11 16 19 21 22 24 31 37 39 44 52 57 65 71 **P**6 **S** NetCare Health Systems, Inc., Nashville, TN	33	10	84	1686	22	13657	0	—	—	214

Hospital, Address, Telephone, Administrator, Approval, Facility, and Physician Codes, Health Care System, Network	Classi-fication Codes		Utilization Data					Expense (thousands) of dollars		
★ American Hospital Association (AHA) membership □ Joint Commission on Accreditation of Healthcare Organizations (JCAHO) accreditation + American Osteopathic Healthcare Association (AOHA) membership ○ American Osteopathic Association (AOA) accreditation △ Commission on Accreditation of Rehabilitation Facilities (CARF) accreditation Control codes 61, 63, 64, 71, 72 and 73 indicate hospitals listed by AOHA, but not registered by AHA. For definition of numerical codes, see page A4	Control	Service	Staffed Beds	Admissions	Census	Outpatient Visits	Births	Total	Payroll	Personnel

INDIANOLA—Sunflower County

⊠ SOUTH SUNFLOWER COUNTY HOSPITAL, 121 East Baker Street, Zip 38751–2498; tel. 601/887–5235; H. J. Blessitt, Administrator **A**1 9 10 **F**7 11 19 21 22 37 40 44 65 71 **P**1	13	10	69	2183	25	10856	407	—	—	155

IUKA—Tishomingo County

□ IUKA HOSPITAL, 1777 Curtis Drive, Zip 38852–1001, Mailing Address: P.O. Box 860, Zip 38852–0860; tel. 601/423–6051; Daniel Perryman, Administrator **A**1 9 10 **F**8 11 12 14 15 16 17 19 21 22 24 27 32 33 37 39 41 44 45 46 49 65 67 68 71 73 **P**3 5 6 **S** North Mississippi Health Services, Inc., Tupelo, MS	23	10	48	1926	26	23708	0	7927	3425	123

JACKSON—Hinds and Rankin County

BAPTIST BEHAVIORAL HEALTH See Mississippi Baptist Health Systems

⊠ CENTRAL MISSISSIPPI MEDICAL CENTER, (Formerly Methodist Healthcare), 1850 Chadwick Drive, Zip 39204–3479, Mailing Address: P.O. Box 59001, Zip 39204–9001; tel. 601/376–1000; Joseph J. Mullany, Chief Executive Officer **A**1 2 5 9 10 **F**7 8 10 11 14 15 16 17 19 21 22 23 31 32 35 37 38 39 40 42 43 44 45 46 47 48 49 51 52 54 58 63 64 65 67 71 73 74 **P**8 **S** Health Management Associates, Naples, FL	23	10	317	11014	202	64163	1276	—	—	1381
□ CHARTER BEHAVIORAL HEALTH SYSTEM, 3531 Lakeland Drive, Zip 39208–9794, Mailing Address: P.O. Box 4297, Zip 39296–4297; tel. 601/939–9030; Rick H. Gray, Ph.D., Chief Executive Officer **A**1 9 10 **F**2 3 15 22 52 53 54 55 56 58 65 **S** Magellan Health Services, Atlanta, GA	32	22	111	2164	81	0	0	—	—	193
⊠ G.V. MONTGOMERY VETERANS AFFAIRS MEDICAL CENTER, 1500 East Woodrow Wilson Drive, Zip 39216–5199; tel. 601/364–1201; Richard P. Miller, Director (Total facility includes 120 beds in nursing home–type unit) (Nonreporting) **A**1 2 3 5 8 **S** Department of Veterans Affairs, Washington, DC Web address: www.visn16.med.va.gov	45	10	443	—		—		—		

METHODIST HEALTHCARE See Central Mississippi Medical Center

⊠ MISSISSIPPI BAPTIST HEALTH SYSTEMS, (Formerly Mississippi Baptist Medical Center), (Includes Baptist Behavioral Health, 5354 I–55 South Frontage Road, Zip 39212; tel. 601/372–9788; D. Preston Smith, Jr., Administrator), 1225 North State Street, Zip 39202–2002; tel. 601/968–1000; Kurt W. Metzner, President and Chief Executive Officer (Nonreporting) **A**1 2 3 5 9 10	23	10	631	—		—		—		

MISSISSIPPI CRIPPLED CHILDREN'S T. AND T. CENTER See University Hospitals and Clinics, University of Mississippi Medical Center

⊠ MISSISSIPPI HOSPITAL RESTORATIVE CARE, (RESTORATIVE CARE), 1225 North State Street, Zip 39202–2097, Mailing Address: P.O. Box 23695, Zip 39225–3695; tel. 601/968–1000; Sallye M. Wilcox, Ph.D., R.N., Executive Director **A**1 **F**2 10 11 12 14 15 16 17 19 20 21 22 23 24 27 31 32 33 35 37 39 41 42 43 45 47 63 66 67 71 73 74 **P**7 8	23	49	25	200	17	0	0	6259	2311	73
⊠ MISSISSIPPI METHODIST HOSPITAL AND REHABILITATION CENTER, 1350 Woodrow Wilson Drive, Zip 39216–5198; tel. 601/981–2611; Mark A. Adams, President and Chief Executive Officer **A**1 5 9 10 **F**1 2 3 7 8 9 10 11 12 17 19 20 21 22 23 24 26 27 31 32 33 35 37 38 39 40 41 42 43 44 45 46 47 48 49 50 51 52 53 54 55 56 57 58 59 60 61 63 64 65 66 67 68 69 70 71 72 73 74 Web address: www.mmhcehab.org	23	46	121	1696	84	3571	0	36219	16308	576

RIVER OAKS EAST See Women's Hospital at River Oaks

⊠ RIVER OAKS HOSPITAL, 1030 River Oaks Drive, Zip 39208–9729, Mailing Address: P.O. Box 5100, Zip 39296–5100; tel. 601/932–1030; John J. Cleary, President and Chief Executive Officer **A**1 10 **F**7 8 11 12 15 16 19 20 21 22 27 33 37 38 39 40 41 42 44 45 46 47 52 63 65 71 73 74 **S** Health Management Associates, Naples, FL	33	10	109	6111	72	15453	1312	49497	19586	456
⊠ ST. DOMINIC–JACKSON MEMORIAL HOSPITAL, 969 Lakeland Drive, Zip 39216–4699; tel. 601/982–0121; Claude W. Harbarger, President **A**1 2 3 5 9 10 **F**2 3 8 10 11 12 16 17 19 20 23 24 31 33 35 37 39 42 43 44 45 48 49 51 52 53 54 55 56 57 58 59 63 65 67 71 72 73 **P**8 Web address: www.stdom.com	23	10	571	14204	320	236317	0	115337	49730	1928
⊠ UNIVERSITY HOSPITALS AND CLINICS, UNIVERSITY OF MISSISSIPPI MEDICAL CENTER, (Includes Mississippi Crippled Children's T. and T. Center, 777 Lakeland Drive, Zip 39216; tel. 601/366–6442; Larry E. Tuminello, Director), 2500 North State Street, Zip 39216–4505; tel. 601/984–4100; Frederick Woodrell, Director **A**1 2 3 5 8 9 10 **F**1 8 9 10 11 12 15 16 19 20 21 22 23 31 35 37 38 39 40 41 42 43 44 45 47 48 49 51 52 54 55 56 57 58 61 63 64 65 66 67 68 69 70 71 73 **P**6 **S** Quorum Health Group/Quorum Health Resources, Inc., Brentwood, TN	12	10	610	23155	437	179892	3264	216728	92897	2951
□ WOMEN'S HOSPITAL AT RIVER OAKS, (Formerly River Oaks East), 1026 North Flowood Drive, Zip 39208–9599, Mailing Address: P.O. Box 4546, Zip 39296–4546; tel. 601/932–1000; Carl Etter, Executive Director **A**1 9 10 **F**7 8 11 12 15 16 17 19 20 21 22 27 37 38 39 40 41 42 44 45 46 47 48 51 52 64 65 71 73 74 **S** Health Management Associates, Naples, FL	33	10	76	3087	36	304	1493	19870	8427	214

KEESLER AFB—Harrison County

⊠ U. S. AIR FORCE MEDICAL CENTER KEESLER, 301 Fisher Street, Room 1A132, Zip 39534–2519; tel. 228/377–6510; Colonel Randall W. Hartley, Administrator (Nonreporting) **A**1 2 3 5 **S** Department of the Air Force, Bowling AFB, DC Web address: www.81mdg06.keesler.af.mil/index.cgi	41	10	185	—		—		—		

KILMICHAEL—Montgomery County

KILMICHAEL HOSPITAL, 301 Lamar Avenue, Zip 39747–0188, Mailing Address: P.O. Box 188, Zip 39747–0188; tel. 601/262–4311; Clint Gee, III, Chief Executive Officer **A**9 10 **F**15 16 22 27 **P**8	13	10	19	606	9	3495	0	1940	523	50

Hospital, Address, Telephone, Administrator, Approval, Facility, and Physician Codes, Health Care System, Network	Classi-fication Codes		Utilization Data					Expense (thousands) of dollars		
★ American Hospital Association (AHA) membership □ Joint Commission on Accreditation of Healthcare Organizations (JCAHO) accreditation + American Osteopathic Healthcare Association (AOHA) membership ○ American Osteopathic Association (AOA) accreditation △ Commission on Accreditation of Rehabilitation Facilities (CARF) accreditation Control codes 61, 63, 64, 71, 72 and 73 indicate hospitals listed by AOHA, but not registered by AHA. For definition of numerical codes, see page A4	Control	Service	Staffed Beds	Admissions	Census	Outpatient Visits	Births	Total	Payroll	Personnel

KOSCIUSKO—Attala County

MONTFORT JONES MEMORIAL HOSPITAL, Highway 12 West, Zip 39090–3209, Mailing Address: Box 677, Zip 39090–0677; tel. 601/289–4311; Thomas Bland, Administrator **A**9 10 **F**2 7 8 11 15 19 20 21 22 26 33 37 40 44 47 48 49 57 65 71

| | 13 | 10 | 72 | 2190 | 40 | 19711 | 228 | — | — | 193 |

LAUREL—Jones County

⊞ SOUTH CENTRAL REGIONAL MEDICAL CENTER, (Includes South Central Extended Care, Ivy Street, Ellisville, Zip 39437; tel. 601/477–9159), 1220 Jefferson Street, Zip 39440–4374, Mailing Address: P.O. Box 607, Zip 39441–0607; tel. 601/426–4000; G. Douglas Higginbotham, Executive Director (Total facility includes 60 beds in nursing home–type unit) **A**1 9 10 **F**2 7 8 10 11 14 15 16 17 19 20 21 22 23 24 26 27 32 33 35 37 39 40 41 42 44 45 46 48 49 52 57 63 64 65 66 67 70 71 73 74 **P**3 8

| | 13 | 10 | 266 | 10137 | 200 | 77023 | 1011 | 53906 | 23942 | 1137 |

LEXINGTON—Holmes County

⊞ METHODIST HEALTHCARE MIDDLE MISSISSIPPI HOSPITAL, 239 Bowling Green Road, Zip 39095–9332; tel. 601/834–1321; James K. Greer, Administrator **A**1 10 **F**7 8 19 21 22 27 40 44 46 65 71 73 **S** Methodist Healthcare, Memphis, TN

| | 23 | 10 | 80 | 2145 | 32 | 15042 | 146 | 88364 | 36845 | 129 |

LOUISVILLE—Winston County

WINSTON MEDICAL CENTER, 562 East Main Street, Zip 39339–2742, Mailing Address: P.O. Box 967, Zip 39339–0967; tel. 601/773–6211; W. Dale Saulters, Administrator (Total facility includes 120 beds in nursing home–type unit) **A**9 10 **F**8 11 19 22 32 37 44 57 64 65 71 73

| | 23 | 10 | 185 | 1401 | 142 | 21125 | 0 | — | — | 213 |

LUCEDALE—George County

GEORGE COUNTY HOSPITAL, 859 Winter Street, Zip 39452–6603, Mailing Address: P.O. Box 607, Zip 39452–0607; tel. 601/947–3161; Paul A. Gardner, CPA, Administrator **A**9 10 **F**1 2 7 8 9 11 12 15 16 17 19 21 22 24 26 27 32 33 35 36 37 38 39 40 41 42 44 45 46 47 48 49 51 52 61 64 65 66 67 68 70 71 72 73 74 **P**8

| | 13 | 10 | 53 | 2592 | 25 | 27181 | 154 | 17144 | 8308 | 282 |

MACON—Noxubee County

★ NOXUBEE GENERAL HOSPITAL, 606 North Jefferson Street, Zip 39341–2236, Mailing Address: P.O. Box 480, Zip 39341–0480; tel. 601/726–4231; Arthur Nester, Jr., Administrator (Total facility includes 60 beds in nursing home–type unit) **A**9 10 **F**2 8 9 11 15 20 22 26 31 37 38 40 44 47 48 52 64 65 70 73

| | 13 | 10 | 109 | 1031 | 74 | 9670 | 0 | — | — | 133 |

MAGEE—Simpson County

MAGEE GENERAL HOSPITAL, 300 S.E. Third Avenue, Zip 39111–3698; tel. 601/849–5070; Althea H. Crumpton, Administrator **A**9 10 **F**19 21 22 31 44 49 57 63 65 71 73

| | 23 | 10 | 64 | 2277 | 35 | 29652 | 1 | 9322 | 3852 | 180 |

MAGNOLIA—Pike County

BEACHAM MEMORIAL HOSPITAL, 205 North Cherry Street, Zip 39652–2819; tel. 601/783–2351; Marilyn Speed, Administrator **A**9 10 **F**16 20 64 65 71

| | 23 | 10 | 37 | 1189 | 25 | 4475 | 0 | 3606 | 1701 | 72 |

MARKS—Quitman County

QUITMAN COUNTY HOSPITAL AND NURSING HOME, 340 Getwell Drive, Zip 38646–9785; tel. 601/326–8031; Richard E. Waller, M.D., Interim Administrator (Total facility includes 60 beds in nursing home–type unit) **A**9 10 **F**2 7 9 10 11 14 15 16 19 20 22 23 26 33 36 37 38 40 43 44 45 46 47 48 49 52 64 65 69 71 73

| | 33 | 10 | 96 | 1075 | 79 | 8238 | 0 | — | — | 164 |

MCCOMB—Pike County

⊞ SOUTHWEST MISSISSIPPI REGIONAL MEDICAL CENTER, 215 Marion Avenue, Zip 39648–2798, Mailing Address: P.O. Box 1307, Zip 39648–1307; tel. 601/249–5500; Norman M. Price, FACHE, Administrator **A**1 9 10 **F**7 8 10 11 15 16 17 19 20 21 22 31 32 35 37 40 42 44 45 46 48 49 60 63 64 65 67 70 71 73 74 **P**6

| | 15 | 10 | 130 | 6986 | 109 | 52253 | 846 | 51335 | 22583 | 898 |

MEADVILLE—Franklin County

FRANKLIN COUNTY MEMORIAL HOSPITAL, Hospital Road, Zip 39653, Mailing Address: P.O. Box 636, Zip 39653–0636; tel. 601/384–5801; Semmes Ross, Jr., Administrator **A**9 10 **F**2 12 14 15 17 19 22 26 27 44 45 48 49 52 57 59 65 67 71

| | 13 | 10 | 41 | 1194 | 24 | 3261 | 0 | 7368 | 2968 | 85 |

MENDENHALL—Simpson County

SIMPSON GENERAL HOSPITAL, 1842 Simpson Highway 149, Zip 39114–3592; tel. 601/847–2221; Wayne Harris, Administrator **A**9 10 **F**15 16 17 19 21 22 24 26 31 32 44 45 46 48 49 57 65 67 71 73 **P**5

| | 13 | 10 | 49 | 1335 | 26 | 9413 | 1 | 7715 | 3370 | 153 |

MERIDIAN—Lauderdale County

EAST MISSISSIPPI STATE HOSPITAL, 4555 Highland Park Drive, Zip 39307–5498, Mailing Address: Box 4128, West Station, Zip 39304–4128; tel. 601/482–6186; Ramiro J. Martinez, M.D., Director (Total facility includes 226 beds in nursing home–type unit) **F**2 12 14 15 16 20 26 46 52 53 57 64 65 73 **S** Mississippi State Department of Mental Health, Jackson, MS

| | 12 | 22 | 633 | 1348 | 575 | 0 | 0 | 40293 | 23671 | 1102 |

⊞ JEFF ANDERSON REGIONAL MEDICAL CENTER, 2124 14th Street, Zip 39301–4093; tel. 601/553–6000; Mark D. McPhail, Chief Executive Officer **A**1 9 10 **F**7 8 10 11 12 14 15 16 17 19 20 21 22 23 24 31 35 37 38 40 41 42 43 44 45 46 47 48 49 52 60 63 65 66 67 71 73 **P**7 8

| | 23 | 10 | 260 | 9056 | 138 | 43495 | 779 | — | — | 797 |

□ LAUREL WOOD CENTER, 5000 Highway 39 North, Zip 39303–1021; tel. 601/483–6211; John Chioco, Chief Executive Officer **A**1 9 10 **F**2 3 12 17 35 39 45 46 52 53 54 55 57 59 65 67 71 **P**6

| | 33 | 22 | 79 | 534 | 18 | 0 | 0 | — | — | 100 |

⊞ RILEY MEMORIAL HOSPITAL, 1102 21st Avenue, Zip 39301–4096, Mailing Address: P.O. Box 1810, Zip 39302–1810; tel. 601/693–2511; Carl Etter, Chief Executive Officer **A**1 9 10 **F**2 7 8 9 10 11 12 16 17 19 20 21 22 23 24 31 32 35 37 39 40 41 42 44 45 46 47 48 49 51 52 61 63 65 67 71 73 74 **P**7 8 **S** Health Management Associates, Naples, FL

| | 33 | 10 | 180 | 4591 | 100 | 11272 | 368 | 30009 | 14844 | 684 |

Hospital, Address, Telephone, Administrator, Approval, Facility, and Physician Codes, Health Care System, Network	Classification Codes		Utilization Data					Expense (thousands) of dollars		
	Control	Service	Staffed Beds	Admissions	Census	Outpatient Visits	Births	Total	Payroll	Personnel

★ American Hospital Association (AHA) membership
□ Joint Commission on Accreditation of Healthcare Organizations (JCAHO) accreditation
+ American Osteopathic Healthcare Association (AOHA) membership
○ American Osteopathic Association (AOA) accreditation
△ Commission on Accreditation of Rehabilitation Facilities (CARF) accreditation
Control codes 61, 63, 64, 71, 72 and 73 indicate hospitals listed by AOHA, but not registered by AHA. For definition of numerical codes, see page A4

Hospital	Control	Service	Staffed Beds	Admissions	Census	Outpatient Visits	Births	Total	Payroll	Personnel
⊠ RUSH FOUNDATION HOSPITAL, 1314 19th Avenue, Zip 39301–4195; tel. 601/483–0011; Wallace Strickland, Administrator **A**1 9 10 **F**1 2 7 8 9 10 11 12 15 16 17 19 20 21 22 23 24 26 27 31 32 33 36 37 38 39 40 41 42 43 44 45 46 47 48 49 51 52 60 61 63 64 65 66 67 68 69 71 72 73 74 **P**3 5 6 8	23	10	195	9650	132	21918	1046	65954	25146	1525
MONTICELLO—Lawrence County										
LAWRENCE COUNTY HOSPITAL, Highway 84 East, Zip 39654–0788, Mailing Address: P.O. Box 788, Zip 39654–0788; tel. 601/587–4051; Deborah Roberts, Administrator **A**9 10 **F**2 9 11 17 20 21 22 32 37 38 45 46 57 65 71	13	10	53	1279	26	5452	0	—	—	146
NATCHEZ—Adams County										
□ NATCHEZ COMMUNITY HOSPITAL, 129 Jefferson Davis Boulevard, Zip 39120–5100, Mailing Address: P.O. Box 1203, Zip 39121–1203; tel. 601/445–6200; Raymond Bane, Executive Director **A**1 9 10 **F**7 8 10 11 14 16 19 21 22 23 31 35 37 40 42 44 46 49 65 71 73 **P**1 6 8 **S** Health Management Associates, Naples, FL	33	10	101	3375	42	24751	530	—	—	252
⊠ NATCHEZ REGIONAL MEDICAL CENTER, Seargent S Prentiss Drive, Zip 39120, Mailing Address: P.O. Box 1488, Zip 39121–1488; tel. 601/443–2100; Karen A. Fiducia, Interim Chief Executive Officer **A**1 9 10 **F**7 8 11 12 14 15 16 17 19 21 22 33 35 37 38 39 40 41 42 44 45 48 49 63 65 66 67 71 73 74 **S** Quorum Health Group/Quorum Health Resources, Inc., Brentwood, TN	13	10	121	4508	66	29734	496	30248	13212	408
NEW ALBANY—Union County										
⊠ BAPTIST MEMORIAL HOSPITAL–UNION COUNTY, 200 Highway 30 West, Zip 38652–3197; tel. 601/538–7631; John Tompkins, Administrator **A**1 9 10 **F**7 8 11 12 15 17 19 20 21 22 32 35 37 39 40 44 45 46 48 49 63 64 65 67 71 73 74 **S** Baptist Memorial Health Care Corporation, Memphis, TN	21	10	153	5520	61	32356	978	26533	8200	342
OCEAN SPRINGS—Jackson County										
□ OCEAN SPRINGS HOSPITAL, 3109 Bienville Boulevard, Zip 39564–4361; tel. 228/818–1111; Dwight Rimes, Administrator **A**1 **F**2 7 8 10 11 12 14 15 16 17 19 20 21 22 23 27 31 32 33 35 37 39 40 41 42 43 44 47 48 52 63 64 65 67 71 **P**3 8 **S** Singing River Hospital System, Gautier, MS	13	10	124	5559	84	91315	432	—	—	566
OKOLONA—Chickasaw County										
★ OKOLONA COMMUNITY HOSPITAL, (Includes SHEARER–RICHARDSON MEMORIAL NURSING HOME), Rockwell Drive, Zip 38860–0420, Mailing Address: P.O. Box 420, Zip 38860–0420; tel. 601/447–3311; Brenda Wise, Administrator (Total facility includes 66 beds in nursing home–type unit) **A**9 10 **F**20 23 31 32 33 35 48 60 64 65 71 73	23	10	76	129	68	0	0	2412	1239	75
OLIVE BRANCH—De Soto County										
□ CHARTER PARKWOOD BEHAVIORAL HEALTH SYSTEM, 8135 Goodman Road, Zip 38654–2199; tel. 601/895–4900; M. Andrew Mayo, Chief Executive Officer **A**1 10 **F**2 3 8 11 12 15 16 17 22 24 27 33 35 37 39 42 44 47 50 52 53 54 55 56 58 59 63 64 65 67 71 72 **S** Magellan Health Services, Atlanta, GA	33	22	66	1227	42	0	0	—	—	71
OXFORD—Lafayette County										
⊠ BAPTIST MEMORIAL HOSPITAL–NORTH MISSISSIPPI, 2301 South Lamar Boulevard, Zip 38655–5338, Mailing Address: P.O. Box 946, Zip 38655–0946; tel. 601/232–8100; James Hahn, Administrator **A**1 9 10 **F**7 8 10 11 12 14 15 16 17 19 20 21 22 23 24 32 33 35 37 40 41 42 43 44 45 46 47 48 52 58 64 65 66 67 71 72 73 74 **P**3 4 5 7 **S** Baptist Memorial Health Care Corporation, Memphis, TN	23	10	204	9729	149	56075	847	—	—	752
PASCAGOULA—Jackson County										
⊠ SINGING RIVER HOSPITAL, 2809 Denny Avenue, Zip 39581–5301; tel. 228/809–5000; Lynn Truelove, Administrator **A**1 2 9 10 **F**2 3 7 8 10 11 12 14 15 16 17 19 20 21 22 23 27 31 32 33 35 37 39 40 41 42 43 44 47 48 52 54 55 56 57 63 64 65 67 71 **P**3 8 **S** Singing River Hospital System, Gautier, MS Web address: www.srhshealth.com	13	10	282	12399	207	190809	950	—	—	1689
PHILADELPHIA—Neshoba County										
⊠ CHOCTAW HEALTH CENTER, Highway 16 West, Zip 39350, Mailing Address: Route 7, Box R–50, Zip 39350; tel. 601/656–2211; James D. Wallace, Executive Director (Nonreporting) **A**1 10 **S** U. S. Public Health Service Indian Health Service, Rockville, MD	47	10	35	—						
★ NESHOBA COUNTY GENERAL HOSPITAL, 1001 Holland Avenue, Zip 39350–2161, Mailing Address: P.O. Box 648, Zip 39350–0648; tel. 601/663–1200; Lawrence Graeber, Administrator (Total facility includes 118 beds in nursing home–type unit) **A**9 10 **F**8 19 21 22 26 27 31 33 35 44 48 57 64 65 71 73 **S** Quorum Health Group/Quorum Health Resources, Inc., Brentwood, TN	13	10	192	2112	148	32713	1	—	—	322
PICAYUNE—Pearl River County										
★ CROSBY MEMORIAL HOSPITAL, 801 Goodyear Boulevard, Zip 39466–3221, Mailing Address: P.O. Box 909, Zip 39466–0909; tel. 601/798–4711; Fred Woody, Administrator **A**9 10 **F**2 7 8 11 14 15 16 17 19 20 21 22 24 26 27 31 32 33 35 36 37 39 40 41 42 44 45 48 49 52 55 57 58 65 66 67 68 71 73 74 **P**4 **S** New American Healthcare Corporation, Brentwood, TN Web address: www.CROSBYHOSPITAL.COM	23	10	71	2842	38	32890	329	16011	6905	242
PONTOTOC—Pontotoc County										
PONTOTOC HOSPITAL AND EXTENDED CARE FACILITY, 176 South Main Street, Zip 38863–3311, Mailing Address: P.O. Box 790, Zip 38863–0790; tel. 601/489–5510; Fred B. Hood, Administrator (Total facility includes 44 beds in nursing home–type unit) **A**9 10 **F**8 15 16 17 20 22 27 32 33 36 39 45 46 48 49 64 65 67 71 73 **P**3 8 **S** North Mississippi Health Services, Inc., Tupelo, MS	23	10	71	658	59	12253	0	7289	3024	129

Hospital, Address, Telephone, Administrator, Approval, Facility, and Physician Codes, Health Care System, Network	Classi-fication Codes		Utilization Data					Expense (thousands) of dollars		
★ American Hospital Association (AHA) membership □ Joint Commission on Accreditation of Healthcare Organizations (JCAHO) accreditation + American Osteopathic Healthcare Association (AOHA) membership ○ American Osteopathic Association (AOA) accreditation △ Commission on Accreditation of Rehabilitation Facilities (CARF) accreditation Control codes 61, 63, 64, 71, 72 and 73 indicate hospitals listed by AOHA, but not registered by AHA. For definition of numerical codes, see page A4	Control	Service	Staffed Beds	Admissions	Census	Outpatient Visits	Births	Total	Payroll	Personnel

POPLARVILLE—Pearl River County

PEARL RIVER COUNTY HOSPITAL, 305 West Moody Street, Zip 39470–7242, Mailing Address: P.O. Box 392, Zip 39470–0392; tel. 601/795–4543; Dorothy C. Bilbo, Administrator (Total facility includes 66 beds in nursing home–type unit) **A**9 10 **F**15 16 46 48 49 64 65 71 73

| | 13 | 10 | 90 | 695 | 74 | 0 | 0 | — | — | 207 |

PORT GIBSON—Claiborne County

★ CLAIBORNE COUNTY HOSPITAL, 123 McComb Avenue, Zip 39150–2915, Mailing Address: P.O. Box 1004, Zip 39150–1004; tel. 601/437–5141; Wanda C. Fleming, Administrator and Chief Executive Officer **A**9 10 **F**16 17 19 22 35 40 44 45 46 49 52 64 65 71 73

| | 13 | 10 | 32 | 710 | 11 | 3510 | 3 | 3426 | 1155 | 73 |

PRENTISS—Jefferson Davis County

PRENTISS REGIONAL HOSPITAL AND EXTENDED CARE FACILITIES, 1102 Rose Street, Zip 39474; tel. 601/792–4276; Mike Boleware, Administrator (Total facility includes 60 beds in nursing home–type unit) **A**9 10 **F**8 11 12 14 15 16 17 19 22 26 45 46 57 64 65 71

| | 23 | 10 | 101 | 981 | 73 | 13417 | 1 | — | — | 173 |

QUITMAN—Clarke County

★ H. C. WATKINS MEMORIAL HOSPITAL, 605 South Archusa Avenue, Zip 39355–2398; tel. 601/776–6925; Thomas G. Bartlett, President and Chief Executive Officer (Total facility includes 11 beds in nursing home–type unit) **A**9 10 **F**2 8 11 19 21 22 35 37 44 48 49 52 64 65 71 73 **S** Quorum Health Group/Quorum Health Resources, Inc., Brentwood, TN

| | 23 | 10 | 43 | 1177 | 32 | 7131 | 0 | — | — | 140 |

RICHTON—Perry County

★ PERRY COUNTY GENERAL HOSPITAL, 206 Bay Avenue, Zip 39476, Mailing Address: P.O. Drawer Y, Zip 39476; tel. 601/788–6316; Bobby Welborn, Administrator (Total facility includes 66 beds in nursing home–type unit) **A**9 10 **F**15 17 20 22 32 44 48 57 64 65 71

| | 13 | 10 | 88 | 511 | 75 | 4402 | 0 | 4736 | 2408 | 144 |

RIPLEY—Tippah County

⊞ TIPPAH COUNTY HOSPITAL, 1005 City Avenue North, Zip 38663–0499; tel. 601/837–9221; Jerry Green, Administrator (Total facility includes 40 beds in nursing home–type unit) **A**1 9 10 **F**8 11 15 16 19 21 22 24 26 31 37 44 47 52 64 65 71 **S** Baptist Memorial Health Care Corporation, Memphis, TN

| | 13 | 10 | 110 | 1541 | 59 | 19738 | 0 | 8692 | 4507 | 203 |

RULEVILLE—Sunflower County

NORTH SUNFLOWER COUNTY HOSPITAL, 840 North Oak Avenue, Zip 38771–0369, Mailing Address: P.O. Box 369, Zip 38771–0369; tel. 601/756–2711; Robert Crook, Administrator (Total facility includes 42 beds in nursing home–type unit) **A**9 10 **F**2 3 15 16 22 32 40 44 52 57 64 65 71 **P**8

| | 13 | 10 | 86 | 1123 | 66 | 4782 | 17 | — | — | 192 |

SENATOBIA—Tate County

□ SENATOBIA COMMUNITY HOSPITAL, 401 Getwell Drive, Zip 38668–2213, Mailing Address: P.O. Box 648, Zip 38668–0648; tel. 601/562–3100; Dan Aranda, Chief Executive Officer **A**1 9 10 **F**7 8 12 16 19 20 22 26 31 33 40 44 45 46 48 52 65 71 **S** Paracelsus Healthcare Corporation, Houston, TX

| | 33 | 10 | 52 | 1167 | 16 | 16177 | 85 | 6841 | 2761 | 106 |

SOUTHAVEN—De Soto County

⊞ △ BAPTIST MEMORIAL HOSPITAL–DESOTO, 7601 Southcrest Parkway, Zip 38671–4742; tel. 601/349–4000; Melvin E. Walker, Administrator (Total facility includes 120 beds in nursing home–type unit) **A**1 7 9 10 **F**2 3 7 8 10 11 12 14 15 16 17 19 20 21 22 23 24 26 27 31 32 33 35 37 38 39 40 41 42 43 44 45 46 48 49 51 52 53 54 55 56 57 58 59 60 63 64 65 66 67 69 71 72 73 74 **P**1 3 8 **S** Baptist Memorial Health Care Corporation, Memphis, TN

| | 23 | 10 | 260 | 6428 | 187 | 44617 | 965 | 35259 | 13912 | 660 |

STARKVILLE—Oktibbeha County

⊞ OKTIBBEHA COUNTY HOSPITAL, 400 Hospital Road, Zip 39759–2163, Mailing Address: Drawer 1506, Zip 39760–1506; tel. 601/323–4320; Arthur C. Kelly, Administrator and Chief Executive Officer **A**1 9 10 **F**7 8 11 12 14 15 16 17 19 20 21 22 24 31 33 35 37 40 41 44 46 47 48 49 52 63 65 66 67 69 71 73

| | 13 | 10 | 96 | 3826 | 48 | 62593 | 1094 | 24225 | 11948 | 443 |

TUPELO—Lee County

□ △ NORTH MISSISSIPPI MEDICAL CENTER, 830 South Gloster Street, Zip 38801–4934; tel. 601/841–3000; Jeffrey B. Barber, Dr.PH, President and Chief Executive Officer (Total facility includes 100 beds in nursing home–type unit) **A**1 2 5 7 9 10 **F**2 3 7 8 10 11 12 14 15 16 17 19 21 22 23 24 26 32 33 35 37 38 39 40 41 42 43 44 45 46 47 48 49 51 52 53 55 57 58 59 60 63 64 65 66 67 71 73 74 **P**3 5 6 **S** North Mississippi Health Services, Inc., Tupelo, MS

| | 23 | 10 | 724 | 27399 | 531 | 108298 | 2327 | 240925 | 98734 | 3926 |

TYLERTOWN—Walthall County

WALTHALL COUNTY GENERAL HOSPITAL, 100 Hospital Drive, Zip 39667–2099; tel. 601/876–2122; Jimmy Graves, Administrator **A**9 10 **F**8 15 19 20 22 32 35 44 46 49 52 57 65 71 73

| | 13 | 10 | 49 | 1778 | 28 | 17412 | 0 | 7655 | 3429 | 128 |

UNION—Newton County

LAIRD HOSPITAL, 25117 Highway 15, Zip 39365–9099; tel. 601/774–8214; Georgia Buchanan, President **A**9 10 **F**8 19 21 22 32 35 37 41 44 46 48 49 63 65 71 73

| | 33 | 10 | 50 | 1730 | 27 | 14550 | 2 | 18579 | 10438 | 242 |

VICKSBURG—Warren County

⊞ PARKVIEW REGIONAL MEDICAL CENTER, 100 McAuley Drive, Zip 39180–2897, Mailing Address: P.O. Box 590, Zip 39181–0590; tel. 601/631–2131; Florence Jones, Administrator (Total facility includes 17 beds in nursing home–type unit) **A**1 2 9 10 **F**2 3 7 8 10 11 12 19 21 22 23 26 32 33 35 36 37 38 39 40 42 44 45 46 49 52 53 54 55 56 57 58 59 64 65 71 73 74 **P**1 2 **S** Quorum Health Group/Quorum Health Resources, Inc., Brentwood, TN

| | 33 | 10 | 197 | 6911 | 118 | 17325 | 980 | 47303 | 16333 | 607 |

⊞ VICKSBURG MEDICAL CENTER, 1111 North Frontage Road, Zip 39180; tel. 601/619–3800; Rob Followell, Chief Operating Officer and Administrator **A**1 9 10 **F**1 2 3 7 8 9 10 11 12 14 16 17 19 20 21 22 23 24 26 27 31 32 33 35 36 37 38 39 40 41 42 43 44 45 46 47 48 49 51 52 53 54 55 56 57 58 59 60 61 64 65 66 67 68 69 71 72 73 74 **P**7 **S** Columbia/HCA Healthcare Corporation, Nashville, TN

| | 33 | 10 | 154 | 4121 | 95 | 32036 | 336 | 26164 | 10678 | 383 |

Hospital, Address, Telephone, Administrator, Approval, Facility, and Physician Codes, Health Care System, Network	Classi-fication Codes		Utilization Data					Expense (thousands) of dollars		
★ American Hospital Association (AHA) membership □ Joint Commission on Accreditation of Healthcare Organizations (JCAHO) accreditation + American Osteopathic Healthcare Association (AOHA) membership ○ American Osteopathic Association (AOA) accreditation △ Commission on Accreditation of Rehabilitation Facilities (CARF) accreditation Control codes 61, 63, 64, 71, 72 and 73 indicate hospitals listed by AOHA, but not registered by AHA. For definition of numerical codes, see page A4	Control	Service	Staffed Beds	Admissions	Census	Outpatient Visits	Births	Total	Payroll	Personnel

WATER VALLEY—Yalobusha County

YALOBUSHA GENERAL HOSPITAL, Highway 7 South, Zip 38965, Mailing Address: P.O. Box 728, Zip 38965–0728; tel. 601/473–1411; John R. Jones, Administrator (Total facility includes 65 beds in nursing home–type unit) **A**9 10 **F**12 14 19 20 39 41 48 64 65 71 73 **P**4 7

| | 13 | 10 | 91 | 747 | 73 | 286 | 0 | — | — | 133 |

WAYNESBORO—Wayne County

WAYNE GENERAL HOSPITAL, 950 Matthew Drive, Zip 39367–2590, Mailing Address: P.O. Box 1249, Zip 39367–1249; tel. 601/735–5151; Donald Hemeter, Administrator **A**9 10 **F**7 8 15 17 19 20 21 22 24 31 32 33 37 39 40 44 45 47 49 63 65 71 73

| | 13 | 10 | 80 | 3920 | 52 | 33739 | 337 | — | — | 351 |

WEST POINT—Clay County

CLAY COUNTY MEDICAL CENTER, 835 Medical Center Drive, Zip 39773–9320; tel. 601/495–2300; David M. Reid, Administrator **A**9 10 **F**7 8 11 15 16 17 19 20 22 24 33 37 39 40 41 42 44 45 46 48 49 51 61 63 65 66 67 71 73 74 **S** North Mississippi Health Services, Inc., Tupelo, MS

| | 23 | 10 | 60 | 4065 | 38 | 34986 | 423 | 14478 | 6662 | 219 |

WHITFIELD—Rankin County

⊞ MISSISSIPPI STATE HOSPITAL, (Includes Whitfield Medical Surgical Hospital, Oak Circle, Zip 39193; tel. 601/351–8023), Zip 39193–0157; tel. 601/351–8000; James G. Chastain, Director (Total facility includes 451 beds in nursing home–type unit) **A**1 10 **F**2 7 8 9 10 11 12 15 17 19 20 21 22 23 27 31 35 37 38 39 40 41 42 43 44 45 46 47 48 49 52 53 54 55 56 57 58 59 60 61 64 65 66 68 69 71 73 74 **P**1 **S** Mississippi State Department of Mental Health, Jackson, MS

| | 12 | 22 | 1299 | 1734 | 1230 | 3873 | 0 | — | — | 1901 |

WIGGINS—Stone County

STONE COUNTY HOSPITAL, 1434 East Central Avenue, Zip 39577; tel. 601/928–6600; Regina Moore, Interim Chief Executive Officer **A**9 10 **F**8 14 15 16 17 19 21 22 33 37 41 44 45 49 65 71 73 **S** NetCare Health Systems, Inc., Nashville, TN

| | 33 | 10 | 50 | 1289 | 15 | 11957 | 0 | — | — | 130 |

WINONA—Montgomery County

TYLER HOLMES MEMORIAL HOSPITAL, 409 Tyler Holmes Drive, Zip 38967–1599; tel. 601/283–4114; Gregory S. Mullen, Administrator **A**9 10 **F**15 16 17 19 21 22 26 31 32 33 36 40 44 46 52 57 61 65 71 **P**8

| | 13 | 10 | 49 | 1206 | 24 | 15716 | 41 | 7565 | 3041 | 153 |

YAZOO CITY—Yazoo County

KING'S DAUGHTERS HOSPITAL, 823 Grand Avenue, Zip 39194–3233; tel. 601/746–2261; Noel W. Hart, Administrator **A**9 10 **F**8 11 14 16 19 20 21 22 24 31 36 37 44 46 65 71 73

| | 23 | 10 | 51 | 1726 | 32 | 33737 | 0 | 10628 | — | 175 |

MISSOURI

Resident population 5,439 (in thousands)
Resident population in metro areas 67.0%
Birth rate per 1,000 population 13.7
65 years and over 13.7%
Percent of persons without health insurance 13.2%

Hospital, Address, Telephone, Administrator, Approval, Facility, and Physician Codes, Health Care System, Network	Classi-fication Codes		Utilization Data					Expense (thousands) of dollars		
★ American Hospital Association (AHA) membership ☐ Joint Commission on Accreditation of Healthcare Organizations (JCAHO) accreditation + American Osteopathic Healthcare Association (AOHA) membership ○ American Osteopathic Association (AOA) accreditation △ Commission on Accreditation of Rehabilitation Facilities (CARF) accreditation Control codes 61, 63, 64, 71, 72 and 73 indicate hospitals listed by AOHA, but not registered by AHA. For definition of numerical codes, see page A4	Control	Service	Staffed Beds	Admissions	Census	Outpatient Visits	Births	Total	Payroll	Personnel

ALBANY—Gentry County
★ GENTRY COUNTY MEMORIAL HOSPITAL, 705 North College Street, Zip 64402–1499; tel. 660/726–3941; John W. Richmond, President and Chief Executive Officer (Total facility includes 10 beds in nursing home–type unit) **A**9 10 **F**8 12 15 16 17 19 20 21 22 26 28 29 30 32 33 34 35 37 41 42 44 45 46 49 51 61 63 64 65 66 67 71 73 74 **P**6
Web address: www.gcmh.org

| | | 23 | 10 | 35 | 968 | 17 | 12566 | 0 | 6014 | 2907 | 112 |

APPLETON CITY—St. Clair County
ELLETT MEMORIAL HOSPITAL, 610 North Ohio Avenue, Zip 64724–1609; tel. 660/476–2111; Sandy Morlan, Administrator **A**9 10 **F**15 16 19 22 29 35 41 44 49 65 71 **P**5

| | | 16 | 10 | 25 | 424 | 5 | 2328 | 0 | 1708 | 905 | 45 |

AURORA—Lawrence County
AURORA COMMUNITY HOSPITAL, 500 Porter Street, Zip 65605–2399; tel. 417/678–2122; Don Buchanan, Chief Operating Officer **A**10 **F**7 8 11 12 15 17 19 21 22 24 27 28 29 30 32 34 36 37 39 40 41 44 45 46 49 64 65 67 71 73 **P**6

| | | 14 | 10 | 31 | 1478 | 14 | 21412 | 287 | 9963 | 5266 | 194 |

BELTON—Cass County
★ RESEARCH BELTON HOSPITAL, 17065 South 71 Highway, Zip 64012–2165; tel. 816/348–1200; Daniel F. Sheehan, Administrator (Total facility includes 7 beds in nursing home–type unit) **A**9 **F**1 2 3 4 5 6 7 8 9 10 11 12 13 14 15 16 17 18 19 20 21 22 23 24 26 28 29 30 31 32 33 34 35 37 38 39 40 41 42 43 44 46 47 48 49 52 53 54 55 56 57 58 59 60 61 63 64 65 69 70 71 73 74 **P**5 8 **S** Health Midwest, Kansas City, MO
Web address: www.healthmidwest.org/hospitals/rbh/shtml

| | | 23 | 10 | 47 | 1505 | 19 | 21885 | 0 | 13601 | 5691 | 137 |

BETHANY—Harrison County
HARRISON COUNTY COMMUNITY HOSPITAL, 2600 Miller Street, Zip 64424, Mailing Address: P.O. Box 428, Zip 64424–0428; tel. 660/425–2211; Dan P. Broyles, Administrator **A**9 10 **F**2 6 8 13 14 15 16 17 19 20 21 22 24 26 27 28 29 30 31 32 33 34 36 37 39 41 42 44 45 46 48 49 51 53 54 55 56 57 58 59 60 62 63 64 65 66 67 68 69 71 73 74 **P**5

| | | 16 | 10 | 21 | 867 | 9 | 22106 | 0 | 5180 | 2334 | 98 |

BLUE SPRINGS—Jackson County
⊞ △ ST. MARY'S HOSPITAL OF BLUE SPRINGS, 201 West R. D. Mize Road, Zip 64014; tel. 816/228–5900; Gordon Docking, Senior Executive Officer **A**1 7 9 10 **F**4 6 7 8 10 11 12 15 16 17 19 20 21 22 24 25 26 28 29 30 31 32 33 34 35 37 38 39 40 41 42 43 44 45 46 48 49 60 63 64 65 66 67 71 72 73 **P**1 5 6 **S** Carondelet Health System, Saint Louis, MO

| | | 23 | 10 | 112 | 4556 | 61 | 51132 | 931 | 43845 | 17816 | 439 |

BOLIVAR—Polk County
⊞ CITIZENS MEMORIAL HOSPITAL, 1500 North Oakland, Zip 65613–3099; tel. 417/326–6000; Donald J. Babb, Chief Executive Officer **A**1 9 10 **F**7 8 14 15 16 17 19 21 22 26 27 28 29 30 31 32 33 34 35 37 39 40 41 42 44 45 46 49 51 52 56 57 58 65 66 67 70 71 73 74 **P**6

| | | 16 | 10 | 74 | 2700 | 31 | 29489 | 344 | 24933 | 9900 | 449 |

BONNE TERRE—St. Francois County
PARKLAND HEALTH CENTER–BONNE TERRE See Parkland Health Center, Farmington

BOONVILLE—Cooper County
⊞ COOPER COUNTY MEMORIAL HOSPITAL, 17651 B Highway, Zip 65233–2839, Mailing Address: P.O. Box 88, Zip 65233–0088; tel. 660/882–7461; Wilbert E. Meyer, Administrator and Chief Executive Officer (Total facility includes 24 beds in nursing home–type unit) **A**1 9 10 **F**8 12 14 15 16 17 19 22 24 28 29 30 32 34 35 39 41 42 44 49 54 64 65 67 71 73

| | | 13 | 10 | 49 | 779 | 32 | 16310 | 0 | 7075 | 3384 | 147 |

BRANSON—Taney County
⊞ SKAGGS COMMUNITY HEALTH CENTER, Business Highway 65 and Skaggs Road, Zip 65616–2035, Mailing Address: P.O. Box 650, Zip 65615–0650; tel. 417/335–7000; Bob D. Phillips, Administrator (Total facility includes 23 beds in nursing home–type unit) **A**1 9 10 **F**7 8 12 14 15 16 17 18 19 21 22 23 26 27 28 29 30 31 32 33 34 35 37 39 40 41 42 44 45 46 49 51 54 64 65 67 69 70 71 73 **P**8

| | | 23 | 10 | 99 | 4995 | 58 | 111080 | 491 | 42368 | 18764 | 592 |

BRIDGETON—St. Louis County
ST. VINCENT'S PSYCHIATRIC DIVISION See DePaul Health Center, Saint Louis

BROOKFIELD—Linn County
⊞ GENERAL JOHN J. PERSHING MEMORIAL HOSPITAL, 130 East Lockling Avenue, Zip 64628–0130, Mailing Address: P.O. Box 408, Zip 64628–0408; tel. 660/258–2222; Phil Hamilton, R.N., Chief Executive Officer **A**9 10 **F**8 12 14 15 16 17 19 22 24 25 28 29 30 31 32 33 35 39 40 41 42 44 46 49 51 65 71 72 73

| | | 23 | 10 | 34 | 841 | 7 | 45068 | 20 | 9378 | 4526 | 195 |

BUTLER—Bates County
BATES COUNTY MEMORIAL HOSPITAL, 615 West Nursery Street, Zip 64730–0370; tel. 660/679–4135; Bob S. Edwards, Jr., Chief Executive Officer (Total facility includes 12 beds in nursing home–type unit) **A**9 10 **F**7 8 12 14 16 19 21 22 24 28 29 30 32 33 34 35 37 39 40 41 44 45 46 49 64 65 71 73

| | | 13 | 10 | 52 | 1943 | 28 | 17183 | 31 | 11154 | 4592 | 170 |

Hospital, Address, Telephone, Administrator, Approval, Facility, and Physician Codes, Health Care System, Network	Classi-fication Codes		Utilization Data					Expense (thousands) of dollars		
★ American Hospital Association (AHA) membership □ Joint Commission on Accreditation of Healthcare Organizations (JCAHO) accreditation + American Osteopathic Healthcare Association (AOHA) membership ○ American Osteopathic Association (AOA) accreditation △ Commission on Accreditation of Rehabilitation Facilities (CARF) accreditation Control codes 61, 63, 64, 71, 72 and 73 indicate hospitals listed by AOHA, but not registered by AHA. For definition of numerical codes, see page A4	Control	Service	Staffed Beds	Admissions	Census	Outpatient Visits	Births	Total	Payroll	Personnel

CAMERON—Clinton County

CAMERON COMMUNITY HOSPITAL, 1015 West Fourth Street, Zip 64429–1498; tel. 816/632–2101; Joseph F. Abrutz, Jr., Administrator **A**9 10 **F**8 11 12 14 15 16 17 19 20 22 24 26 27 28 29 30 31 32 33 34 35 37 39 42 44 46 49 52 54 57 58 64 65 66 67 71 73 **P**6	23	10	48	1693	26	34456	0	18168	8143	312

CAPE GIRARDEAU—Cape Girardeau County

✖ SAINT FRANCIS MEDICAL CENTER, 211 St. Francis Drive, Zip 63703–8399; tel. 573/331–3000; Don K. Rhodes, Interim President and Chief Executive Officer (Total facility includes 26 beds in nursing home–type unit) **A**1 2 10 **F**4 5 8 10 11 12 13 15 16 17 19 20 21 22 23 24 27 28 29 30 31 32 34 35 37 39 41 42 43 44 45 46 47 48 49 63 64 65 66 67 71 72 73 74 **P**8	23	10	264	7227	131	64539	0	84725	35008	1166
✖ SOUTHEAST MISSOURI HOSPITAL, 1701 Lacey Street, Zip 63701–5299; tel. 573/334–4822; James W. Wente, CPA, CHE, Administrator (Total facility includes 20 beds in nursing home–type unit) **A**1 2 10 **F**4 7 8 10 11 12 13 15 16 17 18 19 20 21 22 24 28 29 30 31 32 33 34 35 36 37 38 39 40 41 42 43 44 45 47 49 52 55 56 57 60 63 64 65 67 68 71 73 **Web address:** www.sehosp.org	23	10	244	9461	133	105345	1449	96530	35690	1303

CARROLLTON—Carroll County

CARROLL COUNTY MEMORIAL HOSPITAL, 1502 North Jefferson Street, Zip 64633–1999; tel. 816/542–1695; Jerry Dover, Chief Executive Officer **A**9 10 **F**1 8 15 16 19 20 22 26 28 29 30 31 32 33 34 36 39 41 42 44 46 49 64 65 71 73 **P**6	23	10	50	376	32	11473	1	3335	1669	73

CARTHAGE—Jasper County

★ MCCUNE–BROOKS HOSPITAL, 627 West Centennial Avenue, Zip 64836–0677; tel. 417/358–8121; Robert Y. Copeland, Jr., Chief Executive Officer (Total facility includes 7 beds in nursing home–type unit) **A**9 10 **F**8 19 22 26 28 29 30 32 33 35 36 37 39 44 52 57 64 65 66 67 71	14	10	57	1852	31	47989	0	17512	7923	292

CASSVILLE—Barry County

SOUTH BARRY COUNTY MEMORIAL HOSPITAL, 94 Main Street, Zip 65625–1610; tel. 417/847–4115; Deborah Stubbs, Chief Executive Officer **A**10 **F**8 19 22 24 28 29 30 32 33 34 39 41 44 49 51 64 71 **P**1 5	16	10	18	726	7	39720	0	6729	2629	102

CHESTERFIELD—St. Louis County

✖ ST. LUKE'S HOSPITAL, 232 South Woods Mill Road, Zip 63017–3480; tel. 314/434–1500; Gary R. Olson, President (Total facility includes 126 beds in nursing home–type unit) **A**1 2 3 5 9 10 **F**1 2 3 4 5 6 7 8 9 10 11 12 13 14 15 16 17 18 19 20 21 22 23 24 25 26 27 28 29 30 31 32 33 34 35 36 37 38 39 40 41 42 43 44 45 46 47 48 49 51 52 53 54 55 56 57 58 59 60 61 62 63 64 65 66 67 68 69 70 71 72 73 74 **P**8 **S** Sisters of Mercy Health System–St. Louis, Saint Louis, MO	21	10	495	17874	304	151443	2669	174346	80488	2038

CHILLICOTHE—Livingston County

✖ HEDRICK MEDICAL CENTER, 100 Central Avenue, Zip 64601–1599; tel. 660/646–1480; James K. Johnson, Chief Executive Officer **A**1 9 10 **F**7 12 14 15 16 17 18 19 22 28 29 30 32 33 34 35 36 37 39 40 41 42 44 45 46 49 55 58 64 65 67 71 73 **S** Health Midwest, Kansas City, MO	23	10	80	1480	21	28710	390	14642	6317	223

CLINTON—Henry County

✖ GOLDEN VALLEY MEMORIAL HOSPITAL, 1600 North Second Street, Zip 64735–1197; tel. 660/885–5511; Randy S. Wertz, Administrator (Total facility includes 12 beds in nursing home–type unit) **A**1 9 10 **F**7 8 14 15 16 17 19 21 22 28 29 30 31 32 33 35 37 39 40 41 42 44 49 52 53 54 55 56 57 58 59 63 64 65 66 67 71 73 74	16	10	106	3702	52	11146	336	24742	11847	399

COLUMBIA—Boone County

✖ BOONE HOSPITAL CENTER, 1600 East Broadway, Zip 65201–5897; tel. 573/815–8000; Michael Shirk, President and Senior Executive Officer (Total facility includes 33 beds in nursing home–type unit) **A**1 2 3 5 9 10 **F**4 7 8 10 12 14 15 16 17 19 21 22 24 25 26 28 29 30 31 32 33 34 35 37 38 39 40 41 42 43 44 45 46 48 49 52 54 55 56 57 58 59 60 61 63 64 65 67 69 71 72 73 74 **P**3 5 8 **S** BJC Health System, Saint Louis, MO **Web address:** www.boone.org	23	10	327	13432	216	91149	1575	128128	48225	1435
✖ △ COLUMBIA REGIONAL HOSPITAL, 404 Keene Street, Zip 65201–6698; tel. 573/875–9000; Bruce Eady, Chief Executive Officer **A**1 2 5 7 9 10 **F**4 7 8 10 12 14 15 16 18 19 20 21 22 23 26 28 29 30 31 32 34 35 37 39 40 41 42 44 45 46 48 49 52 53 57 63 64 65 66 67 69 71 72 73 74 **P**5 8 **S** TENET Healthcare Corporation, Santa Barbara, CA	33	10	265	4571	75	13729	191	59667	20473	659
ELLIS FISCHEL CANCER CENTER See University Hospitals and Clinics										
✖ HARRY S. TRUMAN MEMORIAL VETERANS HOSPITAL, 800 Hospital Drive, Zip 65201–5297; tel. 573/814–6300; Gary L. Campbell, Director (Total facility includes 41 beds in nursing home–type unit) **A**1 2 3 5 8 **F**3 4 5 8 10 11 12 14 16 17 19 20 21 22 26 27 28 29 30 31 32 33 34 35 37 39 41 42 43 44 45 46 48 49 51 52 54 55 56 57 58 59 60 63 64 65 67 68 69 71 72 73 74 **P**6 **S** Department of Veterans Affairs, Washington, DC	45	10	161	3973	97	94987	0	76934	38287	931
□ MID MISSOURI MENTAL HEALTH CENTER, 3 Hospital Drive, Zip 65201–5296; tel. 573/884–1300; Dennis R. Canote, Chief Executive Officer **A**1 3 5 10 **F**15 16 29 52 53 54 55 56 57 58 59 **P**6	12	22	69	1716	54	7318	0	14858	7670	263
□ △ UNIVERSITY HOSPITALS AND CLINICS, (Includes Ellis Fischel Cancer Center, 115 Business Loop 70 West, Zip 65203; tel. 573/882–5460; Keith Weinhold, Director), One Hospital Drive, Zip 65212–0001; tel. 573/882–4141; Patsy J. Hart, Executive Director **A**1 2 3 5 7 8 9 10 **F**2 4 5 7 8 9 10 11 12 14 16 17 18 19 20 21 22 23 24 25 26 27 28 29 30 31 32 34 35 37 38 39 40 41 42 43 44 45 46 47 48 49 50 51 52 53 54 55 56 57 58 59 60 61 63 65 66 67 68 69 70 71 72 73 74 **P**1	12	10	383	12963	216	431180	1432	218346	90921	3438

Hospital, Address, Telephone, Administrator, Approval, Facility, and Physician Codes, Health Care System, Network	Classi-fication Codes		Utilization Data					Expense (thousands) of dollars		
★ American Hospital Association (AHA) membership □ Joint Commission on Accreditation of Healthcare Organizations (JCAHO) accreditation + American Osteopathic Healthcare Association (AOHA) membership ○ American Osteopathic Association (AOA) accreditation △ Commission on Accreditation of Rehabilitation Facilities (CARF) accreditation Control codes 61, 63, 64, 71, 72 and 73 indicate hospitals listed by AOHA, but not registered by AHA. For definition of numerical codes, see page A4	Control	Service	Staffed Beds	Admissions	Census	Outpatient Visits	Births	Total	Payroll	Personnel

CREVE COEUR—St. Louis County
BARNES–JEWISH WEST COUNTY HOSPITAL See Saint Louis

CRYSTAL CITY—Jefferson County

□ JEFFERSON MEMORIAL HOSPITAL, Highway 61 South, Zip 63019, Mailing Address: P.O. Box 350, Zip 63019–0350; tel. 314/933–1000; Mark S. Brodeur, Chief Executive Officer (Total facility includes 185 beds in nursing home–type unit) **A**1 9 10 **F**2 3 4 6 7 8 10 12 15 16 17 19 21 22 23 24 25 27 28 29 30 31 32 33 34 35 37 39 40 41 42 43 44 46 48 49 52 53 54 55 56 57 58 59 60 62 63 64 65 66 67 71 72 73 | 23 | 10 | 393 | 8197 | 253 | 84368 | 802 | 69992 | 33409 | 1282

DEXTER—Stoddard County

DEXTER MEMORIAL HOSPITAL, 1200 North One Mile Road, Zip 63841–1099; tel. 573/624–5566; Randal Tennison, Administrator **A**9 10 **F**8 11 12 15 19 20 22 25 26 28 29 30 31 32 33 34 37 39 41 44 45 48 49 51 63 64 65 67 71 72 73 **S** NetCare Health Systems, Inc., Nashville, TN | 23 | 10 | 48 | 749 | 9 | 31408 | 0 | 10463 | 5029 | 181

DONIPHAN—Ripley County

RIPLEY COUNTY MEMORIAL HOSPITAL, 109 Plum Street, Zip 63935–1299; tel. 573/996–2141; Charles Ray Freeman, Administrator **A**9 10 **F**8 14 15 16 17 19 22 28 29 30 32 33 34 41 44 45 46 49 51 71 | 13 | 10 | 26 | 516 | 10 | 6525 | 0 | 4181 | 1667 | 99

EL DORADO SPRINGS—Cedar County

CEDAR COUNTY MEMORIAL HOSPITAL, 1401 South Park Street, Zip 64744–2096; tel. 417/876–2511; Jackie Boyles, Administrator **A**10 **F**7 8 15 16 17 19 22 24 28 29 30 31 32 33 34 36 39 40 41 46 49 64 65 67 68 71 73 74 **P**6 | 13 | 10 | 34 | 875 | 9 | 5971 | 95 | 5590 | 3051 | 112

EXCELSIOR SPRINGS—Clay County

□ EXCELSIOR SPRINGS MEDICAL CENTER, 1700 Rainbow Boulevard, Zip 64024–1190; tel. 816/630–6081; Sally S. Nance, Chief Executive Officer (Total facility includes 80 beds in nursing home–type unit) **A**1 9 10 **F**6 8 12 14 15 16 17 19 22 26 27 28 29 30 32 33 34 35 36 37 39 41 42 44 45 46 49 64 65 67 71 73 | 14 | 10 | 104 | 756 | 83 | 18677 | 0 | 11216 | 5283 | 136

FAIRFAX—Atchison County

COMMUNITY HOSPITAL ASSOCIATION, Highway 59, Zip 64446–0107; tel. 660/686–2211; Larry S. Goodloe, Administrator **A**9 10 **F**7 8 19 20 22 29 30 32 33 34 35 37 39 40 41 42 44 46 49 58 64 65 71 | 23 | 10 | 42 | 724 | 20 | 13642 | 53 | 5091 | 2076 | 109

FARMINGTON—St. Francois County

+ ○ MINERAL AREA REGIONAL MEDICAL CENTER, 1212 Weber Road, Zip 63640–3309; tel. 573/701–7304; Kerry L. Noble, Chief Executive Officer (Total facility includes 10 beds in nursing home–type unit) **A**9 10 11 12 13 **F**1 2 3 7 8 12 14 15 16 17 18 19 20 21 22 27 28 29 30 31 32 33 34 35 37 39 40 41 42 44 45 46 49 53 54 55 56 57 58 59 64 65 66 67 70 71 72 73 **P**6 8 | 23 | 10 | 120 | 3952 | 50 | 63001 | 408 | 32803 | 13970 | 513

★ PARKLAND HEALTH CENTER, (Includes Parkland Health Center–Bonne Terre, 7245 Vo–Tech Road, Bonne Terre, Zip 63628; tel. 573/358–1400), 1101 West Liberty Street, Zip 63640–1997; tel. 573/756–6451; Richard L. Conklin, President **A**1 9 10 **F**4 7 8 12 14 15 16 17 18 19 20 21 22 24 25 28 29 30 31 32 33 34 35 36 37 39 40 41 42 44 45 46 49 51 53 54 55 56 57 58 63 65 66 67 69 71 72 73 **P**5 6 7 **S** BJC Health System, Saint Louis, MO | 23 | 10 | 94 | 3235 | 33 | 63439 | 426 | 26351 | 10818 | 408

□ SOUTHEAST MISSOURI MENTAL HEALTH CENTER, 1010 West Columbia, Zip 63640–2997; tel. 573/218–6792; Donald L. Barton, Superintendent **A**1 10 **F**14 15 16 17 22 24 28 29 39 41 45 46 52 56 59 65 67 73 | 12 | 22 | 196 | 1695 | 171 | 1032 | 0 | 27852 | 15393 | 601

FLORISSANT—St. Louis County
CHRISTIAN HOSPITAL NORTHWEST See Christian Hospital Northeast–Northwest, Saint Louis

FORT LEONARD WOOD—Pulaski County

★ GENERAL LEONARD WOOD ARMY COMMUNITY HOSPITAL, 126 Missouri Avenue, Zip 65473–8952; tel. 573/596–0414; Lieutenant Colonel Julie Martin, Administrator **A**1 2 **F**1 2 3 4 5 6 7 8 9 10 11 12 13 14 15 16 17 18 19 20 21 22 23 24 25 26 27 28 29 30 31 32 33 34 35 36 37 38 39 40 41 42 43 44 45 46 47 48 49 50 51 52 53 54 55 56 57 58 59 60 61 62 63 64 65 66 67 68 69 70 71 72 73 74 **S** Department of the Army, Office of the Surgeon General, Falls Church, VA
Web address: www.webglwach.leonardwood.amedd.army.mil | 42 | 10 | 97 | 2267 | 23 | 272568 | 369 | 53897 | 22647 | 931

FREDERICKTOWN—Madison County

MADISON MEDICAL CENTER, 100 South Wood at West College, Zip 63645, Mailing Address: P.O. Box 431, Zip 63645–0431; tel. 573/783–3341; Floyd D. Bounds, Administrator (Total facility includes 123 beds in nursing home–type unit) **A**9 10 **F**7 8 14 15 16 17 19 22 29 30 32 34 37 39 40 41 44 46 49 51 64 65 71 | 13 | 10 | 143 | 468 | 125 | 18945 | 57 | 8925 | 4373 | 230

FULTON—Callaway County

□ CALLAWAY COMMUNITY HOSPITAL, 9 South Hospital Drive, Zip 65251–2513; tel. 573/642–3376; Gerald M. Torba, Chief Executive Officer **A**1 9 10 **F**7 8 13 14 15 16 17 19 22 24 25 28 29 30 32 34 35 37 39 40 41 42 44 46 49 65 67 71 73 | 23 | 10 | 31 | 1257 | 16 | 22011 | 153 | 10971 | 4254 | 121

□ FULTON STATE HOSPITAL, 600 East Fifth Street, Zip 65251–1798; tel. 573/592–4100; Felix T. Vincenz, Ph.D., Acting Superintendent (Total facility includes 24 beds in nursing home–type unit) **A**1 10 **F**2 3 12 16 18 20 26 27 28 29 30 39 41 45 46 51 52 53 55 57 58 65 67 73 **P**6 | 12 | 22 | 508 | 672 | 482 | 0 | 0 | 55915 | 32260 | 1262

Hospital, Address, Telephone, Administrator, Approval, Facility, and Physician Codes, Health Care System, Network	Classi-fication Codes		Utilization Data					Expense (thousands) of dollars		
	Control	Service	Staffed Beds	Admissions	Census	Outpatient Visits	Births	Total	Payroll	Personnel

★ American Hospital Association (AHA) membership
□ Joint Commission on Accreditation of Healthcare Organizations (JCAHO) accreditation
+ American Osteopathic Healthcare Association (AOHA) membership
○ American Osteopathic Association (AOA) accreditation
△ Commission on Accreditation of Rehabilitation Facilities (CARF) accreditation
Control codes 61, 63, 64, 71, 72 and 73 indicate hospitals listed by AOHA, but not registered by AHA. For definition of numerical codes, see page A4

HANNIBAL—Marion County

⊠ HANNIBAL REGIONAL HOSPITAL, Highway 36 West, Zip 63401, Mailing Address: P.O. Box 551, Zip 63401–0551; tel. 573/248–1300; John C. Grossmeier, President and Chief Executive Officer **A**1 2 9 10 **F**7 8 10 14 15 16 17 18 19 20 22 23 28 29 30 31 32 34 35 37 39 40 41 42 44 45 46 49 52 54 55 56 57 58 59 61 63 65 66 67 71 73 74 **P**1 6 | 23 | 10 | 105 | 5206 | 66 | 66487 | 597 | 43604 | 18082 | 634

HARRISONVILLE—Cass County

⊠ CASS MEDICAL CENTER, 1800 East Mechanic Street, Zip 64701–2099; tel. 816/884–3291; Alan O. Freeman, Chief Executive Officer **A**1 9 10 **F**8 12 14 15 16 19 20 21 22 28 29 30 33 34 35 37 39 41 42 44 45 46 49 51 52 53 54 55 57 58 63 65 66 67 71 73 **P**7 **S** Health Midwest, Kansas City, MO | 13 | 10 | 35 | 1323 | 18 | 16731 | 0 | — | — | 181

HAYTI—Pemiscot County

PEMISCOT MEMORIAL HEALTH SYSTEM, Highway 61 and Reed, Zip 63851, Mailing Address: P.O. Box 489, Zip 63851–0489; tel. 573/359–1372; Darrell Jean, Administrator and Chief Executive Officer (Total facility includes 116 beds in nursing home–type unit) **A**9 10 **F**2 3 7 8 9 11 12 15 16 19 21 22 26 27 28 29 30 31 32 34 35 36 37 38 39 40 41 44 46 47 49 51 53 54 55 56 57 58 64 65 69 71 72 73 74 **P**6 8 | 13 | 10 | 179 | 5912 | 134 | 56329 | 196 | 25578 | 12997 | 638

HERMANN—Gasconade County

HERMANN AREA DISTRICT HOSPITAL, Mailing Address: P.O. Box 470, Zip 65041–0470; tel. 573/486–2191; Dan McKinney, Administrator **A**9 10 **F**8 12 15 16 17 19 21 22 28 29 30 32 33 34 35 36 39 40 41 42 44 46 49 64 65 71 73 **P**6 | 16 | 10 | 41 | 375 | 24 | 11112 | 8 | 5014 | 2279 | 106

HOUSTON—Texas County

TEXAS COUNTY MEMORIAL HOSPITAL, 1333 Sam Houston Boulevard, Zip 65483–2046; tel. 417/967–3311; William L. Sword, President and Chief Executive Officer **A**9 10 **F**7 8 12 16 19 20 22 24 25 27 28 29 30 31 32 33 34 36 37 39 40 41 44 45 46 49 51 64 65 71 73 **P**6 | 13 | 10 | 66 | 2109 | 23 | 10667 | 292 | 9910 | 4364 | 226

INDEPENDENCE—Jackson County

⊠ INDEPENDENCE REGIONAL HEALTH CENTER, 1509 West Truman Road, Zip 64050–3498; tel. 816/836–8100; Michael W. Chappelow, President and Chief Executive Officer (Total facility includes 70 beds in nursing home–type unit) **A**1 2 9 10 **F**1 2 3 4 5 6 7 8 9 10 11 12 13 15 16 17 18 19 20 21 22 23 24 26 27 28 29 30 31 32 33 34 35 36 37 38 39 40 41 42 43 44 45 46 47 48 49 51 52 53 54 56 57 58 60 61 63 64 65 66 67 70 71 73 74 **P**6 **S** Health Midwest, Kansas City, MO | 33 | 10 | 329 | 7984 | 161 | 76834 | 498 | 113331 | 34450 | 936

⊠ MEDICAL CENTER OF INDEPENDENCE, 17203 East 23rd Street, Zip 64057–1899; tel. 816/478–5000; J. Kent Howard, President and Chief Executive Officer (Total facility includes 9 beds in nursing home–type unit) **A**1 9 10 **F**1 2 3 4 5 7 8 9 10 11 12 13 14 15 16 17 18 19 20 21 22 23 24 25 26 27 28 29 30 31 32 33 34 35 36 37 38 39 40 41 42 43 44 45 46 47 48 49 51 52 53 54 55 56 57 58 59 60 61 63 64 65 66 67 68 69 70 71 73 74 **P**1 5 **S** Health Midwest, Kansas City, MO | 23 | 10 | 123 | 4531 | 58 | 42142 | 857 | 33899 | 15352 | 373

JEFFERSON CITY—Cole County

□ + ○ △ CAPITAL REGION MEDICAL CENTER, 1125 Madison Street, Zip 65101–5227; tel. 573/635–7141; Edward F. Farnsworth, President (Total facility includes 20 beds in nursing home–type unit) **A**1 7 10 11 12 13 **F**1 3 4 5 7 8 9 10 11 12 13 14 15 16 17 18 19 21 22 23 24 25 26 28 29 30 31 32 33 34 35 36 37 38 39 40 41 42 43 44 45 46 47 48 49 50 53 54 55 56 57 58 59 60 63 64 65 66 67 70 71 72 73 74 **P**8 | 23 | 10 | 134 | 5937 | 94 | 87650 | 397 | — | — | 1124

⊠ ST. MARYS HEALTH CENTER, 100 St. Marys Medical Plaza, Zip 65101–1601; tel. 573/761–7000; Mark R. Taylor, President (Total facility includes 10 beds in nursing home–type unit) **A**1 2 9 10 **F**4 7 8 10 12 14 15 16 17 18 19 20 21 22 24 28 29 30 31 32 33 34 35 37 39 40 41 42 43 44 45 46 48 49 51 52 53 54 55 56 57 58 59 60 63 64 65 67 70 71 72 73 74 **P**1 4 7 **S** SSM Health Care, Saint Louis, MO | 23 | 10 | 167 | 8537 | 103 | 128496 | 1096 | 81325 | 33310 | 1022

JOPLIN—Newton County

⊠ + ○ FREEMAN HEALTH SYSTEM, (Includes Freeman Hospital East, 932 East 34th Street, Zip 64804–3999; Freeman Hospital West, 1102 West 32nd Street), 1102 West 32nd Street, Zip 64804–3599; tel. 417/623–2801; Gary D. Duncan, President and Chief Executive Officer (Total facility includes 32 beds in nursing home–type unit) **A**1 2 9 10 11 12 13 **F**2 3 4 5 7 8 10 12 13 14 15 16 17 18 19 20 21 22 23 26 27 28 29 30 31 32 33 34 35 37 38 39 40 41 42 43 44 45 46 48 49 51 52 53 54 55 56 57 58 59 60 61 64 65 66 67 70 71 72 73 74 **P**1 6 | 23 | 10 | 266 | 10949 | 150 | 166467 | 2393 | 142762 | 69101 | 1781

Web address: www.freemanhospitals.org

⊠ △ ST. JOHN'S REGIONAL MEDICAL CENTER, 2727 McClelland Boulevard, Zip 64804–1694; tel. 417/781–2727; Gary L. Rowe, President and Chief Executive Officer (Total facility includes 10 beds in nursing home–type unit) **A**1 2 7 9 10 **F**4 7 8 10 11 12 14 15 16 17 18 19 20 21 22 23 25 27 28 29 30 31 32 33 34 35 36 37 39 40 41 42 43 44 45 46 48 49 51 52 53 54 55 56 57 58 59 60 64 65 66 67 68 70 71 72 73 74 **P**1 6 7 **S** Catholic Health Initiatives, Denver, CO | 23 | 10 | 367 | 14461 | 218 | 256386 | 643 | 156095 | 57347 | 1994

Web address: www.stj.com

Hospital, Address, Telephone, Administrator, Approval, Facility, and Physician Codes, Health Care System, Network	Classification Codes		Utilization Data					Expense (thousands) of dollars		
	Control	Service	Staffed Beds	Admissions	Census	Outpatient Visits	Births	Total	Payroll	Personnel

★ American Hospital Association (AHA) membership
□ Joint Commission on Accreditation of Healthcare Organizations (JCAHO) accreditation
+ American Osteopathic Healthcare Association (AOHA) membership
○ American Osteopathic Association (AOA) accreditation
△ Commission on Accreditation of Rehabilitation Facilities (CARF) accreditation
Control codes 61, 63, 64, 71, 72 and 73 indicate hospitals listed by AOHA, but not registered by AHA. For definition of numerical codes, see page A4

KANSAS CITY—Jackson County

✶ BAPTIST MEDICAL CENTER, 6601 Rockhill Road, Zip 64131–1197; tel. 816/276–7000; Darrell W. Moore, President and Chief Executive Officer (Total facility includes 23 beds in nursing home–type unit) **A**1 2 3 5 9 10 **F**1 2 3 4 5 7 8 10 11 12 13 15 16 17 18 19 20 21 22 23 24 25 26 27 28 29 30 31 32 33 34 35 36 37 38 39 40 41 42 43 44 45 46 48 49 51 52 53 54 55 56 57 58 59 60 61 63 64 65 66 67 68 69 70 71 72 73 74 **P**1 4 5 7 **S** Health Midwest, Kansas City, MO

| | 23 | 10 | 265 | 10663 | 166 | 62080 | 1634 | 102076 | 44502 | 1178 |

✶ CHILDREN'S MERCY HOSPITAL, 2401 Gillham Road, Zip 64108–9898; tel. 816/234–3000; Randall L. O'Donnell, Ph.D., President and Chief Executive Officer **A**1 2 3 5 8 9 10 **F**4 5 9 10 12 13 15 16 17 19 20 21 22 25 28 29 31 32 34 35 38 39 41 42 43 44 45 46 47 49 51 54 58 60 65 67 68 70 71 73 **P**4 5 6

Web address: www.childrens–mercy.org

| | 23 | 50 | 184 | 8639 | 129 | 232928 | 0 | 171467 | 87953 | 2489 |

□ CRITTENTON, 10918 Elm Avenue, Zip 64134–4199; tel. 816/765–6600; Gary L. Watson, FACHE, Senior Executive Officer **A**1 10 **F**2 3 11 12 14 15 17 18 28 29 30 34 37 38 39 40 45 46 48 52 53 54 55 56 58 59 64 65 67 73 **P**8 **S** Saint Luke's Shawnee Mission Health System, Kansas City, MO

| | 23 | 52 | 113 | 954 | 79 | 16123 | 0 | 12342 | 7307 | 184 |

✶ + ○ PARK LANE MEDICAL CENTER, 5151 Raytown Road, Zip 64133–2199; tel. 816/358–8000; Derell Taloney, President and Chief Executive Officer (Total facility includes 15 beds in nursing home–type unit) **A**1 9 10 11 12 13 **F**1 2 3 4 5 7 9 10 11 12 14 15 16 17 18 19 20 21 22 23 24 25 26 27 28 29 30 31 32 33 34 35 36 37 38 39 40 41 42 43 44 45 46 47 48 49 51 52 53 54 55 56 57 58 59 60 61 63 64 65 66 67 68 69 70 71 72 73 74 **P**1 4 5 7 **S** Health Midwest, Kansas City, MO

| | 23 | 10 | 83 | 2411 | 42 | 56578 | 0 | 24216 | 11381 | 316 |

★ △ REHABILITATION INSTITUTE, 3011 Baltimore, Zip 64108–3465; tel. 816/751–7900; Ronald L. Herrick, President **A**7 9 10 **F**1 2 3 4 5 6 7 8 9 10 11 12 13 14 15 16 17 18 19 20 22 23 24 25 26 27 28 29 30 31 32 33 34 36 37 39 40 41 42 43 44 45 46 47 48 49 51 52 53 54 55 56 57 58 59 60 61 64 65 66 67 68 69 70 71 72 73 74 **P**2 5 8 **S** Health Midwest, Kansas City, MO

| | 23 | 46 | 36 | 343 | 14 | 12718 | 0 | 13079 | 7675 | 245 |

✶ RESEARCH MEDICAL CENTER, 2316 East Meyer Boulevard, Zip 64132–1199; tel. 816/276–4000; Steven R. Newton, President and Chief Executive Officer (Total facility includes 35 beds in nursing home–type unit) **A**1 2 3 5 9 10 **F**1 2 3 4 5 7 9 10 11 12 13 14 15 16 17 18 19 20 21 22 23 24 25 26 27 28 29 30 31 32 33 34 35 36 37 38 39 40 41 42 43 44 45 46 47 48 49 51 52 53 54 55 56 57 58 59 60 61 63 64 65 66 67 68 69 70 71 72 73 74 **P**1 6 **S** Health Midwest, Kansas City, MO

Web address: www.healthmidwest.org

| | 23 | 10 | 491 | 14556 | 258 | 70939 | 1821 | 178886 | 73988 | 1974 |

✶ RESEARCH PSYCHIATRIC CENTER, 2323 East 63rd Street, Zip 64130–3495; tel. 816/444–8161; Todd Krass, Administrator and Chief Executive Officer **A**1 10 **F**1 2 3 4 5 6 7 8 9 10 11 12 13 15 16 17 18 19 20 22 23 24 25 26 27 28 29 30 31 32 33 34 35 36 37 38 39 40 41 42 43 44 45 46 47 48 49 50 51 52 53 54 55 56 57 58 59 60 61 62 63 64 65 66 67 68 69 70 71 72 73 74 **P**4 5 7 8 **S** Columbia/HCA Healthcare Corporation, Nashville, TN

| | 33 | 22 | 100 | 1825 | 43 | 5220 | 0 | 8817 | 4481 | 108 |

✶ SAINT JOSEPH HEALTH CENTER, 1000 Carondelet Drive, Zip 64114–4673; tel. 816/942–4400; Andrew W. Allen, Interim President and Chief Executive Officer **A**1 2 5 9 10 **F**4 5 7 8 10 12 13 15 16 17 19 21 22 24 28 29 30 31 32 33 34 35 37 38 39 40 41 42 43 44 45 46 48 49 60 63 65 66 67 70 71 72 73 **P**1 3 5 6 **S** Carondelet Health System, Saint Louis, MO

| | 23 | 10 | 267 | 10886 | 170 | 122045 | 1763 | 115761 | 41704 | 1188 |

✶ SAINT LUKE'S HOSPITAL, 4400 Wornall Road, Zip 64111–3238; tel. 816/932–2000; G. Richard Hastings, President and Chief Executive Officer (Total facility includes 30 beds in nursing home–type unit) **A**1 2 3 8 9 10 **F**2 3 4 5 7 8 10 11 12 13 14 15 16 17 18 19 20 21 22 24 25 26 27 28 29 30 31 32 33 34 35 37 38 39 40 41 42 43 44 45 46 48 49 51 52 53 54 55 56 57 58 59 60 61 63 64 65 66 67 68 69 70 71 72 73 74 **P**6 8 **S** Saint Luke's Shawnee Mission Health System, Kansas City, MO

Web address: www.dia.net/mercy

| | 23 | 10 | 510 | 20103 | 337 | 146692 | 2804 | — | — | 2587 |

□ SAINT LUKE'S NORTHLAND HOSPITAL, 5830 N.W. Barry Road, Zip 64154; tel. 816/891–6000; N. Gary Wages, Senior Executive Officer **A**1 **F**2 3 4 5 6 7 8 10 11 12 13 14 15 16 17 18 19 20 21 22 24 25 26 27 28 29 30 31 32 33 34 35 36 37 38 39 40 41 42 43 44 45 46 47 48 49 50 51 52 53 54 55 56 57 58 59 60 61 63 64 65 66 67 69 70 71 72 73 74 **P**6 8 **S** Saint Luke's Shawnee Mission Health System, Kansas City, MO

| | 23 | 10 | 58 | 3398 | 35 | 36293 | 872 | 30839 | 12646 | 318 |

ST. MARY'S HOSPITAL See Trinity Lutheran Hospital

✶ TRINITY LUTHERAN HOSPITAL, (Includes St. Mary's Hospital, 101 Memorial Drive, Zip 64108; tel. 816/751–4600), 3030 Baltimore Avenue, Zip 64108–3404; tel. 816/751–4600; Ronald A. Ommen, President and Chief Executive Officer (Total facility includes 30 beds in nursing home–type unit) **A**1 2 3 5 9 10 **F**1 2 3 4 5 6 7 8 10 11 12 13 14 15 16 17 19 20 21 22 27 28 29 30 31 32 33 34 35 36 37 38 40 44 45 46 48 49 51 52 53 54 55 56 57 60 61 64 65 66 67 68 71 72 73 74 **P**1 5 6 **S** Health Midwest, Kansas City, MO

| | 21 | 10 | 334 | 7201 | 130 | 143214 | 0 | — | 39108 | 914 |

★ △ TRUMAN MEDICAL CENTER–EAST, 7900 Lee's Summit Road, Zip 64139–1241; tel. 816/373–4415; Donald R. Smithburg, Administrator (Total facility includes 212 beds in nursing home–type unit) **A**3 5 7 9 10 **F**3 7 8 10 11 12 13 14 15 16 17 18 19 20 21 22 25 26 27 29 30 31 32 34 35 37 38 39 40 41 42 44 45 46 48 49 51 52 53 54 55 56 57 58 59 61 64 65 66 70 71 72 73 74 **S** Truman Medical Center, Kansas City, MO

| | 23 | 10 | 302 | 4133 | 248 | 104669 | 862 | 48456 | 23157 | 759 |

Hospital, Address, Telephone, Administrator, Approval, Facility, and Physician Codes, Health Care System, Network	Classi-fication Codes		Utilization Data					Expense (thousands) of dollars		
★ American Hospital Association (AHA) membership □ Joint Commission on Accreditation of Healthcare Organizations (JCAHO) accreditation + American Osteopathic Healthcare Association (AOHA) membership ○ American Osteopathic Association (AOA) accreditation △ Commission on Accreditation of Rehabilitation Facilities (CARF) accreditation Control codes 61, 63, 64, 71, 72 and 73 indicate hospitals listed by AOHA, but not registered by AHA. For definition of numerical codes, see page A4	Control	Service	Staffed Beds	Admissions	Census	Outpatient Visits	Births	Total	Payroll	Personnel
☒ TRUMAN MEDICAL CENTER–WEST, 2301 Holmes Street, Zip 64108–2677; tel. 816/556–3000; Cathy Disch, Director Operations (Total facility includes 18 beds in nursing home–type unit) **A**1 2 3 5 8 9 10 **F**3 7 8 10 11 16 17 18 19 20 21 22 25 27 28 30 31 32 34 35 37 38 39 40 41 42 43 44 45 46 48 49 51 53 54 55 56 57 58 59 60 61 63 64 65 66 68 70 71 73 74 **P**6 7 **S** Truman Medical Center, Kansas City, MO	23	10	215	11004	175	289270	1966	121952	61217	1501
□ TWO RIVERS PSYCHIATRIC HOSPITAL, 5121 Raytown Road, Zip 64133–2141; tel. 816/356–5688; Linda Berridge, Chief Executive Officer **A**1 10 **F**12 14 16 17 18 26 27 29 39 41 45 46 52 53 54 55 56 57 59 65 67 **S** Universal Health Services, Inc., King of Prussia, PA **Web address:** www.torivershospital.com	33	22	80	1187	37	0	0	8348	3268	98
□ VALUEMARK BEHAVIORAL HEALTHCARE SYSTEM OF KANSAS CITY, 4800 N.W. 88th Street, Zip 64154–2757; tel. 816/436–3900; John Hunter, Chief Executive Officer (Total facility includes 38 beds in nursing home–type unit) **A**1 10 **F**12 15 16 17 18 19 26 27 29 32 34 35 39 41 52 53 54 55 56 57 58 59 65 67 **S** ValueMark Healthcare Systems, Inc., Atlanta, GA	33	22	72	530	39	0	0	—	—	145
□ VENCOR HOSPITAL–KANSAS CITY, (VENTILATOR LONG TERM CARE), 8701 Troost Avenue, Zip 64131–3495; tel. 816/995–2000; Robert F. Berry, Administrator (Total facility includes 16 beds in nursing home–type unit) **A**1 10 **F**12 14 16 19 21 22 26 27 29 34 35 37 39 41 42 45 46 50 52 60 63 64 65 67 71 73 **P**5 **S** Vencor, Incorporated, Louisville, KY	33	49	110	472	56	383	0	—	—	275
☒ VETERANS AFFAIRS MEDICAL CENTER, 4801 Linwood Boulevard, Zip 64128–2295; tel. 816/861–4700; Hugh F. Doran, Director **A**1 2 3 5 8 **F**1 2 3 4 5 6 7 10 11 12 14 16 17 18 19 20 21 22 23 24 26 28 29 30 32 33 34 35 37 39 41 42 43 44 45 46 48 49 51 52 54 55 56 57 58 59 60 63 65 67 71 73 74 **S** Department of Veterans Affairs, Washington, DC	45	10	165	5502	152	232016	0	—	—	1269
□ WESTERN MISSOURI MENTAL HEALTH CENTER, 600 East 22nd Street, Zip 64108–2675; tel. 816/512–4000; Gloria Joseph, Superintendent **A**1 3 5 10 **F**2 3 6 12 15 16 17 18 19 21 22 24 27 28 29 30 35 39 41 45 46 52 53 54 55 56 57 58 63 65 67 71 73 **P**6	12	22	107	2558	82	46420	0	25681	17548	655
KENNETT—Dunklin County										
☒ TWIN RIVERS REGIONAL MEDICAL CENTER, 1301 First Street, Zip 63857–2508; tel. 573/888–4522; John W. Sanders, Chief Executive Officer **A**1 9 10 **F**7 8 11 12 13 15 16 17 19 21 22 23 24 27 28 29 30 32 33 34 35 37 39 40 42 44 46 48 49 52 53 56 65 71 73 **P**7 **S** TENET Healthcare Corporation, Santa Barbara, CA	33	10	116	2864	35	99768	259	18121	7483	364
KIRKSVILLE—Adair County										
□ + ○ NORTHEAST REGIONAL MEDICAL CENTER–JEFFERSON CAMPUS, (Includes Northeast Regional Medical Center–Patterson Campus, 112 East Patterson Avenue, tel. 660/785–1000), 315 South Osteopathy, Zip 63501–8599, Mailing Address: P.O. Box C8502, Zip 63501–8599; tel. 660/785–1100; Charles M. Boughton, Chief Executive Officer (Total facility includes 14 beds in nursing home–type unit) **A**1 9 10 11 12 13 **F**4 5 7 8 10 12 14 15 16 17 18 19 20 21 22 24 28 29 30 31 32 34 35 37 39 40 41 42 44 45 46 48 49 54 63 64 65 66 67 70 71 **P**5	33	10	164	5445	66	155947	561	—	—	695
LAKE SAINT LOUIS—St. Charles County										
★ ST. JOSEPH HOSPITAL WEST, 100 Medical Plaza, Zip 63367–1395; tel. 314/625–5200; Kevin F. Kast, President (Total facility includes 11 beds in nursing home–type unit) **A**9 10 **F**2 3 4 5 6 7 8 10 11 12 13 14 15 16 17 18 19 20 21 22 23 24 25 26 28 29 30 31 32 33 34 35 37 38 39 40 41 42 43 44 45 46 47 48 49 51 52 53 54 55 56 57 58 59 60 61 63 64 65 66 67 68 69 71 72 73 74 **P**1 **S** SSM Health Care, Saint Louis, MO	23	10	59	2643	30	41859	604	21924	10319	200
LAMAR—Barton County										
★ BARTON COUNTY MEMORIAL HOSPITAL, Second and Gulf Streets, Zip 64759–0626; tel. 417/682–6081; Ronald Morton, Administrator **A**10 **F**7 8 11 15 16 19 20 21 22 28 29 30 32 33 34 37 39 40 41 44 46 48 49 64 65 66 67 71 72	13	10	42	1078	14	31724	95	7857	3365	124
LEBANON—Laclede County										
☒ BREECH REGIONAL MEDICAL CENTER, 100 Hospital Drive, Zip 65536–2317, Mailing Address: P.O. Box N, Zip 65536–2317; tel. 417/533–6100; Gary W. Pulsipher, President **A**1 9 10 **F**7 8 17 18 19 20 21 22 27 28 29 30 32 33 34 35 37 39 40 41 44 46 49 64 65 66 71 73 **S** Sisters of Mercy Health System–St. Louis, Saint Louis, MO	23	10	35	1460	15	28558	221	9104	5391	199
LEES SUMMIT—Jackson County										
☒ LEE'S SUMMIT HOSPITAL, 530 North Murray Road, Zip 64081–1497; tel. 816/969–6000; John L. Jacobson, President and Chief Executive Officer **A**1 9 10 **F**2 3 4 5 8 9 10 11 12 14 15 17 18 19 21 22 23 24 25 26 27 28 29 30 32 33 34 35 36 37 38 39 41 42 43 44 45 46 47 48 49 51 52 53 54 55 56 57 58 59 60 61 64 65 66 67 69 71 72 73 74 **P**4 5 7 8 **S** Health Midwest, Kansas City, MO	23	10	83	3177	39	59448	0	26263	11748	298
LEXINGTON—Lafayette County										
☒ LAFAYETTE REGIONAL HEALTH CENTER, 1500 State Street, Zip 64067–1199; tel. 660/259–2203; Jeffrey S. Tarrant, Administrator **A**1 9 10 **F**7 8 12 15 16 19 22 29 30 34 35 37 39 40 41 42 44 45 46 49 51 65 71 73 **P**1 5 7 **S** Health Midwest, Kansas City, MO	23	10	37	1480	16	17165	1	11057	4366	134
LIBERTY—Clay County										
☒ LIBERTY HOSPITAL, 2525 Glenn Hendren Drive, Zip 64069–1002, Mailing Address: P.O. Box 1002, Zip 64069–1002; tel. 816/781–7200; Joseph W. Crossett, Administrator (Total facility includes 26 beds in nursing home–type unit) **A**1 9 10 **F**4 5 7 8 10 15 16 17 19 21 22 23 26 27 28 29 30 32 33 34 35 36 37 38 39 40 41 42 44 48 49 60 64 65 67 70 71 73 **P**5 **Web address:** www.Libertyhospital.org	16	10	168	7630	112	68870	712	62753	28050	919

Hospital, Address, Telephone, Administrator, Approval, Facility, and Physician Codes, Health Care System, Network	Classi-fication Codes		Utilization Data					Expense (thousands) of dollars		
★ American Hospital Association (AHA) membership ☐ Joint Commission on Accreditation of Healthcare Organizations (JCAHO) accreditation + American Osteopathic Healthcare Association (AOHA) membership ○ American Osteopathic Association (AOA) accreditation △ Commission on Accreditation of Rehabilitation Facilities (CARF) accreditation Control codes 61, 63, 64, 71, 72 and 73 indicate hospitals listed by AOHA, but not registered by AHA. For definition of numerical codes, see page A4	Control	Service	Staffed Beds	Admissions	Census	Outpatient Visits	Births	Total	Payroll	Personnel

LOUISIANA—Pike County

⊞ PIKE COUNTY MEMORIAL HOSPITAL, 2305 West Georgia Street, Zip 63353–0020; tel. 573/754–5531; Gregory C. Reed, Administrator **A**1 9 10 **F**8 12 14 15 16 19 22 27 28 29 30 34 35 39 40 44 49 65 67 71 73 **P**8 **S** SSM Health Care, Saint Louis, MO

| | 13 | 10 | 31 | 891 | 9 | 15132 | 66 | 7559 | 3570 | 121 |

MACON—Macon County

SAMARITAN MEMORIAL HOSPITAL, 1205 North Jackson Street, Zip 63552; tel. 816/385–3151; Bernard A. Orman, Jr., Administrator **A**10 **F**3 7 8 10 12 15 16 17 18 19 22 23 24 26 28 29 30 31 32 33 34 35 39 40 41 42 44 45 49 51 52 54 57 65 66 67 69 71 73 **P**3

| | 13 | 10 | 28 | 1039 | 15 | 26291 | 121 | 9569 | 3903 | 164 |

MARSHALL—Saline County

★ FITZGIBBON HOSPITAL, 2305 South 65 Highway, Zip 65340–0250, Mailing Address: P.O. Box 250, Zip 65340–0250; tel. 660/886–7431; Ronald A. Ott, Chief Executive Officer (Total facility includes 13 beds in nursing home–type unit) **A**9 10 **F**7 8 15 16 17 19 21 22 24 27 28 29 30 32 33 34 35 37 39 40 41 44 46 49 63 64 65 66 67 71 74 **P**1

| | 23 | 10 | 57 | 2044 | 26 | 75797 | 316 | 22169 | 10599 | 364 |

MARYVILLE—Nodaway County

⊞ ST. FRANCIS HOSPITAL AND HEALTH SERVICES, 2016 South Main Street, Zip 64468–2693; tel. 660/562–2600; Michael Baumgartner, President **A**1 9 10 **F**7 8 10 12 14 15 16 18 19 20 21 22 28 29 30 32 33 34 35 39 40 44 49 52 54 55 56 57 58 59 64 65 67 71 73 **P**5 6 7 8 **S** SSM Health Care, Saint Louis, MO

| | 23 | 10 | 54 | 2131 | 22 | 58103 | 309 | 15938 | 7946 | 322 |

MEMPHIS—Scotland County

○ SCOTLAND COUNTY MEMORIAL HOSPITAL, Sigler Avenue, Zip 63555, Mailing Address: Route 1, Box 53, Zip 63555; tel. 660/465–8511; Marcia R. Dial, Administrator **A**9 10 11 **F**5 7 8 12 13 14 15 16 17 18 19 20 22 25 26 28 29 30 32 33 34 36 37 39 40 41 42 44 45 46 48 49 51 64 65 66 67 71 74 **P**6

| | 16 | 10 | 32 | 430 | 5 | 14637 | 50 | 3784 | 1625 | 96 |

MEXICO—Audrain County

⊞ AUDRAIN MEDICAL CENTER, 620 East Monroe Street, Zip 65265–0858; tel. 573/581–1760; Douglas R. Trembath, President and Chief Executive Officer (Total facility includes 40 beds in nursing home–type unit) **A**1 9 10 **F**3 7 8 10 12 13 14 15 16 17 18 19 20 21 22 25 26 27 28 29 30 32 33 34 35 37 39 40 41 42 44 45 46 49 51 52 53 54 55 56 57 58 59 64 65 66 67 68 71 73 74 **P**2

Web address: www.amc–healthcare.org

| | 23 | 10 | 154 | 4636 | 84 | 93981 | 243 | 50251 | 22234 | 704 |

MILAN—Sullivan County

★ ○ SULLIVAN COUNTY MEMORIAL HOSPITAL, 630 West Third Street, Zip 63556–1098; tel. 660/265–4212; Martha Gragg, Chief Executive Officer (Total facility includes 12 beds in nursing home–type unit) **A**10 11 **F**12 13 14 15 16 17 19 20 22 24 28 29 30 34 39 41 44 49 51 64 65 71

| | 13 | 10 | 38 | 182 | 25 | 14517 | 0 | 2933 | 1640 | 86 |

MOBERLY—Randolph County

⊞ MOBERLY REGIONAL MEDICAL CENTER, 1515 Union Avenue, Zip 65270–9449, Mailing Address: P.O. Box 3000, Zip 65270–3000; tel. 660/263–8400; Daniel E. McKay, Chief Executive Officer (Total facility includes 21 beds in nursing home–type unit) **A**1 9 10 **F**1 7 8 10 11 12 15 16 17 18 19 20 21 22 24 26 27 28 29 30 32 33 34 37 39 40 41 44 45 46 49 51 52 54 57 59 64 65 66 67 68 70 71 72 73 74 **S** Community Health Systems, Inc., Brentwood, TN

| | 33 | 10 | 92 | 3253 | 41 | 43157 | 261 | 21802 | 7859 | 289 |

MONETT—Barry County

COX MONETT HOSPITAL, 801 Lincoln Avenue, Zip 65708–1698; tel. 417/354–1400; Gregory D. Johnson, Administrator **A**9 10 **F**3 8 12 15 16 17 18 19 20 22 25 26 27 28 29 30 32 33 34 37 39 41 42 44 45 46 49 51 53 54 55 56 57 63 64 65 66 67 71 72 73 **P**1 8 **S** Cox Health System, Springfield, MO

| | 23 | 10 | 53 | 975 | 12 | 46067 | 0 | 8986 | 4453 | 180 |

MOUNT VERNON—Lawrence County

☐ △ MISSOURI REHABILITATION CENTER, 600 North Main, Zip 65712–1099; tel. 417/466–3711; Charles A. Drewel, Director **A**1 7 10 **F**3 6 19 21 26 27 29 30 31 33 34 37 39 41 42 46 48 49 51 58 64 65 67 71 73 **P**6

| | 12 | 10 | 135 | 539 | 70 | 28487 | 0 | 19774 | 11257 | 422 |

MOUNTAIN VIEW—Howell County

⊞ ST. FRANCIS HOSPITAL, Highway 60, Zip 65548, Mailing Address: P.O. Box 82, Zip 65548–0082; tel. 417/934–2246; Gary W. Jordan, President and Chief Executive Officer **A**1 9 10 **F**8 14 15 19 22 28 29 32 33 34 39 40 49 65 70 71 72 **P**6 **S** Sisters of Mercy Health System–St. Louis, Saint Louis, MO

| | 23 | 10 | 20 | 476 | 5 | 20559 | 0 | 4017 | 1609 | 95 |

NEOSHO—Newton County

FREEMAN NEOSHO HOSPITAL, 113 West Hickory Street, Zip 64850–1799; tel. 417/455–4352; Phil Willcoxon, Administrator **A**9 10 **F**2 3 4 5 7 8 9 10 11 12 13 15 17 19 21 22 26 27 28 29 30 31 32 33 34 35 37 38 39 40 41 42 43 44 45 46 47 48 49 51 52 53 54 55 56 57 58 59 61 63 64 65 66 70 71 72 73 74 **P**1 4 7

| | 23 | 10 | 54 | 1961 | 29 | 39313 | 0 | 18186 | 5298 | 227 |

NEVADA—Vernon County

☐ HEARTLAND BEHAVIORAL HEALTH SERVICES, 1500 West Ashland Street, Zip 64772–1710; tel. 417/667–2666; Ed Goosman, Chief Executive Officer **A**1 10 **F**14 26 29 52 53 54 55 56 57 65 **P**8 **S** Ramsay Health Care, Inc., Coral Gables, FL

| | 33 | 22 | 30 | 472 | 17 | 1134 | 0 | 7984 | 3524 | 54 |

⊞ NEVADA REGIONAL MEDICAL CENTER, 800 South Ash Street, Zip 64772–3223; tel. 417/667–3355; Robert B. Ohlen, President and Chief Executive Officer (Total facility includes 14 beds in nursing home–type unit) **A**1 9 10 **F**7 8 14 15 16 17 19 20 22 23 25 27 28 29 30 31 32 33 34 35 40 42 44 46 49 64 65 66 71 73 **S** Quorum Health Group/Quorum Health Resources, Inc., Brentwood, TN

| | 14 | 10 | 85 | 2381 | 29 | 28688 | 324 | 17330 | 7144 | 259 |

Hospital, Address, Telephone, Administrator, Approval, Facility, and Physician Codes, Health Care System, Network	Classi-fication Codes		Utilization Data					Expense (thousands) of dollars		
★ American Hospital Association (AHA) membership □ Joint Commission on Accreditation of Healthcare Organizations (JCAHO) accreditation + American Osteopathic Healthcare Association (AOHA) membership ○ American Osteopathic Association (AOA) accreditation △ Commission on Accreditation of Rehabilitation Facilities (CARF) accreditation Control codes 61, 63, 64, 71, 72 and 73 indicate hospitals listed by AOHA, but not registered by AHA. For definition of numerical codes, see page A4	Control	Service	Staffed Beds	Admissions	Census	Outpatient Visits	Births	Total	Payroll	Personnel

NORTH KANSAS CITY—Clay County

⊠ NORTH KANSAS CITY HOSPITAL, 2800 Clay Edwards Drive, Zip 64116–3281; tel. 816/691–2000; David R. Carpenter, FACHE, President and Chief Executive Officer (Total facility includes 39 beds in nursing home–type unit) **A**1 9 10 **F**3 4 7 8 9 10 11 12 15 16 17 18 19 20 21 22 23 28 29 30 32 33 34 35 36 37 38 39 40 41 42 43 44 46 47 48 49 52 54 55 56 57 59 60 63 64 65 67 70 71 72 73 **P**6 — 14 10 350 15679 248 94995 1739 138175 57602 1608

OSAGE BEACH—Camden County

⊠ LAKE OF THE OZARKS GENERAL HOSPITAL, 54 Hospital Drive, Zip 65065–9699; tel. 573/348–8000; Michael E. Henze, Chief Executive Officer (Total facility includes 10 beds in nursing home–type unit) **A**1 9 10 **F**4 7 8 10 11 12 14 15 16 17 19 20 21 22 23 28 29 30 32 33 34 35 37 39 40 41 42 43 44 45 46 49 63 64 65 66 67 70 71 73 74 **P**6 — 23 10 94 4339 54 54624 621 48450 17733 556
Web address: www.lakeoftheozarkhospital.com

OSCEOLA—St. Clair County

⊠ SAC–OSAGE HOSPITAL, Junction Highways 13 & Business 13, Zip 64776, Mailing Address: P.O. Box 426, Zip 64776–0426; tel. 417/646–8181; Terry E. Erwine, Administrator **A**1 9 10 **F**7 8 15 16 19 22 28 29 30 31 33 34 37 39 40 41 42 44 45 46 49 64 65 67 71 73 — 16 10 47 1308 20 5888 43 5645 3011 114

PERRYVILLE—Perry County

□ PERRY COUNTY MEMORIAL HOSPITAL, 434 North West Street, Zip 63775–1398; tel. 314/547–2536; Ralph Paulding, President and Chief Executive Officer **A**1 9 10 **F**1 7 8 12 15 16 17 18 19 22 23 24 25 26 27 28 29 30 32 34 35 39 40 41 44 49 53 58 63 64 65 66 67 68 71 72 73 — 13 10 47 1017 14 33275 152 11666 5272 229

PILOT KNOB—Iron County

⊠ ARCADIA VALLEY HOSPITAL, Highway 21, Zip 63663, Mailing Address: P.O. Box 548, Zip 63663–0548; tel. 573/546–3924; H. Clark Duncan, Administrator (Total facility includes 24 beds in nursing home–type unit) **A**1 9 10 **F**8 12 14 15 16 17 19 20 22 25 26 27 28 29 30 32 33 34 35 37 39 41 44 46 49 64 65 67 71 73 **P**8 **S** SSM Health Care, Saint Louis, MO — 23 10 50 763 35 35944 1 8491 3826 133

POPLAR BLUFF—Butler County

□ △ DOCTORS REGIONAL MEDICAL CENTER, 621 Pine Boulevard, Zip 63901; tel. 573/686–4111; Kerry L. Noble, Chief Executive Officer (Total facility includes 15 beds in nursing home–type unit) **A**1 2 7 9 10 **F**2 3 7 8 10 12 15 16 17 18 19 20 21 22 23 24 25 28 29 30 31 32 33 34 35 37 39 40 41 42 44 45 46 48 49 51 52 53 54 55 56 57 58 59 64 65 66 67 71 72 73 74 — 33 10 186 5684 80 25242 471 37231 13330 591

⊠ JOHN J. PERSHING VETERANS AFFAIRS MEDICAL CENTER, 1500 North Westwood Boulevard, Zip 63901–3318; tel. 573/686–4151; Nancy Arnold, Director (Total facility includes 40 beds in nursing home–type unit) **A**1 2 3 7 8 14 15 16 17 19 20 21 22 25 26 27 28 29 30 31 32 34 35 37 39 41 42 44 45 46 49 51 52 64 65 71 72 73 74 **S** Department of Veterans Affairs, Washington, DC — 45 10 48 1129 49 76370 0 30976 13997 352

⊠ LUCY LEE HOSPITAL, 2620 North Westwood Boulevard, Zip 63901–2341, Mailing Address: P.O. Box 88, Zip 63901–2341; tel. 573/785–7721; Brian T. Flynn, Chief Executive Officer (Total facility includes 24 beds in nursing home–type unit) **A**1 2 10 **F**4 7 8 11 12 15 17 19 20 21 22 24 26 28 29 30 31 32 34 35 37 39 40 41 42 44 45 46 48 49 60 63 64 65 66 67 71 72 73 74 **P**1 7 **S** TENET Healthcare Corporation, Santa Barbara, CA — 33 10 173 7559 103 89564 1167 46800 14562 878
Web address: www.tenethealth.com

POTOSI—Washington County

WASHINGTON COUNTY MEMORIAL HOSPITAL, 300 Health Way, Zip 63664–1499; tel. 573/438–5451; Clarence E. Lay, Administrator **A**9 10 **F**8 14 15 16 17 19 22 25 26 28 29 30 32 34 35 37 39 41 44 46 49 65 67 71 72 73 — 13 10 42 665 7 26622 0 8013 3375 164

RICHMOND—Ray County

RAY COUNTY MEMORIAL HOSPITAL, 904 Wollard Boulevard, Zip 64085–2243; tel. 816/470–5432; Tommy L. Hicks, Administrator (Total facility includes 11 beds in nursing home–type unit) **A**9 10 **F**8 15 19 22 29 32 33 34 35 37 41 42 44 49 64 65 71 73 — 13 10 50 1340 20 7704 0 10293 4724 182

ROLLA—Phelps County

⊠ ○ △ PHELPS COUNTY REGIONAL MEDICAL CENTER, 1000 West Tenth Street, Zip 65401–2905; tel. 573/364–3100; David Ross, Chief Executive Officer (Total facility includes 32 beds in nursing home–type unit) **A**1 7 9 10 11 12 **F**1 2 3 7 8 10 12 15 16 17 18 19 20 21 22 23 27 28 29 30 31 32 33 34 35 36 37 39 40 41 42 44 46 48 49 52 53 54 55 56 57 58 59 60 63 64 65 66 67 70 71 72 73 74 **P**3 — 13 10 214 7619 118 109919 832 53078 23174 929

SAINT CHARLES—St. Charles County

□ BHC SPIRIT OF ST. LOUIS HOSPITAL, 5931 Highway 94 South, Zip 63304–5601; tel. 314/441–7300; Greg Panter, Interim Chief Executive Officer **A**1 9 10 **F**1 2 3 12 18 29 34 52 53 54 55 56 58 59 65 67 **S** Behavioral Healthcare Corporation, Nashville, TN — 33 22 104 544 51 0 0 5605 3384 120

⊠ ST. JOSEPH HEALTH CENTER, 300 First Capitol Drive, Zip 63301–2835; tel. 314/947–5000; Kevin F. Kast, President (Total facility includes 19 beds in nursing home–type unit) **A**1 2 9 10 **F**2 3 4 5 7 8 10 11 12 14 15 16 17 18 19 20 21 22 23 24 25 26 28 29 30 31 32 33 34 35 37 38 39 40 41 42 43 44 45 46 47 48 49 51 52 53 54 55 56 57 58 59 60 61 62 64 65 66 67 68 69 70 71 72 73 74 **P**1 **S** SSM Health Care, Saint Louis, MO — 23 10 176 10827 137 — 837 85246 35344 990

Hospital, Address, Telephone, Administrator, Approval, Facility, and Physician Codes, Health Care System, Network	Classi-fication Codes		Utilization Data					Expense (thousands) of dollars		
★ American Hospital Association (AHA) membership □ Joint Commission on Accreditation of Healthcare Organizations (JCAHO) accreditation + American Osteopathic Healthcare Association (AOHA) membership ○ American Osteopathic Association (AOA) accreditation △ Commission on Accreditation of Rehabilitation Facilities (CARF) accreditation Control codes 61, 63, 64, 71, 72 and 73 indicate hospitals listed by AOHA, but not registered by AHA. For definition of numerical codes, see page A4	Control	Service	Staffed Beds	Admissions	Census	Outpatient Visits	Births	Total	Payroll	Personnel

SAINT JOSEPH—Buchanan County

Hospital	Control	Service	Staffed Beds	Admissions	Census	Outpatient Visits	Births	Total	Payroll	Personnel
✠ △ HEARTLAND REGIONAL MEDICAL CENTER, (Includes Heartland Hospital East, 5325 Faraon Street, Zip 64506; Heartland Hospital West, 801 Faraon Street, Zip 64501; tel. 816/271–7111), 5325 Faraon Street, Zip 64506–3398; tel. 816/271–6000; Lowell C. Kruse, Chief Executive Officer (Total facility includes 220 beds in nursing home–type unit) **A**1 2 5 7 9 10 **F**4 5 7 8 10 11 12 13 14 15 16 17 19 21 22 23 25 26 27 28 29 30 31 32 33 34 35 37 39 40 41 42 43 44 45 46 48 49 51 52 54 55 56 57 60 64 65 66 70 71 73 74 **P**6	23	10	504	18269	377	486305	1609	—	—	2153
□ NORTHWEST MISSOURI PSYCHIATRIC REHABILITATION CENTER, (Includes Woodson Childrens Psychiatric Hospital, 3400 Frederick, Zip 64506–2913; tel. 816/387–2320), 3505 Frederick Avenue, Zip 64506; tel. 816/378–2300; Ron Dittemore, Ed.D., Superintendent **A**1 10 **F**15 29 52 53 54 55 56 57 73 WOODSON CHILDRENS PSYCHIATRIC HOSPITAL See Northwest Missouri Psychiatric Rehabilitation Center	12	22	120	180	112	79	0	19668	11552	427

SAINT LOUIS—St. Louis County

Hospital	Control	Service	Staffed Beds	Admissions	Census	Outpatient Visits	Births	Total	Payroll	Personnel
✠ ALEXIAN BROTHERS HOSPITAL, 3933 South Broadway, Zip 63118–9984; tel. 314/865–3333; Glenn Appelbaum, Senior Vice President (Total facility includes 40 beds in nursing home–type unit) **A**1 9 10 **F**2 3 4 5 7 8 9 10 11 12 13 15 16 17 18 19 20 21 22 25 26 27 28 29 30 31 32 33 34 37 38 39 40 41 42 43 44 45 46 47 48 49 51 52 53 54 55 56 57 58 59 60 63 64 65 66 67 70 71 72 73 74 **P**5 6 7 8 **S** Sisters of Mercy Health System–St. Louis, Saint Louis, MO	23	10	203	5119	83	42584	0	39984	19003	579
✠ △ BARNES–JEWISH HOSPITAL, One Barnes–Jewish Hospital Plaza, Zip 63110–1094; tel. 314/747–3000; Peter L. Slavin, M.D., President **A**1 2 3 5 7 8 9 10 **F**1 2 3 4 5 6 7 8 9 10 11 12 13 14 15 16 17 18 19 20 21 22 23 24 25 26 27 28 29 30 31 32 33 34 35 36 37 38 39 40 41 42 43 44 45 46 47 48 49 50 51 52 53 54 55 56 57 58 59 60 61 62 63 64 65 66 67 68 69 70 71 72 73 74 **P**1 4 5 6 7 8 **S** BJC Health System, Saint Louis, MO	23	10	927	46715	747	182460	3819	696133	296637	7797
✠ BARNES–JEWISH WEST COUNTY HOSPITAL, 12634 Olive Boulevard, Zip 63141–6354; tel. 314/996–8000; William Behrendt, Interim President (Total facility includes 10 beds in nursing home–type unit) **A**1 9 10 **F**1 2 3 4 5 6 7 8 9 10 11 12 13 15 16 17 18 19 20 21 22 23 24 25 26 27 28 29 30 31 32 33 34 35 36 37 38 39 40 41 42 43 44 45 46 47 48 49 50 51 52 53 54 55 56 57 58 59 60 61 62 63 64 65 66 67 68 69 70 71 72 73 74 **P**1 5 7 8 **S** BJC Health System, Saint Louis, MO	23	10	91	2779	38	35304	0	34161	10853	289
✠ △ BETHESDA GENERAL HOSPITAL, 3655 Vista Avenue, Zip 63110–2594; tel. 314/772–9200; Joseph J. Brinker, Chief Executive Officer (Total facility includes 28 beds in nursing home–type unit) **A**1 5 7 9 10 **F**1 4 6 8 10 12 19 20 22 23 26 27 28 29 30 32 33 34 35 36 37 39 41 44 46 48 49 50 52 55 56 57 58 59 62 63 64 65 67 71 72	23	10	118	778	33	1440	0	14185	6284	187
✠ CARDINAL GLENNON CHILDREN'S HOSPITAL, 1465 South Grand Boulevard, Zip 63104–1095; tel. 314/577–5600; Douglas A. Ries, President **A**1 3 5 9 **F**2 3 4 5 6 9 10 12 13 14 15 16 17 18 19 20 21 22 23 24 25 27 28 29 30 31 32 33 34 35 38 39 41 42 43 44 45 46 47 48 49 50 51 52 53 54 55 56 58 59 60 63 65 66 67 68 69 70 71 72 73 74 **P**8 **S** SSM Health Care, Saint Louis, MO	23	50	172	7456	108	156265	0	96093	39654	1121
✠ △ CHRISTIAN HOSPITAL NORTHEAST-NORTHWEST, (Includes Christian Hospital Northwest, 1225 Graham Road, Florissant, Zip 63031; tel. 314/953–6000), 11133 Dunn Road, Zip 63136–6192; tel. 314/653–5000; John O'Shaughnessy, President and Senior Executive Officer (Total facility includes 36 beds in nursing home–type unit) **A**1 2 7 9 10 **F**1 2 3 4 5 6 7 8 9 10 11 12 13 14 15 16 17 18 19 20 21 22 23 24 25 27 28 29 30 31 32 33 34 35 36 37 38 39 40 41 42 43 44 45 46 47 48 49 50 52 53 54 55 56 57 58 59 60 61 62 63 64 65 66 67 68 70 71 72 73 74 **P**5 7 8 **S** BJC Health System, Saint Louis, MO **Web address:** www.bjc.org	23	10	563	22668	318	190659	1720	—	—	2370
✠ △ COMPTON HEIGHTS HOSPITAL, (Formerly Lafayette–Grand Hospital), 3545 Lafayette Avenue, Zip 63104–9984; tel. 314/865–6500; Lee Stoll, Chief Executive Officer (Total facility includes 86 beds in nursing home–type unit) **A**1 7 9 10 **F**8 10 14 15 19 21 22 26 27 29 32 33 34 35 37 41 42 44 48 49 52 56 57 59 64 65 71 73 **P**8 **S** TENET Healthcare Corporation, Santa Barbara, CA DEACONESS CENTRAL HOSPITAL See Forest Park Hospital DEACONESS WEST HOSPITAL See Des Peres Hospital	33	10	214	4382	104	28289	0	40170	19280	633
✠ DEPAUL HEALTH CENTER, (Includes ST, ANNE'S SKILLED NURSING DIVISION; DePaul Hospital, Bridgeton; St. Vincent's Psychiatric Division, Bridgeton), 12303 DePaul Drive, Zip 63044–2588; tel. 314/344–6000; Robert G. Porter, President (Total facility includes 52 beds in nursing home–type unit) **A**1 2 9 10 **F**2 3 4 7 8 9 10 11 12 13 14 15 16 17 18 19 20 21 22 24 25 26 27 28 29 30 31 32 33 34 35 36 37 38 39 40 41 42 43 44 45 46 47 48 49 51 52 53 54 55 56 57 58 59 60 63 64 65 66 67 68 69 70 71 73 74 **S** SSM Health Care, Saint Louis, MO	21	10	272	11441	182	102900	871	103044	39733	1225
★ + ○ DES PERES HOSPITAL, (Formerly Deaconess West Hospital), (Includes Metropolitan Medical Center–West), 2345 Dougherty Ferry Road, Zip 63122–3313; tel. 314/768–3000; Michele C. Meyer, Interim Chief Executive Officer **A**9 10 11 12 13 **F**3 4 5 7 8 9 10 12 13 15 16 17 18 19 21 22 25 26 27 29 31 32 33 34 35 36 37 39 40 41 42 43 44 45 46 47 48 49 51 52 54 55 56 57 58 59 60 61 62 63 64 65 66 67 71 72 73 74 **S** TENET Healthcare Corporation, Santa Barbara, CA	33	10	93	2827	39	31515	0	40556	18915	430

Hospital, Address, Telephone, Administrator, Approval, Facility, and Physician Codes, Health Care System, Network	Classi-fication Codes		Utilization Data					Expense (thousands) of dollars		
	Control	Service	Staffed Beds	Admissions	Census	Outpatient Visits	Births	Total	Payroll	Personnel

★ American Hospital Association (AHA) membership
□ Joint Commission on Accreditation of Healthcare Organizations (JCAHO) accreditation
+ American Osteopathic Healthcare Association (AOHA) membership
○ American Osteopathic Association (AOA) accreditation
△ Commission on Accreditation of Rehabilitation Facilities (CARF) accreditation
Control codes 61, 63, 64, 71, 72 and 73 indicate hospitals listed by AOHA, but not registered by AHA. For definition of numerical codes, see page A4

Hospital	Control	Service	Staffed Beds	Admissions	Census	Outpatient Visits	Births	Total	Payroll	Personnel
⊠ △ FOREST PARK HOSPITAL, (Formerly Deaconess Central Hospital), 6150 Oakland Avenue, Zip 63139–3297; tel. 314/768–3000; Glennon K. McFadden, Chief Executive Officer (Total facility includes 20 beds in nursing home–type unit) **A**1 2 3 5 7 9 10 12 **F**1 2 3 4 7 8 10 11 12 14 15 16 17 19 21 22 23 26 27 29 30 32 33 34 35 36 37 40 41 42 43 44 48 49 51 52 54 55 56 57 58 59 60 62 63 64 65 66 67 71 72 73 74 **P**5 6 8 **S** TENET Healthcare Corporation, Santa Barbara, CA	33	10	296	12681	195	85319	1669	114515	52380	1498
LAFAYETTE–GRAND HOSPITAL See Compton Heights Hospital										
LUTHERAN MEDICAL CENTER See SouthPointe Hospital										
METROPOLITAN MEDICAL CENTER–WEST See Des Peres Hospital										
□ METROPOLITAN ST. LOUIS PSYCHIATRIC CENTER, 5351 Delmar, Zip 63112–3198; tel. 314/877–0500; Gregory L. Dale, Chief Executive Officer **A**1 3 5 10 **F**1 2 3 6 12 14 17 18 19 20 22 29 35 39 41 45 46 52 55 56 57 58 59 64 65 67 73 **P**6	12	22	125	1848	107	5161	0	18741	10729	373
MISSOURI BAPTIST MEDICAL CENTER See Town and Country										
○ NORMANDY COMMUNITY HOSPITAL, 7840 Natural Bridge Road, Zip 63121; tel. 314/382–6400; Thomas G. Walther, Administrator (Nonreporting) **A**10 11	32	10	80	—	—	—	—	—	—	—
□ SAINT LOUIS UNIVERSITY HOSPITAL, 3635 Vista at Grand Boulevard, Zip 63110–0250, Mailing Address: P.O. Box 15250, Zip 63110–0250; tel. 314/577–8000; Leona D. Stoll, Chief Executive Officer **A**1 3 5 8 9 10 **F**2 3 4 5 7 8 10 11 12 14 15 16 17 19 20 21 22 23 25 26 27 28 29 30 31 32 33 34 35 36 37 39 40 41 42 43 44 45 46 48 49 50 51 52 53 54 55 56 57 58 59 60 61 62 63 64 65 66 67 69 70 71 72 73 74 **P**1 5 **S** TENET Healthcare Corporation, Santa Barbara, CA	33	10	303	11160	179	137124	0	172754	66754	2003
⊠ SHRINERS HOSPITALS FOR CHILDREN, ST. LOUIS, 2001 South Lindbergh Boulevard, Zip 63131–3597; tel. 314/432–3600; Carolyn P. Golden, Administrator **A**1 3 5 **F**12 14 15 19 27 28 29 30 34 35 41 45 46 49 51 63 65 66 67 73 **S** Shriners Hospitals for Children, Tampa, FL	23	57	80	2183	33	12606	0	—	—	237
⊠ SOUTHPOINTE HOSPITAL, (Formerly Lutheran Medical Center), 2639 Miami Street, Zip 63118–3999; tel. 314/772–1456; Doug Doris, Chief Executive Officer (Total facility includes 30 beds in nursing home–type unit) **A**1 6 9 10 **F**1 2 3 4 7 8 10 12 14 15 16 17 18 19 20 21 22 26 27 28 29 30 31 32 33 34 35 37 39 40 41 42 44 45 46 48 49 51 52 53 54 55 56 57 58 59 60 61 63 64 65 66 67 71 73 74 **P**6 **S** TENET Healthcare Corporation, Santa Barbara, CA	33	10	243	5665	129	118984	344	42473	22245	637
⊠ △ SSM REHAB, 6420 Clayton Road, Suite 600, Zip 63117–1861; tel. 314/768–5300; Melinda Clark, President (Total facility includes 20 beds in nursing home–type unit) **A**1 7 9 10 **F**12 14 16 17 28 30 32 41 48 49 64 65 66 67 73 **P**1 8 **S** SSM Health Care, Saint Louis, MO	21	46	100	1371	58	99458	0	34513	19491	457
⊠ ST. ANTHONY'S MEDICAL CENTER, 10010 Kennerly Road, Zip 63128–2185; tel. 314/525–1000; David P. Seifert, President (Total facility includes 96 beds in nursing home–type unit) **A**1 9 10 **F**1 2 3 4 5 7 8 9 10 11 12 13 14 15 16 17 18 19 20 21 22 23 24 25 26 27 28 29 30 31 32 33 34 35 36 37 38 39 40 41 42 43 44 45 46 47 48 49 51 52 53 54 55 56 57 58 59 60 61 63 64 65 66 67 68 69 70 71 72 73 74 **P**6 8 **S** Sisters of Mercy Health System–St. Louis, Saint Louis, MO	23	10	685	25878	401	181008	1526	186559	81137	2525
⊠ △ ST. JOHN'S MERCY MEDICAL CENTER, (Includes St. John's Mercy Hospital, 200 Madison Avenue, Washington, Zip 63090; tel. 314/239–8000), 615 South New Ballas Road, Zip 63141–8277; tel. 314/569–6000; Mark Weber, FACHE, President (Total facility includes 22 beds in nursing home–type unit) **A**1 2 3 5 7 8 9 10 **F**2 3 5 6 7 8 9 10 11 12 13 14 15 16 17 18 19 20 21 22 23 24 25 26 27 28 29 30 31 32 33 34 35 36 37 38 39 40 41 42 43 44 45 46 47 48 49 50 51 52 53 54 55 56 57 58 59 60 61 63 64 65 66 67 68 70 71 72 73 74 **P**1 2 3 4 5 6 7 8 **S** Sisters of Mercy Health System–St. Louis, Saint Louis, MO	23	10	898	36425	451	412358	7632	—	—	4451
⊠ ST. JOSEPH HOSPITAL OF KIRKWOOD, 525 Couch Avenue, Zip 63122–5594; tel. 314/966–1500; Carla S. Baum, President (Total facility includes 44 beds in nursing home–type unit) **A**1 2 9 10 **F**2 3 4 5 7 8 9 10 11 12 13 14 15 16 17 18 19 20 21 22 23 24 26 27 28 29 30 31 32 33 34 35 36 37 38 39 40 41 42 43 44 45 47 48 49 52 53 54 55 56 57 58 59 60 61 63 64 65 66 67 68 69 70 71 72 73 74 **P**6 8 **S** SSM Health Care, Saint Louis, MO	23	10	213	6585	97	86089	742	58970	26726	806
⊠ △ ST. LOUIS CHILDREN'S HOSPITAL, (PEDIATRIC–GENERAL), One Children's Place, Zip 63110–1077; tel. 314/454–6000; Ted W. Frey, President **A**1 3 5 7 8 9 10 **F**2 3 4 5 6 7 8 9 10 11 12 13 14 15 16 17 18 19 20 21 22 23 24 25 26 27 28 29 30 31 32 33 34 35 36 37 38 39 40 41 42 43 44 45 46 47 48 49 50 51 52 53 54 55 56 57 58 59 60 61 62 63 64 65 66 67 68 69 70 71 72 73 74 **P**1 4 **S** BJC Health System, Saint Louis, MO Web address: www.STLOUISCHILDRENS.ORG	23	50	235	10515	157	117815	0	165566	69741	1790
□ ST. LOUIS PSYCHIATRIC REHABILITATION CENTER, 5300 Arsenal Street, Zip 63139–1494; tel. 314/644–8000; Roberta Gardine, Chief Executive Officer **A**1 10 **F**12 20 24 29 30 39 52 54 55 65 73 **P**6	12	22	212	36	210	0	0	27724	16526	639
⊠ ST. MARY'S HEALTH CENTER, 6420 Clayton Road, Zip 63117–1811; tel. 314/768–8000; Michael E. Zilm, President (Total facility includes 50 beds in nursing home–type unit) **A**1 2 3 5 8 9 10 **F**2 3 4 5 7 8 10 11 12 13 14 15 16 17 18 19 20 21 22 23 24 25 28 29 30 31 32 33 34 35 36 37 38 39 40 41 42 43 44 45 46 47 48 49 51 52 53 54 55 56 57 58 59 60 61 63 64 65 66 67 68 69 71 72 73 74 **P**6 8 **S** SSM Health Care, Saint Louis, MO	23	10	441	18222	268	164175	2212	136795	54946	1425
⊠ VETERANS AFFAIRS MEDICAL CENTER, 1 Jefferson Barracks Drive, Zip 63125–4199; tel. 314/652–4100; Linda Kurz, Acting Director (Total facility includes 114 beds in nursing home–type unit) **A**1 2 3 5 **F**2 3 4 5 8 10 12 15 16 18 19 21 22 24 26 29 31 32 34 35 37 41 46 49 50 52 54 56 57 58 59 60 63 64 65 69 71 73 **S** Department of Veterans Affairs, Washington, DC	45	10	355	8606	335	326240	0	—	—	2636

Hospital, Address, Telephone, Administrator, Approval, Facility, and Physician Codes, Health Care System, Network	Classi-fication Codes		Utilization Data					Expense (thousands) of dollars		
★ American Hospital Association (AHA) membership □ Joint Commission on Accreditation of Healthcare Organizations (JCAHO) accreditation + American Osteopathic Healthcare Association (AOHA) membership ○ American Osteopathic Association (AOA) accreditation △ Commission on Accreditation of Rehabilitation Facilities (CARF) accreditation Control codes 61, 63, 64, 71, 72 and 73 indicate hospitals listed by AOHA, but not registered by AHA. For definition of numerical codes, see page A4	Control	Service	Staffed Beds	Admissions	Census	Outpatient Visits	Births	Total	Payroll	Personnel

SAINT PETERS—St. Charles County

⊞ BARNES–JEWISH ST. PETERS HOSPITAL, 10 Hospital Drive, Zip 63376–1659; tel. 314/916–9000; Carm Moceri, President (Total facility includes 8 beds in nursing home–type unit) **A**1 9 10 **F**7 8 10 12 14 15 16 17 19 21 22 27 28 29 30 31 32 33 34 35 37 39 40 41 42 44 45 46 49 63 64 65 66 67 71 72 73 74 **P**5 6 8 **S** BJC Health System, Saint Louis, MO	23	10	84	4541	47	83571	1059	38220	16743	460

SALEM—Dent County

SALEM MEMORIAL DISTRICT HOSPITAL, Highway 72 North, Zip 65560, Mailing Address: P.O. Box 774, Zip 65560; tel. 573/729–6626; Dennis P. Pryor, Administrator (Total facility includes 18 beds in nursing home–type unit) **A**9 10 **F**7 8 12 15 16 19 22 27 28 29 30 32 33 34 39 40 41 44 45 46 49 64 65 66 71 73	16	10	46	1347	31	17665	99	8518	3456	150

SEDALIA—Pettis County

⊞ BOTHWELL REGIONAL HEALTH CENTER, 601 East 14th Street, Zip 65301–1706, Mailing Address: P.O. Box 1706, Zip 65302–1706; tel. 660/826–8833; James T. Rank, Administrator **A**1 9 10 **F**4 7 8 10 11 15 16 19 20 21 22 23 29 30 32 33 34 35 37 39 40 41 42 44 49 52 53 56 57 60 65 66 67 70 71 72 74	14	10	147	5878	79	42279	627	—	—	663

SIKESTON—Scott County

□ MISSOURI DELTA MEDICAL CENTER, 1008 North Main Street, Zip 63801–5099; tel. 573/471–1600; Charles D. Ancell, President (Total facility includes 14 beds in nursing home–type unit) **A**1 9 10 **F**3 4 5 6 7 8 10 12 14 15 16 17 18 19 20 21 22 23 24 25 26 27 28 29 30 32 33 34 35 36 37 39 40 41 42 43 44 45 46 49 51 52 54 56 57 58 59 60 62 63 64 65 66 67 69 71 72 73 74	23	10	154	4859	71	80918	544	36749	16361	573

SMITHVILLE—Clay County

⊞ SAINT LUKE'S NORTHLAND HOSPITAL–SMITHVILLE CAMPUS, 601 South 169 Highway, Zip 64089–9334; tel. 816/532–3700; Don Sipes, Senior Executive Officer (Total facility includes 16 beds in nursing home–type unit) **A**1 9 10 **F**2 3 4 5 6 7 8 10 11 12 13 15 16 17 18 19 20 21 22 23 24 25 26 27 28 29 30 31 32 33 34 35 36 37 38 39 40 41 42 43 44 45 46 48 49 50 51 52 53 54 55 56 57 58 59 60 61 63 64 65 66 67 68 69 70 71 72 73 74 **P**6 8 **S** Saint Luke's Shawnee Mission Health System, Kansas City, MO **Web address:** www.saint–lukes.org	23	10	59	935	20	3443	0	7663	3463	164

SPRINGFIELD—Greene County

⊞ COX HOSPITAL SOUTH, (Formerly Columbia Hospital North and South), 1000 East Walnut Lawn, Zip 65807–7399; tel. 417/882–4700; Michelle Fischer, Administrator **A**1 10 **F**3 8 15 17 19 22 28 29 30 32 34 37 41 44 46 49 57 58 59 65 67 71 73 **S** Cox Health System, Springfield, MO	33	10	140	2119	81	15899	0	—	—	345
⊞ △ COX MEDICAL CENTER, (Includes Lester E. Cox Medical Center North, 1423 North Jefferson Avenue, Zip 65802; tel. 417/269–3000; Lester E. Cox Medical Center South, 3801 South National Avenue, Zip 65807; tel. 417/269–6000), 1423 North Jefferson Street, Zip 65802–1988; tel. 417/269–3000; Larry D. Wallis, President and Chief Executive Officer (Total facility includes 43 beds in nursing home–type unit) **A**1 2 3 6 7 9 10 **F**2 3 4 6 7 8 10 11 12 14 15 16 17 18 19 21 22 23 24 25 26 27 28 29 30 31 32 34 35 36 37 38 39 40 41 42 43 44 45 46 47 48 49 51 52 53 54 55 56 57 58 59 60 61 63 64 65 66 67 70 71 72 73 74 **P**6 8 **S** Cox Health System, Springfield, MO	23	10	521	25667	388	960162	3302	251369	104828	4499
□ LAKELAND REGIONAL HOSPITAL, 440 South Market Street, Zip 65806–2090; tel. 417/865–5581; John William Thompson, Ph.D., President and Chief Executive Officer **A**1 10 **F**12 14 18 19 22 25 29 34 35 39 46 52 53 54 55 56 58 59 64 65 67 71 **P**5 6	33	22	88	1858	79	4884	0	10826	5939	188
⊞ △ ST. JOHN'S REGIONAL HEALTH CENTER, 1235 East Cherokee Street, Zip 65804–2263; tel. 417/885–2000; Robert T. Brodhead, Interim Chief Executive Officer (Total facility includes 62 beds in nursing home–type unit) **A**1 2 6 7 10 **F**3 4 5 7 8 9 10 11 12 13 14 15 16 17 18 19 20 21 22 23 24 27 28 29 30 32 33 34 35 36 37 38 39 40 41 42 43 44 45 46 47 48 49 51 52 53 54 55 56 57 58 59 60 63 64 65 66 67 68 69 70 71 72 73 74 **P**6 **S** Sisters of Mercy Health System–St. Louis, Saint Louis, MO	23	10	734	29300	426	280726	2491	254961	117849	3803
□ U. S. MEDICAL CENTER FOR FEDERAL PRISONERS, 1900 West Sunshine Street, Zip 65807–2240, Mailing Address: P.O. Box 4000, Zip 65808–4000; tel. 417/862–7041; R. H. Rison, Warden (Nonreporting) **A**1	48	10	587	—				—	—	—

STE. GENEVIEVE—Ste. Genevieve County

STE. GENEVIEVE COUNTY MEMORIAL HOSPITAL, Highways 61 and 32, Zip 63670–0468; tel. 573/883–2751; Joseph Moss, Administrator **A**9 10 **F**7 8 12 15 16 17 18 19 20 22 23 26 28 29 30 32 33 34 35' 37 39 40 41 42 44 45 49 65 67 71 73 74 **P**6	13	10	34	1585	21	77459	50	14099	6753	250

SULLIVAN—Crawford County

★ MISSOURI BAPTIST HOSPITAL OF SULLIVAN, 751 Sappington Bridge Road, Zip 63080–2354, Mailing Address: P.O. Box 190, Zip 63080–0190; tel. 573/468–4186; Davis D. Skinner, President (Total facility includes 6 beds in nursing home–type unit) **A**9 10 **F**7 8 12 14 15 16 17 18 19 20 21 22 26 27 28 29 30 31 32 33 34 35 37 39 40 41 42 44 45 46 49 51 58 64 65 71 73 **P**5 6 8 **S** BJC Health System, Saint Louis, MO	23	10	46	1556	18	73831	161	16535	6929	242

TOWN AND COUNTRY—St. Louis County

⊞ MISSOURI BAPTIST MEDICAL CENTER, 3015 North Ballas Road, Zip 63131–2374; tel. 314/996–5000; Mark A. Eustis, President **A**1 2 6 9 10 **F**1 2 3 4 5 6 7 8 9 10 11 12 13 15 16 17 18 19 20 21 22 23 24 25 26 27 28 29 30 31 32 33 34 35 36 37 38 39 40 41 42 43 44 45 46 47 48 49 50 51 52 53 54 55 56 57 58 59 60 61 62 63 64 65 66 67 68 69 70 71 72 73 74 **P**1 5 6 7 **S** BJC Health System, Saint Louis, MO	23	10	372	17164	233	279628	3152	182497	71338	2008

Hospital, Address, Telephone, Administrator, Approval, Facility, and Physician Codes, Health Care System, Network	Classi-fication Codes		Utilization Data					Expense (thousands) of dollars		
★ American Hospital Association (AHA) membership □ Joint Commission on Accreditation of Healthcare Organizations (JCAHO) accreditation + American Osteopathic Healthcare Association (AOHA) membership ○ American Osteopathic Association (AOA) accreditation △ Commission on Accreditation of Rehabilitation Facilities (CARF) accreditation Control codes 61, 63, 64, 71, 72 and 73 indicate hospitals listed by AOHA, but not registered by AHA. For definition of numerical codes, see page A4	Control	Service	Staffed Beds	Admissions	Census	Outpatient Visits	Births	Total	Payroll	Personnel

TRENTON—Grundy County

□ WRIGHT MEMORIAL HOSPITAL, 701 East First Street, Zip 64683–0648, Mailing Address: P.O. Box 628, Zip 64683–0628; tel. 660/359–5621; Ralph G. Goodrich, Senior Executive Officer **A**1 9 10 **F**7 8 11 14 15 16 17 19 22 26 27 28 29 30 32 33 34 37 39 40 41 42 44 49 51 56 58 64 65 71 73 **P**1 **S** Saint Luke's Shawnee Mission Health System, Kansas City, MO

| | 23 | 10 | 38 | 758 | 8 | 18113 | 128 | 8357 | 4221 | 144 |

TROY—Lincoln County

□ LINCOLN COUNTY MEMORIAL HOSPITAL, 1000 East Cherry Street, Zip 63379–1599; tel. 314/528–8551; Floyd B. Dowell, Jr., Administrator (Total facility includes 8 beds in nursing home–type unit) **A**1 9 10 **F**8 11 12 15 16 17 19 20 22 23 25 28 29 30 32 33 34 35 37 39 41 44 45 46 49 64 65 66 67 71 **P**8

| | 13 | 10 | 36 | 1454 | 20 | 48207 | 0 | 15795 | 7440 | 218 |

WARRENSBURG—Johnson County

□ WESTERN MISSOURI MEDICAL CENTER, 403 Burkarth Road, Zip 64093–3101; tel. 660/747–2500; Gregory B. Vinardi, President and Chief Executive Officer (Total facility includes 11 beds in nursing home–type unit) **A**1 9 10 **F**7 8 12 13 14 15 16 19 20 21 22 23 28 29 30 31 32 33 34 35 36 37 39 40 41 42 44 45 46 61 64 65 66 67 68 70 71 73 74 **P**6

| | 13 | 10 | 69 | 2656 | 29 | 46201 | 589 | 19787 | 9593 | 322 |

WASHINGTON—Franklin County

ST. JOHN'S MERCY HOSPITAL See St. John's Mercy Medical Center, Saint Louis

WENTZVILLE—St. Charles County

□ DOCTORS HOSPITAL, 500 Medical Drive, Zip 63385–0711; tel. 314/327–1000; Barry A. Papania, President and Chief Executive Officer (Total facility includes 27 beds in nursing home–type unit) **A**1 9 10 **F**7 8 12 14 15 16 19 21 22 23 26 29 30 32 33 34 35 37 39 40 41 42 44 46 49 52 56 57 63 64 65 67 70 71 72 73 74 **S** New American Healthcare Corporation, Brentwood, TN

| | 33 | 10 | 90 | 2206 | 26 | 11289 | 91 | 19319 | 7042 | 186 |

WEST PLAINS—Howell County

☒ OZARKS MEDICAL CENTER, 1100 Kentucky Avenue, Zip 65775–2029, Mailing Address: P.O. Box 1100, Zip 65775–1100; tel. 417/256–9111; Charles R. Brackney, President and Chief Executive Officer (Total facility includes 16 beds in nursing home–type unit) **A**1 9 10 **F**3 6 7 8 10 12 14 15 16 18 19 21 22 23 28 29 30 31 32 33 34 35 37 39 40 41 42 44 45 46 49 52 53 54 55 56 57 58 60 63 64 65 66 67 71 72 73 74 **P**8

| | 23 | 10 | 120 | 5457 | 64 | 38329 | 738 | 49487 | 23810 | 929 |

MONTANA

Resident population 880 (in thousands)
Resident population in metro areas 23.5%
Birth rate per 1,000 population 12.8
65 years and over 13.2%
Percent of persons without health insurance 13.6%

Hospital, Address, Telephone, Administrator, Approval, Facility, and Physician Codes, Health Care System, Network	Classi-fication Codes		Utilization Data					Expense (thousands) of dollars		
	Control	Service	Staffed Beds	Admissions	Census	Outpatient Visits	Births	Total	Payroll	Personnel

★ American Hospital Association (AHA) membership
□ Joint Commission on Accreditation of Healthcare Organizations (JCAHO) accreditation
+ American Osteopathic Healthcare Association (AOHA) membership
○ American Osteopathic Association (AOA) accreditation
△ Commission on Accreditation of Rehabilitation Facilities (CARF) accreditation
Control codes 61, 63, 64, 71, 72 and 73 indicate hospitals listed by AOHA, but not registered by AHA. For definition of numerical codes, see page A4

ANACONDA—Deer Lodge County										
★ COMMUNITY HOSPITAL OF ANACONDA, 401 West Pennsylvania Street, Zip 59711–1999; tel. 406/563–8500; Sam J. Allen, Administrator (Total facility includes 67 beds in nursing home–type unit) **A**9 10 **F**3 6 7 8 10 11 12 13 16 17 18 19 20 22 24 26 27 28 31 32 33 34 35 37 39 40 41 44 45 49 53 54 55 56 57 58 61 62 64 65 66 67 68 71 73 **P**3 **S** Quorum Health Group/Quorum Health Resources, Inc., Brentwood, TN	23	10	92	1079	69	145938	48	10181	4948	161
BAKER—Fallon County										
FALLON MEDICAL COMPLEX, 202 South 4th Street West, Zip 59313–0820, Mailing Address: P.O. Box 820, Zip 59313–0820; tel. 406/778–3331; David Espeland, Chief Executive Officer (Total facility includes 40 beds in nursing home–type unit) **A**9 10 **F**7 8 10 11 14 15 16 17 19 20 22 26 28 29 31 32 34 35 36 37 39 40 42 44 49 51 62 64 67 71 **P**6 8	23	10	52	289	40	22970	18	4936	2576	116
BIG SANDY—Chouteau County										
★ BIG SANDY MEDICAL CENTER, Mailing Address: P.O. Box 530, Zip 59520–0530; tel. 406/378–2188; Harry Bold, Administrator (Total facility includes 22 beds in nursing home–type unit) **A**9 10 **F**15 16 22 32 34 49 64	23	10	30	47	23	5015	0	1248	667	31
BIG TIMBER—Sweet Grass County										
PIONEER MEDICAL CENTER, 301 West Seventh Avenue, Zip 59011, Mailing Address: P.O. Box 1228, Zip 59011–1228; tel. 406/932–4603; Cody Langbehn, Administrator (Total facility includes 52 beds in nursing home–type unit) **A**10 **F**1 14 20 22 30 33 34 36 44 49 64 65 71	13	10	60	137	48	3646	0	2530	1325	70
BILLINGS—Yellowstone County										
⊞ DEACONESS BILLINGS CLINIC, 2800 10th Avenue North, Zip 59101–0799, Mailing Address: P.O. Box 37000, Zip 59107–7000; tel. 406/657–4000; Nicholas J. Wolter, M.D., Chief Executive Officer (Total facility includes 90 beds in nursing home–type unit) **A**1 3 9 10 **F**3 4 10 11 12 15 16 17 18 19 21 22 23 26 27 28 29 30 31 34 37 41 42 43 44 45 46 49 51 52 53 54 55 56 57 58 59 60 61 62 64 65 66 67 70 71 72 73 74 **P**3 8 **Web address:** www.billingsclinic.org	23	10	306	9979	245	539482	0	163928	73168	1721
⊞ △ SAINT VINCENT HOSPITAL AND HEALTH CENTER, 1233 North 30th Street, Zip 59101–0165, Mailing Address: P.O. Box 35200, Zip 59107–5200; tel. 406/657–7000; Patrick M. Hermanson, Senior Executive Officer (Total facility includes 28 beds in nursing home–type unit) **A**1 7 9 10 **F**4 6 7 8 10 12 13 14 15 16 17 18 19 21 22 23 26 28 29 30 31 33 34 35 37 38 39 40 41 42 43 44 45 46 49 51 60 61 64 65 66 67 68 70 71 72 73 74 **P**6 8 **S** Sisters of Charity of Leavenworth Health Services Corporation, Leavenworth, KS **Web address:** www.svhhc.org	21	10	257	13037	169	175515	1889	112017	47040	1393
BOZEMAN—Gallatin County										
★ BOZEMAN DEACONESS HOSPITAL, 915 Highland Boulevard, Zip 59715–6999; tel. 406/585–5000; John A. Nordwick, President and Chief Executive Officer (Nonreporting) **A**9 10	23	10	70	—	—	—	—	—	—	—
BROWNING—Glacier County										
⊞ U. S. PUBLIC HEALTH SERVICE BLACKFEET COMMUNITY HOSPITAL, Mailing Address: P.O. Box 760, Zip 59417–0760; tel. 406/338–6100; Reis Fisher, Service Unit Director (Nonreporting) **A**1 10 **S** U. S. Public Health Service Indian Health Service, Rockville, MD	47	10	25	—	—	—	—	—	—	—
BUTTE—Silver Bow County										
⊞ ST. JAMES COMMUNITY HOSPITAL, 400 South Clark Street, Zip 59701–2328, Mailing Address: P.O. Box 3300, Zip 59702–3300; tel. 406/723–2500; Robert Rodgers, Administrator and Senior Executive Officer **A**1 9 10 **F**7 10 12 14 15 17 19 21 22 23 24 26 28 34 35 37 39 40 41 42 44 45 46 49 60 63 64 65 66 67 70 71 **S** Sisters of Charity of Leavenworth Health Services Corporation, Leavenworth, KS	23	10	100	4377	63	40376	510	38982	15200	431
CHESTER—Liberty County										
LIBERTY COUNTY HOSPITAL AND NURSING HOME, Mailing Address: P.O. Box 705, Zip 59522–0705; tel. 406/759–5181; Douglas Faus, Administrator (Total facility includes 53 beds in nursing home–type unit) **A**9 10 **F**1 7 8 11 22 32 34 37 40 44 49 64 65 71	13	10	64	362	52	5102	18	3101	1471	77
CHOTEAU—Teton County										
TETON MEDICAL CENTER, 915 Fourth Street N.W., Zip 59422–9123; tel. 406/466–5763; Lorin C. MacKay, Administrator (Total facility includes 42 beds in nursing home–type unit) **A**10 **F**1 8 16 22 28 31 33 44 49 64	16	10	46	128	33	5712	0	2271	1184	52
CIRCLE—McCone County										
MCCONE COUNTY MEDICAL ASSISTANCE FACILITY, Mailing Address: P.O. Box 48, Zip 59215–0048; tel. 406/485–3381; Mack N. Simpson, Administrator (Total facility includes 30 beds in nursing home–type unit) **A**10 **F**1 13 14 17 20 21 22 27 28 32 36 39 64 65 73	23	10	38	96	26	2282	0	1304	629	31

Hospital, Address, Telephone, Administrator, Approval, Facility, and Physician Codes, Health Care System, Network	Classi-fication Codes		Utilization Data					Expense (thousands) of dollars		
	Control	Service	Staffed Beds	Admissions	Census	Outpatient Visits	Births	Total	Payroll	Personnel

★ American Hospital Association (AHA) membership
□ Joint Commission on Accreditation of Healthcare Organizations (JCAHO) accreditation
+ American Osteopathic Healthcare Association (AOHA) membership
○ American Osteopathic Association (AOA) accreditation
△ Commission on Accreditation of Rehabilitation Facilities (CARF) accreditation
Control codes 61, 63, 64, 71, 72 and 73 indicate hospitals listed by AOHA, but not registered by AHA. For definition of numerical codes, see page A4

COLUMBUS—Stillwater County

STILLWATER COMMUNITY HOSPITAL, 44 West Fourth Avenue North, Zip 59019, Mailing Address: P.O. Box 959, Zip 59019–0959; tel. 406/322–5316; Tim Russell, Administrator (Total facility includes 10 beds in nursing home–type unit) **A**9 10 **F**7 8 12 13 15 17 21 22 26 28 30 32 33 39 40 44 49 62 64 65 67 71	23	10	23	205	11	6084	32	2371	1186	39

CONRAD—Pondera County

★ PONDERA MEDICAL CENTER, 805 Sunset Boulevard, Zip 59425–1721, Mailing Address: P.O. Box 757, Zip 59425–0757; tel. 406/278–3211; Barry W. Singleton, FACHE, Chief Executive Officer **A**9 10 **F**1 7 8 15 19 21 22 28 32 41 44 46 49 51 64 65 71 73	23	10	79	875	66	7071	25	5948	3105	165

CROW AGENCY—Big Horn County

✉ U. S. PUBLIC HEALTH SERVICE INDIAN HOSPITAL, Mailing Address: P.O. Box 9, Zip 59022–0009; tel. 406/638–2626; Tennyson Doney, Service Unit Director (Nonreporting) **A**1 10 **S** U. S. Public Health Service Indian Health Service, Rockville, MD	47	10	24	—	—	—	—	—	—	—

CULBERTSON—Roosevelt County

★ ROOSEVELT MEMORIAL MEDICAL CENTER, 818 Second Avenue East, Zip 59218, Mailing Address: P.O. Box 419, Zip 59218–0419; tel. 406/787–6281; Walter Busch, Administrator (Total facility includes 44 beds in nursing home–type unit) **A**10 **F**15 22 26 27 28 30 32 34 36 39 46 49 51 64 65 71 73 **P**6	23	10	54	281	40	839	0	2192	1337	64

CUT BANK—Glacier County

★ GLACIER COUNTY MEDICAL CENTER, 802 Second Street S.E., Zip 59427–3331; tel. 406/873–2251; Dale E. Polla, Administrator (Total facility includes 39 beds in nursing home–type unit) **A**9 10 **F**7 11 12 13 14 15 16 17 19 20 22 27 28 30 32 33 37 39 40 42 44 64 65 67 71 73 **P**5 **S** Quorum Health Group/Quorum Health Resources, Inc., Brentwood, TN	13	10	59	425	38	14159	45	5280	2333	104

DEER LODGE—Powell County

★ POWELL COUNTY MEMORIAL HOSPITAL, 1101 Texas Avenue, Zip 59722–1828; tel. 406/846–2212; Connie Huber, R.N., Chief Executive Officer (Total facility includes 16 beds in nursing home–type unit) **A**9 10 **F**14 15 16 37 40 64 **S** Brim Healthcare, Inc., Brentwood, TN	23	10	35	289	15	6092	26	4358	2038	83

DILLON—Beaverhead County

★ BARRETT MEMORIAL HOSPITAL, 1260 South Atlantic Street, Zip 59725–3597; tel. 406/683–3000; John M. Mootry, Chief Executive Officer **A**9 10 **F**7 8 11 14 15 16 19 20 21 28 29 30 32 33 35 37 39 40 42 44 61 63 64 65 67 71 73 **P**8 **S** Brim Healthcare, Inc., Brentwood, TN **Web address:** www.barretthospital.org	16	10	22	984	8	20709	93	9430	3872	132

ENNIS—Madison County

MADISON VALLEY HOSPITAL, 217 North Main Street, Zip 59729–0397, Mailing Address: P.O. Box 397, Zip 59729–0397; tel. 406/682–4222; Pete Brekhus, Chief Executive Officer **A**9 10 **F**22 26 37 44 71 **P**5	23	10	9	108	1	4306	0	1469	834	30

FORSYTH—Rosebud County

★ ROSEBUD HEALTH CARE CENTER, 383 North 17th Avenue, Zip 59327; tel. 406/356–2161; John M. Chioutsis, Chief Executive Officer (Total facility includes 55 beds in nursing home–type unit) **A**9 10 **F**8 11 26 28 30 32 37 44 64 67 71 73 **P**5 6 **S** Brim Healthcare, Inc., Brentwood, TN	23	10	75	378	57	9485	0	3945	2044	91

FORT BENTON—Chouteau County

MISSOURI RIVER MEDICAL CENTER, 1501 St. Charles Street, Zip 59442–0249, Mailing Address: P.O. Box 249, Zip 59442–0249; tel. 406/622–3331; Jay Pottenger, Administrator (Total facility includes 45 beds in nursing home–type unit) **A**9 10 **F**6 21 22 25 31 32 64 65	16	10	52	151	37	10019	0	3214	1812	88

FORT HARRISON—Lewis and Clark County

✉ VETERANS AFFAIRS MONTANA HEALTHCARE SYSTEM, Highway 12 and William Street, Zip 59636; tel. 406/442–6410; Joseph Underkofler, Director (Total facility includes 30 beds in nursing home–type unit) **A**1 9 **F**3 4 7 8 10 11 12 14 15 16 19 20 21 22 24 25 26 28 29 30 31 32 33 34 35 36 37 39 42 44 45 46 49 51 52 54 56 57 58 60 64 65 67 70 71 73 **P**6 **S** Department of Veterans Affairs, Washington, DC **Web address:** www.ft–harrison.va.gov	45	10	45	2007	37	119759	0	33203	22423	514

GLASGOW—Valley County

□ FRANCES MAHON DEACONESS HOSPITAL, 621 Third Street South, Zip 59230–2699; tel. 406/228–4351; Randall G. Holom, Chief Executive Officer **A**1 3 9 10 **F**8 11 15 19 21 22 26 28 31 32 34 42 44 50 54 65	23	10	32	1095	11	26139	103	11909	4919	206

GLENDIVE—Dawson County

□ GLENDIVE MEDICAL CENTER, 202 Prospect Drive, Zip 59330–1999; tel. 406/365–3306; Paul Hanson, Chief Executive Officer (Total facility includes 75 beds in nursing home–type unit) **A**1 9 10 **F**6 8 14 15 17 18 19 21 22 26 28 30 31 32 33 34 35 36 37 39 40 41 42 44 46 49 64 65 67 70 73 **P**7 8 **Web address:** www.gmc.org	23	10	101	724	74	16842	74	9180	4342	184

GREAT FALLS—Cascade County

✉ △ BENEFIS HEALTH CARE, (Includes Benefis Health Care–East Campus, 1101 26th Street, Zip 59405; Benefis Health Care–West Campus, 500 15th Avenue South, Zip 59405), 500 15th Avenue South, Zip 59403–4389; tel. 406/455–5000; Lloyd V. Smith, President and Chief Executive Officer (Total facility includes 140 beds in nursing home–type unit) **A**1 2 7 9 10 **F**2 3 4 7 8 10 11 12 14 15 17 19 21 22 23 24 26 28 30 31 32 33 34 35 37 38 40 41 42 43 44 45 48 49 51 52 53 54 55 56 57 58 59 60 64 65 66 67 71 **P**5 **S** Providence Services, Spokane, WA **Web address:** www.benefis.org	21	10	304	11895	311	—	1274	130244	56713	1549

Hospital, Address, Telephone, Administrator, Approval, Facility, and Physician Codes, Health Care System, Network	Classi-fication Codes		Utilization Data					Expense (thousands) of dollars		
★ American Hospital Association (AHA) membership □ Joint Commission on Accreditation of Healthcare Organizations (JCAHO) accreditation + American Osteopathic Healthcare Association (AOHA) membership ○ American Osteopathic Association (AOA) accreditation △ Commission on Accreditation of Rehabilitation Facilities (CARF) accreditation Control codes 61, 63, 64, 71, 72 and 73 indicate hospitals listed by AOHA, but not registered by AHA. For definition of numerical codes, see page A4	Control	Service	Staffed Beds	Admissions	Census	Outpatient Visits	Births	Total	Payroll	Personnel

HAMILTON—Ravalli County

Hospital	Control	Service	Staffed Beds	Admissions	Census	Outpatient Visits	Births	Total	Payroll	Personnel
★ MARCUS DALY MEMORIAL HOSPITAL, 1200 Westwood Drive, Zip 59840–2395; tel. 406/363–2211; John M. Bartos, Administrator **A**9 10 **F**7 8 14 15 16 17 19 22 28 29 30 32 33 35 41 42 44 45 48 49 65 67 71 **P**8	23	10	48	1623	17	31815	139	16555	8951	310

HARDIN—Big Horn County

Hospital	Control	Service	Staffed Beds	Admissions	Census	Outpatient Visits	Births	Total	Payroll	Personnel
★ BIG HORN COUNTY MEMORIAL HOSPITAL, 17 North Miles Avenue, Zip 59034–0430, Mailing Address: P.O. Box 430, Zip 59034–0430; tel. 406/665–2310; Robert G. Notarianni, Chief Executive Officer (Total facility includes 37 beds in nursing home–type unit) **A**9 10 **F**6 7 8 12 14 15 17 22 26 28 30 32 39 44 49 62 64 65 68 71 **S** Brim Healthcare, Inc., Brentwood, TN	23	10	53	521	38	5777	42	4014	2050	87

HARLEM—Blaine County

Hospital	Control	Service	Staffed Beds	Admissions	Census	Outpatient Visits	Births	Total	Payroll	Personnel
★ U. S. PUBLIC HEALTH SERVICE INDIAN HOSPITAL, Rural Route 1, Box 67, Zip 59526; tel. 406/353–3100; Charles D. Plumage, Director (Total facility includes 37 beds in nursing home–type unit) **A**10 **S** U. S. Public Health Service Indian Health Service, Rockville, MD	23	10	53	443	38	5777	42	4014	2050	87

HARLOWTON—Wheatland County

Hospital	Control	Service	Staffed Beds	Admissions	Census	Outpatient Visits	Births	Total	Payroll	Personnel
★ WHEATLAND MEMORIAL HOSPITAL, 530 Third Street North, Zip 59036, Mailing Address: P.O. Box 287, Zip 59036–0287; tel. 406/632–4351; Craig E. Aasved, Administrator (Total facility includes 36 beds in nursing home–type unit) **A**9 10 **F**1 3 4 5 6 7 8 9 10 11 12 13 14 15 16 17 18 19 20 21 22 24 25 26 27 28 30 31 32 33 34 35 36 37 38 39 40 41 42 43 44 45 46 47 49 50 51 53 54 55 56 57 58 59 60 61 64 65 66 67 68 69 71 72 73 74 **P**7 8 **S** Quorum Health Group/Quorum Health Resources, Inc., Brentwood, TN	13	10	54	188	37	4050	0	3047	1622	71

HAVRE—Hill County

Hospital	Control	Service	Staffed Beds	Admissions	Census	Outpatient Visits	Births	Total	Payroll	Personnel
✚ NORTHERN MONTANA HOSPITAL, 30 13th Street, Zip 59501–5222, Mailing Address: P.O. Box 1231, Zip 59501–1231; tel. 406/265–2211; David Henry, Chief Executive Officer (Total facility includes 167 beds in nursing home–type unit) **A**1 9 10 **F**2 3 6 7 8 15 16 19 21 22 28 30 32 33 35 37 40 41 44 52 53 56 58 59 64 65 66 67 70 71 73 **P**6 **S** Brim Healthcare, Inc., Brentwood, TN	23	10	259	3513	166	70255	454	35306	17302	513

HELENA—Lewis and Clark County

Hospital	Control	Service	Staffed Beds	Admissions	Census	Outpatient Visits	Births	Total	Payroll	Personnel
✚ SHODAIR CHILDREN'S HOSPITAL, 2755 Colonial Drive, Zip 59601, Mailing Address: P.O. Box 5539, Zip 59604–5539; tel. 406/444–7500; Jack Casey, Administrator **A**1 9 10 **F**15 16 52 53 55 58 59 61 64 65	23	52	22	218	34	6575	0	6318	3732	146
✚ ST. PETER'S HOSPITAL, 2475 Broadway, Zip 59601; tel. 406/442–2480; Robert W. Ladenburger, President (Total facility includes 8 beds in nursing home–type unit) **A**1 9 10 **F**7 8 10 12 13 14 15 16 17 19 21 22 23 28 29 30 32 33 34 35 37 38 39 40 41 42 44 45 49 52 54 55 56 58 59 60 63 64 65 66 67 71 73 74 **P**8	23	10	54	4699	44	73180	748	46829	20623	471

KALISPELL—Flathead County

Hospital	Control	Service	Staffed Beds	Admissions	Census	Outpatient Visits	Births	Total	Payroll	Personnel
✚ △ KALISPELL REGIONAL MEDICAL CENTER, (Includes Pathways Treatment Center, 200 Heritage Way, Zip 59901; tel. 406/756–3950), 310 Sunnyview Lane, Zip 59901–3199; tel. 406/752–5111; Velinda Stevens, President and Chief Executive Officer **A**1 7 9 10 **F**1 2 3 4 7 8 10 11 12 15 16 17 18 19 20 21 22 24 26 28 30 31 32 33 34 35 37 39 40 41 42 44 45 46 48 49 52 53 54 55 56 57 58 59 60 63 64 65 66 67 68 71 73 **P**5 6 7 8 **Web address:** www.krmc.org	23	10	142	5986	70	128762	778	52086	21755	721

LEWISTOWN—Fergus County

Hospital	Control	Service	Staffed Beds	Admissions	Census	Outpatient Visits	Births	Total	Payroll	Personnel
★ CENTRAL MONTANA MEDICAL CENTER, 408 Wendell Avenue, Zip 59457–2261, Mailing Address: P.O. Box 580, Zip 59457–0580; tel. 406/538–7711; David M. Faulkner, Chief Executive Officer and Administrator (Total facility includes 85 beds in nursing home–type unit) **A**9 10 **F**1 7 8 13 14 15 16 19 21 22 24 26 28 30 32 33 34 35 37 39 40 42 44 49 56 63 64 65 66 67 70 71 **S** Quorum Health Group/Quorum Health Resources, Inc., Brentwood, TN	23	10	124	1373	96	30520	131	14369	6968	250

LIBBY—Lincoln County

Hospital	Control	Service	Staffed Beds	Admissions	Census	Outpatient Visits	Births	Total	Payroll	Personnel
★ ST. JOHN'S LUTHERAN HOSPITAL, 350 Louisiana Avenue, Zip 59923–2198; tel. 406/293–7761; Richard L. Palagi, Chief Executive Officer **A**9 10 **F**6 7 8 11 14 17 19 22 28 29 30 32 33 37 39 40 41 42 44 49 51 65 66 67 71 72 73 **P**6 7 **S** Brim Healthcare, Inc., Brentwood, TN **Web address:** www.libby.org/sjlh	23	10	26	1035	10	25356	108	7675	3388	129

LIVINGSTON—Park County

Hospital	Control	Service	Staffed Beds	Admissions	Census	Outpatient Visits	Births	Total	Payroll	Personnel
★ LIVINGSTON MEMORIAL HOSPITAL, 504 South 13th Street, Zip 59047–3798; tel. 406/222–3541; Richard V. Brown, Chief Executive Officer **A**9 10 **F**7 8 11 12 13 15 16 17 19 21 22 24 28 29 30 32 33 34 37 40 41 42 44 49 63 66 67 71	23	10	32	1194	11	23859	150	9327	4475	200

MALTA—Phillips County

Hospital	Control	Service	Staffed Beds	Admissions	Census	Outpatient Visits	Births	Total	Payroll	Personnel
PHILLIPS COUNTY MEDICAL CENTER, 417 South Fourth East, Zip 59538, Mailing Address: P.O. Box 640, Zip 59538–0640; tel. 406/654–1100; Larry E. Putnam, Administrator **A**9 10 **F**14 15 22 28 30 32 44 49 66 71	23	10	14	124	1	5346	0	2379	1183	55

MILES CITY—Custer County

Hospital	Control	Service	Staffed Beds	Admissions	Census	Outpatient Visits	Births	Total	Payroll	Personnel
✚ HOLY ROSARY HEALTH CENTER, 2600 Wilson Street, Zip 59301–5094; tel. 406/233–2600; H. Ray Gibbons, FACHE, Administrator and Senior Executive Officer (Total facility includes 107 beds in nursing home–type unit) **A**1 9 10 **F**2 3 7 8 12 13 14 15 16 17 19 21 22 24 27 28 30 32 35 36 37 39 40 42 44 48 53 54 55 56 57 58 63 64 65 67 71 72 **S** Sisters of Charity of Leavenworth Health Services Corporation, Leavenworth, KS	21	10	151	2470	92	24428	209	19039	8300	196

MISSOULA—Missoula County

Hospital	Control	Service	Staffed Beds	Admissions	Census	Outpatient Visits	Births	Total	Payroll	Personnel
✚ △ COMMUNITY MEDICAL CENTER, 2827 Fort Missoula Road, Zip 59801; tel. 406/728–4100; Grant M. Winn, President **A**1 7 9 10	23	10	117	5007	67	173099	1379	51688	27089	637

Hospital, Address, Telephone, Administrator, Approval, Facility, and Physician Codes, Health Care System, Network	Classi-fication Codes		Utilization Data					Expense (thousands) of dollars		
★ American Hospital Association (AHA) membership □ Joint Commission on Accreditation of Healthcare Organizations (JCAHO) accreditation + American Osteopathic Healthcare Association (AOHA) membership ○ American Osteopathic Association (AOA) accreditation △ Commission on Accreditation of Rehabilitation Facilities (CARF) accreditation Control codes 61, 63, 64, 71, 72 and 73 indicate hospitals listed by AOHA, but not registered by AHA. For definition of numerical codes, see page A4	Control	Service	Staffed Beds	Admissions	Census	Outpatient Visits	Births	Total	Payroll	Personnel

Hospital	Control	Service	Staffed Beds	Admissions	Census	Outpatient Visits	Births	Total	Payroll	Personnel
⊠ ST. PATRICK HOSPITAL, 500 West Broadway, Zip 59802–4096, Mailing Address: Box 4587, Zip 59806–4587; tel. 406/543–7271; Lawrence L. White, Jr., President (Total facility includes 18 beds in nursing home–type unit) **A**1 2 9 10 **F**2 3 4 10 12 14 15 16 17 19 21 22 23 24 27 29 30 32 33 34 35 37 39 41 42 43 44 45 49 52 53 54 55 56 57 58 59 60 63 64 65 66 67 68 69 70 71 72 73 **P**7 **S** Providence Services, Spokane, WA **Web address:** www.saintpatrick.org	21	10	213	9241	125	103614	0	89838	35109	1064
PHILIPSBURG—Granite County										
GRANITE COUNTY MEMORIAL HOSPITAL AND NURSING HOME, Mailing Address: P.O. Box 729, Zip 59858–0729; tel. 406/859–3271; Doris White Gilbertson, Administrator (Total facility includes 32 beds in nursing home–type unit) **A**10 **F**1 15 20 22 32 33 34 49 51 64 65 71 **P**5	13	10	35	30	28	2383	0	1321	734	38
PLAINS—Sanders County										
★ CLARK FORK VALLEY HOSPITAL, Mailing Address: P.O. Box 768, Zip 59859–0768; tel. 406/826–3601; Mary Anne Peterson, Interim Administrator (Total facility includes 28 beds in nursing home–type unit) **A**9 10 **F**8 14 15 16 19 22 28 32 34 37 40 44 49 64 71 **P**6	23	10	44	780	35	24278	—	7242	3734	139
PLENTYWOOD—Sheridan County										
SHERIDAN MEMORIAL HOSPITAL, 440 West Laurel Avenue, Zip 59254–1596; tel. 406/765–1420; Ella Gutzke, Administrator (Total facility includes 78 beds in nursing home–type unit) **A**9 10 **F**7 8 14 15 16 19 20 22 26 28 30 31 32 34 36 37 40 41 44 46 49 64 67 68 71 73	23	10	93	653	72	731	23	5025	2674	50
POLSON—Lake County										
⊠ ST. JOSEPH HOSPITAL, Skyline Drive and 14th Avenue, Zip 59860, Mailing Address: P.O. Box 1010, Zip 59860–1010; tel. 406/883–5377; John W. Glueckert, President **A**1 9 10 **F**7 8 15 19 22 24 32 40 44 65 73 **S** Providence Services, Spokane, WA	21	10	22	690	5	15711	61	5341	2360	108
POPLAR—Roosevelt County										
POPLAR COMMUNITY HOSPITAL See Northeast Montana Health Services, Wolf Point										
RED LODGE—Carbon County										
★ BEARTOOTH HOSPITAL AND HEALTH CENTER, 600 West 20th Street, Zip 59068, Mailing Address: P.O. Box 590, Zip 59068–0590; tel. 406/446–2345; Kelley Evans, Administrator (Total facility includes 30 beds in nursing home–type unit) **A**9 10	23	10	56	452	31	11405	25	3829	2337	82
RONAN—Lake County										
★ ST. LUKE COMMUNITY HOSPITAL, 107 Sixth Avenue S.W., Zip 59864–2634; tel. 406/676–4441; Shane Roberts, Administrator (Total facility includes 75 beds in nursing home–type unit) **A**9 10 **F**1 7 8 14 15 16 22 28 30 31 34 40 41 44 64 71 **P**6	23	10	99	854	70	60212	128	11090	6090	192
ROUNDUP—Musselshell County										
★ ROUNDUP MEMORIAL HOSPITAL, 1202 Third Street West, Zip 59072–1816, Mailing Address: P.O. Box 40, Zip 59072–0040; tel. 406/323–2302; Dave McIvor, Administrator (Total facility includes 37 beds in nursing home–type unit) **A**9 10 **F**1 15 22 32 64 71 **S** Brim Healthcare, Inc., Brentwood, TN	23	10	54	353	37	4484	0	3467	1796	88
SCOBEY—Daniels County										
DANIELS MEMORIAL HOSPITAL, 105 Fifth Avenue East, Zip 59263, Mailing Address: P.O. Box 400, Zip 59263–0400; tel. 406/487–2296; Glenn Haugo, Administrator (Total facility includes 48 beds in nursing home–type unit) (Nonreporting) **A**9 10	23	10	54	—	—	—	—	—	—	—
SHELBY—Toole County										
MARIAS MEDICAL CENTER, 640 Park Drive, Zip 59474–1663, Mailing Address: P.O. Box 915, Zip 59474–0915; tel. 406/434–3200; Jerry Morasko, Administrator (Total facility includes 68 beds in nursing home–type unit) **A**9 10 **Web address:** www.mariasmedicalcenter.org	13	10	84	890	71	9653	83	7837	2431	157
SHERIDAN—Madison County										
RUBY VALLEY HOSPITAL, 220 East Crofoot Street, Zip 59749, Mailing Address: P.O. Box 336, Zip 59749–0336; tel. 406/842–5453; Steve Lang, Administrator **A**9 10 **F**22 32 49	16	10	8	167	1	8380	0	1316	797	30
SIDNEY—Richland County										
SIDNEY HEALTH CENTER, 216 14th Avenue S.W., Zip 59270–3586; tel. 406/488–2100; Donald J. Rush, Chief Executive Officer (Nonreporting) **A**9 10	23	10	42	—	—	—	—	—	—	—
SUPERIOR—Mineral County										
★ MINERAL COMMUNITY HOSPITAL, Roosevelt and Brooklyn, Zip 59872, Mailing Address: P.O. Box 66, Zip 59872–0066; tel. 406/822–4841; Steven Smoot, Chief Executive Officer (Total facility includes 20 beds in nursing home–type unit) (Nonreporting) **A**9 10 **S** Brim Healthcare, Inc., Brentwood, TN	23	10	30	—	—	—	—	—	—	—
TERRY—Prairie County										
★ PRAIRIE COMMUNITY MEDICAL ASSISTANCE FACILITY, 312 South Adams Avenue, Zip 59349–0156, Mailing Address: P.O. Box 156, Zip 59349–0156; tel. 406/635–5511; James R. Mantz, Administrator (Total facility includes 19 beds in nursing home–type unit) **A**10 **F**8 13 15 22 26 28 36 51 64	16	10	21	34	18	1566	0	1098	621	33
TOWNSEND—Broadwater County										
BROADWATER HEALTH CENTER, 110 North Oak Street, Zip 59644–2306; tel. 406/266–3186; James Holcomb, Chief Executive Officer (Total facility includes 35 beds in nursing home–type unit) **A**9 10 **F**14 15 22 32 39 49 64 65 67	23	10	44	182	38	—	1	2193	1028	67

Hospital, Address, Telephone, Administrator, Approval, Facility, and Physician Codes, Health Care System, Network	Classi-fication Codes		Utilization Data					Expense (thousands) of dollars		
★ American Hospital Association (AHA) membership ☐ Joint Commission on Accreditation of Healthcare Organizations (JCAHO) accreditation + American Osteopathic Healthcare Association (AOHA) membership ○ American Osteopathic Association (AOA) accreditation △ Commission on Accreditation of Rehabilitation Facilities (CARF) accreditation Control codes 61, 63, 64, 71, 72 and 73 indicate hospitals listed by AOHA, but not registered by AHA. For definition of numerical codes, see page A4	Control	Service	Staffed Beds	Admissions	Census	Outpatient Visits	Births	Total	Payroll	Personnel

WARM SPRINGS—Deer Lodge County

MONTANA STATE HOSPITAL, Zip 59756; tel. 406/693–7000; Carl Keener, M.D., Medical Director (Total facility includes 30 beds in nursing home–type unit) **F**52 57 64 65 **P**6	12	22	170	402	182	0	0	—	12000	402

WHITE SULPHUR SPRINGS—Meagher County

MOUNTAINVIEW MEDICAL CENTER, 16 West Main Street, Zip 59645, Mailing Address: P.O. Box Q, Zip 59645; tel. 406/547–3321; Greg Nielsen, Administrator (Total facility includes 31 beds in nursing home–type unit) **A**9 10 **F**13 26 28 39 49 64 **P**6	23	10	37	158	21	—	0	1803	1052	50

WHITEFISH—Flathead County

★ NORTH VALLEY HOSPITAL, 6575 Highway 93 South, Zip 59937; tel. 406/863–2501; Kenneth E. S. Platou, Chief Executive Officer (Total facility includes 56 beds in nursing home–type unit) **A**9 10 **F**1 7 8 17 19 22 26 28 30 33 34 37 40 41 44 46 49 64 65 66 71 72 73 **P**5 **S** Quorum Health Group/Quorum Health Resources, Inc., Brentwood, TN **Web address:** www.nvhosp.org	23	10	99	1422	71	40536	161	14067	6799	179

WOLF POINT—Roosevelt County

NORTHEAST MONTANA HEALTH SERVICES, (Includes Poplar Community Hospital, H and Court Avenue, Poplar, Zip 59255, Mailing Address: P.O. Box 38, Zip 59255; tel. 406/768–3452; Trinity Hospital, 315 Knapp Street, Zip 59201; tel. 406/653–2100), 315 Knapp Street, Zip 59201–1898; tel. 406/653–2110; Margaret Norgaard, Administrator (Total facility includes 82 beds in nursing home–type unit) **A**9 10 **F**1 7 14 15 16 22 26 28 30 32 36 37 40 42 44 45 46 62 64 65 68 71 **P**6	23	10	117	978	72	14817	167	7919	4483	223

NEBRASKA

Resident population 1,663 (in thousands)
Resident population in metro areas 50.9%
Birth rate per 1,000 population 14.2
65 years and over 13.7%
Percent of persons without health insurance 11.4%

Hospital, Address, Telephone, Administrator, Approval, Facility, and Physician Codes, Health Care System, Network	Classi-fication Codes		Utilization Data					Expense (thousands) of dollars		
★ American Hospital Association (AHA) membership □ Joint Commission on Accreditation of Healthcare Organizations (JCAHO) accreditation + American Osteopathic Healthcare Association (AOHA) membership ○ American Osteopathic Association (AOA) accreditation △ Commission on Accreditation of Rehabilitation Facilities (CARF) accreditation Control codes 61, 63, 64, 71, 72 and 73 indicate hospitals listed by AOHA, but not registered by AHA. For definition of numerical codes, see page A4	Control	Service	Staffed Beds	Admissions	Census	Outpatient Visits	Births	Total	Payroll	Personnel

AINSWORTH—Brown County
BROWN COUNTY HOSPITAL, 945 East Zero Street, Zip 69210–1547; tel. 402/387–2800; David Hartberg, Administrator **A**9 10 **F**7 14 16 22 25 32 34 41 44 51

| | 13 | 10 | 25 | 225 | 8 | 6849 | 31 | 2201 | 1055 | 56 |

ALBION—Boone County
★ BOONE COUNTY HEALTH CENTER, 723 West Fairview Street, Zip 68620–1725, Mailing Address: P.O. Box 151, Zip 68620–0151; tel. 402/395–2191; Gayle E. Primrose, Administrator **A**9 10 **F**2 3 7 8 11 15 16 17 19 22 24 25 26 28 30 31 32 33 34 35 37 39 40 41 42 44 45 48 49 51 52 53 54 55 57 58 64 65 66 67 71 73 **P**6

| | 13 | 10 | 20 | 763 | 8 | 45277 | 92 | 7220 | 4179 | 152 |

ALLIANCE—Box Butte County
□ BOX BUTTE GENERAL HOSPITAL, 2101 Box Butte Avenue, Zip 69301–0810, Mailing Address: P.O. Box 810, Zip 69301–0810; tel. 308/762–6660; Terrance J. Padden, Administrator **A**1 9 10 **F**3 7 8 12 13 14 15 17 18 19 22 24 26 28 29 30 33 34 35 36 37 39 40 41 42 44 45 46 49 51 52 56 61 64 65 66 67 68 71 72 73

| | 13 | 10 | 44 | 834 | 9 | 17224 | 129 | 6766 | 3263 | 114 |

ALMA—Harlan County
★ HARLAN COUNTY HEALTH SYSTEM, (Formerly Harlan County Hospital), 717 North Brown Street, Zip 68920–0836, Mailing Address: P.O. Box 836, Zip 68920–0836; tel. 308/928–2151; Allen Van Driel, Administrator **A**9 10 **F**8 15 16 19 21 22 31 32 33 34 44 49 71 **P**6 8 **S** Great Plains Health Alliance, Inc., Phillipsburg, KS

| | 13 | 10 | 25 | 281 | 8 | 11241 | 0 | 2252 | 1169 | 38 |

ATKINSON—Holt County
WEST HOLT MEMORIAL HOSPITAL, 406 Legion Street, Zip 68713–0200, Mailing Address: Rural Route 1, Box 200, Zip 68713–0200; tel. 402/925–2811; Mel L. Snow, Administrator **A**9 10 **F**4 7 8 10 14 15 16 17 18 19 22 25 26 28 29 30 34 35 40 41 42 43 44 45 49 51 58 60 61 65 69 71 74 **P**6

| | 23 | 10 | 18 | 422 | 4 | 8795 | 15 | 4206 | 1496 | 65 |

AUBURN—Nemaha County
★ NEMAHA COUNTY HOSPITAL, 2022 13th Street, Zip 68305–1799; tel. 402/274–4366; Glen E. Krueger, Administrator **A**9 10 **F**8 11 14 15 16 19 22 28 30 33 34 35 37 41 42 44 45 49 60 64 71

| | 13 | 10 | 30 | 500 | 6 | 18039 | 1 | 3526 | 1626 | 74 |

AURORA—Hamilton County
MEMORIAL HOSPITAL, 1423 Seventh Street, Zip 68818–1197; tel. 402/694–3171; Eldon A. Wall, Administrator (Total facility includes 53 beds in nursing home–type unit) **A**9 10 **F**7 8 15 19 22 23 28 30 32 33 34 36 37 39 40 41 42 44 49 64 65 66 71 **P**6

| | 23 | 10 | 78 | 633 | 53 | 16149 | 81 | 8200 | 4464 | 154 |

BASSETT—Rock County
ROCK COUNTY HOSPITAL, 102 East South Street, Zip 68714, Mailing Address: P.O. Box 100, Zip 68714–0100; tel. 402/684–3366; David Stephenson, Administrator (Total facility includes 30 beds in nursing home–type unit) **A**9 10 **F**19 22 44 64 71

| | 13 | 10 | 47 | 485 | 32 | 5899 | 1 | 2293 | 1433 | 84 |

BEATRICE—Gage County
✠ BEATRICE COMMUNITY HOSPITAL AND HEALTH CENTER, 1110 North Tenth Street, Zip 68310–2039, Mailing Address: P.O. Box 278, Zip 68310–0278; tel. 402/228–3344; Kenneth J. Zimmerman, Administrator (Total facility includes 78 beds in nursing home–type unit) **A**1 9 10 **F**7 8 11 15 16 17 19 21 22 23 28 30 32 33 35 36 37 40 41 44 48 49 62 64 65 67 71 73

| | 23 | 10 | 108 | 1231 | 87 | 7997 | 151 | 16713 | 8242 | 330 |

BENKELMAN—Dundy County
DUNDY COUNTY HOSPITAL, 1313 North Cheyenne Street, Zip 69021, Mailing Address: P.O. Box 626, Zip 69021–0626; tel. 308/423–2204; Marlo L. Miller, Administrator **A**9 10 **F**8 13 15 17 19 21 22 24 27 28 29 30 35 37 40 41 42 43 44 49 51 63 65 71 73 74 **P**4 7

| | 13 | 10 | 14 | 310 | 4 | 7722 | 14 | 3036 | 1406 | 62 |

BLAIR—Washington County
✠ MEMORIAL COMMUNITY HOSPITAL AND HEALTH SYSTEM, 810 North 22nd Street, Zip 68008–1199, Mailing Address: P.O. Box 250, Zip 68008–0250; tel. 402/426–2182; Robert Omer, President and Chief Executive Officer **A**1 9 10 **F**7 8 14 15 16 17 18 19 22 28 30 32 33 34 35 36 39 40 41 44 45 46 49 64 65 67 71 73 **P**6

| | 23 | 10 | 33 | 1058 | 11 | 75999 | 121 | 12337 | 7192 | 261 |

BRIDGEPORT—Morrill County
MORRILL COUNTY COMMUNITY HOSPITAL, 1313 S Street, Zip 69336–0579, Mailing Address: P.O. Box 579, Zip 69336–0579; tel. 308/262–1616; Julia Morrow, Administrator (Nonreporting) **A**9 10

| | 13 | 10 | 20 | — | — | — | — | — | — | — |

BROKEN BOW—Custer County
JENNIE M. MELHAM MEMORIAL MEDICAL CENTER, 145 Memorial Drive, Zip 68822–1378, Mailing Address: P.O. Box 250, Zip 68822–0250; tel. 308/872–6891; Michael J. Steckler, Chief Executive Officer (Total facility includes 77 beds in nursing home–type unit) **A**9 10 **F**6 7 8 17 19 21 22 24 28 30 32 33 34 35 44 62 64 65 71

| | 23 | 10 | 116 | 1086 | 81 | 10047 | 98 | 6996 | 3406 | 177 |

Hospital, Address, Telephone, Administrator, Approval, Facility, and Physician Codes, Health Care System, Network	Classi-fication Codes		Utilization Data					Expense (thousands) of dollars		
★ American Hospital Association (AHA) membership □ Joint Commission on Accreditation of Healthcare Organizations (JCAHO) accreditation + American Osteopathic Healthcare Association (AOHA) membership ○ American Osteopathic Association (AOA) accreditation △ Commission on Accreditation of Rehabilitation Facilities (CARF) accreditation Control codes 61, 63, 64, 71, 72 and 73 indicate hospitals listed by AOHA, but not registered by AHA. For definition of numerical codes, see page A4	Control	Service	Staffed Beds	Admissions	Census	Outpatient Visits	Births	Total	Payroll	Personnel

CALLAWAY—Custer County

★ CALLAWAY DISTRICT HOSPITAL, 211 Kimball, Zip 68825–0100, Mailing Address: P.O. Box 100, Zip 68825–0100; tel. 308/836–2228; Marvin Neth, Administrator **A**9 10 **F**11 15 16 19 22 33 37 40 44 64 71 **P**3 — 16 10 12 244 3 6500 6 1357 585 28

CAMBRIDGE—Furnas County

★ TRI–VALLEY HEALTH SYSTEM, West Highway 6 and 34, Zip 69022–0488, Mailing Address: P.O. Box 488, Zip 69022–0488; tel. 308/697–3329; Jerry W. Harris, Interim Chief Executive Officer (Total facility includes 36 beds in nursing home–type unit) (Nonreporting) **A**9 10 **S** Brim Healthcare, Inc., Brentwood, TN — 23 10 56 — — — — — — —

CENTRAL CITY—Merrick County

LITZENBERG MEMORIAL COUNTY HOSPITAL, 1715 26th Street, Zip 68826–9620, Mailing Address: Route 2, Box 1, Zip 68826–0001; tel. 308/946–3015; Mike R. Bowman, Administrator (Total facility includes 46 beds in nursing home–type unit) **A**9 10 **F**6 7 8 14 15 16 19 21 22 24 32 34 35 36 41 42 44 48 49 64 65 66 71 73 **P**5 — 13 10 64 516 50 14319 41 5013 2599 127

CHADRON—Dawes County

★ CHADRON COMMUNITY HOSPITAL AND HEALTH SERVICES, 821 Morehead Street, Zip 69337–2599; tel. 308/432–5586; Harold L. Krueger, Jr., Chief ExecutiveOfficer **A**9 10 **F**1 6 7 8 12 13 15 16 17 18 19 22 28 30 31 32 33 37 39 40 44 48 49 61 62 64 65 66 71 73 **P**5 8 — 23 10 32 692 10 6705 109 6618 2804 125

COLUMBUS—Platte County

▣ COLUMBUS COMMUNITY HOSPITAL, 3020 18th Street, Zip 68601–4214, Mailing Address: P.O. Box 819, Zip 68602–0819; tel. 402/564–7118; Donald H. Zornes, Administrator (Total facility includes 19 beds in nursing home–type unit) **A**1 9 10 **F**7 8 10 11 12 15 16 17 19 20 21 22 23 28 30 31 32 33 34 35 36 37 38 39 40 41 44 45 46 49 52 64 65 67 71 73 **P**8 — 23 10 73 2300 38 53189 505 17870 7552 261

COZAD—Dawson County

COZAD COMMUNITY HOSPITAL, 300 East 12th Street, Zip 69130–1505, Mailing Address: P.O. Box 108, Zip 69130–0108; tel. 308/784–2261; Lyle E. Davis, Administrator **A**9 10 **F**7 8 19 22 24 30 32 33 36 37 39 40 44 49 51 65 71 **P**3 — 16 10 21 932 4 5470 56 5414 3001 68

CREIGHTON—Knox County

CREIGHTON AREA HEALTH SERVICES, 1503 Main Street, Zip 68729–0186, Mailing Address: P.O. Box 186, Zip 68729–0186; tel. 402/358–3322; Paul Hurd, Chief Executive Officer (Total facility includes 46 beds in nursing home–type unit) **A**9 10 **F**1 7 8 15 16 17 19 22 27 28 30 32 34 35 37 39 40 41 42 44 64 65 67 71 **P**8 — 14 10 76 433 50 5518 13 3615 1880 94

CRETE—Saline County

★ CRETE MUNICIPAL HOSPITAL, 1540 Grove Street, Zip 68333–0220, Mailing Address: P.O. Box 220, Zip 68333–0220; tel. 402/826–6800; Joseph W. Lohrman, Administrator (Total facility includes 22 beds in nursing home–type unit) **A**9 10 **F**7 8 14 15 16 19 22 32 42 44 64 71 73
Web address: www.creteabc.org — 14 10 57 694 44 18922 56 5446 2592 95

DAVID CITY—Butler County

BUTLER COUNTY HEALTH CARE CENTER, 372 South Ninth Street, Zip 68632–2199; tel. 402/367–3115; Roger Reamer, Administrator **A**9 10 **F**1 3 7 8 14 15 16 17 19 20 22 24 27 28 30 32 33 34 35 36 39 40 42 44 45 46 49 51 58 62 64 65 66 67 71 73 — 13 10 31 689 10 18765 91 4060 2061 81

FAIRBURY—Jefferson County

★ JEFFERSON COMMUNITY HEALTH CENTER, 2200 H Street, Zip 68352–1119, Mailing Address: P.O. Box 277, Zip 68352–0277; tel. 402/729–3351; Bill Welch, Administrator (Total facility includes 41 beds in nursing home–type unit) **A**9 10 **F**7 8 10 16 17 19 20 22 24 26 28 29 30 32 33 35 39 41 42 44 45 46 49 64 65 66 67 71 73 — 23 10 65 456 42 10611 41 5699 2711 123

FALLS CITY—Richardson County

★ COMMUNITY MEDICAL CENTER, 2307 Barada Street, Zip 68355–1599; tel. 402/245–2428; Victor Lee, Chief Executive Officer and Administrator **A**9 10 **F**7 8 15 16 17 19 21 22 26 28 30 32 33 34 35 42 44 49 63 65 66 74 **P**6 **S** Great Plains Health Alliance, Inc., Phillipsburg, KS — 23 10 35 1035 17 21350 61 7207 3136 126

FRANKLIN—Franklin County

★ FRANKLIN COUNTY MEMORIAL HOSPITAL, 1406 Q Street, Zip 68939–0315, Mailing Address: P.O. Box 315, Zip 68939–0315; tel. 308/425–6221; Jerrell F. Gerdes, Administrator **A**9 10 **F**8 14 15 16 19 20 22 24 27 28 30 31 32 33 34 35 42 44 65 70 71 **P**6 — 13 10 20 230 5 5238 3 2606 1488 67

FREMONT—Dodge County

▣ FREMONT AREA MEDICAL CENTER, 450 East 23rd Street, Zip 68025–2387; tel. 402/721–1610; Vincent J. O'Connor, Jr., President and Chief Executive Officer (Total facility includes 162 beds in nursing home–type unit) **A**1 2 9 10 **F**1 7 8 11 15 16 17 19 21 22 26 27 28 29 30 31 32 33 34 35 37 39 40 41 42 44 45 46 48 49 60 63 64 65 66 67 71 72 73 **P**8 — 13 10 262 3945 197 63557 451 38398 20059 625

FRIEND—Saline County

WARREN MEMORIAL HOSPITAL, 905 Second Street, Zip 68359–1198; tel. 402/947–2541; Joseph W. Lohrman, Administrator (Total facility includes 58 beds in nursing home–type unit) **A**9 10 **F**1 6 7 8 14 15 16 22 28 30 32 33 34 36 41 44 49 51 64 70 — 14 10 73 133 48 5320 6 2097 1175 58

GENEVA—Fillmore County

FILLMORE COUNTY HOSPITAL, 1325 H Street, Zip 68361–1325, Mailing Address: P.O. Box 193, Zip 68361–0193; tel. 402/759–3167; Larry Eichelberger, Chief Executive Officer (Total facility includes 20 beds in nursing home–type unit) **A**9 10 **F**3 7 8 11 12 13 15 16 17 19 20 22 24 26 27 28 29 30 31 32 33 34 35 36 37 39 40 41 42 44 45 46 49 61 64 65 66 67 71 73 — 13 10 53 441 30 8545 34 3995 1809 78

Hospital, Address, Telephone, Administrator, Approval, Facility, and Physician Codes, Health Care System, Network	Classi-fication Codes		Utilization Data					Expense (thousands) of dollars		
	Control	Service	Staffed Beds	Admissions	Census	Outpatient Visits	Births	Total	Payroll	Personnel

★ American Hospital Association (AHA) membership
□ Joint Commission on Accreditation of Healthcare Organizations (JCAHO) accreditation
+ American Osteopathic Healthcare Association (AOHA) membership
○ American Osteopathic Association (AOA) accreditation
△ Commission on Accreditation of Rehabilitation Facilities (CARF) accreditation
Control codes 61, 63, 64, 71, 72 and 73 indicate hospitals listed by AOHA, but not registered by AHA. For definition of numerical codes, see page A4

GENOA—Nance County

GENOA COMMUNITY HOSPITAL, 706 Ewing Avenue, Zip 68640, Mailing Address: P.O. Box 310, Zip 68640–0310; tel. 402/993–2283; Wade H. Edwards, Administrator (Total facility includes 59 beds in nursing home–type unit) (Nonreporting) **A**9 10

| | 14 | 10 | 99 | — | — | — | — | — | — | — |

GORDON—Sheridan County

★ GORDON MEMORIAL HOSPITAL DISTRICT, 300 East Eighth Street, Zip 69343–9990; tel. 308/282–0401; Gladys Phemister, Chief Executive Officer **A**9 10 **F**1 3 6 7 8 11 15 16 17 19 22 28 30 32 37 40 44 49 61 64 71 **P**6
Web address: www.ci.gordon.ne.us/

| | 16 | 10 | 40 | 875 | 49 | 18322 | 48 | 6212 | 3235 | 137 |

GOTHENBURG—Dawson County

★ GOTHENBURG MEMORIAL HOSPITAL, 910 20th Street, Zip 69138–1237, Mailing Address: P.O. Box 469, Zip 69138–0469; tel. 308/537–3661; John H. Johnson, Chief Executive Officer (Total facility includes 37 beds in nursing home–type unit) **A**9 10 **F**7 8 19 22 24 29 30 32 33 34 37 40 41 42 44 45 48 49 51 64 65 67 71

| | 16 | 10 | 49 | 312 | 37 | 9743 | 60 | 3305 | 1588 | 102 |

GRAND ISLAND—Hall County

✠ ST. FRANCIS MEDICAL CENTER, (Includes Saint Francis Memorial Health Center, 2116 West Faidley Avenue, Zip 68803), 2620 West Faidley Avenue, Zip 68803–4297, Mailing Address: P.O. Box 9804, Zip 68802–9804; tel. 308/384–4600; Michael R. Gloor, FACHE, President and Chief Executive Officer (Total facility includes 36 beds in nursing home–type unit) **A**1 2 3 5 9 10 **F**2 3 4 7 8 10 11 12 15 16 17 19 20 21 22 23 27 28 30 32 33 34 35 37 38 39 40 41 42 44 49 54 58 60 62 64 65 66 67 71 73 **P**8 **S** Catholic Health Initiatives, Denver, CO
Web address: www.sfmc–gi.org

| | 23 | 10 | 198 | 6443 | 98 | 72490 | 910 | 63184 | 26718 | 850 |

GRANT—Perkins County

PERKINS COUNTY HEALTH SERVICES, (Includes GOLDEN OURS CONVALESCENT HOME), 900 Lincoln Avenue, Zip 69140–9799, Mailing Address: Rural Route 1, Box 26, Zip 69140–9799; tel. 308/352–7200; Carol A. Abbuhl, Chief Executive Officer (Total facility includes 64 beds in nursing home–type unit) **A**9 10 **F**7 11 19 22 26 28 32 33 34 40 42 44 49 64 65 67 71 **P**6

| | 16 | 10 | 84 | 695 | 63 | 9587 | 33 | 4915 | 2690 | 135 |

HASTINGS—Adams County

□ HASTINGS REGIONAL CENTER, 4200 West Second Street, Zip 68901–9700, Mailing Address: P.O. Box 579, Zip 68902–0579; tel. 402/462–1971; Michael J. Sheehan, Administrator (Nonreporting) **A**1 10

| | 12 | 49 | 232 | — | — | — | — | — | — | — |

✠ MARY LANNING MEMORIAL HOSPITAL, 715 North St. Joseph Avenue, Zip 68901–4497; tel. 402/461–5110; W. Michael Kearney, President (Total facility includes 20 beds in nursing home–type unit) **A**1 2 9 10 **F**3 7 8 10 11 13 15 16 17 19 20 21 22 23 24 28 30 31 32 33 34 35 36 37 38 39 40 41 42 44 45 46 49 51 52 53 54 55 56 57 58 59 60 62 64 65 66 67 70 71 73 74 **P**6
Web address: www.mlmh.org

| | 23 | 10 | 125 | 4975 | 62 | 37436 | 663 | 43268 | 20514 | 707 |

HEBRON—Thayer County

★ THAYER COUNTY HEALTH SERVICES, 120 Park Avenue, Zip 68370–2019, Mailing Address: P.O. Box 49, Zip 68370–0049; tel. 402/768–6041; Larry E. Leaming, Administrator **A**9 10 **F**7 8 13 15 17 19 20 22 28 30 32 33 34 35 39 40 41 42 44 46 49 51 64 65 66 67 71 73 74 **P**6

| | 13 | 10 | 14 | 464 | 4 | 20623 | 40 | 5034 | 2324 | 98 |

HENDERSON—York County

HENDERSON HEALTH CARE SERVICES, 1621 Front Street, Zip 68371–0217, Mailing Address: P.O. Box 217, Zip 68371–0217; tel. 402/723–4512; Mark Neubacher, Chief Executive Officer (Total facility includes 42 beds in nursing home–type unit) **A**9 10 **F**1 6 7 14 15 19 22 27 30 32 34 36 44 49 51 57 62 64 65 71 74 **P**8

| | 23 | 10 | 59 | 209 | 42 | 14590 | 9 | 3680 | 2176 | 42 |

HOLDREGE—Phelps County

✠ PHELPS MEMORIAL HEALTH CENTER, 1220 Miller Street, Zip 68949–0828, Mailing Address: P.O. Box 828, Zip 68949–0828; tel. 308/995–2211; Jerome Seigfried, Jr., Chief Executive Officer **A**1 9 10 **F**7 8 10 13 14 15 16 17 19 21 22 28 30 32 33 34 35 37 39 40 41 44 45 46 49 65 66 67 71 73 **S** Quorum Health Group/Quorum Health Resources, Inc., Brentwood, TN

| | 23 | 10 | 28 | 1538 | 17 | 18978 | 149 | 9558 | 4186 | 150 |

IMPERIAL—Chase County

CHASE COUNTY COMMUNITY HOSPITAL, 600 West 12th Street, Zip 69033–0819, Mailing Address: P.O. Box 819, Zip 69033–0819; tel. 308/882–7111; Ed Hackman, Administrator **A**9 10 **F**7 8 14 15 16 17 19 22 25 26 28 30 33 34 42 44 49 67 71 74

| | 13 | 10 | 12 | 577 | 6 | 13162 | 56 | 2929 | 1432 | 57 |

KEARNEY—Buffalo County

✠ △ GOOD SAMARITAN HEALTH SYSTEMS, (Includes Richard H. Young Psychiatric Hospital, 4600 17th Avenue, Zip 68847; tel. 308/865–2000), 10 East 31st Street, Zip 68847–2926, Mailing Address: P.O. Box 1990, Zip 68848–1990; tel. 308/865–7100; William Wilson Hendrickson, President and Chief Executive Officer (Total facility includes 20 beds in nursing home–type unit) **A**1 2 3 5 7 9 10 **F**1 2 3 4 5 7 8 10 11 12 14 15 16 17 19 21 22 23 24 27 28 29 30 32 33 34 35 36 37 38 39 40 41 42 43 44 45 46 48 49 52 53 54 56 57 58 59 60 64 65 66 67 68 70 71 73 **P**6 8 **S** Catholic Health Initiatives, Denver, CO

| | 21 | 10 | 267 | 8340 | 140 | 60992 | 865 | 90091 | 37494 | 1294 |

KIMBALL—Kimball County

KIMBALL COUNTY HOSPITAL, 505 South Burg Street, Zip 69145–1398; tel. 308/235–3621; Gerri Linn, Administrator **A**9 10 **F**19 22 30 32 40 41 44 49 51 71 73 **P**8

| | 13 | 10 | 20 | 239 | 4 | 6024 | 30 | 2389 | 1101 | 42 |

Hospital, Address, Telephone, Administrator, Approval, Facility, and Physician Codes, Health Care System, Network	Classi-fication Codes		Utilization Data					Expense (thousands) of dollars		
★ American Hospital Association (AHA) membership □ Joint Commission on Accreditation of Healthcare Organizations (JCAHO) accreditation + American Osteopathic Healthcare Association (AOHA) membership ○ American Osteopathic Association (AOA) accreditation △ Commission on Accreditation of Rehabilitation Facilities (CARF) accreditation Control codes 61, 63, 64, 71, 72 and 73 indicate hospitals listed by AOHA, but not registered by AHA. For definition of numerical codes, see page A4	Control	Service	Staffed Beds	Admissions	Census	Outpatient Visits	Births	Total	Payroll	Personnel

LEXINGTON—Dawson County

✠ TRI–COUNTY AREA HOSPITAL, 13th and Erie Streets, Zip 68850–0980, Mailing Address: P.O. Box 980, Zip 68850–0980; tel. 308/324–5651; Calvin A. Hiner, Administrator **A**1 9 10 **F**8 10 14 15 16 17 19 21 22 24 28 29 30 32 33 34 35 39 40 41 42 44 45 46 49 50 62 64 65 66 67 71

| | 16 | 10 | 37 | 1475 | 15 | 20225 | 251 | 8252 | 3749 | — |

LINCOLN—Lancaster County

✠ BRYANLGH MEDICAL CENTER, (Includes Bryan Memorial–BryanLGH–East, 1600 South 48th Street; Lincoln General–BryanLGH–West, 2300 South 16th Street, Zip 68502–3781; tel. 402/475–1011), 1600 South 48th Street, Zip 68506–1299; tel. 402/489–0200; Craig M. Ames, President and Chief Operating Officer (Total facility includes 35 beds in nursing home–type unit) **A**1 2 3 5 9 10 **F**2 4 7 8 10 11 12 15 16 17 18 19 21 22 26 27 28 29 30 31 32 34 35 37 40 42 43 44 45 46 48 49 52 53 54 55 56 57 58 59 60 63 64 65 66 67 68 70 71 73 **P**8
Web address: www.bryanlgh.org
LINCOLN DIVISION See Veterans Affairs Greater Nebraska Health Care System
LINCOLN GENERAL–BRYANLGH–WEST See BryanLGH Medical Center

| | 23 | 10 | 523 | 21699 | 270 | — | 2178 | 243307 | 96419 | 2956 |

□ LINCOLN REGIONAL CENTER, West Prospector Place and Folsom, Zip 68522–2299, Mailing Address: P.O. Box 94949, Zip 68509–4949; tel. 402/471–4444; Barbara Ramsey, Ph.D., Chief Executive Officer **A**1 10 **F**14 15 16 20 27 41 52 53 54 55 56 57 58 59 65 67 73 **P**6
Web address: www.hhs.state.ne.us

| | 12 | 22 | 194 | 324 | 192 | 0 | 0 | 20420 | 13002 | 473 |

△ MADONNA REHABILITATION HOSPITAL, 5401 South Street, Zip 68506–2134; tel. 402/489–7102; Marsha Lommel Halpern, President and Chief Executive Officer (Total facility includes 177 beds in nursing home–type unit) **A**7 9 10 **F**1 12 14 15 16 17 24 27 28 29 30 32 34 39 41 45 46 48 49 64 65 67 73 **P**6
Web address: www.madonna.org

| | 21 | 46 | 252 | 1619 | 219 | 27737 | 0 | 33469 | 20423 | 696 |

✠ SAINT ELIZABETH REGIONAL MEDICAL CENTER, (Formerly St Elizabeth Community Health Center), 555 South 70th Street, Zip 68510–2494; tel. 402/489–7181; Robert J. Lanik, President **A**1 2 3 5 9 10 **F**4 7 8 9 10 11 12 14 15 16 19 22 23 28 30 31 32 33 35 37 38 40 41 42 43 44 46 49 65 66 67 71 72 73 **S** Catholic Health Initiatives, Denver, CO
Web address: www.stez.org

| | 21 | 10 | 170 | 7155 | 93 | 81412 | 1790 | 84576 | 33544 | 1341 |

✠ VETERANS AFFAIRS GREATER NEBRASKA HEALTH CARE SYSTEM, (Includes Lincoln Division), 600 South 70th Street, Zip 68510–2493; tel. 402/489–3802; David Asper, Director (Total facility includes 76 beds in nursing home–type unit) **A**1 3 **F**3 8 11 12 15 16 19 20 21 22 25 27 28 29 30 33 34 37 41 42 44 45 46 49 51 52 54 58 64 65 71 73 74 **S** Department of Veterans Affairs, Washington, DC

| | 45 | 10 | 129 | 1587 | 87 | 130270 | 0 | — | 24491 | 572 |

LYNCH—Boyd County

★ NIOBRARA VALLEY HOSPITAL, Mailing Address: P.O. Box 118, Zip 68746–0118; tel. 402/569–2451; E. R. Testerman, Administrator **A**9 10 **F**7 8 19 22 26 28 30 32 34 39 40 44 45 49 61 64 71 **P**5 6

| | 23 | 10 | 20 | 329 | 4 | 401 | 2 | 1989 | 947 | 40 |

MCCOOK—Red Willow County

✠ COMMUNITY HOSPITAL, 1301 East H Street, Zip 69001–1328, Mailing Address: P.O. Box 1328, Zip 69001–1328; tel. 308/345–2650; Gary Bieganski, President **A**1 9 10 **F**7 8 11 14 15 17 19 21 22 23 28 30 32 34 35 37 40 44 45 49 64 65 71 73 74

| | 23 | 10 | 44 | 1337 | 18 | 39042 | 150 | 11519 | 4887 | 152 |

MINDEN—Kearney County

★ KEARNEY COUNTY HEALTH SERVICES, (Formerly Kearney County Community Hospital), 727 East First Street, Zip 68959–1700; tel. 308/832–1440; Joanne J. Petrik, Interim Administrator (Total facility includes 50 beds in nursing home–type unit) **A**9 10 **F**7 15 22 28 30 32 33 34 37 39 40 41 44 51 64 65 71 73 **P**3 6

| | 13 | 10 | 72 | 173 | 49 | 6102 | 11 | 3632 | 2227 | 99 |

NEBRASKA CITY—Otoe County

★ ST. MARY'S HOSPITAL, 1314 Third Avenue, Zip 68410–1999; tel. 402/873–3321; Daniel J. Kelly, President and Chief Executive Officer **A**9 10 **F**3 7 8 15 16 19 22 32 33 35 36 37 39 40 41 44 46 63 64 65 71 73 **S** Catholic Health Initiatives, Denver, CO

| | 21 | 10 | 28 | 517 | 7 | 24957 | 105 | 4880 | 2044 | 89 |

NELIGH—Antelope County

★ ANTELOPE MEMORIAL HOSPITAL, 102 West Ninth Street, Zip 68756–0229, Mailing Address: P.O. Box 229, Zip 68756–0229; tel. 402/887–4151; Jack W. Green, Administrator **A**9 10 **F**7 8 15 17 19 22 24 30 32 35 39 40 42 44 45 46 49 64 65 71

| | 23 | 10 | 45 | 697 | 14 | 11394 | 28 | 4742 | 2232 | 90 |

NORFOLK—Madison County

✠ FAITH REGIONAL HEALTH SERVICES, (Includes East Campus, 1500 Koenigstein Avenue, Zip 68701, Mailing Address: East Campus, Zip 68701; tel. 402/371–3402; West Campus, 2700 Norfolk Avenue, Zip 68701; tel. 402/371–4880), 2700 Norfolk Avenue, Zip 68702–0869, Mailing Address: P.O. BOX 869, Zip 68702–0869; tel. 402/644–7201; Robert L. Driewer, Chief Executive Officer (Total facility includes 99 beds in nursing home–type unit) **A**1 9 10 **F**3 7 8 10 12 14 15 16 17 19 20 21 22 23 28 29 30 32 33 35 37 39 40 41 44 45 49 52 56 60 64 65 66 67 71 72 73 **P**8 **S** Missionary Benedictine Sisters American Province, Norfolk, NE

| | 23 | 10 | 225 | 6112 | 131 | 51368 | 840 | 48994 | 22717 | 825 |

□ NORFOLK REGIONAL CENTER, 1700 North Victory Road, Zip 68701–6859, Mailing Address: P.O. Box 1209, Zip 68702–1209; tel. 402/370–3400 **A**1 10 **F**3 12 15 17 18 27 32 34 52 54 55 57 58 59 65 67 73

| | 12 | 22 | 174 | 358 | 170 | — | 0 | 12497 | 7920 | 325 |

Hospital, Address, Telephone, Administrator, Approval, Facility, and Physician Codes, Health Care System, Network	Classi-fication Codes		Utilization Data					Expense (thousands) of dollars		
★ American Hospital Association (AHA) membership □ Joint Commission on Accreditation of Healthcare Organizations (JCAHO) accreditation + American Osteopathic Healthcare Association (AOHA) membership ○ American Osteopathic Association (AOA) accreditation △ Commission on Accreditation of Rehabilitation Facilities (CARF) accreditation Control codes 61, 63, 64, 71, 72 and 73 indicate hospitals listed by AOHA, but not registered by AHA. For definition of numerical codes, see page A4	Control	Service	Staffed Beds	Admissions	Census	Outpatient Visits	Births	Total	Payroll	Personnel

NORTH PLATTE—Lincoln County

⊠ GREAT PLAINS REGIONAL MEDICAL CENTER, 601 West Leota Street, Zip 69101–6598, Mailing Address: P.O. Box 1167, Zip 69103–1167; tel. 308/534–9310; Lucinda A. Bradley, President **A**1 2 3 5 9 10 **F**3 7 8 10 11 12 15 19 21 22 23 28 32 33 34 35 37 39 40 41 42 44 46 49 52 53 56 58 59 60 65 66 67 71 73 **P**8 **S** Quorum Health Group/Quorum Health Resources, Inc., Brentwood, TN	23	10	99	4856	49	98990	501	45942	19036	569

O'NEILL—Holt County

⊠ AVERA ST. ANTHONY'S HOSPITAL, (Formerly St. Anthony's Hospital), Second and Adams Streets, Zip 68763–1597; tel. 402/336–2611; Ronald J. Cork, President and Chief Executive Officer **A**1 9 10 **F**7 8 12 15 16 17 18 19 22 26 28 29 30 31 32 34 35 39 40 41 42 44 45 49 54 65 66 67 71 73 **P**1 6 **S** Avera Health, Yankton, SD	21	10	29	951	7	18282	122	7426	2611	105

OAKLAND—Burt County

OAKLAND MEMORIAL HOSPITAL, 601 East Second Street, Zip 68045–1499; tel. 402/685–5601; Karen Vlach, Administrator **A**9 10 **F**8 12 14 19 22 28 30 32 33 34 36 37 39 41 42 44 46 51 64 71 73 **P**5 6	16	10	23	189	4	6662	0	2254	1201	42

OFFUTT AFB—Sarpy County

⊠ EHRLING BERGQUIST HOSPITAL, 2501 Capehart Road, Zip 68113–2160; tel. 402/294–7312; Colonel John R. Sheehan, USAF, MSC, Deputy Commander (Nonreporting) **A**1 3 5 **S** Department of the Air Force, Bowling AFB, DC	41	10	45	—	—	—	—	—	—	—

OGALLALA—Keith County

★ OGALLALA COMMUNITY HOSPITAL, 300 East Tenth Street, Zip 69153–1509; tel. 308/284–4011; Linda Morris, Administrator **A**9 10 **F**7 8 11 12 13 15 16 17 19 21 22 25 28 30 32 33 34 37 40 42 44 49 51 58 64 67 68 71 72 **P**6 **S** Lutheran Health Systems, Fargo, ND	23	10	29	715	7	26999	68	7543	—	125

OMAHA—Douglas County

⊠ ALEGENT HEALTH BERGAN MERCY MEDICAL CENTER, 7500 Mercy Road, Zip 68124; tel. 402/343–4410; Charles J. Marr, Chief Executive Officer (Total facility includes 241 beds in nursing home–type unit) **A**1 2 3 5 9 10 **F**1 2 3 4 6 7 8 10 11 12 13 14 15 16 17 18 19 20 21 22 23 24 25 26 27 28 30 31 32 33 34 35 37 38 39 40 41 42 43 44 45 46 48 49 51 52 53 54 55 56 57 58 59 60 62 63 64 65 66 67 68 71 72 73 74 **P**6 8 **S** Catholic Health Initiatives, Denver, CO	21	10	549	14657	387	116336	2342	142466	58382	2014
ALEGENT HEALTH CENTER FOR MENTAL HEALTH, (Formerly St. Joseph Center for Mental Health), 819 Dorcas Street, Zip 68108–1198; tel. 402/449–4000; Robert C. Caldwell, Chief Operating Officer (Nonreporting) **A**3 5 9	33	22	115	—	—	—	—	—	—	—
⊠ △ ALEGENT HEALTH IMMANUEL MEDICAL CENTER, 6901 North 72nd Street, Zip 68122–1799; tel. 402/572–2121; Randall W. Smith, Chief Operating Officer (Total facility includes 200 beds in nursing home–type unit) **A**1 2 5 7 9 10 **F**1 2 3 4 6 7 8 10 11 12 13 14 15 16 17 18 19 20 21 22 23 24 25 26 27 28 29 30 31 32 33 34 35 37 38 39 40 41 42 43 44 45 46 48 49 50 51 52 53 54 55 56 57 58 59 60 62 63 64 65 66 67 68 71 72 73 74 **P**6 8	21	10	542	11523	385	187228	856	125429	47283	1628
□ BOYS TOWN NATIONAL RESEARCH HOSPITAL, 555 North 30th Street, Zip 68131–2198; tel. 402/498–6511; John K. Arch, Administrator **A**1 3 9 10 **F**14 15 16 17 25 44 45 46 51 53 55 **P**6 **Web address:** www.boystown.org/btnrh	23	50	14	1530	4	119853	0	—	—	309
⊠ CHILDREN'S HOSPITAL, 8301 Dodge Street, Zip 68114–4199; tel. 402/354–5400; Gary A. Perkins, President and Chief Executive Officer **A**1 3 5 9 10 **F**10 12 15 17 19 21 22 23 28 29 32 34 35 38 39 42 43 44 45 47 60 63 65 67 71 72 73 **P**8 **Web address:** www.childrens-omaha.com	23	50	100	5312	71	70427	0	64513	27575	740
○ DOUGLAS COUNTY HOSPITAL, 4102 Woolworth Avenue, Zip 68105–1899; tel. 402/444–7000; James C. Tourville, Administrator (Total facility includes 272 beds in nursing home–type unit) (Nonreporting) **A**10 11	13	49	329	—	—	—	—	—	—	—
★ METHODIST RICHARD YOUNG, (Includes Richard H. Young Memorial Hospital), 415 South 25th Avenue, Zip 68131–3619; tel. 402/354–6600; Sandra C. Carson, FACHE, Senior Vice President **A**5 9 10 **F**2 3 4 7 8 10 11 12 15 16 17 18 19 21 22 23 26 28 29 30 32 33 34 35 37 38 39 40 41 42 43 44 45 47 48 49 51 52 53 56 57 58 59 60 61 62 64 65 66 67 68 70 71 72 73 74 **P**1 7 **Web address:** www.bestcare.org	21	22	97	1591	52		0	13928	7413	248
□ NEBRASKA HEALTH SYSTEM, (Includes Nebraska Health System, 4350 Dewey Avenue, Mailing Address: 4350 Dewey Avnue, Zip 68105–1018; Nebraska Health System, 600 South 42nd Street, Zip 68198–4085; tel. 402/559–4000), 4350 Dewey Avenue, Zip 68105–1018, Mailing Address: 987400 Nebraska Medical Center, Zip 68198–7400; tel. 402/552–2552; Louis W. Burgher, M.D., Ph.D., President and Chief Executive Officer (Nonreporting) **A**1 2 3 5 8 9 10	23	10	543	—	—	—	—	—	—	—
⊠ △ NEBRASKA METHODIST HOSPITAL, 8303 Dodge Street, Zip 68114–4199; tel. 402/354–4000; John Martin Fraser, President and Chief Executive Officer **A**1 2 3 7 9 10 **F**3 4 6 7 8 10 11 12 14 15 16 17 18 19 20 21 22 23 24 26 27 28 29 30 31 32 33 34 35 37 38 39 40 41 42 43 44 45 47 48 49 51 52 53 54 55 56 58 59 60 61 62 64 65 66 67 69 70 71 72 73 74 **P**6 7 8 RICHARD H. YOUNG MEMORIAL HOSPITAL See Methodist Richard Young ST. JOSEPH CENTER FOR MENTAL HEALTH See Alegent Health Center for Mental Health	23	10	359	13306	166	162982	3220	165097	69914	2024
⊠ ST. JOSEPH HOSPITAL, 601 North 30th Street, Zip 68131–2197; tel. 402/449–5021; J. Richard Stanko, President and Chief Executive Officer **A**1 3 5 8 10 **F**4 7 8 10 11 12 16 19 20 21 22 24 25 31 34 35 37 38 40 41 42 43 44 46 47 49 51 60 63 64 65 68 70 71 72 73 74 **P**2 7 8 **S** TENET Healthcare Corporation, Santa Barbara, CA	33	10	277	9915	145	57967	883	101581	32772	1067

Hospital, Address, Telephone, Administrator, Approval, Facility, and Physician Codes, Health Care System, Network	Classi-fication Codes		Utilization Data					Expense (thousands) of dollars		
★ American Hospital Association (AHA) membership □ Joint Commission on Accreditation of Healthcare Organizations (JCAHO) accreditation + American Osteopathic Healthcare Association (AOHA) membership ○ American Osteopathic Association (AOA) accreditation △ Commission on Accreditation of Rehabilitation Facilities (CARF) accreditation Control codes 61, 63, 64, 71, 72 and 73 indicate hospitals listed by AOHA, but not registered by AHA. For definition of numerical codes, see page A4	Control	Service	Staffed Beds	Admissions	Census	Outpatient Visits	Births	Total	Payroll	Personnel

Hospital	Control	Service	Staffed Beds	Admissions	Census	Outpatient Visits	Births	Total	Payroll	Personnel
⊠ VETERANS AFFAIRS MEDICAL CENTER, 4101 Woolworth Avenue, Zip 68105–1873; tel. 402/449–0600; John J. Phillips, Director **A**1 3 5 8 **F**2 3 4 8 10 12 17 19 20 21 22 23 26 28 30 31 34 35 37 39 41 42 43 44 45 46 49 50 51 52 54 56 57 58 59 60 63 65 67 68 71 73 74 **P**1 **S** Department of Veterans Affairs, Washington, DC	45	10	122	3231	71	147361	0	74934	41696	900
ORD—Valley County										
★ VALLEY COUNTY HOSPITAL, 217 Westridge Drive, Zip 68862–1675; tel. 308/728–3211; Colleen Chapp, Interim Chief Executive Officer and Administrator (Total facility includes 70 beds in nursing home–type unit) **A**9 10 **F**7 8 11 14 15 19 20 22 24 27 30 32 33 34 35 40 44 64 65 71	13	10	77	551	69	12818	47	6812	2968	164
OSCEOLA—Polk County										
ANNIE JEFFREY MEMORIAL COUNTY HEALTH CENTER, 531 Beebe Street, Zip 68651, Mailing Address: P.O. Box 428, Zip 68651–0428; tel. 402/747–2031; Carol E. Jones, Administrator **A**9 10 **F**7 8 14 15 16 17 19 22 24 28 29 30 32 33 34 35 36 39 40 41 44 45 49 51 64 65 66 71 73 **P**6	13	10	21	289	2	14731	27	2588	1320	57
OSHKOSH—Garden County										
GARDEN COUNTY HOSPITAL, 1100 West Second Street, Zip 69154, Mailing Address: P.O. Box 320, Zip 69154–0320; tel. 308/772–3283; Diana Stevens, Administrator (Total facility includes 36 beds in nursing home–type unit) **A**9 10 **F**1 3 8 13 14 17 18 19 22 24 26 28 30 32 34 44 49 51 53 54 55 56 57 58 59 61 64 65 66 67 70 71 72 74	13	10	46	212	34	1711	0	2260	1258	65
OSMOND—Pierce County										
★ OSMOND GENERAL HOSPITAL, 5th and Maple Street, Zip 68765–0429, Mailing Address: P.O. Box 429, Zip 68765–0429; tel. 402/748–3393; Celine M. Mlady, Chief Executive Officer **A**9 10 **F**1 8 11 15 19 22 30 32 33 34 35 36 37 44 47 62 64 65 71 **P**6 8	23	10	30	737	26	5798	0	3092	1768	71
PAPILLION—Sarpy County										
⊠ ALEGENT–HEALTH MIDLANDS COMMUNITY HOSPITAL, (Formerly Midlands Community Hospital), 11111 South 84th Street, Zip 68046–4157; tel. 402/593–3000; Diana Smalley, Chief Operating Officer **A**1 2 9 10 **F**1 2 3 4 6 7 8 10 11 12 14 15 16 17 18 19 20 21 22 23 24 25 26 27 28 29 30 31 32 33 34 35 37 38 39 40 41 42 43 44 45 46 48 49 50 51 52 53 54 55 56 57 58 59 60 62 63 64 65 66 67 68 71 72 73 74 **P**6 8	21	10	160	3339	50	18894	451	19902	8029	279
PAWNEE CITY—Pawnee County										
PAWNEE COUNTY MEMORIAL HOSPITAL, 600 I Street, Zip 68420–3001, Mailing Address: P.O. Box 313, Zip 68420–0313; tel. 402/852–2231; James A. Kubik, Administrator (Nonreporting) **A**9 10	13	10	21	—	—	—	—	—	—	—
PENDER—Thurston County										
★ PENDER COMMUNITY HOSPITAL, 603 Earl Street, Zip 68047–0100, Mailing Address: P.O. Box 100, Zip 68047–0100; tel. 402/385–3083; Roger Mazour, Administrator **A**9 10 **F**7 8 11 19 22 34 35 40 41 42 44 49 64 65 71 **P**7 **S** Mercy Health Services, Farmington Hills, MI	33	10	30	807	9	9266	65	3953	1627	76
PLAINVIEW—Pierce County										
PLAINVIEW PUBLIC HOSPITAL, 705 North Third Street, Zip 68769, Mailing Address: P.O. Box 489, Zip 68769–0489; tel. 402/582–4245; Donald T. Naiberk, Administrator and Chief Executive Officer (Nonreporting) **A**9 10	14	10	19	—	—	—	—	—	—	—
RED CLOUD—Webster County										
WEBSTER COUNTY COMMUNITY HOSPITAL, Sixth Avenue and Franklin Street, Zip 68970–0465; tel. 402/746–2291; Terry L. Hoffart, Administrator **A**9 10 **F**8 19 28 35 37 41 44 49 66 71 73 **P**3	13	10	16	213	5	669	0	1639	669	33
SAINT PAUL—Howard County										
★ HOWARD COUNTY COMMUNITY HOSPITAL, 1102 Kendall Street, Zip 68873–1536, Mailing Address: P.O. Box 406, Zip 68873–0406; tel. 308/754–4421; Russell W. Swigart, Administrator **A**9 10 **F**7 14 19 22 33 34 35 44 49 65 70 71 **P**6	13	10	36	384	20	—	48	3396	1704	82
SARGENT—Custer County										
GOLI MEDICAL CENTER, 1201 West Main Street, Zip 68874; tel. 308/527–3414; Rajitha Goli, M.D., Administrator and Chief Executive Officer (Nonreporting) **A**9 10	16	10	18	—	—	—	—	—	—	—
SCHUYLER—Colfax County										
ALEGENT HEALTH–MEMORIAL HOSPITAL, 104 West 17th Street, Zip 68661–1396; tel. 402/352–2441; Asa B. Wilson, Administrator (Total facility includes 32 beds in nursing home–type unit) **A**9 10 **F**7 8 12 15 16 17 22 26 28 30 31 32 33 34 36 39 40 42 44 48 49 56 64 65 66 67 71	23	10	50	424	35	17400	71	5552	3211	118
SCOTTSBLUFF—Scotts Bluff County										
⊠ REGIONAL WEST MEDICAL CENTER, 4021 Avenue B, Zip 69361–4695; tel. 308/635–3711; David M. Nitschke, President and Chief Executive Officer (Total facility includes 24 beds in nursing home–type unit) **A**1 2 3 5 9 10 **F**1 7 8 10 12 14 15 16 17 18 19 21 22 23 24 28 30 32 33 34 35 36 37 38 39 40 41 42 44 45 46 48 49 52 53 54 55 56 57 58 59 60 63 64 65 66 67 70 71 73 **P**4 5 6 7	23	10	202	6084	77	40092	741	58555	25255	807
SEWARD—Seward County										
MEMORIAL HEALTH CARE SYSTEMS, 300 North Columbia Avenue, Zip 68434–9907; tel. 402/643–2971; Ronald D. Waltz, Chief Executive Officer (Total facility includes 120 beds in nursing home–type unit) **A**9 10 **F**1 7 8 12 15 16 17 19 22 24 26 27 28 30 32 33 34 35 39 44 45 46 49 51 64 65 66 71 73 **P**6 **Web address:** www.mhcs–seward.org	23	10	154	782	134	17620	98	12781	6896	269

Hospital, Address, Telephone, Administrator, Approval, Facility, and Physician Codes, Health Care System, Network	Classi-fication Codes		Utilization Data					Expense (thousands) of dollars		
	Control	Service	Staffed Beds	Admissions	Census	Outpatient Visits	Births	Total	Payroll	Personnel

★ American Hospital Association (AHA) membership
□ Joint Commission on Accreditation of Healthcare Organizations (JCAHO) accreditation
+ American Osteopathic Healthcare Association (AOHA) membership
○ American Osteopathic Association (AOA) accreditation
△ Commission on Accreditation of Rehabilitation Facilities (CARF) accreditation
Control codes 61, 63, 64, 71, 72 and 73 indicate hospitals listed by AOHA, but not registered by AHA. For definition of numerical codes, see page A4

SIDNEY—Cheyenne County

★ MEMORIAL HEALTH CENTER, 645 Osage Street, Zip 69162–1799; tel. 308/254–5825; Rex D. Walk, Chief Executive Officer (Total facility includes 70 beds in nursing home–type unit) (Nonreporting) **A**9 10 — Control 23, Service 10, Staffed Beds 102

SUPERIOR—Nuckolls County

BRODSTONE MEMORIAL HOSPITAL, 520 East Tenth Street, Zip 68978–1225, Mailing Address: P.O. Box 187, Zip 68978–0187; tel. 402/879–3281; Ronald D. Waggoner, Administrator and Chief Executive Officer **A**9 10 **F**7 8 19 20 22 27 32 33 34 35 36 37 40 41 44 49 64 65 71 — Control 23, Service 10, Staffed Beds 49, Admissions 697, Census 11, Outpatient Visits 14344, Births 44, Total 5793, Payroll 2401, Personnel 109

SYRACUSE—Otoe County

COMMUNITY MEMORIAL HOSPITAL, 1579 Midland Street, Zip 68446–9732, Mailing Address: P.O. Box N, Zip 68446; tel. 402/269–2795; Al Klaasmeyer, Administrator **A**9 10 **F**7 8 12 14 17 19 20 21 22 24 27 29 30 32 33 35 39 40 44 45 49 51 64 71 **P**6 — Control 16, Service 10, Staffed Beds 18, Admissions 199, Census 2, Outpatient Visits 23557, Births 15, Total 2801, Payroll 1251, Personnel 57

TECUMSEH—Johnson County

★ JOHNSON COUNTY HOSPITAL, 202 High Street, Zip 68450–0599, Mailing Address: P.O. Box 599, Zip 68450–0599; tel. 402/335–3361; John E. Keelan, Administrator **A**9 10 **F**1 7 8 14 15 16 17 19 22 28 32 33 34 35 37 40 41 42 44 49 51 63 71 — Control 13, Service 10, Staffed Beds 22, Admissions 332, Census 3, Outpatient Visits 6709, Births 28, Total 2303, Payroll 965, Personnel 55

TILDEN—Antelope County

TILDEN COMMUNITY HOSPITAL, Second and Pine Streets, Zip 68781, Mailing Address: P.O. Box 340, Zip 68781–0340; tel. 402/368–5343; LuAnn Barr, Administrator (Nonreporting) **A**9 10 — Control 23, Service 10, Staffed Beds 20

VALENTINE—Cherry County

★ CHERRY COUNTY HOSPITAL, Highway 12 and Green Street, Zip 69201–0410; tel. 402/376–2525; Brent A. Peterson, Administrator **A**9 10 **F**8 10 11 14 15 16 19 21 22 28 29 32 34 35 37 40 42 44 46 64 70 71 — Control 13, Service 10, Staffed Beds 28, Admissions 735, Census 8, Outpatient Visits 6892, Births 262, Total 4629, Payroll 2071, Personnel 73

WAHOO—Saunders County

SAUNDERS COUNTY HEALTH SERVICE, 805 West Tenth Street, Zip 68066–1102, Mailing Address: P.O. Box 185, Zip 68066–0185; tel. 402/443–4191; Michael Boyles, Administrator (Total facility includes 73 beds in nursing home–type unit) **A**9 10 **F**12 15 16 17 19 22 24 27 28 32 33 35 39 44 48 64 65 **P**6 — Control 13, Service 10, Staffed Beds 103, Admissions 232, Census 82, Outpatient Visits 13346, Births 0, Total 4464, Payroll 2586, Personnel 151

WAYNE—Wayne County

PROVIDENCE MEDICAL CENTER, 1200 Providence Road, Zip 68787–1299; tel. 402/375–3800; Marcile Thomas, Administrator **A**9 10 **F**7 8 14 15 16 19 22 24 32 33 35 36 42 44 49 65 66 71 **S** Missionary Benedictine Sisters American Province, Norfolk, NE — Control 21, Service 10, Staffed Beds 34, Admissions 971, Census 12, Outpatient Visits 11093, Births 101, Total 5452, Payroll 2440, Personnel 80

WEST POINT—Cuming County

★ ST. FRANCIS MEMORIAL HOSPITAL, 430 North Monitor Street, Zip 68788–1595; tel. 402/372–2404; Ronald O. Briggs, President (Total facility includes 70 beds in nursing home–type unit) **A**9 10 **F**1 6 7 8 15 19 22 24 30 32 33 34 35 40 41 42 44 48 49 56 64 65 66 71 73 **P**6 **S** Franciscan Sisters of Christian Charity HealthCare Ministry, Inc, Manitowoc, WI — Control 21, Service 10, Staffed Beds 102, Admissions 681, Census 75, Outpatient Visits 57305, Births 104, Total 9011, Payroll 4684, Personnel 153

WINNEBAGO—Thurston County

⊞ U. S. PUBLIC HEALTH SERVICE INDIAN HOSPITAL, Highway 7577, Zip 68071; tel. 402/878–2231; Donald Lee, Service Unit Director (Nonreporting) **A**1 10 **S** U. S. Public Health Service Indian Health Service, Rockville, MD — Control 47, Service 10, Staffed Beds 30

YORK—York County

★ YORK GENERAL HOSPITAL, 2222 Lincoln Avenue, Zip 68467–1095; tel. 402/362–0445; Charles K. Schulz, Chief Executive Officer **A**9 10 **F**7 8 11 12 15 16 17 19 20 21 22 24 28 30 32 33 34 35 37 39 40 41 42 44 46 48 49 63 64 65 66 67 71 73 74 **P**5
Web address: www.yorkhospital.org — Control 23, Service 10, Staffed Beds 41, Admissions 1154, Census 13, Outpatient Visits 31601, Births 147, Total 9397, Payroll 4174, Personnel 153

NEVADA

Resident population 1,747 (in thousands)
Resident population in metro areas 78.6%
Birth rate per 1,000 population 16.4
65 years and over 11.5%
Percent of persons without health insurance 15.6%

Hospital, Address, Telephone, Administrator, Approval, Facility, and Physician Codes, Health Care System, Network	Classi- fication Codes		Utilization Data					Expense (thousands) of dollars		
★ American Hospital Association (AHA) membership □ Joint Commission on Accreditation of Healthcare Organizations (JCAHO) accreditation + American Osteopathic Healthcare Association (AOHA) membership ○ American Osteopathic Association (AOA) accreditation △ Commission on Accreditation of Rehabilitation Facilities (CARF) accreditation Control codes 61, 63, 64, 71, 72 and 73 indicate hospitals listed by AOHA, but not registered by AHA. For definition of numerical codes, see page A4	Control	Service	Staffed Beds	Admissions	Census	Outpatient Visits	Births	Total	Payroll	Personnel
BATTLE MOUNTAIN—Lander County										
BATTLE MOUNTAIN GENERAL HOSPITAL, 535 South Humboldt Street, Zip 89820–1988; tel. 702/635–2550; Kathy Ancho, Administrator (Nonreporting) **A**10	13	10	14	—	—	—	—	—	—	—
BOULDER CITY—Clark County										
BOULDER CITY HOSPITAL, 901 Adams Boulevard, Zip 89005–2299; tel. 702/293–4111; Kim O. Crandell, Chief Executive Officer and Administrator (Total facility includes 47 beds in nursing home–type unit) (Nonreporting) **A**9 10	23	10	67	—	—	—	—	—	—	—
CARSON CITY—Carson City County										
⊞ CARSON TAHOE HOSPITAL, 775 Fleischmann Way, Zip 89702, Mailing Address: P.O. Box 2168, Zip 89702–2168; tel. 775/882–1361; Steve Smith, Chief Executive Officer **A**1 9 10 **F**1 2 3 7 10 12 14 15 17 18 19 21 22 25 26 28 29 30 31 32 34 35 37 39 40 42 44 45 46 48 49 51 52 53 54 55 56 57 58 59 60 63 65 67 68 71 72 73 74	13	10	128	7207	73	96839	718	57860	23860	703
ELKO—Elko County										
⊞ ELKO GENERAL HOSPITAL, 1297 College Avenue, Zip 89801–3499; tel. 775/753–1999; Richard L. Kilburn, Chief Executive Officer **A**1 9 10 **F**12 15 16 17 19 21 22 25 28 29 35 39 40 44 45 56 65 66 67 71 73 **S** Province Healthcare Corporation, Brentwood, TN	33	10	50	2413	33	44583	672	14426	5821	275
ELY—White Pine County										
□ WILLIAM BEE RIRIE HOSPITAL, 1500 Avenue H, Zip 89301–2699; tel. 702/289–3001; Robert A. Morasko, Chief Executive Officer (Nonreporting) **A**1 9 10	13	10	40	—	—	—	—	—	—	—
FALLON—Churchill County										
⊞ CHURCHILL COMMUNITY HOSPTIAL, 801 East Williams Avenue, Zip 89406–3052; tel. 702/423–3151; Jeffrey Feike, Administrator **A**1 9 10 **F**7 8 12 15 16 17 19 21 22 28 32 34 35 37 40 42 44 48 49 70 71 73 **P**4 6 7 **S** Lutheran Health Systems, Fargo, ND	23	10	40	2331	20	—	422	—	—	230
HAWTHORNE—Mineral County										
MOUNT GRANT GENERAL HOSPITAL, First and A Street, Zip 89415, Mailing Address: P.O. Box 1510, Zip 89415–1510; tel. 702/945–2461; Richard Munger, Administrator (Total facility includes 20 beds in nursing home–type unit) (Nonreporting) **A**9 10	46	10	35	—	—	—	—	—	—	—
HENDERSON—Clark County										
⊞ ST. ROSE DOMINICAN HOSPITAL, 102 Lake Mead Drive, Zip 89015–5524; tel. 702/564–2622; Rod A. Davis, President and Chief Executive Officer **A**1 9 10 **F**7 8 10 12 13 15 16 17 19 21 22 25 28 29 30 32 34 35 37 40 41 42 44 45 49 64 65 66 67 71 72 73 74 **P**5 7 **S** Catholic Healthcare West, San Francisco, CA	23	10	143	7622	85	—	1563	55149	24411	649
LAS VEGAS—Clark County										
□ BHC MONTEVISTA HOSPITAL, 5900 West Rochelle Avenue, Zip 89103–3327; tel. 702/364–1111; Darryl S. Dubroca, Chief Executive Officer and Administrator (Nonreporting) **A**1 10 **S** Behavioral Healthcare Corporation, Nashville, TN	33	22	80	—	—	—	—	—	—	—
□ CHARTER BEHAVIORAL HEALTH SYSTEM OF NEVADA, 7000 West Spring Mountain Road, Zip 89117–3816; tel. 702/876–4357; Alan G. Chapman, Chief Executive Officer (Nonreporting) **A**1 10 **S** Magellan Health Services, Atlanta, GA	33	22	84	—	—	—	—	—	—	—
COLUMBIA SUNRISE HOSPITAL See Sunrise Hospital and Medical Center										
COLUMBIA SUNRISE MOUNTAINVIEW HOSPITAL See Mountainview Hospital										
□ DESERT SPRINGS HOSPITAL, 2075 East Flamingo Road, Zip 89119–5121, Mailing Address: P.O. Box 19204, Zip 89132–9204; tel. 702/733–8800; John Lloyd Hummer, Chief Executive Officer (Nonreporting) **A**1 10 **S** Universal Health Services, Inc., King of Prussia, PA	33	10	225	—	—	—	—	—	—	—
⊞ MIKE O'CALLAGHAN FEDERAL HOSPITAL, 4700 Las Vegas Boulevard North, Suite 2419, Zip 89191–6601; tel. 702/653–2000; Colonel Jack A. Gupton, MSC, USAF, Administrator **A**1 **F**1 3 4 5 6 7 8 10 12 13 17 18 19 20 21 22 23 24 26 27 29 30 31 32 33 34 35 37 39 40 41 42 43 44 45 46 49 51 53 54 55 56 57 58 59 60 61 65 66 67 69 70 71 72 73 74 **P**1 **S** Department of the Air Force, Bowling AFB, DC	41	10	94	4396	51	185501	537	39900	—	750
★ MOUNTAINVIEW HOSPITAL, (Formerly Columbia Sunrise Mountainview Hospital), 3100 North Tenaya Way, Zip 89128; tel. 702/255–5000; Mark J. Howard, President and Chief Executive Officer (Nonreporting) **A**10 **S** Columbia/HCA Healthcare Corporation, Nashville, TN **Web address:** www.mountainview–hospital.com	33	10	120	—	—	—	—	—	—	—
⊞ △ SUNRISE HOSPITAL AND MEDICAL CENTER, (Formerly Columbia Sunrise Hospital), 3186 Maryland Parkway, Zip 89109–2306, Mailing Address: P.O. Box 98530, Zip 89193–8530; tel. 702/731–8000; Jerald F. Mitchell, President and Chief Executive Officer **A**1 2 3 5 7 9 10 **F**4 7 8 10 11 12 14 15 16 19 21 22 29 34 35 37 38 40 41 42 43 44 47 48 49 60 64 65 66 68 71 73 **S** Columbia/HCA Healthcare Corporation, Nashville, TN **Web address:** www.sunrise.columbia.net	33	10	675	38234	525	122186	5437	248877	104171	2663
THC – LAS VEGAS HOSPITAL See Vencor Hospital–Las Vegas										

Hospital, Address, Telephone, Administrator, Approval, Facility, and Physician Codes, Health Care System, Network	Classi-fication Codes		Utilization Data					Expense (thousands) of dollars		
★ American Hospital Association (AHA) membership □ Joint Commission on Accreditation of Healthcare Organizations (JCAHO) accreditation + American Osteopathic Healthcare Association (AOHA) membership ○ American Osteopathic Association (AOA) accreditation △ Commission on Accreditation of Rehabilitation Facilities (CARF) accreditation Control codes 61, 63, 64, 71, 72 and 73 indicate hospitals listed by AOHA, but not registered by AHA. For definition of numerical codes, see page A4	Control	Service	Staffed Beds	Admissions	Census	Outpatient Visits	Births	Total	Payroll	Personnel

Hospital	Control	Service	Staffed Beds	Admissions	Census	Outpatient Visits	Births	Total	Payroll	Personnel
□ UNIVERSITY MEDICAL CENTER, 1800 West Charleston Boulevard, Zip 89102–2386; tel. 702/383–2000; William R. Hale, Chief Executive Officer (Nonreporting) **A**1 2 3 5 10	13	10	506	—	—	—	—	—	—	—
□ VALLEY HOSPITAL MEDICAL CENTER, 620 Shadow Lane, Zip 89106–4194; tel. 702/388–4000; Roger Collins, Chief Executive Officer and Managing Director (Nonreporting) **A**1 9 10 **S** Universal Health Services, Inc., King of Prussia, PA	33	10	365	—	—	—	—	—	—	—
□ VENCOR HOSPITAL–LAS VEGAS, (Formerly THC – Las Vegas Hospital), 5100 West Sahara Avenue, Zip 89102–3436; tel. 702/871–1418 (Nonreporting) **A**1 10 **S** Vencor, Incorporated, Louisville, KY	33	49	52	—	—	—	—	—	—	—
★ VETERANS AFFAIRS SOUTHERN NEVADA HEALTHCARE SYSTEM, (Formerly Veterans Affairs Medical Center), 1700 Vegas Drive, Zip 89106; tel. 702/636–3000; Ramon J. Reevey, Director (Nonreporting) **A**5 **S** Department of Veterans Affairs, Washington, DC	45	10	100	—	—	—	—	—	—	—
LOVELOCK—Pershing County										
★ PERSHING GENERAL HOSPITAL, 855 Sixth Street, Zip 89419, Mailing Address: P.O. Box 661, Zip 89419–0661; tel. 702/273–2621; Jon Smith, Administrator (Total facility includes 25 beds in nursing home–type unit) (Nonreporting) **A**9 10 **S** Lutheran Health Systems, Fargo, ND	16	10	34	—	—	—	—	—	—	—
NORTH LAS VEGAS—Clark County										
⊞ LAKE MEAD HOSPITAL MEDICAL CENTER, 1409 East Lake Mead Boulevard, Zip 89030–7197; tel. 702/649–7711; Randall Hempling, Administrator **A**1 10 **F**1 2 7 10 11 12 14 15 16 19 22 25 28 34 35 37 40 41 42 44 46 52 57 59 64 65 71 73 **S** TENET Healthcare Corporation, Santa Barbara, CA **Web address:** www.tenethealth.com	33	10	184	8300	104	37650	1234	43139	18144	456
OWYHEE—Elko County										
⊞ U. S. PUBLIC HEALTH SERVICE OWYHEE COMMUNITY HEALTH FACILITY, Mailing Address: P.O. Box 130, Zip 89832–0130; tel. 775/757–2415; Walden Townsend, Service Unit Director (Nonreporting) **A**1 10 **S** U. S. Public Health Service Indian Health Service, Rockville, MD	46	10	15	—	—	—	—	—	—	—
RENO—Washoe County										
□ BHC WEST HILLS HOSPITAL, 1240 East Ninth Street, Zip 89512–2997, Mailing Address: P.O. Box 30012, Zip 89520–0012; tel. 775/323–0478; Pamela McCullough Broughton, Chief Executive Officer **A**1 3 5 10 **F**1 3 15 16 52 53 54 55 56 57 58 59 **S** Behavioral Healthcare Corporation, Nashville, TN	33	22	95	1646	· 44	5440	0	7315	4004	258
BHC WILLOW SPRINGS RESIDENTIAL TREATMENT CENTER, 690 Edison Way, Zip 89502–4135; tel. 775/858–3303; Robert Bartlett, Administrator **F**15 52 53 **P**8 **S** Behavioral Healthcare Corporation, Nashville, TN	33	52	68	136	45	0	0	4868	2822	90
⊞ IOANNIS A. LOUGARIS VETERANS AFFAIRS MEDICAL CENTER, 1000 Locust Street, Zip 89520–0111; tel. 702/786–7200; Gary R. Whitfield, Director (Total facility includes 60 beds in nursing home–type unit) **A**1 3 5 **F**1 3 4 6 8 10 12 16 17 19 20 21 22 25 26 27 29 30 31 32 33 34 35 37 42 43 44 45 46 49 50 51 52 54 57 58 59 64 65 67 68 71 72 73 74 **P**6 **S** Department of Veterans Affairs, Washington, DC	45	10	140	3059	113	129669	0	64435	33115	708
⊞ △ SAINT MARY'S REGIONAL MEDICAL CENTER, 235 West Sixth Street, Zip 89520–0108; tel. 702/323–2041; Jeff K. Bills, Chief Executive Officer **A**1 7 9 10 **F**3 4 7 8 10 11 12 13 15 16 17 19 20 21 22 24 25 26 28 29 30 32 33 34 35 37 38 39 40 41 42 43 44 45 46 48 49 53 54 56 58 59 60 63 64 65 67 70 71 72 73 74 **P**5 6 **Web address:** www.saintmarysreno.com	21	10	238	12810	173	—	2352	127192	48524	1793
⊞ WASHOE MEDICAL CENTER, 77 Pringle Way, Zip 89520–0109; tel. 775/982–4100; Robert B. Burn, President and Chief Executive Officer (Total facility includes 19 beds in nursing home–type unit) (Nonreporting) **A**1 2 3 5 9 10 **Web address:** www.washoehealth.com	23	10	436	—	—	—	—	—	—	—
SPARKS—Washoe County										
□ NEVADA MENTAL HEALTH INSTITUTE, 480 Galletti Way, Zip 89431–5574; tel. 702/688–2001; David Rosin, M.D., Medical Director **A**1 3 5 10 **F**6 12 34 52 55 56 57 58 59 65 **P**6	12	22	52	1347	52	—	0	14398	7145	203
□ NORTHERN NEVADA MEDICAL CENTER, 2375 East Prater Way, Zip 89434–9645; tel. 702/331–7000; James R. Pagels, Chief Executive Officer and Managing Director **A**1 10 **F**8 12 14 15 16 17 19 21 22 23 26 27 28 29 30 34 35 37 44 46 48 49 51 52 55 56 57 58 59 65 66 71 72 73 74 **P**5 7 **S** Universal Health Services, Inc., King of Prussia, PA **Web address:** www.nnmc.com	32	10	100	2504	40	45638	0	27361	10022	380
TONOPAH—Nye County										
NYE REGIONAL MEDICAL CENTER, 825 South Main Street, Zip 89049, Mailing Address: P.O. Box 391, Zip 89049–0391; tel. 702/482–6233; Malinda Lewis, Administrator (Total facility includes 24 beds in nursing home–type unit) (Nonreporting) **A**9 10	13	10	45	—	—	—	—	—	—	—
WINNEMUCCA—Humboldt County										
★ HUMBOLDT GENERAL HOSPITAL, 118 East Haskell Street, Zip 89445–3299; tel. 775/623–5222; Byron Quinton, Administrator (Total facility includes 30 beds in nursing home–type unit) **A**9 10 **F**3 7 8 14 15 19 22 35 37 40 44 64 65 71 73 **P**5	16	10	52	798	34	24617	334	10114	3973	141
YERINGTON—Lyon County										
SOUTH LYON MEDICAL CENTER, Surprise at Whitacre Avenue, Zip 89447, Mailing Address: P.O. Box 940, Zip 89447–0940; tel. 702/463–2301; Joan S. Hall, R.N., Administrator (Total facility includes 30 beds in nursing home–type unit) (Nonreporting) **A**9 10	23	10	44	—	—	—	—	—	—	—

NEW HAMPSHIRE

Resident population 1,185 (in thousands)
Resident population in metro areas 58.6%
Birth rate per 1,000 population 12.8
65 years and over 12.1%
Percent of persons without health insurance 9.5%

Hospital, Address, Telephone, Administrator, Approval, Facility, and Physician Codes, Health Care System, Network	Classi-fication Codes		Utilization Data					Expense (thousands) of dollars		
★ American Hospital Association (AHA) membership □ Joint Commission on Accreditation of Healthcare Organizations (JCAHO) accreditation + American Osteopathic Healthcare Association (AOHA) membership ○ American Osteopathic Association (AOA) accreditation △ Commission on Accreditation of Rehabilitation Facilities (CARF) accreditation Control codes 61, 63, 64, 71, 72 and 73 indicate hospitals listed by AOHA, but not registered by AHA. For definition of numerical codes, see page A4	Control	Service	Staffed Beds	Admissions	Census	Outpatient Visits	Births	Total	Payroll	Personnel

BERLIN—Coos County

✠ ANDROSCOGGIN VALLEY HOSPITAL, 59 Page Hill Road, Zip 03570–3531; tel. 603/752–2200; Donald F. Saunders, President **A**1 9 10 **F**7 8 15 16 19 21 22 26 28 29 30 31 32 33 34 35 37 39 40 41 42 44 49 51 52 54 55 56 57 58 64 65 67 70 71 73 74 **P**3 — 23 10 | 64 | 2094 | 37 | 42175 | 99 | 19349 | 8560 | 269

CLAREMONT—Sullivan County

★ VALLEY REGIONAL HOSPITAL, 243 Elm Street, Zip 03743–2099; tel. 603/542–7771; Donald R. Holl, President **A**9 10 **F**1 3 6 7 8 12 13 15 16 17 18 19 21 22 23 24 25 27 28 29 30 32 33 34 35 37 39 40 41 42 44 45 49 51 52 54 55 56 57 58 59 63 64 65 66 67 70 71 72 73 74 **P**7
Web address: www.vrh.org — 23 10 | 43 | 1582 | 18 | 61064 | 240 | 23104 | 11073 | 403

COLEBROOK—Coos County

★ UPPER CONNECTICUT VALLEY HOSPITAL, Corliss Lane, Zip 03576–9533, Mailing Address: RFD 2, Box 13, Zip 03576–9533; tel. 603/237–4971; Deanna S. Howard, Chief Executive Officer **A**9 10 **F**7 8 13 14 15 16 17 19 22 28 29 30 32 37 39 40 41 42 44 56 65 67 71
Web address: www.hitchcock.org/pages/tha — 23 10 | 20 | 491 | 5 | 17842 | 49 | 5324 | 2363 | 118

CONCORD—Merrimack County

✠ CONCORD HOSPITAL, 250 Pleasant Street, Zip 03301–2598; tel. 603/225–2711; Michael B. Green, President and Chief Executive Officer **A**1 2 3 5 9 10 **F**3 4 6 7 8 10 11 12 13 14 15 16 17 19 20 21 22 23 24 25 26 29 30 31 33 34 35 37 39 40 41 42 43 44 45 49 51 52 53 54 55 56 57 58 59 61 63 65 66 67 68 70 71 72 73 74 **P**6 7
Web address: www.crhc.org — 23 10 | 176 | 8918 | 123 | 211012 | 1300 | 98099 | 46218 | 1459

□ △ HEALTHSOUTH REHABILITATION HOSPITAL, 254 Pleasant Street, Zip 03301–2508; tel. 603/226–9800; Lori Manor, Administrator (Nonreporting) **A**1 7 10 **S** HEALTHSOUTH Corporation, Birmingham, AL — 33 46 | 50 | — | — | — | — | — | — | —

□ NEW HAMPSHIRE HOSPITAL, 36 Clinton Street, Zip 03301–3861; tel. 603/271–5200; Chester G. Batchelder, Superintendent (Total facility includes 49 beds in nursing home–type unit) **A**1 3 5 10 **F**14 15 16 20 26 31 39 41 45 46 52 53 54 55 57 64 65 67 73 **P**6 — 12 22 | 261 | 1176 | 208 | 0 | 0 | 41316 | 23827 | 801

DERRY—Rockingham County

✠ PARKLAND MEDICAL CENTER, One Parkland Drive, Zip 03038–2750; tel. 603/432–1500; Scott W. Goodspeed, President and Chief Executive Officer **A**1 2 9 10 **F**7 8 12 16 17 19 22 23 27 28 29 30 34 35 37 39 40 42 44 45 46 49 51 65 67 71 73 74 **S** Columbia/HCA Healthcare Corporation, Nashville, TN
Web address: www.parklandmc.com — 33 10 | 53 | 3124 | 36 | 61933 | 638 | 31802 | 14090 | 422

DOVER—Strafford County

✠ WENTWORTH–DOUGLASS HOSPITAL, 789 Central Avenue, Zip 03820–2589; tel. 603/740–2801; Gregory J. Walker, Chief Executive Officer **A**1 2 9 10 **F**5 7 8 10 12 13 14 15 16 17 19 21 22 23 24 26 28 29 30 31 32 33 34 35 37 39 40 41 42 44 45 46 49 51 60 61 63 65 66 67 70 71 72 73 74 **P**5 8
Web address: www.wdhospital.com — 23 10 | 115 | 4264 | 49 | 73179 | 586 | 51168 | 22106 | 589

DUBLIN—Cheshire County

BEECH HILL HOSPITAL, New Harrisville Road, Zip 03444, Mailing Address: P.O. Box 254, Zip 03444–0254; tel. 603/563–8511; Matt Feehrey, Chief Executive Officer **F**2 3 16 17 22 67 **P**6 — 31 82 | 50 | 826 | 29 | 1839 | 0 | 3851 | 2335 | 65

EXETER—Rockingham County

✠ EXETER HOSPITAL, 10 Buzell Avenue, Zip 03833–2515; tel. 603/778–7311; Kevin J. Callahan, President and Chief Executive Officer **A**1 2 9 10 **F**4 7 8 10 12 13 14 15 16 17 19 20 21 22 23 24 25 26 27 28 29 30 31 32 33 34 35 37 39 40 41 42 44 45 46 49 51 53 54 56 57 58 60 61 63 64 65 66 67 70 71 72 73 74 **P**1 — 23 10 | 80 | 4370 | 163 | 76540 | 828 | 60483 | 25493 | 617

FRANKLIN—Merrimack County

✠ FRANKLIN REGIONAL HOSPITAL, 15 Aiken Avenue, Zip 03235–1299; tel. 603/934–2060; Walter A. Strauch, Executive Director **A**1 9 10 **F**7 8 14 15 16 17 19 22 28 29 30 32 33 34 37 40 41 44 45 46 49 51 54 56 57 64 65 67 71 73 74 **P**8
Web address: www.frh.org — 23 10 | 49 | 1795 | 27 | 42388 | 120 | 18015 | 9472 | 284

GREENFIELD—Hillsborough County

CROTCHED MOUNTAIN REHABILITATION CENTER, 1 Verney Drive, Zip 03047–5000; tel. 603/547–3311; Major W. Wheelock, President (Total facility includes 62 beds in nursing home–type unit) **F**6 12 20 24 27 28 39 48 49 53 64 65 73
Web address: www.cmf.org — 23 46 | 146 | 34 | 100 | 0 | 0 | 20319 | 12195 | 419

HAMPSTEAD—Rockingham County

□ HAMPSTEAD HOSPITAL, 218 East Road, Zip 03841–2228; tel. 603/329–5311; Phillip J. Kubiak, President (Nonreporting) **A**1 10
Web address: www.hampstead hospital.com — 33 22 | 99 | — | — | — | — | — | — | —

Hospital, Address, Telephone, Administrator, Approval, Facility, and Physician Codes, Health Care System, Network	Classi-fication Codes		Utilization Data					Expense (thousands) of dollars		
★ American Hospital Association (AHA) membership □ Joint Commission on Accreditation of Healthcare Organizations (JCAHO) accreditation + American Osteopathic Healthcare Association (AOHA) membership ○ American Osteopathic Association (AOA) accreditation △ Commission on Accreditation of Rehabilitation Facilities (CARF) accreditation Control codes 61, 63, 64, 71, 72 and 73 indicate hospitals listed by AOHA, but not registered by AHA. For definition of numerical codes, see page A4	Control	Service	Staffed Beds	Admissions	Census	Outpatient Visits	Births	Total	Payroll	Personnel

KEENE—Cheshire County

☒ △ CHESHIRE MEDICAL CENTER, 580 Court Street, Zip 03431–1718; tel. 603/355–2000; Robert J. Langlais, President and Chief Executive Officer **A**1 2 7 9 10 **F**1 7 8 11 12 14 15 16 17 18 19 20 21 23 24 27 28 29 30 31 32 33 34 35 36 39 40 41 42 44 45 46 48 49 52 53 54 55 56 57 58 59 60 63 65 66 67 70 71 73 74 **P**1
Web address: www.cheshire–med.com

| | 23 | 10 | 141 | 5031 | 74 | 70665 | 460 | 44037 | 20121 | 662 |

LACONIA—Belknap County

★ LAKES REGION GENERAL HOSPITAL, 80 Highland Street, Zip 03246–3298; tel. 603/524–3211; Thomas Clairmont, President **A**2 9 10 **F**1 3 4 7 8 10 12 13 14 15 16 17 19 20 22 23 24 26 28 30 31 33 34 35 37 40 41 42 44 45 49 52 53 54 55 56 57 63 65 67 70 71 72 73 74 **P**6 8
Web address: www.lrgh.org

| | 23 | 10 | 117 | 5079 | 68 | 40659 | 531 | 57961 | 27954 | 785 |

LANCASTER—Coos County

☒ WEEKS MEMORIAL HOSPITAL, 173 Middle Street, Zip 03584; tel. 603/788–4911; Scott W. Howe, Chief Executive Officer **A**1 9 10 **F**7 12 14 15 16 17 19 21 22 26 28 29 30 31 32 33 34 37 39 40 41 42 44 46 49 56 65 66 67 68 71 73 **P**6
Web address: www.weeks.hitchcock.org

| | 23 | 10 | 38 | 1049 | 17 | 65468 | 86 | 14132 | 7596 | 228 |

LEBANON—Grafton County

★ ALICE PECK DAY MEMORIAL HOSPITAL, 125 Mascoma Street, Zip 03766–2650; tel. 603/448–3121; Robert A. Mesropian, President and Chief Executive Officer (Total facility includes 50 beds in nursing home–type unit) **A**9 10 **F**6 7 8 12 13 14 15 16 17 19 21 22 25 26 28 29 30 33 34 35 39 40 41 42 44 45 46 49 51 62 64 65 67 70 71 **P**8

| | 23 | 10 | 72 | 1041 | 55 | 30949 | 210 | 16596 | 8810 | 248 |

☒ MARY HITCHCOCK MEMORIAL HOSPITAL, One Medical Center Drive, Zip 03756–0001; tel. 603/650–5000; James W. Varnum, President **A**1 3 5 8 9 10 **F**3 4 7 8 10 11 12 14 15 16 17 19 21 23 26 27 28 29 30 31 32 33 34 35 36 37 38 39 40 41 42 43 44 45 46 47 48 49 51 52 53 54 56 57 58 59 60 61 63 65 66 67 68 70 71 72 73 74 **P**3
Web address: www.hitchcock.org/pages/tha/ucvh.html

| | 23 | 10 | 322 | 17515 | 237 | 394621 | 984 | 236881 | 85182 | 2952 |

LITTLETON—Grafton County

☒ LITTLETON REGIONAL HOSPITAL, 262 Cottage Street, Zip 03561–4101; tel. 603/444–7731; Robert S. Pearson, Administrator **A**1 2 9 10 **F**7 8 14 15 16 17 19 21 22 23 27 28 29 30 31 33 34 35 37 39 40 41 42 44 46 49 60 61 65 69 71 73 74 **S** Quorum Health Group/Quorum Health Resources, Inc., Brentwood, TN
Web address: www.littletonhospital.org

| | 23 | 10 | 49 | 1341 | 13 | 33664 | 231 | 17811 | 7575 | 219 |

MANCHESTER—Hillsborough County

☒ △ CATHOLIC MEDICAL CENTER, 100 McGregor Street, Zip 03102–3770; tel. 603/668–3545; Allyson Pitman Giles, President and Chief Executive Officer **A**1 7 9 10 **F**1 2 3 4 5 6 7 8 10 11 12 14 15 16 17 18 19 20 21 22 23 24 26 28 29 30 31 32 33 34 35 37 39 41 42 43 44 45 46 48 49 52 54 56 57 58 59 60 65 66 67 71 72 73 74 **P**7 8

| | 23 | 10 | 213 | 8490 | 139 | 55712 | 0 | 117287 | 34808 | 936 |

☒ ELLIOT HOSPITAL, One Elliot Way, Zip 03103; tel. 603/663–2090; Douglas F. Dean, Jr., President and Chief Executive Officer **A**1 2 9 10 **F**1 3 4 5 6 7 8 10 12 13 14 15 16 17 18 19 20 21 22 23 24 26 27 28 29 30 31 32 33 34 35 37 38 39 40 41 42 43 44 45 46 49 51 52 54 55 56 57 58 59 60 61 62 63 65 66 67 70 71 72 73 74 **P**7 8

| | 23 | 10 | 225 | 10287 | 124 | 111138 | 2517 | 108497 | 38309 | 890 |

☒ VETERANS AFFAIRS MEDICAL CENTER, 718 Smyth Road, Zip 03104–4098; tel. 603/624–4366; Paul J. McCool, Director (Total facility includes 120 beds in nursing home–type unit) **A**1 **F**1 2 3 8 11 12 16 19 20 21 22 25 26 28 30 31 32 33 34 37 39 41 42 44 45 46 49 51 54 55 56 58 64 65 67 71 73 74 **P**6 **S** Department of Veterans Affairs, Washington, DC

| | 45 | 10 | 157 | 1794 | 139 | 103440 | 0 | 47460 | 22066 | 461 |

NASHUA—Hillsborough County

□ CHARTER BROOKSIDE BEHAVIORAL HEALTH SYSTEM OF NEW ENGLAND, 29 Northwest Boulevard, Zip 03063–4005; tel. 603/886–5000; T. Mark Gallagher, Chief Executive Officer (Nonreporting) **A**1 10 **S** Magellan Health Services, Atlanta, GA

| | 33 | 22 | 100 | — | — | — | — | — | — | — |

☒ SOUTHERN NEW HAMPSHIRE MEDICAL CENTER, 8 Prospect Street, Zip 03060, Mailing Address: P.O. Box 2014, Zip 03061–2014; tel. 603/577–2000; Thomas E. Wilhelmsen, Jr., President and Chief Executive Officer **A**1 2 9 10 **F**1 3 7 8 10 12 13 14 15 16 17 18 19 21 22 23 27 28 29 30 31 32 33 34 35 37 38 39 40 41 42 44 45 46 49 51 52 53 54 55 56 57 58 59 60 61 63 65 66 67 70 71 72 73 74 **P**6 8
Web address: www.snhmc.org

| | 23 | 10 | 171 | 6486 | 66 | 135023 | 1446 | 65837 | 32032 | 926 |

☒ △ ST. JOSEPH HOSPITAL, 172 Kinsley Street, Zip 03061; tel. 603/882–3000; Peter B. Davis, President and Chief Executive Officer **A**1 2 6 7 9 10 **F**1 2 3 7 8 10 11 12 13 14 15 16 17 18 19 20 21 22 23 25 26 27 28 29 30 31 32 33 34 35 39 40 41 42 44 48 49 52 57 58 60 63 65 67 70 71 73 74 **P**6 8 **S** Covenant Health Systems, Inc., Lexington, MA
Web address: www.nh–healthcare.org

| | 21 | 10 | 135 | 5529 | 79 | 136210 | 858 | 60666 | 28507 | 740 |

NEW LONDON—Merrimack County

☒ NEW LONDON HOSPITAL, 270 County Road, Zip 03257–4570; tel. 603/526–2911; Maureen McNamara, President and Chief Executive Officer (Total facility includes 58 beds in nursing home–type unit) **A**1 9 10 **F**7 8 12 13 14 15 16 17 18 19 20 22 24 25 28 30 32 33 34 35 36 37 39 40 41 42 44 45 49 51 61 64 65 66 67 71 72 73 74 **P**8

| | 23 | 10 | 93 | 1313 | 71 | 172062 | 129 | 18828 | 9622 | 283 |

Hospital, Address, Telephone, Administrator, Approval, Facility, and Physician Codes, Health Care System, Network	Classi-fication Codes		Utilization Data					Expense (thousands) of dollars		
★ American Hospital Association (AHA) membership □ Joint Commission on Accreditation of Healthcare Organizations (JCAHO) accreditation + American Osteopathic Healthcare Association (AOHA) membership ○ American Osteopathic Association (AOA) accreditation △ Commission on Accreditation of Rehabilitation Facilities (CARF) accreditation Control codes 61, 63, 64, 71, 72 and 73 indicate hospitals listed by AOHA, but not registered by AHA. For definition of numerical codes, see page A4	Control	Service	Staffed Beds	Admissions	Census	Outpatient Visits	Births	Total	Payroll	Personnel

NORTH CONWAY—Carroll County

MEMORIAL HOSPITAL, 3073 Main Street, Zip 03860–5001, Mailing Address: P.O. Box 5001, Zip 03860–5001; tel. 603/356–5461; Gary R. Poquette, FACHE, Executive Director (Total facility includes 45 beds in nursing home–type unit) **A**9 10 **F**1 7 8 12 14 15 16 17 19 20 21 22 28 29 30 34 35 37 40 41 42 44 45 46 49 56 63 64 65 67 70 71 73 74 **P**3 — 23 10 80 1516 60 32692 205 17964 7129 254

PETERBOROUGH—Hillsborough County

✠ MONADNOCK COMMUNITY HOSPITAL, 452 Old Street Road, Zip 03458–1295; tel. 603/924–7191; Peter L. Gosline, Chief Executive Officer **A**1 9 10 **F**4 7 8 12 14 15 16 17 18 19 20 22 26 28 30 31 32 33 34 36 37 39 40 41 42 43 44 45 46 49 51 52 55 56 57 58 59 65 67 70 71 73 74 — 23 10 62 1824 23 70058 401 17031 7655 247

PLYMOUTH—Grafton County

SPEARE MEMORIAL HOSPITAL, 16 Hospital Road, Zip 03264–1199; tel. 603/536–1120; David L. Pearse, President **A**9 10 **F**7 8 11 13 14 15 17 19 20 22 30 33 37 39 40 41 42 44 49 63 65 67 71 73 **P**8 — 23 10 28 969 9 40919 113 12255 6378 176
Web address: www.spearehospital.com

PORTSMOUTH—Rockingham County

✠ PORTSMOUTH REGIONAL HOSPITAL AND PAVILION, (Includes Portsmouth Pavilion), 333 Borthwick Avenue, Zip 03801–7004; tel. 603/436–5110; William J. Schuler, Chief Executive Officer **A**1 9 10 **F**3 4 7 8 10 11 12 13 17 18 19 21 22 23 24 26 28 30 32 33 34 35 37 39 40 41 42 43 44 49 52 53 56 57 58 59 63 65 71 72 73 74 **P**1 6 8 **S** Columbia/HCA Healthcare Corporation, Nashville, TN — 33 10 179 6945 102 95633 962 — — 797

ROCHESTER—Strafford County

✠ FRISBIE MEMORIAL HOSPITAL, 11 Whitehall Road, Zip 03867–3297; tel. 603/332–5211; Alvin D. Felgar, President and Chief Executive Officer **A**1 2 9 10 **F**3 7 8 10 11 15 16 17 19 21 22 26 30 31 33 34 35 37 39 40 41 42 44 46 49 51 52 54 55 57 58 63 65 66 67 71 73 74 **P**3 5 6 8 — 23 10 70 3060 38 56626 551 33098 14298 408
Web address: www.frisbiehospital.com

SALEM—Rockingham County

□ △ NORTHEAST REHABILITATION HOSPITAL, 70 Butler Street, Zip 03079; tel. 603/893–2900; John F. Prochilo, Chief Executive Officer and Administrator **A**1 7 10 **F**5 9 12 13 14 15 16 17 24 28 29 32 34 39 41 45 48 49 64 65 66 67 73 — 33 46 80 1170 64 109261 0 26130 12856 439
Web address: www.rehabnet.com

WOLFEBORO—Carroll County

★ HUGGINS HOSPITAL, 240 South Main Street, Zip 03894–4411, Mailing Address: P.O. Box 912, Zip 03894–0912; tel. 603/569–7500; Leslie N. H. MacLeod, President (Total facility includes 27 beds in nursing home–type unit) **A**9 10 **F**1 6 7 8 16 19 20 22 26 28 29 30 34 37 40 41 44 46 51 62 63 64 65 67 71 73 74 **P**8 — 23 10 82 1761 53 50488 121 17426 7930 254
Web address: www.higginshospital.org

WOODSVILLE—Grafton County

✠ COTTAGE HOSPITAL, Swiftwater Road, Zip 03785–2001, Mailing Address: P.O. Box 2001, Zip 03785–2001; tel. 603/747–2761; Reginald J. Lavoie, Administrator **A**1 2 9 10 **F**7 8 15 16 19 22 35 36 37 40 41 42 44 49 54 64 65 71 72 73 74 **P**8 — 23 10 34 1003 12 38384 73 10790 5961 164

NEW JERSEY

Resident population 8,115 (in thousands)
Resident population in metro areas 98.4%
Birth rate per 1,000 population 14.5
65 years and over 13.7%
Percent of persons without health insurance 16.7%

Hospital, Address, Telephone, Administrator, Approval, Facility, and Physician Codes, Health Care System, Network	Classi-fication Codes		Utilization Data					Expense (thousands) of dollars		
	Control	Service	Staffed Beds	Admissions	Census	Outpatient Visits	Births	Total	Payroll	Personnel

★ American Hospital Association (AHA) membership
□ Joint Commission on Accreditation of Healthcare Organizations (JCAHO) accreditation
+ American Osteopathic Healthcare Association (AOHA) membership
○ American Osteopathic Association (AOA) accreditation
△ Commission on Accreditation of Rehabilitation Facilities (CARF) accreditation
Control codes 61, 63, 64, 71, 72 and 73 indicate hospitals listed by AOHA, but not registered by AHA. For definition of numerical codes, see page A4

ANCORA—Atlantic County

□ ANCORA PSYCHIATRIC HOSPITAL, 202 Spring Garden Road, Zip 08037–9699; tel. 609/561–1700; Yvonne A. Pressley, Chief Executive Officer (Nonreporting) **A**1 10 **S** Division of Mental Health Services, Department of Human Services, State of New Jersey, Trenton, NJ — 12 22 625 — — — — — — — —

ATLANTIC CITY—Atlantic County

⊠ ATLANTIC CITY MEDICAL CENTER, 1925 Pacific Avenue, Zip 08401–6713; tel. 609/345–4000; David P. Tilton, President and Chief Executive Officer (Total facility includes 14 beds in nursing home–type unit) **A**1 2 3 9 10 **F**3 8 10 11 12 13 14 15 16 17 18 19 21 22 25 26 27 28 29 30 31 32 33 34 35 37 38 40 41 42 44 45 47 48 49 51 52 53 54 55 56 57 58 59 60 61 63 64 65 67 68 70 71 72 73 74 **P**6 — 23 10 402 25662 326 — 2164 188472 82727 2040
Web address: www.atlanticare.org

BAYONNE—Hudson County

⊠ BAYONNE HOSPITAL, 29 East 29th Street, Zip 07002–4699; tel. 201/858–5000; Michael R. D'Agnes, President and Chief Executive Officer **A**1 2 6 9 10 **F**1 3 7 8 10 11 12 13 15 16 17 18 19 20 21 22 26 27 28 29 30 32 33 34 35 37 40 41 42 44 46 49 51 52 53 54 55 56 57 58 59 60 61 63 64 65 67 68 71 73 74 **P**7 — 23 10 278 9438 184 167948 566 87384 38629 1379
Web address: www.bayonnehospital.com

BELLE MEAD—Somerset County

⊠ CARRIER FOUNDATION, County Route 601, P.O. Box 147, Zip 08502–0147; tel. 908/281–1000; C. Richard Sarle, President and Chief Executive Officer **A**1 10 **F**1 2 3 12 15 16 17 25 26 30 34 45 52 53 54 55 56 57 58 59 67 68 73 **P**1 — 23 22 166 3792 117 64365 0 35602 14371 415
Web address: www.carrier.org

BELLEVILLE—Essex County

⊠ CLARA MAASS HEALTH SYSTEM, 1 Clara Maass Drive, Zip 07109–3557; tel. 973/450–2000; Thomas A. Biga, Executive Director (Total facility includes 179 beds in nursing home–type unit) (Nonreporting) **A**1 2 9 10 **S** Saint Barnabas Health Care System, West Orange, NJ — 23 10 644 — — — — — — —

BERKELEY HEIGHTS—Union County

★ RUNNELLS SPECIALIZED HOSPITAL OF UNION COUNTY, 40 Watchung Way, Zip 07922–2618; tel. 908/771–5700; Joseph W. Sharp, Administrator (Total facility includes 300 beds in nursing home–type unit) (Nonreporting) **A**10 — 13 49 345 — — — — — — —
Web address: www.unioncoutynj.org/runells

BERLIN—Camden County

★ WEST JERSEY HOSPITAL–BERLIN, 100 Townsend Avenue, Zip 08009–9035; tel. 609/322–3100; Ellen Guarnieri, Executive Director **A**9 **F**1 2 3 5 7 8 10 12 13 14 15 16 17 19 20 21 22 25 26 27 28 29 30 32 33 34 35 36 37 38 39 40 41 42 44 45 46 49 51 60 61 64 65 66 67 71 72 73 74 **P**5 7 **S** Virtua Health, Marlton, NJ — 23 10 79 3631 51 21231 0 26103 13066 368

BLACKWOOD—Camden County

□ CAMDEN COUNTY HEALTH SERVICES CENTER, (LONG TERM CARE), Woodbury–Turnersville Road, Zip 08012–2799, Mailing Address: P.O. Box 1639, Zip 08012–2799; tel. 609/374–6600; Stanford A. Alliker, Chief Executive Officer (Total facility includes 291 beds in nursing home–type unit) **A**1 9 10 **F**1 14 15 16 19 21 26 27 28 31 35 50 51 52 54 55 56 57 63 64 65 67 73 — 13 49 441 1156 429 0 0 38246 16472 442

BOONTON TOWNSHIP—Morris County

SAINT CLARE'S HOSPITAL/BOONTON TOWNSHIP See Saint Clare's Health Services, Denville

BRICK TOWNSHIP—Ocean County

BRICK HOSPITAL DIVISION See Meridian Health System, Neptune

BRIDGETON—Cumberland County

⊠ SOUTH JERSEY HOSPITAL, (Includes South Jersey Hospital–Bridgeton, 333 Irving Avenue, tel. 609/451–6600; South Jersey Hospital–Elmer, West Front Street, Elmer, Zip 08318–0516, Mailing Address: P.O. Box 1090, Zip 08318–1090; tel. 609/358–2341; South Jersey Hospital–Millville, 1200 North High, Millville, Zip 08332–2586; tel. 609/825–3500), 333 Irving Avenue, Zip 08302–2100; tel. 609/451–6600; Chester B. Kaletkowski, President and Chief Executive Officer **A**1 2 9 10 **F**3 7 8 12 14 15 16 17 18 19 20 21 22 24 25 29 30 32 33 34 37 39 40 41 42 44 45 46 49 52 53 54 55 56 57 58 59 60 65 66 67 68 71 73 **S** South Jersey Health System, Bridgeton, NJ — 23 10 340 11956 199 241675 786 114827 52797 1506
Web address: www.sjhs.com

BROWNS MILLS—Burlington County

⊠ DEBORAH HEART AND LUNG CENTER, (SPECIALTY HEART & LUNG CENTER), 200 Trenton Road, Zip 08015–1799; tel. 609/893–6611; John R. Ernst, Executive Director **A**1 3 5 9 10 13 **F**4 10 14 17 19 21 27 28 29 30 34 37 43 50 63 65 67 71 73 **P**6 — 23 49 161 5070 94 28067 0 119419 63760 1288
Web address: www.deborah.org

Hospital, Address, Telephone, Administrator, Approval, Facility, and Physician Codes, Health Care System, Network	Classi-fication Codes		Utilization Data					Expense (thousands) of dollars		
★ American Hospital Association (AHA) membership □ Joint Commission on Accreditation of Healthcare Organizations (JCAHO) accreditation + American Osteopathic Healthcare Association (AOHA) membership ○ American Osteopathic Association (AOA) accreditation △ Commission on Accreditation of Rehabilitation Facilities (CARF) accreditation Control codes 61, 63, 64, 71, 72 and 73 indicate hospitals listed by AOHA, but not registered by AHA. For definition of numerical codes, see page A4	Control	Service	Staffed Beds	Admissions	Census	Outpatient Visits	Births	Total	Payroll	Personnel

CAMDEN—Camden County

☒ △ OUR LADY OF LOURDES MEDICAL CENTER, 1600 Haddon Avenue, Zip 08103–3117; tel. 609/757–3500; Alexander J. Hatala, President and Chief Executive Officer **A**1 3 5 7 9 10 12 13 **F**4 7 8 10 11 12 13 14 15 16 17 18 19 20 21 22 26 28 29 30 31 32 33 34 35 36 37 38 40 41 42 43 44 45 46 48 49 51 52 54 55 56 57 58 61 63 65 67 68 69 70 71 73 74 **P**6 7 **S** Catholic Health East, Newtown Square, PA
Web address: www.lourdesnet.org

| | 23 | 10 | 327 | 15136 | 277 | 189021 | 1312 | 162016 | 70756 | 1985 |

☒ THE COOPER HEALTH SYSTEM, One Cooper Plaza, Zip 08103–1489; tel. 609/342–2000; Leslie D. Hirsch, Acting President and Chief Executive Officer (Nonreporting) **A**1 2 3 5 8 9 10 13
Web address: www.cooperhealth.org

| | 23 | 10 | 370 | — | — | — | — | — | — | — |

☒ WEST JERSEY HOSPITAL–CAMDEN, 1000 Atlantic Avenue, Zip 08104–1595; tel. 609/246–3000; Carolyn M. Ballard, Executive Director **A**1 2 3 5 9 10 **F**1 2 3 5 7 8 10 12 13 14 15 16 17 19 20 21 22 25 26 27 28 29 30 33 34 35 36 37 38 39 40 41 42 44 45 46 49 51 60 61 64 65 66 67 71 72 73 74 **P**5 7 **S** Virtua Health, Marlton, NJ

| | 23 | 10 | 94 | 4143 | 64 | 47339 | 0 | 43360 | 21704 | 663 |

CAPE MAY COURT HOUSE—Cape May County

☒ BURDETTE TOMLIN MEMORIAL HOSPITAL, 2 Stone Harbor Boulevard, Zip 08210–9990; tel. 609/463–2000; Thomas L. Scott, FACHE, President and Chief Executive Officer **A**1 9 10 **F**3 7 8 12 13 14 15 16 17 18 19 20 21 22 24 27 28 30 32 33 35 37 39 40 41 42 44 45 46 49 51 56 58 65 67 68 71 73 **P**7
Web address: www.btmh.com

| | 23 | 10 | 206 | 10015 | 160 | 110589 | 646 | 61622 | 30087 | 962 |

CEDAR GROVE—Essex County

□ ESSEX COUNTY HOSPITAL CENTER, 125 Fairview Avenue, Zip 07009–1399; tel. 973/228–8200; Muriel M. Shore, Ed.D., R.N., Chief Executive Officer **A**1 10 **F**12 18 20 26 41 46 52 57 65 73

| | 13 | 22 | 400 | 500 | 343 | 0 | 0 | — | 29527 | 624 |

CHERRY HILL—Camden County

★ + ○ KENNEDY MEMORIAL HOSPITALS–UNIVERSITY MEDICAL CENTER, (Includes Kennedy Memorial Hospital, 18 East Laurel Road, Stratford, Zip 08084; tel. 609/346–6000; Kennedy Memorial Hospital, 435 Hurffville–Cross Keys Road, Turnersville, Zip 08012; tel. 609/582–2500), 2201 Chapel Avenue West, Zip 08002–2048; tel. 609/488–6500; Joseph W. Devine, Vice President, Hospital Services **A**9 10 11 12 13 **F**2 3 7 8 10 12 13 14 15 16 17 18 19 20 21 22 26 27 29 30 31 32 33 34 35 37 38 39 40 41 44 45 46 49 51 52 53 54 55 56 57 58 59 61 62 63 64 65 66 67 71 73 74

| | 23 | 10 | 458 | 22700 | 290 | 360000 | 1823 | 187376 | 81605 | 1986 |

DENVILLE—Morris County

☒ SAINT CLARE'S HEALTH SERVICES, (Formerly Northwest Covenant Medical Center), (Includes Saint Clare's Hospital/Boonton Township, 130 Powerville Road, Boonton Township, Zip 07005; tel. 201/625–6000; Saint Clare's Hospital/Denville, 25 Pocono Road, Zip 07834; tel. 201/625–6000; Saint Clare's Hospital/Sussex, 20 Walnut Street, Sussex, Zip 07461; tel. 201/702–2200; St. Clare's Hospital/Dover, 400 West Blackwell Street, Dover, Zip 07801–3311; tel. 201/989–3000), 25 Pocono Road, Zip 07834–2995; tel. 973/625–6000; Kathryn J. McDonagh, President and Chief Executive Officer (Total facility includes 141 beds in nursing home–type unit) **A**1 2 9 10 **F**1 2 3 6 7 8 10 12 13 14 15 16 17 18 19 20 21 22 23 24 25 26 27 28 29 30 32 33 35 36 37 39 40 41 42 44 46 49 51 52 53 54 55 56 57 58 59 60 62 64 65 66 67 68 70 71 72 73 74 **P**1 5 6 7 **S** Marian Health System, Tulsa, OK
Web address: www.saintclares.org

| | 21 | 10 | 657 | 23815 | 456 | 167830 | 2145 | 217690 | 102521 | 2369 |

DOVER—Morris County

ST. CLARE'S HOSPITAL/DOVER See Saint Clare's Health Services, Denville

EAST ORANGE—Essex County

☒ EAST ORANGE GENERAL HOSPITAL, 300 Central Avenue, Zip 07019–2819; tel. 973/672–8400; Claude D. Watts, Jr., President and Chief Executive Officer **A**1 10 **F**2 3 8 12 13 15 16 17 18 19 21 22 25 26 30 31 32 33 34 35 37 41 42 44 46 49 52 53 54 55 56 57 66 67 69 71 73 74

| | 23 | 10 | 238 | 7722 | 193 | 78475 | 3 | — | 39263 | 845 |

☒ VETERANS AFFAIRS NEW JERSEY HEALTH CARE SYSTEM, (Includes East Orange Division, 385 Tremont Avenue, tel. 973/676–1000; Lyons Division, 151 Knollcroft Road, Lyons, Zip 07939–9998; tel. 908/647–0180), 385 Tremont Avenue, Zip 07018–1095; tel. 973/676–1000; Kenneth H. Mizrach, Director (Total facility includes 360 beds in nursing home–type unit) **A**1 2 3 5 8 **F**1 2 3 8 10 11 12 17 18 19 20 21 22 24 25 26 28 29 30 31 32 34 35 37 39 41 42 44 45 46 48 49 51 52 54 56 57 58 59 60 63 64 65 67 71 73 74 **P**6 **S** Department of Veterans Affairs, Washington, DC

| | 45 | 10 | 930 | 6081 | 493 | 394345 | 0 | 252185 | 143864 | 3130 |

EDISON—Middlesex County

★ △ JFK JOHNSON REHABILITATION INSTITUTE, 65 James Street, Zip 08818–3059; tel. 732/321–7050; Scott Gebhard, Senior Vice President Operations (Nonreporting) **A**7 10 **S** Solaris Health System, Edison, NJ

| | 23 | 46 | 92 | — | — | — | — | — | — | — |

☒ JFK MEDICAL CENTER, 65 James Street, Zip 08818–3947; tel. 732/321–7000; John P. McGee, President and Chief Executive Officer (Nonreporting) **A**1 2 3 5 9 **S** Solaris Health System, Edison, NJ
Web address: www.jfkhs.org

| | 23 | 10 | 380 | — | — | — | — | — | — | — |

ELIZABETH—Union County

☒ ELIZABETH GENERAL MEDICAL CENTER, 925 East Jersey Street, Zip 07201–2728; tel. 908/289–8600; David A. Fletcher, President and Chief Executive Officer (Total facility includes 136 beds in nursing home–type unit) **A**1 2 3 5 6 9 10 **F**1 3 7 8 10 12 14 15 16 17 18 19 20 21 22 26 28 29 30 31 33 34 37 39 40 41 42 44 45 49 51 52 53 54 55 56 57 58 59 60 64 65 67 71 73 74
Web address: www.egmc.org

| | 23 | 10 | 401 | 9172 | 313 | 264536 | — | 122810 | 62529 | 1472 |

Hospital, Address, Telephone, Administrator, Approval, Facility, and Physician Codes, Health Care System, Network	Classification Codes		Utilization Data					Expense (thousands) of dollars		
	Control	Service	Staffed Beds	Admissions	Census	Outpatient Visits	Births	Total	Payroll	Personnel

★ American Hospital Association (AHA) membership
□ Joint Commission on Accreditation of Healthcare Organizations (JCAHO) accreditation
+ American Osteopathic Healthcare Association (AOHA) membership
○ American Osteopathic Association (AOA) accreditation
△ Commission on Accreditation of Rehabilitation Facilities (CARF) accreditation
Control codes 61, 63, 64, 71, 72 and 73 indicate hospitals listed by AOHA, but not registered by AHA. For definition of numerical codes, see page A4

Hospital	Control	Service	Staffed Beds	Admissions	Census	Outpatient Visits	Births	Total	Payroll	Personnel
✸ ST. ELIZABETH HOSPITAL, 225 Williamson Street, Zip 07202–3600; tel. 908/527–5000; Sister Elizabeth Ann Maloney, President and Chief Executive Officer (Total facility includes 20 beds in nursing home–type unit) **A**1 2 3 9 10 **F**3 7 8 10 11 12 13 14 15 16 17 19 21 22 24 26 27 28 30 31 32 33 34 35 37 39 40 41 44 45 49 54 60 63 64 65 67 68 71 73 74 **P**7	21	10	284	12017	172	116314	1123	95004	41395	1076
ELMER—Salem County										
SOUTH JERSEY HOSPITAL–ELMER See South Jersey Hospital, Bridgeton										
ENGLEWOOD—Bergen County										
✸ ENGLEWOOD HOSPITAL AND MEDICAL CENTER, 350 Engle Street, Zip 07631–1898; tel. 201/894–3000; Daniel A. Kane, President and Chief Executive Officer (Nonreporting) **A**1 2 3 5 6 9 10	23	10	318							
FLEMINGTON—Hunterdon County										
✸ HUNTERDON MEDICAL CENTER, 2100 Wescott Drive, Zip 08822–4604; tel. 908/788–6100; Robert P. Wise, President and Chief Executive Officer **A**1 2 3 5 9 10 **F**1 3 7 8 10 12 13 14 15 16 17 18 19 21 22 24 25 26 28 29 30 31 32 33 34 35 37 39 40 41 42 44 45 46 49 51 52 53 54 55 56 57 58 59 61 65 67 68 71 73 74 **P**1 5 7 Web address: www.hunterdonhealthcare.org	23	10	176	7406	103	227598	1285	86884	44669	1265
FLORHAM PARK—Morris County										
✸ ATLANTIC HEALTH SYSTEM, (Includes General Hospital Center at Passaic, 350 Boulevard, Passaic, Zip 07055–2800; tel. 973/365–4300; Marie Cassese, R.N., President; Morristown Memorial Hospital, 100 Madison Avenue, Morristown, Zip 07962–1956; tel. 973/971–5000; Jean M. McMahon, R.N., President; Mountainside Hospital, Bay and Highland Avenues, Montclair, Zip 07042–4898; tel. 973/429–6000; Robert A. Silver, President; Overlook Hospital, 99 Beauvoir Avenue, Summit, Zip 07902–0220; tel. 908/522–2000; David H. Freed, President; 325 Columbia Turnpike, Zip 07932–0959; Mailing Address: P.O. Box 959, Zip 07932–0959; tel. 973/660–3100; Richard P. Oths, President and Chief Executive Officer (Total facility includes 410 beds in nursing home–type unit) **A**1 2 3 5 6 8 10 **F**2 3 4 5 7 8 10 11 12 13 15 16 17 18 19 20 21 22 24 25 26 27 28 29 30 31 32 33 34 35 36 37 38 39 40 41 42 43 44 45 46 47 48 49 51 52 53 54 55 56 57 58 59 60 61 64 65 66 67 68 70 71 72 73 74 **P**4 5 6 7 Web address: www.ATLANTICHEALTH.ORG	23	10	1404	67368	1316	742039	7856	734298	350752	6891
FREEHOLD—Monmouth County										
✸ CENTRASTATE HEALTHCARE SYSTEM, 901 West Main Street, Zip 07728–2549; tel. 732/431–2000; Thomas H. Litz, FACHE, President and Chief Executive Officer **A**1 9 10 **F**3 7 8 11 12 13 14 15 16 17 18 19 22 23 25 26 28 29 30 32 33 34 35 37 39 40 41 42 44 45 46 49 51 52 54 55 56 58 61 62 64 65 66 67 68 71 72 73 74 **P**5 8	23	10	241	9581	149	119309	1317	82211	38848	1418
GLEN GARDNER—Hunterdon County										
□ SENATOR GARRETT T. W. HAGEDORN GERO PSYCHIATRIC HOSPITAL, 200 Sanitorium Road, Zip 08826–9752; tel. 908/537–2141; Donald A. Bruckman, Acting Chief Executive Officer (Nonreporting) **A**1 10 **S** Division of Mental Health Services, Department of Human Services, State of New Jersey, Trenton, NJ	12	22	181	—	—	—	—	—	—	—
GREYSTONE PARK—Morris County										
✸ GREYSTONE PARK PSYCHIATRIC HOSPITAL, Central Avenue, Zip 07950, Mailing Address: P.O. Box A, Zip 07950; tel. 973/538–1800; Michael Greenstein, Chief Executive Officer (Nonreporting) **A**1 10 **S** Division of Mental Health Services, Department of Human Services, State of New Jersey, Trenton, NJ	12	22	605	—	—	—	—	—	—	—
HACKENSACK—Bergen County										
✸ HACKENSACK UNIVERSITY MEDICAL CENTER, (Includes Hasbrouck Heights Ambulatory Care Facility, Hasbrouck Heights), 30 Prospect Avenue, Zip 07601–1991; tel. 201/996–2000; John P. Ferguson, FACHE, President and Chief Executive Officer **A**1 2 3 5 8 9 10 **F**3 4 5 7 8 10 11 12 13 14 15 16 17 18 19 20 21 22 24 25 26 27 28 29 30 31 32 33 34 36 37 38 39 40 41 42 43 44 45 46 47 49 51 52 53 54 55 56 57 58 59 60 61 65 66 67 68 69 70 71 72 73 74 **P**5 7 8	23	10	556	53486	522	1689152	3894	436873	201998	4574
HACKETTSTOWN—Warren County										
✸ HACKETTSTOWN COMMUNITY HOSPITAL, 651 Willow Grove Street, Zip 07840–1798; tel. 908/852–5100; Gene C. Milton, President and Chief Executive Officer **A**1 9 10 **F**3 7 8 12 14 15 16 19 20 21 22 24 26 28 29 30 33 34 35 36 37 39 40 41 42 44 45 46 49 58 65 66 67 71 73 74	21	10	106	4095	54	43029	548	32106	14616	419
HAMILTON—Mercer County										
□ ROBERT WOOD JOHNSON UNIVERSITY HOSPITAL AT HAMILTON, One Hamilton Health Place, Zip 08690–3599; tel. 609/586–7900; Christy Stephenson, Chief Administrative Officer **A**1 10 **F**1 7 8 10 12 14 15 16 17 19 20 21 22 26 27 28 29 30 32 33 34 35 36 37 39 40 41 42 44 45 46 49 51 60 61 63 64 65 67 71 72 73 74 **P**6 7 Web address: www.rwjhamilton.org	23	10	160	6546	94	—	572	55851	23088	—
HAMMONTON—Atlantic County										
✸ WILLIAM B. KESSLER MEMORIAL HOSPITAL, 600 South White Horse Pike, Zip 08037–2099; tel. 609/561–6700; Warren E. Gager, Chief Executive Officer **A**1 9 10 **F**8 11 12 14 15 16 19 20 21 22 24 27 30 31 32 34 37 39 41 42 44 45 46 49 51 63 65 66 67 71 73	23	10	96	3404	60	195780	0	—	—	468
HOBOKEN—Hudson County										
□ ST. MARY HOSPITAL, 308 Willow Avenue, Zip 07030–3889; tel. 201/418–1000; Robert S. Chaloner, President and Chief Executive Officer **A**1 3 9 10 **F**3 8 12 17 18 19 21 22 23 26 27 28 30 31 34 37 40 41 42 44 46 47 49 52 53 54 55 56 57 58 59 61 71 72 73 **P**3 4 7 8 **S** Franciscan Health Partnership, Inc., Latham, NY	23	10	328	8853	144	128026	1070	82604	40998	977

Hospital, Address, Telephone, Administrator, Approval, Facility, and Physician Codes, Health Care System, Network	Classi-fication Codes		Utilization Data					Expense (thousands) of dollars		
★ American Hospital Association (AHA) membership □ Joint Commission on Accreditation of Healthcare Organizations (JCAHO) accreditation + American Osteopathic Healthcare Association (AOHA) membership ○ American Osteopathic Association (AOA) accreditation △ Commission on Accreditation of Rehabilitation Facilities (CARF) accreditation Control codes 61, 63, 64, 71, 72 and 73 indicate hospitals listed by AOHA, but not registered by AHA. For definition of numerical codes, see page A4	Control	Service	Staffed Beds	Admissions	Census	Outpatient Visits	Births	Total	Payroll	Personnel

HOLMDEL—Monmouth County

✠ BAYSHORE COMMUNITY HOSPITAL, 727 North Beers Street, Zip 07733–1598; tel. 732/739–5900; Thomas Goldman, President and Chief Executive Officer (Total facility includes 13 beds in nursing home–type unit) **A**1 9 10 **F**1 3 6 8 10 11 12 15 16 17 18 19 20 21 22 24 26 28 29 30 31 33 34 35 36 37 39 44 45 46 49 51 53 56 57 58 62 63 64 65 67 71 72 73 **P**5 7
Web address: www.bchs.com

| | 23 | 10 | 181 | 8496 | 146 | 47571 | 0 | 64889 | 30176 | 901 |

IRVINGTON—Essex County

✠ IRVINGTON GENERAL HOSPITAL, 832 Chancellor Avenue, Zip 07111–0709; tel. 973/399–6000; Paul A. Mertz, Executive Director (Nonreporting) **A**1 9 10 **S** Saint Barnabas Health Care System, West Orange, NJ

| | 23 | 10 | 157 | — | — | — | — | — | — | — |

JERSEY CITY—Hudson County

✠ CHRIST HOSPITAL, 176 Palisade Avenue, Zip 07306–1196, Mailing Address: P.O. Box J–1, Zip 07306–1196; tel. 201/795–8200; Daniel R. Connell, President (Nonreporting) **A**1 2 6 9 10 13
Web address: www.christhospital.org

| | 23 | 10 | 358 | — | — | — | — | — | — | — |

□ GREENVILLE HOSPITAL, 1825 John F. Kennedy Boulevard, Zip 07305–2198; tel. 201/547–6100; Jonathan M. Metsch, Dr.PH, President and Chief Executive Officer (Nonreporting) **A**1 9 10 **S** Liberty Healthcare System, Jersey City, NJ

| | 23 | 10 | 86 | — | — | — | — | — | — | — |

✠ JERSEY CITY MEDICAL CENTER, 50 Baldwin Avenue, Zip 07304–3199; tel. 201/915–2000; Jonathan M. Metsch, Dr.PH, President and Chief Executive Officer (Nonreporting) **A**1 2 3 5 9 10 **S** Liberty Healthcare System, Jersey City, NJ

| | 23 | 10 | 487 | — | — | — | — | — | — | — |

□ ST. FRANCIS HOSPITAL, 25 McWilliams Place, Zip 07302–1698; tel. 201/418–1000; Robert S. Chaloner, President and Chief Executive Officer **A**1 6 9 10 **F**2 3 5 8 11 17 18 19 20 21 22 23 24 27 28 30 31 32 34 35 37 41 42 44 46 47 48 49 51 52 53 54 56 57 58 59 60 61 65 67 68 70 71 72 73 **P**3 4 7 8 **S** Franciscan Health Partnership, Inc., Latham, NY

| | 23 | 10 | 238 | 4363 | 115 | 47594 | 0 | 47398 | 24303 | 557 |

KEARNY—Hudson County

✠ WEST HUDSON HOSPITAL, 206 Bergen Avenue, Zip 07032–3399; tel. 201/955–7051; Carmen Bruce Alecci, Executive Director (Total facility includes 46 beds in nursing home–type unit) **A**1 9 10 **F**8 12 15 16 17 18 19 21 22 27 28 29 30 32 33 34 35 37 39 41 42 44 46 49 54 56 63 64 65 71 73 **P**5 **S** Saint Barnabas Health Care System, West Orange, NJ

| | 23 | 10 | 217 | 3982 | 130 | 37912 | 0 | 36142 | 17080 | 482 |

LAKEWOOD—Ocean County

✠ KIMBALL MEDICAL CENTER, 600 River Avenue, Zip 08701–5281; tel. 732/363–1900; Joanne Carrocino, Executive Director **A**1 9 10 **F**1 2 3 4 5 6 7 8 9 10 11 12 13 14 15 16 17 18 19 20 21 22 24 25 26 27 28 29 30 31 32 33 34 35 36 37 39 40 41 42 43 44 45 46 47 49 51 52 53 54 55 56 57 58 59 60 61 64 65 66 67 68 69 71 72 73 74 **P**5 7 **S** Saint Barnabas Health Care System, West Orange, NJ
Web address: www.sbhcs.com

| | 23 | 10 | 248 | 11174 | 187 | 146873 | 1050 | 101747 | 47994 | 1377 |

LAWRENCEVILLE—Mercer County

✠ △ ST. LAWRENCE REHABILITATION CENTER, 2381 Lawrenceville Road, Zip 08648; tel. 609/896–9500; Charles L. Brennan, Chief Executive Officer **A**1 7 10 **F**1 12 14 17 21 25 27 34 36 41 46 48 49 64 65 67 73

| | 21 | 46 | 116 | 1966 | 95 | 20481 | 0 | 17923 | 10731 | 300 |

LIVINGSTON—Essex County

✠ ○ SAINT BARNABAS MEDICAL CENTER, 94 Old Short Hills Road, Zip 07039–5668; tel. 973/322–5000; Vincent D. Joseph, Executive Director **A**1 2 3 5 8 9 10 11 **F**3 4 5 7 8 9 10 11 12 13 14 15 16 17 18 19 20 21 22 23 24 25 26 28 29 30 31 32 33 34 35 37 38 40 41 42 43 44 46 47 49 51 52 53 54 55 56 57 58 59 60 61 63 65 66 67 69 71 72 73 74 **P**1 5 **S** Saint Barnabas Health Care System, West Orange, NJ

| | 23 | 10 | 571 | 30542 | 483 | 176606 | 6890 | 359946 | 166333 | 2898 |

LONG BRANCH—Monmouth County

✠ MONMOUTH MEDICAL CENTER, 300 Second Avenue, Zip 07740–6303; tel. 732/222–5200; Frank J. Vozos, M.D., FACS, Executive Director (Nonreporting) **A**1 2 3 5 8 9 10 **S** Saint Barnabas Health Care System, West Orange, NJ

| | 23 | 10 | 435 | — | — | — | — | — | — | — |

LYONS—Somerset County

LYONS DIVISION See Veterans Affairs New Jersey Health Care System, East Orange

MANAHAWKIN—Ocean County

✠ SOUTHERN OCEAN COUNTY HOSPITAL, 1140 Route 72 West, Zip 08050–2499; tel. 609/978–8900; Joseph P. Coyle, President and Chief Executive Officer **A**1 2 9 10 **F**3 7 8 12 13 14 15 16 17 19 21 22 24 25 26 28 29 30 32 33 34 35 37 40 42 44 45 46 49 56 63 64 65 66 67 68 71 73 74 **P**1 5 7

| | 23 | 10 | 120 | 5604 | 79 | 90076 | 32 | 46641 | 18090 | 527 |

MARLTON—Burlington County

✠ WEST JERSEY HOSPITAL–MARLTON, 90 Brick Road, Zip 08053–9697; tel. 609/355–6000; Leroy J. Rosenberg, Executive Director **A**1 9 10 **F**1 2 3 5 7 8 10 12 13 14 15 16 17 19 20 21 22 25 26 27 28 29 30 32 33 34 35 36 37 38 39 40 41 42 44 45 46 49 51 60 61 64 65 66 67 71 72 73 74 **P**5 7 **S** Virtua Health, Marlton, NJ
Web address: www.wjhs.org

| | 23 | 10 | 177 | 8289 | 108 | 34521 | 0 | 61377 | 30723 | 892 |

MILLVILLE—Cumberland County

SOUTH JERSEY HOSPITAL–MILLVILLE See South Jersey Hospital, Bridgeton

MONTCLAIR—Essex County

MOUNTAINSIDE HOSPITAL See Atlantic Health System, Florham Park

Hospital, Address, Telephone, Administrator, Approval, Facility, and Physician Codes, Health Care System, Network	Classi-fication Codes		Utilization Data					Expense (thousands) of dollars		
★ American Hospital Association (AHA) membership □ Joint Commission on Accreditation of Healthcare Organizations (JCAHO) accreditation + American Osteopathic Healthcare Association (AOHA) membership ○ American Osteopathic Association (AOA) accreditation △ Commission on Accreditation of Rehabilitation Facilities (CARF) accreditation Control codes 61, 63, 64, 71, 72 and 73 indicate hospitals listed by AOHA, but not registered by AHA. For definition of numerical codes, see page A4	Control	Service	Staffed Beds	Admissions	Census	Outpatient Visits	Births	Total	Payroll	Personnel

MORRISTOWN—Morris County

MORRISTOWN MEMORIAL HOSPITAL See Atlantic Health System, Florham Park

MOUNT HOLLY—Burlington County

□ VIRTUA–MEMORIAL HOSPITAL BURLINGTON COUNTY, (Formerly Memorial Hospital of Burlington County), 175 Madison Avenue, Zip 08060–2099; tel. 609/267–0700; Donald I. Brunn, President and Chief Executive Officer **A**1 2 3 5 9 10 **F**5 7 8 11 12 13 14 15 16 17 19 21 22 25 26 28 30 31 32 34 35 37 39 40 41 42 44 45 46 49 51 52 54 55 57 60 61 65 67 71 73 74 **P**2 4 5 7 **S** Virtua Health, Marlton, NJ
Web address: www.virtua.org

| | 23 | 10 | 348 | 16087 | 207 | 223536 | 1888 | 125716 | 51977 | 0 |

MOUNTAINSIDE—Union County

★ △ CHILDREN'S SPECIALIZED HOSPITAL, (Includes Children's Specialized Hospital–Ocean, 94 Stevens Road, Toms River, Zip 08755–1237; tel. 732/914–1100), 150 New Providence Road, Zip 07091–2590; tel. 908/233–3720; Richard B. Ahlfeld, President (Total facility includes 41 beds in nursing home–type unit) **A**1 7 10 **F**12 15 17 20 25 27 29 30 34 39 45 46 48 49 51 54 64 65 67 73

| | 23 | 56 | 117 | 269 | 79 | 99625 | 0 | 35414 | 19921 | 470 |

NEPTUNE—Monmouth County

★ △ MERIDIAN HEALTH SYSTEM, (Includes Brick Hospital Division, 425 Jack Martin Boulevard, Brick Township, Zip 08724; tel. 908/840–2200; Jersey Shore Medical Center, 1945 Route 33, Zip 07754–0397; tel. 908/775–5500; Medical Center of Ocean County, 2121 Edgewater Place, Point Pleasant, Zip 08742–2290; tel. 908/892–1100; Point Pleasant Hospital Division, 2121 Edgewater Place, Point Pleasant, Zip 08742; tel. 908/892–1100; Riverview Medical Center, 1 Riverview Plaza, Red Bank, Zip 07701–9982; tel. 908/741–2700), 1945 State Highway 33, Zip 07753; tel. 732/775–5500; John K. Lloyd, Chief Executive Officer (Nonreporting) **A**1 2 3 5 7 8 9 10

| | 23 | 10 | 1269 | — | — | — | — | — | — | — |

NEW BRUNSWICK—Middlesex County

HURTADO HEALTH CENTER, 11 Bishop Place, Zip 08901–1180; tel. 732/932–8429; Susan Skalsky, M.D., Director (Nonreporting)

| | 12 | 11 | 27 | — | — | — | — | — | — | — |

★ ROBERT WOOD JOHNSON UNIVERSITY HOSPITAL, 1 Robert Wood Johnson Place, Zip 08903–2601; tel. 732/828–3000; Harvey A. Holzberg, President and Chief Executive Officer **A**1 2 3 5 8 9 10 **F**1 2 3 4 5 6 7 8 10 11 12 13 14 15 16 17 19 20 21 22 23 24 25 26 27 28 29 30 31 32 33 34 35 37 39 40 41 42 43 44 45 46 47 49 51 52 53 54 55 56 57 58 59 61 62 63 64 65 66 67 68 70 71 72 73 74 **P**4 5 7 8
Web address: www.rwjuh.edu

| | 23 | 10 | 425 | 30876 | 400 | — | 1259 | — | — | — |

ST. PETER'S MEDICAL CENTER See St. Peter's University Hospital

★ ST. PETER'S UNIVERSITY HOSPITAL, (Formerly St. Peter's Medical Center), 254 Easton Avenue, Zip 08901–1780, Mailing Address: P.O. Box 591, Zip 08903–0591; tel. 732/745–8600; John E. Matuska, President and Chief Executive Officer (Total facility includes 20 beds in nursing home–type unit) **A**1 2 3 5 9 10 **F**1 3 7 8 10 11 12 13 14 15 16 17 19 20 21 22 23 25 26 27 28 29 30 31 32 34 35 37 38 39 40 41 42 44 45 46 47 49 51 54 55 56 58 60 61 62 64 65 66 67 68 71 73 74 **P**1 2 7

| | 21 | 10 | 406 | 22096 | 308 | 180751 | 6671 | 203945 | 88993 | 2301 |

NEWARK—Essex County

□ COLUMBUS HOSPITAL, 495 North 13th Street, Zip 07107–1397; tel. 973/268–1400; John G. Magliaro, President and Chief Executive Officer (Nonreporting) **A**1 9 10

| | 23 | 10 | 206 | — | — | — | — | — | — | — |

★ ○ NEWARK BETH ISRAEL MEDICAL CENTER, 201 Lyons Avenue, Zip 07112–2027; tel. 973/926–7000; Paul A. Mertz, Executive Director **A**1 2 3 5 8 9 10 11 12 13 **F**1 4 5 6 8 9 10 11 12 13 15 16 17 18 19 20 21 22 23 25 26 27 28 29 30 31 32 33 34 35 37 38 39 40 41 42 43 44 45 46 47 49 50 51 52 53 54 55 56 57 58 59 60 61 63 64 65 66 67 68 69 71 72 73 74 **P**6 8 **S** Saint Barnabas Health Care System, West Orange, NJ

| | 23 | 10 | 490 | 20852 | 383 | 282135 | 3090 | 306570 | 134822 | 2930 |

□ SAINT JAMES HOSPITAL OF NEWARK, 155 Jefferson Street, Zip 07105; tel. 973/589–1300; Ceu Cirne–Neves, Administrator (Nonreporting) **A**1 3 9 10 **S** Cathedral Healthcare System, Inc., Newark, NJ

| | 21 | 10 | 189 | — | — | — | — | — | — | — |

□ △ SAINT MICHAEL'S MEDICAL CENTER, 268 Dr. Martin Luther King Jr. Boulevard, Zip 07102–2094; tel. 973/877–5000; Barbara Loughney, Administrator **A**1 3 5 7 9 10 12 13 **F**3 4 6 7 8 10 11 12 13 14 15 16 17 18 19 20 21 22 24 25 26 27 28 29 30 31 32 33 34 35 37 39 40 41 42 43 44 45 46 49 50 51 53 54 56 58 59 60 63 65 66 67 71 73 74 **P**1 **S** Cathedral Healthcare System, Inc., Newark, NJ
Web address: www.cathedralhealthcare.org

| | 21 | 10 | 299 | 11303 | 201 | 83345 | 774 | 142188 | 62884 | 1276 |

★ UNIVERSITY OF MEDICINE AND DENTISTRY OF NEW JERSEY–UNIVERSITY HOSPITAL, 150 Bergen Street, Zip 07103–2406; tel. 973/972–4300; Daniel L. Marcantuono, FACHE, Acting Vice President and Chief Executive Officer **A**1 2 3 5 8 9 10 **F**3 4 7 8 10 12 13 15 16 17 18 19 20 21 22 23 24 25 26 27 28 29 30 31 34 35 37 38 39 40 41 42 43 44 47 49 51 52 53 54 55 56 57 58 59 60 61 65 66 67 68 69 71 73 74 **P**5

| | 12 | 10 | 498 | 17063 | 341 | 288971 | 1964 | 326659 | 170129 | 3096 |

NEWTON—Sussex County

★ △ NEWTON MEMORIAL HOSPITAL, 175 High Street, Zip 07860–1004; tel. 973/383–2121; Dennis H. Collette, President and Chief Executive Officer **A**1 2 7 9 10 **F**3 7 8 12 14 15 16 17 18 19 20 21 22 27 28 29 30 31 35 36 37 39 40 41 42 44 45 46 48 49 51 52 53 54 55 56 57 58 59 61 63 65 67 71 73 **P**5 8

| | 23 | 10 | 162 | 8731 | 100 | 174395 | 856 | 58439 | 26292 | 598 |

Hospital, Address, Telephone, Administrator, Approval, Facility, and Physician Codes, Health Care System, Network	Classi-fication Codes		Utilization Data					Expense (thousands) of dollars		
★ American Hospital Association (AHA) membership □ Joint Commission on Accreditation of Healthcare Organizations (JCAHO) accreditation + American Osteopathic Healthcare Association (AOHA) membership ○ American Osteopathic Association (AOA) accreditation △ Commission on Accreditation of Rehabilitation Facilities (CARF) accreditation Control codes 61, 63, 64, 71, 72 and 73 indicate hospitals listed by AOHA, but not registered by AHA. For definition of numerical codes, see page A4	Control	Service	Staffed Beds	Admissions	Census	Outpatient Visits	Births	Total	Payroll	Personnel

NORTH BERGEN—Hudson County

✠ PALISADES GENERAL HOSPITAL, 7600 River Road, Zip 07047–6217; tel. 201/854–5000; Bruce J. Markowitz, President and Chief Executive Officer **A**1 9 10 **F**3 8 12 15 16 17 19 22 24 26 27 28 29 30 35 37 39 40 41 42 44 45 49 56 58 65 67 71 73 **P**5
Web address: www.palisadesmedical.org

| | 23 | 10 | 202 | 8141 | 135 | 44376 | 1506 | 59036 | 27742 | 661 |

OLD BRIDGE—Middlesex County

OLD BRIDGE DIVISION See Raritan Bay Medical Center, Perth Amboy

ORANGE—Essex County

✠ HOSPITAL CENTER AT ORANGE, (Includes New Jersey Orthopedic Hospital Unit; Orange Memorial Hospital Unit), 188 South Essex Avenue, Zip 07051; tel. 973/266–2200; James E. Romer, President and Chief Executive Officer **A**1 2 3 5 9 10 **F**2 3 4 6 7 8 9 10 11 12 14 15 16 17 19 21 22 26 27 28 29 30 31 32 34 35 36 37 38 39 40 41 42 43 44 45 46 47 49 51 52 53 54 55 56 57 58 59 60 61 63 64 65 66 67 71 73 74

| | 23 | 10 | 160 | 5835 | 133 | 117875 | 439 | 60118 | 28503 | 714 |

PARAMUS—Bergen County

✠ BERGEN REGIONAL MEDICAL CENTER, 230 East Ridgewood Avenue, Zip 07652–4131; tel. 201/967–4000; Fred S. Sganga, President and Chief Executive Officer (Total facility includes 610 beds in nursing home–type unit) **A**1 3 5 6 9 10 **F**1 2 3 8 11 14 15 16 17 19 20 21 22 26 27 28 30 31 33 34 37 39 44 45 46 49 51 52 53 54 55 56 57 58 59 63 64 65 67 68 71 73 74 **P**6 8
Web address: www.bergenregional.com

| | 13 | 10 | 1039 | 8251 | 844 | 61822 | 0 | 142947 | 71374 | 1793 |

PASSAIC—Passaic County

✠ BETH ISRAEL HOSPITAL, 70 Parker Avenue, Zip 07055–7000; tel. 973/365–5000; Jeffrey S. Moll, President and Chief Executive Officer (Total facility includes 13 beds in nursing home–type unit) **A**1 2 9 10 **F**8 10 11 12 13 14 15 16 17 19 21 22 26 27 28 29 30 31 32 33 34 35 37 39 41 42 44 45 46 49 51 59 60 61 63 64 65 67 68 71 72 73 74
Web address: www.pbih.org

| | 23 | 10 | 223 | 6335 | 132 | 67556 | 0 | 52342 | 23059 | 1016 |

GENERAL HOSPITAL CENTER AT PASSAIC See Atlantic Health System, Florham Park

✠ ST. MARY'S HOSPITAL, 211 Pennington Avenue, Zip 07055–4698; tel. 973/470–3000; Patricia Peterson, President and Chief Executive Officer **A**1 10 **F**2 4 5 6 7 8 9 10 11 12 13 14 15 16 17 18 19 21 22 25 26 27 28 29 30 31 32 33 34 35 36 37 38 39 40 41 42 43 44 45 46 47 48 49 51 52 53 54 55 56 57 58 59 60 62 64 65 67 70 71 72 73 74 **P**1 5

| | 21 | 10 | 229 | 5449 | 100 | 97111 | 853 | 55017 | 25741 | 724 |

PATERSON—Passaic County

✠ BARNERT HOSPITAL, 680 Broadway Street, Zip 07514–1472; tel. 973/977–6600; Dominick R. Calgi, President and Chief Executive Officer (Total facility includes 12 beds in nursing home–type unit) **A**1 9 10 **F**1 3 4 6 7 8 12 14 15 16 17 19 21 22 26 27 28 29 30 31 34 35 36 37 39 40 41 42 44 45 46 49 51 52 53 54 55 56 58 59 65 67 68 71 73 74 **P**5 8

| | 23 | 10 | 194 | 6117 | 102 | 350382 | 717 | 67466 | 30781 | 646 |

✠ ○ △ ST. JOSEPH'S HOSPITAL AND MEDICAL CENTER, 703 Main Street, Zip 07503–2691; tel. 973/754–2000; Patrick R. Wardell, President and Chief Executive Officer (Total facility includes 141 beds in nursing home–type unit) (Nonreporting) **A**1 2 3 5 7 8 9 10 11 12 13
Web address: www.sjhmc.org

| | 21 | 10 | 621 | — | — | — | — | — | — | — |

PEAPACK—Somerset County

✠ △ MATHENY SCHOOL AND HOSPITAL, (HABILITATION), Main Street, Zip 07977, Mailing Address: P.O. Box 339, Zip 07977–0339; tel. 908/234–0011; Steven M. Proctor, President **A**1 7 10 **F**1 6 12 15 16 17 20 27 32 34 49 51 54 64 65 73

| | 23 | 49 | 87 | 53 | 79 | 400 | 0 | 16872 | 10673 | 327 |

PERTH AMBOY—Middlesex County

✠ RARITAN BAY MEDICAL CENTER, (Includes Old Bridge Division, One Hospital Plaza, Old Bridge, Zip 08857; tel. 732/360–1000; Perth Amboy Division, 530 New Brunswick Avenue, tel. 732/442–3700), 530 New Brunswick Avenue, Zip 08861–3685; tel. 732/442–3700; Keith H. McLaughlin, President and Chief Executive Officer **A**1 3 5 6 9 10 **F**2 3 4 6 7 8 10 11 12 14 15 16 17 18 19 21 22 23 25 27 28 29 30 31 32 33 34 35 36 37 39 40 42 44 46 49 51 52 54 55 56 58 61 63 65 67 68 71 73 74 **P**7 8
Web address: www.rbmc.org

| | 23 | 10 | 365 | 13703 | 277 | 198263 | 873 | 137935 | 70398 | 1700 |

PHILLIPSBURG—Warren County

✠ WARREN HOSPITAL, 185 Roseberry Street, Zip 08865–9955; tel. 908/859–6700; Jeffrey C. Goodwin, President and Chief Executive Officer **A**1 2 3 5 9 10 12 13 **F**2 3 7 8 10 11 12 14 15 16 17 19 20 22 25 26 27 29 30 31 34 35 36 37 39 40 41 42 44 45 46 48 49 51 52 54 56 57 65 66 67 68 69 71 73 **P**5

| | 23 | 10 | 193 | 5837 | 102 | 55145 | 343 | 59370 | 28864 | 850 |

PISCATAWAY—Middlesex County

UNIVERSITY OF MEDICINE AND DENTISTRY OF NEW JERSEY, UNIVERSITY BEHAVIORAL HEALTHCARE, 671 Hoes Lane, Zip 08854–5633, Mailing Address: P.O. Box 1392, Zip 08855–1392; tel. 732/235–5900; Christopher O. Kosseff, Vice President and Chief Executive Officer (Nonreporting) **A**3 5 10

| | 12 | 22 | 64 | — | — | — | — | — | — | — |

PLAINFIELD—Union County

✠ MUHLENBERG REGIONAL MEDICAL CENTER, 1200 Park Avenue, Zip 07061; tel. 908/668–2000; John R. Kopicki, President and Chief Executive Officer (Total facility includes 23 beds in nursing home–type unit) **A**1 3 5 6 9 10 **F**1 3 7 8 10 11 12 14 15 16 17 19 20 21 22 24 27 28 29 30 31 32 33 35 37 39 40 41 42 44 45 46 48 49 51 52 53 54 55 56 57 58 59 60 63 64 65 66 67 69 71 72 73 **P**5 7 8 **S** Solaris Health System, Edison, NJ

| | 23 | 10 | 303 | 13505 | 198 | 201064 | 1411 | 107242 | 54610 | 1449 |

Hospital, Address, Telephone, Administrator, Approval, Facility, and Physician Codes, Health Care System, Network	Classi-fication Codes		Utilization Data					Expense (thousands) of dollars		
★ American Hospital Association (AHA) membership □ Joint Commission on Accreditation of Healthcare Organizations (JCAHO) accreditation + American Osteopathic Healthcare Association (AOHA) membership ○ American Osteopathic Association (AOA) accreditation △ Commission on Accreditation of Rehabilitation Facilities (CARF) accreditation Control codes 61, 63, 64, 71, 72 and 73 indicate hospitals listed by AOHA, but not registered by AHA. For definition of numerical codes, see page A4	Control	Service	Staffed Beds	Admissions	Census	Outpatient Visits	Births	Total	Payroll	Personnel

POINT PLEASANT—Ocean County

MEDICAL CENTER OF OCEAN COUNTY See Meridian Health System, Neptune

POINT PLEASANT HOSPITAL DIVISION See Meridian Health System, Neptune

POMONA—Atlantic County

★ △ BACHARACH INSTITUTE FOR REHABILITATION, (Formerly Bacharach Rehabilitation Hospital), 61 West Jimmy Leeds Road, Zip 08240–0723, Mailing Address: P.O. Box 723, Zip 08240–0723; tel. 609/652–7000; Richard J. Kathrins, Administrator and Chief Executive Officer (Nonreporting) **A**1 7 10 Web address: www.bacharach.org | 23 | 46 | 80 | — | — | — | — | — | — | —

POMPTON PLAINS—Morris County

★ CHILTON MEMORIAL HOSPITAL, 97 West Parkway, Zip 07444–1696; tel. 973/831–5000; James J. Doyle, Jr., President and Chief Executive Officer **A**1 2 9 10 **F**7 8 10 12 13 14 15 16 17 19 20 21 22 26 28 29 30 31 32 33 34 35 37 38 39 40 41 42 44 47 49 51 52 53 54 55 56 57 60 63 65 66 67 71 72 73 74 **P**5 8 | 23 | 10 | 256 | 10060 | 137 | 94341 | 1467 | 79660 | 35648 | 803

PRINCETON—Mercer County

★ MEDICAL CENTER AT PRINCETON, (Includes Acute General Hospital, Merwick Unit–Extended Care and Rehabilitation, Princeton House Unit–Community Mental Health and Substance Abuse), 253 Witherspoon Street, Zip 08540–3213; tel. 609/497–4000; Dennis W. Doody, President and Chief Executive Officer (Total facility includes 93 beds in nursing home–type unit) **A**1 2 3 5 9 10 **F**1 2 3 7 8 10 11 12 14 15 16 17 18 19 20 21 22 26 27 28 29 30 31 32 33 34 35 37 39 40 41 42 44 45 46 48 49 52 54 55 56 57 58 59 60 63 64 65 67 71 73 **P**7 8 | 23 | 10 | 392 | 15797 | 300 | 221829 | 1517 | 121049 | 57704 | 1870

RAHWAY—Union County

★ RAHWAY HOSPITAL, 865 Stone Street, Zip 07065–2797; tel. 732/381–4200; Kirk C. Tice, President and Chief Executive Officer (Total facility includes 16 beds in nursing home–type unit) **A**1 9 10 **F**3 4 7 8 10 11 12 13 14 15 16 17 18 19 21 22 23 26 27 28 29 30 31 32 33 34 35 37 39 40 42 44 45 46 49 51 53 56 57 60 63 64 65 67 68 70 71 72 73 74 **P**1 5 Web address: www.rahwayhospital.com | 23 | 10 | 232 | 9326 | 174 | 64234 | 776 | 76367 | 33580 | 765

RED BANK—Monmouth County

RIVERVIEW MEDICAL CENTER See Meridian Health System, Neptune

RIDGEWOOD—Bergen County

★ VALLEY HOSPITAL, 223 North Van Dien Avenue, Zip 07450–9982; tel. 201/447–8000; Audrey Meyers, President **A**1 2 9 10 **F**3 4 7 8 10 11 12 13 14 15 16 17 19 20 21 22 24 25 26 28 29 30 31 32 33 34 35 36 37 38 39 40 41 42 43 44 45 46 49 51 52 53 54 55 56 57 58 60 61 64 65 66 67 68 71 72 73 74 Web address: www.valleyhealth.com | 23 | 10 | 412 | 38119 | 371 | 185463 | 3093 | 204064 | 101034 | 2350

SALEM—Salem County

★ MEMORIAL HOSPITAL OF SALEM COUNTY, 310 Woodstown Road, Zip 08079–2080; tel. 609/935–1000; Denise R. Williams, President and Chief Executive Officer **A**1 2 9 10 **F**7 8 12 14 15 16 17 19 20 21 22 28 30 31 32 33 34 35 36 37 39 40 41 42 44 46 49 54 56 64 65 67 71 73 74 **P**5 6 7 Web address: www.salemhosp.org | 23 | 10 | 122 | 4821 | 67 | 153304 | 427 | 46058 | 23849 | 600

SECAUCUS—Hudson County

□ MEADOWLANDS HOSPITAL MEDICAL CENTER, 55 Meadowland Parkway, Zip 07096–1580; tel. 201/392–3100; Paul V. Cavalli, M.D., President (Total facility includes 30 beds in nursing home–type unit) **A**1 9 10 **F**3 7 8 10 11 12 13 15 17 18 19 20 21 22 24 29 30 31 32 33 35 37 39 40 41 42 44 46 48 49 53 54 55 56 57 58 59 61 63 65 66 67 70 71 73 74 **S** Liberty Healthcare System, Jersey City, NJ | 23 | 10 | 173 | 6783 | 105 | 75834 | 1116 | 46207 | 22856 | 560

SOMERS POINT—Atlantic County

★ SHORE MEMORIAL HOSPITAL, 1 East New York Avenue, Zip 08244–2387; tel. 609/653–3500; Richard A. Pitman, President **A**1 2 9 10 **F**3 7 8 12 14 15 16 19 21 22 26 28 29 30 31 32 33 35 37 39 40 41 44 45 46 49 51 60 63 64 65 67 71 73 74 **P**5 7 Web address: www.shorememorial.org | 23 | 10 | 171 | 9923 | 144 | 93026 | 1147 | 105677 | 44103 | 1229

SOMERVILLE—Somerset County

★ SOMERSET MEDICAL CENTER, 110 Rehill Avenue, Zip 08876–2598; tel. 908/685–2200; Michael A. Turner, President and Chief Executive Officer **A**1 2 3 5 9 10 **F**3 7 8 10 11 12 15 16 17 19 21 22 23 26 27 28 30 31 32 33 35 37 39 40 41 42 44 46 49 51 52 54 55 56 57 58 59 65 67 71 73 **P**5 Web address: www.somersetmc.org | 23 | 10 | 297 | 12796 | 179 | 140235 | 1335 | 115464 | 55469 | 1339

SOUTH AMBOY—Middlesex County

★ MEMORIAL MEDICAL CENTER AT SOUTH AMBOY, 540 Bordentown Avenue, Zip 08879–1598; tel. 732/721–1000; Irv J. Diamond, Chief Executive Officer **A**1 9 10 **F**3 8 11 12 14 15 16 17 18 19 21 22 27 28 30 36 39 41 42 44 46 49 52 53 54 55 56 57 58 59 65 67 71 73 | 23 | 10 | 161 | 3088 | 67 | 55483 | 0 | 28869 | 16229 | 524

STRATFORD—Camden County

KENNEDY MEMORIAL HOSPITAL See Kennedy Memorial Hospitals–University Medical Center, Cherry Hill

SUMMIT—Union County

□ CHARTER BEHAVIORAL HEALTH SYSTEM OF NEW JERSEY–SUMMIT, 19 Prospect Street, Zip 07902–0100; tel. 908/522–7000; James Gallagner, Chief Executive Officer (Nonreporting) **A**1 10 **S** Magellan Health Services, Atlanta, GA | 33 | 22 | 90 | — | — | — | — | — | — | —

OVERLOOK HOSPITAL See Atlantic Health System, Florham Park

Hospital, Address, Telephone, Administrator, Approval, Facility, and Physician Codes, Health Care System, Network	Classi-fication Codes		Utilization Data					Expense (thousands) of dollars		
★ American Hospital Association (AHA) membership □ Joint Commission on Accreditation of Healthcare Organizations (JCAHO) accreditation + American Osteopathic Healthcare Association (AOHA) membership ○ American Osteopathic Association (AOA) accreditation △ Commission on Accreditation of Rehabilitation Facilities (CARF) accreditation Control codes 61, 63, 64, 71, 72 and 73 indicate hospitals listed by AOHA, but not registered by AHA. For definition of numerical codes, see page A4	Control	Service	Staffed Beds	Admissions	Census	Outpatient Visits	Births	Total	Payroll	Personnel

SUSSEX—Sussex County
SAINT CLARE'S HOSPITAL/SUSSEX See Saint Clare's Health Services, Denville
TEANECK—Bergen County

⊞ HOLY NAME HOSPITAL, 718 Teaneck Road, Zip 07666–4281; tel. 201/833–3000; Michael Maron, President and Chief Executive Officer **A**1 2 6 9 10 **F**1 7 8 10 12 13 14 15 16 17 19 20 21 22 26 27 28 29 30 32 33 34 35 37 39 40 41 42 44 45 46 49 52 54 60 65 67 68 71 73 74 **P**6 8 **Web address:** www.holyname.org	23	10	341	15774	224	238139	1733	123078	64324	1257

TOMS RIVER—Ocean County
CHILDREN'S SPECIALIZED HOSPITAL–OCEAN See Children's Specialized Hospital, Mountainside

⊞ COMMUNITY MEDICAL CENTER, 99 Route 37 West, Zip 08755–6423; tel. 732/557–8000; Kevin R. Burchill, Executive Director **A**1 2 9 10 **F**1 3 6 7 8 10 11 12 13 14 15 16 17 18 19 20 21 22 24 25 26 27 28 29 30 31 32 33 34 35 36 37 39 40 41 42 44 45 46 49 51 52 54 55 56 57 58 59 60 61 63 64 65 66 67 68 71 72 73 74 **P**2 **S** Saint Barnabas Health Care System, West Orange, NJ **Web address:** www.sbhcs.com	23	10	435	21963	340	217593	1913	199465	86581	2166
□ △ HEALTHSOUTH REHABILITATION HOSPITAL OF NEW JERSEY, 14 Hospital Drive, Zip 08755–6470; tel. 732/244–3100; Patricia Ostaszewski, Chief Executive Officer and Administrator (Total facility includes 63 beds in nursing home–type unit) (Nonreporting) **A**1 7 9 10 **S** HEALTHSOUTH Corporation, Birmingham, AL	33	46	155	—	—	—	—	—	—	—

TRENTON—Mercer County

⊞ CAPITAL HEALTH SYSTEM, (Includes Capital Health System at Fuld, 750 Brunswick Avenue, Zip 08638–4174; tel. 609/394–6000; Capital Health System at Mercer, 446 Bellevue Avenue), 446 Bellevue Avenue, Zip 08618–4597, Mailing Address: P.O. Box 1658, Zip 08607–1658; tel. 609/394–4000; Alireza Maghazehe, Chief Executive Officer **A**1 2 3 5 6 9 10 **F**1 3 7 8 10 11 12 13 15 16 17 18 19 20 21 22 26 27 28 29 30 31 32 33 34 35 36 37 38 39 40 41 42 44 45 46 49 51 52 54 55 56 58 59 60 61 63 65 66 67 68 70 71 72 73 74 **P**5	23	10	491	20013	323	460095	2815	207270	93884	2979
⊞ ST. FRANCIS MEDICAL CENTER, 601 Hamilton Avenue, Zip 08629–1986; tel. 609/599–5000; Judith M. Persichilli, President and Chief Executive Officer **A**1 2 3 5 6 9 10 **F**4 7 8 10 11 12 14 15 16 19 21 22 23 26 27 28 29 30 31 32 33 34 35 36 37 40 42 43 44 45 46 49 51 52 54 55 56 58 59 60 63 65 67 68 71 72 73 74 **P**5 6 7 8 **S** Catholic Health Initiatives, Denver, CO	21	10	214	7523	119	139542	291	81463	37644	885
⊞ TRENTON PSYCHIATRIC HOSPITAL, Sullivan Way, Zip 08625, Mailing Address: P.O. Box 7500, West Trenton, Zip 08628–7500; tel. 609/633–1500; Joseph Jupin, Jr., Chief Executive Officer (Nonreporting) **A**1 3 10 **S** Division of Mental Health Services, Department of Human Services, State of New Jersey, Trenton, NJ	12	22	379	—	—	—	—	—	—	—

TURNERSVILLE—Camden County
KENNEDY MEMORIAL HOSPITAL See Kennedy Memorial Hospitals–University Medical Center, Cherry Hill
UNION—Union County

⊞ + ○ UNION HOSPITAL, 1000 Galloping Hill Road, Zip 07083–1652; tel. 908/687–1900; Kathryn W. Coyne, Executive Director and Chief Operating Officer **A**1 2 9 10 11 12 13 **F**1 2 3 4 7 8 9 10 11 12 14 15 17 18 19 20 21 22 25 26 27 28 29 30 31 32 33 34 35 37 38 39 40 41 42 43 44 45 46 47 49 52 53 54 55 56 58 60 64 65 66 69 71 72 73 **P**5 **S** Saint Barnabas Health Care System, West Orange, NJ **Web address:** www.sbhcs.com	23	10	148	5986	109	—	0	64251	28537	1015

VINELAND—Cumberland County

⊞ NEWCOMB MEDICAL CENTER, 65 South State Street, Zip 08360–4893; tel. 609/691–9000; Chester B. Kaletkowski, President and Chief Executive Officer (Nonreporting) **A**1 2 9 10 **S** South Jersey Health System, Bridgeton, NJ	23	10	139	—	—	—	—	—	—	—
□ VINELAND DEVELOPMENTAL CENTER HOSPITAL, 1676 East Landis Avenue, Zip 08361–2992; tel. 609/696–6200; Judith L. Sisti, MS, Administrator (Nonreporting) **A**1 10	12	12	100	—	—	—	—	—	—	—

VOORHEES—Camden County

⊞ WEST JERSEY HOSPITAL–VOORHEES, 101 Carnie Boulevard, Zip 08043–1597; tel. 609/325–3000; Joan T. Meyers, R.N., Executive Director **A**1 3 5 9 **F**1 2 3 5 7 8 10 12 13 14 15 16 17 19 20 21 22 25 26 27 28 29 30 32 33 34 35 36 37 38 39 40 41 42 44 45 46 49 51 56 58 60 61 64 65 67 71 72 73 74 **P**5 7 **S** Virtua Health, Marlton, NJ **Web address:** www.wjhs.org	23	10	244	16370	182	67569	5119	114006	57066	1559

WAYNE—Passaic County

⊞ WAYNE GENERAL HOSPITAL, 224 Hamburg Turnpike, Zip 07470–2100; tel. 973/942–6900; Kenneth H. Kozloff, Executive Director **A**1 9 10 **F**1 7 8 11 12 13 15 16 17 19 21 22 23 25 26 27 28 30 31 32 33 34 37 39 40 41 42 44 45 46 49 51 60 63 65 67 71 73 **P**5 8 **S** Saint Barnabas Health Care System, West Orange, NJ	23	10	170	7254	115	129781	876	71625	33462	900

WEST ORANGE—Essex County

⊞ △ KESSLER INSTITUTE FOR REHABILITATION, (Includes East Orange Facility, West Orange Facility, Saddle Brook Facility and Welkind Facility), 1199 Pleasant Valley Way, Zip 07052–1419; tel. 973/731–3600; Robert Brehm, President **A**1 3 5 7 10 **F**1 12 15 16 27 39 41 48 49 54 64 65 66 73 **P**6 **Web address:** www.kessler–rehab.com	33	46	322	5239	284	—	0	87577	50541	1066

Hospital, Address, Telephone, Administrator, Approval, Facility, and Physician Codes, Health Care System, Network	Classi-fication Codes		Utilization Data					Expense (thousands) of dollars		
★ American Hospital Association (AHA) membership □ Joint Commission on Accreditation of Healthcare Organizations (JCAHO) accreditation + American Osteopathic Healthcare Association (AOHA) membership ○ American Osteopathic Association (AOA) accreditation △ Commission on Accreditation of Rehabilitation Facilities (CARF) accreditation Control codes 61, 63, 64, 71, 72 and 73 indicate hospitals listed by AOHA, but not registered by AHA. For definition of numerical codes, see page A4	Control	Service	Staffed Beds	Admissions	Census	Outpatient Visits	Births	Total	Payroll	Personnel

WESTAMPTON TOWNSHIP—Burlington County

□ HAMPTON HOSPITAL, Rancocas Road, Zip 08073, Mailing Address: P.O. Box 7000, Zip 08073; tel. 609/267–7000; Joanne Wilson, Chief Executive Officer (Nonreporting) **A**1 10 **S** Hospital Group of America, Wayne, PA
— 33 22 83 — — — — — — — —

WESTWOOD—Bergen County

✠ PASCACK VALLEY HOSPITAL, 250 Old Hook Road, Zip 07675–3181; tel. 201/358–3000; Louis R. Ycre, Jr., FACHE, President and Chief Executive Officer **A**1 2 9 10 **F**7 8 10 11 14 15 16 17 19 20 21 22 24 26 27 28 29 30 31 32 33 34 35 36 37 38 39 40 41 42 44 45 46 49 51 53 54 55 57 58 59 60 61 65 66 67 68 71 72 73 74 **P**1 5 7
23 10 206 16438 142 114475 922 90376 42684 979

WILLINGBORO—Burlington County

✠ RANCOCAS HOSPITAL, (Formerly Allegheny University Hospital, Rancocas), 218–A Sunset Road, Zip 08046–1162; tel. 609/835–2900; Joseph Flamini, Chief Executive Officer **A**1 2 9 10 13 **F**3 7 8 10 11 12 15 16 17 19 20 21 22 26 28 30 33 35 37 40 41 42 43 44 46 49 51 52 54 56 57 58 59 60 61 63 65 66 67 71 73 74 **S** Catholic Health East, Newtown Square, PA
23 10 237 10065 159 144441 1300 74769 33217 929

WOODBRIDGE—Middlesex County

WOODBRIDGE DEVELOPMENT CENTER, Rahway Avenue, Zip 07095, Mailing Address: P.O. Box 189, Zip 07095; tel. 908/499–5951; Amy R. Bailon, M.D., Medical Director (Nonreporting)
12 12 125

WOODBURY—Gloucester County

✠ UNDERWOOD–MEMORIAL HOSPITAL, 509 North Broad Street, Zip 08096–1697, Mailing Address: P.O. Box 359, Zip 08096–7359; tel. 856/845–0100; Steven W. Jackmuff, President and Chief Executive Officer **A**1 3 9 10 **F**1 7 8 10 11 12 15 16 17 18 19 20 21 22 25 26 27 28 30 31 32 34 35 37 39 40 41 42 44 49 51 52 54 56 57 58 59 63 64 65 67 71 73 74 **P**6
23 10 239 10858 147 110937 1253 83722 40696 1124

WYCKOFF—Bergen County

✠ CHRISTIAN HEALTH CARE CENTER, (Formerly Ramapo Ridge Psychiatric Hospital), 301 Sicomac Avenue, Zip 07481–2194; tel. 201/848–5200; Douglas A. Struyk, President and Chief Executive Officer (Nonreporting) **A**1 10
Web address: www.chccnj.org
23 22 80 — — — — — — — —

NEW MEXICO

Resident population 1,737 (in thousands)
Resident population in metro areas 55.9%
Birth rate per 1,000 population 16
65 years and over 11.2%
Percent of persons without health insurance 22.3%

Hospital, Address, Telephone, Administrator, Approval, Facility, and Physician Codes, Health Care System, Network	Classi-fication Codes		Utilization Data					Expense (thousands) of dollars		
	Control	Service	Staffed Beds	Admissions	Census	Outpatient Visits	Births	Total	Payroll	Personnel

★ American Hospital Association (AHA) membership
□ Joint Commission on Accreditation of Healthcare Organizations (JCAHO) accreditation
+ American Osteopathic Healthcare Association (AOHA) membership
○ American Osteopathic Association (AOA) accreditation
△ Commission on Accreditation of Rehabilitation Facilities (CARF) accreditation
Control codes 61, 63, 64, 71, 72 and 73 indicate hospitals listed by AOHA, but not registered by AHA. For definition of numerical codes, see page A4

ALAMOGORDO—Otero County

Hospital	Control	Service	Staffed Beds	Admissions	Census	Outpatient Visits	Births	Total	Payroll	Personnel
✠ GERALD CHAMPION MEMORIAL HOSPITAL, 1209 Ninth Street, Zip 88310; tel. 505/439–2100; Carl W. Mantey, Administrator **A**1 9 10 **F**7 8 14 15 16 19 21 22 23 24 28 30 33 34 35 37 40 42 44 65 66 67 71 73 **P**5 **S** Quorum Health Group/Quorum Health Resources, Inc., Brentwood, TN	23	10	73	3613	37	57896	737	26358	8714	295

ALBUQUERQUE—Bernalillo County

Hospital	Control	Service	Staffed Beds	Admissions	Census	Outpatient Visits	Births	Total	Payroll	Personnel
★ CARRIE TINGLEY HOSPITAL, 1127 University Boulevard N.E., Zip 87102–1715; tel. 505/272–5200; Robert T. Maruca, Administrator **A**3 5 9 10 **F**2 3 4 8 9 10 11 12 13 17 18 19 20 22 25 26 28 30 31 32 33 34 35 37 38 39 40 41 42 43 44 45 46 47 48 49 51 52 53 54 55 56 57 58 59 60 61 65 66 67 68 70 71 72 73 74 **P**3 **S** University of New Mexico, Albuquerque, NM	12	56	20	307	6	8873	0	11234	4584	136
□ CHARTER HEIGHTS BEHAVIORAL HEALTH SYSTEM, (Includes Charter Heights Behavioral Health System Northeast, 103 Hospital Loop N.E., Zip 87109; Charter Heights Behavioral Health System Southeast, 5901 Zuni Road S.E., Zip 87108; tel. 505/265–8800), 103 Hospital Loop N.E., Zip 87109–2115; tel. 505/883–8777; Joseph R. Brunson, Chief Executive Officer (Nonreporting) **A**1 9 10 **S** Magellan Health Services, Atlanta, GA	33	22	172	—	—	—	—	—	—	—
DESERT HILLS HOSPITAL, 5310 Sequoia Road N.W., Zip 87120–1249; tel. 505/836–7330; Carol Bickelman, President and Chief Executive Officer (Nonreporting)	33	22	35	—	—	—	—	—	—	—
□ △ HEALTHSOUTH REHABILITATION CENTER, 7000 Jefferson N.E., Zip 87109–4357; tel. 505/344–9478; Darby Brockette, Administrator (Nonreporting) **A**1 7 9 10 **S** HEALTHSOUTH Corporation, Birmingham, AL	33	46	60	—	—	—	—	—	—	—
□ LOVELACE HEALTH SYSTEM, 5400 Gibson Boulevard S.E., Zip 87108–4763; tel. 505/262–7000; Martin Hickey, M.D., Chief Executive Officer (Nonreporting) **A**1 2 3 5 9 10	33	10	147	—	—	—	—	—	—	—
□ MEMORIAL PSYCHIATRIC HOSPITAL, 806 Central Avenue S.E., Zip 87102–3671, Mailing Address: P.O. Box 26568, Zip 87125–6568; tel. 505/247–0220; Richard B. Hiester, Administrator **A**1 10 **F**3 14 16 52 53 55 57 58 59 65	32	22	58	606	30	0	0	—	—	119
✠ PRESBYTERIAN HOSPITAL, (Formerly Presbyterian Healthcare Services), 1100 Central Avenue S.E., Zip 87106–4934, Mailing Address: P.O. Box 26666, Zip 87125–6666; tel. 505/841–1234; James Jeppson, Administrator (Nonreporting) **A**1 2 3 5 9 10 **S** Presbyterian Healthcare Services, Albuquerque, NM **Web address:** www.phs.org	23	10	424	—	—	—	—	—	—	—
★ PRESBYTERIAN KASEMAN HOSPITAL, 8300 Constitution Avenue N.E., Zip 87110–7624, Mailing Address: P.O. Box 26666, Zip 87125–6666; tel. 505/291–2000; Robert A. Garcia, Administrator (Nonreporting) **A**9 10 **S** Presbyterian Healthcare Services, Albuquerque, NM	23	10	120	—	—	—	—	—	—	—
✠ PUBLIC HEALTH SERVICE INDIAN HOSPITAL, 801 Vassar Drive N.E., Zip 87106–2799; tel. 505/248–4000; Cheri Lyon, Service Unit Director (Nonreporting) **A**1 10 **S** U. S. Public Health Service Indian Health Service, Rockville, MD	47	10	28	—	—	—	—	—	—	—
✠ ST. JOSEPH MEDICAL CENTER, 601 Martin Luther King Jr. Drive N.E., Zip 87102, Mailing Address: P.O. Box 25555, Zip 87125–0555; tel. 505/727–8000; Steven J. Smith, President (Total facility includes 24 beds in nursing home–type unit) **A**1 2 5 9 10 **F**1 3 4 7 8 10 11 12 14 15 17 19 21 22 23 26 27 28 30 32 34 35 36 37 39 41 42 43 44 45 46 49 51 54 56 57 58 60 61 63 64 65 67 71 72 73 74 **P**5 **S** Catholic Health Initiatives, Denver, CO	21	10	218	10742	155	64796	0	69963	29590	1011
✠ ST. JOSEPH NORTHEAST HEIGHTS HOSPITAL, 4701 Montgomery Boulevard N.E., Zip 87109–1251, Mailing Address: P.O. Box 25555, Zip 87125–0555; tel. 505/727–7800; C. Vincent Townsend, Jr., Vice President **A**1 9 10 **F**1 4 7 8 10 12 14 15 19 21 22 23 26 27 30 32 33 34 35 36 37 39 40 41 42 43 44 46 49 51 54 60 61 63 65 67 68 70 71 72 73 74 **P**5 **S** Catholic Health Initiatives, Denver, CO	21	10	87	3959	37	39317	1515	16206	7444	244
★ △ ST. JOSEPH REHABILITATION HOSPITAL AND OUTPATIENT CENTER, 505 Elm Street N.E., Zip 87102–2500, Mailing Address: P.O. Box 25555, Zip 87125–5555; tel. 505/727–4700; Mary Lou Coors, Administrator (Total facility includes 17 beds in nursing home–type unit) **A**7 9 10 **F**1 3 4 7 8 10 12 14 15 19 21 22 26 27 28 30 32 33 34 35 36 39 41 42 43 44 45 46 48 49 51 54 56 57 58 60 61 63 64 65 67 71 72 73 74 **P**5 **S** Catholic Health Initiatives, Denver, CO	21	46	63	961	45	3495	0	8392	4971	214
✠ ST. JOSEPH WEST MESA HOSPITAL, 10501 Golf Course Road N.W., Zip 87114–5000, Mailing Address: P.O. Box 25555, Zip 87125–0555; tel. 505/727–2000; C. Vincent Townsend, Jr., Vice President (Total facility includes 22 beds in nursing home–type unit) **A**1 9 10 **F**3 4 7 8 10 12 14 15 17 19 21 22 23 26 27 30 32 33 34 35 36 39 42 43 44 46 49 51 52 54 56 57 58 60 61 63 64 65 67 71 72 73 74 **P**5 **S** Catholic Health Initiatives, Denver, CO	21	10	74	2322	44	31965	174	12413	5888	164

Hospital, Address, Telephone, Administrator, Approval, Facility, and Physician Codes, Health Care System, Network	Classification Codes		Utilization Data					Expense (thousands) of dollars		
	Control	Service	Staffed Beds	Admissions	Census	Outpatient Visits	Births	Total	Payroll	Personnel

★ American Hospital Association (AHA) membership
□ Joint Commission on Accreditation of Healthcare Organizations (JCAHO) accreditation
+ American Osteopathic Healthcare Association (AOHA) membership
○ American Osteopathic Association (AOA) accreditation
△ Commission on Accreditation of Rehabilitation Facilities (CARF) accreditation
Control codes 61, 63, 64, 71, 72 and 73 indicate hospitals listed by AOHA, but not registered by AHA. For definition of numerical codes, see page A4

Hospital	Control	Service	Staffed Beds	Admissions	Census	Outpatient Visits	Births	Total	Payroll	Personnel
⊞ UNIVERSITY HOSPITAL, 2211 Lomas Boulevard N.E., Zip 87106–2745; tel. 505/272–2121; Stephen W. McKernan, Chief Executive Officer **A**1 2 3 5 8 9 10 12 **F**3 4 5 7 8 9 10 12 14 15 16 17 19 21 22 23 24 26 28 29 30 31 32 33 34 35 37 38 40 41 42 43 44 45 46 47 49 54 55 58 60 61 63 65 66 67 68 70 71 72 73 74 **S** University of New Mexico, Albuquerque, NM **Web address:** www.unm.edu	12	10	271	20367	262	394200	3258	214827	88296	2445
★ UNIVERSITY OF NEW MEXICO CHILDREN'S PSYCHIATRIC HOSPITAL, 1001 Yale Boulevard N.E., Zip 87131–3830; tel. 505/272–2945; Christina B. Gunn, Chief Executive Officer **A**5 **F**12 14 17 28 52 53 55 58 59 65 67 **P**6 **S** University of New Mexico, Albuquerque, NM **Web address:** www.cph.unm.edu	12	52	55	428	37	20755	0	10656	5982	243
★ UNIVERSITY OF NEW MEXICO MENTAL HEALTH CENTER, 2600 Marble N.E., Zip 87131–2600; tel. 505/272–2263; Stephen W. McKernan, Chief Executive Officer (Nonreporting) **A**5 9 **S** University of New Mexico, Albuquerque, NM **Web address:** www.mhc.unm.edu	13	22	60	—	—	—	—	—	—	—
□ VENCOR HOSPITAL – ALBUQUERQUE, 700 High Street N.E., Zip 87102–2565; tel. 505/242–4444; Jeanne Koester, Chief Executive Officer **A**1 5 10 **F**12 15 22 26 27 28 37 41 65 67 **P**8 **S** Vencor, Incorporated, Louisville, KY	33	10	58	440	39	—	0	12379	5057	146
⊞ VETERANS AFFAIRS MEDICAL CENTER, 1501 San Pedro S.E., Zip 87108–5138; tel. 505/265–1711; Norman E. Browne, Director (Total facility includes 36 beds in nursing home–type unit) **A**1 2 3 5 8 9 **F**1 2 3 4 5 8 10 12 17 18 19 20 21 22 23 25 26 27 28 29 30 31 32 33 34 35 37 39 41 42 43 44 45 46 48 49 51 52 54 55 56 57 58 63 64 65 67 71 73 74 **S** Department of Veterans Affairs, Washington, DC **Web address:** www.va.gov	45	10	209	5414	173	374828	0	147263	71406	1701
ARTESIA—Eddy County										
⊞ ARTESIA GENERAL HOSPITAL, 702 North 13th Street, Zip 88210–1199; tel. 505/748–3333; Anthony J. Plantier, Administrator **A**1 9 10 **F**7 8 12 14 15 17 19 22 32 33 34 36 39 44 46 49 65 71 **S** Presbyterian Healthcare Services, Albuquerque, NM	16	10	20	510	6	31643	4	7578	3579	112
CANNON AFB—Curry County										
★ U. S. AIR FORCE HOSPITAL, 208 West Casablanca Avenue, Zip 88103–5300; tel. 505/784–6318; Major John Sell, MSC, USAF, Administrator **F**1 2 3 4 5 7 8 9 10 11 12 17 18 19 20 22 23 24 28 29 31 34 35 37 38 39 40 41 42 43 44 46 47 48 49 52 53 54 55 58 59 60 64 65 69 70 71 73 74 **S** Department of the Air Force, Bowling AFB, DC	41	10	10	316	3	56319	137	20231	—	288
CARLSBAD—Eddy County										
⊞ CARLSBAD MEDICAL CENTER, (Formerly Columbia Medical Center of Carlsbad), 2430 West Pierce Street, Zip 88220–3597; tel. 505/887–4100; Thomas McClintock, Chief Executive Officer **A**1 9 10 **F**7 8 12 14 15 16 17 18 19 20 21 22 23 26 27 28 30 31 34 35 37 38 39 40 41 42 44 45 46 48 49 54 56 60 63 64 65 67 71 73 74 **P**8 **S** Triad Hospitals, Inc., Dallas, TX **Web address:** www.columbia.com	33	10	131	4151	47	56488	731	27575	12564	438
CLAYTON—Union County										
★ UNION COUNTY GENERAL HOSPITAL, 301 Harding Street, Zip 88415–3321, Mailing Address: P.O. Box 489, Zip 88415–0489; tel. 505/374–2585; W. C. McElhannon, Administrator (Nonreporting) **A**9 10 **S** Brim Healthcare, Inc., Brentwood, TN	33	10	28	—	—	—	—	—	—	—
CLOVIS—Curry County										
⊞ PLAINS REGIONAL MEDICAL CENTER, 2100 North Thomas Street, Zip 88101–9412, Mailing Address: P.O. Box 1688, Zip 88101–1688; tel. 505/769–2141; Gordon Aird, Interim Administrator **A**1 9 10 **F**7 8 19 21 22 23 26 28 32 33 34 35 36 37 39 40 41 42 44 49 50 56 60 61 64 65 67 71 72 73 74 **S** Presbyterian Healthcare Services, Albuquerque, NM	23	10	74	5444	58	96738	1030	30213	11676	436
CROWNPOINT—McKinley County										
⊞ U. S. PUBLIC HEALTH SERVICE INDIAN HOSPITAL, Mailing Address: P.O. Box 358, Zip 87313–0358; tel. 505/786–5291; Anita Muneta, Chief Executive Officer **A**1 10 **F**3 7 12 13 15 16 17 18 20 22 26 28 30 31 32 34 39 40 46 49 51 53 54 55 61 65 67 68 71 72 74 **P**8 **S** U. S. Public Health Service Indian Health Service, Rockville, MD	47	10	32	991	11	47268	140	10793	—	263
DEMING—Luna County										
★ MIMBRES MEMORIAL HOSPITAL, 900 West Ash Street, Zip 88030–4098, Mailing Address: P.O. Box 710, Zip 88031–0710; tel. 505/546–2761; Timothy E. Schmidt, Chief Executive Officer (Total facility includes 70 beds in nursing home–type unit) (Nonreporting) **A**9 10 **S** Community Health Systems, Inc., Brentwood, TN	33	10	119	—	—	—	—	—	—	—
ESPANOLA—Rio Arriba County										
⊞ ESPANOLA HOSPITAL, 1010 Spruce Street, Zip 87532–2746; tel. 505/753–7111; Marcella A. Romero, Administrator **A**1 9 10 **F**7 8 12 14 15 16 19 22 28 32 35 37 40 44 46 49 51 65 71 72 73 **P**3 5 8 **S** Presbyterian Healthcare Services, Albuquerque, NM	23	10	80	2367	18	39932	302	17894	8540	295
FARMINGTON—San Juan County										
⊞ SAN JUAN REGIONAL MEDICAL CENTER, (Includes Interface Rehabilitation Hospital, 525 South Schwartz, Zip 87401; tel. 505/327–3422; Jeff Hamblen, Administrator), 801 West Maple Street, Zip 87401–5698; tel. 505/325–5011; Donald R. Carlson, President and Chief Executive Officer (Total facility includes 15 beds in nursing home–type unit) **A**1 2 9 10 **F**3 7 8 10 12 13 15 16 17 19 21 22 23 25 28 29 34 35 37 40 41 42 44 45 49 53 54 56 58 59 60 63 64 65 67 70 71 72 73 74 **P**4 5 8	23	10	168	7533	92	101678	1044	71795	33306	979

Hospital, Address, Telephone, Administrator, Approval, Facility, and Physician Codes, Health Care System, Network	Classi-fication Codes		Utilization Data					Expense (thousands) of dollars		
★ American Hospital Association (AHA) membership □ Joint Commission on Accreditation of Healthcare Organizations (JCAHO) accreditation + American Osteopathic Healthcare Association (AOHA) membership ○ American Osteopathic Association (AOA) accreditation △ Commission on Accreditation of Rehabilitation Facilities (CARF) accreditation Control codes 61, 63, 64, 71, 72 and 73 indicate hospitals listed by AOHA, but not registered by AHA. For definition of numerical codes, see page A4	Control	Service	Staffed Beds	Admissions	Census	Outpatient Visits	Births	Total	Payroll	Personnel

FORT SUMNER—De Baca County

★ DEBACA GENERAL HOSPITAL, 500 North Tenth Street, Zip 88119, Mailing Address: P.O. Box 349, Zip 88119–0349; tel. 505/355–2414; Dick L. Stout, Chief Executive Officer and Administrator **A**9 10 **F**22 28 30 32 34 64 **P**6	13	10	17	199	1	—	0	1933	869	32

GALLUP—McKinley County

⊞ GALLUP INDIAN MEDICAL CENTER, 516 East Nizhoni Boulevard, Zip 87301–5748, Mailing Address: P.O. Box 1337, Zip 87305–1337; tel. 505/722–1000; Timothy G. Fleming, M.D., Chief Executive Officer **A**1 10 **F**8 12 16 17 19 20 21 22 25 34 35 37 40 44 46 49 51 53 56 58 **P**6 **S** U. S. Public Health Service Indian Health Service, Rockville, MD	47	10	99	5826	60	211603	1003	58619	35541	808
⊞ REHOBOTH MCKINLEY CHRISTIAN HOSPITAL, 1901 Red Rock Drive, Zip 87301–1901; tel. 505/863–7000; David J. Baltzer, President **A**1 9 10 **F**2 3 7 8 12 14 15 16 17 18 19 22 28 29 30 32 33 34 35 39 40 41 44 49 51 52 53 54 55 56 58 59 64 65 67 71 73 74 **P**5 6 **Web address:** www.rmch.org	23	10	113	2829	54	163535	360	38854	19037	552

GRANTS—Cibola County

⊞ CIBOLA GENERAL HOSPITAL, 1212 Bonita Avenue, Zip 87020–2104; tel. 505/287–4446; Walter Topp, III, Administrator **A**1 9 10 **F**7 15 16 19 22 28 37 40 44 45 46 65 71 **P**8 **S** Quorum Health Group/Quorum Health Resources, Inc., Brentwood, TN	13	10	22	958	8	10016	179	6798	—	—

HOBBS—Lea County

⊞ LEA REGIONAL HOSPITAL, (Formerly Columbia Lea Regional Hospital), 5419 North Lovington Highway, Zip 88240–9125, Mailing Address: P.O. Box 3000, Zip 88240–3000; tel. 505/392–6581; Bill Gresco, Administrator **A**1 9 10 **F**7 8 12 14 15 16 19 21 22 23 25 30 34 35 37 40 44 48 49 51 52 54 56 57 58 63 64 65 67 70 71 73 **P**1 **S** Triad Hospitals, Inc., Dallas, TX	33	10	141	4955	59	21197	843	23976	10869	405

HOLLOMAN AFB—Otero County

⊞ U. S. AIR FORCE HOSPITAL, 280 First Street, Zip 88330–8273; tel. 505/475–5587; Colonel Marilyn J. Abu–Ghusson, USAF, Commander (Nonreporting) **A**1 **S** Department of the Air Force, Bowling AFB, DC	41	10	7	—	—	—	—	—	—	—

KIRTLAND AFB—Bernalillo County

★ U. S. AIR FORCE HOSPITAL–KIRTLAND, 2050A Second Street S.E., Zip 87117–5559; tel. 505/846–3547; Colonel Jimmie M. Smith, USAF, Commander (Nonreporting) **A**3 5 **S** Department of the Air Force, Bowling AFB, DC	41	10	10	—	—	—	—	—	—	—

LAS CRUCES—Dona Ana County

□ BHC MESILLA VALLEY HOSPITAL, 3751 Del Rey Boulevard, Zip 88012–8526, Mailing Address: P.O. Box 429, Zip 88004–0429; tel. 505/382–3500; Alison Druck, R.N., Ed.D., Chief Executive Officer **A**1 10 **F**2 3 12 14 15 16 17 18 25 26 31 34 45 46 52 53 54 55 56 57 58 59 65 67 **P**8 **S** Behavioral Healthcare Corporation, Nashville, TN	33	22	84	757	70	840	0	7661	3162	143
⊞ MEMORIAL MEDICAL CENTER, 2450 South Telshor Boulevard, Zip 88011–5076; tel. 505/522–8641; Steven L. Smith, President and Chief Executive Officer **A**1 3 5 9 10 **F**4 7 8 10 12 15 19 21 22 28 35 37 40 42 43 44 49 50 52 56 64 65 70 71 72 73 74 **Web address:** www.mmclc.org	15	10	228	9519	163	91193	1816	82111	32412	1192

LAS VEGAS—San Miguel County

□ LAS VEGAS MEDICAL CENTER, 3795 Hot Springs Boulevard, Zip 87701, Mailing Address: P.O. Box 1388, Zip 87701–1388; tel. 505/454–2100; Felix Alderele, Administrator (Total facility includes 166 beds in nursing home–type unit) **A**1 **F**12 14 15 16 17 18 20 41 45 49 52 53 54 55 56 57 58 64 65 67 **P**6	12	22	348	623	282	45600	0	35702	21807	1012
⊞ NORTHEASTERN REGIONAL HOSPITAL, 1235 Eighth Street, Zip 87701–4254, Mailing Address: P.O. Box 248, Zip 87701–0238; tel. 505/425–6751; Jerry B. Scott, Chief Executive Officer **A**1 9 10 **F**7 8 12 13 14 15 16 19 22 23 24 28 30 35 37 40 41 44 49 65 71 **P**8 **S** Brim Healthcare, Inc., Brentwood, TN	23	10	54	2496	28	43275	377	14760	6368	279

LOS ALAMOS—Los Alamos County

⊞ LOS ALAMOS MEDICAL CENTER, 3917 West Road, Zip 87544–2293; tel. 505/662–4201; Paul J. Wilson, Administrator **A**1 9 10 **F**1 2 3 4 5 6 7 8 9 10 11 12 13 14 15 16 17 18 19 20 21 22 23 24 25 26 27 28 29 30 31 32 33 34 35 36 37 38 39 40 41 42 43 44 45 46 47 48 49 50 51 52 53 54 55 56 57 58 59 60 61 62 63 64 65 66 67 69 70 71 72 73 74 **P**5 7 8 **S** Lutheran Health Systems, Fargo, ND	23	10	47	1539	14	85542	232	18848	6494	268

LOVINGTON—Lea County

⊞ NOR–LEA GENERAL HOSPITAL, 1600 North Main Avenue, Zip 88260–2871; tel. 505/396–6611; David R. Jordan, Ph.D., Administrator and Chief Executive Officer **A**1 9 10 **F**19 22 28 32 33 34 39 41 44 65 71 **S** Lubbock Methodist Hospital System, Lubbock, TX	16	10	28	565	4	18714	0	5686	—	182

MESCALERO—Otero County

⊞ U. S. PUBLIC HEALTH SERVICE INDIAN HOSPITAL, Mailing Address: Box 210, Zip 88340–0210; tel. 505/671–4441; Jo Ann Skaggs, Service Unit Director (Nonreporting) **A**1 10 **S** U. S. Public Health Service Indian Health Service, Rockville, MD	47	10	13	—	—	—	—	—	—	—

RATON—Colfax County

★ MINERS' COLFAX MEDICAL CENTER, (Includes Miners' Hospital of New Mexico), 200 Hospital Drive, Zip 87740–2099; tel. 505/445–3661; David Antle, Chief Executive Officer (Total facility includes 30 beds in nursing home–type unit) (Nonreporting) **A**9 10	13	10	68							

Hospital, Address, Telephone, Administrator, Approval, Facility, and Physician Codes, Health Care System, Network	Classi-fication Codes		Utilization Data					Expense (thousands) of dollars		
★ American Hospital Association (AHA) membership □ Joint Commission on Accreditation of Healthcare Organizations (JCAHO) accreditation + American Osteopathic Healthcare Association (AOHA) membership ○ American Osteopathic Association (AOA) accreditation △ Commission on Accreditation of Rehabilitation Facilities (CARF) accreditation Control codes 61, 63, 64, 71, 72 and 73 indicate hospitals listed by AOHA, but not registered by AHA. For definition of numerical codes, see page A4	Control	Service	Staffed Beds	Admissions	Census	Outpatient Visits	Births	Total	Payroll	Personnel

ROSWELL—Chaves County

⊠ EASTERN NEW MEXICO MEDICAL CENTER, 405 West Country Club Road, Zip 88201–9981; tel. 505/622–8170; Ronald J. Shafer, President and Chief Executive Officer (Nonreporting) **A**1 9 10 **S** Community Health Systems, Inc., Brentwood, TN
Web address: www.enmmc.com

| | 13 | 10 | 168 | — | — | — | — | — | — | — |

□ △ SOUTHERN NEW MEXICO REHABILITATION CENTER, (Includes Pecos Valley Lodge), 31 Gail Harris Avenue, Zip 88201–8134; tel. 505/347–5491; Donald D. Miller, Executive Director **A**1 7 10 **F**2 3 14 15 16 48 49

| | 12 | 46 | 35 | 509 | 26 | 4853 | 0 | 6357 | 3043 | 119 |

RUIDOSO—Lincoln County

⊠ LINCOLN COUNTY MEDICAL CENTER, 211 Sudderth Drive, Zip 88345–6043, Mailing Address: P.O. Box 8000, Zip 88345–8000; tel. 505/257–7381; James P. Gibson, Administrator **A**1 9 10 **F**2 3 4 5 6 7 8 9 10 11 12 13 14 15 16 17 18 19 20 22 24 26 28 29 30 31 32 33 34 37 38 39 40 41 42 43 44 46 47 48 49 52 53 54 56 58 64 70 71 73 **P**2 8 **S** Presbyterian Healthcare Services, Albuquerque, NM

| | 23 | 10 | 31 | 721 | 5 | 44841 | 247 | 12066 | 5752 | 185 |

SAN FIDEL—Cibola County

⊠ ACOMA–CANONCITO–LAGUNA HOSPITAL, Mailing Address: P.O. Box 130, Zip 87049–0130; tel. 505/552–6634; Richard L. Zephier, Ph.D., Service Unit Director **A**1 10 **F**2 8 10 12 13 14 15 16 17 18 20 22 25 26 27 28 34 41 46 49 51 61 65 67 71 72 74 **S** U. S. Public Health Service Indian Health Service, Rockville, MD

| | 47 | 10 | 15 | 477 | 7 | 77427 | 0 | — | — | 240 |

SANTA FE—Santa Fe County

□ BHC PINON HILLS HOSPITAL, 313 Camino Alire, Zip 87501–2319; tel. 505/988–8003; Jerry Smith, Chief Executive Officer (Nonreporting) **A**1 10 **S** Behavioral Healthcare Corporation, Nashville, TN

| | 33 | 22 | 34 | — | — | — | — | — | — | — |

⊠ PHS SANTA FE INDIAN HOSPITAL, 1700 Cerrillos Road, Zip 87505–3554; tel. 505/988–9821; Lawrence A. Jordan, Director **A**1 10 **F**7 8 10 13 15 16 19 20 21 22 25 26 28 30 31 32 34 35 39 40 42 43 44 45 49 51 53 56 58 60 61 65 69 70 71 74 **S** U. S. Public Health Service Indian Health Service, Rockville, MD

| | 47 | 10 | 39 | 1357 | 14 | 53108 | 286 | 13465 | — | 267 |

⊠ △ ST. VINCENT HOSPITAL, 455 St. Michael's Drive, Zip 87505–7663, Mailing Address: P.O. Box 2107, Zip 87504–2107; tel. 505/983–3361; William W. Webster, Interim President and Chief Executive Officer (Nonreporting) **A**1 2 5 7 9 10
Web address: www.stvin.org

| | 23 | 10 | 198 | — | — | — | — | — | — | — |

SANTA TERESA—Dona Ana County

□ ALLIANCE HOSPITAL OF SANTA TERESA, 100 Laura Court, Zip 88008, Mailing Address: P.O. Box 6, Las Cruces, Zip 88008–0006; tel. 505/589–0033; Michele Irwin, Administrator (Nonreporting) **A**1 10 **S** Bowdon Corporate Offices, Atlanta, GA

| | 33 | 22 | 72 | — | — | — | — | — | — | — |

SHIPROCK—San Juan County

⊠ NORTHERN NAVAJO MEDICAL CENTER, Mailing Address: P.O. Box 160, Zip 87420–0160; tel. 505/368–6001; Dee Hutchison, Chief Executive Officer **A**1 10 **F**1 2 3 4 5 6 7 8 9 10 11 12 13 15 16 17 19 20 21 22 23 25 26 27 28 29 30 31 32 33 34 35 37 38 39 40 42 43 44 45 46 47 48 49 51 52 53 54 56 57 58 59 60 61 64 65 67 68 69 70 71 72 74 **P**6 **S** U. S. Public Health Service Indian Health Service, Rockville, MD

| | 44 | 10 | 59 | 3733 | 37 | 201898 | 829 | 60303 | 26864 | 783 |

SILVER CITY—Grant County

⊠ GILA REGIONAL MEDICAL CENTER, 1313 East 32nd Street, Zip 88061; tel. 505/538–4000; Polly Pine, Administrator **A**1 9 10 **F**7 8 16 17 19 21 22 30 32 33 35 37 40 41 42 44 49 52 53 56 58 65 68 71 **P**3 5 **S** Quorum Health Group/Quorum Health Resources, Inc., Brentwood, TN

| | 13 | 10 | 59 | 3453 | 31 | 67237 | 558 | 27407 | 13311 | 346 |

SOCORRO—Socorro County

⊠ SOCORRO GENERAL HOSPITAL, 1202 Highway 60 West, Zip 87801, Mailing Address: P.O. Box 1009, Zip 87801–1009; tel. 505/835–1140; Jeff Dye, Administrator on **A**1 9 10 **F**7 8 17 19 22 28 30 32 33 35 40 41 44 49 68 71 **P**1 4 5 6 8 **S** Presbyterian Healthcare Services, Albuquerque, NM

| | 23 | 10 | 30 | 638 | 5 | 16375 | 174 | 7945 | 3730 | 179 |

TAOS—Taos County

⊠ HOLY CROSS HOSPITAL, 1397 Weimer Road, Zip 87571, Mailing Address: P.O. Box DD, Zip 87571; tel. 505/758–8883; Warren K. Spellman, Administrator **A**1 9 10 **F**7 8 14 15 17 19 22 28 35 37 39 40 44 45 49 52 71 72 **P**3 8 **S** Quorum Health Group/Quorum Health Resources, Inc., Brentwood, TN

| | 23 | 10 | 34 | 1889 | 17 | 41918 | 289 | 14325 | 5459 | 181 |

TRUTH OR CONSEQUENCES—Sierra County

⊠ SIERRA VISTA HOSPITAL, 800 East Ninth Avenue, Zip 87901–1961; tel. 505/894–2111; Domenica Rush, Administrator **A**1 9 10 **F**15 16 19 22 32 34 44 58 65 67 71 73 **P**6

| | 15 | 10 | 32 | 396 | 3 | 45452 | 29 | 5883 | 2606 | 119 |

TUCUMCARI—Quay County

★ DR. DAN C. TRIGG MEMORIAL HOSPITAL, 301 East Miel De Luna Avenue, Zip 88401–3810, Mailing Address: P.O. Box 608, Zip 88401–0608; tel. 505/461–0141; Dell Willis, Administrator (Nonreporting) **A**9 10 **S** Presbyterian Healthcare Services, Albuquerque, NM

| | 23 | 10 | 37 | — | — | — | — | — | — | — |

ZUNI—McKinley County

⊠ U. S. PUBLIC HEALTH SERVICE INDIAN HOSPITAL, Mailing Address: P.O. Box 467, Zip 87327–0467; tel. 505/782–4431; Jean Othole, Service Unit Director **A**1 10 **F**1 3 4 5 6 7 8 10 13 14 15 16 18 19 20 21 24 26 27 28 30 35 40 50 53 54 55 56 57 58 59 60 63 64 69 72 **S** U. S. Public Health Service Indian Health Service, Rockville, MD

| | 47 | 10 | 24 | 848 | 9 | 5068 | 114 | — | — | 181 |

NEW YORK

Resident population 18,175 (in thousands)
Resident population in metro areas 91.8%
Birth rate per 1,000 population 15
65 years and over 13.4%
Percent of persons without health insurance 17%

Hospital, Address, Telephone, Administrator, Approval, Facility, and Physician Codes, Health Care System, Network	Classification Codes		Utilization Data					Expense (thousands) of dollars		
	Control	Service	Staffed Beds	Admissions	Census	Outpatient Visits	Births	Total	Payroll	Personnel

★ American Hospital Association (AHA) membership
☐ Joint Commission on Accreditation of Healthcare Organizations (JCAHO) accreditation
+ American Osteopathic Healthcare Association (AOHA) membership
○ American Osteopathic Association (AOA) accreditation
△ Commission on Accreditation of Rehabilitation Facilities (CARF) accreditation
Control codes 61, 63, 64, 71, 72 and 73 indicate hospitals listed by AOHA, but not registered by AHA. For definition of numerical codes, see page A4

ALBANY—Albany County

Hospital	Control	Service	Staffed Beds	Admissions	Census	Outpatient Visits	Births	Total	Payroll	Personnel
✠ ALBANY MEDICAL CENTER, 43 New Scotland Avenue, Zip 12208–3478; tel. 518/262–3125; Mary A. Nolan, R.N., MS, Executive Vice President Care Delivery and General Director **A**1 2 3 5 8 9 10 **F**4 7 8 10 11 12 15 16 17 19 20 21 22 26 28 30 31 32 34 35 37 38 39 40 41 42 43 44 45 46 47 48 49 51 52 53 54 55 56 57 58 59 60 61 63 65 68 70 71 72 73 74 **P**6 **Web address:** www.amc.edu	23	10	574	23674	445	302285	2372	285006	94647	2918
✠ CAPITAL DISTRICT PSYCHIATRIC CENTER, 75 New Scotland Avenue, Zip 12208–3474; tel. 518/447–9611; Jesse Nixon, Jr., Ph.D., Director (Nonreporting) **A**1 3 5 10 **S** New York State Department of Mental Health, Albany, NY	12	22	200	—	—	—	—	—	—	—
☐ CHILD'S HOSPITAL, 25 Hackett Boulevard, Zip 12208–3499; tel. 518/242–1200; Stephen J. Lauko, Chief Executive Officer (Nonreporting) **A**1 3 5 9 10	23	45	20	—	—	—	—	—	—	—
☐ MEMORIAL HOSPITAL, 600 Northern Boulevard, Zip 12204–1083; tel. 518/471–3221; Norman E. Dascher, Jr., Chief Executive Officer (Nonreporting) **A**1 6 9 10 **Web address:** www.nehealth.com	23	10	165	—	—	—	—	—	—	—
✠ ST. PETER'S HOSPITAL, 315 South Manning Boulevard, Zip 12208–1789; tel. 518/525–1550; Steven P. Boyle, President and Chief Executive Officer (Nonreporting) **A**1 2 3 5 9 10 **S** Catholic Health East, Newtown Square, PA	23	10	437	—	—	—	—	—	—	—
✠ △ VETERANS AFFAIRS MEDICAL CENTER, 113 Holland Avenue, Zip 12208–3473; tel. 518/462–3311; Clyde Parkis, Director (Total facility includes 50 beds in nursing home–type unit) **A**1 2 3 5 7 8 9 **F**1 3 4 8 10 11 12 15 16 17 18 19 20 21 22 25 26 28 29 30 31 32 33 34 35 37 39 41 42 44 45 46 48 49 51 52 54 55 56 57 58 59 60 63 64 65 67 71 73 74 **S** Department of Veterans Affairs, Washington, DC	45	10	158	3756	85	251143	0	116644	73571	—

ALEXANDRIA BAY—Jefferson County

Hospital	Control	Service	Staffed Beds	Admissions	Census	Outpatient Visits	Births	Total	Payroll	Personnel
☐ E. J. NOBLE HOSPITAL SAMARITAN, 19 Fuller Street, Zip 13607; tel. 315/482–2511; Richard A. Brooks, Administrator and Chief Operating Officer (Total facility includes 27 beds in nursing home–type unit) (Nonreporting) **A**1 9 10	23	10	52	—	—	—	—	—	—	—

AMITYVILLE—Suffolk County

Hospital	Control	Service	Staffed Beds	Admissions	Census	Outpatient Visits	Births	Total	Payroll	Personnel
☐ BRUNSWICK GENERAL HOSPITAL, (Includes Brunswick Hall, 80 Louden Avenue, Zip 11701–2735; tel. 516/789–7100; Brunswick Physical Medicine and Rehabilitation Hospital, 366 Broadway), 366 Broadway, Zip 11701–9820; tel. 516/789–7000; Benjamin M. Stein, M.D., President (Total facility includes 94 beds in nursing home–type unit) **A**1 9 10 **F**1 8 11 15 16 17 19 21 22 26 27 28 30 32 33 35 37 39 42 44 46 48 49 52 53 54 55 56 57 58 64 65 67 71 73	33	10	474	7085	336	143804	0	74233	38945	1195
☐ SOUTH OAKS HOSPITAL, 400 Sunrise Highway, Zip 11701; tel. 516/264–4000; Patrick R. Martore, Chief Executive Officer (Nonreporting) **A**1 9 10 **Web address:** www.southoaks.com	33	22	334	—	—	—	—	—	—	—

AMSTERDAM—Montgomery County

Hospital	Control	Service	Staffed Beds	Admissions	Census	Outpatient Visits	Births	Total	Payroll	Personnel
✠ AMSTERDAM MEMORIAL HOSPITAL, 4988 State Highway 30, Zip 12010–1699; tel. 518/842–3100; Cornelio R. Catena, President and Chief Executive Officer (Total facility includes 160 beds in nursing home–type unit) **A**1 9 10 **F**1 8 11 12 13 14 15 17 19 20 21 22 24 25 26 27 29 30 34 35 37 39 41 42 44 45 48 49 64 65 66 67 68 71 73 74 **S** Quorum Health Group/Quorum Health Resources, Inc., Brentwood, TN	23	10	242	2462	191	67708	0	30999	12781	482
✠ ST. MARY'S HOSPITAL, 427 Guy Park Avenue, Zip 12010–1095; tel. 518/842–1900; Peter E. Capobianco, President and Chief Executive Officer **A**1 9 10 **F**2 3 7 8 11 12 13 14 15 16 17 18 19 22 25 26 27 28 29 30 31 32 33 35 37 39 40 41 42 44 45 46 48 49 51 52 53 54 55 56 57 58 61 65 66 67 71 73 74 **P**8 **S** Carondelet Health System, Saint Louis, MO **Web address:** www.smha.org	21	10	143	4939	80	184974	660	42728	22909	673

AUBURN—Cayuga County

Hospital	Control	Service	Staffed Beds	Admissions	Census	Outpatient Visits	Births	Total	Payroll	Personnel
✠ AUBURN MEMORIAL HOSPITAL, 17 Lansing Street, Zip 13021–1943; tel. 315/255–7011; Christopher J. Rogers, Administrator (Total facility includes 80 beds in nursing home–type unit) **A**1 5 9 10 **F**7 8 11 12 14 15 16 19 22 25 33 34 37 40 44 49 52 54 56 64 65 66 67 71 72 73	23	10	306	7507	203	112389	620	54940	26992	827

BATAVIA—Genesee County

GENESEE MEMORIAL HOSPITAL See United Memorial Medical Center–North Street
ST JEROME HOSPITAL See United Memorial Medical Center–Bank Street

Hospital	Control	Service	Staffed Beds	Admissions	Census	Outpatient Visits	Births	Total	Payroll	Personnel
✠ UNITED MEMORIAL MEDICAL CENTER–BANK STREET, (Formerly St Jerome Hospital), 16 Bank Street, Zip 14020–2260; tel. 716/343–3131; Gary DeLisle, Interim Chief Executive Officer **A**1 9 10 **F**2 5 8 11 14 15 16 17 18 19 22 25 28 29 30 32 33 34 35 37 41 44 51 60 62 65 71 73	21	10	82	2365	53	75110	0	21515	9668	339
✠ UNITED MEMORIAL MEDICAL CENTER–NORTH STREET, (Formerly Genesee Memorial Hospital), 127 North Street, Zip 14020–1697; tel. 716/343–6030; Gary DeLisle, Interim Chief Executive Officer (Nonreporting) **A**1 9 10	23	10	70	—	—	—	—	—	—	—

Hospital, Address, Telephone, Administrator, Approval, Facility, and Physician Codes, Health Care System, Network	Classi-fication Codes		Utilization Data					Expense (thousands) of dollars		
	Control	Service	Staffed Beds	Admissions	Census	Outpatient Visits	Births	Total	Payroll	Personnel

★ American Hospital Association (AHA) membership
☐ Joint Commission on Accreditation of Healthcare Organizations (JCAHO) accreditation
+ American Osteopathic Healthcare Association (AOHA) membership
○ American Osteopathic Association (AOA) accreditation
△ Commission on Accreditation of Rehabilitation Facilities (CARF) accreditation
Control codes 61, 63, 64, 71, 72 and 73 indicate hospitals listed by AOHA, but not registered by AHA. For definition of numerical codes, see page A4

Hospital	Control	Service	Staffed Beds	Admissions	Census	Outpatient Visits	Births	Total	Payroll	Personnel
★ VETERANS AFFAIRS WESTERN NEW YORK HEALTHCARE SYSTEM–BATAVIA DIVISION, 222 Richmond Avenue, Zip 14020–1288; tel. 716/343–7500; Richard S. Droske, Director (Total facility includes 70 beds in nursing home–type unit) (Nonreporting) **A**5 9 **S** Department of Veterans Affairs, Washington, DC	45	10	158	—	—	—	—	—	—	—
BATH—Steuben County										
☒ IRA DAVENPORT MEMORIAL HOSPITAL, 7571 State Route 54, Zip 14810–9533; tel. 607/776–8500; James B. Watson, Chief Executive Officer (Total facility includes 120 beds in nursing home–type unit) (Nonreporting) **A**1 9 10	23	10	186	—	—	—	—	—	—	—
☒ VETERANS AFFAIRS MEDICAL CENTER, (LONG TERM ACUTE CARE), 76 Veterans Avenue, Zip 14810–0842; tel. 607/776–2111; John F. Dunn, Jr., Acting Director (Total facility includes 380 beds in nursing home–type unit) **A**1 9 **F**3 12 14 15 16 17 19 20 22 24 25 26 28 29 30 31 32 33 34 39 44 45 46 49 51 52 54 55 56 57 58 59 64 65 67 71 73 74 **P**6 **S** Department of Veterans Affairs, Washington, DC	45	49	426	2016	356	90135	0	42817	23527	632
BAY SHORE—Suffolk County										
☒ SOUTHSIDE HOSPITAL, 301 East Main Street, Zip 11706–8458; tel. 516/968–3000; Theodore A. Jospe, President **A**1 3 5 9 10 **F**2 3 4 7 8 10 11 12 13 14 15 16 17 18 19 20 21 22 24 25 26 27 28 29 30 31 32 33 34 35 37 39 40 41 42 44 45 46 48 49 51 52 54 55 56 57 58 60 61 63 65 66 67 68 71 73 74 **P**2 5 7 **S** North Shore– Long Island Jewish Health System, Great Neck, NY	23	10	356	14469	280	88282	2101	124398	69013	1565
BEACON—Dutchess County										
☒ CRAIG HOUSE CENTER, Howland Avenue, Zip 12508; tel. 914/831–1200; Linda Achber, Acting Chief Executive Officer (Nonreporting) **A**1 10	33	22	61	—	—	—	—	—	—	—
BELLEROSE—Queens County, See New York City										
BETHPAGE—Nassau County										
☐ NEW ISLAND HOSPITAL, (Formerly Mid–Island Hospital), 4295 Hempstead Turnpike, Zip 11714–5769; tel. 516/579–6000; Robert J. Reed, President (Nonreporting) **A**1 9 10	33	10	223	—	—	—	—	—	—	—
BINGHAMTON—Broome County										
BINGHAMTON GENERAL HOSPITAL See United Health Services Hospitals–Binghamton										
☒ BINGHAMTON PSYCHIATRIC CENTER, 425 Robinson Street, Zip 13901–4198; tel. 607/724–1391; Margaret R. Dugan, Executive Director **A**1 10 **F**15 20 25 39 46 52 53 57 58 59 65 67 73 **P**6 **S** New York State Department of Mental Health, Albany, NY	12	22	216	166	202	45375	0	23669	—	542
☒ OUR LADY OF LOURDES MEMORIAL HOSPITAL, 169 Riverside Drive, Zip 13905–4198; tel. 607/798–5111; John D. O'Neil, President and Chief Executive Officer **A**1 2 9 10 **F**5 7 8 12 14 15 16 17 19 21 22 23 24 25 26 27 28 29 30 31 32 33 34 35 36 37 39 40 41 42 44 45 46 49 51 53 55 58 60 63 65 66 67 68 71 72 73 74 **P**5 6 7 **S** Daughters of Charity National Health System, Saint Louis, MO Web address: www.lourdes.com	21	10	184	9236	151	855884	1117	108558	48974	1239
☒ ○ UNITED HEALTH SERVICES HOSPITALS–BINGHAMTON, (Includes Binghamton General Hospital, 10–42 Mitchell Avenue; Medicenter, 600 High Avenue, Endicott, Zip 13760; tel. 607/754–7171; Wilson Memorial Regional Medical Center, 33–57 Harrison Street, Johnson City, Zip 13790), 10–42 Mitchell Avenue, Zip 13903; tel. 607/763–6000; Matthew J. Salanger, President and Chief Executive Officer **A**1 2 3 5 8 9 10 11 12 **F**1 2 3 4 6 7 8 9 10 11 12 13 14 15 16 17 18 19 20 21 22 26 28 29 30 31 32 34 37 38 39 40 41 42 43 44 45 46 48 49 51 52 54 55 56 57 58 60 61 62 64 65 66 67 70 71 72 73 74 **P**1 Web address: www.uhs.net	23	10	516	19265	362	219786	1622	198009	79044	2406
BRENTWOOD—Suffolk County										
☒ PILGRIM PSYCHIATRIC CENTER, (Includes Kings Park Psychiatric Center, 998 Crooked Hill Road, tel. 516/761–3500; Alan M. Weinstock, MS, Chief Executive Officer), 998 Crooked Hill Road, Zip 11717–1087; tel. 516/761–3500; Kathleen Kelly, Chief Executive Officer (Nonreporting) **A**1 5 10 **S** New York State Department of Mental Health, Albany, NY	12	22	744	—	—	—	—	—	—	—
BROCKPORT—Monroe County										
☒ LAKESIDE MEMORIAL HOSPITAL, 156 West Avenue, Zip 14420–1286; tel. 716/395–6095; Robert W. Harris, President **A**1 9 10 **F**2 3 4 7 8 9 10 11 14 15 16 17 19 21 22 23 28 30 33 35 37 38 39 40 41 42 43 44 45 46 47 48 50 52 53 54 55 56 57 58 59 60 63 64 65 67 69 70 71 72 73	23	10	72	2602	47	16471	403	—	—	323
BRONX—Bronx County, See New York City										
BRONXVILLE—Westchester County										
☒ LAWRENCE HOSPITAL, 55 Palmer Avenue, Zip 10708–3491; tel. 914/787–1000; Roger G. Dvorak, President **A**1 2 9 10 **F**7 8 11 12 15 16 17 19 21 22 26 30 32 33 34 35 36 37 38 39 40 41 42 44 45 46 49 54 63 65 66 67 71 73 74 **P**5 Web address: www.lawrencehealth.org	23	10	232	9034	154	104322	1560	71371	38007	897
BROOKLYN—Kings County, See New York City										
BUFFALO—Erie County										
☐ BRYLIN HOSPITALS, 1263 Delaware Avenue, Zip 14209–2497; tel. 716/886–8200; Eric D. Pleskow, President and Chief Executive Officer (Nonreporting) **A**1 9 10 Web address: www.brylin.com	33	22	150	—	—	—	—	—	—	—

Hospital, Address, Telephone, Administrator, Approval, Facility, and Physician Codes, Health Care System, Network	Classi-fication Codes		Utilization Data					Expense (thousands) of dollars		
★ American Hospital Association (AHA) membership □ Joint Commission on Accreditation of Healthcare Organizations (JCAHO) accreditation + American Osteopathic Healthcare Association (AOHA) membership ○ American Osteopathic Association (AOA) accreditation △ Commission on Accreditation of Rehabilitation Facilities (CARF) accreditation Control codes 61, 63, 64, 71, 72 and 73 indicate hospitals listed by AOHA, but not registered by AHA. For definition of numerical codes, see page A4	Control	Service	Staffed Beds	Admissions	Census	Outpatient Visits	Births	Total	Payroll	Personnel
✸ BUFFALO GENERAL HOSPITAL, 100 High Street, Zip 14203–1154; tel. 716/845–5600; John E. Friedlander, President and Chief Executive Officer (Total facility includes 242 beds in nursing home–type unit) (Nonreporting) **A**1 3 5 8 9 10 **S** KALEIDA Health, Buffalo, NY	23	10	965	—	—	—	—	—	—	—
✸ BUFFALO PSYCHIATRIC CENTER, 400 Forest Avenue, Zip 14213–1298; tel. 716/885–2261; George Molnar, M.D., Executive Director **A**1 10 **F**1 3 4 5 6 7 8 9 10 11 12 15 16 17 18 19 20 21 22 23 24 25 26 27 28 29 30 31 35 37 39 40 41 42 43 44 45 46 48 49 50 51 52 54 55 56 57 58 59 60 61 63 64 65 67 69 70 71 73 **P**1 **S** New York State Department of Mental Health, Albany, NY **Web address:** www.omh.state.ny.us	12	22	260	195	255	80283	—	48794	33100	795
□ CHILDREN'S HOSPITAL, 219 Bryant Street, Zip 14222–2099; tel. 716/878–7000; Joseph A. Ruffolo, President and Chief Executive Officer (Nonreporting) **A**1 3 5 9 10 **S** KALEIDA Health, Buffalo, NY	23	59	313	—	—	—	—	—	—	—
□ ERIE COUNTY MEDICAL CENTER, 462 Grider Street, Zip 14215–3098; tel. 716/898–3000; Paul J. Candino, Chief Executive Officer (Total facility includes 794 beds in nursing home–type unit) **A**1 3 5 9 10 **F**2 3 4 8 9 10 11 12 13 14 15 16 17 18 19 20 21 22 25 26 27 28 30 31 32 33 34 35 37 39 41 42 43 44 46 48 49 51 52 53 54 55 56 57 58 63 64 65 67 68 70 71 73 74 **P**5 **Web address:** www.ecmc.edu	13	10	1211	13669	1109	286745	0	195615	99351	2037
□ MERCY HOSPITAL, 565 Abbott Road, Zip 14220–2095; tel. 716/826–7000; John P. Davanzo, President and Chief Executive Officer (Total facility includes 74 beds in nursing home–type unit) **A**1 3 5 9 10 **F**2 3 4 6 7 8 9 10 11 12 14 15 17 18 19 20 21 22 23 25 26 27 28 29 30 31 32 33 34 35 36 37 38 39 40 41 42 43 44 45 46 47 48 49 51 52 53 54 55 56 57 58 59 60 61 62 63 64 65 66 67 68 71 72 73 74 **P**5 8 **S** Catholic Health East, Newtown Square, PA **Web address:** www.mercywny.org	21	10	457	13364	312	289501	2556	113172	53960	1496
✸ MILLARD FILLMORE GATES CIRCLE HOSPITAL, (Formerly Millard Fillmore Health System), (Includes Millard Fillmore Suburban Hospital, 1540 Maple Road, Williamsville, Zip 14221; tel. 716/688–3100), 3 Gates Circle, Zip 14209–9986; tel. 716/887–4600; Joyce Korzen, R.N., Chief Operating Officer (Total facility includes 75 beds in nursing home–type unit) (Nonreporting) **A**1 3 5 6 9 10 **S** KALEIDA Health, Buffalo, NY **Web address:** www.mfhs.edu	23	10	588	—	—	—	—	—	—	—
□ ROSWELL PARK CANCER INSTITUTE, (COMPREHENSIVE CANCER CENTER), Elm and Carlton Streets, Zip 14263–0001; tel. 716/845–2300; David C. Hohn, M.D., President and Chief Executive Officer **A**1 2 3 5 8 9 10 **F**8 12 14 15 16 17 19 20 21 25 28 29 30 31 32 33 34 35 37 39 41 42 44 45 46 49 53 54 60 63 65 67 68 71 73 **P**6 **Web address:** www.rpci.med.buffalo.edu	12	49	137	4584	83	97122	0	—	—	1276
□ SHEEHAN MEMORIAL HOSPITAL, 425 Michigan Avenue, Zip 14203–2297; tel. 716/848–2000; Olivia Smith–Blackwell, M.D., M.P.H., President and Chief Executive Officer (Nonreporting) **A**1 9 10	23	10	109	—	—	—	—	—	—	—
✸ SISTERS OF CHARITY HOSPITAL OF BUFFALO, 2157 Main Street, Zip 14214–2692; tel. 716/862–1000; Patrick J. Wiles, President and Chief Executive Officer (Total facility includes 80 beds in nursing home–type unit) **A**1 2 3 5 6 9 10 12 13 **F**1 2 3 4 7 8 9 10 11 12 13 14 15 16 17 18 19 20 21 22 25 26 27 28 29 30 31 32 33 34 35 36 37 38 39 40 41 42 43 44 45 46 47 48 49 50 51 52 53 54 55 56 57 58 59 60 61 63 64 65 66 67 68 70 71 72 73 74 **P**3 8 **Web address:** www.sisters–buffalo.org	21	10	297	12067	287	387382	3005	106231	48688	1809
✸ VETERANS AFFAIRS WESTERN NEW YORK HEALTHCARE SYSTEM–BUFFALO DIVISION, 3495 Bailey Avenue, Zip 14215–1129; tel. 716/834–9200; William F. Feeley, Director (Total facility includes 120 beds in nursing home–type unit) **A**1 2 3 5 8 9 **F**1 3 4 8 10 11 12 17 18 19 20 21 22 24 25 26 27 28 29 30 31 32 33 34 35 37 39 41 42 43 44 45 46 49 50 51 52 54 55 56 57 58 59 60 61 63 64 65 67 68 71 72 73 74 **S** Department of Veterans Affairs, Washington, DC	45	10	250	5432	265	412121	0	142416	94425	1622
✸ WESTERN NEW YORK CHILDREN'S PSYCHIATRIC CENTER, 1010 East and West Road, Zip 14224–3698; tel. 716/674–9730; Jed M. Cohen, Acting Executive Director **A**1 **F**12 17 18 20 22 25 39 44 47 52 53 54 55 56 58 59 65 67 73 **S** New York State Department of Mental Health, Albany, NY	12	52	46	78	39	11279	—	—	—	166
CAMBRIDGE—Washington County										
□ MARY MCCLELLAN HOSPITAL, One Myrtle Avenue, Zip 12816–1098; tel. 518/252–2540; Kathleen Lacasse, Chief Executive Officer (Total facility includes 40 beds in nursing home–type unit) **A**1 9 10 **F**7 8 12 14 15 19 21 22 25 30 33 34 37 39 40 41 44 48 49 51 64 65 66 67 71 73 74 **P**5 6	23	10	114	1358	54	84671	138	15076	8967	328
CANANDAIGUA—Ontario County										
✸ F. F. THOMPSON HEALTH SYSTEM, 350 Parrish Street, Zip 14424–1793; tel. 716/396–6000; Linda M. Janczak, President and Chief Executive Officer (Total facility includes 188 beds in nursing home–type unit) **A**1 3 9 10 **F**1 7 8 12 14 15 16 17 19 21 22 25 27 28 29 30 33 34 35 37 39 40 41 42 44 45 49 64 65 66 67 71 72 73 74 **P**5 6 **Web address:** www.ffth.com	23	10	301	4537	247	155593	694	49577	25988	887
✸ VETERANS AFFAIRS MEDICAL CENTER, 400 Fort Hill Avenue, Zip 14424–1197; tel. 716/394–2000; W. David Smith, Director (Total facility includes 150 beds in nursing home–type unit) (Nonreporting) **A**1 5 **S** Department of Veterans Affairs, Washington, DC	45	49	626	—	—	—	—	—	—	—

Hospital, Address, Telephone, Administrator, Approval, Facility, and Physician Codes, Health Care System, Network	Classi-fication Codes		Utilization Data					Expense (thousands) of dollars		
	Control	Service	Staffed Beds	Admissions	Census	Outpatient Visits	Births	Total	Payroll	Personnel

★ American Hospital Association (AHA) membership
□ Joint Commission on Accreditation of Healthcare Organizations (JCAHO) accreditation
+ American Osteopathic Healthcare Association (AOHA) membership
○ American Osteopathic Association (AOA) accreditation
△ Commission on Accreditation of Rehabilitation Facilities (CARF) accreditation
Control codes 61, 63, 64, 71, 72 and 73 indicate hospitals listed by AOHA, but not registered by AHA. For definition of numerical codes, see page A4

CARMEL—Putnam County

| ARMS ACRES, 75 Seminary Hill Road, Zip 10512–1921; tel. 914/225–3400; Edward Spauster, Ph.D., Executive Director (Nonreporting) | 33 | 82 | 129 | — | — | — | — | — | — | — |
| ✠ PUTNAM HOSPITAL CENTER, Stoneleigh Avenue, Zip 10512–9948; tel. 914/279–5711; Rodney N. Huebbers, President and Chief Executive Officer (Nonreporting) **A**1 9 10 | 23 | 10 | 164 | — | — | — | — | — | — | — |

CARTHAGE—Jefferson County

| □ CARTHAGE AREA HOSPITAL, 1001 West Street, Zip 13619–9703; tel. 315/493–1000; Walter S. Becker, Administrator (Total facility includes 30 beds in nursing home–type unit) **A** 9 10 **F**7 8 12 14 15 16 17 19 21 22 28 29 30 34 39 40 41 44 45 48 49 51 64 65 67 71 73 74 | 23 | 10 | 78 | 1931 | 50 | 53937 | 253 | 12714 | 6642 | 247 |

CASTLE POINT—Dutchess County

VETERAN AFFAIRS HUDSON VALLEY HEALTH CARE SYSTEM–CASTLE POINT DIVISION See Veterans Affairs Hudson Valley Health Care System–F.D. Roosevelt Hospital, Montrose

CHEEKTOWAGA—Erie County

| ✠ ST. JOSEPH HOSPITAL, 2605 Harlem Road, Zip 14225–4097; tel. 716/891–2400; Patrick J. Wiles, President and Chief Executive Officer **A**1 9 10 **F**3 5 7 8 10 11 12 14 15 16 19 20 22 28 29 30 31 32 33 35 37 39 41 42 43 44 45 46 49 50 51 53 60 63 65 69 71 73 74 **P**3 5 6 **S** Catholic Health East, Newtown Square, PA Web address: www.sjh.org | 23 | 10 | 208 | 5624 | 99 | 183333 | 0 | 48871 | 23094 | 644 |

CLIFTON SPRINGS—Ontario County

| ✠ CLIFTON SPRINGS HOSPITAL AND CLINIC, 2 Coulter Road, Zip 14432–1189; tel. 315/462–1311; John P. Galati, President and Chief Executive Officer (Total facility includes 108 beds in nursing home–type unit) (Nonreporting) **A**1 9 10 | 23 | 10 | 262 | — | — | — | — | — | — | — |

COBLESKILL—Schoharie County

| □ BASSETT HOSPITAL OF SCHOHARIE COUNTY, 41 Grandview Drive, Zip 12043–1331; tel. 518/234–2511; Donald W. Massey, Administrator (Nonreporting) **A**1 9 10 | 23 | 10 | 40 | — | — | — | — | — | — | — |

COOPERSTOWN—Otsego County

| ✠ MARY IMOGENE BASSETT HOSPITAL, One Atwell Road, Zip 13326–1394; tel. 607/547–3100; William F. Streck, M.D., President and Chief Executive Officer **A**1 2 3 5 8 9 10 **F**7 8 10 12 14 15 16 19 20 21 22 24 25 29 30 31 34 35 37 39 40 41 42 44 45 46 49 51 52 53 54 55 56 58 59 60 61 63 65 66 67 70 71 73 **P**6 Web address: www.bassethealthcare.org/ | 23 | 10 | 180 | 7791 | 106 | 422202 | 571 | 140341 | 75796 | 1927 |

CORNING—Steuben County

| ✠ CORNING HOSPITAL, 176 Denison Parkway East, Zip 14830–2899; tel. 607/937–7200; John E. Pignatore, President and Chief Executive Officer (Total facility includes 120 beds in nursing home–type unit) **A**1 9 10 **F**1 7 8 14 15 16 19 21 22 35 37 40 42 44 49 51 64 65 66 67 71 73 74 Web address: www.corninghospital.com | 23 | 10 | 264 | 5592 | 192 | 90992 | 468 | 38233 | 18236 | 531 |

CORNWALL—Orange County

| ✠ CORNWALL HOSPITAL, 19 Laurel Avenue, Zip 12518–1499; tel. 914/534–7711; Louis H. Smith, Executive Vice President and Administrator **A**1 9 10 **F**8 14 15 16 17 19 20 22 26 27 28 29 30 35 37 42 44 49 52 54 56 57 63 65 67 68 71 73 **S** Greater Hudson Valley Health System, Newburgh, NY | 23 | 10 | 125 | 4132 | 85 | 54399 | 0 | 31869 | 16851 | 446 |

CORTLAND—Cortland County

| ✠ CORTLAND MEMORIAL HOSPITAL, 134 Homer Avenue, Zip 13045–0960; tel. 607/756–3500; Thomas H. Carman, President and Chief Executive Officer (Total facility includes 82 beds in nursing home–type unit) **A**1 9 10 **F**1 7 8 12 15 17 19 21 22 24 26 28 30 32 35 37 40 41 44 45 46 49 52 54 56 63 64 65 66 67 71 73 74 | 23 | 10 | 193 | 5487 | 162 | 89978 | 653 | 43405 | 20599 | 740 |

CORTLANDT MANOR—Westchester County

| ✠ HUDSON VALLEY HOSPITAL CENTER, 1980 Crompond Road, Zip 10567; tel. 914/737–9000; John C. Federspiel, President and Chief Executive Officer **A**1 9 10 **F**3 7 8 12 14 15 16 17 18 19 21 22 25 26 28 30 34 35 37 39 40 41 42 44 49 65 66 67 70 71 73 **P**5 8 Web address: www.hvhc.org | 23 | 10 | 120 | 5918 | 77 | 77059 | 1070 | 49756 | 22750 | 548 |

CUBA—Allegany County

| □ CUBA MEMORIAL HOSPITAL, 140 West Main Street, Zip 14727–1398; tel. 716/968–2000; Darlene D. Bainbridge, Chief Executive Officer (Total facility includes 61 beds in nursing home–type unit) (Nonreporting) **A**1 9 | 23 | 10 | 87 | — | — | — | — | — | — | — |

DANSVILLE—Livingston County

| ✠ NICHOLAS H. NOYES MEMORIAL HOSPITAL, 111 Clara Barton Street, Zip 14437–9527; tel. 716/335–6001; James Wissler, President and Chief Executive Officer **A**1 9 10 **F**8 16 17 19 22 35 36 37 39 40 44 49 58 65 71 73 **P**3 | 23 | 10 | 49 | 2145 | 25 | 96782 | 250 | 19633 | 9370 | 319 |

DOBBS FERRY—Westchester County

| □ COMMUNITY HOSPITAL AT DOBBS FERRY, 128 Ashford Avenue, Zip 10522–1896; tel. 914/693–0700; Thomas E. Green, President and Chief Executive Officer (Nonreporting) **A**1 9 10 | 23 | 10 | 50 | — | — | — | — | — | — | — |

DUNKIRK—Chautauqua County

| ✠ BROOKS MEMORIAL HOSPITAL, 529 Central Avenue, Zip 14048–2599; tel. 716/366–1111; Richard H. Ketcham, President **A**1 9 10 **F**7 8 12 17 19 21 22 26 28 29 30 32 34 35 36 37 40 42 44 46 49 60 65 71 73 74 **P**5 Web address: www.brookshospital.org | 23 | 10 | 133 | 2906 | 47 | 90992 | 486 | 24678 | 10989 | 359 |

Hospital, Address, Telephone, Administrator, Approval, Facility, and Physician Codes, Health Care System, Network	Classi-fication Codes		Utilization Data					Expense (thousands) of dollars		
★ American Hospital Association (AHA) membership □ Joint Commission on Accreditation of Healthcare Organizations (JCAHO) accreditation + American Osteopathic Healthcare Association (AOHA) membership ○ American Osteopathic Association (AOA) accreditation △ Commission on Accreditation of Rehabilitation Facilities (CARF) accreditation Control codes 61, 63, 64, 71, 72 and 73 indicate hospitals listed by AOHA, but not registered by AHA. For definition of numerical codes, see page A4	Control	Service	Staffed Beds	Admissions	Census	Outpatient Visits	Births	Total	Payroll	Personnel

EAST MEADOW—Nassau County

□ NASSAU COUNTY MEDICAL CENTER, 2201 Hempstead Turnpike, Zip 11554–1854; tel. 516/572–0123; Jerald C. Newman, Chief Executive Officer (Total facility includes 809 beds in nursing home–type unit) (Nonreporting) **A**1 2 3 5 8 9 10 12

| | 13 | 10 | 1384 | — | — | — | — | — | — | — |

ELIZABETHTOWN—Essex County

✠ ELIZABETHTOWN COMMUNITY HOSPITAL, Park Street, Zip 12932–0277, Mailing Address: P.O. Box 277, Zip 12932–0277; tel. 518/873–6377; Douglas G. Cushing, Administrator (Nonreporting) **A**1 9 10

| | 23 | 10 | 25 | — | — | — | — | — | — | — |

ELLENVILLE—Ulster County

□ ELLENVILLE COMMUNITY HOSPITAL, Route 209, Zip 12428–0668, Mailing Address: P.O. Box 668, Zip 12428–0668; tel. 914/647–6400; Judith Durr, Interim Chief Executive Officer (Nonreporting) **A**1 9 10

| | 23 | 10 | 31 | — | — | — | — | — | — | — |

ELMHURST—Queens County, See New York City

ELMIRA—Chemung County

✠ ARNOT OGDEN MEDICAL CENTER, 600 Roe Avenue, Zip 14905–1629; tel. 607/737–4100; Anthony J. Cooper, President and Chief Executive Officer (Total facility includes 40 beds in nursing home–type unit) **A**1 2 6 9 10 **F**4 7 8 10 11 12 15 16 17 19 21 22 25 26 27 28 29 30 31 34 35 37 38 39 40 41 42 43 44 45 46 49 51 54 60 61 63 64 65 67 68 70 71 72 73 74 **P**6
Web address: www.aomc.org

| | 23 | 10 | 247 | 7777 | 168 | 199311 | 1354 | 89010 | 43503 | 1238 |

✠ ELMIRA PSYCHIATRIC CENTER, 100 Washington Street, Zip 14901–2898; tel. 607/737–4739; George A. Roets, Director **A**1 10 **F**14 16 18 20 28 30 52 53 55 57 58 65 67 73 **P**1 **S** New York State Department of Mental Health, Albany, NY

| | 12 | 22 | 103 | 323 | 105 | 37250 | 0 | — | — | 350 |

✠ ST. JOSEPH'S HOSPITAL, (Includes Twin Tiers Rehabilitation Center), 555 East Market Street, Zip 14902–1512; tel. 607/733–6541; Sister Marie Castagnaro, President and Chief Executive Officer (Total facility includes 31 beds in nursing home–type unit) **A**1 2 9 10 **F**2 3 8 9 11 12 15 16 17 18 19 21 22 26 28 29 30 31 33 34 35 37 39 41 42 44 45 46 48 49 51 52 54 55 56 57 58 62 64 65 66 67 68 69 70 71 73 74 **S** Carondelet Health System, Saint Louis, MO
Web address: www.stjosephs.org

| | 21 | 10 | 224 | 5280 | 152 | 99695 | 0 | — | — | 772 |

ENDICOTT—Broome County

MEDICENTER See United Health Services Hospitals–Binghamton, Binghamton

FAR ROCKAWAY—Queens County, See New York City

FLUSHING—Queens County, See New York City

FOREST HILLS—Queens County, See New York City

FORT DRUM—Jefferson County

★ WILCOX ARMY COMMUNITY HOSPITAL, Zip 13602–5004 (Nonreporting) **S** Department of the Army, Office of the Surgeon General, Falls Church, VA

| | 42 | 10 | 30 | — | — | — | — | — | — | — |

FULTON—Oswego County

✠ ALBERT LINDLEY LEE MEMORIAL HOSPITAL, 510 South Fourth Street, Zip 13069–2994; tel. 315/592–2224; Dennis A. Casey, Executive Director **A**1 9 10 **F**3 4 8 10 16 19 20 21 22 25 29 30 31 32 34 37 41 42 44 45 51 53 54 55 56 57 58 59 63 65 66 67 69 71 73

| | 23 | 10 | 67 | 2337 | 39 | 48807 | 0 | 15762 | 9022 | 289 |

GENEVA—Ontario County

✠ GENEVA GENERAL HOSPITAL, 196 North Street, Zip 14456–1694; tel. 315/787–4000; James J. Dooley, President (Total facility includes 343 beds in nursing home–type unit) **A**1 6 9 10 **F**1 2 4 7 8 10 12 13 14 15 16 17 19 20 21 22 25 26 27 28 29 30 31 32 33 34 35 36 37 39 40 41 42 44 45 46 48 49 54 56 62 64 65 67 69 71 72 73 74

| | 23 | 10 | 479 | 4677 | 404 | 233240 | 672 | 51970 | 25967 | 938 |

GLEN COVE—Nassau County

✠ NORTH SHORE UNIVERSITY HOSPITAL AT GLEN COVE, 101 St. Andrews Lane, Zip 11542; tel. 516/674–7300; Mark R. Stenzler, Vice President Administration (Nonreporting) **A**1 2 3 5 9 10 **S** North Shore– Long Island Jewish Health System, Great Neck, NY

| | 23 | 10 | 265 | — | — | — | — | — | — | — |

GLEN OAKS—Queens County, See New York City

GLENS FALLS—Warren County

□ GLENS FALLS HOSPITAL, 100 Park Street, Zip 12801–9898; tel. 518/792–3151; David G. Kruczlnicki, President and Chief Executive Officer (Nonreporting) **A**1 2 9 10
Web address: www.glensfallshosp.org

| | 23 | 10 | 410 | — | — | — | — | — | — | — |

GLOVERSVILLE—Fulton County

□ NATHAN LITTAUER HOSPITAL AND NURSING HOME, 99 East State Street, Zip 12078–1293; tel. 518/725–8621; Thomas J. Dowd, President (Total facility includes 84 beds in nursing home–type unit) **A**1 5 9 10 **F**3 4 7 8 12 14 15 16 17 19 20 21 22 26 28 29 30 31 32 33 34 35 37 39 40 41 42 44 45 46 49 51 53 54 55 56 57 58 61 64 65 67 71 73 74
Web address: www.nlh.org

| | 23 | 10 | 208 | 4660 | 135 | 129598 | 376 | 37957 | 19553 | 607 |

GOSHEN—Orange County

✠ ARDEN HILL HOSPITAL, 4 Harriman Drive, Zip 10924–2499; tel. 914/294–5441; Wayne Becker, Interim Chief Executive Officer (Nonreporting) **A**1 9 10
Web address: www.ardenhill.org

| | 23 | 10 | 176 | — | — | — | — | — | — | — |

GOUVERNEUR—St. Lawrence County

□ EDWARD JOHN NOBLE HOSPITAL OF GOUVERNEUR, 77 West Barney Street, Zip 13642–1090; tel. 315/287–1000; Charles P. Conole, FACHE, Administrator **A**1 9 10 **F**7 8 9 11 12 13 14 15 16 17 18 19 21 22 26 28 29 30 31 32 33 34 35 37 38 39 40 41 42 43 44 45 46 47 49 52 53 54 56 57 60 61 65 71 74 **P**5
Web address: www.ejnoble.northnet.org

| | 23 | 10 | 47 | 1566 | 24 | 27337 | 117 | 10637 | 5566 | 224 |

Hospital, Address, Telephone, Administrator, Approval, Facility, and Physician Codes, Health Care System, Network	Classi-fication Codes		Utilization Data					Expense (thousands) of dollars		
★ American Hospital Association (AHA) membership □ Joint Commission on Accreditation of Healthcare Organizations (JCAHO) accreditation + American Osteopathic Healthcare Association (AOHA) membership ○ American Osteopathic Association (AOA) accreditation △ Commission on Accreditation of Rehabilitation Facilities (CARF) accreditation Control codes 61, 63, 64, 71, 72 and 73 indicate hospitals listed by AOHA, but not registered by AHA. For definition of numerical codes, see page A4	Control	Service	Staffed Beds	Admissions	Census	Outpatient Visits	Births	Total	Payroll	Personnel

GOWANDA—Cattaraugus County

□ TRI–COUNTY MEMORIAL HOSPITAL, 100 Memorial Drive, Zip 14070–1194; tel. 716/532–3377; Diane J. Osika, Chief Executive Officer **A**1 9 10 **F**1 2 3 4 5 6 7 8 9 10 11 12 13 14 15 16 17 18 19 20 21 22 23 24 25 26 27 28 30 31 32 33 34 35 37 38 39 41 42 43 44 45 46 47 48 49 50 51 52 53 54 55 56 57 58 59 60 61 64 65 67 68 69 70 71 72 73 74 **S** KALEIDA Health, Buffalo, NY

	23	10	65	1458	32	45625	0	10860	6245	201

GREENPORT—Suffolk County

□ EASTERN LONG ISLAND HOSPITAL, 201 Manor Place, Zip 11944–1298; tel. 516/477–1000; John M. Gwiazda, President and Chief Executive Officer **A**1 9 10 **F**2 3 8 11 14 15 16 19 21 22 24 26 27 30 31 34 35 37 39 41 42 44 45 46 49 52 56 57 60 65 66 67 71 73
Web address: www.elih.com

	23	10	80	2473	56	21922	0	17957	9789	194

HAMILTON—Madison County

✉ COMMUNITY MEMORIAL HOSPITAL, 150 Broad Street, Zip 13346–9518; tel. 315/824–1100; David Felton, President and Chief Executive Officer (Total facility includes 40 beds in nursing home–type unit) (Nonreporting) **A**1 9 10

	23	10	84	—	—	—	—	—	—	—

HARRIS—Sullivan County

✉ COMMUNITY GENERAL HOSPITAL OF SULLIVAN COUNTY, Bushville Road, Zip 12742, Mailing Address: P.O. Box 800, Zip 12742–0800; tel. 914/794–3300; Brian Buonanni, Chief Executive Officer (Total facility includes 60 beds in nursing home–type unit) (Nonreporting) **A**1 2 9 10

	23	10	304	—	—	—	—	—	—	—

HEMPSTEAD—Nassau County

□ ISLAND MEDICAL CENTER, 800 Front Street, Zip 11550–4600; tel. 516/560–1200; Leonard Polonsky, interim Chief Executive Officer (Nonreporting) **A**1 9 10

	32	10	213	—	—	—	—	—	—	—

HOLLISWOOD—Queens County, See New York City

HORNELL—Steuben County

□ ST. JAMES MERCY HOSPITAL, 411 Canisteo Street, Zip 14843–2197; tel. 607/324–8000; William G. Connors, President and Chief Executive Officer (Total facility includes 55 beds in nursing home–type unit) (Nonreporting) **A**1 6 9 10 **S** Catholic Health East, Newtown Square, PA
Web address: www.sjmh.org

	23	10	200	—	—	—	—	—	—	—

HUDSON—Columbia County

□ COLUMBIA MEMORIAL HOSPITAL, (Includes Columbia–Greene Long Term Care, 161 Jefferson Heights, Catskill, Zip 12414; tel. 518/943–6363), 71 Prospect Avenue, Zip 12534–2900; tel. 518/828–8039; Jane Ehrlich, President and Chief Executive Officer (Total facility includes 120 beds in nursing home–type unit) (Nonreporting) **A**1 9 10
Web address: www.cmn.net.org

	23	10	251	—	—	—	—	—	—	—

HUNTINGTON—Suffolk County

✉ HUNTINGTON HOSPITAL, 270 Park Avenue, Zip 11743–2799; tel. 516/351–2200; J. Ronald Gaudreault, President and Chief Executive Officer **A**1 2 3 9 10 **F**4 7 8 11 14 15 16 19 21 22 25 26 28 30 34 36 37 39 40 42 44 46 52 54 60 61 63 65 67 70 71 73 74 **P**5 7 8 **S** North Shore– Long Island Jewish Health System, Great Neck, NY
Web address: www.hunthosp.org

	23	10	265	12375	214	96288	1911	103798	56329	1294

HUNTINGTON STATION—Suffolk County

✉ SAGAMORE CHILDREN'S PSYCHIATRIC CENTER, 197 Half Hollow Road, Zip 11746; tel. 516/673–7700; Robert Schweitzer, Ed.D., Executive Director **A**1 **F**12 14 15 16 17 19 21 22 32 35 39 45 46 52 53 54 55 58 59 65 71 73 **S** New York State Department of Mental Health, Albany, NY

	12	52	69	240	65	27464	0	12649	—	247

ILION—Herkimer County

MOHAWK VALLEY DIVISION See St. Luke's Memorial Hospital Center, Utica

IRVING—Chautauqua County

○ LAKE SHORE HOSPITAL, 845 Route 5 and 20, Zip 14081–9716; tel. 716/934–2654; James B. Foster, Chief Executive Officer (Total facility includes 160 beds in nursing home–type unit) **A**9 10 11 **F**1 8 12 15 17 19 22 30 32 33 34 35 37 44 45 49 52 56 64 65 69 71 73 **P**8
Web address: www.lakeshorehosp.org

	23	10	222	1862	189	44818	0	23422	10161	406

ITHACA—Tompkins County

✉ CAYUGA MEDICAL CENTER AT ITHACA, 101 Dates Drive, Zip 14850–1383; tel. 607/274–4011; Bonnie H. Howell, President and Chief Executive Officer **A**1 2 5 10 **F**7 8 12 13 14 15 16 17 18 19 21 22 24 25 28 31 32 33 34 35 36 37 39 40 41 42 44 46 48 49 52 54 56 60 63 65 66 67 71 72 73 74 **P**5 7 8
Web address: www.cayugamed.org

	23	10	145	5952	90	150728	769	46782	20735	638

JACKSON HEIGHTS—Queens County, See New York City
JAMAICA—Queens County, See New York City
JAMESTOWN—Chautauqua County

✉ WOMAN'S CHRISTIAN ASSOCIATION HOSPITAL, 207 Foote Avenue, Zip 14702–9975; tel. 716/487–0141; Betsy T. Wright, President and Chief Executive Officer **A**1 2 9 10 **F**2 3 7 8 12 13 14 15 16 17 18 19 20 21 22 25 27 28 29 30 31 33 34 35 37 39 40 41 42 44 45 46 48 49 51 52 53 54 55 56 57 58 59 60 65 66 67 68 71 73 74 **P**5

	23	10	255	9492	200	215291	787	75579	38358	1144

JOHNSON CITY—Broome County

WILSON MEMORIAL REGIONAL MEDICAL CENTER See United Health Services Hospitals–Binghamton, Binghamton

Hospital, Address, Telephone, Administrator, Approval, Facility, and Physician Codes, Health Care System, Network	Classi-fication Codes		Utilization Data					Expense (thousands) of dollars		
★ American Hospital Association (AHA) membership ☐ Joint Commission on Accreditation of Healthcare Organizations (JCAHO) accreditation + American Osteopathic Healthcare Association (AOHA) membership ○ American Osteopathic Association (AOA) accreditation △ Commission on Accreditation of Rehabilitation Facilities (CARF) accreditation Control codes 61, 63, 64, 71, 72 and 73 indicate hospitals listed by AOHA, but not registered by AHA. For definition of numerical codes, see page A4	Control	Service	Staffed Beds	Admissions	Census	Outpatient Visits	Births	Total	Payroll	Personnel

KATONAH—Westchester County

☒ FOUR WINDS HOSPITAL, 800 Cross River Road, Zip 10536–3549; tel. 914/763–8151; Samuel C. Klagsbrun, M.D., Executive Medical Director **A**1 10 **F**3 12 14 15 16 17 19 21 22 26 27 35 41 50 52 53 54 55 56 57 58 59 63 65 67 71 73 **P**3 4 7
Web address: www.fourwinds.com

| | 33 | 22 | 175 | 2119 | 152 | 7458 | 0 | — | — | 592 |

KENMORE—Erie County

☐ KENMORE MERCY HOSPITAL, 2950 Elmwood Avenue, Zip 14217–1390; tel. 716/447–6100; Sister Mary Joel Schimscheiner, Chief Executive Officer **A**1 9 10 **F**3 5 6 8 10 11 12 14 15 16 17 18 19 20 22 23 25 26 28 29 30 32 33 34 35 36 39 41 42 44 45 46 49 51 61 62 65 66 71 72 73 74 **P**5 **S** Catholic Health East, Newtown Square, PA

| | 21 | 10 | 184 | 6872 | 124 | 162140 | 0 | 60274 | 25772 | 836 |

KINGSTON—Ulster County

☒ BENEDICTINE HOSPITAL, 105 Marys Avenue, Zip 12401–5894; tel. 914/338–2500; Thomas A. Dee, President and Chief Executive Officer (Nonreporting) **A**1 2 3 5 9 10

| | 21 | 10 | 222 | — | — | — | — | — | — | — |

☐ KINGSTON HOSPITAL, 396 Broadway, Zip 12401–4692; tel. 914/331–3131; Anthony P. Marmo, Chief Executive Officer (Nonreporting) **A**1 3 5 9 10

| | 23 | 10 | 140 | — | — | — | — | — | — | — |

LACKAWANNA—Erie County

☒ OUR LADY OF VICTORY HOSPITAL, 55 Melroy Road, Zip 14218–1687; tel. 716/825–8000; John P. Davanzo, President and Chief Executive Officer (Total facility includes 10 beds in nursing home–type unit) (Nonreporting) **A**1 9 10

| | 21 | 10 | 232 | — | — | — | — | — | — | — |

LEWISTON—Niagara County

☒ MOUNT ST. MARY'S HOSPITAL OF NIAGARA FALLS, 5300 Military Road, Zip 14092–1997; tel. 716/297–4800; Angelo G. Calbone, President and Chief Executive Officer **A**1 9 10 **F**2 3 7 8 11 14 15 16 17 19 20 22 25 30 31 35 37 39 40 44 46 49 51 56 59 61 65 67 71 73 **S** Daughters of Charity National Health System, Saint Louis, MO

| | 21 | 10 | 179 | 4877 | 95 | 209136 | 408 | 40079 | 16418 | 473 |

LITTLE FALLS—Herkimer County

☒ LITTLE FALLS HOSPITAL, 140 Burwell Street, Zip 13365–1725; tel. 315/823–1000; David S. Armstrong, Jr., Administrator (Total facility includes 34 beds in nursing home–type unit) **A**1 9 10 **F**1 4 6 7 8 10 11 12 13 14 15 16 17 19 20 21 22 24 25 26 27 28 29 30 31 33 34 35 37 38 39 40 41 42 43 44 45 46 47 49 51 52 53 54 55 56 60 61 63 64 65 66 67 68 71 72 73 74 **P**5

| | 23 | 10 | 134 | 3586 | 91 | 68977 | 286 | 19237 | 10864 | 426 |

LITTLE NECK—Queens County, See New York City
LOCKPORT—Niagara County

☒ LOCKPORT MEMORIAL HOSPITAL, 521 East Avenue, Zip 14094–3299; tel. 716/514–5700; Erich J. Wolters, President and Chief Executive Officer (Nonreporting) **A**1 9 10

| | 23 | 10 | 134 | — | — | — | — | — | — | — |

LONG BEACH—Nassau County

☒ LONG BEACH MEDICAL CENTER, 455 East Bay Drive, Zip 11561–2300, Mailing Address: P.O. Box 300, Zip 11561–2300; tel. 516/897–1000; Martin F. Nester, Jr., Chief Executive Officer (Total facility includes 200 beds in nursing home–type unit) **A**1 9 10 12 13 **F**3 4 5 8 11 14 15 16 17 18 19 20 21 22 26 27 28 29 30 31 32 34 35 37 39 42 44 45 46 48 49 51 52 53 54 55 56 57 58 63 64 65 66 67 68 71 73 74 **P**8
Web address: www.lbmc.org

| | 23 | 10 | 363 | 5845 | 326 | 184743 | 0 | 76277 | 39040 | 957 |

LONG ISLAND CITY—Queens County, See New York City
LOWVILLE—Lewis County

☒ LEWIS COUNTY GENERAL HOSPITAL, 7785 North State Street, Zip 13367–1297; tel. 315/376–5200; Ernest R. McNeely, Jr., Chief Executive Officer and Administrator (Total facility includes 160 beds in nursing home–type unit) **A**1 9 10 **F**1 7 8 15 16 19 21 22 26 27 28 30 32 33 34 37 40 41 42 44 45 46 49 51 64 65 66 67 71 73 74 **P**8 **S** Brim Healthcare, Inc., Brentwood, TN

| | 13 | 10 | 214 | 2211 | 175 | 40143 | 250 | 21495 | 9810 | 330 |

MALONE—Franklin County

☒ ALICE HYDE HOSPITAL ASSOCIATION, 115 Park Street, Zip 12953–0729, Mailing Address: P.O. Box 729, Zip 12953–0729; tel. 518/483–3000; John W. Johnson, President and Chief Executive Officer (Total facility includes 75 beds in nursing home–type unit) **A**1 9 10 **F**1 3 7 8 12 13 15 17 18 19 20 22 23 26 28 30 32 33 34 35 36 37 39 40 41 42 44 46 54 56 57 58 60 64 65 67 71 73
Web address: www.northnet.org/ahha

| | 23 | 10 | 153 | 3486 | 115 | 57952 | 257 | 26156 | 13669 | 487 |

MANHASSET—Nassau County

MANHASSET AMBULATORY CARE PAVILION See Long Island Jewish Medical Center, New York

☒ NORTH SHORE UNIVERSITY HOSPITAL, 300 Community Drive, Zip 11030–3876; tel. 516/562–0100; John S. T. Gallagher, Chief Executive Officer (Total facility includes 256 beds in nursing home–type unit) **A**1 2 3 5 8 9 10 **F**1 2 3 4 5 7 8 10 11 12 13 14 15 16 17 18 19 20 21 22 23 25 26 27 28 29 30 31 32 33 34 35 36 37 38 39 40 41 42 43 44 45 46 47 48 49 50 51 52 53 54 55 56 57 58 60 61 63 64 65 66 67 68 70 71 72 73 74 **P**2 5 6 8 **S** North Shore–Long Island Jewish Health System, Great Neck, NY

| | 23 | 10 | 705 | 41877 | 908 | 466388 | 5492 | 718176 | 335613 | 4625 |

MANHATTAN—New York County, See New York City
MARGARETVILLE—Delaware County

☐ MARGARETVILLE MEMORIAL HOSPITAL, Route 28, Zip 12455, Mailing Address: P.O. Box 200, Zip 12455–0200; tel. 914/586–2631; Roger A. Masse, Chief Executive Officer **A**1 9 10 **F**19 21 22 37 44 49 65 67 71 73

| | 23 | 10 | 22 | 587 | 6 | 24869 | 0 | 6100 | 3311 | 120 |

Hospital, Address, Telephone, Administrator, Approval, Facility, and Physician Codes, Health Care System, Network	Classi-fication Codes		Utilization Data					Expense (thousands) of dollars		
★ American Hospital Association (AHA) membership □ Joint Commission on Accreditation of Healthcare Organizations (JCAHO) accreditation + American Osteopathic Healthcare Association (AOHA) membership ○ American Osteopathic Association (AOA) accreditation △ Commission on Accreditation of Rehabilitation Facilities (CARF) accreditation Control codes 61, 63, 64, 71, 72 and 73 indicate hospitals listed by AOHA, but not registered by AHA. For definition of numerical codes, see page A4	Control	Service	Staffed Beds	Admissions	Census	Outpatient Visits	Births	Total	Payroll	Personnel

MASSENA—St. Lawrence County

□ MASSENA MEMORIAL HOSPITAL, One Hospital Drive, Zip 13662-1097; tel. 315/764-1711; Charles F. Fahd, II, Chief Executive Officer **A**1 9 10 **F**1 5 6 7 8 11 12 13 14 15 16 17 19 20 21 22 23 24 25 26 27 28 29 30 32 33 35 36 37 39 40 41 42 44 45 48 49 51 61 65 71 73 74 **P**5

| | | 14 | 10 | 50 | 2893 | 34 | 93951 | 211 | 21599 | 10655 | 293 |

MEDINA—Orleans County

✠ MEDINA MEMORIAL HOSPITAL, 200 Ohio Street, Zip 14103-1095; tel. 716/798-2000; James Sinner, Chief Executive Officer (Total facility includes 30 beds in nursing home–type unit) **A**1 9 10 **F**7 8 12 13 14 15 16 17 19 21 25 27 28 29 30 32 33 34 37 40 41 42 44 45 46 48 49 51 56 64 67 68 70 71 73 74 **P**5 **S** Quorum Health Group/Quorum Health Resources, Inc., Brentwood, TN

| 23 | 10 | 101 | 2593 | 62 | 82401 | 209 | 22554 | 10138 | 375 |

MIDDLETOWN—Orange County

✠ △ HORTON MEDICAL CENTER, 60 Prospect Avenue, Zip 10940-4133; tel. 914/343-2424; Jeffrey D. Hirsch, Executive Vice President and Administrator **A**1 2 7 9 10 **F**3 7 8 11 12 14 15 16 17 19 21 22 28 30 34 35 37 39 40 42 44 46 48 49 51 56 60 61 63 65 67 71 73 74 **P**1 5 **S** Greater Hudson Valley Health System, Newburgh, NY

| 23 | 10 | 168 | 10617 | 157 | 142219 | 1482 | 85719 | 42765 | 887 |

✠ MIDDLETOWN PSYCHIATRIC CENTER, 122 Dorothea Dix Drive, Zip 10940-6198; tel. 914/342-5511; James H. Bopp, Executive Director **A**1 10 **F**2 3 4 8 9 11 12 14 15 16 18 19 20 21 22 25 26 27 30 31 35 37 39 40 41 42 43 44 45 46 48 52 55 56 57 58 59 60 64 65 67 70 71 73 **S** New York State Department of Mental Health, Albany, NY

| 12 | 22 | 205 | 168 | 214 | 45883 | 0 | 28586 | — | 501 |

MINEOLA—Nassau County

✠ WINTHROP–UNIVERSITY HOSPITAL, 259 First Street, Zip 11501; tel. 516/663-2200; Daniel P. Walsh, President and Chief Executive Officer **A**1 2 3 5 8 9 10 **F**3 4 7 8 10 12 13 14 15 16 17 18 19 21 22 26 27 29 30 31 32 34 35 37 38 39 40 41 42 43 44 45 46 49 53 54 55 56 57 58 60 61 63 65 67 68 70 71 73 74 **P**5

| 23 | 10 | 467 | 26713 | 460 | 210247 | 5042 | 289069 | 141744 | 2913 |

MONTOUR FALLS—Schuyler County

✠ SCHUYLER HOSPITAL, 220 Steuben Street, Zip 14865-9709; tel. 607/535-7121; Robert Mincemoyer, President and Chief Executive Officer (Total facility includes 120 beds in nursing home–type unit) (Nonreporting) **A**1 9 10
Web address: www.schuylerhsopital.org

| 23 | 10 | 169 | — | — | — | — | — | — | — |

MONTROSE—Westchester County

✠ VETERANS AFFAIRS HUDSON VALLEY HEALTH CARE SYSTEM–F.D. ROOSEVELT HOSPITAL, (Includes Veteran Affairs Hudson Valley Health Care System–Castle Point Division, Castle Point, Zip 12511-9999; tel. 914/831-2000; Veterans Affairs Hudson Valley Health Care System–Montrose Division, Zip 10548), Mailing Address: P.O. Box 100, Zip 10548-0110; tel. 914/737-4400; Michael A. Sabo, Director (Total facility includes 258 beds in nursing home–type unit) **A**1 3 5 9 **F**2 12 14 15 16 17 19 20 21 22 24 25 26 27 29 30 31 32 34 39 41 42 44 45 46 49 51 52 54 55 56 57 58 59 61 63 64 65 67 71 72 73 74 **S** Department of Veterans Affairs, Washington, DC

| 45 | 22 | 651 | 3699 | 629 | 217007 | 0 | 119185 | 73230 | 1628 |

MOUNT KISCO—Westchester County

✠ NORTHERN WESTCHESTER HOSPITAL CENTER, 400 Main Street, Zip 10549-3477; tel. 914/666-1200; Donald W. Davis, President **A**1 2 9 10 **F**7 8 11 12 15 16 17 19 21 22 26 28 29 30 31 33 34 35 37 38 39 40 41 42 44 45 46 49 52 53 54 55 56 57 60 61 65 67 71 73 74 **P**7 8
Web address: www.nwhc.net

| 23 | 10 | 185 | 9151 | 140 | 61812 | 1898 | 83156 | 40274 | 952 |

MOUNT VERNON—Westchester County

□ MOUNT VERNON HOSPITAL, 12 North Seventh Avenue, Zip 10550-2098; tel. 914/664-8000; Richard L. Petrillo, M.D., Executive Director **A**1 3 5 6 9 10 **F**1 2 3 4 7 8 9 10 11 12 13 15 16 17 19 21 22 26 27 29 30 31 32 33 34 35 37 38 39 40 41 42 43 44 45 47 48 49 52 53 54 55 56 57 58 59 60 61 64 65 67 70 71 73 74 **P**1 5

| 23 | 10 | 148 | 6983 | 125 | 40215 | 577 | 56084 | 29453 | 779 |

NEW HAMPTON—Orange County

□ MID–HUDSON PSYCHIATRIC CENTER, Route 17M, Zip 10958, Mailing Address: P.O. Box 158, Zip 10958-0158; tel. 914/374-3171; Richard Bennett, Executive Director **A**1 10 **F**2 4 8 9 11 12 18 19 20 21 22 24 27 29 30 31 35 37 38 39 40 41 42 43 44 45 46 48 50 52 54 55 60 63 64 65 67 70 71 **P**6
Web address: www.omh.state.ny.us

| 12 | 22 | 277 | 321 | 287 | 0 | 0 | — | — | 567 |

NEW HYDE PARK—Queens County, See New York City

NEW ROCHELLE—Westchester County

✠ SOUND SHORE MEDICAL CENTER OF WESTCHESTER, 16 Guion Place, Zip 10802; tel. 914/632-5000; John R. Spicer, President and Chief Executive Officer (Total facility includes 150 beds in nursing home–type unit) **A**1 2 3 5 8 9 10 **F**1 3 8 10 14 15 16 17 18 19 21 22 26 27 28 29 30 31 32 33 34 35 36 37 39 40 41 42 44 45 46 48 49 51 53 54 55 56 57 58 59 60 61 63 64 65 66 67 68 70 71 72 73 **P**4 5 6 7 8
Web address: www.ssmc.org

| 23 | 10 | 257 | 11154 | 181 | 204743 | 1118 | 110393 | 55215 | 1187 |

NEW YORK (Includes all hospitals located within the five boroughs)
  BRONX - Bronx County (Mailing Address - Bronx)
  BROOKLYN - Kings County (Mailing Address - Brooklyn)
  MANHATTAN - New York County (Mailing Address - New York)
  QUEENS - Queens County (Mailing Addresses - Bellerose, Elmhurst, Far Rockaway, Flushing, Forest Hills, Glen Oaks, Holliswood, Jackson Heights, Jamaica, Little Neck, Long Island City, New Hyde Park, and Queens Village)
  RICHMOND VALLEY - Richmond County (Mailing Address - Staten Island)
  BAYLEY SETON CAMPUS See Sisters of Charity Medical Center

Hospital, Address, Telephone, Administrator, Approval, Facility, and Physician Codes, Health Care System, Network	Classi-fication Codes		Utilization Data					Expense (thousands) of dollars		
★ American Hospital Association (AHA) membership □ Joint Commission on Accreditation of Healthcare Organizations (JCAHO) accreditation + American Osteopathic Healthcare Association (AOHA) membership ○ American Osteopathic Association (AOA) accreditation △ Commission on Accreditation of Rehabilitation Facilities (CARF) accreditation Control codes 61, 63, 64, 71, 72 and 73 indicate hospitals listed by AOHA, but not registered by AHA. For definition of numerical codes, see page A4	Control	Service	Staffed Beds	Admissions	Census	Outpatient Visits	Births	Total	Payroll	Personnel

✠ BELLEVUE HOSPITAL CENTER, (Includes Bellevue Comprehensive General Care, Bellevue Physical Medicine and Rehabilitation Services, Bellevue Psychiatric Services, Bellevue Tuberculosis Services, Comprehensive Ambulatory Care Services: Level I Trauma Center), 462 First Avenue, Zip 10016–9198, Mailing Address: 462 First Avenue, ME–8, Zip 10016–9198; tel. 212/562–4141; Carlos Perez, Executive Director **A**1 2 3 5 9 10 **F**1 2 3 4 7 8 10 11 12 13 14 15 16 17 18 19 20 21 22 23 25 26 27 28 29 30 31 32 34 35 37 38 39 40 41 42 43 44 45 46 47 48 49 51 52 53 54 55 56 57 58 59 60 61 64 65 66 67 68 70 71 72 73 74 **P**6 **S** New York City Health and Hospitals Corporation, New York, NY	14	10	811	25135	729	553442	2013	326317	226127	4876
✠ BETH ISRAEL MEDICAL CENTER, (Includes Beth Israel Medical Center–Herbert and Nell Singer Division, 170 East End Avenue, Zip 10128; tel. 212/870–9000; Beth Israel Medical Center–Kings Highway Division, 3201 Kings Highway, Zip 11234; tel. 718/252–3000), First Avenue and 16th Street, Zip 10003–3803; tel. 212/420–2000; Matthew E. Fink, M.D., President and Chief Executive Officer **A**1 3 5 6 8 9 10 **F**2 3 4 7 8 9 10 11 12 13 14 15 16 17 18 19 20 21 22 23 25 26 28 29 30 31 32 33 34 35 36 37 38 39 40 41 42 43 44 45 46 47 49 50 51 52 53 54 55 56 57 58 59 60 61 63 64 65 66 67 68 70 71 72 73 74 **P**5 6 7 8 **S** Continuum Health Partners, New York, NY **Web address:** www.bethisraelny.org BETH ISRAEL MEDICAL CENTER–KINGS HIGHWAY DIVISION See Beth Israel Medical Center	23	10	1254	54440	1006	508752	5460	835219	421397	8536
✠ BRONX CHILDREN'S PSYCHIATRIC CENTER, 1000 Waters Place, Bronx, Zip 10461–2799; tel. 718/892–0808; E. Richard Feinberg, M.D., Executive Director (Nonreporting) **A**1 3 **S** New York State Department of Mental Health, Albany, NY	12	52	75	—	—	—	—	—	—	—
✠ BRONX PSYCHIATRIC CENTER, 1500 Waters Place, Bronx, Zip 10461–2796; tel. 718/931–0600; LeRoy Carmichael, Executive Director (Nonreporting) **A**1 3 5 10 **S** New York State Department of Mental Health, Albany, NY	12	22	658	—	—	—	—	—	—	—
✠ BRONX–LEBANON HOSPITAL CENTER, (Includes Concourse Division, 1650 Grand Concourse, Zip 10457; tel. 212/590–1800; Fulton Division, 1276 Fulton Avenue, Zip 10456; tel. 718/590–1800), 1276 Fulton Avenue, Bronx, Zip 10456–3499; tel. 718/590–1800; Miguel A. Fuentes, President and Chief Executive Officer (Nonreporting) **A**1 2 3 5 8 9 10	23	10	576	—	—	—	—	—	—	—
□ BROOKDALE HOSPITAL MEDICAL CENTER, Linden Boulevard at Brookdale Plaza, Brooklyn, Zip 11212–3198; tel. 718/240–5000; Frank J. Maddalena, President and Chief Executive Officer (Total facility includes 448 beds in nursing home–type unit) (Nonreporting) **A**1 3 5 8 9 10 12 **Web address:** www.brookdalehospital.org	23	10	1048	—	—	—	—	—	—	—
✠ BROOKLYN HOSPITAL CENTER, (Includes Caledonian Campus, 100 Parkside Avenue, Zip 11226; tel. 718/940–2000; Downtown Campus, 121 DeKalb Avenue, Zip 11201), 121 DeKalb Avenue, Brooklyn, Zip 11201–5493; tel. 718/250–8005; Frederick D. Alley, President and Chief Executive Officer **A**1 2 3 5 8 9 10 **F**1 2 4 7 8 10 11 12 13 15 16 17 19 20 21 22 25 26 27 28 29 30 31 32 33 34 35 37 38 39 40 41 42 43 44 45 46 47 49 51 53 54 55 56 57 58 59 60 61 63 64 65 67 68 70 71 73 74 **P**5 **S** New York & Presbyterian Healthcare, New York, NY BROOKLYN JEWISH DIVISION See Interfaith Medical Center	23	10	653	27071	477	203483	3985	275814	151172	3359
✠ CABRINI MEDICAL CENTER, 227 East 19th Street, Zip 10003–2600; tel. 212/995–6000; Jeffrey Frerichs, President and Chief Executive Officer **A**1 2 3 5 8 9 10 **F**2 8 11 12 14 15 16 17 19 21 22 23 25 26 27 28 29 30 31 32 33 34 35 37 39 41 42 44 46 48 49 51 52 54 56 58 59 60 63 65 70 71 73 74 **P**5 8 **Web address:** www.cabrininy.org CALEDONIAN CAMPUS See Brooklyn Hospital Center	21	10	319	11609	264	74196	0	169986	90420	1789
✠ CALVARY HOSPITAL, (SPECIALTY TREATMENT HOSPITAL–ONCOLOGY), 1740 Eastchester Road, Bronx, Zip 10461–2392; tel. 718/863–6900; Frank A. Calamari, President and Chief Executive Officer **A**1 9 10 **F**8 14 16 19 20 21 22 32 33 34 39 41 42 45 54 60 65 67 73 **Web address:** www.calvaryhospital.org	21	49	200	2434	170	19038	0	52548	30705	631
✠ CATHOLIC MEDICAL CENTERS, (Includes Holy Family Home, 1740 84th Street, Brooklyn, Zip 11214; tel. 718/232–3666; Mary Immaculate Hospital, 152–11 89th Avenue, Zip 11432; tel. 718/558–2000; Monsignor James H Fitzpatrick Pavilion for Skilled Nursing Care, 152–11 89th Avenue, Zip 11432; tel. 718/558–2800; St. John's Queens Hospital, 90–02 Queens Boulevard, Flushing, Zip 11373; tel. 718/558–1000; Sister ; St. Joseph's Hospital, 158–40 79th Avenue, Flushing, Zip 11366; tel. 718/558–6200; St. Mary's Hospital of Brooklyn, 170 Buffalo Avenue, Brooklyn, Zip 11213; tel. 718/221–3000), 88–25 153rd Street, Jamaica, Zip 11432–3731; tel. 718/558–6900; William D. McGuire, President and Chief Executive Officer (Total facility includes 603 beds in nursing home–type unit) **A**1 2 3 5 8 9 10 **F**2 3 5 8 11 12 14 15 16 17 18 19 20 21 22 23 25 26 28 30 31 32 33 34 35 37 38 39 40 41 42 44 45 46 47 49 51 58 59 60 64 65 66 67 68 70 71 72 73 74 **P**5	21	10	1432	40644	1249	1233564	4427	—	—	5572
✠ COLER MEMORIAL HOSPITAL, Roosevelt Island, Zip 10044; tel. 212/848–6000; Samuel Lehrfeld, Executive Director (Total facility includes 775 beds in nursing home–type unit) **A**1 10 **F**20 26 31 33 41 46 48 54 64 65 71 73 **S** New York City Health and Hospitals Corporation, New York, NY CONCOURSE DIVISION See Bronx–Lebanon Hospital Center	14	48	1025	874	928	0	0	—	56822	1279

Hospital, Address, Telephone, Administrator, Approval, Facility, and Physician Codes, Health Care System, Network	Classification Codes		Utilization Data					Expense (thousands) of dollars		
	Control	Service	Staffed Beds	Admissions	Census	Outpatient Visits	Births	Total	Payroll	Personnel

★ American Hospital Association (AHA) membership
☐ Joint Commission on Accreditation of Healthcare Organizations (JCAHO) accreditation
+ American Osteopathic Healthcare Association (AOHA) membership
○ American Osteopathic Association (AOA) accreditation
△ Commission on Accreditation of Rehabilitation Facilities (CARF) accreditation
Control codes 61, 63, 64, 71, 72 and 73 indicate hospitals listed by AOHA, but not registered by AHA. For definition of numerical codes, see page A4

Hospital	Control	Service	Staffed Beds	Admissions	Census	Outpatient Visits	Births	Total	Payroll	Personnel
⊠ CONEY ISLAND HOSPITAL, 2601 Ocean Parkway, Brooklyn, Zip 11235–7795; tel. 718/616–3000; William Walsh, Executive Director **A**1 3 5 9 10 **F**3 4 5 8 10 11 12 14 15 16 17 18 19 20 21 22 23 25 26 27 28 30 31 32 34 35 37 39 40 41 42 44 46 48 49 51 52 53 54 55 56 57 58 59 60 61 65 67 68 70 71 73 74 **P**6 **S** New York City Health and Hospitals Corporation, New York, NY	14	10	409	15993	343	367967	1300	200274	115343	2452
CORNERSTONE OF MEDICAL ARTS CENTER HOSPITAL, 57 West 57th Street, Zip 10019–2802; tel. 212/755–0200; Norman J. Sokolow, Chairman and Chief Executive Officer **A**9 **F**2 3 12 15 16 17 27 46 54 58 59 65 68 **Web address:** www.nyee.edu	33	82	222	5100	86	16000	0	13750	6800	150
⊠ CREEDMOOR PSYCHIATRIC CENTER, Jamaica, Mailing Address: 80–45 Winchester Boulevard, Queens Village, Zip 11427–2199; tel. 718/264–3300; Charlotte Seltzer, Chief Executive Officer **A**1 3 10 **F**12 15 16 20 52 58 65 73 **S** New York State Department of Mental Health, Albany, NY	12	22	524	378	551	216000	0	9687	—	1265
⊠ DOCTORS' HOSPITAL OF STATEN ISLAND, 1050 Targee Street, Staten Island, Zip 10304–4499; tel. 718/390–1400; Stephen N. F. Anderson, Director (Nonreporting) **A**1 9 10	33	10	117	—	—	—	—	—	—	—
DOWNTOWN CAMPUS See Brooklyn Hospital Center										
⊠ △ ELMHURST HOSPITAL CENTER, 79–01 Broadway, Elmhurst, Zip 11373; tel. 718/334–4000; Pete Velez, Executive Director **A**1 2 3 5 7 8 9 10 **F**2 3 4 5 7 8 9 10 11 12 13 14 15 16 17 18 19 20 21 22 23 25 26 27 28 29 30 31 32 33 34 35 37 38 39 40 41 42 43 44 45 46 47 48 49 50 51 52 53 54 55 56 57 58 59 60 61 63 64 65 66 67 68 69 70 71 73 74 **P**6 **S** New York City Health and Hospitals Corporation, New York, NY	14	10	525	21835	434	586920	4232	245843	163812	3655
FLUSHING HOSPITAL MEDICAL CENTER See New York Flushing Hospital Medical Center										
FULTON DIVISION See Bronx–Lebanon Hospital Center										
⊠ △ GOLDWATER MEMORIAL HOSPITAL, Franklin D. Roosevelt Island, Zip 10044; tel. 212/318–8000; Samuel Lehrfeld, Executive Director (Total facility includes 574 beds in nursing home–type unit) **A**1 3 5 7 10 **F**19 22 26 31 41 46 48 54 64 65 71 73 **S** New York City Health and Hospitals Corporation, New York, NY **Web address:** www.coler–goldwater.org	14	48	991	968	873	0	0	—	57966	1253
⊠ GRACIE SQUARE HOSPITAL, 420 East 76th Street, Zip 10021–3104; tel. 212/988–4400; Frank Bruno, Chief Executive Officer **A**1 9 10 **F**3 14 15 16 39 46 52 57 59 65 **P**1 5 **S** New York & Presbyterian Healthcare, New York, NY	23	22	130	2422	113	39707	0	25178	13875	312
⊠ △ HARLEM HOSPITAL CENTER, (Includes Harlem General Care Unit and Harlem Psychiatric Unit), 506 Lenox Avenue, Zip 10037–1894; tel. 212/939–1000; John M. Palmer, Ph.D., Executive Director (Nonreporting) **A**1 2 3 5 7 8 9 10 **S** New York City Health and Hospitals Corporation, New York, NY	14	10	414	—	—	—	—	—	—	—
HILLSIDE HOSPITAL See Long Island Jewish Medical Center										
⊠ HOLLISWOOD HOSPITAL, 87–37 Palermo Street, Holliswood, Zip 11423; tel. 718/776–8181; Jeffrey Borenstein, M.D., Chief Executive Officer and Medical Director **A**1 9 10 **F**12 15 26 52 53 54 55 56 57 58 59 65	33	22	100	2445	90	—	0	16224	7295	32
⊠ △ HOSPITAL FOR JOINT DISEASES ORTHOPAEDIC INSTITUTE, 301 East 17th Street, Zip 10003–3890; tel. 212/598–6000; John N. Kastanis, FACHE, President and Chief Executive Officer **A**1 3 5 7 9 10 **F**4 5 7 8 10 11 12 13 14 15 16 17 19 20 22 23 24 25 26 28 29 30 31 32 33 34 35 37 38 39 40 41 42 43 44 45 46 47 48 49 50 51 52 53 54 55 56 57 58 59 60 61 64 65 66 68 71 72 73 74 **P**5 **Web address:** www.hjd.edu	23	47	163	5959	126	67896	0	122771	53281	1054
⊠ HOSPITAL FOR SPECIAL SURGERY, 535 East 70th Street, Zip 10021–4898; tel. 212/606–1000; John R. Reynolds, President and Chief Executive Officer **A**1 3 5 6 8 9 10 **F**1 2 3 4 5 6 7 8 9 10 11 12 13 14 15 16 17 18 19 20 21 22 23 24 25 26 27 28 29 30 31 32 33 34 35 36 37 38 39 40 41 42 43 44 45 46 47 48 49 50 51 52 53 54 55 56 57 58 59 60 61 63 64 65 66 67 68 70 71 72 73 74 **P**5 8 **S** New York & Presbyterian Healthcare, New York, NY **Web address:** www.hss.edu	23	47	138	7438	106	169813	0	170686	69671	1685
☐ INTERFAITH MEDICAL CENTER, (Includes Brooklyn Jewish Division, 555 Prospect Place, Zip 11238; tel. 718/935–7000; St. John's Episcopal Hospital Division, 1545 Atlantic Avenue, Zip 11213; tel. 718/604–6000), 555 Prospect Place, Brooklyn, Zip 11238–4299; tel. 718/935–7000; Corbett A. Price, Chief Executive Officer **A**1 3 5 6 9 10 **F**2 3 4 7 8 9 10 11 12 13 15 16 17 18 19 20 21 22 25 26 28 29 30 31 32 33 34 35 37 38 39 40 42 43 44 46 47 49 52 54 56 57 58 59 60 61 64 65 67 71 73 74	23	10	385	14861	357	226445	1000	176348	100223	1647
⊠ JACOBI MEDICAL CENTER, Pelham Parkway South and Eastchester Road, Bronx, Zip 10461–1197; tel. 718/918–5000; Joseph S. Orlando, Executive Director **A**1 3 5 8 9 10 **F**2 3 4 7 8 9 10 11 12 13 14 15 16 17 18 19 20 21 22 25 26 28 29 30 31 32 33 34 35 37 38 39 40 41 42 43 44 45 46 47 48 49 51 52 53 54 55 56 57 58 59 60 61 64 65 67 68 70 71 73 74 **P**3 **S** New York City Health and Hospitals Corporation, New York, NY **Web address:** www.nychhc.org	14	10	549	19360	425	428314	2277	209745	170371	3176
⊠ JAMAICA HOSPITAL MEDICAL CENTER, 8900 Van Wyck Expressway, Jamaica, Zip 11418–2832; tel. 718/206–6000; David P. Rosen, President **A**1 3 5 9 10 12 13 **F**4 7 8 10 11 12 14 15 16 17 18 19 20 21 22 24 25 26 27 28 30 31 32 34 35 37 38 40 41 42 43 44 47 48 49 51 52 54 55 56 57 58 60 61 63 64 65 66 67 68 70 71 72 73 74 **P**5 7 **Web address:** www.Jamaicahospital.org	23	10	365	19590	332	338812	3123	229016	116209	2676

Hospital, Address, Telephone, Administrator, Approval, Facility, and Physician Codes, Health Care System, Network	Classi-fication Codes		Utilization Data					Expense (thousands) of dollars		
★ American Hospital Association (AHA) membership □ Joint Commission on Accreditation of Healthcare Organizations (JCAHO) accreditation + American Osteopathic Healthcare Association (AOHA) membership ○ American Osteopathic Association (AOA) accreditation △ Commission on Accreditation of Rehabilitation Facilities (CARF) accreditation Control codes 61, 63, 64, 71, 72 and 73 indicate hospitals listed by AOHA, but not registered by AHA. For definition of numerical codes, see page A4	Control	Service	Staffed Beds	Admissions	Census	Outpatient Visits	Births	Total	Payroll	Personnel
⊞ KINGS COUNTY HOSPITAL CENTER, 451 Clarkson Avenue, Brooklyn, Zip 11203–2097; tel. 718/245–3131; Jean G. Leon, R.N., Senior Vice President **A**1 2 3 5 9 10 **F**1 2 3 4 5 7 8 11 12 13 15 16 17 18 19 20 21 22 23 24 25 27 28 29 30 31 34 37 38 39 40 41 42 44 45 46 47 48 49 50 51 52 53 54 55 56 58 60 61 63 65 66 68 70 71 72 73 74 **P**6 **S** New York City Health and Hospitals Corporation, New York, NY	14	10	728	25275	632	706212	2205	291968	218925	4661
⊞ KINGSBORO PSYCHIATRIC CENTER, 681 Clarkson Avenue, Brooklyn, Zip 11203–2199; tel. 718/221–7395; John M. Palmer, Ph.D., Director (Nonreporting) **A**1 3 5 10 **S** New York State Department of Mental Health, Albany, NY	12	22	400	—		—		—		—
⊞ △ KINGSBROOK JEWISH MEDICAL CENTER, 585 Schenectady Avenue, Brooklyn, Zip 11203–1891; tel. 718/604–5000; Milton M. Gutman, Chief Executive Officer (Total facility includes 538 beds in nursing home–type unit) **A**1 3 5 7 9 10 **F**1 8 11 12 14 15 16 17 19 21 22 25 26 27 28 29 30 32 33 34 35 37 39 41 44 45 46 48 49 51 52 54 55 57 58 64 65 71 73 **P**5	23	10	864	8900	779	129009	—	174292	96635	2036
⊞ LENOX HILL HOSPITAL, 100 East 77th Street, Zip 10021–1883; tel. 212/434–2000; Gladys George, President and Chief Executive Officer **A**1 3 5 8 9 10 **F**3 4 5 7 8 10 11 12 13 14 15 16 17 18 19 20 21 22 24 25 26 27 28 29 30 31 32 34 35 37 38 39 40 41 42 43 44 45 46 47 49 51 52 53 54 55 56 57 58 60 61 63 65 66 67 68 71 72 73 74 **P**1 5 7 8	23	10	616	26457	489	278383	3792	327924	155515	3145
⊞ LINCOLN MEDICAL AND MENTAL HEALTH CENTER, 234 East 149th Street, Bronx, Zip 10451–9998; tel. 718/579–5700; Jose R. Sanchez, Executive Director **A**1 3 9 10 **F**3 7 8 11 12 13 14 15 16 17 18 19 20 22 25 26 27 28 29 30 31 32 34 37 39 40 42 44 45 46 47 51 52 53 54 55 56 57 58 60 61 65 68 70 71 72 73 74 **P**5 **S** New York City Health and Hospitals Corporation, New York, NY	14	10	330	20356	296	468643	3093	285628	145415	2933
⊞ LONG ISLAND COLLEGE HOSPITAL, 339 Hicks Street, Brooklyn, Zip 11201–5509; tel. 718/780–1000; Peter A. Kelly, Interim President and Chief Executive Officer **A**1 2 3 5 8 9 10 **F**2 3 5 7 8 10 11 12 13 14 15 16 17 18 19 20 21 22 23 25 26 27 28 30 31 32 33 34 35 37 38 39 40 41 42 44 46 47 48 49 51 52 53 54 55 56 57 58 59 60 61 65 66 67 71 72 73 74 **P**5 **S** Continuum Health Partners, New York, NY **Web address:** www.lich.org	23	10	419	19630	349	178241	2974	237436	119485	2694
⊞ △ LONG ISLAND JEWISH MEDICAL CENTER, (Includes Hillside Hospital, 75–59 263rd Street, Glen Oaks, Zip 11004; tel. 718/470–8000; Manhasset Ambulatory Care Pavilion, 1554 Northern Boulevard, Manhasset, Zip 11030; tel. 516/365–2070; Schneider Children's Hospital, 270–05 76th Avenue, Zip 11040; tel. 718/470–3000), 270–05 76th Avenue, New Hyde Park, Zip 11040–1496; tel. 718/470–7000; David R. Dantzker, M.D., President **A**1 2 3 5 7 8 9 10 13 **F**1 2 3 4 5 6 7 8 10 11 12 13 14 15 16 17 18 19 20 21 22 23 25 26 27 28 29 30 31 32 34 35 36 37 38 39 40 41 42 43 44 45 46 47 48 49 50 51 52 53 54 55 56 57 58 59 60 61 63 64 65 66 67 68 70 71 72 73 74 **P**2 5 6 8 **S** North Shore– Long Island Jewish Health System, Great Neck, NY **Web address:** www.lij.edu	23	10	784	34757	706	511800	—	571319	301514	5520
⊞ LUTHERAN MEDICAL CENTER, 150 55th Street, Brooklyn, Zip 11220–2570; tel. 718/630–7000; Dominic J. Lodato, Interim President (Nonreporting) **A**1 3 5 9 10 12 13 **Web address:** www.LMCMC.COM	23	10	433	—		—		—		—
⊞ MAIMONIDES MEDICAL CENTER, 4802 Tenth Avenue, Brooklyn, Zip 11219–2916; tel. 718/283–6000; Stanley Brezenoff, President **A**1 3 5 8 9 10 12 13 **F**1 4 7 8 10 11 12 13 14 15 16 17 18 19 20 21 22 25 26 27 28 30 31 32 34 35 37 38 39 40 41 42 43 44 46 47 49 51 52 53 54 56 57 58 59 61 62 63 65 66 67 68 69 71 72 73 **P**5 7 8	23	10	668	29972	557	206006	4503	430200	217112	4007
⊞ MANHATTAN EYE, EAR AND THROAT HOSPITAL, 210 East 64th Street, Zip 10021–9885; tel. 212/838–9200; George A. Sarkar, Ph.D., JD, Executive Director **A**1 3 5 9 10 **F**14 15 16 22 44 65 67 68 73 **Web address:** www.meeth.org	23	45	30	2540	11	96464	0	41983	17832	470
⊞ MANHATTAN PSYCHIATRIC CENTER–WARD'S ISLAND, 600 East 125th Street, Zip 10035–9998; tel. 212/369–0500; Eileen Consilvio, R.N., MS, Executive Director (Nonreporting) **A**1 3 5 10 **S** New York State Department of Mental Health, Albany, NY	12	22	745	—		—		—		—
MARY IMMACULATE HOSPITAL See Catholic Medical Centers										
⊞ MEMORIAL HOSPITAL FOR CANCER AND ALLIED DISEASES, 1275 York Avenue, Zip 10021–6094; tel. 212/639–2000; John R. Gunn, Executive Vice President (Nonreporting) **A**1 2 3 5 8 9 10	23	49	404	—		—		—		—
⊞ METROPOLITAN HOSPITAL CENTER, (Includes Metropolitan General Care Unit, Metropolitan Drug Detoxification and Metropolitan Psychiatric Unit), 1901 First Avenue, Zip 10029–7496; tel. 212/423–6262; Jose R. Sanchez, Executive Director **A**1 3 5 8 9 10 **F**1 2 3 7 8 10 11 12 13 14 15 16 17 18 19 20 21 22 25 26 27 28 29 30 31 32 34 35 37 38 39 40 41 42 44 45 46 47 48 49 51 52 53 54 55 56 57 58 59 60 61 63 65 71 73 74 **S** New York City Health and Hospitals Corporation, New York, NY	14	10	351	13318	336	401378	1893	218385	119131	2849
⊞ MONTEFIORE MEDICAL CENTER, (Includes Jack D Weiler Hospital of Albert Einstein College of Medicine, 1825 Eastchester Road, Zip 10461–2373; tel. 718/904–2000; Loeb Center Nursing Rehabilitation, 111 East 210th Street), 111 East 210th Street, Bronx, Zip 10467–2490; tel. 718/920–4321; Spencer Foreman, M.D., President (Total facility includes 80 beds in nursing home–type unit) **A**1 2 3 5 8 9 10 **F**3 4 7 8 10 11 12 13 15 16 17 19 20 21 22 23 25 26 28 29 30 31 32 33 34 35 37 38 39 40 41 42 43 44 45 46 48 49 50 51 52 53 54 55 56 57 58 59 60 61 63 64 65 66 67 68 71 73 74 **P**5 7 **Web address:** www.montefiore.org	23	10	1032	44388	805	771234	3745	1057487	541884	9484

Hospital, Address, Telephone, Administrator, Approval, Facility, and Physician Codes, Health Care System, Network	Classi-fication Codes		Utilization Data					Expense (thousands) of dollars		
★ American Hospital Association (AHA) membership □ Joint Commission on Accreditation of Healthcare Organizations (JCAHO) accreditation + American Osteopathic Healthcare Association (AOHA) membership ○ American Osteopathic Association (AOA) accreditation △ Commission on Accreditation of Rehabilitation Facilities (CARF) accreditation Control codes 61, 63, 64, 71, 72 and 73 indicate hospitals listed by AOHA, but not registered by AHA. For definition of numerical codes, see page A4	Control	Service	Staffed Beds	Admissions	Census	Outpatient Visits	Births	Total	Payroll	Personnel

Hospital	Control	Service	Staffed Beds	Admissions	Census	Outpatient Visits	Births	Total	Payroll	Personnel
⊠ MOUNT SINAI–NYU HOSPITALS/HEALTH SYSTEM, (Includes Mount Sinai Medical Center, One Gustave L. Levy Place, Zip 10029–6574; tel. 212/241–6500; Mount Sinai–NYU Medical Center, 550 First Avenue, Zip 10016–4576; tel. 212/263–7300; Theresa A. Bischoff, Deputy Provost and Executive Vice President; Rusk Institute), One Gustave Levy Place, Zip 10019–6574; tel. 212/241–6500; John W. Rowe, M.D., President (Nonreporting) **A**1 3 5 8 9 10	23	10	1860	—	—	—	—	—	—	—
⊠ NEW YORK COMMUNITY HOSPITAL, 2525 Kings Highway, Brooklyn, Zip 11229–1798; tel. 718/692–5300; Lin H. Mo, President and Chief Executive Officer (Nonreporting) **A**1 9 10 **S** New York & Presbyterian Healthcare, New York, NY	23	10	134	—	—	—	—	—	—	—
⊠ NEW YORK EYE AND EAR INFIRMARY, 310 East 14th Street, Zip 10003–4201; tel. 212/979–4000; Joseph P. Corcoran, President and Chief Executive Officer **A**1 3 5 9 10 **F**12 13 17 19 20 25 28 30 34 44 51 60 65 67 68 70 71 73 **P**8	23	45	30	1752	10	162216	0	52196	25904	594
⊠ NEW YORK FLUSHING HOSPITAL MEDICAL CENTER, (Formerly Flushing Hospital Medical Center), 45th Avenue at Parsons Boulevard, Flushing, Zip 11355–2100; tel. 718/670–5000; Stephen S. Mills, President and Chief Executive Officer **A**1 3 5 9 10 **F**2 3 4 7 8 10 11 12 13 14 15 16 17 18 19 20 21 22 25 28 29 30 31 32 34 35 37 38 39 40 42 43 44 45 46 49 51 53 54 55 57 58 60 61 65 67 70 71 73 **P**5 **S** New York & Presbyterian Healthcare, New York, NY	23	10	250	13355	213	117361	2683	132011	66808	1404
⊠ NEW YORK HOSPITAL MEDICAL CENTER OF QUEENS, 56–45 Main Street, Flushing, Zip 11355–5000; tel. 718/670–1231; Stephen S. Mills, President and Chief Executive Officer **A**1 2 3 5 9 10 **F**3 4 8 9 10 11 12 13 14 15 16 17 18 19 20 21 22 24 25 26 27 28 29 30 31 32 33 34 35 37 39 40 41 42 43 44 45 46 47 49 51 52 53 54 58 60 61 64 65 66 67 70 71 73 74 **P**3 4 5 7 **S** New York & Presbyterian Healthcare, New York, NY **Web address:** www.nyhq.org	23	10	457	21884	373	286149	2486	254185	117360	2384
NEW YORK HOSPITAL, CORNELL UNIVERSITY MEDICAL CENTER See New York Presbyterian Hospital										
⊠ NEW YORK METHODIST HOSPITAL, 506 Sixth Street, Brooklyn, Zip 11215–3645; tel. 718/780–3000; Mark J. Mundy, President and Chief Executive Officer **A**1 2 3 5 8 9 10 **F**5 7 8 10 11 12 13 14 16 17 19 21 22 25 26 28 30 31 32 34 35 37 38 40 41 42 44 45 46 48 49 51 52 56 57 58 60 61 63 65 66 67 70 71 72 73 74 **P**5 7 **S** New York & Presbyterian Healthcare, New York, NY **Web address:** www.nym.org	23	10	560	22383	469	268679	3308	247211	120119	2606
⊠ △ NEW YORK PRESBYTERIAN HOSPITAL, (Includes New York Hospital, Cornell University Medical Center, Mailing Address: 525 East 68th Street, Zip 10021–4885; New York Hospital, Westchester Division; Payne Whitney Psychiatric Clinic; Presbyterian Hospital in the City of New York, Columbia–Presbyterian Medical Center, Zip 10032–3784; tel. 212/305–2500), 525 East 68th Street, Zip 10021–4885; tel. 212/746–5454; David B. Skinner, M.D., Vice Chairman and Chief Executive Officer; William T. Speck, President and Chief Operating Officer **A**1 2 3 5 7 8 9 10 **F**1 2 3 4 5 6 7 8 9 10 11 12 13 14 15 16 17 18 19 20 21 22 23 24 25 26 27 28 29 30 31 32 33 34 35 36 37 38 39 40 41 42 43 44 45 46 47 48 49 50 51 52 53 54 55 56 57 58 59 60 61 63 64 65 66 67 68 70 71 72 73 74 **P**1 2 4 5 7 **S** New York & Presbyterian Healthcare, New York, NY	23	10	2278	80883	1751	1003542	9273	1482020	702341	
⊠ NEW YORK STATE PSYCHIATRIC INSTITUTE, 1051 Riverside Drive, Zip 10032–2695; tel. 212/543–5000; John M. Oldham, M.D., Director **A**1 3 5 10 **F**14 15 16 52 53 55 57 58 59 **S** New York State Department of Mental Health, Albany, NY	12	22	58	439	50	50992	0	—	—	—
□ NEW YORK UNIVERSITY DOWNTOWN HOSPITAL, 170 William Street, Zip 10038–2649; tel. 212/312–5000; Leonard A. Aubrey, President and Chief Executive Officer **A**1 3 5 9 10 **F**3 7 8 12 16 17 19 20 22 25 26 28 29 30 31 32 34 37 39 40 43 44 45 46 49 51 56 65 66 71 73 74 **P**5 7 8 **Web address:** www.nyudh.med.nyu.edu	23	10	148	8297	112	98921	1860	107354	56134	1018
NEW YORK UNIVERSITY HOSPITALS CENTER See Mount Sinai–NYU Medical Center										
⊠ NORTH CENTRAL BRONX HOSPITAL, 3424 Kossuth Avenue, Bronx, Zip 10467–2489; tel. 718/519–3500; Arthur Wagner, Chief Operating Officer **A**1 3 5 9 10 **F**2 3 4 7 8 9 10 11 12 13 14 15 16 17 19 20 21 22 25 26 28 29 30 31 32 33 34 35 37 38 40 41 42 43 44 45 46 47 48 49 51 52 53 54 55 56 57 58 59 60 61 64 65 67 68 70 71 73 74 **P**3 **S** New York City Health and Hospitals Corporation, New York, NY	14	10	255	9846	198	247427	3199	117144	82962	1499
⊠ NORTH GENERAL HOSPITAL, 1879 Madison Avenue, Zip 10035–2745; tel. 212/423–4000; Thomas P. Long, Executive Vice President **A**1 3 5 9 10 **F**1 2 3 4 5 6 8 9 10 12 13 14 15 16 17 18 19 20 21 22 23 25 26 27 28 29 30 31 32 33 34 35 36 37 38 39 40 41 42 43 44 45 46 47 48 49 50 51 52 53 54 55 56 57 58 59 61 62 63 64 65 66 67 69 70 71 72 73 74 **P**7 8	23	10	200	6122	114	98072	0	102431	46728	1020
⊠ NORTH SHORE UNIVERSITY HOSPITAL–FOREST HILLS, Flushing, Mailing Address: 102–01 66th Road, Zip 11375; tel. 718/830–4000; Andrew J. Mitchell, Vice President, Administration (Nonreporting) **A**1 2 5 9 10 **S** North Shore– Long Island Jewish Health System, Great Neck, NY	23	10	231							
⊠ OUR LADY OF MERCY MEDICAL CENTER, (Includes Florence D'Urso Pavilion, 1870 Pelham Parkway South, Zip 10461; tel. 212/430–6000), 600 East 233rd Street, Bronx, Zip 10466–2697; tel. 718/920–9000; Gary S. Horan, FACHE, President and Chief Executive Officer **A**1 2 3 5 8 9 10 **F**3 4 7 8 11 12 13 14 15 16 17 20 22 25 26 28 30 31 32 34 36 37 38 39 40 42 44 45 46 49 51 52 54 56 57 58 60 61 62 65 66 67 68 71 73 74 **P**1 5 **S** Our Lady of Mercy Healthcare System, Inc., New York, NY **Web address:** www.ourladyofmercy.com	21	10	478	17852	373	292514	2674	—	—	2377

Hospital, Address, Telephone, Administrator, Approval, Facility, and Physician Codes, Health Care System, Network	Classi-fication Codes		Utilization Data					Expense (thousands) of dollars		
	Control	Service	Staffed Beds	Admissions	Census	Outpatient Visits	Births	Total	Payroll	Personnel

★ American Hospital Association (AHA) membership
□ Joint Commission on Accreditation of Healthcare Organizations (JCAHO) accreditation
+ American Osteopathic Healthcare Association (AOHA) membership
○ American Osteopathic Association (AOA) accreditation
△ Commission on Accreditation of Rehabilitation Facilities (CARF) accreditation
Control codes 61, 63, 64, 71, 72 and 73 indicate hospitals listed by AOHA, but not registered by AHA. For definition of numerical codes, see page A4

□ PARKWAY HOSPITAL, 70–35 113th Street, Flushing, Zip 11375; tel. 718/990–4100; Paul E. Svensson, Chief Executive Officer (Nonreporting) **A**1 9 10	33	10	251	—	—	—	—	—	—	—
□ ○ PENINSULA HOSPITAL CENTER, 51–15 Beach Channel Drive, Far Rockaway, Zip 11691–1074; tel. 718/945–7100; Robert V. Levine, President and Chief Executive Officer **A**1 9 10 11 12 13 **F**8 11 15 16 17 18 19 20 21 22 26 27 32 33 34 35 37 39 41 42 44 45 46 49 51 54 56 60 63 67 69 70 71 73 **P**5 8 PRESBYTERIAN HOSPITAL IN THE CITY OF NEW YORK See New York Presbyterian Hospital	23	10	235	5834	149	80928	—	65899	37670	1136
✠ QUEENS CHILDREN'S PSYCHIATRIC CENTER, 74–03 Commonwealth Boulevard, Jamaica, Zip 11426–1890; tel. 718/264–4506; Gloria Faretra, M.D., Executive Director (Nonreporting) **A**1 **S** New York State Department of Mental Health, Albany, NY	12	52	106	—	—	—	—	—	—	—
✠ QUEENS HOSPITAL CENTER, 82–68 164th Street, Jamaica, Zip 11432–1104; tel. 718/883–3000; Gladiola Sampson, Executive Director **A**1 2 3 5 9 10 **F**2 3 7 8 11 12 13 14 15 16 17 18 19 20 21 22 26 28 29 30 31 32 33 34 35 37 38 39 40 41 42 44 45 46 48 49 51 52 53 54 55 56 57 58 59 65 67 68 71 73 74 **P**6 **S** New York City Health and Hospitals Corporation, New York, NY	14	10	276	12889	250	301907	1361	141538	103697	2338
□ ROCKEFELLER UNIVERSITY HOSPITAL, (CLINICAL RESEARCH), 1230 York Avenue, Zip 10021–6399; tel. 212/327–8000; Emil Gotschlich, M.D., Vice President Medical Sciences **A**1 3 9 10 **F**65 Web address: www.clinfo.rockefeller.edu	23	49	40	358	8	4694	0	—	—	58
✠ SAINT VINCENTS HOSPITAL AND MEDICAL CENTER, (Formerly Saint Vincent's Hospital Medical Center of New York), (Includes Saint Vincents Hospital, 275 North Street, Zip 10528; tel. 914/925–5300), 153 West 11th Street, Zip 10011–8397; tel. 212/604–7000; Karl P. Adler, M.D., President and Chief Executive Officer **A**1 2 3 5 6 8 9 10 **F**3 4 7 8 10 11 12 13 16 17 18 19 20 21 22 25 26 28 29 30 31 32 34 35 36 37 38 39 40 41 42 43 44 45 46 48 49 50 51 52 53 54 55 56 57 58 60 61 63 65 66 67 68 70 71 73 74 **P**8 **S** Sisters of Charity Center, New York, NY SCHNEIDER CHILDREN'S HOSPITAL See Long Island Jewish Medical Center	21	10	580	22126	470	456360	1602	382885	190719	3411
✠ SISTERS OF CHARITY MEDICAL CENTER, (Includes Bayley Seton Campus, 75 Vanderbilt Avenue, Zip 10304–3850; tel. 718/354–6000; St Vincent's Campus, 355 Bard Avenue), 355 Bard Avenue, Staten Island, Zip 10310–1699; tel. 718/876–1234; Dominick M. Stanzione, Chief Operating Officer and Executive Vice President **A**1 2 3 5 6 9 10 **F**1 2 3 4 5 6 7 8 10 11 12 13 14 15 16 17 18 19 20 21 22 23 25 26 27 28 29 30 31 32 33 34 35 37 38 39 40 41 42 43 44 45 46 47 48 49 51 52 53 54 55 56 57 58 59 60 61 62 64 65 66 67 68 69 70 71 72 73 74 **P**7 Web address: www.schsi.org	21	10	568	26529	426	370360	3662	299477	129527	2771
✠ SOUTH BEACH PSYCHIATRIC CENTER, 777 Seaview Avenue, Staten Island, Zip 10305–3499; tel. 718/667–2300; Lucy Sarkis, M.D., Executive Director (Nonreporting) **A**1 10 **S** New York State Department of Mental Health, Albany, NY	12	22	325	—	—	—	—	—	—	—
□ ○ ST. BARNABAS HOSPITAL, 183rd Street and Third Avenue, Bronx, Zip 10457–9998, Mailing Address: 4422 Third Avenue, Zip 10457–9998; tel. 718/960–9000; Ronald Gade, M.D., President (Nonreporting) **A**1 3 5 9 10 11 12 13	23	10	458	—	—	—	—	—	—	—
□ ST. CLARE'S HOSPITAL AND HEALTH CENTER, 415 West 51st Street, Zip 10019–6394; tel. 212/586–1500; James A. Rutherford, President and Chief Executive Officer (Nonreporting) **A**1 9 10 12 ST. JOHN'S EPISCOPAL HOSPITAL DIVISION See Interfaith Medical Center	21	10	236	—	—	—	—	—	—	—
✠ ○ ST. JOHN'S EPISCOPAL HOSPITAL–SOUTH SHORE, 327 Beach 19th Street, Far Rockaway, Zip 11691–4424; tel. 718/869–7000; Nancy Simmons, Administrator (Nonreporting) **A**1 3 5 9 11 12 13 **S** Episcopal Health Services Inc., Uniondale, NY ST. JOHN'S QUEENS HOSPITAL See Catholic Medical Centers ST. JOSEPH'S HOSPITAL See Catholic Medical Centers	21	10	314	—	—	—	—	—	—	—
✠ ST. LUKE'S–ROOSEVELT HOSPITAL CENTER, (Includes Roosevelt Hospital, 1000 Tenth Avenue, Zip 10019; tel. 212/523–4000; St. Luke's Hospital Center, 1111 Amsterdam Avenue, tel. 212/523–4000), 1111 Amsterdam Avenue, Zip 10025; tel. 212/523–4300; Sigurd H. Ackerman, M.D., President and Chief Executive Officer **A**1 3 5 8 9 10 **F**2 3 4 5 7 8 10 11 12 13 14 15 16 17 18 19 20 21 22 25 26 28 29 30 31 32 33 34 35 37 38 39 40 41 42 43 44 45 46 48 49 51 52 53 54 55 56 57 58 59 60 61 63 65 66 67 68 70 71 73 74 **P**4 5 6 7 8 **S** Continuum Health Partners, New York, NY Web address: www.wehealnewyork.org ST. MARY'S HOSPITAL OF BROOKLYN See Catholic Medical Centers	23	10	724	36347	664	495543	4510	620864	279845	5649
□ △ STATEN ISLAND UNIVERSITY HOSPITAL, 475 Seaview Avenue, Staten Island, Zip 10305–9998; tel. 718/226–9000; Rick J. Varone, President (Nonreporting) **A**1 2 3 5 7 9 10 **S** North Shore– Long Island Jewish Health System, Great Neck, NY	23	10	617	—	—	—	—	—	—	—
UNION HOSPITAL OF THE BRONX, 260 East 188th Street, Bronx, Zip 10458; tel. 718/220–2020; Ronald Gade, M.D., President (Nonreporting) **A**9 10	23	10	197	—	—	—	—	—	—	—
✠ UNIVERSITY HOSPITAL OF BROOKLYN–STATE UNIVERSITY OF NEW YORK HEALTH SCIENCE CENTER AT BROOKLYN, 445 Lenox Road, Brooklyn, Zip 11203–2098; tel. 718/270–2404; Percy Allen, II, FACHE, Vice President Hospital Affairs and Chief Executive Officer **A**1 2 3 5 8 9 10 **F**4 5 7 8 10 11 12 13 14 15 16 17 18 19 20 21 22 25 27 28 29 30 31 34 35 37 38 40 41 42 43 44 45 46 47 48 49 50 51 52 53 54 55 56 58 59 60 61 63 65 66 67 68 71 72 73 74 Web address: www.hscbklyn.edu	12	10	376	10921	219	201607	1576	—	102398	1970

Hospital, Address, Telephone, Administrator, Approval, Facility, and Physician Codes, Health Care System, Network	Classi- fication Codes		Utilization Data					Expense (thousands) of dollars		
★ American Hospital Association (AHA) membership □ Joint Commission on Accreditation of Healthcare Organizations (JCAHO) accreditation + American Osteopathic Healthcare Association (AOHA) membership ○ American Osteopathic Association (AOA) accreditation △ Commission on Accreditation of Rehabilitation Facilities (CARF) accreditation Control codes 61, 63, 64, 71, 72 and 73 indicate hospitals listed by AOHA, but not registered by AHA. For definition of numerical codes, see page A4	Control	Service	Staffed Beds	Admissions	Census	Outpatient Visits	Births	Total	Payroll	Personnel
✠ VETERANS AFFAIRS MEDICAL CENTER, 800 Poly Place, Brooklyn, Zip 11209–7104; tel. 718/630–3500; John J. Donnellan, Jr., Director (Total facility includes 181 beds in nursing home–type unit) **A**1 3 5 8 **F**1 2 3 4 5 8 10 11 14 15 16 17 18 19 20 21 22 23 24 25 26 27 28 30 31 32 34 35 37 39 41 42 43 44 45 46 49 51 52 54 55 56 57 58 59 60 61 63 64 65 67 69 71 72 73 74 **P**6 **S** Department of Veterans Affairs, Washington, DC **Web address:** www.vaww.va.gov/	45	10	399	6644	366	410826	0	194559	96529	2110
✠ VETERANS AFFAIRS MEDICAL CENTER, 130 West Kingsbridge Road, Bronx, Zip 10468–3992; tel. 718/584–9000; Maryann Musumeci, Director (Total facility includes 112 beds in nursing home–type unit) **A**1 2 3 5 8 **F**3 8 10 11 12 15 16 17 19 20 21 22 23 25 26 27 28 29 30 31 32 33 34 35 37 39 41 42 44 45 46 49 50 51 52 55 56 57 58 59 60 64 65 67 71 72 73 74 **P**6 **S** Department of Veterans Affairs, Washington, DC	45	10	328	4075	302	280491	0	147910	99099	1471
✠ VETERANS AFFAIRS MEDICAL CENTER, 423 East 23rd Street, Zip 10010–5050; tel. 212/686–7500; John J. Donnellan, Jr., Director **A**1 2 3 5 8 **F**1 3 4 6 8 10 11 16 17 18 19 20 21 22 23 24 25 26 27 28 29 30 31 32 33 34 35 37 39 41 42 43 44 45 46 48 49 50 51 52 54 55 56 57 58 60 63 64 65 67 71 73 74 **S** Department of Veterans Affairs, Washington, DC	45	10	201	5417	172	336578	0	175887	90885	1658
□ VICTORY MEMORIAL HOSPITAL, 9036 Seventh Avenue, Brooklyn, Zip 11228–3625; tel. 718/630–1234; Krishin L. Bhatia, Administrator (Total facility includes 150 beds in nursing home–type unit)	23	10	410	—	—	—	—	—	—	—
□ WESTCHESTER SQUARE MEDICAL CENTER, 2475 St. Raymond Avenue, Bronx, Zip 10461–3198; tel. 718/430–7300; Alan Kopman, President and Chief Executive Officer **A**1 9 10 **F**2 3 4 8 9 10 11 17 19 21 22 25 29 31 32 34 35 37 40 41 42 43 44 46 47 48 49 51 52 53 54 55 56 57 58 59 60 61 65 66 68 70 71 73 74 **P**1 5	33	10	205	6956	150	41186	0	53322	26676	612
□ WESTERN QUEENS COMMUNITY HOSPITAL, 25–10 30th Avenue, Astoria Station, Long Island City, Zip 11102–2495; tel. 718/932–1000; Elliot J. Simon, FACHE, Chief Operating Officer (Nonreporting) **A**1 9 10	33	10	208	—	—	—	—	—	—	—
✠ WOODHULL MEDICAL AND MENTAL HEALTH CENTER, 760 Broadway Street, Brooklyn, Zip 11206–5383; tel. 718/963–8000; Cynthia Carrington–Murray, R.N., MS, Executive Director **A**1 3 9 10 **F**1 2 3 7 8 10 12 13 14 15 16 17 18 19 20 21 22 24 25 26 27 28 29 30 31 34 37 39 40 42 44 46 48 49 51 52 53 54 55 56 57 58 59 60 61 63 65 67 68 70 71 72 73 74 **P**6 **S** New York City Health and Hospitals Corporation, New York, NY	14	10	358	16585	358	333824	1342	—	118121	2510
✠ ○ WYCKOFF HEIGHTS MEDICAL CENTER, 374 Stockholm Street, Brooklyn, Zip 11237–4099; tel. 718/963–7102; Dominick J. Gio, President and Chief Executive Officer **A**1 3 5 9 10 11 13 **F**7 8 11 15 16 17 19 20 21 22 26 28 30 31 32 34 37 38 39 40 42 44 46 49 51 60 65 67 71 **S** New York & Presbyterian Healthcare, New York, NY	23	10	324	16268	267	198168	1642	153133	73233	1598
NEWARK—Wayne County										
✠ VIAHEALTH OF WAYNE, (Includes Myers Campus, 6600 Middle Road, Sodus, Zip 14551–0310; tel. 315/483–3000; Newark–Wayne Campus, Driving Park Avenue, tel. 315/332–2022, Driving Park Avenue, Zip 14513, Mailing Address: P.O. Box 111, Zip 14513–0111; tel. 315/332–2022; W. Neil Stroman, President (Total facility includes 180 beds in nursing home–type unit) **A**1 9 10 **F**1 7 8 12 17 19 21 22 28 30 34 37 40 44 48 49 52 53 54 55 56 57 58 61 63 64 65 71 73 74 **P**5 **S** Via Health, Rochester, NY	23	10	267	3850	225	112203	529	44015	18945	578
NEWBURGH—Orange County										
□ ST. LUKE'S HOSPITAL, 70 Dubois Street, Zip 12550–4898, Mailing Address: P.O. Box 631, Zip 12550–0631; tel. 914/561–4400; Laurence E. Kelly, Executive Vice President and Administrator **A**1 9 10 **F**1 3 8 11 12 14 15 16 17 19 21 22 23 25 26 27 28 29 30 31 34 35 37 38 39 40 42 44 45 46 48 49 51 52 54 55 56 57 58 59 60 61 62 63 64 65 66 67 71 73 74 **P**8 **S** Greater Hudson Valley Health System, Newburgh, NY **Web address:** www.stlukeshospital.org	23	10	184	8926	126	110000	1172	58626	28483	779
NEWFANE—Niagara County										
INTER–COMMUNITY MEMORIAL HOSPITAL, 2600 William Street, Zip 14108–1093; tel. 716/778–5111; Clare A. Haar, Chief Executive Officer **A**9 10 **F**7 8 11 14 15 16 17 19 20 21 22 25 26 28 29 30 32 34 35 37 39 40 41 42 44 45 46 49 51 61 64 65 71 72 73 74 **P**5 8	23	10	71	2280	32	56291	154	14281	7670	227
NIAGARA FALLS—Niagara County										
□ NIAGARA FALLS MEMORIAL MEDICAL CENTER, 621 Tenth Street, Zip 14302–0708, Mailing Address: P.O. Box 708, Zip 14302–0708; tel. 716/278–4000; Angelo G. Calbone, President and Chief Executive Officer (Nonreporting) **A**1 3 5 9 10	23	10	288	—	—	—	—	—	—	—
NORTH TARRYTOWN—Westchester County										
PHELPS MEMORIAL HOSPITAL CENTER See Sleepy Hollow										
NORTH TONAWANDA—Niagara County										
□ DE GRAFF MEMORIAL HOSPITAL, 445 Tremont Street, Zip 14120–0750, Mailing Address: P.O. Box 0750, Zip 14120–0750; tel. 716/694–4500; Marcia B. Gutfeld, Vice President and Chief Operating Officer (Total facility includes 80 beds in nursing home–type unit) (Nonreporting) **A**1 9 10 **S** KALEIDA Health, Buffalo, NY	23	10	210	—	—	—	—	—	—	—
NORTHPORT—Suffolk County										
✠ VETERANS AFFAIRS MEDICAL CENTER, 79 Middleville Road, Zip 11768–2293; tel. 516/261–4400; Mary A. Dowling, Director (Total facility includes 170 beds in nursing home–type unit) **A**1 2 3 5 8 **F**2 3 4 8 10 11 12 15 16 19 20 21 22 23 25 26 27 29 31 32 33 34 35 37 39 41 42 43 44 45 46 48 49 51 52 54 55 56 57 58 59 60 61 63 64 65 67 69 71 72 73 74 **P**6 **S** Department of Veterans Affairs, Washington, DC	45	10	659	4800	418	285640	0	—	94527	1594

Hospital, Address, Telephone, Administrator, Approval, Facility, and Physician Codes, Health Care System, Network	Classi-fication Codes		Utilization Data					Expense (thousands) of dollars		
	Control	Service	Staffed Beds	Admissions	Census	Outpatient Visits	Births	Total	Payroll	Personnel

★ American Hospital Association (AHA) membership
□ Joint Commission on Accreditation of Healthcare Organizations (JCAHO) accreditation
+ American Osteopathic Healthcare Association (AOHA) membership
○ American Osteopathic Association (AOA) accreditation
△ Commission on Accreditation of Rehabilitation Facilities (CARF) accreditation
Control codes 61, 63, 64, 71, 72 and 73 indicate hospitals listed by AOHA, but not registered by AHA. For definition of numerical codes, see page A4

NORWICH—Chenango County

□ CHENANGO MEMORIAL HOSPITAL, 179 North Broad Street, Zip 13815–1097; tel. 607/337–4111; Frank W. Mirabito, President (Total facility includes 80 beds in nursing home–type unit) **A**1 9 10 **F**7 8 12 15 16 17 19 20 21 22 26 28 30 31 32 34 37 39 40 41 42 44 45 46 49 51 61 63 64 65 67 71 73 74 **P**6 7 8 — 23 10 | 138 | 2316 | 107 | 215616 | 292 | 34692 | 16418 | 545

NYACK—Rockland County

✠ NYACK HOSPITAL, 160 North Midland Avenue, Zip 10960–1998; tel. 914/348–2000; Greger C. Anderson, President and Chief Executive Officer **A**1 2 9 10 **F**2 3 7 9 11 12 14 15 16 17 18 19 21 22 30 31 32 34 35 37 39 40 41 42 44 45 46 48 49 50 54 65 70 71 73 74 **P**1 5 7 — 23 10 | 317 | 12763 | 212 | 328212 | 1198 | 118674 | 52773 | 1112

OCEANSIDE—Nassau County

✠ SOUTH NASSAU COMMUNITIES HOSPITAL, 2445 Oceanside Road, Zip 11572–1500; tel. 516/763–2030; Joseph A. Quagliata, President and Chief Executive Officer **A**1 2 3 5 9 10 **F**4 7 8 9 10 11 12 14 15 16 17 18 19 21 22 26 27 28 29 30 31 32 34 35 37 38 39 40 41 42 43 44 45 46 47 49 51 52 53 54 55 56 57 58 59 60 63 65 66 67 68 70 71 73 74 **P**3 5 7 — 23 10 | 356 | 12441 | 268 | 169700 | 1194 | 106595 | 54568 | 1384

OGDENSBURG—St. Lawrence County

□ HEPBURN MEDICAL CENTER, 214 King Street, Zip 13669–1192; tel. 315/393–3600; Lorraine B. Kabot, FACHE, President and Chief Executive Officer (Total facility includes 29 beds in nursing home–type unit) **A**1 9 10 **F**4 7 8 14 15 16 17 18 19 21 22 23 24 25 26 28 29 30 31 33 34 35 39 40 42 44 45 46 49 51 52 54 55 56 58 60 63 64 65 67 68 69 71 73 74 — 23 10 | 149 | 4474 | 73 | 109770 | 391 | 31789 | 16539 | 458

✠ ST. LAWRENCE PSYCHIATRIC CENTER, 1 Chimney Point Drive, Zip 13669–2291; tel. 315/393–3000; John R. Scott, Director **A**1 10 **F**3 4 5 6 7 8 10 12 13 18 19 20 21 22 23 24 28 31 32 33 35 36 42 43 44 45 46 49 50 52 53 54 55 56 57 58 59 60 63 69 70 71 73 **S** New York State Department of Mental Health, Albany, NY — 12 22 | 120 | 250 | 119 | 34623 | 0 | — | 20900 | 464

OLEAN—Cattaraugus County

□ OLEAN GENERAL HOSPITAL, 515 Main Street, Zip 14760–9912; tel. 716/373–2600; Robert A. Catalano, M.D., President and Chief Executive Officer **A**1 3 6 9 10 **F**7 8 9 11 12 15 16 18 19 21 22 27 30 32 33 34 35 38 39 40 41 42 44 45 46 47 49 52 54 56 57 63 64 65 67 71 73 — 23 10 | 209 | 7044 | 104 | 144257 | 718 | 46776 | 22636 | 799

ONEIDA—Madison County

✠ ONEIDA HEALTHCARE CENTER, 321 Genesee Street, Zip 13421–0321; tel. 315/363–6000; Richard G. Smith, Chief Executive Officer (Total facility includes 160 beds in nursing home–type unit) **A**1 9 10 **F**7 8 11 14 15 16 19 21 22 25 28 29 34 37 39 40 41 44 45 46 63 64 65 71 73 **P**1 — 23 10 | 261 | 3133 | 198 | 101256 | 464 | 36695 | 16759 | 562

ONEONTA—Otsego County

✠ AURELIA OSBORN FOX MEMORIAL HOSPITAL, 1 Norton Avenue, Zip 13820–2697; tel. 607/432–2000; John R. Remillard, President (Total facility includes 130 beds in nursing home–type unit) **A**1 9 10 **F**1 7 8 11 12 14 15 16 17 18 19 21 22 23 24 25 26 28 29 30 32 34 35 36 37 39 40 41 42 44 45 46 49 51 52 53 54 55 56 57 58 60 63 64 65 71 73 74 **P**5 **S** Quorum Health Group/Quorum Health Resources, Inc., Brentwood, TN **Web address:** www.foxcarenetwork.com — 23 10 | 246 | 4389 | 203 | 166197 | 334 | 49559 | 23440 | 617

ORANGEBURG—Rockland County

✠ ROCKLAND CHILDREN'S PSYCHIATRIC CENTER, 599 Convent Road, Zip 10962; tel. 914/359–7400; Marcia Werby, Administrator (Nonreporting) **A**1 3 **S** New York State Department of Mental Health, Albany, NY — 12 52 | 54 | — | — | — | — | — | — | —

✠ ROCKLAND PSYCHIATRIC CENTER, 140 Old Orangeburg Road, Zip 10962–0071; tel. 914/359–1000; James H. Bopp, Executive Director **A**1 5 10 **F**12 17 18 20 52 56 57 58 59 65 67 73 **S** New York State Department of Mental Health, Albany, NY — 12 22 | 470 | 668 | 399 | 134646 | 0 | 83588 | 57000 | 1152

OSSINING—Westchester County

OSSINING CORRECTIONAL FACILITIES HOSPITAL, 354 Hunter Street, Zip 10562–5498; tel. 914/941–0108; Benjamin I. Dyett, M.D., Director (Nonreporting) — 12 11 | 25 | — | — | — | — | — | — | —

□ STONY LODGE HOSPITAL, 40 Croton Dam Road, Zip 10562–2644, Mailing Address: P.O. Box 1250, Briarcliff Manor, Zip 10510–1250; tel. 914/941–7400; Kevin F. Czipo, Executive Director **A**1 10 **F**52 53 **P**6 **Web address:** www.stonylodge.com — 33 22 | 61 | 948 | 58 | 0 | 0 | 10794 | 5970 | 183

OSWEGO—Oswego County

✠ OSWEGO HOSPITAL, 110 West Sixth Street, Zip 13126–9985; tel. 315/349–5511; Corte J. Spencer, Chief Executive Officer (Total facility includes 44 beds in nursing home–type unit) **A**1 9 10 **F**3 7 8 11 12 14 15 16 19 21 22 25 30 31 32 33 35 36 37 40 41 44 49 51 52 53 54 55 56 57 58 59 63 64 65 67 69 71 72 73 74 **P**6 — 23 10 | 208 | 4644 | 114 | 244445 | 708 | 36466 | 17854 | 534

PATCHOGUE—Suffolk County

✠ BROOKHAVEN MEMORIAL HOSPITAL MEDICAL CENTER, 101 Hospital Road, Zip 11772–9998; tel. 516/654–7100; Thomas Ockers, President and Chief Executive Officer **A**1 9 10 **F**3 7 8 11 14 15 16 17 19 21 22 24 25 28 30 31 32 33 34 36 37 39 40 41 42 44 45 54 56 58 61 65 67 70 71 73 74 — 23 10 | 321 | 11164 | 199 | — | 876 | 106144 | 52376 | 1232

PENN YAN—Yates County

✠ SOLDIERS AND SAILORS MEMORIAL HOSPITAL OF YATES COUNTY, 418 North Main Street, Zip 14527–1085; tel. 315/531–2000; James J. Dooley, President and Chief Executive Officer (Total facility includes 152 beds in nursing home–type unit) **A**1 9 10 **F**1 8 13 14 15 16 17 19 22 25 26 28 29 30 34 37 41 44 51 52 53 54 55 56 57 58 64 65 67 71 73 74 **P**6 — 23 10 | 217 | 1579 | 176 | 38706 | 0 | 21200 | 10612 | 412

Hospital, Address, Telephone, Administrator, Approval, Facility, and Physician Codes, Health Care System, Network	Classi-fication Codes		Utilization Data					Expense (thousands) of dollars		
★ American Hospital Association (AHA) membership □ Joint Commission on Accreditation of Healthcare Organizations (JCAHO) accreditation + American Osteopathic Healthcare Association (AOHA) membership ○ American Osteopathic Association (AOA) accreditation △ Commission on Accreditation of Rehabilitation Facilities (CARF) accreditation Control codes 61, 63, 64, 71, 72 and 73 indicate hospitals listed by AOHA, but not registered by AHA. For definition of numerical codes, see page A4	Control	Service	Staffed Beds	Admissions	Census	Outpatient Visits	Births	Total	Payroll	Personnel

PLAINVIEW—Nassau County

✱ NORTH SHORE UNIVERSITY HOSPITAL AT PLAINVIEW, 888 Old Country Road, Zip 11803–4978; tel. 516/719–3000; Deborah Tascone, R.N., MS, Vice President for Administration (Nonreporting) **A**1 2 9 10 **S** North Shore– Long Island Jewish Health System, Great Neck, NY	23	10	279	—	—	—	—	—	—	—

PLATTSBURGH—Clinton County

✱ CHAMPLAIN VALLEY PHYSICIANS HOSPITAL MEDICAL CENTER, 75 Beekman Street, Zip 12901–1493; tel. 518/561–2000; Kevin J. Carroll, President (Total facility includes 54 beds in nursing home–type unit) **A**1 2 5 9 10 **F**7 8 10 11 12 13 15 16 19 20 21 22 23 24 25 28 29 30 32 33 34 35 36 37 39 40 41 42 44 46 49 51 52 56 60 64 65 67 70 71 72 73 74 Web address: www.cvph.org	23	10	400	9778	229	211675	904	91960	45986	1289

POMONA—Rockland County

□ DOCTOR ROBERT L. YEAGER HEALTH CENTER, (Includes Summit Park Hospital–Rockland County Infirmary), 50 Sanatorium Road, Zip 10970–3554; tel. 914/364–2700; Peter T. Fella, Commissioner (Total facility includes 300 beds in nursing home–type unit) (Nonreporting) **A**1 10	13	49	408	—	—	—	—	—	—	—

PORT CHESTER—Westchester County

✱ UNITED HOSPITAL MEDICAL CENTER, 406 Boston Post Road, Zip 10573–7300; tel. 914/934–3000; Kevin Dahill, President and Chief Executive Officer (Total facility includes 40 beds in nursing home–type unit) **A**1 5 9 10 **F**1 2 3 7 8 10 11 12 14 15 16 17 19 21 22 26 27 28 30 32 33 35 36 37 38 39 40 41 44 45 46 49 52 53 54 55 56 57 58 59 64 65 71 73 74 **P**5 **S** New York & Presbyterian Healthcare, New York, NY Web address: www.uhmc.com	23	10	191	7231	154	44336	966	78675	34594	770

PORT JEFFERSON—Suffolk County

✱ JOHN T. MATHER MEMORIAL HOSPITAL, 75 North Country Road, Zip 11777–2190; tel. 516/473–1320; Kenneth D. Roberts, President **A**1 2 9 10 **F**2 3 7 8 11 14 16 17 19 20 21 22 27 28 30 32 33 34 35 36 37 38 39 40 41 42 44 45 46 48 49 52 53 56 57 58 59 60 61 63 65 66 67 71 73 74 **P**5 6 8 Web address: www.matherhospital.com	23	10	235	10002	199	105510	0	98777	46597	1204
✱ ST. CHARLES HOSPITAL AND REHABILITATION CENTER, 200 Belle Terre Road, Zip 11777; tel. 516/474–6000; Barry T. Zeman, President and Chief Executive Officer **A**1 2 5 9 10 **F**2 3 5 7 8 11 12 13 14 15 16 17 19 20 22 24 25 26 27 28 30 32 33 34 35 36 37 38 39 40 41 42 44 45 46 48 49 51 53 54 55 56 58 59 63 65 66 67 71 73 74 **P**5 6 8	21	10	291	9486	248	204743	2000	102831	53581	1193

PORT JERVIS—Orange County

□ MERCY COMMUNITY HOSPITAL, 160 East Main Street, Zip 12771–2245, Mailing Address: P.O. Box 1014, Zip 12771–1014; tel. 914/856–5351; Michael Parmer, M.D., Site Administrator (Total facility includes 46 beds in nursing home–type unit) **A**1 2 9 10 **F**2 7 8 12 14 15 16 17 19 20 21 22 27 28 30 31 32 33 34 35 37 39 40 42 44 46 49 52 54 56 64 65 67 71 73 **P**5 **S** Franciscan Health Partnership, Inc., Latham, NY	21	10	187	4193	114	64771	205	35998	17136	527

POTSDAM—St. Lawrence County

✱ CANTON–POTSDAM HOSPITAL, 50 Leroy Street, Zip 13676–1799; tel. 315/265–3300; Bruce C. Potter, President **A**1 9 10 **F**2 3 7 8 14 15 16 19 21 22 23 25 28 29 30 35 39 40 44 46 49 63 65 66 70 71 73 Web address: www.potsdam.ny.us/cph	23	10	94	3829	62	95397	352	28727	14386	481

POUGHKEEPSIE—Dutchess County

✱ HUDSON RIVER PSYCHIATRIC CENTER, 373 North Road, Zip 12601–1197; tel. 914/452–8000; James Regan, Ph.D., Chief Executive Officer (Nonreporting) **A**1 5 10 **S** New York State Department of Mental Health, Albany, NY	12	22	460	—	—	—	—	—	—	—
□ △ SAINT FRANCIS HOSPITAL, (Includes Saint Francis Hospital–Beacon, 60 Delavan Avenue, Beacon, Zip 12508; tel. 914/831–3500), 35 North Road, Zip 12601–1399; tel. 914/471–2000; Sister M. Ann Elizabeth, President **A**1 3 7 9 10 **F**2 3 7 8 10 11 12 13 14 15 16 17 19 20 21 22 23 26 27 28 29 30 31 32 33 34 35 37 38 39 40 41 42 44 45 46 48 49 51 52 53 54 55 56 57 58 60 61 63 65 66 67 70 71 72 73 74 Web address: www.saintfrancishospital.com	21	10	314	11011	253	273224	0	114271	57439	1461
✱ VASSAR BROTHERS HOSPITAL, 45 Reade Place, Zip 12601–3990; tel. 914/454–8500; Ronald T. Mullahey, President **A**1 2 3 9 10 **F**7 8 10 11 12 14 15 16 17 19 20 21 22 27 28 30 31 32 33 34 37 38 39 40 42 44 45 46 60 61 65 67 71 73 74	23	10	252	13225	188	159928	2468	96030	42847	889

QUEENS—Queens County, See New York City
QUEENS VILLAGE—Queens County, See New York City
RHINEBECK—Dutchess County

✱ NORTHERN DUTCHESS HOSPITAL, 10 Springbrook Avenue, Zip 12572–5002, Mailing Address: P.O. Box 5002, Zip 12572–5002; tel. 914/876–3001; Michael C. Mazzarella, President and Chief Executive Officer **A**1 9 10 **F**2 4 7 8 10 11 12 15 16 18 19 20 21 22 24 26 30 31 32 33 34 35 37 39 40 41 42 43 44 46 49 52 53 54 55 58 59 60 62 64 65 67 69 71 73	23	10	68	2547	38	41139	56	22115	9549	337

RICHMOND VALLEY—Richmond County, See New York City
RIVERHEAD—Suffolk County

✱ CENTRAL SUFFOLK HOSPITAL, 1300 Roanoke Avenue, Zip 11901–2028; tel. 516/548–6000; Joseph F. Turner, President (Total facility includes 60 beds in nursing home–type unit) **A**1 9 10 **F**4 7 8 12 14 15 16 19 21 22 28 29 30 32 34 35 40 42 44 45 46 49 64 65 67 71 72 73 **P**7 Web address: www.centralsuffolkhospital.org	23	10	196	4924	144	69134	205	52328	25820	603

Hospital, Address, Telephone, Administrator, Approval, Facility, and Physician Codes, Health Care System, Network	Classi-fication Codes		Utilization Data					Expense (thousands) of dollars		
★ American Hospital Association (AHA) membership □ Joint Commission on Accreditation of Healthcare Organizations (JCAHO) accreditation + American Osteopathic Healthcare Association (AOHA) membership ○ American Osteopathic Association (AOA) accreditation △ Commission on Accreditation of Rehabilitation Facilities (CARF) accreditation Control codes 61, 63, 64, 71, 72 and 73 indicate hospitals listed by AOHA, but not registered by AHA. For definition of numerical codes, see page A4	Control	Service	Staffed Beds	Admissions	Census	Outpatient Visits	Births	Total	Payroll	Personnel

ROCHESTER—Monroe County

☒ GENESEE HOSPITAL, 224 Alexander Street, Zip 14607–4055; tel. 716/263–6000; William R. Holman, President **A**1 2 3 5 8 9 10 **F**1 3 4 5 6 7 8 10 11 12 13 14 16 17 18 19 20 21 22 24 25 26 28 29 30 32 33 34 35 37 39 40 41 42 43 44 46 47 49 51 52 53 54 55 56 58 59 60 61 65 67 68 70 71 72 73 74 **S** Via Health, Rochester, NY | 23 | 10 | 325 | 12677 | 255 | — | 2236 | — | — | 2713

☒ HIGHLAND HOSPITAL OF ROCHESTER, 1000 South Avenue, Zip 14620–2782; tel. 716/473–2200; Steven I. Goldstein, President and Chief Executive Officer **A**1 2 3 5 9 10 **F**1 2 3 4 6 7 8 9 10 11 12 14 15 16 17 19 20 22 25 26 27 28 29 30 31 32 34 35 37 38 40 41 42 43 44 45 46 47 48 49 51 52 53 54 55 56 58 59 60 61 64 67 68 70 71 72 73 74 **P**7 | 23 | 10 | 180 | 7998 | 110 | 301547 | 1943 | 101602 | 52181 | 1266

☒ PARK RIDGE HOSPITAL, 1555 Long Pond Road, Zip 14626–4182; tel. 716/723–7000; Martin E. Carlin, President **A**1 2 9 10 **F**1 2 3 6 7 8 10 11 12 13 14 15 16 17 18 19 20 21 22 24 26 28 30 31 32 34 35 37 39 41 42 44 45 46 49 51 53 54 55 56 57 58 59 60 61 62 64 65 66 67 68 69 71 72 73 74 **P**5 6 8 **S** Daughters of Charity National Health System, Saint Louis, MO
Web address: www.parkridgehs.org | 23 | 10 | 239 | 8856 | 181 | 345427 | 0 | 108564 | 50754 | 1178

☒ ROCHESTER GENERAL HOSPITAL, 1425 Portland Avenue, Zip 14621–3099; tel. 716/338–4000; Richard S. Constantino, M.D., President (Nonreporting) **A**1 2 3 5 6 8 9 10 **S** Via Health, Rochester, NY
Web address: www.viahealth.org/ | 23 | 10 | 476 | — | — | — | — | — | — | —

☒ ROCHESTER PSYCHIATRIC CENTER, 1111 Elmwood Avenue, Zip 14620–3005; tel. 716/473–3230; Bryan F. Rudes, Executive Director (Nonreporting) **A**1 3 5 9 10 **S** New York State Department of Mental Health, Albany, NY | 12 | 22 | 288 | — | — | — | — | — | — | —

☒ △ ST. MARY'S HOSPITAL, 89 Genesee Street, Zip 14611–3285; tel. 716/464–3000; Stewart Putnam, President **A**1 2 3 5 7 9 10 **F**1 2 3 6 8 10 12 13 14 15 16 17 18 19 20 21 22 24 26 28 30 32 34 35 37 39 41 42 44 45 46 48 49 51 52 53 54 55 56 57 58 59 61 62 64 65 66 67 68 71 72 73 74 **P**5 6 7 8 **S** Daughters of Charity National Health System, Saint Louis, MO
Web address: www.unityhealth.org | 21 | 10 | 73 | 4219 | 102 | 545990 | 534 | 96634 | 43447 | 1040

☒ △ STRONG MEMORIAL HOSPITAL OF THE UNIVERSITY OF ROCHESTER, 601 Elmwood Avenue, Zip 14642–0002; tel. 716/275–2100; Steven I. Goldstein, General Director and Chief Executive Officer **A**1 3 5 7 8 9 10 **F**3 4 5 6 7 8 9 10 11 12 13 14 15 16 17 18 19 20 21 22 23 24 26 27 28 29 30 31 32 33 34 35 36 37 38 39 40 41 42 43 44 45 46 47 48 49 50 51 52 53 54 55 56 57 58 59 60 61 62 63 64 65 66 67 68 70 71 72 73 74 **P**6 8 | 23 | 10 | 658 | 28704 | 543 | 315472 | 3751 | 398756 | 185177 | 6588

ROCKVILLE CENTRE—Nassau County

☒ MERCY MEDICAL CENTER, 1000 North Village Avenue, Zip 11570–1098; tel. 516/255–0111; Vincent DiRubbio, President and Chief Executive Officer **A**1 2 3 9 10 **F**3 4 7 8 9 10 11 12 14 15 16 17 19 21 22 23 26 28 30 31 32 33 34 35 37 38 40 41 42 43 44 46 48 49 52 54 55 56 57 58 59 60 63 64 65 66 67 68 70 71 73 74 **P**6 8 | 21 | 10 | 342 | 13983 | 280 | 186814 | 2140 | 135051 | 65639 | 1669

ROME—Oneida County

☒ ROME MEMORIAL HOSPITAL, 1500 North James Street, Zip 13440–2898; tel. 315/338–7000; Alvin C. White, President and Chief Executive Officer (Total facility includes 82 beds in nursing home–type unit) **A**1 9 10 **F**3 4 7 8 10 11 12 13 14 15 16 18 19 20 21 22 28 29 30 31 32 33 34 35 36 37 38 39 40 41 42 43 44 45 46 48 49 51 52 53 54 55 56 57 59 60 61 63 64 65 66 67 68 70 71 72 73 74 **P**5
Web address: www.romehosp.com | 23 | 10 | 211 | 5263 | 155 | 130695 | 563 | 41410 | 20536 | 764

ROSLYN—Nassau County

☒ ST. FRANCIS HOSPITAL, 100 Port Washington Boulevard, Zip 11576–1348; tel. 516/562–6000; Alan D. Guerci, M.D., Interim President and Chief Executive Officer **A**1 5 9 10 **F**3 4 7 8 10 11 12 14 15 16 17 19 20 21 22 24 25 30 32 33 34 35 36 37 39 41 42 43 44 45 46 49 50 54 56 57 58 59 60 63 65 66 67 69 71 73 74 **P**1 5
Web address: www.st franciscenter.com | 23 | 10 | 279 | 15243 | 313 | 88234 | 0 | 201427 | 89720 | 1767

RYE—Westchester County

☒ RYE HOSPITAL CENTER, 754 Boston Post Road, Zip 10580–2724; tel. 914/967–4567; Jack C. Schoenholtz, M.D., Medical Director, Administrator and President **A**1 10 **F**19 20 21 22 35 45 50 52 53 55 57 60 63 65 71 73 | 33 | 22 | 34 | 151 | 29 | 0 | 0 | 4659 | 2070 | 51

SARANAC LAKE—Franklin County

☒ ADIRONDACK MEDICAL CENTER, Lake Colby Drive, Zip 12983, Mailing Address: P.O. Box 471, Zip 12983–0471; tel. 518/891–4141; Chandler M. Ralph, Chief Executive Officer **A**1 9 10 **F**7 8 12 14 15 16 17 19 21 28 31 33 35 36 37 40 41 42 44 49 51 63 64 65 66 70 73 **P**5 8 **S** Brim Healthcare, Inc., Brentwood, TN
Web address: www.northnet.org/adirondackmedcenter | 23 | 10 | 75 | 3347 | 49 | 101892 | 258 | 31260 | 15114 | 391

SARATOGA SPRINGS—Saratoga County

☒ SARATOGA HOSPITAL, 211 Church Street, Zip 12866–1003; tel. 518/587–3222; David Andersen, President and Chief Executive Officer (Total facility includes 72 beds in nursing home–type unit) **A**1 9 10 **F**7 8 11 12 14 15 16 17 18 19 21 22 26 28 30 33 34 35 37 39 40 41 42 44 46 49 51 52 53 54 55 56 57 64 65 67 71 73 74 **P**5 | 23 | 10 | 191 | 6422 | 171 | 121840 | 764 | 53186 | 25264 | 858

SCHENECTADY—Schenectady County

□ BELLEVUE WOMAN'S HOSPITAL, 2210 Troy Road, Zip 12309–4797; tel. 518/346–9400; Michael A. Mangini, Administrator and Chief Executive Officer (Nonreporting) **A**1 9 10 | 33 | 44 | 55 | — | — | — | — | — | — | —

Hospital, Address, Telephone, Administrator, Approval, Facility, and Physician Codes, Health Care System, Network	Classification Codes		Utilization Data					Expense (thousands) of dollars		
	Control	Service	Staffed Beds	Admissions	Census	Outpatient Visits	Births	Total	Payroll	Personnel

★ American Hospital Association (AHA) membership
□ Joint Commission on Accreditation of Healthcare Organizations (JCAHO) accreditation
+ American Osteopathic Healthcare Association (AOHA) membership
○ American Osteopathic Association (AOA) accreditation
△ Commission on Accreditation of Rehabilitation Facilities (CARF) accreditation
Control codes 61, 63, 64, 71, 72 and 73 indicate hospitals listed by AOHA, but not registered by AHA. For definition of numerical codes, see page A4

Hospital	Control	Service	Staffed Beds	Admissions	Census	Outpatient Visits	Births	Total	Payroll	Personnel
CONIFER PARK, 79 Glenridge Road, Zip 12302; tel. 518/399–6446; Jack Duffy, Executive Director **F**2 3 16 65 67 74 **P**6	33	82	225	2447	120	—	0	—	—	186
⊠ ELLIS HOSPITAL, 1101 Nott Street, Zip 12308–2487; tel. 518/243–4000; G. B. Serrill, President and Chief Executive Officer (Total facility includes 82 beds in nursing home–type unit) **A**1 2 3 5 6 9 10 **F**3 4 5 6 7 8 10 11 12 13 14 15 16 17 18 19 20 21 22 23 24 25 26 28 29 30 31 32 33 34 35 37 39 40 41 42 43 44 45 46 49 51 52 53 54 55 56 57 58 59 60 61 62 63 64 65 66 67 70 71 73 74 **S** Quorum Health Group/Quorum Health Resources, Inc., Brentwood, TN Web address: www.shine.org	23	10	450	11744	283	240769	437	117910	52320	1576
□ ST. CLARE'S HOSPITAL OF SCHENECTADY, 600 McClellan Street, Zip 12304–1090; tel. 518/382–2000; Paul J. Chodkowski, President and Chief Executive Officer **A**1 3 5 9 10 12 **F**7 8 12 13 14 15 16 17 19 20 21 22 23 24 25 28 30 33 34 35 37 39 40 41 44 45 46 49 51 65 71 73 74 **P**3	21	10	200	6296	94	154824	812	58347	28215	862
⊠ △ SUNNYVIEW HOSPITAL AND REHABILITATION CENTER, 1270 Belmont Avenue, Zip 12308–2104; tel. 518/382–4500; Bradford M. Goodwin, President and Chief Executive Officer **A**1 3 5 7 9 10 **F**12 14 15 16 19 21 24 26 28 29 34 35 41 48 49 50 53 54 63 65 67 71 73 **P**5 6 Web address: www.shine.org	23	46	104	1790	76	37612	0	22402	13602	382
SEAFORD—Nassau County										
+ ○ MASSAPEQUA GENERAL HOSPITAL, 750 Hicksville Road, Zip 11783–1300; Mailing Address: P.O. Box 20, Zip 11783–0020; tel. 516/520–6000; John P. Breen, Chief Executive Officer (Nonreporting) **A**9 10 11 12 13	33	10	122							
SIDNEY—Delaware County										
⊠ THE HOSPITAL, 43 Pearl Street West, Zip 13838–1399; tel. 607/561–2153; Russell A. Test, Administrator and Chief Executive Officer (Total facility includes 40 beds in nursing home–type unit) **A**1 9 10 **F**7 8 12 14 15 16 17 19 22 25 26 28 29 30 32 33 34 37 39 40 41 44 46 49 51 64 65 67 71 72 73 **S** Brim Healthcare, Inc., Brentwood, TN Web address: www.thehospital.org	14	10	87	1697	58	40614	143	13012	6469	229
SLEEPY HOLLOW—Westchester County										
⊠ PHELPS MEMORIAL HOSPITAL CENTER, 701 North Broadway, Zip 10591–1096; tel. 914/366–3000; Keith F. Safian, President and Chief Executive Officer **A**1 9 10 **F**2 3 4 5 7 8 10 11 12 14 15 16 17 18 19 20 21 22 26 27 28 29 30 31 32 33 34 35 36 37 39 40 41 42 43 44 45 46 48 49 51 52 53 54 55 56 57 58 59 60 61 63 64 65 66 67 68 69 70 71 72 73 74 **P**5 Web address: www.phelpshospital.org	23	10	235	8165	139	120313	872	65807	35753	791
SMITHTOWN—Suffolk County										
⊠ ST. JOHN'S EPISCOPAL HOSPITAL–SMITHTOWN, 50 Route 25–A, Zip 11787–1398; tel. 516/862–3000; James M. Wilson, Regional Administrator (Nonreporting) **A**1 9 **S** Episcopal Health Services Inc., Uniondale, NY	21	10	366							
□ ST. JOHN'S EPISCOPAL MEDICAL HEALTHCARE CENTER, 498 Smithtown By–Pass, Zip 11787–5018; tel. 516/361–4000; Michael Chiarello, Administrator (Nonreporting) **A**1 9 10	21	10	112							
SODUS—Wayne County										
MYERS CAMPUS See ViaHealth of Wayne, Newark										
SOUTHAMPTON—Suffolk County										
□ SOUTHAMPTON HOSPITAL, 240 Meeting House Lane, Zip 11968–5090; tel. 516/726–8555; Thomas B. Doolan, Acting President and Chief Executive Officer (Nonreporting) **A**1 9 10	23	10	127							
SPRINGVILLE—Erie County										
BERTRAND CHAFFEE HOSPITAL, 224 East Main Street, Zip 14141–1497; tel. 716/592–2871; Steve Krisiak, Chief Executive Officer (Nonreporting) **A**9 10	23	10	49							
STAR LAKE—St. Lawrence County										
★ CLIFTON–FINE HOSPITAL, Oswegatchie Trail, Zip 13690, Mailing Address: P.O. Box 10, Zip 13690–0010; tel. 315/848–3351; Rodney C. Boula, Administrator and Chief Executive Officer (Nonreporting) **A**9 10 Web address: www.northnet.org	16	10	20							
STATEN ISLAND—Richmond County, See New York City										
STONY BROOK—Suffolk County										
⊠ UNIVERSITY HOSPITAL, State University of New York, Zip 11794–8410; tel. 516/689–8333; Michael A. Maffetone, Director and Chief Executive Officer **A**1 2 3 5 8 9 10 **F**4 7 8 9 10 11 12 13 14 15 16 17 18 19 20 21 22 23 25 26 28 29 30 31 34 35 37 38 39 40 41 42 43 44 45 46 47 49 51 52 53 54 55 56 57 58 59 60 61 63 64 65 66 67 68 70 71 72 73 74 Web address: www.uhmc.sunysb.edu	12	10	504	24288	374	587144	3511	320738	148732	3781
SUFFERN—Rockland County										
□ GOOD SAMARITAN HOSPITAL, 255 Lafayette Avenue, Zip 10901–4869; tel. 914/368–5000; James A. Martin, Chief Executive Officer (Nonreporting) **A**1 2 9 10 **S** Franciscan Health Partnership, Inc., Latham, NY	21	10	308							
SYOSSET—Nassau County										
⊠ NORTH SHORE UNIVERSITY HOSPITAL AT SYOSSET, 221 Jericho Turnpike, Zip 11791–4567; tel. 516/496–6400; Deborah Tascone, R.N., MS, Vice President of Administration (Nonreporting) **A**1 3 9 10 **S** North Shore– Long Island Jewish Health System, Great Neck, NY	23	10	186							
SYRACUSE—Onondaga County										
□ BENJAMIN RUSH CENTER, 650 South Salina Street, Zip 13202–3524; tel. 315/476–2161; Norman J. Lesswing, Ph.D., Administrator and Chief Executive Officer (Nonreporting) **A**1 9 10	31	22	107							

Hospital, Address, Telephone, Administrator, Approval, Facility, and Physician Codes, Health Care System, Network	Classi-fication Codes		Utilization Data					Expense (thousands) of dollars		
	Control	Service	Staffed Beds	Admissions	Census	Outpatient Visits	Births	Total	Payroll	Personnel

★ American Hospital Association (AHA) membership
□ Joint Commission on Accreditation of Healthcare Organizations (JCAHO) accreditation
+ American Osteopathic Healthcare Association (AOHA) membership
○ American Osteopathic Association (AOA) accreditation
△ Commission on Accreditation of Rehabilitation Facilities (CARF) accreditation
Control codes 61, 63, 64, 71, 72 and 73 indicate hospitals listed by AOHA, but not registered by AHA. For definition of numerical codes, see page A4

⊠ COMMUNITY–GENERAL HOSPITAL OF GREATER SYRACUSE, 4900 Broad Road, Zip 13215; tel. 315/492–5011; Kent A. Arnold, President (Total facility includes 50 beds in nursing home–type unit) **A**1 3 5 9 10 **F**4 7 8 12 14 19 21 22 25 26 28 29 30 31 33 34 37 39 40 41 42 44 49 52 53 54 55 64 65 71 73 **P**5 6 7 **Web address:** www.cgh.org	23	10	322	10820	203	126046	1459	79804	34900	1062
⊠ CROUSE HOSPITAL, 736 Irving Avenue, Zip 13210–1690; tel. 315/470–7111; Kent A. Arnold, President and Chief Executive Officer **A**1 3 5 9 10 12 **F**2 3 4 7 8 10 12 13 14 15 16 17 18 19 20 21 22 25 26 27 28 29 30 31 32 34 35 37 38 39 40 42 44 45 46 49 53 54 55 58 60 65 66 67 69 70 71 72 73 74 **P**1 5 7 **Web address:** www.crouse.org	23	10	407	22580	336	51662	3677	172330	74760	2308
⊠ RICHARD H. HUTCHINGS PSYCHIATRIC CENTER, 620 Madison Street, Zip 13210–2319; tel. 315/473–4980; Bryan F. Rudes, Executive Director **A**1 3 5 10 **F**12 14 15 16 18 28 52 53 54 55 56 57 58 59 65 73 **P**6 **S** New York State Department of Mental Health, Albany, NY	12	22	136	301	132	38861	0	—	—	509
□ ST. JOSEPH'S HOSPITAL HEALTH CENTER, 301 Prospect Avenue, Zip 13203–1895; tel. 315/448–5111; Theodore M. Pasinski, President (Nonreporting) **A**1 3 5 6 9 10 **S** Sisters of the 3rd Franciscan Order, Syracuse, NY **Web address:** www.SJHSYR.ORG	21	10	431	—	—	—	—	—	—	—
⊠ UNIVERSITY HOSPITAL–SUNY HEALTH SCIENCE CENTER AT SYRACUSE, 750 East Adams Street, Zip 13210–2399; tel. 315/464–5540; Ben Moore, III, Executive Director **A**1 3 5 8 9 10 **F**4 8 9 10 11 12 15 16 17 19 20 21 22 23 25 26 28 29 30 31 34 35 37 39 41 42 43 44 45 46 47 48 49 52 53 54 55 56 57 58 59 60 61 63 65 66 67 68 70 71 72 73 74 **P**5 6 7 **Web address:** www.universityhospital.org/	12	10	356	14210	305	251284	0	222043	103601	2662
⊠ VETERANS AFFAIRS MEDICAL CENTER, 800 Irving Avenue, Zip 13210–2796; tel. 315/476–7461; Philip P. Thomas, Director (Total facility includes 50 beds in nursing home–type unit) **A**1 3 5 8 **F**1 3 8 10 12 17 19 20 22 23 25 26 27 28 30 31 32 34 35 37 42 44 45 46 48 49 51 52 55 56 57 58 59 60 63 64 65 71 72 73 74 **S** Department of Veterans Affairs, Washington, DC	45	10	129	2256	104	225536	0	85648	53876	1039
TICONDEROGA—Essex County										
□ MOSES LUDINGTON HOSPITAL, 2 Wicker Street, Zip 12883–1097; tel. 518/585–2831; Diane M. Hart, Chief Executive Officer (Nonreporting) **A**1 9 10	23	10	39	—	—	—	—	—	—	—
TROY—Rensselaer County										
□ SAMARITAN HOSPITAL, 2215 Burdett Avenue, Zip 12180–2475; tel. 518/271–3300; Paul A. Milton, Chief Operating Officer (Nonreporting) **A**1 6 9 10 **Web address:** www.nehealth.com	23	10	272	—	—	—	—	—	—	—
⊠ SETON HEALTH SYSTEM, (Includes Seton Health System–St. Mary's Hospital, 1300 Massachusetts Avenue, Zip 12180), 1300 Massachusetts Avenue, Zip 12180–1695; tel. 518/268–5000; Mark A. Donovan, M.D., President and Chief Executive Officer (Nonreporting) **A**1 9 10 **S** Daughters of Charity National Health System, Saint Louis, MO **Web address:** www.setonhealth.org	21	10	344	—	—	—	—	—	—	—
UTICA—Oneida County										
⊠ FAXTON HOSPITAL, 1676 Sunset Avenue, Zip 13502–5475; tel. 315/738–6200; Andrew E. Peterson, President and Chief Executive Officer **A**1 2 9 10 **F**1 3 4 7 8 10 11 12 15 17 19 20 21 22 23 26 28 29 30 32 33 34 35 36 37 38 39 40 41 42 43 44 46 48 49 51 52 56 60 64 65 67 68 70 71 72 73 74	23	10	166	5364	104	105010	0	48037	21072	685
⊠ MOHAWK VALLEY PSYCHIATRIC CENTER, 1400 Noyes, Zip 13502–3803; tel. 315/797–6800; Sarah F. Rudes, Executive Director (Nonreporting) **A**1 10 **S** New York State Department of Mental Health, Albany, NY	12	22	614	—	—	—	—	—	—	—
⊠ ST. ELIZABETH MEDICAL CENTER, 2209 Genesee Street, Zip 13501–5999; tel. 315/798–8100; Sister Rose Vincent, President and Chief Executive Officer **A**1 3 6 9 10 12 **F**4 7 10 11 12 13 14 15 16 18 19 21 22 28 30 33 34 35 37 38 39 40 42 43 44 49 51 52 53 54 55 56 57 58 63 65 66 67 70 71 72 73 74 **P**6 **S** Sisters of the 3rd Franciscan Order, Syracuse, NY **Web address:** www.stemc.org	21	10	166	8102	133	259411	0	74444	36384	1242
⊠ ST. LUKE'S MEMORIAL HOSPITAL CENTER, (Includes Allen–Calder Skilled Nursing Facility; Mohawk Valley Division, 295 West Main Street, Ilion, Zip 13357–1599; tel. 315/895–7474), Mailing Address: P.O. Box 479, Zip 13503–0479; tel. 315/798–6000; Andrew E. Peterson, President and Chief Executive Officer (Total facility includes 124 beds in nursing home–type unit) **A**1 9 10 **F**1 3 4 7 8 10 11 12 15 17 19 20 21 22 23 26 28 29 30 32 33 34 35 36 37 38 39 40 41 42 43 44 48 49 51 52 56 57 60 61 63 64 65 67 69 70 71 72 73 74	23	10	390	13229	303	128373	1987	83900	40048	1200
VALHALLA—Westchester County										
⊠ BLYTHEDALE CHILDREN'S HOSPITAL, 95 Bradhurst Avenue, Zip 10595–1697; tel. 914/592–7555; Robert Stone, President **A**1 10 **F**14 15 16 20 24 28 29 30 34 39 41 45 46 48 49 53 54 55 58 65 66 67 71 73 **P**6 **Web address:** www.blythedale.org	23	56	92	304	76	18367	0	23325	14684	329
□ WESTCHESTER MEDICAL CENTER, Valhalla Campus, Zip 10595; tel. 914/493–7000; Edward A. Stolzenberg, President and Chief Executive Officer (Total facility includes 399 beds in nursing home–type unit) **A**1 2 3 5 8 9 10 **F**1 3 4 7 8 9 10 11 12 13 15 16 17 18 19 20 21 22 23 24 26 27 28 29 30 31 32 33 34 35 37 38 39 40 41 42 43 44 45 46 47 48 49 50 51 52 53 54 55 56 57 58 59 60 61 63 64 65 66 67 68 70 71 72 73 74 **P**5	13	10	1040	22725	925	150962	1183	391478	162387	3252

Hospital, Address, Telephone, Administrator, Approval, Facility, and Physician Codes, Health Care System, Network	Classi-fication Codes		Utilization Data					Expense (thousands) of dollars		
★ American Hospital Association (AHA) membership □ Joint Commission on Accreditation of Healthcare Organizations (JCAHO) accreditation + American Osteopathic Healthcare Association (AOHA) membership ○ American Osteopathic Association (AOA) accreditation △ Commission on Accreditation of Rehabilitation Facilities (CARF) accreditation Control codes 61, 63, 64, 71, 72 and 73 indicate hospitals listed by AOHA, but not registered by AHA. For definition of numerical codes, see page A4	Control	Service	Staffed Beds	Admissions	Census	Outpatient Visits	Births	Total	Payroll	Personnel

VALLEY STREAM—Nassau County

✠ FRANKLIN HOSPITAL MEDICAL CENTER, 900 Franklin Avenue, Zip 11580–2190; tel. 516/256–6000; William Kowalewski, President and Chief Executive Officer (Total facility includes 120 beds in nursing home–type unit) **A**1 2 9 10 **F**1 2 3 4 6 7 8 9 10 11 12 13 14 15 16 17 18 19 20 21 22 23 25 26 27 28 29 30 31 32 33 34 35 36 37 38 39 40 41 42 43 44 45 46 47 48 49 50 51 52 53 54 55 56 57 58 59 60 61 62 63 64 65 66 67 68 70 71 72 73 74 **P**5 8 **S** North Shore– Long Island Jewish Health System, Great Neck, NY | 23 | 10 | 425 | 9383 | 317 | 33306 | 467 | 81695 | 41228 | 995

WALTON—Delaware County

□ DELAWARE VALLEY HOSPITAL, 1 Titus Place, Zip 13856–1498; tel. 607/865–2100; David J. Polge, President and Chief Executive Officer **A**1 9 10 **F**2 7 8 14 15 16 17 19 21 22 25 26 27 28 30 37 39 40 41 42 44 49 51 61 63 65 67 71 73 74 **P**6 | 23 | 10 | 42 | 1300 | 18 | 31822 | 167 | 10789 | 6015 | 187

WARSAW—Wyoming County

□ WYOMING COUNTY COMMUNITY HOSPITAL, 400 North Main Street, Zip 14569–1097; tel. 716/786–2233; Lucille K. Sheedy, Administrator and Chief Executive Officer (Total facility includes 160 beds in nursing home–type unit) **A**1 9 10 **F**7 8 12 13 14 15 16 17 19 20 21 22 25 30 32 33 34 35 37 40 41 42 44 48 49 52 64 65 74 **P**4 7
Web address: www.wycol.com/wyoming_county | 13 | 10 | 262 | 3417 | 206 | 43860 | 404 | 22626 | 11392 | 504

WARWICK—Orange County

□ ST. ANTHONY COMMUNITY HOSPITAL, 15 Maple Avenue, Zip 10990–5180; tel. 914/986–2276; James A. Martin, President and Chief Executive Officer (Nonreporting) **A**1 9 10 **S** Franciscan Health Partnership, Inc., Latham, NY | 21 | 10 | 73 | — | — | — | — | — | — | —

WATERTOWN—Jefferson County

□ SAMARITAN MEDICAL CENTER, 830 Washington Street, Zip 13601–4066, Mailing Address: P.O. Box 517, Zip 13601–0517; tel. 315/785–4000; David E. Tinker, President and Chief Executive Officer **A**1 9 10 12 **F**1 2 3 7 8 11 12 14 15 16 17 18 19 21 22 23 25 26 27 28 29 30 31 32 34 35 37 38 39 40 42 44 45 46 48 49 51 52 53 54 55 56 57 58 60 64 65 66 67 71 72 73 74 **P**5 6 7 | 23 | 10 | 178 | 10147 | 153 | 108571 | 1658 | 80743 | 41691 | 1093

WELLSVILLE—Allegany County

✠ JONES MEMORIAL HOSPITAL, 191 North Main Street, Zip 14895–1197, Mailing Address: P.O. Box 72, Zip 14895–0072; tel. 716/593–1100; William M. DiBerardino, FACHE, President and Chief Executive Officer **A**1 9 10 **F**7 8 11 12 14 15 16 17 19 21 22 28 29 30 35 36 37 39 40 41 42 43 44 45 46 49 51 65 66 67 71 73 74 **P**8
Web address: www.jmhny.org | 23 | 10 | 70 | 3010 | 32 | 64164 | 370 | 20085 | 8802 | 297

WEST HAVERSTRAW—Rockland County

✠ HELEN HAYES HOSPITAL, Route 9W, Zip 10993–1195; tel. 914/786–4000; Magdalena Ramirez, Chief Executive Officer **A**1 5 9 10 **F**3 4 5 7 8 10 11 12 13 14 15 16 17 18 19 20 21 22 23 24 27 28 31 32 33 34 35 36 37 38 39 40 41 42 43 44 46 47 48 49 50 51 52 53 54 55 56 57 58 59 60 61 63 64 65 66 67 68 70 71 72 73 74
Web address: www.helenhayeshospital.org | 12 | 46 | 155 | 2090 | 127 | 19267 | 0 | 53310 | 23122 | 644

WEST ISLIP—Suffolk County

✠ GOOD SAMARITAN HOSPITAL MEDICAL CENTER, 1000 Montauk Highway, Zip 11795–4958; tel. 516/376–3000; Richard J. Murphy, Chief Executive Officer (Total facility includes 100 beds in nursing home–type unit) (Nonreporting) **A**1 2 9 10 12 13 | 21 | 10 | 525 | — | — | — | — | — | — | —

WEST POINT—Orange County

✠ KELLER ARMY COMMUNITY HOSPITAL, U.S. Military Academy, Zip 10996–1197; tel. 914/938–4837; Lieutenant Colonel Kenneth Franklin, Deputy Commander for Clinical Services **A**1 3 9 **F**2 3 4 7 8 9 10 11 12 13 14 15 16 17 19 20 21 22 23 25 26 27 28 29 30 31 32 33 34 35 37 38 39 40 41 42 43 44 45 46 47 48 49 51 52 53 54 55 56 57 58 59 60 61 64 65 66 67 68 70 71 72 73 74 **S** Department of the Army, Office of the Surgeon General, Falls Church, VA
Web address: www.wramc.amedd.army.mil.wp | 42 | 10 | 44 | 588 | 5 | 163219 | 185 | 41724 | 22185 | 482

WESTFIELD—Chautauqua County

★ WESTFIELD MEMORIAL HOSPITAL, 189 East Main Street, Zip 14787–1195; tel. 716/326–4921; Barbara A. Malinowski, Administrator and Chief Executive Officer **A**9 10 **F**4 7 8 10 14 15 16 17 19 21 22 28 30 32 33 34 35 40 42 43 44 49 51 53 56 58 59 60 65 67 70 71 72 73 **P**1
Web address: www.wmhinc.org | 23 | 10 | 32 | 809 | 8 | 33453 | 165 | 6829 | 3318 | 115

WHITE PLAINS—Westchester County

✠ △ BURKE REHABILITATION HOSPITAL, 785 Mamaroneck Avenue, Zip 10605–2593; tel. 914/597–2500; Mary Beth Walsh, M.D., Chief Executive Officer **A**1 5 7 10 **F**5 20 26 30 34 39 46 48 49 65 66 67 73 | 23 | 46 | 150 | 2240 | 126 | 18500 | 0 | 38463 | 21529 | 518

NEW YORK HOSPITAL, WESTCHESTER DIVISION See New York Presbyterian Hospital, New York

□ ST. AGNES HOSPITAL, (Includes Children's Rehabilitation Center), 305 North Street, Zip 10605–2299; tel. 914/681–4500; Gary S. Horan, FACHE, President and Chief Executive Officer **A**1 3 5 9 10 **F**2 3 5 7 8 11 12 13 14 15 16 17 18 19 20 22 26 27 28 30 31 32 34 35 36 37 39 40 41 42 44 45 46 47 49 51 53 54 55 56 57 58 60 61 62 65 66 67 68 71 73 **P**5 8 **S** Our Lady of Mercy Healthcare System, Inc., New York, NY
Web address: www.saintagneshospital.com | 21 | 10 | 142 | 6029 | 90 | 122370 | 602 | — | — | 709

Hospital, Address, Telephone, Administrator, Approval, Facility, and Physician Codes, Health Care System, Network	Classi-fication Codes		Utilization Data					Expense (thousands) of dollars		
★ American Hospital Association (AHA) membership □ Joint Commission on Accreditation of Healthcare Organizations (JCAHO) accreditation + American Osteopathic Healthcare Association (AOHA) membership ○ American Osteopathic Association (AOA) accreditation △ Commission on Accreditation of Rehabilitation Facilities (CARF) accreditation Control codes 61, 63, 64, 71, 72 and 73 indicate hospitals listed by AOHA, but not registered by AHA. For definition of numerical codes, see page A4	Control	Service	Staffed Beds	Admissions	Census	Outpatient Visits	Births	Total	Payroll	Personnel

	Control	Service	Staffed Beds	Admissions	Census	Outpatient Visits	Births	Total	Payroll	Personnel
✠ WHITE PLAINS HOSPITAL CENTER, Davis Avenue and Post Road, Zip 10601–4699; tel. 914/681–0600; Jon B. Schandler, President and Chief Executive Officer **A**1 2 5 9 10 **F**3 7 8 11 12 14 15 16 17 19 20 21 22 26 28 29 30 31 32 33 35 37 39 40 41 42 44 45 46 49 50 51 52 53 54 56 58 63 65 67 70 71 73 **P**2 5 7 8 **Web address:** www.wphospital.com	23	10	307	12029	210	156647	1756	110163	54714	1239
WILLIAMSVILLE—Erie County MILLARD FILLMORE SUBURBAN HOSPITAL See Millard Fillmore Gates Circle Hospital, Buffalo										
YONKERS—Westchester County										
✠ ST. JOHN'S RIVERSIDE HOSPITAL, 967 North Broadway, Zip 10701–1399; tel. 914/964–4444; James Foy, President and Chief Executive Officer **A**1 6 9 10 **F**3 7 8 10 14 15 16 17 18 19 21 22 24 25 27 28 29 30 31 32 33 34 35 36 37 39 40 41 42 43 44 45 49 51 60 61 65 66 67 71 73 74 **P**5 8 **Web address:** www.riversidehealth.org	23	10	235	10268	162	90363	1912	69528	40441	985
✠ ST. JOSEPH'S MEDICAL CENTER, 127 South Broadway, Zip 10701–4080; tel. 914/378–7000; Sister Mary Linehan, President (Total facility includes 200 beds in nursing home–type unit) **A**1 3 5 9 10 **F**1 2 3 4 8 9 10 11 12 13 14 15 16 17 18 19 20 21 22 23 26 27 28 30 31 32 33 34 35 37 38 39 40 41 42 43 44 46 47 49 50 51 52 53 54 56 57 58 60 64 65 67 68 70 71 72 73 74 **P**5 8 **S** Sisters of Charity Center, New York, NY **Web address:** www.stjosephs.org	21	10	394	7349	347	249957	0	109976	50725	793
✠ YONKERS GENERAL HOSPITAL, Two Park Avenue, Zip 10703–3497; tel. 914/964–7300; Tibisay A. Guzman, Executive Vice President and Chief Operating Officer **A**1 9 10 **F**2 3 14 15 16 17 18 19 21 31 34 37 41 42 44 45 54 60 63 65 71 73	23	10	190	5644	119	198967	0	39981	25810	657

NORTH CAROLINA

Resident population 7,546 (in thousands)
Resident population in metro areas 64.8%
Birth rate per 1,000 population 14.1
65 years and over 12.5%
Percent of persons without health insurance 16%

Hospital, Address, Telephone, Administrator, Approval, Facility, and Physician Codes, Health Care System, Network	Classi-fication Codes		Utilization Data					Expense (thousands) of dollars		
	Control	Service	Staffed Beds	Admissions	Census	Outpatient Visits	Births	Total	Payroll	Personnel

★ American Hospital Association (AHA) membership
□ Joint Commission on Accreditation of Healthcare Organizations (JCAHO) accreditation
+ American Osteopathic Healthcare Association (AOHA) membership
○ American Osteopathic Association (AOA) accreditation
△ Commission on Accreditation of Rehabilitation Facilities (CARF) accreditation
Control codes 61, 63, 64, 71, 72 and 73 indicate hospitals listed by AOHA, but not registered by AHA. For definition of numerical codes, see page A4

Hospital, Address, Telephone, Administrator, Approval, Facility, and Physician Codes, Health Care System, Network	Control	Service	Staffed Beds	Admissions	Census	Outpatient Visits	Births	Total	Payroll	Personnel
AHOSKIE—Hertford County										
⊠ ROANOKE–CHOWAN HOSPITAL, 500 South Academy Street, Zip 27910, Mailing Address: P.O. Box 1385, Zip 27910–1385; tel. 252/209–3000; Susan S. Lassiter, President and Chief Executive Officer **A**1 3 9 10 **F**7 8 10 12 13 15 16 19 20 21 22 24 28 30 32 33 35 37 40 41 42 44 46 49 51 52 54 56 57 58 63 65 67 71 72 73 **P**7 8 Web address: www.rch.uhseast.com	23	10	118	4517	58	209453	449	31119	14067	631
ALBEMARLE—Stanly County										
⊠ STANLY MEMORIAL HOSPITAL, 301 Yadkin Street, Zip 28001, Mailing Address: P.O. Box 1489, Zip 28002–1489; tel. 704/984–4000; Roy M. Hinson, CHE, President and Chief Executive Officer **A**1 9 10 **F**1 7 8 10 11 12 15 19 20 21 22 23 26 28 30 31 32 34 35 36 37 39 40 41 42 44 45 46 48 49 51 52 53 55 56 57 64 65 66 67 71 73 **P**6 Web address: www.stanly.org	23	10	119	4990	61	86718	645	36138	14070	482
ANDREWS—Cherokee County										
□ DISTRICT MEMORIAL HOSPITAL, 71 Whitaker Lane, Zip 28901–9229; tel. 704/321–1291; Daniel C. White, Chief Executive Officer (Total facility includes 25 beds in nursing home–type unit) **A**1 10 **F**1 8 12 14 15 16 19 22 25 28 29 30 32 33 34 35 37 41 42 44 46 49 51 64 65 71 73 **P**5 6 8	23	10	50	1157	37	22046	0	11683	6338	228
ASHEBORO—Randolph County										
⊠ RANDOLPH HOSPITAL, 364 White Oak Street, Zip 27203, Mailing Address: P.O. Box 1048, Zip 27204–1048; tel. 336/625–5151; Robert E. Morrison, President **A**1 9 10 **F**7 8 12 14 15 16 17 19 20 21 22 26 28 30 32 34 35 37 39 40 41 42 44 49 63 65 71 73	23	10	105	5415	53	126770	680	41487	19260	591
ASHEVILLE—Buncombe County										
□ CHARTER ASHEVILLE BEHAVIORAL HEALTH SYSTEM, 60 Caledonia Road, Zip 28803–2555, Mailing Address: P.O. Box 5534, Zip 28813–5534; tel. 704/253–3681; Tammy B. Wood, Chief Executive Officer (Nonreporting) **A**1 9 10 **S** Magellan Health Services, Atlanta, GA	33	22	139	—	—	—	—	—	—	—
MEMORIAL MISSION HOSPITAL See Mission St. Joseph's Health										
⊠ MISSION ST. JOSEPH'S HEALTH, (Includes Memorial Mission Hospital, 509 Biltmore Avenue; St. Joseph's Hospital, 428 Biltmore Avenue, Zip 28801–9839; tel. 828/255–3100), 509 Biltmore Avenue, Zip 28801–4690; tel. 828/255–4000; Robert F. Burgin, President and Chief Executive Officer (Total facility includes 25 beds in nursing home–type unit) (Nonreporting) **A**1 2 3 5 9 10 Web address: www.msj.org	23	10	700	—	—	—	—	—	—	—
ST. JOSEPH'S HOSPITAL See Mission St. Joseph's Health										
⊠ △ THOMS REHABILITATION HOSPITAL, 68 Sweeten Creek Road, Zip 28803–1599, Mailing Address: P.O. Box 15025, Zip 28813–0025; tel. 828/274–2400; Dennis A. Giles, President **A**1 7 10 **F**1 12 14 15 16 26 32 33 41 48 49 62 64 65 66 67 73 **P**1	23	46	100	1362	66	34242	0	27118	13112	338
⊠ VETERANS AFFAIRS MEDICAL CENTER, 1100 Tunnel Road, Zip 28805–2087; tel. 828/298–7911; James A. Christian, Director (Total facility includes 120 beds in nursing home–type unit) (Nonreporting) **A**1 3 5 **S** Department of Veterans Affairs, Washington, DC Web address: www.va.gov	45	10	389	—	—	—	—	—	—	—
BANNER ELK—Avery County										
CHARLES A. CANNON JR. MEMORIAL HOSPITAL See Charles A. Cannon Jr, Memorial Hospital, Crossnore										
BELHAVEN—Beaufort County										
PUNGO DISTRICT HOSPITAL, 202 East Water Street, Zip 27810–9998; tel. 919/943–2111; Thomas O. Miller, Administrator **A**9 10 **F**7 8 17 19 22 27 37 39 40 42 44 49 64 67 71	23	10	42	1635	32	8848	0	9346	4897	186
BLACK MOUNTAIN—Buncombe County										
JULIAN F. KEITH ALCOHOL AND DRUG ABUSE TREATMENT CENTER, 301 Tabernacle Road, Zip 28711–2599; tel. 828/669–3402; William A. Rafter, Director (Nonreporting) **A**10 Web address: www.jfkadatc.net	12	82	110	—	—	—	—	—	—	—
BLOWING ROCK—Watauga County										
⊠ BLOWING ROCK HOSPITAL, (Includes Dr. Charles Davant Rehabilitation and Extended Care Center), Chestnut Street, Zip 28605–0148, Mailing Address: Box 148, Zip 28605–0148; tel. 828/295–3136; Patricia Gray, Administrator and Chief Executive Officer (Total facility includes 72 beds in nursing home–type unit) **A**1 9 10 **F**1 16 19 21 22 26 27 28 32 41 44 46 64 65 71	23	10	100	429	76	49961	0	6131	3626	179
BOILING SPRINGS—Cleveland County										
CRAWLEY MEMORIAL HOSPITAL, 315 West College Avenue, Zip 28017, Mailing Address: P.O. Box 996, Zip 28017–0996; tel. 704/434–9466; Gail McKillop, President (Nonreporting) **A**10 **S** Carolinas HealthCare System, Charlotte, NC	23	10	51	—	—	—	—	—	—	—

Hospital, Address, Telephone, Administrator, Approval, Facility, and Physician Codes, Health Care System, Network	Classi-fication Codes		Utilization Data					Expense (thousands) of dollars		
★ American Hospital Association (AHA) membership □ Joint Commission on Accreditation of Healthcare Organizations (JCAHO) accreditation + American Osteopathic Healthcare Association (AOHA) membership ○ American Osteopathic Association (AOA) accreditation △ Commission on Accreditation of Rehabilitation Facilities (CARF) accreditation Control codes 61, 63, 64, 71, 72 and 73 indicate hospitals listed by AOHA, but not registered by AHA. For definition of numerical codes, see page A4	Control	Service	Staffed Beds	Admissions	Census	Outpatient Visits	Births	Total	Payroll	Personnel

BOONE—Watauga County

☒ WATAUGA MEDICAL CENTER, Deerfield Road, Zip 28607–2600, Mailing Address: P.O. Box 2600, Zip 28607–2600; tel. 828/262–4100; Richard G. Sparks, President (Total facility includes 10 beds in nursing home–type unit) **A**1 2 9 10 **F**7 8 10 12 15 16 17 19 21 22 23 24 28 29 30 32 35 37 38 40 42 44 45 60 64 65 67 68 71 73 **P**3 8
Web address: www.wataugamc.org

| | 23 | 10 | 105 | 4891 | 60 | 40333 | 544 | 40687 | 17412 | 617 |

BREVARD—Transylvania County

☒ TRANSYLVANIA COMMUNITY HOSPITAL, Hospital Drive, Zip 28712–1116, Mailing Address: Box 1116, Zip 28712–1116; tel. 828/884–9111; Robert J. Bednarek, President and Chief Executive Officer (Total facility includes 10 beds in nursing home–type unit) **A**1 10 **F**2 3 7 8 11 12 14 15 16 17 19 21 22 23 27 28 29 30 32 33 34 35 36 39 40 41 42 44 46 49 63 64 65 67 71 73 74 **P**5 8

| | 23 | 10 | 90 | 2327 | 41 | 37436 | 219 | 23250 | 11975 | 347 |

BRYSON CITY—Swain County

□ SWAIN COUNTY HOSPITAL, 45 Plateau Street, Zip 28713–6784; tel. 704/488–2155; James M. Kirby, Administrator **A**1 9 10 **F**8 12 14 15 16 17 19 22 27 30 32 33 34 35 39 41 42 44 48 49 56 65 71 73 **P**7 8
Web address: www.westcare.org

| | 23 | 10 | 42 | 788 | 26 | 13956 | 0 | 6807 | 3130 | 81 |

BURGAW—Pender County

★ PENDER MEMORIAL HOSPITAL, 507 Freemont Street, Zip 28425; tel. 910/259–5451; Ronald J. Vigus, Chief Executive Officer (Total facility includes 43 beds in nursing home–type unit) **A**9 10 **F**8 15 16 19 22 26 28 32 33 35 37 41 44 49 64 71 73 **S** Quorum Health Group/Quorum Health Resources, Inc., Brentwood, TN

| | 13 | 10 | 86 | 1263 | 52 | 26542 | 0 | 11447 | 5949 | — |

BURLINGTON—Alamance County

☒ ALAMANCE REGIONAL MEDICAL CENTER, 1240 Huffman Mill Road, Zip 27216–0202, Mailing Address: P.O. Box 202, Zip 27216–0202; tel. 336/538–7000; Thomas E. Ryan, President (Total facility includes 81 beds in nursing home–type unit) **A**1 2 9 10 **F**2 3 4 7 8 10 12 14 15 16 17 19 20 21 22 23 26 27 28 29 30 31 32 33 34 35 37 39 40 41 42 44 45 46 48 49 52 53 54 55 56 57 58 59 60 61 63 64 65 66 67 68 71 73 74 **P**5
Web address: www.armc.com

| | 23 | 10 | 319 | 9257 | 191 | 102785 | 1175 | 88657 | 36405 | 1231 |

BUTNER—Granville County

□ JOHN UMSTEAD HOSPITAL, (Includes Alcohol and Drug Abuse Treatment Center, 205 West E Street, Zip 27509; tel. 919/575–7928; Cliff Hood, Director), 1003 12th Street, Zip 27509–1626; tel. 919/575–7211; Patricia L. Christian, R.N., Ph.D., Director (Total facility includes 30 beds in nursing home–type unit) **A**1 3 5 **F**20 37 41 52 53 54 55 56 57 58 64 65 73 **P**1

| | 12 | 22 | 593 | 4637 | 464 | 2313 | 0 | — | 41657 | 1333 |

CAMP LEJEUNE—Onslow County

☒ NAVAL HOSPITAL, Mailing Address: P.O. Box 10100, Zip 28547–0100; tel. 910/450–4300; Captain Thomas R. Collison, Commanding Officer **A**1 **F**3 8 12 13 15 17 18 19 20 21 22 24 25 27 28 29 30 31 34 35 37 39 40 41 44 45 46 49 51 52 55 56 57 61 65 66 71 73 74 **P**1 **S** Department of Navy, Washington, DC

| | 43 | 10 | 102 | 4179 | 32 | 459761 | 1151 | 45097 | — | 1136 |

CARY—Wake County

WESTERN WAKE MEDICAL CENTER See Wake Medical Center, Raleigh

CHAPEL HILL—Orange County

☒ △ UNIVERSITY OF NORTH CAROLINA HOSPITALS, (Includes North Carolina Children's and Women's Hospital; North Carolina Neurosciences Hospital), 101 Manning Drive, Zip 27514–4220; tel. 919/966–4131; Eric B. Munson, President and Chief Executive Officer **A**1 2 3 5 7 8 9 10 **F**2 4 5 7 8 9 10 11 12 13 14 15 16 17 19 20 21 22 26 30 31 32 33 34 35 37 38 39 40 41 42 43 44 45 46 47 48 49 51 52 53 54 55 56 57 58 60 61 63 65 66 67 68 70 71 72 73 74 **P**1 5 6 7
Web address: www.med.unc.edu

| | 12 | 10 | 670 | 28131 | 476 | 701387 | 2335 | 388421 | 161264 | 4368 |

CHARLOTTE—Mecklenburg County

AMETHYST, 1715 Sharon Road West, Zip 28210–5663, Mailing Address: P.O. Box 32861, Zip 28232–2861; tel. 704/554–8373; Steven G. Johnson, Administrator **A**9 10 **F**1 2 3 4 5 6 7 8 9 10 11 12 13 14 15 16 17 18 19 20 21 22 23 24 25 26 27 28 29 30 31 32 33 34 35 37 38 39 40 41 42 43 44 45 46 47 48 49 50 51 52 53 54 55 56 58 59 60 61 62 63 64 65 66 67 68 70 71 72 73 74

| | 16 | 82 | 76 | 504 | 32 | 15831 | 0 | 8153 | 4474 | 131 |

☒ CAROLINAS MEDICAL CENTER, 1000 Blythe Boulevard, Zip 28203–5871, Mailing Address: P.O. Box 32861, Zip 28232–2861; tel. 704/355–2000; Paul S. Franz, President **A**1 2 3 5 8 9 10 **F**1 2 3 4 5 6 7 8 9 10 11 12 13 14 15 17 18 19 20 21 22 23 24 25 26 27 28 29 30 31 32 33 34 35 36 37 38 39 40 41 42 43 44 45 46 47 48 49 50 51 52 53 54 55 56 57 58 59 60 61 63 64 65 66 67 68 70 71 72 73 74 **P**3 6 **S** Carolinas HealthCare System, Charlotte, NC
Web address: www.carolinas.org

| | 16 | 10 | 736 | 37051 | 613 | 308019 | 5497 | 509099 | 194081 | 6386 |

☒ △ CHARLOTTE INSTITUTE OF REHABILITATION, 1100 Blythe Boulevard, Zip 28203–5864; tel. 704/355–4300; Don Gabriel, Administrator **A**1 3 7 9 10 **F**1 2 3 4 5 6 7 8 9 10 11 12 13 14 17 18 19 20 21 22 23 24 25 26 27 28 29 30 31 32 33 34 35 36 37 38 39 40 41 42 43 44 45 46 47 48 49 50 51 52 53 54 55 56 57 58 59 60 61 63 64 65 66 67 68 70 71 72 73 74 **P**3 6 **S** Carolinas HealthCare System, Charlotte, NC

| | 16 | 46 | 118 | 2011 | 95 | 43799 | 0 | 29285 | 17240 | 433 |

☒ △ MERCY HOSPITAL, (Includes Mercy Hospital South, 10628 Park Road, Pineville, Zip 28210; tel. 704/543–2025; Bill Brown, Administrator), 2001 Vail Avenue, Zip 28207–1289; tel. 704/379–5100; C. Curtis Copenhaver, President **A**1 6 7 9 10 **F**2 3 4 8 10 11 12 14 15 16 19 21 22 28 30 31 32 35 37 39 43 44 46 48 49 63 65 67 71 73 **S** Carolinas HealthCare System, Charlotte, NC

| | 16 | 10 | 224 | 7861 | 132 | 50612 | 0 | 70263 | 30369 | 835 |

Hospital, Address, Telephone, Administrator, Approval, Facility, and Physician Codes, Health Care System, Network	Classi-fication Codes		Utilization Data					Expense (thousands) of dollars		
	Control	Service	Staffed Beds	Admissions	Census	Outpatient Visits	Births	Total	Payroll	Personnel

★ American Hospital Association (AHA) membership
□ Joint Commission on Accreditation of Healthcare Organizations (JCAHO) accreditation
+ American Osteopathic Healthcare Association (AOHA) membership
○ American Osteopathic Association (AOA) accreditation
△ Commission on Accreditation of Rehabilitation Facilities (CARF) accreditation
Control codes 61, 63, 64, 71, 72 and 73 indicate hospitals listed by AOHA, but not registered by AHA. For definition of numerical codes, see page A4

Hospital	Control	Service	Staffed Beds	Admissions	Census	Outpatient Visits	Births	Total	Payroll	Personnel
✖ PRESBYTERIAN HOSPITAL, (Formerly Presbyterian Healthcare), 200 Hawthorne Lane, Zip 28204–2528, Mailing Address: P.O. Box 33549, Zip 28233–3549; tel. 704/384–4000; Thomas R. Revels, President and Chief Executive Officer (Total facility includes 301 beds in nursing home–type unit) **A**1 2 6 9 10 **F**3 4 5 7 8 10 11 12 13 15 17 18 19 21 22 23 25 27 28 29 30 31 32 33 34 35 37 38 39 40 41 42 43 44 45 46 47 49 51 52 53 54 55 56 57 58 59 60 61 63 64 65 67 68 70 71 73 74 **P**1 2 6 **S** Novant Health, Winston Salem, NC **Web address:** www.phsc.com	23	10	853	30349	682	135184	4228	299307	127023	—
★ PRESBYTERIAN SPECIALTY HOSPITAL, 1600 East Third Street, Zip 28204–3282, Mailing Address: P.O. Box 34425, Zip 28234–4425; tel. 704/384–6000; Patricia Mabe, Vice President and Chief Nursing Officer (Nonreporting) **A**9 10 **S** Novant Health, Winston Salem, NC	23	45	15	—	—	—	—	—	—	—
✖ PRESBYTERIAN–ORTHOPAEDIC HOSPITAL, 1901 Randolph Road, Zip 28207–1195; tel. 704/375–6792; Grayce M. Crockett, Administrator (Nonreporting) **A**1 9 10 **S** Novant Health, Winston Salem, NC	33	47	166	—	—	—	—	—	—	—
□ UNIVERSITY HOSPITAL, 8800 North Tryon Street, Zip 28262–8415, Mailing Address: P.O. Box 560727, Zip 28256–0727; tel. 704/548–6000; W. Spencer Lilly, Administrator **A**1 9 10 **F**4 6 7 8 10 12 14 16 19 20 21 22 24 28 29 30 31 32 34 35 37 39 40 41 42 43 44 49 50 51 53 54 55 56 57 58 59 60 61 63 65 66 67 68 70 71 72 73 74 **P**6 7 **S** Carolinas HealthCare System, Charlotte, NC	16	10	122	5896	57	78232	1650	42005	17693	461
CHEROKEE—Swain County										
✖ U. S. PUBLIC HEALTH SERVICE INDIAN HOSPITAL, Hospital Road, Zip 28719, Mailing Address: Hospital Road, Caller Box C–26, Zip 28719; tel. 828/497–9163; Edwin McLemore, Administrator (Nonreporting) **A**1 10 **S** U. S. Public Health Service Indian Health Service, Rockville, MD	47	10	30	—	—	—	—	—	—	—
CHERRY POINT—Craven County										
✖ NAVAL HOSPITAL, Mailing Address: PSC Box 8023, Zip 28533–0023; tel. 252/466–0266; Captain Jones A. Bold, Commanding Officer **A**1 **F**8 12 16 20 22 29 30 34 39 40 41 44 45 49 51 58 67 71 74 **S** Department of Navy, Washington, DC	43	10	23	1203	10	159881	579	17773	3428	349
CLINTON—Sampson County										
✖ SAMPSON REGIONAL MEDICAL CENTER, (Formerly Sampson County Memorial Hospital), 607 Beaman Street, Zip 28328–2697, Mailing Address: Drawer 258, Zip 28329–0258; tel. 910/592–8511; Lee Pridgen, Jr., Administrator (Total facility includes 30 beds in nursing home–type unit) **A**1 9 10 **F**7 8 14 15 16 19 22 32 35 37 40 44 46 49 64 65 71 **Web address:** www.scmh.com	13	10	146	4338	76	46704	298	33711	16424	554
CLYDE—Haywood County										
✖ HAYWOOD REGIONAL MEDICAL CENTER, 262 Leroy George Drive, Zip 28721–9434; tel. 828/456–7311; David O. Rice, President (Total facility includes 20 beds in nursing home–type unit) **A**1 9 10 **F**7 8 10 12 13 14 15 16 17 19 21 22 23 24 28 29 30 32 33 35 37 39 40 41 42 44 45 46 49 51 54 56 60 65 67 71 72 73 74 **P**3 6 8 **Web address:** www.haymed.org	16	10	111	4973	67	79927	299	45825	20409	696
COLUMBUS—Polk County										
□ ST. LUKE'S HOSPITAL, 220 Hospital Drive, Zip 28722–9473; tel. 704/894–3311; C. Cameron Highsmith, Jr., President and Chief Executive Officer (Nonreporting) **A**1 10	23	10	73	—	—	—	—	—	—	—
CONCORD—Cabarrus County										
✖ NORTHEAST MEDICAL CENTER, 920 Church Street North, Zip 28025–2983; tel. 704/783–3000; Laurence C. Hinsdale, President and Chief Executive Officer **A**1 2 3 5 6 9 10 **F**4 7 8 10 11 14 15 16 19 21 22 24 29 32 33 35 37 38 40 41 42 43 44 46 58 60 61 65 71 72 73 74	23	10	338	17421	201	557566	2124	174527	78184	2425
CROSSNORE—Avery County										
✖ CHARLES A. CANNON JR, MEMORIAL HOSPITAL, (Includes Charles A. Cannon Jr. Memorial Hospital, 805 Shawneehaw Avenue, Banner Elk, Zip 28604–9724, Mailing Address: P.O. Box 8, Zip 28604–0008; tel. 828/898–5111), One Crossnore Drive, Zip 28616, Mailing Address: Drawer 470, Zip 28616; tel. 828/733–1736; Edward C. Greene, Jr., President (Total facility includes 10 beds in nursing home–type unit) **A**1 9 10 **F**7 8 19 21 22 28 33 35 37 40 44 52 56 57 64 65 71 73 **P**6	23	10	90	3125	36	—	165	28767	11560	532
DANBURY—Stokes County										
✖ STOKES–REYNOLDS MEMORIAL HOSPITAL, Mailing Address: P.O. Box 10, Zip 27016–0010; tel. 336/593–2831; Sandra D. Priddy, President (Total facility includes 40 beds in nursing home–type unit) **A**1 9 10 **F**3 8 14 15 16 19 22 25 33 37 44 64 65 71 72 73 **P**6 **Web address:** www.bgsm.edu/stokes	21	10	93	897	72	23083	0	11366	5311	206
DUNN—Harnett County										
□ BETSY JOHNSON REGIONAL HOSPITAL, 800 Tilghman Drive, Zip 28334–5599, Mailing Address: Drawer 1706, Zip 28335–1706; tel. 910/892–7161; Shannon D. Brown, President **A**1 9 10 **F**7 8 14 17 19 20 22 28 35 37 39 40 41 44 49 63 65 67 71 73 **Web address:** www.BJRH.org	23	10	72	3899	42	53892	709	23372	11416	391
DURHAM—Durham County										
✖ DUKE UNIVERSITY MEDICAL CENTER, (Includes Duke University Hospital), Erwin Road, Zip 27710, Mailing Address: P.O. Box 3708, Zip 27710–3708; tel. 919/684–8111; Michael D. Israel, Chief Executive Officer and Vice Chancellor **A**1 2 3 5 8 9 10 **F**3 4 5 7 8 9 10 11 12 13 15 16 17 18 19 20 21 22 23 24 26 28 29 30 31 35 37 38 39 40 41 42 43 44 45 46 47 48 49 50 51 52 53 54 55 56 57 58 59 60 61 63 65 66 67 68 70 71 72 73 74	23	10	878	37400	673	879080	2719	654380	238995	6102

Hospital, Address, Telephone, Administrator, Approval, Facility, and Physician Codes, Health Care System, Network	Classi-fication Codes		Utilization Data					Expense (thousands) of dollars		
	Control	Service	Staffed Beds	Admissions	Census	Outpatient Visits	Births	Total	Payroll	Personnel

★ American Hospital Association (AHA) membership
☐ Joint Commission on Accreditation of Healthcare Organizations (JCAHO) accreditation
+ American Osteopathic Healthcare Association (AOHA) membership
○ American Osteopathic Association (AOA) accreditation
△ Commission on Accreditation of Rehabilitation Facilities (CARF) accreditation
Control codes 61, 63, 64, 71, 72 and 73 indicate hospitals listed by AOHA, but not registered by AHA. For definition of numerical codes, see page A4

Hospital	Control	Service	Staffed Beds	Admissions	Census	Outpatient Visits	Births	Total	Payroll	Personnel
✠ DURHAM REGIONAL HOSPITAL, 3643 North Roxboro Road, Zip 27704–2763; tel. 919/470–4000; Richard L. Myers, President and Chief Executive Officer **A**1 3 5 6 9 10 **F**3 4 7 8 10 11 12 15 16 17 19 21 22 23 24 25 26 27 28 29 30 31 32 34 35 37 39 40 41 42 43 44 45 46 49 51 52 53 54 55 56 57 58 59 60 63 65 67 71 72 73 74 **P**1 **Web address:** www.dchc.org	23	10	185	13763	168	91463	1861	123766	53667	1709
NORTH CAROLINA EYE AND EAR HOSPITAL, 1110 West Main Street, Zip 27701–2000; tel. 919/682–9341; H. Ed Jones, Chief Executive Officer (Nonreporting) **A**9 10	33	45	24	—	—	—	—	—	—	—
✠ VETERANS AFFAIRS MEDICAL CENTER, 508 Fulton Street, Zip 27705–3897; tel. 919/286–0411; Michael B. Phaup, Director (Total facility includes 120 beds in nursing home–type unit) **A**1 3 5 8 **F**3 4 8 10 11 14 15 16 19 20 21 22 26 27 28 29 30 31 32 34 35 37 39 41 42 43 44 45 46 49 51 52 54 55 56 57 58 60 63 64 65 67 68 71 73 74 **P**6 **S** Department of Veterans Affairs, Washington, DC	45	10	235	6517	236	179880	0	138246	62602	1325
EDEN—Rockingham County										
✠ MOREHEAD MEMORIAL HOSPITAL, 117 East King's Highway, Zip 27288–5299; tel. 336/623–9711; Robert Enders, President (Total facility includes 128 beds in nursing home–type unit) **A**1 2 9 10 **F**7 8 12 13 15 16 17 19 21 22 23 26 28 30 32 34 35 37 39 40 41 42 45 46 49 51 60 63 64 65 66 67 68 71 73 74 **P**6 8 **S** Quorum Health Group/Quorum Health Resources, Inc., Brentwood, TN **Web address:** www.morehead.org	23	10	236	5882	187	97107	766	41779	19971	712
EDENTON—Chowan County										
✠ CHOWAN HOSPITAL, 211 Virginia Road, Zip 27932–0629, Mailing Address: P.O. Box 629, Zip 27932–0629; tel. 252/482–8451; Barbara R. Cale, Administrator (Total facility includes 40 beds in nursing home–type unit) **A**1 9 10 **F**7 8 12 14 15 16 17 19 20 21 22 28 30 31 32 33 34 37 39 40 41 42 44 45 46 49 52 54 56 58 59 64 65 67 71 73 74 **P**3	13	10	111	2415	59	22924	388	18772	9408	390
ELIZABETH CITY—Pasquotank County										
✠ ALBEMARLE HOSPITAL, 1144 North Road Street, Zip 27909, Mailing Address: P.O. Box 1587, Zip 27906–1587; tel. 252/335–0531; Philip D. Bagby, President and Chief Executive Officer **A**1 9 10 **F**7 8 10 11 12 16 17 19 20 21 22 23 24 28 29 30 34 35 37 39 40 41 42 44 45 46 49 60 65 67 71 73	13	10	147	7451	115	80557	786	53304	23813	744
ELIZABETHTOWN—Bladen County										
✠ BLADEN COUNTY HOSPITAL, 501 South Poplar Street, Zip 28337–0398, Mailing Address: P.O. Box 398, Zip 28337–0398; tel. 910/862–5100; Leo A. Petit, Jr., Chief Executive Officer (Total facility includes 10 beds in nursing home–type unit) **A**1 9 10 **F**7 8 11 15 16 17 19 21 22 25 27 28 29 30 32 33 34 35 37 39 40 44 45 49 64 65 67 71 72 73 **P**1 7 **Web address:** www.bchn.org	13	10	58	1867	30	38752	259	15233	6901	276
ELKIN—Surry County										
✠ HUGH CHATHAM MEMORIAL HOSPITAL, Parkwood Drive, Zip 28621–0560, Mailing Address: P.O. Box 560, Zip 28621–0560; tel. 336/527–7000; Richard D. Osmus, Chief Executive Officer (Total facility includes 120 beds in nursing home–type unit) **A**1 9 10 **F**6 7 8 10 12 14 15 16 19 21 22 26 28 30 32 33 34 35 37 39 40 41 42 44 45 49 51 61 62 63 64 65 66 67 71 73 74 **P**1 3 **S** Quorum Health Group/Quorum Health Resources, Inc., Brentwood, TN	23	10	201	4527	170	42475	358	33454	15400	594
ERWIN—Harnett County										
✠ GOOD HOPE HOSPITAL, 410 Denim Drive, Zip 28339–0668, Mailing Address: P.O. Box 668, Zip 28339–0668; tel. 910/897–6151; Donald E. Annis, Chief Executive Officer (Nonreporting) **A**1 10 **S** Quorum Health Group/Quorum Health Resources, Inc., Brentwood, TN **Web address:** www.goodhopehospital.org	23	10	72	—	—	—	—	—	—	—
FAYETTEVILLE—Cumberland County										
BEHAVIORAL HEALTH CARE OF CAPE FEAR VALLEY HEALTH SYSTEM, (Formerly Cumberland Hospital), 3425 Melrose Road, Zip 28304–1695; tel. 910/609–3000; James P. Sprouse, Associate Administrator for Psychiatric Services **A**10 **F**1 2 3 4 7 8 10 11 12 14 15 16 17 19 20 21 22 23 25 26 28 29 30 31 32 33 34 35 37 38 39 40 41 42 43 44 45 46 49 52 53 54 55 56 57 58 59 60 63 65 67 71 73 **P**6 **Web address:** www.capefearvalley.com	13	22	120	2184	56	35038	0	17787	—	227
✠ △ CAPE FEAR VALLEY HEALTH SYSTEM, 1638 Owen Drive, Zip 28304–3431, Mailing Address: P.O. Box 2000, Zip 28302–2000; tel. 910/609–4000; John T. Carlisle, Chief Executive Officer **A**1 2 3 5 7 9 10 **F**2 3 4 7 8 10 11 12 15 16 17 19 21 22 26 28 29 31 32 33 34 37 38 40 41 42 43 44 45 46 48 49 51 52 53 56 58 59 60 65 67 71 73 74 **P**6 **Web address:** www.capefearvalley.com	13	10	424	21110	390	349431	4240	—	—	3296
CUMBERLAND HOSPITAL See Behavioral Health Care of Cape Fear Valley Health System										
✠ HIGHSMITH–RAINEY MEMORIAL HOSPITAL, 150 Robeson Street, Zip 28301–5570; tel. 910/609–1000; Joel F. Engles, Chief Executive Officer **A**1 10 **F**7 8 11 12 14 15 16 19 21 22 28 30 35 37 39 40 44 46 49 63 71 73 **P**1 2 4 5 6 7 8 **S** Columbia/HCA Healthcare Corporation, Nashville, TN	33	10	133	3675	47	24733	277	26968	12697	404
✠ VETERANS AFFAIRS MEDICAL CENTER, 2300 Ramsey Street, Zip 28301–3899; tel. 910/822–7059; Richard J. Baltz, Director (Total facility includes 39 beds in nursing home–type unit) **A**1 **F**1 3 8 14 15 16 17 19 20 21 22 24 26 27 28 29 30 31 32 34 35 37 39 41 44 45 46 49 51 52 55 56 57 58 61 64 65 67 71 73 74 **P**6 **S** Department of Veterans Affairs, Washington, DC	45	10	159	3525	139	160913	0	53214	28541	661

Hospital, Address, Telephone, Administrator, Approval, Facility, and Physician Codes, Health Care System, Network	Classi-fication Codes		Utilization Data					Expense (thousands) of dollars		
★ American Hospital Association (AHA) membership □ Joint Commission on Accreditation of Healthcare Organizations (JCAHO) accreditation + American Osteopathic Healthcare Association (AOHA) membership ○ American Osteopathic Association (AOA) accreditation △ Commission on Accreditation of Rehabilitation Facilities (CARF) accreditation Control codes 61, 63, 64, 71, 72 and 73 indicate hospitals listed by AOHA, but not registered by AHA. For definition of numerical codes, see page A4	Control	Service	Staffed Beds	Admissions	Census	Outpatient Visits	Births	Total	Payroll	Personnel

FLETCHER—Henderson County

★ ○ PARK RIDGE HOSPITAL, Naples Road, Zip 28732, Mailing Address: P.O. Box 1569, Zip 28732–1569; tel. 828/684–8501; Michael V. Gentry, President **A**1 10 11 **F**7 8 10 11 12 14 15 19 21 22 23 32 33 35 37 39 40 41 44 46 49 52 53 56 57 59 65 67 71 73 **P**5 6 **S** Adventist Health System Sunbelt Health Care Corporation, Winter Park, FL
Web address: www.ahss.org

| | 23 | 10 | 92 | 3512 | 52 | 41021 | 404 | 35547 | 16472 | 532 |

FORT BRAGG—Cumberland County

★ WOMACK ARMY MEDICAL CENTER, Normandy Drive, Zip 28307–5000; tel. 910/432–4802; Colonel Thomas H. Auer, Commander **A**1 3 5 **F**2 3 4 7 8 10 12 13 14 15 16 17 18 19 20 21 22 23 24 25 28 29 30 31 32 33 34 35 37 38 39 40 41 42 43 44 45 46 48 49 50 51 52 53 54 55 56 57 58 59 60 61 63 65 66 67 68 69 70 71 73 74 **P**1 **S** Department of the Army, Office of the Surgeon General, Falls Church, VA

| | 42 | 10 | 173 | 8348 | 62 | 893179 | 2470 | — | — | 1878 |

FRANKLIN—Macon County

★ ANGEL MEDICAL CENTER, Riverview and White Oak Streets, Zip 28734, Mailing Address: P.O. Box 1209, Zip 28744; tel. 828/524–8411; Michael E. Zuliani, Chief Executive Officer **A**1 9 10 **F**7 8 12 15 17 19 21 22 23 28 32 33 34 35 37 39 41 42 44 46 49 63 65 67 71 72 74 **S** Quorum Health Group/Quorum Health Resources, Inc., Brentwood, TN

| | 23 | 10 | 59 | 2491 | 25 | 45277 | 196 | 24859 | 11669 | 369 |

FUQUAY–VARINA—Wake County

SOUTHERN WAKE HOSPITAL See Wake Medical Center, Raleigh

GASTONIA—Gaston County

★ GASTON MEMORIAL HOSPITAL, 2525 Court Drive, Zip 28054–2142, Mailing Address: P.O. Box 1747, Zip 28053–1747; tel. 704/834–2000; Wayne F. Shovelin, President and Chief Executive Officer **A**1 2 9 10 **F**3 4 6 7 8 10 11 12 14 15 16 17 18 19 20 21 22 23 24 28 29 30 32 33 34 35 37 39 40 41 42 43 44 45 46 49 52 53 54 55 56 57 58 59 60 63 65 67 70 71 72 73 74

| | 23 | 10 | 348 | 18150 | 238 | 120247 | 2385 | 132962 | 59295 | 2300 |

GOLDSBORO—Wayne County

□ CHERRY HOSPITAL, 201 Stevens Mill Road, Zip 27530–1057; tel. 919/731–3200; Liston G. Edwards, Director (Total facility includes 173 beds in nursing home–type unit) **A**1 3 5 10 **F**14 15 16 20 26 52 53 57 64 65 73 **P**6
Web address: www.ddhs.state.nc.us/mhddsas/cherry.htm

| | 12 | 22 | 662 | 2470 | 506 | — | 0 | 57029 | 39401 | 1240 |

★ WAYNE MEMORIAL HOSPITAL, 2700 Wayne Memorial Drive, Zip 27534–8001, Mailing Address: P.O. Box 8001, Zip 27533–8001; tel. 919/736–1110; James W. Hubbell, President and Chief Executive Officer **A**1 2 9 10 **F**7 8 10 12 14 15 17 19 21 22 23 26 29 30 31 32 33 34 35 37 38 39 40 41 42 44 45 46 49 52 53 54 55 56 57 59 60 63 65 66 67 71 73
Web address: www.waynehealth.org

| | 23 | 10 | 262 | 11916 | 171 | 133242 | 1550 | 84739 | 36614 | 1176 |

GREENSBORO—Guilford County

□ CHARTER GREENSBORO BEHAVIORAL HEALTH SYSTEM, 700 Walter Reed Drive, Zip 27403–1129, Mailing Address: P.O. Box 10399, Zip 27404–0399; tel. 336/852–4821; Nancy Reaves, Chief Executive Officer (Nonreporting) **A**1 9 10 **S** Magellan Health Services, Atlanta, GA

| | 33 | 22 | 68 | — | — | — | — | — | — | — |

★ △ MOSES CONE HEALTH SYSTEM, (Includes Moses H. Cone Memorial Hospital, 1200 North Elm Street, Zip 27401; tel. 910/574–7000; Wesley Long Community Hospital, 501 North Elam Avenue, Zip 27403–1199, Mailing Address: P.O. Box 2747, Zip 27402–2747; tel. 910/854–6100; Women's Hospital of Greensboro, 801 Green Valley Road, Zip 27408; tel. 910/574–6500), 1200 North Elm Street, Zip 27401–1020; tel. 336/832–1000; Dennis R. Barry, President (Total facility includes 290 beds in nursing home–type unit) **A**1 2 3 5 7 8 9 10 **F**4 7 8 10 11 12 13 14 15 16 17 19 20 21 22 23 25 26 27 28 29 30 31 32 33 34 35 37 38 39 40 41 42 43 44 45 46 48 49 52 54 55 57 59 60 61 64 65 66 67 70 71 73 74 **P**1 7
Web address: www.mosescone.com

| | 23 | 10 | 1112 | 38955 | 852 | 372363 | 5485 | 335951 | 153131 | 4695 |

□ VENCOR HOSPITAL–GREENSBORO, 2401 Southside Boulevard, Zip 27406–3311; tel. 336/271–2800; Leanne Fiorentino, Chief Executive Officer (Total facility includes 65 beds in nursing home–type unit) (Nonreporting) **A**1 10 **S** Vencor, Incorporated, Louisville, KY

| | 33 | 49 | 124 | — | — | — | — | — | — | — |

WESLEY LONG COMMUNITY HOSPITAL See Moses Cone Health System
WOMEN'S HOSPITAL OF GREENSBORO See Moses Cone Health System

GREENVILLE—Pitt County

★ △ PITT COUNTY MEMORIAL HOSPITAL–UNIVERSITY HEALTH SYSTEMS OF EASTERN CAROLINA, 2100 Stantonsburg Road, Zip 27835–6028, Mailing Address: Box 6028, Zip 27835–6028; tel. 252/816–4451; Dave C. McRae, President and Chief Executive Officer **A**1 2 3 5 7 8 9 10 **F**4 7 8 10 11 12 13 14 15 16 17 19 20 21 22 24 25 26 27 28 29 30 31 32 33 34 35 37 38 39 40 41 42 43 44 45 46 47 48 49 51 52 53 54 55 56 57 58 59 60 61 63 64 65 67 68 70 71 72 73 74 **P**1 5 7 8
Web address: www.pcmh.com

| | 23 | 10 | 684 | 32871 | 549 | 200965 | 3221 | 332032 | 148074 | 4742 |

WALTER B. JONES ALCOHOL AND DRUG ABUSE TREATMENT CENTER, 2577 West Fifth Street, Zip 27834–7813; tel. 252/830–3426; Phillip A. Mooring, Director (Nonreporting) **A**10

| | 12 | 82 | 76 | — | — | — | — | — | — | — |

HAMLET—Richmond County

□ HAMLET HOSPITAL, Rice and Vance Streets, Zip 28345, Mailing Address: P.O. Box 1109, Zip 28345–1109; tel. 910/582–3611; Nancy C. Fodi, Executive Director **A**1 10 **F**12 15 19 22 26 28 30 35 37 39 41 44 45 46 49 52 56 59 65 71 73 **S** Health Management Associates, Naples, FL

| | 33 | 10 | 64 | 3094 | 39 | 16719 | 0 | 9705 | 5524 | 198 |

Hospital, Address, Telephone, Administrator, Approval, Facility, and Physician Codes, Health Care System, Network	Classi-fication Codes		Utilization Data					Expense (thousands) of dollars		
	Control	Service	Staffed Beds	Admissions	Census	Outpatient Visits	Births	Total	Payroll	Personnel

★ American Hospital Association (AHA) membership
□ Joint Commission on Accreditation of Healthcare Organizations (JCAHO) accreditation
+ American Osteopathic Healthcare Association (AOHA) membership
○ American Osteopathic Association (AOA) accreditation
△ Commission on Accreditation of Rehabilitation Facilities (CARF) accreditation
Control codes 61, 63, 64, 71, 72 and 73 indicate hospitals listed by AOHA, but not registered by AHA. For definition of numerical codes, see page A4

HENDERSON—Vance County

✠ △ MARIA PARHAM HOSPITAL, 566 Ruin Creek Road, Zip 27536–2957; tel. 252/438–4143; Philip S. Lakernick, President and Chief Executive Officer (Nonreporting) **A**1 7 9 10 Web address: www.mphosp.org	23	10	93	—	—	—	—	—	—	—

HENDERSONVILLE—Henderson County

✠ MARGARET R. PARDEE MEMORIAL HOSPITAL, 715 Fleming Street, Zip 28791–2563; tel. 828/696–1000; Frank J. Aaron, Jr., Chief Executive Officer (Total facility includes 40 beds in nursing home–type unit) **A**1 2 3 9 10 **F**1 7 8 11 12 14 15 16 17 19 21 22 23 26 28 29 30 32 34 35 36 37 40 41 42 44 45 46 49 51 52 54 55 56 57 58 59 60 61 63 64 65 67 71 72 73 74 **P**1 5 6 8 Web address: www.pardee–med.org	13	10	223	8103	140	123268	624	61702	28646	949

HICKORY—Catawba County

✠ CATAWBA MEMORIAL HOSPITAL, 810 Fairgrove Church Road S.E., Zip 28602–9643; tel. 828/326–3000; J. Anthony Rose, President and Chief Executive Officer **A**1 9 10 **F**7 8 10 14 15 16 17 19 21 22 23 24 26 27 28 30 33 34 35 37 40 41 42 44 45 48 49 52 54 56 57 58 60 61 65 66 67 71 72 73 74 **P**8 Web address: www.catawbamemorial.org	13	10	183	8138	112	163045	1454	79810	35745	994
✠ △ FRYE REGIONAL MEDICAL CENTER, (Includes Frye Regional Medical Center–South Campus, tel. 704/328–2226), 420 North Center Street, Zip 28601–5049; tel. 828/322–6070; Dennis Phillips, Chief Executive Officer (Total facility includes 17 beds in nursing home–type unit) **A**1 7 9 10 **F**2 3 7 8 10 11 12 13 14 15 16 17 18 19 20 21 22 23 24 25 26 28 29 30 31 32 33 34 35 37 38 39 40 41 42 43 44 45 48 49 51 52 53 54 55 56 57 58 63 64 65 66 67 71 73 74 **P**1 **S** TENET Healthcare Corporation, Santa Barbara, CA	33	10	355	12487	214	142656	941	—	—	1569

HIGH POINT—Guilford County

✠ HIGH POINT REGIONAL HEALTH SYSTEM, 601 North Elm Street, Zip 27262–4398, Mailing Address: P.O. Box HP–5, Zip 27261; tel. 336/884–8400; Jeffrey S. Miller, President (Total facility includes 30 beds in nursing home–type unit) **A**1 2 9 10 **F**2 3 4 5 7 8 10 11 12 13 14 15 16 17 18 19 20 21 22 23 24 25 26 27 28 29 30 31 32 33 34 35 36 37 39 40 41 42 43 44 45 46 49 52 54 55 57 58 59 60 64 65 66 67 68 71 72 73 74 **P**5 8	23	10	306	16158	226	77864	1806	116783	47702	1554

HIGHLANDS—Macon County

✠ HIGHLANDS–CASHIERS HOSPITAL, Hospital Drive, Zip 28741, Mailing Address: P.O. Drawer 190, Zip 28741–0190; tel. 828/526–1200; Jack A. Calloway, Chief Executive Officer (Total facility includes 72 beds in nursing home–type unit) **A**1 10 **F**8 14 16 19 20 22 28 30 32 33 36 41 44 49 64 65 71 72	23	10	96	640	81	—	0	8416	4090	140

JACKSONVILLE—Onslow County

□ BRYNN MARR BEHAVIORAL HEALTHCARE SYSTEM, 192 Village Drive, Zip 28546–7299; tel. 910/577–1400; Dale Armstrong, Chief Executive Officer (Nonreporting) **A**1 10 **S** Ramsay Health Care, Inc., Coral Gables, FL	33	22	76	—	—	—	—	—	—	—
✠ ONSLOW MEMORIAL HOSPITAL, 317 Western Boulevard, Zip 28540, Mailing Address: P.O. Box 1358, Zip 28540–1358; tel. 910/577–2281; Douglas Kramer, Chief Executive Officer (Nonreporting) **A**1 9 10	16	10	133	—	—	—	—	—	—	—

JEFFERSON—Ashe County

✠ ASHE MEMORIAL HOSPITAL, 200 Hospital Avenue, Zip 28640; tel. 336/246–7101; R. D. Williams, Administrator and Chief Executive Officer (Total facility includes 60 beds in nursing home–type unit) **A**1 9 10 **F**7 8 14 15 16 19 22 24 28 29 34 35 39 40 41 44 45 49 64 65 71 73 **S** Quorum Health Group/Quorum Health Resources, Inc., Brentwood, TN Web address: www.ashememorial.org	23	10	115	1958	82	32162	126	14237	6631	269

KENANSVILLE—Duplin County

✠ DUPLIN GENERAL HOSPITAL, 401 North Main Street, Zip 28349–9989, Mailing Address: P.O. Box 278, Zip 28349–0278; tel. 910/296–0941; Richard E. Harrell, President and Chief Executive Officer (Total facility includes 20 beds in nursing home–type unit) **A**1 9 10 **F**7 8 14 15 16 17 19 21 22 26 31 35 37 39 40 41 42 44 49 51 52 55 56 57 64 65 71 73 74 **P**6 Web address: www.dgh.org	23	10	80	3097	58	31507	557	17052	8143	326

KINGS MOUNTAIN—Cleveland County

□ KINGS MOUNTAIN HOSPITAL, 706 West King Street, Zip 28086–2708, Mailing Address: P.O. Box 339, Zip 28086–0339; tel. 704/739–3601; Hank Neal, Administrator (Total facility includes 10 beds in nursing home–type unit) **A**1 9 10 **F**8 11 14 15 16 19 22 37 41 44 49 52 56 64 65 71 73 **S** Carolinas HealthCare System, Charlotte, NC	16	10	72	2196	35	54865	0	10351	5124	201

KINSTON—Lenoir County

CASWELL CENTER, 2415 West Vernon Avenue, Zip 28501–3321; tel. 919/559–5222; Jim S. Woodall, Director (Nonreporting)	12	62	829	—	—	—	—	—	—	—
✠ LENOIR MEMORIAL HOSPITAL, 100 Airport Road, Zip 28501, Mailing Address: P.O. Box 1678, Zip 28503–1678; tel. 252/522–7000; Gary E. Black, President and Chief Executive Officer (Total facility includes 26 beds in nursing home–type unit) **A**1 2 9 10 **F**6 7 10 12 14 15 16 17 19 20 21 22 24 26 28 29 30 31 32 35 37 39 40 41 42 44 45 46 48 49 59 60 64 65 67 70 71 72 73	13	10	245	9013	128	66504	754	63797	28422	969

LAURINBURG—Scotland County

✠ SCOTLAND MEMORIAL HOSPITAL, 500 Lauchwood Drive, Zip 28352–5599; tel. 910/291–7000; Gregory C. Wood, Chief Executive Officer (Total facility includes 50 beds in nursing home–type unit) **A**1 9 10 **F**2 3 7 8 10 12 13 14 15 16 17 19 22 26 27 28 30 32 33 34 35 37 40 41 42 44 45 46 49 51 54 55 56 57 58 60 61 64 65 66 67 68 71 72 73 74 **P**8 Web address: www.scotlandhealth.org	23	10	174	4466	106	78480	666	43898	17739	682

Hospital, Address, Telephone, Administrator, Approval, Facility, and Physician Codes, Health Care System, Network	Classi-fication Codes		Utilization Data					Expense (thousands) of dollars		
★ American Hospital Association (AHA) membership □ Joint Commission on Accreditation of Healthcare Organizations (JCAHO) accreditation + American Osteopathic Healthcare Association (AOHA) membership ○ American Osteopathic Association (AOA) accreditation △ Commission on Accreditation of Rehabilitation Facilities (CARF) accreditation Control codes 61, 63, 64, 71, 72 and 73 indicate hospitals listed by AOHA, but not registered by AHA. For definition of numerical codes, see page A4	Control	Service	Staffed Beds	Admissions	Census	Outpatient Visits	Births	Total	Payroll	Personnel

LENOIR—Caldwell County

✉ CALDWELL MEMORIAL HOSPITAL, 321 Mulberry Street S.W., Zip 28645–5720, Mailing Address: P.O. Box 1890, Zip 28645–1890; tel. 828/757–5100; Frederick L. Soule, President and Chief Executive Officer (Total facility includes 10 beds in nursing home–type unit) **A**1 9 10 **F**7 8 10 12 15 16 17 19 21 22 30 35 37 39 40 41 42 44 46 49 59 64 65 66 67 71 72 73 74 **P**5 6 8 — 23 10 | 68 | 4056 | 38 | 167552 | 573 | 37558 | 19064 | 697

LEXINGTON—Davidson County

✉ LEXINGTON MEMORIAL HOSPITAL, 250 Hospital Drive, Zip 27292, Mailing Address: P.O. Box 1817, Zip 27293–1817; tel. 336/248–5161; John A. Cashion, FACHE, President **A**1 9 10 **F**3 7 8 10 12 15 16 19 22 25 29 30 32 34 35 37 39 40 41 42 44 45 46 49 51 53 54 55 56 58 59 63 65 67 71 72 73 **P**2 3 5 8 — 23 10 | 87 | 4121 | 45 | 78696 | 686 | 32516 | 14705 | 481

Web address: www.lmh.hbocvan.com

LINCOLNTON—Lincoln County

□ LINCOLN MEDICAL CENTER, 200 Gamble Drive, Zip 28092–0677, Mailing Address: Box 677, Zip 28093–0677; tel. 704/735–3071; Peter W. Acker, President and Chief Executive Officer **A**1 9 10 **F**7 8 12 14 17 19 21 22 26 27 28 30 32 34 35 36 39 40 41 44 49 65 66 67 68 71 73 74 **P**3 5 7 — 23 10 | 75 | 3917 | 53 | 25703 | 444 | 31981 | 14815 | 493

Web address: www.lincolnmedical.org

LOUISBURG—Franklin County

□ FRANKLIN REGIONAL MEDICAL CENTER, 100 Hospital Drive, Zip 27549–2256, Mailing Address: P.O. Box 609, Zip 27549–0609; tel. 919/496–5131; Ann Barnhart, Executive Director **A**1 9 10 **F**8 10 11 15 16 17 19 22 23 28 29 30 32 34 35 37 41 44 45 46 49 52 54 56 65 66 67 70 71 73 **S** Health Management Associates, Naples, FL — 33 10 | 85 | 2506 | 33 | 27244 | 0 | 11480 | 5829 | 222

LUMBERTON—Robeson County

✉ SOUTHEASTERN REGIONAL MEDICAL CENTER, 300 West 27th Street, Zip 28358–3017, Mailing Address: P.O. Box 1408, Zip 28359–1408; tel. 910/671–5000; J. L. Welsh, Jr., President and Chief Executive Officer **A**1 9 10 **F**1 2 3 5 6 7 8 10 12 15 16 17 19 21 22 23 28 29 30 31 32 33 34 35 37 38 39 40 41 42 44 45 46 48 49 51 53 56 57 60 65 66 67 71 72 73 **P**8 — 23 10 | 281 | 12240 | 184 | 165966 | 1616 | 89243 | 40456 | 1786

MARION—McDowell County

✉ MCDOWELL HOSPITAL, 100 Rankin Drive, Zip 28752–4989, Mailing Address: P.O. Box 730, Zip 28752–0730; tel. 828/659–5000; Jeffrey M. Judd, President and Chief Executive Officer **A**1 9 10 **F**7 8 12 14 16 17 19 21 22 23 24 25 28 30 33 35 37 42 44 45 46 49 63 65 67 71 73 74 **P**6 — 23 10 | 65 | 2843 | 31 | 56945 | 342 | 20011 | 9148 | 321

MATTHEWS—Mecklenburg County

★ PRESBYTERIAN HOSPITAL-MATTHEWS, 1500 Matthews Township Parkway, Zip 28105, Mailing Address: P.O. Box 3310, Zip 28106–3310; tel. 704/384–6500; Mark R. Farmer, Vice President and Administrator **A**9 10 **F**3 4 5 7 8 10 11 12 13 15 17 18 19 21 22 23 25 26 27 28 29 30 31 32 33 34 35 37 39 40 41 42 43 44 45 46 47 49 51 52 53 54 55 56 57 58 59 60 61 63 64 65 67 70 71 73 74 **P**1 2 6 **S** Novant Health, Winston Salem, NC — 23 10 | 76 | 4097 | 35 | — | 1258 | 16619 | 11775 | 320

MCCAIN—Hoke County

MCCAIN CORRECTIONAL HOSPITAL, Mailing Address: P.O. Box 5118, Zip 28361–5118; tel. 910/944–2351; F. David Hubbard, Superintendent (Nonreporting) — 12 11 | 81 | — | — | — | — | — | — | —

MOCKSVILLE—Davie County

✉ DAVIE COUNTY HOSPITAL, 223 Hospital Street, Zip 27028–2038, Mailing Address: P.O. Box 1209, Zip 27028–1209; tel. 336/751–8100; Mike Kimel, Administrator **A**1 9 10 **F**8 15 16 17 19 22 32 34 35 37 39 41 44 49 65 71 **P**3 5 6 8 **S** Novant Health, Winston Salem, NC — 23 10 | 32 | 731 | 9 | 15060 | 0 | 8340 | 4138 | 135

Web address: www.novanthealth.org

MONROE—Union County

✉ UNION REGIONAL MEDICAL CENTER, 600 Hospital Drive, Zip 28112–6000, Mailing Address: P.O. Box 5003, Zip 28111–5003; tel. 704/283–3100; John W. Roberts, President and Chief Executive Officer (Total facility includes 66 beds in nursing home–type unit) **A**1 9 10 **F**2 3 4 5 6 7 8 10 11 12 13 14 15 17 18 19 20 21 22 23 24 26 27 28 29 30 31 32 34 35 36 39 40 41 42 43 44 45 46 49 50 51 53 56 57 58 59 60 61 63 64 65 66 67 68 70 71 72 73 74 **S** Carolinas HealthCare System, Charlotte, NC — 16 10 | 223 | 6813 | 136 | 73912 | 1032 | 47052 | 21321 | 713

Web address: www.carolinas.org

MOORESVILLE—Iredell County

□ LAKE NORMAN REGIONAL MEDICAL CENTER, 610 East Center Avenue, Zip 28115, Mailing Address: P.O. Box 360, Zip 28115–0360; tel. 704/663–1113; P. Paul Smith, Jr., Executive Director **A**1 10 **F**7 8 10 12 14 15 16 17 19 21 22 23 25 26 27 28 30 32 34 35 36 37 39 40 41 42 44 45 46 49 51 65 67 71 73 74 **P**8 **S** Health Management Associates, Naples, FL — 33 10 | 111 | 3636 | 42 | 36596 | 403 | — | — | 332

MOREHEAD CITY—Carteret County

✉ CARTERET GENERAL HOSPITAL, 3500 Arendell Street, Zip 28557–2901, Mailing Address: P.O. Box 1619, Zip 28557–1619; tel. 252/247–1616; F. A. Odell, III, FACHE, President (Total facility includes 104 beds in nursing home–type unit) **A**1 9 10 **F**7 8 11 14 15 16 17 19 21 22 28 30 32 33 39 40 42 44 45 46 49 60 63 64 65 67 71 72 73 — 13 10 | 225 | 5875 | 176 | 60790 | 580 | 44388 | 20460 | 575

MORGANTON—Burke County

□ BROUGHTON HOSPITAL, 1000 South Sterling Street, Zip 28655–3999; tel. 828/433–2111; Seth P. Hunt, Jr., Director and Chief Executive Officer **A**1 10 **F**19 20 21 28 35 46 52 53 57 60 63 64 65 67 71 73 — 12 22 | 622 | 3628 | 515 | 0 | 0 | 90735 | 40421 | 1355

Web address: www.broughtonhospital.org

Hospital, Address, Telephone, Administrator, Approval, Facility, and Physician Codes, Health Care System, Network	Classi- fication Codes		Utilization Data					Expense (thousands) of dollars		
★ American Hospital Association (AHA) membership □ Joint Commission on Accreditation of Healthcare Organizations (JCAHO) accreditation + American Osteopathic Healthcare Association (AOHA) membership ○ American Osteopathic Association (AOA) accreditation △ Commission on Accreditation of Rehabilitation Facilities (CARF) accreditation Control codes 61, 63, 64, 71, 72 and 73 indicate hospitals listed by AOHA, but not registered by AHA. For definition of numerical codes, see page A4	Control	Service	Staffed Beds	Admissions	Census	Outpatient Visits	Births	Total	Payroll	Personnel
✠ GRACE HOSPITAL, 2201 South Sterling Street, Zip 28655–4058; tel. 828/438–2000; V. Otis Wilson, Jr., President (Total facility includes 120 beds in nursing home–type unit) **A**1 9 10 **F**7 8 10 12 13 15 17 19 21 22 23 24 28 30 32 34 35 37 39 40 41 42 44 49 52 54 55 56 57 58 59 60 62 63 64 65 67 71 72 73 **P**1 **Web address:** www.gracehcs.org	23	10	269	5808	180	104537	833	52391	23888	862
MOUNT AIRY—Surry County										
✠ NORTHERN HOSPITAL OF SURRY COUNTY, 830 Rockford Street, Zip 27030–5365, Mailing Address: P.O. Box 1101, Zip 27030–1101; tel. 336/719–7000; William B. James, Chief Executive Officer (Total facility includes 13 beds in nursing home–type unit) **A**1 9 10 **F**7 8 10 12 15 16 17 19 20 22 26 28 29 30 32 33 34 35 37 40 41 42 44 45 49 56 64 65 67 71 73 74 **S** Quorum Health Group/Quorum Health Resources, Inc., Brentwood, TN	16	10	103	5145	54	62926	671	40900	17652	561
MURPHY—Cherokee County										
✠ MURPHY MEDICAL CENTER, 4130 U.S. Highway 64 East, Zip 28906–7917; tel. 828/837–8161; Mike Stevenson, Administrator (Total facility includes 120 beds in nursing home–type unit) **A**1 10 **F**7 8 14 15 16 19 21 22 28 29 30 34 35 37 41 42 44 49 60 63 64 65 67 71 72 73 **P**5 8 **Web address:** www.grove.net/mmc	23	10	170	2464	139	28219	275	19568	9306	391
NEW BERN—Craven County										
□ △ CRAVEN REGIONAL MEDICAL AUTHORITY, 2000 Neuse Boulevard, Zip 28560–3499, Mailing Address: P.O. Box 12157, Zip 28561–2157; tel. 252/633–8111; Raymond Budrys, Chief Executive Officer **A**1 2 7 9 10 **F**4 7 8 10 11 12 14 15 16 19 21 22 23 25 26 27 28 29 30 31 32 34 35 37 39 40 41 43 44 48 49 52 55 56 57 59 60 63 64 65 66 71 73 74	16	10	258	12807	188	122591	1133	108666	43669	1338
NORTH WILKESBORO—Wilkes County										
✠ WILKES REGIONAL MEDICAL CENTER, 1370 West D Street, Zip 28659–3506, Mailing Address: P.O. Box 609, Zip 28659–0609; tel. 336/651–8100; David L. Henson, Chief Executive Officer (Total facility includes 10 beds in nursing home–type unit) (Nonreporting) **A**1 9 10 **Web address:** www.wfubmc.edu	14	10	130	—	—	—	—	—	—	—
OXFORD—Granville County										
✠ GRANVILLE MEDICAL CENTER, 1010 College Street, Zip 27565–2507, Mailing Address: Box 947, Zip 27565–0947; tel. 919/690–3000; Joe W. Pollard, Jr., Chief Executive Officer (Total facility includes 80 beds in nursing home–type unit) **A**1 9 10 **F**1 7 8 12 14 17 19 21 22 26 28 30 32 34 35 37 40 41 42 44 49 59 60 64 65 66 67 71 73 **P**8 **S** Quorum Health Group/Quorum Health Resources, Inc., Brentwood, TN	13	10	128	1849	90	—	526	16486	7564	284
PINEHURST—Moore County										
✠ △ FIRSTHEALTH MOORE REGIONAL HOSPITAL, (Formerly Moore Regional Hospital), 155 Memorial Drive, Zip 28374, Mailing Address: P.O. Box 3000, Zip 28374–3000; tel. 910/215–1000; Charles T. Frock, President and Chief Executive Officer **A**1 2 7 9 10 **F**2 3 4 7 8 10 11 12 14 15 16 17 19 20 21 22 23 24 25 26 27 28 29 30 31 32 33 34 35 37 38 39 40 41 42 43 44 45 46 47 48 49 51 52 54 55 56 57 58 59 60 63 64 65 67 71 72 73 74 **P**6 7	23	10	371	17630	285	118425	1587	160840	68638	2095
PLYMOUTH—Washington County										
✠ WASHINGTON COUNTY HOSPITAL, 958 U.S. Highway 64 East, Zip 27962–9591; tel. 252/793–4135; Lawrence H. McAvoy, Administrator **A**1 9 10 **F**12 14 15 16 19 22 35 42 44 45 71 **S** Quorum Health Group/Quorum Health Resources, Inc., Brentwood, TN	13	10	33	1164	16	18069	0	8314	3714	146
RALEIGH—Wake County										
CENTRAL PRISON HOSPITAL, 1300 Western Boulevard, Zip 27606–2148; tel. 919/733–0800; Robert Reardon, Hospital Services Administrator **F**2 3 4 8 9 10 11 12 16 18 19 20 22 23 25 27 28 30 31 33 34 35 37 38 39 40 41 42 43 44 48 49 51 52 54 55 56 58 60 64 65 67 71 74 **P**6	12	11	229	3183	206	7642	0	19252	8590	202
□ DOROTHEA DIX HOSPITAL, 820 South Boylan Avenue, Zip 27603–2176; tel. 919/733–5324; Michael S. Pedneau, Director (Nonreporting) **A**1 3 5 10	12	22	442	—	—	—	—	—	—	—
✠ HOLLY HILL/ CHARTER BEHAVIORAL HEALTH SYSTEM, 3019 Falstaff Road, Zip 27610–1812; tel. 919/250–7000; James B. Brawley, Chief Executive Officer **A**1 9 10 **F**3 52 53 54 55 56 57 58 59 **S** Columbia/HCA Healthcare Corporation, Nashville, TN	32	22	108	2424	61	9733	0	—	—	130
✠ RALEIGH COMMUNITY HOSPITAL, 3400 Wake Forest Road, Zip 27609–7373, Mailing Address: P.O. Box 28280, Zip 27611–8280; tel. 919/954–3000; James E. Raynor, Chief Executive Officer **A**1 9 10 **F**7 12 14 15 19 21 22 24 30 31 34 35 37 39 40 41 42 44 49 52 57 59 64 65 66 71 73 **P**3 6 7	23	10	168	5922	83	65029	722	—	—	571
✠ REX HEALTHCARE, 4420 Lake Boone Trail, Zip 27607–6599; tel. 919/784–3100; James W. Albright, President and Chief Executive Officer (Total facility includes 140 beds in nursing home–type unit) **A**1 2 9 10 **F**4 8 10 11 12 15 16 17 19 21 22 24 25 26 28 29 30 32 33 34 35 37 38 40 42 43 44 49 51 60 64 67 71 72 73 74 **P**1 6 **Web address:** www.rexhealth.com	23	10	534	27907	395	560038	5120	226568	106743	2825
WAKE COUNTY ALCOHOLISM TREATMENT CENTER, 3000 Falstaff Road, Zip 27610–1897; tel. 919/250–1500; Roy Nickell, Director Substance Abuse Services **A**10 **F**2 3 12 16 27 54 56 58 65 67 **P**5	13	82	34	836	26	15463	0	—	3470	124

Hospital, Address, Telephone, Administrator, Approval, Facility, and Physician Codes, Health Care System, Network	Classification Codes		Utilization Data					Expense (thousands) of dollars		
★ American Hospital Association (AHA) membership □ Joint Commission on Accreditation of Healthcare Organizations (JCAHO) accreditation + American Osteopathic Healthcare Association (AOHA) membership ○ American Osteopathic Association (AOA) accreditation △ Commission on Accreditation of Rehabilitation Facilities (CARF) accreditation Control codes 61, 63, 64, 71, 72 and 73 indicate hospitals listed by AOHA, but not registered by AHA. For definition of numerical codes, see page A4	Control	Service	Staffed Beds	Admissions	Census	Outpatient Visits	Births	Total	Payroll	Personnel

⊠ △ WAKE MEDICAL CENTER, (Includes Eastern Wake Day Hospital, 320 Hospital Road, Zebulon, Zip 27597; tel. 919/269–7406; Southern Wake Hospital, 400 West Ranson Street, Fuquay–Varina, Zip 27526; tel. 919/552–2206; Western Wake Medical Center, 1900 Kildaire Farm Road, Cary, Zip 27511; tel. 919/233–2300), 3000 New Bern Avenue, Zip 27610–1295; tel. 919/250–8000; Raymond L. Champ, President (Total facility includes 37 beds in nursing home–type unit) **A**1 3 5 7 9 10 **F**4 7 8 10 11 12 13 14 15 17 18 19 20 21 22 23 24 25 28 30 31 32 34 35 37 38 39 40 41 42 43 44 45 47 48 49 51 63 64 65 66 67 70 71 72 73 74 **P**3 7 **Web address:** www.wakemed.org	23	10	692	30903	553	394377	4457	289333	130933	3935
REIDSVILLE—Rockingham County										
⊠ ANNIE PENN HOSPITAL, 618 South Main Street, Zip 27320–5094; tel. 336/634–1010; Susan H. Fitzgibbon, President and Chief Executive Officer (Total facility includes 42 beds in nursing home–type unit) **A**1 9 10 **F**7 8 12 15 16 19 22 23 28 32 33 34 35 36 37 40 41 42 44 45 46 49 64 65 67 71 73 **S** Carolinas HealthCare System, Charlotte, NC	23	10	126	3873	81	—	382	30523	13252	444
ROANOKE RAPIDS—Halifax County										
⊠ HALIFAX REGIONAL MEDICAL CENTER, 250 Smith Church Road, Zip 27870–4914, Mailing Address: P.O. Box 1089, Zip 27870–1089; tel. 252/535–8011; M. E. Gilstrap, President and Chief Executive Officer **A**1 9 10 **F**7 8 12 14 15 17 18 19 20 21 22 23 28 30 31 34 35 36 37 40 42 44 45 46 49 51 52 53 55 56 57 58 60 63 65 67 71 72 73 74 **Web address:** www.halifaxrmc.org	23	10	157	7199	107	79356	721	49157	21071	727
ROCKINGHAM—Richmond County										
⊠ RICHMOND MEMORIAL HOSPITAL, 925 Long Drive, Zip 28379–4815; tel. 910/417–3000; David G. Hohl, Chief Executive Officer (Total facility includes 51 beds in nursing home–type unit) **A**1 9 10 **F**1 7 8 10 12 14 15 16 17 19 22 23 28 30 32 34 35 37 40 41 44 45 46 49 64 65 67 71 73 74 **P**7	23	10	151	5146	87	41887	551	35871	17560	615
ROCKY MOUNT—Nash County										
⊠ NASH HEALTH CARE SYSTEMS, 2460 Curtis Ellis Drive, Zip 27804–2297; tel. 252/443–8000; Richard Kirk Toomey, President and Chief Executive Officer **A**1 2 9 10 **F**2 3 7 8 10 11 12 13 14 15 16 17 18 19 20 21 22 23 24 25 28 29 30 31 32 33 34 35 36 37 39 40 41 42 44 45 46 49 52 53 54 55 56 57 58 59 60 63 65 66 67 71 72 73 74 **P**6 7 **Web address:** www.nhcs.org	13	10	273	13414	206	103902	1427	104209	47312	1437
ROXBORO—Person County										
⊠ PERSON MEMORIAL HOSPITAL, 615 Ridge Road, Zip 27573–4630; tel. 336/599–2121; Regis Cabonor, Administrator (Total facility includes 60 beds in nursing home–type unit) **A**1 9 10 **F**7 8 12 14 17 19 21 22 28 30 34 35 37 39 40 41 42 44 49 56 58 64 66 67 71 73 74	23	10	110	1708	56	37190	158	14664	6572	298
RUTHERFORDTON—Rutherford County										
⊠ RUTHERFORD HOSPITAL, 288 South Ridgecrest Avenue, Zip 28139–3097; tel. 828/286–5000; Robert D. Jones, President (Total facility includes 150 beds in nursing home–type unit) **A**1 9 10 **F**7 8 10 14 15 16 19 21 22 23 28 30 32 34 35 37 40 41 42 44 45 46 49 50 52 54 55 56 58 59 64 65 67 71 73 74 **S** Quorum Health Group/Quorum Health Resources, Inc., Brentwood, TN	23	10	261	5502	208	109493	609	47858	22309	833
SALISBURY—Rowan County										
⊠ ROWAN REGIONAL MEDICAL CENTER, 612 Mocksville Avenue, Zip 28144–2799; tel. 704/638–1000; James M. Freeman, Chief Executive Officer **A**1 9 10 **F**2 3 7 8 10 11 12 14 16 19 21 22 33 35 37 40 44 46 49 52 59 71 **P**1 **Web address:** www.rowan.org	23	10	222	11584	149	53561	953	79216	35937	1094
⊠ VETERANS AFFAIRS MEDICAL CENTER, 1601 Brenner Avenue, Zip 28144–2559; tel. 704/638–9000; Timothy May, Director (Total facility includes 300 beds in nursing home–type unit) **A**1 5 **F**2 3 4 8 10 12 14 15 17 19 20 21 23 24 25 26 27 28 30 31 32 34 35 37 41 42 44 45 46 49 51 52 54 56 57 58 59 61 63 64 65 67 70 71 73 74 **S** Department of Veterans Affairs, Washington, DC	45	22	551	2946	275	150950	0	104406	53813	1249
SANFORD—Lee County										
⊠ CENTRAL CAROLINA HOSPITAL, 1135 Carthage Street, Zip 27330; tel. 919/774–2100; L. Glenn Davis, Executive Director **A**1 9 10 **F**7 8 10 12 14 15 16 19 20 21 22 23 24 28 30 31 34 35 36 37 39 40 41 42 44 46 49 52 65 71 72 73 74 **P**1 7 **S** TENET Healthcare Corporation, Santa Barbara, CA **Web address:** www.tenethealth.com/centralcarolina	33	10	137	5975	72	55929	882	35718	15965	552
SCOTLAND NECK—Halifax County										
OUR COMMUNITY HOSPITAL, 921 Junior High Road, Zip 27874–0405, Mailing Address: Box 405, Zip 27874–0405; tel. 919/826–4144; Thomas K. Majure, Administrator (Total facility includes 60 beds in nursing home–type unit) (Nonreporting) **A**10	23	10	100	—	—	—	—	—	—	—
SEYMOUR JOHNSON AFB—Wayne County										
★ U. S. AIR FORCE HOSPITAL SEYMOUR JOHNSON, 1050 Jabara Avenue, Zip 27531–5300; tel. 919/722–0001; Colonel Michael Lischak, MC, USAF, Commander (Nonreporting) **S** Department of the Air Force, Bowling AFB, DC	41	10	41	—	—	—	—	—	—	—
SHELBY—Cleveland County										
⊠ CLEVELAND REGIONAL MEDICAL CENTER, 201 Grover Street, Zip 28150–3940; tel. 704/487–3000; John Young, President and Chief Executive Officer (Total facility includes 120 beds in nursing home–type unit) **A**1 2 9 10 **F**7 8 10 11 12 13 15 16 17 18 19 20 21 22 23 25 26 28 29 30 31 32 33 34 35 37 38 39 40 41 42 44 45 46 47 48 49 51 54 56 60 64 67 68 70 71 73 **P**5 **S** Carolinas HealthCare System, Charlotte, NC	16	10	308	9483	235	68841	1192	74068	31911	1104

Hospital, Address, Telephone, Administrator, Approval, Facility, and Physician Codes, Health Care System, Network	Classi-fication Codes		Utilization Data					Expense (thousands) of dollars		
★ American Hospital Association (AHA) membership □ Joint Commission on Accreditation of Healthcare Organizations (JCAHO) accreditation + American Osteopathic Healthcare Association (AOHA) membership ○ American Osteopathic Association (AOA) accreditation △ Commission on Accreditation of Rehabilitation Facilities (CARF) accreditation Control codes 61, 63, 64, 71, 72 and 73 indicate hospitals listed by AOHA, but not registered by AHA. For definition of numerical codes, see page A4	Control	Service	Staffed Beds	Admissions	Census	Outpatient Visits	Births	Total	Payroll	Personnel

SILER CITY—Chatham County

☒ CHATHAM HOSPITAL, West Third Street and Ivy Avenue, Zip 27344–2343, Mailing Address: P.O. Box 649, Zip 27344; tel. 919/663–2113; Woodrow W. Hathaway, Jr., Chief Executive Officer **A**1 9 10 **F**11 12 15 17 19 22 28 35 39 44 49 59 65 70 71 73 **S** Quorum Health Group/Quorum Health Resources, Inc., Brentwood, TN — 23 10 | 35 | 1049 | 14 | 15430 | 0 | 7072 | 3236 | 135

SMITHFIELD—Johnston County

☒ JOHNSTON MEMORIAL HOSPITAL, 509 North Bright Leaf Boulevard, Zip 27577–1376, Mailing Address: P.O. Box 1376, Zip 27577–1376; tel. 919/934–8171; Leland E. Farnell, President **A**1 9 10 **F**7 8 10 14 15 16 19 20 21 22 23 25 28 30 32 33 34 35 36 37 40 42 44 49 51 52 54 56 57 65 68 71 72 73 **P**6 **S** Quorum Health Group/Quorum Health Resources, Inc., Brentwood, TN — 13 10 | 127 | 4782 | 63 | 165902 | 707 | 38964 | 18610 | 630

SOUTHPORT—Brunswick County

☒ J. ARTHUR DOSHER MEMORIAL HOSPITAL, 924 Howe Street, Zip 28461–3099; tel. 910/457–3800; Edgar Haywood, III, Administrator **A**1 10 **F**14 15 16 19 22 26 28 32 34 35 41 44 49 65 67 71 — 16 10 | 40 | 1343 | 14 | 12813 | 0 | 11773 | 4792 | 176

SPARTA—Alleghany County

☒ ALLEGHANY MEMORIAL HOSPITAL, 233 Doctors Street, Zip 28675–0009, Mailing Address: P.O. Box 9, Zip 28675–0009; tel. 336/372–5511; James Yarborough, Chief Executive Officer **A**1 9 10 **F**1 4 7 8 10 12 14 15 16 17 19 20 22 30 32 33 34 35 40 41 42 43 44 64 65 70 71 **S** Quorum Health Group/Quorum Health Resources, Inc., Brentwood, TN — 23 10 | 46 | 1534 | 21 | 8408 | 29 | 8824 | 4430 | 172

SPRUCE PINE—Mitchell County

□ SPRUCE PINE COMMUNITY HOSPITAL, 125 Hospital Drive, Zip 28777–3035, Mailing Address: P.O. Drawer 9, Zip 28777–0009; tel. 704/765–4201; Keith S. Holtsclaw, Chief Executive Officer **A**1 9 10 **F**7 11 12 15 16 17 19 20 22 24 28 30 32 34 35 40 41 42 44 48 49 51 64 65 67 71 73 **P**5 — 23 10 | 45 | 2008 | 19 | 35413 | 180 | 10084 | 6187 | 209

STATESVILLE—Iredell County

☒ DAVIS MEDICAL CENTER, (Formerly Columbia Davis Medical Center), 218 Old Mocksville Road, Zip 28625, Mailing Address: P.O. Box 1823, Zip 28687–1823; tel. 704/873–0281; R. Alan Larson, Chief Executive Officer (Total facility includes 13 beds in nursing home–type unit) (Nonreporting) **A**1 10 **S** NetCare Health Systems, Inc., Nashville, TN — 33 10 | 132 | — | — | — | — | — | — | —

☒ IREDELL MEMORIAL HOSPITAL, 557 Brookdale Drive, Zip 28677–1828, Mailing Address: P.O. Box 1828, Zip 28687–1828; tel. 704/873–5661; S. Arnold Nunnery, President and Chief Executive Officer (Total facility includes 48 beds in nursing home–type unit) **A**1 2 9 10 **F**7 8 10 11 12 13 14 15 16 17 19 21 22 23 28 29 30 31 32 33 35 37 40 41 42 44 45 46 49 51 53 54 55 56 57 58 59 60 63 64 65 67 71 73 74 **P**6 — 23 10 | 202 | 8325 | 107 | 138535 | 1017 | 67090 | 32217 | 830

SUPPLY—Brunswick County

☒ BRUNSWICK COMMUNITY HOSPITAL, (Formerly Columbia Brunswick Hospital), 1 Medical Center Drive, Zip 28462–3350, Mailing Address: P.O. Box 139, Zip 28462–0139; tel. 910/755–8121; C. Mark Gregson, Chief Executive Officer (Nonreporting) **A**1 9 10 **S** NetCare Health Systems, Inc., Nashville, TN — 33 10 | 56 | — | — | — | — | — | — | —

SYLVA—Jackson County

☒ HARRIS REGIONAL HOSPITAL, 68 Hospital Road, Zip 28779–2795; tel. 828/586–7000; Mark Leonard, Chief Executive Officer (Total facility includes 100 beds in nursing home–type unit) **A**1 10 **F**7 8 12 15 16 17 19 21 22 23 27 28 29 30 32 33 34 35 37 39 40 41 42 44 45 46 49 56 60 63 64 65 71 72 73 74 **P**7 8
Web address: www.westcare.org — 23 10 | 175 | 4488 | 143 | 50083 | 742 | 41342 | 18865 | 741

TARBORO—Edgecombe County

☒ HERITAGE HOSPITAL, 111 Hospital Drive, Zip 27886–2011; tel. 252/641–7700; Janet Mullaney, President (Total facility includes 10 beds in nursing home–type unit) **A**1 9 10 **F**7 8 12 15 16 19 20 21 22 23 24 28 29 30 35 37 40 41 42 44 46 48 49 64 65 66 67 71 73 **P**1 7 8 — 23 10 | 127 | 4944 | 57 | 24933 | 655 | 22002 | 10811 | 392

TAYLORSVILLE—Alexander County

☒ ALEXANDER COMMUNITY HOSPITAL, 326 Third Street S.W., Zip 28681–3096; tel. 828/632–4282; Joe W. Pollard, Jr., Chief Executive Officer **A**1 9 10 **F**8 11 15 16 17 19 21 22 28 30 35 40 41 44 46 49 57 59 64 65 67 71 — 23 10 | 39 | 895 | 11 | 14202 | 0 | 7137 | 2751 | 97

THOMASVILLE—Davidson County

☒ COMMUNITY GENERAL HOSPITAL OF THOMASVILLE, 207 Old Lexington Road, Zip 27360, Mailing Address: P.O. Box 789, Zip 27361–0789; tel. 336/472–2000; Lynn Ingram Boggs, President and Chief Executive Officer (Total facility includes 15 beds in nursing home–type unit) **A**1 9 10 **F**7 8 10 11 12 15 16 17 19 21 22 28 30 31 34 35 36 37 39 40 41 42 44 45 46 49 52 56 57 58 63 64 65 67 68 71 72 73 74 **P**5 **S** Novant Health, Winston Salem, NC
Web address: www.cghp.org — 23 10 | 123 | 4734 | 55 | 77705 | 623 | 24494 | 12864 | 384

TROY—Montgomery County

□ FIRSTHEALTH MONTGOMERY MEMORIAL HOSPITAL, 520 Allen Street, Zip 27371–2802, Mailing Address: P.O. Box 486, Zip 27371–0486; tel. 910/572–1301; Kerry A. Hensley, R.N., Administrator (Total facility includes 51 beds in nursing home–type unit) **A**1 9 10 **F**8 14 15 16 17 19 20 22 24 26 27 30 32 33 41 44 49 51 53 58 64 65 71 73 74 **P**3 — 23 10 | 66 | 718 | 51 | 20635 | 0 | 8490 | 4708 | 168

VALDESE—Burke County

☒ VALDESE GENERAL HOSPITAL, Mailing Address: P.O. Box 700, Zip 28690–0700; tel. 828/874–2251; Lloyd E. Wallace, President and Chief Executive Officer (Total facility includes 120 beds in nursing home–type unit) **A**1 2 10 **F**7 8 10 11 12 14 15 16 17 19 21 22 23 26 28 30 34 35 37 39 40 41 42 44 45 46 49 60 62 63 64 65 70 71 73 **P**8 **S** Carolinas HealthCare System, Charlotte, NC — 16 10 | 199 | 3439 | 153 | 31575 | 370 | 29384 | 12960 | 570

Hospital, Address, Telephone, Administrator, Approval, Facility, and Physician Codes, Health Care System, Network	Classification Codes		Utilization Data					Expense (thousands) of dollars		
	Control	Service	Staffed Beds	Admissions	Census	Outpatient Visits	Births	Total	Payroll	Personnel

★ American Hospital Association (AHA) membership
☐ Joint Commission on Accreditation of Healthcare Organizations (JCAHO) accreditation
+ American Osteopathic Healthcare Association (AOHA) membership
○ American Osteopathic Association (AOA) accreditation
△ Commission on Accreditation of Rehabilitation Facilities (CARF) accreditation
Control codes 61, 63, 64, 71, 72 and 73 indicate hospitals listed by AOHA, but not registered by AHA. For definition of numerical codes, see page A4

WADESBORO—Anson County

✖ ANSON COMMUNITY HOSPITAL, (Formerly Anson County Hospital and Skilled Nursing Facilities), 500 Morven Road, Zip 28170–2745; tel. 704/694–5131; Frederick G. Thompson, Ph.D., Administrator and Chief Executive Officer (Total facility includes 95 beds in nursing home–type unit) **A**1 9 10 **F**8 12 14 15 16 17 19 21 22 26 28 29 30 34 41 42 44 45 46 49 64 65 67 71 **S** Carolinas HealthCare System, Charlotte, NC	16	10	125	1673	108	26731	0	15139	7449	301

WASHINGTON—Beaufort County

✖ BEAUFORT COUNTY HOSPITAL, 628 East 12th Street, Zip 27889–3498; tel. 252/975–4100; Kenneth E. Ragland, Administrator **A**1 9 10 **F**3 7 8 11 12 14 15 16 18 19 20 21 22 24 27 28 29 30 32 33 34 35 36 39 41 42 43 44 45 46 49 51 52 54 55 56 57 62 65 66 67 69 70 71 72 73 74 **P**3 5	23	10	103	3527	52	45907	351	28986	14310	464

WHITEVILLE—Columbus County

✖ COLUMBUS COUNTY HOSPITAL, 500 Jefferson Street, Zip 28472–9987; tel. 910/642–8011; William S. Clark, Chief Executive Officer (Nonreporting) **A**1 9 10 **S** Quorum Health Group/Quorum Health Resources, Inc., Brentwood, TN **Web address:** www.cchospital.com	23	10	117	—	—	—	—	—	—	—

WILLIAMSTON—Martin County

✖ MARTIN GENERAL HOSPITAL, 310 South McCaskey Road, Zip 27892–2150, Mailing Address: P.O. Box 1128, Zip 27892–1128; tel. 252/809–6121; Scott M. Landrum, Chief Executive Officer (Nonreporting) **A**1 3 9 10 **S** Community Health Systems, Inc., Brentwood, TN	13	10	49	—	—	—	—	—	—	—

WILMINGTON—New Hanover County

✖ CAPE FEAR MEMORIAL HOSPITAL, 5301 Wrightsville Avenue, Zip 28403–6599; tel. 910/452–8100; C. Mark Gregson, Chief Executive Officer (Nonreporting) **A**1 10	33	10	109	—	—	—	—	—	—	—
✖ △ NEW HANOVER REGIONAL MEDICAL CENTER, 2131 South 17th Street, Zip 28401–7483, Mailing Address: P.O. Box 9000, Zip 28402–9000; tel. 910/343–7000; William K. Atkinson, II, Ph.D., Chief Executive Officer **A**1 3 5 7 9 10 **F**4 5 6 7 8 10 11 12 14 15 16 17 18 19 21 22 23 25 26 27 28 29 30 31 32 33 34 35 37 38 39 40 42 43 44 45 46 48 49 51 52 53 54 55 56 57 58 59 60 61 63 64 65 66 67 68 70 71 73 74 **P**7 **Web address:** www.nhrmc.org	13	10	546	26039	403	56395	2521	247058	103566	3054

WILSON—Wilson County

✖ WILSON MEMORIAL HOSPITAL, 1705 South Tarboro Street, Zip 27893–3428; tel. 252/399–8040; Christopher T. Durrer, President and Chief Executive Officer **A**1 9 10 **F**1 7 8 10 12 15 16 17 19 20 22 23 28 29 30 32 33 34 35 36 37 40 41 42 44 45 46 49 52 53 54 55 56 58 64 65 67 71 73 **P**6 **Web address:** www.wilsonmemorial.com	23	10	221	7995	100	122882	1329	61186	25114	843

WINDSOR—Bertie County

★ BERTIE MEMORIAL HOSPITAL, 401 Sterlingworth Street, Zip 27983–1726, Mailing Address: P.O. Box 40, Zip 27983–1726; tel. 252/794–3141; Anthony F. Mullen, Administrator **A**9 10 **F**8 15 19 22 28 34 44 65 71 73	23	10	16	356	6	17140	0	4743	2074	87

WINSTON–SALEM—Forsyth County

AMOS COTTAGE REHABILITATION HOSPITAL, 3325 Silas Creek Parkway, Zip 27103–3089; tel. 336/774–2400; Douglas M. Cody, Administrator (Nonreporting) **A**10	23	56	31	—	—	—	—	—	—	—
☐ CHARTER BEHAVIORAL HEALTH SYSTEM OF WINSTON–SALEM, (Formerly Charter Hospital of Winston–Salem), 3637 Old Vineyard Road, Zip 27104–4835; tel. 336/768–7710; Michael J. Carney, Chief Executive Officer **A**1 10 **F**2 3 15 52 53 54 55 56 57 58 59 **P**6 **S** Magellan Health Services, Atlanta, GA	33	22	111	1600	60	—	0	—	—	145
✖ △ FORSYTH MEDICAL CENTER, (Formerly Forsyth Memorial Hospital), 3333 Silas Creek Parkway, Zip 27103–3090; tel. 336/718–5000; Gregory J. Beier, President (Total facility includes 22 beds in nursing home–type unit) **A**1 2 3 5 7 9 10 **F**3 4 5 7 8 10 11 12 13 14 15 16 17 19 20 21 22 23 24 25 26 28 29 30 32 33 34 35 37 38 39 40 41 42 43 44 45 46 48 49 51 52 54 55 57 58 59 60 64 65 66 67 71 72 73 74 **P**4 5 7 8 **S** Novant Health, Winston Salem, NC **Web address:** www.novanthealth.org	23	10	680	32422	517	123429	6197	193049	95711	2840
✖ MEDICAL PARK HOSPITAL, 1950 South Hawthorne Road, Zip 27103–3993, Mailing Address: P.O. Box 24728, Zip 27114–4728; tel. 336/718–0600; Eduard R. Koehler, Administrator **A**1 2 9 10 **F**2 3 4 7 8 9 10 11 12 14 15 16 17 19 20 21 22 24 25 26 27 28 29 30 31 32 33 34 35 37 38 39 40 41 42 43 44 45 46 47 48 49 51 52 54 55 56 57 58 59 60 63 64 65 66 67 71 72 73 74 **P**6 **S** Novant Health, Winston Salem, NC	23	10	59	2061	17	11511	0	18247	6651	221
✖ △ NORTH CAROLINA BAPTIST HOSPITAL, Medical Center Boulevard, Zip 27157; tel. 336/716–2011; Len B. Preslar, Jr., President and Chief Executive Officer (Total facility includes 49 beds in nursing home–type unit) **A**1 2 3 5 7 8 9 10 **F**3 4 5 8 9 10 11 12 13 14 15 16 17 19 20 21 22 23 24 25 26 27 28 29 30 31 32 33 34 35 36 37 38 39 40 41 42 43 44 45 46 47 48 49 50 51 52 53 54 55 56 57 58 59 60 61 63 64 65 66 67 68 70 71 72 73 74 **P**4 6 7 **Web address:** www.wfubmc.edu	23	10	821	29139	607	126015	—	412800	189277	5547

YADKINVILLE—Yadkin County

✖ HOOTS MEMORIAL HOSPITAL, 624 West Main Street, Zip 27055–7804, Mailing Address: P.O. Box 68, Zip 27055–0068; tel. 336/679–2041; Lance C. Labine, President **A**1 9 10 **F**3 8 12 15 16 19 22 28 30 31 32 33 34 35 37 44 49 59 71 73 **P**6 **Web address:** www.bgsm.edu/hoots/	13	10	26	672	8	16921	0	7064	3457	110

ZEBULON—Wake County

EASTERN WAKE DAY HOSPITAL See Wake Medical Center, Raleigh

NORTH DAKOTA

Resident population 638 (in thousands)
Resident population in metro areas 43.1%
Birth rate per 1,000 population 13.2
65 years and over 14.4%
Percent of persons without health insurance 9.8%

Hospital, Address, Telephone, Administrator, Approval, Facility, and Physician Codes, Health Care System, Network	Classi-fication Codes		Utilization Data					Expense (thousands) of dollars		
	Control	Service	Staffed Beds	Admissions	Census	Outpatient Visits	Births	Total	Payroll	Personnel

★ American Hospital Association (AHA) membership
□ Joint Commission on Accreditation of Healthcare Organizations (JCAHO) accreditation
+ American Osteopathic Healthcare Association (AOHA) membership
○ American Osteopathic Association (AOA) accreditation
△ Commission on Accreditation of Rehabilitation Facilities (CARF) accreditation
Control codes 61, 63, 64, 71, 72 and 73 indicate hospitals listed by AOHA, but not registered by AHA. For definition of numerical codes, see page A4.

ASHLEY—McIntosh County
★ ASHLEY MEDICAL CENTER, 612 North Center Avenue, Zip 58413–0556; tel. 701/288–3433; Lieutenant Kathleen Hoeft, Administrator and Chief Executive Officer (Total facility includes 44 beds in nursing home–type unit) (Nonreporting) **A**9 10

	23	10	70	—	—	—	—	—	—	—

BELCOURT—Rolette County
✠ U. S. PUBLIC HEALTH SERVICE INDIAN HOSPITAL, Mailing Address: P.O. Box 160, Zip 58316–0160; tel. 701/477–6111; Ray Grandbois, M.P.H., Service Unit Director (Nonreporting) **A**1 5 10 **S** U. S. Public Health Service Indian Health Service, Rockville, MD

	47	10	42	—	—	—	—	—	—	—

BISMARCK—Burleigh County
✠ △ MEDCENTER ONE, 300 North Seventh Street, Zip 58501–4439, Mailing Address: P.O. Box 5525, Zip 58506–5525; tel. 701/323–6000; Terrance G. Brosseau, President and Chief Executive Officer (Total facility includes 21 beds in nursing home–type unit) **A**1 2 3 5 7 9 10 **F**2 3 4 5 7 8 10 11 12 13 14 15 16 17 18 19 20 21 22 23 24 26 27 28 29 30 31 32 33 34 35 36 37 38 39 40 41 42 43 44 45 46 47 48 49 51 52 53 54 55 56 57 58 59 60 61 62 63 64 65 66 67 68 70 71 72 73 74 **P**6
Web address: www.medcenterone.com

	23	10	230	7623	129	423993	542	135387	72370	1586

✠ △ ST. ALEXIUS MEDICAL CENTER, 900 East Broadway, Zip 58501–4586, Mailing Address: P.O. Box 5510, Zip 58506–5510; tel. 701/224–7000; Richard A. Tschider, FACHE, Administrator and Chief Executive Officer (Nonreporting) **A**1 2 3 5 7 9 10 **S** Benedictine Sisters of the Annunciation, Bismarck, ND
Web address: www.st.alexius.org

	21	10	269	—	—	—	—	—	—	—

BOTTINEAU—Bottineau County
ST. ANDREW'S HEALTH CENTER, 316 Ohmer Street, Zip 58318–1018; tel. 701/228–2255; Keith Korman, President (Total facility includes 32 beds in nursing home–type unit) **A**5 9 10 **F**6 7 14 15 16 19 22 26 27 28 30 32 36 39 40 44 49 53 54 55 57 62 63 64 65 66 71 73 **P**5 **S** Sisters of Mary of the Presentation Health Corporation, Fargo, ND

	23	10	67	461	41	6000	8	3503	1569	80

BOWMAN—Bowman County
ST. LUKE'S TRI–STATE HOSPITAL, 202 Sixth Avenue S.W., Zip 58623–0009, Mailing Address: P.O. Drawer C, Zip 58623; tel. 701/523–5265; Jim Opdahl, Administrator **A**9 10 **F**8 15 17 19 22 28 35 37 44 49 51 53 54 57 64 65 66 71 74 **P**6

	23	10	34	372	10	3871	0	2537	1117	52

CANDO—Towner County
★ TOWNER COUNTY MEDICAL CENTER, Highway 281 N, Box 6888, Zip 58324–0688; tel. 701/968–4411; Timothy J. Tracy, Chief Executive Officer (Total facility includes 10 beds in nursing home–type unit) (Nonreporting) **A**9 10

	23	10	32	—	—	—	—	—	—	—

CARRINGTON—Foster County
★ CARRINGTON HEALTH CENTER, 800 North Fourth Street, Zip 58421–1217; tel. 701/652–3141; Brian J. McDermott, President and Chief Executive Officer (Total facility includes 40 beds in nursing home–type unit) **A**9 10 **F**7 8 15 16 19 22 26 28 30 32 34 35 44 49 51 64 65 67 71 73 **P**4 7 **S** Catholic Health Initiatives, Denver, CO

	21	10	70	831	49	32208	57	8185	3111	151

CAVALIER—Pembina County
★ PEMBINA COUNTY MEMORIAL HOSPITAL AND WEDGEWOOD MANOR, 301 Mountain Street East, Zip 58220–4015; tel. 701/265–8461; George A. Rohrich, Administrator (Total facility includes 60 beds in nursing home–type unit) (Nonreporting) **A**9 10 **S** Lutheran Health Systems, Fargo, ND

	23	10	89	—	—	—	—	—	—	—

COOPERSTOWN—Griggs County
GRIGGS COUNTY HOSPITAL AND NURSING HOME, 1200 Roberts Avenue, Zip 58425, Mailing Address: P.O. Box 728, Zip 58425–0728; tel. 701/797–2221; Bruce D. Bowersox, Administrator and Chief Executive Officer (Total facility includes 58 beds in nursing home–type unit) (Nonreporting) **A**9 10

	23	10	69	—	—	—	—	—	—	—

CROSBY—Divide County
ST. LUKE'S HOSPITAL, 702 First Street Southwest, Zip 58730–0010; tel. 701/965–6384; Leslie O. Urvand, Administrator **A**9 10 **F**8 11 14 19 22 28 29 30 32 34 36 44 45 46 49 71

	23	10	29	280	5	3203	0	2358	962	44

DEVILS LAKE—Ramsey County
✠ MERCY HOSPITAL, 1031 Seventh Street, Zip 58301–2798; tel. 701/662–2131; Marlene Krein, President and Chief Executive Officer **A**1 9 10 **F**7 11 14 15 16 17 19 21 22 28 29 30 31 32 33 35 37 39 40 42 44 45 46 49 65 67 68 71 73 **P**5 **S** Catholic Health Initiatives, Denver, CO

	23	10	35	1645	17	12939	250	10903	5000	164

DICKINSON—Stark County
✠ ST. JOSEPH'S HOSPITAL AND HEALTH CENTER, 30 Seventh Street West, Zip 58601–4399; tel. 701/225–7200; Greg Hanson, President and Chief Executive Officer **A**1 9 10 **F**5 6 15 16 17 19 21 24 30 32 33 34 35 36 37 40 41 44 45 46 52 53 54 55 56 57 58 59 63 65 66 67 70 71 73 **S** Catholic Health Initiatives, Denver, CO
Web address: www.stjosehospital.org

	21	10	90	2871	44	30352	340	23651	9853	350

Hospital, Address, Telephone, Administrator, Approval, Facility, and Physician Codes, Health Care System, Network	Classification Codes		Utilization Data					Expense (thousands) of dollars		
	Control	Service	Staffed Beds	Admissions	Census	Outpatient Visits	Births	Total	Payroll	Personnel

★ American Hospital Association (AHA) membership
□ Joint Commission on Accreditation of Healthcare Organizations (JCAHO) accreditation
+ American Osteopathic Healthcare Association (AOHA) membership
○ American Osteopathic Association (AOA) accreditation
△ Commission on Accreditation of Rehabilitation Facilities (CARF) accreditation
Control codes 61, 63, 64, 71, 72 and 73 indicate hospitals listed by AOHA, but not registered by AHA. For definition of numerical codes, see page A4

ELGIN—Grant County

	Control	Service	Staffed Beds	Admissions	Census	Outpatient Visits	Births	Total	Payroll	Personnel
JACOBSON MEMORIAL HOSPITAL CARE CENTER, 601 East Street North, Zip 58533–0376; tel. 701/584–2792; Jacqueline Seibel, Administrator (Total facility includes 25 beds in nursing home–type unit) (Nonreporting) **A**9 10	23	10	50	—	—	—	—	—	—	—

FARGO—Cass County

	Control	Service	Staffed Beds	Admissions	Census	Outpatient Visits	Births	Total	Payroll	Personnel
□ △ DAKOTA HEARTLAND HEALTH SYSTEM, 1720 South University Drive, Zip 58103–4994; tel. 701/280–4100; Louis Kauffman, President and Chief Executive Officer (Total facility includes 16 beds in nursing home–type unit) (Nonreporting) **A**1 2 3 5 7 9 10 **S** Paracelsus Healthcare Corporation, Houston, TX **Web address:** www.dakotahealthland.com	32	10	203							
⊠ △ MERITCARE HEALTH SYSTEM, 720 Fourth Street North, Zip 58122–0002; tel. 701/234–6000; Roger Gilbertson, M.D., President (Total facility includes 24 beds in nursing home–type unit) **A**1 2 3 5 7 8 9 10 **F**3 4 7 8 10 11 12 14 15 16 19 21 22 23 24 25 26 28 29 30 31 32 33 34 35 37 38 39 40 41 42 43 44 45 46 47 48 49 51 52 53 54 55 56 57 58 59 60 61 63 65 66 67 68 70 71 72 73 74 **P**6 **Web address:** www.meritcare.com	21	10	311	12883	188	44013	1600	149549	56085	1628
⊠ VETERANS AFFAIRS MEDICAL AND REGIONAL OFFICE CENTER, 2101 Elm Street, Zip 58102–2498; tel. 701/232–3241; Douglas M. Kenyon, Director (Total facility includes 50 beds in nursing home–type unit) **A**1 3 5 9 **F**3 8 12 17 18 19 20 21 22 26 27 28 30 31 32 33 35 37 39 41 42 44 45 46 49 51 52 54 55 56 57 58 59 60 63 64 65 67 71 73 74 **S** Department of Veterans Affairs, Washington, DC	45	10	113	2709	94	86134	0	46417	24359	530

FORT YATES—Sioux County

	Control	Service	Staffed Beds	Admissions	Census	Outpatient Visits	Births	Total	Payroll	Personnel
⊠ U. S. PUBLIC HEALTH SERVICE INDIAN HOSPITAL, N 10 North River Road, Zip 58538, Mailing Address: P.O. Box J, Zip 58538; tel. 701/854–3831; Terry Pourier, Service Unit Director (Nonreporting) **A**1 5 10 **S** U. S. Public Health Service Indian Health Service, Rockville, MD	47	10	14	—	—	—	—	—	—	—

GARRISON—McLean County

	Control	Service	Staffed Beds	Admissions	Census	Outpatient Visits	Births	Total	Payroll	Personnel
★ GARRISON MEMORIAL HOSPITAL, 407 Third Avenue S.E., Zip 58540–0039; tel. 701/463–2275; Richard Spilovoy, Administrator (Total facility includes 24 beds in nursing home–type unit) **A**5 9 10 **F**8 14 15 16 19 32 33 35 49 64 65 66 70 71 **P**6 8 **S** Benedictine Sisters of the Annunciation, Bismarck, ND	21	10	30	301	33	8840	1	2907	1537	70

GRAFTON—Walsh County

	Control	Service	Staffed Beds	Admissions	Census	Outpatient Visits	Births	Total	Payroll	Personnel
⊠ UNITY MEDICAL CENTER, 164 West 13th Street, Zip 58237–1896; tel. 701/352–1620; Everett A. Butler, Chief Executive Officer **A**1 5 9 10 **F**7 8 15 16 17 19 21 22 28 30 32 33 34 35 40 41 42 44 46 49 51 65 70 71 73 **P**6	23	10	17	939	7	26762	46	4724	2661	90

GRAND FORKS—Grand Forks County

	Control	Service	Staffed Beds	Admissions	Census	Outpatient Visits	Births	Total	Payroll	Personnel
⊠ △ ALTRU HEALTH SYSTEM, (Includes Altru Hospital, 1200 South Columbia Road, tel. 701/780–5000; Altru Health Institute, 1300 South Columbia Road, tel. 701/780–2311), 1000 South Columbia Road, Zip 58201; tel. 701/780–5000; Gregory Gerloff, Chief Executive Officer **A**1 2 3 5 7 9 10 **F**2 3 4 5 6 7 8 10 12 13 14 15 16 17 18 19 21 22 23 24 26 27 28 29 30 31 32 33 34 35 36 37 38 39 40 41 42 43 44 45 46 48 49 50 51 52 53 54 55 56 57 58 59 60 61 62 63 65 66 67 70 71 72 73 74 **P**2 **Web address:** www.altru.org	23	10	259	10618	149	83397	1297	199611	105438	2491

GRAND FORKS AFB—Grand Forks County

	Control	Service	Staffed Beds	Admissions	Census	Outpatient Visits	Births	Total	Payroll	Personnel
⊠ U. S. AIR FORCE HOSPITAL, Grand Forks SAC, Zip 58205–6332, Mailing Address: Grand Forks SAC, 220 G. Street, Zip 58205–6332; tel. 701/747–5391; Lieutenant Colonel Robert J. Rennie, Administrator **A**1 5 9 **F**7 8 15 16 17 18 19 20 22 27 28 29 30 32 33 34 35 36 39 40 41 42 43 44 45 46 49 51 53 54 56 57 58 59 60 65 67 68 70 71 72 73 74 **S** Department of the Air Force, Bowling AFB, DC	41	44	12	298	2	64240	217	16795	—	226

HARVEY—Wells County

	Control	Service	Staffed Beds	Admissions	Census	Outpatient Visits	Births	Total	Payroll	Personnel
★ ST. ALOISIUS MEDICAL CENTER, 325 East Brewster Street, Zip 58341–1605; tel. 701/324–4651; Ronald J. Volk, President (Total facility includes 116 beds in nursing home–type unit) **A**5 9 10 **F**3 7 8 19 22 28 30 32 33 35 37 40 41 42 44 49 53 54 58 64 65 67 71 73 74 **S** Sisters of Mary of the Presentation Health Corporation, Fargo, ND	21	10	165	826	128	7278	20	7401	4000	130

HAZEN—Mercer County

	Control	Service	Staffed Beds	Admissions	Census	Outpatient Visits	Births	Total	Payroll	Personnel
★ SAKAKAWEA MEDICAL CENTER, 510 Eighth Avenue N.E., Zip 58545–4637; tel. 701/748–2225; Edwin E. Hurysz, Chief Executive Officer **A**5 9 10 **F**3 7 8 11 15 16 19 22 26 28 30 32 33 35 37 39 40 44 45 62 64 65 66 67 71 73 **P**6	23	10	32	577	8	13484	41	5103	2026	113

HETTINGER—Adams County

	Control	Service	Staffed Beds	Admissions	Census	Outpatient Visits	Births	Total	Payroll	Personnel
□ WEST RIVER REGIONAL MEDICAL CENTER, 1000 Highway 12, Zip 58639–7530, Mailing Address: Rural Route 2, Box 124, Zip 58639–0124; tel. 701/567–4561; Jim K. Long, CPA, Administrator and Chief Executive Officer **A**1 5 9 10 **F**7 8 11 12 13 15 16 17 18 19 20 21 22 26 27 28 29 30 32 34 35 37 39 40 41 42 44 45 46 49 58 62 63 64 65 66 67 70 71 73 74 **P**3	23	10	43	1600	20	8865	116	14103	4959	201

HILLSBORO—Traill County

	Control	Service	Staffed Beds	Admissions	Census	Outpatient Visits	Births	Total	Payroll	Personnel
HILLSBORO MEDICAL CENTER, 12 Third Street S.E., Zip 58045–4821, Mailing Address: P.O. Box 609, Zip 58045–0609; tel. 701/436–4501; Bruce D. Bowersox, Administrator (Total facility includes 50 beds in nursing home–type unit) (Nonreporting) **A**5 9 10	23	10	74	—	—	—	—	—	—	—

JAMESTOWN—Stutsman County

	Control	Service	Staffed Beds	Admissions	Census	Outpatient Visits	Births	Total	Payroll	Personnel
⊠ JAMESTOWN HOSPITAL, 419 Fifth Street N.E., Zip 58401–3360; tel. 701/252–1050; Richard W. Hall, President **A**1 5 9 10 **F**7 8 15 16 19 21 22 30 31 32 33 34 35 37 39 40 41 45 46 49 56 61 63 64 65 67 71 73 **Web address:** www.jamestownhospital.com	23	10	56	1945	25	44415	237	14464	6961	240

Hospital, Address, Telephone, Administrator, Approval, Facility, and Physician Codes, Health Care System, Network	Classi-fication Codes		Utilization Data					Expense (thousands) of dollars		
	Control	Service	Staffed Beds	Admissions	Census	Outpatient Visits	Births	Total	Payroll	Personnel

Approval codes legend:
★ American Hospital Association (AHA) membership
□ Joint Commission on Accreditation of Healthcare Organizations (JCAHO) accreditation
+ American Osteopathic Healthcare Association (AOHA) membership
○ American Osteopathic Association (AOA) accreditation
△ Commission on Accreditation of Rehabilitation Facilities (CARF) accreditation
Control codes 61, 63, 64, 71, 72 and 73 indicate hospitals listed by AOHA, but not registered by AHA. For definition of numerical codes, see page A4

Hospital, Address, Telephone, Administrator, Approval, Facility, and Physician Codes, Health Care System, Network	Control	Service	Staffed Beds	Admissions	Census	Outpatient Visits	Births	Total	Payroll	Personnel
□ NORTH DAKOTA STATE HOSPITAL, 1624 23rd Street S.E., Zip 58401, Mailing Address: P.O. Box 476, Zip 58402–0476; tel. 701/253–3650; Alex Schweitzer, Superintendent and Chief Executive Officer (Nonreporting) **A**1 5 9 10	12	22	280	—	—	—	—	—	—	—
KENMARE—Ward County										
★ KENMARE COMMUNITY HOSPITAL, 317 First Avenue N.W., Zip 58746–7104, Mailing Address: P.O. Box 697, Zip 58746–0697; tel. 701/385–4296; Verlin D. Buechler, Administrator and Chief Executive Officer (Total facility includes 12 beds in nursing home–type unit) (Nonreporting) **A**9 10 **S** Quorum Health Group/Quorum Health Resources, Inc., Brentwood, TN	30	48	42	—	—	—	—	—	—	—
LANGDON—Cavalier County										
★ CAVALIER COUNTY MEMORIAL HOSPITAL, 909 Second Street, Zip 58249–2499; tel. 701/256–6100; Daryl J. Wilkens, Administrator **A**5 9 10 **F**7 8 11 14 15 17 19 22 28 29 30 32 33 34 37 39 40 42 44 49 51 65 71 **P**6	23	10	28	531	6	16377	24	3080	1679	67
LINTON—Emmons County										
LINTON HOSPITAL, 518 North Broadway, Zip 58552–7308, Mailing Address: P.O. Box 850, Zip 58552–0850; tel. 701/254–4511; Dale Aman, Administrator **A**5 9 10 **F**6 8 16 19 21 22 30 32 33 35 36 37 40 44 49 62 65 70 71 73	23	10	25	371	4	6560	8	3078	1744	75
LISBON—Ransom County										
★ LISBON MEDICAL CENTER, 905 Main Street, Zip 58054–0353, Mailing Address: P.O. Box 353, Zip 58054–0353; tel. 701/683–5241; Michael Matthews, Administrator (Total facility includes 45 beds in nursing home–type unit) (Nonreporting) **A**5 9 10 **S** Lutheran Health Systems, Fargo, ND **Web address:** www.lhsnet.com	23	10	70	—	—	—	—	—	—	—
MAYVILLE—Traill County										
★ UNION HOSPITAL, 42 Sixth Avenue S.E., Zip 58257–1598; tel. 701/786–3800; Roger Baier, Chief Executive Officer **A**5 9 10 **F**2 3 7 8 14 15 16 19 21 22 24 26 31 32 34 39 40 44 48 52 58 61 64 65 70 71 **Web address:** www.unionhospital.com	23	10	28	473	7	8056	18	2861	1383	56
MCVILLE—Nelson County										
COMMUNITY HOSPITAL IN NELSON COUNTY, 200 Main Street, Zip 58254, Mailing Address: P.O. Box 365, Zip 58254–0365; tel. 701/322–4328; Jim Opdahl, Administrator (Nonreporting) **A**9 10	23	10	19	—	—	—	—	—	—	—
MINOT—Ward County										
⊞ △ TRINITY HEALTH, (Formerly Trinity Medical Center), Burdick Expressway at Main Street, Zip 58701–5020, Mailing Address: P.O. Box 5020, Zip 58702–5020; tel. 701/857–5000; Terry G. Hoff, President (Total facility includes 294 beds in nursing home–type unit) **A**1 2 3 5 7 9 10 **F**1 3 4 7 8 10 12 13 14 15 16 17 19 21 22 24 25 26 28 30 31 32 33 34 35 37 38 39 40 41 42 43 44 45 46 48 49 51 53 54 55 56 57 58 59 61 62 63 64 65 66 67 68 70 71 72 73 74 **P**1 3 4 5 6	23	10	472	6073	369	43093	572	104363	51755	1386
⊞ U. S. AIR FORCE REGIONAL HOSPITAL, 10 Missile Avenue, Zip 58705–5024; tel. 701/723–5103; Colonel David L. Clark, Commander **A**1 5 9 **F**8 12 13 15 16 19 20 22 24 27 28 29 30 35 39 40 44 45 46 49 51 55 58 61 65 67 71 73 74 **S** Department of the Air Force, Bowling AFB, DC	41	10	15	495	4	83929	250	9508	1489	—
⊞ UNIMED MEDICAL CENTER, 407 3rd Street S.E., Zip 58702–5001; tel. 701/857–2000; Michael L. Mullins, Chief Executive Officer **A**1 2 3 5 9 10 **F**2 3 4 7 8 10 12 14 16 17 18 19 20 21 22 27 28 29 30 32 33 35 37 38 40 41 42 43 44 45 46 49 52 53 54 55 56 57 58 59 60 63 65 67 70 71 73 74 **P**6 **S** Quorum Health Group/Quorum Health Resources, Inc., Brentwood, TN	33	10	160	4875	65	41997	409	49338	21929	615
NORTHWOOD—Grand Forks County										
★ NORTHWOOD DEACONESS HEALTH CENTER, 4 North Park Street, Zip 58267–0190; tel. 701/587–6060; Larry E. Feickert, Chief Administrative Officer (Total facility includes 112 beds in nursing home–type unit) **A**9 10 **F**1 7 11 15 17 19 20 22 24 26 27 34 35 36 37 39 40 44 45 46 49 51 60 64 71 72 73 74 **P**5	21	10	124	342	95	3741	16	5563	3144	125
OAKES—Dickey County										
⊞ OAKES COMMUNITY HOSPITAL, 314 South Eighth Street, Zip 58474–2099; tel. 701/742–3291; Bradley D. Burris, President and Chief Executive Officer **A**1 9 10 **F**7 8 11 13 15 17 19 21 22 24 28 32 33 35 40 41 42 44 45 49 54 63 65 66 71 **P**5 **S** Catholic Health Initiatives, Denver, CO	21	10	30	715	8	18350	59	8362	2749	—
PARK RIVER—Walsh County										
★ ST. ANSGAR'S HEALTH CENTER, 115 Vivian Street, Zip 58270–0708; tel. 701/284–7500; Michael D. Mahrer, President **A**9 10 **F**7 14 15 16 19 22 27 30 32 33 34 35 41 44 54 65 71 **S** Catholic Health Initiatives, Denver, CO	21	10	20	588	10	8484	30	3799	1582	67
RICHARDTON—Stark County										
RICHARDTON HEALTH CENTER, 212 Third Avenue West, Zip 58652–7103, Mailing Address: P.O. Box H, Zip 58652; tel. 701/974–3304; Kurt Waldbillig, Chief Executive Officer **A**9 10 **F**8 11 14 15 16 22 24 26 28 36 46 48 65 73 **P**5	23	10	26	68	0	338	0	2504	629	35
ROLLA—Rolette County										
PRESENTATION MEDICAL CENTER, 213 Second Avenue N.E., Zip 58367–7153, Mailing Address: P.O. Box 759, Zip 58367–0759; tel. 701/477–3161; Kimber Wraalstad, Chief Executive Officer (Total facility includes 48 beds in nursing home–type unit) **A**9 10 **F**7 8 13 15 17 19 22 24 28 30 32 34 36 39 40 41 42 44 45 46 49 53 54 57 58 64 65 66 70 71 73 74 **S** Sisters of Mary of the Presentation Health Corporation, Fargo, ND	21	10	102	892	55	7158	80	6430	3429	145
RUGBY—Pierce County										
★ HEART OF AMERICA MEDICAL CENTER, 800 Main Avenue South, Zip 58368–2198; tel. 701/776–5261; Jerry E. Jurena, Executive Director (Total facility includes 198 beds in nursing home–type unit) **A**9 10 **F**3 7 8 17 19 21 22 24 26 28 31 32 34 36 37 39 40 41 44 49 62 64 65 66 67 71 73 **Web address:** www.hamc.com	23	10	218	932	202	21390	82	11273	5624	240

Hospital, Address, Telephone, Administrator, Approval, Facility, and Physician Codes, Health Care System, Network	Classi-fication Codes		Utilization Data					Expense (thousands) of dollars		
★ American Hospital Association (AHA) membership □ Joint Commission on Accreditation of Healthcare Organizations (JCAHO) accreditation + American Osteopathic Healthcare Association (AOHA) membership ○ American Osteopathic Association (AOA) accreditation △ Commission on Accreditation of Rehabilitation Facilities (CARF) accreditation Control codes 61, 63, 64, 71, 72 and 73 indicate hospitals listed by AOHA, but not registered by AHA. For definition of numerical codes, see page A4	Control	Service	Staffed Beds	Admissions	Census	Outpatient Visits	Births	Total	Payroll	Personnel

STANLEY—Mountrail County

MOUNTRAIL COUNTY MEDICAL CENTER, 502 Third Street S.E., Zip 58784–4323, Mailing Address: P.O. Box 399, Zip 58784–0399; tel. 701/628–2424; Mitch Leupp, Administrator **A**9 10 **F**8 15 19 21 22 28 32 33 36 44 49 65 71 **P**6 — 23 10 25 115 4 5697 1 919 469 30

TIOGA—Williams County

★ TIOGA MEDICAL CENTER, 810 North Welo Street, Zip 58852–0159, Mailing Address: P.O. Box 159, Zip 58852–0159; tel. 701/664–3305; Lowell D. Herfindahl, President and Chief Executive Officer (Total facility includes 30 beds in nursing home–type unit) (Nonreporting) **A**9 10 — 23 10 59 — — — — — — —

TURTLE LAKE—McLean County

COMMUNITY MEMORIAL HOSPITAL, 220 Fifth Avenue, Zip 58575, Mailing Address: P.O. Box 280, Zip 58575–0280; tel. 701/448–2331; Dan Odegaard, Administrator **A**9 10 **F**1 15 19 22 24 30 32 33 44 49 64 66 70 71 — 21 10 23 154 7 3465 0 1119 657 40

VALLEY CITY—Barnes County

⊠ MERCY HOSPITAL, 570 Chautauqua Boulevard, Zip 58072–3199; tel. 701/845–6400; Jane Bissel, President and Chief Executive Officer **A**1 9 10 **F**1 7 8 11 15 19 22 26 29 30 32 34 35 37 39 40 44 49 64 65 66 70 71 73 **S** Catholic Health Initiatives, Denver, CO — 21 10 50 996 35 15734 101 7098 3805 134

WATFORD CITY—McKenzie County

★ MCKENZIE COUNTY MEMORIAL HOSPITAL, 516 North Main Street, Zip 58854–0548, Mailing Address: P.O. Box 548, Zip 58854–0548; tel. 701/842–3000; Colette Anderson, Administrator **A**9 10 **F**8 15 16 19 22 24 28 30 32 39 41 44 49 64 65 66 71 **P**5 — 23 10 24 181 5 1179 0 1858 763 38

WILLISTON—Williams County

⊠ MERCY MEDICAL CENTER, 1301 15th Avenue West, Zip 58801–3896; tel. 701/774–7400; M. Thomas Mitchell, President and Chief Executive Officer **A**1 9 10 **F**2 3 7 8 12 15 17 19 21 22 24 28 30 32 33 34 35 37 39 40 41 42 44 46 49 51 52 53 54 55 56 57 58 59 60 63 65 66 67 71 73 **P**6 **S** Catholic Health Initiatives, Denver, CO
Web address: www.dia.net/mercy — 21 10 93 2640 40 33782 305 26658 12753 427

WISHEK—McIntosh County

★ WISHEK COMMUNITY HOSPITAL AND CLINICS, 1007 Fourth Avenue South, Zip 58495, Mailing Address: P.O. Box 647, Zip 58495–0647; tel. 701/452–2326; C. Gary Kopp, Administrator **A**9 10 **F**11 14 15 16 19 21 25 30 32 34 37 44 45 48 49 64 65 67 70 71 **P**6 8
Web address: www.wchc.com — 23 10 22 474 5 11727 0 3920 2060 80

OHIO

Resident population 11,209 (in thousands)
Resident population in metro areas 80.8%
Birth rate per 1,000 population 13.8
65 years and over 13.4%
Percent of persons without health insurance 11.5%

Hospital, Address, Telephone, Administrator, Approval, Facility, and Physician Codes, Health Care System, Network	Classi-fication Codes		Utilization Data					Expense (thousands) of dollars		
★ American Hospital Association (AHA) membership □ Joint Commission on Accreditation of Healthcare Organizations (JCAHO) accreditation + American Osteopathic Healthcare Association (AOHA) membership ○ American Osteopathic Association (AOA) accreditation △ Commission on Accreditation of Rehabilitation Facilities (CARF) accreditation Control codes 61, 63, 64, 71, 72 and 73 indicate hospitals listed by AOHA, but not registered by AHA. For definition of numerical codes, see page A4	Control	Service	Staffed Beds	Admissions	Census	Outpatient Visits	Births	Total	Payroll	Personnel

AKRON—Summit County

AKRON CITY HOSPITAL See Summa Health System

✠ AKRON GENERAL MEDICAL CENTER, 400 Wabash Avenue, Zip 44307–2433; tel. 330/384–6000; Alan J. Bleyer, President **A**1 2 3 5 9 10 **F**4 7 8 10 11 12 14 16 19 21 22 23 24 25 26 27 28 29 30 31 32 33 34 35 37 39 40 41 42 43 44 45 46 49 51 52 54 55 56 58 59 60 61 63 65 66 67 69 70 71 72 73 74 **P**7 8 **Web address:** www.agmc.org	23	10	473	25027	342	391608	3309	246517	111435	2713
✠ CHILDREN'S HOSPITAL MEDICAL CENTER OF AKRON, (REGIONAL BURN UNIT), One Perkins Square, Zip 44308–1062; tel. 330/379–8200; William H. Considine, President **A**1 3 5 8 9 10 **F**1 2 3 4 7 8 9 10 11 12 13 14 15 16 17 18 19 20 21 22 23 24 25 26 27 28 29 30 31 32 33 34 35 37 38 39 40 41 43 44 45 46 47 48 49 51 52 53 54 55 56 58 59 60 61 63 64 65 66 67 68 70 71 72 73 74 **P**6 8 **Web address:** www.akronchildrens.org	23	50	200	6925	103	234936	1	118736	56794	1716
✠ △ EDWIN SHAW HOSPITAL FOR REHABILITATION, 1621 Flickinger Road, Zip 44312–4495; tel. 330/784–1271; Daniel K. Church, Ph.D., President and Chief Executive Officer (Total facility includes 49 beds in nursing home–type unit) **A**1 7 10 **F**2 3 14 15 17 20 24 34 36 46 48 49 64 65 67 73	15	46	188	2175	88	—	0	26189	14681	421

SAINT THOMAS HOSPITAL See Summa Health System

✠ SUMMA HEALTH SYSTEM, (Includes Akron City Hospital, 525 East Market Street, Zip 44309–2090, Mailing Address: P.O. Box 2090, Zip 44309–2090; tel. 330/375–3000; Saint Thomas Hospital, 444 North Main Street, Zip 44310; tel. 330/375–3000), Albert F. Gilbert, Ph.D., President and Chief Executive Officer **A**1 2 3 5 8 9 10 **F**2 3 4 5 7 8 9 10 11 12 13 14 15 16 17 18 19 20 21 22 23 24 25 26 27 28 29 30 31 32 33 34 35 36 37 38 39 40 41 42 43 44 45 46 47 48 49 50 51 52 53 54 56 57 58 59 60 61 63 64 65 66 67 68 70 71 72 73 74 **P**1 2 3 5 6 8 **Web address:** www.summahealth.org	23	10	590	32043	430	451366	3417	—	—	2531

ALLIANCE—Stark County

□ △ ALLIANCE COMMUNITY HOSPITAL, 264 East Rice Street, Zip 44601–4399; tel. 330/829–4000; Stanley W. Jonas, Chief Executive Officer (Total facility includes 78 beds in nursing home–type unit) (Nonreporting) **A**1 2 7 9 10 **Web address:** www.achosp.org	23	10	206	—	—	—	—	—	—	—

AMHERST—Lorain County

✠ EMH AMHERST HOSPITAL, 254 Cleveland Avenue, Zip 44001–1699; tel. 440/988–6000; Kevin C. Martin, President and Chief Executive Officer **A**1 10 **F**4 7 8 10 11 14 15 16 19 21 22 25 26 28 30 32 34 35 36 37 38 39 40 41 42 43 44 45 46 49 51 52 56 57 59 63 65 66 67 69 71 72 73 74 **P**7 8	23	10	40	1029	12	30365	164	10454	4508	146

ASHLAND—Ashland County

✠ SAMARITAN REGIONAL HEALTH SYSTEM, 1025 Center Street, Zip 44805–4098; tel. 419/289–0491; William C. Kelley, Jr., FACHE, President and Chief Executive Officer **A**1 9 10 **F**7 8 12 13 15 16 17 19 21 22 25 28 30 32 34 35 37 40 41 42 44 45 46 49 52 57 58 63 65 66 67 71 73 **Web address:** www.samho.org	23	10	70	3282	38	131740	547	40614	15885	461

ASHTABULA—Ashtabula County

✠ ASHTABULA COUNTY MEDICAL CENTER, 2420 Lake Avenue, Zip 44004–4993; tel. 440/997–2262; R. D. Richardson, President and Chief Executive Officer (Nonreporting) **A**1 9 10 **Web address:** www.acmchealth.org	23	10	163	—	—	—	—	—	—	—

ATHENS—Athens County

✠ + O'BLENESS MEMORIAL HOSPITAL, 55 Hospital Drive, Zip 45701–2302; tel. 740/593–5551; Richard F. Castrop, President **A**1 9 10 12 13 **F**7 8 14 17 19 20 21 22 23 26 28 30 31 32 33 34 35 37 39 40 42 44 45 46 48 49 51 56 63 65 67 71 72 73 **Web address:** www.obleness.org	23	10	75	2538	25	64773	499	24868	10509	313

SOUTHEAST PSYCHIATRIC HOSPITAL See Appalachian Psychiatric Healthcare System, Cambridge

BARBERTON—Summit County

✠ BARBERTON CITIZENS HOSPITAL, 155 Fifth Street N.E., Zip 44203–3398; tel. 330/745–1611; Ronald J. Elder, President (Total facility includes 50 beds in nursing home–type unit) **A**1 2 3 5 9 10 **F**7 8 10 11 12 15 16 19 21 22 23 26 28 29 30 32 34 35 37 39 40 41 42 44 45 46 48 49 51 52 56 57 64 65 66 71 73 **P**8 **S** Quorum Health Group/Quorum Health Resources, Inc., Brentwood, TN **Web address:** www.barbhosp.com	33	10	251	9089	176	326272	845	71231	35966	972

BARNESVILLE—Belmont County

✠ BARNESVILLE HOSPITAL ASSOCIATION, 639 West Main Street, Zip 43713–1096, Mailing Address: P.O. Box 309, Zip 43713–0309; tel. 740/425–3941; Richard L. Doan, Chief Executive Officer **A**1 9 10 **F**8 12 14 15 16 17 19 21 22 28 30 31 32 33 34 36 37 39 41 44 45 46 49 54 56 65 67 71 73 **P**6	23	10	55	2131	32	28823	0	13185	6489	279

Hospital, Address, Telephone, Administrator, Approval, Facility, and Physician Codes, Health Care System, Network	Classification Codes		Utilization Data					Expense (thousands) of dollars		
	Control	Service	Staffed Beds	Admissions	Census	Outpatient Visits	Births	Total	Payroll	Personnel

★ American Hospital Association (AHA) membership
□ Joint Commission on Accreditation of Healthcare Organizations (JCAHO) accreditation
+ American Osteopathic Healthcare Association (AOHA) membership
○ American Osteopathic Association (AOA) accreditation
△ Commission on Accreditation of Rehabilitation Facilities (CARF) accreditation
Control codes 61, 63, 64, 71, 72 and 73 indicate hospitals listed by AOHA, but not registered by AHA. For definition of numerical codes, see page A4

BATAVIA—Clermont County

□ CLERMONT MERCY HOSPITAL, 3000 Hospital Drive, Zip 45103–1998; tel. 513/732–8200; Fred L. Kolb, President **A**1 9 10 **F**6 7 8 10 12 14 15 16 17 19 21 22 24 26 28 29 30 32 33 34 35 37 41 42 44 45 46 49 52 53 57 58 59 60 62 63 65 66 67 71 72 73 74 **P**6 8 **S** Catholic Healthcare Partners, Cincinnati, OH
Web address: www.mercy.health–partners.org
| | 21 | 10 | 133 | 4838 | 57 | 157646 | 0 | 44610 | 20087 | 503 |

BEDFORD—Cuyahoga County

✠ UHHS BEDFORD MEDICAL CENTER, 44 Blaine Avenue, Zip 44146–2799; tel. 440/439–2000; Arlene A. Rak, R.N., President (Nonreporting) **A**1 9 10 **S** University Hospitals Health System, Cleveland, OH
| | 23 | 10 | 110 | — | — | — | — | — | — | — |

BELLAIRE—Belmont County

✠ BELMONT COMMUNITY HOSPITAL, 4697 Harrison Street, Zip 43906, Mailing Address: P.O. Box 653, Zip 43906–0653; tel. 740/671–1200; Gary R. Gould, FACHE, Chief Executive Officer **A**1 9 10 **F**4 7 8 10 12 13 15 16 17 19 20 22 23 24 25 26 27 28 29 30 32 34 35 37 39 40 41 42 43 44 45 48 49 51 52 56 59 60 61 65 66 67 70 71 73 74 **P**1 6 7
| | 23 | 10 | 79 | 2347 | 37 | 37856 | 166 | 15270 | 8297 | 283 |

BELLEFONTAINE—Logan County

✠ MARY RUTAN HOSPITAL, 205 Palmer Avenue, Zip 43311–2298; tel. 937/592–4015; Ewing H. Crawfis, President (Nonreporting) **A**1 3 9 10
| | 23 | 10 | 72 | — | — | — | — | — | — | — |

BELLEVUE—Sandusky County

✠ BELLEVUE HOSPITAL, 811 Northwest Street, Zip 44811, Mailing Address: P.O. Box 8004, Zip 44811–8004; tel. 419/483–4040; Michael K. Winthrop, President **A**1 2 9 10 **F**7 8 15 16 19 21 22 23 26 27 30 31 32 33 34 35 37 40 41 42 44 49 57 63 65 66 67 71 73 **P**7 8
Web address: www.bellevuehospital.com
| | 23 | 10 | 48 | 2022 | 20 | 39620 | 363 | 19794 | 8499 | 258 |

BOWLING GREEN—Wood County

✠ WOOD COUNTY HOSPITAL, 950 West Wooster Street, Zip 43402–2699; tel. 419/354–8900; Michael A. Miesle, Administrator **A**1 9 10 **F**7 8 10 14 15 16 19 21 22 23 28 31 33 34 35 36 37 39 40 41 42 44 49 58 63 65 66 67 70 71 73 **P**8
| | 23 | 10 | 98 | 3620 | 40 | 88981 | 446 | 28247 | 13419 | 408 |

BRYAN—Williams County

□ COMMUNITY HOSPITALS OF WILLIAMS COUNTY, (Includes Bryan Hospital, 433 West High Street, Zip 43506; tel. 419/636–1131; Montpelier Hospital, Snyder and Lincoln Avenue, Montpelier, Zip 43543; tel. 419/485–3154), 433 West High Street, Zip 43506–1680; tel. 419/636–1131; Rusty O. Brunicardi, President (Nonreporting) **A**1 2 9 10
| | 23 | 10 | 121 | — | — | — | — | — | — | — |

BUCYRUS—Crawford County

✠ BUCYRUS COMMUNITY HOSPITAL, 629 North Sandusky Avenue, Zip 44820–0627, Mailing Address: Box 627, Zip 44820–0627; tel. 419/562–4677; LaMar L. Wyse, Chief Executive Officer **A**1 9 10 **F**8 15 17 19 21 22 28 30 32 33 34 35 36 37 39 41 42 44 46 49 63 65 71 73 **P**2 3 5 6 7 **S** OhioHealth, Columbus, OH
| | 23 | 10 | 47 | 963 | 10 | 41196 | 0 | 12376 | 4977 | 150 |

CADIZ—Harrison County

✠ HARRISON COMMUNITY HOSPITAL, 951 East Market Street, Zip 43907–9749; tel. 740/942–4631; Terry Carson, Chief Executive Officer **A**1 9 10 **F**8 11 17 19 20 21 22 24 28 30 32 34 35 37 39 44 45 48 49 65 67 70 71 73 74
Web address: www.harrisoncommunity.com
| | 23 | 10 | 48 | 718 | 22 | 13596 | 0 | 6937 | 3274 | 154 |

CAMBRIDGE—Guernsey County

□ APPALACHIAN PSYCHIATRIC HEALTHCARE SYSTEM, (Includes Southeast Psychiatric Hospital, 100 Hospital Drive, Athens, Zip 45701–2301; tel. 614/594–5000; Mark F. McGee, M.D., Chief Clinical Officer), 66737 Old 21 Road North, Zip 43725–9298; tel. 740/439–1371; Stephen C. Pierson, Ph.D., Chief Executive Officer **A**1 10 **F**12 14 15 39 41 45 52 54 55 56 57 65 67 73
| | 12 | 22 | 120 | 783 | 103 | 0 | 0 | — | — | — |

✠ SOUTHEASTERN OHIO REGIONAL MEDICAL CENTER, 1341 North Clark Street, Zip 43725–0610, Mailing Address: P.O. Box 610, Zip 43725–0610; tel. 740/439–3561; Philip E. Hearing, President and Chief Executive Officer (Total facility includes 20 beds in nursing home–type unit) **A**1 2 9 10 **F**7 8 12 14 15 16 17 19 22 28 29 30 32 34 35 37 39 40 41 44 46 49 63 64 65 66 67 71 73 74 **P**6 8
| | 23 | 10 | 113 | 4497 | 51 | 78928 | 349 | 35714 | 15066 | 551 |

CANTON—Stark County

✠ AULTMAN HOSPITAL, 2600 Sixth Street S.W., Zip 44710–1799; tel. 330/452–9911; Richard J. Pryce, President (Nonreporting) **A**1 2 3 5 6 10
| | 23 | 10 | 736 | — | — | — | — | — | — | — |

✠ △ MERCY MEDICAL CENTER, 1320 Mercy Drive N.W., Zip 44708–2641; tel. 330/489–1000; Norman W. Wengerd, Interim President and Chief Executive Officer **A**1 2 3 5 7 9 10 **F**3 4 7 8 10 11 12 14 15 16 17 19 21 22 24 26 27 28 29 30 32 33 34 35 37 38 39 40 41 42 43 44 45 46 48 49 50 52 53 54 55 56 57 58 59 60 63 65 66 68 70 71 72 73 74 **S** Sisters of Charity of St. Augustine Health System, Cleveland, OH
| | 32 | 10 | 374 | 16119 | 244 | 466283 | 1777 | 145526 | 65105 | 2145 |

CHAGRIN FALLS—Cuyahoga County

□ BHC WINDSOR HOSPITAL, 115 East Summit Street, Zip 44022–2750; tel. 440/247–5300; Donald K. Sykes, Jr., Chief Executive Officer (Nonreporting) **A**1 10 **S** Behavioral Healthcare Corporation, Nashville, TN
| | 33 | 22 | 50 | — | — | — | — | — | — | — |

CHARDON—Geauga County

□ △ HEATHER HILL HOSPITAL AND HEALTH CARE CENTER, (LONG TERM HOSPITAL), 12340 Bass Lake Road, Zip 44024–8327; tel. 440/285–4040; Robert Glenn Harr, President (Total facility includes 194 beds in nursing home–type unit) **A**1 7 10 **F**1 12 14 15 17 26 27 29 30 32 33 34 39 41 45 48 49 57 58 64 65 66 67 73
| | 23 | 49 | 250 | 1120 | 214 | 1955 | 0 | 23308 | 11900 | 418 |

Hospital, Address, Telephone, Administrator, Approval, Facility, and Physician Codes, Health Care System, Network	Classi-fication Codes		Utilization Data					Expense (thousands) of dollars		

	Control	Service	Staffed Beds	Admissions	Census	Outpatient Visits	Births	Total	Payroll	Personnel

Legend:
★ American Hospital Association (AHA) membership
□ Joint Commission on Accreditation of Healthcare Organizations (JCAHO) accreditation
+ American Osteopathic Healthcare Association (AOHA) membership
○ American Osteopathic Association (AOA) accreditation
△ Commission on Accreditation of Rehabilitation Facilities (CARF) accreditation
Control codes 61, 63, 64, 71, 72 and 73 indicate hospitals listed by AOHA, but not registered by AHA. For definition of numerical codes, see page A4

Hospital	Control	Service	Staffed Beds	Admissions	Census	Outpatient Visits	Births	Total	Payroll	Personnel
✖ UHHS GEAUGA REGIONAL HOSPITAL, 13207 Ravenna Road, Zip 44024–9012; tel. 440/269–6000; Richard J. Frenchie, President and Chief Executive Officer (Total facility includes 21 beds in nursing home–type unit) **A**1 2 9 10 **F**7 8 11 12 14 15 16 19 20 21 22 28 30 32 33 34 35 37 39 40 41 42 44 45 46 49 52 54 56 57 63 64 65 66 67 71 73 74 **P**4 5 7 8 **S** University Hospitals Health System, Cleveland, OH Web address: www.uhhs.com/geauga/index.html	23	10	126	4915	61	68029	714	37779	16298	386
CHILLICOTHE—Ross County										
✖ ADENA HEALTH SYSTEM, 272 Hospital Road, Zip 45601–0708; tel. 740/779–7500; Allen V. Rupiper, President **A**1 2 9 10 **F**3 7 8 10 12 14 15 16 17 19 21 22 25 26 28 29 30 31 32 33 34 35 37 39 40 41 42 44 45 46 48 49 51 52 53 54 55 56 57 58 59 60 63 65 66 67 68 71 72 73 74 **P**6 8 Web address: www.adena.org	23	10	161	7997	82	160959	1096	87027	36574	979
✖ VETERANS AFFAIRS MEDICAL CENTER, 17273 State Route 104, Zip 45601–0999; tel. 740/773–1141; Michael W. Walton, Director (Total facility includes 162 beds in nursing home–type unit) **A**1 5 **F**1 3 8 12 15 17 19 20 21 22 26 27 28 29 30 31 32 33 35 37 39 41 44 46 49 51 52 54 55 56 57 58 59 64 65 67 71 73 74 **P**6 **S** Department of Veterans Affairs, Washington, DC Web address: www.bright.net/~vachilli	45	22	324	4233	287	135162	0	76042	43674	1129
CINCINNATI—Hamilton County										
□ BETHESDA NORTH HOSPITAL, 10500 Montgomery Road, Zip 45242–4415; tel. 513/745–1111; John S. Prout, President and Chief Executive Officer **A**1 9 10 **F**1 2 3 4 6 7 8 10 11 12 15 16 17 18 19 21 22 23 24 25 26 27 28 29 30 31 32 33 34 35 37 38 39 40 41 42 43 44 45 46 48 49 51 52 53 54 55 56 57 58 59 60 61 62 63 64 65 66 67 68 70 71 72 73 **P**3 7 **S** Bethesda Hospital, Inc., Cincinnati, OH Web address: www.trihealth.com	23	10	245	15021	152	186016	2840	—	—	—
□ △ BETHESDA OAK HOSPITAL, 619 Oak Street, Zip 45206–1690; tel. 513/569–6111; Linda D. Schaffner, R.N., Vice President and Administrator **A**1 2 3 5 7 9 10 **F**1 2 3 4 6 7 8 10 11 12 15 16 17 18 19 21 22 23 24 25 26 27 28 29 30 31 32 33 34 35 37 38 39 40 41 42 43 44 45 46 48 49 51 52 53 54 55 56 57 58 59 60 61 62 63 64 65 66 67 68 70 71 72 73 **P**3 7 **S** Bethesda Hospital, Inc., Cincinnati, OH Web address: www.trihealth.com	23	10	116	5955	46	79452	2356	—	—	—
✖ △ CHILDREN'S HOSPITAL MEDICAL CENTER, (Includes Division of Adolescent Medicine, Cincinnati Center for Developmental Disorders, and Convalescent Hospital for Children; Children's Hospital), 3333 Burnet Avenue, Zip 45229–3039; tel. 513/636–4200; James M. Anderson, President and Chief Executive Officer **A**1 2 3 5 7 8 9 10 **F**3 5 10 12 13 15 16 17 18 19 20 21 22 25 28 29 31 32 33 34 35 38 39 42 43 44 45 46 47 48 49 51 52 53 54 55 56 58 60 63 65 66 67 68 70 71 72 73 **P**1 Web address: www.chmcc.org	23	50	299	14131	200	411171	0	234263	83048	3377
✖ △ CHRIST HOSPITAL, 2139 Auburn Avenue, Zip 45219–2989; tel. 513/585–2000; Richard L. Seim, Senior Vice President (Total facility includes 20 beds in nursing home–type unit) **A**1 2 3 5 6 7 9 10 **F**2 3 4 5 7 8 9 10 11 12 13 14 15 16 17 18 19 20 21 22 24 25 26 27 28 29 30 31 32 33 34 35 36 37 38 39 40 41 42 43 44 45 46 48 49 50 51 52 53 54 55 56 57 58 59 60 61 63 64 65 66 67 68 70 71 72 73 74 **P**6 8 **S** Health Alliance of Greater Cincinnati, Cincinnati, OH	23	10	483	25242	315	150660	3486	257381	101741	2863
□ △ DEACONESS HOSPITAL, 311 Straight Street, Zip 45219–1099; tel. 513/559–2100; E. Anthony Woods, President (Total facility includes 20 beds in nursing home–type unit) (Nonreporting) **A**1 7 9 10 Web address: www.Deaconess–healthcare.com	23	10	219	—	—	—	—	—	—	—
✖ △ DRAKE CENTER, 151 West Galbraith Road, Zip 45216–1096; tel. 513/948–2500; Roberta J. Bradford, President and Chief Executive Officer (Total facility includes 204 beds in nursing home–type unit) **A**1 3 5 7 9 10 **F**12 14 15 16 17 19 20 24 25 26 27 28 29 30 31 35 39 41 45 46 48 49 50 54 55 57 58 64 65 66 67 71 73 **P**5 6 Web address: www.drakecenter.com	23	46	288	1113	236	20151	0	44316	21070	629
✖ △ FRANCISCAN HOSPITAL–MOUNT AIRY CAMPUS, 2446 Kipling Avenue, Zip 45239–6650; tel. 513/853–5000; R. Christopher West, President (Total facility includes 20 beds in nursing home–type unit) **A**1 2 3 5 7 9 10 **F**2 6 7 8 10 11 12 14 15 16 17 19 21 22 24 25 26 28 30 31 32 33 34 35 36 37 39 40 41 42 44 46 48 49 51 52 53 56 57 58 59 62 64 65 66 71 72 73 74 **S** Catholic Healthcare Partners, Cincinnati, OH	21	10	240	10449	132	109230	695	—	—	1288
□ △ FRANCISCAN HOSPITAL–WESTERN HILLS CAMPUS, 3131 Queen City Avenue, Zip 45238–2396; tel. 513/389–5000; R. Christopher West, President **A**1 2 7 9 10 **F**3 6 7 8 10 11 12 14 15 16 17 19 21 22 24 25 26 28 30 31 32 33 34 35 36 37 39 40 41 42 44 46 48 49 52 53 56 57 58 59 62 64 65 66 71 72 73 74 **S** Catholic Healthcare Partners, Cincinnati, OH	21	10	224	9478	141	52489	0	—	—	910
✖ △ GOOD SAMARITAN HOSPITAL, 375 Dixmyth Avenue, Zip 45220–2489; tel. 513/872–1400; John S. Prout, President and Chief Executive Officer (Total facility includes 15 beds in nursing home–type unit) **A**1 2 3 5 6 7 8 9 10 **F**1 2 3 4 6 7 8 10 11 12 13 15 16 17 18 19 21 22 23 24 25 26 27 28 29 30 31 32 33 34 35 37 38 39 40 41 42 43 44 45 46 48 49 51 52 53 54 55 56 57 58 59 60 61 62 63 64 65 66 67 68 70 71 72 73 **P**3 7 **S** Catholic Health Initiatives, Denver, CO Web address: www.trihealth.com	21	10	441	21582	270	165281	5098	184275	81150	2121

Hospital, Address, Telephone, Administrator, Approval, Facility, and Physician Codes, Health Care System, Network	Classi-fication Codes		Utilization Data					Expense (thousands) of dollars		
	Control	Service	Staffed Beds	Admissions	Census	Outpatient Visits	Births	Total	Payroll	Personnel

★ American Hospital Association (AHA) membership
□ Joint Commission on Accreditation of Healthcare Organizations (JCAHO) accreditation
+ American Osteopathic Healthcare Association (AOHA) membership
○ American Osteopathic Association (AOA) accreditation
△ Commission on Accreditation of Rehabilitation Facilities (CARF) accreditation
   Control codes 61, 63, 64, 71, 72 and 73 indicate hospitals listed by AOHA, but not registered by AHA. For definition of numerical codes, see page A4

Hospital	Control	Service	Staffed Beds	Admissions	Census	Outpatient Visits	Births	Total	Payroll	Personnel
⊠ △ JEWISH HOSPITAL KENWOOD, 4777 East Galbraith Road, Zip 45236; tel. 513/686–3000; M. Aurora Lambert, Senior Vice President **A**1 2 3 5 7 9 10 **F**2 3 4 5 7 8 9 10 11 12 13 14 15 16 17 18 19 20 21 22 24 25 26 27 28 29 30 31 32 33 34 35 36 37 38 39 40 41 42 43 44 45 46 48 49 50 51 52 53 54 55 56 57 58 59 60 61 63 64 65 66 67 68 70 71 72 73 74 **P**6 8 **S** Health Alliance of Greater Cincinnati, Cincinnati, OH	23	10	142	10853	139	115671	809	121713	49948	1173
□ MERCY HOSPITAL ANDERSON, 7500 State Road, Zip 45255–2492; tel. 513/624–4500; Fred L. Kolb, President **A**1 2 9 10 **F**6 7 8 10 12 14 15 16 17 19 21 22 24 26 28 29 30 32 33 34 35 37 39 40 41 42 44 45 46 49 60 62 63 65 66 67 71 72 73 74 **P**6 8 **S** Catholic Healthcare Partners, Cincinnati, OH	21	10	156	9147	89	114402	1921	72505	27016	722
□ PAULINE WARFIELD LEWIS CENTER, 1101 Summit Road, Zip 45237–2652; tel. 513/948–3600; Elizabeth Banks, Chief Executive Officer (Nonreporting) **A**1 10 **Web address:** www.prime/prime.htm	12	22	357	—	—	—	—	—	—	—
⊠ SHRINERS HOSPITALS FOR CHILDREN, SHRINERS BURNS HOSPITAL, CINCINNATI, (PEDIATRIC BURN INJURIES), 3229 Burnet Avenue, Zip 45229–3095; tel. 513/872–6000; Ronald R. Hitzler, Administrator **A**1 **F**9 12 19 21 35 41 44 45 46 50 54 56 63 65 69 71 73 **S** Shriners Hospitals for Children, Tampa, FL	23	59	30	785	20	4863	0	—	—	297
⊠ UNIVERSITY HOSPITAL, 234 Goodman Street, Zip 45219–2316; tel. 513/558–1000; Elliot G. Cohen, Senior Vice President **A**1 2 3 5 8 9 10 **F**2 3 4 5 7 8 9 10 11 12 13 14 15 16 17 18 19 20 21 22 24 25 26 27 28 29 30 31 32 33 34 35 36 37 38 39 40 41 42 43 44 45 46 47 48 49 50 51 52 53 54 55 56 57 58 59 60 61 63 64 65 66 67 68 70 71 72 73 74 **P**6 8 **S** Health Alliance of Greater Cincinnati, Cincinnati, OH	23	10	411	20497	314	246847	1953	321742	114934	3223
⊠ VETERANS AFFAIRS MEDICAL CENTER, 3200 Vine Street, Zip 45220–2288; tel. 513/861–3100; Gary N. Nugent, Medical Director (Total facility includes 64 beds in nursing home–type unit) (Nonreporting) **A**1 3 5 8 **S** Department of Veterans Affairs, Washington, DC	45	10	240	—	—	—	—	—	—	—

CIRCLEVILLE—Pickaway County

Hospital	Control	Service	Staffed Beds	Admissions	Census	Outpatient Visits	Births	Total	Payroll	Personnel
⊠ BERGER HEALTH SYSTEM, 600 North Pickaway Street, Zip 43113–1499; tel. 740/474–2126; Brian R. Colfack, CHE, President and Chief Executive Officer **A**1 9 10 **F**7 8 12 13 14 15 16 17 19 21 22 27 28 29 30 32 33 34 35 37 39 40 41 42 44 45 46 48 49 51 65 66 67 70 71 72 73 74 **P**3 **Web address:** www.bergerhealth.com	15	10	86	1982	25	62568	38	25325	8508	315

CLEVELAND—Cuyahoga County

Hospital	Control	Service	Staffed Beds	Admissions	Census	Outpatient Visits	Births	Total	Payroll	Personnel
CAMPUS HOSPITAL OF CLEVELAND, 18120 Puritas Road, Zip 44135–3896; tel. 216/476–0222; Joan Curran, Administrator (Nonreporting) **A**9 10 CLEVELAND CAMPUS See Northcoast Behavioral Healthcare System, Northfield	33	82	60	—	—	—	—	—	—	—
⊠ △ CLEVELAND CLINIC FOUNDATION, (Formerly Cleveland Clinic Hospital), 9500 Euclid Avenue, Zip 44195–5108; tel. 216/444–2200; Frank L. Lordeman, Chief Operating Officer **A**1 2 3 5 7 8 9 10 **F**2 3 4 5 7 8 9 10 11 12 13 14 15 16 17 19 20 21 22 23 24 25 26 27 28 29 30 31 32 33 34 35 37 38 39 40 41 42 43 44 45 46 47 48 49 50 51 52 53 54 55 56 57 58 59 60 61 63 64 65 66 67 68 70 71 72 73 74 **P**1 3 5 6 **Web address:** www.ccf.org	23	10	933	45246	724	1520823	2425	661463	306825	12342
□ DEACONESS HOSPITAL OF CLEVELAND, 4229 Pearl Road, Zip 44109–4218; tel. 216/459–6300; Wayne G. Deschambeau, Chief Executive Officer (Total facility includes 15 beds in nursing home–type unit) (Nonreporting) **A**1 2 10	32	10	212	—	—	—	—	—	—	—
⊠ △ FAIRVIEW HOSPITAL, 18101 Lorain Avenue, Zip 44111–5656; tel. 216/476–7000; Louis P. Caravella, M.D., Chief Executive Officer (Total facility includes 35 beds in nursing home–type unit) **A**1 2 3 5 6 7 9 10 **F**1 4 5 7 8 10 11 12 14 15 16 17 19 21 22 24 26 27 28 29 30 32 33 34 35 36 37 38 39 40 41 42 43 44 45 46 48 49 51 52 54 56 57 58 59 60 63 64 65 66 67 70 71 72 73 74 **P**1 6 **S** Fairview Hospital System, Cleveland, OH	23	10	437	16482	235	326998	3321	157863	76603	2028
⊠ GRACE HOSPITAL, 2307 West 14th Street, Zip 44113–3698; tel. 216/687–1500; Robert P. Range, President and Chief Executive Officer **A**1 9 10 **F**8 14 15 16 26 27 28 29 30 32 34 37 39 41 44 45 46 49 51 65 71 72 73 **Web address:** www.transcare.org	23	10	57	398	28	18438	0	12820	6274	168
⊠ HEALTH HILL HOSPITAL FOR CHILDREN, Mailing Address: 2801 Martin Luther King Jr. Drive, Zip 44104–3865; tel. 216/721–5400; Thomas A. Rathbone, President **A**1 10 **F**3 4 7 8 10 12 13 14 15 16 17 18 19 20 21 22 23 24 25 27 28 29 30 31 32 34 35 39 41 42 43 44 45 46 49 50 51 54 55 58 59 60 61 63 65 66 67 68 71 72 73 74 **P**6 **Web address:** www.healthhill.org	23	56	46	189	19	10177	0	12694	7977	177
□ △ LUTHERAN HOSPITAL, 1730 West 25th Street, Zip 44113; tel. 216/696–4300; Jack E. Bell, Chief Operating Officer (Total facility includes 20 beds in nursing home–type unit) **A**1 7 9 10 **F**1 4 5 7 8 10 11 12 14 15 16 17 19 21 22 23 26 27 28 29 33 34 35 37 38 39 40 41 42 43 44 46 48 49 52 54 55 57 58 59 63 64 65 66 67 70 71 72 73 74 **P**1 6 **S** Fairview Hospital System, Cleveland, OH	23	10	204	4283	82	105958	0	51031	23853	636
□ MERIDIA HILLCREST HOSPITAL, 6780 Mayfield Road, Zip 44124–2202; tel. 216/449–4500; Catherine B. Leary, R.N., Chief Operating Officer **A**1 2 3 9 10 **F**2 3 4 7 8 10 11 12 13 14 15 16 17 19 21 22 23 24 25 26 27 28 29 30 31 33 34 35 36 37 38 39 40 41 42 43 44 45 46 47 48 49 51 52 54 55 57 58 59 60 61 63 64 65 66 67 68 70 71 72 73 74 **P**1 3 4 7 8 **S** Meridia Health System, Cleveland, OH **Web address:** www.meridia.com	23	10	305	15884	191	202006	2805	135372	49960	1395

Hospital, Address, Telephone, Administrator, Approval, Facility, and Physician Codes, Health Care System, Network	Classi-fication Codes		Utilization Data					Expense (thousands) of dollars		
★ American Hospital Association (AHA) membership □ Joint Commission on Accreditation of Healthcare Organizations (JCAHO) accreditation + American Osteopathic Healthcare Association (AOHA) membership ○ American Osteopathic Association (AOA) accreditation △ Commission on Accreditation of Rehabilitation Facilities (CARF) accreditation Control codes 61, 63, 64, 71, 72 and 73 indicate hospitals listed by AOHA, but not registered by AHA. For definition of numerical codes, see page A4	Control	Service	Staffed Beds	Admissions	Census	Outpatient Visits	Births	Total	Payroll	Personnel
□ MERIDIA HURON HOSPITAL, 13951 Terrace Road, Zip 44112–4399; tel. 216/761–3300; Beverly Lozar, Chief Operating Officer (Total facility includes 20 beds in nursing home–type unit) **A**1 2 3 5 6 9 10 **F**2 3 4 7 8 10 11 12 13 14 15 16 17 19 21 22 23 24 25 26 27 28 29 30 31 33 34 35 36 37 38 40 41 42 43 44 45 46 47 48 49 51 52 54 55 56 57 58 59 60 61 63 64 65 66 67 68 70 71 72 73 74 **P**1 3 4 7 8 **S** Meridia Health System, Cleveland, OH **Web address:** www.meridia.com	23	10	163	5633	94	47329	0	56931	25858	656
⊠ △ METROHEALTH MEDICAL CENTER, 2500 MetroHealth Drive, Zip 44109–1998; tel. 216/778–7800; Terry R. White, President and Chief Executive Officer (Total facility includes 291 beds in nursing home–type unit) (Nonreporting) **A**1 2 3 5 7 8 9 10 **Web address:** www.metrohealth.org	13	10	811	—	—	—	—	—	—	—
□ MT. SINAI MEDICAL CENTER, One Mt Sinai Drive, Zip 44106–4198; tel. 216/421–3400; Geoffrey Moebins, Chief Operating Officer (Nonreporting) **A**1 2 3 5 8 9 10 RAINBOW BABIES AND CHILDREN'S HOSPITAL See University Hospitals of Cleveland	23	10	344	—	—	—	—	—	—	—
⊠ SAINT LUKE'S MEDICAL CENTER, 11311 Shaker Boulevard, Zip 44104–3805; tel. 216/368–7000; Alan H. Channing, Chief Executive Officer **A**1 3 5 9 10 **F**1 3 4 5 7 8 10 12 13 14 15 16 17 19 20 21 22 25 26 27 28 30 31 32 33 34 35 36 38 39 40 41 42 43 44 45 46 49 51 52 53 54 55 56 57 58 59 60 61 63 65 67 68 70 71 73 74 **P**6 **S** Columbia/HCA Healthcare Corporation, Nashville, TN **Web address:** www.cn.com/stlukes	32	10	165	6600	96	100728	401	85037	30124	724
□ SAINT MICHAEL HOSPITAL, 5163 Broadway Avenue, Zip 44127–1532; tel. 216/429–8000; Geoffrey D. Moebius, President and Chief Executive Officer (Total facility includes 55 beds in nursing home–type unit) (Nonreporting) **A**1 2 10	33	10	199	—	—	—	—	—	—	—
⊠ ○ ST. JOHN WEST SHORE HOSPITAL, 29000 Center Ridge Road, Zip 44145–5219; tel. 440/835–8000; Fred M. DeGrandis, President and Chief Executive Officer (Nonreporting) **A**1 10 11 12 **S** Sisters of Charity of St. Augustine Health System, Cleveland, OH	33	10	183	—	—	—	—	—	—	—
⊠ ST. VINCENT CHARITY HOSPITAL, 2351 East 22nd Street, Zip 44115–3111; tel. 216/861–6200; Alan H. Channing, Chief Executive Officer (Nonreporting) **A**1 2 3 5 9 10 **S** Sisters of Charity of St. Augustine Health System, Cleveland, OH	33	10	266	—	—	—	—	—	—	—
⊠ △ UNIVERSITY HOSPITALS OF CLEVELAND, (Includes Alfred and Norma Lerner Tower, Bolwell Health Center, Hanna Pavilion, Lakeside Hospital, Samuel Mather Pavilion; Rainbow Babies and Children's Hospital; University MacDonald Women's Hospital), 11100 Euclid Avenue, Zip 44106–2602; tel. 216/844–1000; Farah M. Walters, President and Chief Executive Officer (Total facility includes 50 beds in nursing home–type unit) **A**1 2 3 5 7 8 9 10 **F**2 3 4 5 7 8 10 11 12 13 14 16 17 18 19 20 21 22 23 24 25 26 27 28 29 30 31 32 33 34 35 36 37 38 39 40 41 42 43 44 45 46 47 48 49 50 51 52 53 54 55 56 57 58 59 60 61 63 64 65 66 67 68 70 71 72 73 74 **P**3 5 6 7 **S** University Hospitals Health System, Cleveland, OH **Web address:** www.uhhs.com/uhhs/eeauga/index.html UNIVERSITY MACDONALD WOMEN'S HOSPITAL See University Hospitals of Cleveland	23	10	747	37869	601	699865	4726	—	—	5467
⊠ VETERANS AFFAIRS MEDICAL CENTER, 10701 East Boulevard, Zip 44106–1702; tel. 216/791–3800; Richard S. Citron, Acting Director (Total facility includes 195 beds in nursing home–type unit) (Nonreporting) **A**1 3 5 8 **S** Department of Veterans Affairs, Washington, DC	45	10	817	—	—	—	—	—	—	—
COLDWATER—Mercer County										
⊠ MERCER COUNTY JOINT TOWNSHIP COMMUNITY HOSPITAL, 800 West Main Street, Zip 45828–1698; tel. 419/678–2341; James W. Isaacs, Chief Executive Officer **A**1 9 10 **F**7 8 15 16 17 19 21 22 25 28 30 32 33 35 37 40 41 44 46 63 65 66 67 71 72 73	16	10	58	2398	23	108093	395	20128	8769	284
COLUMBUS—Franklin County										
⊠ ARTHUR G. JAMES CANCER HOSPITAL AND RICHARD J. SOLOVE RESEARCH INSTITUTE, (Formerly Arthur G. James Cancer Hospital and Research Institute), (ACUTE CARE CANCER HOSPITAL), 300 West Tenth Avenue, Zip 43210–1240; tel. 614/293–5485; David E. Schuller, M.D., Chief Executive Officer **A**1 2 3 5 8 9 10 **F**1 3 4 5 7 8 9 10 11 12 13 14 15 16 17 18 19 20 21 22 24 25 26 28 29 30 31 32 33 34 35 37 38 39 41 42 43 44 45 46 48 49 51 52 53 54 55 56 57 58 59 60 61 63 65 66 67 68 70 71 72 73 74 **P**5 **Web address:** www.jamesline.com	12	49	120	5933	95	90536	0	105044	26159	1503
⊠ △ CHILDREN'S HOSPITAL, 700 Children's Drive, Zip 43205–2696; tel. 614/722–2000; Thomas N. Hansen, M.D., Chief Executive Officer **A**1 2 3 5 7 9 10 **F**4 10 12 13 14 19 20 21 22 25 27 28 29 31 32 33 34 35 38 39 41 42 43 44 45 46 47 48 49 51 54 55 56 58 63 65 67 68 70 71 72 73 **P**8 **Web address:** www.childrenscolumbus.org COLUMBUS CAMPUS See Twin Valley Psychiatric System, Dayton	23	50	281	10594	156	338315	0	174354	72756	2491
□ △ COLUMBUS COMMUNITY HOSPITAL, 1430 South High Street, Zip 43207–1093; tel. 614/445–5000; Michael L. Brown, Interim Chief Executive Officer (Nonreporting) **A**1 7 9 10	32	10	118	—	—	—	—	—	—	—
⊠ + ○ △ DOCTORS HOSPITAL, (Includes Doctors Hospital West, 5100 West Broad Street, Zip 43228; tel. 614/297–4000), 1087 Dennison Avenue, Zip 43201–3496; tel. 614/297–4000; John A. Bowers, Executive Vice President and Chief Operating Officer (Nonreporting) **A**1 7 9 10 11 12 13 **S** OhioHealth, Columbus, OH **Web address:** www.doctorshospital.org	23	10	380	—	—	—	—	—	—	—

Hospital, Address, Telephone, Administrator, Approval, Facility, and Physician Codes, Health Care System, Network	Classification Codes		Utilization Data					Expense (thousands) of dollars		
	Control	Service	Staffed Beds	Admissions	Census	Outpatient Visits	Births	Total	Payroll	Personnel

Approval/membership key:

★ American Hospital Association (AHA) membership
□ Joint Commission on Accreditation of Healthcare Organizations (JCAHO) accreditation
+ American Osteopathic Healthcare Association (AOHA) membership
○ American Osteopathic Association (AOA) accreditation
△ Commission on Accreditation of Rehabilitation Facilities (CARF) accreditation
Control codes 61, 63, 64, 71, 72 and 73 indicate hospitals listed by AOHA, but not registered by AHA. For definition of numerical codes, see page A4

Hospital	Control	Service	Staffed Beds	Admissions	Census	Outpatient Visits	Births	Total	Payroll	Personnel
✠ GRANT/RIVERSIDE METHODIST HOSPITALS–GRANT CAMPUS, 111 South Grant Avenue, Zip 43215–1898; tel. 614/566–9000; David P. Blom, President **A**1 3 5 8 9 10 **F**1 2 3 4 7 8 10 11 12 14 15 16 17 18 19 20 21 22 23 24 25 26 27 28 29 30 31 32 33 34 35 37 38 39 40 41 42 43 44 45 46 48 49 51 52 53 54 55 56 57 58 59 60 61 63 64 65 66 67 68 70 71 72 73 74 **P**2 3 4 5 6 7 8 **S** OhioHealth, Columbus, OH **Web address:** www.ohiohealth.com	21	10	459	19211	242	151985	2749	184137	75900	1902
✠ GRANT/RIVERSIDE METHODIST HOSPITALS–RIVERSIDE CAMPUS, 3535 Olentangy River Road, Zip 43214–3998; tel. 614/566–5000; David P. Blom, President **A**1 2 3 5 8 9 10 **F**1 2 3 4 7 8 10 11 12 14 15 16 17 18 19 20 21 22 23 24 25 26 27 28 29 30 31 32 33 34 35 37 38 39 40 41 42 43 44 45 46 48 49 51 52 53 54 55 56 57 58 59 60 61 63 64 65 66 67 70 71 72 73 74 **P**2 3 4 5 6 7 8 **S** OhioHealth, Columbus, OH **Web address:** www.ohiohealth.com	21	10	812	39403	495	217749	5998	378059	167809	4513
✠ MOUNT CARMEL HEALTH SYSTEM, (Includes Mount Carmel East Hospital, 6001 East Broad Street, Zip 43213; tel. 614/234–6000; Mount Carmel Medical Center, 793 West State Street, Zip 43222; tel. 614/234–5000; St. Ann's Hospital, 500 South Cleveland Avenue, Westerville, Zip 43081–8998; tel. 614/898–4000), Mailing Address: 793 West State Street, Zip 43222–1551; tel. 614/234–5423; Joseph Calvaruso, Chief Executive Officer (Total facility includes 14 beds in nursing home–type unit) **A**1 2 3 5 9 10 **F**2 4 7 8 9 10 11 12 15 16 17 19 21 22 23 25 26 27 28 29 30 31 32 33 34 35 36 37 38 39 40 41 42 43 44 45 46 48 49 50 51 52 54 55 56 57 58 59 60 64 65 66 67 70 71 72 73 74 **P**1 2 3 5 6 7 **S** Holy Cross Health System Corporation, South Bend, IN **Web address:** www.mchs.com	21	10	1036	43676	520	517239	7590	446245	188981	5017
✠ OHIO STATE UNIVERSITY HOSPITAL EAST, (Formerly Park Medical Center), 1492 East Broad Street, Zip 43205–1546; tel. 614/251–3000; Larry Anstine, Chief Operating Officer (Total facility includes 20 beds in nursing home–type unit) **A**1 2 3 9 10 **F**2 3 4 8 10 12 14 15 16 19 21 22 24 26 27 28 29 30 32 34 35 37 41 42 44 45 49 51 52 57 60 64 65 71 72 73 74	33	10	165	5693	86	37815	0	—	—	557
✠ △ OHIO STATE UNIVERSITY MEDICAL CENTER, 410 West 10th Avenue, Zip 43210–1240; tel. 614/293–8000; R. Reed Fraley, Associate Vice President for Health Sciences and Chief Executive Officer **A**1 3 5 7 8 9 10 **F**1 3 4 5 7 8 9 10 11 12 14 15 16 17 18 19 20 21 22 23 24 25 26 28 29 30 31 32 33 34 35 37 38 39 40 41 42 43 44 45 46 48 49 51 52 53 54 55 56 57 58 59 60 61 63 65 66 67 68 70 71 72 73 74	12	10	551	25838	393	278229	3373	348093	132140	3756
PARK MEDICAL CENTER See Ohio State University Hospital East										
CONNEAUT—Ashtabula County										
✠ UHHS BROWN MEMORIAL HOSPITAL, 158 West Main Road, Zip 44030–2039, Mailing Address: P.O. Box 648, Zip 44030–0648; tel. 440/593–1131; Gerard D. Klein, President (Nonreporting) **A**1 9 10 **S** University Hospitals Health System, Cleveland, OH	23	10	51	—	—	—	—	—	—	—
COSHOCTON—Coshocton County										
□ COSHOCTON COUNTY MEMORIAL HOSPITAL, 1460 Orange Street, Zip 43812–6330, Mailing Address: P.O. Box 1330, Zip 43812–6330; tel. 740/622–6411; Gregory M. Nowak, Administrator and Chief Executive Officer (Total facility includes 61 beds in nursing home–type unit) (Nonreporting) **A**1 9 10	23	10	151	—	—	—	—	—	—	—
CRESTLINE—Crawford County										
CRESTLINE HOSPITAL See MedCentral Health System, Mansfield										
CUYAHOGA FALLS—Summit County										
+ ○ △ CUYAHOGA FALLS GENERAL HOSPITAL, 1900 23rd Street, Zip 44223–1499; tel. 330/971–7000; Fred Anthony, President and Chief Executive Officer **A**7 10 11 12 13 **F**7 8 12 14 15 16 17 19 20 22 27 28 30 32 35 37 39 40 41 42 44 49 51 52 56 57 58 59 63 65 67 71 72 73 74 **P**3 8	23	10	144	4101	55	78615	547	49893	23053	634
DAYTON—Montgomery County										
✠ CHILDREN'S MEDICAL CENTER, One Children's Plaza, Zip 45404–1815; tel. 937/226–8300; Laurence P. Harkness, President and Chief Executive Officer **A**1 3 5 8 9 10 **F**10 12 13 14 15 16 17 19 20 22 25 27 28 29 30 31 32 33 34 35 38 39 41 44 45 46 47 49 51 53 54 55 58 65 67 68 71 72 73 **Web address:** www.cmcdayton.org	23	50	155	6142	79	209101	0	80131	36184	978
DAYTON CAMPUS See Twin Valley Psychiatric System										
□ △ FRANCISCAN MEDICAL CENTER–DAYTON CAMPUS, One Franciscan Way, Zip 45408–1498; tel. 937/229–6000; Duane L. Erwin, Chief Executive Officer (Total facility includes 30 beds in nursing home–type unit) **A**1 2 3 5 7 9 10 **F**1 4 6 7 8 10 11 12 14 15 16 17 19 20 21 22 24 25 26 27 28 29 30 31 32 34 35 37 39 40 41 42 43 44 45 46 48 49 51 52 53 54 55 56 58 59 60 62 64 65 66 67 70 71 72 73 74 **P**6 8 **S** Franciscan Health Partnership, Inc., Latham, NY	21	10	321	13726	216	280994	957	136100	63200	1604
✠ GOOD SAMARITAN HOSPITAL AND HEALTH CENTER, 2222 Philadelphia Drive, Zip 45406–1813; tel. 937/278–2612; K. Douglas Deck, President and Chief Executive Officer **A**1 2 3 5 9 10 **F**2 3 4 6 7 8 9 10 11 12 14 15 16 17 18 19 20 21 22 23 25 26 28 29 30 31 32 33 34 35 37 38 39 40 41 42 43 44 45 46 48 49 51 52 53 54 55 56 57 58 59 60 62 63 64 65 66 67 68 70 71 72 73 74 **P**6 8 **S** Catholic Health Initiatives, Denver, CO	21	10	324	16917	214	185604	1556	166933	74491	2023
○ GRANDVIEW HOSPITAL AND MEDICAL CENTER, (Includes Southview Hospital and Family Health Center, 1997 Miamisburg–Centerville Road, Zip 45459–3800; tel. 937/439–6000), 405 Grand Avenue, Zip 45405–4796; tel. 937/226–3200; Richard J. Minor, President and Chief Executive Officer (Nonreporting) **A**9 10 11 12 13 **Web address:** www.gvh-svh.org	23	10	320	—	—	—	—	—	—	—
KETTERING YOUTH SERVICES See Kettering Medical Center, Kettering										

Hospital, Address, Telephone, Administrator, Approval, Facility, and Physician Codes, Health Care System, Network	Classi-fication Codes		Utilization Data					Expense (thousands) of dollars		
★ American Hospital Association (AHA) membership □ Joint Commission on Accreditation of Healthcare Organizations (JCAHO) accreditation + American Osteopathic Healthcare Association (AOHA) membership ○ American Osteopathic Association (AOA) accreditation △ Commission on Accreditation of Rehabilitation Facilities (CARF) accreditation Control codes 61, 63, 64, 71, 72 and 73 indicate hospitals listed by AOHA, but not registered by AHA. For definition of numerical codes, see page A4	Control	Service	Staffed Beds	Admissions	Census	Outpatient Visits	Births	Total	Payroll	Personnel

▣ △ MIAMI VALLEY HOSPITAL, One Wyoming Street, Zip 45409–2763; tel. 937/208–8000; William M. Thornton, Presdent and Chief Executive Officer **A**1 2 3 5 7 8 9 10 **F**1 2 3 4 7 8 9 10 11 12 14 15 16 17 18 19 20 21 22 23 24 25 26 27 28 29 30 31 32 33 34 35 36 37 38 39 40 41 42 43 44 45 46 48 49 51 53 54 55 56 57 58 59 60 61 63 65 66 67 68 70 71 72 73 74 **P**5 8	23	10	714	27783	378	552954	5673	302051	131988	3769
□ TWIN VALLEY PSYCHIATRIC SYSTEM, (Includes Columbus Campus, 1960 West Broad Street, Columbus, Zip 43223–1295; tel. 614/752–0333; Dayton Campus, 2611 Wayne Avenue, tel. 937/258–0440), 2611 Wayne Avenue, Zip 45420–1800; tel. 937/258–0440; James Ignelzi, Chief Executive Officer (Nonreporting) **A**1 10	12	22	504	—	—	—	—	—	—	—
▣ VETERANS AFFAIRS MEDICAL CENTER, 4100 West Third Street, Zip 45428–1002; tel. 937/268–6511; Steven M. Cohen, M.D., Director (Total facility includes 265 beds in nursing home–type unit) **A**1 3 5 8 **F**1 3 8 10 12 15 19 20 21 22 24 25 26 28 29 30 31 32 33 34 35 37 39 41 42 44 45 46 48 49 51 52 54 58 60 63 64 65 67 71 73 **P**6 **S** Department of Veterans Affairs, Washington, DC	45	10	539	5223	544	213338	0	117444	73381	1851
DEFIANCE—Defiance County										
▣ DEFIANCE HOSPITAL, 1206 East Second Street, Zip 43512–2495; tel. 419/783–6955; Robert J. Coholich, President **A**1 9 10 **F**7 8 11 15 16 19 21 22 27 28 29 30 32 35 36 37 39 40 42 44 45 46 49 52 55 56 57 58 59 63 65 67 71 73 **P**1 7 **S** ProMedica Health System, Toledo, OH **Web address:** www.promedica.org	23	10	80	2845	29	30354	505	24804	9357	285
DELAWARE—Delaware County										
□ △ GRADY MEMORIAL HOSPITAL, 561 West Central Avenue, Zip 43015–1485; tel. 740/369–8711; Everett P. Weber, Jr., President and Chief Executive Officer (Nonreporting) **A**1 2 7 9 10	23	10	84	—	—	—	—	—	—	—
DENNISON—Tuscarawas County										
▣ TWIN CITY HOSPITAL, 819 North First Street, Zip 44621–1098; tel. 740/922–2800; Cheryl Hicks, Chief Executive Officer **A**1 9 10 **F**8 11 12 14 16 17 19 20 22 28 29 30 32 33 34 37 39 41 44 45 46 48 49 51 63 64 65 66 71 73 74 **P**7 **Web address:** www.web1.tusco.net/tchosp	23	10	30	558	7	—	0	6220	2719	120
DOVER—Tuscarawas County										
▣ UNION HOSPITAL, 659 Boulevard, Zip 44622–2077; tel. 330/343–3311; William W. Harding, President and Chief Executive Officer **A**1 9 10 **F**7 8 14 15 16 17 19 21 22 28 30 32 33 34 35 36 37 39 40 42 44 49 53 54 55 56 57 58 63 65 66 67 71 73	23	10	104	4518	47	173503	790	37550	15544	513
EAST LIVERPOOL—Columbiana County										
▣ EAST LIVERPOOL CITY HOSPITAL, 425 West Fifth Street, Zip 43920–2498; tel. 330/385–7200; Melvin R. Creeley, President (Total facility includes 20 beds in nursing home–type unit) **A**1 9 10 **F**1 7 8 11 13 15 16 19 21 22 26 28 30 32 34 35 37 38 39 40 41 42 44 45 46 49 52 54 56 57 58 63 64 65 67 71 72 **P**8	23	10	198	8842	88	65665	452	38703	17259	531
ELYRIA—Lorain County										
▣ EMH REGIONAL MEDICAL CENTER, 630 East River Street, Zip 44035–5902; tel. 440/329–7500; Kevin C. Martin, President and Chief Executive Officer **A**1 2 9 10 **F**4 7 8 10 11 14 15 16 19 21 22 23 25 26 28 30 32 33 34 35 37 38 39 40 41 42 43 44 49 51 52 55 56 59 63 65 66 67 69 71 72 73 74 **P**7 8 **Web address:** www.emh–healthcare.org	23	10	296	11908	139	207407	988	103281	37252	1068
EUCLID—Cuyahoga County										
□ △ EUCLID HOSPITAL, (Formerly Meridia Euclid Hospital), 18901 Lake Shore Boulevard, Zip 44119–1090; tel. 216/531–9000; Denise Zeman, Chief Operating Officer (Total facility includes 40 beds in nursing home–type unit) **A**1 2 7 9 10 **F**2 3 4 7 8 10 11 12 13 14 15 16 17 19 21 22 24 25 26 27 28 29 30 31 33 34 35 36 37 38 40 41 42 43 44 45 46 47 48 49 50 52 54 55 56 57 58 59 60 61 63 64 65 66 67 70 71 72 73 74 **P**1 3 4 7 8 **S** Meridia Health System, Cleveland, OH **Web address:** www.meridia.com	23	10	187	6787	142	52060	416	51860	24343	650
FAIRFIELD—Butler County										
MERCY HOSPITAL OF FAIRFIELD See Mercy Hospital, Hamilton										
FINDLAY—Hancock County										
▣ BLANCHARD VALLEY HEALTH ASSOCIATION SYSTEM, (Includes Blanchard Valley Regional Health Center–Bluffton Campus, 139 Garau Street, Bluffton, Zip 45817–0048; tel. 419/358–9010; Blanchard Valley Regional Health Center–Findlay Campus, 145 West Wallace Street, tel. 419/423–4500; Clifford R. Lehman, President), 145 West Wallace Street, Zip 45840–1299; tel. 419/423–4500; William E. Ruse, FACHE, President and Chief Executive Officer **A**1 9 10 **F**1 6 7 8 10 11 12 13 14 15 16 17 19 21 22 25 26 28 29 30 32 33 34 35 36 40 41 42 44 45 46 49 51 52 59 60 62 64 65 66 67 71 72 73 **P**6 **Web address:** www.bvrh.org	23	10	192	7663	82	182979	1292	62839	28184	941
FOSTORIA—Hancock County										
▣ FOSTORIA COMMUNITY HOSPITAL, 501 Van Buren Street, Zip 44830–0907, Mailing Address: P.O. Box 907, Zip 44830–0907; tel. 419/435–7734; Brad A. Higgins, President and Chief Executive Officer **A**1 9 10 **F**7 8 14 15 16 17 19 21 22 24 27 28 29 30 31 32 34 35 36 37 39 40 42 44 45 46 49 63 65 66 67 68 70 71 72 73 **Web address:** www.fchosp.com	23	10	50	1347	12	35352	216	15440	5937	187

Hospital, Address, Telephone, Administrator, Approval, Facility, and Physician Codes, Health Care System, Network	Classification Codes		Utilization Data					Expense (thousands) of dollars		
★ American Hospital Association (AHA) membership □ Joint Commission on Accreditation of Healthcare Organizations (JCAHO) accreditation + American Osteopathic Healthcare Association (AOHA) membership ○ American Osteopathic Association (AOA) accreditation △ Commission on Accreditation of Rehabilitation Facilities (CARF) accreditation Control codes 61, 63, 64, 71, 72 and 73 indicate hospitals listed by AOHA, but not registered by AHA. For definition of numerical codes, see page A4	Control	Service	Staffed Beds	Admissions	Census	Outpatient Visits	Births	Total	Payroll	Personnel

FREMONT—Sandusky County

⊠ MEMORIAL HOSPITAL, 715 South Taft Avenue, Zip 43420–3200; tel. 419/332–7321; John A. Gorman, Chief Executive Officer **A**1 9 10 **F**1 7 8 14 15 16 17 19 21 27 29 30 32 33 34 35 36 37 39 40 41 42 44 45 49 52 54 55 57 58 59 65 71 73 74 **P**6 8 **S** Quorum Health Group/Quorum Health Resources, Inc., Brentwood, TN | 23 | 10 | 114 | 3187 | 31 | 36159 | 516 | 32012 | 12534 | 372

GALION—Crawford County

⊠ GALION COMMUNITY HOSPITAL, 269 Portland Way South, Zip 44833–2399; tel. 419/468–4841; Lyndon J. Christman, Administrator and Chief Operating Officer (Total facility includes 33 beds in nursing home–type unit) **A**1 9 10 **F**7 8 14 15 16 17 19 21 22 28 30 32 33 35 36 37 40 41 42 44 49 63 64 65 67 71 73 74 **P**3 4 7 **S** OhioHealth, Columbus, OH | 23 | 10 | 109 | 2133 | 31 | 42962 | 455 | 18064 | 6778 | 241

GALLIPOLIS—Gallia County

⊠ △ HOLZER MEDICAL CENTER, 100 Jackson Pike, Zip 45631–1563; tel. 740/446–5000; Charles I. Adkins, Jr., President **A**1 2 7 9 10 **F**7 8 11 12 15 16 17 19 21 22 23 24 25 26 28 29 30 32 33 35 37 39 40 41 42 44 46 48 49 58 60 63 64 65 67 71 73 74 **P**5
Web address: www.holzer.org | 23 | 10 | 269 | 6366 | 76 | 66094 | 855 | 48641 | 19823 | 768

GARFIELD HEIGHTS—Cuyahoga County

⊠ △ MARYMOUNT HOSPITAL, 12300 McCracken Road, Zip 44125–2975; tel. 216/581–0500; Thomas J. Trudell, President and Chief Executive Officer **A**1 2 6 7 10 **F**3 4 6 7 8 10 12 14 15 16 17 18 19 21 22 23 25 27 28 30 31 32 33 34 35 36 37 39 40 41 42 43 44 46 48 49 51 52 53 54 55 56 57 58 59 62 63 64 65 66 67 69 71 72 73 74 **P**1 3 6 7 | 21 | 10 | 220 | 8785 | 141 | 138941 | 1024 | 90437 | 39729 | 1077

GENEVA—Ashtabula County

⊠ UHHS–MEMORIAL HOSPITAL OF GENEVA, 870 West Main Street, Zip 44041–1295; tel. 440/466–1141; Gerard D. Klein, Chief Executive Officer **A**1 9 10 **F**8 12 14 15 16 17 19 22 28 29 30 35 37 41 44 45 46 49 63 67 71 73 **P**7 **S** University Hospitals Health System, Cleveland, OH | 23 | 10 | 35 | 1055 | 12 | 44776 | 0 | 11952 | 4289 | 180

GEORGETOWN—Brown County

⊠ BROWN COUNTY GENERAL HOSPITAL, 425 Home Street, Zip 45121–1407; tel. 937/378–6121; David T. Wallace, President and Chief Executive Officer **A**1 9 10 **F**3 7 8 14 19 21 22 28 32 33 35 37 40 41 42 44 45 46 53 54 55 56 57 58 59 63 65 69 71 73 **P**6 **S** Quorum Health Group/Quorum Health Resources, Inc., Brentwood, TN
Web address: www.bcgh.org | 13 | 10 | 53 | 1744 | 15 | 51876 | 422 | 15970 | 6669 | 245

GREEN SPRINGS—Sandusky County

⊠ △ ST. FRANCIS HEALTH CARE CENTRE, (LONG TERM ACUTE CARE), 401 North Broadway, Zip 44836–9653; tel. 419/639–2626; Dan Schwanke, Executive Director (Total facility includes 150 beds in nursing home–type unit) **A**1 7 9 10 **F**12 14 15 16 26 27 31 34 39 41 46 49 57 58 64 65 67 73 **S** ProMedica Health System, Toledo, OH | 21 | 49 | 186 | 482 | 106 | 7038 | 0 | 13246 | 5063 | 153

GREENFIELD—Highland County

⊠ △ GREENFIELD AREA MEDICAL CENTER, 545 South Street, Zip 45123–1400; tel. 937/981–2116; Mark E. Marchetti, Chief Executive Officer **A**1 7 9 10 **F**8 12 14 15 16 17 18 19 22 28 29 30 32 33 35 36 41 44 46 48 49 65 71 72 73 **S** Quorum Health Group/Quorum Health Resources, Inc., Brentwood, TN | 23 | 10 | 36 | 858 | 16 | 24631 | 0 | 9520 | 3670 | 123

GREENVILLE—Darke County

□ WAYNE HOSPITAL, 835 Sweitzer Street, Zip 45331–1077; tel. 937/548–1141; Raymond E. Laughlin, Jr., President and Chief Executive Officer **A**1 9 10 **F**7 11 15 17 19 21 22 34 35 40 44 45 49 65 71 73 **P**8 | 23 | 10 | 92 | 2945 | 37 | 63553 | 468 | 26101 | 11078 | 356

HAMILTON—Butler County

⊠ FORT HAMILTON HOSPITAL, (Formerly Fort Hamilton–Hughes Memorial Hospital), 630 Eaton Avenue, Zip 45013–2770; tel. 513/867–2000; James A. Kingsbury, President and Chief Executive Officer **A**1 2 9 10 **F**2 3 4 5 7 8 9 10 11 12 13 14 15 16 17 18 19 20 21 22 23 24 25 26 27 28 29 30 31 32 33 34 35 36 37 38 39 40 41 42 43 44 45 46 48 49 50 51 52 53 54 55 56 57 58 59 60 61 63 64 65 66 67 68 70 71 72 73 74 **P**7 8 **S** Health Alliance of Greater Cincinnati, Cincinnati, OH | 23 | 10 | 181 | 8167 | 100 | 97582 | 1170 | 62308 | 26215 | 782

□ MERCY HOSPITAL, (Includes Mercy Hospital of Fairfield, 3000 Mack Road, Fairfield; Mercy Hospital of Hamilton, 100 Riverfront Plaza), Mailing Address: P.O. Box 418, Zip 45012–0418; tel. 513/867–6400; David A. Ferrell, President (Total facility includes 53 beds in nursing home–type unit) **A**1 2 9 10 **F**1 4 6 7 8 10 12 14 15 16 17 19 21 22 24 25 26 27 28 29 30 32 33 34 35 36 37 39 40 41 42 44 45 46 48 49 62 63 64 65 66 67 71 72 73 74 **P**6 8 **S** Catholic Healthcare Partners, Cincinnati, OH
Web address: www.mercy.health–partners.org | 21 | 10 | 248 | 10486 | 146 | 198162 | 1109 | 87723 | 35803 | 1017

HICKSVILLE—Defiance County

□ COMMUNITY MEMORIAL HOSPITAL, 208 North Columbus Street, Zip 43526–1299; tel. 419/542–6692; Deryl E. Gulliford, Ph.D., Administrator **A**1 10 **F**14 15 16 17 19 22 24 27 28 30 31 32 33 34 35 36 39 40 41 44 45 46 49 51 55 66 67 71 72 73 74 **P**6 | 16 | 10 | 24 | 483 | 4 | 15258 | 92 | 6122 | 3076 | 108

HILLSBORO—Highland County

⊠ HIGHLAND DISTRICT HOSPITAL, 1275 North High Street, Zip 45133–8571; tel. 937/393–6100; Charles H. Bair, Chief Executive Officer **A**1 9 10 **F**7 8 12 14 15 16 17 19 22 35 40 41 42 44 46 49 65 66 68 71 73 | 16 | 10 | 51 | 2296 | 23 | 29767 | 387 | 20567 | 8337 | 285

Hospital, Address, Telephone, Administrator, Approval, Facility, and Physician Codes, Health Care System, Network	Classi-fication Codes		Utilization Data					Expense (thousands) of dollars		
★ American Hospital Association (AHA) membership □ Joint Commission on Accreditation of Healthcare Organizations (JCAHO) accreditation + American Osteopathic Healthcare Association (AOHA) membership ○ American Osteopathic Association (AOA) accreditation △ Commission on Accreditation of Rehabilitation Facilities (CARF) accreditation Control codes 61, 63, 64, 71, 72 and 73 indicate hospitals listed by AOHA, but not registered by AHA. For definition of numerical codes, see page A4	Control	Service	Staffed Beds	Admissions	Census	Outpatient Visits	Births	Total	Payroll	Personnel

IRONTON—Lawrence County

□ RIVER VALLEY HEALTH SYSTEM, (Includes Behavioral Health–Portsmouth Campus, 2201 25th Street, Portsmouth, Zip 45662–3252; tel. 614/354–2804; Rick E. Harlow, Vice President Behavioral Health), 2228 South Ninth Street, Zip 45638–2526; tel. 614/532–3231; Terry L. Vanderhoof, President and Chief Executive Officer (Total facility includes 11 beds in nursing home–type unit) **A**1 9 10 **F**7 8 17 19 21 22 25 30 32 34 35 37 40 44 46 52 56 58 59 63 64 65 71 72 73

| | 13 | 10 | 219 | 3236 | 54 | 30895 | 144 | 10439 | 13436 | 699 |

KENTON—Hardin County

⊞ HARDIN MEMORIAL HOSPITAL, 921 East Franklin Street, Zip 43326–2099, Mailing Address: P.O. Box 710, Zip 43326–0710; tel. 419/673–0761; Don J. Sabol, Chief Executive Officer **A**1 9 10 **F**1 3 4 5 7 8 10 12 13 14 15 16 17 18 19 20 21 22 23 24 25 26 27 28 29 30 31 32 33 34 35 36 37 39 40 41 42 43 44 45 46 49 50 51 53 54 55 56 57 58 59 60 61 62 63 65 66 67 69 71 72 73 74 **P**3 5 **S** OhioHealth, Columbus, OH

| | 23 | 10 | 51 | 1872 | 27 | 47473 | 141 | 14094 | 5652 | 258 |

KETTERING—Montgomery County

⊞ KETTERING MEDICAL CENTER, (Includes Charles F. Kettering Memorial Hospital, 3535 Southern Boulevard, Zip 45429; tel. 513/298–4331; Kettering Youth Services, 5350 Lamme Road, Dayton, Zip 45439; tel. 513/299–9511; Sycamore Hospital, 2150 Leiter Road, Miamisburg, Zip 45342; tel. 513/866–0551), 3535 Southern Boulevard, Zip 45429–1221; tel. 937/298–4331; Francisco J. Perez, President and Chief Executive Officer **A**1 2 3 5 8 9 10 **F**3 4 5 6 7 8 10 12 14 15 16 17 19 21 22 26 27 28 29 30 32 34 35 37 38 39 40 41 42 43 44 45 46 49 50 51 52 53 54 55 56 57 58 59 60 62 63 65 66 67 71 73 74 **P**8
Web address: www.ketthealth.com

| | 21 | 10 | 410 | 17636 | 206 | 164968 | 1903 | 213839 | 92971 | 2787 |

LAKEWOOD—Cuyahoga County

⊞ LAKEWOOD HOSPITAL, 14519 Detroit Avenue, Zip 44107–4383; tel. 216/521–4200; Revonda L. Shumaker, R.N., President and Chief Executive Officer (Total facility includes 45 beds in nursing home–type unit) **A**1 2 10 **F**1 2 3 4 5 7 8 9 10 11 12 13 14 15 16 17 18 19 20 21 22 23 24 25 26 27 28 29 30 31 32 33 34 35 36 37 38 39 40 41 42 43 44 45 46 47 48 49 50 51 52 53 54 55 56 57 58 59 60 61 63 64 65 66 67 68 70 71 72 73 74 **P**2 6 7 8

| | 23 | 10 | 283 | 9552 | 153 | 134237 | 461 | 105675 | 43498 | 1236 |

LANCASTER—Fairfield County

⊞ △ FAIRFIELD MEDICAL CENTER, 401 North Ewing Street, Zip 43130–3371; tel. 740/687–8000; Creighton E. Likes, Jr., President and Chief Executive Officer (Total facility includes 24 beds in nursing home–type unit) **A**1 7 9 10 **F**2 3 7 8 10 12 14 15 16 17 18 19 21 22 24 25 26 28 29 30 32 34 35 37 39 40 41 42 44 46 48 49 51 52 53 54 55 56 57 58 59 60 63 64 65 66 67 70 71 73 74 **P**4 7

| | 23 | 10 | 196 | 10630 | 122 | 197908 | 1342 | 86456 | 35873 | 1167 |

LIMA—Allen County

⊞ △ LIMA MEMORIAL HOSPITAL, 1001 Bellefontaine Avenue, Zip 45804–2894; tel. 419/228–3335; John B. White, President and Chief Executive Officer **A**1 2 7 10 **F**4 7 8 10 11 12 14 15 19 21 22 23 26 28 29 30 31 32 34 35 36 37 39 40 41 42 43 44 45 46 48 49 52 54 55 56 57 59 60 63 64 65 66 67 71 73 74 **P**3 7 8

| | 23 | 10 | 328 | 7952 | 116 | 145345 | 550 | 80448 | 33038 | 961 |

□ OAKWOOD CORRECTIONAL FACILITY, 3200 North West Street, Zip 45801–2000; tel. 419/225–8052; Christopher Yanai, M.D., Warden and Chief Executive Officer **A**1 **F**12 14 15 16 17 18 27 30 31 39 45 46 51 52 54 55 56 57 58 65 67 73 74

| | 12 | 22 | 131 | 255 | 95 | 562 | 0 | 20561 | 12880 | 320 |

□ △ ST. RITA'S MEDICAL CENTER, 730 West Market Street, Zip 45801–4670; tel. 419/227–3361; James P. Reber, President **A**1 2 7 9 10 **F**2 3 4 7 8 10 11 12 14 15 16 17 18 19 20 21 22 23 24 25 26 28 29 30 31 32 33 34 35 37 38 39 40 41 42 43 44 46 48 49 51 52 53 54 55 56 57 58 59 60 63 64 65 66 67 71 72 73 74 **P**8 **S** Catholic Healthcare Partners, Cincinnati, OH
Web address: www.mercy.com\srmc

| | 21 | 10 | 320 | 12788 | 158 | 265243 | 1991 | 137358 | 59559 | 1706 |

LODI—Medina County

⊞ LODI COMMUNITY HOSPITAL, 225 Elyria Street, Zip 44254–1096; tel. 330/948–1222; Thomas L. Lockard, President and Chief Executive Officer (Total facility includes 7 beds in nursing home–type unit) (Nonreporting) **A**1 5 10

| | 23 | 10 | 21 | — | — | — | — | — | — | — |

LOGAN—Hocking County

⊞ HOCKING VALLEY COMMUNITY HOSPITAL, Route 2, State Route 664, Zip 43138–0966, Mailing Address: Box 966, Zip 43138–0966; tel. 740/385–5631; Larry Willard, Administrator (Total facility includes 30 beds in nursing home–type unit) (Nonreporting) **A**1 9 10

| | 13 | 10 | 92 | — | — | — | — | — | — | — |

LONDON—Madison County

⊞ MADISON COUNTY HOSPITAL, 210 North Main Street, Zip 43140–1115; tel. 740/852–1372; Stuart W. Williams, Interim Chief Executive Officer (Total facility includes 11 beds in nursing home–type unit) **A**1 9 10 **F**3 7 8 11 14 15 16 17 19 22 23 24 25 26 28 29 30 31 32 33 34 35 36 37 39 40 41 42 44 48 49 52 53 54 58 59 64 65 66 67 68 71 73 74 **P**6

| | 23 | 10 | 46 | 1849 | 36 | 20049 | 183 | 20350 | 9078 | 314 |

LORAIN—Lorain County

□ △ LORAIN COMMUNITY/ST. JOSEPH REGIONAL HEALTH CENTER, (Includes Lorain Community/St. Joseph Health Center—East Campus, 205 West 20th Street, Zip 44052–3794; tel. 216/233–1000; Lorain Community/St. Joseph Regional Health Center–West Campus, tel. 216/960–3000), 3700 Kolbe Road, Zip 44053–1697; tel. 216/960–3000; Brian C. Lockwood, President and Chief Executive Officer (Total facility includes 16 beds in nursing home–type unit) (Nonreporting) **A**1 2 7 9 10 **S** Catholic Healthcare Partners, Cincinnati, OH

| | 23 | 10 | 303 | — | — | — | — | — | — | — |

Hospital, Address, Telephone, Administrator, Approval, Facility, and Physician Codes, Health Care System, Network	Classi-fication Codes		Utilization Data					Expense (thousands) of dollars		
★ American Hospital Association (AHA) membership □ Joint Commission on Accreditation of Healthcare Organizations (JCAHO) accreditation + American Osteopathic Healthcare Association (AOHA) membership ○ American Osteopathic Association (AOA) accreditation △ Commission on Accreditation of Rehabilitation Facilities (CARF) accreditation Control codes 61, 63, 64, 71, 72 and 73 indicate hospitals listed by AOHA, but not registered by AHA. For definition of numerical codes, see page A4	Control	Service	Staffed Beds	Admissions	Census	Outpatient Visits	Births	Total	Payroll	Personnel

MANSFIELD—Richland County

☒ MEDCENTRAL HEALTH SYSTEM, (Includes Crestline Hospital, 291 Heiser Court, Crestline, Zip 44827–1453; tel. 419/683–1212; Susan Brown, Site Administrator and Nursing Director; Mansfield Hospital, 335 Glessner Avenue, tel. 419/526–8000; Paul Kautz, M.D., Vice President and Chief Operating Officer; Shelby Hospital, 20 Morris Road, Shelby, Zip 44875–0608; tel. 419/342–5015; Ron Distl, Vice President and Chief Operating Officer), 335 Glessner Avenue, Zip 44903–2265; tel. 419/526–8000; James E. Meyer, President and Chief Executive Officer **A**1 2 6 9 10 **F**2 3 4 7 8 10 11 12 15 16 17 19 20 21 22 23 25 28 29 30 31 32 33 34 35 37 39 40 41 42 43 44 45 46 48 49 52 53 54 55 56 57 58 60 63 65 66 67 70 71 72 73 74 **P**5 7 8
Web address: www.medcentral.org | 23 | 10 | 309 | 12871 | 199 | 173144 | 1352 | 112932 | 53685 | 1663 |

☒ RICHLAND HOSPITAL, 1451 Lucas Road, Zip 44901–0637, Mailing Address: P.O. Box 637, Zip 44901–0637; tel. 419/589–5511; Sylvester Cocuzza, Administrator (Nonreporting) **A**1 9 10 | 23 | 22 | 92 | — | — | — | — | — | — | — |

MARIETTA—Washington County

☒ △ MARIETTA MEMORIAL HOSPITAL, 401 Matthew Street, Zip 45750–1699; tel. 740/374–1400; Larry J. Unroe, President **A**1 7 9 10 **F**2 3 4 7 8 10 11 14 15 16 17 19 21 22 23 24 26 27 28 29 30 31 32 33 34 35 37 39 40 41 42 44 45 46 48 49 52 54 55 56 58 59 60 63 64 65 66 67 71 72 73 74 **P**8
Web address: www.mmhospital.org | 23 | 10 | 130 | 5534 | 70 | 136675 | 737 | 47824 | 21379 | 730 |

★ + ○ SELBY GENERAL HOSPITAL, 1106 Colegate Drive, Zip 45750–1323; tel. 740/373–0582; Richard C. Sommer, Interim Chief Executive Officer **A**10 11 12 13 **F**2 7 8 15 16 19 21 22 26 30 34 35 36 37 39 40 41 42 44 49 51 54 57 58 59 62 63 65 72 73 74 **P**6 8 **S** Quorum Health Group/Quorum Health Resources, Inc., Brentwood, TN
Web address: www.selby.wscc.edu | 23 | 10 | 52 | 1718 | 21 | 31684 | 66 | 16348 | 6868 | 181 |

MARION—Marion County

☒ △ MARION GENERAL HOSPITAL, 1000 McKinley Park Drive, Zip 43302–6397; tel. 740/383–8400; Frank V. Swinehart, President and Chief Executive Officer **A**1 2 7 9 10 **F**1 7 8 10 15 16 17 19 21 22 28 30 31 32 33 34 35 37 39 40 41 42 44 45 46 48 49 52 53 54 55 56 57 58 59 60 65 67 71 73 74 **P**7 8 **S** OhioHealth, Columbus, OH
Web address: www.mariongeneral.org | 23 | 10 | 133 | 6098 | 69 | 99828 | 898 | 65340 | 27063 | 833 |

□ MEDCENTER HOSPITAL, 1050 Delaware Avenue, Zip 43302–6459; tel. 740/383–8000; Cheryl Herbert, President (Nonreporting) **A**1 9 10 | 23 | 10 | 86 | — | — | — | — | — | — | — |

MARTINS FERRY—Belmont County

☒ EAST OHIO REGIONAL HOSPITAL, 90 North Fourth Street, Zip 43935–1648; tel. 740/633–1100; Brian K. Felici, Vice President and Administrator (Total facility includes 94 beds in nursing home–type unit) **A**1 9 10 **F**2 3 5 7 8 10 11 12 14 15 16 17 18 19 21 22 23 24 25 26 27 28 29 30 31 32 34 35 37 39 40 41 42 43 44 45 46 47 48 49 51 52 53 54 55 56 57 58 59 60 61 63 64 65 66 67 71 72 73 74 **P**6 8 | 23 | 10 | 165 | 3765 | 127 | 139067 | 104 | 40870 | 17640 | 556 |

MARYSVILLE—Union County

□ MEMORIAL HOSPITAL, 500 London Avenue, Zip 43040–1594; tel. 937/644–6115; Danny L. Boggs, President and Chief Executive Officer (Total facility includes 95 beds in nursing home–type unit) **A**1 9 10 **F**7 8 12 14 15 16 19 21 22 24 27 28 30 32 34 35 36 37 39 40 41 42 44 46 49 63 64 65 66 67 71 73 **P**7 | 13 | 10 | 145 | 2552 | 103 | 171368 | 567 | 34748 | 14933 | 509 |

MASSILLON—Stark County

★ + ○ DOCTORS HOSPITAL OF STARK COUNTY, 400 Austin Avenue N.W., Zip 44646–3554; tel. 330/837–7200; Thomas E. Cecconi, Chief Executive Officer **A**2 9 10 11 12 13 **F**7 8 10 12 14 15 16 19 21 22 23 26 27 30 32 34 37 39 40 41 42 44 45 46 48 49 51 52 54 57 59 65 67 71 73 74 **P**7 8 **S** Quorum Health Group/Quorum Health Resources, Inc., Brentwood, TN
Web address: www.drshospital.com | 33 | 10 | 110 | 4827 | 61 | 65146 | 358 | 41681 | 18726 | 519 |

☒ △ MASSILLON COMMUNITY HOSPITAL, 875 Eighth Street N.E., Zip 44646–8503, Mailing Address: P.O. Box 805, Zip 44648–8503; tel. 330/832–8761; Mervin F. Strine, President and Chief Executive Officer (Total facility includes 20 beds in nursing home–type unit) **A**1 7 9 10 **F**2 3 4 7 8 10 11 12 15 16 17 19 20 21 22 23 24 26 28 29 30 31 32 34 35 37 39 40 41 42 44 45 46 48 49 52 57 59 63 64 65 67 71 73 **P**6
Web address: www.mchosp.org | 23 | 10 | 179 | 4649 | 65 | 105622 | 231 | 41624 | 20034 | 543 |

□ MASSILLON PSYCHIATRIC CENTER, 3000 Erie Street, Zip 44646–7993, Mailing Address: Box 540, Zip 44648–0540; tel. 330/833–3135; Cathy L. Cincinat, Chief Executive Officer (Nonreporting) **A**1 10 | 12 | 22 | 184 | — | — | — | — | — | — | — |

MAUMEE—Lucas County

CHARTER HOSPITAL OF TOLEDO See Focus Healthcare of Ohio

□ FOCUS HEALTHCARE OF OHIO, (Formerly Charter Hospital of Toledo), 1725 Timber Line Road, Zip 43537–4015; tel. 419/891–9333; Dennis J. Sajdak, Chief Executive Officer (Nonreporting) **A**1 10 **S** Magellan Health Services, Atlanta, GA | 33 | 52 | 38 | — | — | — | — | — | — | — |

☒ ST. LUKE'S HOSPITAL, 5901 Monclova Road, Zip 43537–1899; tel. 419/893–5911; Frank J. Bartell, III, President and Chief Executive Officer (Total facility includes 26 beds in nursing home–type unit) **A**1 2 9 10 **F**7 8 10 12 14 15 17 19 21 22 23 27 28 30 34 35 36 37 40 41 42 44 45 46 49 54 63 64 65 66 67 68 71 73 **P**8
Web address: www.stlukeshospital.com | 23 | 10 | 180 | 8983 | 106 | 132417 | 561 | 83726 | 37243 | 971 |

Hospital, Address, Telephone, Administrator, Approval, Facility, and Physician Codes, Health Care System, Network	Classi-fication Codes		Utilization Data					Expense (thousands) of dollars		
★ American Hospital Association (AHA) membership □ Joint Commission on Accreditation of Healthcare Organizations (JCAHO) accreditation + American Osteopathic Healthcare Association (AOHA) membership ○ American Osteopathic Association (AOA) accreditation △ Commission on Accreditation of Rehabilitation Facilities (CARF) accreditation Control codes 61, 63, 64, 71, 72 and 73 indicate hospitals listed by AOHA, but not registered by AHA. For definition of numerical codes, see page A4	Control	Service	Staffed Beds	Admissions	Census	Outpatient Visits	Births	Total	Payroll	Personnel

MEDINA—Medina County

□ △ MEDINA GENERAL HOSPITAL, 1000 East Washington Street, Zip 44256–2170; tel. 330/725–1000; Gary D. Hallman, President and Chief Executive Officer **A**1 2 7 9 10 **F**7 8 12 13 14 15 17 19 20 21 22 28 30 34 35 37 39 40 41 42 44 49 51 61 65 66 67 71 72 73 74 **P**8 — 23 10 | 118 | 5006 | 57 | 150862 | 912 | 54549 | 24908 | 896

MIAMISBURG—Montgomery County

SYCAMORE HOSPITAL See Kettering Medical Center, Kettering

MIDDLEBURG HEIGHTS—Cuyahoga County

☒ SOUTHWEST GENERAL HEALTH CENTER, 18697 Bagley Road, Zip 44130–3497; tel. 440/816–8000; L. Jon Schurmeier, President and Chief Executive Officer **A**1 2 10 **F**1 2 3 4 5 6 7 8 9 10 11 12 13 14 15 16 17 18 19 20 21 22 23 24 25 26 27 28 29 30 31 32 33 34 35 37 38 39 40 41 42 43 44 45 46 47 48 49 50 52 53 54 55 56 57 58 59 60 62 63 64 65 66 67 68 70 71 72 73 74 **P**6 8 Web address: www.swgeneral.com — 23 10 | 293 | 13001 | 181 | 258864 | 1504 | 126915 | 58374 | 1583

MIDDLETOWN—Butler County

☒ △ MIDDLETOWN REGIONAL HOSPITAL, 105 McKnight Drive, Zip 45044–4838; tel. 513/424–2111; Douglas W. McNeill, FACHE, President and Chief Executive Officer **A**1 2 7 9 10 **F**4 7 8 10 12 13 15 16 17 19 21 22 23 24 28 29 30 32 33 35 36 37 39 40 41 42 44 46 48 49 52 53 54 55 56 57 58 59 63 65 66 71 73 74 **P**6 8 Web address: www.middletownhospital.org — 23 10 | 183 | 7824 | 90 | 147144 | 1086 | 78341 | 32969 | 827

MILLERSBURG—Holmes County

□ JOEL POMERENE MEMORIAL HOSPITAL, 981 Wooster Road, Zip 44654–1094; tel. 330/674–1015; P. W. Smith, Jr., Administrator and Chief Executive Officer **A**1 9 10 **F**7 8 14 15 19 22 32 35 37 40 41 44 49 65 66 71 73 **P**5 6 — 13 10 | 38 | 1829 | 16 | 25272 | 562 | 14116 | 5060 | 189

MONTPELIER—Williams County

MONTPELIER HOSPITAL See Community Hospitals of Williams County, Bryan

MOUNT GILEAD—Morrow County

☒ MORROW COUNTY HOSPITAL, 651 West Marion Road, Zip 43338–1096; tel. 419/946–5015; Alan C. Pauley, Administrator (Total facility includes 38 beds in nursing home–type unit) **A**1 9 10 **F**1 7 8 14 15 16 17 19 22 28 30 32 33 34 35 36 37 39 40 41 42 44 49 51 64 65 66 71 73 **P**7 8 **S** OhioHealth, Columbus, OH — 13 10 | 75 | 974 | 39 | 31148 | 111 | 11445 | 3863 | 192

MOUNT VERNON—Knox County

☒ KNOX COMMUNITY HOSPITAL, 1330 Coshocton Road, Zip 43050–1495; tel. 740/393–9000; Robert G. Polahar, Chief Executive Officer **A**1 9 10 **F**7 15 16 19 22 32 35 36 37 40 42 44 46 52 59 63 65 71 73 **P**8 **S** Quorum Health Group/Quorum Health Resources, Inc., Brentwood, TN — 23 10 | 75 | 4289 | 47 | 73719 | 391 | 35814 | 13707 | 476

NAPOLEON—Henry County

☒ HENRY COUNTY HOSPITAL, 11–600 State Road 424, Zip 43545–9399; tel. 419/592–4015; Kimberly Bordenkircher, Interim Chief Executive Officer **A**1 9 10 **F**3 7 8 11 12 14 15 19 20 24 28 29 30 34 35 37 39 40 41 42 44 45 46 49 53 58 64 65 66 70 71 73 74 — 23 10 | 34 | 866 | 11 | — | 118 | 10311 | 4191 | 148

NELSONVILLE—Athens County

★ + ○ DOCTORS HOSPITAL OF NELSONVILLE, 1950 Mount Saint Mary Drive, Zip 45764–1193; tel. 740/753–1931; Mark R. Seckinger, Administrator (Total facility includes 45 beds in nursing home–type unit) (Nonreporting) **A**10 11 **S** OhioHealth, Columbus, OH — 23 10 | 70 | — | — | — | — | — | — | —

NEWARK—Licking County

☒ LICKING MEMORIAL HOSPITAL, 1320 West Main Street, Zip 43055–3699; tel. 740/348–4000; William J. Andrews, President **A**1 9 10 **F**2 3 7 8 10 11 12 14 15 16 17 19 21 22 28 31 32 35 37 40 41 42 44 45 49 50 52 54 55 56 57 58 59 61 63 65 67 71 73 74 **P**6 — 23 10 | 239 | 6826 | 67 | 195768 | 1063 | 50908 | 26635 | 1084

NORTHFIELD—Summit County

□ NORTHCOAST BEHAVIORAL HEALTHCARE SYSTEM, (Includes Cleveland Campus, 1708 Southpoint Drive, Cleveland, Zip 44109–1999; tel. 216/787–0500; George P. Gintoli, Chief Executive Officer; Northfield Campus, 1756 Sagamore Road, tel. 330/467–7131; Toledo Campus, 930 South Detroit Avenue, Toledo, Zip 43614–2701; tel. 419/381–1881; George P. Gintoli, Chief Executive Officer), 1756 Sagamore Road, Zip 44067; tel. 330/467–7131; George P. Gintoli, Chief Executive Officer **A**1 5 10 **F**14 15 20 27 41 46 52 55 57 65 67 73 **P**6 — 12 22 | 359 | 1914 | 308 | 0 | 0 | — | — | 920

NORWALK—Huron County

☒ + ○ FISHER–TITUS MEDICAL CENTER, 272 Benedict Avenue, Zip 44857–2374; tel. 419/668–8101; Patrick J. Martin, President and Chief Executive Officer (Total facility includes 69 beds in nursing home–type unit) **A**1 2 9 10 11 **F**4 6 7 8 12 15 16 17 19 20 21 22 23 26 27 28 29 30 32 35 36 37 39 40 41 42 44 45 54 56 62 63 64 65 66 67 71 73 74 **P**2 7 Web address: www.fisher–titus.com — 23 10 | 143 | 3716 | 96 | 61671 | 675 | 38121 | 17357 | 527

OAK HILL—Jackson County

☒ OAK HILL COMMUNITY MEDICAL CENTER, 350 Charlotte Avenue, Zip 45656–1326; tel. 740/682–7717; Robert A. Bowers, Chief Executive Officer (Total facility includes 24 beds in nursing home–type unit) **A**1 10 **F**15 19 22 25 28 30 32 33 37 39 41 44 49 51 52 57 64 65 71 **P**6 — 23 10 | 58 | 571 | 33 | 15511 | 0 | — | — | 107

OBERLIN—Lorain County

☒ ALLEN MEMORIAL HOSPITAL, 200 West Lorain Street, Zip 44074–1077; tel. 440/775–1211; James H. Schaum, President and Chief Executive Officer (Total facility includes 16 beds in nursing home–type unit) **A**1 10 **F**7 8 12 13 14 15 17 19 20 21 22 26 28 29 30 31 32 34 35 36 37 39 40 41 44 45 49 61 64 65 66 70 71 72 73 — 23 10 | 91 | 1953 | 26 | 22093 | 264 | 16363 | 7348 | 208

Hospital, Address, Telephone, Administrator, Approval, Facility, and Physician Codes, Health Care System, Network	Classi-fication Codes		Utilization Data					Expense (thousands) of dollars		
★ American Hospital Association (AHA) membership □ Joint Commission on Accreditation of Healthcare Organizations (JCAHO) accreditation + American Osteopathic Healthcare Association (AOHA) membership ○ American Osteopathic Association (AOA) accreditation △ Commission on Accreditation of Rehabilitation Facilities (CARF) accreditation Control codes 61, 63, 64, 71, 72 and 73 indicate hospitals listed by AOHA, but not registered by AHA. For definition of numerical codes, see page A4	Control	Service	Staffed Beds	Admissions	Census	Outpatient Visits	Births	Total	Payroll	Personnel

OREGON—Lucas County

□ ST. CHARLES MERCY HOSPITAL, 2600 Navarre Avenue, Zip 43616–3297; tel. 419/698–7479; Cathleen K. Nelson, President and Chief Executive Officer (Total facility includes 20 beds in nursing home–type unit) **A**1 2 9 10 **F**2 3 4 7 8 9 10 11 12 13 14 15 16 17 19 21 22 23 24 25 26 27 28 30 31 32 33 34 35 36 37 38 39 40 41 42 43 44 45 46 47 48 49 51 52 53 54 56 57 58 59 60 62 63 64 65 66 67 68 69 70 71 72 73 74 **P**1 3 6 **S** Catholic Healthcare Partners, Cincinnati, OH | 21 | 10 | 309 | 11702 | 166 | 210810 | 900 | 105992 | 55057 | 1451

ORRVILLE—Wayne County

⌧ DUNLAP MEMORIAL HOSPITAL, 832 South Main Street, Zip 44667–2208; tel. 330/682–3010; Lynn V. Horner, President and Chief Executive Officer **A**1 9 10 **F**7 8 19 21 22 27 28 29 30 35 39 40 41 42 44 45 46 49 63 65 71 73 | 23 | 10 | 38 | 792 | 6 | 27576 | 246 | 9941 | 4042 | 146

OXFORD—Butler County

⌧ MCCULLOUGH–HYDE MEMORIAL HOSPITAL, 110 North Poplar Street, Zip 45056–1292; tel. 513/523–2111; Richard A. Daniels, President and Chief Executive Officer **A**1 9 10 **F**7 8 12 14 15 16 17 19 21 22 27 28 30 32 33 34 35 36 37 39 40 41 42 44 49 63 65 66 67 71 72 73
Web address: www.mhmh.org | 23 | 10 | 44 | 2691 | 22 | 57405 | 477 | 24841 | 11031 | 291

PAINESVILLE—Lake County

⌧ △ LAKE HOSPITAL SYSTEM, 10 East Washington, Zip 44077–3472; tel. 216/354–2400; Cynthia Ann Moore–Hardy, President and Chief Executive Officer **A**1 2 7 9 10 **F**4 7 8 10 12 13 14 15 16 17 18 19 20 21 22 25 26 27 28 29 30 31 32 33 34 35 36 37 38 39 40 41 42 43 44 45 46 49 60 63 64 65 66 67 71 72 73 74 **P**1 3
Web address: www.lhs.net | 23 | 10 | 374 | 13487 | 175 | 365097 | 1304 | 136500 | 54800 | —

PARMA—Cuyahoga County

⌧ △ PARMA COMMUNITY GENERAL HOSPITAL, 7007 Powers Boulevard, Zip 44129–5495; tel. 440/888–1800; Thomas A. Selden, President and Chief Executive Officer (Total facility includes 27 beds in nursing home–type unit) **A**1 2 7 9 10 **F**1 7 8 10 11 12 13 14 16 17 19 21 22 24 26 27 28 29 30 32 33 34 36 37 39 40 41 42 44 45 46 48 49 52 55 57 58 59 63 64 65 66 67 71 73 **P**1 6 | 23 | 10 | 261 | 11813 | 193 | 153143 | 686 | 93176 | 42804 | 1193

PAULDING—Paulding County

⌧ PAULDING COUNTY HOSPITAL, 11558 State Road 111, Zip 45879–9220; tel. 419/399–4080; Gary W. Adkins, Interim Chief Executive Officer **A**1 9 10 **F**7 8 19 21 22 28 30 32 34 35 36 39 40 41 44 49 51 64 65 71 72 73 **P**7 **S** Quorum Health Group/Quorum Health Resources, Inc., Brentwood, TN
Web address: www.bright.net/pch | 13 | 10 | 51 | 720 | 6 | 32339 | 109 | 9999 | 4491 | 143

POMEROY—Meigs County

□ VETERANS MEMORIAL HOSPITAL OF MEIGS COUNTY, 115 East Memorial Drive, Zip 45769–9572; tel. 740/992–2104; Robert Bowers, Administrator (Total facility includes 40 beds in nursing home–type unit) **A**1 10 **F**14 15 16 19 22 28 32 33 34 39 41 42 44 45 52 57 64 65 71 73 | 23 | 10 | 69 | 263 | 42 | 17442 | 0 | — | — | —

PORT CLINTON—Ottawa County

□ H. B. MAGRUDER MEMORIAL HOSPITAL, 615 Fulton Street, Zip 43452–2034; tel. 419/734–3131; David R. Norwine, President and Chief Executive Officer **A**1 9 10 **F**8 12 14 15 16 17 19 21 22 28 30 34 36 37 39 42 44 45 46 49 51 63 65 66 67 71 73 **P**6 8 | 23 | 10 | 33 | 1714 | 16 | 66211 | 0 | 16037 | 6783 | 221

PORTSMOUTH—Scioto County

BEHAVIORAL HEALTH–PORTSMOUTH CAMPUS See River Valley Health System, Ironton

⌧ △ SOUTHERN OHIO MEDICAL CENTER, (Includes Mercy Hospital, 1248 Kinneys Lane, Zip 45662; Scioto Memorial Hospital, 1805 27th Street, Zip 45662), 1805 27th Street, Zip 45662–2400; tel. 740/354–5000; Randal M. Arnett, President and Chief Executive Officer **A**1 7 9 10 12 13 **F**1 7 8 14 15 17 18 19 20 21 22 23 24 25 26 28 29 30 31 32 33 34 35 36 37 39 40 41 42 44 45 46 48 49 51 54 55 56 58 60 61 62 63 65 66 67 68 71 72 73 74 **P**3 **S** OhioHealth, Columbus, OH
Web address: www.somc.org | 23 | 10 | 281 | 10779 | 150 | 209873 | 1453 | 98117 | 43930 | 1637

RAVENNA—Portage County

⌧ ROBINSON MEMORIAL HOSPITAL, 6847 North Chestnut Street, Zip 44266–1204, Mailing Address: P.O. Box 1204, Zip 44266–1204; tel. 330/297–0811; Stephen Colecchi, President and Chief Executive Officer **A**1 2 5 9 10 **F**7 8 10 11 12 13 15 16 17 19 21 22 23 24 25 26 28 29 30 31 32 33 34 35 37 39 40 41 42 44 45 46 49 52 54 55 56 59 60 61 63 65 66 67 70 71 72 73 74 **P**6 8 | 13 | 10 | 131 | 8256 | 99 | 93535 | 915 | 88868 | 38468 | 1078

RICHMOND HEIGHTS—Cuyahoga County

+ ○ PHS MT. SINAI MEDICAL CENTER EAST, 27100 Chardon Road, Zip 44143–1198; tel. 440/585–6500; Linton Sharpnack, Chief Executive Officer (Nonreporting) **A**9 10 11 12 13 | 23 | 10 | 98 | — | — | — | — | — | — | —

ROCK CREEK—Ashtabula County

GLENBEIGH HEALTH SOURCES, Route 45, Zip 44084, Mailing Address: P.O. Box 298, Zip 44084–0298; tel. 440/563–3400; Patricia Weston–Hall, Executive Director **A**9 10 **F**2 3 15 16 **P**5
Web address: www.glenbeigh.com | 23 | 82 | 80 | 934 | 23 | — | 0 | — | — | 55

SAINT CLAIRSVILLE—Belmont County

□ BHC FOX RUN HOSPITAL, 67670 Traco Drive, Zip 43950–9375; tel. 740/695–2131; Charles L. Visalli, Chief Executive Officer (Nonreporting) **A**1 10 **S** Behavioral Healthcare Corporation, Nashville, TN | 33 | 22 | 65 | — | — | — | — | — | — | —

Hospital, Address, Telephone, Administrator, Approval, Facility, and Physician Codes, Health Care System, Network	Classi-fication Codes		Utilization Data					Expense (thousands) of dollars		
★ American Hospital Association (AHA) membership □ Joint Commission on Accreditation of Healthcare Organizations (JCAHO) accreditation + American Osteopathic Healthcare Association (AOHA) membership ○ American Osteopathic Association (AOA) accreditation △ Commission on Accreditation of Rehabilitation Facilities (CARF) accreditation Control codes 61, 63, 64, 71, 72 and 73 indicate hospitals listed by AOHA, but not registered by AHA. For definition of numerical codes, see page A4	Control	Service	Staffed Beds	Admissions	Census	Outpatient Visits	Births	Total	Payroll	Personnel

SAINT MARYS—Auglaize County

⊠ JOINT TOWNSHIP DISTRICT MEMORIAL HOSPITAL, 200 St. Clair Street, Zip 45885–2400; tel. 419/394–3387; James R. Chick, President (Total facility includes 23 beds in nursing home–type unit) **A**1 9 10 **F**7 8 12 14 15 16 17 19 21 22 25 27 28 29 30 32 33 34 35 37 39 40 41 44 46 49 51 64 65 66 67 71 73 74
Web address: www.jtdmh.com

| | 23 | 10 | 91 | 3992 | 51 | 65710 | 315 | 29797 | 12562 | 444 |

SALEM—Columbiana County

⊠ SALEM COMMUNITY HOSPITAL, 1995 East State Street, Zip 44460–0121; tel. 330/332–1551; Howard E. Rohleder, Administrator and Chief Executive Officer (Total facility includes 15 beds in nursing home–type unit) **A**1 5 9 10 **F**7 8 10 12 14 15 16 19 21 22 28 30 34 35 36 37 39 40 41 42 44 49 51 63 64 65 67 71 73

| | 23 | 10 | 123 | 5367 | 69 | 76449 | 478 | 46541 | 23464 | 669 |

SANDUSKY—Erie County

□ + ○ △ FIRELANDS COMMUNITY HOSPITAL, 1101 Decatur Street, Zip 44870–3335; tel. 419/626–7400; Dennis A. Sokol, President and Chief Executive Officer (Nonreporting) **A**1 2 7 9 10 11 12 13

| | 23 | 10 | 232 | — | — | — | — | — | — | — |

⊠ PROVIDENCE HOSPITAL, 1912 Hayes Avenue, Zip 44870–4736; tel. 419/621–7000; Sister Nancy Linenkugel, FACHE, President and Chief Executive Officer (Total facility includes 46 beds in nursing home–type unit) **A**1 2 6 10 **F**2 3 6 7 8 10 11 12 14 15 16 17 18 19 21 22 23 25 26 27 28 29 30 31 32 33 34 35 37 39 40 41 42 44 45 46 48 49 52 53 54 55 56 57 58 59 60 63 64 65 66 67 71 73 74 **P**3 8 **S** Franciscan Services Corporation, Sylvania, OH
Web address: www.providencehealth.org

| | 21 | 10 | 170 | 3851 | 85 | 78255 | 271 | 42761 | 18172 | 618 |

SHELBY—Richland County

SHELBY HOSPITAL See MedCentral Health System, Mansfield

SIDNEY—Shelby County

⊠ WILSON MEMORIAL HOSPITAL, 915 West Michigan Street, Zip 45365–2491; tel. 937/498–2311; Thomas J. Boecker, President and Chief Executive Officer (Total facility includes 62 beds in nursing home–type unit) **A**1 9 10 **F**7 8 12 14 15 16 19 21 22 28 30 32 33 34 35 37 39 40 41 44 45 46 49 52 57 64 65 67 71 **P**6

| | 23 | 10 | 142 | 3473 | 94 | 106305 | 515 | 39808 | 16814 | 484 |

SPRINGFIELD—Clark County

⊠ COMMUNITY HOSPITAL, 2615 East High Street, Zip 45505–1422, Mailing Address: Box 1228, Zip 45501–1228; tel. 937/325–0531; Neal E. Kresheck, President (Total facility includes 41 beds in nursing home–type unit) **A**1 6 9 10 **F**6 7 8 10 11 12 13 14 15 16 17 19 21 22 24 26 27 28 29 30 31 32 33 34 35 36 37 39 40 41 42 44 45 46 49 51 60 63 64 65 66 67 68 71 72 73 74

| | 23 | 10 | 200 | 9483 | 138 | 126730 | 1918 | 79296 | 34958 | 1338 |

□ △ MERCY MEDICAL CENTER, 1343 North Fountain Boulevard, Zip 45501–1380; tel. 937/390–5000; Teresa Richle, Interim Senior Vice President Acute Care Operations (Total facility includes 20 beds in nursing home–type unit) (Nonreporting) **A**1 2 5 7 9 10 **S** Catholic Healthcare Partners, Cincinnati, OH

| | 21 | 10 | 218 | — | — | — | — | — | — | — |

STEUBENVILLE—Jefferson County

⊠ TRINITY HEALTH SYSTEM, (Includes Trinity Medical Center East, 380 Summit Avenue, tel. 740/283–7000; Trinity Medical Center West, 4000 Johnson Road, Zip 43952–2393; tel. 740/264–8000), 380 Summit Avenue, Zip 43952–2699; tel. 740/283–7000; Fred B. Brower, President and Chief Executive Officer (Nonreporting) **A**1 2 6 9 10 **S** Franciscan Services Corporation, Sylvania, OH
Web address: www.trinityhealth.com

| | 21 | 10 | 533 | — | — | — | — | — | — | — |

SYLVANIA—Lucas County

⊠ △ FLOWER HOSPITAL, 5200 Harroun Road, Zip 43560–2196; tel. 419/824–1444; Randall Kelley, President (Total facility includes 244 beds in nursing home–type unit) **A**1 3 5 7 9 10 **F**2 3 4 5 6 7 8 10 11 12 13 14 15 16 17 18 19 20 21 22 23 24 25 26 27 28 29 30 31 32 34 35 37 38 39 40 41 42 43 44 45 46 47 48 49 51 52 53 54 55 56 57 58 59 60 61 62 63 64 65 66 67 70 71 73 74 **P**1 7 **S** ProMedica Health System, Toledo, OH
Web address: www.promedica.org

| | 23 | 10 | 487 | 10482 | 373 | 78710 | 1065 | 96016 | 45187 | 1331 |

TIFFIN—Seneca County

□ MERCY HOSPITAL, 485 West Market Street, Zip 44883–0727, Mailing Address: P.O. Box 727, Zip 44883–0727; tel. 419/447–3130; Mark Shugarman, President **A**1 9 10 **F**4 7 8 11 12 14 15 16 17 19 21 22 26 27 28 29 30 31 32 34 35 36 39 40 41 42 44 45 46 49 51 60 62 63 65 67 68 70 71 73 **P**8 **S** Catholic Healthcare Partners, Cincinnati, OH

| | 21 | 10 | 60 | 2504 | 24 | 68819 | 426 | 26351 | 11084 | 437 |

TOLEDO—Lucas County

□ △ MEDICAL COLLEGE OF OHIO HOSPITALS, 3000 Arlington Avenue, Zip 43614–5805; tel. 419/383–4000; Frank S. McCullough, M.D., President **A**1 2 3 5 7 8 10 **F**4 5 8 10 12 13 14 15 16 17 19 20 21 22 24 25 26 28 30 31 34 35 37 41 42 43 44 45 46 48 49 51 52 53 55 58 59 60 61 65 66 67 68 70 71 73 74 **P**4 7

| | 12 | 10 | 210 | 8188 | 142 | 202244 | 0 | 131017 | 52872 | 1674 |

Web address: www.mco.edu

⊠ ○ RIVERSIDE MERCY HOSPITAL, (Formerly Riverside Hospital), 1600 North Superior Street, Zip 43604–2199; tel. 419/729–6000; Scott E. Shook, President (Total facility includes 12 beds in nursing home–type unit) (Nonreporting) **A**1 2 9 10 11 **S** Catholic Healthcare Partners, Cincinnati, OH

| | 23 | 10 | 162 | — | — | — | — | — | — | — |

Hospital, Address, Telephone, Administrator, Approval, Facility, and Physician Codes, Health Care System, Network	Classi-fication Codes		Utilization Data					Expense (thousands) of dollars		
★ American Hospital Association (AHA) membership ☐ Joint Commission on Accreditation of Healthcare Organizations (JCAHO) accreditation + American Osteopathic Healthcare Association (AOHA) membership ○ American Osteopathic Association (AOA) accreditation △ Commission on Accreditation of Rehabilitation Facilities (CARF) accreditation Control codes 61, 63, 64, 71, 72 and 73 indicate hospitals listed by AOHA, but not registered by AHA. For definition of numerical codes, see page A4	Control	Service	Staffed Beds	Admissions	Census	Outpatient Visits	Births	Total	Payroll	Personnel

	Control	Service	Staffed Beds	Admissions	Census	Outpatient Visits	Births	Total	Payroll	Personnel
☐ ○ ST. VINCENT MERCY MEDICAL CENTER, 2213 Cherry Street, Zip 43608-2691; tel. 419/251-3232; Steven L. Mickus, President and Chief Executive Officer **A**1 2 3 5 6 9 10 11 12 13 14 15 16 17 19 21 22 23 24 25 26 27 28 29 30 31 32 34 35 36 37 38 39 40 41 42 43 44 46 47 48 49 51 53 54 55 56 57 58 59 60 62 63 64 65 66 67 68 70 71 72 73 74 **P**1 6 **S** Catholic Healthcare Partners, Cincinnati, OH **Web address:** www.mercyweb.org	21	10	483	19237	287	249354	1597	327143	153838	4242
⊠ THE TOLEDO HOSPITAL, 2142 North Cove Boulevard, Zip 43606-3896; tel. 419/471-4000; Barbara Steele, President **A**1 2 3 5 8 9 10 **F**2 3 4 5 6 7 8 10 11 12 13 14 15 16 17 18 19 20 21 22 23 24 25 26 27 28 29 30 31 32 34 35 37 38 39 40 41 42 43 44 45 46 47 48 49 51 52 53 54 55 56 57 58 59 60 61 62 63 64 65 66 67 68 70 71 73 74 **P**1 7 **S** ProMedica Health System, Toledo, OH **Web address:** www.promedica.org TOLEDO CAMPUS See Northcoast Behavioral Healthcare System, Northfield	23	10	561	24809	347	288415	4065	305857	135781	3242
TROY—Miami County										
☐ △ UPPER VALLEY MEDICAL CENTER, (Includes Dettmer Hospital, 3130 North Dixie Highway, Zip 45373-1039; tel. 937/440-7500), 3130 North Dixie Highway, Zip 45373; tel. 937/440-7500; David J. Meckstroth, President and Chief Executive Officer (Total facility includes 16 beds in nursing home–type unit) (Nonreporting) **A**1 2 7 9 10 **Web address:** www.uvmc.com	23	10	392	—	—	—	—	—	—	—
UPPER SANDUSKY—Wyandot County										
★ WYANDOT MEMORIAL HOSPITAL, 885 North Sandusky Avenue, Zip 43351-1098; tel. 419/294-4991; Joseph A. D'Ettorre, Chief Executive Officer **A**9 10 **F**7 8 11 12 15 16 19 21 22 28 30 33 34 35 36 40 41 42 44 45 46 56 63 71 73 **P**6	16	10	31	964	10	40826	109	11142	4176	137
URBANA—Champaign County										
MERCY MEMORIAL HOSPITAL, 904 Scioto Street, Zip 43078-2200; tel. 937/653-5231; Richard Rogers, Senior Vice President (Nonreporting) **A**9 10 **S** Catholic Healthcare Partners, Cincinnati, OH	21	10	20	—	—	—	—	—	—	—
VAN WERT—Van Wert County										
⊠ VAN WERT COUNTY HOSPITAL, 1250 South Washington Street, Zip 45891-2599; tel. 419/238-2390; Mark J. Minick, President and Chief Executive Officer **A**1 9 10 **F**7 8 11 12 13 14 15 16 17 19 22 26 28 29 30 35 37 39 40 41 42 44 46 63 65 66 71 73 **P**7 8 **Web address:** www.vanwerthospital.org	23	10	100	1973	17	103144	319	20760	8485	239
WADSWORTH—Medina County										
☐ WADSWORTH–RITTMAN HOSPITAL, 195 Wadsworth Road, Zip 44281-9505; tel. 330/334-1504; James W. Brumlow, Jr., President and Chief Executive Officer **A**1 10 **F**8 19 21 22 26 28 30 32 34 35 37 39 40 41 42 44 45 46 48 49 56 63 65 67 71 74 **P**1 2 5 7 8	23	10	64	2241	32	55206	169	19630	9101	281
WARREN—Trumbull County										
FORUM HEALTH–TRUMBULL MEMORIAL See Trumbull Memorial Hospital										
⊠ HILLSIDE REHABILITATION HOSPITAL, 8747 Squires Lane N.E., Zip 44484-1649; tel. 330/841-3700; Margaret Edwards, Chief Operating Officer **A**1 5 9 10 **F**4 6 7 8 10 11 12 14 15 16 17 19 21 22 25 26 28 29 30 32 33 34 35 36 37 38 39 40 41 42 43 44 45 46 47 48 49 51 52 53 54 55 56 57 58 60 64 65 66 67 71 72 73 74 **P**7 8 **S** Forum Health, Youngstown, OH	23	46	47	680	43	966	0	10184	4901	221
☐ ○ ST. JOSEPH HEALTH CENTER, 667 Eastland Avenue S.E., Zip 44484-4531; tel. 330/841-4000; Robert W. Shroder, Vice President Operations (Total facility includes 11 beds in nursing home–type unit) **A**1 2 9 10 11 12 13 **F**2 3 6 7 8 10 12 14 15 16 19 21 22 23 26 27 28 29 30 32 33 34 35 36 37 39 40 41 42 43 44 45 46 49 51 52 54 55 56 58 59 60 63 64 65 66 67 68 70 71 72 73 74 **P**8 **S** Catholic Healthcare Partners, Cincinnati, OH **Web address:** www.hmhs.org	21	10	136	7667	87	130691	776	62584	24687	668
⊠ TRUMBULL MEMORIAL HOSPITAL, (Formerly Forum Health–Trumbull Memorial), 1350 East Market Street, Zip 44482-6628; tel. 330/841-9011; Gary E. Kaatz, Chief Operating Officer **A**1 2 5 9 10 **F**3 4 6 7 8 10 11 12 13 14 15 16 17 18 19 21 22 23 24 25 26 28 29 30 31 32 33 34 35 37 38 39 40 41 42 43 44 47 48 49 51 52 56 57 60 63 64 65 66 67 71 73 **P**7 8 **S** Forum Health, Youngstown, OH	23	10	279	12263	152	200253	1026	111906	51012	1514
WARRENSVILLE HEIGHTS—Morgan County										
☐ + ○ △ MERIDIA SOUTH POINTE HOSPITAL, 4110 Warrensville Center Road, Zip 44122-7099; tel. 216/491-6000; Kathleen A. Rice, Chief Operating Officer **A**1 2 7 9 10 11 12 13 **F**2 3 4 7 8 10 11 12 13 14 15 16 17 18 19 21 22 23 24 25 26 27 28 29 30 31 32 33 34 35 36 37 38 39 40 41 42 43 44 45 46 47 48 49 50 51 52 54 55 56 57 58 59 60 61 63 64 65 66 67 68 70 71 72 73 74 **P**1 3 4 7 8 **S** Meridia Health System, Cleveland, OH **Web address:** www.southpointgme.com	23	10	178	6367	90	107052	0	69674	30298	837
WASHINGTON COURT HOUSE—Lucas County										
⊠ FAYETTE COUNTY MEMORIAL HOSPITAL, 1430 Columbus Avenue, Zip 43160-1791; tel. 740/335-1210; Francis G. Albarano, Administrator **A**1 9 10 **F**7 8 12 14 15 17 19 20 21 22 27 28 29 30 32 33 34 35 36 39 40 41 42 44 45 46 56 65 66 67 71 73 **S** Quorum Health Group/Quorum Health Resources, Inc., Brentwood, TN	13	10	35	1452	14	52779	303	16361	6844	216
WAUSEON—Fulton County										
⊠ FULTON COUNTY HEALTH CENTER, 725 South Shoop Avenue, Zip 43567-1701; tel. 419/335-2015; E. Dean Beck, Administrator (Total facility includes 86 beds in nursing home–type unit) **A**1 2 9 10 **F**3 6 7 8 14 15 19 21 22 24 28 30 35 36 37 39 40 41 42 44 49 52 55 56 58 59 64 65 66 67 71 73	23	10	172	2428	101	116691	314	22719	10161	437

Hospital, Address, Telephone, Administrator, Approval, Facility, and Physician Codes, Health Care System, Network	Classi-fication Codes		Utilization Data					Expense (thousands) of dollars		
	Control	Service	Staffed Beds	Admissions	Census	Outpatient Visits	Births	Total	Payroll	Personnel

★ American Hospital Association (AHA) membership
□ Joint Commission on Accreditation of Healthcare Organizations (JCAHO) accreditation
+ American Osteopathic Healthcare Association (AOHA) membership
○ American Osteopathic Association (AOA) accreditation
△ Commission on Accreditation of Rehabilitation Facilities (CARF) accreditation
Control codes 61, 63, 64, 71, 72 and 73 indicate hospitals listed by AOHA, but not registered by AHA. For definition of numerical codes, see page A4

WAVERLY—Pike County

□ PIKE COMMUNITY HOSPITAL, 100 Dawn Lane, Zip 45690–9664; tel. 740/947–2186; Richard E. Sobota, President and Chief Executive Officer **A**1 9 10 **F**8 15 16 17 19 21 22 26 27 28 29 30 32 33 34 37 39 41 44 45 46 49 63 65 71 72 73 **P**5

| | 23 | 10 | 40 | 806 | 8 | 37838 | 0 | 8205 | 4187 | 163 |

WEST UNION—Adams County

□ ADAMS COUNTY HOSPITAL, 210 North Wilson Drive, Zip 45693–1574; tel. 937/544–5571; Linda Niles, Interim Chief Executive Officer (Total facility includes 18 beds in nursing home–type unit) (Nonreporting) **A**1 9 10

| | 13 | 10 | 49 | — | — | — | — | — | — | — |

WESTERVILLE—Franklin County

ST. ANN'S HOSPITAL See Mount Carmel Health System, Columbus

WILLARD—Huron County

□ MERCY HOSPITAL–WILLARD, 110 East Howard Street, Zip 44890–1611; tel. 419/933–2931; Dale E. Thornton, President **A**1 9 10 **F**7 8 15 16 19 22 23 28 29 30 32 33 34 35 36 37 40 41 42 44 46 58 63 65 66 67 71 73 **P**3 8 **S** Catholic Healthcare Partners, Cincinnati, OH

| | 21 | 10 | 30 | 818 | 7 | 44878 | 127 | 13085 | 5553 | 187 |

WILLOUGHBY—Lake County

□ UHHS LAURELWOOD HOSPITAL, 35900 Euclid Avenue, Zip 44094–4648; tel. 440/953–3000; Farshid Afsarifard, Ph.D., President **A**1 9 10 **F**2 3 4 8 10 11 12 15 16 17 18 19 21 22 26 32 34 35 37 38 40 42 43 44 45 46 48 49 50 51 52 53 54 55 56 57 58 59 60 63 65 66 67 68 71 73 **P**5 6 **S** University Hospitals Health System, Cleveland, OH

| | 23 | 22 | 70 | 3187 | 77 | 44313 | 0 | 13320 | 6819 | 334 |

WILMINGTON—Clinton County

□ CLINTON MEMORIAL HOSPITAL, 610 West Main Street, Zip 45177–2194; tel. 937/382–6611; Thomas F. Kurtz, Jr., President and Chief Executive Officer (Total facility includes 12 beds in nursing home–type unit) **A**1 2 3 9 10 **F**4 7 8 15 16 17 18 19 20 21 22 24 25 26 28 29 30 31 32 33 34 35 36 37 39 40 41 42 44 45 46 49 51 54 58 60 64 65 66 67 71 73 74 **P**1

| | 13 | 10 | 93 | 4283 | 45 | 144311 | 564 | 45466 | 20846 | 481 |

WOOSTER—Wayne County

□ WOOSTER COMMUNITY HOSPITAL, 1761 Beall Avenue, Zip 44691–2342; tel. 330/263–8100; William E. Sheron, Chief Executive Officer (Nonreporting) **A**1 2 9 10 **S** Quorum Health Group/Quorum Health Resources, Inc., Brentwood, TN

| | 14 | 10 | 90 | — | — | — | — | — | — | — |

WORTHINGTON—Franklin County

□ HARDING HOSPITAL, 445 East Granville Road, Zip 43085–3195; tel. 614/885–5381; S. R. Thorward, M.D., President and Chief Executive Officer (Nonreporting) **A**1 3 5 9 10

| | 23 | 22 | 56 | — | — | — | — | — | — | — |

WRIGHT–PATTERSON AFB—Greene County

✠ U. S. AIR FORCE MEDICAL CENTER WRIGHT–PATTERSON, 4881 Sugar Maple Drive, Zip 45433–5529; tel. 937/257–0940; Brigadier General Joseph Kelley, Commander (Nonreporting) **A**1 2 3 5 **S** Department of the Air Force, Bowling AFB, DC

| | 41 | 10 | 135 | — | — | — | — | — | — | — |

XENIA—Greene County

✠ △ GREENE MEMORIAL HOSPITAL, 1141 North Monroe Drive, Zip 45385–1600; tel. 937/372–8011; Michael R. Stephens, President (Total facility includes 12 beds in nursing home–type unit) **A**1 2 5 7 9 10 **F**2 3 6 7 8 10 12 15 16 17 19 21 22 25 26 27 28 30 32 33 34 35 36 37 39 40 41 42 44 45 46 48 49 51 52 53 54 55 56 57 58 59 60 62 63 64 65 66 67 70 71 72 73 74 **P**6 7 8
Web address: www.greene–memorial.org

| | 23 | 10 | 150 | 4304 | 63 | 121215 | 272 | 44190 | 17944 | 675 |

YOUNGSTOWN—Mahoning County

□ BHC BELMONT PINES HOSPITAL, 615 Churchill–Hubbard Road, Zip 44505–1379; tel. 330/759–2700; Edward Nasca, Chief Executive Officer (Nonreporting) **A**1 9 10 **S** Behavioral Healthcare Corporation, Nashville, TN
Web address: www.belmontpines.com

| | 33 | 22 | 77 | — | — | — | — | — | — | — |

FORUM HEALTH See Western Reserve Care System
NORTHSIDE MEDICAL CENTER See Western Reserve Care System

□ △ ST. ELIZABETH HEALTH CENTER, 1044 Belmont Avenue, Zip 44501, Mailing Address: P.O. Box 1790, Zip 44501–1790; tel. 330/746–7211; Robert W. Shroder, Executive Vice President Operations (Total facility includes 30 beds in nursing home–type unit) **A**1 2 3 5 6 7 8 9 10 **F**3 4 6 7 8 10 11 12 14 15 16 17 18 19 20 21 22 24 25 26 27 28 29 30 31 32 34 35 37 38 39 40 41 42 43 44 46 48 49 51 52 54 55 56 57 58 59 60 61 63 64 65 66 67 68 70 71 72 73 74 **P**8 **S** Catholic Healthcare Partners, Cincinnati, OH

| | 21 | 10 | 339 | 19140 | 292 | 241260 | 2004 | 164251 | 71928 | 1987 |

TOD CHILDREN'S HOSPITAL See Western Reserve Care System

✠ △ WESTERN RESERVE CARE SYSTEM, (Formerly Forum Health), (Includes Northside Medical Center, 500 Gypsy Lane, Zip 44501–0240; tel. 330/747–1444; Tod Children's Hospital, 500 Gypsy Lane, Zip 44501–0240; tel. 330/747–6700), 345 Oak Hill Avenue, Zip 44501–0990, Mailing Address: P.O. Box 990, Zip 44501–0990; tel. 330/747–0777; Charles A. Johns, President and Chief Executive Officer (Total facility includes 26 beds in nursing home–type unit) **A**1 2 3 7 8 9 10 **F**2 3 4 6 7 8 10 11 12 13 14 15 16 17 18 19 20 21 22 23 24 25 26 27 28 29 30 31 32 33 34 35 36 37 38 39 40 41 42 43 44 45 46 47 48 49 51 52 53 54 55 56 57 58 59 60 63 64 65 66 67 68 71 72 73 74 **P**7 8 **S** Forum Health, Youngstown, OH

| | 23 | 10 | 371 | 17309 | 262 | 278858 | 1841 | 199599 | 85843 | 2369 |

+ ○ YOUNGSTOWN OSTEOPATHIC HOSPITAL, 1319 Florencedale Avenue, Zip 44505–2795, Mailing Address: P.O. Box 1258, Zip 44501–1258; tel. 330/744–9200; William P. Lawrence, President and Chief Executive Officer (Nonreporting) **A**10 11 12 13

| | 23 | 10 | 88 | — | — | — | — | — | — | — |

Hospital, Address, Telephone, Administrator, Approval, Facility, and Physician Codes, Health Care System, Network	Classi-fication Codes		Utilization Data					Expense (thousands) of dollars		
	Control	Service	Staffed Beds	Admissions	Census	Outpatient Visits	Births	Total	Payroll	Personnel

ZANESVILLE—Muskingum County

⊠ △ GENESIS HEALTHCARE SYSTEM, (Includes Bethesda Hospital, 2951 Maple Avenue, Zip 43701–1465; tel. 614/454–4000; Charles D. Hunter, Executive Vice President and Chief Operating Officer; Good Samaritan Medical and Rehabilitation Center, 800 Forest Avenue), 800 Forest Avenue, Zip 43701–2881; tel. 740/454–5000; Thomas L. Sieber, President and Chief Executive Officer (Total facility includes 44 beds in nursing home–type unit) **A**1 2 7 9 10 **F**1 3 7 8 10 11 12 13 14 15 16 17 19 21 22 23 24 25 26 28 29 30 31 32 33 34 35 36 37 39 40 41 42 44 45 46 47 48 49 51 52 53 54 55 56 57 58 59 60 61 64 65 71 72 73 74 **P**8 **S** Franciscan Sisters of Christian Charity HealthCare Ministry, Inc, Manitowoc, WI

	23	10	467	17126	244	311831	1995	140744	63998	2013

OKLAHOMA

Resident population 3,347 (in thousands)
Resident population in metro areas 59.4%
Birth rate per 1,000 population 13.9
65 years and over 13.4%
Percent of persons without health insurance 17%

Hospital, Address, Telephone, Administrator, Approval, Facility, and Physician Codes, Health Care System, Network	Classi-fication Codes		Utilization Data					Expense (thousands) of dollars		
★ American Hospital Association (AHA) membership □ Joint Commission on Accreditation of Healthcare Organizations (JCAHO) accreditation + American Osteopathic Healthcare Association (AOHA) membership ○ American Osteopathic Association (AOA) accreditation △ Commission on Accreditation of Rehabilitation Facilities (CARF) accreditation Control codes 61, 63, 64, 71, 72 and 73 indicate hospitals listed by AOHA, but not registered by AHA. For definition of numerical codes, see page A4	Control	Service	Staffed Beds	Admissions	Census	Outpatient Visits	Births	Total	Payroll	Personnel

ADA—Pontotoc County

✚ CARL ALBERT INDIAN HEALTH FACILITY, 1001 North Country Club Road, Zip 74820–2847; tel. 580/436–3980; Bruce A. Bennett, Administrator (Nonreporting) **A**1 10 **S** U. S. Public Health Service Indian Health Service, Rockville, MD	47	10	53	—	—	—	—	—	—	—
□ ROLLING HILLS HOSPITAL, 1000 Rolling Hills Lane, Zip 74820–9415; tel. 580/436–3600; Darnell Powell, Executive Director **A**1 10 **F**2 7 8 10 11 15 16 19 21 22 29 35 37 40 46 48 53 54 55 56 57 59 63 65 **P**6	33	22	40	579	31	0	0	4510	1975	74
✚ △ VALLEY VIEW REGIONAL HOSPITAL, 430 North Monta Vista, Zip 74820–4610; tel. 580/332–2323; Philip Fisher, President and Chief Executive Officer **A**1 2 7 9 10 **F**7 8 11 14 15 17 19 21 22 23 27 28 30 32 34 35 36 37 38 39 40 42 44 45 46 48 49 60 63 65 67 70 71 72 73	23	10	139	6064	80	50878	630	42703	16313	646

ALTUS—Jackson County

✚ JACKSON COUNTY MEMORIAL HOSPITAL, 1200 East Pecan Street, Zip 73521–6192, Mailing Address: Box 8190, Zip 73522–8190; tel. 580/482–4781; William G. Wilson, President and Chief Executive Officer (Total facility includes 25 beds in nursing home–type unit) **A**1 9 10 **F**6 7 8 15 16 17 19 21 22 23 28 29 30 32 33 34 35 36 37 39 40 41 42 44 45 46 48 49 51 56 58 59 62 64 65 66 67 70 71 73 **P**6	16	10	101	4397	67	46482	381	32547	14991	577
✚ U. S. AIR FORCE HOSPITAL ALTUS, Altus AFB, Zip 73523–5005; tel. 580/481–7347; Colonel David L. Clark, USAF, Commander **A**1 **F**3 7 8 17 18 20 25 27 28 29 39 40 44 45 46 49 62 63 65 67 68 71 72 73 **S** Department of the Air Force, Bowling AFB, DC	41	10	15	436	3	—	162			

ALVA—Woods County

★ SHARE MEDICAL CENTER, 800 Share Drive, Zip 73717–3699, Mailing Address: P.O. Box 727, Zip 73717–0727; tel. 580/327–2800; Barbara Oestmann, Chief Executive Officer (Total facility includes 80 beds in nursing home–type unit) **A**9 10 **F**1 7 8 12 14 15 16 19 20 21 22 28 32 33 34 36 40 42 44 46 51 53 55 56 57 64 65 67 73 **S** Quorum Health Group/Quorum Health Resources, Inc., Brentwood, TN	16	10	117	988	81	11642	56	7676	3789	108

ANADARKO—Caddo County

ANADARKO MUNICIPAL HOSPITAL, 1002 Central Boulevard East, Zip 73005–4496; tel. 405/247–2551; Alan Riffel, Acting Administrator (Nonreporting) **A**9 10	14	10	49	—	—	—	—	—	—	—

ANTLERS—Pushmataha County

PUSHMATAHA COUNTY–TOWN OF ANTLERS HOSPITAL AUTHORITY, 510 East Main Street, Zip 74523–3262, Mailing Address: P.O. Box 518, Zip 74523–3262; tel. 580/298–3342; Les Alexander, Administrator **A**9 10 **F**1 2 3 4 5 6 7 8 9 10 11 12 13 14 15 16 17 18 19 20 21 22 23 24 25 26 27 28 29 30 31 32 33 34 35 36 37 38 39 40 41 42 43 44 45 46 47 48 49 50 51 52 53 54 55 56 57 58 59 60 61 62 63 64 65 66 67 68 69 70 71 72 73 74 **P**5	16	10	46	1621	23	5789	0	7091	3420	78

ARDMORE—Carter County

✚ MERCY MEMORIAL HEALTH CENTER, 1011 14th Street N.W., Zip 73401–1889; tel. 580/223–5400; Bobby G. Thompson, President and Chief Executive Officer **A**1 10 **F**3 7 8 10 12 14 15 16 17 19 20 21 22 23 26 28 29 30 31 32 34 35 37 40 41 42 44 45 46 48 49 52 54 55 56 57 59 60 64 65 67 71 72 73 **P**8 **S** Sisters of Mercy Health System–St. Louis, Saint Louis, MO **Web address:** www.mercyok.com	21	10	199	7435	109	80557	830	51521	19658	846

ATOKA—Atoka County

★ ATOKA MEMORIAL HOSPITAL, 1501 South Virginia Avenue, Zip 74525–3298; tel. 580/889–3333; Paul David Moore, Administrator **A**9 10 **F**12 19 22 27 32 34 37 49 63 **S** Quorum Health Group/Quorum Health Resources, Inc., Brentwood, TN	13	10	25	559	8	6508	1	—	—	—

BARTLESVILLE—Washington County

✚ JANE PHILLIPS MEDICAL CENTER, 3500 East Frank Phillips Boulevard, Zip 74006–2409; tel. 918/333–7200; Larry Minden, Chief Executive Officer (Total facility includes 61 beds in nursing home–type unit) (Nonreporting) **A**1 2 5 9 10	23	10	212	—	—	—	—	—	—	—

BEAVER—Beaver County

BEAVER COUNTY MEMORIAL HOSPITAL, 212 East Eighth Street, Zip 73932, Mailing Address: P.O. Box 640, Zip 73932–0640; tel. 580/625–4551; La Vern Melton, Administrator **A**9 10 **F**8 22 27 44 65 71 **P**6	16	10	24	188	2	—	27	1836	906	49

BETHANY—Oklahoma County

✚ BETHANY HOSPITAL, (Formerly Integris Bethany Hospital), 7600 N.W. 23rd Street, Zip 73008–4900; tel. 405/787–3450; David Lundquist, Chief Executive Officer **A**1 9 10 **F**10 12 15 16 19 22 37 44 51 52 57 65 71 73	23	10	70	877	15	0	0	6846	3003	0

BLACKWELL—Kay County

★ BLACKWELL REGIONAL HOSPITAL, 710 South 13th Street, Zip 74631–3700; tel. 580/363–2311; Greg Martin, Administrator and Chief Executive Officer **A**9 10 **F**7 8 14 19 32 34 35 40 44 49 65 71 73 **P**6 7 **S** INTEGRIS Health, Oklahoma City, OK	23	10	34	1409	17	12889	108	7156	2999	123

Hospital, Address, Telephone, Administrator, Approval, Facility, and Physician Codes, Health Care System, Network	Classi-fication Codes		Utilization Data					Expense (thousands) of dollars		
	Control	Service	Staffed Beds	Admissions	Census	Outpatient Visits	Births	Total	Payroll	Personnel

★ American Hospital Association (AHA) membership
□ Joint Commission on Accreditation of Healthcare Organizations (JCAHO) accreditation
+ American Osteopathic Healthcare Association (AOHA) membership
○ American Osteopathic Association (AOA) accreditation
△ Commission on Accreditation of Rehabilitation Facilities (CARF) accreditation
Control codes 61, 63, 64, 71, 72 and 73 indicate hospitals listed by AOHA, but not registered by AHA. For definition of numerical codes, see page A4

BOISE CITY—Cimarron County

CIMARRON MEMORIAL HOSPITAL, 100 South Ellis Street, Zip 73933; tel. 580/544–2501; Ronny Lathrop, Chief Executive Officer and Administrator (Total facility includes 41 beds in nursing home–type unit) **A**9 10 **F**1 7 8 22 25 28 32 33 39 40 44 49 64 71 **P**6	13	10	61	194	36	6241	46	3901	1675	88

BRISTOW—Creek County

★ BRISTOW MEMORIAL HOSPITAL, Seventh and Spruce Streets, Zip 74010, Mailing Address: P.O. Box 780, Zip 74010–0780; tel. 918/367–2215; William L. Legate, Administrator **A**9 10 **F**8 11 15 16 17 19 22 28 30 32 33 34 44 49 65 71 73 **S** Hillcrest HealthCare System, Tulsa, OK	33	10	16	206	2	22201	0	2652	1281	54

BROKEN ARROW—Tulsa County

□ BROKEN ARROW MEDICAL CENTER, 3000 South Elm Place, Zip 74012–7952; tel. 918/455–3535; Bruce Switzer, Administrator **A**1 9 10 **F**2 3 4 7 8 10 11 12 13 15 16 17 18 19 21 22 23 24 25 28 29 30 32 33 35 37 38 39 40 41 42 43 44 45 47 48 49 52 60 64 65 67 69 70 71 73 74 **Web address:** www.stfrancis.com	23	10	71	1036	21	15749	1	10672	4920	345

BUFFALO—Harper County

★ HARPER COUNTY COMMUNITY HOSPITAL, Highway 64 North, Zip 73834, Mailing Address: P.O. Box 60, Zip 73834–0060; tel. 580/735–2555; P. Jane McDowell, Administrator **A**10 **F**8 15 17 22 28 29 30 33 36 39 40 44 46 49 64 71	13	10	25	296	6	1139	17	1545	814	51

CARNEGIE—Caddo County

★ CARNEGIE TRI–COUNTY MUNICIPAL HOSPITAL, 102 North Broadway, Zip 73015, Mailing Address: P.O. Box 97, Zip 73015–0097; tel. 580/654–1050; Phil Hawkins, Administrator **A**9 10 **F**15 16 22 27 32 40 49 51 **P**5 6	14	10	22	590	6	1802	22	2227	1162	66

CHEYENNE—Roger Mills County

★ ROGER MILLS MEMORIAL HOSPITAL, Fifth and L. L Males Avenue, Zip 73628, Mailing Address: P.O. Box 219, Zip 73628–0219; tel. 580/497–3336; Marilyn Bryan, Administrator **A**9 10 **F**22 28 30 32 33 40 44 65	13	10	15	154	2	—	1	2405	1378	25

CHICKASHA—Grady County

⊞ GRADY MEMORIAL HOSPITAL, 2220 North Iowa Avenue, Zip 73018–2738; tel. 405/224–2300; Roger R. Boid, Administrator (Total facility includes 11 beds in nursing home–type unit) **A**1 9 10 **F**7 11 12 19 20 21 22 23 28 30 32 34 35 37 39 40 41 44 49 56 63 64 65 67 71 73	16	10	147	3276	42	24727	380	24501	11615	347

CLAREMORE—Rogers County

⊞ CLAREMORE REGIONAL HOSPITAL, (Formerly Columbia Claremore Regional Hospital), 1202 North Muskogee Place, Zip 74017–3036; tel. 918/341–2556; Ken Seidel, Executive Director **A**1 9 10 **F**1 6 7 8 10 11 12 13 17 18 19 20 22 23 25 26 27 28 29 30 33 34 40 41 42 43 44 45 49 50 51 52 54 55 56 57 58 59 63 64 65 66 67 68 71 72 73 74 **S** Triad Hospitals, Inc., Dallas, TX	33	10	68	3879	48	43095	644	—	—	—
⊞ U. S. PUBLIC HEALTH SERVICE COMPREHENSIVE INDIAN HEALTH FACILITY, 101 South Moore Avenue, Zip 74017–5091; tel. 918/342–6434; John Daugherty, Jr., Service Unit Director **A**1 5 10 **F**8 15 16 20 22 34 37 40 44 49 51 61 65 71 **P**6 **S** U. S. Public Health Service Indian Health Service, Rockville, MD	47	10	46	2221	24	146943	652	5111	3064	375

CLEVELAND—Pawnee County

★ CLEVELAND AREA HOSPITAL, 1401 West Pawnee Street, Zip 74020–3019; tel. 918/358–2501; Thomas Henton, President and Chief Executive Officer **A**9 10 **F**8 15 19 21 22 27 28 32 34 44 46 49 65 66 68 71 73 **P**1 3 7 8 **S** Hillcrest HealthCare System, Tulsa, OK	23	10	17	273	4	8931	0	—	—	77

CLINTON—Custer County

⊞ INTERGRIS CLINTON REGIONAL HOSPITAL, 100 North 30th Street, Zip 73601–3117, Mailing Address: P.O. Box 1569, Zip 73601–1569; tel. 580/323–2363; Jerry Jones, Administrator (Nonreporting) **A**1 9 10 **S** INTEGRIS Health, Oklahoma City, OK	14	10	49	—	—	—	—	—	—	—
⊞ U. S. PUBLIC HEALTH SERVICE INDIAN HOSPITAL, Mailing Address: Route 1, Box 3060, Zip 73601–9303; tel. 580/323–2884; Thedis V. Mitchell, Director **A**1 10 **F**2 3 4 5 7 8 9 10 11 12 13 14 15 16 17 19 20 22 27 28 30 31 34 36 37 38 39 40 42 43 44 46 47 48 49 52 53 54 56 59 60 64 65 67 69 70 71 72 74 **P**6 **S** U. S. Public Health Service Indian Health Service, Rockville, MD	47	10	11	254	3	31212	0	5922	3394	102

COALGATE—Coal County

★ HURLEY HEALTH CENTER, (Formerly Mary Hurley Hospital), 6 North Covington Street, Zip 74538–2002, Mailing Address: P.O. Box 326, Zip 74538; tel. 580/927–2327; Dan A. Clements, Chief Executive Officer (Total facility includes 75 beds in nursing home–type unit) (Nonreporting) **A**9 10 **S** Hillcrest HealthCare System, Tulsa, OK	23	10	95	—	—	—	—	—	—	—

CORDELL—Washita County

★ CORDELL MEMORIAL HOSPITAL, 1220 North Glenn English Street, Zip 73632–2099; tel. 580/832–3339; Charles H. Greene, Jr., Administrator **A**9 10 **F**11 15 22 28 30 44 71	14	10	28	533	5	4500	0	2085	902	49

CUSHING—Payne County

⊞ CUSHING REGIONAL HOSPITAL, 1027 East Cherry Street, Zip 74023–4101, Mailing Address: P.O. Box 1409, Zip 74023–1409; tel. 918/225–2915; Ron Cackler, President and Chief Executive Officer **A**1 9 10 **F**1 3 12 15 17 19 21 22 25 26 28 29 30 32 33 36 37 40 41 42 44 45 46 49 52 54 55 56 57 58 59 64 65 66 67 71 73 **P**8 **S** Quorum Health Group/Quorum Health Resources, Inc., Brentwood, TN	14	10	75	2814	40	18118	417	14009	6178	242

DRUMRIGHT—Creek County

★ DRUMRIGHT MEMORIAL HOSPITAL, 501 South Lou Allard Drive, Zip 74030–4899; tel. 918/352–2525; James L. Clough, Administrator **A**9 10 **F**8 15 16 19 22 25 32 35 44 71 73 **P**1 4 5 8 **S** INTEGRIS Health, Oklahoma City, OK	23	10	15	439	5	4515	0	3730	2108	77

Hospital, Address, Telephone, Administrator, Approval, Facility, and Physician Codes, Health Care System, Network	Classi-fication Codes		Utilization Data					Expense (thousands) of dollars		
★ American Hospital Association (AHA) membership □ Joint Commission on Accreditation of Healthcare Organizations (JCAHO) accreditation + American Osteopathic Healthcare Association (AOHA) membership ○ American Osteopathic Association (AOA) accreditation △ Commission on Accreditation of Rehabilitation Facilities (CARF) accreditation Control codes 61, 63, 64, 71, 72 and 73 indicate hospitals listed by AOHA, but not registered by AHA. For definition of numerical codes, see page A4	Control	Service	Staffed Beds	Admissions	Census	Outpatient Visits	Births	Total	Payroll	Personnel

DUNCAN—Stephens County

⊞ DUNCAN REGIONAL HOSPITAL, 1407 North Whisenant Drive, Zip 73533–1650, Mailing Address: P.O. Box 2000, Zip 73534–2000; tel. 580/252–5300; David Robertson, Chief Executive Officer (Total facility includes 16 beds in nursing home–type unit) **A**1 9 10 **F**7 8 11 14 15 16 17 19 21 22 28 30 32 33 35 37 39 40 41 44 45 48 49 64 65 66 67 71 73 **P**8

| | 23 | 10 | 100 | 4242 | 52 | 51554 | 487 | 29001 | 13553 | 336 |

DURANT—Bryan County

□ MEDICAL CENTER OF SOUTHEASTERN OKLAHOMA, 1800 University Boulevard, Zip 74701–3006, Mailing Address: P.O. Box 1207, Zip 74702–1207; tel. 580/924–3080; Jacquelyn Harms, Executive Director **A**1 9 10 **F**7 8 10 12 14 17 19 21 22 23 28 30 32 34 35 37 40 41 44 45 46 49 63 65 67 70 71 73 74 **P**8 **S** Health Management Associates, Naples, FL

| | 33 | 10 | 103 | 5485 | 56 | 31165 | 692 | — | — | 354 |

EDMOND—Oklahoma County

⊞ EDMOND MEDICAL CENTER, 1 South Bryant Street, Zip 73034–4798; tel. 405/341–6100; Stanley D. Tatum, Chief Executive Officer **A**1 9 10 **F**4 7 8 9 10 11 12 14 15 16 17 18 19 20 21 22 24 25 26 28 29 30 31 33 34 35 37 38 40 41 42 43 44 45 46 48 49 51 52 53 54 55 56 58 59 60 61 64 65 66 67 68 71 72 73 74 **P**1 5 7 8 **S** Columbia/HCA Healthcare Corporation, Nashville, TN

| | 33 | 10 | 81 | 2616 | 41 | 32896 | 93 | 27403 | 9651 | 256 |

HORIZON SPECIALTY HOSPITAL, 1100 East Ninth Street, Zip 73034–5755; tel. 405/341–8150; Joe Smithers, Administrator (Nonreporting) **A**10

| | 33 | 49 | 43 | — | — | — | — | — | — | — |

EL RENO—Canadian County

★ PARK VIEW HOSPITAL, 2115 Parkview Drive, Zip 73036–2199, Mailing Address: P.O. Box 129, Zip 73036–0129; tel. 405/262–2640; Lex Smith, Administrator **A**9 10 **F**7 12 14 15 16 17 19 20 22 28 29 30 32 33 34 35 37 39 40 44 45 48 49 56 58 64 65 67 71 73

| | 16 | 10 | 54 | 1697 | 20 | 18792 | 179 | 12940 | 6817 | 275 |

ELK CITY—Beckham County

⊞ GREAT PLAINS REGIONAL MEDICAL CENTER, 1705 West Second Street, Zip 73644–4496, Mailing Address: P.O. Box 2339, Zip 73648–2339; tel. 580/225–2511; Pat James, Interim Chief Executive Officer **A**1 9 10 **F**8 11 12 14 15 16 17 19 20 21 22 23 26 27 28 29 30 32 34 35 37 39 40 41 42 44 45 46 49 51 52 53 54 55 56 57 58 60 63 64 65 66 67 71 73 74 **P**8

| | 23 | 10 | 82 | 2200 | 46 | 31481 | 211 | 22927 | 10383 | 351 |

ENID—Garfield County

□ INTEGRIS BASS BEHAVIORAL HEALTH SYSTEM, 2216 South Van Buren Street, Zip 73703–8299; tel. 580/234–2220; James Hutchison, Director (Nonreporting) **A**1 **S** Ramsay Health Care, Inc., Coral Gables, FL

| | 33 | 22 | 50 | — | — | — | — | — | — | — |

⊞ INTEGRIS BASS BAPTIST HEALTH CENTER, 600 South Monroe Street, Zip 73701, Mailing Address: P.O. Box 3168, Zip 73702–3168; tel. 580/233–2300; William E. Mosteller, Jr., Interim Administrator **A**1 3 5 9 10 **F**2 7 8 10 12 15 16 19 21 22 26 28 29 30 31 32 33 34 35 36 37 38 39 40 41 42 44 48 52 53 54 55 56 57 60 63 64 66 67 71 72 73 74 **P**6 7 **S** INTEGRIS Health, Oklahoma City, OK

| | 23 | 10 | 207 | 5810 | 113 | 41150 | 773 | 48328 | 22265 | 823 |

⊞ △ ST. MARY'S MERCY HOSPITAL, 305 South Fifth Street, Zip 73701–5899, Mailing Address: Box 232, Zip 73702–0232; tel. 580/233–6100; Frank Lopez, FACHE, President and Chief Executive Officer **A**1 2 3 5 7 9 10 **F**7 8 10 12 14 15 16 17 19 21 22 23 24 25 28 30 31 32 34 35 36 37 39 40 41 42 44 45 48 49 64 65 67 71 73 74 **P**1 4 5 6 7 **S** Sisters of Mercy Health System–St. Louis, Saint Louis, MO **Web address:** www.mercyok.com

| | 21 | 10 | 137 | 5534 | 97 | 88298 | 279 | 48840 | 17483 | 561 |

EUFAULA—Mcintosh County

COMMUNITY HOSPITAL–LAKEVIEW, 1 Hospital Drive, Zip 74432, Mailing Address: P.O. Box 629, Zip 74432–0629; tel. 918/689–2535; Daniel J. Schaetzle, Administrator **A**9 10 **F**8 14 15 16 19 21 22 28 32 34 44 46 67 71 73

| | 33 | 10 | 33 | 366 | 3 | 9315 | 0 | 3153 | 1250 | 58 |

FAIRFAX—Osage County

★ FAIRFAX MEMORIAL HOSPITAL, Taft Avenue and Highway 18, Zip 74637, Mailing Address: P.O. Box 219, Zip 74637–0219; tel. 918/642–3291; Annabeth Murray, Administrator **A**9 10 **F**8 19 22 28 32 33 34 44 71 **S** Hillcrest HealthCare System, Tulsa, OK

| | 23 | 10 | 21 | 291 | 3 | 3325 | 0 | 2434 | 1159 | 35 |

FAIRVIEW—Major County

FAIRVIEW HOSPITAL, 523 East State Road, Zip 73737–1498; tel. 580/227–3721; Mark Harrel, Administrator (Nonreporting) **A**9 10

| | 14 | 10 | 31 | — | — | — | — | — | — | — |

FORT SILL—Comanche County

⊞ REYNOLDS ARMY COMMUNITY HOSPITAL, 4301 Mow–way Street, Zip 73503–6300; tel. 580/458–3000; Colonel Gary Ripple, Commander (Nonreporting) **A**1 **S** Department of the Army, Office of the Surgeon General, Falls Church, VA

| | 42 | 10 | 116 | — | — | — | — | — | — | — |

FORT SUPPLY—Woodward County

WESTERN STATE PSYCHIATRIC CENTER, 1222 10th Street, Suite 211, Zip 73841–0001; tel. 580/571–3233; Steve Norwood, Executive Director **A**9 10 **F**2 12 14 15 18 20 25 28 30 31 39 46 52 53 54 55 56 57 58 59 65 67 **S** Oklahoma State Department of Mental Health and Substance Abuse Services, Oklahoma City, OK

| | 12 | 22 | 156 | 954 | 99 | 46370 | 0 | — | — | 244 |

FREDERICK—Tillman County

★ MEMORIAL HOSPITAL, 319 East Josephine, Zip 73542–2299; tel. 580/335–7565; Douglas K. Weaver, Chief Executive Officer **A**9 10 **F**12 15 17 19 22 26 27 28 30 32 33 34 44 46 51 53 54 55 58 62 65 71

| | 16 | 10 | 30 | 846 | 9 | 3028 | 2 | 4586 | 1989 | 79 |

Hospital, Address, Telephone, Administrator, Approval, Facility, and Physician Codes, Health Care System, Network	Classification Codes		Utilization Data					Expense (thousands) of dollars		
★ American Hospital Association (AHA) membership □ Joint Commission on Accreditation of Healthcare Organizations (JCAHO) accreditation + American Osteopathic Healthcare Association (AOHA) membership ○ American Osteopathic Association (AOA) accreditation △ Commission on Accreditation of Rehabilitation Facilities (CARF) accreditation Control codes 61, 63, 64, 71, 72 and 73 indicate hospitals listed by AOHA, but not registered by AHA. For definition of numerical codes, see page A4	Control	Service	Staffed Beds	Admissions	Census	Outpatient Visits	Births	Total	Payroll	Personnel

GROVE—Delaware County

⊞ INTEGRIS GROVE GENERAL HOSPITAL, 1310 South Main Street, Zip 74344–1310; tel. 918/786–2243; Dee Renshaw, Administrator **A**1 9 10 **F**7 8 12 13 14 15 16 17 19 20 22 28 32 34 41 42 44 46 49 62 64 65 66 70 71 73 **P**5 8 **S** INTEGRIS Health, Oklahoma City, OK
Web address: www.ohs.com

	23	10	72	3385	44	56226	194	23022	11046	341

GUTHRIE—Logan County

⊞ LOGAN HOSPITAL AND MEDICAL CENTER, Highway 33 West at Academy Road, Zip 73044, Mailing Address: P.O. Box 1017, Zip 73044–1017; tel. 405/282–6700; Judy Feuquay, Chief Executive Officer **A**1 9 10 **F**8 14 15 16 19 20 21 22 28 30 32 44 49 51 64 67 71 73 **S** Quorum Health Group/Quorum Health Resources, Inc., Brentwood, TN

	13	10	32	965	13	11219	0	8660	4102	116

GUYMON—Texas County

★ MEMORIAL HOSPITAL OF TEXAS COUNTY, 520 Medical Drive, Zip 73942–4438; tel. 580/338–6515; Kevin Cox, Administrator **A**9 10 **F**7 8 11 12 13 14 15 17 18 19 21 22 28 29 30 31 32 33 35 36 37 39 40 44 46 47 49 66 71 74

	13	10	35	2101	20	14234	274	11528	4365	169

HENRYETTA—Okmulgee County

⊞ HENRYETTA MEDICAL CENTER, Dewey Bartlett and Main Streets, Zip 74437, Mailing Address: P.O. Box 1269, Zip 74437–1269; tel. 918/652–4463; James P. Bailey, President and Chief Executive Officer **A**1 9 10 **F**1 2 3 4 5 6 7 8 9 10 11 12 13 14 15 16 17 18 19 20 21 22 23 24 25 26 27 28 29 30 31 32 33 34 35 36 37 38 39 40 41 42 43 44 45 46 47 48 49 50 51 52 53 54 55 56 57 58 59 60 61 62 63 64 65 66 67 68 69 71 72 73 74 **S** Quorum Health Group/Quorum Health Resources, Inc., Brentwood, TN

	23	10	46	1101	20	—	0	7544	3350	111

HOBART—Kiowa County

★ ELKVIEW GENERAL HOSPITAL, 429 West Elm Street, Zip 73651–1699; tel. 580/726–3324; J. W. Finch, Jr., Administrator **A**9 10 **F**7 8 12 15 19 20 21 22 26 30 32 42 44 49 56 63 65 71 73

	16	10	40	1322	18	7963	96	6789	3698	188

HOLDENVILLE—Hughes County

★ HOLDENVILLE GENERAL HOSPITAL, 100 Crestview Drive, Zip 74848–9700; tel. 405/379–6631; Shawn Morrow, Chief Executive Officer and Administrator **A**9 10 **F**19 22 28 32 34 42 44 63 72 **S** Quorum Health Group/Quorum Health Resources, Inc., Brentwood, TN

	14	10	27	621	7	—	1	—	—	—

HOLLIS—Harmon County

★ HARMON MEMORIAL HOSPITAL, 400 East Chestnut Street, Zip 73550–2030, Mailing Address: P.O. Box 791, Zip 73550–0791; tel. 580/688–3363; Al Allee, Administrator **A**9 10 **F**22 32 65 71

	16	10	11	336	4	2706	0	1755	1088	43

HUGO—Choctaw County

★ CHOCTAW MEMORIAL HOSPITAL, 1405 East Kirk Road, Zip 74743–3603; tel. 580/326–6414; L. Eugene Matthews, Administrator **A**9 10 **F**15 19 22 28 30 32 44 71

	16	10	38	1092	12	5172	0	5417	2194	107

IDABEL—Mccurtain County

★ MCCURTAIN MEMORIAL HOSPITAL, 1301 Lincoln Road, Zip 74745–7341; tel. 580/286–7623; Claude E. Camp, III, Chief Executive Officer (Nonreporting) **A**9 10 **S** Quorum Health Group/Quorum Health Resources, Inc., Brentwood, TN

	23	10	89	—	—	—	—	—	—	—

KINGFISHER—Kingfisher County

★ KINGFISHER REGIONAL HOSPITAL, 500 South Ninth Street, Zip 73750–3528, Mailing Address: P.O. Box 59, Zip 73750–0059; tel. 405/375–3141; Daryle Voss, Chief Executive Officer **A**9 10 **F**7 8 19 22 28 30 32 34 40 44 46 49 51 64 65 71 73 **S** Quorum Health Group/Quorum Health Resources, Inc., Brentwood, TN

	23	10	38	1415	16	38923	126	8137	3714	113

LAWTON—Comanche County

⊞ COMANCHE COUNTY MEMORIAL HOSPITAL, 3401 Gore Boulevard, Zip 73505–0129, Mailing Address: Box 129, Zip 73502–0129; tel. 580/355–8620; Randall K. Segler, Chief Executive Officer **A**1 2 9 10 **F**4 6 7 8 10 11 12 14 15 16 18 19 20 21 22 25 27 28 29 30 31 32 34 35 37 39 40 41 42 43 44 45 46 48 49 52 53 54 55 57 58 59 60 62 63 64 65 66 67 68 70 71

	16	10	343	9068	155	63593	1032	115873	47732	1353

MEMORIAL PAVILION, 1602 S.W. 82nd Street, Zip 73505–9099; tel. 580/357–7827; Jim Ivey, Administrator (Nonreporting) **A**10

	33	22	99	—	—	—	—	—	—	—

⊞ △ SOUTHWESTERN MEDICAL CENTER, 5602 S.W. Lee Boulevard, Zip 73505–9635, Mailing Address: P.O. Box 7290, Zip 73506–7290; tel. 580/531–4700; Thomas L. Rine, President and Chief Executive Officer **A**1 2 7 9 10 **F**7 8 10 12 14 15 16 17 19 21 22 26 28 30 34 35 37 39 40 41 42 44 48 49 51 52 57 59 60 63 65 70 71 72 73 74 **P**1 7 **S** Columbia/HCA Healthcare Corporation, Nashville, TN
Web address: www.columbia–swmc.com

	33	10	139	3966	54	62136	427	40499	11907	428

⊞ U. S. PUBLIC HEALTH SERVICE INDIAN HOSPITAL, 1515 Lawrie Tatum Road, Zip 73507–3099; tel. 580/353–0350; George E. Howell, Service Unit Director (Nonreporting) **A**1 10 **S** U. S. Public Health Service Indian Health Service, Rockville, MD

	47	10	44	—	—	—	—	—	—	—

MADILL—Marshall County

MARSHALL MEMORIAL HOSPITAL, 1 Hospital Drive, Zip 73446, Mailing Address: P.O. Box 827, Zip 73446–0827; tel. 405/795–3384; Norma Howard, Administrator **A**9 10 **F**8 15 16 22 28 30 32 33 40 44 65 71 **S** INTEGRIS Health, Oklahoma City, OK

	13	10	25	749	10	11426	22	4453	2341	81

Hospital, Address, Telephone, Administrator, Approval, Facility, and Physician Codes, Health Care System, Network	Classi-fication Codes		Utilization Data					Expense (thousands) of dollars		
★ American Hospital Association (AHA) membership □ Joint Commission on Accreditation of Healthcare Organizations (JCAHO) accreditation + American Osteopathic Healthcare Association (AOHA) membership ○ American Osteopathic Association (AOA) accreditation △ Commission on Accreditation of Rehabilitation Facilities (CARF) accreditation Control codes 61, 63, 64, 71, 72 and 73 indicate hospitals listed by AOHA, but not registered by AHA. For definition of numerical codes, see page A4	Control	Service	Staffed Beds	Admissions	Census	Outpatient Visits	Births	Total	Payroll	Personnel

MANGUM—Greer County

MANGUM CITY HOSPITAL, One Wickersham Drive, Zip 73554, Mailing Address: P.O. Box 280, Zip 73554–0280; tel. 580/782–3353; Danny Avery, Administrator **A**9 10 **F**14 15 16 19 28 32 33 34 40 44 49 70 71 73

| | 14 | 10 | 24 | 554 | 6 | 0 | 32 | 3192 | 1793 | 44 |

MARIETTA—Love County

★ MERCY HEALTH LOVE COUNTY, 300 Wanda Street, Zip 73448–1200; tel. 580/276–3347; Richard Barker, Administrator (Nonreporting) **A**10

| | 13 | 10 | 30 | — | — | — | — | — | — | — |

MCALESTER—Pittsburg County

⊠ △ MCALESTER REGIONAL HEALTH CENTER, One Clark Bass Boulevard, Zip 74501–4267, Mailing Address: P.O. Box 1228, Zip 74502–1228; tel. 918/426–1800; Joel W. Tate, FACHE, Chief Executive Officer **A**1 7 9 10 **F**2 3 4 6 7 8 10 12 15 16 17 18 19 21 22 23 26 27 28 30 31 32 33 34 35 36 37 39 40 41 42 44 45 46 48 49 52 63 64 65 66 67 71 73

| | 16 | 10 | 197 | 4741 | 69 | — | 613 | 37694 | 15608 | 620 |

MIAMI—Ottawa County

⊠ INTEGRIS BAPTIST REGIONAL HEALTH CENTER, 200 Second Street S.W., Zip 74354–6830, Mailing Address: P.O. Box 1207, Zip 74355–1207; tel. 918/540–7100; Steven G. Kelly, Administrator **A**1 9 10 **F**7 8 12 13 14 15 16 17 19 21 22 23 26 27 28 29 30 31 32 35 36 37 39 40 41 42 45 46 49 51 52 56 57 60 62 63 64 65 66 67 71 72 73 74 **P**1 2 3 4 5 7 8 **S** INTEGRIS Health, Oklahoma City, OK
Web address: www.integris-health.com

| | 23 | 10 | 123 | 4368 | 69 | 50625 | 329 | 32713 | 15631 | 492 |

□ WILLOW CREST HOSPITAL, 130 A Street S.W., Zip 74354–6800; tel. 918/542–1836; Anne G. Anthony, Administrator and Chief Executive Officer (Nonreporting) **A**1 10
Web address: www.willowcresthospital.com

| | 33 | 22 | 50 | — | — | — | — | — | — | — |

MIDWEST CITY—Oklahoma County

⊠ MIDWEST REGIONAL MEDICAL CENTER, 2825 Parklawn Drive, Zip 73110–4258; tel. 405/610–4411; Peter Lawson, Chief Executive Officer **A**1 2 9 10 **F**4 7 8 10 11 12 14 15 16 19 21 22 26 27 28 29 32 35 37 40 41 42 43 44 46 49 51 52 54 55 56 57 60 64 65 66 67 71 73 74 **P**1 7 **S** Health Management Associates, Naples, FL

| | 33 | 10 | 214 | 10626 | 136 | 92414 | 990 | 95492 | 29296 | 845 |

MUSKOGEE—Muskogee County

⊠ △ MUSKOGEE REGIONAL MEDICAL CENTER, 300 Rockefeller Drive, Zip 74401–5081; tel. 918/682–5501; Bill R. Kennedy, President and Chief Executive Officer **A**1 2 7 9 10 **F**19 32 40 44 46 48 49 52 54 56 57 58 59 65 71 72 73

| | 16 | 10 | 222 | 11050 | 171 | 41250 | 1052 | 65001 | 27877 | 1021 |

⊠ VETERANS AFFAIRS MEDICAL CENTER, 1011 Honor Heights Drive, Zip 74401–1399; tel. 918/683–3261; Allen J. Colston, Director **A**1 3 5 **F**3 12 16 19 20 21 22 27 28 30 32 33 35 37 42 44 46 49 51 64 65 67 71 72 73 74 **P**6 **S** Department of Veterans Affairs, Washington, DC
Web address: www.visn16.med.va.gov

| | 45 | 10 | 50 | 2331 | 46 | 161674 | 0 | 59358 | 32318 | 610 |

NORMAN—Cleveland County

□ GRIFFIN MEMORIAL HOSPITAL, 900 East Main Street, Zip 73071–5305, Mailing Address: P.O. Box 151, Zip 73070–0151; tel. 405/321–4880; Don Bowen, Superintendent **A**1 3 5 9 10 **F**19 20 22 27 29 34 35 44 46 50 52 55 56 57 63 65 71 73 **P**6 **S** Oklahoma State Department of Mental Health and Substance Abuse Services, Oklahoma City, OK

| | 12 | 22 | 182 | 1987 | 149 | 6129 | 0 | 24661 | 14495 | 551 |

J. D. MCCARTY CENTER FOR CHILDREN WITH DEVELOPMENTAL DISABILITIES, 1125 East Alameda, Zip 73071–5264; tel. 405/321–4830; Curtis A. Peters, Chief Executive Officer **A**10 **F**12 16 17 20 34 39 46 48 49 65 67 73
Web address: www.jdmc.org

| | 12 | 56 | 42 | 216 | 30 | 2699 | 0 | 5072 | 3254 | 125 |

⊠ NORMAN REGIONAL HOSPITAL, 901 North Porter Street, Zip 73071–6482, Mailing Address: P.O. Box 1308, Zip 73070–1308; tel. 405/321–1700; Max Lauderdale, Chief Executive Officer **A**1 2 9 10 **F**3 4 7 8 10 12 14 15 16 17 18 19 20 21 22 24 25 27 28 29 30 31 32 34 35 36 37 39 40 41 42 43 44 45 46 48 49 51 52 53 54 55 57 58 59 60 63 64 65 66 67 70 71 72 73 74 **P**1 7

| | 16 | 10 | 271 | 12497 | 169 | 236009 | 1533 | 102458 | 44854 | 1219 |

NOWATA—Nowata County

JANE PHILLIPS NOWATA HEALTH CENTER, 237 South Locust Street, Zip 74048–0426, Mailing Address: P.O. Box 426, Zip 74048–0426; tel. 918/273–3102; Maggie Blevins, Administrator **A**9 10 **F**2 22 44 71 73

| | 33 | 10 | 34 | 421 | 11 | 2222 | 0 | 1605 | 539 | 21 |

OKEENE—Blaine County

OKEENE MUNICIPAL HOSPITAL, 207 East F Street, Zip 73763, Mailing Address: P.O. Box 489, Zip 73763–0489; tel. 580/822–4417; Debbie Howe, Administrator (Total facility includes 21 beds in nursing home–type unit) **A**9 10 **F**6 7 8 12 19 22 28 30 32 36 40 44 49 64 71

| | 14 | 10 | 56 | 521 | 29 | 1724 | 71 | 2987 | 1594 | 83 |

OKEMAH—Okfuskee County

★ CREEK NATION COMMUNITY HOSPITAL, 309 North 14th Street, Zip 74859–2099; tel. 918/623–1424; Frank H. Wahpepah, M.P.H., Administrator (Nonreporting) **A**9 10 **S** U. S. Public Health Service Indian Health Service, Rockville, MD

| | 47 | 10 | 34 | — | — | — | — | — | — | — |

OKLAHOMA CITY—Oklahoma County

⊠ △ BONE AND JOINT HOSPITAL, 1111 North Dewey Avenue, Zip 73103–2615; tel. 405/552–9100; James A. Hyde, Administrator (Nonreporting) **A**1 3 5 7 9 10 **S** SSM Health Care, Saint Louis, MO

| | 23 | 47 | 89 | — | — | — | — | — | — | — |

CHILDREN'S HOSPITAL OF OKLAHOMA See University Health Partners

⊠ DEACONESS HOSPITAL, 5501 North Portland Avenue, Zip 73112–2099; tel. 405/604–6000; Paul Dougherty, President and Chief Executive Officer (Total facility includes 22 beds in nursing home–type unit) **A**1 2 9 10 **F**4 7 8 10 11 12 14 15 16 17 19 21 22 23 26 28 30 31 32 33 34 35 37 38 40 42 43 44 45 46 48 49 50 52 54 55 56 57 58 59 60 62 64 65 67 71 73 **P**1

| | 23 | 10 | 219 | 10850 | 153 | 68437 | 1721 | 72497 | 32007 | 1142 |

Hospital, Address, Telephone, Administrator, Approval, Facility, and Physician Codes, Health Care System, Network	Classi-fication Codes		Utilization Data					Expense (thousands) of dollars		
★ American Hospital Association (AHA) membership □ Joint Commission on Accreditation of Healthcare Organizations (JCAHO) accreditation + American Osteopathic Healthcare Association (AOHA) membership ○ American Osteopathic Association (AOA) accreditation △ Commission on Accreditation of Rehabilitation Facilities (CARF) accreditation Control codes 61, 63, 64, 71, 72 and 73 indicate hospitals listed by AOHA, but not registered by AHA. For definition of numerical codes, see page A4	Control	Service	Staffed Beds	Admissions	Census	Outpatient Visits	Births	Total	Payroll	Personnel

Hospital	Control	Service	Staffed Beds	Admissions	Census	Outpatient Visits	Births	Total	Payroll	Personnel
□ △ HEALTHSOUTH REHABILITATION HOSPITAL, 700 N.W. Seventh Street, Zip 73102–1295; tel. 405/553–1192; Hank Ross, Chief Executive Officer (Nonreporting) **A**1 7 10 **S** HEALTHSOUTH Corporation, Birmingham, AL	33	46	46	—	—	—	—	—	—	—
HIGH POINTE, 6501 N.E. 50th Street, Zip 73141–9613; tel. 405/424–3383; Johnny J. Smith, Chief Executive Officer (Nonreporting) **A**10 **S** Century Healthcare Corporation, Tulsa, OK	33	22	68	—	—	—	—	—	—	—
★ + ○ HILLCREST HEALTH CENTER, 2129 S.W. 59th Street, Zip 73119–7001; tel. 405/685–6671; Ray Brazier, President **A**9 10 11 12 13 **F**1 2 3 4 5 6 7 8 9 10 11 12 13 14 15 16 17 18 19 20 21 22 23 24 25 26 27 28 29 30 31 32 33 34 35 36 37 38 39 40 41 42 43 44 45 46 47 48 49 50 51 52 53 54 55 56 57 58 59 60 61 62 63 64 65 66 67 68 69 70 71 72 73 74 **P**8 **S** SSM Health Care, Saint Louis, MO	21	10	141	7443	78	101449	850	42286	17625	592
⊠ INTEGRIS BAPTIST MEDICAL CENTER, 3300 N.W. Expressway, Zip 73112–4481; tel. 405/949–3011; Thomas R. Rice, FACHE, President and Chief Operating Officer **A**1 2 3 5 9 10 **F**1 2 3 4 7 8 9 10 11 12 13 14 15 16 17 18 19 20 21 22 23 24 25 26 27 28 29 30 31 32 33 34 35 37 38 39 40 41 42 43 44 45 46 47 49 51 52 53 54 55 56 57 58 59 60 61 63 64 65 66 67 68 69 70 71 72 73 74 **P**1 7 **S** INTEGRIS Health, Oklahoma City, OK **Web address:** www.integris–health.com	23	10	506	21840	300	—	2272	238998	86589	2328
⊠ △ INTEGRIS SOUTHWEST MEDICAL CENTER, 4401 South Western, Zip 73109–3441; tel. 405/636–7000; Thomas R. Rice, FACHE, President and Chief Operating Officer (Total facility includes 39 beds in nursing home–type unit) **A**1 2 7 9 10 **F**2 3 4 5 7 8 9 10 11 12 14 15 16 17 19 21 22 24 26 27 28 29 30 32 33 34 35 36 37 38 39 40 41 42 43 44 45 46 47 48 49 50 51 52 53 54 55 56 57 58 59 60 61 63 64 65 66 67 69 71 73 74 **P**6 7 8 **S** INTEGRIS Health, Oklahoma City, OK	23	10	302	11928	226	130995	934	110466	44551	1376
⊠ △ MERCY HEALTH CENTER, 4300 West Memorial Road, Zip 73120–8362; tel. 405/755–1515; Michael J. Packnett, President and Chief Executive Officer **A**1 2 7 9 10 **F**3 4 7 8 10 11 12 15 16 17 18 19 21 22 24 26 27 28 29 30 31 32 33 34 35 36 37 38 39 40 41 42 43 44 45 47 48 49 50 52 53 60 64 65 67 71 73 74 **P**1 4 6 7 **S** Sisters of Mercy Health System–St. Louis, Saint Louis, MO	21	10	304	12814	180	173688	1561	111359	46302	1207
□ NORTHWEST SURGICAL HOSPITAL, (SURGICAL–ORTHOPEDIC), 9204 North May Avenue, Zip 73120–4419; tel. 405/848–1918; William Federman, Chief Executive Officer **A**1 10 **F**22 44	33	49	9	433	7	2170	0	5374	1435	31
PRESBYTERIAN HOSPITAL See University Health Partners										
⊠ △ ST. ANTHONY HOSPITAL, 1000 North Lee Street, Zip 73102–1080, Mailing Address: P.O. Box 205, Zip 73101–0205; tel. 405/272–7000; Valinda Rutledge, President (Total facility includes 43 beds in nursing home–type unit) **A**1 2 3 5 7 9 10 **F**1 2 3 4 7 8 10 11 12 15 16 17 19 20 21 22 24 25 26 28 29 30 31 34 35 37 39 40 41 42 43 44 45 48 49 51 52 53 54 55 56 57 58 59 60 64 65 66 67 69 71 73 74 **P**8 **S** SSM Health Care, Saint Louis, MO	21	10	408	14553	243	289099	1009	141703	56682	1866
⊠ UNIVERSITY HEALTH PARTNERS, (Includes Children's Hospital of Oklahoma, 940 N.E. 13th Street, Zip 73104; tel. 405/271–6165; Presbyterian Hospital, 700 N.E. 13th Street, Zip 73104–5070; tel. 405/271–5100; University Hospital, 920 N.E. 13th Street, Zip 73104; tel. 405/271–4700), 6501 North Broadway, Suite 200, Zip 73116; tel. 405/879–0900; David L. Dunlap, Chief Executive Officer (Nonreporting) **A**1 2 3 5 8 9 10	33	10	614	—	—	—	—	—	—	—
UNIVERSITY HOSPITAL See University Health Partners										
⊠ VETERANS AFFAIRS MEDICAL CENTER, 921 N.E. 13th Street, Zip 73104–5028; tel. 405/270–0501; Steven J. Gentling, Director (Total facility includes 40 beds in nursing home–type unit) (Nonreporting) **A**1 3 5 8 **S** Department of Veterans Affairs, Washington, DC	45	10	277	—	—	—	—	—	—	—
OKMULGEE—Okmulgee County										
GEORGE NIGH REHABILITATION INSTITUTE, 900 East Airport Road, Zip 74447–9762, Mailing Address: P.O. Box 1118, Zip 74447–1118; tel. 918/756–9211; Mitchell Townsend, Administrator (Total facility includes 13 beds in nursing home–type unit) **A**10 **F**15 16 19 21 34 35 41 48 49 64 65 71 73 **P**8	12	46	33	357	20	5367	0	5779	2680	110
□ OKMULGEE MEMORIAL HOSPITAL, (Formerly OMH Medical Center), 1401 Morris Drive, Zip 74447–6419, Mailing Address: P.O. Box 1038, Zip 74447–1038; tel. 918/756–4233; David D. Rasmussen, Administrator **A**1 9 10 **F**4 7 8 11 12 15 16 19 21 22 26 28 30 32 33 37 38 40 44 52 57 63 65 71 73	23	10	66	2388	31	—	451	14034	6249	201
PAULS VALLEY—Garvin County										
PAULS VALLEY GENERAL HOSPITAL, 100 Valley Drive, Zip 73075–0368, Mailing Address: Box 368, Zip 73075–0368; tel. 405/238–5501; Charles Johnston, Administrator (Total facility includes 8 beds in nursing home–type unit) **A**9 10 **F**7 8 19 22 28 32 37 40 41 44 49 53 59 64 65 71	14	10	50	1453	22	49375	44	8778	4273	161
PAWHUSKA—Osage County										
PAWHUSKA HOSPITAL, 1101 East 15th Street, Zip 74056–1920; tel. 918/287–3232; Samuel T. Guild, Administrator (Nonreporting) **A**9 10	14	10	19	—	—	—	—	—	—	—
PAWNEE—Pawnee County										
★ PAWNEE MUNICIPAL HOSPITAL, 1212 Fourth Street, Zip 74058–4046, Mailing Address: P.O. Box 467, Zip 74058–0467; tel. 918/762–2577; John Ketring, Administrator **A**9 10 **F**19 22 28 32 33 44 49 65 66 71 73 **S** INTEGRIS Health, Oklahoma City, OK	23	10	32	723	7	2459	0	—	—	—

Hospital, Address, Telephone, Administrator, Approval, Facility, and Physician Codes, Health Care System, Network	Classification Codes		Utilization Data					Expense (thousands) of dollars		
★ American Hospital Association (AHA) membership □ Joint Commission on Accreditation of Healthcare Organizations (JCAHO) accreditation + American Osteopathic Healthcare Association (AOHA) membership ○ American Osteopathic Association (AOA) accreditation △ Commission on Accreditation of Rehabilitation Facilities (CARF) accreditation Control codes 61, 63, 64, 71, 72 and 73 indicate hospitals listed by AOHA, but not registered by AHA. For definition of numerical codes, see page A4	Control	Service	Staffed Beds	Admissions	Census	Outpatient Visits	Births	Total	Payroll	Personnel

PERRY—Noble County

✠ PERRY MEMORIAL HOSPITAL, 501 14th Street, Zip 73077–5099; tel. 580/336–3541; Joe Duerr, Chief Executive Officer **A**1 10 **F**8 12 15 19 22 28 30 32 33 41 42 44 49 65 71 73 **P**8 **S** Quorum Health Group/Quorum Health Resources, Inc., Brentwood, TN

| | 16 | 10 | 28 | 828 | 12 | 25363 | 0 | 5304 | 2429 | 86 |

PONCA CITY—Kay County

✠ ST. JOSEPH REGIONAL MEDICAL CENTER OF NORTHERN OKLAHOMA, 14th Street and Hartford Avenue, Zip 74601–2035, Mailing Address: Box 1270, Zip 74602–1270; tel. 580/765–3321; Garry L. England, President and Chief Executive Officer (Total facility includes 10 beds in nursing home–type unit) **A**1 9 10 **F**7 8 14 15 16 17 18 19 21 22 23 24 27 28 29 30 32 33 34 35 36 37 40 42 44 49 52 54 56 60 62 63 64 65 66 67 71 73 **P**5 6 7 **S** Via Christi Health System, Wichita, KS

| | 21 | 10 | 90 | 3152 | 40 | 58108 | 537 | 26834 | 10766 | 355 |

POTEAU—Le Flore County

✠ EASTERN OKLAHOMA MEDICAL CENTER, 105 Wall Street, Zip 74953, Mailing Address: P.O. Box 1148, Zip 74953–1148; tel. 918/647–8161; Craig R. Cudworth, Chief Executive Officer **A**1 9 10 **F**7 8 14 17 19 21 22 23 26 28 30 32 33 34 37 39 40 42 44 49 53 55 63 65 71 73 **P**1 8 **S** Quorum Health Group/Quorum Health Resources, Inc., Brentwood, TN

| | 23 | 10 | 72 | 3314 | 30 | 17296 | 479 | 14260 | 6782 | 275 |

PRAGUE—Lincoln County

★ PRAGUE MUNICIPAL HOSPITAL, 1322 Klabzuba Avenue, Zip 74864, Mailing Address: P.O. Drawer S, Zip 74864; tel. 405/567–4922; Chris Mattingly, Chief Executive Officer **A**9 10 **F**19 21 22 28 29 30 32 34 35 44 50 63 64 71 **P**6 **S** Hillcrest HealthCare System, Tulsa, OK

| | 14 | 10 | 19 | 217 | 6 | 9970 | 0 | 2373 | 1166 | 46 |

PRYOR—Mayes County

✠ MAYES COUNTY MEDICAL CENTER, 129 North Kentucky Street, Zip 74361–4211, Mailing Address: P.O. Box 278, Zip 74362–0278; tel. 918/825–1600; W. Charles Jordan, Administrator **A**1 9 10 **F**7 8 17 19 22 28 30 32 33 34 39 40 41 44 46 65 67 71 73 **S** INTEGRIS Health, Oklahoma City, OK

| | 23 | 10 | 34 | 1078 | 14 | — | 6 | — | — | — |

PURCELL—McClain County

★ PURCELL MUNICIPAL HOSPITAL, 1500 North Green Avenue, Zip 73080–1699, Mailing Address: P.O. Box 511, Zip 73080–0511; tel. 405/527–6524; Curtis R. Pryor, Administrator **A**9 10 **F**7 12 14 16 17 19 22 25 28 30 32 40 42 44 45 46 49 56 65 67 71 **P**8 **S** Quorum Health Group/Quorum Health Resources, Inc., Brentwood, TN

| | 14 | 10 | 20 | 1427 | 14 | 28259 | 91 | 7972 | 3507 | 145 |

SALLISAW—Sequoyah County

SEQUOYAH MEMORIAL HOSPITAL, 213 East Redwood Street, Zip 74955–2811, Mailing Address: P.O. Box 505, Zip 74955–0505; tel. 918/774–1100; Ruth Ann Roark, Administrator (Nonreporting) **A**10

| | 15 | 10 | 41 | — | — | — | — | — | — | — |

SAPULPA—Creek County

✠ BARTLETT MEMORIAL MEDICAL CENTER, 519 South Division Street, Zip 74066–4501, Mailing Address: P.O. Box 1368, Zip 74067–1368; tel. 918/224–4280; W. D. Robinson, Chief Executive Officer **A**1 9 10 **F**8 15 16 17 19 20 21 22 28 30 32 33 34 37 42 44 45 46 48 49 64 65 71 73 **P**5 **S** Marian Health System, Tulsa, OK

| | 21 | 10 | 113 | 2014 | 29 | 13147 | 0 | 14474 | 5559 | 181 |

SAYRE—Beckham County

★ SAYRE MEMORIAL HOSPITAL, 501 East Washington Street, Zip 73662, Mailing Address: P.O. Box 680, Zip 73662; tel. 580/928–5541; Larry Anderson, Administrator **A**9 10 **F**7 8 16 19 22 28 30 32 34 44 49 65 71 73 **P**6 **S** Quorum Health Group/Quorum Health Resources, Inc., Brentwood, TN

| | 23 | 10 | 46 | 1180 | 14 | 21731 | 129 | 6419 | 3393 | 114 |

SEILING—Dewey County

SEILING HOSPITAL, Highway 60 N.E., Zip 73663, Mailing Address: P.O. Box 720, Zip 73663–0720; tel. 580/922–7361; Jane McDowell, Administrator **A**9 10 **F**19 22 28 32 41 49 71

| | 14 | 10 | 18 | 409 | 5 | 4389 | 0 | 1907 | 1039 | 34 |

SEMINOLE—Seminole County

★ SEMINOLE MEDICAL CENTER, (Formerly Seminole Municipal Hospital), 2401 Wrangler Boulevard, Zip 74868; tel. 405/303–4000; Stephen R. Schoaps, Chief Executive Officer **A**9 10 **F**7 8 12 15 16 17 19 22 28 30 37 40 41 44 46 49 65 67 70 71 **P**1 2 7 **S** Columbia/HCA Healthcare Corporation, Nashville, TN

| | 33 | 10 | 32 | 418 | 4 | 8732 | 32 | 4867 | 1618 | 113 |

SHATTUCK—Ellis County

★ NEWMAN MEMORIAL HOSPITAL, 905 South Main Street, Zip 73858–9602; tel. 580/938–2551; Gary W. Mitchell, Chief Executive Officer **A**9 10 **F**7 8 15 17 19 22 24 32 34 35 36 37 40 42 44 49 65 70 71 73

| | 23 | 10 | 27 | 1033 | 11 | 26200 | 84 | 7373 | 3502 | 105 |

SHAWNEE—Pottawatomie County

✠ MISSION HILL MEMORIAL HOSPITAL, 1900 South Gordon Cooper Drive, Zip 74801–8600; tel. 405/273–2240; Thomas G. Honaker, III, Administrator **A**1 9 10 **F**7 8 10 15 19 20 21 22 30 32 33 35 37 39 40 41 44 49 61 65 71 73 74 **P**8 **S** SSM Health Care, Saint Louis, MO

| | 32 | 10 | 49 | 1754 | 17 | 13357 | 254 | 10125 | 4416 | 157 |

✠ SHAWNEE REGIONAL HOSPITAL, 1102 West MacArthur Street, Zip 74804–1744; tel. 405/273–2270; Robert F. Maynard, Chief Executive Officer **A**1 2 9 10 **F**7 8 10 12 14 15 16 17 19 21 22 26 28 30 32 33 35 37 39 40 42 44 45 49 60 63 64 65 66 67 71 73 74

| | 23 | 10 | 126 | 3858 | 47 | 51517 | 747 | 25952 | 11247 | 398 |

SPENCER—Oklahoma County

✠ INTEGRIS MENTAL HEALTH SYSTEM–SPENCER, 2601 North Spencer Road, Zip 73084–3699, Mailing Address: P.O. Box 11137, Oklahoma City, Zip 73136–0137; tel. 405/427–2441; Murali Krishna, M.D., President and Chief Operating Officer (Nonreporting) **A**1 9 10 **S** INTEGRIS Health, Oklahoma City, OK

| | 23 | 22 | 44 | — | — | — | — | — | — | — |

Hospital, Address, Telephone, Administrator, Approval, Facility, and Physician Codes, Health Care System, Network	Classi-fication Codes		Utilization Data						Expense (thousands) of dollars		
★ American Hospital Association (AHA) membership □ Joint Commission on Accreditation of Healthcare Organizations (JCAHO) accreditation + American Osteopathic Healthcare Association (AOHA) membership ○ American Osteopathic Association (AOA) accreditation △ Commission on Accreditation of Rehabilitation Facilities (CARF) accreditation Control codes 61, 63, 64, 71, 72 and 73 indicate hospitals listed by AOHA, but not registered by AHA. For definition of numerical codes, see page A4	Control	Service	Staffed Beds	Admissions	Census	Outpatient Visits	Births	Total	Payroll	Personnel

	Control	Service	Staffed Beds	Admissions	Census	Outpatient Visits	Births	Total	Payroll	Personnel
STIGLER—Haskell County										
★ HASKELL COUNTY HEALTHCARE SYSTEM, 401 N.W. H Street, Zip 74462–1625; tel. 918/967–4682; Stacy D. Holland, Administrator and Chief Executive Officer **A**9 10 **F**17 19 25 27 28 30 32 33 34 39 41 42 44 49 65 70 71 72 73 **P**5	13	10	31	770	10	11211	0	5624	3261	177
STILLWATER—Payne County										
⊠ STILLWATER MEDICAL CENTER, 1323 West Sixth Avenue, Zip 74074–4399, Mailing Address: P.O. Box 2408, Zip 74076–2408; tel. 405/372–1480; Jerry G. Moeller, President and Chief Executive Officer (Total facility includes 18 beds in nursing home–type unit) **A**1 9 10 **F**8 10 14 15 16 19 20 21 22 23 31 32 33 34 35 36 37 40 42 44 46 49 56 63 64 65 71 73 **P**8 **Web address:** www.stilwater–medical.org	16	10	93	4578	66	55279	793	39242	16704	582
SULPHUR—Murray County										
ARBUCKLE MEMORIAL HOSPITAL, 2011 West Broadway Street, Zip 73086–4221; tel. 580/622–2161; Kenneth R. Ross, Chief Executive Officer **A**9 10 **F**8 14 15 16 22 34 52 56 65 71	13	10	35	1301	14	5007	2	2975	1675	62
TAHLEQUAH—Cherokee County										
⊠ TAHLEQUAH CITY HOSPITAL, 1400 East Downing Street, Zip 74464–3324, Mailing Address: P.O. Box 1008, Zip 74465–1008; tel. 918/456–0641; Gary L. Jepson, Chief Executive Officer **A**1 9 10 **F**7 8 14 15 16 19 21 22 26 28 30 32 34 35 37 40 44 45 49 52 57 63 65 71 73	16	10	86	2869	31	34901	321	17640	8138	305
⊠ WILLIAM W. HASTINGS INDIAN HOSPITAL, 100 South Bliss Avenue, Zip 74464–3399; tel. 918/458–3100; Hickory Starr, Jr., Administrator **A**1 10 **F**7 10 12 13 15 19 20 22 28 31 34 37 39 40 44 52 53 54 55 56 57 58 59 71 73 **P**6 **S** U. S. Public Health Service Indian Health Service, Rockville, MD	47	10	60	3630	30	202639	1024	24583	15844	445
TALIHINA—La Flore County										
⊠ CHOCTAW NATION INDIAN HOSPITAL, Rural Route 2, Box 1725, Zip 74571–9517; tel. 918/567–2211; Rosemary Hooser, Administrator **A**1 10 **F**7 8 10 12 15 16 19 20 21 22 23 25 26 27 28 29 30 31 32 33 34 35 36 39 40 41 42 43 44 45 46 49 50 51 53 54 55 56 57 58 60 61 63 65 66 67 68 69 71 72 73 74 **S** U. S. Public Health Service Indian Health Service, Rockville, MD	47	10	44	1263	14	62928	225	—	—	265
TISHOMINGO—Johnston County										
JOHNSTON MEMORIAL HOSPITAL, 1000 South Byrd Street, Zip 73460–3299; tel. 580/371–2327; Connie Pedersen, Administrator **A**9 10 **F**1 3 4 5 6 7 8 10 11 12 13 17 18 19 20 21 22 23 24 25 26 27 28 29 30 31 32 33 34 35 36 37 39 41 42 43 44 45 46 49 50 53 54 55 56 57 58 59 60 61 62 63 64 65 66 67 68 69 70 71 72 73	13	10	27	641	6	—	19	—	—	—
TULSA—Tulsa County										
BROOKHAVEN HOSPITAL, 201 South Garnett Road, Zip 74128–1800; tel. 918/438–4257; Rolf B. Gainer, Chief Executive Officer and Administrator **A**9 10 **F**3 12 16 18 19 20 21 22 24 27 30 34 35 41 43 44 45 46 49 52 54 55 56 57 58 59 60 62 63 65 66 67 68 70 71 72	33	22	40	466	23	992	0	—	—	87
□ CANCER TREATMENT CENTERS OF AMERICA–TULSA, (Formerly Memorial Medical Center and Cancer Treatment Center–Tulsa), 2408 East 81st Street, Zip 74137–4210; tel. 918/496–5000; Joseph A. Gagliardi, President and Chief Executive Officer **A**1 2 10 **F**8 12 14 15 16 19 21 27 28 29 30 34 35 37 39 41 42 44 45 46 49 60 63 67 73 **P**6 **S** Cancer Treatment Centers of America, Arlington Heights, IL	33	10	72	434	20	30454	0	23059	4761	344
⊠ CHILDREN'S MEDICAL CENTER, 5300 East Skelly Drive, Zip 74135–6599, Mailing Address: P.O. Box 35648, Zip 74153–0648; tel. 918/664–6600; Donald A. Lorack, Jr., President and Chief Executive Officer **A**1 3 5 9 10 **F**7 8 10 12 16 17 18 19 21 22 24 26 28 29 30 32 33 34 35 41 44 45 46 49 50 51 53 54 55 56 57 58 59 60 61 65 66 67 68 71 72 73 74 **P**6 **S** Hillcrest HealthCare System, Tulsa, OK	33	52	90	734	72	147578	0	21055	14217	432
COLUMBIA DOCTORS HOSPITAL See Doctors Hospital										
COLUMBIA SPECIALTY HOSPITAL OF TULSA See Hillcrest Specialty Hospital										
★ CONTINUOUS CARE CENTER OF TULSA, (LONG TERM ACUTE CARE), 1923 South Utica Avenue, Zip 74105, Mailing Address: 1755 South Utica Avenue, Zip 74105; tel. 918/749–8930; Raymond L. Replogle, President and Chief Executive Officer **A**10 **F**11 12 14 15 16 19 21 22 26 35 37 41 65 71	23	49	28	316	22	0	0	7145	2503	72
⊠ DOCTORS HOSPITAL, (Formerly Columbia Doctors Hospital), 2323 South Harvard Avenue, Zip 74114–3370; tel. 918/744–4000; Kenneth Noteboom, Chief Executive Officer **A**1 9 10 **F**2 4 7 8 10 12 17 19 21 22 23 25 26 27 30 32 34 35 37 40 41 42 43 44 46 48 49 52 53 57 59 60 63 64 65 67 71 73 **P**1 7 **S** Hillcrest HealthCare System, Tulsa, OK **Web address:** www.columbia.net	33	10	121	3324	60	17885	815	24833	10821	478
⊠ △ HILLCREST MEDICAL CENTER, 1120 South Utica, Zip 74104–4090; tel. 918/579–1000; Donald A. Lorack, Jr., President and Chief Executive Officer **A**1 2 3 5 7 9 10 **F**2 3 4 6 7 8 9 10 11 12 13 14 15 16 17 18 19 21 22 23 24 25 26 27 28 29 30 31 32 33 34 35 37 38 39 40 41 42 43 44 46 47 48 49 50 51 52 53 54 55 56 57 58 59 60 61 62 63 64 65 66 67 68 69 70 71 72 73 74 **P**3 5 6 8 **S** Hillcrest HealthCare System, Tulsa, OK **Web address:** www.hillcrest.com	23	10	439	19372	289	103570	3876	176934	71249	2242
⊠ HILLCREST SPECIALTY HOSPITAL, (Formerly Columbia Specialty Hospital of Tulsa), (LONG TERM CARE), 2408 East 81st Street, 2500, Zip 74137–4210; tel. 918/491–2400; Kenneth Noteboom, Chief Executive Officer **A**1 10 **F**1 2 3 4 7 8 10 11 12 17 18 19 21 22 26 27 28 29 30 31 32 33 34 35 37 39 40 41 42 43 44 45 46 48 49 51 52 55 57 58 59 60 64 65 66 67 69 71 72 73 74 **P**5 7 8 **S** Hillcrest HealthCare System, Tulsa, OK **Web address:** www.columbia.net	33	49	45	201	15	0	0	6658	2746	59

Hospital, Address, Telephone, Administrator, Approval, Facility, and Physician Codes, Health Care System, Network	Classi-fication Codes		Utilization Data					Expense (thousands) of dollars		
★ American Hospital Association (AHA) membership □ Joint Commission on Accreditation of Healthcare Organizations (JCAHO) accreditation + American Osteopathic Healthcare Association (AOHA) membership ○ American Osteopathic Association (AOA) accreditation △ Commission on Accreditation of Rehabilitation Facilities (CARF) accreditation Control codes 61, 63, 64, 71, 72 and 73 indicate hospitals listed by AOHA, but not registered by AHA. For definition of numerical codes, see page A4	Control	Service	Staffed Beds	Admissions	Census	Outpatient Visits	Births	Total	Payroll	Personnel

□ LAUREATE PSYCHIATRIC CLINIC AND HOSPITAL, 6655 South Yale Avenue, Zip 74136–3329; tel. 918/481–4000; John L. Fleming, M.D., Interim Chief Executive Officer (Nonreporting) **A**1 3 5 9 10	23	22	75	—	—	—	—	—	—	—
MEMORIAL MEDICAL CENTER AND CANCER TREATMENT CENTER–TULSA See Cancer Treatment Centers of America–Tulsa										
PARKSIDE HOSPITAL, 1620 East 12th Street, Zip 74120–5499; tel. 918/582–2131; Paul Greever, Chief Executive Officer **A**3 5 10 **F**1 2 3 12 14 17 18 30 52 53 54 55 56 58 59 65 73 **P**6	23	22	40	1316	22	71848	0	12747	7441	54
⊞ SAINT FRANCIS HOSPITAL, 6161 South Yale Avenue, Zip 74136–1992; tel. 918/494–2200; Donna Rheault, Chief Operating Officer (Total facility includes 40 beds in nursing home–type unit) **A**1 2 3 5 8 9 10 **F**3 4 7 8 10 11 12 13 15 16 17 18 19 20 21 22 24 28 29 30 31 32 33 34 35 36 37 38 39 40 41 42 43 44 45 46 47 48 49 53 54 55 56 57 58 59 60 63 64 65 66 67 68 69 71 73 74 **P**6 8 **Web address:** www.saintfrancis.com	23	10	584	33245	410	382548	3545	254133	107677	4146
SHADOW MOUNTAIN HOSPITAL See The Brown Schools at Shadow Mountain										
⊞ △ ST. JOHN MEDICAL CENTER, 1923 South Utica Avenue, Zip 74104–5445; tel. 918/744–2345; David Pynn, President and Chief Executive Officer **A**1 2 3 5 7 9 10 **F**1 2 3 4 7 8 10 11 12 14 15 16 17 18 19 20 21 22 23 24 25 26 27 28 29 30 31 32 33 34 35 37 38 39 40 41 42 43 44 45 47 48 49 51 52 54 55 56 57 58 59 60 62 64 65 66 67 68 69 70 71 72 73 74 **P**5 6 7 **S** Marian Health System, Tulsa, OK **Web address:** www.sjmc.org	21	10	552	23176	401	118441	2336	212418	78807	4683
□ THE BROWN SCHOOLS AT SHADOW MOUNTAIN, (Formerly Shadow Mountain Hospital), 6262 South Sheridan Road, Zip 74133–4099; tel. 918/492–8200; Nancy J. Cranton, Chief Executive Officer (Nonreporting) **A**1 **S** Healthcare America, Inc., Austin, TX	33	52	100	—	—	—	—	—	—	—
⊞ + ○ △ TULSA REGIONAL MEDICAL CENTER, 744 West Ninth Street, Zip 74127–9990; tel. 918/599–5900; Steve Dobbs, Executive Vice President and Chief Executive Officer **A**1 7 9 10 11 12 13 **F**3 4 7 8 10 11 12 14 17 18 19 21 22 23 25 26 30 31 33 35 36 37 38 39 40 41 42 43 44 49 52 53 54 55 56 57 58 59 60 64 65 66 67 69 70 71 73 **P**8 **S** Hillcrest HealthCare System, Tulsa, OK	33	10	255	9187	163	32791	786	101954	34612	1149
VINITA—Craig County										
⊞ CRAIG GENERAL HOSPITAL, 735 North Foreman Street, Zip 74301–1418, Mailing Address: Box 326, Zip 74301–0326; tel. 918/256–7551; B. Joe Gunn, FACHE, Administrator and Chief Executive Officer **A**1 9 10 **F**7 8 11 12 15 16 19 21 22 28 30 32 33 34 35 36 40 42 44 49 62 71 73	16	10	36	1100	14	23293	115	8889	3939	142
□ EASTERN STATE HOSPITAL, Mailing Address: P.O. Box 69, Zip 74301–0069; tel. 918/256–7841; William T. Burkett, Chief Executive Officer **A**1 9 10 **F**14 15 16 20 22 24 27 29 30 31 39 41 45 46 52 55 56 65 73 **P**1 **S** Oklahoma State Department of Mental Health and Substance Abuse Services, Oklahoma City, OK	12	22	314	1780	244	0	0	—	16868	626
WAGONER—Wagoner County										
⊞ WAGONER COMMUNITY HOSPITAL, 1200 West Cherokee, Zip 74467–4681, Mailing Address: Box 407, Zip 74477–0407; tel. 918/485–5514; John W. Crawford, Chief Executive Officer **A**1 9 10 **F**7 8 12 14 15 16 19 20 21 22 24 26 28 29 30 31 34 37 40 42 44 45 46 49 51 52 54 55 56 65 71 73 74 **P**8 **S** Hillcrest HealthCare System, Tulsa, OK	33	10	100	2079	28	10039	104	16266	5777	131
WATONGA—Blaine County										
★ WATONGA MUNICIPAL HOSPITAL, 500 North Nash Boulevard, Zip 73772–0370, Mailing Address: Box 370, Zip 73772–0370; tel. 580/623–7211; Terry Buckner, Administrator **A**9 10 **F**11 19 20 22 28 30 32 33 34 44 49 65 71 **P**6 **S** Quorum Health Group/Quorum Health Resources, Inc., Brentwood, TN	16	10	23	734	9	12195	2	5315	2852	114
WAURIKA—Jefferson County										
★ JEFFERSON COUNTY HOSPITAL, Highway 70 and 81, Zip 73573, Mailing Address: P.O. Box 90, Zip 73573–0090; tel. 580/228–2344; Richard Tallon, Administrator **A**9 10 **F**11 19 22 28 32 44 49 53 58 71 73	13	10	30	539	10	16590	0	2610	1431	60
WEATHERFORD—Custer County										
★ SOUTHWESTERN MEMORIAL HOSPITAL, 215 North Kansas Street, Zip 73096–5499; tel. 580/772–5551; Ronnie D. Walker, President **A**9 10 **F**7 8 15 16 19 28 34 35 44 71 73	16	10	46	791	7	11315	207	5096	2272	110
WILBURTON—Latimer County										
LATIMER COUNTY GENERAL HOSPITAL, 806 Highway 2 North, Zip 74578–3698; tel. 918/465–2391; M. Sue Turner, Administrator **A**9 10 **F**19 22 28 32 44 71 **P**5	13	10	33	595	6	4856	0	2862	1510	38
WOODWARD—Woodward County										
⊞ WOODWARD HOSPITAL AND HEALTH CENTER, 900 17th Street, Zip 73801–2423; tel. 580/256–5511; Joel A. Hart, Chief Executive Officer **A**1 9 10 **F**7 8 11 14 15 16 19 21 22 23 32 33 35 37 40 41 42 44 49 52 57 64 65 67 71 72 73 **P**5 6 **S** Quorum Health Group/Quorum Health Resources, Inc., Brentwood, TN	23	10	68	1975	30	18597	263	19184	7541	290

OREGON

Resident population 3,282 (in thousands)
Resident population in metro areas 68.5%
Birth rate per 1,000 population 13.6
65 years and over 13.3%
Percent of persons without health insurance 15.3%

Hospital, Address, Telephone, Administrator, Approval, Facility, and Physician Codes, Health Care System, Network	Classification Codes		Utilization Data					Expense (thousands) of dollars		
★ American Hospital Association (AHA) membership □ Joint Commission on Accreditation of Healthcare Organizations (JCAHO) accreditation + American Osteopathic Healthcare Association (AOHA) membership ○ American Osteopathic Association (AOA) accreditation △ Commission on Accreditation of Rehabilitation Facilities (CARF) accreditation Control codes 61, 63, 64, 71, 72 and 73 indicate hospitals listed by AOHA, but not registered by AHA. For definition of numerical codes, see page A4	Control	Service	Staffed Beds	Admissions	Census	Outpatient Visits	Births	Total	Payroll	Personnel

ALBANY—Linn County

✠ ALBANY GENERAL HOSPITAL, 1046 West Sixth Avenue, Zip 97321–1999; tel. 541/812–4000; Richard J. Delano, President **A**1 2 9 10 **F**7 8 10 12 15 17 19 21 22 28 29 30 32 33 34 35 37 39 40 41 42 44 46 49 51 54 59 60 65 66 67 68 70 71 72 73 74 **P**6

| | 23 | 10 | 71 | 2026 | 30 | 38699 | 758 | 30293 | 13110 | 413 |

ASHLAND—Jackson County

✠ ASHLAND COMMUNITY HOSPITAL, 280 Maple Street, Zip 97520, Mailing Address: P.O. Box 98, Zip 97520; tel. 541/482–2441; James R. Watson, Administrator **A**1 9 10 **F**1 6 7 8 12 14 16 17 19 22 23 28 30 32 34 36 37 39 40 41 44 45 46 65 67 70 71 **P**5

| | 23 | 10 | 49 | 1553 | 15 | 25649 | 299 | 15489 | 7674 | 178 |

ASTORIA—Clatsop County

✠ COLUMBIA MEMORIAL HOSPITAL, 2111 Exchange Street, Zip 97103; tel. 503/325–4321; Terry O. Finklein, Chief Executive Officer **A**1 9 10 **F**7 8 16 17 19 21 22 28 30 32 33 34 37 39 40 41 42 44 49 65 67 68 70 71 73 74 **P**8

| | 23 | 10 | 37 | 2075 | 17 | 44635 | 338 | 17254 | 8164 | 231 |

BAKER CITY—Baker County

✠ ST. ELIZABETH HEALTH SERVICES, 3325 Pocahontas Road, Zip 97814; tel. 541/523–6461; Robert T. Mannix, Jr., President and Chief Operations Officer (Total facility includes 98 beds in nursing home–type unit) (Nonreporting) **A**1 9 10 **S** Catholic Health Initiatives, Denver, CO

| | 21 | 10 | 134 | — | — | — | — | — | — | — |

BANDON—Coos County

★ SOUTHERN COOS GENERAL HOSPITAL, 900 11th Street S.E., Zip 97411; tel. 541/347–2426; James A. Wathen, Chief Executive Officer **A**9 10 **F**8 14 15 17 20 22 28 32 34 44 49 64 65 71

| | 16 | 10 | 18 | 159 | 2 | 8293 | 0 | 2875 | 1470 | 54 |

BEND—Deschutes County

✠ ST. CHARLES MEDICAL CENTER, 2500 N.E. Neff Road, Zip 97701–6015; tel. 541/382–4321; James T. Lussier, President and Chief Executive Officer (Nonreporting) **A**1 2 3 9 10

| | 23 | 10 | 181 | — | — | — | — | — | — | — |

BURNS—Harney County

HARNEY DISTRICT HOSPITAL, 557 West Washington Street, Zip 97720–1497; tel. 503/573–7281; David L. Harman, Administrator **A**9 10 **F**7 17 19 22 28 30 40 44 49 56 70 71 **P**5

| | 16 | 10 | 36 | 457 | 3 | 16899 | 61 | 4658 | 2060 | 59 |

CLACKAMAS—Clackamas County

✠ KAISER SUNNYSIDE MEDICAL CENTER, 10180 S.E. Sunnyside Road, Zip 97015–9303; tel. 503/652–2880; Kathleen S. Wegener, Chief Executive Officer **A**1 2 10 **F**2 3 4 7 8 9 10 11 12 13 16 18 19 20 21 22 23 24 26 27 28 29 30 31 32 33 34 35 37 38 39 40 41 42 43 44 45 46 47 48 49 50 52 53 54 55 56 57 58 59 60 61 63 64 65 66 67 69 70 71 72 73 74 **S** Kaiser Foundation Hospitals, Oakland, CA

| | 23 | 10 | 178 | 11794 | 122 | 271673 | 1633 | — | — | 1142 |

COOS BAY—Coos County

✠ BAY AREA HOSPITAL, 1775 Thompson Road, Zip 97420–2198; tel. 541/269–8111; Dale Jessup, President and Chief Executive Officer **A**1 2 9 10 **F**7 8 11 12 14 16 17 19 21 22 23 28 29 30 31 32 33 34 35 37 39 40 41 42 44 45 46 49 52 53 54 56 60 65 67 70 71 **P**5

| | 16 | 10 | 114 | 7630 | 77 | 28679 | 608 | 51652 | 25959 | 635 |

COQUILLE—Coos County

COQUILLE VALLEY HOSPITAL, 940 East Fifth Street, Zip 97423; tel. 541/396–3101; Edna J. Cotner, Administrator **A**9 10 **F**7 8 15 16 22 32 40 44 67 71 **P**5

| | 16 | 10 | 20 | 475 | 4 | 9140 | 49 | 4040 | 1722 | 80 |

CORVALLIS—Benton County

✠ GOOD SAMARITAN HOSPITAL CORVALLIS, 3600 N.W. Samaritan Drive, Zip 97330, Mailing Address: P.O. Box 1068, Zip 97339; tel. 541/757–5111; Larry A. Mullins, President and Chief Executive Officer **A**1 2 9 10 **F**4 7 8 10 12 14 15 16 17 19 20 21 22 23 29 30 31 32 34 35 37 39 40 41 42 43 44 45 46 49 51 52 54 55 56 57 58 60 63 65 66 67 70 71 73 74 **P**6

| | 23 | 10 | 127 | 6624 | 74 | 170598 | 1059 | 70986 | 34891 | 631 |

DALLAS—Polk County

□ VALLEY COMMUNITY HOSPITAL, 550 S.E. Clay Street, Zip 97338, Mailing Address: P.O. Box 378, Zip 97338; tel. 503/623–8301; Stephen A. Bowles, President **A**1 9 10 **F**3 7 12 14 15 17 19 21 23 35 40 44 49 66 70 71 73

| | 23 | 10 | 44 | 1379 | 12 | 26300 | 177 | 13503 | 7520 | 192 |

ENTERPRISE—Wallowa County

★ WALLOWA MEMORIAL HOSPITAL, 401 East First Street, Zip 97828, Mailing Address: P.O. Box 460, Zip 97828; tel. 541/426–3111; Kim Dahlman, Chief Executive Officer (Total facility includes 32 beds in nursing home–type unit) (Nonreporting) **A**9 10

| | 16 | 10 | 55 | — | — | — | — | — | — | — |

EUGENE—Lane County

✠ △ SACRED HEART MEDICAL CENTER, 1255 Hilyard Street, Zip 97401, Mailing Address: P.O. Box 10905, Zip 97440; tel. 541/686–7300; Judy Hodgson, Administrator **A**1 2 7 9 10 **F**4 7 8 10 11 12 14 15 16 17 19 21 22 24 25 26 28 29 30 32 33 34 35 37 38 40 41 42 43 44 45 48 49 51 52 56 60 61 65 67 70 71 72 73 74 **P**6 **S** PeaceHealth, Bellevue, WA
Web address: www.peacehealth.com

| | 21 | 10 | 395 | 19788 | 240 | 212567 | 2354 | 215928 | 83720 | 2784 |

Hospital, Address, Telephone, Administrator, Approval, Facility, and Physician Codes, Health Care System, Network	Classi-fication Codes		Utilization Data					Expense (thousands) of dollars		
★ American Hospital Association (AHA) membership □ Joint Commission on Accreditation of Healthcare Organizations (JCAHO) accreditation + American Osteopathic Healthcare Association (AOHA) membership ○ American Osteopathic Association (AOA) accreditation △ Commission on Accreditation of Rehabilitation Facilities (CARF) accreditation Control codes 61, 63, 64, 71, 72 and 73 indicate hospitals listed by AOHA, but not registered by AHA. For definition of numerical codes, see page A4	Control	Service	Staffed Beds	Admissions	Census	Outpatient Visits	Births	Total	Payroll	Personnel
SERENITY LANE, 616 East 16th, Zip 97401; tel. 541/687–1110; Neil H. McNaughton, Executive Director and Administrator (Nonreporting)	23	82	55	—	—	—	—	—	—	—
FLORENCE—Lane County										
✚ PEACE HARBOR HOSPITAL, 400 Ninth Street, Zip 97439, Mailing Address: P.O. Box 580, Zip 97439; tel. 541/997–8412; James Barnhart, Administrator **A**1 9 10 **F**7 8 14 15 16 19 21 22 30 32 33 35 37 40 44 49 65 70 71 73 **P**6 **S** PeaceHealth, Bellevue, WA	21	10	21	1238	12	37964	74	14365	6622	158
FOREST GROVE—Washington County										
TUALITY FOREST GROVE HOSPITAL See Tuality Healthcare, Hillsboro										
GOLD BEACH—Curry County										
CURRY GENERAL HOSPITAL, 94220 Fourth Street, Zip 97444–9990; tel. 541/247–6621; Randall J. Scholten, Chief Executive Officer **A**9 10 **F**7 8 13 14 15 16 17 19 25 27 28 30 34 40 44 46 51 56 67 70 71 72 73 74 **P**1	16	10	24	516	5	14981	96	4946	2327	93
GRANTS PASS—Josephine County										
✚ THREE RIVERS COMMUNITY HOSPITAL AND HEALTH CENTER, (Includes Dimmick Campus, 715 N.W. Dimmick Street, tel. 541/476–6831; Washington Campus, 1505 N.W. Washington Boulevard, Zip 97526; tel. 541/479–7531), 715 N.W. Dimmick Street, Zip 97526–1596; tel. 541/476–6831; Paul Janke, Chief Operating Officer (Nonreporting) **A**1 9 10 **S** Asante Health System, Medford, OR	23	10	150	—	—	—	—	—	—	—
GRESHAM—Multnomah County										
✚ LEGACY MOUNT HOOD MEDICAL CENTER, 24800 S.E. Stark, Zip 97030–0154; tel. 503/667–1122; Thomas S. Parker, Site Administrator **A**1 2 9 10 **F**2 3 4 7 8 9 10 11 12 13 14 15 16 17 18 19 21 22 23 24 25 26 28 29 30 31 32 33 34 35 37 38 39 40 41 42 43 44 45 46 47 48 49 50 51 52 53 54 55 56 57 58 59 60 61 63 64 65 67 68 70 71 72 73 74 **S** Legacy Health System, Portland, OR **Web address:** www.legacyhealth.org	23	10	86	3358	28	44344	685	28630	12946	351
HEPPNER—Morrow County										
PIONEER MEMORIAL HOSPITAL, 564 East Pioneer Drive, Zip 97836, Mailing Address: P.O. Box 9, Zip 97836; tel. 541/676–9133; Sheila Dahlman, Interim Administrator (Total facility includes 32 beds in nursing home–type unit) **A**10 **F**11 20 22 25 32 64 70 71	16	10	43	156	27	5989	—	4931	2543	73
HERMISTON—Umatilla County										
✚ GOOD SHEPHERD COMMUNITY HOSPITAL, 610 N.W. 11th Street, Zip 97838–9696; tel. 541/567–6483; Dennis E. Burke, President **A**1 9 10 **F**7 8 14 15 16 19 22 23 28 29 30 32 33 34 35 37 39 40 44 45 46 51 65 67 70 71 73 **P**5 6	23	10	45	2453	21	42096	434	19549	8810	264
HILLSBORO—Washington County										
✚ TUALITY HEALTHCARE, (Includes Tuality Community Hospital, 335 S.E. Eighth Avenue, Mailing Address: P.O. Box 309, Zip 97123; tel. 503/681–1111; Tuality Forest Grove Hospital, 1809 Maple Street, Forest Grove, Zip 97116–1995; tel. 503/357–2173), 335 S.E. Eighth Avenue, Zip 97123; tel. 503/681–1111; Richard Stenson, President and Chief Executive Officer (Total facility includes 18 beds in nursing home–type unit) **A**1 9 10 **F**3 4 7 8 10 12 13 14 16 17 19 21 22 23 24 25 26 27 28 29 30 32 33 34 35 37 39 40 41 42 44 45 49 52 57 58 59 64 65 66 67 71 72 73 74 **P**1 6 7 **Web address:** www.tuality.com	23	10	129	6910	71	128571	1396	66889	28624	799
HOOD RIVER—Hood River County										
✚ HOOD RIVER MEMORIAL HOSPITAL, 13th and May Streets, Zip 97031, Mailing Address: P.O. Box 149, Zip 97031; tel. 541/386–3911; Larry Bowe, JD, Chief Executive Officer **A**1 9 10 **F**1 3 7 8 11 15 16 19 20 21 22 24 29 31 32 33 34 35 37 40 41 42 44 62 65 67 70 71 72 73 **P**8 **S** Sisters of Providence Health System, Seattle, WA	23	10	31	1411	11	37719	359	15013	6457	220
JOHN DAY—Grant County										
★ BLUE MOUNTAIN HOSPITAL, 170 Ford Road, Zip 97845; tel. 541/575–1311; Robert Houser, Chief Executive Officer (Total facility includes 52 beds in nursing home–type unit) **A**9 10 **F**1 7 8 11 19 28 32 34 37 39 40 44 45 48 49 56 64 65 66 67 70 71 **P**5 8 **S** Brim Healthcare, Inc., Brentwood, TN	16	10	73	491	43	15651	60	6660	3102	114
KLAMATH FALLS—Klamath County										
✚ MERLE WEST MEDICAL CENTER, 2865 Daggett Street, Zip 97601–1180; tel. 541/882–6311; Paul R. Stewart, President and Chief Executive Officer (Total facility includes 107 beds in nursing home–type unit) **A**1 2 3 9 10 **F**4 6 7 8 10 12 15 16 17 19 20 21 22 23 24 28 30 31 32 35 37 40 41 42 44 49 51 52 56 58 60 62 63 64 65 66 67 70 71 72 73 **P**6 8 **Web address:** www.mwmc.org	23	10	238	6621	141	148297	855	61400	23314	798
LA GRANDE—Union County										
✚ GRANDE RONDE HOSPITAL, 900 Sunset Drive, Zip 97850, Mailing Address: P.O. Box 3290, Zip 97850; tel. 541/963–8421; James A. Mattes, President (Total facility includes 13 beds in nursing home–type unit) **A**1 9 10 **F**7 8 12 14 15 16 19 21 22 24 32 33 35 37 39 40 41 42 44 49 63 64 65 66 67 70 71 73 **P**1	23	10	62	2038	24	36546	299	21417	10066	298
LAKEVIEW—Lake County										
LAKE DISTRICT HOSPITAL, 700 South J Street, Zip 97630–1679; tel. 503/947–2114; Richard T. Moore, Administrator (Total facility includes 47 beds in nursing home–type unit) (Nonreporting) **A**9 10	16	10	68	—	—	—	—	—	—	—
LEBANON—Linn County										
✚ LEBANON COMMUNITY HOSPITAL, 525 North Santiam Highway, Zip 97355, Mailing Address: P.O. Box 739, Zip 97355–0739; tel. 541/258–2101; Steven W. Jasperson, Executive Vice President Operations **A**1 9 10 **F**6 7 8 12 14 15 19 22 24 28 29 32 33 34 35 37 40 41 44 45 46 49 62 65 67 70 71 73 **P**6	23	10	49	3640	33	61324	314	24931	12345	507

Hospital, Address, Telephone, Administrator, Approval, Facility, and Physician Codes, Health Care System, Network	Classi-fication Codes		Utilization Data					Expense (thousands) of dollars		
★ American Hospital Association (AHA) membership □ Joint Commission on Accreditation of Healthcare Organizations (JCAHO) accreditation + American Osteopathic Healthcare Association (AOHA) membership ○ American Osteopathic Association (AOA) accreditation △ Commission on Accreditation of Rehabilitation Facilities (CARF) accreditation Control codes 61, 63, 64, 71, 72 and 73 indicate hospitals listed by AOHA, but not registered by AHA. For definition of numerical codes, see page A4	Control	Service	Staffed Beds	Admissions	Census	Outpatient Visits	Births	Total	Payroll	Personnel

LINCOLN CITY—Lincoln County

☒ NORTH LINCOLN HOSPITAL, 3043 N.E. 28th Street, Zip 97367–4523, Mailing Address: P.O. Box 767, Zip 97367–0767; tel. 541/994–3661; David C. Bigelow, Chief Executive Officer **A**1 10 **F**7 8 19 21 22 23 28 30 32 33 35 37 40 44 49 65 67 70 71 73 **P**5	16	10	30	1348	12	66920	190	18822	10127	272

MADRAS—Jefferson County

★ MOUNTAIN VIEW HOSPITAL DISTRICT, 470 N.E. A Street, Zip 97741; tel. 541/475–3882; Eric Alexander, Interim Administrator (Total facility includes 68 beds in nursing home–type unit) (Nonreporting) **A**9 10	16	10	102	—	—	—	—	—	—	—

MCMINNVILLE—Yamhill County

☒ WILLIAMETTE VALLEY MEDICAL CENTER, (Formerly Columbia Williamette Valley Medical Center), 2700 Three Mile Lane, Zip 97128–6498; tel. 503/472–6131; Rosemari Davis, Chief Executive Officer (Nonreporting) **A**1 9 10 **S** Triad Hospitals, Inc., Dallas, TX **Web address:** www.columbia.net	33	10	67	—	—	—	—	—	—	—

MEDFORD—Jackson County

☒ PROVIDENCE MEDFORD MEDICAL CENTER, 1111 Crater Lake Avenue, Zip 97504–6241; tel. 541/732–5000; Charles T. Wright, Chief Executive, Southern Oregon Service Area **A**1 2 9 10 **F**1 4 7 8 10 12 13 14 15 16 17 19 22 23 26 27 28 29 30 31 32 33 34 35 37 39 40 41 42 44 45 46 48 49 56 63 65 67 70 71 73 74 **P**4 5 6 7 **S** Sisters of Providence Health System, Seattle, WA **Web address:** www.providence.org	21	10	117	5450	60	298827	532	55310	25832	701
☒ ROGUE VALLEY MEDICAL CENTER, 2825 East Barnett Road, Zip 97504–8332; tel. 541/608–4900; Mark W. Folger, FACHE, Senior Vice President (Nonreporting) **A**1 2 9 10 **S** Asante Health System, Medford, OR	23	10	249	—	—	—	—	—	—	—

MILWAUKIE—Clackamas County

☒ PROVIDENCE MILWAUKIE HOSPITAL, 10150 S.E. 32nd Avenue, Zip 97222–6593; tel. 503/513–8300; Janice Burger, Operations Administrator (Total facility includes 29 beds in nursing home–type unit) **A**1 2 9 10 **F**1 2 3 4 5 7 8 9 10 11 12 14 15 16 17 19 20 22 23 24 26 29 31 32 33 34 35 37 38 39 40 41 42 43 44 48 49 50 51 52 53 54 55 56 57 58 59 60 62 64 65 66 67 68 70 71 72 73 74 **P**5 6 **S** Sisters of Providence Health System, Seattle, WA	21	10	56	3276	35	113677	398	28670	11263	322

NEWBERG—Yamhill County

☒ PROVIDENCE NEWBERG HOSPITAL, 501 Villa Road, Zip 97132; tel. 503/537–1555; Mark W. Meinert, CHE, Chief Executive, Yamhill Service Area **A**1 9 10 **F**1 7 8 11 12 13 14 15 16 17 19 21 22 26 27 28 29 32 33 35 39 40 41 42 44 45 49 65 67 70 71 72 73 74 **P**5 **S** Sisters of Providence Health System, Seattle, WA	21	10	35	1335	11	72492	232	16276	7448	206

NEWPORT—Lincoln County

☒ PACIFIC COMMUNITIES HEALTH DISTRICT, 930 S.W. Abbey Street, Zip 97365–4820, Mailing Address: P.O. Box 945, Zip 97365–4820; tel. 541/265–2244; Michael R. Fraser, Administrator (Nonreporting) **A**1 10	16	10	41	—	—	—	—	—	—	—

ONTARIO—Malheur County

☒ HOLY ROSARY MEDICAL CENTER, 351 S.W. Ninth Street, Zip 97914–2693; tel. 541/881–7000; Bruce Jensen, Chief Executive Officer and Team Leader **A**1 9 10 **F**7 8 11 14 16 19 20 21 22 25 28 30 31 32 33 35 39 40 41 42 44 45 46 49 63 65 66 70 71 72 73 **P**5 **S** Catholic Health Initiatives, Denver, CO	21	10	74	3757	33	48571	694	29239	11328	375

OREGON CITY—Clackamas County

☒ WILLAMETTE FALLS HOSPITAL, 1500 Division Street, Zip 97045–1597; tel. 503/656–1631; Robert A. Steed, President **A**1 2 9 10 **F**7 8 15 16 19 21 22 25 29 30 32 33 34 35 37 39 40 41 42 44 45 49 51 65 66 67 71 72 73 **P**5 8	23	10	91	5839	42	60732	1058	45870	22326	429

PENDLETON—Umatilla County

EASTERN OREGON PSYCHIATRIC CENTER, 2575 Westgate, Zip 97801; tel. 541/276–4511; Maxine Stone, Interim Superintendent (Nonreporting) **A**10	12	22	60	—	—	—	—	—	—	—
☒ ST. ANTHONY HOSPITAL, 1601 S.E. Court Avenue, Zip 97801–3297; tel. 541/276–5121; Jeffrey S. Drop, President and Chief Executive Officer **A**1 2 9 10 **F**7 8 11 12 14 15 17 19 20 21 22 23 24 26 27 28 29 30 32 33 34 35 37 39 40 41 42 44 46 49 51 63 65 66 67 70 71 73 **P**5 **S** Catholic Health Initiatives, Denver, CO	21	10	49	2022	19	21704	454	22625	9370	302

PORTLAND—Multnomah County

☒ ADVENTIST MEDICAL CENTER, 10123 S.E. Market, Zip 97216–2599; tel. 503/257–2500; Deryl L. Jones, President **A**1 2 3 9 10 **F**2 3 4 7 8 10 12 14 15 16 17 19 21 22 23 24 28 29 30 32 33 34 35 37 39 40 41 42 44 45 46 49 52 53 54 55 56 57 58 59 60 61 65 66 67 71 72 73 74 **P**5 7 **S** Adventist Health, Roseville, CA **Web address:** www.adventisthealthnw.com	21	10	214	9546	113	101455	1421	99698	46654	1479
DOERNBECHER CHILDREN'S HOSPITAL See OHSU Hospital										
★ ○ EASTMORELAND HOSPITAL, 2900 S.E. Steele Street, Zip 97202; tel. 503/234–0411; J. Phillip Young, Chief Executive Officer (Nonreporting) **A**9 10 11 12 13 **S** New American Healthcare Corporation, Brentwood, TN	33	10	77	—	—	—	—	—	—	—
GOOD SAMARITAN HOSPITAL AND MEDICAL CENTER See Legacy Good Samaritan Hospital and Medical Center										
☒ △ LEGACY EMANUEL HOSPITAL AND HEALTH CENTER, 2801 North Gantenbein Avenue, Zip 97227–1674; tel. 503/413–2200; Stephani White, Vice President and Site Administrator **A**1 3 5 7 9 10 **F**2 3 4 7 8 9 10 11 12 13 14 16 17 18 19 21 22 23 24 25 26 28 29 30 31 32 33 34 35 38 39 40 41 42 43 44 45 46 47 48 49 50 51 52 53 54 55 56 57 58 59 60 61 63 64 65 67 68 70 71 72 73 74 **S** Legacy Health System, Portland, OR **Web address:** www.legacyhealth.org	23	10	359	18060	239	220395	2380	186763	86652	2360

Hospital, Address, Telephone, Administrator, Approval, Facility, and Physician Codes, Health Care System, Network	Classi-fication Codes		Utilization Data					Expense (thousands) of dollars		
★ American Hospital Association (AHA) membership □ Joint Commission on Accreditation of Healthcare Organizations (JCAHO) accreditation + American Osteopathic Healthcare Association (AOHA) membership ○ American Osteopathic Association (AOA) accreditation △ Commission on Accreditation of Rehabilitation Facilities (CARF) accreditation Control codes 61, 63, 64, 71, 72 and 73 indicate hospitals listed by AOHA, but not registered by AHA. For definition of numerical codes, see page A4	Control	Service	Staffed Beds	Admissions	Census	Outpatient Visits	Births	Total	Payroll	Personnel
⊠ LEGACY GOOD SAMARITAN HOSPITAL AND MEDICAL CENTER, (Includes Good Samaritan Hospital and Medical Center; Rehabilitation Institute of Oregon), 1015 N.W. 22nd Avenue, Zip 97210; tel. 503/413–7711 **A**1 2 3 5 9 10 **F**2 3 4 7 8 9 10 11 12 13 14 15 16 17 18 19 21 22 23 24 25 26 28 29 30 31 32 33 34 35 37 38 39 40 41 42 43 44 45 46 47 48 49 50 51 52 53 54 55 56 57 58 59 60 61 63 64 65 67 68 70 71 72 73 74 **S** Legacy Health System, Portland, OR **Web address:** www.legacyhealth.org	23	10	294	12151	173	243080	1579	150009	61631	1437
⊠ OHSU HOSPITAL, (Formerly Oregon Health Sciences University Hospital), (Includes Doernbecher Children's Hospital), 3181 S.W. Sam Jackson Park Road, Zip 97201–3098; tel. 503/494–8311; Roy G. Vinyard, II, President and Chief Executive Officeer **A**1 2 3 5 8 9 10 **F**3 4 5 7 8 10 11 12 13 14 15 16 17 18 19 20 21 22 23 24 25 26 28 29 30 31 32 33 34 35 37 38 39 40 41 42 43 44 45 46 47 49 51 52 53 54 55 56 57 58 60 61 63 65 66 67 68 69 70 71 72 73 74 **P**6 **Web address:** www.ohsu.edu	16	10	352	20478	288	411672	2429	337377	125465	3528
OREGON HEALTH SCIENCES UNIVERSITY HOSPITAL See OHSU Hospital										
□ PACIFIC GATEWAY HOSPITAL AND COUNSELING CENTER, 1345 S.E. Harney, Zip 97202; tel. 503/234–5353; Robert Marshall, Chief Executive Officer **A**1 10 **F**2 12 14 15 16 17 52 53 54 55 56 57 64 65 **P**8 **S** Behavioral Healthcare Corporation, Nashville, TN	33	22	66	1255	30	0	0	5393	3426	80
⊠ △ PROVIDENCE PORTLAND MEDICAL CENTER, 4805 N.E. Glisan Street, Zip 97213–2967; tel. 503/215–1111; David T. Underriner, Operations Administrator (Total facility includes 20 beds in nursing home–type unit) **A**1 2 3 5 7 9 10 **F**1 3 4 5 6 7 8 10 11 12 14 15 16 17 18 19 21 22 23 24 25 26 27 28 29 30 31 32 33 34 35 37 38 39 40 41 42 43 44 45 48 49 50 51 52 53 54 55 56 57 58 59 60 62 64 65 66 67 68 71 72 73 74 **P**5 6 **S** Sisters of Providence Health System, Seattle, WA **Web address:** www.providence.org	21	10	380	21879	244	588470	2394	226484	91972	2506
⊠ PROVIDENCE ST. VINCENT MEDICAL CENTER, 9205 S.W. Barnes Road, Zip 97225–6661; tel. 503/216–1234; Donald Elsom, Operations Administrator **A**1 2 3 5 9 10 **F**1 3 4 5 6 7 8 10 11 12 14 15 16 17 18 19 21 22 23 24 25 26 28 29 30 31 32 33 34 35 37 38 39 40 41 42 43 44 45 46 48 49 50 51 52 53 54 56 57 58 60 62 63 64 65 66 67 68 71 72 73 74 **P**5 6 **S** Sisters of Providence Health System, Seattle, WA **Web address:** www.phsworld.phsor.org	21	10	442	25976	299	634700	5246	265381	103041	2954
REHABILITATION INSTITUTE OF OREGON See Legacy Good Samaritan Hospital and Medical Center										
⊠ SHRINERS HOSPITALS FOR CHILDREN, PORTLAND, 3101 S.W. Sam Jackson Park Road, Zip 97201; tel. 503/241–5090; Nancy Jones, Administrator (Nonreporting) **A**1 3 5 **S** Shriners Hospitals for Children, Tampa, FL	23	57	25	—	—	—	—	—	—	—
⊠ VETERANS AFFAIRS MEDICAL CENTER, 3710 S.W. U.S. Veterans Hospital Road, Zip 97201; tel. 503/220–8262; James Tuchschmidt, M.D., Chief Executive Officer (Total facility includes 72 beds in nursing home–type unit) **A**1 2 3 5 8 **F**1 2 3 4 8 10 11 12 14 16 17 19 20 21 22 23 24 25 26 27 28 29 30 31 32 33 34 35 37 39 41 42 43 44 45 46 48 49 51 52 54 55 56 57 58 59 60 63 64 65 67 68 71 73 74 **P**6 **S** Department of Veterans Affairs, Washington, DC	45	10	303	7881	220	312019	0	186680	91868	2125
⊠ WOODLAND PARK HOSPITAL, 10300 N.E. Hancock, Zip 97220; tel. 503/257–5500; J. Phillip Young, Assistant Administrator Operations (Nonreporting) **A**1 10 **S** New American Healthcare Corporation, Brentwood, TN	33	10	123	—	—	—	—	—	—	—
PRINEVILLE—Crook County										
PIONEER MEMORIAL HOSPITAL, 1201 North Elm Street, Zip 97754; tel. 541/447–6254; Donald J. Wee, Executive Director **A**9 10 **F**1 7 8 15 16 17 19 22 29 32 33 37 39 40 44 46 65 67 70 71 73 **P**5 **S** Lutheran Health Systems, Fargo, ND	23	10	30	959	9	13935	106	8946	4033	130
REDMOND—Deschutes County										
⊠ CENTRAL OREGON DISTRICT HOSPITAL, 1253 North Canal Boulevard, Zip 97756–1395; tel. 541/548–8131; James A. Diegel, CHE, Executive Director **A**1 9 10 **F**7 8 12 14 15 17 19 22 28 29 30 31 32 34 37 39 40 44 45 49 56 65 67 70 71 73 74 **P**7 **S** Lutheran Health Systems, Fargo, ND	16	10	48	2127	15	27088	332	16459	7759	217
REEDSPORT—Douglas County										
LOWER UMPQUA HOSPITAL DISTRICT, 600 Ranch Road, Zip 97467–1795; tel. 541/271–2171; Sandra Reese, Administrator (Total facility includes 28 beds in nursing home–type unit) **A**9 10 **F**7 8 11 15 19 22 26 28 32 33 35 37 40 41 44 49 64 65 70 73	16	10	49	1763	31	13763	39	8549	3759	108
ROSEBURG—Douglas County										
⊠ DOUGLAS COMMUNITY MEDICAL CENTER, 738 West Harvard Avenue, Zip 97470–2996; tel. 541/673–6641; Leslie Paul Luke, Chief Executive Officer **A**1 2 9 10 **F**7 8 9 10 11 12 14 15 16 19 21 22 28 30 32 33 35 38 39 40 41 42 43 44 47 48 49 52 53 57 58 59 60 63 64 65 70 71 74 **P**5 **S** Triad Hospitals, Inc., Dallas, TX	33	10	100	2000	26	37185	97	21720	9098	320
⊠ MERCY MEDICAL CENTER, 2700 Stewart Parkway, Zip 97470–1297; tel. 541/673–0611; Victor J. Fresolone, FACHE, President and Chief Executive Officer **A**1 2 9 10 **F**7 8 10 12 15 16 17 19 21 22 24 26 27 28 30 31 32 33 34 35 37 40 42 44 46 49 52 53 55 56 57 58 59 60 62 65 67 70 71 73 74 **S** Catholic Health Initiatives, Denver, CO **Web address:** www.mercyrose.org	21	10	103	7497	67	155625	861	46758	19100	646

Hospital, Address, Telephone, Administrator, Approval, Facility, and Physician Codes, Health Care System, Network	Classi-fication Codes		Utilization Data					Expense (thousands) of dollars		
	Control	Service	Staffed Beds	Admissions	Census	Outpatient Visits	Births	Total	Payroll	Personnel

✠ VETERANS AFFAIRS ROSEBURG HEALTHCARE SYSTEM, 913 N.W. Garden Valley Boulevard, Zip 97470–6513; tel. 541/440–1000; George Marnell, Director (Total facility includes 90 beds in nursing home–type unit) (Nonreporting) **A**1 **S** Department of Veterans Affairs, Washington, DC	45	10	229	—	—	—	—	—	—	—
SALEM—Marion County										
□ OREGON STATE HOSPITAL, 2600 Center Street N.E., Zip 97310–0530; tel. 503/945–2870; Stanley F. Mazur-Hart, Ph.D., Superintendent (Nonreporting) **A**1 3 5 10 PSYCHIATRIC MEDICINE CENTER See Salem Hospital REGIONAL REHABILITATION CENTER See Salem Hospital	12	22	546	—	—	—	—	—	—	—
✠ SALEM HOSPITAL, (Includes Psychiatric Medicine Center, 1127 Oak Street S.E., Zip 97301; Regional Rehabilitation Center, 2561 Center Street N.E., Zip 97301; tel. 503/370–5986), 665 Winter Street S.E., Zip 97301–3959, Mailing Address: Box 14001, Zip 97309–5014; tel. 503/370–5200; Dennis Noonan, President and Chief Executive Officer (Total facility includes 35 beds in nursing home–type unit) **A**1 2 9 10 **F**3 4 7 8 10 11 12 13 14 15 16 17 19 21 22 26 27 28 29 30 31 32 34 35 37 39 40 41 42 43 44 45 46 48 49 52 53 54 56 57 58 59 60 61 63 64 65 66 67 68 70 71 72 73 Web address: www.salemhospital.org	23	10	395	18205	243	242044	3599	170457	87746	2121
SEASIDE—Clatsop County										
✠ PROVIDENCE SEASIDE HOSPITAL, 725 South Wahanna Road, Zip 97138–7735; tel. 503/717–7000; Ronald Swanson, Chief Executive Officer (Total facility includes 22 beds in nursing home–type unit) **A**1 10 **F**7 8 11 12 14 15 16 19 21 22 25 27 28 30 31 32 33 36 37 39 40 41 42 44 45 49 51 64 65 67 71 73 **P**6 7 **S** Sisters of Providence Health System, Seattle, WA Web address: www.providence.org	21	10	50	1097	23	34258	156	12985	7459	159
SILVERTON—Marion County										
★ SILVERTON HOSPITAL, 342 Fairview Street, Zip 97381; tel. 503/873–1500; William E. Winter, Administrative Director (Nonreporting) **A**9 10 Web address: www.silvertonhospital.org	23	10	38	—	—	—	—	—	—	—
SPRINGFIELD—Lane County										
✠ MCKENZIE–WILLAMETTE HOSPITAL, 1460 G Street, Zip 97477–4197; tel. 541/726–4400; Roy J. Orr, President and Chief Executive Officer **A**1 9 10 **F**1 7 14 15 16 17 19 21 22 26 28 29 30 32 33 37 39 40 41 44 45 49 65 67 70 72 73 74 **P**1 5 Web address: www.mckweb.com	23	10	106	8186	62	104518	1164	53772	25987	847
STAYTON—Marion County										
✠ SANTIAM MEMORIAL HOSPITAL, 1401 North 10th Avenue, Zip 97383; tel. 503/769–2175; Terry L. Fletchall, Administrator **A**1 9 10 **F**7 8 14 15 16 19 22 27 30 34 39 40 44 49 64 65 70 71 74 Web address: www.santiamhospital.com	23	10	40	976	9	22530	141	7319	3198	95
THE DALLES—Wasco County										
✠ MID–COLUMBIA MEDICAL CENTER, 1700 East 19th Street, Zip 97058–3316; tel. 541/296–1111; Mark D. Scott, President **A**1 9 10 **F**6 7 8 10 11 12 13 15 16 17 19 22 23 24 25 28 29 30 31 32 33 35 37 39 40 41 42 44 45 61 65 67 68 71 72 73 74 **P**5 8	23	10	49	2820	24	68586	331	27587	11996	425
TILLAMOOK—Tillamook County										
✠ TILLAMOOK COUNTY GENERAL HOSPITAL, 1000 Third Street, Zip 97141–3430; tel. 503/842–4444; Wendell Hesseltine, President **A**1 9 10 **F**7 14 15 16 19 22 28 30 32 33 35 37 41 44 65 67 71 **S** Adventist Health, Roseville, CA	21	10	30	1404	14	39490	128	18385	8438	231
TUALATIN—Clackamas County										
✠ LEGACY MERIDIAN PARK HOSPITAL, 19300 S.W. 65th Avenue, Zip 97062–9741; tel. 503/692–1212; Jeff Cushing, Vice President and Site Administrator **A**1 2 9 10 **F**2 3 4 7 8 9 10 11 12 13 14 15 16 17 18 19 21 22 23 24 25 26 28 29 30 31 32 33 34 35 37 38 39 40 41 42 43 44 45 46 47 48 49 50 51 52 53 54 55 56 57 58 59 60 61 63 64 65 67 68 70 71 72 73 74 **S** Legacy Health System, Portland, OR Web address: www.legacyhealth.org	23	10	116	7699	66	62520	1466	48611	20340	543

PENNSYLVANIA

Resident population 12,001 (in thousands)
Resident population in metro areas 84.9%
Birth rate per 1,000 population 12.6
65 years and over 15.8%
Percent of persons without health insurance 9.5%

Hospital, Address, Telephone, Administrator, Approval, Facility, and Physician Codes, Health Care System, Network	Classi-fication Codes		Utilization Data					Expense (thousands) of dollars		
★ American Hospital Association (AHA) membership □ Joint Commission on Accreditation of Healthcare Organizations (JCAHO) accreditation + American Osteopathic Healthcare Association (AOHA) membership ○ American Osteopathic Association (AOA) accreditation △ Commission on Accreditation of Rehabilitation Facilities (CARF) accreditation Control codes 61, 63, 64, 71, 72 and 73 indicate hospitals listed by AOHA, but not registered by AHA. For definition of numerical codes, see page A4	Control	Service	Staffed Beds	Admissions	Census	Outpatient Visits	Births	Total	Payroll	Personnel

ABINGTON—Montgomery County

⊠ ABINGTON MEMORIAL HOSPITAL, 1200 Old York Road, Zip 19001–3720; tel. 215/481–2000; Richard L. Jones, Jr., President and Chief Executive Officer **A**1 2 3 5 9 10 **F**1 4 7 8 10 11 14 15 16 17 19 20 21 22 23 24 25 26 27 28 29 30 31 32 33 34 35 36 37 38 39 40 41 42 43 44 46 47 48 49 51 52 53 56 57 58 59 60 61 63 64 65 66 67 68 70 71 73 74
Web address: www.amh.org — 23 10 424 22675 320 332147 3517 270563 131334 3215

ALIQUIPPA—Beaver County

□ UPMC BEAVER VALLEY, 2500 Hospital Drive, Zip 15001–2123; tel. 724/857–1212; Thomas P. Timcho, President (Total facility includes 16 beds in nursing home–type unit) **A**1 9 10 **F**1 2 3 4 5 6 7 8 10 11 12 13 14 15 16 17 18 19 20 21 22 23 24 25 26 27 28 29 30 31 32 33 34 35 36 37 38 39 40 41 42 43 44 45 46 47 48 49 50 51 52 53 54 55 56 57 58 59 60 61 62 63 64 65 66 67 68 70 71 72 73 74 **P**1 6 7 8 **S** UPMC Health System, Pittsburgh, PA — 23 10 104 4858 83 16230 0 35685 16456 510

ALLENTOWN—Lehigh County

□ ALLENTOWN STATE HOSPITAL, 1600 Hanover Avenue, Zip 18103–2408; tel. 610/740–3200; Gregory M. Smith, Chief Executive Officer (Nonreporting) **A**1 9 10 — 12 22 415 — — — — — — —

□ △ GOOD SHEPHERD REHABILITATION HOSPITAL, 543 St. John Street, Zip 18103–3295; tel. 610/776–3120; Sara Gammon, President and Chief Executive Officer **A**1 7 9 10 **F**2 5 10 12 14 15 16 17 19 21 22 23 27 34 35 45 48 49 50 52 54 65 67 71 73 **P**6
Web address: www.goodshepherdrehab.org — 23 46 75 1715 65 257924 0 30494 — 479

⊠ LEHIGH VALLEY HOSPITAL, Cedar Crest Boulevard and I–78, Zip 18103, Mailing Address: P.O. Box 689, Zip 18105–1556; tel. 610/402–8000; Elliot J. Sussman, M.D., President and Chief Executive Officer (Total facility includes 52 beds in nursing home–type unit) **A**1 2 3 5 8 9 10 **F**4 5 6 7 8 9 10 11 12 13 14 15 16 17 18 19 20 21 22 23 24 26 28 29 30 31 32 33 34 35 36 37 38 39 40 41 42 43 44 45 46 49 51 52 53 54 55 56 57 58 59 60 61 63 64 65 66 67 68 70 71 73 74 **P**3 5 7 8
Web address: www.lvhhn.org — 23 10 605 31031 474 410297 3519 340992 143571 3450

⊠ SACRED HEART HOSPITAL, 421 Chew Street, Zip 18102–3490; tel. 610/776–4500; Joseph M. Cimerola, FACHE, President and Chief Executive Officer (Total facility includes 22 beds in nursing home–type unit) **A**1 2 3 5 9 10 **F**4 6 7 8 10 11 12 13 14 15 16 17 19 20 21 22 24 25 26 27 28 29 30 31 32 33 34 35 37 38 39 40 41 42 43 44 45 46 49 51 52 54 55 56 57 58 59 60 63 64 65 67 68 71 73 74 **P**6 8
Web address: www.shh.org — 23 10 241 8055 140 150879 482 70338 29695 1206

ST LUKE'S HOSPITAL–ALLENTOWN CAMPUS See St. Luke's Hospital and Health Network, Bethlehem

ALTOONA—Blair County

ALTOONA CENTER, 1515 Fourth Street, Zip 16601–4595; tel. 814/946–6900; Barry C. Benford, Director (Nonreporting) — 12 62 138 — — — — — — —

⊠ ○ ALTOONA HOSPITAL, 620 Howard Avenue, Zip 16601–4899; tel. 814/946–2011; James W. Barner, President and Chief Executive Officer **A**1 2 3 5 9 10 11 12 **F**2 3 4 7 8 10 11 12 14 15 16 18 19 22 23 25 26 28 30 32 33 35 37 40 41 42 43 44 45 46 52 53 54 55 56 57 58 59 60 71 73 74 **P**1
Web address: www.altoonahosp.org — 23 10 189 12995 183 326509 1266 125178 55124 1464

⊠ BON SECOURS–HOLY FAMILY REGIONAL HEALTH SYSTEM, 2500 Seventh Avenue, Zip 16602–2099; tel. 814/944–1681; Barbara H. Biehner, Chief Executive Officer (Total facility includes 17 beds in nursing home–type unit) **A**1 2 9 10 **F**7 8 10 14 15 16 17 19 21 22 26 27 28 30 31 32 33 35 37 40 41 42 44 45 46 48 49 52 54 57 59 60 64 65 66 67 71 73 **P**5 8 **S** Bon Secours Health System, Inc., Marriottsville, MD — 23 10 161 5464 101 110367 354 48498 21382 601

□ △ HEALTHSOUTH REHABILITATION HOSPITAL OF ALTOONA, 2005 Valley View Boulevard, Zip 16602–4598; tel. 814/944–3535; Scott Filler, Administrator (Nonreporting) **A**1 7 9 10 **S** HEALTHSOUTH Corporation, Birmingham, AL — 33 46 70 — — — — — — —

⊠ JAMES E. VAN ZANDT VETERANS AFFAIRS MEDICAL CENTER, 2907 Pleasant Valley Boulevard, Zip 16602–4377; tel. 814/943–8164; Gerald L. Williams, Director and Chief Executive Officer (Total facility includes 40 beds in nursing home–type unit) **A**1 9 **F**3 8 12 14 15 16 17 19 20 22 25 26 27 28 29 30 31 32 33 34 37 39 44 45 46 49 51 54 58 64 65 67 71 73 74 **P**6 **S** Department of Veterans Affairs, Washington, DC — 45 10 78 1734 73 86376 0 31434 18472 351

AMBLER—Montgomery County

□ HORSHAM CLINIC, 722 East Butler Pike, Zip 19002–2398; tel. 215/643–7800; David A. Baron, D.O., Medical Director (Nonreporting) **A**1 5 9 10 **S** Universal Health Services, Inc., King of Prussia, PA — 33 22 138 — — — — — — —

Hospital, Address, Telephone, Administrator, Approval, Facility, and Physician Codes, Health Care System, Network	Classi-fication Codes		Utilization Data					Expense (thousands) of dollars		
★ American Hospital Association (AHA) membership □ Joint Commission on Accreditation of Healthcare Organizations (JCAHO) accreditation + American Osteopathic Healthcare Association (AOHA) membership ○ American Osteopathic Association (AOA) accreditation △ Commission on Accreditation of Rehabilitation Facilities (CARF) accreditation Control codes 61, 63, 64, 71, 72 and 73 indicate hospitals listed by AOHA, but not registered by AHA. For definition of numerical codes, see page A4	Control	Service	Staffed Beds	Admissions	Census	Outpatient Visits	Births	Total	Payroll	Personnel

ASHLAND—Schuylkill County

□ ASHLAND REGIONAL MEDICAL CENTER, 101 Broad Street, Zip 17921–2198; tel. 717/875–2000; Michael J. Callan, Sr., Chief Executive Officer (Total facility includes 40 beds in nursing home–type unit) **A**1 9 10 **F**8 15 16 17 19 20 21 22 24 26 27 28 29 30 32 33 34 35 37 39 41 42 44 45 46 49 63 64 65 66 67 71 73 74	23	10	116	2958	80	28029	0	14936	7446	322

BALA CYNWYD—Montgomery County

✠ MERCY HEALTH SYSTEM OF SOUTHEASTERN PENNSYLVANIA, (Includes Mercy Fitzgerald Hospital, 1500 South Lansdowne Avenue, Darby, Zip 19023; tel. 610/237–4020; Mercy Hospital of Philadelphia, 5301 Cedar Avenue, Philadelphia, Zip 19143; tel. 215/748–9000), One Bala Plaza, Suite 402, Zip 19004–1401; tel. 610/660–7440; Plato A. Marinakos, President and Chief Executive Officer (Total facility includes 38 beds in nursing home–type unit) **A**1 2 3 5 9 10 **F**2 4 7 8 10 11 12 14 15 16 17 18 19 22 23 25 28 29 30 31 32 33 34 35 36 37 38 39 40 41 42 44 46 48 49 52 54 55 56 57 58 60 64 65 67 71 73 74 **P**1 2 4 5 6 8 **Web address:** www.mercyhealth.org	21	10	535	24652	390	99720	1624	184812	94592	2016

BEAVER—Beaver County

THE MEDICAL CENTER, BEAVER See Valley Medical Facilities, Sewickley

BENSALEM—Bucks County

LIVENGRIN FOUNDATION, 4833 Hulmeville Road, Zip 19020–3099; tel. 215/638–5200; Richard M. Pine, President and Chief Executive Officer (Nonreporting)	23	82	76	—	—	—	—	—	—	—

BERWICK—Columbia County

✠ BERWICK HOSPITAL CENTER, 701 East 16th Street, Zip 18603–2397; tel. 570/759–5000; David R. Sirk, President and Chief Executive Officer (Total facility includes 240 beds in nursing home–type unit) (Nonreporting) **A**1 9 10 **S** Community Health Systems, Inc., Brentwood, TN	23	10	409	—	—	—	—	—	—	—

BETHLEHEM—Northampton County

✠ MUHLENBERG HOSPITAL CENTER, 2545 Schoenersville Road, Zip 18017–7384; tel. 610/861–2200; Elliot J. Sussman, M.D., President and Chief Executive Officer **A**1 9 10 **F**4 7 8 9 10 11 12 13 14 15 16 17 19 20 21 22 25 26 27 28 29 30 32 33 34 35 37 38 39 40 41 42 43 44 45 46 47 48 49 52 53 56 57 58 59 60 62 63 64 65 67 68 70 71 73 74 **P**8	23	10	148	6299	104	116584	0	47177	20794	435
□ + ○ △ ST. LUKE'S HOSPITAL AND HEALTH NETWORK, (Includes St Luke's Hospital–Allentown Campus, 1736 Hamilton Street, Allentown, Zip 18104–5656; tel. 610/770–8300; John M. Sherwood, FACHE, President; St. Luke's Quakertown Hospital, 1021 Park Avenue, Quakertown, Zip 18951–9003; tel. 215/538–4510), 801 Ostrum Street, Zip 18015–1014; tel. 610/954–4000; Richard A. Anderson, President and Chief Executive Officer (Total facility includes 18 beds in nursing home–type unit) **A**1 2 3 5 6 7 8 9 10 11 12 13 **F**3 4 7 8 10 11 12 13 14 15 16 17 19 21 22 23 24 25 26 28 29 30 31 32 33 34 35 37 38 39 40 41 42 43 44 45 49 51 52 54 58 59 60 61 63 64 65 67 71 72 73 74 **P**8 **Web address:** www.slhn–lehighvalley.org	23	10	549	24630	362	402971	2637	215793	100029	2782

BLOOMSBURG—Columbia County

✠ BLOOMSBURG HOSPITAL, 549 East Fair Street, Zip 17815–0340; tel. 570/387–2100; Robert J. Spinelli, Administrator and Chief Executive Officer **A**1 9 10 **F**2 3 7 8 14 15 17 19 21 22 27 28 29 30 32 33 34 35 37 40 41 42 44 46 52 54 55 56 58 59 63 65 66 67 71 73	23	10	117	3578	43	86589	523	25574	10404	374

BRADDOCK—Allegheny County

□ UPMC BRADDOCK, 400 Holland Avenue, Zip 15104–1599; tel. 412/636–5000; Margaret Priselac, R.N., Chief Operating Officer (Total facility includes 30 beds in nursing home–type unit) **A**1 9 10 **F**3 8 12 13 14 15 16 17 18 19 20 21 22 23 27 28 29 30 31 32 33 35 36 37 42 44 52 54 55 56 57 63 64 65 67 68 71 73 **P**8 **S** UPMC Health System, Pittsburgh, PA	23	10	179	6834	110	97744	0	37790	18069	573

BRADFORD—McKean County

✠ BRADFORD REGIONAL MEDICAL CENTER, 116 Interstate Parkway, Zip 16701–0218; tel. 814/368–4143; George E. Leonhardt, President and Chief Executive Officer (Total facility includes 95 beds in nursing home–type unit) (Nonreporting) **A**1 9 10	23	10	216	—	—	—	—	—	—	—

BRIDGEVILLE—Allegheny County

□ MAYVIEW STATE HOSPITAL, 1601 Mayview Road, Zip 15017–1547; tel. 412/257–6500; Shirley J. Dumpman, Superintendent **A**1 5 9 10 **F**14 20 52 57 65 73 **P**6	12	22	509	577	450	0	0	60354	36215	968

BRISTOL—Bucks County

□ LOWER BUCKS HOSPITAL, 501 Bath Road, Zip 19007–3190; tel. 215/785–9200; Nathan Bosk, FACHE, Chief Executive Officer **A**1 9 10 **F**4 7 8 10 11 12 14 15 16 17 18 19 21 22 24 25 28 29 30 32 34 35 37 38 39 40 41 42 43 44 45 46 49 51 52 54 55 58 63 65 66 67 68 71 73 74 **P**1 5 **S** Temple University Health System, Philadelphia, PA	23	10	163	8931	112	141349	1324	68727	27334	868

BROOKVILLE—Jefferson County

✠ BROOKVILLE HOSPITAL, 100 Hospital Road, Zip 15825–1367; tel. 814/849–2312; Warren J. Bassett, FACHE, President **A**1 9 10 **F**7 8 11 14 15 16 17 19 20 21 22 28 30 32 39 40 41 44 45 49 63 65 66 68 71 73 **P**5 **Web address:** www.brookvillehospital.org	23	10	63	2106	22	63156	127	21755	8826	323

BROWNSVILLE—Fayette County

✠ BROWNSVILLE GENERAL HOSPITAL, 125 Simpson Road, Zip 15417–9699; tel. 724/785–7200; Richard D. Constantine, Chief Executive Officer (Total facility includes 21 beds in nursing home–type unit) **A**1 9 10 **F**8 15 16 17 19 21 22 23 26 28 29 30 31 34 35 37 39 41 44 45 46 49 52 53 55 57 59 64 65 67 71 **S** Quorum Health Group/Quorum Health Resources, Inc., Brentwood, TN **Web address:** www.bghlink.com	23	10	115	3226	73	44372	0	20311	9302	272

Hospital, Address, Telephone, Administrator, Approval, Facility, and Physician Codes, Health Care System, Network	Classi-fication Codes		Utilization Data					Expense (thousands) of dollars		
★ American Hospital Association (AHA) membership ☐ Joint Commission on Accreditation of Healthcare Organizations (JCAHO) accreditation + American Osteopathic Healthcare Association (AOHA) membership ○ American Osteopathic Association (AOA) accreditation △ Commission on Accreditation of Rehabilitation Facilities (CARF) accreditation Control codes 61, 63, 64, 71, 72 and 73 indicate hospitals listed by AOHA, but not registered by AHA. For definition of numerical codes, see page A4	Control	Service	Staffed Beds	Admissions	Census	Outpatient Visits	Births	Total	Payroll	Personnel

BRYN MAWR—Montgomery County

BRYN MAWR COLLEGE INFIRMARY, Bryn Mawr College Campus, Zip 19010; tel. 610/526–7360; Kay Kerr, M.D., Medical Director (Nonreporting)

| | 23 | 11 | 7 | — | — | — | — | — | — | — |

☒ BRYN MAWR HOSPITAL, 130 South Bryn Mawr Avenue, Zip 19010–3160; tel. 610/526–3000; Kenneth Hanover, President and Chief Executive Officer (Total facility includes 17 beds in nursing home–type unit) **A**1 2 3 5 9 10 **F**4 5 7 8 10 11 12 15 16 17 19 20 22 27 28 29 30 31 32 33 35 36 37 38 39 40 41 42 43 44 45 49 51 52 53 54 55 56 57 58 59 60 61 63 64 65 67 68 71 73 74 **P**1 3 5 8 **S** Jefferson Health System, Wayne, PA
Web address: www.jeffersonhealth.org

| | 23 | 10 | 300 | 14247 | 198 | 126249 | 1951 | 145994 | 54106 | 1470 |

BUTLER—Butler County

☒ BUTLER HEALTH SYSTEM, 911 East Brady Street, Zip 16001–4646; tel. 724/284–4408; Joseph A. Stewart, Chief Executive Officer (Total facility includes 19 beds in nursing home–type unit) **A**1 9 10 **F**2 3 4 7 8 10 11 12 13 14 15 16 17 19 21 22 23 24 27 28 31 32 33 35 37 40 44 46 49 52 54 56 57 63 64 65 67 71 **P**4 5 7

| | 23 | 10 | 239 | 9780 | 146 | 220270 | 922 | 66515 | 30588 | 1004 |

☒ VETERANS AFFAIRS MEDICAL CENTER, (EXTENDED CARE & PRIMARY MED), 325 New Castle Road, Zip 16001–2480; tel. 724/287–4781; Michael E. Moreland, Director (Total facility includes 106 beds in nursing home–type unit) **A**1 **F**1 3 4 8 10 14 15 16 17 19 20 21 22 23 24 26 27 28 30 31 32 34 35 37 39 41 42 43 44 45 46 49 51 52 54 56 57 58 60 64 65 67 68 71 73 74 **P**6 **S** Department of Veterans Affairs, Washington, DC
Web address: www.va.gov/station/529–butler

| | 45 | 49 | 170 | 1215 | 159 | 87263 | 0 | 43319 | 21044 | 512 |

CAMP HILL—Cumberland County

☒ HOLY SPIRIT HOSPITAL, 503 North 21st Street, Zip 17011–2288; tel. 717/763–2100; Sister Romaine Niemeyer, President **A**1 5 9 10 **F**2 3 4 7 8 10 12 15 16 17 18 19 21 22 27 28 29 30 31 32 33 34 35 37 38 39 40 41 42 44 46 49 51 52 53 54 55 56 57 58 59 60 63 65 67 68 71 73 74 **P**8
Web address: www.hsh.org

| | 21 | 10 | 265 | 12618 | 182 | 143597 | 866 | 90961 | 46979 | 1474 |

STATE CORRECTIONAL INSTITUTION AT CAMP HILL, 2500 Lisbon Road, Zip 17011, Mailing Address: P.O. Box 200, Zip 17011–0200; tel. 717/737–4531; Kathy Montag, Administrator Health Care (Nonreporting)

| | 12 | 49 | 34 | — | — | — | — | — | — | — |

CANONSBURG—Washington County

☒ ALLEGHENY UNIVERSITY HOSPITALS, CANONSBURG, (Formerly Canonsburg General Hospital), 100 Medical Boulevard, Zip 15317–9762; tel. 724/745–6100; Barbara A. Bensaia, Chief Executive Officer (Total facility includes 28 beds in nursing home–type unit) (Nonreporting) **A**1 9 10 **S** Allegheny University Hospitals–West, Pittsburgh, PA

| | 23 | 10 | 120 | — | — | — | — | — | — | — |

CARBONDALE—Lackawanna County

☒ MARIAN COMMUNITY HOSPITAL, 100 Lincoln Avenue, Zip 18407–2170; tel. 570/281–1000; Sister Jean Coughlin, President and Chief Executive Officer (Nonreporting) **A**1 9 10

| | 21 | 10 | 99 | — | — | — | — | — | — | — |

CARLISLE—Cumberland County

☒ CARLISLE HOSPITAL AND HEALTH SERVICES, (Formerly Carlisle Hospital), 246 Parker Street, Zip 17013–3618; tel. 717/249–1212; Michael J. Halstead, President and Chief Executive Officer **A**1 9 10 **F**6 7 8 9 13 15 16 17 18 19 21 22 31 32 33 34 35 37 38 39 40 41 42 44 45 46 47 49 51 52 53 54 55 56 57 58 59 60 61 62 64 65 67 70 71 72 73 74 **P**8 **S** Quorum Health Group/Quorum Health Resources, Inc., Brentwood, TN
Web address: www.chhs.org

| | 23 | 10 | 166 | 7174 | 89 | 150979 | 649 | 55568 | 25066 | 702 |

CENTRE HALL—Centre County

☐ MEADOWS PSYCHIATRIC CENTER, Mailing Address: Rural Delivery 1, Box 259, Zip 16828–9798; tel. 814/364–2161; Joseph Barszczewski, Chief Executive Officer and Managing Director **A**1 9 10 **F**15 16 52 53 54 55 56 57 58 59 **P**7 **S** Universal Health Services, Inc., King of Prussia, PA

| | 33 | 22 | 101 | 1838 | 85 | — | 0 | 16219 | 8190 | 307 |

CHAMBERSBURG—Franklin County

☒ △ CHAMBERSBURG HOSPITAL, 112 North Seventh Street, Zip 17201–6005, Mailing Address: P.O. Box 6005, Zip 17201–6005; tel. 717/267–3000; Norman B. Epstein, President (Total facility includes 18 beds in nursing home–type unit) **A**1 2 7 9 10 **F**1 2 3 7 8 10 11 12 14 15 16 17 18 19 20 21 22 23 24 25 26 27 28 29 30 31 32 33 34 35 37 38 39 40 41 42 44 45 46 47 48 49 51 52 54 55 56 57 58 59 60 63 64 65 66 67 68 69 71 73 74 **P**6 8
Web address: www.summithealth.org

| | 23 | 10 | 205 | 10843 | 150 | 189879 | 1128 | 81213 | 38440 | 1006 |

CHESTER—Delaware County

KEYSTONE CENTER, 2001 Providence Avenue, Zip 19013–5504; tel. 610/876–9000; Jimmy Patton, Chief Executive Officer and Managing Director (Nonreporting) **S** Universal Health Services, Inc., King of Prussia, PA

| | 33 | 82 | 76 | — | — | — | — | — | — | — |

CLARION—Clarion County

★ + ○ CLARION HOSPITAL, One Hospital Drive, Zip 16214–8599; tel. 814/226–9500; Donald D. Evans, President and Chief Executive Officer **A**9 10 11 12 13 **F**7 8 19 21 22 24 33 34 35 40 41 42 44 64 71 73 **P**7 **S** Quorum Health Group/Quorum Health Resources, Inc., Brentwood, TN
Web address: www.pen.com/clarionhospital

| | 23 | 10 | 86 | 3666 | 39 | 83568 | 383 | 21922 | 9927 | 369 |

☐ CLARION PSYCHIATRIC CENTER, 2 Hospital Drive, Zip 16214–9424, Mailing Address: Rural Delivery 3, Box 188, Zip 16214–9424; tel. 814/226–9545; Michael R. Keefer, CHE, Administrator and Chief Executive Officer (Nonreporting) **A**1 9 10 **S** Universal Health Services, Inc., King of Prussia, PA

| | 33 | 22 | 52 | — | — | — | — | — | — | — |

Hospital, Address, Telephone, Administrator, Approval, Facility, and Physician Codes, Health Care System, Network	Classification Codes		Utilization Data					Expense (thousands) of dollars		
	Control	Service	Staffed Beds	Admissions	Census	Outpatient Visits	Births	Total	Payroll	Personnel

★ American Hospital Association (AHA) membership
□ Joint Commission on Accreditation of Healthcare Organizations (JCAHO) accreditation
+ American Osteopathic Healthcare Association (AOHA) membership
○ American Osteopathic Association (AOA) accreditation
△ Commission on Accreditation of Rehabilitation Facilities (CARF) accreditation
Control codes 61, 63, 64, 71, 72 and 73 indicate hospitals listed by AOHA, but not registered by AHA. For definition of numerical codes, see page A4

CLARKS SUMMIT—Lackawanna County

□ CLARKS SUMMIT STATE HOSPITAL, 1451 Hillside Drive, Zip 18411–9505; tel. 717/586–2011; Thomas P. Comerford, Jr., Superintendent **A**1 9 10 **F**1 2 8 10 11 12 14 16 17 18 19 20 21 26 27 28 30 35 37 39 40 42 44 45 46 48 52 54 55 56 57 60 61 64 65 67 71 73 **P**6	12	22	428	78	249	0	0	34140	19994	507

CLEARFIELD—Clearfield County

□ CLEARFIELD HOSPITAL, 809 Turnpike Avenue, Zip 16830–1232, Mailing Address: P.O. Box 992, Zip 16830–0992; tel. 814/765–5341; Kent C. Hess, Interim Chief Executive Officer (Total facility includes 9 beds in nursing home–type unit) **A**1 9 10 **F**7 8 10 12 14 15 16 17 19 21 22 23 25 28 29 30 32 33 34 35 36 37 39 40 41 42 44 45 46 49 51 63 64 65 66 67 71 73 **Web address:** www.clearfieldhospital.org	23	10	101	4516	62	205063	467	45251	20823	588

COAL TOWNSHIP—Northumberland County

⊠ SHAMOKIN AREA COMMUNITY HOSPITAL, 4200 Hospital Road, Zip 17866–9697; tel. 570/644–4200; John Wiercinski, President and Chief Executive Officer (Total facility includes 15 beds in nursing home–type unit) **A**1 9 10 **F**8 12 14 15 16 17 18 19 21 22 26 28 30 31 33 34 35 37 39 41 44 46 49 52 54 57 59 64 65 66 67 71 73 **P**1	23	10	61	1677	20	45017	0	13392	5058	194

COALDALE—Schuylkill County

⊠ MINER'S MEMORIAL MEDICAL CENTER, 360 West Ruddle Street, Zip 18218–0067, Mailing Address: P.O. Box 67, Zip 18218–0067; tel. 570/645–2131; William J. Crossin, President and Chief Executive Officer (Total facility includes 48 beds in nursing home–type unit) (Nonreporting) **A**1 9 10	23	10	110	—	—	—	—	—	—	—

COATESVILLE—Chester County

⊠ BRANDYWINE HOSPITAL, 201 Reeceville Road, Zip 19320–1536; tel. 610/383–8000; James H. Thornton, Jr., President and Chief Executive Officer (Total facility includes 20 beds in nursing home–type unit) **A**1 2 9 10 **F**7 8 10 12 13 14 15 16 17 18 19 20 21 22 24 25 26 27 28 29 30 31 32 33 34 35 36 37 39 40 41 42 44 45 46 49 50 51 52 56 57 59 60 61 63 64 65 66 67 70 71 72 73 74 **P**8 **Web address:** www.brandywinehospital.com	23	10	178	7681	104	116161	707	67332	31218	807
⊠ VETERANS AFFAIRS MEDICAL CENTER, 1400 Black Horse Hill Road, Zip 19320–2097; tel. 610/384–7711; Gary W. Devansky, Chief Executive Officer (Total facility includes 200 beds in nursing home–type unit) **A**1 **F**1 2 6 12 15 16 17 18 19 20 26 27 28 30 31 32 34 39 41 44 45 46 49 51 52 56 57 58 59 61 64 65 67 71 72 73 74 **P**6 **S** Department of Veterans Affairs, Washington, DC	45	22	721	3703	552	115692	0	77537	45899	1153

COLUMBIA—Lancaster County

⊠ LANCASTER GENERAL HOSPITAL–SUSQUEHANNA DIVISION, 306 North Seventh Street, Zip 17512–2132, Mailing Address: P.O. Box 926, Zip 17512–0926; tel. 717/684–2841; Scott A. Berlucchi, President and Chief Executive Officer **A**1 9 10 **F**2 3 8 14 15 16 17 19 22 28 32 33 34 39 41 44 45 46 49 51 65 66 67 71 74	23	10	74	1520	29	—	0	8565	3766	149

CONNELLSVILLE—Fayette County

⊠ HIGHLANDS HOSPITAL, 401 East Murphy Avenue, Zip 15425–2700; tel. 724/628–1500; Michael J. Evans, Chief Executive Officer **A**1 9 10 **F**7 8 12 16 17 19 21 22 26 28 29 30 31 32 33 35 37 39 40 41 42 44 46 49 52 53 54 55 56 57 59 60 63 64 65 67 71 73 74 **P**6 8 **S** Fay–West Health System, Mount Pleasant, PA	23	10	87	2892	50	55646	0	18253	7706	240

CORRY—Erie County

⊠ CORRY MEMORIAL HOSPITAL, 612 West Smith Street, Zip 16407–1152; tel. 814/664–4641; Joseph T. Hodges, President (Nonreporting) **A**1 9 10 **S** Quorum Health Group/Quorum Health Resources, Inc., Brentwood, TN	23	10	55	—	—	—	—	—	—	—

COUDERSPORT—Potter County

⊠ CHARLES COLE MEMORIAL HOSPITAL, 1001 East Second Street, Zip 16915–9762; tel. 814/274–9300; David B. Acker, Chief Executive Officer (Total facility includes 50 beds in nursing home–type unit) (Nonreporting) **A**1 9 10	23	10	120	—	—	—	—	—	—	—

DANVILLE—Montour County

□ DANVILLE STATE HOSPITAL, 200 State Hospital Drive, Zip 17821–9198; tel. 570/271–4500; Paul J. Gritman, Superintendent (Total facility includes 30 beds in nursing home–type unit) **A**1 10 **F**1 2 3 4 5 6 7 8 9 10 11 12 13 17 18 19 20 21 22 23 24 25 26 27 28 29 30 31 32 33 34 35 36 37 38 39 40 41 42 43 44 45 46 47 48 49 50 51 52 53 54 55 56 57 58 59 60 61 62 63 64 65 66 67 69 70 71 72 73 74 **P**6	12	22	272	106	238	0	0	29079	18629	441
⊠ GEISINGER MEDICAL CENTER, 100 North Academy Avenue, Zip 17822–0150; tel. 570/271–6211; Nancy L. Rizzo, Senior Vice President, Operations (Nonreporting) **A**1 2 3 5 6 8 9 10 12 13 **S** Penn State Geisinger Health System, Harrisburg, PA **Web address:** www.psghs.edu	23	10	548	—	—	—	—	—	—	—

DEVON—Chester County

DEVEREUX FOUNDATION–FRENCH CENTER, 123 Old Lancaster Road, Zip 19333–1439, Mailing Address: P.O. Box 400, Zip 19333–0400; tel. 610/964–3215; Richard Warden, Executive Director (Total facility includes 84 beds in nursing home–type unit) (Nonreporting)	23	59	110	—	—	—	—	—	—	—

DOWNINGTOWN—Chester County

★ ST. JOHN VIANNEY HOSPITAL, 151 Woodbine Road, Zip 19335–3057; tel. 610/269–2600; Louis D. Horvath, Administrator (Nonreporting) **Web address:** www.sjvcenter.org	21	22	54	—	—	—	—	—	—	—

Hospital, Address, Telephone, Administrator, Approval, Facility, and Physician Codes, Health Care System, Network	Classi-fication Codes		Utilization Data					Expense (thousands) of dollars		
★ American Hospital Association (AHA) membership □ Joint Commission on Accreditation of Healthcare Organizations (JCAHO) accreditation + American Osteopathic Healthcare Association (AOHA) membership ○ American Osteopathic Association (AOA) accreditation △ Commission on Accreditation of Rehabilitation Facilities (CARF) accreditation Control codes 61, 63, 64, 71, 72 and 73 indicate hospitals listed by AOHA, but not registered by AHA. For definition of numerical codes, see page A4	Control	Service	Staffed Beds	Admissions	Census	Outpatient Visits	Births	Total	Payroll	Personnel

DOYLESTOWN—Bucks County

✠ △ DOYLESTOWN HOSPITAL, 595 West State Street, Zip 18901–2597; tel. 215/345–2200; Richard A. Reif, President and Chief Executive Officer (Total facility includes 297 beds in nursing home–type unit) **A**1 7 9 10 **F**1 4 6 7 8 10 12 13 14 15 16 17 18 19 20 21 22 23 25 26 27 28 29 30 31 32 33 34 35 36 37 39 40 41 42 44 45 46 48 49 51 52 54 55 56 57 59 61 62 64 65 67 68 71 73 74 **P**5 8 **Web address:** www.dh.org	23	10	493	9962	360	218907	1154	102579	46596	1596
□ FOUNDATIONS BEHAVIORAL HEALTH, 833 East Butler Avenue, Zip 18901–2280; tel. 215/345–0444; Ronald T. Bernstein, Chief Executive Officer (Nonreporting) **A**1 10	23	22	45	—	—	—	—	—	—	—

DREXEL HILL—Delaware County

✠ ○ △ DELAWARE COUNTY MEMORIAL HOSPITAL, 501 North Lansdowne Avenue, Zip 19026–1114; tel. 610/284–8100; Joan K. Richards, President **A**1 2 5 7 9 10 11 12 **F**1 2 3 4 7 8 9 10 11 12 13 14 15 16 17 18 19 21 22 23 24 26 27 28 29 30 31 32 33 34 35 36 37 38 39 40 41 42 43 44 45 46 48 49 51 52 53 54 55 56 57 58 59 60 61 64 65 66 67 68 69 71 72 73 74 **P**1 **S** Crozer–Keystone Health System, Springfield, PA	23	10	231	10992	170	140037	969	94995	35459	1000

DU BOIS—Clearfield County

□ DUBOIS REGIONAL MEDICAL CENTER, 100 Hospital Avenue, Zip 15801–1440, Mailing Address: P.O. Box 447, Zip 15801–0447; tel. 814/371–2200; Raymond A. Graeca, President and Chief Executive Officer (Total facility includes 14 beds in nursing home–type unit) **A**1 2 9 10 **F**7 8 10 13 14 15 16 17 19 21 22 23 25 26 27 28 29 30 32 33 34 35 37 38 39 40 41 42 44 46 48 49 51 52 53 54 55 56 57 58 60 61 64 65 66 67 71 73 **P**6 8 **Web address:** www.drmc.org	23	10	203	7982	117	243943	652	70965	35620	1052

EAGLEVILLE—Montgomery County

★ EAGLEVILLE HOSPITAL, 100 Eagleville Road, Zip 19408–0045, Mailing Address: P.O. Box 45, Zip 19408–0045; tel. 610/539–6000; Kendria Kurtz, Chief Executive Officer **A**9 10 **F**2 12 14 15 17 22 29 31 39 54 55 56 65 67 73 74 **P**6 **Web address:** www.eaglevillehospital.org	23	82	100	1966	64	0	0	12260	6448	249

EAST STROUDSBURG—Monroe County

✠ POCONO MEDICAL CENTER, 206 East Brown Street, Zip 18301–3006; tel. 570/421–4000; Marilyn R. Rettaliata, President and Chief Executive Officer (Total facility includes 23 beds in nursing home–type unit) **A**1 2 9 10 **F**7 8 11 12 13 15 19 20 21 22 25 30 31 34 35 37 39 40 41 42 44 45 46 49 52 54 56 60 64 65 67 71 73 74 **Web address:** www.pmchealthsystem.org	23	10	215	9785	154	147169	882	70405	34400	933

EASTON—Northampton County

✠ △ EASTON HOSPITAL, 250 South 21st Street, Zip 18042–3892; tel. 610/250–4000; Donna Mulholland, President and Chief Executive Officer **A**1 2 3 5 7 9 10 12 13 **F**4 7 8 10 12 14 15 16 17 19 20 21 22 28 29 30 31 32 33 34 35 36 37 38 39 40 41 42 43 44 45 46 48 49 51 54 55 56 58 59 60 63 65 67 71 73 74 **P**6 7 8 **Web address:** www.eastonhospital.org	23	10	248	12598	215	228124	653	119497	55702	1493

ELKINS PARK—Montgomery County

✠ ELKINS PARK HOSPITAL, (Formerly Allegheny University Hospital, Elkins Park), 60 East Township Line Road, Zip 19027–2220; tel. 215/663–6000; Richard Centafont, Interim Chief Executive Officer (Nonreporting) **A**1 3 5 9 10 **S** TENET Healthcare Corporation, Santa Barbara, CA **Web address:** www.auhs.edu	23	10	158	—	—	—	—	—	—	—

ELLWOOD CITY—Lawrence County

ELLWOOD CITY HOSPITAL, 724 Pershing Street, Zip 16117–1474; tel. 724/752–0081; Herbert S. Skuba, President (Total facility includes 23 beds in nursing home–type unit) (Nonreporting) **A**9 10	23	10	118	—	—	—	—	—	—	—

EPHRATA—Lancaster County

□ EPHRATA COMMUNITY HOSPITAL, 169 Martin Avenue, Zip 17522–1724, Mailing Address: P.O. Box 1002, Zip 17522–1002; tel. 717/733–0311; John M. Porter, Jr., President and Chief Executive Officer (Total facility includes 15 beds in nursing home–type unit) **A**1 9 10 **F**7 8 11 14 15 16 17 19 21 22 26 30 31 32 33 34 35 36 37 39 40 41 42 44 45 46 49 51 52 53 54 55 56 57 58 63 64 65 67 71 73 74 **P**8	23	10	124	6347	78	174299	627	45712	22592	650

ERIE—Erie County

✠ HAMOT MEDICAL CENTER, 201 State Street, Zip 16550–0002; tel. 814/877–6000; John T. Malone, President and Chief Executive Officer (Total facility includes 35 beds in nursing home–type unit) **A**1 2 3 5 9 10 **F**3 4 6 7 8 10 12 14 15 16 17 18 19 21 22 23 24 26 27 28 29 30 31 32 33 34 35 36 37 38 39 40 41 42 43 44 45 46 49 50 51 52 53 54 55 56 58 59 60 61 62 63 64 65 66 67 68 70 71 72 73 74 **P**6 7 8 **Web address:** www.hamot.org	23	10	375	14835	210	102567	1548	140002	54798	2212
□ △ HEALTHSOUTH LAKE ERIE INSTITUTE OF REHABILITATION, 137 West Second Street, Zip 16507–1403; tel. 814/453–5602; Louis M. Condrasky, Chief Executive Officer (Total facility includes 27 beds in nursing home–type unit) (Nonreporting) **A**1 7 9 10 **S** HEALTHSOUTH Corporation, Birmingham, AL	33	46	99	—	—	—	—	—	—	—
□ △ HEALTHSOUTH REHABILITATION HOSPITAL OF ERIE, (Formerly HEALTHSOUTH Great Lakes Rehabilitation Hospital), 143 East Second Street, Zip 16507–1595; tel. 814/878–1200; Louis M. Condrasky, Chief Executive Officer (Nonreporting) **A**1 7 9 **S** HEALTHSOUTH Corporation, Birmingham, AL	33	46	108	—	—	—	—	—	—	—

Hospital, Address, Telephone, Administrator, Approval, Facility, and Physician Codes, Health Care System, Network	Classi-fication Codes		Utilization Data					Expense (thousands) of dollars		
★ American Hospital Association (AHA) membership □ Joint Commission on Accreditation of Healthcare Organizations (JCAHO) accreditation + American Osteopathic Healthcare Association (AOHA) membership ○ American Osteopathic Association (AOA) accreditation △ Commission on Accreditation of Rehabilitation Facilities (CARF) accreditation Control codes 61, 63, 64, 71, 72 and 73 indicate hospitals listed by AOHA, but not registered by AHA. For definition of numerical codes, see page A4	Control	Service	Staffed Beds	Admissions	Census	Outpatient Visits	Births	Total	Payroll	Personnel

Hospital	Control	Service	Staffed Beds	Admissions	Census	Outpatient Visits	Births	Total	Payroll	Personnel
★ ○ METRO HEALTH CENTER, 252 West 11th Street, Zip 16501–9964; tel. 814/870–3400; Debra M. Dragovan, Chief Executive Officer **A**9 10 11 12 13 **F**7 8 14 15 16 19 21 22 30 34 35 37 40 44 46 63 65 71 72 73 **P**8 **Web address:** www.metrohealth.org	23	10	112	2454	28	44685	241	18480	6688	234
+ ○ MILLCREEK COMMUNITY HOSPITAL, 5515 Peach Street, Zip 16509–2695; tel. 814/864–4031; Mary L. Eckert, President and Chief Executive Officer **A**9 10 11 12 13 **F**2 7 8 10 14 15 16 19 22 35 37 40 44 51 65 71 72 73	23	10	101	3178	37	46015	210	19798	7835	267
□ SAINT VINCENT HEALTH CENTER, 232 West 25th Street, Zip 16544–0001; tel. 814/452–5000; Sister Catherine Manning, President and Chief Executive Officer (Total facility includes 14 beds in nursing home–type unit) **A**1 3 5 9 10 **F**3 4 7 8 10 11 12 13 14 15 16 17 18 19 20 21 22 29 30 32 33 34 35 37 38 40 41 42 43 44 45 46 48 49 51 52 54 56 57 58 60 64 65 67 70 71 73 74 **P**5 6 **Web address:** www.svhs.org	23	10	450	16307	245	214850	1697	138752	55262	1769
✣ SHRINERS HOSPITALS FOR CHILDREN, ERIE, 1645 West 8th Street, Zip 16505–5007; tel. 814/875–8700; Richard W. Brzuz, Administrator **A**1 3 **F**5 12 13 15 16 17 27 28 29 30 34 45 46 47 48 49 64 65 71 73 **S** Shriners Hospitals for Children, Tampa, FL	23	57	30	884	11	9330	0	—	—	128
✣ VETERANS AFFAIRS MEDICAL CENTER, 135 East 38th Street, Zip 16504–1559; tel. 814/860–2576; Stephen M. Lucas, Chief Executive Officer (Total facility includes 9 beds in nursing home–type unit) **A**1 9 **F**2 3 4 8 10 11 14 15 16 17 18 19 20 21 22 26 27 28 29 30 31 33 34 35 37 39 41 42 43 44 45 46 48 49 51 52 54 55 56 57 58 59 60 64 65 67 68 71 73 74 **P**6 **S** Department of Veterans Affairs, Washington, DC **Web address:** www.erie.net/~vamcerie	45	10	61	1319	32	99500	0	37096	17054	422
EVERETT—Bedford County										
✣ UPMC BEDFORD MEMORIAL, 10455 Lincoln Highway, Zip 15537–7046; tel. 814/623–6161; James C. Vreeland, FACHE, President and Chief Executive Officer **A**1 9 10 **F**3 4 6 7 10 12 13 14 15 16 17 18 19 20 21 22 23 26 27 28 29 30 31 32 33 34 35 36 37 39 40 41 42 43 44 45 49 50 51 53 54 55 56 57 58 59 60 62 63 65 66 67 70 71 73 **P**3 7 8 **S** UPMC Health System, Pittsburgh, PA **Web address:** www.bedford.org	23	10	59	1968	18	80030	290	19353	8309	287
FARRELL—Mercer County										
SHENANGO VALLEY CAMPUS See UPMC Horizon, Greenville										
FORT WASHINGTON—Montgomery County										
□ NORTHWESTERN INSTITUTE, 450 Bethlehem Pike, Zip 19034–0209; tel. 215/641–5300; Joseph Roynan, Administrator (Nonreporting) **A**1 9 10	33	22	146	—	—	—	—	—	—	—
FRANKLIN—Venango County										
□ NORTHWEST MEDICAL CENTERS, (Includes Northwest Medical Center–Franklin Campus, 1 Spruce Street, Zip 16323; tel. 814/437–7000; Northwest Medical Center–Oil City Campus, 174 East Bissell Avenue, Oil City, Zip 16301–0568, Mailing Address: P.O. Box 1068, Zip 16301–0568; tel. 814/677–1711), 1 Spruce Street, Zip 16323–2544; tel. 814/437–7000; Neil E. Todhunter, Chief Executive Officer **A**1 2 9 10 **F**3 4 7 8 13 15 17 19 21 22 23 28 30 34 35 36 37 39 40 41 42 44 48 49 52 54 55 56 57 58 59 60 63 64 65 66 71 72 73 **P**7 8 **Web address:** www.northwesthealthsystem.org	23	10	176	8050	103	—	426	60379	27892	857
GETTYSBURG—Adams County										
✣ GETTYSBURG HOSPITAL, 147 Gettys Street, Zip 17325–0786; tel. 717/334–2121; Steven W. Renner, President and Chief Executive Officer (Total facility includes 23 beds in nursing home–type unit) **A**1 9 10 **F**3 4 7 8 14 15 16 17 19 21 22 23 28 30 32 33 34 37 39 40 41 42 44 46 49 56 64 65 66 67 71 73 74 **P**6 8 **Web address:** www.gettysburghosp.org	23	10	99	4401	53	106162	528	38885	18428	551
GLENSIDE—Montgomery County										
✣ △ CHESTNUT HILL REHABILITATION HOSPITAL, 8601 Stenton Avenue, Zip 19038–8312; tel. 215/233–6200; James B. McCaslin, Director (Total facility includes 34 beds in nursing home–type unit) **A**1 7 10 **F**1 5 6 7 8 12 13 14 15 16 17 19 20 21 22 26 27 28 29 30 31 32 33 34 35 36 39 41 42 44 45 46 48 49 50 51 54 56 57 60 61 62 63 64 65 66 67 69 71 73 74 **P**4 5 7	23	46	81	1731	69	13898	0	14675	6113	205
GREENSBURG—Westmoreland County										
✣ WESTMORELAND REGIONAL HOSPITAL, 532 West Pittsburgh Street, Zip 15601–2239; tel. 724/832–4000; Joseph J. Peluso, President and Chief Executive Officer (Total facility includes 46 beds in nursing home–type unit) **A**1 2 9 10 **F**2 3 4 7 8 10 11 12 13 14 16 17 19 20 21 22 23 25 26 27 28 29 30 31 32 33 34 35 37 38 39 40 41 42 43 44 45 46 48 49 52 53 54 55 56 57 58 59 60 61 63 64 65 67 68 71 73 74 **P**1 **Web address:** www.westmoreland.org	23	10	345	13581	213	224197	835	96151	45558	1440
GREENVILLE—Mercer County										
□ UPMC HORIZON, (Formerly Horizon Hospital System), (Includes Greenville Campus, 110 North Main Street, Zip 16125–1795; tel. 724/588–2100; Shenango Valley Campus, 2200 Memorial Drive, Farrell, Zip 16121–1398; tel. 724/981–3500), J. Larry Heinike, President and Chief Executive Officer (Total facility includes 28 beds in nursing home–type unit) (Nonreporting) **A**1 2 9 10 12 **S** UPMC Health System, Pittsburgh, PA **Web address:** www.hhs.org	23	10	286	—	—	—	—	—	—	—

Hospital, Address, Telephone, Administrator, Approval, Facility, and Physician Codes, Health Care System, Network	Classi-fication Codes		Utilization Data					Expense (thousands) of dollars		
★ American Hospital Association (AHA) membership □ Joint Commission on Accreditation of Healthcare Organizations (JCAHO) accreditation + American Osteopathic Healthcare Association (AOHA) membership ○ American Osteopathic Association (AOA) accreditation △ Commission on Accreditation of Rehabilitation Facilities (CARF) accreditation Control codes 61, 63, 64, 71, 72 and 73 indicate hospitals listed by AOHA, but not registered by AHA. For definition of numerical codes, see page A4	Control	Service	Staffed Beds	Admissions	Census	Outpatient Visits	Births	Total	Payroll	Personnel

GROVE CITY—Mercer County

+ ○ UNITED COMMUNITY HOSPITAL, 631 North Broad Street Extension, Zip 16127–9703; tel. 724/458–5442; Robert J. Turner, Administrator (Total facility includes 20 beds in nursing home–type unit) **A**9 10 11 **F**3 7 8 14 15 16 17 19 20 21 22 28 30 32 33 34 35 37 39 40 41 42 44 45 49 56 60 63 64 65 67 70 71 73 **Web address:** www.pathways.net/uch	23	10	104	3496	51	65295	323	24510	10334	340

HANOVER—York County

□ HANOVER HOSPITAL, 300 Highland Avenue, Zip 17331–2297; tel. 717/637–3711; William R. Walb, President and Chief Executive Officer **A**1 9 10 **F**4 7 8 10 11 12 13 15 16 17 18 19 20 21 22 25 27 28 30 31 32 33 34 35 37 39 40 41 42 44 45 46 49 63 65 66 67 71 73 **P**8 **Web address:** www.hanoverhospital.org	23	10	101	5735	64	134168	619	49540	22100	685

HARRISBURG—Dauphin County

COMMUNITY GENERAL OSTEOPATHIC HOSPITAL See PinnacleHealth System										
□ EDGEWATER PSYCHIATRIC CENTER, 1829 North Front Street, Zip 17102–2213; tel. 717/238–8666; Stephen C. Blanchard, Director (Nonreporting) **A**1 9 10	23	22	26	—	—	—	—	—	—	—
□ HARRISBURG STATE HOSPITAL, 2101 Cameron Street, Zip 17105–1300, Mailing Address: Pouch A, Zip 17105–1300; tel. 717/772–7455; Bruce Darney, Superintendent **A**1 9 10 **F**8 12 20 26 30 46 52 55 57 65 73 **P**6	12	22	366	152	352	0	0	36243	21662	586
PINNACLEHEALTH AT COMMUNITY GENERAL OSTEOPATHIC HOSPITAL See PinnacleHealth System										
⊞ + ○ PINNACLEHEALTH SYSTEM, (Includes PinnacleHealth at Community General Osteopathic Hospital, 4300 Londonderry Road, Zip 17109–5397; tel. 717/652–3000; PinnacleHealth at Harrisburg Hospital, 111 South Front Street, Zip 17101–2099; tel. 717/782–3131; PinnacleHealth at Polyclinic Hospital, 2601 North Third Street, Zip 17110–2098; tel. 717/782–4141; PinnacleHealth at Seidle Memorial Hospital, 120 South Filbert Street, Mechanicsburg, Zip 17055–6591; tel. 717/795–6760; Susan A. Edwards, Senior Vice President for Operations), 17 South Market Square, Zip 17101–2003, Mailing Address: P.O. Box 8700, Zip 17105–8700; tel. 717/782–5678; John S. Cramer, FACHE, President and Chief Executive Officer (Total facility includes 123 beds in nursing home–type unit) **A**1 2 3 5 9 10 11 12 13 **F**1 3 4 6 7 8 10 11 12 14 15 16 17 19 20 21 22 23 26 28 29 30 31 32 33 34 35 36 38 39 40 41 42 43 44 45 46 48 49 51 52 53 54 56 57 58 59 60 61 62 63 64 65 67 71 72 73 74 **P**1 5 6 **Web address:** www.pinnaclehealth.org	23	10	857	34368	604	489708	4545	329434	148091	5017

HAVERTOWN—Delaware County

□ MERCY COMMUNITY HOSPITAL, 2000 Old West Chester Pike, Zip 19083–2712; tel. 610/853–7000; George F. McLaughlin, Chief Executive Officer **A**1 9 10 **F**1 2 3 7 8 12 14 15 16 17 19 21 22 25 26 27 28 30 32 33 34 35 37 40 41 42 44 45 46 49 54 56 57 59 60 61 62 64 65 66 67 71 73 74 **P**8 **S** Catholic Health East, Newtown Square, PA	21	10	97	4053	48	49776	0	26262	12196	328

HAZLETON—Luzerne County

⊞ HAZLETON GENERAL HOSPITAL, 700 East Broad Street, Zip 18201–6897; tel. 570/450–4357; E. Richard Moore, President **A**1 9 10 **F**7 8 12 14 15 16 17 19 21 22 24 27 28 29 30 31 32 34 35 36 37 39 40 41 42 44 45 46 49 51 52 54 55 56 57 61 63 64 65 66 67 71 73 74 **Web address:** www.ghha.org	23	10	152	5412	109	43877	0	35992	15096	537
⊞ HAZLETON–ST. JOSEPH MEDICAL CENTER, 687 North Church Street, Zip 18201–3198; tel. 570/459–4444; Bernard C. Rudegeair, President and Chief Executive Officer (Total facility includes 11 beds in nursing home–type unit) (Nonreporting) **A**1 9 10 **Web address:** www.ghha.org	21	10	122	—	—	—	—	—	—	—

HERSHEY—Dauphin County

⊞ △ PENN STATE GEISINGER HEALTH SYSTEM–MILTON S. HERSHEY MEDICAL CENTER, 500 University Drive, Zip 17033–0850, Mailing Address: P.O. Box 850, Zip 17033–0850; tel. 717/531–8521; Theodore E. Townsend, Senior Vice President, Operations **A**1 2 3 5 7 8 9 10 **F**3 4 5 7 8 10 12 13 14 15 16 17 19 21 22 23 24 25 26 27 28 29 30 31 32 34 35 37 38 39 40 41 42 43 44 45 46 47 48 49 51 52 53 54 55 56 57 58 59 60 61 63 65 66 67 68 70 71 72 73 74 **P**1 **S** Penn State Geisinger Health System, Harrisburg, PA **Web address:** www.collmed.psu.edu/	23	10	455	20453	375	402743	1192	313534	150702	5044

HONESDALE—Wayne County

⊞ WAYNE MEMORIAL HOSPITAL, 601 Park Street, Zip 18431–1445; tel. 570/253–8100; G. Richard Garman, Executive Director **A**1 9 10 **F**1 7 8 15 16 17 19 21 22 23 24 25 27 28 30 31 32 33 35 37 39 40 41 42 44 45 49 53 55 56 57 58 64 65 66 67 68 71 73 **P**8 **Web address:** www.wmh.org	23	10	95	3991	58	114417	448	33656	14497	510

HUNTINGDON—Huntingdon County

⊞ J. C. BLAIR MEMORIAL HOSPITAL, 1225 Warm Springs Avenue, Zip 16652–2398; tel. 814/643–2290; Richard E. D'Alberto, Chief Executive Officer **A**1 9 10 **F**7 8 16 19 22 28 34 35 37 40 44 45 46 49 52 54 58 59 65 66 71 73 **S** Quorum Health Group/Quorum Health Resources, Inc., Brentwood, TN **Web address:** www.JCBlair.Org	23	10	104	3525	45	68846	296	27613	11527	349

INDIANA—Indiana County

⊞ INDIANA HOSPITAL, 835 Hospital Road, Zip 15701–3650, Mailing Address: P.O. Box 788, Zip 15701–0788; tel. 724/357–7000; Stephen A. Wolfe, President and Chief Executive Officer (Total facility includes 18 beds in nursing home–type unit) **A**1 9 10 **F**3 7 8 12 13 14 15 16 17 19 20 21 22 24 25 26 28 30 32 33 34 35 37 40 41 42 44 45 49 52 54 56 57 58 60 63 64 65 67 71 73	23	10	148	6595	88	184512	652	51824	26968	802

Hospital, Address, Telephone, Administrator, Approval, Facility, and Physician Codes, Health Care System, Network	Classi-fication Codes		Utilization Data					Expense (thousands) of dollars		
★ American Hospital Association (AHA) membership □ Joint Commission on Accreditation of Healthcare Organizations (JCAHO) accreditation + American Osteopathic Healthcare Association (AOHA) membership ○ American Osteopathic Association (AOA) accreditation △ Commission on Accreditation of Rehabilitation Facilities (CARF) accreditation Control codes 61, 63, 64, 71, 72 and 73 indicate hospitals listed by AOHA, but not registered by AHA. For definition of numerical codes, see page A4	Control	Service	Staffed Beds	Admissions	Census	Outpatient Visits	Births	Total	Payroll	Personnel

JEANNETTE—Westmoreland County

□ JEANNETTE DISTRICT MEMORIAL HOSPITAL, 600 Jefferson Avenue, Zip 15644–2504; tel. 724/527–3551; Robert J. Bulger, President and Chief Executive Officer (Total facility includes 11 beds in nursing home–type unit) **A**1 9 10 **F**4 7 8 12 15 16 19 21 22 29 30 35 37 40 41 42 44 45 46 48 49 64 65 67 71 73 **P**8 **Web address:** www.jdmh.org/	23	10	137	5037	77	80806	418	34892	16201	495
□ MONSOUR MEDICAL CENTER, 70 Lincoln Way East, Zip 15644–3167; tel. 724/527–1511; William T. Abraham, Interim Chief Executive Officer **A**1 9 10 **F**2 8 10 12 14 15 16 18 19 22 26 29 30 31 32 37 39 42 44 52 53 57 65 70 71 73	23	10	137	2428	60	36009	0	23287	10630	318

JERSEY SHORE—Lycoming County

⊠ JERSEY SHORE HOSPITAL, 1020 Thompson Street, Zip 17740–1794; tel. 570/398–0100; Louis A. Ditzel, Jr., President and Chief Executive Officer **A**1 9 10 **F**8 11 12 13 14 15 16 17 19 21 22 23 28 29 30 33 34 35 36 37 39 41 44 45 49 51 63 64 65 66 67 69 71 73 **P**6 **S** Quorum Health Group/Quorum Health Resources, Inc., Brentwood, TN	23	10	49	1141	11	74095	0	12448	5259	201

JOHNSTOWN—Cambria County

⊠ CONEMAUGH MEMORIAL MEDICAL CENTER, (Formerly Memorial Medical Center), (Includes Good Samaritan Medical Center, 1020 Franklin Street, Zip 15905–4186; tel. 814/533–1000), 1086 Franklin Street, Zip 15905–4305; tel. 814/534–9000; Steven E. Tucker, President **A**1 2 3 5 6 9 10 12 **F**2 3 4 6 7 8 10 11 12 13 14 15 16 17 18 19 20 21 22 23 24 25 26 27 28 29 30 31 32 33 34 35 37 38 39 40 41 42 43 44 45 46 48 49 51 52 53 54 55 56 57 58 59 60 62 63 64 65 67 70 71 72 73 74 **P**4 6 8 **Web address:** www.conemaugh.org GOOD SAMARITAN MEDICAL CENTER See Conemaugh Memorial Medical Center LEE HOSPITAL See UPMC Lee Regional MEMORIAL MEDICAL CENTER See Conemaugh Memorial Medical Center	23	10	450	16157	269	127976	916	195193	73616	2370
□ UPMC LEE REGIONAL, (Formerly Lee Hospital), 320 Main Street, Zip 15901–1694; tel. 814/533–0123; David R. Davis, President and Chief Executive Officer (Total facility includes 18 beds in nursing home–type unit) (Nonreporting) **A**1 2 9 10 **S** UPMC Health System, Pittsburgh, PA **Web address:** www.city page.com/lee	23	10	224	—	—	—	—	—	—	—

KANE—McKean County

KANE COMMUNITY HOSPITAL, North Fraley Street, Zip 16735, Mailing Address: Rural Route 2, Box 230, Zip 16733–9654; tel. 814/837–8585; J. Gary Rhodes, Chief Executive Officer **A**9 10 **F**3 8 11 12 14 15 16 17 19 22 25 27 28 29 30 32 34 37 41 42 44 48 49 51 54 56 61 64 65 67 71 74 **P**6 **Web address:** www.kanehosp.com	23	10	35	1359	18	22804	0	8907	4136	141

KINGSTON—Luzerne County

NESBITT MEMORIAL HOSPITAL See Wyoming Valley Health Care System, Wilkes–Barre

KITTANNING—Armstrong County

□ ARMSTRONG COUNTY MEMORIAL HOSPITAL, One Nolte Drive, Zip 16201–8808; tel. 724/543–8500; Jack D. Hoard, President and Chief Executive Officer (Total facility includes 25 beds in nursing home–type unit) **A**1 2 9 10 **F**7 8 10 11 12 14 15 17 19 21 22 28 29 30 32 34 35 37 39 40 41 42 44 46 49 50 51 52 53 54 55 56 57 60 63 64 65 66 67 71 73 **P**5	23	10	210	7104	114	136340	504	45105	20993	729

LAFAYETTE HILL—Montgomery County

□ EUGENIA HOSPITAL, 660 Thomas Road, Zip 19444–1199; tel. 215/836–7700; John P. Ash, FACHE, President and Chief Executive Officer (Nonreporting) **A**1 9 10	33	22	126	—	—	—	—	—	—	—

LANCASTER—Lancaster County

+ ○ COMMUNITY HOSPITAL OF LANCASTER, 1100 East Orange Street, Zip 17602–3218, Mailing Address: P.O. Box 3002, Zip 17604–3002; tel. 717/397–3711; Mark C. Barabas, President **A**9 10 11 12 13 **F**7 8 10 12 14 15 16 17 19 20 21 22 25 28 29 30 31 32 33 34 35 37 39 40 41 42 44 48 49 51 52 54 56 63 64 65 66 67 71 73 74 **P**8 **Web address:** www.chol.org	23	10	116	5046	61	81414	668	42045	17193	667
□ △ LANCASTER GENERAL HOSPITAL, 555 North Duke Street, Zip 17604–3555, Mailing Address: P.O. Box 3555, Zip 17604–3555; tel. 717/290–5511; Mark A. Brazitis, President (Total facility includes 30 beds in nursing home–type unit) **A**1 2 3 5 6 7 9 10 **F**3 4 7 8 10 12 13 14 15 16 17 19 20 21 22 30 32 33 34 35 37 38 39 40 41 42 43 44 45 46 48 49 51 52 53 54 56 58 60 61 63 64 65 66 67 68 70 71 73 74	23	10	493	24167	309	490153	2868	218251	102510	2787
⊠ △ ST. JOSEPH HOSPITAL, 250 College Avenue, Zip 17604, Mailing Address: P.O. Box 3509, Zip 17604–3509; tel. 717/291–8211; John Kerr Tolmie, President and Chief Executive Officer (Total facility includes 19 beds in nursing home–type unit) (Nonreporting) **A**1 2 7 9 10 **S** Catholic Health Initiatives, Denver, CO **Web address:** www.chieast.org	21	10	256	—	—	—	—	—	—	—

LANGHORNE—Bucks County

BUCKS COUNTY CAMPUS See Frankford Hospital of the City of Philadelphia, Philadelphia

⊠ ST. MARY MEDICAL CENTER, Langhorne–Newtown Road, Zip 19047–1295; tel. 215/750–2000; Gregory T. Wozniak, President and Chief Executive Officer **A**1 2 9 10 **F**4 7 8 10 11 12 13 14 15 16 17 19 21 22 24 25 26 28 30 32 35 37 38 39 40 41 42 43 44 46 48 49 56 60 63 65 66 67 70 71 73 74 **S** Catholic Health Initiatives, Denver, CO	21	10	244	12342	159	—	1392	97965	41528	1019

Hospital, Address, Telephone, Administrator, Approval, Facility, and Physician Codes, Health Care System, Network	Classi-fication Codes		Utilization Data					Expense (thousands) of dollars		
★ American Hospital Association (AHA) membership □ Joint Commission on Accreditation of Healthcare Organizations (JCAHO) accreditation + American Osteopathic Healthcare Association (AOHA) membership ○ American Osteopathic Association (AOA) accreditation △ Commission on Accreditation of Rehabilitation Facilities (CARF) accreditation Control codes 61, 63, 64, 71, 72 and 73 indicate hospitals listed by AOHA, but not registered by AHA. For definition of numerical codes, see page A4	Control	Service	Staffed Beds	Admissions	Census	Outpatient Visits	Births	Total	Payroll	Personnel

LANSDALE—Montgomery County

☒ NORTH PENN HOSPITAL, 100 Medical Campus Drive, Zip 19446–1200; tel. 215/368–2100; Robert H. McKay, President (Total facility includes 18 beds in nursing home–type unit) **A**1 2 9 10 **F**1 7 8 11 12 15 17 19 21 22 28 29 30 32 33 36 37 39 40 42 44 45 46 49 63 64 65 67 71 73 — 23 10 107 4970 60 95968 678 40165 17525 564

LATROBE—Westmoreland County

☒ LATROBE AREA HOSPITAL, 121 West Second Avenue, Zip 15650–1096; tel. 724/537–1000; Douglas A. Clark, Executive Director (Total facility includes 20 beds in nursing home–type unit) **A**1 2 3 5 9 10 **F**5 7 8 10 11 12 13 14 15 16 17 18 19 21 22 24 25 27 28 29 30 31 32 33 34 35 37 39 40 41 42 44 45 49 51 52 53 54 55 56 58 59 60 63 64 65 67 68 71 73 74 **P**6 **Web address:** www.lah.com — 23 10 232 12279 163 308181 818 99246 45632 1273

LEBANON—Lebanon County

☒ GOOD SAMARITAN HOSPITAL, Fourth and Walnut Streets, Zip 17042, Mailing Address: P.O. Box 1281, Zip 17042–1281; tel. 717/270–7500; Robert J. Longo, President and Chief Executive Officer (Total facility includes 19 beds in nursing home–type unit) **A**1 3 5 9 10 **F**3 4 7 8 10 12 14 15 16 17 18 19 20 21 22 24 27 30 31 32 33 34 35 37 39 40 41 42 44 48 49 51 53 54 55 56 57 58 59 60 63 64 65 66 67 71 72 73 74 **P**8 **Web address:** www.gshleb.com — 23 10 175 9344 134 173374 1052 72828 32535 961

☒ VETERANS AFFAIRS MEDICAL CENTER, 1700 South Lincoln Avenue, Zip 17042–7529; tel. 717/272–6621; Charleen R. Szabo, FACHE, Chief Executive Officer **A**1 3 5 9 **F**2 3 4 12 15 16 17 19 20 22 25 26 27 28 30 31 32 33 34 37 39 41 42 44 45 46 49 51 52 54 56 57 58 59 64 65 67 71 72 73 74 **S** Department of Veterans Affairs, Washington, DC **Web address:** www.va.gov — 45 10 321 2694 121 150557 0 80269 40484 1009

LEHIGHTON—Carbon County

☒ GNADEN HUETTEN MEMORIAL HOSPITAL, 211 North 12th Street, Zip 18235–1138; tel. 610/377–1300; Robert J. Clark, FACHE, President and Chief Executive Officer (Total facility includes 91 beds in nursing home–type unit) **A**1 9 10 **F**7 8 12 14 15 16 17 19 20 21 22 25 26 27 28 30 32 33 35 36 37 39 40 41 42 44 45 46 48 49 52 53 54 55 56 57 59 61 64 65 67 71 73 74 **P**3 8 — 23 10 202 3594 138 112689 317 31739 14788 469

LEWISBURG—Union County

EVANGELICAL COMMUNITY HOSPITAL, One Hospital Drive, Zip 17837–9314; tel. 717/522–2000; Michael Daniloff, President (Nonreporting) **A**9 10 — 23 10 115 — — — — — — —

U. S. PENITENTIARY INFIRMARY, Route 7, Zip 17837–9303; tel. 717/523–1251; Arnold Reyes, Administrator (Nonreporting) — 48 11 17 — — — — — — —

LEWISTOWN—Mifflin County

☒ LEWISTOWN HOSPITAL, 400 Highland Avenue, Zip 17044–1198; tel. 717/248–5411; A. Gordon McAleer, FACHE, President and Chief Executive Officer **A**1 2 9 10 **F**3 7 8 11 14 15 16 17 19 20 21 22 26 30 31 32 33 34 35 37 39 40 41 42 44 49 52 53 54 55 56 57 58 60 63 71 73 **P**3 6 **Web address:** www.lewistownhospital.org — 23 10 179 7830 94 129938 679 45397 22499 782

LOCK HAVEN—Clinton County

☒ LOCK HAVEN HOSPITAL, 24 Cree Drive, Zip 17745–2699; tel. 570/893–5000; Gary R. Rhoads, President and Chief Executive Officer (Total facility includes 120 beds in nursing home–type unit) (Nonreporting) **A**1 9 10 **S** Quorum Health Group/Quorum Health Resources, Inc., Brentwood, TN — 23 10 195 — — — — — — —

MALVERN—Chester County

☒ △ BRYN MAWR REHABILITATION HOSPITAL, 414 Paoli Pike, Zip 19355–3300, Mailing Address: P.O. Box 3007, Zip 19355–3300; tel. 610/251–5400 (Total facility includes 23 beds in nursing home–type unit) **A**1 7 9 10 **F**2 3 4 5 6 7 8 9 10 11 12 13 14 15 16 17 18 19 20 21 22 24 25 26 27 28 29 30 31 32 33 34 35 36 37 38 39 40 41 42 43 44 45 46 47 48 49 50 51 52 53 54 55 56 57 58 59 60 61 64 65 66 67 68 70 71 72 73 74 **S** Jefferson Health System, Wayne, PA — 23 46 141 2718 118 — 0 31400 15984 526

□ DEVEREUX MAPLETON PSYCHIATRIC INSTITUTE–MAPLETON CENTER, 655 Sugartown Road, Zip 19355–0297, Mailing Address: Box 297, Zip 19355–0297; tel. 610/296–6923; Richard Warden, Executive Director (Nonreporting) **A**1 **S** Devereux Foundation, Villanova, PA — 23 22 13 — — — — — — —

MALVERN INSTITUTE, 940 King Road, Zip 19355–3167; tel. 610/647–0330; Thomas Cain, Administrator and Chief Executive Officer (Nonreporting) **A**9 — 33 82 40 — — — — — — —

MCCONNELLSBURG—Fulton County

★ FULTON COUNTY MEDICAL CENTER, 216 South First Street, Zip 17233–1399; tel. 717/485–3155; Robert B. Murray, III, President and Chief Executive Officer (Total facility includes 57 beds in nursing home–type unit) (Nonreporting) **A**9 10 — 23 10 96 — — — — — — —

MCKEES ROCKS—Allegheny County

☒ OHIO VALLEY GENERAL HOSPITAL, 25 Heckel Road, Zip 15136–1694; tel. 412/777–6161; William Provenzano, President **A**1 6 9 10 **F**4 7 8 10 12 13 14 15 16 17 18 19 21 22 23 25 26 28 29 30 32 33 34 35 36 37 40 41 42 44 45 46 49 51 61 65 67 71 72 73 **P**5 **S** Quorum Health Group/Quorum Health Resources, Inc., Brentwood, TN — 23 10 103 4655 64 90790 411 41310 15494 471

MCKEESPORT—Allegheny County

☒ UPMC MCKEESPORT, (Formerly McKeesport Hospital), 1500 Fifth Avenue, Zip 15132–2482; tel. 412/664–2000; Ronald H. Ott, President and Chief Executive Officer (Total facility includes 28 beds in nursing home–type unit) (Nonreporting) **A**1 3 5 9 10 **S** UPMC Health System, Pittsburgh, PA — 23 10 320 — — — — — — —

Hospital, Address, Telephone, Administrator, Approval, Facility, and Physician Codes, Health Care System, Network	Classi-fication Codes		Utilization Data					Expense (thousands) of dollars		
★ American Hospital Association (AHA) membership □ Joint Commission on Accreditation of Healthcare Organizations (JCAHO) accreditation + American Osteopathic Healthcare Association (AOHA) membership ○ American Osteopathic Association (AOA) accreditation △ Commission on Accreditation of Rehabilitation Facilities (CARF) accreditation Control codes 61, 63, 64, 71, 72 and 73 indicate hospitals listed by AOHA, but not registered by AHA. For definition of numerical codes, see page A4	Control	Service	Staffed Beds	Admissions	Census	Outpatient Visits	Births	Total	Payroll	Personnel

MEADOWBROOK—Montgomery County

□ HOLY REDEEMER HOSPITAL AND MEDICAL CENTER, 1648 Huntingdon Pike, Zip 19046–8099; tel. 215/947–3000; Mark T. Jones, President (Total facility includes 15 beds in nursing home–type unit) **A**1 5 9 10 **F**6 7 8 10 11 12 13 14 15 16 17 19 22 23 24 25 27 28 29 30 31 32 33 34 35 36 38 39 40 41 42 44 46 48 49 51 58 62 64 65 66 67 71 73 **P**6
Web address: www.holyredeemer.com
| 23 | 10 | 230 | 12082 | 147 | 141704 | 1709 | 81509 | 32823 | 1004 |

MEADVILLE—Crawford County

✦ MEADVILLE MEDICAL CENTER, (Includes Meadville City Hospital, 751 Liberty Street, Zip 16335; tel. 814/333–5000; Spencer Hospital, 1034 Grove Street, Zip 16335), 751 Liberty Street, Zip 16335–2555; tel. 814/333–5000; Anthony J. DeFail, President and Chief Executive Officer (Total facility includes 32 beds in nursing home–type unit) **A**1 2 9 10 **F**2 3 7 8 12 15 16 17 19 21 22 24 32 33 35 40 41 42 44 45 46 48 49 51 52 53 56 58 59 63 64 65 66 67 71 73 74 **P**6 7 8
| 23 | 10 | 289 | 8711 | 141 | 118820 | 606 | 63119 | 26587 | 880 |

MECHANICSBURG—Cumberland County

□ △ HEALTHSOUTH REHABILITATION OF MECHANICSBURG, 175 Lancaster Boulevard, Zip 17055–0736, Mailing Address: P.O. Box 2016, Zip 17055–2016; tel. 717/691–3700; Melissa Kutz, Administrator and Chief Executive Officer (Nonreporting) **A**1 7 9 10 **S** HEALTHSOUTH Corporation, Birmingham, AL
PINNACLEHEALTH AT SEIDLE MEMORIAL HOSPITAL See PinnacleHealth System, Harrisburg
| 33 | 46 | 103 | — | — | — | — | — | — | — |

MEDIA—Delaware County

✦ RIDDLE MEMORIAL HOSPITAL, 1068 West Baltimore Pike, Zip 19063–5177; tel. 610/566–9400; Donald L. Laughlin, President (Total facility includes 23 beds in nursing home–type unit) **A**1 2 9 10 **F**3 5 6 7 8 10 12 13 14 15 16 17 19 20 21 22 24 26 28 30 31 32 33 34 35 37 38 39 40 41 42 44 45 46 49 50 61 62 64 65 66 67 71 73 74 **P**6 7
Web address: www.riddlehospital.org
| 23 | 10 | 177 | 9930 | 141 | 94209 | 899 | 64401 | 30965 | 840 |

MEYERSDALE—Somerset County

✦ MEYERSDALE MEDICAL CENTER, 200 Hospital Drive, Zip 15552–1247; tel. 814/634–5911; Mary L. Libengood, President **A**1 9 10 **F**8 14 15 16 17 19 22 28 30 32 37 44 49 63 65 67 71 73
| 23 | 10 | 20 | 501 | 7 | 21398 | 0 | 4985 | 2410 | 96 |

MONONGAHELA—Washington County

✦ MONONGAHELA VALLEY HOSPITAL, 1163 Country Club Road, Rt 88, Zip 15063–1095; tel. 724/258–1000; Anthony M. Lombardi, President and Chief Executive Officer (Total facility includes 15 beds in nursing home–type unit) **A**1 2 9 10 **F**2 5 6 7 8 10 11 13 14 15 16 17 19 20 21 22 23 26 27 28 29 30 31 32 33 34 35 37 39 40 41 42 44 45 46 48 49 52 53 54 55 56 57 60 61 63 64 65 66 67 68 71 73 74 **P**8
Web address: www.monvalleyhospital.com
| 23 | 10 | 262 | 11109 | 194 | 183817 | 541 | 72803 | 34353 | 1048 |

MONROEVILLE—Allegheny County

✦ ALLEGHENY UNIVERSITY HOSPITALS, FORBES REGIONAL, 2570 Haymaker Road, Zip 15146–3592; tel. 412/858–2000; Dana W. Ramish, FACHE, President and Chief Executive Officer (Total facility includes 25 beds in nursing home–type unit) **A**1 2 3 5 9 10 **F**7 8 10 12 14 15 16 17 19 21 22 24 26 27 28 29 30 32 33 34 35 36 37 39 40 41 42 44 45 46 49 52 56 57 59 60 61 63 64 65 66 67 70 71 73 **P**6 **S** Allegheny University Hospitals–West, Pittsburgh, PA
| 23 | 10 | 342 | 13869 | 198 | 84074 | 1343 | 105880 | 45551 | 1150 |

□ HEALTHSOUTH GREATER PITTSBURGH REHABILITATION HOSPITAL, 2380 McGinley Road, Zip 15146–4400; tel. 412/856–2400; Faith A. Deigan, Administrator and Chief Executive Officer **A**1 9 10 **F**1 12 14 15 16 17 19 20 27 34 35 39 41 42 44 45 46 48 49 65 66 67 71 73 **P**5 **S** HEALTHSOUTH Corporation, Birmingham, AL
Web address: www.healthsouth.com
| 33 | 46 | 89 | 1378 | 79 | 28944 | 0 | 23427 | 9046 | 280 |

MONTROSE—Susquehanna County

ENDLESS MOUNTAIN HEALTH SYSTEMS, 1 Grow Avenue, Zip 18801–1199; tel. 570/278–3801; Rex Catlin, Chief Executive Officer **A**9 10 **F**8 14 16 17 19 22 26 32 37 44 49 65 67 71 **P**4 7
Web address: www.emhs.org
| 23 | 10 | 32 | 1037 | 11 | 34954 | 0 | 6646 | 2628 | 117 |

MOUNT GRETNA—Lebanon County

□ PHILHAVEN, BAHAVIORAL HEALTHCARE SERVICES, 283 South Butler Road, Zip 17064, Mailing Address: P.O. Box 550, Zip 17064–0550; tel. 717/273–8871; LaVern J. Yutzy, Chief Executive Officer **A**1 9 10 **F**14 15 32 52 53 54 55 56 57 58 59 73 74 **P**6
Web address: www.philhaven.com
| 21 | 22 | 83 | 1594 | 49 | 57420 | 0 | 23110 | 15189 | 507 |

MOUNT PLEASANT—Westmoreland County

✦ FRICK HOSPITAL, 508 South Church Street, Zip 15666–1790; tel. 724/547–1500; Rodney L. Gunderson, Chief Executive Officer (Total facility includes 18 beds in nursing home–type unit) **A**1 2 9 10 **F**7 8 10 11 12 14 15 16 17 18 19 20 21 22 26 28 29 30 31 32 34 35 37 39 40 41 42 44 46 49 52 53 54 55 56 57 58 59 60 63 64 65 66 67 68 71 73 **P**8 **S** Fay–West Health System, Mount Pleasant, PA
| 23 | 10 | 171 | 6061 | 95 | 100677 | 454 | 40204 | 19324 | 561 |

MUNCY—Lycoming County

MUNCY VALLEY HOSPITAL See Susquehanna Health System, Williamsport

NANTICOKE—Luzerne County

MERCY SPECIAL CARE HOSPITAL, 128 West Washington Street, Zip 18634–3113; tel. 570/735–5000; Robert D. Williams, Administrator (Nonreporting) **A**9 10 **S** Catholic Healthcare Partners, Cincinnati, OH
| 23 | 49 | 38 | — | — | — | — | — | — | — |

Hospital, Address, Telephone, Administrator, Approval, Facility, and Physician Codes, Health Care System, Network	Classi-fication Codes		Utilization Data					Expense (thousands) of dollars		
★ American Hospital Association (AHA) membership □ Joint Commission on Accreditation of Healthcare Organizations (JCAHO) accreditation + American Osteopathic Healthcare Association (AOHA) membership ○ American Osteopathic Association (AOA) accreditation △ Commission on Accreditation of Rehabilitation Facilities (CARF) accreditation Control codes 61, 63, 64, 71, 72 and 73 indicate hospitals listed by AOHA, but not registered by AHA. For definition of numerical codes, see page A4	Control	Service	Staffed Beds	Admissions	Census	Outpatient Visits	Births	Total	Payroll	Personnel

NATRONA HEIGHTS—Allegheny County

⊠ ALLEGHENY UNIVERSITY HOSPITALS, ALLEGHENY VALLEY, 1301 Carlisle Street, Zip 15065–1192; tel. 724/224–5100; Joseph Calig, President and Chief Executive Officer (Total facility includes 21 beds in nursing home–type unit) **A**1 2 9 10 **F**3 7 8 10 11 12 15 16 17 19 21 22 28 29 30 31 32 33 34 35 36 37 39 40 41 42 44 45 49 51 52 54 56 57 60 61 63 64 65 66 67 71 72 73 74 **S** Allegheny University Hospitals–West, Pittsburgh, PA

| | 23 | 10 | 268 | 9558 | 156 | 144303 | 548 | 77414 | 33324 | 915 |

NEW CASTLE—Lawrence County

⊠ △ JAMESON HOSPITAL, 1211 Wilmington Avenue, Zip 16105–2595; tel. 724/658–9001; Thomas White, President and Chief Executive Officer (Total facility includes 20 beds in nursing home–type unit) **A**1 2 6 7 9 10 **F**6 7 8 10 11 12 13 14 15 16 17 19 20 21 22 23 26 28 29 30 32 34 35 37 39 40 41 42 44 45 48 49 57 59 60 61 63 64 65 66 67 71 72 73 74 **P**3 7 8
Web address: www.jamesonhealthsystem.com

| | 23 | 10 | 160 | 6551 | 103 | 197926 | 547 | 59880 | 26618 | 1164 |

⊠ ST. FRANCIS HOSPITAL OF NEW CASTLE, 1000 South Mercer Street, Zip 16101–4673; tel. 724/658–3511; Sister Donna Zwigart, FACHE, Chief Executive Officer (Total facility includes 45 beds in nursing home–type unit) **A**1 6 9 10 **F**2 3 5 7 8 11 12 13 14 15 16 17 18 19 20 21 22 23 26 27 28 29 30 31 32 33 34 35 39 40 41 42 44 45 46 48 49 52 53 54 55 56 57 58 59 60 61 62 63 64 65 67 71 72 73 74 **P**5 6 **S** St. Francis Health System, Pittsburgh, PA
Web address: www.w.sfhs.edu

| | 23 | 10 | 187 | 4230 | 99 | 74857 | 145 | 35083 | 14937 | 755 |

NEW KENSINGTON—Westmoreland County

□ CITIZENS GENERAL HOSPITAL, 651 Fourth Avenue, Zip 15068–6591; tel. 724/337–3541; Edward M. Klaman, Acting Chief Executive Officer (Total facility includes 20 beds in nursing home–type unit) **A**1 2 6 9 10 **F**6 7 8 12 14 16 19 20 21 22 23 27 28 29 30 32 33 35 37 39 40 41 42 44 49 57 59 60 64 65 67 70 71 73

| | 23 | 10 | 136 | 4815 | 79 | 80560 | 316 | 44631 | 17129 | 569 |

NORRISTOWN—Montgomery County

□ MONTGOMERY COUNTY EMERGENCY SERVICE, 50 Beech Drive, Zip 19401, Mailing Address: P.O. Box 3005, Zip 19404–3005; tel. 610/279–6100; Rocio Nell, M.D., Chief Executive Officer and Medical Director (Nonreporting) **A**1 10

| | 23 | 22 | 53 | — | — | — | — | — | — | — |

⊠ MONTGOMERY HOSPITAL, 1301 Powell Street, Zip 19401, Mailing Address: P.O. Box 992, Zip 19404–0992; tel. 610/270–2000; Timothy M. Casey, President and Chief Executive Officer (Total facility includes 19 beds in nursing home–type unit) **A**1 2 3 5 9 10 **F**4 7 8 10 11 12 14 15 16 17 19 21 22 23 26 27 28 29 30 31 32 33 34 35 37 38 39 40 41 42 43 44 45 46 49 51 52 54 55 56 57 58 59 60 61 64 65 66 67 68 71 73 74 **P**5 6 7
Web address: www.mont–hosp.com

| | 23 | 10 | 213 | 10269 | 128 | 128464 | 665 | 76001 | 35150 | 1005 |

□ NORRISTOWN STATE HOSPITAL, 1001 Sterigere Street, Zip 19401–5399; tel. 215/270–1000; Albert R. Di Dario, Superintendent **A**1 5 9 10 **F**2 14 20 24 46 52 57 65 73

| | 12 | 22 | 859 | 531 | 405 | 0 | 0 | 75023 | 45294 | 1248 |

+ ○ SUBURBAN GENERAL HOSPITAL, 2701 DeKalb Pike, Zip 19401–1820; tel. 610/278–2000; Edward R. Solvibile, President (Nonreporting) **A**2 9 10 11 12 13 **S** Catholic Health East, Newtown Square, PA

| | 23 | 10 | 106 | — | — | — | — | — | — | — |

⊠ VALLEY FORGE MEDICAL CENTER AND HOSPITAL, 1033 West Germantown Pike, Zip 19403–3998; tel. 610/539–8500; Marian W. Colcher, President **A**1 9 10 **F**2 12 16 22 31 39 54 65 67 **P**6

| | 33 | 82 | 70 | 1498 | 45 | — | 0 | 5380 | 4328 | 125 |

NORTH WARREN—Warren County

□ WARREN STATE HOSPITAL, 33 Main Drive, Zip 16365–5099; tel. 814/723–5500; Carmen N. Ferranto, Chief Executive Officer **A**1 10 **F**8 14 15 16 20 22 42 44 52 57 65 73

| | 12 | 22 | 333 | 284 | 265 | 0 | 0 | 32096 | 19567 | 523 |

OAKDALE—Allegheny County

□ VENCOR HOSPITAL–PITTSBURGH, 7777 Steubenville Pike, Zip 15071–3409; tel. 412/494–5500; Patricia B. Speak, Administrator (Nonreporting) **A**1 9 10 **S** Vencor, Incorporated, Louisville, KY

| | 33 | 49 | 63 | — | — | — | — | — | — | — |

OIL CITY—Venango County

NORTHWEST MEDICAL CENTER–OIL CITY CAMPUS See Northwest Medical Centers, Franklin

OREFIELD—Lehigh County

★ NATIONAL HOSPITAL FOR KIDS IN CRISIS, 5300 Kids Peace Drive, Zip 18069–9101; tel. 610/799–8800; John P. Peter, President and Chief Executive Officer **A**9 10 **F**15 16 28 52 53 54 55 56 58 59 **P**6
Web address: www.kidspeace.org

| | 23 | 52 | 72 | 1225 | 53 | 0 | 0 | 14556 | 5085 | 158 |

PALMERTON—Carbon County

□ PALMERTON HOSPITAL, 135 Lafayette Avenue, Zip 18071–9990; tel. 610/826–3141; Peter L. Kern, President and Chief Executive Officer (Nonreporting) **A**1 9 10
Web address: www.palmertonhospital.com

| | 23 | 10 | 70 | — | — | — | — | — | — | — |

PAOLI—Chester County

★ PAOLI MEMORIAL HOSPITAL, 255 West Lancaster Avenue, Zip 19301–1792; tel. 610/648–1000; C. Barry Dykes, Senior Vice President **A**2 9 10 **F**1 2 3 4 5 6 7 8 9 10 11 12 13 15 16 17 18 19 20 21 22 23 25 26 27 28 29 30 31 32 33 34 35 36 37 38 39 40 41 42 43 44 45 46 47 48 49 50 51 52 53 54 55 56 57 58 59 60 61 62 63 64 65 66 67 68 69 71 72 73 74 **P**3 7 **S** Jefferson Health System, Wayne, PA
Web address: www.mlhs.org

| | 23 | 10 | 129 | 7793 | 85 | 97470 | 789 | 55248 | 20886 | 590 |

Hospital, Address, Telephone, Administrator, Approval, Facility, and Physician Codes, Health Care System, Network	Classi-fication Codes		Utilization Data					Expense (thousands) of dollars		
	Control	Service	Staffed Beds	Admissions	Census	Outpatient Visits	Births	Total	Payroll	Personnel

★ American Hospital Association (AHA) membership
□ Joint Commission on Accreditation of Healthcare Organizations (JCAHO) accreditation
+ American Osteopathic Healthcare Association (AOHA) membership
○ American Osteopathic Association (AOA) accreditation
△ Commission on Accreditation of Rehabilitation Facilities (CARF) accreditation
Control codes 61, 63, 64, 71, 72 and 73 indicate hospitals listed by AOHA, but not registered by AHA. For definition of numerical codes, see page A4

PECKVILLE—Lackawanna County

| MID–VALLEY HOSPITAL, 1400 Main Street, Zip 18452–2009; tel. 570/383–5500; Gerard H. Warner, Jr., Chief Executive Officer **A**9 10 **F**8 14 15 16 17 19 21 22 28 30 32 33 34 37 39 42 44 46 49 65 71 73 **P**3 8 Web address: www.mid–valleyhospital.baweb.com/ | 23 | 10 | 40 | 1206 | 18 | 29013 | 0 | 10305 | 4274 | 169 |

PHILADELPHIA—Philadelphia County

| ⊞ ALBERT EINSTEIN MEDICAL CENTER, (Includes Moss Rehabilitation Hospital, 1200 West Tabor Road, Zip 19141–3099; tel. 215/456–9070), 5501 Old York Road, Zip 19141–3098; tel. 215/456–7890; Martin Goldsmith, President (Total facility includes 102 beds in nursing home–type unit) (Nonreporting) **A**1 2 3 5 8 9 10 13 **S** Albert Einstein Healthcare Network, Philadelphia, PA | 23 | 10 | 701 | — | | | | | | |

ALLEGHENY UNIVERSITY HOSPITAL, CITY AVENUE See City Avenue Hospital
ALLEGHENY UNVERSITY HOSPITAL, GRADUATE See Graduate Hospital
ALLEGHENY UNVERSITY HOSPITAL, MEDICAL COLLEGE OF PENNSYLVANIA HOSPITAL See Medical College of Pennsylvania Hospital
ALLEGHENY UNVERSITY HOSPITAL, PARKVIEW See Parkview Hospital

⊞ BELMONT CENTER FOR COMPREHENSIVE TREATMENT, 4200 Monument Road, Zip 19131–1625; tel. 215/877–2000; Jack H. Dembow, General Director and Vice President (Nonreporting) **A**1 3 5 9 10 **S** Albert Einstein Healthcare Network, Philadelphia, PA	23	22	146	—						
□ CHARTER FAIRMOUNT BEHAVIORAL HEALTH SYSTEM, 561 Fairthorne Avenue, Zip 19128–2499; tel. 215/487–4000; Diane Kiddy, Chief Executive Officer **A**1 9 10 **F**14 52 53 55 56 57 59 **P**6 **S** Magellan Health Services, Atlanta, GA	32	22	136	4431	96	12243	0	13285	7565	195
⊞ CHESTNUT HILL HEALTHCARE, 8835 Germantown Avenue, Zip 19118–2765; tel. 215/248–8200; Cary F. Leptuck, President and Chief Executive Officer **A**1 3 5 9 10 **F**7 8 12 13 15 16 17 19 21 22 29 33 35 36 37 40 41 42 44 46 49 51 60 65 71 73 74 **P**2 5 7 Web address: www.chh.org	23	10	189	8235	95	103550	1057	61683	26289	869
□ CHILDREN'S HOSPITAL OF PHILADELPHIA, 34th Street and Civic Center Boulevard, Zip 19104–4399; tel. 215/590–1000; Edmond F. Notebaert, President (Nonreporting) **A**1 2 3 5 8 9 10 Web address: www.chop.edu	23	50	304	—						
□ CHILDREN'S SEASHORE HOUSE, 3405 Civic Center Boulevard, Zip 19104–4302; tel. 215/895–3600; Richard W. Shepherd, President and Chief Executive Officer (Nonreporting) **A**1 3 5 9 10 Web address: www.children's–seashore.org	33	56	77	—						
★ + ○ CITY AVENUE HOSPITAL, (Formerly Allegheny University Hospital, City Avenue), 4150 City Avenue, Zip 19131–1610; tel. 215/871–1000; Andrea F. Gilbert, Chief Executive Officer (Nonreporting) **A**9 10 11 12 13 **S** TENET Healthcare Corporation, Santa Barbara, CA	23	10	195	—						

EASTERN PENNSYLVANIA PSYCHIATRIC INSTITUTE See Medical College of Pennsylvania Hospital

| ⊞ EPISCOPAL HOSPITAL, (Includes George L. Harrison Memorial House), 100 East Lehigh Avenue, Zip 19125–1098; tel. 215/427–7000; Mark T. Bateman, Executive Director (Total facility includes 35 beds in nursing home–type unit) (Nonreporting) **A**1 2 3 5 6 9 10 | 23 | 10 | 218 | — | | | | | | |
| ⊞ FOX CHASE CANCER CENTER–AMERICAN ONCOLOGIC HOSPITAL, (ONCOLOGY), 7701 Burholme Avenue, Zip 19111–2412; tel. 215/728–6900; Robert C. Young, M.D., President **A**1 2 3 5 8 9 10 **F**8 12 14 15 16 17 18 19 20 21 28 29 30 31 32 33 34 35 37 39 41 42 44 45 46 49 50 54 60 65 67 68 71 73 74 **P**6 Web address: www.fccc.edu | 23 | 49 | 74 | 3510 | 54 | 41086 | 0 | 60331 | 18536 | 508 |

FRANKFORD CAMPUS See Frankford Hospital of the City of Philadelphia

⊞ + ○ FRANKFORD HOSPITAL OF THE CITY OF PHILADELPHIA, (Includes Bucks County Campus, 380 North Oxford Valley Road, Langhorne, Zip 19047–8399; tel. 215/949–5000; Frankford Campus, Frankford Avenue and Wakeling Street, Zip 19124; tel. 215/831–2000, Torresdale Campus), Knights and Red Lion Roads, Zip 19114–1486; tel. 215/612–4000; Roy A. Powell, President (Total facility includes 35 beds in nursing home–type unit) **A**1 3 5 8 9 10 11 12 13 **F**2 7 8 10 11 12 13 14 15 16 17 19 21 22 23 26 29 30 31 32 33 34 35 36 37 38 39 40 41 42 43 44 45 46 48 49 51 52 56 57 59 60 61 63 64 65 68 71 73 74 **P**3 **S** Jefferson Health System, Wayne, PA	23	10	490	25435	351	—	2045	209899	95481	2652
□ FRIEDMAN HOSPITAL OF THE HOME FOR THE JEWISH AGED, 5301 Old York Road, Zip 19141–2996; tel. 215/456–2900; Frank Podietz, President (Total facility includes 538 beds in nursing home–type unit) **A**1 9 10 **F**1 2 3 4 5 6 7 8 9 10 11 12 13 15 16 17 18 19 20 21 22 23 24 25 26 28 29 30 31 32 33 34 35 36 37 38 39 40 41 42 43 44 45 46 47 48 49 50 51 52 53 54 55 56 57 58 59 60 61 62 63 64 65 66 67 68 70 71 72 73 74 **P**6	23	10	566	986	532	66338	0	49350	26572	791
⊞ FRIENDS HOSPITAL, 4641 Roosevelt Boulevard, Zip 19124–2399; tel. 215/831–4600; Wayne A. Mugrauer, Chief Executive Officer (Nonreporting) **A**1 3 9 10	23	22	192	—						
⊞ GERMANTOWN HOSPITAL AND COMMUNITY HEALTH SERVICES, (Formerly Germantown Hospital and Medical Center), One Penn Boulevard, Zip 19144–1498; tel. 215/951–8000; David A. Ricci, President and Chief Executive Officer (Total facility includes 22 beds in nursing home–type unit) (Nonreporting) **A**1 5 9 10 **S** Jefferson Health System, Wayne, PA	23	10	158	—						

GIRARD MEDICAL CENTER See North Philadelphia Health System

Hospital, Address, Telephone, Administrator, Approval, Facility, and Physician Codes, Health Care System, Network	Classi-fication Codes		Utilization Data					Expense (thousands) of dollars		
★ American Hospital Association (AHA) membership □ Joint Commission on Accreditation of Healthcare Organizations (JCAHO) accreditation + American Osteopathic Healthcare Association (AOHA) membership ○ American Osteopathic Association (AOA) accreditation △ Commission on Accreditation of Rehabilitation Facilities (CARF) accreditation Control codes 61, 63, 64, 71, 72 and 73 indicate hospitals listed by AOHA, but not registered by AHA. For definition of numerical codes, see page A4	Control	Service	Staffed Beds	Admissions	Census	Outpatient Visits	Births	Total	Payroll	Personnel
⊞ GRADUATE HOSPITAL, (Formerly Allegheny University Hospital, Graduate), One Graduate Plaza, Zip 19146–1407; tel. 215/893–2000; Christopher DiCicco, Chief Executive Officer (Nonreporting) **A**1 2 3 5 8 9 10 **S** TENET Healthcare Corporation, Santa Barbara, CA	23	10	198	—	—	—	—	—	—	—
⊞ HAHNEMANN UNIVERSITY HOSPITAL, Broad and Vine Streets, Zip 19102–1192; tel. 215/762–7000; Michael P. Halter, Chief Executive Officer (Nonreporting) **A**1 2 3 5 8 9 10 **S** TENET Healthcare Corporation, Santa Barbara, CA **Web address:** www.auhs.edu	23	10	540	—	—	—	—	—	—	—
⊞ △ HOSPITAL OF THE UNIVERSITY OF PENNSYLVANIA, 3400 Spruce Street, Zip 19104–4204; tel. 215/662–4000; Thomas E. Beeman, Senior Vice President, Operations **A**1 3 5 7 8 9 10 **F**1 2 3 4 5 7 8 10 11 12 14 15 16 17 18 19 20 21 22 23 25 26 27 28 29 30 31 32 33 34 35 37 38 39 40 41 42 43 44 45 46 48 49 50 51 52 53 54 55 56 57 58 59 60 61 63 64 65 66 67 68 70 71 73 74 **P**1 4 5 6 7 **S** University of Pennsylvania Health System, Philadelphia, PA **Web address:** www.upenn.edu	23	10	659	31859	545	562167	2703	646464	221718	7261
⊞ JEANES HOSPITAL, 7600 Central Avenue, Zip 19111–2499; tel. 215/728–2000; G. Roger Martin, President and Chief Executive Officer (Total facility includes 24 beds in nursing home–type unit) **A**1 9 10 **F**1 7 8 12 14 15 16 17 19 20 21 22 26 28 30 32 33 35 37 38 39 40 41 42 44 46 48 49 60 61 64 65 67 71 73 74 **S** Temple University Health System, Philadelphia, PA **Web address:** www.jeanes.com	23	10	206	6544	148	96272	681	71380	—	934
□ JOHN F. KENNEDY MEMORIAL HOSPITAL, Langdon Street and Cheltenham Avenue, Zip 19124–1098; tel. 215/831–7000; Stephen H. Saks, Chief Executive Officer (Nonreporting) **A**1 9 10	23	10	141	—	—	—	—	—	—	—
□ KENSINGTON HOSPITAL, 136 West Diamond Street, Zip 19122–1721; tel. 215/426–8100; Eileen Hause, Chief Executive Officer (Nonreporting) **A**1 9 10	23	10	45	—	—	—	—	—	—	—
⊞ △ MAGEE REHABILITATION HOSPITAL, Six Franklin Plaza, Zip 19102–1177; tel. 215/587–3099; William E. Staas, Jr., President and Medical Director **A**1 3 7 9 10 **F**12 14 15 16 25 28 39 41 45 48 49 65 67 **P**4 7 **S** Jefferson Health System, Wayne, PA **Web address:** www.mageerehab.org	23	46	96	1400	72	39441	0	29387	16444	393
⊞ MEDICAL COLLEGE OF PENNSYLVANIA HOSPITAL, (Formerly Allegheny Unversity Hospital, Medical College of Pennsylvania Hospital), (Includes Eastern Pennsylvania Psychiatric Institute, 3200 Henry Avenue, Zip 19129; tel. 215/842–4000), 3300 Henry Avenue, Zip 19129–1121; tel. 215/842–6000; Richard S. Freeman, Chief Executive Officer (Nonreporting) **A**1 2 3 5 8 9 10 **S** TENET Healthcare Corporation, Santa Barbara, CA	23	10	369	—	—	—	—	—	—	—
METHODIST HOSPITAL See Thomas Jefferson University Hospital										
⊞ △ NAZARETH HOSPITAL, 2601 Holme Avenue, Zip 19152–2007; tel. 215/335–6000; Gregory T. Wozniak, President and Chief Executive Officer (Total facility includes 28 beds in nursing home–type unit) **A**1 7 9 10 **F**8 11 12 14 15 16 17 19 21 22 24 27 28 30 31 32 33 34 35 37 39 40 41 42 44 45 46 48 49 52 54 56 57 60 63 64 65 67 71 73 74 **P**7 8 **S** Catholic Health Initiatives, Denver, CO	23	10	222	10232	162	151204	103	65480	30802	730
NEUMANN MEDICAL CENTER See Temple East, Neumann Medical Center										
□ NORTH PHILADELPHIA HEALTH SYSTEM, (Includes Girard Medical Center, Girard Avenue at Eighth Street, Zip 19122; tel. 215/787–2000; Gloria Zankowski, Senior Vice President and Chief Executive Officer; St. Joseph's Hospital, 16th Street and Girard Avenue, Zip 19130; tel. 215/787–9000; Catherine Kutzler, R.N., Senior Vice President and Chief Executive Officer), 16th Street and Girard Avenue, Zip 19130–1615; tel. 215/787–9000; George J. Walmsley, III, President and Chief Executive Officer (Nonreporting) **A**1 5 9 10 12 13 **S** Catholic Health East, Newtown Square, PA	23	10	315	—	—	—	—	—	—	—
NORTHEASTERN HOSPITAL OF PHILADELPHIA, 2301 East Allegheny Avenue, Zip 19134–4497; tel. 215/291–3000; Lynn Holder, Associate Director (Nonreporting) **A**5 6 9 10 **S** Temple University Health System, Philadelphia, PA	23	10	166	—	—	—	—	—	—	—
★ ○ PARKVIEW HOSPITAL, (Formerly Allegheny Unversity Hospital, Parkview), 1331 East Wyoming Avenue, Zip 19124–3808; tel. 215/537–7400; Ernest N. Perilli, Chief Executive Officer (Total facility includes 19 beds in nursing home–type unit) (Nonreporting) **A**9 11 13 **S** TENET Healthcare Corporation, Santa Barbara, CA	23	10	165	—	—	—	—	—	—	—
⊞ PENNSYLVANIA HOSPITAL, 800 Spruce Street, Zip 19107–6192; tel. 215/829–3000; Timothy O. Morgan, Executive Director **A**1 2 3 5 8 9 10 **F**1 2 3 4 5 6 7 8 10 11 12 13 14 15 16 17 18 19 20 21 22 23 24 25 26 27 28 29 30 31 32 33 34 35 37 38 39 40 41 42 43 44 45 46 48 49 50 51 52 53 54 55 56 57 58 59 60 61 63 64 65 66 67 68 70 71 73 74 **P**1 6 **S** University of Pennsylvania Health System, Philadelphia, PA **Web address:** www.pahosp.com	23	10	346	16384	247	189681	3618	199835	89699	2417
□ PRESBYTERIAN MEDICAL CENTER OF THE UNIVERSITY OF PENNSYLVANIA HEALTH SYSTEM, 51 North 39th Street, Zip 19104–2640; tel. 215/662–8000; Michele M. Volpe, Executive Director (Total facility includes 20 beds in nursing home–type unit) (Nonreporting) **A**1 3 5 6 9 10 **S** University of Pennsylvania Health System, Philadelphia, PA **Web address:** www.health.upenn.edu/pmc	23	10	325	—	—	—	—	—	—	—
□ ROXBOROUGH MEMORIAL HOSPITAL, 5800 Ridge Avenue, Zip 19128–1737; tel. 215/483–9900; John J. Donnelly, Jr., President and Chief Executive Officer (Total facility includes 24 beds in nursing home–type unit) (Nonreporting) **A**1 6 9 10	23	10	129	—	—	—	—	—	—	—

Hospital, Address, Telephone, Administrator, Approval, Facility, and Physician Codes, Health Care System, Network	Classification Codes		Utilization Data					Expense (thousands) of dollars		
	Control	Service	Staffed Beds	Admissions	Census	Outpatient Visits	Births	Total	Payroll	Personnel

★ American Hospital Association (AHA) membership
□ Joint Commission on Accreditation of Healthcare Organizations (JCAHO) accreditation
+ American Osteopathic Healthcare Association (AOHA) membership
○ American Osteopathic Association (AOA) accreditation
△ Commission on Accreditation of Rehabilitation Facilities (CARF) accreditation
Control codes 61, 63, 64, 71, 72 and 73 indicate hospitals listed by AOHA, but not registered by AHA. For definition of numerical codes, see page A4

	Control	Service	Staffed Beds	Admissions	Census	Outpatient Visits	Births	Total	Payroll	Personnel
�włk SHRINERS HOSPITALS FOR CHILDREN, PHILADELPHIA, 3551 North Broad Street, Zip 19140–4105; tel. 215/430–4000; Sharon J. Rajnic, Administrator **A**1 3 5 **F**12 14 15 17 19 20 29 30 34 35 45 49 54 58 65 66 67 71 73 **S** Shriners Hospitals for Children, Tampa, FL	23	57	59	836	35	7964	0	—	—	265
✻ ○ ST. AGNES MEDICAL CENTER, 1900 South Broad Street, Zip 19145–2304; tel. 215/339–4100; Sister Margaret T. Sullivan, President, Chief Executive Officer and Chief Operating Officer (Total facility includes 19 beds in nursing home–type unit) **A**1 3 5 9 10 11 **F**9 11 12 17 19 22 24 27 28 30 32 34 37 41 42 44 48 49 64 65 71 73 74 **P**5 7 8 **S** Catholic Health Initiatives, Denver, CO	21	10	172	5578	110	51463	0	52611	23387	515
✻ ST. CHRISTOPHER'S HOSPITAL FOR CHILDREN, (PEDIATRIC), Erie Avenue at Front Street, Zip 19134–1095; tel. 215/427–5000; Calvin Bland, President and Chief Executive Officer **A**1 3 5 8 9 10 **F**1 2 3 4 5 7 8 9 10 11 12 13 14 15 16 17 18 19 20 21 22 25 26 27 28 29 30 31 32 34 35 37 38 39 40 41 42 43 44 45 46 47 48 49 51 52 53 54 55 56 57 58 59 60 61 65 66 67 68 70 71 73 74 **P**3 6 7 **S** TENET Healthcare Corporation, Santa Barbara, CA **Web address:** www.allegheny.edu	23	59	130	9253	114	98026	0	—	—	1136
ST. JOSEPH'S HOSPITAL See North Philadelphia Health System										
□ TEMPLE EAST, NEUMANN MEDICAL CENTER, (Formerly Neumann Medical Center), 1741 Frankford Avenue, Zip 19125–2495; tel. 215/291–2000; Lynn Holder, Executive Director (Nonreporting) **A**1 9 10 **S** Temple University Health System, Philadelphia, PA **Web address:** www.neumann.org	23	10	166	—	—	—	—	—	—	—
□ TEMPLE UNIVERSITY HOSPITAL, Broad and Ontario Streets, Zip 19140–5192; tel. 215/707–2000; Paul Boehringer, Executive Director (Total facility includes 16 beds in nursing home–type unit) **A**1 2 3 5 8 9 10 **F**1 4 5 6 7 8 10 11 12 13 14 15 16 17 18 19 20 21 22 23 24 25 26 27 28 29 30 31 32 33 34 35 37 38 39 40 41 42 43 44 45 46 48 49 50 51 52 54 55 56 57 58 59 60 61 62 63 64 65 66 67 69 70 71 72 73 74 **P**3 4 5 6 7 **S** Temple University Health System, Philadelphia, PA **Web address:** www.allcet.com/tuhs/index.htm	23	10	398	21186	340	157291	1945	273969	113790	2558
✻ △ THOMAS JEFFERSON UNIVERSITY HOSPITAL, (Includes Methodist Hospital, 2301 South Broad Street, Zip 19148; tel. 215/952–9000; Thomas Jefferson University Hospital–Ford Road Campus, 3905 Ford Road, Zip 19131; tel. 215/578–3630), 111 South 11th Street, Zip 19107–5096; tel. 215/955–7022; Thomas J. Lewis, President and Chief Executive Officer (Total facility includes 210 beds in nursing home–type unit) **A**1 2 3 5 6 7 8 9 10 **F**1 2 3 4 5 6 7 8 10 11 12 13 15 16 17 18 19 20 21 22 23 24 25 26 27 28 29 30 31 32 33 34 35 36 37 38 39 40 41 42 43 44 45 46 47 48 49 51 52 53 54 55 56 57 58 60 61 63 64 65 66 67 68 70 71 73 74 **P**2 3 7 8 **S** Jefferson Health System, Wayne, PA **Web address:** www.jeffersonhealth.org	23	10	992	35178	742	750969	3112	582487	238695	5664
TORRESDALE CAMPUS See Frankford Hospital of the City of Philadelphia										
□ VENCOR HOSPITAL–PHILADELPHIA, (LONG TERM ACUTE CARE), 6129 Palmetto Street, Zip 19111–5729; tel. 215/722–8555; Debra Condon, Administrator **A**1 10 **F**37 65 71 **S** Vencor, Incorporated, Louisville, KY	33	49	52	302	39	0	0	15463	5262	125
✻ VETERANS AFFAIRS MEDICAL CENTER, University and Woodland Avenues, Zip 19104–4594; tel. 215/823–5800; Michael J. Sullivan, Director (Total facility includes 180 beds in nursing home–type unit) (Nonreporting) **A**1 3 5 8 9 **S** Department of Veterans Affairs, Washington, DC	45	10	656	—	—	—	—	—	—	—
✻ WILLS EYE HOSPITAL, (EYE HOSPITAL), 900 Walnut Street, Zip 19107–5598; tel. 215/928–3000; D. McWilliams Kessler, Executive Director **A**1 3 5 9 10 **F**2 3 4 5 7 8 9 10 11 12 13 14 15 16 17 18 19 20 21 22 23 24 25 26 27 28 29 30 31 32 33 34 35 37 38 39 40 41 42 43 44 45 46 47 48 49 50 51 52 53 54 55 56 57 58 59 60 61 63 65 66 67 68 70 71 72 73 74 **Web address:** www.jeffline.tju.edu/wills	23	49	115	4620	49	58361	0	63564	25296	631
PHOENIXVILLE—Chester County										
✻ PHOENIXVILLE HOSPITAL OF THE UNIVERSITY OF PENNSYLVANIA HEALTH SYSTEM, 140 Nutt Road, Zip 19460–0809, Mailing Address: P.O. Box 809, Zip 19460–0809; tel. 610/983–1000; Richard E. Seagrave, Executive Director and Chief Operating Officer (Total facility includes 21 beds in nursing home–type unit) **A**1 9 10 **F**3 4 7 8 10 11 13 14 15 16 17 19 20 21 22 23 26 29 30 31 32 33 34 35 37 38 39 40 41 42 43 44 46 49 54 55 56 60 61 63 64 65 66 67 68 70 71 73 74 **P**4 6 **S** University of Pennsylvania Health System, Philadelphia, PA	23	10	127	6106	60	95695	1158	45142	19359	600
PITTSBURGH—Allegheny County										
✻ ALLEGHENY UNIVERSITY HOSPITALS–FORBES METROPOLITAN, (LONG TERM ACUTE CARE), 225 Penn Avenue, Zip 15221–2173; tel. 412/247–2424; April A. Stevens, R.N., Vice President and Administrator **A**1 9 10 **F**4 7 8 10 12 13 15 16 17 19 20 21 22 24 25 26 27 28 29 30 31 32 33 34 35 36 39 41 42 43 44 45 46 48 49 50 51 52 54 55 56 57 58 59 60 61 63 64 65 66 67 68 70 71 72 73 74 **P**6 **S** Allegheny University Hospitals–West, Pittsburgh, PA	23	49	155	1305	101	20973	0	32350	13514	307
✻ ALLEGHENY UNIVERSITY HOSPITALS, ALLEGHENY GENERAL, 320 East North Avenue, Zip 15212–4756; tel. 412/359–3131; Connie M. Cibrone, President and Chief Executive Officer (Total facility includes 60 beds in nursing home–type unit) **A**1 2 3 5 8 9 10 **F**3 4 7 8 10 11 12 13 14 15 16 17 18 19 20 22 23 24 25 26 27 28 30 31 32 33 34 35 37 38 39 40 41 42 43 44 45 46 47 49 51 52 53 54 55 56 57 58 60 61 63 64 65 66 67 68 70 71 73 74 **S** Allegheny University Hospitals–West, Pittsburgh, PA **Web address:** www.allhealth.edu	23	10	552	31182	468	449607	1935	513247	168536	5031

Hospital, Address, Telephone, Administrator, Approval, Facility, and Physician Codes, Health Care System, Network	Classi-fication Codes		Utilization Data					Expense (thousands) of dollars		
	Control	Service	Staffed Beds	Admissions	Census	Outpatient Visits	Births	Total	Payroll	Personnel

★ American Hospital Association (AHA) membership
□ Joint Commission on Accreditation of Healthcare Organizations (JCAHO) accreditation
+ American Osteopathic Healthcare Association (AOHA) membership
○ American Osteopathic Association (AOA) accreditation
△ Commission on Accreditation of Rehabilitation Facilities (CARF) accreditation
Control codes 61, 63, 64, 71, 72 and 73 indicate hospitals listed by AOHA, but not registered by AHA. For definition of numerical codes, see page A4

Hospital	Control	Service	Staffed Beds	Admissions	Census	Outpatient Visits	Births	Total	Payroll	Personnel
★ CHILDREN'S HOME OF PITTSBURGH, (NEONATAL/PEDIATRIC SPECIALTY), 5618 Kentucky Avenue, Zip 15232–2606; tel. 412/441–4884; Pamela R. Schanwald, Chief Executive Officer **A**9 10 **F**16 19 21 31 32 33 35 41 45 46 50 63 65 71 73	23	59	10	134	7	0	0	2019	903	38
□ CHILDREN'S HOSPITAL OF PITTSBURGH, 3705 Fifth Avenue at De Soto Street, Zip 15213–2583; tel. 412/692–5325; Ronald L. Violi, President and Chief Executive Officer (Nonreporting) **A**1 2 3 5 8 9 10	23	50	235	—	—	—	—	—	—	—
EYE AND EAR HOSPITAL OF PITTSBURGH See UPMC Presbyterian										
□ △ HEALTHSOUTH HARMARVILLE REHABILITATION HOSPITAL, Guys Run Road, Zip 15238–0460, Mailing Address: Box 11460, Guys Run Road, Zip 15238–0460; tel. 412/781–5700; Frank G. DeLisi, III, CHE, Chief Executive Officer and Director Operations (Total facility includes 40 beds in nursing home–type unit) (Nonreporting) **A**1 3 7 9 10 **S** HEALTHSOUTH Corporation, Birmingham, AL	33	46	202	—	—	—	—	—	—	—
✶ MAGEE–WOMENS HOSPITAL, 300 Halket Street, Zip 15213–3180; tel. 412/641–1000; Irma E. Goertzen, President and Chief Executive Officer **A**1 2 3 5 8 9 10 **F**7 8 12 13 14 15 16 17 19 21 22 25 27 28 29 30 32 34 35 37 38 39 40 42 44 45 46 49 60 61 63 65 67 68 71 73 74 **P**6 8	23	44	261	12816	131	385434	7990	113046	47662	1544
□ △ MERCY HOSPITAL OF PITTSBURGH, 1400 Locust Street, Zip 15219–5166; tel. 412/232–8111; J. Penn Krause, Executive Vice President Operations (Total facility includes 37 beds in nursing home–type unit) **A**1 2 3 5 6 7 8 9 10 12 **F**4 6 7 8 9 10 11 12 13 14 15 16 17 18 19 20 21 22 23 24 25 26 27 28 29 30 31 32 33 34 35 37 38 39 40 41 42 43 44 45 46 47 48 49 51 52 53 54 55 56 57 58 60 61 63 64 65 67 68 70 71 72 73 74 **P**5 8 **S** Catholic Health East, Newtown Square, PA	23	10	422	17867	294	253872	1130	217713	73831	2152
□ MERCY PROVIDENCE HOSPITAL, 1004 Arch Street, Zip 15212–5235; tel. 412/323–5600; Sister Kathi Sweeney, Administrator **A**1 9 10 **F**8 11 14 15 16 17 18 19 20 21 22 24 28 29 30 31 34 35 39 41 45 46 48 49 52 54 55 56 58 60 63 65 67 71 72 73 **P**5 8 **S** Catholic Health East, Newtown Square, PA	23	10	120	4413	70	18533	0	25504	9548	306
MONTEFIORE HOSPITAL See UPMC Presbyterian										
PODIATRY HOSPITAL OF PITTSBURGH, 215 South Negley Avenue, Zip 15206–3594; tel. 412/661–0814; Joseph S. Noviello, Chief Executive Officer (Nonreporting) **A**9 10	23	49	13	—	—	—	—	—	—	—
SHADYSIDE HOSPITAL See UPMC Shadyside										
□ SOUTH HILLS HEALTH SYSTEM, 565 Coal Valley Road, Zip 15236–0119, Mailing Address: Box 18119, Zip 15236–0119; tel. 412/469–5000; William R. Jennings, President and Chief Executive Officer (Total facility includes 74 beds in nursing home–type unit) (Nonreporting) **A**1 9 10 **Web address:** www.shhspgh.org	23	10	466	—	—	—	—	—	—	—
□ SOUTHWOOD PSYCHIATRIC HOSPITAL, 2575 Boyce Plaza Road, Zip 15241–3925; tel. 412/257–2290; Alan A. Axelson, M.D., Chief Executive Officer (Nonreporting) **A**1 9 **S** FHC Health Systems, Norfolk, VA	33	52	50	—	—	—	—	—	—	—
✶ ST. CLAIR MEMORIAL HOSPITAL, 1000 Bower Hill Road, Zip 15243–1873; tel. 412/561–4900; Benjamin E. Snead, President and Chief Executive Officer (Total facility includes 26 beds in nursing home–type unit) **A**1 2 9 10 **F**1 2 4 5 6 7 8 10 11 12 13 14 15 16 17 18 19 21 22 23 24 25 26 27 28 29 30 31 32 33 34 35 37 38 39 40 41 42 43 44 45 46 49 52 54 55 56 57 58 59 60 61 63 64 65 67 68 71 73 74 **P**3 8	23	10	286	12188	177	148147	1341	90936	42303	1244
✶ ○ ST. FRANCIS CENTRAL HOSPITAL, 1200 Centre Avenue, Zip 15219–3507; tel. 412/562–3000; Robin Z. Mohr, Chief Executive Officer (Total facility includes 19 beds in nursing home–type unit) **A**1 9 10 11 12 13 **F**2 3 4 5 7 8 10 11 12 13 14 17 18 19 20 21 22 23 25 26 27 28 29 30 31 32 34 35 37 39 40 41 42 43 44 45 46 48 49 50 51 52 53 54 55 56 57 58 59 60 61 62 63 64 65 66 67 71 72 73 74 **P**5 6 **S** St. Francis Health System, Pittsburgh, PA **Web address:** www.sfhs.edu	23	10	136	4234	73	62209	0	40258	16338	464
✶ △ ST. FRANCIS MEDICAL CENTER, 400 45th Street, Zip 15201–1198; tel. 412/622–4343; Sister Florence Brandt, Chief Executive Officer (Total facility includes 320 beds in nursing home–type unit) **A**1 2 3 5 6 7 8 9 10 **F**2 3 4 5 7 8 10 11 12 14 17 19 20 21 22 23 24 25 26 27 28 29 30 31 32 34 35 37 39 40 41 42 43 44 45 46 48 49 50 51 52 53 54 55 56 57 58 59 60 63 64 65 66 67 68 71 72 73 74 **P**5 7 8 **S** St. Francis Health System, Pittsburgh, PA	23	10	832	17639	622	296417	622	196130	86871	2662
STATE CORRECTIONAL INSTITUTION HOSPITAL, Doerr Street, Zip 15233, Mailing Address: Box 99901, Zip 15233; tel. 412/761–1955; Joseph Morrash, Administrator (Nonreporting)	12	11	27	—	—	—	—	—	—	—
□ SUBURBAN GENERAL HOSPITAL, 100 South Jackson Avenue, Zip 15202–3428; tel. 412/734–6000; James M. Collins, President and Chief Executive Officer (Total facility includes 25 beds in nursing home–type unit) **A**1 9 10 **F**4 7 8 9 10 11 12 13 14 15 16 17 18 19 20 21 22 23 26 27 28 30 31 32 33 34 35 37 38 40 41 42 43 44 45 46 48 49 51 52 54 56 57 60 61 63 64 65 67 68 71 73 74 **P**7 8	23	10	143	4208	85	45000	0	30384	13618	530
★ △ THE CHILDREN'S INSTITUTE OF PITTSBURGH, 6301 Northumberland Street, Zip 15217–1396; tel. 412/420–2400; John A. Wilson, President and Chief Executive Officer **A**7 9 10 **F**12 14 15 16 17 34 41 46 48 49 53 65 73 **Web address:** www.amazingkids.org	23	46	38	86	23	5364	0	4345	2537	169
UNIVERSITY OF PITTSBURGH MEDICAL CENTER See UPMC Presbyterian										
UNIVERSITY OF PITTSBURGH MEDICAL CENTER–PASSAVANT See UPMC Passavant										

Hospital, Address, Telephone, Administrator, Approval, Facility, and Physician Codes, Health Care System, Network	Classi-fication Codes		Utilization Data					Expense (thousands) of dollars		
★ American Hospital Association (AHA) membership □ Joint Commission on Accreditation of Healthcare Organizations (JCAHO) accreditation + American Osteopathic Healthcare Association (AOHA) membership ○ American Osteopathic Association (AOA) accreditation △ Commission on Accreditation of Rehabilitation Facilities (CARF) accreditation Control codes 61, 63, 64, 71, 72 and 73 indicate hospitals listed by AOHA, but not registered by AHA. For definition of numerical codes, see page A4	Control	Service	Staffed Beds	Admissions	Census	Outpatient Visits	Births	Total	Payroll	Personnel
□ UPMC PASSAVANT, (Formerly University of Pittsburgh Medical Center–Passavant), 9100 Babcock Boulevard, Zip 15237–5815; tel. 412/367–6700; Raymond J. Beck, President and Chief Executive Officer (Total facility includes 24 beds in nursing home–type unit) **A**1 9 10 **F**1 2 3 4 5 6 7 8 10 11 12 13 14 15 16 17 18 19 20 21 22 23 24 25 26 27 28 29 30 31 32 33 34 35 36 37 38 39 40 41 42 43 44 45 46 47 48 49 50 51 52 53 54 55 56 57 58 59 60 61 62 63 64 65 66 67 68 70 71 72 73 74 **P**1 5 6 7 8 **S** UPMC Health System, Pittsburgh, PA	23	10	193	9619	147	157525	0	78785	37480	1148
⊠ UPMC PRESBYTERIAN, (Formerly University of Pittsburgh Medical Center), (Includes Eye and Ear Hospital of Pittsburgh, 200 Lothrop Street, Zip 15213–2592; tel. 412/647–2345; Montefiore Hospital, 200 Lothrop Street, Zip 15213; tel. 412/647–2345; UPMC Presbyterian Hospital, 200 Lothrop Street, Zip 15213; tel. 412/647–2345; Western Psychiatric Institute and Clinic, 3811 O'Hara Street, Zip 15213–2593; tel. 412/624–2100), Henry A. Mordoh, President (Total facility includes 23 beds in nursing home–type unit) **A**1 2 3 5 8 9 **F**1 2 3 4 5 6 7 8 10 11 12 13 14 15 16 17 18 19 20 21 22 23 24 25 26 27 28 29 30 31 32 33 34 35 36 37 38 39 40 41 42 43 44 45 46 47 48 49 50 51 52 53 54 55 56 57 58 59 60 61 62 63 64 65 66 67 68 70 71 72 73 74 **P**1 6 7 **S** UPMC Health System, Pittsburgh, PA **Web address:** www.upmc.edu	23	10	782	33240	655	1194646	0	673135	208063	6756
⊠ UPMC SHADYSIDE, (Formerly Shadyside Hospital), 5230 Centre Avenue, Zip 15232–1304; tel. 412/623–2121; Henry A. Mordoh, President (Total facility includes 145 beds in nursing home–type unit) (Nonreporting) **A**1 2 3 5 9 10 **S** UPMC Health System, Pittsburgh, PA **Web address:** www.upmc.edu	23	10	508	—	—	—	—	—	—	—
□ UPMC SOUTH SIDE, 2000 Mary Street, Zip 15203–2095; tel. 412/488–5550; Marcie S. Caplan, Acting Chief Executive Officer (Total facility includes 29 beds in nursing home–type unit) **A**1 9 10 **F**1 2 3 4 5 6 7 8 10 11 12 13 14 15 16 17 18 19 20 21 22 23 24 25 26 27 28 29 30 31 32 33 34 35 36 37 38 39 40 41 42 43 44 45 46 47 48 49 50 51 52 53 54 55 56 57 58 59 60 61 62 63 64 65 66 67 68 70 71 72 73 74 **P**1 6 7 **S** UPMC Health System, Pittsburgh, PA **Web address:** www.upmc.edu	23	10	165	5386	105	19896	0	35707	15593	447
⊠ UPMC ST. MARGARET, 815 Freeport Road, Zip 15215–3301; tel. 412/784–4000; Stanley J. Kevish, President (Total facility includes 22 beds in nursing home–type unit) **A**1 2 3 5 6 8 9 10 **F**5 6 8 10 12 15 16 17 19 20 21 22 25 26 28 29 30 31 32 33 34 35 37 39 41 42 44 45 46 48 49 54 56 57 58 60 62 64 65 66 67 68 71 73 **P**8 **S** UPMC Health System, Pittsburgh, PA	23	10	223	8992	137	110893	0	82151	30065	928
⊠ VETERANS AFFAIRS PITTSBURGH HEALTHCARE SYSTEM, (Includes Veterans Affairs Medical Center, 7180 Highland Drive, Zip 15206–1297; tel. 412/365–4900; Veterans Affairs Medical Center, University Drive C, tel. 412/688–6000), Delafield Road, Zip 15240–1001; tel. 412/784–3900; Thomas A. Cappello, Director (Total facility includes 300 beds in nursing home–type unit) **A**1 2 3 5 8 **F**1 3 4 5 9 10 11 12 14 16 17 18 19 20 21 22 23 24 26 27 28 29 30 31 32 33 34 35 37 39 40 41 42 43 44 45 46 49 50 51 52 54 55 56 57 58 59 60 63 64 65 67 68 71 73 74 **P**6 **S** Department of Veterans Affairs, Washington, DC **Web address:** www.pitt.edu	45	49	889	9189	989	359625	0	203004	106417	2347
⊠ WESTERN PENNSYLVANIA HOSPITAL, 4800 Friendship Avenue, Zip 15224–1722; tel. 412/578–5000; Charles M. O'Brien, Jr., President and Chief Executive Officer **A**1 2 3 5 6 8 9 10 12 **F**1 4 7 8 9 10 11 12 13 14 15 16 17 18 19 20 21 22 23 26 27 28 30 34 35 37 38 40 41 42 43 44 45 46 48 49 51 52 54 56 57 60 61 63 64 65 67 68 71 73 74 **P**7 8 **Web address:** www.westpennhospital.org WESTERN PSYCHIATRIC INSTITUTE AND CLINIC See UPMC Presbyterian	23	10	512	17702	304	150977	1913	211928	87909	2291
PLEASANT GAP—Centre County										
□ △ HEALTHSOUTH NITTANY VALLEY REHABILITATION HOSPITAL, 550 West College Avenue, Zip 16823–8808; tel. 814/359–3421; Mary Jane Hawkins, Administrator and Chief Executive Officer (Nonreporting) **A**1 7 9 10 **S** HEALTHSOUTH Corporation, Birmingham, AL	33	46	88	—	—	—	—	—	—	—
POTTSTOWN—Montgomery County										
⊠ POTTSTOWN MEMORIAL MEDICAL CENTER, 1600 East High Street, Zip 19464–5008; tel. 610/327–7000; John J. Buckley, President and Chief Executive Officer (Total facility includes 21 beds in nursing home–type unit) **A**1 2 9 10 **F**7 8 10 12 14 15 16 17 19 20 21 22 24 26 27 30 32 34 35 36 37 39 40 41 42 44 45 46 49 51 52 56 57 60 63 64 65 66 67 71 73 74 **P**6 **Web address:** www.pmmctr.org	23	10	212	8871	118	157444	850	71208	33477	954
POTTSVILLE—Schuylkill County										
⊠ GOOD SAMARITAN REGIONAL MEDICAL CENTER, 700 East Norwegian Street, Zip 17901–2798; tel. 570/621–4000; Gino J. Pazzaglini, President and Chief Executive Officer **A**1 2 5 9 10 **F**3 4 7 8 11 12 14 15 16 19 22 26 28 30 31 32 33 34 35 36 37 39 40 41 42 44 45 46 60 65 67 71 73 74 **P**6 **S** Daughters of Charity National Health System, Saint Louis, MO **Web address:** www.goodsamrmc.com	21	10	153	7871	126	132787	350	50094	23932	711
⊠ △ POTTSVILLE HOSPITAL AND WARNE CLINIC, 420 South Jackson Street, Zip 17901–3692; tel. 570/621–5000; Donald R. Gintzig, President and Chief Executive Officer **A**1 2 6 7 9 10 **F**7 8 12 13 14 15 16 17 19 20 21 22 23 26 27 28 30 31 32 33 34 35 37 39 40 41 42 44 45 48 49 52 53 55 56 57 58 65 66 71 73 74 **S** Quorum Health Group/Quorum Health Resources, Inc., Brentwood, TN **Web address:** www.pottsville.com/hospital	23	10	196	6372	123	80214	603	46631	21343	772

Hospital, Address, Telephone, Administrator, Approval, Facility, and Physician Codes, Health Care System, Network	Classi-fication Codes		Utilization Data					Expense (thousands) of dollars		
★ American Hospital Association (AHA) membership □ Joint Commission on Accreditation of Healthcare Organizations (JCAHO) accreditation + American Osteopathic Healthcare Association (AOHA) membership ○ American Osteopathic Association (AOA) accreditation △ Commission on Accreditation of Rehabilitation Facilities (CARF) accreditation Control codes 61, 63, 64, 71, 72 and 73 indicate hospitals listed by AOHA, but not registered by AHA. For definition of numerical codes, see page A4	Control	Service	Staffed Beds	Admissions	Census	Outpatient Visits	Births	Total	Payroll	Personnel

PUNXSUTAWNEY—Jefferson County

□ PUNXSUTAWNEY AREA HOSPITAL, 81 Hillcrest Drive, Zip 15767–2616; tel. 814/938–1800; Daniel D. Blough, Jr., Chief Executive Officer (Total facility includes 14 beds in nursing home–type unit) **A**1 9 10 **F**7 8 14 15 16 19 20 21 22 30 31 32 34 37 39 40 42 44 49 64 65 71
Web address: www.pah.org

| | 23 | 10 | 65 | 2117 | 27 | 92134 | 226 | 18510 | 7506 | 286 |

QUAKERTOWN—Bucks County

ST. LUKE'S QUAKERTOWN HOSPITAL See St. Luke's Hospital and Health Network, Bethlehem

READING—Berks County

□ △ HEALTHSOUTH READING REHABILITATION HOSPITAL, 1623 Morgantown Road, Zip 19607–9455; tel. 610/796–6000; Tammy L. Ober, Administrator and Chief Executive Officer (Total facility includes 19 beds in nursing home–type unit) **A**1 7 9 10 **F**12 14 15 16 26 27 39 48 49 64 65 67 73 **S** HEALTHSOUTH Corporation, Birmingham, AL
Web address: www.rdgrehab.com

| | 33 | 46 | 95 | 1592 | 61 | 21880 | 0 | — | 9840 | 245 |

⊞ READING HOSPITAL AND MEDICAL CENTER, Sixth Avenue and Spruce Street, Zip 19611–1428, Mailing Address: P.O. Box 16052, Zip 19612–6052; tel. 610/988–8000; Charles Sullivan, President and Chief Executive Officer **A**1 2 3 5 9 10 **F**3 4 6 7 8 10 12 13 14 15 16 17 18 19 20 21 22 23 25 26 28 29 30 31 34 35 37 38 39 40 41 42 43 44 45 46 48 49 51 52 53 54 55 56 57 58 59 60 61 62 65 66 67 68 71 72 73 74 **P**8
Web address: www.readinghospital.org

| | 23 | 10 | 565 | 28584 | 408 | 585323 | 2930 | 221315 | 101348 | 2880 |

★ ST. JOSEPH MEDICAL CENTER, Twelth and Walnut Streets, Zip 19603–0316, Mailing Address: P.O. Box 316, Zip 19603–0316; tel. 610/378–2000; Christopher B. Rumpf, M.D., Interim President (Total facility includes 25 beds in nursing home–type unit) (Nonreporting) **A**3 5 9 10 12 **S** Catholic Health Initiatives, Denver, CO
Web address: www.chi–east.org/

| | 21 | 10 | 417 | — | | | | | | |

RENOVO—Clinton County

BUCKTAIL MEDICAL CENTER, 1001 Pine Street, Zip 17764–1618; tel. 570/923–1000; Lennea F. Brown, Administrator (Total facility includes 41 beds in nursing home–type unit) (Nonreporting) **A**9 10

| | 23 | 10 | 50 | — | | | | | | |

RIDGWAY—Elk County

□ ELK COUNTY REGIONAL MEDICAL CENTER, 94 Hospital Street, Zip 15853; tel. 814/776–6111; Richard J. Bruno, Senior Vice President (Nonreporting) **A**1 9 10

| | 23 | 10 | 52 | — | | | | | | |

RIDLEY PARK—Delaware County

TAYLOR HOSPITAL See Crozer–Chester Medical Center, Upland

ROARING SPRING—Blair County

⊞ NASON HOSPITAL, 105 Nason Drive, Zip 16673–1202; tel. 814/224–2141; John P. Kinney, President and Chief Executive Officer **A**1 5 9 10 **F**7 8 15 19 21 22 23 28 29 30 32 33 34 35 37 40 44 45 49 65 67 71 73

| | 23 | 10 | 40 | 1644 | 19 | 50472 | 250 | 14204 | 5965 | 198 |

SAINT MARYS—Elk County

⊞ ST. MARYS REGIONAL MEDICAL CENTER, 763 Johnsonburg Road, Zip 15857–3417; tel. 814/781–7500; Paul A. DeSantis, President (Total facility includes 138 beds in nursing home–type unit) **A**1 9 10 **F**7 8 12 14 15 16 17 19 21 22 23 28 29 30 32 33 35 37 39 40 41 42 44 45 46 49 62 64 65 66 71 73 74

| | 23 | 10 | 204 | 3500 | 164 | 68992 | 354 | 30308 | 14319 | 535 |

SAYRE—Bradford County

⊞ ROBERT PACKER HOSPITAL, 1 Guthrie Square, Zip 18840–1698; tel. 570/888–6666; William F. Vanaskie, President and Chief Executive Officer (Nonreporting) **A**1 2 3 5 9 10 **S** Guthrie Healthcare System, Sayre, PA
Web address: www.inet.guthrie.org

| | 23 | 10 | 265 | — | | | | | | |

SCRANTON—Lackawanna County

⊞ △ ALLIED SERVICES REHABILITATION HOSPITAL, 475 Morgan Highway, Zip 18501–1130; tel. 570/348–1300; James L. Brady, President **A**1 7 9 10 **F**1 3 5 6 14 15 16 17 24 25 27 32 34 35 39 41 45 46 48 49 53 54 55 56 58 62 64 65 66 67 71 73 74 **P**5 6

| | 23 | 46 | 117 | 2153 | 89 | 16599 | 0 | 31009 | 14809 | 502 |

⊞ COMMUNITY MEDICAL CENTER, 1800 Mulberry Street, Zip 18510; tel. 570/969–8000; C. Richard Hartman, M.D., President and Chief Executive Officer (Total facility includes 20 beds in nursing home–type unit) **A**1 3 9 10 **F**1 4 7 8 10 11 12 13 14 15 16 17 18 19 21 22 23 25 26 27 28 29 30 31 33 34 35 37 38 39 40 41 42 43 44 45 46 49 51 52 53 54 55 56 57 58 59 60 61 64 65 67 70 71 72 73 74 **P**5 8

| | 23 | 10 | 276 | 12504 | 200 | 109135 | 1736 | 97495 | 39865 | 1113 |

□ MERCY HOSPITAL OF SCRANTON, 746 Jefferson Avenue, Zip 18501–1624; tel. 717/348–7100; Susan Petula, President (Total facility includes 22 beds in nursing home–type unit) **A**1 2 3 5 9 10 **F**4 7 8 10 11 12 13 15 16 17 19 21 22 23 24 26 28 29 32 33 34 35 37 39 40 41 42 43 44 49 51 60 63 64 65 67 68 71 73 74 **P**8 **S** Catholic Healthcare Partners, Cincinnati, OH

| | 21 | 10 | 265 | 11747 | 199 | 247839 | 923 | 110052 | 43892 | 1333 |

⊞ MOSES TAYLOR HOSPITAL, 700 Quincy Avenue, Zip 18510–1724; tel. 570/340–2100; Harold E. Anderson, Chief Executive Officer (Total facility includes 32 beds in nursing home–type unit) (Nonreporting) **A**1 3 5 9 10
Web address: www.mth.org

| | 23 | 10 | 222 | — | | | | | | |

SELLERSVILLE—Bucks County

⊞ △ GRAND VIEW HOSPITAL, 700 Lawn Avenue, Zip 18960–1576; tel. 215/453–4000; Stuart H. Fine, Chief Executive Officer **A**1 2 7 9 10 **F**2 3 7 8 11 12 13 15 16 17 19 21 22 23 24 26 28 29 30 31 32 33 34 36 37 40 41 42 44 45 46 49 52 53 54 56 57 58 59 60 63 65 66 67 71 73 74 **P**1

| | 23 | 10 | 174 | 8802 | 112 | 144448 | 1119 | 69822 | 33053 | 1075 |

Hospital, Address, Telephone, Administrator, Approval, Facility, and Physician Codes, Health Care System, Network	Classi-fication Codes		Utilization Data					Expense (thousands) of dollars		
★ American Hospital Association (AHA) membership □ Joint Commission on Accreditation of Healthcare Organizations (JCAHO) accreditation + American Osteopathic Healthcare Association (AOHA) membership ○ American Osteopathic Association (AOA) accreditation △ Commission on Accreditation of Rehabilitation Facilities (CARF) accreditation Control codes 61, 63, 64, 71, 72 and 73 indicate hospitals listed by AOHA, but not registered by AHA. For definition of numerical codes, see page A4	Control	Service	Staffed Beds	Admissions	Census	Outpatient Visits	Births	Total	Payroll	Personnel

SEWICKLEY—Allegheny County

⊠ △ D. T. WATSON REHABILITATION HOSPITAL, 301 Camp Meeting Road, Zip 15143–8773; tel. 412/741–9500; Robert N. Gibson, President and Chief Executive Officer **A**1 7 9 10 **F**12 16 48 49 65 73 **P**6
Web address: www.dtwatson.org

| | 23 | 46 | 44 | 410 | 20 | 16600 | 0 | 11089 | 6149 | 154 |

⊠ VALLEY MEDICAL FACILITIES, (Includes Sewickley Valley Hospital, (A Division of Valley Medical Facilities), 720 Blackburn Road, Zip 15143–1459; tel. 412/741–6600; The Medical Center, Beaver, 1000 Dutch Ridge Road, Beaver, Zip 15009–9727; tel. 724/728–7000), 720 Blackburn Road, Zip 15143–1498; tel. 412/741–6600; James C. Cooper, Chief Operating Officer (Total facility includes 34 beds in nursing home–type unit) (Nonreporting) **A**1 2 5 6 9 10

| | 23 | 10 | 654 | — | — | — | — | — | — | — |

SHARON—Mercer County

⊠ △ SHARON REGIONAL HEALTH SYSTEM, 740 East State Street, Zip 16146–3395; tel. 724/983–3911; Wayne W. Johnston, President and Chief Executive Officer (Total facility includes 40 beds in nursing home–type unit) **A**1 2 6 7 9 10 **F**3 7 8 10 11 13 15 16 17 19 21 22 23 24 25 26 28 29 30 32 33 34 35 38 39 40 41 42 44 45 48 49 51 52 53 54 55 56 57 58 59 60 63 64 65 66 67 70 71 72 73 74 **P**6 7 8
Web address: www.schs–pa.org

| | 23 | 10 | 234 | 8560 | 126 | — | 685 | 76449 | 36557 | 1190 |

SHICKSHINNY—Luzerne County

CLEAR BROOK LODGE, Bethel Road, Zip 18655, Mailing Address: Rural Delivery 2, Box 2166, Zip 18655; tel. 717/864–3116; Dave Lombard, President and Chief Executive Officer (Nonreporting)

| | 23 | 82 | 65 | — | — | — | — | — | — | — |

SOMERSET—Somerset County

⊠ SOMERSET HOSPITAL CENTER FOR HEALTH, 225 South Center Avenue, Zip 15501–2088; tel. 814/443–5000; Michael J. Farrell, Chief Executive Officer (Total facility includes 15 beds in nursing home–type unit) **A**1 2 9 10 **F**1 3 7 8 10 12 13 14 15 16 19 20 21 22 23 26 28 29 30 31 32 33 34 35 37 39 40 41 42 44 46 49 52 53 54 55 56 57 58 59 64 65 66 67 71 72 73 74 **P**6
Web address: www.somersethospital.com

| | 23 | 10 | 132 | 4670 | 74 | 124247 | 552 | 34900 | 14710 | 506 |

SPANGLER—Cambria County

⊠ MINERS HOSPITAL NORTHERN CAMBRIA, 2205 Crawford Avenue, Zip 15775, Mailing Address: P.O. Box 490, Zip 15775–0490; tel. 814/948–7171; Roger P. Winn, Chief Executive Officer (Nonreporting) **A**1 9 10

| | 23 | 10 | 40 | — | — | — | — | — | — | — |

SPRINGFIELD—Delaware County

SPRINGFIELD HOSPITAL See Crozer–Chester Medical Center, Upland

STATE COLLEGE—Centre County

⊠ CENTRE COMMUNITY HOSPITAL, 1800 East Park Avenue, Zip 16803–6797; tel. 814/231–7000; Lance H. Rose, FACHE, President and Chief Executive Officer (Total facility includes 16 beds in nursing home–type unit) **A**1 2 9 10 **F**7 8 11 14 15 16 17 19 21 23 28 30 31 32 33 34 35 37 39 40 41 42 44 46 49 52 54 56 57 60 61 63 64 65 70 71 73
Web address: www.cch1.org

| | 23 | 10 | 186 | 8580 | 115 | 119066 | 1124 | 57161 | 26227 | 708 |

SUNBURY—Northumberland County

⊠ SUNBURY COMMUNITY HOSPITAL, 350 North Eleventh Street, Zip 17801–0737; tel. 570/286–3333; Nicholas A. Prisco, Chief Executive Officer (Total facility includes 29 beds in nursing home–type unit) **A**1 9 10 **F**7 8 11 12 13 14 15 16 17 19 21 22 24 26 28 29 30 31 33 34 35 36 39 40 41 42 44 45 49 61 64 65 67 68 71 73 74 **P**8
Web address: www.sunburyhospital.com

| | 23 | 10 | 100 | 2904 | 53 | 78950 | 140 | 21835 | 10732 | 382 |

SUSQUEHANNA—Susquehanna County

BARNES–KASSON COUNTY HOSPITAL, 400 Turnpike Street, Zip 18847–1638; tel. 717/853–3135; Sara C. Iveson, Executive Director (Total facility includes 58 beds in nursing home–type unit) **A**9 10 **F**7 8 12 13 16 17 19 20 22 27 30 32 34 35 36 37 40 41 42 44 49 51 63 64 65 68 71 73
Web address: www.barnes–kasson.org

| | 23 | 10 | 105 | 1739 | 86 | 23261 | 121 | 12486 | 6049 | 220 |

TITUSVILLE—Crawford County

★ TITUSVILLE AREA HOSPITAL, 406 West Oak Street, Zip 16354–1404; tel. 814/827–1851; Anthony J. Nasralla, FACHE, President and Chief Executive Officer (Nonreporting) **A**9 10

| | 23 | 10 | 90 | — | — | — | — | — | — | — |

TORRANCE—Westmoreland County

□ TORRANCE STATE HOSPITAL, Torrance Road, Zip 15779–0111, Mailing Address: P.O. Box 111, Zip 15779–0111; tel. 724/459–8000; Richard A. Stillwagon, Superintendent **A**1 10 **F**8 14 15 16 20 22 27 52 57 65 73

| | 12 | 22 | 352 | 123 | 316 | 0 | 0 | 34150 | 20060 | 563 |

TOWANDA—Bradford County

⊠ MEMORIAL HOSPITAL, One Hospital Drive, Zip 18848–9702; tel. 570/265–2191; Gary A. Baker, President (Total facility includes 44 beds in nursing home–type unit) **A**1 9 10 **F**1 7 8 9 12 16 17 19 21 22 28 30 32 33 34 35 37 38 39 40 41 45 46 64 65 66 67 70 71 73 **S** Quorum Health Group/Quorum Health Resources, Inc., Brentwood, TN

| | 23 | 10 | 93 | 2406 | 69 | 27436 | 293 | 17538 | 8101 | 294 |

TROY—Bradford County

★ ○ TROY COMMUNITY HOSPITAL, 100 John Street, Zip 16947–0036; tel. 570/297–2121; Mark Webster, President **A**9 10 11 **F**1 4 6 7 8 10 11 12 14 15 17 19 20 21 22 23 24 26 27 28 29 30 31 32 33 35 37 40 41 42 43 44 45 46 47 49 50 52 54 55 58 60 61 63 64 65 66 67 70 71 73 74 **S** Guthrie Healthcare System, Sayre, PA

| | 23 | 10 | 35 | 451 | 24 | 27106 | 1 | 9387 | 4361 | 103 |

Hospital, Address, Telephone, Administrator, Approval, Facility, and Physician Codes, Health Care System, Network	Classi-fication Codes		Utilization Data					Expense (thousands) of dollars		
★ American Hospital Association (AHA) membership □ Joint Commission on Accreditation of Healthcare Organizations (JCAHO) accreditation + American Osteopathic Healthcare Association (AOHA) membership ○ American Osteopathic Association (AOA) accreditation △ Commission on Accreditation of Rehabilitation Facilities (CARF) accreditation Control codes 61, 63, 64, 71, 72 and 73 indicate hospitals listed by AOHA, but not registered by AHA. For definition of numerical codes, see page A4	Control	Service	Staffed Beds	Admissions	Census	Outpatient Visits	Births	Total	Payroll	Personnel

TUNKHANNOCK—Wyoming County

✠ TYLER MEMORIAL HOSPITAL, 880 State Road 6 West, Zip 18657–6149; tel. 570/836–2161; William M. Milligan, Jr., President and Chief Executive Officer **A**1 2 9 10 **F**7 8 12 14 15 16 17 19 21 22 24 28 30 32 33 35 37 39 40 41 42 44 45 46 49 65 71 73 74

| | 23 | 10 | 60 | 2371 | 22 | 43727 | 272 | 16312 | 7132 | 248 |

TYRONE—Blair County

✠ TYRONE HOSPITAL, One Hospital Drive, Zip 16686–1810; tel. 814/684–1255; Philip J. Stoner, Chief Executive Officer (Nonreporting) **A**1 9 10 **S** Quorum Health Group/Quorum Health Resources, Inc., Brentwood, TN

| | 23 | 10 | 59 | — | — | — | — | — | — | — |

UNION CITY—Erie County

✠ UNION CITY MEMORIAL HOSPITAL, 130 North Main Street, Zip 16438–1094, Mailing Address: P.O. Box 111, Zip 16438–0111; tel. 814/438–1000; Thomas McLoughlin, President and Chief Executive Officer **A**1 9 10 **F**8 12 13 14 15 16 18 19 20 22 25 28 29 30 32 33 34 37 39 41 44 45 46 49 65 67 71 73 **P**3 7
Web address: www.svhs.org

| | 23 | 10 | 23 | 760 | 12 | 18990 | 0 | 5089 | 2435 | 81 |

UNIONTOWN—Fayette County

✠ UNIONTOWN HOSPITAL, 500 West Berkeley Street, Zip 15401–5596; tel. 724/430–5000; Paul Bacharach, President and Chief Executive Officer (Total facility includes 19 beds in nursing home–type unit) **A**1 2 9 10 **F**7 8 10 14 15 16 19 21 22 23 30 32 33 34 35 37 39 40 42 44 48 49 63 64 65 71 72 73 **P**6

| | 23 | 10 | 206 | 9762 | 144 | 172959 | 954 | 65823 | 28103 | 869 |

UPLAND—Delaware County

✠ ○ △ CROZER–CHESTER MEDICAL CENTER, (Includes Springfield Hospital, 190 West Sproul Road, Springfield, Zip 19064–2097; tel. 610/328–8700; Gwendolyn A. Smith, R.N., Vice President; Taylor Hospital, 175 East Chester Pike, Ridley Park, Zip 19078–2212; tel. 610/595–6000; Diane C. Miller, President and Chief Operating Officer), One Medical Center Boulevard, Zip 19013–3995; tel. 610/447–2000; Joan K. Richards, President **A**1 2 3 5 7 8 9 10 11 12 13 **F**1 2 3 4 7 8 9 10 11 12 13 14 15 16 17 18 19 21 22 23 24 26 27 28 29 30 31 32 33 34 35 36 37 38 39 40 41 42 43 44 45 46 48 49 51 52 53 54 55 56 57 58 59 60 61 63 64 65 66 67 68 69 70 71 72 73 74 **P**1 **S** Crozer–Keystone Health System, Springfield, PA

| | 23 | 10 | 589 | 24246 | 375 | 470914 | 2221 | 280320 | 115612 | 3249 |

WARMINSTER—Bucks County

✠ WARMINSTER HOSPITAL, (Formerly Allegheny University Hospitals, Bucks County), 225 Newtown Road, Zip 18974–5221; tel. 215/441–6600; Jeffrey Yarnel, Chief Executive Officer (Nonreporting) **A**1 3 5 9 10 **S** TENET Healthcare Corporation, Santa Barbara, CA
Web address: www.auhs.edu

| | 23 | 10 | 132 | — | — | — | — | — | — | — |

WARREN—Warren County

WARREN GENERAL HOSPITAL, 2 Crescent Park West, Zip 16365–2111, Mailing Address: P.O. Box 68, Zip 16365–2111; tel. 814/723–3300; Alton M. Schadt, Executive Director (Total facility includes 16 beds in nursing home–type unit) **A**9 10 **F**2 3 7 8 19 20 21 22 23 28 29 30 32 33 34 35 37 40 41 42 44 46 49 51 52 53 54 55 56 57 58 59 60 63 64 65 66 71 73
Web address: www.wgh.org
WARREN STATE HOSPITAL See North Warren

| | 23 | 10 | 109 | 3310 | 44 | 57487 | 339 | 31451 | 14190 | 466 |

WASHINGTON—Washington County

✠ WASHINGTON HOSPITAL, 155 Wilson Avenue, Zip 15301–3398; tel. 724/225–7000; Telford W. Thomas, President and Chief Executive Officer (Total facility includes 17 beds in nursing home–type unit) **A**1 2 3 5 6 9 10 **F**4 7 8 10 11 12 13 14 15 16 17 19 20 21 22 23 25 26 28 30 32 33 34 35 37 39 40 41 42 43 44 45 49 51 52 54 55 56 57 59 60 61 63 64 65 66 67 68 71 73 74 **P**1 7 8
Web address: www.welnet.org

| | 23 | 10 | 246 | 13439 | 182 | — | 1096 | 132496 | 64480 | 1532 |

WAYNESBORO—Franklin County

✠ WAYNESBORO HOSPITAL, 501 East Main Street, Zip 17268–2394; tel. 717/765–4000; Norman B. Epstein, President (Nonreporting) **A**1 5 9 10
Web address: www.summithealth.org

| | 23 | 10 | 62 | — | — | — | — | — | — | — |

WAYNESBURG—Greene County

✠ GREENE COUNTY MEMORIAL HOSPITAL, Seventh Street and Bonar Avenue, Zip 15370–1697; tel. 724/627–3101; Raoul Walsh, Chief Executive Officer (Total facility includes 20 beds in nursing home–type unit) **A**1 9 10 **F**8 13 14 15 16 19 21 22 23 26 28 30 31 32 34 35 37 41 42 44 46 49 52 55 64 65 67 71 73 74 **P**1 **S** Quorum Health Group/Quorum Health Resources, Inc., Brentwood, TN

| | 23 | 10 | 60 | 2711 | 44 | 39437 | 0 | 23459 | 8594 | 290 |

WELLSBORO—Tioga County

✠ SOLDIERS AND SAILORS MEMORIAL HOSPITAL, 32–36 Central Avenue, Zip 16901–1899; tel. 570/724–1631; Jan E. Fisher, R.N., Executive Director **A**1 9 10 **F**1 5 7 8 11 14 15 16 17 19 21 22 25 26 28 30 32 33 35 36 37 39 40 41 44 46 49 51 52 53 54 55 56 57 58 59 61 62 64 65 66 71 73

| | 23 | 10 | 97 | 3251 | 38 | — | 306 | 23188 | 10136 | 380 |

WERNERSVILLE—Berks County

□ WERNERSVILLE STATE HOSPITAL, Route 422, Zip 19565–0300, Mailing Address: P.O. Box 300, Zip 19565–0300; tel. 610/670–4111; Kenneth W. Ehrhart, Superintendent **A**1 9 10 **F**4 8 10 19 20 21 24 31 35 39 42 43 44 45 46 49 52 57 60 65 71 73

| | 12 | 22 | 332 | 209 | 302 | 0 | 0 | — | — | 552 |

WEST CHESTER—Chester County

✠ CHESTER COUNTY HOSPITAL, 701 East Marshall Street, Zip 19380–4412; tel. 610/431–5000; H. L. Perry Pepper, President (Total facility includes 20 beds in nursing home–type unit) **A**1 2 6 9 10 **F**7 8 10 11 12 14 15 16 17 19 21 22 24 26 28 29 30 32 33 34 35 36 37 38 39 40 41 42 44 45 46 47 49 51 60 63 64 65 66 67 71 73 74 **P**4 6 7 8

| | 23 | 10 | 224 | 10298 | 119 | 313387 | 2047 | 83842 | 37930 | 1130 |

Hospital, Address, Telephone, Administrator, Approval, Facility, and Physician Codes, Health Care System, Network	Classi-fication Codes		Utilization Data					Expense (thousands) of dollars		
★ American Hospital Association (AHA) membership □ Joint Commission on Accreditation of Healthcare Organizations (JCAHO) accreditation + American Osteopathic Healthcare Association (AOHA) membership ○ American Osteopathic Association (AOA) accreditation △ Commission on Accreditation of Rehabilitation Facilities (CARF) accreditation Control codes 61, 63, 64, 71, 72 and 73 indicate hospitals listed by AOHA, but not registered by AHA. For definition of numerical codes, see page A4	Control	Service	Staffed Beds	Admissions	Census	Outpatient Visits	Births	Total	Payroll	Personnel

WEST GROVE—Chester County

□ SOUTHERN CHESTER COUNTY MEDICAL CENTER, 1015 West Baltimore Pike, Zip 19390–9499; tel. 610/869–1000; Scott K. Phillips, President and Chief Executive Officer (Total facility includes 25 beds in nursing home–type unit) **A**1 9 10 **F**3 6 8 12 14 15 16 17 18 19 21 22 30 31 32 33 34 35 37 39 41 42 44 49 51 53 54 55 56 57 58 62 64 65 67 71 73 **P**1

| | 23 | 10 | 71 | 2617 | 37 | 40631 | 0 | 27252 | 10808 | 420 |

WILKES–BARRE—Luzerne County

CLEAR BROOK MANOR, Road 10 East Northampton Street, Zip 18702; tel. 717/823–1171; Donald Noll, Director (Nonreporting)

| | 23 | 82 | 50 | — | — | — | — | — | — | — |

□ FIRST HOSPITAL WYOMING VALLEY, 149 Dana Street, Zip 18702–4825; tel. 717/829–7900; John Malia, Director (Nonreporting) **A**1 9 10

| | 33 | 22 | 96 | — | — | — | — | — | — | — |

✖ △ JOHN HEINZ INSTITUTE OF REHABILITATION MEDICINE, 150 Mundy Street, Zip 18702–6830; tel. 570/826–3800; Thomas E. Pugh, Vice President Rehabilitation Services **A**1 7 9 10 **F**12 14 15 16 17 27 28 34 39 41 45 46 48 49 65 67 73
Web address: www.alliedservices.org

| | 23 | 46 | 112 | 2195 | 96 | 116048 | 0 | 34664 | 15653 | 463 |

□ MERCY HOSPITAL OF WILKES–BARRE, 25 Church Street, Zip 18765–0999; Mailing Address: P.O. Box 658, Zip 18765–0658; tel. 570/826–3100 (Nonreporting) **A**1 9 10 **S** Catholic Healthcare Partners, Cincinnati, OH

| | 21 | 10 | 173 | — | — | — | — | — | — | — |

✖ PENN STATE GEISINGER WYOMING VALLEY MEDICAL CENTER, 1000 East Mountain Drive, Zip 18711–0027; tel. 570/826–7300; Conrad W. Schintz, Senior Vice–President Operations **A**1 2 9 10 **F**3 7 8 11 12 14 15 16 19 21 22 28 29 30 34 35 37 39 40 41 42 44 45 46 48 49 54 56 60 63 65 67 70 73 **P**3 6 8 **S** Penn State Geisinger Health System, Harrisburg, PA

| | 23 | 10 | 124 | 5892 | 82 | 170273 | 525 | 54879 | 20347 | 662 |

✖ VETERANS AFFAIRS MEDICAL CENTER, 1111 East End Boulevard, Zip 18711–0026; tel. 570/824–3521; Reedes Hurt, Chief Executive Officer (Total facility includes 165 beds in nursing home–type unit) **A**1 2 3 5 9 **F**1 2 3 4 5 6 8 10 11 12 14 15 16 17 18 19 20 21 22 23 24 25 26 27 28 30 31 32 33 34 35 37 39 41 42 43 44 45 46 49 50 51 52 54 55 56 57 58 59 60 63 64 65 67 68 71 73 74 **S** Department of Veterans Affairs, Washington, DC

| | 45 | 10 | 289 | 3975 | 261 | 227251 | — | — | — | 1016 |

WILKES–BARRE GENERAL HOSPITAL See Wyoming Valley Health Care System

✖ WYOMING VALLEY HEALTH CARE SYSTEM, (Includes Nesbitt Memorial Hospital, 562 Wyoming Avenue, Kingston, Zip 18704–3784; tel. 717/283–7000; Wilkes–Barre General Hospital, 575 North River Street, Zip 18764), 575 North River Street, Zip 18764–0001; tel. 570/829–8111; Patricia Finan, President and Chief Executive Officer (Total facility includes 26 beds in nursing home–type unit) **A**1 5 9 **F**2 3 4 6 7 8 9 10 11 12 13 14 15 16 17 18 19 20 21 22 24 25 27 28 29 30 32 33 34 35 37 39 40 41 42 43 44 46 49 52 53 54 55 56 57 58 59 60 62 63 64 65 66 67 68 71 72 73 74 **P**8

| | 23 | 10 | 442 | 20695 | 349 | 447204 | 1815 | 203292 | 82484 | 2640 |

WILLIAMSBURG—Blair County

CHARTER BEHAVIORAL HEALTH SYSTEM AT COVE FORGE, New Beginnings Road, P.O. Box B, Zip 16693; tel. 814/832–2121; Jonathan Wolf, Chief Executive Officer (Nonreporting) **S** Magellan Health Services, Atlanta, GA

| | 33 | 82 | 100 | — | — | — | — | — | — | — |

WILLIAMSPORT—Lycoming County

✖ △ SUSQUEHANNA HEALTH SYSTEM, (Includes Divine Providence Hospital, 1100 Grampian Boulevard, Zip 17701–1995; tel. 717/320–7006; Muncy Valley Hospital, 215 East Water Street, Muncy, Zip 17756–8700; tel. 717/546–8282; Williamsport Hospital and Medical Center, 777 Rural Avenue, Zip 17701–3198; tel. 717/321–1000; Steven P. Johnson, Senior Vice President and Chief Operating Officer), 1001 Grampian Boulevard, Zip 17701–1946; tel. 570/320–7000; Donald R. Creamer, President and Chief Executive Officer (Total facility includes 129 beds in nursing home–type unit) **A**1 2 3 5 6 7 9 10 **F**1 3 4 5 7 8 10 11 12 13 14 15 16 17 19 20 21 22 23 24 25 26 27 28 29 30 31 32 33 34 35 37 39 40 41 42 43 44 45 46 48 49 51 52 53 54 55 56 57 58 59 60 61 63 64 65 66 67 68 71 72 73 74 **P**3 7 8
Web address: www.shscares.org

| | 23 | 10 | 495 | 14011 | 302 | 493194 | 1284 | 144498 | 59978 | 2140 |

WILLOW GROVE—Montgomery County

□ HUNTINGTON HOSPITAL, 240 Fitzwatertown Road, Zip 19090–2399; tel. 215/657–4010; Alan I. Stevens, Administrator (Nonreporting) **A**1 9 10

| | 23 | 22 | 31 | — | — | — | — | — | — | — |

WINDBER—Somerset County

□ WINDBER HOSPITAL, 600 Somerset Avenue, Zip 15963–1331; tel. 814/467–6611; Nicholas Jacobs, Executive Director **A**1 9 10 **F**2 3 4 7 8 9 10 11 12 15 16 17 18 19 21 22 23 25 26 27 28 29 30 32 33 34 35 37 38 39 40 41 42 43 44 45 46 47 48 49 52 53 54 55 56 57 58 59 60 63 64 65 67 70 71 72 73 74 **P**7 8
Web address: www.conemaugh.org

| | 23 | 10 | 67 | 2280 | 27 | 43922 | 164 | 18263 | 7300 | 264 |

WYNNEWOOD—Montgomery County

★ LANKENAU HOSPITAL, 100 Lancaster Avenue West, Zip 19096–3411; tel. 610/645–2000; William McCune, Senior Vice President, Operations **A**2 3 5 9 10 **F**1 3 4 5 7 8 10 12 13 14 15 16 17 18 19 20 21 22 23 24 25 26 27 28 29 30 31 32 33 34 35 36 37 38 39 40 41 42 43 44 45 46 48 49 51 52 53 54 55 56 57 58 59 60 61 63 64 65 66 67 68 71 73 74 **P**3 7 **S** Jefferson Health System, Wayne, PA
Web address: www.jeffersonhealth.org

| | 23 | 10 | 314 | 13876 | 216 | 110820 | 1723 | 165223 | 60686 | 1696 |

YORK—York County

□ △ HEALTHSOUTH REHABILITATION HOSPITAL OF YORK, 1850 Normandie Drive, Zip 17404–1534; tel. 717/767–6941; Cheryl Fleming, Chief Executive Officer (Nonreporting) **A**1 7 9 10 **S** HEALTHSOUTH Corporation, Birmingham, AL

| | 33 | 48 | 88 | — | — | — | — | — | — | — |

Hospital, Address, Telephone, Administrator, Approval, Facility, and Physician Codes, Health Care System, Network	Classi-fication Codes		Utilization Data					Expense (thousands) of dollars		
★ American Hospital Association (AHA) membership □ Joint Commission on Accreditation of Healthcare Organizations (JCAHO) accreditation + American Osteopathic Healthcare Association (AOHA) membership ○ American Osteopathic Association (AOA) accreditation △ Commission on Accreditation of Rehabilitation Facilities (CARF) accreditation Control codes 61, 63, 64, 71, 72 and 73 indicate hospitals listed by AOHA, but not registered by AHA. For definition of numerical codes, see page A4	Control	Service	Staffed Beds	Admissions	Census	Outpatient Visits	Births	Total	Payroll	Personnel
★ + ○ MEMORIAL HOSPITAL, 325 South Belmont Street, Zip 17403–2609, Mailing Address: P.O. Box 15118, Zip 17405–5118; tel. 717/843–8623; Sally J. Dixon, President and Chief Executive Officer **A**9 10 11 12 13 **F**7 8 10 12 14 15 16 17 19 21 22 23 25 26 28 30 32 33 34 35 36 37 39 40 41 42 44 45 49 51 52 53 54 56 57 58 63 65 66 67 71 73 74 **P**6	23	10	126	5806	65	68263	470	44838	21784	627
⊠ YORK HOSPITAL, 1001 South George Street, Zip 17405–3645; tel. 717/851–2345; Brian A. Gragnolati, President **A**1 2 3 5 8 9 10 **F**3 4 7 8 10 11 12 13 14 15 16 17 18 19 20 21 22 23 25 26 28 30 31 32 33 34 35 37 38 39 40 41 42 43 44 45 46 49 51 52 53 54 55 56 57 58 59 60 61 63 65 67 69 70 71 72 73 74 **P**6 **S** South Central Community Health, York, PA **Web address:** www.yorkhealth.org	23	10	434	23187	302	611733	2880	227840	107739	3012

RHODE ISLAND

Resident population 988 (in thousands)
Resident population in metro areas 94.0%
Birth rate per 1,000 population 12.9
65 years and over 15.8%
Percent of persons without health insurance 9.9%

Hospital, Address, Telephone, Administrator, Approval, Facility, and Physician Codes, Health Care System, Network	Classi-fication Codes		Utilization Data					Expense (thousands) of dollars		
★ American Hospital Association (AHA) membership □ Joint Commission on Accreditation of Healthcare Organizations (JCAHO) accreditation + American Osteopathic Healthcare Association (AOHA) membership ○ American Osteopathic Association (AOA) accreditation △ Commission on Accreditation of Rehabilitation Facilities (CARF) accreditation Control codes 61, 63, 64, 71, 72 and 73 indicate hospitals listed by AOHA, but not registered by AHA. For definition of numerical codes, see page A4	Control	Service	Staffed Beds	Admissions	Census	Outpatient Visits	Births	Total	Payroll	Personnel

CRANSTON—Providence County

□ ELEANOR SLATER HOSPITAL, (Includes Institute of Mental Health–Rhode Island Medical Center, Howard Avenue, Howard, Zip 02920, Mailing Address: Box 8281, Cranston, Zip 02920–0281; tel. 401/464–2495; Betty A. Fielder, Clinical Administrative Officer; Rhode Island Medical Center, Mailing Address: Box 8269, Zip 02920; tel. 401/464–3085), 111 Howard Avenue, Zip 02920–3001, Mailing Address: P.O. Box 8269, Zip 02920–8269; tel. 401/464–3085; Richard H. Freeman, Chief Executive Officer **A**1 9 10 **F**19 20 21 26 31 35 42 52 57 64 65 68 71 73 **P**6

| | 12 | 10 | 452 | 304 | 462 | 0 | 0 | 95668 | 49616 | 1212 |

EAST PROVIDENCE—Providence County

✠ EMMA PENDLETON BRADLEY HOSPITAL, 1011 Veterans Memorial Parkway, Zip 02915–5099; tel. 401/432–1000; Daniel J. Wall, President and Chief Executive Officer **A**1 3 5 9 10 **F**14 15 16 18 29 52 53 54 55 56 58 59 65 **S** Lifespan Corporation, Providence, RI

| | 23 | 59 | 60 | 864 | 46 | 26815 | 0 | 23051 | 15493 | 503 |

HOWARD—Providence County

INSTITUTE OF MENTAL HEALTH–RHODE ISLAND MEDICAL CENTER See Eleanor Slater Hospital, Cranston

NEWPORT—Newport County

✠ △ NEWPORT HOSPITAL, 11 Friendship Street, Zip 02840–2299; tel. 401/846–6400; Arthur J. Sampson, President and Chief Executive Officer **A**1 2 7 9 10 **F**7 8 11 12 13 16 17 19 22 25 26 28 29 30 34 35 36 37 39 40 41 42 44 45 46 48 49 51 52 56 57 59 64 65 67 71 73 **P**3 6 7 **S** Lifespan Corporation, Providence, RI
Web address: www.lifespan.org

| | 23 | 10 | 110 | 5939 | 83 | 100403 | 736 | 53826 | 24932 | 584 |

NORTH PROVIDENCE—Providence County

OUR LADY OF FATIMA HOSPITAL See St. Joseph Health Services of Rhode Island

✠ ST. JOSEPH HEALTH SERVICES OF RHODE ISLAND, (Includes Our Lady of Fatima Hospital, 200 High Service Avenue, Zip 02904; St. Joseph Hospital for Specialty Care, 21 Peace Street, Providence, Zip 02907; tel. 401/456–3000), 200 High Service Avenue, Zip 02904–5199; tel. 401/456–3000; H. John Keimig, President and Chief Executive Officer (Total facility includes 20 beds in nursing home–type unit) **A**1 6 9 10 **F**6 8 11 12 16 17 18 19 20 21 22 23 26 27 28 30 31 32 33 34 35 37 39 41 42 44 46 48 49 51 52 54 56 57 58 59 60 64 65 67 69 71 72 73 74 **P**5
Web address: www.saintjosephri.com

| | 21 | 10 | 272 | 11425 | 228 | 221819 | 422 | 116026 | 61522 | 1500 |

PAWTUCKET—Providence County

✠ △ MEMORIAL HOSPITAL OF RHODE ISLAND, 111 Brewster Street, Zip 02860–4499; tel. 401/729–2000; Francis R. Dietz, President **A**1 2 3 5 7 8 9 10 **F**1 2 3 4 7 8 9 10 11 12 13 16 17 19 21 22 25 26 27 28 30 31 32 33 34 35 36 37 38 39 40 41 42 43 44 45 47 48 49 51 52 53 54 56 57 58 59 60 61 64 65 66 67 70 71 72 73 74 **P**1

| | 23 | 10 | 197 | 7699 | 115 | 84627 | 746 | 109128 | 61516 | 1380 |

PROVIDENCE—Providence County

✠ BUTLER HOSPITAL, 345 Blackstone Boulevard, Zip 02906–4829; tel. 401/455–6200; Patricia R. Recupero, JD, M.D., President and Chief Executive Officer **A**1 3 5 9 10 **F**2 3 4 7 8 10 11 12 15 17 18 19 20 21 22 25 26 27 28 29 30 31 32 33 34 35 37 38 39 40 41 42 44 45 46 48 49 51 52 53 54 55 56 57 58 59 61 63 65 66 67 71 73 74 **P**5 6 8 **S** Care New England Health System, Providence, RI
Web address: www.butler.org

| | 23 | 22 | 105 | 4951 | 91 | 48319 | 0 | 37957 | 24544 | 563 |

✠ MIRIAM HOSPITAL, 164 Summit Avenue, Zip 02906–2895; tel. 401/793–2500; Edward M. Schottland, Senior Vice President and Chief Operating Officer **A**1 2 3 5 8 9 10 **F**2 4 5 8 9 10 11 12 13 14 15 16 17 18 19 20 21 22 23 24 25 26 28 29 30 31 32 33 34 35 37 39 41 42 43 44 45 47 49 51 52 53 54 55 56 57 58 59 60 63 64 65 66 67 68 70 71 73 74 **P**3 8 **S** Lifespan Corporation, Providence, RI

| | 23 | 10 | 198 | 12016 | 168 | 141949 | 0 | 112256 | 56004 | 1260 |

✠ RHODE ISLAND HOSPITAL, 593 Eddy Street, Zip 02903–4900; tel. 401/444–4000; Steven D. Baron, President and Chief Executive Officer **A**1 2 3 5 8 9 10 **F**4 5 8 10 11 12 13 14 15 16 17 18 19 20 21 22 23 24 26 28 29 30 31 32 33 34 35 37 39 41 42 43 44 45 46 47 49 51 52 53 54 55 56 57 58 59 60 63 65 66 67 68 70 71 73 74 **P**3 6 8 **S** Lifespan Corporation, Providence, RI

| | 23 | 10 | 677 | 28756 | 462 | 522870 | 0 | 341239 | 177145 | 4301 |

✠ ROGER WILLIAMS MEDICAL CENTER, 825 Chalkstone Avenue, Zip 02908–4735; tel. 401/456–2000; Robert A. Urciuoli, President and Chief Executive Officer **A**1 2 3 5 8 9 10 **F**3 6 8 10 12 14 15 16 17 19 21 22 23 26 28 29 30 31 32 34 35 37 39 41 42 44 46 49 51 54 58 60 63 64 65 67 68 71 73 **P**3 5 8
Web address: www.rwmc.com

| | 23 | 10 | 146 | 7600 | 111 | 117834 | 0 | 82103 | 39422 | 1055 |

ST. JOSEPH HOSPITAL FOR SPECIALTY CARE See St. Joseph Health Services of Rhode Island, North Providence

Hospital, Address, Telephone, Administrator, Approval, Facility, and Physician Codes, Health Care System, Network	Classi-fication Codes		Utilization Data					Expense (thousands) of dollars		
★ American Hospital Association (AHA) membership □ Joint Commission on Accreditation of Healthcare Organizations (JCAHO) accreditation + American Osteopathic Healthcare Association (AOHA) membership ○ American Osteopathic Association (AOA) accreditation △ Commission on Accreditation of Rehabilitation Facilities (CARF) accreditation Control codes 61, 63, 64, 71, 72 and 73 indicate hospitals listed by AOHA, but not registered by AHA. For definition of numerical codes, see page A4	Control	Service	Staffed Beds	Admissions	Census	Outpatient Visits	Births	Total	Payroll	Personnel
✖ VETERANS AFFAIRS MEDICAL CENTER, 830 Chalkstone Avenue, Zip 02908–4799; tel. 401/457–3042; James P. Cody, Acting Director **A**1 3 5 **F**1 3 4 8 9 10 12 14 15 16 17 18 19 20 21 22 23 25 26 27 28 29 30 31 32 33 34 35 37 39 41 42 43 44 46 49 50 51 52 54 55 56 58 61 63 64 65 67 68 71 72 73 74 **S** Department of Veterans Affairs, Washington, DC	45	10	78	3078	66	227079	0	72138	32141	781
✖ WOMEN AND INFANTS HOSPITAL OF RHODE ISLAND, 101 Dudley Street, Zip 02905–2499; tel. 401/274–1100; Thomas G. Parris, Jr., President **A**1 3 5 8 9 10 **F**2 3 4 5 7 8 10 11 12 13 15 16 17 18 19 20 21 22 23 24 25 26 27 28 29 30 31 32 33 34 35 37 38 39 40 41 42 43 44 45 46 47 48 49 51 52 53 54 55 56 57 58 59 61 63 65 66 67 68 70 71 73 74 **P**5 6 8 **S** Care New England Health System, Providence, RI **Web address:** www.wihri,org	23	44	197	13591	168	58729	8909	144416	76843	1693
WAKEFIELD—Washington County										
✖ SOUTH COUNTY HOSPITAL, 100 Kenyon Avenue, Zip 02879–4299; tel. 401/782–8000; Patrick L. Muldoon, President and Chief Executive Officer **A**1 9 10 **F**1 3 7 8 11 12 13 15 16 17 18 19 20 21 22 24 25 26 27 28 29 30 31 32 33 34 35 36 37 39 40 41 42 44 45 46 49 51 53 54 55 56 57 58 59 63 65 66 67 71 72 73 74 **P**5 7 8 **Web address:** www.schospital.com	23	10	100	4798	57	114184	545	44675	21412	594
WARWICK—Kent County										
✖ △ KENT COUNTY MEMORIAL HOSPITAL, 455 Tollgate Road, Zip 02886–2770; tel. 401/737–7000; Robert E. Baute, M.D., President and Chief Executive Officer **A**1 2 7 9 10 **F**2 3 4 7 8 10 11 12 15 16 17 18 19 20 21 22 25 26 27 28 29 30 31 32 33 34 35 37 38 39 40 41 42 44 45 46 48 49 51 52 53 54 55 56 57 58 59 60 61 63 65 66 67 71 73 74 **P**5 6 8 **S** Care New England Health System, Providence, RI	23	10	326	13782	222	164776	1128	131477	71530	1659
WESTERLY—Washington County										
✖ WESTERLY HOSPITAL, 25 Wells Street, Zip 02891–2934; tel. 401/596–6000; Michael K. Lally, President and Chief Executive Officer **A**1 9 10 **F**1 7 8 9 12 17 19 21 22 26 28 30 31 34 35 36 37 39 40 41 42 44 45 46 48 49 51 54 56 57 63 65 66 67 68 70 71 72 73 74 **P**8	23	10	125	4284	55	323240	497	45865	21361	420
WOONSOCKET—Providence County										
✖ LANDMARK MEDICAL CENTER, (Includes Landmark Medical Center–Fogarty Unit, Eddie Dowling Highway, North Smithfield, Zip 02896; tel. 401/766–0800; Landmark Medical Center–Woonsocket Unit, 115 Cass Avenue, Zip 02895; tel. 401/769–4100), 115 Cass Avenue, Zip 02895–4731; tel. 401/769–4100; Gary J. Gaube, President (Total facility includes 19 beds in nursing home–type unit) **A**1 9 10 **F**7 8 15 16 19 20 21 22 23 26 28 29 30 32 33 34 35 37 39 40 41 42 44 45 48 49 52 53 54 55 56 57 58 63 64 65 67 71 72 73 **P**6 7 8	23	10	173	6566	94	200068	415	74162	35382	644

SOUTH CAROLINA

Resident population 3,836 (in thousands)
Resident population in metro areas 67.1%
Birth rate per 1,000 population 13.9
65 years and over 12.1%
Percent of persons without health insurance 17.1%

Hospital, Address, Telephone, Administrator, Approval, Facility, and Physician Codes, Health Care System, Network	Classi-fication Codes		Utilization Data					Expense (thousands) of dollars		
★ American Hospital Association (AHA) membership □ Joint Commission on Accreditation of Healthcare Organizations (JCAHO) accreditation + American Osteopathic Healthcare Association (AOHA) membership ○ American Osteopathic Association (AOA) accreditation △ Commission on Accreditation of Rehabilitation Facilities (CARF) accreditation Control codes 61, 63, 64, 71, 72 and 73 indicate hospitals listed by AOHA, but not registered by AHA. For definition of numerical codes, see page A4	Control	Service	Staffed Beds	Admissions	Census	Outpatient Visits	Births	Total	Payroll	Personnel

ABBEVILLE—Abbeville County

★ ABBEVILLE COUNTY MEMORIAL HOSPITAL, 901 West Greenwood Street, Zip 29620–0887, Mailing Address: P.O. Box 887, Zip 29620–0887; tel. 864/459–5011; Bruce P. Bailey, Administrator **A**9 10 **F**7 8 11 12 15 17 19 22 26 27 28 30 32 34 35 37 40 41 44 45 46 48 49 56 63 64 65 69 71 73 74 **P**8 **S** Quorum Health Group/Quorum Health Resources, Inc., Brentwood, TN

| 13 | 10 | 42 | 1026 | 12 | 24719 | 159 | 10174 | 5111 | 187 |

AIKEN—Aiken County

☒ AIKEN REGIONAL MEDICAL CENTERS, (Includes Aurora Pavilion, 655 Medical Park Drive, Zip 29801, Mailing Address: P.O. Box 1073, Zip 29802; tel. 803/641–5900), 302 University Parkway, Zip 29801–2757, Mailing Address: P.O. Box 1117, Zip 29802–1117; tel. 803/641–5000; Richard H. Satcher, Chief Executive Officer **A**1 2 9 10 **F**2 3 4 7 8 10 11 12 14 15 16 17 19 21 22 23 25 26 27 28 31 32 33 34 35 37 39 40 41 42 43 44 45 46 48 49 52 53 54 55 56 57 58 59 60 63 65 67 68 69 70 71 73 74 **P**8 **S** Universal Health Services, Inc., King of Prussia, PA

| 33 | 10 | 269 | 11503 | 145 | 60101 | 1102 | 91549 | 29871 | 787 |

ANDERSON—Anderson County

☒ ANDERSON AREA MEDICAL CENTER, 800 North Fant Street, Zip 29621–5793; tel. 864/261–1000; John A. Miller, Jr., President **A**1 2 3 5 9 10 **F**2 3 7 8 10 11 12 13 14 15 16 17 19 21 22 23 24 25 26 27 28 29 30 31 32 34 35 37 40 41 42 44 45 46 47 48 49 52 53 54 55 56 57 58 60 61 63 65 66 67 69 70 71 73 74 **P**7 8

| 21 | 10 | 364 | 17840 | 271 | 420486 | 1884 | 172150 | 72160 | 2497 |

BAMBERG—Bamberg County

☒ BAMBERG COUNTY MEMORIAL HOSPITAL AND NURSING CENTER, North and McGee Streets, Zip 29003–0507, Mailing Address: P.O. Box 507, Zip 29003–0507; tel. 803/245–4321; Warren E. Hammett, Administrator (Total facility includes 44 beds in nursing home–type unit) (Nonreporting) **A**1 9 10

| 13 | 10 | 84 | | | | | | | |

BARNWELL—Barnwell County

☒ BARNWELL COUNTY HOSPITAL, 811 Reynolds Road, Zip 29812; tel. 803/259–1000; J. L. Dozier, Jr., FACHE, Chief Executive Officer **A**1 9 10 **F**8 16 17 19 21 22 26 28 30 31 33 34 37 44 45 48 49 64 65 69 71 73 **P**7 8

| 13 | 10 | 33 | 860 | 12 | 23816 | — | 7311 | 2820 | 136 |

BEAUFORT—Beaufort County

☒ BEAUFORT MEMORIAL HOSPITAL, 955 Ribaut Road, Zip 29902–5441, Mailing Address: P.O. Box 1068, Zip 29901–1068; tel. 843/522–5200; David E. Brown, President and Chief Executive Officer (Total facility includes 44 beds in nursing home–type unit) **A**1 9 10 **F**7 8 14 15 16 17 19 21 22 23 24 28 30 31 32 33 34 35 37 39 40 41 44 45 46 49 54 55 56 57 59 63 64 65 66 69 71 73 74

| 13 | 10 | 185 | 7660 | 103 | 31254 | 1302 | 55976 | 22886 | 760 |

☒ NAVAL HOSPITAL, 1 Pinckney Boulevard, Zip 29902–6148; tel. 803/525–5301; Captain Clint E. Adams, MC, USN, Commanding Officer (Nonreporting) **A**1 5 **S** Department of Navy, Washington, DC

| 43 | 10 | 20 | | | | | | | |

BENNETTSVILLE—Marlboro County

☒ MARLBORO PARK HOSPITAL, 1138 Cheraw Highway, Zip 29512–0738, Mailing Address: P.O. Box 738, Zip 29512–0738; tel. 843/479–2881; Stephen Chapman, Chief Executive Officer (Total facility includes 7 beds in nursing home–type unit) **A**1 9 10 **F**7 8 11 15 17 19 21 22 23 28 30 31 33 35 37 39 40 41 44 45 50 52 55 57 59 63 64 65 69 71 73 74 **P**2 8 **S** Community Health Systems, Inc., Brentwood, TN

| 32 | 10 | 105 | 2419 | 32 | 15166 | 207 | 19364 | 7105 | 214 |

CAMDEN—Kershaw County

☒ KERSHAW COUNTY MEDICAL CENTER, Haile and Roberts Streets, Zip 29020–7003, Mailing Address: P.O. Box 7003, Zip 29020–7003; tel. 803/432–4311; Donnie J. Weeks, President and Chief Executive Officer **A**1 9 10 **F**2 3 4 6 7 8 9 10 11 14 15 16 17 19 20 21 22 25 26 27 28 29 30 32 33 34 35 36 37 38 39 40 41 42 43 44 45 47 48 49 53 54 55 56 57 58 59 60 62 63 64 65 67 68 69 71 73 74

| 13 | 10 | 100 | 4487 | 56 | 73477 | 353 | 39816 | 17224 | 530 |

CHARLESTON—Charleston County

☒ BON SECOURS–ST. FRANCIS XAVIER HOSPITAL, 2095 Henry Tecklenburg Drive, Zip 29414–0001, Mailing Address: P.O. Box 160001, Zip 29414–0001; tel. 803/402–1000; Allen P. Carroll, Chief Executive Officer (Total facility includes 22 beds in nursing home–type unit) (Nonreporting) **A**1 9 10 **S** Bon Secours Health System, Inc., Marriottsville, MD

| 21 | 10 | 147 | | | | | | | |

☒ △ CHARLESTON MEMORIAL HOSPITAL, 326 Calhoun Street, Zip 29401–1189; tel. 803/953–8300; Thomas F. Moore, Administrator **A**1 3 5 7 9 10 **F**4 8 10 11 14 16 17 19 22 23 31 32 35 37 44 45 49 54 56 60 65 69 71 73 74 **P**5 8
Web address: www.musc.edu

| 13 | 10 | 117 | 1408 | 42 | 41439 | — | 39576 | 11616 | 362 |

□ CHARTER HOSPITAL OF CHARLESTON, 2777 Speissegger Drive, Zip 29405–8299; tel. 803/747–5830; Anne Battin, Administrator **A**1 10 **F**2 3 17 19 21 28 34 35 41 45 46 52 53 54 55 56 57 58 59 65 67 71 **S** Magellan Health Services, Atlanta, GA

| 33 | 22 | 70 | 803 | 24 | 2174 | — | 9156 | 3804 | 116 |

COLUMBIA TRIDENT MEDICAL CENTER See Trident Medical Center

Hospital, Address, Telephone, Administrator, Approval, Facility, and Physician Codes, Health Care System, Network	Classi-fication Codes		Utilization Data					Expense (thousands) of dollars		
★ American Hospital Association (AHA) membership □ Joint Commission on Accreditation of Healthcare Organizations (JCAHO) accreditation + American Osteopathic Healthcare Association (AOHA) membership ○ American Osteopathic Association (AOA) accreditation △ Commission on Accreditation of Rehabilitation Facilities (CARF) accreditation Control codes 61, 63, 64, 71, 72 and 73 indicate hospitals listed by AOHA, but not registered by AHA. For definition of numerical codes, see page A4	Control	Service	Staffed Beds	Admissions	Census	Outpatient Visits	Births	Total	Payroll	Personnel
⊠ △ MUSC MEDICAL CENTER OF MEDICAL UNIVERSITY OF SOUTH CAROLINA, 171 Ashley Avenue, Zip 29425; tel. 843/792–2300; Stuart Smith, Vice President Clinical Operations and Executive Director **A**1 2 3 5 7 8 9 10 **F**2 3 4 5 6 7 8 9 10 11 12 13 14 15 16 17 18 19 20 21 22 23 24 25 26 27 28 30 31 32 33 34 35 36 37 38 39 40 41 42 43 44 45 46 47 48 49 50 51 52 53 54 55 56 57 58 59 60 61 62 63 65 66 67 68 69 70 71 73 74 **Web address:** www.musc.edu	12	10	572	25195	419	549868	1988	379558	143152	3657
NAVAL HOSPITAL See North Charleston										
⊠ RALPH H. JOHNSON VETERANS AFFAIRS MEDICAL CENTER, (Formerly Veterans Affairs Medical Center), 109 Bee Street, Zip 29401–5703; tel. 843/577–5011; R. J. Vogel, Chief Executive Officer (Nonreporting) **A**1 2 3 5 8 **S** Department of Veterans Affairs, Washington, DC	45	10	161	—	—	—	—	—	—	—
⊠ ROPER HOSPITAL, 316 Calhoun Street, Zip 29401–1125; tel. 843/724–2000; Edward L. Berdick, President and Chief Executive Officer (Nonreporting) **A**1 2 6 9 10 **S** Carolinas HealthCare System, Charlotte, NC	23	10	398	—	—	—	—	—	—	—
⊠ ROPER HOSPITAL NORTH, 2750 Speissegger Drive, Zip 29405–8294; tel. 843/745–2800; John C. Hales, Jr., FACHE, President and Chief Executive Officer (Nonreporting) **A**1 9 10 **S** Carolinas HealthCare System, Charlotte, NC	23	10	104	—	—	—	—	—	—	—
⊠ TRIDENT MEDICAL CENTER, (Formerly Columbia Trident Medical Center), 9330 Medical Plaza Drive, Zip 29406–9195; tel. 843/797–7000; Michael P. Joyce, President and Chief Executive Officer (Nonreporting) **A**1 2 9 10 **S** Columbia/HCA Healthcare Corporation, Nashville, TN	33	10	286	—	—	—	—	—	—	—
VETERANS AFFAIRS MEDICAL CENTER See Ralph H. Johnson Veterans Affairs Medical Center										
CHERAW—Chesterfield County										
⊠ CHESTERFIELD GENERAL HOSPITAL, Highway 9 West, Zip 29520, Mailing Address: P.O. Box 151, Zip 29520–0151; tel. 843/537–7881; Chris Wolf, Chief Executive Officer (Total facility includes 7 beds in nursing home–type unit) **A**1 9 10 **F**6 7 8 11 13 14 15 16 17 19 21 22 23 26 27 28 30 31 32 33 34 35 37 38 39 40 41 44 45 46 47 48 49 51 63 64 65 69 71 73 **P**8 **S** Community Health Systems, Inc., Brentwood, TN	33	10	66	2291	22	32284	275	17770	6140	206
CHESTER—Chester County										
□ CHESTER COUNTY HOSPITAL AND NURSING CENTER, 1 Medical Park Drive, Zip 29706–9799; tel. 803/581–9400; William H. Bundy, Chief Executive Officer **A**1 9 10 **F**4 7 8 10 11 15 16 17 18 19 21 22 26 27 28 30 31 32 33 34 35 36 37 38 39 40 41 42 43 44 45 46 49 50 53 60 62 63 64 65 67 68 69 71 73 74	13	10	70	2986	40	17154	200	24624	10750	308
CLINTON—Laurens County										
⊠ LAURENS COUNTY HEALTHCARE SYSTEM, (Includes Laurens County Hospital, Mailing Address: P.O. Box 976, Zip 29325; tel. 803/833–9100), Highway 76 West, Zip 29325, Mailing Address: P.O. Box 976, Zip 29325–0976; tel. 864/833–9100; Michael A. Kozar, Chief Executive Officer **A**1 9 10 **F**7 8 11 13 14 15 16 17 19 21 22 23 28 30 31 32 33 34 35 37 39 40 41 44 45 46 49 55 56 57 59 65 67 69 71 74 **P**8 **S** Quorum Health Group/Quorum Health Resources, Inc., Brentwood, TN **Web address:** www.lchcs.org	16	10	85	3625	54	60325	428	26751	10553	398
WHITTEN CENTER INFIRMARY, Whitten Center, Zip 29325, Mailing Address: Drawer 239, Zip 29325; tel. 864/833–2733; George Dellaportas, M.D., Director Professional Services (Nonreporting)	12	12	24	—	—	—	—	—	—	—
COLUMBIA—Richland County										
COLUMBIA PROVIDENCE HOSPITAL See Providence Hospital										
⊠ △ HEALTHSOUTH REHABILITATION HOSPITAL, 2935 Colonial Drive, Zip 29203–6811; tel. 803/254–7777; Debbie W. Johnston, Director Operations **A**1 7 10 **F**12 17 24 26 27 34 39 41 45 46 48 49 65 66 67 71 73 **S** HEALTHSOUTH Corporation, Birmingham, AL	33	46	87	1453	74	10121	—	13515	6781	233
MIDLANDS CENTER, 8301 Farrow Road, Zip 29203–3294; tel. 803/935–7508; Ronald P. Childs, FACHE, Health Services Administrator (Nonreporting)	12	12	24	—	—	—	—	—	—	—
⊠ PALMETTO BAPTIST MEDICAL CENTER/COLUMBIA, Taylor at Marion Street, Zip 29220; tel. 803/296–5010; James M. Bridges, Executive Vice President and Chief Operating Officer **A**1 2 9 10 **F**2 7 8 10 11 12 14 15 16 17 19 21 22 23 25 26 28 30 31 32 33 34 35 37 38 39 40 41 42 44 45 46 47 48 49 52 53 54 55 56 57 58 59 60 63 65 67 69 71 73 74 **P**7 **S** Palmetto Health Alliance, Columbia, SC **Web address:** www.bhsc.hbocvan.com	23	10	369	18489	259	203942	3217	174559	73396	2088
⊠ PALMETTO RICHLAND MEMORIAL HOSPITAL, Five Richland Medical Park Drive, Zip 29203, Mailing Address: P.O. Box 2266, Zip 29203–2266; tel. 803/434–7000; B. Daniel Paysinger, M.D., Chief Operating Officer **A**1 2 3 5 8 9 10 **F**1 2 3 4 8 9 10 11 12 13 15 16 17 19 20 21 22 23 24 25 26 27 28 29 30 31 32 33 34 35 37 38 39 40 41 42 43 44 45 46 47 48 49 51 52 53 54 55 56 57 58 59 60 61 63 65 66 67 68 69 70 71 73 74 **S** Palmetto Health Alliance, Columbia, SC **Web address:** www.rmh.edu	13	10	595	28708	514	338318	3093	376637	145846	4224
⊠ PROVIDENCE HOSPITAL, (Formerly Columbia Providence Hospital), 2435 Forest Drive, Zip 29204–2098; tel. 803/256–5300; Stephen A. Purves, CHE, President and Chief Executive Officer (Total facility includes 19 beds in nursing home–type unit) **A**1 9 10 **F**4 8 10 11 14 15 16 17 19 20 21 22 25 28 29 30 31 34 35 37 41 43 44 45 46 49 54 63 65 67 69 71 73 **S** Sisters of Charity of St. Augustine Health System, Cleveland, OH **Web address:** www.provhosp.com	32	10	235	11133	188	78447	—	111242	38709	1060

Hospital, Address, Telephone, Administrator, Approval, Facility, and Physician Codes, Health Care System, Network	Classification Codes		Utilization Data					Expense (thousands) of dollars		
	Control	Service	Staffed Beds	Admissions	Census	Outpatient Visits	Births	Total	Payroll	Personnel

Approval key:

★ American Hospital Association (AHA) membership
□ Joint Commission on Accreditation of Healthcare Organizations (JCAHO) accreditation
+ American Osteopathic Healthcare Association (AOHA) membership
○ American Osteopathic Association (AOA) accreditation
△ Commission on Accreditation of Rehabilitation Facilities (CARF) accreditation
Control codes 61, 63, 64, 71, 72 and 73 indicate hospitals listed by AOHA, but not registered by AHA. For definition of numerical codes, see page A4

Hospital	Control	Service	Staffed Beds	Admissions	Census	Outpatient Visits	Births	Total	Payroll	Personnel
□ SOUTH CAROLINA STATE HOSPITAL, 2100 Bull Street, Zip 29202, Mailing Address: P.O. Box 119, Zip 29202–0119; tel. 803/898–2261; Jaime E. Condom, M.D., Director (Nonreporting) **A**1	12	22	350	—	—	—	—	—	—	—
⊠ WILLIAM JENNINGS BRYAN DORN VETERANS MEDICAL CENTER, 6439 Garners Ferry Road, Zip 29209–1639; tel. 803/776–4000; Brian Heckert, Medical Center Director **A**1 2 3 5 **F**2 6 8 10 11 16 17 19 20 21 22 25 26 27 30 31 32 33 34 35 37 41 42 44 45 46 48 49 51 52 54 55 56 57 58 59 60 63 65 67 69 70 71 73 74 **S** Department of Veterans Affairs, Washington, DC	45	10	156	3851	155	11634	—	108211	64641	1266
□ WILLIAM S. HALL PSYCHIATRIC INSTITUTE, 1800 Colonial Drive, Zip 29203–6827, Mailing Address: P.O. Box 202, Zip 29202–0202; tel. 803/898–1725; Dalmer P. Sercy, Director **A**1 3 5 10 **F**1 8 13 20 22 27 34 39 44 45 46 49 52 53 54 55 56 57 58 65 73	12	22	215	990	156	0	—	29162	—	539
CONWAY—Horry County										
□ CHARTER SANDS BEHAVIORAL HEALTH SYSTEM OF CONWAY, 152 Waccamaw Medical Park Drive, Zip 29526–8922; tel. 803/347–7156; Dale Armstrong, Chief Executive Officer **A**1 10 **F**2 15 16 17 25 28 39 41 45 46 52 53 54 55 56 57 58 59 65 67 **P**5 **S** Magellan Health Services, Atlanta, GA	33	22	48	779	22	—	—	6425	3018	114
⊠ CONWAY HOSPITAL, 300 Singleton Ridge Road, Zip 29526, Mailing Address: P.O. Box 829, Zip 29528–0829; tel. 843/347–7111; Philip A. Clayton, President and Chief Executive Officer (Total facility includes 88 beds in nursing home–type unit) **A**1 9 10 **F**7 8 10 14 15 16 17 19 21 22 23 28 30 31 32 33 35 37 39 40 44 45 48 49 63 65 67 69 70 71 73 74	23	10	227	8672	179	76841	1059	51452	18706	743
DARLINGTON—Darlington County										
WILSON MEDICAL CENTER See McLeod Regional Medical Center, Florence										
DILLON—Dillon County										
⊠ SAINT EUGENE MEDICAL CENTER, 301 East Jackson Street, Zip 29536–2509, Mailing Address: P.O. Box 1327, Zip 29536–1327; tel. 843/774–4111; Ronald W. Webb, President (Total facility includes 13 beds in nursing home–type unit) **A**1 9 10 **F**7 8 10 11 13 16 17 19 21 22 23 24 28 30 31 33 34 35 37 40 41 44 45 46 48 49 51 63 65 66 67 68 69 71 73 74 **P**1 8	23	10	117	5042	51	29146	327	21604	9168	304
EASLEY—Pickens County										
⊠ PALMETTO BAPTIST MEDICAL CENTER EASLEY, 200 Fleetwood Drive, Zip 29640–2076, Mailing Address: P.O. Box 2129, Zip 29641–2129; tel. 864/855–7200; Roddey E. Gettys, III, Executive Vice President (Total facility includes 13 beds in nursing home–type unit) **A**1 9 10 **F**7 8 11 13 14 15 16 17 19 20 21 22 23 26 28 29 30 31 34 35 36 37 39 40 41 44 45 46 48 49 62 64 65 67 69 71 73 74 **S** Palmetto Health Alliance, Columbia, SC	23	10	106	4201	52	31034	654	32927	13472	476
EDGEFIELD—Edgefield County										
⊠ EDGEFIELD COUNTY HOSPITAL, 300 Ridge Medical Plaza, Zip 29824; tel. 803/637–3174; W. Joseph Seel, Administrator **A**1 9 10 **F**8 13 15 16 17 19 22 26 27 28 30 32 33 39 41 44 45 48 49 51 64 65 66 67 68 69 71 74	13	10	40	735	8	9893	—	6198	2887	130
FAIRFAX—Allendale County										
★ ALLENDALE COUNTY HOSPITAL, Highway 278 West, Zip 29827–0278, Mailing Address: Box 218, Zip 29827–0218; tel. 803/632–3311; M. K. Hiatt, Administrator (Total facility includes 44 beds in nursing home–type unit) **A**9 10 **F**7 8 15 16 19 22 28 30 31 33 40 41 44 49 64 65 67 69 71 74	13	10	80	711	49	20389	195	6288	2210	114
FLORENCE—Florence County										
⊠ △ CAROLINAS HOSPITAL SYSTEM, (Includes Bruce Hospital System, 121 East Cedar Street, Zip 29501; Florence General Hospital, 512 South Irby Street, Zip 29501–5210; tel. 803/661–3000), 805 Pamplico Highway, Zip 29505, Mailing Address: P.O. Box 100550, Zip 29501–0550; tel. 843/674–5000; David A. McClellan, Chief Executive Officer (Total facility includes 44 beds in nursing home–type unit) **A**1 7 9 10 **F**2 3 4 10 11 13 14 15 16 17 19 20 21 22 23 24 25 26 27 28 29 30 31 32 33 34 35 37 38 39 40 41 43 44 45 47 48 49 51 53 55 57 58 60 62 63 65 66 67 69 71 73 74 **S** Quorum Health Group/Quorum Health Resources, Inc., Brentwood, TN **Web address:** www.carolinashospital.com	33	10	340	12658	213	129649	—	119177	46906	1296
□ HEALTHSOUTH REHABILITATION HOSPITAL, 900 East Cheves Street, Zip 29506–2704; tel. 843/679–9000; Dennis A. Lofe, FACHE, Chief Executive Officer **A**1 10 **F**4 8 10 11 12 13 17 19 22 23 24 25 26 28 29 30 31 32 33 34 35 37 38 39 40 41 43 44 45 46 47 48 49 53 55 56 57 58 65 66 67 69 71 73 **S** HEALTHSOUTH Corporation, Birmingham, AL	33	46	88	1204	71	8843	—	12564	6015	213
⊠ MCLEOD REGIONAL MEDICAL CENTER, (Includes Wilson Medical Center, 701 Cashua Ferry Road, Darlington, Zip 29532, Mailing Address: Box 1859, Zip 29540; tel. 803/395–1100; Debbie Locklair, Administrator), 555 East Cheves Street, Zip 29506–2617, Mailing Address: P.O. Box 100551, Zip 29501–0551; tel. 843/667–2000; J. Bruce Barragan, President and Chief Executive Officer **A**1 2 3 5 9 10 **F**2 3 4 7 8 9 10 11 12 13 14 15 16 17 19 20 21 22 23 24 25 27 28 29 30 31 32 33 34 35 37 38 39 40 41 42 43 44 45 46 47 48 49 51 52 53 54 55 56 57 58 59 60 63 65 66 67 68 69 70 71 73 74 **P**7	23	10	411	21756	336	182971	2088	226747	82993	2696
FORT JACKSON—Richland County										
⊠ MONCRIEF ARMY COMMUNITY HOSPITAL, Mailing Address: P.O. Box 500, Zip 29207–5720; tel. 803/751–2284; Colonel Dale Carroll, Commander (Nonreporting) **A**1 2 **S** Department of the Army, Office of the Surgeon General, Falls Church, VA	42	10	91	—	—	—	—	—	—	—
GAFFNEY—Cherokee County										
□ UPSTATE CAROLINA MEDICAL CENTER, 1530 North Limestone Street, Zip 29340–4738; tel. 864/487–1500; Nancy C. Fodi, Executive Director **A**1 9 10 **F**7 8 11 12 14 15 17 19 21 22 24 28 30 34 35 37 39 40 41 44 45 46 48 49 65 66 71 73 74 **P**8 **S** Health Management Associates, Naples, FL	33	10	125	3543	41	39959	302	23749	9293	294

Hospital, Address, Telephone, Administrator, Approval, Facility, and Physician Codes, Health Care System, Network	Classi-fication Codes		Utilization Data					Expense (thousands) of dollars		
★ American Hospital Association (AHA) membership □ Joint Commission on Accreditation of Healthcare Organizations (JCAHO) accreditation + American Osteopathic Healthcare Association (AOHA) membership ○ American Osteopathic Association (AOA) accreditation △ Commission on Accreditation of Rehabilitation Facilities (CARF) accreditation Control codes 61, 63, 64, 71, 72 and 73 indicate hospitals listed by AOHA, but not registered by AHA. For definition of numerical codes, see page A4	Control	Service	Staffed Beds	Admissions	Census	Outpatient Visits	Births	Total	Payroll	Personnel

GEORGETOWN—Georgetown County

⊞ GEORGETOWN MEMORIAL HOSPITAL, 606 Black River Road, Zip 29440–3368, Mailing Address: Drawer 1718, Zip 29442–1718; tel. 843/527–7000; Paul D. Gatens, Sr., Administrator **A**1 9 10 **F**2 5 7 8 9 10 11 14 15 16 17 19 21 22 23 24 25 26 28 29 30 31 34 35 37 40 41 42 44 45 46 47 48 49 54 56 59 60 61 63 65 66 68 69 70 71 73 74 **S** Quorum Health Group/Quorum Health Resources, Inc., Brentwood, TN	23	10	131	7676	91	92052	748	49390	17706	555

GREENVILLE—Greenville County

⊞ △ GREENVILLE MEMORIAL HOSPITAL, (Includes Marshall I. Pickens Hospital; Roger C. Peace Rehabilitation Hospital), 701 Grove Road, Zip 29605–4295; tel. 864/455–7000; J. Bland Burkhardt, Jr., Senior Vice President and Administrator (Total facility includes 48 beds in nursing home–type unit) **A**1 2 5 7 8 9 10 **F**2 3 4 7 8 10 11 12 13 14 15 16 17 19 21 22 24 25 26 27 28 29 30 31 32 33 34 35 37 38 39 40 41 42 43 44 45 46 47 48 49 51 52 53 54 55 56 57 58 59 60 61 63 65 66 67 68 69 70 71 73 74 **P**2 6 8 **S** Greenville Hospital System, Greenville, SC	23	10	850	34457	625	387858	4785	—	—	3591
⊞ SHRINERS HOSPITALS FOR CHILDREN, GREENVILLE, 950 West Faris Road, Zip 29605–4277; tel. 864/271–3444; Gary F. Fraley, Administrator **A**1 3 5 **F**15 19 21 22 27 28 30 34 37 38 41 45 47 48 49 50 53 63 65 69 70 71 73 **S** Shriners Hospitals for Children, Tampa, FL	33	57	50	967	18	15428	0	—	—	213
⊞ △ ST. FRANCIS HEALTH SYSTEM, One St. Francis Drive, Zip 29601–3207; tel. 864/255–1000; Richard C. Neugent, President and Chief Executive Officer **A**1 2 7 10 **F**2 3 4 8 10 11 12 13 15 16 17 19 21 22 23 24 25 28 29 30 31 32 33 34 35 37 38 39 40 41 42 43 44 45 46 48 49 52 53 55 57 58 59 60 63 65 66 67 69 71 73 74 **P**1 2 6 **Web address:** www.stfrancishealth.com	23	10	225	9446	169	214212	0	90723	42976	1358
W. J. BARGE MEMORIAL HOSPITAL, Wade Hampton Boulevard, Zip 29614; tel. 803/242–5100; Aras Pundys, Administrator **F**7 22 27 30 34 40 44 45 49 74	23	11	79	1560	12	7014	1	3111	728	44

GREENWOOD—Greenwood County

⊞ SELF MEMORIAL HOSPITAL, 1325 Spring Street, Zip 29646–3860; tel. 864/227–4111; M. John Heydel, President and Chief Executive Officer **A**1 2 3 5 9 10 **F**2 7 8 11 13 14 15 16 17 18 19 20 21 22 23 24 25 26 28 29 30 31 32 33 34 35 37 38 39 40 41 42 44 45 46 47 48 49 51 52 53 54 55 56 57 58 60 63 65 66 67 68 69 70 71 73 74 **P**5 8	23	10	363	11278	171	147704	1705	95050	45339	1461

GREER—Greenville County

★ ALLEN BENNETT HOSPITAL, (Includes Roger Huntington Nursing Center), 313 Memorial Drive, Zip 29650–1521; tel. 864/848–8130; Michael W. Massey, Administrator (Total facility includes 88 beds in nursing home–type unit) **A**9 10 **F**2 3 4 5 7 8 10 11 12 13 14 15 16 17 18 19 21 22 24 26 27 28 29 30 31 32 33 34 35 37 38 39 40 41 42 43 44 45 46 47 48 49 51 53 54 55 56 57 58 59 60 61 63 65 66 67 68 69 70 71 73 74 **P**2 6 8 **S** Greenville Hospital System, Greenville, SC	23	10	146	2974	124	69631	353	26777	10747	297
□ CHARTER GREENVILLE BEHAVIORAL HEALTH SYSTEM, 2700 East Phillips Road, Zip 29650–4816; tel. 864/968–6300; William L. Callison, Chief Executive Officer **A**1 10 **F**2 3 15 16 17 27 28 34 45 52 53 54 55 56 57 58 59 65 67 **S** Magellan Health Services, Atlanta, GA	33	22	66	1902	42	0	0	8016	3328	95

HARTSVILLE—Darlington County

□ BYERLY HOSPITAL, 413 East Carolina Avenue, Zip 29550–4309; tel. 843/339–2100; Page Vaughan, Executive Director **A**1 9 10 **F**7 8 11 13 15 16 17 19 21 22 24 28 30 31 35 36 37 40 45 46 49 63 65 66 67 68 69 71 **S** Health Management Associates, Naples, FL	33	10	100	5354	60	49007	572	26411	9418	389

HILTON HEAD ISLAND—Beaufort County

⊞ HILTON HEAD MEDICAL CENTER AND CLINICS, 25 Hospital Center Boulevard, Zip 29926–2738, Mailing Address: P.O. Box 21117, Zip 29925–1117; tel. 843/681–6122; Dennis Ray Bruns, President and Chief Executive Officer (Total facility includes 15 beds in nursing home–type unit) **A**1 9 10 **F**1 4 6 7 8 9 10 11 12 15 16 17 19 20 21 22 24 25 26 27 28 29 30 31 33 34 35 36 37 38 39 40 41 42 44 45 46 47 48 49 51 52 53 54 55 56 57 58 59 64 65 66 67 69 70 71 73 74 **S** TENET Healthcare Corporation, Santa Barbara, CA **Web address:** www.tenethealth.com	32	10	79	4247	44	92492	402	—	—	402

KINGSTREE—Williamsburg County

⊞ CAROLINAS HOSPITAL SYSTEM–KINGSTREE, 500 Nelson Boulevard, Zip 29556–4027, Mailing Address: P.O. Drawer 568, Zip 29556–0568; tel. 843/354–9661; David T. Boucher, Chief Executive Officer (Nonreporting) **A**1 9 10 **S** Quorum Health Group/Quorum Health Resources, Inc., Brentwood, TN	33	10	47	—	—	—	—	—	—	—

LAKE CITY—Florence County

⊞ CAROLINAS HOSPITAL SYSTEM–LAKE CITY, 258 North Ron McNair Boulevard, Zip 29560–1029, Mailing Address: P.O. Box 1029, Zip 29560–1029; tel. 843/394–2036; David T. Boucher, Chief Executive Officer (Nonreporting) **A**1 9 10 **S** Quorum Health Group/Quorum Health Resources, Inc., Brentwood, TN	33	10	40	—	—	—	—	—	—	—

LANCASTER—Lancaster County

⊞ SPRINGS MEMORIAL HOSPITAL, 800 West Meeting Street, Zip 29720–2298; tel. 803/286–1214; Robert M. Luther, Chief Executive Officer **A**1 9 10 **F**2 3 7 8 10 15 16 17 19 21 22 23 28 30 31 32 33 34 35 37 40 41 44 45 48 49 60 65 69 71 73 74 **P**8 **S** Community Health Systems, Inc., Brentwood, TN	33	10	169	6028	91	29185	632	49136	15678	620

Hospital, Address, Telephone, Administrator, Approval, Facility, and Physician Codes, Health Care System, Network	Classi-fication Codes		Utilization Data					Expense (thousands) of dollars		
★ American Hospital Association (AHA) membership □ Joint Commission on Accreditation of Healthcare Organizations (JCAHO) accreditation + American Osteopathic Healthcare Association (AOHA) membership ○ American Osteopathic Association (AOA) accreditation △ Commission on Accreditation of Rehabilitation Facilities (CARF) accreditation Control codes 61, 63, 64, 71, 72 and 73 indicate hospitals listed by AOHA, but not registered by AHA. For definition of numerical codes, see page A4	Control	Service	Staffed Beds	Admissions	Census	Outpatient Visits	Births	Total	Payroll	Personnel

LOCKHART—Union County

| ★ HOPE HOSPITAL, 102 Hope Drive, Zip 29364, Mailing Address: P.O. Box 280, Zip 29364–0280; tel. 864/545–6500; Mildred W. Purvis, Administrator **F**28 45 | 13 | 10 | 10 | 126 | 2 | 0 | — | 624 | 337 | 12 |

LORIS—Horry County

| ✠ LORIS COMMUNITY HOSPITAL, 3655 Mitchell Street, Zip 29569–2827; tel. 843/716–7000; J. Timothy Browne, Chief Executive Officer (Total facility includes 88 beds in nursing home–type unit) **A**1 9 10 **F**7 8 11 14 15 16 17 19 21 22 24 28 30 31 32 33 34 35 37 39 40 41 44 45 46 49 63 64 65 66 68 69 70 71 74
Web address: www.lorishealthcaresystem.com | 16 | 10 | 193 | 3649 | 132 | 69208 | 421 | 33719 | 13685 | 555 |

MANNING—Clarendon County

| ✠ CLARENDON MEMORIAL HOSPITAL, 10 Hospital Street, Zip 29102, Mailing Address: P.O. Box 550, Zip 29102–0550; tel. 803/435–8463; Edward R. Frye, Jr., Administrator **A**1 9 10 **F**7 8 11 14 15 16 17 18 19 20 21 22 25 26 30 31 32 33 34 35 36 37 39 40 41 44 45 49 54 65 68 69 71 73 74 **P**8 | 16 | 10 | 56 | 2021 | 31 | 87280 | 331 | 18812 | 8934 | 309 |

MOUNT PLEASANT—Charleston County

| ✠ EAST COOPER REGIONAL MEDICAL CENTER, 1200 Johnnie Dodds Boulevard, Zip 29464–3294; tel. 843/881–0100; Jack Dusenbery, President **A**1 9 10 **F**7 8 10 11 15 16 17 19 22 23 24 25 28 30 31 32 34 35 37 39 40 41 44 45 48 49 56 61 65 66 69 70 71 73 74 **P**6 **S** TENET Healthcare Corporation, Santa Barbara, CA | 33 | 10 | 112 | 3875 | 41 | 81891 | 1241 | — | — | 427 |

MULLINS—Marion County

| ✠ MARION COUNTY MEDICAL CENTER, 2829 East Highway 76, Zip 29574, Mailing Address: P.O. Drawer 1150, Marion, Zip 29571–1150; tel. 843/431–2000; Thomas E. Fuller, Executive Director (Total facility includes 92 beds in nursing home–type unit) **A**1 9 10 **F**2 3 4 6 7 8 10 11 13 15 16 17 18 19 20 21 22 23 24 25 26 27 28 30 31 32 33 34 35 36 37 38 39 40 41 43 44 45 47 48 49 51 52 53 54 55 56 57 58 59 60 64 65 66 67 68 69 70 71 73 74 **P**5
Web address: www.mcmed.org | 16 | 10 | 216 | 7156 | 176 | 23589 | 506 | 35815 | 12918 | 532 |

MYRTLE BEACH—Horry County

| ✠ GRAND STRAND REGIONAL MEDICAL CENTER, (Formerly Columbia Grand Strand Medical Center), 809 82nd Parkway, Zip 29572–1413; tel. 803/692–1100; Doug White, Chief Executive Officer (Total facility includes 18 beds in nursing home–type unit) **A**1 2 9 10 **F**4 8 10 11 12 13 14 15 16 17 19 21 22 23 24 25 26 28 30 31 32 33 34 35 37 39 40 41 43 44 45 46 48 49 60 63 64 65 66 67 69 70 71 73 74 **S** Columbia/HCA Healthcare Corporation, Nashville, TN | 33 | 10 | 186 | 10517 | 118 | 128849 | 762 | — | — | 783 |

NEWBERRY—Newberry County

| ✠ NEWBERRY COUNTY MEMORIAL HOSPITAL, 2669 Kinard Street, Zip 29108–0497, Mailing Address: P.O. Box 497, Zip 29108–0497; tel. 803/276–7570; Lynn W. Beasley, President and Chief Executive Officer **A**1 9 10 **F**7 8 11 12 13 14 15 16 17 19 21 22 25 26 27 28 29 30 31 37 39 40 41 44 45 47 48 49 59 65 69 71 73 74 **P**8 **S** Quorum Health Group/Quorum Health Resources, Inc., Brentwood, TN | 13 | 10 | 65 | 2101 | 26 | 28752 | 255 | 17076 | 6898 | 267 |

NORTH CHARLESTON—Charleston County

| ✠ NAVAL HOSPITAL, 3600 Rivers Avenue, Zip 29405; tel. 803/743–7000; Captain John M. Mateczun, Commanding Officer **A**1 3 5 **F**1 2 3 4 5 6 8 9 10 11 12 13 14 16 17 18 19 20 21 23 24 25 26 28 29 30 31 32 33 34 35 37 38 39 40 41 42 43 44 45 46 47 48 49 51 52 53 54 55 56 57 58 59 60 61 65 66 69 71 73 74 **P**5 6 **S** Department of Navy, Washington, DC
Web address: www.nhchasn.med.navy.mil | 43 | 10 | 32 | 749 | 7 | 142483 | 0 | 34942 | 10059 | 738 |

ORANGEBURG—Orangeburg County

| ✠ REGIONAL MEDICAL CENTER OF ORANGEBURG AND CALHOUN COUNTIES, 3000 St. Matthews Road, Zip 29118–1470; tel. 803/533–2200; Thomas C. Dandridge, President **A**1 2 9 10 **F**2 3 4 5 6 7 8 9 10 11 13 15 16 17 18 19 20 21 22 23 24 26 27 28 30 31 32 33 34 35 36 37 38 39 40 41 42 43 44 45 46 47 48 49 50 51 52 53 54 55 56 57 58 59 60 61 62 63 65 66 67 68 69 70 71 73 74 **P**8 **S** Quorum Health Group/Quorum Health Resources, Inc., Brentwood, TN | 13 | 10 | 295 | 10787 | 167 | 43108 | 1457 | 79199 | 33837 | 1031 |

PICKENS—Pickens County

| ✠ CANNON MEMORIAL HOSPITAL, 123 West G. Acker Drive, Zip 29671, Mailing Address: P.O. Box 188, Zip 29671–0188; tel. 864/878–4791; Norman G. Rentz, President and Chief Executive Officer **A**1 9 10 **F**8 11 13 14 17 19 22 25 26 28 30 31 34 35 37 44 45 49 65 69 71 **P**8 | 23 | 10 | 42 | 1099 | 14 | 28466 | 0 | 9629 | 4193 | 159 |

RIDGELAND—Jasper County

| LOW COUNTRY GENERAL HOSPITAL, Highway 278, Zip 29936, Mailing Address: Drawer 400, Zip 29936–0400; tel. 843/726–8111; Jeffrey L. White, Chief Executive Officer **A**9 10 **F**2 3 4 5 6 8 9 10 11 13 14 15 16 17 18 19 20 21 22 23 24 25 26 27 28 30 31 32 33 34 35 36 37 38 39 40 41 42 43 44 45 46 47 48 49 50 51 52 53 54 55 56 57 58 59 60 61 63 65 66 67 68 69 70 71 73 74 | 23 | 10 | 31 | 662 | 8 | 7655 | 43 | 4043 | 2264 | 50 |

ROCK HILL—York County

| ✠ PIEDMONT HEALTHCARE SYSTEM, 222 Herlong Avenue, Zip 29732–1952; tel. 803/329–1234; Charles F. Miller, Interim President **A**1 9 10 **F**3 4 7 8 10 11 12 15 16 17 19 21 22 25 26 27 28 30 31 34 35 37 38 39 40 41 43 44 45 46 49 51 52 53 54 55 56 57 58 59 60 65 67 69 70 71 73 74 **S** TENET Healthcare Corporation, Santa Barbara, CA | 33 | 10 | 276 | 12669 | 175 | 128408 | 1373 | 111552 | 35788 | 1302 |

SENECA—Oconee County

| ✠ OCONEE MEMORIAL HOSPITAL, (Includes Lila Doyle Nursing Care Facility), 298 Memorial Drive, Zip 29672; tel. 864/882–3351; W. H. Hudson, President (Total facility includes 79 beds in nursing home–type unit) **A**1 9 10 **F**7 8 11 13 14 15 16 17 19 21 22 23 28 29 30 31 33 34 35 37 40 41 44 45 49 65 67 69 71 73 | 23 | 10 | 190 | 7543 | 159 | 88510 | 611 | 57969 | 23381 | 886 |

Hospital, Address, Telephone, Administrator, Approval, Facility, and Physician Codes, Health Care System, Network	Classi-fication Codes		Utilization Data					Expense (thousands) of dollars		
★ American Hospital Association (AHA) membership □ Joint Commission on Accreditation of Healthcare Organizations (JCAHO) accreditation + American Osteopathic Healthcare Association (AOHA) membership ○ American Osteopathic Association (AOA) accreditation △ Commission on Accreditation of Rehabilitation Facilities (CARF) accreditation Control codes 61, 63, 64, 71, 72 and 73 indicate hospitals listed by AOHA, but not registered by AHA. For definition of numerical codes, see page A4	Control	Service	Staffed Beds	Admissions	Census	Outpatient Visits	Births	Total	Payroll	Personnel

SHAW AFB—Sumter County

☒ U. S. AIR FORCE HOSPITAL SHAW, 431 Meadowlark Street, Zip 29152–5319; tel. 803/895–6324; Lieutenant Colonel Donald Taylor, Administrator **A**1 **F**2 3 4 7 8 9 10 11 13 16 17 18 19 20 22 23 24 28 29 30 34 35 37 38 39 40 41 42 43 44 45 46 47 48 49 50 51 52 53 54 55 56 58 59 60 61 63 65 66 67 68 69 71 73 74 **S** Department of the Air Force, Bowling AFB, DC

41	10	16	992	7	138660	318	—	—	414

SIMPSONVILLE—Greenville County

★ HILLCREST HOSPITAL, 729 S.E. Main Street, Zip 29681–3280; tel. 864/967–6100; Mark Slyter, Administrator **A**9 10 **F**2 3 4 8 10 11 12 13 14 15 16 17 19 21 22 25 26 27 28 29 30 31 32 33 34 35 37 38 39 40 41 42 43 44 45 46 47 48 49 52 53 54 55 56 57 58 59 60 61 63 65 67 68 69 71 73 **P**2 6 8 **S** Greenville Hospital System, Greenville, SC

23	10	46	1451	18	61557	0	17018	6152	153

SPARTANBURG—Spartanburg County

☒ △ MARY BLACK HEALTH SYSTEM, 1700 Skylyn Drive, Zip 29307–1061, Mailing Address: P.O. Box 3217, Zip 29304–3217; tel. 864/573–3000; William W. Fox, Chief Executive Officer **A**1 7 9 10 **F**7 8 10 11 12 13 17 19 21 22 23 25 28 30 31 34 35 37 39 40 41 42 44 45 46 48 49 57 63 64 65 67 69 71 73 74 **P**4 8 **S** Quorum Health Group/Quorum Health Resources, Inc., Brentwood, TN

33	10	210	7066	108	118345	1062	57492	22396	700

★ SPARTANBURG HOSPITAL FOR RESTORATIVE CARE, 389 Serpentine Drive, Zip 29303; tel. 864/560–3280; Anita M. Butler, Administrator (Nonreporting) **A**10 **S** Spartanburg Regional Healthcare System, Spartanburg, SC

16	10	45	—	—	—	—	—	—	—

☒ SPARTANBURG REGIONAL MEDICAL CENTER, 101 East Wood Street, Zip 29303–3016; tel. 864/560–6000; Joseph Michael Oddis, President (Nonreporting) **A**1 2 3 5 9 10 **S** Spartanburg Regional Healthcare System, Spartanburg, SC

16	10	471	—	—	—	—	—	—	—

SUMMERVILLE—Dorchester County

★ SUMMERVILLE MEDICAL CENTER, 295 Midland Parkway, Zip 29485–8104; tel. 843/832–5100; Steven M. Anderson, Chief Executive Officer (Nonreporting) **A**9 **S** Columbia/HCA Healthcare Corporation, Nashville, TN

33	10	99	—	—	—	—	—	—	—

SUMTER—Sumter County

☒ TUOMEY HEALTHCARE SYSTEM, 129 North Washington Street, Zip 29150–4983; tel. 803/778–9000; Jay Cox, President and Chief Executive Officer (Total facility includes 18 beds in nursing–type unit) **A**1 9 10 **F**2 4 7 8 10 11 14 15 16 17 19 21 22 23 24 25 26 28 29 30 32 33 34 35 37 38 40 41 42 43 44 45 46 47 48 49 51 52 53 56 57 60 63 65 66 67 69 71 73 74 **P**8 **S** Quorum Health Group/Quorum Health Resources, Inc., Brentwood, TN
Web address: www.tuomey.com

21	10	239	11738	219	68903	1322	86930	36663	1220

TRAVELERS REST—Greenville County

□ SPRING BROOK BEHAVIORAL HEALTHCARE SYSTEM, One Chestnut Way, Zip 29690–1005, Mailing Address: P.O. Box 1005, Zip 29690–1005; tel. 864/834–8013; Shawn J. O'Connor, Chief Executive Officer **A**1 10 **F**17 19 21 22 25 26 27 31 34 35 45 46 48 49 52 53 54 55 56 57 58 59 65 70 71

33	22	44	180	8	0	0	—	—	84

UNION—Union County

☒ WALLACE THOMSON HOSPITAL, 322 West South Street, Zip 29379–2857, Mailing Address: P.O. Box 789, Zip 29379–0789; tel. 864/429–2600; Harrell L. Connelly, Chief Executive Officer (Total facility includes 113 beds in nursing home–type unit) **A**1 9 10 **F**8 17 19 22 27 28 30 32 34 35 36 37 39 40 41 44 45 46 49 60 63 64 65 69 71 73 74 **S** Quorum Health Group/Quorum Health Resources, Inc., Brentwood, TN

16	10	220	4269	169	44168	169	25935	9925	464

VARNVILLE—Hampton County

★ HAMPTON REGIONAL MEDICAL CENTER, 503 Carolina Avenue West, Zip 29944, Mailing Address: P.O. Box 338, Zip 29944–0338; tel. 803/943–2771; Dave H. Hamill, President and Chief Executive Officer **A**9 10 **F**8 14 15 16 17 19 22 28 30 34 41 44 45 49 64 65 69 71 73 74

23	10	36	541	6	16654	1	—	—	108

WALTERBORO—Colleton County

☒ COLLETON MEDICAL CENTER, 501 Robertson Boulevard, Zip 29488–5714; tel. 843/549–2000; Rebecca T. Brewer, CHE, Chief Executive Officer (Total facility includes 15 beds in nursing home–type unit) **A**1 9 10 **F**7 8 10 12 13 17 19 21 22 23 25 26 28 30 34 35 37 39 40 41 44 45 46 48 49 51 63 64 65 67 68 71 73 74 **S** Columbia/HCA Healthcare Corporation, Nashville, TN

33	10	131	4609	71	29772	359	29530	10399	372

WEST COLUMBIA—Lexington County

□ CHARTER RIVERS BEHAVIORAL HEALTH SYSTEM, 2900 Sunset Boulevard, Zip 29169–3422; tel. 803/796–9911; R. Andy Hanner, Chief Executive Officer **A**1 10 **F**2 3 14 15 16 17 19 25 26 27 28 34 35 45 49 52 53 54 55 56 57 59 65 73 **S** Magellan Health Services, Atlanta, GA

33	22	66	1504	30	4098	—	7299	3100	78

☒ LEXINGTON MEDICAL CENTER, 2720 Sunset Boulevard, Zip 29169–4816; tel. 803/791–2000; Michael J. Biediger, President **A**1 9 10 **F**7 8 10 11 12 13 15 16 17 18 19 20 21 22 24 25 26 28 30 31 33 34 35 37 38 39 40 41 42 44 45 46 48 49 51 60 63 65 66 67 69 70 71 73 74 **Web address:** www.lexmed.com

16	10	273	14111	179	188319	2259	122237	50594	1541

WINNSBORO—Fairfield County

☒ FAIRFIELD MEMORIAL HOSPITAL, 102 U.S. Highway 321 By–Pass North, Zip 29180, Mailing Address: P.O. Box 620, Zip 29180–0620; tel. 803/635–5548; Brent R. Lammers, Administrator **A**1 9 10 **F**8 14 15 16 17 19 22 28 29 30 32 33 34 39 41 42 44 45 49 64 65 67 69 71 73

13	10	33	826	10	20893	0	9891	4165	185

WOODRUFF—Spartanburg County

★ B.J. WORKMAN MEMORIAL HOSPITAL, 751 East Georgia Street, Zip 29388, Mailing Address: P.O. Box 699, Zip 29388–0699; tel. 864/476–8122; G. Curtis Walker, R.N., Administrator (Nonreporting) **A**9 10 **S** Spartanburg Regional Healthcare System, Spartanburg, SC

13	10	32	—	—	—	—	—	—	—

SOUTH DAKOTA

Resident population 738 (in thousands)
Resident population in metro areas 33.1%
Birth rate per 1,000 population 14.4
65 years and over 14.3%
Percent of persons without health insurance 9.5%

Hospital, Address, Telephone, Administrator, Approval, Facility, and Physician Codes, Health Care System, Network	Classi-fication Codes		Utilization Data					Expense (thousands) of dollars		
	Control	Service	Staffed Beds	Admissions	Census	Outpatient Visits	Births	Total	Payroll	Personnel

★ American Hospital Association (AHA) membership
□ Joint Commission on Accreditation of Healthcare Organizations (JCAHO) accreditation
+ American Osteopathic Healthcare Association (AOHA) membership
○ American Osteopathic Association (AOA) accreditation
△ Commission on Accreditation of Rehabilitation Facilities (CARF) accreditation
Control codes 61, 63, 64, 71, 72 and 73 indicate hospitals listed by AOHA, but not registered by AHA. For definition of numerical codes, see page A4

Hospital	Control	Service	Staffed Beds	Admissions	Census	Outpatient Visits	Births	Total	Payroll	Personnel
ABERDEEN—Brown County										
⊞ △ AVERA ST. LUKE'S, (Formerly St Luke's Midland Regional Medical Center), 305 South State Street, Zip 57402–4450; tel. 605/622–5000; Dale J. Stein, President and Chief Executive Officer (Total facility includes 81 beds in nursing home–type unit) **A**1 2 7 9 10 **F**1 2 3 6 7 8 10 11 12 14 15 16 17 22 23 26 28 30 31 32 33 34 36 37 39 40 41 42 48 52 64 **P**6 8 **S** Avera Health, Yankton, SD **Web address:** www.averastlukes.org	21	10	224	6238	164	166701	699	67009	28911	942
ST LUKE'S MIDLAND REGIONAL MEDICAL CENTER See Avera St. Luke's										
ARMOUR—Douglas County										
DOUGLAS COUNTY MEMORIAL HOSPITAL, 708 Eighth Street, Zip 57313–2102; tel. 605/724–2159; Angelia K. Henry, Administrator **A**10 **F**7 15 16 19 22 26 28 30 32 33 34 35 36 39 41 42 44 49 66 71	23	10	9	280	2	5768	10	1613	827	41
BOWDLE—Edmunds County										
★ BOWDLE HOSPITAL, 9051 West Fifth Street, Zip 57428–0566; tel. 605/285–6146; Bryan Breitling, Administrator and Chief Executive Officer (Total facility includes 41 beds in nursing home–type unit) **A**9 10 **F**8 15 19 22 24 27 30 32 33 34 40 44 64 65 71	14	10	61	403	42	6175	13	3143	1555	67
BRITTON—Marshall County										
MARSHALL COUNTY HEALTHCARE CENTER, 413 Ninth Street, Zip 57430–0230, Mailing Address: Box 230, Zip 57430–0230; tel. 605/448–2253; Stephanie Lulewicz, Administrator **A**9 10 **F**6 14 15 16 19 22 28 30 32 34 49 51 71 **S** Avera Health, Yankton, SD	23	10	20	485	8	7995	0	2464	788	72
BROOKINGS—Brookings County										
★ BROOKINGS HOSPITAL, 300 22nd Avenue, Zip 57006–2496; tel. 605/696–9000; David B. Johnson, Administrator (Total facility includes 79 beds in nursing home–type unit) **A**10 **F**7 12 14 16 17 19 22 26 27 28 30 32 33 35 36 37 39 40 44 45 46 64 67 71 73	14	10	140	2017	96	39346	301	14551	7801	201
BURKE—Gregory County										
COMMUNITY MEMORIAL HOSPITAL, Eighth and Jackson, Zip 57523, Mailing Address: P.O. Box 319, Zip 57523–0319; tel. 605/775–2621; Carol A. Varland, Chief Executive Officer **A**9 10 **F**16 19 22 32 33 35 **S** Avera Health, Yankton, SD	23	10	16	334	9	2198	0	1981	—	48
CANTON—Lincoln County										
★ CANTON–INWOOD MEMORIAL HOSPITAL, 440 North Hiawatha Drive, Zip 57013–9404; tel. 605/987–2621; John Devick, Chief Executive Officer (Nonreporting) **A**9 10 **S** Sioux Valley Hospitals and Health System, Sioux Falls, SD	23	10	25	—	—	—	—	—	—	—
CHAMBERLAIN—Brule County										
★ MID DAKOTA HOSPITAL, 300 South Byron Boulevard, Zip 57325–9741; tel. 605/734–5511; Earl N. Sheehy, Administrator **A**9 10 **F**7 8 17 19 22 28 30 37 41 44 49 65 71 **S** Sioux Valley Hospitals and Health System, Sioux Falls, SD	23	10	54	1464	13	8713	67	7033	3085	115
CLEAR LAKE—Deuel County										
★ DEUEL COUNTY MEMORIAL HOSPITAL, (RURAL PRIMARY CARE HOSPITAL), 701 Third Avenue South, Zip 57226–1037, Mailing Address: P.O. Box 1037, Zip 57226–1037; tel. 605/874–2141; Robert J. Salmon, Administrator (Total facility includes 10 beds in nursing home–type unit) **A**9 10 **F**6 8 13 15 16 17 19 20 21 22 24 30 32 36 49 51 63 64 65 71 **P**6 **S** Sioux Valley Hospitals and Health System, Sioux Falls, SD	23	49	16	229	4	4019	0	1830	988	49
CUSTER—Custer County										
CUSTER COMMUNITY HOSPITAL, 1039 Montgomery Street, Zip 57730–1397; tel. 605/673–2229; Jason Petik, Administrator **A**10 **F**6 7 8 14 15 19 22 25 28 32 33 39 40 41 51 57 65 71 72 **P**7 8	23	10	10	211	4	17595	14	2700	1609	53
DE SMET—Kingsbury County										
DE SMET MEMORIAL HOSPITAL, 306 Prairie Avenue S.W., Zip 57231–9499; tel. 605/854–3329; John L. Single, Chief Executive Officer and Administrator **A**9 10 **F**8 14 15 16 19 22 30 32 44 49 65 71	14	10	13	276	4	8341	0	1334	570	17
DEADWOOD—Lawrence County										
★ NORTHERN HILLS GENERAL HOSPITAL, 61 Charles Street, Zip 57732–1303; tel. 605/578–2313; Richard G. Soukup, Chief Executive Officer **A**9 10 **F**1 3 7 8 15 16 19 22 24 28 29 30 32 33 35 36 37 39 40 41 44 49 53 54 55 57 58 64 65 66 71	23	10	18	514	6	9821	47	5448	2651	99
DELL RAPIDS—Minnehaha County										
DELL AREA HEALTH CENTER, (Formerly Dell Rapids Community Hospital), 909 North Iowa Street, Zip 57022–1231; tel. 605/428–5431 (Total facility includes 50 beds in nursing home–type unit) **A**9 10 **F**7 8 11 17 20 22 24 30 34 39 40 44 49 64 71 73	23	10	79	645	17	6767	34	3454	1721	122
EAGLE BUTTE—Dewey County										
⊞ U. S. PUBLIC HEALTH SERVICE INDIAN HOSPITAL, Mailing Address: P.O. Box 1012, Zip 57625–1012; tel. 605/964–3001; Donald D. Annis, Service Unit Director **A**1 10 **F**1 3 4 5 6 7 8 10 12 13 14 15 18 19 20 21 22 23 24 25 26 27 28 29 30 31 32 33 34 35 36 39 40 41 42 43 44 45 46 49 50 51 53 54 55 56 57 58 59 60 61 62 63 65 66 67 69 70 71 72 73 74 **S** U. S. Public Health Service Indian Health Service, Rockville, MD	47	10	23	777	5	52946	78	6762	3602	87

Hospital, Address, Telephone, Administrator, Approval, Facility, and Physician Codes, Health Care System, Network	Classi-fication Codes		Utilization Data					Expense (thousands) of dollars		
★ American Hospital Association (AHA) membership □ Joint Commission on Accreditation of Healthcare Organizations (JCAHO) accreditation + American Osteopathic Healthcare Association (AOHA) membership ○ American Osteopathic Association (AOA) accreditation △ Commission on Accreditation of Rehabilitation Facilities (CARF) accreditation Control codes 61, 63, 64, 71, 72 and 73 indicate hospitals listed by AOHA, but not registered by AHA. For definition of numerical codes, see page A4	Control	Service	Staffed Beds	Admissions	Census	Outpatient Visits	Births	Total	Payroll	Personnel

ELLSWORTH AFB—Meade County

☒ U. S. AIR FORCE HOSPITAL, 2900 Doolittle Drive, Zip 57706; tel. 605/385–3201; Colonel Farley Howell, Commanding Officer (Nonreporting) **A**1 **S** Department of the Air Force, Bowling AFB, DC **Web address:** www.elsworth.af.mil/~medge/index.htm

| | 41 | 10 | 31 | — | — | — | — | — | — | — |

EUREKA—McPherson County

EUREKA COMMUNITY HEALTH SERVICES, (Formerly Eureka Community Hospital), 410 Ninth Street, Zip 57437–0517; tel. 605/284–2661; Robert A. Dockter, Administrator **A**9 10 **F**6 8 15 16 17 19 22 32 35 44 49 65 66 71 **S** Avera Health, Yankton, SD

| | 23 | 10 | 6 | 244 | 3 | 7453 | 0 | 1168 | 520 | 30 |

FAULKTON—Faulk County

FAULK COUNTY MEMORIAL HOSPITAL, (CRITICAL ACCESS HOSPITAL), 911 St. John Street, Zip 57438, Mailing Address: P.O. Box 100, Zip 57438–0100; tel. 605/598–6263; Patricia Kadlec, Administrator **A**9 10 **F**6 11 12 14 15 16 19 22 27 30 32 34 39 41 51 62 65 71

| | 13 | 49 | 19 | 171 | 7 | 5922 | 0 | 1359 | 632 | 27 |

FLANDREAU—Moody County

★ FLANDREAU MUNICIPAL HOSPITAL, 214 North Prairie Avenue, Zip 57028–1243; tel. 605/997–2433; Curtis Hohman, Interim Administrator (Nonreporting) **A**9 10 **S** Avera Health, Yankton, SD

| | 14 | 10 | 18 | — | — | — | — | — | — | — |

FORT MEADE—Meade County

☒ VETERANS AFFAIRS BLACK HILLS HEALTH CARE SYSTEM, (Includes Veterans Affairs Medical Center, 500 North Fifth Street, Hot Springs, Zip 57747; tel. 605/745–2052), 113 Comanche Road, Zip 57741–1099; tel. 605/347–2511; Peter P. Henry, Director (Total facility includes 104 beds in nursing home–type unit) **A**1 5 **F**2 3 12 16 17 19 20 21 22 25 26 27 28 29 30 32 33 34 35 37 39 41 42 44 45 46 48 49 51 52 58 64 65 67 68 71 73 74 **S** Department of Veterans Affairs, Washington, DC

| | 45 | 10 | 163 | 2672 | 157 | 173791 | 0 | 74809 | 39023 | 918 |

FREEMAN—Hutchinson County

★ FREEMAN COMMUNITY HOSPITAL, 510 East Eighth Street, Zip 57029–0370, Mailing Address: P.O. Box 370, Zip 57029–0370; tel. 605/925–4000; James M. Krehbiel, Chief Executive Officer (Total facility includes 59 beds in nursing home–type unit) **A**9 10 **F**1 7 8 14 15 16 17 19 22 26 27 28 29 30 32 33 34 35 36 37 39 40 41 42 44 45 48 49 62 63 64 65 66 67 68 71 73 **P**4 7

| | 23 | 10 | 85 | 467 | 64 | 9495 | 34 | 4758 | 2513 | 106 |

GETTYSBURG—Potter County

★ GETTYSBURG MEDICAL CENTER, 606 East Garfield, Zip 57442–1398; tel. 605/765–2480; Mark Schmidt, Administrator (Total facility includes 54 beds in nursing home–type unit) (Nonreporting) **A**10 **S** Catholic Health Initiatives, Denver, CO

| | 23 | 10 | 61 | — | — | — | — | — | — | — |

GREGORY—Gregory County

★ GREGORY COMMUNITY HOSPITAL, 400 Park Street, Zip 57533–0400, Mailing Address: Box 408, Zip 57533–0408; tel. 605/835–8394; Carol A. Varland, Chief Executive Officer (Total facility includes 58 beds in nursing home–type unit) **A**9 10 **F**1 7 8 12 14 15 16 19 20 21 22 24 26 27 28 29 30 32 35 37 40 41 42 44 45 46 58 64 65 66 67 71 **S** Lutheran Health Systems, Fargo, ND

| | 23 | 10 | 84 | 814 | 66 | 21215 | 37 | 5987 | 2890 | 135 |

HOT SPRINGS—Fall River County

VETERANS AFFAIRS MEDICAL CENTER See Veterans Affairs Black Hills Health Care System, Fort Meade

HOVEN—Potter County

★ HOLY INFANT HOSPITAL, Main Street, Zip 57450–0158, Mailing Address: P.O. Box 158, Zip 57450–0158; tel. 605/948–2262; Jeff Marlette, Administrator (Nonreporting) **A**9 10

| | 23 | 10 | 22 | — | — | — | — | — | — | — |

HURON—Beadle County

☒ HURON REGIONAL MEDICAL CENTER, 172 Fourth Street S.E., Zip 57350–2590; tel. 605/353–6200; John L. Single, Chief Executive Officer **A**1 9 10 **F**7 8 14 15 16 19 21 22 24 30 32 33 34 35 37 39 40 41 44 45 49 56 65 66 71 73 **S** Quorum Health Group/Quorum Health Resources, Inc., Brentwood, TN

| | 23 | 10 | 61 | 2700 | 29 | 44202 | 256 | 19064 | 7771 | 245 |

LEMMON—Perkins County

FIVE COUNTIES HOSPITAL, 401 Sixth Avenue West, Zip 57638–1318, Mailing Address: P.O. Box 479, Zip 57638–0479; tel. 605/374–3871; Helen S. Lindquist, Administrator (Total facility includes 52 beds in nursing home–type unit) **A**9 10 **F**22 64

| | 23 | 10 | 56 | 54 | 43 | 4305 | 0 | 1803 | 903 | 44 |

MADISON—Lake County

☒ MADISON COMMUNITY HOSPITAL, 917 North Washington Avenue, Zip 57042–1696; tel. 605/256–6551; Tamara Miller, Administrator (Nonreporting) **A**1 9 10

| | 23 | 10 | 49 | — | — | — | — | — | — | — |

MARTIN—Bennett County

BENNETT COUNTY HEALTHCARE CENTER, (Formerly Bennett County Community Hospital), Merriman Star Route, Zip 57551, Mailing Address: P.O. Box 70–D, Zip 57551; tel. 605/685–6622; John L. Jacobs, Administrator (Total facility includes 48 beds in nursing home–type unit) **A**9 10 **F**7 8 22 28 32 34 40 49 64

| | 13 | 10 | 68 | 386 | 49 | 1529 | 6 | 3132 | 1711 | 79 |

MILBANK—Grant County

□ ST. BERNARD'S PROVIDENCE HOSPITAL, (Includes St. William Home for the Aged), 901 East Virgil Avenue, Zip 57252–2124, Mailing Address: P.O. Box 432, Zip 57252–0432; tel. 605/432–4538; Sister Genevieve Karels, Administrator (Total facility includes 82 beds in nursing home–type unit) **A**1 9 10 **F**6 7 8 14 15 16 19 22 30 32 33 34 35 37 40 49 64 71

| | 21 | 10 | 117 | 542 | 85 | 5545 | 44 | 5898 | 2104 | 145 |

Hospital, Address, Telephone, Administrator, Approval, Facility, and Physician Codes, Health Care System, Network	Classi-fication Codes		Utilization Data					Expense (thousands) of dollars		
★ American Hospital Association (AHA) membership □ Joint Commission on Accreditation of Healthcare Organizations (JCAHO) accreditation + American Osteopathic Healthcare Association (AOHA) membership ○ American Osteopathic Association (AOA) accreditation △ Commission on Accreditation of Rehabilitation Facilities (CARF) accreditation Control codes 61, 63, 64, 71, 72 and 73 indicate hospitals listed by AOHA, but not registered by AHA. For definition of numerical codes, see page A4	Control	Service	Staffed Beds	Admissions	Census	Outpatient Visits	Births	Total	Payroll	Personnel

MILLER—Hand County

★ HAND COUNTY MEMORIAL HOSPITAL, 300 West Fifth Street, Zip 57362–1238; tel. 605/853–2421; Clarence A. Lee, Administrator **A**10 **F**3 6 8 11 12 13 14 15 16 17 19 20 21 22 26 27 28 29 30 32 34 36 39 41 42 44 45 46 49 53 54 58 63 65 66 67 68 70 71 73 74 **P**1 3 4 5 6 7 8 **S** Avera Health, Yankton, SD

| | 23 | 10 | 21 | 484 | 8 | 3286 | 0 | 2625 | 1207 | 68 |

MITCHELL—Davison County

⊠ AVERA QUEEN OF PEACE, (Formerly Queen of Peace Hospital), 525 North Foster, Zip 57301–2999; tel. 605/995–2000; Ronald L. Jacobson, President and Chief Executive Officer (Total facility includes 84 beds in nursing home–type unit) **A**1 9 10 **F**1 3 7 8 12 14 15 16 17 19 20 22 23 24 26 27 28 30 32 33 34 35 36 37 39 40 41 42 44 45 49 56 62 64 65 66 67 71 73 74 **P**6 **S** Avera Health, Yankton, SD

| | 21 | 10 | 183 | 4172 | 123 | 73559 | 479 | 33361 | 15406 | 455 |

MOBRIDGE—Walworth County

★ MOBRIDGE REGIONAL HOSPITAL, 1401 Tenth Avenue West, Zip 57601–1199, Mailing Address: P.O. Box 580, Zip 57601–0580; tel. 605/845–3693; John M. Kutch, Chief Executive Officer (Total facility includes 16 beds in nursing home–type unit) **A**9 10 **F**6 7 8 14 15 16 19 22 24 26 28 29 30 31 32 33 34 35 37 39 40 44 45 49 56 57 62 64 65 66 67 70 71 **P**6
Web address: www.cam–walnet.com/~mrh/

| | 23 | 10 | 64 | 793 | 11 | 11914 | 35 | 7023 | 3762 | 134 |

PARKSTON—Hutchinson County

★ AVERA ST. BENEDICT HEALTH CENTER, (Formerly St Benedict Health Center), Glynn Drive, Zip 57366, Mailing Address: P.O. Box B, Zip 57366; tel. 605/928–3311; Gale Walker, Administrator (Total facility includes 75 beds in nursing home–type unit) (Nonreporting) **A**9 10 **S** Avera Health, Yankton, SD
Web address: www.parkston.com

| | 21 | 10 | 105 | — | — | — | — | — | — | — |

PHILIP—Haakon County

HANS P. PETERSON MEMORIAL HOSPITAL, 603 West Pine, Zip 57567, Mailing Address: P.O. Box 790, Zip 57567–0790; tel. 605/859–2511; David Dick, Administrator (Total facility includes 36 beds in nursing home–type unit) **A**9 10 **F**6 19 20 21 22 30 32 39 64 65 **P**6

| | 23 | 10 | 66 | 347 | 52 | 1677 | 9 | 2538 | 1300 | 99 |

PIERRE—Hughes County

⊠ ST. MARY'S HEALTHCARE CENTER, (Formerly St. Mary's Hospital), 800 East Dakota Avenue, Zip 57501–3313; tel. 605/224–3100; James D. M. Russell, Chief Executive Officer (Total facility includes 105 beds in nursing home–type unit) **A**1 9 10 **F**8 14 15 16 19 22 30 32 33 34 35 36 37 40 41 42 44 49 62 64 65 66 71 73 **P**5 **S** Catholic Health Initiatives, Denver, CO
Web address: www.st-marys.com

| | 23 | 10 | 191 | 2900 | 125 | 15510 | 366 | 21054 | 10423 | 303 |

PINE RIDGE—Shannon County

⊠ U. S. PUBLIC HEALTH SERVICE INDIAN HOSPITAL, Mailing Address: P.O. Box 1201, Zip 57770–1201; tel. 605/867–5131; Vern F. Donnell, Service Unit Director (Nonreporting) **A**1 10 **S** U. S. Public Health Service Indian Health Service, Rockville, MD

| | 47 | 10 | 46 | — | — | — | — | — | — | — |

PLATTE—Charles Mix County

★ PLATTE COMMUNITY MEMORIAL HOSPITAL, 609 East Seventh, Zip 57369–2123, Mailing Address: P.O. Box 200, Zip 57369–0200; tel. 605/337–3364; Mark Burket, Chief Executive Officer (Total facility includes 48 beds in nursing home–type unit) **A**9 10 **F**1 6 8 11 14 15 16 17 19 22 24 30 32 33 34 36 39 41 42 44 49 64 65 71 73 **S** Avera Health, Yankton, SD

| | 23 | 10 | 63 | 344 | 54 | 1581 | 21 | 3738 | 2305 | 94 |

RAPID CITY—Pennington County

⊠ INDIAN HEALTH SERVICE HOSPITAL, 3200 Canyon Lake Drive, Zip 57702–8197; tel. 605/355–2280; Michelle Leach, Director **A**1 10 **F**2 3 8 9 11 13 15 16 19 20 21 22 27 28 29 30 34 35 37 38 39 40 41 42 43 44 45 46 47 48 49 50 51 52 53 54 55 56 57 58 59 61 62 63 64 65 66 67 69 70 71 72 73 74 **S** U. S. Public Health Service Indian Health Service, Rockville, MD

| | 44 | 10 | 32 | 544 | 11 | 59271 | 0 | 11381 | 3740 | 159 |

⊠ RAPID CITY REGIONAL HOSPITAL SYSTEM OF CARE, 353 Fairmont Boulevard, Zip 57701–7393, Mailing Address: P.O. Box 6000, Zip 57709–6000; tel. 605/341–1000; Adil M. Ameer, President and Chief Executive Officer **A**1 2 3 5 9 10 **F**1 4 6 7 8 10 12 14 15 16 19 21 22 23 28 30 32 33 35 37 38 40 41 42 43 44 46 47 48 49 52 53 55 57 58 59 60 65 66 67 71 73 **P**1 6 7
Web address: www.rcrh.org

| | 23 | 10 | 360 | 15500 | 233 | 112263 | 1612 | 154173 | 65843 | 1787 |

REDFIELD—Spink County

COMMUNITY MEMORIAL HOSPITAL, 110 West Tenth Avenue, Zip 57469–0420, Mailing Address: P.O. Box 420, Zip 57469–0420; tel. 605/472–1111; Daniel Keierleber, Administrator **A**9 10 **F**7 8 14 16 19 22 26 30 32 34 36 37 40 41 44 46 49 51 71 **P**6

| | 14 | 10 | 25 | 532 | 8 | 15523 | 3 | 4217 | 2421 | 85 |

ROSEBUD—Todd County

⊠ U. S. PUBLIC HEALTH SERVICE INDIAN HOSPITAL, Highway 18, Soldier Creek Road, Zip 57570; tel. 605/747–2231; Gayla J. Twiss, Service Unit Director **A**1 10 **F**2 3 4 7 8 9 10 11 12 14 15 16 17 18 19 20 21 22 23 27 28 29 30 31 32 34 35 37 38 40 41 42 43 44 46 47 48 49 50 52 53 54 55 56 57 58 59 60 61 63 64 65 66 67 69 70 71 74 **P**6 **S** U. S. Public Health Service Indian Health Service, Rockville, MD

| | 47 | 10 | 35 | 997 | 8 | 75264 | 21 | 20841 | 9018 | 221 |

SCOTLAND—Bon Homme County

★ LANDMANN–JUNGMAN MEMORIAL HOSPITAL, 600 Billars Street, Zip 57059–2026; tel. 605/583–2226; William H. Koellner, Administrator **A**9 10 **F**8 14 15 16 19 22 24 28 32 33 34 35 36 39 44 46 49 51 62 65 71 73

| | 23 | 10 | 19 | 324 | 4 | 5474 | 7 | 2442 | 1090 | 47 |

Hospital, Address, Telephone, Administrator, Approval, Facility, and Physician Codes, Health Care System, Network	Classi-fication Codes		Utilization Data					Expense (thousands) of dollars		
★ American Hospital Association (AHA) membership □ Joint Commission on Accreditation of Healthcare Organizations (JCAHO) accreditation + American Osteopathic Healthcare Association (AOHA) membership ○ American Osteopathic Association (AOA) accreditation △ Commission on Accreditation of Rehabilitation Facilities (CARF) accreditation Control codes 61, 63, 64, 71, 72 and 73 indicate hospitals listed by AOHA, but not registered by AHA. For definition of numerical codes, see page A4	Control	Service	Staffed Beds	Admissions	Census	Outpatient Visits	Births	Total	Payroll	Personnel

SIOUX FALLS—Minnehaha County

☒ △ AVERA MCKENNAN HOSPITAL, (Formerly McKennan Hospital), 800 East 21st Street, Zip 57105–1096, Mailing Address: P.O. Box 5045, Zip 57117–5045; tel. 605/322–8000; Fredrick Slunecka, President and Chief Executive Officer (Total facility includes 196 beds in nursing home–type unit) **A**1 2 3 5 7 9 10 **F**3 4 5 6 7 8 9 10 11 12 13 14 15 16 17 18 19 21 22 23 24 25 26 27 28 29 30 31 32 33 34 35 37 38 39 40 41 42 43 44 45 46 47 48 49 51 52 53 54 55 56 57 58 59 60 61 62 63 64 65 66 67 68 70 71 73 74 **P**1 6 **S** Avera Health, Yankton, SD **Web address:** www.mckennan.com	21	10	521	14928	411	408973	1152	181732	77769	1990
CHILDRENS CARE HOSPITAL AND SCHOOL, (CHILDREN'S SPECIALTY HOSPITAL), 2501 West 26th Street, Zip 57105–2498; tel. 605/782–2300; Charisse S. Oland, President and Chief Executive Officer **F**12 14 15 16 17 27 34 48 49 64 65 73 **Web address:** www.cchs.org	23	59	96	48	74	0	0	10654	6671	272
☒ ROYAL C. JOHNSON VETERANS MEMORIAL HOSPITAL, 2501 West 22nd Street, Zip 57105–1394, Mailing Address: P.O. Box 5046, Zip 57117–5046; tel. 605/336–3230; R. Vincent Crawford, Director (Total facility includes 65 beds in nursing home–type unit) **A**1 3 5 **F**1 2 3 8 11 12 15 16 17 19 20 21 22 26 27 28 29 30 31 32 33 34 35 37 39 41 42 44 45 46 48 49 52 54 56 57 58 59 63 64 65 67 71 73 74 **P**6 **S** Department of Veterans Affairs, Washington, DC	45	10	110	3499	92	95278	0	43529	19703	645
☒ △ SIOUX VALLEY HOSPITAL, (Includes Sioux Valley Behavioral Health, 2812 South Louise Avenue, Zip 57106–4309; tel. 605/361–8111), 1100 South Euclid Avenue, Zip 57105–0496, Mailing Address: P.O. Box 5039, Zip 57117–5039; tel. 605/333–1000; Becky Nelson, President **A**1 2 3 5 7 9 10 **F**3 4 7 8 10 11 12 14 15 16 17 18 19 20 21 22 24 25 26 27 28 29 30 31 32 33 34 35 37 38 39 40 41 42 43 44 45 46 47 48 49 51 52 53 54 55 56 58 61 65 66 67 70 71 72 73 74 **P**6 **S** Sioux Valley Hospitals and Health System, Sioux Falls, SD	23	10	503	18700	284	164699	2024	192343	85788	2970

SISSETON—Roberts County

★ COTEAU DES PRAIRIES HOSPITAL, 205 Orchard Drive, Zip 57262–2398; tel. 605/698–7647; Bill Nelson, Administrator and Chief Executive Officer (Nonreporting) **A**9 10	23	10	27	—	—	—	—	—	—	—
☒ U. S. PUBLIC HEALTH SERVICE INDIAN HOSPITAL, Chestnut Street, Zip 57262, Mailing Address: P.O. Box 189, Zip 57262–0189; tel. 605/698–7606; Richard Huff, Administrator **A**1 10 **F**8 12 13 14 15 16 19 20 22 27 30 31 33 34 44 46 61 65 67 71 74 **S** U. S. Public Health Service Indian Health Service, Rockville, MD **Web address:** www.home.aberdeen.his.gov	47	10	18	342	3	32173	0	3844	—	63

SPEARFISH—Lawrence County

★ LOOKOUT MEMORIAL HOSPITAL, 1440 North Main Street, Zip 57783–1504; tel. 605/642–2617; Deb J. Krmpotic, R.N., Administrator **A**9 10 **F**1 6 7 8 11 12 14 15 16 19 21 22 27 28 30 32 33 34 35 36 37 39 40 41 42 44 45 46 49 61 62 63 64 65 66 67 71 73 **P**6 **S** Lutheran Health Systems, Fargo, ND	23	10	32	1697	15	38662	288	10258	4214	239

STURGIS—Meade County

★ STURGIS COMMUNITY HEALTH CARE CENTER, 949 Harmon Street, Zip 57785–2452; tel. 605/347–2536; Deb J. Krmpotic, R.N., Administrator (Total facility includes 84 beds in nursing home–type unit) **A**9 10 **F**7 8 12 14 15 16 19 22 32 33 35 40 41 44 64 67 71 **S** Lutheran Health Systems, Fargo, ND	23	10	114	1048	92	18345	107	8387	3942	109

TYNDALL—Bon Homme County

★ ST. MICHAEL'S HOSPITAL, Douglas Street and Broadway, Zip 57066, Mailing Address: P.O. Box 27, Zip 57066–0027; tel. 605/589–3341; Carol Deurmier, Chief Executive Officer (Total facility includes 9 beds in nursing home–type unit) **A**10 **F**7 8 14 15 16 19 22 30 32 33 35 37 40 44 45 56 58 64 65 66 71 **P**4 7	21	10	34	371	16	16317	21	2639	1483	55

VERMILLION—Clay County

★ SIOUX VALLEY VERMILLION CAMPUS, 20 South Plum Street, Zip 57069–3346; tel. 605/624–2611; Larry W. Veitz, Chief Executive Officer (Total facility includes 66 beds in nursing home–type unit) **A**9 10 **F**3 7 8 14 16 17 19 22 28 29 30 32 33 34 35 39 41 42 44 45 46 49 62 64 65 66 67 71 73 **P**4 7 **S** Sioux Valley Hospitals and Health System, Sioux Falls, SD	23	10	95	942	69	17395	67	7209	3404	118

VIBORG—Turner County

★ PIONEER MEMORIAL HOSPITAL AND HEALTH SERVICES, 315 North Washington Street, Zip 57070, Mailing Address: P.O. Box 368, Zip 57070–0368; tel. 605/326–5161; Georgia Pokorney, Chief Executive Officer (Total facility includes 52 beds in nursing home–type unit) **A**10 **F**1 3 4 6 7 8 9 10 11 13 15 19 20 21 22 24 26 28 30 32 33 34 35 36 37 38 39 40 41 42 43 44 45 47 49 51 60 62 64 65 66 67 70 71 74 **P**5 **S** Sioux Valley Hospitals and Health System, Sioux Falls, SD	23	10	64	408	54	10716	4	4544	2257	67

WAGNER—Charles Mix County

★ WAGNER COMMUNITY MEMORIAL HOSPITAL, Third and Walnut, Zip 57380, Mailing Address: P.O. Box 280, Zip 57380–0280; tel. 605/384–3611; Arlene C. Bich, Administrator **A**9 10 **F**7 11 15 16 19 22 26 28 29 30 32 33 34 37 40 44 45 49 51 62 64 65 70 71	23	10	20	652	6	6944	0	2936	1284	52

WATERTOWN—Codington County

☒ PRAIRIE LAKES HOSPITAL AND CARE CENTER, 400 Tenth Avenue N.W., Zip 57201–6210, Mailing Address: P.O. Box 1210, Zip 57201–1210; tel. 605/882–7000; Edmond L. Weiland, President and Chief Executive Officer (Total facility includes 51 beds in nursing home–type unit) **A**1 2 9 10 **F**7 8 14 15 16 17 19 22 29 32 33 34 35 37 39 40 41 42 44 45 46 49 56 58 64 65 66 67 71 73 74 **S** Sioux Valley Hospitals and Health System, Sioux Falls, SD **Web address:** www.prairielakes.com	23	10	119	2962	80	66002	601	29465	11049	371

Hospital, Address, Telephone, Administrator, Approval, Facility, and Physician Codes, Health Care System, Network	Classi-fication Codes		Utilization Data					Expense (thousands) of dollars		
★ American Hospital Association (AHA) membership □ Joint Commission on Accreditation of Healthcare Organizations (JCAHO) accreditation + American Osteopathic Healthcare Association (AOHA) membership ○ American Osteopathic Association (AOA) accreditation △ Commission on Accreditation of Rehabilitation Facilities (CARF) accreditation Control codes 61, 63, 64, 71, 72 and 73 indicate hospitals listed by AOHA, but not registered by AHA. For definition of numerical codes, see page A4	Control	Service	Staffed Beds	Admissions	Census	Outpatient Visits	Births	Total	Payroll	Personnel

WEBSTER—Day County

★ LAKE AREA HOSPITAL, North First Street, Zip 57274, Mailing Address: P.O. Box 489, Zip 57274–0489; tel. 605/345–3336; Donald J. Finn, Administrator **A**9 10 **F**7 8 11 12 15 16 19 21 22 28 30 31 40 44 45 49 71 **P**5 **S** Sioux Valley Hospitals and Health System, Sioux Falls, SD

| | 23 | 10 | 26 | 517 | 7 | — | 3 | 3245 | 1342 | 62 |

WESSINGTON SPRINGS—Jerauld County

WESKOTA MEMORIAL MEDICAL CENTER, 604 First Street N.E., Zip 57382, Mailing Address: P.O. Box 429, Zip 57382; tel. 605/539–1201; Kayleen R. Lee, Chief Executive Officer **A**9 10 **F**7 15 16 19 22 30 32 49 67 71 **P**5

| | 23 | 10 | 28 | 431 | 7 | 3476 | 13 | 1501 | 790 | 39 |

WINNER—Tripp County

★ WINNER REGIONAL HEALTHCARE CENTER, 745 East Eighth Street, Zip 57580–2677, Mailing Address: P.O. Box 745, Zip 57580–0745; tel. 605/842–7100; Rebecca L. Cooper, Interim Chief Executive Officer (Total facility includes 81 beds in nursing home–type unit) **A**9 10 **F**7 8 11 14 15 16 17 19 21 22 24 26 28 29 30 32 33 34 35 36 39 40 41 42 44 49 50 61 64 66 68 71 **S** Sioux Valley Hospitals and Health System, Sioux Falls, SD

| | 23 | 10 | 116 | 946 | 90 | 9400 | 168 | 9851 | 4757 | 126 |

YANKTON—Yankton County

✠ △ AVERA SACRED HEART HEALTH SERVICES, (Formerly Sacred Heart Health Services), 501 Summit Avenue, Zip 57078–3899; tel. 605/668–8000; Pamela J. Rezac, President and Chief Executive Officer (Total facility includes 113 beds in nursing home–type unit) **A**1 2 7 9 10 **F**1 6 7 8 10 11 12 14 15 16 17 19 21 22 23 24 26 28 29 30 32 33 34 35 36 37 39 41 42 44 45 46 48 60 63 65 66 67 71 73 **P**3 7 **S** Avera Health, Yankton, SD

| | 21 | 10 | 257 | 5419 | 181 | 23800 | 648 | 56715 | 16482 | 484 |

TENNESSEE

Resident population 5,431 (in thousands)
Resident population in metro areas 66.6%
Birth rate per 1,000 population 13.9
65 years and over 12.5%
Percent of persons without health insurance 15.2%

Hospital, Address, Telephone, Administrator, Approval, Facility, and Physician Codes, Health Care System, Network	Classi-fication Codes		Utilization Data					Expense (thousands) of dollars		
★ American Hospital Association (AHA) membership □ Joint Commission on Accreditation of Healthcare Organizations (JCAHO) accreditation + American Osteopathic Healthcare Association (AOHA) membership ○ American Osteopathic Association (AOA) accreditation △ Commission on Accreditation of Rehabilitation Facilities (CARF) accreditation Control codes 61, 63, 64, 71, 72 and 73 indicate hospitals listed by AOHA, but not registered by AHA. For definition of numerical codes, see page A4	Control	Service	Staffed Beds	Admissions	Census	Outpatient Visits	Births	Total	Payroll	Personnel

ASHLAND CITY—Cheatham County

★ CHEATHAM MEDICAL CENTER, (Formerly Columbia Cheatham Medical Center), 313 North Main Street, Zip 37015–1358; tel. 615/792–3030; Rick Wallace, FACHE, Chief Executive Officer and Administrator **A**9 **F**12 14 15 16 19 22 28 44 45 46 49 51 54 56 57 65 66 71 73 **P**7 **S** Columbia/HCA Healthcare Corporation, Nashville, TN **Web address:** www.columbia.net	33	10	29	817	7	11812	0	5520	2902	80

ATHENS—McMinn County

⊞ ATHENS REGIONAL MEDICAL CENTER, 1114 West Madison Avenue, Zip 37303–4150, Mailing Address: P.O. Box 250, Zip 37371–0250; tel. 423/745–1411; John R. Workman, Chief Executive Officer **A**1 9 10 **F**7 8 11 14 15 16 17 19 21 22 23 24 26 28 30 34 35 37 39 40 41 42 44 45 49 58 63 65 67 71 73 **P**7 **S** Columbia/HCA Healthcare Corporation, Nashville, TN **Web address:** www.columbiachat.com	33	10	91	2406	23	54984	313	15928	7191	260

BOLIVAR—Hardeman County

⊞ BOLIVAR GENERAL HOSPITAL, 650 Nuckolls Road, Zip 38008–1500; tel. 901/658–3100; George L. Austin, Administrator (Nonreporting) **A**1 9 10 **S** West Tennessee Healthcare, Jackson, TN	23	10	47	—	—	—	—	—	—	—

BRISTOL—Sullivan County

⊞ WELLMONT BRISTOL REGIONAL MEDICAL CENTER, 1 Medical Park Boulevard, Zip 37620–7434; tel. 423/844–4200; Randall M. Olson, Administrator (Total facility includes 30 beds in nursing home–type unit) **A**1 2 3 5 9 10 **F**1 4 6 7 8 10 11 12 14 15 16 17 19 20 21 22 23 24 25 26 28 29 30 31 32 33 34 35 37 39 40 41 42 43 44 45 46 49 50 51 52 53 55 56 57 58 59 60 63 64 65 66 67 70 71 72 73 74 **P**1 4 5 6 7 **S** Quorum Health Group/Quorum Health Resources, Inc., Brentwood, TN **Web address:** www.wellmont.org	23	10	275	11680	173	—	817	101654	41442	1618

BROWNSVILLE—Haywood County

⊞ METHODIST HEALTHCARE–BROWNSVILLE HOSPITAL, (Formerly Methodist–Haywood Park Hospital), 2545 North Washington Avenue, Zip 38012–1697; tel. 901/772–4110; Sandra Bailey, Administrator **A**1 9 10 **F**1 2 3 4 5 6 7 8 9 10 11 12 13 15 16 17 18 19 20 21 22 23 24 25 26 27 28 29 30 31 32 33 34 35 36 37 38 39 40 41 42 43 44 45 46 47 48 49 50 51 52 53 54 55 56 57 58 59 60 61 62 64 65 66 67 68 70 71 72 73 74 **P**3 5 7 **S** Methodist Healthcare, Memphis, TN	21	10	44	1152	14	13005	186	4814	2312	72

CAMDEN—Benton County

⊞ CAMDEN GENERAL HOSPITAL, 175 Hospital Drive, Zip 38320–1617; tel. 901/584–6135; John M. Carruth, Administrator (Total facility includes 10 beds in nursing home–type unit) **A**1 9 10 **F**14 15 16 19 22 28 44 64 71 **P**5 8 **S** West Tennessee Healthcare, Jackson, TN	16	10	34	616	31	14976	0	2954	1970	75

CARTHAGE—Smith County

⊞ FRANK T. RUTHERFORD MEMORIAL HOSPITAL, (Includes Carthage General Hospital; Trousdale Medical Center, 500 Church Street, Hartsville, Zip 37074, Mailing Address: P.O. Box 319, Carthage, Zip 37030; tel. 615/374–2221), 130 Lebanon Highway, Zip 37030–2955, Mailing Address: P.O. Box 319, Zip 37030–0319; tel. 615/735–9815; Wayne Winfree, Chief Executive Officer **A**1 9 10 **F**2 3 7 8 12 15 16 17 19 22 28 30 32 35 39 40 41 44 45 49 53 54 58 63 65 67 68 71 73 **P**7	23	10	54	2331	27	30491	49	15095	8003	338
⊞ SMITH COUNTY MEMORIAL HOSPITAL, 158 Hospital Drive, Zip 37030–1096; tel. 615/735–1560; Jerry H. Futrell, Chief Executive Officer **A**1 9 10 **F**7 8 12 14 15 16 19 22 26 28 35 40 44 49 52 57 65 71 73 **P**8 **S** LifePoint Hospitals, Inc., Nashville, TN	33	10	40	1489	20	13032	116	10031	3762	121

CELINA—Clay County

□ CUMBERLAND RIVER HOSPITAL NORTH, 100 Old Jefferson Street, Zip 38551; tel. 931/243–3581; Patrick J. Gray, Chief Executive Officer (Total facility includes 8 beds in nursing home–type unit) (Nonreporting) **A**1 9 10 **S** Paracelsus Healthcare Corporation, Houston, TX	33	10	66	—	—	—	—	—	—	—

CENTERVILLE—Hickman County

□ BAPTIST HICKMAN COMMUNITY HOSPITAL, 135 East Swan Street, Zip 37033–1446; tel. 615/729–4271; Jack M. Keller, Administrator (Total facility includes 40 beds in nursing home–type unit) **A**1 9 10 **F**8 14 15 16 19 22 28 30 32 33 34 49 59 64 65 71	23	10	65	576	45	9012	0	6729	2728	69

CHATTANOOGA—Hamilton County

COLUMBIA PARKRIDGE MEDICAL CENTER See Parkridge Medical Center

⊞ ERLANGER HEALTH SYSTEM, (Includes Erlanger North Hospital, 632 Morrison Springs Road, Zip 37415; tel. 615/778–3300; T. C. Thompson Children's Hospital, 910 Blackford Street, Zip 37403; tel. 615/778–6011; Willie D. Miller Eye Center), 975 East Third Street, Zip 37403–2112; tel. 423/778–7000; Dennis Pettigrew, President and Chief Executive Officer (Nonreporting) **A**1 2 3 5 9 10	16	10	536	—	—	—	—	—	—	—

Hospital, Address, Telephone, Administrator, Approval, Facility, and Physician Codes, Health Care System, Network	Classi-fication Codes		Utilization Data					Expense (thousands) of dollars		
	Control	Service	Staffed Beds	Admissions	Census	Outpatient Visits	Births	Total	Payroll	Personnel

Approval / membership key:
★ American Hospital Association (AHA) membership
□ Joint Commission on Accreditation of Healthcare Organizations (JCAHO) accreditation
+ American Osteopathic Healthcare Association (AOHA) membership
○ American Osteopathic Association (AOA) accreditation
△ Commission on Accreditation of Rehabilitation Facilities (CARF) accreditation
Control codes 61, 63, 64, 71, 72 and 73 indicate hospitals listed by AOHA, but not registered by AHA. For definition of numerical codes, see page A4

Hospital	Control	Service	Staffed Beds	Admissions	Census	Outpatient Visits	Births	Total	Payroll	Personnel
□ HEALTHSOUTH CHATTANOOGA REHABILITATION HOSPITAL, 2412 McCallie Avenue, Zip 37404–3398; tel. 423/698–0221; Susan Heath, Chief Executive Officer (Nonreporting) A1 9 10 S HEALTHSOUTH Corporation, Birmingham, AL Web address: www.healthsouth.com	33	46	69	—	—	—	—	—	—	—
⌧ MEMORIAL HOSPITAL, 2525 De Sales Avenue, Zip 37404–3322; tel. 423/495–2525; L. Clark Taylor, Jr., President and Chief Executive Officer (Total facility includes 15 beds in nursing home–type unit) (Nonreporting) A1 2 3 5 9 10 S Catholic Health Initiatives, Denver, CO Web address: www.memorial.org	21	10	287	—	—	—	—	—	—	—
⌧ MEMORIAL NORTH PARK HOSPITAL, 2051 Hamill Road, Zip 37343–4096; tel. 423/870–6100; Sean S. McMurray, CHE, Administrator (Nonreporting) A1 9 10 S Catholic Health Initiatives, Denver, CO	23	10	83	—	—	—	—	—	—	—
□ MOCCASIN BEND MENTAL HEALTH INSTITUTE, 100 Moccasin Bend Road, Zip 37405–4496; tel. 423/785–3400; Russell K. Vatter, Superintendent (Total facility includes 91 beds in nursing home–type unit) A1 10 F16 43 46 52 53 65 73	12	22	172	1633	145	0	0	16504	10698	401
⌧ PARKRIDGE MEDICAL CENTER, (Formerly Columbia Parkridge Medical Center), (Includes East Ridge Hospital, 941 Spring Creek Road, East Ridge, Zip 37412; tel. 423/855–3500; Brenda M. Waltz, CHE, Chief Executive Officer; Valley Behavioral Health System, 2200 Morris Hill Road, Zip 37421; tel. 423/499–1204; Philip R. Cook, Chief Executive Officer, 2333 McCallie Avenue, Zip 37404–3285; tel. 423/493–1486; Niels P. Vernegaard, President (Total facility includes 28 beds in nursing home–type unit) (Nonreporting) A1 9 10 S Columbia/HCA Healthcare Corporation, Nashville, TN Web address: www.columbia.net	33	10	517	—	—	—	—	—	—	—
⌧ △ SISKIN HOSPITAL FOR PHYSICAL REHABILITATION, One Siskin Plaza, Zip 37403–1306; tel. 423/634–1200; Robert P. Main, President and Chief Executive Officer A1 7 9 10 F12 14 16 20 25 27 34 39 41 48 49 64 65 66 67 73 Web address: www.siskinrehab.org	23	46	80	1156	70	14246	0	23016	12616	318
T. C. THOMPSON CHILDREN'S HOSPITAL See Erlanger Health System										
VALLEY BEHAVIORAL HEALTH SYSTEM See Parkridge Medical Center										
□ VENCOR HOSPITAL–CHATTANOOGA, 709 Walnut Street, Zip 37402–1961; tel. 423/266–7721; Steven E. McGraw, Administrator (Nonreporting) A1 10 S Vencor, Incorporated, Louisville, KY	33	49	43	—	—	—	—	—	—	—
WILLIE D. MILLER EYE CENTER See Erlanger Health System										
CLARKSVILLE—Montgomery County										
⌧ GATEWAY HEALTH SYSTEM, (Formerly Clarksville Memorial Hospital), 1771 Madison Street, Zip 37043–4900, Mailing Address: P.O. Box 3160, Zip 37043–3160; tel. 931/552–6622; James Lee Decker, President and Chief Executive Officer (Total facility includes 29 beds in nursing home–type unit) A1 9 10 F7 8 10 14 15 16 19 21 22 28 30 31 32 33 34 35 36 37 38 39 40 42 44 45 46 49 52 56 57 59 60 64 65 71 73 P2 5 Web address: www.crhs.com	23	10	199	8918	139	90282	1285	73622	29816	978
CLEVELAND—Bradley County										
⌧ BRADLEY MEMORIAL HOSPITAL, 2305 Chambliss Avenue N.W., Zip 37311, Mailing Address: P.O. Box 3060, Zip 37320–3060; tel. 423/559–6000; Jim Whitlock, Administrator A1 9 10 F7 8 10 12 14 15 16 19 21 22 23 28 30 32 33 34 35 37 39 40 41 42 44 45 49 60 65 67 71 73 74	13	10	174	7553	80	107187	1147	69336	28629	846
⌧ CLEVELAND COMMUNITY HOSPITAL, 2800 Westside Drive N.W., Zip 37312–3599; tel. 423/339–4100; Marty Smith, Chief Executive Officer (Nonreporting) A1 9 10 S Community Health Systems, Inc., Brentwood, TN	33	10	70	—	—	—	—	—	—	—
COLLIERVILLE—Shelby County										
BAPTIST MEMORIAL HOSPITAL–COLLIERVILLE See Baptist Memorial Hospital, Memphis										
COLUMBIA—Maury County										
⌧ MAURY REGIONAL HOSPITAL, 1224 Trotwood Avenue, Zip 38401–4823; tel. 931/381–1111; William R. Walter, Chief Executive Officer (Nonreporting) A1 9 10 Web address: www.mauryregional.com	13	10	275	—	—	—	—	—	—	—
COOKEVILLE—Putnam County										
⌧ COOKEVILLE REGIONAL MEDICAL CENTER, 142 West Fifth Street, Zip 38501–1760, Mailing Address: P.O. Box 340, Zip 38503–0340; tel. 931/528–2541; Tod N. Lambert, Administrator and Chief Executive Officer (Nonreporting) A1 9 10	14	10	158	—	—	—	—	—	—	—
COPPERHILL—Polk County										
□ COPPER BASIN MEDICAL CENTER, State Highway 68, Zip 37317, Mailing Address: P.O. Box 990, Zip 37317–0990; tel. 423/496–5511; Grady Scott, President and Chief Executive Officer (Nonreporting) A1 9 10	23	10	44	—	—	—	—	—	—	—
COVINGTON—Tipton County										
⌧ BAPTIST MEMORIAL HOSPITAL–TIPTON, 1995 Highway 51 South, Zip 38019–3635; tel. 901/476–2621; Glenn Baker, Administrator A1 9 10 F7 8 12 14 15 16 19 22 23 28 29 30 31 32 33 35 38 39 40 44 45 46 49 61 65 67 71 S Baptist Memorial Health Care Corporation, Memphis, TN	23	10	48	2843	30	38039	454	20201	6104	259
CROSSVILLE—Cumberland County										
⌧ CUMBERLAND MEDICAL CENTER, 421 South Main Street, Zip 38555–5031; tel. 931/484–9511; Edwin S. Anderson, President (Total facility includes 16 beds in nursing home–type unit) A1 9 10 F7 8 10 11 12 15 16 19 21 22 23 24 28 29 32 35 37 39 40 41 42 44 48 49 51 60 64 65 67 71 73 Web address: www.cmchealthcare.org	23	10	177	6593	77	64040	566	39514	19925	751

Hospital, Address, Telephone, Administrator, Approval, Facility, and Physician Codes, Health Care System, Network	Classi-fication Codes		Utilization Data					Expense (thousands) of dollars		
	Control	Service	Staffed Beds	Admissions	Census	Outpatient Visits	Births	Total	Payroll	Personnel

★ American Hospital Association (AHA) membership
□ Joint Commission on Accreditation of Healthcare Organizations (JCAHO) accreditation
+ American Osteopathic Healthcare Association (AOHA) membership
○ American Osteopathic Association (AOA) accreditation
△ Commission on Accreditation of Rehabilitation Facilities (CARF) accreditation
Control codes 61, 63, 64, 71, 72 and 73 indicate hospitals listed by AOHA, but not registered by AHA. For definition of numerical codes, see page A4

DAYTON—Rhea County
★ RHEA MEDICAL CENTER, 7900 Rhea County Highway, Zip 37321–5912; tel. 423/775–1121; Kennedy L. Croom, Jr., Administrator and Chief Executive Officer (Total facility includes 89 beds in nursing home–type unit) **A**9 10 **F**15 19 22 35 37 44 49 64 71 **S** Quorum Health Group/Quorum Health Resources, Inc., Brentwood, TN

| | 13 | 10 | 131 | 1152 | 97 | 35308 | 0 | 12434 | 5350 | 169 |

DICKSON—Dickson County
⊞ HORIZON MEDICAL CENTER, 111 Highway 70 East, Zip 37055–2033; tel. 615/441–2357; Rick Wallace, FACHE, Chief Executive Officer and Administrator (Total facility includes 26 beds in nursing home–type unit) **A**1 9 10 **F**7 8 10 12 14 15 16 19 21 22 26 28 30 32 33 34 35 37 39 40 41 42 44 45 46 49 51 52 56 57 64 65 66 71 72 73 74 **P**7 **S** Columbia/HCA Healthcare Corporation, Nashville, TN
Web address: www.columbia.net

| | 33 | 10 | 176 | 3868 | 49 | 51846 | 463 | 27399 | 11727 | 341 |

DYERSBURG—Dyer County
⊞ METHODIST HEALTHCARE– DYERSBURG HOSPITAL, (Formerly Methodist Hospital of Dyersburg), 400 Tickle Street, Zip 38024–3182; tel. 901/285–2410; Richard McCormick, Administrator **A**1 9 10 **F**7 8 11 12 14 15 19 21 22 23 27 28 30 32 33 35 40 44 45 46 49 60 65 71 73 **P**5 7 8 **S** Methodist Healthcare, Memphis, TN
Web address: www.methodisthealth.org

| | 23 | 10 | 105 | 4277 | 41 | 42273 | 648 | 29468 | 11264 | 328 |

EAST RIDGE—Hamilton County
EAST RIDGE HOSPITAL See Parkridge Medical Center, Chattanooga

ELIZABETHTON—Carter County
□ SYCAMORE SHOALS HOSPITAL, (Formerly Columbia Sycamore Shoals Hospital), 1501 West Elk Avenue, Zip 37643–1368; tel. 423/542–1300; Scott Williams, Chief Executive Officer (Total facility includes 12 beds in nursing home–type unit) **A**1 9 10 **F**3 4 7 8 10 12 13 14 15 16 17 18 19 20 21 22 23 24 25 26 27 28 29 30 31 32 33 34 35 37 39 40 41 42 43 44 45 46 47 49 51 54 55 56 57 58 59 60 61 63 64 65 66 67 68 70 71 72 73 74 **P**5 7 8 **S** Mountain States Health Alliance, Johnson City, TN

| | 23 | 10 | 112 | 2250 | 26 | 54183 | 458 | 19244 | 6416 | 253 |

ERIN—Houston County
⊞ TRINITY HOSPITAL, (Formerly Columbia Trinity Hospital), 353 Main Street, Zip 37061–0489, Mailing Address: P.O. Box 489, Zip 37061–0489; tel. 931/289–4211; Jay Woodall, Chief Executive Officer **A**1 9 10 **F**7 12 15 16 19 20 22 28 30 35 40 44 49 66 71 **P**7 **S** LifePoint Hospitals, Inc., Nashville, TN

| | 33 | 10 | 28 | 1399 | 13 | 12574 | 55 | — | — | 104 |

ERWIN—Unicoi County
⊞ UNICOI COUNTY MEMORIAL HOSPITAL, 100 Greenway Circle, Zip 37650–2196, Mailing Address: P.O. Box 802, Zip 37650–0802; tel. 423/743–3141; James L. McMackin, Chief Executive Officer (Total facility includes 46 beds in nursing home–type unit) **A**1 9 10 **F**8 14 15 16 19 22 28 30 32 39 41 44 49 64 65 66 71 **P**5

| | 15 | 10 | 84 | 978 | 57 | 24640 | 0 | 9708 | 4402 | 180 |

ETOWAH—McMinn County
⊞ WOODS MEMORIAL HOSPITAL DISTRICT, Highway 411 North, Zip 37331, Mailing Address: P.O. Box 410, Zip 37331–0410; tel. 423/263–3600; Guy Hazlett, FACHE, Chief Executive Officer (Total facility includes 88 beds in nursing home–type unit) (Nonreporting) **A**1 9 10

| | 13 | 10 | 160 | — | — | — | — | — | — | — |

FAYETTEVILLE—Lincoln County
⊞ LINCOLN COUNTY HEALTH FACILITIES, 700 West Maple Street, Zip 37334–3202; tel. 931/438–1111; Gary G. Kendrick, Chief Executive Officer **A**1 9 10 **F**7 8 11 15 17 19 21 22 24 26 27 28 32 33 34 35 37 40 41 42 44 49 57 67 71 73 **S** Quorum Health Group/Quorum Health Resources, Inc., Brentwood, TN

| | 13 | 10 | 51 | 2097 | 21 | 33626 | 238 | 11431 | 5915 | 252 |

FRANKLIN—Williamson County
⊞ WILLIAMSON MEDICAL CENTER, 2021 Carothers Road, Zip 37067–5822, Mailing Address: P.O. Box 681600, Zip 37068–1600; tel. 615/791–0500; Ronald G. Joyner, Chief Executive Officer **A**1 9 10 **F**4 7 8 10 19 21 22 23 28 30 33 34 35 37 40 42 44 45 46 49 54 56 63 65 66 67 71 73 **P**6
Web address: www.williamsonmedicalcntr.org

| | 13 | 10 | 121 | 5219 | 63 | 102586 | 655 | 52395 | 21016 | 713 |

GALLATIN—Sumner County
⊞ △ SUMNER REGIONAL MEDICAL CENTER, 555 Hartsville Pike, Zip 37066–2449, Mailing Address: P.O. Box 1558, Zip 37066–1558; tel. 615/452–4210; William T. Sugg, President and Chief Executive Officer (Total facility includes 10 beds in nursing home–type unit) **A**1 7 9 10 **F**7 8 10 12 13 14 15 16 17 19 21 22 24 27 28 30 32 33 34 35 37 38 39 40 41 42 44 45 46 48 49 56 60 64 65 66 67 68 71 72 73 74

| | 23 | 10 | 155 | 4209 | 61 | 102995 | 682 | 46124 | 18687 | 628 |

GERMANTOWN—Shelby County
□ △ BAPTIST REHABILITATION–GERMANTOWN, 2100 Exeter Road, Zip 38138; tel. 901/757–1350; Paula Gisler, Administrator **A**1 7 9 10 **F**2 3 4 5 7 8 9 10 11 12 14 15 16 17 18 19 20 21 22 23 24 25 26 27 28 29 30 32 33 34 35 37 38 40 41 42 43 44 45 46 47 48 49 50 51 52 53 54 55 56 57 58 59 60 61 63 64 65 66 67 68 70 71 72 73 74 **P**8 **S** Baptist Memorial Health Care Corporation, Memphis, TN
METHODIST HOSPITAL GERMANTOWN See Methodist Healthcare–Memphis Hospital, Memphis

| | 21 | 46 | 75 | 1325 | 43 | 5121 | 0 | 18861 | 7390 | 262 |

GREENEVILLE—Greene County
⊞ LAUGHLIN MEMORIAL HOSPITAL, 1420 Tusculum Boulevard, Zip 37745; tel. 423/787–5000; Charles H. Whitfield, Jr., President and Chief Executive Officer (Total facility includes 90 beds in nursing home–type unit) **A**1 9 10 **F**7 8 15 16 17 19 21 22 26 28 32 34 35 37 40 41 44 45 46 49 60 63 64 65 66 67 71 73 74

| | 23 | 10 | 230 | 5494 | 146 | 55740 | 499 | 32896 | 12483 | 434 |

Hospital, Address, Telephone, Administrator, Approval, Facility, and Physician Codes, Health Care System, Network	Classi-fication Codes		Utilization Data					Expense (thousands) of dollars		
	Control	Service	Staffed Beds	Admissions	Census	Outpatient Visits	Births	Total	Payroll	Personnel

★ American Hospital Association (AHA) membership
□ Joint Commission on Accreditation of Healthcare Organizations (JCAHO) accreditation
+ American Osteopathic Healthcare Association (AOHA) membership
○ American Osteopathic Association (AOA) accreditation
△ Commission on Accreditation of Rehabilitation Facilities (CARF) accreditation
Control codes 61, 63, 64, 71, 72 and 73 indicate hospitals listed by AOHA, but not registered by AHA. For definition of numerical codes, see page A4

☒ TAKOMA ADVENTIST HOSPITAL, 401 Takoma Avenue, Zip 37743–4668; tel. 423/639–3151; Carlyle L. E. Walton, President (Nonreporting) **A**1 9 10 **S** Adventist Health System Sunbelt Health Care Corporation, Winter Park, FL	21	10	80	—	—	—	—	—	—	—
HARRIMAN—Roane County										
□ ROANE MEDICAL CENTER, 412 Devonia Street, Zip 37748, Mailing Address: P.O. Box 489, Zip 37748–0489; tel. 423/882–1323; Jim Gann, Administrator **A**1 9 10 **F**8 10 15 16 17 19 22 24 27 28 29 30 35 37 44 65 67 71 73 74 **P**8 **Web address:** www.kornet.org/r_health	14	10	85	4182	43	51266	2	23045	9626	371
HARTSVILLE—Trousdale County										
TROUSDALE MEDICAL CENTER See Frank T. Rutherford Memorial Hospital, Carthage										
HENDERSONVILLE—Sumner County										
☒ HENDERSONVILLE HOSPITAL, 355 New Shackle Island Road, Zip 37075–2393; tel. 615/264–4000; Robert Klein, Chief Executive Officer (Total facility includes 10 beds in nursing home–type unit) **A**1 9 10 **F**7 8 10 12 14 15 16 19 21 22 26 28 29 30 34 35 37 40 44 45 46 49 53 54 55 56 57 58 60 63 64 65 66 67 71 73 74 **P**7 **S** Columbia/HCA Healthcare Corporation, Nashville, TN	33	10	68	2851	32	63276	562	—	8574	275
HERMITAGE—Davidson County										
☒ SUMMIT MEDICAL CENTER, 5655 Frist Boulevard, Zip 37076–2053; tel. 615/316–3000; Bryan K. Dearing, Chief Executive Officer (Total facility includes 34 beds in nursing home–type unit) **A**1 9 10 **F**3 4 6 7 8 9 10 11 12 14 15 16 17 18 19 20 21 22 23 26 27 28 29 30 31 32 33 34 35 37 38 40 41 42 43 44 45 46 47 48 49 50 51 52 53 54 55 56 57 58 59 60 61 62 63 64 65 66 67 68 70 71 72 73 74 **P**5 7 8 **S** Columbia/HCA Healthcare Corporation, Nashville, TN	33	10	204	9263	120	87014	1260	56002	25358	750
HUMBOLDT—Gibson County										
☒ HUMBOLDT GENERAL HOSPITAL, 3525 Chere Carol Road, Zip 38343–3699; tel. 901/784–0301; Bill Kail, Administrator **A**1 9 10 **F**7 8 12 14 15 16 17 19 22 28 30 32 33 40 44 49 65 66 71 73 **S** West Tennessee Healthcare, Jackson, TN **Web address:** www.wth.net	15	10	46	1208	16	20054	119	5110	2553	88
HUNTINGDON—Carroll County										
☒ BAPTIST MEMORIAL HOSPITAL–HUNTINGDON, 631 R. B. Wilson Drive, Zip 38344–1675; tel. 901/986–4461; Susan M. Breeden, Administrator (Nonreporting) **A**1 9 10 **S** Baptist Memorial Health Care Corporation, Memphis, TN	21	10	70	—	—	—	—	—	—	—
JACKSON—Madison County										
COLUMBIA REGIONAL HOSPITAL OF JACKSON See Methodist LeBonheur Healthcare–Jackson										
☒ △ JACKSON–MADISON COUNTY GENERAL HOSPITAL, 708 West Forest Avenue, Zip 38301–3855; tel. 901/425–5000; James T. Moss, President and Chief Executive Officer (Total facility includes 85 beds in nursing home–type unit) (Nonreporting) **A**1 2 3 5 7 9 10 **S** West Tennessee Healthcare, Jackson, TN	16	10	567	—	—	—	—	—	—	—
☒ METHODIST LEBONHEUR HEALTHCARE–JACKSON, (Formerly Columbia Regional Hospital of Jackson), 367 Hospital Boulevard, Zip 38305–4518, Mailing Address: P.O. Box 3310, Zip 38303–0310; tel. 901/661–2000; Tim Brady, Chief Executive Officer (Nonreporting) **A**1 9 10 **S** Methodist Healthcare, Memphis, TN **Web address:** www.regionalhospital.com	33	10	103	—	—	—	—	—	—	—
★ PATHWAYS OF TENNESSEE, 238 Summar Drive, Zip 38301–3982; tel. 901/935–8200; John D. Rudnick, Jr., FACHE, Executive Director (Nonreporting) **A**10 **S** West Tennessee Healthcare, Jackson, TN	23	22	57	—	—	—	—	—	—	—
JAMESTOWN—Fentress County										
□ FENTRESS COUNTY GENERAL HOSPITAL, Highway 52 West, Zip 38556, Mailing Address: P.O. Box 1500, Zip 38556; tel. 931/879–8171; Patrick J. Gray, Chief Executive Officer (Total facility includes 13 beds in nursing home–type unit) (Nonreporting) **A**1 9 10 **S** Paracelsus Healthcare Corporation, Houston, TX	33	10	73	—	—	—	—	—	—	—
JASPER—Marion County										
☒ GRANDVIEW MEDICAL CENTER, (Formerly Columbia South Pittsburg Hospital), 1000 Highway 28, Zip 37347; tel. 423/837–9500; Phil Rowland, Chief Executive Officer (Nonreporting) **A**1 9 10 **S** Columbia/HCA Healthcare Corporation, Nashville, TN	33	10	47	—	—	—	—	—	—	—
JEFFERSON CITY—Jefferson County										
□ JEFFERSON MEMORIAL HOSPITAL, 1800 Bishop Avenue, Zip 37760–1992, Mailing Address: P.O. Box 560, Zip 37760–0560; tel. 423/475–2091; Michael C. Hicks, President and Chief Executive Officer **A**1 9 10 **F**8 12 15 16 19 21 22 25 28 32 34 37 39 40 44 46 49 51 65 67 71 73 **S** Catholic Healthcare Partners, Cincinnati, OH **Web address:** www.mercy.com/stmarys	23	10	22	1623	19	24638	1	11878	4954	184
JELLICO—Campbell County										
☒ JELLICO COMMUNITY HOSPITAL, 188 Hospital Lane, Zip 37762–4400; tel. 423/784–7252; Jimm Bunch, President and Chief Executive Officer **A**1 9 10 **F**7 10 14 15 16 19 21 22 32 35 37 40 41 44 46 49 65 71 **P**8 **S** Adventist Health System Sunbelt Health Care Corporation, Winter Park, FL **Web address:** www.ahss.org	23	10	54	2023	20	29054	255	15182	5408	223
JOHNSON CITY—Washington County										
□ △ JAMES H. AND CECILE C. QUILLEN REHABILITATION HOSPITAL, (Formerly Northeast Tennessee Rehabilitation Hospital), 2511 Wesley Street, Zip 37601–1723; tel. 423/283–0700; John Turner, Chief Executive Officer **A**1 7 9 10 **F**1 2 3 4 7 8 10 12 13 14 15 16 17 19 20 21 22 23 24 25 26 27 28 29 30 31 32 33 34 35 37 38 39 40 41 42 43 44 45 46 47 48 49 51 52 54 55 56 57 58 59 60 61 63 64 65 66 67 68 70 71 72 73 74 **P**5 7 8 **S** Mountain States Health Alliance, Johnson City, TN	23	46	60	517	25	2413	0	7777	3370	122

Hospital, Address, Telephone, Administrator, Approval, Facility, and Physician Codes, Health Care System, Network	Classi-fication Codes		Utilization Data					Expense (thousands) of dollars		
★ American Hospital Association (AHA) membership □ Joint Commission on Accreditation of Healthcare Organizations (JCAHO) accreditation + American Osteopathic Healthcare Association (AOHA) membership ○ American Osteopathic Association (AOA) accreditation △ Commission on Accreditation of Rehabilitation Facilities (CARF) accreditation Control codes 61, 63, 64, 71, 72 and 73 indicate hospitals listed by AOHA, but not registered by AHA. For definition of numerical codes, see page A4	Control	Service	Staffed Beds	Admissions	Census	Outpatient Visits	Births	Total	Payroll	Personnel

★ △ JOHNSON CITY MEDICAL CENTER, (Formerly Johnson City Medical Center Hospital), 400 North State of Franklin Road, Zip 37604–6094; tel. 423/431–6111; Dennis Vonderfecht, President and Chief Executive Officer **A**2 3 5 7 8 9 10 **F**2 3 4 7 8 10 12 13 14 15 16 17 18 19 20 21 22 23 24 25 26 27 28 29 30 31 32 33 34 35 37 38 39 40 41 42 43 44 45 46 47 48 49 51 52 53 54 55 56 58 59 60 63 64 65 66 67 68 70 71 72 73 74 **P**7 8 **S** Mountain States Health Alliance, Johnson City, TN **Web address:** www.jcmc.com	23	10	407	18196	300	157838	1351	165390	61773	2719
□ JOHNSON CITY SPECIALTY HOSPITAL, 203 East Watauga Avenue, Zip 37601–4651; tel. 423/926–1111; Gary Varner, Interim Chief Executive Officer **A**1 9 10 **F**2 3 4 7 8 10 11 12 14 15 16 17 19 22 23 24 26 28 29 30 32 35 37 38 40 41 42 43 44 48 49 52 53 54 55 56 57 58 59 60 61 65 66 67 68 70 71 73 74 **P**4 5 8 **S** Mountain States Health Alliance, Johnson City, TN **Web address:** www.columbia.net	23	45	49	1053	8	14739	637	10097	3570	114
NORTHEAST TENNESSEE REHABILITATION HOSPITAL See James H. and Cecile C. Quillen Rehabilitation Hospital										
WOODRIDGE HOSPITAL, 403 State of Franklin Road, Zip 37604–6009; tel. 423/928–7111; Donald Larkin, Ph.D., Administrator **A**3 5 9 10 **F**1 2 3 12 14 15 16 18 45 52 53 54 55 56 57 58 59 65 67 **Web address:** www.frontier	23	22	65	3556	53	—	0	5961	3296	119
KINGSPORT—Sullivan County										
□ △ HEALTHSOUTH REHABILITATION HOSPITAL, 113 Cassel Drive, Zip 37660–3775; tel. 423/246–7240; Terry R. Maxhimer, Regional Vice President (Nonreporting) **A**1 7 9 10 **S** HEALTHSOUTH Corporation, Birmingham, AL	33	46	50	—	—	—	—	—	—	—
□ INDIAN PATH MEDICAL CENTER, (Formerly Columbia Indian Path Medical Center), (Includes Indian Path Pavilion, 2300 Pavilion Drive, Zip 37660–4672; tel. 423/378–7500), 2000 Brookside Drive, Zip 37660–4604; tel. 423/392–7000; Randy Cook, Administrator **A**1 9 10 **F**2 3 4 7 8 10 12 13 17 18 19 20 21 22 23 24 25 27 28 29 30 31 32 33 34 35 37 39 40 41 42 43 44 45 46 49 51 52 54 55 56 57 58 59 60 61 63 64 65 66 67 68 70 71 72 73 74 **P**5 7 8 **S** Mountain States Health Alliance, Johnson City, TN	23	10	196	4440	76	91271	294	46564	17759	524
⊞ WELLMONT HOLSTON VALLEY MEDICAL CENTER, West Ravine Street, Zip 37662–0224; Mailing Address: Box 238, Zip 37662–0224; tel. 423/224–4000; Louis H. Bremer, President and Chief Executive Officer (Total facility includes 35 beds in nursing home–type unit) **A**1 2 3 5 9 10 **F**1 4 6 7 8 10 11 12 14 15 16 19 21 22 26 28 30 31 32 33 34 35 37 38 39 40 41 42 43 44 46 47 49 63 64 65 66 69 70 71 73 74 **S** Quorum Health Group/Quorum Health Resources, Inc., Brentwood, TN	23	10	380	16718	231	137445	1646	150187	60195	1674
KNOXVILLE—Knox County										
⊞ △ BAPTIST HOSPITAL OF EAST TENNESSEE, 137 Blount Avenue S.E., Zip 37920–1643, Mailing Address: P.O. Box 1788, Zip 37901–1788; tel. 423/632–5011; Jon Foster, Executive Vice President and Administrator **A**1 2 7 9 10 **F**3 4 7 8 10 11 12 14 15 16 17 18 19 20 21 22 26 27 28 29 30 31 32 33 34 35 37 39 40 41 42 43 44 45 46 48 49 51 52 54 55 56 57 58 59 60 61 65 67 68 71 73 74 **P**8 **S** Baptist Health System of Tennessee, Knoxville, TN	21	10	299	13172	218	101224	524	130438	52237	1620
□ EAST TENNESSEE CHILDREN'S HOSPITAL, 2018 Clinch Avenue, Zip 37916–2393, Mailing Address: P.O. Box 15010, Zip 37901–5010; tel. 423/541–8000; Robert F. Koppel, President and Chief Executive Officer **A**1 9 10 **F**10 15 16 19 22 32 34 35 38 39 41 42 44 45 46 47 48 49 51 60 65 70 71 73 **P**8 **Web address:** www.etch.com	23	50	103	4671	62	79434	0	47482	22608	963
⊞ △ FORT SANDERS REGIONAL MEDICAL CENTER, 1901 Clinch Avenue S.W., Zip 37916–2394; tel. 423/541–1111; James R. Burkhart, FACHE, Administrator (Total facility includes 24 beds in nursing home–type unit) **A**1 2 6 7 9 10 **F**2 3 4 7 8 10 11 12 14 15 16 17 18 19 21 22 23 24 25 26 27 28 29 30 31 32 33 34 35 37 39 40 41 42 43 44 45 46 48 49 52 53 54 55 56 57 58 59 60 61 63 64 65 66 67 71 73 74 **P**6 7 **S** Covenant Health, Knoxville, TN	23	10	406	17327	279	287295	2562	131047	51383	1808
⊞ FORT SANDERS–PARKWEST MEDICAL CENTER, 9352 Park West Boulevard, Zip 37923–4387, Mailing Address: P.O. Box 22993, Zip 37933–0993; tel. 423/694–5700; James R. Burkhart, FACHE, President and Chief Executive Officer **A**1 2 9 10 **F**1 2 4 7 8 10 11 12 14 15 16 17 19 21 22 23 24 25 28 29 30 31 32 33 34 35 37 39 40 41 42 43 44 45 46 48 49 50 51 52 53 57 60 63 64 65 66 67 71 73 74 **P**1 **S** Covenant Health, Knoxville, TN	23	10	280	12005	162	85259	904	100645	33140	1063
□ LAKESHORE MENTAL HEALTH INSTITUTE, 5908 Lyons View Drive, Zip 37919–7598; tel. 423/450–5200; Richard Lee Thomas, Superintendent (Nonreporting) **A**1 10	12	22	277	—	—	—	—	—	—	—
□ △ ST. MARY'S HEALTH SYSTEM, 900 East Oak Hill Avenue, Zip 37917–4556; tel. 423/545–8000; Richard C. Williams, President and Chief Executive Officer (Total facility includes 25 beds in nursing home–type unit) (Nonreporting) **A**1 2 3 7 9 10 **S** Catholic Healthcare Partners, Cincinnati, OH	21	10	300	—	—	—	—	—	—	—
⊞ UNIVERSITY OF TENNESSEE MEMORIAL HOSPITAL, 1924 Alcoa Highway, Zip 37920–6900; tel. 423/544–9000; Thomas M. Kish, Executive Director **A**1 2 3 9 10 **F**4 7 8 10 11 12 14 16 17 19 20 21 22 23 24 31 32 33 34 35 37 38 40 41 42 43 44 45 46 47 49 50 51 53 54 60 61 64 65 67 68 70 71 73 74 **P**2 4 5 7 8	12	10	439	19276	297	404686	2888	248183	109054	3285

Hospital, Address, Telephone, Administrator, Approval, Facility, and Physician Codes, Health Care System, Network	Classi- fication Codes		Utilization Data					Expense (thousands) of dollars		
★ American Hospital Association (AHA) membership □ Joint Commission on Accreditation of Healthcare Organizations (JCAHO) accreditation + American Osteopathic Healthcare Association (AOHA) membership ○ American Osteopathic Association (AOA) accreditation △ Commission on Accreditation of Rehabilitation Facilities (CARF) accreditation Control codes 61, 63, 64, 71, 72 and 73 indicate hospitals listed by AOHA, but not registered by AHA. For definition of numerical codes, see page A4	Control	Service	Staffed Beds	Admissions	Census	Outpatient Visits	Births	Total	Payroll	Personnel

LA FOLLETTE—Campbell County

☒ LA FOLLETTE MEDICAL CENTER, East Avenue, Zip 37766, Mailing Address: P.O. Box 1301, Zip 37766–1301; tel. 423/562–2211; Nicholas P. Lewis, Administrator (Total facility includes 98 beds in nursing home–type unit) (Nonreporting) **A**1 9 10 — 14 10 148 — — — — — — —

LAFAYETTE—Macon County

☒ MACON COUNTY GENERAL HOSPITAL, 204 Medical Drive, Zip 37083–1799, Mailing Address: P.O. Box 378, Zip 37083–0378; tel. 615/666–2147; Dennis A. Wolford, FACHE, Administrator **A**1 9 10 **F**14 15 16 19 22 28 30 44 51 65 71 **S** Quorum Health Group/Quorum Health Resources, Inc., Brentwood, TN — 23 10 43 850 10 12222 0 4888 1886 80

LAWRENCEBURG—Lawrence County

☒ CROCKETT HOSPITAL, U.S. Highway 43 South, Zip 38464–0847, Mailing Address: P.O. Box 847, Zip 38464–0847; tel. 931/762–6571; Jack S. Buck, Chief Executive Officer **A**1 9 10 **F**7 8 10 12 13 14 15 16 17 18 19 20 21 22 28 29 30 34 35 37 39 40 41 44 45 46 48 49 51 65 66 67 68 71 74 **P**7 **S** LifePoint Hospitals, Inc., Nashville, TN — 33 10 98 2839 34 40256 183 14020 6853 271

LEBANON—Wilson County

☒ UNIVERSITY MEDICAL CENTER, (Includes McFarland Specialty Hospital, 500 Park Avenue, Zip 37087–3720; tel. 615/449–0500), 1411 Baddour Parkway, Zip 37087–2573; tel. 615/444–8262; Larry W. Keller, Chief Executive Officer **A**1 9 10 **F**7 8 10 12 19 20 21 22 28 30 32 35 37 40 41 42 44 46 48 49 52 54 55 56 57 59 60 63 64 65 66 67 71 73 74 **P**5 6 7 **S** TENET Healthcare Corporation, Santa Barbara, CA — 33 10 225 7570 115 139485 824 56994 21983 764

LEWISBURG—Marshall County

□ MARSHALL MEDICAL CENTER, 1080 North Ellington Parkway, Zip 37091–2227, Mailing Address: P.O. Box 1609, Zip 37091–1609; tel. 931/359–6241; Steve C. Hoelscher, Administrator **A**1 9 10 **F**8 14 15 16 19 21 22 28 29 30 32 34 35 37 39 41 44 45 46 49 65 66 71 73 **P**5 — 13 10 77 1249 13 28577 1 10183 4245 145

LEXINGTON—Henderson County

☒ METHODIST HEALTHCARE–LEXINGTON HOSPITAL, (Formerly Methodist Hospital of Lexington), 200 West Church Street, Zip 38351–2014; tel. 901/968–3646; Eugene Ragghianti, Administrator (Nonreporting) **A**1 9 10 **S** Methodist Healthcare, Memphis, TN — 21 10 32 — — — — — — —

LINDEN—Perry County

BAPTIST PERRY COMMUNITY HOSPITAL, Highway 13 South, Zip 37096, Mailing Address: Route 10, Box 8, Zip 37096; tel. 931/589–2121; Gary C. Morse, Chief Executive Officer and Administrator (Nonreporting) **A**9 10 — 23 10 53 — — — — — — —

LIVINGSTON—Overton County

☒ LIVINGSTON REGIONAL HOSPITAL, (Formerly Columbia Livingston Regional Hospital), 315 Oak Street, Zip 38570, Mailing Address: P.O. Box 550, Zip 38570–0550; tel. 931/823–5611; Timothy W. McGill, Chief Executive Officer (Total facility includes 15 beds in nursing home–type unit) **A**1 9 10 **F**7 8 12 14 15 16 19 20 22 28 30 32 35 37 39 40 42 44 49 64 65 66 67 71 73 74 **P**7 8 **S** LifePoint Hospitals, Inc., Nashville, TN — 33 10 88 3364 43 28527 301 18271 6704 257

LOUDON—Loudon County

☒ FORT SANDERS LOUDON MEDICAL CENTER, 1125 Grove Street, Zip 37774–1512, Mailing Address: P.O. Box 217, Zip 37774–0217; tel. 423/458–8222; Martha O'Regan Chill, President and Chief Administrative Officer (Nonreporting) **A**1 9 10 **S** Covenant Health, Knoxville, TN — 23 10 50 — — — — — — —

LOUISVILLE—Blount County

PENINSULA HOSPITAL, 2347 Jones Bend Road, Zip 37777–5213, Mailing Address: P.O. Box 2000, Zip 37777–2000; tel. 423/970–9800; David H. McReynolds, Chief Operating Officer and Administrator **A**9 10 **F**2 3 4 5 6 7 8 10 11 12 13 14 15 16 17 18 19 20 21 22 24 25 26 27 28 29 30 31 32 33 34 35 37 39 40 41 42 43 44 45 46 47 48 49 50 51 52 53 54 55 56 57 58 59 60 61 62 63 64 65 66 67 68 71 72 73 74 — 23 22 155 2928 83 — 0 9660 5017 186

MADISON—Davidson County

☒ NASHVILLE MEMORIAL HOSPITAL, 612 West Due West Avenue, Zip 37115–4474; tel. 615/865–3511; Allyn R. Harris, Chief Executive Officer (Nonreporting) **A**1 2 5 9 10 **S** Columbia/HCA Healthcare Corporation, Nashville, TN — 33 10 250 — — — — — — —

☒ △ TENNESSEE CHRISTIAN MEDICAL CENTER, (Includes Tennessee Christian Medical Center – Portland, 105 Redbud Drive, Portland, Zip 37148), 500 Hospital Drive, Zip 37115–5032; tel. 615/865–2373; Clint Kreitner, President and Chief Executive Officer (Total facility includes 50 beds in nursing home–type unit) (Nonreporting) **A**1 7 9 10 **S** Adventist Health System Sunbelt Health Care Corporation, Winter Park, FL — 21 10 288 — — — — — — —

MANCHESTER—Coffee County

★ COFFEE MEDICAL CENTER, 1001 McArthur Drive, Zip 37355–2455, Mailing Address: P.O. Box 1079, Zip 37355–1079; tel. 931/728–3586; Edward A. Perdue, Chief Executive Officer (Total facility includes 72 beds in nursing home–type unit) **A**9 10 **F**8 17 19 22 26 33 34 40 41 44 49 64 65 67 71 — 16 10 108 810 77 10353 0 6543 2781 87

★ ○ MEDICAL CENTER OF MANCHESTER, 481 Interstate Drive, Zip 37355–3108, Mailing Address: P.O. Box 1409, Zip 37355–1409; tel. 931/728–6354; David C. Wilson, Chief Executive Officer (Nonreporting) **A**9 10 11 **S** TENET Healthcare Corporation, Santa Barbara, CA — 33 10 49 — — — — — — —

MARTIN—Weakley County

☒ METHODIST HEALTHCARE–VOLUNTEER HOSPITAL, (Formerly Columbia Volunteer General Hospital), 161 Mount Pelia Road, Zip 38237–0967, Mailing Address: P.O. Box 967, Zip 38237–0967; tel. 901/587–4261; R. Coleman Foss, Chief Executive Officer (Nonreporting) **A**1 9 10 **S** Methodist Healthcare, Memphis, TN — 33 10 65 — — — — — — —

Hospital, Address, Telephone, Administrator, Approval, Facility, and Physician Codes, Health Care System, Network	Classi-fication Codes		Utilization Data					Expense (thousands) of dollars		
★ American Hospital Association (AHA) membership □ Joint Commission on Accreditation of Healthcare Organizations (JCAHO) accreditation + American Osteopathic Healthcare Association (AOHA) membership ○ American Osteopathic Association (AOA) accreditation △ Commission on Accreditation of Rehabilitation Facilities (CARF) accreditation Control codes 61, 63, 64, 71, 72 and 73 indicate hospitals listed by AOHA, but not registered by AHA. For definition of numerical codes, see page A4	Control	Service	Staffed Beds	Admissions	Census	Outpatient Visits	Births	Total	Payroll	Personnel

MARYVILLE—Blount County

☒ BLOUNT MEMORIAL HOSPITAL, 907 East Lamar Alexander Parkway, Zip 37804–5016; tel. 423/983–7211; Joseph M. Dawson, Administrator (Total facility includes 30 beds in nursing home–type unit) **A**1 2 6 9 10 **F**2 3 4 7 8 10 11 12 13 14 15 16 17 18 19 21 22 23 24 25 28 29 30 31 32 33 34 35 37 39 41 42 44 46 49 52 54 55 56 58 59 60 63 64 65 66 67 70 71 73 **P**8

| | 13 | 10 | 173 | 7390 | 87 | 151328 | 610 | 76153 | 33048 | 1094 |

MCKENZIE—Carroll County

☒ METHODIST HEALTHCARE – MCKENZIE HOSPITAL, (Formerly Methodist Hospital of McKenzie), 161 Hospital Drive, Zip 38201–1636; tel. 901/352–5344; Richard McCormick, Administrator **A**1 9 10 **F**7 8 14 19 22 28 30 32 33 39 40 41 44 46 49 64 66 71 73 **S** Methodist Healthcare, Memphis, TN

| | 21 | 10 | 27 | 919 | 8 | 15422 | 335 | 7519 | 3511 | 137 |

MCMINNVILLE—Warren County

☒ RIVER PARK HOSPITAL, 1559 Sparta Road, Zip 37110–1316; tel. 931/815–4000; Terry J. Gunn, Chief Executive Officer (Nonreporting) **A**1 9 10 **S** Columbia/HCA Healthcare Corporation, Nashville, TN
 Web address: www.columbia.net

| | 33 | 10 | 90 | — | — | — | — | — | — | — |

MEMPHIS—Shelby County

☒ BAPTIST MEMORIAL HOSPITAL, (Includes Baptist Memorial Hospital East, 6019 Walnut Grove Road, Zip 38119; tel. 901/226–5000; Baptist Memorial Hospital Rehabilitation Center; Baptist Memorial Hospital–Collierville, 1500 West Poplar Avenue, Collierville, Zip 38017; tel. 901/227–8140; James Vandersteeg, Vice President and Administrator), 899 Madison Avenue, Zip 38146–0001; tel. 901/227–2727; Stephen Curtis Reynolds, President and Chief Executive Officer (Total facility includes 70 beds in nursing home–type unit) **A**1 2 3 5 6 9 10 **F**2 3 4 7 8 10 11 12 14 15 16 17 18 19 20 21 22 23 24 25 26 28 29 30 31 32 33 34 35 37 38 39 40 41 42 43 44 45 46 48 49 51 52 53 54 55 56 57 58 59 60 63 64 65 66 67 68 70 71 72 73 74 **S** Baptist Memorial Health Care Corporation, Memphis, TN

| | 21 | 10 | 1072 | 44140 | 790 | 198529 | 5572 | 227899 | 131273 | 4022 |

□ CHARTER LAKESIDE BEHAVIORAL HEALTH SYSTEM, 2911 Brunswick Road, Zip 38133–4199, Mailing Address: P.O. Box 341308, Zip 38134–1308; tel. 901/377–4700; Rob S. Waggener, Chief Executive Officer (Nonreporting) **A**1 9 10 **S** Magellan Health Services, Atlanta, GA

| | 33 | 22 | 174 | — | — | — | — | — | — | — |

□ DELTA MEDICAL CENTER, 3000 Getwell Road, Zip 38118–2299; tel. 901/369–8500; Larry D. Walker, Chief Executive Officer **A**1 9 10 **F**2 3 8 12 17 19 21 22 26 28 30 34 35 37 39 44 49 51 52 57 58 59 65 67 71 **S** New American Healthcare Corporation, Brentwood, TN

| | 33 | 10 | 134 | 2839 | 65 | 20770 | 0 | 23780 | 9785 | 259 |

□ HEALTHSOUTH REHABILITATION HOSPITAL, 1282 Union Avenue, Zip 38104–3414; tel. 901/722–2000; Jerry Gray, Administrator **A**1 9 10 **F**5 12 16 19 21 22 32 34 45 48 49 50 58 63 65 71 **S** HEALTHSOUTH Corporation, Birmingham, AL
 LE BONHEUR CHILDREN'S MEDICAL CENTER See Methodist Healthcare–Memphis Hospital

| | 32 | 46 | 80 | 1691 | 75 | 16994 | 0 | 15798 | 7498 | 203 |

□ MEMPHIS MENTAL HEALTH INSTITUTE, 865 Poplar Avenue, Zip 38105–4626, Mailing Address: P.O. Box 40966, Zip 38174–0966; tel. 901/524–1201; Russell M. Davidson, Superintendent **A**1 5 9 10 **F**2 3 26 39 45 46 52 55 56 57 65 66 73

| | 12 | 22 | 135 | 1707 | 98 | 304 | 0 | 12601 | 7471 | 263 |

☒ METHODIST HEALTHCARE–MEMPHIS HOSPITAL, (Formerly Methodist Hospitals of Memphis), (Includes Le Bonheur Children's Medical Center, One Children's Plaza, Zip 38103–2893; tel. 901/572–3000; James E. Shmerling, President; Methodist Hospital Germantown, 7691 Poplar, Germantown, Zip 38138, Mailing Address: P.O. Box 381588, Zip 38138; tel. 901/754–6418; David G. Baytos, Administrator; Methodist Hospitals of Memphis–Central; Methodist Hospitals of Memphis–South Unit, 1300 Wesley Drive, Zip 38116; tel. 901/346–3700; Cecelia Sawyer, Administrator; Methodist North–J. Harris Hospital, 3960 New Covington Pike, Zip 38128; tel. 901/372–5200), 1265 Union Avenue, Zip 38104–3499; tel. 901/726–7000; David L. Ramsey, President (Total facility includes 24 beds in nursing home–type unit) **A**1 2 3 5 6 9 10 **F**2 3 4 5 7 8 10 11 12 13 15 16 17 18 19 20 21 22 23 24 25 26 27 28 30 31 32 33 34 35 37 38 40 41 42 43 44 45 46 47 49 51 52 53 54 57 59 60 61 63 64 65 66 67 68 70 71 72 73 74 **P**6 7 8 **S** Methodist Healthcare, Memphis, TN
 Web address: www.methodisthealth.org

| | 23 | 10 | 1201 | 57354 | 873 | 348038 | 7543 | 510732 | 223532 | 7156 |

□ REGIONAL MEDICAL CENTER AT MEMPHIS, 877 Jefferson Avenue, Zip 38103–2897; tel. 901/545–7100; Bruce W. Steinhauer, M.D., President and Chief Executive Officer **A**1 2 3 5 6 8 9 10 **F**7 8 9 12 14 15 16 17 19 21 22 25 27 28 29 30 31 34 35 37 38 39 40 41 42 44 46 49 51 56 60 61 65 68 70 71 72 73 74

| | 23 | 10 | 383 | 14055 | 234 | 139623 | 3718 | 178407 | 64585 | 1599 |

☒ SAINT FRANCIS HOSPITAL, 5959 Park Avenue, Zip 38119–5198, Mailing Address: P.O. Box 171808, Zip 38187–1808; tel. 901/765–1000; David L. Archer, Chief Executive Officer (Total facility includes 42 beds in nursing home–type unit) **A**1 2 3 5 9 10 **F**2 3 4 7 8 10 12 14 19 21 22 23 24 26 27 28 30 31 32 33 34 35 37 39 40 42 43 44 45 46 48 49 52 53 57 59 60 63 64 65 67 70 71 73 74 **P**5 7 8 **S** TENET Healthcare Corporation, Santa Barbara, CA

| | 33 | 10 | 558 | 18305 | 330 | 177403 | 1481 | 130894 | 52916 | 1653 |

☒ ST. JUDE CHILDREN'S RESEARCH HOSPITAL, (PEDIATRIC HEMATOLOGY ONCOLOGY), 332 North Lauderdale Street, Zip 38105–2794; tel. 901/495–3300; Arthur W. Nienhuis, M.D., Director **A**1 2 3 5 9 10 **F**16 18 19 20 21 31 34 35 39 42 44 45 46 47 49 54 56 60 63 65 67 68 71 73 **P**6
 Web address: www.web.stjude.org

| | 23 | 59 | 54 | 2122 | 41 | 44077 | 0 | 170688 | 72012 | 1809 |

Hospital, Address, Telephone, Administrator, Approval, Facility, and Physician Codes, Health Care System, Network	Classi-fication Codes		Utilization Data					Expense (thousands) of dollars		
	Control	Service	Staffed Beds	Admissions	Census	Outpatient Visits	Births	Total	Payroll	Personnel

★ American Hospital Association (AHA) membership
□ Joint Commission on Accreditation of Healthcare Organizations (JCAHO) accreditation
+ American Osteopathic Healthcare Association (AOHA) membership
○ American Osteopathic Association (AOA) accreditation
△ Commission on Accreditation of Rehabilitation Facilities (CARF) accreditation
Control codes 61, 63, 64, 71, 72 and 73 indicate hospitals listed by AOHA, but not registered by AHA. For definition of numerical codes, see page A4

Hospital	Control	Service	Staffed Beds	Admissions	Census	Outpatient Visits	Births	Total	Payroll	Personnel
□ UNIVERSITY OF TENNESSEE BOWLD HOSPITAL, 951 Court Avenue, Zip 38103–2898; tel. 901/448–4000; Jeffrey R. Woodside, M.D., Executive Director (Nonreporting) **A**1 2 3 5 9 10	12	10	111	—	—	—	—	—	—	—
⊞ VETERANS AFFAIRS MEDICAL CENTER, 1030 Jefferson Avenue, Zip 38104–2193; tel. 901/523–8990; K. L. Mulholland, Jr., Director **A**1 2 3 5 8 **F**3 4 5 6 7 8 10 11 12 14 15 16 17 18 19 20 21 22 23 24 25 26 27 28 29 30 31 32 33 34 35 37 39 41 42 43 44 45 46 49 51 52 54 55 56 57 58 59 60 61 62 64 65 67 68 70 71 72 73 74 **P**6 **S** Department of Veterans Affairs, Washington, DC	45	10	274	7636	232	260095	0	146139	77201	1899
MILAN—Gibson County										
⊞ MILAN GENERAL HOSPITAL, 4039 South Highland, Zip 38358; tel. 901/686–1591; Alfred P. Taylor, Administrator and Chief Executive Officer (Total facility includes 13 beds in nursing home–type unit) **A**1 9 10 **F**8 11 14 15 16 17 19 22 26 30 34 41 44 49 52 57 64 65 66 71 72 73 **S** West Tennessee Healthcare, Jackson, TN	16	10	62	1033	26	14498	0	6992	2662	85
MORRISTOWN—Hamblen County										
⊞ △ LAKEWAY REGIONAL HOSPITAL, 726 McFarland Street, Zip 37814–3990; tel. 423/586–2302; Robert B. Wampler, CPA, Chief Executive Officer (Nonreporting) **A**1 7 9 10 **S** Community Health Systems, Inc., Brentwood, TN	33	10	135	—	—	—	—	—	—	—
□ △ MORRISTOWN–HAMBLEN HOSPITAL, 908 West Fourth North Street, Zip 37816, Mailing Address: P.O. Box 1178, Zip 37816; tel. 423/586–4231; Richard L. Clark, Administrator and Chief Executive Officer (Nonreporting) **A**1 7 9 10	23	10	143	—	—	—	—	—	—	—
MOUNTAIN HOME—Washington County										
⊞ JAMES H. QUILLEN VETERANS AFFAIRS MEDICAL CENTER, Zip 37684–4000; tel. 423/926–1171; Carl J. Gerber, M.D., Ph.D., Director (Total facility includes 120 beds in nursing home–type unit) **A**1 2 3 5 8 **F**1 9 10 11 12 14 16 17 18 19 20 21 22 24 25 26 27 28 29 30 31 32 33 34 35 36 37 39 41 42 43 44 45 46 48 49 51 52 54 55 56 57 58 59 60 62 64 65 67 68 69 71 73 74 **P**6 **S** Department of Veterans Affairs, Washington, DC	45	10	322	5151	257	227633	0	101455	57567	1344
MURFREESBORO—Rutherford County										
⊞ ALVIN C. YORK VETERANS AFFAIRS MEDICAL CENTER, 3400 Lebanon Pike, Zip 37129–1236; tel. 615/867–6100; Richard S. Citron, Acting Director (Total facility includes 166 beds in nursing home–type unit) (Nonreporting) **A**1 3 5 **S** Department of Veterans Affairs, Washington, DC **Web address:** www.va.gov/murfreesboro.htm	45	10	637	—	—	—	—	—	—	—
⊞ MIDDLE TENNESSEE MEDICAL CENTER, 400 North Highland Avenue, Zip 37130–3854, Mailing Address: P.O. Box 1178, Zip 37133–1178; tel. 615/849–4100; Arthur W. Hastings, President and Chief Executive Officer **A**1 9 10 **F**7 8 10 11 14 15 16 19 21 22 24 26 31 32 33 35 37 39 40 42 44 45 46 49 60 65 66 71 73 74 **P**5 **Web address:** www.mtmc.org	21	10	193	10603	112	118317	1805	72420	28623	1051
NASHVILLE—Davidson County										
⊞ BAPTIST HOSPITAL, 2000 Church Street, Zip 37236–0002; tel. 615/329–5555; Erie Chapman, III, President and Chief Executive Officer **A**1 2 3 5 9 10 **F**4 5 7 8 10 11 12 14 16 17 19 21 22 23 24 25 26 28 30 31 32 33 34 35 37 38 39 40 41 42 43 44 45 46 48 49 50 60 61 64 65 66 67 68 71 72 73 74 **P**5 **Web address:** www.baptist–hosp.org/	23	10	563	27281	382	305148	4548	260515	101709	2943
⊞ △ CENTENNIAL MEDICAL CENTER AND PARTHENON PAVILION, 2300 Patterson Street, Zip 37203–1528; tel. 615/342–1000; Larry Kloess, President (Total facility includes 24 beds in nursing home–type unit) (Nonreporting) **A**1 2 3 5 7 9 10 **S** Columbia/HCA Healthcare Corporation, Nashville, TN COLUMBIA SOUTHERN HILLS MEDICAL CENTER See Southern Hills Medical Center	33	10	680	—	—	—	—	—	—	—
⊞ METROPOLITAN NASHVILLE GENERAL HOSPITAL, 1818 Albion Street, Zip 37208; tel. 615/341–4000; Roxane Stitzer, Ph.D., Chief Executive Officer **A**1 2 3 5 6 9 10 **F**7 8 10 13 14 15 16 17 19 20 21 22 23 27 30 31 34 35 37 38 39 40 42 44 46 49 51 53 54 55 56 57 58 59 60 61 65 70 71 73	15	10	124	4961	71	84459	791	52495	26159	756
□ MIDDLE TENNESSEE MENTAL HEALTH INSTITUTE, 221 Stewarts Ferry Pike, Zip 37214–3325; tel. 615/902–7535; Joseph W. Carobene, Superintendent (Total facility includes 40 beds in nursing home–type unit) **A**1 3 10 **F**14 15 16 20 21 39 41 45 52 53 54 55 56 57 64 65 73	12	22	283	2331	236	0	0	26529	16693	670
★ NASHVILLE METROPOLITAN BORDEAUX HOSPITAL, 1414 County Hospital Road, Zip 37218–3001; tel. 615/862–7000; Wayne Hayes, Administrator (Total facility includes 525 beds in nursing home–type unit) **A**10 **F**15 20 26 27 28 41 46 64 65 67 73 **P**1	23	48	565	661	475	0	0	32260	18386	628
□ △ NASHVILLE REHABILITATION HOSPITAL, 610 Gallatin Road, Zip 37206–3225; tel. 615/226–4330; Jane Andrews, Administrator and Chief Executive Officer (Nonreporting) **A**1 7 9 10	33	46	28	—	—	—	—	—	—	—
⊞ PSYCHIATRIC HOSPITAL AT VANDERBILT, 1601 23rd Avenue South, Zip 37212–3198; tel. 615/320–7770; Richard A. Bangert, Chief Executive Officer and Administrator **A**1 3 10 **F**2 3 15 16 17 19 21 22 35 50 52 53 54 55 56 57 58 59 65 70 71 **S** Columbia/HCA Healthcare Corporation, Nashville, TN	32	22	88	2344	44	5551	0	9107	4287	146
⊞ SOUTHERN HILLS MEDICAL CENTER, (Formerly Columbia Southern Hills Medical Center), 391 Wallace Road, Zip 37211–4859; tel. 615/781–4000; Jeffrey Whitehorn, Chief Executive Officer (Total facility includes 20 beds in nursing home–type unit) **A**1 9 10 **F**1 2 3 4 5 7 8 10 11 12 13 14 15 16 17 18 19 20 21 22 23 24 25 26 28 29 30 31 33 35 37 38 39 40 41 42 43 44 45 48 49 50 51 52 53 54 55 56 57 58 59 63 64 65 66 67 68 70 71 72 73 74 **P**1 6 7 8 **S** Columbia/HCA Healthcare Corporation, Nashville, TN **Web address:** www.columbia.net	33	10	140	6588	81	69179	1132	46547	21370	562

Hospital, Address, Telephone, Administrator, Approval, Facility, and Physician Codes, Health Care System, Network	Classi-fication Codes		Utilization Data					Expense (thousands) of dollars		
★ American Hospital Association (AHA) membership ☐ Joint Commission on Accreditation of Healthcare Organizations (JCAHO) accreditation + American Osteopathic Healthcare Association (AOHA) membership ○ American Osteopathic Association (AOA) accreditation △ Commission on Accreditation of Rehabilitation Facilities (CARF) accreditation Control codes 61, 63, 64, 71, 72 and 73 indicate hospitals listed by AOHA, but not registered by AHA. For definition of numerical codes, see page A4	Control	Service	Staffed Beds	Admissions	Census	Outpatient Visits	Births	Total	Payroll	Personnel
✠ ST. THOMAS HEALTH SERVICES, (Formerly St. Thomas Hospital), 4220 Harding Road, Zip 37205–2095, Mailing Address: P.O. Box 380, Zip 37202–0380; tel. 615/222–2111; John Lucas, M.D., President and Chief Executive Officer (Nonreporting) **A**1 2 3 5 9 10 **S** Daughters of Charity National Health System, Saint Louis, MO	21	10	514	—	—	—	—	—	—	—
✠ VANDERBILT UNIVERSITY HOSPITAL, 1161 21st Avenue South, Zip 37232–2102; tel. 615/322–5000; Norman B. Urmy, Executive Vice President Clinical Affairs (Total facility includes 23 beds in nursing home–type unit) (Nonreporting) **A**1 2 3 5 8 9 10	23	10	576	—	—	—	—	—	—	—
✠ VETERANS AFFAIRS MEDICAL CENTER, 1310 24th Avenue South, Zip 37212–2637; tel. 615/327–5332; William A. Mountcastle, Director **A**1 2 3 5 8 **F**1 2 3 4 8 10 12 16 17 18 19 20 21 22 25 26 28 29 30 31 32 33 34 35 37 39 41 42 43 44 45 46 48 49 50 51 52 56 57 58 59 60 63 64 65 67 68 71 73 74 **P**6 **S** Department of Veterans Affairs, Washington, DC **Web address:** www.nashville.med.va.gov	45	10	161	6040	143	188785	0	129386	56572	1317
NEWPORT—Cocke County										
☐ BAPTIST HOSPITAL OF COCKE COUNTY, 435 Second Street, Zip 37821–3799; tel. 423/625–2200; Wayne Buckner, Administrator (Total facility includes 56 beds in nursing home–type unit) **A**1 9 10 **F**7 8 15 16 19 20 21 22 26 28 29 30 34 35 39 40 41 44 45 46 49 61 63 64 65 71 73 **P**1 **S** Baptist Health System of Tennessee, Knoxville, TN **Web address:** www.baptistoneword.org/	21	10	109	2313	77	41430	291	19469	7697	265
OAK RIDGE—Anderson County										
☐ METHODIST MEDICAL CENTER OF OAK RIDGE, 990 Oak Ridge Turnpike, Zip 37830–6976, Mailing Address: P.O. Box 2529, Zip 37831–2529; tel. 423/481–1000; Daniel J. Bonk, President and Chief Administrative Officer **A**1 2 9 10 **F**2 3 4 7 8 10 12 14 15 16 17 19 21 22 28 30 32 33 34 35 37 39 40 41 42 43 44 45 46 49 51 52 54 55 56 57 58 59 60 61 63 64 65 66 67 71 73 74 **P**7 **S** Covenant Health, Knoxville, TN	23	10	295	12703	177	175254	1223	104661	46351	1498
RIDGEVIEW PSYCHIATRIC HOSPITAL AND CENTER, 240 West Tyrone Road, Zip 37830–6571; tel. 423/482–1076; Robert J. Benning, Chief Executive Officer (Nonreporting) **A**10	23	22	20	—	—	—	—	—	—	—
ONEIDA—Scott County										
✠ SCOTT COUNTY HOSPITAL, 18797 Alberta Avenue, Zip 37841–4939, Mailing Address: P.O. Box 4939, Zip 37841–4939; tel. 423/569–8521; Peter T. Petruzzi, Chief Executive Officer **A**1 9 10 **F**3 7 8 11 12 15 16 19 22 28 31 34 37 40 41 44 46 49 52 53 54 56 57 58 59 64 65 71 73 **S** Community Health Systems, Inc., Brentwood, TN	33	10	77	2444	26	18699	20	9009	4304	187
PARIS—Henry County										
✠ HENRY COUNTY MEDICAL CENTER, 301 Tyson Avenue, Zip 38242–4544, Mailing Address: Box 1030, Zip 38242–1030; tel. 901/644–8537; Thomas H. Gee, Administrator (Total facility includes 174 beds in nursing home–type unit) **A**1 9 10 **F**7 8 11 15 16 19 20 21 22 23 24 26 27 28 30 32 33 34 35 37 39 40 41 42 44 46 49 52 53 54 55 56 57 59 60 63 64 65 66 67 68 71 73 **P**5	16	10	269	4578	219	57161	311	30378	14416	439
PARSONS—Decatur County										
☐ DECATUR COUNTY GENERAL HOSPITAL, 969 Tennessee Avenue South, Zip 38363–0250, Mailing Address: Box 250, Zip 38363–0250; tel. 901/847–3031; Larry N. Lindsey, Administrator and Chief Executive Officer (Nonreporting) **A**1 9 10	13	10	40	—	—	—	—	—	—	—
PIKEVILLE—Bledsoe County										
☐ BLEDSOE COUNTY GENERAL HOSPITAL, 128 Wheelertown Road, Zip 37367, Mailing Address: P.O. Box 699, Zip 37367–0699; tel. 423/447–2112; Gary Burton, Chief Executive Officer (Nonreporting) **A**1 9 10 **S** Paracelsus Healthcare Corporation, Houston, TX	33	10	26	—	—	—	—	—	—	—
PORTLAND—Sumner County										
TENNESSEE CHRISTIAN MEDICAL CENTER – PORTLAND See Tennessee Christian Medical Center, Madison										
PULASKI—Giles County										
✠ HILLSIDE HOSPITAL, (Formerly Columbia Hillside Hospital), 1265 East College Street, Zip 38478–4541; tel. 931/363–7531; James H. Edmondson, Chief Executive Officer and Administrator (Nonreporting) **A**1 9 10 **S** LifePoint Hospitals, Inc., Nashville, TN	16	10	85	—	—	—	—	—	—	—
RIPLEY—Lauderdale County										
✠ BAPTIST MEMORIAL HOSPITAL–LAUDERDALE, 326 Asbury Road, Zip 38063–9701; tel. 901/221–2200; Joe Hunsucker, Administrator **A**1 9 10 **F**2 3 8 15 16 19 22 26 28 30 32 33 34 37 39 44 45 46 49 52 53 54 55 56 57 58 59 65 71 73 **S** Baptist Memorial Health Care Corporation, Memphis, TN **Web address:** www.bmhcc.org	21	10	70	945	13	18157	0	7751	3001	129
ROGERSVILLE—Hawkins County										
✠ HAWKINS COUNTY MEMORIAL HOSPITAL, 851 Locust Street, Zip 37857; tel. 423/272–2671; R. Frank Testerman, Administrator **A**1 9 10 **F**8 15 17 19 22 28 30 32 44 45 49 64 65 69 71 73	13	10	50	1228	18	36818	0	7401	3333	146
SAVANNAH—Hardin County										
☐ HARDIN COUNTY GENERAL HOSPITAL, 2006 Wayne Road, Zip 38372–2294; tel. 901/925–4954; Charlotte Burns, Administrator and Chief Executive Officer (Total facility includes 73 beds in nursing home–type unit) (Nonreporting) **A**1 9 10	13	10	130	—	—	—	—	—	—	—

Hospital, Address, Telephone, Administrator, Approval, Facility, and Physician Codes, Health Care System, Network	Classi-fication Codes		Utilization Data					Expense (thousands) of dollars		
★ American Hospital Association (AHA) membership □ Joint Commission on Accreditation of Healthcare Organizations (JCAHO) accreditation + American Osteopathic Healthcare Association (AOHA) membership ○ American Osteopathic Association (AOA) accreditation △ Commission on Accreditation of Rehabilitation Facilities (CARF) accreditation Control codes 61, 63, 64, 71, 72 and 73 indicate hospitals listed by AOHA, but not registered by AHA. For definition of numerical codes, see page A4	Control	Service	Staffed Beds	Admissions	Census	Outpatient Visits	Births	Total	Payroll	Personnel

SELMER—McNairy County

☒ METHODIST HEALTHCARE–MCNAIRY HOSPITAL, (Formerly McNairy County General Hospital), 705 East Poplar Avenue, Zip 38375–1748; tel. 901/645–3221; John R. Borden, Administrator (Nonreporting) **A**1 9 10 **S** Methodist Healthcare, Memphis, TN

| | 13 | 10 | 86 | — | — | — | — | — | — | — |

SEVIERVILLE—Sevier County

☒ FORT SANDERS–SEVIER MEDICAL CENTER, 709 Middle Creek Road, Zip 37862–5016, Mailing Address: P.O. Box 8005, Zip 37864–8005; tel. 423/429–6100; Ellen Wilhoit, Administrator (Total facility includes 54 beds in nursing home–type unit) **A**1 9 10 **F**7 8 10 12 15 16 19 21 22 28 30 31 32 33 35 37 40 41 44 45 49 63 64 67 71 73 **P**7 **S** Covenant Health, Knoxville, TN

| | 23 | 10 | 100 | 2562 | 78 | 67216 | 517 | 20312 | 8300 | 338 |

SEWANEE—Franklin County

EMERALD–HODGSON HOSPITAL See Southern Tennessee Medical Center, Winchester

SHELBYVILLE—Bedford County

□ BEDFORD COUNTY MEDICAL CENTER, (Formerly Bedford County General Hospital), 845 Union Street, Zip 37160–9971; tel. 931/685–5433; Richard L. Graham, Administrator (Total facility includes 107 beds in nursing home–type unit) (Nonreporting) **A**1 9 10

| | 13 | 10 | 180 | — | — | — | — | — | — | — |

SMITHVILLE—DeKalb County

☒ BAPTIST DEKALB HOSPITAL, 520 West Main Street, Zip 37166–0840, Mailing Address: P.O. Box 640, Zip 37166–0640; tel. 615/597–7171; Dennis Smock, Chief Executive Officer **A**1 9 10 **F**7 8 10 12 15 17 18 19 22 26 28 29 30 35 37 39 40 42 44 46 49 57 65 71 73

| | 32 | 10 | 52 | 1769 | 17 | 13862 | 103 | 10269 | 4104 | 138 |

SOMERVILLE—Fayette County

☒ METHODIST HEALTHCARE – FAYETTE HOSPITAL, 214 Lakeview Drive, Zip 38068; tel. 901/465–0532; Michael Blome', Administrator **A**1 9 10 **F**1 2 3 4 5 6 7 8 9 10 11 12 13 14 15 16 17 18 19 21 22 23 24 25 26 27 28 29 30 31 32 33 34 35 36 37 38 39 40 41 42 43 44 45 46 47 48 49 50 51 52 53 54 55 56 57 58 59 60 61 62 63 64 65 66 67 68 70 71 72 73 74 **P**1 2 4 5 6 7 8 **S** Methodist Healthcare, Memphis, TN
Web address: www.methodisthealth.org

| | 21 | 10 | 38 | 948 | 8 | 14834 | 124 | 5212 | 2355 | 134 |

SPARTA—White County

☒ WHITE COUNTY COMMUNITY HOSPITAL, 401 Sewell Road, Zip 38583–1299; tel. 931/738–9211; David Conejo, Chief Executive Officer (Nonreporting) **A**1 9 10 **S** Community Health Systems, Inc., Brentwood, TN

| | 33 | 10 | 60 | — | — | — | — | — | — | — |

SPRINGFIELD—Robertson County

□ NORTH CREST MEDICAL CENTER, 100 North Crest Drive, Zip 37172–2984; tel. 615/384–2411; William A. Kenley, President and Chief Executive Officer **A**1 9 10 **F**7 8 10 12 14 15 16 19 21 22 30 32 33 35 37 40 41 42 44 45 46 54 58 65 67 71 72 73 74
Web address: www.columbia.net

| | 23 | 10 | 100 | 3879 | 49 | 44584 | 511 | 34124 | 12373 | 399 |

SWEETWATER—Monroe County

☒ SWEETWATER HOSPITAL, 304 Wright Street, Zip 37874–2897; tel. 423/337–6171; Scott Bowman, Administrator (Nonreporting) **A**1 9 10

| | 23 | 10 | 59 | — | — | — | — | — | — | — |

TAZEWELL—Claiborne County

☒ CLAIBORNE COUNTY HOSPITAL, 1850 Old Knoxville Road, Zip 37879–3625, Mailing Address: P.O. Box 219, Zip 37879–0219; tel. 423/626–4211; Michael T. Hutchins, Administrator (Total facility includes 50 beds in nursing home–type unit) **A**1 9 10 **F**12 15 16 17 19 22 27 30 32 33 34 35 37 39 41 44 45 46 49 64 65 71 73

| | 13 | 10 | 110 | 2615 | 79 | 79464 | 0 | 13391 | 6476 | 347 |

TRENTON—Gibson County

☒ GIBSON GENERAL HOSPITAL, 200 Hospital Drive, Zip 38382–3300; tel. 901/855–7900; Kelly R. Yenawine, Administrator **A**1 9 10 **F**2 8 14 15 16 19 21 22 28 30 32 33 34 44 49 65 71 73 **P**1 **S** West Tennessee Healthcare, Jackson, TN
Web address: www.wth.net

| | 15 | 10 | 42 | 838 | 10 | 16106 | 0 | 4332 | 1977 | 68 |

TULLAHOMA—Coffee County

☒ HARTON REGIONAL MEDICAL CENTER, 1801 North Jackson Street, Zip 37388–2201, Mailing Address: P.O. Box 460, Zip 37388–0460; tel. 931/393–3000; David C. Wilson, Chief Executive Officer (Nonreporting) **A**1 9 10 **S** TENET Healthcare Corporation, Santa Barbara, CA
Web address: www.tenethealth.com\harton\

| | 33 | 10 | 137 | — | — | — | — | — | — | — |

UNION CITY—Obion County

☒ BAPTIST MEMORIAL HOSPITAL–UNION CITY, 1201 Bishop Street, Zip 38261–5403, Mailing Address: P.O. Box 310, Zip 38281–0310; tel. 901/884–8601; Mike Perryman, Administrator (Nonreporting) **A**1 9 10 **S** Baptist Memorial Health Care Corporation, Memphis, TN
Web address: www.columbia.net

| | 23 | 10 | 133 | — | — | — | — | — | — | — |

WAVERLY—Humphreys County

BAPTIST THREE RIVERS HOSPITAL, 451 Highway 13 South, Zip 37185–2149, Mailing Address: P.O. Box 437, Zip 37185–2149; tel. 931/296–4203; Donald W. James, DPH, Administrator (Total facility includes 4 beds in nursing home–type unit) **A**9 10 **F**8 14 15 16 19 21 22 28 30 44 46 51 57 64 65 71 73

| | 32 | 10 | 46 | 580 | 8 | 23070 | 0 | 5950 | 2541 | 74 |

WAYNESBORO—Wayne County

□ WAYNE MEDICAL CENTER, 103 J. V. Mangubat Drive, Zip 38485, Mailing Address: P.O. Box 580, Zip 38485–0580; tel. 931/722–5411; Shirley Harder, Chief Executive Officer (Total facility includes 61 beds in nursing home–type unit) (Nonreporting) **A**1 9 10

| | 23 | 10 | 110 | — | — | — | — | — | — | — |

Hospital, Address, Telephone, Administrator, Approval, Facility, and Physician Codes, Health Care System, Network	Classi-fication Codes		Utilization Data					Expense (thousands) of dollars		
★ American Hospital Association (AHA) membership □ Joint Commission on Accreditation of Healthcare Organizations (JCAHO) accreditation + American Osteopathic Healthcare Association (AOHA) membership ○ American Osteopathic Association (AOA) accreditation △ Commission on Accreditation of Rehabilitation Facilities (CARF) accreditation Control codes 61, 63, 64, 71, 72 and 73 indicate hospitals listed by AOHA, but not registered by AHA. For definition of numerical codes, see page A4	Control	Service	Staffed Beds	Admissions	Census	Outpatient Visits	Births	Total	Payroll	Personnel

WESTERN INSTITUTE—Hardeman County

□ WESTERN MENTAL HEALTH INSTITUTE, Highway 64 West, Zip 38074; tel. 901/658–5141; Elizabeth Littlefield, Ed.D., Superintendent **A**1 10 **F**15 52 53 56 57

| | 12 | 22 | 247 | 1340 | 230 | 0 | 0 | 23023 | 15787 | 580 |

WINCHESTER—Franklin County

☒ SOUTHERN TENNESSEE MEDICAL CENTER, (Includes Emerald–Hodgson Hospital, University Avenue, Sewanee, Zip 37375; tel. 615/598–5691), 185 Hospital Road, Zip 37398–2468; tel. 931/967–8200; Kenneth E. Alexander, Chief Executive Officer (Total facility includes 66 beds in nursing home–type unit) **A**1 9 10 **F**7 8 10 12 15 19 21 22 26 29 30 34 35 39 40 41 42 44 45 49 52 57 64 65 66 67 71 73 **P**6 7 8 **S** LifePoint Hospitals, Inc., Nashville, TN

| | 33 | 10 | 211 | 4645 | 107 | 53730 | 472 | 26539 | 10013 | 398 |

WOODBURY—Cannon County

☒ STONES RIVER HOSPITAL, 324 Doolittle Road, Zip 37190–1139; tel. 615/563–4001; Bill Patterson, Interim Administrator **A**1 9 10 **F**8 12 14 15 16 17 19 21 22 26 28 29 30 35 39 41 42 44 46 49 51 52 57 58 59 63 65 71 73 **P**5 8 **S** Columbia/HCA Healthcare Corporation, Nashville, TN
Web address: www.wth.net

| | 33 | 10 | 55 | 1350 | 16 | 14859 | 0 | 9716 | 3812 | 130 |

TEXAS

Resident population 19,760 (in thousands)
Resident population in metro areas 81.5%
Birth rate per 1,000 population 17.2
65 years and over 10.1%
Percent of persons without health insurance 24.3%

Hospital, Address, Telephone, Administrator, Approval, Facility, and Physician Codes, Health Care System, Network	Classi-fication Codes		Utilization Data					Expense (thousands) of dollars		
★ American Hospital Association (AHA) membership □ Joint Commission on Accreditation of Healthcare Organizations (JCAHO) accreditation + American Osteopathic Healthcare Association (AOHA) membership ○ American Osteopathic Association (AOA) accreditation △ Commission on Accreditation of Rehabilitation Facilities (CARF) accreditation Control codes 61, 63, 64, 71, 72 and 73 indicate hospitals listed by AOHA, but not registered by AHA. For definition of numerical codes, see page A4	Control	Service	Staffed Beds	Admissions	Census	Outpatient Visits	Births	Total	Payroll	Personnel

ABILENE—Taylor County

☒ ABILENE REGIONAL MEDICAL CENTER, 6250 Highway 83–84 at Antilley Road, Zip 79606–5299; tel. 915/695–9900; Woody Gilliland, Chief Executive Officer (Total facility includes 20 beds in nursing home–type unit) **A**1 9 10 **F**4 7 8 10 12 14 15 16 17 19 21 22 23 24 25 26 27 28 29 30 32 34 35 37 38 39 40 42 43 44 45 46 49 51 61 63 64 65 67 71 72 73 74 **P**3 **S** Quorum Health Group/Quorum Health Resources, Inc., Brentwood, TN **Web address:** www.abilene.com/armc	33	10	157	7517	104	37251	1269	57745	22114	703
☒ △ HENDRICK HEALTH SYSTEM, 1242 North 19th Street, Zip 79601–2316; tel. 915/670–2000; Michael C. Waters, FACHE, President (Total facility includes 49 beds in nursing home–type unit) **A**1 7 9 10 **F**4 5 6 7 8 10 11 12 15 16 17 19 20 21 22 23 24 25 26 27 28 29 30 31 32 33 34 35 37 39 40 41 42 43 44 45 46 47 48 49 51 56 60 62 63 64 65 66 67 70 71 73 74 **P**6 7 8 **Web address:** www.abilene.com/hmc/	21	10	410	14625	243	144428	1234	133866	58782	2688
☒ U. S. AIR FORCE HOSPITAL, 7th Medical Group, Dyess AFB, Zip 79607–1367; tel. 915/696–5429; Major John G. Wiseman, Administrator (Nonreporting) **A**1 **S** Department of the Air Force, Bowling AFB, DC	41	10	20	—	—	—	—	—	—	—

ALICE—Jim Wells County

☒ ALICE REGIONAL HOSPITAL, 300 East Third Street, Zip 78332–4794; tel. 361/664–4376; Abraham Martinez, Chief Executive Officer (Total facility includes 17 beds in nursing home–type unit) **A**1 9 10 **F**3 8 10 12 14 15 16 17 18 19 21 22 23 25 26 30 33 34 35 37 39 40 41 42 44 46 49 51 52 53 54 55 57 58 61 64 65 66 67 70 71 73 74 **P**7 8 **S** Triad Hospitals, Inc., Dallas, TX	32	10	120	5070	68	68130	371	35410	10618	352

ALPINE—Brewster County

★ BIG BEND REGIONAL MEDICAL CENTER, 801 East Brown Street, Zip 79830–3209; tel. 915/837–3447; Don Edd Green, Chief Executive Officer **A**9 10 **F**12 15 19 22 32 40 44 65 70 71 73 **S** Community Health Systems, Inc., Brentwood, TN **Web address:** www.overland.net/~bbrmc	16	10	25	1344	11	20651	217	8725	4398	127

ALVIN—Brazoria County

ALVIN MEDICAL CENTER See Clear Lake Regional Medical Center, Webster

AMARILLO—Potter County

☒ △ BAPTIST ST. ANTHONY HEALTH SYSTEM, 1600 Wallace Boulevard, Zip 79106–1799; tel. 806/358–5800; John D. Hicks, President and Chief Executive Officer **A**1 2 3 5 7 9 10 **F**4 7 8 10 11 12 14 15 16 17 19 20 21 22 23 25 27 28 30 34 35 36 37 38 39 40 41 42 43 44 45 46 47 51 63 65 66 67 68 71 72 73 74 **P**3 7	21	10	385	21850	248	131838	1950	—	—	2244
□ IHS OF AMARILLO, 5601 Plum Creek Drive, Zip 79124; tel. 806/351–1000; Neal Duncan, Executive Director **A**1 10 **F**12 15 16 27 49 65 67 73	33	48	20	163	9	5518	0	3877	2751	149
☒ NORTHWEST TEXAS HEALTHCARE SYSTEM, (Includes Psychiatric Pavilion, 7201 Evans, Zip 79106), 1501 South Coulter Avenue, Zip 79106–1790, Mailing Address: P.O. Box 1110, Zip 79175–1110; tel. 806/354–1000; Michael A. Callahan, Chief Executive Officer **A**1 3 5 10 **F**2 3 4 7 8 10 11 12 13 14 15 16 17 18 19 20 21 22 24 25 26 29 30 31 34 35 37 38 39 40 41 42 43 44 45 46 47 49 51 52 53 54 55 56 57 58 59 63 64 65 66 67 70 71 73 74 **P**6 **S** Universal Health Services, Inc., King of Prussia, PA **Web address:** www.nwths.com	33	10	345	14403	196	226656	2308	146894	47024	1538
PSYCHIATRIC PAVILION See Northwest Texas Healthcare System										
☒ VETERANS AFFAIRS MEDICAL CENTER, 6010 Amarillo Boulevard West, Zip 79106–1992; tel. 806/354–7801; Wallace M. Hopkins, FACHE, Director (Total facility includes 120 beds in nursing home–type unit) (Nonreporting) **A**1 2 3 5 **S** Department of Veterans Affairs, Washington, DC	45	10	218	—	—	—	—	—	—	—

ANAHUAC—Chambers County

BAYSIDE COMMUNITY HOSPITAL, 200 Hospital Drive, Zip 77514, Mailing Address: P.O. Box 398, Zip 77514–0398; tel. 409/267–3143; Stephen M. Goode, Executive Director **A**9 10 **F**22 28 32 44 **P**6	16	10	12	257	3	1871	0	3230	1573	56

ANDREWS—Andrews County

☒ PERMIAN GENERAL HOSPITAL, Northeast By–Pass, Zip 79714, Mailing Address: P.O. Box 2108, Zip 79714–2108; tel. 915/523–2200; Randy R. Richards, Chief Executive Officer **A**1 9 10 **F**7 8 12 14 15 16 17 18 19 20 21 22 24 28 30 32 34 35 38 39 40 41 44 45 46 49 51 65 67 70 71 73 **P**7	13	10	71	1358	12	43029	271	12503	5368	243

ANGLETON—Brazoria County

☒ ANGLETON–DANBURY GENERAL HOSPITAL, 132 East Hospital Drive, Zip 77515–4197; tel. 409/849–7721; David A. Bleakney, Administrator **A**1 9 10 **F**7 8 12 14 15 16 19 21 22 24 28 29 30 31 34 37 40 44 45 46 49 51 65 66 67 71 73 **P**5 **Web address:** www.adgh.org	16	10	24	2840	27	31534	516	19997	6601	248

Hospital, Address, Telephone, Administrator, Approval, Facility, and Physician Codes, Health Care System, Network	Classi-fication Codes		Utilization Data					Expense (thousands) of dollars		
★ American Hospital Association (AHA) membership □ Joint Commission on Accreditation of Healthcare Organizations (JCAHO) accreditation + American Osteopathic Healthcare Association (AOHA) membership ○ American Osteopathic Association (AOA) accreditation △ Commission on Accreditation of Rehabilitation Facilities (CARF) accreditation Control codes 61, 63, 64, 71, 72 and 73 indicate hospitals listed by AOHA, but not registered by AHA. For definition of numerical codes, see page A4	Control	Service	Staffed Beds	Admissions	Census	Outpatient Visits	Births	Total	Payroll	Personnel

ANSON—Jones County

★ ANSON GENERAL HOSPITAL, 101 Avenue J, Zip 79501–2198; tel. 915/823–3231; Dudley R. White, Administrator (Total facility includes 8 beds in nursing home–type unit) **A**9 10 **F**19 20 22 24 32 35 44 49 71 73 **P**3 8

| | 14 | 10 | 30 | 793 | 12 | 20491 | 0 | 5122 | 2393 | 153 |

ARANSAS PASS—San Patricio County

⊠ NORTH BAY HOSPITAL, (Formerly Columbia North Bay Hospital), 1711 West Wheeler Avenue, Zip 78336–4536; tel. 361/758–8585; John Krogness, Chief Executive Officer **A**1 9 10 **F**7 12 15 16 19 22 28 30 34 35 37 40 44 51 52 57 59 65 71 73 **P**7 8 **S** Columbia/HCA Healthcare Corporation, Nashville, TN

| | 33 | 10 | 69 | 2125 | 29 | 31614 | 248 | 17468 | 7235 | 202 |

ARLINGTON—Tarrant County

⊠ ARLINGTON MEMORIAL HOSPITAL, 800 West Randol Mill Road, Zip 76012–2503; tel. 817/548–6100; Wayne N. Clark, President and Chief Executive Officer **A**1 9 10 **F**4 7 8 10 11 12 14 15 16 19 21 22 23 24 35 37 38 40 42 43 44 49 50 65 67 71 73 74 **P**1 **S** Texas Health Resources, Irving, TX

| | 23 | 10 | 338 | 16575 | 199 | 115909 | 2820 | 114529 | 45128 | 1479 |

□ BHC MILLWOOD HOSPITAL, 1011 North Cooper Street, Zip 76011–5517; tel. 817/261–3121; Wayne Hallford, Chief Executive Officer **A**1 10 **F**3 12 14 22 25 27 34 46 52 53 54 56 58 59 65 67 **P**8 **S** Behavioral Healthcare Corporation, Nashville, TN

| | 33 | 22 | 82 | 1431 | 29 | 7065 | 0 | 6326 | 2972 | 101 |

COLUMBIA MEDICAL CENTER OF ARLINGTON See Medical Center of Arlington

□ △ HEALTHSOUTH REHABILITATION HOSPITAL OF ARLINGTON, 3200 Matlock Road, Zip 76015–2911; tel. 817/468–4000; S. Denise Borroni, Administrator and Chief Executive Officer (Total facility includes 18 beds in nursing home–type unit) (Nonreporting) **A**1 7 10 **S** HEALTHSOUTH Corporation, Birmingham, AL

| | 33 | 46 | 60 | — | — | — | — | — | — | — |

⊠ △ MEDICAL CENTER OF ARLINGTON, (Formerly Columbia Medical Center of Arlington), 3301 Matlock Road, Zip 76015–2998; tel. 817/465–3241; Michael R. Burroughs, FACHE, President and Chief Executive Officer **A**1 7 9 10 **F**1 2 3 4 7 8 10 12 14 15 17 19 20 21 22 26 27 28 29 30 31 32 33 34 35 37 38 39 40 41 42 43 44 45 46 48 49 52 53 54 55 56 57 58 59 65 71 73 74 **P**5 6 **S** Columbia/HCA Healthcare Corporation, Nashville, TN
Web address: www.medicalcenterarlington.com

| | 33 | 10 | 178 | 8112 | 106 | 66679 | 2159 | 68743 | 21396 | 541 |

□ VENCOR ARLINGTON, TEXAS, 1000 North Cooper Street, Zip 76011–5540; tel. 817/543–0200 **A**1 10 **F**12 14 16 17 26 28 37 41 65 70 **S** Vencor, Incorporated, Louisville, KY

| | 33 | 10 | 80 | 344 | 29 | 725 | 0 | 9233 | 4155 | 118 |

ASPERMONT—Stonewall County

★ STONEWALL MEMORIAL HOSPITAL, U.S. Highway 380 & 83 North, Zip 79502, Mailing Address: P.O. Box C, Zip 79502; tel. 940/989–3551; Judy Ingram, Acting Administrator (Total facility includes 2 beds in nursing home–type unit) **A**9 10 **F**8 12 15 16 19 21 28 32 33 34 35 39 50 63 64 71 **P**6

| | 16 | 10 | 16 | 172 | 2 | 661 | 0 | — | — | 55 |

ATHENS—Henderson County

⊠ EAST TEXAS MEDICAL CENTER ATHENS, 2000 South Palestine Street, Zip 75751–5610; tel. 903/675–2216; Patrick L. Wallace, Administrator **A**1 9 10 **F**8 12 15 19 21 22 23 27 28 30 32 37 40 42 44 49 59 65 66 67 70 71 72 **P**7 **S** East Texas Medical Center Regional Healthcare System, Tyler, TX

| | 23 | 10 | 108 | 5691 | 64 | 87580 | 817 | 36190 | 12240 | 374 |

ATLANTA—Cass County

★ ATLANTA MEMORIAL HOSPITAL, Highway 77 at South Williams, Zip 75551, Mailing Address: P.O. Box 1049, Zip 75551–1049; tel. 903/799–3000; Tom Crow, Administrator (Total facility includes 8 beds in nursing home–type unit) **A**9 10 **F**7 8 15 16 17 19 26 27 28 30 32 33 37 39 40 42 43 44 46 52 57 59 61 64 65 70 71 **P**8

| | 16 | 10 | 52 | 1989 | 27 | — | 175 | 10502 | 4456 | 199 |

BROOKS HOSPITAL, 230 North Louise Street, Zip 75551–2589, Mailing Address: P.O. Box 1069, Zip 75551–1069; tel. 903/796–2873; Jesse Brooks, M.D., Administrator **F**1 3 4 5 6 7 8 10 12 13 17 18 19 20 21 22 23 24 25 26 27 28 29 30 31 32 33 34 35 36 39 41 42 43 44 45 46 49 50 51 53 54 55 56 57 58 59 60 61 62 63 65 66 67 69 70 71 72 73 74 **P**1 2 3 4 5 6 8

| | 33 | 10 | 22 | 45 | 0 | 19 | 0 | — | — | 33 |

AUSTIN—Travis County

AUSTIN DIAGNOSTIC MEDICAL CENTER See North Austin Medical Center

□ AUSTIN STATE HOSPITAL, 4110 Guadalupe Street, Zip 78751–4296; tel. 512/452–0381; Diane Faucher, Superintendent **A**1 3 10 **F**11 20 37 40 41 52 53 55 56 57 65 73
Web address: www.mhmr.state.tx.us

| | 12 | 22 | 308 | 2303 | 255 | 0 | 0 | — | — | — |

⊠ BRACKENRIDGE HOSPITAL, (Includes Children's Hospital of Austin, tel. 512/324–8000; Patrick Shumaker, Administrator), 601 East 15th Street, Zip 78701–1996; tel. 512/324–7000; Susan McClernon, Administrator **A**1 2 3 9 10 **F**2 3 4 7 8 10 11 12 13 15 16 17 19 21 22 23 25 26 28 29 30 31 32 34 35 37 38 39 40 41 42 43 44 46 47 49 51 52 53 54 56 57 58 59 60 61 63 64 65 66 67 68 70 71 72 73 74 **P**5 6 8 **S** Daughters of Charity National Health System, Saint Louis, MO

| | 21 | 10 | 291 | 14566 | 188 | 156129 | 2783 | 136008 | 55825 | 1334 |

□ △ BROWN SCHOOLS REHABILITATION CENTER, 1106 West Dittmar, Zip 78745–9990, Mailing Address: P.O. Box 150459, Zip 78715–0459; tel. 512/444–4835; Kay Peck, Chief Executive Officer **A**1 7 10 **F**12 15 16 34 39 41 45 46 49 52 53 55 58 65 **S** Healthcare America, Inc., Austin, TX

| | 33 | 22 | 60 | 92 | 58 | 1775 | 0 | 8882 | 5192 | 216 |

□ CHARTER BEHAVIORAL HEALTH SYSTEM OF AUSTIN, 8402 Cross Park Drive, Zip 78754–4588, Mailing Address: P.O. Box 140585, Zip 78714–0585; tel. 870/837–1800; Armin Steege, Chief Executive Officer **A**1 9 10 **F**2 3 12 14 15 16 19 21 25 35 46 52 53 54 55 56 58 59 65 67 71 **P**5 7 **S** Magellan Health Services, Atlanta, GA

| | 32 | 22 | 29 | 995 | 19 | 4273 | 0 | 4880 | 2404 | 76 |

Hospital, Address, Telephone, Administrator, Approval, Facility, and Physician Codes, Health Care System, Network	Classi-fication Codes		Utilization Data					Expense (thousands) of dollars		
★ American Hospital Association (AHA) membership □ Joint Commission on Accreditation of Healthcare Organizations (JCAHO) accreditation + American Osteopathic Healthcare Association (AOHA) membership ○ American Osteopathic Association (AOA) accreditation △ Commission on Accreditation of Rehabilitation Facilities (CARF) accreditation Control codes 61, 63, 64, 71, 72 and 73 indicate hospitals listed by AOHA, but not registered by AHA. For definition of numerical codes, see page A4	Control	Service	Staffed Beds	Admissions	Census	Outpatient Visits	Births	Total	Payroll	Personnel

Hospital	Control	Service	Staffed Beds	Admissions	Census	Outpatient Visits	Births	Total	Payroll	Personnel
CHRISTOPHER HOUSE, 2820 East Martin Luther King, Zip 78702; tel. 512/322-0747 (Nonreporting)	23	49	15	—	—	—	—	—	—	—
□ △ HEALTHSOUTH REHABILITATION HOSPITAL OF AUSTIN, 1215 Red River Street, Zip 78701, Mailing Address: P.O. Box 13366, Zip 78711-3366; tel. 512/474-5700; William O. Mitchell, Jr., Chief Executive Officer (Total facility includes 20 beds in nursing home–type unit) **A**1 7 9 10 **F**12 15 16 46 48 49 64 67 73 **S** HEALTHSOUTH Corporation, Birmingham, AL	33	46	80	1573	60	34736	0	14818	6587	245
✚ NORTH AUSTIN MEDICAL CENTER, (Formerly Austin Diagnostic Medical Center), 12221 MoPac Expressway North, Zip 78758-2483; tel. 512/901-1000; Donald H. Wilkerson, Chief Executive Officer (Total facility includes 18 beds in nursing home–type unit) **A**1 10 **F**1 2 3 4 7 8 10 11 12 14 15 16 17 18 19 20 21 22 23 24 25 27 28 29 30 31 32 34 35 37 38 39 40 41 42 43 44 45 46 48 49 52 53 54 55 57 58 59 60 61 63 64 65 66 67 68 71 72 73 74 **P**1 3 7 8 **S** Columbia/HCA Healthcare Corporation, Nashville, TN **Web address:** www.columbia.stdavids.com	32	10	150	7591	97	189748	602	91793	27134	745
✚ SETON MEDICAL CENTER, 1201 West 38th Street, Zip 78705-1056; tel. 512/324-1000; Gregory R. Angle, Administrator **A**1 2 9 10 **F**2 3 4 7 8 10 11 12 13 15 16 17 19 21 22 23 25 26 28 29 30 31 32 34 35 37 38 39 40 41 42 43 44 46 47 49 51 52 53 54 56 57 58 59 60 61 63 64 65 66 67 68 70 71 72 73 74 **P**5 6 8 **S** Daughters of Charity National Health System, Saint Louis, MO **Web address:** www.seton.org	21	10	490	26469	347	433023	5430	242052	103479	2887
✚ SETON SHOAL CREEK HOSPITAL, 3501 Mills Avenue, Zip 78731-6391; tel. 512/452-0361; Gail M. Oberta, Administrator and Chief Executive Officer **A**1 9 10 **F**2 3 4 7 8 10 12 13 15 16 17 19 21 23 25 26 28 29 30 31 32 34 35 37 38 39 40 41 42 43 44 46 47 49 51 52 53 54 56 57 58 59 60 61 63 64 65 66 67 68 70 71 72 73 74 **P**1 5 6 8 **S** Daughters of Charity National Health System, Saint Louis, MO	21	22	118	268	23	1941	0	927	488	95
□ SPECIALTY HOSPITAL OF AUSTIN, (LONG TERM ACUTE CARE), 4207 Burnet Road, Zip 78756-3396; tel. 512/706-1900; William R. Cook, Chief Executive Officer **A**1 10 **F**19 22 27 35 37 60 64 65 71	33	49	76	560	44	0	0	12612	5804	199
✚ ST. DAVID'S MEDICAL CENTER, 919 East 32nd Street, Zip 78705-2709, Mailing Address: P.O. Box 4039, Zip 78765-4039; tel. 512/476-7111; Cole C. Eslyn, Chief Executive Officer **A**1 2 9 10 **F**1 2 3 4 7 8 10 12 14 15 16 17 19 21 22 23 24 25 26 27 28 29 30 31 32 33 34 35 37 38 39 40 41 42 43 44 45 46 48 49 52 53 54 57 58 59 60 61 63 64 65 66 67 68 70 71 72 73 74 **P**8 **S** Columbia/HCA Healthcare Corporation, Nashville, TN **Web address:** www.columbia.net	32	10	296	17350	225	64189	4480	125869	50054	1988
✚ ST. DAVID'S PAVILION, 1025 East 32nd Street, Zip 78765; tel. 512/867-5800; Cole C. Eslyn, Chief Executive Officer **A**1 9 10 **F**1 3 4 7 8 10 12 14 15 16 17 18 19 21 22 23 24 25 26 27 28 29 30 31 32 33 34 35 37 38 39 40 41 42 43 44 45 46 48 49 52 53 54 55 57 58 59 60 61 63 64 65 66 67 68 70 71 72 73 74 **P**8 **S** Columbia/HCA Healthcare Corporation, Nashville, TN **Web address:** www.columbia.net	32	22	38	1615	27	6695	0	8966	3026	—
✚ △ ST. DAVID'S REHABILITATION CENTER, 1005 East 32nd Street, Zip 78705-2705, Mailing Address: P.O. Box 4270, Zip 78765-4270; tel. 512/867-5100; Cole C. Eslyn, Chief Executive Officer (Total facility includes 37 beds in nursing home–type unit) **A**1 7 9 10 **F**1 2 3 4 7 8 10 12 14 15 16 17 18 19 21 22 23 24 25 26 27 28 29 30 31 32 33 34 35 37 38 39 40 41 42 43 44 45 46 48 49 52 53 54 55 57 58 59 60 61 63 64 65 66 67 68 70 71 72 73 74 **P**8 **S** Columbia/HCA Healthcare Corporation, Nashville, TN **Web address:** www.columbia.net	32	46	104	1800	73	39584	0	21385	10292	—
✚ ST. DAVID'S SOUTH HOSPITAL, (Formerly Columbia St David's South Hospital), 901 West Ben White Boulevard, Zip 78704-6903; tel. 512/447-2211; Richard W. Klusmann, Chief Executive Officer **A**1 9 10 **F**4 5 7 8 10 11 12 15 16 19 21 22 23 28 30 32 35 37 40 41 42 43 44 49 60 64 65 71 73 74 **P**1 **S** Columbia/HCA Healthcare Corporation, Nashville, TN	33	10	164	8950	111	133551	1058	72181	28481	669
AZLE—Tarrant County										
✚ HARRIS METHODIST NORTHWEST, 108 Denver Trail, Zip 76020-3697; tel. 817/444-8600; Larry Thompson, Vice President and Administrator (Total facility includes 8 beds in nursing home–type unit) **A**1 9 10 **F**1 2 3 4 7 8 9 10 11 12 13 14 15 16 17 18 19 21 22 23 24 25 26 28 29 30 31 32 33 35 37 38 39 40 41 42 43 44 45 46 47 48 49 50 52 53 54 55 56 57 58 59 60 61 63 64 65 66 67 68 70 71 72 73 74 **S** Texas Health Resources, Irving, TX **Web address:** www.hmhs.com	23	10	44	1296	14	22168	0	12251	5081	166
BALLINGER—Runnels County										
BALLINGER MEMORIAL HOSPITAL, 608 Avenue B, Zip 76821-2499; tel. 915/365-2531; Robert E. Vernor, Administrator **A**9 10 **F**14 15 16 22 24 26 28 31 32 65 70 71 73	16	10	16	355	4	8151	0	2513	1358	59
BAY CITY—Matagorda County										
✚ MATAGORDA GENERAL HOSPITAL, 1115 Avenue G, Zip 77414-3544; tel. 409/245-6383; Wendell H. Baker, Jr., Chief Executive Officer **A**1 9 10 **F**4 7 8 10 12 16 18 19 22 23 26 27 28 30 31 32 33 34 35 37 39 40 41 42 43 44 48 49 52 54 57 58 65 70 71 73 74 **P**5 **S** Matagorda County Hospital District, Bay City, TX	16	10	67	2395	25	20766	389	25822	10228	431
BAYTOWN—Harris County										
□ BAYCOAST MEDICAL CENTER, 1700 James Bowie Drive, Zip 77520-3386; tel. 281/420-6100; Walter J. Ornsteen, President and Chief Executive Officer (Total facility includes 20 beds in nursing home–type unit) **A**1 9 10 **F**7 8 11 12 14 15 16 19 20 21 22 23 28 29 30 33 35 37 39 40 41 42 44 45 46 48 49 63 64 65 71 72 73 74 **P**5 7 **S** Paracelsus Healthcare Corporation, Houston, TX	33	10	191	2637	33	28880	468	19963	9142	209

Hospital, Address, Telephone, Administrator, Approval, Facility, and Physician Codes, Health Care System, Network	Classi-fication Codes		Utilization Data					Expense (thousands) of dollars		
★ American Hospital Association (AHA) membership ☐ Joint Commission on Accreditation of Healthcare Organizations (JCAHO) accreditation + American Osteopathic Healthcare Association (AOHA) membership ○ American Osteopathic Association (AOA) accreditation △ Commission on Accreditation of Rehabilitation Facilities (CARF) accreditation Control codes 61, 63, 64, 71, 72 and 73 indicate hospitals listed by AOHA, but not registered by AHA. For definition of numerical codes, see page A4	Control	Service	Staffed Beds	Admissions	Census	Outpatient Visits	Births	Total	Payroll	Personnel

	Control	Service	Staffed Beds	Admissions	Census	Outpatient Visits	Births	Total	Payroll	Personnel
✖ △ SAN JACINTO METHODIST HOSPITAL, 4401 Garth Road, Zip 77521–3160; tel. 281/420–8600; William Simmons, President and Chief Executive Officer (Total facility includes 45 beds in nursing home–type unit) **A**1 3 5 7 9 10 **F**3 4 7 8 10 12 15 17 18 19 20 21 22 23 26 27 28 30 32 33 34 35 37 39 40 41 42 44 45 46 48 49 51 52 54 55 56 57 58 59 60 63 64 65 67 68 71 73 **P**3 7 8 **S** Methodist Health Care System, Houston, TX **Web address:** www.methodisthealth.com\sanjacinto	21	10	231	10108	144	150392	1320	76271	32274	1229
BEAUMONT—Jefferson County										
✖ BAPTIST HOSPITAL OF SOUTHEAST TEXAS, College and 11th Streets, Zip 77701, Mailing Address: Drawer 1591, Zip 77704–1591; tel. 409/835–3781; David N. Parmer, President and Chief Executive Officer (Total facility includes 31 beds in nursing home–type unit) **A**1 5 9 10 **F**4 7 8 10 12 19 20 21 22 23 27 28 30 32 33 35 37 41 42 43 44 45 46 48 49 51 60 64 65 67 71 72 73 **P**3 5	21	10	206	6475	108	46709	0	43162	19531	682
✖ BEAUMONT MEDICAL AND SURGICAL HOSPITAL, (Formerly Columbia Beaumont Medical Center), (Includes Fannin Pavilion of Beaumont Regional Medical Center, 3250 Fannin Street, Zip 77701; tel. 409/833–1411), 3080 College, Zip 77701–4689, Mailing Address: P.O. Box 5817, Zip 77726–5817; tel. 409/833–1411; Luis G. Silva, Chief Executive Officer and Regional Administrator **A**1 9 10 **F**2 3 7 8 12 14 15 16 19 20 22 26 27 30 31 35 37 40 41 42 44 45 52 53 54 55 56 57 58 59 64 65 67 70 71 73 74 **P**7 **S** Columbia/HCA Healthcare Corporation, Nashville, TN	33	10	372	6098	98	34639	1264	37971	17582	534
✖ CHRISTUS ST. ELIZABETH HOSPITAL, (Formerly St Elizabeth Hospital), 2830 Calder Avenue, Zip 77702, Mailing Address: P.O. Box 5405, Zip 77726–5405; tel. 409/892–7171; Edward W. Myers, Chief Executive Officer (Total facility includes 27 beds in nursing home–type unit) **A**1 2 5 9 10 **F**4 7 8 10 11 12 13 14 15 16 17 19 20 21 22 24 26 27 28 29 30 31 32 33 34 35 37 38 39 40 41 42 43 44 45 46 47 48 49 51 60 63 64 65 67 71 72 73 74 **P**3 5 6 7 8 **S** Christus Health, Houston, TX FANNIN PAVILION OF BEAUMONT REGIONAL MEDICAL CENTER See Beaumont Medical and Surgical Hospital	21	10	468	22819	287	152037	2346	182881	75774	2054
☐ △ HEALTHSOUTH REHABILITATION HOSPITAL OF BEAUMONT, 3340 Plaza 10 Boulevard, Zip 77707; tel. 409/835–0835; Michael Hagen, Administrator **A**1 7 10 **F**12 17 24 25 27 28 34 48 49 57 65 67 73 **P**5 **S** HEALTHSOUTH Corporation, Birmingham, AL ST ELIZABETH HOSPITAL See Christus St. Elizabeth Hospital	32	46	61	761	41	18952	0	11892	5429	135
BEDFORD—Tarrant County										
✖ HARRIS METHODIST–HEB, (Includes Harris Methodist–Springwood, 1608 Hospital Parkway, Zip 76022; tel. 817/355–7700), 1600 Hospital Parkway, Zip 76022–6913, Mailing Address: P.O. Box 669, Zip 76095–0669; tel. 817/685–4000; Jack McCabe, Senior Vice President and Administrator (Total facility includes 15 beds in nursing home–type unit) **A**1 2 9 10 **F**2 3 4 7 8 10 12 14 15 16 17 18 19 21 22 23 24 26 27 28 30 31 32 33 34 35 37 38 39 40 41 42 43 44 45 46 48 49 52 53 54 55 56 57 58 59 60 64 65 67 71 73 74 **P**2 5 7 **S** Texas Health Resources, Irving, TX **Web address:** www.hmhs.com	21	10	184	10596	116	74218	1618	89959	38427	1138
BEEVILLE—Bee County										
✖ CHRISTUS SPOHN HOSPITAL BEEVILLE, (Formerly Spohn Bee County Hospital), 1500 East Houston Street, Zip 78102; tel. 361/354–2125; David S. Wagner, Vice President and Administrator **A**1 9 10 **F**7 8 14 15 16 17 19 21 22 23 28 32 33 34 35 37 40 44 45 46 49 57 60 65 66 67 70 71 73 **P**3 5 8 **S** Christus Health, Houston, TX	21	10	69	4304	40	88350	444	22104	10008	301
BELLVILLE—Austin County										
☐ BELLVILLE GENERAL HOSPITAL, 44 North Cummings Street, Zip 77418–1347; tel. 409/865–3141; Bob Ellzey, Administrator **A**1 9 10 **F**8 12 19 21 22 26 28 30 32 34 35 44 49 60 66 71 72 **P**3	16	10	32	810	9	12381	135	6471	2427	100
BIG LAKE—Reagan County										
REAGAN MEMORIAL HOSPITAL, 805 North Main Street, Zip 76932–3999; tel. 915/884–2561; Ron Galloway, Administrator (Total facility includes 48 beds in nursing home–type unit) **A**9 10 **F**15 22 24 26 28 30 32 49 64 66	16	10	62	74	26	1459	0	2376	1319	58
BIG SPRING—Howard County										
☐ BIG SPRING STATE HOSPITAL, Lamesa Highway, Zip 79720, Mailing Address: P.O. Box 231, Zip 79721–0231; tel. 915/267–8216; Edward Moughon, Superintendent **A**1 10 **F**14 15 16 17 18 19 20 22 26 35 44 45 49 52 53 55 56 57 65 71 73 **Web address:** www.mhmr.state.tx.us	12	22	241	903	188	0	0	27829	16013	—
✖ SCENIC MOUNTAIN MEDICAL CENTER, 1601 West 11th Place, Zip 79720–4198; tel. 915/263–1211; Loren F. Chandler, Interim Chief Executive Officer **A**1 9 10 **F**7 8 10 11 12 16 17 19 21 22 26 28 30 32 34 35 37 40 41 44 45 46 49 52 57 63 64 65 70 71 73 **P**7 **S** Community Health Systems, Inc., Brentwood, TN **Web address:** www.smmccare.com	33	10	128	4220	49	19464	258	18523	8728	307
✖ VETERANS AFFAIRS MEDICAL CENTER, 300 Veterans Boulevard, Zip 79720–5500; tel. 915/263–7361; Cary D. Brown, Director (Total facility includes 40 beds in nursing home–type unit) (Nonreporting) **A**1 2 3 5 **S** Department of Veterans Affairs, Washington, DC	45	10	189	—	—	—	—	—	—	—
BONHAM—Fannin County										
✖ NORTHEAST MEDICAL CENTER, 504 Lipscomb Boulevard, Zip 75418–4096, Mailing Address: P.O. Drawer C, Zip 75418–4096; tel. 903/583–8585; Gwen S. Eddleman, R.N., Interim Chief Executive Officer (Total facility includes 10 beds in nursing home–type unit) **A**1 9 10 **F**8 12 15 19 21 22 28 30 32 34 35 37 41 44 49 64 65 67 69 71 **S** Community Health Systems, Inc., Brentwood, TN	32	10	46	1342	19	12812	0	11333	4464	—

Hospital, Address, Telephone, Administrator, Approval, Facility, and Physician Codes, Health Care System, Network	Classi-fication Codes		Utilization Data					Expense (thousands) of dollars		
★ American Hospital Association (AHA) membership □ Joint Commission on Accreditation of Healthcare Organizations (JCAHO) accreditation + American Osteopathic Healthcare Association (AOHA) membership ○ American Osteopathic Association (AOA) accreditation △ Commission on Accreditation of Rehabilitation Facilities (CARF) accreditation Control codes 61, 63, 64, 71, 72 and 73 indicate hospitals listed by AOHA, but not registered by AHA. For definition of numerical codes, see page A4	Control	Service	Staffed Beds	Admissions	Census	Outpatient Visits	Births	Total	Payroll	Personnel

SAM RAYBURN MEMORIAL VETERANS CENTER See Veterans Affairs North Texas Health Care System, Dallas

BORGER—Hutchinson County

⊞ GOLDEN PLAINS COMMUNITY HOSPITAL, 200 South McGee Street, Zip 79007–0495; tel. 806/273–1100; Norman Lambert, Chief Executive Officer **A**1 10 **F**7 8 12 15 16 19 22 23 28 32 34 35 37 39 40 44 46 49 65 66 70 71 73
Web address: www.borger.com

| | 16 | 10 | 48 | 1276 | 12 | 17027 | 176 | 10742 | 4464 | 188 |

BOWIE—Montague County

★ BOWIE MEMORIAL HOSPITAL, 705 East Greenwood Avenue, Zip 76230–3199; tel. 940/872–1126; Joyce Crumpler, R.N., Administrator **A**9 10 **F**14 15 16 19 22 28 32 33 37 44 49 65 70 71

| | 16 | 10 | 44 | 1478 | 21 | 47071 | 0 | 9361 | 4715 | 184 |

BRADY—McCulloch County

HEART OF TEXAS MEMORIAL HOSPITAL, Nine Road, Zip 76825–1150, Mailing Address: P.O. Box 1150, Zip 76825–1150; tel. 915/597–2901; Windell M. McCord, Administrator **A**9 10 **F**19 22 24 28 32 44 49 51 70 71 73

| | 16 | 10 | 27 | 864 | 9 | 21724 | 0 | 4868 | 2213 | 93 |

BRECKENRIDGE—Stephens County

STEPHENS MEMORIAL HOSPITAL, 200 South Geneva Street, Zip 76424–4799; tel. 817/559–2241; James Reese, CHE, Administrator **A**9 10 **F**7 8 15 16 19 22 24 26 28 30 32 34 35 36 40 41 42 44 49 51 65 70 71

| | 13 | 10 | 33 | 974 | 12 | 34010 | 27 | 6030 | 3049 | 125 |

BRENHAM—Washington County

⊞ TRINITY COMMUNITY MEDICAL CENTER OF BRENHAM, 700 Medical Parkway, Zip 77833–5498; tel. 409/836–6173; John L. Simms, President and Chief Executive Officer **A**1 9 10 **F**7 14 15 16 17 19 21 23 26 28 30 32 37 40 44 49 65 70 71 **S** Franciscan Services Corporation, Sylvania, OH
Web address: www.trinitymed.com

| | 21 | 10 | 60 | 2167 | 24 | 37071 | 346 | 16441 | 6951 | 224 |

BROWNFIELD—Terry County

⊞ BROWNFIELD REGIONAL MEDICAL CENTER, 705 East Felt, Zip 79316–3439; tel. 806/637–3551; Mike Click, Administrator **A**1 9 10 **F**7 8 14 15 16 17 19 22 24 28 29 30 31 32 34 37 40 44 46 49 65 70 71 73

| | 16 | 10 | 42 | 680 | 9 | 48696 | 119 | 7550 | 3921 | 160 |

BROWNSVILLE—Cameron County

⊞ BROWNSVILLE MEDICAL CENTER, 1040 West Jefferson Street, Zip 78520–5829, Mailing Address: P.O. Box 3590, Zip 78523–3590; tel. 956/544–1400; John M. Chubb, Chief Executive Officer **A**1 9 10 **F**4 7 8 10 12 15 16 19 22 24 28 30 32 35 37 38 40 41 43 44 45 46 49 51 53 54 55 56 57 58 59 64 65 70 71 73 74 **P**3 4 7 8 **S** TENET Healthcare Corporation, Santa Barbara, CA

| | 32 | 10 | 205 | 11067 | 164 | 47523 | 2615 | 74051 | 26900 | 843 |

⊞ VALLEY REGIONAL MEDICAL CENTER, 100A Alton Gloor Boulevard, Zip 78526, Mailing Address: P.O. Box 3710, Zip 78521–3710; tel. 956/350–7101; Charles F. Sexton, Chief Executive Officer **A**1 9 10 **F**4 7 8 10 12 14 15 16 17 19 21 22 27 28 30 34 35 37 38 39 40 41 43 44 46 48 49 65 67 71 73 74 **P**7 **S** Columbia/HCA Healthcare Corporation, Nashville, TN
Web address: www.columbia.net

| | 32 | 10 | 177 | 7369 | 105 | 64055 | 2113 | 51189 | 21510 | 646 |

BROWNWOOD—Brown County

⊞ BROWNWOOD REGIONAL MEDICAL CENTER, (Formerly Columbia Brownwood Medical Center), 1501 Burnet Drive, Zip 76801–5933, Mailing Address: P.O. Box 760, Zip 76804–0760; tel. 915/646–8541; Tim Lancaster, Chief Executive Officer (Total facility includes 20 beds in nursing home–type unit) **A**1 9 10 **F**7 8 10 12 14 15 16 17 19 21 22 24 25 26 28 30 32 33 34 35 36 37 39 40 41 42 44 45 46 48 49 51 52 54 57 60 63 64 65 67 71 73 74 **P**3 **S** Triad Hospitals, Inc., Dallas, TX

| | 33 | 10 | 164 | 6863 | 98 | 123470 | 723 | 43472 | 17827 | 653 |

BRYAN—Brazos County

⊞ ST. JOSEPH REGIONAL HEALTH CENTER, 2801 Franciscan Drive, Zip 77802–2599; tel. 409/776–3777; Sister Gretchen Kunz, President and Chief Executive Officer (Total facility includes 30 beds in nursing home–type unit) **A**1 3 5 9 10 **F**3 4 7 8 10 11 12 13 14 15 16 17 19 21 22 23 25 26 27 28 29 30 31 32 33 35 37 39 40 41 42 43 44 45 46 48 49 51 52 54 55 58 60 63 64 65 66 67 71 72 73 **P**8 **S** Franciscan Services Corporation, Sylvania, OH

| | 21 | 10 | 283 | 14840 | 199 | 211017 | 2401 | 128147 | 51058 | 1614 |

BURLESON—Johnson County

⊞ HUGULEY MEMORIAL MEDICAL CENTER, 11801 South Freeway, Zip 76028, Mailing Address: P.O. Box 6337, Fort Worth, Zip 76115–6337; tel. 817/293–9110; Peter M. Weber, President and Chief Executive Officer (Total facility includes 33 beds in nursing home–type unit) **A**1 9 10 **F**3 7 8 10 11 12 13 14 15 16 17 19 21 22 23 24 26 28 29 30 32 33 34 35 37 39 40 41 42 44 45 46 49 51 52 54 55 56 57 58 59 60 62 63 64 65 67 71 73 74 **P**1 3 6 7 **S** Adventist Health System Sunbelt Health Care Corporation, Winter Park, FL

| | 21 | 10 | 169 | 7718 | 105 | 80953 | 1016 | 66027 | 26103 | 881 |

BURNET—Burnet County

⊞ SETON HIGHLAND LAKES, Highway 281 South, Zip 78611, Mailing Address: P.O. Box 1219, Zip 78611–0840; tel. 512/756–6000; Terry R. Andris, CHE, Administrator **A**1 9 10 **F**8 12 15 16 19 21 22 28 30 32 33 34 39 42 44 49 59 63 64 65 67 71 **P**8 **S** Daughters of Charity National Health System, Saint Louis, MO

| | 21 | 10 | 26 | 1010 | 10 | 22863 | 0 | 9050 | 3985 | 143 |

CALDWELL—Burleson County

★ BURLESON ST. JOSEPH HEALTH CENTER, 1101 Woodson Drive, Zip 77836–1052, Mailing Address: P.O. Drawer 360, Zip 77836–0360; tel. 409/567–3245; William H. Craig, President and Chief Executive Officer **A**9 10 **F**8 13 14 15 16 17 19 21 22 25 26 28 29 30 32 34 46 49 65 71 73 **P**5 7 8 **S** Franciscan Services Corporation, Sylvania, OH
Web address: www.st–joseph.org/

| | 21 | 10 | 30 | 293 | 8 | 8344 | 1 | 4678 | 2022 | 55 |

Hospital, Address, Telephone, Administrator, Approval, Facility, and Physician Codes, Health Care System, Network	Classi-fication Codes		Utilization Data					Expense (thousands) of dollars		
	Control	Service	Staffed Beds	Admissions	Census	Outpatient Visits	Births	Total	Payroll	Personnel

★ American Hospital Association (AHA) membership
□ Joint Commission on Accreditation of Healthcare Organizations (JCAHO) accreditation
+ American Osteopathic Healthcare Association (AOHA) membership
○ American Osteopathic Association (AOA) accreditation
△ Commission on Accreditation of Rehabilitation Facilities (CARF) accreditation
Control codes 61, 63, 64, 71, 72 and 73 indicate hospitals listed by AOHA, but not registered by AHA. For definition of numerical codes, see page A4

CAMERON—Milam County
CENTRAL TEXAS HOSPITAL, 806 North Crockett Avenue, Zip 76520–2599; tel. 254/697–6591; Jodi Beauregard, Administrator **A**9 10 **F**12 17 19 21 22 25 27 28 29 33 34 44 48 49 64 71 72 73 **S** NetCare Health Systems, Inc., Nashville, TN
| 33 | 10 | 44 | 474 | 6 | 15831 | 1 | 2626 | 1032 | 57 |

CANADIAN—Hemphill County
HEMPHILL COUNTY HOSPITAL, 1020 South Fourth Street, Zip 79014–3315; tel. 806/323–6422; Robert Ezzell, Administrator **A**9 **F**1 8 12 18 20 21 22 26 32 33 34 36 45 46 49 51 56 65 67 70 71 73
| 16 | 10 | 19 | 210 | 3 | 12135 | 0 | 3598 | 1523 | 58 |

CARRIZO SPRINGS—Dimmit County
DIMMIT COUNTY MEMORIAL HOSPITAL, 704 Hospital Drive, Zip 78834–3836; tel. 830/876–2424; Ernest Flores, Jr., Administrator **A**9 10 **F**7 8 14 15 16 19 22 28 32 34 40 44 46 49 61 70 71
| 13 | 10 | 35 | 1077 | 11 | 16855 | 144 | 7258 | 3022 | 138 |

CARROLLTON—Denton County
⊞ TRINITY MEDICAL CENTER, 4343 North Josey Lane, Zip 75010–4691; tel. 972/492–1010; Craig E. Sims, President (Total facility includes 12 beds in nursing home–type unit) **A**1 9 10 **F**4 7 8 10 12 14 15 16 17 19 20 21 22 23 25 26 28 29 30 33 34 35 37 38 39 40 41 42 43 44 46 49 54 61 63 64 65 66 67 70 71 72 73 74 **P**5 **S** TENET Healthcare Corporation, Santa Barbara, CA
Web address: www.tenethealth.com
| 33 | 10 | 144 | 5868 | 54 | 80800 | 1821 | 40543 | 16527 | 432 |

CARTHAGE—Panola County
□ EAST TEXAS MEDICAL CENTER CARTHAGE, 409 Cottage Road, Zip 75633–1466, Mailing Address: P.O. Box 549, Zip 75633–0549; tel. 903/693–3841; Gary Mikeal Hudson, Administrator **A**1 9 10 **F**8 16 19 22 32 37 44 65 70 71 73 **S** East Texas Medical Center Regional Healthcare System, Tyler, TX
| 23 | 10 | 30 | 958 | 13 | 25581 | 0 | 8341 | 3757 | 144 |

CENTER—Shelby County
□ MEMORIAL HOSPITAL OF CENTER, 602 Hurst Street, Zip 75935–3414, Mailing Address: P.O. Box 1749, Zip 75935–1749; tel. 409/598–2781; Robert V. Deen, Chief Executive Officer (Total facility includes 10 beds in nursing home–type unit) **A**1 9 10 **F**8 14 15 16 19 21 22 32 36 41 42 44 49 57 64 65 70 71 73 **P**8 **S** New American Healthcare Corporation, Brentwood, TN
| 33 | 10 | 46 | 1574 | 19 | — | 123 | 10540 | 4308 | 163 |

CENTER POINT—Kerr County
□ STARLITE VILLAGE HOSPITAL, Elm Pass Road, Zip 78010, Mailing Address: P.O. Box 317, Zip 78010–0317; tel. 830/634–2212; Marion Black, Administrator **A**1 10 **F**2 3 18 22 34 39 52 56 57 58 65 67 **P**5
| 33 | 82 | 42 | 661 | 19 | 3037 | 0 | 3400 | 1699 | 84 |

CHILDRESS—Childress County
□ CHILDRESS REGIONAL MEDICAL CENTER, Highway 83 North, Zip 79201, Mailing Address: P.O. Box 1030, Zip 79201–1030; tel. 940/937–6371; Frances T. Smith, Administrator **A**1 9 10 **F**8 12 13 14 15 16 17 19 21 22 23 26 27 28 29 30 31 32 33 34 39 40 44 45 46 49 51 65 66 67 70 71 73 74
| 16 | 10 | 35 | 916 | 8 | 22180 | 203 | 8061 | 3974 | 163 |

CHILLICOTHE—Hardeman County
CHILLICOTHE HOSPITAL DISTRICT, 303 Avenue I, Zip 79225, Mailing Address: P.O. Box 370, Zip 79225–0370; tel. 817/852–5131; Linda Hall, Administrator **A**9 10 **F**12 14 15 16 19 21 22 28 30 32 35 44 69 70 71
| 16 | 10 | 12 | 79 | 1 | 326 | 0 | 1148 | 560 | 25 |

CLARKSVILLE—Red River County
⊞ EAST TEXAS MEDICAL CENTER–CLARKSVILLE, 3000 Highway 82 West, Zip 75426, Mailing Address: P.O. Box 1270, Zip 75426–1270; tel. 903/427–3851; Terry Cutler, Administrator and Chief Operating Officer **A**1 9 10 **F**8 14 15 19 22 28 30 32 34 37 39 44 45 46 49 65 67 70 71 73 **P**8 **S** East Texas Medical Center Regional Healthcare System, Tyler, TX
| 16 | 10 | 36 | 1833 | 18 | 23959 | 0 | 7420 | 2679 | 110 |

CLEBURNE—Johnson County
⊞ WALLS REGIONAL HOSPITAL, 201 Walls Drive, Zip 76031–1008; tel. 817/641–2551; Brent D. Magers, FACHE, Executive Director and Senior Vice President (Total facility includes 12 beds in nursing home–type unit) **A**1 9 10 **F**3 4 7 8 10 12 13 14 15 16 17 19 21 22 24 26 28 29 30 31 32 33 34 35 37 39 40 41 42 44 45 46 49 51 53 54 55 56 58 59 60 61 63 64 65 66 67 68 70 71 73 74 **P**5 **S** Texas Health Resources, Irving, TX
Web address: www.hmhs.com
| 21 | 10 | 112 | 4236 | 50 | 83930 | 668 | 31818 | 12515 | 388 |

CLEVELAND—Liberty County
⊞ CLEVELAND REGIONAL MEDICAL CENTER, 300 East Crockett Street, Zip 77327–4062, Mailing Address: P.O. Box 1688, Zip 77328–1688; tel. 281/593–1811; Deborah Hopps, Interim Chief Executive Officer (Total facility includes 11 beds in nursing home–type unit) **A**1 9 10 **F**7 8 10 12 15 16 19 21 22 27 28 30 32 34 35 37 39 40 42 44 46 49 64 65 66 71 73 **P**7 **S** Community Health Systems, Inc., Brentwood, TN
Web address: www.crmcr.com
| 32 | 10 | 93 | 3240 | 38 | 48565 | 459 | 21231 | 9162 | 290 |

CLIFTON—Bosque County
★ GOODALL–WITCHER HEALTHCARE, (Formerly Goodall–Witcher Hospital), 101 South Avenue T, Zip 76634–1897, Mailing Address: P.O. Box 549, Zip 76634–0549; tel. 254/675–8322; Jim B. Smith, President and Chief Executive Officer (Total facility includes 30 beds in nursing home–type unit) **A**9 10 **F**7 8 15 19 21 22 30 32 34 37 40 44 49 64 65 70 71 73 **P**3
Web address: www.gwhf.org
| 23 | 10 | 70 | 1349 | 43 | 6377 | 173 | 11637 | 4783 | 223 |

COLEMAN—Coleman County
COLEMAN COUNTY MEDICAL CENTER, 310 South Pecos Street, Zip 76834–4159; tel. 915/625–2135; Michael Morris, Administrator **A**9 10 **F**14 15 16 19 22 24 30 32 34 35 36 39 44 49 71 73
| 16 | 10 | 27 | 1842 | 16 | 5371 | 33 | 6208 | 2823 | 161 |

Hospital, Address, Telephone, Administrator, Approval, Facility, and Physician Codes, Health Care System, Network	Classi- fication Codes		Utilization Data					Expense (thousands) of dollars		
★ American Hospital Association (AHA) membership □ Joint Commission on Accreditation of Healthcare Organizations (JCAHO) accreditation + American Osteopathic Healthcare Association (AOHA) membership ○ American Osteopathic Association (AOA) accreditation △ Commission on Accreditation of Rehabilitation Facilities (CARF) accreditation Control codes 61, 63, 64, 71, 72 and 73 indicate hospitals listed by AOHA, but not registered by AHA. For definition of numerical codes, see page A4	Control	Service	Staffed Beds	Admissions	Census	Outpatient Visits	Births	Total	Payroll	Personnel

COLLEGE STATION—Brazos County

⊠ COLLEGE STATION MEDICAL CENTER, 1604 Rock Prairie Road, Zip 77845–8345, Mailing Address: P.O. Box 10000, Zip 77842–3500; tel. 409/764–5100; Thomas W. Jackson, Chief Executive Officer (Total facility includes 10 beds in nursing home–type unit) **A**1 5 9 10 **F**7 8 10 12 15 16 19 21 22 23 24 30 31 35 37 38 40 41 44 49 64 65 71 **P**8 **S** Triad Hospitals, Inc., Dallas, TX **Web address:** www.columbia.net	33	10	119	3186	36	47564	585	26642	11506	308

COLORADO CITY—Mitchell County

★ MITCHELL COUNTY HOSPITAL, 1543 Chestnut Street, Zip 79512–3998; tel. 915/728–3431; Roland K. Rickard, Administrator **A**9 10 **F**7 8 12 14 15 16 17 19 22 24 30 32 33 44 46 49 64 65 70 71 73 **P**5 **S** Lubbock Methodist Hospital System, Lubbock, TX	16	10	25	878	10	4552	76	9726	5336	228

COLUMBUS—Colorado County

□ COLUMBUS COMMUNITY HOSPITAL, 110 Shult Drive, Zip 78934–3010, Mailing Address: P.O. Box 865, Zip 78934–0865; tel. 409/732–2371; Robert Thomas, Administrator (Nonreporting) **A**1 9 10	23	10	36	—	—	—	—	—	—	—

COMANCHE—Comanche County

COMANCHE COMMUNITY HOSPITAL, 211 South Austin Street, Zip 76442–3224; tel. 915/356–5241; W. Evan Moore, Administrator **A**9 10 **F**15 16 19 21 22 24 30 32 33 34 35 44 49 56 65 70 71	16	10	16	601	9	32975	0	5058	2458	92

COMMERCE—Hunt County

PRESBYTERIAN HOSPITAL OF COMMERCE See Hunt Memorial Hospital District, Greenville

CONROE—Montgomery County

⊠ CONROE REGIONAL MEDICAL CENTER, (Formerly Columbia Conroe Regional Medical Center), 504 Medical Boulevard, Zip 77304, Mailing Address: P.O. Box 1538, Zip 77305–1538; tel. 409/539–1111; Russell Meyers, Chief Executive Officer (Total facility includes 12 beds in nursing home–type unit) **A**1 3 9 10 **F**4 7 8 10 11 12 14 15 16 19 21 22 26 28 29 30 34 35 37 38 39 40 41 42 43 44 45 48 49 51 60 63 64 65 67 70 71 73 74 **P**7 8 **S** Columbia/HCA Healthcare Corporation, Nashville, TN **Web address:** www.columbia.net	33	10	244	12903	151	98143	1855	72778	31222	888

CORPUS CHRISTI—Nueces County

□ CHARTER BEHAVIORAL HEALTH SYSTEM–CORPUS CHRISTI, 3126 Rodd Field Road, Zip 78414–3901; tel. 361/993–8893; John S. Lacy, Chief Executive Officer **A**1 9 10 **F**3 15 16 17 52 53 54 55 56 57 58 59 **S** Magellan Health Services, Atlanta, GA	32	22	80	1611	33	3894	0	7649	2829	71
⊠ △ CHRISTUS SPOHN HEALTH SYSTEM, (Formerly Spohn Health System), 1702 Santa Fe, Zip 78404; tel. 512/881–3400; Jake Henry, Jr., President (Total facility includes 54 beds in nursing home–type unit) **A**1 2 7 9 10 **F**4 7 8 10 11 12 14 15 16 17 19 21 22 23 24 26 28 29 30 31 32 33 34 35 37 39 40 41 42 43 44 45 46 48 49 51 52 57 60 64 65 66 67 68 71 73 74 **P**3 5 8 **S** Christus Health, San Antonio, TX	21	10	432	14263	268	130257	0	121440	46639	1639
⊠ CHRISTUS SPOHN HOSPITAL MEMORIAL, (Formerly Spohn Memorial Hospital), 2606 Hospital Boulevard, Zip 78405–1818, Mailing Address: Box 5280, Zip 78465–5280; tel. 361/902–4000; Steven R. Kamber, Vice President and Administrator **A**1 3 9 10 **F**4 7 8 9 10 11 12 14 15 16 17 18 19 20 21 22 23 24 26 27 28 29 30 31 32 33 34 35 37 39 40 42 43 44 46 49 51 52 53 54 55 56 57 58 59 60 65 66 67 69 70 71 72 73 74 **P**3 5 8 **S** Christus Health, San Antonio, TX	21	10	273	9049	151	160486	902	97675	40626	1190

COLUMBIA BAYVIEW PSYCHIATRIC CENTER See Corpus Christi Medical Center–Bayview Psychiatric Center

COLUMBIA DOCTORS REGIONAL MEDICAL CENTER See Corpus Christi Medical Center

COLUMBIA NORTHWEST HOSPITAL See Northwest Regional Hospital

⊠ CORPUS CHRISTI MEDICAL CENTER, (Formerly Columbia Doctors Regional Medical Center), 3315 South Alameda Street, Zip 78411–1883, Mailing Address: P.O. Box 3828, Zip 78463–3828; tel. 361/857–1400; Steven Woerner, Chief Executive Officer (Total facility includes 26 beds in nursing home–type unit) (Nonreporting) **A**1 9 10 **S** Columbia/HCA Healthcare Corporation, Nashville, TN **Web address:** www.columbia.net	32	10	237	—	—	—	—	—	—	—
⊠ CORPUS CHRISTI MEDICAL CENTER BAY AREA, (Formerly Columbia Bay Area Medical Center), 7101 South Padre Island Drive, Zip 78412–4999; tel. 361/985–1200; Steven Woerner, Chief Executive Officer (Total facility includes 42 beds in nursing home–type unit) **A**1 9 10 12 13 **F**2 3 4 7 8 9 10 11 12 14 15 16 17 18 19 20 21 22 23 25 27 28 29 30 31 34 35 37 38 39 40 41 42 43 44 45 46 49 52 53 54 55 56 57 58 59 60 61 64 65 66 67 68 71 72 73 74 **P**3 5 8 **S** Columbia/HCA Healthcare Corporation, Nashville, TN	32	10	534	19645	270	90929	4046	128396	50889	1580
⊠ CORPUS CHRISTI MEDICAL CENTER–BAYVIEW PSYCHIATRIC CENTER, (Formerly Columbia Bayview Psychiatric Center), 6226 Saratoga Boulevard, Zip 78414–3421; tel. 361/993–9700; Janie L. Harwood, Administrator (Nonreporting) **A**1 9 10 **S** Columbia/HCA Healthcare Corporation, Nashville, TN **Web address:** www.columbia.net	33	22	40	—	—	—	—	—	—	—
⊠ DRISCOLL CHILDREN'S HOSPITAL, 3533 South Alameda Street, Zip 78411–1785, Mailing Address: P.O. Box 6530, Zip 78466–6530; tel. 512/694–5000; Stephen Hough, Interim President and Chief Executive Officer **A**1 3 5 9 10 **F**4 5 10 12 14 15 16 17 19 21 22 25 27 28 29 30 31 32 33 34 35 38 39 41 42 43 44 45 47 49 51 53 54 58 60 63 65 66 67 68 71 72 73 74 **Web address:** www.driscollchildrens.org	23	50	188	6623	104	84537	0	70990	34772	1233

Hospital, Address, Telephone, Administrator, Approval, Facility, and Physician Codes, Health Care System, Network	Classi-fication Codes		Utilization Data					Expense (thousands) of dollars		
★ American Hospital Association (AHA) membership □ Joint Commission on Accreditation of Healthcare Organizations (JCAHO) accreditation + American Osteopathic Healthcare Association (AOHA) membership ○ American Osteopathic Association (AOA) accreditation △ Commission on Accreditation of Rehabilitation Facilities (CARF) accreditation Control codes 61, 63, 64, 71, 72 and 73 indicate hospitals listed by AOHA, but not registered by AHA. For definition of numerical codes, see page A4	Control	Service	Staffed Beds	Admissions	Census	Outpatient Visits	Births	Total	Payroll	Personnel

★ NAVAL HOSPITAL, 10651 E Street, Zip 78419–5131; tel. 512/961–2688; Captain Elizabeth R. Barker, Commanding Officer (Nonreporting) **S** Department of Navy, Washington, DC **Web address:** www.nhcc.med.navy.mil	43	10	25	—	—	—	—	—	—	—
✖ NORTHWEST REGIONAL HOSPITAL, (Formerly Columbia Northwest Hospital), 13725 Farm to Market Road 624, Zip 78410–5199; tel. 512/767–4300; Winston Borland, Chief Executive Officer (Total facility includes 7 beds in nursing home–type unit) **A**1 9 10 **F**8 15 19 20 21 22 24 25 28 31 34 35 37 41 44 48 49 63 64 65 66 67 71 **S** Columbia/HCA Healthcare Corporation, Nashville, TN	33	10	64	2600	40	203490	0	33247	15921	451
✖ △ REHABILITATION HOSPITAL OF SOUTH TEXAS, (Formerly Columbia Rehabilitation Hospital), 6226 Saratoga Boulevard, Zip 78414–3421; tel. 361/991–9690; Kevin N. Fowler, Chief Executive Officer (Total facility includes 14 beds in nursing home–type unit) **A**1 7 9 10 **F**2 3 7 8 10 12 14 15 16 19 20 21 22 25 26 27 28 29 30 31 32 34 35 37 38 39 40 41 42 43 44 45 48 49 52 53 54 55 56 57 58 59 64 65 68 71 73 74 **P**5 8 **S** Columbia/HCA Healthcare Corporation, Nashville, TN SPOHN HEALTH SYSTEM See Christus Spohn Health System SPOHN MEMORIAL HOSPITAL See Christus Spohn Hospital Memorial	32	46	40	612	26	6338	0	7894	4252	134
CORSICANA—Navarro County										
✖ NAVARRO REGIONAL HOSPITAL, 3201 West Highway 22, Zip 75110; tel. 903/654–6800; Nancy A. Byrnes, Chief Executive Officer **A**1 9 10 **F**4 7 8 10 12 14 15 16 19 20 22 23 27 28 30 31 33 35 37 39 40 41 42 44 48 49 57 64 65 71 73 **P**3 7 8 **S** Triad Hospitals, Inc., Dallas, TX **Web address:** www.columbia.net	32	10	144	4051	60	35602	537	29169	10246	339
CRANE—Crane County										
★ CRANE MEMORIAL HOSPITAL, 1310 South Alford Street, Zip 79731–3899; tel. 915/558–3555; Stan Wiley, Administrator **A**10 **F**6 8 14 15 16 20 22 27 28 29 30 31 32 33 34 39 44 51 71 72	13	10	28	168	1	7514	0	2790	1233	37
CROCKETT—Houston County										
✖ EAST TEXAS MEDICAL CENTER CROCKETT, 1100 Loop 304 East, Zip 75835–1810; tel. 409/544–2002; Nelda K. Welch, Administrator **A**1 9 10 **F**7 8 13 14 15 16 17 19 21 22 25 27 28 30 31 32 34 35 37 39 40 41 42 44 46 48 49 51 63 65 66 67 70 71 73 **P**3 7 **S** East Texas Medical Center Regional Healthcare System, Tyler, TX	23	10	68	2317	29	59601	110	15293	6632	202
CROSBYTON—Crosby County										
★ CROSBYTON CLINIC HOSPITAL, 710 West Main Street, Zip 79322–2143; tel. 806/675–2382; Michael Johnson, Administrator and Chief Executive Officer **A**9 10 **F**2 3 4 6 7 8 10 11 12 15 16 17 18 19 20 21 22 24 26 28 29 30 32 34 35 37 38 39 40 41 42 43 44 45 46 47 48 49 51 52 53 54 55 57 58 59 60 64 65 71 73 74 **P**6 **S** St. Joseph Health System, Orange, CA	23	10	35	661	9	23649	0	4164	2004	81
CUERO—De Witt County										
✖ CUERO COMMUNITY HOSPITAL, 2550 North Esplanade Street, Zip 77954–4716; tel. 512/275–6191; James E. Buckner, Jr., Administrator **A**1 10 **F**7 8 14 15 16 19 21 22 25 28 30 31 32 34 35 37 39 40 41 44 45 49 51 59 65 66 70 71 73 **Web address:** www.cuerohosp.org	16	10	49	2745	35	127001	170	20149	8557	387
DALHART—Dallam County										
□ COON MEMORIAL HOSPITAL AND HOME, 1411 Denver Avenue, Zip 79022–4809; tel. 806/249–4571; Leroy Schaffner, Chief Executive Officer **A**1 10 **F**7 17 19 26 28 32 33 34 36 40 44 45 49 70 71 73	16	10	23	540	5	13681	53	6441	2777	107
DALLAS—Dallas County										
A. WEBB ROBERTS HOSPITAL See Baylor University Medical Center AMERICAN TRANSITIONAL CARE HOSPITAL–DALLAS/FORT WORTH See SSH Dallas/Fort Worth										
★ BAYLOR CENTER FOR RESTORATIVE CARE, 3504 Swiss Avenue, Zip 75204–6224; tel. 214/820–9700; Gerry Brueckner, R.N., Executive Director **A**9 10 **F**3 4 5 7 8 10 11 12 13 14 15 16 19 21 22 23 24 25 26 29 30 31 32 33 34 35 37 38 42 43 44 45 46 47 48 49 50 52 53 54 56 57 58 59 60 61 63 64 65 66 67 68 70 71 73 74 **P**3 5 7 8 **S** Baylor Health Care System, Dallas, TX **Web address:** www.baylordallas.edu/	23	10	72	755	56	0	0	9997	4870	134
★ △ BAYLOR INSTITUTE FOR REHABILITATION, 3505 Gaston Avenue, Zip 75246–2018; tel. 214/826–7030; Laura J. Lycan, Executive Director (Nonreporting) **A**3 7 10 **S** Baylor Health Care System, Dallas, TX **Web address:** www.bhcs.com	21	46	92	—	—	—	—	—	—	—
✖ BAYLOR UNIVERSITY MEDICAL CENTER, (Includes A. Webb Roberts Hospital; Erik and Margaret Jonsson Hospital; George W. Truett Memorial Hospital; Karl and Esther Hoblitzelle Memorial Hospital), 3500 Gaston Avenue, Zip 75246–2088; tel. 214/820–0111; M. Tim Parris, Executive Vice President and Chief Operating Officer **A**1 2 3 5 8 9 10 **F**3 4 5 7 8 10 11 12 13 15 17 18 19 20 21 22 23 24 25 26 28 29 30 31 32 33 34 35 36 37 38 39 40 41 42 43 44 45 46 48 49 51 52 54 55 56 57 58 59 60 61 63 64 65 66 67 68 70 71 72 73 74 **P**1 **S** Baylor Health Care System, Dallas, TX **Web address:** www.bhcs.com	23	10	891	35864	580	392654	4323	419448	156285	4709
✖ CHARLTON METHODIST HOSPITAL, 3500 West Wheatland Road, Zip 75237, Mailing Address: Box 225357, Zip 75222–5357; tel. 214/947–7500; David L. Knocke, CHE, Executive Director **A**1 3 9 10 **S** Methodist Hospitals of Dallas, Dallas, TX **Web address:** www.mhd.com	23	10	134	8962	110	—	1655	—	—	—

Hospital, Address, Telephone, Administrator, Approval, Facility, and Physician Codes, Health Care System, Network	Classi-fication Codes		Utilization Data					Expense (thousands) of dollars		
★ American Hospital Association (AHA) membership □ Joint Commission on Accreditation of Healthcare Organizations (JCAHO) accreditation + American Osteopathic Healthcare Association (AOHA) membership ○ American Osteopathic Association (AOA) accreditation △ Commission on Accreditation of Rehabilitation Facilities (CARF) accreditation Control codes 61, 63, 64, 71, 72 and 73 indicate hospitals listed by AOHA, but not registered by AHA. For definition of numerical codes, see page A4	Control	Service	Staffed Beds	Admissions	Census	Outpatient Visits	Births	Total	Payroll	Personnel

	Control	Service	Staffed Beds	Admissions	Census	Outpatient Visits	Births	Total	Payroll	Personnel
⊠ CHILDREN'S MEDICAL CENTER OF DALLAS, 1935 Motor Street, Zip 75235–7794; tel. 214/456–7000; George D. Farr, President and Chief Executive Officer **A**1 2 3 5 8 9 10 **F**4 10 12 13 14 15 16 17 18 19 20 21 22 25 27 28 30 31 32 34 35 39 41 42 43 44 45 46 47 49 51 52 53 54 55 56 58 59 63 65 66 67 68 70 71 72 73 **Web address:** www.childrens.com	23	50	224	12353	162	249714	0	185373	90722	2220
COLUMBIA MEDICAL CENTER–DALLAS SOUTHWEST See Dallas Southwest Medical Center										
DALLAS COUNTY HOSPITAL DISTRICT, PARKLAND HEALTH AND HOSPITAL SYSTEM See Parkland Health and Hospital System										
⊠ ○ DALLAS SOUTHWEST MEDICAL CENTER, (Formerly Columbia Medical Center–Dallas Southwest), 2929 South Hampton Road, Zip 75224–3026; tel. 214/330–4611; James B. Warren, Chief Executive Officer **A**1 9 10 11 12 13 **F**1 2 3 4 5 6 7 8 9 10 11 12 13 14 15 16 17 18 19 20 21 22 23 24 25 26 27 28 29 30 31 32 33 34 35 36 37 38 39 40 41 42 43 44 45 46 47 48 49 50 51 52 53 54 55 56 57 58 59 60 61 62 63 64 65 66 67 68 70 71 72 73 74 **P**1 5 7 **S** Columbia/HCA Healthcare Corporation, Nashville, TN	32	10	107	2865	31	33079	340	28600	9216	245
⊠ DOCTORS HOSPITAL OF DALLAS, 9440 Poppy Drive, Zip 75218–3694; tel. 214/324–6100; Robert S. Freymuller, Chief Executive Officer (Total facility includes 25 beds in nursing home–type unit) **A**1 9 10 **F**2 4 7 8 9 10 12 14 15 16 17 19 20 21 22 23 26 27 28 29 31 32 33 34 35 37 38 40 41 42 43 44 45 46 47 48 49 52 55 56 57 58 59 60 63 64 65 66 67 70 71 72 73 74 **P**5 7 **S** TENET Healthcare Corporation, Santa Barbara, CA **Web address:** www.tenethealth.com/doctorsdallas	32	10	204	8063	125	82135	474	58240	23415	641
ERIK AND MARGARET JONSSON HOSPITAL See Baylor University Medical Center										
GEORGE W. TRUETT MEMORIAL HOSPITAL See Baylor University Medical Center										
GREEN OAKS HOSPITAL, 7808 Clodus Fields Drive, Zip 75251–2206; tel. 972/991–9504; Dennis Wade, Administrator **A**9 **F**2 3 12 14 15 16 34 52 53 54 56 57 58 59 65 67 **P**8 **S** Columbia/HCA Healthcare Corporation, Nashville, TN **Web address:** www.koala.com	32	22	106	5250	70	14632	0	15111	7752	227
□ △ HEALTHSOUTH MEDICAL CENTER, 2124 Research Row, Zip 75235–2504; tel. 214/904–6100; Robert M. Smart, Area Manager and Chief Executive Officer **A**1 7 10 **F**12 14 16 19 24 25 27 28 33 34 35 39 41 42 44 45 46 48 49 54 65 66 67 71 73 **S** HEALTHSOUTH Corporation, Birmingham, AL	33	46	106	1156	51	—	0	15533	7689	220
KARL AND ESTHER HOBLITZELLE MEMORIAL HOSPITAL See Baylor University Medical Center										
★ MARY SHIELS HOSPITAL, 3515 Howell Street, Zip 75204–2895; tel. 214/443–3000; Rob Shiels, Administrator **A**9 10 **F**34 44 45 46 49	33	10	15	335	2	2429	0	6012	2809	62
⊠ △ MEDICAL CITY DALLAS HOSPITAL, 7777 Forest Lane, Zip 75230–2598; tel. 972/566–7000; Stephen Corbeil, President and Chief Executive Officer (Total facility includes 34 beds in nursing home–type unit) **A**1 2 7 9 10 **F**3 4 7 8 10 11 12 14 16 17 18 19 20 21 22 23 26 28 29 30 31 33 34 35 37 38 39 40 41 42 43 44 45 46 47 48 49 50 51 53 54 55 56 57 58 59 60 61 63 64 65 66 67 68 71 73 74 **P**5 7 **S** Columbia/HCA Healthcare Corporation, Nashville, TN **Web address:** www.columbia.net	33	10	511	21855	313	130642	3851	237566	81063	2791
⊠ △ METHODIST MEDICAL CENTER, 1441 North Beckley Avenue, Zip 75203–1201, Mailing Address: Box 655999, Zip 75265–5999; tel. 214/947–8181; Kim Hollon, FACHE, Executive Director **A**1 2 3 5 7 8 9 10 **F**4 7 8 10 11 12 14 15 16 17 19 21 22 23 24 25 26 27 28 29 30 31 34 35 37 38 39 40 41 42 43 44 45 46 48 49 51 60 61 63 64 65 66 67 68 70 71 73 74 **P**1 7 **S** Methodist Hospitals of Dallas, Dallas, TX **Web address:** www.mhd.com	23	10	362	15195	275	135962	2113	144613	62210	1699
□ △ NORTH DALLAS REHABILITATION HOSPITAL, 8383 Meadow Road, Zip 75231–3798; tel. 214/891–0880; Tricia Heath, R.N., Administrator and Chief Executive Officer (Nonreporting) **A**1 7 10	33	46	36	—	—	—	—	—	—	—
OUR CHILDREN'S HOUSE AT BAYLOR, (Formerly Pediatric Center for Restorative Care), 3301 Swiss Avenue, Zip 75204–6219; tel. 214/820–9838; Geraldine Brueckner, Administrator **A**10 **F**3 4 7 8 9 10 11 12 13 15 16 17 19 21 22 23 24 25 26 27 28 29 30 31 32 33 35 37 38 39 41 42 43 44 45 46 47 50 53 54 55 56 57 59 61 63 64 65 66 67 68 70 71 73 74 **P**1 3 5 7 **Web address:** www.baylordallas.edu/	23	50	17	163	15	12035	0	5214	3078	73
⊠ PARKLAND HEALTH AND HOSPITAL SYSTEM, (Formerly Dallas County Hospital District, Parkland Health and Hospital System), 5201 Harry Hines Boulevard, Zip 75235–7731; tel. 214/590–8000; Ron J. Anderson, M.D., President and Chief Executive Officer **A**1 2 3 5 8 9 10 **F**4 5 7 8 9 10 11 12 14 15 16 17 18 19 20 21 22 23 24 25 26 27 28 29 30 31 34 35 37 38 39 40 41 42 43 44 45 46 48 49 51 52 54 55 56 57 58 59 60 61 63 65 67 68 70 71 72 73 74	16	10	688	38858	521	892598	13480	576699	208568	7295
PEDIATRIC CENTER FOR RESTORATIVE CARE See Our Children's House at Baylor										
⊠ △ PRESBYTERIAN HOSPITAL OF DALLAS, 8200 Walnut Hill Lane, Zip 75231–4402; tel. 214/345–6789; Mark H. Merrill, Executive Director (Total facility includes 78 beds in nursing home–type unit) **A**1 2 3 5 7 9 10 **F**1 3 4 5 6 7 8 10 11 12 13 14 15 16 17 18 19 20 21 22 23 24 25 26 27 28 29 30 31 32 33 34 35 36 37 38 39 40 41 42 43 44 45 46 48 49 51 52 53 54 55 56 57 58 59 60 61 62 63 64 65 67 68 71 72 73 74 **P**2 5 6 **S** Texas Health Resources, Irving, TX **Web address:** www.texashealth.org	23	10	667	25660	403	280666	5002	281614	109174	3065

Hospital, Address, Telephone, Administrator, Approval, Facility, and Physician Codes, Health Care System, Network	Classi-fication Codes		Utilization Data					Expense (thousands) of dollars		
★ American Hospital Association (AHA) membership ☐ Joint Commission on Accreditation of Healthcare Organizations (JCAHO) accreditation + American Osteopathic Healthcare Association (AOHA) membership ○ American Osteopathic Association (AOA) accreditation △ Commission on Accreditation of Rehabilitation Facilities (CARF) accreditation Control codes 61, 63, 64, 71, 72 and 73 indicate hospitals listed by AOHA, but not registered by AHA. For definition of numerical codes, see page A4	Control	Service	Staffed Beds	Admissions	Census	Outpatient Visits	Births	Total	Payroll	Personnel
☒ RHD MEMORIAL MEDICAL CENTER, Seven Medical Parkway, Zip 75381, Mailing Address: P.O. Box 819094, Zip 75381–9094; tel. 972/247–1000; Craig E. Sims, President and Chief Executive Officer **A**1 10 **F**4 7 8 10 12 14 15 16 17 19 20 21 22 23 25 26 28 29 30 32 33 34 35 37 39 40 41 42 43 44 45 46 49 54 61 63 65 66 67 70 71 73 74 **P**5 **S** TENET Healthcare Corporation, Santa Barbara, CA **Web address:** www.tenethealth.com	33	10	150	4175	50	53748	480	44526	16902	420
☐ SSH DALLAS/FORT WORTH, (Formerly American Transitional Care Hospital–Dallas/Fort Worth), (LONG TERM ACUTE CARE), 10 Medical Parkway, Suite 205, Zip 75234; tel. 972/488–9167; LouAnn O. Mathews, Administrator **A**1 10 **F**12 19 22 31 35 65 71	33	49	36	149	11	0	0	5460	1807	37
☒ ST. PAUL MEDICAL CENTER, 5909 Harry Hines Boulevard, Zip 75235–6285; tel. 214/879–1000; Frank Tiedemann, President and Chief Executive Officer **A**1 2 3 5 8 9 10 **F**1 3 4 5 7 8 10 11 12 13 15 16 17 18 19 20 21 22 23 24 25 26 27 28 29 30 31 32 33 34 35 37 38 39 40 41 42 43 44 45 46 48 49 50 51 52 53 54 55 56 57 58 59 60 61 62 63 64 65 66 67 68 70 71 73 74 **P**2 5 7 **S** Texas Health Resources, Irving, TX	21	10	348	13362	213	128600	2401	143818	57416	1658
☒ TEXAS SCOTTISH RITE HOSPITAL FOR CHILDREN, 2222 Welborn Street, Zip 75219–9982, Mailing Address: Box 190567, Zip 75219–0567; tel. 214/559–5000; J. C. Montgomery, Jr., President **A**1 3 5 **F**5 12 19 20 34 39 41 45 46 65 67 71 73 **P**6	23	57	64	2331	26	39083	0	—	—	592
☐ TIMBERLAWN MENTAL HEALTH SYSTEM, 4600 Samuell Boulevard, Zip 75228–6800, Mailing Address: P.O. Box 151489, Zip 75315–1489; tel. 214/381–7181; Debra S. Lowrance, R.N., Chief Executive Officer and Managing Director **A**1 9 10 **F**2 3 12 15 17 22 25 34 46 48 52 53 54 55 56 57 58 59 65 67 **S** Universal Health Services, Inc., King of Prussia, PA **Web address:** www.timberlawn.com	33	22	124	2600	59	21903	0	11688	4286	183
○ TRI-CITY HEALTH CENTRE, 7525 Scyene Road, Zip 75227–5677; tel. 214/381–7171; Gerald D. Neal, Chief Executive Officer **A**10 11 13 **F**3 7 8 12 14 15 16 17 19 21 22 25 26 27 28 30 34 35 37 39 40 41 42 44 46 49 52 57 58 68 70 72 73	23	10	131	3222	45	23876	427	32173	10076	457
☐ VENCOR HOSPITAL – DALLAS, (LONG TERM ACUTE CARE), 9525 Greenville Avenue, Zip 75243; tel. 214/355–2600; Dorothy J. Elford, Executive Director and Administrator **A**1 10 **F**19 22 35 37 65 71 **S** Vencor, Incorporated, Louisville, KY	32	49	76	453	48	8	0	14218	6962	246
☒ VETERANS AFFAIRS NORTH TEXAS HEALTH CARE SYSTEM, (Includes Sam Rayburn Memorial Veterans Center, 1201 East Ninth Street, Bonham, Zip 75418–4091; tel. 903/583–2111), 4500 South Lancaster Road, Zip 75216–7167; tel. 214/742–8387; Alan G. Harper, Director (Total facility includes 240 beds in nursing home–type unit) (Nonreporting) **A**1 2 3 5 8 **S** Department of Veterans Affairs, Washington, DC	45	10	1031	—	—	—	—	—	—	—
☐ △ ZALE LIPSHY UNIVERSITY HOSPITAL, 5151 Harry Hines Boulevard, Zip 75235–7786; tel. 214/590–3000; Robert B. Smith, President and Chief Executive Officer **A**1 3 5 7 8 9 10 **F**4 8 10 12 14 15 19 22 28 29 30 32 34 35 37 41 42 43 44 45 46 48 52 54 56 57 59 60 64 65 67 71 73	23	10	147	5727	112	11161	0	86452	29759	761
DE LEON—Comanche County										
★ DE LEON HOSPITAL, 407 South Texas Avenue, Zip 76444–1947, Mailing Address: P.O. Box 319, Zip 76444–0319; tel. 254/893–2011; Michael K. Hare, Administrator **A**9 10 **F**8 14 15 19 22 28 30 32 33 34 37 42 44 49 58 65 71 73 **S** Brim Healthcare, Inc., Brentwood, TN	16	10	14	908	12	18913	0	5265	2269	78
DE SOTO—Dallas County										
☐ CEDARS HOSPITAL, 2000 North Old Hickory Trail, Zip 75115–2242; tel. 972/298–7323; Don P. Johnson, Administrator **A**1 10 **F**2 3 26 34 45 52 53 54 55 56 57 58 59 65 **Web address:** www.lakeviewsystem.com	33	22	76	723	22	2274	0	6621	2468	95
☐ HAVEN HOSPITAL, 800 Kirnwood Drive, Zip 75115–2092; tel. 972/709–3700; Sheila C. Kelly, R.N., MS, Chief Executive Officer **A**1 10 **F**2 3 15 16 52 53 56 57 58 59 **S** Magellan Health Services, Atlanta, GA	32	22	27	905	19	5212	0	5988	2950	74
DECATUR—Wise County										
☒ DECATUR COMMUNITY HOSPITAL, 2000 South FM 51, Zip 76234–9295; tel. 940/627–5921; Stephen M. Summers, CPA, Chief Executive Officer (Total facility includes 10 beds in nursing home–type unit) **A**1 9 10 **F**7 8 12 14 15 16 19 22 24 28 32 37 40 41 44 49 63 64 65 66 67 70 71 **Web address:** www.decaturcommunity.com	16	10	69	3431	36	71523	381	17409	8953	312
DEL RIO—Val Verde County										
☒ VAL VERDE REGIONAL MEDICAL CENTER, 801 Bedell Avenue, Zip 78840–4185, Mailing Address: P.O. Box 1527, Zip 78840–1527; tel. 830/775–8566; Don Griffin, Chief Executive Officer **A**1 9 10 **F**7 8 10 12 15 16 19 21 22 28 30 32 33 34 35 36 37 39 40 44 45 46 49 51 65 70 71 73 74 **P**5	16	10	76	3878	39	49866	946	11154	9896	386
DENISON—Grayson County										
☒ TEXOMA HEALTHCARE SYSTEM, 1000 Memorial Drive, Zip 75020–2035, Mailing Address: P.O. Box 890, Zip 75021–9988; tel. 903/416–4000; Arthur L. Hohenberger, FACHE, President and Chief Executive Officer **A**1 2 9 10 **F**3 4 7 8 10 11 12 14 15 16 17 19 21 22 23 25 26 27 28 29 30 32 33 34 35 37 39 40 41 42 43 44 45 46 48 49 51 52 53 54 56 57 58 59 60 65 66 67 71 73 74 **P**3 5	23	10	205	8110	116	53492	428	74741	30891	1172

Hospital, Address, Telephone, Administrator, Approval, Facility, and Physician Codes, Health Care System, Network	Classification Codes		Utilization Data					Expense (thousands) of dollars		
★ American Hospital Association (AHA) membership □ Joint Commission on Accreditation of Healthcare Organizations (JCAHO) accreditation + American Osteopathic Healthcare Association (AOHA) membership ○ American Osteopathic Association (AOA) accreditation △ Commission on Accreditation of Rehabilitation Facilities (CARF) accreditation Control codes 61, 63, 64, 71, 72 and 73 indicate hospitals listed by AOHA, but not registered by AHA. For definition of numerical codes, see page A4	Control	Service	Staffed Beds	Admissions	Census	Outpatient Visits	Births	Total	Payroll	Personnel

DENTON—Denton County

Hospital	Control	Service	Staffed Beds	Admissions	Census	Outpatient Visits	Births	Total	Payroll	Personnel
⊞ DENTON COMMUNITY HOSPITAL, 207 North Bonnie Brae Street, Zip 76201–3798; tel. 940/898–7000; Timothy Charles, Chief Executive Officer **A**1 9 10 **F**7 8 10 12 14 16 17 19 21 22 28 30 31 32 33 34 35 37 39 40 41 42 44 49 56 63 65 66 67 71 73 74 **P**5 **S** NetCare Health Systems, Inc., Nashville, TN **Web address:** www.dentonhospital.com	33	10	110	5623	62	35882	920	30497	12571	409
⊞ DENTON REGIONAL MEDICAL CENTER, 4405 North Interstate 35, Zip 76207–3499; tel. 940/566–4000; Bob Haley, Chief Executive Officer (Total facility includes 25 beds in nursing home–type unit) **A**1 9 10 **F**4 7 8 10 12 16 19 20 21 22 23 28 30 33 34 35 36 37 40 41 42 43 44 48 49 52 57 59 60 64 65 71 73 74 **S** Columbia/HCA Healthcare Corporation, Nashville, TN	32	10	271	6381	100	71663	851	49237	20500	634

DENVER CITY—Yoakum County

Hospital	Control	Service	Staffed Beds	Admissions	Census	Outpatient Visits	Births	Total	Payroll	Personnel
★ YOAKUM COUNTY HOSPITAL, 412 Mustang Avenue, Zip 79323–2750, Mailing Address: P.O. Drawer 1130, Zip 79323–1130; tel. 806/592–5484; Edward Rodgers, Chief Executive Officer **A**9 10 **F**6 12 15 17 28 29 30 34 37 39 40 44 49 65 70 71 73 **P**5 **S** St. Joseph Health System, Orange, CA	13	10	24	416	3	5364	65	4406	1407	59

DIMMITT—Castro County

Hospital	Control	Service	Staffed Beds	Admissions	Census	Outpatient Visits	Births	Total	Payroll	Personnel
PLAINS MEMORIAL HOSPITAL, 310 West Halsell Street, Zip 79027–1846, Mailing Address: P.O. Box 278, Zip 79027–0278; tel. 806/647–2191; Joseph F. Sloan, CHE, Chief Executive Officer **A**9 10 **F**8 12 14 15 17 19 22 28 32 33 36 39 40 41 44 49 52 57 58 59 65 70 71 73	16	10	36	407	7	55216	40	7288	3294	173

DUMAS—Moore County

Hospital	Control	Service	Staffed Beds	Admissions	Census	Outpatient Visits	Births	Total	Payroll	Personnel
⊞ MOORE COUNTY HOSPITAL DISTRICT, 224 East Second Street, Zip 79029–3808; tel. 806/935–7171; Scott R. Brown, Administrator and Chief Executive Officer (Total facility includes 60 beds in nursing home–type unit) **A**1 9 10 **F**6 7 8 14 15 16 17 19 20 22 26 27 28 30 31 32 33 35 36 37 39 40 41 44 45 46 49 51 65 67 69 70 71 72 73 74 **P**8	16	10	118	1716	78	26757	439	13873	6124	254

EAGLE LAKE—Colorado County

Hospital	Control	Service	Staffed Beds	Admissions	Census	Outpatient Visits	Births	Total	Payroll	Personnel
□ RICE MEDICAL CENTER, 600 South Austin Road, Zip 77434–3298, Mailing Address: P.O. Box 277, Zip 77434–0277; tel. 409/234–5571; David N. Keith, Chief Executive Officer **A**1 10 **F**2 7 8 14 15 16 19 22 24 26 28 30 32 35 37 40 44 49 59 65 70 71 73 **P**6	16	10	32	688	7	15753	109	6068	2339	94

EAGLE PASS—Maverick County

Hospital	Control	Service	Staffed Beds	Admissions	Census	Outpatient Visits	Births	Total	Payroll	Personnel
★ FORT DUNCAN MEDICAL CENTER, 350 South Adams Street, Zip 78852; tel. 830/773–5321; Don Spaulding, Administrator and Chief Executive Officer **A**6 9 10 **F**8 15 16 17 19 22 25 28 30 32 34 35 37 40 44 45 46 49 65 70 71 73 **S** Quorum Health Group/Quorum Health Resources, Inc., Brentwood, TN	16	10	69	4508	46	26914	961	23495	8604	288

EASTLAND—Eastland County

Hospital	Control	Service	Staffed Beds	Admissions	Census	Outpatient Visits	Births	Total	Payroll	Personnel
EASTLAND MEMORIAL HOSPITAL, 304 South Daugherty Street, Zip 76448–2609, Mailing Address: P.O. Box 897, Zip 76448–0897; tel. 254/629–2601; John Yeary, Administrator **A**9 10 **F**8 14 15 16 19 21 22 24 26 28 29 30 32 34 40 44 48 49 70 71	16	10	38	1238	12	21450	126	6266	3162	151

EDEN—Concho County

Hospital	Control	Service	Staffed Beds	Admissions	Census	Outpatient Visits	Births	Total	Payroll	Personnel
CONCHO COUNTY HOSPITAL, 614 Eaker Street, Zip 76837, Mailing Address: Drawer L, Zip 76837; tel. 915/869–5911; Joe Brosig, Administrator **A**9 10 **F**1 2 3 4 5 6 7 8 9 10 11 12 13 14 16 17 18 19 20 21 22 23 24 25 26 27 28 29 30 31 33 34 35 36 37 38 39 40 41 42 43 44 47 48 49 50 51 52 53 54 55 56 57 58 59 60 61 62 63 64 65 66 67 69 70 71 72 73 74 **P**5	16	10	20	290	4	10465	0	1695	955	37

EDINBURG—Hidalgo County

Hospital	Control	Service	Staffed Beds	Admissions	Census	Outpatient Visits	Births	Total	Payroll	Personnel
⊞ EDINBURG REGIONAL MEDICAL CENTER, (Formerly Edinburg Hospital), 333 West Freddy Gonzalez Drive, Zip 78539–6199; tel. 956/383–6211; Chris Smolik, Chief Executive Officer **A**1 9 10 **F**1 4 6 7 8 10 12 14 15 16 17 19 21 22 23 24 27 28 29 30 34 35 37 39 40 41 42 43 44 45 46 48 49 51 52 53 54 55 56 57 58 59 60 61 63 65 66 67 70 71 73 74 **P**1 3 7 **S** Universal Health Services, Inc., King of Prussia, PA **Web address:** www.uhsermc.com	33	10	163	7048	94	—	1989	41337	17022	594

EDNA—Jackson County

Hospital	Control	Service	Staffed Beds	Admissions	Census	Outpatient Visits	Births	Total	Payroll	Personnel
JACKSON COUNTY HOSPITAL, 1013 South Wells Street, Zip 77957–4098; tel. 361/782–5241; Marcella V. Henke, Administrator and Chief Executive Officer **A**9 10 **F**14 15 16 22 26 32 33 34 36 39 44 70	16	10	31	397	5	—	0	4958	1599	62

EL CAMPO—Wharton County

Hospital	Control	Service	Staffed Beds	Admissions	Census	Outpatient Visits	Births	Total	Payroll	Personnel
□ EL CAMPO MEMORIAL HOSPITAL, 303 Sandy Corner Road, Zip 77437–9535; tel. 409/543–6251; Steve Gularte, Administrator **A**1 9 10 **F**7 12 15 16 17 19 21 22 24 26 27 28 29 30 32 34 37 39 41 44 45 46 49 51 59 65 66 67 71	16	10	42	788	10	15363	0	9521	3528	140

EL PASO—El Paso County

Hospital	Control	Service	Staffed Beds	Admissions	Census	Outpatient Visits	Births	Total	Payroll	Personnel
★ COLUMBIA BEHAVIORAL CENTER, 1155 Idaho Street, Zip 79902–1699; tel. 915/544–4000; Serena Pickman, Director **A**9 **F**2 3 4 7 8 10 11 12 14 15 16 18 19 20 21 22 23 24 25 26 27 28 30 31 33 34 35 37 38 40 42 43 44 45 46 47 48 49 52 53 54 55 56 57 58 59 60 63 64 65 66 67 71 73 74 **P**6 **S** Columbia/HCA Healthcare Corporation, Nashville, TN **Web address:** www.columbia–elp.com	32	22	37	864	10	4091	0	5175	2187	47
⊞ COLUMBIA MEDICAL CENTER WEST, 1801 North Oregon Street, Zip 79902–3591; tel. 915/521–1200; Hank Hernandez, Chief Executive Officer (Total facility includes 18 beds in nursing home–type unit) **A**1 2 9 10 **F**2 3 4 7 8 10 11 12 14 15 16 18 19 20 21 22 23 24 25 26 28 30 31 32 33 34 35 37 38 40 41 42 43 44 46 47 48 49 51 52 53 54 55 56 57 58 59 60 63 64 65 66 67 69 71 73 74 **P**6 **S** Columbia/HCA Healthcare Corporation, Nashville, TN **Web address:** www.columbia–hca.com	32	10	221	8818	123	69439	1432	78196	29407	815

Hospital, Address, Telephone, Administrator, Approval, Facility, and Physician Codes, Health Care System, Network	Classi-fication Codes		Utilization Data					Expense (thousands) of dollars		
★ American Hospital Association (AHA) membership □ Joint Commission on Accreditation of Healthcare Organizations (JCAHO) accreditation + American Osteopathic Healthcare Association (AOHA) membership ○ American Osteopathic Association (AOA) accreditation △ Commission on Accreditation of Rehabilitation Facilities (CARF) accreditation Control codes 61, 63, 64, 71, 72 and 73 indicate hospitals listed by AOHA, but not registered by AHA. For definition of numerical codes, see page A4	Control	Service	Staffed Beds	Admissions	Census	Outpatient Visits	Births	Total	Payroll	Personnel

	Control	Service	Staffed Beds	Admissions	Census	Outpatient Visits	Births	Total	Payroll	Personnel
✇ COLUMBIA MEDICAL CENTER–EAST, 10301 Gateway West, Zip 79925–7798; tel. 915/595–9000; Douglas A. Matney, Senior Vice President Operations (Total facility includes 29 beds in nursing home–type unit) **A**1 9 10 **F**2 3 4 7 8 10 11 12 15 16 17 18 19 21 22 23 24 25 26 27 28 29 30 31 32 33 34 35 37 38 39 40 41 42 43 44 45 46 47 48 49 52 53 54 55 56 57 58 59 60 63 64 65 66 67 68 71 73 74 **P**5 7 **S** Columbia/HCA Healthcare Corporation, Nashville, TN **Web address:** www.columbia wtd.com	32	10	299	14232	211	107096	2355	103005	40503	1005
★ △ COLUMBIA REHABILITATION HOSPITAL, 300 Waymore Drive, Zip 77902–1628; tel. 915/577–2600; Cristina Huerta, Administrative Director (Nonreporting) **A**7 **S** Columbia/HCA Healthcare Corporation, Nashville, TN	33	46	40	—	—	—	—	—	—	—
✇ PROVIDENCE MEMORIAL HOSPITAL, 2001 North Oregon Street, Zip 79902–3368; tel. 915/577–6011; L. Marcus Fry, Jr., Chief Executive Officer (Total facility includes 64 beds in nursing home–type unit) **A**1 2 5 9 10 **F**4 7 8 10 11 12 15 16 17 19 20 21 22 25 28 29 30 33 34 35 36 37 38 39 40 41 42 43 44 45 46 47 49 60 61 63 64 65 67 68 70 71 73 74 **P**1 7 **S** TENET Healthcare Corporation, Santa Barbara, CA	32	10	379	16250	241	174164	3180	147378	59647	1584
□ R. E. THOMASON GENERAL HOSPITAL, 4815 Alameda Avenue, Zip 79905–2794; Mailing Address: P.O. Box 20009, Zip 79998–0009; tel. 915/544–1200; Pete T. Duarte, Chief Executive Officer **A**1 2 3 5 9 10 **F**4 8 10 14 15 16 17 19 20 21 22 23 25 27 28 30 31 33 35 37 38 39 40 41 42 43 44 45 46 49 51 54 60 61 63 65 66 68 70 71 72 73	16	10	267	13083	184	421742	5081	124858	44287	1368
✇ △ RIO VISTA PHYSICAL REHABILITATION HOSPITAL, 1740 Curie Drive, Zip 79902–2900; tel. 915/544–3399; Patsy A. Parker, Administrator and Chief Executive Officer (Total facility includes 27 beds in nursing home–type unit) **A**1 7 10 **F**4 5 7 8 9 10 11 12 14 15 16 17 19 21 22 25 27 28 30 34 35 37 38 40 41 42 43 44 46 47 48 49 60 63 64 65 68 71 73 74 **P**3 5 7 8 **S** TENET Healthcare Corporation, Santa Barbara, CA	33	46	100	1521	55	35275	0	20383	11649	322
✇ SIERRA MEDICAL CENTER, 1625 Medical Center Drive, Zip 79902–5044; tel. 915/747–4000; Thomas E. Casaday, President and Chief Executive Officer **A**1 2 9 10 **F**4 7 8 10 11 12 15 16 17 19 20 21 22 28 29 30 31 33 34 35 36 37 38 39 40 41 42 43 44 45 46 47 48 49 60 63 64 65 66 67 68 71 73 74 **P**7 8 **S** TENET Healthcare Corporation, Santa Barbara, CA	32	10	328	12333	165	106116	2486	132736	41955	1252
□ SOUTHWESTERN GENERAL HOSPITAL, 1221 North Cotton, Zip 79902–3096; tel. 915/496–9600; Stephen J. Campbell, Administrator **A**1 9 10 **F**7 8 15 16 17 19 21 22 28 30 34 35 37 40 44 49 63 65 70 71 74	32	10	102	1809	19	22713	169	13532	6174	213
✇ WILLIAM BEAUMONT ARMY MEDICAL CENTER, 5005 North Piedras Street, Zip 79920–5001; tel. 915/569–2121; Colonel Jimmy Sanders, Chief of Staff (Nonreporting) **A**1 2 3 5 **S** Department of the Army, Office of the Surgeon General, Falls Church, VA	42	10	209	—	—	—	—	—	—	—
ELDORADO—Schleicher County										
SCHLEICHER COUNTY MEDICAL CENTER, 305 Mertzon Highway, Zip 76936, Mailing Address: Box V, Zip 76936; tel. 915/853–2507; Ann Fagan–Cook, Administrator **A**9 **F**22 26 28 33 39 41 49 65 70 73 **P**6	16	10	16	62	5	4404	0	1429	709	40
ELECTRA—Wichita County										
ELECTRA MEMORIAL HOSPITAL, 1207 South Bailey Street, Zip 76360–3221, Mailing Address: P.O. Box 1112, Zip 76360–1112; tel. 940/495–3981; Jan A. Reed, CPA, Administrator and Chief Executive Officer **A**9 10 **F**8 13 15 19 21 22 26 28 30 32 34 41 44 49 51 65 66 68 70 71 73 74	16	10	23	628	7	14749	0	3399	1710	64
FAIRFIELD—Freestone County										
EAST TEXAS MEDICAL CENTER–FAIRFIELD, (Formerly Fairfield Memorial Hospital), 125 Newman Street, Zip 75840–1499; tel. 903/389–2121; David Kuhn, Administrator **A**9 10 **F**7 15 16 19 21 22 28 30 37 40 44 70 71 **P**7 **S** East Texas Medical Center Regional Healthcare System, Tyler, TX	23	10	19	274	6	22974	23	2643	1044	86
FLORESVILLE—Wilson County										
WILSON MEMORIAL HOSPITAL, 1301 Hospital Boulevard, Zip 78114–2798; tel. 830/393–3122; Robert Duffield, Administrator **A**9 10 **F**8 12 14 16 17 19 21 22 28 29 30 32 33 34 39 44 45 46 49 65 66 67 71 73	16	10	30	745	10	43874	0	6255	2847	103
FORT HOOD—Bell County										
✇ DARNALL ARMY COMMUNITY HOSPITAL, 36000 Darnall Loop, Zip 76544–4752; tel. 254/288–8000; Colonel Kenneth L. Farmer, Jr., Commander (Nonreporting) **A**1 2 3 5 **S** Department of the Army, Office of the Surgeon General, Falls Church, VA	42	10	169	—	—	—	—	—	—	—
FORT STOCKTON—Pecos County										
✇ PECOS COUNTY MEMORIAL HOSPITAL, Sanderson Highway, Zip 79735, Mailing Address: P.O. Box 1648, Zip 79735–1648; tel. 915/336–2241; David B. Shaw, Administrator and Chief Executive Officer **A**1 9 10 **F**7 8 12 13 14 15 16 17 19 22 24 27 28 29 30 32 34 39 40 44 45 46 49 51 61 65 67 70 71 72 73	13	10	31	841	10	33759	191	10122	4562	162
FORT WORTH—Tarrant County										
□ ALL SAINTS EPISCOPAL HOSPITAL OF FORT WORTH, 1400 Eighth Avenue, Zip 76104–4192, Mailing Address: P.O. Box 31, Zip 76101–0031; tel. 817/926–2544; James P. Schuessler, President and Chief Executive Officer **A**1 2 9 10 **F**3 4 7 8 10 11 12 14 15 16 17 19 21 22 24 25 26 28 29 30 32 33 34 35 37 38 39 40 41 42 43 44 45 46 48 49 52 54 55 56 57 58 59 60 61 64 65 66 67 69 71 72 73 74 **P**6 7 8	23	10	269	12390	175	58588	1302	106060	41035	1237
ALL SAINTS HOSPITAL–CITYVIEW, 7100 Oakmont Boulevard, Zip 76132–3999; tel. 817/346–5870; Deborah P. Allbach, R.N., Chief Executive Officer **F**1 2 3 4 7 8 10 11 12 13 14 15 16 17 19 20 21 22 23 24 26 28 29 30 32 33 34 35 37 38 39 40 41 42 43 44 45 46 48 49 51 52 53 54 55 56 57 58 59 60 63 64 65 66 67 71 72 73 74 **P**5 6 7 **Web address:** www.allsaints.com	23	10	43	1851	15	27821	657	14310	5399	142

Hospital, Address, Telephone, Administrator, Approval, Facility, and Physician Codes, Health Care System, Network	Classification Codes		Utilization Data					Expense (thousands) of dollars		
	Control	Service	Staffed Beds	Admissions	Census	Outpatient Visits	Births	Total	Payroll	Personnel

★ American Hospital Association (AHA) membership
□ Joint Commission on Accreditation of Healthcare Organizations (JCAHO) accreditation
+ American Osteopathic Healthcare Association (AOHA) membership
○ American Osteopathic Association (AOA) accreditation
△ Commission on Accreditation of Rehabilitation Facilities (CARF) accreditation
Control codes 61, 63, 64, 71, 72 and 73 indicate hospitals listed by AOHA, but not registered by AHA. For definition of numerical codes, see page A4

Hospital	Control	Service	Staffed Beds	Admissions	Census	Outpatient Visits	Births	Total	Payroll	Personnel
□ COOK CHILDREN'S MEDICAL CENTER, 801 Seventh Avenue, Zip 76104–2796; tel. 817/885–4000; Russell K. Tolman, President and Chief Executive Officer **A**1 2 3 9 10 **F**10 12 13 14 15 16 17 18 19 20 21 22 25 27 28 29 30 31 32 34 35 38 39 41 42 43 44 45 46 47 48 49 51 52 53 55 56 58 59 60 63 65 66 67 68 70 71 72 73 **P**3 4 6	23	50	181	7150	121	161391	0	132332	51392	1605
★ △ HARRIS CONTINUED CARE HOSPITAL, (LONG TERM CARE), 1301 Pennsylvania Avenue, 4th Floor, Zip 76104–2190, Mailing Address: P.O. Box 3471, Zip 76113–3471; tel. 817/878–5500; Larry Thompson, Senior Vice President and Executive Director **A**7 10 **F**2 3 4 7 8 10 11 12 16 17 18 19 21 22 23 24 26 27 28 29 30 31 32 33 34 35 37 38 39 40 41 42 43 44 45 46 48 49 50 52 53 54 55 56 58 59 60 61 63 64 65 66 67 68 70 71 72 73 74 **P**2 5 7 **S** Texas Health Resources, Irving, TX **Web address:** www.hmhs.com	21	49	10	75	8	0	0	7323	1219	30
⊠ HARRIS METHODIST FORT WORTH, 1301 Pennsylvania Avenue, Zip 76104–2895; tel. 817/882–2000; Barclay E. Berdan, Chief Executive Officer (Total facility includes 19 beds in nursing home–type unit) **A**1 2 3 9 10 **F**2 4 7 8 10 11 12 14 15 16 17 19 20 21 22 23 24 28 29 30 32 33 35 37 38 39 40 41 42 43 44 46 47 48 49 52 54 56 60 64 65 67 68 70 71 73 **P**3 5 **S** Texas Health Resources, Irving, TX **Web address:** www.hmhs.com	21	10	502	24301	364	108294	5335	221730	94178	2817
⊠ HARRIS METHODIST SOUTHWEST, 6100 Harris Parkway, Zip 76132–4199; tel. 817/346–5050; Stansel Harvey, Senior Executive Vice President, Executive Director/Administrator (Total facility includes 8 beds in nursing home–type unit) **A**1 9 10 **F**2 3 4 7 8 10 12 13 14 15 16 17 18 19 20 21 22 23 24 26 27 28 29 30 31 32 33 34 35 37 39 40 41 42 43 44 45 46 47 48 49 50 51 52 53 54 55 56 57 58 59 60 61 62 63 64 65 66 67 68 71 72 73 74 **P**2 3 5 7 8 **S** Texas Health Resources, Irving, TX **Web address:** www.hmhs.com	21	10	85	4603	43	77925	1722	41764	15282	470
□ △ HEALTHSOUTH REHABILITATION HOSPITAL OF FORT WORTH, 1212 West Lancaster Avenue, Zip 76102–4510; tel. 817/870–2336; S. Denise Borroni, Administrator and Chief Executive Officer **A**1 7 9 10 **F**12 16 27 34 41 42 48 49 54 65 66 67 **S** HEALTHSOUTH Corporation, Birmingham, AL **Web address:** www.healthsouth.com	33	46	60	788	41	7908	0	6982	3714	138
□ △ HEALTHSOUTH REHABILITATION HOSPITAL–CITYVIEW, 6701 Oakmont Boulevard, Zip 76132–2957; tel. 817/370–4700; S. Denise Borroni, Administrator and Chief Executive Officer **A**1 7 9 10 **F**14 15 27 46 48 49 66 67 **S** HEALTHSOUTH Corporation, Birmingham, AL	33	46	62	704	41	12988	0	10028	5319	158
□ JPS HEALTH NETWORK, (Formerly Tarrant County Hospital District), (Includes John Peter Smith Hospital), 1500 South Main Street, Zip 76104–4941; tel. 817/921–3431; Anthony J. Alcini, President and Chief Executive Officer (Total facility includes 15 beds in nursing home–type unit) **A**1 3 5 6 9 10 **F**7 8 12 13 14 15 16 17 19 20 21 22 25 26 27 28 30 31 32 34 35 36 37 38 39 40 41 42 43 44 46 49 50 51 52 54 55 56 58 59 61 63 64 65 67 68 70 71 72 73 74 **P**3 **S** Tarrant County Hospital District, Fort Worth, TX **Web address:** www.jpshealthnet.org	16	10	293	19016	229	338140	4733	—	—	2968
□ + ○ △ OSTEOPATHIC MEDICAL CENTER OF TEXAS, 1000 Montgomery Street, Zip 76107–2691; tel. 817/731–4311; Ron Stephen, Executive Vice President and Administrator (Total facility includes 12 beds in nursing home–type unit) **A**1 7 9 10 11 12 13 **F**4 7 8 10 11 12 13 14 15 16 17 19 21 22 23 24 25 26 27 28 29 30 31 32 34 35 37 39 40 41 42 43 44 46 48 49 52 53 54 55 56 57 59 61 64 65 66 67 70 71 72 73 **P**5 7 **Web address:** www.ohst.com	23	10	193	7839	143	79054	754	83943	32024	914
⊠ △ PLAZA MEDICAL CENTER OF FORT WORTH, 900 Eighth Avenue, Zip 76104–3986; tel. 817/347–5857; Stephen Bernstein, FACHE, Chief Executive Officer (Nonreporting) **A**1 7 9 10 **S** Columbia/HCA Healthcare Corporation, Nashville, TN **Web address:** www.columbia.net	33	10	289	—	—	—	—	—	—	—
TARRANT COUNTY PSYCHIATRIC CENTER, 1527 Hemphill Street, Zip 76104–4789; tel. 817/923–6467; Connie Oliverson Perra, Director (Nonreporting)	16	22	39	—	—	—	—	—	—	—
TRINITY SPRINGS PAVILION, 1500 South Main Street, Zip 76104–4917; tel. 817/927–3636; Robert N. Bourassa, Executive Director (Nonreporting) **S** Tarrant County Hospital District, Fort Worth, TX	16	52	34	—	—	—	—	—	—	—
VENCOR HOSPITAL–FORT WORTH SOUTHWEST, (LONG TERM ACUTE CARE), 7800 Oakmont Boulevard, Zip 76132–4299; tel. 817/346–0094; Robert L. McNew, Administrator **F**12 16 22 27 34 49 65 **S** Vencor, Incorporated, Louisville, KY	33	49	80	316	29		0	9603	3987	91
FREDERICKSBURG—Gillespie County										
⊠ HILL COUNTRY MEMORIAL HOSPITAL, 1020 Kerrville Road, Zip 78624, Mailing Address: P.O. Box 835, Zip 78624–0835; tel. 830/997–4353; Jeff A. Bourgeois, Chief Executive Officer **A**1 9 10 **F**7 8 10 15 16 17 19 21 22 23 24 30 32 33 35 37 39 40 41 42 44 49 63 64 65 66 67 70 71 73 **P**8	23	10	59	3322	39	46992	390	24764	10652	419
FRIONA—Parmer County										
PARMER COUNTY COMMUNITY HOSPITAL, 1307 Cleveland Street, Zip 79035–1121; tel. 806/250–2754; Bill J. Neely, Administrator **A**10 **F**15 19 22 30 32 33 34 36 39 71	23	10	34	297	2	6992	0	3124	1284	52

Hospital, Address, Telephone, Administrator, Approval, Facility, and Physician Codes, Health Care System, Network	Classi-fication Codes		Utilization Data					Expense (thousands) of dollars		
★ American Hospital Association (AHA) membership □ Joint Commission on Accreditation of Healthcare Organizations (JCAHO) accreditation + American Osteopathic Healthcare Association (AOHA) membership ○ American Osteopathic Association (AOA) accreditation △ Commission on Accreditation of Rehabilitation Facilities (CARF) accreditation Control codes 61, 63, 64, 71, 72 and 73 indicate hospitals listed by AOHA, but not registered by AHA. For definition of numerical codes, see page A4	Control	Service	Staffed Beds	Admissions	Census	Outpatient Visits	Births	Total	Payroll	Personnel

GAINESVILLE—Cooke County

GAINESVILLE MEMORIAL HOSPITAL, 1016 Ritchey Street, Zip 76240–3539; tel. 940/665–1751; William S. Abbott, Administrator (Total facility includes 10 beds in nursing home–type unit) **A**9 10 **F**8 14 15 16 17 18 19 22 30 32 33 34 35 39 40 41 42 44 49 60 63 64 65 67 70 71 73 **P**8	16	10	50	2032	22	13626	279	14944	5557	279

GALVESTON—Galveston County

⊠ SHRINERS HOSPITALS FOR CHILDREN, GALVESTON BURNS HOSPITAL, (PEDIATRIC BURN CARE), 815 Market Street, Zip 77550–2725; tel. 409/770–6600; John A. Swartwout, Administrator **A**1 3 5 **F**9 12 19 34 35 44 54 65 71 73 **S** Shriners Hospitals for Children, Tampa, FL **Web address:** www.shrinershq.org	23	59	30	1060	21	3014	0	20942	9093	284
⊠ △ UNIVERSITY OF TEXAS MEDICAL BRANCH HOSPITALS, 301 University Boulevard, Zip 77555–0138; tel. 409/772–1011; David S. Lopez, FACHE, Senior Executive Director **A**1 2 3 5 7 8 9 10 **F**1 4 5 7 8 9 10 11 12 15 16 17 19 20 21 22 23 24 25 26 27 28 29 30 31 32 33 34 35 37 38 39 40 41 42 43 44 45 46 47 48 49 51 52 53 54 55 56 57 58 59 60 61 63 65 66 67 68 71 72 73 74 **P**5 6 **S** University of Texas System, Austin, TX **Web address:** www.utmb.edu	12	10	894	33609	564	878078	4279	449514	189803	5559

GARLAND—Dallas County

⊠ BAYLOR MEDICAL CENTER AT GARLAND, 2300 Marie Curie Boulevard, Zip 75042–5706; tel. 972/487–5000; John B. McWhorter, III, Executive Director (Total facility includes 20 beds in nursing home–type unit) **A**1 3 9 10 **F**4 5 7 8 10 11 12 15 16 17 19 20 21 22 23 24 26 27 28 29 30 31 32 33 34 35 37 38 39 40 41 42 43 44 45 46 47 48 49 50 51 53 54 55 56 60 61 63 64 65 66 67 68 70 71 74 **P**6 7 8 **S** Baylor Health Care System, Dallas, TX	23	10	186	9063	121	133514	1584	84268	32712	—
⊠ GARLAND COMMUNITY HOSPITAL, 2696 West Walnut Street, Zip 75042–6499; tel. 972/276–7116; Gene Miller, Chief Executive Officer **A**1 9 10 **F**1 2 3 17 19 21 22 26 27 28 32 35 37 41 44 52 54 55 56 57 58 59 63 65 70 71 73 **P**4 7 **S** TENET Healthcare Corporation, Santa Barbara, CA	32	10	113	2549	37	50923	0	27634	11767	349

GATESVILLE—Coryell County

□ CORYELL MEMORIAL HOSPITAL, 1507 West Main Street, Zip 76528–1098, Mailing Address: P.O. Box 659, Zip 76528–0659; tel. 254/248–6300; David Byrom, Administrator **A**1 10 **F**6 14 15 16 19 28 32 37 44 49 51 62 65 67 70 71 73 **P**4 **Web address:** www.cmhos.org	16	10	48	1008	13	—	0	10416	5193	244

GEORGETOWN—Williamson County

⊠ GEORGETOWN HEALTHCARE SYSTEM, 2000 Scenic Drive, Zip 78626–7793; tel. 512/930–5338; Kenneth W. Poteete, President and Chief Executive Officer (Total facility includes 9 beds in nursing home–type unit) **A**1 9 10 **F**7 8 14 15 16 19 21 22 28 30 32 34 35 37 39 40 41 42 44 49 64 65 66 67 70 71 73	23	10	65	3120	28	39090	776	24449	11337	404

GLEN ROSE—Somervell County

⊠ GLEN ROSE MEDICAL CENTER, 1021 Holden Street, Zip 76043–4937, Mailing Address: P.O. Box 2099, Zip 76043–2099; tel. 254/897–2215; Gary A. Marks, Administrator **A**1 9 10 **F**8 14 15 19 21 22 23 26 27 28 30 33 34 41 44 49 50 51 56 64 65 70 71	13	10	16	579	6	5333	0	7239	2681	130

GONZALES—Gonzales County

★ MEMORIAL HOSPITAL, Highway 90A By–Pass, Zip 78629, Mailing Address: P.O. Box 587, Zip 78629–0587; tel. 830/672–7581; Douglas Langley, Administrator **A**10 **F**8 14 15 16 17 18 19 22 28 29 30 32 33 34 37 39 40 41 42 44 46 49 51 59 65 66 67 70 71 **P**8	16	10	34	1273	15	21139	135	10241	4428	182
⊠ △ WARM SPRINGS REHABILITATION HOSPITAL, Mailing Address: P.O. Box 58, Zip 78629–0058; tel. 830/672–6592; John W. Davis, Administrator **A**1 7 10 **F**15 16 41 48 49 65	23	46	68	693	53	15924	0	11620	5095	183

GRAHAM—Young County

★ GRAHAM REGIONAL MEDICAL CENTER, (Formerly Graham General Hospital), 1301 Montgomery Road, Zip 76450–4224, Mailing Address: P.O. Box 1390, Zip 76450–1390; tel. 940/549–3400; Blake Kretz, Administrator **A**10 **F**7 8 12 15 16 19 22 28 29 32 33 35 36 40 41 42 44 57 65 66 70 71 73 **P**5 **Web address:** www.grahamrmc.com	14	10	38	1575	15	104398	220	12215	5306	182

GRANBURY—Hood County

⊠ LAKE GRANBURY MEDICAL CENTER, 1310 Paluxy Road, Zip 76048–5699; tel. 817/573–2683; Mike Pruitt, Chief Executive Officer **A**1 9 10 **F**7 8 12 14 15 16 19 21 22 24 30 32 33 34 35 37 39 40 41 42 44 45 46 49 63 64 65 67 69 71 73 **S** Community Health Systems, Inc., Brentwood, TN	33	10	49	1713	20	23513	153	17409	6579	206

GRAND PRAIRIE—Dallas County

⊠ + ○ DALLAS–FORT WORTH MEDICAL CENTER, 2709 Hospital Boulevard, Zip 75051–1083; tel. 972/641–5000; Robert A. Ficken, Chief Executive Officer (Total facility includes 11 beds in nursing home–type unit) **A**1 9 10 11 12 13 **F**4 7 8 10 12 15 16 17 19 21 22 23 24 26 27 28 30 32 34 35 37 38 39 40 41 44 46 48 49 51 52 57 61 64 65 71 73 74 **P**5 **S** Quorum Health Group/Quorum Health Resources, Inc., Brentwood, TN **Web address:** www.dfwmedicalcenter.com	23	10	162	4198	64	54171	837	46651	17283	440

GRAND SALINE—Van Zandt County

★ COZBY–GERMANY HOSPITAL, 707 North Waldrip Street, Zip 75140–1555; tel. 903/962–4242; William Rowton, Chief Executive Officer **A**9 10 **F**8 19 22 32 33 34 44 57 59 65 70 71	23	10	16	376	4	4981	2	2839	1452	62

Hospital, Address, Telephone, Administrator, Approval, Facility, and Physician Codes, Health Care System, Network	Classi-fication Codes		Utilization Data					Expense (thousands) of dollars		
	Control	Service	Staffed Beds	Admissions	Census	Outpatient Visits	Births	Total	Payroll	Personnel

★ American Hospital Association (AHA) membership
□ Joint Commission on Accreditation of Healthcare Organizations (JCAHO) accreditation
+ American Osteopathic Healthcare Association (AOHA) membership
○ American Osteopathic Association (AOA) accreditation
△ Commission on Accreditation of Rehabilitation Facilities (CARF) accreditation
Control codes 61, 63, 64, 71, 72 and 73 indicate hospitals listed by AOHA, but not registered by AHA. For definition of numerical codes, see page A4

GRAPEVINE—Tarrant County

☒ BAYLOR MEDICAL CENTER AT GRAPEVINE, 1650 West College Street, Zip 76051–1650; tel. 817/329–2500; Mark C. Hood, Executive Director (Total facility includes 9 beds in nursing home–type unit) **A**1 9 10 **F**1 3 4 5 7 8 10 12 14 15 16 17 18 19 20 21 22 23 24 25 26 27 28 29 30 31 32 33 34 35 36 37 39 40 41 42 43 44 45 46 49 50 51 53 54 55 56 57 58 59 60 61 63 64 65 66 67 68 71 73 74 **S** Baylor Health Care System, Dallas, TX — 21 | 10 | 97 | 4997 | 51 | 48385 | 1356 | 41572 | 17360 | 637

□ CHARTER GRAPEVINE BEHAVIORAL HEALTH SYSTEM, 2300 William D. Tate Avenue, Zip 76051–9964; tel. 817/481–1900; Sandra C. Podley, Chief Executive Officer **A**1 9 10 **F**1 2 3 12 16 19 22 27 35 46 48 52 53 54 55 56 57 58 59 65 67 70 71 **S** Magellan Health Services, Atlanta, GA — 32 | 22 | 80 | 1839 | 35 | 11615 | 0 | 9755 | 3414 | 64

GREENVILLE—Hunt County

□ GLEN OAKS HOSPITAL, 301 East Division, Zip 75402; tel. 903/454–6000; Thomas E. Rourke, Administrator **A**1 9 10 **F**2 16 22 26 34 52 53 54 55 56 57 58 59 65 67 **S** Universal Health Services, Inc., King of Prussia, PA — 33 | 22 | 54 | 1038 | 22 | 4044 | 0 | 4017 | 2314 | 75

☒ HUNT MEMORIAL HOSPITAL DISTRICT, (Includes Presbyterian Hospital of Commerce, 2900 Sterling Hart Drive, Commerce, Zip 75428; tel. 903/886–3161; Presbyterian Hospital of Greenville), 4215 Joe Ramsey Boulevard, Zip 75401–7899, Mailing Address: P.O. Drawer 1059, Zip 75403–1059; tel. 903/408–5000; Richard Carter, Chief Executive Officer (Total facility includes 15 beds in nursing home–type unit) **A**1 9 10 **F**7 8 12 14 15 16 19 21 22 28 29 30 32 34 35 37 39 40 41 44 45 46 49 64 65 67 70 71 72 73 **P**8
Web address: www.hmhd.org — 16 | 10 | 147 | 6222 | 73 | 63503 | 782 | 44765 | 20121 | 630

GROESBECK—Limestone County

LIMESTONE MEDICAL CENTER, 701 McClintic Street, Zip 76642–2105; tel. 254/729–3281; Penny Gray, Administrator and Chief Executive Officer **A**9 10 **F**15 16 19 21 22 28 32 34 39 46 49 51 59 65 70 71 73 — 16 | 10 | 15 | 267 | 2 | 14661 | 0 | 3974 | 1816 | 24

GROVES—Jefferson County

★ + ○ DOCTORS HOSPITAL, 5500 39th Street, Zip 77619–9805; tel. 409/962–5733; John Isbell, Chief Executive Officer (Total facility includes 6 beds in nursing home–type unit) **A**9 10 11 12 13 **F**8 10 12 14 15 19 21 22 26 28 30 34 35 37 41 44 46 49 51 52 57 59 60 63 64 65 66 71 73 **P**8 — 23 | 10 | 78 | 2318 | 31 | 20051 | — | 22442 | 7806 | 211

HALE CENTER—Hale County

☒ HI–PLAINS HOSPITAL, 203 West Fourth Street, Zip 79041, Mailing Address: P.O. Box 1260, Zip 79041–1260; tel. 806/839–2471; Gordon H. Russell, Administrator (Total facility includes 44 beds in nursing home–type unit) **A**1 9 10 **F**7 16 19 21 32 40 44 49 65 70 71 **P**8
Web address: www.texasonline.net/hiplains — 23 | 10 | 84 | 530 | 52 | 2155 | 78 | 5430 | 2798 | 141

HALLETTSVILLE—Lavaca County

LAVACA MEDICAL CENTER, 1400 North Texana Street, Zip 77964–2099; tel. 512/798–3671; James Vanek, Administrator **A**10 **F**8 19 22 24 28 33 34 44 70 71 73 — 16 | 10 | 36 | 645 | 7 | 14837 | 0 | 7296 | 2547 | 99

HAMLIN—Jones County

HAMLIN MEMORIAL HOSPITAL, 632 Northwest Second Street, Zip 79520–3831, Mailing Address: P.O. Box 400, Zip 79520–0400; tel. 915/576–3646; Charley C. Latham, Administrator **A**9 10 **F**15 16 19 22 24 26 28 32 35 36 44 49 71 **P**6 — 16 | 10 | 23 | 529 | 7 | 5782 | 1 | 3446 | 1350 | 81

HARLINGEN—Cameron County

□ RIO GRANDE STATE CENTER, 1401 South Rangerville Road, Zip 78552–7638; tel. 956/425–8900; Sonia Hernandez–Keeble, Director **A**1 **F**24 28 39 45 46 52 55 56 57 65 67 73
Web address: www.mhmr.state.tx.us — 12 | 22 | 60 | 1006 | 42 | 0 | 0 | 10458 | 5488 |

☒ SOUTH TEXAS HOSPITAL, 1301 Rangerville Road, Zip 78552–7609, Mailing Address: P.O. Box 592, Zip 78551–0592; tel. 956/423–3420; Mary Diaz, R.N., Ed.D., Interim Director **A**1 10 **F**8 12 14 15 16 17 19 20 21 27 28 29 30 31 34 35 39 41 44 45 46 49 51 65 71 73 74 **P**6 **S** Texas Department of Health, Austin, TX
Web address: www.tdh.texas.gov — 12 | 10 | 60 | 512 | 31 | 31402 | 0 | 14011 | 6806 | 268

☒ VALLEY BAPTIST MEDICAL CENTER, 2101 Pease Street, Zip 78550–8307, Mailing Address: P.O. Drawer 2588, Zip 78551–2588; tel. 956/389–1100; Ben M. McKibbens, President **A**1 2 3 5 9 10 **F**4 7 8 10 12 13 15 16 17 18 19 22 23 26 28 29 30 32 33 35 37 38 39 40 41 42 43 44 45 47 48 49 50 60 70 71 73 **P**3 8 — 21 | 10 | 361 | 20782 | 221 | 111376 | 3945 | 170734 | 67885 | 2261

HASKELL—Haskell County

HASKELL MEMORIAL HOSPITAL, 1 North Avenue N, Zip 79521–5499, Mailing Address: P.O. Box 1117, Zip 79521–1117; tel. 817/864–2621; Bill Nemir, Administrator **A**9 10 **F**14 15 16 17 19 22 24 25 27 28 29 30 32 33 35 36 44 46 49 66 71 73 **P**1 — 16 | 10 | 30 | 402 | 4 | — | 0 | 2603 | 1202 | 56

HEMPHILL—Sabine County

★ SABINE COUNTY HOSPITAL, Highway 83 West, Zip 75948, Mailing Address: P.O. Box 750, Zip 75948–0750; tel. 409/787–3300; Edith McCauley, Administrator **A**9 10 **F**15 19 20 22 28 32 34 40 41 44 49 56 57 58 65 70 71 — 16 | 10 | 36 | 565 | 5 | 8871 | 18 | 3796 | 1443 | 54

HENDERSON—Rusk County

☒ HENDERSON MEMORIAL HOSPITAL, 300 Wilson Street, Zip 75652–5956; tel. 903/657–7541; George T. Roberts, Jr., Chief Executive Officer (Total facility includes 16 beds in nursing home–type unit) **A**1 9 10 **F**7 8 12 15 16 19 20 22 28 29 30 31 32 34 35 37 39 40 44 45 46 49 63 64 65 70 71 74 **P**8 **S** Quorum Health Group/Quorum Health Resources, Inc., Brentwood, TN — 23 | 10 | 96 | 3466 | 42 | 53330 | 443 | 21499 | 10202 | 336

Hospital, Address, Telephone, Administrator, Approval, Facility, and Physician Codes, Health Care System, Network	Classi-fication Codes		Utilization Data					Expense (thousands) of dollars		
★ American Hospital Association (AHA) membership □ Joint Commission on Accreditation of Healthcare Organizations (JCAHO) accreditation + American Osteopathic Healthcare Association (AOHA) membership ○ American Osteopathic Association (AOA) accreditation △ Commission on Accreditation of Rehabilitation Facilities (CARF) accreditation Control codes 61, 63, 64, 71, 72 and 73 indicate hospitals listed by AOHA, but not registered by AHA. For definition of numerical codes, see page A4	Control	Service	Staffed Beds	Admissions	Census	Outpatient Visits	Births	Total	Payroll	Personnel

HENRIETTA—Clay County

CLAY COUNTY MEMORIAL HOSPITAL, 310 West South Street, Zip 76365–3399; tel. 940/538–5621; Edward E. Browning, Chief Executive Officer and Administrator **A**9 10 **F**7 19 22 26 30 32 34 40 44 49 57 70 71 **P**8

| | 16 | 10 | 25 | 393 | 4 | 8814 | 9 | 3383 | 1538 | 55 |

HEREFORD—Deaf Smith County

⊞ HEREFORD REGIONAL MEDICAL CENTER, 801 East Third Street, Zip 79045–5727, Mailing Address: P.O. Box 1858, Zip 79045–1858; tel. 806/364–2141; John S. Studsrud, Administrator **A**1 9 10 **F**7 8 12 13 14 15 16 17 18 19 21 22 25 28 30 31 32 33 34 35 37 40 41 44 45 46 49 65 67 70 71 73 74

| | 16 | 10 | 36 | 1052 | 9 | 33943 | 287 | 10756 | 5247 | 182 |

HILLSBORO—Hill County

⊞ HILL REGIONAL HOSPITAL, 101 Circle Drive, Zip 76645–2670; tel. 254/582–8425; Jan McClure, Chief Executive Officer (Total facility includes 23 beds in nursing home–type unit) **A**1 9 10 **F**7 12 15 16 19 22 26 30 34 35 37 40 41 44 45 46 49 52 57 63 64 70 71 73 **S** Community Health Systems, Inc., Brentwood, TN

| | 33 | 10 | 80 | 1969 | 26 | 20828 | 203 | 11376 | 4351 | 160 |

HONDO—Medina County

MEDINA COMMUNITY HOSPITAL, 3100 Avenue East, Zip 78861–3599; tel. 830/741–4677; Elwood E. Currier, Jr., CHE, Administrator **A**9 10 **F**7 8 12 14 15 19 21 24 27 28 29 32 33 34 40 41 42 44 46 49 65 70 71 **P**4 7

| | 15 | 10 | 27 | 927 | 8 | 85009 | 180 | 15230 | 6987 | 254 |

HOUSTON—Harris County

AMERICAN TRANSITIONAL HOSPITAL See Select Specialty Hospital

⊞ BAYOU CITY MEDICAL CENTER, (Includes North Campus, 4200 Portsmouth Street, tel. 713/623–2500; Steve Altmiller, Chief Executive Officer; South Campus, 6700 Bellaire at Tarnef, Zip 77074–4999, Mailing Address: P.O. Box 740389, Zip 77274–0389; tel. 713/774–7611), 4200 Portsmouth Street, Zip 77027–6899; tel. 713/623–2500; Steve Altmiller, Chief Executive Officer (Total facility includes 15 beds in nursing home–type unit) **A**1 9 10 **F**2 4 7 8 10 12 14 15 16 17 19 20 21 22 26 27 28 29 30 31 32 33 34 35 37 38 40 41 42 43 44 45 46 48 49 50 51 52 53 54 55 56 57 60 66 67 71 73 74 **P**5 7 8 **S** TENET Healthcare Corporation, Santa Barbara, CA

| | 33 | 10 | 283 | 7776 | 129 | 82023 | 1357 | 74065 | 28577 | 815 |

⊞ BELLAIRE MEDICAL CENTER, (Formerly Columbia Bellaire Medical Center), 5314 Dashwood Street, Zip 77081–4689; tel. 713/512–1200; Walter Leleux, Chief Executive Officer (Total facility includes 15 beds in nursing home–type unit) **A**1 9 10 **F**1 2 3 4 5 7 8 10 11 12 14 15 16 17 19 21 22 23 24 25 26 28 29 30 32 33 34 35 37 38 39 40 41 42 43 44 45 46 47 48 49 51 52 53 54 55 56 57 58 59 60 61 64 65 66 67 71 72 73 74 **P**2 4 5 6 7 8 **S** Columbia/HCA Healthcare Corporation, Nashville, TN
Web address: www.columbia.net

| | 33 | 10 | 202 | 4992 | 76 | — | 1516 | 39170 | 16516 | 436 |

BEN TAUB GENERAL HOSPITAL See Harris County Hospital District

CASA, A SPECIAL HOSPITAL, (SPECIAL HOSPITAL SUBACUTE CARE), 1803 Old Spanish Trail, Zip 77054–2001; tel. 713/796–2272; Gretchen Thorp, R.N., Administrator **A**10 **F**12 15 31 42 65 73

| | 32 | 49 | 40 | 763 | 20 | 0 | 0 | 2932 | 1250 | 57 |

⊞ △ CHRISTUS ST. JOSEPH HOSPITAL, (Formerly St Joseph Hospital), 1919 LaBranch Street, Zip 77002; tel. 713/757–1000; Sally E. Jeffcoat, Chief Executive Officer (Total facility includes 29 beds in nursing home–type unit) **A**1 2 3 5 7 9 10 **F**2 3 4 7 8 10 12 13 14 15 16 17 18 19 21 22 23 26 28 29 30 31 32 33 34 35 37 38 39 40 41 42 43 44 45 46 48 49 51 52 54 55 56 57 59 60 61 63 64 65 66 67 68 70 71 72 73 74 **P**1 5 **S** Christus Health, Houston, TX
Web address: www.stjoe.sch.org

| | 23 | 10 | 443 | 17989 | 272 | 133501 | 4259 | 165568 | 70615 | 1768 |

COLUMBIA BELLAIRE MEDICAL CENTER See Bellaire Medical Center

□ CYPRESS CREEK HOSPITAL, 17750 Cali Drive, Zip 77090–2700; tel. 713/586–7600; Terry Scovill, Administrator **A**1 9 10 **F**3 14 15 16 52 53 56 57 58 59 **S** Healthcare America, Inc., Austin, TX
Web address: www.brownschools.com

| | 33 | 22 | 80 | 2040 | 47 | 4007 | 0 | 8466 | 4501 | 172 |

⊞ △ CYPRESS FAIRBANKS MEDICAL CENTER, 10655 Steepletop Drive, Zip 77065–4297; tel. 281/890–4285; Bill Klier, Chief Executive Officer (Total facility includes 14 beds in nursing home–type unit) (Nonreporting) **A**1 7 9 10 **S** TENET Healthcare Corporation, Santa Barbara, CA
Web address: www.tenethealth.com/cypressfairbanks

| | 33 | 10 | 136 | — | — | — | — | — | — | — |

⊞ DIAGNOSTIC CENTER HOSPITAL, 6447 Main Street, Zip 77030–1595; tel. 713/790–0790; William A. Gregory, Chief Executive Officer (Total facility includes 25 beds in nursing home–type unit) **A**1 10 **F**2 4 7 8 9 10 11 12 15 16 17 18 19 20 21 22 23 24 27 28 29 30 31 32 33 34 35 37 38 39 40 41 42 43 44 45 46 47 48 49 50 51 52 54 55 57 58 60 61 63 64 65 66 67 68 71 73 **P**1 3 **S** Methodist Health Care System, Houston, TX
Web address: www.tmh.tmc.edi/

| | 23 | 10 | 115 | 3349 | 60 | 6648 | 0 | 38094 | 13811 | 406 |

★ DOCTORS HOSPITAL AIRLINE, (Formerly Columbia Doctors Hospital Airline), 5815 Airline Drive, Zip 77076–4996; tel. 281/765–2600; Joe G. Baldwin, Chief Executive Officer (Nonreporting) **S** Columbia/HCA Healthcare Corporation, Nashville, TN

| | 32 | 10 | 114 | — | — | — | — | — | — | — |

⊞ DOCTORS HOSPITAL–TIDWELL, 510 West Tidwell Road, Zip 77091–4399; tel. 713/691–1111; John H. Styles, Jr., Administrator **A**1 9 10 **F**8 12 14 19 21 22 28 30 35 37 39 41 45 46 49 65 71

| | 32 | 10 | 69 | 2704 | 38 | 11839 | 0 | 17963 | 7222 | 370 |

⊞ EAST HOUSTON REGIONAL MEDICAL CENTER, (Formerly Columbia East Houston Medical Center), 13111 East Freeway, Zip 77015; tel. 713/393–2000; Merrily Walters, Administrator **A**1 9 10 **F**2 3 4 5 7 8 10 11 12 14 15 16 18 19 21 22 23 24 25 26 28 29 30 32 33 34 35 37 38 39 40 41 42 43 44 45 46 47 48 49 51 52 53 55 56 57 58 59 60 61 64 65 66 67 71 72 73 74 **P**2 4 5 6 7 8 **S** Columbia/HCA Healthcare Corporation, Nashville, TN

| | 33 | 10 | 121 | 5845 | 60 | 57495 | 1139 | 38994 | 16153 | 446 |

Hospital, Address, Telephone, Administrator, Approval, Facility, and Physician Codes, Health Care System, Network	Classi-fication Codes		Utilization Data					Expense (thousands) of dollars		
	Control	Service	Staffed Beds	Admissions	Census	Outpatient Visits	Births	Total	Payroll	Personnel

★ American Hospital Association (AHA) membership
□ Joint Commission on Accreditation of Healthcare Organizations (JCAHO) accreditation
+ American Osteopathic Healthcare Association (AOHA) membership
○ American Osteopathic Association (AOA) accreditation
△ Commission on Accreditation of Rehabilitation Facilities (CARF) accreditation
Control codes 61, 63, 64, 71, 72 and 73 indicate hospitals listed by AOHA, but not registered by AHA. For definition of numerical codes, see page A4

□ FOREST SPRINGS HOSPITAL, 1120 Cypress Station, Zip 77090–3031; tel. 281/893–7200; Deo Shanker, CPA, Chief Executive Officer **A**1 9 **F**2 3 19 21 27 35 52 53 54 55 56 57 58 59 65 **S** Cambridge International, Inc,, Houston, TX	33	22	48	340	9	1884	0	2724	1277	51
□ HARRIS COUNTY HOSPITAL DISTRICT, (Includes Ben Taub General Hospital, 1504 Taub Loop, Zip 77030; tel. 713/793–2300; Lyndon B Johnson General Hospital, 5656 Kelley, Zip 77026; tel. 713/636–5000; Margo Hilliard, M.D., Senior Vice President; Quentin Mease Hospital, 3601 North MacGregor, Zip 77004; tel. 713/528–1499), 2525 Holly Hall Street, Zip 77054–4108, Mailing Address: P.O. Box 66769, Zip 77266–6769; tel. 713/746–6400 (Total facility includes 24 beds in nursing home–type unit) **A**1 2 3 5 8 9 10 **F**3 4 7 8 10 11 12 14 15 17 18 19 21 22 25 26 27 30 31 32 34 35 37 38 40 42 43 44 47 48 49 52 56 58 59 60 61 63 64 65 67 70 71 73 **P**6	16	10	894	41081	652	911823	11373	447392	164644	5034
⊠ HARRIS COUNTY PSYCHIATRIC CENTER, 2800 South MacGregor Way, Zip 77021–1000, Mailing Address: P.O. Box 20249, Zip 77225–0249; tel. 713/741–5000; Robert W. Guynn, M.D., Executive Director **A**1 3 5 9 10 **F**3 12 14 15 16 19 21 27 35 41 46 50 52 53 54 55 56 57 58 59 63 65 67 71 73 **S** University of Texas System, Austin, TX **Web address:** www.uth.tmc.edu	12	22	193	5390	139	1311	0	30695	14799	426
□ △ HEALTHSOUTH HOUSTON REHABILITATION INSTITUTE, 17506 Red Oak Drive, Zip 77090–7721, Mailing Address: P.O. Box 73684, Zip 77273–3684; tel. 281/580–1212; Anne R. Leon, Chief Executive Officer (Total facility includes 14 beds in nursing home–type unit) (Nonreporting) **A**1 7 9 10 **S** HEALTHSOUTH Corporation, Birmingham, AL	33	46	80	—	—	—	—	—	—	—
⊠ HERMANN HOSPITAL, 6411 Fannin, Zip 77030–1501; tel. 713/704–4000; James E. Eastham, Senior Vice President and Chief Executive Officer (Total facility includes 15 beds in nursing home–type unit) **A**1 3 5 8 9 10 **F**2 3 4 6 7 8 9 10 11 12 15 16 17 19 20 21 22 23 24 25 26 27 28 29 30 31 32 33 34 35 36 37 38 39 40 41 42 43 44 45 46 47 48 49 50 51 52 53 54 55 56 57 58 59 60 61 62 63 64 65 66 67 68 70 71 72 73 74 **P**5 **S** Memorial Hermann Healthcare System, Houston, TX	23	10	624	23831	391	301090	2921	367979	133943	3238
⊠ HOUSTON NORTHWEST MEDICAL CENTER, 710 FM 1960 West, Zip 77090–3496; tel. 281/440–1000; James Kelly, Chief Executive Officer (Total facility includes 20 beds in nursing home–type unit) **A**1 2 9 10 **F**3 4 7 8 10 12 15 16 17 19 20 21 22 23 24 27 28 29 30 31 32 34 35 37 38 40 41 42 43 44 45 46 49 52 54 56 57 58 59 60 63 64 65 67 71 72 73 74 **P**8 **S** TENET Healthcare Corporation, Santa Barbara, CA **Web address:** www.houstonnorthwestmed.com	32	10	408	18338	209	433251	3558	138833	56961	1490
□ INTRACARE MEDICAL CENTER HOSPITAL, 7601 Fannin Street, Zip 77054–1905; tel. 713/790–0949; Alice Hiniker, Ph.D., Administrator **A**1 10 **F**2 3 19 21 27 35 52 53 54 55 56 58 65 **S** Cambridge International, Inc,, Houston, TX	33	22	100	1063	33	7212	0	7869	3372	113
LYNDON B JOHNSON GENERAL HOSPITAL See Harris County Hospital District										
⊠ MEMORIAL HERMAN BEHAVIORAL HEALTH CENTER, (Formerly Memorial Spring Shadows Glen), 2801 Gessner, Zip 77080–2599; tel. 713/462–4000; Sue E. Green, Vice President and Chief Executive Officer **A**1 9 **F**2 3 4 6 7 8 9 10 11 12 15 16 17 19 20 21 22 23 24 25 26 27 28 29 30 31 32 33 34 35 36 37 38 39 40 41 42 43 44 45 46 47 48 49 50 51 52 53 54 55 56 57 58 59 60 61 62 63 64 65 66 67 68 70 71 72 73 74 **P**5 **S** Memorial Hermann Healthcare System, Houston, TX **Web address:** www.mhcs.org	23	22	108	2896	68	799	0	15793	6827	205
⊠ MEMORIAL HOSPITAL SOUTHWEST, 7600 Beechnut, Zip 77074–1850; tel. 713/776–5000; Lynn Schroth, Chief Executive Officer (Total facility includes 89 beds in nursing home–type unit) **A**1 2 3 5 9 10 **F**2 3 4 6 7 8 9 10 11 12 15 16 17 19 20 21 22 23 24 25 26 27 28 29 30 31 32 33 34 35 36 37 38 39 40 41 42 43 44 45 46 47 48 49 50 51 52 53 54 55 56 57 58 59 60 61 62 63 64 65 66 67 68 70 71 72 73 74 **P**5 **S** Memorial Hermann Healthcare System, Houston, TX **Web address:** www.mhcs.org	23	10	886	41826	564	273089	6358	303549	101774	3189
⊠ MEMORIAL HOSPITAL–MEMORIAL CITY, 920 Frostwood Drive, Zip 77024–9173; tel. 713/932–3000; Jerel T. Humphrey, Vice President, Chief Executive Officer and Administrator (Total facility includes 24 beds in nursing home–type unit) **A**1 2 6 9 10 **F**2 3 4 6 7 8 9 10 11 12 15 16 17 19 20 21 22 23 24 25 26 27 28 29 30 31 32 33 34 35 36 37 38 39 40 41 42 43 44 45 46 47 48 49 50 51 52 53 54 55 56 57 58 59 60 61 62 63 64 65 66 67 68 70 71 72 73 74 **P**5 **S** Memorial Hermann Healthcare System, Houston, TX **Web address:** www.mhcs.org	23	10	340	16051	186	90714	3520	113285	30150	1012
★ MEMORIAL REHABILITATION HOSPITAL, 3043 Gessner Drive, Zip 77080–2597; tel. 713/462–2515; Roger Truskoloski, Vice President and Chief Executive Officer (Total facility includes 24 beds in nursing home–type unit) **F**2 3 4 6 7 8 9 10 11 12 15 16 17 19 20 21 22 23 24 25 26 27 28 29 30 31 33 34 35 36 37 38 39 40 41 42 43 44 45 46 47 48 49 50 51 52 53 54 55 56 57 58 59 60 61 62 63 64 65 66 67 68 70 71 72 73 74 **P**5 **S** Memorial Hermann Healthcare System, Houston, TX **Web address:** www.mhcs.com	23	46	106	754	44	2747	0	14402	4699	146
NORTH CAMPUS See Bayou City Medical Center										
⊠ NORTH HOUSTON MEDICAL CENTER, (Formerly Columbia North Houston Medical Center), 233 West Parker Road, Zip 77076–2999; tel. 281/765–2600; Joe G. Baldwin, Chief Executive Officer **A**1 9 10 **F**2 3 4 5 7 8 10 11 12 14 15 16 17 19 20 21 22 23 24 25 26 27 28 29 30 32 33 34 35 37 38 39 40 41 42 43 44 45 46 47 48 49 51 52 53 55 56 57 58 59 60 61 64 65 66 67 70 71 72 73 74 **P**2 4 5 6 7 8 **S** Columbia/HCA Healthcare Corporation, Nashville, TN	33	10	109	7178	88	51158	1414	44175	20627	356

Hospital, Address, Telephone, Administrator, Approval, Facility, and Physician Codes, Health Care System, Network	Classification Codes		Utilization Data					Expense (thousands) of dollars		
	Control	Service	Staffed Beds	Admissions	Census	Outpatient Visits	Births	Total	Payroll	Personnel

Approval symbols:

★ American Hospital Association (AHA) membership
□ Joint Commission on Accreditation of Healthcare Organizations (JCAHO) accreditation
+ American Osteopathic Healthcare Association (AOHA) membership
○ American Osteopathic Association (AOA) accreditation
△ Commission on Accreditation of Rehabilitation Facilities (CARF) accreditation
Control codes 61, 63, 64, 71, 72 and 73 indicate hospitals listed by AOHA, but not registered by AHA. For definition of numerical codes, see page A4

Hospital	Control	Service	Staffed Beds	Admissions	Census	Outpatient Visits	Births	Total	Payroll	Personnel
NORTHSIDE GENERAL HOSPITAL, 2807 Little York Road, Zip 77093–3495; tel. 713/697–7777; Carole A. Veloso, President and Chief Executive Officer **A**9 10 **F**12 14 15 16 17 19 21 22 28 30 34 37 42 44 46 49 61 65 71	33	10	39	1479	15	7063	1	7069	4447	125
★ △ PARK PLAZA HOSPITAL, 1313 Hermann Drive, Zip 77004–7092; tel. 713/527–5000; Robert L. Quist, Chief Executive Officer (Total facility includes 40 beds in nursing home–type unit) **A**1 2 3 5 7 9 10 **F**4 7 8 10 12 14 15 16 17 19 21 22 26 28 30 31 32 34 35 37 40 41 42 43 44 45 46 48 49 52 57 60 61 63 64 65 67 71 73 **P**5 7 8 **S** TENET Healthcare Corporation, Santa Barbara, CA *Web address:* www.tenethealth.com	32	10	370	9443	175	55899	1032	92058	33097	886
QUENTIN MEASE HOSPITAL See Harris County Hospital District										
□ RIVERSIDE GENERAL HOSPITAL, 3204 Ennis Street, Zip 77004–3299; tel. 713/526–2441; Earnest Gibson, III, Administrator (Nonreporting) **A**1 9 10	23	82	56	—	—	—	—	—	—	—
★ △ ROSEWOOD MEDICAL CENTER, (Formerly Columbia Rosewood Medical Center), 9200 Westheimer Road, Zip 77063–3599; tel. 713/780–7000; Maura Walsh, Chief Executive Officer (Total facility includes 18 beds in nursing home–type unit) **A**1 7 9 10 **F**2 3 4 5 7 8 10 11 12 14 16 17 18 19 20 21 22 23 24 25 26 27 28 29 30 31 32 33 34 35 37 38 39 40 41 42 43 44 45 46 47 48 49 51 52 53 54 55 56 57 58 59 60 61 63 64 65 66 67 71 72 73 74 **P**2 4 5 6 7 8 **S** Columbia/HCA Healthcare Corporation, Nashville, TN	33	10	184	4896	69	43447	491	36643	15358	368
SAM HOUSTON MEMORIAL HOSPITAL See Spring Branch Medical Center										
□ SELECT SPECIALTY HOSPITAL, (Formerly American Transitional Hospital), 6447 Main Street, Zip 77030, Mailing Address: 6500 Fannin Street, Suite 907, Zip 77030; tel. 713/791–9393; Ron J. MacLaren, Chief Executive Officer (Nonreporting) **A**1 10	33	49	34	—	—	—	—	—	—	—
SHARPSTOWN GENERAL HOSPITAL See Bayou City Medical Center										
★ SHRINERS HOSPITALS FOR CHILDREN, HOUSTON, 6977 Main Street, Zip 77030–3701; tel. 713/797–1616; Steven B. Reiter, Administrator **A**1 3 5 **F**5 9 12 17 19 20 22 27 28 34 35 39 44 45 47 48 49 51 54 64 65 67 71 73 **P**6 **S** Shriners Hospitals for Children, Tampa, FL	23	57	40	784	18	10306	0	—	—	185
SOUTH CAMPUS See Bayou City Medical Center										
★ SPECIALTY HOSPITAL OF HOUSTON, (LONG TERM ACUTE CARE), 5556 Gasmer Drive, Zip 77035–4598; tel. 713/551–5300; Shelley R. Cochran, Interim Chief Executive Officer **A**1 10 **F**12 14 15 16 19 21 26 27 35 37 39 44 45 46 49 50 51 59 63 65 71	33	49	54	302	35	0	0	15893	6510	236
★ △ SPRING BRANCH MEDICAL CENTER, (Includes Sam Houston Memorial Hospital, 1615 Hillendahl, Zip 77055; tel. 713/932–5500), 8850 Long Point Road, Zip 77055–3082; tel. 713/467–6555; Pat Currie, Chief Executive Officer (Total facility includes 39 beds in nursing home–type unit) **A**1 2 7 9 10 **F**2 3 4 5 7 8 10 11 12 14 15 16 17 19 21 22 23 24 25 26 28 29 30 31 32 33 34 35 37 38 39 40 41 42 43 44 45 46 47 48 49 51 52 53 55 56 57 58 59 60 61 64 65 66 67 71 72 73 74 **P**2 4 5 6 7 8 **S** Columbia/HCA Healthcare Corporation, Nashville, TN	33	10	318	11416	152	77088	1400	—	33122	845
□ SSH HEIGHTS HOSPITAL, (LONG TERM ACUTE CARE), 1917 Ashland Street, Zip 77008–3994; tel. 713/861–6161 **A**1 9 10 **F**12 16 19 21 26 27 35 37 41 42 48 50 65 67 71	33	49	170	1052	91	151	0	22495	10501	425
ST JOSEPH HOSPITAL See Christus St. Joseph Hospital										
★ △ ST. LUKE'S EPISCOPAL HEALTH SYSTEM, (Formerly St. Luke's Episcopal Hospital), 6720 Bertner Avenue, Zip 77030–2697, Mailing Address: Box 20269, Zip 77225–0269; tel. 713/791–1000; Michael K. Jhin, President and Chief Executive Officer **A**1 2 3 5 7 8 9 10 **F**4 7 8 10 11 12 14 15 16 17 19 21 22 25 26 28 29 30 32 34 35 37 39 40 41 42 43 44 45 46 48 49 51 54 56 61 63 64 65 67 68 71 73 74 **P**5 7 8 *Web address:* www.sleh.com	21	10	637	30749	439	183876	2377	349197	136125	3489
★ TEXAS CHILDREN'S HOSPITAL, 6621 Fannin Street, Zip 77030–2399, Mailing Address: Box 300630, Zip 77230–0630; tel. 713/770–1000; Mark A. Wallace, Executive Director and Chief Executive Officer **A**1 3 5 8 9 10 **F**4 5 10 12 13 15 16 17 19 20 21 22 24 25 29 30 31 32 34 35 38 39 41 42 43 44 45 46 47 49 51 54 55 58 60 63 65 66 67 68 70 71 72 73 **P**5 7 *Web address:* www.txchildrens.org	23	50	374	18010	319	377791	0	280122	129390	2984
★ TEXAS ORTHOPEDIC HOSPITAL, (Formerly Columbia Texas Orthopedic Hospital), 7401 South Main Street, Zip 77030–4509; tel. 713/799–8600; Beryl Ramsey, Chief Executive Officer (Total facility includes 9 beds in nursing home–type unit) **A**1 9 10 **F**2 3 4 5 7 8 10 11 12 14 16 17 19 21 22 23 24 25 26 28 29 30 32 33 34 35 37 38 39 40 41 42 43 44 45 46 47 48 49 51 52 53 55 56 57 58 59 60 61 64 65 66 67 71 72 73 74 **P**2 4 5 6 7 8 **S** Columbia/HCA Healthcare Corporation, Nashville, TN *Web address:* www.columbia.net	32	47	49	1719	17	31860	0	23351	9081	232
★ △ THE INSTITUTE FOR REHABILITATION AND RESEARCH, 1333 Moursund, Zip 77030–3405; tel. 713/799–5000; Louisa F. Adelung, President and Chief Executive Officer **A**1 3 5 7 9 10 **F**12 16 19 20 21 22 29 34 35 41 44 45 46 48 49 64 65 66 67 71 73 **P**5 *Web address:* www.tmc.edu/tirr	23	46	70	796	53	21845	0	30928	11975	293
★ △ THE METHODIST HOSPITAL, 6565 Fannin Street, Zip 77030–2707; tel. 713/790–3311; R. G. Girotto, Executive Vice President and Chief Operating Officer (Total facility includes 25 beds in nursing home–type unit) **A**1 2 3 5 7 8 10 **F**2 3 4 5 7 8 9 10 11 12 14 15 16 17 18 19 20 21 22 23 26 27 28 29 30 31 32 33 34 35 36 37 40 41 42 43 44 45 46 48 49 51 52 54 55 56 57 58 59 60 61 63 64 65 66 67 68 71 73 74 **P**2 3 5 **S** Methodist Health Care System, Houston, TX *Web address:* www.methodisthealth.com	23	10	879	35098	626	305082	2953	484482	173181	4605

Hospital, Address, Telephone, Administrator, Approval, Facility, and Physician Codes, Health Care System, Network	Classi-fication Codes		Utilization Data					Expense (thousands) of dollars		
	Control	Service	Staffed Beds	Admissions	Census	Outpatient Visits	Births	Total	Payroll	Personnel

★ American Hospital Association (AHA) membership
□ Joint Commission on Accreditation of Healthcare Organizations (JCAHO) accreditation
+ American Osteopathic Healthcare Association (AOHA) membership
○ American Osteopathic Association (AOA) accreditation
△ Commission on Accreditation of Rehabilitation Facilities (CARF) accreditation
Control codes 61, 63, 64, 71, 72 and 73 indicate hospitals listed by AOHA, but not registered by AHA. For definition of numerical codes, see page A4

Hospital	Control	Service	Staffed Beds	Admissions	Census	Outpatient Visits	Births	Total	Payroll	Personnel
✠ THE WOMAN'S HOSPITAL OF TEXAS, 7600 Fannin Street, Zip 77054–1900; tel. 713/790–1234; Linda B. Russell, President **A**1 5 9 10 **F**2 3 4 5 7 8 10 11 12 17 19 21 22 23 24 25 26 28 29 30 32 33 34 35 37 38 39 40 41 42 43 44 45 46 47 48 49 51 52 53 55 56 57 58 59 60 61 64 65 66 67 71 72 73 74 **P**8 **S** Columbia/HCA Healthcare Corporation, Nashville, TN **Web address:** www.columbia.net	33	44	162	10519	129	28335	6575	68777	31807	734
TWELVE OAKS HOSPITAL See Bayou City Medical Center										
✠ UNIVERSITY OF TEXAS M. D. ANDERSON CANCER CENTER, (COMPREHENSIVE CANCER CENTER), 1515 Holcombe Boulevard, Box 91, Zip 77030–4095; tel. 713/792–6000; John Mendelsohn, M.D., President and Chief Executive Officer **A**1 2 3 5 8 9 10 **F**8 12 14 15 16 17 19 20 21 22 25 28 29 30 34 35 37 39 41 42 44 45 46 48 49 53 54 55 56 58 60 63 65 67 68 71 73 **P**5 6 **S** University of Texas System, Austin, TX **Web address:** www.mdanderson.org	12	49	437	15920	335	499627	0	775353	365376	8418
✠ VENCOR HOSPITAL–HOUSTON, 6441 Main Street, Zip 77030–1596; tel. 713/790–0500; Bob Stein, Executive Director (Nonreporting) **A**1 10 **S** Vencor, Incorporated, Louisville, KY **Web address:** www.vencor.com	32	10	94	—	—	—	—	—	—	—
✠ VETERANS AFFAIRS MEDICAL CENTER, 2002 Holcombe Boulevard, Zip 77030–4298; tel. 713/791–1414; David Whatley, Director (Total facility includes 120 beds in nursing home–type unit) (Nonreporting) **A**1 3 5 8 **S** Department of Veterans Affairs, Washington, DC	45	10	859	—	—	—	—	—	—	—
✠ △ WEST HOUSTON MEDICAL CENTER, 12141 Richmond Avenue, Zip 77082–2499; tel. 281/558–3444; Jeffrey S. Holland, Chief Executive Officer (Total facility includes 18 beds in nursing home–type unit) **A**1 7 9 10 **F**2 3 4 5 7 8 10 11 12 14 15 16 17 19 20 21 22 23 24 25 26 28 29 30 32 33 34 35 37 38 39 40 41 42 43 44 45 46 47 48 49 51 52 53 55 56 57 58 59 60 61 64 65 66 67 71 72 73 74 **P**2 4 5 6 7 8 **S** Columbia/HCA Healthcare Corporation, Nashville, TN **Web address:** www.columbia.net	33	10	169	6859	88	53418	1346	49540	19538	484
□ WEST OAKS HOSPITAL, 6500 Hornwood Drive, Zip 77074–5095; tel. 713/995–0909; Terry Scovill, Chief Executive Officer **A**1 10 **F**1 2 3 15 16 19 21 22 26 27 34 35 39 50 52 53 54 55 56 57 58 59 60 63 67 70 **S** Healthcare America, Inc., Austin, TX	33	22	144	3634	62	9107	0	11921	5746	228
HUMBLE—Harris County										
□ △ HEALTHSOUTH REHABILITATION HOSPITAL, 19002 McKay Drive, Zip 77338–5701; tel. 281/446–6148; Darrell L. Pile, Administrator **A**1 7 10 **F**12 14 15 16 19 24 26 27 32 34 35 39 44 45 46 48 49 65 66 67 71 **S** HEALTHSOUTH Corporation, Birmingham, AL	33	46	60	594	31	6430	0	6739	3175	115
✠ NORTHEAST MEDICAL CENTER HOSPITAL, 18951 Memorial North, Zip 77338–4297; tel. 281/540–7700; Syble F. Missildine, Administrator (Total facility includes 16 beds in nursing home–type unit) **A**1 2 9 10 **F**1 3 4 5 7 8 10 11 12 13 15 16 17 18 19 20 21 22 23 24 25 26 27 28 29 30 31 32 33 34 35 36 37 39 40 41 42 43 44 45 46 47 48 49 51 53 54 55 56 57 58 59 60 61 62 63 64 65 66 67 68 69 70 71 72 73 74 **P**1 8 **Web address:** www.nemch.org	16	10	204	9310	117	110956	1315	77784	30568	795
HUNT—Kerr County										
LA HACIENDA TREATMENT CENTER, FM 1340, Zip 78024, Mailing Address: P.O. Box 1, Zip 78024–0001; tel. 830/238–4222; Frank J. Sadlack, Ph.D., Executive Director **F**2 12 46 67 **P**1 **Web address:** www.lahacienda.com	32	82	10	596	6	0	0	1224	641	—
HUNTSVILLE—Walker County										
✠ HUNTSVILLE MEMORIAL HOSPITAL, 485 I–45 South, Zip 77340–4362, Mailing Address: P.O. Box 4001, Zip 77342–4001; tel. 409/291–3411; Ralph E. Beaty, Administrator (Total facility includes 11 beds in nursing home–type unit) **A**1 6 9 10 **F**7 8 14 16 19 21 22 25 28 29 30 32 34 35 37 40 41 44 49 57 64 65 66 67 70 71 73 **S** Quorum Health Group/Quorum Health Resources, Inc., Brentwood, TN **Web address:** www.huntsvillememorial.com	33	10	130	2999	36	73506	469	28321	12490	368
IRAAN—Pecos County										
□ PECOS COUNTY GENERAL HOSPITAL, 305 West Fifth Street, Zip 79744, Mailing Address: P.O. Box 665, Zip 79744–2057; tel. 915/639–2871; David B. Shaw, Administrator and Chief Executive Officer **A**1 9 10 **F**8 14 15 16 22 28 30 34 39 44 45 49 51 65 70 71	13	10	13	295	3	5753	0	2415	593	25
IRVING—Dallas County										
✠ BAYLOR MEDICAL CENTER AT IRVING, 1901 North MacArthur Boulevard, Zip 75061–2291; tel. 972/579–8100; Michael F. O'Keefe, FACHE, Executive Director (Total facility includes 18 beds in nursing home–type unit) **A**1 2 9 10 **F**1 4 7 8 10 11 12 15 16 17 19 20 21 22 23 25 26 27 28 30 31 32 33 34 35 37 39 40 41 42 43 44 45 46 48 49 51 54 56 60 63 64 65 66 67 71 72 73 74 **P**8 **S** Baylor Health Care System, Dallas, TX **Web address:** www.bhcs.com/irving	21	10	235	12981	160	94522	2333	111907	51537	1492
JACKSBORO—Jack County										
✠ FAITH COMMUNITY HOSPITAL, 717 Magnolia Street, Zip 76458–1111; tel. 940/567–6633; Don Hopkins, Administrator **A**9 10 **F**15 19 22 28 32 33 41 44 49 64 65 70 71 **P**6	16	10	18	524	5	15241	0	3568	1614	72

Hospital, Address, Telephone, Administrator, Approval, Facility, and Physician Codes, Health Care System, Network	Classification Codes		Utilization Data					Expense (thousands) of dollars		
★ American Hospital Association (AHA) membership □ Joint Commission on Accreditation of Healthcare Organizations (JCAHO) accreditation + American Osteopathic Healthcare Association (AOHA) membership ○ American Osteopathic Association (AOA) accreditation △ Commission on Accreditation of Rehabilitation Facilities (CARF) accreditation Control codes 61, 63, 64, 71, 72 and 73 indicate hospitals listed by AOHA, but not registered by AHA. For definition of numerical codes, see page A4	Control	Service	Staffed Beds	Admissions	Census	Outpatient Visits	Births	Total	Payroll	Personnel

JACKSONVILLE—Cherokee County

★ EAST TEXAS MEDICAL CENTER JACKSONVILLE, 501 South Ragsdale Street, Zip 75766–2413; tel. 903/541–5000; Steve Bowen, President (Total facility includes 18 beds in nursing home–type unit) **A**9 10 **F**7 8 15 17 19 20 21 22 23 24 28 34 35 37 40 41 44 46 49 51 57 64 65 66 67 71 73 74 **P**1 7 **S** East Texas Medical Center Regional Healthcare System, Tyler, TX

| | 23 | 10 | 83 | 2795 | 42 | 50453 | 441 | 23680 | 10012 | 296 |

JASPER—Jasper County

⊞ JASPER MEMORIAL HOSPITAL, 1275 Marvin Hancock Drive, Zip 75951–4995; tel. 409/384–5461; George N. Miller, Jr., Chief Executive Officer **A**1 6 9 10 **F**7 8 12 14 15 16 17 19 22 25 26 28 29 30 31 32 34 35 37 40 44 45 46 48 49 51 65 70 71 73 **P**5 8 **S** Christus Health, Houston, TX

| | 21 | 10 | 54 | 2525 | 22 | 43644 | 394 | 13780 | 6399 | 241 |

JOURDANTON—Atascosa County

□ TRI-CITY COMMUNITY HOSPITAL, 1604 Highway 97 East, Zip 78026, Mailing Address: P.O. Box 189, Zip 78026–0189; tel. 830/769–3515; S. Allan Smith, Administrator **A**1 9 10 **F**8 16 18 19 20 21 22 26 28 30 32 33 34 35 39 41 42 44 46 49 57 58 65 66 71 72 **P**5

| | 32 | 10 | 30 | 1909 | 18 | 86987 | 1 | — | — | 250 |

JUNCTION—Kimble County

KIMBLE HOSPITAL, 2101 Main Street, Zip 76849–2101; tel. 915/446–3321; Jamie R. Jacoby, Administrator **A**9 10 **F**22 24 26 32 34 39 49 70 71

| | 16 | 10 | 15 | 283 | 3 | 14912 | 0 | 2902 | 1363 | 58 |

KATY—Fort Bend County

⊞ KATY MEDICAL CENTER, 5602 Medical Center Drive, Zip 77494–6399; tel. 281/392–1111; Brian S. Barbe, Chief Executive Officer **A**1 9 10 **F**2 3 4 5 7 8 10 11 12 16 17 19 20 21 22 24 25 26 28 29 30 31 33 34 35 36 37 38 39 40 41 42 43 44 45 46 47 48 49 51 52 53 55 57 58 59 60 61 64 65 66 67 71 72 73 74 **P**2 4 5 6 7 8 **S** Columbia/HCA Healthcare Corporation, Nashville, TN

| | 33 | 10 | 73 | 3856 | 34 | 51612 | 715 | 21718 | 10611 | 301 |

KAUFMAN—Kaufman County

⊞ PRESBYTERIAN HOSPITAL OF KAUFMAN, 850 Highway 243 West, Zip 75142–9998, Mailing Address: P.O. Box 310, Zip 75142–0310; tel. 972/932–7200; Michael J. McBride, CHE, Senior Vice President and Executive Director (Total facility includes 6 beds in nursing home–type unit) **A**1 9 10 **F**7 8 15 16 17 19 21 22 27 28 34 37 40 42 44 51 61 64 65 71 73 **S** Texas Health Resources, Irving, TX

| | 23 | 10 | 68 | 2720 | 31 | 59358 | 332 | 21836 | 8732 | 290 |

KENEDY—Karnes County

OTTO KAISER MEMORIAL HOSPITAL, 3349 South Highway 181, Zip 78119–5240; tel. 830/583–3401; Harold L. Boening, Administrator **A**9 10 **F**19 22 32 37 44 49 71

| | 16 | 10 | 30 | 401 | 4 | 30776 | 0 | 4487 | 1969 | 80 |

KERMIT—Winkler County

MEMORIAL HOSPITAL, 821 Jeffee Drive, Zip 79745–4696, Mailing Address: Drawer H, Zip 79745–6008; tel. 915/586–5864; Judene Willhelm, Administrator **A**9 10 **F**13 22 49 70 71

| | 13 | 10 | 16 | 498 | 6 | 9229 | 0 | 3667 | 1643 | 72 |

KERRVILLE—Kerr County

□ KERRVILLE STATE HOSPITAL, 721 Thompson Drive, Zip 78028–5154; tel. 830/896–2211; Gloria P. Olsen, Ph.D., Superintendent **A**1 10 **F**14 15 16 20 22 26 30 39 45 52 56 57 65 67 73
Web address: www.mhmr.state.tx.us
KERVILLE DIVISION See South Texas Veterans Health Care System, San Antonio

| | 12 | 22 | 217 | 562 | 169 | 0 | 0 | 25532 | 15473 | — |

⊞ SID PETERSON MEMORIAL HOSPITAL, 710 Water Street, Zip 78028–5398; tel. 830/896–4200; Frederic W. Hall, Jr., Administrator (Total facility includes 28 beds in nursing home–type unit) **A**1 9 10 **F**4 7 8 11 12 14 15 16 19 21 22 23 28 30 32 34 35 40 41 42 44 45 46 49 62 64 65 71 73 74 **P**8
Web address: www.spmh.com

| | 23 | 10 | 130 | 5969 | 87 | 77608 | 390 | 32012 | 15807 | 491 |

KILGORE—Gregg County

★ ROY H. LAIRD MEMORIAL HOSPITAL, 1612 South Henderson Boulevard, Zip 75662–3594; tel. 903/984–3505; Roderick G. La Grone, President **A**9 10 **F**7 8 19 21 22 26 30 32 34 35 39 40 41 44 45 49 70 71 73 74

| | 14 | 10 | 51 | 1075 | 10 | 25346 | 358 | 13473 | 5758 | 189 |

KILLEEN—Bell County

⊞ METROPLEX ADVENTIST HOSPITAL, 2201 South Clear Creek Road, Zip 76542–9305; tel. 254/526–7523; Kenneth A. Finch, Chief Executive Officer (Total facility includes 13 beds in nursing home–type unit) **A**1 9 10 **F**7 8 10 12 14 15 16 17 19 21 22 23 28 29 30 32 34 35 37 39 40 41 42 44 45 46 49 52 53 54 55 56 57 59 63 64 65 67 71 72 73 **P**8 **S** Adventist Health System Sunbelt Health Care Corporation, Winter Park, FL

| | 21 | 10 | 213 | 6699 | 87 | 93516 | 746 | 51746 | 18582 | 721 |

KINGSVILLE—Kleberg County

⊞ CHRISTUS SPOHN HOSPITAL KLEBERG, (Formerly Spohn Kleberg Memorial Hospital), 1311 General Cavazos Boulevard, Zip 78363–1197, Mailing Address: P.O. Box 1197, Zip 78363–1197; tel. 361/595–1661; Ernesto M. Flores, Jr., Administrator (Total facility includes 15 beds in nursing home–type unit) **A**1 9 10 **F**7 8 12 14 15 16 19 21 22 28 30 31 32 33 34 35 37 39 40 41 42 44 46 49 51 53 54 55 56 58 59 60 64 65 66 67 68 70 71 73 **P**3 5 8 **S** Christus Health, San Antonio, TX

| | 21 | 10 | 100 | 6383 | 80 | 81502 | 412 | 30349 | 14267 | 465 |

KINGWOOD—Harris County

□ CHARTER BEHAVIORAL HEALTH SYSTEM OF SOUTHEAST TEXAS–KINGWOOD, 2001 Ladbrook Drive, Zip 77339–3004; tel. 281/358–4501; Ramona Key, Chief Executive Officer **A**1 10 **F**2 3 12 15 18 27 46 52 53 55 56 57 58 59 65 67 **S** Magellan Health Services, Atlanta, GA

| | 33 | 22 | 80 | 1206 | 22 | 3220 | 0 | 5276 | 2448 | 62 |

Hospital, Address, Telephone, Administrator, Approval, Facility, and Physician Codes, Health Care System, Network	Classi-fication Codes		Utilization Data					Expense (thousands) of dollars		
	Control	Service	Staffed Beds	Admissions	Census	Outpatient Visits	Births	Total	Payroll	Personnel

★ American Hospital Association (AHA) membership
□ Joint Commission on Accreditation of Healthcare Organizations (JCAHO) accreditation
+ American Osteopathic Healthcare Association (AOHA) membership
○ American Osteopathic Association (AOA) accreditation
△ Commission on Accreditation of Rehabilitation Facilities (CARF) accreditation
Control codes 61, 63, 64, 71, 72 and 73 indicate hospitals listed by AOHA, but not registered by AHA. For definition of numerical codes, see page A4.

Hospital	Control	Service	Staffed Beds	Admissions	Census	Outpatient Visits	Births	Total	Payroll	Personnel
✠ KINGWOOD MEDICAL CENTER, (Formerly Columbia Kingwood Medical Center), 22999 U.S. Highway 59, Zip 77339; tel. 281/359–7500; Charles D. Schuetz, Chief Executive Officer **A**1 9 10 **F**2 3 4 6 7 8 9 10 11 12 13 14 15 16 17 18 19 20 21 22 23 24 25 26 27 28 29 30 31 32 33 34 35 36 37 38 39 40 41 42 43 44 45 46 47 48 49 50 51 52 53 54 55 56 57 58 59 60 61 62 63 64 65 66 67 68 70 71 72 73 74 **P**1 2 5 7 **S** Columbia/HCA Healthcare Corporation, Nashville, TN	33	10	153	6652	88	55155	863	45128	20268	530
LA GRANGE—Fayette County										
✠ FAYETTE MEMORIAL HOSPITAL, 543 North Jackson Street, Zip 78945–2040; tel. 409/968–3166; J. L. Flotte', Interim Chief Executive Officer and Administrator **A**1 9 10 **F**7 8 12 14 15 16 17 19 21 22 26 28 29 30 32 33 34 35 39 40 41 42 44 46 49 51 65 71 73 74	23	10	45	2062	25	68254	231	12542	5360	225
LACKLAND AFB—Bexar County										
✠ WILFORD HALL MEDICAL CENTER, 2200 Bergquist Drive, Zip 78236–5300; tel. 210/292–7353; Colonel Arthur E. Aenchbacher, Jr., Administrator (Nonreporting) **A**1 2 3 5 **S** Department of the Air Force, Bowling AFB, DC	41	10	715	—	—	—	—	—	—	—
LAKE JACKSON—Brazoria County										
✠ △ BRAZOSPORT MEMORIAL HOSPITAL, 100 Medical Drive, Zip 77566–9983; tel. 409/297–4411; Wesley W. Oswald, Chief Executive Officer **A**1 2 7 9 10 **F**2 3 7 8 10 12 15 16 19 21 22 23 30 32 35 36 37 40 41 42 44 48 52 53 56 57 58 59 60 64 65 67 71 73 74 **P**8 **S** Quorum Health Group/Quorum Health Resources, Inc., Brentwood, TN **Web address:** www.brazosportmemorial.com	23	10	156	5814	62	23065	732	36699	15604	522
LAMESA—Dawson County										
MEDICAL ARTS HOSPITAL, 1600 North Bryan Avenue, Zip 79331; tel. 806/872–2183; Karl R. Stinson, CHE, Chief Executive Officer **A**9 10 **F**7 8 12 14 15 16 17 19 22 28 30 32 34 40 44 46 49 65 70 71 73	13	10	44	819	8	16849	94	8490	4423	211
LANCASTER—Dallas County										
✠ MEDICAL CENTER AT LANCASTER, (Formerly Columbia Medical Center), 2600 West Pleasant Run Road, Zip 75146–1199; tel. 972/223–9600; Ernest C. Lynch, III, Chief Executive Officer **A**1 9 10 **F**2 3 4 7 8 10 11 12 13 14 16 17 19 20 21 22 23 25 26 27 28 30 33 34 35 38 39 40 41 42 43 44 46 47 49 52 53 54 55 56 57 58 59 61 63 65 66 67 68 71 72 73 74 **P**5 **S** Columbia/HCA Healthcare Corporation, Nashville, TN **Web address:** www.columbia–hca.com	33	10	79	2546	35	29876	234	19788	9768	233
LAREDO—Webb County										
✠ DOCTORS HOSPITAL OF LAREDO, (Formerly Columbia Doctors Hospital of Laredo), 500 East Mann Road, Zip 78041–2699; tel. 956/723–1131; Benjamin Everett, Chief Executive Officer (Total facility includes 6 beds in nursing home–type unit) **A**1 9 10 **F**8 10 12 15 16 18 19 21 22 25 28 29 30 32 34 35 37 38 39 40 42 44 49 60 63 64 65 71 73 74 **P**8 **S** Universal Health Services, Inc., King of Prussia, PA **Web address:** www.columbia.net	32	10	117	5706	63	78944	1790	32903	13508	445
✠ MERCY REGIONAL MEDICAL CENTER, 1515 Logan Avenue, Zip 78040–4617; Mailing Address: Drawer 2068, Zip 78044–2068; tel. 956/718–6222; Mark S. Stauder, President and Chief Executive Officer (Total facility includes 47 beds in nursing home–type unit) **A**1 9 10 **F**4 7 8 10 11 12 13 14 15 16 17 19 21 22 23 25 27 28 30 31 32 34 35 37 38 39 40 42 43 44 45 46 47 48 49 51 52 63 64 65 70 71 72 73 74 **P**8 **S** Sisters of Mercy Health System–St. Louis, Saint Louis, MO **Web address:** www.mhst.smhs.com	21	10	320	14608	210	184478	3717	111656	39358	1277
LEAGUE CITY—Galveston County										
□ DEVEREUX TEXAS TREATMENT NETWORK, 1150 Devereux Drive, Zip 77573–2043; tel. 281/335–1000; L. Gail Atkinson, Executive Director (Nonreporting) **A**1 10 **S** Devereux Foundation, Villanova, PA **Web address:** www.devereux.org	23	22	88	—	—	—	—	—	—	—
LEVELLAND—Hockley County										
✠ COVENANT HOSPITAL–LEVELLAND, (Formerly Methodist Hospital–Levelland), 1900 South College Avenue, Zip 79336–6508; tel. 806/894–4963; Jerry Osburn, Administrator **A**1 9 10 **F**7 8 14 15 16 17 19 20 21 22 28 29 30 31 32 33 34 36 39 40 43 44 45 46 49 51 53 54 55 56 57 58 59 65 70 71 73 **P**7 **S** St. Joseph Health System, Orange, CA	21	10	44	1339	15	17142	254	10501	3439	163
LEWISVILLE—Denton County										
✠ MEDICAL CENTER OF LEWISVILLE, 500 West Main, Zip 75057–3699; tel. 972/420–1000; Raymond M. Dunning, Jr., Chief Executive Officer **A**1 9 10 **F**4 7 8 19 32 33 35 37 40 41 42 44 49 64 65 66 70 71 73 74 **S** Columbia/HCA Healthcare Corporation, Nashville, TN **Web address:** www.lewisvillemedical.com	33	10	116	6695	76	61115	1248	43135	19822	594
LIBERTY—Liberty County										
□ LIBERTY–DAYTON HOSPITAL, 1353 North Travis Street, Zip 77575–1353; tel. 409/336–7316; Sean Stricker, Administrator **A**1 9 10 **F**19 21 22 32 33 34 44 49 68 71 73 **P**5	33	10	35	812	8	20857	0	6745	2814	86
LIBERTY HILL—Williamson County										
MERIDELL ACHIEVEMENT CENTER, 12550 West Highway 29, Zip 78642, Mailing Address: P.O. Box 87, Zip 78642–0087; tel. 800/366–8656; Trish Mitchell, Chief Executive Officer (Nonreporting) **S** Universal Health Services, Inc., King of Prussia, PA	33	52	78	—	—	—	—	—	—	—

Hospital, Address, Telephone, Administrator, Approval, Facility, and Physician Codes, Health Care System, Network	Classi-fication Codes		Utilization Data					Expense (thousands) of dollars		
	Control	Service	Staffed Beds	Admissions	Census	Outpatient Visits	Births	Total	Payroll	Personnel

★ American Hospital Association (AHA) membership
□ Joint Commission on Accreditation of Healthcare Organizations (JCAHO) accreditation
+ American Osteopathic Healthcare Association (AOHA) membership
○ American Osteopathic Association (AOA) accreditation
△ Commission on Accreditation of Rehabilitation Facilities (CARF) accreditation
Control codes 61, 63, 64, 71, 72 and 73 indicate hospitals listed by AOHA, but not registered by AHA. For definition of numerical codes, see page A4

LINDEN—Cass County

LINDEN MUNICIPAL HOSPITAL, 404 North Kaufman Street, Zip 75563–5235; tel. 903/756–5561; Richard D. Arnold, Administrator **A**9 10 **F**8 16 19 20 22 32 37 44 46 49 71 — 16 10 39 762 14 3645 0 5619 2778 103

LITTLEFIELD—Lamb County

⊞ LAMB HEALTHCARE CENTER, 1500 South Sunset, Zip 79339–4899; tel. 806/385–6411; Randall A. Young, Administrator **A**1 9 10 **F**7 15 16 17 19 22 28 30 32 33 34 36 39 40 44 45 46 64 65 68 70 71 74 **S** Lubbock Methodist Hospital System, Lubbock, TX — 13 10 41 1082 15 10859 103 5584 2767 123

LIVINGSTON—Polk County

□ MEMORIAL MEDICAL CENTER, 602 East Church Street, Zip 77351–1257, Mailing Address: P.O. Box 1257, Zip 77351–1257; tel. 409/327–4381; James C. Dickson, Administrator **A**1 9 10 **F**7 8 15 19 22 28 30 34 39 40 44 63 65 70 73 **S** Memorial Health System of East Texas, Lufkin, TX — 23 10 28 1552 11 37372 142 9137 3951 86

LLANO—Llano County

⊞ LLANO MEMORIAL HEALTHCARE SYSTEM, 200 West Ollie Street, Zip 78643–2628; tel. 915/247–5040; Ernest Parisi, Administrator and Chief Executive Officer **A**1 9 10 **F**7 8 15 16 17 19 21 22 28 30 32 33 40 41 42 44 49 51 65 71
Web address: www.LlANOMEMORIAL.ORG — 13 10 30 1597 13 98415 308 14667 5754 241

LOCKNEY—Floyd County

W. J. MANGOLD MEMORIAL HOSPITAL, 320 North Main Street, Zip 79241–0037, Mailing Address: Box 37, Zip 79241–0037; tel. 806/652–3373; Sharon Hunt, Administrator **A**9 10 **F**7 15 16 19 22 28 34 40 44 49 51 61 70 71 — 16 10 27 569 5 24724 124 3384 1729 84

LONGVIEW—Gregg County

⊞ △ GOOD SHEPHERD MEDICAL CENTER, 700 East Marshall Avenue, Zip 75601–5571; tel. 903/236–2000; Jerry D. Adair, President and Chief Executive Officer (Total facility includes 25 beds in nursing home–type unit) **A**1 7 9 10 **F**4 7 8 10 12 14 15 16 17 19 20 21 22 23 25 26 27 28 29 30 31 32 34 35 37 39 40 41 42 43 44 45 46 47 48 49 51 56 60 63 64 65 66 67 69 71 72 73 74 **P**1 — 23 10 320 17312 243 141638 1784 136790 55683 1695

⊞ LONGVIEW REGIONAL MEDICAL CENTER, 2901 North Fourth Street, Zip 75605–5191, Mailing Address: P.O. Box 14000, Zip 75607–4000; tel. 903/758–1818; Vicki L. Romero, Chief Executive Officer (Total facility includes 20 beds in nursing home–type unit) **A**1 9 10 **F**4 7 8 10 12 15 16 17 18 19 20 21 22 23 28 30 34 35 37 39 40 41 42 43 44 45 46 48 49 60 63 64 65 66 67 71 73 74 **P**7 8 **S** Triad Hospitals, Inc., Dallas, TX
Web address: www.columbia.net/index.html — 33 10 164 4769 64 43544 526 40112 17899 558

LUBBOCK—Lubbock County

□ CHARTER PLAINS BEHAVIORAL HEALTH SYSTEM, 801 North Quaker Avenue, Zip 79416–2408, Mailing Address: P.O. Box 10560, Zip 79408–0560; tel. 806/744–5505; Earl W. Balzen, R.N., Chief Executive Officer and Administrator **A**1 5 9 10 **F**2 3 12 15 16 34 46 52 53 54 56 57 58 59 65 67 **S** Magellan Health Services, Atlanta, GA — 32 22 80 825 18 2588 0 4752 2207 68

★ COVENANT CHILDREN'S HOSPITAL, (Formerly Methodist Children's Hospital), 3610 21st Street, Zip 79410–1218; tel. 806/784–5040; George H. McCleskey, President and Chief Executive Officer **A**9 10 **F**4 7 8 10 12 14 15 16 17 19 21 22 23 24 26 27 30 31 32 35 38 39 41 42 43 44 45 47 49 60 65 66 67 68 70 71 73 74 **P**3 5 6 **S** St. Joseph Health System, Orange, CA
Web address: www.methlube.org — 21 50 73 1675 19 15221 0 — — 63

⊞ △ COVENANT MEDICAL CENTER, (Formerly Methodist Hospital), 3615 19th Street, Zip 79410–1201, Mailing Address: Box 1201, Zip 79408–1201; tel. 806/792–1011; George H. McCleskey, President and Chief Executive Officer **A**1 2 6 7 9 10 **F**4 7 8 10 11 12 14 15 16 17 19 21 22 23 24 26 27 30 31 32 35 37 39 40 41 42 43 44 45 48 64 65 66 67 68 70 71 73 74 **P**3 5 6 **S** St. Joseph Health System, Orange, CA
Web address: www.methlub.org — 21 10 520 20809 351 91835 1709 240730 86428 2317

⊞ △ COVENANT MEDICAL CENTER–LAKESIDE, (Formerly St Mary of the Plains Hospital), 4000 24th Street, Zip 79410–1894; tel. 806/796–6000; Charley O. Trimble, President and Chief Executive Officer **A**1 3 5 7 9 10 **F**2 3 4 7 8 10 11 12 14 15 16 17 19 20 21 22 23 25 28 29 30 31 32 34 35 37 38 39 40 41 42 43 44 45 46 47 48 49 52 56 59 60 61 64 65 67 71 72 73 74 **P**6 **S** St. Joseph Health System, Orange, CA — 21 10 410 14377 254 602638 1141 217600 56624 2122

⊞ HIGHLAND MEDICAL CENTER, 2412 50th Street, Zip 79412–2494; tel. 806/788–4060; John D. Brock, Chief Executive Officer **A**1 2 9 10 **F**7 8 12 15 16 17 19 20 21 22 28 30 34 35 39 40 41 42 44 46 48 49 64 65 71 72 73 74 **S** Community Health Systems, Inc., Brentwood, TN — 33 10 123 1981 22 17521 922 16941 5987 203

□ IHS HOSPITAL OF LUBBOCK, (Formerly Horizon Specialty Hospital), 1409 9th Street, Zip 79401–2601; tel. 806/767–9133; Steve Grappe, Administrator **A**1 10 **F**12 27 65 — 33 46 30 256 19 0 0 5123 1578 82

METHODIST CHILDREN'S HOSPITAL See Covenant Children's Hospital
METHODIST HOSPITAL See Covenant Medical Center
ST MARY OF THE PLAINS HOSPITAL See Covenant Medical Center–Lakeside

⊞ UNIVERSITY MEDICAL CENTER, 602 Indiana Avenue, Zip 79415–3364, Mailing Address: P.O. Box 5980, Zip 79408–5980; tel. 806/743–3111; James P. Courtney, President and Chief Executive Officer (Total facility includes 17 beds in nursing home–type unit) **A**1 2 3 5 9 10 **F**4 7 8 9 10 11 12 15 17 19 20 21 22 23 28 29 30 31 32 33 35 37 38 39 40 41 42 43 44 46 47 48 49 56 60 63 64 65 66 67 68 70 71 73 74
Web address: www.teamumc.org — 16 10 318 15762 187 158297 2084 103848 45537 1564

Hospital, Address, Telephone, Administrator, Approval, Facility, and Physician Codes, Health Care System, Network	Classi-fication Codes		Utilization Data					Expense (thousands) of dollars		
★ American Hospital Association (AHA) membership □ Joint Commission on Accreditation of Healthcare Organizations (JCAHO) accreditation + American Osteopathic Healthcare Association (AOHA) membership ○ American Osteopathic Association (AOA) accreditation △ Commission on Accreditation of Rehabilitation Facilities (CARF) accreditation Control codes 61, 63, 64, 71, 72 and 73 indicate hospitals listed by AOHA, but not registered by AHA. For definition of numerical codes, see page A4	Control	Service	Staffed Beds	Admissions	Census	Outpatient Visits	Births	Total	Payroll	Personnel

LUFKIN—Angelina County

⊠ MEMORIAL MEDICAL CENTER OF EAST TEXAS, 1201 West Frank Avenue, Zip 75904–3357, Mailing Address: P.O. Box 1447, Zip 75902–1447; tel. 409/634–8111; Gary Lex Whatley, President and Chief Executive Officer (Total facility includes 30 beds in nursing home–type unit) **A**1 2 9 10 **F**1 7 8 10 12 14 15 16 17 18 19 21 22 23 24 26 27 28 29 30 31 32 33 34 35 37 39 40 41 42 44 45 46 48 49 51 52 54 55 56 58 59 60 64 65 66 67 70 71 72 73 74 **P**5 6 7 8 **S** Memorial Health System of East Texas, Lufkin, TX

| | | 23 | 10 | 233 | 10412 | 169 | 119339 | 551 | 67168 | 27556 | 932 |

⊠ WOODLAND HEIGHTS MEDICAL CENTER, 505 South John Redditt Drive, Zip 75904, Mailing Address: P.O. Box 150610, Zip 75915–0610; tel. 409/634–8311; Don H. McBride, Chief Executive Officer (Total facility includes 16 beds in nursing home–type unit) **A**1 9 10 **F**4 7 8 10 11 12 15 16 19 21 22 23 25 28 30 34 35 39 40 43 44 45 46 64 65 66 71 73 74 **P**5 8 **S** Triad Hospitals, Inc., Dallas, TX

| | | 33 | 10 | 110 | 5595 | 80 | 42989 | 628 | 31938 | 13490 | 478 |

LULING—Caldwell County

★ SETON EDGAR B. DAVIS HOSPITAL, (Formerly Edgar B. Davis Memorial Hospital), 130 Hays Street, Zip 78648–3207, Mailing Address: P.O. Box 510, Zip 78648–0510; tel. 830/875–5643; Neal Kelley, Administrator (Total facility includes 6 beds in nursing home–type unit) **A**9 10 **F**19 21 22 27 32 34 35 44 49 57 60 64 65 70 71 73

| | | 14 | 10 | 21 | 1041 | 12 | 33116 | 80 | 6937 | 2946 | 119 |

MADISONVILLE—Madison County

⊠ MADISON ST. JOSEPH HEALTH CENTER, 100 West Cross Street, Zip 77864–0698, Mailing Address: Box 698, Zip 77864–0698; tel. 409/348–2631; Reed Edmundson, Interim Administrator **A**1 9 10 **F**7 8 14 15 16 19 20 21 22 25 28 30 32 34 40 44 49 51 58 65 71 73 **P**6 **S** Franciscan Services Corporation, Sylvania, OH

| | | 21 | 10 | 35 | 1075 | 14 | 42462 | 122 | 10096 | 5313 | 254 |

MANSFIELD—Tarrant County

□ VENCOR HOSPITAL–MANSFIELD, (Formerly Mansfield General Hospital), (Includes Vencor Hospital – Fort Worth West, 815 Eighth Avenue, Fort Worth, Zip 76104; tel. 817/332–4812), 1802 Highway 157 North, Zip 76063–9555; tel. 817/473–6101; Bill Grey, Administrator **A**1 10 **F**12 16 19 22 26 34 37 44 49 65 70 71 73 **S** Vencor, Incorporated, Louisville, KY

| | | 32 | 48 | 115 | 938 | 62 | — | 1 | 23055 | 9209 | 311 |

MARLIN—Falls County

CENTRAL TEXAS VETERANS AFFAIRS HEALTH CARE SYSTEM, MARLIN INTEGRATED CLINICAL FACILITY See Central Texas Veterans Affairs Healthcare System, Temple

FALLS COMMUNITY HOSPITAL AND CLINIC, 322 Coleman Street, Zip 76661–2358, Mailing Address: Box 60, Zip 76661–0060; tel. 254/803–3561; Willis L. Reese, Administrator **A**10 **F**8 15 16 19 21 22 26 28 30 39 57 70 71 **P**5

| | | 23 | 10 | 36 | 1296 | 15 | 65502 | 3 | 6859 | 2185 | 123 |

MARSHALL—Harrison County

⊠ MARSHALL REGIONAL MEDICAL CENTER, 811 South Washington Avenue, Zip 75670–5336, Mailing Address: P.O. Box 1599, Zip 75671–1599; tel. 903/927–6000; Thomas N. Cammack, Jr., Chief Executive Officer (Total facility includes 10 beds in nursing home–type unit) **A**1 9 10 **F**7 8 12 17 19 21 22 23 24 28 30 32 34 35 37 39 40 41 44 46 49 63 64 65 66 71

| | | 23 | 10 | 101 | 3279 | 40 | 74898 | 624 | 29461 | 12589 | 353 |

MCALLEN—Hidalgo County

□ CHARTER PALMS BEHAVIORAL HEALTH SYSTEM, 1421 East Jackson Avenue, Zip 78501–1602, Mailing Address: P.O. Box 5239, Zip 78502–5239; tel. 956/631–5421; Leslie Bingham, Chief Executive Officer **A**1 9 10 **F**2 3 14 15 16 19 34 35 52 53 56 57 58 59 65 71 **S** Magellan Health Services, Atlanta, GA

| | | 32 | 22 | 40 | 1233 | 26 | 290 | 0 | 5072 | 2273 | 74 |

□ MCALLEN MEDICAL CENTER, 301 West Expressway 83, Zip 78503; tel. 956/632–4000; Daniel P. McLean, Executive Director **A**1 3 9 10 **F**2 4 6 7 8 10 12 14 15 16 19 21 22 23 24 25 28 29 30 34 35 37 38 39 40 41 42 43 44 45 46 47 49 51 52 53 54 55 56 57 58 59 60 61 64 65 66 67 71 73 **P**3 7 8 **S** Universal Health Services, Inc., King of Prussia, PA
Web address: www.uhsmmc.com

| | | 32 | 10 | 455 | 21446 | 336 | 84730 | 5469 | 129877 | 53127 | 1647 |

⊠ RIO GRANDE REGIONAL HOSPITAL, (Formerly Columbia Rio Grande Regional Hospital), 101 East Ridge Road, Zip 78503–1299; tel. 956/632–6000; Randall M. Everts, Chief Executive Officer **A**1 9 10 **F**4 7 8 10 11 12 17 19 20 21 22 23 25 26 28 29 30 34 35 37 38 39 40 41 42 43 44 46 49 60 65 67 71 73 74 **P**8 **S** Columbia/HCA Healthcare Corporation, Nashville, TN
Web address: www.columbia.net

| | | 32 | 10 | 216 | 11082 | 140 | 77554 | 2315 | 61848 | 25607 | 791 |

MCCAMEY—Upton County

MCCAMEY HOSPITAL, Highway 305 South, Zip 79752, Mailing Address: P.O. Box 1200, Zip 79752–1200; tel. 915/652–8626; Bill Boswell, Chief Executive Officer (Total facility includes 30 beds in nursing home–type unit) **A**9 10 **F**22 28 32 34 44 49 64

| | | 16 | 10 | 46 | 45 | 29 | 5581 | 0 | 4328 | 1956 | 50 |

MCKINNEY—Collin County

⊠ NORTH CENTRAL MEDICAL CENTER, (Formerly Medical Center of McKinney), (Includes Westpark Surgery Center, 130 South Central Expressway, Zip 75070; tel. 972/548–5300), 4500 Medical Center Drive, Zip 75069–3499; tel. 972/547–8000; Dale Mulder, Chief Executive Officer (Total facility includes 18 beds in nursing home–type unit) **A**1 9 10 **F**7 10 12 15 16 17 19 22 25 26 35 37 40 41 42 44 48 49 52 57 58 59 60 64 65 71 73 74 **P**7 **S** Columbia/HCA Healthcare Corporation, Nashville, TN
Web address: www.columbia.net

| | | 32 | 10 | 215 | 6329 | 80 | 78522 | 1029 | 41729 | 18244 | 579 |

Hospital, Address, Telephone, Administrator, Approval, Facility, and Physician Codes, Health Care System, Network	Classi-fication Codes		Utilization Data					Expense (thousands) of dollars		
★ American Hospital Association (AHA) membership □ Joint Commission on Accreditation of Healthcare Organizations (JCAHO) accreditation + American Osteopathic Healthcare Association (AOHA) membership ○ American Osteopathic Association (AOA) accreditation △ Commission on Accreditation of Rehabilitation Facilities (CARF) accreditation Control codes 61, 63, 64, 71, 72 and 73 indicate hospitals listed by AOHA, but not registered by AHA. For definition of numerical codes, see page A4	Control	Service	Staffed Beds	Admissions	Census	Outpatient Visits	Births	Total	Payroll	Personnel

MEMPHIS—Hall County

HALL COUNTY HOSPITAL, 1800 North Boykin Drive, Zip 79245–2039; tel. 806/259–3504; Jody Dixon, Administrator **A**9 10 **F**8 15 16 22 28 32 33 39 49 51 71 **P**6	16	10	20	345	3	7463	0	2355	1160	54

MESQUITE—Dallas County

□ MEDICAL CENTER OF MESQUITE, 1011 North Galloway Avenue, Zip 75149–2433; tel. 214/320–7000; Terry J. Fontenot, President and Chief Executive Officer **A**1 9 10 **F**4 7 8 10 12 14 15 16 17 19 21 22 26 29 30 34 35 37 38 39 40 42 43 44 49 57 63 64 65 71 73 74 **P**8 **S** Paracelsus Healthcare Corporation, Houston, TX	33	10	176	5759	73	55876	377	47771	16657	313
□ MESQUITE COMMUNITY HOSPITAL, 3500 Interstate 30, Zip 75150–2696; tel. 972/698–3300; Raymond P. De Blasi, Chief Executive Officer (Total facility includes 13 beds in nursing home–type unit) **A**1 9 10 **F**7 8 10 14 15 16 19 20 21 22 26 31 32 33 35 37 39 40 44 49 52 57 64 65 71 73	32	10	128	5546	63	61920	1275	32425	14288	464

MEXIA—Limestone County

□ PARKVIEW REGIONAL HOSPITAL, 312 East Glendale Street, Zip 76667–3608; tel. 254/562–5332; Tim Adams, Administrator and Chief Executive Officer **A**1 9 10 **F**7 8 12 14 15 16 19 21 22 28 29 30 32 34 35 37 40 41 44 45 46 48 49 65 66 70 71 73 **P**4 7 **S** Province Healthcare Corporation, Brentwood, TN	32	10	44	1916	29	27702	164	16411	5191	203

MIDLAND—Midland County

⊠ △ MEMORIAL HOSPITAL AND MEDICAL CENTER, (Includes Memorial Rehabilitation Hospital, Zip 79704; tel. 915/520–2333), 2200 West Illinois Avenue, Zip 79701–6499; tel. 915/685–1111; Harold Rubin, President and Chief Executive Officer (Total facility includes 17 beds in nursing home–type unit) **A**1 2 3 5 7 9 10 **F**3 4 7 8 10 11 12 14 15 16 17 18 19 21 22 23 27 28 29 30 33 34 35 37 38 40 41 42 43 44 47 48 49 51 56 60 63 64 65 66 67 68 71 72 73 74 **P**8	16	10	276	11050	185	135594	1498	121850	39195	1174
□ WESTWOOD MEDICAL CENTER, 4214 Andrews Highway, Zip 79703–4861; tel. 915/522–2273; Michael S. Potter, President and Chief Executive Officer **A**1 9 10 **F**1 2 3 4 5 6 7 8 9 10 11 12 13 14 16 17 18 19 20 21 23 24 25 26 27 28 29 30 31 32 33 34 35 36 37 38 39 40 41 42 43 44 45 46 47 48 49 50 51 52 53 54 55 56 57 58 59 60 61 62 63 64 65 66 67 68 69 70 71 72 73 74 **P**1 2 3 4 5 6 7 8 **S** Paracelsus Healthcare Corporation, Houston, TX **Web address:** www.westwoodmed.com	33	10	86	2106	22	21307	291	27442	7601	233

MINERAL WELLS—Palo Pinto County

⊠ PALO PINTO GENERAL HOSPITAL, 400 S.W. 25th Avenue, Zip 76067–9685; tel. 940/325–7891; Patricia Dorris, Chief Executive Officer **A**1 9 10 **F**4 7 8 12 13 14 15 16 19 21 22 24 28 29 30 32 33 35 36 37 39 40 41 42 44 45 46 49 51 65 66 67 70 71 73 74	16	10	44	2826	33	30323	419	21614	10281	381

MISSION—Hidalgo County

⊠ MISSION HOSPITAL, 900 South Bryan Road, Zip 78572–6613; tel. 956/580–9000; Paul H. Ballard, Chief Executive Officer **A**1 9 10 **F**4 7 8 10 11 12 15 16 17 19 21 22 26 28 29 30 35 37 38 39 40 41 42 44 45 46 47 49 51 52 65 70 71 73 **P**1 3 6 7 8 **S** Quorum Health Group/Quorum Health Resources, Inc., Brentwood, TN **Web address:** www.missionhosp.com	23	10	110	5310	65	32723	1072	39465	16159	511

MISSOURI CITY—Fort Bend County

⊠ FORT BEND MEDICAL CENTER, 3803 FM 1092 at Highway 6, Zip 77459; tel. 281/403–4800; Rod Brace, Chief Executive Officer (Total facility includes 5 beds in nursing home–type unit) **A**1 9 10 **F**2 3 4 5 7 8 10 11 12 15 16 17 19 20 21 22 23 24 25 26 28 29 30 32 33 34 35 37 38 39 40 41 42 43 44 45 46 47 48 49 50 51 52 53 55 56 57 58 59 60 61 64 65 66 67 71 72 73 74 **P**2 4 5 6 7 8 **S** Columbia/HCA Healthcare Corporation, Nashville, TN **Web address:** www.columbia.net	33	10	65	2830	32	49223	364	22971	8937	256

MONAHANS—Ward County

⊠ WARD MEMORIAL HOSPITAL, 406 South Gary Street, Zip 79756–4798, Mailing Address: P.O. Box 40, Zip 79756–0040; tel. 915/943–2511; Joe Wright, Administrator **A**1 9 10 **F**1 2 3 4 5 6 7 8 9 10 11 12 13 14 15 17 18 19 20 21 22 23 24 25 26 27 28 29 30 31 32 33 34 35 36 37 39 40 41 42 43 44 45 46 47 48 49 50 51 52 53 54 55 56 57 58 59 60 61 62 63 64 65 66 67 69 70 71 72 73 74	13	10	36	828	7	11247	77	6875	3333	115

MORTON—Cochran County

★ COCHRAN MEMORIAL HOSPITAL, 201 East Grant Street, Zip 79346–3444; tel. 806/266–5565; Paul McKinney, Administrator **A**9 10 **F**22 28 32 70 **P**5	16	10	15	213	1	1037	0	2451	1293	75

MOUNT PLEASANT—Titus County

⊠ TITUS REGIONAL MEDICAL CENTER, 2001 North Jefferson Avenue, Zip 75455–2398; tel. 903/577–6000; Steven K. Jacobson, Chief Executive Officer (Total facility includes 6 beds in nursing home–type unit) **A**1 9 10 **F**7 8 10 15 16 17 19 21 22 23 28 30 32 34 35 37 39 40 44 48 49 64 65 71 73 74 **P**8 **S** Quorum Health Group/Quorum Health Resources, Inc., Brentwood, TN	16	10	92	5468	70	140854	986	46368	20498	748

MOUNT VERNON—Franklin County

⊠ EAST TEXAS MEDICAL CENTER–MOUNT VERNON, Highway 37 South, Zip 75457, Mailing Address: P.O. Box 477, Zip 75457–0477; tel. 903/537–4552; Jerry Edwards, CHE, Administrator **A**1 9 10 **F**8 12 13 15 16 17 19 20 22 26 27 28 29 30 32 34 39 44 59 70 71 72 **P**7 8 **S** East Texas Medical Center Regional Healthcare System, Tyler, TX	23	10	30	813	7	19321	0	6146	2667	76

Hospital, Address, Telephone, Administrator, Approval, Facility, and Physician Codes, Health Care System, Network	Classi- fication Codes		Utilization Data					Expense (thousands) of dollars		
	Control	Service	Staffed Beds	Admissions	Census	Outpatient Visits	Births	Total	Payroll	Personnel

★ American Hospital Association (AHA) membership
☐ Joint Commission on Accreditation of Healthcare Organizations (JCAHO) accreditation
+ American Osteopathic Healthcare Association (AOHA) membership
○ American Osteopathic Association (AOA) accreditation
△ Commission on Accreditation of Rehabilitation Facilities (CARF) accreditation
Control codes 61, 63, 64, 71, 72 and 73 indicate hospitals listed by AOHA, but not registered by AHA. For definition of numerical codes, see page A4

MUENSTER—Cooke County

MUENSTER MEMORIAL HOSPITAL, 605 North Maple Street, Zip 76252–2424, Mailing Address: P.O. Box 370, Zip 76252–0370; tel. 940/759–2271; Jack R. Endres, Administrator **A**9 10 **F**7 8 15 19 20 21 22 28 30 32 33 40 44 49 65 67 70 71 **P**8

| | 16 | 10 | 18 | 424 | 4 | 19558 | 81 | 3748 | 1871 | 65 |

MULESHOE—Bailey County

★ MULESHOE AREA MEDICAL CENTER, 708 South First Street, Zip 79347–3627; tel. 806/272–4524; Jim G. Bone, Interim Administrator **A**9 10 **F**7 16 19 22 25 28 29 30 32 40 44 70 71 73 **S** Lubbock Methodist Hospital System, Lubbock, TX

| | 16 | 10 | 25 | 574 | 5 | 34347 | 52 | 4857 | 2400 | 104 |

NACOGDOCHES—Nacogdoches County

☒ NACOGDOCHES MEDICAL CENTER, 4920 N.E. Stallings, Zip 75961–1200, Mailing Address: P.O. Box 631604, Zip 75963–1604; tel. 409/568–3380; Glenn A. Robinson, Chief Executive Officer **A**1 9 10 **F**4 7 8 10 12 15 16 17 19 20 21 22 23 26 28 29 30 32 33 34 35 37 39 40 41 42 43 44 46 49 60 65 67 71 73 74 **P**5 **S** TENET Healthcare Corporation, Santa Barbara, CA
Web address: www.tenethealth.com/nacogdoches

| | 32 | 10 | 150 | 6807 | 81 | — | 698 | 37740 | 16424 | 525 |

☐ △ NACOGDOCHES MEMORIAL HOSPITAL, 1204 North Mound Street, Zip 75961–4061; tel. 409/568–8520; G. W. Jones, Administrator **A**1 7 9 10 **F**4 7 8 10 14 15 16 19 21 22 23 28 30 31 32 33 34 35 37 40 41 42 43 44 45 48 49 63 64 65 67 71 73 **P**8

| | 16 | 10 | 155 | 5851 | 91 | 41612 | 818 | 48983 | 19393 | 678 |

☐ PINELANDS HOSPITAL, 4632 Northeast Stallings Drive, Zip 75961–1617, Mailing Address: P.O. Box 1004, Zip 79563–1004; tel. 409/560–5900; Steve Scott, Chief Executive Officer **A**1 9 10 **F**12 15 18 26 52 53 54 55 56 57 58 59 65 67 **P**1 5 7

| | 33 | 22 | 38 | 539 | 13 | 400 | 0 | 3038 | 1463 | 54 |

NASSAU BAY—Harris County

☒ ST. JOHN HOSPITAL, 18300 St. John Drive, Zip 77058; tel. 281/333–5503; Thomas Permetti, Chief Executive Officer (Total facility includes 24 beds in nursing home–type unit) **A**1 9 10 **F**2 3 5 7 8 9 10 11 12 14 15 16 17 18 19 20 21 22 24 28 30 31 32 33 34 35 36 37 38 39 40 41 42 44 45 46 47 48 49 50 51 52 53 54 55 56 57 58 59 60 61 63 64 65 66 67 68 71 72 73 74 **P**5 6 7 8 **S** Christus Health, Houston, TX

| | 23 | 10 | 135 | 5087 | 50 | 114614 | 687 | 44455 | 17369 | 575 |

NAVASOTA—Grimes County

GRIMES ST. JOSEPH HEALTH CENTER, 210 South Judson Street, Zip 77868–3704, Mailing Address: P.O. Box 1390, Zip 77868–1390; tel. 409/825–6585; Molly Hurst, Administrative Director (Total facility includes 12 beds in nursing home–type unit) (Nonreporting) **A**9
Web address: www.st–joseph.org

| | 33 | 10 | 47 | — | — | — | — | — | — | — |

NEDERLAND—Jefferson County

☒ MID–JEFFERSON HOSPITAL, Highway 365 and 27th Street, Zip 77627–6288, Mailing Address: P.O. Box 1917, Zip 77627–1917; tel. 409/727–2321; Wilson J. Weber, Chief Executive Officer (Total facility includes 18 beds in nursing home–type unit) **A**1 5 9 10 **F**7 8 12 13 15 16 17 19 21 22 28 29 30 31 32 34 37 40 44 45 46 51 64 71 73 74 **P**3 7 **S** TENET Healthcare Corporation, Santa Barbara, CA
Web address: www.tenethealth.com/lakepointe

| | 32 | 10 | 138 | 3212 | 38 | 58227 | 452 | 17959 | 7292 | 264 |

NEW BRAUNFELS—Comal County

☒ MCKENNA MEMORIAL HOSPITAL, 600 North Union Avenue, Zip 78130; tel. 830/606–9111; Bill Morton, President and Chief Executive Officer **A**1 9 10 **F**7 8 11 12 15 16 17 19 20 21 22 23 24 25 27 28 30 32 33 34 35 37 39 40 41 42 44 45 46 48 49 51 54 56 58 63 65 72 73 74 **P**1

| | 23 | 10 | 89 | 5096 | 56 | 32004 | 700 | 35940 | 15625 | 608 |

NOCONA—Montague County

★ NOCONA GENERAL HOSPITAL, 100 Park Street, Zip 76255–3616; tel. 940/825–3235; Jamers Brasier, Administrator **A**9 10 **F**8 12 15 16 19 20 22 26 28 32 34 39 40 42 44 49 51 58 65 70 71 73

| | 16 | 10 | 38 | 1187 | 11 | 16225 | 95 | 6340 | 3096 | 119 |

NORTH RICHLAND HILLS—Tarrant County

☒ NORTH HILLS HOSPITAL, (Formerly Columbia North Hills Hospital), 4401 Booth Calloway Road, Zip 76180–7399; tel. 817/284–1431; Randy Moresi, Chief Executive Officer **A**1 9 10 **F**4 7 8 10 11 12 15 16 19 21 22 23 24 28 29 30 32 33 34 35 37 39 40 41 42 43 44 45 46 48 49 64 65 67 71 73 74 **P**3 5 7 8 **S** Columbia/HCA Healthcare Corporation, Nashville, TN
Web address: www.columbia.net

| | 32 | 10 | 133 | 5293 | 69 | 60726 | 779 | 41910 | 18115 | 430 |

ODESSA—Ector County

☒ MEDICAL CENTER HOSPITAL, 500 West Fourth Street, Zip 79761–5059, Mailing Address: P.O. Drawer 7239, Zip 79760–7239; tel. 915/640–4000; J. Michael Stephans, Administrator (Total facility includes 25 beds in nursing home–type unit) **A**1 2 3 5 9 10 **F**4 7 8 10 11 12 16 17 19 21 22 23 25 30 33 34 35 37 38 39 40 42 43 44 46 49 50 51 53 56 58 59 60 63 64 65 71 73 **P**8

| | 16 | 10 | 324 | 13493 | 232 | 136141 | 1529 | 140152 | 47384 | 1581 |

☒ ODESSA REGIONAL HOSPITAL, 520 East Sixth Street, Zip 79761–4565, Mailing Address: P.O. Box 4859, Zip 79760–4859; tel. 915/334–8200; Lex A. Guinn, Chief Executive Officer **A**1 9 10 **F**7 8 10 12 15 16 19 22 27 28 29 30 34 36 37 38 39 40 44 45 46 65 67 70 71 73 74 **P**8 **S** TENET Healthcare Corporation, Santa Barbara, CA
Web address: www.orh.net

| | 32 | 44 | 44 | 4169 | 46 | 56772 | 1469 | 24879 | 10460 | 345 |

OLNEY—Young County

★ HAMILTON HOSPITAL, 903 West Hamilton Street, Zip 76374–1725, Mailing Address: P.O. Box 158, Zip 76374–0158; tel. 940/564–5521; William R. Smith, Administrator (Nonreporting) **A**9 10

| | 16 | 10 | 46 | — | — | — | — | — | — | — |

Hospital, Address, Telephone, Administrator, Approval, Facility, and Physician Codes, Health Care System, Network	Classification Codes		Utilization Data					Expense (thousands) of dollars		
	Control	Service	Staffed Beds	Admissions	Census	Outpatient Visits	Births	Total	Payroll	Personnel

★ American Hospital Association (AHA) membership
□ Joint Commission on Accreditation of Healthcare Organizations (JCAHO) accreditation
+ American Osteopathic Healthcare Association (AOHA) membership
○ American Osteopathic Association (AOA) accreditation
△ Commission on Accreditation of Rehabilitation Facilities (CARF) accreditation
Control codes 61, 63, 64, 71, 72 and 73 indicate hospitals listed by AOHA, but not registered by AHA. For definition of numerical codes, see page A4

ORANGE—Orange County

□ BAPTIST HOSPITAL–ORANGE, 608 Strickland Drive, Zip 77630–4717; tel. 409/883–9361; Kevin T. Coleman, Administrator (Total facility includes 16 beds in nursing home–type unit) **A**1 9 10 **F**7 8 12 15 16 17 19 21 22 26 27 28 30 31 32 34 35 37 40 41 44 48 49 64 65 67 70 71 73 **P**8

| | 23 | 10 | 120 | 3863 | 57 | 54032 | 199 | 24747 | 10207 | 369 |

PALACIOS—Matagorda County

★ WAGNER GENERAL HOSPITAL, 310 Green Street, Zip 77465–3214, Mailing Address: P.O. Box 859, Zip 77465–0859; tel. 512/972–2511; Kevin Hecht, Director **A**9 10 **F**15 16 22 28 30 32 34 49 **P**6 **S** Matagorda County Hospital District, Bay City, TX

| | 16 | 10 | 6 | 42 | 1 | 3615 | 0 | 1303 | 768 | 16 |

PALESTINE—Anderson County

□ MEMORIAL MOTHER FRANCES HOSPITAL, (Formerly Memorial Hospital), 4000 South Loop 256, Zip 75801–8467, Mailing Address: P.O. Box 4070, Zip 75802–4070; tel. 903/731–5000; Randell G. Stokes, Chief Executive Officer **A**1 9 10 **F**7 8 10 11 19 21 22 24 28 30 32 34 35 39 40 44 45 46 48 63 65 67 71 **P**3 4 7 **S** Province Healthcare Corporation, Brentwood, TN
Web address: www.mmfh.org

| | 32 | 10 | 84 | 3071 | 41 | 47776 | 303 | 23346 | 8521 | — |

⊠ △ TRINITY VALLEY MEDICAL CENTER, 2900 South Loop 256, Zip 75801–6958; tel. 903/731–1000; Larry C. Bozeman, Chief Executive Officer (Total facility includes 12 beds in nursing home–type unit) **A**1 7 9 10 **F**7 8 10 12 15 16 19 20 21 22 23 27 28 30 32 34 35 37 40 41 44 45 46 48 49 52 55 56 57 63 64 65 67 70 71 73 74 **S** TENET Healthcare Corporation, Santa Barbara, CA

| | 33 | 10 | 150 | 4170 | 53 | 58392 | 667 | 31372 | 12053 | 401 |

PAMPA—Gray County

⊠ PAMPA REGIONAL MEDICAL CENTER, (Formerly Columbia Medical Center), One Medical Plaza, Zip 79065; tel. 806/665–3721; Phillip E. Fowler, Interim Chief Executive Officer (Total facility includes 24 beds in nursing home–type unit) **A**1 9 10 **F**7 8 10 12 14 15 16 19 21 22 23 26 28 30 34 35 37 39 40 41 44 46 49 52 57 61 64 65 71 73 **P**8 **S** Triad Hospitals, Inc., Dallas, TX
Web address: www.cmcp.com

| | 33 | 10 | 107 | 3003 | 40 | — | 289 | 21325 | 9098 | 260 |

PARIS—Lamar County

⊠ MCCUISTION REGIONAL MEDICAL CENTER, 865 Deshong Drive, Zip 75462–2097, Mailing Address: P.O. Box 160, Zip 75461–0160; tel. 903/737–1111; Michael J. McBride, CHE, Senior Vice President and Executive Director **A**1 9 10 **F**7 8 10 12 14 15 16 17 19 21 22 23 24 27 28 29 30 31 32 33 34 35 37 40 41 42 44 45 46 49 60 65 66 67 71 73 74 **P**1 2 6 7 8 **S** Texas Health Resources, Irving, TX

| | 23 | 10 | 158 | 6728 | 69 | 49171 | 738 | 33753 | 14653 | 516 |

⊠ ST. JOSEPH'S HOSPITAL AND HEALTH CENTER, 820 Clarksville Street, Zip 75460–9070, Mailing Address: P.O. Box 9070, Zip 75461–9070; tel. 903/785–4521; Monty E. McLaurin, President **A**1 9 10 **F**4 8 10 12 14 15 16 17 19 21 22 23 24 26 28 29 30 31 32 33 34 35 37 39 41 42 43 44 46 48 49 51 52 54 55 56 57 58 59 60 65 66 67 71 73 **P**3 7 8 **S** Christus Health, San Antonio, TX
Web address: www.stjosephhc.com

| | 21 | 10 | 175 | 7252 | 112 | 48505 | 0 | 50748 | 21172 | 743 |

PASADENA—Harris County

⊠ △ BAYSHORE MEDICAL CENTER, (Formerly Columbia Bayshore Medical Center), 4000 Spencer Highway, Zip 77504–1294; tel. 713/359–2000; Donald L. Stewart, Chief Executive Officer (Total facility includes 36 beds in nursing home–type unit) **A**1 2 7 9 10 **F**2 3 4 5 7 8 10 11 12 14 15 16 17 19 20 21 22 23 24 25 26 27 28 29 30 32 33 34 35 37 38 39 40 41 42 43 44 45 46 47 48 49 51 52 53 54 55 56 57 58 59 60 61 64 65 66 67 68 70 71 72 73 74 **P**1 2 4 5 6 7 8 **S** Columbia/HCA Healthcare Corporation, Nashville, TN

| | 33 | 10 | 296 | 13928 | 170 | 139956 | 1931 | 90277 | 33779 | 968 |

⊠ MEMORIAL HOSPITAL PASADENA, 906 East Southmore Avenue, Zip 77502–1124, Mailing Address: P.O. Box 1879, Zip 77502–1879; tel. 713/477–0411; Dennis M. Knox, Vice President and Chief Executive Officer (Total facility includes 21 beds in nursing home–type unit) **A**1 9 10 **F**2 3 4 6 7 8 9 10 11 12 15 16 17 19 20 21 22 23 24 25 26 27 28 29 30 31 32 33 34 35 36 37 38 39 40 41 42 43 44 46 47 48 49 50 51 52 53 54 55 56 57 58 59 60 61 62 63 64 65 66 67 68 70 71 72 73 74 **P**5 **S** Memorial Hermann Healthcare System, Houston, TX
Web address: www.mhcs.org

| | 23 | 10 | 172 | 5479 | 65 | 36334 | 1201 | 37133 | 12873 | 411 |

PEARSALL—Frio County

FRIO HOSPITAL, 320 Berry Ranch Road, Zip 78061–3998; tel. 830/334–3617; Alan D. Holmes, Chief Executive Officer **A**9 10 **F**7 8 15 16 19 22 28 32 44 49 70 71

| | 23 | 10 | 22 | 796 | 8 | 13971 | 224 | 5385 | 2464 | 87 |

PECOS—Reeves County

★ REEVES COUNTY HOSPITAL, 2323 Texas Street, Zip 79772–7338; tel. 915/447–3551; Charles N. Butts, Interim Chief Executive Officer **A**9 10 **F**7 14 19 22 28 32 37 40 44 46 49 65 70 71 **S** Lubbock Methodist Hospital System, Lubbock, TX
Web address: www.rchd.org

| | 16 | 10 | 44 | 763 | 9 | 12331 | 116 | 6103 | 2583 | 113 |

PERRYTON—Ochiltree County

OCHILTREE GENERAL HOSPITAL, 3101 Garrett Drive, Zip 79070–5393; tel. 806/435–3606; Wallace N. Boyd, Administrator **A**10 **F**7 8 12 15 16 17 19 21 22 28 29 30 32 33 34 36 37 40 44 49 65 67 70 71 73 74 **P**1

| | 16 | 10 | 45 | 1071 | 12 | 18304 | 205 | 6308 | 3268 | 109 |

PITTSBURG—Camp County

⊠ EAST TEXAS MEDICAL CENTER PITTSBURG, 414 Quitman Street, Zip 75686–1032; tel. 903/856–6663; W. Perry Henderson, Administrator **A**1 9 10 **F**8 19 21 22 25 32 44 70 71 73 **P**5 7 **S** East Texas Medical Center Regional Healthcare System, Tyler, TX

| | 23 | 10 | 42 | 1337 | 20 | 29272 | 0 | 10720 | 4638 | 172 |

Hospital, Address, Telephone, Administrator, Approval, Facility, and Physician Codes, Health Care System, Network	Classi-fication Codes		Utilization Data					Expense (thousands) of dollars		
★ American Hospital Association (AHA) membership □ Joint Commission on Accreditation of Healthcare Organizations (JCAHO) accreditation + American Osteopathic Healthcare Association (AOHA) membership ○ American Osteopathic Association (AOA) accreditation △ Commission on Accreditation of Rehabilitation Facilities (CARF) accreditation Control codes 61, 63, 64, 71, 72 and 73 indicate hospitals listed by AOHA, but not registered by AHA. For definition of numerical codes, see page A4	Control	Service	Staffed Beds	Admissions	Census	Outpatient Visits	Births	Total	Payroll	Personnel

PLAINVIEW—Hale County

⊠ COVENANT HOSPITAL PLAINVIEW, (Formerly Methodist Hospital Plainview), 2601 Dimmitt Road, Zip 79072–1833; tel. 806/296–5531; Joe S. Langford, Chief Executive Officer **A**1 9 10 **F**2 3 7 8 10 12 14 15 16 17 18 19 20 21 22 23 25 28 30 31 32 34 35 36 37 39 40 41 42 44 45 46 49 51 52 53 54 56 57 58 59 65 66 67 70 71 72 73 **P**3 7 **S** St. Joseph Health System, Orange, CA | 21 | 10 | 34 | 2291 | 26 | 76770 | 502 | 21128 | 6737 | 275

PLANO—Collin County

□ △ HEALTHSOUTH PLANO REHABILITATION HOSPITAL, (Formerly HEALTHSOUTH Rehabilitation Hospital–Plano), 2800 West 15th Street, Zip 75075–7526; tel. 972/612–9000; Tracy Nixon, Chief Executive Officer **A**1 7 10 **F**1 5 12 15 16 19 21 24 26 27 35 39 41 42 48 49 50 54 58 65 66 67 71 73 **P**5 **S** HEALTHSOUTH Corporation, Birmingham, AL | 32 | 46 | 62 | 883 | 53 | 41730 | 0 | 13332 | 6557 | 192

⊠ MEDICAL CENTER OF PLANO, 3901 West 15th Street, Zip 75075–7799; tel. 972/596–6800; Harvey L. Fishero, President and Chief Executive Officer (Total facility includes 20 beds in nursing home–type unit) **A**1 2 9 10 **F**4 7 8 10 11 12 14 15 16 17 19 21 22 23 24 28 30 31 32 33 34 35 37 38 40 41 42 43 44 45 46 49 50 63 64 65 66 67 71 73 74 **P**5 7 **S** Columbia/HCA Healthcare Corporation, Nashville, TN | 33 | 10 | 265 | 14773 | 178 | 57824 | 3740 | 97658 | 38171 | 1030

⊠ PRESBYTERIAN HOSPITAL OF PLANO, 6200 West Parker Road, Zip 75093–7914; tel. 972/608–8000; Philip M. Wentworth, FACHE, Senior Vice President and Executive Director **A**1 9 10 **F**7 8 12 14 15 16 17 19 21 22 27 28 29 30 32 33 34 35 37 39 40 44 46 49 61 63 64 65 66 67 71 72 73 74 **P**8 **S** Texas Health Resources, Irving, TX
Web address: www.texashealth.org | 23 | 10 | 91 | 7004 | 68 | 57207 | 2049 | 67548 | 22638 | 643

PORT ARTHUR—Jefferson County

⊠ CHRISTUS ST. MARY HOSPITAL, (Formerly St Mary Hospital), 3600 Gates Boulevard, Zip 77642–3601, Mailing Address: P.O. Box 3696, Zip 77643–3696; tel. 409/985–7431; Jeffrey Webster, Chief Executive Officer **A**1 3 5 9 10 **F**3 4 7 8 10 12 14 15 16 17 19 21 22 24 25 27 30 32 34 35 37 39 40 41 42 43 44 45 46 49 52 54 55 56 57 58 59 60 64 65 67 71 73 74 **P**1 3 4 5 6 7 8 **S** Christus Health, Houston, TX | 21 | 10 | 223 | 9480 | 119 | 110133 | 759 | 66821 | 26975 | 816

⊠ PARK PLACE MEDICAL CENTER, 3050 39th Street, Zip 77642–5535, Mailing Address: P.O. Box 1648, Zip 77641–1648; tel. 409/983–4951; Wilson J. Weber, Chief Executive Officer (Total facility includes 21 beds in nursing home–type unit) **A**1 9 10 **F**2 4 7 8 10 12 15 16 17 19 21 22 23 27 28 29 30 34 35 37 38 40 41 42 43 44 45 46 48 51 60 64 65 67 71 72 73 74 **P**3 7 **S** TENET Healthcare Corporation, Santa Barbara, CA
ST MARY HOSPITAL See Christus St. Mary Hospital | 32 | 10 | 219 | 4692 | 73 | 23561 | 522 | 35584 | 14776 | 449

PORT LAVACA—Calhoun County

⊠ MEMORIAL MEDICAL CENTER, 815 North Virginia Street, Zip 77979–3025, Mailing Address: P.O. Box 25, Zip 77979–0025; tel. 361/552–6713; Bob L. Bybee, President and Chief Executive Officer **A**1 9 10 **F**3 7 8 14 15 16 19 21 22 26 28 30 32 33 34 35 37 38 39 40 41 44 49 57 59 65 67 68 70 71 | 13 | 10 | 35 | 1472 | 17 | 31038 | 233 | — | — | 275

QUANAH—Hardeman County

HARDEMAN COUNTY MEMORIAL HOSPITAL, 402 Mercer Street, Zip 79252–4026, Mailing Address: P.O. Box 90, Zip 79252–0090; tel. 940/663–2795; Charles Hurt, Administrator **A**9 10 **F**15 19 21 22 27 30 32 34 44 65 70 71 73 **P**6 | 16 | 10 | 23 | 237 | 5 | 18492 | 0 | 2358 | 1150 | 53

QUITMAN—Wood County

□ EAST TEXAS MEDICAL CENTER–QUITMAN, (Formerly East Texas Medical Center – Wood County at Quitman), 117 Winnsboro Street, Zip 75783–2144, Mailing Address: P.O. Box 1000, Zip 75783–1000; tel. 903/763–4505; Marion W. Stanberry, Administrator **A**1 9 10 **F**7 8 12 14 15 16 19 21 22 28 30 42 44 46 67 70 71 73 **P**2 3 7 8 **S** East Texas Medical Center Regional Healthcare System, Tyler, TX | 16 | 10 | 17 | 931 | 17 | 6352 | 51 | 2210 | 1950 | 120

RANKIN—Upton County

RANKIN HOSPITAL DISTRICT, 1105 Elizabeth Street, Zip 79778, Mailing Address: P.O. Box 327, Zip 79778–0327; tel. 915/693–2443; John Paul Loyless, Administrator **A**9 10 **F**14 15 16 17 22 32 34 39 46 51 | 16 | 10 | 20 | 36 | 0 | 8616 | 1 | 1671 | 854 | 22

REFUGIO—Refugio County

⊠ REFUGIO COUNTY MEMORIAL HOSPITAL, 107 Swift Street, Zip 78377–2425; tel. 512/526–2321; William G. Jones, Administrator **A**1 9 10 **F**14 15 16 17 19 22 31 34 36 39 44 45 46 49 51 57 71 73 **P**2 | 16 | 10 | 20 | 287 | 4 | 13305 | 0 | 5652 | 1953 | 96

RICHARDSON—Dallas County

□ BAYLOR/ RICHARDSON MEDICAL CENTER, 401 West Campbell Road, Zip 75080–3499; tel. 972/498–4000; Ronald L. Boring, President and Chief Executive Officer (Total facility includes 16 beds in nursing home–type unit) **A**1 9 10 **F**2 3 4 7 8 9 10 11 12 13 16 17 18 19 20 21 22 23 25 28 30 31 32 33 34 35 37 38 39 40 41 42 43 44 45 46 47 48 49 52 53 54 55 56 57 58 59 60 61 63 64 65 66 67 68 70 71 72 73 74 **P**5 6 8
Web address: www.baylordallas.edu | 16 | 10 | 113 | 6178 | 65 | 55320 | 782 | 46278 | 18228 | 536

RICHMOND—Fort Bend County

□ POLLY RYON MEMORIAL HOSPITAL, 1705 Jackson Street, Zip 77469–3289; tel. 281/341–3000; Sam L. Steffee, Executive Director and Chief Executive Officer (Total facility includes 34 beds in nursing home–type unit) **A**1 9 10 **F**7 8 14 15 16 19 21 22 23 31 32 33 34 35 37 40 41 42 44 46 49 64 65 66 67 70 71 73 **P**5 8
Web address: www.pollyryon.org | 16 | 10 | 159 | 4496 | 63 | 39908 | 732 | 29922 | 13457 | 379

Hospital, Address, Telephone, Administrator, Approval, Facility, and Physician Codes, Health Care System, Network	Classi-fication Codes		Utilization Data					Expense (thousands) of dollars		
★ American Hospital Association (AHA) membership □ Joint Commission on Accreditation of Healthcare Organizations (JCAHO) accreditation + American Osteopathic Healthcare Association (AOHA) membership ○ American Osteopathic Association (AOA) accreditation △ Commission on Accreditation of Rehabilitation Facilities (CARF) accreditation Control codes 61, 63, 64, 71, 72 and 73 indicate hospitals listed by AOHA, but not registered by AHA. For definition of numerical codes, see page A4	Control	Service	Staffed Beds	Admissions	Census	Outpatient Visits	Births	Total	Payroll	Personnel

RIO GRANDE CITY—Starr County

★ STARR COUNTY MEMORIAL HOSPITAL, Rural Route 1, Zip 78582–9801, Mailing Address: P.O. Box 78, Zip 78582–0078; tel. 956/487–5561; Thalia H. Munoz, Administrator **A**9 10 **F**7 14 15 16 19 20 22 28 30 40 44 65 70 71

	16	10	44	2056	20	52520	833	9654	4620	229

ROCKDALE—Milam County

RICHARDS MEMORIAL HOSPITAL, 1700 Brazos Street, Zip 76567–2517, Mailing Address: Drawer 1010, Zip 76567–1010; tel. 512/446–2513; Edward F. Lynch, Administrator **A**9 10 **F**8 12 14 15 16 19 22 25 26 28 30 32 33 34 41 44 51 57 59 60 64 70 71 73 **P**5

	16	10	30	487	7	6686	2	4745	1776	71

ROTAN—Fisher County

FISHER COUNTY HOSPITAL DISTRICT, Roby Highway, Zip 79546, Mailing Address: Drawer F, Zip 79546; tel. 915/735–2256; Ella Raye Helms, Administrator (Total facility includes 10 beds in nursing home–type unit) **A**9 10 **F**13 15 16 17 19 24 28 30 32 34 35 39 49 51 64 65 70 71 73 **P**6 **S** Lubbock Methodist Hospital System, Lubbock, TX

	16	10	23	299	11	17915	0	4557	2096	72

ROUND ROCK—Williamson County

⊠ ROUND ROCK HOSPITAL, 2400 Round Rock Avenue, Zip 78681–4097; tel. 512/341–1000; Deborah L. Ryle, Chief Executive Officer **A**1 9 10 **F**7 8 12 14 15 16 19 21 22 23 28 29 30 34 35 37 39 40 42 44 46 49 64 65 71 73 74 **P**1 5 7 **S** Columbia/HCA Healthcare Corporation, Nashville, TN
Web address: www.columbia–stdavids.com

	32	10	64	3611	37	44900	994	24548	10807	282

ROWLETT—Rockwall County

⊠ LAKE POINTE MEDICAL CENTER, 6800 Scenic Drive, Zip 75088, Mailing Address: P.O. Box 1550, Zip 75030–1550; tel. 972/412–2273; Kenneth R. Teel, Administrator **A**1 9 10 **F**7 8 11 12 13 16 17 19 20 22 24 28 29 32 33 34 35 37 39 40 41 42 44 45 49 64 65 66 67 71 72 73 74 **P**8 **S** TENET Healthcare Corporation, Santa Barbara, CA
Web address: www.tenethealth.com/lakepointe

	33	10	92	5167	47	73013	628	28372	13640	380

RUSK—Cherokee County

□ EAST TEXAS MEDICAL CENTER RUSK, 500 North Bonner Street, Zip 75785, Mailing Address: P.O. Box 317, Zip 75785–0317; tel. 903/683–2273; Brenda Copley, Acting Administrator **A**1 9 10 **F**8 12 14 15 16 17 19 21 22 23 26 28 29 30 31 32 34 35 39 44 45 46 49 50 51 63 65 70 71 73 74 **P**7 **S** East Texas Medical Center Regional Healthcare System, Tyler, TX

	23	10	25	730	6	34860	0	6497	2763	135

□ RUSK STATE HOSPITAL, Jacksonville Highway North, Zip 75785, Mailing Address: P.O. Box 318, Zip 75785–0318; tel. 903/683–3421; Harold R. Parrish, Superintendent **A**1 10 **F**14 15 16 19 20 21 26 27 28 30 31 35 44 45 46 52 54 55 56 57 65 67 71 73
Web address: www.mhmr.state.tx.us

	12	22	380	2083	342	0	0	—	—	—

SAN ANGELO—Tom Green County

□ RIVER CREST HOSPITAL, 1636 Hunters Glen Road, Zip 76901–5016; tel. 915/949–5722; Larry Grimes, Managing Director **A**1 9 10 **F**2 3 12 13 15 16 17 19 21 22 26 27 28 30 35 41 46 49 50 52 53 54 55 56 57 58 59 63 65 67 71 **P**5 **S** Universal Health Services, Inc., King of Prussia, PA

	33	22	80	1442	26	1378	0	4479	2155	58

⊠ △ SAN ANGELO COMMUNITY MEDICAL CENTER, (Formerly Columbia Medical Center), 3501 Knickerbocker Road, Zip 76904–7698; tel. 915/949–9511; Samuel G. Feazell, Chief Executive Officer **A**1 2 7 9 10 **F**2 3 4 5 7 8 10 11 12 13 14 15 16 17 19 20 21 22 23 24 26 28 29 30 31 32 33 34 35 37 38 39 40 41 42 43 44 45 46 48 49 51 52 53 54 56 57 58 59 60 61 63 64 65 66 67 71 72 73 74 **P**8 **S** Triad Hospitals, Inc., Dallas, TX

	32	10	135	5526	68	65947	947	51283	18129	576

⊠ △ SHANNON MEDICAL CENTER, (Includes Shannon Medical Center– St. John's Campus, 2018 Pulliam Street, Zip 76905–5197; tel. 915/659–7100), 120 East Harris Street, Zip 76903–5976; tel. 915/653–6741; Lawrence Leonard, President and Chief Executive Officer (Total facility includes 22 beds in nursing home–type unit) **A**1 2 7 9 10 **F**2 3 4 7 10 11 12 14 15 16 17 18 19 21 22 24 25 27 28 29 30 32 34 35 37 39 40 41 42 43 44 45 46 47 48 49 52 54 55 56 57 58 59 60 63 64 65 66 67 71 72 73 74 **P**3
Web address: www.shannonhealth.com

	23	10	268	12485	176	104941	1269	103244	39898	1415

SAN ANTONIO—Bexar County

⊠ BAPTIST MEDICAL CENTER, 111 Dallas Street, Zip 78205–1230; tel. 210/297–7000; Perry Willmore, Vice President Operations (Total facility includes 31 beds in nursing home–type unit) (Nonreporting) **A**1 2 3 5 6 9 10 **S** Baptist Health System, San Antonio, TX
Web address: www.baptisthealthsystem.org

	21	10	481	—	—	—	—	—	—	—

⊠ BROOKE ARMY MEDICAL CENTER, Fort Sam Houston, Zip 78234–6200; tel. 210/916–4141; Colonel Joseph P. Gonzales, MS, USA, Chief of Staff (Nonreporting) **A**1 2 3 5 9 **S** Department of the Army, Office of the Surgeon General, Falls Church, VA

	42	10	464	—	—	—	—	—	—	—

□ CHARTER REAL BEHAVIORAL HEALTH SYSTEM, 8550 Huebner Road, Zip 78240–1897, Mailing Address: P.O. Box 380157, Zip 78280–0157; tel. 210/699–8585; James M. Hunt, Chief Executive Officer **A**1 9 10 **F**1 2 3 12 14 15 16 18 26 27 34 39 52 53 54 55 56 57 58 59 65 67 **S** Magellan Health Services, Atlanta, GA

	32	22	90	1353	23	4546	0	7442	2772	75

⊠ △ CHRISTUS SANTA ROSA HEALTH CARE, (Formerly Santa Rosa Health Care Corporation), 519 West Houston Street, Zip 78207–3108; tel. 210/704–2011; William C. Finlayson, President and Chief Exeecutive Officer **A**1 2 3 5 7 9 10 **F**2 3 4 7 8 10 11 12 13 14 15 16 17 18 19 20 21 22 23 25 26 27 28 29 30 31 32 33 34 35 37 38 39 40 41 42 43 44 45 46 47 48 49 51 52 53 54 55 56 57 58 59 60 61 63 64 65 66 67 68 70 71 72 73 74 **P**5 6 7 **S** Christus Health, San Antonio, TX

	21	10	609	22909	398	186076	3774	215141	87904	2745

Hospital, Address, Telephone, Administrator, Approval, Facility, and Physician Codes, Health Care System, Network	Classi-fication Codes		Utilization Data					Expense (thousands) of dollars		
	Control	Service	Staffed Beds	Admissions	Census	Outpatient Visits	Births	Total	Payroll	Personnel

★ American Hospital Association (AHA) membership
□ Joint Commission on Accreditation of Healthcare Organizations (JCAHO) accreditation
+ American Osteopathic Healthcare Association (AOHA) membership
○ American Osteopathic Association (AOA) accreditation
△ Commission on Accreditation of Rehabilitation Facilities (CARF) accreditation
Control codes 61, 63, 64, 71, 72 and 73 indicate hospitals listed by AOHA, but not registered by AHA. For definition of numerical codes, see page A4

Hospital	Control	Service	Staffed Beds	Admissions	Census	Outpatient Visits	Births	Total	Payroll	Personnel
□ △ HEALTHSOUTH REHABILITATION INSTITUTE OF SAN ANTONIO, 9119 Cinnamon Hill, Zip 78240–5401; tel. 210/691–0737; Diane B. Lampe, Administrator and Chief Executive Officer **A**1 7 9 10 **F**5 12 14 15 16 19 21 25 26 27 35 41 42 44 46 48 49 50 63 65 66 67 71 73 **S** HEALTHSOUTH Corporation, Birmingham, AL	33	46	108	1501	77	20322	0	16809	6292	253
□ HORIZON SPECIALTY HOSPITAL, (LONG TERM ACUTE CARE), 7310 Oak Manor Drive, Zip 78229–4509; tel. 210/308–0261; Peggy Wood, Administrator **A**1 10 **F**12 14 16 19 21 26 27 28 31 32 33 35 39 45 46 48 50 63 65 71	33	49	25	282	24	0	0	4799	2257	65
✠ METHODIST AMBULATORY SURGERY HOSPITAL, (SURGICAL SPECIALTY), 9150 Huebner Road, Zip 78240–1545; tel. 210/691–0800; Elaine F. Morris, Administrator (Total facility includes 16 beds in nursing home–type unit) **A**1 10 **F**2 4 7 8 10 11 12 13 17 18 19 21 22 23 24 25 26 27 28 29 30 32 33 34 35 37 38 39 40 41 42 43 44 45 46 47 48 49 51 52 54 55 57 59 60 61 64 65 67 68 70 71 73 74 **P**8 **S** Columbia/HCA Healthcare Corporation, Nashville, TN	33	49	37	683	9	13025	0	15870	5023	120
★ METHODIST WOMEN'S AND CHILDREN'S HOSPITAL, 8109 Fredericksburg Road, Zip 78229–3383; tel. 210/692–5000; Arthur E. Marlin, M.D., Chief Executive Officer (Nonreporting) **A**9 **S** Columbia/HCA Healthcare Corporation, Nashville, TN **Web address:** www.mhshealthcare.com	32	10	150	—	—	—	—	—	—	—
✠ METROPOLITAN METHODIST HOSPITAL, 1310 McCullough Avenue, Zip 78212–2617; tel. 210/208–2200; Mark L. Bernard, Chief Executive Officer (Total facility includes 16 beds in nursing home–type unit) **A**1 9 10 **F**2 3 4 5 7 8 10 11 12 13 14 15 16 17 18 19 20 21 22 23 24 25 26 27 28 29 30 31 33 35 37 38 39 40 41 42 43 44 45 46 47 48 49 53 54 55 56 57 58 59 60 61 63 64 65 66 67 68 70 71 73 **P**2 3 5 7 8 **S** Columbia/HCA Healthcare Corporation, Nashville, TN **Web address:** www.mhshealthcare.com	32	10	228	11072	130	39811	2541	68623	26837	787
□ MISSION VISTA BEHAVIORAL HEALTH SYSTEM, 14747 Jones Maltsberger, Zip 78247–3713; tel. 210/490–0000; Holly Minnis, Chief Executive Officer **A**1 9 10 **F**2 3 12 14 15 16 18 22 26 34 45 46 52 54 56 57 58 59 65 67 **P**6 **S** Ramsay Health Care, Inc., Coral Gables, FL	33	22	16	479	11	5317	0	2979	1581	31
□ NIX HEALTH CARE SYSTEM, 414 Navarro Street, Zip 78205–2522; tel. 210/271–1800; John F. Strieby, President and Chief Executive Officer (Total facility includes 17 beds in nursing home–type unit) **A**1 3 9 10 **F**4 7 8 10 12 19 21 26 27 28 30 32 33 34 35 37 39 40 42 43 44 45 46 48 49 50 52 57 59 60 63 64 65 66 67 68 71 73 74 **P**1 3	33	10	149	3513	60	99692	581	38788	15570	467
NORTH CENTRAL BAPTIST HOSPITAL, 520 Madison Oak Drive, Zip 78258–3912; Dan Brown, Administrator (Nonreporting) **S** Baptist Health System, San Antonio, TX	21	10	50	—	—	—	—	—	—	—
NORTHEAST BAPTIST HOSPITAL, 8811 Village Drive, Zip 78217–5440; tel. 210/653–2330; Dan Brown, Administrator (Nonreporting) **A**3 9 **S** Baptist Health System, San Antonio, TX	21	10	210	—	—	—	—	—	—	—
✠ NORTHEAST METHODIST HOSPITAL, 12412 Judson Road, Zip 78233–3272, Mailing Address: P.O. Box 659510, Zip 78265–9510; tel. 210/650–4949; Mark L. Bernard, Chief Executive Officer (Total facility includes 10 beds in nursing home–type unit) **A**1 9 10 **F**2 3 4 5 7 8 10 11 12 13 14 15 16 17 18 19 20 21 22 23 24 25 26 27 28 29 30 31 33 34 35 37 38 39 40 41 42 43 44 45 46 47 48 49 52 53 54 55 56 57 58 59 60 61 63 64 65 66 67 68 70 71 72 73 74 **P**2 3 5 7 8 **S** Columbia/HCA Healthcare Corporation, Nashville, TN **Web address:** www.mhshealthcare.com	32	10	99	3528	49	46136	1	30021	12169	345
✠ SAN ANTONIO COMMUNITY HOSPITAL, 8026 Floyd Curl Drive, Zip 78229–3915; tel. 210/692–8110; James C. Scoggin, Jr., Chief Executive Officer (Total facility includes 20 beds in nursing home–type unit) **A**1 3 5 9 10 **F**2 3 4 7 8 10 11 12 13 14 15 16 17 18 19 20 21 22 23 25 26 27 28 29 30 31 32 33 34 35 37 38 39 40 41 42 43 44 45 46 47 48 49 52 54 55 57 58 59 60 61 63 64 65 66 67 68 70 71 72 73 74 **P**2 5 7 8 **S** Columbia/HCA Healthcare Corporation, Nashville, TN **Web address:** www.mhshealthcare.com	32	10	291	6408	100	64145	0	64586	24136	637
□ SAN ANTONIO STATE HOSPITAL, 6711 South New Braunfels, Zip 78223–3009, Mailing Address: Box 23991, Highland Hills Station, Zip 78223–0991; tel. 210/531–7711; Robert C. Arizpe, Superintendent **A**1 10 **F**6 8 12 17 18 20 27 28 29 30 45 46 52 53 54 55 56 65 67 73 **Web address:** www.mhmr.state.tx.us	12	22	416	2044	356	0	0	—	—	—
SANTA ROSA HEALTH CARE CORPORATION See Christus Santa Rosa Health Care										
✠ SOUTH TEXAS VETERANS HEALTH CARE SYSTEM, (Includes Kerville Division, 3600 Memorial Boulevard, Kerville, Zip 78028; tel. 210/896–2020; San Antonio Division, 7400 Merton Minter Boulevard, tel. 210/617–5140; Jose R. Coronado, FACHE, Director), 7400 Merton Minter Boulevard, Zip 78284–5799; tel. 210/617–5140; Jose R. Coronado, FACHE, Director (Total facility includes 274 beds in nursing home–type unit) (Nonreporting) **A**1 2 5 8 **S** Department of Veterans Affairs, Washington, DC	45	10	1112	—	—	—	—	—	—	—
SOUTHEAST BAPTIST HOSPITAL, 4214 East Southcross Boulevard, Zip 78222–3740; tel. 210/297–3000; Kevin Walters, Administrator (Nonreporting) **A**9 **S** Baptist Health System, San Antonio, TX	21	10	153	—	—	—	—	—	—	—
✠ △ SOUTHWEST GENERAL HOSPITAL, 7400 Barlite Boulevard, Zip 78224–1399; tel. 210/921–2000; Keith Swinney, Chief Executive Officer (Total facility includes 23 beds in nursing home–type unit) **A**1 7 10 **F**7 8 10 12 14 15 16 17 19 20 22 27 28 33 35 37 40 41 42 44 45 46 48 49 52 54 56 57 64 65 67 70 71 73 74 **S** TENET Healthcare Corporation, Santa Barbara, CA **Web address:** www.tenethealth.comswgh	33	10	200	5788	106	47889	1173	46005	23741	594

Hospital, Address, Telephone, Administrator, Approval, Facility, and Physician Codes, Health Care System, Network	Classi-fication Codes		Utilization Data					Expense (thousands) of dollars		
★ American Hospital Association (AHA) membership □ Joint Commission on Accreditation of Healthcare Organizations (JCAHO) accreditation + American Osteopathic Healthcare Association (AOHA) membership ○ American Osteopathic Association (AOA) accreditation △ Commission on Accreditation of Rehabilitation Facilities (CARF) accreditation Control codes 61, 63, 64, 71, 72 and 73 indicate hospitals listed by AOHA, but not registered by AHA. For definition of numerical codes, see page A4	Control	Service	Staffed Beds	Admissions	Census	Outpatient Visits	Births	Total	Payroll	Personnel

SOUTHWEST MENTAL HEALTH CENTER, 8535 Tom Slick, Zip 78229–3363; tel. 210/616–0300; Frederick W. Hines, President (Nonreporting) **A**5 9 **Web address:** www.smhc.org	23	52	80	—	—	—	—	—	—	—
⊠ SOUTHWEST TEXAS METHODIST HOSPITAL, 7700 Floyd Curl Drive, Zip 78229–3993; tel. 210/575–4000; James C. Scoggin, Jr., Chief Executive Officer (Total facility includes 38 beds in nursing home–type unit) **A**1 2 3 5 9 10 **F**2 3 4 7 8 10 11 12 13 14 15 16 17 18 19 20 21 22 23 25 26 27 28 29 30 31 33 34 35 37 38 39 40 41 42 43 44 45 46 47 48 49 52 53 54 55 56 57 58 59 60 61 63 64 65 66 67 68 70 71 72 73 74 **P**2 3 5 7 8 **S** Columbia/HCA Healthcare Corporation, Nashville, TN **Web address:** www.mhshealthcare.com	32	10	774	33023	443	177592	8201	263873	109391	3144
□ ST. LUKE'S BAPTIST HOSPITAL, 7930 Floyd Curl Drive, Zip 78229–0100; tel. 210/692–8703 (Total facility includes 29 beds in nursing home–type unit) (Nonreporting) **A**1 3 5 9 **S** Baptist Health System, San Antonio, TX	21	10	219	—	—	—	—	—	—	—
□ TEXAS CENTER FOR INFECTIOUS DISEASE, 2303 S.E. Military Drive, Zip 78223–3597; tel. 210/534–8857; James N. Elkins, FACHE, Director **A**1 9 10 **F**19 20 21 22 24 27 31 34 39 41 44 46 51 54 65 67 71 73 **P**1 **S** Texas Department of Health, Austin, TX	12	33	109	178	65	9502	0	13429	7597	269
⊠ UNIVERSITY HEALTH SYSTEM, (Includes University Health Center – Downtown, tel. 210/358–3400; University Hospital, tel. 210/358–4000), 4502 Medical Drive, Zip 78229–4493; tel. 210/358–4000; John A. Guest, President and Chief Executive Officer **A**1 2 3 5 8 9 10 **F**1 3 4 7 8 10 11 12 13 14 15 16 17 18 19 20 21 22 23 25 26 27 28 29 30 31 32 34 35 37 38 39 40 41 42 43 44 45 46 47 48 49 51 52 53 54 55 56 57 58 60 61 63 65 66 67 68 70 71 72 73 74 **P**1 **Web address:** www.universityhealthsystem.com	16	10	547	19604	313	492287	2734	319479	104291	4091
⊠ △ WARM SPRINGS & BAPTIST REHABILITATION HOSPITAL, 5101 Medical Drive, Zip 78229–6098; tel. 210/616–0100; James L. Ashbaugh, Regional Director of Operations **A**1 3 7 10 **F**12 15 16 19 27 32 35 41 48 49 65 71 73 **Web address:** www.warmsprings.org	23	46	64	1128	53	17640	0	17490	6643	157
SAN AUGUSTINE—San Augustine County										
MEMORIAL MEDICAL CENTER OF SAN AUGUSTINE, 511 East Hospital Street, Zip 75972–2121, Mailing Address: P.O. Box 658, Zip 75972–0658; tel. 409/275–3446; Terry Napper, Administrator **A**9 10 **F**6 8 11 12 14 15 16 17 19 20 22 24 26 27 28 30 32 34 36 37 39 40 41 44 46 48 49 51 52 64 65 71 **P**6 7 8 **S** Memorial Health System of East Texas, Lufkin, TX	23	10	16	522	4	27730	0	3543	1675	56
SAN BENITO—Cameron County										
□ DOLLY VINSANT MEMORIAL HOSPITAL, 400 East U.S. Highway 77, Zip 78586–5310, Mailing Address: P.O. Box 42, Zip 78586–0042; tel. 956/399–1313; Mark Dooley, Chief Executive Officer **A**1 9 10 **F**8 12 14 15 16 19 20 21 22 28 30 34 35 37 39 44 45 49 66 71 72 73 **S** New American Healthcare Corporation, Brentwood, TN	33	10	49	1211	11	—	0	8211	3080	192
SAN MARCOS—Hays County										
⊠ CENTRAL TEXAS MEDICAL CENTER, 1301 Wonder World Drive, Zip 78666–7544; tel. 512/353–8979; Ken Bacon, President and Chief Executive Officer (Total facility includes 5 beds in nursing home–type unit) **A**1 9 10 **F**7 8 10 12 14 15 16 17 19 20 21 22 24 28 29 30 32 33 35 37 39 40 41 44 45 46 49 64 65 66 67 71 73 **P**6 8 **S** Adventist Health System Sunbelt Health Care Corporation, Winter Park, FL	21	10	113	4236	44	59211	940	35643	12513	492
SEGUIN—Guadalupe County										
⊠ GUADALUPE VALLEY HOSPITAL, 1215 East Court Street, Zip 78155–5189; tel. 830/379–2411; Don L. Richey, Administrator (Total facility includes 19 beds in nursing home–type unit) **A**1 9 10 **F**3 7 8 12 14 15 18 19 21 22 23 26 31 32 33 34 35 37 40 41 42 44 45 46 49 53 55 57 58 59 63 64 65 66 67 70 71 73 **P**1 **Web address:** www.gvh.com	15	10	94	4969	62	61311	661	33581	15885	617
SEMINOLE—Gaines County										
★ MEMORIAL HOSPITAL, 209 N.W. Eighth Street, Zip 79360–3447; tel. 915/758–5811; Steve Beck, Chief Executive Officer and Administrator **A**9 10 **F**3 7 8 12 13 14 15 16 17 18 19 20 21 22 24 26 28 29 30 32 33 34 35 39 40 41 44 45 46 49 51 53 54 55 56 59 61 65 66 67 70 71 73 74	16	10	33	757	8	32162	134	10319	3269	146
SEYMOUR—Baylor County										
★ SEYMOUR HOSPITAL, 200 Stadium Drive, Zip 76380–2344; tel. 940/888–5572; Charles Norris, Administrator **A**9 10 **F**1 19 22 26 27 28 30 32 34 37 40 41 44 49 59 64 65 67 70 71 **P**6	16	10	34	694	12	25727	40	6266	2641	114
SHAMROCK—Wheeler County										
SHAMROCK GENERAL HOSPITAL, 1000 South Main Street, Zip 79079–2896; tel. 806/256–2114; Wiley M. Fires, Administrator (Total facility includes 8 beds in nursing home–type unit) **A**9 10 **F**12 22 32 33 44 61 64 70 73	16	10	30	543	11	29768	1	2957	1521	68
SHEPPARD AFB—Wichita County										
⊠ U. S. AIR FORCE REGIONAL HOSPITAL–SHEPPARD, 149 Hart Street, Suite 1, Zip 76311–3478; tel. 940/676–2010; Colonel Richard D. Maddox, Administrator (Nonreporting) **A**1 **S** Department of the Air Force, Bowling AFB, DC	41	10	65	—	—	—	—	—	—	—
SHERMAN—Grayson County										
COLUMBIA MEDICAL CENTER OF SHERMAN See Community Medical Center Sherman										

Hospital, Address, Telephone, Administrator, Approval, Facility, and Physician Codes, Health Care System, Network	Classi-fication Codes		Utilization Data					Expense (thousands) of dollars		
★ American Hospital Association (AHA) membership □ Joint Commission on Accreditation of Healthcare Organizations (JCAHO) accreditation + American Osteopathic Healthcare Association (AOHA) membership ○ American Osteopathic Association (AOA) accreditation △ Commission on Accreditation of Rehabilitation Facilities (CARF) accreditation Control codes 61, 63, 64, 71, 72 and 73 indicate hospitals listed by AOHA, but not registered by AHA. For definition of numerical codes, see page A4	Control	Service	Staffed Beds	Admissions	Census	Outpatient Visits	Births	Total	Payroll	Personnel
⊞ COMMUNITY MEDICAL CENTER SHERMAN, (Formerly Columbia Medical Center of Sherman), 1111 Gallagher Road, Zip 75090–1798; tel. 903/870–7000; John F. Adams, Chief Executive Officer **A**1 9 10 **F**7 8 12 15 19 21 22 23 26 28 29 30 31 32 33 34 35 37 40 41 42 44 45 46 48 49 50 52 57 58 63 64 65 67 71 73 74 **P**5 **S** Triad Hospitals, Inc., Dallas, TX **Web address:** www.columbia–hca.com	33	10	160	3070	44	35891	326	22479	10324	304
⊞ △ WILSON N. JONES REGIONAL HEALTH SYSTEM, 500 North Highland Avenue, Zip 75092–7354, Mailing Address: P.O. Box 1258, Zip 75091–1258; tel. 903/870–4611; K. Steven Rowley, CHE, President and Chief Executive Officer (Total facility includes 29 beds in nursing home–type unit) (Nonreporting) **A**1 7 9 10 **Web address:** www.wnjrhs.org	23	10	197	—	—	—	—	—	—	—
SMITHVILLE—Bastrop County										
SMITHVILLE HOSPITAL, Ninth and Mills Streets, Zip 78957, Mailing Address: P.O. Box 359, Zip 78957–0359; tel. 512/237–3214; James W. Langford, Administrator **A**9 10 **F**8 19 22 31 34 37 44 71 73	16	10	24	1237	10	8639	0	8927	3992	190
SNYDER—Scurry County										
⊞ D. M. COGDELL MEMORIAL HOSPITAL, 1700 Cogdell Boulevard, Zip 79549–6198; tel. 915/573–6374; Jeff Reecer, Chief Executive Officer (Total facility includes 25 beds in nursing home–type unit) **A**1 9 10 **F**7 8 12 14 15 16 17 19 20 21 22 24 25 26 28 30 32 33 34 37 39 40 41 44 45 46 49 64 65 66 67 70 71 73 **P**6 **S** St. Joseph Health System, Orange, CA	13	10	64	1080	37	60117	126	12240	5436	244
SONORA—Sutton County										
LILLIAN M. HUDSPETH MEMORIAL HOSPITAL, 308 Hudspeth Avenue, Zip 76950–3399, Mailing Address: P.O. Box 455, Zip 76950–0455; tel. 915/387–2521; Joe Hendrus, Administrator **A**9 10 **F**14 15 22 28 49 70	16	10	13	210	4	—	0	1780	751	44
SPEARMAN—Hansford County										
★ HANSFORD HOSPITAL, 707 South Roland Street, Zip 79081–3441; tel. 806/659–2535; Allen R. Alberty, Chief Executive Officer **A**9 10 **F**8 13 14 15 16 22 26 27 28 30 32 33 34 36 42 49 64 65 71 73	16	10	28	235	2	7643	0	2584	1229	43
STAMFORD—Jones County										
STAMFORD MEMORIAL HOSPITAL, Highway 6 East, Zip 79553, Mailing Address: P.O. Box 911, Zip 79553–0911; tel. 915/773–2725; Sam H. Raney, Interim Administrator **A**9 10 **F**15 19 20 22 24 32 35 44 49 70 71 **P**5	16	10	35	299	4	2817	0	3554	1936	77
STANTON—Martin County										
MARTIN COUNTY HOSPITAL DISTRICT, 610 North St. Peter Street, Zip 79782, Mailing Address: P.O. Box 640, Zip 79782–0640; tel. 915/756–3345; Rick Jacobus, Administrator **A**9 10 **F**15 16 22 40 44 70 71 **P**5	16	10	21	331	5	4137	16	4042	1689	64
STEPHENVILLE—Erath County										
⊞ HARRIS METHODIST–ERATH COUNTY, 411 North Belknap Street, Zip 76401–3415, Mailing Address: P.O. Box 1399, Zip 76401–1399; tel. 254/965–1500; Ronald E. Dorris, Senior Vice President and Executive Director **A**1 9 10 **F**7 12 15 16 19 20 21 22 23 26 28 29 30 31 32 33 34 35 37 39 40 41 42 44 45 46 49 50 61 63 65 66 67 70 71 73 74 **P**2 5 7 **S** Texas Health Resources, Irving, TX **Web address:** www.hmhs.com	21	10	75	2948	33	15075	352	17447	6715	227
SUGAR LAND—Fort Bend County										
⊞ METHODIST HEALTH CENTER–SUGAR LAND, (Formerly Sugar Land Health Center), 16655 S.W. Freeway, Zip 77479; tel. 281/274–8000; Joan Damon, Administrator **A**1 **F**7 16 19 22 30 34 35 40 44 65 71 73 **P**2 3 4 5 6 **S** Methodist Health Care System, Houston, TX	21	10	22	374	3	8370	96	—	5112	127
SULPHUR SPRINGS—Hopkins County										
⊞ HOPKINS COUNTY MEMORIAL HOSPITAL, 115 Airport Road, Zip 75482–0115; tel. 903/885–7671; Richard L. Goddard, Chief Executive Officer **A**1 9 10 **F**7 8 14 15 16 19 22 28 30 31 32 33 34 35 37 40 44 46 49 57 65 67 70 71 73 **Web address:** www.hcmhospital.org	16	10	90	4186	42	41943	943	21448	10517	365
SWEENY—Brazoria County										
□ SWEENY COMMUNITY HOSPITAL, 305 North McKinney Street, Zip 77480–2895; tel. 409/548–3311; Herbert A. Turk, FACHE, Administrator **A**1 9 10 **F**14 15 17 19 22 32 35 36 37 44 46 49 59 65 67 71	16	10	19	210	2	3502	0	6438	3125	102
SWEETWATER—Nolan County										
⊞ ROLLING PLAINS MEMORIAL HOSPITAL, 200 East Arizona Street, Zip 79556–7199, Mailing Address: P.O. Box 690, Zip 79556–0690; tel. 915/235–1701; Thomas F. Kennedy, Administrator **A**1 9 10 **F**7 8 14 15 16 19 20 21 22 24 26 31 32 33 34 35 37 40 44 46 49 65 67 70 71 73	16	10	54	1833	28	26977	256	11396	4988	215
TAHOKA—Lynn County										
LYNN COUNTY HOSPITAL DISTRICT, Brownfield Highway, Zip 79373–1310, Mailing Address: Box 1310, Zip 79373–1310; tel. 806/998–4533; Louise Landers, Administrator (Nonreporting) **A**9 10	16	10	24	—	—	—	—	—	—	—
TAYLOR—Williamson County										
□ JOHNS COMMUNITY HOSPITAL, 305 Mallard Lane, Zip 76574–1208; tel. 512/352–7611; Ernest Balla, Administrator **A**1 9 10 **F**8 14 15 16 19 21 22 27 28 30 32 34 37 44 45 49 51 65 71 **P**6 **Web address:** www.spinoza.pub–lib.ci.taylor.tx.us	23	10	48	1346	30	27591	0	8974	4937	163

Hospital, Address, Telephone, Administrator, Approval, Facility, and Physician Codes, Health Care System, Network	Classi-fication Codes		Utilization Data					Expense (thousands) of dollars		
★ American Hospital Association (AHA) membership □ Joint Commission on Accreditation of Healthcare Organizations (JCAHO) accreditation + American Osteopathic Healthcare Association (AOHA) membership ○ American Osteopathic Association (AOA) accreditation △ Commission on Accreditation of Rehabilitation Facilities (CARF) accreditation Control codes 61, 63, 64, 71, 72 and 73 indicate hospitals listed by AOHA, but not registered by AHA. For definition of numerical codes, see page A4	Control	Service	Staffed Beds	Admissions	Census	Outpatient Visits	Births	Total	Payroll	Personnel

TEMPLE—Bell County

✠ CENTRAL TEXAS VETERANS AFFAIRS HEALTHCARE SYSTEM, (Includes Central Texas Veterans Affairs Health Care System, 4800 Memorial Drive, Waco, Zip 76711–1397; tel. 817/752–6581; Central Texas Veterans Affairs Health Care System, Marlin Integrated Clinical Facility, 1016 Ward Street, Marlin, Zip 76661–2162; tel. 817/778–4811; Olin E. Teague Veterans' Center), 1901 South First Street, Zip 76504–7493; tel. 254/778–4811; Dean Billick, Director (Total facility includes 320 beds in nursing home–type unit) (Nonreporting) **A**1 2 3 5 **S** Department of Veterans Affairs, Washington, DC	45	10	1852	—	—	—	—	—	—	—
✠ KING'S DAUGHTERS HOSPITAL, 1901 S.W. H. K. Dodgen Loop, Zip 76502–1896; tel. 254/771–8600; Tucker Bonner, President (Total facility includes 8 beds in nursing home–type unit) **A**1 9 10 **F**7 14 15 16 19 20 21 22 27 28 30 31 32 33 34 35 37 39 40 41 42 44 45 49 56 63 64 65 67 71 73 Web address: www.kdhosp.org	23	10	116	2748	29	32649	488	23616	10249	385
OLIN E. TEAGUE VETERANS' CENTER See Central Texas Veterans Affairs Healthcare System										
✠ △ SCOTT AND WHITE MEMORIAL HOSPITAL, 2401 South 31st Street, Zip 76508–0002; tel. 254/724–2111; Dick Sweeden, Administrator (Total facility includes 52 beds in nursing home–type unit) **A**1 2 3 5 7 8 9 10 **F**1 2 3 4 7 8 10 11 12 14 15 16 17 19 20 21 22 23 25 26 27 28 29 30 31 32 33 35 37 38 40 41 42 43 44 45 46 47 48 49 52 53 54 56 57 58 59 60 61 64 65 66 67 68 71 72 73 74 Web address: www.swinfo.tamu.edu	23	10	463	21387	290	103248	2448	232117	163897	3554

TERRELL—Kaufman County

✠ MEDICAL CENTER AT TERRELL, 1551 Highway 34 South, Zip 75160–4833; tel. 972/563–7611; Ronald J. Ensor, Chief Executive Officer (Total facility includes 18 beds in nursing home–type unit) **A**1 9 10 **F**7 8 12 15 16 19 21 22 34 35 37 39 40 41 44 45 46 48 49 64 65 71 73 **S** Triad Hospitals, Inc., Dallas, TX	33	10	131	2864	38	31910	137	19626	7010	248
□ TERRELL STATE HOSPITAL, 1200 East Brin Street, Zip 75160–2938, Mailing Address: P.O. Box 70, Zip 75160–0070; tel. 972/563–6452; Beatrice Butler, Superintendent **A**1 3 5 9 10 **F**1 3 4 5 6 7 8 9 10 11 12 14 15 16 17 18 19 20 21 22 23 26 27 28 29 30 31 35 36 37 38 39 40 41 42 43 44 45 46 47 48 49 50 52 53 54 55 56 57 59 60 63 65 67 68 71 73 Web address: www.mhmr.state.tx.us	12	22	425	1803	325	0	0	—	—	—

TEXARKANA—Bowie County

✠ △ CHRISTUS ST. MICHAEL HEALTH SYSTEM, (Formerly St. Michael Health Care Center), (Includes Christus St. Michael Rehabilitation Hospital, 2400 St. Michael Drive, Zip 75503; tel. 903/614–4000; Deanna Hinterberger, Administrator), 2600 St. Michael Drive, Zip 75503–2372; tel. 903/614–1000; Don A. Beeler, President and Chief Executive Officer (Total facility includes 30 beds in nursing home–type unit) **A**1 2 7 9 10 **F**1 4 7 8 10 11 12 13 14 15 16 17 19 21 22 23 24 25 26 27 28 30 32 33 34 35 37 39 40 41 42 43 44 46 48 49 50 51 57 58 60 61 63 64 65 66 67 68 71 72 73 74 **P**3 7 8 **S** Christus Health, Houston, TX Web address: www.smhcc.org	21	10	319	14826	243	145956	733	119399	49832	1710
□ △ HEALTHSOUTH REHABILITATION HOSPITAL OF TEXARKANA, 515 West 12th Street, Zip 75501–4416; tel. 903/793–0088; Jeffrey A. Livingston, Chief Executive Officer **A**1 7 9 10 **F**14 15 16 22 46 48 49 65 66 **S** HEALTHSOUTH Corporation, Birmingham, AL	33	46	60	980	53	12064	0	12431	5416	198
✠ WADLEY REGIONAL MEDICAL CENTER, 1000 Pine Street, Zip 75501–5170, Mailing Address: Box 1878, Zip 75504–1878; tel. 903/798–8000; Hugh R. Hallgren, President and Chief Executive Officer **A**1 2 3 5 9 10 **F**4 7 8 10 12 13 15 16 17 19 21 22 23 24 25 27 28 29 30 31 32 33 34 35 37 39 40 41 42 43 44 45 46 50 60 63 64 65 66 71 72 73 74 **P**8	23	10	342	11939	166	114095	1545	96416	37735	1217

TEXAS CITY—Galveston County

✠ △ MAINLAND MEDICAL CENTER, (Formerly Columbia Mainland Medical Center), 6801 E F Lowry Expressway, Zip 77591; tel. 409/938–5000; Alice G. Adams, Administrator (Total facility includes 30 beds in nursing home–type unit) **A**1 5 7 9 10 **F**2 3 4 5 7 8 10 11 12 14 15 16 17 18 19 20 21 22 23 24 25 26 28 29 30 31 32 33 34 35 37 38 39 40 41 42 43 44 45 46 47 48 49 51 52 53 54 55 56 57 58 59 60 61 64 65 66 67 71 72 73 74 **P**5 **S** Columbia/HCA Healthcare Corporation, Nashville, TN Web address: www.columbia.net	33	10	182	7727	93	93385	560	47700	20724	571

THE WOODLANDS—Montgomery County

✠ MEMORIAL HOSPITAL–THE WOODLANDS, 9250 Pinecroft Drive, Zip 77380–3225; tel. 281/364–2300; Steve Sanders, Vice President and Chief Executive Officer **A**1 9 **F**2 3 4 6 7 8 9 10 11 12 15 16 17 19 20 21 22 23 24 25 26 27 28 29 30 31 32 33 34 35 37 38 39 40 41 42 43 44 45 46 47 48 49 50 51 52 53 54 55 56 57 58 59 60 61 62 63 64 65 66 67 68 70 71 72 73 74 **P**5 **S** Memorial Hermann Healthcare System, Houston, TX Web address: www.mhhs.org	23	10	73	5405	43	42762	1961	28352	10453	353

THROCKMORTON—Throckmorton County

THROCKMORTON COUNTY MEMORIAL HOSPITAL, 802 North Minter Street, Zip 76483, Mailing Address: P.O. Box 729, Zip 76483–0729; tel. 940/849–2151; Charles Norris, Administrator (Nonreporting) **A**9 10	13	10	20	—	—	—	—	—	—	—

Hospital, Address, Telephone, Administrator, Approval, Facility, and Physician Codes, Health Care System, Network	Classi-fication Codes		Utilization Data					Expense (thousands) of dollars		
	Control	Service	Staffed Beds	Admissions	Census	Outpatient Visits	Births	Total	Payroll	Personnel

★ American Hospital Association (AHA) membership
□ Joint Commission on Accreditation of Healthcare Organizations (JCAHO) accreditation
+ American Osteopathic Healthcare Association (AOHA) membership
○ American Osteopathic Association (AOA) accreditation
△ Commission on Accreditation of Rehabilitation Facilities (CARF) accreditation
Control codes 61, 63, 64, 71, 72 and 73 indicate hospitals listed by AOHA, but not registered by AHA. For definition of numerical codes, see page A4

TOMBALL—Harris County

⊠ △ TOMBALL REGIONAL HOSPITAL, 605 Holderrieth Street, Zip 77375–0889, Mailing Address: Box 889, Zip 77377–0889; tel. 281/351–1623; Robert F. Schaper, President and Chief Executive Officer (Total facility includes 18 beds in nursing home–type unit) **A**1 7 9 10 **F**4 7 8 10 11 12 15 16 19 21 22 23 24 29 30 32 33 34 35 37 39 40 41 42 43 44 45 48 49 52 54 56 57 58 59 64 65 66 71 73 **P**8
Web address: www.tomballhospital.org

| | 16 | 10 | 128 | 7064 | 117 | 85279 | 596 | 60640 | 20987 | 834 |

TRINITY—Trinity County

EAST TEXAS MEDICAL CENTER TRINITY, 900 Prospect Drive, Zip 75862–0471, Mailing Address: P.O. Box 471, Zip 75862–0471; tel. 409/594–3541; James C. Whitmire, CHE, Administrator **A**9 10 **F**15 16 22 28 32 33 34 65 70 73 **P**3 7 **S** East Texas Medical Center Regional Healthcare System, Tyler, TX

| | 23 | 10 | 22 | 519 | 7 | 29839 | 0 | 4935 | 2231 | 78 |

TULIA—Swisher County

★ SWISHER MEMORIAL HOSPITAL DISTRICT, 539 Southeast Second, Zip 79088–2403, Mailing Address: P.O. Box 808, Zip 79088–0808; tel. 806/995–3581; Jeffrey Madison, Chief Executive Officer **A**9 10 **F**6 8 12 13 15 17 18 19 22 25 26 28 29 30 31 32 33 34 45 46 49 65 71 73 **P**6 **S** St. Joseph Health System, Orange, CA

| | 16 | 10 | 26 | 165 | 6 | 6891 | 0 | 2271 | 1294 | 60 |

TYLER—Smith County

DOCTORS MEMORIAL HOSPITAL, 1400 West Southwest Loop 323, Zip 75701; tel. 903/561–3771; Olie E. Clem, Chief Executive Officer **A**9 10 **F**4 10 12 15 19 22 26 28 32 35 42 43 44 45 46 60 71 **P**7 8

| | 23 | 10 | 46 | 1176 | 14 | 6228 | 110 | 6056 | 3113 | 93 |

□ EAST TEXAS MEDICAL CENTER REHABILITATION CENTER, 701 Olympic Plaza Circle, Zip 75701–1996; tel. 903/596–3000; Eddie L. Howard, Vice President and Chief Operating Officer **A**1 10 **F**2 3 4 7 8 9 10 11 12 14 15 16 19 21 22 24 27 28 29 30 32 34 35 37 39 40 41 42 43 44 48 49 52 53 54 55 57 58 59 60 64 65 66 67 68 70 71 73 74 **P**7 **S** East Texas Medical Center Regional Healthcare System, Tyler, TX

| | 23 | 46 | 49 | 855 | 43 | 44362 | 0 | 18673 | 8600 | 195 |

⊠ △ EAST TEXAS MEDICAL CENTER TYLER, (Includes East Texas Medical Center Behavioral Health Center, 4101 University Boulevard, Zip 75701–6600; tel. 903/566–8668), 1000 South Beckham Street, Zip 75701–1996, Mailing Address: Box 6400, Zip 75711–6400; tel. 903/597–0351; Robert B. Evans, Administrator and Chief Executive Officer (Total facility includes 34 beds in nursing home–type unit) **A**1 2 7 9 10 **F**2 3 4 7 8 10 11 12 14 16 19 21 22 23 24 26 27 28 30 34 35 37 39 40 41 42 43 44 49 52 53 54 55 56 57 58 59 60 63 64 65 66 68 70 71 72 73 **P**6 7 8 **S** East Texas Medical Center Regional Healthcare System, Tyler, TX

| | 23 | 10 | 369 | 17512 | 247 | 230006 | 613 | 207328 | 70842 | 2758 |

□ △ HEALTHSOUTH REHABILITATION HOSPITAL–TYLER, 3131 Troup Highway, Zip 75701–8352; tel. 903/510–7000; Sharla Anderson, Interim Chief Executive Officer **A**1 7 10 **F**12 14 15 16 19 21 22 28 30 34 35 39 41 46 48 49 65 66 67 71 73 **S** HEALTHSOUTH Corporation, Birmingham, AL

| | 32 | 46 | 63 | 1038 | 53 | 9785 | 0 | 11277 | 5332 | 184 |

⊠ TRINITY MOTHER FRANCES HEALTH SYSTEM, 800 East Dawson, Zip 75701–2093; tel. 903/593–8441; J. Lindsey Bradley, Jr., FACHE, President and Chief Administrative Officer (Total facility includes 17 beds in nursing home–type unit) **A**1 2 3 9 10 **F**4 7 8 10 11 12 13 14 15 17 18 19 20 21 22 23 24 25 28 29 30 31 32 34 35 37 40 41 42 43 44 45 46 48 49 51 52 56 60 61 64 65 66 67 68 70 71 72 73 74 **P**2 5 6 7 8
Web address: www.trimofran.org

| | 23 | 10 | 308 | 16544 | 215 | 233099 | 2352 | 202341 | 74956 | 1916 |

⊠ UNIVERSITY OF TEXAS HEALTH CENTER AT TYLER, 11937 Highway 271, Zip 75708–3154; tel. 903/877–3451; Ronald F. Garvey, M.D., President (Total facility includes 24 beds in nursing home–type unit) **A**1 3 9 10 **F**4 8 10 12 13 14 15 16 17 19 22 26 29 30 31 34 35 37 39 41 42 43 44 46 49 51 63 64 65 66 71 73 74 **P**6 **S** University of Texas System, Austin, TX

| | 12 | 10 | 136 | 3601 | 82 | 118518 | 0 | 67704 | 39079 | 1199 |

UVALDE—Uvalde County

★ UVALDE COUNTY HOSPITAL AUTHORITY, 1025 Garner Field Road, Zip 78801–1025; tel. 830/278–6251; Ben M. Durr, Administrator **A**9 10 **F**7 8 10 12 15 16 19 21 22 25 28 32 33 34 35 37 40 41 44 45 49 63 65 70 71 72 73 **P**5

| | 16 | 10 | 51 | 2659 | 29 | 49013 | 585 | 17319 | 8145 | 358 |

VAN HORN—Culberson County

CULBERSON HOSPITAL DISTRICT, Eisenhower–Farm Market Road 2185, Zip 79855, Mailing Address: P.O. Box 609, Zip 79855–0609; tel. 915/283–2760; J. Scott Hensley, Ph.D., Chief Executive Officer **A**9 10 **F**7 14 15 16 22 31 40 44 49 71 **P**8

| | 16 | 10 | 25 | 114 | 1 | 1722 | 5 | 2062 | 855 | 57 |

VERNON—Wilbarger County

□ WILBARGER GENERAL HOSPITAL, 920 Hillcrest Drive, Zip 76384–3196; tel. 817/552–9351; Larry Parsons, Administrator **A**1 9 10 **F**7 8 12 14 15 16 19 22 26 28 29 30 32 34 40 44 45 46 49 51 58 65 67 71 **P**5

| | 16 | 10 | 49 | 1880 | 28 | 97151 | 124 | 10243 | 4439 | 218 |

VICTORIA—Victoria County

⊠ CITIZENS MEDICAL CENTER, 2701 Hospital Drive, Zip 77901–5749; tel. 361/573–9181; David P. Brown, Administrator (Total facility includes 20 beds in nursing home–type unit) **A**1 2 9 10 **F**4 7 8 10 11 12 14 15 16 17 18 19 21 22 23 25 26 28 29 30 31 32 34 35 37 39 41 42 43 44 45 46 47 49 50 52 54 55 56 57 59 60 63 64 65 71 73 **P**8
Web address: www.citizensmedicalcenter.com

| | 13 | 10 | 251 | 8812 | 130 | 69785 | 307 | 81198 | 28340 | 993 |

⊠ DETAR HOSPITAL, 506 East San Antonio Street, Zip 77901–6060, Mailing Address: Box 2089, Zip 77902–2089; tel. 512/575–7441; William R. Blanchard, Chief Executive Officer (Total facility includes 20 beds in nursing home–type unit) **A**1 9 10 **F**4 7 8 10 14 15 16 19 20 22 24 25 26 27 28 29 30 32 33 35 37 39 40 41 42 43 44 45 46 47 48 49 52 57 64 65 71 73 74 **P**3 7 8 **S** Triad Hospitals, Inc., Dallas, TX
Web address: www.detar.com

| | 33 | 10 | 217 | 6242 | 80 | 88347 | 943 | 46029 | 19893 | 576 |

Hospital, Address, Telephone, Administrator, Approval, Facility, and Physician Codes, Health Care System, Network	Classi-fication Codes		Utilization Data					Expense (thousands) of dollars		
★ American Hospital Association (AHA) membership □ Joint Commission on Accreditation of Healthcare Organizations (JCAHO) accreditation + American Osteopathic Healthcare Association (AOHA) membership ○ American Osteopathic Association (AOA) accreditation △ Commission on Accreditation of Rehabilitation Facilities (CARF) accreditation Control codes 61, 63, 64, 71, 72 and 73 indicate hospitals listed by AOHA, but not registered by AHA. For definition of numerical codes, see page A4	Control	Service	Staffed Beds	Admissions	Census	Outpatient Visits	Births	Total	Payroll	Personnel

	Control	Service	Staffed Beds	Admissions	Census	Outpatient Visits	Births	Total	Payroll	Personnel
□ VICTORIA REGIONAL MEDICAL CENTER, 101 Medical Drive, Zip 77904–3198; tel. 512/573–6100; Aston Hecker, Chief Executive Officer **A**1 9 10 **F**3 7 12 14 15 16 19 21 22 28 29 30 31 34 35 37 40 44 45 46 49 52 53 54 55 56 57 58 59 65 67 71 73 **S** Triad Hospitals, Inc., Dallas, TX	33	10	122	3929	47	41883	476	29371	10851	326

WACO—McLennan County

CENTRAL TEXAS VETERANS AFFAIRS HEALTH CARE SYSTEM See Central Texas Veterans Affairs Healthcare System, Temple

	Control	Service	Staffed Beds	Admissions	Census	Outpatient Visits	Births	Total	Payroll	Personnel
★ △ HILLCREST BAPTIST MEDICAL CENTER, 3000 Herring Avenue, Zip 76708–3299, Mailing Address: Box 5100, Zip 76708–0100; tel. 254/202–2000; Richard E. Scott, President **A**1 2 3 5 7 9 10 **F**1 4 5 7 8 10 11 12 13 15 16 17 19 21 22 23 24 25 26 27 28 29 30 31 32 33 34 35 37 38 39 40 41 42 43 44 45 46 48 49 51 56 60 63 65 66 67 68 70 71 72 73 74 **P**6 7 8 **Web address:** www.hillcrest.net	21	10	260	13984	176	218464	3076	113421	44228	1426
★ PROVIDENCE HEALTH CENTER, 6901 Medical Parkway, Zip 76712–7998, Mailing Address: P.O. Box 2589, Zip 76702–2589; tel. 254/751–4000; Kent A. Keahey, President and Chief Executive Officer (Total facility includes 209 beds in nursing home–type unit) **A**1 2 3 5 9 10 **F**2 3 4 6 7 8 10 12 14 15 16 17 18 19 21 22 23 26 28 30 31 32 33 34 35 37 39 40 42 43 44 49 52 53 54 55 56 57 58 59 63 64 65 67 70 71 73 74 **P**8 **S** Daughters of Charity National Health System, Saint Louis, MO **Web address:** www.providence–waco.org	21	10	427	9354	294	67750	417	72287	28405	820

WAXAHACHIE—Ellis County

	Control	Service	Staffed Beds	Admissions	Census	Outpatient Visits	Births	Total	Payroll	Personnel
★ BAYLOR MEDICAL CENTER–ELLIS COUNTY, (Includes Baylor Medical Center – Ellis County, 803 West Lampasas Street, Ennis, Zip 75119; tel. 972/875–0900), 1405 West Jefferson Street, Zip 75165–2275; tel. 972/923–7000; James Michael Lee, Executive Director **A**1 9 10 **F**7 8 12 15 19 22 24 27 30 32 33 35 36 37 39 40 41 42 44 49 64 65 66 71 73 **P**5 6 **S** Baylor Health Care System, Dallas, TX **Web address:** www.baylordallas.edu	23	10	83	5115	53	63560	1002	40213	17882	538

WEATHERFORD—Parker County

	Control	Service	Staffed Beds	Admissions	Census	Outpatient Visits	Births	Total	Payroll	Personnel
★ CAMPBELL HEALTH SYSTEM, 713 East Anderson Street, Zip 76086–9971; tel. 817/596–8751; John B. Millstead, Chief Executive Officer **A**1 9 10 **F**7 8 12 14 15 16 17 19 21 22 23 24 28 30 32 33 35 36 37 39 40 41 44 49 65 67 70 71 73 **P**8 **S** Quorum Health Group/Quorum Health Resources, Inc., Brentwood, TN	16	10	67	3745	36	54649	607	26010	10626	395

WEBSTER—Harris County

	Control	Service	Staffed Beds	Admissions	Census	Outpatient Visits	Births	Total	Payroll	Personnel
★ CLEAR LAKE REGIONAL MEDICAL CENTER, (Includes Alvin Medical Center, 301 Medic Lane, Alvin, Zip 77511–5597; tel. 281/331–6141), 500 Medical Center Boulevard, Zip 77598–4286; tel. 281/338–3110; Donald A. Shaffett, Chief Executive Officer (Total facility includes 39 beds in nursing home–type unit) **A**1 2 9 10 **F**2 3 4 5 7 8 10 11 12 14 15 16 17 19 21 22 23 24 25 26 28 29 30 32 33 34 35 37 38 39 40 41 42 43 44 45 46 47 48 49 51 52 53 55 56 57 58 59 60 61 64 65 66 67 71 72 73 74 **P**2 4 5 6 7 8 **S** Columbia/HCA Healthcare Corporation, Nashville, TN	33	10	375	17406	203	91825	2918	85754	38179	1093

WEIMAR—Colorado County

	Control	Service	Staffed Beds	Admissions	Census	Outpatient Visits	Births	Total	Payroll	Personnel
□ COLORADO–FAYETTE MEDICAL CENTER, 400 Youens Drive, Zip 78962–9561; tel. 409/725–9531; Randy Bacus, Chief Executive Officer (Total facility includes 14 beds in nursing home–type unit) **A**1 9 10 **F**8 12 19 22 28 32 41 44 49 59 63 64 65 71	23	10	38	1823	30	31498	0	8720	3648	142

WELLINGTON—Collingsworth County

	Control	Service	Staffed Beds	Admissions	Census	Outpatient Visits	Births	Total	Payroll	Personnel
COLLINGSWORTH GENERAL HOSPITAL, 1014 15th Street, Zip 79095–3704; tel. 806/447–2521; S. Beth Caison, Administrator **A**9 10 **F**8 12 13 14 15 16 19 22 26 27 28 30 32 39 44 46 49 65 71 74 **P**6	16	10	20	294	5	17936	0	2547	1360	65

WESLACO—Hidalgo County

	Control	Service	Staffed Beds	Admissions	Census	Outpatient Visits	Births	Total	Payroll	Personnel
★ KNAPP MEDICAL CENTER, 1401 East Eighth Street, Zip 78596–6640, Mailing Address: P.O. Box 1110, Zip 78599–1110; tel. 956/968–8567; Robert W. Vanderveer, Chief Executive Officer and Administrator (Total facility includes 18 beds in nursing home–type unit) **A**1 9 10 **F**7 8 14 15 16 17 19 20 21 22 26 27 28 30 32 33 34 35 37 39 40 42 44 45 46 49 63 64 65 67 70 71 73 74	23	10	233	10978	124	55484	1770	67938	26489	990

WEST—McLennan County

	Control	Service	Staffed Beds	Admissions	Census	Outpatient Visits	Births	Total	Payroll	Personnel
□ WEST COMMUNITY HOSPITAL, 501 Meadow Drive, Zip 76691–1018, Mailing Address: P.O. Box 478, Zip 76691–0478; tel. 817/826–7000; Betty York, Executive Director **A**1 9 10 **F**15 16 19 22 30 32 34 44 46 51 65 71 73 **P**6 7 8	21	10	21	416	6	20248	0	3800	1575	63

WHARTON—Wharton County

	Control	Service	Staffed Beds	Admissions	Census	Outpatient Visits	Births	Total	Payroll	Personnel
★ GULF COAST MEDICAL CENTER, 1400 Highway 59, Zip 77488–3004, Mailing Address: P.O. Box 3004, Zip 77488–3004; tel. 409/532–2500; Michael D. Murphy, Chief Executive Officer (Total facility includes 20 beds in nursing home–type unit) **A**1 2 9 10 **F**7 10 12 14 15 16 19 21 22 30 37 40 41 42 44 45 46 48 60 63 64 65 70 71 73 74 **S** Triad Hospitals, Inc., Dallas, TX **Web address:** www.gulfcoastmedical.com	33	10	161	3932	58	54027	623	27159	12841	364

WHEELER—Wheeler County

	Control	Service	Staffed Beds	Admissions	Census	Outpatient Visits	Births	Total	Payroll	Personnel
PARKVIEW HOSPITAL, 1000 Sweetwater Street, Zip 79096, Mailing Address: P.O. Box 1030, Zip 79096–1030; tel. 806/826–5581; B. W. Robertson, Administrator **A**9 10 **F**8 14 15 16 17 19 22 32 40 46 65 71	16	10	25	503	10	11005	0	3078	1533	67

WHITNEY—Hill County

	Control	Service	Staffed Beds	Admissions	Census	Outpatient Visits	Births	Total	Payroll	Personnel
LAKE WHITNEY MEDICAL CENTER, 200 North San Jacinto Street, Zip 76692–2388, Mailing Address: P.O. Box 458, Zip 76692–0458; tel. 254/694–3165; Ruth Ann Crow, Administrator (Nonreporting) **A**9 10	16	10	48	—	—	—	—	—	—	—

Hospital, Address, Telephone, Administrator, Approval, Facility, and Physician Codes, Health Care System, Network	Classi-fication Codes		Utilization Data					Expense (thousands) of dollars		
★ American Hospital Association (AHA) membership □ Joint Commission on Accreditation of Healthcare Organizations (JCAHO) accreditation + American Osteopathic Healthcare Association (AOHA) membership ○ American Osteopathic Association (AOA) accreditation △ Commission on Accreditation of Rehabilitation Facilities (CARF) accreditation Control codes 61, 63, 64, 71, 72 and 73 indicate hospitals listed by AOHA, but not registered by AHA. For definition of numerical codes, see page A4	Control	Service	Staffed Beds	Admissions	Census	Outpatient Visits	Births	Total	Payroll	Personnel

WICHITA FALLS—Wichita County

□ RED RIVER HOSPITAL, 1505 Eighth Street, Zip 76301–3106; tel. 940/322–3171; Ricky Powell, Chief Executive Officer **A**1 9 10 **F**2 3 12 19 26 39 52 53 56 57 58 59 65 67

| | 31 | 22 | 50 | 948 | 28 | 89 | 0 | 5520 | 2647 | 77 |

⊠ UNITED REGIONAL HEALTH CARE SYSTEM, (Includes United Regional Health Care System–Eighth Street Campus, 1600 Eighth Street, Zip 76301–3164; United Regional Health Care System–Eleventh Street Campus, 1600 11th Street, Zip 76301–9988; tel. 940/764–0055; David D. Whitaker, FACHE, President and Chief Operating Officer), 1600 Tenth Street, Zip 76301; tel. 940/764–3055; Jeffrey E. Hausler, Vice Chairman and Chief Executive Officer (Total facility includes 37 beds in nursing home–type unit) **A**1 2 3 5 9 10 **F**4 7 8 10 11 12 13 14 15 16 17 19 20 21 22 23 27 28 29 30 31 32 33 35 37 39 40 41 42 43 44 45 46 49 56 60 61 63 64 65 67 68 71 72 73 74 **P**3

| | 23 | 10 | 403 | 17476 | 254 | 126263 | 1913 | 136249 | 54352 | 2526 |

□ WICHITA FALLS STATE HOSPITAL, 6515 Lake Road, Zip 76308–5419, Mailing Address: Box 300, Zip 76307–0300; tel. 940/692–1220; James E. Smith, Superintendent **A**1 10 **F**15 16 20 39 41 45 46 52 53 57 65 73
Web address: www.mhmr.state.tx.us

| | 12 | 22 | 371 | 1386 | 313 | 0 | 0 | 38792 | 23286 | — |

WINNIE—Chambers County

□ MEDICAL CENTER OF WINNIE, Broadway at Campbell Road, Zip 77665, Mailing Address: P.O. Box 208, Zip 77665–0208; tel. 409/296–2131; John W. Beauchamp, Chief Executive Officer (Nonreporting) **A**1 9 10

| | 23 | 10 | 49 | — | — | — | — | — | — | — |

WINNSBORO—Wood County

⊠ PRESBYTERIAN HOSPITAL OF WINNSBORO, 719 West Coke Road, Zip 75494–3098, Mailing Address: P.O. Box 628, Zip 75494–0628; tel. 903/342–5227; Dan Noteware, Senior Vice President and Executive Director (Total facility includes 8 beds in nursing home–type unit) **A**1 9 10 **F**8 12 15 16 17 19 21 22 27 28 29 30 35 37 39 44 46 49 64 65 67 71 73 **P**1 2 3 4 **S** Texas Health Resources, Irving, TX

| | 23 | 10 | 46 | 1235 | 19 | 31190 | 0 | 12862 | 5469 | 133 |

WINTERS—Runnels County

NORTH RUNNELS HOSPITAL, East Highway 53, Zip 79567, Mailing Address: P.O. Box 185, Zip 79567–0185; tel. 915/754–4553; Scott A. Anderson, Administrator **A**9 10 **F**19 22 28 30 32 33 35 44 71

| | 16 | 10 | 21 | 210 | 2 | 15037 | 0 | 2861 | 1649 | 64 |

WOODVILLE—Tyler County

TYLER COUNTY HOSPITAL, 1100 West Bluff Street, Zip 75979–4799, Mailing Address: P.O. Box 549, Zip 75979–0549; tel. 409/283–8141; James W. Gainey, R.N., Administrator **A**6 9 10 **F**6 7 8 14 19 22 28 30 32 34 44 49 71 73

| | 16 | 10 | 26 | 1028 | 12 | 15967 | 1 | 4948 | 2320 | 106 |

YOAKUM—Lavaca County

⊠ YOAKUM COMMUNITY HOSPITAL, 1200 Carl Ramert Drive, Zip 77995–4198, Mailing Address: P.O. Box 753, Zip 77995–0753; tel. 361/293–2321; Jeff R. Egbert, Chief Executive Officer **A**1 9 10 **F**7 8 12 14 15 16 17 19 20 22 26 28 30 32 34 35 37 39 40 44 45 49 51 65 67 68 70 71 73

| | 23 | 10 | 28 | 987 | 11 | 16427 | 158 | 9154 | 3778 | 182 |

UTAH

Resident population 2,100 (in thousands)
Resident population in metro areas 73.5%
Birth rate per 1,000 population 20.3
65 years and over 8.7%
Percent of persons without health insurance 12.0%

Hospital, Address, Telephone, Administrator, Approval, Facility, and Physician Codes, Health Care System, Network	Classi-fication Codes		Utilization Data					Expense (thousands) of dollars		
★ American Hospital Association (AHA) membership □ Joint Commission on Accreditation of Healthcare Organizations (JCAHO) accreditation + American Osteopathic Healthcare Association (AOHA) membership ○ American Osteopathic Association (AOA) accreditation △ Commission on Accreditation of Rehabilitation Facilities (CARF) accreditation Control codes 61, 63, 64, 71, 72 and 73 indicate hospitals listed by AOHA, but not registered by AHA. For definition of numerical codes, see page A4	Control	Service	Staffed Beds	Admissions	Census	Outpatient Visits	Births	Total	Payroll	Personnel

AMERICAN FORK—Utah County

☒ AMERICAN FORK HOSPITAL, 170 North 1100 East, Zip 84003–9787; tel. 801/763–3300; Keith N. Alexander, Administrator and Chief Operating Officer (Total facility includes 12 beds in nursing home–type unit) **A**1 9 10 **F**4 7 8 10 11 12 13 14 15 16 17 18 19 20 21 22 24 25 28 29 30 31 32 33 34 35 36 37 38 39 40 41 42 43 44 45 46 47 48 49 51 52 53 54 55 56 57 58 59 60 61 64 65 66 67 68 70 71 72 73 74 **P**5 6 **S** Intermountain Health Care, Inc., Salt Lake City, UT
Web address: www.ihc.com

| | 23 | 10 | 72 | 4510 | 30 | 95728 | 2333 | 24784 | 11378 | 407 |

BEAVER—Beaver County

BEAVER VALLEY HOSPITAL, 85 North 400 East, Zip 84713, Mailing Address: P.O. Box 1670, Zip 84713–1670; tel. 435/438–2531; Craig Val Davidson, CHE, Administrator (Total facility includes 24 beds in nursing home–type unit) **A**9 10 **F**7 14 15 16 19 22 28 32 44 46 49 64 65 71 73

| | 14 | 10 | 36 | 799 | 29 | 7829 | 102 | 4349 | 1884 | 85 |

BOUNTIFUL—Davis County

☒ LAKEVIEW HOSPITAL, 630 East Medical Drive, Zip 84010–4996; tel. 801/292–6231; Craig Preston, Chief Executive Officer (Total facility includes 10 beds in nursing home–type unit) **A**1 9 10 **F**2 7 8 10 11 12 14 15 16 18 19 21 22 24 26 28 30 35 37 39 40 41 42 44 45 46 49 52 53 56 57 64 65 67 71 73 74 **P**5 **S** Columbia/HCA Healthcare Corporation, Nashville, TN
Web address: www.columbia.net

| | 33 | 10 | 90 | 3416 | 38 | 54918 | 694 | 30806 | 10904 | 416 |

BRIGHAM CITY—Box Elder County

☒ BRIGHAM CITY COMMUNITY HOSPITAL, 950 South Medical Drive, Zip 84302–3090; tel. 435/734–9471; Tad A. Morley, Chief Executive Officer **A**1 9 10 **F**7 8 11 12 14 15 19 21 22 28 30 34 35 37 39 40 41 44 65 73 **S** Columbia/HCA Healthcare Corporation, Nashville, TN
Web address: www.columbia.net

| | 33 | 10 | 49 | 1375 | 9 | 17879 | 516 | 10356 | 4297 | 156 |

CEDAR CITY—Iron County

☒ VALLEY VIEW MEDICAL CENTER, 595 South 75 East, Zip 84720–3462; tel. 435/586–6587; Craig M. Smedley, Administrator **A**1 9 10 **F**7 8 12 15 19 21 22 28 29 32 37 40 41 44 46 49 64 65 67 71 73 74 **P**6 **S** Intermountain Health Care, Inc., Salt Lake City, UT

| | 23 | 10 | 36 | 2025 | 14 | 68031 | 697 | 15216 | 6230 | 188 |

DELTA—Millard County

★ DELTA COMMUNITY MEDICAL CENTER, 126 South White Sage Avenue, Zip 84624–8937; tel. 435/864–5591; James E. Beckstrand, Administrator **A**9 10 **F**1 3 6 7 8 14 17 22 26 28 29 32 33 34 39 40 44 45 46 48 49 53 54 55 56 57 58 64 66 71 73 74 **P**6 7 **S** Intermountain Health Care, Inc., Salt Lake City, UT

| | 23 | 10 | 20 | 361 | 4 | 11202 | 115 | 3310 | 1422 | 49 |

FILLMORE—Millard County

★ FILLMORE COMMUNITY MEDICAL CENTER, 674 South Highway 99, Zip 84631–5013; tel. 435/743–5591; James E. Beckstrand, Administrator **A**9 10 **F**7 8 11 14 15 18 22 26 28 29 32 33 34 37 39 40 44 47 48 49 51 64 65 71 73 **P**6 **S** Intermountain Health Care, Inc., Salt Lake City, UT
Web address: www.ihc.com

| | 23 | 10 | 20 | 267 | 14 | 28263 | 43 | 2806 | 1139 | 55 |

GUNNISON—Sanpete County

★ GUNNISON VALLEY HOSPITAL, 64 East 100 North, Zip 84634, Mailing Address: P.O. Box 759, Zip 84634–0759; tel. 435/528–7246; Greg Rosenvall, Administrator **A**9 10 **F**7 19 21 22 32 34 44 49 71 **P**5 **S** Rural Health Management Corporation, Nephi, UT

| | 13 | 10 | 21 | 816 | 8 | 31958 | 215 | 6256 | 2622 | 93 |

HEBER CITY—Wasatch County

★ WASATCH COUNTY HOSPITAL, 55 South 500 East, Zip 84032–1999; tel. 435/654–2500; Randall K. Probst, Administrator **A**9 10 **F**7 8 14 15 16 17 19 20 22 24 26 28 29 30 32 33 36 37 39 40 41 44 45 49 65 67 71 73 **S** Intermountain Health Care, Inc., Salt Lake City, UT

| | 23 | 10 | 20 | 440 | 4 | 20957 | 167 | 4344 | 1656 | 42 |

HILL AFB—Davis County

★ U. S. AIR FORCE HOSPITAL, 7321 11th Street, Zip 84056–5012; tel. 801/777–5457; Colonel John A. Reyburn, Jr., Commander (Nonreporting) **A**9 **S** Department of the Air Force, Bowling AFB, DC
Web address: www.75mdg.hill.af.mil

| | 41 | 10 | 15 | — | — | — | — | — | — | — |

KANAB—Kane County

KANE COUNTY HOSPITAL, 355 North Main Street, Zip 84741–3238; tel. 801/644–5811; Mike Sinclair, Administrator (Nonreporting) **A**9 10

| | 16 | 10 | 33 | — | — | — | — | — | — | — |

LAYTON—Davis County

□ DAVIS HOSPITAL AND MEDICAL CENTER, 1600 West Antelope Drive, Zip 84041–1142; tel. 801/825–9561; Bruce A. Baldwin, Chief Executive Officer **A**1 9 10 **F**4 7 8 10 12 14 15 16 17 19 21 22 26 28 29 30 33 34 35 37 38 39 40 42 44 45 46 49 52 57 60 64 65 66 71 72 73 74 **P**6 **S** Paracelsus Healthcare Corporation, Houston, TX

| | 33 | 10 | 126 | 5948 | 56 | 73935 | 1928 | 31019 | 14253 | 431 |

Hospital, Address, Telephone, Administrator, Approval, Facility, and Physician Codes, Health Care System, Network	Classi-fication Codes		Utilization Data					Expense (thousands) of dollars		
★ American Hospital Association (AHA) membership □ Joint Commission on Accreditation of Healthcare Organizations (JCAHO) accreditation + American Osteopathic Healthcare Association (AOHA) membership ○ American Osteopathic Association (AOA) accreditation △ Commission on Accreditation of Rehabilitation Facilities (CARF) accreditation Control codes 61, 63, 64, 71, 72 and 73 indicate hospitals listed by AOHA, but not registered by AHA. For definition of numerical codes, see page A4	Control	Service	Staffed Beds	Admissions	Census	Outpatient Visits	Births	Total	Payroll	Personnel

LOGAN—Cache County

☒ LOGAN REGIONAL HOSPITAL, 1400 North 500 East, Zip 84341–2455; tel. 435/716–1000; Richard Smith, Administrator (Total facility includes 15 beds in nursing home–type unit) **A**1 9 10 **F**3 11 15 16 19 21 24 26 28 29 30 32 33 34 35 37 39 40 41 44 49 51 52 53 54 56 57 58 59 64 65 66 67 71 72 73 74 **P**6 7 **S** Intermountain Health Care, Inc., Salt Lake City, UT
Web address: www.ihc.com | 23 | 10 | 112 | 7463 | 63 | 165929 | 2262 | 46098 | 22880 | 644 |

MIDVALE—Salt Lake County

HIGHLAND RIDGE HOSPITAL, 175 West 7200 South, Zip 84047; tel. 801/272–9851 **F**2 3 15 **S** Pioneer Behavioral Health, Peabody, MA | 33 | 82 | 32 | 478 | 20 | — | 0 | 3247 | 1430 | 50 |

MILFORD—Beaver County

★ MILFORD VALLEY MEMORIAL HOSPITAL, 451 North Main Street, Zip 84751–0640, Mailing Address: P.O. Box 640, Zip 84751–0640; tel. 435/387–2411; John E. Gledhill, Administrator **A**9 10 **F**1 2 3 4 5 6 7 8 9 10 11 12 13 14 15 16 17 18 19 20 21 22 23 24 25 26 27 28 29 30 31 32 33 34 35 36 37 38 39 40 41 42 43 44 45 46 47 48 49 50 51 52 53 54 55 56 57 58 59 60 61 62 63 64 65 66 67 69 70 71 72 73 74 **P**5 6 **S** Rural Health Management Corporation, Nephi, UT | 16 | 10 | 34 | 475 | 20 | 1296 | 24 | 3712 | 1869 | 97 |

MOAB—Grand County

★ ALLEN MEMORIAL HOSPITAL, 719 West 400 North Street, Zip 84532–2297, Mailing Address: P.O. Box 998, Zip 84532–0998; tel. 435/259–7191; Charles A. Davis, Administrator and Chief Executive Officer **A**9 10 **F**7 14 19 22 28 30 32 33 40 44 46 65 71 **S** Rural Health Management Corporation, Nephi, UT | 16 | 10 | 38 | 724 | 8 | 6605 | 86 | 6714 | 3185 | 153 |

MONTICELLO—San Juan County

★ SAN JUAN HOSPITAL, 364 West First North, Zip 84535, Mailing Address: P.O. Box 308, Zip 84535–0308; tel. 435/587–2116; Reid M. Wood, Executive Director (Nonreporting) **A**9 10 | 16 | 10 | 26 | — | — | — | — | — | — | — |

MOUNT PLEASANT—Sanpete County

★ SANPETE VALLEY HOSPITAL, 1100 South Medical Drive, Zip 84647–2222; tel. 435/462–2441; George Winn, Administrator **A**9 10 **F**7 8 12 14 15 16 17 19 22 28 30 32 33 39 44 46 49 64 71 **P**6 **S** Intermountain Health Care, Inc., Salt Lake City, UT | 23 | 10 | 20 | 548 | 10 | 64212 | 112 | 5392 | 1860 | 84 |

NEPHI—Juab County

★ CENTRAL VALLEY MEDICAL CENTER, 549 North 400 East, Zip 84648–1226; tel. 435/623–1242; Mark R. Stoddard, President **A**9 10 **F**7 8 19 22 28 30 32 34 39 40 44 49 51 64 70 71 **P**6 **S** Rural Health Management Corporation, Nephi, UT | 23 | 10 | 22 | 676 | 5 | 52569 | 93 | 7049 | 2652 | 111 |

OGDEN—Weber County

☒ MCKAY–DEE HOSPITAL CENTER, 3939 Harrison Boulevard, Zip 84409–2386, Mailing Address: Box 9370, Zip 84409–0370; tel. 801/398–2800; Patricia Harrington, Administrator and Chief Operating Officer **A**1 2 3 5 9 10 **F**2 3 4 7 8 10 11 12 14 15 17 18 19 21 22 24 25 26 28 29 30 31 32 33 34 35 37 38 39 40 41 42 43 44 45 48 49 51 52 53 54 55 56 57 58 59 61 64 65 66 67 70 71 72 73 74 **S** Intermountain Health Care, Inc., Salt Lake City, UT
Web address: www.ihc.com | 23 | 10 | 293 | 13952 | 186 | 469121 | 3237 | 136228 | 63818 | 1857 |

☒ OGDEN REGIONAL MEDICAL CENTER, 5475 South 500 East, Zip 84405–6978; tel. 801/479–2111; Steven B. Bateman, Chief Executive Officer **A**1 2 9 10 **F**2 3 4 7 8 10 11 12 13 14 15 16 17 18 19 20 21 22 24 26 28 29 30 31 34 35 37 38 39 40 41 42 43 44 45 46 48 51 52 53 54 55 56 57 58 59 60 64 65 67 68 70 71 73 74 **P**5 6 7 8 **S** Columbia/HCA Healthcare Corporation, Nashville, TN
Web address: www.columbia.net | 33 | 10 | 179 | 6614 | 77 | 57178 | 1853 | 60332 | 21664 | 716 |

OREM—Utah County

★ OREM COMMUNITY HOSPITAL, 331 North 400 West, Zip 84057–1999; tel. 801/224–4080; Kim Nielsen, Administrator and Chief Operating Officer **A**9 10 **F**4 7 8 10 11 12 13 14 15 16 17 18 19 20 21 22 24 25 26 28 29 30 31 32 33 34 35 36 37 38 39 40 41 42 43 44 45 46 47 48 49 51 52 53 54 55 56 57 58 59 60 61 64 65 66 67 68 70 71 72 73 74 **P**6 **S** Intermountain Health Care, Inc., Salt Lake City, UT | 23 | 10 | 20 | 1647 | 9 | 58482 | 1419 | 10357 | 4712 | 132 |

PANGUITCH—Garfield County

★ GARFIELD MEMORIAL HOSPITAL AND CLINICS, 200 North 400 East, Zip 84759, Mailing Address: P.O. Box 389, Zip 84759–0389; tel. 435/676–8811; Eric Packer, Administrator **A**9 10 **F**7 12 17 22 25 32 39 40 44 46 48 49 64 65 71 73 **P**6 **S** Intermountain Health Care, Inc., Salt Lake City, UT | 23 | 10 | 44 | 528 | 28 | 29126 | 40 | 4244 | 2270 | 69 |

PAYSON—Utah County

☒ MOUNTAIN VIEW HOSPITAL, 1000 East 100 North, Zip 84651–1690; tel. 801/465–9201; Kevin Johnson, Chief Executive Officer **A**1 9 10 **F**2 3 4 6 7 8 9 10 11 12 14 15 16 17 18 19 20 21 22 23 26 28 30 32 33 34 35 36 37 38 39 40 41 44 45 46 47 48 49 51 52 53 54 55 56 57 58 59 60 64 65 66 67 70 71 73 74 **P**5 **S** Columbia/HCA Healthcare Corporation, Nashville, TN | 33 | 10 | 126 | 3960 | 39 | 51630 | 1144 | 28648 | 10418 | 352 |

PRICE—Carbon County

☒ CASTLEVIEW HOSPITAL, 300 North Hospital Drive, Zip 84501–4200; tel. 435/637–4800; Jeff Frandsen, Chief Executive Officer (Total facility includes 8 beds in nursing home–type unit) **A**1 9 10 **F**7 8 11 14 15 16 19 21 22 27 28 29 30 35 37 38 40 44 46 51 61 63 64 65 66 70 71 73 74 **P**7 8 **S** LifePoint Hospitals, Inc., Nashville, TN | 33 | 10 | 60 | 2205 | 20 | 66708 | 417 | 17790 | 6763 | 300 |

Hospital, Address, Telephone, Administrator, Approval, Facility, and Physician Codes, Health Care System, Network	Classi- fication Codes		Utilization Data					Expense (thousands) of dollars		
★ American Hospital Association (AHA) membership □ Joint Commission on Accreditation of Healthcare Organizations (JCAHO) accreditation + American Osteopathic Healthcare Association (AOHA) membership ○ American Osteopathic Association (AOA) accreditation △ Commission on Accreditation of Rehabilitation Facilities (CARF) accreditation Control codes 61, 63, 64, 71, 72 and 73 indicate hospitals listed by AOHA, but not registered by AHA. For definition of numerical codes, see page A4	Control	Service	Staffed Beds	Admissions	Census	Outpatient Visits	Births	Total	Payroll	Personnel

PROVO—Utah County

□ UTAH STATE HOSPITAL, 1300 East Center Street, Zip 84606–3554, Mailing Address: P.O. Box 270, Zip 84603–0270; tel. 801/344–4400; Mark I. Payne, Superintendent **A**1 10 **F**14 15 16 20 26 41 52 53 55 56 57 65 73 **P**6	12	22	343	380	311	0	0	31002	17478	782
⊠ △ UTAH VALLEY REGIONAL MEDICAL CENTER, 1034 North 500 West, Zip 84604–3337; tel. 801/373–7850; Mary Ann Young, R.N., Administrator (Total facility includes 14 beds in nursing home–type unit) **A**1 2 3 7 9 10 **F**4 7 8 10 11 12 13 14 15 16 17 18 19 20 21 22 24 25 26 28 29 30 31 32 33 34 35 36 37 38 39 40 41 42 43 44 45 46 48 49 51 52 53 54 55 56 57 58 60 61 64 65 66 67 68 70 71 72 73 74 **P**6 **S** Intermountain Health Care, Inc., Salt Lake City, UT	23	10	314	17792	216	310252	3753	160489	73430	2311

RICHFIELD—Sevier County

⊠ SEVIER VALLEY HOSPITAL, 1100 North Main Street, Zip 84701–1843; tel. 435/896–8271; Gary E. Beck, Administrator **A**1 9 10 **F**7 8 12 14 15 16 17 19 21 22 28 29 30 32 33 34 35 39 40 41 44 48 49 51 64 65 71 73 **P**3 5 6 **S** Intermountain Health Care, Inc., Salt Lake City, UT	23	10	27	1352	10	15922	229	10137	3686	160

ROOSEVELT—Duchesne County

★ UINTAH BASIN MEDICAL CENTER, 250 West 300 North, 75–2, Zip 84066; tel. 435/722–6163; Bradley D. LeBaron, Administrator and Chief Executive Officer **A**9 10 **F**7 8 11 14 15 16 19 21 22 28 30 31 37 39 40 44 46 48 49 51 56 61 64 66 67 71 73 74 **P**5 7 8	13	10	42	1987	14	33435	397	17668	6197	252

SAINT GEORGE—Washington County

⊠ DIXIE REGIONAL MEDICAL CENTER, 544 South 400 East, Zip 84770–3799; tel. 435/688–4000; L. Steven Wilson, Administrator **A**1 2 9 10 **F**7 8 10 12 15 16 19 21 22 28 29 30 32 33 34 35 37 39 40 42 44 49 52 59 60 65 67 71 72 73 74 **P**5 **S** Intermountain Health Care, Inc., Salt Lake City, UT **Web address:** www.ihc.com	23	10	116	8142	86	226983	1871	64649	25378	752

SALT LAKE CITY—Salt Lake County

□ BHC OLYMPUS VIEW HOSPITAL, 1430 East 4500 South, Zip 84117–4208; tel. 801/272–8000; Barry W. Woodward, Administrator (Nonreporting) **A**1 10 **S** Behavioral Healthcare Corporation, Nashville, TN	33	22	82	—	—	—	—	—	—	—
⊠ COTTONWOOD HOSPITAL MEDICAL CENTER, 5770 South 300 East, Zip 84107–6186; tel. 801/262–3461; Douglas R. Fonnesbeck, Administrator and Chief Executive Officer **A**1 2 9 10 **F**1 2 3 4 5 6 7 8 9 10 11 12 13 14 15 16 17 18 19 20 21 22 23 24 25 26 27 28 29 30 31 32 33 34 35 36 37 38 39 40 41 42 43 44 45 46 47 48 49 51 52 53 54 55 56 57 58 59 60 61 62 63 64 65 66 67 68 70 71 72 73 74 **P**3 4 5 6 **S** Intermountain Health Care, Inc., Salt Lake City, UT **Web address:** www.ihc.com	23	10	162	11242	95	348315	3513	92163	39736	1488
⊠ △ LDS HOSPITAL, Eighth Avenue and C Street, Zip 84143–0001; tel. 801/408–1100; Richard M. Cagen, Chief Executive Officer and Administrator (Total facility includes 32 beds in nursing home–type unit) **A**1 2 3 5 7 9 10 **F**2 3 4 7 8 10 11 12 14 15 16 17 18 19 21 22 24 25 26 28 29 30 31 32 33 34 35 37 38 40 41 42 43 44 45 46 47 48 49 51 52 53 54 55 56 57 58 59 60 61 64 65 66 67 68 70 71 72 73 74 **P**6 **S** Intermountain Health Care, Inc., Salt Lake City, UT **Web address:** www.ihcweb.co.ihc.com	23	10	412	25971	331	567518	4480	271870	117488	3252
□ PIONEER VALLEY HOSPITAL, 3460 South Pioneer Parkway, Zip 84120–2648; tel. 801/964–3100; Keith Tintle, Chief Executive Officer (Nonreporting) **A**1 2 9 10 **S** Paracelsus Healthcare Corporation, Houston, TX	33	10	127	—	—	—	—	—	—	—
⊠ PRIMARY CHILDREN'S MEDICAL CENTER, (PEDIATRICS MED/SURG REHAB PSYC), 100 North Medical Drive, Zip 84113–1100; tel. 801/588–2000; Joseph R. Horton, Chief Executive Officer and Administrator **A**1 3 5 9 10 **F**2 3 4 5 7 8 10 11 12 13 14 15 17 19 20 21 22 24 25 26 30 31 32 34 35 37 38 39 40 41 42 43 44 45 46 47 48 49 51 52 53 54 55 56 57 58 59 60 61 63 64 65 66 67 68 70 71 72 73 74 **S** Intermountain Health Care, Inc., Salt Lake City, UT	23	59	183	9708	149	104214	0	139579	67618	1805
□ SALT LAKE REGIONAL MEDICAL CENTER, 1050 East South Temple, Zip 84102–1599; tel. 801/350–4111; Kay Matsumura, Chief Executive Officer **A**1 2 3 5 9 10 **F**4 7 8 10 11 12 14 15 16 17 19 21 22 26 31 34 35 37 38 39 40 41 42 43 44 45 46 48 49 50 51 56 63 65 66 67 70 71 73 74 **P**7 **S** Paracelsus Healthcare Corporation, Houston, TX	33	10	138	6305	64	195772	1766	64377	22223	495
⊠ SHRINERS HOSPITALS FOR CHILDREN–INTERMOUNTAIN, Fairfax Road and Virginia Street, Zip 84103–4399; tel. 801/536–3500; J. Craig Patchin, Administrator **A**1 3 5 **F**12 19 34 35 39 41 47 49 54 65 67 71 73 **P**5 6 **S** Shriners Hospitals for Children, Tampa, FL **Web address:** www.shriners.com	23	57	40	1086	21	5798	0	—	—	181
⊠ ST. MARK'S HOSPITAL, 1200 East 3900 South, Zip 84124–1390; tel. 801/268–7111; John Hanshaw, Chief Executive Officer **A**1 2 3 9 10 **F**4 7 8 10 11 12 14 15 16 17 19 21 22 23 25 26 27 28 29 30 32 34 35 37 39 40 41 42 43 44 45 46 53 55 58 59 60 63 64 65 71 72 73 74 **P**4 5 7 **S** Columbia/HCA Healthcare Corporation, Nashville, TN **Web address:** www.columbia.net	33	10	229	15791	170	195639	3151	112968	36245	1148
⊠ △ UNIVERSITY OF UTAH HOSPITALS AND CLINICS, 50 North Medical Drive, Zip 84132–0002; tel. 801/581–2380; Christine St. Andre, Executive Director **A**1 2 3 5 7 8 9 10 **F**4 7 8 9 10 11 12 14 17 18 19 20 21 22 23 25 26 28 30 31 32 34 35 37 38 39 40 41 42 43 44 45 46 48 49 51 52 54 56 57 60 61 63 64 65 66 67 68 70 71 72 73 74 **P**5 **Web address:** www.med.utah.edu/	12	10	358	16811	293	433120	2923	261968	99641	3399

Hospital, Address, Telephone, Administrator, Approval, Facility, and Physician Codes, Health Care System, Network	Classi-fication Codes		Utilization Data					Expense (thousands) of dollars		
	Control	Service	Staffed Beds	Admissions	Census	Outpatient Visits	Births	Total	Payroll	Personnel

★ American Hospital Association (AHA) membership
☐ Joint Commission on Accreditation of Healthcare Organizations (JCAHO) accreditation
+ American Osteopathic Healthcare Association (AOHA) membership
○ American Osteopathic Association (AOA) accreditation
△ Commission on Accreditation of Rehabilitation Facilities (CARF) accreditation
Control codes 61, 63, 64, 71, 72 and 73 indicate hospitals listed by AOHA, but not registered by AHA. For definition of numerical codes, see page A4

Hospital	Control	Service	Staffed Beds	Admissions	Census	Outpatient Visits	Births	Total	Payroll	Personnel
☐ UNIVERSITY OF UTAH NEUROPSYCHIATRIC INSTITUTE, 501 Chipeta Way, Zip 84108–1225; tel. 801/583–2500; Ross Van Vranken, Chief Executive Officer **A**1 3 5 10 **F**1 2 3 12 14 15 16 17 19 21 26 35 45 46 52 53 54 55 56 57 58 59 65 67 68	23	22	90	1985	49	16153	0	13971	7079	232
⊞ VETERANS AFFAIRS MEDICAL CENTER, 500 Foothill Drive, Zip 84148–0002; tel. 801/582–1565; James R. Floyd, Medical Center Director **A**1 2 3 5 8 9 **F**3 4 8 10 12 14 15 16 17 18 19 20 21 22 23 24 25 26 27 28 29 30 31 32 33 34 35 37 39 41 42 43 44 45 46 49 50 51 52 54 55 56 57 58 60 61 63 64 65 67 68 71 73 74 **S** Department of Veterans Affairs, Washington, DC	45	10	138	1252	27	226467	0	121663	57512	1470

SANDY—Salt Lake County

Hospital	Control	Service	Staffed Beds	Admissions	Census	Outpatient Visits	Births	Total	Payroll	Personnel
⊞ ALTA VIEW HOSPITAL, 9660 South 1300 East, Zip 84094–3793; tel. 801/501–2600; Wes Thompson, Administrator and Chief Executive Officer **A**1 9 10 **F**1 2 3 4 5 6 7 8 9 10 11 12 13 14 15 16 17 18 19 20 21 22 23 24 25 26 27 28 29 30 31 32 33 34 35 36 37 38 39 40 41 42 43 44 45 46 47 48 49 51 52 53 54 55 56 57 58 59 60 61 62 63 64 65 66 67 68 70 71 72 73 74 **P**3 4 5 6 **S** Intermountain Health Care, Inc., Salt Lake City, UT **Web address:** www.ihc.com	23	10	72	4909	35	160982	1890	38370	16449	606
☐ △ HEALTHSOUTH REHABILITATION HOSPITAL OF UTAH, 8074 South 1300 East, Zip 84094–0743; tel. 801/561–3400; Richard M. Richards, Administrator (Total facility includes 36 beds in nursing home–type unit) **A**1 7 9 10 **F**1 12 15 16 26 30 32 34 41 42 45 48 49 64 65 73 **P**5 **S** HEALTHSOUTH Corporation, Birmingham, AL	33	46	58	1657	52	—	0	—	5391	148

TOOELE—Tooele County

Hospital	Control	Service	Staffed Beds	Admissions	Census	Outpatient Visits	Births	Total	Payroll	Personnel
★ TOOELE VALLEY REGIONAL MEDICAL CENTER, 211 South 100 East, Zip 84074–2794; tel. 435/882–1697; Brent Cope, Chief Executive Officer (Total facility includes 84 beds in nursing home–type unit) **A**9 10 **F**7 8 14 15 18 19 20 22 28 30 32 33 34 37 39 40 41 44 49 51 53 54 56 64 65 67 70 71 74 **S** Community Health Systems, Inc., Brentwood, TN	16	10	107	1220	76	10784	156	14159	5741	279

TREMONTON—Box Elder County

Hospital	Control	Service	Staffed Beds	Admissions	Census	Outpatient Visits	Births	Total	Payroll	Personnel
★ BEAR RIVER VALLEY HOSPITAL, 440 West 600 North, Zip 84337–2497; tel. 435/257–7441; Robert F. Jex, Administrator (Total facility includes 38 beds in nursing home–type unit) **A**9 10 **F**7 12 14 15 17 20 22 28 30 32 33 40 44 46 49 64 71 73 **S** Intermountain Health Care, Inc., Salt Lake City, UT	23	10	58	612	40	9793	71	4262	2164	71

VERNAL—Uintah County

Hospital	Control	Service	Staffed Beds	Admissions	Census	Outpatient Visits	Births	Total	Payroll	Personnel
⊞ ASHLEY VALLEY MEDICAL CENTER, (Formerly Columbia Ashley Valley Medical Center), 151 West 200 North, Zip 84078–1907; tel. 435/789–3342; Ronald J. Perry, Chief Executive Officer **A**1 9 10 **F**7 8 12 15 19 21 22 28 30 32 35 37 39 40 44 46 66 71 **P**5 7 8 **S** LifePoint Hospitals, Inc., Nashville, TN **Web address:** www.avmc–hospital.com	33	10	29	1429	12	34927	284	13729	4775	182

WEST JORDAN—Salt Lake County

Hospital	Control	Service	Staffed Beds	Admissions	Census	Outpatient Visits	Births	Total	Payroll	Personnel
COPPER HILLS YOUTH CENTER, 5899 West Rivendell Drive, Zip 84088–5700, Mailing Address: P.O. Box 459, Zip 84084–0459; tel. 801/561–3377; Sandy Podley, Chief Executive Officer **A**9 10 **F**14 15 16 52 53 59 **S** Children's Comprehensive Services, Inc., Nashville, TN	33	52	80	263	55	—	0	—	—	—
☐ JORDAN VALLEY HOSPITAL, 3580 West 9000 South, Zip 84088–8811; tel. 801/561–8888; Jeffrey J. Manley, Chief Executive Officer (Nonreporting) **A**1 9 10 **S** Paracelsus Healthcare Corporation, Houston, TX	33	10	50	—	—	—	—	—	—	—

WOODS CROSS—Davis County

Hospital	Control	Service	Staffed Beds	Admissions	Census	Outpatient Visits	Births	Total	Payroll	Personnel
☐ BENCHMARK BEHAVIORAL HEALTH SYSTEMS, 592 West 1350 South, Zip 84087–1665; tel. 801/299–5300; Richard O. Hurt, Ph.D., Chief Executive Officer **A**1 9 10 **F**1 14 15 16 22 52 53 57 59 65 67 **P**8 **S** Ramsay Health Care, Inc., Coral Gables, FL	33	22	68	49	79	784	0	7365	—	262

VERMONT

Resident population 591 (in thousands)
Resident population in metro areas 27.6%
Birth rate per 1,000 population 11.6
65 years and over 12.3%
Percent of persons without health insurance 11.1%

Hospital, Address, Telephone, Administrator, Approval, Facility, and Physician Codes, Health Care System, Network	Classi-fication Codes		Utilization Data					Expense (thousands) of dollars		
★ American Hospital Association (AHA) membership □ Joint Commission on Accreditation of Healthcare Organizations (JCAHO) accreditation + American Osteopathic Healthcare Association (AOHA) membership ○ American Osteopathic Association (AOA) accreditation △ Commission on Accreditation of Rehabilitation Facilities (CARF) accreditation Control codes 61, 63, 64, 71, 72 and 73 indicate hospitals listed by AOHA, but not registered by AHA. For definition of numerical codes, see page A4	Control	Service	Staffed Beds	Admissions	Census	Outpatient Visits	Births	Total	Payroll	Personnel

BARRE—Washington County

★ CENTRAL VERMONT MEDICAL CENTER, Fisher Road, Zip 05641–9060, Mailing Address: P.O. Box 547, Zip 05641–0547; tel. 802/371–4100; Daria V. Mason, Chief Executive Officer (Total facility includes 153 beds in nursing home–type unit) **A**1 9 10 **F**7 8 11 14 15 16 17 19 20 21 22 23 27 28 30 31 34 35 37 39 40 41 42 44 45 46 48 49 51 52 54 56 57 61 63 64 65 66 71 72 73 74 **P**1 6
Web address: www.central–vt.com/web/cvmc

| 23 | 10 | 294 | 3906 | 201 | 76405 | 463 | 45491 | 21055 | 524 |

BENNINGTON—Bennington County

★ SOUTHWESTERN VERMONT MEDICAL CENTER, 100 Hospital Drive East, Zip 05201–5013; tel. 802/442–6361; Harvey M. Yorke, President and Chief Executive Officer **A**1 2 9 10 **F**1 2 3 4 7 8 10 11 12 13 14 15 16 17 19 21 22 25 26 27 28 29 30 32 33 34 35 36 37 39 40 41 42 44 45 46 48 49 51 52 54 55 56 57 58 59 60 63 64 65 66 67 69 70 71 72 73 74 **P**6 8

| 23 | 10 | 84 | 4401 | 46 | 143990 | 413 | 40197 | 18898 | 627 |

BRATTLEBORO—Windham County

★ BRATTLEBORO MEMORIAL HOSPITAL, 9 Belmont Avenue, Zip 05301–3498; tel. 802/257–0341; Brian R. Mitteer, President **A**1 9 10 **F**7 8 11 14 15 16 17 19 21 22 24 28 30 31 35 37 39 40 41 42 44 46 49 63 65 67 71 73
Web address: www.sover.net/~bmh

| 23 | 10 | 61 | 2318 | 27 | — | 345 | 23157 | 9639 | 272 |

★ BRATTLEBORO RETREAT, Anna Marsh Lane, Zip 05301, Mailing Address: P.O. Box 803, Zip 05302–0803; tel. 802/257–7785; Richard T. Palmisano, II, R.N., MS, Chief Executive Officer (Total facility includes 99 beds in nursing home–type unit) **A**1 5 10 **F**3 12 15 25 26 27 52 53 54 55 56 57 58 59 64 65 67 73 **P**7
Web address: www.bratretreat.org

| 23 | 22 | 177 | 2280 | 130 | 15666 | 0 | 26892 | — | 434 |

BURLINGTON—Chittenden County

★ FLETCHER ALLEN HEALTH CARE, (Includes Fanny Allen Campus, 101 College Parkway, Colchester, Zip 05446–3035; tel. 802/655–1234; Medical Center Hospital Campus, Colchester Avenue, Zip 05401; tel. 802/656–2345), 111 Colchester Avenue, Zip 05401–1429; tel. 802/656–2345; William V. Boettcher, Chief Executive Officer **A**1 2 3 5 8 9 10 **F**2 3 4 7 8 9 10 11 12 13 14 15 16 17 18 19 20 21 22 23 25 26 28 29 30 31 32 33 34 35 37 38 39 40 41 42 43 44 45 46 47 48 49 51 52 53 54 55 56 57 58 59 60 63 64 65 66 67 68 70 71 72 73 **P**1 8
Web address: www.fahc.org

| 23 | 10 | 481 | 19141 | 320 | 372354 | 2215 | — | — | 3140 |

MIDDLEBURY—Addison County

★ PORTER HOSPITAL, 115 Porter Drive, Zip 05753–8606; tel. 802/388–4701; James L. Daily, President (Total facility includes 118 beds in nursing home–type unit) **A**1 9 10 **F**8 14 16 17 19 21 22 26 28 30 35 37 39 40 42 44 45 46 49 51 63 64 65 67 71 73 74
Web address: www.addisonindependent.com/porter

| 23 | 10 | 163 | 1428 | 132 | 62651 | 321 | 22283 | 10329 | 458 |

MORRISVILLE—Lamoille County

★ COPLEY HOSPITAL, 528 Washington Highway, Zip 05661–9209; tel. 802/888–4231; Carolyn C. Roberts, President **A**1 9 10 **F**7 8 11 14 15 16 17 19 21 22 28 29 30 33 34 36 37 38 39 40 42 44 46 48 49 53 58 64 65 66 67 71 73 **P**8
Web address: www.copleyhealthsystems.org

| 23 | 10 | 41 | 1714 | 21 | 48021 | 248 | 17891 | 7686 | 265 |

NEWPORT—Orleans County

★ NORTH COUNTRY HOSPITAL AND HEALTH CENTER, 189 Prouty Drive, Zip 05855–9329; tel. 802/334–7331; Sidney A. Toll, President **A**1 9 10 **F**7 8 16 17 19 21 22 28 29 30 35 37 39 40 41 42 44 45 46 49 51 58 65 67 71 73 74 **P**6

| 23 | 10 | 27 | 1971 | 19 | — | 201 | 21747 | 11374 | 310 |

RANDOLPH—Orange County

★ GIFFORD MEDICAL CENTER, 44 South Main Street, Zip 05060, Mailing Address: P.O. Box 2000, Zip 05060–2000; tel. 802/728–4441; David H. Gregg, Jr., President (Total facility includes 41 beds in nursing home–type unit) **A**1 2 9 10 **F**1 7 8 11 12 13 14 15 16 17 19 21 22 25 26 27 28 29 30 32 33 34 39 40 41 42 44 45 46 49 51 53 54 55 56 57 58 59 64 65 66 67 71 72 73 74 **P**6
Web address: www.giffordmed.com

| 23 | 10 | 93 | 1335 | 48 | 22012 | 233 | 17344 | 9478 | 277 |

RUTLAND—Rutland County

★ RUTLAND REGIONAL MEDICAL CENTER, 160 Allen Street, Zip 05701–4595; tel. 802/775–7111; Thomas W. Huebner, President and Chief Executive Officer **A**1 2 9 10 **F**4 6 7 8 12 13 14 15 16 19 21 22 23 28 30 31 34 35 37 39 40 41 42 44 45 46 48 49 52 54 55 56 58 59 60 63 65 66 67 70 71 72 73 **P**5 8
Web address: www.rrmc.org

| 23 | 10 | 132 | 6288 | 82 | 108648 | 593 | 67495 | 31339 | 743 |

SAINT ALBANS—Franklin County

★ NORTHWESTERN MEDICAL CENTER, 131 Fairfield Street, Zip 05478–1734, Mailing Address: P.O. Box 1370, Zip 05478–1370; tel. 802/524–5911; Peter A. Hofstetter, Chief Executive Officer **A**1 2 9 10 **F**7 8 12 14 15 16 17 18 19 22 28 29 30 34 35 36 37 39 40 41 44 45 46 48 49 65 67 71 72 73 **P**8 **S** Quorum Health Group/Quorum Health Resources, Inc., Brentwood, TN
Web address: www.nmcinc.org

| 23 | 10 | 70 | 2165 | 22 | 24320 | 789 | 23287 | 10334 | 302 |

Hospital, Address, Telephone, Administrator, Approval, Facility, and Physician Codes, Health Care System, Network	Classi-fication Codes		Utilization Data					Expense (thousands) of dollars		
★ American Hospital Association (AHA) membership □ Joint Commission on Accreditation of Healthcare Organizations (JCAHO) accreditation + American Osteopathic Healthcare Association (AOHA) membership ○ American Osteopathic Association (AOA) accreditation △ Commission on Accreditation of Rehabilitation Facilities (CARF) accreditation Control codes 61, 63, 64, 71, 72 and 73 indicate hospitals listed by AOHA, but not registered by AHA. For definition of numerical codes, see page A4	Control	Service	Staffed Beds	Admissions	Census	Outpatient Visits	Births	Total	Payroll	Personnel

SAINT JOHNSBURY—Caledonia County

☒ NORTHEASTERN VERMONT REGIONAL HOSPITAL, Hospital Drive, Zip 05819–9962, Mailing Address: P.O. Box 905, Zip 05819–9962; tel. 802/748–8141; Paul R. Bengtson, Chief Executive Officer **A**1 9 10 **F**7 8 12 14 15 16 17 19 21 22 29 30 31 34 37 39 40 41 42 44 45 46 49 53 54 56 58 63 65 66 71 72 73 74 **P**7 **S** Quorum Health Group/Quorum Health Resources, Inc., Brentwood, TN

	23	10	28	1650	15	75195	289	20618	9075	268

SPRINGFIELD—Windsor County

☒ SPRINGFIELD HOSPITAL, 25 Ridgewood Road, Zip 05156–2003, Mailing Address: P.O. Box 2003, Zip 05156–2003; tel. 802/885–2151; Glenn D. Cordner, Chief Executive Officer **A**1 9 10 **F**1 7 8 12 14 15 16 19 21 22 25 26 28 31 34 35 37 39 40 41 44 49 52 56 57 63 65 67 71 72 73 **P**4 7

Web address: www.multiplan.com/mplpghosp.dbm?

	23	10	50	2334	26	42541	244	20766	7689	271

TOWNSHEND—Windham County

★ GRACE COTTAGE HOSPITAL, (Includes Stratton House Nursing Home), Route 35, Zip 05353–0216, Mailing Address: P.O. Box 216, Zip 05353–0216; tel. 802/365–7357; Albert LaRochelle, Administrator (Total facility includes 30 beds in nursing home–type unit) **A**9 10 **F**1 7 16 22 27 33 36 40 41 44 49 51 58 64 65 73 **P**6

	23	10	48	378	40	10663	12	4191	2369	81

WATERBURY—Washington County

VERMONT STATE HOSPITAL, 103 South Main Street, Zip 05671–2501; tel. 802/241–1000; Bertold Francke, M.D., Interim Executive Director **A**9 10 **F**20 52 65 73 **P**6

	12	22	68	304	54	0	0	9529	5318	179

WHITE RIVER JUNCTION—Windsor County

☒ VETERANS AFFAIRS MEDICAL CENTER, North Hartland Road, Zip 05009–0001; tel. 802/295–9363; Gary M. De Gasta, Center Director **A**1 3 5 8 9 **F**3 19 20 22 27 30 32 37 41 42 44 46 49 51 52 54 57 58 59 64 65 73 74 **S** Department of Veterans Affairs, Washington, DC

Web address: www.wrjva1.hitchcock.org

	45	10	60	2303	51	121979	0	—	—	—

WINDSOR—Windsor County

★ MT. ASCUTNEY HOSPITAL AND HEALTH CENTER, County Road, Rural Route 1, Box 6, Zip 05089–9702; tel. 802/674–6711; Richard Slusky, Administrator (Total facility includes 66 beds in nursing home–type unit) **A**9 10 **F**8 12 14 15 16 17 20 22 26 27 29 30 31 32 33 34 36 37 39 41 44 45 46 48 49 54 56 58 64 65 67 71 73 **P**6

Web address: www.mtascutneyhosp

	23	10	99	1047	80	18617	0	11835	6055	236

VIRGINIA

Resident population 6,791 (in thousands)
Resident population in metro areas 76.5%
Birth rate per 1,000 population 14
65 years and over 11.2%
Percent of persons without health insurance 12.5%

Hospital, Address, Telephone, Administrator, Approval, Facility, and Physician Codes, Health Care System, Network	Classi-fication Codes		Utilization Data					Expense (thousands) of dollars		
★ American Hospital Association (AHA) membership □ Joint Commission on Accreditation of Healthcare Organizations (JCAHO) accreditation + American Osteopathic Healthcare Association (AOHA) membership ○ American Osteopathic Association (AOA) accreditation △ Commission on Accreditation of Rehabilitation Facilities (CARF) accreditation Control codes 61, 63, 64, 71, 72 and 73 indicate hospitals listed by AOHA, but not registered by AHA. For definition of numerical codes, see page A4	Control	Service	Staffed Beds	Admissions	Census	Outpatient Visits	Births	Total	Payroll	Personnel

ABINGDON—Washington County

✚ JOHNSTON MEMORIAL HOSPITAL, 351 Court Street N.E., Zip 24210–2921; tel. 540/676–7000; Clark R. Beil, Chief Executive Officer **A**1 2 9 10 **F**3 4 7 8 10 11 12 14 15 16 17 19 20 21 22 25 26 27 28 30 31 32 33 34 35 37 38 39 40 41 42 44 45 46 48 49 51 52 56 57 59 63 65 66 67 69 71 72 73 74 **P**8
Web address: www.jmh.org
| | 23 | 10 | 135 | 5047 | 66 | 77031 | 726 | 36722 | 15616 | 574 |

ALEXANDRIA—Independent City County

✚ INOVA ALEXANDRIA HOSPITAL, 4320 Seminary Road, Zip 22304–1594; tel. 703/504–3000; H. Patrick Walters, Administrator **A**1 2 3 5 9 10 **F**3 4 6 7 8 10 12 13 15 16 17 19 21 22 24 25 27 28 29 30 31 32 34 35 37 38 39 40 41 42 43 44 45 46 49 51 52 53 54 55 56 57 58 59 60 61 63 65 66 67 68 70 71 72 73 74 **P**1 4 6 7 8 **S** Inova Health System, Falls Church, VA
Web address: www.inova.com
| | 23 | 10 | 316 | 14827 | 206 | 99710 | 3275 | 112863 | 55105 | 1333 |

✚ △ INOVA MOUNT VERNON HOSPITAL, 2501 Parker's Lane, Zip 22306–3209; tel. 703/664–7000; Susan Herbert, Administrator **A**1 2 3 7 9 10 **F**1 3 4 6 7 8 10 11 12 13 14 15 16 17 19 21 22 23 25 26 27 28 30 31 32 33 34 35 36 37 38 39 40 41 42 43 44 45 46 47 48 49 51 52 53 54 55 56 57 58 59 60 61 62 63 64 65 66 67 68 70 71 72 73 74 **P**1 2 7 8 **S** Inova Health System, Falls Church, VA
Web address: www.inova.com
| | 23 | 10 | 229 | 8176 | 146 | 63220 | 0 | 78088 | 33142 | 747 |

ARLINGTON—Arlington County

✚ ARLINGTON HOSPITAL, 1701 North George Mason Drive, Zip 22205–3698; tel. 703/558–5000; James B. Cole, President and Chief Executive Officer (Nonreporting) **A**1 2 3 5 9 10 **S** Columbia/HCA Healthcare Corporation, Nashville, TN
| | 32 | 10 | 256 | — | — | — | — | ✖ | ✖ | ✖ |

✚ △ COLUMBIA PENTAGON CITY HOSPITAL, 2455 Army Navy Drive, Zip 22206–2999; tel. 703/920–6700; Thomas Anderson, Chief Executive Officer (Nonreporting) **A**1 5 7 9 10 **S** Columbia/HCA Healthcare Corporation, Nashville, TN
Web address: www.columbia.net
| | 33 | 10 | 102 | — | — | — | — | ✖ | ✖ | ✖ |

□ HOSPICE OF NORTHERN VIRGINIA, (HOSPICE), 4715 North 15th Street, Zip 22205; tel. 703/525–7070; David J. English, President and Chief Executive Officer **A**1 10 **F**12 14 15 16 17 28 31 32 33 64 65 67 73 **P**6
Web address: www.hospiceonline.org
| | 23 | 49 | 15 | 114 | 2 | 0 | 0 | 2173 | 1300 | 266 |

□ NORTHERN VIRGINIA COMMUNITY HOSPITAL, (Formerly Vencor Hospital–Arlington), 601 South Carlin Springs Road, Zip 22204–1096; tel. 703/671–1200; Mark Aanonson, Administrator **A**1 5 9 10 **F**8 10 11 12 15 19 21 22 37 39 41 42 44 46 48 49 56 58 59 71 73 **S** Vencor, Incorporated, Louisville, KY
Web address: www.vencorhospital–arlington.com
| | 33 | 10 | 175 | 2756 | 57 | 12601 | 0 | 35178 | 14131 | 351 |

BEDFORD—Independent City County

✚ CARILION BEDFORD MEMORIAL HOSPITAL, 1613 Oakwood Street, Zip 24523–0688, Mailing Address: P.O. Box 688, Zip 24523–0688; tel. 540/586–2441; Howard Ainsley, Vice President and Hospital Director (Total facility includes 111 beds in nursing home–type unit) **A**1 9 10 **F**1 7 8 11 12 14 15 16 17 18 19 22 27 28 29 30 32 33 37 39 40 41 42 44 49 51 52 53 54 56 60 63 64 65 67 71 73 74 **P**6 **S** Carilion Health System, Roanoke, VA
| | 23 | 10 | 161 | 1701 | 120 | 11184 | 231 | 18097 | 8137 | 308 |

BIG STONE GAP—Wise County

✚ WELLMONT LONESOME PINE HOSPITAL, (Formerly Lonesome Pine Hospital), 1990 Holton Avenue East, Zip 24219–0230; tel. 540/523–3111; Paul A. Bishop, Administrator **A**1 9 10 **F**7 8 12 14 15 16 17 18 19 22 23 26 27 28 30 32 33 34 36 37 39 40 42 44 46 49 56 63 64 65 66 71 73 74 **P**1 3 4 5 6 7 **S** Quorum Health Group/Quorum Health Resources, Inc., Brentwood, TN
| | 23 | 10 | 53 | 1853 | 21 | 21888 | 224 | 14687 | 6489 | 221 |

BLACKSBURG—Montgomery County

✚ MONTGOMERY REGIONAL HOSPITAL, 3700 South Main Street, Zip 24060–7081, Mailing Address: P.O. Box 90004, Zip 24062–9004; tel. 540/953–5101; David R. Williams, Chief Executive Officer (Total facility includes 11 beds in nursing home–type unit) **A**1 9 10 **F**2 3 4 7 8 10 11 12 14 15 16 17 18 19 21 22 23 24 26 28 29 30 31 34 35 37 39 40 41 42 43 44 45 46 47 48 49 51 52 53 54 55 56 57 58 59 60 61 63 64 65 66 67 70 71 72 73 74 **P**8 **S** Columbia/HCA Healthcare Corporation, Nashville, TN
Web address: www.montreghosp.com
| | 33 | 10 | 115 | 4903 | 55 | 53779 | 596 | 33040 | 11811 | 417 |

BURKEVILLE—Nottoway County

□ PIEDMONT GERIATRIC HOSPITAL, Mailing Address: P.O. Box 427, Zip 23922–0427; tel. 804/767–4401; Willard R. Pierce, Jr., Director (Nonreporting) **A**1 9 10 **S** Virginia Department of Mental Health, Richmond, VA
| | 12 | 49 | 210 | — | — | — | — | — | — | — |

CATAWBA—Roanoke County

□ CATAWBA HOSPITAL, Mailing Address: P.O. Box 200, Zip 24070–0200; tel. 540/375–4200; James S. Reinhard, M.D., Director **A**1 9 10 **F**14 15 16 19 20 26 35 45 46 52 57 65 73 **P**6 **S** Virginia Department of Mental Health, Richmond, VA
| | 12 | 22 | 171 | 314 | 136 | 0 | 0 | 15641 | 9384 | 337 |

Hospital, Address, Telephone, Administrator, Approval, Facility, and Physician Codes, Health Care System, Network	Classi-fication Codes		Utilization Data					Expense (thousands) of dollars		
★ American Hospital Association (AHA) membership □ Joint Commission on Accreditation of Healthcare Organizations (JCAHO) accreditation + American Osteopathic Healthcare Association (AOHA) membership ○ American Osteopathic Association (AOA) accreditation △ Commission on Accreditation of Rehabilitation Facilities (CARF) accreditation Control codes 61, 63, 64, 71, 72 and 73 indicate hospitals listed by AOHA, but not registered by AHA. For definition of numerical codes, see page A4	Control	Service	Staffed Beds	Admissions	Census	Outpatient Visits	Births	Total	Payroll	Personnel

CHARLOTTESVILLE—Independent City County

□ CHARTER BEHAVIORAL HEALTH SYSTEM OF CHARLOTTESVILLE, 2101 Arlington Boulevard, Zip 22903–1593; tel. 804/977–1120; Wayne Adams, Chief Executive Officer (Nonreporting) **A**1 9 10 **S** Magellan Health Services, Atlanta, GA	33	22	62	—	—	—	—	—	—	—
⊠ MARTHA JEFFERSON HOSPITAL, 459 Locust Avenue, Zip 22902–9940; tel. 804/982–7000; James E. Haden, President and Chief Executive Officer **A**1 2 9 10 **F**7 8 10 11 12 14 15 16 17 19 21 22 23 24 28 29 30 32 33 34 35 39 40 41 42 44 46 49 60 63 65 68 71 73 74 **P**1 4 7 **Web address:** www.marthajefferson.org	23	10	156	9045	91	87067	1408	76858	35706	1060
⊠ UNIVERSITY OF VIRGINIA MEDICAL CENTER, Jefferson Park Avenue, Zip 22908, Mailing Address: P.O. Box 10050, Zip 22906–0050; tel. 804/924–0211; William E. Carter, Jr., Senior Associate Vice President for Operations **A**1 2 3 5 8 9 10 **F**3 4 5 7 8 9 10 11 12 13 15 16 17 18 19 20 21 22 23 25 26 27 28 29 30 31 32 33 34 35 37 38 39 40 41 42 43 44 45 46 47 48 49 51 52 53 54 55 56 57 58 59 60 61 63 65 66 67 68 70 71 72 73 74 **P**3 **Web address:** www.med.virginia.edu	12	10	595	27839	452	514509	1522	444458	158708	5295

CHESAPEAKE—Independent City County

⊠ CHESAPEAKE GENERAL HOSPITAL, 736 Battlefield Boulevard North, Zip 23320–4941, Mailing Address: P.O. Box 2028, Zip 23327–2028; tel. 757/312–8121; Donald S. Buckley, FACHE, President **A**1 2 5 9 10 **F**1 6 7 8 10 16 17 19 22 23 24 26 28 30 32 33 34 35 36 37 39 40 41 42 44 46 49 52 57 59 60 61 63 65 67 71 73 74 **Web address:** www.chealth.com	16	10	260	14432	202	144853	3135	106523	48903	1544

CLINTWOOD—Dickenson County

□ DICKENSON COUNTY MEDICAL CENTER, Hospital Drive, Zip 24228, Mailing Address: P.O. Box 1390, Zip 24228–1390; tel. 540/926–0300; Benjamin A. Peak, Chief Executive Officer **A**1 9 10 **F**8 14 19 22 26 28 30 32 37 44 51 65 67 71 73 74 **P**6 **Web address:** www.dcmc.mounet.com	33	10	41	1319	18	41617	0	8686	4021	157

CULPEPER—Culpeper County

⊠ CULPEPER MEMORIAL HOSPITAL, 501 Sunset Lane, Zip 22701–3917, Mailing Address: Box 592, Zip 22701–0592; tel. 540/829–4100; H. Lee Kirk, Jr., President and Chief Executive Officer (Nonreporting) **A**1 9 10	23	10	70	—	—	—	—	—	—	—

DANVILLE—Independent City County

⊠ DANVILLE REGIONAL MEDICAL CENTER, 142 South Main Street, Zip 24541–2922; tel. 804/799–2100; Larry T. DePriest, President (Total facility includes 60 beds in nursing home–type unit) **A**1 2 3 5 6 9 10 **F**2 3 6 7 8 10 11 12 14 15 16 17 19 21 22 25 28 29 30 31 32 33 34 35 37 39 40 41 42 44 45 46 48 49 51 52 54 55 56 58 59 60 61 62 63 64 65 67 71 72 73 74 **P**6 8 **Web address:** www.danvilleregional.org	23	10	312	11826	200	271389	1219	88953	36433	1143
□ SOUTHERN VIRGINIA MENTAL HEALTH INSTITUTE, 382 Taylor Drive, Zip 24541–4023; tel. 804/799–6220; Constance N. Fletcher, Ph.D., Director **A**1 9 10 **F**15 52 **S** Virginia Department of Mental Health, Richmond, VA	12	22	96	872	95	0	0	8412	5618	181

EMPORIA—Independent City County

⊠ GREENSVILLE MEMORIAL HOSPITAL, 214 Weaver Avenue, Zip 23847–1482; tel. 804/348–2000; Gerald R. Lundberg, Interim Chief Executive Officer (Total facility includes 65 beds in nursing home–type unit) **A**1 9 10 **F**7 8 12 14 16 19 21 22 27 28 30 32 34 35 37 40 42 44 45 46 49 64 65 71 73 **S** Community Health Systems, Inc., Brentwood, TN	23	10	144	3062	103	39689	121	21265	9753	312

FAIRFAX—Independent City County

⊠ INOVA FAIR OAKS HOSPITAL, 3600 Joseph Siewick Drive, Zip 22033–1709; tel. 703/391–3600; William A. Brown, Vice President and Administrator (Nonreporting) **A**1 2 5 9 10 **S** Inova Health System, Falls Church, VA	23	10	133	—	—	—	—	—	—	—

FALLS CHURCH—Independent City County

⊠ DOMINION HOSPITAL, 2960 Sleepy Hollow Road, Zip 22044–2001; tel. 703/536–2000; Barbara D. S. Hekimian, Chief Executive Officer **A**1 9 10 **F**15 17 18 52 53 54 55 56 57 58 59 65 67 **P**2 4 7 **S** Columbia/HCA Healthcare Corporation, Nashville, TN	33	22	100	2121	61	1955	0	12714	5913	157
⊠ INOVA FAIRFAX HOSPITAL, 3300 Gallows Road, Zip 22042–3300; tel. 703/698–1110; Steven E. Brown, Administrator **A**1 2 3 5 8 9 10 **F**1 3 4 6 7 8 10 11 12 13 14 16 17 19 21 22 25 28 29 30 31 32 34 35 36 37 38 39 40 41 42 43 44 45 46 47 49 50 51 52 53 54 55 56 57 58 59 60 61 63 65 66 67 68 70 71 72 73 74 **P**1 4 6 7 8 **S** Inova Health System, Falls Church, VA **Web address:** www.inova.com	23	10	656	45447	593	108260	9710	410074	171377	3902
□ NORTHERN VIRGINIA MENTAL HEALTH INSTITUTE, 3302 Gallows Road, Zip 22042–3398; tel. 703/207–7110; John Russotto, Facility Director (Nonreporting) **A**1 9 10 **S** Virginia Department of Mental Health, Richmond, VA	12	22	62	—	—	—	—	—	—	—

FARMVILLE—Prince Edward County

⊠ SOUTHSIDE COMMUNITY HOSPITAL, 800 Oak Street, Zip 23901–1199; tel. 804/392–8811; John H. Greer, President **A**1 9 10 **F**7 8 14 15 16 19 20 22 32 35 37 40 41 42 44 45 46 49 65 66 71 73 **S** Carilion Health System, Roanoke, VA	23	10	88	4364	43	43718	360	27125	12365	422

FISHERSVILLE—Augusta County

□ AUGUSTA HEALTH CARE, 96 Medical Center Drive, Zip 22939, Mailing Address: P.O. Box 1000, Zip 22939–1000; tel. 540/932–4000; Richard H. Graham, President and Chief Executive Officer **A**1 2 10 **F**1 2 3 7 8 10 12 14 15 16 17 19 20 21 22 23 24 26 27 28 29 30 31 32 33 34 35 36 37 39 40 41 42 44 45 46 48 49 51 52 53 54 55 56 57 58 59 63 64 65 66 67 70 71 72 73 **P**1 **Web address:** www.augustamed.com	23	10	221	11492	130	245199	1032	90897	39670	1336

Hospital, Address, Telephone, Administrator, Approval, Facility, and Physician Codes, Health Care System, Network	Classi-fication Codes		Utilization Data					Expense (thousands) of dollars		
★ American Hospital Association (AHA) membership □ Joint Commission on Accreditation of Healthcare Organizations (JCAHO) accreditation + American Osteopathic Healthcare Association (AOHA) membership ○ American Osteopathic Association (AOA) accreditation △ Commission on Accreditation of Rehabilitation Facilities (CARF) accreditation Control codes 61, 63, 64, 71, 72 and 73 indicate hospitals listed by AOHA, but not registered by AHA. For definition of numerical codes, see page A4	Control	Service	Staffed Beds	Admissions	Census	Outpatient Visits	Births	Total	Payroll	Personnel

△ WOODROW WILSON REHABILITATION CENTER, Mailing Address: P.O. Box 1500, Zip 22939–1500; tel. 540/332–7000; David J. Schwemer, Administrator (Nonreporting) **A**7 9 10	12	46	30	—	—	—	—	—	—	—
FORT BELVOIR—Fairfax County										
✠ DEWITT ARMY COMMUNITY HOSPITAL, 9501 Farrell Road, Zip 22060–5901; tel. 703/805–0510; Colonel James W. Martin, Commander (Nonreporting) **A**1 3 5 **S** Department of the Army, Office of the Surgeon General, Falls Church, VA	42	10	62	—	—	—	—	—	—	—
FRANKLIN—Independent City County										
✠ SOUTHAMPTON MEMORIAL HOSPITAL, 100 Fairview Drive, Zip 23851–1206, Mailing Address: P.O. Box 817, Zip 23851–0817; tel. 757/569–6100; Edward J. Patnesky, President and Chief Executive Officer (Total facility includes 131 beds in nursing home–type unit) **A**1 9 10 **F**3 6 7 8 12 14 15 16 17 19 21 22 23 28 30 32 33 34 35 37 39 40 41 42 44 46 49 53 54 55 56 57 58 62 64 65 66 67 71 73 74 **P**8	23	10	203	2880	152	51872	258	28046	13350	485
FREDERICKSBURG—Independent City County										
✠ MARY WASHINGTON HOSPITAL, 1001 Sam Perry Boulevard, Zip 22401–3354; tel. 540/899–1100; Fred M. Rankin, III, President and Chief Executive Officer **A**1 2 9 10 **F**2 3 4 6 7 8 10 11 12 14 15 16 17 18 19 21 22 23 25 26 28 29 30 31 32 33 34 35 36 37 38 39 40 41 42 43 44 45 46 49 52 53 54 55 56 57 58 59 60 62 63 64 65 66 67 68 71 72 73 **P**5 6 8	23	10	328	16153	213	159485	2543	139673	54462	1606
FRONT ROYAL—Warren County										
✠ WARREN MEMORIAL HOSPITAL, 1000 Shenandoah Avenue, Zip 22630–3598; tel. 540/636–0300; Charlie M. Horton, President (Total facility includes 40 beds in nursing home–type unit) **A**1 9 10 **F**7 8 12 15 16 17 19 21 22 27 28 30 32 33 34 37 39 40 41 44 45 46 49 63 64 65 67 71 72 73 74 **P**5 8 **S** Valley Health System, Winchester, VA	23	10	95	1780	63	33100	136	19798	9412	260
GALAX—Independent City County										
✠ TWIN COUNTY REGIONAL HOSPITAL, 200 Hospital Drive, Zip 24333–2283; tel. 540/236–8181; Marcus G. Kuhn, President and Chief Executive Officer **A**1 9 10 **F**7 8 10 11 12 14 15 16 17 18 19 21 22 24 28 29 30 32 33 34 35 39 40 41 44 46 49 52 56 57 58 59 64 65 67 71 73 74 **P**5	23	10	89	4333	52	35900	417	33775	14551	498
GLOUCESTER—Gloucester County										
□ RIVERSIDE WALTER REED HOSPITAL, 7519 Hospital Drive, Zip 23061–4178, Mailing Address: P.O. Box 1130, Zip 23061–1130; tel. 804/693–8800; Grady W. Philips, III, Vice President and Administrator **A**1 9 10 **F**1 2 3 4 6 7 8 10 11 12 13 14 15 16 17 18 19 20 22 23 24 25 26 27 28 29 30 31 32 33 34 35 37 39 40 41 42 43 44 45 46 48 49 51 52 53 54 55 56 57 58 59 60 61 62 63 64 65 66 67 70 71 72 73 74 **P**6 **S** Riverside Health System, Newport News, VA	23	10	71	1803	29	96109	0	15435	7347	245
GRUNDY—Buchanan County										
✠ BUCHANAN GENERAL HOSPITAL, Mailing Address: Route 5, Box 20, Zip 24614–9611; tel. 540/935–1000; John West, Administrator **A**1 9 10 **F**8 15 16 19 21 22 23 28 30 32 35 37 41 42 44 49 63 65 71 73 **P**8 **S** Quorum Health Group/Quorum Health Resources, Inc., Brentwood, TN	23	10	144	4822	55	55031	0	25020	10280	360
HAMPTON—Independent City County										
✠ PENINSULA BEHAVIORAL CENTER, 2244 Executive Drive, Zip 23666–2430; tel. 757/827–1001; Steuart A. Kimmeth, Chief Executive Officer (Nonreporting) **A**1 9 10 **S** Columbia/HCA Healthcare Corporation, Nashville, TN	33	22	60	—	—	—	—	—	—	—
✠ SENTARA HAMPTON GENERAL HOSPITAL, 3120 Victoria Boulevard, Zip 23661–1585, Mailing Address: Drawer 640, Zip 23669–0640; tel. 757/727–7000; Russell Kenwood, Administrator (Total facility includes 26 beds in nursing home–type unit) **A**1 2 9 10 **F**4 6 7 8 10 11 12 15 16 19 22 23 24 25 26 27 30 32 33 34 35 36 37 40 41 42 43 44 46 49 51 60 64 66 68 70 71 72 74 **P**2 6 **S** Sentara Health System, Norfolk, VA **Web address:** www.sentara.com	23	10	178	8501	142	176203	968	73635	26663	856
✠ U. S. AIR FORCE HOSPITAL, 45 Pine Street, Zip 23665–2080; tel. 757/764–6969; Colonel Glenn R. Willauer, Administrator (Nonreporting) **A**1 **S** Department of the Air Force, Bowling AFB, DC	41	10	59	—	—	—	—	—	—	—
✠ VETERANS AFFAIRS MEDICAL CENTER, 100 Emancipation Drive, Zip 23667–0001; tel. 757/722–9961; Bettye W. Story, Ph.D., Director (Total facility includes 120 beds in nursing home–type unit) (Nonreporting) **A**1 2 3 5 8 **S** Department of Veterans Affairs, Washington, DC **Web address:** www.152.128.127.205	45	10	670	—	—	—	—	—	—	—
HARRISONBURG—Independent City County										
✠ ROCKINGHAM MEMORIAL HOSPITAL, 235 Cantrell Avenue, Zip 22801–3293; tel. 540/433–4100; Carter Melton, President **A**1 2 9 10 **F**3 7 8 10 11 12 13 14 15 16 17 18 19 20 21 22 23 24 25 28 29 30 31 32 33 34 35 39 40 41 42 44 45 46 49 52 54 55 56 57 58 59 60 63 65 66 67 68 71 73 74 **P**8	23	10	266	11490	136	124055	1626	94466	44467	1275
HOPEWELL—Independent City County										
✠ JOHN RANDOLPH MEDICAL CENTER, 411 West Randolph Road, Zip 23860, Mailing Address: P.O. Box 971, Zip 23860; tel. 804/541–1600; Daniel J. Wetta, Jr., Chief Executive Officer (Total facility includes 124 beds in nursing home–type unit) (Nonreporting) **A**1 9 10 **S** Columbia/HCA Healthcare Corporation, Nashville, TN	33	10	271	—	—	—	—	—	—	—
HOT SPRINGS—Bath County										
★ BATH COUNTY COMMUNITY HOSPITAL, Route 220, Zip 24445, Mailing Address: Drawer Z, Zip 24445; tel. 540/839–7000; Harry M. Lowd, III, President **A**9 10 **F**8 15 22 30 32 33 34 36 37 39 45 49 56 65 67 71 73	23	10	25	451	7	13986	0	5654	2489	84

Hospital, Address, Telephone, Administrator, Approval, Facility, and Physician Codes, Health Care System, Network	Classi-fication Codes		Utilization Data					Expense (thousands) of dollars		
★ American Hospital Association (AHA) membership □ Joint Commission on Accreditation of Healthcare Organizations (JCAHO) accreditation + American Osteopathic Healthcare Association (AOHA) membership ○ American Osteopathic Association (AOA) accreditation △ Commission on Accreditation of Rehabilitation Facilities (CARF) accreditation Control codes 61, 63, 64, 71, 72 and 73 indicate hospitals listed by AOHA, but not registered by AHA. For definition of numerical codes, see page A4	Control	Service	Staffed Beds	Admissions	Census	Outpatient Visits	Births	Total	Payroll	Personnel

KILMARNOCK—Lancaster County

⊠ RAPPAHANNOCK GENERAL HOSPITAL, 101 Harris Drive, Zip 22482, Mailing Address: P.O. Box 1449, Zip 22482–1449; tel. 804/435–8000; James M. Holmes, President and Chief Executive Officer **A**1 9 10 **F**7 8 12 14 15 16 19 20 21 22 23 26 28 30 31 32 34 35 37 39 40 41 42 44 45 46 49 54 56 59 65 66 67 71 73 **P**3 4 7	23	10	76	2725	33	25721	257	23056	11104	363

LEBANON—Russell County

⊠ RUSSELL COUNTY MEDICAL CENTER, Carroll and Tate Streets, Zip 24266–4510; tel. 540/889–1224; David L. Brash, Chief Executive Officer **A**1 9 10 **F**7 8 12 14 15 16 18 19 20 22 25 26 28 32 34 35 37 39 40 41 44 49 51 52 54 56 57 65 70 71 73 **S** Community Health Systems, Inc., Brentwood, TN	33	10	78	3435	43	75150	0	21554	6174	250

LEESBURG—Loudoun County

□ CHARTER BEHAVIORAL HEALTH SYSTEM AT SPRINGWOOD, 42009 Charter Springwood Lane, Zip 20176–6269; tel. 703/777–0800; Craig S. Juengling, Chief Executive Officer (Nonreporting) **A**1 9 10 **S** Magellan Health Services, Atlanta, GA	33	22	77	—	—	—	—	—	—	—
★ GRAYDON MANOR, 801 Children's Center Road S.W., Zip 20175–2598; tel. 703/777–3485; Bernard J. Haberlein, Executive Director **F**52 53 55 58	23	52	43	47	38	1724	0	5205	3425	108
⊠ LOUDOUN HOSPITAL CENTER, 44045 Riverside Parkway, Zip 20176–2799; tel. 703/858–6000; G. T. Dunlop Ecker, President and Chief Executive Officer **A**1 2 9 10 **F**3 7 8 12 14 15 16 17 19 21 22 25 26 29 30 31 33 34 35 36 37 39 40 41 42 44 49 52 53 54 55 56 57 58 59 60 63 65 67 71 72 73 **P**6 8 **Web address:** www.loudounhospital.org	23	10	92	5806	112	46249	1124	65995	27499	550

LEXINGTON—Independent City County

⊠ STONEWALL JACKSON HOSPITAL, 1 Health Circle, Zip 24450–2492; tel. 540/462–1200; Robert E. Huch, President (Total facility includes 50 beds in nursing home–type unit) **A**1 9 10 **F**7 8 14 15 16 19 21 22 27 28 30 32 33 34 35 36 39 40 41 44 46 49 63 64 65 66 71 73	23	10	130	1748	69	51906	232	16622	7541	328

LOW MOOR—Alleghany County

⊠ ALLEGHANY REGIONAL HOSPITAL, (Formerly Columbia Alleghany Regional Hospital), One ARH Lane, Zip 24457, Mailing Address: P.O. Box 7, Zip 24457–0007; tel. 540/862–6011; Ward W. Stevens, CHE, Chief Executive Officer **A**1 9 10 12 13 **F**7 8 12 14 15 16 19 20 21 22 28 30 34 35 36 37 40 42 44 46 56 63 65 71 73 **S** Columbia/HCA Healthcare Corporation, Nashville, TN **Web address:** www.columbia.net	33	10	156	4004	49	68931	295	24741	10231	353

LURAY—Page County

⊠ PAGE MEMORIAL HOSPITAL, 200 Memorial Drive, Zip 22835–1005; tel. 540/743–4561; Donald J. Morgan, Administrator **A**1 9 10 **F**14 15 16 19 22 25 27 30 32 33 34 35 41 44 49 63 65 67 71 73	23	10	54	1593	17	29216	0	11233	5962	201

LYNCHBURG—Independent City County

⊠ LYNCHBURG GENERAL HOSPITAL, 1901 Tate Springs Road, Zip 24501–1167; tel. 804/947–3000; L. Darrell Powers, President (Total facility includes 130 beds in nursing home–type unit) **A**1 2 5 6 9 10 **F**1 3 4 8 10 11 14 15 16 17 18 19 20 21 22 23 24 25 26 28 29 30 32 33 34 35 37 41 42 43 44 49 53 54 55 56 57 58 59 60 63 64 65 67 71 72 73 74 **P**6 7 8 **S** Centra Health, Inc., Lynchburg, VA **Web address:** www.centrahealth.com	23	10	350	12400	302	103918	0	104812	50457	1195
⊠ △ VIRGINIA BAPTIST HOSPITAL, 3300 Rivermont Avenue, Zip 24503–9989; tel. 804/947–4000; Thomas C. Jividen, Senior Vice President (Total facility includes 36 beds in nursing home–type unit) **A**1 5 7 9 10 **F**1 2 3 4 8 10 11 14 15 16 17 18 19 20 21 22 24 25 26 27 28 29 30 32 33 34 35 37 38 40 41 42 43 44 48 49 52 53 54 55 56 57 58 59 60 63 64 65 67 71 72 73 74 **P**8 **S** Centra Health, Inc., Lynchburg, VA **Web address:** www.centrahealth.com	23	10	322	9640	223	43465	2336	84057	47231	1062

MADISON HEIGHTS—Amherst County

CENTRAL VIRGINIA TRAINING CENTER, 210 East Colony Road, Zip 24572–2005, Mailing Address: P.O. Box 1098, Lynchburg, Zip 24505–1098; tel. 804/947–6326; Judy Dudley, Director (Total facility includes 104 beds in nursing home–type unit) (Nonreporting) **A**10 **S** Virginia Department of Mental Health, Richmond, VA	12	62	1112	—	—	—	—	—	—	—

MANASSAS—Independent City County

⊠ PRINCE WILLIAM HOSPITAL, 8700 Sudley Road, Zip 20110–4418, Mailing Address: Box 2610, Zip 20108–0867; tel. 703/369–8000; Kenneth B. Swenson, President **A**1 2 9 10 **F**3 6 7 8 11 12 14 15 16 17 18 19 21 22 23 24 26 28 29 30 32 33 35 40 41 42 44 45 46 49 52 53 54 55 56 57 58 59 62 63 65 67 71 74 **P**8 **Web address:** www.pwhs.org	23	10	130	7541	73	91148	1396	59484	26306	813

MARION—Smyth County

⊠ SMYTH COUNTY COMMUNITY HOSPITAL, 565 Radio Hill Road, Zip 24354–3526, Mailing Address: P.O. Box 880, Zip 24354–0880; tel. 540/782–1234; Roger W. Cooper, President (Total facility includes 125 beds in nursing home–type unit) **A**1 9 10 **F**6 7 8 12 19 21 22 23 28 30 32 35 37 40 42 44 45 49 63 64 65 71 **S** Carilion Health System, Roanoke, VA	23	10	279	3275	154	40619	301	30930	13605	546
□ SOUTHWESTERN VIRGINIA MENTAL HEALTH INSTITUTE, 502 East Main Street, Zip 24354–3390; tel. 540/783–1200; Gerald E. Deans, Director (Nonreporting) **A**1 9 10 **S** Virginia Department of Mental Health, Richmond, VA	12	22	266	—	—	—	—	—	—	—

Hospital, Address, Telephone, Administrator, Approval, Facility, and Physician Codes, Health Care System, Network	Classi-fication Codes		Utilization Data					Expense (thousands) of dollars		
★ American Hospital Association (AHA) membership □ Joint Commission on Accreditation of Healthcare Organizations (JCAHO) accreditation + American Osteopathic Healthcare Association (AOHA) membership ○ American Osteopathic Association (AOA) accreditation △ Commission on Accreditation of Rehabilitation Facilities (CARF) accreditation Control codes 61, 63, 64, 71, 72 and 73 indicate hospitals listed by AOHA, but not registered by AHA. For definition of numerical codes, see page A4	Control	Service	Staffed Beds	Admissions	Census	Outpatient Visits	Births	Total	Payroll	Personnel

MARTINSVILLE—Independent City County

⊞ MEMORIAL HOSPITAL OF MARTINSVILLE AND HENRY COUNTY, 320 Hospital Drive, Zip 24112–1981, Mailing Address: Box 4788, Zip 24115–4788; tel. 540/666–7200; Joseph Roach, Chief Executive Officer **A**1 2 9 10 **F**7 8 10 14 15 16 19 21 22 23 28 29 30 31 32 33 35 39 40 41 42 44 45 46 49 52 54 55 56 58 59 60 63 65 67 71 73 74 **S** Quorum Health Group/Quorum Health Resources, Inc., Brentwood, TN
Web address: www.martinsvillehospital.org

| | 23 | 10 | 152 | 7231 | 96 | 183842 | 521 | 57596 | 25532 | 805 |

MECHANICSVILLE—Hanover County

⊞ MEMORIAL REGIONAL MEDICAL CENTER, (Formerly Richmond Memorial Hospital), 8260 Atlee Road, Zip 23116, Mailing Address: P.O. Box 26783, Richmond, Zip 23261–6783; tel. 804/764–6102; Michael Robinson, Executive Vice President and Administrator (Total facility includes 20 beds in nursing home–type unit) (Nonreporting) **A**1 2 5 6 9 10 **S** Bon Secours Health System, Inc., Marriottsville, MD

| | 23 | 10 | 272 | — | — | — | — | — | — | — |

NASSAWADOX—Northampton County

⊞ SHORE MEMORIAL HOSPITAL, 9507 Hospital Avenue, Zip 23413–1821, Mailing Address: P.O. Box 17, Zip 23413–0017; tel. 757/414–8000; Richard A. Brvenik, President and Chief Executive Officer (Total facility includes 13 beds in nursing home–type unit) **A**1 5 9 10 **F**3 7 8 12 13 14 15 16 17 18 19 21 22 25 26 27 28 29 30 31 32 33 34 35 36 37 39 40 41 42 44 45 46 49 51 52 53 54 55 56 57 58 61 63 64 65 66 67 68 69 70 71 72 73 74 **P**6
Web address: www.shorehealthservices.org

| | 23 | 10 | 123 | 5016 | 82 | 54173 | 467 | 31052 | 16200 | 632 |

NEW KENT—New Kent County

□ △ CUMBERLAND, A BROWN SCHOOLS HOSPITAL FOR CHILDREN AND ADOLESCENTS, 9407 Cumberland Road, Zip 23124–2029; tel. 804/966–2242; Ernest C. Priddy, III, Chief Executive Officer (Nonreporting) **A**1 7 10 **S** Healthcare America, Inc., Austin, TX

| | 33 | 56 | 84 | — | — | — | — | — | — | — |

NEWPORT NEWS—Independent City County

⊞ MARY IMMACULATE HOSPITAL, (Includes St. Francis Nursing Center), 2 Bernardine Drive, Zip 23602–4499; tel. 757/886–6000; Cynthia B. Farrand, Executive Vice President and Administrator **A**1 5 9 10 **F**3 4 7 8 10 12 14 15 16 17 19 21 22 25 27 28 29 30 32 33 34 35 37 38 39 40 41 42 44 45 49 59 63 64 65 67 71 72 73 74 **P**1 7 8 **S** Bon Secours Health System, Inc., Marriottsville, MD
Web address: www.mihospital.com

| | 21 | 10 | 110 | 6328 | 71 | 67846 | 1586 | 46134 | 16883 | 485 |

⊞ MCDONALD ARMY COMMUNITY HOSPITAL, Jefferson Avenue, Fort Eustis, Zip 23604–5548; tel. 757/314–7501; Colonel George Weightman, Commander (Nonreporting) **A**1 **S** Department of the Army, Office of the Surgeon General, Falls Church, VA

| | 42 | 10 | 30 | — | — | — | — | — | — | — |

NEWPORT NEWS GENERAL HOSPITAL, 5100 Marshall Avenue, Zip 23605–2600, Mailing Address: P.O. Box 5769, Zip 23605–5769; tel. 804/247–7200; Lissa B. Hays, Chief Operating Officer (Nonreporting) **A**5 9 10

| | 23 | 10 | 126 | — | — | — | — | — | — | — |

⊞ RIVERSIDE REGIONAL MEDICAL CENTER, (Includes Riverside Psychiatric Institute), 500 J. Clyde Morris Boulevard, Zip 23601–1976; tel. 757/594–2000; Gerald R. Brink, President and Chief Executive Officer **A**1 2 3 5 6 9 10 **F**1 2 3 4 6 7 8 10 11 12 13 14 15 16 17 18 19 20 21 22 23 24 25 26 27 28 29 30 31 32 33 34 35 37 39 40 41 42 43 44 45 46 48 49 51 52 53 54 55 56 57 58 59 60 61 62 63 64 65 66 67 70 71 72 73 74 **P**6 **S** Riverside Health System, Newport News, VA

| | 23 | 10 | 576 | 17390 | 233 | 256884 | 2351 | 147296 | 56879 | 1801 |

□ WOODSIDE HOSPITAL, 17579 Warwick Boulevard, Zip 23603–1343; tel. 757/888–0400; Robert J. Lehmann, Chief Executive Officer (Nonreporting) **A**1 9 10

| | 33 | 22 | 68 | — | — | — | — | — | — | — |

NORFOLK—Independent City County

⊞ BON SECOURS–DEPAUL MEDICAL CENTER, 150 Kingsley Lane, Zip 23505–4650; tel. 757/889–5000; David J. McCombs, Executive Vice President and Administrator (Nonreporting) **A**1 2 3 5 9 10 **S** Bon Secours Health System, Inc., Marriottsville, MD

| | 21 | 10 | 202 | — | — | — | — | — | — | — |

⊞ CHILDREN'S HOSPITAL OF THE KING'S DAUGHTERS, 601 Children's Lane, Zip 23507–1971; tel. 757/668–7700; Robert I. Bonar, Jr., President and Chief Executive Officer **A**1 2 3 5 9 10 **F**10 12 13 14 15 16 17 19 21 22 27 29 30 31 32 33 34 35 38 39 41 42 43 44 45 46 47 49 51 53 54 55 58 60 65 67 68 71 72 73 **P**1 7
Web address: www.chkd.org

| | 23 | 50 | 137 | 5479 | 116 | 113988 | 0 | 92281 | 41165 | 1931 |

★ LAKE TAYLOR HOSPITAL, 1309 Kempsville Road, Zip 23502–2286; tel. 757/461–5001; David B. Tate, Jr., President and Chief Executive Officer (Total facility includes 226 beds in nursing home–type unit) **A**9 10 **F**14 20 31 54 57 64 65 73 **S** Riverside Health System, Newport News, VA
Web address: www.laketaylor.org

| | 16 | 48 | 330 | 517 | 257 | 0 | 0 | 15645 | 7547 | 303 |

□ NORFOLK COMMUNITY HOSPITAL, 2539 Corprew Avenue, Zip 23504–3994; tel. 757/628–1400; Phillip D. Brooks, President (Nonreporting) **A**1 5 9 10

| | 23 | 10 | 103 | — | — | — | — | — | — | — |

□ NORFOLK PSYCHIATRIC CENTER, 860 Kempsville Road, Zip 23502–3980; tel. 757/461–4565; J. Frank Gallagher, III, Administrator (Nonreporting) **A**1 9 10 **S** Magellan Health Services, Atlanta, GA

| | 33 | 22 | 77 | — | — | — | — | — | — | — |

★ SENTARA LEIGH HOSPITAL, 830 Kempsville Road, Zip 23502–3981; tel. 757/466–6000; Darleen S. Anderson, R.N., MSN, Site Administrator **A**3 5 9 10 **F**1 3 4 7 8 9 10 11 12 14 15 16 17 18 19 21 22 23 24 25 26 27 28 29 30 31 32 33 34 35 36 37 38 39 40 41 42 43 44 45 46 47 48 49 51 52 53 54 55 56 57 58 59 60 61 62 63 64 65 66 67 68 71 72 73 74 **P**5 6 7 **S** Sentara Health System, Norfolk, VA
Web address: www.sentara.com

| | 23 | 10 | 214 | 11007 | 134 | 94881 | 1470 | 73306 | 25762 | 876 |

Hospital, Address, Telephone, Administrator, Approval, Facility, and Physician Codes, Health Care System, Network	Classification Codes		Utilization Data					Expense (thousands) of dollars		
	Control	Service	Staffed Beds	Admissions	Census	Outpatient Visits	Births	Total	Payroll	Personnel

★ American Hospital Association (AHA) membership
□ Joint Commission on Accreditation of Healthcare Organizations (JCAHO) accreditation
+ American Osteopathic Healthcare Association (AOHA) membership
○ American Osteopathic Association (AOA) accreditation
△ Commission on Accreditation of Rehabilitation Facilities (CARF) accreditation
Control codes 61, 63, 64, 71, 72 and 73 indicate hospitals listed by AOHA, but not registered by AHA. For definition of numerical codes, see page A4

Hospital	Control	Service	Beds	Admissions	Census	Outpatient	Births	Total	Payroll	Personnel
✠ SENTARA NORFOLK GENERAL HOSPITAL, 600 Gresham Drive, Zip 23507–1999; tel. 757/668–3000; Mark R. Gavens, President **A**1 2 3 5 6 8 9 10 **F**1 3 4 6 7 8 9 10 11 12 13 14 15 16 17 18 19 21 23 24 25 26 27 28 29 30 31 32 33 34 35 36 37 38 39 40 41 42 43 44 45 46 47 48 49 51 52 53 54 55 56 57 58 59 60 61 62 63 64 65 66 67 68 70 71 72 73 74 **P**5 6 7 **S** Sentara Health System, Norfolk, VA Web address: www.sentara.com	23	10	479	22829	348	165490	2579	226914	76605	2817
NORTON—Independent City County										
□ NORTON COMMUNITY HOSPITAL, 100 15th Street N.W., Zip 24273–1699; tel. 540/679–9600 **A**1 9 10 **F**7 8 12 14 15 16 17 19 20 21 22 23 24 25 26 28 30 31 32 33 34 35 37 39 40 41 44 45 46 48 49 60 63 64 65 66 67 68 71 72 73 74 **P**6 8 Web address: www.nchosp.org	23	10	59	4667	57	50206	472	24092	9625	309
✠ ST. MARY'S HOSPITAL, Third Street N.E., Zip 24273–1131, Mailing Address: P.O. Box 620, Zip 24273–0620; tel. 540/679–9100; Gary L. DelForge, Administrator (Total facility includes 44 beds in nursing home–type unit) **A**1 9 10 **F**2 3 7 8 12 13 14 15 16 17 19 20 21 22 25 26 28 29 30 32 34 35 37 40 41 42 44 45 46 51 52 53 55 56 57 58 63 64 65 66 67 71 73 **P**6 Web address: www.st–maryshospital.com	23	10	98	3256	76	44918	79	22464	9717	407
PEARISBURG—Giles County										
✠ CARILION GILES MEMORIAL HOSPITAL, 1 Taylor Avenue, Zip 24134–1932; tel. 540/921–6000; Morris D. Reece, Administrator and Chief Executive Officer (Total facility includes 21 beds in nursing home–type unit) **A**1 9 10 **F**8 12 14 15 16 17 19 21 27 28 29 30 32 33 34 35 37 39 41 42 44 45 46 49 50 51 56 57 58 59 60 61 62 63 64 65 66 67 68 70 71 72 73 74 **P**1 2 3 4 5 6 7 8 **S** Carilion Health System, Roanoke, VA	23	10	53	1452	37	27641	0	13643	6830	—
PENNINGTON GAP—Lee County										
✠ LEE COUNTY COMMUNITY HOSPITAL, West Morgan Avenue, Zip 24277, Mailing Address: P.O. Box 70, Zip 24277–0070; tel. 540/546–1440; James L. Davis, Chief Executive Officer (Nonreporting) **A**1 9 10	23	10	80	—	—	—	—	—	—	—
PETERSBURG—Independent City County										
□ CENTRAL STATE HOSPITAL, 26317 West Washington Street, Zip 23803, Mailing Address: P.O. Box 4030, Zip 23803–4030; tel. 804/524–7000; Larry L. Latham, Director **A**1 5 9 10 **F**14 15 16 52 53 54 55 **P**6 **S** Virginia Department of Mental Health, Richmond, VA	12	22	516	1238	438	0	0	—	—	796
✠ POPLAR SPRINGS HOSPITAL, 350 Poplar Drive, Zip 23805–4657; tel. 804/733–6874; Anthony J. Vadella, Chief Executive Officer (Nonreporting) **A**1 9 10 Web address: www.poplarsprings.com	33	22	100	—	—	—	—	—	—	—
✠ SOUTHSIDE REGIONAL MEDICAL CENTER, 801 South Adams Street, Zip 23803–5133; tel. 804/862–5000; David S. Dunham, President (Total facility includes 20 beds in nursing home–type unit) **A**1 6 9 10 **F**7 8 10 12 14 15 16 19 20 21 22 23 25 28 29 30 32 34 35 37 39 40 41 42 44 45 46 49 52 54 55 56 57 59 60 63 64 65 67 71 72 73 **P**8 **S** Quorum Health Group/Quorum Health Resources, Inc., Brentwood, TN Web address: www.srmconline.com	16	10	268	12807	191	163722	1358	85524	40116	1336
PORTSMOUTH—Independent City County										
✠ △ MARYVIEW HOSPITAL, 3636 High Street, Zip 23707–3236; tel. 757/398–2200; Wayne Jones, Executive Vice President and Administrator (Total facility includes 120 beds in nursing home–type unit) **A**1 2 3 5 7 9 10 **F**3 4 6 7 8 10 11 12 14 15 16 17 18 19 21 25 26 28 29 30 31 32 33 34 35 36 37 39 40 41 42 43 44 45 46 49 52 53 54 55 56 57 58 59 60 61 63 64 65 66 67 68 71 72 73 74 **P**6 8 **S** Bon Secours Health System, Inc., Marriottsville, MD Web address: www.bonsecours.com	23	10	441	15022	321	301154	1080	105897	45523	2015
✠ NAVAL MEDICAL CENTER, 620 John Paul Jones Circle, Zip 23708–2197; tel. 757/953–7424; Rear Admiral Marion Balsam, MC, USN, Commander **A**1 2 3 5 **F**3 4 5 8 10 11 12 14 15 16 19 20 21 22 23 24 25 28 29 30 31 34 35 37 38 39 40 41 42 44 45 46 49 50 51 52 54 56 58 59 60 61 63 65 66 67 71 73 74 **S** Department of Navy, Washington, DC Web address: www.164.167.49.190/	43	10	310	14038	159	1383696	2853	—	—	4724
PULASKI—Independent City County										
✠ PULASKI COMMUNITY HOSPITAL, 2400 Lee Highway, Zip 24301–0759, Mailing Address: P.O. Box 759, Zip 24301–0759; tel. 540/994–8100; Jack Nunley, Chief Executive Officer (Total facility includes 12 beds in nursing home–type unit) **A**1 9 10 **F**7 8 12 14 15 16 19 21 22 28 30 35 37 40 41 42 44 45 56 60 63 64 65 70 71 73 **P**8 **S** Columbia/HCA Healthcare Corporation, Nashville, TN Web address: www.pch–va.com	33	10	62	3544	48	35221	151	21233	8867	342
RADFORD—Independent City County										
✠ △ CARILION NEW RIVER VALLEY MEDICAL CENTER, (Formerly Carilion Radford Community Hospital), 2900 Tyler Road, Zip 24141–2430, Mailing Address: P.O. Box 5, Zip 24141–0005; tel. 540/731–2000; Virginia Ousley, Director (Total facility includes 27 beds in nursing home–type unit) **A**1 7 9 10 **F**2 3 4 8 10 11 12 13 14 15 16 17 18 19 20 21 22 23 24 27 28 30 31 32 33 34 35 36 37 39 40 41 42 44 45 46 48 49 51 52 53 54 55 56 57 58 59 64 65 67 70 71 72 73 74 **P**8 **S** Carilion Health System, Roanoke, VA	23	10	158	4929	72	34821	743	47426	17254	606

Hospital, Address, Telephone, Administrator, Approval, Facility, and Physician Codes, Health Care System, Network	Classi-fication Codes		Utilization Data					Expense (thousands) of dollars		
★ American Hospital Association (AHA) membership □ Joint Commission on Accreditation of Healthcare Organizations (JCAHO) accreditation + American Osteopathic Healthcare Association (AOHA) membership ○ American Osteopathic Association (AOA) accreditation △ Commission on Accreditation of Rehabilitation Facilities (CARF) accreditation Control codes 61, 63, 64, 71, 72 and 73 indicate hospitals listed by AOHA, but not registered by AHA. For definition of numerical codes, see page A4	Control	Service	Staffed Beds	Admissions	Census	Outpatient Visits	Births	Total	Payroll	Personnel

⊠ CARILION SAINT ALBANS HOSPITAL, Route 11, Lee Highway, Zip 24143, Mailing Address: P.O. Box 3608, Zip 24143–3608; tel. 540/639–2481; Janet McKinney Crawford, Vice President and Administrator **A**1 9 10 **F**3 12 14 15 16 52 53 54 56 57 58 59 65 73 **P**8 **S** Carilion Health System, Roanoke, VA **Web address:** www.carilion.com	23	22	68	1734	29	17321	0	8350	4291	150
RESTON—Fairfax County										
⊠ COLUMBIA RESTON HOSPITAL CENTER, 1850 Town Center Parkway, Zip 20190–3298; tel. 703/689–9000; William A. Adams, President and Chief Executive Officer **A**1 2 5 9 10 **F**7 8 10 14 15 16 19 22 23 24 30 32 35 37 39 40 41 42 44 49 65 66 73 **P**1 4 7 **S** Columbia/HCA Healthcare Corporation, Nashville, TN **Web address:** www.columbia.net	33	10	121	9904	83	102568	2021	48723	23719	477
RICHLANDS—Tazewell County										
⊠ CLINCH VALLEY MEDICAL CENTER, (Formerly Columbia Clinch Valley Medical Center), 2949 West Front Street, Zip 24641–2099; tel. 540/596–6000; James W. Thweatt, Chief Executive Officer (Total facility includes 22 beds in nursing home–type unit) **A**1 9 10 **F**3 7 8 10 11 12 14 15 17 19 20 21 22 23 28 29 30 31 34 35 37 39 40 41 42 44 45 46 48 49 58 60 63 64 65 67 71 73 **S** Columbia/HCA Healthcare Corporation, Nashville, TN **Web address:** www.ccvmc.com	33	10	200	6304	77	43591	535	33650	12003	451
RICHMOND—Independent City County										
⊠ BON SECOURS ST. MARY'S HOSPITAL, 5801 Bremo Road, Zip 23226–1900; tel. 804/285–2011; Ann E. Honeycutt, Executive Vice President and Administrator (Nonreporting) **A**1 2 3 5 9 10 **S** Bon Secours Health System, Inc., Marriottsville, MD	21	10	391	—	—	—	—	—	—	—
⊠ BON SECOURS–RICHMOND COMMUNITY HOSPITAL, 1500 North 28th Street, Zip 23223–5396, Mailing Address: Box 27184, Zip 23261–7184; tel. 804/225–1700; Samuel F. Lillard, Executive Vice President and Administrator (Nonreporting) **A**1 9 10 **S** Bon Secours Health System, Inc., Marriottsville, MD	23	10	88	—	—	—	—	—	—	—
⊠ BON SECOURS–STUART CIRCLE, 413 Stuart Circle, Zip 23220–3799; tel. 804/358–7051; Edward Gerardo, Executive Vice President and Administrator (Nonreporting) **A**1 9 10 **S** Bon Secours Health System, Inc., Marriottsville, MD	21	10	158	—	—	—	—	—	—	—
□ CAPITOL MEDICAL CENTER, 701 West Grace Street, Zip 23220–4191; tel. 804/775–4100; Priscilla J. Shuler, Chief Executive Officer (Nonreporting) **A**1 9 10 **S** Paracelsus Healthcare Corporation, Houston, TX	33	10	131	—	—	—	—	—	—	—
□ CHARTER WESTBROOK BEHAVIORAL HEALTH SYSTEM, 1500 Westbrook Avenue, Zip 23227–3399; tel. 804/266–9671; Stephen P. Fahey, Administrator (Nonreporting) **A**1 9 10 **S** Magellan Health Services, Atlanta, GA	33	22	210	—	—	—	—	—	—	—
⊠ △ CHILDREN'S HOSPITAL, 2924 Brook Road, Zip 23220–1298; tel. 804/321–7474; Leslie G. Wyatt, Administrator **A**1 3 5 7 9 **F**15 16 19 20 25 27 44 46 49 65 67 73 **Web address:** www.childrenshosp–richmond.org	23	56	18	373	6	39703	0	16080	8000	231
⊠ △ CHIPPENHAM AND JOHNSTON–WILLIS HOSPITALS, (Includes Chippenham Medical Center, 7101 Jahnke Road, Zip 23225; tel. 804/320–3911; Johnston–Willis Hospital, 1401 Johnston–Willis Drive, Zip 23235; tel. 804/330–2000), 7101 Jahnke Road, Zip 23225–4044; tel. 804/320–3911; Marilyn B. Tavenner, Chief Executive Officer **A**1 2 3 5 7 9 10 **F**1 3 4 7 8 10 11 12 14 15 16 17 18 19 21 22 23 24 25 26 27 28 29 30 33 34 35 37 38 39 40 41 42 43 44 45 46 47 48 49 51 52 53 54 55 56 57 58 59 60 61 63 65 66 67 68 70 71 73 74 **P**5 6 7 8 **S** Columbia/HCA Healthcare Corporation, Nashville, TN	33	10	748	28211	424	217606	3107	185062	83053	2569
□ △ HEALTHSOUTH MEDICAL CENTER, 7700 East Parham Road, Zip 23294–4301; tel. 804/747–5600; Charles A. Stark, CHE, Administrator, Chief Executive Officer and Regional Vice President **A**1 2 5 7 10 **F**5 8 10 11 12 14 15 16 17 19 20 21 22 23 25 26 27 28 29 30 31 33 34 35 37 39 41 42 44 45 46 48 49 51 54 55 56 57 58 63 65 66 67 71 73 74 **S** HEALTHSOUTH Corporation, Birmingham, AL **Web address:** www.healthsouth–richmond.com	33	10	147	4159	68	32556	0	39875	13826	445
□ HEALTHSOUTH REHABILITATION HOSPITAL OF VIRGINIA, 5700 Fitzhugh Avenue, Zip 23226–1800; tel. 804/288–5700; Jeff Ruskan, Administrator **A**1 9 10 **F**8 10 12 14 15 16 19 21 22 25 26 27 30 34 35 41 42 44 48 49 50 51 63 65 66 67 71 73 74 **P**5 **S** HEALTHSOUTH Corporation, Birmingham, AL	33	46	40	1893	33	9002	0	6923	3532	106
⊠ HENRICO DOCTORS' HOSPITAL, 1602 Skipwith Road, Zip 23229–5298; tel. 804/289–4500; Patrick W. Farrell, Chief Executive Officer **A**1 2 9 10 **F**2 3 4 5 7 8 10 11 12 14 15 16 17 19 21 22 23 24 27 28 29 33 34 35 36 37 38 39 40 41 42 43 44 47 48 49 50 52 53 54 55 56 57 58 59 61 63 64 65 66 67 68 70 71 73 74 **P**5 **S** Columbia/HCA Healthcare Corporation, Nashville, TN	33	10	340	14182	199	101957	3399	108891	47363	988
⊠ HUNTER HOLMES MCGUIRE VETERANS AFFAIRS MEDICAL CENTER, 1201 Broad Rock Boulevard, Zip 23249–0002; tel. 804/675–5000; James W. Dudley, Director (Total facility includes 80 beds in nursing home–type unit) **A**1 2 3 5 8 **F**2 3 4 8 10 11 12 15 16 17 19 20 21 22 26 27 28 30 31 33 34 35 37 39 41 42 43 44 45 46 48 49 50 51 52 54 55 56 57 58 60 61 63 64 65 67 68 70 71 72 73 74 **S** Department of Veterans Affairs, Washington, DC	45	10	404	10100	349	263779	0	159070	80172	1927

Hospital, Address, Telephone, Administrator, Approval, Facility, and Physician Codes, Health Care System, Network	Classification Codes		Utilization Data					Expense (thousands) of dollars		
★ American Hospital Association (AHA) membership □ Joint Commission on Accreditation of Healthcare Organizations (JCAHO) accreditation + American Osteopathic Healthcare Association (AOHA) membership ○ American Osteopathic Association (AOA) accreditation △ Commission on Accreditation of Rehabilitation Facilities (CARF) accreditation Control codes 61, 63, 64, 71, 72 and 73 indicate hospitals listed by AOHA, but not registered by AHA. For definition of numerical codes, see page A4	Control	Service	Staffed Beds	Admissions	Census	Outpatient Visits	Births	Total	Payroll	Personnel

Hospital	Control	Service	Staffed Beds	Admissions	Census	Outpatient Visits	Births	Total	Payroll	Personnel
JOHNSTON–WILLIS HOSPITAL See Chippenham and Johnston–Willis Hospitals										
★ △ MEDICAL COLLEGE OF VIRGINIA HOSPITALS, VIRGINIA COMMONWEALTH UNIVERSITY, 401 North 12th Street, Zip 23219, Mailing Address: P.O. Box 980510, Zip 23298–0510; tel. 804/828–9000; Carl R. Fischer, Associate Vice President and Chief Executive Officer **A**1 2 3 5 7 8 9 10 **F**3 4 7 8 9 10 11 12 14 15 16 17 18 19 20 21 22 23 24 25 26 27 28 29 30 31 32 34 35 37 38 39 40 41 42 43 44 45 46 47 48 49 51 52 53 54 56 57 58 59 60 61 63 65 66 67 68 70 71 72 73 74 **P**4 7 Web address: www.vcu.edu	16	10	703	29456	509	404492	2395	412132	168166	4806
★ RETREAT HOSPITAL, 2621 Grove Avenue, Zip 23220–4308; tel. 804/254–5100; Paul L. Baldwin, Chief Executive Officer (Nonreporting) **A**1 2 9 10 **S** Columbia/HCA Healthcare Corporation, Nashville, TN	33	10	146	—	—	—	—	—	—	—
★ RICHMOND EYE AND EAR HOSPITAL, 1001 East Marshall Street, Zip 23219–1993; tel. 804/775–4500; James W. Worrell, Chief Executive Officer **A**1 9 10 **F**14 44 **S** Quorum Health Group/Quorum Health Resources, Inc., Brentwood, TN	23	45	32	454	2	6493	0	8421	3152	101
□ △ SHELTERING ARMS REHABILITATION HOSPITAL, 1311 Palmyra Avenue, Zip 23227–4418; tel. 804/342–4100; Jack A. Carroll, Ph.D., President **A**1 7 9 10 **F**14 15 19 24 25 27 28 29 30 35 41 46 48 49 65 66 71 **P**6	23	46	40	1043	34	59783	0	21899	13431	296
□ VALUEMARK WEST END BEHAVIORAL HEALTHCARE SYSTEM, 12800 West Creek Parkway, Zip 23238–1116; tel. 804/784–2200; James D. McBeath, Chief Executive Officer (Nonreporting) **A**1 9 10 **S** ValueMark Healthcare Systems, Inc., Atlanta, GA	33	22	84	—	—	—	—	—	—	—
ROANOKE—Independent City County										
★ △ CARILION MEDICAL CENTER, (Formerly Carilion Roanoke Memorial Hospital), (Includes Carilion Roanoke Community Hospital, 101 Elm Avenue S.E., Zip 24013–2230, Mailing Address: P.O. Box 12946, Zip 24029–2946; tel. 540/985–8000; Roanoke Memorial Rehabilitation Center, South Jefferson and McClanahan Streets, Mailing Address: P.O. Box 13367, Zip 24033; Belleview at Jefferson Street, Zip 24014, Mailing Address: P.O. Box 13367, Zip 24033–3367; tel. 540/981–7000; Lucas A. Snipes, FACHE, Director **A**1 2 3 5 6 7 9 10 **F**2 3 4 7 8 10 11 12 13 15 16 17 18 19 20 21 22 23 24 25 26 27 28 29 30 31 32 33 34 35 37 38 39 40 41 42 43 44 45 46 47 48 49 51 52 53 54 55 56 57 58 59 60 61 63 64 65 66 67 70 71 72 73 74 **P**2 7 8 **S** Carilion Health System, Roanoke, VA Web address: www.carilion.com	23	10	677	29844	442	—	2747	314234	115214	3791
ROCKY MOUNT—Franklin County										
★ CARILION FRANKLIN MEMORIAL HOSPITAL, 180 Floyd Avenue, Zip 24151–1389; tel. 540/483–5277; Matthew J. Perry, Director **A**1 9 10 **F**7 8 15 16 17 19 22 30 32 33 37 39 40 41 42 44 49 65 67 71 73 **P**2 7 8 **S** Carilion Health System, Roanoke, VA Web address: www.carilion.com	23	10	37	2601	21	22429	218	15775	6600	231
SALEM—Independent City County										
★ △ LEWIS–GALE MEDICAL CENTER, (Includes Lewis–Gale Pavilion, 1902 Braeburn Drive, Zip 24153–7391; tel. 703/772–2800), 1900 Electric Road, Zip 24153–7494; tel. 540/776–4000; William B. Downey, Administrator (Nonreporting) **A**1 2 7 9 10 **S** Columbia/HCA Healthcare Corporation, Nashville, TN	33	10	521	—	—	—	—	—	—	—
MOUNT REGIS CENTER, 405 Kimball Avenue, Zip 24153–6299; tel. 703/389–4761; Gail S. Basham, Chief Operating Officer (Nonreporting) **S** Pioneer Behavioral Health, Peabody, MA	23	82	25	—	—	—	—	—	—	—
★ VETERANS AFFAIRS MEDICAL CENTER, 1970 Roanoke Boulevard, Zip 24153; tel. 540/982–2463; Stephen L. Lemons, Ed.D., Director (Total facility includes 90 beds in nursing home–type unit) **A**1 2 3 5 8 **F**1 2 3 4 8 10 11 12 14 15 16 17 19 20 22 23 24 25 26 27 28 30 31 34 35 37 39 41 42 43 44 45 46 49 51 52 54 55 56 57 58 59 60 64 65 67 68 71 73 74 **S** Department of Veterans Affairs, Washington, DC Web address: www.vaww.salem.med.va.gov	45	10	387	5703	290	228508	0	105189	56868	1335
SOUTH BOSTON—Independent City County										
★ HALIFAX REGIONAL HOSPITAL, 2204 Wilborn Avenue, Zip 24592–1638; tel. 804/575–3100; Chris A. Lumsden, Chief Executive Officer (Total facility includes 19 beds in nursing home–type unit) **A**1 9 10 **F**7 8 10 12 14 15 16 17 19 20 21 22 28 29 30 31 32 34 35 37 40 41 44 45 46 49 59 63 64 65 66 71 73 **P**7 8 **S** Quorum Health Group/Quorum Health Resources, Inc., Brentwood, TN	23	10	157	5651	88	52350	558	44528	18267	557
SOUTH HILL—Mecklenburg County										
★ COMMUNITY MEMORIAL HEALTHCENTER, 125 Buena Vista Circle, Zip 23970–0090, Mailing Address: P.O. Box 90, Zip 23970–0090; tel. 804/447–3151; W. Scott Burnette, President (Total facility includes 161 beds in nursing home–type unit) **A**1 9 10 **F**2 3 7 8 12 13 14 15 16 17 19 21 22 23 26 28 30 31 32 33 34 35 36 37 39 40 41 42 44 45 46 49 51 52 56 57 58 59 63 64 65 66 67 71 72 73 74 **P**3 8 Web address: www.cmh–sh.org	23	10	284	5415	223	86419	310	37412	22133	604
STAUNTON—Independent City County										
DE JARNETTE CENTER, 1355 Richmond Road, Zip 24401–1091, Mailing Address: Box 2309, Zip 24402–2309; tel. 540/332–2100; Andrea C. Newsome, FACHE, Director **A**3 9 **F**2 7 8 9 10 11 12 13 14 15 16 17 19 20 21 22 23 24 25 28 29 30 31 32 35 37 39 40 41 42 43 44 45 46 47 48 49 50 51 52 53 54 55 56 58 60 61 63 64 65 66 67 69 70 71 73 74 **P**6 **S** Virginia Department of Mental Health, Richmond, VA	12	52	48	464	36	0	0	—	4029	126

Hospital, Address, Telephone, Administrator, Approval, Facility, and Physician Codes, Health Care System, Network	Classi-fication Codes		Utilization Data					Expense (thousands) of dollars		
★ American Hospital Association (AHA) membership □ Joint Commission on Accreditation of Healthcare Organizations (JCAHO) accreditation + American Osteopathic Healthcare Association (AOHA) membership ○ American Osteopathic Association (AOA) accreditation △ Commission on Accreditation of Rehabilitation Facilities (CARF) accreditation Control codes 61, 63, 64, 71, 72 and 73 indicate hospitals listed by AOHA, but not registered by AHA. For definition of numerical codes, see page A4	Control	Service	Staffed Beds	Admissions	Census	Outpatient Visits	Births	Total	Payroll	Personnel

Hospital	Control	Service	Staffed Beds	Admissions	Census	Outpatient Visits	Births	Total	Payroll	Personnel
□ WESTERN STATE HOSPITAL, 1301 Richmond Avenue, Zip 24401–9146, Mailing Address: P.O. Box 2500, Zip 24402–2500; tel. 540/332–8000; Lynwood F. Harding, Director **A**1 9 10 **F**2 4 5 8 9 10 11 12 19 20 21 22 23 26 27 30 31 35 37 39 40 41 42 43 44 46 48 49 50 52 57 60 63 65 67 71 73 **S** Virginia Department of Mental Health, Richmond, VA	12	22	369	1015	376	0	0	39783	25580	824
STUART—Patrick County										
⊠ PATRICK COMMUNITY HOSPITAL, (Formerly Patrick Community Memorial Hospital), 18688 Jeb Stuart Highway, Zip 24171–9512; tel. 540/694–3151; John M. Faulkner, FACHE, President and Chief Executive Officer (Total facility includes 25 beds in nursing home–type unit) **A**1 9 10 **F**7 8 12 14 15 16 17 19 22 28 30 32 33 36 37 39 40 41 44 46 49 64 65 71 73	23	10	59	1067	33	18413	126	10866	5674	208
SUFFOLK—Independent City County										
⊠ LOUISE OBICI MEMORIAL HOSPITAL, 1900 North Main Street, Zip 23434–4323, Mailing Address: P.O. Box 1100, Zip 23439–1100; tel. 757/934–4000; William C. Giermak, President and Chief Executive Officer (Nonreporting) **A**1 2 5 6 9 10	23	10	164	—	—	—	—	—	—	—
TAPPAHANNOCK—Essex County										
□ RIVERSIDE TAPPAHANNOCK HOSPITAL, 618 Hospital Road, Zip 22560; tel. 804/443–3311; Elizabeth J. Martin, Vice President and Administrator (Total facility includes 25 beds in nursing home–type unit) (Nonreporting) **A**1 9 10 **S** Riverside Health System, Newport News, VA	23	10	100	—	—	—	—	—	—	—
TAZEWELL—Tazewell County										
⊠ TAZEWELL COMMUNITY HOSPITAL, 141 Ben Bolt Avenue, Zip 24651–9700; tel. 540/988–2506; Craig B. James, President and Chief Executive Officer **A**1 9 10 **F**8 15 19 22 30 32 34 35 37 44 46 71 73 **P**1 **S** Carilion Health System, Roanoke, VA	23	10	38	1285	15	22428	0	8351	3440	138
VIRGINIA BEACH—Independent City County										
⊠ SENTARA BAYSIDE HOSPITAL, 800 Independence Boulevard, Zip 23455–6076; tel. 757/363–6100; Virginia Bogue, Site Administrator **A**1 5 9 10 **F**1 3 4 6 7 8 9 10 11 12 13 14 15 16 17 18 19 21 22 23 24 25 26 27 28 29 30 31 32 33 34 35 36 37 38 39 40 41 42 43 44 46 47 48 49 51 52 53 54 55 56 57 58 59 60 61 62 63 64 65 66 67 68 70 71 72 73 74 **P**6 **S** Sentara Health System, Norfolk, VA **Web address:** www.sentara.com	23	10	116	5920	65	56496	1199	41509	13279	497
⊠ SENTARA VIRGINIA BEACH GENERAL HOSPITAL, (Formerly Virginia Beach General Hospital), 1060 First Colonial Road, Zip 23454–9000; tel. 757/481–8000; Robert L. Graves, Administrator **A**1 2 3 5 9 10 **F**1 3 4 6 7 8 9 10 11 12 13 14 15 16 17 18 19 21 22 23 24 25 26 27 28 29 30 31 32 33 34 35 36 37 38 39 40 41 42 43 44 45 46 47 48 49 51 52 53 54 55 56 57 58 59 60 61 62 63 64 65 66 67 68 70 71 72 73 74 **P**2 5 6 7 8 **S** Sentara Health System, Norfolk, VA **Web address:** www.tidehealth.com	23	10	274	12036	159	156358	2218	97777	39010	1083
WARRENTON—Fauquier County										
⊠ FAUQUIER HOSPITAL, 500 Hospital Drive, Zip 20186–3099; tel. 540/349–0531; Rodger H. Baker, President and Chief Executive Officer **A**1 9 10 **F**6 7 8 12 14 15 16 17 19 21 22 26 28 29 30 32 33 34 35 37 39 40 41 42 44 45 46 49 63 65 66 67 71 73 **Web address:** www.fauquierhospital.org	23	10	83	4545	43	56708	537	37760	18599	571
WILLIAMSBURG—Independent City County										
□ EASTERN STATE HOSPITAL, Mailing Address: P.O. Box 8791, Zip 23187–8791; tel. 757/253–5161; John M. Favret, Director **A**1 5 9 10 **F**7 14 19 20 21 24 26 28 30 35 39 41 46 52 54 55 56 57 60 64 65 71 73 **S** Virginia Department of Mental Health, Richmond, VA	12	22	581	1282	505	—	0	56853	36275	1241
⊠ WILLIAMSBURG COMMUNITY HOSPITAL, 301 Monticello Avenue, Zip 23187–8700, Mailing Address: Box 8700, Zip 23187–8700; tel. 757/259–6000; Les A. Donahue, President and Chief Executive Officer (Nonreporting) **A**1 2 5 9 10 **S** Sentara Health System, Norfolk, VA **Web address:** www.sentara.com	23	10	100	—	—	—	—	—	—	—
WINCHESTER—Independent City County										
⊠ WINCHESTER MEDICAL CENTER, 1840 Amherst Street, Zip 22601–2540, Mailing Address: P.O. Box 3340, Zip 22604–3340; tel. 540/722–8000; George B. Caley, President **A**1 2 9 10 **F**4 7 8 10 11 12 14 15 16 17 19 21 22 23 28 29 30 31 32 33 34 35 36 37 38 39 40 41 42 43 44 46 48 49 52 53 54 55 56 58 59 60 63 65 67 71 72 73 **P**5 7 8 **S** Valley Health System, Winchester, VA **Web address:** www.valleyhealthlink.com	23	10	376	20521	273	190799	1825	157003	71095	1858
WOODBRIDGE—Prince William County										
⊠ POTOMAC HOSPITAL, 2300 Opitz Boulevard, Zip 22191–3399; tel. 703/670–1313; William Mason Moss, President **A**1 2 9 10 **F**6 7 8 10 11 12 14 15 16 17 19 21 22 28 29 30 31 33 34 35 37 38 39 40 41 42 44 46 49 51 52 54 55 56 57 58 59 60 62 63 65 67 71 73 74 **P**5 **Web address:** www.pwcweb.com/potomachospital	23	10	153	7991	88	132033	1907	63812	28762	677
WOODSTOCK—Shenandoah County										
⊠ SHENANDOAH MEMORIAL HOSPITAL, 759 South Main Street, Zip 22664–1127, Mailing Address: P.O. Box 508, Zip 22664–0508; tel. 540/459–4021; Floyd Heater, Chief Executive Officer (Total facility includes 34 beds in nursing home–type unit) **A**1 9 10 **F**3 4 7 8 10 12 14 15 16 17 19 21 22 23 24 26 27 28 30 32 34 35 37 39 40 41 44 45 46 49 50 52 53 54 55 56 57 58 60 63 64 65 66 69 70 71 73 **Web address:** www.shenmemhosp.com	23	10	129	2402	58	62416	203	20403	9446	310

Hospital, Address, Telephone, Administrator, Approval, Facility, and Physician Codes, Health Care System, Network	Classi-fication Codes		Utilization Data					Expense (thousands) of dollars		
★ American Hospital Association (AHA) membership □ Joint Commission on Accreditation of Healthcare Organizations (JCAHO) accreditation + American Osteopathic Healthcare Association (AOHA) membership ○ American Osteopathic Association (AOA) accreditation △ Commission on Accreditation of Rehabilitation Facilities (CARF) accreditation Control codes 61, 63, 64, 71, 72 and 73 indicate hospitals listed by AOHA, but not registered by AHA. For definition of numerical codes, see page A4	Control	Service	Staffed Beds	Admissions	Census	Outpatient Visits	Births	Total	Payroll	Personnel

WYTHEVILLE—Wythe County

☒ WYTHE COUNTY COMMUNITY HOSPITAL, 600 West Ridge Road, Zip 24382–1099; tel. 540/228–0200; Larry H. Chewning, III, Chief Executive Officer (Total facility includes 8 beds in nursing home–type unit) **A**1 2 9 10 **F**7 8 11 12 13 14 15 16 17 19 21 22 25 26 27 28 29 30 32 33 34 35 37 39 40 41 42 44 45 48 49 51 61 64 65 66 67 71 73 74 **S** Carilion Health System, Roanoke, VA
Web address: www.wcch.org

	23	10	90	2958	42	48248	227	22400	9954	362

WASHINGTON

Resident population 5,689 (in thousands)
Resident population in metro areas 80.5%
Birth rate per 1,000 population 14.2
65 years and over 11.5%
Percent of persons without health insurance 13.5%

Hospital, Address, Telephone, Administrator, Approval, Facility, and Physician Codes, Health Care System, Network	Classi-fication Codes		Utilization Data					Expense (thousands) of dollars		
	Control	Service	Staffed Beds	Admissions	Census	Outpatient Visits	Births	Total	Payroll	Personnel

★ American Hospital Association (AHA) membership
□ Joint Commission on Accreditation of Healthcare Organizations (JCAHO) accreditation
+ American Osteopathic Healthcare Association (AOHA) membership
○ American Osteopathic Association (AOA) accreditation
△ Commission on Accreditation of Rehabilitation Facilities (CARF) accreditation
Control codes 61, 63, 64, 71, 72 and 73 indicate hospitals listed by AOHA, but not registered by AHA. For definition of numerical codes, see page A4

ABERDEEN—Grays Harbor County

✉ GRAYS HARBOR COMMUNITY HOSPITAL, 915 Anderson Drive, Zip 98520; tel. 360/532–8330; Michael J. Madden, Administrator (Total facility includes 60 beds in nursing home–type unit) **A**1 9 10 **F**2 3 7 12 16 19 22 32 35 37 40 44 49 54 56 64 65 70 71 73	23	10	172	4514	101	70780	552	40338	19324	543

ANACORTES—Skagit County

✉ ISLAND HEALTH NORTHWEST, (Formerly Island Hospital Northwest), 1211 24th Street, Zip 98221–2590; tel. 360/299–1300; C. Philip Sandifer, Chief Executive Officer **A**1 2 9 10 **F**7 8 12 14 15 16 17 19 21 22 24 28 30 31 32 34 35 37 39 40 42 44 46 49 51 65 67 68 70 71 73 74 **P**7 8 Web address: www.island–health.org	16	10	43	1982	18	55164	232	25321	13083	310

ARLINGTON—Snohomish County

✉ CASCADE VALLEY HOSPITAL, NORTH SNOHOMISH COUNTY HEALTH SYSTEM, 330 South Stillaguamish Avenue, Zip 98223–1642; tel. 360/435–2133; Robert D. Campbell, Jr., Administrator **A**1 9 10 **F**7 8 12 15 19 22 34 35 37 40 42 44 71 74 **P**6 8	16	10	48	1956	15	34197	443	19299	9219	219

AUBURN—King County

□ AUBURN REGIONAL MEDICAL CENTER, 202 North Division, Plaza One, Zip 98001–4908; tel. 253/833–7711; Michael M. Gherardini, Chief Executive Officer and Managing Director (Nonreporting) **A**1 2 9 10 **S** Universal Health Services, Inc., King of Prussia, PA	33	10	100	—	—	—	—	—	—	—

BELLEVUE—King County

✉ OVERLAKE HOSPITAL MEDICAL CENTER, 1035 116th Avenue N.E., Zip 98004; tel. 425/688–5000; Kenneth D. Graham, President and Chief Executive Officer **A**1 2 9 10 **F**4 7 8 10 11 12 14 15 16 17 19 21 22 23 26 34 35 37 39 40 41 42 43 44 45 46 48 49 52 53 54 57 58 59 60 65 66 67 70 71 72 73 74 **P**6 Web address: www.overlakehospital.org	23	10	233	14464	156	139425	3116	127438	57267	1243

BELLINGHAM—Whatcom County

✉ △ ST. JOSEPH HOSPITAL, 2901 Squalicum Parkway, Zip 98225–1898; tel. 360/734–5400; Nancy J. Bitting, Chief Executive Officer **A**1 2 7 9 10 **F**1 2 3 4 5 7 8 10 11 12 13 14 15 16 17 19 21 22 23 26 27 28 29 30 31 34 35 37 38 39 40 41 42 43 44 45 46 47 48 49 50 51 52 55 56 58 60 61 63 65 66 67 68 70 71 72 73 **P**7 **S** PeaceHealth, Bellevue, WA Web address: www.peacehealth	23	10	189	11319	120	84932	1948	101941	44300	1039

BREMERTON—Kitsap County

✉ HARRISON MEMORIAL HOSPITAL, 2520 Cherry Street, Zip 98310–4270; tel. 360/377–3911; David W. Gitch, President and Chief Executive Officer **A**1 2 9 10 **F**4 7 8 10 12 14 15 16 17 19 21 22 23 25 26 27 28 29 30 31 32 33 34 35 37 39 40 41 42 44 45 46 49 52 53 54 55 56 57 58 60 61 65 67 70 71 72 73 74 **P**1 Web address: www.harrisonhospital.org	23	10	252	11971	119	109578	1668	88080	43657	965
✉ NAVAL HOSPITAL, Boone Road, Zip 98312–1898; tel. 360/475–4000; Captain Gregg S. Parker, Commanding Officer **A**1 5 **F**3 7 8 11 12 13 16 19 20 21 22 24 27 28 30 34 35 37 39 40 41 42 44 45 46 48 49 51 54 55 56 58 59 63 65 67 71 73 74 **P**5 **S** Department of Navy, Washington, DC Web address: www.nh_bremerton.med.navy.mil	43	44	91	2859	26	351599	814	46126	12011	—

BREWSTER—Okanogan County

★ OKANOGAN–DOUGLAS COUNTY HOSPITAL, 507 Hospital Way, Zip 98812, Mailing Address: P.O. Box 577, Zip 98812; tel. 509/689–2517; Howard M. Gamble, Administrator **A**9 10 **F**6 7 8 12 19 22 24 28 34 37 40 44 47 48 49 70 71	16	10	43	1106	9	10441	192	7392	3707	136

CENTRALIA—Lewis County

✉ PROVIDENCE CENTRALIA HOSPITAL, 914 South Scheuber Road, Zip 98531; tel. 360/736–2803; Steve Burdick, Administrator (Total facility includes 63 beds in nursing home–type unit) **A**1 2 9 10 **F**3 7 8 11 12 14 15 16 19 20 21 22 26 28 29 30 31 34 35 39 40 41 42 44 45 46 48 49 51 62 64 65 66 67 71 72 73 74 **P**8 **S** Sisters of Providence Health System, Seattle, WA	21	10	142	4864	96	126160	600	42013	21847	544

CHELAN—Chelan County

LAKE CHELAN COMMUNITY HOSPITAL, 503 East Highland Avenue, Zip 98816, Mailing Address: Box 908, Zip 98816; tel. 509/682–2531; Larry Peterson, Chief Executive Officer **A**9 10 **F**2 3 7 19 22 32 33 36 40 44 52 65 67 68 70 71 73	16	10	30	739	11	—	112	7131	3812	100

CHEWELAH—Stevens County

★ ST. JOSEPH'S HOSPITAL, 500 East Webster Street, Zip 99109, Mailing Address: P.O. Box 197, Zip 99109; tel. 509/935–8211; Gary V. Peck, Chief Executive Officer (Total facility includes 40 beds in nursing home–type unit) (Nonreporting) **A**9 10 **S** Providence Services, Spokane, WA	21	10	65	—	—	—	—	—	—	—

CLARKSTON—Asotin County

□ TRI–STATE MEMORIAL HOSPITAL, 1221 Highland Avenue, Zip 99403–0189, Mailing Address: P.O. Box 189, Zip 99403–0189; tel. 509/758–5511; Joseph K. Lillard, Administrator **A**1 9 10 **F**8 14 15 17 19 22 28 32 33 37 44 65 67 69 71 72 73 Web address: www.tri–satehospital.com	23	10	41	1136	14	32485	0	14312	5804	184

Hospital, Address, Telephone, Administrator, Approval, Facility, and Physician Codes, Health Care System, Network	Classi-fication Codes		Utilization Data					Expense (thousands) of dollars		
★ American Hospital Association (AHA) membership □ Joint Commission on Accreditation of Healthcare Organizations (JCAHO) accreditation + American Osteopathic Healthcare Association (AOHA) membership ○ American Osteopathic Association (AOA) accreditation △ Commission on Accreditation of Rehabilitation Facilities (CARF) accreditation Control codes 61, 63, 64, 71, 72 and 73 indicate hospitals listed by AOHA, but not registered by AHA. For definition of numerical codes, see page A4	Control	Service	Staffed Beds	Admissions	Census	Outpatient Visits	Births	Total	Payroll	Personnel

COLFAX—Whitman County

★ WHITMAN HOSPITAL AND MEDICAL CENTER, 1200 West Fairview, Zip 99111–9579; tel. 509/397–3435; Gordon C. McLean, Administrator (Nonreporting) **A**9 10
Web address: www.whitmanhospital.com

| | 13 | 10 | 32 | — | — | — | — | — | — | — |

COLVILLE—Stevens County

⊞ MOUNT CARMEL HOSPITAL, 982 East Columbia Street, Zip 99114–0351, Mailing Address: Box 351, Zip 99114–0351; tel. 509/684–2561; Gloria Cooper, Chief Executive Officer **A**1 3 9 10 **F**7 8 12 14 15 16 19 22 34 35 37 40 41 44 45 46 49 56 67 70 71 **P**8 **S** Providence Services, Spokane, WA

| | 21 | 10 | 32 | 1459 | 12 | 28792 | 199 | 12775 | 5733 | 135 |

COUPEVILLE—Island County

⊞ WHIDBEY GENERAL HOSPITAL, 101 North Main Street, Zip 98239–0400, Mailing Address: P.O. Box 400, Zip 98239–0400; tel. 360/678–7656; Scott Rhine, Administrator (Nonreporting) **A**1 2 9 10
Web address: www.whidbeygen.comwghosp

| | 16 | 10 | 51 | — | — | — | — | — | — | — |

DAVENPORT—Lincoln County

★ LINCOLN HOSPITAL, 10 Nichols Street, Zip 99122; tel. 509/725–7101; Kenneth J. Hall, Administrator (Total facility includes 71 beds in nursing home–type unit) **A**9 10 **F**6 7 8 12 15 19 22 26 27 30 34 39 40 41 44 49 64 65 66 71 73 **P**5

| | 16 | 10 | 95 | 585 | 65 | 14444 | 24 | 8214 | 4207 | 170 |

DAYTON—Columbia County

DAYTON GENERAL HOSPITAL, 1012 South Third Street, Zip 99328; tel. 509/382–2531; Oral R. Compson, Administrator (Nonreporting) **A**9 10

| | 16 | 10 | 18 | — | — | — | — | — | — | — |

DEER PARK—Spokane County

★ DEER PARK HOSPITAL, (Formerly Deer Park Health Center and Hospital), East 1015 D Street, Zip 99006, Mailing Address: P.O. Box 742, Zip 99006; tel. 509/276–5061; Garvin Olson, Chief Operating Officer (Nonreporting) **A**9 10 **S** Providence Services, Spokane, WA

| | 33 | 10 | 26 | — | — | — | — | — | — | — |

EDMONDS—Snohomish County

⊞ STEVENS HEALTHCARE, 21601 76th Avenue West, Zip 98026–7506; tel. 425/640–4000; Steve C. McCary, President and Chief Executive Officer **A**1 2 9 10 **F**1 4 7 8 10 16 17 18 19 20 21 22 25 26 27 28 29 30 31 34 35 37 39 40 41 42 44 45 46 49 51 52 53 54 55 56 57 58 59 60 65 66 67 70 71 73 74 **P**1 6 7

| | 16 | 10 | 134 | 8127 | 85 | 371685 | 1649 | 93532 | 43519 | 1070 |

ELLENSBURG—Kittitas County

KITTITAS VALLEY COMMUNITY HOSPITAL, 603 South Chestnut Street, Zip 98926; tel. 509/962–7302; Eric Jensen, Administrator **A**3 9 10 **F**7 8 11 15 16 17 19 22 24 26 29 32 33 35 36 37 39 40 41 44 49 65 67 70 71 73

| | 16 | 10 | 37 | 1702 | 14 | 43382 | 229 | 14724 | 7033 | 195 |

ENUMCLAW—King County

ENUMCLAW COMMUNITY HOSPITAL, (Formerly Community Memorial Hospital), 1450 Battersby Avenue, Zip 98022, Mailing Address: P.O. Box 218, Zip 98022–0218; tel. 360/825–2505; Dennis A. Popp, Administrator and Chief Executive Officer (Nonreporting) **A**9 10

| | 23 | 10 | 29 | — | — | — | — | — | — | — |

EPHRATA—Grant County

★ COLUMBIA BASIN HOSPITAL, 200 Southeast Boulevard, Zip 98823–1997; tel. 509/754–4631; Allen L. Beach, Administrator (Total facility includes 29 beds in nursing home–type unit) **A**9 10 **F**6 8 14 22 28 30 49 64 65 67 70 71 **P**5 6

| | 16 | 10 | 58 | 319 | 46 | 13578 | 0 | 6586 | 2847 | 114 |

EVERETT—Snohomish County

⊞ △ PROVIDENCE GENERAL MEDICAL CENTER, (Includes Providence General Medical Center – Colby Campus, 14th and Colby Avenue, Mailing Address: P.O. Box 1147, Zip 98206; tel. 206/261–2000; Providence General Medical Center – Pacific Campus, Pacific and Nassau Streets, Zip 98201; tel. 206/258–7123), 1321 Colby Street, Zip 98206, Mailing Address: P.O. Box 1067, Zip 98206–1067; tel. 425/261–2000; Mel Pyne, Administrator **A**1 2 7 9 10 **F**2 3 4 7 8 10 12 14 15 16 19 21 22 23 24 25 26 28 29 31 32 33 34 35 37 38 39 40 41 42 43 44 45 46 48 49 50 51 53 54 55 56 60 63 65 66 67 68 70 71 73 74 **S** Sisters of Providence Health System, Seattle, WA

| | 23 | 10 | 262 | 17127 | 162 | 454161 | 3197 | 161254 | 67778 | 1694 |

FAIRCHILD AFB—Spokane County

★ U. S. AIR FORCE HOSPITAL, 701 Hospital Loop, Zip 99011–8701; tel. 509/247–5217; Major Scott F. Wardell, Administrator (Nonreporting) **S** Department of the Air Force, Bowling AFB, DC

| | 41 | 10 | 35 | — | — | — | — | — | — | — |

FEDERAL WAY—King County

★ ST. FRANCIS HOSPITAL, 34515 Ninth Avenue South, Zip 98003–9710; tel. 253/927–9700; Joseph W. Wilczek, President and Chief Executive Officer (Nonreporting) **A**2 9 10 **S** Catholic Health Initiatives, Denver, CO

| | 21 | 10 | 67 | — | — | — | — | — | — | — |

FORKS—Clallam County

FORKS COMMUNITY HOSPITAL, 530 Bogachiel Way, Zip 98331–9699; tel. 360/374–6271; Janet A. Hays, Administrator (Total facility includes 36 beds in nursing home–type unit) **A**9 10 **F**1 3 7 8 13 14 15 16 17 21 22 26 28 29 30 31 39 40 41 44 45 49 51 58 64 65 67 70 71 73 74 **P**6

| | 16 | 10 | 53 | 368 | 34 | 14910 | 82 | 9963 | 5122 | 171 |

GOLDENDALE—Klickitat County

KLICKITAT VALLEY HOSPITAL, 310 South Roosevelt, Zip 98620, Mailing Address: P.O. Box 5, Zip 98620; tel. 509/773–4022; Ron Ingraham, Administrator **A**3 9 10 **F**7 14 15 16 17 22 28 29 30 32 33 34 40 41 44 49 56 64 65 70 71 72 **P**5 6 8

| | 16 | 10 | 15 | 525 | 3 | 16789 | 66 | 5103 | 3670 | 100 |

GRAND COULEE—Grant County

★ COULEE COMMUNITY HOSPITAL, 411 Fortuyn Road, Zip 99133–8718; tel. 509/633–1753; Charlotte Lang, Administrator (Total facility includes 29 beds in nursing home–type unit) **A**9 10 **F**7 8 15 19 21 22 44 64 71 72 **P**3 **S** Brim Healthcare, Inc., Brentwood, TN

| | 16 | 10 | 48 | 412 | 26 | 25256 | 40 | 5709 | 2300 | 116 |

Hospital, Address, Telephone, Administrator, Approval, Facility, and Physician Codes, Health Care System, Network	Classi-fication Codes		Utilization Data					Expense (thousands) of dollars		
★ American Hospital Association (AHA) membership □ Joint Commission on Accreditation of Healthcare Organizations (JCAHO) accreditation + American Osteopathic Healthcare Association (AOHA) membership ○ American Osteopathic Association (AOA) accreditation △ Commission on Accreditation of Rehabilitation Facilities (CARF) accreditation Control codes 61, 63, 64, 71, 72 and 73 indicate hospitals listed by AOHA, but not registered by AHA. For definition of numerical codes, see page A4	Control	Service	Staffed Beds	Admissions	Census	Outpatient Visits	Births	Total	Payroll	Personnel

ILWACO—Pacific County

★ OCEAN BEACH HOSPITAL, First and Fir, Zip 98624, Mailing Address: P.O. Drawer H, Zip 98624; tel. 360/642–3181; Pamela Ott, R.N., Administrator (Nonreporting) **A**9 10

| | 16 | 10 | 14 | — | — | — | — | — | — | — |

KENNEWICK—Benton County

⊠ KENNEWICK GENERAL HOSPITAL, 900 South Auburn Street, Zip 99336–0128, Mailing Address: Box 6128, Zip 99336; tel. 509/586–6111; Tom Nielsen, Administrator **A**1 2 9 10 **F**1 7 8 10 12 15 16 19 21 22 31 32 34 35 37 39 40 41 42 44 45 46 60 65 67 70 71 72 73 74 **P**7

| | 16 | 10 | 70 | 4549 | 37 | 85267 | 1173 | 36939 | 16225 | 404 |

KIRKLAND—King County

□ BHC FAIRFAX HOSPITAL, 10200 N.E. 132nd Street, Zip 98034; tel. 425/821–2000; Michelle Egerer, Chief Executive Officer (Nonreporting) **A**1 9 10 **S** Behavioral Healthcare Corporation, Nashville, TN

| | 33 | 22 | 133 | — | — | — | — | — | — | — |

⊠ EVERGREEN COMMUNITY HEALTH CENTER, 12040 N.E. 128th Street, Zip 98034; tel. 425/899–1000; Andrew Fallat, FACHE, Chief Executive Officer (Total facility includes 17 beds in nursing home–type unit) **A**1 2 9 10 **F**4 7 8 10 11 12 13 14 15 16 19 21 22 23 24 26 27 29 30 32 33 34 35 37 39 40 41 42 44 45 49 50 54 56 57 58 60 64 65 67 68 70 71 73 **P**6
Web address: www.evergreenhealthnet.org

| | 16 | 10 | 149 | 10166 | 85 | 188674 | 3346 | 107642 | 50129 | 1327 |

LAKEWOOD—Pierce County

★ ST. CLARE HOSPITAL, 11315 Bridgeport Way S.W., Zip 98499–0998, Mailing Address: P.O. Box 99998, Zip 98499–0998; tel. 253/588–1711; Joseph W. Wilczek, President and Chief Executive Officer (Nonreporting) **A**10 **S** Catholic Health Initiatives, Denver, CO

| | 23 | 10 | 60 | — | — | — | — | — | — | — |

LONGVIEW—Cowlitz County

⊠ ST. JOHN MEDICAL CENTER, 1615 Delaware Street, Zip 98632, Mailing Address: P.O. Box 3002, Zip 98632–0302; tel. 360/414–2000; Mark E. McGourty, Regional Chief Executive Officer (Nonreporting) **A**1 2 9 10 **S** PeaceHealth, Bellevue, WA

| | 23 | 10 | 178 | — | — | — | — | — | — | — |

MCCLEARY—Grays Harbor County

★ MARK REED HOSPITAL, 322 South Birch Street, Zip 98557; tel. 360/495–3244; Jean E. Roberts, Administrator (Nonreporting) **A**9 10 **S** Sisters of Providence Health System, Seattle, WA

| | 16 | 10 | 7 | — | — | — | — | — | — | — |

MEDICAL LAKE—Spokane County

□ EASTERN STATE HOSPITAL, Fir and Maple, Zip 99022–0045, Mailing Address: P.O. Box A, Zip 99022–0045; tel. 509/299–4351; C. Jan Gregg, Chief Executive Officer **A**1 10 **F**14 15 16 20 27 52 54 55 56 57 65 73 **P**6

| | 12 | 22 | 302 | 1009 | 300 | 0 | 0 | 40689 | 24811 | 595 |

MONROE—Snohomish County

⊠ VALLEY GENERAL HOSPITAL, 14701 179th S.E., Zip 98272, Mailing Address: P.O. Box 646, Zip 98272–0646; tel. 360/794–7497; Eric Buckland, CHE, Chief Executive Officer **A**1 9 10 **F**2 3 7 8 11 15 16 17 19 21 22 23 24 26 28 30 31 34 37 40 44 46 49 52 53 56 57 58 64 65 66 67 68 70 71 73

| | 16 | 10 | 59 | 2040 | 27 | 25912 | 402 | 17895 | 8011 | 222 |

MORTON—Lewis County

★ MORTON GENERAL HOSPITAL, 521 Adams Street, Zip 98356, Mailing Address: Drawer C, Zip 98356–0019; tel. 360/496–5112; Mike Lee, Superintendent (Total facility includes 30 beds in nursing home–type unit) **A**9 10 **F**7 8 15 16 19 22 26 34 40 44 65 70 71 72 73 **S** Sisters of Providence Health System, Seattle, WA

| | 16 | 10 | 48 | 447 | 33 | 11185 | 31 | 6499 | 2965 | 100 |

MOSES LAKE—Grant County

⊠ SAMARITAN HEALTHCARE, 801 East Wheeler Road, Zip 98837–1899; tel. 509/765–5606; Keith J. Baldwin, Administrator **A**1 9 10 **F**7 11 15 16 17 19 21 22 25 28 29 30 34 35 37 39 40 41 44 45 46 49 51 65 66 67 70 71 72 73
Web address: www.samaritanhealthcare.com

| | 16 | 10 | 50 | 2697 | 21 | 39214 | 939 | 27713 | 13228 | 368 |

MOUNT VERNON—Skagit County

⊠ AFFILIATED HEALTH SERVICES, (Includes Skagit Valley Hospital, Gregg A. Davidson, Associate Administrator and Chief Operating Officer; United General Hospital, 1971 Highway 20, Sedro Woolley, Zip 98284, Mailing Address: P.O. Box 1376, Zip 98273–1376; tel. 360/856–6021), 1415 Kincaid Street, Zip 98274, Mailing Address: P.O. Box 1376, Zip 98273–1376; tel. 360/424–4111; Patrick R. Mahoney, Chief Executive Officer **A**1 9 10 **F**4 5 7 8 10 11 12 14 15 16 17 19 21 22 23 26 28 29 30 32 33 34 35 37 39 40 41 42 44 46 49 52 54 56 57 58 59 60 63 64 65 67 68 70 71 73 74
Web address: www.affiliatedhealth.org

| | 16 | 10 | 194 | 6970 | 72 | 113277 | 1340 | 80061 | 35073 | 864 |

NEWPORT—Pend Oreille County

NEWPORT COMMUNITY HOSPITAL, 714 West Pine, Zip 99156; tel. 509/447–2441; John R. White, Administrator (Total facility includes 50 beds in nursing home–type unit) (Nonreporting) **A**9 10

| | 16 | 10 | 74 | — | — | — | — | — | — | — |

OAK HARBOR—Island County

⊠ NAVAL HOSPITAL, 3475 North Saratoga Street, Zip 98278–8800; tel. 360/257–9500; Captain Michael W. Benway, Commanding Officer (Nonreporting) **A**1 **S** Department of Navy, Washington, DC

| | 43 | 10 | 25 | — | — | — | — | — | — | — |

ODESSA—Lincoln County

★ ODESSA MEMORIAL HOSPITAL, 502 East Amende, Zip 99159, Mailing Address: P.O. Box 368, Zip 99159–0368; tel. 509/982–2611; Carol Schott, Administrator (Total facility includes 23 beds in nursing home–type unit) (Nonreporting) **A**9 10

| | 16 | 10 | 40 | — | — | — | — | — | — | — |

Hospital, Address, Telephone, Administrator, Approval, Facility, and Physician Codes, Health Care System, Network	Classi-fication Codes		Utilization Data					Expense (thousands) of dollars		
★ American Hospital Association (AHA) membership □ Joint Commission on Accreditation of Healthcare Organizations (JCAHO) accreditation + American Osteopathic Healthcare Association (AOHA) membership ○ American Osteopathic Association (AOA) accreditation △ Commission on Accreditation of Rehabilitation Facilities (CARF) accreditation Control codes 61, 63, 64, 71, 72 and 73 indicate hospitals listed by AOHA, but not registered by AHA. For definition of numerical codes, see page A4	Control	Service	Staffed Beds	Admissions	Census	Outpatient Visits	Births	Total	Payroll	Personnel
OLYMPIA—Thurston County										
★□ CAPITAL MEDICAL CENTER, 3900 Capital Mall Drive S.W., Zip 98502–8654, Mailing Address: P.O. Box 19002, Zip 98507–0013; tel. 360/754–5858; Joseph Sharp, Chief Executive Officer (Total facility includes 9 beds in nursing home–type unit) **A**1 2 9 10 **F**4 7 8 10 11 12 15 16 17 19 21 22 23 28 30 31 34 35 37 40 41 42 44 49 60 64 67 71 73 **P**5 **S** Columbia/HCA Healthcare Corporation, Nashville, TN	32	10	110	4213	45	77922	594	44894	16210	437
★□ △ PROVIDENCE ST. PETER HOSPITAL, 413 Lilly Road N.E., Zip 98506–5116; tel. 360/491–9480; C. Scott Bond, Administrator **A**1 2 3 5 7 9 10 **F**2 3 4 7 8 10 11 12 15 17 18 19 20 21 22 23 24 25 26 27 28 29 30 31 32 33 34 35 37 39 40 41 42 43 44 45 46 48 49 51 52 53 54 55 56 57 58 59 60 62 63 64 65 67 70 71 73 **P**7 8 **S** Sisters of Providence Health System, Seattle, WA **Web address:** www.providence.org	21	10	315	15535	173	243468	1915	149208	70559	1820
OMAK—Okanogan County										
★ MID–VALLEY HOSPITAL, 810 Jasmine, Zip 98841, Mailing Address: P.O. Box 793, Zip 98841; tel. 509/826–1760; Michael D. Billing, Administrator **A**3 9 10 **F**7 8 12 14 15 16 19 21 31 35 37 40 44 46 49 51 70 71	16	10	32	1237	10	12420	267	11998	5584	108
OTHELLO—Adams County										
★ OTHELLO COMMUNITY HOSPITAL, 315 North 14th Street, Zip 99344; tel. 509/488–2636; Jerry Lane, Administrator **A**9 10 **F**7 8 19 28 34 36 37 40 41 44 70 71	16	10	32	871	5	22086	381	5713	3034	76
PASCO—Franklin County										
★□ △ LOURDES MEDICAL CENTER, 520 North Fourth Avenue, Zip 99301, Mailing Address: P.O. Box 2568, Zip 99302; tel. 509/547–7704; Thomas Corley, Chief Executive Officer (Total facility includes 21 beds in nursing home–type unit) **A**1 2 7 9 10 **F**2 3 7 8 11 14 15 16 17 19 21 22 23 30 32 33 35 37 40 41 42 44 45 48 49 52 53 54 55 56 57 58 59 64 65 66 67 70 71 72 73 **P**7 **S** Carondelet Health System, Saint Louis, MO **Web address:** www.cbvcp.com\healthcenter	21	10	132	3820	54	118699	631	37720	17560	406
POMEROY—Garfield County										
GARFIELD COUNTY MEMORIAL HOSPITAL, 66th North Sixth Street, Zip 99347–0880, Mailing Address: P.O. Box 880, Zip 99347; tel. 509/843–1591; Pat Richardson, Interim Administrator (Total facility includes 40 beds in nursing home–type unit) (Nonreporting) **A**9 10	16	10	54	—	—	—	—	—	—	—
PORT ANGELES—Clallam County										
□ OLYMPIC MEMORIAL HOSPITAL, 939 Caroline Street, Zip 98362–3997; tel. 360/417–7000; Michael Glenn, Administrator (Total facility includes 125 beds in nursing home–type unit) **A**1 2 9 10 **F**7 8 11 14 15 16 17 19 21 22 24 28 29 30 32 34 37 40 42 44 45 46 49 51 60 64 65 70 71 73 74 **P**3 **Web address:** www.OMHNET.COM	16	10	203	5063	151	89846	579	50023	23695	637
PORT TOWNSEND—Jefferson County										
★ JEFFERSON GENERAL HOSPITAL, 834 Sheridan, Zip 98368; tel. 360/385–2200; Victor J. Dirksen, Administrator **A**10 **F**7 8 10 11 12 13 15 16 19 21 22 23 24 27 28 29 30 31 32 33 37 39 40 41 44 45 49 65 66 67 68 71 73 **P**8 **Web address:** www.jgh.org	16	10	35	1672	12	36471	141	15235	7586	207
PROSSER—Benton County										
★ PROSSER MEMORIAL HOSPITAL, 723 Memorial Street, Zip 99350–1593; tel. 509/786–2222; James Tavary, Administrator (Total facility includes 36 beds in nursing home–type unit) **A**9 10 **F**7 8 22 26 31 32 40 41 42 44 49 64 65 71 73 74	16	10	50	755	36	5568	403	7410	3264	131
PULLMAN—Whitman County										
□ PULLMAN MEMORIAL HOSPITAL, N.E. 1125 Washington Avenue, Zip 99163–4742; tel. 509/332–2541; Scott K. Adams, Chief Executive Officer **A**1 9 10 **F**1 2 3 4 5 6 7 8 9 10 11 12 14 15 16 17 18 19 20 21 22 23 24 26 27 28 29 30 31 32 33 34 35 36 37 38 39 40 41 42 43 44 45 46 47 48 49 51 53 54 55 56 57 58 59 60 61 62 63 64 65 66 67 69 70 71 72 73 **P**8	16	10	36	1055	7	36316	267	13265	5670	150
PUYALLUP—Pierce County										
★□ △ GOOD SAMARITAN COMMUNITY HEALTHCARE, 407 14th Avenue S.E., Zip 98372–0192, Mailing Address: Box 1247, Zip 98371–0192; tel. 253/848–6661; David K. Hamry, President **A**1 2 7 9 10 **F**1 6 7 11 12 14 15 16 17 18 19 21 22 24 25 26 28 29 30 32 33 34 37 38 39 40 41 42 44 45 46 48 49 51 53 54 55 56 57 58 59 60 62 63 65 66 67 68 70 71 72 73 **P**1 6 7	21	10	211	9494	123	376292	1401	118894	70210	1686
QUINCY—Grant County										
QUINCY VALLEY MEDICAL CENTER, 908 Tenth Avenue S.W., Zip 98848; tel. 509/787–3531; Alan MacPhee, Administrator (Total facility includes 22 beds in nursing home–type unit) (Nonreporting) **A**9 10	13	10	38	—	—	—	—	—	—	—
REDMOND—King County										
★ THE EASTSIDE HOSPITAL, 2700 152nd Avenue N.E., Zip 98052–5560; tel. 425/883–5151; Patricia Kennedy–Scott, Northern Region Vice President (Nonreporting)	23	10	125	—	—	—	—	—	—	—
RENTON—King County										
★□ VALLEY MEDICAL CENTER, 400 South 43rd Street, Zip 98055–9987; tel. 425/228–3450; Richard D. Roodman, Chief Executive Officer (Total facility includes 39 beds in nursing home–type unit) (Nonreporting) **A**1 2 3 5 9 10 **Web address:** www.valleymed.org	16	10	196	—	—	—	—	—	—	—

Hospital, Address, Telephone, Administrator, Approval, Facility, and Physician Codes, Health Care System, Network	Classi-fication Codes		Utilization Data					Expense (thousands) of dollars		
★ American Hospital Association (AHA) membership □ Joint Commission on Accreditation of Healthcare Organizations (JCAHO) accreditation + American Osteopathic Healthcare Association (AOHA) membership ○ American Osteopathic Association (AOA) accreditation △ Commission on Accreditation of Rehabilitation Facilities (CARF) accreditation Control codes 61, 63, 64, 71, 72 and 73 indicate hospitals listed by AOHA, but not registered by AHA. For definition of numerical codes, see page A4	Control	Service	Staffed Beds	Admissions	Census	Outpatient Visits	Births	Total	Payroll	Personnel

REPUBLIC—Ferry County

FERRY COUNTY MEMORIAL HOSPITAL, 36 Klondike Road, Zip 99166; tel. 509/775–3333; Nancy McIntyre, Administrator (Total facility includes 14 beds in nursing home–type unit) **A**9 10 **F**2 7 8 9 10 11 12 15 16 17 18 19 20 22 26 27 28 29 30 31 32 33 35 36 37 38 39 40 41 43 44 45 47 48 49 51 52 53 54 55 56 57 58 59 60 61 62 64 65 66 67 71 73 74	16	10	25	299	13	7256	9	2926	1360	51

RICHLAND—Benton County

★ △ KADLEC MEDICAL CENTER, 888 Swift Boulevard, Zip 99352–9974; tel. 509/946–4611; Marcel Loh, President and Chief Executive Officer **A**1 2 7 9 10 **F**1 7 8 10 12 14 15 16 19 21 22 23 31 32 35 37 38 39 40 41 42 44 45 46 48 49 51 60 65 70 71 72 73 **S** Quorum Health Group/Quorum Health Resources, Inc., Brentwood, TN **Web address:** www.kadlecmed.com	23	10	124	5869	65	66669	1148	62095	25499	547
★ LOURDES COUNSELING CENTER, 1175 Carondelet Drive, Zip 99352–1175; tel. 509/943–9104; Thomas Corley, Chief Executive Officer (Nonreporting) **A**1 9 10 **S** Carondelet Health System, Saint Louis, MO	21	22	32	—	—	—	—	—	—	—

RITZVILLE—Adams County

EAST ADAMS RURAL HOSPITAL, 903 South Adams Street, Zip 99169–2298; tel. 509/659–1200; James G. Parrish, Administrator (Nonreporting) **A**9 10	16	10	17							

SEATTLE—King County

★ △ CHILDREN'S HOSPITAL AND REGIONAL MEDICAL CENTER, 4800 Sand Point Way N.E., Zip 98105, Mailing Address: Box 5371, Zip 98105–0371; tel. 206/526–2000; Treuman Katz, President and Chief Executive Officer **A**1 2 3 5 7 8 9 10 **F**5 10 12 13 14 15 16 17 19 20 21 22 25 28 29 30 34 35 38 39 42 43 44 45 46 47 48 49 51 52 53 54 55 56 58 59 60 61 65 66 67 68 70 71 72 73 **P**6	23	50	208	11020	148	150002	0	156035	63968	1491
★ △ HARBORVIEW MEDICAL CENTER, 325 Ninth Avenue, Box 359717, Zip 98104–2499; tel. 206/731–3000; David E. Jaffe, Executive Director and Chief Executive Officer **A**1 3 5 7 8 9 10 **F**3 4 5 7 8 9 10 11 12 13 14 15 16 17 18 19 20 21 22 23 25 26 27 28 30 31 33 34 35 37 39 41 42 43 44 46 48 49 50 51 52 53 54 55 56 57 58 59 60 65 66 67 68 70 71 72 73 74 **P**3 **Web address:** www.washington.edu/medical/hmc/index.html	13	10	340	14537	282	360421	0	291089	124660	2931
★ △ HIGHLINE COMMUNITY HOSPITAL, (Includes Highline Specialty Center, 12844 Military Road Fork, Tukwila, Zip 98168; Mark Benedum, Administrator), 16251 Sylvester Road S.W., Zip 98166–0657; tel. 206/244–9970; Paul Tucker, Administrator (Total facility includes 30 beds in nursing home–type unit) (Nonreporting) **A**1 2 7 10	23	10	203							
★ △ NORTHWEST HOSPITAL, 1550 North 115th Street, Zip 98133–8498; tel. 206/364–0500; C. W. Schneider, President and Chief Executive Officer (Total facility includes 42 beds in nursing home–type unit) (Nonreporting) **A**1 2 3 7 9 10 **Web address:** www.nwhweb	23	10	238	—	—	—	—	—	—	—
★ △ PROVIDENCE SEATTLE MEDICAL CENTER, 500 17th Avenue, Zip 98122, Mailing Address: P.O. Box 34008, Zip 98124–1008; tel. 206/320–2000; Nancy A. Giunto, FACHE, Operations Administrator (Total facility includes 51 beds in nursing home–type unit) **A**1 2 3 5 7 9 10 **F**1 2 4 6 7 8 9 10 11 12 14 15 16 17 19 21 22 26 27 28 29 30 31 32 33 34 35 37 38 39 40 41 42 43 44 45 46 47 48 49 51 52 54 55 56 57 58 59 60 61 62 64 65 66 67 68 71 72 73 74 **P**5 6 7 **S** Sisters of Providence Health System, Seattle, WA	21	10	310	14780	205	115822	1749	160037	72852	1910
□ REGIONAL HOSPITAL FOR RESPIRATORY AND COMPLEX CARE, 12844 Military Road South, Zip 98168; tel. 206/248–4548; James C. Cannon, Administrator and Chief Executive Officer (Nonreporting) **A**1 10	23	49	27	—	—	—	—	—	—	—
□ SCHICK SHADEL HOSPITAL, 12101 Ambaum Boulevard S.W., Zip 98146–2699, Mailing Address: Box 48149, Zip 98148–0149; tel. 206/244–8100; Marvy Schmidt, Administrator (Nonreporting) **A**1 9 10	33	82	63	—	—	—	—	—	—	—
★ SWEDISH HEALTH SERVICES, (Includes Swedish Medical Center–Ballard, Northwest Market and Barnes, Zip 98107–1507, Mailing Address: Box 70707, Zip 98107; tel. 206/782–2700), 747 Broadway Avenue, Zip 98122–4307; tel. 206/386–6000; Richard H. Peterson, President and Chief Executive Officer (Nonreporting) **A**1 2 3 5 9 10 **Web address:** www.swedish.org	23	10	597							
★ △ UNIVERSITY OF WASHINGTON MEDICAL CENTER, 1959 Northeast Pacific Street, Box 356151, Zip 98195–6151; tel. 206/598–3300; Robert H. Muilenburg, Executive Director **A**1 2 3 5 7 8 9 10 **F**4 5 7 8 10 14 15 16 19 20 21 22 25 28 29 30 31 34 35 37 38 39 40 41 42 43 44 45 46 48 49 50 51 52 54 55 56 57 58 59 60 61 63 65 66 68 71 72 73 74 **P**6 **Web address:** www.washington.edu/medical	12	10	348	15117	265	314580	1700	295920	121156	3148
□ VENCOR HOSPITAL SEATTLE, (Formerly Vencor Seattle Hospital), (LONG TERM ACUTE CARE), 10560 Fifth Avenue N.E., Zip 98125–0977; tel. 206/364–2050; Jim Steinruck, CHE, Administrator and Chief Executive Officer **A**1 9 10 **F**12 16 65 **S** Vencor, Incorporated, Louisville, KY **Web address:** www.vencor.com	33	49	49	200	23	360	0	10392	4569	83
★ △ VETERANS AFFAIRS PUGET SOUND HEALTH CARE SYSTEM, (Includes Veterans Affairs Puget Sound Health Care System–American Lake Division, Tacoma, Zip 98493; tel. 206/582–8440), 1660 South Columbian Way, Zip 98108–1597; tel. 206/762–1010; Timothy B. Williams, Director (Total facility includes 132 beds in nursing home–type unit) (Nonreporting) **A**1 3 5 7 8 9 **S** Department of Veterans Affairs, Washington, DC	45	10	557	—	—	—	—	—	—	—

Hospital, Address, Telephone, Administrator, Approval, Facility, and Physician Codes, Health Care System, Network	Classi-fication Codes		Utilization Data					Expense (thousands) of dollars		
★ American Hospital Association (AHA) membership □ Joint Commission on Accreditation of Healthcare Organizations (JCAHO) accreditation + American Osteopathic Healthcare Association (AOHA) membership ○ American Osteopathic Association (AOA) accreditation △ Commission on Accreditation of Rehabilitation Facilities (CARF) accreditation Control codes 61, 63, 64, 71, 72 and 73 indicate hospitals listed by AOHA, but not registered by AHA. For definition of numerical codes, see page A4	Control	Service	Staffed Beds	Admissions	Census	Outpatient Visits	Births	Total	Payroll	Personnel

Hospital	Control	Service	Staffed Beds	Admissions	Census	Outpatient Visits	Births	Total	Payroll	Personnel
⊠ △ VIRGINIA MASON MEDICAL CENTER, 1100 Ninth Avenue, Zip 98101, Mailing Address: P.O. Box 900, Zip 98111–0900; tel. 206/223–6600; J. Michael Rona, President (Nonreporting) A1 2 3 5 7 9 10 **Web address:** www.vmmc.org	44	10	280	—	—	—	—	—	—	—

SEDRO WOOLLEY—Skagit County

UNITED GENERAL HOSPITAL See Affiliated Health Services, Mount Vernon

SHELTON—Mason County

Hospital	Control	Service	Staffed Beds	Admissions	Census	Outpatient Visits	Births	Total	Payroll	Personnel
□ MASON GENERAL HOSPITAL, 901 Mountainview Drive, Zip 98584, Mailing Address: P.O. Box 1668, Zip 98584; tel. 360/426–1611; G. Robert Appel, Administrator (Nonreporting) A1 9 10	16	10	68	—	—	—	—	—	—	—

SOUTH BEND—Pacific County

Hospital	Control	Service	Staffed Beds	Admissions	Census	Outpatient Visits	Births	Total	Payroll	Personnel
WILLAPA HARBOR HOSPITAL, 800 Alder Street, Zip 98586–0438, Mailing Address: P.O. Box 438, Zip 98586–0438; tel. 360/875–5526; Moe Chaudry, Administrator (Nonreporting) A9 10	16	10	18	—	—	—	—	—	—	—

SPOKANE—Spokane County

Hospital	Control	Service	Staffed Beds	Admissions	Census	Outpatient Visits	Births	Total	Payroll	Personnel
□ DEACONESS MEDICAL CENTER–SPOKANE, 800 West Fifth Avenue, Zip 99204, Mailing Address: P.O. Box 248, Zip 99210–0248; tel. 509/458–5800 A1 2 3 5 9 10 F1 2 3 4 5 6 7 8 9 10 11 12 15 16 17 18 19 20 21 22 23 24 25 26 27 28 29 30 31 32 33 34 35 36 37 38 39 40 41 42 43 44 45 47 48 49 50 51 52 53 54 55 56 57 58 59 60 61 64 65 66 67 68 70 71 72 73 P8 S Empire Health Services, Spokane, WA	23	10	326	12786	170	131921	2595	135718	52227	1382
⊠ HOLY FAMILY HOSPITAL, North 5633 Lidgerwood Avenue, Zip 99207; tel. 509/482–0111; Cathy J. Simchuk, Interim Chief Executive Officer A1 2 9 10 F1 2 3 4 7 8 9 10 11 12 15 16 19 21 22 23 26 27 28 29 30 32 33 35 37 38 39 40 41 42 43 44 45 46 47 48 49 51 52 53 54 55 56 57 58 59 60 63 64 65 66 67 68 70 71 72 73 74 S Providence Services, Spokane, WA **Web address:** www.holy–family.org	21	10	190	8303	89	72287	1026	65245	29634	—
⊠ SACRED HEART MEDICAL CENTER, West 101 Eighth Avenue, Zip 99220, Mailing Address: P.O. Box 2555, Zip 99220; tel. 509/455–3040; Ryland P. Davis, President (Nonreporting) A1 2 3 5 9 10 S Providence Services, Spokane, WA	21	10	607	—	—	—	—	—	—	—
⊠ SHRINERS HOSPITALS FOR CHILDREN–SPOKANE, 911 West Fifth Avenue, Zip 99204–2901, Mailing Address: P.O. Box 2472, Zip 99210–2472; tel. 509/455–7844; Charles R. Young, Administrator A1 3 F12 14 15 16 17 20 46 48 49 65 73 S Shriners Hospitals for Children, Tampa, FL	23	57	30	756	12	7615	0	—	—	132
□ △ ST. LUKES REHABILITATION INSTITUTE, 711 South Cowley Street, Zip 99202; tel. 509/838–4771; Thomas M. Fritz, Administrator (Nonreporting) A1 7 9 10	23	46	72	—	—	—	—	—	—	—
□ VALLEY HOSPITAL AND MEDICAL CENTER, 12606 East Mission Avenue, Zip 99216–9969; tel. 509/924–6650; Michael T. Liepman, Chief Operating Officer (Nonreporting) A1 2 9 10 S Empire Health Services, Spokane, WA	23	10	117	—	—	—	—	—	—	—
⊠ VETERANS AFFAIRS MEDICAL CENTER, North 4815 Assembly Street, Zip 99205–6197; tel. 509/327–0200; Joseph M. Manley, Director (Total facility includes 60 beds in nursing home–type unit) (Nonreporting) A1 S Department of Veterans Affairs, Washington, DC	45	10	192	—	—	—	—	—	—	—

SUNNYSIDE—Yakima County

Hospital	Control	Service	Staffed Beds	Admissions	Census	Outpatient Visits	Births	Total	Payroll	Personnel
★ + ○ SUNNYSIDE COMMUNITY HOSPITAL, 10th and Tacoma Avenue, Zip 98944, Mailing Address: P.O. Box 719, Zip 98944–0719; tel. 509/837–1650; Jon D. Smiley, Chief Executive Officer A2 9 10 11 F7 8 12 14 17 19 20 21 22 23 28 29 30 32 33 34 35 37 39 40 42 44 45 46 51 65 67 68 70 71 73 P4 7 S Brim Healthcare, Inc., Brentwood, TN **Web address:** www.televar.com/sch	23	10	34	1752	16	48105	526	17984	7588	174

TACOMA—Pierce County

ALLENMORE HOSPITAL See Tacoma General Hospital

Hospital	Control	Service	Staffed Beds	Admissions	Census	Outpatient Visits	Births	Total	Payroll	Personnel
⊠ MADIGAN ARMY MEDICAL CENTER, Zip 98431–5000; tel. 253/968–1110; Brigadier General Mack C. Hill, Commanding General A1 2 3 5 F3 4 7 8 10 12 13 14 15 16 17 19 20 21 22 26 27 29 30 31 34 35 37 38 39 40 41 42 43 44 45 46 49 50 51 52 53 54 55 56 57 58 60 61 63 65 66 67 70 71 72 73 74 S Department of the Army, Office of the Surgeon General, Falls Church, VA **Web address:** www.mamc.amedd.army.mil	42	10	172	8872	117	817244	1802	122360	56000	2969
□ MARY BRIDGE CHILDREN'S HOSPITAL AND HEALTH CENTER, 317 Martin Luther King Jr. Way, Zip 98405–0299, Mailing Address: Box 5299, Zip 98405–0299; tel. 253/403–1400; Diane Cecchettini, Executive Vice President A1 3 5 9 10 F1 4 7 8 10 11 12 13 14 17 18 19 21 22 23 25 26 28 29 30 31 32 33 34 35 37 38 39 40 41 42 43 44 47 49 50 51 54 60 61 63 65 67 70 71 72 73 74 P2 5 S MultiCare Health System, Tacoma, WA **Web address:** www.multicare.com	23	50	72	3132	33	164651	0	35519	16654	383
⊠ PUGET SOUND HOSPITAL, 215 South 36th Street, Zip 98408, Mailing Address: P.O. Box 11412, Zip 98411–0412; tel. 253/474–0561; Bruce Brandler, Chief Executive Officer (Nonreporting) A1 9 10	33	10	146	—	—	—	—	—	—	—

ST. CLARE HOSPITAL See Lakewood

Hospital	Control	Service	Staffed Beds	Admissions	Census	Outpatient Visits	Births	Total	Payroll	Personnel
⊠ △ ST. JOSEPH MEDICAL CENTER, 1717 South J Street, Zip 98405, Mailing Address: P.O. Box 2197, Zip 98401–2197; tel. 253/627–4101; Joseph W. Wilczek, President and Chief Executive Officer (Nonreporting) A1 2 7 9 10 S Catholic Health Initiatives, Denver, CO	21	10	271	—	—	—	—	—	—	—

Hospital, Address, Telephone, Administrator, Approval, Facility, and Physician Codes, Health Care System, Network	Classi-fication Codes		Utilization Data					Expense (thousands) of dollars		
★ American Hospital Association (AHA) membership □ Joint Commission on Accreditation of Healthcare Organizations (JCAHO) accreditation + American Osteopathic Healthcare Association (AOHA) membership ○ American Osteopathic Association (AOA) accreditation △ Commission on Accreditation of Rehabilitation Facilities (CARF) accreditation Control codes 61, 63, 64, 71, 72 and 73 indicate hospitals listed by AOHA, but not registered by AHA. For definition of numerical codes, see page A4	Control	Service	Staffed Beds	Admissions	Census	Outpatient Visits	Births	Total	Payroll	Personnel

✠ TACOMA GENERAL HOSPITAL, (Includes Allenmore Hospital, South 19th and Union Avenue, Zip 98405, Mailing Address: P.O. Box 11414, Zip 98411–0414; tel. 253/403–2323), 315 Martin Luther King Jr. Way, Zip 98405–0299, Mailing Address: P.O. Box 5299, Zip 98405–0299; tel. 253/403–1000; Diane Cecchettini, Executive Vice President **A**1 2 3 5 9 10 **F**1 4 7 8 10 11 12 13 17 18 19 21 22 25 26 28 29 30 31 33 34 35 37 38 39 40 41 42 43 44 45 46 47 49 50 51 54 60 61 63 65 67 68 70 71 72 73 74 **P**5 6 **S** MultiCare Health System, Tacoma, WA **Web address:** www.multicare.com	23	10	365	20128	233	401331	3425	202287	79108	1863
VETERANS AFFAIRS PUGET SOUND HEALTH CARE SYSTEM–AMERICAN LAKE DIVISION See Veterans Affairs Puget Sound Health Care System, Seattle										
□ WESTERN STATE HOSPITAL, 9601 Steilacoom Boulevard S.W., Zip 98498; tel. 253/582–8900; Pat Terry, Ph.D., Acting Chief Executive Officer (Nonreporting) **A**1 9 10	12	22	835	—	—	—	—	—	—	—
TONASKET—Okanogan County										
NORTH VALLEY HOSPITAL, Second and Western, Zip 98855, Mailing Address: P.O. Box 488, Zip 98855; tel. 509/486–2151; Warner H. Bartleson, Administrator (Total facility includes 70 beds in nursing home–type unit) (Nonreporting) **A**9 10	16	10	92	—	—	—	—	—	—	—
TOPPENISH—Yakima County										
✠ PROVIDENCE TOPPENISH HOSPITAL, 502 West Fourth Avenue, Zip 98948, Mailing Address: P.O. Box 672, Zip 98948–0672; tel. 509/865–3105; Larry Anthony, Administrator **A**1 9 10 **F**7 8 14 15 16 17 19 21 22 32 33 34 37 40 41 44 46 51 65 67 70 71 73 74 **P**6 **S** Sisters of Providence Health System, Seattle, WA	21	10	48	2227	19	59309	609	14004	6137	163
VANCOUVER—Clark County										
✠ △ SOUTHWEST WASHINGTON MEDICAL CENTER, (Includes Vancouver Memorial Campus, 3400 Main Street, Zip 98663; tel. 206/696–5000), 400 N.E. Mother Joseph Place, Zip 98664, Mailing Address: P.O. Box 1600, Zip 98668; tel. 360/256–2000; Geoffrey N. Lang, President and Chief Executive Officer **A**1 2 3 7 9 10 **F**4 7 8 10 11 12 14 15 16 17 19 21 22 28 29 30 31 32 33 34 35 37 39 40 41 42 43 44 45 46 48 49 51 52 54 55 56 57 58 59 60 65 66 67 70 71 72 73 **P**1 5 **Web address:** www.swmedctr.com	23	10	310	18534	170	189075	4342	159554	77591	1780
WALLA WALLA—Walla Walla County										
✠ JONATHAN M. WAINWRIGHT MEMORIAL VETERANS AFFAIRS MEDICAL CENTER, 77 Wainwright Drive, Zip 99362–3994; tel. 509/525–5200 (Total facility includes 30 beds in nursing home–type unit) **A**1 **F**2 3 12 14 16 17 19 20 22 27 30 31 37 46 51 52 54 56 58 59 64 65 67 73 **P**6 **S** Department of Veterans Affairs, Washington, DC	45	10	46	1455	67	48500	0	—	—	318
✠ △ ST. MARY MEDICAL CENTER, 401 West Poplar Street, Zip 99362, Mailing Address: Box 1477, Zip 99362–0312; tel. 509/525–3320; John A. Isely, President **A**1 2 7 9 10 **F**7 8 14 19 22 28 30 31 32 35 37 38 39 40 41 42 44 48 49 52 56 57 58 60 65 70 71 73 74 **P**6 **S** Providence Services, Spokane, WA	21	10	107	3899	54	64155	491	49196	24891	666
STATE PENITENTIARY HOSPITAL, Mailing Address: Box 520, Zip 99362; tel. 509/525–3610; Barbara Croft, Health Care Manager (Nonreporting)	12	11	36	—	—	—	—	—	—	—
✠ WALLA WALLA GENERAL HOSPITAL, 1025 South Second Avenue, Zip 99362, Mailing Address: Box 1398, Zip 99362–0480; Morre Dean, President (Nonreporting) **A**1 2 9 10 **S** Adventist Health, Roseville, CA	21	10	72	—	—	—	—	—	—	—
WENATCHEE—Chelan County										
✠ CENTRAL WASHINGTON HOSPITAL, 1201 South Miller Street, Zip 98801–1948, Mailing Address: Box 1887, Zip 98807–1887; tel. 509/662–1511; John T. Evans, Jr., President and Chief Executive Officer **A**1 9 10 **F**4 7 8 10 11 12 14 15 16 17 19 22 23 28 29 32 33 34 35 36 37 38 39 40 41 42 44 45 51 64 65 67 70 71 73 74 **P**8	23	10	133	7211	84	112782	1360	64250	32032	735
WHITE SALMON—Klickitat County										
SKYLINE HOSPITAL, 211 Skyline Drive, Zip 98672–0099, Mailing Address: Box 99, Zip 98672–0099; tel. 509/493–1101; Lynn Milnes, Administrator and Chief Executive Officer **A**9 10 **F**7 8 9 10 11 15 16 22 28 33 34 37 38 40 44 47 51 64 70 **P**5	16	10	24	750	6	12733	135	5768	3091	105
YAKIMA—Yakima County										
✠ △ PROVIDENCE YAKIMA MEDICAL CENTER, 110 South Ninth Avenue, Zip 98902–3397; tel. 509/575–5000; Barbara A. Hood, Chief Executive Officer **A**1 2 3 7 9 10 **F**4 7 8 10 11 14 15 16 17 19 21 22 23 28 29 30 32 33 34 35 37 40 41 42 43 44 45 46 48 49 51 62 63 64 65 67 70 71 73 74 **P**6 **S** Sisters of Providence Health System, Seattle, WA **Web address:** www.providence.org	21	10	169	6263	82	216255	597	84653	37196	833
✠ YAKIMA VALLEY MEMORIAL HOSPITAL, 2811 Tieton Drive, Zip 98902–3799; tel. 509/575–8000; Richard W. Linneweh, Jr., President and Chief Executive Officer **A**1 2 3 9 10 **F**7 8 10 12 13 14 15 16 17 19 21 22 28 29 30 32 33 34 35 37 38 39 40 41 42 44 45 46 49 52 54 58 60 63 64 65 66 67 70 71 73 74 **P**4	23	10	210	10467	105	170853	2298	86242	35169	943

WEST VIRGINIA

Resident population 1,811 (in thousands)
Resident population in metro areas 42.2%
Birth rate per 1,000 population 11.6
65 years and over 15.1%
Percent of persons without health insurance 14.9%

Hospital, Address, Telephone, Administrator, Approval, Facility, and Physician Codes, Health Care System, Network	Classi-fication Codes		Utilization Data					Expense (thousands) of dollars		
★ American Hospital Association (AHA) membership □ Joint Commission on Accreditation of Healthcare Organizations (JCAHO) accreditation + American Osteopathic Healthcare Association (AOHA) membership ○ American Osteopathic Association (AOA) accreditation △ Commission on Accreditation of Rehabilitation Facilities (CARF) accreditation Control codes 61, 63, 64, 71, 72 and 73 indicate hospitals listed by AOHA, but not registered by AHA. For definition of numerical codes, see page A4	Control	Service	Staffed Beds	Admissions	Census	Outpatient Visits	Births	Total	Payroll	Personnel

BECKLEY—Raleigh County

□ BECKLEY APPALACHIAN REGIONAL HOSPITAL, 306 Stanaford Road, Zip 25801–3142; tel. 304/255–3000; David R. Lyon, Administrator **A**1 9 10 **F**1 3 4 8 11 12 15 16 17 18 19 21 22 26 28 29 30 31 32 35 37 39 42 44 49 52 53 54 55 56 57 58 59 63 65 71 73 **P**6 **S** Appalachian Regional Healthcare, Lexington, KY

| | 23 | 10 | 173 | 7791 | 136 | 24011 | 0 | 44794 | 13778 | 743 |

⊠ RALEIGH GENERAL HOSPITAL, (Formerly Columbia Raleigh General Hospital), 1710 Harper Road, Zip 25801–3397; tel. 304/256–4100; David B. Darden, Chief Executive Officer (Nonreporting) **A**1 9 10 13 **S** Columbia/HCA Healthcare Corporation, Nashville, TN

| | 30 | 10 | 303 | — | — | — | — | — | — | — |

⊠ VETERANS AFFAIRS MEDICAL CENTER, 200 Veterans Avenue, Zip 25801–6499; tel. 304/255–2121; Gerard P. Husson, Director (Total facility includes 50 beds in nursing home–type unit) **A**1 **F**3 8 16 17 19 20 22 28 33 34 35 37 42 44 45 46 49 51 56 58 60 63 64 65 71 73 74 **P**6 **S** Department of Veterans Affairs, Washington, DC

| | 45 | 10 | 90 | 1788 | 32 | 74926 | 0 | 33660 | 17118 | 393 |

BERKELEY SPRINGS—Morgan County

★ MORGAN COUNTY WAR MEMORIAL HOSPITAL, 1124 Fairfax Street, Zip 25411–1718; tel. 304/258–1234; David A. Sweeney, FACHE, Administrator (Total facility includes 16 beds in nursing home–type unit) **A**9 10 **F**8 15 16 20 22 27 30 32 33 34 44 45 46 49 64 65 67 71 73 **S** Valley Health System, Winchester, VA

| | 13 | 10 | 44 | 1115 | 31 | 19884 | 0 | 7556 | 3082 | 114 |

BLUEFIELD—Mercer County

⊠ BLUEFIELD REGIONAL MEDICAL CENTER, 500 Cherry Street, Zip 24701–3390; tel. 304/327–1100; Eugene P. Pawlowski, President **A**1 9 10 **F**7 8 10 11 12 13 14 15 16 19 21 22 24 30 32 34 35 37 39 40 41 42 44 49 50 60 63 64 65 71 72 73 **P**8
Web address: www.bluefield.org

| | 23 | 10 | 265 | 8965 | 139 | 125707 | 837 | 66729 | 29282 | 951 |

⊠ ST. LUKE'S HOSPITAL, (Formerly Columbia St. Luke's Hospital), 1333 Southview Drive, Zip 24701–4399, Mailing Address: P.O. Box 1190, Zip 24701–1190; tel. 304/327–2900; Deane E. Beamer, President and Chief Executive Officer **A**1 9 10 **F**8 12 14 15 16 19 21 22 23 26 30 32 35 37 39 41 44 49 54 56 63 65 67 71 73 **P**5 7 **S** Columbia/HCA Healthcare Corporation, Nashville, TN
Web address: www.columbiastlukes.com

| | 33 | 10 | 79 | 1898 | 10 | 23579 | 0 | 13008 | 5274 | 194 |

BUCKEYE—Pocahontas County

★ POCAHONTAS MEMORIAL HOSPITAL, Mailing Address: Rural Route 2, Box 52 W, Zip 24924; tel. 304/799–7400; Ivan Withers, Chief Executive Officer **A**9 10 **F**8 14 15 16 19 21 22 26 28 29 30 32 34 41 44 45 46 49 51 65 71 72 73

| | 13 | 10 | 27 | 742 | 17 | 25063 | 0 | 4234 | 1684 | 92 |

BUCKHANNON—Upshur County

⊠ ST. JOSEPH'S HOSPITAL OF BUCKHANNON, (Formerly St. Joseph's Hospital), Amalia Drive, Zip 26201–2222; tel. 304/473–2000; Wayne B. Griffith, FACHE, Chief Executive Officer (Total facility includes 16 beds in nursing home–type unit) **A**1 9 10 **F**2 7 8 11 12 14 15 16 17 19 22 24 27 28 29 30 32 33 34 35 37 39 40 42 44 45 46 49 52 55 56 57 58 59 64 65 67 70 71 73 **P**7 8

| | 23 | 10 | 95 | 2281 | 36 | 61600 | 243 | 17918 | 7077 | 286 |

CHARLESTON—Kanawha County

⊠ △ CHARLESTON AREA MEDICAL CENTER, (Includes General Division, 501 Morris Street, Zip 25301, Mailing Address: Box 1393, Zip 25325; tel. 304/348–5432; Memorial Division, 3200 Maccorkle Avenue S.E., Zip 25304; tel. 304/348–5432; Women and Children's Hospital, 800 Pennsylvania Avenue, Zip 25302; tel. 304/348–5432; 501 Morris Street, Zip 25301–1300, Mailing Address: P.O. Box 1547, Zip 25326–1547; tel. 304/348–5432; Robert L. Savage, President and Chief Executive Officer (Total facility includes 20 beds in nursing home–type unit) **A**1 2 3 5 7 8 9 10 **F**3 4 5 6 7 8 10 11 12 13 14 15 16 17 18 19 20 21 22 23 24 25 26 27 28 29 30 31 32 33 34 35 36 37 38 39 40 41 42 43 44 45 46 47 48 49 51 52 53 54 55 56 57 58 59 60 61 63 64 65 66 67 68 70 71 72 73 74 **P**3 4 6 7 **S** Camcare, Inc., Charleston, WV
Web address: www.camcare.com

| | 23 | 10 | 784 | 36550 | 603 | 430000 | 3200 | 399800 | 145300 | 4640 |

⊠ EYE AND EAR CLINIC OF CHARLESTON, 1306 Kanawha Boulevard East, Zip 25301, Mailing Address: P.O. Box 2271, Zip 25328–2271; tel. 304/343–4371; W. Allen Shelton, II, Administrator and Chief Executive Officer **A**1 9 10 **F**1 2 3 4 5 6 7 8 10 11 12 13 17 18 19 20 21 22 23 24 25 26 27 28 29 30 31 32 34 35 37 38 39 40 41 42 43 44 45 46 47 48 49 50 51 52 53 54 55 56 57 58 59 60 61 63 64 65 66 67 68 70 71 72 73 74 **P**3 4 5 8
Web address: www.eyeandearclinicwv.com

| | 33 | 45 | 26 | 46 | 0 | 5185 | 0 | 5456 | 2186 | 74 |

GENERAL DIVISION See Charleston Area Medical Center

⊠ HIGHLAND HOSPITAL, 300 56th Street S.E., Zip 25304–2361, Mailing Address: P.O. Box 4107, Zip 25364–4107; tel. 304/926–1600; David M. McWatters, Administrator **A**1 5 9 10 **F**16 25 26 28 29 32 39 52 53 54 55 56 57 58 59 65 **P**5 6
Web address: www.highlandhosp.com

| | 23 | 22 | 58 | 817 | 23 | 5791 | 0 | 7715 | 3532 | 162 |

MEMORIAL DIVISION See Charleston Area Medical Center

Hospital, Address, Telephone, Administrator, Approval, Facility, and Physician Codes, Health Care System, Network	Classi-fication Codes		Utilization Data					Expense (thousands) of dollars		
★ American Hospital Association (AHA) membership □ Joint Commission on Accreditation of Healthcare Organizations (JCAHO) accreditation + American Osteopathic Healthcare Association (AOHA) membership ○ American Osteopathic Association (AOA) accreditation △ Commission on Accreditation of Rehabilitation Facilities (CARF) accreditation Control codes 61, 63, 64, 71, 72 and 73 indicate hospitals listed by AOHA, but not registered by AHA. For definition of numerical codes, see page A4	Control	Service	Staffed Beds	Admissions	Census	Outpatient Visits	Births	Total	Payroll	Personnel
⊠ SAINT FRANCIS HOSPITAL, 333 Laidley Street, Zip 25301–1628, Mailing Address: P.O. Box 471, Zip 25322–0471; tel. 304/347–6500; Dan Lauffer, Chief Executive Officer (Total facility includes 30 beds in nursing home–type unit) (Nonreporting) **A**1 9 10 **S** Columbia/HCA Healthcare Corporation, Nashville, TN WOMEN AND CHILDREN'S HOSPITAL See Charleston Area Medical Center	33	10	155	—	—	—	—	—	—	—
CLARKSBURG—Harrison County										
⊠ LOUIS A. JOHNSON VETERANS AFFAIRS MEDICAL CENTER, 1 Medical Center Drive, Zip 26301–4199; tel. 304/623–3461; Michael W. Neusch, FACHE, Director (Nonreporting) **A**1 2 3 5 9 **S** Department of Veterans Affairs, Washington, DC	45	10	160	—	—	—	—	—	—	—
⊠ UNITED HOSPITAL CENTER, Route 19 South, Zip 26301, Mailing Address: P.O. Box 1680, Zip 26302–1680; tel. 304/624–2121; Bruce C. Carter, President (Total facility includes 51 beds in nursing home–type unit) **A**1 2 3 5 9 10 12 13 **F**2 3 6 7 8 10 11 12 16 18 19 20 21 22 23 25 28 30 32 33 34 35 37 40 41 42 44 45 46 49 51 52 53 54 55 56 57 58 60 62 63 64 65 67 71 73 **P**4 **S** West Virginia United Health System, Fairmont, WV **Web address:** www.uhcwv.org	23	10	360	13044	255	324274	873	99269	40753	1276
ELKINS—Randolph County										
⊠ DAVIS MEMORIAL HOSPITAL, Gorman Avenue and Reed Street, Zip 26241, Mailing Address: P.O. Box 1484, Zip 26241–1484; tel. 304/636–3300; Robert L. Hammer, II, Chief Executive Officer **A**1 9 10 **F**2 3 4 6 7 8 9 10 11 16 19 21 22 23 24 25 26 27 28 29 30 31 32 33 34 35 36 37 38 39 40 41 42 43 44 46 47 48 49 50 52 53 54 55 56 57 58 59 60 63 64 65 69 70 71 73 **P**7 8 **S** West Virginia United Health System, Fairmont, WV **Web address:** www.davishealthcare.com	23	10	115	5949	78	132579	506	46183	19040	635
FAIRMONT—Marion County										
⊠ FAIRMONT GENERAL HOSPITAL, 1325 Locust Avenue, Zip 26554–1435; tel. 304/367–7100; Richard W. Graham, FACHE, President (Total facility includes 55 beds in nursing home–type unit) **A**1 9 10 **F**2 3 7 8 10 11 12 16 17 19 21 22 23 28 29 30 32 35 36 39 40 41 42 44 46 49 52 53 54 55 56 57 58 59 63 64 65 66 67 71 73 74 **P**7 8 **S** Quorum Health Group/Quorum Health Resources, Inc., Brentwood, TN **Web address:** www.fghi.com	23	10	211	6649	125	138888	561	48260	19839	—
GASSAWAY—Braxton County										
★ BRAXTON COUNTY MEMORIAL HOSPITAL, 100 Hoylman Drive, Zip 26624–9320; tel. 304/364–5156; Tony E. Atkins, Administrator **A**9 10 **F**8 13 15 16 17 19 21 22 24 28 29 31 32 34 44 49 51 61 65 71 74 **S** Camcare, Inc., Charleston, WV **Web address:** www.pihn.org	23	10	30	786	6	21678	1	6785	3292	114
GLEN DALE—Marshall County										
⊠ REYNOLDS MEMORIAL HOSPITAL, 800 Wheeling Avenue, Zip 26038–1697; tel. 304/845–3211; John Sicurella, Chief Executive Officer (Total facility includes 20 beds in nursing home–type unit) **A**1 6 9 10 **F**1 3 7 8 15 16 17 19 21 22 24 26 28 29 30 32 33 34 35 37 39 40 41 42 44 45 46 49 53 54 55 56 57 58 59 60 63 64 65 70 71 73 **P**8 **Web address:** www.reymem.com	23	10	140	3348	58	72077	123	29781	12213	421
GRAFTON—Taylor County										
□ GRAFTON CITY HOSPITAL, 500 Market Street, Zip 26354–1187; tel. 304/265–0400; Gary R. Willmon, Administrator (Total facility includes 72 beds in nursing home–type unit) **A**1 9 10 **F**8 11 12 14 15 16 19 21 22 24 25 26 28 29 30 32 33 34 37 39 42 44 45 46 49 51 54 64 65 66 68 70 71 72 73 74 **P**3 **Web address:** www.gchospital@aol.com	14	10	106	1373	83	14867	0	10087	4900	241
GRANTSVILLE—Calhoun County										
MINNIE HAMILTON HEALTHCARE CENTER, High Street, Zip 26147, Mailing Address: Route 1, Box 1A, Zip 26147; tel. 304/354–9244; Barbara Lay, Administrator (Total facility includes 24 beds in nursing home–type unit) **A**9 **F**8 13 15 16 17 18 19 20 21 22 24 25 28 29 30 31 32 34 39 45 49 51 64 65 67 70 71 73 74 **P**6	23	10	49	370	21	28023	0	5294	3008	138
HINTON—Summers County										
□ SUMMERS COUNTY APPALACHIAN REGIONAL HOSPITAL, Terrace Street, Zip 25951, Mailing Address: Drawer 940, Zip 25951–0940; tel. 304/466–1000; Rocco K. Massey, Administrator (Total facility includes 24 beds in nursing home–type unit) **A**1 9 10 **F**8 12 14 15 16 17 19 22 28 30 32 34 35 37 44 46 49 51 64 65 71 73 74 **S** Appalachian Regional Healthcare, Lexington, KY **Web address:** www.arh.org	23	10	50	790	38	54172	0	9119	4402	146
HUNTINGTON—Cabell County										
⊠ CABELL HUNTINGTON HOSPITAL, 1340 Hal Greer Boulevard, Zip 25701–0195; tel. 304/526–2000; W. Don Smith, II, President and Chief Executive Officer (Total facility includes 15 beds in nursing home–type unit) **A**1 3 5 9 10 **F**2 3 4 7 8 9 10 11 12 15 16 17 19 20 21 22 23 26 28 29 30 31 32 34 35 37 38 39 40 41 42 43 44 45 46 47 49 51 52 53 54 55 57 59 60 61 63 64 65 66 67 70 71 73 74 **P**8 **Web address:** www.chhi.org	23	10	293	14520	180	210426	2289	113330	49756	1399
⊠ COLUMBIA RIVER PARK HOSPITAL, 1230 Sixth Avenue, Zip 25701–2312, Mailing Address: P.O. Box 1875, Zip 25719–1875; tel. 304/526–9111; Scott C. Stamm, Chief Executive Officer **A**1 9 10 **F**1 16 17 18 22 28 30 52 53 54 55 56 57 58 59 **S** Columbia/HCA Healthcare Corporation, Nashville, TN **Web address:** www.columbia.net	33	22	125	1865	54	0	0	9828	4355	174

Hospital, Address, Telephone, Administrator, Approval, Facility, and Physician Codes, Health Care System, Network	Classi-fication Codes		Utilization Data					Expense (thousands) of dollars		
	Control	Service	Staffed Beds	Admissions	Census	Outpatient Visits	Births	Total	Payroll	Personnel

★ American Hospital Association (AHA) membership
□ Joint Commission on Accreditation of Healthcare Organizations (JCAHO) accreditation
+ American Osteopathic Healthcare Association (AOHA) membership
○ American Osteopathic Association (AOA) accreditation
△ Commission on Accreditation of Rehabilitation Facilities (CARF) accreditation
Control codes 61, 63, 64, 71, 72 and 73 indicate hospitals listed by AOHA, but not registered by AHA. For definition of numerical codes, see page A4

□ △ HEALTHSOUTH HUNTINGTON REHABILITATION HOSPITAL, 6900 West Country Club Drive, Zip 25705–2000; tel. 304/733–1060; John Forester, Chief Operating Officer (Nonreporting) **A**1 7 10 **S** HEALTHSOUTH Corporation, Birmingham, AL	33	46	40	—	—	—	—	—	—	—
✠ ST. MARY'S HOSPITAL, 2900 First Avenue, Zip 25702–1272; tel. 304/526–1234; J. Thomas Jones, Executive Director (Total facility includes 38 beds in nursing home–type unit) **A**1 2 3 5 6 9 10 **F**3 4 7 8 10 11 12 15 16 17 19 21 22 23 26 28 29 30 32 34 35 37 39 40 41 42 43 44 45 46 49 51 52 53 54 55 56 57 59 60 63 64 65 67 70 71 73 74 **P**2 8 Web address: www.st-marys.org	21	10	403	16343	263	132363	666	144299	55759	1685
✠ VETERANS AFFAIRS MEDICAL CENTER, 1540 Spring Valley Drive, Zip 25704–9300; tel. 304/429–6741; David N. Pennington, Chief Executive Officer **A**1 3 5 9 **F**1 2 3 4 6 8 11 12 15 16 17 18 19 20 21 22 23 25 26 27 28 29 30 31 32 33 35 37 39 41 42 43 44 45 46 49 50 51 52 54 55 56 57 58 59 60 63 64 65 67 69 71 73 74 **S** Department of Veterans Affairs, Washington, DC Web address: www.va.gov/station	45	10	80	3396	63	178493	0	—	—	687
HURRICANE—Putnam County										
✠ PUTNAM GENERAL HOSPITAL, 1400 Hospital Drive, Zip 25526–9210, Mailing Address: P.O. Box 900, Zip 25526–0900; tel. 304/757–1700; Patsy Hardy, Administrator **A**1 9 10 **F**7 8 12 14 15 16 19 21 22 23 28 30 32 33 35 39 40 41 44 46 49 56 65 66 71 73 **S** Columbia/HCA Healthcare Corporation, Nashville, TN Web address: www.columbia-hca.com	33	10	64	2861	38	47271	6	20773	8600	272
KEYSER—Mineral County										
□ POTOMAC VALLEY HOSPITAL, 167 South Mineral Street, Zip 26726–2699; tel. 304/788–3141; Larry Abrams, Administrator **A**1 9 10 **F**8 11 14 19 21 22 29 30 31 32 33 37 44 49 63 65 67 71 73	33	10	42	1991	18	46587	0	13065	4543	187
KINGWOOD—Preston County										
✠ PRESTON MEMORIAL HOSPITAL, 300 South Price Street, Zip 26537–1495; tel. 304/329–1400; Charles Lonchar, President and Chief Executive Officer **A**1 9 10 **F**2 3 7 8 12 17 19 21 22 28 30 32 34 35 39 40 41 44 49 63 65 67 71 73 74 **P**8 **S** Quorum Health Group/Quorum Health Resources, Inc., Brentwood, TN	23	10	60	1139	14	39971	159	10358	4822	199
LOGAN—Logan County										
★ GUYAN VALLEY HOSPITAL, (CRITICAL ACCESS HOSPITAL), 396 Dingess Street, Zip 25601–3695; tel. 304/792–1700; Phillip Belcher, Administrator **F**7 8 11 12 15 16 19 20 21 22 25 30 32 34 35 37 39 40 41 42 44 45 46 49 51 58 64 65 67 70 71 73 74 **P**4 7	23	49	15	263	9	9525	0	4918	2531	97
□ LOGAN GENERAL HOSPITAL, 20 Hospital Drive, Zip 25601–3473; tel. 304/792–1101; Ted A. Hatfield, Chief Executive Officer **A**1 10 13 **F**11 15 16 19 21 22 30 34 35 40 41 42 44 49 54 55 56 65 71 73 **P**6	23	10	132	6852	88	178773	451	69974	35745	866
MADISON—Boone County										
✠ BOONE MEMORIAL HOSPITAL, 701 Madison Avenue, Zip 25130–1699; tel. 304/369–1230; Tommy H. Mullins, Administrator **A**1 9 10 **F**14 15 16 19 21 22 32 33 35 44 49 64 65 71 Web address: www.wvbmh.com	13	10	38	735	15	35773	0	6688	2697	120
MAN—Logan County										
□ MAN ARH HOSPITAL, 700 East McDonald Avenue, Zip 25635–1011; tel. 304/583–8421; Erica McDonald, Administrator **A**1 9 10 **F**8 12 14 15 16 17 19 21 22 25 28 29 30 32 33 34 35 37 44 49 51 55 58 63 65 71 73 **P**6 **S** Appalachian Regional Healthcare, Lexington, KY	23	10	46	875	8	51294	0	12754	5842	219
MARTINSBURG—Berkeley County										
✠ CITY HOSPITAL, Dry Run Road, Zip 25401, Mailing Address: P.O. Box 1418, Zip 25402–1418; tel. 304/264–1000; Peter L. Mulford, Administrator (Total facility includes 19 beds in nursing home–type unit) **A**1 2 3 9 10 **F**1 2 3 7 8 12 16 17 18 19 23 24 26 28 30 31 32 33 34 35 37 39 40 41 42 44 45 46 49 52 53 54 57 58 59 64 65 66 67 70 71 74 **P**8 **S** Quorum Health Group/Quorum Health Resources, Inc., Brentwood, TN	23	10	143	6562	90	106745	836	49853	20515	625
✠ VETERANS AFFAIRS MEDICAL CENTER, Charles Town Road, Zip 25401–0205; tel. 304/263–0811; George Moore, Director (Total facility includes 148 beds in nursing home–type unit) **A**1 3 5 9 **F**2 3 4 5 8 10 15 16 19 20 21 22 23 24 25 26 28 30 31 32 33 34 35 37 39 41 42 43 44 45 46 49 50 51 52 54 55 56 57 58 59 60 61 63 64 65 66 67 70 71 72 73 74 **S** Department of Veterans Affairs, Washington, DC Web address: www.va.gov/visn5	45	10	566	4325	494	196981	0	81586	55172	1170
MONTGOMERY—Fayette County										
✠ MONTGOMERY GENERAL HOSPITAL, 401 Sixth Avenue, Zip 25136–0270, Mailing Address: P.O. Box 270, Zip 25136–0270; tel. 304/442–5151; William R. Laird, IV, President and Chief Executive Officer (Total facility includes 44 beds in nursing home–type unit) **A**1 10 **F**8 12 15 16 17 19 22 28 30 32 34 35 37 44 46 49 51 64 65 66 67 71 73 **P**6 8 Web address: www.mghwv.org	23	10	99	1651	57	57159	0	22065	9525	250
MORGANTOWN—Monongalia County										
□ CHESTNUT RIDGE HOSPITAL, 930 Chestnut Ridge Road, Zip 26505–2854; tel. 304/293–4000; Lawrence J. Drake, Chief Executive Officer **A**1 5 9 10 **F**2 3 9 11 15 19 21 22 35 37 38 40 47 48 52 53 54 56 57 58 59 70 71 **P**6 **S** Ramsay Health Care, Inc., Coral Gables, FL	33	22	70	1222	44	3697	0	6447	3005	134

Hospital, Address, Telephone, Administrator, Approval, Facility, and Physician Codes, Health Care System, Network	Classi-fication Codes		Utilization Data					Expense (thousands) of dollars		
★ American Hospital Association (AHA) membership □ Joint Commission on Accreditation of Healthcare Organizations (JCAHO) accreditation + American Osteopathic Healthcare Association (AOHA) membership ○ American Osteopathic Association (AOA) accreditation △ Commission on Accreditation of Rehabilitation Facilities (CARF) accreditation Control codes 61, 63, 64, 71, 72 and 73 indicate hospitals listed by AOHA, but not registered by AHA. For definition of numerical codes, see page A4	Control	Service	Staffed Beds	Admissions	Census	Outpatient Visits	Births	Total	Payroll	Personnel

□ △ HEALTHSOUTH MOUNTAINVIEW REGIONAL REHABILITATION HOSPITAL, 1160 Van Voorhis Road, Zip 26505–3435; tel. 304/598–1100; Sharon Noro, Chief Executive Officer (Nonreporting) **A**1 7 10 **S** HEALTHSOUTH Corporation, Birmingham, AL **Web address:** www.healthsouth.com	33	46	80	—	—	—	—	—	—	—
⊞ MONONGALIA GENERAL HOSPITAL, 1200 J. D. Anderson Drive, Zip 26505–3486; tel. 304/598–1200; Robert P. Ritz, Chief Executive Officer (Total facility includes 20 beds in nursing home–type unit) **A**1 3 5 9 10 **F**4 6 7 8 10 11 12 13 14 15 16 17 19 21 22 23 24 25 28 29 30 31 32 33 34 35 37 39 42 43 44 46 49 51 54 60 61 62 63 65 66 67 71 72 73 74 **Web address:** www.monhealthsys.org	23	10	182	7668	105	104777	532	71082	30906	870
⊞ WEST VIRGINIA UNIVERSITY HOSPITALS, Medical Center Drive, Zip 26506–4749; tel. 304/598–4000; Bruce McClymonds, President (Total facility includes 20 beds in nursing home–type unit) **A**1 2 3 5 8 9 10 **F**2 3 4 7 8 10 11 12 17 18 19 20 21 22 23 25 26 28 29 30 31 32 33 34 35 37 38 40 41 42 43 44 45 46 47 49 50 51 52 53 54 55 56 57 58 59 60 61 63 64 65 66 67 68 70 71 73 74 **P**6 8 **S** West Virginia United Health System, Fairmont, WV **Web address:** www.wvhealth.wvu.edu	23	10	401	12812	238	380732	1302	194740	71411	2506
NEW MARTINSVILLE—Wetzel County										
⊞ WETZEL COUNTY HOSPITAL, 3 East Benjamin Drive, Zip 26155–2758; tel. 304/455–8000; Alvin R. Lawson, JD, Chief Executive Officer (Total facility includes 10 beds in nursing home–type unit) **A**1 9 10 **F**7 8 13 14 15 16 17 19 21 22 24 28 32 34 37 39 41 44 45 49 51 64 65 67 70 71 73 **P**6	13	10	63	1643	19	46639	167	14156	5918	182
OAK HILL—Fayette County										
⊞ PLATEAU MEDICAL CENTER, 430 Main Street, Zip 25901–3455; tel. 304/469–8600; Hank Woodson, Administrator (Nonreporting) **A**1 9 10 **S** Camcare, Inc., Charleston, WV	33	10	79	—	—	—	—	—	—	—
PARKERSBURG—Wood County										
⊞ CAMDEN–CLARK MEMORIAL HOSPITAL, 800 Garfield Avenue, Zip 26101–5378, Mailing Address: P.O. Box 718, Zip 26102–0718; tel. 304/424–2111; Thomas J. Corder, President and Chief Executive Officer (Total facility includes 25 beds in nursing home–type unit) **A**1 2 9 10 **F**7 8 12 14 15 16 17 19 21 22 23 24 28 29 30 32 33 34 35 39 40 42 44 45 46 49 60 63 64 65 67 71 73 74 **P**7 **Web address:** www.ccmh.org	23	10	238	10681	140	247691	828	84179	33921	1121
□ △ HEALTHSOUTH WESTERN HILLS REGIONAL REHABILITATION HOSPITAL, 3 Western Hills Drive, Zip 26101–8122, Mailing Address: P.O. Box 1428, Zip 26102–1428; tel. 304/420–1300; Thomas Heller, Administrator (Nonreporting) **A**1 7 10 **S** HEALTHSOUTH Corporation, Birmingham, AL	33	46	40	—	—	—	—	—	—	—
⊞ ST. JOSEPH'S HOSPITAL, 1824 Murdoch Avenue, Zip 26101–3246, Mailing Address: P.O. Box 327, Zip 26102–0327; tel. 304/424–4111; Stephens M. Mundy, Chief Executive Officer (Total facility includes 35 beds in nursing home–type unit) **A**1 9 10 **F**2 3 7 8 10 11 12 14 15 16 17 19 22 23 25 26 27 28 29 30 31 32 34 35 37 39 40 41 42 44 46 48 49 52 53 55 56 57 59 63 64 65 66 67 71 72 73 74 **P**7 **Web address:** www.wvha.com/web/sjh	32	10	294	8190	124	155640	513	56688	23569	767
PETERSBURG—Grant County										
★ GRANT MEMORIAL HOSPITAL, Route 55 West, Zip 26847, Mailing Address: P.O. Box 1019, Zip 26847–1019; tel. 304/257–1026; Robert L. Harman, Administrator (Total facility includes 10 beds in nursing home–type unit) **A**9 10 **F**7 8 12 13 15 17 19 21 22 26 28 29 30 32 33 34 35 37 40 42 44 49 58 64 65 70 71 74	13	10	61	2371	35	76104	291	19097	8220	324
PHILIPPI—Barbour County										
BROADDUS HOSPITAL, College Hill, Zip 26416–1051; tel. 304/457–1760; Susannah Higgins, Chief Executive Officer (Total facility includes 60 beds in nursing home–type unit) **A**9 **F**8 12 13 14 15 16 17 19 22 26 27 28 32 33 34 42 44 49 51 54 57 58 64 65 73 74 **P**7 8 **S** West Virginia United Health System, Fairmont, WV	23	10	72	385	60	21435	0	5899	2961	139
POINT PLEASANT—Mason County										
⊞ PLEASANT VALLEY HOSPITAL, 2520 Valley Drive, Zip 25550–2083; tel. 304/675–4340; Michael G. Sellards, Executive Director (Total facility includes 100 beds in nursing home–type unit) **A**1 9 10 **F**7 8 12 14 15 16 17 19 22 23 24 28 30 32 33 34 35 37 39 40 41 42 44 48 49 58 63 64 65 67 71 73 **P**8 **Web address:** www.pvalley.org	23	10	201	4512	129	73611	174	39025	18594	630
PRINCETON—Mercer County										
□ △ HEALTHSOUTH SOUTHERN HILLS REHABILITATION HOSPITAL, 120 Twelfth Street, Zip 24740–2312; tel. 304/487–8000; Ken Howell, Administrator **A**1 7 10 **F**5 12 14 15 16 17 19 20 22 24 25 26 27 28 29 30 34 35 41 44 45 46 48 49 54 55 57 58 65 66 67 71 73 74 **S** HEALTHSOUTH Corporation, Birmingham, AL **Web address:** www.healthsouth.com	33	46	46	735	40	16713	0	10755	4308	135
⊞ PRINCETON COMMUNITY HOSPITAL, 12th Street, Zip 24740–1369, Mailing Address: P.O. Box 1369, Zip 24740–1369; tel. 304/487–7000; Daniel C. Dunmyer, Chief Executive Officer (Total facility includes 23 beds in nursing home–type unit) **A**1 2 9 10 **F**3 4 7 8 10 11 12 14 15 16 17 19 20 21 22 23 24 26 28 30 31 32 34 35 37 39 40 41 42 44 45 46 49 51 52 53 54 55 56 57 58 60 63 64 65 66 67 68 71 73 **P**1 4 7	14	10	213	8830	130	143667	405	61053	27519	927

Hospital, Address, Telephone, Administrator, Approval, Facility, and Physician Codes, Health Care System, Network	Classi-fication Codes		Utilization Data					Expense (thousands) of dollars		
★ American Hospital Association (AHA) membership □ Joint Commission on Accreditation of Healthcare Organizations (JCAHO) accreditation + American Osteopathic Healthcare Association (AOHA) membership ○ American Osteopathic Association (AOA) accreditation △ Commission on Accreditation of Rehabilitation Facilities (CARF) accreditation Control codes 61, 63, 64, 71, 72 and 73 indicate hospitals listed by AOHA, but not registered by AHA. For definition of numerical codes, see page A4	Control	Service	Staffed Beds	Admissions	Census	Outpatient Visits	Births	Total	Payroll	Personnel

RANSON—Jefferson County

⊞ JEFFERSON MEMORIAL HOSPITAL, 300 South Preston Street, Zip 25438–1699; tel. 304/728–1600; Jon D. Applebaum, Administrator **A**1 5 9 10 **F**7 8 14 15 16 17 19 21 22 28 32 34 35 37 39 40 41 42 44 45 46 49 64 65 66 67 70 71 72 73 **P**8

| | 23 | 10 | 58 | 2201 | 23 | 54538 | 221 | 19570 | 9152 | 309 |

RICHWOOD—Nicholas County

RICHWOOD AREA COMMUNITY HOSPITAL, Riverside Addition, Zip 26261; tel. 304/846–2573; D. Parker Haddix, Chief Executive Officer (Nonreporting) **A**9

| | 23 | 10 | 6 | — | — | — | — | — | — | — |

RIPLEY—Jackson County

⊞ JACKSON GENERAL HOSPITAL, Pinnell Street, Zip 25271, Mailing Address: P.O. Box 720, Zip 25271–0720; tel. 304/372–2731; Richard L. Rohaley, President and Chief Executive Officer **A**1 9 10 **F**7 8 11 14 15 16 19 21 22 28 32 34 35 37 40 41 44 49 65 66 71 72

| | 23 | 10 | 82 | 2682 | 37 | 36541 | 144 | 19908 | 9640 | 317 |

ROMNEY—Hampshire County

□ HAMPSHIRE MEMORIAL HOSPITAL, 549 Center Avenue, Zip 26757–1199; tel. 304/822–4561; Roberta D. McCauley, Chief Executive Officer (Total facility includes 30 beds in nursing home–type unit) **A**1 9 10 **F**8 14 15 16 19 22 31 32 44 49 65 71 **P**4 7

| | 33 | 10 | 47 | 778 | 35 | 30563 | 0 | 6484 | 2481 | — |

RONCEVERTE—Greenbrier County

⊞ ○ GREENBRIER VALLEY MEDICAL CENTER, 202 Maplewood Avenue, Zip 24970–0497, Mailing Address: P.O. Box 497, Zip 24970–0497; tel. 304/647–4411; Donald D. Sandoval, FACHE, Chief Executive Officer **A**1 9 10 11 13 **F**7 8 12 14 16 19 21 22 23 26 28 29 30 31 32 33 34 35 37 39 40 42 44 45 46 49 60 63 65 71 73 **S** NetCare Health Systems, Inc., Nashville, TN

| | 33 | 10 | 122 | 4122 | 54 | 36183 | 449 | 23810 | 9500 | 365 |

SISTERSVILLE—Tyler County

SISTERSVILLE GENERAL HOSPITAL, 314 South Wells Street, Zip 26175–1098; tel. 304/652–2611; F. David Richardson, Ph.D., Administrator **A**9 **F**8 15 16 22 24 28 30 32 33 41 44 49 64 65 71 73
Web address: www.wvha.com/web/sjh

| | 14 | 10 | 12 | 186 | 2 | 25233 | 0 | 3767 | 2010 | 75 |

SOUTH CHARLESTON—Kanawha County

⊞ THOMAS MEMORIAL HOSPITAL, 4605 MacCorkle Avenue S.W., Zip 25309–1398; tel. 304/766–3600; Stephen P. Dexter, Chief Executive Officer **A**1 3 5 9 10 **F**2 3 7 8 11 14 15 16 17 19 21 22 23 26 27 28 29 30 32 34 35 36 37 38 39 40 41 42 44 45 49 52 53 54 55 56 57 58 59 60 63 64 65 66 67 71 72 73 74 **P**7
Web address: www.outtasiteinc.com/thomas

| | 23 | 10 | 216 | 8824 | 129 | 192813 | 585 | 77841 | 30689 | 886 |

SPENCER—Roane County

⊞ ROANE GENERAL HOSPITAL, 200 Hospital Drive, Zip 25276–1060; tel. 304/927–4444; Lewis Newberry, Interim Chief Executive Officer (Total facility includes 9 beds in nursing home–type unit) **A**1 9 10 **F**1 7 8 17 19 21 28 30 32 34 40 44 45 64 65 70 71 73

| | 23 | 10 | 55 | 1262 | 25 | 26072 | 136 | 11615 | 6154 | 230 |

SUMMERSVILLE—Nicholas County

★ SUMMERSVILLE MEMORIAL HOSPITAL, 400 Fairview Heights Road, Zip 26651–0400; tel. 304/872–2891; Ron Hancock, Interim Administrator (Total facility includes 52 beds in nursing home–type unit) **A**9 10 **F**4 7 8 17 19 21 22 25 26 34 35 37 40 42 44 49 64 65 67 70 71 72 73

| | 14 | 10 | 109 | 1979 | 75 | 55810 | 208 | 19621 | 8765 | 307 |

WEBSTER SPRINGS—Webster County

★ WEBSTER COUNTY MEMORIAL HOSPITAL, (CRITICAL ACCESS HOSPITAL), 324 Miller Mountain Drive, Zip 26288–1087; tel. 304/847–5682; Stephen M. Gavalchik, Administrator **A**9 **F**14 15 16 17 22 24 28 29 30 32 34 41 44 51 65 71 **P**6

| | 13 | 49 | 15 | 282 | 2 | 24840 | 1 | 4751 | 2748 | 101 |

WEIRTON—Brooke County

⊞ WEIRTON MEDICAL CENTER, 601 Colliers Way, Zip 26062–5091; tel. 304/797–6000; Donald Muhlenthaler, FACHE, President and Chief Executive Officer (Total facility includes 33 beds in nursing home–type unit) **A**1 9 10 **F**3 5 7 8 10 11 12 13 14 15 16 17 19 20 21 22 24 25 26 27 28 29 30 31 32 33 34 35 39 40 41 42 44 45 49 51 52 53 54 55 56 57 58 59 63 64 65 66 67 69 70 71 73 74 **P**8
Web address: www.weirtonmedical.com

| | 23 | 10 | 240 | 7241 | 112 | 111531 | 269 | 51955 | 23712 | 781 |

WESTON—Lewis County

⊞ STONEWALL JACKSON MEMORIAL HOSPITAL, Mailing Address: Route 4, Box 10, Zip 26452; tel. 304/269–8000; David D. Shaffer, Chief Executive Officer (Total facility includes 10 beds in nursing home–type unit) **A**1 9 10 **F**7 8 14 15 16 19 20 21 22 28 30 32 35 37 40 41 42 44 49 64 65 66 67 70 71 **P**8

| | 23 | 10 | 70 | 3321 | 48 | 71710 | 286 | 17647 | 8289 | 272 |

□ WILLIAM R. SHARPE JR. HOSPITAL, Route 33 West, Zip 26452, Mailing Address: P.O. Box 1127, Zip 26452–1127; tel. 304/269–1210; Jack C. Clohan, Jr., Administrator **A**1 5 10 **F**14 15 16 27 45 46 52 54 55 56 57 65 67 73 **P**6

| | 12 | 22 | 150 | 1321 | 126 | 0 | 0 | 19170 | 8041 | 415 |

WHEELING—Ohio County

⊞ OHIO VALLEY MEDICAL CENTER, 2000 Eoff Street, Zip 26003–3870; tel. 304/234–0123; Thomas P. Galinski, President and Chief Executive Officer (Total facility includes 172 beds in nursing home–type unit) **A**1 2 3 5 9 10 13 **F**3 5 7 8 10 11 12 14 15 16 17 18 19 21 22 23 24 25 26 27 28 29 30 31 32 34 35 37 39 40 41 42 44 45 46 47 48 49 51 52 53 54 55 56 57 58 59 60 61 63 64 65 66 67 71 72 73 74 **P**6 8

| | 23 | 10 | 385 | 7141 | 238 | 113397 | 540 | 67864 | 28768 | 923 |

⊞ WHEELING, 1 Medical Park, Zip 26003–0708; tel. 304/243–3000; Donald H. Hofreuter, M.D., Administrator and Chief Executive Officer (Total facility includes 24 beds in nursing home–type unit) **A**1 2 3 5 9 10 **F**3 4 7 8 10 11 12 13 15 16 17 19 21 22 23 24 25 26 27 28 29 30 31 32 34 35 37 39 40 41 42 43 44 45 46 49 51 53 54 55 56 57 58 59 60 63 64 65 66 67 70 71 72 73 74 **P**8
Web address: www.wheelinghosp.com

| | 23 | 10 | 276 | 10908 | 151 | 260162 | 1200 | 122351 | 52354 | 1693 |

Hospital, Address, Telephone, Administrator, Approval, Facility, and Physician Codes, Health Care System, Network	Classi-fication Codes		Utilization Data					Expense (thousands) of dollars		
★ American Hospital Association (AHA) membership □ Joint Commission on Accreditation of Healthcare Organizations (JCAHO) accreditation + American Osteopathic Healthcare Association (AOHA) membership ○ American Osteopathic Association (AOA) accreditation △ Commission on Accreditation of Rehabilitation Facilities (CARF) accreditation Control codes 61, 63, 64, 71, 72 and 73 indicate hospitals listed by AOHA, but not registered by AHA. For definition of numerical codes, see page A4	Control	Service	Staffed Beds	Admissions	Census	Outpatient Visits	Births	Total	Payroll	Personnel

WILLIAMSON—Mingo County

□ WILLIAMSON MEMORIAL HOSPITAL, 859 Alderson Street, Zip 25661–3215, Mailing Address: P.O. Box 1980, Zip 25661–1980; tel. 304/235–2500; William Kinzley, Chief Executive Officer **A**1 9 10 **F**7 8 12 15 16 19 21 22 23 28 30 31 32 35 37 39 41 42 44 46 49 65 66 71 **P**6 8 **S** Health Management Associates, Naples, FL	33	10	76	3817	48	36921	222	23198	8397	289

WISCONSIN

Resident population 5,224 (in thousands)
Resident population in metro areas 66.9%
Birth rate per 1,000 population 13.2
65 years and over 13.2%
Percent of persons without health insurance 8.4%

Hospital, Address, Telephone, Administrator, Approval, Facility, and Physician Codes, Health Care System, Network	Classification Codes		Utilization Data					Expense (thousands) of dollars		
	Control	Service	Staffed Beds	Admissions	Census	Outpatient Visits	Births	Total	Payroll	Personnel

★ American Hospital Association (AHA) membership
□ Joint Commission on Accreditation of Healthcare Organizations (JCAHO) accreditation
+ American Osteopathic Healthcare Association (AOHA) membership
○ American Osteopathic Association (AOA) accreditation
△ Commission on Accreditation of Rehabilitation Facilities (CARF) accreditation
Control codes 61, 63, 64, 71, 72 and 73 indicate hospitals listed by AOHA, but not registered by AHA. For definition of numerical codes, see page A4

AMERY—Polk County

Hospital	Control	Service	Staffed Beds	Admissions	Census	Outpatient Visits	Births	Total	Payroll	Personnel
✖ AMERY REGIONAL MEDICAL CENTER, (Formerly Apple River Hospital), 225 Scholl Court, Zip 54001–1292; tel. 715/268–8000; Michael Karuschak, Jr., Chief Executive Officer (Nonreporting) **A**1 9 10 **S** Quorum Health Group/Quorum Health Resources, Inc., Brentwood, TN	23	10	10	—	—	—	—	—	—	—

ANTIGO—Langlade County

Hospital	Control	Service	Staffed Beds	Admissions	Census	Outpatient Visits	Births	Total	Payroll	Personnel
□ LANGLADE MEMORIAL HOSPITAL, 112 East Fifth Avenue, Zip 54409–2796; tel. 715/623–2331; David R. Schneider, Executive Director **A**1 9 10 **F**1 2 3 4 7 8 9 11 12 16 19 21 22 32 33 34 35 36 37 38 39 40 42 43 44 45 47 49 52 63 65 66 71 74	21	10	43	1679	18	28306	213	18401	8115	271

APPLETON—Outagamie County

Hospital	Control	Service	Staffed Beds	Admissions	Census	Outpatient Visits	Births	Total	Payroll	Personnel
★ APPLETON MEDICAL CENTER, 1818 North Meade Street, Zip 54911–3496; tel. 920/731–4101; Robert H. Malte, Senior Vice President **A**2 3 5 9 10 **F**2 3 4 6 7 8 10 11 12 14 16 18 19 21 22 23 24 32 34 35 36 37 38 39 40 41 42 43 44 45 46 48 49 52 53 54 55 56 57 58 59 60 62 65 66 70 71 72 74 **P**6 8 **S** United Health Group, Appleton, WI **Web address:** www.unitedhealth.org	23	10	146	7273	83	87722	1255	73780	32159	843
✖ △ ST. ELIZABETH HOSPITAL, 1506 South Oneida Street, Zip 54915–1397; tel. 920/738–2000; Otto L. Cox, President (Nonreporting) **A**1 2 3 5 7 10 **S** Wheaton Franciscan Services, Inc., Wheaton, IL	21	10	155	—	—	—	—	—	—	—

ARCADIA—Trempealeau County

Hospital	Control	Service	Staffed Beds	Admissions	Census	Outpatient Visits	Births	Total	Payroll	Personnel
✖ FRANCISCAN SKEMP HEALTHCARE–ARCADIA CAMPUS, 464 South St. Joseph Avenue, Zip 54612–1401; tel. 608/323–3341; Robert M. Tracey, Administrator (Total facility includes 75 beds in nursing home–type unit) **A**1 10 **F**2 3 7 14 16 18 19 22 32 33 34 40 41 44 45 46 49 52 58 64 65 66 71 **P**6 **S** Franciscan Skemp Healthcare, La Crosse, WI	21	10	101	375	76	15755	56	—	—	—

ASHLAND—Ashland County

Hospital	Control	Service	Staffed Beds	Admissions	Census	Outpatient Visits	Births	Total	Payroll	Personnel
✖ MEMORIAL MEDICAL CENTER, 1615 Maple Lane, Zip 54806–3689; tel. 715/682–4563; Daniel J. Hymans, President (Nonreporting) **A**1 9 10 **Web address:** www.ashlandmmc.com	23	10	101	—	—	—	—	—	—	—

BALDWIN—St. Croix County

Hospital	Control	Service	Staffed Beds	Admissions	Census	Outpatient Visits	Births	Total	Payroll	Personnel
★ BALDWIN HOSPITAL, 730 10th Avenue, Zip 54002–0300; tel. 715/684–3311; Richard L. Range, Chief Executive Officer (Nonreporting) **A**9 10 **Web address:** www.baldwinhospital.com	23	10	29	—	—	—	—	—	—	—

BARABOO—Sauk County

Hospital	Control	Service	Staffed Beds	Admissions	Census	Outpatient Visits	Births	Total	Payroll	Personnel
✖ ST. CLARE HOSPITAL AND HEALTH SERVICES, 707 14th Street, Zip 53913–1597; tel. 608/356–1400; David B. Jordahl, FACHE, President **A**1 3 10 **F**2 3 7 8 11 12 14 16 18 19 21 22 24 31 32 33 34 35 36 37 39 40 41 42 44 45 46 49 53 58 63 65 66 71 **S** SSM Health Care, Saint Louis, MO **Web address:** www.stclare.com	21	10	76	2459	24	44520	296	20309	9882	248

BARRON—Barron County

Hospital	Control	Service	Staffed Beds	Admissions	Census	Outpatient Visits	Births	Total	Payroll	Personnel
□ BARRON MEDICAL CENTER–MAYO HEALTH SYSTEM, (Formerly Barron Memorial Medical Center and Skilled Nursing Facility), 1222 Woodland Avenue, Zip 54812–1798; tel. 715/537–3186; Mark D. Wilson, Administrator (Total facility includes 50 beds in nursing home–type unit) **A**1 9 10 **F**7 8 9 11 12 14 16 19 22 24 34 36 37 39 40 41 44 45 46 47 49 54 55 56 57 58 62 64 65 66 71 72 **S** Mayo Foundation, Rochester, MN	23	10	92	1302	60	21837	72	—	—	—

BEAVER DAM—Dodge County

Hospital	Control	Service	Staffed Beds	Admissions	Census	Outpatient Visits	Births	Total	Payroll	Personnel
✖ BEAVER DAM COMMUNITY HOSPITALS, 707 South University Avenue, Zip 53916–3089; tel. 920/887–7181; John R. Landdeck, President (Total facility includes 123 beds in nursing home–type unit) (Nonreporting) **A**1 9 10	23	10	216	—	—	—	—	—	—	—

BELOIT—Rock County

Hospital	Control	Service	Staffed Beds	Admissions	Census	Outpatient Visits	Births	Total	Payroll	Personnel
□ △ BELOIT MEMORIAL HOSPITAL, 1969 West Hart Road, Zip 53511–2299; tel. 608/364–5011; Gregory K. Britton, President and Chief Executive Officer **A**1 7 9 10 **F**2 3 4 5 7 8 9 10 11 12 16 18 19 21 22 23 31 32 33 34 35 37 38 39 40 41 42 43 44 45 46 47 48 49 50 52 53 54 55 56 57 58 59 60 63 65 66 70 71 72 74 **P**1 **Web address:** www.beloitmemorialhospital.org	23	10	124	4953	68	130577	661	47769	22739	711

BERLIN—Green Lake County

Hospital	Control	Service	Staffed Beds	Admissions	Census	Outpatient Visits	Births	Total	Payroll	Personnel
□ BERLIN MEMORIAL HOSPITAL, (Formerly Community Health Network), (Includes Juliette Manor Nursing Home, Community Clinics), 225 Memorial Drive, Zip 54923–1295; tel. 920/361–1313; Craig W. C. Schmidt, President and Chief Executive Officer (Total facility includes 106 beds in nursing home–type unit) (Nonreporting) **A**1 9 10	23	10	167	—	—	—	—	—	—	—

BLACK RIVER FALLS—Jackson County

Hospital	Control	Service	Staffed Beds	Admissions	Census	Outpatient Visits	Births	Total	Payroll	Personnel
□ BLACK RIVER MEMORIAL HOSPITAL, 711 West Adams Street, Zip 54615–9113; tel. 715/284–5361; Stanley J. Gaynor, Chief Executive Officer and Administrator (Nonreporting) **A**1 9 10	23	10	38	—	—	—	—	—	—	—

Hospital, Address, Telephone, Administrator, Approval, Facility, and Physician Codes, Health Care System, Network	Classi-fication Codes		Utilization Data					Expense (thousands) of dollars		
★ American Hospital Association (AHA) membership □ Joint Commission on Accreditation of Healthcare Organizations (JCAHO) accreditation + American Osteopathic Healthcare Association (AOHA) membership ○ American Osteopathic Association (AOA) accreditation △ Commission on Accreditation of Rehabilitation Facilities (CARF) accreditation Control codes 61, 63, 64, 71, 72 and 73 indicate hospitals listed by AOHA, but not registered by AHA. For definition of numerical codes, see page A4	Control	Service	Staffed Beds	Admissions	Census	Outpatient Visits	Births	Total	Payroll	Personnel

BLOOMER—Chippewa County

| ⊞ BLOOMER COMMUNITY MEMORIAL HOSPITAL AND THE MAPLEWOOD, 1501 Thompson Street, Zip 54724–1299; tel. 715/568–2000; John Perushek, Administrator (Total facility includes 75 beds in nursing home–type unit) **A**1 9 10 **F**1 7 8 9 14 16 19 21 22 32 33 34 40 41 42 44 48 49 53 54 56 57 58 64 65 71 74 **S** Mayo Foundation, Rochester, MN | 23 | 10 | 101 | 596 | 84 | 7804 | 54 | — | — | — |

BOSCOBEL—Grant County

| BOSCOBEL AREA HEALTH CARE, 205 Parker Street, Zip 53805–1698; tel. 608/375–4112; Steven T. Moburg, Administrator (Total facility includes 85 beds in nursing home–type unit) (Nonreporting) **A**10 | 23 | 10 | 131 | — | — | — | — | — | — | — |

BROOKFIELD—Waukesha County

| ⊞ △ ELMBROOK MEMORIAL HOSPITAL, 19333 West North Avenue, Zip 53045–4198; tel. 414/785–2000; Kimry A. Johnsrud, President **A**1 7 9 10 **F**2 3 4 5 6 7 8 10 11 12 18 19 21 22 23 31 32 33 34 35 36 37 38 39 40 41 42 43 44 45 46 48 49 52 53 54 55 56 57 58 59 60 62 63 65 66 70 71 74 **P**2 5 7 8 **S** Wheaton Franciscan Services, Inc., Wheaton, IL | 21 | 10 | 136 | 6438 | 70 | 75306 | 994 | 55061 | 21314 | 434 |

BURLINGTON—Racine County

| ⊞ MEMORIAL HOSPITAL CORPORATION OF BURLINGTON, (Includes Aurora Medical Center, 10400 75th Street, Kenosha, Zip 53142; tel. 414/697–7000; Seonaid A. Ritz, R.N., Site Administrator), 252 McHenry Street, Zip 53105–1828; tel. 414/767–6000; Loren J. Anderson, Executive Vice President **A**1 9 10 **F**7 8 9 10 11 12 16 18 19 21 22 23 34 35 37 39 40 41 42 44 45 46 48 56 65 71 74 **S** Aurora Health Care, Milwaukee, WI | 23 | 10 | 87 | 2931 | 31 | 82241 | 540 | 32912 | 12948 | 330 |

CHILTON—Calumet County

| ⊞ CALUMET MEDICAL CENTER, 614 Memorial Drive, Zip 53014–1597; tel. 920/849–2386; Lea Whitby, President **A**1 9 10 **F**3 8 10 11 12 16 18 19 21 22 32 33 34 35 36 37 39 41 42 44 45 46 47 49 53 54 55 56 57 58 59 65 66 70 71 74 | 23 | 10 | 53 | 584 | 7 | 29882 | 0 | 9092 | 4093 | 138 |

CHIPPEWA FALLS—Chippewa County

| ⊞ ST. JOSEPH'S HOSPITAL, 2661 County Highway I, Zip 54729–1498; tel. 715/723–1811; David B. Fish, Executive Vice President and Administrator **A**1 9 10 **F**2 3 7 8 11 12 14 16 19 21 22 32 33 34 36 37 39 40 41 42 44 45 46 47 56 65 71 **S** Hospital Sisters Health System, Springfield, IL | 21 | 10 | 127 | 3336 | 50 | 56742 | 398 | 28999 | 14655 | 394 |

COLUMBUS—Columbia County

| ⊞ COLUMBUS COMMUNITY HOSPITAL, 1515 Park Avenue, Zip 53925; tel. 920/623–2200; Charles Smith, Administrator (Nonreporting) **A**1 10 | 23 | 10 | 53 | — | — | — | — | — | — | — |

CUBA CITY—Grant County

| CUBA CITY MEDICAL CENTER See Southwest Health Center, Platteville | | | | | | | | | | |

CUMBERLAND—Barron County

| □ CUMBERLAND MEMORIAL HOSPITAL, 1110 Seventh Avenue, Zip 54829, Mailing Address: P.O. Box 37, Zip 54829–0037; tel. 715/822–2741; Carol Kellermann, Acting Administrator (Total facility includes 71 beds in nursing home–type unit) **A**1 10 **F**2 7 12 16 19 21 22 32 34 35 39 40 41 42 44 45 46 52 54 56 57 58 62 63 64 65 66 70 71 **P**5 6 | 23 | 10 | 131 | 1464 | 86 | 7729 | 67 | — | — | — |

DARLINGTON—Lafayette County

| MEMORIAL HOSPITAL OF LAFAYETTE COUNTY, 800 Clay Street, Zip 53530–1228, Mailing Address: P.O. Box 70, Zip 53530–0070; tel. 608/776–4466; Sherry Kudronowicz, Administrator **A**10 **F**2 3 7 8 14 19 22 34 35 40 44 45 46 48 49 52 56 65 71 | 13 | 10 | 28 | 364 | 3 | 17671 | 42 | 4144 | 1500 | 61 |

DODGEVILLE—Iowa County

| ⊞ MEMORIAL HOSPITAL OF IOWA COUNTY, 825 South Iowa Street, Zip 53533–1999; tel. 608/935–2711; Ray Marmorstone, Chief Executive Officer (Total facility includes 44 beds in nursing home–type unit) (Nonreporting) **A**1 9 10 **S** Brim Healthcare, Inc., Brentwood, TN | 23 | 10 | 82 | — | — | — | — | — | — | — |

DURAND—Pepin County

| CHIPPEWA VALLEY HOSPITAL AND OAKVIEW CARE CENTER, 1220 Third Avenue West, Zip 54736–1600, Mailing Address: P.O. Box 224, Zip 54736–0224; tel. 715/672–4211; Douglas R. Peterson, President and Chief Executive Officer (Total facility includes 58 beds in nursing home–type unit) **A**9 10 **F**7 8 19 22 24 34 36 39 40 44 45 48 49 64 65 71 **S** Adventist Health System Sunbelt Health Care Corporation, Winter Park, FL | 21 | 10 | 83 | 784 | 76 | 10352 | 36 | — | — | — |

EAGLE RIVER—Vilas County

| ★ EAGLE RIVER MEMORIAL HOSPITAL, 201 Hospital Road, Zip 54521–8835; tel. 715/479–7411; Patricia L. Richardson, Chief Executive Officer **A**9 10 **F**2 3 6 7 8 11 12 14 16 19 21 22 24 32 33 34 35 36 39 40 41 42 44 45 46 48 49 52 62 65 66 71 74 | 23 | 10 | 9 | 360 | 5 | 16805 | 0 | 7437 | 3519 | 115 |

EAU CLAIRE—Eau Claire County

| □ LUTHER HOSPITAL, 1221 Whipple Street, Zip 54702–4105; tel. 715/838–3311; William Rupp, M.D., President and Chief Executive Officer **A**1 2 3 5 9 10 **F**3 4 7 8 9 10 11 12 19 21 22 24 32 33 34 35 37 38 39 40 41 42 43 44 45 46 47 48 52 53 54 55 56 57 58 59 60 63 65 66 70 71 74 **S** Mayo Foundation, Rochester, MN | 23 | 10 | 179 | 8048 | 92 | 121131 | 907 | 70314 | 29804 | 1015 |
| ⊞ △ SACRED HEART HOSPITAL, 900 West Clairemont Avenue, Zip 54701–5105; tel. 715/839–4121; Stephen F. Ronstrom, Executive Vice President and Administrator (Nonreporting) **A**1 2 3 5 7 9 10 **S** Hospital Sisters Health System, Springfield, IL
Web address: www.sacredhearthospital–ec.org | 21 | 10 | 261 | — | — | — | — | — | — | — |

Hospital, Address, Telephone, Administrator, Approval, Facility, and Physician Codes, Health Care System, Network	Classi-fication Codes		Utilization Data					Expense (thousands) of dollars		
★ American Hospital Association (AHA) membership □ Joint Commission on Accreditation of Healthcare Organizations (JCAHO) accreditation + American Osteopathic Healthcare Association (AOHA) membership ○ American Osteopathic Association (AOA) accreditation △ Commission on Accreditation of Rehabilitation Facilities (CARF) accreditation Control codes 61, 63, 64, 71, 72 and 73 indicate hospitals listed by AOHA, but not registered by AHA. For definition of numerical codes, see page A4	Control	Service	Staffed Beds	Admissions	Census	Outpatient Visits	Births	Total	Payroll	Personnel

EDGERTON—Rock County

MEMORIAL COMMUNITY HOSPITAL, 313 Stoughton Road, Zip 53534–1198; tel. 608/884–3441; Charles E. Bruhn, Chief Executive Officer (Total facility includes 61 beds in nursing home–type unit) (Nonreporting) **A**9 10 **S** Brim Healthcare, Inc., Brentwood, TN
| | | 23 | 10 | 115 | — | | — | | — | — | — |

ELKHORN—Walworth County

⊠ △ LAKELAND MEDICAL CENTER, West 3985 County Road NN, Zip 53121, Mailing Address: P.O. Box 1002, Zip 53121–1002; tel. 414/741–2000; Loren J. Anderson, Executive Vice President **A**1 7 9 10 **F**2 3 7 8 11 12 16 19 21 22 34 35 37 39 40 41 42 44 45 46 52 53 54 56 58 59 63 65 66 71 72 74 **P**5 **S** Aurora Health Care, Milwaukee, WI
| | | 23 | 10 | 78 | 3372 | 37 | 55815 | 475 | 31279 | 12638 | 392 |

FOND DU LAC—Fond Du Lac County

□ △ AGNESIAN HEALTHCARE, 430 East Division Street, Zip 54935–0385; tel. 920/929–2300; Robert A. Fale, President **A**1 2 7 9 10 **F**1 2 3 4 5 7 8 10 11 12 16 18 19 21 23 31 32 33 34 35 36 37 39 40 41 42 43 44 45 48 49 52 53 54 55 56 57 58 59 60 63 64 65 66 70 71 72 74 **P**3
Web address: www.agnesian.com
| | | 21 | 10 | 179 | 6525 | 80 | 194449 | 936 | 92361 | 36194 | 1066 |

FORT ATKINSON—Jefferson County

⊠ FORT ATKINSON MEMORIAL HEALTH SERVICES, 611 East Sherman Avenue, Zip 53538–1998; tel. 920/568–5000; John C. Albaugh, President and Chief Executive Officer (Total facility includes 28 beds in nursing home–type unit) **A**1 9 10 **F**3 7 8 9 11 12 16 19 21 22 23 24 32 33 34 35 37 39 40 41 42 44 45 46 47 48 49 54 58 63 64 65 66 71 72 74 **P**6 7
| | | 23 | 10 | 102 | 4145 | 54 | 75083 | 469 | | | |

FRIENDSHIP—Adams County

□ ADAMS COUNTY MEMORIAL HOSPITAL AND NURSING CARE UNIT, 402 West Lake Street, Zip 53934–9699, Mailing Address: P.O. Box 40, Zip 53934–0040; tel. 608/339–3331; Steven R. Nockerts, Administrator and Chief Executive Officer (Total facility includes 18 beds in nursing home–type unit) **A**1 9 10 **F**1 2 3 8 12 16 18 19 21 22 32 33 34 35 39 41 44 45 48 49 55 56 57 58 64 65 66 71 **P**5
| | | 23 | 10 | 58 | 655 | 28 | 35500 | 0 | | | |

GRANTSBURG—Burnett County

★ BURNETT MEDICAL CENTER, 257 West St. George Avenue, Zip 54840–7827; tel. 715/463–5353; Timothy J. Wick, Chief Executive Officer (Total facility includes 53 beds in nursing home–type unit) **A**9 10 **F**1 7 8 14 16 19 21 22 34 35 39 40 41 42 44 45 46 48 49 64 65 66 71 72 **S** Brim Healthcare, Inc., Brentwood, TN
| | | 23 | 10 | 70 | 773 | 59 | 9789 | 55 | — | — | — |

GREEN BAY—Brown County

⊠ BELLIN HOSPITAL, 744 South Webster Avenue, Zip 54301–3581, Mailing Address: P.O. Box 23400, Zip 54305–3400; tel. 920/433–3500; George Kerwin, President **A**1 9 10 **F**4 7 8 10 11 14 16 19 21 23 24 32 33 34 35 37 39 40 41 42 43 44 45 46 63 65 66 71 72 **P**5 6
Web address: www.bellin.org
| | | 21 | 10 | 180 | 9803 | 99 | 373172 | 1914 | 122457 | 60161 | 1749 |

□ BELLIN PSYCHIATRIC CENTER, 301 East St. Joseph Street, Zip 54301–2241, Mailing Address: P.O. Box 23725, Zip 54305–3725; tel. 920/433–3630; Robert W. Fry, President **A**1 10 **F**2 3 11 14 19 21 34 35 45 48 50 52 53 54 55 56 57 58 59 63 65 71
Web address: www.bellin.org
| | | 21 | 22 | 60 | 1304 | 26 | 20100 | 0 | 7314 | 4000 | 94 |

BROWN COUNTY MENTAL HEALTH CENTER, 2900 St. Anthony Drive, Zip 54311–5899; tel. 414/468–1136; Mark Quam, Executive Director **A**10 **F**2 3 12 18 34 39 52 53 54 55 56 57 58 65
| | | 13 | 22 | 74 | 1599 | 30 | 15419 | 0 | 7070 | 4198 | 136 |

⊠ ST. MARY'S HOSPITAL MEDICAL CENTER, 1726 Shawano Avenue, Zip 54303–3282; tel. 920/498–4200; James G. Coller, Executive Vice President and Administrator **A**1 9 10 **F**7 8 11 16 19 21 22 24 33 34 35 36 37 39 40 42 44 45 46 47 56 63 65 70 71 74 **S** Hospital Sisters Health System, Springfield, IL
Web address: www.stmgb.org
| | | 21 | 10 | 119 | 4591 | 50 | 75276 | 570 | 41539 | 17749 | 494 |

⊠ △ ST. VINCENT HOSPITAL, 835 South Van Buren Street, Zip 54307–3508, Mailing Address: P.O. Box 13508, Zip 54307–3508; tel. 920/433–0111; Joseph J. Neidenbach, Executive Vice President and Administrator (Nonreporting) **A**1 2 7 9 10 **S** Hospital Sisters Health System, Springfield, IL
Web address: www.stvgb.org
| | | 21 | 10 | 353 | — | | — | | — | — | — |

GREENFIELD—Milwaukee County

□ VENCOR HOSPITAL–MILWAUKEE, (Formerly THC–Milwaukee), 5017 South 110th Street, Zip 53228; tel. 414/427–8282; Daniel R. West, Administrator **A**1 9 10 **F**4 6 10 12 16 18 19 21 22 32 35 37 39 41 42 44 45 46 48 49 50 54 57 63 65 71 **S** Vencor, Incorporated, Louisville, KY
| | | 33 | 10 | 34 | 230 | 25 | 4 | 0 | 10469 | 4383 | 124 |

HARTFORD—Washington County

⊠ HARTFORD MEMORIAL HOSPITAL, 1032 East Sumner Street, Zip 53027–1698; tel. 414/673–2300; Mark Schwartz, Administrator **A**1 9 10 **F**1 7 8 11 12 14 16 19 21 22 24 32 33 34 35 36 37 39 40 41 42 44 45 49 63 64 65 66 70 71 74 **S** Aurora Health Care, Milwaukee, WI
| | | 23 | 10 | 71 | 1830 | 32 | 54585 | 256 | 20770 | 8796 | 280 |

HAYWARD—Sawyer County

⊠ HAYWARD AREA MEMORIAL HOSPITAL AND NURSING HOME, 11040 State Road 77, Zip 54843, Mailing Address: Route 3, Box 3999, Zip 54843–3999; tel. 715/634–8911; Barbara A. Peickert, R.N., Chief Executive Officer (Total facility includes 76 beds in nursing home–type unit) (Nonreporting) **A**1 9 10
| | | 23 | 10 | 117 | — | | — | | — | — | — |

Hospital, Address, Telephone, Administrator, Approval, Facility, and Physician Codes, Health Care System, Network	Classi-fication Codes		Utilization Data					Expense (thousands) of dollars		
★ American Hospital Association (AHA) membership □ Joint Commission on Accreditation of Healthcare Organizations (JCAHO) accreditation + American Osteopathic Healthcare Association (AOHA) membership ○ American Osteopathic Association (AOA) accreditation △ Commission on Accreditation of Rehabilitation Facilities (CARF) accreditation Control codes 61, 63, 64, 71, 72 and 73 indicate hospitals listed by AOHA, but not registered by AHA. For definition of numerical codes, see page A4	Control	Service	Staffed Beds	Admissions	Census	Outpatient Visits	Births	Total	Payroll	Personnel

HAZEL GREEN—Grant County

HAZEL GREEN HOSPITAL See Southwest Health Center, Platteville

HILLSBORO—Vernon County

★ ST. JOSEPH'S MEMORIAL HOSPITAL AND NURSING HOME, 400 Water Avenue, Zip 54634–0527, Mailing Address: P.O. Box 527, Zip 54634–0527; tel. 608/489–2211; Nancy Bauman, Chief Executive Officer (Total facility includes 65 beds in nursing home–type unit) (Nonreporting) **A**10 **S** Brim Healthcare, Inc., Brentwood, TN

| | 21 | 10 | 85 | — | — | — | — | — | — | — |

HUDSON—St. Croix County

□ HUDSON MEDICAL CENTER, 400 Wisconsin Street, Zip 54016–1600; tel. 715/386–9321; Marian M. Furlong, R.N., Chief Executive Officer **A**1 9 10 **F**1 3 7 8 11 12 14 16 19 21 22 24 32 33 34 35 36 37 39 40 41 42 44 45 46 48 49 54 65 66 71 **P**4 7

| | 23 | 10 | 39 | 1114 | 17 | 17060 | 172 | 9406 | 4396 | 137 |

JANESVILLE—Rock County

✠ MERCY HEALTH SYSTEM, 1000 Mineral Point Avenue, Zip 53545–5003, Mailing Address: P.O. Box 5003, Zip 53547–5003; tel. 608/756–6000; Javon R. Bea, President and Chief Executive Officer (Nonreporting) **A**1 2 3 9 10

| | 23 | 10 | 216 | | | | | | | |

KENOSHA—Kenosha County

✠ KENOSHA HOSPITAL AND MEDICAL CENTER, 6308 Eighth Avenue, Zip 53143–5082; tel. 414/656–2011; Richard O. Schmidt, Jr., President and Chief Executive Officer **A**1 9 10 **F**4 5 7 8 10 11 12 14 16 19 21 22 23 24 31 32 33 34 35 36 37 38 39 40 41 42 43 44 45 46 48 49 56 63 65 66 70 71 72 74 **P**6 8 **S** Horizon Healthcare, Inc., Milwaukee, WI

| | 23 | 10 | 116 | 6402 | 67 | 136533 | 977 | 73552 | 36210 | 818 |

✠ ST. CATHERINE'S HOSPITAL, 3556 Seventh Avenue, Zip 53140–2595; tel. 414/656–2011; Richard O. Schmidt, Jr., President and Chief Executive Officer (Nonreporting) **A**1 2 3 9 10 **S** Wheaton Franciscan Services, Inc., Wheaton, IL

| | 21 | 10 | 148 | | | | | | | |

KEWAUNEE—Kewaunee County

✠ ST. MARY'S KEWAUNEE AREA MEMORIAL HOSPITAL, 810 Lincoln Street, Zip 54216; tel. 920/388–2210; Cathie A. Kocourek, Acting Administrator **A**1 9 10 **F**7 8 22 32 33 34 39 40 44 45 46 65 71 72 **S** Aurora Health Care, Milwaukee, WI

| | 23 | 10 | 18 | 284 | 3 | 15935 | 27 | 3371 | 1922 | 64 |

LA CROSSE—La Crosse County

✠ FRANCISCAN SKEMP HEALTHCARE–LA CROSSE CAMPUS, 700 West Avenue South, Zip 54601–4783; tel. 608/785–0940; Glenn Forbes, M.D., President and Chief Executive Officer **A**1 2 3 10 **F**2 3 4 6 7 8 9 10 11 12 16 18 19 21 22 23 24 32 33 34 35 36 37 38 39 40 41 42 43 44 45 46 47 48 49 52 53 54 55 56 57 58 59 60 62 65 66 70 71 72 74 **P**8 **S** Franciscan Skemp Healthcare, La Crosse, WI
Web address: www.mayo.edu/fsh/

| | 21 | 10 | 213 | 8794 | 105 | 79752 | 718 | 68050 | 31394 | 947 |

✠ △ LUTHERAN HOSPITAL–LA CROSSE, 1910 South Avenue, Zip 54601–9980; tel. 608/785–0530; Philip J. Dahlberg, M.D., President **A**1 2 5 7 8 9 10 **F**2 3 4 5 6 7 9 10 11 12 14 16 18 19 21 22 23 31 32 33 34 35 36 37 38 39 40 41 42 43 44 45 46 47 48 49 52 53 54 55 56 57 58 59 60 62 63 65 66 70 71 72 74
Web address: www.gundluth.org

| | 23 | 10 | 286 | 13442 | 155 | 106966 | 1556 | 138177 | 59711 | 1728 |

LADYSMITH—Rusk County

RUSK COUNTY MEMORIAL HOSPITAL AND NURSING HOME, 900 College Avenue West, Zip 54848–2116; tel. 715/532–5561; J. Michael Shaw, Administrator (Total facility includes 99 beds in nursing home–type unit) **A**10 **F**2 3 7 8 9 11 14 16 19 22 34 37 38 39 40 42 44 45 48 52 53 54 55 56 57 58 59 64 65 70 71

| | 13 | 10 | 134 | 1058 | 102 | 25638 | 124 | — | — | — |

LANCASTER—Grant County

✠ GRANT REGIONAL HEALTH CENTER, 507 South Monroe Street, Zip 53813–2099; tel. 608/723–2143; Larry D. Rentfro, FACHE, President and Chief Executive Officer **A**1 10 **F**7 8 14 16 19 22 24 32 33 34 35 37 39 40 41 42 44 45 48 63 65 66 71 72 74 **P**5 **S** Brim Healthcare, Inc., Brentwood, TN

| | 23 | 10 | 28 | 634 | 6 | 20274 | 101 | 7301 | 3154 | 108 |

MADISON—Dane County

□ MENDOTA MENTAL HEALTH INSTITUTE, 301 Troy Drive, Zip 53704–1599; tel. 608/243–2500; Steve Watters, Chief Executive Officer **A**1 3 5 10 **F**2 12 18 22 34 39 45 46 52 53 54 55 56 57 58 65 **P**6

| | 12 | 22 | 257 | 759 | 221 | 13237 | 0 | 38227 | 23366 | 664 |

✠ △ MERITER HOSPITAL, (Includes Meriter–Capitol), 202 South Park Street, Zip 53715–1599; tel. 608/267–6000; Terri L. Potter, President and Chief Executive Officer **A**1 3 5 7 10 **F**1 2 3 4 5 6 7 8 9 10 11 12 16 19 21 22 23 24 32 33 34 35 36 37 38 39 40 41 42 43 44 45 46 47 48 49 52 53 54 55 56 57 58 59 60 62 65 66 70 71 72 74
Web address: www.meriter.com

| | 23 | 10 | 375 | 14364 | 195 | 139332 | 3331 | 150467 | 62095 | 1511 |

✠ ST. MARYS HOSPITAL MEDICAL CENTER, 707 South Mills Street, Zip 53715–0450; tel. 608/251–6100; Gerald W. Lefert, President **A**1 3 5 10 **F**1 4 7 8 10 11 12 16 18 19 21 22 23 24 32 33 34 35 37 38 39 40 41 42 43 44 45 46 47 49 52 54 55 56 57 60 65 70 71 **S** SSM Health Care, Saint Louis, MO
Web address: www.ssmhc.com

| | 23 | 10 | 303 | 16819 | 207 | 47273 | 2846 | 137630 | 55571 | 1233 |

✠ △ UNIVERSITY OF WISCONSIN HOSPITAL AND CLINICS, (Includes University of Wisconsin Children's Hospital), 600 Highland Avenue, Zip 53792–0002; tel. 608/263–6400; Gordon M. Derzon, Chief Executive Officer **A**1 3 5 7 8 9 10 **F**3 4 5 8 9 10 11 12 14 16 19 21 22 23 24 31 32 34 35 37 39 40 41 42 43 44 45 46 47 48 49 50 52 53 54 55 56 57 58 60 63 65 66 70 71 72 74
Web address: www.biostat.wisc.edu/

| | 23 | 10 | 474 | 20852 | 337 | 458750 | 0 | 316303 | 128905 | 3909 |

Hospital, Address, Telephone, Administrator, Approval, Facility, and Physician Codes, Health Care System, Network	Classi-fication Codes		Utilization Data					Expense (thousands) of dollars		
★ American Hospital Association (AHA) membership □ Joint Commission on Accreditation of Healthcare Organizations (JCAHO) accreditation + American Osteopathic Healthcare Association (AOHA) membership ○ American Osteopathic Association (AOA) accreditation △ Commission on Accreditation of Rehabilitation Facilities (CARF) accreditation Control codes 61, 63, 64, 71, 72 and 73 indicate hospitals listed by AOHA, but not registered by AHA. For definition of numerical codes, see page A4	Control	Service	Staffed Beds	Admissions	Census	Outpatient Visits	Births	Total	Payroll	Personnel

⊠ WILLIAM S. MIDDLETON MEMORIAL VETERANS HOSPITAL, 2500 Overlook Terrace, Zip 53705–2286; tel. 608/256–1901; Nathan L. Geraths, Director (Nonreporting) **A**1 3 5 **S** Department of Veterans Affairs, Washington, DC	45	10	200	—	—	—	—	—	—	—
MANITOWOC—Manitowoc County										
⊠ △ HOLY FAMILY MEMORIAL MEDICAL CENTER, 2300 Western Avenue, Zip 54220, Mailing Address: P.O. Box 1450, Zip 54221–1450; tel. 920/684–2011; Daniel B. McGinty, President and Chief Executive Officer **A**1 7 9 10 **F**1 2 3 7 8 10 11 12 14 16 19 21 22 23 32 33 34 35 36 37 39 40 41 42 44 45 48 49 50 52 53 55 56 58 59 60 63 65 66 71 **P**6 **S** Franciscan Sisters of Christian Charity HealthCare Ministry, Inc, Manitowoc, WI **Web address:** www.hfmhealth.org	21	10	176	5814	74	159386	465	62049	30233	897
MARINETTE—Marinette County										
⊠ BAY AREA MEDICAL CENTER, 3100 Shore Drive, Zip 54143–4297; tel. 715/735–6621; Rick Ament, President and Chief Executive Officer **A**1 9 10 **F**3 7 8 11 12 18 19 21 22 34 35 37 39 40 41 42 44 45 46 47 49 52 54 55 57 58 60 65 66 71 72 74	23	10	115	4505	56	47691	379	38136	18125	436
MARSHFIELD—Wood County										
NORWOOD HEALTH CENTER, 1600 North Chestnut Avenue, Zip 54449–1499; tel. 715/384–2188; Randy Bestul, Administrator **A**10 **F**12 52 53 57 58 65	13	22	19	472	7	0	0	1467	911	43
⊠ △ SAINT JOSEPH'S HOSPITAL, 611 St. Joseph Avenue, Zip 54449–1898; tel. 715/387–1713; Michael A. Schmidt, President and Chief Executive Officer **A**1 2 3 5 7 10 **F**2 3 4 5 6 7 9 10 11 14 16 19 21 22 23 31 32 33 34 35 36 37 38 39 40 41 42 43 44 45 46 47 48 49 52 53 56 57 58 59 60 63 65 66 70 71 74 **P**8 **S** Marian Health System, Tulsa, OK	21	10	524	16451	248	135203	1226	157725	60239	1849
MAUSTON—Juneau County										
□ MILE BLUFF MEDICAL CENTER, 1050 Division Street, Zip 53948–1997; tel. 608/847–6161; Daniel N. Manders, President and Chief Executive Officer (Total facility includes 60 beds in nursing home–type unit) **A**1 10 **F**7 8 16 19 21 22 32 33 34 35 39 40 41 42 44 45 46 49 62 63 64 65 66 71 72 **P**6	23	10	97	2030	77	53230	215	—	—	—
MEDFORD—Taylor County										
⊠ MEMORIAL HOSPITAL OF TAYLOR COUNTY, (Includes Memorial Nursing Home), 135 South Gibson Street, Zip 54451–1696; tel. 715/748–8100; Greg Roraff, President and Chief Executive Officer (Total facility includes 104 beds in nursing home–type unit) **A**1 9 10 **F**1 6 7 8 11 16 19 21 22 32 34 35 37 40 41 44 45 46 49 54 56 63 64 65 71 **P**4 7	23	10	153	1092	115	26308	167	—	—	—
MENOMONEE FALLS—Waukesha County										
⊠ △ COMMUNITY MEMORIAL HOSPITAL, W180 N8085 Town Hall Road, Zip 53051, Mailing Address: P.O. Box 408, Zip 53052–0408; tel. 414/251–1000; Robert Eugene Drisner, President and Chief Executive Officer (Nonreporting) **A**1 2 7 9 10 **S** Horizon Healthcare, Inc., Milwaukee, WI **Web address:** www.communitymemorial.com	23	10	153	—	—	—	—	—	—	—
MENOMONIE—Dunn County										
□ MYRTLE WERTH HOSPITAL–MAYO HEALTH SYSTEM, 2321 Stout Road, Zip 54751–2397; tel. 715/235–5531; Thomas Miller, III, Chief Executive Officer **A**1 3 9 10 **F**7 8 11 16 19 21 22 34 35 37 39 40 41 44 45 48 63 65 66 71	23	10	55	1547	13	31681	272	9563	4439	159
MEQUON—Ozaukee County										
⊠ ST. MARY'S HOSPITAL OZAUKEE, 13111 North Port Washington Road, Zip 53097–2416; tel. 414/243–7300; Therese B. Pandl, Senior Vice President and Chief Operating Officer (Nonreporting) **A**1 9 10 **S** Daughters of Charity National Health System, Saint Louis, MO **Web address:** www.columbia–stmarys.com	21	10	82	—	—	—	—	—	—	—
MERRILL—Lincoln County										
⊠ GOOD SAMARITAN HEALTH CENTER OF MERRILL, 601 Center Avenue South, Zip 54452–3404; tel. 715/536–5511; Michael Hammer, President and Chief Executive Officer **A**1 9 10 **F**1 3 4 5 7 8 9 10 11 12 14 18 19 21 22 23 32 33 34 35 36 37 39 40 41 42 44 45 47 49 53 54 55 56 57 58 59 65 66 70 71 74 **S** Catholic Health Initiatives, Denver, CO	21	10	63	1362	20	43279	173	11342	5165	160
MILWAUKEE—Milwaukee County										
CHARTER HOSPITAL OF MILWAUKEE, 11101 West Lincoln Avenue, Zip 53227–1166; tel. 414/327–3000; Robert Kwech, Chief Executive Officer (Nonreporting) **A**9 10 **S** Magellan Health Services, Atlanta, GA	33	22	80	—	—	—	—	—	—	—
⊠ CHILDREN'S HOSPITAL OF WISCONSIN, 9000 West Wisconsin Avenue, Zip 53226–4810, Mailing Address: P.O. Box 1997, Zip 53201–1997; tel. 414/266–2000; Jon E. Vice, President and Chief Executive Officer **A**1 3 5 8 9 10 **F**4 5 9 10 11 12 16 19 21 22 23 31 32 33 34 35 38 39 41 42 43 44 45 46 47 48 49 52 53 54 56 58 60 63 65 66 70 71 72 **P**4 **Web address:** www.chw.org	23	50	222	18188	167	191188	0	159037	53302	1498
⊠ CLEMENT J. ZABLOCKI VETERANS AFFAIRS MEDICAL CENTER, 5000 West National Avenue, Zip 53295; tel. 414/384–2000; Glen W. Grippen, Director (Total facility includes 196 beds in nursing home–type unit) (Nonreporting) **A**1 2 3 5 8 **S** Department of Veterans Affairs, Washington, DC	45	10	566	—	—	—	—	—	—	—
⊠ △ COLUMBIA HOSPITAL, 2025 East Newport Avenue, Zip 53211–2990; tel. 414/961–3300; Susan Henckel, Executive Vice President and Chief Executive Officer **A**1 2 3 5 7 9 10 **F**2 3 4 5 7 8 9 10 11 12 14 16 18 19 21 22 23 24 31 32 33 34 35 37 38 39 40 41 42 43 44 45 46 47 48 49 52 53 54 55 56 57 58 59 60 63 65 66 70 71 72 74 **P**6 **S** Horizon Healthcare, Inc., Milwaukee, WI	23	10	334	10800	155	271308	1121	134504	54102	1392

Hospital, Address, Telephone, Administrator, Approval, Facility, and Physician Codes, Health Care System, Network	Classi-fication Codes		Utilization Data					Expense (thousands) of dollars		
★ American Hospital Association (AHA) membership □ Joint Commission on Accreditation of Healthcare Organizations (JCAHO) accreditation + American Osteopathic Healthcare Association (AOHA) membership ○ American Osteopathic Association (AOA) accreditation △ Commission on Accreditation of Rehabilitation Facilities (CARF) accreditation Control codes 61, 63, 64, 71, 72 and 73 indicate hospitals listed by AOHA, but not registered by AHA. For definition of numerical codes, see page A4	Control	Service	Staffed Beds	Admissions	Census	Outpatient Visits	Births	Total	Payroll	Personnel
☒ △ FROEDTERT MEMORIAL LUTHERAN HOSPITAL, 9200 West Wisconsin Avenue, Zip 53226–3596, Mailing Address: P.O. Box 26099, Zip 53226–3596; tel. 414/259–3000; William D. Petasnick, President **A**1 2 3 5 7 8 9 10 **F**1 3 4 5 7 8 10 11 12 14 16 19 21 22 23 31 32 33 34 35 36 37 38 39 40 41 42 43 44 45 46 48 49 52 54 55 56 57 58 60 62 63 65 66 70 71 72 74 **S** Horizon Healthcare, Inc., Milwaukee, WI	23	10	467	18236	349	343665	745	283084	78770	2232
☒ MILWAUKEE COUNTY MENTAL HEALTH DIVISION, 9455 Watertown Plank Road, Zip 53226–3559; tel. 414/257–6995; M. Kathleen Eilers, Administrator (Total facility includes 216 beds in nursing home–type unit) **A**1 3 5 10 **F**2 3 7 9 11 12 14 18 19 21 22 31 34 35 38 39 40 42 44 46 47 48 49 52 53 56 57 58 59 64 65 70 71 72	13	22	372	3496	339	17182	0	—	—	—
MILWAUKEE PSYCHIATRIC HOSPITAL See Wauwatosa										
○ NORTHWEST GENERAL HOSPITAL, 5310 West Capitol Drive, Zip 53216–2299; tel. 414/447–8543; C. Dennis Barr, President and Chief Executive Officer **A**10 11 **F**2 3 8 12 19 21 22 34 35 37 39 41 42 44 45 48 49 63 65 71 72	23	10	98	2274	30	26813	0	12306	6524	212
☒ △ SACRED HEART REHABILITATION INSTITUTE, 2350 North Lake Drive, Zip 53211–4507, Mailing Address: P.O. Box 392, Zip 53201–0392; tel. 414/298–6700; William H. Lange, Administrator and Senior Vice President **A**1 7 10 **F**12 14 16 19 21 34 35 39 41 45 46 48 49 54 57 65 66 71 **P**1 5 6 **S** Daughters of Charity National Health System, Saint Louis, MO	21	46	59	744	28	21568	0	17872	9208	163
☒ △ SINAI SAMARITAN MEDICAL CENTER, 945 North 12th Street, Zip 53233–1337, Mailing Address: P.O. Box 342, Zip 53201–0342; tel. 414/219–2000; Leonard E. Wilk, Administrator **A**1 2 3 5 7 8 9 10 **F**1 2 3 4 5 7 8 10 11 12 14 16 18 19 21 22 23 24 31 32 33 34 35 36 37 38 39 40 41 42 43 44 45 46 47 48 49 52 53 54 55 56 57 58 59 60 62 63 65 66 70 71 72 74 **P**4 6 **S** Aurora Health Care, Milwaukee, WI **Web address:** www.aurorahealthcare.com	23	10	316	13480	163	273338	3356	190522	65038	1786
☒ △ ST. FRANCIS HOSPITAL, 3237 South 16th Street, Zip 53215–4592; tel. 414/647–5000; Gregory A. Banaszynski, President **A**1 2 5 7 9 10 **F**2 3 4 5 6 7 8 9 10 11 12 14 16 18 19 21 22 23 32 33 34 35 36 37 38 39 40 41 42 43 44 45 46 48 49 53 54 55 56 57 58 59 60 62 63 65 66 70 71 72 74 **P**5 6 8 **S** Wheaton Franciscan Services, Inc., Wheaton, IL	23	10	260	13133	171	108504	1675	121425	42035	1173
☒ ST. JOSEPH'S HOSPITAL, 5000 West Chambers Street, Zip 53210–9988; tel. 414/447–2000; Patricia A. Kaldor, R.N., President (Nonreporting) **A**1 2 3 5 9 10 **S** Wheaton Franciscan Services, Inc., Wheaton, IL **Web address:** www.covhealth.org	21	10	484	—	—	—	—	—	—	—
☒ △ ST. LUKE'S MEDICAL CENTER, (Includes St. Luke's South Shore, 5900 South Lake Drive, Cudahy, Zip 53110–8903; tel. 414/769–9000; Lee Jaeger, Administrator), 2900 West Oklahoma Avenue, Zip 53215–4330, Mailing Address: P.O. Box 2901, Zip 53201–2901; tel. 414/649–6000; Mark S. Wiener, Administrator **A**1 2 3 5 7 8 9 10 **F**1 2 3 4 5 6 7 8 10 11 12 14 16 18 19 21 22 23 24 31 32 33 34 35 36 37 38 39 40 41 42 43 44 45 46 47 48 49 52 53 54 55 56 57 58 59 60 62 63 65 66 70 71 72 74 **P**4 6 **S** Aurora Health Care, Milwaukee, WI	23	10	765	30295	465	363229	1272	408824	127775	3511
☒ ST. MARY'S HOSPITAL, 2323 North Lake Drive, Zip 53211–9682, Mailing Address: P.O. Box 503, Zip 53201–0503; tel. 414/291–1000; Charles C. Lobeck, Chief Executive Officer **A**1 2 3 5 9 10 **F**3 4 7 8 9 10 11 12 14 16 18 19 21 22 32 34 35 37 38 39 40 41 42 43 44 45 53 54 57 58 59 63 65 66 71 72 74 **P**8 **S** Daughters of Charity National Health System, Saint Louis, MO **Web address:** www.columbia–stmarys.com	21	10	257	8966	130	300482	2483	131827	65547	1737
☒ △ ST. MICHAEL HOSPITAL, 2400 West Villard Avenue, Zip 53209–4999; tel. 414/527–8000; Jeffrey K. Jenkins, President (Total facility includes 22 beds in nursing home–type unit) **A**1 2 3 5 7 9 10 **F**2 3 4 7 8 10 11 12 14 16 18 19 21 22 23 24 32 33 34 35 37 38 39 40 41 42 43 44 45 46 48 49 52 53 54 55 56 57 58 59 60 63 64 65 66 70 71 72 74 **P**6 **S** Wheaton Franciscan Services, Inc., Wheaton, IL	21	10	212	8893	130	101588	981	—	—	—
VENCOR HOSPITAL–MILWAUKEE, 5700 West Layton Avenue, Zip 53202; tel. 414/325–5900; E. Kay Gray, Interim Administrator (Nonreporting) **A**10 **S** Vencor, Incorporated, Louisville, KY	33	49	60	—	—	—	—	—	—	—
MONROE—Green County										
□ THE MONROE CLINIC, 515 22nd Avenue, Zip 53566–1598; tel. 608/324–1000; Kenneth Blount, President and Chief Executive Officer **A**1 9 10 **F**3 5 7 8 10 11 14 16 18 19 21 22 23 24 32 33 34 35 37 39 40 41 42 44 45 46 47 48 49 53 54 56 57 58 63 65 66 71 72 74 **P**6 8	21	10	117	3611	40	221740	390	60044	31749	716
NEENAH—Winnebago County										
☒ △ THEDA CLARK MEDICAL CENTER, 130 Second Street, Zip 54956–2883, Mailing Address: P.O. Box 2021, Zip 54957–2021; tel. 920/729–3100; Robert H. Malte, Senior Vice President **A**1 7 9 10 **F**2 3 4 5 6 7 8 10 11 12 14 16 18 19 21 22 23 24 32 34 35 36 37 38 39 40 41 42 43 44 45 46 48 49 52 53 54 55 56 57 58 59 60 62 65 66 70 71 72 74 **P**6 8 **S** United Health Group, Appleton, WI **Web address:** www.unitedhealth.org	23	10	216	8762	118	63087	1280	73364	34198	906
NEILLSVILLE—Clark County										
MEMORIAL MEDICAL CENTER, (Includes Neillsville Memorial Home), 216 Sunset Place, Zip 54456–1799; tel. 715/743–3101; Glen E. Grady, Administrator (Total facility includes 140 beds in nursing home–type unit) **A**9 10 **F**3 6 7 8 16 19 21 22 32 34 35 39 40 41 42 44 45 46 49 62 64 65 71 72 **P**6	23	10	169	1105	122	45410	33	—	—	—

Hospital, Address, Telephone, Administrator, Approval, Facility, and Physician Codes, Health Care System, Network	Classi-fication Codes		Utilization Data					Expense (thousands) of dollars		
	Control	Service	Staffed Beds	Admissions	Census	Outpatient Visits	Births	Total	Payroll	Personnel

★ American Hospital Association (AHA) membership
□ Joint Commission on Accreditation of Healthcare Organizations (JCAHO) accreditation
+ American Osteopathic Healthcare Association (AOHA) membership
○ American Osteopathic Association (AOA) accreditation
△ Commission on Accreditation of Rehabilitation Facilities (CARF) accreditation
Control codes 61, 63, 64, 71, 72 and 73 indicate hospitals listed by AOHA, but not registered by AHA. For definition of numerical codes, see page A4

NEW LONDON—Outagamie County

☒ NEW LONDON FAMILY MEDICAL CENTER, 1405 Mill Street, Zip 54961–2155, Mailing Address: P.O. Box 307, Zip 54961–0307; tel. 920/982–5330; Paul E. Gurgel, President and Chief Executive Officer **A**1 9 10 **F**7 8 11 19 21 22 34 35 37 39 40 41 44 45 48 49 66 71 72

| | 23 | 10 | 39 | 1234 | 12 | 51690 | 166 | 11062 | 4966 | 150 |

NEW RICHMOND—St. Croix County

★ HOLY FAMILY HOSPITAL, 535 Hospital Road, Zip 54017–1495; tel. 715/246–2101; Jean M. Needham, President **A**9 10 **F**7 8 12 14 16 18 19 22 24 32 34 35 36 37 38 39 40 41 42 44 45 46 48 49 65 66 71

| | 21 | 10 | 20 | 1048 | 13 | 12177 | 128 | 7203 | 3306 | 86 |

OCONOMOWOC—Waukesha County

☒ △ OCONOMOWOC MEMORIAL HOSPITAL, 791 Summit Avenue, Zip 53066–3896; tel. 414/569–9400; Douglas Guy, President and Chief Executive Officer (Nonreporting) **A**1 7 9 10 **S** ProHealth Care, Waukesha, WI

| | 23 | 10 | 73 | | | | | | | |

□ ROGERS MEMORIAL HOSPITAL, 34700 Valley Road, Zip 53066–4599; tel. 414/646–4411; David L. Moulthrop, Ph.D., President and Chief Executive Officer **A**1 9 10 **F**3 12 14 16 18 19 34 35 39 45 46 52 53 54 55 56 57 58 59 65
Web address: www.rogershospital.org

| | 23 | 22 | 90 | 1049 | 64 | 5601 | 0 | 13555 | 7761 | 216 |

OCONTO—Oconto County

OCONTO MEMORIAL HOSPITAL, 405 First Street, Zip 54153–1299; tel. 920/834–8800; Lee W. Bennett, Chief Executive Officer (Nonreporting) **A**9 10

| | 23 | 10 | 17 | — | — | — | — | — | — | — |

OCONTO FALLS—Oconto County

COMMUNITY MEMORIAL HOSPITAL, 855 South Main Street, Zip 54154–1296; tel. 920/846–3444; Tom Thompson, Administrator (Nonreporting) **A**10 **S** Brim Healthcare, Inc., Brentwood, TN

| | 23 | 10 | 26 | — | — | — | — | — | — | — |

OSCEOLA—Polk County

OSCEOLA MEDICAL CENTER, 301 River Street, Zip 54020, Mailing Address: P.O. Box 218, Zip 54020–0218; tel. 715/294–2111; Jeffrey K. Meyer, Administrator and Chief Executive Officer (Total facility includes 40 beds in nursing home–type unit) **A**9 10 **F**7 8 11 19 22 32 33 34 40 41 42 44 45 46 48 49 64 65 71 **P**5

| | 23 | 10 | 59 | 587 | 45 | 20277 | 64 | | | |

OSHKOSH—Winnebago County

☒ △ MERCY MEDICAL CENTER, 631 Hazel Street, Zip 54901–4680, Mailing Address: P.O. Box 1100, Zip 54902–1100; tel. 920/236–2000; Otto L. Cox, President **A**1 2 7 9 10 **F**3 4 5 7 8 9 10 11 12 18 19 21 22 23 32 33 34 35 36 37 40 41 42 43 44 45 46 47 48 49 52 53 54 55 56 57 58 63 65 66 70 71 72 **P**6

| | 21 | 10 | 226 | 7740 | 103 | 366804 | 954 | 86871 | 38739 | 1001 |

OSSEO—Trempealeau County

OSSEO AREA HOSPITAL AND NURSING HOME, 13025 Eighth Street, Zip 54758, Mailing Address: P.O. Box 70, Zip 54758–0070; tel. 715/597–3121; Bradley D. Groseth, Administrator (Total facility includes 61 beds in nursing home–type unit) **A**10 **F**1 11 19 22 33 34 41 44 45 46 47 49 62 63 64 65 71 **S** Mayo Foundation, Rochester, MN

| | 23 | 10 | 76 | 179 | 63 | 8585 | 0 | — | — | — |

PARK FALLS—Price County

☒ FLAMBEAU HOSPITAL, 98 Sherry Avenue, Zip 54552–1467, Mailing Address: P.O. Box 310, Zip 54552–0310; tel. 715/762–2484; Curtis A. Johnson, Administrator **A**1 10 **F**7 8 11 12 16 19 21 22 24 32 33 34 36 37 39 40 41 44 45 46 48 49 65 66 71 72 **S** Marian Health System, Tulsa, OK

| | 23 | 10 | 42 | 1112 | 12 | 20894 | 107 | 9881 | 4641 | 165 |

PLATTEVILLE—Grant County

☒ SOUTHWEST HEALTH CENTER, (Includes Cuba City Medical Center, 808 South Washington Street, Cuba City, Zip 53807; tel. 608/744–2161; Hazel Green Hospital, 2110 Church Street, Hazel Green, Zip 53811; tel. 608/854–2231), 250 Camp Street, Zip 53818–1703; tel. 608/348–2331; Anne K. Klawiter, President and Chief Executive Officer (Total facility includes 95 beds in nursing home–type unit) **A**1 10 **F**6 7 8 14 16 19 22 32 33 34 35 36 39 40 44 45 52 57 64 65 71 **S** Brim Healthcare, Inc., Brentwood, TN
Web address: www.southwesthealth.org

| | 23 | 10 | 165 | 1301 | 114 | 19096 | 165 | | | |

PLYMOUTH—Sheboygan County

☒ VALLEY VIEW MEDICAL CENTER, 901 Reed Street, Zip 53073–2409; tel. 920/893–1771; T. Gregg Watson, Administrator (Total facility includes 60 beds in nursing home–type unit) (Nonreporting) **A**1 9 10 **S** Aurora Health Care, Milwaukee, WI

| | 23 | 10 | 92 | | | | | | | |

PORT WASHINGTON—Ozaukee County

ST. MARY'S HOSPITAL OZAUKEE See Mequon

PORTAGE—Columbia County

☒ DIVINE SAVIOR HOSPITAL AND NURSING HOME, 1015 West Pleasant Street, Zip 53901–9987, Mailing Address: P.O. Box 387, Zip 53901–0387; tel. 608/742–4131; Michael Decker, President and Chief Executive Officer (Total facility includes 124 beds in nursing home–type unit) **A**1 10 **F**2 3 7 8 11 14 16 19 21 22 32 34 35 36 37 39 40 41 42 44 45 46 47 48 49 56 63 64 65 66 70 71 **P**6

| | 21 | 10 | 186 | 1990 | 131 | 42090 | 174 | — | — | — |

PRAIRIE DU CHIEN—Crawford County

☒ PRAIRIE DU CHIEN MEMORIAL HOSPITAL, 705 East Taylor Street, Zip 53821–2196; tel. 608/326–2431; Harold W. Brown, Chief Executive Officer **A**1 9 10 **F**1 2 3 6 7 8 11 12 14 16 19 22 32 33 34 35 36 37 39 40 41 42 44 45 46 49 53 54 56 58 59 62 64 65 71 72

| | 23 | 10 | 43 | 1760 | 33 | 20732 | 203 | 12149 | 6298 | 203 |

PRAIRIE DU SAC—Sauk County

□ SAUK PRAIRIE MEMORIAL HOSPITAL, 80 First Street, Zip 53578–1550; tel. 608/643–3311; Bobbe Teigen, Administrator **A**1 10 **F**2 7 8 11 12 14 16 19 21 22 24 31 32 33 34 35 36 37 39 40 41 42 44 45 48 49 54 56 63 65 66 70 71 72 **P**8
Web address: www.spmh.org

| | 23 | 10 | 36 | 2175 | 19 | 41258 | 221 | 22517 | 11058 | 307 |

Hospital, Address, Telephone, Administrator, Approval, Facility, and Physician Codes, Health Care System, Network	Classi- fication Codes		Utilization Data					Expense (thousands) of dollars		
★ American Hospital Association (AHA) membership □ Joint Commission on Accreditation of Healthcare Organizations (JCAHO) accreditation + American Osteopathic Healthcare Association (AOHA) membership ○ American Osteopathic Association (AOA) accreditation △ Commission on Accreditation of Rehabilitation Facilities (CARF) accreditation Control codes 61, 63, 64, 71, 72 and 73 indicate hospitals listed by AOHA, but not registered by AHA. For definition of numerical codes, see page A4	Control	Service	Staffed Beds	Admissions	Census	Outpatient Visits	Births	Total	Payroll	Personnel

RACINE—Racine County

☒ △ SAINT MARY'S MEDICAL CENTER, 3801 Spring Street, Zip 53405–1690; tel. 414/636–4011; Kenneth R. Buser, President **A**1 2 3 7 9 10 **F**2 3 4 7 8 10 11 12 14 16 19 21 22 23 24 32 33 34 35 37 38 39 40 41 42 43 44 45 46 47 48 49 52 53 54 55 56 57 58 59 60 65 66 71 72 74 **P**6 **S** Wheaton Franciscan Services, Inc., Wheaton, IL
| 21 | 10 | 179 | 9412 | 132 | 200327 | 0 | 93816 | 39501 | 1271 |

★ ST. LUKE'S MEMORIAL HOSPITAL, 1320 Wisconsin Avenue, Zip 53403–1987; tel. 414/636–2011; Kenneth R. Buser, President (Total facility includes 50 beds in nursing home–type unit) **A**5 9 10 **F**2 3 4 7 8 10 11 12 14 16 18 19 21 22 23 24 32 33 34 35 38 39 40 41 42 43 44 45 46 47 48 49 52 53 54 55 56 57 58 59 60 64 65 66 71 72 74 **P**6 **S** Wheaton Franciscan Services, Inc., Wheaton, IL
| 23 | 10 | 187 | 4991 | 117 | 92216 | 2020 | — | — | — |

REEDSBURG—Sauk County

□ REEDSBURG AREA MEDICAL CENTER, 2000 North Dewey Street, Zip 53959–1097; tel. 608/524–6487; George L. Johnson, President (Total facility includes 50 beds in nursing home–type unit) **A**1 10 **F**4 7 8 10 11 12 16 18 19 21 22 24 32 33 34 35 36 37 39 40 41 42 44 45 47 49 64 65 66 70 71 72 **P**6
| 23 | 10 | 88 | 2106 | 70 | 42945 | 213 | — | — | — |

RHINELANDER—Oneida County

☒ SACRED HEART–ST. MARY'S HOSPITALS, (Includes Sacred Heart Hospital, 216 North Seventh Street, Tomahawk, Zip 54487; tel. 715/453–7700; St. Mary's Hospital), 1044 Kabel Avenue, Zip 54501–3998; tel. 715/369–6600; Kevin J. O'Donnell, President and Chief Executive Officer **A**1 10 **F**2 3 7 8 11 12 16 19 22 23 24 32 33 34 35 36 37 39 40 41 42 44 45 46 49 52 53 54 55 56 57 58 59 60 63 65 66 71 **S** Marian Health System, Tulsa, OK
Web address: www.ministryhealth.org
| 21 | 10 | 52 | 4766 | 54 | 48930 | 407 | 39850 | 19242 | 618 |

RICE LAKE—Barron County

☒ LAKEVIEW MEDICAL CENTER, 1100 North Main Street, Zip 54868–1238; tel. 715/234–1515; Edward H. Wolf, Chief Executive Officer **A**1 9 10 **F**7 11 16 19 22 23 24 32 33 34 35 36 37 39 40 41 42 44 45 49 63 65 66 71
| 23 | 10 | 69 | 2712 | 25 | 23944 | 439 | 20209 | 10124 | 264 |

RICHLAND CENTER—Richland County

□ RICHLAND HOSPITAL, 431 North Park Street, Zip 53581–1899; tel. 608/647–6321; Thomas J. Werner, Administrator **A**1 10 **F**3 7 8 10 11 19 21 22 32 34 35 36 37 39 40 41 42 44 45 54 55 56 58 65 66 70 71
| 23 | 10 | 38 | 1630 | 18 | 15290 | 187 | 13077 | 6204 | 222 |

RIPON—Fond Du Lac County

☒ RIPON MEDICAL CENTER, 933 Newbury Street, Zip 54971–1798, Mailing Address: P.O. Box 390, Zip 54971–0390; tel. 920/748–3101; Jon W. Baker, Chief Executive Officer **A**1 9 10 **F**7 8 11 12 16 19 21 22 24 34 35 36 37 39 40 41 42 44 45 46 47 49 54 58 63 65 66 70 71 72 74 **S** Brim Healthcare, Inc., Brentwood, TN
Web address: www.riponmedicalcenter.com
| 23 | 10 | 29 | 1082 | 11 | 29463 | 88 | 10804 | 4469 | 135 |

RIVER FALLS—St. Croix County

☒ RIVER FALLS AREA HOSPITAL, 1629 East Division Street, Zip 54022–1571; tel. 715/425–6155; Sharon Whelan, Administrator **A**1 9 10 **F**7 11 14 16 19 21 22 24 32 33 34 35 36 37 39 40 44 45 46 47 48 49 65 66 71 72 **S** Allina Health System, Minneapolis, MN
| 23 | 10 | 36 | 1112 | 10 | 10509 | 231 | 10459 | 3891 | 96 |

SAINT CROIX FALLS—Polk County

□ ST. CROIX VALLEY MEMORIAL HOSPITAL, 204 South Adams Street, Zip 54024–9400; tel. 715/483–3261; Steve L. Urosevich, Chief Executive Officer **A**1 9 10 **F**2 3 6 7 8 11 18 19 21 22 24 32 33 34 35 37 40 41 42 44 45 46 47 49 52 53 54 56 57 58 63 65 66 70 71 74
| 23 | 10 | 69 | 1979 | 16 | 27862 | 274 | 13696 | 6067 | 186 |

SHAWANO—Shawano County

☒ SHAWANO MEDICAL CENTER, 309 North Bartlette Street, Zip 54166–0477; tel. 715/526–2111; John J. Kestly, Administrator **A**1 9 10 **F**7 8 10 11 14 16 19 21 22 32 33 34 35 37 39 40 44 45 46 48 56 63 65 66 71 74 **P**5 **S** Brim Healthcare, Inc., Brentwood, TN
| 23 | 10 | 46 | 2273 | 21 | 41091 | 357 | 15710 | 7014 | 223 |

SHEBOYGAN—Sheboygan County

☒ △ SHEBOYGAN MEMORIAL MEDICAL CENTER, 2629 North Seventh Street, Zip 53083–4998; tel. 920/451–5000; T. Gregg Watson, Administrator (Total facility includes 60 beds in nursing home–type unit) **A**1 2 7 9 10 **F**2 3 4 5 7 8 10 11 12 16 19 21 22 23 23 33 34 35 36 37 39 40 41 42 44 45 46 48 49 52 53 54 55 56 57 58 60 62 64 65 66 71 72 74 **S** Aurora Health Care, Milwaukee, WI
| 23 | 10 | 219 | 6285 | 124 | 63139 | 992 | — | — | — |

☒ △ ST. NICHOLAS HOSPITAL, 1601 North Taylor Drive, Zip 53081–2496; tel. 920/459–8300; Michael J. Stenger, Executive Vice President and Administrator **A**1 2 7 9 10 **F**7 8 10 11 12 14 16 18 19 21 22 23 24 32 33 34 35 36 37 39 40 41 42 44 45 46 48 49 53 54 56 60 63 64 65 66 70 71 72 74 **P**5 **S** Hospital Sisters Health System, Springfield, IL
Web address: www.stnicholashospital.org
| 21 | 10 | 185 | 3321 | 47 | 58382 | 379 | 33093 | 13082 | 418 |

SHELL LAKE—Washburn County

□ INDIANHEAD MEDICAL CENTER, 113 Fourth Avenue West, Zip 54871; tel. 715/468–7833; Paul Naglosky, Administrator **A**1 9 10 **F**7 11 19 22 32 34 35 37 40 42 44 45 46 65 71
| 33 | 10 | 49 | 619 | 7 | 7373 | 21 | 3788 | 1673 | 67 |

SPARTA—Monroe County

☒ FRANCISCAN SKEMP HEALTHCARE–SPARTA CAMPUS, 310 West Main Street, Zip 54656–2171; tel. 608/269–2132; William P. Sexton, Administrator (Total facility includes 30 beds in nursing home–type unit) **A**1 10 **F**2 7 8 12 14 16 19 22 32 33 34 39 40 41 44 45 46 49 64 65 66 70 71 74 **P**6 **S** Franciscan Skemp Healthcare, La Crosse, WI
| 21 | 10 | 59 | 796 | 40 | 38099 | 131 | — | — | — |

Hospital, Address, Telephone, Administrator, Approval, Facility, and Physician Codes, Health Care System, Network	Classi-fication Codes		Utilization Data					Expense (thousands) of dollars		
★ American Hospital Association (AHA) membership □ Joint Commission on Accreditation of Healthcare Organizations (JCAHO) accreditation + American Osteopathic Healthcare Association (AOHA) membership ○ American Osteopathic Association (AOA) accreditation △ Commission on Accreditation of Rehabilitation Facilities (CARF) accreditation Control codes 61, 63, 64, 71, 72 and 73 indicate hospitals listed by AOHA, but not registered by AHA. For definition of numerical codes, see page A4	Control	Service	Staffed Beds	Admissions	Census	Outpatient Visits	Births	Total	Payroll	Personnel

SPOONER—Washburn County

⊠ SPOONER HEALTH SYSTEM, (Formerly Community Memorial Hospital), 819 Ash Street, Zip 54801–1299; tel. 715/635–2111; Michael Schafer, Chief Executive Officer (Total facility includes 90 beds in nursing home–type unit) **A**1 9 10 **F**2 7 8 11 12 16 19 21 22 32 33 34 36 40 41 42 44 45 48 49 50 63 64 65 66 71 **S** Brim Healthcare, Inc., Brentwood, TN

| | 23 | 10 | 136 | 1097 | 99 | 20798 | 94 | — | — | — |

STANLEY—Chippewa County

⊠ VICTORY MEDICAL CENTER, 230 East Fourth Avenue, Zip 54768–1298; tel. 715/644–5571; Cynthia Eichman, Chief Executive Officer and Administrator (Total facility includes 86 beds in nursing home–type unit) **A**1 10 **F**1 8 11 16 19 21 22 32 33 39 41 44 45 46 49 56 64 65 66 71 72 **P**6 **S** Marian Health System, Tulsa, OK

| | 21 | 10 | 127 | 690 | 84 | 21916 | 0 | — | — | — |

STEVENS POINT—Portage County

⊠ SAINT MICHAEL'S HOSPITAL, 900 Illinois Avenue, Zip 54481–3196; tel. 715/346–5000; Jeffrey L. Martin, President and Chief Executive Officer **A**1 9 10 **F**2 3 7 11 14 16 19 21 22 23 32 33 34 35 36 37 38 39 40 41 42 44 45 46 47 49 52 53 54 55 56 57 59 63 65 66 71 72 **S** Marian Health System, Tulsa, OK
Web address: www.smhosp.org

| | 21 | 10 | 114 | 4530 | 47 | 77293 | 700 | 45518 | 21411 | 554 |

STOUGHTON—Dane County

□ STOUGHTON HOSPITAL ASSOCIATION, 900 Ridge Street, Zip 53589–1896; tel. 608/873–6611; Terrence Brenny, President **A**1 9 10 **F**1 8 11 14 19 22 31 32 33 34 35 37 41 42 44 45 46 48 49 52 54 57 63 65 66 71 72

| | 23 | 10 | 40 | 1198 | 18 | 31599 | 0 | 14013 | 5449 | 174 |

STURGEON BAY—Door County

⊠ DOOR COUNTY MEMORIAL HOSPITAL, 323 South 18th Avenue, Zip 54235–1495; tel. 920/743–5566; Gerald M. Worrick, President and Chief Executive Officer (Total facility includes 30 beds in nursing home–type unit) (Nonreporting) **A**1 9 10
Web address: www.doorcounty-wi.com

| | 23 | 10 | 77 | — | — | — | — | — | — | — |

SUPERIOR—Douglas County

□ ST. MARY'S HOSPITAL OF SUPERIOR, 3500 Tower Avenue, Zip 54880–5395; tel. 715/392–8281; Delores E. Schultz, R.N., Administrator **A**1 9 10 **F**8 11 12 14 16 19 21 22 32 33 34 35 37 39 41 42 44 45 46 48 49 65 71 72 **S** Benedictine Health System, Duluth, MN

| | 23 | 10 | 42 | 1288 | 13 | 47390 | 0 | 11815 | 5597 | 173 |

TOMAH—Monroe County

□ TOMAH MEMORIAL HOSPITAL, 321 Butts Avenue, Zip 54660–1412; tel. 608/372–2181; Philip Stuart, Administrator **A**1 9 10 **F**2 3 7 9 11 12 16 19 22 32 33 34 35 36 38 39 40 41 42 44 45 52 58 63 65 66 71 72

| | 23 | 10 | 45 | 989 | 11 | 25405 | 192 | 9709 | 4398 | 142 |

⊠ VETERANS AFFAIRS MEDICAL CENTER, 500 East Veterans Street, Zip 54660; tel. 608/372–3971; Stan Johnson, Medical Center Director (Total facility includes 100 beds in nursing home–type unit) (Nonreporting) **A**1 **S** Department of Veterans Affairs, Washington, DC

| | 45 | 22 | 569 | — | — | — | — | — | — | — |

TOMAHAWK—Lincoln County

SACRED HEART HOSPITAL See Sacred Heart–St. Mary's Hospitals, Rhinelander

TWO RIVERS—Manitowoc County

⊠ TWO RIVERS COMMUNITY HOSPITAL AND HAMILTON MEMORIAL HOME, 2500 Garfield Street, Zip 54241–2399; tel. 920/793–1178; Cathie A. Kocourek, Acting Administrator (Total facility includes 85 beds in nursing home–type unit) **A**1 9 10 **F**7 8 10 11 12 14 16 19 21 22 32 33 34 35 36 37 39 40 41 44 45 46 47 48 49 64 65 71 **S** Aurora Health Care, Milwaukee, WI

| | 23 | 10 | 138 | 1541 | 96 | 22435 | 244 | — | — | — |

VIROQUA—Vernon County

VERNON MEMORIAL HOSPITAL, 507 South Main Street, Zip 54665–2096; tel. 608/637–2101; Garith W. Steiner, Chief Executive Officer **A**10 **F**3 7 8 12 14 16 19 22 24 32 33 34 39 40 41 42 44 45 46 49 54 55 56 57 58 65 66 70 71

| | 23 | 10 | 18 | 1670 | 15 | 57652 | 161 | 13375 | 6894 | 168 |

WATERTOWN—Dodge County

⊠ WATERTOWN MEMORIAL HOSPITAL, 125 Hospital Drive, Zip 53098–3384; tel. 920/261–4210; John P. Kosanovich, President **A**1 10 **F**1 3 6 7 8 11 12 16 19 21 22 32 33 34 35 36 37 39 40 41 44 45 46 47 49 56 58 62 63 65 66 70 71 72 74 **P**6 8

| | 23 | 10 | 45 | 2187 | 25 | 76983 | 299 | 25128 | 12067 | 337 |

WAUKESHA—Waukesha County

⊠ △ WAUKESHA MEMORIAL HOSPITAL, 725 American Avenue, Zip 53188–5099; tel. 414/544–2011; Rexford W. Titus, III, President and Chief Executive Officer **A**1 2 3 5 7 9 10 **F**2 3 4 6 7 8 10 11 12 14 16 19 21 22 23 24 32 33 34 35 36 37 38 39 40 41 42 43 44 45 47 48 49 52 53 54 55 56 57 58 59 60 62 63 65 66 70 71 72 74 **P**1 5 6 7 **S** ProHealth Care, Waukesha, WI
Web address: www.phci.org

| | 23 | 10 | 294 | 12392 | 166 | 232899 | 2153 | 146014 | 53263 | 1423 |

WAUPACA—Waupaca County

⊠ RIVERSIDE MEDICAL CENTER, 800 Riverside Drive, Zip 54981–1999; tel. 715/258–1000; Craig A. Kantos, Chief Executive Officer **A**1 9 10 **F**7 8 9 10 11 19 21 22 23 34 35 37 40 41 42 44 45 46 47 48 52 57 63 65 71 74 **S** Quorum Health Group/Quorum Health Resources, Inc., Brentwood, TN

| | 23 | 10 | 40 | 1773 | 18 | 47018 | 238 | 16590 | 7265 | 210 |

WAUPUN—Fond Du Lac County

⊠ WAUPUN MEMORIAL HOSPITAL, 620 West Brown Street, Zip 53963–1799; tel. 920/324–5581; James E. Baer, FACHE, President **A**1 9 10 **F**1 4 7 8 10 11 16 18 19 21 22 23 32 33 34 35 36 37 39 40 41 44 45 47 49 65 66 71 72

| | 21 | 10 | 49 | 1216 | 11 | 50012 | 93 | 12841 | 5249 | 157 |

WAUSAU—Marathon County

NORTH CENTRAL HEALTH CARE FACILITIES, 1100 Lakeview Drive, Zip 54403–6799; tel. 715/848–4600; Tim Steller, Chief Executive Officer (Total facility includes 356 beds in nursing home–type unit) **A**10 **F**2 3 12 18 19 22 34 35 39 45 48 49 52 53 54 55 56 57 58 59 64 65

| | 13 | 22 | 406 | 1187 | 362 | 111922 | 0 | — | — | — |

Hospital, Address, Telephone, Administrator, Approval, Facility, and Physician Codes, Health Care System, Network	Classi-fication Codes		Utilization Data					Expense (thousands) of dollars		
★ American Hospital Association (AHA) membership □ Joint Commission on Accreditation of Healthcare Organizations (JCAHO) accreditation + American Osteopathic Healthcare Association (AOHA) membership ○ American Osteopathic Association (AOA) accreditation △ Commission on Accreditation of Rehabilitation Facilities (CARF) accreditation Control codes 61, 63, 64, 71, 72 and 73 indicate hospitals listed by AOHA, but not registered by AHA. For definition of numerical codes, see page A4	Control	Service	Staffed Beds	Admissions	Census	Outpatient Visits	Births	Total	Payroll	Personnel

☒ △ WAUSAU HOSPITAL, 333 Pine Ridge Boulevard, Zip 54401–4187, Mailing Address: P.O. Box 1847, Zip 54402–1847; tel. 715/847–2121; Paul A. Spaude, President and Chief Executive Officer **A**1 2 3 5 7 9 10 **F**2 3 4 7 8 9 10 11 16 19 21 22 23 32 33 34 35 37 39 40 41 42 43 44 45 46 47 48 49 52 53 54 56 57 58 59 60 63 65 70 71 **P**6 **Web address:** www.wausauhospital.org	23	10	212	11052	134	74791	1367	116460	44330	1262
WAUWATOSA—Milwaukee County										
+ ○ LAKEVIEW HOSPITAL, 10010 West Bluemound Road, Zip 53226; tel. 414/259–7200; J. E. Race, Administrator and Chief Executive Officer (Nonreporting) **A**9 10 11	23	10	72	—	—	—	—	—	—	—
☒ MILWAUKEE PSYCHIATRIC HOSPITAL, 1220 Dewey Avenue, Zip 53213–2598; tel. 414/454–6600; James A. Moore, Administrator **A**1 3 5 9 10 **F**1 2 3 4 5 6 7 8 9 10 11 12 14 16 18 19 21 22 23 24 31 32 33 34 35 36 38 39 40 41 42 43 44 45 46 47 48 49 50 52 53 54 55 56 57 58 59 60 62 63 65 66 70 71 72 74 **P**4 6 **S** Aurora Health Care, Milwaukee, WI	23	22	75	1683	52	22711	0	13695	5939	194
WEST ALLIS—Milwaukee County										
□ CHARTER BEHAVIORAL HEALTH SYSTEM OF MILWAUKEE/WEST ALLIS, 11101 West Lincoln Avenue, Zip 53227; tel. 414/327–3000; Ron Escarda, Chief Executive Officer (Nonreporting) **A**1	33	22	80	—	—	—	—	—	—	—
☒ WEST ALLIS MEMORIAL HOSPITAL, 8901 West Lincoln Avenue, Zip 53227–0901, Mailing Address: P.O. Box 27901, Zip 53227–0901; tel. 414/328–6000; Richard A. Kellar, Administrator **A**1 2 9 10 **F**1 2 3 4 5 6 7 8 10 11 12 16 18 19 21 22 23 32 33 34 35 36 37 38 39 40 41 42 43 44 45 48 49 52 53 54 55 56 57 58 59 60 62 63 65 66 71 72 **P**2 4 5 6 **S** Aurora Health Care, Milwaukee, WI	23	10	158	6757	97	110088	642	77083	32800	881
WEST BEND—Washington County										
☒ ST. JOSEPH'S COMMUNITY HOSPITAL OF WEST BEND, 551 South Silverbrook Drive, Zip 53095–3898; tel. 414/334–5533; Gregory T. Burns, Executive Director **A**1 9 10 **F**2 7 8 11 12 14 16 18 19 21 22 23 34 35 36 37 39 40 41 42 44 45 47 49 52 54 57 63 65 70 71 **P**6	23	10	121	5038	54	48318	806	30290	14653	427
WHITEHALL—Trempealeau County										
TRI–COUNTY MEMORIAL HOSPITAL, 18601 Lincoln Street, Zip 54773–0065, Mailing Address: P.O. Box 65, Zip 54773–0065; tel. 715/538–4361; Ronald B. Fields, President (Total facility includes 68 beds in nursing home–type unit) **A**9 10 **F**3 4 5 6 7 8 10 11 14 16 19 21 22 31 32 33 34 35 36 37 39 41 42 43 44 45 46 48 49 50 53 54 55 56 57 58 59 60 63 64 65 66 71 72 74	23	10	92	554	70	10535	0	—	—	—
WILD ROSE—Waushara County										
WILD ROSE COMMUNITY MEMORIAL HOSPITAL, 601 Grove Avenue, Zip 54984, Mailing Address: P.O. Box 243, Zip 54984–0243; tel. 414/622–3257; Donald Caves, President **A**9 10 **F**2 3 6 8 12 16 18 19 22 32 33 34 39 40 41 44 45 48 49 53 54 55 56 57 58 65 66 71 74	23	10	26	361	4	10994	25	4284	1759	89
WINNEBAGO—Winnebago County										
□ WINNEBAGO MENTAL HEALTH INSTITUTE, Mailing Address: P.O. Box 9, Zip 54985–0009; tel. 920/235–4910; Joann O'Connor, Director **A**1 10 **F**2 4 7 8 10 11 19 22 24 35 40 41 44 45 46 47 48 50 52 53 55 56 63 65 70 71 72 **P**6	12	22	330	896	258	299	0	33941	20778	667
WISCONSIN RAPIDS—Wood County										
☒ RIVERVIEW HOSPITAL ASSOCIATION, (Includes Riverview Manor), 410 Dewey Street, Zip 54494–4724, Mailing Address: P.O. Box 8080, Zip 54495–8080; tel. 715/423–6060; Celse A. Berard, President (Total facility includes 118 beds in nursing home–type unit) **A**1 9 10 **F**2 7 8 10 11 19 21 22 34 35 36 37 39 40 42 44 45 47 48 49 52 54 63 64 65 66 70 71 **Web address:** www.rhahealthcare.org	23	10	197	3385	136	34744	614	—	—	—
WOODRUFF—Oneida County										
☒ HOWARD YOUNG MEDICAL CENTER, 240 Maple Street, Zip 54568, Mailing Address: P.O. Box 470, Zip 54568–0470; tel. 715/356–8000; Patricia L. Richardson, President and Chief Executive Officer **A**1 9 10 **F**3 6 7 8 9 11 12 18 19 21 22 23 24 32 33 34 35 37 39 40 41 42 44 45 46 47 48 49 56 58 63 65 66 71	23	10	65	4301	45	32637	299	—	—	—

WYOMING

Resident population 481 (in thousands)
Resident population in metro areas 29.7%
Birth rate per 1,000 population 13
65 years and over 11.3%
Percent of persons without health insurance 13.5%

Hospital, Address, Telephone, Administrator, Approval, Facility, and Physician Codes, Health Care System, Network	Classi-fication Codes		Utilization Data					Expense (thousands) of dollars		
★ American Hospital Association (AHA) membership □ Joint Commission on Accreditation of Healthcare Organizations (JCAHO) accreditation + American Osteopathic Healthcare Association (AOHA) membership ○ American Osteopathic Association (AOA) accreditation △ Commission on Accreditation of Rehabilitation Facilities (CARF) accreditation Control codes 61, 63, 64, 71, 72 and 73 indicate hospitals listed by AOHA, but not registered by AHA. For definition of numerical codes, see page A4	Control	Service	Staffed Beds	Admissions	Census	Outpatient Visits	Births	Total	Payroll	Personnel

AFTON—Lincoln County

★ STAR VALLEY HOSPITAL, 110 Hospital Lane, Zip 83110–0579, Mailing Address: P.O. Box 579, Zip 83110–0579; tel. 307/886–5800; Alberto Vasquez, Administrator (Total facility includes 24 beds in nursing home–type unit) **A**9 10 **F**7 8 12 14 15 16 22 25 28 30 32 34 40 41 44 46 49 64 65 71 73 **P**6 **S** Intermountain Health Care, Inc., Salt Lake City, UT
Web address: www.ihc.com

	16	10	39	559	24	28669	66	4396	2307	79

BUFFALO—Johnson County

□ JOHNSON COUNTY HEALTHCARE CENTER, (Formerly Johnson County Memorial Hospital), 497 West Lott Street, Zip 82834–1691; tel. 307/684–5521; Sandy Ward, Administrator (Total facility includes 50 beds in nursing home–type unit) **A**1 9 10 **F**7 8 19 22 26 28 32 33 37 40 44 45 49 64 65 71

	16	10	65	551	53	11558	58	7316	3828	154

CASPER—Natrona County

⊠ △ WYOMING MEDICAL CENTER, 1233 East Second Street, Zip 82601–2988; tel. 307/577–7201; Michael E. Schrader, President and Chief Executive Officer **A**1 3 7 9 10 **F**3 4 7 8 10 12 14 15 16 17 19 21 22 23 25 27 28 30 31 32 34 35 37 39 40 41 42 43 44 45 46 48 49 51 60 61 63 65 67 71 73 74 **P**6
Web address: www.wmcnet.org

	23	10	154	7210	82	63857	851	78787	31396	930

CHEYENNE—Laramie County

⊠ U. S. AIR FORCE HOSPITAL, 6900 Alden Drive, Zip 82005–3913; tel. 307/773–2045; Major Brenda Bullard, Administrator (Nonreporting) **A**1 9 **S** Department of the Air Force, Bowling AFB, DC

	41	10	15	—	—	—	—	—	—	—

⊠ UNITED MEDICAL CENTER, (Includes De Paul Hospital, 2600 East 18th Street, Zip 82001–5511; tel. 307/634–2273), 214 East 23rd Street, Zip 82001–3790; tel. 307/634–2273; Jon M. Gates, Chief Executive Officer **A**1 3 9 10 **F**3 4 7 8 10 11 12 15 16 17 19 21 22 23 24 28 30 32 33 35 37 40 41 42 43 44 46 48 49 52 53 54 55 56 57 58 59 60 63 64 65 67 71 73 74

	13	10	163	7514	88	157968	845	62830	26995	868

⊠ VETERANS AFFAIRS MEDICAL CENTER, 2360 East Pershing Boulevard, Zip 82001–5392; tel. 307/778–7550; Richard Fry, Director (Total facility includes 50 beds in nursing home–type unit) **A**1 9 **F**2 3 4 8 10 11 12 16 17 18 19 20 21 22 23 26 27 28 30 31 32 33 34 35 37 39 41 42 43 44 46 48 49 51 52 54 55 56 58 60 61 64 65 67 68 71 73 74 **P**6 **S** Department of Veterans Affairs, Washington, DC

	45	10	71	1040	60	65290	0	25638	—	329

CODY—Park County

⊠ WEST PARK HOSPITAL, 707 Sheridan Avenue, Zip 82414; tel. 307/527–7501; Douglas A. McMillan, Administrator and Chief Executive Officer (Total facility includes 140 beds in nursing home–type unit) **A**1 9 10 **F**2 3 7 8 12 15 16 17 18 19 20 21 22 26 27 28 30 32 33 34 35 37 39 40 41 42 44 45 46 48 49 51 55 56 60 64 65 66 67 70 71 72 73 **P**8 **S** Quorum Health Group/Quorum Health Resources, Inc., Brentwood, TN

	16	10	179	1764	117	49257	223	24808	11052	416

DOUGLAS—Converse County

★ MEMORIAL HOSPITAL OF CONVERSE COUNTY, 111 South Fifth Street, Zip 82633–2490; tel. 307/358–2122; Fred F. Schroeder, Administrator **A**9 10 **F**1 2 3 4 5 6 7 8 9 10 12 13 15 16 17 18 19 20 21 22 23 24 25 26 28 29 30 31 32 33 34 35 36 39 40 41 42 43 44 45 46 47 48 49 50 51 52 53 54 55 56 57 58 59 60 61 62 64 65 66 67 69 70 71 73 74 **P**5

	13	10	34	456	4	18052	72	6605	2680	111

EVANSTON—Uinta County

⊠ EVANSTON REGIONAL HOSPITAL, 190 Arrowhead Drive, Zip 82930–9266; tel. 307/789–3636; Robert W. Allen, Administrator **A**1 9 10 **F**7 8 12 15 16 17 19 20 22 28 29 30 32 33 35 37 39 40 44 46 49 65 67 70 71 73 **S** Intermountain Health Care, Inc., Salt Lake City, UT

	23	10	38	1050	9	44387	247	9340	3525	121

WYOMING STATE HOSPITAL, 830 Highway 150 South, Zip 82931–5341, Mailing Address: P.O. Box 177, Zip 82931–0177; tel. 307/789–3464; Pablo Hernandez, M.D., Administrator **A**10 **F**3 12 14 15 16 17 20 29 34 46 52 53 54 55 56 57 58 65 67 73 **P**6

	12	22	122	449	111	—	0	15994	9440	451

GILLETTE—Campbell County

⊠ CAMPBELL COUNTY MEMORIAL HOSPITAL, 501 South Burma Avenue, Zip 82716–3426, Mailing Address: P.O. Box 3011, Zip 82717–3011; tel. 307/682–8811; David Crow, Chief Executive Officer **A**1 9 10 **F**3 7 8 11 12 14 15 16 17 18 19 22 24 28 30 32 35 36 37 39 40 41 42 44 45 46 47 49 52 53 55 56 57 58 59 65 66 67 71 73 **P**8
Web address: www.ccmh.net

	16	10	86	2642	26	71785	497	31515	13913	439

JACKSON—Teton County

□ ST. JOHN'S HOSPITAL AND LIVING CENTER, 625 East Broadway Street, Zip 83001, Mailing Address: P.O. Box 428, Zip 83001–0428; tel. 307/733–3636; John Valiante, Chief Executive Officer (Total facility includes 60 beds in nursing home–type unit) **A**1 9 10 **F**7 8 12 14 16 17 19 22 24 28 29 32 33 34 35 37 39 40 42 44 45 46 48 49 51 56 59 64 65 67 71 73

	16	10	102	2100	74	10151	263	31182	13707	568

Hospital, Address, Telephone, Administrator, Approval, Facility, and Physician Codes, Health Care System, Network	Classi-fication Codes		Utilization Data					Expense (thousands) of dollars		
★ American Hospital Association (AHA) membership □ Joint Commission on Accreditation of Healthcare Organizations (JCAHO) accreditation + American Osteopathic Healthcare Association (AOHA) membership ○ American Osteopathic Association (AOA) accreditation △ Commission on Accreditation of Rehabilitation Facilities (CARF) accreditation Control codes 61, 63, 64, 71, 72 and 73 indicate hospitals listed by AOHA, but not registered by AHA. For definition of numerical codes, see page A4	Control	Service	Staffed Beds	Admissions	Census	Outpatient Visits	Births	Total	Payroll	Personnel

KEMMERER—Lincoln County

★ SOUTH LINCOLN MEDICAL CENTER, 711 Onyx Street, Zip 83101–3214, Mailing Address: P.O. Box 390, Zip 83101–0390; tel. 307/877–4401; Marla Shelby, Administrator and Chief Executive Officer **A**9 10 **F**7 8 22 28 32 40 44 49 66

| | 16 | 10 | 16 | 308 | 5 | 16065 | 31 | 4834 | 2213 | 81 |

LANDER—Fremont County

□ LANDER VALLEY MEDICAL CENTER, 1320 Bishop Randall Drive, Zip 82520–3996; tel. 307/332–4420; Andrew Gramlich, Chief Executive Officer (Total facility includes 21 beds in nursing home–type unit) **A**1 9 10 **F**2 3 7 8 10 12 15 16 19 20 21 22 26 28 30 32 33 34 35 36 37 39 40 41 44 45 46 49 53 54 55 56 57 58 63 64 65 67 71 73 74 **P**5 **S** New American Healthcare Corporation, Brentwood, TN
Web address: www.landerhospital.com

| | 33 | 10 | 102 | 2340 | 29 | 15352 | 182 | 13893 | 7258 | 289 |

LARAMIE—Albany County

✠ IVINSON MEMORIAL HOSPITAL, 255 North 30th Street, Zip 82070–5195; tel. 307/742–2141; J. Michael Boyd, Chief Executive Officer (Total facility includes 13 beds in nursing home–type unit) **A**1 9 10 **F**3 7 8 12 14 15 16 17 18 19 21 22 26 28 29 30 33 34 35 37 39 40 41 44 45 46 49 52 54 55 56 57 58 61 63 64 65 67 68 70 71 73 74 **P**5 8
Web address: www.ivinsonhospital.org

| | 16 | 10 | 74 | 2732 | 24 | 43912 | 427 | 26854 | 11735 | 363 |

LOVELL—Big Horn County

★ NORTH BIG HORN HOSPITAL, 1115 Lane 12, Zip 82431–9580, Mailing Address: P.O. Box 518, Zip 82431–0518; tel. 307/548–2771; Michael R. Piper, Administrator (Total facility includes 95 beds in nursing home–type unit) **A**9 10 **F**1 8 12 14 15 16 17 22 24 26 28 30 31 32 34 37 39 44 45 46 49 51 64 65 66 67 71 73
Web address: www.nbhh.com

| | 16 | 10 | 112 | 371 | 89 | 8319 | 0 | 6898 | 3887 | 182 |

LUSK—Niobrara County

NIOBRARA COUNTY HOSPITAL DISTRICT, 921 Ballencee Avenue, Zip 82225, Mailing Address: P.O. Box 780, Zip 82225–0780; tel. 307/334–2711; Jeffrey L. Neuberger, Administrator (Total facility includes 36 beds in nursing home–type unit) (Nonreporting) **A**9 10

| | 16 | 10 | 46 | — | — | — | — | — | — | — |

NEWCASTLE—Weston County

WESTON COUNTY HEALTH SERVICES, 1124 Washington Street, Zip 82701–2996; tel. 307/746–4491; Jack Brinkers, CHE, Administrator (Total facility includes 51 beds in nursing home–type unit) **A**9 10 **F**7 8 11 15 16 19 22 28 32 35 37 39 40 44 49 64 67 71

| | 13 | 10 | 73 | 352 | 48 | 10388 | 51 | 4626 | 2255 | 98 |

POWELL—Park County

✠ POWELL HOSPITAL, 777 Avenue H, Zip 82435–2296; tel. 307/754–2267; Rod Barton, Chief Executive Officer (Total facility includes 100 beds in nursing home–type unit) **A**1 9 10 **F**7 8 14 16 17 21 22 26 28 29 30 32 33 34 35 37 39 40 41 44 48 49 50 51 64 65 66 67 71 73 **P**1 **S** Brim Healthcare, Inc., Brentwood, TN
Web address: www.wir.net/powell–hospital

| | 23 | 10 | 140 | 995 | 106 | 15504 | 219 | 11971 | 6367 | 245 |

RAWLINS—Carbon County

MEMORIAL HOSPITAL OF CARBON COUNTY, 2221 West Elm Street, Zip 82301–5108; tel. 307/324–2221; Richard Johnson, Chief Executive Officer (Total facility includes 10 beds in nursing home–type unit) (Nonreporting) **A**9 10

| | 13 | 10 | 45 | — | — | — | — | — | — | — |

RIVERTON—Fremont County

COLUMBIA RIVERTON MEMORIAL HOSPITAL See Riverton Memorial Hospital

✠ RIVERTON MEMORIAL HOSPITAL, (Formerly Columbia Riverton Memorial Hospital), 2100 West Sunset Drive, Zip 82501–2274; tel. 307/856–4161 **A**1 9 10 **F**7 8 11 14 15 16 19 21 22 28 30 31 32 33 35 37 39 40 44 45 46 49 65 70 71 73 **P**7 **S** LifePoint Hospitals, Inc., Nashville, TN
Web address: www.riverton–hospital.com

| | 33 | 10 | 59 | 1860 | 18 | 29499 | 247 | 12898 | 5227 | 224 |

ROCK SPRINGS—Sweetwater County

✠ MEMORIAL HOSPITAL OF SWEETWATER COUNTY, 1200 College Drive, Zip 82901–5868, Mailing Address: Box 1359, Zip 82902–1359; tel. 307/362–3711; John M. Ferry, Executive Director **A**1 9 10 **F**7 8 12 14 15 16 17 19 20 22 28 30 33 35 36 37 39 40 42 44 45 46 49 65 70 71 73

| | 13 | 10 | 99 | 2254 | 20 | 82884 | 518 | 22472 | 9172 | 318 |

SHERIDAN—Sheridan County

□ MEMORIAL HOSPITAL OF SHERIDAN COUNTY, 1401 West Fifth Street, Zip 82801–2799; tel. 307/672–1000; T. Marvin Goldman, Administrator **A**1 9 10 **F**7 8 11 14 15 19 21 22 23 28 32 33 35 37 40 42 44 46 49 56 60 65 67 71 73 74

| | 13 | 10 | 60 | 2513 | 30 | 38450 | 266 | 22156 | 10910 | 350 |

✠ VETERANS AFFAIRS MEDICAL CENTER, 1898 Fort Road, Zip 82801–8320; tel. 307/672–3473; Maureen Humphrys, Director (Total facility includes 50 beds in nursing home–type unit) **A**1 9 **F**3 8 11 12 15 16 19 20 21 22 24 25 26 27 28 30 32 34 35 39 41 44 45 46 49 51 52 54 56 57 58 59 60 64 65 67 71 73 74 **P**6 **S** Department of Veterans Affairs, Washington, DC

| | 45 | 22 | 121 | 1465 | 125 | 46191 | 0 | 30942 | 16589 | 423 |

SUNDANCE—Crook County

CROOK COUNTY MEDICAL SERVICES DISTRICT, 713 Oak Street, Zip 82729, Mailing Address: P.O. Box 517, Zip 82729–0517; tel. 307/283–3501; Don A. Nelson, Administrator (Total facility includes 32 beds in nursing home–type unit) **A**9 10 **F**1 14 15 16 22 28 32 33 45 46 49 64 65 71 73 **P**6

| | 16 | 10 | 48 | 239 | 36 | 3605 | 0 | 3722 | 2012 | 87 |

THERMOPOLIS—Hot Springs County

✠ HOT SPRINGS COUNTY MEMORIAL HOSPITAL, 150 East Arapahoe Street, Zip 82443–2498; tel. 307/864–3121; Edward G. Leake, Chief Executive Officer **A**1 9 10 **F**7 8 15 19 22 28 32 34 37 40 44 45 48 63 65 71

| | 13 | 10 | 49 | 1144 | 11 | 10607 | 51 | 6934 | 3005 | 92 |

Hospital, Address, Telephone, Administrator, Approval, Facility, and Physician Codes, Health Care System, Network	Classi-fication Codes		Utilization Data					Expense (thousands) of dollars		
★ American Hospital Association (AHA) membership □ Joint Commission on Accreditation of Healthcare Organizations (JCAHO) accreditation + American Osteopathic Healthcare Association (AOHA) membership ○ American Osteopathic Association (AOA) accreditation △ Commission on Accreditation of Rehabilitation Facilities (CARF) accreditation Control codes 61, 63, 64, 71, 72 and 73 indicate hospitals listed by AOHA, but not registered by AHA. For definition of numerical codes, see page A4	Control	Service	Staffed Beds	Admissions	Census	Outpatient Visits	Births	Total	Payroll	Personnel

TORRINGTON—Goshen County

✠ COMMUNITY HOSPITAL, 2000 Campbell Drive, Zip 82240–1597; tel. 307/532–4181; Charles Myers, Administrator **A**1 9 10 **F**7 8 11 12 17 19 22 26 28 30 32 34 35 36 37 39 42 44 49 64 65 66 67 71 **S** Lutheran Health Systems, Fargo, ND	23	10	36	1266	19	36436	120	7225	3258	165

WHEATLAND—Platte County

✠ PLATTE COUNTY MEMORIAL HOSPITAL, 201 14th Street, Zip 82201–3201, Mailing Address: P.O. Box 848, Zip 82201–0848; tel. 307/322–3636; Dana K. Barnett, Administrator (Total facility includes 43 beds in nursing home–type unit) **A**1 9 10 **F**7 8 12 14 15 16 19 22 28 29 34 35 37 44 64 65 71 73 **S** Lutheran Health Systems, Fargo, ND	23	10	86	1108	67	29428	78	5727	2500	148

WORLAND—Washakie County

✠ WASHAKIE MEMORIAL HOSPITAL, 400 South 15th Street, Zip 82401–3531, Mailing Address: P.O. Box 700, Zip 82401–0700; tel. 307/347–3221; James Kiser, Administrator **A**1 9 10 **F**7 8 12 15 16 17 19 22 28 30 32 34 35 37 40 41 42 44 49 64 65 67 71 73 **P**7 **S** Lutheran Health Systems, Fargo, ND	23	10	30	1052	11	38418	84	8744	3913	120

Hospital, Address, Telephone, Administrator, Approval, Facility, and Physician Codes, Health Care System, Network	Classi-fication Codes		Utilization Data					Expense (thousands) of dollars		
	Control	Service	Staffed Beds	Admissions	Census	Outpatient Visits	Births	Total	Payroll	Personnel

- ★ American Hospital Association (AHA) membership
- ☐ Joint Commission on Accreditation of Healthcare Organizations (JCAHO) accreditation
- ＋ American Osteopathic Healthcare Association (AOHA) membership
- ○ American Osteopathic Association (AOA) accreditation
- △ Commission on Accreditation of Rehabilitation Facilities (CARF) accreditation
  Control codes 61, 63, 64, 71, 72 and 73 indicate hospitals listed by AOHA, but not registered by AHA. For definition of numerical codes, see page A4

AMERICAN SAMOA

PAGO PAGO—American Samoa County

Hospital	Control	Service	Staffed Beds	Admissions	Census	Outpatient Visits	Births	Total	Payroll	Personnel
LYNDON B. JOHNSON TROPICAL MEDICAL CENTER, Zip 96799; tel. 684/633–1222; Iotamo T. Saleapaga, M.D., Director Health (Nonreporting) A10	12	10	125	—	—	—	—	—	—	—

GUAM

AGANA—Guam County

Hospital	Control	Service	Staffed Beds	Admissions	Census	Outpatient Visits	Births	Total	Payroll	Personnel
☒ U. S. NAVAL HOSPITAL, Mailing Address: PSC 490, Box 7607, FPO, AP, Zip 96538–1600; tel. 671/344–9340; Captain David Wheeler, Sr., Chief Executive Officer (Nonreporting) A1 S Department of Navy, Washington, DC	43	10	55							

TAMUNING—Guam County

Hospital	Control	Service	Staffed Beds	Admissions	Census	Outpatient Visits	Births	Total	Payroll	Personnel
GUAM MEMORIAL HOSPITAL AUTHORITY, 850 Governor Carlos G. Camacho Road, Zip 96911; tel. 671/647–2211; Tyrone J. Taitano, Administrator (Total facility includes 29 beds in nursing home–type unit) F7 8 16 19 22 31 34 35 37 38 39 40 44 45 46 47 48 49 63 64 65 68 71	12	10	186	11647	148	—	3699	64979	32757	842

MARSHALL ISLANDS

KWAJALEIN ISLAND—Marshall Islands County

Hospital	Control	Service	Staffed Beds	Admissions	Census	Outpatient Visits	Births	Total	Payroll	Personnel
KWAJALEIN HOSPITAL, U.S. Army Kwajalein Atoll, Zip 96960, Mailing Address: Box 1702, APO, AP, Zip 96555–5000; tel. 805/355–2225; Mike Mathews, Administrator (Nonreporting) S Department of the Army, Office of the Surgeon General, Falls Church, VA	42	10	14	—	—	—	—	—	—	—

PUERTO RICO

AGUADILLA—Aguadilla County

Hospital	Control	Service	Staffed Beds	Admissions	Census	Outpatient Visits	Births	Total	Payroll	Personnel
☒ AGUADILLA GENERAL HOSPITAL, Carr Aguadilla San Juan, Zip 00605, Mailing Address: P.O. Box 4036, Zip 00605; tel. 787/891–3000; William Rodriguez Castro, Executive Director (Nonreporting) A1 9 10 S Puerto Rico Department of Health, San Juan, PR	12	10	110	—	—	—	—	—	—	—

AIBONITO—Aibonito County

Hospital	Control	Service	Staffed Beds	Admissions	Census	Outpatient Visits	Births	Total	Payroll	Personnel
★ MENNONITE GENERAL HOSPITAL, Jose Vasquez, Zip 00705, Mailing Address: P.O. Box 1379, Zip 00705; tel. 787/735–8001; Domingo Torres Zayas, CHE, Executive Director A9 10 F19 22 33 34 35 39 40 42 44 49 56 58 65 71 73	23	10	131	9543	106	76393	1112	28132	10947	737

ARECIBO—Arecibo County

Hospital	Control	Service	Staffed Beds	Admissions	Census	Outpatient Visits	Births	Total	Payroll	Personnel
★ ARECIBO REGIONAL HOSPITAL, 129 San Luis Avenue, Zip 00612, Mailing Address: P.O. Box 659, Zip 00613; tel. 787/878–7272; Samuel Monroig, Vice President for Administration (Nonreporting) A9 10 S Puerto Rico Department of Health, San Juan, PR	12	10	183	—	—	—	—	—	—	—
HOSPITAL DR. SUSONI, 55 Nicomedes Rivera Street, Zip 00612, Mailing Address: P.O. Box 145200, Zip 00614; tel. 787/878–1010; Hector Barreto, M.D., Director (Nonreporting) A9 10	33	10	138	—	—	—	—	—	—	—
★ HOSPITAL EL BUEN PASTOR, 52 De Diego, Zip 00612, Mailing Address: P.O. Box 413, Zip 00612; tel. 787/878–2730; Julio Galarce, Administrator (Nonreporting)	33	10	72	—	—	—	—	—	—	—

ARROYO—Arroyo County

Hospital	Control	Service	Staffed Beds	Admissions	Census	Outpatient Visits	Births	Total	Payroll	Personnel
★ LAFAYETTE HOSPITAL, Central Lafayette, Zip 00714, Mailing Address: P.O. Box 207, Zip 00714; tel. 787/839–3232; Francisco Santiago–Vega, Consultor A9 10 F14 15 16 19 44 64 65 71	33	10	40	2428	25	—	172	4770	1417	109

BAYAMON—Bayamon County

Hospital	Control	Service	Staffed Beds	Admissions	Census	Outpatient Visits	Births	Total	Payroll	Personnel
☒ HOSPITAL HERMANOS MELENDEZ, Route 2, KM 11–7, Zip 00960, Mailing Address: P.O. Box 306, Zip 00960; tel. 787/785–9784; Tomas Martinez, Administrator A1 9 10 F11 19 22 37 40 44 49 63 65 71 73	33	10	211	14244	178	52299	2032	36346	12724	639
★ HOSPITAL MATILDE BRENES, Extension Hermanas Davila, Zip 00960, Mailing Address: P.O. Box 2957, Zip 00960; tel. 809/786–6315; Manuel J. Vazquez, Administrator (Nonreporting) A9 10	33	10	95	—	—	—	—	—	—	—

Hospital, Address, Telephone, Administrator, Approval, Facility, and Physician Codes, Health Care System, Network	Classi-fication Codes		Utilization Data					Expense (thousands) of dollars		
	Control	Service	Staffed Beds	Admissions	Census	Outpatient Visits	Births	Total	Payroll	Personnel

★ American Hospital Association (AHA) membership
□ Joint Commission on Accreditation of Healthcare Organizations (JCAHO) accreditation
+ American Osteopathic Healthcare Association (AOHA) membership
○ American Osteopathic Association (AOA) accreditation
△ Commission on Accreditation of Rehabilitation Facilities (CARF) accreditation
Control codes 61, 63, 64, 71, 72 and 73 indicate hospitals listed by AOHA, but not registered by AHA. For definition of numerical codes, see page A4

Hospital	Control	Service	Staffed Beds	Admissions	Census	Outpatient Visits	Births	Total	Payroll	Personnel
✠ HOSPITAL SAN PABLO, Calle San Cruz 70, Zip 00961, Mailing Address: P.O. Box 236, Zip 00960; tel. 787/740–4747; Jorge De Jesus, Executive Director (Nonreporting) **A**1 3 5 9 10 **S** Universal Health Services, Inc., King of Prussia, PA	33	10	364	—	—	—	—	—	—	—
✠ HOSPITAL UNIVERSITARIO DR. RAMON RUIZ ARNAU, Avenue Laurel, Santa Juanita, Zip 00956; tel. 787/787–5151; Nilda E. Diaz, Executive Director **A**1 3 5 9 10 **F**1 3 5 7 8 11 13 17 18 19 21 22 27 28 29 30 31 34 35 37 38 39 40 41 42 47 49 50 53 56 57 58 63 65 73 **P**8 **S** Puerto Rico Department of Health, San Juan, PR	16	10	340	12251	195	115260	4260	—	—	875
✠ MEPSI CENTER, Carretera Numero 2 K 8–2, Zip 00959–6089, Mailing Address: Carretera Numero 2 K. 8–2, Zip 00960–6089; tel. 787/793–3030; Manuel G. Mendez, Operating Trustee **A**1 9 10 **F**1 2 14 15 16 17 19 26 34 35 41 46 49 52 53 54 55 57 59 65 71	33	22	450	4587	140	—	0	16236	7131	399

CAGUAS—Caguas County

Hospital	Control	Service	Staffed Beds	Admissions	Census	Outpatient Visits	Births	Total	Payroll	Personnel
✠ CAGUAS REGIONAL HOSPITAL, Carretera Caguas A Cidra, Zip 00725, Mailing Address: P.O. Box 5729, Zip 00726; tel. 787/744–2500; Noemi Davis Marte, M.D., Medical Director (Nonreporting) **A**1 3 5 9 10 **S** Puerto Rico Department of Health, San Juan, PR	12	10	256	—	—	—	—	—	—	—
□ HOSPITAL INTERAMERICANO DE MEDICINA AVANZADA, Avenida Luis Munoz Marin, Zip 00726, Mailing Address: Apartado 4980, Zip 00726; tel. 787/743–3434; Carlos M. Pineiro, President **A**1 9 10 **F**4 8 10 11 15 16 19 21 22 25 33 35 37 38 39 40 43 44 47 49 52 53 59 63 65 67 71 73	33	10	333	16972	308	125301	2321	60908	15371	1154

CAROLINA—Carolina County

Hospital	Control	Service	Staffed Beds	Admissions	Census	Outpatient Visits	Births	Total	Payroll	Personnel
✠ HOSPITAL DR. FEDERICO TRILLA, 65th Infanteria, KM 8 3, Zip 00984, Mailing Address: P.O. Box 3869, Zip 00984; tel. 787/757–1800; Ivon Millon, Chief Executive Officer (Nonreporting) **A**1 3 5 9 10	33	10	220	—	—	—	—	—	—	—

CASTANER—Lares County

Hospital	Control	Service	Staffed Beds	Admissions	Census	Outpatient Visits	Births	Total	Payroll	Personnel
★ CASTANER GENERAL HOSPITAL, KM 64–2, Route 135, Zip 00631, Mailing Address: P.O. Box 1003, Zip 00631; tel. 787/829–5010; Domingo Monroig, Administrator (Nonreporting) **A**9 10	23	10	24	—	—	—	—	—	—	—

CAYEY—Cayey County

Hospital	Control	Service	Staffed Beds	Admissions	Census	Outpatient Visits	Births	Total	Payroll	Personnel
★ HOSPITAL MENONITA DE CAYEY, 4 H. Mendoza Street, Zip 00737, Mailing Address: P.O. Box 373130, Zip 00737; tel. 787/263–1001; Domingo Torres–Zayas, Executive Director (Nonreporting) **A**9 10	23	10	50	—	—	—	—	—	—	—

CIDRA—Cidra County

Hospital	Control	Service	Staffed Beds	Admissions	Census	Outpatient Visits	Births	Total	Payroll	Personnel
✠ FIRST HOSPITAL PANAMERICANO, State Road 787 KM 1 5, Zip 00739, Mailing Address: P.O. Box 1398, Zip 00739; tel. 787/739–5555; Jorge Torres, Executive Director **A**1 5 10 **F**2 15 16 26 52 53 54 55 56 57 58 59 65 67 **S** FHC Health Systems, Norfolk, VA	33	22	155	6421	148	—	0	14362	7796	416

FAJARDO—Fajardo County

Hospital	Control	Service	Staffed Beds	Admissions	Census	Outpatient Visits	Births	Total	Payroll	Personnel
DR. JOSE RAMOS LEBRON HOSPITAL, General Valero Avenue, #194, Zip 00738, Mailing Address: P.O. Box 1028, Zip 00738; tel. 787/863–0505; Maria Elena Rodriguez, Executive Administrator **A**9 10 **F**2 16 19 22 37 39 40 44 65 **S** Universal Health Services, Inc., King of Prussia, PA	33	10	107	1801	32	—	57	—	—	384
★ HOSPITAL DOCTOR GUBERN, (Formerly Doctors Gubern's Hospital), (Includes Dr. Gubern's Hospital, General Valero Avenue 267 & 261, Mailing Address: Box 846, Zip 00738; tel. 809/792–3495; Antonio R. Barcelo, Director), 110 Antonio R. Barcelo, Zip 00738, Mailing Address: P.O. Box 846, Zip 00738–0846; tel. 787/863–0669; Edwin Sueiro, Executive Director (Nonreporting) **A**9 10 **S** United Medical Corporation, Windermere, FL	33	10	51	—	—	—	—	—	—	—

GUAYAMA—Guayama County

Hospital	Control	Service	Staffed Beds	Admissions	Census	Outpatient Visits	Births	Total	Payroll	Personnel
✠ DR. ALEJANDRO BUITRAGO–GUAYAMA AREA HOSPITAL, Avenue Pedro Albesus, Zip 00784, Mailing Address: Call Box 1006, Zip 00785–1006; tel. 787/864–4300; Carlos Rodriguez Mateo, M.D., Medical Director (Nonreporting) **A**1 9 10	12	10	155	—	—	—	—	—	—	—
★ HOSPITAL SANTA ROSA, Veterans Avenue, Zip 00784, Mailing Address: P.O. Box 10008, Zip 00785; tel. 787/864–0101; Herson E. Morales, Executive Director **A**9 10 **F**7 10 16 19 22 35 37 40 44 71	23	10	89	3832	38	28280	483	5239	3007	215

HUMACAO—Humacao County

Hospital	Control	Service	Staffed Beds	Admissions	Census	Outpatient Visits	Births	Total	Payroll	Personnel
□ FONT MARTELO HOSPITAL, 3 Font Martelo Street, Zip 00792, Mailing Address: P.O. Box 639, Zip 00792–0639; tel. 787/852–2424; Julio A. Ortiz, M.D., Chairman (Nonreporting) **A**1 9 10	33	10	64	—	—	—	—	—	—	—
HOSPITAL DR. DOMINGUEZ, 300 Font Martelo Street, Zip 00791, Mailing Address: P.O. Box 699, Zip 00792; tel. 787/852–0505; Rogelio Diaz–Reyes, Administrator (Nonreporting) **A**9 10	33	10	54	—	—	—	—	—	—	—
★ HOSPITAL SUB–REGIONAL DR. VICTOR R. NUNEZ, Avenida Tejas, Expreso Cruz Ortiz Stella, Zip 00791; tel. 787/852–2727; Ahmed Alvarez Pabon, Executive Director (Nonreporting) **A**10 **S** Puerto Rico Department of Health, San Juan, PR	12	10	83	—	—	—	—	—	—	—
★ RYDER MEMORIAL HOSPITAL, 355 Font Martelo Street, Zip 00792, Mailing Address: P.O. Box 859, Zip 00792–0859; tel. 787/852–0768; Saturnino Pena Flores, Executive Director (Total facility includes 62 beds in nursing home–type unit) **A**9 10 **F**1 8 11 14 16 17 19 20 22 25 28 30 31 32 33 34 35 37 39 40 41 42 44 45 49 51 58 62 63 64 65 68 71 73 **P**8	23	10	206	9816	146	138848	1143	40993	17738	1193

MANATI—Manati County

Hospital	Control	Service	Staffed Beds	Admissions	Census	Outpatient Visits	Births	Total	Payroll	Personnel
★ CLINICA SAN AGUSTIN, Route 2, KM 49–5, Zip 00674, Mailing Address: P.O. Box 991, Zip 00674; tel. 787/854–2091; Astrid Abreu, Administrator **A**9 10 **F**15 16 22 39 44 45 51 58 65 71 **P**5 8	33	10	12	1144	13	—	88	2749	885	68

Hospital, Address, Telephone, Administrator, Approval, Facility, and Physician Codes, Health Care System, Network	Classi-fication Codes		Utilization Data					Expense (thousands) of dollars		
★ American Hospital Association (AHA) membership □ Joint Commission on Accreditation of Healthcare Organizations (JCAHO) accreditation + American Osteopathic Healthcare Association (AOHA) membership ○ American Osteopathic Association (AOA) accreditation △ Commission on Accreditation of Rehabilitation Facilities (CARF) accreditation Control codes 61, 63, 64, 71, 72 and 73 indicate hospitals listed by AOHA, but not registered by AHA. For definition of numerical codes, see page A4	Control	Service	Staffed Beds	Admissions	Census	Outpatient Visits	Births	Total	Payroll	Personnel

⊠ DOCTORS CENTER, KM 47–7, Zip 00674, Mailing Address: P.O. Box 30532, Zip 00674; tel. 787/854–1795; Carla Blanco, Administrator (Nonreporting) **A**1 3 9 10	33	10	150	—	—	—	—	—	—	—
MAYAGUEZ—Mayaguez County										
⊠ BELLA VISTA HOSPITAL, State Road 349, Zip 00680, Mailing Address: P.O. Box 1750, Zip 00681; tel. 787/834–6000; Ruth M. Ortiz, Chief Operating Officer (Nonreporting) **A**1 3 9 10 **S** Adventist Health System Sunbelt Health Care Corporation, Winter Park, FL	21	10	157	—	—	—	—	—	—	—
CLINICA ESPANOLA, Barrio La Quinta, Zip 00680, Mailing Address: P.O. Box 490, Zip 00681–0490; tel. 787/832–0442; Emigdio Inigo-Agostini, M.D., Board President (Nonreporting) **A**9 10	33	10	69	—	—	—	—	—	—	—
⊠ DR. RAMON E. BETANCES HOSPITAL–MAYAGUEZ MEDICAL CENTER BRANCH, 410 Hostos Avenue, Zip 00680; tel. 787/834–8686; Maria Del Pilar Rodriguez, Administrator **A**1 3 5 10 **F**8 19 20 22 30 34 37 38 39 40 42 47 60 65 70 71 **P**1 6 **S** Puerto Rico Department of Health, San Juan, PR	12	10	206	8384	110	116142	1890	—	—	1036
★ HOSPITAL PEREA, 15 Basora Street, Zip 00681, Mailing Address: P.O. Box 170, Zip 00681; tel. 787/834–0101; Ramon Lopez, Administrator (Nonreporting) **A**10 **S** United Medical Corporation, Windermere, FL	33	10	82	—	—	—	—	—	—	—
PONCE—Ponce County										
⊠ DR. PILA'S HOSPITAL, Avenida Las Americas, Zip 00731, Mailing Address: P.O. Box 1910, Zip 00733–1910; tel. 787/848–5600; Miguel J. Bustelo, Executive Director **A**1 3 5 9 10 **F**4 7 14 15 16 19 21 22 23 28 30 32 34 37 40 41 44 46 49 50 51 62 63 65 71	23	10	177	9751	136	148825	850	37210	11254	586
⊠ HOSPITAL DE DAMAS, Ponce by Pass, Zip 00731; tel. 787/840–8686; Roberto A. Rentas, Administrator (Total facility includes 28 beds in nursing home–type unit) (Nonreporting) **A**1 3 5 9 10	23	10	334	—	—	—	—	—	—	—
⊠ HOSPITAL EPISCOPAL SAN LUCAS, Guadalupe Street, Zip 00731, Mailing Address: P.O. Box 2027, Zip 00733; tel. 787/840–4545; Guillermo J. Martin, Executive Director **A**1 3 5 10 **F**4 7 10 11 15 16 19 21 22 27 31 32 34 37 38 40 44 45 49 50 63 64 65 **P**8	21	10	168	8552	137	27121	504	35085	11507	666
⊠ HOSPITAL ONCOLOGICO ANDRES GRILLASCA, Centro Medico De Ponce, Zip 00733, Mailing Address: P.O. Box 1324, Zip 00733; tel. 787/848–0800; Santiago Rivera, Executive Administrator (Nonreporting) **A**1 2 5 9 10	23	49	53	—	—	—	—	—	—	—
⊠ PONCE REGIONAL HOSPITAL, 917 Tito Castro Avenue, Zip 00731; tel. 787/844–2080; Julio Andino Rodriguez, Executive Director **A**1 3 5 9 10 **F**4 8 10 11 15 16 19 20 22 27 34 35 37 38 39 40 43 44 47 49 65 **S** Puerto Rico Department of Health, San Juan, PR	16	10	307	13586	184	173507	3139	—	15391	—
SAN GERMAN—San German County										
⊠ HOSPITAL DE LA CONCEPCION, 41 Luna Street, Zip 00683, Mailing Address: P.O. Box 285, Zip 00683–0285; tel. 787/892–1860; Jaime F. Maestre Grau, Executive Director **A**1 2 3 5 9 10 **F**14 15 16 19 22 27 35 37 40 44 46 49 50 54 60 63 65 71 **P**5	21	10	123	6719	93	—	428	22199	8964	593
SAN JUAN—San Juan County										
⊠ ASHFORD PRESBYTERIAN COMMUNITY HOSPITAL, 1451 Ashford Avenue Condado, Zip 00907, Mailing Address: P.O. Box 9020032, Zip 00902–0032; tel. 787/721–2160; Pedro J. Gonzalez, Executive Director (Nonreporting) **A**1 9 10	23	10	180	—	—	—	—	—	—	—
⊠ AUXILIO MUTUO HOSPITAL, Ponce De Leon Avenue, Zip 00919, Mailing Address: P.O. Box 191227, Zip 00919–1227; tel. 787/758–2000; Ivan E. Colon, Administrator (Nonreporting) **A**1 9 10	23	10	402	—	—	—	—	—	—	—
⊠ BHC HOSPITAL SAN JUAN CAPESTRANO, Mailing Address: Rural Route 2, Box 11, Zip 00926; tel. 787/760–0222; Laura Vargas, Administrator and Chief Executive Officer (Nonreporting) **A**1 10 **S** Behavioral Healthcare Corporation, Nashville, TN	33	22	88	—	—	—	—	—	—	—
⊠ CARDIOVASCULAR CENTER OF PUERTO RICO AND THE CARIBBEAN, Americo Mirada Centro Medico, Zip 00936, Mailing Address: P.O. Box 366528, Zip 00936–6528; tel. 787/754–8500; Marilyn Perez de Vazquez, Executive Director (Nonreporting) **A**1 10	12	49	192	—	—	—	—	—	—	—
DOCTORS HOSPITAL, 1395 San Rafael Street, Zip 00910, Mailing Address: Box 11338, Santurce Station, Zip 00910; tel. 809/723–2950; Georgina Mattei de Collazo, Executive Director (Nonreporting) **A**9 10	33	10	96	—	—	—	—	—	—	—
FUNDACION HOSPITAL METROPOLITAN See Hospital Metropolitan										
⊠ HOSPITAL DEL MAESTRO, 550 Sergio Cuevas, Zip 00918, Mailing Address: P.O. Box 364708, Zip 00936–4708; tel. 787/758–8383; Luisa Rivera Lugaro, Administrator (Nonreporting) **A**1 10	23	10	214	—	—	—	—	—	—	—
⊠ HOSPITAL METROPOLITAN, (Formerly Fundacion Hospital Metropolitan), 1785 Route 21, Zip 00922, Mailing Address: P.O. Box 11981, Zip 00922; tel. 787/782–9999; Henry Ruberte, Executive Director (Nonreporting) **A**1 9	23	10	119	—	—	—	—	—	—	—
★ HOSPITAL PAVIA–HATO REY, (Formerly Hato Rey Community Hospital), Mailing Address: 435 Ponce De Leon, Hato Rey, Zip 00917; tel. 787/754–0909; Jorge De Jesus, Executive Director (Nonreporting) **A**9 10 **S** United Medical Corporation, Windermere, FL	33	10	105	—	—	—	—	—	—	—
⊠ HOSPITAL PAVIA–SANTURCE, 1462 Asia Street, Zip 00909, Mailing Address: Box 11137, Santurce Station, Zip 00910; tel. 787/727–6060; Jorge De Jesus, Executive Director (Nonreporting) **A**1 9 10 **S** United Medical Corporation, Windermere, FL	33	10	183	—	—	—	—	—	—	—

Hospital, Address, Telephone, Administrator, Approval, Facility, and Physician Codes, Health Care System, Network	Classi-fication Codes		Utilization Data					Expense (thousands) of dollars		
	Control	Service	Staffed Beds	Admissions	Census	Outpatient Visits	Births	Total	Payroll	Personnel

★ American Hospital Association (AHA) membership
□ Joint Commission on Accreditation of Healthcare Organizations (JCAHO) accreditation
+ American Osteopathic Healthcare Association (AOHA) membership
○ American Osteopathic Association (AOA) accreditation
△ Commission on Accreditation of Rehabilitation Facilities (CARF) accreditation
Control codes 61, 63, 64, 71, 72 and 73 indicate hospitals listed by AOHA, but not registered by AHA. For definition of numerical codes, see page A4

	Control	Service	Staffed Beds	Admissions	Census	Outpatient Visits	Births	Total	Payroll	Personnel
★ HOSPITAL SAN FRANCISCO, 371 De Diego Avenue, Zip 00923, Mailing Address: P.O. Box 29025, Zip 00929–0025; tel. 787/767–2528; Domingo Nevarez, Executive Director **A**10 **F**4 8 10 11 12 14 15 16 19 22 28 35 37 38 40 42 43 44 45 46 47 64 65 71 73 **S** Universal Health Services, Inc., King of Prussia, PA	33	10	150	8064	129	79750	0	28776	10760	790
⊠ I. GONZALEZ MARTINEZ ONCOLOGIC HOSPITAL, Puerto Rico Medical Center, Hato Rey, Zip 00935, Mailing Address: P.O. Box 191811, Zip 00919–1811; tel. 787/765–2382; Celia Molano, Executive Director (Nonreporting) **A**1 2 3 5 9 10	23	49	80	—	—	—	—	—	—	—
★ INDUSTRIAL HOSPITAL, Puerto Rico Medical Center, Zip 00936, Mailing Address: P.O. Box 5028, Zip 00936; tel. 787/764–3660; Domingo Velez, Administrator **A**5 **F**4 9 19 20 21 22 27 33 34 35 37 39 41 43 44 45 48 49 50 63 65 67 69 70 71 72 **P**5	12	10	125	3953	88	206164	—	—	—	701
★ SAN CARLOS GENERAL HOSPITAL, 1822 Ponce De Leon Avenue, Zip 00919, Mailing Address: Call Box 8410, Zip 00910–8410; tel. 787/727–5858; Pedro J. Gonzalez, Executive Director (Total facility includes 8 beds in nursing home–type unit) (Nonreporting) **A**9 10	33	10	66	—	—	—	—	—	—	—
★ SAN JORGE CHILDREN'S HOSPITAL, 258 San Jorge Avenue, Zip 00912; tel. 787/727–1000; Domingo Cruz Vivaldi, Administrator (Nonreporting) **A**9 **S** United Medical Corporation, Windermere, FL	33	50	85	—	—	—	—	—	—	—
⊠ SAN JUAN CITY HOSPITAL, Puerto Rico Medical Center, Zip 00928, Mailing Address: Apartado 21405, Rio Piedras, Zip 00928; tel. 787/766–2222; Maritza Espinosa, Chief Executive Officer **A**1 3 5 10 **F**1 2 3 4 5 6 7 8 9 10 11 12 13 14 15 16 17 18 19 20 21 22 23 24 26 27 28 29 30 31 32 33 34 35 36 37 38 39 40 41 42 43 44 45 46 47 48 49 50 51 52 53 54 55 56 57 58 59 60 61 62 63 64 65 66 67 68 69 70 71 72 73 74 **P**6	14	10	311	11576	193	68075	3740	—	—	1098
★ STATE PSYCHIATRIC HOSPITAL, Monacillos Avenue, Zip 00936, Mailing Address: Call Box 2100, Caparra Heights Station, Zip 00922–2100; tel. 787/766–4646; Guadalupe Alvarez, Administrator (Nonreporting) **A**3 **S** Puerto Rico Department of Health, San Juan, PR	12	22	425	—	—	—	—	—	—	—
★ U. S. NAVAL HOSPITAL, Roosevelt Roads, Mailing Address: P.O. Box 3007, FPO, AA, Zip 34051–8100; tel. 787/865–5762; Captain G. R. Brown, Commanding Officer (Nonreporting) **S** Department of Navy, Washington, DC	43	10	35	—	—	—	—	—	—	—
⊠ UNIVERSITY HOSPITAL, Puerto Rico Medical Center, Rio Piedras Station, Zip 00935; tel. 787/754–3633; Betty Ocasio, Executive Director (Nonreporting) **A**1 2 3 5 9 10 **S** Puerto Rico Department of Health, San Juan, PR	12	10	297	—	—	—	—	—	—	—
⊠ UNIVERSITY PEDIATRIC HOSPITAL, Mailing Address: Call Box 191079, Zip 00910–1079; tel. 787/756–3198; Sylvia Mercado, Chief Executive Officer (Nonreporting) **A**1 3 5 9 10	12	50	135	—	—	—	—	—	—	—
⊠ VETERANS AFFAIRS MEDICAL CENTER, One Veterans Plaza, Zip 00927–5800; tel. 787/766–5665; James A. Palmer, Director (Total facility includes 120 beds in nursing home–type unit) (Nonreporting) **A**1 2 3 5 8 **S** Department of Veterans Affairs, Washington, DC	45	10	693	—	—	—	—	—	—	—
VEGA BAJA—Vega Baja County										
★ WILMA N. VAZQUEZ MEDICAL CENTER, KM 395 Road 2, Call Box 7001, Zip 00694; tel. 787/858–1580; Ramon J. Vilar, Administrator (Total facility includes 20 beds in nursing home–type unit) **A**9 10 **F**19 22 27 35 37 44 49 64 65 71 **P**8	33	10	130	4541	57	28318	36	10092	—	231
YAUCO—Yauco County										
⊠ BELLA VISTA SOUTHWEST HOSPITAL, (Formerly Hospital De Area De Yauco), Carretera 128 KM 1 0, Zip 00698, Mailing Address: P.O. Box 68, Zip 00698; tel. 787/856–2105; Nemuel O. Artiles, Chief Executive Officer (Nonreporting) **A**1 5 10	12	10	123	—	—	—	—	—	—	—

VIRGIN ISLANDS

	Control	Service	Staffed Beds	Admissions	Census	Outpatient Visits	Births	Total	Payroll	Personnel
CHRISTIANSTED—St. Croix County										
⊠ GOVERNOR JUAN F. LOUIS HOSPITAL, 4007 Estate Diamond Ruby, Zip 00820–4421; tel. 340/778–6311; George H. McCoy, Chief Executive Officer **A**1 10 **F**4 10 11 12 15 16 17 19 20 22 27 28 30 34 37 38 40 44 46 49 51 52 56 57 64 65 67 71 73	12	10	197	5051	96	24765	970	—	—	592
SAINT THOMAS—St. Thomas County										
ROY LESTER SCHNEIDER HOSPITAL, 9048 Sugar Estate, Charlotte Amalie, Zip 00802; tel. 809/776–8311; Judy Magras, Acting Chief Executive Officer (Nonreporting) **A**10	12	10	133	—	—	—	—	—	—	—

U.S. Government Hospitals
Outside the United States, by Area

GERMANY

Heidelberg: ★ U. S. Army Hospital, APO, AE 09014
Landstuhl: ★ Landstuhl Army Regional Medical Center, APO, AE 09180
Wurzburg: ★ U. S. Army Hospital, APO, USAMEDDAC Wurzburg, AE 09244

ICELAND

Keflavilk: ★ U. S. Naval Hospital–Keflavilk, FPO, PSC 1003, Box 8, AE 09728–0308

ITALY

Naples: ★ U. S. Naval Hospital, FPO, AE 09619

JAPAN

Yokosuka: ★ U. S. Naval Hospital, FPO, Box 1487, AP 96350

KOREA

Seoul: ★ U. S. Army Community Hospital Seoul, APO, AP 96205
Yongsan: Medcom 18th Commander, Facilities Division Eamc L EM, APO, AP 96205

PANAMA

Ancon: ★ Gorgas Army Hospital, APO, AA 34004

SPAIN

Rota: ★ U. S. Naval Hospital, Rota, FPO, PSC 819, Box 18, AE 09645–2500

TAIWAN

Taipei: U. S. Naval Hospital Taipei, Taipei, No 300 Shin–Pai Road, Sec 2

★Indicates membership in the American Hospital Association

This section is an index of all hospitals in alphabetical order by hospital name, followed by the city, state and page reference to the hospital's listing in Section A.

A

A. G. HOLLEY STATE HOSPITAL, LANTANA, FL, p. A88
A. WEBB ROBERTS HOSPITAL, DALLAS, TEXAS, p. A399
ABBEVILLE COUNTY MEMORIAL HOSPITAL, ABBEVILLE, SC, p. A370
ABBEVILLE GENERAL HOSPITAL, ABBEVILLE, LA, p. A177
ABBOTT NORTHWESTERN HOSPITAL, MINNEAPOLIS, MN, p. A225
ABERDEEN–MONROE COUNTY HOSPITAL, ABERDEEN, MS, p. A231
ABILENE REGIONAL MEDICAL CENTER, ABILENE, TX, p. A392
ABINGTON MEMORIAL HOSPITAL, ABINGTON, PA, p. A347
ABRAHAM LINCOLN MEMORIAL HOSPITAL, LINCOLN, IL, p. A128
ABROM KAPLAN MEMORIAL HOSPITAL, KAPLAN, LA, p. A180
ACADIA HOSPITAL, BANGOR, ME, p. A187
ACADIA–ST. LANDRY HOSPITAL, CHURCH POINT, LA, p. A178
ACOMA–CANONCITO–LAGUNA HOSPITAL, SAN FIDEL, NM, p. A280
ACUTE GENERAL HOSPITAL, MERWICK UNIT–EXTENDED CARE AND REHABILITATION, PRINCETON HOUSE UNIT–COMMUNITY MENTAL HEALTH AND SUBSTANCE ABUSE, p. A274
ADAIR COUNTY MEMORIAL HOSPITAL, GREENFIELD, IA, p. A150
ADAMS COUNTY HOSPITAL, WEST UNION, OH, p. A331
ADAMS COUNTY MEMORIAL HOSPITAL, DECATUR, IN, p. A137
ADAMS COUNTY MEMORIAL HOSPITAL AND NURSING CARE UNIT, FRIENDSHIP, WI, p. A458
ADCARE HOSPITAL OF WORCESTER, WORCESTER, MA, p. A205
ADDISON COMMUNITY HOSPITAL, ADDISON, MI, p. A206
ADDISON GILBERT HOSPITAL, GLOUCESTER, MASSACHUSETTS, p. A197
ADENA HEALTH SYSTEM, CHILLICOTHE, OH, p. A319
ADIRONDACK MEDICAL CENTER, SARANAC LAKE, NY, p. A297
ADVENTIST MEDICAL CENTER, PORTLAND, OR, p. A344
AFFILIATED HEALTH SERVICES, MOUNT VERNON, WA, p. A445
AGNESIAN HEALTHCARE, FOND DU LAC, WI, p. A458
AGUADILLA GENERAL HOSPITAL, AGUADILLA, PR, p. A469
AIKEN REGIONAL MEDICAL CENTERS, AIKEN, SC, p. A370
AKRON CITY HOSPITAL, AKRON, OHIO, p. A317
AKRON GENERAL MEDICAL CENTER, AKRON, OH, p. A317
ALAMANCE REGIONAL MEDICAL CENTER, BURLINGTON, NC, p. A303
ALAMEDA COUNTY MEDICAL CENTER, SAN LEANDRO, CA, p. A61
ALAMEDA COUNTY MEDICAL CENTER–HIGHLAND CAMPUS, OAKLAND, CA, p. A54
ALAMEDA HOSPITAL, ALAMEDA, CA, p. A36
ALASKA NATIVE MEDICAL CENTER, ANCHORAGE, AK, p. A20
ALASKA PSYCHIATRIC INSTITUTE, ANCHORAGE, AK, p. A20
ALASKA REGIONAL HOSPITAL, ANCHORAGE, AK, p. A20
ALBANY AREA HOSPITAL AND MEDICAL CENTER, ALBANY, MN, p. A220
ALBANY GENERAL HOSPITAL, ALBANY, OR, p. A342
ALBANY MEDICAL CENTER, ALBANY, NY, p. A281
ALBEMARLE HOSPITAL, ELIZABETH CITY, NC, p. A305
ALBERT EINSTEIN MEDICAL CENTER, PHILADELPHIA, PA, p. A358
ALBERT LEA MEDICAL CENTER, ALBERT LEA, MN, p. A220
ALBERT LINDLEY LEE MEMORIAL HOSPITAL, FULTON, NY, p. A285
ALCOHOL AND DRUG ABUSE TREATMENT CENTER, BUTNER, NORTH CAROLINA, p. A303
ALEDA E. LUTZ VETERANS AFFAIRS MEDICAL CENTER, SAGINAW, MI, p. A216
ALEGENT HEALTH BERGAN MERCY MEDICAL CENTER, OMAHA, NE, p. A260
ALEGENT HEALTH CENTER FOR MENTAL HEALTH, OMAHA, NE, p. A260
ALEGENT HEALTH COMMUNITY MEMORIAL HOSPITAL, MISSOURI VALLEY, IA, p. A152
ALEGENT HEALTH IMMANUEL MEDICAL CENTER, OMAHA, NE, p. A260
ALEGENT HEALTH MERCY HOSPITAL, COUNCIL BLUFFS, IA, p. A147
ALEGENT HEALTH–MEMORIAL HOSPITAL, SCHUYLER, NE, p. A261
ALEGENT–HEALTH MIDLANDS COMMUNITY HOSPITAL, PAPILLION, NE, p. A261

ALEXANDER COMMUNITY HOSPITAL, TAYLORSVILLE, NC, p. A311
ALEXIAN BROTHERS BEHAVIORAL HEALTH HOSPITAL, HOFFMAN ESTATES, IL, p. A127
ALEXIAN BROTHERS HOSPITAL, SAINT LOUIS, MO, p. A247
ALEXIAN BROTHERS HOSPITAL, SAN JOSE, CA, p. A60
ALEXIAN BROTHERS MEDICAL CENTER, ELK GROVE VILLAGE, IL, p. A124
ALFRED AND NORMA LERNER TOWER, BOLWELL HEALTH CENTER, HANNA PAVILION, LAKESIDE HOSPITAL, SAMUEL MATHER PAVILION, RAINBOW BABIES AND CHILDREN'S HOSPITAL, CLEVELAND, OHIO, p. A321
UNIVERSITY MACDONALD WOMEN'S HOSPITAL, CLEVELAND, OHIO, p. A321
ALFRED I.DUPONT HOSPITAL FOR CHILDREN, WILMINGTON, DE, p. A78
ALHAMBRA HOSPITAL, ALHAMBRA, CA, p. A36
ALICE HYDE HOSPITAL ASSOCIATION, MALONE, NY, p. A287
ALICE PECK DAY MEMORIAL HOSPITAL, LEBANON, NH, p. A266
ALICE REGIONAL HOSPITAL, ALICE, TX, p. A392
ALL CHILDREN'S HOSPITAL, SAINT PETERSBURG, FL, p. A94
ALL SAINTS EPISCOPAL HOSPITAL OF FORT WORTH, FORT WORTH, TX, p. A403
ALL SAINTS HOSPITAL–CITYVIEW, FORT WORTH, TX, p. A403
ALLEGAN GENERAL HOSPITAL, ALLEGAN, MI, p. A206
ALLEGHANY MEMORIAL HOSPITAL, SPARTA, NC, p. A311
ALLEGHANY REGIONAL HOSPITAL, LOW MOOR, VA, p. A436
ALLEGHENY UNIVERSITY HOSPITALS–FORBES METROPOLITAN, PITTSBURGH, PA, p. A360
ALLEGHENY UNIVERSITY HOSPITALS, ALLEGHENY GENERAL, PITTSBURGH, PA, p. A360
ALLEGHENY UNIVERSITY HOSPITALS, ALLEGHENY VALLEY, NATRONA HEIGHTS, PA, p. A357
ALLEGHENY UNIVERSITY HOSPITALS, CANONSBURG, CANONSBURG, PA, p. A349
ALLEGHENY UNIVERSITY HOSPITALS, FORBES REGIONAL, MONROEVILLE, PA, p. A356
ALLEN BENNETT HOSPITAL, GREER, SC, p. A373
ALLEN COUNTY HOSPITAL, IOLA, KS, p. A159
ALLEN MEMORIAL HOSPITAL, OBERLIN, OH, p. A327
ALLEN MEMORIAL HOSPITAL, WATERLOO, IA, p. A154
ALLEN MEMORIAL HOSPITAL, MOAB, UT, p. A428
ALLEN PARISH HOSPITAL, KINDER, LA, p. A180
ALLEN–CALDER SKILLED NURSING FACILITY, MOHAWK VALLEY DIVISION, ILION, NEW YORK, p. A299
ALLENDALE COUNTY HOSPITAL, FAIRFAX, SC, p. A372
ALLENMORE HOSPITAL, TACOMA, WASHINGTON, p. A449
ALLENTOWN STATE HOSPITAL, ALLENTOWN, PA, p. A347
ALLIANCE COMMUNITY HOSPITAL, ALLIANCE, OH, p. A317
ALLIANCE HOSPITAL OF SANTA TERESA, SANTA TERESA, NM, p. A280
ALLIED SERVICES REHABILITATION HOSPITAL, SCRANTON, PA, p. A363
ALPENA GENERAL HOSPITAL, ALPENA, MI, p. A206
ALTA BATES MEDICAL CENTER–ASHBY CAMPUS, BERKELEY, CA, p. A38
ALTA BATES MEDICAL CENTER–HERRICK CAMPUS, BERKELEY, CALIFORNIA, p. A38
ALTA DISTRICT HOSPITAL, DINUBA, CA, p. A41
ALTA VIEW HOSPITAL, SANDY, UT, p. A430
ALTON MEMORIAL HOSPITAL, ALTON, IL, p. A118
ALTON MENTAL HEALTH CENTER, ALTON, IL, p. A118
ALTOONA CENTER, ALTOONA, PA, p. A347
ALTOONA HOSPITAL, ALTOONA, PA, p. A347
ALTRU HEALTH SYSTEM, GRAND FORKS, ND, p. A314
ALTRU HOSPITAL, GRAND FORKS, NORTH DAKOTA, p. A314
ALTRUA HEALTH INSTITUTE, GRAND FORKS, NORTH DAKOTA, p. A314
ALVARADO HOSPITAL MEDICAL CENTER, SAN DIEGO, CA, p. A59
ALVIN C. YORK VETERANS AFFAIRS MEDICAL CENTER, MURFREESBORO, TN, p. A388
ALVIN MEDICAL CENTER, ALVIN, TEXAS, p. A425
AMERICAN FORK HOSPITAL, AMERICAN FORK, UT, p. A427
AMERICAN LEGION HOSPITAL, CROWLEY, LA, p. A179
AMERY REGIONAL MEDICAL CENTER, AMERY, WI, p. A456
AMETHYST, CHARLOTTE, NC, p. A303
AMOS COTTAGE REHABILITATION HOSPITAL, WINSTON–SALEM, NC, p. A312
AMSTERDAM MEMORIAL HOSPITAL, AMSTERDAM, NY, p. A281
ANACAPA HOSPITAL, PORT HUENEME, CA, p. A56
ANADARKO MUNICIPAL HOSPITAL, ANADARKO, OK, p. A333
ANAHEIM GENERAL HOSPITAL, ANAHEIM, CA, p. A36

ANAHEIM MEMORIAL MEDICAL CENTER, ANAHEIM, CA, p. A36
ANAMOSA COMMUNITY HOSPITAL, ANAMOSA, IA, p. A146
ANCORA PSYCHIATRIC HOSPITAL, ANCORA, NJ, p. A268
ANDALUSIA REGIONAL HOSPITAL, ANDALUSIA, AL, p. A11
ANDERSON AREA MEDICAL CENTER, ANDERSON, SC, p. A370
ANDERSON COUNTY HOSPITAL, GARNETT, KS, p. A158
ANDERSON HOSPITAL, MARYVILLE, IL, p. A129
ANDREW MCFARLAND MENTAL HEALTH CENTER, SPRINGFIELD, IL, p. A133
ANDROSCOGGIN VALLEY HOSPITAL, BERLIN, NH, p. A265
ANGEL MEDICAL CENTER, FRANKLIN, NC, p. A306
ANGLETON–DANBURY GENERAL HOSPITAL, ANGLETON, TX, p. A392
ANNA JAQUES HOSPITAL, NEWBURYPORT, MA, p. A202
ANNE ARUNDEL MEDICAL CENTER, ANNAPOLIS, MD, p. A191
ANNIE JEFFREY MEMORIAL COUNTY HEALTH CENTER, OSCEOLA, NE, p. A261
ANNIE PENN HOSPITAL, REIDSVILLE, NC, p. A310
ANOKA–METROPOLITAN REGIONAL TREATMENT CENTER, ANOKA, MN, p. A220
ANSON COMMUNITY HOSPITAL, WADESBORO, NC, p. A312
ANSON GENERAL HOSPITAL, ANSON, TX, p. A393
ANTELOPE MEMORIAL HOSPITAL, NELIGH, NE, p. A259
ANTELOPE VALLEY HOSPITAL, LANCASTER, CA, p. A46
APPALACHIAN PSYCHIATRIC HEALTHCARE SYSTEM, CAMBRIDGE, OH, p. A318
APPLETON MEDICAL CENTER, APPLETON, WI, p. A456
APPLETON MUNICIPAL HOSPITAL AND NURSING HOME, APPLETON, MN, p. A220
APPLING HEALTHCARE SYSTEM, BAXLEY, GA, p. A101
ARBORVIEW HOSPITAL, WARREN, MI, p. A218
ARBOUR H. R. I. HOSPITAL, BROOKLINE, MA, p. A199
ARBOUR HOSPITAL, BOSTON, MA, p. A197
ARBUCKLE MEMORIAL HOSPITAL, SULPHUR, OK, p. A340
ARCADIA VALLEY HOSPITAL, PILOT KNOB, MO, p. A246
ARDEN HILL HOSPITAL, GOSHEN, NY, p. A285
ARECIBO REGIONAL HOSPITAL, ARECIBO, PR, p. A469
ARH REGIONAL MEDICAL CENTER, HAZARD, KY, p. A170
ARIZONA STATE HOSPITAL, PHOENIX, AZ, p. A24
ARKANSAS CHILDREN'S HOSPITAL, LITTLE ROCK, AR, p. A32
ARKANSAS METHODIST HOSPITAL, PARAGOULD, AR, p. A34
ARKANSAS STATE HOSPITAL, LITTLE ROCK, AR, p. A32
ARKANSAS VALLEY REGIONAL MEDICAL CENTER, LA JUNTA, CO, p. A71
ARLINGTON HOSPITAL, ARLINGTON, VA, p. A433
ARLINGTON MEMORIAL HOSPITAL, ARLINGTON, TX, p. A393
ARLINGTON MUNICIPAL HOSPITAL, ARLINGTON, MN, p. A220
ARMS ACRES, CARMEL, NY, p. A284
ARMSTRONG COUNTY MEMORIAL HOSPITAL, KITTANNING, PA, p. A354
ARNOLD MEMORIAL HEALTH CARE CENTER, ADRIAN, MN, p. A220
ARNOLD PALMER HOSPITAL FOR CHILDREN AND WOMEN; M. D. ANDERSON CANCER CENTER AND SAND LAKE HOSPITAL, p. A92
ARNOT OGDEN MEDICAL CENTER, ELMIRA, NY, p. A285
AROOSTOOK HEALTH CENTER, MARS HILL, MAINE, p. A189
AROOSTOOK MEDICAL CENTER, PRESQUE ISLE, ME, p. A189
ARROWHEAD COMMUNITY HOSPITAL AND MEDICAL CENTER, GLENDALE, AZ, p. A23
ARROWHEAD REGIONAL MEDICAL CENTER, COLTON, CA, p. A40
ARROYO GRANDE COMMUNITY HOSPITAL, ARROYO GRANDE, CA, p. A36
ARTESIA GENERAL HOSPITAL, ARTESIA, NM, p. A278
ARTHUR G. JAMES CANCER HOSPITAL AND RICHARD J. SOLOVE RESEARCH INSTITUTE, COLUMBUS, OH, p. A321
ARTHUR R. GOULD MEMORIAL HOSPITAL, PRESQUE ISLE, MAINE, p. A189
ASCENSION HOSPITAL AND BEHAVIORAL HEALTH SERVICES, GONZALES, LA, p. A179
ASHE MEMORIAL HOSPITAL, JEFFERSON, NC, p. A307
ASHFORD PRESBYTERIAN COMMUNITY HOSPITAL, SAN JUAN, PR, p. A471
ASHLAND COMMUNITY HOSPITAL, ASHLAND, OR, p. A342
ASHLAND HEALTH CENTER, ASHLAND, KS, p. A156
ASHLAND REGIONAL MEDICAL CENTER, ASHLAND, PA, p. A348
ASHLEY COUNTY MEDICAL CENTER, CROSSETT, AR, p. A30
ASHLEY MEDICAL CENTER, ASHLEY, ND, p. A313
ASHLEY VALLEY MEDICAL CENTER, VERNAL, UT, p. A430
ASHTABULA COUNTY MEDICAL CENTER, ASHTABULA, OH, p. A317

C

D

E

F

FALLS COMMUNITY HOSPITAL AND CLINIC, MARLIN, TX, p. A414
FALLS MEMORIAL HOSPITAL, INTERNATIONAL FALLS, MN, p. A224
FALLSTON GENERAL HOSPITAL, FALLSTON, MD, p. A194
FALMOUTH HOSPITAL, FALMOUTH, MA, p. A200
FAMILY HEALTH WEST, FRUITA, CO, p. A70
FANNIN PAVILION OF BEAUMONT REGIONAL MEDICAL CENTER, BEAUMONT, TEXAS, p. A395
FANNIN REGIONAL HOSPITAL, BLUE RIDGE, GA, p. A101
FANNY ALLEN CAMPUS, COLCHESTER, VERMONT, p. A431
FARIBAULT REGIONAL CENTER, FARIBAULT, MN, p. A223
FAULK COUNTY MEMORIAL HOSPITAL, FAULKTON, SD, p. A377
FAULKNER HOSPITAL, BOSTON, MA, p. A198
FAUQUIER HOSPITAL, WARRENTON, VA, p. A441
FAWCETT MEMORIAL HOSPITAL, PORT CHARLOTTE, FL, p. A93
FAXTON HOSPITAL, UTICA, NY, p. A299
FAYETTE COUNTY HOSPITAL, VANDALIA, IL, p. A134
FAYETTE COUNTY MEMORIAL HOSPITAL, WASHINGTON COURT HOUSE, OH, p. A330
FAYETTE MEDICAL CENTER, FAYETTE, AL, p. A14
FAYETTE MEMORIAL HOSPITAL, CONNERSVILLE, IN, p. A137
FAYETTE MEMORIAL HOSPITAL, LA GRANGE, TX, p. A412
FEATHER RIVER HOSPITAL, PARADISE, CA, p. A55
FEDERAL MEDICAL CENTER, LEXINGTON, KY, p. A171
FENTRESS COUNTY GENERAL HOSPITAL, JAMESTOWN, TN, p. A384
FERGUS FALLS REGIONAL TREATMENT CENTER, FERGUS FALLS, MN, p. A223
FERGUSON CAMPUS, GRAND RAPIDS, MICHIGAN, p. A211
FERRELL HOSPITAL, ELDORADO, IL, p. A124
FERRY COUNTY MEMORIAL HOSPITAL, REPUBLIC, WA, p. A447
FIELD MEMORIAL COMMUNITY HOSPITAL, CENTREVILLE, MS, p. A232
FIELDSTONE CENTER, BATTLE CREEK, MICHIGAN, p. A206
FILLMORE COMMUNITY MEDICAL CENTER, FILLMORE, UT, p. A427
FILLMORE COUNTY HOSPITAL, GENEVA, NE, p. A257
FINLEY HOSPITAL, DUBUQUE, IA, p. A149
FIRELANDS COMMUNITY HOSPITAL, SANDUSKY, OH, p. A329
FIRST CARE MEDICAL SERVICES, FOSSTON, MN, p. A223
FIRST HOSPITAL PANAMERICANO, CIDRA, PR, p. A470
FIRST HOSPITAL VALLEJO, VALLEJO, CA, p. A66
FIRST HOSPITAL WYOMING VALLEY, WILKES-BARRE, PA, p. A366
FIRSTHEALTH MONTGOMERY MEMORIAL HOSPITAL, TROY, NC, p. A311
FIRSTHEALTH MOORE REGIONAL HOSPITAL, PINEHURST, NC, p. A309
FISHER COUNTY HOSPITAL DISTRICT, ROTAN, TX, p. A419
FISHER-TITUS MEDICAL CENTER, NORWALK, OH, p. A327
FISHERMEN'S HOSPITAL, MARATHON, FL, p. A89
FITZGIBBON HOSPITAL, MARSHALL, MO, p. A245
FIVE COUNTIES HOSPITAL, LEMMON, SD, p. A377
FLAGET MEMORIAL HOSPITAL, BARDSTOWN, KY, p. A167
FLAGLER HOSPITAL, SAINT AUGUSTINE, FL, p. A94
FLAGLER HOSPITAL-WEST, SAINT AUGUSTINE, FLORIDA, p. A94
FLAGSTAFF MEDICAL CENTER, FLAGSTAFF, AZ, p. A22
FLAMBEAU HOSPITAL, PARK FALLS, WI, p. A462
FLANDREAU MUNICIPAL HOSPITAL, FLANDREAU, SD, p. A377
FLEMING COUNTY HOSPITAL, FLEMINGSBURG, KY, p. A168
FLETCHER ALLEN HEALTH CARE, BURLINGTON, VT, p. A431
FLINT RIVER COMMUNITY HOSPITAL, MONTEZUMA, GA, p. A108
FLORALA MEMORIAL HOSPITAL, FLORALA, AL, p. A14
FLORENCE D'URSO PAVILION, NEW YORK, NEW YORK, p. A292
FLORENCE GENERAL HOSPITAL, FLORENCE, SOUTH CAROLINA, p. A372
FLORENCE HOSPITAL, FLORENCE, AL, p. A14
FLORIDA CENTER FOR ADDICTIONS AND DUAL DISORDERS, AVON PARK, FL, p. A81
FLORIDA HOSPITAL, ORLANDO, FL, p. A91
FLORIDA HOSPITAL EAST ORLANDO, ORLANDO, FLORIDA, p. A91
FLORIDA HOSPITAL HEARTLAND DIVISION, SEBRING, FL, p. A95
FLORIDA HOSPITAL KISSIMMEE, KISSIMMEE, FLORIDA, p. A91
FLORIDA HOSPITAL WATERMAN, EUSTIS, FL, p. A84
FLORIDA HOSPITAL-ALTAMONTE, ALTAMONTE SPRINGS, FLORIDA, p. A91
FLORIDA HOSPITAL-APOPKA, APOPKA, FLORIDA, p. A91
FLORIDA KEYS MEMORIAL HOSPITAL, KEY WEST, FLORIDA, p. A87
FLORIDA MEDICAL CENTER HOSPITAL, FORT LAUDERDALE, FL, p. A84
FLORIDA STATE HOSPITAL, CHATTAHOOCHEE, FL, p. A82
FLOWER HOSPITAL, SYLVANIA, OH, p. A329
FLOWERS HOSPITAL, DOTHAN, AL, p. A13
FLOYD COUNTY MEMORIAL HOSPITAL, CHARLES CITY, IA, p. A147
FLOYD MEDICAL CENTER, ROME, GA, p. A109

FLOYD MEMORIAL HOSPITAL AND HEALTH SERVICES, NEW ALBANY, IN, p. A143
FLOYD VALLEY HOSPITAL, LE MARS, IA, p. A151
FOCUS HEALTHCARE OF OHIO, MAUMEE, OH, p. A326
FONT MARTELO HOSPITAL, HUMACAO, PR, p. A470
FOOTHILL PRESBYTERIAN HOSPITAL-MORRIS L. JOHNSTON MEMORIAL, GLENDORA, CA, p. A44
FOREST HOSPITAL, DES PLAINES, IL, p. A124
FOREST PARK HOSPITAL, SAINT LOUIS, MO, p. A248
FOREST SPRINGS HOSPITAL, HOUSTON, TX, p. A408
FOREST VIEW HOSPITAL, GRAND RAPIDS, MI, p. A210
FORKS COMMUNITY HOSPITAL, FORKS, WA, p. A444
FORREST GENERAL HOSPITAL, HATTIESBURG, MS, p. A233
FORSYTH MEDICAL CENTER, WINSTON-SALEM, NC, p. A312
FORT ATKINSON MEMORIAL HEALTH SERVICES, FORT ATKINSON, WI, p. A458
FORT BEND MEDICAL CENTER, MISSOURI CITY, TX, p. A415
FORT DEFIANCE INDIAN HEALTH SERVICE HOSPITAL, FORT DEFIANCE, AZ, p. A23
FORT DUNCAN MEDICAL CENTER, EAGLE PASS, TX, p. A402
FORT HAMILTON HOSPITAL, HAMILTON, OH, p. A324
FORT LOGAN HOSPITAL, STANFORD, KY, p. A175
FORT MADISON COMMUNITY HOSPITAL, FORT MADISON, IA, p. A149
FORT SANDERS LOUDON MEDICAL CENTER, LOUDON, TN, p. A386
FORT SANDERS REGIONAL MEDICAL CENTER, KNOXVILLE, TN, p. A385
FORT SANDERS-PARKWEST MEDICAL CENTER, KNOXVILLE, TN, p. A385
FORT SANDERS-SEVIER MEDICAL CENTER, SEVIERVILLE, TN, p. A390
FORT WALTON BEACH MEDICAL CENTER, FORT WALTON BEACH, FL, p. A85
FORT WASHINGTON HOSPITAL, FORT WASHINGTON, MD, p. A194
45TH STREET MENTAL HEALTH CENTER, WEST PALM BEACH, FL, p. A97
FOSTORIA COMMUNITY HOSPITAL, FOSTORIA, OH, p. A323
FOUNDATIONS BEHAVIORAL HEALTH, DOYLESTOWN, PA, p. A351
FOUNTAIN VALLEY REGIONAL HOSPITAL AND MEDICAL CENTER, FOUNTAIN VALLEY, CA, p. A42
FOUR WINDS HOSPITAL, KATONAH, NY, p. A287
FOX CHASE CANCER CENTER-AMERICAN ONCOLOGIC HOSPITAL, PHILADELPHIA, PA, p. A358
FRAMINGHAM UNION HOSPITAL, FRAMINGHAM, MASSACHUSETTS, p. A200
FRANCES MAHON DEACONESS HOSPITAL, GLASGOW, MT, p. A252
FRANCISCAN CHILDREN'S HOSPITAL AND REHABILITATION CENTER, BOSTON, MA, p. A198
FRANCISCAN HOSPITAL-MOUNT AIRY CAMPUS, CINCINNATI, OH, p. A319
FRANCISCAN HOSPITAL-WESTERN HILLS CAMPUS, CINCINNATI, OH, p. A319
FRANCISCAN MEDICAL CENTER-DAYTON CAMPUS, DAYTON, OH, p. A322
FRANCISCAN SKEMP HEALTHCARE-ARCADIA CAMPUS, ARCADIA, WI, p. A456
FRANCISCAN SKEMP HEALTHCARE-LA CROSSE CAMPUS, LA CROSSE, WI, p. A459
FRANCISCAN SKEMP HEALTHCARE-SPARTA CAMPUS, SPARTA, WI, p. A463
FRANK R. HOWARD MEMORIAL HOSPITAL, WILLITS, CA, p. A67
FRANK T. RUTHERFORD MEMORIAL HOSPITAL, CARTHAGE, TN, p. A381
FRANKFORD CAMPUS, PHILADELPHIA, PENNSYLVANIA, p. A358
FRANKFORD HOSPITAL OF THE CITY OF PHILADELPHIA, PHILADELPHIA, PA, p. A358
FRANKFORT REGIONAL MEDICAL CENTER, FRANKFORT, KY, p. A169
FRANKLIN COUNTY MEDICAL CENTER, PRESTON, ID, p. A116
FRANKLIN COUNTY MEMORIAL HOSPITAL, MEADVILLE, MS, p. A235
FRANKLIN COUNTY MEMORIAL HOSPITAL, FRANKLIN, NE, p. A257
FRANKLIN FOUNDATION HOSPITAL, FRANKLIN, LA, p. A179
FRANKLIN GENERAL HOSPITAL, HAMPTON, IA, p. A150
FRANKLIN HOSPITAL AND SKILLED NURSING CARE UNIT, BENTON, IL, p. A119
FRANKLIN HOSPITAL MEDICAL CENTER, VALLEY STREAM, NY, p. A300
FRANKLIN MEDICAL CENTER, GREENFIELD, MA, p. A201
FRANKLIN MEDICAL CENTER, WINNSBORO, LA, p. A186
FRANKLIN MEMORIAL HOSPITAL, FARMINGTON, ME, p. A188
FRANKLIN REGIONAL HOSPITAL, FRANKLIN, NH, p. A265
FRANKLIN REGIONAL MEDICAL CENTER, LOUISBURG, NC, p. A308

FRANKLIN SQUARE HOSPITAL CENTER, BALTIMORE, MD, p. A191
FRANKLIN-SIMPSON MEMORIAL HOSPITAL, FRANKLIN, KY, p. A169
FRAZIER REHABILITATION CENTER, LOUISVILLE, KY, p. A172
FREDERICK MEMORIAL HOSPITAL, FREDERICK, MD, p. A194
FREDONIA REGIONAL HOSPITAL, FREDONIA, KS, p. A158
FREEMAN COMMUNITY HOSPITAL, FREEMAN, SD, p. A377
FREEMAN HEALTH SYSTEM, JOPLIN, MO, p. A242
FREEMAN HOSPITAL EAST, JOPLIN, MISSOURI, p. A242
FREEMAN HOSPITAL WEST, JOPLIN, MISSOURI, p. A242
FREEMAN NEOSHO HOSPITAL, NEOSHO, MO, p. A245
FREEPORT MEMORIAL HOSPITAL, FREEPORT, IL, p. A125
FREMONT AREA MEDICAL CENTER, FREMONT, NE, p. A257
FREMONT MEDICAL CENTER, YUBA CITY, CA, p. A67
FRENCH HOSPITAL MEDICAL CENTER, SAN LUIS OBISPO, CA, p. A61
FRESNO COMMUNITY HOSPITAL AND MEDICAL CENTER, FRESNO, CA, p. A43
FRESNO SURGERY CENTER-THE HOSPITAL FOR SURGERY, FRESNO, CA, p. A43
FRICK HOSPITAL, MOUNT PLEASANT, PA, p. A356
FRIEDMAN HOSPITAL OF THE HOME FOR THE JEWISH AGED, PHILADELPHIA, PA, p. A358
FRIENDS HOSPITAL, PHILADELPHIA, PA, p. A358
FRIO HOSPITAL, PEARSALL, TX, p. A417
FRISBIE MEMORIAL HOSPITAL, ROCHESTER, NH, p. A267
FROEDTERT MEMORIAL LUTHERAN HOSPITAL, MILWAUKEE, WI, p. A461
FRYE REGIONAL MEDICAL CENTER, HICKORY, NC, p. A307
FRYE REGIONAL MEDICAL CENTER-SOUTH CAMPUS, HICKORY, NORTH CAROLINA, p. A307
FULLER MEMORIAL HOSPITAL, SOUTH ATTLEBORO, MA, p. A204
FULTON COUNTY HEALTH CENTER, WAUSEON, OH, p. A330
FULTON COUNTY HOSPITAL, SALEM, AR, p. A34
FULTON COUNTY MEDICAL CENTER, MCCONNELLSBURG, PA, p. A355
FULTON DIVISION, NEW YORK, NEW YORK, p. A289
FULTON STATE HOSPITAL, FULTON, MO, p. A241

G

G. PIERCE WOOD MEMORIAL HOSPITAL, ARCADIA, FL, p. A81
G.V. MONTGOMERY VETERANS AFFAIRS MEDICAL CENTER, JACKSON, MS, p. A234
GADSDEN COMMUNITY HOSPITAL, QUINCY, FL, p. A94
GADSDEN REGIONAL MEDICAL CENTER, GADSDEN, AL, p. A14
GAINESVILLE MEMORIAL HOSPITAL, GAINESVILLE, TX, p. A405
GALENA-STAUSS HOSPITAL, GALENA, IL, p. A125
GALESBURG COTTAGE HOSPITAL, GALESBURG, IL, p. A125
GALION COMMUNITY HOSPITAL, GALION, OH, p. A324
GALLUP INDIAN MEDICAL CENTER, GALLUP, NM, p. A279
GARDEN CITY HOSPITAL, GARDEN CITY, MI, p. A210
GARDEN COUNTY HOSPITAL, OSHKOSH, NE, p. A261
GARDEN GROVE HOSPITAL AND MEDICAL CENTER, GARDEN GROVE, CA, p. A43
GARDEN PARK COMMUNITY HOSPITAL, GULFPORT, MS, p. A233
GARDENVIEW NURSING HOME, p. A224
GARFIELD COUNTY MEMORIAL HOSPITAL, POMEROY, WA, p. A446
GARFIELD MEDICAL CENTER, MONTEREY PARK, CA, p. A53
GARFIELD MEMORIAL HOSPITAL AND CLINICS, PANGUITCH, UT, p. A428
GARLAND COMMUNITY HOSPITAL, GARLAND, TX, p. A405
GARRARD COUNTY MEMORIAL HOSPITAL, LANCASTER, KY, p. A170
GARRETT COUNTY MEMORIAL HOSPITAL, OAKLAND, MD, p. A195
GARRISON MEMORIAL HOSPITAL, GARRISON, ND, p. A314
GARY MEMORIAL HOSPITAL, BREAUX BRIDGE, LA, p. A178
GASTON MEMORIAL HOSPITAL, GASTONIA, NC, p. A306
GATEWAY HEALTH SYSTEM, CLARKSVILLE, TN, p. A382
GATEWAY REGIONAL HEALTH SYSTEM, MOUNT STERLING, KY, p. A173
GATEWAYS HOSPITAL AND MENTAL HEALTH CENTER, LOS ANGELES, CA, p. A48
GAYLORD HOSPITAL, WALLINGFORD, CT, p. A77
GEARY COMMUNITY HOSPITAL, JUNCTION CITY, KS, p. A160
GEISINGER MEDICAL CENTER, DANVILLE, PA, p. A350
GENERAL DIVISION, CHARLESTON, WEST VIRGINIA, p. A450
GENERAL HOSPITAL, EUREKA, CA, p. A41
GENERAL HOSPITAL, LOS ANGELES, CALIFORNIA, p. A49
GENERAL HOSPITAL CENTER AT PASSAIC, PASSAIC, NEW JERSEY, p. A270

GENERAL JOHN J. PERSHING MEMORIAL HOSPITAL, BROOKFIELD, MO, p. A239

GENERAL LEONARD WOOD ARMY COMMUNITY HOSPITAL, FORT LEONARD WOOD, MO, p. A241

GENESEE HOSPITAL, ROCHESTER, NY, p. A297

GENESIS HEALTHCARE SYSTEM, ZANESVILLE, OH, p. A332

GENESIS MEDICAL CENTER, DAVENPORT, IA, p. A148

GENESIS MEDICAL CENTER–EAST CAMPUS, DAVENPORT, IOWA, p. A148

GENESIS MEDICAL CENTER–WEST CAMPUS, DAVENPORT, IOWA, p. A148

GENESYS REGIONAL MEDICAL CENTER, GRAND BLANC, MI, p. A210

GENEVA GENERAL HOSPITAL, GENEVA, NY, p. A285

GENOA COMMUNITY HOSPITAL, GENOA, NE, p. A258

GENTRY COUNTY MEMORIAL HOSPITAL, ALBANY, MO, p. A239

GEORGE A. ZELLER MENTAL HEALTH CENTER, PEORIA, IL, p. A131

GEORGE COUNTY HOSPITAL, LUCEDALE, MS, p. A235

GEORGE E. WEEMS MEMORIAL HOSPITAL, APALACHICOLA, FL, p. A81

GEORGE L. HARRISON MEMORIAL HOUSE, p. A358

GEORGE L. MEE MEMORIAL HOSPITAL, KING CITY, CA, p. A45

GEORGE NIGH REHABILITATION INSTITUTE, OKMULGEE, OK, p. A338

GEORGE W. TRUETT MEMORIAL HOSPITAL, DALLAS, TEXAS, p. A399

GEORGE WASHINGTON UNIVERSITY HOSPITAL, WASHINGTON, DC, p. A79

GEORGETOWN COMMUNITY HOSPITAL, GEORGETOWN, KY, p. A169

GEORGETOWN HEALTHCARE SYSTEM, GEORGETOWN, TX, p. A405

GEORGETOWN MEMORIAL HOSPITAL, GEORGETOWN, SC, p. A373

GEORGETOWN UNIVERSITY HOSPITAL, WASHINGTON, DC, p. A79

GEORGIA MENTAL HEALTH INSTITUTE, ATLANTA, GA, p. A100

GEORGIA REGIONAL HOSPITAL AT ATLANTA, DECATUR, GA, p. A104

GEORGIA REGIONAL HOSPITAL AT AUGUSTA, AUGUSTA, GA, p. A101

GEORGIA REGIONAL HOSPITAL AT SAVANNAH, SAVANNAH, GA, p. A109

GEORGIANA HOSPITAL, GEORGIANA, AL, p. A15

GERALD CHAMPION MEMORIAL HOSPITAL, ALAMOGORDO, NM, p. A277

GERBER MEMORIAL HOSPITAL, FREMONT, MI, p. A210

GERMANTOWN HOSPITAL AND COMMUNITY HEALTH SERVICES, PHILADELPHIA, PA, p. A358

GETTYSBURG HOSPITAL, GETTYSBURG, PA, p. A352

GETTYSBURG MEDICAL CENTER, GETTYSBURG, SD, p. A377

GIBSON AREA HOSPITAL AND HEALTH SERVICES, GIBSON CITY, IL, p. A125

GIBSON COMMUNITY HOSPITAL NURSING HOME, p. A125

GIBSON GENERAL HOSPITAL, PRINCETON, IN, p. A143

GIBSON GENERAL HOSPITAL, TRENTON, TN, p. A390

GIFFORD MEDICAL CENTER, RANDOLPH, VT, p. A431

GILA REGIONAL MEDICAL CENTER, SILVER CITY, NM, p. A280

GILLETTE CHILDREN'S SPECIALTY HEALTHCARE, SAINT PAUL, MN, p. A228

GILMORE MEMORIAL HOSPITAL, AMORY, MS, p. A231

GIRARD MEDICAL CENTER, PHILADELPHIA, PENNSYLVANIA, p. A359

GLACIAL RIDGE HOSPITAL, GLENWOOD, MN, p. A223

GLACIER COUNTY MEDICAL CENTER, CUT BANK, MT, p. A252

GLADES GENERAL HOSPITAL, BELLE GLADE, FL, p. A81

GLADYS SPELLMAN SPECIALTY HOSPITAL AND NURSING CENTER, CHEVERLY, MD, p. A193

GLEN OAKS HOSPITAL, GREENVILLE, TX, p. A406

GLEN ROSE MEDICAL CENTER, GLEN ROSE, TX, p. A405

GLENBEIGH HEALTH SOURCES, ROCK CREEK, OH, p. A328

GLENBROOK HOSPITAL, GLENVIEW, ILLINOIS, p. A125

GLENCOE AREA HEALTH CENTER, GLENCOE, MN, p. A223

GLENDALE ADVENTIST MEDICAL CENTER, GLENDALE, CA, p. A43

GLENDALE MEMORIAL HOSPITAL AND HEALTH CENTER, GLENDALE, CA, p. A43

GLENDIVE MEDICAL CENTER, GLENDIVE, MT, p. A252

GLENN MEDICAL CENTER, WILLOWS, CA, p. A67

GLENOAKS HOSPITAL, GLENDALE HEIGHTS, IL, p. A126

GLENS FALLS HOSPITAL, GLENS FALLS, NY, p. A285

GLENWOOD REGIONAL MEDICAL CENTER, WEST MONROE, LA, p. A186

GLENWOOD STATE HOSPITAL SCHOOL, GLENWOOD, IA, p. A150

GNADEN HUETTEN MEMORIAL HOSPITAL, LEHIGHTON, PA, p. A355

GOLDEN OURS CONVALESCENT HOME, p. A258

GOLDEN PLAINS COMMUNITY HOSPITAL, BORGER, TX, p. A396

GOLDEN VALLEY MEMORIAL HOSPITAL, CLINTON, MO, p. A240

GOLDWATER MEMORIAL HOSPITAL, NEW YORK, NY, p. A290

GOLETA VALLEY COTTAGE HOSPITAL, SANTA BARBARA, CA, p. A62

GOLI MEDICAL CENTER, SARGENT, NE, p. A261

GOOD HOPE HOSPITAL, ERWIN, NC, p. A305

GOOD SAMARITAN COMMUNITY HEALTHCARE, PUYALLUP, WA, p. A446

GOOD SAMARITAN HEALTH CENTER OF MERRILL, MERRILL, WI, p. A460

GOOD SAMARITAN HEALTH SYSTEMS, KEARNEY, NE, p. A258

GOOD SAMARITAN HOSPITAL, SUFFERN, NY, p. A298

GOOD SAMARITAN HOSPITAL, LEBANON, PA, p. A355

GOOD SAMARITAN HOSPITAL, CINCINNATI, OH, p. A319

GOOD SAMARITAN HOSPITAL, VINCENNES, IN, p. A145

GOOD SAMARITAN HOSPITAL, DOWNERS GROVE, IL, p. A124

GOOD SAMARITAN HOSPITAL, SAN JOSE, CA, p. A60

GOOD SAMARITAN HOSPITAL, BAKERSFIELD, CA, p. A37

GOOD SAMARITAN HOSPITAL, LOS ANGELES, CA, p. A48

GOOD SAMARITAN HOSPITAL AND HEALTH CENTER, DAYTON, OH, p. A322

GOOD SAMARITAN HOSPITAL AND MEDICAL CENTER, PORTLAND, OREGON, p. A345

GOOD SAMARITAN HOSPITAL CORVALLIS, CORVALLIS, OR, p. A342

GOOD SAMARITAN HOSPITAL MEDICAL CENTER, WEST ISLIP, NY, p. A300

GOOD SAMARITAN HOSPITAL OF MARYLAND, BALTIMORE, MD, p. A191

GOOD SAMARITAN MEDICAL AND REHABILITATION CENTER, ZANESVILLE, OHIO, p. A332

GOOD SAMARITAN MEDICAL CENTER, BROCKTON, MA, p. A199

GOOD SAMARITAN MEDICAL CENTER, JOHNSTOWN, PENNSYLVANIA, p. A354

GOOD SAMARITAN MEDICAL CENTER, WEST PALM BEACH, FL, p. A97

GOOD SAMARITAN MEDICAL CENTER – CUSHING CAMPUS, BROCKTON, MASSACHUSETTS, p. A199

GOOD SAMARITAN REGIONAL HEALTH CENTER, MOUNT VERNON, IL, p. A130

GOOD SAMARITAN REGIONAL MEDICAL CENTER, POTTSVILLE, PA, p. A362

GOOD SAMARITAN REGIONAL MEDICAL CENTER, PHOENIX, AZ, p. A24

GOOD SHEPHERD COMMUNITY HOSPITAL, HERMISTON, OR, p. A343

GOOD SHEPHERD HOSPITAL, BARRINGTON, IL, p. A118

GOOD SHEPHERD MEDICAL CENTER, LONGVIEW, TX, p. A413

GOOD SHEPHERD REHABILITATION HOSPITAL, ALLENTOWN, PA, p. A347

GOODALL–WITCHER HEALTHCARE, CLIFTON, TX, p. A397

GOODING COUNTY MEMORIAL HOSPITAL, GOODING, ID, p. A115

GOODLAND REGIONAL MEDICAL CENTER, GOODLAND, KS, p. A158

GORDON HOSPITAL, CALHOUN, GA, p. A102

GORDON MEMORIAL HOSPITAL DISTRICT, GORDON, NE, p. A258

GOSHEN GENERAL HOSPITAL, GOSHEN, IN, p. A139

GOTHENBURG MEMORIAL HOSPITAL, GOTHENBURG, NE, p. A258

GOTTLIEB MEMORIAL HOSPITAL, MELROSE PARK, IL, p. A129

GOVE COUNTY MEDICAL CENTER, QUINTER, KS, p. A163

GOVERNOR JUAN F. LOUIS HOSPITAL, CHRISTIANSTED, VI, p. A472

GRACE COTTAGE HOSPITAL, TOWNSHEND, VT, p. A432

GRACE HOSPITAL, MORGANTON, NC, p. A309

GRACE HOSPITAL, CLEVELAND, OH, p. A320

GRACE HOSPITAL, DETROIT, MI, p. A208

GRACEVILLE HEALTH CENTER, GRACEVILLE, MN, p. A223

GRACEWOOD STATE SCHOOL AND HOSPITAL, GRACEWOOD, GA, p. A105

GRACIE SQUARE HOSPITAL, NEW YORK, NY, p. A290

GRADUATE HOSPITAL, PHILADELPHIA, PA, p. A359

GRADY GENERAL HOSPITAL, CAIRO, GA, p. A102

GRADY MEMORIAL HOSPITAL, ATLANTA, GA, p. A100

GRADY MEMORIAL HOSPITAL, DELAWARE, OH, p. A323

GRADY MEMORIAL HOSPITAL, CHICKASHA, OK, p. A334

GRAFTON CITY HOSPITAL, GRAFTON, WV, p. A451

GRAHAM COUNTY HOSPITAL, HILL CITY, KS, p. A159

GRAHAM HOSPITAL, CANTON, IL, p. A119

GRAHAM REGIONAL MEDICAL CENTER, GRAHAM, TX, p. A405

GRANADA HILLS COMMUNITY HOSPITAL, LOS ANGELES, CA, p. A48

GRAND RIVER HOSPITAL DISTRICT, RIFLE, CO, p. A72

GRAND STRAND REGIONAL MEDICAL CENTER, MYRTLE BEACH, SC, p. A374

GRAND VIEW HOSPITAL, SELLERSVILLE, PA, p. A363

GRAND VIEW HOSPITAL, IRONWOOD, MI, p. A212

GRANDE RONDE HOSPITAL, LA GRANDE, OR, p. A343

GRANDVIEW HOSPITAL AND MEDICAL CENTER, DAYTON, OH, p. A322

GRANDVIEW MEDICAL CENTER, JASPER, TN, p. A384

GRANITE COUNTY MEMORIAL HOSPITAL AND NURSING HOME, PHILIPSBURG, MT, p. A254

GRANITE FALLS MUNICIPAL HOSPITAL AND MANOR, GRANITE FALLS, MN, p. A223

GRANT COUNTY HEALTH CENTER, ELBOW LAKE, MN, p. A222

GRANT HOSPITAL, CHICAGO, IL, p. A120

GRANT MEMORIAL HOSPITAL, PETERSBURG, WV, p. A453

GRANT REGIONAL HEALTH CENTER, LANCASTER, WI, p. A459

GRANT/RIVERSIDE METHODIST HOSPITALS–GRANT CAMPUS, COLUMBUS, OH, p. A322

GRANT/RIVERSIDE METHODIST HOSPITALS–RIVERSIDE CAMPUS, COLUMBUS, OH, p. A322

GRANVILLE MEDICAL CENTER, OXFORD, NC, p. A309

GRAPE COMMUNITY HOSPITAL, HAMBURG, IA, p. A150

GRATIOT COMMUNITY HOSPITAL, ALMA, MI, p. A206

GRAVETTE MEDICAL CENTER HOSPITAL, GRAVETTE, AR, p. A31

GRAYDON MANOR, LEESBURG, VA, p. A436

GRAYS HARBOR COMMUNITY HOSPITAL, ABERDEEN, WA, p. A443

GREAT LAKES REHABILITATION HOSPITAL, SOUTHFIELD, MI, p. A217

GREAT PLAINS REGIONAL MEDICAL CENTER, NORTH PLATTE, NE, p. A260

GREAT PLAINS REGIONAL MEDICAL CENTER, ELK CITY, OK, p. A335

GREATER BALTIMORE MEDICAL CENTER, BALTIMORE, MD, p. A191

GREATER COMMUNITY HOSPITAL, CRESTON, IA, p. A148

GREATER EL MONTE COMMUNITY HOSPITAL, SOUTH EL MONTE, CA, p. A63

GREATER SOUTHEAST COMMUNITY HOSPITAL, WASHINGTON, DC, p. A79

GREELEY COUNTY HOSPITAL, TRIBUNE, KS, p. A165

GREEN HOSPITAL OF SCRIPPS CLINIC, LA JOLLA, CA, p. A45

GREEN OAKS HOSPITAL, DALLAS, TX, p. A400

GREENBRIER BEHAVIORAL HEALTH SYSTEM, COVINGTON, LA, p. A179

GREENBRIER HOSPITAL, BROOKSVILLE, FL, p. A82

GREENBRIER VALLEY MEDICAL CENTER, RONCEVERTE, WV, p. A454

GREENE COUNTY GENERAL HOSPITAL, LINTON, IN, p. A142

GREENE COUNTY HOSPITAL, EUTAW, AL, p. A14

GREENE COUNTY MEDICAL CENTER, JEFFERSON, IA, p. A151

GREENE COUNTY MEMORIAL HOSPITAL, WAYNESBURG, PA, p. A365

GREENE MEMORIAL HOSPITAL, XENIA, OH, p. A331

GREENFIELD AREA MEDICAL CENTER, GREENFIELD, OH, p. A324

GREENLEAF CENTER, VALDOSTA, GA, p. A111

GREENSVILLE MEMORIAL HOSPITAL, EMPORIA, VA, p. A434

GREENVIEW REGIONAL HOSPITAL, BOWLING GREEN, KY, p. A167

GREENVILLE CAMPUS, GREENVILLE, PENNSYLVANIA, p. A352

GREENVILLE HOSPITAL, JERSEY CITY, NJ, p. A271

GREENVILLE MEMORIAL HOSPITAL, GREENVILLE, SC, p. A373

GREENWICH HOSPITAL, GREENWICH, CT, p. A74

GREENWOOD COUNTY HOSPITAL, EUREKA, KS, p. A158

GREENWOOD LEFLORE HOSPITAL, GREENWOOD, MS, p. A233

GREGORY COMMUNITY HOSPITAL, GREGORY, SD, p. A377

GRENADA LAKE MEDICAL CENTER, GRENADA, MS, p. A233

GREYSTONE PARK PSYCHIATRIC HOSPITAL, GREYSTONE PARK, NJ, p. A270

GRIFFIN HOSPITAL, DERBY, CT, p. A74

GRIFFIN MEMORIAL HOSPITAL, NORMAN, OK, p. A337

GRIGGS COUNTY HOSPITAL AND NURSING HOME, COOPERSTOWN, ND, p. A313

GRIMES ST. JOSEPH HEALTH CENTER, NAVASOTA, TX, p. A416

GRINNELL REGIONAL MEDICAL CENTER, GRINNELL, IA, p. A150

GRISELL MEMORIAL HOSPITAL DISTRICT ONE, RANSOM, KS, p. A163

GRITMAN MEDICAL CENTER, MOSCOW, ID, p. A116

GROSSMONT HOSPITAL, LA MESA, CA, p. A46

GROVE HILL MEMORIAL HOSPITAL, GROVE HILL, AL, p. A15

GRUNDY COUNTY MEMORIAL HOSPITAL, GRUNDY CENTER, IA, p. A150

GUADALUPE VALLEY HOSPITAL, SEGUIN, TX, p. A421

GUAM MEMORIAL HOSPITAL AUTHORITY, TAMUNING, GU, p. A469

GULF BREEZE HOSPITAL, GULF BREEZE, FL, p. A85

GULF COAST HOSPITAL, FORT MYERS, FL, p. A84

GULF COAST MEDICAL CENTER, PANAMA CITY, FL, p. A92

GULF COAST MEDICAL CENTER, BILOXI, MS, p. A231

GULF COAST MEDICAL CENTER, WHARTON, TX, p. A425

GULF COAST TREATMENT CENTER, FORT WALTON BEACH, FL, p. A85

GULF OAKS HOSPITAL, BILOXI, MISSISSIPPI, p. A231

GULF PINES HOSPITAL, PORT SAINT JOE, FL, p. A93

I

J

M

PARKLAND HEALTH AND HOSPITAL SYSTEM, DALLAS, TX, p. A400
PARKLAND HEALTH CENTER, FARMINGTON, MO, p. A241
PARKLAND HEALTH CENTER–BONNE TERRE, BONNE TERRE, MISSOURI, p. A241
PARKLAND MEDICAL CENTER, DERRY, NH, p. A265
PARKRIDGE MEDICAL CENTER, CHATTANOOGA, TN, p. A382
PARKSIDE HOSPITAL, TULSA, OK, p. A341
PARKVIEW COMMUNITY HOSPITAL MEDICAL CENTER, RIVERSIDE, CA, p. A57
PARKVIEW HOSPITAL, BRUNSWICK, ME, p. A188
PARKVIEW HOSPITAL, PHILADELPHIA, PA, p. A359
PARKVIEW HOSPITAL, FORT WAYNE, IN, p. A138
PARKVIEW HOSPITAL, WHEELER, TX, p. A425
PARKVIEW MEDICAL CENTER, PUEBLO, CO, p. A72
PARKVIEW REGIONAL HOSPITAL, MEXIA, TX, p. A415
PARKVIEW REGIONAL MEDICAL CENTER, VICKSBURG, MS, p. A237
PARKWAY HOSPITAL, NEW YORK, NY, p. A293
PARKWAY MEDICAL CENTER, LITHIA SPRINGS, GA, p. A106
PARKWAY MEDICAL CENTER HOSPITAL, DECATUR, AL, p. A13
PARKWAY REGIONAL HOSPITAL, FULTON, KY, p. A169
PARKWAY REGIONAL MEDICAL CENTER, NORTH MIAMI BEACH, FL, p. A91
PARMA COMMUNITY GENERAL HOSPITAL, PARMA, OH, p. A328
PARMER COUNTY COMMUNITY HOSPITAL, FRIONA, TX, p. A404
PARRISH MEDICAL CENTER, TITUSVILLE, FL, p. A97
PARSONS STATE HOSPITAL AND TRAINING CENTER, PARSONS, KS, p. A163
PASCACK VALLEY HOSPITAL, WESTWOOD, NJ, p. A276
PASCO COMMUNITY HOSPITAL, DADE CITY, FL, p. A83
PASSAVANT AREA HOSPITAL, JACKSONVILLE, IL, p. A127
PATHWAYS OF TENNESSEE, JACKSON, TN, p. A384
PATHWAYS TREATMENT CENTER, KALISPELL, MONTANA, p. A253
PATRICK COMMUNITY HOSPITAL, STUART, VA, p. A441
PATTIE A. CLAY HOSPITAL, RICHMOND, KY, p. A175
PATTON STATE HOSPITAL, PATTON, CA, p. A56
PAUL B. HALL REGIONAL MEDICAL CENTER, PAINTSVILLE, KY, p. A174
PAUL OLIVER MEMORIAL HOSPITAL, FRANKFORT, MI, p. A210
PAULDING COUNTY HOSPITAL, PAULDING, OH, p. A328
PAULINE WARFIELD LEWIS CENTER, CINCINNATI, OH, p. A320
PAULS VALLEY GENERAL HOSPITAL, PAULS VALLEY, OK, p. A338
PAWHUSKA HOSPITAL, PAWHUSKA, OK, p. A338
PAWNEE COUNTY MEMORIAL HOSPITAL, PAWNEE CITY, NE, p. A261
PAWNEE MUNICIPAL HOSPITAL, PAWNEE, OK, p. A338
PAYNE WHITNEY PSYCHIATRIC CLINIC, NEW YORK, NEW YORK, p. A292
PAYNESVILLE AREA HEALTH CARE SYSTEM, PAYNESVILLE, MN, p. A226
PAYSON REGIONAL MEDICAL CENTER, PAYSON, AZ, p. A24
PEACE HARBOR HOSPITAL, FLORENCE, OR, p. A343
PEACH REGIONAL MEDICAL CENTER, FORT VALLEY, GA, p. A105
PEACHTREE REGIONAL HOSPITAL, NEWNAN, GA, p. A108
PEARL RIVER COUNTY HOSPITAL, POPLARVILLE, MS, p. A237
PECOS COUNTY GENERAL HOSPITAL, IRAAN, TX, p. A410
PECOS COUNTY MEMORIAL HOSPITAL, FORT STOCKTON, TX, p. A403
PECOS VALLEY LODGE, ROSWELL, NEW MEXICO, p. A280
PEKIN HOSPITAL, PEKIN, IL, p. A131
PELLA REGIONAL HEALTH CENTER, PELLA, IA, p. A153
PEMBINA COUNTY MEMORIAL HOSPITAL AND WEDGEWOOD MANOR, CAVALIER, ND, p. A313
PEMBROKE HOSPITAL, PEMBROKE, MA, p. A203
PEMISCOT MEMORIAL HEALTH SYSTEM, HAYTI, MO, p. A242
PENDER COMMUNITY HOSPITAL, PENDER, NE, p. A261
PENDER MEMORIAL HOSPITAL, BURGAW, NC, p. A303
PENDLETON MEMORIAL METHODIST HOSPITAL, NEW ORLEANS, LA, p. A183
PENINSULA BEHAVIORAL CENTER, HAMPTON, VA, p. A435
PENINSULA HOSPITAL, LOUISVILLE, TN, p. A386
PENINSULA HOSPITAL, BURLINGAME, CALIFORNIA, p. A38
PENINSULA HOSPITAL CENTER, NEW YORK, NY, p. A293
PENINSULA REGIONAL MEDICAL CENTER, SALISBURY, MD, p. A196
PENN STATE GEISINGER HEALTH SYSTEM–MILTON S. HERSHEY MEDICAL CENTER, HERSHEY, PA, p. A353
PENN STATE GEISINGER WYOMING VALLEY MEDICAL CENTER, WILKES–BARRE, PA, p. A366
PENNOCK HOSPITAL, HASTINGS, MI, p. A211
PENNSYLVANIA HOSPITAL, PHILADELPHIA, PA, p. A359
PENOBSCOT BAY MEDICAL CENTER, ROCKPORT, ME, p. A189
PENOBSCOT VALLEY HOSPITAL, LINCOLN, ME, p. A189
PENROSE COMMUNITY HOSPITAL, COLORADO SPRINGS, COLORADO, p. A69
PENROSE HOSPITAL, COLORADO SPRINGS, COLORADO, p. A69

PENROSE–ST. FRANCIS HEALTH SERVICES, COLORADO SPRINGS, CO, p. A69
PEOPLE'S MEMORIAL HOSPITAL OF BUCHANAN COUNTY, INDEPENDENCE, IA, p. A150
PERHAM MEMORIAL HOSPITAL AND HOME, PERHAM, MN, p. A227
PERKINS COUNTY HEALTH SERVICES, GRANT, NE, p. A258
PERMIAN GENERAL HOSPITAL, ANDREWS, TX, p. A392
PERRY COUNTY GENERAL HOSPITAL, RICHTON, MS, p. A237
PERRY COUNTY MEMORIAL HOSPITAL, TELL CITY, IN, p. A144
PERRY COUNTY MEMORIAL HOSPITAL, PERRYVILLE, MO, p. A246
PERRY HOSPITAL, PERRY, GA, p. A108
PERRY MEMORIAL HOSPITAL, PRINCETON, IL, p. A132
PERRY MEMORIAL HOSPITAL, PERRY, OK, p. A339
PERSHING GENERAL HOSPITAL, LOVELOCK, NV, p. A264
PERSON MEMORIAL HOSPITAL, ROXBORO, NC, p. A310
PERTH AMBOY DIVISION, PERTH AMBOY, NEW JERSEY, p. A273
PETALUMA VALLEY HOSPITAL, PETALUMA, CA, p. A56
PETERSBURG MEDICAL CENTER, PETERSBURG, AK, p. A21
PHELPS COUNTY REGIONAL MEDICAL CENTER, ROLLA, MO, p. A246
PHELPS MEMORIAL HEALTH CENTER, HOLDREGE, NE, p. A258
PHELPS MEMORIAL HOSPITAL CENTER, SLEEPY HOLLOW, NY, p. A298
PHENIX REGIONAL HOSPITAL, PHENIX CITY, AL, p. A17
PHILHAVEN, BAHAVIORAL HEALTHCARE SERVICES, MOUNT GRETNA, PA, p. A356
PHILLIPS COUNTY HOSPITAL, PHILLIPSBURG, KS, p. A163
PHILLIPS COUNTY MEDICAL CENTER, MALTA, MT, p. A253
PHILLIPS EYE INSTITUTE, MINNEAPOLIS, MN, p. A225
PHOEBE PUTNEY MEMORIAL HOSPITAL, ALBANY, GA, p. A99
PHOENIX BAPTIST HOSPITAL AND MEDICAL CENTER, PHOENIX, AZ, p. A25
PHOENIX CHILDREN'S HOSPITAL, PHOENIX, AZ, p. A25
PHOENIX MEMORIAL HEALTH SYSTEM, PHOENIX, AZ, p. A25
PHOENIX REGIONAL MEDICAL CENTER, PHOENIX, AZ, p. A25
PHOENIXVILLE HOSPITAL OF THE UNIVERSITY OF PENNSYLVANIA HEALTH SYSTEM, PHOENIXVILLE, PA, p. A360
PHS MT. SINAI MEDICAL CENTER EAST, RICHMOND HEIGHTS, OH, p. A328
PHS SANTA FE INDIAN HOSPITAL, SANTA FE, NM, p. A280
PHYSICIANS HOSPITAL, NEW ORLEANS, LA, p. A184
PICKENS COUNTY MEDICAL CENTER, CARROLLTON, AL, p. A13
PIEDMONT GERIATRIC HOSPITAL, BURKEVILLE, VA, p. A433
PIEDMONT HEALTHCARE SYSTEM, ROCK HILL, SC, p. A374
PIEDMONT HOSPITAL, ATLANTA, GA, p. A100
PIGGOTT COMMUNITY HOSPITAL, PIGGOTT, AR, p. A34
PIKE COMMUNITY HOSPITAL, WAVERLY, OH, p. A331
PIKE COUNTY MEMORIAL HOSPITAL, LOUISIANA, MO, p. A245
PIKE COUNTY MEMORIAL HOSPITAL, MURFREESBORO, AR, p. A33
PIKEVILLE UNITED METHODIST HOSPITAL OF KENTUCKY, PIKEVILLE, KY, p. A174
PILGRIM PSYCHIATRIC CENTER, BRENTWOOD, NY, p. A282
PINCKNEYVILLE COMMUNITY HOSPITAL, PINCKNEYVILLE, IL, p. A132
PINE GROVE HOSPITAL, LOS ANGELES, CA, p. A50
PINE MEDICAL CENTER, SANDSTONE, MN, p. A228
PINE REST CHRISTIAN MENTAL HEALTH SERVICES, GRAND RAPIDS, MI, p. A211
PINECREST REHABILITATION HOSPITAL, DELRAY BEACH, FL, p. A83
PINELAKE REGIONAL HOSPITAL, MAYFIELD, KY, p. A173
PINELANDS HOSPITAL, NACOGDOCHES, TX, p. A416
PINEVILLE COMMUNITY HOSPITAL ASSOCIATION, PINEVILLE, KY, p. A174
PINNACLEHEALTH AT COMMUNITY GENERAL OSTEOPATHIC HOSPITAL, HARRISBURG, PENNSYLVANIA, p. A353
PINNACLEHEALTH AT HARRISBURG HOSPITAL, HARRISBURG, PENNSYLVANIA, p. A353
PINNACLEHEALTH AT POLYCLINIC HOSPITAL, HARRISBURG, PENNSYLVANIA, p. A353
PINNACLEHEALTH AT SEIDLE MEMORIAL HOSPITAL, MECHANICSBURG, PENNSYLVANIA, p. A353
PINNACLEHEALTH SYSTEM, HARRISBURG, PA, p. A353
PIONEER MEDICAL CENTER, BIG TIMBER, MT, p. A251
PIONEER MEMORIAL HOSPITAL, HEPPNER, OR, p. A343
PIONEER MEMORIAL HOSPITAL, PRINEVILLE, OR, p. A345
PIONEER MEMORIAL HOSPITAL AND HEALTH SERVICES, VIBORG, SD, p. A379
PIONEER VALLEY HOSPITAL, SALT LAKE CITY, UT, p. A429
PIONEERS HOSPITAL OF RIO BLANCO COUNTY, MEEKER, CO, p. A72
PIONEERS MEMORIAL HEALTHCARE DISTRICT, BRAWLEY, CA, p. A38
PIPESTONE COUNTY MEDICAL CENTER, PIPESTONE, MN, p. A227

PITT COUNTY MEMORIAL HOSPITAL–UNIVERSITY HEALTH SYSTEMS OF EASTERN CAROLINA, GREENVILLE, NC, p. A306
PLACENTIA LINDA HOSPITAL, PLACENTIA, CA, p. A56
PLAINS MEMORIAL HOSPITAL, DIMMITT, TX, p. A402
PLAINS REGIONAL MEDICAL CENTER, CLOVIS, NM, p. A278
PLAINVIEW PUBLIC HOSPITAL, PLAINVIEW, NE, p. A261
PLAINVILLE RURAL HOSPITAL DISTRICT NUMBER ONE, PLAINVILLE, KS, p. A163
PLANTATION GENERAL HOSPITAL, PLANTATION, FL, p. A93
PLATEAU MEDICAL CENTER, OAK HILL, WV, p. A453
PLATTE COMMUNITY MEMORIAL HOSPITAL, PLATTE, SD, p. A378
PLATTE COUNTY MEMORIAL HOSPITAL, WHEATLAND, WY, p. A468
PLATTE VALLEY MEDICAL CENTER, BRIGHTON, CO, p. A68
PLAZA MEDICAL CENTER OF FORT WORTH, FORT WORTH, TX, p. A404
PLEASANT VALLEY HOSPITAL, POINT PLEASANT, WV, p. A453
PLUMAS DISTRICT HOSPITAL, QUINCY, CA, p. A56
POCAHONTAS COMMUNITY HOSPITAL, POCAHONTAS, IA, p. A153
POCAHONTAS MEMORIAL HOSPITAL, BUCKEYE, WV, p. A450
POCATELLO REGIONAL MEDICAL CENTER, POCATELLO, ID, p. A116
POCONO MEDICAL CENTER, EAST STROUDSBURG, PA, p. A351
PODIATRY HOSPITAL OF PITTSBURGH, PITTSBURGH, PA, p. A361
POH MEDICAL CENTER, PONTIAC, MI, p. A215
POINT PLEASANT HOSPITAL DIVISION, POINT PLEASANT, NEW JERSEY, p. A272
POINTE COUPEE GENERAL HOSPITAL, NEW ROADS, LA, p. A184
POLK MEDICAL CENTER, CEDARTOWN, GA, p. A102
POLLY RYON MEMORIAL HOSPITAL, RICHMOND, TX, p. A418
POMERADO HOSPITAL, POWAY, CA, p. A56
POMONA VALLEY HOSPITAL MEDICAL CENTER, POMONA, CA, p. A56
PONCE REGIONAL HOSPITAL, PONCE, PR, p. A471
PONDERA MEDICAL CENTER, CONRAD, MT, p. A252
PONTOTOC HOSPITAL AND EXTENDED CARE FACILITY, PONTOTOC, MS, p. A236
POPLAR COMMUNITY HOSPITAL, POPLAR, MONTANA, p. A255
POPLAR SPRINGS HOSPITAL, PETERSBURG, VA, p. A438
PORT HURON HOSPITAL, PORT HURON, MI, p. A216
PORTAGE HEALTH SYSTEM, HANCOCK, MI, p. A211
PORTER ADVENTIST HOSPITAL, DENVER, CO, p. A69
PORTER HOSPITAL, MIDDLEBURY, VT, p. A431
PORTER MEMORIAL HOSPITAL, VALPARAISO, IN, p. A145
PORTERVILLE DEVELOPMENTAL CENTER, PORTERVILLE, CA, p. A56
PORTSMOUTH PAVILION, PORTSMOUTH, NEW HAMPSHIRE, p. A267
PORTSMOUTH REGIONAL HOSPITAL AND PAVILION, PORTSMOUTH, NH, p. A267
POTOMAC HOSPITAL, WOODBRIDGE, VA, p. A441
POTOMAC VALLEY HOSPITAL, KEYSER, WV, p. A452
POTTSTOWN MEMORIAL MEDICAL CENTER, POTTSTOWN, PA, p. A362
POTTSVILLE HOSPITAL AND WARNE CLINIC, POTTSVILLE, PA, p. A362
POUDRE VALLEY HOSPITAL, FORT COLLINS, CO, p. A70
POWELL CONVALESCENT CENTER, DES MOINES, IOWA, p. A148
POWELL COUNTY MEMORIAL HOSPITAL, DEER LODGE, MT, p. A252
POWELL HOSPITAL, POWELL, WY, p. A467
PRAGUE MUNICIPAL HOSPITAL, PRAGUE, OK, p. A339
PRAIRIE COMMUNITY MEDICAL ASSISTANCE FACILITY, TERRY, MT, p. A254
PRAIRIE DU CHIEN MEMORIAL HOSPITAL, PRAIRIE DU CHIEN, WI, p. A462
PRAIRIE LAKES HOSPITAL AND CARE CENTER, WATERTOWN, SD, p. A379
PRAIRIE VIEW, NEWTON, KS, p. A162
PRATT REGIONAL MEDICAL CENTER, PRATT, KS, p. A163
PRATTVILLE BAPTIST HOSPITAL, PRATTVILLE, AL, p. A18
PRECEDENT HEALTH CENTER, DENVER, CO, p. A69
PRENTICE WOMEN'S HOSPITAL, CHICAGO, ILLINOIS, p. A121
PRENTISS REGIONAL HOSPITAL AND EXTENDED CARE FACILITIES, PRENTISS, MS, p. A237
PRESBYTERIAN HOSPITAL, CHARLOTTE, NC, p. A304
PRESBYTERIAN HOSPITAL, OKLAHOMA CITY, OKLAHOMA, p. A338
PRESBYTERIAN HOSPITAL, ALBUQUERQUE, NM, p. A277
PRESBYTERIAN HOSPITAL IN THE CITY OF NEW YORK, NEW YORK, NEW YORK, p. A292
PRESBYTERIAN HOSPITAL OF COMMERCE, COMMERCE, TEXAS, p. A406
PRESBYTERIAN HOSPITAL OF DALLAS, DALLAS, TX, p. A400

Q

R

RICHARD H. YOUNG PSYCHIATRIC HOSPITAL, KEARNEY, NEBRASKA, p. A258
RICHARD L. ROUDEBUSH VETERANS AFFAIRS MEDICAL CENTER, INDIANAPOLIS, IN, p. A140
RICHARDS MEMORIAL HOSPITAL, ROCKDALE, TX, p. A419
RICHARDSON MEDICAL CENTER, RAYVILLE, LA, p. A185
RICHARDTON HEALTH CENTER, RICHARDTON, ND, p. A315
RICHLAND HOSPITAL, MANSFIELD, OH, p. A326
RICHLAND HOSPITAL, RICHLAND CENTER, WI, p. A463
RICHLAND MEMORIAL HOSPITAL, OLNEY, IL, p. A131
RICHLAND PARISH HOSPITAL–DELHI, DELHI, LA, p. A179
RICHMOND EYE AND EAR HOSPITAL, RICHMOND, VA, p. A440
RICHMOND MEMORIAL HOSPITAL, ROCKINGHAM, NC, p. A310
RICHMOND STATE HOSPITAL, RICHMOND, IN, p. A144
RICHWOOD AREA COMMUNITY HOSPITAL, RICHWOOD, WV, p. A454
RIDDLE MEMORIAL HOSPITAL, MEDIA, PA, p. A356
RIDGECREST HOSPITAL, CLAYTON, GA, p. A102
RIDGECREST REGIONAL HOSPITAL, RIDGECREST, CA, p. A57
RIDGEVIEW INSTITUTE, SMYRNA, GA, p. A109
RIDGEVIEW MEDICAL CENTER, WACONIA, MN, p. A229
RIDGEVIEW PSYCHIATRIC HOSPITAL AND CENTER, OAK RIDGE, TN, p. A389
RILEY HOSPITAL FOR CHILDRERN, INDIANAPOLIS, INDIANA, p. A140
RILEY MEMORIAL HOSPITAL, MERIDIAN, MS, p. A235
RINGGOLD COUNTY HOSPITAL, MOUNT AYR, IA, p. A152
RIO GRANDE REGIONAL HOSPITAL, MCALLEN, TX, p. A414
RIO GRANDE STATE CENTER, HARLINGEN, TX, p. A406
RIO VISTA PHYSICAL REHABILITATION HOSPITAL, EL PASO, TX, p. A403
RIPLEY COUNTY MEMORIAL HOSPITAL, DONIPHAN, MO, p. A241
RIPON MEDICAL CENTER, RIPON, WI, p. A463
RIVENDELL BEHAVIORAL HEALTH SERVICES, BENTON, AR, p. A29
RIVENDELL OF MICHIGAN, SAINT JOHNS, MI, p. A216
RIVER CREST HOSPITAL, SAN ANGELO, TX, p. A419
RIVER FALLS AREA HOSPITAL, RIVER FALLS, WI, p. A463
RIVER OAKS HOSPITAL, JACKSON, MS, p. A234
RIVER OAKS HOSPITAL, NEW ORLEANS, LA, p. A184
RIVER PARISHES HOSPITAL, LA PLACE, LA, p. A181
RIVER PARK HOSPITAL, MCMINNVILLE, TN, p. A387
RIVER VALLEY HEALTH SYSTEM, IRONTON, OH, p. A325
RIVER WEST MEDICAL CENTER, PLAQUEMINE, LA, p. A185
RIVEREDGE HOSPITAL, FOREST PARK, IL, p. A125
RIVERLAND MEDICAL CENTER, FERRIDAY, LA, p. A179
RIVERSIDE COMMUNITY HOSPITAL, RIVERSIDE, CA, p. A57
RIVERSIDE COUNTY REGIONAL MEDICAL CENTER, MORENO VALLEY, CA, p. A53
RIVERSIDE GENERAL HOSPITAL, HOUSTON, TX, p. A409
RIVERSIDE HEALTH SYSTEM, WICHITA, KS, p. A165
RIVERSIDE MEDICAL CENTER, KANKAKEE, IL, p. A128
RIVERSIDE MEDICAL CENTER, WAUPACA, WI, p. A464
RIVERSIDE MEDICAL CENTER, FRANKLINTON, LA, p. A179
RIVERSIDE MERCY HOSPITAL, TOLEDO, OH, p. A329
RIVERSIDE OSTEOPATHIC HOSPITAL, TRENTON, MI, p. A218
RIVERSIDE PSYCHIATRIC INSTITUTE, p. A437
RIVERSIDE REGIONAL MEDICAL CENTER, NEWPORT NEWS, VA, p. A437
RIVERSIDE TAPPAHANNOCK HOSPITAL, TAPPAHANNOCK, VA, p. A441
RIVERSIDE WALTER REED HOSPITAL, GLOUCESTER, VA, p. A435
RIVERTON MEMORIAL HOSPITAL, RIVERTON, WY, p. A467
RIVERVALLEY BEHAVIORAL HEALTH HOSPITAL, OWENSBORO, KY, p. A174
RIVERVIEW HEALTHCARE ASSOCIATION, CROOKSTON, MN, p. A222
RIVERVIEW HOSPITAL, NOBLESVILLE, IN, p. A143
RIVERVIEW HOSPITAL ASSOCIATION, WISCONSIN RAPIDS, WI, p. A465
RIVERVIEW HOSPITAL FOR CHILDREN, MIDDLETOWN, CT, p. A75
RIVERVIEW MANOR, p. A465
RIVERVIEW MEDICAL CENTER, RED BANK, NEW JERSEY, p. A272
RIVERVIEW MEDICAL CENTER, GONZALES, LA, p. A179
RIVERVIEW REGIONAL MEDICAL CENTER, GADSDEN, AL, p. A15
RIVERWOOD HEALTH CARECENTER, AITKIN, MN, p. A220
ROANE GENERAL HOSPITAL, SPENCER, WV, p. A454
ROANE MEDICAL CENTER, HARRIMAN, TN, p. A384
ROANOKE MEMORIAL REHABILITATION CENTER, ROANOKE, VIRGINIA, p. A440
ROANOKE–CHOWAN HOSPITAL, AHOSKIE, NC, p. A302
ROBERT F. KENNEDY MEDICAL CENTER, HAWTHORNE, CA, p. A44
ROBERT PACKER HOSPITAL, SAYRE, PA, p. A363

ROBERT WOOD JOHNSON UNIVERSITY HOSPITAL, NEW BRUNSWICK, NJ, p. A272
ROBERT WOOD JOHNSON UNIVERSITY HOSPITAL AT HAMILTON, HAMILTON, NJ, p. A270
ROBINSON MEMORIAL HOSPITAL, RAVENNA, OH, p. A328
ROCHELLE COMMUNITY HOSPITAL, ROCHELLE, IL, p. A132
ROCHESTER GENERAL HOSPITAL, ROCHESTER, NY, p. A297
ROCHESTER METHODIST HOSPITAL, ROCHESTER, MN, p. A227
ROCHESTER PSYCHIATRIC CENTER, ROCHESTER, NY, p. A297
ROCK COUNTY HOSPITAL, BASSETT, NE, p. A256
ROCK CREEK CENTER, LEMONT, IL, p. A128
ROCKCASTLE HOSPITAL AND RESPIRATORY CARE CENTER, MOUNT VERNON, KY, p. A174
ROCKDALE HOSPITAL, CONYERS, GA, p. A103
ROCKEFELLER UNIVERSITY HOSPITAL, NEW YORK, NY, p. A293
ROCKFORD CENTER, NEWARK, DE, p. A78
ROCKFORD MEMORIAL HOSPITAL, ROCKFORD, IL, p. A132
ROCKINGHAM MEMORIAL HOSPITAL, HARRISONBURG, VA, p. A435
ROCKLAND CHILDREN'S PSYCHIATRIC CENTER, ORANGEBURG, NY, p. A295
ROCKLAND PSYCHIATRIC CENTER, ORANGEBURG, NY, p. A295
ROCKVILLE GENERAL HOSPITAL, VERNON ROCKVILLE, CT, p. A77
ROGER C. PEACE REHABILITATION HOSPITAL, GREENVILLE, SOUTH CAROLINA, p. A373
ROGER HUNTINGTON NURSING CENTER, p. A373
ROGER MILLS MEMORIAL HOSPITAL, CHEYENNE, OK, p. A334
ROGER WILLIAMS MEDICAL CENTER, PROVIDENCE, RI, p. A368
ROGERS CITY REHABILITATION HOSPITAL, ROGERS CITY, MI, p. A216
ROGERS MEMORIAL HOSPITAL, OCONOMOWOC, WI, p. A462
ROGUE VALLEY MEDICAL CENTER, MEDFORD, OR, p. A344
ROLLING HILLS HOSPITAL, ADA, OK, p. A333
ROLLING PLAINS MEMORIAL HOSPITAL, SWEETWATER, TX, p. A422
ROME MEMORIAL HOSPITAL, ROME, NY, p. A297
ROOSEVELT HOSPITAL, NEW YORK, NEW YORK, p. A293
ROOSEVELT MEMORIAL MEDICAL CENTER, CULBERTSON, MT, p. A252
ROOSEVELT WARM SPRINGS INSTITUTE FOR REHABILITATION, WARM SPRINGS, GA, p. A111
ROPER HOSPITAL, CHARLESTON, SC, p. A371
ROPER HOSPITAL NORTH, CHARLESTON, SC, p. A371
ROSE MEDICAL CENTER, DENVER, CO, p. A69
ROSEAU AREA HOSPITAL AND HOMES, ROSEAU, MN, p. A227
ROSEBUD HEALTH CARE CENTER, FORSYTH, MT, p. A252
ROSELAND COMMUNITY HOSPITAL, CHICAGO, IL, p. A122
ROSEWOOD MEDICAL CENTER, HOUSTON, TX, p. A409
ROSS SKILLED NURSING FACILITY, p. A187
ROSWELL PARK CANCER INSTITUTE, BUFFALO, NY, p. A283
ROTARY REHABILITATION HOSPITAL, MOBILE, ALABAMA, p. A16
ROUND ROCK HOSPITAL, ROUND ROCK, TX, p. A419
ROUNDUP MEMORIAL HOSPITAL, ROUNDUP, MT, p. A254
ROUTT MEMORIAL HOSPITAL, STEAMBOAT SPRINGS, CO, p. A73
ROWAN REGIONAL MEDICAL CENTER, SALISBURY, NC, p. A310
ROXBOROUGH MEMORIAL HOSPITAL, PHILADELPHIA, PA, p. A359
ROY H. LAIRD MEMORIAL HOSPITAL, KILGORE, TX, p. A411
ROY LESTER SCHNEIDER HOSPITAL, SAINT THOMAS, VI, p. A472
ROYAL C. JOHNSON VETERANS MEMORIAL HOSPITAL, SIOUX FALLS, SD, p. A379
RUBY VALLEY HOSPITAL, SHERIDAN, MT, p. A254
RUMFORD COMMUNITY HOSPITAL, RUMFORD, ME, p. A189
RUNNELLS SPECIALIZED HOSPITAL OF UNION COUNTY, BERKELEY HEIGHTS, NJ, p. A268
RUSH COUNTY MEMORIAL HOSPITAL, LA CROSSE, KS, p. A160
RUSH FOUNDATION HOSPITAL, MERIDIAN, MS, p. A236
RUSH MEMORIAL HOSPITAL, RUSHVILLE, IN, p. A144
RUSH NORTH SHORE MEDICAL CENTER, SKOKIE, IL, p. A133
RUSH–COPLEY MEDICAL CENTER, AURORA, IL, p. A118
RUSH–PRESBYTERIAN–ST. LUKE'S MEDICAL CENTER, CHICAGO, IL, p. A122
RUSK COUNTY MEMORIAL HOSPITAL AND NURSING HOME, LADYSMITH, WI, p. A459
RUSK INSTITUTE, NEW YORK, NEW YORK, p. A292
RUSK STATE HOSPITAL, RUSK, TX, p. A419
RUSSELL COUNTY HOSPITAL, RUSSELL SPRINGS, KY, p. A175
RUSSELL COUNTY MEDICAL CENTER, LEBANON, VA, p. A436
RUSSELL MEDICAL CENTER, ALEXANDER CITY, AL, p. A11
RUSSELL REGIONAL HOSPITAL, RUSSELL, KS, p. A163
RUSSELLVILLE HOSPITAL, RUSSELLVILLE, AL, p. A18
RUTHERFORD HOSPITAL, RUTHERFORDTON, NC, p. A310
RUTLAND REGIONAL MEDICAL CENTER, RUTLAND, VT, p. A431
RYDER MEMORIAL HOSPITAL, HUMACAO, PR, p. A470
RYE HOSPITAL CENTER, RYE, NY, p. A297

S

SABETHA COMMUNITY HOSPITAL, SABETHA, KS, p. A164
SABINE COUNTY HOSPITAL, HEMPHILL, TX, p. A406
SABINE MEDICAL CENTER, MANY, LA, p. A182
SAC–OSAGE HOSPITAL, OSCEOLA, MO, p. A246
SACRED HEART HOSPITAL, ALLENTOWN, PA, p. A347
SACRED HEART HOSPITAL, CUMBERLAND, MD, p. A194
SACRED HEART HOSPITAL, CHICAGO, IL, p. A122
SACRED HEART HOSPITAL, EAU CLAIRE, WI, p. A457
SACRED HEART HOSPITAL, TOMAHAWK, WISCONSIN, p. A463
SACRED HEART HOSPITAL OF PENSACOLA, PENSACOLA, FL, p. A93
SACRED HEART MEDICAL CENTER, SPOKANE, WA, p. A448
SACRED HEART MEDICAL CENTER, EUGENE, OR, p. A342
SACRED HEART REHABILITATION INSTITUTE, MILWAUKEE, WI, p. A461
SACRED HEART–ST. MARY'S HOSPITALS, RHINELANDER, WI, p. A463
SADDLEBACK MEMORIAL MEDICAL CENTER, LAGUNA HILLS, CA, p. A46
SAGAMORE CHILDREN'S PSYCHIATRIC CENTER, HUNTINGTON STATION, NY, p. A286
SAGE MEMORIAL HOSPITAL, GANADO, AZ, p. A23
SAINT AGNES MEDICAL CENTER, FRESNO, CA, p. A43
SAINT ALPHONSUS REGIONAL MEDICAL CENTER, BOISE, ID, p. A114
SAINT ANNE'S HOSPITAL, FALL RIVER, MA, p. A200
SAINT ANTHONY HOSPITAL, CHICAGO, IL, p. A122
SAINT ANTHONY MEDICAL CENTER, ROCKFORD, IL, p. A133
SAINT ANTHONY MEMORIAL HEALTH CENTERS, MICHIGAN CITY, IN, p. A142
SAINT ANTHONY'S HEALTH CENTER, ALTON, IL, p. A118
SAINT BARNABAS MEDICAL CENTER, LIVINGSTON, NJ, p. A271
SAINT CLARE'S HEALTH SERVICES, DENVILLE, NJ, p. A269
SAINT CLARE'S HOSPITAL, ALTON, ILLINOIS, p. A118
SAINT CLARE'S HOSPITAL/BOONTON TOWNSHIP, BOONTON TOWNSHIP, NEW JERSEY, p. A269
SAINT CLARE'S HOSPITAL/DENVILLE, DENVILLE, NEW JERSEY, p. A269
SAINT CLARE'S HOSPITAL/SUSSEX, SUSSEX, NEW JERSEY, p. A269
SAINT ELIZABETH REGIONAL MEDICAL CENTER, LINCOLN, NE, p. A259
SAINT EUGENE MEDICAL CENTER, DILLON, SC, p. A372
SAINT FRANCIS HOSPITAL, POUGHKEEPSIE, NY, p. A296
SAINT FRANCIS HOSPITAL, CHARLESTON, WV, p. A451
SAINT FRANCIS HOSPITAL, MEMPHIS, TN, p. A387
SAINT FRANCIS HOSPITAL, TULSA, OK, p. A341
SAINT FRANCIS HOSPITAL AND HEALTH CENTER, BLUE ISLAND, IL, p. A119
SAINT FRANCIS HOSPITAL AND MEDICAL CENTER, HARTFORD, CT, p. A75
SAINT FRANCIS HOSPITAL–BEACON, BEACON, NEW YORK, p. A296
SAINT FRANCIS MEDICAL CENTER, PEORIA, IL, p. A131
SAINT FRANCIS MEDICAL CENTER, CAPE GIRARDEAU, MO, p. A240
SAINT FRANCIS MEMORIAL HEALTH CENTER, GRAND ISLAND, NEBRASKA, p. A258
SAINT FRANCIS MEMORIAL HOSPITAL, SAN FRANCISCO, CA, p. A60
SAINT JAMES HOSPITAL, PONTIAC, IL, p. A132
SAINT JAMES HOSPITAL OF NEWARK, NEWARK, NJ, p. A272
SAINT JOHN HOSPITAL, LEAVENWORTH, KS, p. A160
SAINT JOHN'S HEALTH SYSTEM, ANDERSON, IN, p. A136
SAINT JOHN'S HOSPITAL AND HEALTH CENTER, SANTA MONICA, CA, p. A62
SAINT JOSEPH COMMUNITY HOSPITAL, NEW HAMPTON, IA, p. A152
SAINT JOSEPH HEALTH CENTER, KANSAS CITY, MO, p. A243
SAINT JOSEPH HOSPITAL, BELVIDERE, IL, p. A119
SAINT JOSEPH HOSPITAL, LEXINGTON, KY, p. A171
SAINT JOSEPH HOSPITAL, EUREKA, CA, p. A42
SAINT JOSEPH HOSPITAL EAST, LEXINGTON, KY, p. A171
SAINT JOSEPH MERCY HEALTH SYSTEM, ANN ARBOR, MI, p. A206
SAINT JOSEPH'S HOSPITAL, MARSHFIELD, WI, p. A460
SAINT JOSEPH'S HOSPITAL OF ATLANTA, ATLANTA, GA, p. A100
SAINT JOSEPH'S REGIONAL MEDICAL CENTER–PLYMOUTH CAMPUS, PLYMOUTH, IN, p. A143
SAINT JOSEPH'S REGIONAL MEDICAL CENTER–SOUTH BEND CAMPUS, SOUTH BEND, IN, p. A144
SAINT LOUIS UNIVERSITY HOSPITAL, SAINT LOUIS, MO, p. A248
SAINT LOUISE HOSPITAL, MORGAN HILL, CA, p. A53

U

V

W

WALLACE THOMSON HOSPITAL, UNION, SC, p. A375
WALLOWA MEMORIAL HOSPITAL, ENTERPRISE, OR, p. A342
WALLS REGIONAL HOSPITAL, CLEBURNE, TX, p. A397
WALTER B. JONES ALCOHOL AND DRUG ABUSE TREATMENT CENTER, GREENVILLE, NC, p. A306
WALTER KNOX MEMORIAL HOSPITAL, EMMETT, ID, p. A115
WALTER O. BOSWELL MEMORIAL HOSPITAL, SUN CITY, AZ, p. A26
WALTER OLIN MOSS REGIONAL MEDICAL CENTER, LAKE CHARLES, LA, p. A181
WALTER P. REUTHER PSYCHIATRIC HOSPITAL, WESTLAND, MI, p. A219
WALTER REED ARMY MEDICAL CENTER, WASHINGTON, DC, p. A80
WALTHALL COUNTY GENERAL HOSPITAL, TYLERTOWN, MS, p. A237
WALTON MEDICAL CENTER, MONROE, GA, p. A107
WALTON REGIONAL HOSPITAL, DE FUNIAK SPRINGS, FL, p. A83
WALTON REHABILITATION HOSPITAL, AUGUSTA, GA, p. A101
WAMEGO CITY HOSPITAL, WAMEGO, KS, p. A165
WARD MEMORIAL HOSPITAL, MONAHANS, TX, p. A415
WARM SPRINGS & BAPTIST REHABILITATION HOSPITAL, SAN ANTONIO, TX, p. A421
WARM SPRINGS REHABILITATION HOSPITAL, GONZALES, TX, p. A405
WARMINSTER HOSPITAL, WARMINSTER, PA, p. A365
WARNER BROWN HOSPITAL, EL DORADO, ARKANSAS, p. A30
WARRACK MEDICAL CENTER HOSPITAL, SANTA ROSA, CA, p. A63
WARREN G. MAGNUSON CLINICAL CENTER, NATIONAL INSTITUTES OF HEALTH, BETHESDA, MD, p. A193
WARREN GENERAL HOSPITAL, WARREN, PA, p. A365
WARREN HOSPITAL, PHILLIPSBURG, NJ, p. A273
WARREN MEMORIAL HOSPITAL, FRONT ROYAL, VA, p. A435
WARREN MEMORIAL HOSPITAL, FRIEND, NE, p. A257
WARREN STATE HOSPITAL, NORTH WARREN, PA, p. A357
WASATCH COUNTY HOSPITAL, HEBER CITY, UT, p. A427
WASECA MEDICAL CENTER, WASECA, MN, p. A229
WASHAKIE MEMORIAL HOSPITAL, WORLAND, WY, p. A468
WASHBURN REGIONAL HEALTH CENTER, WASHBURN, MAINE, p. A189
WASHINGTON ADVENTIST HOSPITAL, TAKOMA PARK, MD, p. A196
WASHINGTON CAMPUS, GRANTS PASS, OREGON, p. A343
WASHINGTON COUNTY HEALTH SYSTEM, HAGERSTOWN, MD, p. A194
WASHINGTON COUNTY HOSPITAL, PLYMOUTH, NC, p. A309
WASHINGTON COUNTY HOSPITAL, NASHVILLE, IL, p. A130
WASHINGTON COUNTY HOSPITAL, WASHINGTON, IA, p. A154
WASHINGTON COUNTY HOSPITAL, WASHINGTON, KS, p. A165
WASHINGTON COUNTY INFIRMARY AND NURSING HOME, CHATOM, AL, p. A13
WASHINGTON COUNTY MEMORIAL HOSPITAL, SALEM, IN, p. A144
WASHINGTON COUNTY MEMORIAL HOSPITAL, POTOSI, MO, p. A246
WASHINGTON COUNTY REGIONAL HOSPITAL, SANDERSVILLE, GA, p. A109
WASHINGTON HOSPITAL, WASHINGTON, PA, p. A365
WASHINGTON HOSPITAL CENTER, WASHINGTON, DC, p. A80
WASHINGTON MEDICAL CENTER, CULVER CITY, CA, p. A40
WASHINGTON REGIONAL MEDICAL CENTER, FAYETTEVILLE, AR, p. A30
WASHINGTON TOWNSHIP HEALTH CARE DISTRICT, FREMONT, CA, p. A42
WASHINGTON–ST. TAMMANY REGIONAL MEDICAL CENTER, BOGALUSA, LA, p. A178
WASHOE MEDICAL CENTER, RENO, NV, p. A264
WATAUGA MEDICAL CENTER, BOONE, NC, p. A303
WATERBURY HOSPITAL, WATERBURY, CT, p. A77
WATERTOWN MEMORIAL HOSPITAL, WATERTOWN, WI, p. A464
WATONGA MUNICIPAL HOSPITAL, WATONGA, OK, p. A341
WATSONVILLE COMMUNITY HOSPITAL, WATSONVILLE, CA, p. A66
WAUKESHA MEMORIAL HOSPITAL, WAUKESHA, WI, p. A464
WAUPUN MEMORIAL HOSPITAL, WAUPUN, WI, p. A464
WAUSAU HOSPITAL, WAUSAU, WI, p. A465
WAVERLY MUNICIPAL HOSPITAL, WAVERLY, IA, p. A155
WAYNE COUNTY HOSPITAL, MONTICELLO, KY, p. A173
WAYNE COUNTY HOSPITAL, CORYDON, IA, p. A147
WAYNE GENERAL HOSPITAL, WAYNE, NJ, p. A275
WAYNE GENERAL HOSPITAL, WAYNESBORO, MS, p. A238
WAYNE HOSPITAL, GREENVILLE, OH, p. A324
WAYNE MEDICAL CENTER, WAYNESBORO, TN, p. A390
WAYNE MEMORIAL HOSPITAL, HONESDALE, PA, p. A353
WAYNE MEMORIAL HOSPITAL, GOLDSBORO, NC, p. A306
WAYNE MEMORIAL HOSPITAL, JESUP, GA, p. A106
WAYNESBORO HOSPITAL, WAYNESBORO, PA, p. A365
WEBSTER COUNTY COMMUNITY HOSPITAL, RED CLOUD, NE, p. A261

WEBSTER COUNTY MEMORIAL HOSPITAL, WEBSTER SPRINGS, WV, p. A454
WEBSTER HEALTH SERVICES, EUPORA, MS, p. A233
WEDOWEE HOSPITAL, WEDOWEE, AL, p. A19
WEED ARMY COMMUNITY HOSPITAL, FORT IRWIN, CA, p. A42
WEEKS MEMORIAL HOSPITAL, LANCASTER, NH, p. A266
WEINER MEMORIAL MEDICAL CENTER, MARSHALL, MN, p. A225
WEIRTON MEDICAL CENTER, WEIRTON, WV, p. A454
WEISBROD MEMORIAL COUNTY HOSPITAL, EADS, CO, p. A70
WELBORN MEMORIAL BAPTIST HOSPITAL, EVANSVILLE, IN, p. A138
WELLINGTON REGIONAL MEDICAL CENTER, WEST PALM BEACH, FL, p. A98
WELLMONT BRISTOL REGIONAL MEDICAL CENTER, BRISTOL, TN, p. A381
WELLMONT HOLSTON VALLEY MEDICAL CENTER, KINGSPORT, TN, p. A385
WELLMONT LONESOME PINE HOSPITAL, BIG STONE GAP, VA, p. A433
WELLS COMMUNITY HOSPITAL, BLUFFTON, IN, p. A136
WELLSPRING FOUNDATION, BETHLEHEM, CT, p. A74
WELLSTAR COBB HOSPITAL, AUSTELL, GA, p. A101
WELLSTAR DOUGLAS HOSPITAL, DOUGLASVILLE, GA, p. A104
WELLSTAR KENNESTONE HOSPITAL, MARIETTA, GA, p. A107
WELLSTAR PAULDING HOSPITAL, DALLAS, GA, p. A103
WELLSTAR WINDY HILL HOSPITAL, MARIETTA, GA, p. A107
WENTWORTH–DOUGLASS HOSPITAL, DOVER, NH, p. A265
WERNERSVILLE STATE HOSPITAL, WERNERSVILLE, PA, p. A365
WESKOTA MEMORIAL MEDICAL CENTER, WESSINGTON SPRINGS, SD, p. A380
WESLEY LONG COMMUNITY HOSPITAL, GREENSBORO, NORTH CAROLINA, p. A306
WESLEY MEDICAL CENTER, HATTIESBURG, MS, p. A233
WESLEY MEDICAL CENTER, WICHITA, KS, p. A166
WESLEY REHABILITATION HOSPITAL, WICHITA, KS, p. A166
WESLEY WOODS CENTER OF EMORY UNIVERSITY, ATLANTA, GA, p. A100
WEST ALLIS MEMORIAL HOSPITAL, WEST ALLIS, WI, p. A465
WEST ANAHEIM MEDICAL CENTER, ANAHEIM, CA, p. A36
WEST BOCA MEDICAL CENTER, BOCA RATON, FL, p. A81
WEST BRANCH REGIONAL MEDICAL CENTER, WEST BRANCH, MI, p. A219
WEST CALCASIEU CAMERON HOSPITAL, SULPHUR, LA, p. A186
WEST CAMPUS, NORFOLK, NEBRASKA, p. A259
WEST CARROLL MEMORIAL HOSPITAL, OAK GROVE, LA, p. A184
WEST CENTRAL COMMUNITY HOSPITAL, CLINTON, IN, p. A137
WEST COMMUNITY HOSPITAL, WEST, TX, p. A425
WEST FELICIANA PARISH HOSPITAL, SAINT FRANCISVILLE, LA, p. A185
WEST FLORIDA REGIONAL MEDICAL CENTER, PENSACOLA, FL, p. A93
WEST GEORGIA HEALTH SYSTEM, LA GRANGE, GA, p. A106
WEST HAVEN DIVISION, WEST HAVEN, CONNECTICUT, p. A77
WEST HILLS HOSPITAL AND MEDICAL CENTER, LOS ANGELES, CA, p. A51
WEST HOLT MEMORIAL HOSPITAL, ATKINSON, NE, p. A256
WEST HOUSTON MEDICAL CENTER, HOUSTON, TX, p. A410
WEST HUDSON HOSPITAL, KEARNY, NJ, p. A271
WEST JEFFERSON MEDICAL CENTER, MARRERO, LA, p. A182
WEST JERSEY HOSPITAL–BERLIN, BERLIN, NJ, p. A268
WEST JERSEY HOSPITAL–CAMDEN, CAMDEN, NJ, p. A269
WEST JERSEY HOSPITAL–MARLTON, MARLTON, NJ, p. A271
WEST JERSEY HOSPITAL–VOORHEES, VOORHEES, NJ, p. A275
WEST OAKS HOSPITAL, HOUSTON, TX, p. A410
WEST PACES MEDICAL CENTER, ATLANTA, GA, p. A100
WEST PARK HOSPITAL, CODY, WY, p. A466
WEST RIVER REGIONAL MEDICAL CENTER, HETTINGER, ND, p. A314
WEST SHORE HOSPITAL, MANISTEE, MI, p. A214
WEST SUBURBAN HOSPITAL MEDICAL CENTER, OAK PARK, IL, p. A131
WEST VALLEY MEDICAL CENTER, CALDWELL, ID, p. A114
WEST VIRGINIA UNIVERSITY HOSPITALS, MORGANTOWN, WV, p. A453
WESTBOROUGH STATE HOSPITAL, WESTBOROUGH, MA, p. A205
WESTBRIDGE TREATMENT CENTER, PHOENIX, AZ, p. A25
WESTBROOK COMMUNITY HOSPITAL, WESTBROOK, ME, p. A190
WESTBROOK HEALTH CENTER, WESTBROOK, MN, p. A229
WESTCHESTER GENERAL HOSPITAL, MIAMI, FL, p. A90
WESTCHESTER MEDICAL CENTER, VALHALLA, NY, p. A299
WESTCHESTER SQUARE MEDICAL CENTER, NEW YORK, NY, p. A294
WESTERLY HOSPITAL, WESTERLY, RI, p. A369
WESTERN ARIZONA REGIONAL MEDICAL CENTER, BULLHEAD CITY, AZ, p. A22
WESTERN BAPTIST HOSPITAL, PADUCAH, KY, p. A174

WESTERN MARYLAND CENTER, HAGERSTOWN, MD, p. A195
WESTERN MEDICAL CENTER HOSPITAL ANAHEIM, ANAHEIM, CA, p. A36
WESTERN MEDICAL CENTER–SANTA ANA, SANTA ANA, CA, p. A62
WESTERN MENTAL HEALTH INSTITUTE, WESTERN INSTITUTE, TN, p. A391
WESTERN MISSOURI MEDICAL CENTER, WARRENSBURG, MO, p. A250
WESTERN MISSOURI MENTAL HEALTH CENTER, KANSAS CITY, MO, p. A244
WESTERN NEW YORK CHILDREN'S PSYCHIATRIC CENTER, BUFFALO, NY, p. A283
WESTERN PENNSYLVANIA HOSPITAL, PITTSBURGH, PA, p. A362
WESTERN PLAINS REGIONAL HOSPITAL, DODGE CITY, KS, p. A157
WESTERN PSYCHIATRIC INSTITUTE AND CLINIC, PITTSBURGH, PENNSYLVANIA, p. A362
WESTERN QUEENS COMMUNITY HOSPITAL, NEW YORK, NY, p. A294
WESTERN RESERVE CARE SYSTEM, YOUNGSTOWN, OH, p. A331
WESTERN STATE HOSPITAL, STAUNTON, VA, p. A441
WESTERN STATE HOSPITAL, HOPKINSVILLE, KY, p. A170
WESTERN STATE HOSPITAL, TACOMA, WA, p. A449
WESTERN STATE PSYCHIATRIC CENTER, FORT SUPPLY, OK, p. A335
WESTERN WAKE MEDICAL CENTER, CARY, NORTH CAROLINA, p. A310
WESTFIELD MEMORIAL HOSPITAL, WESTFIELD, NY, p. A300
WESTLAKE COMMUNITY HOSPITAL, MELROSE PARK, IL, p. A129
WESTLAKE REGIONAL HOSPITAL, COLUMBIA, KY, p. A168
WESTMORELAND REGIONAL HOSPITAL, GREENSBURG, PA, p. A352
WESTON COUNTY HEALTH SERVICES, NEWCASTLE, WY, p. A467
WESTPARK SURGERY CENTER, MCKINNEY, TEXAS, p. A414
WESTSIDE REGIONAL MEDICAL CENTER, PLANTATION, FL, p. A93
WESTVIEW HOSPITAL, INDIANAPOLIS, IN, p. A140
WESTWOOD LODGE HOSPITAL, WESTWOOD, MA, p. A205
WESTWOOD MEDICAL CENTER, MIDLAND, TX, p. A415
WETZEL COUNTY HOSPITAL, NEW MARTINSVILLE, WV, p. A453
WHEATLAND MEMORIAL HOSPITAL, HARLOWTON, MT, p. A253
WHEATON COMMUNITY HOSPITAL, WHEATON, MN, p. A229
WHEELER COUNTY HOSPITAL, GLENWOOD, GA, p. A105
WHEELING HOSPITAL, WHEELING, WV, p. A454
WHIDBEY GENERAL HOSPITAL, COUPEVILLE, WA, p. A444
WHIDDEN MEMORIAL HOSPITAL, EVERETT, MASSACHUSETTS, p. A202
WHITE COMMUNITY HOSPITAL, AURORA, MN, p. A220
WHITE COUNTY COMMUNITY HOSPITAL, SPARTA, TN, p. A390
WHITE COUNTY MEDICAL CENTER, CARMI, IL, p. A119
WHITE COUNTY MEDICAL CENTER, SEARCY, AR, p. A34
WHITE COUNTY MEMORIAL HOSPITAL, MONTICELLO, IN, p. A142
WHITE MEMORIAL MEDICAL CENTER, LOS ANGELES, CA, p. A51
WHITE MOUNTAIN REGIONAL MEDICAL CENTER, SPRINGERVILLE, AZ, p. A26
WHITE PLAINS HOSPITAL CENTER, WHITE PLAINS, NY, p. A301
WHITE RIVER MEDICAL CENTER, BATESVILLE, AR, p. A29
WHITESBURG APPALACHIAN REGIONAL HOSPITAL, WHITESBURG, KY, p. A175
WHITFIELD MEDICAL SURGICAL HOSPITAL, WHITFIELD, MISSISSIPPI, p. A238
WHITING FORENSIC DIVISION OF CONNECTICUT VALLEY HOSPITAL, MIDDLETOWN, CONNECTICUT, p. A75
WHITINSVILLE MEDICAL CENTER, WHITINSVILLE, MASSACHUSETTS, p. A202
WHITLEY MEMORIAL HOSPITAL, COLUMBIA CITY, IN, p. A137
WHITMAN HOSPITAL AND MEDICAL CENTER, COLFAX, WA, p. A444
WHITTEN CENTER INFIRMARY, CLINTON, SC, p. A371
WHITTIER HOSPITAL MEDICAL CENTER, WHITTIER, CA, p. A67
WHITTIER REHABILITATION HOSPITAL, HAVERHILL, MA, p. A201
WICHITA COUNTY HOSPITAL, LEOTI, KS, p. A161
WICHITA COUNTY HOSPITAL LONG TERM CARE, LEOTI, KANSAS, p. A161
WICHITA FALLS STATE HOSPITAL, WICHITA FALLS, TX, p. A426
WICKENBURG REGIONAL HOSPITAL, WICKENBURG, AZ, p. A27
WILBARGER GENERAL HOSPITAL, VERNON, TX, p. A424
WILCOX ARMY COMMUNITY HOSPITAL, FORT DRUM, NY, p. A285
WILCOX MEMORIAL HOSPITAL, LIHUE, HI, p. A113
WILD ROSE COMMUNITY MEMORIAL HOSPITAL, WILD ROSE, WI, p. A465

Y

Z

Index of Health Care Professionals

This section is an index of the key health care professionals for the hospitals and/or health care systems listed in this publication. The index is in alphabetical order, by individual, followed by the title, institutional affiliation, city, state and page reference to the hospital and/or health care system listing in section A and/or B.

A

AANONSON, Mark, Administrator, Northern Virginia Community Hospital, Arlington, VA, p. A433

AARON Jr., Frank J., Chief Executive Officer, Margaret R. Pardee Memorial Hospital, Hendersonville, NC, p. A307

AASVED, Craig E., Administrator, Wheatland Memorial Hospital, Harlowton, MT, p. A253

ABBOTT, William S., Administrator, Gainesville Memorial Hospital, Gainesville, TX, p. A405

ABBUHL, Carol A., Chief Executive Officer, Perkins County Health Services, Grant, NE, p. A258

ABRAHAM, Mathew, Chief Executive Officer, Antelope Valley Hospital, Lancaster, CA, p. A46

ABRAHAM, William T., Interim Chief Executive Officer, Monsour Medical Center, Jeannette, PA, p. A354

ABRAMS, Larry, Administrator, Potomac Valley Hospital, Keyser, WV, p. A452

ABREU, Astrid, Administrator, Clinica San Agustin, Manati, PR, p. A470

ABRUTZ Jr., Joseph F., Administrator, Cameron Community Hospital, Cameron, MO, p. A240

ABU–GHUSSON, Marilyn J., USAF, Commander, U. S. Air Force Hospital, Holloman AFB, NM, p. A279

ACHBER, Linda, Acting Chief Executive Officer, Craig House Center, Beacon, NY, p. A282

ACKER, David B., Chief Executive Officer, Charles Cole Memorial Hospital, Coudersport, PA, p. A350

ACKER, Peter W., President and Chief Executive Officer, Lincoln Medical Center, Lincolnton, NC, p. A308

ACKERMAN, Sigurd H., M.D., President and Chief Executive Officer, St. Luke's–Roosevelt Hospital Center, New York, NY, p. A293

ACKLEY, Michael, Administrator, Fergus Falls Regional Treatment Center, Fergus Falls, MN, p. A223

ACKLEY, Richard Michael, Administrator and Chief Executive Officer, Forest Hospital, Des Plaines, IL, p. A124

ADAIR, Jerry D., President and Chief Executive Officer, Good Shepherd Medical Center, Longview, TX, p. A413

ADAMS, Alice G., Administrator, Mainland Medical Center, Texas City, TX, p. A423

ADAMS, Charles T., President and Chief Executive Officer, Chatuge Regional Hospital and Nursing Home, Hiawassee, GA, p. A106

ADAMS, Daniel F., President and Chief Executive Officer, Presbyterian Intercommunity Hospital, Whittier, CA, p. A67

ADAMS, Harry F., Administrator, Washington Medical Center, Culver City, CA, p. A40

ADAMS, Jerry W., President, Sumter Regional Hospital, Americus, GA, p. A99

ADAMS, John F., Chief Executive Officer, Community Medical Center Sherman, Sherman, TX, p. A422

ADAMS, Judy, Administrator and Chief Executive Officer, Little River Memorial Hospital, Ashdown, AR, p. A29

ADAMS, Mark, Chief Executive Officer, West Valley Medical Center, Caldwell, ID, p. A114

ADAMS, Mark A., President and Chief Executive Officer, Mississippi Methodist Hospital and Rehabilitation Center, Jackson, MS, p. A234

ADAMS, Richard, Ph.D., Administrator, BHC Cedar Vista Hospital, Fresno, CA, p. A43

ADAMS, Robert W., President and Chief Executive Officer, St. Agnes Healthcare, Baltimore, MD, p. A192

ADAMS, Scott K., Chief Executive Officer, Pullman Memorial Hospital, Pullman, WA, p. A446

ADAMS, Tim, Administrator and Chief Executive Officer, Parkview Regional Hospital, Mexia, TX, p. A415

ADAMS, Wayne, Chief Executive Officer, Charter Behavioral Health System of Charlottesville, Charlottesville, VA, p. A434

ADAMS, William A., President and Chief Executive Officer, Columbia Reston Hospital Center, Reston, VA, p. A439

ADAMS, Clint E., USN, Commanding Officer, Naval Hospital, Beaufort, SC, p. A370

ADAMS, Nancy R., Commander, Tripler Army Medical Center, Honolulu, HI, p. A112

ADDISON, Wilfred J., President and Chief Executive Officer, Inland Hospital, Waterville, ME, p. A190

ADELUNG, Louisa F., President and Chief Executive Officer, The Institute for Rehabilitation and Research, Houston, TX, p. A409

ADKINS, Gary W., Interim Chief Executive Officer, Paulding County Hospital, Paulding, OH, p. A328

ADKINS, Scott D., Administrator, Bleckley Memorial Hospital, Cochran, GA, p. A102

ADKINS Jr., Charles I., President, Holzer Medical Center, Gallipolis, OH, p. A324

ADLER, Karl P., M.D., President and Chief Executive Officer, Saint Vincents Hospital and Medical Center, New York, NY, p. A293

AENCHBACHER Jr., Arthur E., Administrator, Wilford Hall Medical Center, Lackland AFB, TX, p. A412

AFSARIFARD, Farshid, Ph.D., President, UHHS Laurelwood Hospital, Willoughby, OH, p. A331

AHLFELD, Richard B., President, Children's Specialized Hospital, Mountainside, NJ, p. A272

AINSLEY, Howard, Vice President and Hospital Director, Carilion Bedford Memorial Hospital, Bedford, VA, p. A433

AINSWORTH, Larry K., President and Chief Executive Officer, St. Joseph Hospital, Orange, CA, p. A55

AIRD, Gordon, Interim Administrator, Plains Regional Medical Center, Clovis, NM, p. A278

AKERS, Cynthia O., R.N., Administrator, Hamilton County Hospital, Syracuse, KS, p. A164

ALBARANO, Francis G., Administrator, Fayette County Memorial Hospital, Washington Court House, OH, p. A330

ALBAUGH, John C., President and Chief Executive Officer, Fort Atkinson Memorial Health Services, Fort Atkinson, WI, p. A458

ALBERT, Anna, Chief Executive Officer, U. S. Public Health Service Phoenix Indian Medical Center, Phoenix, AZ, p. A25

ALBERTY, Allen R., Chief Executive Officer, Hansford Hospital, Spearman, TX, p. A422

ALBRIGHT, James W., President and Chief Executive Officer, Rex Healthcare, Raleigh, NC, p. A309

ALCHESAY–NACHU, Carla, Service Unit Director, U. S. Public Health Service Indian Hospital, Whiteriver, AZ, p. A27

ALCINI, Anthony J.
  President and Chief Executive Officer, JPS Health Network, Fort Worth, TX, p. A404
  President and Chief Executive Officer, Tarrant County Hospital District, Fort Worth, TX, p. B143

ALDERELE, Felix, Administrator, Las Vegas Medical Center, Las Vegas, NM, p. A279

ALDRED, Richard, Chief Administrative Officer, St. Dominic's Hospital, Manteca, CA, p. A51

ALECCI, Carmen Bruce, Executive Director, West Hudson Hospital, Kearny, NJ, p. A271

ALEMAN, Ralph A., Chief Executive Officer, Miami Heart Institute and Medical Center, Miami, FL, p. A90

ALENDER, James, Acting President and Chief Executive Officer, Howard Community Hospital, Kokomo, IN, p. A141

ALEXANDER, Eric, Interim Administrator, Mountain View Hospital District, Madras, OR, p. A344

ALEXANDER, Gordon L., M.D., Senior Vice President and Administrator, Fairview–University Medical Center, Minneapolis, MN, p. A225

ALEXANDER, Keith N., Administrator and Chief Operating Officer, American Fork Hospital, American Fork, UT, p. A427

ALEXANDER, Kenneth E., Chief Executive Officer, Southern Tennessee Medical Center, Winchester, TN, p. A391

ALEXANDER, Les, Administrator, Pushmataha County–Town of Antlers Hospital Authority, Antlers, OK, p. A333

ALEXANDER, Michael, President and Chief Executive Officer, Candler County Hospital, Metter, GA, p. A107

ALFORD, Wendell, Administrator, Madison Parish Hospital, Tallulah, LA, p. A186

ALLBACH, Deborah P., R.N., Chief Executive Officer, All Saints Hospital–Cityview, Fort Worth, TX, p. A403

ALLEE, Al, Administrator, Harmon Memorial Hospital, Hollis, OK, p. A336

ALLEN, Andrew W., Interim President and Chief Executive Officer, Saint Joseph Health Center, Kansas City, MO, p. A243

ALLEN, John, President and Chief Executive Officer, Spencer Municipal Hospital, Spencer, IA, p. A154

ALLEN, Richard L., President and Chief Executive Officer, Mercy Health Center of Manhattan, New York, KS, p. A161

ALLEN, Robert W., Administrator, Evanston Regional Hospital, Evanston, WY, p. A466

ALLEN, Sam J., Administrator, Community Hospital of Anaconda, Anaconda, MT, p. A251

ALLEN, Terry H., Executive Director, 45th Street Mental Health Center, West Palm Beach, FL, p. A97

ALLEN, Timothy, Chief Executive Officer, Charter Behavioral Health System of Southern California/Mission Viejo, Mission Viejo, CA, p. A52

ALLEN, Mark L., USAF, Administrator, U. S. Air Force Hospital, Columbus, MS, p. A232

ALLEN II, Percy, FACHE, Vice President Hospital Affairs and Chief Executive Officer, University Hospital of Brooklyn–State University of New York Health Science Center at Brooklyn, New York, NY, p. A293

ALLEY, Frederick D., President and Chief Executive Officer, Brooklyn Hospital Center, New York, NY, p. A289

ALLEY, Richard S., Executive Vice President and Chief Executive Officer, Arrowhead Community Hospital and Medical Center, Glendale, AZ, p. A23

ALLIKER, Stanford A., Chief Executive Officer, Camden County Health Services Center, Blackwood, NJ, p. A268

ALLMAN, Roger J., Chief Executive Officer, King's Daughters' Hospital, Madison, IN, p. A142

ALTMILLER, Steve, Chief Executive Officer, Bayou City Medical Center, Houston, TX, p. A407

ALTON, Aaron, President, Sisters of Mary of the Presentation Health Corporation, Fargo, ND, p. B138

ALVAREZ, Frank D., President and Chief Executive Officer, Tucson Medical Center, Tucson, AZ, p. A27

ALVAREZ, Guadalupe, Administrator, State Psychiatric Hospital, San Juan, PR, p. A472

ALVIN, William R., President, Henry Ford Wyandotte Hospital, Wyandotte, MI, p. A219

AMAN, Dale, Administrator, Linton Hospital, Linton, ND, p. A315

AMEEN, David J., President and Chief Executive Officer, Saint Mary's Health Services, Grand Rapids, MI, p. A211

AMEER, Adil M., President and Chief Executive Officer, Rapid City Regional Hospital System of Care, Rapid City, SD, p. A378

AMENT, Rick, President and Chief Executive Officer, Bay Area Medical Center, Marinette, WI, p. A460

AMES, Craig M., President and Chief Operating Officer, BryanLGH Medical Center, Lincoln, NE, p. A259

AMMON, Donald R., President, Adventist Health, Roseville, CA, p. B59

AMOS, James L., President, Margaret Mary Community Hospital, Batesville, IN, p. A136

AMOS, Helen, President and Chief Executive Officer, Mercy Medical Center, Baltimore, MD, p. A192

AMSTUTZ, Terry L., CHE, Chief Executive Officer and Administrator, Medical Center of Calico Rock, Calico Rock, AR, p. A29

ANAEBONAM, Nneka, Administrator, Isham Health Center, Andover, MA, p. A197

ANASTASIO, Lance W., President, Winter Haven Hospital, Winter Haven, FL, p. A98

ANCELL, Charles D., President, Missouri Delta Medical Center, Sikeston, MO, p. A249

ANCHO, Kathy, Administrator, Battle Mountain General Hospital, Battle Mountain, NV, p. A263

ANDERSEN, David, President and Chief Executive Officer, Saratoga Hospital, Saratoga Springs, NY, p. A297

ANDERSEN, Edward, President and Chief Executive Officer, CGH Medical Center, Sterling, IL, p. A134

ANDERSEN, Howard C., Interim Chief Executive Officer, Cumberland County Hospital, Burkesville, KY, p. A167

ANDERSON, Chris, Chief Executive Officer, Singing River Hospital System, Gautier, MS, p. B136

ANDERSON, Colette, Administrator, McKenzie County Memorial Hospital, Watford City, ND, p. A316

ANDERSON, Daniel K., Senior Vice President and Administrator, Fairview Lakes Regional Medical Center, Wyoming, MN, p. A230

ANDERSON, Darleen S., MSN, Site Administrator, Sentara Leigh Hospital, Norfolk, VA, p. A437

ANDERSON, David S., FACHE, Administrator, Lassen Community Hospital, Susanville, CA, p. A64

ANDERSON, Edwin S., President, Cumberland Medical Center, Crossville, TN, p. A382

ANDERSON, Greger C., President and Chief Executive Officer, Nyack Hospital, Nyack, NY, p. A295

ANDERSON, H. William, Administrator, Baxter County Regional Hospital, Mountain Home, AR, p. A33

ANDERSON, Harold E., Chief Executive Officer, Moses Taylor Hospital, Scranton, PA, p. A363

ANDERSON, J. Kendall, President and Chief Executive Officer, JM/MD Health System, Walnut Creek, CA, p. A66

ANDERSON, James M., President and Chief Executive Officer, Children's Hospital Medical Center, Cincinnati, OH, p. A319

ANDERSON, John, Administrator, Selma Baptist Hospital, Selma, AL, p. A18

ANDERSON, Larry, Administrator, Sayre Memorial Hospital, Sayre, OK, p. A339

ANDERSON, Loren J.
Executive Vice President, Lakeland Medical Center, Elkhorn, WI, p. A458
Executive Vice President, Memorial Hospital Corporation of Burlington, Burlington, WI, p. A457

ANDERSON, Melinda, Administrator, LAC–Olive View–UCLA Medical Center, Los Angeles, CA, p. A49

ANDERSON, Paul J., Administrator, Ortonville Area Health Services, Ortonville, MN, p. A226

ANDERSON, Richard A., President and Chief Executive Officer, St. Luke's Hospital and Health Network, Bethlehem, PA, p. A348

ANDERSON, Ron J., M.D., President and Chief Executive Officer, Parkland Health and Hospital System, Dallas, TX, p. A400

ANDERSON, Scott A., Administrator, North Runnels Hospital, Winters, TX, p. A426

ANDERSON, Scott R., President and Chief Executive Officer, North Memorial Health Care, Robbinsdale, MN, p. A227

ANDERSON, Sharla, Interim Chief Executive Officer, HEALTHSOUTH Rehabilitation Hospital–Tyler, Tyler, TX, p. A424

ANDERSON, Stephen N. F., Director, Doctors' Hospital of Staten Island, New York, NY, p. A290

ANDERSON, Steven M., Chief Executive Officer, Summerville Medical Center, Summerville, SC, p. A375

ANDERSON, Thomas, Chief Executive Officer, Columbia Pentagon City Hospital, Arlington, VA, p. A433

ANDERSON, Mary Jo, Senior Vice President, Hospital Operations, Scripps Health, San Diego, CA, p. B135

ANDREWS, Jane, Administrator and Chief Executive Officer, Nashville Rehabilitation Hospital, Nashville, TN, p. A388

ANDREWS, Norman J., Chief Executive Officer, Oak Valley District Hospital, Oakdale, CA, p. A54

ANDREWS, William J., President, Licking Memorial Hospital, Newark, OH, p. A327

ANDRIS, Terry R., CHE, Administrator, Seton Highland Lakes, Burnet, TX, p. A396

ANDRON, Thomas, Chief Executive Officer, Kremmling Memorial Hospital, Kremmling, CO, p. A71

ANDRUS, Michael G., Administrator and Chief Executive Officer, Franklin County Medical Center, Preston, ID, p. A116

ANDRUS, Terry W., President, East Alabama Medical Center, Opelika, AL, p. A17

ANEL, Manuel, M.D., Administrator and Chief Executive Officer, Long Beach Doctors Hospital, Long Beach, CA, p. A47

ANGERMEIER, Ingo, FACHE, Administrator and Chief Executive Officer, LSU Medical Center–University Hospital, Shreveport, LA, p. A185

ANGLE, Gregory R., Administrator, Seton Medical Center, Austin, TX, p. A394

ANNIS, Donald D., Service Unit Director, U. S. Public Health Service Indian Hospital, Eagle Butte, SD, p. A376

ANNIS, Donald E., Chief Executive Officer, Good Hope Hospital, Erwin, NC, p. A305

ANSTINE, Larry, Chief Operating Officer, Ohio State University Hospital East, Columbus, OH, p. A322

ANTHONY, Anne G., Administrator and Chief Executive Officer, Willow Crest Hospital, Miami, OK, p. A337

ANTHONY, Fred, President and Chief Executive Officer, Cuyahoga Falls General Hospital, Cuyahoga Falls, OH, p. A322

ANTHONY, Larry, Administrator, Providence Toppenish Hospital, Toppenish, WA, p. A449

ANTLE, David, Chief Executive Officer, Miners' Colfax Medical Center, Raton, NM, p. A279

ANTWINE, Brenda, Administrator, HEALTHSOUTH Rehabilitation Hospital of Jonesboro, Jonesboro, AR, p. A31

APPEL, G. Robert, Administrator, Mason General Hospital, Shelton, WA, p. A448

APPELBAUM, Glenn, Senior Vice President, Alexian Brothers Hospital, Saint Louis, MO, p. A247

APPLEBAUM, Jon D., Administrator, Jefferson Memorial Hospital, Ranson, WV, p. A454

APRATO, Peter P., Administrator and Chief Operating Officer, Robert F. Kennedy Medical Center, Hawthorne, CA, p. A44

ARANDA, Dan, Chief Executive Officer, Senatobia Community Hospital, Senatobia, MS, p. A237

ARANT, Marie E., Interim Chief Executive Officer, Millinocket Regional Hospital, Millinocket, ME, p. A189

ARBUCKLE, Barry S., Ph.D.
Chief Executive Officer, Orange Coast Memorial Medical Center, Fountain Valley, CA, p. A42
Chief Executive Officer, Saddleback Memorial Medical Center, Laguna Hills, CA, p. A46

ARCH, John K., Administrator, Boys Town National Research Hospital, Omaha, NE, p. A260

ARCHBELL, Larry J., Vice President Operations, University Community Hospital–Carrollwood, Tampa, FL, p. A97

ARCHER, David L., Chief Executive Officer, Saint Francis Hospital, Memphis, TN, p. A387

ARCHER III, William R., M.D., Commissioner, Texas Department of Health, Austin, TX, p. B147

ARCIDI, Alfred, M.D., President, Whittier Rehabilitation Hospital, Haverhill, MA, p. A201

AREHART, Michael, Chief Executive Officer, Twin Falls Clinic Hospital, Twin Falls, ID, p. A117

ARISMENDI, Luis, M.D., Administrator, Dameron Hospital, Stockton, CA, p. A64

ARIZPE, Robert C., Superintendent, San Antonio State Hospital, San Antonio, TX, p. A420

ARMSTRONG, Dale
Chief Executive Officer, Brynn Marr Behavioral Healthcare System, Jacksonville, NC, p. A307
Chief Executive Officer, Charter Sands Behavioral Health System of Conway, Conway, SC, p. A372

ARMSTRONG Jr., David S., Administrator, Little Falls Hospital, Little Falls, NY, p. A287

ARNETT, Randal M., President and Chief Executive Officer, Southern Ohio Medical Center, Portsmouth, OH, p. A328

ARNOLD, Kent A.
President, Community–General Hospital of Greater Syracuse, Syracuse, NY, p. A299
President and Chief Executive Officer, Crouse Hospital, Syracuse, NY, p. A299

ARNOLD, Margo, Administrator, Mercy Westside Hospital, Taft, CA, p. A64

ARNOLD, Nancy, Director, John J. Pershing Veterans Affairs Medical Center, Poplar Bluff, MO, p. A246

ARNOLD, Richard D., Administrator, Linden Municipal Hospital, Linden, TX, p. A413

ARNOLD, Thomas B., Director, Veterans Affairs Medical Center, Iron Mountain, MI, p. A212

ARP, James, Chief Executive Officer, Colorado River Medical Center, Needles, CA, p. A53

ARTILES, Nemuel O., Chief Executive Officer, Bella Vista Southwest Hospital, Yauco, PR, p. A472

ASAY, Grant, Chief Executive Officer, Sitka Community Hospital, Sitka, AK, p. A21

ASBE, Vickie, Administrator, Anamosa Community Hospital, Anamosa, IA, p. A146

ASH, James L.
President and Chief Executive Officer, Cottage Health System, Santa Barbara, CA, p. B86
President and Chief Executive Officer, Santa Barbara Cottage Hospital, Santa Barbara, CA, p. A62
President and Chief Executive Officer, Santa Ynez Valley Cottage Hospital, Solvang, CA, p. A63

ASH, John P., FACHE, President and Chief Executive Officer, Eugenia Hospital, Lafayette Hill, PA, p. A354

ASH, Richard M., Chief Executive Officer, Northern Itasca Health Care Center, Bigfork, MN, p. A221

ASHBAUGH, James L., Regional Director of Operations, Warm Springs & Baptist Rehabilitation Hospital, San Antonio, TX, p. A421

ASHKIN, David, M.D., Medical Executive Director, A. G. Holley State Hospital, Lantana, FL, p. A88

ASHWORTH, Ronald B., Chief Executive Officer, Sisters of Mercy Health System–St. Louis, Saint Louis, MO, p. B138

ASPER, David, Director, Veterans Affairs Greater Nebraska Health Care System, Lincoln, NE, p. A259

ASSELL, William C., President and Chief Executive Officer, St. Joseph's Mercy Hospital, Centerville, IA, p. A147

ATKINS, Tony E., Administrator, Braxton County Memorial Hospital, Gassaway, WV, p. A451

ATKINSON, Allan, Chief Executive Officer, Winneshiek County Memorial Hospital, Decorah, IA, p. A148

ATKINSON, L. Gail, Executive Director, Devereux Texas Treatment Network, League City, TX, p. A412

ATKINSON, Robert P., President and Chief Executive Officer, Jefferson Regional Medical Center, Pine Bluff, AR, p. A34

ATKINSON II, William K., Ph.D., Chief Executive Officer, New Hanover Regional Medical Center, Wilmington, NC, p. A312

AUBERT, Harry, Chief Executive Officer, Lost Rivers District Hospital, Arco, ID, p. A114

AUBREY, Leonard A., President and Chief Executive Officer, New York University Downtown Hospital, New York, NY, p. A292

AUER, Thomas H., Commander, Womack Army Medical Center, Fort Bragg, NC, p. A306

AUSMAN, Dan F., Chief Executive Officer, Irvine Medical Center, Irvine, CA, p. A45

AUSTIN, George L., Administrator, Bolivar General Hospital, Bolivar, TN, p. A381

AUSTIN, James D., CHE
Administrator, Kalkaska Memorial Health Center, Kalkaska, MI, p. A213
Administrator, Paul Oliver Memorial Hospital, Frankfort, MI, p. A210

AUSTIN, L. Joe, Chief Executive Officer, Huntsville Hospital, Huntsville, AL, p. A15

AUSTIN, Robert S., President, Gunnison Valley Hospital, Gunnison, CO, p. A71

AVERS, John M., Chief Executive Officer, White County Memorial Hospital, Monticello, IN, p. A142

AVERY, Danny, Administrator, Mangum City Hospital, Mangum, OK, p. A337

AXELSON, Alan A., M.D., Chief Executive Officer, Southwood Psychiatric Hospital, Pittsburgh, PA, p. A361

AYRES, Larry J., Administrator and Chief Executive Officer, Pointe Coupee General Hospital, New Roads, LA, p. A184

B

BABB, Donald J., Chief Executive Officer, Citizens Memorial Hospital, Bolivar, MO, p. A239

BACHARACH, Paul, President and Chief Executive Officer, Uniontown Hospital, Uniontown, PA, p. A365

BACON, Ken, President and Chief Executive Officer, Central Texas Medical Center, San Marcos, TX, p. A421

BACUS, Randy, Chief Executive Officer, Colorado–Fayette Medical Center, Weimar, TX, p. A425

BADGER Jr., Theodore J., Chief Executive Officer, Beauregard Memorial Hospital, De Ridder, LA, p. A179

BAER, James E., FACHE, President, Waupun Memorial Hospital, Waupun, WI, p. A464

BAGBY, Philip D., President and Chief Executive Officer, Albemarle Hospital, Elizabeth City, NC, p. A305

BAGGERLY, Gregory C., USAF, Commander, U. S. Air Force Hospital, MacDill AFB, FL, p. A88

BAHL, Barry I., Director, Veterans Affairs Medical Center, Saint Cloud, MN, p. A227

BAIER, Roger, Chief Executive Officer, Union Hospital, Mayville, ND, p. A315

BAILEY, Bruce P., Administrator, Abbeville County Memorial Hospital, Abbeville, SC, p. A370

BAILEY, Carl W., Chief Executive Officer, Florence Hospital, Florence, AL, p. A14

BAILEY, David, Chief Executive Officer, Healthsouth Rehabilitation Hospital of Kokomo, Kokomo, IN, p. A141

BAILEY, G. Owen, Administrator, Thomas Hospital, Fairhope, AL, p. A14

BAILEY, James P., President and Chief Executive Officer, Henryetta Medical Center, Henryetta, OK, p. A336

BAILEY, Sandra, Administrator, Methodist Healthcare–Brownsville Hospital, Brownsville, TN, p. A381

BAILON, Amy R., M.D., Medical Director, Woodbridge Development Center, Woodbridge, NJ, p. A276

BAINBRIDGE, Darlene D., Chief Executive Officer, Cuba Memorial Hospital, Cuba, NY, p. A284

BAIR, Charles H., Chief Executive Officer, Highland District Hospital, Hillsboro, OH, p. A324

BAIRD, Marvin L., Executive Director, Adams County Memorial Hospital, Decatur, IN, p. A137

BAKER, Bob M., President and Chief Executive Officer, Gratiot Community Hospital, Alma, MI, p. A206

BAKER, Gary A., President, Memorial Hospital, Towanda, PA, p. A364

BAKER, Glenn, Administrator, Baptist Memorial Hospital–Tipton, Covington, TN, p. A382

BAKER, Harry M., Chief Executive Officer, Cross County Hospital, Wynne, AR, p. A35

BAKER, Jeannie, Administrator, Shands at Starke, Starke, FL, p. A95

BAKER, John A., Chief Executive Officer, Methodist Behavioral Resources, New Orleans, LA, p. A183

BAKER, Jon W., Chief Executive Officer, Ripon Medical Center, Ripon, WI, p. A463

BAKER, Rod L., President and Chief Executive Officer, Parrish Medical Center, Titusville, FL, p. A97

BAKER, Rodger H., President and Chief Executive Officer, Fauquier Hospital, Warrenton, VA, p. A441

BAKER Jr., Wendell H.
District Administrator, Matagorda County Hospital District, Bay City, TX, p. B114
Chief Executive Officer, Matagorda General Hospital, Bay City, TX, p. A394

BAKST, Michael D., Ph.D., Executive Director, Community Memorial Hospital of San Buenaventura, Ventura, CA, p. A66

BALDWIN, Bruce A., Chief Executive Officer, Davis Hospital and Medical Center, Layton, UT, p. A427

BALDWIN, Gilda
Chief Executive Officer, Southern Winds Hospital, Hialeah, FL, p. A86
Chief Executive Officer, Westchester General Hospital, Miami, FL, p. A90

BALDWIN, Joe G.
Chief Executive Officer, Doctors Hospital Airline, Houston, TX, p. A407
Chief Executive Officer, North Houston Medical Center, Houston, TX, p. A408

BALDWIN, Keith J., Administrator, Samaritan Healthcare, Moses Lake, WA, p. A445

BALDWIN, Paul L., Chief Executive Officer, Retreat Hospital, Richmond, VA, p. A440

BALIK, M. Barbara, Ed.D., Administrator, United Hospital, Saint Paul, MN, p. A228

BALL, Donald M., President, Jackson Hospital and Clinic, Montgomery, AL, p. A17

BALLA, Ernest, Administrator, Johns Community Hospital, Taylor, TX, p. A422

BALLANTYNE III, Reginald M., President, PMH Health Resources, Inc., Phoenix, AZ, p. B125

BALLARD, Bryan M., Chief Executive Officer, Mendocino Coast District Hospital, Fort Bragg, CA, p. A42

BALLARD, Carolyn M., Executive Director, West Jersey Hospital–Camden, Camden, NJ, p. A269

BALLARD, Paul H., Chief Executive Officer, Mission Hospital, Mission, TX, p. A415

BALLARD, Susan, Administrator, Menifee Valley Medical Center, Sun City, CA, p. A64

BALLARD, William J., Chief Executive Officer, Children's Comprehensive Services, Inc., Nashville, TN, p. B77

BALSAM, Marion, USN, Commander, Naval Medical Center, Portsmouth, VA, p. A438

BALTZ, Richard J., Director, Veterans Affairs Medical Center, Fayetteville, NC, p. A305

BALTZER, David J., President, Rehoboth McKinley Christian Hospital, Gallup, NM, p. A279

BALZEN, Earl W., R.N., Chief Executive Officer and Administrator, Charter Plains Behavioral Health System, Lubbock, TX, p. A413

BAN Jr., Albert, Administrator, Thomasville Infirmary, Thomasville, AL, p. A18

BANASZYNSKI, Gregory A., President, St. Francis Hospital, Milwaukee, WI, p. A461

BANE, Raymond, Executive Director, Natchez Community Hospital, Natchez, MS, p. A236

BANGERT, Richard A., Chief Executive Officer and Administrator, Psychiatric Hospital at Vanderbilt, Nashville, TN, p. A388

BANGS, Kathryn A., President and Chief Executive Officer, Clinton Memorial Hospital, Saint Johns, MI, p. A216

BANK, Kendall C., Administrator, Northfield Hospital, Northfield, MN, p. A226

BANKS, Elizabeth, Chief Executive Officer, Pauline Warfield Lewis Center, Cincinnati, OH, p. A320

BARABAS, Mark C., President, Community Hospital of Lancaster, Lancaster, PA, p. A354

BARBAKOW, Jeffrey, Chairman and Chief Executive Officer, TENET Healthcare Corporation, Santa Barbara, CA, p. B143

BARBATO, Anthony L., M.D., President and Chief Executive Officer, Loyola University Medical Center, Maywood, IL, p. A129

BARBE, Brian S., Chief Executive Officer, Katy Medical Center, Katy, TX, p. A411

BARBER, Jeffrey B., Dr.PH
President and Chief Executive Officer, North Mississippi Health Services, Inc., Tupelo, MS, p. B120
President and Chief Executive Officer, North Mississippi Medical Center, Tupelo, MS, p. A237

BARBER, Mike, Facility Service Integrator, Clovis Community Medical Center, Clovis, CA, p. A39

BARBER, Steve, Administrator, Dorminy Medical Center, Fitzgerald, GA, p. A105

BARBERA, Sal A., FACHE, Administrator, South Florida State Hospital, Pembroke Pines, FL, p. A93

BARBINI, Gerald J., Administrator and Chief Executive Officer, Hubbard Regional Hospital, Webster, MA, p. A205

BARCO, Lawrence F., President, MidMichigan Medical Center–Clare, Clare, MI, p. A208

BARD, Thomas, Chief Executive Officer, Spring Hill Regional Hospital, Spring Hill, FL, p. A95

BARKER, Richard, Administrator, Mercy Health Love County, Marietta, OK, p. A337

BARKER, Elizabeth R., Commanding Officer, Naval Hospital, Corpus Christi, TX, p. A399

BARNER, James W., President and Chief Executive Officer, Altoona Hospital, Altoona, PA, p. A347

BARNETT, Dana K., Administrator, Platte County Memorial Hospital, Wheatland, WY, p. A468

BARNETT, Gary L., President and Chief Executive Officer, Sarah Bush Lincoln Health Center, Mattoon, IL, p. A129

BARNETT, Rick J., Executive Vice President and Chief Operating Officer, Mercy Medical Center Mount Shasta, Mount Shasta, CA, p. A53

BARNETT, Timothy, Chief Executive Officer, Yavapai Regional Medical Center, Prescott, AZ, p. A25

BARNHART, Ann, Executive Director, Franklin Regional Medical Center, Louisburg, NC, p. A308

BARNHART, James, Administrator, Peace Harbor Hospital, Florence, OR, p. A343

BARON, David A., D.O., Medical Director, Horsham Clinic, Ambler, PA, p. A347

BARON, Steven D., President and Chief Executive Officer, Rhode Island Hospital, Providence, RI, p. A368

BARR, C. Dennis, President and Chief Executive Officer, Northwest General Hospital, Milwaukee, WI, p. A461

BARR, LuAnn, Administrator, Tilden Community Hospital, Tilden, NE, p. A262

BARRAGAN, J. Bruce, President and Chief Executive Officer, McLeod Regional Medical Center, Florence, SC, p. A372

BARRETO, Hector, M.D., Director, Hospital Dr. Susoni, Arecibo, PR, p. A469

BARRETT, Susan, President and Chief Executive Officer, St. Mary–Rogers Memorial Hospital, Rogers, AR, p. A34

BARRON, Steven R., President and Chief Executive Officer, Alexian Brothers Hospital, San Jose, CA, p. A60

BARROW, William F., President and Chief Executive Officer, De Soto Regional Health System, Mansfield, LA, p. A182

BARRY, Dennis R., President, Moses Cone Health System, Greensboro, NC, p. A306

BARRY, R. Michael, Administrator, Plumas District Hospital, Quincy, CA, p. A56

BARRY, Suzanne, Administrator and Chief Operating Officer, Hartgrove Hospital, Chicago, IL, p. A120

BARSZCZEWSKI, Joseph, Chief Executive Officer and Managing Director, Meadows Psychiatric Center, Centre Hall, PA, p. A349

BARTELL III, Frank J., President and Chief Executive Officer, St. Luke's Hospital, Maumee, OH, p. A326

BARTELS, Bruce M., President, South Central Community Health, York, PA, p. B140

BARTER, James T., M.D., Director, Metropolitan Children and Adolescent Institute, Chicago, IL, p. A121

BARTLESON, Warner H., Administrator, North Valley Hospital, Tonasket, WA, p. A449

BARTLETT, John D., Chief Executive Officer, Palms of Pasadena Hospital, Saint Petersburg, FL, p. A94

BARTLETT, John T., Director, Searcy Hospital, Mount Vernon, AL, p. A17

BARTLETT, Robert, Administrator, BHC Willow Springs Residential Treatment Center, Reno, NV, p. A264

BARTLETT, Thomas G., President and Chief Executive Officer, H. C. Watkins Memorial Hospital, Quitman, MS, p. A237

BARTON, Donald L., Superintendent, Southeast Missouri Mental Health Center, Farmington, MO, p. A241

BARTON, Larry O., President, Western Baptist Hospital, Paducah, KY, p. A174

BARTON, Rod, Chief Executive Officer, Powell Hospital, Powell, WY, p. A467

BARTOS, John M., Administrator, Marcus Daly Memorial Hospital, Hamilton, MT, p. A253

BARTZ, Daniel R., Chief Executive Officer, Cloud County Health Center, Concordia, KS, p. A157

BASH, Robert R., Administrator, Booneville Community Hospital, Booneville, AR, p. A29

BASHAM, Gail S., Chief Operating Officer, Mount Regis Center, Salem, VA, p. A440

BASLER, Jack, President, Henry County Memorial Hospital, New Castle, IN, p. A143

BASS, Adrianne Black, Administrator, University of Southern California–Kenneth Norris Jr. Cancer Hospital, Los Angeles, CA, p. A51

BASSETT, Warren J., FACHE, President, Brookville Hospital, Brookville, PA, p. A348

BASTONE, Peter F., President and Chief Executive Officer, Mission Hospital Regional Medical Center, Mission Viejo, CA, p. A52

BATAL, Lucille M., Administrator, Baldpate Hospital, Haverhill, MA, p. A201

BATCHELDER, Chester G., Superintendent, New Hampshire Hospital, Concord, NH, p. A265

BATEMAN, Mark T., Executive Director, Episcopal Hospital, Philadelphia, PA, p. A358

BATEMAN, Steven B., Chief Executive Officer, Ogden Regional Medical Center, Ogden, UT, p. A428

BATES, Jonathan R., M.D., President and Chief Executive Officer, Arkansas Children's Hospital, Little Rock, AR, p. A32

BATES, Rodney, Administrator, Logan County Hospital, Oakley, KS, p. A162

BATT, Richard A., President and Chief Executive Officer, Franklin Memorial Hospital, Farmington, ME, p. A188

BATTIN, Anne, Administrator, Charter Hospital of Charleston, Charleston, SC, p. A370

BATULIS, Scott, Vice President and Administrator, HealthEast Bethesda Rehabilitation Hospital, Saint Paul, MN, p. A228

BAUER, Clifford J., Chief Executive Officer, Hialeah Hospital, Hialeah, FL, p. A85

BAUER, Ken, Chief Executive Officer, Michael Reese Hospital and Medical Center, Chicago, IL, p. A121

BAUM, Carla S., President, St. Joseph Hospital of Kirkwood, Saint Louis, MO, p. A248

BAUMAN, Nancy, Chief Executive Officer, St. Joseph's Memorial Hospital and Nursing Home, Hillsboro, WI, p. A459

BAUMGARDNER, Brian P., Administrator, Bartow Memorial Hospital, Bartow, FL, p. A81

BAUMGART, Kris, Chief Executive Officer, Stewart Memorial Community Hospital, Lake City, IA, p. A151

BAUMGARTNER, Michael, President, St. Francis Hospital and Health Services, Maryville, MO, p. A245

BAUTE, Robert E., M.D., President and Chief Executive Officer, Kent County Memorial Hospital, Warwick, RI, p. A369

BEA, Javon R., President and Chief Executive Officer, Mercy Health System, Janesville, WI, p. A459

BEACH, Allen L., Administrator, Columbia Basin Hospital, Ephrata, WA, p. A444

BEAMAN Jr., Charles D., President, Palmetto Health Alliance, Columbia, SC, p. B123

BEAMER, Deane E., President and Chief Executive Officer, St. Luke's Hospital, Bluefield, WV, p. A450

BEAR, Lawrence P., Administrator, Jersey Community Hospital, Jerseyville, IL, p. A127

BEARD, Les, Chief Executive Officer, Eastside Medical Center, Snellville, GA, p. A110

BEARDSLEY, David L., Administrator, University Behavioral Center, Orlando, FL, p. A92

BEASLEY, Lynn W., President and Chief Executive Officer, Newberry County Memorial Hospital, Newberry, SC, p. A374

BEATTY, Margaret, President, Sisters of Mercy of the Americas–Regional Community of Baltimore, Baltimore, MD, p. B138

BEATY, Ralph E., Administrator, Huntsville Memorial Hospital, Huntsville, TX, p. A410

BEAUCHAMP, John W., Chief Executive Officer, Medical Center of Winnie, Winnie, TX, p. A426

BEAUCHAMP, Philip K., FACHE
President and Chief Executive Officer, Morton Plant Hospital, Clearwater, FL, p. A82
President and Chief Executive Officer, Morton Plant Mease Health Care, Dunedin, FL, p. B118

BEAULIEU, Gerald, Acting President and Chief Executive Officer, Columbia Hospital for Women Medical Center, Washington, DC, p. A79

BEAUREGARD, Jodi, Administrator, Central Texas Hospital, Cameron, TX, p. A397

BEBOW, Gary, Administrator and Chief Executive Officer, White River Medical Center, Batesville, AR, p. A29

BECHTOLD, Gregg A., President and Chief Executive Officer, Johnson Memorial Hospital, Franklin, IN, p. A139

BECK, E. Dean, Administrator, Fulton County Health Center, Wauseon, OH, p. A330

BECK, Gary E., Administrator, Sevier Valley Hospital, Richfield, UT, p. A429

BECK, Judi, Administrator and Chief Executive Officer, Mayers Memorial Hospital District, Fall River Mills, CA, p. A42

BECK, Lawrence M., President, Good Samaritan Hospital of Maryland, Baltimore, MD, p. A191

BECK, Raymond J., President and Chief Executive Officer, UPMC Passavant, Pittsburgh, PA, p. A362

BECK, Steve, Chief Executive Officer and Administrator, Memorial Hospital, Seminole, TX, p. A421

BECK, Walter, Chief Executive Officer, George L. Mee Memorial Hospital, King City, CA, p. A45

BECKER, Michael, Executive Director, Devereux Hospital and Children's Center of Florida, Melbourne, FL, p. A89

BECKER, Walter S., Administrator, Carthage Area Hospital, Carthage, NY, p. A284

BECKER, Wayne, Interim Chief Executive Officer, Arden Hill Hospital, Goshen, NY, p. A285

BECKMAN, Gregory L., President and Chief Executive Officer, McLaren Regional Medical Center, Flint, MI, p. A210

BECKSTRAND, James E.
Administrator, Delta Community Medical Center, Delta, UT, p. A427
Administrator, Fillmore Community Medical Center, Fillmore, UT, p. A427

BEDNAREK, Robert J., President and Chief Executive Officer, Transylvania Community Hospital, Brevard, NC, p. A303

BEELER, Don A., President and Chief Executive Officer, Christus St. Michael Health System, Texarkana, TX, p. A423

BEEMAN, Barry G., President and Chief Executive Officer, Atlantic General Hospital, Berlin, MD, p. A193

BEEMAN, Thomas E., Senior Vice President, Operations, Hospital of the University of Pennsylvania, Philadelphia, PA, p. A359

BEGLEY, Bruce D., Executive Director, Methodist Hospital, Henderson, KY, p. A170

BEHNKE, Bruce, Administrator, Kaiser Foundation Hospital, Honolulu, HI, p. A112

BEHRENDT, William, Interim President, Barnes–Jewish West County Hospital, Saint Louis, MO, p. A247

BEHRENS, B. Lyn
President, Loma Linda University Health Sciences Center, Loma Linda, CA, p. B110
President, Loma Linda University Medical Center, Loma Linda, CA, p. A47

BEHRMANN, John, Administrator and Chief Executive Officer, Kentfield Rehabilitation Hospital, Kentfield, CA, p. A45

BEIER, Gregory J., President, Forsyth Medical Center, Winston–Salem, NC, p. A312

BEIL, Clark R., Chief Executive Officer, Johnston Memorial Hospital, Abingdon, VA, p. A433

BEIRNE, Frank, Chief Executive Officer, Samaritan Hospital, Lexington, KY, p. A171

BELCHER, Phillip, Administrator, Guyan Valley Hospital, Logan, WV, p. A452

BELL, David C., Chief Operating Officer, BHC Sand Hill Behavioral Healthcare, Gulfport, MS, p. A233

BELL, Jack E., Chief Operating Officer, Lutheran Hospital, Cleveland, OH, p. A320

BEN, Nella, Chief Executive Officer, U. S. Public Health Service Indian Hospital, San Carlos, AZ, p. A26

BENFER, David W., President and Chief Executive Officer, Hospital of Saint Raphael, New Haven, CT, p. A76

BENFORD, Barry C., Director, Altoona Center, Altoona, PA, p. A347

BENGTSON, Paul R., Chief Executive Officer, Northeastern Vermont Regional Hospital, Saint Johnsbury, VT, p. A432

BENN, David P., President and Chief Executive Officer, Memorial Hospitals Association, Modesto, CA, p. A52

BENNETT, Bruce A., Administrator, Carl Albert Indian Health Facility, Ada, OK, p. A333

BENNETT, John, President and Chief Executive Officer, Shelby Memorial Hospital, Shelbyville, IL, p. A133

BENNETT, Lee W., Chief Executive Officer, Oconto Memorial Hospital, Oconto, WI, p. A462

BENNETT, Richard, Executive Director, Mid–Hudson Psychiatric Center, New Hampton, NY, p. A288

BENNING, Robert J., Chief Executive Officer, Ridgeview Psychiatric Hospital and Center, Oak Ridge, TN, p. A389

BENSAIA, Barbara A., Chief Executive Officer, Allegheny University Hospitals, Canonsburg, Canonsburg, PA, p. A349

BENSON, M. J., USN, Commanding Officer, Naval Hospital, Jacksonville, FL, p. A86

BENTLEY, Brian S., Administrator, Sutter Merced Medical Center, Merced, CA, p. A52

BENTON, Earnest E., Chief Executive Officer, Minnie G. Boswell Memorial Hospital, Greensboro, GA, p. A105

BENTON, Lowell S., Executive Director, Woodland Medical Center, Cullman, AL, p. A13

BENWAY, Michael W., Commanding Officer, Naval Hospital, Oak Harbor, WA, p. A445

BERARD, Celse A., President, Riverview Hospital Association, Wisconsin Rapids, WI, p. A465

BERAULT, John S., Chief Executive Officer, Medical Center of Louisiana at New Orleans, New Orleans, LA, p. A183

BERDAN, Barclay E., Chief Executive Officer, Harris Methodist Fort Worth, Fort Worth, TX, p. A404

BERDICK, Edward L., President and Chief Executive Officer, Roper Hospital, Charleston, SC, p. A371

BERGENFELD, Joel, Chief Executive Officer, Florida Medical Center Hospital, Fort Lauderdale, FL, p. A84

BERGER, Susan, Prioress, Benedictine Sisters of the Annunciation, Bismarck, ND, p. B67

BERGLING, Richard Q., Administrator and Chief Executive Officer, Plainville Rural Hospital District Number One, Plainville, KS, p. A163

BERGREN, Jeff, Chief Executive Officer and Administrator, BHC Streamwood Hospital, Streamwood, IL, p. A134

BERLUCCHI, Scott A., President and Chief Executive Officer, Lancaster General Hospital–Susquehanna Division, Columbia, PA, p. A350

BERMAN, Seth, President and Chief Executive Officer, Hall–Brooke Hospital, A Division of Hall–Brooke Foundation, Westport, CT, p. A77

BERNARD, Mark L.
Chief Executive Officer, Metropolitan Methodist Hospital, San Antonio, TX, p. A420
Chief Executive Officer, Northeast Methodist Hospital, San Antonio, TX, p. A420

BERNARD, Patricia, R.N., Administrator, Osborne County Memorial Hospital, Osborne, KS, p. A162

BERNARD, Peter J.
President and Chief Executive Officer, Caritas Medical Center, Louisville, KY, p. A172
President and Chief Executive Officer, Caritas Peace Center, Louisville, KY, p. A172

BERND, David L., President and Chief Executive Officer, Sentara Health System, Norfolk, VA, p. B135

BERNSTEIN, Martin B., Chief Executive Officer, Northern Maine Medical Center, Fort Kent, ME, p. A188

BERNSTEIN, Ronald T., Chief Executive Officer, Foundations Behavioral Health, Doylestown, PA, p. A351

BERNSTEIN, Stephen, FACHE, Chief Executive Officer, Plaza Medical Center of Fort Worth, Fort Worth, TX, p. A404

BERO, Joan A., Regional Vice President and Chief Operating Officer, O'Connor Hospital, San Jose, CA, p. A61

BERRETT, Britt, Chief Executive Officer, Sharp Chula Vista Medical Center, Chula Vista, CA, p. A39

BERRIDGE, Linda, Chief Executive Officer, Two Rivers Psychiatric Hospital, Kansas City, MO, p. A244

BERRY, Robert F., Administrator, Vencor Hospital–Kansas City, Kansas City, MO, p. A244

BERTEAU, Robert, Chief Executive Officer, ValueMark Behavioral Healthcare System of Florida, Orlando, FL, p. A92

BERTRAM, Donna L., R.N., Administrator, Penrose–St. Francis Health Services, Colorado Springs, CO, p. A69

BESTUL, Randy, Administrator, Norwood Health Center, Marshfield, WI, p. A460

BESWICK, Melinda D., President, California Hospital Medical Center, Los Angeles, CA, p. A48

BETJEMANN, John H., President, Methodist Hospitals, Gary, IN, p. A139

BETTS, Peter J., President and Chief Executive Officer, East Jefferson General Hospital, Metairie, LA, p. A182

BEVERLY, Douglas H., CHE, Chief Operating Officer, St. Clair Regional Hospital, Pell City, AL, p. A17

BEVERLY, Ken B., President and Chief Executive Officer, Archbold Medical Center, Thomasville, GA, p. B62

BEVINS, O. David, Chief Executive Officer, Kentucky River Medical Center, Jackson, KY, p. A170

BEYER, Robert L., President and Chief Executive Officer, Saint Joseph's Regional Medical Center–South Bend Campus, South Bend, IN, p. A144

BHATIA, Krishin L., Administrator, Victory Memorial Hospital, New York, NY, p. A294

BIANCHI, Charles A., President, Hillsdale Community Health Center, Hillsdale, MI, p. A211

BICH, Arlene C., Administrator, Wagner Community Memorial Hospital, Wagner, SD, p. A379

BICKELMAN, Carol, President and Chief Executive Officer, Desert Hills Hospital, Albuquerque, NM, p. A277

BICKLING, J. Allan, Chief Executive Officer, Edward W. McCready Memorial Hospital, Crisfield, MD, p. A193

BIEDIGER, Michael J., President, Lexington Medical Center, West Columbia, SC, p. A375

BIEGANSKI, Gary, President, Community Hospital, McCook, NE, p. A259

BIEHNER, Barbara H., Chief Executive Officer, Bon Secours–Holy Family Regional Health System, Altoona, PA, p. A347

BIESTER, Doris J., R.N., President and Chief Executive Officer, Children's Hospital, Denver, CO, p. A69

BIGA, Thomas A., Executive Director, Clara Maass Health System, Belleville, NJ, p. A268

BIGELOW, David C., Chief Executive Officer, North Lincoln Hospital, Lincoln City, OR, p. A344

BIGLEY, Robert F., Administrator, Dale Medical Center, Ozark, AL, p. A17

BIHLDORFF, John P., President and Chief Executive Officer, Newton–Wellesley Hospital, Newton Lower Falls, MA, p. A202

BILBO, Dorothy C., Administrator, Pearl River County Hospital, Poplarville, MS, p. A237

BILL, Charles E., CHE, Chief Executive Officer, Cobre Valley Community Hospital, Claypool, AZ, p. A22

BILLICK, Dean, Director, Central Texas Veterans Affairs Healthcare System, Temple, TX, p. A423

BILLING, Michael D., Administrator, Mid–Valley Hospital, Omak, WA, p. A446

BILLS, Jeff K., Chief Executive Officer, Saint Mary's Regional Medical Center, Reno, NV, p. A264

BILLS, Robert C., President and Vice Chairman, Valley Presbyterian Hospital, Los Angeles, CA, p. A51

BING, William W., Administrator, Morehouse General Hospital, Bastrop, LA, p. A177

BINGHAM, Leslie, Chief Executive Officer, Charter Palms Behavioral Health System, McAllen, TX, p. A414

BIRCHELL, Bruce K., Chief Executive Officer, Morton County Health System, Elkhart, KS, p. A157

BIRDZELL, JoAnn
President and Chief Executive Officer, St. Catherine Hospital, East Chicago, IN, p. A137
President and Chief Executive Officer, St. Elizabeth's Hospital, Chicago, IL, p. A122

BIRDZELL, John R., FACHE, Chief Executive Officer, Bedford Regional Medical Center, Bedford, IN, p. A136

BIRKHOLZ, Peter, Administrator and Chief Executive Officer, Cordova Community Medical Center, Cordova, AK, p. A20

BISCARO, Ron, Administrator and Chief Operating Officer, St. Francis Medical Center of Santa Barbara, Santa Barbara, CA, p. A62

BISCHALANEY, George, President and Chief Executive Officer, Eden Medical Center, Castro Valley, CA, p. A38

BISCONE, Mark A., Executive Director, Waldo County General Hospital, Belfast, ME, p. A187

BISHOP, Marvin O., Administrator, Weisbrod Memorial County Hospital, Eads, CO, p. A70

BISHOP, Paul A., Administrator, Wellmont Lonesome Pine Hospital, Big Stone Gap, VA, p. A433

BISSEL, Jane, President and Chief Executive Officer, Mercy Hospital, Valley City, ND, p. A316

BITTING, Nancy J., Chief Executive Officer, St. Joseph Hospital, Bellingham, WA, p. A443

BJELLA, Karmon, Chief Executive Officer, Muscatine General Hospital, Muscatine, IA, p. A152

BLACK, Gary E., President and Chief Executive Officer, Lenoir Memorial Hospital, Kinston, NC, p. A307

BLACK, Glenn, Associate Vice President and Chief Operating Officer, Kingswood Hospital, Ferndale, MI, p. A210

BLACK, Marion, Administrator, Starlite Village Hospital, Center Point, TX, p. A397

BLAIR, John E., Chief Executive, Ravenswood Hospital Medical Center, Chicago, IL, p. A121

BLAIR, Mardian J., President, Adventist Health System Sunbelt Health Care Corporation, Winter Park, FL, p. B59

BLAIR, Phillip C., Interim Administrator, White County Medical Center, Carmi, IL, p. A119

BLAKLEY, Scott F., Chief Executive Officer, Charter Brentwood Behavioral Health System, Shreveport, LA, p. A185

BLANCHARD, Stephen C., Director, Edgewater Psychiatric Center, Harrisburg, PA, p. A353

BLANCHARD, William R., Chief Executive Officer, DeTar Hospital, Victoria, TX, p. A424

BLANCHETTE, Edward A., M.D., Director, Connecticut Department of Correction's Hospital, Somers, CT, p. A76

BLANCO, Carla, Administrator, Doctors Center, Manati, PR, p. A471

BLAND, Calvin, President and Chief Executive Officer, St. Christopher's Hospital for Children, Philadelphia, PA, p. A360

BLAND, Edward C., President and Chief Executive Officer, Healdsburg General Hospital, Healdsburg, CA, p. A44

BLAND, Thomas, Administrator, Montfort Jones Memorial Hospital, Kosciusko, MS, p. A235

BLASBAND, Charles A., Chief Executive Officer, Citrus Memorial Hospital, Inverness, FL, p. A86

BLASKO Jr., Joseph, President and Chief Executive Officer, Christus Health, San Antonio, TX, p. B77

BLAYLOCK, Darrell, Chief Executive Officer, Lakeview Regional Medical Center, Covington, LA, p. A179

BLEAKNEY, David A., Administrator, Angleton–Danbury General Hospital, Angleton, TX, p. A392

BLEIBERG, Efrain, M.D., President and Chief of Staff, C. F. Menninger Memorial Hospital, Topeka, KS, p. A164

BLESSING, William H., President, Mary Free Bed Hospital and Rehabilitation Center, Grand Rapids, MI, p. A210

BLESSITT, H. J., Administrator, South Sunflower County Hospital, Indianola, MS, p. A234

BLEVINS, Maggie, Administrator, Jane Phillips Nowata Health Center, Nowata, OK, p. A337

BLEYER, Alan J., President, Akron General Medical Center, Akron, OH, p. A317

BLODGETT, Ruth P., Chief Operating Officer, Berkshire Medical Center, Pittsfield, MA, p. A203

BLOM, David P.
President, Grant/Riverside Methodist Hospitals–Grant Campus, Columbus, OH, p. A322
President, Grant/Riverside Methodist Hospitals–Riverside Campus, Columbus, OH, p. A322

BLOME', Michael, Administrator, Methodist Healthcare – Fayette Hospital, Somerville, TN, p. A390

BLOUGH Jr., Daniel D., Chief Executive Officer, Punxsutawney Area Hospital, Punxsutawney, PA, p. A363

BLOUNT, Kenneth, President and Chief Executive Officer, The Monroe Clinic, Monroe, WI, p. A461

BLUFORD, John W., Executive Director and Chief Executive Officer, Truman Medical Center, Kansas City, MO, p. B148

BLUM, James G., Administrator, Tyler Healthcare Center, Tyler, MN, p. A229

BLUM, Joanne M., Administrator, Veterans Home and Hospital, Rocky Hill, CT, p. A76

BOARDMAN, Debra, Chief Executive Officer, Riverwood Health CareCenter, Aitkin, MN, p. A220

BOBBS, Kathy, Chief Executive Officer, Riverview Medical Center, Gonzales, LA, p. A179

BOBELDYK, Jerry, Administrator, Murray County Memorial Hospital, Slayton, MN, p. A228

BOECKER, Thomas J., President and Chief Executive Officer, Wilson Memorial Hospital, Sidney, OH, p. A329

BOEHLER, Sharron D., Commissioner, Oklahoma State Department of Mental Health and Substance Abuse Services, Oklahoma City, OK, p. B122

BOEHRINGER, Paul, Executive Director, Temple University Hospital, Philadelphia, PA, p. A360

BOENING, Harold L., Administrator, Otto Kaiser Memorial Hospital, Kenedy, TX, p. A411

BOETTCHER, William V., Chief Executive Officer, Fletcher Allen Health Care, Burlington, VT, p. A431

BOFF, Michael G., President, Trillium Hospital, Albion, MI, p. A206

BOGAN, James, Chief Executive Officer, Portage Health System, Hancock, MI, p. A211

BOGGS, Danny L., President and Chief Executive Officer, Memorial Hospital, Marysville, OH, p. A326

BOGGS, Lynn Ingram, President and Chief Executive Officer, Community General Hospital of Thomasville, Thomasville, NC, p. A311

BOGUE, Virginia, Site Administrator, Sentara Bayside Hospital, Virginia Beach, VA, p. A441

BOHL, Jim, President and Chief Executive Officer, Doctors Hospital, Springfield, IL, p. A133

BOHNE', Mary S., Administrator, Sandypines, Tequesta, FL, p. A97

BOID, Roger R., Administrator, Grady Memorial Hospital, Chickasha, OK, p. A334

BOLD, Harry, Administrator, Big Sandy Medical Center, Big Sandy, MT, p. A251

BOLD, Jones A., Commanding Officer, Naval Hospital, Cherry Point, NC, p. A304

BOLEWARE, Mike, Administrator, Prentiss Regional Hospital and Extended Care Facilities, Prentiss, MS, p. A237

BONAR Jr., Robert I., President and Chief Executive Officer, Children's Hospital of The King's Daughters, Norfolk, VA, p. A437

BOND, C. Scott, Administrator, Providence St. Peter Hospital, Olympia, WA, p. A446

BONE, Jim G., Interim Administrator, Muleshoe Area Medical Center, Muleshoe, TX, p. A416

BONK, Daniel J., President and Chief Administrative Officer, Methodist Medical Center of Oak Ridge, Oak Ridge, TN, p. A389

BONNER, Tucker, President, King's Daughters Hospital, Temple, TX, p. A423

BOONE, Richard, Executive Director, Crawford Memorial Hospital, Van Buren, AR, p. A35

BOOR, Leon J., Chief Executive Officer and Administrator, Memorial Hospital, Abilene, KS, p. A156

BOOTH, Patrick M., President, Winona Community Memorial Hospital, Winona, MN, p. A230

BOOTH, Peter G., President, Henrietta D. Goodall Hospital, Sanford, ME, p. A190

BOPP, James H.
Executive Director, Middletown Psychiatric Center, Middletown, NY, p. A288
Executive Director, Rockland Psychiatric Center, Orangeburg, NY, p. A295

BORDEN, John R., Administrator, Methodist Healthcare–McNairy Hospital, Selmer, TN, p. A390

BORDENKIRCHER, Kimberly, Interim Chief Executive Officer, Henry County Hospital, Napoleon, OH, p. A327

BORENSTEIN, Jeffrey, M.D., Chief Executive Officer and Medical Director, Holliswood Hospital, New York, NY, p. A290

BORIES Jr., Robert F., FACHE, Administrator, Shriners Hospitals for Children, Shriners Burns Hospital–Boston, Boston, MA, p. A198

BORING, Ronald L., President and Chief Executive Officer, Baylor/ Richardson Medical Center, Richardson, TX, p. A418

BORLAND, Winston, Chief Executive Officer, Northwest Regional Hospital, Corpus Christi, TX, p. A399

BORRONI, S. Denise
Administrator and Chief Executive Officer, HEALTHSOUTH Rehabilitation Hospital of Arlington, Arlington, TX, p. A393
Administrator and Chief Executive Officer, HEALTHSOUTH Rehabilitation Hospital of Fort Worth, Fort Worth, TX, p. A404
Administrator and Chief Executive Officer, HEALTHSOUTH Rehabilitation Hospital–Cityview, Fort Worth, TX, p. A404

BOSK, Nathan, FACHE, Chief Executive Officer, Lower Bucks Hospital, Bristol, PA, p. A348

BOSSARD, Karen L., Administrator, Greene County Medical Center, Jefferson, IA, p. A151

BOSTICK, Roy D., Director, E. A. Conway Medical Center, Monroe, LA, p. A182

BOSWELL, Bill, Chief Executive Officer, McCamey Hospital, McCamey, TX, p. A414

BOUCHER, David T.
Chief Executive Officer, Carolinas Hospital System–Kingstree, Kingstree, SC, p. A373
Chief Executive Officer, Carolinas Hospital System–Lake City, Lake City, SC, p. A373

BOUFFARD, Rodney, Superintendent, Augusta Mental Health Institute, Augusta, ME, p. A187

BOUGHTON, Charles M., Chief Executive Officer, Northeast Regional Medical Center–Jefferson Campus, Kirksville, MO, p. A244

BOUIS, Charles, President and Chief Executive Officer, Edward A. Utlaut Memorial Hospital, Greenville, IL, p. A126

BOULA, Rodney C., Administrator and Chief Executive Officer, Clifton–Fine Hospital, Star Lake, NY, p. A298

BOULENGER, Bo, Chief Executive Officer, Homestead Hospital, Homestead, FL, p. A86

BOUNDS, Floyd D., Administrator, Madison Medical Center, Fredericktown, MO, p. A241

BOUR, Thomas C., Administrator, Mayo Clinic Hospital, Phoenix, AZ, p. A25

BOURASSA, Robert N., Executive Director, Trinity Springs Pavilion, Fort Worth, TX, p. A404

BOURGEOIS, Jeff A., Chief Executive Officer, Hill Country Memorial Hospital, Fredericksburg, TX, p. A404

BOURGEOIS Jr., Milton D., Administrator, St. Anne General Hospital, Raceland, LA, p. A185

BOVENDER Jr., Jack O., President and Chief Operating Officer, Columbia/HCA Healthcare Corporation, Nashville, TN, p. B78

BOWE, Larry, JD, Chief Executive Officer, Hood River Memorial Hospital, Hood River, OR, p. A343

BOWEN, Claire L., President, Fairview Hospital, Great Barrington, MA, p. A200

BOWEN, Don, Superintendent, Griffin Memorial Hospital, Norman, OK, p. A337

BOWEN, Steve, President, East Texas Medical Center Jacksonville, Jacksonville, TX, p. A411

BOWERS, John A., Executive Vice President and Chief Operating Officer, Doctors Hospital, Columbus, OH, p. A321

BOWERS, Robert, Administrator, Veterans Memorial Hospital of Meigs County, Pomeroy, OH, p. A328

BOWERS, Robert A., Chief Executive Officer, Oak Hill Community Medical Center, Oak Hill, OH, p. A327

BOWERSOX, Bruce D.
Administrator and Chief Executive Officer, Griggs County Hospital and Nursing Home, Cooperstown, ND, p. A313
Administrator, Hillsboro Medical Center, Hillsboro, ND, p. A314

BOWLES, Stephen A., President, Valley Community Hospital, Dallas, OR, p. A342

BOWLING, John S., President and Chief Executive Officer, South Georgia Medical Center, Valdosta, GA, p. A111

BOWMAN, Leslie C., Regional Administrator, Ancillary Services and Site Administrator, Detroit Receiving Hospital and University Health Center, Detroit, MI, p. A208

BOWMAN, Mike R., Administrator, Litzenberg Memorial County Hospital, Central City, NE, p. A257

BOWMAN, Scott, Administrator, Sweetwater Hospital, Sweetwater, TN, p. A390

BOYD, Charles E., Administrator, Doctors' Hospital of Shreveport, Shreveport, LA, p. A185

BOYD, Christopher L., Chief Executive Officer and Managing Director, Inland Valley Regional Medical Center, Wildomar, CA, p. A67

BOYD, J. Michael, Chief Executive Officer, Ivinson Memorial Hospital, Laramie, WY, p. A467

BOYD, Wallace N., Administrator, Ochiltree General Hospital, Perryton, TX, p. A417

BOYER, Gregory E., Chief Executive Officer, Wellington Regional Medical Center, West Palm Beach, FL, p. A98

BOYLE, Steven P., President and Chief Executive Officer, St. Peter's Hospital, Albany, NY, p. A281

BOYLES, Jackie, Administrator, Cedar County Memorial Hospital, El Dorado Springs, MO, p. A241

BOYLES, Michael, Administrator, Saunders County Health Service, Wahoo, NE, p. A262

BOZEMAN, Larry C., Chief Executive Officer, Trinity Valley Medical Center, Palestine, TX, p. A417

BRABAND, Jon D., Chief Executive Officer, Glencoe Area Health Center, Glencoe, MN, p. A223

BRACE, Rod, Chief Executive Officer, Fort Bend Medical Center, Missouri City, TX, p. A415

BRACKIN, D. Wayne, Chief Executive Officer, South Miami Hospital, Miami, FL, p. A90

BRACKNEY, Charles R., President and Chief Executive Officer, Ozarks Medical Center, West Plains, MO, p. A250

BRADDOM, Randall L., M.D., Chief Executive Officer and Medical Director, Wishard Health Services, Indianapolis, IN, p. A140

BRADEL, William T., Executive Director, Sacred Heart Hospital, Cumberland, MD, p. A194

BRADFORD, Donald L., Chief Executive Officer, Gadsden Community Hospital, Quincy, FL, p. A94

BRADFORD, Roberta J., President and Chief Executive Officer, Drake Center, Cincinnati, OH, p. A319

BRADLEY, David K., Chief Executive Officer, Geary Community Hospital, Junction City, KS, p. A160

BRADLEY, Lucinda A., President, Great Plains Regional Medical Center, North Platte, NE, p. A260

BRADLEY Jr., J. Lindsey, FACHE, President and Chief Administrative Officer, Trinity Mother Frances Health System, Tyler, TX, p. A424

BRADSHAW, Dorothy A., Director, Deer's Head Center, Salisbury, MD, p. A196

BRADY, Barry, Administrator, Ozark Health Medical Center, Clinton, AR, p. A30

BRADY, James L., President, Allied Services Rehabilitation Hospital, Scranton, PA, p. A363

BRADY, Patrick R., Chief Executive Officer, Sutter Roseville Medical Center, Roseville, CA, p. A57

BRADY, Tim, Chief Executive Officer, Methodist LeBonheur Healthcare–Jackson, Jackson, TN, p. A384

BRAILSFORD, Tammie McMann, Administrator and Chief Operating Officer, St. Mary Medical Center, Long Beach, CA, p. A47

BRAMLETT Jr., E. Chandler
President and Chief Executive Officer, Infirmary Health System, Inc., Mobile, AL, p. B105
President and Chief Executive Officer, Mobile Infirmary Medical Center, Mobile, AL, p. A16

BRANAMAN, A. Ray, Administrator, Mary Breckinridge Hospital, Hyden, KY, p. A170

BRANCO, Patrick, Administrator, Divine Providence Health Center, Ivanhoe, MN, p. A224

BRANDLER, Bruce, Chief Executive Officer, Puget Sound Hospital, Tacoma, WA, p. A448

BRANDON, David, Chief Executive Officer, Fayette Memorial Hospital, Connersville, IN, p. A137

BRANDT, Stephen, President and Chief Executive Officer, West Florida Regional Medical Center, Pensacola, FL, p. A93

BRANDT, Florence, Chief Executive Officer, St. Francis Medical Center, Pittsburgh, PA, p. A361

BRANTLEY, Cheryl Y., Administrator, South Florida Evaluation and Treatment Center, Miami, FL, p. A90

BRASH, David L., Chief Executive Officer, Russell County Medical Center, Lebanon, VA, p. A436

BRASIER, Jamers, Administrator, Nocona General Hospital, Nocona, TX, p. A416

BRASS, Alan W., FACHE, President and Chief Executive Officer, ProMedica Health System, Toledo, OH, p. B125

BRAUN, Greg
Administrator, Harmony Community Hospital, Harmony, MN, p. A224
Administrator, Tweeten Lutheran Health Care Center, Spring Grove, MN, p. A228

BRAWLEY, James B., Chief Executive Officer, Holly Hill/ Charter Behavioral Health System, Raleigh, NC, p. A309

BRAZIER, Ray, President, Hillcrest Health Center, Oklahoma City, OK, p. A338

BRAZITIS, Mark A., President, Lancaster General Hospital, Lancaster, PA, p. A354

BREEDEN, Susan M., Administrator, Baptist Memorial Hospital–Huntingdon, Huntingdon, TN, p. A384

BREEN, John P., Chief Executive Officer, Massapequa General Hospital, Seaford, NY, p. A298

BREEN, Michael F., President, St. John NorthEast Community Hospital, Detroit, MI, p. A209

BREGANT Jr., Robert E., Administrator, Ransom Memorial Hospital, Ottawa, KS, p. A162

BREHE, Deborah, Chief Executive Officer, Mission Bay Hospital, San Diego, CA, p. A59

BREHM, Robert, President, Kessler Institute for Rehabilitation, West Orange, NJ, p. A275

BREITLING, Bryan, Administrator and Chief Executive Officer, Bowdle Hospital, Bowdle, SD, p. A376

BREKHUS, Pete, Chief Executive Officer, Madison Valley Hospital, Ennis, MT, p. A252

BREMER, Louis H., President and Chief Executive Officer, Wellmont Holston Valley Medical Center, Kingsport, TN, p. A385

BRENNAN, Charles L., Chief Executive Officer, St. Lawrence Rehabilitation Center, Lawrenceville, NJ, p. A271

BRENNAN, Darlene, Chief Executive Officer, BHC East Lake Hospital, New Orleans, LA, p. A183

BRENNAN, Donald A., President and Chief Executive Officer, Daughters of Charity National Health System, Saint Louis, MO, p. B86

BRENNY, Terrence, President, Stoughton Hospital Association, Stoughton, WI, p. A464

BRESSANELLI, Leo A., President and Chief Executive Officer, Genesis Medical Center, Davenport, IA, p. A148

BRETT, C. William, Ph.D., President and Chief Executive Officer, Windmoor Healthcare of Clearwater, Clearwater, FL, p. A82

BREWER, Gary L., Chief Executive Officer, Valley View Hospital, Glenwood Springs, CO, p. A70

BREWER, Jeff, President, Walker Baptist Medical Center, Jasper, AL, p. A16

BREWER, Rebecca T., CHE, Chief Executive Officer, Colleton Medical Center, Walterboro, SC, p. A375

BREWER, Sally, Vice President and Administrator, Memorial Hospital at Exeter, Exeter, CA, p. A42

BREZENOFF, Stanley, President, Maimonides Medical Center, New York, NY, p. A291

BRIDGES, James M., Executive Vice President and Chief Operating Officer, Palmetto Baptist Medical Center/Columbia, Columbia, SC, p. A371

BRIGGS, Ronald O., President, St. Francis Memorial Hospital, West Point, NE, p. A262

BRILEY, Ellen, Administrator and Chief Executive Officer, Elba General Hospital, Elba, AL, p. A14

BRIMHALL, Dennis C., President, University of Colorado Hospital, Denver, CO, p. A70

BRINGHURST, John F., Administrator, Petersburg Medical Center, Petersburg, AK, p. A21

BRINK, Gerald R., President and Chief Executive Officer, Riverside Regional Medical Center, Newport News, VA, p. A437

BRINKER, Joseph J., Chief Executive Officer, Bethesda General Hospital, Saint Louis, MO, p. A247

BRINKERS, Jack, CHE, Administrator, Weston County Health Services, Newcastle, WY, p. A467

BRINKERT, William K., President, St. John of God Hospital, Brighton, MA, p. A199

BRITT, John H., Executive Director, Massachusetts Hospital School, Canton, MA, p. A200

BRITTON, Gregory K., President and Chief Executive Officer, Beloit Memorial Hospital, Beloit, WI, p. A456

BROCCOLINO, Victor A., President and Chief Executive Officer, Howard County General Hospital, Columbia, MD, p. A193

BROCK, John D., Chief Executive Officer, Highland Medical Center, Lubbock, TX, p. A413

BROCKETTE, Darby, Administrator, HEALTHSOUTH Rehabilitation Center, Albuquerque, NM, p. A277

BROCKMANN, William F., President and Chief Executive Officer, Caylor–Nickel Medical Center, Bluffton, IN, p. A136

BRODEUR, Mark S., Chief Executive Officer, Jefferson Memorial Hospital, Crystal City, MO, p. A241

BRODHEAD, Robert T., Interim Chief Executive Officer, St. John's Regional Health Center, Springfield, MO, p. A249

BRODY, Robert J., President and Chief Executive Officer, St. Francis Hospital and Health Centers, Beech Grove, IN, p. A136

BRODY, Sue G.
President and Chief Executive Officer, Bayfront Medical Center, Saint Petersburg, FL, p. A94
President and Chief Executive Officer, St. Anthony's Hospital, Saint Petersburg, FL, p. A94

BROGAN, Alanna, Chief Operating Officer, Petaluma Valley Hospital, Petaluma, CA, p. A56

BROOKS, Jesse, M.D., Administrator, Brooks Hospital, Atlanta, TX, p. A393

BROOKS, Phillip D., President, Norfolk Community Hospital, Norfolk, VA, p. A437

BROOKS, Richard A., Administrator and Chief Operating Officer, E. J. Noble Hospital Samaritan, Alexandria Bay, NY, p. A281

BROOKS III, J. Milton, Administrator, Pineville Community Hospital Association, Pineville, KY, p. A174

BROSIG, Joe, Administrator, Concho County Hospital, Eden, TX, p. A402

BROSSEAU, Terrance G., President and Chief Executive Officer, MedCenter One, Bismarck, ND, p. A313

BROTHERTON, Thomas J., Administrator, Shriners Hospitals for Children, Honolulu, Honolulu, HI, p. A112

BROTHMAN, Daniel, Chief Executive Officer, Western Medical Center–Santa Ana, Santa Ana, CA, p. A62

BROTMAN, Martin, M.D., President and Chief Executive Officer, California Pacific Medical Center, San Francisco, CA, p. A60

BROUGHTON, Pamela McCullough, Chief Executive Officer, BHC West Hills Hospital, Reno, NV, p. A264

BROWER, Fred B., President and Chief Executive Officer, Trinity Health System, Steubenville, OH, p. A329

BROWN, Carl D., Administrator, Lakeview Community Hospital, Eufaula, AL, p. A14

BROWN, Cary D., Director, Veterans Affairs Medical Center, Big Spring, TX, p. A395

BROWN, Cynthia K., R.N., Chief Executive Officer, BHC Canyon Ridge Hospital, Chino, CA, p. A39

BROWN, Dan
Administrator, North Central Baptist Hospital, San Antonio, TX, p. A420
Administrator, Northeast Baptist Hospital, San Antonio, TX, p. A420

BROWN, David E., President and Chief Executive Officer, Beaufort Memorial Hospital, Beaufort, SC, p. A370

BROWN, David P., Administrator, Citizens Medical Center, Victoria, TX, p. A424

BROWN, Donald G., Chief Executive Officer, Community Memorial Hospital, Monmouth, IL, p. A129

BROWN, H. Thomas, Administrator, Cobb Memorial Hospital, Royston, GA, p. A109

BROWN, Harold W., Chief Executive Officer, Prairie du Chien Memorial Hospital, Prairie Du Chien, WI, p. A462

BROWN, Henry A., Chief Executive Officer, Doctors Hospital of Hyde Park, Chicago, IL, p. A120

BROWN, Lennea F., Administrator, Bucktail Medical Center, Renovo, PA, p. A363

BROWN, Luella, Service Unit Director, U. S. Public Health Service Indian Hospital, Cass Lake, MN, p. A221

BROWN, Michael L., Interim Chief Executive Officer, Columbus Community Hospital, Columbus, OH, p. A321

BROWN, Murray L., Administrator, Neosho Memorial Regional Medical Center, Chanute, KS, p. A156

BROWN, Patricia W., Executive Director, Savannas Hospital, Port St. Lucie, FL, p. A94

BROWN, Rex H., President, Hillsboro Area Hospital, Hillsboro, IL, p. A127

BROWN, Richard V., Chief Executive Officer, Livingston Memorial Hospital, Livingston, MT, p. A253

BROWN, Richard W., President and Chief Executive Officer, Health Midwest, Kansas City, MO, p. B100

BROWN, Robert A., Senior Vice President and Chief Operating Officer, Addison Community Hospital, Addison, MI, p. A206

BROWN, Scott R., Administrator and Chief Executive Officer, Moore County Hospital District, Dumas, TX, p. A402

BROWN, Shannon D., President, Betsy Johnson Regional Hospital, Dunn, NC, p. A304

BROWN, Steven E., Administrator, Inova Fairfax Hospital, Falls Church, VA, p. A434

BROWN, Terry, Administrator and Chief Executive Officer, HEALTHSOUTH Lakeshore Rehabilitation Hospital, Birmingham, AL, p. A12

BROWN, William A., Vice President and Administrator, Inova Fair Oaks Hospital, Fairfax, VA, p. A434

BROWN, G. R., Commanding Officer, U. S. Naval Hospital, Roosevelt Roads, PR, p. A472

BROWNE, J. Timothy, Chief Executive Officer, Loris Community Hospital, Loris, SC, p. A374

BROWNE, Norman E., Director, Veterans Affairs Medical Center, Albuquerque, NM, p. A278

BROWNING, Edward E., Chief Executive Officer and Administrator, Clay County Memorial Hospital, Henrietta, TX, p. A407

BROWNLEE, Walter W., President and Chief Executive Officer, Jefferson County Hospital, Fairfield, IA, p. A149

BROYLES, Dan P., Administrator, Harrison County Community Hospital, Bethany, MO, p. A239

BRUCE, Sandra B., President and Chief Executive Officer, Saint Alphonsus Regional Medical Center, Boise, ID, p. A114

BRUCKMAN, Donald A., Acting Chief Executive Officer, Senator Garrett T. W. Hagedorn Gero Psychiatric Hospital, Glen Gardner, NJ, p. A270

BRUECKNER, Geraldine, Administrator, Our Children's House at Baylor, Dallas, TX, p. A400

BRUECKNER, Gerry, R.N., Executive Director, Baylor Center for Restorative Care, Dallas, TX, p. A399

BRUHN, Charles E., Chief Executive Officer, Memorial Community Hospital, Edgerton, WI, p. A458

BRUM, Joseph G., President and Chief Executive Officer, Henry Medical Center, Stockbridge, GA, p. A110

BRUMITT, Jerry D., President and Chief Executive Officer, Saint John's Health System, Anderson, IN, p. A136

BRUMLOW Jr., James W., President and Chief Executive Officer, Wadsworth–Rittman Hospital, Wadsworth, OH, p. A330

BRUNDIGE, James E., Administrator, Haxtun Hospital District, Haxtun, CO, p. A71

BRUNICARDI, Rusty O., President, Community Hospitals of Williams County, Bryan, OH, p. A318

BRUNN, Donald I., President and Chief Executive Officer, Virtua–Memorial Hospital Burlington County, Mount Holly, NJ, p. A272

BRUNO, Frank, Chief Executive Officer, Gracie Square Hospital, New York, NY, p. A290

BRUNO, Richard J., Senior Vice President, Elk County Regional Medical Center, Ridgway, PA, p. A363

BRUNS, Dennis Ray, President and Chief Executive Officer, Hilton Head Medical Center and Clinics, Hilton Head Island, SC, p. A373

BRUNSON, Joseph R., Chief Executive Officer, Charter Heights Behavioral Health System, Albuquerque, NM, p. A277

BRVENIK, Richard A., President and Chief Executive Officer, Shore Memorial Hospital, Nassawadox, VA, p. A437

BRYAN, Jay, Chief Executive Officer, Lakeshore Community Hospital, Shelby, MI, p. A217

BRYAN, Margaret, Administrator, Shriners Hospitals for Children, Northern California, Sacramento, CA, p. A58

BRYAN, Marilyn, Administrator, Roger Mills Memorial Hospital, Cheyenne, OK, p. A334

BRYAN, Peter K., Chief Executive Officer, Kern Medical Center, Bakersfield, CA, p. A37

BRZUZ, Richard W., Administrator, Shriners Hospitals for Children, Erie, Erie, PA, p. A352

BUCHANAN, A. C., President and Chief Executive Officer, Rapides Regional Medical Center, Alexandria, LA, p. A177

BUCHANAN, Don, Chief Operating Officer, Aurora Community Hospital, Aurora, MO, p. A239

BUCHANAN, Georgia, President, Laird Hospital, Union, MS, p. A237

BUCK, Jack S., Chief Executive Officer, Crockett Hospital, Lawrenceburg, TN, p. A386

BUCK, William G., President and Chief Executive Officer, Pasco Community Hospital, Dade City, FL, p. A83

BUCKLAND, Eric, CHE, Chief Executive Officer, Valley General Hospital, Monroe, WA, p. A445

BUCKLEY, Donald S., FACHE, President, Chesapeake General Hospital, Chesapeake, VA, p. A434

BUCKLEY, Howard R., President, Mercy Hospital Portland, Portland, ME, p. A189

BUCKLEY, Jeffrey L., President and Chief Executive Officer, Gateway Regional Health System, Mount Sterling, KY, p. A173

BUCKLEY, John J., President and Chief Executive Officer, Pottstown Memorial Medical Center, Pottstown, PA, p. A362

BUCKLEY Jr., John J., President, Southern Illinois Hospital Services, Carbondale, IL, p. B140

BUCKNER, Terry, Administrator, Watonga Municipal Hospital, Watonga, OK, p. A341

BUCKNER, Wayne, Administrator, Baptist Hospital of Cocke County, Newport, TN, p. A389

BUCKNER Jr., James E., Administrator, Cuero Community Hospital, Cuero, TX, p. A399

BUDNICK, Michael J., Administrator and Chief Executive Officer, Gibson General Hospital, Princeton, IN, p. A143

BUDRYS, Raymond, Chief Executive Officer, Craven Regional Medical Authority, New Bern, NC, p. A309

BUECHLER, Verlin D., Administrator and Chief Executive Officer, Kenmare Community Hospital, Kenmare, ND, p. A315

BUHRMANN, Henry J., President and Chief Executive Officer, Marin General Hospital, Greenbrae, CA, p. A44

BULGER, Robert J., President and Chief Executive Officer, Jeannette District Memorial Hospital, Jeannette, PA, p. A354

BULL, Jayne R., Administrator, Leelanau Memorial Health Center, Northport, MI, p. A215

BULLARD, Brenda, Administrator, U. S. Air Force Hospital, Cheyenne, WY, p. A466

BULLOCK, Scott B., President, MaineGeneral Medical Center–Waterville Campus, Waterville, ME, p. A190

BUNCH, Jimm
President and Chief Executive Officer, Jellico Community Hospital, Jellico, TN, p. A384
Chief Executive Officer, Memorial Hospital, Manchester, KY, p. A173

BUNDY, William H., Chief Executive Officer, Chester County Hospital and Nursing Center, Chester, SC, p. A371

BUNKER, Stephen P., President and Chief Operating Officer, Holmes Regional Medical Center, Melbourne, FL, p. A89

BUONANNI, Brian, Chief Executive Officer, Community General Hospital of Sullivan County, Harris, NY, p. A286

BURCHILL, Kevin R., Executive Director, Community Medical Center, Toms River, NJ, p. A275

BURD, Ronald P., President and Chief Executive Officer, Devereux Foundation, Villanova, PA, p. B94

BURDICK, Steve, Administrator, Providence Centralia Hospital, Centralia, WA, p. A443

BURDIN Jr., John J., President and Chief Executive Officer, Lafayette General Medical Center, Lafayette, LA, p. A181

BURFEIND, Raymond F., President, Covenant Medical Center, Waterloo, IA, p. A155

BURFITT, Gregory H., President and Chief Executive Officer, Brookwood Medical Center, Birmingham, AL, p. A11

BURGER, Janice, Operations Administrator, Providence Milwaukie Hospital, Milwaukie, OR, p. A344

BURGESS, Roger M., Administrator, St. Francis Hospital, Escanaba, MI, p. A209

BURGHER, Louis W., Ph.D., President and Chief Executive Officer, Nebraska Health System, Omaha, NE, p. A260

BURGIN, Robert F., President and Chief Executive Officer, Mission St. Joseph's Health, Asheville, NC, p. A302

BURGIO, David E., FACHE, President and Chief Executive Officer, Berea Hospital, Berea, KY, p. A167

BURKE, Dennis E., President, Good Shepherd Community Hospital, Hermiston, OR, p. A343

BURKET, Mark, Chief Executive Officer, Platte Community Memorial Hospital, Platte, SD, p. A378

BURKETT, William T., Chief Executive Officer, Eastern State Hospital, Vinita, OK, p. A341

BURKHARD, Thomas, Commanding Officer, Naval Hospital, Camp Pendleton, CA, p. A38

BURKHARDT Jr., J. Bland, Senior Vice President and Administrator, Greenville Memorial Hospital, Greenville, SC, p. A373

BURKHART, James R., FACHE
Administrator, Fort Sanders Regional Medical Center, Knoxville, TN, p. A385
President and Chief Executive Officer, Fort Sanders–Parkwest Medical Center, Knoxville, TN, p. A385

BURN, Robert B., President and Chief Executive Officer, Washoe Medical Center, Reno, NV, p. A264

BURNETTE, W. Scott, President, Community Memorial Healthcenter, South Hill, VA, p. A440

BURNS, Charlotte, Administrator and Chief Executive Officer, Hardin County General Hospital, Savannah, TN, p. A389

BURNS, Dennis R., Administrator and Chief Executive Officer, Sonoma Valley Hospital, Sonoma, CA, p. A63

BURNS, Gregory T., Executive Director, St. Joseph's Community Hospital of West Bend, West Bend, WI, p. A465

BURNS, Randall P., Director and Chief Executive Officer, Alaska Psychiatric Institute, Anchorage, AK, p. A20

BURRIS, Bradley D., President and Chief Executive Officer, Oakes Community Hospital, Oakes, ND, p. A315

BURROUGHS, Michael R., FACHE, President and Chief Executive Officer, Medical Center of Arlington, Arlington, TX, p. A393

BURROWS, Jack A., Administrator, Clarke County Hospital, Osceola, IA, p. A153

BURTON, Gary, Chief Executive Officer, Bledsoe County General Hospital, Pikeville, TN, p. A389

BURTON, W. R., Administrator, Memorial Hospital at Gulfport, Gulfport, MS, p. A233

BURZYNSKI, Cheryl A., President, Bay Special Care, Bay City, MI, p. A207

BUSCH, Walter, Administrator, Roosevelt Memorial Medical Center, Culbertson, MT, p. A252

BUSER, Kenneth R.
President, Saint Mary's Medical Center, Racine, WI, p. A463
President, St. Luke's Memorial Hospital, Racine, WI, p. A463

BUSH, Mark E., Executive Vice President, MidMichigan Medical Center–Gladwin, Gladwin, MI, p. A210

BUSHMAIER, Jim E., Administrator and Chief Executive Officer, Stuttgart Regional Medical Center, Stuttgart, AR, p. A35

BUSTELO, Miguel J., Executive Director, Dr. Pila's Hospital, Ponce, PR, p. A471

BUTIKOFER, Lon D., Ph.D., Administrator and Chief Executive Officer, Regional Medical Center of Northeast Iowa and Delaware County, Manchester, IA, p. A151

BUTLER, Anita M., Administrator, Spartanburg Hospital for Restorative Care, Spartanburg, SC, p. A375

BUTLER, Beatrice, Superintendent, Terrell State Hospital, Terrell, TX, p. A423

BUTLER, Everett A., Chief Executive Officer, Unity Medical Center, Grafton, ND, p. A314

BUTLER, Frank, Director, University of Kentucky Hospital, Lexington, KY, p. A171

BUTLER, Peter W., President and Chief Executive Officer, Methodist Health Care System, Houston, TX, p. B117

BUTLER, Jeffrey L., Administrator, Malcolm Grow Medical Center, Andrews AFB, MD, p. A191

BUTLER, Joe W., Deputy Commander Administration, Martin Army Community Hospital, Fort Benning, GA, p. A105

BUTTS, Charles N., Interim Chief Executive Officer, Reeves County Hospital, Pecos, TX, p. A417

BUURMAN, Rita K., Chief Executive Officer, Sabetha Community Hospital, Sabetha, KS, p. A164

BYBEE, Bob L., President and Chief Executive Officer, Memorial Medical Center, Port Lavaca, TX, p. A418

BYRNE, Frank D., M.D., President, Parkview Hospital, Fort Wayne, IN, p. A138

BYRNES, Nancy A., Chief Executive Officer, Navarro Regional Medical Center, Corsicana, TX, p. A399

BYROM, David, Administrator, Coryell Memorial Hospital, Gatesville, TX, p. A405

C

CABONOR, Regis, Administrator, Person Memorial Hospital, Roxboro, NC, p. A310

CACKLER, Ron, President and Chief Executive Officer, Cushing Regional Hospital, Cushing, OK, p. A334

CAGEN, Richard M., Chief Executive Officer and Administrator, LDS Hospital, Salt Lake City, UT, p. A429

CAGLE, Brooks, Chief Executive Officer, Charter Cypress Behavioral Health System, Lafayette, LA, p. A181

CAHILL, Patricia A., President and Chief Executive Officer, Catholic Health Initiatives, Denver, CO, p. B73

CAIN, Margaret C., Chief Executive Officer, North Suburban Medical Center, Thornton, CO, p. A73

CAIN, R. Mark, Executive Director, Southwest Regional Medical Center, Little Rock, AR, p. A32

CAIN, Thomas, Administrator and Chief Executive Officer, Malvern Institute, Malvern, PA, p. A355

CAISON, S. Beth, Administrator, Collingsworth General Hospital, Wellington, TX, p. A425

CALAMARI, Frank A., President and Chief Executive Officer, Calvary Hospital, New York, NY, p. A289

CALBONE, Angelo G.
President and Chief Executive Officer, Mount St. Mary's Hospital of Niagara Falls, Lewiston, NY, p. A287
President and Chief Executive Officer, Niagara Falls Memorial Medical Center, Niagara Falls, NY, p. A294

CALDERIN, Carolina, Chief Executive Officer, Pan American Hospital, Miami, FL, p. A90

CALDERONE, John, Ph.D., Chief Executive Officer, Corona Regional Medical Center, Corona, CA, p. A40

CALDWELL, Darren, Chief Executive Officer, Drew Memorial Hospital, Monticello, AR, p. A33

CALDWELL, Harvey G., Administrator and Chief Executive Officer, Brainerd Regional Human Services Center, Brainerd, MN, p. A221

CALDWELL, Robert C., Chief Operating Officer, Alegent Health Center for Mental Health, Omaha, NE, p. A260

CALE, Barbara R., Administrator, Chowan Hospital, Edenton, NC, p. A305

CALEY, George B., President, Winchester Medical Center, Winchester, VA, p. A441

CALGI, Dominick R., President and Chief Executive Officer, Barnert Hospital, Paterson, NJ, p. A273

CALHOUN, Jean, Administrator, Metropolitan Hospital, Atlanta, GA, p. A100

CALHOUN, Kevin P., President and Chief Executive Officer, Bell Memorial Hospital, Ishpeming, MI, p. A212

CALICO, Forrest, M.D., President, Appalachian Regional Healthcare, Lexington, KY, p. B61

CALIG, Joseph, President and Chief Executive Officer, Allegheny University Hospitals, Allegheny Valley, Natrona Heights, PA, p. A357

CALLAHAN, Keith L., Executive Vice President and Administrator, St. Mary's Hospital, Decatur, IL, p. A123

CALLAHAN, Kevin J., President and Chief Executive Officer, Exeter Hospital, Exeter, NH, p. A265

CALLAHAN, Michael A., Chief Executive Officer, Northwest Texas Healthcare System, Amarillo, TX, p. A392

CALLAN Sr., Michael J., Chief Executive Officer, Ashland Regional Medical Center, Ashland, PA, p. A348

CALLISON, William L., Chief Executive Officer, Charter Greenville Behavioral Health System, Greer, SC, p. A373

CALLOWAY, Jack A., Chief Executive Officer, Highlands–Cashiers Hospital, Highlands, NC, p. A307

CALVARUSO, Joseph, Chief Executive Officer, Mount Carmel Health System, Columbus, OH, p. A322

CAMERON, Marie, FACHE, President and Chief Executive Officer, Southwest Hospital and Medical Center, Atlanta, GA, p. A100

CAMERON, Richard, M.D., Administrator, Harbor View Mercy Hospital, Fort Smith, AR, p. A31

CAMMACK Jr., Thomas N., Chief Executive Officer, Marshall Regional Medical Center, Marshall, TX, p. A414

CAMP III, Claude E., Chief Executive Officer, McCurtain Memorial Hospital, Idabel, OK, p. A336

CAMPBELL, Al, Chief Executive Officer, Southeast Colorado Hospital and Long Term Care, Springfield, CO, p. A72

CAMPBELL, Bruce C., President and Chief Executive Officer, Illinois Masonic Medical Center, Chicago, IL, p. A121

CAMPBELL, C. Scott, Executive Director, Bulloch Memorial Hospital, Statesboro, GA, p. A110

CAMPBELL, Deborah, Administrator, Thomas H. Boyd Memorial Hospital, Carrollton, IL, p. A119

CAMPBELL, Gary L., Director, Harry S. Truman Memorial Veterans Hospital, Columbia, MO, p. A240

CAMPBELL, Katharine Ann, Administrator, Harms Memorial Hospital District, American Falls, ID, p. A114

CAMPBELL, Ronald L., Chief Executive Officer, Walton Medical Center, Monroe, GA, p. A107

CAMPBELL, Stephen J., Administrator, Southwestern General Hospital, El Paso, TX, p. A403

CAMPBELL, Wayne, Chief Executive Officer, Fort Walton Beach Medical Center, Fort Walton Beach, FL, p. A85

CAMPBELL, William E., Ph.D., Superintendent, Glenwood State Hospital School, Glenwood, IA, p. A150

CAMPBELL Jr., Robert D., Administrator, Cascade Valley Hospital, North Snohomish County Health System, Arlington, WA, p. A443

CAMPEAU, Jerry, Inteirm Chief Executive Officer, White Mountain Regional Medical Center, Springerville, AZ, p. A26

CANDINO, Paul J., Chief Executive Officer, Erie County Medical Center, Buffalo, NY, p. A283

CANNON, James C., Administrator and Chief Executive Officer, Regional Hospital for Respiratory and Complex Care, Seattle, WA, p. A447

CANOTE, Dennis R., Chief Executive Officer, Mid Missouri Mental Health Center, Columbia, MO, p. A240

CANTRELL, Gary, President and Chief Executive Officer, St. Lucie Medical Center, Port St. Lucie, FL, p. A94

CANTWELL, Jerry, Administrator, Delta County Memorial Hospital, Delta, CO, p. A69

CAPLAN, Marcie S., Acting Chief Executive Officer, UPMC South Side, Pittsburgh, PA, p. A362

CAPOBIANCO, Peter E., President and Chief Executive Officer, St. Mary's Hospital, Amsterdam, NY, p. A281

CAPPELLO, Thomas A., Director, Veterans Affairs Pittsburgh Healthcare System, Pittsburgh, PA, p. A362

CARAVELLA, Louis P., M.D., Chief Executive Officer, Fairview Hospital, Cleveland, OH, p. A320

CARBONE, Davide M., Chief Executive Officer, Aventura Hospital and Medical Center, Miami, FL, p. A89

CARDA, Timothy L., Chief Executive Officer, Tustin Hospital and Medical Center, Tustin, CA, p. A65

CARL, Gerald E.
Administrator, Arnold Memorial Health Care Center, Adrian, MN, p. A220
Administrator, Luverne Community Hospital, Luverne, MN, p. A224

CARLE, Chris, Administrator, St. Elizabeth Medical Center–Grant County, Williamstown, KY, p. A175

CARLIN, Martin E., President, Park Ridge Hospital, Rochester, NY, p. A297

CARLISLE, John T., Chief Executive Officer, Cape Fear Valley Health System, Fayetteville, NC, p. A305

CARLSON, Brian J., President and Chief Executive Officer, Lake View Memorial Hospital, Two Harbors, MN, p. A229

CARLSON, Debra, Acting Administrator, First Care Medical Services, Fosston, MN, p. A223

CARLSON, Donald R., President and Chief Executive Officer, San Juan Regional Medical Center, Farmington, NM, p. A278

CARLSON, Greg L., President and Chief Executive Officer, Owensboro Mercy Health System, Owensboro, KY, p. A174

CARLSON, Roland R., Chief Executive Officer, Valley West Community Hospital, Sandwich, IL, p. A133

CARLSTEDT, Nancy S., President, Bloomington Hospital, Bloomington, IN, p. A136

CARMAN, Thomas H., President and Chief Executive Officer, Cortland Memorial Hospital, Cortland, NY, p. A284

CARMICHAEL, LeRoy, Executive Director, Bronx Psychiatric Center, New York, NY, p. A289

CARNEY, Christopher M., President and Chief Executive Officer, Bon Secours Health System, Inc., Marriottsville, MD, p. B67

CARNEY, Michael J., Chief Executive Officer, Charter Behavioral Health System of Winston–Salem, Winston–Salem, NC, p. A312

CAROBENE, Joseph W., Superintendent, Middle Tennessee Mental Health Institute, Nashville, TN, p. A388

CAROSELLI, Joseph P., Administrator, Idaho Elks Rehabilitation Hospital, Boise, ID, p. A114

CARPENTER, David R., FACHE, President and Chief Executive Officer, North Kansas City Hospital, North Kansas City, MO, p. A246

CARR, C. Larry, Regional Executive Vice President and President, Bakersfield Memorial Hospital, Bakersfield, CA, p. A37

CARR, Wiley N., President and Chief Executive Officer, Porter Memorial Hospital, Valparaiso, IN, p. A145

CARRAWAY, Robert M., M.D., Chairman and Chief Executive Officer, Carraway Methodist Health System, Birmingham, AL, p. B72

CARRELL, Jan V., Chief Executive Officer and Administrator, Montrose Memorial Hospital, Montrose, CO, p. A72

CARRINGTON–MURRAY, Cynthia, MS, Executive Director, Woodhull Medical and Mental Health Center, New York, NY, p. A294

CARROCINO, Joanne, Executive Director, Kimball Medical Center, Lakewood, NJ, p. A271

CARROLL, Allen P., Chief Executive Officer, Bon Secours–St. Francis Xavier Hospital, Charleston, SC, p. A370

CARROLL, Jack A., Ph.D., President, Sheltering Arms Rehabilitation Hospital, Richmond, VA, p. A440

CARROLL, James J., Administrator, Cloquet Community Memorial Hospital, Cloquet, MN, p. A221

CARROLL, Kevin J., President, Champlain Valley Physicians Hospital Medical Center, Plattsburgh, NY, p. A296

CARROLL, Michael W., Administrator, Richland Parish Hospital–Delhi, Delhi, LA, p. A179

CARROLL, Dale, Commander, Moncrief Army Community Hospital, Fort Jackson, SC, p. A372

CARRUTH, John M., Administrator, Camden General Hospital, Camden, TN, p. A381

CARSON, Mitchell C., President, Ball Memorial Hospital, Muncie, IN, p. A143

CARSON, Randy, Chief Executive Officer, North Georgia Medical Center, Ellijay, GA, p. A104

CARSON, Sandra C., FACHE, Senior Vice President, Methodist Richard Young, Omaha, NE, p. A260

CARSON, Terry, Chief Executive Officer, Harrison Community Hospital, Cadiz, OH, p. A318

CARTER, Bruce C., President, United Hospital Center, Clarksburg, WV, p. A451

CARTER, Michael C., Chief Executive Officer, Anaheim Memorial Medical Center, Anaheim, CA, p. A36

CARTER, Richard, Chief Executive Officer, Hunt Memorial Hospital District, Greenville, TX, p. A406

CARTER Jr., William E., Senior Associate Vice President for Operations, University of Virginia Medical Center, Charlottesville, VA, p. A434

CARUSO, Frank T., Chief Executive Officer, Hoopeston Community Memorial Hospital, Hoopeston, IL, p. A127

CARY, Roger C., President and Chief Executive Officer, Midwestern Regional Medical Center, Zion, IL, p. A135

CASADAY, Thomas E., President and Chief Executive Officer, Sierra Medical Center, El Paso, TX, p. A403

CASALOU, Robert F., Interim President and Chief Executive Officer, Providence Hospital and Medical Centers, Southfield, MI, p. A217

CASE, Edward B., Executive Vice President and Chief Operating Officer, BJC Health System, Saint Louis, MO, p. B67

CASEY, Dennis A., Executive Director, Albert Lindley Lee Memorial Hospital, Fulton, NY, p. A285

CASEY, Jack, Administrator, Shodair Children's Hospital, Helena, MT, p. A253

CASEY, Marsha N., President, St. Vincent Hospitals and Health Services, Indianapolis, IN, p. A140

CASEY, Timothy M., President and Chief Executive Officer, Montgomery Hospital, Norristown, PA, p. A357

CASEY, William J.
Administrator, Kingsburg District Hospital, Kingsburg, CA, p. A45
Chief Executive Officer, Sanger General Hospital, Sanger, CA, p. A61

CASHION, John A., FACHE, President, Lexington Memorial Hospital, Lexington, NC, p. A308

CASSELS, William H., Administrator, DCH Regional Medical Center, Tuscaloosa, AL, p. A18

CASSIDY, James E., President and Chief Executive Officer, St. Mary's Regional Medical Center, Lewiston, ME, p. A189

CASTAGNARO, Marie, President and Chief Executive Officer, St. Joseph's Hospital, Elmira, NY, p. A285

CASTRO, William Rodriguez, Executive Director, Aguadilla General Hospital, Aguadilla, PR, p. A469

CASTROP, Richard F., President, O'Bleness Memorial Hospital, Athens, OH, p. A317

CATALANO, Robert A., M.D., President and Chief Executive Officer, Olean General Hospital, Olean, NY, p. A295

CATALDO, Vince A., Administrator, Prevost Memorial Hospital, Donaldsonville, LA, p. A179

CATELLIER, Julie A., Director, Veterans Affairs Medical Center, Biloxi, MS, p. A231

CATENA, Cornelio R., President and Chief Executive Officer, Amsterdam Memorial Hospital, Amsterdam, NY, p. A281

CATHEY, Shawn, Administrator, Dardanelle Hospital, Dardanelle, AR, p. A11

CATHEY Jr., James E., Chief Executive Officer, North Oaks Medical Center, Hammond, LA, p. A180

CATLIN, Rex, Chief Executive Officer, Endless Mountain Health Systems, Montrose, PA, p. A356

CAVALLI, Paul V., M.D., President, Meadowlands Hospital Medical Center, Secaucus, NJ, p. A274

CAVES, Donald, President, Wild Rose Community Memorial Hospital, Wild Rose, WI, p. A465

CECCHETTINI, Diane
Executive Vice President, Mary Bridge Children's Hospital and Health Center, Tacoma, WA, p. A448
Executive Vice President, MultiCare Health System, Tacoma, WA, p. B118
Executive Vice President, Tacoma General Hospital, Tacoma, WA, p. A449

CECCHINI, Marina, Chief Executive Officer, Charter Indianapolis Behavioral Health System, Indianapolis, IN, p. A140

CECCONI, Thomas E., Chief Executive Officer, Doctors Hospital of Stark County, Massillon, OH, p. A326

CECERO, David M., President and Chief Executive Officer, West Suburban Hospital Medical Center, Oak Park, IL, p. A131

CENAC, Louis, M.D., Administrator, St. Helena Parish Hospital, Greensburg, LA, p. A179

CENTAFONT, Richard, Interim Chief Executive Officer, Elkins Park Hospital, Elkins Park, PA, p. A351

CERCEO, Richard, Administrator, Vencor Hospital–Chicago Central, Chicago, IL, p. A123

CERNY, Ralph J., President and Chief Executive Officer, Munson Medical Center, Traverse City, MI, p. A218

CETTI, Janet E., President and Chief Executive Officer, San Diego Hospice, San Diego, CA, p. A59

CHADDIC, Jim, Chief Executive Officer, Goodland Regional Medical Center, Goodland, KS, p. A158

CHADWICK, Elizabeth M., JD, Executive Director, Devereux Georgia Treatment Network, Kennesaw, GA, p. A106

CHAFFIN, Terry, President and Chief Executive Officer, Fawcett Memorial Hospital, Port Charlotte, FL, p. A93

CHALONER, Robert S.
President and Chief Executive Officer, St. Francis Hospital, Jersey City, NJ, p. A271
President and Chief Executive Officer, St. Mary Hospital, Hoboken, NJ, p. A270

CHAMBERS, Cory, President and Chief Executive Officer, Shady Grove Adventist Hospital, Rockville, MD, p. A196

CHAMBERS, Matthew, Chief Executive Officer, Three Rivers Area Hospital, Three Rivers, MI, p. A218

CHAMP, Raymond L., President, Wake Medical Center, Raleigh, NC, p. A310

CHANDLER, Brue, President and Chief Executive Officer, Saint Joseph's Hospital of Atlanta, Atlanta, GA, p. A100

CHANDLER, Loren F., Interim Chief Executive Officer, Scenic Mountain Medical Center, Big Spring, TX, p. A395

CHANEY, Dennis R., Administrator, Morgan County Appalachian Regional Hospital, West Liberty, KY, p. A175

CHANNING, Alan H.
Chief Executive Officer, Saint Luke's Medical Center, Cleveland, OH, p. A321
Chief Executive Officer, St. Vincent Charity Hospital, Cleveland, OH, p. A321

CHAPMAN, Alan G., Chief Executive Officer, Charter Behavioral Health System of Nevada, Las Vegas, NV, p. A263

CHAPMAN, Richard, Administrator, Trigg County Hospital, Cadiz, KY, p. A167

CHAPMAN, Robert C., FACHE, President and Chief Executive Officer, Eastern Health System, Inc., Birmingham, AL, p. B95

CHAPMAN, Stephen, Chief Executive Officer, Marlboro Park Hospital, Bennettsville, SC, p. A370

CHAPMAN, Thomas W., President and Chief Executive Officer, Children's Hospital for Sick Children, Washington, DC, p. A79

CHAPMAN III, Erie, President and Chief Executive Officer, Baptist Hospital, Nashville, TN, p. A388

CHAPP, Colleen, Interim Chief Executive Officer and Administrator, Valley County Hospital, Ord, NE, p. A261

CHAPPELOW, Michael W., President and Chief Executive Officer, Independence Regional Health Center, Independence, MO, p. A242

CHARLES, Timothy, Chief Executive Officer, Denton Community Hospital, Denton, TX, p. A402

CHARMEL, Patrick, President and Chief Executive Officer, Griffin Hospital, Derby, CT, p. A74

CHASE, Howard M., FACHE, President and Chief Executive Officer, Methodist Hospitals of Dallas, Dallas, TX, p. B117

CHASON, Robert E., Interim Director, University of California, Davis Medical Center, Sacramento, CA, p. A58

CHASTAIN, James G., Director, Mississippi State Hospital, Whitfield, MS, p. A238

CHAUDRY, Moe, Administrator, Willapa Harbor Hospital, South Bend, WA, p. A448

CHENSVOLD, Debrah, President, Palmer Lutheran Health Center, West Union, IA, p. A155

CHERAMIE, Lane M., Chief Executive Officer, Lady of the Sea General Hospital, Cut Off, LA, p. A179

CHERRY Jr., Vincent T., Administrator, Stringfellow Memorial Hospital, Anniston, AL, p. A11

CHESNUT, Arden, Administrator, J. Paul Jones Hospital, Camden, AL, p. A13

CHESTER, Sandra M., Chief Executive Officer, Whittier Hospital Medical Center, Whittier, CA, p. A67

CHEWNING III, Larry H., Chief Executive Officer, Wythe County Community Hospital, Wytheville, VA, p. A442

CHIARAMONTE, Francis P., M.D., President and Chief Executive Officer, Southern Maryland Hospital, Clinton, MD, p. A193

CHIARELLO, Michael, Administrator, St. John's Episcopal Medical Healthcare Center, Smithtown, NY, p. A298

CHICK, James R., President, Joint Township District Memorial Hospital, Saint Marys, OH, p. A329

CHILDERS Jr., Leo F., FACHE, President, Good Samaritan Regional Health Center, Mount Vernon, IL, p. A130

CHILDS, Ronald P., FACHE, Health Services Administrator, Midlands Center, Columbia, SC, p. A371

CHILL, Martha O'Regan, President and Chief Administrative Officer, Fort Sanders Loudon Medical Center, Loudon, TN, p. A386

CHILTON, Harold E., Chief Executive Officer, Twin Cities Community Hospital, Templeton, CA, p. A64

CHIOCO, John, Chief Executive Officer, Laurel Wood Center, Meridian, MS, p. A235

CHIOUTSIS, John M., Chief Executive Officer, Rosebud Health Care Center, Forsyth, MT, p. A252

CHIRCOP, Marc, Chief Executive Officer, Daviess County Hospital, Washington, IN, p. A145

CHMIEL, Katherine, MSN, Administrator and Chief Operating Officer, Taunton State Hospital, Taunton, MA, p. A204

CHODKOWSKI, Paul J., President and Chief Executive Officer, St. Clare's Hospital of Schenectady, Schenectady, NY, p. A298

CHRISTENSEN, Jay, Administrator, Pocahontas Community Hospital, Pocahontas, IA, p. A153

CHRISTIAN, James A., Director, Veterans Affairs Medical Center, Asheville, NC, p. A302

CHRISTIAN, Patricia L., Ph.D., Director, John Umstead Hospital, Butner, NC, p. A303

CHRISTIANSEN, Gary, President and Chief Executive Officer, Carondelet Health System, Saint Louis, MO, p. B71

CHRISTIANSEN, Kevin, Administrator, Vencor Hospital – Tucson, Tucson, AZ, p. A27

CHRISTIANSON, Clark P.
Senior Vice President and Administrator, Memorial Hospital–Flagler, Bunnell, FL, p. A82
Senior Vice President and Administrator, Memorial Hospital–Ormond Beach, Ormond Beach, FL, p. A92

CHRISTIANSON, Delano, Administrator, St. Michael's Hospital, Sauk Centre, MN, p. A228

CHRISTIE, Arthur P., Administrator, Houston Medical Center, Warner Robins, GA, p. A111

CHRISTISON, Earl L., Administrator, Pocatello Regional Medical Center, Pocatello, ID, p. A116

CHRISTMAN, Lyndon J., Administrator and Chief Operating Officer, Galion Community Hospital, Galion, OH, p. A324

CHRISTOPHER, William T., President and Chief Executive Officer, Lawrence & Memorial Hospital, New London, CT, p. A76

CHROMIK, James R., Regional Vice President, Administration, North Broward Medical Center, Pompano Beach, FL, p. A93

CHRZAN, Robert A., President and Chief Executive Officer, The New Children's Hospital, Baltimore, MD, p. A192

CHUBB, John M., Chief Executive Officer, Brownsville Medical Center, Brownsville, TX, p. A396

CHURCH, Daniel K., Ph.D., President and Chief Executive Officer, Edwin Shaw Hospital for Rehabilitation, Akron, OH, p. A317

CHURCH Jr., John D., Director, Veterans Affairs Medical Center, New Orleans, LA, p. A184

CHURCHILL, Timothy A., President, Stephens Memorial Hospital, Norway, ME, p. A189

CIBRAN, Bert, President and Chief Operating Officer, Ramsay Health Care, Inc., Coral Gables, FL, p. B133

CIBRONE, Connie M., President and Chief Executive Officer, Allegheny University Hospitals, Allegheny General, Pittsburgh, PA, p. A360

CIERLIK, Gregory A., President and Chief Executive Officer, Louis A. Weiss Memorial Hospital, Chicago, IL, p. A121

CIMEROLA, Joseph M., FACHE, President and Chief Executive Officer, Sacred Heart Hospital, Allentown, PA, p. A347

CINCINAT, Cathy L., Chief Executive Officer, Massillon Psychiatric Center, Massillon, OH, p. A326

CIRNE–NEVES, Ceu, Administrator, Saint James Hospital of Newark, Newark, NJ, p. A272

CITRON, Richard S.
Acting Director, Alvin C. York Veterans Affairs Medical Center, Murfreesboro, TN, p. A388
Acting Director, Veterans Affairs Medical Center, Cleveland, OH, p. A321

CLAFFEY, Patricia, Executive Director, McPherson Hospital, Howell, MI, p. A212

CLAIRMONT, Thomas, President, Lakes Region General Hospital, Laconia, NH, p. A266

CLARK, Douglas A., Executive Director, Latrobe Area Hospital, Latrobe, PA, p. A355

CLARK, Ira C., President, Jackson Memorial Hospital, Miami, FL, p. A89

CLARK, M. Victoria, Chief Executive Officer, Palo Verde Hospital, Blythe, CA, p. A38

CLARK, Melinda, President, SSM Rehab, Saint Louis, MO, p. A248

CLARK, Michael, Chief Executive Officer, Logan Memorial Hospital, Russellville, KY, p. A175

CLARK, Richard L., Administrator and Chief Executive Officer, Morristown–Hamblen Hospital, Morristown, TN, p. A388

CLARK, Robert J., FACHE, President and Chief Executive Officer, Gnaden Huetten Memorial Hospital, Lehighton, PA, p. A355

CLARK, Thom, President and Chief Executive Officer, Saints Memorial Medical Center, Lowell, MA, p. A201

CLARK, Thomas A., Chief Executive Officer, Wells Community Hospital, Bluffton, IN, p. A136

CLARK, Wayne N., President and Chief Executive Officer, Arlington Memorial Hospital, Arlington, TX, p. A393

CLARK, William S., Chief Executive Officer, Columbus County Hospital, Whiteville, NC, p. A312

CLARK, David L., USAF, Commander, U. S. Air Force Hospital Altus, Altus, OK, p. A333

CLARK, David L., Commander, U. S. Air Force Regional Hospital, Minot, ND, p. A315

CLARK Jr., Ralph H., President, Helen Keller Hospital, Sheffield, AL, p. A18

CLARKE, Richard W., Chief Executive Officer, Emanuel County Hospital, Swainsboro, GA, p. A110

CLARKE, Robert T.
President and Chief Executive Officer, Memorial Health System, Springfield, IL, p. B115
President and Chief Executive Officer, Memorial Medical Center, Springfield, IL, p. A134

CLASSEN, Howard H., Chief Executive Officer, Natividad Medical Center, Salinas, CA, p. A58

CLAYTON, Kent G.
Chief Executive Officer, Coastal Communities Hospital, Santa Ana, CA, p. A61
Chief Executive Officer, Santa Ana Hospital Medical Center, Santa Ana, CA, p. A62

CLAYTON, Philip A., President and Chief Executive Officer, Conway Hospital, Conway, SC, p. A372

CLEARWATER, William J., Vice President and Site Administrator, St. John's Pleasant Valley Hospital, Camarillo, CA, p. A38

CLEARY, John J., President and Chief Executive Officer, River Oaks Hospital, Jackson, MS, p. A234

CLEM, Olie E., Chief Executive Officer, Doctors Memorial Hospital, Tyler, TX, p. A424

CLEMENT, Mark C., President and Chief Executive Officer, Holy Cross Hospital, Chicago, IL, p. A120

CLEMENTS, Dan A., Chief Executive Officer, Hurley Health Center, Coalgate, OK, p. A334

CLEMENTS, Larry E., Administrator, Wildwood Lifestyle Center and Hospital, Wildwood, GA, p. A111

CLENDENIN, Phillip A., Chief Executive Officer, Greenview Regional Hospital, Bowling Green, KY, p. A167

CLIBORNE, James, Chief Operating Officer, Kelsey Memorial Hospital, Lakeview, MI, p. A213

CLICK, Mike, Administrator, Brownfield Regional Medical Center, Brownfield, TX, p. A396

CLINE, Phillip E., Administrator, Providence Kodiak Island Medical Center, Kodiak, AK, p. A21

CLOHAN Jr., Jack C., Administrator, William R. Sharpe Jr. Hospital, Weston, WV, p. A454

CLOUGH, James L., Administrator, Drumright Memorial Hospital, Drumright, OK, p. A334

CLOUGH, Jeanette G., President and Chief Executive Officer, Mount Auburn Hospital, Cambridge, MA, p. A199

COATES, Cliff, Chief Executive Officer, Sutter Medical Center, Santa Rosa, Santa Rosa, CA, p. A63

COATES, David M., Ph.D., President and Chief Executive Officer, Spectrum Health–Reed City Campus, Reed City, MI, p. A216

COATS, Rodney M., President and Chief Executive Officer, Washington County Memorial Hospital, Salem, IN, p. A144

COBB, Terrell M., Executive Director, Greenwood Leflore Hospital, Greenwood, MS, p. A233

COCHRAN, Barry S.
President, Cherokee Baptist Medical Center, Centre, AL, p. A13
President, DeKalb Baptist Medical Center, Fort Payne, AL, p. A14

COCHRAN, Shelley R., Interim Chief Executive Officer, Specialty Hospital of Houston, Houston, TX, p. A409

COCUZZA, Sylvester, Administrator, Richland Hospital, Mansfield, OH, p. A326

CODY, Douglas M., Administrator, Amos Cottage Rehabilitation Hospital, Winston–Salem, NC, p. A312

CODY, James P., Acting Director, Veterans Affairs Medical Center, Providence, RI, p. A369

COE, Isaac S., Interim Administrator, Iberia General Hospital and Medical Center, New Iberia, LA, p. A183

COE, William G., Executive Vice President and Chief Executive Officer, La Paz Regional Hospital, Parker, AZ, p. A24

COHEN, Bruce M., M.D., President and Psychiatrist–in–Chief, McLean Hospital, Belmont, MA, p. A197

COHEN, Elliot G., Senior Vice President, University Hospital, Cincinnati, OH, p. A320

COHEN, Jed M., Acting Executive Director, Western New York Children's Psychiatric Center, Buffalo, NY, p. A283

COHEN, Kenneth B., Director and Administrator, Riverside County Regional Medical Center, Moreno Valley, CA, p. A53

COHEN, Philip A.
Chief Executive Officer, Garfield Medical Center, Monterey Park, CA, p. A53
Interim Chief Executive Officer, Monterey Park Hospital, Monterey Park, CA, p. A53

COHEN, Steven M., M.D., Director, Veterans Affairs Medical Center, Dayton, OH, p. A323

COHOLICH, Robert J., President, Defiance Hospital, Defiance, OH, p. A323

COKER Jr., Robert J., Administrator, Greene County Hospital, Eutaw, AL, p. A14

COLBY, Dan, President and Chief Executive Officer, Harvard Memorial Hospital, Harvard, IL, p. A126

COLCHER, Marian W., President, Valley Forge Medical Center and Hospital, Norristown, PA, p. A357

COLE, Geoffrey F., President and Chief Executive Officer, Emerson Hospital, Concord, MA, p. A200

COLE, Harry, Interim Administrator, Georgiana Hospital, Georgiana, AL, p. A15

COLE, James B., President and Chief Executive Officer, Arlington Hospital, Arlington, VA, p. A433

COLE, James M., President and Chief Executive Officer, Cleo Wallace Centers Hospital, Westminster, CO, p. A73

COLECCHI, Stephen, President and Chief Executive Officer, Robinson Memorial Hospital, Ravenna, OH, p. A328

COLEMAN, Curt, Chief Executive Officer, Jackson County Public Hospital, Maquoketa, IA, p. A151

COLEMAN, Dan C., President and Chief Executive Officer, John C. Lincoln Health Network, Phoenix, AZ, p. A24

COLEMAN, James, Director, Kalamazoo Regional Psychiatric Hospital, Kalamazoo, MI, p. A213

COLEMAN, Kevin T., Administrator, Baptist Hospital–Orange, Orange, TX, p. A417

COLES, Bettie L., R.N., Senior Vice President, Kaiser Foundation Hospital, Oakland, CA, p. A54

COLFACK, Brian R., CHE, President and Chief Executive Officer, Berger Health System, Circleville, OH, p. A320

COLLER, James G., Executive Vice President and Administrator, St. Mary's Hospital Medical Center, Green Bay, WI, p. A458

COLLETTE, Dennis H., President and Chief Executive Officer, Newton Memorial Hospital, Newton, NJ, p. A272

COLLIER, C. Thomas, President and Chief Executive Officer, Sierra Nevada Memorial Hospital, Grass Valley, CA, p. A44

COLLING, Kenneth F., Senior Vice President and Area Manager, Kaiser Foundation Hospital, San Diego, CA, p. A59

COLLINS, Dale, President and Chief Executive Officer, Baptist Health System of Tennessee, Knoxville, TN, p. B64

COLLINS, James M., President and Chief Executive Officer, Suburban General Hospital, Pittsburgh, PA, p. A361

COLLINS, Jeffrey A., Chief Executive Officer, Sun Coast Hospital, Largo, FL, p. A88

COLLINS, Michael F., M.D.
President, Caritas Christi Health Care, Boston, MA, p. B71
President, St. Elizabeth's Medical Center of Boston, Brighton, MA, p. A199

COLLINS, Michael L., Chief Executive Officer, Seven Rivers Community Hospital, Crystal River, FL, p. A83

COLLINS, Roger, Chief Executive Officer and Managing Director, Valley Hospital Medical Center, Las Vegas, NV, p. A264

COLLINS, Thomas J., President and Chief Executive Officer, Memorial Health Services, Long Beach, CA, p. B114

COLLISON, Thomas R., Commanding Officer, Naval Hospital, Camp Lejeune, NC, p. A303

COLOMBO, Armando, Chief Executive Officer, HEALTHSOUTH Rehabilitation Hospital of Tallahassee, Tallahassee, FL, p. A96

COLON, Ivan E., Administrator, Auxilio Mutuo Hospital, San Juan, PR, p. A471

COLSTON, Allen J., Director, Veterans Affairs Medical Center, Muskogee, OK, p. A337

COLVERT, Charles C., President, Shelby Baptist Medical Center, Alabaster, AL, p. A11

COLVIN, Robert A., President and Chief Executive Officer, Memorial Health System, Savannah, GA, p. A109

COLWELL, Loretto Marie, President and Chief Executive Officer, St. Francis Hospital and Medical Center, Topeka, KS, p. A165

COMER, W. Jefferson, FACHE, Chief Executive Officer, Northwest Medical Center, Tucson, AZ, p. A27

COMERFORD Jr., Thomas P., Superintendent, Clarks Summit State Hospital, Clarks Summit, PA, p. A350

COMPSON, Oral R., Administrator, Dayton General Hospital, Dayton, WA, p. A444

COMSTOCK, John M., Chief Executive Officer, Sioux Valley Memorial Hospital, Cherokee, IA, p. A147

CONDOM, Jaime E., M.D., Director, South Carolina State Hospital, Columbia, SC, p. A372

CONDON, Debra, Administrator, Vencor Hospital–Philadelphia, Philadelphia, PA, p. A360

CONDRASKY, Louis M.
Chief Executive Officer, HEALTHSOUTH Lake Erie Institute of Rehabilitation, Erie, PA, p. A351
Chief Executive Officer, HEALTHSOUTH Rehabilitation Hospital of Erie, Erie, PA, p. A351

CONEJO, David, Chief Executive Officer, White County Community Hospital, Sparta, TN, p. A390

CONELL, Marge, R.N., Administrator, Ellinwood District Hospital, Ellinwood, KS, p. A157

CONGER, Rex D., President and Chief Executive Officer, Iroquois Memorial Hospital and Resident Home, Watseka, IL, p. A134

CONKLIN, Richard L., President, Parkland Health Center, Farmington, MO, p. A241

CONN, Kevin R., Administrator, HEALTHSOUTH Sunrise Rehabilitation Hospital, Fort Lauderdale, FL, p. A84

CONNELL, Daniel R., President, Christ Hospital, Jersey City, NJ, p. A271

CONNELLY, Harrell L., Chief Executive Officer, Wallace Thomson Hospital, Union, SC, p. A375

CONNELLY, Michael D., President and Chief Executive Officer, Catholic Healthcare Partners, Cincinnati, OH, p. B74

CONNORS, William G., President and Chief Executive Officer, St. James Mercy Hospital, Hornell, NY, p. A286

CONOLE, Charles P., FACHE, Administrator, Edward John Noble Hospital of Gouverneur, Gouverneur, NY, p. A285

CONSIDINE, William H., President, Children's Hospital Medical Center of Akron, Akron, OH, p. A317

CONSILVIO, Eileen, MS, Executive Director, Manhattan Psychiatric Center–Ward's Island, New York, NY, p. A291

CONSTANTINE, Richard D., Chief Executive Officer, Brownsville General Hospital, Brownsville, PA, p. A348

CONSTANTINO, Richard S., M.D., President, Rochester General Hospital, Rochester, NY, p. A297

CONTE, William A., Director, Edith Nourse Rogers Memorial Veterans Hospital, Bedford, MA, p. A197

CONTI, Vincent S., President and Chief Executive Officer, Maine Medical Center, Portland, ME, p. A189

CONWAY, Jerry, Chief Executive Officer, BHC Vista Del Mar Hospital, Ventura, CA, p. A66

CONZEMIUS, James D., President, Flagler Hospital, Saint Augustine, FL, p. A94

COOK, E. Tim, Chief Executive Officer, Osceola Regional Medical Center, Kissimmee, FL, p. A87

COOK, Jack M., President and Chief Executive Officer, Health Alliance of Greater Cincinnati, Cincinnati, OH, p. B99

COOK, Randy, Administrator, Indian Path Medical Center, Kingsport, TN, p. A385

COOK, William R., Chief Executive Officer, Specialty Hospital of Austin, Austin, TX, p. A394

COOKE, Paula Tamme, Chief Executive Officer, Central State Hospital, Louisville, KY, p. A172

COOPER, Anthony J., President and Chief Executive Officer, Arnot Ogden Medical Center, Elmira, NY, p. A285

COOPER, Chad, Administrator, Sleepy Eye Municipal Hospital, Sleepy Eye, MN, p. A228

COOPER, Donald C., Director, Veterans Affairs Central Iowa Health Care System, Des Moines, IA, p. A149

COOPER, Gerson I., President, Botsford General Hospital, Farmington Hills, MI, p. A209

COOPER, Gloria, Chief Executive Officer, Mount Carmel Hospital, Colville, WA, p. A444

COOPER, James C., Chief Operating Officer, Valley Medical Facilities, Sewickley, PA, p. A364

COOPER, Maxine T.
Chief Executive Officer, Chapman Medical Center, Orange, CA, p. A54
Chief Executive Officer, Placentia Linda Hospital, Placentia, CA, p. A56

COOPER, Paul S., Chief Executive Officer, South Jersey Health System, Bridgeton, NJ, p. B140

COOPER, Rebecca L., Interim Chief Executive Officer, Winner Regional Healthcare Center, Winner, SD, p. A380

COOPER, Robert, Chief Executive Officer, Marshalltown Medical and Surgical Center, Marshalltown, IA, p. A152

COOPER, Roger W., President, Smyth County Community Hospital, Marion, VA, p. A436

COORS, Mary Lou, Administrator, St. Joseph Rehabilitation Hospital and Outpatient Center, Albuquerque, NM, p. A277

COPE, Brent, Chief Executive Officer, Tooele Valley Regional Medical Center, Tooele, UT, p. A430

COPELAN, H. Neil, President and Chief Executive Officer, South Fulton Medical Center, East Point, GA, p. A104

COPELAND Jr., Robert Y., Chief Executive Officer, McCune–Brooks Hospital, Carthage, MO, p. A240

COPENHAVER, C. Curtis, President, Mercy Hospital, Charlotte, NC, p. A303

COPLEY, Brenda, Acting Administrator, East Texas Medical Center Rusk, Rusk, TX, p. A419

CORBEIL, Stephen, President and Chief Executive Officer, Medical City Dallas Hospital, Dallas, TX, p. A400

CORBETT, Clifford L., President and Chief Executive Officer, Morris Hospital, Morris, IL, p. A129

CORCORAN, Joseph P., President and Chief Executive Officer, New York Eye and Ear Infirmary, New York, NY, p. A292

CORDER, Thomas J., President and Chief Executive Officer, Camden–Clark Memorial Hospital, Parkersburg, WV, p. A453

CORDNER, Glenn D., Chief Executive Officer, Springfield Hospital, Springfield, VT, p. A432

CORDOVA, Richard D., Senior Vice President, Kaiser Foundation Hospital, Hayward, CA, p. A44

COREY, Jack M., President, DeKalb Memorial Hospital, Auburn, IN, p. A136

CORK, Ronald J., President and Chief Executive Officer, Avera St. Anthony's Hospital, O'Neill, NE, p. A260

CORLEY, Thomas
Chief Executive Officer, Lourdes Counseling Center, Richland, WA, p. A447
Chief Executive Officer, Lourdes Medical Center, Pasco, WA, p. A446

CORLEY, William E., President, Community Hospitals Indianapolis, Indianapolis, IN, p. A140

CORLISS, Pam
Chief Executive Officer, Atlantic Medical Center–Daytona, Daytona Beach, FL, p. A83
Chief Executive Officer, Atlantic Medical Center–Ormond, Ormond Beach, FL, p. A92

CORMIER, Richard, Ph.D., Chief Executive Officer, Conejos County Hospital, La Jara, CO, p. A71

CORNISH, Helen K., Director, Veterans Affairs Medical Center–Lexington, Lexington, KY, p. A171

CORONADO, Jose R., FACHE, Director, South Texas Veterans Health Care System, San Antonio, TX, p. A420

CORVINO, Frank A., President and Chief Executive Officer, Greenwich Hospital, Greenwich, CT, p. A74

CORY, Clarence, President, Ottumwa Regional Health Center, Ottumwa, IA, p. A153

COSTA, Mark, President, Little Company of Mary Hospital, Torrance, CA, p. A64

COSTELLO, Bud, Administrator and Chief Executive Officer, Macon Northside Hospital, Macon, GA, p. A107

COTNER, Edna J., Administrator, Coquille Valley Hospital, Coquille, OR, p. A342

COUCH, Ken, President, Summit Hospital Corporation, Atlanta, GA, p. B142

COUGHLIN, Jean, President and Chief Executive Officer, Marian Community Hospital, Carbondale, PA, p. A349

COURAGE Jr., Kenneth F., Chief Executive Officer, Psychiatric Institute of Washington, Washington, DC, p. A79

COURTNEY, Curtis B., Chief Executive Officer, Meadowview Regional Medical Center, Maysville, KY, p. A173

COURTNEY, James P., President and Chief Executive Officer, University Medical Center, Lubbock, TX, p. A413

COUSER, David G., FACHE, Administrator, Audubon County Memorial Hospital, Audubon, IA, p. A146

COVA, Charles J., Executive Vice President and Chief Operating Officer, Marian Medical Center, Santa Maria, CA, p. A62

COVERT, Michael H., FACHE, President and Chief Executive Officer, Sarasota Memorial Hospital, Sarasota, FL, p. A95

COVERT, Rob, President and Chief Executive Officer, Oaklawn Hospital, Marshall, MI, p. A214

COVEY, Laird, Chief Executive Officer, Northern Cumberland Memorial Hospital, Bridgton, ME, p. A188

COVINGTON, Steven, Superintendent, Madison State Hospital, Madison, IN, p. A142

COX, Jay, President and Chief Executive Officer, Tuomey Healthcare System, Sumter, SC, p. A375

COX, Keith, CHE, Chief Executive Officer, Charter Behavioral Health System, Mobile, AL, p. A16

COX, Kevin, Administrator, Memorial Hospital of Texas County, Guymon, OK, p. A336

COX, Leigh, Chief Executive Officer, Navapache Regional Medical Center, Show Low, AZ, p. A26

COX, Otto L.
President, Mercy Medical Center, Oshkosh, WI, p. A462
President, St. Elizabeth Hospital, Appleton, WI, p. A456

COX Sr., Arthur J., Director, Florida Center for Addictions and Dual Disorders, Avon Park, FL, p. A81

COYLE, Joseph P., President and Chief Executive Officer, Southern Ocean County Hospital, Manahawkin, NJ, p. A271

COYNE, Kathryn W., Executive Director and Chief Operating Officer, Union Hospital, Union, NJ, p. A275

CRABTREE, Douglas, Chief Executive Officer, Eastern Idaho Regional Medical Center, Idaho Falls, ID, p. A115

CRAIG, Larry, Chief Executive Officer, Jane Todd Crawford Hospital, Greensburg, KY, p. A169

CRAIG, William H., President and Chief Executive Officer, Burleson St. Joseph Health Center, Caldwell, TX, p. A396

CRAIGIN, Jane, Chief Executive Officer, St. Vincent Williamsport Hospital, Williamsport, IN, p. A145

CRAMER, John S., FACHE, President and Chief Executive Officer, PinnacleHealth System, Harrisburg, PA, p. A353

CRANDALL, David, President and Chief Executive Officer, Hospital for Special Care, New Britain, CT, p. A75

CRANDELL, Kim O., Chief Executive Officer and Administrator, Boulder City Hospital, Boulder City, NV, p. A263

CRANE, Margaret W., Chief Executive Officer, Barlow Respiratory Hospital, Los Angeles, CA, p. A48

CRANSTON, Henry J., Chief Executive Officer, HEALTHSOUTH Sea Pines Rehabilitation Hospital, Melbourne, FL, p. A89

CRANTON, Nancy J., Chief Executive Officer, The Brown Schools at Shadow Mountain, Tulsa, OK, p. A341

CRAWFIS, Ewing H., President, Mary Rutan Hospital, Bellefontaine, OH, p. A318

CRAWFORD, David E., FACHE, Executive Vice President and Chief Operating Officer, Medical Center East, Birmingham, AL, p. A12

CRAWFORD, Janet McKinney, Vice President and Administrator, Carilion Saint Albans Hospital, Radford, VA, p. A439

CRAWFORD, John W., Chief Executive Officer, Wagoner Community Hospital, Wagoner, OK, p. A341

CRAWFORD, R. Vincent, Director, Royal C. Johnson Veterans Memorial Hospital, Sioux Falls, SD, p. A379

CREAMER, Donald R., President and Chief Executive Officer, Susquehanna Health System, Williamsport, PA, p. A366

CREEDEN Jr., Francis V., President and Chief Executive Officer, Providence Medical Center, Kansas City, KS, p. A160

CREELEY, Melvin R., President, East Liverpool City Hospital, East Liverpool, OH, p. A323

CRESS, Michael D., Administrator, Vencor Hospital–San Diego, San Diego, CA, p. A59

CREWS, James C., President and Chief Executive Officer, Samaritan Health System, Phoenix, AZ, p. B134

CRIPE, Kimberly C., Chief Executive Officer, Children's Hospital of Orange County, Orange, CA, p. A54

CROCKETT, Grayce M., Administrator, Presbyterian–Orthopaedic Hospital, Charlotte, NC, p. A304

CROFT, Barbara, Health Care Manager, State Penitentiary Hospital, Walla Walla, WA, p. A449

CRONBERG, Chris, Chief Executive Officer, Northern Cochise Community Hospital, Willcox, AZ, p. A27

CRONE, William G., President and Chief Executive Officer, Naples Community Hospital, Naples, FL, p. A90

CRONEN, Kathleen
Chief Executive Officer, Charter North Star Behavioral Health System, Anchorage, AK, p. A20
Chief Executive Officer, Charter North Star Behavioral Health System, Anchorage, AK, p. A20

CRONIN, John C. J., President and Chief Executive Officer, North Adams Regional Hospital, North Adams, MA, p. A203

CROOK, Robert, Administrator, North Sunflower County Hospital, Ruleville, MS, p. A237

CROOM Jr., Kennedy L., Administrator and Chief Executive Officer, Rhea Medical Center, Dayton, TN, p. A383

CROPPER, Douglas P.
Vice President and Administrator, HealthEast St. John's Hospital, Maplewood, MN, p. A225
Vice President and Administrator, HealthEast St. Joseph's Hospital, Saint Paul, MN, p. A228

CROSSETT, Joseph W., Administrator, Liberty Hospital, Liberty, MO, p. A244

CROSSIN, William J., President and Chief Executive Officer, Miner's Memorial Medical Center, Coaldale, PA, p. A350

CROUCH, Matthew, Chief Executive Officer, Charter Anchor Hospital, Atlanta, GA, p. A99

CROW, David, Chief Executive Officer, Campbell County Memorial Hospital, Gillette, WY, p. A466

CROW, Ruth Ann, Administrator, Lake Whitney Medical Center, Whitney, TX, p. A425

CROW, Tom, Administrator, Atlanta Memorial Hospital, Atlanta, TX, p. A393

CROWDER, Jerry W., President and Chief Executive Officer, Bradford Health Services, Birmingham, AL, p. B68

CROWELL, Eric, President and Chief Executive Officer, Trinity Medical Center–West Campus, Rock Island, IL, p. A132

CROWELL, Lynn, Chief Executive Officer, Arkansas Valley Regional Medical Center, La Junta, CO, p. A71

CROWLEY, Thomas, President, St. Elizabeth Hospital, Wabasha, MN, p. A229

CROWTHER, Bruce K., President and Chief Executive Officer, Northwest Community Healthcare, Arlington Heights, IL, p. A118

CRUICKSHANK, James A., Chief Executive Officer, University Hospital and Medical Center, Tamarac, FL, p. A96

CRUMPLER, Joyce, R.N., Administrator, Bowie Memorial Hospital, Bowie, TX, p. A396

CRUMPTON, Althea H., Administrator, Magee General Hospital, Magee, MS, p. A235

CUCCI, Edward A., President and Chief Executive Officer, Swedish Covenant Hospital, Chicago, IL, p. A122

CUDWORTH, Craig R., Chief Executive Officer, Eastern Oklahoma Medical Center, Poteau, OK, p. A339

CULBERSON, David, Chief Executive Officer, West Anaheim Medical Center, Anaheim, CA, p. A36

CULLEN, James J., President and Chief Executive Officer, St. Joseph Medical Center, Towson, MD, p. A196

CULLEN, Sheila M., Director, Veterans Affairs Medical Center, San Francisco, CA, p. A60

CULLEY, James R., Administrator, Valdez Community Hospital, Valdez, AK, p. A21

CULVERN, Rita, Administrator, Jefferson Hospital, Louisville, GA, p. A106

CUMMING, Irene M., Chief Executive Officer, University of Kansas Medical Center, Kansas City, KS, p. A160

CUMMINGS, Bruce D., Chief Executive Officer, Blue Hill Memorial Hospital, Blue Hill, ME, p. A187

CUPPLES, John E., Chief Executive Officer, Spaulding Rehabilitation Hospital, Boston, MA, p. A198

CURLEY, Terrence, Administrator, Saint Louise Hospital, Morgan Hill, CA, p. A53

CURRAN, Joan, Administrator, Campus Hospital of Cleveland, Cleveland, OH, p. A320

CURRIE, Pat, Chief Executive Officer, Spring Branch Medical Center, Houston, TX, p. A409

CURRIER Jr., Elwood E., CHE, Administrator, Medina Community Hospital, Hondo, TX, p. A407

CURRY, Robert H., Senior Vice President and Chief Executive Officer, Thunderbird Samaritan Medical Center, Glendale, AZ, p. A23

CURTIS, Jeff, President and Chief Executive Officer, H.S.C. Medical Center, Malvern, AR, p. A33

CUSANO, Philip D., President and Chief Executive Officer, Stamford Hospital, Stamford, CT, p. A77

CUSHING, Douglas G., Administrator, Elizabethtown Community Hospital, Elizabethtown, NY, p. A285

CUSHING, Jeff, Vice President and Site Administrator, Legacy Meridian Park Hospital, Tualatin, OR, p. A346

CUSTER–MITCHELL, Marilyn J., Administrator, West Central Community Hospital, Clinton, IN, p. A137

CUTLER, Terry, Administrator and Chief Operating Officer, East Texas Medical Center–Clarksville, Clarksville, TX, p. A397

CZIPO, Kevin F., Executive Director, Stony Lodge Hospital, Ossining, NY, p. A295

D

D'AGNES, Michael R., President and Chief Executive Officer, Bayonne Hospital, Bayonne, NJ, p. A268

D'ALBERTO, Richard E., Chief Executive Officer, J. C. Blair Memorial Hospital, Huntingdon, PA, p. A353

D'ERAMO, David, President and Chief Executive Officer, Saint Francis Hospital and Medical Center, Hartford, CT, p. A75

D'ETTORRE, Joseph A., Chief Executive Officer, Wyandot Memorial Hospital, Upper Sandusky, OH, p. A330

DAGUE, James O., President, Goshen General Hospital, Goshen, IN, p. A139

DAHILL, Kevin, President and Chief Executive Officer, United Hospital Medical Center, Port Chester, NY, p. A296

DAHLBERG, Edwin E., President, St. Luke's Regional Medical Center, Boise, ID, p. A114

DAHLBERG, Philip J., M.D., President, Lutheran Hospital–La Crosse, La Crosse, WI, p. A459

DAHLMAN, Kim, Chief Executive Officer, Wallowa Memorial Hospital, Enterprise, OR, p. A342

DAHLMAN, Sheila, Interim Administrator, Pioneer Memorial Hospital, Heppner, OR, p. A343

DAIKEN, Michael E., Administrator, DeQuincy Memorial Hospital, DeQuincy, LA, p. A179

DAILY, James L., President, Porter Hospital, Middlebury, VT, p. A431

DAL CIELO, William J., Chief Executive Officer, Alameda Hospital, Alameda, CA, p. A36

DALE, Gregory L., Chief Executive Officer, Metropolitan St. Louis Psychiatric Center, Saint Louis, MO, p. A248

DALTON, John, President and Chief Executive Officer, Deaconess–Glover Hospital Corporation, Needham, MA, p. A202

DALTON Jr., James E., President and Chief Executive Officer, Quorum Health Group/Quorum Health Resources, Inc., Brentwood, TN, p. B127

DALY, Michael J., President, Baystate Health System, Inc., Springfield, MA, p. B65

DAMON, Joan, Administrator, Methodist Health Center–Sugar Land, Sugar Land, TX, p. A422

DAMORE, Joseph F., President and Chief Executive Officer, Sparrow Health System, Lansing, MI, p. A213

DAMPIER, Bobby H., Chief Executive Officer, Regional Medical Center of Hopkins County, Madisonville, KY, p. A173

DANDRIDGE, Thomas C., President, Regional Medical Center of Orangeburg and Calhoun Counties, Orangeburg, SC, p. A374

DANIEL, Steven G., Administrator, Bob Wilson Memorial Grant County Hospital, Ulysses, KS, p. A165

DANIELS, Gary J., Ph.D., Superintendent, Parsons State Hospital and Training Center, Parsons, KS, p. A163

DANIELS, John D., President and Chief Executive Officer, St. Luke's Regional Medical Center, Sioux City, IA, p. A154

DANIELS, Richard A., President and Chief Executive Officer, McCullough–Hyde Memorial Hospital, Oxford, OH, p. A328

DANILOFF, Michael, President, Evangelical Community Hospital, Lewisburg, PA, p. A355

DANIS, Allen, Acting Administrator, Deaconess Waltham Hospital, Waltham, MA, p. A204

DANTZKER, David R., M.D., President, Long Island Jewish Medical Center, New York, NY, p. A291

DARDEN, David B., Chief Executive Officer, Raleigh General Hospital, Beckley, WV, p. A450

DARLING, Rudy, President and Chief Executive Officer, Carroll Regional Medical Center, Berryville, AR, p. A29

DARNEY, Bruce, Superintendent, Harrisburg State Hospital, Harrisburg, PA, p. A353

DASCHER Jr., Norman E., Chief Executive Officer, Memorial Hospital, Albany, NY, p. A281

DATTALO, Thomas J., Chief Executive Officer, Riveredge Hospital, Forest Park, IL, p. A125

DAUBY, Randall W., Interim Administrator, Hamilton Memorial Hospital District, McLeansboro, IL, p. A129

DAUGHERTY, Charles R., Administrator, Baptist Memorial Hospital–Forrest City, Forrest City, AR, p. A30

DAUGHERTY, Thomas E., Administrator, Mecosta County General Hospital, Big Rapids, MI, p. A207

DAUGHERTY Jr., John, Service Unit Director, U. S. Public Health Service Comprehensive Indian Health Facility, Claremore, OK, p. A334

DAVANZO, John P.
President and Chief Executive Officer, Mercy Hospital, Buffalo, NY, p. A283
President and Chief Executive Officer, Our Lady of Victory Hospital, Lackawanna, NY, p. A287

DAVE, Bhasker J., M.D., Superintendent, Mental Health Institute, Independence, IA, p. A150

DAVIDGE, Robert C., Chief Executive Officer, Our Lady of the Lake Regional Medical Center, Baton Rouge, LA, p. A178

DAVIDSON, Craig Val, CHE, Administrator, Beaver Valley Hospital, Beaver, UT, p. A427

DAVIDSON, Russell M., Superintendent, Memphis Mental Health Institute, Memphis, TN, p. A387

DAVIES, Donald T., Commander, U. S. Air Force Hospital, Vandenberg AFB, CA, p. A66

DAVIS, Aleen S., Chief Executive Officer, Charter Behavioral Health System of Atlanta at Peachford, Atlanta, GA, p. A99

DAVIS, Charles A., Administrator and Chief Executive Officer, Allen Memorial Hospital, Moab, UT, p. A428

DAVIS, David R., President and Chief Executive Officer, UPMC Lee Regional, Johnstown, PA, p. A354

DAVIS, Donald W., President, Northern Westchester Hospital Center, Mount Kisco, NY, p. A288

DAVIS, Gary, Service Unit Director, U. S. Public Health Service Indian Hospital, Parker, AZ, p. A24

DAVIS, Glen C., Administrator, Grady General Hospital, Cairo, GA, p. A102

DAVIS, Hervey, Administrator, Dr. John Warner Hospital, Clinton, IL, p. A123

DAVIS, James L., Chief Executive Officer, Lee County Community Hospital, Pennington Gap, VA, p. A438

DAVIS, John W., Administrator, Warm Springs Rehabilitation Hospital, Gonzales, TX, p. A405

DAVIS, L. Glenn, Executive Director, Central Carolina Hospital, Sanford, NC, p. A310

DAVIS, Lary, President, Sonora Community Hospital, Sonora, CA, p. A63

DAVIS, Lora, Administrator, Perry Hospital, Perry, GA, p. A108

DAVIS, Lyle E., Administrator, Cozad Community Hospital, Cozad, NE, p. A257

DAVIS, Pamela Meyer, President and Chief Executive Officer, Edward Hospital, Naperville, IL, p. A130

DAVIS, Paul, Administrator, Gove County Medical Center, Quinter, KS, p. A163

DAVIS, Peter B., President and Chief Executive Officer, St. Joseph Hospital, Nashua, NH, p. A266

DAVIS, Robert L., President and Chief Executive Officer, North Oakland Medical Centers, Pontiac, MI, p. A215

DAVIS, Rod A., President and Chief Executive Officer, St. Rose Dominican Hospital, Henderson, NV, p. A263

DAVIS, Ronald D., Chief Executive Officer, Washington County Hospital, Washington, IA, p. A154

DAVIS, Rosemari, Chief Executive Officer, Williamette Valley Medical Center, McMinnville, OR, p. A344

DAVIS, Ryland P., President, Sacred Heart Medical Center, Spokane, WA, p. A448

DAVIS Jr., Ray H., Chief Executive Officer, Calais Regional Hospital, Calais, ME, p. A188

DAWES, Christopher G., President, Lucile Salter Packard Children's Hospital at Stanford, Palo Alto, CA, p. A55

DAWES, Dennis W., President, Hendricks Community Hospital, Danville, IN, p. A137

DAWSON, George W., President, Centra Health, Inc., Lynchburg, VA, p. B76

DAWSON, Joseph M., Administrator, Blount Memorial Hospital, Maryville, TN, p. A387

DAWSON, Lynn, Chief Executive Officer, Spalding Rehabilitation Hospital, Aurora, CO, p. A68

DE BLASI, Raymond P., Chief Executive Officer, Mesquite Community Hospital, Mesquite, TX, p. A415

DE GASTA, Gary M., Center Director, Veterans Affairs Medical Center, White River Junction, VT, p. A432

DE JEAN, Julie, Administrator and Chief Executive Officer, Kansas Rehabilitation Hospital, Topeka, KS, p. A165

DE JESUS, Jorge
Executive Director, Hospital Pavia–Hato Rey, San Juan, PR, p. A471
Executive Director, Hospital Pavia–Santurce, San Juan, PR, p. A471
Executive Director, Hospital San Pablo, Bayamon, PR, p. A470

DE MELECIO, Carmen Feliciano, M.D., Secretary of Health, Puerto Rico Department of Health, San Juan, PR, p. B126

DE VOSS, Gerald, Acting Administrator, Duane L. Waters Hospital, Jackson, MI, p. A212

DEAN, Harrison M., Senior Vice President and Administrator, Baptist Memorial Medical Center, North Little Rock, AR, p. A33

DEAN, Morre, President, Walla Walla General Hospital, Walla Walla, WA, p. A449

DEAN, Rhonda, Chief Executive Officer, El Dorado Hospital, Tucson, AZ, p. A27

DEAN Jr., Douglas F., President and Chief Executive Officer, Elliot Hospital, Manchester, NH, p. A266

DEANS, Gerald E., Director, Southwestern Virginia Mental Health Institute, Marion, VA, p. A436

DEARING, Bryan K., Chief Executive Officer, Summit Medical Center, Hermitage, TN, p. A384

DEARTH, Jim, M.D., Chief Executive Officer, Children's Hospital of Alabama, Birmingham, AL, p. A12

DEBOER, Michael D.
President and Chief Executive Officer, Baptist Health, Montgomery, AL, p. B63
President and Chief Executive Officer, Baptist Medical Center, Montgomery, AL, p. A16

DEBRUCE, Lucinda, Chief Executive Officer, Charter Behavioral Health System of Little Rock, Maumelle, AR, p. A33

DECK, K. Douglas, President and Chief Executive Officer, Good Samaritan Hospital and Health Center, Dayton, OH, p. A322

DECKER, Dale A., President and Chief Executive Officer, Sierra Vista Regional Health Center, Sierra Vista, AZ, p. A26

DECKER, James Lee, President and Chief Executive Officer, Gateway Health System, Clarksville, TN, p. A382

DECKER, Michael, President and Chief Executive Officer, Divine Savior Hospital and Nursing Home, Portage, WI, p. A462

DEE, Thomas A., President and Chief Executive Officer, Benedictine Hospital, Kingston, NY, p. A287

DEEMS, Andrew W., President and Chief Executive Officer, Eisenhower Memorial Hospital and Betty Ford Center at Eisenhower, Rancho Mirage, CA, p. A56

DEEN, Robert V., Chief Executive Officer, Memorial Hospital of Center, Center, TX, p. A397

DEFAIL, Anthony J., President and Chief Executive Officer, Meadville Medical Center, Meadville, PA, p. A356

DEFAUW, Thomas David, President and Chief Executive Officer, Rockford Memorial Hospital, Rockford, IL, p. A132

DEGEORGE–SMITH, Ellen, Director, Veterans Affairs Medical Center, Augusta, GA, p. A101

DEGINA Jr., Anthony M., Chief Executive Officer, Plantation General Hospital, Plantation, FL, p. A93

DEGRAAF, Douglas P., Chief Executive Officer, Winter Park Memorial Hospital, Winter Park, FL, p. A98

DEGRANDIS, Fred M., President and Chief Executive Officer, St. John West Shore Hospital, Cleveland, OH, p. A321

DEHNE, Marvin L., Lead Administrator, Mercy Hospital, Coon Rapids, MN, p. A222

DEIGAN, Faith A., Administrator and Chief Executive Officer, HEALTHSOUTH Greater Pittsburgh Rehabilitation Hospital, Monroeville, PA, p. A356

DEIKER, Tom, Ph.D., Superintendent, Mental Health Institute, Cherokee, IA, p. A147

DEL MAURO, Ronald, President and Chief Executive Officer, Saint Barnabas Health Care System, West Orange, NJ, p. B134

DELA CRUZ, Romel, Administrator, Hale Ho'ola Hamakua, Honokaa, HI, p. A112

DELANO, Richard J., President, Albany General Hospital, Albany, OR, p. A342

DELFORGE, Gary L., Administrator, St. Mary's Hospital, Norton, VA, p. A438

DELISI III, Frank G., CHE, Chief Executive Officer and Director Operations, HEALTHSOUTH Harmarville Rehabilitation Hospital, Pittsburgh, PA, p. A361

DELISLE, Gary
Interim Chief Executive Officer, United Memorial Medical Center–Bank Street, Batavia, NY, p. A281
Interim Chief Executive Officer, United Memorial Medical Center–North Street, Batavia, NY, p. A281

DELLAPORTAS, George, M.D., Director Professional Services, Whitten Center Infirmary, Clinton, SC, p. A371

DELLAROCCO, Paul J.
President and Chief Executive Officer, Franciscan Children's Hospital and Rehabilitation Center, Boston, MA, p. A198
President and Chief Executive Officer, Jewish Memorial Hospital and Rehabilitation Center, Boston, MA, p. A198

DEMBOW, Jack H., General Director and Vice President, Belmont Center for Comprehensive Treatment, Philadelphia, PA, p. A358

DEMORALES, Jon, Executive Director, Atascadero State Hospital, Atascadero, CA, p. A37

DENARDO, John J., Director, Veterans Affairs Edward Hines, Jr. Hospital, Hines, IL, p. A127

DENEY, Robert A., Chief Executive Officer, Charter Behavioral Health System of San Diego, San Diego, CA, p. A59

DENNIS, Daniel, Administrator, Wray Community District Hospital, Wray, CO, p. A73

DENTON, Jack L., President, Eaton Rapids Community Hospital, Eaton Rapids, MI, p. A209

DENTON, Mary M., Administrator, LaSalle General Hospital, Jena, LA, p. A180

DOVER, Jerry, Chief Executive Officer, Carroll County Memorial Hospital, Carrollton, MO, p. A240

DOWD, Thomas J., President, Nathan Littauer Hospital and Nursing Home, Gloversville, NY, p. A285

DOWDELL, Thomas C., Executive Director, Memorial Hospital and Medical Center of Cumberland, Cumberland, MD, p. A193

DOWELL Jr., Floyd B., Administrator, Lincoln County Memorial Hospital, Troy, MO, p. A250

DOWLING, Mary A., Director, Veterans Affairs Medical Center, Northport, NY, p. A294

DOWN, Philip, President, Doctors Community Hospital, Lanham, MD, p. A195

DOWNEY, William B., Administrator, Lewis–Gale Medical Center, Salem, VA, p. A440

DOWNING, Samuel W., Chief Executive Officer, Salinas Valley Memorial Healthcare System, Salinas, CA, p. A58

DOWNS, Martin, Facility Director, Lincoln Developmental Center, Lincoln, IL, p. A128

DOYLE Jr., James J., President and Chief Executive Officer, Chilton Memorial Hospital, Pompton Plains, NJ, p. A274

DOZIER Jr., J. L., FACHE, Chief Executive Officer, Barnwell County Hospital, Barnwell, SC, p. A370

DOZORETS, Ronald I., M.D., Chairman, FHC Health Systems, Norfolk, VA, p. B96

DRAGOVAN, Debra M., Chief Executive Officer, Metro Health Center, Erie, PA, p. A352

DRAKE, Lawrence J., Chief Executive Officer, Chestnut Ridge Hospital, Morgantown, WV, p. A452

DREW, John A., President and Chief Executive Officer, Athens Regional Medical Center, Athens, GA, p. A99

DREW, W. David, President and Chief Executive Officer, Atchison Hospital, Atchison, KS, p. A156

DREWA, Marcus E., President and Chief Executive Officer, Methodist Medical Center, Jacksonville, FL, p. A86

DREWEL, Charles A., Director, Missouri Rehabilitation Center, Mount Vernon, MO, p. A245

DRIEWER, Robert L., Chief Executive Officer, Faith Regional Health Services, Norfolk, NE, p. A259

DRISKILL Jr., Thomas M., President and Chief Executive Officer, Hawaii Health Systems Corporation, Honolulu, HI, p. B99

DRISNER, Robert Eugene, President and Chief Executive Officer, Community Memorial Hospital, Menomonee Falls, WI, p. A460

DROBOT, Michael D., President and Chief Executive Officer, Pacific Hospital of Long Beach, Long Beach, CA, p. A47

DROP, Jeffrey S., President and Chief Executive Officer, St. Anthony Hospital, Pendleton, OR, p. A344

DROSKE, Richard S., Director, Veterans Affairs Western New York Healthcare System–Batavia Division, Batavia, NY, p. A282

DRUCK, Alison, Ed.D., Chief Executive Officer, BHC Mesilla Valley Hospital, Las Cruces, NM, p. A279

DRUCKER, Steven C., President and Chief Executive Officer, Loretto Hospital, Chicago, IL, p. A121

DRUE, Margi, Administrator, Kahi Mohala, Ewa Beach, HI, p. A112

DUARTE, Pete T., Chief Executive Officer, R. E. Thomason General Hospital, El Paso, TX, p. A403

DUBROCA, Darryl S., Chief Executive Officer and Administrator, BHC Montevista Hospital, Las Vegas, NV, p. A263

DUDLEY, James W., Director, Hunter Holmes McGuire Veterans Affairs Medical Center, Richmond, VA, p. A439

DUDLEY, Judy, Director, Central Virginia Training Center, Madison Heights, VA, p. A436

DUERR, Joe, Chief Executive Officer, Perry Memorial Hospital, Perry, OK, p. A339

DUFFIELD, Robert, Administrator, Wilson Memorial Hospital, Floresville, TX, p. A403

DUFFY, Charles, President, Decatur County Memorial Hospital, Greensburg, IN, p. A139

DUFFY, Jack, Executive Director, Conifer Park, Schenectady, NY, p. A298

DUFFY, William F., Chief Executive Officer, Cranberry Specialty Hospital of Plymouth County, Middleboro, MA, p. A202

DUGAN, Margaret R., Executive Director, Binghamton Psychiatric Center, Binghamton, NY, p. A282

DUKE, Lance B., FACHE
President and Chief Executive Officer, Phenix Regional Hospital, Phenix City, AL, p. A17
President and Chief Executive Officer, The Medical Center, Columbus, GA, p. A103

DUMPMAN, Shirley J., Superintendent, Mayview State Hospital, Bridgeville, PA, p. A348

DUNAWAY, Clay, Administrator, Walter Olin Moss Regional Medical Center, Lake Charles, LA, p. A181

DUNCAN, Gary D., President and Chief Executive Officer, Freeman Health System, Joplin, MO, p. A242

DUNCAN, H. Clark, Administrator, Arcadia Valley Hospital, Pilot Knob, MO, p. A246

DUNCAN, Neal, Executive Director, IHS of Amarillo, Amarillo, TX, p. A392

DUNHAM, David S., President, Southside Regional Medical Center, Petersburg, VA, p. A438

DUNLAP, David L., Chief Executive Officer, University Health Partners, Oklahoma City, OK, p. A338

DUNMYER, Daniel C., Chief Executive Officer, Princeton Community Hospital, Princeton, WV, p. A453

DUNN, Joseph W., Ph.D.
Chief Executive Officer, Daniel Freeman Marina Hospital, Venice, CA, p. A66
Chief Executive Officer, Daniel Freeman Memorial Hospital, Inglewood, CA, p. A45

DUNN, James, Commander, Munson Army Health Center, Fort Leavenworth, KS, p. A158

DUNN Jr., John F., Acting Director, Veterans Affairs Medical Center, Bath, NY, p. A282

DUNNE, Deborah, Administrator, Scripps Memorial Hospital East County, El Cajon, CA, p. A41

DUNNING Jr., Raymond M., Chief Executive Officer, Medical Center of Lewisville, Lewisville, TX, p. A412

DUPUIS, Burton, Administrator, Gary Memorial Hospital, Breaux Bridge, LA, p. A178

DURHAM, Jeffrey L., Chief Executive Officer, Mediplex Rehabilitation Hospital, Bowling Green, KY, p. A167

DURR, Ben M., Administrator, Uvalde County Hospital Authority, Uvalde, TX, p. A424

DURR, Judith, Interim Chief Executive Officer, Ellenville Community Hospital, Ellenville, NY, p. A285

DURRER, Christopher T., President and Chief Executive Officer, Wilson Memorial Hospital, Wilson, NC, p. A312

DUSENBERY, Jack, President, East Cooper Regional Medical Center, Mount Pleasant, SC, p. A374

DUTCHER, Phillip C.
President and Chief Executive Officer, Good Samaritan Medical Center, West Palm Beach, FL, p. A97
President and Chief Executive Officer, St. Mary's Hospital, West Palm Beach, FL, p. A97

DVORAK, Roger G., President, Lawrence Hospital, Bronxville, NY, p. A282

DWOZAN, C. Richard, President, Habersham County Medical Center, Demorest, GA, p. A104

DYAR, David C., President and Administrator, Westview Hospital, Indianapolis, IN, p. A140

DYE, Jeff, Administrator, Socorro General Hospital, Socorro, NM, p. A280

DYER, Rebecca T., Administrator, Union General Hospital, Blairsville, GA, p. A101

DYETT, Benjamin I., M.D., Director, Ossining Correctional Facilities Hospital, Ossining, NY, p. A295

DYKES, Bradford W., Chief Executive Officer, Perry County Memorial Hospital, Tell City, IN, p. A144

DYKES, C. Barry, Senior Vice President, Paoli Memorial Hospital, Paoli, PA, p. A357

DYKES Sr., Kenneth E., Administrator and Chief Executive Officer, Gulf Pines Hospital, Port Saint Joe, FL, p. A93

DYKSTERHOUSE, Trevor J., President and Chief Executive Officer, Northwest Suburban Community Hospital, Belvidere, IL, p. A119

DYKSTRA, Janet, Chief Executive Officer, Osceola Community Hospital, Sibley, IA, p. A154

E

EADS, John S., Administrator, Washington County Infirmary and Nursing Home, Chatom, AL, p. A13

EADY, Bruce, Chief Executive Officer, Columbia Regional Hospital, Columbia, MO, p. A240

EAGAR Jr., Dan M., Administrator, Bessemer Carraway Medical Center, Bessemer, AL, p. A11

EASTHAM, James E., Senior Vice President and Chief Executive Officer, Hermann Hospital, Houston, TX, p. A408

EATON, Fred R., Administrator, Bannock Regional Medical Center, Pocatello, ID, p. A116

EATON, R. Philip, M.D., Vice President Health Scences, University of New Mexico, Albuquerque, NM, p. B152

EAZELL, Dale E., Ph.D., President and Chief Executive Officer, Casa Colina Hospital for Rehabilitative Medicine, Pomona, CA, p. A56

EBAUGH, Elaine O., Chief Executive Officer, HEALTHSOUTH Rehabilitation Hospital, Largo, FL, p. A88

ECHELARD, Paul D., Administrator, Pinecrest Rehabilitation Hospital, Delray Beach, FL, p. A83

ECKENHOFF, Edward A., President and Chief Executive Officer, National Rehabilitation Hospital, Washington, DC, p. A79

ECKER, G. T. Dunlop, President and Chief Executive Officer, Loudoun Hospital Center, Leesburg, VA, p. A436

ECKERT, Mary L., President and Chief Executive Officer, Millcreek Community Hospital, Erie, PA, p. A352

ECTON, Doris, Administrator and Chief Executive Officer, Nicholas County Hospital, Carlisle, KY, p. A168

EDDLEMAN, Gwen S., R.N., Interim Chief Executive Officer, Northeast Medical Center, Bonham, TX, p. A395

EDMISSON, Jete, President and Chief Executive Officer, Illini Community Hospital, Pittsfield, IL, p. A132

EDMONDSON, James H., Chief Executive Officer and Administrator, Hillside Hospital, Pulaski, TN, p. A389

EDMUNDSON, Reed, Interim Administrator, Madison St. Joseph Health Center, Madisonville, TX, p. A414

EDWARDS, Jerry, CHE, Administrator, East Texas Medical Center–Mount Vernon, Mount Vernon, TX, p. A415

EDWARDS, John R., Administrator and Chief Executive Officer, Pacific Alliance Medical Center, Los Angeles, CA, p. A50

EDWARDS, Liston G., Director, Cherry Hospital, Goldsboro, NC, p. A306

EDWARDS, Margaret, Chief Operating Officer, Hillside Rehabilitation Hospital, Warren, OH, p. A330

EDWARDS, Mark, Chief Executive Officer, Massac Memorial Hospital, Metropolis, IL, p. A129

EDWARDS, Sal A., Chief Executive Officer, Charter Behavioral Health System–East Valley, Chandler, AZ, p. A22

EDWARDS, Samuel, Associate Administrator Hospital Services, Ventura County Medical Center, Ventura, CA, p. A66

EDWARDS, Wade H., Administrator, Genoa Community Hospital, Genoa, NE, p. A258

EDWARDS Jr., Bob S., Chief Executive Officer, Bates County Memorial Hospital, Butler, MO, p. A239

EGBERT, Jeff R., Chief Executive Officer, Yoakum Community Hospital, Yoakum, TX, p. A426

EGERER, Michelle, Chief Executive Officer, BHC Fairfax Hospital, Kirkland, WA, p. A445

EHRHARDT, Bill E., Executive Director, Bowdon Corporate Offices, Atlanta, GA, p. B68

EHRHART, Kenneth W., Superintendent, Wernersville State Hospital, Wernersville, PA, p. A365

EHRLICH, Jane, President and Chief Executive Officer, Columbia Memorial Hospital, Hudson, NY, p. A286

EICHELBERGER, Larry, Chief Executive Officer, Fillmore County Hospital, Geneva, NE, p. A257

EICHER, Kim D., President and Chief Executive Officer, Rehabilitation Hospital of Indiana, Indianapolis, IN, p. A140

EICHMAN, Cynthia, Chief Executive Officer and Administrator, Victory Medical Center, Stanley, WI, p. A464

EILERMAN, Ted, President, St. Elizabeth Medical Center, Granite City, IL, p. A126

EILERS, M. Kathleen, Administrator, Milwaukee County Mental Health Division, Milwaukee, WI, p. A461

EISENMANN, Claudia A., Director Operations, HEALTHSOUTH Rehabilitation Hospital of Fort Smith, Fort Smith, AR, p. A31

EISNER, Nina W., Chief Executive Officer, The Pavilion, Champaign, IL, p. A120

EKDAHL, Patricia, Chief Executive Officer, Norton Spring View Hospital, Lebanon, KY, p. A170

ELDER, Ronald J., President, Barberton Citizens Hospital, Barberton, OH, p. A317

ELDREDGE, Clifford M., President and Chief Executive Officer, Vail Valley Medical Center, Vail, CO, p. A73

ELEGANT, Bruce M., President and Chief Executive Officer, Oak Park Hospital, Oak Park, IL, p. A130

ELFORD, Dorothy J., Executive Director and Administrator, Vencor Hospital – Dallas, Dallas, TX, p. A401

ELHAJ, Ali A., President and Chief Exective Officer, Acadia Hospital, Bangor, ME, p. A187

ELIZABETH, M. Ann, President, Saint Francis Hospital, Poughkeepsie, NY, p. A296

ELKINS, James N., FACHE, Director, Texas Center for Infectious Disease, San Antonio, TX, p. A421

ELLERMAN, Michael P., Administrator, Washington County Hospital, Nashville, IL, p. A130

ELLIOTT, Maurice W., Chief Executive Officer, Methodist Healthcare, Memphis, TN, p. B117

ELLIS, Dan, Administrator, Horn Memorial Hospital, Ida Grove, IA, p. A150

ELLIS, Elmer G., President and Chief Executive Officer, East Texas Medical Center Regional Healthcare System, Tyler, TX, p. B94

ELLIS, Hayden, Administrator, Villa Feliciana Medical Complex, Jackson, LA, p. A180

ELLZEY, Bob, Administrator, Bellville General Hospital, Bellville, TX, p. A395

ELROD, James K., President and Chief Executive Officer, Willis–Knighton Medical Center, Shreveport, LA, p. A185

ELSOM, Donald, Operations Administrator, Providence St. Vincent Medical Center, Portland, OR, p. A345

EMGE, Joann, Chief Executive Officer, Sparta Community Hospital, Sparta, IL, p. A133

ENDERS, Robert, President, Morehead Memorial Hospital, Eden, NC, p. A305

ENDRES, Jack R., Administrator, Muenster Memorial Hospital, Muenster, TX, p. A416

ENGELKEN, Joseph T., Chief Executive Officer, Community Hospital Onaga, Onaga, KS, p. A162

ENGER, Mark M.
Senior Vice President and Administrator, Fairview Ridges Hospital, Burnsville, MN, p. A221
Senior Vice President and Administrator, Fairview Southdale Hospital, Minneapolis, MN, p. A225

ENGHOLM, Kari L., Administrator and Chief Executive Officer, Dallas County Hospital, Perry, IA, p. A153

ENGLAND, Garry L., President and Chief Executive Officer, St. Joseph Regional Medical Center of Northern Oklahoma, Ponca City, OK, p. A339

ENGLERTH, Ladonna, Administrator, East Carroll Parish Hospital, Lake Providence, LA, p. A181

ENGLES, Joel F., Chief Executive Officer, Highsmith–Rainey Memorial Hospital, Fayetteville, NC, p. A305

ENGLISH, David J., President and Chief Executive Officer, Hospice of Northern Virginia, Arlington, VA, p. A433

ENSOR, Ronald J., Chief Executive Officer, Medical Center at Terrell, Terrell, TX, p. A423

EPSTEIN, Norman B.
President, Chambersburg Hospital, Chambersburg, PA, p. A349
President, Waynesboro Hospital, Waynesboro, PA, p. A365

ERB–GUNDEL, Myrna, Administrator, Adair County Memorial Hospital, Greenfield, IA, p. A150

ERGLE Jr., F. W., Administrator, Tallahatchie General Hospital, Charleston, MS, p. A232

ERICH, Kevin R., President, Frank R. Howard Memorial Hospital, Willits, CA, p. A67

ERICKSON, Tyler A., Chief Executive Officer, Wahiawa General Hospital, Wahiawa, HI, p. A113

ERMSHAR, Edwin L., President and Chief Executive Officer, Lindsay District Hospital, Lindsay, CA, p. A46

ERNE, Michael H., President, Mercy American River/Mercy San Juan Hospital, Carmichael, CA, p. A38

ERNST, John R., Executive Director, Deborah Heart and Lung Center, Browns Mills, NJ, p. A268

ERWIN, Duane L., Chief Executive Officer, Franciscan Medical Center–Dayton Campus, Dayton, OH, p. A322

ERWINE, Terry E., Administrator, Sac–Osage Hospital, Osceola, MO, p. A246

ESCARDA, Ron, Chief Executive Officer, Charter Behavioral Health System of Milwaukee/West Allis, West Allis, WI, p. A465

ESLYN, Cole C.
Chief Executive Officer, St. David's Medical Center, Austin, TX, p. A394
Chief Executive Officer, St. David's Pavilion, Austin, TX, p. A394
Chief Executive Officer, St. David's Rehabilitation Center, Austin, TX, p. A394

ESPELAND, David, Chief Executive Officer, Fallon Medical Complex, Baker, MT, p. A251

ESPINOSA, Maritza, Chief Executive Officer, San Juan City Hospital, San Juan, PR, p. A472

ESTEP, Barbara, Administrator, Long Term Care Hospital at Jackson, Montgomery, AL, p. A17

ETHEREDGE, H. Rex, President and Chief Executive Officer, Memorial Hospital of Jacksonville, Jacksonville, FL, p. A86

ETTER, Carl
Chief Executive Officer, Riley Memorial Hospital, Meridian, MS, p. A235
Executive Director, Women's Hospital at River Oaks, Jackson, MS, p. A234

ETTLINGER, Roy A.
Chief Executive Officer, Arbour H. R. I. Hospital, Brookline, MA, p. A199
Chief Executive Officer, Arbour Hospital, Boston, MA, p. A197

EUSTIS, Mark A., President, Missouri Baptist Medical Center, Town and Country, MO, p. A249

EVANS, Donald D., President and Chief Executive Officer, Clarion Hospital, Clarion, PA, p. A349

EVANS, Kelley, Administrator, Beartooth Hospital and Health Center, Red Lodge, MT, p. A254

EVANS, Michael J., Chief Executive Officer, Highlands Hospital, Connellsville, PA, p. A350

EVANS, Robert B., Administrator and Chief Executive Officer, East Texas Medical Center Tyler, Tyler, TX, p. A424

EVANS Jr., John T., President and Chief Executive Officer, Central Washington Hospital, Wenatchee, WA, p. A449

EVERETT, Benjamin, Chief Executive Officer, Doctors Hospital of Laredo, Laredo, TX, p. A412

EVERTS, Randall M., Chief Executive Officer, Rio Grande Regional Hospital, McAllen, TX, p. A414

EWELL, Bobby E., Executive Director, Professional Rehabilitation Hospital, Ferriday, LA, p. A179

EZZELL, Robert, Administrator, Hemphill County Hospital, Canadian, TX, p. A397

F

FAAS, Michael D., President and Chief Executive Officer, Metropolitan Hospital, Grand Rapids, MI, p. A210

FAGAN–COOK, Ann, Administrator, Schleicher County Medical Center, Eldorado, TX, p. A403

FAGERSTROM, Charles, Vice President, Norton Sound Regional Hospital, Nome, AK, p. A21

FAHD II, Charles F., Chief Executive Officer, Massena Memorial Hospital, Massena, NY, p. A288

FAHEY, Stephen P., Administrator, Charter Westbrook Behavioral Health System, Richmond, VA, p. A439

FAHRENBACHER, Fritz, President and Chief Executive Officer, Lee Memorial Hospital, Dowagiac, MI, p. A209

FAILE, Gene, Chief Executive Officer, Glades General Hospital, Belle Glade, FL, p. A81

FAILING, Ann C., President, Church Hospital Corporation, Baltimore, MD, p. A191

FAILING, Richard J., Chief Executive Officer, Kittson Memorial Healthcare Center, Hallock, MN, p. A223

FAIRCHILD, Wayne, Chief Executive Officer, Kahuku Hospital, Kahuku, HI, p. A113

FAIRMAN, John A., Executive Director, District of Columbia General Hospital, Washington, DC, p. A79

FAJA, Garry C.
President and Chief Executive Officer, Saint Joseph Mercy Health System, Ann Arbor, MI, p. A206
President and Chief Executive Officer, Saline Community Hospital, Saline, MI, p. A217

FAJT, John D., Executive Director, Putnam County Hospital, Greencastle, IN, p. A139

FALAST, Earl F., Medical Center Director, Veterans Affairs Medical Center, Marion, IL, p. A128

FALATKO, Michael J., President and Chief Executive Officer, Doctors Hospital of Jackson, Jackson, MI, p. A212

FALE, Randall J., FACHE, President and Chief Executive Officer, St. Joseph's Regional Health Center, Hot Springs, AR, p. A31

FALE, Robert A., President, Agnesian HealthCare, Fond Du Lac, WI, p. A458

FALLAT, Andrew, FACHE, Chief Executive Officer, Evergreen Community Health Center, Kirkland, WA, p. A445

FALLER, Barbara, Administrator, Chowchilla District Memorial Hospital, Chowchilla, CA, p. A39

FAMA, Cheryl A., Administrator, Vice President and Chief Operating Officer, Saint Francis Memorial Hospital, San Francisco, CA, p. A60

FANNING Jr., Robert R., Chief Executive Officer, Beverly Hospital, Beverly, MA, p. A197

FANTASIA, Saverio C., Chief Financial Officer, St. Elizabeths Hospital, Washington, DC, p. A80

FARBER, Nancy D., Chief Executive Officer, Washington Township Health Care District, Fremont, CA, p. A42

FARETRA, Gloria, M.D., Executive Director, Queens Children's Psychiatric Center, New York, NY, p. A293

FARMER, Mark R., Vice President and Administrator, Presbyterian Hospital–Matthews, Matthews, NC, p. A308

FARMER Jr., Kenneth L., Commander, Darnall Army Community Hospital, Fort Hood, TX, p. A403

FARNELL, Leland E., President, Johnston Memorial Hospital, Smithfield, NC, p. A311

FARNSWORTH, Edward F., President, Capital Region Medical Center, Jefferson City, MO, p. A242

FARR, George D., President and Chief Executive Officer, Children's Medical Center of Dallas, Dallas, TX, p. A400

FARRAND, Cynthia B., Executive Vice President and Administrator, Mary Immaculate Hospital, Newport News, VA, p. A437

FARRELL, Michael J., Chief Executive Officer, Somerset Hospital Center for Health, Somerset, PA, p. A364

FARRELL, Patrick W., Chief Executive Officer, Henrico Doctors' Hospital, Richmond, VA, p. A439

FARRIS, James R., CHE, Chief Executive Officer, Wabash General Hospital District, Mount Carmel, IL, p. A130

FARROW, Randall A., Administrator, Mille Lacs Health System, Onamia, MN, p. A226

FARROW, Shelby, Administrator, California Medical Facility, Vacaville, CA, p. A65

FAUCHER, Diane, Superintendent, Austin State Hospital, Austin, TX, p. A393

FAULK, A. Donald, FACHE, President, Medical Center of Central Georgia, Macon, GA, p. A107

FAULKNER, Charlie, President, Princeton Baptist Medical Center, Birmingham, AL, p. A12

FAULKNER, David M., Chief Executive Officer and Administrator, Central Montana Medical Center, Lewistown, MT, p. A253

FAULKNER, John M., FACHE, President and Chief Executive Officer, Patrick Community Hospital, Stuart, VA, p. A441

FAULKNER, Tom, Chief Executive Officer, Hillsboro Community Medical Center, Hillsboro, KS, p. A159

FAULWELL, James A., Administrator, Grundy County Memorial Hospital, Grundy Center, IA, p. A150

FAUS, Douglas, Administrator, Liberty County Hospital and Nursing Home, Chester, MT, p. A251

FAUST, Bill D., Administrator, Floyd County Memorial Hospital, Charles City, IA, p. A147

FAVRET, John M., Director, Eastern State Hospital, Williamsburg, VA, p. A441

FAWZY, Fawzy I., M.D., Medical Director, University of California Los Angeles Neuropsychiatric Hospital, Los Angeles, CA, p. A50

FAY, Juliette, President and Chief Executive Officer, Charles River Hospital, Wellesley, MA, p. A205

FEARS, John R., Director, Carl T. Hayden Veterans Affairs Medical Center, Phoenix, AZ, p. A24

FEAZELL, Samuel G., Chief Executive Officer, San Angelo Community Medical Center, San Angelo, TX, p. A419

FECHTEL Jr., Edward J., President and Chief Executive Officer, St. Mary's Health Care System, Athens, GA, p. A99

FEDERMAN, William, Chief Executive Officer, Northwest Surgical Hospital, Oklahoma City, OK, p. A338

FEDERSPIEL, John C., President and Chief Executive Officer, Hudson Valley Hospital Center, Cortlandt Manor, NY, p. A284

FEDYK, Mark F., Administrator, Morrison Community Hospital, Morrison, IL, p. A129

FEEHREY, Matt, Chief Executive Officer, Beech Hill Hospital, Dublin, NH, p. A265

FEELEY, William F., Director, Veterans Affairs Western New York Healthcare System–Buffalo Division, Buffalo, NY, p. A283

FEICKERT, Larry E., Chief Administrative Officer, Northwood Deaconess Health Center, Northwood, ND, p. A315

FEIKE, Jeffrey, Administrator, Churchill Community Hosptial, Fallon, NV, p. A263

FEILER, Kenneth H., President and Chief Executive Officer, Rose Medical Center, Denver, CO, p. A69

FEINBERG, E. Richard, M.D., Executive Director, Bronx Children's Psychiatric Center, New York, NY, p. A289

FEIT, Marcelina, President and Chief Executive Officer, ValleyCare Memorial Hospital, Livermore, CA, p. A46

FEIT, Marcy
Chief Executive Officer, ValleyCare Health System, Pleasanton, CA, p. B153
Chief Executive Officer, ValleyCare Medical Center, Pleasanton, CA, p. A56

FELDMAN, Mitchell S., Chief Executive Officer, Delray Medical Center, Delray Beach, FL, p. A83

FELDT, Roger D., FACHE, President and Chief Executive Officer, Saline Memorial Hospital, Benton, AR, p. A29

FELGAR, Alvin D., President and Chief Executive Officer, Frisbie Memorial Hospital, Rochester, NH, p. A267

FELICI, Brian K., Vice President and Administrator, East Ohio Regional Hospital, Martins Ferry, OH, p. A326

FELLA, Peter T., Commissioner, Doctor Robert L. Yeager Health Center, Pomona, NY, p. A296

FELTON, David, President and Chief Executive Officer, Community Memorial Hospital, Hamilton, NY, p. A286

FENCEL, Michael M., Chief Executive Officer, Brandon Regional Hospital, Brandon, FL, p. A82

FENSKE, Candace, Administrator, Madelia Community Hospital, Madelia, MN, p. A225

FENTON, John V., Chief Executive Officer, Queen of Angels–Hollywood Presbyterian Medical Center, Los Angeles, CA, p. A50

FERGUSON, John P., FACHE, President and Chief Executive Officer, Hackensack University Medical Center, Hackensack, NJ, p. A270

FERNANDEZ, Andres, Facility Services Integrator and Administrator, University Medical Center, Fresno, CA, p. A43

FERRANTE, Anthony A., M.D., President and Chief Executive Officer, Elmcrest Behavioral Health Network, Portland, CT, p. A76

FERRANTO, Carmen N., Chief Executive Officer, Warren State Hospital, North Warren, PA, p. A357

FERRELL, David A., President, Mercy Hospital, Hamilton, OH, p. A324

FERRY, John M., Executive Director, Memorial Hospital of Sweetwater County, Rock Springs, WY, p. A467

FERRY, Thomas P., Administrator and Chief Executive, Alfred I.duPont Hospital for Children, Wilmington, DE, p. A78

FERRY, William A., Administrator, Vermilion Hospital, Lafayette, LA, p. A181

FETH, Joseph S., Chief Executive Officer, Provena Health, Frankfort, IL, p. B125

FETTERS, Larry S., Administrator and Chief Operating Officer, Foothill Presbyterian Hospital–Morris L. Johnston Memorial, Glendora, CA, p. A44

FEUQUAY, Judy, Chief Executive Officer, Logan Hospital and Medical Center, Guthrie, OK, p. A336

FEURER, Russell E., Chief Executive, Good Shepherd Hospital, Barrington, IL, p. A118

FEURIG, Thomas L., President and Chief Executive Officer, St. Joseph Mercy Oakland, Pontiac, MI, p. A215

FICKEN, Robert A., Chief Executive Officer, Dallas–Fort Worth Medical Center, Grand Prairie, TX, p. A405

FICKES, Cathy, R.N., Chief Executive Officer, Mission Community Hospital–San Fernando Campus, San Fernando, CA, p. A59

FICKLEN, Susan, Administrator, George E. Weems Memorial Hospital, Apalachicola, FL, p. A81

FICKLIN, Dennis E., Chief Executive Officer, Family Health West, Fruita, CO, p. A70

FIDLER, John E., FACHE
Chief Executive Officer, Chico Community Hospital, Chico, CA, p. A39
Chief Executive Officer, Lancaster Community Hospital, Lancaster, CA, p. A46

FIDUCIA, Karen A., Interim Chief Executive Officer, Natchez Regional Medical Center, Natchez, MS, p. A236

FIELD, Carol, Senior Corporate Director and Administrator, Carondelet Holy Cross Hospital, Nogales, AZ, p. A24

FIELD, Robyn, Ph.D., Chief Operating Officer, HEALTHSOUTH Bakersfield Rehabilitation Hospital, Bakersfield, CA, p. A37

FIELDS, Donnie, Administrator, Whitesburg Appalachian Regional Hospital, Whitesburg, KY, p. A175

FIELDS, Ronald B., President, Tri–County Memorial Hospital, Whitehall, WI, p. A465

FIKE, Ruthita J.
Administrator, Littleton Adventist Hospital, Littleton, CO, p. A72
Administrator, Porter Adventist Hospital, Denver, CO, p. A69

FILLER, Scott, Administrator, HEALTHSOUTH Rehabilitation Hospital of Altoona, Altoona, PA, p. A347

FINAN, Patricia, President and Chief Executive Officer, Wyoming Valley Health Care System, Wilkes–Barre, PA, p. A366

FINAN Jr., John J., President and Chief Executive Officer, Franciscan Missionaries of Our Lady Health System, Inc., Baton Rouge, LA, p. B96

FINCH, Kenneth A., Chief Executive Officer, Metroplex Adventist Hospital, Killeen, TX, p. A411

FINCH Jr., J. W., Administrator, Elkview General Hospital, Hobart, OK, p. A336

FINE, Stuart H., Chief Executive Officer, Grand View Hospital, Sellersville, PA, p. A363

FINK, Matthew E., M.D., President and Chief Executive Officer, Beth Israel Medical Center, New York, NY, p. A289

FINKLEIN, Terry O., Chief Executive Officer, Columbia Memorial Hospital, Astoria, OR, p. A342

FINLAYSON, William C., President and Chief Exeuctive Officer, Christus Santa Rosa Health Care, San Antonio, TX, p. A419

FINLEY, Ed, Administrator, Wichita County Hospital, Leoti, KS, p. A161

FINN, Donald J., Administrator, Lake Area Hospital, Webster, SD, p. A380

FINNEGAN, Andrew J., CHE, Administrator, Brooks County Hospital, Quitman, GA, p. A108

FINUCANE, Mark, Director Health Services, Los Angeles County–Department of Health Services, Los Angeles, CA, p. B110

FINZEN, Terry S., President, Regions Hospital, Saint Paul, MN, p. A228

FIORENTINO, Leanne, Chief Executive Officer, Vencor Hospital–Greensboro, Greensboro, NC, p. A306

FIRES, Wiley M., Administrator, Shamrock General Hospital, Shamrock, TX, p. A421

FISCHER, Carl R., Associate Vice President and Chief Executive Officer, Medical College of Virginia Hospitals, Virginia Commonwealth University, Richmond, VA, p. A440

FISCHER, Michelle, Administrator, Cox Hospital South, Springfield, MO, p. A249

FISCHER, Robert W., President, Northwest Hospital Center, Randallstown, MD, p. A195

FISH, David B., Executive Vice President and Administrator, St. Joseph's Hospital, Chippewa Falls, WI, p. A457

FISH, Robert H.
President and Chief Executive Officer, North Coast Health Care Centers, Santa Rosa, CA, p. A63
President and Chief Executive Officer, Santa Rosa Memorial Hospital, Santa Rosa, CA, p. A63

FISHER, Donald Joe, Administrator, King's Daughters Hospital, Greenville, MS, p. A233

FISHER, Jan E., R.N., Executive Director, Soldiers and Sailors Memorial Hospital, Wellsboro, PA, p. A365

FISHER, Philip, President and Chief Executive Officer, Valley View Regional Hospital, Ada, OK, p. A333

FISHER, Reis, Service Unit Director, U. S. Public Health Service Blackfeet Community Hospital, Browning, MT, p. A251

FISHERO, Harvey L., President and Chief Executive Officer, Medical Center of Plano, Plano, TX, p. A418

FITCH Sr., Carl W., President and Chief Executive Officer, Wesley Medical Center, Wichita, KS, p. A166

FITZGERALD, Gerald D., President and Chief Executive Officer, Oakwood Healthcarer, Inc., Dearborn, MI, p. B122

FITZGIBBON, Susan H., President and Chief Executive Officer, Annie Penn Hospital, Reidsville, NC, p. A310

FITZPATRICK, Daniel, Chief Executive Officer, Harlan ARH Hospital, Harlan, KY, p. A170

FITZPATRICK, James G., Administrator and Chief Executive Officer, Kossuth Regional Health Center, Algona, IA, p. A146

FLAHERTY, Tom, Assistant Administrator, Los Angeles County Central Jail Hospital, Los Angeles, CA, p. A49

FLAIG, William G., Administrator, Douglas County Hospital, Alexandria, MN, p. A220

FLAKE, Glenn M., Executive Director, Newnan Hospital, Newnan, GA, p. A108

FLAMINI, Joseph, Chief Executive Officer, Rancocas Hospital, Willingboro, NJ, p. A276

FLEISCHMANN, Larry, M.D., Interim Senior Vice President, Children's Hospital of Michigan, Detroit, MI, p. A208

FLEMING, Cheryl, Chief Executive Officer, HEALTHSOUTH Rehabilitation Hospital of York, York, PA, p. A366

FLEMING, John L., M.D., Interim Chief Executive Officer, Laureate Psychiatric Clinic and Hospital, Tulsa, OK, p. A341

FLEMING, Timothy G., M.D., Chief Executive Officer, Gallup Indian Medical Center, Gallup, NM, p. A279

FLEMING, Wanda C., Administrator and Chief Executive Officer, Claiborne County Hospital, Port Gibson, MS, p. A237

FLESSNER, Arnold, Administrator, Waverly Municipal Hospital, Waverly, IA, p. A155

FLETCHALL, Terry L., Administrator, Santiam Memorial Hospital, Stayton, OR, p. A346

FLETCHER, Allen P., President and Chief Executive Officer, Northeast Alabama Regional Medical Center, Anniston, AL, p. A11

FLETCHER, Constance N., Ph.D., Director, Southern Virginia Mental Health Institute, Danville, VA, p. A434

FLETCHER, David A., President and Chief Executive Officer, Elizabeth General Medical Center, Elizabeth, NJ, p. A269

FLETCHER, Donald C.
President and Chief Executive Officer, Blue Water Health Services Corporation, Port Huron, MI, p. B67
President and Chief Executive Officer, Port Huron Hospital, Port Huron, MI, p. A216

FLORES, Saturnino Pena, Executive Director, Ryder Memorial Hospital, Humacao, PR, p. A470

FLORES Jr., Ernest, Administrator, Dimmit County Memorial Hospital, Carrizo Springs, TX, p. A397

FLORES Jr., Ernesto M., Administrator, Christus Spohn Hospital Kleberg, Kingsville, TX, p. A411

FLOTTE', J. L., Interim Chief Executive Officer and Administrator, Fayette Memorial Hospital, La Grange, TX, p. A412

FLOWERS, Randel, Ph.D., Administrator, Clinton County Hospital, Albany, KY, p. A167

FLOYD, James R., Medical Center Director, Veterans Affairs Medical Center, Salt Lake City, UT, p. A430

FLYNN, Brian T., Chief Executive Officer, Lucy Lee Hospital, Poplar Bluff, MO, p. A246

FLYNN, Patrick D., President and Chief Executive Officer, Washington Regional Medical Center, Fayetteville, AR, p. A30

FLYNN Jr., James H., President and Chief Executive Officer, Franciscan Health Partnership, Inc., Latham, NY, p. B96

FODI, Nancy C.
Executive Director, Hamlet Hospital, Hamlet, NC, p. A306
Executive Director, Upstate Carolina Medical Center, Gaffney, SC, p. A372

FOJTASEK, Georgia R., President and Chief Executive Officer, W. A. Foote Memorial Hospital, Jackson, MI, p. A212

FOLGER, Mark W., FACHE, Senior Vice President, Rogue Valley Medical Center, Medford, OR, p. A344

FOLGER, W. Neath, M.D., President and Chief Executive Officer, Immanuel St. Joseph's–Mayo Health System, Mankato, MN, p. A225

FOLLOWELL, Rob, Chief Operating Officer and Administrator, Vicksburg Medical Center, Vicksburg, MS, p. A237

FONNESBECK, Douglas R., Administrator and Chief Executive Officer, Cottonwood Hospital Medical Center, Salt Lake City, UT, p. A429

FONTENOT, Teri G., President and Chief Executive Officer, Woman's Hospital, Baton Rouge, LA, p. A178

FONTENOT, Terry J., President and Chief Executive Officer, Medical Center of Mesquite, Mesquite, TX, p. A415

FORBES, Glenn, M.D.
President and Chief Executive Officer, Franciscan Skemp Healthcare, La Crosse, WI, p. B97
President and Chief Executive Officer, Franciscan Skemp Healthcare–La Crosse Campus, La Crosse, WI, p. A459

FORD, Raymond L., President and Chief Executive Officer, Glenwood Regional Medical Center, West Monroe, LA, p. A186

FORD, W. Raymond C., Chief Executive Officer, Specialty Hospital Jacksonville, Jacksonville, FL, p. A86

FOREMAN, Robert, Associate Administrator, Brooksville Regional Hospital, Brooksville, FL, p. A82

FOREMAN, Spencer, M.D., President, Montefiore Medical Center, New York, NY, p. A291

FORESTER, John, Chief Operating Officer, HEALTHSOUTH Huntington Rehabilitation Hospital, Huntington, WV, p. A452

FORMIGONI, Ugo, Metro–West Network Manager, John J. Madden Mental Health Center, Hines, IL, p. A127

FORNOFF, Gerald A., Chief Executive Officer, Lakeside Hospital, Metairie, LA, p. A182

FOSDICK, Glenn A., President and Chief Executive Officer, Hurley Medical Center, Flint, MI, p. A210

FOSS, R. Coleman, Chief Executive Officer, Methodist Healthcare–Volunteer Hospital, Martin, TN, p. A386

FOSSUM, John, Administrator, Ely–Bloomenson Community Hospital, Ely, MN, p. A222

FOSTER, Allen, Administrator, Mizell Memorial Hospital, Opp, AL, p. A17

FOSTER, James B., Chief Executive Officer, Lake Shore Hospital, Irving, NY, p. A286

FOSTER, Jon, Executive Vice President and Administrator, Baptist Hospital of East Tennessee, Knoxville, TN, p. A385

FOSTER, Randall S., Administrator and Chief Executive Officer, LAC–King–Drew Medical Center, Los Angeles, CA, p. A49

FOSTER, James H., Commander, U. S. Air Force Hospital, Panama City, FL, p. A92

FOSTER, Robert T., Deputy Commander for Administration, Ireland Army Community Hospital, Fort Knox, KY, p. A169

FOSTER Jr., Charles L., FACHE, President and Chief Executive Officer, West Georgia Health System, La Grange, GA, p. A106

FOUGEROUSSE, Frank G., President and Chief Executive Officer, Wirth Regional Hospital, Oakland City, IN, p. A143

FOWLER, Kevin N., Chief Executive Officer, Rehabilitation Hospital of South Texas, Corpus Christi, TX, p. A399

FOWLER, Phillip E., Interim Chief Executive Officer, Pampa Regional Medical Center, Pampa, TX, p. A417

FOX, David S., President, Central DuPage Hospital, Winfield, IL, p. A135

FOX, Rosemary, Vice President and Chief Operating Officer, St. Mary's Medical Center, San Francisco, CA, p. A60

FOX, Ted, Administrator and Chief Executive Officer, El Centro Regional Medical Center, El Centro, CA, p. A41

FOX, William W., Chief Executive Officer, Mary Black Health System, Spartanburg, SC, p. A375

FOY, James, President and Chief Executive Officer, St. John's Riverside Hospital, Yonkers, NY, p. A301

FRAGALA, M. Richard, M.D., Superintendent, Clifton T. Perkins Hospital Center, Jessup, MD, p. A195

FRAIZER, Frederic L., President and Chief Executive Officer, St. Mary's Medical Center, Saginaw, MI, p. A216

FRALEY, Gary F., Administrator, Shriners Hospitals for Children, Greenville, Greenville, SC, p. A373

FRALEY, R. Reed, Associate Vice President for Health Sciences and Chief Executive Officer, Ohio State University Medical Center, Columbus, OH, p. A322

FRANCES, Richard J., M.D., President and Medical Director, Silver Hill Hospital, New Canaan, CT, p. A75

FRANCKE, Bertold, M.D., Interim Executive Director, Vermont State Hospital, Waterbury, VT, p. A432

FRANDSEN, Jeff, Chief Executive Officer, Castleview Hospital, Price, UT, p. A428

FRANK, Iris C., Administrator, Sutter Maternity and Surgery Center of Santa Cruz, Santa Cruz, CA, p. A62

FRANK, Merrill A., Chief Executive Officer, Rangely District Hospital, Rangely, CO, p. A72

FRANKENFIELD, Sheri, Chief Executive Officer, Jay County Hospital, Portland, IN, p. A143

FRANKLIN, James P., Administrator, Hillcrest Hospital, Calhoun City, MS, p. A232

FRANKLIN, Kenneth, Deputy Commander for Clinical Services, Keller Army Community Hospital, West Point, NY, p. A300

FRANZ, Charles C., Chief Executive Officer, South Peninsula Hospital, Homer, AK, p. A20

FRANZ, Paul S., President, Carolinas Medical Center, Charlotte, NC, p. A303

FRARACCIO, Robert D., Chief Executive Officer, Clark Regional Medical Center, Winchester, KY, p. A176

FRASCHETTI, Robert J., President and Chief Executive Officer, St. Jude Medical Center, Fullerton, CA, p. A43

FRASER, James, Chief Executive Officer, Davenport Medical Center, Davenport, IA, p. A148

FRASER, John Martin, President and Chief Executive Officer, Nebraska Methodist Hospital, Omaha, NE, p. A260

FRASER, Michael R., Administrator, Pacific Communities Health District, Newport, OR, p. A344

FRECH, Terrance R., Chief Executive Officer, Effingham Hospital, Springfield, GA, p. A110

FREDERIC, Donald J., Chief Executive Officer, Crossroads Community Hospital, Mount Vernon, IL, p. A130

FREEBORN, Lisa J., R.N., Administrator, Trego County–Lemke Memorial Hospital, Wakeeney, KS, p. A165

FREEBURG, Eric, Administrator, Memorial Hospital, Chester, IL, p. A120

FREELAND, Franklin, Ed.D., Chief Executive Officer, Fort Defiance Indian Health Service Hospital, Fort Defiance, AZ, p. A23

FREEMAN, Alan O., Chief Executive Officer, Cass Medical Center, Harrisonville, MO, p. A242

FREEMAN, Carol B., Chief Executive Officer, Huntington Beach Hospital, Huntington Beach, CA, p. A45

FREEMAN, Charles Ray, Administrator, Ripley County Memorial Hospital, Doniphan, MO, p. A241

FREEMAN, James M., Chief Executive Officer, Rowan Regional Medical Center, Salisbury, NC, p. A310

FREEMAN, Richard H., Chief Executive Officer, Eleanor Slater Hospital, Cranston, RI, p. A368

FREEMAN, Richard S., Chief Executive Officer, Medical College of Pennsylvania Hospital, Philadelphia, PA, p. A359

FRENCH III, George E., Chief Executive Officer, Minden Medical Center, Minden, LA, p. A182

FRENCHIE, Richard J., President and Chief Executive Officer, UHHS Geauga Regional Hospital, Chardon, OH, p. A319

FRERICHS, Jeffrey, President and Chief Executive Officer, Cabrini Medical Center, New York, NY, p. A289

FRESOLONE, Victor J., FACHE, President and Chief Executive Officer, Mercy Medical Center, Roseburg, OR, p. A345

FREY, Mark A., President and Chief Executive Officer, Alexian Brothers Behavioral Health Hospital, Hoffman Estates, IL, p. A127

FREY, Ted W., President, St. Louis Children's Hospital, Saint Louis, MO, p. A248

FREYMULLER, Robert S., Chief Executive Officer, Doctors Hospital of Dallas, Dallas, TX, p. A400

FREYSINGER, Edward E., Administrator, Oakwood Hospital–Heritage Center, Taylor, MI, p. A217

FRIED, Jeffrey M., FACHE, President and Chief Executive Officer, Beebe Medical Center, Lewes, DE, p. A78

FRIEDELL, Peter E., M.D., President, Jackson Park Hospital and Medical Center, Chicago, IL, p. A121

FRIEDLANDER, John E.
President and Chief Executive Officer, Buffalo General Hospital, Buffalo, NY, p. A283
President and Chief Executive Officer, KALEIDA Health, Buffalo, NY, p. B108

FRIEDMAN, Diane, R.N., President and Chief Executive Officer, Provena Covenant Medical Center, Urbana, IL, p. A134

FRIEDMAN, Steven H., Ph.D., Executive Vice President, Methodist Hospital of Chicago, Chicago, IL, p. A121

FRIEDRICH III, Daniel J., President and Chief Executive Officer, St. Petersburg General Hospital, Saint Petersburg, FL, p. A95

FRIES, Jack, President, St. Luke's Hospital, San Francisco, CA, p. A60

FRIESWICK, Gail, President, Falmouth Hospital, Falmouth, MA, p. A200

FRIESWICK, Gail M., Ed.D., President and Chief Executive Officer, Cape Cod Hospital, Hyannis, MA, p. A201

FRIGO, John S., President, Rush North Shore Medical Center, Skokie, IL, p. A133

FRITTS, Rosemary, Administrator, Pike County Memorial Hospital, Murfreesboro, AR, p. A33

FRITZ, Michael H., President, Carle Foundation Hospital, Urbana, IL, p. A134

FRITZ, Thomas M., Administrator, St. Lukes Rehabilitation Institute, Spokane, WA, p. A448

FROBENIUS, John, President and Chief Executive Officer, St. Cloud Hospital, Saint Cloud, MN, p. A227

FROCK, Charles T., President and Chief Executive Officer, FirstHealth Moore Regional Hospital, Pinehurst, NC, p. A309

FRONZA Jr., Leo F., President and Chief Executive Officer, Elmhurst Memorial Hospital, New York, IL, p. A124

FRY, Richard, Director, Veterans Affairs Medical Center, Cheyenne, WY, p. A466

FRY, Robert W., President, Bellin Psychiatric Center, Green Bay, WI, p. A458

FRY, Willis F., Administrator, Illinois Valley Community Hospital, Peru, IL, p. A132

FRY Jr., L. Marcus, Chief Executive Officer, Providence Memorial Hospital, El Paso, TX, p. A403

FRYE Jr., Edward R., Administrator, Clarendon Memorial Hospital, Manning, SC, p. A374

FUENTES, Miguel A., President and Chief Executive Officer, Bronx–Lebanon Hospital Center, New York, NY, p. A289

FUHRMAN, Andrew, Chief Executive Officer, BHC Fort Lauderdale Hospital, Fort Lauderdale, FL, p. A84

FULFORD, Richard C., Administrator, Gulf Breeze Hospital, Gulf Breeze, FL, p. A85

FULKS, Jerry, Chief Executive Officer, Lanier Park Hospital, Gainesville, GA, p. A105

FULL, James M., Chief Executive Officer, Randolph County Hospital and Health Services, Winchester, IN, p. A145

FULLER, David W., Chief Executive Officer, Lane Memorial Hospital, Zachary, LA, p. A186

FULLER, Thomas E., Executive Director, Marion County Medical Center, Mullins, SC, p. A374

FULTON, Matthew S.
Senior Vice President and Administrator, St. Anthony Central Hospital, Denver, CO, p. A70
Chief Executive Officer, St. Anthony North Hospital, Westminster, CO, p. A73

FULTS, Kendall R., Chief Operating Officer, Central Valley General Hospital, Hanford, CA, p. A44

FUMAI, Frank L., President and Chief Executive Officer, Cathedral Healthcare System, Inc., Newark, NJ, p. B72

FUNDINGSLAND, Donald W., Chief Executive Officer, ProHealth Care, Waukesha, WI, p. B125

FUNK, Lawrence J., Executive Administrator, Laguna Honda Hospital and Rehabilitation Center, San Francisco, CA, p. A60

FUNK, Michael J., Chief Executive Officer, North Ottawa Community Hospital, Grand Haven, MI, p. A210

FUQUA, David G., R.N., Chief Executive Officer, Marshall County Hospital, Benton, KY, p. A167

FURLONG, Marian M., R.N., Chief Executive Officer, Hudson Medical Center, Hudson, WI, p. A459

FURSTMAN, Marc A., Chief Executive Officer, Los Angeles Metropolitan Medical Center, Los Angeles, CA, p. A49

FUTRELL, Jerry H., Chief Executive Officer, Smith County Memorial Hospital, Carthage, TN, p. A381

FYBEL, Gary G., President and Chief Executive Officer, Saint Joseph Hospital, Eureka, CA, p. A42

G

GABARRO, Ralph, Chief Executive Officer, Mayo Regional Hospital, Dover–Foxcroft, ME, p. A188

GABOW, Patricia A., M.D., Chief Executive Officer and Medical Director, Denver Health Medical Center, Denver, CO, p. A69

GABRIEL, Don, Administrator, Charlotte Institute of Rehabilitation, Charlotte, NC, p. A303

GADE, Ronald, M.D.
President, St. Barnabas Hospital, New York, NY, p. A293
President, Union Hospital of the Bronx, New York, NY, p. A293

GAFFNEY, Betty, Senior Vice President and Administrator, St. Joseph Memorial Hospital, Murphysboro, IL, p. A130

GAGEN, Thomas C.
Senior Vice President, Green Hospital of Scripps Clinic, La Jolla, CA, p. A45
Senior Vice President and Regional Administrator, Scripps Memorial Hospital–La Jolla, La Jolla, CA, p. A46

GAGER, Warren E., Chief Executive Officer, William B. Kessler Memorial Hospital, Hammonton, NJ, p. A270

GAGLIARDI, Joseph A., President and Chief Executive Officer, Cancer Treatment Centers of America–Tulsa, Tulsa, OK, p. A340

GAINER, Rolf B., Chief Executive Officer and Administrator, Brookhaven Hospital, Tulsa, OK, p. A340

GAINEY, James W., R.N., Administrator, Tyler County Hospital, Woodville, TX, p. A426

GAINTNER, J. Richard, M.D., Chief Executive Officer, Shands HealthCare, Gainesville, FL, p. B135

GALARCE, Julio, Administrator, Hospital El Buen Pastor, Arecibo, PR, p. A469

GALATI, John P., President and Chief Executive Officer, Clifton Springs Hospital and Clinic, Clifton Springs, NY, p. A284

GALINSKI, Thomas P., President and Chief Executive Officer, Ohio Valley Medical Center, Wheeling, WV, p. A454

GALLACHER, Michael R., President and Chief Executive Officer, Sharon Hospital, Sharon, CT, p. A76

GALLAGHER, John S. T.
Chief Executive Officer, North Shore University Hospital, Manhasset, NY, p. A287
Chief Executive Officer, North Shore– Long Island Jewish Health System, Great Neck, NY, p. B121

GALLAGHER, T. Mark, Chief Executive Officer, Charter Brookside Behavioral Health System of New England, Nashua, NH, p. A266

GALLAGHER III, J. Frank, Administrator, Norfolk Psychiatric Center, Norfolk, VA, p. A437

GALLAGNER, James, Chief Executive Officer, Charter Behavioral Health System of New Jersey–Summit, Summit, NJ, p. A274

GALLATI, Todd, Chief Executive Officer, Lake City Medical Center, Lake City, FL, p. A87

GALLIN, John I., M.D., Director, Warren G. Magnuson Clinical Center, National Institutes of Health, Bethesda, MD, p. A193

GALLOWAY, Ron, Administrator, Reagan Memorial Hospital, Big Lake, TX, p. A395

GAMACHE, Edward L., Administrator, Deckerville Community Hospital, Deckerville, MI, p. A208

GAMBLE, Howard M., Administrator, Okanogan–Douglas County Hospital, Brewster, WA, p. A443

GAMBRELL Jr., Edward C., Administrator, Stephens County Hospital, Toccoa, GA, p. A110

GAMEL, Richard B., Chief Executive Officer, Citizens Medical Center, Colby, KS, p. A157

GAMMIERE, Thomas A., Senior Vice President and Regional Administrator, Scripps Mercy Hospital, San Diego, CA, p. A59

GAMMON, Sara, President and Chief Executive Officer, Good Shepherd Rehabilitation Hospital, Allentown, PA, p. A347

GANDY, Patrick W., Chief Executive Officer, Sabine Medical Center, Many, LA, p. A182

GANDY Jr., M. P., Chief Executive Officer, Santa Rosa Medical Center, Milton, FL, p. A90

GANN, Jim, Administrator, Roane Medical Center, Harriman, TN, p. A384

GANS, Bruce M., M.D., Senior Vice President, Rehabilitation Institute of Michigan, Detroit, MI, p. A209

GANTZ, Daniel L., President, Fayette County Hospital, Vandalia, IL, p. A134

GARBER, Jeff, Administrator and Chief Executive Officer, HEALTHSOUTH Rehabilitation Hospital of Sarasota, Sarasota, FL, p. A95

GARCIA, Louis O., President and Chief Executive Officer, Aurora Regional Medical Center, Aurora, CO, p. A68

GARCIA, Martha, Chief Executive Officer, Coral Gables Hospital, Coral Gables, FL, p. A82

GARCIA, Robert A., Administrator, Presbyterian Kaseman Hospital, Albuquerque, NM, p. A277

GARDINE, Roberta, Chief Executive Officer, St. Louis Psychiatric Rehabilitation Center, Saint Louis, MO, p. A248

GARDNER, James B., President, Huron Memorial Hospital, Bad Axe, MI, p. A206

GARDNER, Jonathan H., Chief Executive Officer, Veterans Affairs Medical Center, Tucson, AZ, p. A27

GARDNER, Paul A., CPA, Administrator, George County Hospital, Lucedale, MS, p. A235

GARDNER Jr., James E., Chief Executive Officer, Christus St. Patrick Hospital, Lake Charles, LA, p. A181

GARFUNKEL, Sanford M., Director, Veterans Affairs Medical Center, Washington, DC, p. A80

GARLEB, Pat, Administrator, Hospital of the California Institution for Men, Chino, CA, p. A39

GARMAN, G. Richard, Executive Director, Wayne Memorial Hospital, Honesdale, PA, p. A353

GARNAS, David, Administrator, Wickenburg Regional Hospital, Wickenburg, AZ, p. A27

GARNER, Douglas, Chief Executive Officer, Magnolia Regional Health Center, Corinth, MS, p. A232

GARNER, Gerald J., Chairman of the Board, Coast Plaza Doctors Hospital, Norwalk, CA, p. A54

GARRETT, Bruce, Administrator and Chief Executive Officer, Russell Regional Hospital, Russell, KS, p. A163

GARRETT, Vernon G., Chief Executive Officer, BHC Intermountain Hospital, Boise, ID, p. A114

GARRIGAN, Michael E., FACHE, President and Chief Executive Officer, St. Francis Hospital, Columbus, GA, p. A103

GARVEY, Ronald F., M.D., President, University of Texas Health Center at Tyler, Tyler, TX, p. A424

GASCHO, Dwight, President and Chief Executive Officer, Scheurer Hospital, Pigeon, MI, p. A215

GASCHO, Gale E.
Chief Executive Officer, Arroyo Grande Community Hospital, Arroyo Grande, CA, p. A36
Chief Executive Officer, French Hospital Medical Center, San Luis Obispo, CA, p. A61

GATENS Sr., Paul D., Administrator, Georgetown Memorial Hospital, Georgetown, SC, p. A373

GATES, Jon M., Chief Executive Officer, United Medical Center, Cheyenne, WY, p. A466

GATES, Monica P., FACHE, Chief Executive Officer, Slidell Memorial Hospital and Medical Center, Slidell, LA, p. A186

GATES, Truman L., President and Chief Executive Officer, Desert Regional Medical Center, Palm Springs, CA, p. A55

GATHRIGHT, Dan, Senior Vice President and Administrator, Baptist Medical Center Arkadelphia, Arkadelphia, AR, p. A29

GATMAITAN, Alfonso W., Chief Executive Officer, Tipton County Memorial Hospital, Tipton, IN, p. A145

GAUBE, Gary J., President, Landmark Medical Center, Woonsocket, RI, p. A369

GAUDREAULT, J. Ronald, President and Chief Executive Officer, Huntington Hospital, Huntington, NY, p. A286

GAUSE, Garry L., Chief Executive Officer, Lloyd Noland Hospital and Health System, Fairfield, AL, p. A14

GAUTHIER, Bonnie B., Chief Executive Officer, Hebrew Home and Hospital, West Hartford, CT, p. A77

GAVALCHIK, Stephen M., Administrator, Webster County Memorial Hospital, Webster Springs, WV, p. A454

GAVENS, Mark R., President, Sentara Norfolk General Hospital, Norfolk, VA, p. A438

GAYNOR, Stanley J., Chief Executive Officer and Administrator, Black River Memorial Hospital, Black River Falls, WI, p. A456

GEARY, George A., President, Milton Hospital, Milton, MA, p. A202

GEBHARD, Scott, Senior Vice President Operations, JFK Johnson Rehabilitation Institute, Edison, NJ, p. A269

GEE, Roland D., Chief Executive Officer, Guttenberg Municipal Hospital, Guttenberg, IA, p. A150

GEE, Thomas H., Administrator, Henry County Medical Center, Paris, TN, p. A389

GEE III, Clint, Chief Executive Officer, Kilmichael Hospital, Kilmichael, MS, p. A234

GEHANT, David P., President and Chief Executive Officer, Boulder Community Hospital, Boulder, CO, p. A68

GEIER, G. Richard, M.D., Chief Executive Officer, Olmsted Medical Center, Rochester, MN, p. A227

GEISSLER, Frederick, Chief Executive Officer, Grand View Hospital, Ironwood, MI, p. A212

GELLER, Harold S., President, Perry Memorial Hospital, Princeton, IL, p. A132

GENTILE, Larry, Chief Executive Officer, Redgate Memorial Hospital, Long Beach, CA, p. A47

GENTLING, Steven J., Director, Veterans Affairs Medical Center, Oklahoma City, OK, p. A338

GENTRY, Lee, President, Lawrence Memorial Hospital, Walnut Ridge, AR, p. A35

GENTRY, Michael V., President, Park Ridge Hospital, Fletcher, NC, p. A306

GENTRY–YOUNG, Stacey, Chief Executive Officer, Pine Grove Hospital, Los Angeles, CA, p. A50

GEORGE, Alan E., Administrator, Camden Medical Center, Saint Marys, GA, p. A109

GEORGE, Dennis L., Chief Executive Officer, Coffey County Hospital, Burlington, KS, p. A156

GEORGE, Gladys, President and Chief Executive Officer, Lenox Hill Hospital, New York, NY, p. A291

GEPFORD, Jon W., President and Chief Executive Officer, Parkview Hospital, Brunswick, ME, p. A188

GERARDO, Edward, Executive Vice President and Administrator, Bon Secours–Stuart Circle, Richmond, VA, p. A439

GERATHS, Nathan L., Director, William S. Middleton Memorial Veterans Hospital, Madison, WI, p. A460

GERBER, Carl J., Ph.D., Director, James H. Quillen Veterans Affairs Medical Center, Mountain Home, TN, p. A388

GERDES, Jerrell F., Administrator, Franklin County Memorial Hospital, Franklin, NE, p. A257

GERLACH, George, Administrator, Granite Falls Municipal Hospital and Manor, Granite Falls, MN, p. A223

GERLACH, John R., Chief Executive Officer and Administrator, DeKalb Medical Center, Decatur, GA, p. A104

GERLACH, Matthew S., Chief Executive Officer and President, Beverly Hospital, Montebello, CA, p. A52

GERLOFF, Gregory, Chief Executive Officer, Altru Health System, Grand Forks, ND, p. A314

GETTYS III, Roddey E., Executive Vice President, Palmetto Baptist Medical Center Easley, Easley, SC, p. A372

GHERARDINI, Michael M., Chief Executive Officer and Managing Director, Auburn Regional Medical Center, Auburn, WA, p. A443

GHEZZI, Lee, Administrator, Windmoor Healthcare of Miami, Miami, FL, p. A90

GHOLSTON, Linda J., Chief Executive Officer, Grenada Lake Medical Center, Grenada, MS, p. A233

GIANNUNZIO, Diane D., President, Southwest Rehabilitation Hospital, Battle Creek, MI, p. A207

GIBBONS, H. Ray, FACHE, Administrator and Senior Executive Vice President, Holy Rosary Health Center, Miles City, MT, p. A253

GIBBS, Henry T., Administrator and Chief Executive Officer, Hancock Memorial Hospital, Sparta, GA, p. A110

GIBSON, James P., Administrator, Lincoln County Medical Center, Ruidoso, NM, p. A280

GIBSON, Robert N., President and Chief Executive Officer, D. T. Watson Rehabilitation Hospital, Sewickley, PA, p. A364

GIBSON, Thomas J., Administrator, University of South Alabama Knollwood Park Hospital, Mobile, AL, p. A16

GIBSON III, Earnest, Administrator, Riverside General Hospital, Houston, TX, p. A409

GIDDINGS, Lucille C., CHE, President and Chief Executive Officer, Nantucket Cottage Hospital, Nantucket, MA, p. A202

GIERMAK, William C., President and Chief Executive Officer, Louise Obici Memorial Hospital, Suffolk, VA, p. A441

GIESECKE, Stephan A., MSC, Commander, U. S. Air Force Hospital Moody, Moody AFB, GA, p. A108

GILBERT, Albert F., Ph.D., President and Chief Executive Officer, Summa Health System, Akron, OH, p. A317

GILBERT, Andrea F., Chief Executive Officer, City Avenue Hospital, Philadelphia, PA, p. A358

GILBERT, Brian D., Chief Executive Officer, Wrangell Medical Center, Wrangell, AK, p. A21

GILBERT, George E., M.P.H., President and Chief Executive Officer, Greater Southeast Healthcare System, Washington, DC, p. B98

GILBERT, Thomas D.
President and Chief Executive Officer, Dunwoody Medical Center, Atlanta, GA, p. A100
Chief Executive Officer, Northlake Regional Medical Center, Tucker, GA, p. A111
President and Chief Executive Officer, West Paces Medical Center, Atlanta, GA, p. A100

GILBERT, William L., Chief Executive Officer, San Jose Medical Center, San Jose, CA, p. A61

GILBERTSON, Doris White, Administrator, Granite County Memorial Hospital and Nursing Home, Philipsburg, MT, p. A254

GILBERTSON, Gerry, Administrator, Fairmont Community Hospital, Fairmont, MN, p. A222

GILBERTSON, Roger, M.D., President, MeritCare Health System, Fargo, ND, p. A314

GILES, Allyson Pitman, President and Chief Executive Officer, Catholic Medical Center, Manchester, NH, p. A266

GILES, Dennis A., President, Thoms Rehabilitation Hospital, Asheville, NC, p. A302

GILLEN, Michael J., Administrator, Sterling Regional Medcenter, Sterling, CO, p. A73

GILLIARD, Ronald M., FACHE, Administrator, Mitchell County Hospital, Camilla, GA, p. A102

GILLIHAN, Kerry G., President and Chief Executive Officer, Cardinal Hill Rehabilitation Hospital, Lexington, KY, p. A171

GILLILAND, Woody, Chief Executive Officer, Abilene Regional Medical Center, Abilene, TX, p. A392

GILLS, Karl B., Administrator, North Colorado Medical Center, Greeley, CO, p. A71

GILMORE, Beverly, Chief Executive Officer, South Valley Hospital, Gilroy, CA, p. A43

GILROY, Gretchen, President and Chief Executive Officer, St. Francis Medical Center–West, Ewa Beach, HI, p. A112

GILSTRAP, M. E., President and Chief Executive Officer, Halifax Regional Medical Center, Roanoke Rapids, NC, p. A310

GINTOLI, George P., Chief Executive Officer, Northcoast Behavioral Healthcare System, Northfield, OH, p. A327

GINTZIG, Donald R., President and Chief Executive Officer, Pottsville Hospital and Warne Clinic, Pottsville, PA, p. A362

GIO, Dominick J., President and Chief Executive Officer, Wyckoff Heights Medical Center, New York, NY, p. A294

GIROTTO, R. G., Executive Vice President and Chief Operating Officer, The Methodist Hospital, Houston, TX, p. A409

GISLER, Paula, Administrator, Baptist Rehabilitation–Germantown, Germantown, TN, p. A383

GITCH, David W., President and Chief Executive Officer, Harrison Memorial Hospital, Bremerton, WA, p. A443

GIUNTO, Nancy A., FACHE, Operations Administrator, Providence Seattle Medical Center, Seattle, WA, p. A447

GLATT, Marie Damian, President, Sisters of Charity of Leavenworth Health Services Corporation, Leavenworth, KS, p. B137

GLAVIS, Edward S., Administrator, Kaiser Foundation Hospital, Fresno, CA, p. A43

GLEDHILL, John E., Administrator, Milford Valley Memorial Hospital, Milford, UT, p. A428

GLENN, Michael, Administrator, Olympic Memorial Hospital, Port Angeles, WA, p. A446

GLOOR, Michael R., FACHE, President and Chief Executive Officer, St. Francis Medical Center, Grand Island, NE, p. A258

GLOSSY, Bernard, President and Chief Executive Officer, Verdugo Hills Hospital, Glendale, CA, p. A44

GLUECKERT, John W., President, St. Joseph Hospital, Polson, MT, p. A254

GODDARD, Richard L., Chief Executive Officer, Hopkins County Memorial Hospital, Sulphur Springs, TX, p. A422

GOERING, Melvin, Chief Executive Officer, Prairie View, Newton, KS, p. A162

GOERTZEN, Irma E., President and Chief Executive Officer, Magee–Womens Hospital, Pittsburgh, PA, p. A361

GOESER, Stephen L., Administrator, Shelby County Myrtue Memorial Hospital, Harlan, IA, p. A150

GOFF, James A., FACHE, Director, Veterans Affairs Palo Alto Health Care System, Palo Alto, CA, p. A55

GOLD, Larry M., President and Chief Executive Officer, Connecticut Children's Medical Center, Hartford, CT, p. A74

GOLD, Richard, Chief Executive Officer, West Boca Medical Center, Boca Raton, FL, p. A81

GOLDBERG, Donald H., President, New England Sinai Hospital and Rehabilitation Center, Stoughton, MA, p. A204

GOLDBERG, Edward M., President and Chief Executive Officer, St. Alexius Medical Center, Hoffman Estates, IL, p. A127

GOLDEN, Carolyn P., Administrator, Shriners Hospitals for Children, St. Louis, Saint Louis, MO, p. A248

GOLDFARB, Saul, President and Chief Executive Officer, Gateways Hospital and Mental Health Center, Los Angeles, CA, p. A48

GOLDMAN, T. Marvin, Administrator, Memorial Hospital of Sheridan County, Sheridan, WY, p. A467

GOLDMAN, Thomas, President and Chief Executive Officer, Bayshore Community Hospital, Holmdel, NJ, p. A271

GOLDSMITH, Martin
President, Albert Einstein Healthcare Network, Philadelphia, PA, p. B60
President, Albert Einstein Medical Center, Philadelphia, PA, p. A358

GOLDSTEIN, Gary W., M.D., President, Kennedy Krieger Children's Hospital, Baltimore, MD, p. A192

GOLDSTEIN, Steven, Ph.D., President and Chief Executive Officer, Chestnut Lodge Hospital, Rockville, MD, p. A196

GOLDSTEIN, Steven I.
President and Chief Executive Officer, Highland Hospital of Rochester, Rochester, NY, p. A297
General Director and Chief Executive Officer, Strong Memorial Hospital of the University of Rochester, Rochester, NY, p. A297

GOLI, Rajitha, M.D., Administrator and Chief Executive Officer, Goli Medical Center, Sargent, NE, p. A261

GOLSON, Allen, Chief Executive Officer, Palmyra Medical Centers, Albany, GA, p. A99

GONZALES, Joseph P., USA, Chief of Staff, Brooke Army Medical Center, San Antonio, TX, p. A419

GONZALEZ, Arthur A., Dr.PH, President and Chief Executive Officer, Tri-City Medical Center, Oceanside, CA, p. A54

GONZALEZ, Pedro J.
Executive Director, Ashford Presbyterian Community Hospital, San Juan, PR, p. A471
Executive Director, San Carlos General Hospital, San Juan, PR, p. A472

GONZALEZ, William G.
President and Chief Executive Officer, Spectrum Health, Grand Rapids, MI, p. B141
Pres, Spectrum Health–Downtown Campus, Grand Rapids, MI, p. A211
President, Spectrum Health–East Campus, Grand Rapids, MI, p. A211

GOODE, Galen, Chief Executive Officer, Hamilton Center, Terre Haute, IN, p. A144

GOODE, Stephen M., Executive Director, Bayside Community Hospital, Anahuac, TX, p. A392

GOODLOE, Larry S., Administrator, Community Hospital Association, Fairfax, MO, p. A241

GOODMAN, Carol L., Administrator and Chief Executive Officer, Union County Hospital District, Anna, IL, p. A118

GOODMAN, Norman B., President and Chief Executive Officer, Brockton Hospital, Brockton, MA, p. A199

GOODMAN, Terry, Executive Director, Miami Jewish Home and Hospital for Aged, Miami, FL, p. A90

GOODRICH, Ralph G., Senior Executive Officer, Wright Memorial Hospital, Trenton, MO, p. A250

GOODSPEED, Ronald B., M.P.H., President, Southcoast Hospitals Group, Fall River, MA, p. A200

GOODSPEED, Scott W., President and Chief Executive Officer, Parkland Medical Center, Derry, NH, p. A265

GOODWIN, Bradford M., President and Chief Executive Officer, Sunnyview Hospital and Rehabilitation Center, Schenectady, NY, p. A298

GOODWIN, Jeffrey C., President and Chief Executive Officer, Warren Hospital, Phillipsburg, NJ, p. A273

GOODWIN, Phillip H., President and Chief Executive Officer, Camcare, Inc., Charleston, WV, p. B70

GOODWIN, Robert P., President and Chief Executive Officer, Lourdes Hospital, Paducah, KY, p. A174

GOOSMAN, Ed, Chief Executive Officer, Heartland Behavioral Health Services, Nevada, MO, p. A245

GORDON, William G., Chief Executive Officer, Barton Memorial Hospital, South Lake Tahoe, CA, p. A63

GORE, Gary R., Chief Executive Officer, Marshall Medical Center North, Guntersville, AL, p. A15

GORMAN, John A., Chief Executive Officer, Memorial Hospital, Fremont, OH, p. A324

GOSLINE, Peter L., Chief Executive Officer, Monadnock Community Hospital, Peterborough, NH, p. A267

GOSS, Allan S., Director, Veterans Affairs Medical Center, Alexandria, LA, p. A177

GOTSCHLICH, Emil, M.D., Vice President Medical Sciences, Rockefeller University Hospital, New York, NY, p. A293

GOTTSCHALK, M. Therese, President, Marian Health System, Tulsa, OK, p. B113

GOULD, Gary R., FACHE, Chief Executive Officer, Belmont Community Hospital, Bellaire, OH, p. A318

GOUX, L. Rene', Chief Executive Officer, Doctors Hospital of Jefferson, Metairie, LA, p. A182

GOUX, Rene, Chief Executive Officer, St. Charles General Hospital, New Orleans, LA, p. A184

GOVENDER, Pamela, Chief Operating Officer, Great Lakes Rehabilitation Hospital, Southfield, MI, p. A217

GOWING, Robert E.
Interim Administrator, Atmore Community Hospital, Atmore, AL, p. A11
Administrator, Jay Hospital, Jay, FL, p. A87

GRADY, Glen E., Administrator, Memorial Medical Center, Neillsville, WI, p. A461

GRADY, Phillip L., Chief Executive Officer, King's Daughters Medical Center, Brookhaven, MS, p. A231

GRAEBER, Lawrence, Administrator, Neshoba County General Hospital, Philadelphia, MS, p. A236

GRAECA, Raymond A., President and Chief Executive Officer, DuBois Regional Medical Center, Du Bois, PA, p. A351

GRAGG, Martha, Chief Executive Officer, Sullivan County Memorial Hospital, Milan, MO, p. A245

GRAGNOLATI, Brian A., President, York Hospital, York, PA, p. A367

GRAH, John, Administrator, Scripps Hospital–Chula Vista, Chula Vista, CA, p. A39

GRAHAM, George W., President, Torrance Memorial Medical Center, Torrance, CA, p. A65

GRAHAM, John A., President and Chief Executive Officer, Sherman Hospital, Elgin, IL, p. A124

GRAHAM, Kenneth D., President and Chief Executive Officer, Overlake Hospital Medical Center, Bellevue, WA, p. A443

GRAHAM, Larry M., Chief Executive Officer, Chalmette Medical Center, Chalmette, LA, p. A178

GRAHAM, Richard H., President and Chief Executive Officer, Augusta Health Care, Fishersville, VA, p. A434

GRAHAM, Richard L., Administrator, Bedford County Medical Center, Shelbyville, TN, p. A390

GRAHAM, Richard W., FACHE, President, Fairmont General Hospital, Fairmont, WV, p. A451

GRAJEWSKI, Timothy J., President and Chief Executive Officer, St. John Hospital and Medical Center, Detroit, MI, p. A209

GRAMLICH, Andrew, Chief Executive Officer, Lander Valley Medical Center, Lander, WY, p. A467

GRAND, Gary S., Chief Executive Officer, Central Louisiana State Hospital, Pineville, LA, p. A184

GRANDBOIS, Ray, M.P.H., Service Unit Director, U. S. Public Health Service Indian Hospital, Belcourt, ND, p. A313

GRANGER, Keith, President and Chief Executive Officer, Flowers Hospital, Dothan, AL, p. A13

GRAPPE, Steve, Administrator, IHS Hospital of Lubbock, Lubbock, TX, p. A413

GRAVES, Jimmy, Administrator, Walthall County General Hospital, Tylertown, MS, p. A237

GRAVES, John T., President and Chief Executive Officer, St. Joseph's Hospital, Huntingburg, IN, p. A139

GRAVES, Philip G., Administrator, Hutchinson Area Health Care, Hutchinson, MN, p. A224

GRAVES, Robert L., Administrator, Sentara Virginia Beach General Hospital, Virginia Beach, VA, p. A441

GRAY, David L., President, Hardin Memorial Hospital, Elizabethtown, KY, p. A168

GRAY, E. Kay, Interim Administrator, Vencor Hospital–Milwaukee, Milwaukee, WI, p. A461

GRAY, Jerry, Administrator, HEALTHSOUTH Rehabilitation Hospital, Memphis, TN, p. A387

GRAY, Patricia, Administrator and Chief Executive Officer, Blowing Rock Hospital, Blowing Rock, NC, p. A302

GRAY, Patrick J.
Chief Executive Officer, Cumberland River Hospital North, Celina, TN, p. A381
Chief Executive Officer, Fentress County General Hospital, Jamestown, TN, p. A384

GRAY, Penny, Administrator and Chief Executive Officer, Limestone Medical Center, Groesbeck, TX, p. A406

GRAY, Rick H., Ph.D., Chief Executive Officer, Charter Behavioral Health System, Jackson, MS, p. A234

GRAY Jr., Clinton, Administrator, Maniilaq Health Center, Kotzebue, AK, p. A21

GRAY Jr., George H., Director, Central Arkansas Veterans Affairs Healthcare System, Little Rock, AR, p. A32

GRAYBILL, Scott R., Chief Executive Officer and Administrator, Community Hospital of Bremen, Bremen, IN, p. A137

GREEN, David R., Administrator, Corcoran District Hospital, Corcoran, CA, p. A40

GREEN, Don Edd, Chief Executive Officer, Big Bend Regional Medical Center, Alpine, TX, p. A392

GREEN, Jack W., Administrator, Antelope Memorial Hospital, Neligh, NE, p. A259

GREEN, Jerry, Administrator, Tippah County Hospital, Ripley, MS, p. A237

GREEN, John H., Administrator, West Feliciana Parish Hospital, Saint Francisville, LA, p. A185

GREEN, Michael B., President and Chief Executive Officer, Concord Hospital, Concord, NH, p. A265

GREEN, Patrick, Administrator, Morgan Memorial Hospital, Madison, GA, p. A107

GREEN, Sue E., Vice President and Chief Executive Officer, Memorial Herman Behavioral Health Center, Houston, TX, p. A408

GREEN, Thomas E., President and Chief Executive Officer, Community Hospital at Dobbs Ferry, Dobbs Ferry, NY, p. A284

GREEN, Warren A., President and Chief Executive Officer, LifeBridge Health, Baltimore, MD, p. B109

GREENE, William M., FACHE, President, Santa Paula Memorial Hospital, Santa Paula, CA, p. A62

GREENE Jr., Charles H., Administrator, Cordell Memorial Hospital, Cordell, OK, p. A334

GREENE Jr., Edward C., President, Charles A. Cannon Jr, Memorial Hospital, Crossnore, NC, p. A304

GREENSPAN, Benn, President and Chief Executive Officer, Mount Sinai Hospital Medical Center of Chicago, Chicago, IL, p. A121

GREENSTEIN, Michael, Chief Executive Officer, Greystone Park Psychiatric Hospital, Greystone Park, NJ, p. A270

GREENWELL, Maryann J., Chief Executive Officer, Ridgecrest Hospital, Clayton, GA, p. A102

GREENWOOD, Kay, MS, Facility Director, North Alabama Regional Hospital, Decatur, AL, p. A13

GREER, James K., Administrator, Methodist Healthcare Middle Mississippi Hospital, Lexington, MS, p. A235

GREER, John H., President, Southside Community Hospital, Farmville, VA, p. A434

GREEVER, Paul, Chief Executive Officer, Parkside Hospital, Tulsa, OK, p. A341

GREGG, C. Jan, Chief Executive Officer, Eastern State Hospital, Medical Lake, WA, p. A445

GREGG Jr., David H., President, Gifford Medical Center, Randolph, VT, p. A431

GREGORY, Mary Jo
Chief Executive Officer, St. Luke's Medical Center, Phoenix, AZ, p. A25
Chief Executive Officer, Tempe St. Luke's Hospital, Tempe, AZ, p. A26

GREGORY, Samuel S., Administrator, Upson Regional Medical Center, Thomaston, GA, p. A110

GREGORY, William A., Chief Executive Officer, Diagnostic Center Hospital, Houston, TX, p. A407

GREGSON, C. Mark
Chief Executive Officer, Brunswick Community Hospital, Supply, NC, p. A311
Chief Executive Officer, Cape Fear Memorial Hospital, Wilmington, NC, p. A312

GRESCO, Bill, Administrator, Lea Regional Hospital, Hobbs, NM, p. A279

GREY, Bill, Administrator, Vencor Hospital–Mansfield, Mansfield, TX, p. A414

GREY, Joel E., Administrator, Sutter Auburn Faith Community Hospital, Auburn, CA, p. A37

GRIFFIN, Debra L., Administrator, Humphreys County Memorial Hospital, Belzoni, MS, p. A231

GRIFFIN, Don, Ph.D., President and Chief Executive Officer, Regional Medical Center–Bayonet Point, Hudson, FL, p. A86

GRIFFIN, Don, Chief Executive Officer, Val Verde Regional Medical Center, Del Rio, TX, p. A401

GRIFFITH, Dennis, Vice President, Decatur General Hospital–West, Decatur, AL, p. A13

GRIFFITH, Greg, Chief Executive Officer, Memorial Hospital of Adel, Adel, GA, p. A99

GRIFFITH, Richard L., President and Chief Executive Officer, Queen's Health Systems, Honolulu, HI, p. B127

GRIFFITH, Wayne B., FACHE, Chief Executive Officer, St. Joseph's Hospital of Buckhannon, Buckhannon, WV, p. A450

GRIFFITHS, Kathleen S., President and Chief Executive Officer, Chelsea Community Hospital, Chelsea, MI, p. A208

GRIMES, Jonathan D., Chief Executive Officer, Straub Clinic and Hospital, Honolulu, HI, p. A112

GRIMES, Larry, Managing Director, River Crest Hospital, San Angelo, TX, p. A419

GRIMES, Teresa F., Administrator, Jackson Medical Center, Jackson, AL, p. A15

GRIMES III, Thomas F., Executive Vice President and Chief Operating Officer, St. Elizabeth Community Hospital, Red Bluff, CA, p. A57

GRIMM, Steve, CHE, Chief Executive Officer, Summit Hospital, Baton Rouge, LA, p. A178

GRIPPEN, Glen W., Director, Clement J. Zablocki Veterans Affairs Medical Center, Milwaukee, WI, p. A460

GRISSLER, Brian G., President and Chief Executive Officer, Suburban Hospital, Bethesda, MD, p. A193

GRISWOLD, Rosanne U., President and Chief Executive Officer, Charlotte Hungerford Hospital, Torrington, CT, p. A77

GRITMAN, Paul J., Superintendent, Danville State Hospital, Danville, PA, p. A350

GRONEWALD, John E., Chief Operating Officer, Ridgeview Institute, Smyrna, GA, p. A109

GROSETH, Bradley D., Administrator, Osseo Area Hospital and Nursing Home, Osseo, WI, p. A462

GROSS, Dan, Chief Executive Officer, Sharp Memorial Hospital, San Diego, CA, p. A59

GROSS, Joseph W., President and Chief Executive Officer, St. Elizabeth Medical Center–North, Covington, KY, p. A168

GROSS, Kevin, Chief Executive Officer, Presbyterian–St. Luke's Medical Center, Denver, CO, p. A69

GROSSMEIER, John C., President and Chief Executive Officer, Hannibal Regional Hospital, Hannibal, MO, p. A242

GROTNES, Milford, Interim Administrator, Decatur County Hospital, Leon, IA, p. A151

GROVER Sr., Bradley K., FACHE, President and Chief Executive Officer, Northside Hospital and Heart Institute, Saint Petersburg, FL, p. A94

GRUBER, Norman F., President and Chief Executive Officer, Palomar Pomerado Health System, San Diego, CA, p. B123

GRUNDSTROM, David A., Administrator, New Ulm Medical Center, New Ulm, MN, p. A226

GRUSSING, Mel, Administrator, LAC–High Desert Hospital, Lancaster, CA, p. A46

GUARNIERI, Ellen, Executive Director, West Jersey Hospital–Berlin, Berlin, NJ, p. A268

GUENTHER, Charles, Administrator, Eastern Plumas District Hospital, Portola, CA, p. A56

GUERCI, Alan D., M.D., Interim President and Chief Executive Officer, St. Francis Hospital, Roslyn, NY, p. A297

GUEST, John A., President and Chief Executive Officer, University Health System, San Antonio, TX, p. A421

GUILD, Samuel T., Administrator, Pawhuska Hospital, Pawhuska, OK, p. A338

GUINN, Lex A., Chief Executive Officer, Odessa Regional Hospital, Odessa, TX, p. A416

GULARTE, Steve, Administrator, El Campo Memorial Hospital, El Campo, TX, p. A402

GULEY, Michael G., Chief Executive Officer, Bon Secours–Venice Hospital, Venice, FL, p. A97

GULICK, Margaret S., President and Chief Executive Officer, Memorial Healthcare Center, Owosso, MI, p. A215

GULLIFORD, Deryl E., Ph.D., Administrator, Community Memorial Hospital, Hicksville, OH, p. A324

GUNDERSON, Rodney L.
Chief Executive Officer, Fay–West Health System, Mount Pleasant, PA, p. B96
Chief Executive Officer, Frick Hospital, Mount Pleasant, PA, p. A356

GUNN, B. Joe, FACHE, Administrator and Chief Executive Officer, Craig General Hospital, Vinita, OK, p. A341

GUNN, Christina B., Chief Executive Officer, University of New Mexico Children's Psychiatric Hospital, Albuquerque, NM, p. A278

GUNN, John R., Executive Vice President, Memorial Hospital for Cancer and Allied Diseases, New York, NY, p. A291

GUNN, Terry J., Chief Executive Officer, River Park Hospital, McMinnville, TN, p. A387

GUPTON, Jack A., USAF, Administrator, Mike O'Callaghan Federal Hospital, Las Vegas, NV, p. A263

GURGEL, Paul E., President and Chief Executive Officer, New London Family Medical Center, New London, WI, p. A462

GUSTAFSON, Philip P., Administrator, San Ramon Regional Medical Center, San Ramon, CA, p. A61

GUTFELD, Marcia B., Vice President and Chief Operating Officer, De Graff Memorial Hospital, North Tonawanda, NY, p. A294

GUTHMILLER, Martin W., Administrator, Orange City Hospital and Clinic, Orange City, IA, p. A153

GUTHRIE, Deborah S., Chief Executive Officer, Parkway Medical Center, Lithia Springs, GA, p. A106

GUTMAN, Milton M., Chief Executive Officer, Kingsbrook Jewish Medical Center, New York, NY, p. A291

GUTZKE, Ella, Administrator, Sheridan Memorial Hospital, Plentywood, MT, p. A254

GUY, Alan C., President and Chief Executive Officer, Covenant Health, Knoxville, TN, p. B86

GUY, Douglas, President and Chief Executive Officer, Oconomowoc Memorial Hospital, Oconomowoc, WI, p. A462

GUYNN, Robert W., M.D., Executive Director, Harris County Psychiatric Center, Houston, TX, p. A408

GUZMAN, Tibisay A., Executive Vice President and Chief Operating Officer, Yonkers General Hospital, Yonkers, NY, p. A301

GWIAZDA, John M., President and Chief Executive Officer, Eastern Long Island Hospital, Greenport, NY, p. A286

GYSIN, Joyce, Administrator, Surprise Valley Community Hospital, Cedarville, CA, p. A39

H

HAAR, Clare A., Chief Executive Officer, Inter–Community Memorial Hospital, Newfane, NY, p. A294

HABERLEIN, Bernard J., Executive Director, Graydon Manor, Leesburg, VA, p. A436

HACHENBERG, Dennis A., Senior Executive Officer, Anderson County Hospital, Garnett, KS, p. A158

HACKER, Richard, Interim Administrator, Russell County Hospital, Russell Springs, KY, p. A175

HACKMAN, Ed, Administrator, Chase County Community Hospital, Imperial, NE, p. A258

HADDIX, D. Parker, Chief Executive Officer, Richwood Area Community Hospital, Richwood, WV, p. A454

HADDLE, Michael A., Chief Executive Officer and Chief Financial Officer, Burke County Hospital, Waynesboro, GA, p. A111

HADEN, James E., President and Chief Executive Officer, Martha Jefferson Hospital, Charlottesville, VA, p. A434

HAGEL, Sonja, Chief Executive Officer, Brotman Medical Center, Culver City, CA, p. A40

HAGEN, David F., President and Chief Executive Officer, Roseau Area Hospital and Homes, Roseau, MN, p. A227

HAGEN, Michael, Administrator, HEALTHSOUTH Rehabilitation Hospital of Beaumont, Beaumont, TX, p. A395

HAHN, James, Administrator, Baptist Memorial Hospital–North Mississippi, Oxford, MS, p. A236

HAILS, Robert, Chief Executive Officer, Charter Beacon, Fort Wayne, IN, p. A138

HALE, William R., Chief Executive Officer, University Medical Center, Las Vegas, NV, p. A264

HALES Jr., John C., FACHE, President and Chief Executive Officer, Roper Hospital North, Charleston, SC, p. A371

HALEY, Bob, Chief Executive Officer, Denton Regional Medical Center, Denton, TX, p. A402

HALKO, Mavis B., Administrator, Lakeshore Community Hospital, Dadeville, AL, p. A13

HALL, Amanda M., Administrator, Smith Hospital, Hahira, GA, p. A105

HALL, Cindy, Administrator, Eastern Ozarks Regional Health System, Cherokee Village, AR, p. A29

HALL, Dennis A., President, Baptist Health System, Birmingham, AL, p. B63

HALL, Herbert L., Chief Executive Officer, Wellspring Foundation, Bethlehem, CT, p. A74

HALL, Joan S., R.N., Administrator, South Lyon Medical Center, Yerington, NV, p. A264

HALL, Kenneth J., Administrator, Lincoln Hospital, Davenport, WA, p. A444

HALL, Kimbrough, Chief Executive Officer, Charter Behavioral Health System of Arizona/Desert Vista, Mesa, AZ, p. A23

HALL, Linda, Administrator, Chillicothe Hospital District, Chillicothe, TX, p. A397

HALL, Marcia K., Chief Executive Officer, Sharp Coronado Hospital, Coronado, CA, p. A40

HALL, Philo D., Interim Chief Executive Officer, Down East Community Hospital, Machias, ME, p. A189

HALL, Richard W., President, Jamestown Hospital, Jamestown, ND, p. A314

HALL, Roger L., Chief Executive Officer, North Okaloosa Medical Center, Crestview, FL, p. A83

HALL, Titus, Chief Executive Officer, Wuesthoff Hospital, Rockledge, FL, p. A94

HALL Jr., Frederic W., Administrator, Sid Peterson Memorial Hospital, Kerrville, TX, p. A411

HALLFORD, Wayne, Chief Executive Officer, BHC Millwood Hospital, Arlington, TX, p. A393

HALLGREN, Hugh R., President and Chief Executive Officer, Wadley Regional Medical Center, Texarkana, TX, p. A423

HALLMAN, Gary D., President and Chief Executive Officer, Medina General Hospital, Medina, OH, p. A327

HALLMAN, Susan, Administrator, Inner Harbour Hospitals, Douglasville, GA, p. A104

HALLONQUIST, Frances A., Chief Executive Officer, Kapiolani Medical Center for Women and Children, Honolulu, HI, p. A112

HALM, Barry J., President and Chief Executive Officer, Benedictine Health System, Duluth, MN, p. B66

HALPERN, Marsha Lommel, President and Chief Executive Officer, Madonna Rehabilitation Hospital, Lincoln, NE, p. A259

HALSETH, Michael J., President and Chief Executive Officer, Valley Health System, Winchester, VA, p. B153

HALSTEAD, Michael J., President and Chief Executive Officer, Carlisle Hospital and Health Services, Carlisle, PA, p. A349

HALTER, Michael P., Chief Executive Officer, Hahnemann University Hospital, Philadelphia, PA, p. A359

HAMILL, Dave H., President and Chief Executive Officer, Hampton Regional Medical Center, Varnville, SC, p. A375

HAMILTON, Daniel, Chief Executive Officer, Pennock Hospital, Hastings, MI, p. A211

HAMILTON, Dennis L., Chief Executive Officer, Freeport Memorial Hospital, Freeport, IL, p. A125

HAMILTON, Phil, R.N., Chief Executive Officer, General John J. Pershing Memorial Hospital, Brookfield, MO, p. A239

HAMILTON, Richard C., Administrator, Eldora Regional Medical Center, Eldora, IA, p. A149

HAMILTON, Theresa, Chief Executive Officer, Vencor Hospital–Los Angeles, Los Angeles, CA, p. A51

HAMMACK, Stanley K., Administrator, USA Children's and Women's Hospital, Mobile, AL, p. A16

HAMMER, Michael, President and Chief Executive Officer, Good Samaritan Health Center of Merrill, Merrill, WI, p. A460

HAMMER, Pat, Chief Executive Officer, Ten Broeck Hospital, Louisville, KY, p. A172

HAMMER II, Robert L., Chief Executive Officer, Davis Memorial Hospital, Elkins, WV, p. A451

HAMMETT, Warren E., Administrator, Bamberg County Memorial Hospital and Nursing Center, Bamberg, SC, p. A370

HAMMOND, Joe, Administrator, Eureka Springs Hospital, Eureka Springs, AR, p. A30

HAMMOND Jr., Robert L., Executive Director, Rankin Medical Center, Brandon, MS, p. A231

HAMNER, David, Administrator, Hardtner Medical Center, Olla, LA, p. A184

HAMRY, David K., President, Good Samaritan Community Healthcare, Puyallup, WA, p. A446

HANCOCK, Edward H., President, Nanticoke Memorial Hospital, Seaford, DE, p. A78

HANCOCK, Ron, Interim Administrator, Summersville Memorial Hospital, Summersville, WV, p. A454

HANKO, James F., President and Chief Executive Officer, North Country Regional Hospital, Bemidji, MN, p. A220

HANNAN, David T., President and Chief Executive Officer, South Shore Hospital, South Weymouth, MA, p. A204

HANNER, R. Andy, Chief Executive Officer, Charter Rivers Behavioral Health System, West Columbia, SC, p. A375

HANNIG, Virgil
Senior Vice President and Administrator, Franklin Hospital and Skilled Nursing Care Unit, Benton, IL, p. A119
Senior Vice President and Administrator, Herrin Hospital, Herrin, IL, p. A126
Senior Vice President and Administrator, United Mine Workers of America Union Hospital, West Frankfort, IL, p. A135

HANOVER, Kenneth, President and Chief Executive Officer, Bryn Mawr Hospital, Bryn Mawr, PA, p. A349

HANSEN, Edwin L., Vice President, Yukon–Kuskokwim Delta Regional Hospital, Bethel, AK, p. A20

HANSEN, Irwin C., President and Chief Executive Officer, Summit Medical Center, Oakland, CA, p. A54

HANSEN, Thomas N., M.D., Chief Executive Officer, Children's Hospital, Columbus, OH, p. A321

HANSHAW, John, Chief Executive Officer, St. Mark's Hospital, Salt Lake City, UT, p. A429

HANSON, Bryant R., President and Chief Executive Officer, Floyd Memorial Hospital and Health Services, New Albany, IN, p. A143

HANSON, Carl, Administrator, Minidoka Memorial Hospital and Extended Care Facility, Rupert, ID, p. A116

HANSON, Craig, Administrator, St. Luke Hospital, Marion, KS, p. A161

HANSON, Greg, President and Chief Executive Officer, St. Joseph's Hospital and Health Center, Dickinson, ND, p. A313

HANSON, J. Marlin, Administrator, Marshall Medical Center South, Boaz, AL, p. A12

HANSON, Paul, Chief Executive Officer, Glendive Medical Center, Glendive, MT, p. A252

HANSON, Timothy H., President and Chief Executive Officer, HealthEast, Saint Paul, MN, p. B101

HANYAK, Diana C., Chief Executive Officer, Charter Behavioral Health System of Southern California–Corona, Corona, CA, p. A40

HARBARGER, Claude W., President, St. Dominic–Jackson Memorial Hospital, Jackson, MS, p. A234

HARBIN, Henry, M.D., President and Chief Executive Officer, Magellan Health Services, Atlanta, GA, p. B111

HARCOURT Jr., John P., President and Chief Executive Officer, Healthcare America, Inc., Austin, TX, p. B100

HARDER, Shirley, Chief Executive Officer, Wayne Medical Center, Waynesboro, TN, p. A390

HARDING, John R., President and Chief Executive Officer, Florida Hospital Heartland Division, Sebring, FL, p. A95

HARDING, Lynwood F., Director, Western State Hospital, Staunton, VA, p. A441

HARDING, William W., President and Chief Executive Officer, Union Hospital, Dover, OH, p. A323

HARDY, Patsy, Administrator, Putnam General Hospital, Hurricane, WV, p. A452

HARDY, Stephen L., Ph.D., Facility Director, Chester Mental Health Center, Chester, IL, p. A120

HARE, Michael K., Administrator, De Leon Hospital, De Leon, TX, p. A401

HARGRAVE, Alfred E., Administrator, Baptist Medical Center Downtown, Montgomery, AL, p. A16

HARKINS, William D., President and Chief Executive Officer, Ancilla Systems Inc., Hobart, IN, p. B61

HARKNESS, Laurence P., President and Chief Executive Officer, Children's Medical Center, Dayton, OH, p. A322

HARLAN, Thomas M., Chief Executive Officer, Chinese Hospital, San Francisco, CA, p. A60

HARMAN, David L., Administrator, Harney District Hospital, Burns, OR, p. A342

HARMAN, Gerald M., Executive Vice President and Administrator, St. Elizabeth's Hospital, Belleville, IL, p. A118

HARMAN, Richmond M., President and Chief Executive Officer, Martin Memorial Health Systems, Stuart, FL, p. A95

HARMAN, Robert L., Administrator, Grant Memorial Hospital, Petersburg, WV, p. A453

HARMON, Ronald A., M.D., Chief Executive Officer, Albert Lea Medical Center, Albert Lea, MN, p. A220

HARMS, Charles F., Administrator, McKee Medical Center, Loveland, CO, p. A72

HARMS, Jacquelyn, Executive Director, Medical Center of Southeastern Oklahoma, Durant, OK, p. A335

HARPER, Alan G., Director, Veterans Affairs North Texas Health Care System, Dallas, TX, p. A401

HARR, Robert Glenn, President, Heather Hill Hospital and Health Care Center, Chardon, OH, p. A318

HARREL, Mark, Administrator, Fairview Hospital, Fairview, OK, p. A335

HARRELL, David E., Chief Executive Officer, Georgia Baptist Health Care System, Atlanta, GA, p. B97

HARRELL, Richard E., President and Chief Executive Officer, Duplin General Hospital, Kenansville, NC, p. A307

HARRINGTON, Frank, Administrator, Aberdeen–Monroe County Hospital, Aberdeen, MS, p. A231

HARRINGTON, Joseph P., Chief Executive Officer, Lodi Memorial Hospital, Lodi, CA, p. A47

HARRINGTON, Michael L., Chief Executive Officer, Bon Secours–St. Joseph Healthcare Group, Port Charlotte, FL, p. A93

HARRINGTON, Patricia, Administrator and Chief Operating Officer, McKay–Dee Hospital Center, Ogden, UT, p. A428

HARRINGTON, Timothy, President, Victory Memorial Hospital, Waukegan, IL, p. A135

HARRINGTON Jr., Allan, Chief Executive Officer, Tucson General Hospital, Tucson, AZ, p. A27

HARRINGTON Jr., John L., FACHE, Administrator, Vencor Hospital–Phoenix, Phoenix, AZ, p. A25

HARRINGTON Jr., Russell D., President, Baptist Health, Little Rock, AR, p. B63

HARRIS, Allyn R., Chief Executive Officer, Nashville Memorial Hospital, Madison, TN, p. A386

HARRIS, Frank W., President and Chief Executive Officer, Russell Medical Center, Alexander City, AL, p. A11

HARRIS, Jerry W., Interim Chief Executive Officer, Tri–Valley Health System, Cambridge, NE, p. A257

HARRIS, Robert L., President and Chief Executive Officer, Ingalls Hospital, Harvey, IL, p. A126

HARRIS, Robert W., President, Lakeside Memorial Hospital, Brockport, NY, p. A282

HARRIS, Wayne, Administrator, Simpson General Hospital, Mendenhall, MS, p. A235

HARROD, Pat, Chief Executive Officer, Charter Behavioral Health System of Paducah, Paducah, KY, p. A174

HART, Diane M., Chief Executive Officer, Moses Ludington Hospital, Ticonderoga, NY, p. A299

HART, Gerald L., Chief Executive Officer, Magic Valley Regional Medical Center, Twin Falls, ID, p. A117

HART, Joel A., Chief Executive Officer, Woodward Hospital and Health Center, Woodward, OK, p. A341

HART, John M., Chief Executive Officer, Behavioral Healthcare–Columbus, Columbus, IN, p. A137

HART, Noel W., Administrator, King's Daughters Hospital, Yazoo City, MS, p. A238

HART, Patsy J., Executive Director, University Hospitals and Clinics, Columbia, MO, p. A240

HART, Remy, Chief Executive Officer, Los Angeles Community Hospital, Los Angeles, CA, p. A49

HART, Steven, Commanding Officer, Naval Hospital, Lemoore, CA, p. A46

HARTBERG, David, Administrator, Brown County Hospital, Ainsworth, NE, p. A256

HARTLEY, H. William, Chief Executive Officer, Rush Memorial Hospital, Rushville, IN, p. A144

HARTLEY, Randall W., Administrator, U. S. Air Force Medical Center Keesler, Keesler AFB, MS, p. A234

HARTMAN, C. Richard, M.D., President and Chief Executive Officer, Community Medical Center, Scranton, PA, p. A363

HARVEY, Stansel, Senior Executive Vice President, Executive Director/Administrator, Harris Methodist Southwest, Fort Worth, TX, p. A404

HARWOOD, Janie L., Administrator, Corpus Christi Medical Center–Bayview Psychiatric Center, Corpus Christi, TX, p. A398

HASTINGS, Arthur W., President and Chief Executive Officer, Middle Tennessee Medical Center, Murfreesboro, TN, p. A388

HASTINGS, G. Richard
President and Chief Executive Officer, Saint Luke's Hospital, Kansas City, MO, p. A243
President and Chief Executive Officer, Saint Luke's Shawnee Mission Health System, Kansas City, MO, p. B134

HATALA, Alexander J., President and Chief Executive Officer, Our Lady of Lourdes Medical Center, Camden, NJ, p. A269

HATCHER, John M., President, Whitley Memorial Hospital, Columbia City, IN, p. A137

HATFIELD, Ted A., Chief Executive Officer, Logan General Hospital, Logan, WV, p. A452

HATHAWAY, Richard D., Chief Operating Officer, Redbud Community Hospital, Clearlake, CA, p. A39

HATHAWAY Jr., Woodrow W., Chief Executive Officer, Chatham Hospital, Siler City, NC, p. A311

HAUG, William F., FACHE, President and Chief Executive Officer, Motion Picture and Television Fund Hospital and Residential Services, Los Angeles, CA, p. A49

HAUGH, Diana, MS, Superintendent, Larue D. Carter Memorial Hospital, Indianapolis, IN, p. A140

HAUGO, Glenn, Administrator, Daniels Memorial Hospital, Scobey, MT, p. A254

HAUSE, Eileen, Chief Executive Officer, Kensington Hospital, Philadelphia, PA, p. A359

HAUSLER, Jeffrey E., Vice Chairman and Chief Executive Officer, United Regional Health Care System, Wichita Falls, TX, p. A426

HAWKINS, Leslie A., President, Mount Desert Island Hospital, Bar Harbor, ME, p. A187

HAWKINS, Mary Jane, Administrator and Chief Executive Officer, HEALTHSOUTH Nittany Valley Rehabilitation Hospital, Pleasant Gap, PA, p. A362

HAWKINS, Phil, Administrator, Carnegie Tri–County Municipal Hospital, Carnegie, OK, p. A334

HAWKINS, Robert L., Superintendent, Colorado Mental Health Institute at Pueblo, Pueblo, CO, p. A72

HAWKINSON, Curtis, Chief Executive Officer, Keefe Memorial Hospital, Cheyenne Wells, CO, p. A68

HAWLEY, Jess, Administrator, Syringa General Hospital, Grangeville, ID, p. A115

HAWLEY Jr., Robert L., Chief Executive Officer, Bolivar Medical Center, Cleveland, MS, p. A232

HAWTHORNE, Connie, Chief Executive Officer, Medical Center Shoals, Muscle Shoals, AL, p. A17

HAWTHORNE, Douglas D., President and Chief Executive Officer, Texas Health Resources, Irving, TX, p. B147

HAYES, Billy, Administrator, Baptist Hospital, Worth County, Sylvester, GA, p. A110

HAYES, David R., President, Taylor County Hospital, Campbellsville, KY, p. A168

HAYES, Howard A., President and Chief Executive Officer, St. Joseph Regional Medical Center, Lewiston, ID, p. A115

HAYES, Jim M., Executive Vice President and Aministrator, St. Mary's Hospital Warrick, Boonville, IN, p. A136

HAYES, T. Farrell, President, Healthcorp of Tennessee, Inc., Chattanooga, TN, p. B101

HAYES, Thomas P.
Chief Executive Officer, Fremont Medical Center, Yuba City, CA, p. A67
Chief Executive Officer, Fremont–Rideout Health Group, Yuba City, CA, p. B97
Chief Executive Officer, Rideout Memorial Hospital, Marysville, CA, p. A52

HAYES, Wayne, Administrator, Nashville Metropolitan Bordeaux Hospital, Nashville, TN, p. A388

HAYS, Cheryl, Administrator, Lawrence Baptist Medical Center, Moulton, AL, p. A17

HAYS, George E., Senior Executive Officer, Saint Luke's South, Overland Park, KS, p. A163

HAYS, Janet A., Administrator, Forks Community Hospital, Forks, WA, p. A444

HAYS, Lissa B., Chief Operating Officer, Newport News General Hospital, Newport News, VA, p. A437

HAYWARD, John, President and Chief Executive Officer, PeaceHealth, Bellevue, WA, p. B124

HAYWOOD, Thomas L., Chief Executive Officer, Southeast Arizona Medical Center, Douglas, AZ, p. A22

HAYWOOD III, Edgar, Administrator, J. Arthur Dosher Memorial Hospital, Southport, NC, p. A311

HAZLETT, Guy, FACHE, Chief Executive Officer, Woods Memorial Hospital District, Etowah, TN, p. A383

HEAD, William C., USAF, Administrator, U. S. Air Force Regional Hospital, Eglin AFB, FL, p. A83

HEAD, Janice, Vice President and Service Area Manager, Kaiser Foundation Hospital, Anaheim, CA, p. A36

HEADDING, John, Chief Administrative Officer, Mercy Hospital and Health Services, Merced, CA, p. A52

HEADLEY, Elwood J., M.D., System Director, Malcom Randall Veterans Affairs Medical Center, Gainesville, FL, p. A85

HEARD, William C., Administrator and Chief Executive Officer, Cumberland Hall Hospital, Hopkinsville, KY, p. A170

HEARING, Philip E., President and Chief Executive Officer, Southeastern Ohio Regional Medical Center, Cambridge, OH, p. A318

HEATER, Floyd, Chief Executive Officer, Shenandoah Memorial Hospital, Woodstock, VA, p. A441

HEATH, Susan, Chief Executive Officer, HEALTHSOUTH Chattanooga Rehabilitation Hospital, Chattanooga, TN, p. A382

HEATH, Tricia, R.N., Administrator and Chief Executive Officer, North Dallas Rehabilitation Hospital, Dallas, TX, p. A400

HECHT, Kevin, Director, Wagner General Hospital, Palacios, TX, p. A417

HECK III, George L., President and Chief Executive Officer, Coffee Regional Medical Center, Douglas, GA, p. A104

HECKER, Aston, Chief Executive Officer, Victoria Regional Medical Center, Victoria, TX, p. A425

HECKERT, Brian, Medical Center Director, William Jennings Bryan Dorn Veterans Medical Center, Columbia, SC, p. A372

HECKERT Jr., Robert James, MSC, Chief of Staff, Walter Reed Army Medical Center, Washington, DC, p. A80

HEDRIX, Michael D., Administrator, Pine Medical Center, Sandstone, MN, p. A228

HEIN, Joyce Grove, Chief Executive Officer, Lakewood Medical Center, Morgan City, LA, p. A183

HEINIKE, J. Larry, President and Chief Executive Officer, UPMC Horizon, Greenville, PA, p. A352

HEISE, Patrick B., Chief Executive Officer, Community Memorial Hospital, Staunton, IL, p. A134

HEITKAMP, Charlotte, Chief Executive Officer, Jackson Medical Center, Jackson, MN, p. A224

HEITZENRATER, James F., Administrator, Marcum and Wallace Memorial Hospital, Irvine, KY, p. A170

HEKIMIAN, Barbara D. S., Chief Executive Officer, Dominion Hospital, Falls Church, VA, p. A434

HELLER, Thomas, Administrator, HEALTHSOUTH Western Hills Regional Rehabilitation Hospital, Parkersburg, WV, p. A453

HELLERSTEDT, Wayne P., Chief Executive Officer, Helen Newberry Joy Hospital, Newberry, MI, p. A215

HELM, Michael D., President, Sparks Regional Medical Center, Fort Smith, AR, p. A31

HELMS, Ella Raye, Administrator, Fisher County Hospital District, Rotan, TX, p. A419

HELZER, James D., Administrator, Veterans Home of California, Yountville, CA, p. A67

HEMETER, Donald, Administrator, Wayne General Hospital, Waynesboro, MS, p. A238

HEMPLING, Randall, Administrator, Lake Mead Hospital Medical Center, North Las Vegas, NV, p. A264

HENCKEL, Susan, Executive Vice President and Chief Executive Officer, Columbia Hospital, Milwaukee, WI, p. A460

HENDERSON, Cynthia T., M.P.H., Director and Chief Operating Officer, Oak Forest Hospital of Cook County, Oak Forest, IL, p. A130

HENDERSON, Donald, Chief Executive Officer, Byrd Regional Hospital, Leesville, LA, p. A181

HENDERSON, W. Perry, Administrator, East Texas Medical Center Pittsburg, Pittsburg, TX, p. A417

HENDERSON Jr., Donald, Deputy Commander for Administration, Lyster U. S. Army Community Hospital, Fort Rucker, AL, p. A14

HENDLER, Ronald, Chief Executive Officer, Crownsville Hospital Center, Crownsville, MD, p. A193

HENDRICKSON, William Wilson, President and Chief Executive Officer, Good Samaritan Health Systems, Kearney, NE, p. A258

HENDRICKSON, Scott D., Deputy Commander for Administration, Irwin Army Community Hospital, Fort Riley, KS, p. A158

HENDRIX, Wayne, President, Kosciusko Community Hospital, Warsaw, IN, p. A145

HENDRUS, Joe, Administrator, Lillian M. Hudspeth Memorial Hospital, Sonora, TX, p. A422

HENGER, Robert E., Administrator, Carraway Northwest Medical Center, Winfield, AL, p. A19

HENIKOFF, Leo M.
President and Chief Executive Officer, Rush–Presbyterian–St. Luke's Medical Center, Chicago, IL, p. A122
President, Rush–Presbyterian–St. Luke's Medical Center, Chicago, IL, p. B134

HENKE, Marcella V., Administrator and Chief Executive Officer, Jackson County Hospital, Edna, TX, p. A402

HENLEY, Darryl E., Administrator, Dos Palos Memorial Hospital, Dos Palos, CA, p. A41

HENNESSY, Thomas G., Chief Executive Officer, MetroWest Medical Center, Framingham, MA, p. A200

HENRY, Angelia K., Administrator, Douglas County Memorial Hospital, Armour, SD, p. A376

HENRY, David, Chief Executive Officer, Northern Montana Hospital, Havre, MT, p. A253

HENRY, Peter P., Director, Veterans Affairs Black Hills Health Care System, Fort Meade, SD, p. A377

HENRY Jr., Jake, President, Christus Spohn Health System, Corpus Christi, TX, p. A398

HENRY Sr., John Dunklin, FACHE
Chief Executive Officer, Crawford Long Hospital of Emory University, Atlanta, GA, p. A99
Chief Executive Officer, Emory University Hospital, Atlanta, GA, p. A100

HENSHAW, Jim, President and Chief Executive Officer, Gooding County Memorial Hospital, Gooding, ID, p. A115

HENSLEY, J. Scott, Ph.D., Chief Executive Officer, Culberson Hospital District, Van Horn, TX, p. A424

HENSLEY, Kerry A., R.N., Administrator, FirstHealth Montgomery Memorial Hospital, Troy, NC, p. A311

HENSON, Blair W., Administrator, Florala Memorial Hospital, Florala, AL, p. A14

HENSON, David L., Chief Executive Officer, Wilkes Regional Medical Center, North Wilkesboro, NC, p. A309

HENSON, James C., President, United Hospital Corporation, Memphis, TN, p. B150

HENSON, John S., President, Baptist Regional Medical Center, Corbin, KY, p. A168

HENTON, Thomas, President and Chief Executive Officer, Cleveland Area Hospital, Cleveland, OK, p. A334

HENZE, Michael E., Chief Executive Officer, Lake of the Ozarks General Hospital, Osage Beach, MO, p. A246

HERBERT, Cheryl, President, MedCenter Hospital, Marion, OH, p. A326

HERBERT, Susan, Administrator, Inova Mount Vernon Hospital, Alexandria, VA, p. A433

HERFINDAHL, Lowell D., President and Chief Executive Officer, Tioga Medical Center, Tioga, ND, p. A316

HERMAN, Bernard J., President and Chief Executive Officer, Mercy Hospital, Bakersfield, CA, p. A37

HERMAN, Paul
Chief Executive Officer, Mount San Rafael Hospital, Trinidad, CO, p. A73
Chief Executive Officer, San Luis Valley Regional Medical Center, Alamosa, CO, p. A68

HERMANSON, Patrick M., Senior Executive Officer, Saint Vincent Hospital and Health Center, Billings, MT, p. A251

HERNANDEZ, Hank, Chief Executive Officer, Columbia Medical Center West, El Paso, TX, p. A402

HERNANDEZ, Leonard, Administrator and Chief Executive Officer, Holton Community Hospital, Holton, KS, p. A159

HERNANDEZ, Pablo, M.D., Administrator, Wyoming State Hospital, Evanston, WY, p. A466

HERNANDEZ–KEEBLE, Sonia, Director, Rio Grande State Center, Harlingen, TX, p. A406

HERRICK, Ronald L., President, Rehabilitation Institute, Kansas City, MO, p. A243

HERRING, Michael S., Administrator, Samuel Simmonds Memorial Hospital, Barrow, AK, p. A20

HERRON, John M., Administrator, Baptist Medical Center, Cumming, GA, p. A103

HERRON, Thomas L., FACHE, President and Chief Executive Officer, Largo Medical Center, Largo, FL, p. A88

HERVEY, Roger D., Administrator, Galena–Stauss Hospital, Galena, IL, p. A125

HESS, Carolyn K., Administrator, Grape Community Hospital, Hamburg, IA, p. A150

HESS, Kent C., Interim Chief Executive Officer, Clearfield Hospital, Clearfield, PA, p. A350

HESSELMANN, Thomas J., President and Chief Executive Officer, Samaritan Health System, Clinton, IA, p. A147

HESSELTINE, Wendell, President, Tillamook County General Hospital, Tillamook, OR, p. A346

HESTER, Forrest G., President and Chief Executive Officer, Abraham Lincoln Memorial Hospital, Lincoln, IL, p. A128

HETLAGE, C. Kennon, Administrator, Memorial Regional Hospital, Los Angeles, FL, p. A86

HEUSER, Keith E., Chief Executive Officer, Memorial Hospital, Carthage, IL, p. A119

HEYBOER Jr., Lester, President and Chief Executive Officer, HealthSource Saginaw, Saginaw, MI, p. A216

HEYDEL, M. John, President and Chief Executive Officer, Self Memorial Hospital, Greenwood, SC, p. A373

HEYDT, Stuart, M.D., Chief Executive Officer, Penn State Geisinger Health System, Harrisburg, PA, p. B125

HIATT, M. K., Administrator, Allendale County Hospital, Fairfax, SC, p. A372

HICKEY, Martin, M.D., Chief Executive Officer, Lovelace Health System, Albuquerque, NM, p. A277

HICKS, Cheryl, Chief Executive Officer, Twin City Hospital, Dennison, OH, p. A323

HICKS, John D., President and Chief Executive Officer, Baptist St. Anthony Health System, Amarillo, TX, p. A392

HICKS, John R., President and Chief Executive Officer, Platte Valley Medical Center, Brighton, CO, p. A68

HICKS, Kevin J., President and Chief Executive Officer, Overland Park Regional Medical Center, Overland Park, KS, p. A163

HICKS, Michael C., President and Chief Executive Officer, Jefferson Memorial Hospital, Jefferson City, TN, p. A384

HICKS, Tommy L., Administrator, Ray County Memorial Hospital, Richmond, MO, p. A246

HIDDE, A. John, President and Chief Executive Officer, Good Samaritan Hospital, Vincennes, IN, p. A145

HIESTER, Richard B., Administrator, Memorial Psychiatric Hospital, Albuquerque, NM, p. A277

HIETPAS, Bernard G.
Chief Executive Officer, Glenn Medical Center, Willows, CA, p. A67
Administrator, Seneca District Hospital, Chester, CA, p. A39

HIGGINBOTHAM, G. Douglas, Executive Director, South Central Regional Medical Center, Laurel, MS, p. A235

HIGGINS, Brad A., President and Chief Executive Officer, Fostoria Community Hospital, Fostoria, OH, p. A323

HIGGINS, Susannah, Chief Executive Officer, Broaddus Hospital, Philippi, WV, p. A453

HIGHSMITH Jr., C. Cameron, President and Chief Executive Officer, St. Luke's Hospital, Columbus, NC, p. A304

HILL, James C., Chief Executive Officer, Charter Behavioral Health System of Tampa Bay, Tampa, FL, p. A96

HILL, Jim, Chief Executive Officer, Charter Behavioral Health System of Tampa Bay at Largo, Largo, FL, p. A88

HILL, Kent D., Director, Veterans Affairs Medical and Regional Office Center, Wichita, KS, p. A165

HILL, Robert B., President and Chief Executive Officer, Bethesda Memorial Hospital, Boynton Beach, FL, p. A81

HILL, Thomas E.
Chief Executive Officer, WellStar Cobb Hospital, Austell, GA, p. A101
Chief Executive Officer, WellStar Douglas Hospital, Douglasville, GA, p. A104
Chief Executive Officer, WellStar Health System, Marietta, GA, p. B155
Chief Executive Officer, WellStar Kennestone Hospital, Marietta, GA, p. A107
Chief Executive Officer, WellStar Paulding Hospital, Dallas, GA, p. A103
Chief Executive Officer, WellStar Windy Hill Hospital, Marietta, GA, p. A107

HILL, Timothy E., Chief Executive Officer, North Arkansas Regional Medical Center, Harrison, AR, p. A31

HILL, Mack C., Commanding General, Madigan Army Medical Center, Tacoma, WA, p. A448

HILL, John, FACHE, Administrator, David Grant Medical Center, Travis AFB, CA, p. A65

HILLARD, Mark, Chief Executive Officer, Maricopa Medical Center, Phoenix, AZ, p. A24

HILLBOM, Richard, Chief Administrative Officer, Oakwood Hospital Beyer Center–Ypsilanti, Ypsilanti, MI, p. A219

HILLENMEYER, John, President and Chief Executive Officer, Orlando Regional Healthcare System, Orlando, FL, p. B123

HILLIS, David W., President and Chief Executive Officer, Adcare Hospital of Worcester, Worcester, MA, p. A205

HILTZ, Richard S., President and Chief Executive Officer, Mercy Memorial Hospital, Monroe, MI, p. A214

HINCHEY, Paul P.
President and Chief Executive Officer, Candler Hospital, Savannah, GA, p. A109
President and Chief Executive Officer, St. Joseph's Hospital, Savannah, GA, p. A109

HINDS, Bob, Executive Director, Bradford Health Services at Huntsville, Madison, AL, p. A16

HINER, Calvin A., Administrator, Tri–County Area Hospital, Lexington, NE, p. A259

HINES, Frederick W., President, Southwest Mental Health Center, San Antonio, TX, p. A421

HINES, William E., Administrator, Prattville Baptist Hospital, Prattville, AL, p. A18

HINIKER, Alice, Ph.D., Administrator, Intracare Medical Center Hospital, Houston, TX, p. A408

HINO, Raymond T., Chief Executive Officer, Tehachapi Hospital, Tehachapi, CA, p. A64

HINSDALE, Laurence C., President and Chief Executive Officer, NorthEast Medical Center, Concord, NC, p. A304

HINSON, Roy M., CHE, President and Chief Executive Officer, Stanly Memorial Hospital, Albemarle, NC, p. A302

HINTON, J. Philip, M.D.
President and Chief Executive Officer, Community Health System of Northern California, Fresno, CA, p. B84
President and Chief Executive Officer, Fresno Community Hospital and Medical Center, Fresno, CA, p. A43

HINTON, James H., President and Chief Executive Officer, Presbyterian Healthcare Services, Albuquerque, NM, p. B125

HIRSCH, Jeffrey D., Executive Vice President and Administrator, Horton Medical Center, Middletown, NY, p. A288

HIRSCH, Leslie D., Acting President and Chief Executive Officer, The Cooper Health System, Camden, NJ, p. A269

HITCHINGS Jr., Roy A., FACHE, President, Penobscot Bay Medical Center, Rockport, ME, p. A189

HITT, Irving, Administrator, Covington County Hospital, Collins, MS, p. A232

HITZLER, Ronald R., Administrator, Shriners Hospitals for Children, Shriners Burns Hospital, Cincinnati, Cincinnati, OH, p. A320

HOARD, Jack D., President and Chief Executive Officer, Armstrong County Memorial Hospital, Kittanning, PA, p. A354

HODGE Jr., Joseph T., Facility Administrator, Central State Hospital, Milledgeville, GA, p. A107

HODGES, Alan, Interim Chief Executive Officer, Bayou Oaks Behavioral Health System, Houma, LA, p. A180

HODGES, Joseph T., President, Corry Memorial Hospital, Corry, PA, p. A350

HODGSON, Judy, Administrator, Sacred Heart Medical Center, Eugene, OR, p. A342

HOEFT, Kathleen, Administrator and Chief Executive Officer, Ashley Medical Center, Ashley, ND, p. A313

HOELSCHER, Steve C., Administrator, Marshall Medical Center, Lewisburg, TN, p. A386

HOFER, Kathleen, President, St. Mary's Medical Center, Duluth, MN, p. A222

HOFF, David L., Chief Executive Officer, Iron County Community Hospital, Iron River, MI, p. A212

HOFF, Terry G., President, Trinity Health, Minot, ND, p. A315

HOFFART, Terry L., Administrator, Webster County Community Hospital, Red Cloud, NE, p. A261

HOFIUS, Chuck, Administrator, Perham Memorial Hospital and Home, Perham, MN, p. A227

HOFREUTER, Donald H., M.D., Administrator and Chief Executive Officer, Wheeling Hospital, Wheeling, WV, p. A454

HOFSTETTER, Peter A., Chief Executive Officer, Northwestern Medical Center, Saint Albans, VT, p. A431

HOGAN, Karen C., Administrator and Chief Executive Officer, San Diego County Psychiatric Hospital, San Diego, CA, p. A59

HOGAN, Ronald C., Superintendent, Georgia Regional Hospital at Atlanta, Decatur, GA, p. A104

HOGUE, John, Administrator, Covina Valley Community Hospital, West Covina, CA, p. A67

HOHENBERGER, Arthur L., FACHE, President and Chief Executive Officer, Texoma Healthcare System, Denison, TX, p. A401

HOHL, David G., Chief Executive Officer, Richmond Memorial Hospital, Rockingham, NC, p. A310

HOHMAN, Curtis, Interim Administrator, Flandreau Municipal Hospital, Flandreau, SD, p. A377

HOHN, David C., M.D., President and Chief Executive Officer, Roswell Park Cancer Institute, Buffalo, NY, p. A283

HOLCOMB, David M., President and Chief Executive Officer, Jennie Edmundson Memorial Hospital, Council Bluffs, IA, p. A148

HOLCOMB, James, Chief Executive Officer, Broadwater Health Center, Townsend, MT, p. A254

HOLDER, Lynn
Associate Director, Northeastern Hospital of Philadelphia, Philadelphia, PA, p. A359
Executive Director, Temple East, Neumann Medical Center, Philadelphia, PA, p. A360

HOLL, Donald R., President, Valley Regional Hospital, Claremont, NH, p. A265

HOLLAND, J. T., Warden, Federal Medical Center, Lexington, KY, p. A171

HOLLAND, Jeffrey S., Chief Executive Officer, West Houston Medical Center, Houston, TX, p. A410

HOLLAND, John F., President, North Fulton Regional Hospital, Roswell, GA, p. A109

HOLLAND, Stacy D., Administrator and Chief Executive Officer, Haskell County Healthcare System, Stigler, OK, p. A340

HOLLANDER, Sharon Flynn, Chief Executive Officer, Georgetown University Hospital, Washington, DC, p. A79

HOLLON, Kim, FACHE, Executive Director, Methodist Medical Center, Dallas, TX, p. A400

HOLMAN, Donna, Administrator, Jasper Memorial Hospital, Monticello, GA, p. A108

HOLMAN, William R., President, Genesee Hospital, Rochester, NY, p. A297

HOLMES, Alan D., Chief Executive Officer, Frio Hospital, Pearsall, TX, p. A417

HOLMES, James M., President and Chief Executive Officer, Rappahannock General Hospital, Kilmarnock, VA, p. A436

HOLMES, James R., President, Redlands Community Hospital, Redlands, CA, p. A57

HOLMES, Elaine C., USN, Commanding Officer, Naval Hospital, Great Lakes, IL, p. A126

HOLOM, Randall G., Chief Executive Officer, Frances Mahon Deaconess Hospital, Glasgow, MT, p. A252

HOLTER, Lee, Chief Executive Officer, St. James Health Services, Saint James, MN, p. A227

HOLTSCLAW, Keith S., Chief Executive Officer, Spruce Pine Community Hospital, Spruce Pine, NC, p. A311

HOLTZ, John, Administrator, Shriners Hospitals for Children, Tampa, Tampa, FL, p. A96

HOLWERDA, Daniel L., President and Chief Executive Officer, Pine Rest Christian Mental Health Services, Grand Rapids, MI, p. A211

HOLZBERG, Harvey A., President and Chief Executive Officer, Robert Wood Johnson University Hospital, New Brunswick, NJ, p. A272

HONAKER, C. Ray, Chief Executive Officer, St. Thomas More Hospital and Progressive Care Center, Canon City, CO, p. A68

HONAKER III, Thomas G., Administrator, Mission Hill Memorial Hospital, Shawnee, OK, p. A339

HONEYCUTT, Ann E., Executive Vice President and Administrator, Bon Secours St. Mary's Hospital, Richmond, VA, p. A439

HOOD, Barbara A., Chief Executive Officer, Providence Yakima Medical Center, Yakima, WA, p. A449

HOOD, Fred B., Administrator, Pontotoc Hospital and Extended Care Facility, Pontotoc, MS, p. A236

HOOD, Mark C., Executive Director, Baylor Medical Center at Grapevine, Grapevine, TX, p. A406

HOOPER, Jerry, Chief Executive Officer, BHC Pinnacle Pointe Hospital, Little Rock, AR, p. A32

HOOPER, Ross, Chief Executive Officer, Crittenden Memorial Hospital, West Memphis, AR, p. A35

HOOPES, John L., Administrator, Mohave Valley Hospital and Medical Center, Bullhead City, AZ, p. A22

HOOSE, Gregory R., Chief Executive Officer, Straith Hospital for Special Surgery, Southfield, MI, p. A217

HOOSER, Rosemary, Administrator, Choctaw Nation Indian Hospital, Talihina, OK, p. A340

HOOVER, Randall L., Chief Executive Officer, Memorial Medical Center, New Orleans, LA, p. A183

HOPKINS, Don, Administrator, Faith Community Hospital, Jacksboro, TX, p. A410

HOPKINS, Wallace M., FACHE, Director, Veterans Affairs Medical Center, Amarillo, TX, p. A392

HOPPER, Cornelius L., M.D., Vice President Health Affairs, University of California–Systemwide Administration, Oakland, CA, p. B151

HOPPER, Stephen R., President and Chief Executive Officer, McDonough District Hospital, Macomb, IL, p. A128

HOPPS, Deborah, Interim Chief Executive Officer, Cleveland Regional Medical Center, Cleveland, TX, p. A397

HOPSTAD, Kyle, Administrator, Virginia Regional Medical Center, Virginia, MN, p. A229

HORAN, Gary S., FACHE
President and Chief Executive Officer, Our Lady of Mercy Healthcare System, Inc., New York, NY, p. B123
President and Chief Executive Officer, Our Lady of Mercy Medical Center, New York, NY, p. A292
President and Chief Executive Officer, St. Agnes Hospital, White Plains, NY, p. A300

HORN, Jerome H., President and Chief Executive Officer, Vaughan Regional Medical Center, Selma, AL, p. A18

HORN, Linda, Administrator, Sutter Delta Medical Center, Antioch, CA, p. A36

HORNER, Lynn V., President and Chief Executive Officer, Dunlap Memorial Hospital, Orrville, OH, p. A328

HORNER, Seward, President, Riverview Hospital, Noblesville, IN, p. A143

HORTON, Charlie M., President, Warren Memorial Hospital, Front Royal, VA, p. A435

HORTON, Jerrell J., Chief Executive Officer, Greeley County Hospital, Tribune, KS, p. A165

HORTON, Joseph R., Chief Executive Officer and Administrator, Primary Children's Medical Center, Salt Lake City, UT, p. A429

HORVATH, Louis D., Administrator, St. John Vianney Hospital, Downingtown, PA, p. A350

HORWITZ, Theodore H., FACHE, President and Chief Executive Officer, MidState Medical Center, Meriden, CT, p. A75

HOSFELD, Anne, Chief Administrative Officer, Novato Community Hospital, Novato, CA, p. A54

HOSS, James R., Administrator and Chief Operating Officer, St. John's Regional Medical Center, Oxnard, CA, p. A55

HOUGH, Stephen, Interim President and Chief Executive Officer, Driscoll Children's Hospital, Corpus Christi, TX, p. A398

HOUGHTON, Jack F., Chief Executive Officer, Bossier Medical Center, Bossier City, LA, p. A178

HOUSE, Judy G., Chief Executive Officer, BHC Ross Hospital, Kentfield, CA, p. A45

HOUSER, Robert, Chief Executive Officer, Blue Mountain Hospital, John Day, OR, p. A343

HOUSLEY, Charles E., FACHE, Administrator, ARH Regional Medical Center, Hazard, KY, p. A170

HOUSTON, Colleen B., Administrator, Miller County Hospital, Colquitt, GA, p. A102

HOVE, Barton A., Chief Executive Officer, Delta Regional Medical Center, Greenville, MS, p. A233

HOVE, David R., President and Chief Executive Officer, St. Joseph's Area Health Services, Park Rapids, MN, p. A226

HOWARD, Deanna S., Chief Executive Officer, Upper Connecticut Valley Hospital, Colebrook, NH, p. A265

HOWARD, Eddie L., Vice President and Chief Operating Officer, East Texas Medical Center Rehabilitation Center, Tyler, TX, p. A424

HOWARD, J. Kent, President and Chief Executive Officer, Medical Center of Independence, Independence, MO, p. A242

HOWARD, Loy M., Chief Executive Officer, Tanner Medical Center, Carrollton, GA, p. A102

HOWARD, Mark J., President and Chief Executive Officer, Mountainview Hospital, Las Vegas, NV, p. A263

HOWARD, Norma, Administrator, Marshall Memorial Hospital, Madill, OK, p. A336

HOWE, Debbie, Administrator, Okeene Municipal Hospital, Okeene, OK, p. A337

HOWE, G. Edwin, President, Aurora Health Care, Milwaukee, WI, p. B62

HOWE, Scott W., Chief Executive Officer, Weeks Memorial Hospital, Lancaster, NH, p. A266

HOWELL, Bonnie H., President and Chief Executive Officer, Cayuga Medical Center at Ithaca, Ithaca, NY, p. A286

HOWELL, George E., Service Unit Director, U. S. Public Health Service Indian Hospital, Lawton, OK, p. A336

HOWELL, Jeffrey S., Administrator, Madison County Memorial Hospital, Madison, FL, p. A88

HOWELL, Jerry M., Chief Operating Officer, Marion General Hospital, Columbia, MS, p. A232

HOWELL, Ken, Administrator, HEALTHSOUTH Southern Hills Rehabilitation Hospital, Princeton, WV, p. A453

HOWELL, R. Edward, Director and Chief Executive Officer, University of Iowa Hospitals and Clinics, Iowa City, IA, p. A151

HOWELL, Farley, Commanding Officer, U. S. Air Force Hospital, Ellsworth AFB, SD, p. A377

HUBBARD, F. David, Superintendent, McCain Correctional Hospital, McCain, NC, p. A308

HUBBARD III, Richard B., President and Chief Executive Officer, Piedmont Hospital, Atlanta, GA, p. A100

HUBBELL, James W., President and Chief Executive Officer, Wayne Memorial Hospital, Goldsboro, NC, p. A306

HUBER, Connie, R.N., Chief Executive Officer, Powell County Memorial Hospital, Deer Lodge, MT, p. A252

HUCH, Robert E., President, Stonewall Jackson Hospital, Lexington, VA, p. A436

HUDGINS, Thomas J., Administrator, Sullivan County Community Hospital, Sullivan, IN, p. A144

HUDSON, Donald C., Vice President and Chief Operating Officer, Mercy Hospital of Folsom, Folsom, CA, p. A42

HUDSON, Gary Mikeal, Administrator, East Texas Medical Center Carthage, Carthage, TX, p. A397

HUDSON, W. H., President, Oconee Memorial Hospital, Seneca, SC, p. A374

HUDSPETH, Todd, Administrator and Chief Executive Officer, Guthrie County Hospital, Guthrie Center, IA, p. A150

HUEBBERS, Rodney N., President and Chief Executive Officer, Putnam Hospital Center, Carmel, NY, p. A284

HUEBNER, Thomas W., President and Chief Executive Officer, Rutland Regional Medical Center, Rutland, VT, p. A431

HUERTA, Cristina, Administrative Director, Columbia Rehabilitation Hospital, El Paso, TX, p. A403

HUETER, Diana T., President and Chief Executive Officer, St. Vincent Infirmary Medical Center, Little Rock, AR, p. A32

HUEY, Kenneth R., President and Chief Executive Officer, Longmont United Hospital, Longmont, CO, p. A72

HUFF, Richard, Administrator, U. S. Public Health Service Indian Hospital, Sisseton, SD, p. A379

HUFF, William J., Chief Executive Officer, Marshall Browning Hospital, Du Quoin, IL, p. A124

HUGHES Jr., Ned B., President, Gerber Memorial Hospital, Fremont, MI, p. A210

HUMMEL, Joseph W.
Senior Vice President, Kaiser Foundation Hospital, Los Angeles, CA, p. A48
Administrator, Kaiser Foundation Hospital–West Los Angeles, Los Angeles, CA, p. A49

HUMMER, John Lloyd, Chief Executive Officer, Desert Springs Hospital, Las Vegas, NV, p. A263

HUMPHREY, Jerel T., Vice President, Chief Executive Officer and Administrator, Memorial Hospital–Memorial City, Houston, TX, p. A408

HUMPHREY, Robert J., Administrator, Lanier Health Services, Valley, AL, p. A19

HUMPHRYS, Maureen, Director, Veterans Affairs Medical Center, Sheridan, WY, p. A467

HUNKINS, Theresa, Administrator, Vencor Hospital–Tampa, Tampa, FL, p. A97

HUNN, Michael F., Chief Executive Officer, Anaheim General Hospital, Anaheim, CA, p. A36

HUNSUCKER, Joe, Administrator, Baptist Memorial Hospital–Lauderdale, Ripley, TN, p. A389

HUNT, James M., Chief Executive Officer, Charter Real Behavioral Health System, San Antonio, TX, p. A419

HUNT, Roger S., President and Chief Executive Officer, Via Health, Rochester, NY, p. B155

HUNT, Sharon, Administrator, W. J. Mangold Memorial Hospital, Lockney, TX, p. A413

HUNT, William, Chief Operating Officer, Woodland Healthcare, Woodland, CA, p. A67

HUNT Jr., Seth P., Director and Chief Executive Officer, Broughton Hospital, Morganton, NC, p. A308

HUNTER, David C., Chief Executive Officer, Wabash County Hospital, Wabash, IN, p. A145

HUNTER, John, Chief Executive Officer, ValueMark Behavioral Healthcare System of Kansas City, Kansas City, MO, p. A244

HUNTER Jr., Harry, Administrator and Chief Operating Officer, Harbor Oaks Hospital, New Baltimore, MI, p. A215

HUNTLEY, Lee S., Chief Executive Officer, Baptist Hospital of Miami, Miami, FL, p. A89

HUPFELD, Stanley F., President and Chief Executive Officer, INTEGRIS Health, Oklahoma City, OK, p. B105

HURD, Paul, Chief Executive Officer, Creighton Area Health Services, Creighton, NE, p. A257

HURST, Molly, Administrative Director, Grimes St. Joseph Health Center, Navasota, TX, p. A416

HURT, Charles, Administrator, Hardeman County Memorial Hospital, Quanah, TX, p. A418

HURT, Reedes, Chief Executive Officer, Veterans Affairs Medical Center, Wilkes–Barre, PA, p. A366

HURT, Richard O., Ph.D., Chief Executive Officer, Benchmark Behavioral Health Systems, Woods Cross, UT, p. A430

HURYSZ, Edwin E., Chief Executive Officer, Sakakawea Medical Center, Hazen, ND, p. A314

HURZELER, Rosemary Johnson, President and Chief Executive Officer, The Connecticut Hospice, Branford, CT, p. A74

HUSSON, Gerard P., Director, Veterans Affairs Medical Center, Beckley, WV, p. A450

HUTCHENRIDER, Ken, President and Chief Executive Officer, Western Plains Regional Hospital, Dodge City, KS, p. A157

HUTCHINS, Michael T., Administrator, Claiborne County Hospital, Tazewell, TN, p. A390

HUTCHISON, Dee, Chief Executive Officer, Northern Navajo Medical Center, Shiprock, NM, p. A280

HUTCHISON, James, Director, Integris Bass Behavioral Health System, Enid, OK, p. A335

HUTTON, Donald H., FACHE, President and Chief Executive Officer, Brooks Rehabilitation Hospital, Jacksonville, FL, p. A86

HYDE, James A., Administrator, Bone and Joint Hospital, Oklahoma City, OK, p. A337

HYER, Julie, President and Chief Executive Officer, Dominican Hospital, Santa Cruz, CA, p. A62

HYMANS, Daniel J., President, Memorial Medical Center, Ashland, WI, p. A456

HYNES, John J., President and Chief Executive Officer, Care New England Health System, Providence, RI, p. B70

I

ICHINOSE, Calvin M., Administrator, Molokai General Hospital, Kaunakakai, HI, p. A113

IGNELZI, James, Chief Executive Officer, Twin Valley Psychiatric System, Dayton, OH, p. A323

INGALA, Robert J., Chief Executive Officer, Hale Hospital, Haverhill, MA, p. A201

INGHAM, Ray, President and Chief Executive Officer, Witham Memorial Hospital, Lebanon, IN, p. A142

INGRAHAM, Ron, Administrator, Klickitat Valley Hospital, Goldendale, WA, p. A444

INGRAM, Judy, Acting Administrator, Stonewall Memorial Hospital, Aspermont, TX, p. A393

INIGO–AGOSTINI, Emigdio, M.D., Board President, Clinica Espanola, Mayaguez, PR, p. A471

IRBY, Frank, Chief Executive Officer, Raulerson Hospital, Okeechobee, FL, p. A91

IRWIN, Michele, Administrator, Alliance Hospital of Santa Teresa, Santa Teresa, NM, p. A280

IRWIN Jr., Richard M., President and Chief Executive Officer, Health Central, Ocoee, FL, p. A91

ISAACS, James W., Chief Executive Officer, Mercer County Joint Township Community Hospital, Coldwater, OH, p. A321

ISBELL, John, Chief Executive Officer, Doctors Hospital, Groves, TX, p. A406

ISELY, John A., President, St. Mary Medical Center, Walla Walla, WA, p. A449

ISOM, Candace, Interim Administrator, Orange County Hospital, Paoli, IN, p. A143

ISRAEL, Michael D., Chief Executive Officer and Vice Chancellor, Duke University Medical Center, Durham, NC, p. A304

IVERSEN, Dale E., President and Chief Executive Officer, Warrack Medical Center Hospital, Santa Rosa, CA, p. A63

IVES, R. Wayne, Administrator, San Vicente Hospital, Los Angeles, CA, p. A50

IVESON, Sara C., Executive Director, Barnes–Kasson County Hospital, Susquehanna, PA, p. A364

IVEY, Jim, Administrator, Memorial Pavilion, Lawton, OK, p. A336

J

JACKMUFF, Steven W., President and Chief Executive Officer, Underwood–Memorial Hospital, Woodbury, NJ, p. A276

JACKSON, Fred L., Chief Executive Officer, King's Daughters' Medical Center, Ashland, KY, p. A167

JACKSON, Joan, Administrator, Melrose Area Hospital, Melrose, MN, p. A225

JACKSON, Lynn, Administrator, Baptist Meriwether Hospital, Warm Springs, GA, p. A111

JACKSON, Thomas W., Chief Executive Officer, College Station Medical Center, College Station, TX, p. A398

JACKSON, Valerie A.
Chief Executive Officer, East Pointe Hospital, Lehigh Acres, FL, p. A88
Chief Executive Officer, Gulf Coast Hospital, Fort Myers, FL, p. A84

JACKSON, William, President, Charlevoix Area Hospital, Charlevoix, MI, p. A207

JACOBI, Paula, President and Chief Executive Officer, Provena St. Mary's Hospital, Kankakee, IL, p. A127

JACOBS, John L., Administrator, Bennett County Healthcare Center, Martin, SD, p. A377

JACOBS, Nicholas, Executive Director, Windber Hospital, Windber, PA, p. A366

JACOBS, Selby, M.D., Director, Connecticut Mental Health Center, New Haven, CT, p. A75

JACOBSON, John L., President and Chief Executive Officer, Lee's Summit Hospital, Lees Summit, MO, p. A244

JACOBSON, Rod, Administrator, Bear Lake Memorial Hospital, Montpelier, ID, p. A115

JACOBSON, Ronald L., President and Chief Executive Officer, Avera Queen of Peace, Mitchell, SD, p. A378

JACOBSON, Steven K., Chief Executive Officer, Titus Regional Medical Center, Mount Pleasant, TX, p. A415

JACOBUS, Rick, Administrator, Martin County Hospital District, Stanton, TX, p. A422

JACOBY, Jamie R., Administrator, Kimble Hospital, Junction, TX, p. A411

JAEGER, Mark J., CHE, Administrator, Saint John Hospital, Leavenworth, KS, p. A160

JAFFE, David E., Executive Director and Chief Executive Officer, Harborview Medical Center, Seattle, WA, p. A447

JAHN, David B., Administrator and Chief Financial Officer, Schoolcraft Memorial Hospital, Manistique, MI, p. A214

JAMES, Craig B., President and Chief Executive Officer, Tazewell Community Hospital, Tazewell, VA, p. A441

JAMES, Curtis, Acting President and Chief Executive Officer, St. Vincent's Hospital, Birmingham, AL, p. A12

JAMES, David, Chief Executive Officer, Sturgis Hospital, Sturgis, MI, p. A217

JAMES, Donald W., DPH, Administrator, Baptist Three Rivers Hospital, Waverly, TN, p. A390

JAMES, Lisa, Chief Operating Officer, Wesley Rehabilitation Hospital, Wichita, KS, p. A166

JAMES, Pat, Interim Chief Executive Officer, Great Plains Regional Medical Center, Elk City, OK, p. A335

JAMES, William B., Chief Executive Officer, Northern Hospital of Surry County, Mount Airy, NC, p. A309

JAMES Jr., George H., President and Chief Executive Officer, Memorial Hospital, Seymour, IN, p. A144

JANCZAK, Linda M., President and Chief Executive Officer, F. F. Thompson Health System, Canandaigua, NY, p. A283

JANKE, Paul, Chief Operating Officer, Three Rivers Community Hospital and Health Center, Grants Pass, OR, p. A343

JANVRIN, Susan, R.N., Site Leader and Nurse Executive, Kaiser Foundation Hospital, Santa Rosa, CA, p. A62

JARM, Timothy L., President, Jewish Hospital–Shelbyville, Shelbyville, KY, p. A175

JARRETT, James L., Chief Executive Officer, Berrien County Hospital, Nashville, GA, p. A108

JARRY, Jacques, Administrator, Bullock County Hospital, Union Springs, AL, p. A19

JASPERSON, Steven W., Executive Vice President Operations, Lebanon Community Hospital, Lebanon, OR, p. A343

JAUDES, Paula Kienberger, M.D., President and Chief Executive Officer, LaRabida Children's Hospital and Research Center, Chicago, IL, p. A121

JAVIER, John, Administrator, Monrovia Community Hospital, Monrovia, CA, p. A52

JEAN, Darrell, Administrator and Chief Executive Officer, Pemiscot Memorial Health System, Hayti, MO, p. A242

JEANMARD, William C., Chief Executive Officer, Allen Parish Hospital, Kinder, LA, p. A180

JEFFCOAT, Sally E., Chief Executive Officer, Christus St. Joseph Hospital, Houston, TX, p. A407

JENKINS, Jeffrey K., President, St. Michael Hospital, Milwaukee, WI, p. A461

JENKINS Jr., Smith, Acting Chief Executive Officer, Veterans Affairs Medical Center–West Los Angeles, Los Angeles, CA, p. A51

JENNINGS, William A., Chief Operating Officer and Administrator, North Bay Hospital, New Port Richey, FL, p. A91

JENNINGS, William R., President and Chief Executive Officer, South Hills Health System, Pittsburgh, PA, p. A361

JENSEN, Bruce, Chief Executive Officer and Team Leader, Holy Rosary Medical Center, Ontario, OR, p. A344

JENSEN, Eric, Administrator, Kittitas Valley Community Hospital, Ellensburg, WA, p. A444

JEPPSON, James, Administrator, Presbyterian Hospital, Albuquerque, NM, p. A277

JEPSON, Gary L., Chief Executive Officer, Tahlequah City Hospital, Tahlequah, OK, p. A340

JERNIGAN Jr., Robert F., Administrator, South Baldwin Regional Medical Center, Foley, AL, p. A14

JESIOLOWSKI, Craig A., Chief Executive Officer, Gibson Area Hospital and Health Services, Gibson City, IL, p. A125

JESSUP, Dale, President and Chief Executive Officer, Bay Area Hospital, Coos Bay, OR, p. A342

JETER, John H., M.D., President and Chief Executive Officer, Hays Medical Center, Hays, KS, p. A159

JEX, Robert F., Administrator, Bear River Valley Hospital, Tremonton, UT, p. A430

JHIN, Michael K., President and Chief Executive Officer, St. Luke's Episcopal Health System, Houston, TX, p. A409

JIVIDEN, Thomas C., Senior Vice President, Virginia Baptist Hospital, Lynchburg, VA, p. A436

JOHANSON, Blair R., Administrator, Charter Behavioral Health System/Central Georgia, Macon, GA, p. A107

JOHN, Roger S., President and Chief Executive Officer, Great Plains Health Alliance, Inc., Phillipsburg, KS, p. B98

JOHN, Susie, M.D., Chief Executive Officer, Tuba City Indian Medical Center, Tuba City, AZ, p. A27

JOHNS, Charles A., President and Chief Executive Officer, Western Reserve Care System, Youngstown, OH, p. A331

JOHNSON, Curtis A., Administrator, Flambeau Hospital, Park Falls, WI, p. A462

JOHNSON, David B., Administrator, Brookings Hospital, Brookings, SD, p. A376

JOHNSON, Dennis B., Administrator, Tri County Baptist Hospital, La Grange, KY, p. A170

JOHNSON, Don P., Administrator, Cedars Hospital, De Soto, TX, p. A401

JOHNSON, Douglas L., Administrator, Baptist Memorial Hospital–Golden Triangle, Columbus, MS, p. A232

JOHNSON, Doyle K., Administrator, Mercy Hospital, Moundridge, KS, p. A162

JOHNSON, Elizabeth, Chief Executive Officer, Sage Memorial Hospital, Ganado, AZ, p. A23

JOHNSON, George L., President, Reedsburg Area Medical Center, Reedsburg, WI, p. A463

JOHNSON, Gregory D., Administrator, Cox Monett Hospital, Monett, MO, p. A245

JOHNSON, James K., Chief Executive Officer, Hedrick Medical Center, Chillicothe, MO, p. A240

JOHNSON, John C., Chief Executive Officer, Holy Cross Hospital, Fort Lauderdale, FL, p. A84

JOHNSON, John H., Chief Executive Officer, Gothenburg Memorial Hospital, Gothenburg, NE, p. A258

JOHNSON, John W., President and Chief Executive Officer, Alice Hyde Hospital Association, Malone, NY, p. A287

JOHNSON, Karl E., Chief Executive Officer, Mount Graham Community Hospital, Safford, AZ, p. A26

JOHNSON, Kevin, Chief Executive Officer, Mountain View Hospital, Payson, UT, p. A428

JOHNSON, L. Barney, President and Chief Executive Officer, Harbor Hospital Center, Baltimore, MD, p. A191

JOHNSON, LaQuita, Chief Executive Officer, Oakdale Community Hospital, Oakdale, LA, p. A184

JOHNSON, Laurence E., Administrator, Shriners Hospitals for Children, Twin Cities, Minneapolis, MN, p. A225

JOHNSON, Michael, Administrator and Chief Executive Officer, Crosbyton Clinic Hospital, Crosbyton, TX, p. A399

JOHNSON, Paul H., President and Chief Executive Officer, Gaylord Hospital, Wallingford, CT, p. A77

JOHNSON, Richard, Chief Executive Officer, Memorial Hospital of Carbon County, Rawlins, WY, p. A467

JOHNSON, Ronald E., Administrator, Meeker County Memorial Hospital, Litchfield, MN, p. A224

JOHNSON, Stan, Medical Center Director, Veterans Affairs Medical Center, Tomah, WI, p. A464

JOHNSON, Steven G., Administrator, Amethyst, Charlotte, NC, p. A303

JOHNSON, Steven M.

President, Citizens Baptist Medical Center, Talladega, AL, p. A18

President, Coosa Valley Baptist Medical Center, Sylacauga, AL, p. A18

JOHNSON, Thomas M., Chief Executive Officer, Kaweah Delta Health Care District, Visalia, CA, p. A66

JOHNSON, Timothy, M.D., President, Austin Medical Center, Austin, MN, p. A220

JOHNSON, Van R., President and Chief Executive Officer, Sutter Health, Sacramento, CA, p. B142

JOHNSON, Viola L., Chief Executive Officer, Huhukam Memorial Hospital, Sacaton, AZ, p. A26

JOHNSON, William D., President, Lee Memorial Health System, Fort Myers, FL, p. A84

JOHNSON–PHILLIPPE, Sue E., Chief Executive Officer, LakeView Community Hospital, Paw Paw, MI, p. A215

JOHNSRUD, Kimry A., President, Elmbrook Memorial Hospital, Brookfield, WI, p. A457

JOHNSTON, Charles, Administrator, Pauls Valley General Hospital, Pauls Valley, OK, p. A338

JOHNSTON, Debbie W., Director Operations, HEALTHSOUTH Rehabilitation Hospital, Columbia, SC, p. A371

JOHNSTON, R. Joe, President and Chief Executive Officer, Dukes Memorial Hospital, Peru, IN, p. A143

JOHNSTON, Wayne W., President and Chief Executive Officer, Sharon Regional Health System, Sharon, PA, p. A364

JOLLY, Jay P., Administrator and Chief Executive Officer, Clay County Hospital, Brazil, IN, p. A136

JONAS, Stanley W., Chief Executive Officer, Alliance Community Hospital, Alliance, OH, p. A317

JONES, Carol E., Administrator, Annie Jeffrey Memorial County Health Center, Osceola, NE, p. A261

JONES, Deryl L., President, Adventist Medical Center, Portland, OR, p. A344

JONES, Donald J., Administrator, Carraway Burdick West Medical Center, Haleyville, AL, p. A15

JONES, Dwayne, Chief Executive Officer, Fairchild Medical Center, Yreka, CA, p. A67

JONES, Florence, Administrator, Parkview Regional Medical Center, Vicksburg, MS, p. A237

JONES, G. W., Administrator, Nacogdoches Memorial Hospital, Nacogdoches, TX, p. A416

JONES, H. Ed, Chief Executive Officer, North Carolina Eye and Ear Hospital, Durham, NC, p. A305

JONES, J. Thomas, Executive Director, St. Mary's Hospital, Huntington, WV, p. A452

JONES, James S., Director, Veterans Affairs Medical Center, Danville, IL, p. A123

JONES, Jerry, Administrator, Intergris Clinton Regional Hospital, Clinton, OK, p. A334

JONES, John R., Administrator, Yalobusha General Hospital, Water Valley, MS, p. A238

JONES, Lowell

Chief Executive Officer, Marymount Medical Center, London, KY, p. A171

Chief Executive Officer, Our Lady of the Way Hospital, Martin, KY, p. A173

JONES, Mark T., President, Holy Redeemer Hospital and Medical Center, Meadowbrook, PA, p. A356

JONES, Nancy, Administrator, Shriners Hospitals for Children, Portland, Portland, OR, p. A345

JONES, Rex, Chief Executive Officer, Howard Memorial Hospital, Nashville, AR, p. A33

JONES, Robert D., President, Rutherford Hospital, Rutherfordton, NC, p. A310

JONES, Robert T., M.D., President and Chief Executive Officer, Hutcheson Medical Center, Fort Oglethorpe, GA, p. A105

JONES, Wayne, Executive Vice President and Administrator, Maryview Hospital, Portsmouth, VA, p. A438

JONES, William G., Administrator, Refugio County Memorial Hospital, Refugio, TX, p. A418

JONES Jr., Richard L., President and Chief Executive Officer, Abington Memorial Hospital, Abington, PA, p. A347

JORDAHL, David B., FACHE, President, St. Clare Hospital and Health Services, Baraboo, WI, p. A456

JORDAN, Bobby, Chief Executive Officer, Winn Parish Medical Center, Winnfield, LA, p. A186

JORDAN, David R., Ph.D., Administrator and Chief Executive Officer, Nor–Lea General Hospital, Lovington, NM, p. A279

JORDAN, Gary W., President and Chief Executive Officer, St. Francis Hospital, Mountain View, MO, p. A245

JORDAN, J. Larry, Administrator, Homer Memorial Hospital, Homer, LA, p. A180

JORDAN, James, Chief Executive Officer, Kit Carson County Memorial Hospital, Burlington, CO, p. A68

JORDAN, Lawrence A., Director, PHS Santa Fe Indian Hospital, Santa Fe, NM, p. A280

JORDAN, Linda U., Administrator, Clay County Hospital, Ashland, AL, p. A11

JORDAN, W. Charles, Administrator, Mayes County Medical Center, Pryor, OK, p. A339

JORVE, Helen, Chief Executive Officer, Graceville Health Center, Graceville, MN, p. A223

JOSEF, Norma C., M.D., Director, Walter P. Reuther Psychiatric Hospital, Westland, MI, p. A219

JOSEPH, Elliot T., President and Chief Executive Officer, Genesys Regional Medical Center, Grand Blanc, MI, p. A210

JOSEPH, Gloria, Superintendent, Western Missouri Mental Health Center, Kansas City, MO, p. A244

JOSEPH, Michael G., Chief Executive Officer, Westside Regional Medical Center, Plantation, FL, p. A93

JOSEPH, Vincent D., Executive Director, Saint Barnabas Medical Center, Livingston, NJ, p. A271

JOSEY, Brenda, Administrator, Wheeler County Hospital, Glenwood, GA, p. A105

JOSLIN, Tim A., Chief Executive Officer, Doctors Medical Center, Modesto, CA, p. A52

JOSPE, Theodore A., President, Southside Hospital, Bay Shore, NY, p. A282

JOYCE, Michael P., President and Chief Executive Officer, Trident Medical Center, Charleston, SC, p. A371

JOYNER, Ronald G., Chief Executive Officer, Williamson Medical Center, Franklin, TN, p. A383

JUBINSKY, Linda, Chief Executive Officer, Peachtree Regional Hospital, Newnan, GA, p. A108

JUDD, Jeffrey M., President and Chief Executive Officer, McDowell Hospital, Marion, NC, p. A308

JUDD, Russell V., Chief Executive Officer, Payson Regional Medical Center, Payson, AZ, p. A24

JUENEMANN, Jean, Chief Executive Officer, Queen of Peace Hospital, New Prague, MN, p. A226

JUENGLING, Craig S.
Chief Executive Officer, Charter Behavioral Health System at Springwood, Leesburg, VA, p. A436
Chief Executive Officer, Charter Behavioral Health System of Maryland at Potomac Ridge, Rockville, MD, p. A195

JULIUS, John D., Interim Administrator, St. Mary–Corwin Medical Center, Pueblo, CO, p. A72

JUPIN Jr., Joseph, Chief Executive Officer, Trenton Psychiatric Hospital, Trenton, NJ, p. A275

JURENA, Jerry E., Executive Director, Heart of America Medical Center, Rugby, ND, p. A315

K

KAATZ, Gary E.
Executive Vice President and Chief Operating Officer, Forum Health, Youngstown, OH, p. B96
Chief Operating Officer, Trumbull Memorial Hospital, Warren, OH, p. A330

KABOT, Lorraine B., FACHE, President and Chief Executive Officer, Hepburn Medical Center, Ogdensburg, NY, p. A295

KADLEC, Patricia, Administrator, Faulk County Memorial Hospital, Faulkton, SD, p. A377

KAIL, Bill, Administrator, Humboldt General Hospital, Humboldt, TN, p. A384

KAJIWARA, Gary K., President and Chief Executive Officer, Kuakini Medical Center, Honolulu, HI, p. A112

KALDOR, Patricia A., R.N., President, St. Joseph's Hospital, Milwaukee, WI, p. A461

KALETKOWSKI, Chester B.
President and Chief Executive Officer, Newcomb Medical Center, Vineland, NJ, p. A275
President and Chief Executive Officer, South Jersey Hospital, Bridgeton, NJ, p. A268

KALLEN–ZURY, Karen, Chief Executive Officer, Hollywood Pavilion, Los Angeles, FL, p. A86

KAMBER, Steven R., Vice President and Administrator, Christus Spohn Hospital Memorial, Corpus Christi, TX, p. A398

KANE, Daniel A., President and Chief Executive Officer, Englewood Hospital and Medical Center, Englewood, NJ, p. A270

KANN, Denise, Administrator and Chief Operating Officer, HEALTHSOUTH Meridian Point Rehabilitation Hospital, Scottsdale, AZ, p. A26

KANNADY, Donald L., Administrator, Bunkie General Hospital, Bunkie, LA, p. A178

KANTOS, Craig A., Chief Executive Officer, Riverside Medical Center, Waupaca, WI, p. A464

KARAM, Judith Ann, President and Chief Executive Officer, Sisters of Charity of St. Augustine Health System, Cleveland, OH, p. B137

KARELS, Genevieve, Administrator, St. Bernard's Providence Hospital, Milbank, SD, p. A377

KARPF, Michael, M.D., Vice Provost Hospital System and Director Medical Center, University of California Los Angeles Medical Center, Los Angeles, CA, p. A50

KARUSCHAK Jr., Michael, Chief Executive Officer, Amery Regional Medical Center, Amery, WI, p. A456

KASEY, Jay D., President, St. Mary's Medical Center of Evansville, Evansville, IN, p. A138

KASPERIK, Donald J., Commander, Winn Army Community Hospital, Hinesville, GA, p. A106

KAST, Kevin F.
President, St. Joseph Health Center, Saint Charles, MO, p. A246
President, St. Joseph Hospital West, Lake Saint Louis, MO, p. A244

KASTANIS, John N., FACHE, President and Chief Executive Officer, Hospital for Joint Diseases Orthopaedic Institute, New York, NY, p. A290

KASTELIC, Sumiyo E., Director, University of California San Diego Medical Center, San Diego, CA, p. A59

KATHRINS, Richard J., Administrator and Chief Executive Officer, Bacharach Institute for Rehabilitation, Pomona, NJ, p. A274

KATSUDA, Frank, Administrator, Memorial Hospital of Gardena, Gardena, CA, p. A43

KATZ, Stuart A., FACHE, Administrator, Hawarden Community Hospital, Hawarden, IA, p. A150

KATZ, Treuman, President and Chief Executive Officer, Children's Hospital and Regional Medical Center, Seattle, WA, p. A447

KAUFFMAN, Louis, President and Chief Executive Officer, Dakota Heartland Health System, Fargo, ND, p. A314

KAUFMAN, Alan G., Director, Division of Mental Health Services, Department of Human Services, State of New Jersey, Trenton, NJ, p. B94

KAUFMAN, Thomas D., Administrator, Kanabec Hospital, Mora, MN, p. A226

KAYLER, R. S., USN, Commanding Officer, Naval Hospital, Twentynine Palms, CA, p. A65

KEAHEY, Kent A., President and Chief Executive Officer, Providence Health Center, Waco, TX, p. A425

KEARNEY, Daniel, Chief Executive Officer, Charter Behavioral Health System–Orlando, Kissimmee, FL, p. A87

KEARNEY, Jerome R., Chief Executive Officer, BHC College Meadows Hospital, Lenexa, KS, p. A161

KEARNEY, W. Michael, President, Mary Lanning Memorial Hospital, Hastings, NE, p. A258

KEARS, David J., Director, Alameda County Health Care Services Agency, San Leandro, CA, p. B60

KECK, Wade E., Chief Executive Officer, Memorial Health Services, Adel, GA, p. B115

KEEFER, Michael R., CHE, Administrator and Chief Executive Officer, Clarion Psychiatric Center, Clarion, PA, p. A349

KEEHAN, Carol, President, Providence Hospital, Washington, DC, p. A79

KEEL, Barry L., Chief Executive Officer, Andalusia Regional Hospital, Andalusia, AL, p. A11

KEEL, Deborah C., Chief Executive Officer, Kenner Regional Medical Center, Kenner, LA, p. A180

KEELAN, John E., Administrator, Johnson County Hospital, Tecumseh, NE, p. A262

KEELEY, Brian E., President and Chief Executive Officer, Baptist Health System of South Florida, Coral Gables, FL, p. B64

KEEN, Robert C., CHE, President and Chief Executive Officer, Hancock Memorial Hospital and Health Services, Greenfield, IN, p. A139

KEENE, Lee D., President and Chief Executive Officer, Rockcastle Hospital and Respiratory Care Center, Mount Vernon, KY, p. A174

KEENER, Carl, M.D., Medical Director, Montana State Hospital, Warm Springs, MT, p. A255

KEIERLEBER, Daniel, Administrator, Community Memorial Hospital, Redfield, SD, p. A378

KEIMIG, H. John, President and Chief Executive Officer, St. Joseph Health Services of Rhode Island, North Providence, RI, p. A368

KEIR, Douglas C., Chief Executive Officer, McDuffie County Hospital, Thomson, GA, p. A110

KEITH, David N., Chief Executive Officer, Rice Medical Center, Eagle Lake, TX, p. A402

KELLAR, Richard A., Administrator, West Allis Memorial Hospital, West Allis, WI, p. A465

KELLER, Jack M., Administrator, Baptist Hickman Community Hospital, Centerville, TN, p. A381

KELLER, Larry W., Chief Executive Officer, University Medical Center, Lebanon, TN, p. A386

KELLERMANN, Carol, Acting Administrator, Cumberland Memorial Hospital, Cumberland, WI, p. A457

KELLEY, Neal, Administrator, Seton Edgar B. Davis Hospital, Luling, TX, p. A414

KELLEY, Randall, President, Flower Hospital, Sylvania, OH, p. A329

KELLEY, Robert C., President and Chief Executive Officer, Madera Community Hospital, Madera, CA, p. A51

KELLEY, William N., M.D., Chief Executive Officer, University of Pennsylvania Health System, Philadelphia, PA, p. B152

KELLEY, Joseph, Commander, U. S. Air Force Medical Center Wright–Patterson, Wright–Patterson AFB, OH, p. A331

KELLEY Jr., William C., FACHE, President and Chief Executive Officer, Samaritan Regional Health System, Ashland, OH, p. A317

KELLIE, Karen J., President, McCall Memorial Hospital, McCall, ID, p. A115

KELLISON, Jay R., Chief Executive Officer, BHC Walnut Creek Hospital, Walnut Creek, CA, p. A66

KELLOGG, Richard E., Acting Commissioner, Virginia Department of Mental Health, Richmond, VA, p. B155

KELLY, Arthur C., Administrator and Chief Executive Officer, Oktibbeha County Hospital, Starkville, MS, p. A237

KELLY, Daniel J., President and Chief Executive Officer, St. Mary's Hospital, Nebraska City, NE, p. A259

KELLY, Frank J., President and Chief Executive Officer, Danbury Hospital, Danbury, CT, p. A74

KELLY, James, Chief Executive Officer, Houston Northwest Medical Center, Houston, TX, p. A408

KELLY, Jeffrey R., President and Chief Executive Officer, Deaconess–Nashoba Hospital, Ayer, MA, p. A197

KELLY, Kathleen, Chief Executive Officer, Pilgrim Psychiatric Center, Brentwood, NY, p. A282

KELLY, Laurence E., Executive Vice President and Administrator, St. Luke's Hospital, Newburgh, NY, p. A294

KELLY, Patrick, Chief Executive Officer, Charter Behavioral Health System of Northwest Arkansas, Fayetteville, AR, p. A30

KELLY, Peter A., Interim President and Chief Executive Officer, Long Island College Hospital, New York, NY, p. A291

KELLY, Sheila C., MS, Chief Executive Officer, Haven Hospital, De Soto, TX, p. A401

KELLY, Steven G., Administrator, Integris Baptist Regional Health Center, Miami, OK, p. A337

KELLY, Timothy J., M.D., President, Fairbanks Hospital, Indianapolis, IN, p. A140

KELLY, Patrick J., Director, Administration, Naval Hospital, Pensacola, FL, p. A93

KELLY Jr., Winfield M., President and Chief Executive Officer, Dimensions Health Corporation, Largo, MD, p. B94

KENDRICK, Gary G., Chief Executive Officer, Lincoln County Health Facilities, Fayetteville, TN, p. A383

KENLEY, William A., President and Chief Executive Officer, North Crest Medical Center, Springfield, TN, p. A390

KENNEDY, Bill R., President and Chief Executive Officer, Muskogee Regional Medical Center, Muskogee, OK, p. A337

KENNEDY, Christopher S., President and Chief Operating Officer, Health First/Cape Canaveral Hospital, Cocoa Beach, FL, p. A82

KENNEDY, Thomas F., Administrator, Rolling Plains Memorial Hospital, Sweetwater, TX, p. A422

KENNEDY III, Thomas D., President and Chief Executive Officer, Bristol Hospital, Bristol, CT, p. A74

KENNEDY–SCOTT, Patricia, Northern Region Vice President, The Eastside Hospital, Redmond, WA, p. A446

KENNER, Gary, President and Chief Executive Officer, Itasca Medical Center, Grand Rapids, MN, p. A223

KENWOOD, Russell, Administrator, Sentara Hampton General Hospital, Hampton, VA, p. A435

KENYON, Douglas M., Director, Veterans Affairs Medical and Regional Office Center, Fargo, ND, p. A314

KERCORIAN, Robert A., Chief Executive Officer, Havenwyck Hospital, Auburn Hills, MI, p. A206

KERINS Sr., James J., Administrator, Caverna Memorial Hospital, Horse Cave, KY, p. A170

KERN, Cynthia L., Administrator, Edgemont Hospital, Los Angeles, CA, p. A48

KERN, Peter L., President and Chief Executive Officer, Palmerton Hospital, Palmerton, PA, p. A357

KERNER, Michael K., President and Chief Executive Officer, Columbia–Augusta Medical Center, Augusta, GA, p. A100

KERR, Kay, M.D., Medical Director, Bryn Mawr College Infirmary, Bryn Mawr, PA, p. A349

KERR, Michael
Administrator, Bellwood General Hospital, Bellflower, CA, p. A37
Chief Executive Officer, Orange County Community Hospital of Buena Park, Buena Park, CA, p. A38

KERR, William B., Executive Vice President and Chief Operating Officer, Stanford Hospital and Clinics, Stanford, CA, p. A64

KERVIN, David D., Administrator, Richardson Medical Center, Rayville, LA, p. A185

KERWIN, George, President, Bellin Hospital, Green Bay, WI, p. A458

KESSEN, Donald J., Administrator and Chief Executive Officer, Rawlins County Health Center, Atwood, KS, p. A156

KESSINGER, A. Jay, Administrative Director, State Hospital North, Orofino, ID, p. A116

KESSLER, D. McWilliams, Executive Director, Wills Eye Hospital, Philadelphia, PA, p. A360

KESSLER, William E., President, Saint Anthony's Health Center, Alton, IL, p. A118

KESTLY, John J., Administrator, Shawano Medical Center, Shawano, WI, p. A463

KETCHAM, Michael S., Administrator, Manning Regional Healthcare Center, Manning, IA, p. A151

KETCHAM, Richard H., President, Brooks Memorial Hospital, Dunkirk, NY, p. A284

KETRING, John, Administrator, Pawnee Municipal Hospital, Pawnee, OK, p. A338

KEUSENKOTHEN, Thomas, President and Chief Executive Officer, Alexian Brothers Health System, Inc., Elk Grove Village, IL, p. B60

KEVISH, Stanley J., President, UPMC St. Margaret, Pittsburgh, PA, p. A362

KEY, Ramona, Chief Executive Officer, Charter Behavioral Health System of Southeast Texas–Kingwood, Kingwood, TX, p. A411

KHAN, Nasir A., M.D., Director, Bournewood Hospital, Brookline, MA, p. A199

KIDDY, Diane, Chief Executive Officer, Charter Fairmount Behavioral Health System, Philadelphia, PA, p. A358

KIEF, Brian, Administrator, United Hospital District, Blue Earth, MN, p. A221

KIEFER, Joseph N., Administrator, Helen Ellis Memorial Hospital, Tarpon Springs, FL, p. A97

KIELANOWICZ, Marie, Provincial Superior, Sisters of the Holy Family of Nazareth–Sacred Heart Province, Des Plaines, IL, p. B140

KIELMAN, Richard C., President and Chief Executive Officer, Dickinson County Memorial Hospital, Spirit Lake, IA, p. A154

KIELY, Robert Gerard, President and Chief Executive Officer, Middlesex Hospital, Middletown, CT, p. A75

KIER, Aloha, Administrator, Jewell County Hospital, Mankato, KS, p. A161

KILBURN, Richard L., Chief Executive Officer, Elko General Hospital, Elko, NV, p. A263

KILEY, Dennis, President, Gordon Hospital, Calhoun, GA, p. A102

KIMEL, Mike, Administrator, Davie County Hospital, Mocksville, NC, p. A308

KIMMETH, Steuart A., Chief Executive Officer, Peninsula Behavioral Center, Hampton, VA, p. A435

KINDRED, Bryan, President and Chief Executive Officer, DCH Health System, Tuscaloosa, AL, p. B87

KING, Dennis, President, Spring Harbor Hospital, South Portland, ME, p. A190

KING, Joe W., M.D., President, Chief Executive Officer and Medical Director, Desert Hills Center for Youth and Families, Tucson, AZ, p. A27

KING, Larry R., Administrator, Washington–St. Tammany Regional Medical Center, Bogalusa, LA, p. A178

KING, Michael, Administrator, Winslow Memorial Hospital, Winslow, AZ, p. A28

KINGSBURY, James A., President and Chief Executive Officer, Fort Hamilton Hospital, Hamilton, OH, p. A324

KINNEY, Charles S., Chief Executive Officer, Martha's Vineyard Hospital, Oak Bluffs, MA, p. A203

KINNEY, John P., President and Chief Executive Officer, Nason Hospital, Roaring Spring, PA, p. A363

KINZLEY, William, Chief Executive Officer, Williamson Memorial Hospital, Williamson, WV, p. A455

KIRBY, Dale A.
President, College Health Enterprises, Costa Mesa, CA, p. B78
Chief Executive Officer, College Hospital Costa Mesa, Costa Mesa, CA, p. A40

KIRBY, James M., Administrator, Swain County Hospital, Bryson City, NC, p. A303

KIRK, Brian, Chief Executive Officer, Sheridan County Hospital, Hoxie, KS, p. A159

KIRK, Warren J., President and Chief Administrative Officer, Alta Bates Medical Center–Ashby Campus, Berkeley, CA, p. A38

KIRK Jr., H. Lee, President and Chief Executive Officer, Culpeper Memorial Hospital, Culpeper, VA, p. A434

KIRK Jr., William R., President and Chief Executive Officer, Kent & Queen Anne's Hospital, Chestertown, MD, p. A193

KIRN, Galen, Administrator, California Mens Colony Hospital, San Luis Obispo, CA, p. A61

KIROUSIS, Theodore E.
Area Director, Medfield State Hospital, Medfield, MA, p. A202
Area Director, Westborough State Hospital, Westborough, MA, p. A205

KIRSCHNER, Sidney, President and Chief Executive Officer, Northside Hospital, Atlanta, GA, p. A100

KISER, Greg, Chief Executive Officer, Three Rivers Medical Center, Louisa, KY, p. A171

KISER, James, Administrator, Washakie Memorial Hospital, Worland, WY, p. A468

KISH, Thomas M., Executive Director, University of Tennessee Memorial Hospital, Knoxville, TN, p. A385

KITCHEN, Barbara, Chief Executive Officer, Charter Ridge Behavioral Health System, Lexington, KY, p. A171

KITE, Landon, President, Fuller Memorial Hospital, South Attleboro, MA, p. A204

KIZER, Kenneth W., M.P.H., Under Secretary for Health, Department of Veterans Affairs, Washington, DC, p. B90

KLAASMEYER, Al, Administrator, Community Memorial Hospital, Syracuse, NE, p. A262

KLAGSBRUN, Samuel C., M.D., Executive Medical Director, Four Winds Hospital, Katonah, NY, p. A287

KLAMAN, Edward M., Acting Chief Executive Officer, Citizens General Hospital, New Kensington, PA, p. A357

KLAWITER, Anne K., President and Chief Executive Officer, Southwest Health Center, Platteville, WI, p. A462

KLEEFISCH, William B., Chief Executive Officer, Maui Medical Memorial Center, Wailuku, HI, p. A113

KLEIN, Gerard D.
President, UHHS Brown Memorial Hospital, Conneaut, OH, p. A322
Chief Executive Officer, UHHS–Memorial Hospital of Geneva, Geneva, OH, p. A324

KLEIN, Robert, Chief Executive Officer, Hendersonville Hospital, Hendersonville, TN, p. A384

KLEIN, Steven M., President and Chief Executive Officer, North Shore Medical Center, Miami, FL, p. A90

KLEINGLOSS, Steven, Acting Director, Veterans Affairs Medical Center, Minneapolis, MN, p. A226

KLIER, Bill, Chief Executive Officer, Cypress Fairbanks Medical Center, Houston, TX, p. A407

KLIMA, Dennis E., President and Chief Executive Officer, Bayhealth Medical Center, Dover, DE, p. A78

KLIMP, Mary, Administrator and Chief Executive Officer, Falls Memorial Hospital, International Falls, MN, p. A224

KLINGMAN, Dwaine, Administrator, Jefferson County Memorial Hospital, Winchester, KS, p. A166

KLINT, Robert B., M.D., President and Chief Executive Officer, SwedishAmerican Health System, Rockford, IL, p. A133

KLOESS, Larry, President, Centennial Medical Center and Parthenon Pavilion, Nashville, TN, p. A388

KLUN, James A., President, Allegan General Hospital, Allegan, MI, p. A206

KLUSMANN, Richard W., Chief Executive Officer, St. David's South Hospital, Austin, TX, p. A394

KLUTTS, Robert, Chief Executive Officer, Touchette Regional Hospital, Centreville, IL, p. A120

KLUTTZ, James K., President and Chief Executive Officer, Frederick Memorial Hospital, Frederick, MD, p. A194

KMETZ, Thomas D., Chief Administrative Officer, Norton Audubon Hospital, Louisville, KY, p. A172

KNAPP, Dennis L., President, Cameron Memorial Community Hospital, Angola, IN, p. A136

KNAUSS, Albert C., President and Chief Executive Officer, Marion General Hospital, Marion, IN, p. A142

KNEIBERT, Kathryn, Administrator, Kemper Community Hospital, De Kalb, MS, p. A232

KNIGHT, Alan D., President and Chief Executive Officer, Jordan Hospital, Plymouth, MA, p. A203

KNIGHT, Robert, Chief Executive Officer, Kern Valley Hospital District, Lake Isabella, CA, p. A46

KNIGHT, Russell M., President and Chief Executive Officer, Mercy Health Center, Dubuque, IA, p. A149

KNOBLE, James K., President, Methodist Medical Center of Illinois, Peoria, IL, p. A131

KNOCKE, David L., CHE, Executive Director, Charlton Methodist Hospital, Dallas, TX, p. A399

KNODE, Scott, Co–Administrator, Community Memorial Hospital, Sumner, IA, p. A154

KNOX, Dennis M., Vice President and Chief Executive Officer, Memorial Hospital Pasadena, Pasadena, TX, p. A417

KNOX, John E., President, St. John Macomb Hospital, Warren, MI, p. A218

KNOX, Jud, President, York Hospital, York, ME, p. A190

KNUEPPEL, Arthur, Interim President and Chief Executive Officer, Battle Creek Health System, Battle Creek, MI, p. A206

KNUTSON, Fred, Administrator, Chippewa County Montevideo Hospital, Montevideo, MN, p. A226

KOBAN Jr., Michael A., Chief Executive Officer, NetCare Health Systems, Inc., Nashville, TN, p. B118

KOCHIS, Thomas, Administrator, Oakwood Hospital Annapolis Center, Wayne, MI, p. A219

KOCOUREK, Cathie A.
Acting Administrator, St. Mary's Kewaunee Area Memorial Hospital, Kewaunee, WI, p. A459
Acting Administrator, Two Rivers Community Hospital and Hamilton Memorial Home, Two Rivers, WI, p. A464

KOEHLER, Eduard R., Administrator, Medical Park Hospital, Winston–Salem, NC, p. A312

KOELLNER, William H., Administrator, Landmann–Jungman Memorial Hospital, Scotland, SD, p. A378

KOENIG, David Scott, Chief Executive Officer, Olympia Fields Osteopathic Hospital and Medical Center, Olympia Fields, IL, p. A131

KOESTER, Jeanne, Chief Executive Officer, Vencor Hospital – Albuquerque, Albuquerque, NM, p. A278

KOLB, Fred L.
President, Clermont Mercy Hospital, Batavia, OH, p. A318
President, Mercy Hospital Anderson, Cincinnati, OH, p. A320

KOLLARS, Tim, Administrator and Chief Executive Officer, Lincoln Hospital Medical Center, Los Angeles, CA, p. A49

KOLLER, George J., President and Chief Executive Officer, Noble Hospital, Westfield, MA, p. A205

KOORTBOJIAN, George, Interim Administrator, Southern Humboldt Community Healthcare District, Garberville, CA, p. A43

KOOY, Donald C., President and Chief Executive Officer, Lapeer Regional Hospital, Lapeer, MI, p. A213

KOPICKI, John R., President and Chief Executive Officer, Muhlenberg Regional Medical Center, Plainfield, NJ, p. A273

KOPMAN, Alan, President and Chief Executive Officer, Westchester Square Medical Center, New York, NY, p. A294

KOPP, C. Gary, Administrator, Wishek Community Hospital and Clinics, Wishek, ND, p. A316

KOPPEL, Robert F., President and Chief Executive Officer, East Tennessee Children's Hospital, Knoxville, TN, p. A385

KOPPELMAN, Ben, Administrator, Albany Area Hospital and Medical Center, Albany, MN, p. A220

KORBELAK, Kathleen M., President and Chief Executive Officer, St. Joseph Hospital & Health Center, Kokomo, IN, p. A141

KORDICK, Jill, Administrator, Madison County Memorial Hospital, Winterset, IA, p. A155

KORMAN, Keith, President, St. Andrew's Health Center, Bottineau, ND, p. A313

KORNEFF, Allen R., President and Chief Executive Officer, Downey Community Hospital Foundation, Downey, CA, p. A41

KORZEN, Joyce, R.N., Chief Operating Officer, Millard Fillmore Gates Circle Hospital, Buffalo, NY, p. A283

KOSANOVICH, John P., President, Watertown Memorial Hospital, Watertown, WI, p. A464

KOSCHALKE, Patricia Ann, President and Chief Executive Officer, Holy Family Medical Center, Des Plaines, IL, p. A124

KOSSEFF, Christopher O., Vice President and Chief Executive Officer, University of Medicine and Dentistry of New Jersey, University Behavioral Healthcare, Piscataway, NJ, p. A273

KOWAL, Robert P., President and Chief Executive Officer, Greater Baltimore Medical Center, Baltimore, MD, p. A191

KOWALEWSKI, William, President and Chief Executive Officer, Franklin Hospital Medical Center, Valley Stream, NY, p. A300

KOWALSKI, Richard S., Administrator and Chief Executive Officer, St. Mary Medical Center, Galesburg, IL, p. A125

KOZAI, Gerald T., President, St. Francis Medical Center, Lynwood, CA, p. A51

KOZAR, Michael A., Chief Executive Officer, Laurens County Healthcare System, Clinton, SC, p. A371

KOZLOFF, Kenneth H., Executive Director, Wayne General Hospital, Wayne, NJ, p. A275

KRABBENHOFT, Kelby K., President, Sioux Valley Hospitals and Health System, Sioux Falls, SD, p. B136

KRAGE, Oliver D., President and Chief Executive Officer, Roseland Community Hospital, Chicago, IL, p. A122

KRAMER, Douglas, Chief Executive Officer, Onslow Memorial Hospital, Jacksonville, NC, p. A307

KRAMER, Richard J., President and Chief Executive Officer, Catholic Healthcare West, San Francisco, CA, p. B75

KRAMER, Thomas H., President, Deaconess Hospital, Evansville, IN, p. A138

KRAML, Louis, Chief Executive Officer, Bingham Memorial Hospital, Blackfoot, ID, p. A114

KRASS, Todd, Administrator and Chief Executive Officer, Research Psychiatric Center, Kansas City, MO, p. A243

KRAUSE, J. Penn, Executive Vice President Operations, Mercy Hospital of Pittsburgh, Pittsburgh, PA, p. A361

KREHBIEL, James M., Chief Executive Officer, Freeman Community Hospital, Freeman, SD, p. A377

KREIN, Marlene, President and Chief Executive Officer, Mercy Hospital, Devils Lake, ND, p. A313

KREITNER, Clint, President and Chief Executive Officer, Tennessee Christian Medical Center, Madison, TN, p. A386

KRESHECK, Neal E., President, Community Hospital, Springfield, OH, p. A329

KRESSEL, Herbert Yehude, M.D., President, Beth Israel Deaconess Medical Center, Boston, MA, p. A197

KRETZ, Blake, Administrator, Graham Regional Medical Center, Graham, TX, p. A405

KREUZER, Jay E., FACHE, President, Saint Francis Hospital and Health Center, Blue Island, IL, p. A119

KREVANS, Sarah
Administrator, Kaiser Foundation Hospital, Sacramento, CA, p. A58
Senior Vice President, Kaiser Foundation Hospital, Sacramento, CA, p. A58

KRIEGER, Robert M., Chief Executive Officer, Orange Park Medical Center, Orange Park, FL, p. A91

KRISHNA, Murali, M.D., President and Chief Operating Officer, Integris Mental Health System–Spencer, Spencer, OK, p. A339

KRISIAK, Steve, Chief Executive Officer, Bertrand Chaffee Hospital, Springville, NY, p. A298

KRMPOTIC, Deb J., R.N.
Administrator, Lookout Memorial Hospital, Spearfish, SD, p. A379
Administrator, Sturgis Community Health Care Center, Sturgis, SD, p. A379

KROELL Jr., H. Scott, Chief Executive Officer, Liberty Regional Medical Center, Hinesville, GA, p. A106

KROESE, Robert D., Chief Executive Officer, Pella Regional Health Center, Pella, IA, p. A153

KROGNESS, John, Chief Executive Officer, North Bay Hospital, Aransas Pass, TX, p. A393

KROHN, Judith, Ph.D., Chief Executive Officer, Anoka–Metropolitan Regional Treatment Center, Anoka, MN, p. A220

KRUCKEBERG, Karl, Director, Alton Mental Health Center, Alton, IL, p. A118

KRUCZLNICKI, David G., President and Chief Executive Officer, Glens Falls Hospital, Glens Falls, NY, p. A285

KRUEGER, Glen E., Administrator, Nemaha County Hospital, Auburn, NE, p. A256

KRUEGER Jr., Harold L., Chief ExecutiveOfficer, Chadron Community Hospital and Health Services, Chadron, NE, p. A257

KRUPA, Michael P., Ed.D.
Chief Executive Officer, Pembroke Hospital, Pembroke, MA, p. A203
Chief Executive Officer, Westwood Lodge Hospital, Westwood, MA, p. A205

KRUSE, Lowell C., Chief Executive Officer, Heartland Regional Medical Center, Saint Joseph, MO, p. A247

KUBIAK, Phillip J., President, Hampstead Hospital, Hampstead, NH, p. A265

KUBIK, James A., Administrator, Pawnee County Memorial Hospital, Pawnee City, NE, p. A261

KUCZKOWSKI, Claire, Administrator, Pioneers Memorial Healthcare District, Brawley, CA, p. A38

KUDRLE, Venetia, Administrator, St. Francis Regional Medical Center, Shakopee, MN, p. A228

KUDRONOWICZ, Sherry, Administrator, Memorial Hospital of Lafayette County, Darlington, WI, p. A457

KUHN, David, Administrator, East Texas Medical Center–Fairfield, Fairfield, TX, p. A403

KUHN, John F., Chief Executive Officer, Forest View Hospital, Grand Rapids, MI, p. A210

KUHN, Marcus G., President and Chief Executive Officer, Twin County Regional Hospital, Galax, VA, p. A435

KUHN, Rebecca C., President and Chief Executive Officer, Paradise Valley Hospital, Phoenix, AZ, p. A25

KUNTZ, Edward L., Board Chairman, President and Chief Executive Officer, Vencor, Incorporated, Louisville, KY, p. B154

KUNZ, Susan, Administrator, Teton Valley Hospital, Driggs, ID, p. A115

KUNZ, Gretchen, President and Chief Executive Officer, St. Joseph Regional Health Center, Bryan, TX, p. A396

KURTZ, Kendria, Chief Executive Officer, Eagleville Hospital, Eagleville, PA, p. A351

KURTZ, Myers R., Administrator, G. Pierce Wood Memorial Hospital, Arcadia, FL, p. A81

KURTZ Jr., Thomas F., President and Chief Executive Officer, Clinton Memorial Hospital, Wilmington, OH, p. A331

KURZ, Linda, Acting Director, Veterans Affairs Medical Center, Saint Louis, MO, p. A248

KUSS, B. Ann, Chief Executive Officer and Managing Director, River Parishes Hospital, La Place, LA, p. A181

KUTCH, John M., Chief Executive Officer, Mobridge Regional Hospital, Mobridge, SD, p. A378

KUTSUDA, Frank, Administrator and Chief Executive Officer, East Los Angeles Doctors Hospital, Los Angeles, CA, p. A48

KUTZ, Melissa, Administrator and Chief Executive Officer, HEALTHSOUTH Rehabilitation of Mechanicsburg, Mechanicsburg, PA, p. A356

KUYKENDALL, George A., President and Chief Executive Officer, San Antonio Community Hospital, Upland, CA, p. A65

KWECH, Robert, Chief Executive Officer, Charter Hospital of Milwaukee, Milwaukee, WI, p. A460

L

LA GRONE, Roderick G., President, Roy H. Laird Memorial Hospital, Kilgore, TX, p. A411

LAABS, Allison C., Executive Vice President and Administrator, St. John's Hospital, Springfield, IL, p. A134

LABARCA, Laurie, Chief Operating Officer, Via Christi Rehabilitation Center, Wichita, KS, p. A166

LABINE, Lance C., President, Hoots Memorial Hospital, Yadkinville, NC, p. A312

LABONTE, Frank, FACHE, Administrator, Shriners Hospitals for Children, Los Angeles, Los Angeles, CA, p. A50

LABRIOLA, John D., Senior Vice President and Hospital Director, William Beaumont Hospital–Royal Oak, Royal Oak, MI, p. A216

LACASSE, Kathleen, Chief Executive Officer, Mary McClellan Hospital, Cambridge, NY, p. A283

LACKEY, Thomas O., Administrator, North Jackson Hospital, Bridgeport, AL, p. A13

LACONTE, Norman H., President and Chief Executive Officer, Proctor Hospital, Peoria, IL, p. A131

LACROIX, William M., Administrator, Paynesville Area Health Care System, Paynesville, MN, p. A226

LACY, Edward L., Administrator, Baptist Medical Center Heber Springs, Heber Springs, AR, p. A31

LACY, John S., Chief Executive Officer, Charter Behavioral Health System–Corpus Christi, Corpus Christi, TX, p. A398

LACY, Leslie, Administrator, Cheyenne County Hospital, Saint Francis, KS, p. A164

LADA, Stephen C., President and Chief Executive Officer, Central Michigan Community Hospital, Mount Pleasant, MI, p. A214

LADENBURGER, Robert W., President, St. Peter's Hospital, Helena, MT, p. A253

LAFFERTY, Douglas L., President and Chief Executive Officer, San Joaquin Community Hospital, Bakersfield, CA, p. A37

LAFFOON, David C., CHE, Chief Executive Officer, Central Arkansas Hospital, Searcy, AR, p. A34

LAIBLE, Ray, Administrative Director, State Hospital South, Blackfoot, ID, p. A114

LAIRD, Michael J., Chief Executive Officer, Pana Community Hospital, Pana, IL, p. A131

LAIRD IV, William R., President and Chief Executive Officer, Montgomery General Hospital, Montgomery, WV, p. A452

LAKE, Robin E., Chief Executive Officer, Harris Hospital, Newport, AR, p. A33

LAKE, Thomas E., Chief Executive Officer, Pioneers Hospital of Rio Blanco County, Meeker, CO, p. A72

LAKERNICK, Philip S., President and Chief Executive Officer, Maria Parham Hospital, Henderson, NC, p. A307

LALLY, Jeanne, Senior Vice President and Administrator, Fairview Northland Regional Health Care, Princeton, MN, p. A227

LALLY, Michael K., President and Chief Executive Officer, Westerly Hospital, Westerly, RI, p. A369

LAMB, Brent, Administrator, Van Nuys Hospital, Los Angeles, CA, p. A51

LAMBERT, M. Aurora, Senior Vice President, Jewish Hospital Kenwood, Cincinnati, OH, p. A320

LAMBERT, Norman, Chief Executive Officer, Golden Plains Community Hospital, Borger, TX, p. A396

LAMBERT, Terry R., Chief Executive Officer, Newman Memorial County Hospital, Emporia, KS, p. A157

LAMBERT, Tod N., Administrator and Chief Executive Officer, Cookeville Regional Medical Center, Cookeville, TN, p. A382

LAMBERTI, Patrick, Chief Executive Officer, POH Medical Center, Pontiac, MI, p. A215

LAMMERS, Brent R., Administrator, Fairfield Memorial Hospital, Winnsboro, SC, p. A375

LAMOUREUX, Bruce, Chief Executive Officer, Saint John's Hospital and Health Center, Santa Monica, CA, p. A62

LAMPE, Diane B., Administrator and Chief Executive Officer, HEALTHSOUTH Rehabilitation Institute of San Antonio, San Antonio, TX, p. A420

LENNEN, Anthony B., President and Chief Executive Officer, Major Hospital, Shelbyville, IN, p. A144

LENZ, Roger W., Administrator, Hamilton County Public Hospital, Webster City, IA, p. A155

LEON, Anne R., Chief Executive Officer, HEALTHSOUTH Houston Rehabilitation Institute, Houston, TX, p. A408

LEON, Jean G., R.N., Senior Vice President, Kings County Hospital Center, New York, NY, p. A291

LEONARD, Douglas J., Chief Executive Officer, Columbus Regional Hospital, Columbus, IN, p. A137

LEONARD, Kathy, Vice President and Administrator, Bert Fish Medical Center, New Smyrna Beach, FL, p. A91

LEONARD, Lawrence, President and Chief Executive Officer, Shannon Medical Center, San Angelo, TX, p. A419

LEONARD, Mark, Chief Executive Officer, Harris Regional Hospital, Sylva, NC, p. A311

LEONHARD Jr., Robert A., Administrator, Physicians Hospital, New Orleans, LA, p. A184

LEONHARDT, George E., President and Chief Executive Officer, Bradford Regional Medical Center, Bradford, PA, p. A348

LEOPARD, Jimmy, Chief Executive Officer, Medical Park Hospital, Hope, AR, p. A31

LEPTUCK, Cary F., President and Chief Executive Officer, Chestnut Hill HealthCare, Philadelphia, PA, p. A358

LERNER, Holly, Chief Executive Officer, Hollywood Medical Center, Los Angeles, FL, p. A86

LERNER, Wayne M., DPH, President and Chief Executive Officer, Rehabilitation Institute of Chicago, Chicago, IL, p. A122

LERZ, Alfred A., President and Chief Executive Officer, Johnson Memorial Hospital, Stafford Springs, CT, p. A77

LESSWING, Norman J., Ph.D., Administrator and Chief Executive Officer, Benjamin Rush Center, Syracuse, NY, p. A298

LETSON, Robert F., President and Chief Executive Officer, Gilmore Memorial Hospital, Amory, MS, p. A231

LEUPP, Mitch, Administrator, Mountrail County Medical Center, Stanley, ND, p. A316

LEURCK, Stephen O., President and Chief Executive Officer, St. Anthony Medical Center, Crown Point, IN, p. A137

LEVENSON, Marvin W., M.D., Administrator and Chief Operating Officer, Pomerado Hospital, Poway, CA, p. A56

LEVINE, Alan, Chief Executive Officer, Doctor's Memorial Hospital, Perry, FL, p. A93

LEVINE, Peter H., M.D., President and Chief Executive Officer, UMass Memorial Health Care–Memorial Campus, Worcester, MA, p. A205

LEVINE, Robert V., President and Chief Executive Officer, Peninsula Hospital Center, New York, NY, p. A293

LEVINSONN, David, Chief Executive Officer, Sherman Oaks Hospital and Health Center, Los Angeles, CA, p. A50

LEVITSKY, Steven E., Administrator, Vencor Hospital North Shore, Peabody, MA, p. A203

LEVY, Shari E., Administrator, Phillips Eye Institute, Minneapolis, MN, p. A225

LEWGOOD, Tony, Administrator, Shriners Hospitals for Children–Lexington, Lexington, KY, p. A171

LEWIS, Brinsley, Senior Executive Officer, GlenOaks Hospital, Glendale Heights, IL, p. A126

LEWIS, Luther J., Chief Executive Officer, Medical Center of South Arkansas, El Dorado, AR, p. A30

LEWIS, Malinda, Administrator, Nye Regional Medical Center, Tonopah, NV, p. A264

LEWIS, Mary Jo
Chief Executive Officer, Parkway Regional Hospital, Fulton, KY, p. A169
Chief Executive Officer, Pinelake Regional Hospital, Mayfield, KY, p. A173

LEWIS, Nicholas P., Administrator, La Follette Medical Center, La Follette, TN, p. A386

LEWIS, Thomas J., President and Chief Executive Officer, Thomas Jefferson University Hospital, Philadelphia, PA, p. A360

LEWIS, Vickie, Chief Executive Officer, Charter Glade Behavioral Health System, Fort Myers, FL, p. A84

LEWIS, Gordon, Deputy Commander for Administration, Bassett Army Community Hospital, Fort Wainwright, AK, p. A20

LEY, Gary R., President and Chief Executive Officer, Garden City Hospital, Garden City, MI, p. A210

LIBENGOOD, Mary L., President, Meyersdale Medical Center, Meyersdale, PA, p. A356

LIBERTINO, John A., M.D., Chief Executive Officer, Lahey Clinic Hospital, Burlington, MA, p. A199

LIEPMAN, Michael T., Chief Operating Officer, Valley Hospital and Medical Center, Spokane, WA, p. A448

LIEVENSE, William C., President and Chief Executive Officer, Doctors Hospital of Sarasota, Sarasota, FL, p. A95

LIKES Jr., Creighton E., President and Chief Executive Officer, Fairfield Medical Center, Lancaster, OH, p. A325

LILLARD, Joseph K., Administrator, Tri–State Memorial Hospital, Clarkston, WA, p. A443

LILLARD, Samuel F., Executive Vice President and Administrator, Bon Secours–Richmond Community Hospital, Richmond, VA, p. A439

LILLY, W. Spencer, Administrator, University Hospital, Charlotte, NC, p. A304

LINCOLN, David R., President and Chief Executive Officer, Covenant Health Systems, Inc., Lexington, MA, p. B86

LIND, Richard A., President and Chief Executive Officer, Memorial Health Systems, Ormond Beach, FL, p. B115

LINDEN, Todd C., President and Chief Executive Officer, Grinnell Regional Medical Center, Grinnell, IA, p. A150

LINDQUIST, Helen S., Administrator, Five Counties Hospital, Lemmon, SD, p. A377

LINDSEY, Larry N., Administrator and Chief Executive Officer, Decatur County General Hospital, Parsons, TN, p. A389

LINEHAN, Mary, President, St. Joseph's Medical Center, Yonkers, NY, p. A301

LINENKUGEL, Nancy, FACHE, President and Chief Executive Officer, Providence Hospital, Sandusky, OH, p. A329

LINGENFELTER, Wayne M., Ed.D., Administrator and Chief Executive Officer, Vencor Hospital–San Leandro, San Leandro, CA, p. A61

LINGOR, John Daniel, President and Chief Executive Officer, Mount Carmel Medical Center, Pittsburg, KS, p. A163

LINN, Gerri, Administrator, Kimball County Hospital, Kimball, NE, p. A258

LINNELL, Jon, Administrator, North Valley Health Center, Warren, MN, p. A229

LINNEWEH Jr., Richard W., President and Chief Executive Officer, Yakima Valley Memorial Hospital, Yakima, WA, p. A449

LINTJER, Gregory W., President, Elkhart General Hospital, Elkhart, IN, p. A138

LIPSTEIN, Steven, President and Chief Operating Officer, University of Chicago Hospitals, Chicago, IL, p. A123

LISCHAK, Michael, USAF, Commander, U. S. Air Force Hospital Seymour Johnson, Seymour Johnson AFB, NC, p. A310

LISTER, Susan, Chief Executive Officer, Charter Winds Hospital, Athens, GA, p. A99

LITCHFORD, Jim, Executive Director, Spalding Regional Hospital, Griffin, GA, p. A105

LITOS, Dennis M., President and Chief Executive Officer, Ingham Regional Medical Center, Lansing, MI, p. A213

LITTLEFIELD, Elizabeth, Ed.D., Superintendent, Western Mental Health Institute, Western Institute, TN, p. A391

LITTRELL, Nancy, Chief Executive Officer, Woodford Hospital, Versailles, KY, p. A175

LITZ, Thomas H., FACHE, President and Chief Executive Officer, CentraState Healthcare System, Freehold, NJ, p. A270

LIVERMORE, Craig A., President and Chief Executive Officer, Delnor–Community Hospital, Geneva, IL, p. A125

LIVINGSTON, Jeffrey A., Chief Executive Officer, HEALTHSOUTH Rehabilitation Hospital of Texarkana, Texarkana, TX, p. A423

LLOYD, John K., Chief Executive Officer, Meridian Health System, Neptune, NJ, p. A272

LOBECK, Charles C., Chief Executive Officer, St. Mary's Hospital, Milwaukee, WI, p. A461

LOCKARD, Thomas L., President and Chief Executive Officer, Lodi Community Hospital, Lodi, OH, p. A325

LOCKWOOD, Brian C., President and Chief Executive Officer, Lorain Community/St. Joseph Regional Health Center, Lorain, OH, p. A325

LODATO, Dominic J., Interim President, Lutheran Medical Center, New York, NY, p. A291

LODGE, Dale M., President and Chief Executive Officer, Winchester Hospital, Winchester, MA, p. A205

LOEBIG Jr., Wilfred F., President and Chief Executive Officer, Wheaton Franciscan Services, Inc., Wheaton, IL, p. B156

LOEPP Jr., Robert A., Administrator, Lifecare Hospitals, Shreveport, LA, p. A185

LOEWEN, Harold C., President, Oaklawn Psychiatric Center, Inc., Goshen, IN, p. A139

LOFE, Dennis A., FACHE, Chief Executive Officer, HEALTHSOUTH Rehabilitation Hospital, Florence, SC, p. A372

LOGUE, John W., Executive Vice President and Chief Operating Officer, St. Vincent's Medical Center, Jacksonville, FL, p. A87

LOH, Marcel, President and Chief Executive Officer, Kadlec Medical Center, Richland, WA, p. A447

LOHRMAN, Joseph W.
Administrator, Crete Municipal Hospital, Crete, NE, p. A257
Administrator, Warren Memorial Hospital, Friend, NE, p. A257

LOMBARD, Dave, President and Chief Executive Officer, Clear Brook Lodge, Shickshinny, PA, p. A364

LOMBARDI, Anthony M., President and Chief Executive Officer, Monongahela Valley Hospital, Monongahela, PA, p. A356

LONCHAR, Charles, President and Chief Executive Officer, Preston Memorial Hospital, Kingwood, WV, p. A452

LONG, Charles H., Chief Executive Officer, De Queen Regional Medical Center, De Queen, AR, p. A30

LONG, Faye, Administrator, Caldwell Memorial Hospital, Columbia, LA, p. A178

LONG, Jim K., CPA, Administrator and Chief Executive Officer, West River Regional Medical Center, Hettinger, ND, p. A314

LONG, Lawrence C., Chief Executive Officer, Tahoe Forest Hospital District, Truckee, CA, p. A65

LONG, Max, Chief Executive Officer, Walter Knox Memorial Hospital, Emmett, ID, p. A115

LONG, Thomas P., Executive Vice President, North General Hospital, New York, NY, p. A292

LONGACRE, Leslie, Executive Director and Chief Executive Officer, South Lake Hospital, Clermont, FL, p. A82

LONGO, Robert J., President and Chief Executive Officer, Good Samaritan Hospital, Lebanon, PA, p. A355

LOPER, Ouida, Administrator, Choctaw County Medical Center, Ackerman, MS, p. A231

LOPEZ, David S., FACHE, Senior Executive Director, University of Texas Medical Branch Hospitals, Galveston, TX, p. A405

LOPEZ, Frank, FACHE, President and Chief Executive Officer, St. Mary's Mercy Hospital, Enid, OK, p. A335

LOPEZ, Ramon, Administrator, Hospital Perea, Mayaguez, PR, p. A471

LOPMAN, Abe, Executive Director, Orlando Regional Medical Center, Orlando, FL, p. A92

LORACK Jr., Donald A.
President and Chief Executive Officer, Children's Medical Center, Tulsa, OK, p. A340
President and Chief Executive Officer, Hillcrest HealthCare System, Tulsa, OK, p. B103
President and Chief Executive Officer, Hillcrest Medical Center, Tulsa, OK, p. A340

LORDEMAN, Frank L., Chief Operating Officer, Cleveland Clinic Foundation, Cleveland, OH, p. A320

LORE, John S., President and Chief Executive Officer, Sisters of St. Joseph Health System, Ann Arbor, MI, p. B139

LORY, Marc H.
President and Chief Executive Officer, Manchester Memorial Hospital, Manchester, CT, p. A75
President and Chief Executive Officer, Rockville General Hospital, Vernon Rockville, CT, p. A77

LOSOFF, Martin, President and Chief Operating Officer, Rush–Copley Medical Center, Aurora, IL, p. A118

LOTHE, Eric L., President and Chief Executive Officer, Skiff Medical Center, Newton, IA, p. A152

LOTT Jr., Carlos B., Director, John D. Dingell Veterans Affairs Medical Center, Detroit, MI, p. A209

LOUGHNEY, Barbara, Administrator, Saint Michael's Medical Center, Newark, NJ, p. A272

LOUISE, Stella, President and Chief Executive Officer, Saint Mary of Nazareth Hospital Center, Chicago, IL, p. A122

LOVE, Martin, Chief Executive Officer, General Hospital, Eureka, CA, p. A41

LOVEDAY, William J., President and Chief Executive Officer, Clarian Health Partners, Indianapolis, IN, p. A140

LOVELL Jr., Charles D., Chief Executive Officer, Muhlenberg Community Hospital, Greenville, KY, p. A169

LOVETT, Juanice, Chief Executive Officer, Rancho Springs Medical Center, Murrieta, CA, p. A53

LOVING, David E., Chief Executive Officer, Edge Regional Medical Center, Troy, AL, p. A18

LOWD III, Harry M., President, Bath County Community Hospital, Hot Springs, VA, p. A435

LOWE, Phillip, Chief Executive Officer, St. Vincent General Hospital, Leadville, CO, p. A71

LOWRANCE, Debra S., R.N., Chief Executive Officer and Managing Director, Timberlawn Mental Health System, Dallas, TX, p. A401

LOWRY, James R., FACHE, Chief Executive Officer, Colquitt Regional Medical Center, Moultrie, GA, p. A108

LOYLESS, John Paul, Administrator, Rankin Hospital District, Rankin, TX, p. A418

LOZAR, Beverly, Chief Operating Officer, Meridia Huron Hospital, Cleveland, OH, p. A321

LUCAS, John, M.D., President and Chief Executive Officer, St. Thomas Health Services, Nashville, TN, p. A389

LUCAS, Stephen M., Chief Executive Officer, Veterans Affairs Medical Center, Erie, PA, p. A352

LUCK Jr., James V., M.D., Chief Executive Officer and Medical Director, Orthopaedic Hospital, Los Angeles, CA, p. A50

LUGARO, Luisa Rivera, Administrator, Hospital Del Maestro, San Juan, PR, p. A471

LUKE, Leslie Paul, Chief Executive Officer, Douglas Community Medical Center, Roseburg, OR, p. A345

LUKER, Patricia, Chief Executive Officer, Franklin Foundation Hospital, Franklin, LA, p. A179

LUKHARD, Kenneth W., Chief Executive Officer, Princeton Hospital, Orlando, FL, p. A92

LULEWICZ, Stephanie, Administrator, Marshall County Healthcare Center, Britton, SD, p. A376

LUMSDEN, Chris A., Chief Executive Officer, Halifax Regional Hospital, South Boston, VA, p. A440

LUNA, Richard, Chief Executive Officer, Specialty Hospital of Santa Ana, Santa Ana, CA, p. A62

LUND, Mark, Superintendent, Mental Health Institute, Clarinda, IA, p. A147

LUND, Robert S., Administrator, Kaiser Foundation Hospital–Riverside, Riverside, CA, p. A57

LUNDBERG, Gerald R., Interim Chief Executive Officer, Greensville Memorial Hospital, Emporia, VA, p. A434

LUNDQUIST, David, Chief Executive Officer, Bethany Hospital, Bethany, OK, p. A333

LUNDSTROM, Greg, Administrator and Chief Executive Officer, Lindsborg Community Hospital, Lindsborg, KS, p. A161

LUSE, Robert H., Chief Executive Officer, Mariners Hospital, Tavernier, FL, p. A97

LUSSIER, James T., President and Chief Executive Officer, St. Charles Medical Center, Bend, OR, p. A342

LUTHER, Robert M., Chief Executive Officer, Springs Memorial Hospital, Lancaster, SC, p. A373

LUTJEMEIER, Everett, Administrator, Washington County Hospital, Washington, KS, p. A165

LYBARGER, William A., Administrator, Cedar Vale Community Hospital, Cedar Vale, KS, p. A156

LYCAN, Laura J., Executive Director, Baylor Institute for Rehabilitation, Dallas, TX, p. A399

LYNCH, Edward F., Administrator, Richards Memorial Hospital, Rockdale, TX, p. A419

LYNCH III, Ernest C., Chief Executive Officer, Medical Center at Lancaster, Lancaster, TX, p. A412

LYON, Cheri, Service Unit Director, Public Health Service Indian Hospital, Albuquerque, NM, p. A277

LYON, David R., Administrator, Beckley Appalachian Regional Hospital, Beckley, WV, p. A450

LYONS, James F., President and Chief Executive Officer, Cape Cod Healthcare, Inc., Hyannis, MA, p. B70

LYONS, Richard D., President and Chief Executive Officer, Northridge Hospital and Medical Center, Sherman Way Campus, Los Angeles, CA, p. A49

LYSINGER, R. Craig, Administrator, Wabash Valley Hospital, West Lafayette, IN, p. A145

M

MAAS, Lawrence A., Administrator, Sutter Davis Hospital, Davis, CA, p. A40

MABE, Patricia, Vice President and Chief Nursing Officer, Presbyterian Specialty Hospital, Charlotte, NC, p. A304

MABRY, Jerry D., Executive Director, National Park Medical Center, Hot Springs, AR, p. A31

MAC DEVITT, Robert E., Chief Executive Officer, Labette County Medical Center, Parsons, KS, p. A163

MACDOWELL, Barry S., President, Reid Hospital and Health Care Services, Richmond, IN, p. A144

MACKAY, Lorin C., Administrator, Teton Medical Center, Choteau, MT, p. A251

MACLAREN, Ron J., Chief Executive Officer, Select Specialty Hospital, Houston, TX, p. A409

MACLEOD, John L., Administrator and Chief Executive Officer, Otsego Memorial Hospital, Gaylord, MI, p. A210

MACLEOD, Leslie N. H., President, Huggins Hospital, Wolfeboro, NH, p. A267

MACPHEE, Alan, Administrator, Quincy Valley Medical Center, Quincy, WA, p. A446

MACRI, William P., Chief Executive Officer, Franklin–Simpson Memorial Hospital, Franklin, KY, p. A169

MACRITCHIE, Anne M., President and Chief Executive Officer, HEALTHSOUTH Braintree Rehabilitation Hospital, Braintree, MA, p. A199

MADDALENA, Frank J., President and Chief Executive Officer, Brookdale Hospital Medical Center, New York, NY, p. A289

MADDEN, Michael J.
Administrator, Grays Harbor Community Hospital, Aberdeen, WA, p. A443
Chief Executive Officer, Providence Holy Cross Medical Center, Los Angeles, CA, p. A50
Chief Executive Officer, Providence Saint Joseph Medical Center, Burbank, CA, p. A38

MADDEN, Patrick J., President and Chief Executive Officer, Sacred Heart Hospital of Pensacola, Pensacola, FL, p. A93

MADDOCK, Dan S., President, Taylor Regional Hospital, Hawkinsville, GA, p. A106

MADDOX, Jim L., Chief Administrative Officer, North Logan Mercy Hospital, Paris, AR, p. A34

MADDOX, Richard D., Administrator, U. S. Air Force Regional Hospital–Sheppard, Sheppard AFB, TX, p. A421

MADISON, Jeffrey, Chief Executive Officer, Swisher Memorial Hospital District, Tulia, TX, p. A424

MAESTRE GRAU, Jaime F., Executive Director, Hospital De La Concepcion, San German, PR, p. A471

MAFFETONE, Michael A., Director and Chief Executive Officer, University Hospital, Stony Brook, NY, p. A298

MAGEE, James L., Executive Director, Piggott Community Hospital, Piggott, AR, p. A34

MAGERS, Brent D., FACHE, Executive Director and Senior Vice President, Walls Regional Hospital, Cleburne, TX, p. A397

MAGHAZEHE, Alireza, Chief Executive Officer, Capital Health System, Trenton, NJ, p. A275

MAGLIARO, John G., President and Chief Executive Officer, Columbus Hospital, Newark, NJ, p. A272

MAGOON, Patrick M., President and Chief Executive Officer, Children's Memorial Hospital, Chicago, IL, p. A120

MAGRAS, Judy, Acting Chief Executive Officer, Roy Lester Schneider Hospital, Saint Thomas, VI, p. A472

MAHADEVAN, Dev, Administrator, Kaiser Foundation Hospital, Los Angeles, CA, p. A49

MAHAFFEY, Robert, Administrator, Heart of Florida Regional Medical Center, Davenport, FL, p. A83

MAHAN, Stephen, Chief Executive Officer, Ocala Regional Medical Center, Ocala, FL, p. A91

MAHER, Robert J., President, Our Lady of Bellefonte Hospital, Ashland, KY, p. A167

MAHER Jr., Robert E., President and Chief Executive Officer, Saint Vincent Hospital, Worcester, MA, p. A205

MAHN, Edward F., Chief Executive Officer, Ketchikan General Hospital, Ketchikan, AK, p. A21

MAHONEY, Kevin J., President, Wilson Center Psychiatric Facility for Children and Adolescents, Faribault, MN, p. A223

MAHONEY, Michael P., President and Chief Executive Officer, St. Rose Hospital, Hayward, CA, p. A44

MAHONEY, Patrick R., Chief Executive Officer, Affiliated Health Services, Mount Vernon, WA, p. A445

MAHONEY, William K., Chief Executive Officer, Wamego City Hospital, Wamego, KS, p. A165

MAHRER, Michael D., President, St. Ansgar's Health Center, Park River, ND, p. A315

MAIDLOW, Spencer, President, Covenant HealthCare, Saginaw, MI, p. A216

MAIER, Gary, Chief Executive Officer, Chino Valley Medical Center, Chino, CA, p. A39

MAIER, Harry R., President, Memorial Hospital, Belleville, IL, p. A118

MAIER, Vonnie, President and Chief Executive Officer, Huerfano Medical Center, Walsenburg, CO, p. A73

MAIN, Robert P., President and Chief Executive Officer, Siskin Hospital for Physical Rehabilitation, Chattanooga, TN, p. A382

MAJURE, Thomas K., Administrator, Our Community Hospital, Scotland Neck, NC, p. A310

MAKI, James W., Chief Executive Officer, Huntington East Valley Hospital, Glendora, CA, p. A44

MAKOWSKI, Peter E.
President and Chief Executive Officer, Citrus Valley Health Partners, Covina, CA, p. B77
President and Chief Executive Officer, Citrus Valley Medical Center Inter–Community Campus, Covina, CA, p. A40
President and Chief Executive Officer, Citrus Valley Medical Center–Queen of the Valley Campus, West Covina, CA, p. A67

MALIA, John, Director, First Hospital Wyoming Valley, Wilkes–Barre, PA, p. A366

MALINOWSKI, Barbara A., Administrator and Chief Executive Officer, Westfield Memorial Hospital, Westfield, NY, p. A300

MALINOWSKI, Mary Norberta, President, St. Joseph Hospital, Bangor, ME, p. A187

MALLAH, Isaac, President and Chief Executive Officer, St. Joseph's Hospital, Tampa, FL, p. A96

MALMUD, Leon S., M.D., President, Temple University Health System, Philadelphia, PA, p. B143

MALONE, John T., President and Chief Executive Officer, Hamot Medical Center, Erie, PA, p. A351

MALONEY, Elizabeth Ann, President and Chief Executive Officer, St. Elizabeth Hospital, Elizabeth, NJ, p. A270

MALTE, Robert H.
Senior Vice President, Appleton Medical Center, Appleton, WI, p. A456
Senior Vice President, Theda Clark Medical Center, Neenah, WI, p. A461

MAMOON, Wendy, Chief Executive Officer, Rock Creek Center, Lemont, IL, p. A128

MANCHUR, Fred
President and Chief Executive Officer, Glendale Adventist Medical Center, Glendale, CA, p. A43
President and Chief Executive Officer, White Memorial Medical Center, Los Angeles, CA, p. A51

MANCINI, Dorothy J., R.N., Regional Vice President Administration, Imperial Point Medical Center, Fort Lauderdale, FL, p. A84

MANDERNACH, Dianne, Chief Executive Officer, Mercy Hospital and Health Care Center, Moose Lake, MN, p. A226

MANDERS, Daniel N., President and Chief Executive Officer, Mile Bluff Medical Center, Mauston, WI, p. A460

MANDSAGER, Richard, M.D., Administrator, Alaska Native Medical Center, Anchorage, AK, p. A20

MANGINI, Michael A., Administrator and Chief Executive Officer, Bellevue Woman's Hospital, Schenectady, NY, p. A297

MANGION, Richard M., President and Chief Executive Officer, Harrington Memorial Hospital, Southbridge, MA, p. A204

MANLEY, Jeffrey J., Chief Executive Officer, Jordan Valley Hospital, West Jordan, UT, p. A430

MANLEY, Joseph M., Director, Veterans Affairs Medical Center, Spokane, WA, p. A448

MANNING, Richard W., Administrator, South Panola Community Hospital, Batesville, MS, p. A231

MANNING, Catherine, President and Chief Executive Officer, Saint Vincent Health Center, Erie, PA, p. A352

MANNIX Jr., Robert T., President and Chief Operations Officer, St. Elizabeth Health Services, Baker City, OR, p. A342

MANOR, Lori, Administrator, Healthsouth Rehabilitation Hospital, Concord, NH, p. A265

MANSFIELD, Jodi J., Executive Vice President and Chief Operating Officer, Shands at the University of Florida, Gainesville, FL, p. A85

MANTEGAZZA, Peter M., President and Chief Executive Officer, Fairlawn Rehabilitation Hospital, Worcester, MA, p. A205

MANTEY, Carl W., Administrator, Gerald Champion Memorial Hospital, Alamogordo, NM, p. A277

MANTZ, James R., Administrator, Prairie Community Medical Assistance Facility, Terry, MT, p. A254

MANUEL, Mark L., Administrator, Eunice Community Medical Center, Eunice, LA, p. A179

MAPES, Stephen W., Chief Executive Officer, Hayes–Green–Beach Memorial Hospital, Charlotte, MI, p. A207

MAPLES, Ruth, Executive Director, Lanterman Developmental Center, Pomona, CA, p. A56

MARCANTUONO, Daniel L., FACHE, Acting Vice President and Chief Executive Officer, University of Medicine and Dentistry of New Jersey–University Hospital, Newark, NJ, p. A272

MARCELINE, Alex M., Chief Executive Officer, Palms West Hospital, Loxahatchee, FL, p. A88

MARCHETTI, Mark E., Chief Executive Officer, Greenfield Area Medical Center, Greenfield, OH, p. A324

MARCOS, Luis R., M.D., President, New York City Health and Hospitals Corporation, New York, NY, p. B119

MARIE, Donna, Executive Vice President and Chief Executive Officer, Resurrection Medical Center, Chicago, IL, p. A122

MARINAKOS, Plato A., President and Chief Executive Officer, Mercy Health System of Southeastern Pennsylvania, Bala Cynwyd, PA, p. A348

MARION, Ben, Chief Executive Officer, Turning Point Hospital, Moultrie, GA, p. A108

MARK, Richard J., President and Chief Executive Officer, St. Mary's Hospital, East St. Louis, IL, p. A124

MARKHAM, Patricia, Administrator, Cass County Memorial Hospital, Atlantic, IA, p. A146

MARKIEWICZ, Dennis P., Vice President Hospital Operations, Crittenton Hospital, Rochester, MI, p. A216

MARKOS, Dennis R., Chief Executive Officer, Ed Fraser Memorial Hospital, MacClenny, FL, p. A88

MARKOWITZ, Bruce J., President and Chief Executive Officer, Palisades General Hospital, North Bergen, NJ, p. A273

MARKS, Craig J., President and Chief Executive Officer, South Haven Community Hospital, South Haven, MI, p. A217

MARKS, Gary A., Administrator, Glen Rose Medical Center, Glen Rose, TX, p. A405

MARLETTE, Jeff, Administrator, Holy Infant Hospital, Hoven, SD, p. A377

MARLEY, Mark E., Executive Director, Natchitoches Parish Hospital, Natchitoches, LA, p. A183

MARLIN, Arthur E., M.D., Chief Executive Officer, Methodist Women's and Children's Hospital, San Antonio, TX, p. A420

MARMERSTEIN, Peter A., Chief Executive Officer, Parkway Regional Medical Center, North Miami Beach, FL, p. A91

MARMO, Anthony P., Chief Executive Officer, Kingston Hospital, Kingston, NY, p. A287

MARMORSTONE, Ray, Chief Executive Officer, Memorial Hospital of Iowa County, Dodgeville, WI, p. A457

MARNELL, George, Director, Veterans Affairs Roseburg Healthcare System, Roseburg, OR, p. A346

MAROC, Genny, Interim Administrator, Marengo Memorial Hospital, Marengo, IA, p. A152

MARON, Michael, President and Chief Executive Officer, Holy Name Hospital, Teaneck, NJ, p. A275

MARONEY, George, Senior Vice President and Administrator, Memorial Hospital of Carbondale, Carbondale, IL, p. A119

MARQUARDT, Robert C., FACHE, President and Chief Executive Officer, Memorial Medical Center of West Michigan, Ludington, MI, p. A213

MARQUARDT, Dennis, USAF, Commander, U. S. Air Force Hospital, Shreveport, LA, p. A185

MARQUETTE Jr., Gerald Joseph, Chief Executive Officer, Coffeyville Regional Medical Center, Coffeyville, KS, p. A157

MARQUEZ, Michael, Chief Executive Officer, Manatee Memorial Hospital, Bradenton, FL, p. A82

MARR, Charles J.
Chief Executive Officer, Alegent Health Bergan Mercy Medical Center, Omaha, NE, p. A260
Chief Executive Officer, Alegent Health Mercy Hospital, Council Bluffs, IA, p. A147

MARSHALL, John A., President and Chief Executive Officer, Norton Suburban Hospital, Louisville, KY, p. A172

MARSHALL, Michael D.
Chief Executive Officer, HEALTHSOUTH Rehabilitation Hospital of Baton Rouge, Baton Rouge, LA, p. A177
Chief Executive Officer, HEALTHSOUTH Rehabilitation Hospital of South Louisiana, Baton Rouge, LA, p. A177

MARSHALL, Philomena A., R.N., President and Chief Executive Officer, Charles A. Dean Memorial Hospital, Greenville, ME, p. A188

MARSHALL, Robert, Chief Executive Officer, Pacific Gateway Hospital and Counseling Center, Portland, OR, p. A345

MARSTELLER, Brent A., Chief Executive Officer, Gulf Coast Medical Center, Panama City, FL, p. A92

MARTE, Noemi Davis, M.D., Medical Director, Caguas Regional Hospital, Caguas, PR, p. A470

MARTIN, Andria, MS, Director and Vice President Operations, University of Connecticut Health Center, John Dempsey Hospital, Farmington, CT, p. A74

MARTIN, D. Wayne, President and Chief Executive Officer, Crisp Regional Hospital, Cordele, GA, p. A103

MARTIN, Elizabeth J., Vice President and Administrator, Riverside Tappahannock Hospital, Tappahannock, VA, p. A441

MARTIN, G. Roger, President and Chief Executive Officer, Jeanes Hospital, Philadelphia, PA, p. A359

MARTIN, Greg, Administrator and Chief Executive Officer, Blackwell Regional Hospital, Blackwell, OK, p. A333

MARTIN, Guillermo J., Executive Director, Hospital Episcopal San Lucas, Ponce, PR, p. A471

MARTIN, James A.
Chief Executive Officer, Good Samaritan Hospital, Suffern, NY, p. A298
President and Chief Executive Officer, St. Anthony Community Hospital, Warwick, NY, p. A300

MARTIN, Jeffrey L., President and Chief Executive Officer, Saint Michael's Hospital, Stevens Point, WI, p. A464

MARTIN, Kevin C.
President and Chief Executive Officer, EMH Amherst Hospital, Amherst, OH, p. A317
President and Chief Executive Officer, EMH Regional Medical Center, Elyria, OH, p. A323

MARTIN, Neil, President and Chief Executive Officer, Redwood Memorial Hospital, Fortuna, CA, p. A42

MARTIN, Norm, President and Chief Executive Officer, Parkview Community Hospital Medical Center, Riverside, CA, p. A57

MARTIN, Patrick J., President and Chief Executive Officer, Fisher–Titus Medical Center, Norwalk, OH, p. A327

MARTIN, James W., Commander, DeWitt Army Community Hospital, Fort Belvoir, VA, p. A435

MARTIN, Julie, Administrator, General Leonard Wood Army Community Hospital, Fort Leonard Wood, MO, p. A241

MARTIN–SHAW, Carolyn, President, Saint Joseph Community Hospital, New Hampton, IA, p. A152

MARTINEZ, Abraham, Chief Executive Officer, Alice Regional Hospital, Alice, TX, p. A392

MARTINEZ, Charles, Ph.D., Chief Executive Officer, Community Hospital of Huntington Park, Huntington Park, CA, p. A45

MARTINEZ, Ramiro J., M.D., Director, East Mississippi State Hospital, Meridian, MS, p. A235

MARTINEZ, Tomas, Administrator, Hospital Hermanos Melendez, Bayamon, PR, p. A469

MARTINEZ Jr., Fred, Chief Executive Officer, St. Charles Parish Hospital, Luling, LA, p. A181

MARTINEZ–LOPEZ, Lester, Director Health Services, Colonel Florence A. Blanchfield Army Community Hospital, Fort Campbell, KY, p. A169

MARTINSEN, Eric, President, Paradise Valley Hospital, National City, CA, p. A53

MARTORE, Patrick R., Chief Executive Officer, South Oaks Hospital, Amityville, NY, p. A281

MARUCA, Robert T., Administrator, Carrie Tingley Hospital, Albuquerque, NM, p. A277

MASCHING, Frances Marie, President, OSF Healthcare System, Peoria, IL, p. B123

MASON, Bill A., President, Springhill Memorial Hospital, Mobile, AL, p. A16

MASON, Daria V., Chief Executive Officer, Central Vermont Medical Center, Barre, VT, p. A431

MASON, Stephen D., Administrator, Northwest Florida Community Hospital, Chipley, FL, p. A82

MASON Jr., Charles H., President and Chief Executive Officer, Parkview Health System, Fort Wayne, IN, p. B124

MASSA, Lawrence J., Chief Executive Officer, Rice Memorial Hospital, Willmar, MN, p. A230

MASSE, Roger A., Chief Executive Officer, Margaretville Memorial Hospital, Margaretville, NY, p. A287

MASSEY, Donald W., Administrator, Bassett Hospital of Schoharie County, Cobleskill, NY, p. A284

MASSEY, Michael W., Administrator, Allen Bennett Hospital, Greer, SC, p. A373

MASSEY, Rocco K., Administrator, Summers County Appalachian Regional Hospital, Hinton, WV, p. A451

MASTERSON, David, Administrator, St. Vincent Mercy Hospital, Elwood, IN, p. A138

MASTRANGELO, Anthony G., Executive Vice President and Administrator, St. Joseph's Hospital, Highland, IL, p. A126

MATECZUN, John M., Commanding Officer, Naval Hospital, North Charleston, SC, p. A374

MATEO, Carlos Rodriguez, M.D., Medical Director, Dr. Alejandro Buitrago–Guayama Area Hospital, Guayama, PR, p. A470

MATHER, Kelly, Chief Executive Officer, San Leandro Hospital, San Leandro, CA, p. A61

MATHEWS, LouAnn O., Administrator, SSH Dallas/Fort Worth, Dallas, TX, p. A401

MATHEWS, Mike, Administrator, Kwajalein Hospital, Kwajalein Island, MH, p. A469

MATNEY, Douglas A., Senior Vice President Operations, Columbia Medical Center–East, El Paso, TX, p. A403

MATSUMURA, Kay, Chief Executive Officer, Salt Lake Regional Medical Center, Salt Lake City, UT, p. A429

MATTEI DE COLLAZO, Georgina, Executive Director, Doctors Hospital, San Juan, PR, p. A471

MATTES, James A., President, Grande Ronde Hospital, La Grande, OR, p. A343

MATTHEWS, Clint, Chief Executive Officer, Palm Beach Gardens Medical Center, Palm Beach Gardens, FL, p. A92

MATTHEWS, John H., Interim Chief Executive Officer, McCray Memorial Hospital, Kendallville, IN, p. A141

MATTHEWS, L. Eugene, Administrator, Choctaw Memorial Hospital, Hugo, OK, p. A336

MATTHEWS, Michael, Administrator, Lisbon Medical Center, Lisbon, ND, p. A315

MATTINGLY, Chris, Chief Executive Officer, Prague Municipal Hospital, Prague, OK, p. A339

MATTISON, Kenneth R., President and Chief Executive Officer, Florida Hospital Waterman, Eustis, FL, p. A84

MATTISON, Lynne M., FACHE, Interim Administrator, St. Benedicts Family Medical Center, Jerome, ID, p. A115

MATUSKA, John E., President and Chief Executive Officer, St. Peter's University Hospital, New Brunswick, NJ, p. A272

MAURER, Gregory L., Administrator, Elmore Medical Center, Mountain Home, ID, p. A116

MAXHIMER, Terry R., Regional Vice President, HEALTHSOUTH Rehabilitation Hospital, Kingsport, TN, p. A385

MAY, Bill, Chief Executive Officer, Allen County Hospital, Iola, KS, p. A159

MAY, Maurice I., President and Chief Executive Officer, Hebrew Rehabilitation Center for Aged, Boston, MA, p. A198

MAY, Timothy, Director, Veterans Affairs Medical Center, Salisbury, NC, p. A310

MAYA, Victor, Chief Executive Officer, Kendall Medical Center, Miami, FL, p. A89

MAYNARD, Robert F., Chief Executive Officer, Shawnee Regional Hospital, Shawnee, OK, p. A339

MAYO, Jim L., Administrator, Baptist Medical Center–Nassau, Fernandina Beach, FL, p. A84

MAYO, M. Andrew, Chief Executive Officer, Charter Parkwood Behavioral Health System, Olive Branch, MS, p. A236

MAZOUR, Roger, Administrator, Pender Community Hospital, Pender, NE, p. A261

MAZUR–HART, Stanley F., Ph.D., Superintendent, Oregon State Hospital, Salem, OR, p. A346

MAZZARELLA, Michael C., President and Chief Executive Officer, Northern Dutchess Hospital, Rhinebeck, NY, p. A296

MAZZUCA, Phillip J., Chief Executive Officer, Parkway Medical Center Hospital, Decatur, AL, p. A13

MCAFEE Jr., James T., Chairman, President and Chief Executive Officer, ValueMark Healthcare Systems, Inc., Atlanta, GA, p. B153

MCALEER, A. Gordon, FACHE, President and Chief Executive Officer, Lewistown Hospital, Lewistown, PA, p. A355

MCALLISTER, C. C., President and Chief Executive Officer, Ouachita Medical Center, Camden, AR, p. A29

MCAVOY, Lawrence H., Administrator, Washington County Hospital, Plymouth, NC, p. A309

MCBARNETTE, Lorna, Chief Executive Officer, Episcopal Health Services Inc., Uniondale, NY, p. B95

MCBEATH, James D., Chief Executive Officer, ValueMark West End Behavioral Healthcare System, Richmond, VA, p. A440

MCBEE, Marie, Chief Executive Officer, Charter Behavioral Health System at Warwick Manor, East New Market, MD, p. A194

MCBRIDE, Don H., Chief Executive Officer, Woodland Heights Medical Center, Lufkin, TX, p. A414

MCBRIDE, Michael J., CHE
Senior Vice President and Executive Director, McCuistion Regional Medical Center, Paris, TX, p. A417
Senior Vice President and Executive Director, Presbyterian Hospital of Kaufman, Kaufman, TX, p. A411

MCCABE, Jack, Senior Vice President and Administrator, Harris Methodist–HEB, Bedford, TX, p. A395

MCCABE, Steve, Chief Executive Officer, Hill Crest Behavioral Health Services, Birmingham, AL, p. A12

MCCABE Jr., Patrick, Executive Director, Levi Hospital, Hot Springs National Park, AR, p. A31

MCCAFFREY, Michael, Commander, Weed Army Community Hospital, Fort Irwin, CA, p. A42

MCCALL, Gerald A., Senior Vice President and Service Area Manager, Kaiser Foundation Hospital, Fontana, CA, p. A42

MCCARRON, Timothy, Chief Operating Officer, Symmes Hospital and Medical Center, Arlington, MA, p. A197

MCCARY, Steve C., President and Chief Executive Officer, Stevens Healthcare, Edmonds, WA, p. A444

MCCASLIN, James B., Director, Chestnut Hill Rehabilitation Hospital, Glenside, PA, p. A352

MCCAULEY, Edith, Administrator, Sabine County Hospital, Hemphill, TX, p. A406

MCCAULEY, Roberta D., Chief Executive Officer, Hampshire Memorial Hospital, Romney, WV, p. A454

MCCLELLAN, David A., Chief Executive Officer, Carolinas Hospital System, Florence, SC, p. A372

MCCLERNON, Susan, Administrator, Brackenridge Hospital, Austin, TX, p. A393

MCCLESKEY, George H.
President and Chief Executive Officer, Covenant Children's Hospital, Lubbock, TX, p. A413
President and Chief Executive Officer, Covenant Medical Center, Lubbock, TX, p. A413
President and Chief Executive Officer, Lubbock Methodist Hospital System, Lubbock, TX, p. B110

MCCLINTOCK, Thomas, Chief Executive Officer, Carlsbad Medical Center, Carlsbad, NM, p. A278

MCCLINTOCK, William T., FACHE, Chief Executive Officer, Boundary Community Hospital, Bonners Ferry, ID, p. A114

MCCLURE, Jan, Chief Executive Officer, Hill Regional Hospital, Hillsboro, TX, p. A407

MCCLYMONDS, Bruce, President, West Virginia University Hospitals, Morgantown, WV, p. A453

MCCOMBS, David J., Executive Vice President and Administrator, Bon Secours–DePaul Medical Center, Norfolk, VA, p. A437

MCCONAHY, Richard L., Chief Executive Officer, Middle Georgia Hospital, Macon, GA, p. A107

MCCONKEY, David M., Chief Executive, Good Samaritan Hospital, Downers Grove, IL, p. A124

MCCOOL, Paul J.
Acting Director, Veterans Affairs Connecticut Healthcare System–West Haven Division, West Haven, CT, p. A77
Director, Veterans Affairs Medical Center, Manchester, NH, p. A266

MCCORD, Windell M., Administrator, Heart of Texas Memorial Hospital, Brady, TX, p. A396

MCCORKLE, Vincent J., President, Mercy Hospital, Springfield, MA, p. A204

MCCORMACK, J. David, Executive Director, Riverview Regional Medical Center, Gadsden, AL, p. A15

MCCORMICK, James, Superintendent, Richmond State Hospital, Richmond, IN, p. A144

MCCORMICK, John J., Chief Executive Officer, San Bernardino Mountains Community Hospital District, Lake Arrowhead, CA, p. A46

MCCORMICK, Richard
Administrator, Methodist Healthcare – McKenzie Hospital, McKenzie, TN, p. A387
Administrator, Methodist Healthcare– Dyersburg Hospital, Dyersburg, TN, p. A383

MCCOY, George H., Chief Executive Officer, Governor Juan F. Louis Hospital, Christiansted, VI, p. A472

MCCOY, L. Kent, President, Huntington Memorial Hospital, Huntington, IN, p. A139

MCCOY, Mike, Chief Executive Officer, Saint Mary's Regional Medical Center, Russellville, AR, p. A34

MCCOY, Sherman P., Executive Director and Chief Executive Officer, Howard University Hospital, Washington, DC, p. A79

MCCRACKEN, Clyde T., Administrator, Ness County Hospital Number Two, Ness City, KS, p. A162

MCCRAY, Cindy M., Administrator and Chief Executive Officer, Hospital District Number Six of Harper County, Anthony, KS, p. A156

MCCULLOUGH, Frank S., M.D., President, Medical College of Ohio Hospitals, Toledo, OH, p. A329

MCCUNE, William, Senior Vice President, Operations, Lankenau Hospital, Wynnewood, PA, p. A366

MCDERMOTT, Brian J., President and Chief Executive Officer, Carrington Health Center, Carrington, ND, p. A313

MCDONAGH, Kathryn J., President and Chief Executive Officer, Saint Clare's Health Services, Denville, NJ, p. A269

MCDONALD, Erica, Administrator, Man ARH Hospital, Man, WV, p. A452

MCDOUGAL Jr., Tom R., Chief Executive Officer, L. V. Stabler Memorial Hospital, Greenville, AL, p. A15

MCDOWELL, James W., President and Chief Executive Officer, St. Mary's Hospital, Centralia, IL, p. A119

MCDOWELL, Jane, Administrator, Seiling Hospital, Seiling, OK, p. A339

MCDOWELL, P. Jane, Administrator, Harper County Community Hospital, Buffalo, OK, p. A334

MCELHANNON, W. C., Administrator, Union County General Hospital, Clayton, NM, p. A278

MCEWEN, David S., Chief Executive Officer, Marlette Community Hospital, Marlette, MI, p. A214

MCFADDEN, Glennon K., Chief Executive Officer, Forest Park Hospital, Saint Louis, MO, p. A248

MCGEACHEY, Edward J., President and Chief Executive Officer, Southern Maine Medical Center, Biddeford, ME, p. A187

MCGEE, John P.
President and Chief Executive Officer, JFK Medical Center, Edison, NJ, p. A269
President and Chief Executive Officer, Solaris Health System, Edison, NJ, p. B140

MCGILL, Richard M., Administrator, Hale County Hospital, Greensboro, AL, p. A15

MCGILL, Timothy W., Chief Executive Officer, Livingston Regional Hospital, Livingston, TN, p. A386

MCGINTY, Daniel B., President and Chief Executive Officer, Holy Family Memorial Medical Center, Manitowoc, WI, p. A460

MCGLASHAN, Thomas H., M.D., Director and Psychiatrist–in–Chief, Yale Psychiatric Institute, New Haven, CT, p. A76

MCGOUGH, Susan, Administrator, Memorial Hospital, Weiser, ID, p. A117

MCGOURTY, Mark E., Regional Chief Executive Officer, St. John Medical Center, Longview, WA, p. A445

MCGOWAN, Donna, R.N., Administrator, Lane County Hospital, Dighton, KS, p. A157

MCGOWAN, George, FACHE, Chief Executive Officer, Medical Center Blount, Oneonta, AL, p. A17

MCGRATH, Denise B., Chief Executive Officer, HEALTHSOUTH Treasure Coast Rehabilitation Hospital, Vero Beach, FL, p. A97

MCGRAW, Steven E., Administrator, Vencor Hospital–Chattanooga, Chattanooga, TN, p. A382

MCGUIRE, William D., President and Chief Executive Officer, Catholic Medical Centers, New York, NY, p. A289

MCINTYRE, Nancy, Administrator, Ferry County Memorial Hospital, Republic, WA, p. A447

MCINTYRE, Kathleen, President, Little Company of Mary Hospital and Health Care Centers, Evergreen Park, IL, p. A125

MCIVOR, Dave, Administrator, Roundup Memorial Hospital, Roundup, MT, p. A254

MCKAY, Daniel E., Chief Executive Officer, Moberly Regional Medical Center, Moberly, MO, p. A245

MCKAY, Robert H., President, North Penn Hospital, Lansdale, PA, p. A355

MCKERNAN, Stephen W.
Chief Executive Officer, University Hospital, Albuquerque, NM, p. A278
Chief Executive Officer, University of New Mexico Mental Health Center, Albuquerque, NM, p. A278

MCKIBBENS, Ben M., President, Valley Baptist Medical Center, Harlingen, TX, p. A406

MCKILLOP, Gail, President, Crawley Memorial Hospital, Boiling Springs, NC, p. A302

MCKINNEY, Dan, Administrator, Hermann Area District Hospital, Hermann, MO, p. A242

MCKINNEY, Jim, President, Brim Healthcare, Inc., Brentwood, TN, p. B68

MCKINNEY, Paul, Administrator, Cochran Memorial Hospital, Morton, TX, p. A415

MCKINNEY Jr., Buck, Chief Executive Officer, Kiowa District Hospital, Kiowa, KS, p. A160

MCKINNON, Ronald A., Administrator, Benson Hospital, Benson, AZ, p. A22

MCKLEM, Patricia A., Medical Center Director, Veterans Affairs Medical Center, Prescott, AZ, p. A25

MCKROW, Dee, Chief Executive Officer, Hills and Dales General Hospital, Cass City, MI, p. A207

MCLAUGHLIN, George F., Chief Executive Officer, Mercy Community Hospital, Havertown, PA, p. A353

MCLAUGHLIN, Keith H., President and Chief Executive Officer, Raritan Bay Medical Center, Perth Amboy, NJ, p. A273

MCLAURIN, Monty E., President, St. Joseph's Hospital and Health Center, Paris, TX, p. A417

MCLEAN, Daniel P., Executive Director, McAllen Medical Center, McAllen, TX, p. A414

MCLEAN, Gordon C., Administrator, Whitman Hospital and Medical Center, Colfax, WA, p. A444

MCLEMORE, Edwin, Administrator, U. S. Public Health Service Indian Hospital, Cherokee, NC, p. A304

MCLEOD, Richard D., Administrator, Owen County Memorial Hospital, Owenton, KY, p. A174

MCLOUGHLIN, Thomas, President and Chief Executive Officer, Union City Memorial Hospital, Union City, PA, p. A365

MCMACKIN, James L., Chief Executive Officer, Unicoi County Memorial Hospital, Erwin, TN, p. A383

MCMACKIN, Kent W., Administrator, Dooly Medical Center, Vienna, GA, p. A111

MCMANUS, Joseph S., President and Chief Executive Officer, Lawrence General Hospital, Lawrence, MA, p. A201

MCMANUS, Michael Thomas, President, St. Clement Health Services, Red Bud, IL, p. A132

MCMEEKIN, John C., President and Chief Executive Officer, Crozer–Keystone Health System, Springfield, PA, p. B86

MCMILLAN, Douglas A., Administrator and Chief Executive Officer, West Park Hospital, Cody, WY, p. A466

MCMILLIN, Alan E., Chief Executive Officer, Women and Children's Hospital–Lake Charles, Lake Charles, LA, p. A181

MCMULLEN, Ronald B., President, Alton Memorial Hospital, Alton, IL, p. A118

MCMURDO, Timothy B., Chief Executive Officer, San Mateo County General Hospital and Clinics, San Mateo, CA, p. A61

MCMURRAY, Sean S., CHE, Administrator, Memorial North Park Hospital, Chattanooga, TN, p. A382

MCMURTRY, Roger, Chief Mental Health Bureau, Mississippi State Department of Mental Health, Jackson, MS, p. B117

MCNAIR, Mike H., Chief Executive Officer, Hartselle Medical Center, Hartselle, AL, p. A15

MCNAMARA, Maureen, President and Chief Executive Officer, New London Hospital, New London, NH, p. A266

MCNAMARA, Robert, Director, Veterans Affairs Medical Center, Leeds, MA, p. A201

MCNASH, Mark, Operations Officer, Hutzel Hospital, Detroit, MI, p. A209

MCNAUGHTON, Neil H., Executive Director and Administrator, Serenity Lane, Eugene, OR, p. A343

MCNEELY Jr., Ernest R., Chief Executive Officer and Administrator, Lewis County General Hospital, Lowville, NY, p. A287

MCNEIL, Greg R., Administrator, Dallas County Hospital, Fordyce, AR, p. A30

MCNEILL, Douglas W., FACHE, President and Chief Executive Officer, Middletown Regional Hospital, Middletown, OH, p. A327

MCNEW, Robert L., Administrator, Vencor Hospital–Fort Worth Southwest, Fort Worth, TX, p. A404

MCPHAIL, Mark D., Chief Executive Officer, Jeff Anderson Regional Medical Center, Meridian, MS, p. A235

MCQUEEN, Elbert T., Chief Executive Officer, HEALTHSOUTH Central Georgia Rehabilitation Hospital, Macon, GA, p. A107

MCRAE, Dave C., President and Chief Executive Officer, Pitt County Memorial Hospital–University Health Systems of Eastern Carolina, Greenville, NC, p. A306

MCREE, Matt, Administrator, Hart County Hospital, Hartwell, GA, p. A105

MCREYNOLDS, David H., Chief Operating Officer and Administrator, Peninsula Hospital, Louisville, TN, p. A386

MCVEETY, John A., Chief Executive Officer, Alpena General Hospital, Alpena, MI, p. A206

MCWATERS Jr., Joe H., Administrator and Chief Executive Officer, First Hospital Vallejo, Vallejo, CA, p. A66

MCWATTERS, David M., Administrator, Highland Hospital, Charleston, WV, p. A450

MCWHORTER III, John B., Executive Director, Baylor Medical Center at Garland, Garland, TX, p. A405

MEADE, Robert C., Chief Executive Officer, Englewood Community Hospital, Englewood, FL, p. A84

MEADES, LeVern, Administrator, Lallie Kemp Medical Center, Independence, LA, p. A180

MEARIAN, Chase, Administrator, Sierra Valley District Hospital, Loyalton, CA, p. A51

MECHTENBERG, David A., Chief Executive Officer, Ridgecrest Regional Hospital, Ridgecrest, CA, p. A57

MECKLENBURG, Gary A., President and Chief Executive Officer, Northwestern Memorial Hospital, Chicago, IL, p. A121

MECKSTROTH, David J., President and Chief Executive Officer, Upper Valley Medical Center, Troy, OH, p. A330

MEEHAN, John J., President and Chief Executive Officer, Hartford Hospital, Hartford, CT, p. A75

MEEKER, Timothy L., Executive Director, Sonoma Developmental Center, Eldridge, CA, p. A41

MEGARA, John J., Chief Executive Officer, Anacapa Hospital, Port Hueneme, CA, p. A56

MEHL, Edward J., Chief Executive Officer, Lake Region Healthcare Corporation, Fergus Falls, MN, p. A223

MEIER, Ernie, President and Chief Executive Officer, Alaska Regional Hospital, Anchorage, AK, p. A20

MEINERT, Mark W., CHE, Chief Executive, Yamhill Service Area, Providence Newberg Hospital, Newberg, OR, p. A344

MEIS, Fred J., Administrator and Chief Executive Officer, Graham County Hospital, Hill City, KS, p. A159

MELBY, Bernette A., Executive Director, University Health Services, Amherst, MA, p. A197

MELBY, Gina, Chief Executive Officer, Northwest Medical Center, Pompano Beach, FL, p. A93

MELCHIORRE Jr., Joseph E., CHE, Executive Administrator, Shriners Hospitals for Children, Tampa, FL, p. B136

MELIN, Craig N., President and Chief Executive Officer, Cooley Dickinson Hospital, Northampton, MA, p. A203

MELTON, Carter, President, Rockingham Memorial Hospital, Harrisonburg, VA, p. A435

MELTON, John W., Administrator, Baptist Medical Center East, Montgomery, AL, p. A17

MELTON, La Vern, Administrator, Beaver County Memorial Hospital, Beaver, OK, p. A333

MELTON, S. Dean, President and Chief Executive Officer, Morgan County Memorial Hospital, Martinsville, IN, p. A142

MELTZER, Neil M., President and Chief Operating Officer, Sinai Hospital of Baltimore, Baltimore, MD, p. A192

MENAUGH, John E., Chief Executive Officer, Sutter Coast Hospital, Crescent City, CA, p. A40

MENDELSOHN, John, M.D., President and Chief Executive Officer, University of Texas M. D. Anderson Cancer Center, Houston, TX, p. A410

MENDEZ, Lincoln S., Chief Executive Officer, HEALTHSOUTH Doctors' Hospital, Coral Gables, FL, p. A83

MENDEZ, Manuel G., Operating Trustee, Mepsi Center, Bayamon, PR, p. A470

MENTON, Timothy P., Interim Administrator, Broward General Medical Center, Fort Lauderdale, FL, p. A84

MERCADO, Sylvia, Chief Executive Officer, University Pediatric Hospital, San Juan, PR, p. A472

MERCY, Scott, Chairman and Chief Executive Officer, LifePoint Hospitals, Inc., Nashville, TN, p. B109

MEREDITH, Stephen L., Chief Executive Officer, Twin Lakes Regional Medical Center, Leitchfield, KY, p. A171

MERRILL, Mark H., Executive Director, Presbyterian Hospital of Dallas, Dallas, TX, p. A400

MERRITT, Tim E., Chief Executive Officer, Wills Memorial Hospital, Washington, GA, p. A111

MERSON, Michael R., President and Chief Executive Officer, MedStar Health, Columbia, MD, p. B114

MERTZ, Paul A.
Executive Director, Irvington General Hospital, Irvington, NJ, p. A271
Executive Director, Newark Beth Israel Medical Center, Newark, NJ, p. A272

MERWIN, Robert W., Chief Executive Officer, Mills–Peninsula Health Services, Burlingame, CA, p. A38

MESMER, Keith, Chief Executive Officer, Hazel Hawkins Memorial Hospital, Hollister, CA, p. A45

MESROPIAN, Robert A., President and Chief Executive Officer, Alice Peck Day Memorial Hospital, Lebanon, NH, p. A266

MESSER, Bristol, Chief Executive Officer, Trace Regional Hospital, Houston, MS, p. A233

MESSMER, Joseph, President and Chief Executive Officer, Mercy Medical Center, Nampa, ID, p. A116

METIVIER, Roland, Chief Executive Officer, Las Encinas Hospital, Pasadena, CA, p. A55

METSCH, Jonathan M., Dr.PH
President and Chief Executive Officer, Greenville Hospital, Jersey City, NJ, p. A271
President and Chief Executive Officer, Jersey City Medical Center, Jersey City, NJ, p. A271
President and Chief Executive Officer, Liberty Healthcare System, Jersey City, NJ, p. B108

METZLER, Michael W., President, Saint Anne's Hospital, Fall River, MA, p. A200

METZNER, Kurt W., President and Chief Executive Officer, Mississippi Baptist Health Systems, Jackson, MS, p. A234

MEYER, Eugene W., President and Chief Executive Officer, Lawrence Memorial Hospital, Lawrence, KS, p. A160

MEYER, James E., President and Chief Executive Officer, MedCentral Health System, Mansfield, OH, p. A326

MEYER, Jeffrey K., Administrator and Chief Executive Officer, Osceola Medical Center, Osceola, WI, p. A462

MEYER, Kurt, Administrator, Delta Memorial Hospital, Dumas, AR, p. A30

MEYER, Marlis, Division Director, Veterans Affairs Medical Center, Lake City, FL, p. A87

MEYER, Michele C., Interim Chief Executive Officer, Des Peres Hospital, Saint Louis, MO, p. A247

MEYER, Robert F., M.D.
Chief Executive Officer, Samaritan Behavioral Health Center–Scottsdale, Scottsdale, AZ, p. A26
Chief Executive Officer, Samaritan–Wendy Paine O'Brien Treatment Center, Phoenix, AZ, p. A25

MEYER, Wilbert E., Administrator and Chief Executive Officer, Cooper County Memorial Hospital, Boonville, MO, p. A239

MEYERS, Audrey, President, Valley Hospital, Ridgewood, NJ, p. A274

MEYERS, Joan T., R.N., Executive Director, West Jersey Hospital–Voorhees, Voorhees, NJ, p. A275

MEYERS, Mark A.
President and Chief Executive Officer, Garden Grove Hospital and Medical Center, Garden Grove, CA, p. A43
President and Chief Executive Officer, Western Medical Center Hospital Anaheim, Anaheim, CA, p. A36

MEYERS, Russell, Chief Executive Officer, Conroe Regional Medical Center, Conroe, TX, p. A398

MICHAEL, Barry, Chief Executive Officer, Meadows Regional Medical Center, Vidalia, GA, p. A111

MICHAEL, Max, M.D., Chief Executive Officer and Medical Director, Cooper Green Hospital, Birmingham, AL, p. A12

MICHALSKI, Eugene F., Vice President and Director, William Beaumont Hospital–Troy, Troy, MI, p. A218

MICHEL, Jack, M.D., Chief Executive Officer, Larkin Community Hospital, South Miami, FL, p. A95

MICHELL, Dyer T., President, Munroe Regional Medical Center, Ocala, FL, p. A91

MICKOSEFF, Tecla A., Administrator, LAC–Harbor–University of California at Los Angeles Medical Center, Torrance, CA, p. A64

MICKUS, Steven L., President and Chief Executive Officer, St. Vincent Mercy Medical Center, Toledo, OH, p. A330

MIDDLEBROOK, Randy, Chief Executive Officer and Administrator, Aspen Valley Hospital District, Aspen, CO, p. A68

MIESLE, Michael A., Administrator, Wood County Hospital, Bowling Green, OH, p. A318

MIGUEL, Hortense, R.N., Service Unit Director, U. S. Public Health Service Indian Hospital, Winterhaven, CA, p. A67

MIKLAS, Joanne P., Ph.D., Superintendent, Gracewood State School and Hospital, Gracewood, GA, p. A105

MILANES, Carlos, Executive Vice President and Administrator, Palm Springs General Hospital, Hialeah, FL, p. A85

MILBRATH, Michael, Administrator, Waseca Medical Center, Waseca, MN, p. A229

MILES, Paul V., Administrator, Middlesboro Appalachian Regional Hospital, Middlesboro, KY, p. A173

MILEWSKI, Robert, President and Chief Executive Officer, Mount Clemens General Hospital, Mount Clemens, MI, p. A214

MILEY, Dennis C., Administrator, Tri–County Hospital, Wadena, MN, p. A229

MILLBURG, Charles L., CHE, Chief Executive Officer, Shenandoah Memorial Hospital, Shenandoah, IA, p. A154

MILLER, Alan B., President and Chief Executive Officer, Universal Health Services, Inc., King of Prussia, PA, p. B150

MILLER, Blaine K., Administrator, Minneola District Hospital, Minneola, KS, p. A162

MILLER, Charles F., Interim President, Piedmont Healthcare System, Rock Hill, SC, p. A374

MILLER, Charles R.
Chief Executive Officer, Northwest Iowa Health Center, Sheldon, IA, p. A153
President and Chief Operating Officer, Paracelsus Healthcare Corporation, Houston, TX, p. B123

MILLER, Donald D., Executive Director, Southern New Mexico Rehabilitation Center, Roswell, NM, p. A280

MILLER, Emil P., Chief Executive Officer, North Ridge Medical Center, Fort Lauderdale, FL, p. A84

MILLER, Gene, Chief Executive Officer, Garland Community Hospital, Garland, TX, p. A405

MILLER, George E., Chief Executive Officer, North Monroe Hospital, Monroe, LA, p. A182

MILLER, Jeffrey S., President, High Point Regional Health System, High Point, NC, p. A307

MILLER, Kevin J., FACHE, Chief Executive Officer, Medical Center of Southern Indiana, Charlestown, IN, p. A137

MILLER, Kimberly J., CHE, Administrator, Mitchell County Regional Health Center, Osage, IA, p. A153

MILLER, Marlo L., Administrator, Dundy County Hospital, Benkelman, NE, p. A256

MILLER, Richard, Administrator and Chief Executive Officer, Norton County Hospital, Norton, KS, p. A162

MILLER, Richard P.
Director, G.V. Montgomery Veterans Affairs Medical Center, Jackson, MS, p. A234
President and Chief Executive Officer, Virtua Health, Marlton, NJ, p. B155

MILLER, Robert, Chief Executive Officer, Henry County Health Center, Mount Pleasant, IA, p. A152

MILLER, Tamara, Administrator, Madison Community Hospital, Madison, SD, p. A377

MILLER, Thomas D., President and Chief Executive Officer, Lutheran Hospital of Indiana, Fort Wayne, IN, p. A138

MILLER, Thomas O., Administrator, Pungo District Hospital, Belhaven, NC, p. A302

MILLER, Wayne T., Administrator, Behavioral Healthcare of Northern Indiana, Plymouth, IN, p. A143

MILLER, William P., President and Chief Executive Officer, Caro Community Hospital, Caro, MI, p. A207

MILLER III, Thomas, Chief Executive Officer, Myrtle Werth Hospital–Mayo Health System, Menomonie, WI, p. A460

MILLER Jr., George N., Chief Executive Officer, Jasper Memorial Hospital, Jasper, TX, p. A411

MILLER Jr., John A., President, Anderson Area Medical Center, Anderson, SC, p. A370

MILLIGAN Jr., William M., President and Chief Executive Officer, Tyler Memorial Hospital, Tunkhannock, PA, p. A365

MILLIRONS, Dennis C., President and Chief Executive Officer, Riverside Medical Center, Kankakee, IL, p. A128

MILLON, Ivon, Chief Executive Officer, Hospital Dr. Federico Trilla, Carolina, PR, p. A470

MILLS, Fred R., President and Chief Executive Officer, Baptist Health System, San Antonio, TX, p. B63

MILLS, Pete, Chief Executive Officer, Jenkins County Hospital, Millen, GA, p. A107

MILLS, Randy, Chief Executive Officer, Barrow Medical Center, Winder, GA, p. A111

MILLS, Stephen S.
President and Chief Executive Officer, New York Flushing Hospital Medical Center, New York, NY, p. A292
President and Chief Executive Officer, New York Hospital Medical Center of Queens, New York, NY, p. A292

MILLSTEAD, John B., Chief Executive Officer, Campbell Health System, Weatherford, TX, p. A425

MILNES, Lynn, Administrator and Chief Executive Officer, Skyline Hospital, White Salmon, WA, p. A449

MILTON, Gene C., President and Chief Executive Officer, Hackettstown Community Hospital, Hackettstown, NJ, p. A270

MILTON, Paul A., Chief Operating Officer, Samaritan Hospital, Troy, NY, p. A299

MINCEMOYER, Robert, President and Chief Executive Officer, Schuyler Hospital, Montour Falls, NY, p. A288

MINDEN, Larry, Chief Executive Officer, Jane Phillips Medical Center, Bartlesville, OK, p. A333

MINER, Charles B., President and Chief Executive Officer, Meridia Health System, Cleveland, OH, p. B116

MINER, Greg, Administrator, Loring Hospital, Sac City, IA, p. A153

MINICK, Mark J., President and Chief Executive Officer, Van Wert County Hospital, Van Wert, OH, p. A330

MINNICK, Peggy, Administrator, BHC Alhambra Hospital, Rosemead, CA, p. A57

MINNIS, Holly, Chief Executive Officer, Mission Vista Behavioral Health System, San Antonio, TX, p. A420

MINNIS, Vernon, Chief Executive Officer, Hospital District Number Five of Harper County, Harper, KS, p. A159

MINNIX Jr., William L., President and Chief Executive Officer, Wesley Woods Center of Emory University, Atlanta, GA, p. A100

MINOR, Richard J., President and Chief Executive Officer, Grandview Hospital and Medical Center, Dayton, OH, p. A322

MIRABITO, Frank W., President, Chenango Memorial Hospital, Norwich, NY, p. A295

MISENER, Kenneth T., Vice President and Chief Operating Officer, Fairview Hospital System, Cleveland, OH, p. B96

MISHELL, Jeffrey, M.D., Chief Executive Officer, Precedent Health Center, Denver, CO, p. A69

MISHLER, Sheila, Chief Executive Officer, Charter Behavioral Health Systems, Lafayette, IN, p. A141

MISSILDINE, Syble F., Administrator, Northeast Medical Center Hospital, Humble, TX, p. A410

MITCHEL, David M., Chief Executive Officer, Avoyelles Hospital, Marksville, LA, p. A182

MITCHELL, Andrew J., Vice President, Administration, North Shore University Hospital–Forest Hills, New York, NY, p. A292

MITCHELL, Gary W., Chief Executive Officer, Newman Memorial Hospital, Shattuck, OK, p. A339

MITCHELL, Jay, Chief Executive Officer, Massachusetts Respiratory Hospital, Braintree, MA, p. A199

MITCHELL, Jerald F., President and Chief Executive Officer, Sunrise Hospital and Medical Center, Las Vegas, NV, p. A263

MITCHELL, Joseph K., Administrator, Tuolumne General Hospital, Sonora, CA, p. A63

MITCHELL, M. Thomas, President and Chief Executive Officer, Mercy Medical Center, Williston, ND, p. A316

MITCHELL, Sidney E., Executive Director, University of Illinois at Chicago Medical Center, Chicago, IL, p. A123

MITCHELL, Thedis V., Director, U. S. Public Health Service Indian Hospital, Clinton, OK, p. A334

MITCHELL, Timothy W., Chief Executive Officer, HEALTHSOUTH Northern Kentucky Rehabilitation Hospital, Covington, KY, p. A168

MITCHELL, Trish, Chief Executive Officer, Meridell Achievement Center, Liberty Hill, TX, p. A412

MITCHELL Jr., William O., Chief Executive Officer, HEALTHSOUTH Rehabilitation Hospital of Austin, Austin, TX, p. A394

MITCHENER Jr., Charles, Chief Executive Officer, Jacksonville Hospital, Jacksonville, AL, p. A16

MITRICK, Joseph, Administrator, Baptist Medical Center–Beaches, Jacksonville Beach, FL, p. A87

MITTEER, Brian R., President, Brattleboro Memorial Hospital, Brattleboro, VT, p. A431

MIZRACH, Kenneth H., Director, Veterans Affairs New Jersey Health Care System, East Orange, NJ, p. A269

MLADY, Celine M., Chief Executive Officer, Osmond General Hospital, Osmond, NE, p. A261

MO, Lin H., President and Chief Executive Officer, New York Community Hospital, New York, NY, p. A292

MOAKLER, Thomas J., Chief Executive Officer, Houlton Regional Hospital, Houlton, ME, p. A188

MOBURG, Steven T., Administrator, Boscobel Area Health Care, Boscobel, WI, p. A457

MOCERI, Carm, President, Barnes–Jewish St. Peters Hospital, Saint Peters, MO, p. A249

MODDERMAN, Melvin E., Administrator, Lincoln Trail Behavioral Health System, Radcliff, KY, p. A175

MOEBINS, Geoffrey, Chief Operating Officer, Mt. Sinai Medical Center, Cleveland, OH, p. A321

MOEBIUS, Geoffrey D., President and Chief Executive Officer, Saint Michael Hospital, Cleveland, OH, p. A321

MOELLER, Jerry G., President and Chief Executive Officer, Stillwater Medical Center, Stillwater, OK, p. A340

MOEN, Daniel P., President and Chief Executive Officer, Heywood Hospital, Gardner, MA, p. A200

MOEN, Robert A., President and Chief Executive Officer, Emanuel Medical Center, Turlock, CA, p. A65

MOHR, Robin Z., Chief Executive Officer, St. Francis Central Hospital, Pittsburgh, PA, p. A361

MOLANO, Celia, Executive Director, I. Gonzalez Martinez Oncologic Hospital, Hato Rey, PR, p. A472

MOLL, Jeffrey S., President and Chief Executive Officer, Beth Israel Hospital, Passaic, NJ, p. A273

MOLNAR, George, M.D., Executive Director, Buffalo Psychiatric Center, Buffalo, NY, p. A283

MONE, Thomas D., President and Chief Executive Officer, San Gabriel Valley Medical Center, San Gabriel, CA, p. A60

MONGAN, James J., M.D., President, Massachusetts General Hospital, Boston, MA, p. A198

MONGE, Peter W., President and Chief Executive Officer, Montgomery General Hospital, Olney, MD, p. A195

MONROIG, Domingo, Administrator, Castaner General Hospital, Castaner, PR, p. A470

MONROIG, Samuel, Vice President for Administration, Arecibo Regional Hospital, Arecibo, PR, p. A469

MONTAG, Kathy, Administrator Health Care, State Correctional Institution at Camp Hill, Camp Hill, PA, p. A349

MONTES, Lisa K., Administrator and Chief Executive Officer, Del Amo Hospital, Torrance, CA, p. A64

MONTGOMERY II, Raymond W., President and Chief Executive Officer, White County Medical Center, Searcy, AR, p. A34

MONTGOMERY Jr., J. C., President, Texas Scottish Rite Hospital for Children, Dallas, TX, p. A401

MONTION, Robert M., Chief Executive Officer, Tulare District Hospital, Tulare, CA, p. A65

MOONEY, Jimmy, Chief Executive Officer, Willingway Hospital, Statesboro, GA, p. A110

MOORE, Darrell W., President and Chief Executive Officer, Baptist Medical Center, Kansas City, MO, p. A243

MOORE, Duncan, President and Chief Executive Officer, Tallahassee Memorial HealthCare, Tallahassee, FL, p. A96

MOORE, E. Richard, President, Hazleton General Hospital, Hazleton, PA, p. A353

MOORE, George, Director, Veterans Affairs Medical Center, Martinsburg, WV, p. A452

MOORE, James A., Administrator, Milwaukee Psychiatric Hospital, Wauwatosa, WI, p. A465

MOORE, Jason H., President and Chief Executive Officer, John D. Archbold Memorial Hospital, Thomasville, GA, p. A110

MOORE, John, Administrator, Hiawatha Community Hospital, Hiawatha, KS, p. A159

MOORE, Joseph L.
    Director, Veterans Affairs Chicago Health Care System–Lakeside Division, Chicago, IL, p. A123
    Director, Veterans Affairs Chicago Health Care System–West Side Division, Chicago, IL, p. A123

MOORE, Michael T., Chief Executive Officer, SCCI Hospital of Kokomo, Kokomo, IN, p. A141

MOORE, Mindy S., Administrator, Vencor Hospital–Brea, Brea, CA, p. A38

MOORE, Paul David, Administrator, Atoka Memorial Hospital, Atoka, OK, p. A333

MOORE, Regina, Interim Chief Executive Officer, Stone County Hospital, Wiggins, MS, p. A238

MOORE, Richard T., Administrator, Lake District Hospital, Lakeview, OR, p. A343

MOORE, Robert J., CHE, Chief Executive Officer, Pekin Hospital, Pekin, IL, p. A131

MOORE, Roland E.
    Acting Director, Brockton Veterans Affairs Medical Center, Brockton, MA, p. A199
    Acting Medical Center Director, Veterans Affairs Medical Center, Boston, MA, p. A198

MOORE, Terence F., President, MidMichigan Health, Midland, MI, p. B117

MOORE, Thomas F., Administrator, Charleston Memorial Hospital, Charleston, SC, p. A370

MOORE, W. Evan, Administrator, Comanche Community Hospital, Comanche, TX, p. A398

MOORE, Mark D., Deputy Commander and Administrator, Bayne–Jones Army Community Hospital, Fort Polk, LA, p. A179

MOORE III, Ben, Executive Director, University Hospital–SUNY Health Science Center at Syracuse, Syracuse, NY, p. A299

MOORE–HARDY, Cynthia Ann, President and Chief Executive Officer, Lake Hospital System, Painesville, OH, p. A328

MOORING, Phillip A., Director, Walter B. Jones Alcohol and Drug Abuse Treatment Center, Greenville, NC, p. A306

MOOTRY, John M., Chief Executive Officer, Barrett Memorial Hospital, Dillon, MT, p. A252

MORALES, Herson E., Executive Director, Hospital Santa Rosa, Guayama, PR, p. A470

MORASKO, Jerry, Administrator, Marias Medical Center, Shelby, MT, p. A254

MORASKO, Robert A., Chief Executive Officer, William Bee Ririe Hospital, Ely, NV, p. A263

MORDOH, Henry A.
    President, UPMC Presbyterian, Pittsburgh, PA, p. A362
    President, UPMC Shadyside, Pittsburgh, PA, p. A362

MORELAND, L. Pat, Administrator, Hardy Wilson Memorial Hospital, Hazlehurst, MS, p. A233

MORELAND, Michael E., Director, Veterans Affairs Medical Center, Butler, PA, p. A349

MORESI, Randy, Chief Executive Officer, North Hills Hospital, North Richland Hills, TX, p. A416

MORGAN, Charles R., Administrator, Wayne Memorial Hospital, Jesup, GA, p. A106

MORGAN, Craig, Administrator, Knox County Hospital, Barbourville, KY, p. A167

MORGAN, Donald J., Administrator, Page Memorial Hospital, Luray, VA, p. A436

MORGAN, James E., Director, Huey P. Long Medical Center, Pineville, LA, p. A184

MORGAN, John, President, Gottlieb Memorial Hospital, Melrose Park, IL, p. A129

MORGAN, Kelly C., President and Chief Executive Officer, Sierra View District Hospital, Porterville, CA, p. A56

MORGAN, Michael L., President and Chief Executive Officer, St. Edward Mercy Medical Center, Fort Smith, AR, p. A31

MORGAN, Timothy O., Executive Director, Pennsylvania Hospital, Philadelphia, PA, p. A359

MORIN, Paul A., Superintendent, Soldiers' Home in Holyoke, Holyoke, MA, p. A201

MORLAN, Sandy, Administrator, Ellett Memorial Hospital, Appleton City, MO, p. A239

MORLEY, Tad A., Chief Executive Officer, Brigham City Community Hospital, Brigham City, UT, p. A427

MORRASH, Joseph, Administrator, State Correctional Institution Hospital, Pittsburgh, PA, p. A361

MORRIS, Elaine F., Administrator, Methodist Ambulatory Surgery Hospital, San Antonio, TX, p. A420

MORRIS, Leigh E., President and Chief Executive Officer, La Porte Regional Health System, La Porte, IN, p. A141

MORRIS, Linda, Administrator, Ogallala Community Hospital, Ogallala, NE, p. A260

MORRIS, Michael, Administrator, Coleman County Medical Center, Coleman, TX, p. A397

MORRIS, Randall R., Administrator, West Carroll Memorial Hospital, Oak Grove, LA, p. A184

MORRIS, Robert, M.D., Administrator, Hilo Medical Center, Hilo, HI, p. A112

MORRIS III, Joseph E., Chief Executive Officer, Kootenai Medical Center, Coeur D'Alene, ID, p. A115

MORRISON, Ann, R.N., Chief Executive Officer, Sebasticook Valley Hospital, Pittsfield, ME, p. A189

MORRISON, Robert E., President, Randolph Hospital, Asheboro, NC, p. A302

MORROW, Julia, Administrator, Morrill County Community Hospital, Bridgeport, NE, p. A256

MORROW, Shawn, Chief Executive Officer and Administrator, Holdenville General Hospital, Holdenville, OK, p. A336

MORSE, Amy, Chief Executive Officer, New England Rehabilitation Hospital of Portland, Portland, ME, p. A189

MORSE, Gary C., Chief Executive Officer and Administrator, Baptist Perry Community Hospital, Linden, TN, p. A386

MORTON, Bill, President and Chief Executive Officer, McKenna Memorial Hospital, New Braunfels, TX, p. A416

MORTON, Ronald, Administrator, Barton County Memorial Hospital, Lamar, MO, p. A244

MOSCATO, Mary, Chief Executive Officer, HEALTHSOUTH New England Rehabilitation Hospital, Woburn, MA, p. A205

MOSES, Jon, Administrator, Wood River Medical Center, Los Angeles, ID, p. A117

MOSS, Dwayne, Chief Executive Officer, T. J. Samson Community Hospital, Glasgow, KY, p. A169

MOSS, James T.
    President and Chief Executive Officer, Jackson–Madison County General Hospital, Jackson, TN, p. A384
    President, West Tennessee Healthcare, Jackson, TN, p. B156

MOSS, Joseph, Administrator, Ste. Genevieve County Memorial Hospital, Ste. Genevieve, MO, p. A249

MOSS, Paul E., President, Milford Hospital, Milford, CT, p. A75

MOSS, Rod, Chief Executive Officer, HEALTHSOUTH Rehabilitation Hospital of North Alabama, Huntsville, AL, p. A15

MOSS, William Mason, President, Potomac Hospital, Woodbridge, VA, p. A441

MOSTELLER Jr., William E., Interim Administrator, Integris Bass Baptist Health Center, Enid, OK, p. A335

MOTZER, Earl James, FACHE, Chief Executive Officer, The James B. Haggin Memorial Hospital, Harrodsburg, KY, p. A170

MOUGHON, Edward, Superintendent, Big Spring State Hospital, Big Spring, TX, p. A395

MOULTHROP, David L., Ph.D., President and Chief Executive Officer, Rogers Memorial Hospital, Oconomowoc, WI, p. A462

MOUNTCASTLE, William A., Director, Veterans Affairs Medical Center, Nashville, TN, p. A389

MOUSA, Barry L., Chief Executive Officer, Fannin Regional Hospital, Blue Ridge, GA, p. A101

MROSS, Charles D., President, Franklin Square Hospital Center, Baltimore, MD, p. A191

MUDLER, Gordon A., President and Chief Executive Officer, Hackley Health, Muskegon, MI, p. A214

MUELLER, Jens, Chairman, Pacific Health Corporation, Long Beach, CA, p. B123

MUETZEL, Hal, Chief Executive Officer, South Bay Hospital, Sun City Center, FL, p. A95

MUGRAUER, Wayne A., Chief Executive Officer, Friends Hospital, Philadelphia, PA, p. A358

MUHLENTHALER, Donald, FACHE, President and Chief Executive Officer, Weirton Medical Center, Weirton, WV, p. A454

MUILENBURG, Robert H., Executive Director, University of Washington Medical Center, Seattle, WA, p. A447

MULDER, Dale, Chief Executive Officer, North Central Medical Center, McKinney, TX, p. A414

MULDOON, Patrick L., President and Chief Executive Officer, South County Hospital, Wakefield, RI, p. A369

MULFORD, Peter L., Administrator, City Hospital, Martinsburg, WV, p. A452

MULHOLLAND, Donna, President and Chief Executive Officer, Easton Hospital, Easton, PA, p. A351

MULHOLLAND Jr., K. L., Director, Veterans Affairs Medical Center, Memphis, TN, p. A388

MULL, Connie, Chief Executive Officer, Cedar Springs Psychiatric Hospital, Colorado Springs, CO, p. A68

MULLAHEY, Ronald T., President, Vassar Brothers Hospital, Poughkeepsie, NY, p. A296

MULLANEY, Garrell S., Chief Executive Officer, Connecticut Valley Hospital, Middletown, CT, p. A75

MULLANEY, Janet, President, Heritage Hospital, Tarboro, NC, p. A311

MULLANY, Joseph J.
    Chief Executive Officer, Biloxi Regional Medical Center, Biloxi, MS, p. A231
    Chief Executive Officer, Central Mississippi Medical Center, Jackson, MS, p. A234

MULLEN, Anthony F., Administrator, Bertie Memorial Hospital, Windsor, NC, p. A312

MULLEN, Gregory S., Administrator, Tyler Holmes Memorial Hospital, Winona, MS, p. A238

MULLEN, Robert L., Administrator, Rice County Hospital District Number One, Lyons, KS, p. A161

MULLER, A. Gary, FACHE, President and Chief Executive Officer, West Jefferson Medical Center, Marrero, LA, p. A182

MULLER, Ralph W., Chief Executive Officer, University of Chicago Health System, Chicago, IL, p. B152

MULLER, Thomas W., M.D., Superintendent, Northwest Georgia Regional Hospital, Rome, GA, p. A109

MULLINS, Charles B., Executive Vice Chancellor, University of Texas System, Austin, TX, p. B152

MULLINS, Larry A., President and Chief Executive Officer, Good Samaritan Hospital Corvallis, Corvallis, OR, p. A342

MULLINS, Michael L., Chief Executive Officer, UniMed Medical Center, Minot, ND, p. A315

MULLINS, Tommy H., Administrator, Boone Memorial Hospital, Madison, WV, p. A452

MULVIHILL, Debbie, Interim Administrator, Coral Springs Medical Center, Coral Springs, FL, p. A83

MUNDY, Mark J., President and Chief Executive Officer, New York Methodist Hospital, New York, NY, p. A292

MUNDY, Stephens M., Chief Executive Officer, St. Joseph's Hospital, Parkersburg, WV, p. A453

MUNETA, Anita, Chief Executive Officer, U. S. Public Health Service Indian Hospital, Crownpoint, NM, p. A278

MUNGER, Richard, Administrator, Mount Grant General Hospital, Hawthorne, NV, p. A263

MUNOZ, Humberto J., Chief Executive Officer, Sunrise Regional Medical Center, Sunrise, FL, p. A96

MUNOZ, Thalia H., Administrator, Starr County Memorial Hospital, Rio Grande City, TX, p. A419

MUNSON, Eric B., President and Chief Executive Officer, University of North Carolina Hospitals, Chapel Hill, NC, p. A303

MUNTEL, Edward G., Ph.D., President and Chief Executive Officer, NorthKey Community Care, Covington, KY, p. A168

MUNTZ, Timothy, President, St. Margaret's Hospital, Spring Valley, IL, p. A133

MURPHY, Horace W., President and Chief Executive Officer, Washington County Health System, Hagerstown, MD, p. A194

MURPHY, Jim, Chief Executive Officer, Knoxville Area Community Hospital, Knoxville, IA, p. A151

MURPHY, Joyce A., President, Carney Hospital, Dorchester, MA, p. A200

MURPHY, Michael, President and Chief Executive Officer, Sharp Healthcare, San Diego, CA, p. B135

MURPHY, Michael D., Chief Executive Officer, Gulf Coast Medical Center, Wharton, TX, p. A425

MURPHY, Michael W., Ph.D., Director, Veterans Affairs Northern Indiana Health Care System, Fort Wayne, IN, p. A138

MURPHY, Peter J., President and Chief Executive Officer, St. James Hospital and Health Centers, Chicago Heights, IL, p. A123

MURPHY, Richard J., Chief Executive Officer, Good Samaritan Hospital Medical Center, West Islip, NY, p. A300

MURPHY, Christina, Co-Chief Executive Officer, Christus Health, Houston, TX, p. B77

MURRAY, Annabeth, Administrator, Fairfax Memorial Hospital, Fairfax, OK, p. A335

MURRAY, Joan, R.N., Administrator, St. James Parish Hospital, Lutcher, LA, p. A182

MURRAY, T. Michael, President, South Coast Medical Center, South Laguna, CA, p. A63

MURRAY, Thomas J., President, Saint Joseph Hospital, Lexington, KY, p. A171

MURRAY III, Robert B., President and Chief Executive Officer, Fulton County Medical Center, McConnellsburg, PA, p. A355

MURRELL, Joe, Administrator, Vencor Hospital–LaGrange, LaGrange, IN, p. A141

MUSUMECI, Maryann, Director, Veterans Affairs Medical Center, New York, NY, p. A294

MUTCH, Patrick F., President, Laurel Regional Hospital, Laurel, MD, p. A195

MYERS, Charles, Administrator, Community Hospital, Torrington, WY, p. A468

MYERS, Edward W., Chief Executive Officer, Christus St. Elizabeth Hospital, Beaumont, TX, p. A395

MYERS, Gary, Administrator, Mammoth Hospital, Mammoth Lakes, CA, p. A51

MYERS, Michael D., Administrator, Veterans Memorial Hospital, Waukon, IA, p. A155

MYERS, Richard L., President and Chief Executive Officer, Durham Regional Hospital, Durham, NC, p. A305

MYNARK, Richard H., Administrator, Pulaski Memorial Hospital, Winamac, IN, p. A145

N

NABORS, Charles E., FACHE, Administrator and Chief Executive Officer, Bryan W. Whitfield Memorial Hospital, Demopolis, AL, p. A13

NACHTMAN, Frank, Administrator, Marshall Hospital, Placerville, CA, p. A56

NAGELVOORT, Clarence A., President and Chief Executive Officer, Norwegian–American Hospital, Chicago, IL, p. A121

NAGLOSKY, Paul, Administrator, Indianhead Medical Center, Shell Lake, WI, p. A463

NAIBERK, Donald T., Administrator and Chief Executive Officer, Plainview Public Hospital, Plainview, NE, p. A261

NAKAYAMA, Makoto, President, Long Beach Community Medical Center, Long Beach, CA, p. A47

NANCE, Sally S., Chief Executive Officer, Excelsior Springs Medical Center, Excelsior Springs, MO, p. A241

NAPIER, Randy L., President and Chief Executive Officer, Southern Indiana Rehabilitation Hospital, New Albany, IN, p. A143

NAPPER, Rick, Chief Executive Officer, Crittenden County Hospital, Marion, KY, p. A173

NAPPER, Terry, Administrator, Memorial Medical Center of San Augustine, San Augustine, TX, p. A421

NARBUTAS, Virgis, Administrator, Vencor Hospital–Ontario, Ontario, CA, p. A54

NARUM, Larry, President, Provena Saint Joseph Hospital, Elgin, IL, p. A124

NASCA, Edward, Chief Executive Officer, BHC Belmont Pines Hospital, Youngstown, OH, p. A331

NASRALLA, Anthony J., FACHE, President and Chief Executive Officer, Titusville Area Hospital, Titusville, PA, p. A364

NATHAN, David G., M.D., President, Dana–Farber Cancer Institute, Boston, MA, p. A198

NATZKE, Kenneth J., Administrator, St. Joseph Medical Center, Bloomington, IL, p. A119

NAY, Clifford D., Executive Director, Scott Memorial Hospital, Scottsburg, IN, p. A144

NAYLOR III, George F., Chief Executive Officer, Barstow Community Hospital, Barstow, CA, p. A37

NEAL, Gerald D., Chief Executive Officer, Tri–City Health Centre, Dallas, TX, p. A401

NEAL, Hank, Administrator, Kings Mountain Hospital, Kings Mountain, NC, p. A307

NEAL, John C., Regional Administrator and Chief Administrative Officer, Mercy Hospital–Turner Memorial, Ozark, AR, p. A34

NEAMAN, Mark R., President and Chief Executive Officer, Evanston Northwestern Healthcare, Evanston, IL, p. A125

NEEDHAM, Jean M., President, Holy Family Hospital, New Richmond, WI, p. A462

NEEDMAN, Herbert G., Administrator and Chief Executive Officer, Temple Community Hospital, Los Angeles, CA, p. A50

NEELY, Bill J., Administrator, Parmer County Community Hospital, Friona, TX, p. A404

NEELY, Cindy, Administrator, Maude Norton Memorial City Hospital, Columbus, KS, p. A157

NEFF, Mark J., President and Chief Executive Officer, St. Claire Medical Center, Morehead, KY, p. A173

NEIDENBACH, Joseph J., Executive Vice President and Administrator, St. Vincent Hospital, Green Bay, WI, p. A458

NELL, Rocio, M.D., Chief Executive Officer and Medical Director, Montgomery County Emergency Service, Norristown, PA, p. A357

NELSON, Becky, President, Sioux Valley Hospital, Sioux Falls, SD, p. A379

NELSON, Bill, Administrator and Chief Executive Officer, Coteau Des Prairies Hospital, Sisseton, SD, p. A379

NELSON, Brock D.
Chief Executive Officer, Children's Hospital and Clinics, Saint Paul, MN, p. A228
Chief Executive Officer, Children's Hospitals and Clinics, Minneapolis, Minneapolis, MN, p. A225

NELSON, Cathleen K., President and Chief Executive Officer, St. Charles Mercy Hospital, Oregon, OH, p. A328

NELSON, David A., President and Chief Executive Officer, St. Francis Medical Center, Breckenridge, MN, p. A221

NELSON, Don A., Administrator, Crook County Medical Services District, Sundance, WY, p. A467

NELSON, Fred, Administrator, Ontonagon Memorial Hospital, Ontonagon, MI, p. A215

NELSON, James O., Administrator, Buena Vista County Hospital, Storm Lake, IA, p. A154

NELSON, Kenneth W., Superintendent, Bridgewater State Hospital, Bridgewater, MA, p. A199

NELSON, William H., President and Chief Executive Officer, Intermountain Health Care, Inc., Salt Lake City, UT, p. B105

NEMACHECK, William, Chief Executive Officer, Marquette General Health System, Marquette, MI, p. A214

NEMIR, Bill, Administrator, Haskell Memorial Hospital, Haskell, TX, p. A406

NERO, Marshall L., Chief Executive Officer, Elmore Community Hospital, Wetumpka, AL, p. A19

NESTER Jr., Arthur, Administrator, Noxubee General Hospital, Macon, MS, p. A235

NESTER Jr., Martin F., Chief Executive Officer, Long Beach Medical Center, Long Beach, NY, p. A287

NETH, Marvin, Administrator, Callaway District Hospital, Callaway, NE, p. A257

NETHERLAND, Ann, Chief Executive Officer, Franklin Medical Center, Winnsboro, LA, p. A186

NETTLES, Sheila, Administrator, Sedan City Hospital, Sedan, KS, p. A164

NEUBACHER, Mark, Chief Executive Officer, Henderson Health Care Services, Henderson, NE, p. A258

NEUBERGER, Jeffrey L., Administrator, Niobrara County Hospital District, Lusk, WY, p. A467

NEUGENT, Richard C., President and Chief Executive Officer, St. Francis Health System, Greenville, SC, p. A373

NEUSCH, Michael W., FACHE, Director, Louis A. Johnson Veterans Affairs Medical Center, Clarksburg, WV, p. A451

NEUSE, Barbara, Chief Executive Officer, Rockford Center, Newark, DE, p. A78

NEVAREZ, Domingo, Executive Director, Hospital San Francisco, San Juan, PR, p. A472

NEVILL, David, President and Chief Executive Officer, Halstead Hospital, Halstead, KS, p. A158

NEWBERRY, Lewis, Interim Chief Executive Officer, Roane General Hospital, Spencer, WV, p. A454

NEWBERRY, R. Alan, President and Chief Executive Officer, Peninsula Regional Medical Center, Salisbury, MD, p. A196

NEWBOLD, Philip A., President and Chief Executive Officer, Memorial Hospital of South Bend, South Bend, IN, p. A144

NEWCOMB, Sherrie, Administrator, Jenkins Community Hospital, Jenkins, KY, p. A170

NEWHAM, Judeth, R.N., President and Chief Executive Officer, Holland Community Hospital, Holland, MI, p. A212

NEWMAN, Delores, MS, Network Manager, Metro South Network, Tinley Park Mental Health Center, Tinley Park, IL, p. A134

NEWMAN, Douglas A., Administrator and Chief Executive Officer, Stafford District Hospital, Stafford, KS, p. A164

NEWMAN, Jerald C., Chief Executive Officer, Nassau County Medical Center, East Meadow, NY, p. A285

NEWMAN, Robert G., M.D., President, Continuum Health Partners, New York, NY, p. B85

NEWSOME, Andrea C., FACHE, Director, De Jarnette Center, Staunton, VA, p. A440

NEWTON, Steven R., President and Chief Executive Officer, Research Medical Center, Kansas City, MO, p. A243

NICHOLS, Mark, Chief Executive Officer, Polk Medical Center, Cedartown, GA, p. A102

NICHOLS, Ralph, Superintendent, Evansville State Hospital, Evansville, IN, p. A138

NICKELL, Roy, Director Substance Abuse Services, Wake County Alcoholism Treatment Center, Raleigh, NC, p. A309

NICKENS III, John R.
Chief Executive Officer, Century City Hospital, Los Angeles, CA, p. A48
Chief Executive Officer, Midway Hospital Medical Center, Los Angeles, CA, p. A49

NICKERSON, Ruth Marie, President and Chief Executive Officer, Saint Agnes Medical Center, Fresno, CA, p. A43

NIEDERPRUEM, Mark L., Administrator, Shriners Hospitals for Children, Springfield, Springfield, MA, p. A204

NIEHM, Sandy, Administrator, Council Community Hospital and Nursing Home, Council, ID, p. A115

NIELSEN, Greg, Administrator, Mountainview Medical Center, White Sulphur Springs, MT, p. A255

NIELSEN, Kim, Administrator and Chief Operating Officer, Orem Community Hospital, Orem, UT, p. A428

NIELSEN, Tom, Administrator, Kennewick General Hospital, Kennewick, WA, p. A445

NIEMEYER, Romaine, President, Holy Spirit Hospital, Camp Hill, PA, p. A349

O

OLSEN, Gloria P., Ph.D., Superintendent, Kerrville State Hospital, Kerrville, TX, p. A411

OLSEN, Robert T., CHE, President and Chief Executive Officer, Yuma Regional Medical Center, Yuma, AZ, p. A28

OLSON, Garvin, Chief Operating Officer, Deer Park Hospital, Deer Park, WA, p. A444

OLSON, Gary R., President, St. Luke's Hospital, Chesterfield, MO, p. A240

OLSON, JoAline, R.N., President and Chief Executive Officer, St. Helena Hospital, Deer Park, CA, p. A40

OLSON, Lynn W., Administrator and Chief Executive Officer, Regina Medical Center, Hastings, MN, p. A224

OLSON, Nathan C., President and Chief Executive Officer, Hammond–Henry Hospital, Geneseo, IL, p. A125

OLSON, Neva M., Chief Executive Officer, Samuel Mahelona Memorial Hospital, Kapaa, HI, p. A113

OLSON, Randall M., Administrator, Wellmont Bristol Regional Medical Center, Bristol, TN, p. A381

OMER, Robert, President and Chief Executive Officer, Memorial Community Hospital and Health System, Blair, NE, p. A256

OMMEN, Ronald A., President and Chief Executive Officer, Trinity Lutheran Hospital, Kansas City, MO, p. A243

ONG, Jesus M., President, South Shore Hospital, Chicago, IL, p. A122

OPDAHL, Jim
Administrator, Community Hospital in Nelson County, McVille, ND, p. A315
Administrator, St. Luke's Tri–State Hospital, Bowman, ND, p. A313

OPPEGARD, Stanley C., Vice President and Chief Operating Officer, Methodist Hospital of Sacramento, Sacramento, CA, p. A58

ORAVEC Jr., Andrew, Administrator, Community Hospital of New Port Richey, New Port Richey, FL, p. A91

ORFGEN, Lynn C., Chief Executive Officer, NorthShore Regional Medical Center, Slidell, LA, p. A186

ORLANDO, Joseph S., Executive Director, Jacobi Medical Center, New York, NY, p. A290

ORMAN Jr., Bernard A., Administrator, Samaritan Memorial Hospital, Macon, MO, p. A245

ORMOND, Evalyn
Administrator, Sterlington Hospital, Sterlington, LA, p. A186
Administrator, Union General Hospital, Farmerville, LA, p. A179

ORNSTEEN, Walter J., President and Chief Executive Officer, Baycoast Medical Center, Baytown, TX, p. A394

ORR, Jon, Administrator, Mountain View Hospital, Gadsden, AL, p. A15

ORR, Lindell W., Chief Executive Officer, Blake Medical Center, Bradenton, FL, p. A82

ORR, Robert W., Administrator, Good Samaritan Hospital, Bakersfield, CA, p. A37

ORR, Roy J., President and Chief Executive Officer, McKenzie–Willamette Hospital, Springfield, OR, p. A346

ORR, Steven R., Chairman and Chief Executive Officer, Lutheran Health Systems, Fargo, ND, p. B111

ORRICK, Charles H., Administrator, Donalsonville Hospital, Donalsonville, GA, p. A104

ORTIZ, Julio A., M.D., Chairman, Font Martelo Hospital, Humacao, PR, p. A470

ORTIZ, Ruth M., Chief Operating Officer, Bella Vista Hospital, Mayaguez, PR, p. A471

OSBORNE, David W., President and Chief Executive Officer, Norwalk Hospital, Norwalk, CT, p. A76

OSBORNE, Doug, Facility Administrator, Georgia Regional Hospital at Savannah, Savannah, GA, p. A109

OSBORNE, Edward J., Chief Executive Officer, ValueMark–Brawner Behavioral Healthcare System–North, Smyrna, GA, p. A109

OSBORNE, Terry W., Chief Executive Officer, American Legion Hospital, Crowley, LA, p. A179

OSBURN, Jerry, Administrator, Covenant Hospital–Levelland, Levelland, TX, p. A412

OSIKA, Diane J., Chief Executive Officer, Tri–County Memorial Hospital, Gowanda, NY, p. A286

OSMUS, Richard D., Chief Executive Officer, Hugh Chatham Memorial Hospital, Elkin, NC, p. A305

OSSE, John M., Administrator, Mitchell County Hospital, Beloit, KS, p. A156

OSTASZEWSKI, Patricia, Chief Executive Officer and Administrator, HEALTHSOUTH Rehabilitation Hospital of New Jersey, Toms River, NJ, p. A275

OSWALD, Wesley W., Chief Executive Officer, Brazosport Memorial Hospital, Lake Jackson, TX, p. A412

OTAKE, Stanley, Chief Executive Officer, Bellflower Medical Center, Bellflower, CA, p. A37

OTHOLE, Jean, Service Unit Director, U. S. Public Health Service Indian Hospital, Zuni, NM, p. A280

OTHS, Richard P., President and Chief Executive Officer, Atlantic Health System, Florham Park, NJ, p. A270

OTT, Pamela, R.N., Administrator, Ocean Beach Hospital, Ilwaco, WA, p. A445

OTT, Ronald A., Chief Executive Officer, Fitzgibbon Hospital, Marshall, MO, p. A245

OTT, Ronald H., President and Chief Executive Officer, UPMC McKeesport, McKeesport, PA, p. A355

OTTEN, Jeffrey, President, Brigham and Women's Hospital, Boston, MA, p. A197

OUSLEY, Virginia, Director, Carilion New River Valley Medical Center, Radford, VA, p. A438

OWEN, Ed, Chief Executive Officer, BHC Fremont Hospital, Fremont, CA, p. A42

OWEN, Ronald S., Chief Executive Officer, Southeast Alabama Medical Center, Dothan, AL, p. A14

OWEN, Terry, Chief Executive Officer, Emory–Adventist Hospital, Smyrna, GA, p. A109

OWENS, Ben E., President, St. Bernards Regional Medical Center, Jonesboro, AR, p. A32

OWENS, Craig A., President and Chief Operating Officer, Verde Valley Medical Center, Cottonwood, AZ, p. A22

OWENS, Leon, Superintendent, Kansas Neurological Institute, Topeka, KS, p. A165

P

PAAP, Antonie H., President and Chief Executive Officer, Children's Hospital Oakland, Oakland, CA, p. A54

PABON, Ahmed Alvarez, Executive Director, Hospital Sub–Regional Dr. Victor R. Nunez, Humacao, PR, p. A470

PACINI, Carol, Provincialate Superior, Little Company of Mary Sisters Healthcare System, Evergreen Park, IL, p. B109

PACKER, Eric, Administrator, Garfield Memorial Hospital and Clinics, Panguitch, UT, p. A428

PACKER, Richard, Administrator, Cassia Regional Medical Center, Burley, ID, p. A114

PACKER, Steven J., M.D., Chief Executive Officer, Community Hospital of the Monterey Peninsula, Monterey, CA, p. A52

PACKNETT, Michael J., President and Chief Executive Officer, Mercy Health Center, Oklahoma City, OK, p. A338

PADDEN, Terrance J., Administrator, Box Butte General Hospital, Alliance, NE, p. A256

PAGE, David R., President and Chief Executive Officer, Fairview Hospital and Healthcare Services, Minneapolis, MN, p. B96

PAGE, Susan M., President and Chief Executive Officer, Pratt Regional Medical Center, Pratt, KS, p. A163

PAGELS, James R., Chief Executive Officer and Managing Director, Northern Nevada Medical Center, Sparks, NV, p. A264

PAINTER, Laureen, Chief Executive Officer, Christus Coushatta Health Care Center, Coushatta, LA, p. A178

PALACIOS, Edward C., R.N., Acting Chief Executive Officer, Selma District Hospital, Selma, CA, p. A63

PALAGI, Richard L., Chief Executive Officer, St. John's Lutheran Hospital, Libby, MT, p. A253

PALLARI, Robert, President and Chief Executive Officer, Legacy Health System, Portland, OR, p. B108

PALM, SharRay, President and Chief Executive Officer, Lakewood Health Center, Baudette, MN, p. A220

PALMER, James A., Director, Veterans Affairs Medical Center, San Juan, PR, p. A472

PALMER, John M., Ph.D.
Executive Director, Harlem Hospital Center, New York, NY, p. A290
Director, Kingsboro Psychiatric Center, New York, NY, p. A291

PALMER, William H., President, Miller Dwan Medical Center, Duluth, MN, p. A222

PALMISANO II, Richard T., MS, Chief Executive Officer, Brattleboro Retreat, Brattleboro, VT, p. A431

PANDL, Therese B., Senior Vice President and Chief Operating Officer, St. Mary's Hospital Ozaukee, Mequon, WI, p. A460

PANDYA, Ashvin, M.D., Interim Administrator, Southern Inyo County Local Health Care District, Lone Pine, CA, p. A47

PANICEK, John M.
Administrator, Rochester Methodist Hospital, Rochester, MN, p. A227
Administrator, Saint Marys Hospital, Rochester, MN, p. A227

PANIS, Reggie, President, Villaview Community Hospital, San Diego, CA, p. A59

PANTER, Greg, Interim Chief Executive Officer, BHC Spirit of St. Louis Hospital, Saint Charles, MO, p. A246

PAPANIA, Barry A., President and Chief Executive Officer, Doctors Hospital, Wentzville, MO, p. A250

PARENTE, William D., President, St. Vincent Medical Center, Los Angeles, CA, p. A50

PARIS, David, Administrator, Calhoun–Liberty Hospital, Blountstown, FL, p. A81

PARIS, Gregory A., Administrator, Monroe County Hospital, Albia, IA, p. A146

PARIS, Herbert, President, Mid Coast Hospital, Bath, ME, p. A187

PARISI, Ernest, Administrator and Chief Executive Officer, Llano Memorial Healthcare System, Llano, TX, p. A413

PARKER, Douglas M., Chief Executive Officer, Northside Hospital – Cherokee, Canton, GA, p. A102

PARKER, Patsy A., Administrator and Chief Executive Officer, Rio Vista Physical Rehabilitation Hospital, El Paso, TX, p. A403

PARKER, Phillip L.
Administrator, D. W. McMillan Memorial Hospital, Brewton, AL, p. A12
Administrator, Escambia County Health Care Authority, Brewton, AL, p. B95

PARKER, Thomas S., Site Administrator, Legacy Mount Hood Medical Center, Gresham, OR, p. A343

PARKER, Gregg S., Commanding Officer, Naval Hospital, Bremerton, WA, p. A443

PARKIS, Clyde, Director, Veterans Affairs Medical Center, Albany, NY, p. A281

PARKS III, Burton O., Administrator, West Shore Hospital, Manistee, MI, p. A214

PARMER, David N., President and Chief Executive Officer, Baptist Hospital of Southeast Texas, Beaumont, TX, p. A395

PARMER, Michael, M.D., Site Administrator, Mercy Community Hospital, Port Jervis, NY, p. A296

PARRIS, M. Tim, Executive Vice President and Chief Operating Officer, Baylor University Medical Center, Dallas, TX, p. A399

PARRIS, Y. C., Director, Veterans Affairs Medical Center, Birmingham, AL, p. A12

PARRIS Jr., Thomas G., President, Women and Infants Hospital of Rhode Island, Providence, RI, p. A369

PARRISH, Harold R., Superintendent, Rusk State Hospital, Rusk, TX, p. A419

PARRISH, James G., Administrator, East Adams Rural Hospital, Ritzville, WA, p. A447

PARSONS, Larry, Administrator, Wilbarger General Hospital, Vernon, TX, p. A424

PARTON, Gerald L., Chief Executive Officer, Meadowcrest Hospital, Gretna, LA, p. A180

PASINSKI, Theodore M., President, St. Joseph's Hospital Health Center, Syracuse, NY, p. A299

PASSAMA, Gary J., President and Chief Executive Officer, NorthBay Healthcare System, Fairfield, CA, p. B121

PATCHIN, J. Craig, Administrator, Shriners Hospitals for Children–Intermountain, Salt Lake City, UT, p. A429

PATE, Alfred S., Director, Veterans Affairs Medical Center, North Chicago, IL, p. A130

PATNESKY, Edward J., President and Chief Executive Officer, Southampton Memorial Hospital, Franklin, VA, p. A435

PATTEN, Bill, Administrator, Sedgwick County Health Center, Julesburg, CO, p. A71

PATTERSON, Bill, Interim Administrator, Stones River Hospital, Woodbury, TN, p. A391

PATTERSON, Donald E., Administrator, Siloam Springs Memorial Hospital, Siloam Springs, AR, p. A34

PATTERSON, Mike, Administrator, Sylvan Grove Hospital, Jackson, GA, p. A106

PATTON, David W., Ph.D., President and Chief Executive Officer, Wilcox Memorial Hospital, Lihue, HI, p. A113

PATTON, Jimmy, Chief Executive Officer and Managing Director, Keystone Center, Chester, PA, p. A349

PATTULLO, Douglas E., Chief Executive Officer, West Branch Regional Medical Center, West Branch, MI, p. A219

PAUGH, J. William, President and Chief Executive Officer, St. Joseph Hospital, Augusta, GA, p. A101

PAULDING, Ralph, President and Chief Executive Officer, Perry County Memorial Hospital, Perryville, MO, p. A246

PAULEY, Alan C., Administrator, Morrow County Hospital, Mount Gilead, OH, p. A327

PAULSON, Mark E., Administrator, Appleton Municipal Hospital and Nursing Home, Appleton, MN, p. A220

PAUTLER, J. Stephen, CHE, Administrator, Windom Area Hospital, Windom, MN, p. A230

PAWLAK, Paul, President and Chief Executive Officer, Silver Cross Hospital, Joliet, IL, p. A127

PAWLOWSKI, Eugene P., President, Bluefield Regional Medical Center, Bluefield, WV, p. A450

PAYNE, Mark I., Superintendent, Utah State Hospital, Provo, UT, p. A429

PAYSINGER, B. Daniel, M.D., Chief Operating Officer, Palmetto Richland Memorial Hospital, Columbia, SC, p. A371

PAYTON, Larry W., Chief Operating Officer, John F. Kennedy Memorial Hospital, Indio, CA, p. A45

PAZZAGLINI, Gino J., President and Chief Executive Officer, Good Samaritan Regional Medical Center, Pottsville, PA, p. A362

PEAK, Benjamin A., Chief Executive Officer, Dickenson County Medical Center, Clintwood, VA, p. A434

PEAK, James G., Chief Executive Officer, Memorial Hospital and Manor, Bainbridge, GA, p. A101

PEAKS, William E., Chief Executive Officer, Garden Park Community Hospital, Gulfport, MS, p. A233

PEARSE, David L., President, Speare Memorial Hospital, Plymouth, NH, p. A267

PEARSON, Bruce E., Senior Vice President and Chief Executive Officer, Desert Samaritan Medical Center, Mesa, AZ, p. A23

PEARSON, Diane, Administrator, Cook County North Shore Hospital, Grand Marais, MN, p. A223

PEARSON, Robert S., Administrator, Littleton Regional Hospital, Littleton, NH, p. A266

PEARSON, Roger W., Administrator, Ellsworth County Medical Center, Ellsworth, KS, p. A157

PECEVICH, Mark, M.D., Superintendent, Spring Grove Hospital Center, Baltimore, MD, p. A192

PECK, Gary V., Chief Executive Officer, St. Joseph's Hospital, Chewelah, WA, p. A443

PECK, Kay, Chief Executive Officer, Brown Schools Rehabilitation Center, Austin, TX, p. A393

PECK, Richard H.
President and Chief Executive Officer, Coffee Health Group, Florence, AL, p. B78
President and Chief Executive Officer, Eliza Coffee Memorial Hospital, Florence, AL, p. A14

PECK, Theresa
President and Chief Executive Officer, Catholic Health Partners, Chicago, IL, p. B74
President and Chief Executive Officer, Columbus Hospital, Chicago, IL, p. A120
President and Chief Executive Officer, Saint Anthony Hospital, Chicago, IL, p. A122
President and Chief Executive Officer, St. Joseph Hospital, Chicago, IL, p. A122

PECOT, L. J., Chief Executive Officer, Jackson Parish Hospital, Jonesboro, LA, p. A180

PEDERSEN, Connie, Administrator, Johnston Memorial Hospital, Tishomingo, OK, p. A340

PEDERSEN, William L., Chief Executive Officer, St. Peter Regional Treatment Center, Saint Peter, MN, p. A228

PEDNEAU, Michael S., Director, Dorothea Dix Hospital, Raleigh, NC, p. A309

PEED, Nancy, Administrator, Peach Regional Medical Center, Fort Valley, GA, p. A105

PEEK, Scott, Administrator, Chambers Memorial Hospital, Danville, AR, p. A30

PEEPLES, Lewis T., Chief Executive Officer, Jennie Stuart Medical Center, Hopkinsville, KY, p. A170

PEICKERT, Barbara A., R.N., Chief Executive Officer, Hayward Area Memorial Hospital and Nursing Home, Hayward, WI, p. A458

PELHAM, Judith, President and Chief Executive Officer, Mercy Health Services, Farmington Hills, MI, p. B115

PELLEGRINO, Cynthia Miller, Director and Chief Executive Officer, Western Maryland Center, Hagerstown, MD, p. A195

PELLEY, Catherine M., President and Chief Executive Officer, St. Mary Regional Medical Center, Apple Valley, CA, p. A36

PELTZ, Brian, Administrator, Oakwood Hospital Seaway Center, Trenton, MI, p. A218

PELUSO, Joseph J., President and Chief Executive Officer, Westmoreland Regional Hospital, Greensburg, PA, p. A352

PEMBERTON, Thomas Paul, Chief Executive Officer, Tallahassee Community Hospital, Tallahassee, FL, p. A96

PENLAND, Victoria M., Administrator and Chief Operating Officer, Palomar Medical Center, Escondido, CA, p. A41

PENNINGTON, David N., Chief Executive Officer, Veterans Affairs Medical Center, Huntington, WV, p. A452

PENTZ, Thomas R., President and Executive Officer, Lawnwood Regional Medical Center, Fort Pierce, FL, p. A85

PEPPER, H. L. Perry, President, Chester County Hospital, West Chester, PA, p. A365

PERDUE, Edward A., Chief Executive Officer, Coffee Medical Center, Manchester, TN, p. A386

PEREA, Carmen G., R.N., Interim Administrator, Central Arizona Medical Center, Florence, AZ, p. A22

PEREZ, Carlos, Executive Director, Bellevue Hospital Center, New York, NY, p. A289

PEREZ, Francisco J., President and Chief Executive Officer, Kettering Medical Center, Kettering, OH, p. A325

PEREZ, George, Executive Vice President and Chief Operating Officer, Walter O. Boswell Memorial Hospital, Sun City, AZ, p. A26

PEREZ DE VAZQUEZ, Marilyn, Executive Director, Cardiovascular Center of Puerto Rico and the Caribbean, San Juan, PR, p. A471

PERFETTO, Patricia, MSN, Executive Director, Willough at Naples, Naples, FL, p. A90

PERILLI, Ernest N., Chief Executive Officer, Parkview Hospital, Philadelphia, PA, p. A359

PERKINS, Gary A., President and Chief Executive Officer, Children's Hospital, Omaha, NE, p. A260

PERMETTI, Thomas, Chief Executive Officer, St. John Hospital, Nassau Bay, TX, p. A416

PERRA, Connie Oliverson, Director, Tarrant County Psychiatric Center, Fort Worth, TX, p. A404

PERREAULT, Robert A., Director, Veterans Affairs Medical Center, Decatur, GA, p. A104

PERRY, Alan S., Director, Veterans Affairs Medical Center, Fresno, CA, p. A43

PERRY, Bruce M., Chief Executive Officer, Mount Sinai Medical Center, Miami Beach, FL, p. A90

PERRY, George H., Ph.D., Chief Executive Officer, NorthShore Psychiatric Hospital, Slidell, LA, p. A185

PERRY, Matthew J., Director, Carilion Franklin Memorial Hospital, Rocky Mount, VA, p. A440

PERRY, Michael J., Chief Executive Officer, Charter Behavioral Health System of Northwest Indiana, Hobart, IN, p. A139

PERRY, Mike, Chief Executive Officer, Westbridge Treatment Center, Phoenix, AZ, p. A25

PERRY, Ronald J., Chief Executive Officer, Ashley Valley Medical Center, Vernal, UT, p. A430

PERRYMAN, Daniel, Administrator, Iuka Hospital, Iuka, MS, p. A234

PERRYMAN, Margaret, Chief Executive Officer, Gillette Children's Specialty Healthcare, Saint Paul, MN, p. A228

PERRYMAN, Mike, Administrator, Baptist Memorial Hospital–Union City, Union City, TN, p. A390

PERSICHILLI, Judith M., President and Chief Executive Officer, St. Francis Medical Center, Trenton, NJ, p. A275

PERUSHEK, John, Administrator, Bloomer Community Memorial Hospital and the MapleWood, Bloomer, WI, p. A457

PETASNICK, William D., President, Froedtert Memorial Lutheran Hospital, Milwaukee, WI, p. A461

PETER, John P., President and Chief Executive Officer, National Hospital for Kids in Crisis, Orefield, PA, p. A357

PETERS, Curtis A., Chief Executive Officer, J. D. McCarty Center for Children With Developmental Disabilities, Norman, OK, p. A337

PETERS, Douglas S., President and Chief Executive Officer, Jefferson Health System, Wayne, PA, p. B106

PETERS, J. Robert, Executive Director, Memorial Hospital, Colorado Springs, CO, p. A68

PETERSEN, Gary L., Administrator, Crawford County Memorial Hospital, Denison, IA, p. A148

PETERSEN, Keith J., Chief Executive Officer, Southwest Georgia Regional Medical Center, Cuthbert, GA, p. A103

PETERSEN, Thomas A., Vice President and Chief Operating Officer, Mercy General Hospital, Sacramento, CA, p. A58

PETERSON, Andrew E.
President and Chief Executive Officer, Faxton Hospital, Utica, NY, p. A299
President and Chief Executive Officer, St. Luke's Memorial Hospital Center, Utica, NY, p. A299

PETERSON, Bob, Chief Executive Officer, Southwest Memorial Hospital, Cortez, CO, p. A69

PETERSON, Brent A., Administrator, Cherry County Hospital, Valentine, NE, p. A262

PETERSON, Bruce D., Administrator, Mercer County Hospital, Aledo, IL, p. A118

PETERSON, Clayton R., President, Long Prairie Memorial Hospital and Home, Long Prairie, MN, p. A224

PETERSON, David A., President and Chief Executive Officer, Aroostook Medical Center, Presque Isle, ME, p. A189

PETERSON, Douglas R., President and Chief Executive Officer, Chippewa Valley Hospital and Oakview Care Center, Durand, WI, p. A457

PETERSON, Larry, Chief Executive Officer, Lake Chelan Community Hospital, Chelan, WA, p. A443

PETERSON, Leland W., President and Chief Executive Officer, Sun Health Corporation, Sun City, AZ, p. B142

PETERSON, Margare, Ph.D., Administrator, Baton Rouge General Health Center, Baton Rouge, LA, p. A177

PETERSON, Mary Anne, Interim Administrator, Clark Fork Valley Hospital, Plains, MT, p. A254

PETERSON, Patricia, President and Chief Executive Officer, St. Mary's Hospital, Passaic, NJ, p. A273

PETERSON, Randy, President and Chief Executive Officer, Salina Regional Health Center, Salina, KS, p. A164

PETERSON, Richard H., President and Chief Executive Officer, Swedish Health Services, Seattle, WA, p. A447

PETERSON, Robert, Interim Administrator, Grand River Hospital District, Rifle, CO, p. A72

PETERSON, Ronald R.
President, Johns Hopkins Health System, Baltimore, MD, p. B107
President, Johns Hopkins Hospital, Baltimore, MD, p. A192

PETERSON, William D., Administrator, Herington Municipal Hospital, Herington, KS, p. A159

PETIK, Jason, Administrator, Custer Community Hospital, Custer, SD, p. A376

PETIT Jr., Leo A., Chief Executive Officer, Bladen County Hospital, Elizabethtown, NC, p. A305

PETRE, Patrick A., Chief Executive Officer, San Dimas Community Hospital, San Dimas, CA, p. A59

PETRIK, Joanne J., Interim Administrator, Kearney County Health Services, Minden, NE, p. A259

PETRILLO, Richard L., M.D., Executive Director, Mount Vernon Hospital, Mount Vernon, NY, p. A288

PETRINI, Julie A., Senior Vice President and Area Manager, Kaiser Foundation Hospital, San Francisco, CA, p. A60

PETRUZZI, Peter T., Chief Executive Officer, Scott County Hospital, Oneida, TN, p. A389

PETTIGREW, Dennis, President and Chief Executive Officer, Erlanger Health System, Chattanooga, TN, p. A381

PETTRY, Harvey H., President and Chief Executive Officer, Richland Memorial Hospital, Olney, IL, p. A131

PETULA, Susan, President, Mercy Hospital of Scranton, Scranton, PA, p. A363

PFEFFER, Jennifer D., Administrator and Chief Executive Officer, Minnesota Valley Health Center, Le Sueur, MN, p. A224

PFEIFER, Dave, Chief Executive Officer, Valley Hospital, Palmer, AK, p. A21

PFEIFFER, James A.
Chief Operating Officer, Mease Countryside Hospital, Safety Harbor, FL, p. A94
Chief Operating Officer, Mease Hospital Dunedin, Dunedin, FL, p. A83

PFEIFFER, Trudy, Interim Administrator, Baum Harmon Memorial Hospital, Primghar, IA, p. A153

PFITZER, Anthony D., Executive Vice President and Administrator, St. Anthony's Memorial Hospital, Effingham, IL, p. A124

PHAUP, Michael B., Director, Veterans Affairs Medical Center, Durham, NC, p. A305

PHELPS, David E., President and Chief Executive Officer, Berkshire Health Systems, Inc., Pittsfield, MA, p. B67

PHELPS, M. Randell, Administrator, Memorial Hospital, Craig, CO, p. A69

PHEMISTER, Gladys, Chief Executive Officer, Gordon Memorial Hospital District, Gordon, NE, p. A258

PHILIPS III, Grady W., Vice President and Administrator, Riverside Walter Reed Hospital, Gloucester, VA, p. A435

PHILLIPS, Arthur J., Administrator, Caribou Memorial Hospital and Nursing Home, Soda Springs, ID, p. A116

PHILLIPS, Bob D., Administrator, Skaggs Community Health Center, Branson, MO, p. A239

PHILLIPS, Dennis, Chief Executive Officer, Frye Regional Medical Center, Hickory, NC, p. A307

PHILLIPS, Joan, Interim Administrator, Victor Valley Community Hospital, Victorville, CA, p. A66

PHILLIPS, John F., Administrator, Gravette Medical Center Hospital, Gravette, AR, p. A31

PHILLIPS, John J., Director, Veterans Affairs Medical Center, Omaha, NE, p. A261

PHILLIPS, Randy, Chief Executive Officer, Community Hospital, Grand Junction, CO, p. A71

PHILLIPS, Scott K., President and Chief Executive Officer, Southern Chester County Medical Center, West Grove, PA, p. A366

PICHE, William K., Chief Executive Officer, Good Samaritan Hospital, San Jose, CA, p. A60

PICKEN, Paula, Administrator, Stanton County Health Care Facility, Johnson, KS, p. A160

PICKMAN, Serena, Director, Columbia Behavioral Center, El Paso, TX, p. A402

PIEPER, Blaine, Administrator, Ohio County Hospital, Hartford, KY, p. A170

PIERCE, Peggy, Administrator, Calhoun Memorial Hospital, Arlington, GA, p. A99

PIERCE, Randolph J., President and Chief Executive Officer, Boca Raton Community Hospital, Boca Raton, FL, p. A81

PIERCE Jr., Willard R., Director, Piedmont Geriatric Hospital, Burkeville, VA, p. A433

PIERROT, Alan H., M.D., Chief Executive Officer, Fresno Surgery Center–The Hospital for Surgery, Fresno, CA, p. A43

PIERSON, Richard, Executive Director, Clinical Programs, University Hospital of Arkansas, Little Rock, AR, p. A32

PIERSON, Stephen C., Ph.D., Chief Executive Officer, Appalachian Psychiatric Healthcare System, Cambridge, OH, p. A318

PIGNATORE, John E., President and Chief Executive Officer, Corning Hospital, Corning, NY, p. A284

PILE, Darrell L., Administrator, HEALTHSOUTH Rehabilitation Hospital, Humble, TX, p. A410

PILKINGTON III, Albert, Administrator and Chief Executive Officer, Mena Medical Center, Mena, AR, p. A33

PINCKNEY, Frank D., President, Greenville Hospital System, Greenville, SC, p. B98

PINE, Polly, Administrator, Gila Regional Medical Center, Silver City, NM, p. A280

PINE, Richard M., President and Chief Executive Officer, Livengrin Foundation, Bensalem, PA, p. A348

PINEIRO, Carlos M., President, Hospital Interamericano De Medicina Avanzada, Caguas, PR, p. A470

PINKERMAN, Charles F., Administrator, Madison Community Hospital, Madison Heights, MI, p. A213

PINKHAM, Margaret G., President and Chief Executive Officer, St. Andrews Hospital and Healthcare Center, Boothbay Harbor, ME, p. A187

PIPER, Michael R., Administrator, North Big Horn Hospital, Lovell, WY, p. A467

PIPICELLI, Thomas P., President and Chief Executive Officer, William W. Backus Hospital, Norwich, CT, p. A76

PIPKIN, Barry, Chief Executive Officer and Managing Director, Bridgeway, North Little Rock, AR, p. A33

PIRIZ, J. E., Administrator, Memorial Hospital Pembroke, Pembroke Pines, FL, p. A92

PISCIOTTA, James M., Chief Executive Officer, Southwest Connecticut Mental Health System, Bridgeport, CT, p. A74

PITCHFORD, Harold, Executive Director, Porterville Developmental Center, Porterville, CA, p. A56

PITMAN, Richard A., President, Shore Memorial Hospital, Somers Point, NJ, p. A274

PITTMAN, Deanna, Administrator, Wilson County Hospital, Neodesha, KS, p. A162

PIVIROTTO, Gregory A., President and Chief Executive Officer, University Medical Center, Tucson, AZ, p. A27

PLANTIER, Anthony J., Administrator, Artesia General Hospital, Artesia, NM, p. A278

PLATOU, Kenneth E. S., Chief Executive Officer, North Valley Hospital, Whitefish, MT, p. A255

PLATT, Anne, Administrator, East Morgan County Hospital, Brush, CO, p. A68

PLATT, C. James, Chief Executive Officer, Fort Madison Community Hospital, Fort Madison, IA, p. A149

PLATT, Melvin J., Administrator, Worthington Regional Hospital, Worthington, MN, p. A230

PLESKOW, Eric D., President and Chief Executive Officer, Brylin Hospitals, Buffalo, NY, p. A282

PLOWDEN, Moultrie D., CHE
President, Randolph County Hospital, Roanoke, AL, p. A18
President, Wedowee Hospital, Wedowee, AL, p. A19

PLUMAGE, Charles D., Director, U. S. Public Health Service Indian Hospital, Harlem, MT, p. A253

PODIETZ, Frank, President, Friedman Hospital of the Home for the Jewish Aged, Philadelphia, PA, p. A358

PODLEY, Sandra C., Chief Executive Officer, Charter Grapevine Behavioral Health System, Grapevine, TX, p. A406

PODLEY, Sandy, Chief Executive Officer, Copper Hills Youth Center, West Jordan, UT, p. A430

POHREN, Allen E., Administrator, Montgomery County Memorial Hospital, Red Oak, IA, p. A153

POISSON, Keith R., President and Chief Executive Officer, Bethany Medical Center, Kansas City, KS, p. A160

POKORNEY, Georgia, Chief Executive Officer, Pioneer Memorial Hospital and Health Services, Viborg, SD, p. A379

POLAHAR, Robert G., Chief Executive Officer, Knox Community Hospital, Mount Vernon, OH, p. A327

POLGE, David J., President and Chief Executive Officer, Delaware Valley Hospital, Walton, NY, p. A300

POLHEBER, Richard, Chief Executive Officer, Page Hospital, Page, AZ, p. A24

POLL, Max, President and Chief Executive Officer, Scottsdale Healthcare, Scottsdale, AZ, p. B135

POLLA, Dale E., Administrator, Glacier County Medical Center, Cut Bank, MT, p. A252

POLLARD Jr., Joe W.
Chief Executive Officer, Alexander Community Hospital, Taylorsville, NC, p. A311
Chief Executive Officer, Granville Medical Center, Oxford, NC, p. A309

POLLOCK, Rusty, President and Chief Executive Officer, Rehabilitation Institute at Santa Barbara, Santa Barbara, CA, p. A62

POLONSKY, Leonard, interim Chief Executive Officer, Island Medical Center, Hempstead, NY, p. A286

POLUNAS, David M., Administrator and Chief Executive Officer, Heart of Florida Behavioral Center, Lakeland, FL, p. A88

POMA, Frank W., President, St. John River District Hospital, East China, MI, p. A209

POORTEN, Kevin P., Chief Executive Officer, Havasu Regional Medical Center, Lake Havasu City, AZ, p. A23

POPE, James W., Chief Administrative Officer, Norton Southwest Hospital, Louisville, KY, p. A172

POPIEL, Gary W., Executive Vice President and Chief Executive Officer, Bi–County Community Hospital, Warren, MI, p. A218

POPP, Dennis A., Administrator and Chief Executive Officer, Enumclaw Community Hospital, Enumclaw, WA, p. A444

POQUETTE, Gary R., FACHE, Executive Director, Memorial Hospital, North Conway, NH, p. A267

PORTEN, Hank J., President, Holyoke Hospital, Holyoke, MA, p. A201

PORTER, Arthur, M.D., President and Chief Executive Officer, Detroit Medical Center, Detroit, MI, p. B93

PORTER, Bill, President and Chief Executive Officer, Southwest Medical Center, Liberal, KS, p. A161

PORTER, John T., President and Chief Executive Officer, Avera Health, Yankton, SD, p. B62

PORTER, Paul, Chief Operating Officer, Fort Washington Hospital, Fort Washington, MD, p. A194

PORTER, Robert G., President, DePaul Health Center, Saint Louis, MO, p. A247

PORTER, Ronald W., Chief Executive Officer, U.S. FamilyCare Medical Center, Montclair, CA, p. A52

PORTER, Thomas C., President, Morton Hospital and Medical Center, Taunton, MA, p. A204

PORTER Jr., John M., President and Chief Executive Officer, Ephrata Community Hospital, Ephrata, PA, p. A351

PORTEUS, Robert W., President and Chief Executive Officer, Carlinville Area Hospital, Carlinville, IL, p. A119

PORTFLEET, Lori, Chief Executive Officer, Kent Community Hospital, Grand Rapids, MI, p. A210

POSEY, M. Kenneth, FACHE, Administrator, Jasper General Hospital, Bay Springs, MS, p. A231

POSTON, Stuart, President, Murray–Calloway County Hospital, Murray, KY, p. A174

POTEETE, Kenneth W., President and Chief Executive Officer, Georgetown Healthcare System, Georgetown, TX, p. A405

POTTENGER, Jay, Administrator, Missouri River Medical Center, Fort Benton, MT, p. A252

POTTER, Bruce C., President, Canton–Potsdam Hospital, Potsdam, NY, p. A296

POTTER, Michael S., President and Chief Executive Officer, Westwood Medical Center, Midland, TX, p. A415

POTTER, Terri L., President and Chief Executive Officer, Meriter Hospital, Madison, WI, p. A459

POTTER, Bonnie B., Commander, National Naval Medical Center, Bethesda, MD, p. A193

POURIER, Terry, Service Unit Director, U. S. Public Health Service Indian Hospital, Fort Yates, ND, p. A314

POWELL, Darnell, Executive Director, Rolling Hills Hospital, Ada, OK, p. A333

POWELL, Denny W., Chief Executive Officer, Phoenix Regional Medical Center, Phoenix, AZ, p. A25

POWELL, Ricky, Chief Executive Officer, Red River Hospital, Wichita Falls, TX, p. A426

POWELL, Roy A., President, Frankford Hospital of the City of Philadelphia, Philadelphia, PA, p. A358

POWELL, Wilma D., Administrator, North Baldwin Hospital, Bay Minette, AL, p. A11

POWELL Jr., Boone, President, Baylor Health Care System, Dallas, TX, p. B65

POWERS, L. Darrell, President, Lynchburg General Hospital, Lynchburg, VA, p. A436

POWERS, Michael K., Administrator, Fairbanks Memorial Hospital, Fairbanks, AK, p. A20

POWERS, Terry C., Administrator, Fort Logan Hospital, Stanford, KY, p. A175

PRASAD, Manoj K., M.D., President and Chief Executive Officer, Kern Hospital and Medical Center, Warren, MI, p. A218

PRESLAR Jr., Len B., President and Chief Executive Officer, North Carolina Baptist Hospital, Winston–Salem, NC, p. A312

PRESSLEY, Yvonne A., Chief Executive Officer, Ancora Psychiatric Hospital, Ancora, NJ, p. A268

PRESTON, Craig, Chief Executive Officer, Lakeview Hospital, Bountiful, UT, p. A427

PRIBYL, Stephen J., USAF, Administrator, Scott Medical Center, Scott AFB, IL, p. A133

PRICE, Corbett A., Chief Executive Officer, Interfaith Medical Center, New York, NY, p. A290

PRICE, Floyd N., Administrator, Grove Hill Memorial Hospital, Grove Hill, AL, p. A15

PRICE, Kim, Administrator, Belmond Community Hospital, Belmond, IA, p. A146

PRICE, Norman M., FACHE, Administrator, Southwest Mississippi Regional Medical Center, McComb, MS, p. A235

PRICE Jr., Eston, Administrator, Evans Memorial Hospital, Claxton, GA, p. A102

PRICE Jr., Warren T.
Chief Executive Officer, East Louisiana State Hospital, Jackson, LA, p. A180
Chief Executive Officer, Eastern Louisiana Mental Health System/Greenwell Spring Campus, Greenwell Springs, LA, p. A180

PRIDDY, Sandra D., President, Stokes–Reynolds Memorial Hospital, Danbury, NC, p. A304

PRIDDY III, Ernest C., Chief Executive Officer, Cumberland, A Brown Schools Hospital for Children and Adolescents, New Kent, VA, p. A437

PRIDGEN Jr., Lee, Administrator, Sampson Regional Medical Center, Clinton, NC, p. A304

PRIMEAUX, Elizabeth A., Chief Executive Officer, Greater El Monte Community Hospital, South El Monte, CA, p. A63

PRIMROSE, Gayle E., Administrator, Boone County Health Center, Albion, NE, p. A256

PRISCO, Nicholas A., Chief Executive Officer, Sunbury Community Hospital, Sunbury, PA, p. A364

PRISELAC, Margaret, R.N., Chief Operating Officer, UPMC Braddock, Braddock, PA, p. A348

PRISELAC, Thomas M., President and Chief Executive Officer, Cedars–Sinai Medical Center, Los Angeles, CA, p. A48

PRISTER, James Richard, President, R. M. L. Specialty Hospital, Hinsdale, IL, p. A127

PRITCHARD, Eugene, President, Condell Medical Center, Libertyville, IL, p. A128

PRITCHETT, Beverly, Executive Officer, Department of the Army, Office of the Surgeon General, Falls Church, VA, p. B89

PROBST, Randall K., Administrator, Wasatch County Hospital, Heber City, UT, p. A427

PROCHILO, John F., Chief Executive Officer and Administrator, Northeast Rehabilitation Hospital, Salem, NH, p. A267

PROCTOR, Randy, Superintendent, Osawatomie State Hospital, Osawatomie, KS, p. A162

PROCTOR, Steven M., President, Matheny School and Hospital, Peapack, NJ, p. A273

PROUT, John S.
President and Chief Executive Officer, Bethesda Hospital, Inc., Cincinnati, OH, p. B67
President and Chief Executive Officer, Bethesda North Hospital, Cincinnati, OH, p. A319
President and Chief Executive Officer, Good Samaritan Hospital, Cincinnati, OH, p. A319

PROVENZANO, William, President, Ohio Valley General Hospital, McKees Rocks, PA, p. A355

PRUITT, Mike, Chief Executive Officer, Lake Granbury Medical Center, Granbury, TX, p. A405

PRUITT, Paul, Administrator, St. Johns River Hospital, Jacksonville, FL, p. A86

PRUSAK, Thomas K., President, St. Joseph's Medical Center, Brainerd, MN, p. A221

PRYCE, Richard J., President, Aultman Hospital, Canton, OH, p. A318

PRYOR, Curtis R., Administrator, Purcell Municipal Hospital, Purcell, OK, p. A339

PRYOR, Dennis P., Administrator, Salem Memorial District Hospital, Salem, MO, p. A249

PUGH, Richard E., President and Chief Executive Officer, New Milford Hospital, New Milford, CT, p. A76

PUGH, Thomas E., Vice President Rehabilitation Services, John Heinz Institute of Rehabilitation Medicine, Wilkes–Barre, PA, p. A366

PUGLISI Jr., Frank J., Executive Director, Contra Costa Regional Medical Center, Martinez, CA, p. A52

PULSIPHER, Gary W., President, Breech Regional Medical Center, Lebanon, MO, p. A244

PUNDYS, Aras, Administrator, W. J. Barge Memorial Hospital, Greenville, SC, p. A373

PUNG, Dawn S., Administrator, Kau Hospital, Pahala, HI, p. A113

PURCELL Jr., Howard J., President, Community Memorial Hospital, Cheboygan, MI, p. A207

PURVES, Stephen A., CHE, President and Chief Executive Officer, Providence Hospital, Columbia, SC, p. A371

PURVIS, J. Jay, Interim Administrator, Paris Community Hospital, Paris, IL, p. A131

PURVIS, Michael, Executive Vice President and Chief Executive Officer, Phoenix Baptist Hospital and Medical Center, Phoenix, AZ, p. A25

PURVIS, Mildred W., Administrator, Hope Hospital, Lockhart, SC, p. A374

PUTNAM, Larry E., Administrator, Phillips County Medical Center, Malta, MT, p. A253

PUTNAM, Stewart, President, St. Mary's Hospital, Rochester, NY, p. A297

PUTTER, Joshua S., Executive Director, Charlotte Regional Medical Center, Punta Gorda, FL, p. A94

PYLE, Joseph, Administrator, Meadow Wood Behavioral Health System, New Castle, DE, p. A78

PYNE, Mel, Administrator, Providence General Medical Center, Everett, WA, p. A444

PYNN, David, President and Chief Executive Officer, St. John Medical Center, Tulsa, OK, p. A341

Q

QUAGLIATA, Joseph A., President and Chief Executive Officer, South Nassau Communities Hospital, Oceanside, NY, p. A295

QUAM, Mark, Executive Director, Brown County Mental Health Center, Green Bay, WI, p. A458

QUAYE, Beverly S., Administrator, Tustin Rehabilitation Hospital, Tustin, CA, p. A65

QUINLAN, Richard S., President and Chief Executive Officer, Hallmark Health System, Melrose, MA, p. A202

QUINLIVAN, Thomas J.
Administrator, Tracy Area Medical Services, Tracy, MN, p. A229
Administrator, Westbrook Health Center, Westbrook, MN, p. A229

QUINN, Robert G., FACHE, Administrator, U. S. Air Force Hospital, Beale AFB, CA, p. A37

QUINTON, Byron, Administrator, Humboldt General Hospital, Winnemucca, NV, p. A264

QUIST, Robert L., Chief Executive Officer, Park Plaza Hospital, Houston, TX, p. A409

R

RAAB, Daniel J., President and Chief Executive Officer, St. Vincent Memorial Hospital, Taylorville, IL, p. A134

RABUKA, Mickey, Administrator, Murray Medical Center, Chatsworth, GA, p. A102

RACE, J. E., Administrator and Chief Executive Officer, Lakeview Hospital, Wauwatosa, WI, p. A465

RAFFERTY, Patrick W., Administrator, Doctors Hospital of Manteca, Manteca, CA, p. A51

RAFTER, William A., Director, Julian F. Keith Alcohol and Drug Abuse Treatment Center, Black Mountain, NC, p. A302

RAGGHIANTI, Eugene, Administrator, Methodist Healthcare–Lexington Hospital, Lexington, TN, p. A386

RAGGIO, James, Administrator, Lompoc Healthcare District, Lompoc, CA, p. A47

RAGLAND, Kenneth E., Administrator, Beaufort County Hospital, Washington, NC, p. A312

RAHN, Douglas L., Chief Executive Officer, Community Health Center of Branch County, Coldwater, MI, p. A208

RAJNIC, Sharon J., Administrator, Shriners Hospitals for Children, Philadelphia, Philadelphia, PA, p. A360

RAK, Arlene A., R.N., President, UHHS Bedford Medical Center, Bedford, OH, p. A318

RALEY, Ana, Administrator, Hadley Memorial Hospital, Washington, DC, p. A79

RALPH, Chandler M., Chief Executive Officer, Adirondack Medical Center, Saranac Lake, NY, p. A297

RALPH, Stephen A.
President and Chief Executive Officer, Huntington Memorial Hospital, Pasadena, CA, p. A55
President and Chief Executive Officer, Southern California Healthcare Systems, Pasadena, CA, p. B140

RAMIREZ, Magdalena, Chief Executive Officer, Helen Hayes Hospital, West Haverstraw, NY, p. A300

RAMISH, Dana W., FACHE, President and Chief Executive Officer, Allegheny University Hospitals, Forbes Regional, Monroeville, PA, p. A356

RAMPAGE, Bruce E., President and Chief Executive Officer, Saint Anthony Memorial Health Centers, Michigan City, IN, p. A142

RAMSEY, Barbara, Ph.D., Chief Executive Officer, Lincoln Regional Center, Lincoln, NE, p. A259

RAMSEY, Beryl, Chief Executive Officer, Texas Orthopedic Hospital, Houston, TX, p. A409

RAMSEY, David L., President, Methodist Healthcare–Memphis Hospital, Memphis, TN, p. A387

RANEY, James Edward, President and Chief Executive Officer, United Health Group, Appleton, WI, p. B150

RANEY, Sam H., Interim Administrator, Stamford Memorial Hospital, Stamford, TX, p. A422

RANGE, Richard L., Chief Executive Officer, Baldwin Hospital, Baldwin, WI, p. A456

RANGE, Robert P., President and Chief Executive Officer, Grace Hospital, Cleveland, OH, p. A320

RANK, James T., Administrator, Bothwell Regional Health Center, Sedalia, MO, p. A249

RANKIN III, Fred M., President and Chief Executive Officer, Mary Washington Hospital, Fredericksburg, VA, p. A435

RANSDELL, Hart, Chief Executive Officer, Jupiter Medical Center, Jupiter, FL, p. A87

RANSDELL, Lewis A., Administrator, Vencor Hospital–Fort Lauderdale, Fort Lauderdale, FL, p. A84

RAPAPORT, Gary D., Chief Executive Officer, Sutter Tracy Community Hospital, Tracy, CA, p. A65

RAPOPORT, Morton I., M.D., President and Chief Executive Officer, University of Maryland Medical System, Baltimore, MD, p. A192

RAPP, Larry, Chief Medical and Executive Officer, Grant County Health Center, Elbow Lake, MN, p. A222

RAPP, Phillip J., President and Chief Executive Officer, St. Francis at Salina, Salina, KS, p. A164

RASH, Marty, President and Chief Executive Officer, Province Healthcare Corporation, Brentwood, TN, p. B126

RASMUSSEN, David D., Administrator, Okmulgee Memorial Hospital, Okmulgee, OK, p. A338

RASMUSSEN, Kyle, Administrator, Bridges Medical Services, Ada, MN, p. A220

RATHBONE, Thomas A., President, Health Hill Hospital for Children, Cleveland, OH, p. A320

RATHJE, J. C., Administrator, Providence Seward Medical Center, Seward, AK, p. A21

RAU, John, Administrator, Stevens Community Medical Center, Morris, MN, p. A226

RAVENBERG, Larry, Administrator, White Community Hospital, Aurora, MN, p. A220

RAY, William K., President and Chief Executive Officer, Wesley Medical Center, Hattiesburg, MS, p. A233

RAYNOR, James E., Chief Executive Officer, Raleigh Community Hospital, Raleigh, NC, p. A309

READ, J. Larry, President and Chief Executive Officer, University Health Care System, Augusta, GA, p. A101

REAGAN, Jim, M.D., Chief Executive Officer, Morris County Hospital, Council Grove, KS, p. A157

REAMER, Roger, Administrator, Butler County Health Care Center, David City, NE, p. A257

REAMEY, Kirk, Chief Executive Officer, Magnolia Hospital, Magnolia, AR, p. A33

REARDON, Robert, Hospital Services Administrator, Central Prison Hospital, Raleigh, NC, p. A309

REARDON, Timothy F., FACHE, Chief Executive Officer, Yuma District Hospital, Yuma, CO, p. A73

REASBECK, Suzanne, President and Chief Executive Officer, Flaget Memorial Hospital, Bardstown, KY, p. A167

REAVES, Nancy, Chief Executive Officer, Charter Greensboro Behavioral Health System, Greensboro, NC, p. A306

REBER, James P., President, St. Rita's Medical Center, Lima, OH, p. A325

RECUPERO, Patricia R., M.D., President and Chief Executive Officer, Butler Hospital, Providence, RI, p. A368

RECZEK, Stanley, President, Salem Hospital, Salem, MA, p. A203

REDDISH, Robert R., Administrator and Chief Executive Officer, Chicot Memorial Hospital, Lake Village, AR, p. A32

REDDOCH Jr., James F., Director, Bryce Hospital, Tuscaloosa, AL, p. A18

REDMAN, Melvin, President and Chief Operating Officer, Doctors Community Healthcare Corporation, Scottsdale, AZ, p. B94

REECE, David A., President, MidMichigan Medical Center–Midland, Midland, MI, p. A214

REECE, Morris D., Administrator and Chief Executive Officer, Carilion Giles Memorial Hospital, Pearisburg, VA, p. A438

REECER, Jeff, Chief Executive Officer, D. M. Cogdell Memorial Hospital, Snyder, TX, p. A422

REED, Gregory C., Administrator, Pike County Memorial Hospital, Louisiana, MO, p. A245

REED, Harold, Administrator, Fayette Medical Center, Fayette, AL, p. A14

REED, Jan A., CPA, Administrator and Chief Executive Officer, Electra Memorial Hospital, Electra, TX, p. A403

REED, Joy, R.N., Administrator, Ottawa County Health Center, Minneapolis, KS, p. A161

REED, Robert J., President, New Island Hospital, Bethpage, NY, p. A282

REED, Ronald R., President and Chief Executive Officer, Mercy Hospital, Iowa City, IA, p. A150

REED, Steven B., President and Chief Executive Officer, Women's Hospital–Indianapolis, Indianapolis, IN, p. A140

REEDER, Steve, Chief Executive Officer, Helena Regional Medical Center, Helena, AR, p. A31

REEK, Thomas F., Chief Executive Officer, Cuyuna Regional Medical Center, Crosby, MN, p. A222

REES, Ron R., President and Chief Executive Officer, Halifax Community Health System, Daytona Beach, FL, p. A83

REESE, James, CHE, Administrator, Stephens Memorial Hospital, Breckenridge, TX, p. A396

REESE, Sandra, Administrator, Lower Umpqua Hospital District, Reedsport, OR, p. A345

REESE, Willis L., Administrator, Falls Community Hospital and Clinic, Marlin, TX, p. A414

REEVES, Luther E., Chief Executive Officer, Fleming County Hospital, Flemingsburg, KY, p. A168

REEVEY, Ramon J., Director, Veterans Affairs Southern Nevada Healthcare System, Las Vegas, NV, p. A264

REGAN, James, Ph.D., Chief Executive Officer, Hudson River Psychiatric Center, Poughkeepsie, NY, p. A296

REGEHR, Stan, President and Chief Executive Officer, Memorial Hospital, McPherson, KS, p. A161

REGLING, Anne M.
Senior Vice President, Grace Hospital, Detroit, MI, p. A208
Senior Vice President, Sinai Hospital, Detroit, MI, p. A209

REID, David M., Administrator, Clay County Medical Center, West Point, MS, p. A238

REIF, Richard A., President and Chief Executive Officer, Doylestown Hospital, Doylestown, PA, p. A351

REILEY, Peggy, Senior Vice President and Chief Clinical Officer, Scottsdale Healthcare–Osborn, Scottsdale, AZ, p. A26

REINER, Steven S., Administrator, Kearny County Hospital, Lakin, KS, p. A160

REINERTSEN, James, M.D., Chief Executive Officer, CareGroup, Boston, MA, p. B70

REINHARD, James S., M.D., Director, Catawba Hospital, Catawba, VA, p. A433

REINHARDT, J. Rudy, Administrator, Hendry Regional Medical Center, Clewiston, FL, p. A82

REITER, Richard R., Interim Executive Director, Broadlawns Medical Center, Des Moines, IA, p. A148

REITER, Steven B., Administrator, Shriners Hospitals for Children, Houston, Houston, TX, p. A409

REKER, Douglas J., Administrator and Chief Executive Officer, Glacial Ridge Hospital, Glenwood, MN, p. A223

REMBIS, Michael A., FACHE, Chief Executive Officer, Centinela Hospital Medical Center, Inglewood, CA, p. A45

REMBOLDT, Darwin R., President and Chief Executive Officer, Hanford Community Medical Center, Hanford, CA, p. A44

REMILLARD, John R., President, Aurelia Osborn Fox Memorial Hospital, Oneonta, NY, p. A295

RENANDER, Dennis J., President and Chief Executive Officer, Galesburg Cottage Hospital, Galesburg, IL, p. A125

RENFORD, Edward J., President and Chief Executive Officer, Grady Memorial Hospital, Atlanta, GA, p. A100

RENICK, Bill, Administrator, Marshall County Medical Center, Holly Springs, MS, p. A233

RENNER, Steven W., President and Chief Executive Officer, Gettysburg Hospital, Gettysburg, PA, p. A352

RENNIE, Robert J., Administrator, U. S. Air Force Hospital, Grand Forks AFB, ND, p. A314

RENSHAW, Dee, Administrator, Integris Grove General Hospital, Grove, OK, p. A336

RENTAS, Roberto A., Administrator, Hospital De Damas, Ponce, PR, p. A471

RENTFRO, Larry D., FACHE, President and Chief Executive Officer, Grant Regional Health Center, Lancaster, WI, p. A459

RENTZ, Norman G., President and Chief Executive Officer, Cannon Memorial Hospital, Pickens, SC, p. A374

RENZ, Anne, Interim Administrator, Cambridge Medical Center, Cambridge, MN, p. A221

REPLOGLE, Raymond L., President and Chief Executive Officer, Continuous Care Center of Tulsa, Tulsa, OK, p. A340

RESNICK, Peter V., Executive Director, Dearborn County Hospital, Lawrenceburg, IN, p. A142

RETTALIATA, Marilyn R., President and Chief Executive Officer, Pocono Medical Center, East Stroudsburg, PA, p. A351

REVELS, Thomas R., President and Chief Executive Officer, Presbyterian Hospital, Charlotte, NC, p. A304

REYBURN Jr., John A., Commander, U. S. Air Force Hospital, Hill AFB, UT, p. A427

REYES, Arnold, Administrator, U. S. Penitentiary Infirmary, Lewisburg, PA, p. A355

REYNOLDS, John R., President and Chief Executive Officer, Hospital for Special Surgery, New York, NY, p. A290

REYNOLDS, Stephen Curtis
President and Chief Executive Officer, Baptist Memorial Health Care Corporation, Memphis, TN, p. B65
President and Chief Executive Officer, Baptist Memorial Hospital, Memphis, TN, p. A387

REZAC, Pamela J., President and Chief Executive Officer, Avera Sacred Heart Health Services, Yankton, SD, p. A380

RHEAULT, Donna, Chief Operating Officer, Saint Francis Hospital, Tulsa, OK, p. A341

RHEAULT, LeRoy E., President and Chief Executive Officer, Via Christi Health System, Wichita, KS, p. B155

RHINE, Scott, Administrator, Whidbey General Hospital, Coupeville, WA, p. A444

RHINEHART, Jennie R., Administrator and Chief Executive Officer, Community Hospital, Tallassee, AL, p. A18

RHOADS, Gary R., President and Chief Executive Officer, Lock Haven Hospital, Lock Haven, PA, p. A355

RHODES, Don K., Interim President and Chief Executive Officer, Saint Francis Medical Center, Cape Girardeau, MO, p. A240

RHODES, J. Gary, Chief Executive Officer, Kane Community Hospital, Kane, PA, p. A354

RICCI, David A., President and Chief Executive Officer, Germantown Hospital and Community Health Services, Philadelphia, PA, p. A358

RICE, Alan J., President, Simi Valley Hospital and Health Care Services, Simi Valley, CA, p. A63

RICE, David O., President, Haywood Regional Medical Center, Clyde, NC, p. A304

RICE, Kathleen A., Chief Operating Officer, Meridia South Pointe Hospital, Warrensville Heights, OH, p. A330

RICE, Mark, Chief Executive Officer, HEALTHSOUTH North Louisiana Rehabilitation Hospital, Ruston, LA, p. A185

RICE, Thomas R., FACHE
President and Chief Operating Officer, Integris Baptist Medical Center, Oklahoma City, OK, p. A338
President and Chief Operating Officer, Integris Southwest Medical Center, Oklahoma City, OK, p. A338

RICE, Tim, President, Lakewood Health System, Staples, MN, p. A228

RICHARD, Robert J., Administrator, People's Memorial Hospital of Buchanan County, Independence, IA, p. A150

RICHARD, Tracey, Administrator, Dubuis Hospital for Continuing Care, Lake Charles, LA, p. A181

RICHARDS, Joan K.
President, Crozer–Chester Medical Center, Upland, PA, p. A365
President, Delaware County Memorial Hospital, Drexel Hill, PA, p. A351

RICHARDS, Randy R., Chief Executive Officer, Permian General Hospital, Andrews, TX, p. A392

RICHARDS, Richard M., Administrator, HEALTHSOUTH Rehabilitation Hospital of Utah, Sandy, UT, p. A430

RICHARDSON, A. D., Administrator, Hood Memorial Hospital, Amite, LA, p. A177

RICHARDSON, Darrel C., Chief Operating Officer, Kanakanak Hospital, Dillingham, AK, p. A20

RICHARDSON, F. David, Ph.D., Administrator, Sistersville General Hospital, Sistersville, WV, p. A454

RICHARDSON, J. E., Chief Executive Officer, Savoy Medical Center, Mamou, LA, p. A182

RICHARDSON, Mark D., President and Chief Executive Officer, Burlington Medical Center, Burlington, IA, p. A146

RICHARDSON, Pat, Interim Administrator, Garfield County Memorial Hospital, Pomeroy, WA, p. A446

RICHARDSON, Patricia L.
Chief Executive Officer, Eagle River Memorial Hospital, Eagle River, WI, p. A457
President and Chief Executive Officer, Howard Young Medical Center, Woodruff, WI, p. A465

RICHARDSON, R. D., President and Chief Executive Officer, Ashtabula County Medical Center, Ashtabula, OH, p. A317

RICHARDSON, William T., President and Chief Executive Officer, Tift General Hospital, Tifton, GA, p. A110

RICHER, R. David, Administrator, Healthsouth Rehabilitation Hospital of Western Massachusetts, Ludlow, MA, p. A201

RICHEY, Don L., Administrator, Guadalupe Valley Hospital, Seguin, TX, p. A421

RICHLE, Teresa, Interim Senior Vice President Acute Care Operations, Mercy Medical Center, Springfield, OH, p. A329

RICHMOND, John W., President and Chief Executive Officer, Gentry County Memorial Hospital, Albany, MO, p. A239

RICHTER, Thomas, Chief Executive Officer, Madison Hospital, Madison, MN, p. A225

RICKARD, Roland K., Administrator, Mitchell County Hospital, Colorado City, TX, p. A398

RIDDELL, Andrew J., President, Atlanticare Medical Center, Lynn, MA, p. A201

RIDDLE, Brian L., President and Chief Executive Officer, Oconee Regional Medical Center, Milledgeville, GA, p. A107

RIDDLE, Marilyn M., Chief Executive Officer, Olympus Specialty Hospital–Springfield, Springfield, MA, p. A204

RIEDMANN, Gary P., President and Chief Executive Officer, St. Anthony Regional Hospital, Carroll, IA, p. A146

RIEGE, Michael J., Chief Executive Officer, Virginia Gay Hospital, Vinton, IA, p. A154

RIEMER–MATUZAK, Stephanie J., Chief Executive Officer, Mercy Health Services North–Grayling, Grayling, MI, p. A211

RIES, Douglas A., President, Cardinal Glennon Children's Hospital, Saint Louis, MO, p. A247

RIES, William G., President, Lake Forest Hospital, Lake Forest, IL, p. A128

RIFFEL, Alan, Acting Administrator, Anadarko Municipal Hospital, Anadarko, OK, p. A333

RIGDON, Henry, Executive Vice President, Northeast Georgia Medical Center, Gainesville, GA, p. A105

RIGSBY, John P., Administrator, Garrard County Memorial Hospital, Lancaster, KY, p. A170

RILEY, Edward E., Chief Executive Officer, Community Memorial Healthcare, Marysville, KS, p. A161

RIMES, Dwight, Administrator, Ocean Springs Hospital, Ocean Springs, MS, p. A236

RINE, Thomas L., President and Chief Executive Officer, Southwestern Medical Center, Lawton, OK, p. A336

RINEHARDT, Mark, Administrator, Lake City Medical Center, Lake City, MN, p. A224

RINKER, Franklin M., President and Chief Executive Officer, Promina Gwinnett Hospital System, Lawrenceville, GA, p. A106

RIORDAN, William J., President and Chief Executive Officer, St. Vincent's Medical Center, Bridgeport, CT, p. A74

RIPPLE, Gary, Commander, Reynolds Army Community Hospital, Fort Sill, OK, p. A335

RISER, Donna, Administrator, Lackey Memorial Hospital, Forest, MS, p. A233

RISK, Richard R., President and Chief Executive Officer, Advocate Health Care, Oak Brook, IL, p. B60

RISON, R. H., Warden, U. S. Medical Center for Federal Prisoners, Springfield, MO, p. A249

RISSING, Daniel J.
Acting Chief Executive Officer, Christus Schumpert Medical Center, Shreveport, LA, p. A185
Acting Chief Executive Officer, Christus St. Frances Cabrini Hospital, Alexandria, LA, p. A177

RITER, Pamela M., R.N., Administrator, Vencor Hospital–St Petersburg, Saint Petersburg, FL, p. A95

RITZ, Robert P., Chief Executive Officer, Monongalia General Hospital, Morgantown, WV, p. A453

RIVERA, Santiago, Executive Administrator, Hospital Oncologico Andres Grillasca, Ponce, PR, p. A471

RIVERS, Kenneth I., Chief Executive Officer, St. Luke Medical Center, Pasadena, CA, p. A55

RIZZO, Nancy L., Senior Vice President, Operations, Geisinger Medical Center, Danville, PA, p. A350

ROACH, Joseph, Chief Executive Officer, Memorial Hospital of Martinsville and Henry County, Martinsville, VA, p. A437

ROADMAN II, Charles H., Surgeon General, Department of the Air Force, Bowling AFB, DC, p. B88

ROARK, Ruth Ann, Administrator, Sequoyah Memorial Hospital, Sallisaw, OK, p. A339

ROBBINS, Alan H., M.D., President, New England Baptist Hospital, Boston, MA, p. A198

ROBBINS, B. C., Superintendent, Georgia Mental Health Institute, Atlanta, GA, p. A100

ROBBINS, Jonathan H., M.D., President and Chief Executive Officer, Health Alliance Hospitals, Leominster, MA, p. A201

ROBBINS, Wes, Chief Executive Officer, Charter by–the–Sea Behavioral Health System, Saint Simons Island, GA, p. A109

ROBERSON, Madeleine L.
Chief Executive Officer, Medical Center of Southwest Louisiana, Lafayette, LA, p. A181
Chief Executive Officer, Women's and Children's Hospital, Lafayette, LA, p. A181

ROBERTS, Carolyn C., President, Copley Hospital, Morrisville, VT, p. A431

ROBERTS, Deborah, Administrator, Lawrence County Hospital, Monticello, MS, p. A236

ROBERTS, Jean E., Administrator, Mark Reed Hospital, McCleary, WA, p. A445

ROBERTS, John W., President and Chief Executive Officer, Union Regional Medical Center, Monroe, NC, p. A308

ROBERTS, Jonathan, Dr.PH, Chief Executive Officer, Earl K. Long Medical Center, Baton Rouge, LA, p. A177

ROBERTS, Kenneth D., President, John T. Mather Memorial Hospital, Port Jefferson, NY, p. A296

ROBERTS, Pamela W., Administrator, Baptist Memorial Hospital–Booneville, Booneville, MS, p. A231

ROBERTS, Robert D., Interim President and Chief Executive Officer, Pacific Coast Hospital, San Francisco, CA, p. A60

ROBERTS, Shane, Administrator, St. Luke Community Hospital, Ronan, MT, p. A254

ROBERTS, Shirley R., Administrator, Washington County Regional Hospital, Sandersville, GA, p. A109

ROBERTS Jr., George T., Chief Executive Officer, Henderson Memorial Hospital, Henderson, TX, p. A406

ROBERTSON, B. W., Administrator, Parkview Hospital, Wheeler, TX, p. A425

ROBERTSON, David, Chief Executive Officer, Duncan Regional Hospital, Duncan, OK, p. A335

ROBERTSON, Jeffrey J., Chief Executive Officer, Lakeview Hospital, Stillwater, MN, p. A229

ROBERTSON, John L., Chief Executive Officer, Wiregrass Medical Center, Geneva, AL, p. A15

ROBERTSON, Thomas L., President and Chief Executive Officer, Carilion Health System, Roanoke, VA, p. B70

ROBERTSON, William G., Senior Executive Officer, Shawnee Mission Medical Center, Shawnee Mission, KS, p. A164

ROBERTSON Jr., James E., President, Public Hospital of the Town of Salem, Salem, IL, p. A133

ROBERTSTAD, John R.
President and Chief Executive Officer, Bixby Medical Center, Lenawee Health Alliance, Adrian, MI, p. A206
President and Chief Executive Officer, Herrick Memorial Hospital, Lenawee Health Alliance, Tecumseh, MI, p. A218
President and Chief Executive Officer, Lenawee Health Alliance, Adrian, MI, p. B108

ROBINSON, Brian C., Chief Executive Officer, North Florida Regional Medical Center, Gainesville, FL, p. A85

ROBINSON, Edward P., Administrator, Community Hospital, Munster, IN, p. A143

ROBINSON, Glenn A., Chief Executive Officer, Nacogdoches Medical Center, Nacogdoches, TX, p. A416

ROBINSON, Michael, Executive Vice President and Administrator, Memorial Regional Medical Center, Mechanicsville, VA, p. A437

ROBINSON, Phillip D., Chief Executive Officer, J. F. K. Medical Center, Atlantis, FL, p. A81

ROBINSON, Raymond, Chief Operating Officer, Worcester State Hospital, Worcester, MA, p. A205

ROBINSON, Richard F., Director, Veterans Affairs Medical Center, Fayetteville, AR, p. A30

ROBINSON, Virginia B., Administrator, Jefferson County Hospital, Fayette, MS, p. A233

ROBINSON, W. D., Chief Executive Officer, Bartlett Memorial Medical Center, Sapulpa, OK, p. A339

ROBY, William J., Executive Vice President, Mountain Manor Treatment Center, Emmitsburg, MD, p. A194

ROCKWOOD Jr., John M., President, Munson Healthcare, Traverse City, MI, p. B118

RODGERS, Edward, Chief Executive Officer, Yoakum County Hospital, Denver City, TX, p. A402

RODGERS, Robert, Administrator and Senior Executive Officer, St. James Community Hospital, Butte, MT, p. A251

RODRIGUEZ, Joseph, Chief Executive Officer, Concord Hospital, Baton Rouge, LA, p. A177

RODRIGUEZ, Julio Andino, Executive Director, Ponce Regional Hospital, Ponce, PR, p. A471

RODRIGUEZ, Maria Del Pilar, Administrator, Dr. Ramon E. Betances Hospital–Mayaguez Medical Center Branch, Mayaguez, PR, p. A471

RODRIGUEZ, Maria Elena, Executive Administrator, Dr. Jose Ramos Lebron Hospital, Fajardo, PR, p. A470

RODRIGUEZ, Roberto, Executive Director, LAC/University of Southern California Medical Center, Los Angeles, CA, p. A49

RODRIGUEZ, Roy, M.D., Chief Executive Officer, Bayview Hospital and Mental Health System, Chula Vista, CA, p. A39

ROE Jr., Louis G., Administrator, Williamson ARH Hospital, South Williamson, KY, p. A175

ROEBACK, Jason, Chief Executive Officer, HEALTHSOUTH Rehabilitation Institute of Tucson, Tucson, AZ, p. A27

ROEDER, John R., President and Chief Executive Officer, Providence Hospital, Mobile, AL, p. A16

ROETS, George A., Director, Elmira Psychiatric Center, Elmira, NY, p. A285

ROGERS, Charles L., President, Cushing Memorial Hospital, Leavenworth, KS, p. A160

ROGERS, Christopher J., Administrator, Auburn Memorial Hospital, Auburn, NY, p. A281

ROGERS, Richard, Senior Vice President, Mercy Memorial Hospital, Urbana, OH, p. A330

ROGERS, Tracy A., Chief Executive Officer, Lakeland Medical Center, New Orleans, LA, p. A183

ROGERSON, Russell E., Warden, Iowa Medical and Classification Center, Oakdale, IA, p. A152

ROGOLS, Kevin L., President and Chief Executive Officer, Finley Hospital, Dubuque, IA, p. A149

ROHALEY, Richard L., President and Chief Executive Officer, Jackson General Hospital, Ripley, WV, p. A454

ROHALL, Roger, Chief Executive Officer, Rivendell of Michigan, Saint Johns, MI, p. A216

ROHLEDER, Howard E., Administrator and Chief Executive Officer, Salem Community Hospital, Salem, OH, p. A329

ROHRICH, George A., Administrator, Pembina County Memorial Hospital and Wedgewood Manor, Cavalier, ND, p. A313

ROJEK, Kenneth J., Chief Executive, Lutheran General Hospital, Park Ridge, IL, p. A131

ROMER, James E., President and Chief Executive Officer, Hospital Center at Orange, Orange, NJ, p. A273

ROMERO, Dudley, President and Chief Executive Officer, Our Lady of Lourdes Regional Medical Center, Lafayette, LA, p. A181

ROMERO, Marcella A., Administrator, Espanola Hospital, Espanola, NM, p. A278

ROMERO, Vicki L., Chief Executive Officer, Longview Regional Medical Center, Longview, TX, p. A413

ROMOFF, Jeffrey A., President, UPMC Health System, Pittsburgh, PA, p. B152

RONA, J. Michael, President, Virginia Mason Medical Center, Seattle, WA, p. A448

RONSTROM, Stephen F., Executive Vice President and Administrator, Sacred Heart Hospital, Eau Claire, WI, p. A457

ROODMAN, Richard D., Chief Executive Officer, Valley Medical Center, Renton, WA, p. A446

ROONEY, Ronald K., President, Arkansas Methodist Hospital, Paragould, AR, p. A34

ROOS, Mary, President and Chief Executive Officer, St. Joseph Community Hospital, Mishawaka, IN, p. A142

ROOT, Darwin E., Administrator, Harrison Memorial Hospital, Cynthiana, KY, p. A168

ROPCHAN, Rebecca, Administrator, Scripps Memorial Hospital–Encinitas, Encinitas, CA, p. A41

RORAFF, Greg, President and Chief Executive Officer, Memorial Hospital of Taylor County, Medford, WI, p. A460

ROSASCO Jr., Edward J., President and Chief Executive Officer, Mercy Hospital, Miami, FL, p. A89

ROSE, J. Anthony, President and Chief Executive Officer, Catawba Memorial Hospital, Hickory, NC, p. A307

ROSE, Lance H., FACHE, President and Chief Executive Officer, Centre Community Hospital, State College, PA, p. A364

ROSE, Renee, President and Chief Executive Officer, Horizon Healthcare, Inc., Milwaukee, WI, p. B104

ROSEBOROUGH, James W., CHE, Director, Veterans Affairs Medical Center, Ann Arbor, MI, p. A206

ROSEN, David P., President, Jamaica Hospital Medical Center, New York, NY, p. A290

ROSENBERG, Leroy J., Executive Director, West Jersey Hospital–Marlton, Marlton, NJ, p. A271

ROSENTHAL, David S., M.D., Director, Stillman Infirmary, Harvard University Health Services, Cambridge, MA, p. A199

ROSENVALL, Greg, Administrator, Gunnison Valley Hospital, Gunnison, UT, p. A427

ROSIN, David, M.D., Medical Director, Nevada Mental Health Institute, Sparks, NV, p. A264

ROSS, David, Chief Executive Officer, Phelps County Regional Medical Center, Rolla, MO, p. A246

ROSS, Hank, Chief Executive Officer, HEALTHSOUTH Rehabilitation Hospital, Oklahoma City, OK, p. A338

ROSS, James E., FACHE
    Chief Executive Officer, Deaton Specialty Hospital and Home, Baltimore, MD, p. A191
    Chief Executive Officer, James Lawrence Kernan Hospital, Baltimore, MD, p. A191

ROSS, Joseph P.
    President and Chief Executive Officer, Dorchester General Hospital, Cambridge, MD, p. A193
    President and Chief Executive Officer, Memorial Hospital at Easton Maryland, Easton, MD, p. A194

ROSS, Kenneth R., Chief Executive Officer, Arbuckle Memorial Hospital, Sulphur, OK, p. A340

ROSS, Zeff, Administrator, Memorial Hospital West, Pembroke Pines, FL, p. A92

ROSS Jr., Semmes, Administrator, Franklin County Memorial Hospital, Meadville, MS, p. A235

ROSSETTI, Stephen J., Ph.D., President and Chief Executive Officer, Saint Luke Institute, Silver Spring, MD, p. A196

ROSSFELD, John, Administrator, University of Miami Hospital and Clinics, Miami, FL, p. A90

ROSSI, L. J., M.D., Chief Executive Officer, Hopedale Medical Complex, Hopedale, IL, p. A127

ROSSIO, Gary J., Director and Chief Executive Officer, Veterans Affairs Medical Center, San Diego, CA, p. A59

ROTH, William, Chief Executive Officer, HEALTHSOUTH Chesapeake Rehabilitation Hospital, Salisbury, MD, p. A196

ROTHSTEIN, Ronald, Chief Executive Officer, Levindale Hebrew Geriatric Center and Hospital, Baltimore, MD, p. A192

ROTHSTEIN, Ruth M., Chief, Cook County Bureau of Health Services, Chicago, IL, p. B86

ROURKE, Thomas E., Administrator, Glen Oaks Hospital, Greenville, TX, p. A406

ROUSH, Sharon L., Chief Executive Officer, Columbia Hospital, West Palm Beach, FL, p. A97

ROWE, Gary L., President and Chief Executive Officer, St. John's Regional Medical Center, Joplin, MO, p. A242

ROWE, John W., M.D., President, Mount Sinai–NYU Hospitals/Health System, New York, NY, p. A292

ROWLAND, Phil, Chief Executive Officer, Grandview Medical Center, Jasper, TN, p. A384

ROWLEY, K. Steven, CHE, President and Chief Executive Officer, Wilson N. Jones Regional Health System, Sherman, TX, p. A422

ROWTON, William, Chief Executive Officer, Cozby–Germany Hospital, Grand Saline, TX, p. A405

ROYAL, Ramon, President, Brighton Hospital, Brighton, MI, p. A207

ROYAL, Stephen L., President and Chief Executive Officer, Southwest Florida Regional Medical Center, Fort Myers, FL, p. A84

ROYNAN, Joseph, Administrator, Northwestern Institute, Fort Washington, PA, p. A352

ROZEK, Thomas M., President and Chief Executive Officer, Miami Children's Hospital, Miami, FL, p. A90

RUBENSTEIN, David A., Chief Operating Officer, Dwight David Eisenhower Army Medical Center, Fort Gordon, GA, p. A105

RUBERTE, Henry, Executive Director, Hospital Metropolitan, San Juan, PR, p. A471

RUBIN, Harold, President and Chief Executive Officer, Memorial Hospital and Medical Center, Midland, TX, p. A415

RUCKDESCHEL, John C., M.D., Director and Chief Executive Officer, H. Lee Moffitt Cancer Center and Research Institute, Tampa, FL, p. A96

RUDEGEAIR, Bernard C., President and Chief Executive Officer, Hazleton–St. Joseph Medical Center, Hazleton, PA, p. A353

RUDES, Bryan F.
    Executive Director, Richard H. Hutchings Psychiatric Center, Syracuse, NY, p. A299
    Executive Director, Rochester Psychiatric Center, Rochester, NY, p. A297

RUDES, Sarah F., Executive Director, Mohawk Valley Psychiatric Center, Utica, NY, p. A299

RUDNICK Jr., John D., FACHE, Executive Director, Pathways of Tennessee, Jackson, TN, p. A384

RUELAS, Raul D., M.D., Administrator, Gulf Coast Treatment Center, Fort Walton Beach, FL, p. A85

RUFFIN, Edward W., Administrator, Coliseum Psychiatric Hospital, Macon, GA, p. A107

RUFFOLO, Joseph A., President and Chief Executive Officer, Children's Hospital, Buffalo, NY, p. A283

RUGLE, Kenneth, Interim Director, Central Alabama Veteran Affairs Health Care System, Montgomery, AL, p. A17

RUMLEY, Darrell, Service Unit Director and Chief Executive Officer, U. S. Public Health Service Indian Hospital, Sells, AZ, p. A26

RUMPF, Christopher B., M.D., Interim President, St. Joseph Medical Center, Reading, PA, p. A363

RUMPZ, Mary Renetta, FACHE, President and Chief Executive Officer, St. Mary Hospital, Livonia, MI, p. A213

RUNDIO, Robert A.
    Executive Director of Hospital Operations, Mesa Lutheran Hospital, Mesa, AZ, p. A24
    Executive Director of Hospital Operations, Valley Lutheran Hospital, Mesa, AZ, p. A24

RUPIPER, Allen V., President, Adena Health System, Chillicothe, OH, p. A319

RUPP, Stephen C., Chief Operating Officer, Greater Southeast Community Hospital, Washington, DC, p. A79

RUPP, William, M.D., President and Chief Executive Officer, Luther Hospital, Eau Claire, WI, p. A457

RUPPERT, James C., Administrator, Mercy Hospital, Corning, IA, p. A147

RUSE, William E., FACHE, President and Chief Executive Officer, Blanchard Valley Health Association System, Findlay, OH, p. A323

RUSH, Domenica, Administrator, Sierra Vista Hospital, Truth or Consequences, NM, p. A280

RUSH, Donald J., Chief Executive Officer, Sidney Health Center, Sidney, MT, p. A254

RUSHING, R. Lynn, Chief Executive Officer, Brook Lane Psychiatric Center, Hagerstown, MD, p. A194

RUSKAN, Jeff, Administrator, HEALTHSOUTH Rehabilitation Hospital of Virginia, Richmond, VA, p. A439

RUSSEL, Kimberly A., President and Chief Executive Officer, Mary Greeley Medical Center, Ames, IA, p. A146

RUSSELL, Bill, Chief Operating Officer and Administrator, Fair Oaks Hospital, Delray Beach, FL, p. A83

RUSSELL, Daniel F., President and Chief Executive Officer, Catholic Health East, Newtown Square, PA, p. B72

RUSSELL, Gordon H., Administrator, Hi–Plains Hospital, Hale Center, TX, p. A406

RUSSELL, James D. M., Chief Executive Officer, St. Mary's Healthcare Center, Pierre, SD, p. A378

RUSSELL, Linda B., President, The Woman's Hospital of Texas, Houston, TX, p. A410

RUSSELL, Mark R., President and Chief Executive Officer, Hospital Group of America, Wayne, PA, p. B104

RUSSELL, Tim, Administrator, Stillwater Community Hospital, Columbus, MT, p. A252

RUSSELL, Webster T., Chief Executive Officer, South Central Kansas Regional Medical Center, Arkansas City, KS, p. A156

RUSSOTTO, John, Facility Director, Northern Virginia Mental Health Institute, Falls Church, VA, p. A434

RUTENBERG, Jack, Administrator, Villa Maria Hospital, North Miami, FL, p. A91

RUTHERFORD, James A., President and Chief Executive Officer, St. Clare's Hospital and Health Center, New York, NY, p. A293

RUTKOWSKI, Robert, Chief Executive, South Suburban Hospital, Hazel Crest, IL, p. A126

RUTLEDGE, Valinda, President, St. Anthony Hospital, Oklahoma City, OK, p. A338

RUTTER, David E., Administrator, Mahaska County Hospital, Oskaloosa, IA, p. A153

RUYLE, W. Kenneth, Director, Veterans Affairs Medical Center, Tuscaloosa, AL, p. A19

RUZYCKI, Frank C., Executive Director, Roosevelt Warm Springs Institute for Rehabilitation, Warm Springs, GA, p. A111

RYAN, Michael G., President and Chief Executive Officer, St. Francis Specialty Hospital, Monroe, LA, p. A183

RYAN, Michael J., Administrator, Nemaha Valley Community Hospital, Seneca, KS, p. A164

RYAN, Thomas E., President, Alamance Regional Medical Center, Burlington, NC, p. A303

RYAN, Mary Jean, President and Chief Executive Officer, SSM Health Care, Saint Louis, MO, p. B141

RYBA, Thomas L., Chief Executive Officer, Charter Savannah Behavioral Health System, Savannah, GA, p. A109

RYDER, Harry, President and Chief Executive Officer, Union Memorial Hospital, Baltimore, MD, p. A192

RYLE, Deborah L., Chief Executive Officer, Round Rock Hospital, Round Rock, TX, p. A419

S

SABA, Francis M., President and Chief Executive Officer, Milford–Whitinsville Regional Hospital, Milford, MA, p. A202

SABIN, Margaret D., Chief Executive Officer, Routt Memorial Hospital, Steamboat Springs, CO, p. A73

SABIN, Robert H.
    Acting Director, Aleda E. Lutz Veterans Affairs Medical Center, Saginaw, MI, p. A216
    Acting Director, Richard L. Roudebush Veterans Affairs Medical Center, Indianapolis, IN, p. A140

SABO, Michael A., Director, Veterans Affairs Hudson Valley Health Care System–F.D. Roosevelt Hospital, Montrose, NY, p. A288

SABOL, Don J., Chief Executive Officer, Hardin Memorial Hospital, Kenton, OH, p. A325

SACCO, Frank V., FACHE, Chief Executive Officer, Memorial Healthcare System, Los Angeles, FL, p. B115

SACK, Michael V., President and Chief Executive Officer, Union Hospital, Elkton, MD, p. A194

SACKETT, John, Administrator, Avista Adventist Hospital, Louisville, CO, p. A72

SACKETT, Walter, Chief Executive Officer, Sunhealth Specialty Hospital for Denver, Thornton, CO, p. A73

SADAU, Ernie W., President and Chief Executive Officer, Hinsdale Hospital, Hinsdale, IL, p. A127

SADLACK, Frank J., Ph.D., Executive Director, La Hacienda Treatment Center, Hunt, TX, p. A410

SADLER, Blair L., President, Children's Hospital and Health Center, San Diego, CA, p. A59

SADVARY, Thomas J., FACHE, Senior Vice President and Chief Operating Officer, Scottsdale Healthcare–Shea, Scottsdale, AZ, p. A26

SAFIAN, Keith F., President and Chief Executive Officer, Phelps Memorial Hospital Center, Sleepy Hollow, NY, p. A298

SAGO, Glenn R., Administrator, Arkansas State Hospital, Little Rock, AR, p. A32

SAILSBURY, Gene, Administrator and Chief Executive Officer, Crawford County Hospital District One, Girard, KS, p. A158

SAIRLS, Ronnie, Administrator, St. Vincent Rehabilitation Hospital, Sherwood, AR, p. A34

SAJDAK, Dennis J., Chief Executive Officer, Focus Healthcare of Ohio, Maumee, OH, p. A326

SAKS, Stephen H., Chief Executive Officer, John F. Kennedy Memorial Hospital, Philadelphia, PA, p. A359

SALA Jr., Anthony S., Chief Executive Officer, Highland Hospital, Shreveport, LA, p. A185

SALANGER, Matthew J., President and Chief Executive Officer, United Health Services Hospitals–Binghamton, Binghamton, NY, p. A282

SALBER, M. Agnes, Prioress, Missionary Benedictine Sisters American Province, Norfolk, NE, p. B117

SALEAPAGA, Iotamo T., M.D., Director Health, Lyndon B. Johnson Tropical Medical Center, Pago Pago, AS, p. A469

SALISBURY, Roger, Administrator, Hodgeman County Health Center, Jetmore, KS, p. A160

SALMON, Robert J.
  Administrator, Deuel County Memorial Hospital, Clear Lake, SD, p. A376
  Chief Executive Officer, Sioux Valley Canby Campus, Canby, MN, p. A221

SAMET, Kenneth A., President, Washington Hospital Center, Washington, DC, p. A80

SAMPSON, Arthur J., President and Chief Executive Officer, Newport Hospital, Newport, RI, p. A368

SAMPSON, Gladiola, Executive Director, Queens Hospital Center, New York, NY, p. A293

SANCHEZ, Jose R.
  Executive Director, Lincoln Medical and Mental Health Center, New York, NY, p. A291
  Executive Director, Metropolitan Hospital Center, New York, NY, p. A291

SANCHEZ, Roberto, Administrator, Lower Florida Keys Health System, Key West, FL, p. A87

SANDER, Larry J., FACHE, Director, Veterans Affairs Medical Center–Louisville, Louisville, KY, p. A173

SANDERS, John W., Chief Executive Officer, Twin Rivers Regional Medical Center, Kennett, MO, p. A244

SANDERS, Larry, FACHE, Chairman and Chief Executive Officer, Columbus Regional Health System, Columbus, GA, p. B84

SANDERS, Steve, Vice President and Chief Executive Officer, Memorial Hospital–The Woodlands, The Woodlands, TX, p. A423

SANDERS, Jimmy, Chief of Staff, William Beaumont Army Medical Center, El Paso, TX, p. A403

SANDIFER, C. Philip, Chief Executive Officer, Island Health Northwest, Anacortes, WA, p. A443

SANDLIN, Keith, Chief Executive Officer, Columbia Cartersville Medical Center, Cartersville, GA, p. A102

SANDOVAL, Donald D., FACHE, Chief Executive Officer, Greenbrier Valley Medical Center, Ronceverte, WV, p. A454

SANGER, William A., President and Chief Executive Officer, Cancer Treatment Centers of America, Arlington Heights, IL, p. B70

SANNER, Charlotte K., M.D., Director Health Service, Simpson Infirmary, Wellesley College, Wellesley, MA, p. A205

SANTIAGO–VEGA, Francisco, Consultor, Lafayette Hospital, Arroyo, PR, p. A469

SANZO, Anthony M., President and Chief Executive Officer, Allegheny University Hospitals–West, Pittsburgh, PA, p. B60

SANZONE, Raymond D., Executive Director, Tewksbury Hospital, Tewksbury, MA, p. A204

SARDONE, Frank J.
  President and Chief Executive Officer, Bronson Healthcare Group, Inc., Kalamazoo, MI, p. B69
  President and Chief Executive Officer, Bronson Methodist Hospital, Kalamazoo, MI, p. A212
  President, Bronson Vicksburg Hospital, Vicksburg, MI, p. A218

SARKAR, George A., JD, Executive Director, Manhattan Eye, Ear and Throat Hospital, New York, NY, p. A291

SARKIS, Lucy, M.D., Executive Director, South Beach Psychiatric Center, New York, NY, p. A293

SARLE, C. Richard, President and Chief Executive Officer, Carrier Foundation, Belle Mead, NJ, p. A268

SASSER, L. Wayne, Vice President and Administrator, Crenshaw Baptist Hospital, Luverne, AL, p. A16

SATALA, Taylor, Service Unit Director, U. S. Public Health Services Indian Hospital, Keams Canyon, AZ, p. A23

SATCHER, Richard H., Chief Executive Officer, Aiken Regional Medical Centers, Aiken, SC, p. A370

SATO, James, Senior Vice President and Chief Executive Officer, Western Arizona Regional Medical Center, Bullhead City, AZ, p. A22

SATZGER, Bruce G.
  Administrator, Commmunity Hospital of San Bernardino, San Bernardino, CA, p. A58
  Administrator, St. Bernardine Medical Center, San Bernardino, CA, p. A58

SAULS, Randy, Administrator, Louis Smith Memorial Hospital, Lakeland, GA, p. A106

SAULTERS, W. Dale, Administrator, Winston Medical Center, Louisville, MS, p. A235

SAUNDERS, Donald F., President, Androscoggin Valley Hospital, Berlin, NH, p. A265

SAVAGE, Robert L., President and Chief Executive Officer, Charleston Area Medical Center, Charleston, WV, p. A450

SCHADT, Alton M., Executive Director, Warren General Hospital, Warren, PA, p. A365

SCHAENGOLD, Phillip S., JD, Chief Executive Officer, George Washington University Hospital, Washington, DC, p. A79

SCHAETZLE, Daniel J., Administrator, Community Hospital–Lakeview, Eufaula, OK, p. A335

SCHAFER, Michael, Chief Executive Officer, Spooner Health System, Spooner, WI, p. A464

SCHAFFER, Arnold R., President and Chief Executive Officer, Glendale Memorial Hospital and Health Center, Glendale, CA, p. A43

SCHAFFER, Gregory F., Senior Vice President Operations, Johns Hopkins Bayview Medical Center, Baltimore, MD, p. A191

SCHAFFNER, Leroy, Chief Executive Officer, Coon Memorial Hospital and Home, Dalhart, TX, p. A399

SCHAFFNER, Linda D., R.N., Vice President and Administrator, Bethesda Oak Hospital, Cincinnati, OH, p. A319

SCHALLER, Marty, Interim Chief Executive Officer, Copper Queen Community Hospital, Bisbee, AZ, p. A22

SCHANDLER, Jon B., President and Chief Executive Officer, White Plains Hospital Center, White Plains, NY, p. A301

SCHANWALD, Pamela R., Chief Executive Officer, Children's Home of Pittsburgh, Pittsburgh, PA, p. A361

SCHAPER, Robert F., President and Chief Executive Officer, Tomball Regional Hospital, Tomball, TX, p. A424

SCHAPPER, Robert A., Chief Executive Officer, Hollywood Community Hospital of Hollywood, Los Angeles, CA, p. A48

SCHATZLEIN, Michael H., M.D., President and Chief Executive Officer, St. Joseph Hospital, Fort Wayne, IN, p. A138

SCHAUM, James H., President and Chief Executive Officer, Allen Memorial Hospital, Oberlin, OH, p. A327

SCHAUMBURG, John, Administrator, Lanai Community Hospital, Lanai City, HI, p. A113

SCHEFFER, Richard H., President, Wing Memorial Hospital and Medical Centers, Palmer, MA, p. A203

SCHERLIN, Marlys, Chief Executive Officer, Greater Community Hospital, Creston, IA, p. A148

SCHERR, Morris L., Executive Vice President, Taylor Manor Hospital, Ellicott City, MD, p. A194

SCHERTZ, David A.
  Administrator, Saint Anthony Medical Center, Rockford, IL, p. A133
  Administrator, Saint Joseph Hospital, Belvidere, IL, p. A119

SCHIMSCHEINER, Mary Joel, Chief Executive Officer, Kenmore Mercy Hospital, Kenmore, NY, p. A287

SCHINTZ, Conrad W., Senior Vice–President Operations, Penn State Geisinger Wyoming Valley Medical Center, Wilkes–Barre, PA, p. A366

SCHIROS, Judy, Administrator, Campbellton Graceville Hospital, Graceville, FL, p. A85

SCHLAUTMAN, Jacolyn M., Executive Vice President and Administrator, St. Joseph's Hospital, Breese, IL, p. A119

SCHLEGELMILCH, Kurt W., M.D., Director, Veterans Affairs Medical Center, Grand Junction, CO, p. A71

SCHLEUSS, Cheryl M., Chief Executive Officer, Greenbrier Behavioral Health System, Covington, LA, p. A179

SCHMELTER, Robert, President, Community Hospital of Ottawa, Ottawa, IL, p. A131

SCHMIDT, Craig W. C., President and Chief Executive Officer, Berlin Memorial Hospital, Berlin, WI, p. A456

SCHMIDT, Gene E., President, Hutchinson Hospital Corporation, Hutchinson, KS, p. A159

SCHMIDT, Mark, Administrator, Gettysburg Medical Center, Gettysburg, SD, p. A377

SCHMIDT, Marvy, Administrator, Schick Shadel Hospital, Seattle, WA, p. A447

SCHMIDT, Michael A., President and Chief Executive Officer, Saint Joseph's Hospital, Marshfield, WI, p. A460

SCHMIDT, Paul R., CHE, President and Chief Executive Officer, St. Joseph Health System, Tawas City, MI, p. A217

SCHMIDT, Richard T., Executive Director, Decatur Hospital, Decatur, GA, p. A103

SCHMIDT, Steve, Chief Executive Officer, Redding Medical Center, Redding, CA, p. A57

SCHMIDT, Timothy E., Chief Executive Officer, Mimbres Memorial Hospital, Deming, NM, p. A278

SCHMIDT Jr., Richard O.
  President and Chief Executive Officer, Kenosha Hospital and Medical Center, Kenosha, WI, p. A459
  President and Chief Executive Officer, St. Catherine's Hospital, Kenosha, WI, p. A459

SCHNEDLER, Lisa, Administrator, Van Buren County Hospital, Keosauqua, IA, p. A151

SCHNEIDER, Barry S., Chief Executive Officer, Watsonville Community Hospital, Watsonville, CA, p. A66

SCHNEIDER, C. W., President and Chief Executive Officer, Northwest Hospital, Seattle, WA, p. A447

SCHNEIDER, Carol, Chief Executive Officer, Christ Hospital and Medical Center, Oak Lawn, IL, p. A130

SCHNEIDER, Charles F., President, Day Kimball Hospital, Putnam, CT, p. A76

SCHNEIDER, David R., Executive Director, Langlade Memorial Hospital, Antigo, WI, p. A456

SCHNEIDER, Mark E., Chief Executive Officer, Rivendell Behavioral Health Services, Benton, AR, p. A29

SCHNEIDER, Thomas R., Administrator, Shriners Hospitals for Children, Shreveport, LA, p. A185

SCHOAPS, Stephen R., Chief Executive Officer, Seminole Medical Center, Seminole, OK, p. A339

SCHOEN, William J., Chairman and Chief Executive Officer, Health Management Associates, Naples, FL, p. B99

SCHOENHOLTZ, Jack C., M.D., Medical Director, Administrator and President, Rye Hospital Center, Rye, NY, p. A297

SCHOLTEN, Randall J., Chief Executive Officer, Curry General Hospital, Gold Beach, OR, p. A343

SCHON, John, Administrator and Chief Executive Officer, Dickinson County Healthcare System, Iron Mountain, MI, p. A212

SCHOTT, Carol, Administrator, Odessa Memorial Hospital, Odessa, WA, p. A445

SCHOTTLAND, Edward M., Senior Vice President and Chief Operating Officer, Miriam Hospital, Providence, RI, p. A368

SCHRADER, Michael E., President and Chief Executive Officer, Wyoming Medical Center, Casper, WY, p. A466

SCHRAMM, Michael, Administrator, Arlington Municipal Hospital, Arlington, MN, p. A220

SCHRECK, Edward, Chief Executive Officer, USC University Hospital, Los Angeles, CA, p. A51

SCHREEG, Timothy M., President and Chief Executive Officer, Jasper County Hospital, Rensselaer, IN, p. A143

SCHREIVOGEL, Herman, Administrator and Chief Executive Officer, Lincoln Community Hospital and Nursing Home, Hugo, CO, p. A71

SCHROEDER, Fred F., Administrator, Memorial Hospital of Converse County, Douglas, WY, p. A466

SCHROFFEL, Bruce, Chief Operating Officer, University of California San Francisco Medical Center, San Francisco, CA, p. A60

SCHROTH, Lynn, Chief Executive Officer, Memorial Hospital Southwest, Houston, TX, p. A408

SCHRUPP, Richard, President and Chief Executive Officer, Mercy Hospital of Franciscan Sisters, Oelwein, IA, p. A152

SCHUBERT, John D., Administrator and Chief Executive Officer, Pinckneyville Community Hospital, Pinckneyville, IL, p. A132

SCHUESSLER, James P., President and Chief Executive Officer, All Saints Episcopal Hospital of Fort Worth, Fort Worth, TX, p. A403

SCHUETZ, Charles D., Chief Executive Officer, Kingwood Medical Center, Kingwood, TX, p. A412

SCHULER, G. Wayne, Executive Director, Madison County Medical Center, Canton, MS, p. A232

SCHULER, William J., Chief Executive Officer, Portsmouth Regional Hospital and Pavilion, Portsmouth, NH, p. A267

SCHULLER, David E., M.D., Chief Executive Officer, Arthur G. James Cancer Hospital and Richard J. Solove Research Institute, Columbus, OH, p. A321

SCHULTE, James E., Administrator, Redwood Falls Municipal Hospital, Redwood Falls, MN, p. A227

SCHULTZ, Delores E., R.N., Administrator, St. Mary's Hospital of Superior, Superior, WI, p. A464

SCHULTZ, Michael, Chief Executive Officer, Feather River Hospital, Paradise, CA, p. A55

SCHULTZ, Steve C., Administrator, Eye Foundation Hospital, Birmingham, AL, p. A12

SCHULZ, Charles K., Chief Executive Officer, York General Hospital, York, NE, p. A262

SCHULZ, Larry A., President and Chief Executive Officer, St. Gabriel's Hospital, Little Falls, MN, p. A224

SCHURMEIER, L. Jon, President and Chief Executive Officer, Southwest General Health Center, Middleburg Heights, OH, p. A327

SCHUSTER, Emmett, Administrator and Chief Executive Officer, Greenwood County Hospital, Eureka, KS, p. A158

SCHWANKE, Dan, Executive Director, St. Francis Health Care Centre, Green Springs, OH, p. A324

SCHWARM, Tony, President, Clay County Hospital, Flora, IL, p. A125

SCHWARTZ, John N., Chief Executive Officer, Trinity Hospital, Chicago, IL, p. A123

SCHWARTZ, Mark, Administrator, Hartford Memorial Hospital, Hartford, WI, p. A458

SCHWARTZ, Michael J., President and Chief Executive Officer, Alexian Brothers Medical Center, Elk Grove Village,, IL, p. A124

SCHWARTZBERG, Gil, President and Chief Executive Officer, City of Hope National Medical Center, Duarte, CA, p. A41

SCHWARZ, Donald E., Administrator, Vencor Hospital–Boston, Boston, MA, p. A198

SCHWEITZER, Alex, Superintendent and Chief Executive Officer, North Dakota State Hospital, Jamestown, ND, p. A315

SCHWEITZER, Robert, Ed.D., Executive Director, Sagamore Children's Psychiatric Center, Huntington Station, NY, p. A286

SCHWEMER, David J., Administrator, Woodrow Wilson Rehabilitation Center, Fishersville, VA, p. A435

SCHWIENTEK, Barbara, Executive Director, Monticello Big Lake Hospital, Monticello, MN, p. A226

SCIOLA, Anthony, President, Shaughnessy–Kaplan Rehabilitation Hospital, Salem, MA, p. A203

SCOGGIN Jr., James C.
Chief Executive Officer, San Antonio Community Hospital, San Antonio, TX, p. A420
Chief Executive Officer, Southwest Texas Methodist Hospital, San Antonio, TX, p. A421

SCOTT, Camille, Administrator, Benewah Community Hospital, Saint Maries, ID, p. A116

SCOTT, Charles F.
President and Chief Executive Officer, Memorial Hospital of Tampa, Tampa, FL, p. A96
President and Chief Executive Officer, Town and Country Hospital, Tampa, FL, p. A96

SCOTT, Grady, President and Chief Executive Officer, Copper Basin Medical Center, Copperhill, TN, p. A382

SCOTT, Jerry B., Chief Executive Officer, Northeastern Regional Hospital, Las Vegas, NM, p. A279

SCOTT, John R., Director, St. Lawrence Psychiatric Center, Ogdensburg, NY, p. A295

SCOTT, Mark D., President, Mid–Columbia Medical Center, The Dalles, OR, p. A346

SCOTT, Richard E., President, Hillcrest Baptist Medical Center, Waco, TX, p. A425

SCOTT, Steve, Chief Executive Officer, Pinelands Hospital, Nacogdoches, TX, p. A416

SCOTT, Thomas L., FACHE, President and Chief Executive Officer, Burdette Tomlin Memorial Hospital, Cape May Court House, NJ, p. A269

SCOVILL, Terry
Administrator, Cypress Creek Hospital, Houston, TX, p. A407
Chief Executive Officer, West Oaks Hospital, Houston, TX, p. A410

SCRUGGS, Carol, R.N., Interim Administrator, University Hospital and Clinics–Durant, Durant, MS, p. A232

SCURR, David J., Superintendent, Mental Health Institute, Mount Pleasant, IA, p. A152

SEABERG, Lynn, Administrator and Chief Executive Officer, Indian Valley Hospital District, Greenville, CA, p. A44

SEAGRAVE, Richard E., Executive Director and Chief Operating Officer, Phoenixville Hospital of the University of Pennsylvania Health System, Phoenixville, PA, p. A360

SEAL, Ronald, President and Chief Executive Officer, Marion Memorial Hospital, Marion, IL, p. A128

SEALE, Corey A., Chief Executive Officer, Fallbrook Hospital District, Fallbrook, CA, p. A42

SEAVER, Roger E., President and Chief Executive Officer, Northridge Hospital Medical Center–Roscoe Boulevard Campus, Los Angeles, CA, p. A50

SECKINGER, Mark R., Administrator, Doctors Hospital of Nelsonville, Nelsonville, OH, p. A327

SEEL, W. Joseph, Administrator, Edgefield County Hospital, Edgefield, SC, p. A372

SEELY, E. T., Administrator, Ferrell Hospital, Eldorado, IL, p. A124

SEGLER, Randall K., Chief Executive Officer, Comanche County Memorial Hospital, Lawton, OK, p. A336

SEIBEL, Jacqueline, Administrator, Jacobson Memorial Hospital Care Center, Elgin, ND, p. A314

SEIDEL, Ken, Executive Director, Claremore Regional Hospital, Claremore, OK, p. A334

SEIDLER, Richard A., FACHE, Chief Executive Officer, Allen Memorial Hospital, Waterloo, IA, p. A154

SEIFERT, David P., President, St. Anthony's Medical Center, Saint Louis, MO, p. A248

SEIGFREID Jr., Jerome, Chief Executive Officer, Phelps Memorial Health Center, Holdrege, NE, p. A258

SEILER, Edward H., Director, Veterans Affairs Medical Center, West Palm Beach, FL, p. A97

SEILER, Steven L., Senior Vice President and Chief Executive Officer, Good Samaritan Regional Medical Center, Phoenix, AZ, p. A24

SEIM, Richard L., Senior Vice President, Christ Hospital, Cincinnati, OH, p. A319

SEITZ, Stewart R., Chief Executive Officer, Gladys Spellman Specialty Hospital and Nursing Center, Cheverly, MD, p. A193

SELBERG, Jeffrey D.
President and Chief Executive Officer, Exempla Healthcare, Inc., Denver, CO, p. B95
President and Chief Executive Officer, Exempla Lutheran Medical Center, Wheat Ridge, CO, p. A73
President and Chief Executive Officer, Exempla Saint Joseph Hospital, Denver, CO, p. A69

SELDEN, Thomas A., President and Chief Executive Officer, Parma Community General Hospital, Parma, OH, p. A328

SELL, John, USAF, Administrator, U. S. Air Force Hospital, Cannon AFB, NM, p. A278

SELLARDS, Michael G., Executive Director, Pleasant Valley Hospital, Point Pleasant, WV, p. A453

SELTZER, Charlotte, Chief Executive Officer, Creedmoor Psychiatric Center, New York, NY, p. A290

SELZ, Timothy P., President and Chief Executive Officer, Provena Saint Therese Medical Center, Waukegan, IL, p. A135

SENNEFF, Robert G., Chief Executive Officer, DeWitt Community Hospital, De Witt, IA, p. A148

SERAPHINE, Jeffrey G., President and Chief Executive Officer, Georgetown Community Hospital, Georgetown, KY, p. A169

SERCY, Dalmer P., Director, William S. Hall Psychiatric Institute, Columbia, SC, p. A372

SERNULKA, John M., President and Chief Executive Officer, Carroll County General Hospital, Westminster, MD, p. A196

SERRILL, G. B., President and Chief Executive Officer, Ellis Hospital, Schenectady, NY, p. A298

SEWELL, John, Interim Chief Executive Officer, Mercy Health Services–North, Cadillac, MI, p. A207

SEXTON, Charles F., Chief Executive Officer, Valley Regional Medical Center, Brownsville, TX, p. A396

SEXTON, J. Dennis, President, All Children's Hospital, Saint Petersburg, FL, p. A94

SEXTON, James J., President and Chief Executive Officer, North Iowa Mercy Health Center, Mason City, IA, p. A152

SEXTON, Kevin J., President and Chief Executive Officer, Holy Cross Hospital of Silver Spring, Silver Spring, MD, p. A196

SEXTON, William P., Administrator, Franciscan Skemp Healthcare–Sparta Campus, Sparta, WI, p. A463

SEYMOUR, James A., Regional Administrator, Alegent Health Community Memorial Hospital, Missouri Valley, IA, p. A152

SGANGA, Fred S., President and Chief Executive Officer, Bergen Regional Medical Center, Paramus, NJ, p. A273

SHAFER, Ronald J., President and Chief Executive Officer, Eastern New Mexico Medical Center, Roswell, NM, p. A280

SHAFFER, David D., Chief Executive Officer, Stonewall Jackson Memorial Hospital, Weston, WV, p. A454

SHAFFETT, Donald A., Chief Executive Officer, Clear Lake Regional Medical Center, Webster, TX, p. A425

SHANKER, Deo, CPA, Chief Executive Officer, Forest Springs Hospital, Houston, TX, p. A408

SHAPIRO, Edward R., M.D., Medical Director and Chief Executive Officer, Austen Riggs Center, Stockbridge, MA, p. A204

SHAPIRO, Marcia S., Chief Executive Officer, Chicago Lakeshore Hospital, Chicago, IL, p. A120

SHARFSTEIN, Steven S., M.D., President, Medical Director and Chief Executive Officer, Sheppard and Enoch Pratt Hospital, Baltimore, MD, p. A192

SHARMA, Timothy, M.D., President, Cambridge International, Inc,, Houston, TX, p. B69

SHARP, Joseph, Chief Executive Officer, Capital Medical Center, Olympia, WA, p. A446

SHARP, Joseph W., Administrator, Runnells Specialized Hospital of Union County, Berkeley Heights, NJ, p. A268

SHARPE, Diane W., Chief Executive Officer, Charter Behavioral Health System–Palm Springs, Cathedral City, CA, p. A39

SHARPNACK, Linton, Chief Executive Officer, PHS Mt. Sinai Medical Center East, Richmond Heights, OH, p. A328

SHAUGHNESSY, kathy, Chief Operating Officer, Pikeville United Methodist Hospital of Kentucky, Pikeville, KY, p. A174

SHAW, David B.
Administrator and Chief Executive Officer, Pecos County General Hospital, Iraan, TX, p. A410
Administrator and Chief Executive Officer, Pecos County Memorial Hospital, Fort Stockton, TX, p. A403

SHAW, Doug, Administrator, Mad River Community Hospital, Arcata, CA, p. A36

SHAW, Douglas E., President, Jewish Hospital, Louisville, KY, p. A172

SHAW, J. Michael, Administrator, Rusk County Memorial Hospital and Nursing Home, Ladysmith, WI, p. A459

SHAW, Robert C., President and Chief Executive Officer, Los Robles Regional Medical Center, Thousand Oaks, CA, p. A64

SHEAHEN, Mary R., President and Chief Executive Officer, Provena Mercy Center, Aurora, IL, p. A118

SHEAR, Bruce A., President and Chief Executive Officer, Pioneer Behavioral Health, Peabody, MA, p. B125

SHEEDY, Lucille K., Administrator and Chief Executive Officer, Wyoming County Community Hospital, Warsaw, NY, p. A300

SHEEHAN, Daniel F., Administrator, Research Belton Hospital, Belton, MO, p. A239

SHEEHAN, Michael J., Administrator, Hastings Regional Center, Hastings, NE, p. A258

SHEEHAN, John R., MSC, Deputy Commander, Ehrling Bergquist Hospital, Offutt AFB, NE, p. A260

SHEEHY, Earl N., Administrator, Mid Dakota Hospital, Chamberlain, SD, p. A376

SHEETZ, Douglas A., Chief Executive Officer, Keokuk County Health Center, Sigourney, IA, p. A154

SHELBY, Dennis R., Chief Executive Officer, HEALTHSOUTH Rehabilitation Hospital, Fayetteville, AR, p. A30

SHELBY, Marla, Administrator and Chief Executive Officer, South Lincoln Medical Center, Kemmerer, WY, p. A467

SHELDON, Lyle Ernest
President and Chief Executive Officer, Fallston General Hospital, Fallston, MD, p. A194
President and Chief Executive Officer, Harford Memorial Hospital, Havre De Grace, MD, p. A195
President and Chief Executive Officer, Upper Chesapeake Health System, Fallston, MD, p. B153

SHELL, Robert G., Chief Executive Officer, Santa Teresita Hospital, Duarte, CA, p. A41

SHELLY, Vicki, R.N., Interim Administrator, Cascade Medical Center, Cascade, ID, p. A114

SHELTON, Frank, President, Union Hospital, Terre Haute, IN, p. A145

SHELTON, James, Chairman and Chief Executive Officer, Triad Hospitals, Inc., Dallas, TX, p. B147

SHELTON, John, President, Montclair Baptist Medical Center, Birmingham, AL, p. A12

SHELTON II, W. Allen, Administrator and Chief Executive Officer, Eye and Ear Clinic of Charleston, Charleston, WV, p. A450

SHEPARD, R. Coert, President, Anderson Hospital, Maryville, IL, p. A129

SHEPHARD, Bruce, Administrator, Clinch Memorial Hospital, Homerville, GA, p. A106

SHEPHERD, Richard W., President and Chief Executive Officer, Children's Seashore House, Philadelphia, PA, p. A358

SHERMAN, James F., President and Chief Executive Officer, West Hills Hospital and Medical Center, Los Angeles, CA, p. A51

SHERON, William E., Chief Executive Officer, Wooster Community Hospital, Wooster, OH, p. A331

SHERROD, Rhonda, Administrator, Shands at Live Oak, Live Oak, FL, p. A88

SHERVINGTON, Walter W., M.D., Chief Executive Officer, New Orleans Adolescent Hospital, New Orleans, LA, p. A183

SHIELDS, Karen, Chief Operating Officer, Kino Community Hospital, Tucson, AZ, p. A27

SHIELS, Rob, Administrator, Mary Shiels Hospital, Dallas, TX, p. A400

SHIMONO, Jiro R., Director, Delaware Psychiatric Center, New Castle, DE, p. A78

SHIN, Peter, DPM, President and Chief Executive Officer, MedLink Hospital and Nursing Center, Washington, DC, p. A79

SHIRK, Michael, President and Senior Executive Officer, Boone Hospital Center, Columbia, MO, p. A240

SHIRTCLIFF, Christine, Executive Vice President, Mary Lane Hospital, Ware, MA, p. A204

SHOCKNEY, Brian T., President and Chief Executive Officer, Memorial Hospital, Logansport, IN, p. A142

SHOEMAKER, Larry D., M.D., Executive Vice President and Chief Operating Officer, Chandler Regional Hospital, Chandler, AZ, p. A22

SHOOK, Scott E., President, Riverside Mercy Hospital, Toledo, OH, p. A329

SHORE, Muriel M., R.N., Chief Executive Officer, Essex County Hospital Center, Cedar Grove, NJ, p. A269

SHOVELIN, Wayne F., President and Chief Executive Officer, Gaston Memorial Hospital, Gastonia, NC, p. A306

SHRODER, Robert W.
Executive Vice President Operations, St. Elizabeth Health Center, Youngstown, OH, p. A331
Vice President Operations, St. Joseph Health Center, Warren, OH, p. A330

SHUGARMAN, Mark, President, Mercy Hospital, Tiffin, OH, p. A329

SHULER, Priscilla J., Chief Executive Officer, Capitol Medical Center, Richmond, VA, p. A439

SHUMAKER, Revonda L., R.N., President and Chief Executive Officer, Lakewood Hospital, Lakewood, OH, p. A325

SHYAVITZ, Linda, President and Chief Executive Officer, Sturdy Memorial Hospital, Attleboro, MA, p. A197

SICURELLA, John, Chief Executive Officer, Reynolds Memorial Hospital, Glen Dale, WV, p. A451

SIEBER, Thomas L., President and Chief Executive Officer, Genesis HealthCare System, Zanesville, OH, p. A332

SIEGEL, Bruce, M.P.H., President and Chief Executive Officer, Tampa General Healthcare, Tampa, FL, p. A96

SIEGWALD–MAYS, Cheryl, Administrator, Doral Palms Hospital, Miami, FL, p. A89

SIEMEN–MESSING, Pauline, R.N., President and Chief Executive Officer, Harbor Beach Community Hospital, Harbor Beach, MI, p. A211

SIEMERS, Thomas R., Chief Executive Officer, Rebsamen Medical Center, Jacksonville, AR, p. A31

SIEPMAN, Milton R., Ph.D.
President and Chief Executive Officer, Baton Rouge General Medical Center, Baton Rouge, LA, p. A177
President and Chief Executive Officer, General Health System, Baton Rouge, LA, p. B97

SILBERNAGEL, Gilbert, Chief Executive Officer, Sutter Lakeside Hospital, Lakeport, CA, p. A46

SILEBI, Margaret, Director Operations, Kaiser Foundation Hospital–Bellflower, Bellflower, CA, p. A37

SILLEN, Robert, Executive Director, Santa Clara Valley Health and Hospital System, San Jose, CA, p. A61

SILLS, Doug, President and Chief Executive Officer, Central Florida Regional Hospital, Sanford, FL, p. A95

SILVA, Luis G., Chief Executive Officer and Regional Administrator, Beaumont Medical and Surgical Hospital, Beaumont, TX, p. A395

SILVA, William G., Executive Director, Metropolitan State Hospital, Norwalk, CA, p. A54

SILVER, Jack B., M.P.H., Chief Executive Officer, Arizona State Hospital, Phoenix, AZ, p. A24

SILVER, Richard A., Director, James A. Haley Veterans Hospital, Tampa, FL, p. A96

SILVERNALE, Vern, Administrator, Johnson Memorial Health Services, Dawson, MN, p. A222

SILVIA, Clarence J., President and Chief Executive Officer, Bradley Memorial Hospital and Health Center, Southington, CT, p. A76

SIMCHUK, Cathy J., Interim Chief Executive Officer, Holy Family Hospital, Spokane, WA, p. A448

SIMMONS, Nancy, Administrator, St. John's Episcopal Hospital–South Shore, New York, NY, p. A293

SIMMONS, Randy, Administrator, Davis County Hospital, Bloomfield, IA, p. A146

SIMMONS, Stephen H.
Senior Administrator, University of South Alabama Hospitals, Mobile, AL, p. B152
Administrator, University of South Alabama Medical Center, Mobile, AL, p. A16

SIMMONS, W. Clay, Executive Vice President, Bradford Health Services at Birmingham, Birmingham, AL, p. A11

SIMMONS, Wallace R., Chief Executive Officer, Crawford Memorial Hospital, Robinson, IL, p. A132

SIMMONS, William, President and Chief Executive Officer, San Jacinto Methodist Hospital, Baytown, TX, p. A395

SIMMS, John L., President and Chief Executive Officer, Trinity Community Medical Center of Brenham, Brenham, TX, p. A396

SIMON, Elliot J., FACHE, Chief Operating Officer, Western Queens Community Hospital, New York, NY, p. A294

SIMON, Mary Alvera, Administrator, Mercy Hospital of Scott County, Waldron, AR, p. A35

SIMONIN, Steve J., Chief Executive Officer, Community Memorial Hospital, Clarion, IA, p. A147

SIMPATICO, Thomas, M.D., Facility Director and Network System Manager, Chicago–Read Mental Health Center, Chicago, IL, p. A120

SIMPSON, Mack N., Administrator, McCone County Medical Assistance Facility, Circle, MT, p. A251

SIMPSON, Tim, Administrator, Vencor–North Florida, Green Cove Springs, FL, p. A85

SIMS, Craig E.
President and Chief Executive Officer, RHD Memorial Medical Center, Dallas, TX, p. A401
President, Trinity Medical Center, Carrollton, TX, p. A397

SIMS, Norman L., USAF, Commander, U. S. Air Force Hospital Little Rock, Jacksonville, AR, p. A31

SIMS Jr., John H., Director, Veterans Affairs Medical Center, Togus, ME, p. A190

SIMSARIAN, John H., Superintendent, Cedarcrest Hospital, Newington, CT, p. A76

SINCLAIR, Mike, Administrator, Kane County Hospital, Kanab, UT, p. A427

SINGLE, John L.
Chief Executive Officer and Administrator, De Smet Memorial Hospital, De Smet, SD, p. A376
Chief Executive Officer, Huron Regional Medical Center, Huron, SD, p. A377

SINGLETON, Barry W., FACHE, Chief Executive Officer, Pondera Medical Center, Conrad, MT, p. A252

SINGLETON, J. Knox, President and Chief Executive Officer, Inova Health System, Falls Church, VA, p. B105

SINGLETON, Thomas, President and Chief Executive Officer, New American Healthcare Corporation, Brentwood, TN, p. B119

SINNER, James, Chief Executive Officer, Medina Memorial Hospital, Medina, NY, p. A288

SINNOTT, Daniel J., President and Chief Executive Officer, St. Francis Hospital, Wilmington, DE, p. A78

SIPES, Don, Senior Executive Officer, Saint Luke's Northland Hospital–Smithville Campus, Smithville, MO, p. A249

SIPKOSKI, Michael, Executive Vice President and Administrator, St. Francis Hospital, Litchfield, IL, p. A128

SIRK, David R., President and Chief Executive Officer, Berwick Hospital Center, Berwick, PA, p. A348

SISSON, William G., President, Central Baptist Hospital, Lexington, KY, p. A171

SISTI, Judith L., MS, Administrator, Vineland Developmental Center Hospital, Vineland, NJ, p. A275

SISTO, Dennis, President and Chief Executive Officer, Queen of the Valley Hospital, Napa, CA, p. A53

SKAGGS, Jo Ann, Service Unit Director, U. S. Public Health Service Indian Hospital, Mescalero, NM, p. A279

SKALSKY, Susan, M.D., Director, Hurtado Health Center, New Brunswick, NJ, p. A272

SKELLEY, Dennis B., President and Chief Executive Officer, Walton Rehabilitation Hospital, Augusta, GA, p. A101

SKINNER, David B., M.D.
Vice Chairman and Chief Executive Officer, New York & Presbyterian Healthcare, New York, NY, p. B119
Vice Chairman and Chief Executive Officer, New York Presbyterian Hospital, New York, NY, p. A292
SKINNER, Davis D., President, Missouri Baptist Hospital of Sullivan, Sullivan, MO, p. A249
SKINNER, Eileen, Interim Director, Ochsner Foundation Hospital, New Orleans, LA, p. A183
SKOGSBERGH, James H.
President, Iowa Lutheran Hospital, Des Moines, IA, p. A148
President, Iowa Methodist Medical Center, Des Moines, IA, p. A148
SKOMOROCH, Orianna A., Chief Executive Officer, Kauai Veterans Memorial Hospital, Waimea, HI, p. A113
SKUBA, Herbert S., President, Ellwood City Hospital, Ellwood City, PA, p. A351
SKUBIC, Mark, Vice President, Methodist Hospital HealthSystem Minnesota, Saint Louis Park, MN, p. A227
SKVAREK, Joann A., Executive Vice President, Edgewater Medical Center, Chicago, IL, p. A120
SLABACH, Brock A., Administrator, Field Memorial Community Hospital, Centreville, MS, p. A232
SLAGTER, Dean G., Administrator, Renville County Hospital, Olivia, MN, p. A226
SLAUBAUGH, D. Ray, President, Graham Hospital, Canton, IL, p. A119
SLAVIN, Peter L., M.D., President, Barnes–Jewish Hospital, Saint Louis, MO, p. A247
SLIETER Jr., Richard G., Administrator, Weiner Memorial Medical Center, Marshall, MN, p. A225
SLOAN, Gary
Chief Executive Officer, Doctors Medical Center–Pinole Campus, Pinole, CA, p. A56
Chief Executive Officer, Doctors Medical Center–San Pablo Campus, San Pablo, CA, p. A61
SLOAN, Joseph F., CHE, Chief Executive Officer, Plains Memorial Hospital, Dimmitt, TX, p. A402
SLOAN, Robert L., Chief Executive Officer, Sibley Memorial Hospital, Washington, DC, p. A80
SLUNECKA, Fredrick, President and Chief Executive Officer, Avera McKennan Hospital, Sioux Falls, SD, p. A379
SLUSKY, Richard, Administrator, Mt. Ascutney Hospital and Health Center, Windsor, VT, p. A432
SLYTER, Mark, Administrator, Hillcrest Hospital, Simpsonville, SC, p. A375
SMALL, Sandra
Administrator, Kaiser Foundation Hospital, Walnut Creek, CA, p. A66
Senior Vice President and Area Manager, Kaiser Foundation Hospital and Rehabilitation Center, Vallejo, CA, p. A66
SMALLEY, Diana, Chief Operating Officer, Alegent–Health Midlands Community Hospital, Papillion, NE, p. A261
SMART, Dalton L., Administrator, Jennings Community Hospital, North Vernon, IN, p. A143
SMART, Michael, Chief Executive Officer, Alameda County Medical Center–Highland Campus, Oakland, CA, p. A54
SMART, Michael G., Administrator, Alameda County Medical Center, San Leandro, CA, p. A61
SMART, Rob, Chief Executive Officer, Bourbon Community Hospital, Paris, KY, p. A174
SMART, Robert M., Area Manager and Chief Executive Officer, HEALTHSOUTH Medical Center, Dallas, TX, p. A400
SMEDLEY, Craig M., Administrator, Valley View Medical Center, Cedar City, UT, p. A427
SMILEY, Jon D., Chief Executive Officer, Sunnyside Community Hospital, Sunnyside, WA, p. A448
SMILEY, W. David, Chief Executive Officer, San Joaquin Valley Rehabilitation Hospital, Fresno, CA, p. A43
SMITH, Alex B., Ph.D., Executive Director, Terrebonne General Medical Center, Houma, LA, p. A180
SMITH, Bernadette
Chief Operating Officer, Seton Medical Center, Daly City, CA, p. A40
Chief Operating Officer, Seton Medical Center Coastside, Moss Beach, CA, p. A53

SMITH, C. W., President and Chief Executive Officer, Parkview Medical Center, Pueblo, CO, p. A72
SMITH, Charles, Administrator, Columbus Community Hospital, Columbus, WI, p. A457
SMITH, Charles M., M.D.
President and Chief Executive Officer, Christiana Care Corporation, Wilmington, DE, p. B77
President and Chief Executive Officer, Christiana Care, Newark, DE, p. A78
SMITH, Connie, Chief Executive Officer, The Medical Center at Bowling Green, Bowling Green, KY, p. A167
SMITH, Dennis H.
Director, VA Maryland Health Care System–Fort Howard Division, Fort Howard, MD, p. A194
Director, Veterans Affairs Maryland Health Care System–Baltimore Division, Baltimore, MD, p. A192
Director, Veterans Affairs Maryland Health Care System–Perry Point Division, Perry Point, MD, p. A195
SMITH, F. Curtis, President, Massachusetts Eye and Ear Infirmary, Boston, MA, p. A198
SMITH, Frances T., Administrator, Childress Regional Medical Center, Childress, TX, p. A397
SMITH, Gordon, Administrator, Merrill Pioneer Community Hospital, Rock Rapids, IA, p. A153
SMITH, Gregory M., Chief Executive Officer, Allentown State Hospital, Allentown, PA, p. A347
SMITH, H. Gerald, President and Chief Executive Officer, St. Francis Medical Center, Monroe, LA, p. A182
SMITH, Harlan J., President and Chief Executive Officer, Franklin Medical Center, Greenfield, MA, p. A201
SMITH, James E., Superintendent, Wichita Falls State Hospital, Wichita Falls, TX, p. A426
SMITH, Jeffrey H., Ph.D., Superintendent, Logansport State Hospital, Logansport, IN, p. A142
SMITH, Jerry, Chief Executive Officer, BHC Pinon Hills Hospital, Santa Fe, NM, p. A280
SMITH, Jim B., President and Chief Executive Officer, Goodall–Witcher Healthcare, Clifton, TX, p. A397
SMITH, Joe E., Administrator and Chief Executive Officer, DeWitt City Hospital, De Witt, AR, p. A30
SMITH, Johnny J., Chief Executive Officer, High Pointe, Oklahoma City, OK, p. A338
SMITH, Johnson L., Chief Executive Officer and Administrator, St. Anthony's Healthcare Center, Morrilton, AR, p. A33
SMITH, Jon, Administrator, Pershing General Hospital, Lovelock, NV, p. A264
SMITH, Joseph S., Chief Executive Officer, Boone County Hospital, Boone, IA, p. A146
SMITH, Lex, Administrator, Park View Hospital, El Reno, OK, p. A335
SMITH, Lloyd V., President and Chief Executive Officer, Benefis Health Care, Great Falls, MT, p. A252
SMITH, Louis H., Executive Vice President and Administrator, Cornwall Hospital, Cornwall, NY, p. A284
SMITH, Marty, Chief Executive Officer, Cleveland Community Hospital, Cleveland, TN, p. A382
SMITH, Meredith H., Administrator, Dodge County Hospital, Eastman, GA, p. A104
SMITH, Michael N., Director Healthcare Services, San Joaquin General Hospital, French Camp, CA, p. A42
SMITH, Randall W., Chief Operating Officer, Alegent Health Immanuel Medical Center, Omaha, NE, p. A260
SMITH, Randy, Chief Executive Officer, Chilton Medical Center, Clanton, AL, p. A13
SMITH, Raymond N., Chief Executive Officer, Community Hospital of Gardena, Gardena, CA, p. A43
SMITH, Richard, Administrator, Logan Regional Hospital, Logan, UT, p. A428
SMITH, Richard G., Chief Executive Officer, Oneida Healthcare Center, Oneida, NY, p. A295
SMITH, Robbie, Administrator, Higgins General Hospital, Bremen, GA, p. A101
SMITH, Robert B., President and Chief Executive Officer, Zale Lipshy University Hospital, Dallas, TX, p. A401
SMITH, Robert L., President and Chief Executive Officer, Decatur General Hospital, Decatur, AL, p. A13
SMITH, Rodney R., Chief Executive Officer, Putnam Community Medical Center, Palatka, FL, p. A92
SMITH, S. Allan, Administrator, Tri–City Community Hospital, Jourdanton, TX, p. A411

SMITH, Steve, Chief Executive Officer, Carson Tahoe Hospital, Carson City, NV, p. A263
SMITH, Steven J., President, St. Joseph Medical Center, Albuquerque, NM, p. A277
SMITH, Steven L., President and Chief Executive Officer, Memorial Medical Center, Las Cruces, NM, p. A279
SMITH, Stuart, Vice President Clinical Operations and Executive Director, MUSC Medical Center of Medical University of South Carolina, Charleston, SC, p. A371
SMITH, Terry J., Administrator, Bibb Medical Center, Centreville, AL, p. A13
SMITH, Thomas W., President and Chief Executive Officer, Ephraim McDowell Regional Medical Center, Danville, KY, p. A168
SMITH, Tim, President and Chief Executive Officer, Fountain Valley Regional Hospital and Medical Center, Fountain Valley, CA, p. A42
SMITH, Todd A., Chief Executive Officer, Charter Behavioral Health System of Southern California–Charter Oak, Covina, CA, p. A40
SMITH, Tommy J., President and Chief Executive Officer, Baptist Healthcare System, Louisville, KY, p. B64
SMITH, W. David, Director, Veterans Affairs Medical Center, Canandaigua, NY, p. A283
SMITH, Wayne T., President and Chief Executive Officer, Community Health Systems, Inc., Brentwood, TN, p. B84
SMITH, William R., Administrator, Hamilton Hospital, Olney, TX, p. A416
SMITH, Jimmie M., USAF, Commander, U. S. Air Force Hospital–Kirtland, Kirtland AFB, NM, p. A279
SMITH II, W. Don, President and Chief Executive Officer, Cabell Huntington Hospital, Huntington, WV, p. A451
SMITH Jr., P. Paul, Executive Director, Lake Norman Regional Medical Center, Mooresville, NC, p. A308
SMITH Jr., P. W., Administrator and Chief Executive Officer, Joel Pomerene Memorial Hospital, Millersburg, OH, p. A327
SMITH–BLACKWELL, Olivia, M.P.H., President and Chief Executive Officer, Sheehan Memorial Hospital, Buffalo, NY, p. A283
SMITHBURG, Donald R., Administrator, Truman Medical Center–East, Kansas City, MO, p. A243
SMITHERS, Joe, Administrator, Horizon Specialty Hospital, Edmond, OK, p. A335
SMITHMIER, Kenneth L., President and Chief Executive Officer, Decatur Memorial Hospital, Decatur, IL, p. A123
SMOCK, Dennis, Chief Executive Officer, Baptist DeKalb Hospital, Smithville, TN, p. A390
SMOLIK, Chris, Chief Executive Officer, Edinburg Regional Medical Center, Edinburg, TX, p. A402
SMOOT, Steven, Chief Executive Officer, Mineral Community Hospital, Superior, MT, p. A254
SNEAD, Benjamin E., President and Chief Executive Officer, St. Clair Memorial Hospital, Pittsburgh, PA, p. A361
SNEDIGAR, Rudy, Chief Executive Officer, Clarinda Regional Health Center, Clarinda, IA, p. A147
SNIPES, Lucas A., FACHE, Director, Carilion Medical Center, Roanoke, VA, p. A440
SNOW, Mel L., Administrator, West Holt Memorial Hospital, Atkinson, NE, p. A256
SNOWDEN, Raymond W., President and Chief Executive Officer, Memorial Hospital and Health Care Center, Jasper, IN, p. A140
SNYDER, David M., Chief Executive Officer, Thibodaux Regional Medical Center, Thibodaux, LA, p. A186
SOBOTA, Richard E., President and Chief Executive Officer, Pike Community Hospital, Waverly, OH, p. A331
SODERBLOM, Alan, Administrator, Loma Linda University Behavioral Medicine Center, Redlands, CA, p. A57
SODOMKA, Patricia, FACHE, Executive Director, Medical College of Georgia Hospital and Clinics, Augusta, GA, p. A101
SOILEAU, Joseph L., Chief Executive Officer, South Cameron Memorial Hospital, Cameron, LA, p. A178
SOKOL, Dennis A., President and Chief Executive Officer, Firelands Community Hospital, Sandusky, OH, p. A329

SOKOLOW, Norman J., Chairman and Chief Executive Officer, Cornerstone of Medical Arts Center Hospital, New York, NY, p. A290

SOLARE, Frank A., President and Chief Executive Officer, Thorek Hospital and Medical Center, Chicago, IL, p. A122

SOLHEIM, John H., Chief Executive Officer, St. Mary's Regional Health Center, Detroit Lakes, MN, p. A222

SOLNIT, Albert J., M.D., Commissioner, Connecticut Department of Mental Health and Addiction Services, Hartford, CT, p. B85

SOLVIBILE, Edward R., President, Suburban General Hospital, Norristown, PA, p. A357

SOMMER, Richard C., Interim Chief Executive Officer, Selby General Hospital, Marietta, OH, p. A326

SOMMERS, Thomas W., President and Chief Executive Officer, Central Kansas Medical Center, Great Bend, KS, p. A158

SONDECKER, James, Director, St. Joseph's Behavioral Health Center, Stockton, CA, p. A64

SONENREICH, Steven, Chief Executive Officer, Cedars Medical Center, Miami, FL, p. A89

SOPO, Deborah A., Administrator, Vencor Hospital–Metro Detroit, Detroit, MI, p. A209

SOUKUP, Richard G., Chief Executive Officer, Northern Hills General Hospital, Deadwood, SD, p. A376

SOULE, Frederick L., President and Chief Executive Officer, Caldwell Memorial Hospital, Lenoir, NC, p. A308

SOYUGENC, Marjorie Z., President and Chief Executive Officer, Welborn Memorial Baptist Hospital, Evansville, IN, p. A138

SPAETH, Ronald G., President and Chief Executive Officer, Highland Park Hospital, Highland Park, IL, p. A126

SPANG, A. James, Administrator, Shriners Hospitals for Children–Chicago, Chicago, IL, p. A122

SPARKMAN, Dena C., Administrator, McDowell ARH Hospital, McDowell, KY, p. A173

SPARKMAN, Ronald L., Administrator, Jackson County Hospital, Scottsboro, AL, p. A18

SPARKS, Julian, Board Chairman, Marshall County Health Care Authority, Guntersville, AL, p. B113

SPARKS, Richard G., President, Watauga Medical Center, Boone, NC, p. A303

SPARROW, William T., Chief Executive Officer, BHC San Luis Rey Hospital, Encinitas, CA, p. A41

SPARTZ, Gregory G., Chief Executive Officer, Willmar Regional Treatment Center, Willmar, MN, p. A230

SPARTZ, Jeff, Administrator, Hennepin County Medical Center, Minneapolis, MN, p. A225

SPAUDE, Paul A., President and Chief Executive Officer, Wausau Hospital, Wausau, WI, p. A465

SPAULDING, Don, Administrator and Chief Executive Officer, Fort Duncan Medical Center, Eagle Pass, TX, p. A402

SPAUSTER, Edward, Ph.D., Executive Director, Arms Acres, Carmel, NY, p. A284

SPEAK, Patricia B., Administrator, Vencor Hospital–Pittsburgh, Oakdale, PA, p. A357

SPECK, William T., President and Chief Operating Officer, New York Presbyterian Hospital, New York, NY, p. A292

SPEED, Marilyn, Administrator, Beacham Memorial Hospital, Magnolia, MS, p. A235

SPELLMAN, Warren K., Administrator, Holy Cross Hospital, Taos, NM, p. A280

SPENCER, Corte J., Chief Executive Officer, Oswego Hospital, Oswego, NY, p. A295

SPENCER, Herman J., Administrator, Northern Inyo Hospital, Bishop, CA, p. A38

SPICER, John R., President and Chief Executive Officer, Sound Shore Medical Center of Westchester, New Rochelle, NY, p. A288

SPIKE, Colleen A., Administrator, Community Hospital and Health Care Center, Saint Peter, MN, p. A228

SPILOVOY, Richard, Administrator, Garrison Memorial Hospital, Garrison, ND, p. A314

SPINELLI, Robert J., Administrator and Chief Executive Officer, Bloomsburg Hospital, Bloomsburg, PA, p. A348

SPIVEY, David, President and Chief Executive Officer, Mercy Hospital, Detroit, MI, p. A209

SPIVEY, Sue, Administrator, Irwin County Hospital, Ocilla, GA, p. A108

SPOELMAN, Roger, President and Chief Executive Officer, Mercy General Health Partners, Muskegon, MI, p. A214

SPRENGER, Gordon M., President, Allina Health System, Minneapolis, MN, p. B61

SPRENGER, Jay D., USAF, Commander, U. S. Air Force Academy Hospital, USAF Academy, CO, p. A73

SPRINGER, Kay H., Administrator, Steele Memorial Hospital, Salmon, ID, p. A116

SPROUSE, James P., Associate Administrator for Psychiatric Services, Behavioral Health Care of Cape Fear Valley Health System, Fayetteville, NC, p. A305

SPYHALSKI, Richard A., Chief Executive Officer, Northwest Medical Center, Thief River Falls, MN, p. A229

ST. ANDRE, Christine, Executive Director, University of Utah Hospitals and Clinics, Salt Lake City, UT, p. A429

ST. CLAIR, Nelson L., President, Riverside Health System, Newport News, VA, p. B133

ST. GEORGE, George H., Chief Executive Officer, Screven County Hospital, Sylvania, GA, p. A110

STAAS Jr., William E., President and Medical Director, Magee Rehabilitation Hospital, Philadelphia, PA, p. A359

STACEY, Bryan, Administrator, Ashland Health Center, Ashland, KS, p. A156

STACEY, Rulon F., President and Chief Executive Officer, Poudre Valley Hospital, Fort Collins, CO, p. A70

STACK, Edward A., President and Chief Executive Officer, Behavioral Healthcare Corporation, Nashville, TN, p. B65

STAMM, Scott C., Chief Executive Officer, Columbia River Park Hospital, Huntington, WV, p. A451

STAMP, Burl E., Chief Executive Officer, Phoenix Children's Hospital, Phoenix, AZ, p. A25

STAMPOHAR, Jeffry, Chief Executive Officer, Deer River Healthcare Center, Deer River, MN, p. A222

STANBERRY, Marion W., Administrator, East Texas Medical Center–Quitman, Quitman, TX, p. A418

STANDEFFER, Luke, Chief Operating Officer, HEALTHSOUTH Medical Center, Birmingham, AL, p. A12

STANKO, J. Richard, President and Chief Executive Officer, St. Joseph Hospital, Omaha, NE, p. A260

STANLEY, Robert R., Interim Chief Executive Officer, Caldwell County Hospital, Princeton, KY, p. A174

STANZIONE, Dominick M., Chief Operating Officer and Executive Vice President, Sisters of Charity Medical Center, New York, NY, p. A293

STAPLES, Nancy, Administrator, Elgin Mental Health Center, Elgin, IL, p. A124

STARK, Charles A., CHE, Administrator, Chief Executive Officer and Regional Vice President, HEALTHSOUTH Medical Center, Richmond, VA, p. A439

STARNES, Gregory D., Chief Executive Officer, Culver Union Hospital, Crawfordsville, IN, p. A137

STARR, Gerald A., Executive Officer, Delano Regional Medical Center, Delano, CA, p. A41

STARR Jr., Hickory, Administrator, William W. Hastings Indian Hospital, Tahlequah, OK, p. A340

STASIK, Randall, President and Chief Executive Officer, Borgess Medical Center, Kalamazoo, MI, p. A212

STATUTO, Richard, Chief Executive Officer, St. Joseph Health System, Orange, CA, p. B142

STAUDER, Mark S., President and Chief Executive Officer, Mercy Regional Medical Center, Laredo, TX, p. A412

STEADHAM, Mark B., President and Chief Executive Officer, St. Catherine Hospital, Garden City, KS, p. A158

STECKLER, Michael J., Chief Executive Officer, Jennie M. Melham Memorial Medical Center, Broken Bow, NE, p. A256

STEED, Larry N., Administrator, Tanner Medical Center–Villa Rica, Villa Rica, GA, p. A111

STEED, Robert A., President, Willamette Falls Hospital, Oregon City, OR, p. A344

STEEGE, Armin, Chief Executive Officer, Charter Behavioral Health System of Austin, Austin, TX, p. A393

STEELE, Barbara, President, The Toledo Hospital, Toledo, OH, p. A330

STEFANIDES, Christine M., CHE, Interim President and Chief Executive Officer, Civista Health, La Plata, MD, p. A195

STEFFEE, Sam L., Executive Director and Chief Executive Officer, Polly Ryon Memorial Hospital, Richmond, TX, p. A418

STEFFEN, Keith E., Administrator, Saint Francis Medical Center, Peoria, IL, p. A131

STEGBAUER, Thomas, Chief Executive Officer, Gritman Medical Center, Moscow, ID, p. A116

STEIN, Benjamin M., M.D., President, Brunswick General Hospital, Amityville, NY, p. A281

STEIN, Bob, Executive Director, Vencor Hospital–Houston, Houston, TX, p. A410

STEIN, Dale J., President and Chief Executive Officer, Avera St. Luke's, Aberdeen, SD, p. A376

STEIN, Gary M., President and Chief Executive Officer, Touro Infirmary, New Orleans, LA, p. A184

STEIN, Norman V., President, University Community Hospital, Tampa, FL, p. A96

STEIN, Sheldon J., Chief Operating Officer, Mt. Washington Pediatric Hospital, Baltimore, MD, p. A192

STEINER, Garith W., Chief Executive Officer, Vernon Memorial Hospital, Viroqua, WI, p. A464

STEINER, Keith M., Chief Executive Officer, Madison Memorial Hospital, Rexburg, ID, p. A116

STEINHAUER, Bruce W., M.D., President and Chief Executive Officer, Regional Medical Center at Memphis, Memphis, TN, p. A387

STEINHAURER, Gordon L., Chief Executive Officer, BHC Valle Vista Hospital, Greenwood, IN, p. A139

STEINHOFF, Earl J., Chief Executive Officer, Prowers Medical Center, Lamar, CO, p. A71

STEINRUCK, Jim, CHE, Administrator and Chief Executive Officer, Vencor Hospital Seattle, Seattle, WA, p. A447

STEITZ, David P., Chief Executive Officer, Frankfort Regional Medical Center, Frankfort, KY, p. A169

STELLER, Tim, Chief Executive Officer, North Central Health Care Facilities, Wausau, WI, p. A464

STENBERG, Scott, Chief Executive Officer, Sutter Amador Hospital, Jackson, CA, p. A45

STENGER, Michael J., Executive Vice President and Administrator, St. Nicholas Hospital, Sheboygan, WI, p. A463

STENSAGER, Mark, President and Chief Executive Officer, Guthrie Healthcare System, Sayre, PA, p. B99

STENSON, Richard, President and Chief Executive Officer, Tuality Healthcare, Hillsboro, OR, p. A343

STENSRUD, Kirk, Administrator, Hendricks Community Hospital, Hendricks, MN, p. A224

STENZLER, Mark R., Vice President Administration, North Shore University Hospital at Glen Cove, Glen Cove, NY, p. A285

STEPANIK, Mark J., Interim Chief Executive Officer, Mid–America Rehabilitation Hospital, Overland Park, KS, p. A163

STEPHANS, J. Michael, Administrator, Medical Center Hospital, Odessa, TX, p. A416

STEPHEN, Ron, Executive Vice President and Administrator, Osteopathic Medical Center of Texas, Fort Worth, TX, p. A404

STEPHENS, Michael D., President and Chief Executive Officer, Hoag Memorial Hospital Presbyterian, Newport Beach, CA, p. A54

STEPHENS, Michael R., President, Greene Memorial Hospital, Xenia, OH, p. A331

STEPHENS, Terry A., Executive Director, Sierra Tucson, Tucson, AZ, p. A27

STEPHENS Jr., Jack T., President and Chief Executive Officer, Lakeland Regional Medical Center, Lakeland, FL, p. A88

STEPHENSON, Christy, Chief Administrative Officer, Robert Wood Johnson University Hospital at Hamilton, Hamilton, NJ, p. A270

STEPHENSON, David, Administrator, Rock County Hospital, Bassett, NE, p. A256

STEPP, Merle E., President and Chief Executive Officer, Clark Memorial Hospital, Jeffersonville, IN, p. A141

STERN, Ron, Chief Executive Officer, Palmetto General Hospital, Hialeah, FL, p. A86

STEVENS, Alan I., Administrator, Huntington Hospital, Willow Grove, PA, p. A366

STEVENS, April A., R.N., Vice President and Administrator, Allegheny University Hospitals–Forbes Metropolitan, Pittsburgh, PA, p. A360

STEVENS, Diana, Administrator, Garden County Hospital, Oshkosh, NE, p. A261

STEVENS, Essimae, Service Unit Director, U.S. Public Health Service Indian Hospital, Redlake, MN, p. A227

STEVENS, Robert, President and Chief Executive Officer, Ridgeview Medical Center, Waconia, MN, p. A229

STEVENS, Velinda, President and Chief Executive Officer, Kalispell Regional Medical Center, Kalispell, MT, p. A253

STEVENS, Ward W., CHE, Chief Executive Officer, Alleghany Regional Hospital, Low Moor, VA, p. A436

STEVENS Jr., Vernon R., Administrator, Riverland Medical Center, Ferriday, LA, p. A179

STEVENSON, Jerry L.
President and Chief Executive Officer, Mercy Hospital, Fort Scott, KS, p. A158
President and Chief Executive Officer, Mercy Hospital, Independence, KS, p. A159

STEVENSON, Mike, Administrator, Murphy Medical Center, Murphy, NC, p. A309

STEWART, Charles L., Administrator, Northport Medical Center, Northport, AL, p. A17

STEWART, Christine R., President and Chief Executive Officer, Russellville Hospital, Russellville, AL, p. A18

STEWART, Diane Gail, Administrator, Sutter Center for Psychiatry, Sacramento, CA, p. A58

STEWART, Donald L., Chief Executive Officer, Bayshore Medical Center, Pasadena, TX, p. A417

STEWART, Joseph A., Chief Executive Officer, Butler Health System, Butler, PA, p. A349

STEWART, Lawrence C., Director, Veterans Affairs Medical Center, Long Beach, CA, p. A47

STEWART, Paul R., President and Chief Executive Officer, Merle West Medical Center, Klamath Falls, OR, p. A343

STEWART, Shirley A., President and Chief Executive Officer, Tulane University Hospital and Clinic, New Orleans, LA, p. A184

STILLWAGON, Richard A., Superintendent, Torrance State Hospital, Torrance, PA, p. A364

STILLWELL, James M., Director, Impact Drug and Alcohol Treatment Center, Pasadena, CA, p. A55

STINDT, John, Chief Executive Officer, Standish Community Hospital, Standish, MI, p. A217

STINSON, Karl R., CHE, Chief Executive Officer, Medical Arts Hospital, Lamesa, TX, p. A412

STITZER, Roxane, Ph.D., Chief Executive Officer, Metropolitan Nashville General Hospital, Nashville, TN, p. A388

STOCK, Greg K., Chief Executive Officer, Northwest Medical Center, Springdale, AR, p. A34

STOCKTON, Eddy R., Administrator, Wayne County Hospital, Monticello, KY, p. A173

STODDARD, Mark R.
President, Central Valley Medical Center, Nephi, UT, p. A428
President, Rural Health Management Corporation, Nephi, UT, p. B134

STOKER, Teresa, Chief Executive Officer, Hillside Hospital, Atlanta, GA, p. A100

STOKES, Barry S., President and Chief Executive Officer, Edward White Hospital, Saint Petersburg, FL, p. A94

STOKES, Gary L., Chief Executive Officer, Gulf Coast Medical Center, Biloxi, MS, p. A231

STOKES, Randell G., Chief Executive Officer, Memorial Mother Frances Hospital, Palestine, TX, p. A417

STOLL, Lee, Chief Executive Officer, Compton Heights Hospital, Saint Louis, MO, p. A247

STOLL, Leona D., Chief Executive Officer, Saint Louis University Hospital, Saint Louis, MO, p. A248

STOLZENBERG, Edward A., President and Chief Executive Officer, Westchester Medical Center, Valhalla, NY, p. A299

STONE, Ken, Administrator, Vencor Hospital – Central Tampa, Tampa, FL, p. A97

STONE, Maxine, Interim Superintendent, Eastern Oregon Psychiatric Center, Pendleton, OR, p. A344

STONE, Robert, President, Blythedale Children's Hospital, Valhalla, NY, p. A299

STONE, Thomas J., Administrator, St. Tammany Parish Hospital, Covington, LA, p. A179

STONER, Philip J., Chief Executive Officer, Tyrone Hospital, Tyrone, PA, p. A365

STORDAHL, Dean R., Chief Executive Officer, Jerry L. Pettis Memorial Veterans Medical Center, Loma Linda, CA, p. A47

STORMOEN, Paul L., Interim Chief Executive Officer, San Luis Obispo General Hospital, San Luis Obispo, CA, p. A61

STORY, Bettye W., Ph.D., Director, Veterans Affairs Medical Center, Hampton, VA, p. A435

STOUT, Dick L., Chief Executive Officer and Administrator, DeBaca General Hospital, Fort Sumner, NM, p. A279

STOVALL, Ed, Administrative Officer, Northville Psychiatric Hospital, Northville, MI, p. A215

STRANGE, John, President and Chief Executive Officer, St. Luke's Hospital, Duluth, MN, p. A222

STRANKO, Teresa K., Chief Executive Officer, HEALTHSOUTH Rehabilitation Hospital of Central Kentucky, Elizabethtown, KY, p. A168

STRASSHEIM, Dale S., President, BroMenn Healthcare, Normal, IL, p. A130

STRATTON, Terry, Chief Executive Officer, Appling Healthcare System, Baxley, GA, p. A101

STRAUCH, Walter A., Executive Director, Franklin Regional Hospital, Franklin, NH, p. A265

STRECK, William F., M.D., President and Chief Executive Officer, Mary Imogene Bassett Hospital, Cooperstown, NY, p. A284

STREET, Jackie, President, Idaho Falls Recovery Center, Idaho Falls, ID, p. A115

STRICKER, Sean, Administrator, Liberty–Dayton Hospital, Liberty, TX, p. A412

STRICKLAND, Wallace, Administrator, Rush Foundation Hospital, Meridian, MS, p. A236

STRIEBY, John F., President and Chief Executive Officer, Nix Health Care System, San Antonio, TX, p. A420

STRINE, Mervin F., President and Chief Executive Officer, Massillon Community Hospital, Massillon, OH, p. A326

STROMAN, W. Neil, President, ViaHealth of Wayne, Newark, NY, p. A294

STROTE, Ted, Administrator, Stevens County Hospital, Hugoton, KS, p. A159

STROUD, Bridget K., Chief Executive Officer, Faribault Regional Center, Faribault, MN, p. A223

STRUXNESS, Ronald E., Executive Vice President and Chief Executive Officer, Our Lady of the Resurrection Medical Center, Chicago, IL, p. A121

STRUYK, Douglas A., President and Chief Executive Officer, Christian Health Care Center, Wyckoff, NJ, p. A276

STUART, Philip, Administrator, Tomah Memorial Hospital, Tomah, WI, p. A464

STUBBLEFIELD, Alfred G., President, Baptist Health Care Corporation, Pensacola, FL, p. B63

STUBBS, Deborah, Chief Executive Officer, South Barry County Memorial Hospital, Cassville, MO, p. A240

STUDER, Quinton, President, Baptist Hospital, Pensacola, FL, p. A93

STUDSRUD, John S., Administrator, Hereford Regional Medical Center, Hereford, TX, p. A407

STUENKEL, Kurt, FACHE, President and Chief Executive Officer, Floyd Medical Center, Rome, GA, p. A109

STYLES Jr., John H., Administrator, Doctors Hospital–Tidwell, Houston, TX, p. A407

SUDDERS, Marylou, Commissioner, Massachusetts Department of Mental Health, Boston, MA, p. B113

SUEIRO, Edwin, Executive Director, Hospital Doctor Gubern, Fajardo, PR, p. A470

SUGG, William T., President and Chief Executive Officer, Sumner Regional Medical Center, Gallatin, TN, p. A383

SUGIYAMA, Deborah
President, NorthBay Medical Center, Fairfield, CA, p. A42
President, VacaValley Hospital, Vacaville, CA, p. A65

SULLIVAN, Charles, President and Chief Executive Officer, Reading Hospital and Medical Center, Reading, PA, p. A363

SULLIVAN, Michael J., Director, Veterans Affairs Medical Center, Philadelphia, PA, p. A360

SULLIVAN, Margaret T., President, Chief Executive Officer and Chief Operating Officer, St. Agnes Medical Center, Philadelphia, PA, p. A360

SUMLIN, Rene W., Chief Executive Officer and Administrator, Vaughan Perry Hospital, Marion, AL, p. A16

SUMMERS, Stephen M., CPA, Chief Executive Officer, Decatur Community Hospital, Decatur, TX, p. A401

SUMMERS, William L., Executive Director, Patton State Hospital, Patton, CA, p. A56

SUMMERSETT III, James A., FACHE, President and Chief Executive Officer, Conway Regional Medical Center, Conway, AR, p. A30

SUROWITZ, Dale, President and Chief Executive Officer, Encino–Tarzana Regional Medical Center Tarzana Campus, Los Angeles, CA, p. A48

SUSI, Jeffrey L., President and Chief Executive Officer, Indian River Memorial Hospital, Vero Beach, FL, p. A97

SUSSMAN, Elliot J., M.D.
President and Chief Executive Officer, Lehigh Valley Hospital, Allentown, PA, p. A347
President and Chief Executive Officer, Muhlenberg Hospital Center, Bethlehem, PA, p. A348

SUTTERER, Larry J., USAF, Administrator, U. S. Air Force Regional Hospital, Elmendorf AFB, AK, p. A20

SUTTON, Frank, Vice President Hospital Services, Searhc MT. Edgecumbe Hospital, Sitka, AK, p. A21

SUYENAGA, Lee, Chief Executive Officer, Alhambra Hospital, Alhambra, CA, p. A36

SVENSSON, Paul E., Chief Executive Officer, Parkway Hospital, New York, NY, p. A293

SWANSON, Ronald, Chief Executive Officer, Providence Seaside Hospital, Seaside, OR, p. A346

SWARTWOUT, John A., Administrator, Shriners Hospitals for Children, Galveston Burns Hospital, Galveston, TX, p. A405

SWEARINGEN, Lawrence L., President and Chief Executive Officer, Blessing Hospital, Quincy, IL, p. A132

SWEEDEN, Dick, Administrator, Scott and White Memorial Hospital, Temple, TX, p. A423

SWEENEY, David A., FACHE, Administrator, Morgan County War Memorial Hospital, Berkeley Springs, WV, p. A450

SWEENEY, Kathi, Administrator, Mercy Providence Hospital, Pittsburgh, PA, p. A361

SWENSON, Kenneth B., President, Prince William Hospital, Manassas, VA, p. A436

SWIGART, Russell W., Administrator, Howard County Community Hospital, Saint Paul, NE, p. A261

SWINEHART, Frank V., President and Chief Executive Officer, Marion General Hospital, Marion, OH, p. A326

SWINIARSKI, Wayne A., FACHE, Chief Executive Officer, West Calcasieu Cameron Hospital, Sulphur, LA, p. A186

SWINNEY, Keith, Chief Executive Officer, Southwest General Hospital, San Antonio, TX, p. A420

SWISHER, Charles D., President and Chief Executive Officer, Kendrick Memorial Hospital, Mooresville, IN, p. A142

SWITZER, Bruce, Administrator, Broken Arrow Medical Center, Broken Arrow, OK, p. A334

SWORD, Russ D., Interim Administrator, Ashley County Medical Center, Crossett, AR, p. A30

SWORD, William L., President and Chief Executive Officer, Texas County Memorial Hospital, Houston, MO, p. A242

SYKES Jr., Donald K., Chief Executive Officer, BHC Windsor Hospital, Chagrin Falls, OH, p. A318

SYPNIEWSKI, Al, Administrator, Baptist Memorial Hospital–Blytheville, Blytheville, AR, p. A29

SZABO, Charleen R., FACHE, Chief Executive Officer, Veterans Affairs Medical Center, Lebanon, PA, p. A355

T

TADLOCK, Cindy, Interim Administrator, Leake Memorial Hospital, Carthage, MS, p. A232

TAITANO, Tyrone J., Administrator, Guam Memorial Hospital Authority, Tamuning, GU, p. A469

TALLEY, James J., Administrator, Wheaton Community Hospital, Wheaton, MN, p. A229

TALLON, Richard, Administrator, Jefferson County Hospital, Waurika, OK, p. A341

TALLY, James E., Ph.D.
President and Chief Executive Officer, Egleston Children's Hospital, Atlanta, GA, p. A100
President and Chief Executive Officer, ESR Children's Health Care System, Inc., Atlanta, GA, p. B95
President and Chief Executive Officer, Scottish Rite Children's Medical Center, Atlanta, GA, p. A100

TALONEY, Derell, President and Chief Executive Officer, Park Lane Medical Center, Kansas City, MO, p. A243

TAMAR, Earl, Chief Operating Officer, Cape Coral Hospital, Cape Coral, FL, p. A82

TAMLYN, Mary E., Administrator, Mackinac Straits Hospital and Health Center, Saint Ignace, MI, p. A216

TAMME, Susan Stout, President, Baptist Hospital East, Louisville, KY, p. A171

TAN, Bienvenido, M.D., Chief Executive Officer, Newhall Community Hospital, Newhall, CA, p. A53

TAN–LACHICA, Nieves, M.D., Superintendent, Andrew McFarland Mental Health Center, Springfield, IL, p. A133

TANG, Leah, Administrator, Avalon Municipal Hospital and Clinic, Avalon, CA, p. A37

TANKLE, Reva S., Ph.D., Chief Executive Officer, Olympus Specialty Hospital, Waltham, MA, p. A204

TANNER, Anthony J., Executive Vice President, HEALTHSOUTH Corporation, Birmingham, AL, p. B101

TANNER, Gale V., Administrator, Monroe County Hospital, Forsyth, GA, p. A105

TANNER, Laurence A., President and Chief Executive Officer, New Britain General Hospital, New Britain, CT, p. A75

TAPPAN, Hugh C., Chief Executive Officer, Hughston Sports Medicine Hospital, Columbus, GA, p. A103

TARBET, Michele T., R.N., Chief Executive Officer, Grossmont Hospital, La Mesa, CA, p. A46

TARR, Judith, Chief Executive Officer, Miles Memorial Hospital, Damariscotta, ME, p. A188

TARRANT, Jeffrey S., Administrator, Lafayette Regional Health Center, Lexington, MO, p. A244

TASCONE, Deborah, MS
Vice President for Administration, North Shore University Hospital at Plainview, Plainview, NY, p. A296
Vice President of Administration, North Shore University Hospital at Syosset, Syosset, NY, p. A298

TASSE, Joseph, Administrator, Oakwood Hospital and Medical Center–Dearborn, Dearborn, MI, p. A208

TATE, Joel W., FACHE, Chief Executive Officer, McAlester Regional Health Center, McAlester, OK, p. A337

TATE Jr., David B., President and Chief Executive Officer, Lake Taylor Hospital, Norfolk, VA, p. A437

TATUM, Stanley D., Chief Executive Officer, Edmond Medical Center, Edmond, OK, p. A335

TAUSSIG, Lynn M., M.D., President and Chief Executive Officer, National Jewish Medical and Research Center, Denver, CO, p. A69

TAVARY, James, Administrator, Prosser Memorial Hospital, Prosser, WA, p. A446

TAVENNER, Marilyn B., Chief Executive Officer, Chippenham and Johnston–Willis Hospitals, Richmond, VA, p. A439

TAVERNIER, Patrice L., Administrator, Fishermen's Hospital, Marathon, FL, p. A89

TAYLOR, Alfred P., Administrator and Chief Executive Officer, Milan General Hospital, Milan, TN, p. A388

TAYLOR, Barbara, R.N., Interim Administrator, Hemet Valley Medical Center, Hemet, CA, p. A44

TAYLOR, James H., President and Chief Executive Officer, University of Louisville Hospital, Louisville, KY, p. A172

TAYLOR, LeAn, Acting Facility Director, Choate Mental Health and Developmental Center, Anna, IL, p. A118

TAYLOR, Mark R., President, St. Marys Health Center, Jefferson City, MO, p. A242

TAYLOR, Meredith, Administrator, Vencor Hospital–Sacramento, Folsom, CA, p. A42

TAYLOR, Steven L., Chief Executive Officer, Harrison County Hospital, Corydon, IN, p. A137

TAYLOR, Donald, Administrator, U. S. Air Force Hospital Shaw, Shaw AFB, SC, p. A375

TAYLOR Jr., L. Clark, President and Chief Executive Officer, Memorial Hospital, Chattanooga, TN, p. A382

TEAGUE, M. E., Chief Executive Officer, Louisiana State Hospitals, New Orleans, LA, p. B110

TEEL, Kenneth R., Administrator, Lake Pointe Medical Center, Rowlett, TX, p. A419

TEIGEN, Bobbe, Administrator, Sauk Prairie Memorial Hospital, Prairie Du Sac, WI, p. A462

TEMBREULL, John P., Administrator, Baraga County Memorial Hospital, L'Anse, MI, p. A213

TENNANT, Gail, Director, H. Douglas Singer Mental Health and Developmental Center, Rockford, IL, p. A132

TENNISON, Randal, Administrator, Dexter Memorial Hospital, Dexter, MO, p. A241

TERREBONNE, Terry J., Administrator, Jennings American Legion Hospital, Jennings, LA, p. A180

TERRIBERRY, Cynthia, USAF, Commanding Officer, U. S. Air Force Hospital Mountain Home, Mountain Home AFB, ID, p. A116

TERRILL, John, Administrator, Smith County Memorial Hospital, Smith Center, KS, p. A164

TERRY, Micheal, Executive Director, Highlands Regional Medical Center, Sebring, FL, p. A95

TERRY, Pat, Ph.D., Acting Chief Executive Officer, Western State Hospital, Tacoma, WA, p. A449

TESAR, James D., Chief Executive Officer, Flint River Community Hospital, Montezuma, GA, p. A108

TEST, Russell A., Administrator and Chief Executive Officer, The Hospital, Sidney, NY, p. A298

TESTERMAN, E. R., Administrator, Niobrara Valley Hospital, Lynch, NE, p. A259

TESTERMAN, R. Frank, Administrator, Hawkins County Memorial Hospital, Rogersville, TN, p. A389

THACHER, Frederick J., Chairman, Community Care Systems, Inc., Wellesley, MA, p. B84

THEBEAU, Robert S.
President and Chief Executive Officer, Kishwaukee Community Hospital, De Kalb, IL, p. A123
President and Chief Executive Officer, Kishwaukee Health System, De Kalb, IL, p. B108

THEROULT, Thomas N., Administrator, Vencor Hospital–Minneapolis, Golden Valley, MN, p. A223

THIEBEN, William H., Chief Executive Officer, Kewanee Hospital, Kewanee, IL, p. A128

THIER, Samuel O., M.D., President and Chief Executive Officer, Partners HealthCare System, Inc., Boston, MA, p. B124

THODE, Mary Ann, Administrator, Kaiser Foundation Hospital, San Rafael, CA, p. A61

THOMAS, Chris, Administrator and Chief Executive Officer, Hegg Memorial Health Center, Rock Valley, IA, p. A153

THOMAS, James R., Chief Executive Officer, Redmond Regional Medical Center, Rome, GA, p. A109

THOMAS, Lacy, Director, Cook County Hospital, Chicago, IL, p. A120

THOMAS, Marcile, Administrator, Providence Medical Center, Wayne, NE, p. A262

THOMAS, Michael P., Administrator, Meade District Hospital, Meade, KS, p. A161

THOMAS, Philip P., Director, Veterans Affairs Medical Center, Syracuse, NY, p. A299

THOMAS, Richard C., Administrator, Bascom Palmer Eye Institute–Anne Bates Leach Eye Hospital, Miami, FL, p. A89

THOMAS, Richard Lee, Superintendent, Lakeshore Mental Health Institute, Knoxville, TN, p. A385

THOMAS, Richard M., President, Pattie A. Clay Hospital, Richmond, KY, p. A175

THOMAS, Robert, Administrator, Columbus Community Hospital, Columbus, TX, p. A398

THOMAS, Telford W., President and Chief Executive Officer, Washington Hospital, Washington, PA, p. A365

THOMPSON, Anne, Chief Executive Officer, Chestatee Regional Hospital, Dahlonega, GA, p. A103

THOMPSON, Bobby G., President and Chief Executive Officer, Mercy Memorial Health Center, Ardmore, OK, p. A333

THOMPSON, Charolette, Administrator, Tri–Ward General Hospital, Bernice, LA, p. A178

THOMPSON, Frederick G., Ph.D., Administrator and Chief Executive Officer, Anson Community Hospital, Wadesboro, NC, p. A312

THOMPSON, Harriet, Administrator, Hancock County Memorial Hospital, Britt, IA, p. A146

THOMPSON, Jim, Chief Executive Officer, Walton Regional Hospital, De Funiak Springs, FL, p. A83

THOMPSON, John William, Ph.D., President and Chief Executive Officer, Lakeland Regional Hospital, Springfield, MO, p. A249

THOMPSON, Larry
Senior Vice President and Executive Director, Harris Continued Care Hospital, Fort Worth, TX, p. A404
Vice President and Administrator, Harris Methodist Northwest, Azle, TX, p. A394

THOMPSON, Lennis, Chief Executive Officer, Livingston Hospital and Healthcare Services, Salem, KY, p. A175

THOMPSON, Mark E., Chief Executive Officer, Monroe County Medical Center, Tompkinsville, KY, p. A175

THOMPSON, Terry, Chief Executive Officer, Fairfield Memorial Hospital, Fairfield, IL, p. A125

THOMPSON, Tom, Administrator, Community Memorial Hospital, Oconto Falls, WI, p. A462

THOMPSON, Wes, Administrator and Chief Executive Officer, Alta View Hospital, Sandy, UT, p. A430

THOMPSON, William D., Commandant, Lawrence F. Quigley Memorial Hospital, Chelsea, MA, p. A200

THOMSON, Thomas, Chief Executive Officer, Colorado Plains Medical Center, Fort Morgan, CO, p. A70

THORESON, Scott, Administrator, Springfield Medical Center–Mayo Health System, Springfield, MN, p. A228

THORNTON, Dale E., President, Mercy Hospital–Willard, Willard, OH, p. A331

THORNTON, William M., Presdent and Chief Executive Officer, Miami Valley Hospital, Dayton, OH, p. A323

THORNTON Jr., James H., President and Chief Executive Officer, Brandywine Hospital, Coatesville, PA, p. A350

THORP, Gretchen, R.N., Administrator, Casa, A Special Hospital, Houston, TX, p. A407

THORSLAND Jr., Edgar, Director, Veterans Affairs Medical Center, Denver, CO, p. A70

THORWARD, S. R., M.D., President and Chief Executive Officer, Harding Hospital, Worthington, OH, p. A331

THWEATT, James W., Chief Executive Officer, Clinch Valley Medical Center, Richlands, VA, p. A439

TIBBITTS, Tom, President, Trinity Regional Hospital, Fort Dodge, IA, p. A149

TICE, Kirk C., President and Chief Executive Officer, Rahway Hospital, Rahway, NJ, p. A274

TIEDEMANN, Frank, President and Chief Executive Officer, St. Paul Medical Center, Dallas, TX, p. A401

TILLER, Gary L., Chief Executive Officer, Ninnescah Valley Health System, Kingman, KS, p. A160

TILTON, David P., President and Chief Executive Officer, Atlantic City Medical Center, Atlantic City, NJ, p. A268

TIMCHO, Thomas P., President, UPMC Beaver Valley, Aliquippa, PA, p. A347

TINKER, A. James, President and Chief Executive Officer, Mercy Medical Center, Cedar Rapids, IA, p. A147

TINKER, David E., President and Chief Executive Officer, Samaritan Medical Center, Watertown, NY, p. A300

TINTLE, Keith, Chief Executive Officer, Pioneer Valley Hospital, Salt Lake City, UT, p. A429

TIPPETS, Wayne C., Director, Veterans Affairs Medical Center, Boise, ID, p. A114

TITUS III, Rexford W., President and Chief Executive Officer, Waukesha Memorial Hospital, Waukesha, WI, p. A464

TOBIN, John H., President and Chief Executive Officer, Waterbury Hospital, Waterbury, CT, p. A77

TOBIN, Timothy C., Chief Executive Officer, Coliseum Medical Centers, Macon, GA, p. A107

TODHUNTER, Neil E., Chief Executive Officer, Northwest Medical Centers, Franklin, PA, p. A352

TOEBBE, Nelson, Chief Executive Officer, Rockdale Hospital, Conyers, GA, p. A103

TOERING, Marla, Administrator, Sioux Center Community Hospital and Health Center, Sioux Center, IA, p. A154

TOLL, Sidney A., President, North Country Hospital and Health Center, Newport, VT, p. A431

TOLMAN, Russell K., President and Chief Executive Officer, Cook Children's Medical Center, Fort Worth, TX, p. A404

TOLMIE, John Kerr, President and Chief Executive Officer, St. Joseph Hospital, Lancaster, PA, p. A354

TOLOSKY, Mark R., Chief Executive Officer, Baystate Medical Center, Springfield, MA, p. A204

TOMBERLIN, Don E., Interim Administrator, Tattnall Memorial Hospital, Reidsville, GA, p. A108

TOMLON, Kenneth, Interim Chief Executive Officer, St. Mary's Hospital and Medical Center, Grand Junction, CO, p. A71

TOMPKINS, Amelia, Administrator, Hamilton Medical Center, Jasper, FL, p. A87

TOMPKINS, John, Administrator, Baptist Memorial Hospital–Union County, New Albany, MS, p. A236

TOMT, Gene, FACHE, Chief Executive Officer, Bonner General Hospital, Sandpoint, ID, p. A116

TOOMEY, Richard Kirk, President and Chief Executive Officer, Nash Health Care Systems, Rocky Mount, NC, p. A310

TOPP III, Walter, Administrator, Cibola General Hospital, Grants, NM, p. A279

TORBA, Gerald M., Chief Executive Officer, Callaway Community Hospital, Fulton, MO, p. A241

TORCHIA, Jude, Chief Executive Officer, Deering Hospital, Miami, FL, p. A89

TORRES, Diane D., R.N., Executive Director, Sebastian River Medical Center, Sebastian, FL, p. A95

TORRES, Jorge, Executive Director, First Hospital Panamericano, Cidra, PR, p. A470

TORRES–ZAYAS, Domingo, Executive Director, Hospital Menonita De Cayey, Cayey, PR, p. A470

TORRESCANO, Bob, Administrator, North Florida Reception Center Hospital, Lake Butler, FL, p. A87

TOTH, Cynthia M., Administrator, Shands Rehab Hospital, Gainesville, FL, p. A85

TOURVILLE, James C., Administrator, Douglas County Hospital, Omaha, NE, p. A260

TOWNSEND, Mitchell, Administrator, George Nigh Rehabilitation Institute, Okmulgee, OK, p. A338

TOWNSEND, Stanley, Administrator, Stone County Medical Center, Mountain View, AR, p. A33

TOWNSEND, Theodore E., Senior Vice President, Operations, Penn State Geisinger Health System–Milton S. Hershey Medical Center, Hershey, PA, p. A353

TOWNSEND, Walden, Service Unit Director, U. S. Public Health Service Owyhee Community Health Facility, Owyhee, NV, p. A264

TOWNSEND Jr., C. Vincent
  Vice President, St. Joseph Northeast Heights Hospital, Albuquerque, NM, p. A277
  Vice President, St. Joseph West Mesa Hospital, Albuquerque, NM, p. A277

TOY, Joseph A., President and Chief Executive Officer, Eastern State Hospital, Lexington, KY, p. A171

TRACEY, Robert M., Administrator, Franciscan Skemp Healthcare–Arcadia Campus, Arcadia, WI, p. A456

TRACY, Tim, Senior Vice President and Chief Operating Officer, John C Lincoln Hospital–Deer Valley, Phoenix, AZ, p. A24

TRACY, Timothy J., Chief Executive Officer, Towner County Medical Center, Cando, ND, p. A313

TRAHAN, Alcus, Administrator, Acadia–St. Landry Hospital, Church Point, LA, p. A178

TRAHAN, Daniel, Acting Administrator, Leonard J. Chabert Medical Center, Houma, LA, p. A180

TRAHAN, Lyman, Administrator, Abrom Kaplan Memorial Hospital, Kaplan, LA, p. A180

TRAMP, Francis, President, Burgess Health Center, Onawa, IA, p. A152

TRAVERSE, Bruce L., President, Carson City Hospital, Carson City, MI, p. A207

TREFRY, Robert J., President and Chief Executive Officer, Bridgeport Hospital, Bridgeport, CT, p. A74

TREMBATH, Douglas R., President and Chief Executive Officer, Audrain Medical Center, Mexico, MO, p. A245

TRIANA, Milton, President and Chief Executive Officer, St. Mary Medical Center, Hobart, IN, p. A139

TRIEBES, David G., Chief Executive Officer, Wood River Township Hospital, Wood River, IL, p. A135

TRIMBLE, Charley O., President and Chief Executive Officer, Covenant Medical Center–Lakeside, Lubbock, TX, p. A413

TRIMBLE, Deborah C., Administrator, Paul B. Hall Regional Medical Center, Paintsville, KY, p. A174

TRIMM, Robert M., President and Chief Executive Officer, Satilla Regional Medical Center, Waycross, GA, p. A111

TRIMMER, Mary R., President and Chief Executive Officer, Mercy Hospital, Port Huron, MI, p. A216

TROWER, G. Wil, President and Chief Executive Officer, North Broward Hospital District, Fort Lauderdale, FL, p. B120

TRSTENSKY, Jomary, President, Hospital Sisters Health System, Springfield, IL, p. B104

TRUDELL, Thomas J., President and Chief Executive Officer, Marymount Hospital, Garfield Heights, OH, p. A324

TRUELOVE, Lynn, Administrator, Singing River Hospital, Pascagoula, MS, p. A236

TRUJILLO, Michael, M.P.H., Director, U. S. Public Health Service Indian Health Service, Rockville, MD, p. B148

TRULL, David J., President and Chief Executive Officer, Faulkner Hospital, Boston, MA, p. A198

TRUSKOLOSKI, Roger, Vice President and Chief Executive Officer, Memorial Rehabilitation Hospital, Houston, TX, p. A408

TRUSLEY III, James F., Director, Veterans Affairs Medical Center, Dublin, GA, p. A104

TSCHIDER, Richard A., FACHE, Administrator and Chief Executive Officer, St. Alexius Medical Center, Bismarck, ND, p. A313

TSO, Ronald, Chief Executive Officer, Chinle Comprehensive Health Care Facility, Chinle, AZ, p. A22

TUCHSCHMIDT, James, M.D., Chief Executive Officer, Veterans Affairs Medical Center, Portland, OR, p. A345

TUCKER, Edgar L., Director, Veterans Affairs Eastern Kansas Health Care System, Topeka, KS, p. A165

TUCKER, Joseph R., President, St. Claude Medical Center, New Orleans, LA, p. A184

TUCKER, Paul, Administrator, Highline Community Hospital, Seattle, WA, p. A447

TUCKER, Steven E., President, Conemaugh Memorial Medical Center, Johnstown, PA, p. A354

TULLMAN, Stephen M., Chief Administrative Officer, Norton Healthcare, Louisville, KY, p. A172

TUNGATE, Rex A., Administrator, Westlake Regional Hospital, Columbia, KY, p. A168

TURK, Herbert A., FACHE, Administrator, Sweeny Community Hospital, Sweeny, TX, p. A422

TURLEY, Frank, Ph.D., Executive Director, Napa State Hospital, Napa, CA, p. A53

TURNBULL, James, Administrator and Chief Executive Officer, Clara Barton Hospital, Hoisington, KS, p. A159

TURNER, Cindy R., Interim Chief Executive Officer, Bacon County Hospital, Alma, GA, p. A99

TURNER, Howard D., Chief Executive Officer, Heart of the Rockies Regional Medical Center, Salida, CO, p. A72

TURNER, John, Chief Executive Officer, James H. and Cecile C. Quillen Rehabilitation Hospital, Johnson City, TN, p. A384

TURNER, Joseph F., President, Central Suffolk Hospital, Riverhead, NY, p. A296

TURNER, M. Sue, Administrator, Latimer County General Hospital, Wilburton, OK, p. A341

TURNER, Mark, Chief Executive Officer, Ojai Valley Community Hospital, Ojai, CA, p. A54

TURNER, Michael A., President and Chief Executive Officer, Somerset Medical Center, Somerville, NJ, p. A274

TURNER, Robert J., Administrator, United Community Hospital, Grove City, PA, p. A353

TURNEY, Brian, Chief Executive Officer, Kingman Regional Medical Center, Kingman, AZ, p. A23

TURNEY, Dennis, Chief Executive Officer, Community Hospital, Watervliet, MI, p. A218

TUTEN, E. Allen, Administrator, Lincoln General Hospital, Ruston, LA, p. A185

TWISS, Gayla J., Service Unit Director, U. S. Public Health Service Indian Hospital, Rosebud, SD, p. A378

U

UFFER, Mark H., Chief Executive Officer, Arrowhead Regional Medical Center, Colton, CA, p. A40

UHLING, Casey, Chief Executive Officer, St. Mary's Hospital, Cottonwood, ID, p. A115

ULAND, Jonas S., Executive Director, Greene County General Hospital, Linton, IN, p. A142

ULBRICHT, William G., Chief Operating Officer, South Florida Baptist Hospital, Plant City, FL, p. A93

ULICNY, Gary R., Ph.D., President and Chief Executive Officer, Shepherd Center, Atlanta, GA, p. A100

ULLIAN, Elaine S., President and Chief Executive Officer, Boston Medical Center, Boston, MA, p. A197

ULMER, Evonne G., JD, Chief Executive Officer, Ionia County Memorial Hospital, Ionia, MI, p. A212

ULSETH, Randy, Administrator, Community Hospital, Cannon Falls, MN, p. A221

UMBDENSTOCK, Richard J., President and Chief Executive Officer, Providence Services, Spokane, WA, p. B126

UNDERKOFLER, Joseph, Director, Veterans Affairs Montana Healthcare System, Fort Harrison, MT, p. A252

UNDERRINER, David T., Operations Administrator, Providence Portland Medical Center, Portland, OR, p. A345

UNROE, Larry J., President, Marietta Memorial Hospital, Marietta, OH, p. A326

UNRUH, Greg, Chief Executive Officer, Scott County Hospital, Scott City, KS, p. A164

UOMO, Paul Dell, President and Chief Executive Officer, Greater Hudson Valley Health System, Newburgh, NY, p. B98

URCIUOLI, Robert A., President and Chief Executive Officer, Roger Williams Medical Center, Providence, RI, p. A368

URMY, Norman B., Executive Vice President Clinical Affairs, Vanderbilt University Hospital, Nashville, TN, p. A389

UROSEVICH, Steve L., Chief Executive Officer, St. Croix Valley Memorial Hospital, Saint Croix Falls, WI, p. A463

URSO, Susan, Administrator, Mendota Community Hospital, Mendota, IL, p. A129

URVAND, Leslie O., Administrator, St. Luke's Hospital, Crosby, ND, p. A313

USHIJIMA, Arthur A., President and Chief Executive Officer, Queen's Medical Center, Honolulu, HI, p. A112

V

VAAGENES, Carl P., Administrator, Pipestone County Medical Center, Pipestone, MN, p. A227

VADELLA, Anthony J., Chief Executive Officer, Poplar Springs Hospital, Petersburg, VA, p. A438

VALDESPINO, Gustavo, Chief Executive Officer, Suburban Medical Center, Paramount, CA, p. A55

VALDESPINO, Gustavo A.
  Chief Executive Officer, Lakewood Regional Medical Center, Lakewood, CA, p. A46
  Chief Executive Officer, Los Alamitos Medical Center, Los Alamitos, CA, p. A47

VALENTINE, Billy M., Director, Overton Brooks Veterans Affairs Medical Center, Shreveport, LA, p. A185

VALIANTE, John, Chief Executive Officer, St. John's Hospital and Living Center, Jackson, WY, p. A466

VALLIANT, Robert F., Administrator, Bartlett Regional Hospital, Juneau, AK, p. A21

VAN DRIEL, Allen, Administrator, Harlan County Health System, Alma, NE, p. A256

VAN ETTEN, Peter, President and Chief Executive Officer, UCSF Stanford Health Care, San Francisco, CA, p. B150

VAN GORDER, Chris D., Chief Executive Officer, Long Beach Memorial Medical Center, Long Beach, CA, p. A47

VAN LITH, Richard
Chief Executive Officer, Bon Secours Hospital, Grosse Pointe, MI, p. A211
Chief Executive Officer, Cottage Hospital, Grosse Pointe Farms, MI, p. A211

VAN STRATEN, Elizabeth, President and Chief Executive Officer, St. Bernard Hospital and Health Care Center, Chicago, IL, p. A122

VAN VORST, Charles B., President and Chief Executive Officer, Mercy Hospital and Medical Center, Chicago, IL, p. A121

VAN VRANKEN, Ross, Chief Executive Officer, University of Utah Neuropsychiatric Institute, Salt Lake City, UT, p. A430

VANASKIE, William F., President and Chief Executive Officer, Robert Packer Hospital, Sayre, PA, p. A363

VANDENBERG, Patricia, President and Chief Executive Officer, Holy Cross Health System Corporation, South Bend, IN, p. B104

VANDENBROEK, Deborah, President and Chief Executive Officer, Marian Health Center, Sioux City, IA, p. A154

VANDER AARDE, Marjorie, Administrator and Chief Executive Officer, Coalinga Regional Medical Center, Coalinga, CA, p. A39

VANDERHOOF, Terry L., President and Chief Executive Officer, River Valley Health System, Ironton, OH, p. A325

VANDERVEER, Robert W., Chief Executive Officer and Administrator, Knapp Medical Center, Weslaco, TX, p. A425

VANDERVORT, Darryl L., President and Chief Executive Officer, Katherine Shaw Bethea Hospital, Dixon, IL, p. A124

VANEK, James, Administrator, Lavaca Medical Center, Hallettsville, TX, p. A406

VANOURNY, Stephen E., M.D., President and Chief Executive Officer, St. Luke's Hospital, Cedar Rapids, IA, p. A147

VARGAS, Laura, Administrator and Chief Executive Officer, BHC Hospital San Juan Capestrano, San Juan, PR, p. A471

VARLAND, Carol A.
Chief Executive Officer, Community Memorial Hospital, Burke, SD, p. A376
Chief Executive Officer, Gregory Community Hospital, Gregory, SD, p. A377

VARNER, Gary, Interim Chief Executive Officer, Johnson City Specialty Hospital, Johnson City, TN, p. A385

VARNUM, James W., President, Mary Hitchcock Memorial Hospital, Lebanon, NH, p. A266

VARONE, Rick J., President, Staten Island University Hospital, New York, NY, p. A293

VASKELIS, Glenna L., Administrator, Sequoia Hospital, Redwood City, CA, p. A57

VASQUEZ, Alberto, Administrator, Star Valley Hospital, Afton, WY, p. A466

VATTER, Russell K., Superintendent, Moccasin Bend Mental Health Institute, Chattanooga, TN, p. A382

VAUGHAN, Page, Executive Director, Byerly Hospital, Hartsville, SC, p. A373

VAUGHT, Richard H., Administrator, William Newton Memorial Hospital, Winfield, KS, p. A166

VAZQUEZ, Manuel J., Administrator, Hospital Matilde Brenes, Bayamon, PR, p. A469

VECCHIONE, George A., President, Lifespan Corporation, Providence, RI, p. B109

VEENSTRA, Henry A., President, Zeeland Community Hospital, Zeeland, MI, p. A219

VEITZ, Larry W., Chief Executive Officer, Sioux Valley Vermillion Campus, Vermillion, SD, p. A379

VELEZ, Domingo, Administrator, Industrial Hospital, San Juan, PR, p. A472

VELEZ, Pete, Executive Director, Elmhurst Hospital Center, New York, NY, p. A290

VELICK, Stephen H., Chief Executive Officer, Henry Ford Hospital, Detroit, MI, p. A208

VELLINGA, David H., President and Chief Executive Officer, Mercy Hospital Medical Center, Des Moines, IA, p. A149

VELOSO, Carole A., President and Chief Executive Officer, Northside General Hospital, Houston, TX, p. A409

VELTE, Carl J., Chief Executive Officer, Munising Memorial Hospital, Munising, MI, p. A214

VENTURA, N. Lawrence, Superintendent, Bangor Mental Health Institute, Bangor, ME, p. A187

VERMAELEN, Elizabeth A., President, Sisters of Charity Center, New York, NY, p. B137

VERNEGAARD, Niels P., President, Parkridge Medical Center, Chattanooga, TN, p. A382

VERNOR, Robert E., Administrator, Ballinger Memorial Hospital, Ballinger, TX, p. A394

VIATOR, Kyle J., Chief Executive Officer, Dauterive Hospital, New Iberia, LA, p. A183

VICE, Jon E., President and Chief Executive Officer, Children's Hospital of Wisconsin, Milwaukee, WI, p. A460

VICTORY, Ronald D., Administrator, Penobscot Valley Hospital, Lincoln, ME, p. A189

VIGUS, Ronald J., Chief Executive Officer, Pender Memorial Hospital, Burgaw, NC, p. A303

VILAR, Ramon J., Administrator, Wilma N. Vazquez Medical Center, Vega Baja, PR, p. A472

VINARDI, Gregory B., President and Chief Executive Officer, Western Missouri Medical Center, Warrensburg, MO, p. A250

VINCENT, Rose, President and Chief Executive Officer, St. Elizabeth Medical Center, Utica, NY, p. A299

VINCENZ, Felix T., Ph.D., Acting Superintendent, Fulton State Hospital, Fulton, MO, p. A241

VINSON, Daniel M., CPA
Senior Vice President, St. Luke Hospital East, Fort Thomas, KY, p. A169
Senior Vice President, St. Luke Hospital West, Florence, KY, p. A169

VINSON, Roy C., Interim Chief Executive Officer, Central Peninsula General Hospital, Soldotna, AK, p. A21

VINTURELLA, Joseph C., Chief Executive Officer, Southeast Louisiana Hospital, Mandeville, LA, p. A182

VINYARD II, Roy G.
Chief Administrative Officer, Asante Health System, Medford, OR, p. B62
President and Chief Executive Offiecer, OHSU Hospital, Portland, OR, p. A345

VIOLI, Ronald L., President and Chief Executive Officer, Children's Hospital of Pittsburgh, Pittsburgh, PA, p. A361

VISALLI, Charles L., Chief Executive Officer, BHC Fox Run Hospital, Saint Clairsville, OH, p. A328

VIVALDI, Domingo Cruz, Administrator, San Jorge Children's Hospital, San Juan, PR, p. A472

VIVIAN, Talbot N., USAF, Administrator, U. S. Air Force Hospital Luke, Glendale, AZ, p. A23

VLACH, Karen, Administrator, Oakland Memorial Hospital, Oakland, NE, p. A260

VODENICKER, Johnette L., Administrator, Memorial Hospital–West Volusia, De Land, FL, p. A83

VOGEL, R. J., Chief Executive Officer, Ralph H. Johnson Veterans Affairs Medical Center, Charleston, SC, p. A371

VOGT, Allen J., Administrator, Cook Hospital and Convalescent Nursing Care Unit, Cook, MN, p. A222

VOLK, Ronald J., President, St. Aloisius Medical Center, Harvey, ND, p. A314

VOLPE, Michele M., Executive Director, Presbyterian Medical Center of the University of Pennsylvania Health System, Philadelphia, PA, p. A359

VONDERFECHT, Dennis
President and Chief Executive Officer, Johnson City Medical Center, Johnson City, TN, p. A385
President and Chief Executive Officer, Mountain States Health Alliance, Johnson City, TN, p. B118

VONDRAK, Darrell E., Administrator, Palo Alto Health System, Emmetsburg, IA, p. A149

VOSS, Daryle, Chief Executive Officer, Kingfisher Regional Hospital, Kingfisher, OK, p. A336

VOZEL, Gerald F., Administrator and Chief Executive Officer, HEALTHSOUTH Tri–State Rehabilitation Hospital, Evansville, IN, p. A138

VOZOS, Frank J., FACS, Executive Director, Monmouth Medical Center, Long Branch, NJ, p. A271

VREELAND, James C., FACHE, President and Chief Executive Officer, UPMC Bedford Memorial, Everett, PA, p. A352

VYVERBERG, Robert W., Ed.D., Director, George A. Zeller Mental Health Center, Peoria, IL, p. A131

W

WAACK, Ronald L., President, Masonic Geriatric Healthcare Center, Wallingford, CT, p. A77

WADE, Dennis, Administrator, Green Oaks Hospital, Dallas, TX, p. A400

WADE, Linda, Administrator and Director of Operations, HEALTHSOUTH Rehabilitation Hospital of Montgomery, Montgomery, AL, p. A17

WAGES, N. Gary, Senior Executive Officer, Saint Luke's Northland Hospital, Kansas City, MO, p. A243

WAGGENER, Rob S., Chief Executive Officer, Charter Lakeside Behavioral Health System, Memphis, TN, p. A387

WAGGONER, Ronald D., Administrator and Chief Executive Officer, Brodstone Memorial Hospital, Superior, NE, p. A262

WAGNER, Arthur, Chief Operating Officer, North Central Bronx Hospital, New York, NY, p. A292

WAGNER, David S., Vice President and Administrator, Christus Spohn Hospital Beeville, Beeville, TX, p. A395

WAGNER, Henry C., President, Jewish Hospital HealthCare Services, Louisville, KY, p. B107

WAHLMEIER, James, Administrator, Phillips County Hospital, Phillipsburg, KS, p. A163

WAHPEPAH, Frank H., M.P.H., Administrator, Creek Nation Community Hospital, Okemah, OK, p. A337

WAITE, Nancy A., Administrator and Deputy Commander, U. S. Air Force Hospital, Davis–Monthan AFB, AZ, p. A22

WAITE, Marguerite, President and Chief Executive Officer, St. Mary's Hospital, Waterbury, CT, p. A77

WAITE III, Ralph J., Chief Executive Officer, BHC Meadow Wood Hospital, Baton Rouge, LA, p. A177

WAKEFIELD Jr., Robert D., Chief Executive Officer, Lemuel Shattuck Hospital, Boston, MA, p. A198

WAKEMAN, Daniel, Chief Executive Officer, Chippewa County War Memorial Hospital, Sault Ste. Marie, MI, p. A217

WALB, William R., President and Chief Executive Officer, Hanover Hospital, Hanover, PA, p. A353

WALDBILLIG, Kurt, Chief Executive Officer, Richardton Health Center, Richardton, ND, p. A315

WALDROUP, Gerald E., Administrator, Lawrence County Memorial Hospital, Lawrenceville, IL, p. A128

WALK, Rex D., Chief Executive Officer, Memorial Health Center, Sidney, NE, p. A262

WALKER, Benjamin H., Facility Administrator, Georgia Regional Hospital at Augusta, Augusta, GA, p. A101

WALKER, Bethy W., Administrator, Doctors' Hospital of Opelousas, Opelousas, LA, p. A184

WALKER, Betty, Administrator, Vencor Hospital–Sycamore, Sycamore, IL, p. A134

WALKER, G. Curtis, R.N., Administrator, B.J. Workman Memorial Hospital, Woodruff, SC, p. A375

WALKER, Gale, Administrator, Avera St. Benedict Health Center, Parkston, SD, p. A378

WALKER, Gregory J., Chief Executive Officer, Wentworth–Douglass Hospital, Dover, NH, p. A265

WALKER, Henry G., President and Chief Executive Officer, Sisters of Providence Health System, Seattle, WA, p. B138

WALKER, James R., FACHE, President and Chief Executive Officer, North Arundel Hospital, Glen Burnie, MD, p. A194

WALKER, Jerry, Administrator, Leahi Hospital, Honolulu, HI, p. A112

WALKER, John E., Chief Executive Officer, Riverside Medical Center, Franklinton, LA, p. A179

WALKER, Larry D., Chief Executive Officer, Delta Medical Center, Memphis, TN, p. A387

WALKER, Melvin E., Administrator, Baptist Memorial Hospital–Desoto, Southaven, MS, p. A237

WALKER, Polly J., R.N., Interim Chief Executive Officer, Sutter Solano Medical Center, Vallejo, CA, p. A66

WALKER, Robert J., President, Castle Medical Center, Kailua, HI, p. A113

WALKER, Ronnie D., President, Southwestern Memorial Hospital, Weatherford, OK, p. A341

WALKLEY Jr., Philip H., Chief Executive Officer, Regional Medical Center of Northeast Arkansas, Jonesboro, AR, p. A32

WALL, Daniel J., President and Chief Executive Officer, Emma Pendleton Bradley Hospital, East Providence, RI, p. A368

WALL, Eldon A., Administrator, Memorial Hospital, Aurora, NE, p. A256

WALL, Joseph C., Administrator, Kona Community Hospital, Kealakekua, HI, p. A113

WALLACE, Archie T., Chief Executive Officer, Thomas B. Finan Center, Cumberland, MD, p. A194

WALLACE, Charlene, Interim President, Westbrook Community Hospital, Westbrook, ME, p. A190

WALLACE, David T., President and Chief Executive Officer, Brown County General Hospital, Georgetown, OH, p. A324

WALLACE, James D., Executive Director, Choctaw Health Center, Philadelphia, MS, p. A236

WALLACE, Lloyd E., President and Chief Executive Officer, Valdese General Hospital, Valdese, NC, p. A311

WALLACE, Mark A., Executive Director and Chief Executive Officer, Texas Children's Hospital, Houston, TX, p. A409

WALLACE, Michael S., Chief Executive Officer, Lucas County Health Center, Chariton, IA, p. A147

WALLACE, Patrick L., Administrator, East Texas Medical Center Athens, Athens, TX, p. A393

WALLACE, Richard B., Chief Executive Officer, Rabun County Memorial Hospital, Clayton, GA, p. A102

WALLACE, Rick, FACHE
Chief Executive Officer and Administrator, Cheatham Medical Center, Ashland City, TN, p. A381
Chief Executive Officer and Administrator, Horizon Medical Center, Dickson, TN, p. A383

WALLACE, Samuel T., President, Iowa Health System, Des Moines, IA, p. B106

WALLACE, Thomas M., President and Chief Executive Officer, Granada Hills Community Hospital, Los Angeles, CA, p. A48

WALLER, Richard E., M.D., Interim Administrator, Quitman County Hospital and Nursing Home, Marks, MS, p. A235

WALLING, John R.
President and Chief Executive Officer, Lafayette Home Hospital, Lafayette, IN, p. A141
President and Chief Executive Officer, St. Elizabeth Medical Center, Lafayette, IN, p. A141

WALLIS, Larry D.
President and Chief Executive Officer, Cox Health System, Springfield, MO, p. B86
President and Chief Executive Officer, Cox Medical Center, Springfield, MO, p. A249

WALLMAN, Gerald H., Administrator, Doctors Hospital of West Covina, West Covina, CA, p. A67

WALMSLEY III, George J., President and Chief Executive Officer, North Philadelphia Health System, Philadelphia, PA, p. A359

WALSH, Daniel P., President and Chief Executive Officer, Winthrop–University Hospital, Mineola, NY, p. A288

WALSH, Mary Beth, M.D., Chief Executive Officer, Burke Rehabilitation Hospital, White Plains, NY, p. A300

WALSH, Maura, Chief Executive Officer, Rosewood Medical Center, Houston, TX, p. A409

WALSH, Raoul, Chief Executive Officer, Greene County Memorial Hospital, Waynesburg, PA, p. A365

WALSH, William, Executive Director, Coney Island Hospital, New York, NY, p. A290

WALTER, William R., Chief Executive Officer, Maury Regional Hospital, Columbia, TN, p. A382

WALTERS, Farah M.
President and Chief Executive Officer, University Hospitals Health System, Cleveland, OH, p. B151
President and Chief Executive Officer, University Hospitals of Cleveland, Cleveland, OH, p. A321

WALTERS, H. Patrick, Administrator, Inova Alexandria Hospital, Alexandria, VA, p. A433

WALTERS, Kevin, Administrator, Southeast Baptist Hospital, San Antonio, TX, p. A420

WALTERS, Merrily, Administrator, East Houston Regional Medical Center, Houston, TX, p. A407

WALTERS, Robert M., Administrator, St. Luke's Hospital, Jacksonville, FL, p. A87

WALTHER, Thomas G., Administrator, Normandy Community Hospital, Saint Louis, MO, p. A248

WALTON, Carlyle L. E., President, Takoma Adventist Hospital, Greeneville, TN, p. A384

WALTON, Michael W., Director, Veterans Affairs Medical Center, Chillicothe, OH, p. A319

WALTZ, Ronald D., Chief Executive Officer, Memorial Health Care Systems, Seward, NE, p. A261

WALZ, George, CHE, Chief Executive Officer, Breckinridge Memorial Hospital, Hardinsburg, KY, p. A169

WALZ, Patrick T.
Chief Executive Officer, Community Hospital Medical Center, Phoenix, AZ, p. A24
Chief Executive Officer, Mesa General Hospital Medical Center, Mesa, AZ, p. A23

WAMPLER, Robert B., CPA, Chief Executive Officer, Lakeway Regional Hospital, Morristown, TN, p. A388

WARD, Sandy, Administrator, Johnson County Healthcare Center, Buffalo, WY, p. A466

WARDELL, Patrick R., President and Chief Executive Officer, St. Joseph's Hospital and Medical Center, Paterson, NJ, p. A273

WARDELL, Scott F., Administrator, U. S. Air Force Hospital, Fairchild AFB, WA, p. A444

WARDEN, Gail L., President and Chief Executive Officer, Henry Ford Health System, Detroit, MI, p. B103

WARDEN, Richard
Executive Director, Devereux Foundation–French Center, Devon, PA, p. A350
Executive Director, Devereux Mapleton Psychiatric Institute–Mapleton Center, Malvern, PA, p. A355

WARMAN Jr., Harold C., President and Chief Executive Officer, Highlands Regional Medical Center, Prestonsburg, KY, p. A174

WARNER, Donald L., Chief Executive Officer, Arborview Hospital, Warren, MI, p. A218

WARNER Jr., Gerard H., Chief Executive Officer, Mid–Valley Hospital, Peckville, PA, p. A358

WARREN, James B., Chief Executive Officer, Dallas Southwest Medical Center, Dallas, TX, p. A400

WARREN, Larry, Executive Director, University of Michigan Hospitals and Health Centers, Ann Arbor, MI, p. A206

WARREN, Richard M., Chief Executive Officer, El Camino Hospital, Mountain View, CA, p. A53

WARREN, Roger D., M.D., Administrator, Hanover Hospital, Hanover, KS, p. A158

WASHBURN, Melinda, Chief Operating Officer, Saint Joseph Hospital East, Lexington, KY, p. A171

WASSERMAN, Joseph A., President and Chief Executive Officer, Lakeland Medical Center–St. Joseph, Saint Joseph, MI, p. A217

WASSERMAN, Neil H., Chief Executive Officer and Chief Financial Officer, Hawthorn Center, Northville, MI, p. A215

WASSON, Ted D., President and Chief Executive Officer, William Beaumont Hospital Corporation, Royal Oak, MI, p. B156

WATERS, Michael C., FACHE, President, Hendrick Health System, Abilene, TX, p. A392

WATERS, W. Charles, President and Chief Executive Officer, Newton Medical Center, Newton, KS, p. A162

WATERSTON, Judith C., President and Chief Executive Officer, Schwab Rehabilitation Hospital and Care Network, Chicago, IL, p. A122

WATFORD, Rodney C., Administrator, Early Memorial Hospital, Blakely, GA, p. A101

WATHEN, James A., Chief Executive Officer, Southern Coos General Hospital, Bandon, OR, p. A342

WATKINS, John R., Chief Executive Officer, Vencor Hospital – New Orleans, New Orleans, LA, p. A184

WATSON, Duffy, President and Chief Executive Officer, Henry Mayo Newhall Memorial Hospital, Valencia, CA, p. A65

WATSON, Gary L., FACHE, Senior Executive Officer, Crittenton, Kansas City, MO, p. A243

WATSON, James B., Chief Executive Officer, Ira Davenport Memorial Hospital, Bath, NY, p. A282

WATSON, James R., Administrator, Ashland Community Hospital, Ashland, OR, p. A342

WATSON, T. Gregg
Administrator, Sheboygan Memorial Medical Center, Sheboygan, WI, p. A463
Administrator, Valley View Medical Center, Plymouth, WI, p. A462

WATSON, Virgil, Administrator, Sumner County Hospital District One, Caldwell, KS, p. A156

WATTERS, Steve, Chief Executive Officer, Mendota Mental Health Institute, Madison, WI, p. A459

WATTS Jr., Claude D., President and Chief Executive Officer, East Orange General Hospital, East Orange, NJ, p. A268

WAUGH, Patrick D., Chief Executive Officer, St. Luke's Behavioral Health Center, Phoenix, AZ, p. A25

WEADICK, James F., Administrator and Chief Executive Officer, Newton General Hospital, Covington, GA, p. A103

WEATHERLY, Jesse O., President, Cullman Regional Medical Center, Cullman, AL, p. A13

WEAVER, Douglas K., Chief Executive Officer, Memorial Hospital, Frederick, OK, p. A335

WEAVER, Thomas H., FACHE, Director, Veterans Affairs Medical Center, Bay Pines, FL, p. A81

WEAVER, William, Administrator, Bradford Health Services at Oak Mountain, Pelham, AL, p. A17

WEBB, Ronald W., President, Saint Eugene Medical Center, Dillon, SC, p. A372

WEBB Jr., Charles L., Administrator, Charter louisville Behavioral Health System, Louisville, KY, p. A172

WEBER, Mark, FACHE, President, St. John's Mercy Medical Center, Saint Louis, MO, p. A248

WEBER, Peter M., President and Chief Executive Officer, Huguley Memorial Medical Center, Burleson, TX, p. A396

WEBER, Wilson J.
Chief Executive Officer, Mid–Jefferson Hospital, Nederland, TX, p. A416
Chief Executive Officer, Park Place Medical Center, Port Arthur, TX, p. A418

WEBER Jr., Everett P., President and Chief Executive Officer, Grady Memorial Hospital, Delaware, OH, p. A323

WEBSTER, Jeffrey, Chief Executive Officer, Christus St. Mary Hospital, Port Arthur, TX, p. A418

WEBSTER, Mark, President, Troy Community Hospital, Troy, PA, p. A364

WEBSTER, William W., Interim President and Chief Executive Officer, St. Vincent Hospital, Santa Fe, NM, p. A280

WEE, Donald J., Executive Director, Pioneer Memorial Hospital, Prineville, OR, p. A345

WEEKS, Donnie J., President and Chief Executive Officer, Kershaw County Medical Center, Camden, SC, p. A370

WEEKS, Steven Douglas
Senior Vice President and Administrator, Baptist Medical Center, Little Rock, AR, p. A32
Senior Vice President and Administrator, Baptist Rehabilitation Institute, Little Rock, AR, p. A32

WEGENER, Kathleen S., Chief Executive Officer, Kaiser Sunnyside Medical Center, Clackamas, OR, p. A342

WEIGHTMAN, George, Commander, McDonald Army Community Hospital, Newport News, VA, p. A437

WEILAND, Edmond L., President and Chief Executive Officer, Prairie Lakes Hospital and Care Center, Watertown, SD, p. A379

WEILER, Joseph W., President, McKenzie Memorial Hospital, Sandusky, MI, p. A217

WEINBAUM, Barry G., Chief Executive Officer, Alvarado Hospital Medical Center, San Diego, CA, p. A59

WEINBERG, Arnold N., M.D., Director, M. I. T. Medical Department, Cambridge, MA, p. A199

WEINBERG, Barth A., Vice President, Inpatient Rehabilitation, Frazier Rehabilitation Center, Louisville, KY, p. A172

WEINER, Jack, President and Chief Executive Officer, St. Joseph's Mercy Hospitals and Health Services, Clinton Township, MI, p. A208

WEIR, Silas M., Chief Executive Officer, Centura Special Care Hospital, Denver, CO, p. A69

WEISS, Thomas M., Chief Executive Officer, Crestwood Medical Center, Huntsville, AL, p. A15

WELBORN, Bobby, Administrator, Perry County General Hospital, Richton, MS, p. A237

WELCH, Bill, Administrator, Jefferson Community Health Center, Fairbury, NE, p. A257

WELCH, Nelda K., Administrator, East Texas Medical Center Crockett, Crockett, TX, p. A399

WELDING, Theodore, Chief Executive Officer, Vencor Hospital–Coral Gables, Coral Gables, FL, p. A83

WELDON, Jeanette, Acting President and Chief Executive Officer, Windham Community Memorial Hospital, Willimantic, CT, p. A77

WELLINGER, M. Rosita, President and Chief Executive Officer, St. Francis Health System, Pittsburgh, PA, p. B141

WELLMAN, Roxann A., Chief Executive Officer, Minnewaska District Hospital, Starbuck, MN, p. A229

WELLS, Mary Ellen, Administrator, Buffalo Hospital, Buffalo, MN, p. A221

WELLS, Scott, Chief Executive Officer, Franklin General Hospital, Hampton, IA, p. A150

WELSH, John H., Chief Executive Officer, Rumford Community Hospital, Rumford, ME, p. A189

WELSH Jr., J. L., President and Chief Executive Officer, Southeastern Regional Medical Center, Lumberton, NC, p. A308

WENDLING, Jeffrey T., President and Chief Executive Officer, Northern Michigan Hospital, Petoskey, MI, p. A215

WENGERD, Norman W., Interim President and Chief Executive Officer, Mercy Medical Center, Canton, OH, p. A318

WENTE, James W., CHE, Administrator, Southeast Missouri Hospital, Cape Girardeau, MO, p. A240

WENTWORTH, Philip M., FACHE, Senior Vice President and Executive Director, Presbyterian Hospital of Plano, Plano, TX, p. A418

WENTZ, Robert J., President and Chief Executive Officer, Oroville Hospital, Oroville, CA, p. A55

WERBY, Marcia, Administrator, Rockland Children's Psychiatric Center, Orangeburg, NY, p. A295

WERNER, Daniel J., Administrator, Owatonna Hospital, Owatonna, MN, p. A226

WERNER, Thomas J., Administrator, Richland Hospital, Richland Center, WI, p. A463

WERNER, Thomas L., President, Florida Hospital, Orlando, FL, p. A91

WERNER, Todd S., Senior Executive Officer, La Grange Memorial Hospital, La Grange, IL, p. A128

WERNICK, Joel, President and Chief Executive Officer, Phoebe Putney Memorial Hospital, Albany, GA, p. A99

WERTZ, Randy S., Administrator, Golden Valley Memorial Hospital, Clinton, MO, p. A240

WESOLOWSKI, Jaime A., Chief Executive Officer, Oak Hill Hospital, Spring Hill, FL, p. A95

WESP, James H., Administrator, Vencor Hospital–Louisville, Louisville, KY, p. A172

WESSNER, David, President and Chief Executive Officer, HealthSystem Minnesota, Saint Louis Park, MN, p. B103

WEST, Daniel R., Administrator, Vencor Hospital–Milwaukee, Greenfield, WI, p. A458

WEST, John, Administrator, Buchanan General Hospital, Grundy, VA, p. A435

WEST, R. Christopher
President, Franciscan Hospital–Mount Airy Campus, Cincinnati, OH, p. A319
President, Franciscan Hospital–Western Hills Campus, Cincinnati, OH, p. A319

WEST, Richard L., President and Chief Executive Officer, Grant Hospital, Chicago, IL, p. A120

WEST, Steven J., Chief Executive Officer, Blackford County Hospital, Hartford City, IN, p. A139

WESTFALL, Bernard G., President and Chief Executive Officer, West Virginia United Health System, Fairmont, WV, p. B156

WESTIN, Charles A., FACHE, Administrator, Republic County Hospital, Belleville, KS, p. A156

WESTON–HALL, Patricia, Executive Director, Glenbeigh Health Sources, Rock Creek, OH, p. A328

WETTA Jr., Daniel J., Chief Executive Officer, John Randolph Medical Center, Hopewell, VA, p. A435

WHALEN, David, Chief Executive Officer, Twin Cities Hospital, Niceville, FL, p. A91

WHATLEY, David, Director, Veterans Affairs Medical Center, Houston, TX, p. A410

WHATLEY, Gary Lex
President and Chief Executive Officer, Memorial Health System of East Texas, Lufkin, TX, p. B115
President and Chief Executive Officer, Memorial Medical Center of East Texas, Lufkin, TX, p. A414

WHEAT, Richard L., Chief Financial Officer, Clearwater Valley Hospital and Clinics, Orofino, ID, p. A116

WHEELER, Michael K., Director, Veterans Affairs Medical Center, Battle Creek, MI, p. A207

WHEELER, Michael D., MSC, Deputy Commander, Administration, Evans U. S. Army Community Hospital, Fort Carson, CO, p. A70

WHEELER Sr., David, Chief Executive Officer, U. S. Naval Hospital, Agana, GU, p. A469

WHEELOCK, Major W., President, Crotched Mountain Rehabilitation Center, Greenfield, NH, p. A265

WHELAN, Sharon, Administrator, River Falls Area Hospital, River Falls, WI, p. A463

WHELAN–WILLIAMS, Sue, Site Administrator, South Seminole Hospital, Longwood, FL, p. A88

WHIPKEY, Neil, Administrator, Shands at Lake Shore, Lake City, FL, p. A87

WHIPPLE, Ingrid L.
Chief Executive Officer, BHC Heritage Oaks Hospital, Sacramento, CA, p. A57
Chief Executive Officer, BHC Sierra Vista Hospital, Sacramento, CA, p. A58

WHITAKER, E. Berton, President and Chief Executive Officer, Southeast Georgia Regional Medical Center, Brunswick, GA, p. A102

WHITAKER, James B., President, Circles of Care, Melbourne, FL, p. A89

WHITAKER Sr., Harold H., Administrator, Webster Health Services, Eupora, MS, p. A233

WHITBY, Lea, President, Calumet Medical Center, Chilton, WI, p. A457

WHITCOMB, John R., Interim Senior Vice President, Harper Hospital, Detroit, MI, p. A208

WHITE, Alvin C., President and Chief Executive Officer, Rome Memorial Hospital, Rome, NY, p. A297

WHITE, Dale A., Chief Executive Officer, Horton Health Foundation, Horton, KS, p. A159

WHITE, Daniel C., Chief Executive Officer, District Memorial Hospital, Andrews, NC, p. A302

WHITE, Daryl Sue, Chief Executive Officer and Managing Director, River Oaks Hospital, New Orleans, LA, p. A184

WHITE, Doug, Chief Executive Officer, Grand Strand Regional Medical Center, Myrtle Beach, SC, p. A374

WHITE, Dudley R., Administrator, Anson General Hospital, Anson, TX, p. A393

WHITE, Jeffrey L., Chief Executive Officer, Low Country General Hospital, Ridgeland, SC, p. A374

WHITE, John B., President and Chief Executive Officer, Lima Memorial Hospital, Lima, OH, p. A325

WHITE, John R., Administrator, Newport Community Hospital, Newport, WA, p. A445

WHITE, Kevin A., Administrator, Medicine Lodge Memorial Hospital, Medicine Lodge, KS, p. A161

WHITE, Mary M., President and Chief Executive Officer, Swedish Medical Center, Englewood, CO, p. A70

WHITE, Stephani, Vice President and Site Administrator, Legacy Emanuel Hospital and Health Center, Portland, OR, p. A344

WHITE, Terry R., President and Chief Executive Officer, MetroHealth Medical Center, Cleveland, OH, p. A321

WHITE, Thomas, President and Chief Executive Officer, Jameson Hospital, New Castle, PA, p. A357

WHITE, Thomas M., President, Empire Health Services, Spokane, WA, p. B95

WHITE Jr., Lawrence L., President, St. Patrick Hospital, Missoula, MT, p. A254

WHITEHORN, Jeffrey, Chief Executive Officer, Southern Hills Medical Center, Nashville, TN, p. A388

WHITEHOUSE, Edward J., Chief Executive Office, Atlantic Shores Hospital, Fort Lauderdale, FL, p. A84

WHITELEY, Earl S., CHE, Chief Executive Officer, Medical Center Enterprise, Enterprise, AL, p. A14

WHITFIELD, Gary R., Director, Ioannis A. Lougaris Veterans Affairs Medical Center, Reno, NV, p. A264

WHITFIELD Jr., Charles H., President and Chief Executive Officer, Laughlin Memorial Hospital, Greeneville, TN, p. A383

WHITLOCK, Jim, Administrator, Bradley Memorial Hospital, Cleveland, TN, p. A382

WHITMIRE, James C., CHE, Administrator, East Texas Medical Center Trinity, Trinity, TX, p. A424

WHITNEY, Harry E., President and Chief Executive Officer, Santa Marta Hospital, Los Angeles, CA, p. A50

WHITTINGTON, Terry G., Chief Executive Officer and Administrator, Bogalusa Community Medical Center, Bogalusa, LA, p. A178

WICK, Timothy J., Chief Executive Officer, Burnett Medical Center, Grantsburg, WI, p. A458

WIEBE, John F., Chief Executive Officer, Clay County Hospital, Clay Center, KS, p. A157

WIENER, Mark S., Administrator, St. Luke's Medical Center, Milwaukee, WI, p. A461

WIERCINSKI, John, President and Chief Executive Officer, Shamokin Area Community Hospital, Coal Township, PA, p. A350

WIESNER, Gerald, Vice President and Chief Operating Officer, Miami County Medical Center, Paola, KS, p. A163

WIGGINS, Louise, Chief Executive Officer and Administrator, Summit Hospital of Northwest Louisiana, Bossier City, LA, p. A178

WIGGINS, Stephen P., Director, Western State Hospital, Hopkinsville, KY, p. A170

WILBANKS, John F., Senior Vice President and Administrator, Baptist Medical Center, Jacksonville, FL, p. A86

WILCOX, Sallye M., R.N., Executive Director, Mississippi Hospital Restorative Care, Jackson, MS, p. A234

WILCZEK, Joseph W.
President and Chief Executive Officer, St. Clare Hospital, Lakewood, WA, p. A445
President and Chief Executive Officer, St. Francis Hospital, Federal Way, WA, p. A444
President and Chief Executive Officer, St. Joseph Medical Center, Tacoma, WA, p. A448

WILES, Patrick J.
President and Chief Executive Officer, Sisters of Charity Hospital of Buffalo, Buffalo, NY, p. A283
President and Chief Executive Officer, St. Joseph Hospital, Cheektowaga, NY, p. A284

WILES, Paul M., President and Chief Executive Officer, Novant Health, Winston Salem, NC, p. B122

WILEY, Donald J., Senior Vice President and Chief Operating Officer, St. Joseph's Medical Center, Stockton, CA, p. A64

WILEY, Stan, Administrator, Crane Memorial Hospital, Crane, TX, p. A399

WILFORD, Dan S., President and Chief Executive Officer, Memorial Hermann Healthcare System, Houston, TX, p. B115

WILFORD, Ned B., President and Chief Executive Officer, Hamilton Medical Center, Dalton, GA, p. A103

WILHELM, Mary Eileen, President and Chief Executive Officer, Mercy Medical, Daphne, AL, p. A13

WILHELMSEN Jr., Thomas E., President and Chief Executive Officer, Southern New Hampshire Medical Center, Nashua, NH, p. A266

WILHOIT, Ellen, Administrator, Fort Sanders–Sevier Medical Center, Sevierville, TN, p. A390

WILK, Leonard E., Administrator, Sinai Samaritan Medical Center, Milwaukee, WI, p. A461

WILKENS, Daryl J., Administrator, Cavalier County Memorial Hospital, Langdon, ND, p. A315

WILKERSON, Donald H., Chief Executive Officer, North Austin Medical Center, Austin, TX, p. A394

WILKERSON, Larry D., Chief Executive Officer, Augusta Medical Complex, Augusta, KS, p. A156

WILKINS, Patricia S., Administrator, North Caddo Medical Center, Vivian, LA, p. A186

WILKINS, William W., President and Chief Executive Officer, OhioHealth, Columbus, OH, p. B122

WILKINSON, Gary L., Director, Veterans Affairs Medical Center, Iowa City, IA, p. A151

WILKINSON, Steven D., President and Chief Executive Officer, Menorah Medical Center, Overland Park, KS, p. A163

WILL, Daniel, Administrator, Zumbrota Health Care, Zumbrota, MN, p. A230

WILLARD, Larry, Administrator, Hocking Valley Community Hospital, Logan, OH, p. A325

WILLAUER, Glenn R., Administrator, U. S. Air Force Hospital, Hampton, VA, p. A435

WILLCOXON, Phil, Administrator, Freeman Neosho Hospital, Neosho, MO, p. A245

WILLERT, Todd, Administrator, Story County Hospital and Long Term Care Facility, Nevada, IA, p. A152

WILLERT, St. Joan
President and Chief Executive Officer, Carondelet St. Joseph's Hospital, Tucson, AZ, p. A27
President and Chief Executive Officer, Carondelet St. Mary's Hospital, Tucson, AZ, p. A27

WILLETT, Allan Brock, M.D., Director, Colorado Mental Health Institute at Fort Logan, Denver, CO, p. A69

WILLETT, Richard, Chief Executive Officer, Redington–Fairview General Hospital, Skowhegan, ME, p. A190

WILLHELM, Judene, Administrator, Memorial Hospital, Kermit, TX, p. A411

WILLIAMS, Cindy, FACHE, Administrator, Carraway Methodist Medical Center, Birmingham, AL, p. A12

WILLIAMS, David R., Chief Executive Officer, Montgomery Regional Hospital, Blacksburg, VA, p. A433

WILLIAMS, Denise R., President and Chief Executive Officer, Memorial Hospital of Salem County, Salem, NJ, p. A274

WILLIAMS, Gerald L., Director and Chief Executive Officer, James E. Van Zandt Veterans Affairs Medical Center, Altoona, PA, p. A347

WILLIAMS, Miriam K., Administrator, Charter Hospital of Pasco, Lutz, FL, p. A88

WILLIAMS, Oreta, Administrator, Jeff Davis Hospital, Hazlehurst, GA, p. A106

WILLIAMS, R. D., Administrator and Chief Executive Officer, Ashe Memorial Hospital, Jefferson, NC, p. A307

WILLIAMS, Richard C., President and Chief Executive Officer, St. Mary's Health System, Knoxville, TN, p. A385

WILLIAMS, Robert B.
Administrator, Florida State Hospital, Chattahoochee, FL, p. A82
Administrator, Shands at AGH, Gainesville, FL, p. A85

WILLIAMS, Robert D., Administrator, Mercy Special Care Hospital, Nanticoke, PA, p. A356

WILLIAMS, Roby D., Administrator, Hardin County General Hospital, Rosiclare, IL, p. A133

WILLIAMS, Roger, Chief Executive Officer, Carroll County Hospital, Carrollton, KY, p. A168

WILLIAMS, Scott, Chief Executive Officer, Sycamore Shoals Hospital, Elizabethton, TN, p. A383

WILLIAMS, Stephen A.
President, Norton Healthcare, Louisville, KY, p. B121
President and Chief Executive Officer, Norton Healthcare Pavilion, Louisville, KY, p. A172

WILLIAMS, Stuart W., Interim Chief Executive Officer, Madison County Hospital, London, OH, p. A325

WILLIAMS, Timothy B., Director, Veterans Affairs Puget Sound Health Care System, Seattle, WA, p. A447

WILLIAMS, Trude, R.N., Administrator, Pacifica Hospital of the Valley, Los Angeles, CA, p. A50

WILLIAMS III, Raymond, President and Chief Executive Officer, Sumner Regional Medical Center, Wellington, KS, p. A165

WILLIAMS Jr., Elton L., CPA, President, Lake Charles Memorial Hospital, Lake Charles, LA, p. A181

WILLIS, Dell, Administrator, Dr. Dan C. Trigg Memorial Hospital, Tucumcari, NM, p. A280

WILLIS, Yvonne, Administrator, Bowdon Area Hospital, Bowdon, GA, p. A101

WILLMON, Gary R., Administrator, Grafton City Hospital, Grafton, WV, p. A451

WILLMORE, Perry, Vice President Operations, Baptist Medical Center, San Antonio, TX, p. A419

WILLS, Andrew, Chief Executive Officer, Estes Park Medical Center, Estes Park, CO, p. A70

WILMOT, Helen
Administrator, Kaiser Foundation Hospital, Redwood City, CA, p. A57
Administrator, Kaiser Foundation Hospital, Santa Clara, CA, p. A62

WILSON, Asa B., Administrator, Alegent Health–Memorial Hospital, Schuyler, NE, p. A261

WILSON, Bill D., Administrator, Wayne County Hospital, Corydon, IA, p. A147

WILSON, Carole, Administrator, Recovery Inn of Menlo Park, Menlo Park, CA, p. A52

WILSON, Daniel, M.D., Administrator, Meadowbrook Hospital, Gardner, KS, p. A158

WILSON, David C.
Chief Executive Officer, Harton Regional Medical Center, Tullahoma, TN, p. A390
Chief Executive Officer, Medical Center of Manchester, Manchester, TN, p. A386

WILSON, Hugh D., Chief Executive Officer, Doctors Hospital, Columbus, GA, p. A103

WILSON, James M., Regional Administrator, St. John's Episcopal Hospital–Smithtown, Smithtown, NY, p. A298

WILSON, Jim, President and Chief Executive Officer, Susan B. Allen Memorial Hospital, El Dorado, KS, p. A157

WILSON, Joanne, Chief Executive Officer, Hampton Hospital, Westampton Township, NJ, p. A276

WILSON, John A., President and Chief Executive Officer, The Children's Institute of Pittsburgh, Pittsburgh, PA, p. A361

WILSON, John M.
President, Bay Harbor Hospital, Los Angeles, CA, p. A48
President and Chief Executive Officer, San Pedro Peninsula Hospital, Los Angeles, CA, p. A50

WILSON, L. Steven, Administrator, Dixie Regional Medical Center, Saint George, UT, p. A429

WILSON, Mark D., Administrator, Barron Medical Center–Mayo Health System, Barron, WI, p. A456

WILSON, Paul J., Administrator, Los Alamos Medical Center, Los Alamos, NM, p. A279

WILSON, Ralph J., Administrator, Red Bay Hospital, Red Bay, AL, p. A18

WILSON, William G., President and Chief Executive Officer, Jackson County Memorial Hospital, Altus, OK, p. A337

WILSON Jr., V. Otis, President, Grace Hospital, Morganton, NC, p. A309

WINDER, Todd, Administrator, Oneida County Hospital, Malad City, ID, p. A115

WINFREE, Wayne, Chief Executive Officer, Frank T. Rutherford Memorial Hospital, Carthage, TN, p. A381

WINGATE–JONES, Phyllis, President, Prince George's Hospital Center, Cheverly, MD, p. A193

WINKLER, Gordon W., Administrator, Ringgold County Hospital, Mount Ayr, IA, p. A152

WINN, George, Administrator, Sanpete Valley Hospital, Mount Pleasant, UT, p. A428

WINN, Grant M., President, Community Medical Center, Missoula, MT, p. A253

WINN, Roger P., Chief Executive Officer, Miners Hospital Northern Cambria, Spangler, PA, p. A364

WINTER, Jeffrey P., Chief Executive Officer, Riverside Community Hospital, Riverside, CA, p. A57

WINTER, William E., Administrative Director, Silverton Hospital, Silverton, OR, p. A346

WINTHROP, Michael K., President, Bellevue Hospital, Bellevue, OH, p. A318

WISBY, Diane, President and Chief Executive Officer, Goleta Valley Cottage Hospital, Santa Barbara, CA, p. A62

WISE, Brenda, Administrator, Okolona Community Hospital, Okolona, MS, p. A236

WISE, Franklin E., Administrator, Fulton County Hospital, Salem, AR, p. A34

WISE, Robert P., President and Chief Executive Officer, Hunterdon Medical Center, Flemington, NJ, p. A270

WISEMAN, Richard J., Ph.D., Superintendent, Riverview Hospital for Children, Middletown, CT, p. A75

WISEMAN, John G., Administrator, U. S. Air Force Hospital, Abilene, TX, p. A392

WISSINK, Gerald L., President and Chief Executive Officer, Baptist Hospitals and Health Systems, Inc., Phoenix, AZ, p. B64

WISSLER, James, President and Chief Executive Officer, Nicholas H. Noyes Memorial Hospital, Dansville, NY, p. A284

WISSMAN, William W., Interim Executive Director, Dunn Memorial Hospital, Bedford, IN, p. A136

WITHERS, Ivan, Chief Executive Officer, Pocahontas Memorial Hospital, Buckeye, WV, p. A450

WITT, Stephen, Chief Executive Officer, College Hospital, Cerritos, CA, p. A39

WITTEY, Charlotte, Chief Executive Officer, Mahnomen Health Center, Mahnomen, MN, p. A225

WOERNER, Steven
Chief Executive Officer, Corpus Christi Medical Center, Corpus Christi, TX, p. A398
Chief Executive Officer, Corpus Christi Medical Center Bay Area, Corpus Christi, TX, p. A398

WOLF, Chris, Chief Executive Officer, Chesterfield General Hospital, Cheraw, SC, p. A371

WOLF, Edward H., Chief Executive Officer, Lakeview Medical Center, Rice Lake, WI, p. A463

WOLF, James N., Chief Executive Officer, District One Hospital, Faribault, MN, p. A222

WOLF, Jonathan, Chief Executive Officer, Charter Behavioral Health System at Cove Forge, Williamsburg, PA, p. A366

WOLF, Laura J., President, Franciscan Sisters of Christian Charity HealthCare Ministry, Inc, Manitowoc, WI, p. B97

WOLFE, Philip R., Chief Executive Officer, Enloe Medical Center, Chico, CA, p. A39

WOLFE, Stephen A., President and Chief Executive Officer, Indiana Hospital, Indiana, PA, p. A353

WOLFF, Ronald V., President and Chief Executive Officer, Bay Medical Center, Panama City, FL, p. A92

WOLFORD, Dennis A., FACHE, Administrator, Macon County General Hospital, Lafayette, TN, p. A386

WOLFRAM, Patricia L., R.N., Chief Executive Officer, San Clemente Hospital and Medical Center, San Clemente, CA, p. A58

WOLIN, Harry, Administrator and Chief Executive Officer, Mason District Hospital, Havana, IL, p. A126

WOLTER, Nicholas J., M.D., Chief Executive Officer, Deaconess Billings Clinic, Billings, MT, p. A251

WOLTERS, Erich J., President and Chief Executive Officer, Lockport Memorial Hospital, Lockport, NY, p. A287

WOOD, Gregory C., Chief Executive Officer, Scotland Memorial Hospital, Laurinburg, NC, p. A307

WOOD, James B., Chief Executive Officer, Fairview Park Hospital, Dublin, GA, p. A104

WOOD, James R., Chairman and Chief Executive Officer, Maryland General Hospital, Baltimore, MD, p. A192

WOOD, Kenneth R., Administrator, Johnson Regional Medical Center, Clarksville, AR, p. A29

WOOD, Kenneth W.
President and Chief Executive Officer, St. Francis Hospital, Evanston, IL, p. A125
Chief Executive Officer, Westlake Community Hospital, Melrose Park, IL, p. A129

WOOD, Michael B., M.D., President and Chief Executive Officer, Mayo Foundation, Rochester, MN, p. B114

WOOD, Peggy, Administrator, Horizon Specialty Hospital, San Antonio, TX, p. A420

WOOD, Reid M., Executive Director, San Juan Hospital, Monticello, UT, p. A428

WOOD, Tammy B., Chief Executive Officer, Charter Asheville Behavioral Health System, Asheville, NC, p. A302

WOODALL, Jay, Chief Executive Officer, Trinity Hospital, Erin, TN, p. A383

WOODALL, Jim S., Director, Caswell Center, Kinston, NC, p. A307

WOODRELL, Frederick, Director, University Hospitals and Clinics, University of Mississippi Medical Center, Jackson, MS, p. A234

WOODS, Daniel J., Chief Executive Officer, Sartori Memorial Hospital, Cedar Falls, IA, p. A146

WOODS, E. Anthony, President, Deaconess Hospital, Cincinnati, OH, p. A319

WOODS, Frederick L., USAF, Administrator, U. S. Air Force Hospital Dover, Dover, DE, p. A78

WOODSIDE, Jeffrey R., M.D., Executive Director, University of Tennessee Bowld Hospital, Memphis, TN, p. A388

WOODSON, Hank, Administrator, Plateau Medical Center, Oak Hill, WV, p. A453

WOODWARD, Barry W., Administrator, BHC Olympus View Hospital, Salt Lake City, UT, p. A429

WOODY, Fred, Administrator, Crosby Memorial Hospital, Picayune, MS, p. A236

WOOTEN, Richard L., President and Chief Executive Officer, Leesburg Regional Medical Center, Leesburg, FL, p. A88

WORDELMAN, Scott, President and Chief Executive Officer, Fairview Red Wing Hospital, Red Wing, MN, p. A227

WORKMAN, Dennis, M.D., Medical Director, Charter Behavioral Health System of Atlanta, Atlanta, GA, p. A99

WORKMAN, John R., Chief Executive Officer, Athens Regional Medical Center, Athens, TN, p. A381

WORLEY, Steve, President and Chief Executive Officer, Children's Hospital, New Orleans, LA, p. A183

WORRELL, James W., Chief Executive Officer, Richmond Eye and Ear Hospital, Richmond, VA, p. A440

WORRICK, Gerald M., President and Chief Executive Officer, Door County Memorial Hospital, Sturgeon Bay, WI, p. A464

WORSHAM, Sharon, Administrator, Charter Centennial Peaks Behavioral Health System, Louisville, CO, p. A72

WOZNIAK, Gregory T.
President and Chief Executive Officer, Nazareth Hospital, Philadelphia, PA, p. A359
President and Chief Executive Officer, St. Mary Medical Center, Langhorne, PA, p. A354

WRAALSTAD, Kimber, Chief Executive Officer, Presentation Medical Center, Rolla, ND, p. A315

WRAY, Christine R., Chief Executive Officer, St. Mary's Hospital, Leonardtown, MD, p. A195

WRIGHT, Betsy T., President and Chief Executive Officer, Woman's Christian Association Hospital, Jamestown, NY, p. A286

WRIGHT, Brenda, Acting Administrator, McLean County Health Center, Calhoun, KY, p. A168

WRIGHT, Charles T., Chief Executive, Southern Oregon Service Area, Providence Medford Medical Center, Medford, OR, p. A344

WRIGHT, Joe, Administrator, Ward Memorial Hospital, Monahans, TX, p. A415

WRIGHT, Rick, CPA, President and Chief Executive Officer, Keweenaw Memorial Medical Center, Laurium, MI, p. A213

WRIGHT, Robert N., President and Chief Operating Officer, Bay Medical Center, Bay City, MI, p. A207

WRIGHT, Roy W., President and Chief Executive Officer, Des Moines General Hospital, Des Moines, IA, p. A148

WRIGHT, Skip, Administrator, Vencor Hospital–Atlanta, Atlanta, GA, p. A100

WRIGHT, Susan L., Administrator, Greenbrier Hospital, Brooksville, FL, p. A82

WRIGHT, Margaret, President, Palos Community Hospital, Palos Heights, IL, p. A131

WRIGHT–GRIGGS, Stephanie, Chief Operating Officer, Provident Hospital of Cook County, Chicago, IL, p. A121

WUOTILA, Gail, Director Hospital Operations, Kaiser Foundation Hospital, South San Francisco, CA, p. A63

WYATT, Leslie G., Administrator, Children's Hospital, Richmond, VA, p. A439

WYNN, Chester A., President and Chief Executive Officer, Passavant Area Hospital, Jacksonville, IL, p. A127

WYSE, LaMar L., Chief Executive Officer, Bucyrus Community Hospital, Bucyrus, OH, p. A318

X

XINIS, James J., President and Chief Executive Officer, Calvert Memorial Hospital, Prince Frederick, MD, p. A195

Y

YAGER, Jolene, R.N., Administrator, Lincoln County Hospital, Lincoln, KS, p. A161

YANAI, Christopher, M.D., Warden and Chief Executive Officer, Oakwood Correctional Facility, Lima, OH, p. A325

YARBOROUGH, James, Chief Executive Officer, Alleghany Memorial Hospital, Sparta, NC, p. A311

YARBROUGH, David L., JD, Administrator, Chief Financial Officer and Director Patient Service, Trinity Hospital, Weaverville, CA, p. A67

YARBROUGH, Mary G., President and Chief Executive Officer, St. Joseph's Hospital and Medical Center, Phoenix, AZ, p. A25

YARNEL, Jeffrey, Chief Executive Officer, Warminster Hospital, Warminster, PA, p. A365

YCRE Jr., Louis R., FACHE, President and Chief Executive Officer, Pascack Valley Hospital, Westwood, NJ, p. A276

YEAGER, Clifford A., Chief Executive Officer, Winona Memorial Hospital, Indianapolis, IN, p. A140

YEARY, John, Administrator, Eastland Memorial Hospital, Eastland, TX, p. A402

YELLAN, Robert J., Senior Vice President, Huron Valley–Sinai Hospital, Commerce Township, MI, p. A208

YENAWINE, Kelly R., Administrator, Gibson General Hospital, Trenton, TN, p. A390

YIM, Herbert K., Administrator, Kohala Hospital, Kohala, HI, p. A113

YINGST, Thomas E., MSC, Administrator, U. S. Air Force Hospital, Edwards AFB, CA, p. A41

YOCHUM, Richard E., President, Pomona Valley Hospital Medical Center, Pomona, CA, p. A56

YORK, Betty, Executive Director, West Community Hospital, West, TX, p. A425

YORKE, Harvey M., President and Chief Executive Officer, Southwestern Vermont Medical Center, Bennington, VT, p. A431

YOSKO, Kathleen C., President and Chief Executive Officer, Marianjoy Rehabilitation Hospital and Clinics, Wheaton, IL, p. A135

YOUNG, Charles R., Administrator, Shriners Hospitals for Children–Spokane, Spokane, WA, p. A448

YOUNG, J. Phillip
Chief Executive Officer, Eastmoreland Hospital, Portland, OR, p. A344
Assistant Administrator Operations, Woodland Park Hospital, Portland, OR, p. A345

YOUNG, John, President and Chief Executive Officer, Cleveland Regional Medical Center, Shelby, NC, p. A310

YOUNG, Mary Ann, R.N., Administrator, Utah Valley Regional Medical Center, Provo, UT, p. A429

YOUNG, Randall A., Administrator, Lamb Healthcare Center, Littlefield, TX, p. A413

YOUNG, Richard T., President, St. John Detroit Riverview Hospital, Detroit, MI, p. A209

YOUNG, Robert C., M.D., President, Fox Chase Cancer Center–American Oncologic Hospital, Philadelphia, PA, p. A358

YOUNG Jr., Frederick C., President, Pendleton Memorial Methodist Hospital, New Orleans, LA, p. A183

YOUNG Jr., William W., President, Central Maine Medical Center, Lewiston, ME, p. A188

YUTZY, LaVern J., Chief Executive Officer, Philhaven, Bahavioral Healthcare Services, Mount Gretna, PA, p. A356

Z

ZACCAGNINO, Joseph A.
President and Chief Executive Officer, Yale New Haven Health System, New Haven, CT, p. B156
President and Chief Executive Officer, Yale–New Haven Hospital, New Haven, CT, p. A76

ZAGER, Joe, Chief Executive Officer, Monroe County Hospital, Monroeville, AL, p. A16

ZANFINI, Gaetano, Chief Executive Officer, Brea Community Hospital, Brea, CA, p. A38

ZASTROW, Allan, FACHE, Chief Executive Officer, Keokuk Area Hospital, Keokuk, IA, p. A151

ZAYAS, Domingo Torres, CHE, Executive Director, Mennonite General Hospital, Aibonito, PR, p. A469

ZECHMAN Jr., Edwin K., President and Chief Executive Officer, Children's National Medical Center, Washington, DC, p. A79

ZEH, Brian R., Chief Executive Officer, Clinton County Hospital, Frankfort, IN, p. A138

ZEMAN, Barry T., President and Chief Executive Officer, St. Charles Hospital and Rehabilitation Center, Port Jefferson, NY, p. A296

ZEMAN, Denise, Chief Operating Officer, Euclid Hospital, Euclid, OH, p. A323

ZEPHIER, Richard L., Ph.D., Service Unit Director, Acoma–Canoncito–Laguna Hospital, San Fidel, NM, p. A280

ZICHAL, Fran, Chief Executive Officer, Central Community Hospital, Elkader, IA, p. A149

ZIELINSKI, Dennis G., Chief Executive Officer, United Memorial Hospital Association, Greenville, MI, p. A211

ZILM, Michael E., President, St. Mary's Health Center, Saint Louis, MO, p. A248

ZIMMERMAN, Joann, Administrator, Santa Teresa Community Hospital, San Jose, CA, p. A61

ZIMMERMAN, Kenneth J., Administrator, Beatrice Community Hospital and Health Center, Beatrice, NE, p. A256

ZIMMERMAN, Nancy, Administrator, Comanche County Hospital, Coldwater, KS, p. A157

ZIOMEK, Janice, Administrator, Moreno Valley Community Hospital, Moreno Valley, CA, p. A53

ZORNES, Donald H., Administrator, Columbus Community Hospital, Columbus, NE, p. A257

ZUBER, Eugene, Administrator, Newport Hospital and Clinic, Newport, AR, p. A33

ZUBKOFF, William, Ph.D., Chief Executive Officer, South Shore Hospital and Medical Center, Miami Beach, FL, p. A90

ZULIANI, Michael E., Chief Executive Officer, Angel Medical Center, Franklin, NC, p. A306

ZWIGART, Donna, FACHE, Chief Executive Officer, St. Francis Hospital of New Castle, New Castle, PA, p. A357

AHA Membership Categories

The American Hospital Association is primarily an organization of hospitals and related institutions. Its object, according to its bylaws, is "to promote high–quality health care and health services for all the people through leadership in the development of public policy, leadership in the representation and advocacy of hospital and health care organization interests, and leadership in the provision of services to assist hospitals and health care organizations in meeting the health care needs of their communities."

The major source of income for the AHA is its membership dues, which are established by the membership through the House of Delegates. The types of membership are described in the following paragraphs:

Institutional Members

Type I–Hospitals or health services organizations or systems which provide a continuum of integrated, community health resources and which include at least one licensed hospital that is owned, leased, managed or religiously sponsored.

Type I members include hospitals, health care systems, integrated delivery systems, and physician hospital organizations (PHOs) and health maintenance organizations (HMOs) wholly or partially owned by or owning a member hospital or system. A Type I member hospital, health care system or integrated delivery system may, at its decretion and upon approval of a membership application by the Association chief executive officer, extend membership to the health care provider organizations, other than a hospital that it owns, leases, or fully controls.

Type II–Freestanding Health Care Provider Organizations

These are health provider organizations, other than registered hospitals, that provide patient care services, including, but not limited to, ambulatory, preventive, rehabilitative, specialty, post–acute and continuing care, as well as physician groups, health insurance services, and staff and group model health maintenance organizations without a hospital component. Type II members are not owned or controlled by a Type I hospital, health care system or integrated delivery system member. They may, however, be part of an organization eligible for, but not holding, Type I membership.

Type III–Other Organizations

Type III membership includes organizations interested in the objectives of the Association, but not eligible for Type I or Type II membership. Organizations eligible for Type III membership shall include, but not be limited to, associations, societies, foundations, corporations, educational and academic institutions, companies, government agencies, international health providers, and organizations having an interest in and a desire to support the objectives of the Association.

Provisional Members

Hospitals that are in the planning or construction stage and that, on completion, will be eligible for institutional membership type I or type II. Provisional membership may also be granted to applicant institutions that cannot, at present, meet the requirements of type I or type II membership.

Government Institution Group Members

Groups of government hospitals operated by the same unit of government may obtain institutional membership under a group plan. Membership dues are based on a special schedule set forth in the bylaws of the AHA.

Contracting Hospitals

The AHA also provides membership services to certain hospitals that are prevented from holding membership because of legal or other restrictions.

Types IA

Hospitals

U.S. hospitals and hospitals in areas associated with the U.S. that are type IA members of the American Hospital Association are included in the list of hospitals in section A. Canadian types I members of the American Hospital Association are listed below.

Canada

ALBERTA

Edmonton: MISERICORDIA COMMUNITY HEALTH CENTRE, 16940 87th Avenue, Zip T5R 4H5; tel. 780/930–5611; Carl Roy, President
ROYAL ALEXANDRA HOSPITAL, 10240 Kingsway, Zip T5H 3V9; tel. 780/477–4111; Charles W. McDougall, Chief Operating Officer

Lamont: LAMONT HEALTH CARE CENTRE, 5216–53rd Street, Zip T0B 2R0; tel. 780/895–2211; Harold James, Chief Executive Officer

St. Albert: STURGEON COMMUNITY HEALTH CENTRE, 201 Boudreau Road, Zip T8N 6C4; tel. 780/460–6200; Wendy Hill, Senior Vice President

Stony Plain: STONY PLAIN MUNICIPAL HOSPITAL, 4800 55th Avenue, Zip T7Z 1P9; tel. 403/963–2241; Myrene Couves, Administrator

BRITISH COLUMBIA

Langley: LANGLEY MEMORIAL HOSPITAL, 22051 Fraser Highway, Zip V3A 4H4; tel. 604/534–4121; Pat E. Zanon, President and Chief Executive Officer

Vancouver: BRITISH COLUMBIA'S CHILDREN'S HOSPITAL, 4480 Oak Street, Zip V6H 3V4; tel. 604/875–2345; John H. Tegenfeldt, President

MANITOBA

Portage La Prarie: PORTAGE DISTRICT GENERAL HOSPITAL, 524 Fifth Street S.E., Zip R1N 3A8; tel. 204/239–2211; Garry C. Mattin, Executive Director

Winnipeg: RIVERVIEW HEALTH CENTRE, 1 Morley Avenue East, Zip R3L 2P4; tel. 204/452–3411; Norman R. Kasian, President

ST. BONIFACE GENERAL HOSPITAL, 409 Tache Avenue, Zip R2H 2A6; tel. 204/233–8563; Kenneth Tremblay, President and Chief Executive Officer

NOVA SCOTIA

North Sydney: NORTHSIDE HARBOR VIEW HOSPITAL, P.O. Box 399, Zip B2A 3M4; tel. 902/794–8521; Mary S. MacIsaac, Chief Executive Officer

Sydney: CAPE BRETON REGIONAL HOSPITAL, 1482 George Street, Zip B1P 1P3; tel. 902/567–8000; John Malcom, Chief Executive Officer

ONTARIO

Brantford: ST. JOSEPH'S HOSPITAL, 99 Wayne Gretzky Parkway, Zip N3S 6T6; tel. 519/753–8641; Romeo Cercone, President and Chief Executive Officer

Guelph: HOMEWOOD HEALTH CENTER, 150 Delhi Street, Zip N1E 6K9; tel. 519/824–1010; Ronald A. Pond, M.D., President and Chief Executive Officer

London: ST. MARYS' HOSPITAL CAMPUS, P.O. Box 5777, Zip N6A 1Y6; tel. 613/646–6000; Philip C. Hassen, President

North York: BAYCREST CENTRE–GERIATRIC CARE, 3560 Bathurst Street, Zip M6A 2E1; tel. 416/789–5131; Stephen W. Herbert, President and Chief Executive Officer

Ottawa: ROYAL OTTAWA HOSPITAL, 1145 Carling Avenue, Zip K1Z 7K4; tel. 613/722–6521; George F. Langill, Executive Director

Parry Sound: WEST PARRY SOUND HEALTH CENTRE, 10 James Street, Zip P2A 1T3; tel. 705/746–9321; Norman Maciver, Chief Executive Officer

Renfrew: RENFREW VICTORIA HOSPITAL, 499 Raglan Street North, Zip K7V 1P6; tel. 613/432–4851; Randy V. Penney, Executive Director

Strathroy: STRATHROY MIDDLESEX GENERAL HOSPITAL, 395 Carrie Street, Zip N7G 3C9; tel. 519/245–1550; Thomas M. Enright, Executive Director

Sudbury: SUDBURY MEMORIAL HOSPITAL, 865 Regent Street South, Zip P3E 3Y9; tel. 705/671–1000; Esko J. Vainio, Executive Director

Thornhill: SHOULDICE HOSPITAL, P.O. Box 370, Zip L3T 4A3; tel. 905/889–1125; Alan O'Dell, Administrator

Toronto: DOCTORS HOSPITAL, 45 Brunswick Avenue, Zip M5S 2M1; tel. 416/923–5411; Brian McFarlane, President and Chief Executive Officer
MOUNT SINAI HOSPITAL, 600 University Avenue, Zip M5G 1X5; tel. 416/596–4200; Theodore J. Freedman, President and Chief Executive Officer
ST. JOSEPH'S HEALTH CENTRE, 30 the Queensway, Zip M6R 1B5; tel. 416/534–9531; Marilyn Bruner, President and Chief Executive Officer
TORONTO REHABILITATION INSTITUTE, 550 University Avenue, Zip M5G 2A2; tel. 416/597–5111; Mark Rochon, President and Chief Executive Officer
WOMEN'S COLLEGE HOSPITAL, 76 Grenville Street, Zip M5S 1B2; tel. 416/323–6400; Patricia Campbell, President and Chief Executive Officer

QUEBEC

Montreal: CENTRE HOSPITALIER DE L' UNIVERISITE DE MONTREAL, 3840 Saint Urbain Street, Zip H2W 1T8; tel. 514/843–2794; Cecile Cleroux, Executive Director
MONTREAL CHILDREN'S HOSPITAL, 2300 Tupper Street, Zip H3H 1P3; tel. 514/934–4400; Patricia Sheppard, Director
MOUNT SINAI HOSPITAL CENTER, 5690 Cavendish Cote St–Luc', Zip H4W 1S7; tel. 514/369–2222; Joseph Rothbart, Executive Director

Sherbrooke: SHERBROOKE HOSPITAL, 375 Argyle Street, Zip J1J 3H5; tel. 819/569–3661; Daniel Bergeron, Director General

Associated University Programs in Health Administration

ALABAMA

Birmingham: UNIVERSITY OF ALABAMA AT BIRMINGHAM, 1675 University Boulevard, Zip 35294–3361; tel. 205/934–5661; Charles L. Joiner, Ph.D., Dean

ARIZONA

Tempe: SCHOOL OF HEALTH ADMINISTRATION AND POLICY, ARIZONA STATE UNIVERSITY, P.O. Box 874506, Zip 85287–4506; tel. 602/965–7778; Frank G. Williams, Ph.D., Professor

CALIFORNIA

Los Angeles: UCLA SCHOOL OF PUBLIC HEALTH, P.O. Box 951772, Zip 90095–1772; tel. 310/825–2594; Thomas Rice, M.D., Administrator

San Francisco: GOLDEN GATE UNIVERSITY, 536 Mission Street, General Library, Zip 94105; tel. 415/442–0777; Steven Dunlap, Assistant Librarian

DISTRICT OF COLUMBIA

Washington: SCHOOL OF PUBLIC HEALTH AND HEALTH SERVICES, THE GEORGE WASHINGTON UNIVERSITY, 2300 Eye Street, N.W., Suite 106H, Zip 20037; tel. 202/994–3139; Richard F. Southby, Ph.D., Associate Dean Health Services and Friesen Professor of International Health School of Public Health and Health Service

GEORGIA

Atlanta: GEORGIA STATE UNIVERSITY, INSTITUTE OF HEALTH ADMINISTRATION, University Plaza, Zip 30303; tel. 404/651–2000; Everett A. Johnson, Director

ILLINOIS

Carbondale: SOUTHERN ILLINOIS UNIVERSITY, COLLEGE OF APPLIED SCIENCES AND ARTS, Zip 62901; tel. 618/536–6682; Frederic L. Morgan, Ph.D., Chair Health Care Professions

Chicago: UNIVERSITY OF CHICAGO, GRADUATE PROGRAM IN HEALTH ADMINISTRATION AND POLICY, 969 East 60th Street, Zip 60637; tel. 312/753–4191; Edward Lawlor, Ph.D., Director

Evanston: HEALTH SERVICE MANAGEMENT PROGRAM, KELLOGG GRADUATE SCHOOL OF MANAGEMENT, NORTHWESTERN UNIVERSITY, 2001 Sheridan Road, Zip 60208; tel. 847/492–5540; Joel Shalowitz, M.D., Professor and Director

University Park: PROGRAM IN HEALTH SERVICE ADMINISTRATION, SCHOOL OF HEALTH PROFESSIONS, GOVERNORS STATE UNIVERSITY, Zip 60466; tel. 847/534–4030; Sang–O Rhee, Chairman

IOWA

Iowa City: GRADUATE PROGRAM IN HOSPITAL AND HEALTH ADMINISTRATION, UNIVERSITY OF IOWA, 2700 Steindler Building, Zip 52242; tel. 319/356–2593; Douglas Wakefield, Ph.D., Interim Head

MARYLAND

Bethesda: NAVAL SCHOOL OF HEALTH SCIENCES, Naval Medical Command, National Region, Zip 20889–5611; tel. 301/295–1251; Captain Harry Coffey, Commanding Officer

MISSOURI

Saint Louis: PROGRAM IN HOSPITAL AND HEALTH CARE ADMINISTRATION, ST. LOUIS UNIVERSITY, 3663 Lindell Boulevard, Zip 63108; tel. 314/577–8000; Michael Counte, Ph.D., Chairman

WASHINGTON UNIVERSITY, SCHOOL OF MEDICINE, 4547 Clayton Avenue, Zip 63110; tel. 314/362–2477; James O. Hepner, Ph.D., Director Health Administration Program

NEW YORK

Valhalla: NEW YORK MEDICAL COLLEGE, Administration Building, Zip 10595; tel. 914/347–5044; Father Harry C. Barrett, M.P.H., President and Chief Executive Officer

OHIO

Columbus: GRADUATE PROGRAM IN HEALTH SERVICES MANAGEMENT AND POLICY, OHIO STATE UNIVERSITY, 1583 Perry Street, Room 246 Samp, Zip 43210; tel. 614/292–9708; Stephen F. Loebs, Ph.D., Chairman and Associate Professor

OKLAHOMA

Oklahoma City: UNIVERSITY OF OKLAHOMA HEALTH SCIENCE CENTER, DEPARTMENT OF HEALTH ADMINISTRATION AND POLICY, P.O. Box 26901, Zip 73104; tel. 405/271–2114; Keith Curtis, Associate Professor and Interim Chair

PENNSYLVANIA

Philadelphia: TEMPLE UNIVERSITY, DEPARTMENT OF HEALTH ADMINISTRATION, SCHOOL OF BUSINESS ADMINISTRATION, Zip 19122–6083; tel. 215/787–8082; William Aaronson, Professor and Chairman

University Park: PENNSYLVANIA STATE UNIVERSITY, 116 Henderson Building, Zip 16802; tel. 814/863–2859; Diane Brannon, Ph.D., Interim Department Head, Health Policy and Administration

TEXAS

Fort Sam Houston: ARMY–BAYLOR UNIVERSITY PROGRAM IN HEALTH CARE ADMINISTRATION, Academy of Health Sciences–USA, Zip 78234; tel. 512/221–5009

San Antonio: TRINITY UNIVERSITY, 715 Stadium Drive, Suite 58, Zip 78212–7200; tel. 210/736–8107; Niccie McKay, Ph.D., Chairman

Sheppard AFB: U. S. AIR FORCE SCHOOL OF HEALTH CARE SCIENCES, Building 1900, MSTL/114, Academic Library, Zip 76311; tel. 817/851–2511

PUERTO RICO

San Juan: SCHOOL OF PUBLIC HEALTH, P.O. Box 5067, Zip 00936; tel. 809/767–9626; Orlando Nieves, Dean

Hospital Schools of Nursing

ARKANSAS

Little Rock: BAPTIST MEDICAL SYSTEM School of Nursing
Pine Bluff: JEFFERSON REGIONAL MEDICAL CENTER School of Nursing

CALIFORNIA

Los Angeles: LOS ANGELES COUNTY–UNIVERSITY OF SOUTHERN CALIFORNIA MEDICAL CENTER School of Nursing

CONNECTICUT

Bridgeport: ST. VINCENT'S COLLEGE

DELAWARE

Lewes: BEEBE MEDICAL CENTER School of Nursing

GEORGIA

Atlanta: GEORGIA BAPTIST MEDICAL CENTER School of Nursing

ILLINOIS

Canton: GRAHAM HOSPITAL School of Nursing
Chicago: RAVENSWOOD HOSPITAL MEDICAL CENTER, HENRY J. KUTSCH COLLEGE OF NURSING
Danville: LAKEVIEW MEDICAL CENTER School of Nursing
Peoria: METHODIST HOSPITAL OF CENTRAL ILLINOIS School of Nursing

INDIANA

Lafayette: ST. ELIZABETH HOSPITAL MEDICAL CENTER School of Nursing

IOWA

Des Moines: IOWA METHODIST HOSPITAL School of Nursing
MERCY HOSPITAL MEDICAL CENTER School of Nursing
Sioux City: ST. LUKE'S REGIONAL MEDICAL CENTER School of Nursing

LOUISIANA

Baton Rouge: BATON ROUGE GENERAL MEDICAL CENTER School of Nursing
OUR LADY OF LAKE REGIONAL MEDICAL CENTER School of Nursing

MARYLAND

Easton: MEMORIAL HOSPITAL AT EASTON MARYLAND School of Nursing

MASSACHUSETTS

Boston: NEW ENGLAND BAPTIST HOSPITAL School of Nursing
Brockton: BROCKTON HOSPITAL School of Nursing
Medford: LAWRENCE MEMORIAL HOSPITAL OF MEDFORD School of Nursing

Springfield: BAYSTATE MEDICAL CENTER School of Nursing

MISSOURI

Saint Louis: BARNES HOSPITAL School of Nursing
LUTHERAN MEDICAL CENTER School of Nursing
Springfield: LESTER E. COX MEDICAL CENTERS School of Nursing
ST JOHN'S School of Nursing
Town & Country: MISSOURI BAPTIST MEDICAL CENTER School of Nursing

NEBRASKA

Lincoln: BRYAN MEMORIAL HOSPITAL School of Nursing

NEW JERSEY

Camden: OUR LADY OF LOURDES MEDICAL CENTER School of Nursing
Elizabeth: ELIZABETH GENERAL MEDICAL CENTER School of Nursing
Englewood: ENGLEWOOD HOSPITAL AND MEDICAL CENTER School of Nursing
Jersey City: CHRIST HOSPITAL School of Nursing
Montclair: MOUNTAINSIDE HOSPITAL School of Nursing
Plainfield: MUHLENBERG REGIONAL MEDICAL CENTER School of Nursing
Teaneck: HOLY NAME HOSPITAL School of Nursing
Trenton: HELENE FULD MEDICAL CENTER School of Nursing
MERCER MEDICAL CENTER School of Nursing
ST. FRANCIS MEDICAL CENTER School of Nursing

NEW YORK

Buffalo: SISTERS OF CHARITY HOSPITAL School of Nursing
Elmira: ARNOT–OGDEN MEMORIAL HOSPITAL School of Nursing
New York: ST. VINCENT'S HOSPITAL AND MEDICAL CENTER OF NEW YORK School of Nursing
Staten Island: ST. VINCENT'S MEDICAL CENTER School of Nursing
Utica: ST. ELIZABETH HOSPITAL School of Nursing
Yonkers: ST. JOHN'S RIVERSIDE HOSPITAL COCHRAN School of Nursing

NORTH CAROLINA

Charlotte: MERCY HOSPITAL School of Nursing
PRESBYTERIAN HOSPITAL School of Nursing
Concord: CABARRUS COLLEGE OF HEALTH SCIENCES
Durham: WATTS School of Nursing

NORTH DAKOTA

Bismarck: MEDCENTER ONE School of Nursing

OHIO

Canton: AULTMAN HOSPITAL School of Nursing
Cincinnati: CHRIST HOSPITAL School of Nursing
GOOD SAMARITAN HOSPITAL School of Nursing
Cleveland: FAIRVIEW GENERAL HOSPITAL School of Nursing
Sandusky: PROVIDENCE HOSPITAL School of Nursing
Springfield: COMMUNITY HOSPITAL OF SPRINGFIELD AND CLARK COUNTY School of Nursing

PENNSYLVANIA

Johnstown: CONEMAUGH VALLEY MEMORIAL HOSPITAL School of Nursing
New Castle: JAMESON MEMORIAL HOSPITAL School of Nursing
ST. FRANCIS HOSPITAL OF NEW CASTLE School of Nursing
Philadelphia: EPISCOPAL HOSPITAL School of Nursing
METHODIST HOSPITAL School of Nursing
Pittsburgh: SHADYSIDE HOSPITAL School of Nursing
ST. FRANCIS MEDICAL CENTER School of Nursing
ST. MARGARET MEMORIAL HOSPITAL LOUISE SUYDAM MCCLINTIC School of Nursing
WESTERN PENNSYLVANIA HOSPITAL School of Nursing
Pottsville: POTTSVILLE HOSPITAL AND WARNE CLINIC School of Nursing
Sewickley: SEWICKLEY VALLEY HOSPITAL School of Nursing
Sharon: SHARON REGIONAL HEALTH SYSTEM School of Nursing
Washington: WASHINGTON HOSPITAL School of Nursing
West Chester: CHESTER COUNTY HOSPITAL School of Nursing

RHODE ISLAND

North Providence: ST. JOSEPH HOSPITAL School of Nursing

TENNESSEE

Knoxville: FORT SANDERS REGIONAL MEDICAL CENTER School of Nursing
Memphis: BAPTIST COLLEGE OF HEALTH SCIENCES
METHODIST HOSPITALS OF MEMPHIS–CENTRAL School of Nursing
ST. JOSEPH HOSPITAL School of Nursing AT BAPTIST

TEXAS

Lubbock: METHODIST HOSPITAL School of Nursing
San Antonio: BAPTIST MEDICAL CENTER School of Nursing

VIRGINIA

Danville: MEMORIAL HOSPITAL OF DANVILLE School of Nursing
Lynchburg: LYNCHBURG GENERAL–MARSHALL LODGE HOSPITAL School of Nursing
Newport News: RIVERSIDE REGIONAL MEDICAL CENTER School of Nursing
Norfolk: SENTARA NORFOLK GENERAL HOSPITAL School of Nursing
Petersburg: SOUTHSIDE REGIONAL MEDICAL CENTER School of Nursing
Richmond: RICHMOND MEMORIAL HOSPITAL School of Nursing
Suffolk: OBICI HOSPITAL School of Nursing

WEST VIRGINIA

Huntington: ST. MARY'S HOSPITAL School of Nursing

Nonhospital Preacute and Postacute Care Facilities

ALABAMA

Fort McClellan: NOBLE ARMY HEALTH CLINIC, Zip 36205–5083; tel. 205/848–2232
Montgomery: MAXWELL CLINIC, 330 Kirkpatrick Avenue East, Zip 36112–6219; tel. 334/953–7801; Colonel Mary Ann E. Cardinali, USAF, Commander
Redstone Arsenal: FOX ARMY HEALTH CENTER, Zip 35809–7000; tel. 256/876–4147; Major Mark A. Miller, Deputy Commander

ALASKA

Anchorage: DEPARTMENT OF VETERANS AFFAIRS ALASKA MEDICAL AND REGIONAL OFFICE CENTER, 2925 Debarr Road, Zip 99508–2989; tel. 907/257–6930; Alonzo M. Poteet, III, Director
SOUTHCENTRAL FOUNDATION, 4501 Diplomacy Drive, Suite 200, Zip 99508; tel. 907/265–4955; Katherine Grosdidier, President and Chief Executive Officer

ARIZONA

Fort Huachuca: RAYMOND W. BLISS ARMY HEALTH CENTER, Zip 85613–7040; tel. 520/533–2350; Major Christopher Hale, Deputy Commander
Phoenix: JESSE OWENS MEMORIAL MEDICAL CENTER, 325 East Baseline Road, Zip 85040; tel. 602/238–3314; Jeffrey K. Norman, Chief Executive Officer
PMH FAMILY HEALTH CENTER–CAMELBACK, 5040 North 15th Avenue, Zip 85015; tel. 602/266–4381; Jeffrey K. Norman, Chief Executive Officer
PMH FAMILY HEALTH CENTER–WEST MCDOWELL, P.O. Box 21207, Zip 85036–1207; tel. 602/2383314; Jeffrey K. Norman, Chief Executive Officer

ARKANSAS

Little Rock: CENTRAL ARKANSAS RADIATION THERAPY INSTITUTE, P.O. Box 55050, Zip 72215; tel. 501/664–8573; Janice E. Burford, President and Chief Executive Officer

CALIFORNIA

Long Beach: NAVAL MEDICAL CLINIC, Reeves Avenue, Building 831, Zip 90822–5073; tel. 562/521–4201; Captain J. M. Lamdin, Commanding Officer
Los Angeles: DEPARTMENT OF VETERANS AFFAIRS, OUTPATIENT CLINIC, 351 East Temple Street, Room A–102, Zip 90012; tel. 213/253–5000; Jules Morevac, Ph.D., Director
Pleasant Hill: VETERANS AFFAIRS NORTHERN CALIFORNIA HEALTH SYSTEM, 2300 Contra Costa Boulevard, 440, Zip 94523–3961; tel. 510/372–2047; Janet R. Johnson, Chief Acquisitions and Materials Management
Port Hueneme: NAVAL MEDICAL CLINIC, Zip 93043; tel. 805/982–4501
San Francisco: VETERANS AFFAIRS OUTPATIENT CLINIC, 4150 Clement Street, Zip 94121; tel. 415/221–4810; Lawrence C. Stewart, Director
Sepulveda: VETERANS AFFAIRS MEDICAL CENTER, 16111 Plummer Street, Zip 91343; tel. 818/891–7711; Smith Jenkins, Jr., Acting Chief Executive Officer

CONNECTICUT

Groton: NAVAL HOSPITAL, 1 Wahoo Drive, Box 600, Zip 06349–5600; tel. 860/694–3261; Captain Kathleen Hiatt, Deputy Commanding Officer
Newington: VETERANS AFFAIRS MEDICAL CENTER–NEWINGTON CAMPUS, 555 Willard Avenue, Zip 06111–2600; tel. 860/666–6951
Stamford: THE REHABILITATION CENTER, 26 Palmer's Hill Road, Zip 06902; tel. 203/325–1544; Kathleen Murphy, President

DELAWARE

New Castle: CHRISTIANA CARE VISITING NURSE ASSOCIATION, One Reads Way, Zip 19720; tel. 302/323–8200
SCHWEIZER'S THERAPY AND REHABILITATION, 100 Corporate Commons, Suite 1, Zip 19720
Newark: CHRISTIANA CARE IMAGING CENTER, 4751 Ogletown–Stanton Road, Zip 19718
CHRISTIANA SURGICENTER, 4755 Ogletown–Stanton Road, Zip 19718
Wilmington: EUGENE DUPONT PREVENTIVE MEDICINE AND REHABILITATION INSTITUTE
INFUSION SERVICES OF DELAWARE, 1701 Rockland Road, Suite 102, Zip 19803

FLORIDA

Key West: NAVAL REGIONAL MEDICAL CLINIC, Roosevelt Boulevard, Zip 33040; tel. 305/293–4500; Captain F. L. Anzalone, Officer–in–Charge
Miami: VITAS HEALTHCARE CORPORATION, 100 South Biscayne Boulevard, Zip 33131; tel. 305/374–4143; Hugh Westbrook, Chairman and Chief Executive Officer
Riverview: TAMPA BAY ACADEMY, 12012 Boyette Road, Zip 33569; tel. 813/677–6700; Edward C. Hoefle, Administrator

GEORGIA

Calhoun: ALLIANT HEALTH PLANS, INC., 401 South Wall Street, Suite 201, Zip 30701; tel. 706/629–8848; Louis G. Smith, Jr., Chief Executive Officer
GEORGIA HEALTH PLUS, 401 South Wall Street, Suite 201, Zip 30701; tel. 706/629–1833; Louis G. Smith, Jr., Chief Executive Officer
Rome: CENTREX, 420 East Second Avenue, Zip 30161; tel. 706/235–1006; Dee B. Russell, M.D., Chief Executive Officer
COMMUNITY HOSPICECARE, P.O. Box 233, Zip 30162–0233; tel. 706/232–0807; Kurt Stuenkel, FACHE, President and Chief Executive Officer
FLOYD HOME HEALTH AGENCY, P.O. Box 6248, Zip 30162–6248; tel. 706/802–4600; Kurt Stuenkel, FACHE, President and Chief Executive Officer
FLOYD MEDICAL OUTPATIENT SURGERY, P.O. Box 233, Zip 30162–0233; tel. 706/802–2070; Kurt Stuenkel, FACHE, President and Chief Executive Officer
FLOYD REHABILITATION CENTER, P.O. Box 233, Zip 30162–0233; tel. 706/802–2091; Kurt Stuenkel, FACHE, President and Chief Executive Officer

HAWAII

Honolulu: VETERANS AFFAIRS MEDICAL REGIONAL OFFICE, P.O. Box 50188, Zip 96850; tel. 808/541–1582
Pearl Harbor: NAVAL REGIONAL MEDICAL CLINIC, Box 121, Building 1750, Zip 96860–5080; tel. 808/471–3025; Captain Robert Murphy, M.D., MSC, USN, Commanding Officer

KANSAS

Wichita: U. S. AIR FORCE HOSPITAL, 59570 Leavenworth Street, Suite 6E4, Zip 67221–5300; tel. 316/652–5000; Lieutenant Colonel Bruce A. Harma, Administrator

LOUISIANA

New Orleans: NAVAL MEDICAL CLINIC, Zip 70142; tel. 504/678–2400; Lieutenant Colonel Deborah Auth, Director, Administration

MAINE

Damariscotta: MILES MEDICAL GROUP, INC., RR 1, Box 4500, Zip 04543; tel. 207/563–1234; Stacey Miller–Friant, Director

Kennebunk: SOUTHERN MAINE HEALTH AND HOME SERVICES, P.O. Box 739, Zip 04043; tel. 207/985–4767; Elaine Brady, R.N., Executive Director

MARYLAND

Annapolis: NAVAL MEDICAL CLINIC, Zip 21402; tel. 410/293–1330
Baltimore: ST. AGNES HEALTH SERVICES, 900 Caton Avenue, Zip 21229; tel. 410/368–2945; Peter Clay, Senior Vice President Managed Care
ST. AGNES HOME CARE AND HOSPICE, 3421 Benson Avenue, Suite G100, Zip 21227; tel. 410/368–2825; Robin Dowell, Director
Fort George G Meade: KIMBROUGH ARMY COMMUNITY HOSPITAL, Zip 20755; tel. 301/677–4171; Colonel David W. Roberts, Commanding Officer
Patuxent River: NAVAL MEDICAL CLINIC, 47149 Buse Road, Zip 20670–5370; tel. 301/342–1418; Captain Ralph A. Puckett, MC, USN, Commanding Officer

MASSACHUSETTS

Falmouth: GOSNOLD ON CAPE COD, P.O. Box 929, Zip 02541; tel. 508/540–6550; Raymond Tamasi, Chief Executive Officer
Springfield: INFUSION AND RESPIRATORY SERVICES, 211 Carando Drive, Zip 01104; tel. 413/794–4663; Maureen Skipper, Senior Vice President Home and Community Based Services
VISITING NURSE ASSOCIATION AND HOSPICE OF WESTERN NEW ENGLAND, INC., 50 Maple Street, Zip 01105; tel. 413/781–5070; Maureen Skipper, President

MICHIGAN

Big Rapids: MECOSTA HEALTH SERVICES, 413 Mecosta, Zip 49307; tel. 717/796–3200; Thomas E. Daugherty, Administrator
Port Huron: TRI–HOSPITAL E.M.S., 309 Grand River Street, Zip 48060; tel. 313/985–7115; Ken Cummings, Chief Executive Officer
WILLOW ENTERPRISES, INC., 1221 Pine Grove Avenue, Zip 48060; tel. 313/989–3737; James B. Bridge, Chief Executive Officer
Sault Sainte Marie: SAULT SAINTE MARIE TRIBAL HEALTH AND HUMAN SERVICES CENTER, 2864 Ashmun Street, Zip 49783; tel. 906/495–5651; Russell Vizina, Division Director Health

MINNESOTA

Saint Paul: HEALTHEAST CARE, INC., 1690 University Avenue W, Suite 370, Zip 55104–3729; tel. 651/232–5070; Steven N. Burrows, Executive Vice President
HEALTHEAST HOME CARE, INC., 1700 University Avenue, Zip 55104; tel. 651/232–2800; Cathy Barr, Director
HEALTHEAST MEDICAL RESEARCH INSTITUTE, 559 Capitol Boulevard, Zip 55103; tel. 651/232–2300; Timothy H. Hanson, President and Chief Executive Officer

MISSOURI

Independence: SURGI–CARE CENTER OF INDEPENDENCE, 2311 Redwood Avenue, Zip 64057; tel. 816/373–7995; Michael W. Chappelow, President and Chief Executive Officer
Whiteman AFB: U. S. AIR FORCE CLINIC WHITEMAN, 331 Sijan Avenue, Zip 65305–5001; tel. 660/687–1194; Lieutenant Colonel David Wilmot, USAF, MSC, Administrator

MONTANA

Malmstrom AFB: U. S. AIR FORCE CLINIC, Zip 59402–5300; tel. 406/731–3863
Miles City: VETERANS AFFAIRS MEDICAL CENTER, 210 South Winchester Avenue, Zip 59301–4742; tel. 406/232–3060; Richard J. Stanley, Director

NEBRASKA

Grand Island: GRAND ISLAND DIVISION, 2211 North Broadwell Avenue, Zip 68803–2196; tel. 308/382–3660
North Platte: GREAT PLAINS PHO, INC., P.O. Box 1167, Zip 69103; tel. 308/535–7496; Todd Hlavaty, M.D., Chairman

NEW HAMPSHIRE

Portsmouth: NAVAL MEDICAL CLINIC, Building H–1, Zip 03801; tel. 207/439–1000; Captain F. M. Richardson, Commanding Officer

NEW JERSEY

Fort Monmouth: PATTERSON ARMY HEALTH CLINIC, Zip 07703–5607; tel. 908/532–1266; Colonel Dolores Loew, Commander

NEW MEXICO

Fort Bayard: FORT BAYARD MEDICAL CENTER, P.O. Box 36219, Zip 88036; tel. 505/537–3302; Marquita George, Administrator

NEW YORK

Lake Placid: CAMELOT, 50 Riverside Drive, Zip 12946; tel. 518/523–3605; Father Carlos J. Caguiat, FACHE, Vice President
New York: STATE UNIVERSITY OF NEW YORK, UNIVERSITY OPTOMETRIC CENTER, 100 East 24th Street, Zip 10010; tel. 212/780–4930; Richard C. Weber, Executive Director
Rochester: ROCHESTER REHABILITATION CENTER, 1000 Elmwood Avenue, Zip 14620; tel. 716/271–2520; George H. Gieselman, President
Tuckahoe: HOME NURSING ASSOCIATION OF WESTCHESTER, 69 Main Street, Zip 10707; tel. 919/961–2818; Mary Wehrberger, Director

NORTH CAROLINA

Winston Salem: QUALCHOICE OF NORTH CAROLINA, INC., 2000 West First Street, Suite 210, Zip 27104; tel. 910/716–0900; Douglas G. Cueny, President

OHIO

Cleveland: KAISER PERMANENTE, 1001 Lakeside, Zip 44114; tel. 216/362–2000; Jeff Blancett, Vice President
Columbus: HOMEREACH, 404 EWilson Bridge Road, Suite H., Zip 43085; tel. 614/566–0888; Rebecca Zuccarelli, Vice President Home and Hospice Services
OHIOHEALTH GROUP, 300 East Wilson Bridge Road, Zip 43085; tel. 614/566–0123; John Burns, Chief Executive Officer
VETERANS AFFAIRS OUTPATIENT CLINIC, 543 Taylor Avenue, Zip 43203–1278; tel. 614/469–5663

OKLAHOMA

Enid: U. S. AIR FORCE CLINIC, Vance AFB, Building 810, Zip 73705–5000; tel. 405/249–7494; Lieutenant Colonel Andrew F. Love, MSC, USAF, Commander Medical Group
Tinker AFB: U. S. AIR FORCE HOSPITAL TINKER, 5700 Arnold Street, Zip 73145; tel. 405/736–2084; Captain Melvin Alexander, Chief Resources Management Flight
Tulsa: SURGICARE OF TULSA, 4415 South Harvard, Suite 100, Zip 74135; tel. 918/742–2502; Dirk Foxworthy, Executive Vice President

PENNSYLVANIA

Chester: COMMUNITY HOSPITAL, DIVISION OF THE CROZER–CHESTER MEDICAL CENTER, Ninth and Wilson Streets, Zip 19013–2098; tel. 610/494–0700; Joan K. Richards, President
Pittsburgh: HEALTH ASSISTANCE PROGRAM FOR PERSONNEL IN INDUSTRY, 4221 Penn Avenue, Zip 15224; tel. 412/622–4994; Eugene Ginchereau, M.D., Director
York: SOUTH CENTRAL PREFERRED, 1803 Mount Rose Avenue, Zip 17403; tel. 717/741–9511; Charles H. Chodroff, M.D., Executive Director
YORK HEALTH CARE SERVICES, 1001 South George Street, Zip 17405; tel. 717/851–2121; Brian A. Gragnolati, Senior Vice President Operations
YORK HEALTH SYSTEM MEDICAL GROUP, Zip 17403; tel. 717/741–8125; William R. Richards, Executive Director

RHODE ISLAND

Newport: NAVAL HOSPITAL, Zip 02841–1002; tel. 401/841–3915; Captain C. Henderson, III, MSC, USN, Commanding Officer

TEXAS

El Paso: VETERANS AFFAIRS HEALTHCARE CENTER, 5001 North Piedras Street, Zip 79930–4211; tel. 915/564–6100; Edward Valenzuela, Director
Houston: CHAMPION'S RESIDENTIAL TREATMENT CENTER, 14320 Walters Road, Zip 77014; tel. 713/537–5050
WEST HOUSTON SURGICARE, 970 Campbell Road, Zip 77024; tel. 713/461–3547; Edward Downs, Administrator
Laughlin AFB: U. S. AIR FORCE HOSPITAL, 590 Mitchell Boulevard, Zip 78843–5200; tel. 210/298–6311
San Antonio: U. S. AIR FORCE CLINIC BROOKS, Building 615, Zip 78235–5300; tel. 210/536–2087; Major Edward M. Jenkins, Administrator
Webster: BAY AREA SURGICARE CENTER, P.O. Box 201445, Zip 77216–1445; tel. 281/332–2433; Mary Colombo, Administrator

VIRGINIA

Fort Lee: KENNER ARMY HEALTH CLINIC, 700 24th Street, Zip 23801–1716; tel. 804/734–9256
Quantico: NAVAL REGIONAL MEDICAL CLINIC, Zip 22134; tel. 703/640–2236

WISCONSIN

Green Bay: UNITY HOSPICE, P.O. Box 28345, Zip 54324–8345; tel. 920/494–0225; Donald Seibel, Executive Director
Milwaukee: EYE INSTITUTE–MEDICAL COLLEGE OF WISCONSIN, 925 North 87th Street, Zip 53226–3595; tel. 414/456–7800; James N. Browne, Chief Executive Officer

Ambulatory Centers and Home Care Agencies

United States

FLORIDA

NEMOURS CHILDREN'S CLINIC, 807 Nira Street, Jacksonville, Zip 32207; tel. 904/390–3600; Barry P. Sales, Administrator

NEW HAMPSHIRE

DARTMOUTH COLLEGE HEALTH SERVICE, 7 Rope Ferry Road, Hanover, Zip 03755–1421; tel. 603/650–1400; John Turco, M.D., Director

NEW YORK

WESTFALL SURGERY CENTER, 1065 Senator Keating Boulevard, Rochester, Zip 14618; tel. 716/256–1330; Gary J. Scott, Administrative Director

PENNSYLVANIA

CRAIG HOUSE–TECHNOMA, 751 North Negley Avenue, Pittsburgh, Zip 15206; tel. 412/361–2801; Richard L. Kerchnner, Administrator

WISCONSIN

CURATIVE REHABILITATION SERVICES, 1000 North 92nd Street, Wauwatosa, Zip 53226; tel. 414/259–1414; Robert H. Coons, Jr., President

Philippines

DEPARTMENT OF VETERANS AFFAIRS, OUTPATIENT CLINIC, Manila, Zip 96440; tel. 632/521–7116

Blue Cross Plans

United States

ARIZONA

BLUE CROSS AND BLUE SHIELD OF ARIZONA, Box 13466, Phoenix, Zip 85002–3466; tel. 602/864–4400; Robert B. Bulla, President and Chief Executive Officer

FLORIDA

BLUE CROSS AND BLUE SHIELD OF FLORIDA, INC., P.O. Box 1798, Jacksonville, Zip 32231–0014; tel. 904/791–8081; William E. Flaherty, Chairman and Chief Executive Officer

NEW YORK

BLUE CROSS AND BLUE SHIELD OF CENTRAL NEW YORK, Box 4809, Syracuse, Zip 13221–4809; tel. 315/448–3902; H. F. Beacham, III, President

OKLAHOMA

BLUE CROSS AND BLUE SHIELD OF OKLAHOMA, Box 3283, Tulsa, Zip 74102; tel. 918/583–0861; Ronald F. King, President and Chief Executive Officer

PENNSYLVANIA

CAPITAL BLUE CROSS, 2500 Elmerton Avenue, Harrisburg, Zip 17110; tel. 717/541–7000; James M. Mead, President

HIGHMARK BLUE CROSS BLUE SHIELD, 120 Fifth Avenue Place, Suite 3014, Pittsburgh, Zip 15222; tel. 412/544–7646; Sandra R. Tomlinson, Senior Vice President, Provider Affairs

Shared Services Organizations

TEXAS

TEXAS HOSPITAL ASSOCIATION, P.O. Box 15587, Austin, Zip 78761–5587; tel. 512/465–1000; Terry Townsend, FACHE, President and Chief Executive Officer

Other Members

UNITED STATES

Architecture:

BURT HILL KOSAR RITTELMANN ASSOCIATES, 400 Morgan Center, Butler, Pennsylvania Zip 16001–5977; tel. 412/285–4761; John E. Brock, Principal

EARL SWENSSON ASSOCIATES, INC., 2100 West End Avenue, Suite 1200, Nashville, Tennessee Zip 37203; tel. 615/329–9445; Richard L. Miller, President

HENNINGSON, DURHAM AND RICHARDSON, 8404 Indian Hills Drive, Omaha, Nebraska Zip 68114; tel. 402/391–0123; Lynn E. Bonge, Executive Vice President

LEGAT MEDICAL ARCHITECTS, 24 North Chapel, Waukegan, Illinois Zip 60085; tel. 847/605–0234; Casimir Frankiewicz, President

MARSHALL CRAFT ASSOCIATES, INC., 6112 York Road, Baltimore, Maryland Zip 21212; tel. 301/532–3131; Richard S. Abbott, Secretary

MATTHEI AND COLIN ASSOCIATES, 332 South Michigan Avenue, Suite 614, Chicago, Illinois Zip 60604; tel. 312/939–4002; Ronald G. Kobold, Managing Partner

THE RITCHIE ORGANIZATION, 80 Bridge Street, Newton, Massachusetts Zip 02158; tel. 617/969–9400; Wendell R. Morgan, Jr., President

WILLIAM A. BERRY & SON, INC., 100 Conifer Hill Drive, Danvers, Massachusetts Zip 01923; tel. 978/774–1057; Ronda Paradis, Vice President

Behavioral Health Center:

DEVEREUX–VICTORIA, 120 David Wade Drive, Victoria, Texas Zip 77902–2666; tel. 512/575–8271; L. Gail Atkinson, Executive Director

Construction Firm:

HBE CORPORATION, P.O. Box 419039, Saint Louis, Missouri Zip 63141; tel. 314/567–9000; Mike Dolan, Executive Vice President

Consulting Firm:

A.P.M./CSC HEALTHCARE, INC., 1675 Broadway, 18th Floor, New York, New York Zip 10019; tel. 212/903–9300; Karen Flaherty, Coordinator Marketing

ARAMARK HEALTHCARE SUPPORT SERVICES, 1101 Market Street, Philadelphia, Pennsylvania Zip 19107; tel. 215/238–3000; Constance B. Girard–diCarlo, President

ARTHUR ANDERSEN & COMPANY, 33 West Monroe Street, Chicago, Illinois Zip 60603; tel. 312/580–0033; Edward Giniat, Director

BOSTON CONSULTING GROUP, 135 East 57th Street, New York, New York Zip 10022; tel. 212/446–2800; Lurie Regan, Healthcare Researcher

CAMPBELL WILSON, 9400 Central Expressway, Suite 613, Dallas, Texas Zip 75231; tel. 214/373–7077; Danna J. Wilson, Principal

ERNST AND YOUNG, 2001 Market Street, Suite 4000, Philadelphia, Pennsylvania Zip 19103–7096; tel. 215/448–5000; Thomas K. Shaffert, Partner

HAMILTON–KSA, 1355 Peachtree Street N.E., Suite 900, Atlanta, Georgia Zip 30309–0900; tel. 404/892–0321; C. B. Souther, Communication Director

HEALTH DIMENSIONS, 7100 Northland Circle, Suite 205, Minneapolis, Minnesota Zip 55428; Betty Ziebarth, Director

HEALTHCARE FINANCIAL ENTERPRISES, INC., 1475 West Cypress Creek Road, 204, Fort Lauderdale, Florida Zip 33309; tel. 954/772–7878; Peter A. Carvalho, President

MARSHALL ERDMAN & ASSOCIATES, INC., 5117 University Avenue, Madison, Wisconsin Zip 53705; tel. 608/238–0211; Ron R. Halverson, Senior Vice President Sales and Marketing

MCKESSON HBO, 5995 Windward Parkway, Atlanta, Georgia Zip 30305; tel. 404/338–3519; Louise Smith, R.N., Manager, Regulatory Assessment and Operations

---

MMI COMPANIES, INC., 540 Lake Cook Road, Deerfield, Illinois Zip 60015–5290; tel. 847/940–7550; Michelle Cooney, Vice President

PRESS, GANEY ASSOCIATES, INC., 404 Columbia Place, South Bend, Indiana Zip 46601; tel. 219/232–3387; Dennis W. Heck, FACHE, Vice President Corporate Development

RURAL HEALTH CONSULTANTS, 2500 West Sixth, Suite H, Lawrence, Kansas Zip 66049; tel. 785/832–8778; Diann Stogsdill, Senior Consultant

TIBER GROUP, INC., 200 South Wacker Drive, Suite 2620, Chicago, Illinois Zip 60601; tel. 312/609–9935; Davi Hirsch, Chief Operating Officer

TOWERS PERRIN, 100 Summit Lake Drive, Valhalla, New York Zip 10595; tel. 212/309–3400; Leslie Tobias, Information Specialist

VICTOR KRAMER COMPANY, INC., 405 Murray Hill Parkway, Suite 1040, Rutherford, New Jersey Zip 07070; tel. 201/935–0414; Thomas Mara, President

WEST HUDSON, INC., 5230 Pacific Concourse Drive, Suite 400, Dallas, Texas Zip 75240; tel. 972/982–8700; Angela Carver, Administrative Coordinator

WHITMAN GARVEY, INC., 1191 Second Avenue, Suite 1800, Seattle, Washington Zip 98101–2939; tel. 206/628–3763; James T. Whitman, President

YAFFE AND COMPANY, INC., 409 Washington Avenue, Suite 700, Towson, Maryland Zip 21204; tel. 410/494–4100; Rian M. Yaffe, President

Educational Services:

CALIFORNIA COLLEGE FOR HEALTH SCIENCES, 222 West 24th Street, National City, California Zip 91950; tel. 619/477–4800; Dale K. Bean, Program Director

Facilities Management:

JOHNSON CONTROLS, INC., 3354 Perimeter Hill Drive, Suite 105, Franklin, Tennessee Zip 37067; tel. 615/771–1400; C. Patrick Hardwick, Business Development Manager

SERVICEMASTER COMPANY, One Servicemaster Way, Downers Grove, Illinois Zip 60515; tel. 708/964–1300; C. William Pollard, Chairman

Health Care Alliance:

PREMIER, INC., 3 Westbrook Corporate Center, 9th Floor, San Diego, California Zip 92130; tel. 619/481–2727; Richard A. Norling, Chief Executive Officer

UNIVERSITY HEALTH SYSTEM OF NEW JERSEY, 154 West State Street, Trenton, New Jersey Zip 08608; tel. 609/656–9600; Thomas E. Terrill, Ph.D., President

UNIVERSITY HEALTHSYSTEM CONSORTIUM, INC., 2001 Spring Road, Suite 700, Oak Brook, Illinois Zip 60523; tel. 630/954–1700; Robert J. Baker, President and Chief Executive Officer

VHA, INC., P.O. Box 140909, Irving, Texas Zip 75014–0909; tel. 972/830–0000; C. Thomas Smith, President and Chief Executive Officer

Information Systems:

3M HEALTH INFORMATION SYSTEMS, P.O. Box 57900, Murray, Utah Zip 84157; tel. 801/265–4400; Scott Slivka, Marketing Manager

CERNER CORPORATION, 2800 Rockcreek Parkway, Kansas City, Missouri Zip 64117; tel. 816/221–1024; Jack Newman, Jr., Executive Vice President

FIRST COAST SYSTEMS, 6430 Southpoint Parkway, Suite 250, Jacksonville, Florida Zip 32216–0978; tel. 904/296–4200; Charles R. Gibbs, President

SUPERIOR CONSULTANT COMPANY, INC., 4000 Town Center, Suite 1100, Southfield, Michigan Zip 48075; tel. 810/386–8300; Richard D. Helppie, President

VECTOR RESEARCH, INC., P.O. Box 1506, Ann Arbor, Michigan Zip 48106; tel. 313/973–9210; Kevin J. Dombkowski, Program Scientist

---

Insurance Broker:

AETNA RETIREMENT SERVICES, 151 Farmington Avenue–TS41, Hartford, Connecticut Zip 06156; tel. 860/273–6053; Lloyd Duggan, Jr., Market Research Manager

HEALTHCARE UNDERWRITERS MUTUAL INSURANCE COMPANY, 8 British American Boulevard, Latham, New York Zip 12110; tel. 518/786–2700; Gerald J. Cassidy, President and Chief Executive Officer

LOCKTON COMPANIES, 7400 State Line Road, Prairie Village, Kansas Zip 66208; tel. 913/676–9546; Becky Sullivan, Senior Vice President and Unit Manager

PRINCIPAL FINANCIAL GROUP, 711 High Street, Des Moines, Iowa Zip 50392–4620; tel. 515/247–5222; Joan Burns, Technical Senior Consultant

VALIC, 2919 Allen Parkway (L13–05), Houston, Texas Zip 77019; tel. 713/831–5311; Carol Melville, Associate Director, Healthcare Marketing

Investment Broker:

STEPHENS, INC., 111 Center Street, Little Rock, Arkansas Zip 72201; tel. 501/377–8125; Nancy Weaver, Research Analyst

Manufacturer/Supplier:

ABBOTT LABORATORIES, One Abbott Park Road, Abbott Park, Illinois Zip 60064; tel. 847/937–4576; William M. Dwyer, Senior Director Strategic Marketing

ALM SURGICAL EQUIPMENT, INC., 1820 North Lemon Street, Anaheim, California Zip 92801–1009; tel. 714/578–1234; George E. Crispin, President

BAXTER INTERNATIONAL, INC., One Baxter Parkway, Deerfield, Illinois Zip 60015; tel. 847/948–2000; Vernon R. Loucks, Jr., Chief Executive Officer

BFI MEDICAL WASTE SYSTEMS, 757 North Eldridge, Houston, Texas Zip 77077; tel. 713/870–7013; Mike Archer, Director Medical Services

BOSTON SCIENTIFIC CORPORATION, One Boston Scientific Place, Natick, Massachusetts Zip 01760; tel. 508/650–8427; Susan Simpson, Marketing and Research Assistant

GENERAL ELECTRIC MEDICAL SYSTEMS, 3000 North Grandview Boulevard, W451, Milwaukee, Wisconsin Zip 53201–0414; tel. 414/544–3287; Frank Cheng, Manager Market and Group Analysis

HILL–ROM, 1069 State Route 46 East, Batesville, Indiana Zip 47006; tel. 812/934–8285; Fay Bohlke, Marketing

JOHNSON & JOHNSON, 425 Hoes Lane, Piscataway, New Jersey Zip 08855; tel. 732/562–3058; Cathi Brozena, Manager Professional Affairs

MANAGEMENT SCIENCE ASSOCIATES, INC., 4801 Cliff Avenue, Independence, Missouri Zip 64055; tel. 816/795–1947; Kenneth J. McDonald, President

MEDSTAT GROUP/INFORUM, 424 Church Street, Suite 2600, Nashville, Tennessee Zip 37219; tel. 800/829–0600; Kelly Tolson, Director Marketing

MERCK U. S. HUMAN HEALTH, WP35–150, West Point, Pennsylvania Zip 19486; tel. 215/652–5000; Phyllis Rausch, Marketing Associate

MILCARE, INC., A. HERMAN MILLER COMPANY, 8500 Byron Road, Zeeland, Michigan Zip 49464; tel. 616/654–8000; David Reid, Senior Vice President and General Manager

NEMSCHOFF CHAIRS, INC., P.O. Box 129, Sheboygan, Wisconsin Zip 53082–0129; tel. 920/459–1216; David Stinson, Vice President

NOVARTIS PHARMACEUTICALS CORPORATION, 59 Route 10, East Hanover, New Jersey Zip 07936–1080; tel. 973/781–3088; Jeff Sargeant, Associate Director

PFIZER U.S. PHARMACEUTICALS GROUP, 235 East 42nd Street, New York, New York Zip 10017; tel. 212/573–7877; Daniel J. Coakley, Director Trade Development and Industry Affairs

PROCTER & GAMBLE, Two Procter & Gamble Plaza, Cincinnati, Ohio Zip 45202; tel. 513/983–6248; James L. Knepler, Manager Patient Care Professional Relations Health Care Products

SIGMA–TAU PHARMACEUTICALS, INC., 800 South Frederick Avenue, Suite 300, Gaithersburg, Maryland Zip 20877; tel. 301/948–1041; C. Kenneth Mehrling, Executive Vice President and General Manager

Metro Health Care Assn:

HEALTHCARE ASSOCIATION OF SOUTHERN CALIFORNIA, 201 North Figueroa Street, 4th Floor, Los Angeles, California Zip 90071–3322; tel. 213/538–0700; James D. Barber, President

Other:

AMERICA'S BLOOD CENTERS, 725 15th Street N.W., Suite 700, Washington, District of Columbia Zip 20005; tel. 202/393–5725; Jim MacPherson, Executive Director

AMERICAN ASSOCIATION OF NURSE ANESTHETISTS, 222 South Prospect Avenue, Park Ridge, Illinois Zip 60068–4001; tel. 847/692–7050; John F. Garde, Executive Director

AMERICAN BOARD OF MEDICAL SPECIALTIES, 1007 Church Street, Suite 404, Evanston, Illinois Zip 60201–5913; tel. 847/491–9091; Stephen H. Miller, M.D., M.P.H., Executive Vice President

AMERICAN HEALTH PROPERTIES, INC., 6400 South Fiddlers Green Circle, Suite 1800, Englewood, Colorado Zip 80111–4961; tel. 303/796–9793; Greg Schonert, Vice President

AMERICAN SOCIETY OF HOSPITAL PHARMACISTS, 7272 Wisconsin Avenue, Bethesda, Maryland Zip 20814; tel. 301/657–3000; Henri R. Manasse, Ph.D., Sc.D., Executive Vice President and Chief Executive Officer

ARMED FORCES INSTITUTE OF PATHOLOGY, 6825 16th Street N.W., Building 54, Washington, District of Columbia Zip 20306–6000; tel. 202/782–2100; Colonel Michael Dickerson, Director

ARMED FORCES MEDICAL LIBRARY, 5109 Leesburg Pike, Room 670, Falls Church, Virginia Zip 22041–3258; tel. 703/756–8028; D. Zehnpfennig, Administrative Librarian

AVIANT INFORMATION, 1785 Voyager Avenue, Simi Valley, California Zip 93063; tel. 805/578–1777; Keisha Koehler

BEECH STREET, 173 Technology, Irvine, California Zip 92618; tel. 714/727–1359; Doreen Corwin, Vice President Network Development

BERGEN BRUNSWIG CORPORATION, 4000 Metropolitan Drive, Orange, California Zip 92868; tel. 714/385–6903; Shannon J. Jager, Librarian

BIOMATRIX, INC., 65 Railroad Avenue, Ridgefield, New Jersey Zip 07657; tel. 201/945–9550; Barbara A. Rohan, Vice President Public Policy and Reimbursement

BLANK ROME COMISKY AND MCCAULEY, 1200 Four Penn Center Plaza, Philadelphia, Pennsylvania Zip 19103; tel. 215/569–5520; Harry D. Madonna, Attorney

BLUE CROSS AND BLUE SHIELD ASSOCIATION, 225 North Michigan Avenue, Chicago, Illinois Zip 60601–7680; tel. 312/440–6000; Patrick G. Hays, President

BROADCAST MUSIC, INC., 10 Music Square East, Nashville, Tennessee Zip 37203–4399; tel. 615/401–2000; Kathryn D. Crow, Director Industry Development

BUSINESS STRATEGY, INC., 944 52nd Street S.E., Grand Rapids, Michigan Zip 49508; tel. 616/261–2200; Karen Rooney, Marketing Director

CANCER PROGRAM PROFESSIONAL SERVICES, INC., 3110 Society Drive, Claymont, Delaware Zip 19703; tel. 302/798–3978; Edith M. Kutlus, President

CIGNA HEALTHCARE, 1601 Chestnut Street, Suite TL5C, Philadelphia, Pennsylvania Zip 19192; tel. 215/761–1636; Charles Major, Subscription and Publications Manager

COMPUTER TECHNOLOGY ASSOCIATES, INC., 6903 Rockledge Drive, Bethesda, Maryland Zip 20817; tel. 301/581–3200; Robert S. Ardrey, II, Vice President

CONCURRENT TECHNOLOGIES CORPORATION, 320 William Pitt Way, Pittsburgh, Pennsylvania Zip 15238–1329; tel. 412/826–5320; David J. Glaser, Director, CTC Healthcare Systems

CONNECTICUT HOSPITAL ASSOCIATION, Box 90, Wallingford, Connecticut Zip 06492–0090; tel. 203/265–7611; Dennis P. May, President

CRASSOCIATES, INC., 8580 Cinderbed Road, Suite 2400, Newington, Virginia Zip 22122; tel. 703/550–8145; Charles H. Robbins, Chairman and Chief Executive Officer

CROTHALL HEALTHCARE, 955 Chesterbrook Boulevard, Suite 300, Wayne, Pennsylvania Zip 19087; tel. 610/249–0420; Graeme Crothall, President and Chief Executive Officer

CURBELL, INC., ELECTRONICS DIVISION, 7 Cobham Drive, Orchard Park, New York Zip 14127–4180; tel. 716/667–3377; Michael P. Donovan, Marketing Manager

DELOITTE & TOUCHE, 250 East Fifth Street, Suite 2100, Cincinnati, Ohio Zip 45202; tel. 513/723–3228; Julie Lange, Manager Marketing

DEPARTMENT OF AIR FORCE MEDICAL SERVICE, HQ USAF/SG, Bolling AFB, District of Columbia Zip 20332–6188; tel. 202/545–6700

DEPARTMENT OF THE ARMY, OFFICE OF THE SURGEON GENERAL, Rockville, Maryland Zip 20857; tel. 202/690–6467; Rear Admiral Michael Blackwell, Chief of Staff

DEPARTMENT OF THE NAVY, BUREAU OF MEDICINE AND SURGERY, 2300 East Street N.W., Washington, District of Columbia Zip 20372–5300; tel. 202/433–4475

DEPARTMENT OF VETERANS AFFAIRS, 301 Howard Street, Suite 700, San Francisco, California Zip 94105; Linda Pierce, Director, Sierra Pacific Network

DEPARTMENT OF VETERANS AFFAIRS, 810 Vermont Avenue N.W., Washington, District of Columbia Zip 20420; tel. 202/273–5400; Togo West, Secretary

DHHS, PUBLIC HEALTH SERVICE, DIVISION OF INDIAN HEALTH, HEALTH CARE ADMINISTRATION BRANCH, 5600 Fisher Lane, Room 6A–25, Rockville, Maryland Zip 20857; tel. 301/443–1085; Susanne Caviness, M.D., Chief Patient Registration and Quality Management

DIABETES TREATMENT CENTERS OF AMERICA, One Burton Hills Boulevard, Suite 300, Nashville, Tennessee Zip 37215; tel. 615/665–1133; Kathryn J. Kirk, Senior Vice President

DIAMOND CRYSTAL SPECIALTY FOODS, INC., 10 Burlington Avenue, Wilmington, Massachusetts Zip 01887–3997; tel. 978/944–3977; Denise C. Kelly, Marketing Manager

DU PONT CORIAN, P.O. Box 80702, Room 1243, Wilmington, Delaware Zip 19880–0702; tel. 302/999–5447; John Burr, Marketing Manager

EMERGENCY CONSULTANTS, INC., 2240 South Airport Road, Traverse City, Michigan Zip 49684; tel. 800/253–1795; James Johnson, M.D., President

EMERGENCY PRACTICE ASSOCIATES, P.O. Box 1260, Waterloo, Iowa Zip 50704; tel. 319/236–3858; Margo Grimm, Chief Executive Officer

ENVIRO GUARD, LTD., P.O. Box 13666, Research Triangle Pk, North Carolina Zip 27709–3666; tel. 919/363–0550; Dan Farmer, Technical Director

GROUP HEALTH INC., 441 Ninth Avenue, 8th Floor, New York, New York Zip 10001–1601; tel. 212/615–0966; Laurie Nordone, Director

GUIDANT CORPORATION/CPI, 4100 Hamline Avenue North, Saint Paul, Minnesota Zip 55112; tel. 612/582–4017; Eva R. Shipley, Supervisor, Library Information Center

HAWAII MEDICAL SERVICE ASSOCIATION, P.O. Box 860, Honolulu, Hawaii Zip 96808–0860; tel. 808/948–5482; Waynette Wong–Chu, Manager Facility Reimbursement

HAWAII STATE DEPARTMENT OF HEALTH, 3675 Kilauea Avenue, Honolulu, Hawaii Zip 96816; tel. 808/961–4255; Bertrand Kobayashi, Deputy Director

HEALTH CARE PROPERTY INVESTORS, INC., 10990 Wilshire Boulevard, Suite 1200, Newport Beach, California Zip 92660–1875; tel. 213/473–1990; Kenneth B. Roath, President and Chief Executive Officer

HEALTH TOUR, 900 Chelmsford Street, Suite 208, Lowell, Massachusetts Zip 01851–8208; tel. 978/551–4000; William Blank, Vice President Sales

HEALTHCARE FINANCIAL PARTNERS, 2 Wisconsin Circle, 4th Floor, Chevy Case, Maryland Zip 20815; tel. 301/961–1640; Carolyn Small, Marketing Manager

HEALTHTEK SOLUTIONS, INC., 999 Waterside Drive, Suite 1910, Norfolk, Virginia Zip 23510; tel. 757/625–0800; Anthony Montville, President

HOECHST MARION ROUSSEL, 10236 Marion Park Drive, Kansas City, Missouri Zip 64137–1405; tel. 816/966–4000; Matt Kerr, Market Manager

HP3 RESEARCH INSTITUTE, 551 Main Street, 2nd Floor, Bethlehem, Pennsylvania Zip 18018; tel. 610/332–2990; RuthAnn Russo, Chief Executive Officer

INTERNATIONAL ASSOCIATION FOR HEALTHCARE SECURITY AND SAFETY, P.O. Box 637, Lombard, Illinois Zip 60148; tel. 630/953–0990; Nancy Felesena, Executive Assistant

INTERNATIONAL RISK MANAGEMENT, INC., 6480 Rockside Woods Boulevard, S., Cleveland, Ohio Zip 44131; tel. 216/901–2155; Donald J. Kosinski, Senior Vice President

INTERQUAL, INC;., 44 Lafayette Road, North Hampton, New Hampshire Zip 03862; tel. 603/946–7255; Joanne Lamprey, Senior Vice President

J. STEPHENS MAYHUGH AND ASSOCIATES, INC., P.O. Box 3276, Baton Rouge, Louisiana Zip 70821–3276; tel. 800/426–2349; Ron Ellis, Chief Executive Officer

J. T. VAUGHN CONSTRUCTION COMPAYNI, INC., P.O. Box 570787, Houston, Texas Zip 77257–0787; tel. 713/781–3390; Joseph Vaughn, President

JANZEN, JOHNSTON AND ROCKWELL, EMERGENCY MEDICINE MANAGEMENT SERVICES, INC., 4551 Glencoe Avenue, Suite 260, Marina Del Rey, California Zip 90292; tel. 310/301–2030; Richard W. Sanders, Vice President Marketing

MCDONALD'S CORPORATION, 711 Jorie Boulevard, Dept 093, Oak Brook, Illinois Zip 60521; tel. 708/575–3000; Laura Ramirez, Senior Manager Specials

MEDICAL PROTECTIVE COMPANY, 5814 Reed Road, Fort Wayne, Indiana Zip 46835; tel. 219/486–0424; Kathleen M. Roman, Director Risk Management

MODERN HEALTHCARE, 740 North Rush Street, Chicago, Illinois Zip 60611; tel. 312/368–6644; Charles S. Lauer, Corporate Vice President

MORRISON HEALTH CARE, INC., 1955 Lake Park Drive, Suite 400, Smyrna, Georgia Zip 30080–8855; tel. 770/437–3300; Glenn Davenport, President and Chief Executive Officer

NATIONWIDE RETIREMENT SOLUTION, Two Nationwide Plaza, 2nd Floor, Columbus, Ohio Zip 43216; tel. 800/372–0764; Suzanne McEoen, Regional Sales Director

NAVAL REGIONAL MEDICAL CENTER, PSC 1005, Box 36, FPO, APO/FPO Europe Zip 09593–0136

NOVACARE, INC., 1016 West Ninth Avenue, King of Prussia, Pennsylvania Zip 19406; tel. 610/992–7162; Elaine R. Mann, Sales and Marketing Manager

OLYMPUS AMERICA, INC., 2 Corporte Center Drive, Melville, New York Zip 11747; tel. 516/844–5000; Steven K. Wendt, Senior Manager National Accounts

OWEN HEALTHCARE, INC., 9800 Centre Parkway, Suite 1100, Houston, Texas Zip 77036; tel. 713/777–8173; Pam Robinson, Communications Coordinator

PROCTER AND GAMBLE COMPANY, 8700 Mason–Montgomery Road, Box 2071, Mason, Ohio Zip 45040–9462; tel. 513/622–4672; John E. Roney, Associate Director

PROFIT RECOVERY GROUP INTERNATIONAL, 2300 Windy Ridge Parkway, Suite 100, Atlanta, Georgia Zip 30339–8426; Charles Kraft, Marketing Manager

REHABCARE GROUP, INC., 7733 Forsyth Boulevard, Suite 1700, Saint Louis, Missouri Zip 63105–1817; tel. 314/863–7422; Keith L. Goding, Executive Vice President and Chief Development Officer

RURAL/METRO CORPORATION, 8401 East Indian School Road, Scottsdale, Arizona Zip 85251; tel. 602/994–3886; Michel A. Sucher, M.D., Vice President, Medical Affairs

SAINT JOSEPH'S REGIONAL MEDICAL CENTER, P.O. Box 1935, South Bend, Indiana Zip 46634; tel. 219/237–7111; Robert L. Beyer, President and Chief Executive Officer

SCHERING PLOUGH CORPORATION, 2000 Galloping Hill Road, Kenilworth, New Jersey Zip 07033; tel. 908/298–7535; Elizabeth M. Turcotte, Manager Government Affairs

SHARED MEDICAL SYSTEMS, 51 Valley Stream Parkway, Malvern, Pennsylvania Zip 19355; tel. 610/219–3164; Susan B. West, Manager Executive Programs

SOCIAL AND SCIENTIFIC SYSTEMS, 7101 Wisconsin Avenue, Suite 1300, Bethesda, Maryland Zip 20814–4805; tel. 301/986–4870; Katrina Hedlesky, Vice President Computers Division

SPECIALTY LABORATORIES, INC., 2211 Michigan Avenue, Santa Monica, California Zip 90404; tel. 310/828–6543; Susan Bailey, Marketing Manager

STEPHENS, LYNN, KLEIN AND MCNICHOLAS, P.A., 9130 South Dadeland Boulevard, Miami, Florida Zip 33156; tel. 305/670–3700; Oscar J. Cabanas, Partner

TERRY S. WARD AND ASSOCIATES, 5300 Hollister, Suite 200, Houston, Texas Zip 77040; tel. 713/690–1000; Terry S. Ward, President

TEXAS MEDICAL CENTER, 406 Jesse Jones Library Building, Houston, Texas Zip 77030–3303; tel. 713/791–8805; Rhonda K. Simon, Vice President

THE ASSOCIATES – MUNICIPAL FINANCE DIVISION, P.O. Box 650363, Dallas, Texas Zip 75265–0363; tel. 972/652–2767; Ron L. Klein, Vice President Marketing and Sales

THE RENFREW CENTER, 7700 Renfrew Lane, Coconut Creek, Florida Zip 33073; tel. 305/698–9222; Barbara Peterson, Executive Director

TOSHIBA AMERICA MEDICAL SYSTEMS, INC., 2441 Michelle Drive, Tustin, California Zip 92680; tel. 714/730–5000; Catherine M. Eilts, Corporate Marketing and Public Relations Manager

TRILOGY DEVELOPMENT, 6034 West Courtyard Drive, Austin, Texas Zip 78730; tel. 512/425–3546; Kira Dennison, Manager

U. S. ARMY MEDICAL COMMAND, 2050 Worth Road, Suite 3, Fort Sam Houston, Texas Zip 78234; tel. 210/221–2212; Lieutenant General Ronald R. Blanck, MS, Commander

UNITED HOSPITAL FUND OF NEW YORK, 350 Fifth Avenue, 23rd Floor, New York, New York Zip 10118; tel. 212/494–0700; James R. Tallon, Jr., President

VANDERWEIL ENGINEERS, 1055 Maitland Ctr Commons Boulevard, Maitland, Florida Zip 32751; tel. 407/660–0088; Ron Graham, Construction Administrator

VETERANS AFFAIRS CENTRAL REGION OFFICE, P.O. Box 134002, Ann Arbor, Michigan Zip 48113–4002; Linda Belton, Network Director

VETERANS AFFAIRS EASTERN REGION OFFICE, 9600 North Point Road, Fort Howard, Maryland Zip 21052

VETERANS AFFAIRS SOUTHERN REGION, 1461 Lakeover Road, Jackson, Mississippi Zip 39213; tel. 601/364–7920; John R. Higgins, M.D., Network Director

VISITING NURSE ASSOCIATION OF BROOKLYN, 138 South Oxford Street, Brooklyn, New York Zip 11217; tel. 718/230–6950; Jane G. Gould, President and Chief Executive Officer

VISN 1 OFFICE, 200 Spring Road, Building 61, Bedford, Massachusetts Zip 01730

VISN 10 OFFICE, 8600 Governor's Hill Road, 115, Cincinnati, Ohio Zip 45259

VISN 12 OFFICE, Fifth Avenue & Roosevelt Road, Hines, Illinois Zip 60141–5000

VISN 13 OFFICE, One Veterans Drive, Minneapolis, Minnesota Zip 55417

VISN 14 OFFICE, 1055 North 115th Street, Suite 204, Omaha, Nebraska Zip 68154

VISN 15 OFFICE, 4801 Linwood Boulevard, Kansas City, Missouri Zip 64128

VISN 17 OFFICE, 1901 North Highway 360, Suite 350, Grand Prairie, Texas Zip 75050

VISN 18 OFFICE, 6001 South Power Road, Building 237, Mesa, Arizona Zip 85206–0910

VISN 19 OFFICE, 4100 East Mississippi Avenue, 510, Glendale, Colorado Zip 80222

VISN 2 OFFICE, P.O. Box 8980, Albany, New York Zip 12208–0980

VISN 20 OFFICE, P.O. Box 1035, Portland, Oregon Zip 97207

VISN 22 OFFICE, 5901 East Seventh Street, Long Beach, California Zip 90822

VISN 3 OFFICE, 130 West Kingsbridge Road, Building 16, Bronx, New York Zip 10468

VISN 4 OFFICE, Delafield Road, Pittsburgh, Pennsylvania Zip 15240

VISN 6 OFFICE, 849 International Drive, Suite 275, Linthicum Heights, Maryland Zip 21090

VISN 6 OFFICE, 300 Morgan Street, Suite 1402, Durham, North Carolina Zip 27701

VISN 7 OFFICE, 2200 Century Parkway N.E., Suite 260, Atlanta, Georgia Zip 30345–3203

VISN 8 OFFICE, P.O. Box 5007, Bay Pines, Florida Zip 33744

VISN 9 OFFICE, 1310 24th Avenue South, Nashville, Tennessee Zip 37212–2637

WINSTAR TELECOMMUNICATIONS, INC., 101 North Wacker Drive, Suite 1950, Chicago, Illinois Zip 60606; tel. 312/673–9400; Jill Buckenmeyer, National Account Manager

Preferred Provider Org:

U.S.A. MANAGED CARE ORGANIZATION, 7301 North 16th Street, Suite 201, Phoenix, Arizona Zip 85020; tel. 602/371–3880; Karen Bass, Vice President and Chief Administrative Officer

Recruitment Services:

DIVERSIFIED SEARCH COMPANIES, 2005 Market Street, 33rd Floor, Philadelphia, Pennsylvania Zip 19103; tel. 215/732–6666; Judith M. von Seldeneck, Chief Executive Officer

School of Nursing:

NORTHEASTERN HOSPITAL OF PHILADELPHIA SCHOOL OF NURSING, 2301 East Allegheny Avenue, Philadelphia, Pennsylvania Zip 19134; tel. 215/291–3145; Mary Wonbwell, Direcctor, School of Nursing

State Agency for Health:

DEPARTMENT OF HEALTH HOSPITAL AND PATIENT DATA SYSTEMS, CENTER FOR HEALTH STATISTICS, P.O. Box 47811, Olympia, Washington Zip 98504–7811; tel. 360/236–7811; Teresa Jennings, Director

CANADA

Other:

DARCOR CASTERS, 7 Staffordshire Place, Toronto, Ontario Zip M8W 1T1; tel. 416/255–8563; Cyril J. Muhic, Regional Sales Manager

SIGMA ASSISTEL, INC., 1100 Boul Rene–Levesque Quest, Suite 1500, Montreal, Quebec Zip H3B 4N4; tel. 800/465–6390; Louise Des Ormeaux, General Manager

ST. JOSEPH'S HEALTH CARE SYSTEM, P.O. Box 155, LCD 1, Hamilton, Ontario Zip L8L 7V7; tel. 905/528–0138; Brian Guest, Executive Director

FOREIGN

AUSTRALIA

Other:

AUSTRALIAN PRIVATE HOSPITALS ASSOCIATION LTD., P.O. Box 346, Curtin ACT 2605, Ian Chalmers, Executive Director

THE VICTORIAN HEALTHCARE ASSOCIATION LIMITED, P.O. Box 365, South Melbourne, Zip 3205; tel. 613/266–3691; John Popper, Managing Director

BAHAMAS

Other:

PRINCESS MARGARET HOSPITAL, P.O. Box N 3730, Nassau, tel. 809/322–2861; Herbert Brown, Administrator

BAHRAIN

Other:

INTERNATIONAL HOSPITAL OF BAHRAIN, P.O. Box 1084, Manama, F. S. Zeerah, M.D., President

BRAZIL

Consulting Firm:

IHC–HOSPITALIUM, Rua dos Pinheiros, 498–cj, 61, San Paulo, Zip 05422–902; Edson Gomez dos Santos, President

Other:

CLINICA SAO VICENTE, Rua Joao Borges 204 – Gavea, Dogue, Zip 22 451–100; Luiz Roberto Londres, President

PRONTOBABY–HOSPITAL DA CRIANCA, Rua Adolfo Mota No 81, Rio De Janeiro, Mario Eduardo Gulmarseo Viana, Director

SOCIEDADE HOSPITAL SAMARITANO, Rua Conselheiro Brotero, 1486, Sao Paulo, Zip 01232–010; tel. 000/825–1122; Bryan Morgan, Director Superintendente

COLUMBIA

Other:

ASOCIACION COLOMBIANA DE HOSPITALES Y CLINICAS, Carrera 4, No 73–15, Bogota, tel. 091/312–4411; Roberto Esguerra Gutierrez, M.D., President

FUNDACION SANTA FE DE BOGOTA, Calle 116 9–02, Santa Fe De Bogota, Ana Catalina Vesquez Quintero, Manager

GREECE

Other:

DIAGNOSTIC AND THERAPEUTIC CENTRE OF ATHENS HYGEIA, S A, 4 Erythrou Stavrou & Kifissiap, Athens, C. Kitsionas, Executive Director

HOSPITAL AFFILIATES INTERNATIONAL, 332 Kifissias Avenue, Halandri, Athens 152 33, A. Philip Chrysafidis, Senior Consultant

IASO S.A. DIAGNOSTIC THERAPEUTIC AND RESEARCH CENTER, OBSTETRICS AND GYNECOLOGY HOSPITAL, 37–39 Kifissias Avenue, Maroussi Athens, Zip 15123; Constantin Mavros, Ph.D., Managing Director and Chief Executive Officer

ISRAEL

Other:

HADASSAH MEDICAL ORGANIZATION, Box 12000, Jerusalem, Zip 91120; Avi Israeli, M.D., Director General

S.A.R.E.L. SUPPLIES AND SERVICES FOR MEDICINE LTD., 15 Yehuda & Noah Mozes Street, Tel Aviv, Moshe Modai, Ph.D., Chief Executive Officer

JAPAN

Other:

NAVAL REGIONAL MEDICAL CENTER, FPO, Zip 96362

ST. LUKE'S INTERNATIONAL HOSPITAL, 10–1 Akashi–Cho, Chuo–Ku, Tokyo 104, Shigeaki Hinohara, M.D., Honorary President

LEBANON

Other:

AMERICAN UNIVERSITY OF BEIRUT MEDICAL CENTER, 850 Third Avenue, 18th Floor, New York, Zip 10022; Dieter Kuntz, Executive Director

MAKASSED GENERAL HOSPITAL, P.O. Box 6301, Beirut, Moh'd Firikh, Director

SAINT GEORGE HOSPITAL, P.O. Box 166378, Beirut, Ziad Kamel, Assistant Director

MEXICO

Other:

SHRINERS HOSPITAL FOR CHILDREN, Suchil 152, Colonel El Rosario, Mexico City 04380, Araceli Nagore, R.N., Administrator

Other Inpatient Care:

OASIS HOSPITAL, 2247 San Diego Avenue, Suite 235, San Ysidro, Zip 92143; tel. 800/700–1850; Francisco Contreras, Director

NETHERLANDS ANTILLES

Other:

SINT MAARTEN MEDICAL CENTER FOUNDATION, Welgelegen Road 30 Ut 1 Cay Hill, Sint Maarten, Emma Bell–Wynter, M.D., Medical Director

PERU

Other:

ASOCIACION BENEFICA ANGLO AMERICANA, Avenue Alfredo Salazar 3 Era, Lima 27, Gonzalo Garrido–Lecca, Director

SOUTHERN PERU COPPER CORPORATION, 1612 N.W. 84th Avenue, Miami, Zip 33126–1032; Rod G. Guzman, Medical Division Superintendent

PHILIPPINES

Other:

ST. LUKE'S MEDICAL CENTER, 279 East Rodriguez Sr Boulevard, Quezon City, Jose F. G. Ledesma, Chief Executive Officer

SAUDI ARABIA

Other:

ABDUL RAHMAN AL MISHARI GENERAL HOSPITAL, Olaya, Riyadh 11564, Abdul Rahman Al Mishari, M.D., President

ELAJ MEDICAL SERVICES COMPANY, LTD., P.O. Box 51141, Jeddah 21463, Mohamed Amin, Medical Director

MUHAMMAD S BASHARAHIL HOSPITAL, P.O. Box 10505, Makkah, Sameer M. Basharahil, Vice President

SAUDI ARAMCO MEDICAL SERVICES, 9009 West Loop South, MS–549, Houston, Zip 77096; Harris Worchel, Supervisor Information and Image Services

SPAIN

Other:

ESCUELA INTERNACIONAL DE ALTA DIRECCION HOSPITALARIO, Alcala 114, 1, Madrid 28009, Enrique Marochi Rodriguez, Chairman

TAIWAN

Other:

CHANG GUNG MEMORIAL HOSPITAL, 199 Tun Hwa North Road, Taipei, Yi–Chou Chuang, Director Administration Center

MACKAY MEMORIAL HOSPITAL, 92–Sec–2 North Chungshan Road, Taipei, Rick C. C. Huang, Vice Superintendent

TURKEY

Other:

ALKAN HOSPITAL, Birlik Mah, 8 Cad 103 Sokak 10, Cankaya, Ankara, Zip 06552; Oguz Engiz, Chief Executive Officer

AMERICAN HOSPITAL OF ISTANBUL, Guzelbaghe SOK 20, Nisantasi, Istanbul, Zip 80020; George D. Roundtree, Chief Executive Officer

BAYINDIR HEALTH CARE SYSTEM, Maslak Pl Buyukdere Cad 69 K. 8, Ayazaga/Istanbul, Zip 80670; Murat Ornekol, President

ISTANBUL MEMORIAL MEDICAL CENTER, Caglayan Vatan Caddesi, 2/5, Istanbul, Zip 80340; Sarper Tanli, M.D., Medical Director

UNITED ARAB EMIRATES

Other:

AMERICAN HOSPITAL–DUBAI, P.O. Box 59, Dubai, Saeed M. Almulla, Chairman

VENEZUELA

Other:

POLICLINICA METROPOLITANA, C.A., P.O. Box 025255, Miami, Zip 33102–5255; Edgar Escalona, M.D., Medical Director

B

**Networks,
Health Care Systems
and Alliances**

Section B

Introduction

This section includes listings for networks, health care systems and alliances.

Networks

The *AHA Guide* shows listings of networks. A network is defined as a group of hospitals, physicians, other providers, insurers and/or community agencies that work together to coordinate and deliver a broad spectrum of services to their community. Organizations listed represent the lead or hub of the network activity. Networks are listed by state, then alphabetically by name including participating partners.

The network identification process has purposely been designed to capture networks of varying organization type. Sources include but are not limited to the following: *AHA Annual Survey,* national, state and metropolitan associations, national news and periodical searches, and the networks and their health care providers themselves. Therefore, networks are included regardless of whether a hospital or healthcare system is the network lead. When an individual hospital does appear in the listing, it is indicative of the role the hospital plays as the network lead. In addition, the network listing is **not** mutually exclusive of the hospital, health care system or alliance listings within this publication.

Networks are very fluid in their composition as goals evolve and partners change. Therefore, some of the networks included in this listing may have dissolved, reformed, or simply been renamed as this section was being produced for publication.

The network identification process is an ongoing and responsive initiative. As more information is collected and validated, it will be made available in other venues, in addition to the *AHA Guide.* For more information concerning the network identification process, please contact Health Forum LLC, an affiliate of the American Hospital Association at 800/821–2039.

Health Care Systems

To reflect the diversity that exists among health care organizations, this publication uses the term health care system to identify both multihospital and diversified single hospital systems.

Multihospital Systems

A multihospital health care system is two or more hospitals owned, leased, sponsored, or contract managed by a central organization.

Single Hospital Systems

Single, freestanding member hospitals may be categorized as health care systems by bringing into membership three or more, and at least 25 percent, of their owned or leased non–hospital preacute and postacute health care organizations. (For purposes of definition, health care delivery is the availability of professional healthcare staff during all hours of the organization's operations). Organizations provide, or provide and finance, diagnostic, therapeutic, and/or consultative patient or client services that normally precede or follow acute, inpatient, hospitalization; or that serve to prevent or substitute for such hospitalization. These services are provided in either a freestanding facility not eligible for licensure as a hospital understate statue or through one that is a subsidiary of a hospital.

The first part of this section is an alphabetical list of multihospital health care systems. Each system listed contains two or more hospitals, which are listed under the system by state. Data for this section were compiled from the 1998 *Annual Survey* and the membership information base as published in section A of the *AHA Guide.*

One of the following codes appears after the name of each system listed to indicate the type of organizational control reported by that system:

CC	Catholic (Roman) church–related system, not–for–profit
CO	Other church–related system, not–for–profit
NP	Other not–for–profit system, including nonfederal, governmental systems
IO	Investor–owned, for profit system
FG	Federal Government

One of the following codes appears after the name of each hospital to indicate how that hospital is related to the system:

O	Owned
L	Leased
S	Sponsored
CM	Contract–managed

The second part of this section lists health care systems indexed geographically by state and city. Every effort has been made to be as inclusive and accurate as possible. However, as in all efforts of this type, there may be omissions. For further information, write to the section for Health Care Systems, American Hospital Association, One North Franklin, Chicago, IL 60606–3401.

Alliances

An alliance is a formal organization, usually owned by shareholders/members, that works on behalf of its individual members in the provision of services and products and in the promotion of activities and ventures. The organization functions under a set of bylaws or other written rules to which each member agrees to abide.

Alliances are listed alphabetically by name. Its members are listed alphabetically by state, city, and then by member name.

ALABAMA

ALABAMA HEALTH SERVICES
48 Medical Park East Drive Suite 450, Birminham, AL 35235; tel. 205/838-3999; Robert C. Chapman, President & CEO

BROOKWOOD MEDICAL CENTER, 2010 Brookwood Medical Center Drive, Birmingham, AL, Zip 35209; tel. 205/877-1000; Gregory H. Burfitt, President and Chief Executive Officer

LLOYD NOLAND HOSPITAL AND HEALTH SYSTEM, 701 Lloyd Noland Parkway, Fairfield, AL, Zip 35064-2699; tel. 205/783-5106; Garry L. Gause, Chief Executive Officer

MEDICAL CENTER BLOUNT, 150 Gilbreath, Oneonta, AL, Zip 35121-2534, Mailing Address: P.O. Box 1000, Zip 35121-1000; tel. 205/625-3511; George McGowan, FACHE, Chief Executive Officer

MEDICAL CENTER EAST, 50 Medical Park East Drive, Birmingham, AL, Zip 35235-9987; tel. 205/838-3000; David E. Crawford, FACHE, Executive Vice President and Chief Operating Officer

ST. CLAIR REGIONAL HOSPITAL, 2805 Hospital Drive, Pell City, AL, Zip 35125-1499; tel. 205/338-3301; Douglas H. Beverly, CHE, Chief Operating Officer

BAPTIST HEALTH SYSTEM
P.O. Box 830605, Birmingham, AL 35283; tel. 205/968-2155; Carl Sather, Senior Vice President

CHEROKEE BAPTIST MEDICAL CENTER, 400 Northwood Drive, Centre, AL, Zip 35960-1023; tel. 256/927-5531; Barry S. Cochran, President

CITIZENS BAPTIST MEDICAL CENTER, 604 Stone Avenue, Talladega, AL, Zip 35160-2217, Mailing Address: P.O. Box 978, Zip 35161-0978; tel. 256/362-8111; Steven M. Johnson, President

COOSA VALLEY BAPTIST MEDICAL CENTER, 315 West Hickory Street, Sylacauga, AL, Zip 35150-2996; tel. 256/249-5000; Steven M. Johnson, President

CULLMAN REGIONAL MEDICAL CENTER, 1912 Alabama Highway 157, Cullman, AL, Zip 35055, Mailing Address: P.O. Box 1108, Zip 35056-1108; tel. 256/737-2000; Jesse O. Weatherly, President

DEKALB BAPTIST MEDICAL CENTER, 200 Medical Center Drive, Fort Payne, AL, Zip 35968-3415, Mailing Address: P.O. Box 680778, Zip 35968-1608; tel. 256/845-3150; Barry S. Cochran, President

LAWRENCE BAPTIST MEDICAL CENTER, 202 Hospital Street, Moulton, AL, Zip 35650-0039, Mailing Address: P.O. Box 39, Zip 35650-0039; tel. 256/974-2200; Cheryl Hays, Administrator

MARION BAPTIST MEDICAL CENTER, 1256 Military Street South, Hamilton, AL, Zip 35570-5001; tel. 205/921-6200; Evan S. Dillard, President

MONTCLAIR BAPTIST MEDICAL CENTER, 800 Montclair Road, Birmingham, AL, Zip 35213-1984; tel. 205/592-1000; John Shelton, President

PRINCETON BAPTIST MEDICAL CENTER, 701 Princeton Avenue S.W., Birmingham, AL, Zip 35211-1305; tel. 205/783-3000; Charlie Faulkner, President

SHELBY BAPTIST MEDICAL CENTER, 1000 First Street North, Alabaster, AL, Zip 35007-0488, Mailing Address: Box 488, Zip 35007-0488; tel. 205/620-8100; Charles C. Colvert, President

HEALTHGROUP OF ALABAMA
P.O. Box 1246, Madison, AL 35758; tel. 205/772-4155; Edward D. Boston, Chief Executive Officer

ATHENS-LIMESTONE HOSPITAL, 700 West Market Street, Athens, AL, Zip 35611-2457, Mailing Address: P.O. Box 999, Zip 35612-0999; tel. 256/233-9292; Philip E. Dotson, Administrator and Chief Executive Officer

DECATUR GENERAL HOSPITAL, 1201 Seventh Street S.E., Decatur, AL, Zip 35601, Mailing Address: P.O. Box 2239, Zip 35609-2239; tel. 256/341-2000; Robert L. Smith, President and Chief Executive Officer

DECATUR GENERAL HOSPITAL-WEST, 2205 Beltline Road S.W., Decatur, AL, Zip 35601-3687, Mailing Address: P.O. Box 2240, Zip 35609-2240; tel. 205/350-1450; Dennis Griffith, Vice President

ELIZA COFFEE MEMORIAL HOSPITAL, 205 Marengo Street, Florence, AL, Zip 35630-6033, Mailing Address: P.O. Box 818, Zip 35631-0818; tel. 256/768-9191; Richard H. Peck, President and Chief Executive Officer

HUNTSVILLE HOSPITAL, 101 Sivley Road, Huntsville, AL, Zip 35801-4470; tel. 256/517-8020; L. Joe Austin, Chief Executive Officer

T.R. MCDOUGAL & ASSOCIATES
P.O. Box 11126, Montgomery, AL 36111; tel. 334/260-8600; Tommy McDougal, President

BRYAN W. WHITFIELD MEMORIAL HOSPITAL, Highway 80 West, Demopolis, AL, Zip 36732, Mailing Address: P.O. Box 890, Zip 36732-0890; tel. 334/289-4000; Charles E. Nabors, FACHE, Administrator and Chief Executive Officer

UNIVERSITY OF ALABAMA
701 South 20th Street, Birmingham, AL 35233; tel. 205/934-5199; Dr. Michael Geheb, Chief Executive Officer

UNIVERSITY OF ALABAMA HOSPITAL, 619 South 19th Street, Birmingham, AL, Zip 35233-6505; tel. 205/934-4011; Martin Nowak, Interim Executive Director

ALASKA

KETCHIKAN GENERAL HOSPITAL
3100 Tongass Avenue, Ketchikan, AK 99901; tel. 907/225-5171; Ed Mahn, President

CHARTER NORTH STAR BEHAVIORAL HEALTH SYSTEM, 1650 South Bragaw, Anchorage, AK, Zip 99508-3467; tel. 907/258-7575; Kathleen Cronen, Chief Executive Officer

KETCHIKAN GENERAL HOSPITAL, 3100 Tongass Avenue, Ketchikan, AK, Zip 99901-5746; tel. 907/225-5171; Edward F. Mahn, Chief Executive Officer

NORTON SOUND REGIONAL HOSPITAL
P.O. Box 966, Nome, AK 99762; tel. 907/443-3311; H. Mack, Network Contact

NORTON SOUND REGIONAL HOSPITAL, Bering Straits, Nome, AK, Zip 99762, Mailing Address: P.O. Box 966, Zip 99762-0966; tel. 907/443-3311; Charles Fagerstrom, Vice President

ARIZONA

ARIZONA VOLUNTARY HOSPITAL FEDERATION
1430 West Broadway, Suite A110, Tempe, AZ 85282; tel. 602/.96-5622; Lew Harper, Network Contact

BAPTIST HOSPITALS AND HEALTH
2224 West Northern, Phoenix, AZ 85021; tel. 602/246-5800; Michael I. Purvis, Executive Vice President

ARROWHEAD COMMUNITY HOSPITAL AND MEDICAL CENTER, 18701 North 67th Avenue, Glendale, AZ, Zip 85308-5722; tel. 602/561-1000; Richard S. Alley, Executive Vice President and Chief Executive Officer

PHOENIX BAPTIST HOSPITAL AND MEDICAL CENTER, 2000 West Bethany Home Road, Phoenix, AZ, Zip 85015-2110; tel. 602/249-0212; Michael Purvis, Executive Vice President and Chief Executive Officer

WESTERN ARIZONA REGIONAL MEDICAL CENTER, 2735 Silver Creek Road, Bullhead City, AZ, Zip 86442-8303; tel. 520/763-2273; James Sato, Senior Vice President and Chief Executive Officer

CARONDELET INTEGRATED DELIVERY SYSTEM
1601 West St. Mary's Road, Tucson, AZ 85745; tel. 602/622-5833; Sister St. Joan Willert, President

CARONDELET HOLY CROSS HOSPITAL, 1171 West Target Range Road, Nogales, AZ, Zip 85621-2496; tel. 520/287-2771; Carol Field, Senior Corporate Director and Administrator

CARONDELET ST. JOSEPH'S HOSPITAL, 350 North Wilmot Road, Tucson, AZ, Zip 85711-2678; tel. 520/296-3211; Sister St. Joan Willert, President and Chief Executive Officer

CARONDELET ST. MARY'S HOSPITAL, 1601 West St. Mary's Road, Tucson, AZ, Zip 85745-2682; tel. 520/622-5833; Sister St. Joan Willert, President and Chief Executive Officer

LUTHERAN HEALTHCARE NETWORK
500 W. 10th Place Suite 237, Mesa, AZ 85201; tel. 602/461-2157; Don Evans, CEO

MESA LUTHERAN HOSPITAL, 525 West Brown Road, Mesa, AZ, Zip 85201-3299; tel. 602/834-1211; Robert A. Rundio, Executive Director of Hospital Operations

VALLEY LUTHERAN HOSPITAL, 6644 Baywood Avenue, Mesa, AZ, Zip 85206-1797; tel. 602/981-2000; Robert A. Rundio, Executive Director of Hospital Operations

MARICOPA HEALTH SYSTEM
2601 East Roosevelt Street, Phoenix, AZ 85008; tel. 602/267-5011; Anthony Rogers, Director

MARICOPA MEDICAL CENTER, 2601 East Roosevelt Street, Phoenix, AZ, Zip 85008-4956; tel. 602/334-5111; Mark Hillard, Chief Executive Officer

NORTHERN ARIZONA HEALTHCARE
1200 North Beaver Street, Flagstaff, AZ 86001; tel. 520/773-2001; Joseph M. Kortum, President & CEO

VERDE VALLEY MEDICAL CENTER, 269 South Candy Lane, Cottonwood, AZ, Zip 86326; tel. 520/634-2251; Craig A. Owens, President and Chief Operating Officer

SAINT LUKES HEALTH SYSTEM
1500 Mill Ave., Tempe, AZ 85281; tel. 602/784-5509; Mary Gregory, CEO

ST. LUKE'S BEHAVIORAL HEALTH CENTER, 1800 East Van Buren, Phoenix, AZ, Zip 85006-3742; tel. 602/251-8484; Patrick D. Waugh, Chief Executive Officer

ST. LUKE'S MEDICAL CENTER, 1800 East Van Buren Street, Phoenix, AZ, Zip 85006-3742; tel. 602/251-8100; Mary Jo Gregory, Chief Executive Officer

TEMPE ST. LUKE'S HOSPITAL, 1500 South Mill Avenue, Tempe, AZ, Zip 85281-6699; tel. 602/784-5510; Mary Jo Gregory, Chief Executive Officer

SAMARITAN SYSTEM CENTER
1441 North 12th Street, Phoenix, AZ 85006; tel. 602/495-4000; James Crews, President

COLORADO RIVER MEDICAL CENTER, 1401 Bailey Avenue, Needles, CA, Zip 92363; tel. 760/326-4531; James Arp, Chief Executive Officer

DESERT SAMARITAN MEDICAL CENTER, 1400 South Dobson Road, Mesa, AZ, Zip 85202-9879; tel. 602/835-3000; Bruce E. Pearson, Senior Vice President and Chief Executive Officer

GOOD SAMARITAN REGIONAL MEDICAL CENTER, 1111 East McDowell Road, Phoenix, AZ, Zip 85006–2666, Mailing Address: P.O. Box 2989, Zip 85062–2989; tel. 602/239–2000; Steven L. Seiler, Senior Vice President and Chief Executive Officer

HAVASU REGIONAL MEDICAL CENTER, 101 Civic Center Lane, Lake Havasu City, AZ, Zip 86403–5683; tel. 520/855–8185; Kevin P. Poorten, Chief Executive Officer

MARYVALE HOSPITAL MEDICAL CENTER, 5102 West Campbell Avenue, Phoenix, AZ, Zip 85031–1799; tel. 602/848–5000; Art Layne, Chief Executive Officer

SAMARITAN BEHAVIORAL HEALTH CENTER–SCOTTSDALE, 7575 East Earll Drive, Scottsdale, AZ, Zip 85251–6998; tel. 602/941–7500; Robert F. Meyer, M.D., Chief Executive Officer

SAMARITAN–WENDY PAINE O'BRIEN TREATMENT CENTER, 5055 North 34th Street, Phoenix, AZ, Zip 85018–1498; tel. 602/955–6200; Robert F. Meyer, M.D., Chief Executive Officer

SAN CLEMENTE HOSPITAL AND MEDICAL CENTER, 654 Camino De Los Mares, San Clemente, CA, Zip 92673; tel. 949/496–1122; Patricia L. Wolfram, R.N., Chief Executive Officer

THUNDERBIRD SAMARITAN MEDICAL CENTER, 5555 West Thunderbird Road, Glendale, AZ, Zip 85306–4696; tel. 602/588–5555; Robert H. Curry, Senior Vice President and Chief Executive Officer

WHITE MOUNTAIN REGIONAL MEDICAL CENTER, 118 South Mountain Avenue, Springerville, AZ, Zip 85938, Mailing Address: P.O. Box 880, Zip 85938–0880; tel. 520/333–4368; Jerry Campeau, Inteirm Chief Executive Officer

SUN HEALTH CORPORATION
13180 N. 103rd Drive, Sun City, AZ 85351; tel. 623/876–5352; Leland W. Peterson, President & CEO

DEL E. WEBB MEMORIAL HOSPITAL, 14502 West Meeker Boulevard, Sun City West, AZ, Zip 85375–5299, Mailing Address: P.O. Box 5169, Sun City, Zip 85375–5169; tel. 623/214–4000; Thomas C. Dickson, Executive Vice President and Chief Operating Officer

WALTER O. BOSWELL MEMORIAL HOSPITAL, 10401 West Thunderbird Boulevard, Sun City, AZ, Zip 85351–3092, Mailing Address: P.O. Box 1690, Zip 85372–1690; tel. 623/977–7211; George Perez, Executive Vice President and Chief Operating Officer

ARKANSAS

ARKANSAS NETWORK
5106 McClanahan, Suite E., North Little Rock, AR 72116; tel. 501/666–1200; Mike Gross, Network Director

CHICOT MEMORIAL HOSPITAL, 2729 Highway 65 and 82 South, Lake Village, AR, Zip 71653, Mailing Address: P.O. Box 512, Zip 71653–0512; tel. 870/265–5351; Robert R. Reddish, Administrator and Chief Executive Officer

DELTA MEMORIAL HOSPITAL, 300 East Pickens Street, Dumas, AR, Zip 71639–2710, Mailing Address: P.O. Box 887, Zip 71639–0887; tel. 870/382–4303; Kurt Meyer, Administrator

HOWARD MEMORIAL HOSPITAL, 800 West Leslie Street, Nashville, AR, Zip 71852–0381, Mailing Address: Box 381, Zip 71852–0381; tel. 870/845–4400; Rex Jones, Chief Executive Officer

MENA MEDICAL CENTER, 311 North Morrow Street, Mena, AR, Zip 71953–2516; tel. 501/394–6100; Albert Pilkington, III, Administrator and Chief Executive Officer

NORTHWEST MEDICAL CENTER, 609 West Maple Avenue, Springdale, AR, Zip 72764–5394, Mailing Address: P.O. Box 47, Zip 72765–0047; tel. 501/751–5711; Greg K. Stock, Chief Executive Officer

OUACHITA MEDICAL CENTER, 638 California Street, Camden, AR, Zip 71701–4699, Mailing Address: P.O. Box 797, Zip 71701–0797; tel. 870/836–1000; C. C. McAllister, President and Chief Executive Officer

REBSAMEN MEDICAL CENTER, 1400 West Braden Street, Jacksonville, AR, Zip 72076–3788; tel. 501/985–7000; Thomas R. Siemers, Chief Executive Officer

SALINE MEMORIAL HOSPITAL, 1 Medical Park Drive, Benton, AR, Zip 72015–3354; tel. 501/776–6000; Roger D. Feldt, FACHE, President and Chief Executive Officer

SILOAM SPRINGS MEMORIAL HOSPITAL, 205 East Jefferson Street, Siloam Springs, AR, Zip 72761–3697; tel. 501/524–4141; Donald E. Patterson, Administrator

ST. VINCENT INFIRMARY MEDICAL CENTER, Two St. Vincent Circle, Little Rock, AR, Zip 72205–5499; tel. 501/660–3000; Diana T. Hueter, President and Chief Executive Officer

ARKANSAS' FIRST SOURCE
P.O. Box 2181, Little Rock, AR 72203; tel. 501/378–3251; Mike Brown, Vice President

ARKANSAS CHILDREN'S HOSPITAL, 800 Marshall Street, Little Rock, AR, Zip 72202–3591; tel. 501/320–1100; Jonathan R. Bates, M.D., President and Chief Executive Officer

ARKANSAS METHODIST HOSPITAL, 900 West Kingshighway, Paragould, AR, Zip 72450–5942, Mailing Address: P.O. Box 339, Zip 72451–0339; tel. 870/239–7000; Ronald K. Rooney, President

BAPTIST MEDICAL CENTER, 9601 Interstate 630, Exit 7, Little Rock, AR, Zip 72205–7299; tel. 501/202–2000; Steven Douglas Weeks, Senior Vice President and Administrator

BAPTIST MEDICAL CENTER ARKADELPHIA, 3050 Twin Rivers Drive, Arkadelphia, AR, Zip 71923–4299; tel. 870/245–1100; Dan Gathright, Senior Vice President and Administrator

BAPTIST MEDICAL CENTER HEBER SPRINGS, 2319 Highway 110 West, Heber Springs, AR, Zip 72543; tel. 501/206–3000; Edward L. Lacy, Administrator

BAPTIST MEMORIAL HOSPITAL–BLYTHEVILLE, 1520 North Division Street, Blytheville, AR, Zip 72315, Mailing Address: P.O. Box 108, Zip 72316–0108; tel. 870/838–7300; Al Sypniewski, Administrator

BAPTIST MEMORIAL HOSPITAL–FORREST CITY, 1601 Newcastle Road, Forrest City, AR, Zip 72335, Mailing Address: P.O. Box 667, Zip 72336–0667; tel. 870/261–0000; Charles R. Daugherty, Administrator

BAPTIST MEMORIAL HOSPITAL–OSCEOLA, 611 West Lee Avenue, Osceola, AR, Zip 72370–3001, Mailing Address: P.O. Box 607, Zip 72370–0607; tel. 870/563–7000; Joel E. North, Administrator

BAPTIST MEMORIAL MEDICAL CENTER, One Pershing Circle, North Little Rock, AR, Zip 72114–1899; tel. 501/202–3000; Harrison M. Dean, Senior Vice President and Administrator

BAPTIST REHABILITATION INSTITUTE, 9601 Interstate 630, Exit 7, Little Rock, AR, Zip 72205–7249; tel. 501/202–7000; Steven Douglas Weeks, Senior Vice President and Administrator

BAPTIST REHABILITATION–GERMANTOWN, 2100 Exeter Road, Germantown, TN, Zip 38138; tel. 901/757–1350; Paula Gisler, Administrator

BAXTER COUNTY REGIONAL HOSPITAL, 624 Hospital Drive, Mountain Home, AR, Zip 72653–2954; tel. 870/424–1000; H. William Anderson, Administrator

BOONEVILLE COMMUNITY HOSPITAL, 880 West Main Street, Booneville, AR, Zip 72927–3420, Mailing Address: P.O. Box 290, Zip 72927–0290; tel. 501/675–2800; Robert R. Bash, Administrator

BRADLEY COUNTY MEDICAL CENTER, 404 South Bradley Street, Warren, AR, Zip 71671; tel. 870/226–3731; Edward L. Nilles, President and Chief Executive Officer

CARROLL REGIONAL MEDICAL CENTER, 214 Carter Street, Berryville, AR, Zip 72616–4303; tel. 870/423–3355; Rudy Darling, President and Chief Executive Officer

CHAMBERS MEMORIAL HOSPITAL, Highway 10 at Detroit, Danville, AR, Zip 72833, Mailing Address: P.O. Box 639, Zip 72833–0639; tel. 501/495–2241; Scott Peek, Administrator

CHICOT MEMORIAL HOSPITAL, 2729 Highway 65 and 82 South, Lake Village, AR, Zip 71653, Mailing Address: P.O. Box 512, Zip 71653–0512; tel. 870/265–5351; Robert R. Reddish, Administrator and Chief Executive Officer

CONWAY REGIONAL MEDICAL CENTER, 2302 College Avenue, Conway, AR, Zip 72032–6297; tel. 501/329–3831; James A. Summersett, III, FACHE, President and Chief Executive Officer

CRAWFORD MEMORIAL HOSPITAL, East Main & South 20th Streets, Van Buren, AR, Zip 72956, Mailing Address: P.O. Box 409, Zip 72957–0409; tel. 501/474–3401; Richard Boone, Executive Director

CRITTENDEN MEMORIAL HOSPITAL, 200 Tyler Avenue, West Memphis, AR, Zip 72301–4223, Mailing Address: P.O. Box 2248, Zip 72303–2248; tel. 870/735–1500; Ross Hooper, Chief Executive Officer

CROSS COUNTY HOSPITAL, 310 South Falls Boulevard, Wynne, AR, Zip 72396–3013, Mailing Address: P.O. Box 590, Zip 72396–0590; tel. 870/238–3300; Harry M. Baker, Chief Executive Officer

DE QUEEN REGIONAL MEDICAL CENTER, 1306 Collin Raye Drive, De Queen, AR, Zip 71832–2198; tel. 870/584–4111; Charles H. Long, Chief Executive Officer

DELTA MEMORIAL HOSPITAL, 300 East Pickens Street, Dumas, AR, Zip 71639–2710, Mailing Address: P.O. Box 887, Zip 71639–0887; tel. 870/382–4303; Kurt Meyer, Administrator

DEWITT CITY HOSPITAL, Highway 1 and Madison Street, De Witt, AR, Zip 72042, Mailing Address: P.O. Box 32, Zip 72042–0032; tel. 870/946–3571; Joe E. Smith, Administrator and Chief Executive Officer

DREW MEMORIAL HOSPITAL, 778 Scogin Drive, Monticello, AR, Zip 71655–5728; tel. 870/367–2411; Darren Caldwell, Chief Executive Officer

EASTERN OZARKS REGIONAL HEALTH SYSTEM, 122 South Allegheny Drive, Cherokee Village, AR, Zip 72529–7300; tel. 870/257–4101; Cindy Hall, Administrator

EUREKA SPRINGS HOSPITAL, 24 Norris Street, Eureka Springs, AR, Zip 72632–3541; tel. 501/253–7400; Joe Hammond, Administrator

FULTON COUNTY HOSPITAL, Highway 9, Salem, AR, Zip 72576, Mailing Address: P.O. Box 517, Zip 72576–0517; tel. 501/895–2691; Franklin E. Wise, Administrator

GRAVETTE MEDICAL CENTER HOSPITAL, 1101 Jackson Street S.W., Gravette, AR, Zip 72736–0470, Mailing Address: P.O. Box 470, Zip 72736–0470; tel. 501/787–5291; John F. Phillips, Administrator

H.S.C. MEDICAL CENTER, 1001 Schneider Drive, Malvern, AR, Zip 72104–4828; tel. 501/337–4911; Jeff Curtis, President and Chief Executive Officer

HARBOR VIEW MERCY HOSPITAL, 10301 Mayo Road, Fort Smith, AR, Zip 72903–1631, Mailing Address: P.O. Box 17000, Zip 72917–7000; tel. 501/484–5550; Richard Cameron, M.D., Administrator

HARRIS HOSPITAL, 1205 McLain Street, Newport, AR, Zip 72112–3533; tel. 870/523–8911; Robin E. Lake, Chief Executive Officer

HEALTHSOUTH REHABILITATION HOSPITAL OF JONESBORO, 1201 Fleming Avenue, Jonesboro, AR, Zip 72401–4311, Mailing Address: P.O. Box 1680, Zip 72403–1680; tel. 870/932–0440; Brenda Antwine, Administrator

HELENA REGIONAL MEDICAL CENTER, 1801 Martin Luther King Drive, Helena, AR, Zip 72342, Mailing Address: P.O. Box 788, Zip 72342–0788; tel. 870/338–5800; Steve Reeder, Chief Executive Officer

HOWARD MEMORIAL HOSPITAL, 800 West Leslie Street, Nashville, AR, Zip 71852–0381, Mailing Address: Box 381, Zip 71852–0381; tel. 870/845–4400; Rex Jones, Chief Executive Officer

Section B

JEFFERSON REGIONAL MEDICAL CENTER, 1515 West 42nd Avenue, Pine Bluff, AR, Zip 71603–7089; tel. 870/541–7100; Robert P. Atkinson, President and Chief Executive Officer

JOHNSON REGIONAL MEDICAL CENTER, 1100 East Poplar Street, Clarksville, AR, Zip 72830–4419, Mailing Address: P.O. Box 738, Zip 72830–0738; tel. 501/754–5454; Kenneth R. Wood, Administrator

LAWRENCE MEMORIAL HOSPITAL, 1309 West Main, Walnut Ridge, AR, Zip 72476–1430, Mailing Address: P.O. Box 839, Zip 72476–0839; tel. 501/886–1200; Lee Gentry, President

LITTLE RIVER MEMORIAL HOSPITAL, Fifth and Locke Streets, Ashdown, AR, Zip 71822–0577, Mailing Address: P.O. Box 577, Zip 71822–0577; tel. 870/898–5011; Judy Adams, Administrator and Chief Executive Officer

MAGNOLIA HOSPITAL, 101 Hospital Drive, Magnolia, AR, Zip 71753–2416, Mailing Address: Box 629, Zip 71753–0629; tel. 870/235–3000; Kirk Reamey, Chief Executive Officer

MCGEHEE–DESHA COUNTY HOSPITAL, 900 South Third, McGehee, AR, Zip 71654–0351, Mailing Address: Box 351, Zip 71654–0351; tel. 501/222–5600

MEDICAL CENTER OF CALICO ROCK, 103 Grasse Street, Calico Rock, AR, Zip 72519, Mailing Address: P.O. Box 438, Zip 72519–0438; tel. 870/297–3726; Terry L. Amstutz, CHE, Chief Executive Officer and Administrator

MEDICAL CENTER OF SOUTH ARKANSAS, 700 West Grove Street, El Dorado, AR, Zip 71730–4416, Mailing Address: P.O. Box 1998, Zip 71731–1998; tel. 870/864–3200; Luther J. Lewis, Chief Executive Officer

MEDICAL PARK HOSPITAL, 2001 South Main Street, Hope, AR, Zip 71801–8194; tel. 870/777–2323; Jimmy Leopard, Chief Executive Officer

MENA MEDICAL CENTER, 311 North Morrow Street, Mena, AR, Zip 71953–2516; tel. 501/394–6100; Albert Pilkington, III, Administrator and Chief Executive Officer

MERCY HOSPITAL OF SCOTT COUNTY, Highways 71 and 80, Waldron, AR, Zip 72958–9984, Mailing Address: Box 2230, Zip 72958–2230; tel. 501/637–4135; Sister Mary Alvera Simon, Administrator

MERCY HOSPITAL–TURNER MEMORIAL, 801 West River Street, Ozark, AR, Zip 72949–3000; tel. 501/667–4138; John C. Neal, Regional Administrator and Chief Administrative Officer

NEWPORT HOSPITAL AND CLINIC, 2000 McLain Street, Newport, AR, Zip 72112–3697; tel. 870/523–6721; Eugene Zuber, Administrator

NORTH ARKANSAS REGIONAL MEDICAL CENTER, 620 North Willow Street, Harrison, AR, Zip 72601–2994; tel. 870/365–2000; Timothy E. Hill, Chief Executive Officer

NORTH LOGAN MERCY HOSPITAL, 500 East Academy, Paris, AR, Zip 72855–4099; tel. 501/963–6101; Jim L. Maddox, Chief Administrative Officer

OUACHITA MEDICAL CENTER, 638 California Street, Camden, AR, Zip 71701–4699, Mailing Address: P.O. Box 797, Zip 71701–0797; tel. 870/836–1000; C. C. McAllister, President and Chief Executive Officer

OZARK HEALTH MEDICAL CENTER, Highway 65 South, Clinton, AR, Zip 72031, Mailing Address: P.O. Box 206, Zip 72031–0206; tel. 501/745–2401; Barry Brady, Administrator

PIGGOTT COMMUNITY HOSPITAL, 1206 Gordon Duckworth Drive, Piggott, AR, Zip 72454–1911; tel. 870/598–3881; James L. Magee, Executive Director

PIKE COUNTY MEMORIAL HOSPITAL, 315 East 13th Street, Murfreesboro, AR, Zip 71958–9541; tel. 870/285–3182; Rosemary Fritts, Administrator

RANDOLPH COUNTY MEDICAL CENTER, 2801 Medical Center Drive, Pocahontas, AR, Zip 72455–9497; tel. 870/892–6000; Michael G. Layfield, Chief Executive Officer

REBSAMEN MEDICAL CENTER, 1400 West Braden Street, Jacksonville, AR, Zip 72076–3788; tel. 501/985–7000; Thomas R. Siemers, Chief Executive Officer

SAINT MARY'S REGIONAL MEDICAL CENTER, 1808 West Main Street, Russellville, AR, Zip 72801–2724; tel. 501/968–2841; Mike McCoy, Chief Executive Officer

SALINE MEMORIAL HOSPITAL, 1 Medical Park Drive, Benton, AR, Zip 72015–3354; tel. 501/776–6000; Roger D. Feldt, FACHE, President and Chief Executive Officer

SILOAM SPRINGS MEMORIAL HOSPITAL, 205 East Jefferson Street, Siloam Springs, AR, Zip 72761–3697; tel. 501/524–4141; Donald E. Patterson, Administrator

ST. ANTHONY'S HEALTHCARE CENTER, 4 Hospital Drive, Morrilton, AR, Zip 72110–4510; tel. 501/354–3512; Johnson L. Smith, Chief Executive Officer and Administrator

ST. BERNARD'S BEHAVIORAL HEALTH, 2712 East Johnson Avenue, Jonesboro, AR, Zip 72401–1874; tel. 870/932–2800; Andrew DeYoung, Administrator

ST. BERNARDS REGIONAL MEDICAL CENTER, 224 East Matthews Street, Jonesboro, AR, Zip 72401–3156, Mailing Address: P.O. Box 9320, Zip 72403–9320; tel. 870/972–4100; Ben E. Owens, President

ST. EDWARD MERCY MEDICAL CENTER, 7301 Rogers Avenue, Fort Smith, AR, Zip 72903–4189, Mailing Address: P.O. Box 17000, Zip 72917–7000; tel. 501/484–6000; Michael L. Morgan, President and Chief Executive Officer

ST. JOSEPH'S REGIONAL HEALTH CENTER, 300 Werner Street, Hot Springs, AR, Zip 71913–6448, Mailing Address: P.O. Box 29001, Zip 71913–9001; tel. 501/622–1000; Randall J. Fale, FACHE, President and Chief Executive Officer

ST. MARY–ROGERS MEMORIAL HOSPITAL, 1200 West Walnut Street, Rogers, AR, Zip 72756–3599; tel. 501/636–0200; Susan Barrett, President and Chief Executive Officer

STONE COUNTY MEDICAL CENTER, Highway 14 East, Mountain View, AR, Zip 72560, Mailing Address: P.O. Box 510, Zip 72560–0510; tel. 870/269–4361; Stanley Townsend, Administrator

STUTTGART REGIONAL MEDICAL CENTER, North Buerkle Road, Stuttgart, AR, Zip 72160, Mailing Address: P.O. Box 1905, Zip 72160–1905; tel. 870/673–3511; Jim E. Bushmaier, Administrator and Chief Executive Officer

WASHINGTON REGIONAL MEDICAL CENTER, 1125 North College Avenue, Fayetteville, AR, Zip 72703–1994; tel. 501/713–1000; Patrick D. Flynn, President and Chief Executive Officer

WHITE COUNTY MEDICAL CENTER, 3214 East Race, Searcy, AR, Zip 72143–4847; tel. 501/268–6121; Raymond W. Montgomery, II, President and Chief Executive Officer

WHITE RIVER MEDICAL CENTER, 1710 Harrison Street, Batesville, AR, Zip 72501–2197, Mailing Address: P.O. Box 2197, Zip 72503–2197; tel. 870/793–1200; Gary Bebow, Administrator and Chief Executive Officer

BAPTIST HEALTH
9601 Interstate 630, Exit 7, Little Rock, AR 72205; tel. 501/228–0107; Russ Herrington, President

BAPTIST MEDICAL CENTER, 9601 Interstate 630, Exit 7, Little Rock, AR, Zip 72205–7299; tel. 501/202–2000; Steven Douglas Weeks, Senior Vice President and Administrator

BAPTIST MEDICAL CENTER ARKADELPHIA, 3050 Twin Rivers Drive, Arkadelphia, AR, Zip 71923–4299; tel. 870/245–1100; Dan Gathright, Senior Vice President and Administrator

BAPTIST MEMORIAL MEDICAL CENTER, One Pershing Circle, North Little Rock, AR, Zip 72114–1899; tel. 501/202–3000; Harrison M. Dean, Senior Vice President and Administrator

BAPTIST REHABILITATION INSTITUTE, 9601 Interstate 630, Exit 7, Little Rock, AR, Zip 72205–7249; tel. 501/202–7000; Steven Douglas Weeks, Senior Vice President and Administrator

SAINT EDWARD MERCY MEDICAL CENTER
7301 Rogers Avenue, Fort Smith, AR 72917; tel. 501/484–6100; Larry Goss, Vice President

HARBOR VIEW MERCY HOSPITAL, 10301 Mayo Road, Fort Smith, AR, Zip 72903–1631, Mailing Address: P.O. Box 17000, Zip 72917–7000; tel. 501/484–5550; Richard Cameron, M.D., Administrator

MERCY HOSPITAL OF SCOTT COUNTY, Highways 71 and 80, Waldron, AR, Zip 72958–9984, Mailing Address: Box 2230, Zip 72958–2230; tel. 501/637–4135; Sister Mary Alvera Simon, Administrator

MERCY HOSPITAL–TURNER MEMORIAL, 801 West River Street, Ozark, AR, Zip 72949–3000; tel. 501/667–4138; John C. Neal, Regional Administrator and Chief Administrative Officer

NORTH LOGAN MERCY HOSPITAL, 500 East Academy, Paris, AR, Zip 72855–4099; tel. 501/963–6101; Jim L. Maddox, Chief Administrative Officer

ST. EDWARD MERCY MEDICAL CENTER, 7301 Rogers Avenue, Fort Smith, AR, Zip 72903–4189, Mailing Address: P.O. Box 17000, Zip 72917–7000; tel. 501/484–6000; Michael L. Morgan, President and Chief Executive Officer

TENET HEALTHCARE CORP.
12814 Cantrell Rd., Little Rock, AR 72223; tel. 501/219–4260; William Bradley, Senior Vice President

CALIFORNIA

ADVENTIST HEALTH SCIENCES SYSTEM–LOMA LINDA UNIV
11161 Anderson Street, Loma Linda, CA 92350; tel. 909/824–4459; David B. Hinshaw, MD, President

LOMA LINDA UNIVERSITY BEHAVIORAL MEDICINE CENTER, 1710 Barton Road, Redlands, CA, Zip 92373; tel. 909/793–9333; Alan Soderblom, Administrator

LOMA LINDA UNIVERSITY MEDICAL CENTER, 11234 Anderson Street, Loma Linda, CA, Zip 92354–2870, Mailing Address: P.O. Box 2000, Zip 92354–0200; tel. 909/824–0800; B. Lyn Behrens, President

ADVENTIST HEALTH SOUTHERN CALIFORNIA
1505 Wilson Terrace   Suite 220, Glendale, CA 91206; tel. 818/409–8300; Fred Manchur, President & Chief Executive

GLENDALE ADVENTIST MEDICAL CENTER, 1509 Wilson Terrace, Glendale, CA, Zip 91206–4007; tel. 818/409–8000; Fred Manchur, President and Chief Executive Officer

SIMI VALLEY HOSPITAL AND HEALTH CARE SERVICES, 2975 North Sycamore Drive, Simi Valley, CA, Zip 93065–1277; tel. 805/527–2462; Alan J. Rice, President

WHITE MEMORIAL MEDICAL CENTER, 1720 Cesar E Chavez Avenue, Los Angeles, CA, Zip 90033–2481; tel. 323/268–5000; Fred Manchur, President and Chief Executive Officer

CATHOLIC HEALTHCARE WEST
1700 Montgomery Street, San Francisco, CA 94111; tel. 415/397–9000; Debbie Canta, Director of Corporate Communication

DOMINICAN HOSPITAL, 1555 Soquel Drive, Santa Cruz, CA, Zip 95065; tel. 831/462–7700; Sister Julie Hyer, President and Chief Executive Officer

MARK TWAIN ST. JOSEPH'S HOSPITAL, 768 Mountain Ranch Road, San Andreas, CA, Zip 95249–9710; tel. 209/754–2515; Michael P. Lawson, Administrator

MERCY AMERICAN RIVER/MERCY SAN JUAN HOSPITAL, 6501 Coyle Avenue, Carmichael, CA, Zip 95608, Mailing Address: P.O. Box 479, Zip 95608; tel. 916/537–5000; Michael H. Erne, President

MERCY GENERAL HOSPITAL, 4001 J Street, Sacramento, CA, Zip 95819; tel. 916/453–4950; Thomas A. Petersen, Vice President and Chief Operating Officer

MERCY HOSPITAL, 2215 Truxtun Avenue, Bakersfield, CA, Zip 93301, Mailing Address: Box 119, Zip 93302; tel. 661/632–5000; Bernard J. Herman, President and Chief Executive Officer

Section B

MERCY HOSPITAL AND HEALTH SERVICES, 2740 M Street, Merced, CA, Zip 95340–2880; tel. 209/384–6444; John Headding, Chief Administrative Officer

MERCY HOSPITAL OF FOLSOM, 1650 Creekside Drive, Folsom, CA, Zip 95630; tel. 916/983–7400; Donald C. Hudson, Vice President and Chief Operating Officer

MERCY MEDICAL CENTER MOUNT SHASTA, 914 Pine Street, Mount Shasta, CA, Zip 96067, Mailing Address: P.O. Box 239, Zip 96067–0239; tel. 530/926–6111; Rick J. Barnett, Executive Vice President and Chief Operating Officer

MERCY MEDICAL CENTER REDDING, 2175 Rosaline Avenue, Redding, CA, Zip 96001, Mailing Address: P.O. Box 496009, Zip 96049–6009; tel. 530/225–6000; John Di Perry, Jr., Executive Vice President and Chief Operating Officer

METHODIST HOSPITAL OF SACRAMENTO, 7500 Hospital Drive, Sacramento, CA, Zip 95823; tel. 916/423–3000; Stanley C. Oppegard, Vice President and Chief Operating Officer

O'CONNOR HOSPITAL, 2105 Forest Avenue, San Jose, CA, Zip 95128; tel. 408/947–2500; Joan A. Bero, Regional Vice President and Chief Operating Officer

ROBERT F. KENNEDY MEDICAL CENTER, 4500 West 116th Street, Hawthorne, CA, Zip 90250; tel. 310/973–1711; Peter P. Aprato, Administrator and Chief Operating Officer

SAINT FRANCIS MEMORIAL HOSPITAL, 900 Hyde Street, San Francisco, CA, Zip 94109, Mailing Address: Box 7726, Zip 94120–7726; tel. 415/353–6000; Cheryl A. Fama, Administrator, Vice President and Chief Operating Officer

SAINT LOUISE HOSPITAL, 18500 Saint Louise Drive, Morgan Hill, CA, Zip 95037; tel. 408/779–1500; Terrence Curley, Administrator

SEQUOIA HOSPITAL, 170 Alameda De Las Pulgas, Redwood City, CA, Zip 94062; tel. 650/369–5811; Glenna L. Vaskelis, Administrator

SETON MEDICAL CENTER, 1900 Sullivan Avenue, Daly City, CA, Zip 94015; tel. 650/992–4000; Bernadette Smith, Chief Operating Officer

SETON MEDICAL CENTER COASTSIDE, Marine Boulevard and Etheldore Street, Moss Beach, CA, Zip 94038; tel. 650/728–5521; Bernadette Smith, Chief Operating Officer

SIERRA NEVADA MEMORIAL HOSPITAL, 155 Glasson Way, Grass Valley, CA, Zip 95945, Mailing Address: P.O. Box 1029, Zip 95945–1029; tel. 530/274–6000; C. Thomas Collier, President and Chief Executive Officer

ST. BERNARDINE MEDICAL CENTER, 2101 North Waterman Avenue, San Bernardino, CA, Zip 92404; tel. 909/883–8711; Bruce G. Satzger, Administrator

ST. DOMINIC'S HOSPITAL, 1777 West Yosemite Avenue, Manteca, CA, Zip 95337; tel. 209/825–3500; Richard Aldred, Chief Administrative Officer

ST. ELIZABETH COMMUNITY HOSPITAL, 2550 Sister Mary Columba Drive, Red Bluff, CA, Zip 96080–4397; tel. 530/529–8000; Thomas F. Grimes, III, Executive Vice President and Chief Operating Officer

ST. FRANCIS MEDICAL CENTER, 3630 East Imperial Highway, Lynwood, CA, Zip 90262; tel. 310/603–6000; Gerald T. Kozai, President

ST. JOHN'S PLEASANT VALLEY HOSPITAL, 2309 Antonio Avenue, Camarillo, CA, Zip 93010–1459; tel. 805/389–5800; William J. Clearwater, Vice President and Site Administrator

ST. JOHN'S REGIONAL MEDICAL CENTER, 1600 North Rose Avenue, Oxnard, CA, Zip 93030; tel. 805/988–2500; James R. Hoss, Administrator and Chief Operating Officer

ST. JOSEPH'S BEHAVIORAL HEALTH CENTER, 2510 North California Street, Stockton, CA, Zip 95204–5568; tel. 209/948–2100; James Sondecker, Director

ST. JOSEPH'S HOSPITAL AND MEDICAL CENTER, 350 West Thomas Road, Phoenix, AZ, Zip 85013–4496, Mailing Address: P.O. Box 2071, Zip 85001–2071; tel. 602/406–3100; Mary G. Yarbrough, President and Chief Executive Officer

ST. JOSEPH'S MEDICAL CENTER, 1800 North California Street, Stockton, CA, Zip 95204, Mailing Address: P.O. Box 213008, Zip 95213–3008; tel. 209/943–2000; Donald J. Wiley, Senior Vice President and Chief Operating Officer

ST. MARY MEDICAL CENTER, 1050 Linden Avenue, Long Beach, CA, Zip 90801, Mailing Address: P.O. Box 887, Zip 90813–0887; tel. 562/491–9000; Tammie McMann Brailsford, Administrator and Chief Operating Officer

ST. MARY'S MEDICAL CENTER, 450 Stanyan Street, San Francisco, CA, Zip 94117–1079; tel. 415/668–1000; Rosemary Fox, Vice President and Chief Operating Officer

ST. ROSE DOMINICAN HOSPITAL, 102 Lake Mead Drive, Henderson, NV, Zip 89015–5524; tel. 702/564–2622; Rod A. Davis, President and Chief Executive Officer

ST. VINCENT MEDICAL CENTER, 2131 West Third Street, Los Angeles, CA, Zip 90057–0992, Mailing Address: P.O. Box 57992, Zip 90057; tel. 213/484–7111; William D. Parente, President

WOODLAND HEALTHCARE, 1325 Cottonwood Street, Woodland, CA, Zip 95695–5199; tel. 530/662–3961; William Hunt, Chief Operating Officer

CCN, INC
8911 Balboa Avenue, San Diego, CA 92123; tel. 619/278–2273; James Buncher, CEO

CEDARS SINAI MEDICAL CENTER
8700 Beverly Blvd–Rm2802, Los Angeles, CA 90048; tel. 310/855–5711; Thomas Priselac, President/CEO

CEDARS–SINAI MEDICAL CENTER, 8700 Beverly Boulevard, Los Angeles, CA, Zip 90048–1865, Mailing Address: Box 48750, Zip 90048–0750; tel. 310/855–5000; Thomas M. Priselac, President and Chief Executive Officer

EAST BAY MEDICAL NETWORK
2000 Powell Street 9th Flr, Emeryville, CA 94608; tel. 510/450–9850; Belina Rule, Provider Relations

ALAMEDA HOSPITAL, 2070 Clinton Avenue, Alameda, CA, Zip 94501; tel. 510/522–3700; William J. Dal Cielo, Chief Executive Officer

ALTA BATES MEDICAL CENTER–ASHBY CAMPUS, 2450 Ashby Avenue, Berkeley, CA, Zip 94705; tel. 510/204–4444; Warren J. Kirk, President and Chief Administrative Officer

PATTON STATE HOSPITAL, 3102 East Highland Avenue, Patton, CA, Zip 92369; tel. 909/425–7000; William L. Summers, Executive Director

SAN LEANDRO HOSPITAL, 13855 East 14th Street, San Leandro, CA, Zip 94578–0398; tel. 510/357–6500; Kelly Mather, Chief Executive Officer

SUTTER DELTA MEDICAL CENTER, 3901 Lone Tree Way, Antioch, CA, Zip 94509; tel. 925/779–7200; Linda Horn, Administrator

WASHINGTON TOWNSHIP HEALTH CARE DISTRICT, 2000 Mowry Avenue, Fremont, CA, Zip 94538–1716; tel. 510/797–1111; Nancy D. Farber, Chief Executive Officer

ESSENTIAL HEALTHCARE NETWORK
525 North Garfield Park, Montery Park, CA 91754; tel. 818/573–2222; A. Schaffer, Acting Executive Director

COMMUNITY HOSPITAL OF HUNTINGTON PARK, 2623 East Slauson Avenue, Huntington Park, CA, Zip 90255; tel. 323/583–1931; Charles Martinez, Ph.D., Chief Executive Officer

GARFIELD MEDICAL CENTER, 525 North Garfield Avenue, Monterey Park, CA, Zip 91754; tel. 626/573–2222; Philip A. Cohen, Chief Executive Officer

GREATER EL MONTE COMMUNITY HOSPITAL, 1701 South Santa Anita Avenue, South El Monte, CA, Zip 91733–9918; tel. 626/579–7777; Elizabeth A. Primeaux, Chief Executive Officer

PACIFIC ALLIANCE MEDICAL CENTER, 531 West College Street, Los Angeles, CA, Zip 90012–2385; tel. 213/624–8411; John R. Edwards, Administrator and Chief Executive Officer

QUEEN OF ANGELS–HOLLYWOOD PRESBYTERIAN MEDICAL CENTER, 1300 North Vermont Avenue, Los Angeles, CA, Zip 90027–0069; tel. 213/413–3000; John V. Fenton, Chief Executive Officer

ROBERT F. KENNEDY MEDICAL CENTER, 4500 West 116th Street, Hawthorne, CA, Zip 90250; tel. 310/973–1711; Peter P. Aprato, Administrator and Chief Operating Officer

SANTA MARTA HOSPITAL, 319 North Humphreys Avenue, Los Angeles, CA, Zip 90022–1499; tel. 323/266–6500; Harry E. Whitney, President and Chief Executive Officer

ST. FRANCIS MEDICAL CENTER, 3630 East Imperial Highway, Lynwood, CA, Zip 90262; tel. 310/603–6000; Gerald T. Kozai, President

SUBURBAN MEDICAL CENTER, 16453 South Colorado Avenue, Paramount, CA, Zip 90723; tel. 562/531–3110; Gustavo Valdespino, Chief Executive Officer

FREMONT–RIDEOUT HEALTH GROUP
989 Plumas Street, Yuba City, CA 95991; tel. 530/751–4046; Deborah Coulter, Community Development

FREMONT MEDICAL CENTER, 970 Plumas Street, Yuba City, CA, Zip 95991; tel. 530/751–4000; Thomas P. Hayes, Chief Executive Officer

RIDEOUT MEMORIAL HOSPITAL, 726 Fourth Street, Marysville, CA, Zip 95901–2128, Mailing Address: 989 Plumas Street, Yuba City, Zip 95991; tel. 530/749–4300; Thomas P. Hayes, Chief Executive Officer

FRIENDLY HILLS HEALTHCARE NETWORK
501 South Idaho Street, LaHabra, CA 90631; tel. 562/905–5204; Dr. Marvin Rice, Chairman & Chief Executive

PLACENTIA LINDA HOSPITAL, 1301 Rose Drive, Placentia, CA, Zip 92870; tel. 714/993–2000; Maxine T. Cooper, Chief Executive Officer

WHITTIER HOSPITAL MEDICAL CENTER, 9080 Colima Road, Whittier, CA, Zip 90605; tel. 562/907–1541; Sandra M. Chester, Chief Executive Officer

HCP/MULLIKEN MEDICAL CENTERS
26000 Altamont Road, Los Altos Hills, CA 94022–4398; tel. 408/947–2866; Patty Raymond, Director–Manged Care

HEALTH FIRST NETWORK
4020 5th Avenue, 3rd Flr, San Diego, CA 92103; tel. 619/293–0986; Roger Burke, President

PALOMAR MEDICAL CENTER, 555 East Valley Parkway, Escondido, CA, Zip 92025–3084; tel. 760/739–3000; Victoria M. Penland, Administrator and Chief Operating Officer

POMERADO HOSPITAL, 15615 Pomerado Road, Poway, CA, Zip 92064; tel. 619/485–6511; Marvin W. Levenson, M.D., Administrator and Chief Operating Officer

INTERMOUNTAIN HEALTHCARE NETWORK
228 McDowell Street, Alturas, CA 96101; tel. 916/233–5131; Donna Donald, Network Contact

INDIAN VALLEY HOSPITAL DISTRICT, 184 Hot Springs Road, Greenville, CA, Zip 95947; tel. 530/284–7191; Lynn Seaberg, Administrator and Chief Executive Officer

MAYERS MEMORIAL HOSPITAL DISTRICT, Highway 299 East, Fall River Mills, CA, Zip 96028, Mailing Address: Box 459, Zip 96028; tel. 530/336–5511; Judi Beck, Administrator and Chief Executive Officer

MODOC MEDICAL CENTER, 228 McDowell Street, Alturas, CA, Zip 96101; tel. 916/233–5131; -Woody J. Laughnan, Chief Executive Officer

SURPRISE VALLEY COMMUNITY HOSPITAL, Main and Washington Streets, Cedarville, CA, Zip 96104, Mailing Address: P.O. Box 246, Zip 96104–0246; tel. 530/279–6111; Joyce Gysin, Administrator

KAISER FOUNDATION HEALTH PLAN OF NORTHERN CALIFORNIA
1 Kaiser Plaza, Oakland, CA 94612; tel. 510/271–2640; Dr. David Lawrence, CEO

KAISER FOUNDATION HOSPITAL, 2425 Geary Boulevard, San Francisco, CA, Zip 94115; tel. 415/202–2000; Julie A. Petrini, Senior Vice President and Area Manager

KAISER FOUNDATION HOSPITAL, 280 West MacArthur Boulevard, Oakland, CA, Zip 94611; tel. 510/987–1000; Bettie L. Coles, R.N., Senior Vice President

KAISER FOUNDATION HOSPITAL, 1425 South Main Street, Walnut Creek, CA, Zip 94596; tel. 925/295–4000; Sandra Small, Administrator

KAISER FOUNDATION HOSPITAL, 27400 Hesperian Boulevard, Hayward, CA, Zip 94545–4297; tel. 510/784–4313; Richard D. Cordova, Senior Vice President

KAISER FOUNDATION HOSPITAL, 1150 Veterans Boulevard, Redwood City, CA, Zip 94063–2087; tel. 650/299–2000; Helen Wilmot, Administrator

KAISER FOUNDATION HOSPITAL, 6600 Bruceville Road, Sacramento, CA, Zip 95823; tel. 916/688–2430; Sarah Krevans, Senior Vice President

KAISER FOUNDATION HOSPITAL, 99 Montecillo Road, San Rafael, CA, Zip 94903–3397; tel. 415/444–2000; Mary Ann Thode, Administrator

KAISER FOUNDATION HOSPITAL, 900 Kiely Boulevard, Santa Clara, CA, Zip 95051–5386; tel. 408/236–6400; Helen Wilmot, Administrator

KAISER FOUNDATION HOSPITAL, 1200 El Camino Real, South San Francisco, CA, Zip 94080–3299; tel. 650/742–2401; Gail Wuotila, Director Hospital Operations

KAISER FOUNDATION HOSPITAL AND REHABILITATION CENTER, 975 Sereno Drive, Vallejo, CA, Zip 94589; tel. 707/651–1000; Sandra Small, Senior Vice President and Area Manager

REDDING MEDICAL CENTER, 1100 Butte Street, Redding, CA, Zip 96001–0853, Mailing Address: Box 496072, Zip 96049–6072; tel. 530/244–5454; Steve Schmidt, Chief Executive Officer

LITTLE COMPANY OF MARY HEALTH SERVICES
4101 Torrance Boulevard, Torrance, CA 90503; tel. 310/540–7676; James Lester, President

LITTLE COMPANY OF MARY HOSPITAL, 4101 Torrance Boulevard, Torrance, CA, Zip 90503–4698; tel. 310/540–7676; Mark Costa, President

SAN PEDRO PENINSULA HOSPITAL, 1300 West Seventh Street, San Pedro, CA, Zip 90732; tel. 310/832–3311; John M. Wilson, President and Chief Executive Officer

NORTHERN SIERRA RURAL HEALTH
700 Zion Street, Nevada City, CA 95959; tel. 510/470–9091; Speranza Avram, Executive Director

LASSEN COMMUNITY HOSPITAL, 560 Hospital Lane, Susanville, CA, Zip 96130–4809; tel. 530/257–5325; David S. Anderson, FACHE, Administrator

SIERRA VALLEY DISTRICT HOSPITAL, 700 Third Street, Loyalton, CA, Zip 96118, Mailing Address: Box 178, Zip 96118; tel. 530/993–1225; Chase Mearian, Administrator

PROVIDENCE SAINT JOSEPH HEALTH MEDICAL CENTER
501 South Buena Vista Street, Burbank, CA 91505; tel. 818/843–5111; Michael Madden, Chairman

PROVIDENCE HOLY CROSS MEDICAL CENTER, 15031 Rinaldi Street, Mission Hills, CA, Zip 91345–1285; tel. 818/365–8051; Michael J. Madden, Chief Executive Officer

PROVIDENCE SAINT JOSEPH MEDICAL CENTER, 501 South Buena Vista Street, Burbank, CA, Zip 91505–4866; tel. 818/843–5111; Michael J. Madden, Chief Executive Officer

SCRIPPSHEALTH
4275 Campus Point Ct, San Diego, CA 92121; tel. 619/678–6111; Kay Alexander, Executive Assistant

GREEN HOSPITAL OF SCRIPPS CLINIC, 10666 North Torrey Pines Road, La Jolla, CA, Zip 92037–1093; tel. 619/455–9100; Thomas C. Gagen, Senior Vice President

SCRIPPS HOSPITAL–CHULA VISTA, 435 H Street, Chula Vista, CA, Zip 91912–1537, Mailing Address: P.O. Box 1537, Zip 91910–1537; tel. 619/691–7000; John Grah, Administrator

SCRIPPS MEMORIAL HOSPITAL EAST COUNTY, 1688 East Main Street, El Cajon, CA, Zip 92021; tel. 619/440–1122; Deborah Dunne, Administrator

SCRIPPS MEMORIAL HOSPITAL–ENCINITAS, 354 Santa Fe Drive, Encinitas, CA, Zip 92024, Mailing Address: P.O. Box 230817, Zip 92023; tel. 760/753–6501; Rebecca Ropchan, Administrator

SCRIPPS MEMORIAL HOSPITAL–LA JOLLA, 9888 Genesee Avenue, La Jolla, CA, Zip 92037–1276, Mailing Address: P.O. Box 28, Zip 92038–0028; tel. 619/626–4123; Thomas C. Gagen, Senior Vice President and Regional Administrator

SCRIPPS MERCY HOSPITAL, 4077 Fifth Avenue, San Diego, CA, Zip 92103–2180; tel. 619/294–8111; Thomas A. Gammiere, Senior Vice President and Regional Administrator

SHARP HEALTHCARE
3131 Berger Avenue, Suite 100, San Diego, CA 92123; tel. 619/541–4000; Peter K. Ellsworth, President & CEO

GROSSMONT HOSPITAL, 5555 Grossmont Center Drive, La Mesa, CA, Zip 91942, Mailing Address: Box 158, Zip 91944–0158; tel. 619/465–0711; Michele T. Tarbet, R.N., Chief Executive Officer

RANCHO SPRINGS MEDICAL CENTER, 25500 Medical Center Drive, Murrieta, CA, Zip 92562–5966; tel. 909/696–6000; Juanice Lovett, Chief Executive Officer

SHARP CABRILLO HOSPITAL, 3475 Kenyon Street, San Diego, CA, Zip 92110–5067; tel. 619/221–3400; Randi Larsson, Chief Operating Officer and Administrator

SHARP CHULA VISTA MEDICAL CENTER, 751 Medical Center Court, Chula Vista, CA, Zip 91911, Mailing Address: Box 1297, Zip 91912; tel. 619/482–5800; Britt Berrett, Chief Executive Officer

SHARP MEMORIAL HOSPITAL, 7901 Frost Street, San Diego, CA, Zip 92123–2788; tel. 619/541–3400; Dan Gross, Chief Executive Officer

SOUTHERN CALIFORNIA HEALTHCARE SYSTEMS
1300 East Green Street, Pasadena, CA 91106; tel. 626/397–2900; Steve Ralph, President & CEO

HUNTINGTON EAST VALLEY HOSPITAL, 150 West Alosta Avenue, Glendora, CA, Zip 91740–4398; tel. 626/335–0231; James W. Maki, Chief Executive Officer

HUNTINGTON MEMORIAL HOSPITAL, 100 West California Boulevard, Pasadena, CA, Zip 91105, Mailing Address: P.O. Box 7013, Zip 91109–7013; tel. 626/397–5000; Stephen A. Ralph, President and Chief Executive Officer

METHODIST HOSPITAL OF SOUTHERN CALIFORNIA, 300 West Huntington Drive, Arcadia, CA, Zip 91007, Mailing Address: P.O. Box 60016, Zip 91066–6016; tel. 626/445–4441; Dennis M. Lee, President

SUTTER HEALTH
2800 L. Street, Sacramento, CA 95816; tel. 916/733–8800; Van Johnson, President & CEO

ALTA BATES MEDICAL CENTER–ASHBY CAMPUS, 2450 Ashby Avenue, Berkeley, CA, Zip 94705; tel. 510/204–4444; Warren J. Kirk, President and Chief Administrative Officer

CALIFORNIA PACIFIC MEDICAL CENTER, 2333 Buchanan Street, San Francisco, CA, Zip 94115, Mailing Address: P.O. Box 94120; tel. 415/563–4321; Martin Brotman, M.D., President and Chief Executive Officer

DAMERON HOSPITAL, 525 West Acacia Street, Stockton, CA, Zip 95203; tel. 209/944–5550; Luis Arismendi, M.D., Administrator

EDEN MEDICAL CENTER, 20103 Lake Chabot Road, Castro Valley, CA, Zip 94546; tel. 510/537–1234; George Bischalaney, President and Chief Executive Officer

MARIN GENERAL HOSPITAL, 250 Bon Air Road, Greenbrae, CA, Zip 94904, Mailing Address: Box 8010, San Rafael, Zip 94912–8010; tel. 415/925–7000; Henry J. Buhrmann, President and Chief Executive Officer

MEMORIAL HOSPITALS ASSOCIATION, Modesto, CA, Mailing Address: P.O. Box 942, Zip 95353; tel. 209/526–4500; David P. Benn, President and Chief Executive Officer

MILLS–PENINSULA HEALTH SERVICES, 1783 El Camino Real, Burlingame, CA, Zip 94010–3205; tel. 650/696–5400; Robert W. Merwin, Chief Executive Officer

NOVATO COMMUNITY HOSPITAL, 1625 Hill Road, Novato, CA, Zip 94947, Mailing Address: P.O. Box 1108, Zip 94948; tel. 415/897–3111; Anne Hosfeld, Chief Administrative Officer

OAK VALLEY DISTRICT HOSPITAL, 350 South Oak Street, Oakdale, CA, Zip 95361; tel. 209/847–3011; Norman J. Andrews, Chief Executive Officer

SUTTER AMADOR HOSPITAL, 810 Court Street, Jackson, CA, Zip 95642–2379; tel. 209/223–7500; Scott Stenberg, Chief Executive Officer

SUTTER AUBURN FAITH COMMUNITY HOSPITAL, 11815 Education Street, Auburn, CA, Zip 95604, Mailing Address: Box 8992, Zip 95604–8992; tel. 530/888–4518; Joel E. Grey, Administrator

SUTTER CENTER FOR PSYCHIATRY, 7700 Folsom Boulevard, Sacramento, CA, Zip 95826–2608; tel. 916/386–3000; Diane Gail Stewart, Administrator

SUTTER COAST HOSPITAL, 800 East Washington Boulevard, Crescent City, CA, Zip 95531; tel. 707/464–8511; John E. Menaugh, Chief Executive Officer

SUTTER DAVIS HOSPITAL, 2000 Sutter Place, Davis, CA, Zip 95616, Mailing Address: P.O. Box 1617, Zip 95617; tel. 530/756–6440; Lawrence A. Maas, Administrator

SUTTER DELTA MEDICAL CENTER, 3901 Lone Tree Way, Antioch, CA, Zip 94509; tel. 925/779–7200; Linda Horn, Administrator

SUTTER LAKESIDE HOSPITAL, 5176 Hill Road East, Lakeport, CA, Zip 95453–6111; tel. 707/262–5001; Gilbert Silbernagel, Chief Executive Officer

SUTTER MEDICAL CENTER, 5151 F Street, Sacramento, CA, Zip 95819–3295; tel. 916/454–3333; Lou Lazatin, Chief Executive Officer

SUTTER MEDICAL CENTER, SANTA ROSA, 3325 Chanate Road, Santa Rosa, CA, Zip 95404; tel. 707/576–4000; Cliff Coates, Chief Executive Officer

SUTTER MERCED MEDICAL CENTER, 301 East 13th Street, Merced, CA, Zip 95340–6211; tel. 209/385–7000; Brian S. Bentley, Administrator

SUTTER ROSEVILLE MEDICAL CENTER, One Medical Plaza, Roseville, CA, Zip 95661–3477; tel. 916/781–1000; Patrick R. Brady, Chief Executive Officer

SUTTER SOLANO MEDICAL CENTER, 300 Hospital Drive, Vallejo, CA, Zip 94589–2517, Mailing Address: P.O. Box 3189, Zip 94589; tel. 707/554–4444; Polly J. Walker, R.N., Interim Chief Executive Officer

SUTTER TRACY COMMUNITY HOSPITAL, 1420 North Tracy Boulevard, Tracy, CA, Zip 95376–3497; tel. 209/835–1500; Gary D. Rapaport, Chief Executive Officer

Section B

TENET HEALTHCARE CORP
3820 State Street, Santa Barbara, CA 93105;
tel. 805/563–7000; Jeffrey C. Barbakow,
Chairman & CEO

ALVARADO HOSPITAL MEDICAL CENTER, 6655 Alvarado Road, San Diego, CA, Zip 92120–5298; tel. 619/287–3270; Barry G. Weinbaum, Chief Executive Officer

CENTURY CITY HOSPITAL, 2070 Century Park East, Los Angeles, CA, Zip 90067; tel. 310/553–6211; John R. Nickens, III, Chief Executive Officer

COMMUNITY HOSPITAL OF LOS GATOS, 815 Pollard Road, Los Gatos, CA, Zip 95030; tel. 408/378–6131; Daniel P. Doore, Chief Executive Officer

DOCTORS HOSPITAL OF MANTECA, 1205 East North Street, Manteca, CA, Zip 95336; tel. 209/823–3111; Patrick W. Rafferty, Administrator

DOCTORS MEDICAL CENTER, 1441 Florida Avenue, Modesto, CA, Zip 95350–4418, Mailing Address: P.O. Box 4138, Zip 95352–4138; tel. 209/578–1211; Tim A. Joslin, Chief Executive Officer

DOCTORS MEDICAL CENTER–PINOLE CAMPUS, 2151 Appian Way, Pinole, CA, Zip 94564; tel. 510/970–5000; Gary Sloan, Chief Executive Officer

GARDEN GROVE HOSPITAL AND MEDICAL CENTER, 12601 Garden Grove Boulevard, Garden Grove, CA, Zip 92843–1959; tel. 714/741–2700; Mark A. Meyers, President and Chief Executive Officer

GARFIELD MEDICAL CENTER, 525 North Garfield Avenue, Monterey Park, CA, Zip 91754; tel. 626/573–2222; Philip A. Cohen, Chief Executive Officer

IRVINE MEDICAL CENTER, 16200 Sand Canyon Avenue, Irvine, CA, Zip 92618–3714; tel. 949/753–2000; Dan F. Ausman, Chief Executive Officer

JOHN F. KENNEDY MEMORIAL HOSPITAL, 47–111 Monroe Street, Indio, CA, Zip 92201, Mailing Address: P.O. Drawer LLLL, Zip 92202–2558; tel. 760/347–6191; Larry W. Payton, Chief Operating Officer

LAKEWOOD REGIONAL MEDICAL CENTER, 3700 East South Street, Lakewood, CA, Zip 90712; tel. 562/531–2550; Gustavo A. Valdespino, Chief Executive Officer

LOS ALAMITOS MEDICAL CENTER, 3751 Katella Avenue, Los Alamitos, CA, Zip 90720; tel. 562/598–1311; Gustavo A. Valdespino, Chief Executive Officer

PLACENTIA LINDA HOSPITAL, 1301 Rose Drive, Placentia, CA, Zip 92870; tel. 714/993–2000; Maxine T. Cooper, Chief Executive Officer

REDDING MEDICAL CENTER, 1100 Butte Street, Redding, CA, Zip 96001–0853, Mailing Address: Box 496072, Zip 96049–6072; tel. 530/244–5454; Steve Schmidt, Chief Executive Officer

SAN DIMAS COMMUNITY HOSPITAL, 1350 West Covina Boulevard, San Dimas, CA, Zip 91773–0308; tel. 909/599–6811; Patrick A. Petre, Chief Executive Officer

SAN RAMON REGIONAL MEDICAL CENTER, 6001 Norris Canyon Road, San Ramon, CA, Zip 94583; tel. 925/275–9200; Philip P. Gustafson, Administrator

SIERRA VISTA REGIONAL MEDICAL CENTER, 1010 Murray Street, San Luis Obispo, CA, Zip 93405, Mailing Address: Box 1367, Zip 93406–1367; tel. 805/546–7600; Sean O'Neal, Administrator

TWIN CITIES COMMUNITY HOSPITAL, 1100 Las Tablas Road, Templeton, CA, Zip 93465; tel. 805/434–3500; Harold E. Chilton, Chief Executive Officer

UNIHEALTH
4100 West Alameda, Burbank, CA 91505;
tel. 818/238–6000; Terry Hartshorn,
President

CALIFORNIA HOSPITAL MEDICAL CENTER, 1401 South Grand Avenue, Los Angeles, CA, Zip 90015–3063; tel. 213/748–2411; Melinda D. Beswick, President

GLENDALE MEMORIAL HOSPITAL AND HEALTH CENTER, 1420 South Central Avenue, Glendale, CA, Zip 91204–2594; tel. 818/502–2201; Arnold R. Schaffer, President and Chief Executive Officer

LA PALMA INTERCOMMUNITY HOSPITAL, 7901 Walker Street, La Palma, CA, Zip 90623–5850, Mailing Address: P.O. Box 5850, Buena Park, Zip 90622; tel. 714/670–7400; Stephen E. Dixon, President and Chief Executive Officer

LINDSAY DISTRICT HOSPITAL, 740 North Sequoia Avenue, Lindsay, CA, Zip 93247, Mailing Address: Box 40, Zip 93247; tel. 559/562–4955; Edwin L. Ermshar, President and Chief Executive Officer

LONG BEACH COMMUNITY MEDICAL CENTER, 1720 Termino Avenue, Long Beach, CA, Zip 90804; tel. 562/498–1000; Makoto Nakayama, President

MARTIN LUTHER HOSPITAL, 1830 West Romneya Drive, Anaheim, CA, Zip 92801–1854; tel. 714/491–5200; Stephen E. Dixon, President and Chief Executive Officer

NORTHRIDGE HOSPITAL AND MEDICAL CENTER, SHERMAN WAY CAMPUS, 14500 Sherman Circle, Van Nuys, CA, Zip 91405; tel. 818/997–0101; Richard D. Lyons, President and Chief Executive Officer

NORTHRIDGE HOSPITAL MEDICAL CENTER–ROSCOE BOULEVARD CAMPUS, 18300 Roscoe Boulevard, Northridge, CA, Zip 91328; tel. 818/885–8500; Roger E. Seaver, President and Chief Executive Officer

SAN GABRIEL VALLEY MEDICAL CENTER, 438 West Las Tunas Drive, San Gabriel, CA, Zip 91776, Mailing Address: P.O. Box 1507, Zip 91778–1507; tel. 626/289–5454; Thomas D. Mone, President and Chief Executive Officer

SANTA MONICA–UCLA MEDICAL CENTER, 1250 16th Street, Santa Monica, CA, Zip 90404–1200; tel. 310/319–4000

COLORADO

CENTURA PENROSE–ST. FRANCIS
2215 N. Cascade Ave., Colorado Springs, CO
80907; tel. 719/636–8800; Rick O'Connell,
CEO

PENROSE–ST. FRANCIS HEALTH SERVICES, Colorado Springs, CO, Donna L. Bertram, R.N., Administrator

COLUMBIA HEALTHONE
4643 Ulster Street, Englewood, CO 80237;
tel. 303/788–2500; Molly Hagen, Director Planning

COMMUNITY HEALTH PROVIDERS ORGANIZATION
2021 N. 12th Street, Grand Junction, CO
81501; tel. 303/256–6200; Randall Phillips,
CEO

COMMUNITY HOSPITAL, 2021 North 12th Street, Grand Junction, CO, Zip 81501–2999; tel. 970/242–0920; Randy Phillips, Chief Executive Officer

EXEMPLA HEALTHCARE
600 Grant Street, Suite 700, Denver, CO
80203–3525; tel. 303/832–2739; Gary Smith,
Member Services

EXEMPLA LUTHERAN MEDICAL CENTER, 8300 West 38th Avenue, Wheat Ridge, CO, Zip 80033–6005; tel. 303/425–4500; Jeffrey D. Selberg, President and Chief Executive Officer

EXEMPLA SAINT JOSEPH HOSPITAL, 1835 Franklin Street, Denver, CO, Zip 80218–1191; tel. 303/837–7111; Jeffrey D. Selberg, President and Chief Executive Officer

SPALDING REHABILITATION HOSPITAL, 900 Potomac Street, Aurora, CO, Zip 80011–6716; tel. 303/367–1166; Lynn Dawson, Chief Executive Officer

KIDSMART HEALTH PARTNERS, INC.
600 Grant, Suite 404, Denver, CO 80203;
tel. 303/839–1552; Randy Unter, Executive Director

CHILDREN'S HOSPITAL, 1056 East 19th Avenue, Denver, CO, Zip 80218–1088; tel. 303/861–8888; Doris J. Biester, R.N., President and Chief Executive Officer

EXEMPLA LUTHERAN MEDICAL CENTER, 8300 West 38th Avenue, Wheat Ridge, CO, Zip 80033–6005; tel. 303/425–4500; Jeffrey D. Selberg, President and Chief Executive Officer

LITTLETON ADVENTIST HOSPITAL, 7700 South Broadway Street, Littleton, CO, Zip 80122–2628; tel. 303/730–8900; Ruthita J. Fike, Administrator

ST. ANTHONY NORTH HOSPITAL, 2551 West 84th Avenue, Westminster, CO, Zip 80030–3887; tel. 303/426–2151; Matthew S. Fulton, Chief Executive Officer

THE COLORADO NETWORK, INC.
4450 Arapahoe Avenue #200, Boulder, CO
80303; tel. 303/440–5511; John Leavitt,
Executive Director

GRAND RIVER HOSPITAL DISTRICT, 701 East Fifth Street, Rifle, CO, Zip 81650–2970, Mailing Address: P.O. Box 912, Zip 81650–0912; tel. 970/625–1510; Robert Peterson, Interim Administrator

HEART OF THE ROCKIES REGIONAL MEDICAL CENTER, 448 East First Street, Salida, CO, Zip 81201–0429, Mailing Address: P.O. Box 429, Zip 81201–0429; tel. 719/539–6661; Howard D. Turner, Chief Executive Officer

MEMORIAL HOSPITAL, 785 Russell Street, Craig, CO, Zip 81625–9906; tel. 970/824–9411; M. Randell Phelps, Administrator

MONTROSE MEMORIAL HOSPITAL, 800 South Third Street, Montrose, CO, Zip 81401–4291; tel. 970/249–2211; Jan V. Carrell, Chief Executive Officer and Administrator

MOUNT SAN RAFAEL HOSPITAL, 410 Benedicta Avenue, Trinidad, CO, Zip 81082–2093; tel. 719/846–9213; Paul Herman, Chief Executive Officer

PARKVIEW MEDICAL CENTER, 400 West 16th Street, Pueblo, CO, Zip 81003–2781; tel. 719/584–4000; C. W. Smith, President and Chief Executive Officer

PIONEERS HOSPITAL OF RIO BLANCO COUNTY, 345 Cleveland Street, Meeker, CO, Zip 81641–0000; tel. 970/878–5047; Thomas E. Lake, Chief Executive Officer

PROWERS MEDICAL CENTER, 401 Kendall Drive, Lamar, CO, Zip 81052–3993; tel. 719/336–4343; Earl J. Steinhoff, Chief Executive Officer

VALLEY VIEW HOSPITAL, 1906 Blake Avenue, Glenwood Springs, CO, Zip 81601–4259, Mailing Address: P.O. Box 1970, Zip 81602–1970; tel. 970/945–6535; Gary L. Brewer, Chief Executive Officer

THE MEDICAL CENTER OF AURORA
8200 East Belleview Avenue, Suite I200,
Englewood, CO 80111; tel. 303/267–8509;
Chris Ives, Systems Director

NORTH SUBURBAN MEDICAL CENTER, 9191 Grant Street, Thornton, CO, Zip 80229–4341; tel. 303/451–7800; Margaret C. Cain, Chief Executive Officer

PRESBYTERIAN–ST. LUKE'S MEDICAL CENTER, 1719 East 19th Avenue, Denver, CO, Zip 80218–1281; tel. 303/839–6000; Kevin Gross, Chief Executive Officer

ROSE MEDICAL CENTER, 4567 East Ninth Avenue, Denver, CO, Zip 80220–3941; tel. 303/320–2121; Kenneth H. Feiler, President and Chief Executive Officer

SWEDISH MEDICAL CENTER, 501 East Hampden Avenue, Englewood, CO, Zip 80110–0101; tel. 303/788–5000; Mary M. White, President and Chief Executive Officer

CONNECTICUT

DANBURY HEALTH SYSTEMS
24 Hospital Ave., Danbury, CT 06810;
tel. 203/797–7066; Frank J. Kelly,
President & CEO

HARTFORD HEALTH CARE CORPORATION
80 Seymour St. P.O. Box 5037, Hartford, CT
06102–5037; tel. 860/545–1490; George M.
Kyriacou, Vice President, Network
Development

CHARLOTTE HUNGERFORD HOSPITAL, 540 Litchfield
Street, Torrington, CT, Zip 06790, Mailing
Address: P.O. Box 988, Zip 06790–0988;
tel. 860/496–6666; Rosanne U. Griswold,
President and Chief Executive Officer

GAYLORD HOSPITAL, Gaylord Farm Road, Wallingford,
CT, Zip 06492, Mailing Address: P.O. Box 400,
Zip 06492; tel. 203/284–2800; Paul H.
Johnson, President and Chief Executive Officer

HARTFORD HOSPITAL, 80 Seymour Street, Hartford,
CT, Zip 06102–5037, Mailing Address: P.O. Box
5037, Zip 06102–5037; tel. 860/545–5000;
John J. Meehan, President and Chief Executive
Officer

HOSPITAL OF SAINT RAPHAEL, 1450 Chapel Street,
New Haven, CT, Zip 06511–1450;
tel. 203/789–3000; David W. Benfer, President
and Chief Executive Officer

NATCHAUG HOSPITAL, 189 Storrs Road, Mansfield
Center, CT, Zip 06250–1638;
tel. 860/456–1311; Stephen W. Larcen, Ph.D.,
Chief Executive Officer

SAINT FRANCIS HOSPITAL AND MEDICAL CENTER,
114 Woodland Street, Hartford, CT,
Zip 06105–1299; tel. 860/714–4000; David
D'Eramo, President and Chief Executive Officer

SHARON HOSPITAL, 50 Hospital Hill Road, Sharon,
CT, Zip 06069–0789, Mailing Address: P.O. Box
789, Zip 06069–0789; tel. 860/364–4141;
Michael R. Gallacher, President and Chief
Executive Officer

NEW MILFORD HOSPITAL HOLDING
21 Elm Street, New Milford, CT 06776;
tel. 860/350–7200; Richard E. Pugh,
President & CEO

NEW YORK PRESBYTERIAN HOSPITAL, 525 East 68th
Street, New York, NY, Zip 10021–4885;
tel. 212/746–5454; David B. Skinner, M.D., Vice
Chairman and Chief Executive Officer; William T.
Speck, President and Chief Operating Officer

NORWALK HEALTH SERVICES
34 Maple Street, Norwalk, CT 06856;
tel. 203/852–2000; David W. Osborne,
President & CEO

SHARON HOSPITAL
50 Hospital Hill Road, Sharon, CT 06069;
tel. 860/364–4010; Michael R. Gallagher,
(Interim) President/CEO

ST. MARY'S HOSPITAL INTEGRATED DELIVERY
NETWORK
56 Franklin St., Waterbury, CT 06702;
tel. 203/574–6000; J.R. Dobbins, M.S., Exec.
Vice–President Planning

SAINT FRANCIS HOSPITAL AND MEDICAL CENTER,
114 Woodland Street, Hartford, CT,
Zip 06105–1299; tel. 860/714–4000; David
D'Eramo, President and Chief Executive Officer

ST. MARY'S HOSPITAL, 56 Franklin Street, Waterbury,
CT, Zip 06706–1200; tel. 203/574–6000;
Sister Marguerite Waite, President and Chief
Executive Officer

ST. VINCENT'S MEDICAL CENTER
2800 Main Street, Bridgeport, CT 06606;
tel. 203/576–5131; William J. Riordan,
President & CEO

THE GREATER WATERBURY NETWORK
64 Robbins Street, Waterbury, CT 06721;
tel. 203/573–7334; John H. Tobin, President

YALE NEW HAVEN HEALTH SYSTEMS
789 Howard Avenue, New Haven, CT 06519;
tel. 203/688–4242; Gayle Capozzalo, Exec.
Vice President, Strategy & System
Development

BRIDGEPORT HOSPITAL, 267 Grant Street,
Bridgeport, CT, Zip 06610–2875, Mailing
Address: P.O. Box 5000, Zip 06610–0120;
tel. 203/384–3000; Robert J. Trefry, President
and Chief Executive Officer

YALE–NEW HAVEN HOSPITAL, 20 York Street, New
Haven, CT, Zip 06504–3202;
tel. 203/688–4242; Joseph A. Zaccagnino,
President and Chief Executive Officer

DELAWARE

CHRISTIANA CARE CORPORATION
P.O. Box 1668, Wilmington, DE 19899;
tel. 302/733–1321; James F. Caldas, Network
Coordinator

CHRISTIANA CARE, 4755 Ogletown–Stanton Road,
Newark, DE, Zip 19718; tel. 302/733–1000;
Charles M. Smith, M.D., President and Chief
Executive Officer

DELAWARE NETWORK HEALTH PLAN
801 Middlefield Road, Seaford, DE 19973;
tel. 302/629–6611; Edward H. Hancock,
President

NANTICOKE MEMORIAL HOSPITAL, 801 Middleford
Road, Seaford, DE, Zip 19973–3698;
tel. 302/629–6611; Edward H. Hancock,
President

DISTRICT OF COLUMBIA

MEDSTAR HEALTH
5565 Strerrett Place, Colombia, DC 20144;
tel. 202/877–6101; Ken Samet, President

NATIONAL REHABILITATION HOSPITAL, 102 Irving
Street N.W., Washington, DC, Zip 20010–2949;
tel. 202/877–1000; Edward A. Eckenhoff,
President and Chief Executive Officer

WASHINGTON HOSPITAL CENTER, 110 Irving Street
N.W., Washington, DC, Zip 20010–2975;
tel. 202/877–7000; Kenneth A. Samet,
President

FLORIDA

ADVENTIST HEALTH SYSTEM
111 North Orlando Avenue, Winter Park, FL
32789; tel. 497/975–1425; Mardian J. Blair,
President

EAST PASCO MEDICAL CENTER, 7050 Gall
Boulevard, Zephyrhills, FL, Zip 33541–1399;
tel. 813/788–0411; Paul Michael Norman,
President

FLORIDA HOSPITAL, 601 East Rollins Street, Orlando,
FL, Zip 32803–1489; tel. 407/896–6611;
Thomas L. Werner, President

FLORIDA HOSPITAL HEARTLAND DIVISION, 4200
Sun'n Lake Boulevard, Sebring, FL, Zip 33872,
Mailing Address: P.O. Box 9400, Zip 33872;
tel. 941/314–4466; John R. Harding, President
and Chief Executive Officer

FLORIDA HOSPITAL WATERMAN, 201 North Eustis
Street, Eustis, FL, Zip 32726–3488, Mailing
Address: P.O. Box B, Zip 32727–0377;
tel. 352/589–3333; Kenneth R. Mattison,
President and Chief Executive Officer

ALLEGANY HEALTH SYSTEM
6200 Courtney Campbell, Tampa, FL
33607–1458; tel. 813/281–9098; Melinda
Owens, Network Contact

ST. ANTHONY'S HOSPITAL, 1200 Seventh Avenue
North, Saint Petersburg, FL, Zip 33705–1388,
Mailing Address: P.O. Box 12588,
Zip 33733–2588; tel. 727/825–1100; Sue G.
Brody, President and Chief Executive Officer

ST. JOSEPH'S HOSPITAL, 3001 West Martin Luther
King Jr. Boulevard, Tampa, FL,
Zip 33607–6387, Mailing Address: P.O. Box
4227, Zip 33677–4227; tel. 813/870–4000;
Isaac Mallah, President and Chief Executive
Officer

ST. MARY'S HOSPITAL, 901 45th Street, West Palm
Beach, FL, Zip 33407–2495, Mailing Address:
P.O. Box 24620, Zip 33416–4620;
tel. 561/844–6300; Phillip C. Dutcher, President
and Chief Executive Officer

BAPTIST HEALTH CARE, INC
P.O. Box 17500, Pensacola, FL 32522;
tel. 850/469–2338; David Sjoberg, Vice
President of Planning

ATMORE COMMUNITY HOSPITAL, 401 Medical Park
Drive, Atmore, AL, Zip 36502–3091;
tel. 334/368–2500; Robert E. Gowing, Interim
Administrator

BAPTIST HOSPITAL, 1000 West Moreno, Pensacola,
FL, Zip 32501–2393, Mailing Address: P.O. Box
17500, Zip 32522–7500; tel. 850/469–2313;
Quinton Studer, President

D. W. MCMILLAN MEMORIAL HOSPITAL, 1301
Belleville Avenue, Brewton, AL, Zip 36426–1306,
Mailing Address: P.O. Box 908,
Zip 36427–0908; tel. 334/867–8061; Phillip L.
Parker, Administrator

GULF BREEZE HOSPITAL, 1110 Gulf Breeze Parkway,
Gulf Breeze, FL, Zip 32561, Mailing Address:
P.O. Box 159, Zip 32562; tel. 850/934–2000;
Richard C. Fulford, Administrator

JAY HOSPITAL, 221 South Alabama Street, Jay, FL,
Zip 32565–1070, Mailing Address: P.O. Box
397, Zip 32565–0397; tel. 850/675–8000;
Robert E. Gowing, Administrator

MIZELL MEMORIAL HOSPITAL, 702 Main Street, Opp,
AL, Zip 36467–1626, Mailing Address: P.O. Box
1010, Zip 36467–1010; tel. 334/493–3541;
Allen Foster, Administrator

BAPTIST HEALTH SYSTEM
6855 Red Road, Coral Gables, FL 33143;
tel. 305/596–1960; Brian Keeley, President

BAPTIST HOSPITAL OF MIAMI, 8900 North Kendall
Drive, Miami, FL, Zip 33176–2197;
tel. 305/596–1960; Lee S. Huntley, Chief
Executive Officer

HOMESTEAD HOSPITAL, 160 N.W. 13th Street,
Homestead, FL, Zip 33030–4299;
tel. 305/248–3232; Bo Boulenger, Chief
Executive Officer

MARINERS HOSPITAL, 91500 Overseas Highway,
Tavernier, FL, Zip 33070; tel. 305/852–4418;
Robert H. Luse, Chief Executive Officer

SOUTH MIAMI HOSPITAL, 6200 S.W. 73rd Street,
Miami, FL, Zip 33143–9990;
tel. 305/661–4611; D. Wayne Brackin, Chief
Executive Officer

BAPTIST/ST. VINCENT'S HEALTH SYSTEM
800 Prudential Drive, Jacksonville, FL
32207–8244; tel. 904/202–2000; William
Mason, President/CEO

BAPTIST MEDICAL CENTER, 800 Prudential Drive,
Jacksonville, FL, Zip 32207–8203;
tel. 904/202–2000; John F. Wilbanks, Senior
Vice President and Administrator

BAPTIST MEDICAL CENTER–BEACHES, 1350 13th
Avenue South, Jacksonville Beach, FL,
Zip 32250–3205; tel. 904/247–2900; Joseph
Mitrick, Administrator

BAPTIST MEDICAL CENTER–NASSAU, 1250 South
18th Street, Fernandina Beach, FL,
Zip 32034–3098; tel. 904/321–3501; Jim L.
Mayo, Administrator

ST. VINCENT'S MEDICAL CENTER, 1800 Barrs Street,
Jacksonville, FL, Zip 32204–2982, Mailing
Address: P.O. Box 2982, Zip 32203–2982;
tel. 904/308–7300; John W. Logue, Executive
Vice President and Chief Operating Officer

BAY CARE HEALTH NETWORK
17757 U.S. Highway 19, Tampa Bay, FL
34524; tel. 813/535–3335; Bill Norsworthy,
President & CEO

ALL CHILDREN'S HOSPITAL, 801 Sixth Street South,
Saint Petersburg, FL, Zip 33701–4899;
tel. 813/898–7451; J. Dennis Sexton, President

BAYFRONT MEDICAL CENTER, 701 Sixth Street
South, Saint Petersburg, FL, Zip 33701–4891;
tel. 727/823–1234; Sue G. Brody, President
and Chief Executive Officer

BROOKSVILLE REGIONAL HOSPITAL, 55 Ponce De
Leon Boulevard, Brooksville, FL,
Zip 34601–0037, Mailing Address: P.O. Box 37,
Zip 34605–0037; tel. 352/796–5111; Robert
Foreman, Associate Administrator

EAST PASCO MEDICAL CENTER, 7050 Gall
Boulevard, Zephyrhills, FL, Zip 33541–1399;
tel. 813/788–0411; Paul Michael Norman,
President

Networks, Health Care Systems and Alliances **B9**

MANATEE MEMORIAL HOSPITAL, 206 Second Street East, Bradenton, FL, Zip 34208–1000; tel. 941/746–5111; Michael Marquez, Chief Executive Officer

MEASE COUNTRYSIDE HOSPITAL, 3231 McMullen–Booth Road, Safety Harbor, FL, Zip 34695–1098, Mailing Address: P.O. 1098, Zip 34695–1098; tel. 813/725–6111; James A. Pfeiffer, Chief Operating Officer

MEASE HOSPITAL DUNEDIN, 601 Main Street, Dunedin, FL, Zip 34698–5891, Mailing Address: P.O. Box 760, Zip 34697–0760; tel. 727/733–1111; James A. Pfeiffer, Chief Operating Officer

MORTON PLANT HOSPITAL, 323 Jeffords Street, Clearwater, FL, Zip 33756, Mailing Address: P.O. Box 210, Zip 34657–0210; tel. 727/462–7000; Philip K. Beauchamp, FACHE, President and Chief Executive Officer

NORTH BAY HOSPITAL, 6600 Madison Street, New Port Richey, FL, Zip 34652–1900; tel. 727/842–8468; William A. Jennings, Chief Operating Officer and Administrator

SOUTH FLORIDA BAPTIST HOSPITAL, 301 North Alexander Street, Plant City, FL, Zip 33566–9058, Mailing Address: Drawer H, Zip 33564–9058; tel. 813/757–1200; William G. Ulbricht, Chief Operating Officer

SPRING HILL REGIONAL HOSPITAL, 10461 Quality Drive, Spring Hill, FL, Zip 34609; tel. 352/688–8200; Thomas Bard, Chief Executive Officer

ST. ANTHONY'S HOSPITAL, 1200 Seventh Avenue North, Saint Petersburg, FL, Zip 33705–1388, Mailing Address: P.O. Box 12588, Zip 33733–2588; tel. 727/825–1100; Sue G. Brody, President and Chief Executive Officer

ST. JOSEPH'S HOSPITAL, 3001 West Martin Luther King Jr. Boulevard, Tampa, FL, Zip 33607–6387, Mailing Address: P.O. Box 4227, Zip 33677–4227; tel. 813/870–4000; Isaac Mallah, President and Chief Executive Officer

UNIVERSITY COMMUNITY HOSPITAL, 3100 East Fletcher Avenue, Tampa, FL, Zip 33613–4688; tel. 813/971–6000; Norman V. Stein, President

UNIVERSITY COMMUNITY HOSPITAL–CARROLLWOOD, 7171 North Dale Mabry Highway, Tampa, FL, Zip 33614–2699; tel. 813/558–8001; Larry J. Archbell, Vice President Operations

COLUMBIA/HCA N & NE FLORIDA DIVISION
1705 Metropolitan, Talahassee, FL 32308; tel. 850/523–0343; Charles Evans, President

FORT WALTON BEACH MEDICAL CENTER, 1000 Mar–Walt Drive, Fort Walton Beach, FL, Zip 32547–6795; tel. 850/862–1111; Wayne Campbell, Chief Executive Officer

GULF COAST MEDICAL CENTER, 449 West 23rd Street, Panama City, FL, Zip 32405–4593, Mailing Address: P.O. Box 15309, Zip 32406–5309; tel. 850/769–8341; Brent A. Marsteller, Chief Executive Officer

MEMORIAL HOSPITAL OF JACKSONVILLE, 3625 University Boulevard South, Jacksonville, FL, Zip 32216–4240, Mailing Address: P.O. Box 16325, Zip 32216–6325; tel. 904/399–6111; H. Rex Etheredge, President and Chief Executive Officer

NORTH FLORIDA REGIONAL MEDICAL CENTER, 6500 Newberry Road, Gainesville, FL, Zip 32605–4392, Mailing Address: P.O. Box 147006, Zip 32614–7006; tel. 352/333–4000; Brian C. Robinson, Chief Executive Officer

OCALA REGIONAL MEDICAL CENTER, 1431 S.W. First Avenue, Ocala, FL, Zip 34474–4058, Mailing Address: P.O. Box 2200, Zip 34478–2200; tel. 352/401–1000; Stephen Mahan, Chief Executive Officer

ORANGE PARK MEDICAL CENTER, 2001 Kingsley Avenue, Orange Park, FL, Zip 32073–5156; tel. 904/276–8500; Robert M. Krieger, Chief Executive Officer

PUTNAM COMMUNITY MEDICAL CENTER, Highway 20 West, Palatka, FL, Zip 32177, Mailing Address: P.O. Box 778, Zip 32178–0778; tel. 904/328–5711; Rodney R. Smith, Chief Executive Officer

SPECIALTY HOSPITAL JACKSONVILLE, 4901 Richard Street, Jacksonville, FL, Zip 32207; tel. 904/737–3120; W. Raymond C. Ford, Chief Executive Officer

TALLAHASSEE COMMUNITY HOSPITAL, 2626 Capital Medical Boulevard, Tallahassee, FL, Zip 32308–4499; tel. 850/656–5000; Thomas Paul Pemberton, Chief Executive Officer

TWIN CITIES HOSPITAL, 2190 Highway 85 North, Niceville, FL, Zip 32578–1045; tel. 850/678–4131; David Whalen, Chief Executive Officer

WEST FLORIDA REGIONAL MEDICAL CENTER, 8383 North Davis Highway, Pensacola, FL, Zip 32514–6088, Mailing Address: P.O. Box 18900, Zip 32523–8900; tel. 850/494–4000; Stephen Brandt, President and Chief Executive Officer

COLUMBIA/HCA S.W. FLORIDA DIVISION
2000 Main Street, Suite 600, Fort Myers, FL 33901; tel. 813/477–3900; Charles Hall, President

DOCTORS HOSPITAL OF SARASOTA, 5731 Bee Ridge Road, Sarasota, FL, Zip 34233–5056; tel. 941/342–1100; William C. Lievense, President and Chief Executive Officer

EAST POINTE HOSPITAL, 1500 Lee Boulevard, Lehigh Acres, FL, Zip 33936–4897; tel. 941/369–2101; Valerie A. Jackson, Chief Executive Officer

ENGLEWOOD COMMUNITY HOSPITAL, 700 Medical Boulevard, Englewood, FL, Zip 34223–3978; tel. 941/475–6571; Robert C. Meade, Chief Executive Officer

FAWCETT MEMORIAL HOSPITAL, 21298 Olean Boulevard, Port Charlotte, FL, Zip 33952–6765, Mailing Address: P.O. Box 4028, Punta Gorda, Zip 33949–4028; tel. 941/629–1181; Terry Chaffin, President and Chief Executive Officer

GULF COAST HOSPITAL, 13681 Doctors Way, Fort Myers, FL, Zip 33912–4309; tel. 941/768–5000; Valerie A. Jackson, Chief Executive Officer

SOUTHWEST FLORIDA REGIONAL MEDICAL CENTER, 2727 Winkler Avenue, Fort Myers, FL, Zip 33901–9396; tel. 941/939–1147; Stephen L. Royal, President and Chief Executive Officer

COLUMBIA/HCA SOUTH FLORIDA DIVISION
7975 N.W. 154th Street, Suite 400A, Miami Lakes, FL 33016; tel. 305/364–1202; Jamie E. Hopping, President

COLUMBIA/HCA TAMPA BAY DIVISION
6200 Courtney Campbell, Tampa, FL 33607; tel. 813/286–6000; J. Daniel Miller, President

BARTOW MEMORIAL HOSPITAL, 1239 East Main Street, Bartow, FL, Zip 33830–5005, Mailing Address: Box 1050, Zip 33830–1050; tel. 941/533–8111; Brian P. Baumgardner, Administrator

BLAKE MEDICAL CENTER, 2020 59th Street West, Bradenton, FL, Zip 34209–4669, Mailing Address: P.O. Box 25004, Zip 34206–5004; tel. 941/792–6611; Lindell W. Orr, Chief Executive Officer

BRANDON REGIONAL HOSPITAL, 119 Oakfield Drive, Brandon, FL, Zip 33511–5799; tel. 813/681–5551; Michael M. Fencel, Chief Executive Officer

COMMUNITY HOSPITAL OF NEW PORT RICHEY, 5637 Marine Parkway, New Port Richey, FL, Zip 34652–4331, Mailing Address: P.O. Box 996, Zip 34656–0996; tel. 727/848–1733; Andrew Oravec, Jr., Administrator

DOCTORS HOSPITAL OF SARASOTA, 5731 Bee Ridge Road, Sarasota, FL, Zip 34233–5056; tel. 941/342–1100; William C. Lievense, President and Chief Executive Officer

EAST POINTE HOSPITAL, 1500 Lee Boulevard, Lehigh Acres, FL, Zip 33936–4897; tel. 941/369–2101; Valerie A. Jackson, Chief Executive Officer

EDWARD WHITE HOSPITAL, 2323 Ninth Avenue North, Saint Petersburg, FL, Zip 33713–6898, Mailing Address: P.O. Box 12018, Zip 33733–2018; tel. 727/323–1111; Barry S. Stokes, President and Chief Executive Officer

ENGLEWOOD COMMUNITY HOSPITAL, 700 Medical Boulevard, Englewood, FL, Zip 34223–3978; tel. 941/475–6571; Robert C. Meade, Chief Executive Officer

FAWCETT MEMORIAL HOSPITAL, 21298 Olean Boulevard, Port Charlotte, FL, Zip 33952–6765, Mailing Address: P.O. Box 4028, Punta Gorda, Zip 33949–4028; tel. 941/629–1181; Terry Chaffin, President and Chief Executive Officer

GULF COAST HOSPITAL, 13681 Doctors Way, Fort Myers, FL, Zip 33912–4309; tel. 941/768–5000; Valerie A. Jackson, Chief Executive Officer

LARGO MEDICAL CENTER, 201 14th Street S.W., Largo, FL, Zip 33770–3133, Mailing Address: P.O. Box 2905, Zip 33779–2905; tel. 727/588–5200; Thomas L. Herron, FACHE, President and Chief Executive Officer

NORTHSIDE HOSPITAL AND HEART INSTITUTE, 6000 49th Street North, Saint Petersburg, FL, Zip 33709–2145; tel. 727/521–4411; Bradley K. Grover, Sr., Ph.D., FACHE, President and Chief Executive Officer

OAK HILL HOSPITAL, 11375 Cortez Boulevard, Spring Hill, FL, Zip 34611, Mailing Address: P.O. Box 5300, Zip 34611–5300; tel. 352/596–6632; Jaime A. Wesolowski, Chief Executive Officer

REGIONAL MEDICAL CENTER–BAYONET POINT, 14000 Fivay Road, Hudson, FL, Zip 34667–7199; tel. 727/863–2411; Don Griffin, Ph.D., President and Chief Executive Officer

SOUTH BAY HOSPITAL, 4016 State Road 674, Sun City Center, FL, Zip 33573–5298; tel. 813/634–3301; Hal Muetzel, Chief Executive Officer

ST. PETERSBURG GENERAL HOSPITAL, 6500 38th Avenue North, Saint Petersburg, FL, Zip 33710–1629; tel. 727/384–1414; Daniel J. Friedrich, III, President and Chief Executive Officer

WEST FLORIDA REGIONAL MEDICAL CENTER, 8383 North Davis Highway, Pensacola, FL, Zip 32514–6088, Mailing Address: P.O. Box 18900, Zip 32523–8900; tel. 850/494–4000; Stephen Brandt, President and Chief Executive Officer

COMMUNITY CARE NETWORK OF INDIAN RIVER
1000 36th Street, Vero Beach, FL 32960; tel. 407/567–4311; Michael J. O'Grady, Jr, President

INDIAN RIVER MEMORIAL HOSPITAL, 1000 36th Street, Vero Beach, FL, Zip 32960–6592; tel. 561/567–4311; Jeffrey L. Susi, President and Chief Executive Officer

COMMUNITY HEALTH NETWORK OF S FLORIDA
4725 North Federal Highway, Ft Lauderdale, FL 33308; tel. 305/771–8000; Raymond Budrys, President

HOLY CROSS HOSPITAL, 4725 North Federal Highway, Fort Lauderdale, FL, Zip 33308–4668, Mailing Address: P.O. Box 23460, Zip 33307–3460; tel. 954/771–8000; John C. Johnson, Chief Executive Officer

FLORIDA HEALTH CHOICE
800 Meadows Road, Boca Raton, FL 33486; tel. 561/496–0505; W. Brent Casey, President

BETHESDA MEMORIAL HOSPITAL, 2815 South Seacrest Boulevard, Boynton Beach, FL, Zip 33435–7995; tel. 561/737–7733; Robert B. Hill, President and Chief Executive Officer

BOCA RATON COMMUNITY HOSPITAL, 800 Meadows Road, Boca Raton, FL, Zip 33486–2368; tel. 561/393–4002; Randolph J. Pierce, President and Chief Executive Officer

GOOD SAMARITAN MEDICAL CENTER, Flagler Drive at Palm Beach Lakes Boulevard, West Palm Beach, FL, Zip 33401–3499; tel. 561/655–5511; Phillip C. Dutcher, President and Chief Executive Officer

HOLY CROSS HOSPITAL, 4725 North Federal Highway, Fort Lauderdale, FL, Zip 33308–4668, Mailing Address: P.O. Box 23460, Zip 33307–3460; tel. 954/771–8000; John C. Johnson, Chief Executive Officer

MARTIN MEMORIAL HEALTH SYSTEMS, 300 S.E. Hospital Drive, Stuart, FL, Zip 34995–9014, Mailing Address: P.O. Box 9010, Zip 34995–9010; tel. 561/223–5945; Richmond M. Harman, President and Chief Executive Officer

MEMORIAL REGIONAL HOSPITAL, 3501 Johnson Street, Hollywood, FL, Zip 33021–5421; tel. 954/987–2000; C. Kennon Hetlage, Administrator

ST. MARY'S HOSPITAL, 901 45th Street, West Palm Beach, FL, Zip 33407–2495, Mailing Address: P.O. Box 24620, Zip 33416–4620; tel. 561/844–6300; Phillip C. Dutcher, President and Chief Executive Officer

FLORIDA HOSPITAL MEDICAL CENTER
601 East Rollins Street, Orlando, FL 32803; tel. 407/896–6611; Thomas L. Werner, President

FLORIDA HOSPITAL, 601 East Rollins Street, Orlando, FL, Zip 32803–1489; tel. 407/896–6611; Thomas L. Werner, President

FLORIDA HOSPITAL WATERMAN, 201 North Eustis Street, Eustis, FL, Zip 32726–3488, Mailing Address: P.O. Box B, Zip 32727–0377; tel. 352/589–3333; Kenneth R. Mattison, President and Chief Executive Officer

GENESIS HEALTH, INC
3627 University Boulevard S., Jacksonville, FL 32216; tel. 904/391–1201; Douglas Baer, VP, Corp Controller

BROOKS REHABILITATION HOSPITAL, 3599 University Boulevard South, Jacksonville, FL, Zip 32216–4211, Mailing Address: P.O. Box 16406, Zip 32245–6406; tel. 904/858–7600; Donald H. Hutton, FACHE, President and Chief Executive Officer

HEARTLAND RURAL HEALTH NETWORK
2010 East Georgia Street, Bartow, FL 33830; tel. 813/533–1111; Valerie Pfister, Executive Director

LAKE OKEECHOBEE RURAL HEALTH NETWORK, INC.
185 U.S. Highway 27 S., South Bay, FL 33493; tel. 561/993–4221; Andrew Behman, CEO

GLADES GENERAL HOSPITAL, 1201 South Main Street, Belle Glade, FL, Zip 33430–4911; tel. 561/996–6571; Gene Faile, Chief Executive Officer

HENDRY REGIONAL MEDICAL CENTER, 500 West Sugarland Highway, Clewiston, FL, Zip 33440–3094; tel. 941/983–9121; Dick Stanly, Interim Administrator

J. F. K. MEDICAL CENTER, 5301 South Congress Avenue, Atlantis, FL, Zip 33462–1197; tel. 561/965–7300; Phillip D. Robinson, Chief Executive Officer

MARTIN MEMORIAL HEALTH SYSTEMS, 300 S.E. Hospital Drive, Stuart, FL, Zip 34995–9014, Mailing Address: P.O. Box 9010, Zip 34995–9010; tel. 561/223–5945; Richmond M. Harman, President and Chief Executive Officer

ST. MARY'S HOSPITAL, 901 45th Street, West Palm Beach, FL, Zip 33407–2495, Mailing Address: P.O. Box 24620, Zip 33416–4620; tel. 561/844–6300; Phillip C. Dutcher, President and Chief Executive Officer

MEMORIAL HEALTHCARE SYSTEM
3501 Johnson Street, Hollywood, FL 33021; tel. 954/987–2000; Alex Chang, Administrative Resident

MEMORIAL HOSPITAL PEMBROKE, 7800 Sheridan Street, Pembroke Pines, FL, Zip 33024; tel. 954/962–9650; J. E. Piriz, Administrator

MEMORIAL HOSPITAL WEST, 703 North Flamingo Road, Pembroke Pines, FL, Zip 33028; tel. 954/436–5000; Zeff Ross, Administrator

MEMORIAL REGIONAL HOSPITAL, 3501 Johnson Street, Hollywood, FL, Zip 33021–5421; tel. 954/987–2000; C. Kennon Hetlage, Administrator

METHODIST HEALTH SYSTEMS
580 West Eighth Street, Jacksonville, FL 32209; tel. 904/798–8000; Marcus Drewa, President

METHODIST MEDICAL CENTER, 580 West Eighth Street, Jacksonville, FL, Zip 32209–6553; tel. 904/798–8000; Marcus E. Drewa, President and Chief Executive Officer

ORLANDO REGIONAL HEALTHCARE
1414 Kuhl Avenue, Orlando, FL 32806; tel. 407/841–5161; John Hillenmeyer, President & CEO

ORLANDO REGIONAL MEDICAL CENTER, 1414 Kuhl Avenue, Orlando, FL, Zip 32806–2093; tel. 407/841–5111; Abe Lopman, Executive Director

SOUTH LAKE HOSPITAL, 847 Eighth Street, Clermont, FL, Zip 34711–2196; tel. 352/394–4071; Leslie Longacre, Executive Director and Chief Executive Officer

SOUTH SEMINOLE HOSPITAL, 555 West State Road 434, Longwood, FL, Zip 32750–4999; tel. 407/767–1200; Sue Whelan–Williams, Site Administrator

ST. CLOUD HOSPITAL, A DIVISION OF ORLANDO REGIONAL HEALTHCARE, 2906 17th Street, Saint Cloud, FL, Zip 34769–6099; tel. 407/892–2135; Jim Norris, Executive Director

THE HEALTH ADVANTAGE NETWORK
1507 N. Faulkenburg Road, Tampa, FL 33619; tel. 813/663–3700; Tammy Lent, Network Contact

ATLANTIC MEDICAL CENTER–DAYTONA, 400 North Clyde Morris Boulevard, Daytona Beach, FL, Zip 32114–2770, Mailing Address: P.O. Box 9000, Zip 32120–9000; tel. 904/239–5000; Pam Corliss, Chief Executive Officer

AVENTURA HOSPITAL AND MEDICAL CENTER, 20900 Biscayne Boulevard, Miami, FL, Zip 33180–1407; tel. 305/682–7100; Davide M. Carbone, Chief Executive Officer

BLAKE MEDICAL CENTER, 2020 59th Street West, Bradenton, FL, Zip 34209–4669, Mailing Address: P.O. Box 25004, Zip 34206–5004; tel. 941/792–6611; Lindell W. Orr, Chief Executive Officer

BRANDON REGIONAL HOSPITAL, 119 Oakfield Drive, Brandon, FL, Zip 33511–5799; tel. 813/681–5551; Michael M. Fencel, Chief Executive Officer

CEDARS MEDICAL CENTER, 1400 N.W. 12th Avenue, Miami, FL, Zip 33136–1003; tel. 305/325–5511; Steven Sonenreich, Chief Executive Officer

CENTRAL FLORIDA REGIONAL HOSPITAL, 1401 West Seminole Boulevard, Sanford, FL, Zip 32771–6764; tel. 407/321–4500; Doug Sills, President and Chief Executive Officer

COMMUNITY HOSPITAL OF NEW PORT RICHEY, 5637 Marine Parkway, New Port Richey, FL, Zip 34652–4331, Mailing Address: P.O. Box 996, Zip 34656–0996; tel. 727/848–1733; Andrew Oravec, Jr., Administrator

DEERING HOSPITAL, 9333 S.W. 152nd Street, Miami, FL, Zip 33157–1780; tel. 305/256–5100; Jude Torchia, Chief Executive Officer

DOCTORS HOSPITAL OF SARASOTA, 5731 Bee Ridge Road, Sarasota, FL, Zip 34233–5056; tel. 941/342–1100; William C. Lievense, President and Chief Executive Officer

EAST POINTE HOSPITAL, 1500 Lee Boulevard, Lehigh Acres, FL, Zip 33936–4897; tel. 941/369–2101; Valerie A. Jackson, Chief Executive Officer

EDWARD WHITE HOSPITAL, 2323 Ninth Avenue North, Saint Petersburg, FL, Zip 33713–6898, Mailing Address: P.O. Box 12018, Zip 33733–2018; tel. 727/323–1111; Barry S. Stokes, President and Chief Executive Officer

ENGLEWOOD COMMUNITY HOSPITAL, 700 Medical Boulevard, Englewood, FL, Zip 34223–3978; tel. 941/475–6571; Robert C. Meade, Chief Executive Officer

FAWCETT MEMORIAL HOSPITAL, 21298 Olean Boulevard, Port Charlotte, FL, Zip 33952–6765, Mailing Address: P.O. Box 4028, Punta Gorda, Zip 33949–4028; tel. 941/629–1181; Terry Chaffin, President and Chief Executive Officer

FORT WALTON BEACH MEDICAL CENTER, 1000 Mar–Walt Drive, Fort Walton Beach, FL, Zip 32547–6795; tel. 850/862–1111; Wayne Campbell, Chief Executive Officer

GULF COAST HOSPITAL, 13681 Doctors Way, Fort Myers, FL, Zip 33912–4309; tel. 941/768–5000; Valerie A. Jackson, Chief Executive Officer

GULF COAST MEDICAL CENTER, 449 West 23rd Street, Panama City, FL, Zip 32405–4593, Mailing Address: P.O. Box 15309, Zip 32406–5309; tel. 850/769–8341; Brent A. Marsteller, Chief Executive Officer

HAMILTON MEDICAL CENTER, 506 N.W. Fourth Street, Jasper, FL, Zip 32052; tel. 904/792–7200; Amelia Tompkins, Administrator

KENDALL MEDICAL CENTER, 11750 Bird Road, Miami, FL, Zip 33175–3530; tel. 305/223–3000; Victor Maya, Chief Executive Officer

LAKE CITY MEDICAL CENTER, 1050 Commerce Boulevard North, Lake City, FL, Zip 32055–3718; tel. 904/719–9000; Todd Gallati, Chief Executive Officer

LARGO MEDICAL CENTER, 201 14th Street S.W., Largo, FL, Zip 33770–3133, Mailing Address: P.O. Box 2905, Zip 33779–2905; tel. 727/588–5200; Thomas L. Herron, FACHE, President and Chief Executive Officer

LAWNWOOD REGIONAL MEDICAL CENTER, 1700 South 23rd Street, Fort Pierce, FL, Zip 34950–0188; tel. 561/461–4000; Thomas R. Pentz, President and Executive Officer

LUCERNE MEDICAL CENTER, 818 Main Lane, Orlando, FL, Zip 32801; tel. 407/649–6111

MEMORIAL HOSPITAL OF JACKSONVILLE, 3625 University Boulevard South, Jacksonville, FL, Zip 32216–4240, Mailing Address: P.O. Box 16325, Zip 32216–6325; tel. 904/399–6111; H. Rex Etheredge, President and Chief Executive Officer

MEMORIAL HOSPITAL PEMBROKE, 7800 Sheridan Street, Pembroke Pines, FL, Zip 33024; tel. 954/962–9650; J. E. Piriz, Administrator

MIAMI HEART INSTITUTE AND MEDICAL CENTER, 4701 Meridian Avenue, Miami, FL, Zip 33140–2910; tel. 305/674–3114; Ralph A. Aleman, Chief Executive Officer

NORTH FLORIDA REGIONAL MEDICAL CENTER, 6500 Newberry Road, Gainesville, FL, Zip 32605–4392, Mailing Address: P.O. Box 147006, Zip 32614–7006; tel. 352/333–4000; Brian C. Robinson, Chief Executive Officer

NORTH OKALOOSA MEDICAL CENTER, 151 Redstone Avenue S.E., Crestview, FL, Zip 32539–6026; tel. 850/689–8100; Roger L. Hall, Chief Executive Officer

NORTHSIDE HOSPITAL AND HEART INSTITUTE, 6000 49th Street North, Saint Petersburg, FL, Zip 33709–2145; tel. 727/521–4411; Bradley K. Grover, Sr., Ph.D., FACHE, President and Chief Executive Officer

NORTHWEST MEDICAL CENTER, 2801 North State Road 7, Pompano Beach, FL, Zip 33063–5727, Mailing Address: P.O. Box 639002, Margate, Zip 33063–9002; tel. 954/978–4000; Gina Melby, Chief Executive Officer

OAK HILL HOSPITAL, 11375 Cortez Boulevard, Spring Hill, FL, Zip 34611, Mailing Address: P.O. Box 5300, Zip 34611–5300; tel. 352/596–6632; Jaime A. Wesolowski, Chief Executive Officer

OCALA REGIONAL MEDICAL CENTER, 1431 S.W. First Avenue, Ocala, FL, Zip 34474–4058, Mailing Address: P.O. Box 2200, Zip 34478–2200; tel. 352/401–1000; Stephen Mahan, Chief Executive Officer

ORANGE PARK MEDICAL CENTER, 2001 Kingsley Avenue, Orange Park, FL, Zip 32073–5156; tel. 904/276–8500; Robert M. Krieger, Chief Executive Officer

OSCEOLA REGIONAL MEDICAL CENTER, 700 West Oak Street, Kissimmee, FL, Zip 34741–4996, Mailing Address: P.O. Box 422589, Zip 34742–2589; tel. 407/846–2266; E. Tim Cook, Chief Executive Officer

PALMS WEST HOSPITAL, 13001 Southern Boulevard, Loxahatchee, FL, Zip 33470–1150; tel. 561/798–3300; Alex M. Marceline, Chief Executive Officer

PASCO COMMUNITY HOSPITAL, 13100 Fort King Road, Dade City, FL, Zip 33525–5294; tel. 352/521–1100; William G. Buck, President and Chief Executive Officer

PLANTATION GENERAL HOSPITAL, 401 N.W. 42nd Avenue, Plantation, FL, Zip 33317–2882; tel. 954/587–5010; Anthony M. Degina, Jr., Chief Executive Officer

PUTNAM COMMUNITY MEDICAL CENTER, Highway 20 West, Palatka, FL, Zip 32177, Mailing Address: P.O. Box 778, Zip 32178–0778; tel. 904/328–5711; Rodney R. Smith, Chief Executive Officer

RAULERSON HOSPITAL, 1796 Highway 441 North, Okeechobee, FL, Zip 34972, Mailing Address: P.O. Box 1307, Zip 34973–1307; tel. 941/763–2151; Frank Irby, Chief Executive Officer

REGIONAL MEDICAL CENTER–BAYONET POINT, 14000 Fivay Road, Hudson, FL, Zip 34667–7199; tel. 727/863–2411; Don Griffin, Ph.D., President and Chief Executive Officer

SANTA ROSA MEDICAL CENTER, 1450 Berryhill Road, Milton, FL, Zip 32570–4028, Mailing Address: P.O. Box 648, Zip 32572–0648; tel. 850/626–7762; M. P. Gandy, Jr., Chief Executive Officer

SOUTH BAY HOSPITAL, 4016 State Road 674, Sun City Center, FL, Zip 33573–5298; tel. 813/634–3301; Hal Muetzel, Chief Executive Officer

SOUTH SEMINOLE HOSPITAL, 555 West State Road 434, Longwood, FL, Zip 32750–4999; tel. 407/767–1200; Sue Whelan–Williams, Site Administrator

SOUTHWEST FLORIDA REGIONAL MEDICAL CENTER, 2727 Winkler Avenue, Fort Myers, FL, Zip 33901–9396; tel. 941/939–1147; Stephen L. Royal, President and Chief Executive Officer

SPECIALTY HOSPITAL JACKSONVILLE, 4901 Richard Street, Jacksonville, FL, Zip 32207; tel. 904/737–3120; W. Raymond C. Ford, Chief Executive Officer

ST. LUCIE MEDICAL CENTER, 1800 S.E. Tiffany Avenue, Port St. Lucie, FL, Zip 34952–7580; tel. 561/335–4000; Gary Cantrell, President and Chief Executive Officer

ST. PETERSBURG GENERAL HOSPITAL, 6500 38th Avenue North, Saint Petersburg, FL, Zip 33710–1629; tel. 727/384–1414; Daniel J. Friedrich, III, President and Chief Executive Officer

TALLAHASSEE COMMUNITY HOSPITAL, 2626 Capital Medical Boulevard, Tallahassee, FL, Zip 32308–4499; tel. 850/656–5000; Thomas Paul Pemberton, Chief Executive Officer

TWIN CITIES HOSPITAL, 2190 Highway 85 North, Niceville, FL, Zip 32578–1045; tel. 850/678–4131; David Whalen, Chief Executive Officer

UNIVERSITY HOSPITAL AND MEDICAL CENTER, 7201 North University Drive, Tamarac, FL, Zip 33321–2996; tel. 954/721–2200; James A. Cruickshank, Chief Executive Officer

WEST FLORIDA REGIONAL MEDICAL CENTER, 8383 North Davis Highway, Pensacola, FL, Zip 32514–6088, Mailing Address: P.O. Box 18900, Zip 32523–8900; tel. 850/494–4000; Stephen Brandt, President and Chief Executive Officer

WESTSIDE REGIONAL MEDICAL CENTER, 8201 West Broward Boulevard, Plantation, FL, Zip 33324–9937; tel. 954/473–6600; Michael G. Joseph, Chief Executive Officer

WINTER PARK MEMORIAL HOSPITAL, 200 North Lakemont Avenue, Winter Park, FL, Zip 32792–3273; tel. 407/646–7000; Douglas P. DeGraaf, Chief Executive Officer

WINTER HAVEN HOSPITAL
200 Avenue F Northeast, Winter Haven, FL 33881; tel. 941/293–1121; Lance Anastasio, President

LAKE WALES MEDICAL CENTERS, 410 South 11th Street, Lake Wales, FL, Zip 33853–4256, Mailing Address: P.O. Box 3460, Zip 33859–3460; tel. 941/676–1433; Joe M. Connell, Chief Executive Officer

GEORGIA

CHATTAHOOCHIE HEALTH NETWORK
P.O. Box 3274, Gainesville, GA 30505; tel. 404/503–3552; R. Fleming Weaver, Executive Director

LANIER PARK HOSPITAL, 675 White Sulphur Road, Gainesville, GA, Zip 30505, Mailing Address: P.O. Box 1354, Zip 30503–1354; tel. 770/503–3000; Jerry Fulks, Chief Executive Officer

COLUMBUS MEDICAL CENTER
710 Center Street, Columbus, GA 31902–0790; tel. 706/660–6110; Kevin Sass, Vice President of Professional Services

BAPTIST MERIWETHER HOSPITAL, 5995 Spring Street, Warm Springs, GA, Zip 31830, Mailing Address: P.O. Box 8, Zip 31830–0008; tel. 706/655–3331; Lynn Jackson, Administrator

SOUTHWEST GEORGIA REGIONAL MEDICAL CENTER, 109 Randolph Street, Cuthbert, GA, Zip 31740–1338; tel. 912/732–2181; Keith J. Petersen, Chief Executive Officer

THE MEDICAL CENTER, 710 Center Street, Columbus, GA, Zip 31902, Mailing Address: P.O. Box 951, Zip 31902–0951; tel. 706/571–1000; Lance B. Duke, FACHE, President and Chief Executive Officer

WEST GEORGIA HEALTH SYSTEM, 1514 Vernon Road, La Grange, GA, Zip 30240–4199; tel. 706/882–1411; Charles L. Foster, Jr., FACHE, President and Chief Executive Officer

COLUMBUS REGIONAL HEALTHCARE SYSTEM
707 Center Street, P.O. Box 790, Columbus, GA 31902–0790; tel. 706/660–6100; Larry Sanders, Fache, Chairman & CEO

PHENIX REGIONAL HOSPITAL, 1707 21st Avenue, Phenix City, AL, Zip 36867–3753, Mailing Address: P.O. Box 190, Zip 36868–0190; tel. 334/291–8502; Lance B. Duke, FACHE, President and Chief Executive Officer

THE MEDICAL CENTER, 710 Center Street, Columbus, GA, Zip 31902, Mailing Address: P.O. Box 951, Zip 31902–0951; tel. 706/571–1000; Lance B. Duke, FACHE, President and Chief Executive Officer

EMORY UNIVERSITY SYSTEM OF HEALTHCARE AFFILIATE NETWORK
1365 Clifton Road Northeast, Atlanta, GA 30322; tel. 404/778–3623; Don Wells, Director of Business Development

FAIRVIEW PARK HOSPITAL, 200 Industrial Boulevard, Dublin, GA, Zip 31021–2997, Mailing Address: P.O. Box 1408, Zip 31040–1408; tel. 912/275–2000; James B. Wood, Chief Executive Officer

HANCOCK MEMORIAL HOSPITAL, 453 Boland Street, Sparta, GA, Zip 31087–1105, Mailing Address: P.O. Box 490, Zip 31087–0490; tel. 706/444–7006; Henry T. Gibbs, Administrator and Chief Executive Officer

TIFT GENERAL HOSPITAL, 901 East 18th Street, Tifton, GA, Zip 31794–3648, Mailing Address: Drawer 747, Zip 31793–0747; tel. 912/382–7120; William T. Richardson, President and Chief Executive Officer

WESLEY WOODS CENTER OF EMORY UNIVERSITY, 1821 Clifton Road N.E., Atlanta, GA, Zip 30329–5102; tel. 404/728–6200; William L. Minnix, Jr., President and Chief Executive Officer

GEORGIA FIRST NETWORK
150 East Ponce de Leon #320, Decatur, GA 30030; tel. 404/778–4939; Russ Toal, President & CEO

APPLING HEALTHCARE SYSTEM, 301 East Tollison Street, Baxley, GA, Zip 31513–2898; tel. 912/367–9841; Terry Stratton, Chief Executive Officer

ATHENS REGIONAL MEDICAL CENTER, 1199 Prince Avenue, Athens, GA, Zip 30606–2793; tel. 706/549–9977; John A. Drew, President and Chief Executive Officer

BROOKS COUNTY HOSPITAL, 903 North Court Street, Quitman, GA, Zip 31643–1315, Mailing Address: P.O. Box 5000, Zip 31643–5000; tel. 912/263–4171; Andrew J. Finnegan, CHE, Administrator

CAMDEN MEDICAL CENTER, 2000 Dan Proctor Drive, Saint Marys, GA, Zip 31558; tel. 912/576–4200; Alan E. George, Administrator

CANDLER COUNTY HOSPITAL, Cedar Road, Metter, GA, Zip 30439, Mailing Address: P.O. Box 597, Zip 30439–0597; tel. 912/685–5741; Michael Alexander, President and Chief Executive Officer

CANDLER HOSPITAL, 5353 Reynolds Street, Savannah, GA, Zip 31405–6013, Mailing Address: P.O. Box 9787, Zip 31412–9787; tel. 912/692–6000; Paul P. Hinchey, President and Chief Executive Officer

CRAWFORD LONG HOSPITAL OF EMORY UNIVERSITY, 550 Peachtree Street N.E., Atlanta, GA, Zip 30365–2225; tel. 404/686–4411; John Dunklin Henry, Sr., FACHE, Chief Executive Officer

CRISP REGIONAL HOSPITAL, 902 North Seventh Street, Cordele, GA, Zip 31015–5007; tel. 912/276–3100; D. Wayne Martin, President and Chief Executive Officer

EARLY MEMORIAL HOSPITAL, 630 Columbia Street, Blakely, GA, Zip 31723–1798; tel. 912/723–4241; Rodney C. Watford, Administrator

EASTSIDE MEDICAL CENTER, 1700 Medical Way, Snellville, GA, Zip 30078, Mailing Address: P.O. Box 587, Zip 30078–0587; tel. 770/979–0200; Les Beard, Chief Executive Officer

EFFINGHAM HOSPITAL, 459 Highway 119 South, Springfield, GA, Zip 31329–3021, Mailing Address: P.O. Box 386, Zip 31329–0386; tel. 912/754–6451; Terrance R. Frech, Chief Executive Officer

EGLESTON CHILDREN'S HOSPITAL, 1405 Clifton Road N.E., Atlanta, GA, Zip 30322–1101; tel. 404/325–6000; James E. Tally, Ph.D., President and Chief Executive Officer

ELBERT MEMORIAL HOSPITAL, 4 Medical Drive, Elberton, GA, Zip 30635–1897; tel. 706/283–3151; Mark LeNeave, Chief Executive Officer

EMORY UNIVERSITY HOSPITAL, 1364 Clifton Road N.E., Atlanta, GA, Zip 30322–1102; tel. 404/712–7021; John Dunklin Henry, Sr., FACHE, Chief Executive Officer

EMORY–ADVENTIST HOSPITAL, 3949 South Cobb Drive S.E., Smyrna, GA, Zip 30080–6300; tel. 770/434–0710; Terry Owen, Chief Executive Officer

FAIRVIEW PARK HOSPITAL, 200 Industrial Boulevard, Dublin, GA, Zip 31021–2997, Mailing Address: P.O. Box 1408, Zip 31040–1408; tel. 912/275–2000; James B. Wood, Chief Executive Officer

FLOYD MEDICAL CENTER, 304 Turner McCall Boulevard, Rome, GA, Zip 30165–2734, Mailing Address: P.O. Box 233, Zip 30162–0233; tel. 706/802–2000; Kurt Stuenkel, FACHE, President and Chief Executive Officer

GRADY GENERAL HOSPITAL, 1155 Fifth Street S.E., Cairo, GA, Zip 31728–3142, Mailing Address: P.O. Box 360, Zip 31728–0360; tel. 912/377–1150; Glen C. Davis, Administrator

HABERSHAM COUNTY MEDICAL CENTER, Highway 441, Demorest, GA, Zip 30535, Mailing Address: P.O. Box 37, Zip 30535–0037; tel. 706/754–2161; C. Richard Dwozan, President

HIGGINS GENERAL HOSPITAL, 200 Allen Memorial Drive, Bremen, GA, Zip 30110–2012, Mailing Address: P.O. Box 655, Zip 30110–0655; tel. 770/537–5851; Robbie Smith, Administrator

HOUSTON MEDICAL CENTER, 1601 Watson Boulevard, Warner Robins, GA, Zip 31093–3431, Mailing Address: Box 2886, Zip 31099–2886; tel. 912/922–4281; Arthur P. Christie, Administrator

JOHN D. ARCHBOLD MEMORIAL HOSPITAL, Gordon Avenue at Mimosa Drive, Thomasville, GA, Zip 31792–6113, Mailing Address: P.O. Box 1018, Zip 31799–1018; tel. 912/228–2000; Jason H. Moore, President and Chief Executive Officer

LIBERTY REGIONAL MEDICAL CENTER, 462 East G. Parkway, Hinesville, GA, Zip 31313, Mailing Address: P.O. Box 919, Zip 31313; tel. 912/369–9400; H. Scott Kroell, Jr., Chief Executive Officer

LOUIS SMITH MEMORIAL HOSPITAL, 852 West Thigpen Avenue, Lakeland, GA, Zip 31635–1099; tel. 912/482–3110; Randy Sauls, Administrator

MEDICAL CENTER OF CENTRAL GEORGIA, 777 Hemlock Street, Macon, GA, Zip 31201–2155, Mailing Address: P.O. Box 6000, Zip 31208–6000; tel. 912/633–1000; A. Donald Faulk, FACHE, President

MEDICAL COLLEGE OF GEORGIA HOSPITAL AND CLINICS, 1120 15th Street, Augusta, GA, Zip 30912–5000; tel. 706/721–0211; Patricia Sodomka, FACHE, Executive Director

MITCHELL COUNTY HOSPITAL, 90 Stephens Street, Camilla, GA, Zip 31730–1899, Mailing Address: P.O. Box 639, Zip 31730–0639; tel. 912/336–5284; Ronald M. Gilliard, FACHE, Administrator

NEWTON GENERAL HOSPITAL, 5126 Hospital Drive, Covington, GA, Zip 30014; tel. 770/786–7053; James F. Weadick, Administrator and Chief Executive Officer

NORTH FULTON REGIONAL HOSPITAL, 3000 Hospital Boulevard, Roswell, GA, Zip 30076–9930; tel. 770/751–2500; John F. Holland, President

NORTHEAST GEORGIA MEDICAL CENTER, 743 Spring Street N.E., Gainesville, GA, Zip 30501–3899; tel. 770/535–3553; Henry Rigdon, Executive Vice President

NORTHSIDE HOSPITAL, 1000 Johnson Ferry Road N.E., Atlanta, GA, Zip 30342–1611; tel. 404/851–8000; Sidney Kirschner, President and Chief Executive Officer

OCONEE REGIONAL MEDICAL CENTER, 821 North Cobb Street, Milledgeville, GA, Zip 31061–2351, Mailing Address: P.O. Box 690, Zip 31061–0690; tel. 912/454–3500; Brian L. Riddle, President and Chief Executive Officer

PALMYRA MEDICAL CENTERS, 2000 Palmyra Road, Albany, GA, Zip 31702–1908, Mailing Address: P.O. Box 1908, Zip 31702–1908; tel. 912/434–2000; Allen Golson, Chief Executive Officer

SOUTH GEORGIA MEDICAL CENTER, 2501 North Patterson Street, Valdosta, GA, Zip 31602–1735, Mailing Address: P.O. Box 1727, Zip 31603–1727; tel. 912/333–1000; John S. Bowling, President and Chief Executive Officer

SOUTHEAST GEORGIA REGIONAL MEDICAL CENTER, 3100 Kemble Avenue, Brunswick, GA, Zip 31520–4252, Mailing Address: P.O. Box 1518, Zip 31521–1518; tel. 912/264–7000; E. Berton Whitaker, President and Chief Executive Officer

SOUTHERN REGIONAL MEDICAL CENTER, 11 Upper Riverdale Road S.W., Riverdale, GA, Zip 30274–2600; tel. 770/991–8000; Eugene A. Leblond, FACHE, President and Chief Executive Officer

SPALDING REGIONAL HOSPITAL, 601 South Eighth Street, Griffin, GA, Zip 30224–4294, Mailing Address: P.O. Drawer V, Zip 30224–1168; tel. 770/228–2721; Jim Litchford, Executive Director

SUMTER REGIONAL HOSPITAL, 100 Wheatley Drive, Americus, GA, Zip 31709–3799; tel. 912/924–6011; Jerry W. Adams, President

TANNER MEDICAL CENTER, 705 Dixie Street, Carrollton, GA, Zip 30117–3818; tel. 770/836–9666; Loy M. Howard, Chief Executive Officer

TANNER MEDICAL CENTER–VILLA RICA, 601 Dallas Road, Villa Rica, GA, Zip 30180–1202, Mailing Address: P.O. Box 638, Zip 30180–0638; tel. 770/456–3100; Larry N. Steed, Administrator

THE MEDICAL CENTER, 710 Center Street, Columbus, GA, Zip 31902, Mailing Address: P.O. Box 951, Zip 31902–0951; tel. 706/571–1000; Lance B. Duke, FACHE, President and Chief Executive Officer

TIFT GENERAL HOSPITAL, 901 East 18th Street, Tifton, GA, Zip 31794–3648, Mailing Address: Drawer 747, Zip 31793–0747; tel. 912/382–7120; William T. Richardson, President and Chief Executive Officer

UPSON REGIONAL MEDICAL CENTER, 801 West Gordon Street, Thomaston, GA, Zip 30286–2831, Mailing Address: P.O. Box 1059, Zip 30286–1059; tel. 706/647–8111; Samuel S. Gregory, Administrator

WALTON MEDICAL CENTER, 330 Alcovy Street, Monroe, GA, Zip 30655–2140, Mailing Address: P.O. Box 1346, Zip 30655–1346; tel. 770/267–8461; Ronald L. Campbell, Chief Executive Officer

WEST GEORGIA HEALTH SYSTEM, 1514 Vernon Road, La Grange, GA, Zip 30240–4199; tel. 706/882–1411; Charles L. Foster, Jr., FACHE, President and Chief Executive Officer

GRADY HEALTH SYSTEM
   80 Butler Street, Atlanta, GA 30335; tel. 404/616–4307; Edward Renford, President

GRADY MEMORIAL HOSPITAL, 80 Butler Street S.E., Atlanta, GA, Zip 30335–3801, Mailing Address: P.O. Box 26189, Zip 30335–3801; tel. 404/616–4252; Edward J. Renford, President and Chief Executive Officer

NATIONAL CARDIOVASCULAR NETWORK
   6 Concourse Prkwy, #2950, Atlanta, GA 30328; tel. 404/551–5018; Michael Lanzilotta, President

BAPTIST HOSPITAL OF EAST TENNESSEE, 137 Blount Avenue S.E., Knoxville, TN, Zip 37920–1643, Mailing Address: P.O. Box 1788, Zip 37901–1788; tel. 423/632–5011; Jon Foster, Executive Vice President and Administrator

NW GEORGIA HEALTHCARE PARTNERSHIP
   P.O. Box 308, Dalton, GA 30722; tel. 706/272–6013; Nancy Kennedy, Executive Director

HAMILTON MEDICAL CENTER, 1200 Memorial Drive, Dalton, GA, Zip 30720–2529, Mailing Address: P.O. Box 1168, Zip 30722–1168; tel. 706/272–6000; Ned B. Wilford, President and Chief Executive Officer

MURRAY MEDICAL CENTER, 707 Old Ellijay Road, Chatsworth, GA, Zip 30705–2060, Mailing Address: P.O. Box 1406, Zip 30705–1406; tel. 706/695–4564; Mickey Rabuka, Administrator

PROMINA HEALTH SYSTEM, INC.
   2000 South Park Place, Atlanta, GA 30339; tel. 770/956–6455; Mike Britain, Director, System Planning

DECATUR HOSPITAL, 450 North Candler Street, Decatur, GA, Zip 30030–2671, Mailing Address: P.O. Box 40, Zip 30031–0040; tel. 404/377–0221; Richard T. Schmidt, Executive Director

DEKALB MEDICAL CENTER, 2701 North Decatur Road, Decatur, GA, Zip 30033–5995; tel. 404/501–1000; John R. Gerlach, Chief Executive Officer and Administrator

PIEDMONT HOSPITAL, 1968 Peachtree Road N.W., Atlanta, GA, Zip 30309–1231; tel. 404/605–5000; Richard B. Hubbard, III, President and Chief Executive Officer

PROMINA GWINNETT HOSPITAL SYSTEM, Lawrenceville, GA, Mailing Address: P.O. Box 348, Zip 30246–0348; tel. 770/995–4321; Franklin M. Rinker, President and Chief Executive Officer

SOUTHERN REGIONAL MEDICAL CENTER, 11 Upper Riverdale Road S.W., Riverdale, GA, Zip 30274–2600; tel. 770/991–8000; Eugene A. Leblond, FACHE, President and Chief Executive Officer

WELLSTAR COBB HOSPITAL, 3950 Austell Road, Austell, GA, Zip 30106–1121; tel. 770/732–4000; Thomas E. Hill, Chief Executive Officer

WELLSTAR DOUGLAS HOSPITAL, 8954 Hospital Drive, Douglasville, GA, Zip 30134–2282; tel. 770/949–1500; Thomas E. Hill, Chief Executive Officer

WELLSTAR KENNESTONE HOSPITAL, 677 Church Street, Marietta, GA, Zip 30060–1148; tel. 770/793–5000; Thomas E. Hill, Chief Executive Officer

WELLSTAR PAULDING HOSPITAL, 600 West Memorial Drive, Dallas, GA, Zip 30132–1335; tel. 770/445–4411; Thomas E. Hill, Chief Executive Officer

WELLSTAR WINDY HILL HOSPITAL, 2540 Windy Hill Road, Marietta, GA, Zip 30067–8632; tel. 770/644–1000; Thomas E. Hill, Chief Executive Officer

SAINT JOSEPH'S HOSPITAL OF ATLANTA, GA
   5665 Peachtree Dunwoody, Atlanta, GA 30342; tel. 404/851–7543; Brian Tisher, Planning Specialist

SAINT JOSEPH'S HOSPITAL OF ATLANTA, 5665 Peachtree Dunwoody Road N.E., Atlanta, GA, Zip 30342–1764; tel. 404/851–7001; Brue Chandler, President and Chief Executive Officer

SOUTHCARE MEDICAL ALLIANCE
   400 North Creek, Suite 300, Atlanta, GA 30327; tel. 404/231–9911; Ken Bryant, Executive Director

APPLING HEALTHCARE SYSTEM, 301 East Tollison Street, Baxley, GA, Zip 31513–2898; tel. 912/367–9841; Terry Stratton, Chief Executive Officer

ATHENS REGIONAL MEDICAL CENTER, 1114 West Madison Avenue, Athens, TN, Zip 37303–4150, Mailing Address: P.O. Box 250, Zip 37371–0250; tel. 423/745–1411; John R. Workman, Chief Executive Officer

BERRIEN COUNTY HOSPITAL, 1221 East McPherson Street, Nashville, GA, Zip 31639–2326, Mailing Address: P.O. Box 665, Zip 31639–0665; tel. 912/686–7471; James L. Jarrett, Chief Executive Officer

BRADLEY MEMORIAL HOSPITAL, 2305 Chambliss Avenue N.W., Cleveland, TN, Zip 37311, Mailing Address: P.O. Box 3060, Zip 37320–3060; tel. 423/559–6000; Jim Whitlock, Administrator

BULLOCH MEMORIAL HOSPITAL, 500 East Grady Street, Statesboro, GA, Zip 30458–5105, Mailing Address: P.O. Box 1048, Zip 30459–1048; tel. 912/486–1000; C. Scott Campbell, Executive Director

BURKE COUNTY HOSPITAL, 351 Liberty Street, Waynesboro, GA, Zip 30830–9686; tel. 706/554–4435; Michael A. Haddle, Chief Executive Officer and Chief Financial Officer

CANDLER COUNTY HOSPITAL, Cedar Road, Metter, GA, Zip 30439, Mailing Address: P.O. Box 597, Zip 30439–0597; tel. 912/685–5741; Michael Alexander, President and Chief Executive Officer

CANDLER HOSPITAL, 5353 Reynolds Street, Savannah, GA, Zip 31405–6013, Mailing Address: P.O. Box 9787, Zip 31412–9787; tel. 912/692–6000; Paul P. Hinchey, President and Chief Executive Officer

CLEVELAND COMMUNITY HOSPITAL, 2800 Westside Drive N.W., Cleveland, TN, Zip 37312–3599; tel. 423/339–4100; Marty Smith, Chief Executive Officer

COBB MEMORIAL HOSPITAL, 577 Franklin Springs Street, Royston, GA, Zip 30662–3909, Mailing Address: P.O. Box 589, Zip 30662–0589; tel. 706/245–5071; H. Thomas Brown, Administrator

COLISEUM MEDICAL CENTERS, 350 Hospital Drive, Macon, GA, Zip 31213; tel. 912/765–7000; Timothy C. Tobin, Chief Executive Officer

COLUMBIA CARTERSVILLE MEDICAL CENTER, 960 Joe Frank Harris Parkway, Cartersville, GA, Zip 30120, Mailing Address: P.O. Box 200008, Zip 30120–9001; tel. 770/382–1530; Keith Sandlin, Chief Executive Officer

Networks, Health Care Systems and Alliances

Section B

DECATUR HOSPITAL, 450 North Candler Street, Decatur, GA, Zip 30030–2671, Mailing Address: P.O. Box 40, Zip 30031–0040; tel. 404/377–0221; Richard T. Schmidt, Executive Director

DEKALB MEDICAL CENTER, 2701 North Decatur Road, Decatur, GA, Zip 30033–5995; tel. 404/501–1000; John R. Gerlach, Chief Executive Officer and Administrator

DOCTORS HOSPITAL, 616 19th Street, Columbus, GA, Zip 31901–1528, Mailing Address: P.O. Box 2188, Zip 31902–2188; tel. 706/571–4262; Hugh D. Wilson, Chief Executive Officer

DODGE COUNTY HOSPITAL, 715 Griffin Street S.W., Eastman, GA, Zip 31023–2223, Mailing Address: P.O. Box 4309, Zip 31023–4309; tel. 912/374–4000; Meredith H. Smith, Administrator

DOOLY MEDICAL CENTER, 1300 Union Street, Vienna, GA, Zip 31092–7541, Mailing Address: P.O. Box 278, Zip 31092–0278; tel. 912/268–4141; Kent W. McMackin, Administrator

EDGEFIELD COUNTY HOSPITAL, 300 Ridge Medical Plaza, Edgefield, SC, Zip 29824; tel. 803/637–3174; W. Joseph Seel, Administrator

EFFINGHAM HOSPITAL, 459 Highway 119 South, Springfield, GA, Zip 31329–3021, Mailing Address: P.O. Box 386, Zip 31329–0386; tel. 912/754–6451; Terrance R. Frech, Chief Executive Officer

EGLESTON CHILDREN'S HOSPITAL, 1405 Clifton Road N.E., Atlanta, GA, Zip 30322–1101; tel. 404/325–6000; James E. Tally, Ph.D., President and Chief Executive Officer

EMANUEL COUNTY HOSPITAL, 117 Kite Road, Swainsboro, GA, Zip 30401–3231, Mailing Address: P.O. Box 879, Zip 30401–0879; tel. 912/237–9911; Richard W. Clarke, Chief Executive Officer

FAIRVIEW PARK HOSPITAL, 200 Industrial Boulevard, Dublin, GA, Zip 31021–2997, Mailing Address: P.O. Box 1408, Zip 31040–1408; tel. 912/275–2000; James B. Wood, Chief Executive Officer

FLOYD MEDICAL CENTER, 304 Turner McCall Boulevard, Rome, GA, Zip 30165–2734, Mailing Address: P.O. Box 233, Zip 30162–0233; tel. 706/802–2000; Kurt Stuenkel, FACHE, President and Chief Executive Officer

GORDON HOSPITAL, 1035 Red Bud Road, Calhoun, GA, Zip 30701–2082, Mailing Address: P.O. Box 12938, Zip 30703–7013; tel. 706/629–2895; Dennis Kiley, President

GRANDVIEW MEDICAL CENTER, 1000 Highway 28, Jasper, TN, Zip 37347; tel. 423/837–9500; Phil Rowland, Chief Executive Officer

HART COUNTY HOSPITAL, Gibson and Cade Streets, Hartwell, GA, Zip 30643–0280, Mailing Address: P.O. Box 280, Zip 30643–0280; tel. 706/856–6100; Matt McRee, Administrator

HIGGINS GENERAL HOSPITAL, 200 Allen Memorial Drive, Bremen, GA, Zip 30110–2012, Mailing Address: P.O. Box 655, Zip 30110–0655; tel. 770/537–5851; Robbie Smith, Administrator

HILTON HEAD MEDICAL CENTER AND CLINICS, 25 Hospital Center Boulevard, Hilton Head Island, SC, Zip 29926–2738, Mailing Address: P.O. Box 21117, Zip 29925–1117; tel. 843/681–6122; Dennis Ray Bruns, President and Chief Executive Officer

HUTCHESON MEDICAL CENTER, 100 Gross Crescent Circle, Fort Oglethorpe, GA, Zip 30742–3669; tel. 706/858–2000; Robert T. Jones, M.D., President and Chief Executive Officer

JEFFERSON HOSPITAL, 1067 Peachtree Street, Louisville, GA, Zip 30434–1599; tel. 912/625–7000; Rita Culvern, Administrator

LIBERTY REGIONAL MEDICAL CENTER, 462 East G. Parkway, Hinesville, GA, Zip 31313, Mailing Address: P.O. Box 919, Zip 31313; tel. 912/369–9400; H. Scott Kroell, Jr., Chief Executive Officer

LOUIS SMITH MEMORIAL HOSPITAL, 852 West Thigpen Avenue, Lakeland, GA, Zip 31635–1099; tel. 912/482–3110; Randy Sauls, Administrator

MCDUFFIE COUNTY HOSPITAL, 521 Hill Street S.W., Thomson, GA, Zip 30824–2199; tel. 706/595–1411; Douglas C. Keir, Chief Executive Officer

MEADOWS REGIONAL MEDICAL CENTER, 1703 Meadows Lane, Vidalia, GA, Zip 30474–8915, Mailing Address: P.O. Box 1048, Zip 30474–1048; tel. 912/537–8921; Barry Michael, Chief Executive Officer

MEMORIAL HEALTH SYSTEM, 4700 Waters Avenue, Savannah, GA, Zip 31404–6283, Mailing Address: P.O. Box 23089, Zip 31403–3089; tel. 912/350–8000; Robert A. Colvin, President and Chief Executive Officer

MEMORIAL HOSPITAL, 2525 De Sales Avenue, Chattanooga, TN, Zip 37404–3322; tel. 423/495–2525; L. Clark Taylor, Jr., President and Chief Executive Officer

MEMORIAL HOSPITAL AND MANOR, 1500 East Shotwell Street, Bainbridge, GA, Zip 31717–4294; tel. 912/246–3500; James G. Peak, Chief Executive Officer

MEMORIAL NORTH PARK HOSPITAL, 2051 Hamill Road, Chattanooga, TN, Zip 37343–4096; tel. 423/870–6100; Sean S. McMurray, CHE, Administrator

NEWTON GENERAL HOSPITAL, 5126 Hospital Drive, Covington, GA, Zip 30014; tel. 770/786–7053; James F. Weadick, Administrator and Chief Executive Officer

NORTH GEORGIA MEDICAL CENTER, 1362 South Main Street, Ellijay, GA, Zip 30540–0346, Mailing Address: P.O. Box 2239, Zip 30540–0346; tel. 706/276–4741; Randy Carson, Chief Executive Officer

NORTHEAST GEORGIA MEDICAL CENTER, 743 Spring Street N.E., Gainesville, GA, Zip 30501–3899; tel. 770/535–3553; Henry Rigdon, Executive Vice President

NORTHSIDE HOSPITAL, 1000 Johnson Ferry Road N.E., Atlanta, GA, Zip 30342–1611; tel. 404/851–8000; Sidney Kirschner, President and Chief Executive Officer

NORTHSIDE HOSPITAL – CHEROKEE, 201 Hospital Road, Canton, GA, Zip 30114–2408, Mailing Address: P.O. Box 906, Zip 30114–0906; tel. 770/720–5100; Douglas M. Parker, Chief Executive Officer

OCONEE REGIONAL MEDICAL CENTER, 821 North Cobb Street, Milledgeville, GA, Zip 31061–2351, Mailing Address: P.O. Box 690, Zip 31061–0690; tel. 912/454–3500; Brian L. Riddle, President and Chief Executive Officer

PALMYRA MEDICAL CENTERS, 2000 Palmyra Road, Albany, GA, Zip 31702–1908, Mailing Address: P.O. Box 1908, Zip 31702–1908; tel. 912/434–2000; Allen Golson, Chief Executive Officer

PEACHTREE REGIONAL HOSPITAL, 60 Hospital Road, Newnan, GA, Zip 30264, Mailing Address: P.O. Box 2228, Zip 30264–2228; tel. 770/253–1912; Linda Jubinsky, Chief Executive Officer

PHENIX REGIONAL HOSPITAL, 1707 21st Avenue, Phenix City, AL, Zip 36867–3753, Mailing Address: P.O. Box 190, Zip 36868–0190; tel. 334/291–8502; Lance B. Duke, FACHE, President and Chief Executive Officer

PIEDMONT HOSPITAL, 1968 Peachtree Road N.W., Atlanta, GA, Zip 30309–1231; tel. 404/605–5000; Richard B. Hubbard, III, President and Chief Executive Officer

PROMINA GWINNETT HOSPITAL SYSTEM, Lawrenceville, GA, Mailing Address: P.O. Box 348, Zip 30246–0348; tel. 770/995–4321; Franklin M. Rinker, President and Chief Executive Officer

PUTNAM GENERAL HOSPITAL, Lake Oconee Parkway, Eatonton, GA, Zip 31024–4330, Mailing Address: Box 4330, Zip 31024–4330; tel. 706/485–2711; Darrell M. Oglesby, Administrator

RIDGECREST HOSPITAL, 393 Ridgecrest Circle, Clayton, GA, Zip 30525; tel. 706/782–4297; Maryann J. Greenwell, Chief Executive Officer

ROCKDALE HOSPITAL, 1412 Milstead Avenue N.E., Conyers, GA, Zip 30207–9990; tel. 770/918–3000; Nelson Toebbe, Chief Executive Officer

SATILLA REGIONAL MEDICAL CENTER, 410 Darling Avenue, Waycross, GA, Zip 31501–5246, Mailing Address: P.O. Box 139, Zip 31502–0139; tel. 912/283–3030; Robert M. Trimm, President and Chief Executive Officer

SCOTTISH RITE CHILDREN'S MEDICAL CENTER, 1001 Johnson Ferry Road N.E., Atlanta, GA, Zip 30342–1600; tel. 404/256–5252; James E. Tally, Ph.D., President and Chief Executive Officer

SHEPHERD CENTER, 2020 Peachtree Road N.W., Atlanta, GA, Zip 30309–1465; tel. 404/352–2020; Gary R. Ulicny, Ph.D., President and Chief Executive Officer

SISKIN HOSPITAL FOR PHYSICAL REHABILITATION, One Siskin Plaza, Chattanooga, TN, Zip 37403–1306; tel. 423/634–1200; Robert P. Main, President and Chief Executive Officer

SOUTH FULTON MEDICAL CENTER, 1170 Cleveland Avenue, East Point, GA, Zip 30344; tel. 404/305–3500; H. Neil Copelan, President and Chief Executive Officer

SOUTH GEORGIA MEDICAL CENTER, 2501 North Patterson Street, Valdosta, GA, Zip 31602–1735, Mailing Address: P.O. Box 1727, Zip 31603–1727; tel. 912/333–1000; John S. Bowling, President and Chief Executive Officer

SOUTHEAST ALABAMA MEDICAL CENTER, 1108 Ross Clark Circle, Dothan, AL, Zip 36301–3024, Mailing Address: P.O. Box 6987, Zip 36302–6987; tel. 334/793–8111; Ronald S. Owen, Chief Executive Officer

SOUTHEAST GEORGIA REGIONAL MEDICAL CENTER, 3100 Kemble Avenue, Brunswick, GA, Zip 31520–4252, Mailing Address: P.O. Box 1518, Zip 31521–1518; tel. 912/264–7000; E. Berton Whitaker, President and Chief Executive Officer

SOUTHERN REGIONAL MEDICAL CENTER, 11 Upper Riverdale Road S.W., Riverdale, GA, Zip 30274–2600; tel. 770/991–8000; Eugene A. Leblond, FACHE, President and Chief Executive Officer

SPALDING REGIONAL HOSPITAL, 601 South Eighth Street, Griffin, GA, Zip 30224–4294, Mailing Address: P.O. Drawer V, Zip 30224–1168; tel. 770/228–2721; Jim Litchford, Executive Director

ST. MARY'S HEALTH CARE SYSTEM, 1230 Baxter Street, Athens, GA, Zip 30606–3791; tel. 706/548–7581; Edward J. Fechtel, Jr., President and Chief Executive Officer

STEPHENS COUNTY HOSPITAL, 2003 Falls Road, Toccoa, GA, Zip 30577–9700; tel. 706/282–4200; Edward C. Gambrell, Jr., Administrator

SUMTER REGIONAL HOSPITAL, 100 Wheatley Drive, Americus, GA, Zip 31709–3799; tel. 912/924–6011; Jerry W. Adams, President

TANNER MEDICAL CENTER, 705 Dixie Street, Carrollton, GA, Zip 30117–3818; tel. 770/836–9666; Loy M. Howard, Chief Executive Officer

TANNER MEDICAL CENTER–VILLA RICA, 601 Dallas Road, Villa Rica, GA, Zip 30180–1202, Mailing Address: P.O. Box 638, Zip 30180–0638; tel. 770/456–3100; Larry N. Steed, Administrator

TAYLOR REGIONAL HOSPITAL, Macon Highway, Hawkinsville, GA, Zip 31036, Mailing Address: P.O. Box 1297, Zip 31036–1297; tel. 912/783–0200; Dan S. Maddock, President

THE MEDICAL CENTER, 710 Center Street, Columbus, GA, Zip 31902, Mailing Address: P.O. Box 951, Zip 31902–0951; tel. 706/571–1000; Lance B. Duke, FACHE, President and Chief Executive Officer

UNIVERSITY HEALTH CARE SYSTEM, 1350 Walton Way, Augusta, GA, Zip 30901–2629; tel. 706/722–9011; J. Larry Read, President and Chief Executive Officer

UPSON REGIONAL MEDICAL CENTER, 801 West Gordon Street, Thomaston, GA, Zip 30286–2831, Mailing Address: P.O. Box 1059, Zip 30286–1059; tel. 706/647–8111; Samuel S. Gregory, Administrator

VENCOR HOSPITAL–CHATTANOOGA, 709 Walnut Street, Chattanooga, TN, Zip 37402–1961; tel. 423/266–7721; Steven E. McGraw, Administrator

WALTON REHABILITATION HOSPITAL, 1355 Independence Drive, Augusta, GA, Zip 30901–1037; tel. 706/724–7746; Dennis B. Skelley, President and Chief Executive Officer

WASHINGTON COUNTY REGIONAL HOSPITAL, 610 Sparta Highway, Sandersville, GA, Zip 31082–1362, Mailing Address: P.O. Box 636, Zip 31082–0636; tel. 912/552–3901; Shirley R. Roberts, Administrator

WAYNE MEMORIAL HOSPITAL, 865 South First Street, Jesup, GA, Zip 31598, Mailing Address: P.O. Box 408, Zip 31598–0408; tel. 912/427–6811; Charles R. Morgan, Administrator

WELLSTAR COBB HOSPITAL, 3950 Austell Road, Austell, GA, Zip 30106–1121; tel. 770/732–4000; Thomas E. Hill, Chief Executive Officer

WELLSTAR DOUGLAS HOSPITAL, 8954 Hospital Drive, Douglasville, GA, Zip 30134–2282; tel. 770/949–1500; Thomas E. Hill, Chief Executive Officer

WELLSTAR PAULDING HOSPITAL, 600 West Memorial Drive, Dallas, GA, Zip 30132–1335; tel. 770/445–4411; Thomas E. Hill, Chief Executive Officer

WELLSTAR WINDY HILL HOSPITAL, 2540 Windy Hill Road, Marietta, GA, Zip 30067–8632; tel. 770/644–1000; Thomas E. Hill, Chief Executive Officer

ST. JOSEPH/CANDLER HEALTH SYSTEM
5353 Reynolds Street, Savannah, GA 31412;
tel. 912/692–2018; Paul Hinchey, President

APPLING HEALTHCARE SYSTEM, 301 East Tollison Street, Baxley, GA, Zip 31513–2898; tel. 912/367–9841; Terry Stratton, Chief Executive Officer

CANDLER COUNTY HOSPITAL, Cedar Road, Metter, GA, Zip 30439, Mailing Address: P.O. Box 597, Zip 30439–0597; tel. 912/685–5741; Michael Alexander, President and Chief Executive Officer

CANDLER HOSPITAL, 5353 Reynolds Street, Savannah, GA, Zip 31405–6013, Mailing Address: P.O. Box 9787, Zip 31412–9787; tel. 912/692–6000; Paul P. Hinchey, President and Chief Executive Officer

EFFINGHAM HOSPITAL, 459 Highway 119 South, Springfield, GA, Zip 31329–3021, Mailing Address: P.O. Box 386, Zip 31329–0386; tel. 912/754–6451; Terrance R. Frech, Chief Executive Officer

EMORY UNIVERSITY HOSPITAL, 1364 Clifton Road N.E., Atlanta, GA, Zip 30322–1102; tel. 404/712–7021; John Dunklin Henry, Sr., FACHE, Chief Executive Officer

LIBERTY REGIONAL MEDICAL CENTER, 462 East G. Parkway, Hinesville, GA, Zip 31313, Mailing Address: P.O. Box 919, Zip 31313; tel. 912/369–9400; H. Scott Kroell, Jr., Chief Executive Officer

MEADOWS REGIONAL MEDICAL CENTER, 1703 Meadows Lane, Vidalia, GA, Zip 30474–8915, Mailing Address: P.O. Box 1048, Zip 30474–1048; tel. 912/537–8921; Barry Michael, Chief Executive Officer

WILLINGWAY HOSPITAL, 311 Jones Mill Road, Statesboro, GA, Zip 30458–4765; tel. 912/764–6236; Jimmy Mooney, Chief Executive Officer

THE MEDICAL RESOURCE NETWORK, LLC
900 Circle, 75 Prkwy, #1400, Atlanta, GA
30339; tel. 770/980–2340; Mark Mixer,
Executive VP

APPLING HEALTHCARE SYSTEM, 301 East Tollison Street, Baxley, GA, Zip 31513–2898; tel. 912/367–9841; Terry Stratton, Chief Executive Officer

ATHENS REGIONAL MEDICAL CENTER, 1199 Prince Avenue, Athens, GA, Zip 30606–2793; tel. 706/549–9977; John A. Drew, President and Chief Executive Officer

BARNWELL COUNTY HOSPITAL, 811 Reynolds Road, Barnwell, SC, Zip 29812; tel. 803/259–1000; J. L. Dozier, Jr., FACHE, Chief Executive Officer

BERRIEN COUNTY HOSPITAL, 1221 East McPherson Street, Nashville, GA, Zip 31639–2326, Mailing Address: P.O. Box 665, Zip 31639–0665; tel. 912/686–7471; James L. Jarrett, Chief Executive Officer

BROOKS COUNTY HOSPITAL, 903 North Court Street, Quitman, GA, Zip 31643–1315, Mailing Address: P.O. Box 5000, Zip 31643–5000; tel. 912/263–4171; Andrew J. Finnegan, CHE, Administrator

BURKE COUNTY HOSPITAL, 351 Liberty Street, Waynesboro, GA, Zip 30830–9686; tel. 706/554–4435; Michael A. Haddle, Chief Executive Officer and Chief Financial Officer

CALHOUN MEMORIAL HOSPITAL, 209 Academy & Carswell Streets, Arlington, GA, Zip 31713, Mailing Address: Drawer R, Zip 31713; tel. 912/725–4272; Peggy Pierce, Administrator

CANDLER COUNTY HOSPITAL, Cedar Road, Metter, GA, Zip 30439, Mailing Address: P.O. Box 597, Zip 30439–0597; tel. 912/685–5741; Michael Alexander, President and Chief Executive Officer

CANDLER HOSPITAL, 5353 Reynolds Street, Savannah, GA, Zip 31405–6013, Mailing Address: P.O. Box 9787, Zip 31412–9787; tel. 912/692–6000; Paul P. Hinchey, President and Chief Executive Officer

CHEROKEE BAPTIST MEDICAL CENTER, 400 Northwood Drive, Centre, AL, Zip 35960–1023; tel. 256/927–5531; Barry S. Cochran, President

CRISP REGIONAL HOSPITAL, 902 North Seventh Street, Cordele, GA, Zip 31015–5007; tel. 912/276–3100; D. Wayne Martin, President and Chief Executive Officer

DECATUR HOSPITAL, 450 North Candler Street, Decatur, GA, Zip 30030–2671, Mailing Address: P.O. Box 40, Zip 30031–0040; tel. 404/377–0221; Richard T. Schmidt, Executive Director

DEKALB MEDICAL CENTER, 2701 North Decatur Road, Decatur, GA, Zip 30033–5995; tel. 404/501–1000; John R. Gerlach, Chief Executive Officer and Administrator

DODGE COUNTY HOSPITAL, 715 Griffin Street S.W., Eastman, GA, Zip 31023–2223, Mailing Address: P.O. Box 4309, Zip 31023–4309; tel. 912/374–4000; Meredith H. Smith, Administrator

DONALSONVILLE HOSPITAL, Hospital Circle, Donalsonville, GA, Zip 31745, Mailing Address: P.O. Box 677, Zip 31745–0677; tel. 912/524–5217; Charles H. Orrick, Administrator

DOOLY MEDICAL CENTER, 1300 Union Street, Vienna, GA, Zip 31092–7541, Mailing Address: P.O. Box 278, Zip 31092–0278; tel. 912/268–4141; Kent W. McMackin, Administrator

EARLY MEMORIAL HOSPITAL, 630 Columbia Street, Blakely, GA, Zip 31723–1798; tel. 912/723–4241; Rodney C. Watford, Administrator

EDGEFIELD COUNTY HOSPITAL, 300 Ridge Medical Plaza, Edgefield, SC, Zip 29824; tel. 803/637–3174; W. Joseph Seel, Administrator

EFFINGHAM HOSPITAL, 459 Highway 119 South, Springfield, GA, Zip 31329–3021, Mailing Address: P.O. Box 386, Zip 31329–0386; tel. 912/754–6451; Terrance R. Frech, Chief Executive Officer

EGLESTON CHILDREN'S HOSPITAL, 1405 Clifton Road N.E., Atlanta, GA, Zip 30322–1101; tel. 404/325–6000; James E. Tally, Ph.D., President and Chief Executive Officer

EMANUEL COUNTY HOSPITAL, 117 Kite Road, Swainsboro, GA, Zip 30401–3231, Mailing Address: P.O. Box 879, Zip 30401–0879; tel. 912/237–9911; Richard W. Clarke, Chief Executive Officer

FLOYD MEDICAL CENTER, 304 Turner McCall Boulevard, Rome, GA, Zip 30165–2734, Mailing Address: P.O. Box 233, Zip 30162–0233; tel. 706/802–2000; Kurt Stuenkel, FACHE, President and Chief Executive Officer

GORDON HOSPITAL, 1035 Red Bud Road, Calhoun, GA, Zip 30701–2082, Mailing Address: P.O. Box 12938, Zip 30703–7013; tel. 706/629–2895; Dennis Kiley, President

GRADY GENERAL HOSPITAL, 1155 Fifth Street S.E., Cairo, GA, Zip 31728–3142, Mailing Address: P.O. Box 360, Zip 31728–0360; tel. 912/377–1150; Glen C. Davis, Administrator

HAMILTON MEDICAL CENTER, 1200 Memorial Drive, Dalton, GA, Zip 30720–2529, Mailing Address: P.O. Box 1168, Zip 30722–1168; tel. 706/272–6000; Ned B. Wilford, President and Chief Executive Officer

HEALTHSOUTH CENTRAL GEORGIA REHABILITATION HOSPITAL, 3351 Northside Drive, Macon, GA, Zip 31210–2591; tel. 912/471–3536; Elbert T. McQueen, Chief Executive Officer

HIGGINS GENERAL HOSPITAL, 200 Allen Memorial Drive, Bremen, GA, Zip 30110–2012, Mailing Address: P.O. Box 655, Zip 30110–0655; tel. 770/537–5851; Robbie Smith, Administrator

HOUSTON MEDICAL CENTER, 1601 Watson Boulevard, Warner Robins, GA, Zip 31093–3431, Mailing Address: Box 2886, Zip 31099–2886; tel. 912/922–4281; Arthur P. Christie, Administrator

JEFFERSON HOSPITAL, 1067 Peachtree Street, Louisville, GA, Zip 30434–1599; tel. 912/625–7000; Rita Culvern, Administrator

JOHN D. ARCHBOLD MEMORIAL HOSPITAL, Gordon Avenue at Mimosa Drive, Thomasville, GA, Zip 31792–6113, Mailing Address: P.O. Box 1018, Zip 31799–1018; tel. 912/228–2000; Jason H. Moore, President and Chief Executive Officer

LIBERTY REGIONAL MEDICAL CENTER, 462 East G. Parkway, Hinesville, GA, Zip 31313, Mailing Address: P.O. Box 919, Zip 31313; tel. 912/369–9400; H. Scott Kroell, Jr., Chief Executive Officer

MCDUFFIE COUNTY HOSPITAL, 521 Hill Street S.W., Thomson, GA, Zip 30824–2199; tel. 706/595–1411; Douglas C. Keir, Chief Executive Officer

MEDICAL CENTER OF CENTRAL GEORGIA, 777 Hemlock Street, Macon, GA, Zip 31201–2155, Mailing Address: P.O. Box 6000, Zip 31208–6000; tel. 912/633–1000; A. Donald Faulk, FACHE, President

MINNIE G. BOSWELL MEMORIAL HOSPITAL, 1201 Siloam Highway, Greensboro, GA, Zip 30642–2811; tel. 706/453–7331; Earnest E. Benton, Chief Executive Officer

MITCHELL COUNTY HOSPITAL, 90 Stephens Street, Camilla, GA, Zip 31730–1899, Mailing Address: P.O. Box 639, Zip 31730–0639; tel. 912/336–5284; Ronald M. Gilliard, FACHE, Administrator

MONROE COUNTY HOSPITAL, 88 Martin Luther King Jr. Drive, Forsyth, GA, Zip 31029, Mailing Address: P.O. Box 1068, Zip 31029–1068; tel. 912/994–2521; Gale V. Tanner, Administrator

NORTHEAST GEORGIA MEDICAL CENTER, 743 Spring Street N.E., Gainesville, GA, Zip 30501–3899; tel. 770/535–3553; Henry Rigdon, Executive Vice President

NORTHSIDE HOSPITAL, 1000 Johnson Ferry Road N.E., Atlanta, GA, Zip 30342–1611; tel. 404/851–8000; Sidney Kirschner, President and Chief Executive Officer

OCONEE REGIONAL MEDICAL CENTER, 821 North Cobb Street, Milledgeville, GA, Zip 31061–2351, Mailing Address: P.O. Box 690, Zip 31061–0690; tel. 912/454–3500; Brian L. Riddle, President and Chief Executive Officer

PEACH REGIONAL MEDICAL CENTER, 601 North Camellia Boulevard, Fort Valley, GA, Zip 31030–4599; tel. 912/825–8691; Nancy Peed, Administrator

Section B

PERRY HOSPITAL, 1120 Morningside Drive, Perry, GA, Zip 31069–2906, Mailing Address: Drawer 1004, Zip 31069–1004; tel. 912/987–3600; Lora Davis, Administrator

PHENIX REGIONAL HOSPITAL, 1707 21st Avenue, Phenix City, AL, Zip 36867–3753, Mailing Address: P.O. Box 190, Zip 36868–0190; tel. 334/291–8502; Lance B. Duke, FACHE, President and Chief Executive Officer

PHOEBE PUTNEY MEMORIAL HOSPITAL, 417 Third Avenue, Albany, GA, Zip 31701–1828, Mailing Address: P.O. Box 1828, Zip 31703–1828; tel. 912/883–1800; Joel Wernick, President and Chief Executive Officer

PIEDMONT HOSPITAL, 1968 Peachtree Road N.W., Atlanta, GA, Zip 30309–1231; tel. 404/605–5000; Richard B. Hubbard, III, President and Chief Executive Officer

PUTNAM GENERAL HOSPITAL, Lake Oconee Parkway, Eatonton, GA, Zip 31024–4330, Mailing Address: Box 4330, Zip 31024–4330; tel. 706/485–2711; Darrell M. Oglesby, Administrator

SHEPHERD CENTER, 2020 Peachtree Road N.W., Atlanta, GA, Zip 30309–1465; tel. 404/352–2020; Gary R. Ulicny, Ph.D., President and Chief Executive Officer

SOUTH FULTON MEDICAL CENTER, 1170 Cleveland Avenue, East Point, GA, Zip 30344; tel. 404/305–3500; H. Neil Copelan, President and Chief Executive Officer

SOUTH GEORGIA MEDICAL CENTER, 2501 North Patterson Street, Valdosta, GA, Zip 31602–1735, Mailing Address: P.O. Box 1727, Zip 31603–1727; tel. 912/333–1000; John S. Bowling, President and Chief Executive Officer

SOUTHWEST GEORGIA REGIONAL MEDICAL CENTER, 109 Randolph Street, Cuthbert, GA, Zip 31740–1338; tel. 912/732–2181; Keith J. Petersen, Chief Executive Officer

TAYLOR REGIONAL HOSPITAL, Macon Highway, Hawkinsville, GA, Zip 31036, Mailing Address: P.O. Box 1297, Zip 31036–1297; tel. 912/783–0200; Dan S. Maddock, President

THE MEDICAL CENTER, 710 Center Street, Columbus, GA, Zip 31902, Mailing Address: P.O. Box 951, Zip 31902–0951; tel. 706/571–1000; Lance B. Duke, FACHE, President and Chief Executive Officer

UNIVERSITY HEALTH CARE SYSTEM, 1350 Walton Way, Augusta, GA, Zip 30901–2629; tel. 706/722–9011; J. Larry Read, President and Chief Executive Officer

UPSON REGIONAL MEDICAL CENTER, 801 West Gordon Street, Thomaston, GA, Zip 30286–2831, Mailing Address: P.O. Box 1059, Zip 30286–1059; tel. 706/647–8111; Samuel S. Gregory, Administrator

WELLSTAR COBB HOSPITAL, 3950 Austell Road, Austell, GA, Zip 30106–1121; tel. 770/732–4000; Thomas E. Hill, Chief Executive Officer

WELLSTAR DOUGLAS HOSPITAL, 8954 Hospital Drive, Douglasville, GA, Zip 30134–2282; tel. 770/949–1500; Thomas E. Hill, Chief Executive Officer

WELLSTAR KENNESTONE HOSPITAL, 677 Church Street, Marietta, GA, Zip 30060–1148; tel. 770/793–5000; Thomas E. Hill, Chief Executive Officer

WELLSTAR PAULDING HOSPITAL, 600 West Memorial Drive, Dallas, GA, Zip 30132–1335; tel. 770/445–4411; Thomas E. Hill, Chief Executive Officer

WELLSTAR WINDY HILL HOSPITAL, 2540 Windy Hill Road, Marietta, GA, Zip 30067–8632; tel. 770/644–1000; Thomas E. Hill, Chief Executive Officer

WILLINGWAY HOSPITAL, 311 Jones Mill Road, Statesboro, GA, Zip 30458–4765; tel. 912/764–6236; Jimmy Mooney, Chief Executive Officer

UNIVERSITY HEALTH, INC.
1350 Walton Way, Augusta, GA 30911; tel. 706/722–9011; Catherine P. Slade, Assistant Vice President

BARNWELL COUNTY HOSPITAL, 811 Reynolds Road, Barnwell, SC, Zip 29812; tel. 803/259–1000; J. L. Dozier, Jr., FACHE, Chief Executive Officer

BURKE COUNTY HOSPITAL, 351 Liberty Street, Waynesboro, GA, Zip 30830–9686; tel. 706/554–4435; Michael A. Haddle, Chief Executive Officer and Chief Financial Officer

EDGEFIELD COUNTY HOSPITAL, 300 Ridge Medical Plaza, Edgefield, SC, Zip 29824; tel. 803/637–3174; W. Joseph Seel, Administrator

EMANUEL COUNTY HOSPITAL, 117 Kite Road, Swainsboro, GA, Zip 30401–3231, Mailing Address: P.O. Box 879, Zip 30401–0879; tel. 912/237–9911; Richard W. Clarke, Chief Executive Officer

JEFFERSON HOSPITAL, 1067 Peachtree Street, Louisville, GA, Zip 30434–1599; tel. 912/625–7000; Rita Culvern, Administrator

MCDUFFIE COUNTY HOSPITAL, 521 Hill Street S.W., Thomson, GA, Zip 30824–2199; tel. 706/595–1411; Douglas C. Keir, Chief Executive Officer

MINNIE G. BOSWELL MEMORIAL HOSPITAL, 1201 Siloam Highway, Greensboro, GA, Zip 30642–2811; tel. 706/453–7331; Earnest E. Benton, Chief Executive Officer

UNIVERSITY HEALTH CARE SYSTEM, 1350 Walton Way, Augusta, GA, Zip 30901–2629; tel. 706/722–9011; J. Larry Read, President and Chief Executive Officer

WALTON REHABILITATION HOSPITAL, 1355 Independence Drive, Augusta, GA, Zip 30901–1037; tel. 706/724–7746; Dennis B. Skelley, President and Chief Executive Officer

WILLS MEMORIAL HOSPITAL, 120 Gordon Street, Washington, GA, Zip 30673–1602, Mailing Address: P.O. Box 370, Zip 30673–0370; tel. 706/678–2151; Tim E. Merritt, Chief Executive Officer

HAWAII

PACIFIC HEALTH CARE
1946 Young Street, Honolulu, HI 96826; tel. 808/547–9712; Gary Kajiwara, President/CEO

KUAKINI MEDICAL CENTER, 347 North Kuakini Street, Honolulu, HI, Zip 96817–2381; tel. 808/536–2236; Gary K. Kajiwara, President and Chief Executive Officer

ST. FRANCIS MEDICAL CENTER, 2230 Liliha Street, Honolulu, HI, Zip 96817–9979, Mailing Address: P.O. Box 30100, Zip 96820–0100; tel. 808/547–6484; Cynthia Okinaka, Administrator

QUEENS HEALTH SYSTEMS
1099 Alakea, Suite 1100, Honolulu, HI 96813; tel. 808/532–6100; Richard Griffith, President/CEO

MOLOKAI GENERAL HOSPITAL, Kaunakakai, HI, Mailing Address: P.O. Box 408, Zip 96748–0408; tel. 808/553–5331; Calvin M. Ichinose, Administrator

QUEEN'S MEDICAL CENTER, 1301 Punchbowl Street, Honolulu, HI, Zip 96813; tel. 808/538–9011; Arthur A. Ushijima, President and Chief Executive Officer

IDAHO

HEALTH NET
1020 N. Washington, Twin Falls, ID 83301; tel. 208/788–9862; Connie Perry, Coordinator

GOODING COUNTY MEMORIAL HOSPITAL, 1120 Montana Street, Gooding, ID, Zip 83330–1858; tel. 208/934–4433; Jim Henshaw, President and Chief Executive Officer

MAGIC VALLEY REGIONAL MEDICAL CENTER, 650 Addison Avenue West, Twin Falls, ID, Zip 83301–5444, Mailing Address: P.O. Box 409, Zip 83303–0409; tel. 208/737–2000; Gerald L. Hart, Chief Executive Officer

MINIDOKA MEMORIAL HOSPITAL AND EXTENDED CARE FACILITY, 1224 Eighth Street, Rupert, ID, Zip 83350–1599; tel. 208/436–0481; Carl Hanson, Administrator

ST. BENEDICTS FAMILY MEDICAL CENTER, 709 North Lincoln Avenue, Jerome, ID, Zip 83338–1851, Mailing Address: P.O. Box 586, Zip 83338–0586; tel. 208/324–4301; Lynne M. Mattison, FACHE, Interim Administrator

TWIN FALLS CLINIC HOSPITAL, 666 Shoshone Street East, Twin Falls, ID, Zip 83301–6168, Mailing Address: P.O. Box 1233, Zip 83301–1233; tel. 208/733–3700; Michael Arehart, Chief Executive Officer

WOOD RIVER MEDICAL CENTER, Sun Valley Road, Sun Valley, ID, Zip 83353, Mailing Address: P.O. Box 86, Zip 83353–0086; tel. 208/622–3333; Jon Moses, Administrator

NORTH IDAHO HEALTH NETWORK
700 Ironwood Drive, Suite 220, Coeur d'Alene, ID 83814; tel. 208/666–3212; Richard McMaster, Executive Director

BENEWAH COMMUNITY HOSPITAL, 229 South Seventh Street, Saint Maries, ID, Zip 83861–1894; tel. 208/245–5551; Camille Scott, Administrator

BONNER GENERAL HOSPITAL, 520 North Third Avenue, Sandpoint, ID, Zip 83864–0877, Mailing Address: Box 1448, Zip 83864–0877; tel. 208/263–1441; Gene Tomt, FACHE, Chief Executive Officer

BOUNDARY COMMUNITY HOSPITAL, 6640 Kaniksu Street, Bonners Ferry, ID, Zip 83805–7532, Mailing Address: HCR 61, Box 61A, Zip 83805–9500; tel. 208/267–3141; William T. McClintock, FACHE, Chief Executive Officer

KOOTENAI MEDICAL CENTER, 2003 Lincoln Way, Coeur D'Alene, ID, Zip 83814–2677; tel. 208/666–2000; Joseph E. Morris, III, Chief Executive Officer

SHOSHONE MEDICAL CENTER, 3 Jacobs Gulch, Kellogg, ID, Zip 83837–2096; tel. 208/784–1221

ILLINOIS

ADVOCATE HEALTH CARE
2025 Windsor Drive, Oak Brook, IL 60523; tel. 630/572–9393; Richard R. Risk, President & CEO

BETHANY HOSPITAL, 3435 West Van Buren Street, Chicago, IL, Zip 60624–3399; tel. 773/265–7700; Lena Dobbs–Johnson, Chief Executive

CHRIST HOSPITAL AND MEDICAL CENTER, 4440 West 95th Street, Oak Lawn, IL, Zip 60453–2699; tel. 708/425–8000; Carol Schneider, Chief Executive Officer

GOOD SAMARITAN HOSPITAL, 3815 Highland Avenue, Downers Grove, IL, Zip 60515–1590; tel. 630/275–5900; David M. McConkey, Chief Executive

GOOD SHEPHERD HOSPITAL, 450 West Highway 22, Barrington, IL, Zip 60010–1901; tel. 847/381–9600; Russell E. Feurer, Chief Executive

LUTHERAN GENERAL HOSPITAL, 1775 Dempster Street, Park Ridge, IL, Zip 60068–1174; tel. 847/723–2210; Kenneth J. Rojek, Chief Executive

RAVENSWOOD HOSPITAL MEDICAL CENTER, 4550 North Winchester Avenue, Chicago, IL, Zip 60640–5205; tel. 773/878–4300; John E. Blair, Chief Executive

SOUTH SUBURBAN HOSPITAL, 17800 South Kedzie Avenue, Hazel Crest, IL, Zip 60429–0989; tel. 708/799–8000; Robert Rutkowski, Chief Executive

TRINITY HOSPITAL, 2320 East 93rd Street, Chicago, IL, Zip 60617–9984; tel. 773/978–2000; John N. Schwartz, Chief Executive Officer

TRINITY MEDICAL CENTER–WEST CAMPUS, 2701 17th Street, Rock Island, IL, Zip 61201–5393; tel. 309/779–5000; Eric Crowell, President and Chief Executive Officer

ALEXIAN BROTHERS HEALTH SYSTEMS
600 Alexian Way, Elk Grove Village, IL 60007; tel. 708/437–5500; Br Felix Bettendorf, President

ALEXIAN BROTHERS MEDICAL CENTER, 800 Biesterfield Road, Elk Grove Village, IL, Zip 60007–3397; tel. 847/437–5500; Michael J. Schwartz, President and Chief Executive Officer

CATHOLIC HEALTH PARTNERS
2913 North Commonwealth Ave., Chicago, IL 60657; tel. 773/883–7300; Sister Theresa Peck, President & CEO

COLUMBUS HOSPITAL, 2520 North Lakeview Avenue, Chicago, IL, Zip 60614–1895; tel. 773/388–7300; Sister Theresa Peck, President and Chief Executive Officer

SAINT ANTHONY HOSPITAL, 2875 West 19th Street, Chicago, IL, Zip 60623–3596; tel. 773/521–1710; Sister Theresa Peck, President and Chief Executive Officer

ST. JOSEPH HOSPITAL, 2900 North Lake Shore Drive, Chicago, IL, Zip 60657–6274; tel. 773/665–3000; Sister Theresa Peck, President and Chief Executive Officer

COLUMBUS CABRINI MEDICAL SYSTEM
2520 North Lakeview Avenue, Chicago, IL 60614; tel. 312/883–7300; Lee Domanico, CEO

LOUIS A. WEISS MEMORIAL HOSPITAL, 4646 North Marine Drive, Chicago, IL, Zip 60640–1501; tel. 773/878–8700; Gregory A. Cierlik, President and Chief Executive Officer

UNIVERSITY OF CHICAGO HOSPITALS, 5841 South Maryland Avenue, Chicago, IL, Zip 60637–1470; tel. 773/702–1000; Steven Lipstein, President and Chief Operating Officer

FAMILY HEALTH NETWORK, INC.
910 W. Van Buren–6th, Chicago, IL 60607; tel. 312/491–1956; Phillip C. Bradley, President & CEO

MERCY HOSPITAL AND MEDICAL CENTER, 2525 South Michigan Avenue, Chicago, IL, Zip 60616–2477; tel. 312/567–2000; Charles B. Van Vorst, President and Chief Executive Officer

MOUNT SINAI HOSPITAL MEDICAL CENTER OF CHICAGO, California Avenue and 15th Street, Chicago, IL, Zip 60608–1610; tel. 773/542–2000; Benn Greenspan, President and Chief Executive Officer

NORWEGIAN–AMERICAN HOSPITAL, 1044 North Francisco Avenue, Chicago, IL, Zip 60622–2794; tel. 773/292–8200; Clarence A. Nagelvoort, President and Chief Executive Officer

SAINT MARY OF NAZARETH HOSPITAL CENTER, 2233 West Division Street, Chicago, IL, Zip 60622–3086; tel. 312/770–2000; Sister Stella Louise, President and Chief Executive Officer

ST. BERNARD HOSPITAL AND HEALTH CARE CENTER, 326 West 64th Street, Chicago, IL, Zip 60621; tel. 773/962–3900; Sister Elizabeth Van Straten, President and Chief Executive Officer

FREEPORT REGIONAL HEALTH ALLIANCE
1006 West Stephenson, Freeport, IL 61032; tel. 815/235–0272; Shelly Dunham, Director of Managed Care & Employer Services

FREEPORT MEMORIAL HOSPITAL, 1045 West Stephenson Street, Freeport, IL, Zip 61032–4899; tel. 815/235–4131; Dennis L. Hamilton, Chief Executive Officer

MERCER COUNTY HOSPITAL
409 North West Ninth Avenue, Aledo, IL 61231; tel. 309/582–5301; Bruce D. Peterson, Administrator

MERCER COUNTY HOSPITAL, 409 N.W. Ninth Avenue, Aledo, IL, Zip 61231–1296; tel. 309/582–5301; Bruce D. Peterson, Administrator

NORTHWESTERN HEALTH CARE NETWORK
980 North Michigan Ave#1500, Chicago, IL 60611; tel. 312/335–6000; Amy Kosifas, Assistant Vice President

CHILDREN'S MEMORIAL HOSPITAL, 2300 Children's Plaza, Chicago, IL, Zip 60614–3394; tel. 773/880–4000; Patrick M. Magoon, President and Chief Executive Officer

EVANSTON NORTHWESTERN HEALTHCARE, 2650 Ridge Avenue, Evanston, IL, Zip 60201–1797; tel. 847/570–2000; Mark R. Neaman, President and Chief Executive Officer

HIGHLAND PARK HOSPITAL, 718 Glenview Avenue, Highland Park, IL, Zip 60035–2497; tel. 847/432–8000; Ronald G. Spaeth, President and Chief Executive Officer

INGALLS HOSPITAL, One Ingalls Drive, Harvey, IL, Zip 60426–3591; tel. 708/333–2300; Robert L. Harris, President and Chief Executive Officer

NORTHWEST COMMUNITY HEALTHCARE, 800 West Central Road, Arlington Heights, IL, Zip 60005–2392; tel. 847/618–1000; Bruce K. Crowther, President and Chief Executive Officer

NORTHWESTERN MEMORIAL HOSPITAL, Superior Street and Fairbanks Court, Chicago, IL, Zip 60611; tel. 312/926–2000; Gary A. Mecklenburg, President and Chief Executive Officer

SILVER CROSS HOSPITAL, 1200 Maple Road, Joliet, IL, Zip 60432–1497; tel. 815/740–1100; Paul Pawlak, President and Chief Executive Officer

SWEDISH COVENANT HOSPITAL, 5145 North California Avenue, Chicago, IL, Zip 60625–3688; tel. 773/878–8200; Edward A. Cucci, President and Chief Executive Officer

RUSH SYSTEM FOR HEALTH
820 West Jackson, Chicago, IL 60607; tel. 312/942–7091; Lora Fallon, Project Manager

HOLY FAMILY MEDICAL CENTER, 100 North River Road, Des Plaines, IL, Zip 60016–1255; tel. 847/297–1800; Sister Patricia Ann Koschalke, President and Chief Executive Officer

OAK PARK HOSPITAL, 520 South Maple Avenue, Oak Park, IL, Zip 60304–1097; tel. 708/383–9300; Bruce M. Elegant, President and Chief Executive Officer

RIVERSIDE MEDICAL CENTER, 350 North Wall Street, Kankakee, IL, Zip 60901–0749; tel. 815/933–1671; Dennis C. Millirons, President and Chief Executive Officer

RUSH NORTH SHORE MEDICAL CENTER, 9600 Gross Point Road, Skokie, IL, Zip 60076–1257; tel. 847/677–9600; John S. Frigo, President

RUSH–COPLEY MEDICAL CENTER, 2000 Ogden Avenue, Aurora, IL, Zip 60504–4206; tel. 630/978–6200; Martin Losoff, President and Chief Operating Officer

RUSH–PRESBYTERIAN–ST. LUKE'S MEDICAL CENTER, 1653 West Congress Parkway, Chicago, IL, Zip 60612–3833; tel. 312/942–5000; Leo M. Henikoff, M.D. President and Chief Executive Officer

SERVANTCOR
335 East Fifth Avenue, Clifton, IL 60927; tel. 815/937–2034; Joseph F. Feth, President

PROVENA COVENANT MEDICAL CENTER, 1400 West Park Street, Urbana, IL, Zip 61801–2396; tel. 217/337–2000; Diane Friedman, R.N., President and Chief Executive Officer

PROVENA ST. MARY'S HOSPITAL, 500 West Court Street, Kankakee, IL, Zip 60901–3661; tel. 815/937–2400; Paula Jacobi, President and Chief Executive Officer

SOUTHERN ILLINI HEALTHCARE NETWORK
P.O. Box 1588, Mt Vernon, IL 62864; tel. 618/242–5404; Richard Huntington, Executive Director

SWEDISH AMERICAN HEALTH SYSTEM
1313 East State Street, Rockford, IL 61104; tel. 815/968–4400; Katherine Hermansen, Manager–Management Engineering

SWEDISHAMERICAN HEALTH SYSTEM, 1400 Charles Street, Rockford, IL, Zip 61104; tel. 815/968–4400; Robert B. Klint, M.D., President and Chief Executive Officer

SYNERGON HEALTH SYSTEM
520 South Maple Avenue, Oak Park, IL 60160; tel. 708/660–2060; Julie Stasiak, Director of Planning

OAK PARK HOSPITAL, 520 South Maple Avenue, Oak Park, IL, Zip 60304–1097; tel. 708/383–9300; Bruce M. Elegant, President and Chief Executive Officer

WESTLAKE COMMUNITY HOSPITAL, 1225 Lake Street, Melrose Park, IL, Zip 60160–4000; tel. 708/681–3000; Kenneth W. Wood, Chief Executive Officer

THE CARLE FOUNDATION
611 West Park Street, Urbana, IL 61801; tel. 217/383–3311; Karen Shelby, Network Contact

CARLE FOUNDATION HOSPITAL, 611 West Park Street, Urbana, IL, Zip 61801–2595; tel. 217/383–3311; Michael H. Fritz, President

THE PAVILION, 809 West Church Street, Champaign, IL, Zip 61820; tel. 217/373–1700; Nina W. Eisner, Chief Executive Officer

INDIANA

ANCILLA SYSTEMS INC.
1000 S. Lake Park Ave., Hobart, IN 46342; tel. 219/947–8500; Larry Jagrow, Sr. VP System Services Compliance Officer

ST. CATHERINE HOSPITAL, 4321 Fir Street, East Chicago, IN, Zip 46312–3097; tel. 219/392–7000; JoAnn Birdzell, President and Chief Executive Officer

ST. ELIZABETH'S HOSPITAL, 1431 North Claremont Avenue, Chicago, IL, Zip 60622–1791; tel. 312/633–5930; JoAnn Birdzell, President and Chief Executive Officer

ST. JOSEPH COMMUNITY HOSPITAL, 215 West Fourth Street, Mishawaka, IN, Zip 46544–1999; tel. 219/259–2431; Mary Roos, President and Chief Executive Officer

ST. MARY MEDICAL CENTER, 1500 South Lake Park Avenue, Hobart, IN, Zip 46342–6699; tel. 219/942–0551; Milton Triana, President and Chief Executive Officer

ST. MARY'S HOSPITAL, 129 North Eighth Street, East St. Louis, IL, Zip 62201–2999; tel. 618/482–7025; Richard J. Mark, President and Chief Executive Officer

MEMORIAL HEALTH SYSTEM INC
707 North Michigan Street, Suite 100, South Bend, IN 46601; tel. 219/284–3699; David Sage, COO

ELKHART GENERAL HOSPITAL, 600 East Boulevard, Elkhart, IN, Zip 46514–2499, Mailing Address: P.O. Box 1329, Zip 46515–1329; tel. 219/294–2621; Gregory W. Lintjer, President

LA PORTE REGIONAL HEALTH SYSTEM, 1007 Lincolnway, La Porte, IN, Zip 46352–0250, Mailing Address: P.O. Box 250, Zip 46352–0250; tel. 219/326–1234; Leigh E. Morris, President and Chief Executive Officer

LUTHERAN HOSPITAL OF INDIANA, 7950 West Jefferson Boulevard, Fort Wayne, IN, Zip 46804–1677; tel. 219/435–7001; Thomas D. Miller, President and Chief Executive Officer

METHODIST HOSPITAL OF INDIANA
P.O. Box 1367, Indianapolis, IN 46202; tel. 317/929–2000; William J. Loveday, President & CEO

REHABILITATION HOSPITAL OF INDIANA, 4141 Shore Drive, Indianapolis, IN, Zip 46254–2607; tel. 317/329–2000; Kim D. Eicher, President and Chief Executive Officer

MIDWEST HEALTH NET INC
6407 Constitution Drive, Fort Wayne, IN 46804; tel. 219/436–7879; Thomas C. Henry, President

BEDFORD REGIONAL MEDICAL CENTER, 2900 West 16th Street, Bedford, IN, Zip 47421–3583; tel. 812/275–1200; John R. Birdzell, FACHE, Chief Executive Officer

CAMERON MEMORIAL COMMUNITY HOSPITAL, 416 East Maumee Street, Angola, IN, Zip 46703–2015; tel. 219/665–2141; Dennis L. Knapp, President

CAYLOR–NICKEL MEDICAL CENTER, One Caylor–Nickel Square, Bluffton, IN, Zip 46714–2529; tel. 219/824–3500; William F. Brockmann, President and Chief Executive Officer

CLINTON COUNTY HOSPITAL, 1300 South Jackson Street, Frankfort, IN, Zip 46041–3394, Mailing Address: P.O. Box 669, Zip 46041–0669; tel. 765/659–4731; Brian R. Zeh, Chief Executive Officer

DECATUR COUNTY MEMORIAL HOSPITAL, 720 North Lincoln Street, Greensburg, IN, Zip 47240–1398; tel. 812/663–4331; Charles Duffy, President

DEKALB MEMORIAL HOSPITAL, 1316 East Seventh Street, Auburn, IN, Zip 46706–2515, Mailing Address: P.O. Box 542, Zip 46706–0542; tel. 219/925–4600; Jack M. Corey, President

DOCTORS HOSPITAL OF JACKSON, 110 North Elm Avenue, Jackson, MI, Zip 49202–3595; tel. 517/787–1440; Michael J. Falatko, President and Chief Executive Officer

DUKES MEMORIAL HOSPITAL, 275 West 12th Street, Peru, IN, Zip 46970–1698; tel. 765/473–6621; R. Joe Johnston, President and Chief Executive Officer

FISHER–TITUS MEDICAL CENTER, 272 Benedict Avenue, Norwalk, OH, Zip 44857–2374; tel. 419/668–8101; Patrick J. Martin, President and Chief Executive Officer

GREENE COUNTY GENERAL HOSPITAL, Rural Route 1, Box 1000, Linton, IN, Zip 47441–9457; tel. 812/847–2281; Jonas S. Uland, Executive Director

HANCOCK MEMORIAL HOSPITAL AND HEALTH SERVICES, 801 North State Street, Greenfield, IN, Zip 46140–1270, Mailing Address: P.O. Box 827, Zip 46140–0827; tel. 317/462–5544; Robert C. Keen, Ph.D., CHE, President and Chief Executive Officer

HENRY COUNTY HOSPITAL, 11–600 State Road 424, Napoleon, OH, Zip 43545–9399; tel. 419/592–4015; Kimberly Bordenkircher, Interim Chief Executive Officer

HENRY COUNTY MEMORIAL HOSPITAL, 1000 North 16th Street, New Castle, IN, Zip 47362–4319, Mailing Address: P.O. Box 490, Zip 47362–0490; tel. 765/521–0890; Jack Basler, President

HOWARD COMMUNITY HOSPITAL, 3500 South Lafountain Street, Kokomo, IN, Zip 46904–9011; tel. 765/453–0702; James Alender, Acting President and Chief Executive Officer

HUNTINGTON MEMORIAL HOSPITAL, 1215 Etna Avenue, Huntington, IN, Zip 46750–3696; tel. 219/356–3000; L. Kent McCoy, President

JOHNSON MEMORIAL HOSPITAL, 1125 West Jefferson Street, Franklin, IN, Zip 46131–2140, Mailing Address: P.O. Box 549, Zip 46131–0549; tel. 317/736–3300; Gregg A. Bechtold, President and Chief Executive Officer

KOSCIUSKO COMMUNITY HOSPITAL, 2101 East Dubois Drive, Warsaw, IN, Zip 46580–3288; tel. 219/267–3200; Wayne Hendrix, President

LIMA MEMORIAL HOSPITAL, 1001 Bellefontaine Avenue, Lima, OH, Zip 45804–2894; tel. 419/228–3335; John B. White, President and Chief Executive Officer

MCCRAY MEMORIAL HOSPITAL, 951 East Hospital Drive, Kendallville, IN, Zip 46755–2293, Mailing Address: P.O. Box 249, Zip 46755–0249; tel. 219/347–1100; John H. Matthews, Interim Chief Executive Officer

MEDICAL COLLEGE OF OHIO HOSPITALS, 3000 Arlington Avenue, Toledo, OH, Zip 43614–5805; tel. 419/383–4000; Frank S. McCullough, M.D., President

MERCY MEMORIAL HOSPITAL, 740 North Macomb Street, Monroe, MI, Zip 48161–9974, Mailing Address: P.O. Box 67, Zip 48161–0067; tel. 734/241–1700; Richard S. Hiltz, President and Chief Executive Officer

MORGAN COUNTY MEMORIAL HOSPITAL, 2209 John R. Wooden Drive, Martinsville, IN, Zip 46151–1840, Mailing Address: P.O. Box 1717, Zip 46151–1717; tel. 765/342–8441; S. Dean Melton, President and Chief Executive Officer

PARKVIEW HOSPITAL, 2200 Randallia Drive, Fort Wayne, IN, Zip 46805–4699; tel. 219/484–6636; Frank D. Byrne, M.D., President

PAULDING COUNTY HOSPITAL, 11558 State Road 111, Paulding, OH, Zip 45879–9220; tel. 419/399–4080; Gary W. Adkins, Interim Chief Executive Officer

RANDOLPH COUNTY HOSPITAL AND HEALTH SERVICES, 325 South Oak Street, Winchester, IN, Zip 47394–2235, Mailing Address: P.O. Box 407, Zip 47394–0407; tel. 765/584–9001; James M. Full, Chief Executive Officer

RIVERVIEW HOSPITAL, 395 Westfield Road, Noblesville, IN, Zip 46060–1425, Mailing Address: P.O. Box 220, Zip 46061–0220; tel. 317/773–0760; Seward Horner, President

ST. CATHERINE HOSPITAL, 4321 Fir Street, East Chicago, IN, Zip 46312–3097; tel. 219/392–7000; JoAnn Birdzell, President and Chief Executive Officer

ST. ELIZABETH'S HOSPITAL, 1431 North Claremont Avenue, Chicago, IL, Zip 60622–1791; tel. 773/278–2000; JoAnn Birdzell, President and Chief Executive Officer

ST. JOSEPH HOSPITAL, 700 Broadway, Fort Wayne, IN, Zip 46802–1493; tel. 219/425–3000; Michael H. Schatzlein, M.D., President and Chief Executive Officer

ST. MARY MEDICAL CENTER, 1500 South Lake Park Avenue, Hobart, IN, Zip 46342–6699; tel. 219/942–0551; Milton Triana, President and Chief Executive Officer

ST. MARY'S HOSPITAL, 129 North Eighth Street, East St. Louis, IL, Zip 62201–2999; tel. 618/274–1900; Richard J. Mark, President and Chief Executive Officer

THE TOLEDO HOSPITAL, 2142 North Cove Boulevard, Toledo, OH, Zip 43606–3896; tel. 419/471–4000; Barbara Steele, President

TIPTON COUNTY MEMORIAL HOSPITAL, 1000 South Main Street, Tipton, IN, Zip 46072–9799; tel. 765/675–8500; Alfonso W. Gatmaitan, Chief Executive Officer

VAN WERT COUNTY HOSPITAL, 1250 South Washington Street, Van Wert, OH, Zip 45891–2599; tel. 419/238–2390; Mark J. Minick, President and Chief Executive Officer

WABASH COUNTY HOSPITAL, 710 North East Street, Wabash, IN, Zip 46992–1924, Mailing Address: P.O. Box 548, Zip 46992–0548; tel. 219/563–3131; David C. Hunter, Chief Executive Officer

WELLS COMMUNITY HOSPITAL, 1100 South Main Street, Bluffton, IN, Zip 46714–3697; tel. 219/824–3210; Thomas A. Clark, Chief Executive Officer

WESTVIEW HOSPITAL, 3630 Guion Road, Indianapolis, IN, Zip 46222–1699; tel. 317/924–6661; David C. Dyar, President and Administrator

WHITE COUNTY MEMORIAL HOSPITAL, 1101 O'Connor Boulevard, Monticello, IN, Zip 47960–1698; tel. 219/583–7111; John M. Avers, Chief Executive Officer

WHITLEY MEMORIAL HOSPITAL, 353 North Oak Street, Columbia City, IN, Zip 46725–1623; tel. 219/244–6191; John M. Hatcher, President

WITHAM MEMORIAL HOSPITAL, 1124 North Lebanon Street, Lebanon, IN, Zip 46052–1776, Mailing Address: P.O. Box 1200, Zip 46052–3005; tel. 765/482–2700; Ray Ingham, President and Chief Executive Officer

PARKVIEW HEALTH SYSTEM
2200 Randallia drive, Fort Wayne, IN 46805; tel. 219/484–6636; Charles Mason, President & CEO

HUNTINGTON MEMORIAL HOSPITAL, 1215 Etna Avenue, Huntington, IN, Zip 46750–3696; tel. 219/356–3000; L. Kent McCoy, President

PARKVIEW HOSPITAL, 2200 Randallia Drive, Fort Wayne, IN, Zip 46805–4699; tel. 219/484–6636; Frank D. Byrne, M.D., President

WHITLEY MEMORIAL HOSPITAL, 353 North Oak Street, Columbia City, IN, Zip 46725–1623; tel. 219/244–6191; John M. Hatcher, President

SAGAMORE HEALTH NETWORK, INC
11555 North Meridian Suite 400, Carmel, IN 46032; tel. 317/573–2903; Greg Yust, President

ADAMS COUNTY MEMORIAL HOSPITAL, 805 High Street, Decatur, IN, Zip 46733–2311, Mailing Address: P.O. Box 151, Zip 46733–0151; tel. 219/724–2145; Marvin L. Baird, Executive Director

CAMERON MEMORIAL COMMUNITY HOSPITAL, 416 East Maumee Street, Angola, IN, Zip 46703–2015; tel. 219/665–2141; Dennis L. Knapp, President

CLAY COUNTY HOSPITAL, 1206 East National Avenue, Brazil, IN, Zip 47834–2797; tel. 812/448–2675; Jay P. Jolly, Administrator and Chief Executive Officer

CLINTON COUNTY HOSPITAL, 1300 South Jackson Street, Frankfort, IN, Zip 46041–3394, Mailing Address: P.O. Box 669, Zip 46041–0669; tel. 765/659–4731; Brian R. Zeh, Chief Executive Officer

COMMUNITY HOSPITAL OF BREMEN, 411 South Whitlock Street, Bremen, IN, Zip 46506–1699, Mailing Address: P.O. Box 8, Zip 46506–0008; tel. 219/546–2211; Scott R. Graybill, Chief Executive Officer and Administrator

COMMUNITY MEMORIAL HOSPITAL, 208 North Columbus Street, Hicksville, OH, Zip 43526–1299; tel. 419/542–6692; Deryl E. Gulliford, Ph.D., Administrator

DUKES MEMORIAL HOSPITAL, 275 West 12th Street, Peru, IN, Zip 46970–1698; tel. 765/473–6621; R. Joe Johnston, President and Chief Executive Officer

DUNN MEMORIAL HOSPITAL, 1600 23rd Street, Bedford, IN, Zip 47421–4704; tel. 812/275–3331; William W. Wissman, Interim Executive Director

FAIRBANKS HOSPITAL, 8102 Clearvista Parkway, Indianapolis, IN, Zip 46256–4698; tel. 317/849–8222; Timothy J. Kelly, M.D., President

FLOYD MEMORIAL HOSPITAL AND HEALTH SERVICES, 1850 State Street, New Albany, IN, Zip 47150–4997; tel. 812/949–5500; Bryant R. Hanson, President and Chief Executive Officer

GIBSON GENERAL HOSPITAL, 1808 Sherman Drive, Princeton, IN, Zip 47670–1043; tel. 812/385–3401; Michael J. Budnick, Administrator and Chief Executive Officer

GREENE COUNTY GENERAL HOSPITAL, Rural Route 1, Box 1000, Linton, IN, Zip 47441–9457; tel. 812/847–2281; Jonas S. Uland, Executive Director

HANCOCK MEMORIAL HOSPITAL AND HEALTH SERVICES, 801 North State Street, Greenfield, IN, Zip 46140–1270, Mailing Address: P.O. Box 827, Zip 46140–0827; tel. 317/462–5544; Robert C. Keen, Ph.D., CHE, President and Chief Executive Officer

HENDRICKS COMMUNITY HOSPITAL, 1000 East Main Street, Danville, IN, Zip 46122–0409, Mailing Address: P.O. Box 409, Zip 46122–0409; tel. 317/745–4451; Dennis W. Dawes, President

HENRY COUNTY MEMORIAL HOSPITAL, 1000 North 16th Street, New Castle, IN, Zip 47362–4319, Mailing Address: P.O. Box 490, Zip 47362–0490; tel. 765/521–0890; Jack Basler, President

HUNTINGTON MEMORIAL HOSPITAL, 1215 Etna Avenue, Huntington, IN, Zip 46750–3696; tel. 219/356–3000; L. Kent McCoy, President

JOHNSON MEMORIAL HOSPITAL, 1125 West Jefferson Street, Franklin, IN, Zip 46131–2140, Mailing Address: P.O. Box 549, Zip 46131–0549; tel. 317/736–3300; Gregg A. Bechtold, President and Chief Executive Officer

KENDRICK MEMORIAL HOSPITAL, 1201 Hadley Road N.W., Mooresville, IN, Zip 46158–1789; tel. 317/831–1160; Charles D. Swisher, President and Chief Executive Officer

KOSCIUSKO COMMUNITY HOSPITAL, 2101 East Dubois Drive, Warsaw, IN, Zip 46580–3288; tel. 219/267–3200; Wayne Hendrix, President

LA PORTE REGIONAL HEALTH SYSTEM, 1007 Lincolnway, La Porte, IN, Zip 46352–0250, Mailing Address: P.O. Box 250, Zip 46352–0250; tel. 219/326–1234; Leigh E. Morris, President and Chief Executive Officer

MCCRAY MEMORIAL HOSPITAL, 951 East Hospital Drive, Kendallville, IN, Zip 46755–2293, Mailing Address: P.O. Box 249, Zip 46755–0249; tel. 219/347–1100; John H. Matthews, Interim Chief Executive Officer

MEDICAL CENTER OF SOUTHERN INDIANA, 2200 Market Street, Charlestown, IN, Zip 47111–0069, Mailing Address: P.O. Box 69, Zip 47111–0069; tel. 812/256–3301; Kevin J. Miller, FACHE, Chief Executive Officer

MEMORIAL HOSPITAL, 1101 Michigan Avenue, Logansport, IN, Zip 46947–7013, Mailing Address: P.O. Box 7013, Zip 46947–7013; tel. 219/753–7541; Brian T. Shockney, President and Chief Executive Officer

MORGAN COUNTY MEMORIAL HOSPITAL, 2209 John R. Wooden Drive, Martinsville, IN, Zip 46151–1840, Mailing Address: P.O. Box 1717, Zip 46151–1717; tel. 765/342–8441; S. Dean Melton, President and Chief Executive Officer

OAKLAWN PSYCHIATRIC CENTER, INC., 330 Lakeview Drive, Goshen, IN, Zip 46528–9365, Mailing Address: P.O. Box 809, Zip 46527–0809; tel. 219/533–1234; Harold C. Loewen, President

ORANGE COUNTY HOSPITAL, 642 West Hospital Road, Paoli, IN, Zip 47454–0499, Mailing Address: P.O. Box 499, Zip 47454–0499; tel. 812/723–2811; Candace Isom, Interim Administrator

PARKVIEW HOSPITAL, 2200 Randallia Drive, Fort Wayne, IN, Zip 46805–4699; tel. 219/484–6636; Frank D. Byrne, M.D., President

PULASKI MEMORIAL HOSPITAL, 616 East 13th Street, Winamac, IN, Zip 46996–1117; tel. 219/946–6131; Richard H. Mynark, Administrator

PUTNAM COUNTY HOSPITAL, 1542 Bloomington Street, Greencastle, IN, Zip 46135–2297; tel. 765/653–5121; John D. Fajt, Executive Director

RANDOLPH COUNTY HOSPITAL AND HEALTH SERVICES, 325 South Oak Street, Winchester, IN, Zip 47394–2235, Mailing Address: P.O. Box 407, Zip 47394–0407; tel. 765/584–9001; James M. Full, Chief Executive Officer

REHABILITATION HOSPITAL OF INDIANA, 4141 Shore Drive, Indianapolis, IN, Zip 46254–2607; tel. 317/329–2000; Kim D. Eicher, President and Chief Executive Officer

RIVERVIEW HOSPITAL, 395 Westfield Road, Noblesville, IN, Zip 46060–1425, Mailing Address: P.O. Box 220, Zip 46061–0220; tel. 317/773–0760; Seward Horner, President

RUSH MEMORIAL HOSPITAL, 1300 North Main Street, Rushville, IN, Zip 46173–1198; tel. 765/932–4111; H. William Hartley, Chief Executive Officer

SAINT JOHN'S HEALTH SYSTEM, 2015 Jackson Street, Anderson, IN, Zip 46016–4339; tel. 765/649–2511; Jerry D. Brumitt, President and Chief Executive Officer

SAINT JOSEPH'S REGIONAL MEDICAL CENTER–PLYMOUTH CAMPUS, 1915 Lake Avenue, Plymouth, IN, Zip 46563–9905, Mailing Address: P.O. Box 670, Zip 46563–9905; tel. 219/936–3181; Brian E. Dietz, FACHE, Executive Vice President

SAINT JOSEPH'S REGIONAL MEDICAL CENTER–SOUTH BEND CAMPUS, 801 East LaSalle, South Bend, IN, Zip 46617–2800; tel. 219/237–7111; Robert L. Beyer, President and Chief Executive Officer

SAINT MARGARET MERCY HEALTHCARE CENTERS, 5454 Hohman Avenue, Hammond, IN, Zip 46320–1999; tel. 219/933–2074; Eugene C. Diamond, President and Chief Executive Officer

ST. ANTHONY MEDICAL CENTER, 1201 South Main Street, Crown Point, IN, Zip 46307–8483; tel. 219/738–2100; Stephen O. Leurck, President and Chief Executive Officer

ST. CATHERINE HOSPITAL, 4321 Fir Street, East Chicago, IN, Zip 46312–3097; tel. 219/392–7000; JoAnn Birdzell, President and Chief Executive Officer

ST. FRANCIS HOSPITAL AND HEALTH CENTERS, 1600 Albany Street, Beech Grove, IN, Zip 46107–1593; tel. 317/787–3311; Robert J. Brody, President and Chief Executive Officer

ST. JOSEPH HOSPITAL, 700 Broadway, Fort Wayne, IN, Zip 46802–1493; tel. 219/425–3000; Michael H. Schatzlein, M.D., President and Chief Executive Officer

ST. MARY MEDICAL CENTER, 1500 South Lake Park Avenue, Hobart, IN, Zip 46342–6699; tel. 219/942–0551; Milton Triana, President and Chief Executive Officer

ST. MARY'S HOSPITAL WARRICK, 1116 Millis Avenue, Boonville, IN, Zip 47601–0629, Mailing Address: Box 629, Zip 47601–0629; tel. 812/897–4800; Jim M. Hayes, Executive Vice President and Aministrator

ST. MARY'S MEDICAL CENTER OF EVANSVILLE, 3700 Washington Avenue, Evansville, IN, Zip 47750; tel. 812/485–4000; Jay D. Kasey, President

ST. VINCENT HOSPITALS AND HEALTH SERVICES, 2001 West 86th Street, Indianapolis, IN, Zip 46260–1991, Mailing Address: P.O. Box 40970, Zip 46240–0970; tel. 317/338–2345; Marsha N. Casey, President

ST. VINCENT MERCY HOSPITAL, 1331 South A Street, Elwood, IN, Zip 46036–1942; tel. 765/552–4600; David Masterson, Administrator

STARKE MEMORIAL HOSPITAL, 102 East Culver Road, Knox, IN, Zip 46534–2299; tel. 219/772–6231; Kathryn J. Norem, Executive Director

SULLIVAN COUNTY COMMUNITY HOSPITAL, 2200 North Section Street, Sullivan, IN, Zip 47882, Mailing Address: P.O. Box 10, Zip 47882–0010; tel. 812/268–4311; Thomas J. Hudgins, Administrator

TIPTON COUNTY MEMORIAL HOSPITAL, 1000 South Main Street, Tipton, IN, Zip 46072–9799; tel. 765/675–8500; Alfonso W. Gatmaitan, Chief Executive Officer

UNION HOSPITAL, 1606 North Seventh Street, Terre Haute, IN, Zip 47804–2780; tel. 812/238–7000; Frank Shelton, President

WABASH COUNTY HOSPITAL, 710 North East Street, Wabash, IN, Zip 46992–1924, Mailing Address: P.O. Box 548, Zip 46992–0548; tel. 219/563–3131; David C. Hunter, Chief Executive Officer

WELLS COMMUNITY HOSPITAL, 1100 South Main Street, Bluffton, IN, Zip 46714–3697; tel. 219/824–3210; Thomas A. Clark, Chief Executive Officer

WESTVIEW HOSPITAL, 3630 Guion Road, Indianapolis, IN, Zip 46222–1699; tel. 317/924–6661; David C. Dyar, President and Administrator

WHITE COUNTY MEMORIAL HOSPITAL, 1101 O'Connor Boulevard, Monticello, IN, Zip 47960–1698; tel. 219/583–7111; John M. Avers, Chief Executive Officer

WHITLEY MEMORIAL HOSPITAL, 353 North Oak Street, Columbia City, IN, Zip 46725–1623; tel. 219/244–6191; John M. Hatcher, President

WITHAM MEMORIAL HOSPITAL, 1124 North Lebanon Street, Lebanon, IN, Zip 46052–1776, Mailing Address: P.O. Box 1200, Zip 46052–3005; tel. 765/482–2700; Ray Ingham, President and Chief Executive Officer

ST VINCENT COMMUNITY HEALTH NETWORK
2001 W. 86th Street, Indianapolis, IN 40970; tel. 317/338–7000; Marsha Casey, President & CEO

JENNINGS COMMUNITY HOSPITAL, 301 Henry Street, North Vernon, IN, Zip 47265–1097; tel. 812/346–6200; Dalton L. Smart, Administrator

ST. JOSEPH HOSPITAL & HEALTH CENTER, 1907 West Sycamore Street, Kokomo, IN, Zip 46904–9010, Mailing Address: P.O. Box 9010, Zip 46904–9010; tel. 765/452–5611; Kathleen M. Korbelak, President and Chief Executive Officer

ST. VINCENT MERCY HOSPITAL, 1331 South A Street, Elwood, IN, Zip 46036–1942; tel. 765/552–4600; David Masterson, Administrator

ST. VINCENT WILLIAMSPORT HOSPITAL, 412 North Monroe Street, Williamsport, IN, Zip 47993–0215; tel. 765/762–4000; Jane Craigin, Chief Executive Officer

SUBURBAN HEALTH ORGANIZATION
2780 Waterfront Parkway, East Drive, Suite 300, Indianapolis, IN 46214; tel. 317/692–5222; Julie M. Carmichael, President

CLINTON COUNTY HOSPITAL, 1300 South Jackson Street, Frankfort, IN, Zip 46041–3394, Mailing Address: P.O. Box 669, Zip 46041–0669; tel. 765/659–4731; Brian R. Zeh, Chief Executive Officer

HANCOCK MEMORIAL HOSPITAL AND HEALTH SERVICES, 801 North State Street, Greenfield, IN, Zip 46140–1270, Mailing Address: P.O. Box 827, Zip 46140–0827; tel. 317/462–5544; Robert C. Keen, Ph.D., CHE, President and Chief Executive Officer

HENDRICKS COMMUNITY HOSPITAL, 1000 East Main Street, Danville, IN, Zip 46122–0409, Mailing Address: P.O. Box 409, Zip 46122–0409; tel. 317/745–4451; Dennis W. Dawes, President

HENRY COUNTY MEMORIAL HOSPITAL, 1000 North 16th Street, New Castle, IN, Zip 47362–4319, Mailing Address: P.O. Box 490, Zip 47362–0490; tel. 765/521–0890; Jack Basler, President

JOHNSON MEMORIAL HOSPITAL, 1125 West Jefferson Street, Franklin, IN, Zip 46131–2140, Mailing Address: P.O. Box 549, Zip 46131–0549; tel. 317/736–3300; Gregg A. Bechtold, President and Chief Executive Officer

MORGAN COUNTY MEMORIAL HOSPITAL, 2209 John R. Wooden Drive, Martinsville, IN, Zip 46151–1840, Mailing Address: P.O. Box 1717, Zip 46151–1717; tel. 765/342–8441; S. Dean Melton, President and Chief Executive Officer

RIVERVIEW HOSPITAL, 395 Westfield Road, Noblesville, IN, Zip 46060–1425, Mailing Address: P.O. Box 220, Zip 46061–0220; tel. 317/773–0760; Seward Horner, President

TIPTON COUNTY MEMORIAL HOSPITAL, 1000 South Main Street, Tipton, IN, Zip 46072–9799; tel. 765/675–8500; Alfonso W. Gatmaitan, Chief Executive Officer

WESTVIEW HOSPITAL, 3630 Guion Road, Indianapolis, IN, Zip 46222–1699; tel. 317/924–6661; David C. Dyar, President and Administrator

WITHAM MEMORIAL HOSPITAL, 1124 North Lebanon Street, Lebanon, IN, Zip 46052–1776, Mailing Address: P.O. Box 1200, Zip 46052–3005; tel. 765/482–2700; Ray Ingham, President and Chief Executive Officer

IOWA

COVENANT HEALTH SYSTEM
3421 West Ninth Street, Waterloo, IA 50702; tel. 319/272–7302; Raymond Burfeind, President/CEO

GENESIS HEALTH SYSTEM
1227 East Rusholme Street, Davenport, IA 52803; tel. 319/421–6000; Leo Bressanelli, President/CEO

DEWITT COMMUNITY HOSPITAL, 1118 11th Street, De Witt, IA, Zip 52742–1296; tel. 319/659–4200; Robert G. Senneff, Chief Executive Officer

Section B

GENESIS MEDICAL CENTER, 1227 East Rusholme Street, Davenport, IA, Zip 52803–2498; tel. 319/421–1000; Leo A. Bressanelli, President and Chief Executive Officer

ILLINI HOSPITAL, 801 Hospital Road, Silvis, IL, Zip 61282–1893; tel. 309/792–9363; Gary E. Larson, Chief Executive Officer

HEALTH NETWORK OF IOWA
1200 Pleasant Street, Des Moines, IA 50304; tel. 515/241–6201; Jim Zahnd, Senior Vice President

MERCY NETWORK
400 University, Des Moines, IA 50309; tel. 515/247–4277; Sara Drobnick, Vice President

ADAIR COUNTY MEMORIAL HOSPITAL, 609 S.E. Kent Street, Greenfield, IA, Zip 50849–9454; tel. 515/743–2123; Myrna Erb–Gundel, Administrator

AUDUBON COUNTY MEMORIAL HOSPITAL, 515 Pacific Street, Audubon, IA, Zip 50025–1099; tel. 712/563–2611; David G. Couser, FAAMA, FACHE, Administrator

DAVIS COUNTY HOSPITAL, 507 North Madison Street, Bloomfield, IA, Zip 52537–1299; tel. 515/664–2145; Randy Simmons, Administrator

HAMILTON COUNTY PUBLIC HOSPITAL, 800 Ohio Street, Webster City, IA, Zip 50595–2824, Mailing Address: P.O. Box 430, Zip 50595–0430; tel. 515/832–9400; Roger W. Lenz, Administrator

MANNING REGIONAL HEALTHCARE CENTER, 410 Main Street, Manning, IA, Zip 51455–1093; tel. 712/653–2072; Michael S. Ketcham, Administrator

MERCY HOSPITAL MEDICAL CENTER, 400 University Avenue, Des Moines, IA, Zip 50314–3190; tel. 515/247–3121; David H. Vellinga, President and Chief Executive Officer

MONROE COUNTY HOSPITAL, RR 3, Box 314–11, Albia, IA, Zip 52531; tel. 515/932–2134; Gregory A. Paris, Administrator

RINGGOLD COUNTY HOSPITAL, 211 Shellway Drive, Mount Ayr, IA, Zip 50854–1299; tel. 515/464–3226; Gordon W. Winkler, Administrator

ST. ANTHONY REGIONAL HOSPITAL, 311 South Clark Street, Carroll, IA, Zip 51401, Mailing Address: P.O. Box 628, Zip 51401–0628; tel. 712/792–8231; Gary P. Riedmann, President and Chief Executive Officer

ST. JOSEPH'S MERCY HOSPITAL, 1 St. Joseph's Drive, Centerville, IA, Zip 52544; tel. 515/437–4111; William C. Assell, President and Chief Executive Officer

STORY COUNTY HOSPITAL AND LONG TERM CARE FACILITY, 630 Sixth Street, Nevada, IA, Zip 50201–2266; tel. 515/382–2111; Todd Willert, Administrator

WAYNE COUNTY HOSPITAL, 417 South East Street, Corydon, IA, Zip 50060–1860, Mailing Address: P.O. Box 305, Zip 50060–0305; tel. 515/872–2260; Bill D. Wilson, Administrator

NORTH IOWA MERCY HEALTH CENTER
1000 4th Street, Southwest, Mason City, IA 50401; tel. 515/424–7481; James Sexton, President

BELMOND COMMUNITY HOSPITAL, 403 First Street S.E., Belmond, IA, Zip 50421–1201, Mailing Address: P.O. Box 326, Zip 50421–0326; tel. 515/444–3223; Kim Price, Administrator

ELDORA REGIONAL MEDICAL CENTER, 2413 Edgington Avenue, Eldora, IA, Zip 50627–1541; tel. 515/939–5416; Richard C. Hamilton, Administrator

FRANKLIN GENERAL HOSPITAL, 1720 Central Avenue East, Hampton, IA, Zip 50441–1859; tel. 515/456–5000; Scott Wells, Chief Executive Officer

HANCOCK COUNTY MEMORIAL HOSPITAL, 532 First Street N.W., Britt, IA, Zip 50423–0068, Mailing Address: P.O. Box 68, Zip 50423–0068; tel. 515/843–3801; Harriet Thompson, Administrator

KOSSUTH REGIONAL HEALTH CENTER, 1515 South Phillips Street, Algona, IA, Zip 50511–3649; tel. 515/295–2451; James G. Fitzpatrick, Administrator and Chief Executive Officer

MITCHELL COUNTY REGIONAL HEALTH CENTER, 616 North Eighth Street, Osage, IA, Zip 50461–1498; tel. 515/732–6005; Kimberly J. Miller, CHE, Administrator

NORTH IOWA MERCY HEALTH CENTER, 1000 Fourth Street S.W., Mason City, IA, Zip 50401–2800; tel. 515/422–7000; James J. Sexton, President and Chief Executive Officer

REGIONAL HEALTH SERVICES OF HOWARD COUNTY, 235 Eighth Avenue West, Cresco, IA, Zip 52136–1098; tel. 319/547–2101; Elizabeth A. Doty, President and Chief Executive Officer

ST LUKES/IOWA HEALTH SYSTEM
P.O. Box 3026, Cedar Rapids, IA 52406–3026; tel. 319/369–7240; Barry C. Spear, VP Sys Development

IOWA METHODIST MEDICAL CENTER, 1200 Pleasant Street, Des Moines, IA, Zip 50309–9976; tel. 515/241–6212; James H. Skogsbergh, President

MARENGO MEMORIAL HOSPITAL, 300 West May Street, Marengo, IA, Zip 52301–1261, Mailing Address: P.O. Box 228, Zip 52301–0228; tel. 319/642–5543; Genny Maroc, Interim Administrator

VIRGINIA GAY HOSPITAL, 502 North Ninth Avenue, Vinton, IA, Zip 52349–2299; tel. 319/472–6200; Michael J. Riege, Chief Executive Officer

KANSAS

COMMUNITY HEALTH ALLIANCE
8300 Troost Ave., Winchester, KS 64131; tel. 816/276–7580; Steven Ashcroft, Administrator

GEARY COMMUNITY HOSPITAL, Ash and St. Mary's Road, Junction City, KS, Zip 66441, Mailing Address: P.O. Box 490, Zip 66441–0490; tel. 785/238–4131; David K. Bradley, Chief Executive Officer

HOLTON COMMUNITY HOSPITAL, 510 Kansas Avenue, Holton, KS, Zip 66436–1545; tel. 785/364–2116; Leonard Hernandez, Administrator and Chief Executive Officer

HORTON HEALTH FOUNDATION, 240 West 18th Street, Horton, KS, Zip 66439–1245; tel. 785/486–2642; Dale A. White, Chief Executive Officer

JEFFERSON COUNTY MEMORIAL HOSPITAL, 408 Delaware Street, Winchester, KS, Zip 66097–4002, Mailing Address: Rural Route 1, Box 1, Zip 66097–0001; tel. 913/774–4340; Dwaine Klingman, Administrator

MORRIS COUNTY HOSPITAL, 600 North Washington Street, Council Grove, KS, Zip 66846–1499, Mailing Address: P.O. Box 275, Zip 66846–0275; tel. 316/767–6811; Jim Reagan, M.D., Chief Executive Officer

NEMAHA VALLEY COMMUNITY HOSPITAL, 1600 Community Drive, Seneca, KS, Zip 66538–9758; tel. 785/336–6181; Michael J. Ryan, Administrator

GREAT PLAINS HEALTH ALLIANCE
P.O. Box 366, Phillipsburg, KS 67661; tel. 785/543–2111; Roger John, President

ASHLAND HEALTH CENTER, 709 Oak Street, Ashland, KS, Zip 67831, Mailing Address: P.O. Box 188, Zip 67831; tel. 316/635–2241; Bryan Stacey, Administrator

CHEYENNE COUNTY HOSPITAL, 210 West First Street, Saint Francis, KS, Zip 67756, Mailing Address: P.O. Box 547, Zip 67756–0547; tel. 785/332–2104; Leslie Lacy, Administrator

COMMUNITY MEDICAL CENTER, 2307 Barada Street, Falls City, NE, Zip 68355–1599; tel. 402/245–2428; Victor Lee, Chief Executive Officer and Administrator

ELLINWOOD DISTRICT HOSPITAL, 605 North Main Street, Ellinwood, KS, Zip 67526–1440; tel. 316/564–2548; Marge Conell, R.N., Administrator

FREDONIA REGIONAL HOSPITAL, 1527 Madison Street, Fredonia, KS, Zip 66736–1751, Mailing Address: P.O. Box 579, Zip 66736–0579; tel. 316/378–2121; Terry Deschaine, Chief Executive Officer

GREELEY COUNTY HOSPITAL, 506 Third Street, Tribune, KS, Zip 67879, Mailing Address: P.O. Box 338, Zip 67879–0338; tel. 316/376–4221; Jerrell J. Horton, Chief Executive Officer

GRISELL MEMORIAL HOSPITAL DISTRICT ONE, 210 South Vermont, Ransom, KS, Zip 67572–0268, Mailing Address: P.O. Box 268, Zip 67572–0268; tel. 785/731–2231; Kristine Ochs, R.N., Administrator

HARLAN COUNTY HEALTH SYSTEM, 717 North Brown Street, Alma, NE, Zip 68920–0836, Mailing Address: P.O. Box 836, Zip 68920–0836; tel. 308/928–2151; Allen Van Driel, Administrator

HILLSBORO COMMUNITY MEDICAL CENTER, 701 South Main Street, Hillsboro, KS, Zip 67063–9981; tel. 316/947–3114; Tom Faulkner, Chief Executive Officer

KIOWA COUNTY MEMORIAL HOSPITAL, 501 South Walnut Street, Greensburg, KS, Zip 67054–1951; tel. 316/723–3341; CeCe Noll, Administrator

LANE COUNTY HOSPITAL, 243 South Second, Dighton, KS, Zip 67839, Mailing Address: P.O. Box 969, Zip 67839–0969; tel. 316/397–5321; Donna McGowan, R.N., Administrator

LINCOLN COUNTY HOSPITAL, 624 North Second Street, Lincoln, KS, Zip 67455–1738, Mailing Address: P.O. Box 406, Zip 67455–0406; tel. 913/524–4403; Jolene Yager, R.N., Administrator

MEDICINE LODGE MEMORIAL HOSPITAL, 710 North Walnut Street, Medicine Lodge, KS, Zip 67104–1019, Mailing Address: P.O. Drawer C, Zip 67104; tel. 316/886–3771; Kevin A. White, Administrator

MINNEOLA DISTRICT HOSPITAL, 212 Main Street, Minneola, KS, Zip 67865–8511; tel. 316/885–4264; Blaine K. Miller, Administrator

MITCHELL COUNTY HOSPITAL, 400 West Eighth, Beloit, KS, Zip 67420–1605, Mailing Address: P.O. Box 399, Zip 67420–0399; tel. 785/738–2266; John M. Osse, Administrator

OSBORNE COUNTY MEMORIAL HOSPITAL, 424 West New Hampshire Street, Osborne, KS, Zip 67473–0070, Mailing Address: P.O. Box 70, Zip 67473–0070; tel. 785/346–2121; Patricia Bernard, R.N., Administrator

OTTAWA COUNTY HEALTH CENTER, 215 East Eighth, Minneapolis, KS, Zip 67467–1999, Mailing Address: P.O. Box 209, Zip 67467–0209; tel. 785/392–2122; Joy Reed, R.N., Administrator

PHILLIPS COUNTY HOSPITAL, 1150 State Street, Phillipsburg, KS, Zip 67661–1799, Mailing Address: P.O. Box 607, Zip 67661–0607; tel. 785/543–5226; James Wahlmeier, Administrator

RAWLINS COUNTY HEALTH CENTER, 707 Grant Street, Atwood, KS, Zip 67730–4700, Mailing Address: Box 47, Zip 67730–4700; tel. 785/626–3211; Donald J. Kessen, Administrator and Chief Executive Officer

REPUBLIC COUNTY HOSPITAL, 2420 G Street, Belleville, KS, Zip 66935–2499; tel. 785/527–2255; Charles A. Westin, FACHE, Administrator

SABETHA COMMUNITY HOSPITAL, 14th and Oregon Streets, Sabetha, KS, Zip 66534, Mailing Address: P.O. Box 229, Zip 66534; tel. 785/284–2121; Rita K. Buurman, Chief Executive Officer

SATANTA DISTRICT HOSPITAL, 401 South Cheyenne Street, Satanta, KS, Zip 67870, Mailing Address: P.O. Box 159, Zip 67870–0159; tel. 316/649–2761; T. G. Lee, Administrator

SMITH COUNTY MEMORIAL HOSPITAL, 614 South Main Street, Smith Center, KS, Zip 66967–0349, Mailing Address: P.O. Box 349, Zip 66967–0349; tel. 785/282–6845; John Terrill, Administrator

TREGO COUNTY–LEMKE MEMORIAL HOSPITAL, 320 North 13th Street, Wakeeney, KS, Zip 67672–2099; tel. 785/743–2182; Lisa J. Freeborn, R.N., Administrator

HAYS MEDICAL CENTER
201 East 7th Street, Hays, KS 67601; tel. 785/623–5116; Chris Lindberg, Director of Rural Development

CHEYENNE COUNTY HOSPITAL, 210 West First Street, Saint Francis, KS, Zip 67756, Mailing Address: P.O. Box 547, Zip 67756–0547; tel. 785/332–2104; Leslie Lacy, Administrator

DWIGHT D. EISENHOWER VETERANS AFFAIRS MEDICAL CENTER, 4101 South Fourth Street Trafficway, Leavenworth, KS, Zip 66048–5055; tel. 913/682–2000

GRISELL MEMORIAL HOSPITAL DISTRICT ONE, 210 South Vermont, Ransom, KS, Zip 67572–0268, Mailing Address: P.O. Box 268, Zip 67572–0268; tel. 785/731–2231; Kristine Ochs, R.N., Administrator

PHILLIPS COUNTY HOSPITAL, 1150 State Street, Phillipsburg, KS, Zip 67661–1799, Mailing Address: P.O. Box 607, Zip 67661–0607; tel. 785/543–5226; James Wahlmeier, Administrator

PLAINVILLE RURAL HOSPITAL DISTRICT NUMBER ONE, 304 South Colorado Avenue, Plainville, KS, Zip 67663–2505; tel. 785/434–4553; Richard Q. Bergling, Administrator and Chief Executive Officer

RAWLINS COUNTY HEALTH CENTER, 707 Grant Street, Atwood, KS, Zip 67730–4700, Mailing Address: Box 47, Zip 67730–4700; tel. 785/626–3211; Donald J. Kessen, Administrator and Chief Executive Officer

SATANTA DISTRICT HOSPITAL, 401 South Cheyenne Street, Satanta, KS, Zip 67870, Mailing Address: P.O. Box 159, Zip 67870–0159; tel. 316/649–2761; T. G. Lee, Administrator

TREGO COUNTY–LEMKE MEMORIAL HOSPITAL, 320 North 13th Street, Wakeeney, KS, Zip 67672–2099; tel. 785/743–2182; Lisa J. Freeborn, R.N., Administrator

MED–OP
202 Center Avenue, Oakley, KS 06774–8171; tel. 913/672–3540; Andrew Draper, Executive Director

CITIZENS MEDICAL CENTER, 100 East College Drive, Colby, KS, Zip 67701–3799; tel. 785/462–7511; Richard B. Gamel, Chief Executive Officer

DECATUR COUNTY HOSPITAL, 810 West Columbia Street, Oberlin, KS, Zip 67749–2450, Mailing Address: P.O. Box 268, Zip 67749–0268; tel. 785/475–2208; Lynn Doeden, R.N., Interim Administrator

GOODLAND REGIONAL MEDICAL CENTER, 220 West Second Street, Goodland, KS, Zip 67735–1602; tel. 785/899–3625; Jim Chaddic, Chief Executive Officer

GRAHAM COUNTY HOSPITAL, 304 West Prout Street, Hill City, KS, Zip 67642–1435, Mailing Address: P.O. Box 339, Zip 67642–0339; tel. 785/421–2121; Fred J. Meis, Administrator and Chief Executive Officer

HAYS MEDICAL CENTER, 2220 Canterbury Drive, Hays, KS, Zip 67601–2342, Mailing Address: P.O. Box 8100, Zip 67601–8100; tel. 785/623–5000; John H. Jeter, M.D., President and Chief Executive Officer

LOGAN COUNTY HOSPITAL, 211 Cherry Street, Oakley, KS, Zip 67748–1201; tel. 913/672–3211; Rodney Bates, Administrator

NESS COUNTY HOSPITAL NUMBER TWO, 312 East Custer Street, Ness City, KS, Zip 67560–1654; tel. 785/798–2291; Clyde T. McCracken, Administrator

NORTON COUNTY HOSPITAL, 102 East Holme, Norton, KS, Zip 67654–0250, Mailing Address: P.O. Box 250, Zip 67654–0250; tel. 785/877–3351; Richard Miller, Administrator and Chief Executive Officer

PLAINVILLE RURAL HOSPITAL DISTRICT NUMBER ONE, 304 South Colorado Avenue, Plainville, KS, Zip 67663–2505; tel. 785/434–4553; Richard Q. Bergling, Administrator and Chief Executive Officer

SHERIDAN COUNTY HOSPITAL, 826 18th Street, Hoxie, KS, Zip 67740–0167, Mailing Address: P.O. Box 167, Zip 67740–0167; tel. 785/675–3281; Brian Kirk, Chief Executive Officer

SATANTA DISTRICT HOSPITAL
P.O. Box 159, Santana, KS 67870; tel. 316/649–2761; Tom Lee, Administrator

SATANTA DISTRICT HOSPITAL, 401 South Cheyenne Street, Satanta, KS, Zip 67870, Mailing Address: P.O. Box 159, Zip 67870–0159; tel. 316/649–2761; T. G. Lee, Administrator

SOUTHEAST KANSAS NETWORK
1400 W. 4th Street, Coffeyville, KS 67337; tel. 316/251–1200; Jerry Marquette, President

ALLEN COUNTY HOSPITAL, 101 South First Street, Iola, KS, Zip 66749–3505, Mailing Address: P.O. Box 540, Zip 66749–0540; tel. 316/365–1000; Bill May, Chief Executive Officer

COFFEYVILLE REGIONAL MEDICAL CENTER, 1400 West Fourth, Coffeyville, KS, Zip 67337–3306; tel. 316/251–1200; Gerald Joseph Marquette, Jr., Chief Executive Officer

FREDONIA REGIONAL HOSPITAL, 1527 Madison Street, Fredonia, KS, Zip 66736–1751, Mailing Address: P.O. Box 579, Zip 66736–0579; tel. 316/378–2121; Terry Deschaine, Chief Executive Officer

LABETTE COUNTY MEDICAL CENTER, 1902 South U.S. Highway 59, Parsons, KS, Zip 67357–7404, Mailing Address: P.O. Box 956, Zip 67357–0956; tel. 316/421–4880; Robert E. Mac Devitt, Chief Executive Officer

MAUDE NORTON MEMORIAL CITY HOSPITAL, 220 North Pennsylvania Street, Columbus, KS, Zip 66725–1197; tel. 316/429–2545; Cindy Neely, Administrator

MERCY HOSPITAL, 821 Burke Street, Fort Scott, KS, Zip 66701–2497; tel. 316/223–2200; Jerry L. Stevenson, President and Chief Executive Officer

MOUNT CARMEL MEDICAL CENTER, 1102 East Centennial, Pittsburg, KS, Zip 66762–6686; tel. 316/231–6100; John Daniel Lingor, President and Chief Executive Officer

NEOSHO MEMORIAL REGIONAL MEDICAL CENTER, 629 South Plummer, Chanute, KS, Zip 66720–1928; tel. 316/431–4000; Murray L. Brown, Administrator

WILSON COUNTY HOSPITAL, 205 Mill Street, Neodesha, KS, Zip 66757–1817, Mailing Address: P.O. Box 360, Zip 66757–0360; tel. 316/325–2611; Deanna Pittman, Administrator

SUNFLOWER HEALTH NETWORK
400 South Santa Fe, Salina, KS 67401; tel. 913/826–3602; Charlie Greenwood, Network Coordinator

CLAY COUNTY HOSPITAL, 617 Liberty Street, Clay Center, KS, Zip 67432–1599; tel. 785/632–2144; John F. Wiebe, Chief Executive Officer

CLOUD COUNTY HEALTH CENTER, 1100 Highland Drive, Concordia, KS, Zip 66901–3997; tel. 785/243–1234; Daniel R. Bartz, Chief Executive Officer

ELLSWORTH COUNTY MEDICAL CENTER, 1604 Aylward, Ellsworth, KS, Zip 67439–0087, Mailing Address: P.O. Drawer 87, Zip 67439–0087; tel. 785/472–3111; Roger W. Pearson, Administrator

HERINGTON MUNICIPAL HOSPITAL, 100 East Helen Street, Herington, KS, Zip 67449–1697; tel. 785/258–2207; William D. Peterson, Administrator

JEWELL COUNTY HOSPITAL, 100 Crestvue Avenue, Mankato, KS, Zip 66956–2407, Mailing Address: P.O. Box 327, Zip 66956–0327; tel. 785/378–3137; Aloha Kier, Administrator

LINCOLN COUNTY HOSPITAL, 624 North Second Street, Lincoln, KS, Zip 67455–1738, Mailing Address: P.O. Box 406, Zip 67455–0406; tel. 913/524–4403; Jolene Yager, R.N., Administrator

LINDSBORG COMMUNITY HOSPITAL, 605 West Lincoln Street, Lindsborg, KS, Zip 67456–2399; tel. 785/227–3308; Greg Lundstrom, Administrator and Chief Executive Officer

MEMORIAL HOSPITAL, 511 N.E. Tenth Street, Abilene, KS, Zip 67410–2100, Mailing Address: P.O. Box 69, Zip 67410–0069; tel. 785/263–2100; Leon J. Boor, Chief Executive Officer and Administrator

MEMORIAL HOSPITAL, 1000 Hospital Drive, McPherson, KS, Zip 67460–2321; tel. 316/241–2250; Stan Regehr, President and Chief Executive Officer

MITCHELL COUNTY HOSPITAL, 400 West Eighth, Beloit, KS, Zip 67420–1605, Mailing Address: P.O. Box 399, Zip 67420–0399; tel. 785/738–2266; John M. Osse, Administrator

OSBORNE COUNTY MEMORIAL HOSPITAL, 424 West New Hampshire Street, Osborne, KS, Zip 67473–0070, Mailing Address: P.O. Box 70, Zip 67473–0070; tel. 785/346–2121; Patricia Bernard, R.N., Administrator

OTTAWA COUNTY HEALTH CENTER, 215 East Eighth, Minneapolis, KS, Zip 67467–1999, Mailing Address: P.O. Box 209, Zip 67467–0209; tel. 785/392–2122; Joy Reed, R.N., Administrator

REPUBLIC COUNTY HOSPITAL, 2420 G Street, Belleville, KS, Zip 66935–2499; tel. 785/527–2255; Charles A. Westin, FACHE, Administrator

RUSSELL REGIONAL HOSPITAL, 200 South Main Street, Russell, KS, Zip 67665–2997; tel. 785/483–3131; Bruce Garrett, Administrator and Chief Executive Officer

SALINA REGIONAL HEALTH CENTER, 400 South Santa Fe Avenue, Salina, KS, Zip 67401–4198, Mailing Address: P.O. Box 5080, Zip 67401–5080; tel. 785/452–7000; Randy Peterson, President and Chief Executive Officer

SMITH COUNTY MEMORIAL HOSPITAL, 614 South Main Street, Smith Center, KS, Zip 66967–0349, Mailing Address: P.O. Box 349, Zip 66967–0349; tel. 785/282–6845; John Terrill, Administrator

KENTUCKY

BAPTIST HEALTHCARE SYSTEM
4007 Kresge Way, Louisville, KY 40207; tel. 502/896–5000; Tommy Smith, President & CEO

BAPTIST HOSPITAL EAST, 4000 Kresge Way, Louisville, KY, Zip 40207–4676; tel. 502/897–8100; Susan Stout Tamme, President

BAPTIST REGIONAL MEDICAL CENTER, 1 Trillium Way, Corbin, KY, Zip 40701–8420; tel. 606/528–1212; John S. Henson, President

CENTRAL BAPTIST HOSPITAL, 1740 Nicholasville Road, Lexington, KY, Zip 40503; tel. 606/260–6100; William G. Sisson, President

HARDIN MEMORIAL HOSPITAL, 913 North Dixie Avenue, Elizabethtown, KY, Zip 42701–2599; tel. 502/737–1212; David L. Gray, President

TRI COUNTY BAPTIST HOSPITAL, 1025 New Moody Lane, La Grange, KY, Zip 40031–0559; tel. 502/222–5388; Dennis B. Johnson, Administrator

WESTERN BAPTIST HOSPITAL, 2501 Kentucky Avenue, Paducah, KY, Zip 42003–3200; tel. 502/575–2100; Larry O. Barton, President

BLUE GRASS FAMILY HEALTH PLAN
651 Perimeter Drive, Lexington, KY 40517; tel. 606/264–4475; Jim Fritz, CEO

BAPTIST REGIONAL MEDICAL CENTER, 1 Trillium Way, Corbin, KY, Zip 40701–8420; tel. 606/528–1212; John S. Henson, President

BEREA HOSPITAL, 305 Estill Street, Berea, KY, Zip 40403–1909; tel. 606/986–3151; David E. Burgio, FACHE, President and Chief Executive Officer

Section B

BOURBON COMMUNITY HOSPITAL, 9 Linville Drive, Paris, KY, Zip 40361–2196; tel. 606/987–1000; Rob Smart, Chief Executive Officer

CENTRAL BAPTIST HOSPITAL, 1740 Nicholasville Road, Lexington, KY, Zip 40503; tel. 606/260–6100; William G. Sisson, President

CLARK REGIONAL MEDICAL CENTER, West Lexington Avenue, Winchester, KY, Zip 40391, Mailing Address: P.O. Box 630, Zip 40392–0630; tel. 606/745–3500; Robert D. Fraraccio, Chief Executive Officer

FORT LOGAN HOSPITAL, 124 Portman Avenue, Stanford, KY, Zip 40484–1200; tel. 606/365–2187; Terry C. Powers, Administrator

FRANKFORT REGIONAL MEDICAL CENTER, 299 King's Daughters Drive, Frankfort, KY, Zip 40601–4186; tel. 502/875–5240; David P. Steitz, Chief Executive Officer

GARRARD COUNTY MEMORIAL HOSPITAL, 308 West Maple Avenue, Lancaster, KY, Zip 40444–1098; tel. 606/792–6844; John P. Rigsby, Administrator

GEORGETOWN COMMUNITY HOSPITAL, 1140 Lexington Road, Georgetown, KY, Zip 40324–9362; tel. 502/868–1100; Jeffrey G. Seraphine, President and Chief Executive Officer

HARRISON MEMORIAL HOSPITAL, Millersburg Road, Cynthiana, KY, Zip 41031–0250, Mailing Address: P.O. Box 250, Zip 41031–0250; tel. 606/234–2300; Darwin E. Root, Administrator

KNOX COUNTY HOSPITAL, 321 High Street, Barbourville, KY, Zip 40906–1317, Mailing Address: P.O. Box 160, Zip 40906–0160; tel. 606/546–4175; Craig Morgan, Administrator

MARCUM AND WALLACE MEMORIAL HOSPITAL, 60 Mercy Court, Irvine, KY, Zip 40336–1331, Mailing Address: P.O. Box 928, Zip 40336–0928; tel. 606/723–2115; James F. Heitzenrater, Administrator

MARYMOUNT MEDICAL CENTER, 310 East Ninth Street, London, KY, Zip 40741–1299; tel. 606/877–3705; Lowell Jones, Chief Executive Officer

MEADOWVIEW REGIONAL MEDICAL CENTER, 989 Medical Park Drive, Maysville, KY, Zip 41056–8750; tel. 606/759–5311; Curtis B. Courtney, Chief Executive Officer

OWEN COUNTY MEMORIAL HOSPITAL, 330 Roland Avenue, Owenton, KY, Zip 40359–1502; tel. 502/484–3441; Richard D. McLeod, Administrator

PATTIE A. CLAY HOSPITAL, EKU By–Pass, Richmond, KY, Zip 40475, Mailing Address: P.O. Box 1600, Zip 40476–2603; tel. 606/625–3131; Richard M. Thomas, President

SAINT JOSEPH HOSPITAL, One St. Joseph Drive, Lexington, KY, Zip 40504–3754; tel. 606/278–3436; Thomas J. Murray, President

THE JAMES B. HAGGIN MEMORIAL HOSPITAL, 464 Linden Avenue, Harrodsburg, KY, Zip 40330–1862; tel. 606/734–5441; Earl James Motzer, Ph.D., FACHE, Chief Executive Officer

WOODFORD HOSPITAL, 360 Amsden Avenue, Versailles, KY, Zip 40383–1286; tel. 606/873–3111; Nancy Littrell, Chief Executive Officer

CARITAS HEALTH SERVICES
1850 Bluegrass Avenue, Louisville, KY 40215–1199; tel. 502/361–6140; Conrad H. Thorne, Chief of Network Operations

CARITAS MEDICAL CENTER, 1850 Bluegrass Avenue, Louisville, KY, Zip 40215–1199; tel. 502/361–6000; Peter J. Bernard, President and Chief Executive Officer

CARITAS PEACE CENTER, 2020 Newburg Road, Louisville, KY, Zip 40205–1879; tel. 502/451–3330; Peter J. Bernard, President and Chief Executive Officer

CENTERCARE
800 Park Street, Bowling Green, KY 42101; tel. 502/745–1517; John M. Fones, President

BAPTIST HOSPITAL, 2000 Church Street, Nashville, TN, Zip 37236–0002; tel. 615/329–5555; Erie Chapman, III, President and Chief Executive Officer

BAPTIST HOSPITAL EAST, 4000 Kresge Way, Louisville, KY, Zip 40207–4676; tel. 502/897–8100; Susan Stout Tamme, President

BAPTIST REGIONAL MEDICAL CENTER, 1 Trillium Way, Corbin, KY, Zip 40701–8420; tel. 606/528–1212; John S. Henson, President

BEDFORD COUNTY MEDICAL CENTER, 845 Union Street, Shelbyville, TN, Zip 37160–9971; tel. 931/685–5433; Richard L. Graham, Administrator

CAVERNA MEMORIAL HOSPITAL, 1501 South Dixie Street, Horse Cave, KY, Zip 42749–1477; tel. 502/786–2191; James J. Kerins, Sr., Administrator

CENTRAL BAPTIST HOSPITAL, 1740 Nicholasville Road, Lexington, KY, Zip 40503; tel. 606/260–6100; William G. Sisson, President

CHRIST HOSPITAL, 2139 Auburn Avenue, Cincinnati, OH, Zip 45219–2989; tel. 513/585–2000; Richard L. Seim, Senior Vice President

CLINTON COUNTY HOSPITAL, 723 Burkesville Road, Albany, KY, Zip 42602–1654; tel. 606/387–6421; Randel Flowers, Ph.D., Administrator

COFFEE MEDICAL CENTER, 1001 McArthur Drive, Manchester, TN, Zip 37355–2455, Mailing Address: P.O. Box 1079, Zip 37355–1079; tel. 931/728–3586; Edward A. Perdue, Chief Executive Officer

COOKEVILLE REGIONAL MEDICAL CENTER, 142 West Fifth Street, Cookeville, TN, Zip 38501–1760, Mailing Address: P.O. Box 340, Zip 38503–0340; tel. 931/528–2541; Tod N. Lambert, Administrator and Chief Executive Officer

CUMBERLAND COUNTY HOSPITAL, Highway 90 West, Burkesville, KY, Zip 42717–0280, Mailing Address: P.O. Box 280, Zip 42717–0280; tel. 502/864–2511; Howard C. Andersen, Interim Chief Executive Officer

DAUTERIVE HOSPITAL, 600 North Lewis Street, New Iberia, LA, Zip 70560, Mailing Address: P.O. Box 11210, Zip 70562–1210; tel. 318/365–7311; Kyle J. Viator, Chief Executive Officer

DOCTORS' HOSPITAL OF OPELOUSAS, 5101 Highway 167 South, Opelousas, LA, Zip 70570–8975; tel. 318/948–2100; Bethy W. Walker, Administrator

FRANKLIN–SIMPSON MEMORIAL HOSPITAL, Brookhaven Road, Franklin, KY, Zip 42135–2929, Mailing Address: P.O. Box 2929, Zip 42135–2929; tel. 502/586–3253; William P. Macri, Chief Executive Officer

GATEWAY HEALTH SYSTEM, 1771 Madison Street, Clarksville, TN, Zip 37043–4900, Mailing Address: P.O. Box 3160, Zip 37043–3160; tel. 931/552–6622; James Lee Decker, President and Chief Executive Officer

GOOD SAMARITAN HOSPITAL, 375 Dixmyth Avenue, Cincinnati, OH, Zip 45220–2489; tel. 513/872–1400; John S. Prout, President and Chief Executive Officer

HARDIN MEMORIAL HOSPITAL, 913 North Dixie Avenue, Elizabethtown, KY, Zip 42701–2599; tel. 502/737–1212; David L. Gray, President

HARTON REGIONAL MEDICAL CENTER, 1801 North Jackson Street, Tullahoma, TN, Zip 37388–2201, Mailing Address: P.O. Box 460, Zip 37388–0460; tel. 931/393–3000; David C. Wilson, Chief Executive Officer

HEALTHSOUTH REHABILITATION HOSPITAL OF CENTRAL KENTUCKY, 134 Heartland Drive, Elizabethtown, KY, Zip 42701–2778; tel. 502/769–3100; Teresa K. Stranko, Chief Executive Officer

HENDERSONVILLE HOSPITAL, 355 New Shackle Island Road, Hendersonville, TN, Zip 37075–2393; tel. 615/264–4000; Robert Klein, Chief Executive Officer

JEWISH HOSPITAL, 217 East Chestnut Street, Louisville, KY, Zip 40202–1886; tel. 502/587–4011; Douglas E. Shaw, President

LOGAN MEMORIAL HOSPITAL, 1625 South Nashville Road, Russellville, KY, Zip 42276–8834, Mailing Address: P.O. Box 10, Zip 42276–0010; tel. 502/726–4011; Michael Clark, Chief Executive Officer

MACON COUNTY GENERAL HOSPITAL, 204 Medical Drive, Lafayette, TN, Zip 37083–1799, Mailing Address: P.O. Box 378, Zip 37083–0378; tel. 615/666–2147; Dennis A. Wolford, FACHE, Administrator

MEADOWVIEW REGIONAL MEDICAL CENTER, 989 Medical Park Drive, Maysville, KY, Zip 41056–8750; tel. 606/759–5311; Curtis B. Courtney, Chief Executive Officer

MEDICAL CENTER AT SCOTTSVILLE, 456 Burnley Road, Scottsville, KY, Zip 42164–6355; tel. 502/622–2800; Sarah Moore, Vice President

MEDICAL CENTER OF MANCHESTER, 481 Interstate Drive, Manchester, TN, Zip 37355–3108, Mailing Address: P.O. Box 1409, Zip 37355–1409; tel. 931/728–6354; David C. Wilson, Chief Executive Officer

MEDICAL CENTER OF SOUTHWEST LOUISIANA, 2810 Ambassador Caffery Parkway, Lafayette, LA, Zip 70506–5900; tel. 318/981–2949; Madeleine L. Roberson, Chief Executive Officer

MONROE COUNTY MEDICAL CENTER, 529 Capp Harlan Road, Tompkinsville, KY, Zip 42167–1840; tel. 502/487–9231; Mark E. Thompson, Chief Executive Officer

MUHLENBERG COMMUNITY HOSPITAL, 440 Hopkinsville Street, Greenville, KY, Zip 42345–1172, Mailing Address: P.O. Box 387, Zip 42345–0387; tel. 502/338–8000; Charles D. Lovell, Jr., Chief Executive Officer

NASHVILLE MEMORIAL HOSPITAL, 612 West Due West Avenue, Madison, TN, Zip 37115–4474; tel. 615/865–3511; Allyn R. Harris, Chief Executive Officer

NORTH OAKS MEDICAL CENTER, 15790 Medical Center Drive, Hammond, LA, Zip 70403–1436, Mailing Address: P.O. Box 2668, Zip 70404–2668; tel. 504/345–2700; James E. Cathey, Jr., Chief Executive Officer

OHIO COUNTY HOSPITAL, 1211 Main Street, Hartford, KY, Zip 42347–1619; tel. 502/298–7411; Blaine Pieper, Administrator

OWENSBORO MERCY HEALTH SYSTEM, 811 East Parrish Avenue, Owensboro, KY, Zip 42303–3268, Mailing Address: P.O. Box 20007, Zip 42303–0007; tel. 502/688–2000; Greg L. Carlson, President and Chief Executive Officer

PIKEVILLE UNITED METHODIST HOSPITAL OF KENTUCKY, 911 South Bypass, Pikeville, KY, Zip 41501–1595; tel. 606/437–3500; kathy Shaughnessy, Chief Operating Officer

PINELAKE REGIONAL HOSPITAL, 1099 Medical Center Circle, Mayfield, KY, Zip 42066–1179, Mailing Address: P.O. Box 1099, Zip 42066–1099; tel. 502/251–4100; Mary Jo Lewis, Chief Executive Officer

SAINT JOSEPH HOSPITAL, One St. Joseph Drive, Lexington, KY, Zip 40504–3754; tel. 606/278–3436; Thomas J. Murray, President

SOUTHERN TENNESSEE MEDICAL CENTER, 185 Hospital Road, Winchester, TN, Zip 37398–2468; tel. 931/967–8200; Kenneth E. Alexander, Chief Executive Officer

ST. ELIZABETH MEDICAL CENTER–GRANT COUNTY, 238 Barnes Road, Williamstown, KY, Zip 41097–9460; tel. 606/824–2400; Chris Carle, Administrator

ST. ELIZABETH MEDICAL CENTER–NORTH, 401 East 20th Street, Covington, KY, Zip 41014–1585; tel. 606/292–4000; Joseph W. Gross, President and Chief Executive Officer

ST. THOMAS HEALTH SERVICES, 4220 Harding Road, Nashville, TN, Zip 37205–2095, Mailing Address: P.O. Box 380, Zip 37202–0380; tel. 615/222–2111; John Lucas, M.D., President and Chief Executive Officer

SUMNER REGIONAL MEDICAL CENTER, 555 Hartsville Pike, Gallatin, TN, Zip 37066–2449, Mailing Address: P.O. Box 1558, Zip 37066–1558; tel. 615/452–4210; William T. Sugg, President and Chief Executive Officer

T. J. SAMSON COMMUNITY HOSPITAL, 1301 North Race Street, Glasgow, KY, Zip 42141–3483; tel. 502/651–4444; Dwayne Moss, Chief Executive Officer

TAYLOR COUNTY HOSPITAL, 1700 Old Lebanon Road, Campbellsville, KY, Zip 42718–9600; tel. 502/465–3561; David R. Hayes, President

THE JAMES B. HAGGIN MEMORIAL HOSPITAL, 464 Linden Avenue, Harrodsburg, KY, Zip 40330–1862; tel. 606/734–5441; Earl James Motzer, Ph.D., FACHE, Chief Executive Officer

TWIN LAKES REGIONAL MEDICAL CENTER, 910 Wallace Avenue, Leitchfield, KY, Zip 42754–1499; tel. 502/259–9400; Stephen L. Meredith, Chief Executive Officer

UNIVERSITY MEDICAL CENTER, 1411 Baddour Parkway, Lebanon, TN, Zip 37087–2573; tel. 615/444–8262; Larry W. Keller, Chief Executive Officer

WESTLAKE REGIONAL HOSPITAL, Westlake Drive, Columbia, KY, Zip 42728–1149, Mailing Address: P.O. Box 468, Zip 42728–0468; tel. 502/384–4753; Rex A. Tungate, Administrator

WILLIAMSON MEDICAL CENTER, 2021 Carothers Road, Franklin, TN, Zip 37067–5822, Mailing Address: P.O. Box 681600, Zip 37068–1600; tel. 615/791–0500; Ronald G. Joyner, Chief Executive Officer

WOMEN'S AND CHILDREN'S HOSPITAL, 4600 Ambassador Caffery Parkway, Lafayette, LA, Zip 70508–6923, Mailing Address: P.O. Box 88030, Zip 70598–8030; tel. 318/981–9100; Madeleine L. Roberson, Chief Executive Officer

CHA PROVIDER NETWORK, INC.
P.O. Box 24647, Lexington,, KY 40524–4647; tel. 606/323–0285; Sallie J. Carter, Network Account Manager

ARH REGIONAL MEDICAL CENTER, 100 Medical Center Drive, Hazard, KY, Zip 41701–1000; tel. 606/439–6610; Charles E. Housley, FACHE, Administrator

BECKLEY APPALACHIAN REGIONAL HOSPITAL, 306 Stanaford Road, Beckley, WV, Zip 25801–3142; tel. 304/255–3000; David R. Lyon, Administrator

BEREA HOSPITAL, 305 Estill Street, Berea, KY, Zip 40403–1909; tel. 606/986–3151; David E. Burgio, FACHE, President and Chief Executive Officer

BOONE MEMORIAL HOSPITAL, 701 Madison Avenue, Madison, WV, Zip 25130–1699; tel. 304/369–1230; Tommy H. Mullins, Administrator

CABELL HUNTINGTON HOSPITAL, 1340 Hal Greer Boulevard, Huntington, WV, Zip 25701–0195; tel. 304/526–2000; W. Don Smith, II, President and Chief Executive Officer

CARDINAL HILL REHABILITATION HOSPITAL, 2050 Versailles Road, Lexington, KY, Zip 40504–1499; tel. 606/254–5701; Kerry G. Gillihan, President and Chief Executive Officer

CAVERNA MEMORIAL HOSPITAL, 1501 South Dixie Street, Horse Cave, KY, Zip 42749–1477; tel. 502/786–2191; James J. Kerins, Sr., Administrator

CENTRAL BAPTIST HOSPITAL, 1740 Nicholasville Road, Lexington, KY, Zip 40503; tel. 606/260–6100; William G. Sisson, President

CHARTER RIDGE BEHAVIORAL HEALTH SYSTEM, 3050 Rio Dosa Drive, Lexington, KY, Zip 40509–9990; tel. 606/269–2325; Barbara Kitchen, Chief Executive Officer

CHRIST HOSPITAL, 2139 Auburn Avenue, Cincinnati, OH, Zip 45219–2989; tel. 513/585–2000; Richard L. Seim, Senior Vice President

CLAIBORNE COUNTY HOSPITAL, 1850 Old Knoxville Road, Tazewell, TN, Zip 37879–3625, Mailing Address: P.O. Box 219, Zip 37879–0219; tel. 423/626–4211; Michael T. Hutchins, Administrator

CLARK REGIONAL MEDICAL CENTER, West Lexington Avenue, Winchester, KY, Zip 40391, Mailing Address: P.O. Box 630, Zip 40392–0630; tel. 606/745–3500; Robert D. Fraraccio, Chief Executive Officer

CLINTON COUNTY HOSPITAL, 723 Burkesville Road, Albany, KY, Zip 42602–1654; tel. 606/387–6421; Randel Flowers, Ph.D., Administrator

EPHRAIM MCDOWELL REGIONAL MEDICAL CENTER, 217 South Third Street, Danville, KY, Zip 40422–9983; tel. 606/239–1000; Thomas W. Smith, President and Chief Executive Officer

FLEMING COUNTY HOSPITAL, 920 Elizaville Avenue, Flemingsburg, KY, Zip 41041, Mailing Address: P.O. Box 388, Zip 41041–0388; tel. 606/849–5000; Luther E. Reeves, Chief Executive Officer

FORT LOGAN HOSPITAL, 124 Portman Avenue, Stanford, KY, Zip 40484–1200; tel. 606/365–2187; Terry C. Powers, Administrator

FORT SANDERS LOUDON MEDICAL CENTER, 1125 Grove Street, Loudon, TN, Zip 37774–1512, Mailing Address: P.O. Box 217, Zip 37774–0217; tel. 423/458–8222; Martha O'Regan Chill, President and Chief Administrative Officer

FORT SANDERS REGIONAL MEDICAL CENTER, 1901 Clinch Avenue S.W., Knoxville, TN, Zip 37916–2394; tel. 423/541–1111; James R. Burkhart, FACHE, Administrator

FORT SANDERS–PARKWEST MEDICAL CENTER, 9352 Park West Boulevard, Knoxville, TN, Zip 37923–4387, Mailing Address: P.O. Box 22993, Zip 37933–0993; tel. 423/694–5700; James R. Burkhart, FACHE, President and Chief Executive Officer

FORT SANDERS–SEVIER MEDICAL CENTER, 709 Middle Creek Road, Sevierville, TN, Zip 37862–5016, Mailing Address: P.O. Box 8005, Zip 37864–8005; tel. 423/429–6100; Ellen Wilhoit, Administrator

FRANKLIN–SIMPSON MEMORIAL HOSPITAL, Brookhaven Road, Franklin, KY, Zip 42135–2929, Mailing Address: P.O. Box 2929, Zip 42135–2929; tel. 502/586–3253; William P. Macri, Chief Executive Officer

GARRARD COUNTY MEMORIAL HOSPITAL, 308 West Maple Avenue, Lancaster, KY, Zip 40444–1098; tel. 606/792–6844; John P. Rigsby, Administrator

HARDIN MEMORIAL HOSPITAL, 913 North Dixie Avenue, Elizabethtown, KY, Zip 42701–2599; tel. 502/737–1212; David L. Gray, President

HARLAN ARH HOSPITAL, 81 Ball Park Road, Harlan, KY, Zip 40831–1792; tel. 606/573–8100; Daniel Fitzpatrick, Chief Executive Officer

HARRISON MEMORIAL HOSPITAL, Millersburg Road, Cynthiana, KY, Zip 41031–0250, Mailing Address: P.O. Box 250, Zip 41031–0250; tel. 606/234–2300; Darwin E. Root, Administrator

HEALTHSOUTH HUNTINGTON REHABILITATION HOSPITAL, 6900 West Country Club Drive, Huntington, WV, Zip 25705–2000; tel. 304/733–1060; John Forester, Chief Operating Officer

HEALTHSOUTH REHABILITATION HOSPITAL OF CENTRAL KENTUCKY, 134 Heartland Drive, Elizabethtown, KY, Zip 42701–2778; tel. 502/769–3100; Teresa K. Stranko, Chief Executive Officer

HIGHLANDS REGIONAL MEDICAL CENTER, 5000 Kentucky Route 321, Prestonsburg, KY, Zip 41653, Mailing Address: P.O. Box 668, Zip 41653–0668; tel. 606/886–8511; Harold C. Warman, Jr., President and Chief Executive Officer

JANE TODD CRAWFORD HOSPITAL, 202–206 Milby Street, Greensburg, KY, Zip 42743–1100, Mailing Address: P.O. Box 220, Zip 42743–0220; tel. 502/932–4211; Larry Craig, Chief Executive Officer

JENKINS COMMUNITY HOSPITAL, Main Street, Jenkins, KY, Zip 41537–9614, Mailing Address: P.O. Box 472, Zip 41537–0472; tel. 606/832–2171; Sherrie Newcomb, Administrator

JEWISH HOSPITAL, 217 East Chestnut Street, Louisville, KY, Zip 40202–1886; tel. 502/587–4011; Douglas E. Shaw, President

JEWISH HOSPITAL KENWOOD, 4777 East Galbraith Road, Cincinnati, OH, Zip 45236; tel. 513/686–3000; M. Aurora Lambert, Senior Vice President

KENTUCKY RIVER MEDICAL CENTER, 540 Jett Drive, Jackson, KY, Zip 41339–9620; tel. 606/666–6305; O. David Bevins, Chief Executive Officer

KNOX COUNTY HOSPITAL, 321 High Street, Barbourville, KY, Zip 40906–1317, Mailing Address: P.O. Box 160, Zip 40906–0160; tel. 606/546–4175; Craig Morgan, Administrator

MAN ARH HOSPITAL, 700 East McDonald Avenue, Man, WV, Zip 25635–1011; tel. 304/583–8421; Erica McDonald, Administrator

MARCUM AND WALLACE MEMORIAL HOSPITAL, 60 Mercy Court, Irvine, KY, Zip 40336–1331, Mailing Address: P.O. Box 928, Zip 40336–0928; tel. 606/723–2115; James F. Heitzenrater, Administrator

MARY BRECKINRIDGE HOSPITAL, 130 Kate Ireland Drive, Hyden, KY, Zip 41749–0000; tel. 606/672–2901; A. Ray Branaman, Administrator

MARYMOUNT MEDICAL CENTER, 310 East Ninth Street, London, KY, Zip 40741–1299; tel. 606/877–3705; Lowell Jones, Chief Executive Officer

MCDOWELL ARH HOSPITAL, Route 122, McDowell, KY, Zip 41647, Mailing Address: P.O. Box 247, Mc Dowell, Zip 41647–0247; tel. 606/377–3400; Dena C. Sparkman, Administrator

MEDICAL CENTER AT SCOTTSVILLE, 456 Burnley Road, Scottsville, KY, Zip 42164–6355; tel. 502/622–2800; Sarah Moore, Vice President

MEMORIAL HOSPITAL, 401 Memorial Drive, Manchester, KY, Zip 40962–9156; tel. 606/598–5104; Jimm Bunch, Chief Executive Officer

MIDDLESBORO APPALACHIAN REGIONAL HOSPITAL, 3600 West Cumberland Avenue, Middlesboro, KY, Zip 40965–2614, Mailing Address: P.O. Box 340, Zip 40965–0340; tel. 606/242–1101; Paul V. Miles, Administrator

MORGAN COUNTY APPALACHIAN REGIONAL HOSPITAL, 476 Liberty Road, West Liberty, KY, Zip 41472–2049, Mailing Address: P.O. Box 579, Zip 41472–0579; tel. 606/743–3186; Dennis R. Chaney, Administrator

NICHOLAS COUNTY HOSPITAL, 2323 Concrete Road, Carlisle, KY, Zip 40311–9721, Mailing Address: P.O. Box 232, Zip 40311–0232; tel. 606/289–7181; Doris Ecton, Administrator and Chief Executive Officer

OUR LADY OF BELLEFONTE HOSPITAL, St. Christopher Drive, Ashland, KY, Zip 41101, Mailing Address: P.O. Box 789, Zip 41105–0789; tel. 606/833–3333; Robert J. Maher, President

OUR LADY OF THE WAY HOSPITAL, 11022 Main Street, Martin, KY, Zip 41649–0910; tel. 606/285–5181; Lowell Jones, Chief Executive Officer

OWEN COUNTY MEMORIAL HOSPITAL, 330 Roland Avenue, Owenton, KY, Zip 40359–1502; tel. 502/484–3441; Richard D. McLeod, Administrator

PATTIE A. CLAY HOSPITAL, EKU By–Pass, Richmond, KY, Zip 40475, Mailing Address: P.O. Box 1600, Zip 40476–2603; tel. 606/625–3131; Richard M. Thomas, President

PAUL B. HALL REGIONAL MEDICAL CENTER, 625 James S Trimble Boulevard, Paintsville, KY, Zip 41240–1055, Mailing Address: P.O. Box 1487, Zip 41240–1487; tel. 606/789–3511; Deborah C. Trimble, Administrator

PENINSULA HOSPITAL, 2347 Jones Bend Road, Louisville, TN, Zip 37777–5213, Mailing Address: P.O. Box 2000, Zip 37777–2000; tel. 423/970–9800; David H. McReynolds, Chief Operating Officer and Administrator

PINEVILLE COMMUNITY HOSPITAL ASSOCIATION, 850 Riverview Avenue, Pineville, KY, Zip 40977–0850; tel. 606/337–3051; J. Milton Brooks, III, Administrator

ROCKCASTLE HOSPITAL AND RESPIRATORY CARE CENTER, 145 Newcomb Avenue, Mount Vernon, KY, Zip 40456–2733, Mailing Address: P.O. Box 1310, Zip 40456–1310; tel. 606/256–2195; Lee D. Keene, President and Chief Executive Officer

RUSSELL COUNTY HOSPITAL, Dowell Road, Russell Springs, KY, Zip 42642, Mailing Address: P.O. Box 1610, Zip 42642–1610; tel. 502/866–4141; Richard Hacker, Interim Administrator

ST. CLAIRE MEDICAL CENTER, 222 Medical Circle, Morehead, KY, Zip 40351–1180; tel. 606/783–6500; Mark J. Neff, President and Chief Executive Officer

ST. LUKE HOSPITAL EAST, 85 North Grand Avenue, Fort Thomas, KY, Zip 41075–1796; tel. 606/572–3100; Daniel M. Vinson, CPA, Senior Vice President

ST. LUKE HOSPITAL WEST, 7380 Turfway Road, Florence, KY, Zip 41042–1337; tel. 606/525–5200; Daniel M. Vinson, CPA, Senior Vice President

ST. MARY'S HOSPITAL, 2900 First Avenue, Huntington, WV, Zip 25702–1272; tel. 304/526–1234; J. Thomas Jones, Executive Director

SUMMERS COUNTY APPALACHIAN REGIONAL HOSPITAL, Terrace Street, Hinton, WV, Zip 25951, Mailing Address: Drawer 940, Zip 25951–0940; tel. 304/466–1000; Rocco K. Massey, Administrator

TAYLOR COUNTY HOSPITAL, 1700 Old Lebanon Road, Campbellsville, KY, Zip 42718–9600; tel. 502/465–3561; David R. Hayes, President

THE JAMES B. HAGGIN MEMORIAL HOSPITAL, 464 Linden Avenue, Harrodsburg, KY, Zip 40330–1862; tel. 606/734–5441; Earl James Motzer, Ph.D., FACHE, Chief Executive Officer

THREE RIVERS MEDICAL CENTER, Highway 644, Louisa, KY, Zip 41230, Mailing Address: P.O. Box 769, Zip 41230–0769; tel. 606/638–9451; Greg Kiser, Chief Executive Officer

UNIVERSITY HOSPITAL, 234 Goodman Street, Cincinnati, OH, Zip 45219–2316; tel. 513/558–1000; Elliot G. Cohen, Senior Vice President

UNIVERSITY OF KENTUCKY HOSPITAL, 800 Rose Street, Lexington, KY, Zip 40536–0084; tel. 606/323–5000; Frank Butler, Director

WELLMONT HOLSTON VALLEY MEDICAL CENTER, West Ravine Street, Kingsport, TN, Zip 37662–0224, Mailing Address: Box 238, Zip 37662–0224; tel. 423/224–4000; Louis H. Bremer, President and Chief Executive Officer

WELLMONT LONESOME PINE HOSPITAL, 1990 Holton Avenue East, Big Stone Gap, VA, Zip 24219–0230; tel. 540/523–3111; Paul A. Bishop, Administrator

WHITESBURG APPALACHIAN REGIONAL HOSPITAL, 240 Hospital Road, Whitesburg, KY, Zip 41858–1254; tel. 606/633–3600; Donnie Fields, Administrator

WILLIAMSON ARH HOSPITAL, 260 Hospital Drive, South Williamson, KY, Zip 41503–4072; tel. 606/237–1700; Louis G. Roe, Jr., Administrator

WOODFORD HOSPITAL, 360 Amsden Avenue, Versailles, KY, Zip 40383–1286; tel. 606/873–3111; Nancy Littrell, Chief Executive Officer

COMMUNITY CARE NETWORK
110 A. Second Street, Henderson, KY 42420; tel. 502/827–7380; Elizabeth Johnson, Director of Marketing

CALDWELL COUNTY HOSPITAL, 101 Hospital Drive, Princeton, KY, Zip 42445–0410, Mailing Address: Box 410, Zip 42445–0410; tel. 502/365–0300; Robert R. Stanley, Interim Chief Executive Officer

CRITTENDEN COUNTY HOSPITAL, Highway 60 South, Marion, KY, Zip 42064, Mailing Address: P.O. Box 386, Zip 42064–0386; tel. 502/965–1018; Rick Napper, Chief Executive Officer

FRANKLIN–SIMPSON MEMORIAL HOSPITAL, Brookhaven Road, Franklin, KY, Zip 42135–2929, Mailing Address: P.O. Box 2929, Zip 42135–2929; tel. 502/586–3253; William P. Macri, Chief Executive Officer

JENNIE STUART MEDICAL CENTER, 320 West 18th Street, Hopkinsville, KY, Zip 42241–2400, Mailing Address: P.O. Box 2400, Zip 42241–2400; tel. 502/887–0100; Lewis T. Peeples, Chief Executive Officer

LIVINGSTON HOSPITAL AND HEALTHCARE SERVICES, 131 Hospital Drive, Salem, KY, Zip 42078; tel. 502/988–2299; Lennis Thompson, Chief Executive Officer

METHODIST HOSPITAL, 1305 North Elm Street, Henderson, KY, Zip 42420–2775, Mailing Address: P.O. Box 48, Zip 42420–0048; tel. 502/827–7700; Bruce D. Begley, Executive Director

METHODIST HOSPITAL UNION COUNTY, 4604 Highway 60 West, Morganfield, KY, Zip 42437–9570; tel. 502/389–3030; Patrick Donahue, Administrator

MUHLENBERG COMMUNITY HOSPITAL, 440 Hopkinsville Street, Greenville, KY, Zip 42345–1172, Mailing Address: P.O. Box 387, Zip 42345–0387; tel. 502/338–8000; Charles D. Lovell, Jr., Chief Executive Officer

MURRAY–CALLOWAY COUNTY HOSPITAL, 803 Poplar Street, Murray, KY, Zip 42071–2432; tel. 502/762–1100; Stuart Poston, President

REGIONAL MEDICAL CENTER OF HOPKINS COUNTY, 900 Hospital Drive, Madisonville, KY, Zip 42431–1694; tel. 502/825–5100; Bobby H. Dampier, Chief Executive Officer

COMMUNITY HEALTH DELIVERY SYSTEM, INC
2020 Newbrug Road, Louisville, KY 40205; tel. 502/451–3330; Fran Dotson, Network Contact

BAPTIST HOSPITAL EAST, 4000 Kresge Way, Louisville, KY, Zip 40207–4676; tel. 502/897–8100; Susan Stout Tamme, President

BAPTIST REGIONAL MEDICAL CENTER, 1 Trillium Way, Corbin, KY, Zip 40701–8420; tel. 606/528–1212; John S. Henson, President

BRECKINRIDGE MEMORIAL HOSPITAL, 1011 Old Highway 60, Hardinsburg, KY, Zip 40143–2597; tel. 502/756–7000; George Walz, CHE, Chief Executive Officer

CALDWELL COUNTY HOSPITAL, 101 Hospital Drive, Princeton, KY, Zip 42445–0410, Mailing Address: Box 410, Zip 42445–0410; tel. 502/365–0300; Robert R. Stanley, Interim Chief Executive Officer

CARITAS MEDICAL CENTER, 1850 Bluegrass Avenue, Louisville, KY, Zip 40215–1199; tel. 502/361–6000; Peter J. Bernard, President and Chief Executive Officer

CARITAS PEACE CENTER, 2020 Newburg Road, Louisville, KY, Zip 40205–1879; tel. 502/451–3330; Peter J. Bernard, President and Chief Executive Officer

CARROLL COUNTY HOSPITAL, 309 11th Street, Carrollton, KY, Zip 41008–1400; tel. 502/732–4321; Roger Williams, Chief Executive Officer

CAVERNA MEMORIAL HOSPITAL, 1501 South Dixie Street, Horse Cave, KY, Zip 42749–1477; tel. 502/786–2191; James J. Kerins, Sr., Administrator

CENTRAL BAPTIST HOSPITAL, 1740 Nicholasville Road, Lexington, KY, Zip 40503; tel. 606/260–6100; William G. Sisson, President

FLAGET MEMORIAL HOSPITAL, 201 Cathedral Manor, Bardstown, KY, Zip 40004–1299; tel. 502/348–3923; Suzanne Reasbeck, President and Chief Executive Officer

JANE TODD CRAWFORD HOSPITAL, 202–206 Milby Street, Greensburg, KY, Zip 42743–1100, Mailing Address: P.O. Box 220, Zip 42743–0220; tel. 502/932–4211; Larry Craig, Chief Executive Officer

MARYMOUNT MEDICAL CENTER, 310 East Ninth Street, London, KY, Zip 40741–1299; tel. 606/877–3705; Lowell Jones, Chief Executive Officer

NORTON HEALTHCARE, 200 East Chestnut Street, Louisville, KY, Zip 40202–1800, Mailing Address: P.O. Box 35070, Zip 40232–5070; tel. 502/629–8000; Stephen M. Tullman, Chief Administrative Officer

SAINT JOSEPH HOSPITAL, One St. Joseph Drive, Lexington, KY, Zip 40504–3754; tel. 606/278–3436; Thomas J. Murray, President

ST. ELIZABETH MEDICAL CENTER–GRANT COUNTY, 238 Barnes Road, Williamstown, KY, Zip 41097–9460; tel. 606/824–2400; Chris Carle, Administrator

ST. ELIZABETH MEDICAL CENTER–NORTH, 401 East 20th Street, Covington, KY, Zip 41014–1585; tel. 606/292–4000; Joseph W. Gross, President and Chief Executive Officer

TRI COUNTY BAPTIST HOSPITAL, 1025 New Moody Lane, La Grange, KY, Zip 40031–0559; tel. 502/222–5388; Dennis B. Johnson, Administrator

TRIGG COUNTY HOSPITAL, Highway 68 East, Cadiz, KY, Zip 42211, Mailing Address: P.O. Box 312, Zip 42211–0312; tel. 502/522–3215; Richard Chapman, Administrator

TWIN LAKES REGIONAL MEDICAL CENTER, 910 Wallace Avenue, Leitchfield, KY, Zip 42754–1499; tel. 502/259–9400; Stephen L. Meredith, Chief Executive Officer

WESTERN BAPTIST HOSPITAL, 2501 Kentucky Avenue, Paducah, KY, Zip 42003–3200; tel. 502/575–2100; Larry O. Barton, President

JEWISH HOSPITAL HEALTHCARE SERVICES
201 Abraham Flexner Way, Louisville, KY 40202; tel. 502/587–4011; Greg Pugh, Manager Corp. Planning

CLARK MEMORIAL HOSPITAL, 1220 Missouri Avenue, Jeffersonville, IN, Zip 47130–3743, Mailing Address: Box 69, Zip 47131–0069; tel. 812/282–6631; Merle E. Stepp, President and Chief Executive Officer

FRAZIER REHABILITATION CENTER, 220 Abraham Flexner Way, Louisville, KY, Zip 40202–1887; tel. 502/582–7400; Barth A. Weinberg, Vice President, Inpatient Rehabilitation

HARDIN MEMORIAL HOSPITAL, 913 North Dixie Avenue, Elizabethtown, KY, Zip 42701–2599; tel. 502/737–1212; David L. Gray, President

JEWISH HOSPITAL, 217 East Chestnut Street, Louisville, KY, Zip 40202–1886; tel. 502/587–4011; Douglas E. Shaw, President

JEWISH HOSPITAL–SHELBYVILLE, 727 Hospital Drive, Shelbyville, KY, Zip 40065–1699; tel. 502/647–4000; Timothy L. Jarm, President

PATTIE A. CLAY HOSPITAL, EKU By–Pass, Richmond, KY, Zip 40475, Mailing Address: P.O. Box 1600, Zip 40476–2603; tel. 606/625–3131; Richard M. Thomas, President

SAINT JOSEPH HOSPITAL EAST, 150 North Eagle Creek Drive, Lexington, KY, Zip 40509–1807; tel. 606/268–4800; Melinda Washburn, Chief Operating Officer

SCOTT MEMORIAL HOSPITAL, 1415 North Gardner Street, Scottsburg, IN, Zip 47170–0430, Mailing Address: Box 430, Zip 47170–0430; tel. 812/752–8500; Clifford D. Nay, Executive Director

SOUTHERN INDIANA REHABILITATION HOSPITAL, 3104 Blackiston Boulevard, New Albany, IN, Zip 47150–9579; tel. 812/941–8300; Randy L. Napier, President and Chief Executive Officer

TAYLOR COUNTY HOSPITAL, 1700 Old Lebanon Road, Campbellsville, KY, Zip 42718–9600; tel. 502/465–3561; David R. Hayes, President

WASHINGTON COUNTY MEMORIAL HOSPITAL, 911 North Shelby Street, Salem, IN, Zip 47167; tel. 812/883–5881; Rodney M. Coats, President and Chief Executive Officer

NORTON HEALTH CARE, INC.
P.O. Box 35070, Louisville, KY 40232; tel. 502/629–6000; Steven A. Williams, President

NORTON AUDUBON HOSPITAL, One Audubon Plaza Drive, Louisville, KY, Zip 40217–1397, Mailing Address: P.O. Box 17550, Zip 40217–0550; tel. 502/636–7111; Thomas D. Kmetz, Chief Administrative Officer

NORTON HEALTHCARE, 200 East Chestnut Street, Louisville, KY, Zip 40202–1800, Mailing Address: P.O. Box 35070, Zip 40232–5070; tel. 502/629–8000; Stephen M. Tullman, Chief Administrative Officer

NORTON SPRING VIEW HOSPITAL, 320 Loretto Road, Lebanon, KY, Zip 40033–0320; tel. 502/692–3161; Patricia Ekdahl, Chief Executive Officer

NORTON SUBURBAN HOSPITAL, 4001 Dutchmans Lane, Louisville, KY, Zip 40207–4799; tel. 502/893–1000; John A. Marshall, President and Chief Executive Officer

ST ELIZABETH MEDICAL CENTER
1 Medical Village Drive, Edgewood, KY 41017; tel. 606/344–2000; Joseph W. Gross, President & CEO

ST. ELIZABETH MEDICAL CENTER–GRANT COUNTY, 238 Barnes Road, Williamstown, KY, Zip 41097–9460; tel. 606/824–2400; Chris Carle, Administrator

ST. ELIZABETH MEDICAL CENTER–NORTH, 401 East 20th Street, Covington, KY, Zip 41014–1585; tel. 606/292–4000; Joseph W. Gross, President and Chief Executive Officer

VENCOR, INC.
680 S. Forth Street, Louisville, KY 40202; tel. 502/569–7300; Edward Kuntz, CEO

LOUISIANA

FRANCISCAN MISSIONARIES OF OUR LADY
4200 Essen Lane, Baton Rouge, LA 70809; tel. 225/923–2701; John Finan Jr., President & CEO

ABBEVILLE GENERAL HOSPITAL, 118 North Hospital Drive, Abbeville, La, Zip 70510–4077, Mailing Address: P.O. Box 580, Zip 70511–0580; tel. 318/893–5466; Ray A. Landry, Administrator

ABROM KAPLAN MEMORIAL HOSPITAL, 1310 West Seventh Street, Kaplan, LA, Zip 70548–2998; tel. 318/643–8300; Lyman Trahan, Administrator

ACADIA–ST. LANDRY HOSPITAL, 810 South Broadway Street, Church Point, LA, Zip 70525–4497; tel. 318/684–5435; Alcus Trahan, Administrator

AMERICAN LEGION HOSPITAL, 1305 Crowley Rayne Highway, Crowley, LA, Zip 70526–9410; tel. 318/783–3222; Terry W. Osborne, Chief Executive Officer

IBERIA GENERAL HOSPITAL AND MEDICAL CENTER, 2315 East Main Street, New Iberia, LA, Zip 70560–4031, Mailing Address: P.O. Box 13338, Zip 70562–3338; tel. 318/364–0441; Isaac S. Coe, Interim Administrator

JENNINGS AMERICAN LEGION HOSPITAL, 1634 Elton Road, Jennings, LA, Zip 70546–3614; tel. 318/824–2490; Terry J. Terrebonne, Administrator

OPELOUSAS GENERAL HOSPITAL, 520 Prudhomme Lane, Opelousas, LA, Zip 70570–6454, Mailing Address: P.O. Box 1208, Zip 70571–1208; tel. 318/948–3011; Daryl J. Doise, Administrator

OUR LADY OF LOURDES REGIONAL MEDICAL CENTER, 611 St. Landry Street, Lafayette, LA, Zip 70506–4697, Mailing Address: Box 4027, Zip 70502–4027; tel. 318/289–2000; Dudley Romero, President and Chief Executive Officer

OUR LADY OF THE LAKE REGIONAL MEDICAL CENTER, 5000 Hennessy Boulevard, Baton Rouge, LA, Zip 70808–4350; tel. 225/765–6565; Robert C. Davidge, Chief Executive Officer

ST. FRANCIS MEDICAL CENTER, 309 Jackson Street, Monroe, LA, Zip 71201–7498, Mailing Address: P.O. Box 1901, Zip 71210–1901; tel. 318/327–4000; H. Gerald Smith, President and Chief Executive Officer

GENERAL HEALTH SYSTEM
5757 Corporate Boulevard, Baton Rouge, LA 70808; tel. 225/237–1603; Milton Siepman, CEO

LAKEVIEW REGIONAL MEDICAL CENTER
95 East Fairway Drive, Covington, LA 70433; tel. 504/867–3800; Darrell Blaylock, CEO

LAKEVIEW REGIONAL MEDICAL CENTER, 95 East Fairway Drive, Covington, LA, Zip 70433–7507; tel. 504/867–3800; Darrell Blaylock, Chief Executive Officer

LOUISIANA HEALTH CARE AUTHORITY
8550 United Plaza Boulevard, Baton Rouge, LA 70809; tel. 225/922–0488; James Brexlor, Director of Networks

E. A. CONWAY MEDICAL CENTER, 4864 Jackson Street, Monroe, LA, Zip 71202–6497, Mailing Address: P.O. Box 1881, Zip 71210–1881; tel. 318/330–7000; Roy D. Bostick, Director

EARL K. LONG MEDICAL CENTER, 5825 Airline Highway, Baton Rouge, LA, Zip 70805–2498; tel. 225/358–1000; Jonathan Roberts, Dr.PH, Chief Executive Officer

HUEY P. LONG MEDICAL CENTER, 352 Hospital Boulevard, Pineville, LA, Zip 71360, Mailing Address: P.O. Box 5352, Zip 71361–5352; tel. 318/448–0811; James E. Morgan, Director

LALLIE KEMP MEDICAL CENTER, 52579 Highway 51 South, Independence, LA, Zip 70443–2231; tel. 504/878–9421; LeVern Meades, Administrator

LEONARD J. CHABERT MEDICAL CENTER, 1978 Industrial Boulevard, Houma, LA, Zip 70363–7094; tel. 504/873–2200; Daniel Trahan, Acting Administrator

MEDICAL CENTER OF LOUISIANA AT NEW ORLEANS, 2021 Perdido Street, New Orleans, LA, Zip 70112–1396; tel. 504/588–3000; John S. Berault, Chief Executive Officer

UNIVERSITY MEDICAL CENTER, 2390 West Congress Street, Lafayette, LA, Zip 70506–4298, Mailing Address: P.O. Box 69300, Zip 70596–9300; tel. 318/261–6001; Lawrence T. Dorsey, Administrator

WALTER OLIN MOSS REGIONAL MEDICAL CENTER, 1000 Walters Street, Lake Charles, LA, Zip 70605; tel. 318/475–8100; Clay Dunaway, Administrator

WASHINGTON–ST. TAMMANY REGIONAL MEDICAL CENTER, 400 Memphis Street, Bogalusa, LA, Zip 70427–0040, Mailing Address: Box 40, Zip 70429–0040; tel. 504/735–1322; Larry R. King, Administrator

OCHSNER HEALTH PLAN
One Galleria Boulevard, Suite 1224, New Orleans, LA 70001; tel. 504/836–8064; Connie Baer, Vice President of Marketing

BEAUREGARD MEMORIAL HOSPITAL, 600 South Pine Street, De Ridder, LA, Zip 70634–4998, Mailing Address: P.O. Box 730, Zip 70634–0730; tel. 318/462–7100; Theodore J. Badger, Jr., Chief Executive Officer

BUNKIE GENERAL HOSPITAL, Evergreen Highway, Bunkie, LA, Zip 71322, Mailing Address: P.O. Box 380, Zip 71322–0380; tel. 318/346–6681; Donald L. Kannady, Administrator

BYRD REGIONAL HOSPITAL, 1020 West Fertitta Boulevard, Leesville, LA, Zip 71446–4697; tel. 318/239–9041; Donald Henderson, Chief Executive Officer

CHRISTUS SCHUMPERT MEDICAL CENTER, One St. Mary Place, Shreveport, LA, Zip 71101–4399, Mailing Address: P.O. Box 21976, Zip 71120–1076; tel. 318/681–4500; Daniel J. Rissing, Acting Chief Executive Officer

CHRISTUS ST. FRANCES CABRINI HOSPITAL, 3330 Masonic Drive, Alexandria, LA, Zip 71301–3899; tel. 318/487–1122; Daniel J. Rissing, Acting Chief Executive Officer

CHRISTUS ST. PATRICK HOSPITAL, 524 South Ryan Street, Lake Charles, LA, Zip 70601–5799, Mailing Address: P.O. Box 3401, Zip 70602–3401; tel. 318/436–2511; James E. Gardner, Jr., Chief Executive Officer

DE SOTO REGIONAL HEALTH SYSTEM, 207 Jefferson Street, Mansfield, LA, Zip 71052–2603, Mailing Address: P.O. Box 1636, Zip 71052–0672; tel. 318/871–3101; William F. Barrow, President and Chief Executive Officer

HOMER MEMORIAL HOSPITAL, 620 East College Street, Homer, LA, Zip 71040–3202; tel. 318/927–2024; J. Larry Jordan, Administrator

JENNINGS AMERICAN LEGION HOSPITAL, 1634 Elton Road, Jennings, LA, Zip 70546–3614; tel. 318/824–2490; Terry J. Terrebonne, Administrator

LADY OF THE SEA GENERAL HOSPITAL, 200 West 134th Place, Cut Off, LA, Zip 70345–4145; tel. 504/632–6401; Lane M. Cheramie, Chief Executive Officer

LANE MEMORIAL HOSPITAL, 6300 Main Street, Zachary, LA, Zip 70791–9990; tel. 225/658–4000; David W. Fuller, Chief Executive Officer

MINDEN MEDICAL CENTER, 1 Medical Plaza, Minden, LA, Zip 71055–3330; tel. 318/377–2321; George E. French, III, Chief Executive Officer

NATCHITOCHES PARISH HOSPITAL, 501 Keyser Avenue, Natchitoches, LA, Zip 71457–6036, Mailing Address: P.O. Box 2009, Zip 71457–2009; tel. 318/352–1200; Mark E. Marley, Executive Director

NORTHSHORE REGIONAL MEDICAL CENTER, 100 Medical Center Drive, Slidell, LA, Zip 70461–8572; tel. 504/649–7070; Lynn C. Orfgen, Chief Executive Officer

OCHSNER FOUNDATION HOSPITAL, 1516 Jefferson Highway, New Orleans, LA, Zip 70121–2484; tel. 504/842–3000; Eileen Skinner, Interim Director

PENDLETON MEMORIAL METHODIST HOSPITAL, 5620 Read Boulevard, New Orleans, LA, Zip 70127–3154; tel. 504/244–5100; Frederick C. Young, Jr., President

RIVER WEST MEDICAL CENTER, 59355 River West Drive, Plaquemine, LA, Zip 70764–9543; tel. 225/687–9222; Mark Nosacka, Chief Executive Officer

RIVERLAND MEDICAL CENTER, 1700 North E 'E' Wallace Boulevard, Ferriday, LA, Zip 71334, Mailing Address: P.O. Box 111, Zip 71334–0111; tel. 318/757–6551; Vernon R. Stevens, Jr., Administrator

SABINE MEDICAL CENTER, 240 Highland Drive, Many, LA, Zip 71449–3718; tel. 318/256–5691; Patrick W. Gandy, Chief Executive Officer

ST. ANNE GENERAL HOSPITAL, 4608 Highway 1, Raceland, LA, Zip 70394; tel. 504/537–6841; Milton D. Bourgeois, Jr., Administrator

SUMMIT HOSPITAL, 17000 Medical Center Drive, Baton Rouge, LA, Zip 70816–3224; tel. 225/755–4800; Steve Grimm, CHE, Chief Executive Officer

WEST CALCASIEU CAMERON HOSPITAL, 701 East Cypress Street, Sulphur, LA, Zip 70663–5000, Mailing Address: P.O. Box 2509, Zip 70664–2509; tel. 318/527–4240; Wayne A. Swiniarski, FACHE, Chief Executive Officer

WEST JEFFERSON MEDICAL CENTER, 1101 Medical Center Boulevard, Marrero, LA, Zip 70072–3191; tel. 504/347–5511; A. Gary Muller, FACHE, President and Chief Executive Officer

PEOPLES HEALTH NETWORK
111 Veterans Memorial Boulevard, Metaire, LA 70005; tel. 504/837–7374; Roger Friend, Network Contact

TENET HEALTH SYSTEM
111 Veterans Boulevard, Metarie, LA 70005; tel. 504/833–1495; Reynold Jennings, Senior Vice President

DOCTORS HOSPITAL OF JEFFERSON, 4320 Houma Boulevard, Metairie, LA, Zip 70006–2973; tel. 504/849–4000; L. Rene' Goux, Chief Executive Officer

KENNER REGIONAL MEDICAL CENTER, 180 West Esplanade Avenue, Kenner, LA, Zip 70065–6001; tel. 504/468–8600; Deborah C. Keel, Chief Executive Officer

MEADOWCREST HOSPITAL, 2500 Belle Chase Highway, Gretna, LA, Zip 70056–7196; tel. 504/392–3131; Gerald L. Parton, Chief Executive Officer

MEDICAL CENTER OF LOUISIANA AT NEW ORLEANS, 2021 Perdido Street, New Orleans, LA, Zip 70112–1396; tel. 504/588–3000; John S. Berault, Chief Executive Officer

Section B

NORTHSHORE PSYCHIATRIC HOSPITAL, 104 Medical Center Drive, Slidell, LA, Zip 70461–7838; tel. 504/646–5500; George H. Perry, Ph.D., Chief Executive Officer

NORTHSHORE REGIONAL MEDICAL CENTER, 100 Medical Center Drive, Slidell, LA, Zip 70461–8572; tel. 504/649–7070; Lynn C. Orfgen, Chief Executive Officer

ST. CHARLES GENERAL HOSPITAL, 3700 St. Charles Avenue, New Orleans, LA, Zip 70115–4680; tel. 504/899–7441; Rene Goux, Chief Executive Officer

MAINE

BLUE HILL MEMORIAL HOSPITAL
Water Street, Blue Hill, ME 04614;
tel. 207/374–2836; Bruce D. Cummings, CEO

BLUE HILL MEMORIAL HOSPITAL, Water Street, Blue Hill, ME, Zip 04614–0823, Mailing Address: P.O. Box 823, Zip 04614–0823; tel. 207/374–2836; Bruce D. Cummings, Chief Executive Officer

HEALTH NET, INC.
One Merchants Plaza, 5th Floor, Bangor, ME 04401; tel. 207/942–2844; Dale Bradford, CEO (Interim)

ACADIA HOSPITAL, 268 Stillwater Avenue, Bangor, ME, Zip 04401–3945, Mailing Address: P.O. Box 422, Zip 04402–0422; tel. 207/973–6100; Ali A. Elhaj, President and Chief Exective Officer

AROOSTOOK MEDICAL CENTER, 140 Academy Street, Presque Isle, ME, Zip 04769–3171, Mailing Address: P.O. Box 151, Zip 04769–0151; tel. 207/768–4000; David A. Peterson, President and Chief Executive Officer

BLUE HILL MEMORIAL HOSPITAL, Water Street, Blue Hill, ME, Zip 04614–0823, Mailing Address: P.O. Box 823, Zip 04614–0823; tel. 207/374–2836; Bruce D. Cummings, Chief Executive Officer

CHARLES A. DEAN MEMORIAL HOSPITAL, Pritham Avenue, Greenville, ME, Zip 04441–1395, Mailing Address: P.O. Box 1129, Zip 04441–1129; tel. 207/695–2223; Philomena A. Marshall, R.N., President and Chief Executive Officer

EASTERN MAINE MEDICAL CENTER, 489 State Street, Bangor, ME, Zip 04401–6674, Mailing Address: P.O. Box 404, Zip 04402–0404; tel. 207/973–7000; Norman A. Ledwin, President and Chief Executive Officer

INLAND HOSPITAL, 200 Kennedy Memorial Drive, Waterville, ME, Zip 04901–4595; tel. 207/861–3000; Wilfred J. Addison, President and Chief Executive Officer

MILLINOCKET REGIONAL HOSPITAL, 200 Somerset Street, Millinocket, ME, Zip 04462–1298; tel. 207/723–5161; Marie E. Arant, Interim Chief Executive Officer

MOUNT DESERT ISLAND HOSPITAL, Wayman Lane, Bar Harbor, ME, Zip 04609–0008, Mailing Address: P.O. Box 8, Zip 04609–0008; tel. 207/288–5081; Leslie A. Hawkins, President

NORTHERN MAINE MEDICAL CENTER, 143 East Main Street, Fort Kent, ME, Zip 04743–1497; tel. 207/834–3155; Martin B. Bernstein, Chief Executive Officer

SEBASTICOOK VALLEY HOSPITAL, 99 Grove Street, Pittsfield, ME, Zip 04967–1199; tel. 207/487–5141; Ann Morrison, R.N., Chief Executive Officer

SYNERNET INC
222 St. John Street, Suite 329, Portland, ME 04102; tel. 207/771–3456; Susan Homer, Office Manager

BLUE HILL MEMORIAL HOSPITAL, Water Street, Blue Hill, ME, Zip 04614–0823, Mailing Address: P.O. Box 823, Zip 04614–0823; tel. 207/374–2836; Bruce D. Cummings, Chief Executive Officer

FRANKLIN MEMORIAL HOSPITAL, One Hospital Drive, Farmington, ME, Zip 04938–9990; tel. 207/778–6031; Richard A. Batt, President and Chief Executive Officer

HENRIETTA D. GOODALL HOSPITAL, 25 June Street, Sanford, ME, Zip 04073–2645; tel. 207/324–4310; Peter G. Booth, President

INLAND HOSPITAL, 200 Kennedy Memorial Drive, Waterville, ME, Zip 04901–4595; tel. 207/861–3000; Wilfred J. Addison, President and Chief Executive Officer

MERCY HOSPITAL PORTLAND, 144 State Street, Portland, ME, Zip 04101–3795; tel. 207/879–3000; Howard R. Buckley, President

MID COAST HOSPITAL, 1356 Washington Street, Bath, ME, Zip 04530–2897; tel. 207/443–5524; Herbert Paris, President

MILES MEMORIAL HOSPITAL, Bristol Road, Damariscotta, ME, Zip 04543, Mailing Address: Rural Route 2, Box 4500, Zip 04543–9767; tel. 207/563–1234; Judith Tarr, Chief Executive Officer

MOUNT DESERT ISLAND HOSPITAL, Wayman Lane, Bar Harbor, ME, Zip 04609–0008, Mailing Address: P.O. Box 8, Zip 04609–0008; tel. 207/288–5081; Leslie A. Hawkins, President

NORTHERN CUMBERLAND MEMORIAL HOSPITAL, South High Street, Bridgton, ME, Zip 04009, Mailing Address: P.O. Box 230, Zip 04009–0230; tel. 207/647–8841; Laird Covey, Chief Executive Officer

NORTHERN MAINE MEDICAL CENTER, 143 East Main Street, Fort Kent, ME, Zip 04743–1497; tel. 207/834–3155; Martin B. Bernstein, Chief Executive Officer

PENOBSCOT BAY MEDICAL CENTER, 6 Glen Cove Drive, Rockport, ME, Zip 04856–4241; tel. 207/596–8000; Roy A. Hitchings, Jr., FACHE, President

REDINGTON–FAIRVIEW GENERAL HOSPITAL, Fairview Avenue, Skowhegan, ME, Zip 04976, Mailing Address: P.O. Box 468, Zip 04976–0468; tel. 207/474–5121; Richard Willett, Chief Executive Officer

RUMFORD COMMUNITY HOSPITAL, 420 Franklin Street, Rumford, ME, Zip 04276–2145, Mailing Address: P.O. Box 619, Zip 04276–0619; tel. 207/364–4581; John H. Welsh, Chief Executive Officer

SEBASTICOOK VALLEY HOSPITAL, 99 Grove Street, Pittsfield, ME, Zip 04967–1199; tel. 207/487–5141; Ann Morrison, R.N., Chief Executive Officer

SOUTHERN MAINE MEDICAL CENTER, One Medical Center Drive, Biddeford, ME, Zip 04005–9496, Mailing Address: P.O. Box 626, Zip 04005–0626; tel. 207/283–7000; Edward J. McGeachey, President and Chief Executive Officer

ST. JOSEPH HOSPITAL, 360 Broadway, Bangor, ME, Zip 04401–3897, Mailing Address: P.O. Box 403, Zip 04402–0403; tel. 207/262–1000; Sister Mary Norberta Malinowski, President

ST. MARY'S REGIONAL MEDICAL CENTER, 45 Golder Street, Lewiston, ME, Zip 04240–6033, Mailing Address: P.O. Box 291, Zip 04243–0291; tel. 207/777–8100; James E. Cassidy, President and Chief Executive Officer

STEPHENS MEMORIAL HOSPITAL, 181 Main Street, Norway, ME, Zip 04268–1297; tel. 207/743–5933; Timothy A. Churchill, President

WALDO COUNTY GENERAL HOSPITAL, Northport Avenue, Belfast, ME, Zip 04915, Mailing Address: P.O. Box 287, Zip 04915–0287; tel. 207/338–2500; Mark A. Biscone, Executive Director

WESTBROOK COMMUNITY HOSPITAL, 40 Park Road, Westbrook, ME, Zip 04092–3158; tel. 207/854–8464; Charlene Wallace, Interim President

YORK HOSPITAL, 15 Hospital Drive, York, ME, Zip 03909–1099; tel. 207/351–2395; Jud Knox, President

MARYLAND

DIMENSIONS HEALTHCARE SYSTEM
9200 Basil Court, Landover, MD 20785; tel. 410/792–0294; Winfield M. Kelly, Jr, President & CEO

LAUREL REGIONAL HOSPITAL, 7300 Van Dusen Road, Laurel, MD, Zip 20707–9266; tel. 301/725–4300; Patrick F. Mutch, President

PRINCE GEORGE'S HOSPITAL CENTER, 3001 Hospital Drive, Cheverly, MD, Zip 20785–1189; tel. 301/618–2000; Phyllis Wingate–Jones, President

JOHNS HOPKINS HEALTH SYSTEM
600 North Wolfe Street, Baltimore, MD 21287; tel. 410/955–3180; Edward D. Miller, MD, Dean

JOHNS HOPKINS BAYVIEW MEDICAL CENTER, 4940 Eastern Avenue, Baltimore, MD, Zip 21224–2780; tel. 410/550–0100; Gregory F. Schaffer, Senior Vice President Operations

JOHNS HOPKINS HOSPITAL, 600 North Wolfe Street, Baltimore, MD, Zip 21287–0002; tel. 410/955–5000; Ronald R. Peterson, President

KENT & QUEEN ANNE'S HOSPITAL, 100 Brown Street, Chestertown, MD, Zip 21620–1499; tel. 410/778–3300; William R. Kirk, Jr., President and Chief Executive Officer

SUBURBAN HOSPITAL, 8600 Old Georgetown Road, Bethesda, MD, Zip 20814–1497; tel. 301/896–3100; Brian G. Grissler, President and Chief Executive Officer

MARYLAND HEALTH NETWORK
1508 Woodlawn Drive, Suite 13, Baltimore, MD 21044; tel. 410/594–2401; Peter Clay, President

GREATER BALTIMORE MEDICAL CENTER, 6701 North Charles Street, Baltimore, MD, Zip 21204–6892; tel. 410/828–2000; Robert P. Kowal, President and Chief Executive Officer

HOLY CROSS HOSPITAL OF SILVER SPRING, 1500 Forest Glen Road, Silver Spring, MD, Zip 20910–1484; tel. 301/754–7000; Kevin J. Sexton, President and Chief Executive Officer

MONTGOMERY GENERAL HOSPITAL, 18101 Prince Philip Drive, Olney, MD, Zip 20832–1512; tel. 301/774–8882; Peter W. Monge, President and Chief Executive Officer

NORTHWEST HOSPITAL CENTER, 5401 Old Court Road, Randallstown, MD, Zip 21133–5185; tel. 410/521–2200; Robert W. Fischer, President

ST. AGNES HEALTHCARE, 900 Caton Avenue, Baltimore, MD, Zip 21229–5299; tel. 410/368–6000; Robert W. Adams, President and Chief Executive Officer

MEDSTAR HEALTH
2330 West Joppa Road Suite 301, Lutherville, MD 21093; tel. 410/772–6500; John McDaniel, President & CEO

CHURCH HOSPITAL CORPORATION, 100 North Broadway, Baltimore, MD, Zip 21231–1593; tel. 410/522–8000; Ann C. Failing, President

FRANKLIN SQUARE HOSPITAL CENTER, 9000 Franklin Square Drive, Baltimore, MD, Zip 21237–3998; tel. 410/682–7000; Charles D. Mross, President

GOOD SAMARITAN HOSPITAL OF MARYLAND, 5601 Loch Raven Boulevard, Baltimore, MD, Zip 21239–2995; tel. 410/532–8000; Lawrence M. Beck, President

UNION MEMORIAL HOSPITAL, 201 East University Parkway, Baltimore, MD, Zip 21218–2391; tel. 410/554–2000; Harry Ryder, President and Chief Executive Officer

UNIVERSITY OF MARYLAND MEDICAL SYSTEM
14 Univ of Maryland Avenue, Baltimore, MD 21201; tel. 410/328–3322; Morton I. Rapaport, MD, President & CEO

DEATON SPECIALTY HOSPITAL AND HOME, 611 South Charles Street, Baltimore, MD, Zip 21230–3898; tel. 410/547–8500; James E. Ross, FACHE, Chief Executive Officer

JAMES LAWRENCE KERNAN HOSPITAL, 2200 Kernan Drive, Baltimore, MD, Zip 21207–6697; tel. 410/448–2500; James E. Ross, FACHE, Chief Executive Officer

UNIVERSITY OF MARYLAND MEDICAL SYSTEM, 22 South Greene Street, Baltimore, MD, Zip 21201–1595; tel. 410/328–8667; Morton I. Rapaport, M.D., President and Chief Executive Officer

MASSACHUSETTS

BAYSTATE HEALTH SYSTEM
759 Chestnut Street, Springfield, MA 01199;
tel. 413/784-0000; Michael J. Daly,
President & CEO

BAYSTATE MEDICAL CENTER, 759 Chestnut Street, Springfield, MA, Zip 01199-0001; tel. 413/794-0000; Mark R. Tolosky, Chief Executive Officer

FRANKLIN MEDICAL CENTER, 164 High Street, Greenfield, MA, Zip 01301-2613; tel. 413/773-0211; Harlan J. Smith, President and Chief Executive Officer

MARY LANE HOSPITAL, 85 South Street, Ware, MA, Zip 01082-1697; tel. 413/967-6211; Christine Shirtcliff, Executive Vice President

BERKSHIRE HEALTH SYSTEM
725 North Street, Pittsfield, MA 01201;
tel. 413/447-2000; David Phelps, President

BERKSHIRE MEDICAL CENTER, 725 North Street, Pittsfield, MA, Zip 01201-4124; tel. 413/447-2000; Ruth P. Blodgett, Chief Operating Officer

FAIRVIEW HOSPITAL, 29 Lewis Avenue, Great Barrington, MA, Zip 01230-1713; tel. 413/528-0790; Claire L. Bowen, President

BETH ISRAEL HEALTHCARE
330 Brookline Avenue, Boston, MA 02215;
tel. 617/735-2000; Mitchell T. Rabkin,
President

CAPE COD HEALTHCARE, INC.
88 Lewis Bay Road, Hyannisport, MA 02601;
tel. 508/771-1800; Steven Abbott, Chief
Executive Officer

CAPE COD HOSPITAL, 27 Park Street, Hyannis, MA, Zip 02601-5203; tel. 508/771-1800; Gail M. Frieswick, Ed.D., President and Chief Executive Officer

FALMOUTH HOSPITAL, 100 Ter Heun Drive, Falmouth, MA, Zip 02540-2599; tel. 508/457-3500; Gail Frieswick, President

CARITAS CHRISTI HEALTH
736 Cambridge Street, Boston, MA 02135;
tel. 617/789-2500; Michael F. Collins, M.D.,
President & Chief Executive

GOOD SAMARITAN MEDICAL CENTER, 235 North Pearl Street, Brockton, MA, Zip 02401-1794; tel. 508/427-3000; Frank J. Larkin, President and Chief Executive Officer

HOLY FAMILY HOSPITAL AND MEDICAL CENTER, 70 East Street, Methuen, MA, Zip 01844-4597; tel. 978/687-0151; William L. Lane, President

SAINT ANNE'S HOSPITAL, 795 Middle Street, Fall River, MA, Zip 02721-1798; tel. 508/674-5741; Michael W. Metzler, President

ST. ELIZABETH'S MEDICAL CENTER OF BOSTON, 736 Cambridge Street, Brighton, MA, Zip 02135-2997; tel. 617/789-3000; Michael F. Collins, M.D., President

ST. JOHN OF GOD HOSPITAL, 296 Allston Street, Brighton, MA, Zip 02146-1659; tel. 617/277-5750; William K. Brinkert, President

CHILDREN'S HOSPITAL
300 Longwood Avenue, Boston, MA 02115;
tel. 617/355-8555; David S. Weiner, VP of
Network Dev

CHILDREN'S HOSPITAL, 300 Longwood Avenue, Boston, MA, Zip 02115-5737; tel. 617/355-6000; Stephen R. Laverty, President and Chief Operating Officer

CONTINUUM OF CARE NETWORK
57 Union Street, Marlborough, MA 01752;
tel. 508/481-5000; Cheryl Herberg, Network
Coordinator

UMASS MARLBOROUGH HOSPITAL, 57 Union Street, Marlborough, MA, Zip 01752-1297; tel. 508/481-5000; Annette B. Leahy, Chief Executive Officer

FALLON HEALTHCARE SYSTEM
Chestnut Pl, 10 Chestnut Street, Worcester,
MA 01608; tel. 508/799-2100; Margaret
McKenna, Director of Provider Relations

ATHOL MEMORIAL HOSPITAL, 2033 Main Street, Athol, MA, Zip 01331-3598; tel. 978/249-3511; William DiFederico, President

BETH ISRAEL DEACONESS MEDICAL CENTER, 330 Brookline Avenue, Boston, MA, Zip 02215-5491; tel. 617/667-7000; Herbert Yehude Kressel, M.D., President

BRIGHAM AND WOMEN'S HOSPITAL, 75 Francis Street, Boston, MA, Zip 02115-6195; tel. 617/732-5500; Jeffrey Otten, President

CHILDREN'S HOSPITAL, 300 Longwood Avenue, Boston, MA, Zip 02115-5737; tel. 617/355-6000; Stephen R. Laverty, President and Chief Operating Officer

CLINTON HOSPITAL, 201 Highland Street, Clinton, MA, Zip 01510-1096; tel. 978/368-3000; Thomas Devins, President

DANA-FARBER CANCER INSTITUTE, 44 Binney Street, Boston, MA, Zip 02115-6084; tel. 617/632-3000; David G. Nathan, M.D., President

DEACONESS WALTHAM HOSPITAL, Hope Avenue, Waltham, MA, Zip 02254-9116; tel. 781/647-6000; Allen Danis, Acting Administrator

DEACONESS-GLOVER HOSPITAL CORPORATION, 148 Chestnut Street, Needham, MA, Zip 02192-2483; tel. 781/453-3000; John Dalton, President and Chief Executive Officer

DEACONESS-NASHOBA HOSPITAL, 200 Groton Road, Ayer, MA, Zip 01432-3300; tel. 978/784-9000; Jeffrey R. Kelly, President and Chief Executive Officer

HARRINGTON MEMORIAL HOSPITAL, 100 South Street, Southbridge, MA, Zip 01550-4045; tel. 508/765-9771; Richard M. Mangion, President and Chief Executive Officer

HEALTH ALLIANCE HOSPITALS, 60 Hospital Road, Leominster, MA, Zip 01453-8004; tel. 978/466-2000; Jonathan H. Robbins, M.D., President and Chief Executive Officer

HOLY FAMILY HOSPITAL AND MEDICAL CENTER, 70 East Street, Methuen, MA, Zip 01844-4597; tel. 978/687-0151; William L. Lane, President

HUBBARD REGIONAL HOSPITAL, 340 Thompson Road, Webster, MA, Zip 01570-0608; tel. 508/943-2600; Gerald J. Barbini, Administrator and Chief Executive Officer

LAWRENCE GENERAL HOSPITAL, 1 General Street, Lawrence, MA, Zip 01842-0389, Mailing Address: P.O. Box 189, Zip 01842-0389; tel. 978/683-4000; Joseph S. McManus, President and Chief Executive Officer

MASSACHUSETTS GENERAL HOSPITAL, 55 Fruit Street, Boston, MA, Zip 02114-2696; tel. 617/726-2000; James J. Mongan, M.D., President

MILFORD-WHITINSVILLE REGIONAL HOSPITAL, 14 Prospect Street, Milford, MA, Zip 01757-3090; tel. 508/473-1190; Francis M. Saba, President and Chief Executive Officer

NEW ENGLAND BAPTIST HOSPITAL, 125 Parker Hill Avenue, Boston, MA, Zip 02120-3297; tel. 617/754-5800; Alan H. Robbins, M.D., President

SAINT VINCENT HOSPITAL, 25 Winthrop Street, Worcester, MA, Zip 01604-4593; tel. 508/798-1234; Robert E. Maher, Jr., President and Chief Executive Officer

SAINTS MEMORIAL MEDICAL CENTER, One Hospital Drive, Lowell, MA, Zip 01852-1389; tel. 978/458-1411; Thom Clark, President and Chief Executive Officer

UMASS MARLBOROUGH HOSPITAL, 57 Union Street, Marlborough, MA, Zip 01752-1297; tel. 508/481-5000; Annette B. Leahy, Chief Executive Officer

LAHEY NETWORK
41 Mall Road, Burlington, MA 01805;
tel. 718/744-8000; Dr. L. Bertino, President

ATLANTICARE MEDICAL CENTER, 500 Lynnfield Street, Lynn, MA, Zip 01904-1487; tel. 781/581-9200; Andrew J. Riddell, President

LAHEY CLINIC HOSPITAL, 41 Mall Road, Burlington, MA, Zip 01805-0001; tel. 781/744-8330; John A. Libertino, M.D., Chief Executive Officer

MARY HITCHCOCK MEMORIAL HOSPITAL, One Medical Center Drive, Lebanon, NH, Zip 03756-0001; tel. 603/650-5000; James W. Varnum, President

SOUTHERN NEW HAMPSHIRE MEDICAL CENTER, 8 Prospect Street, Nashua, NH, Zip 03060, Mailing Address: P.O. Box 2014, Zip 03061-2014; tel. 603/577-2000; Thomas E. Wilhelmsen, Jr., President and Chief Executive Officer

WING MEMORIAL HOSPITAL AND MEDICAL CENTERS, 40 Wright Street, Palmer, MA, Zip 01069-1138; tel. 413/283-7651; Richard H. Scheffer, President

NEW ENGLAND MEDICAL CENTER
750 Washington Street NEMC Box 451,
Boston, MA 02111; tel. 617/636-9589;
Thomas O'donnell, President

BOSTON MEDICAL CENTER, One Boston Medical Center Place, Boston, MA, Zip 02118-2393; tel. 617/638-8000; Elaine S. Ullian, President and Chief Executive Officer

HALE HOSPITAL, 140 Lincoln Avenue, Haverhill, MA, Zip 01830-6798; tel. 978/374-2000; Robert J. Ingala, Chief Executive Officer

HUBBARD REGIONAL HOSPITAL, 340 Thompson Road, Webster, MA, Zip 01570-0608; tel. 508/943-2600; Gerald J. Barbini, Administrator and Chief Executive Officer

LAHEY CLINIC HOSPITAL, 41 Mall Road, Burlington, MA, Zip 01805-0001; tel. 781/744-8330; John A. Libertino, M.D., Chief Executive Officer

MALDEN MEDICAL CENTER, 100 Hospital Road, Malden, MA, Zip 02148-3591; tel. 781/322-7560

QUINCY HOSPITAL, 114 Whitwell Street, Quincy, MA, Zip 02169-1899; tel. 617/773-6100; Jeffrey Doran, Chief Executive Officer

NORTHEAST HEALTH SYSTEMS
85 Herrick Street, Beverly, MA 01915;
tel. 978/922-3000; Elisabeth Babcock, Vice
President of Network

BEVERLY HOSPITAL, 85 Herrrick Street, Beverly, MA, Zip 01915-1777; tel. 978/922-3000; Robert R. Fanning, Jr., Chief Executive Officer

PARTNERS HEALTHCARE SYSYTEM
32 Fruit Street, Boston, MA 02114;
tel. 617/732-5500; John McGonagle,
Dir-Comm Hlth Servs

BRIGHAM AND WOMEN'S HOSPITAL, 75 Francis Street, Boston, MA, Zip 02115-6195; tel. 617/732-5500; Jeffrey Otten, President

MASSACHUSETTS GENERAL HOSPITAL, 55 Fruit Street, Boston, MA, Zip 02114-2696; tel. 617/726-2000; James J. Mongan, M.D., President

SALEM HOSPITAL, 81 Highland Avenue, Salem, MA, Zip 01970-2768; tel. 978/741-1200; Stanley Reczek, President

SHAUGHNESSY-KAPLAN REHABILITATION HOSPITAL, Dove Avenue, Salem, MA, Zip 01970-2999; tel. 978/745-9000; Anthony Sciola, President

PATHWAY HEALTH NETWORK
1 Deaconess Road, Boston, MA 02215;
tel. 617/632-9967; Susan K. Glazer, VP -
Planning

BETH ISRAEL DEACONESS MEDICAL CENTER, 330 Brookline Avenue, Boston, MA, Zip 02215-5491; tel. 617/667-7000; Herbert Yehude Kressel, M.D., President

DEACONESS WALTHAM HOSPITAL, Hope Avenue, Waltham, MA, Zip 02254-9116; tel. 781/647-6000; Allen Danis, Acting Administrator

DEACONESS-GLOVER HOSPITAL CORPORATION, 148 Chestnut Street, Needham, MA, Zip 02192-2483; tel. 781/453-3000; John Dalton, President and Chief Executive Officer

Section B

DEACONESS–NASHOBA HOSPITAL, 200 Groton Road, Ayer, MA, Zip 01432–3300; tel. 978/784–9000; Jeffrey R. Kelly, President and Chief Executive Officer

MOUNT AUBURN HOSPITAL, 330 Mount Auburn Street, Cambridge, MA, Zip 02138; tel. 617/499–5700; Jeanette G. Clough, President and Chief Executive Officer

NEW ENGLAND BAPTIST HOSPITAL, 125 Parker Hill Avenue, Boston, MA, Zip 02120–3297; tel. 617/754–5800; Alan H. Robbins, M.D., President

SISTERS OF PROVIDENCE HEALTH
85 Spring Street, Springfield, MA 01105; tel. 413/736–5494; Geraldine Noonan, Administrator

MERCY HOSPITAL, 271 Carew Street, Springfield, MA, Zip 01104–2398, Mailing Address: P.O. Box 9012, Zip 01102–9012; tel. 413/748–9000; Vincent J. McCorkle, President

MICHIGAN

BATTLE CREEK HEALTH SYSTEM
300 North Avenue, Battle Creek, MI 49016; tel. 616/966–8000; Arthur Knueppeal, President

BATTLE CREEK HEALTH SYSTEM, 300 North Avenue, Battle Creek, MI, Zip 49016–3396; tel. 616/966–8000; Arthur Knueppel, Interim President and Chief Executive Officer

BORGESS HEALTH ALLIANCE
1521 Gull Road, Kalamazoo, MI 49001; tel. 616/226–7000; Mike Alfred, Executive Director, Business Dev. & Public Relations

BORGESS MEDICAL CENTER, 1521 Gull Road, Kalamazoo, MI, Zip 49001–1640; tel. 616/226–4800; Randall Stasik, President and Chief Executive Officer

COMMUNITY HEALTH CENTER OF BRANCH COUNTY, 274 East Chicago Street, Coldwater, MI, Zip 49036–2088; tel. 517/279–5400; Lieutenant Douglas L. Rahn, Chief Executive Officer

COMMUNITY HOSPITAL, Medical Park Drive, Watervliet, MI, Zip 49098–0158, Mailing Address: P.O. Box 158, Zip 49098–0158; tel. 616/463–3111; Dennis Turney, Chief Executive Officer

DOCTORS HOSPITAL OF JACKSON, 110 North Elm Avenue, Jackson, MI, Zip 49202–3595; tel. 517/787–1440; Michael J. Falatko, President and Chief Executive Officer

HILLSDALE COMMUNITY HEALTH CENTER, 168 South Howell Street, Hillsdale, MI, Zip 49242–2081; tel. 517/437–4451; Charles A. Bianchi, President

LEE MEMORIAL HOSPITAL, 420 West High Street, Dowagiac, MI, Zip 49047–1907; tel. 616/782–8681; Fritz Fahrenbacher, President and Chief Executive Officer

THREE RIVERS AREA HOSPITAL, 1111 West Broadway, Three Rivers, MI, Zip 49093–9362; tel. 616/278–1145; Matthew Chambers, Chief Executive Officer

BUTTERWORTH HEALTH SYSTEM
100 Michigan St. S.E., Grand Rapids, MI 49503; tel. 616/776–2008; Carol Sarosik, Regional VP

CARSON CITY HOSPITAL, 406 East Elm Street, Carson City, MI, Zip 48811–0879, Mailing Address: P.O. Box 879, Zip 48811–0879; tel. 517/584–3131; Bruce L. Traverse, President

GERBER MEMORIAL HOSPITAL, 212 South Sullivan Street, Fremont, MI, Zip 49412–1596; tel. 616/924–3300; Ned B. Hughes, Jr., President

METROPOLITAN HOSPITAL, 1919 Boston Street S.E., Grand Rapids, MI, Zip 49506–4199, Mailing Address: P.O. Box 158, Zip 49501–0158; tel. 616/252–7200; Michael D. Faas, President and Chief Executive Officer

PINE REST CHRISTIAN MENTAL HEALTH SERVICES, 300 68th Street S.E., Grand Rapids, MI, Zip 49501–0165, Mailing Address: P.O. Box 165, Zip 49501–0165; tel. 616/455–5000; Daniel L. Holwerda, President and Chief Executive Officer

SPECTRUM HEALTH–DOWNTOWN CAMPUS, 100 Michigan Street N.E., Grand Rapids, MI, Zip 49503–2551; tel. 616/391–1774; William G. Gonzalez, Pres

UNITED MEMORIAL HOSPITAL ASSOCIATION, 615 South Bower Street, Greenville, MI, Zip 48838–2628; tel. 616/754–4691; Dennis G. Zielinski, Chief Executive Officer

ZEELAND COMMUNITY HOSPITAL, 100 South Pine Street, Zeeland, MI, Zip 49464–1619; tel. 616/772–4644; Henry A. Veenstra, President

DETROIT MEDICAL CENTER
4201 St. Antoine Boulevard, Detroit, MI 48201; tel. 313/745–3605; Douglas Keegan, VP Planning

CHILDREN'S HOSPITAL OF MICHIGAN, 3901 Beaubien Street, Detroit, MI, Zip 48201–9985; tel. 313/745–0073; Larry Fleischmann, M.D., Interim Senior Vice President

DETROIT RECEIVING HOSPITAL AND UNIVERSITY HEALTH CENTER, 4201 St. Antoine Boulevard, Detroit, MI, Zip 48201–2194; tel. 313/745–3603; Leslie C. Bowman, Regional Administrator, Ancillary Services and Site Administrator

GRACE HOSPITAL, 6071 West Outer Drive, Detroit, MI, Zip 48235–2679; tel. 313/966–3525; Anne M. Regling, Senior Vice President

HARPER HOSPITAL, 3990 John R, Detroit, MI, Zip 48201–9027; tel. 313/745–8040; John R. Whitcomb, Interim Senior Vice President

HURON VALLEY–SINAI HOSPITAL, 1 William Carls Drive, Commerce Township, MI, Zip 48382–2201; tel. 248/360–3300; Robert J. Yellan, Senior Vice President

HUTZEL HOSPITAL, 4707 St. Antoine Boulevard, Detroit, MI, Zip 48201–0154; tel. 313/745–7555; Mark McNash, Operations Officer

REHABILITATION INSTITUTE OF MICHIGAN, 261 Mack Boulevard, Detroit, MI, Zip 48201–2495; tel. 313/745–1203; Bruce M. Gans, M.D., Senior Vice President

DETROIT–MACOMB HOSPITAL CORP
11800 East Twelve Mile Road, Warren, MI 48093; tel. 313/573–5000; George P. Karolis, Administrator

ST. JOHN DETROIT RIVERVIEW HOSPITAL, 7733 East Jefferson Avenue, Detroit, MI, Zip 48214–2598; tel. 313/499–4000; Richard T. Young, President

ST. JOHN MACOMB HOSPITAL, 11800 East Twelve Mile Road, Warren, MI, Zip 48093–3494; tel. 810/573–5000; John E. Knox, President

FIRST CHOICE NETWORK
60 Kalamazoo Ave., South Haven, MI 49090; tel. 616/637–1690; Anne Watkins, President

COMMUNITY HOSPITAL, Medical Park Drive, Watervliet, MI, Zip 49098–0158, Mailing Address: P.O. Box 158, Zip 49098–0158; tel. 616/463–3111; Dennis Turney, Chief Executive Officer

LEE MEMORIAL HOSPITAL, 420 West High Street, Dowagiac, MI, Zip 49047–1907; tel. 616/782–8681; Fritz Fahrenbacher, President and Chief Executive Officer

GENESYS HEALTH SYSTEM
302 Kensington Avenue, Flint, MI 48503–2000; tel. 810/762–8675; Mark Harris, Director of Marketing

GREAT LAKES HEALTH NETWORK
P.O. Box 5153, Southfield, MI 48086; tel. 810/356–3460; Barbara Potter, Network Coordinator

BI–COUNTY COMMUNITY HOSPITAL, 13355 East Ten Mile Road, Warren, MI, Zip 48089–2065; tel. 810/759–7300; Gary W. Popiel, Executive Vice President and Chief Executive Officer

BOTSFORD GENERAL HOSPITAL, 28050 Grand River Avenue, Farmington Hills, MI, Zip 48336–5933; tel. 248/471–8000; Gerson I. Cooper, President

GARDEN CITY HOSPITAL, 6245 North Inkster Road, Garden City, MI, Zip 48135–4001; tel. 734/421–3300; Gary R. Ley, President and Chief Executive Officer

MOUNT CLEMENS GENERAL HOSPITAL, 1000 Harrington Boulevard, Mount Clemens, MI, Zip 48043–2992; tel. 810/493–8000; Robert Milewski, President and Chief Executive Officer

POH MEDICAL CENTER, 50 North Perry Street, Pontiac, MI, Zip 48342–2253; tel. 810/338–5000; Patrick Lamberti, Chief Executive Officer

RIVERSIDE OSTEOPATHIC HOSPITAL, 150 Truax Street, Trenton, MI, Zip 48183–2151; tel. 734/676–4200; Dennis R. Lemanski, D.O., Vice President and Chief Executive Officer

ST. JOHN OAKLAND HOSPITAL, 27351 Dequindre, Madison Heights, MI, Zip 48071–3499; tel. 248/967–7000; Robert Deputat, President

HENRY FORD HEALTH SYSTEM
One Ford Place, Detroit, MI 48202; tel. 313/874–3436; Mehul Patel, Admin. Fellow

BI–COUNTY COMMUNITY HOSPITAL, 13355 East Ten Mile Road, Warren, MI, Zip 48089–2065; tel. 810/759–7300; Gary W. Popiel, Executive Vice President and Chief Executive Officer

COTTAGE HOSPITAL, 159 Kercheval Avenue, Grosse Pointe Farms, MI, Zip 48236–3692; tel. 313/640–1000; Richard Van Lith, Chief Executive Officer

HENRY FORD COTTAGE HOSPITAL, 2799 West Grand Boulevard, Detroit, MI, Zip 48202–2689; tel. 313/916–2600; Stephen H. Velick, Chief Executive Officer

HENRY FORD WYANDOTTE HOSPITAL, 2333 Biddle Avenue, Wyandotte, MI, Zip 48192–4693; tel. 734/284–2400; William R. Alvin, President

KINGSWOOD HOSPITAL, 10300 West Eight Mile Road, Ferndale, MI, Zip 48220–2198; tel. 248/398–3200; Glenn Black, Associate Vice President and Chief Operating Officer

RIVERSIDE OSTEOPATHIC HOSPITAL, 150 Truax Street, Trenton, MI, Zip 48183–2151; tel. 734/676–4200; Dennis R. Lemanski, D.O., Vice President and Chief Executive Officer

ST. JOSEPH MERCY OAKLAND, 900 Woodward Avenue, Pontiac, MI, Zip 48341–2985; tel. 248/858–3000; Thomas L. Feurig, President and Chief Executive Officer

ST. JOSEPH'S MERCY HOSPITALS AND HEALTH SERVICES, Clinton Township, MI, Jack Weiner, President and Chief Executive Officer

HOSPITAL NETWORK, INC.
252 East Lovell Street, Box 42, Kalamazoo, MI 49007; tel. 616/341–8888; George Angelidis, President/CEO

ALLEGAN GENERAL HOSPITAL, 555 Linn Street, Allegan, MI, Zip 49010–1594; tel. 616/673–8424; James A. Klun, President

BRONSON METHODIST HOSPITAL, 252 East Lovell Street, Kalamazoo, MI, Zip 49007–5345; tel. 616/341–6000; Frank J. Sardone, President and Chief Executive Officer

BRONSON VICKSBURG HOSPITAL, 13326 North Boulevard, Vicksburg, MI, Zip 49097–1099; tel. 616/649–2321; Frank J. Sardone, President

OAKLAWN HOSPITAL, 200 North Madison Street, Marshall, MI, Zip 49068–1199; tel. 616/781–4271; Rob Covert, President and Chief Executive Officer

STURGIS HOSPITAL, 916 Myrtle, Sturgis, MI, Zip 49091–2001; tel. 616/651–7824; David James, Chief Executive Officer

LAKELAND REGIONAL HEALTH SYSTEM
1234 Napier Avenue, St. Joseph, MI 49085; tel. 616/927–5363; Ben Hill, Marketing Department

BRONSON METHODIST HOSPITAL, 252 East Lovell Street, Kalamazoo, MI, Zip 49007–5345; tel. 616/341–6000; Frank J. Sardone, President and Chief Executive Officer

LAKELAND MEDICAL CENTER–ST. JOSEPH, 1234 Napier Avenue, Saint Joseph, MI, Zip 49085–2112; tel. 616/983–8300; Joseph A. Wasserman, President and Chief Executive Officer

SOUTH HAVEN COMMUNITY HOSPITAL, 955 South Bailey Avenue, South Haven, MI, Zip 49090; tel. 616/637–5271; Craig J. Marks, President and Chief Executive Officer

MUNSON HEALTH CARE SYSTEM
1105 Sixth Street, Traverse City, MI 49684; tel. 616/935–6000; John M. Rockwood, President & CEO

KALKASKA MEMORIAL HEALTH CENTER, 419 South Coral Street, Kalkaska, MI, Zip 49646; tel. 616/258–7500; James D. Austin, CHE, Administrator

LEELANAU MEMORIAL HEALTH CENTER, 215 South High Street, Northport, MI, Zip 49670, Mailing Address: P.O. Box 217, Zip 49670–0217; tel. 616/386–0000; Jayne R. Bull, Administrator

PAUL OLIVER MEMORIAL HOSPITAL, 224 Park Avenue, Frankfort, MI, Zip 49635; tel. 616/352–9621; James D. Austin, CHE, Administrator

MUSKEGON MERCY COM HLTH CARE SYSTEM
1500 East Sherman Boulevard, Muskegon, MI 49443; tel. 616/739–3948; Roger Spoelman, President Partners & Chief Executive

PORT HURON HOSPITAL
1221 Pine Grove Avenue, Port Huron, MI 48060; tel. 810/989–3708; Gary LeRoy, Consultant

PORT HURON HOSPITAL, 1221 Pine Grove Avenue, Port Huron, MI, Zip 48061–5011; tel. 810/987–5000; Donald C. Fletcher, President and Chief Executive Officer

ST. JOHN RIVER DISTRICT HOSPITAL, 4100 River Road, East China, MI, Zip 48054; tel. 810/329–7111; Frank W. Poma, President

ST. JOHN HEALTH SYSTEM
22101 Moross Road, Detroit, MI 48236; tel. 313/343–4000; Mark J. Brady, Sr. Planning Analyst

PORT HURON HOSPITAL, 1221 Pine Grove Avenue, Port Huron, MI, Zip 48061–5011; tel. 810/987–5000; Donald C. Fletcher, President and Chief Executive Officer

ST. JOHN DETROIT RIVERVIEW HOSPITAL, 7733 East Jefferson Avenue, Detroit, MI 48214–2598; tel. 313/499–4000; Richard T. Young, President

ST. JOHN MACOMB HOSPITAL, 11800 East Twelve Mile Road, Warren, MI, Zip 48093–3494; tel. 810/573–5000; John E. Knox, President

ST. JOHN NORTHEAST COMMUNITY HOSPITAL, 4777 East Outer Drive, Detroit, MI, Zip 48234–0401; tel. 313/369–9100; Michael F. Breen, President

ST. JOHN OAKLAND HOSPITAL, 27351 Dequindre, Madison Heights, MI, Zip 48071–3499; tel. 248/967–7000; Robert Deputat, President

ST. JOHN RIVER DISTRICT HOSPITAL, 4100 River Road, East China, MI, Zip 48054; tel. 810/329–7111; Frank W. Poma, President

WILLIAM BEAUMONT HOSPITAL
3601 W. Thirteen Mile Road, Royal Oak, MI 48073–6769; tel. 248/551–6405; Holli Zwar, Planning Specialist

ST. MARY HOSPITAL, 36475 West Five Mile Road, Livonia, MI, Zip 48154–1988; tel. 734/655–4800; Sister Mary Renetta Rumpz, FACHE, President and Chief Executive Officer

WILLIAM BEAUMONT HOSPITAL–ROYAL OAK, 3601 West Thirteen Mile Road, Royal Oak, MI, Zip 48073–6769; tel. 248/551–5000; John D. Labriola, Senior Vice President and Hospital Director

WILLIAM BEAUMONT HOSPITAL–TROY, 44201 Dequindre Road, Troy, MI, Zip 48098–1198; tel. 248/828–5100; Eugene F. Michalski, Vice President and Director

MINNESOTA

AFFILIATED COMMUNITY HEALTH NETWORK, INC
101 Wilmar Avenue S.W., Willmar, MN 56201; tel. 612/231–6719; Burnell J. Mellema MD, President

AVERA MCKENNAN HOSPITAL, 800 East 21st Street, Sioux Falls, SD, Zip 57105–1096, Mailing Address: P.O. Box 5045, Zip 57117–5045; tel. 605/322–8000; Fredrick Slunecka, President and Chief Executive Officer

REDWOOD FALLS MUNICIPAL HOSPITAL, 100 Fallwood Road, Redwood Falls, MN, Zip 56283–1828; tel. 507/637–2907; James E. Schulte, Administrator

RICE MEMORIAL HOSPITAL, 301 Becker Avenue S.W., Willmar, MN, Zip 56201–3395; tel. 320/235–4543; Lawrence J. Massa, Chief Executive Officer

WEINER MEMORIAL MEDICAL CENTER, 300 South Bruce Street, Marshall, MN, Zip 56258–1934; tel. 507/532–9661; Richard G. Slieter, Jr., Administrator

WILLMAR REGIONAL TREATMENT CENTER, North Highway 71, Willmar, MN, Zip 56201–1128, Mailing Address: Box 1128, Zip 56201–1128; tel. 320/231–5100; Gregory G. Spartz, Chief Executive Officer

ALLINA HEALTH SYSTEM
5601 Smetana Drive, Minnetonka, MN 55343; tel. 612/992–3648; Ann Fleischauer, Vice President Physician Communication

ABBOTT NORTHWESTERN HOSPITAL, 800 East 28th Street, Minneapolis, MN, Zip 55407–3799; tel. 612/863–4201; Mark Dixon, Administrator

BUFFALO HOSPITAL, 303 Catlin Street, Buffalo, MN, Zip 55313–1947; tel. 612/682–7180; Mary Ellen Wells, Administrator

CAMBRIDGE MEDICAL CENTER, 701 South Dellwood Street, Cambridge, MN, Zip 55008–1920; tel. 612/689–7700; Anne Renz, Interim Administrator

FAIRMONT COMMUNITY HOSPITAL, 835 Johnson Street, Fairmont, MN, Zip 56031, Mailing Address: P.O. Box 835, Zip 56031–0835; tel. 507/238–8100; Gerry Gilbertson, Administrator

GRANITE FALLS MUNICIPAL HOSPITAL AND MANOR, 345 Tenth Avenue, Granite Falls, MN, Zip 56241–1499; tel. 320/564–3111; George Gerlach, Administrator

HUTCHINSON AREA HEALTH CARE, 1095 Highway 15 South, Hutchinson, MN, Zip 55350–3182; tel. 320/234–5000; Philip G. Graves, Administrator

LONG PRAIRIE MEMORIAL HOSPITAL AND HOME, 20 Ninth Street S.E., Long Prairie, MN, Zip 56347–1404; tel. 320/732–2141; Clayton R. Peterson, President

MILLE LACS HEALTH SYSTEM, 200 North Elm Street, Onamia, MN, Zip 56359–7978; tel. 320/532–3154; Randall A. Farrow, Administrator

NEW ULM MEDICAL CENTER, 1324 Fifth Street North, New Ulm, MN, Zip 56073–1553, Mailing Address: P.O. Box 577, Zip 56073–0577; tel. 507/354–2111; David A. Grundstrom, Administrator

NORTHFIELD HOSPITAL, 801 West First Street, Northfield, MN, Zip 55057–1697; tel. 507/645–6661; Kendall C. Bank, Administrator

OWATONNA HOSPITAL, 903 Oak Street South, Owatonna, MN, Zip 55060–3234; tel. 507/451–3850; Daniel J. Werner, Administrator

PHILLIPS EYE INSTITUTE, 2215 Park Avenue, Minneapolis, MN, Zip 55404–3756; tel. 612/336–6000; Shari E. Levy, Administrator

RIVER FALLS AREA HOSPITAL, 1629 East Division Street, River Falls, WI, Zip 54022–1571; tel. 715/425–6155; Sharon Whelan, Administrator

ST. FRANCIS REGIONAL MEDICAL CENTER, 1455 St. Francis Avenue, Shakopee, MN, Zip 55379–3380; tel. 612/403–3000; Venetia Kudrle, Administrator

STEVENS COUNTY HOSPITAL, 1006 South Jackson Street, Hugoton, KS, Zip 67951–2842, Mailing Address: P.O. Box 10, Zip 67951–0010; tel. 316/544–8511; Ted Strote, Administrator

UNITED HOSPITAL, 333 North Smith Street, Saint Paul, MN, Zip 55102–2389; tel. 651/220–8000; M. Barbara Balik, MSN, Ed.D., Administrator

UNITED HOSPITAL DISTRICT, 515 South Moore Street, Blue Earth, MN, Zip 56013–2158, Mailing Address: P.O. Box 160, Zip 56013–0160; tel. 507/526–3273; Brian Kief, Administrator

CRITERION HEALTHCARE NETWORK
100 Washington Sq, Suite 748, Minneapolis, MN 55401; tel. 612/338–0700; Douglas Shaw, Executive Director

DAKOTA CLINIC
P.O. Box 65460, St. Paul, MN 55164; tel. 701/280–8631; Petrice Balkow Feick, Network Contact

FAIRVIEW HEALTH SYSTEM
2450 Riverside Avenue, Minneapolis, MN 53454; tel. 612/672–6267; Geri Martin, Network Contact

FAIRVIEW NORTHLAND REGIONAL HEALTH CARE, 911 Northland Drive, Princeton, MN, Zip 55371–2173; tel. 612/389–6300; Jeanne Lally, Senior Vice President and Administrator

FAIRVIEW RIDGES HOSPITAL, 201 East Nicollet Boulevard, Burnsville, MN, Zip 55337–5799; tel. 612/892–2000; Mark M. Enger, Senior Vice President and Administrator

FAIRVIEW SOUTHDALE HOSPITAL, 6401 France Avenue South, Minneapolis, MN, Zip 55435–2199; tel. 612/924–5000; Mark M. Enger, Senior Vice President and Administrator

FAIRVIEW–UNIVERSITY MEDICAL CENTER, 2450 Riverside Avenue, Minneapolis, MN, Zip 55454–1400; tel. 612/672–6000; Gordon L. Alexander, M.D., Senior Vice President and Administrator

HEALTHEAST
1450 Energy Park Drive, St. Paul, MN 55108; tel. 612/232–1000; Tim Hanson, President

HEALTHEAST BETHESDA REHABILITATION HOSPITAL, 559 Capitol Boulevard, Saint Paul, MN, Zip 55103–2101; tel. 651/232–2000; Scott Batulis, Vice President and Administrator

HEALTHEAST ST. JOHN'S HOSPITAL, 1575 Beam Avenue, Maplewood, MN, Zip 55109; tel. 651/232–7000; Douglas P. Cropper, Vice President and Administrator

HEALTHEAST ST. JOSEPH'S HOSPITAL, 69 West Exchange Street, Saint Paul, MN, Zip 55102–1053; tel. 651/232–3000; Douglas P. Cropper, Vice President and Administrator

HEALTHPARTNERS
8100 34th Avenue South, Minneapolis, MN 55440; tel. 612/883–5585; George Halverson, President

REGIONS HOSPITAL, 640 Jackson Street, Saint Paul, MN, Zip 55101–2595; tel. 651/221–3456; Terry S. Finzen, President

I–35 CORRIDOR HEALTH NETWORK
760 West Fourth Street, Rush City, MN 55069; tel. 612/358–4708; Lynn Clayton, Administrator

FAIRVIEW–UNIVERSITY MEDICAL CENTER, 2450 Riverside Avenue, Minneapolis, MN, Zip 55454–1400; tel. 612/672–6000; Gordon L. Alexander, M.D., Senior Vice President and Administrator

KANABEC HOSPITAL, 300 Clark Street, Mora, MN, Zip 55051–1590; tel. 320/679–1212; Thomas D. Kaufman, Administrator

MERCY HOSPITAL AND HEALTH CARE CENTER, 710 South Kenwood Avenue, Moose Lake, MN, Zip 55767–9405; tel. 218/485–4481; Dianne Mandernach, Chief Executive Officer

PINE MEDICAL CENTER, 109 Court Avenue South, Sandstone, MN, Zip 55072–5120; tel. 320/245–2212; Michael D. Hedrix, Administrator

Section B

ITASCA PARTNERSHIP FOR QUALITY HEALTHCARE
501 Pokegama Avenue, Grand Rapids, MN
55744; tel. 218/326–7513; Lee Jess, DDS,
President

DEER RIVER HEALTHCARE CENTER, 1002 Comstock
Drive, Deer River, MN, Zip 56636–9700;
tel. 218/246–2900; Jeffry Stampohar, Chief
Executive Officer

ITASCA MEDICAL CENTER, 126 First Avenue S.E.,
Grand Rapids, MN, Zip 55744–3698;
tel. 218/326–3401; Gary Kenner, President and
Chief Executive Officer

NORTHERN ITASCA HEALTH CARE CENTER, 258 Pine
Tree Drive, Bigfork, MN, Zip 56628, Mailing
Address: P.O. Box 258, Zip 56628–0258;
tel. 218/743–3177; Richard M. Ash, Chief
Executive Officer

MAYO FOUNDATION
200 S.W. First Street, Rochester, MN 55905;
tel. 507/284–8860; Dave Sperling, President

LUTHER HOSPITAL, 1221 Whipple Street, Eau Claire,
WI, Zip 54702–4105; tel. 715/838–3311;
William Rupp, M.D., President and Chief
Executive Officer

ROCHESTER METHODIST HOSPITAL, 201 West
Center Street, Rochester, MN, Zip 55902–3084;
tel. 507/266–7890; John M. Panicek,
Administrator

SAINT MARYS HOSPITAL, 1216 Second Street S.W.,
Rochester, MN, Zip 55902–1970;
tel. 507/255–5123; John M. Panicek,
Administrator

MINNESOTA RURAL HEALTH COOPERATIVE
P.O. Box 104, Willmar, MN 56201;
tel. 612/231–3849; Lyle Munneke, MD,
President & Chairperson

APPLETON MUNICIPAL HOSPITAL AND NURSING
HOME, 30 South Behl Street, Appleton, MN,
Zip 56208–1699; tel. 320/289–2422; Mark E.
Paulson, Administrator

CHIPPEWA COUNTY MONTEVIDEO HOSPITAL, 824
North 11th Street, Montevideo, MN,
Zip 56265–1683; tel. 320/269–8877; Fred
Knutson, Administrator

DIVINE PROVIDENCE HEALTH CENTER, 312 East
George Street, Ivanhoe, MN, Zip 56142–0136,
Mailing Address: P.O. Box G., Zip 56142–0136;
tel. 507/694–1414; Patrick Branco,
Administrator

GRACEVILLE HEALTH CENTER, 115 West Second
Street, Graceville, MN, Zip 56240–0157, Mailing
Address: P.O. Box 157, Zip 56240–0157;
tel. 320/748–7223; Helen Jorve, Chief
Executive Officer

GRANITE FALLS MUNICIPAL HOSPITAL AND MANOR,
345 Tenth Avenue, Granite Falls, MN,
Zip 56241–1499; tel. 320/564–3111; George
Gerlach, Administrator

HENDRICKS COMMUNITY HOSPITAL, 503 East Lincoln
Street, Hendricks, MN, Zip 56136–9598;
tel. 507/275–3134; Kirk Stensrud, Administrator

JOHNSON MEMORIAL HEALTH SERVICES, 1282
Walnut Street, Dawson, MN, Zip 56232–2333;
tel. 612/769–4323; Vern Silvernale,
Administrator

MADISON HOSPITAL, 820 Third Avenue, Madison,
MN, Zip 56256–1014, Mailing Address: P.O. Box
184, Zip 56256–0184; tel. 320/598–7556;
Thomas Richter, Chief Executive Officer

ORTONVILLE AREA HEALTH SERVICES, 750 Eastvold
Avenue, Ortonville, MN, Zip 56278–1133;
tel. 320/839–2502; Paul J. Anderson,
Administrator

REDWOOD FALLS MUNICIPAL HOSPITAL, 100
Fallwood Road, Redwood Falls, MN,
Zip 56283–1828; tel. 507/637–2907; James E.
Schulte, Administrator

RENVILLE COUNTY HOSPITAL, 611 East Fairview
Avenue, Olivia, MN, Zip 56277–1397;
tel. 320/523–1261; Dean G. Slagter,
Administrator

RICE MEMORIAL HOSPITAL, 301 Becker Avenue S.W.,
Willmar, MN, Zip 56201–3395;
tel. 320/235–4543; Lawrence J. Massa, Chief
Executive Officer

SIOUX VALLEY CANBY CAMPUS, 112 St. Olaf Avenue
South, Canby, MN, Zip 56220–1433;
tel. 507/223–7277; Robert J. Salmon, Chief
Executive Officer

SWIFT COUNTY–BENSON HOSPITAL, 1815 Wisconsin
Avenue, Benson, MN, Zip 56215–1653;
tel. 320/843–4232; Frank Lawatsch, Chief
Executive Officer

TYLER HEALTHCARE CENTER, 240 Willow Street,
Tyler, MN, Zip 56178–0280;
tel. 507/247–5521; James G. Blum,
Administrator

WEINER MEMORIAL MEDICAL CENTER, 300 South
Bruce Street, Marshall, MN, Zip 56258–1934;
tel. 507/532–9661; Richard G. Slieter, Jr.,
Administrator

NORTHERN LAKES HEALTH CONSORTIUM
600 East Superior Street, Suite 404, Duluth,
MN 55802; tel. 218/727–9393; Terry J. Hill,
Executive Director

CLOQUET COMMUNITY MEMORIAL HOSPITAL, 512
Skyline Boulevard, Cloquet, MN,
Zip 55720–1199; tel. 218/879–4641; James J.
Carroll, Administrator

COOK COUNTY NORTH SHORE HOSPITAL, Gunflint
Trail, Grand Marais, MN, Zip 55604, Mailing
Address: P.O. Box 10, Zip 55604–0010;
tel. 218/387–3040; Diane Pearson,
Administrator

COOK HOSPITAL AND CONVALESCENT NURSING
CARE UNIT, 10 South Fifth Street East, Cook,
MN, Zip 55723–9745; tel. 218/666–5945; Allen
J. Vogt, Administrator

CUMBERLAND MEMORIAL HOSPITAL, 1110 Seventh
Avenue, Cumberland, WI, Zip 54829, Mailing
Address: P.O. Box 37, Zip 54829–0037;
tel. 715/822–2741; Carol Kellermann, Acting
Administrator

CUYUNA REGIONAL MEDICAL CENTER, 320 East Main
Street, Crosby, MN, Zip 56441–1690;
tel. 218/546–7000; Thomas F. Reek, Chief
Executive Officer

DEER RIVER HEALTHCARE CENTER, 1002 Comstock
Drive, Deer River, MN, Zip 56636–9700;
tel. 218/246–2900; Jeffry Stampohar, Chief
Executive Officer

ELY–BLOOMENSON COMMUNITY HOSPITAL, 328
West Conan Street, Ely, MN, Zip 55731–1198;
tel. 218/365–3271; John Fossum, Administrator

FALLS MEMORIAL HOSPITAL, 1400 Highway 71,
International Falls, MN, Zip 56649–2189;
tel. 218/283–4481; Mary Klimp, Administrator
and Chief Executive Officer

FLAMBEAU HOSPITAL, 98 Sherry Avenue, Park Falls,
WI, Zip 54552–1467, Mailing Address: P.O. Box
310, Zip 54552–0310; tel. 715/762–2484;
Curtis A. Johnson, Administrator

GRAND VIEW HOSPITAL, N10561 Grand View Lane,
Ironwood, MI, Zip 49938–9359;
tel. 906/932–2525; Frederick Geissler, Chief
Executive Officer

HAYWARD AREA MEMORIAL HOSPITAL AND NURSING
HOME, 11040 State Road 77, Hayward, WI,
Zip 54843, Mailing Address: Route 3, Box 3999,
Zip 54843–3999; tel. 715/634–8911; Barbara
A. Peickert, R.N., Chief Executive Officer

ITASCA MEDICAL CENTER, 126 First Avenue S.E.,
Grand Rapids, MN, Zip 55744–3698;
tel. 218/326–3401; Gary Kenner, President and
Chief Executive Officer

LAKE VIEW MEMORIAL HOSPITAL, 325 11th Avenue,
Two Harbors, MN, Zip 55616–1298;
tel. 218/834–7300; Brian J. Carlson, President
and Chief Executive Officer

LAKEVIEW MEDICAL CENTER, 1100 North Main
Street, Rice Lake, WI, Zip 54868–1238;
tel. 715/234–1515; Edward H. Wolf, Chief
Executive Officer

MERCY HOSPITAL AND HEALTH CARE CENTER, 710
South Kenwood Avenue, Moose Lake, MN,
Zip 55767–9405; tel. 218/485–4481; Dianne
Mandernach, Chief Executive Officer

MILLE LACS HEALTH SYSTEM, 200 North Elm Street,
Onamia, MN, Zip 56359–7978;
tel. 320/532–3154; Randall A. Farrow,
Administrator

MILLER DWAN MEDICAL CENTER, 502 East Second
Street, Duluth, MN, Zip 55805–1982;
tel. 218/727–8762; William H. Palmer, President

NORTHERN ITASCA HEALTH CARE CENTER, 258 Pine
Tree Drive, Bigfork, MN, Zip 56628, Mailing
Address: P.O. Box 258, Zip 56628–0258;
tel. 218/743–3177; Richard M. Ash, Chief
Executive Officer

ONTONAGON MEMORIAL HOSPITAL, 601 Seventh
Street, Ontonagon, MI, Zip 49953–1496;
tel. 906/884–4134; Fred Nelson, Administrator

PINE MEDICAL CENTER, 109 Court Avenue South,
Sandstone, MN, Zip 55072–5120;
tel. 320/245–2212; Michael D. Hedrix,
Administrator

RIVERWOOD HEALTH CARECENTER, 301 Minnesota
Avenue South, Aitkin, MN, Zip 56431–1626;
tel. 218/927–2121; Debra Boardman, Chief
Executive Officer

SPOONER HEALTH SYSTEM, 819 Ash Street,
Spooner, WI, Zip 54801–1299;
tel. 715/635–2111; Michael Schafer, Chief
Executive Officer

ST. LUKE'S HOSPITAL, 915 East First Street, Duluth,
MN, Zip 55805–2193; tel. 218/726–5555; John
Strange, President and Chief Executive Officer

UNIVERSITY MEDICAL CENTER–MESABI, 750 East
34th Street, Hibbing, MN, Zip 55746–4600;
tel. 218/262–4881; Richard W. Dinter, M.D.,
Chief Operating Officer

VIRGINIA REGIONAL MEDICAL CENTER, 901 Ninth
Street North, Virginia, MN, Zip 55792–2398;
tel. 218/741–3340; Kyle Hopstad, Administrator

WHITE COMMUNITY HOSPITAL, 5211 Highway 110,
Aurora, MN, Zip 55705–1599;
tel. 218/229–2211; Larry Ravenberg,
Administrator

NORTHSTAR HEALTH CONSORTIUM
715 Delmore Drive, Roseau, MN 56751;
tel. 218/463–2500; Dave Hagen, Chairman

KITTSON MEMORIAL HEALTHCARE CENTER, 1010
South Birch Street, Hallock, MN, Zip 56728,
Mailing Address: P.O. Box 700,
Zip 56728–0700; tel. 218/843–3612; Richard
J. Failing, Chief Executive Officer

LAKEWOOD HEALTH CENTER, 600 South Main
Avenue, Baudette, MN, Zip 56623;
tel. 218/634–2120; SharRay Palm, President
and Chief Executive Officer

NORTH VALLEY HEALTH CENTER, 109 South
Minnesota Street, Warren, MN,
Zip 56762–1499; tel. 218/745–4211; Jon
Linnell, Administrator

ROSEAU AREA HOSPITAL AND HOMES, 715 Delmore
Avenue, Roseau, MN, Zip 56751–1599;
tel. 218/463–2500; David F. Hagen, President
and Chief Executive Officer

QUALITY HEALTH ALLIANCE
501 Holly Lane, Mankato, MN 56001;
tel. 507/389–8697; Linda Ridelhuber,
Executive Director

NEW ULM MEDICAL CENTER, 1324 Fifth Street North,
New Ulm, MN, Zip 56073–1553, Mailing
Address: P.O. Box 577, Zip 56073–0577;
tel. 507/354–2111; David A. Grundstrom,
Administrator

SLEEPY EYE MUNICIPAL HOSPITAL, 400 Fourth
Avenue N.W., Sleepy Eye, MN, Zip 56085–1109;
tel. 507/794–3571; Chad Cooper, Administrator

SPRINGFIELD MEDICAL CENTER–MAYO HEALTH
SYSTEM, 625 North Jackson Avenue,
Springfield, MN, Zip 56087–1714, Mailing
Address: P.O. Box 146, Zip 56087–0146;
tel. 507/723–6201; Scott Thoreson,
Administrator

ST. JAMES HEALTH SERVICES, 1207 Sixth Avenue
South, Saint James, MN, Zip 56081–2415;
tel. 507/375–3261; Lee Holter, Chief Executive
Officer

ST. PETER REGIONAL TREATMENT CENTER, 100
Freeman Drive, Saint Peter, MN,
Zip 56082–1599; tel. 507/931–7100; William L.
Pedersen, Chief Executive Officer

UNITED HOSPITAL DISTRICT, 515 South Moore Street, Blue Earth, MN, Zip 56013–2158, Mailing Address: P.O. Box 160, Zip 56013–0160; tel. 507/526–3273; Brian Kief, Administrator

WASECA MEDICAL CENTER, 100 Fifth Avenue N.W., Waseca, MN, Zip 56093–2422; tel. 507/835–1210; Michael Milbrath, Administrator

QUALITY HEALTH NETWORK
910 Main Street, Suite 202, Redwing, MN 55066; tel. 612/388–0750; Jerry Olson, President

FAIRVIEW RED WING HOSPITAL, 1407 West Fourth Street, Red Wing, MN, Zip 55066–2198; tel. 651/388–6721; Scott Wordelman, President and Chief Executive Officer

FAIRVIEW–UNIVERSITY MEDICAL CENTER, 2450 Riverside Avenue, Minneapolis, MN, Zip 55454–1400; tel. 612/672–6000; Gordon L. Alexander, M.D., Senior Vice President and Administrator

SOUTHWEST MINNESOTA HEALTH ALLIANCE
305 East Luverne Street, Luverne, MN 56156; tel. 507/283–2775; Jeff Stevenson, President

LUVERNE COMMUNITY HOSPITAL, 305 East Luverne Street, Luverne, MN, Zip 56156–2519, Mailing Address: P.O. Box 1019, Zip 56156–1019; tel. 507/283–2321; Gerald E. Carl, Administrator

MURRAY COUNTY MEMORIAL HOSPITAL, 2042 Juniper Avenue, Slayton, MN, Zip 56172–1016; tel. 507/836–6111; Jerry Bobeldyk, Administrator

SIOUX VALLEY CANBY CAMPUS, 112 St. Olaf Avenue South, Canby, MN, Zip 56220–1433; tel. 507/223–7277; Robert J. Salmon, Chief Executive Officer

TRACY AREA MEDICAL SERVICES, 251 Fifth Street East, Tracy, MN, Zip 56175–1536; tel. 507/629–3200; Thomas J. Quinlivan, Administrator

WINDOM AREA HOSPITAL, Highways 60 and 71 North, Windom, MN, Zip 56101, Mailing Address: P.O. Box 339, Zip 56101–0339; tel. 507/831–2400; J. Stephen Pautler, CHE, Administrator

WORTHINGTON REGIONAL HOSPITAL, 1018 Sixth Avenue, Worthington, MN, Zip 56187–2202, Mailing Address: P.O. Box 997, Zip 56187–0997; tel. 507/372–2941; Melvin J. Platt, Administrator

MISSISSIPPI

NORTH MISSISSIPPI HEALTH SERVICES
830 South Gloster, Tupelo, MS 38801; tel. 662/841–3148; Len Grice, Marketing Director

CLAY COUNTY MEDICAL CENTER, 835 Medical Center Drive, West Point, MS, Zip 39773–9320; tel. 601/495–2300; David M. Reid, Administrator

IUKA HOSPITAL, 1777 Curtis Drive, Iuka, MS, Zip 38852–1001, Mailing Address: P.O. Box 860, Zip 38852–0860; tel. 601/423–6051; Daniel Perryman, Administrator

NORTH MISSISSIPPI MEDICAL CENTER, 830 South Gloster Street, Tupelo, MS, Zip 38801–4934; tel. 601/841–3000; Jeffrey B. Barber, Dr.PH, President and Chief Executive Officer

PONTOTOC HOSPITAL AND EXTENDED CARE FACILITY, 176 South Main Street, Pontotoc, MS, Zip 38863–3311, Mailing Address: P.O. Box 790, Zip 38863–0790; tel. 601/489–5510; Fred B. Hood, Administrator

WEBSTER HEALTH SERVICES, 500 Highway 9 South, Eupora, MS, Zip 39744; tel. 601/258–6221; Harold H. Whitaker, Sr., Administrator

MISSOURI

BJC HEALTH SYSTEM
4444 Forest Park Av–S500, St. Louis, MO 63108–2259; tel. 314/286–2085; Patrick N. Lee, Management Assoc

ALTON MEMORIAL HOSPITAL, One Memorial Drive, Alton, IL, Zip 62002–6722; tel. 618/463–7311; Ronald B. McMullen, President

BARNES–JEWISH HOSPITAL, One Barnes–Jewish Hospital Plaza, Saint Louis, MO, Zip 63110–1094; tel. 314/747–3000; Peter L. Slavin, M.D., President

BARNES–JEWISH ST. PETERS HOSPITAL, 10 Hospital Drive, Saint Peters, MO, Zip 63376–1659; tel. 314/916–9000; Carm Moceri, President

BARNES–JEWISH WEST COUNTY HOSPITAL, 12634 Olive Boulevard, Saint Louis, MO, Zip 63141–6354; tel. 314/996–8000; William Behrendt, Interim President

BOONE HOSPITAL CENTER, 1600 East Broadway, Columbia, MO, Zip 65201–5897; tel. 573/815–8000; Michael Shirk, President and Senior Executive Officer

CHRISTIAN HOSPITAL NORTHEAST–NORTHWEST, 11133 Dunn Road, Saint Louis, MO, Zip 63136–6192; tel. 314/653–5000; John O'Shaughnessy, President and Senior Executive Officer

CLAY COUNTY HOSPITAL, 700 North Mill Street, Flora, IL, Zip 62839–1823, Mailing Address: P.O. Box 280, Zip 62839–0280; tel. 618/662–2131; Tony Schwarm, President

FAYETTE COUNTY HOSPITAL, Seventh and Taylor Streets, Vandalia, IL, Zip 62471–1296; tel. 618/283–1231; Daniel L. Gantz, President

MISSOURI BAPTIST HOSPITAL OF SULLIVAN, 751 Sappington Bridge Road, Sullivan, MO, Zip 63080–2354, Mailing Address: P.O. Box 190, Zip 63080–0190; tel. 573/468–4186; Davis D. Skinner, President

MISSOURI BAPTIST MEDICAL CENTER, 3015 North Ballas Road, Town and Country, MO, Zip 63131–2374; tel. 314/996–5000; Mark A. Eustis, President

PARKLAND HEALTH CENTER, 1101 West Liberty Street, Farmington, MO, Zip 63640–1997; tel. 573/756–6451; Richard L. Conklin, President

PUBLIC HOSPITAL OF THE TOWN OF SALEM, 1201 Ricker Drive, Salem, IL, Zip 62881–6250, Mailing Address: P.O. Box 1250, Zip 62881–1250; tel. 618/548–3194; James E. Robertson, Jr., President

ST. LOUIS CHILDREN'S HOSPITAL, One Children's Place, Saint Louis, MO, Zip 63110–1077; tel. 314/454–6000; Ted W. Frey, President

CARONDELET HEALTH
P.O. Box 8510, Kansas City, MO 64114; tel. 816/943–2673; Andrew Allen, CEO

MCCUNE–BROOKS HOSPITAL, 627 West Centennial Avenue, Carthage, MO, Zip 64836–0677; tel. 417/358–8121; Robert Y. Copeland, Jr., Chief Executive Officer

ST. JOHN'S REGIONAL MEDICAL CENTER, 2727 McClelland Boulevard, Joplin, MO, Zip 64804–1694; tel. 417/781–2727; Gary L. Rowe, President and Chief Executive Officer

ST. JOSEPH HEALTH CENTER, 300 First Capitol Drive, Saint Charles, MO, Zip 63301–2835; tel. 314/947–5000; Kevin F. Kast, President

ST. MARY'S HOSPITAL OF BLUE SPRINGS, 201 West R. D. Mize Road, Blue Springs, MO, Zip 64014; tel. 816/228–5900; Gordon Docking, Senior Executive Officer

COX HEALTH SYSTEMS
1423 N. Jefferson, Springfield, MO 65802; tel. 417/269–8806; Betty Breshears, Vice President

COX HOSPITAL SOUTH, 3801 S. National, Springfield, MO 65807; tel. 417/269–6000; Norb Bagley, Senior Vice President of Hospital Services

COX MEDICAL CENTER, 1423 N. Jefferson, Springfield, MO 65802; tel. 417/269–3000; John Mentgen, Administrator

COX MONETT HOSPITAL, 801 Lincoln Avenue, Monett, MO, Zip 65708–1698; tel. 417/354–1400; Gregory D. Johnson, Administrator

FREEMAN HEALTH SYSTEMS
1102 W. 32nd, Joplin, MO 64804; tel. 417/623–2801; Gary Duncan, President/CEO

HEALTH MIDWEST
2306 E. Meyer Blvd., B–11, Kansas City, MO 64132; tel. 816/276–9130; Thomas Cransham, Senior Vice President, Strategic Planning

ALLEN COUNTY HOSPITAL, 101 South First Street, Iola, KS, Zip 66749–3505, Mailing Address: P.O. Box 540, Zip 66749–0540; tel. 316/365–1000; Bill May, Chief Executive Officer

BAPTIST MEDICAL CENTER, 6601 Rockhill Road, Kansas City, MO, Zip 64131–1197; tel. 816/276–7000; Darrell W. Moore, President and Chief Executive Officer

CASS MEDICAL CENTER, 1800 East Mechanic Street, Harrisonville, MO, Zip 64701–2099; tel. 816/884–3291; Alan O. Freeman, Chief Executive Officer

HEDRICK MEDICAL CENTER, 100 Central Avenue, Chillicothe, MO, Zip 64601–1599; tel. 660/646–1480; James K. Johnson, Chief Executive Officer

LAFAYETTE REGIONAL HEALTH CENTER, 1500 State Street, Lexington, MO, Zip 64067–1199; tel. 660/259–2203; Jeffrey S. Tarrant, Administrator

LEE'S SUMMIT HOSPITAL, 530 North Murray Road, Lees Summit, MO, Zip 64081–1497; tel. 816/969–6000; John L. Jacobson, President and Chief Executive Officer

MEDICAL CENTER OF INDEPENDENCE, 17203 East 23rd Street, Independence, MO, Zip 64057–1899; tel. 816/478–5000; J. Kent Howard, President and Chief Executive Officer

PARK LANE MEDICAL CENTER, 5151 Raytown Road, Kansas City, MO, Zip 64133–2199; tel. 816/358–8000; Derell Taloney, President and Chief Executive Officer

REHABILITATION INSTITUTE, 3011 Baltimore, Kansas City, MO, Zip 64108–3465; tel. 816/751–7900; Ronald L. Herrick, President

RESEARCH BELTON HOSPITAL, 17065 South 71 Highway, Belton, MO, Zip 64012–2165; tel. 816/348–1200; Daniel F. Sheehan, Administrator

RESEARCH MEDICAL CENTER, 2316 East Meyer Boulevard, Kansas City, MO, Zip 64132–1199; tel. 816/276–4000; Steven R. Newton, President and Chief Executive Officer

RESEARCH PSYCHIATRIC CENTER, 2323 East 63rd Street, Kansas City, MO, Zip 64130–3495; tel. 816/444–8161; Todd Krass, Administrator and Chief Executive Officer

TRINITY LUTHERAN HOSPITAL, 3030 Baltimore Avenue, Kansas City, MO, Zip 64108–3404; tel. 816/751–4600; Ronald A. Ommen, President and Chief Executive Officer

HEARTLAND HEALTH SYSTEM
5325 Faraon Street, St. Joseph, MO 64506; tel. 816/271–6012; Curt Kretzinger, Medical Center Administrator

NORTHWEST MISSOURI HEALTHCARE AGENDA
705 North College Avenue, Albany, MO 64402; tel. 816/726–3941; John Richmond, Chairman

HEARTLAND REGIONAL MEDICAL CENTER, 5325 Faraon Street, St. Joseph, MO 64506; tel. 816/271–6012; Curt Tretzinger, Medical Center Administrator

HEARTLAND REGIONAL MEDICAL CENTER, 5325 Faraon Street, Saint Joseph, MO, Zip 64506–3398; tel. 816/271–6000; Lowell C. Kruse, Chief Executive Officer

SAINT LUKES–SHAWNEE
4400 Wornall, Kansas City, MO 34111; tel. 816/932–2000; G. Richard Hastings, President/CEO

ST LOUIS HEALTH CARE NETWORK
1173 Corporate Lake Drive, St. Louis, MO 63132; tel. 314/989–2000; Sister Mary Jean Ryan, President/CEO

ARCADIA VALLEY HOSPITAL, Highway 21, Pilot Knob, MO, Zip 63663, Mailing Address: P.O. Box 548, Zip 63663–0548; tel. 573/546–3924; H. Clark Duncan, Administrator

CARDINAL GLENNON CHILDREN'S HOSPITAL, 1465 South Grand Boulevard, Saint Louis, MO, Zip 63104–1095; tel. 314/577–5600; Douglas A. Ries, President

DEPAUL HEALTH CENTER, 12303 DePaul Drive, Saint Louis, MO, Zip 63044–2588; tel. 314/344–6000; Robert G. Porter, President

PIKE COUNTY MEMORIAL HOSPITAL, 2305 West Georgia Street, Louisiana, MO, Zip 63353–0020; tel. 573/754–5531; Gregory C. Reed, Administrator

SSM REHAB, 6420 Clayton Road, Suite 600, Saint Louis, MO, Zip 63117–1861; tel. 314/768–5300; Melinda Clark, President

ST. JOSEPH HEALTH CENTER, 300 First Capitol Drive, Saint Charles, MO, Zip 63301–2835; tel. 314/947–5000; Kevin F. Kast, President

ST. JOSEPH HOSPITAL WEST, 100 Medical Plaza, Lake Saint Louis, MO, Zip 63367–1395; tel. 314/625–5200; Kevin F. Kast, President

ST. MARY'S HEALTH CENTER, 6420 Clayton Road, Saint Louis, MO, Zip 63117–1811; tel. 314/768–8000; Michael E. Zilm, President

ST. MARY'S HOSPITAL, 129 North Eighth Street, East St. Louis, IL, Zip 62201–2999; tel. 618/274–1900; Richard J. Mark, President and Chief Executive Officer

UNITY HEALTH
12409 Powers Court Drive, St. Louis, MO 63131; tel. 314/364–3000; Richard S. Slack, Vice President Planning & Marketing

ALEXIAN BROTHERS HOSPITAL, 3933 South Broadway, Saint Louis, MO, Zip 63118–9984; tel. 314/865–3333; Glenn Appelbaum, Senior Vice President

COMMUNITY MEMORIAL HOSPITAL, 400 Caldwell Street, Staunton, IL, Zip 62088–1499; tel. 618/635–2200; Patrick B. Heise, Chief Executive Officer

ST. ANTHONY'S MEDICAL CENTER, 10010 Kennerly Road, Saint Louis, MO, Zip 63128–2185; tel. 314/525–1000; David P. Seifert, President

ST. CLEMENT HEALTH SERVICES, One St. Clement Boulevard, Red Bud, IL, Zip 62278–1194; tel. 618/282–3831; Michael Thomas McManus, President

ST. JOHN'S MERCY MEDICAL CENTER, 615 South New Ballas Road, Saint Louis, MO, Zip 63141–8277; tel. 314/569–6000; Mark Weber, FACHE, President

ST. JOSEPH'S HOSPITAL, 1515 Main Street, Highland, IL, Zip 62249–1656; tel. 618/654–7421; Anthony G. Mastrangelo, Executive Vice President and Administrator

ST. LUKE'S HOSPITAL, 232 South Woods Mill Road, Chesterfield, MO, Zip 63017–3480; tel. 314/434–1500; Gary R. Olson, President

UNIVERSITY OF MISSOURI HEALTH
1 Hospital Drive, Columbia, MO 65201; tel. 573/882–4141; Robert Churchill, Interim Director

MONTANA

MONTANA HEALTH NETWORK INC
11 S. 7th Street, Suite 160, Miles City, MT 59301; tel. 406/232–1420; Janet Bastian, CEO

BEARTOOTH HOSPITAL AND HEALTH CENTER, 600 West 20th Street, Red Lodge, MT, Zip 59068, Mailing Address: P.O. Box 590, Zip 59068–0590; tel. 406/446–2345; Kelley Evans, Administrator

CENTRAL MONTANA MEDICAL CENTER, 408 Wendell Avenue, Lewistown, MT, Zip 59457–2261, Mailing Address: P.O. Box 580, Zip 59457–0580; tel. 406/538–7711; David M. Faulkner, Chief Executive Officer and Administrator

DANIELS MEMORIAL HOSPITAL, 105 Fifth Avenue East, Scobey, MT, Zip 59263, Mailing Address: P.O. Box 400, Zip 59263–0400; tel. 406/487–2296; Glenn Haugo, Administrator

DEACONESS BILLINGS CLINIC, 2800 10th Avenue North, Billings, MT, Zip 59101–0799, Mailing Address: P.O. Box 37000, Zip 59107–7000; tel. 406/657–4000; Nicholas J. Wolter, M.D., Chief Executive Officer

FALLON MEDICAL COMPLEX, 202 South 4th Street West, Baker, MT, Zip 59313–0820, Mailing Address: P.O. Box 820, Zip 59313–0820; tel. 406/778–3331; David Espeland, Chief Executive Officer

FRANCES MAHON DEACONESS HOSPITAL, 621 Third Street South, Glasgow, MT, Zip 59230–2699; tel. 406/228–4351; Randall G. Holom, Chief Executive Officer

GLENDIVE MEDICAL CENTER, 202 Prospect Drive, Glendive, MT, Zip 59330–1999; tel. 406/365–3306; Paul Hanson, Chief Executive Officer

HOLY ROSARY HEALTH CENTER, 2600 Wilson Street, Miles City, MT, Zip 59301–5094; tel. 406/233–2600; H. Ray Gibbons, FACHE, Administrator and Senior Executive Officer

MCCONE COUNTY MEDICAL ASSISTANCE FACILITY, Circle, MT, Mailing Address: P.O. Box 48, Zip 59215–0048; tel. 406/485–3381; Mack N. Simpson, Administrator

NORTHEAST MONTANA HEALTH SERVICES, 315 Knapp Street, Wolf Point, MT, Zip 59201–1898; tel. 406/653–2110; Margaret Norgaard, Administrator

PHILLIPS COUNTY MEDICAL CENTER, 417 South Fourth East, Malta, MT, Zip 59538, Mailing Address: P.O. Box 640, Zip 59538–0640; tel. 406/654–1100; Larry E. Putnam, Administrator

ROOSEVELT MEMORIAL MEDICAL CENTER, 818 Second Avenue East, Culbertson, MT, Zip 59218, Mailing Address: P.O. Box 419, Zip 59218–0419; tel. 406/787–6281; Walter Busch, Administrator

ROUNDUP MEMORIAL HOSPITAL, 1202 Third Street West, Roundup, MT, Zip 59072–1816, Mailing Address: P.O. Box 40, Zip 59072–0040; tel. 406/323–2302; Dave McIvor, Administrator

SHERIDAN MEMORIAL HOSPITAL, 440 West Laurel Avenue, Plentywood, MT, Zip 59254–1596; tel. 406/765–1420; Ella Gutzke, Administrator

SIDNEY HEALTH CENTER, 216 14th Avenue S.W., Sidney, MT, Zip 59270–3586; tel. 406/488–2100; Donald J. Rush, Chief Executive Officer

STILLWATER COMMUNITY HOSPITAL, 44 West Fourth Avenue North, Columbus, MT, Zip 59019, Mailing Address: P.O. Box 959, Zip 59019–0959; tel. 406/322–5316; Tim Russell, Administrator

NORTHERN ROCKIES HEALTHCARE NETWORK
P.O. Box 4587, Missoula, MT 59806; tel. 406/543–7271; Kimberly Rowse, Network Contact

ST. PATRICK HOSPITAL, 500 West Broadway, Missoula, MT, Zip 59802–4096, Mailing Address: Box 4587, Zip 59806–4587; tel. 406/543–7271; Lawrence L. White, Jr., President

NEBRASKA

ALEGENT HEALTH
1010 North 96th Street, Omaha, NE 68114; tel. 402/255–1661; Robert Azar, President of Public Health

ALEGENT HEALTH COMMUNITY MEMORIAL HOSPITAL, 631 North Eighth Street, Missouri Valley, IA, Zip 51555–1199; tel. 712/642–2784; James A. Seymour, Regional Administrator

ALEGENT HEALTH IMMANUEL MEDICAL CENTER, 6901 North 72nd Street, Omaha, NE, Zip 68122–1799; tel. 402/572–2121; Randall W. Smith, Chief Operating Officer

ALEGENT HEALTH MERCY HOSPITAL, 800 Mercy Drive, Council Bluffs, IA, Zip 51503–3128, Mailing Address: P.O. Box 1C, Zip 51502–3001; tel. 712/328–5000; Charles J. Marr, Chief Executive Officer

ALEGENT HEALTH–MEMORIAL HOSPITAL, 104 West 17th Street, Schuyler, NE, Zip 68661–1396; tel. 402/352–2441; Asa B. Wilson, Administrator

MERCY HOSPITAL, 703 Rosary Drive, Corning, IA, Zip 50841, Mailing Address: P.O. Box 368, Zip 50841–0368; tel. 515/322–3121; James C. Ruppert, Administrator

BEHAVIORAL HEALTH SPECIALIST
600 S. 13th St., Norfolk, NE 68701; tel. 402/370–3401; Jackie O'Brien, Referral Specialist

BLUE RIVER VALLEY HEALTH NETWORK
121 S. 13th Suite 700, Lincoln, NE 68508; tel. 402/475–3865; Rick Boucher, Executive Director

ANNIE JEFFREY MEMORIAL COUNTY HEALTH CENTER, 531 Beebe Street, Osceola, NE, Zip 68651, Mailing Address: P.O. Box 428, Zip 68651–0428; tel. 402/747–2031; Carol E. Jones, Administrator

BUTLER COUNTY HEALTH CARE CENTER, 372 South Ninth Street, David City, NE, Zip 68632–2199; tel. 402/367–3115; Roger Reamer, Administrator

CRETE MUNICIPAL HOSPITAL, 1540 Grove Street, Crete, NE, Zip 68333–0220, Mailing Address: P.O. Box 220, Zip 68333–0220; tel. 402/826–6800; Joseph W. Lohrman, Administrator

FILLMORE COUNTY HOSPITAL, 1325 H Street, Geneva, NE, Zip 68361–1325, Mailing Address: P.O. Box 193, Zip 68361–0193; tel. 402/759–3167; Larry Eichelberger, Chief Executive Officer

HENDERSON HEALTH CARE SERVICES, 1621 Front Street, Henderson, NE, Zip 68371–0217, Mailing Address: P.O. Box 217, Zip 68371–0217; tel. 402/723–4512; Mark Neubacher, Chief Executive Officer

LITZENBERG MEMORIAL COUNTY HOSPITAL, 1715 26th Street, Central City, NE, Zip 68826–9620, Mailing Address: Route 2, Box 1, Zip 68826–0001; tel. 308/946–3015; Mike R. Bowman, Administrator

MEMORIAL HEALTH CARE SYSTEMS, 300 North Columbia Avenue, Seward, NE, Zip 68434–9907; tel. 402/643–2971; Ronald D. Waltz, Chief Executive Officer

MEMORIAL HOSPITAL, 1423 Seventh Street, Aurora, NE, Zip 68818–1197; tel. 402/694–3171; Eldon A. Wall, Administrator

SAUNDERS COUNTY HEALTH SERVICE, 805 West Tenth Street, Wahoo, NE, Zip 68066–1102, Mailing Address: P.O. Box 185, Zip 68066–0185; tel. 402/443–4191; Michael Boyles, Administrator

WARREN MEMORIAL HOSPITAL, 905 Second Street, Friend, NE, Zip 68359–1198; tel. 402/947–2541; Joseph W. Lohrman, Administrator

YORK GENERAL HOSPITAL, 2222 Lincoln Avenue, York, NE, Zip 68467–1095; tel. 402/362–0445; Charles K. Schulz, Chief Executive Officer

CENTRAL NEBRASKA PRIMARY
1518 J. Street, Ord, NE 68862; tel. 308/728–3011; Barbara Weems, Foundation President

BOONE COUNTY HEALTH CENTER, 723 West Fairview Street, Albion, NE, Zip 68620–1725, Mailing Address: P.O. Box 151, Zip 68620–0151; tel. 402/395–2191; Gayle E. Primrose, Administrator

VALLEY COUNTY HOSPITAL, 217 Westridge Drive, Ord, NE, Zip 68862–1675; tel. 308/728–3211; Colleen Chapp, Interim Chief Executive Officer and Administrator

HEART HEALTH ALLIANCE
P.O. Box 980, Lexington, NE 68850; tel. 308/324–8358; Ken Foster, Executive Director

BRODSTONE MEMORIAL HOSPITAL, 520 East Tenth Street, Superior, NE, Zip 68978–1225, Mailing Address: P.O. Box 187, Zip 68978–0187; tel. 402/879–3281; Ronald D. Waggoner, Administrator and Chief Executive Officer

Section B

COMMUNITY HOSPITAL, 1301 East H Street, McCook, NE, Zip 69001–1328, Mailing Address: P.O. Box 1328, Zip 69001–1328; tel. 308/345–2650; Gary Bieganski, President

FRANKLIN COUNTY MEMORIAL HOSPITAL, 1406 Q Street, Franklin, NE, Zip 68939–0315, Mailing Address: P.O. Box 315, Zip 68939–0315; tel. 308/425–6221; Jerrell F. Gerdes, Administrator

GOTHENBURG MEMORIAL HOSPITAL, 910 20th Street, Gothenburg, NE, Zip 69138–1237, Mailing Address: P.O. Box 469, Zip 69138–0469; tel. 308/537–3661; John H. Johnson, Chief Executive Officer

GREAT PLAINS REGIONAL MEDICAL CENTER, 601 West Leota Street, North Platte, NE, Zip 69101–6598, Mailing Address: P.O. Box 1167, Zip 69103–1167; tel. 308/534–9310; Lucinda A. Bradley, President

HARLAN COUNTY HEALTH SYSTEM, 717 North Brown Street, Alma, NE, Zip 68920–0836, Mailing Address: P.O. Box 836, Zip 68920–0836; tel. 308/928–2151; Allen Van Driel, Administrator

MARY LANNING MEMORIAL HOSPITAL, 715 North St. Joseph Avenue, Hastings, NE, Zip 68901–4497; tel. 402/461–5110; W. Michael Kearney, President

PHELPS MEMORIAL HEALTH CENTER, 1220 Miller Street, Holdrege, NE, Zip 68949–0828, Mailing Address: P.O. Box 828, Zip 68949–0828; tel. 308/995–2211; Jerome Seigfreid, Jr., Chief Executive Officer

TRI–COUNTY AREA HOSPITAL, 13th and Erie Streets, Lexington, NE, Zip 68850–0980, Mailing Address: P.O. Box 980, Zip 68850–0980; tel. 308/324–5651; Calvin A. Hiner, Administrator

TRI–VALLEY HEALTH SYSTEM, West Highway 6 and 34, Cambridge, NE, Zip 69022–0488, Mailing Address: P.O. Box 488, Zip 69022–0488; tel. 308/697–3329; Jerry W. Harris, Interim Chief Executive Officer

WEBSTER COUNTY COMMUNITY HOSPITAL, Sixth Avenue and Franklin Street, Red Cloud, NE, Zip 68970–0465; tel. 402/746–2291; Terry L. Hoffart, Administrator

HEARTLAND HEALTH ALLIANCE
1600 South 48th Street, Lincoln, NE 68506; tel. 402/483–3111; R. Lynn Wilson, President

BEATRICE COMMUNITY HOSPITAL AND HEALTH CENTER, 1110 North Tenth Street, Beatrice, NE, Zip 68310–2039, Mailing Address: P.O. Box 278, Zip 68310–0278; tel. 402/228–3344; Kenneth J. Zimmerman, Administrator

BOONE COUNTY HEALTH CENTER, 723 West Fairview Street, Albion, NE, Zip 68620–1725, Mailing Address: P.O. Box 151, Zip 68620–0151; tel. 402/395–2191; Gayle E. Primrose, Administrator

BUTLER COUNTY HEALTH CARE CENTER, 372 South Ninth Street, David City, NE, Zip 68632–2199; tel. 402/367–3115; Roger Reamer, Administrator

CHERRY COUNTY HOSPITAL, Highway 12 and Green Street, Valentine, NE, Zip 69201–0410; tel. 402/376–2525; Brent A. Peterson, Administrator

COMMUNITY MEMORIAL HOSPITAL, 1579 Midland Street, Syracuse, NE, Zip 68446–9732, Mailing Address: P.O. Box N, Zip 68446; tel. 402/269–2795; Al Klaasmeyer, Administrator

CRETE MUNICIPAL HOSPITAL, 1540 Grove Street, Crete, NE, Zip 68333–0220, Mailing Address: P.O. Box 220, Zip 68333–0220; tel. 402/826–6800; Joseph W. Lohrman, Administrator

GREAT PLAINS REGIONAL MEDICAL CENTER, 601 West Leota Street, North Platte, NE, Zip 69101–6598, Mailing Address: P.O. Box 1167, Zip 69103–1167; tel. 308/534–9310; Lucinda A. Bradley, President

JENNIE M. MELHAM MEMORIAL MEDICAL CENTER, 145 Memorial Drive, Broken Bow, NE, Zip 68822–1378, Mailing Address: P.O. Box 250, Zip 68822–0250; tel. 308/872–6891; Michael J. Steckler, Chief Executive Officer

MIDLANDS CHOICE
8420 W. Dodge Road, Omaha, NE 68114; tel. 800/605–8259; Ann Bruns, Director

NORTHEAST HEALTH SERVICES
P.O. Box 186, Crighton, NE 68729; tel. 402/358–3322; Paul Hurd, President

OSMOND GENERAL HOSPITAL, 5th and Maple Street, Osmond, NE, Zip 68765–0429, Mailing Address: P.O. Box 429, Zip 68765–0429; tel. 402/748–3393; Celine M. Mlady, Chief Executive Officer

PLAINVIEW PUBLIC HOSPITAL, 705 North Third Street, Plainview, NE, Zip 68769, Mailing Address: P.O. Box 489, Zip 68769–0489; tel. 402/582–4245; Donald T. Naiberk, Administrator and Chief Executive Officer

OSMOND GENERAL HOSPITAL, 5th and Maple Street, Osmond, NE, Zip 68765–0429, Mailing Address: P.O. Box 429, Zip 68765–0429; tel. 402/748–3393; Celine M. Mlady, Chief Executive Officer

RURAL HEALTHCARE NETWORK
821 Morehead Street, Chadron, NE 69337; tel. 308/432–5586; Harold Krueger, CEO

BOX BUTTE GENERAL HOSPITAL, 2101 Box Butte Avenue, Alliance, NE, Zip 69301–0810, Mailing Address: P.O. Box 810, Zip 69301–0810; tel. 308/762–6660; Terrance J. Padden, Administrator

CHADRON COMMUNITY HOSPITAL AND HEALTH SERVICES, 821 Morehead Street, Chadron, NE, Zip 69337–2599; tel. 308/432–5586; Harold L. Krueger, Jr., Chief Executive Officer

CHASE COUNTY COMMUNITY HOSPITAL, 600 West 12th Street, Imperial, NE, Zip 69033–0819, Mailing Address: P.O. Box 819, Zip 69033–0819; tel. 308/882–7111; Ed Hackman, Administrator

GARDEN COUNTY HOSPITAL, 1100 West Second Street, Oshkosh, NE, Zip 69154, Mailing Address: P.O. Box 320, Zip 69154–0320; tel. 308/772–3283; Diana Stevens, Administrator

GORDON MEMORIAL HOSPITAL DISTRICT, 300 East Eighth Street, Gordon, NE, Zip 69343–9990; tel. 308/282–0401; Gladys Phemister, Chief Executive Officer

KIMBALL COUNTY HOSPITAL, 505 South Burg Street, Kimball, NE, Zip 69145–1398; tel. 308/235–3621; Gerri Linn, Administrator

MEMORIAL HEALTH CENTER, 645 Osage Street, Sidney, NE, Zip 69162–1799; tel. 308/254–5825; Rex D. Walk, Chief Executive Officer

MORRILL COUNTY COMMUNITY HOSPITAL, 1313 S Street, Bridgeport, NE, Zip 69336–0579, Mailing Address: P.O. Box 579, Zip 69336–0579; tel. 308/262–1616; Julia Morrow, Administrator

REGIONAL WEST MEDICAL CENTER, 4021 Avenue B, Scottsbluff, NE, Zip 69361–4695; tel. 308/635–3711; David M. Nitschke, President and Chief Executive Officer

SE NEBRASKA HEALTHCARE
245 South 84th Street, Lincoln, NE 68510; tel. 402/486–7320; Dick Waller, Director

WESTERN PLAINS COMMUNITY
302 West 27th Street, Scottsbluff, NE 69361; tel. 308/635–2260; Todd Sorensen, MD

NEVADA

NAHHS
4600 Kietzke Lane Suite A–108, Reno, NV 89502; tel. 775/827–0184; Bill Welch, President

SAINT MARY'S HEALTH NETWORK
235 West Sixth Street, Reno, NV 89520; tel. 775/789–3000; Tamara Bradshaw, Research Assistant

LASSEN COMMUNITY HOSPITAL, 560 Hospital Lane, Susanville, CA, Zip 96130–4809; tel. 530/257–5325; David S. Anderson, FACHE, Administrator

SAINT MARY'S REGIONAL MEDICAL CENTER, 235 West Sixth Street, Reno, NV, Zip 89520–0108; tel. 702/323–2041; Jeff K. Bills, Chief Executive Officer

NEW HAMPSHIRE

CARING COMMUNITY NETWORK OF THE TWIN RIVERS
15 Aiken Ave., Franklin, NH 03235; tel. 603/934–2060; Walter A. Strauch, Chairman

FRANKLIN REGIONAL HOSPITAL, 15 Aiken Avenue, Franklin, NH, Zip 03235–1299; tel. 603/934–2060; Walter A. Strauch, Executive Director

HEALTHLINK
80 Highland Street, Laconia, NH 03246; tel. 603/527–2910; Sharon Swanson, Network Contact

CATHOLIC MEDICAL CENTER, 100 McGregor Street, Manchester, NH, Zip 03102–3770; tel. 603/668–3545; Allyson Pitman Giles, President and Chief Executive Officer

CONCORD HOSPITAL, 250 Pleasant Street, Concord, NH, Zip 03301–2598; tel. 603/225–2711; Michael B. Green, President and Chief Executive Officer

ELLIOT HOSPITAL, One Elliot Way, Manchester, NH, Zip 03103; tel. 603/663–2090; Douglas F. Dean, Jr., President and Chief Executive Officer

LAKES REGION GENERAL HOSPITAL, 80 Highland Street, Laconia, NH, Zip 03246–3298; tel. 603/524–3211; Thomas Clairmont, President

MARY HITCHCOCK MEMORIAL HOSPITAL, One Medical Center Drive, Lebanon, NH, Zip 03756–0001; tel. 603/650–5000; James W. Varnum, President

PARTNERS IN HEALTH
243 Elm Street, Claremont, NH 03743; tel. 603/542–7771; Jane Manning, Chairperson

VALLEY REGIONAL HOSPITAL, 243 Elm Street, Claremont, NH, Zip 03743–2099; tel. 603/542–7771; Donald R. Holl, President

ST JOSEPH HEALTH CARE
172 Kinsley Street, Nashua, NH 03061; tel. 603/882–3000; Peter B. Davis, President

ST. JOSEPH HOSPITAL, 172 Kinsley Street, Nashua, NH, Zip 03061; tel. 603/882–3000; Peter B. Davis, President and Chief Executive Officer

NEW JERSEY

ATLANTICARE HEALTH SYSTEM
6725 Delilah Road, Egg Harbor Township, NJ 08234; tel. 609/272–6311; Dominic S. Moffa, Vice President–Administration

ATLANTIC CITY MEDICAL CENTER, 1925 Pacific Avenue, Atlantic City, NJ, Zip 08401–6713; tel. 609/345–4000; David P. Tilton, President and Chief Executive Officer

CAPE ADVANTAGE HEALTH ALLIANCE
Two Stone Habor Boulevard, Court House, NJ 08210; tel. 609/463–2480; Tom Scott, President & CEO

BURDETTE TOMLIN MEMORIAL HOSPITAL, 2 Stone Harbor Boulevard, Cape May Court House, NJ, Zip 08210–9990; tel. 609/463–2000; Thomas L. Scott, FACHE, President and Chief Executive Officer

CLARA MAASS HEALTH SYSTEM
One Franklin Avenue, Belleville, NJ 07109; tel. 201/450–2000; Robert S. Curtis, President

CLARA MAASS HEALTH SYSTEM, 1 Clara Maass Drive, Belleville, NJ, Zip 07109–3557; tel. 973/450–2000; Thomas A. Biga, Executive Director

COMMUNITY/KIMBALL HEALTH CARE SYSTEM
99 Highway 37 W., Toms River, NJ 08755; tel. 732/349–3450; Mark Pilla, President

COMMUNITY MEDICAL CENTER, 99 Route 37 West, Toms River, NJ, Zip 08755–6423; tel. 732/557–8000; Kevin R. Burchill, Executive Director

FIRST OPTION HEALTH PLAN
2 Bridge Street, Red Bank, NJ 07701; tel. 908/842–5000; John McCarthy, VP Finance

BARNERT HOSPITAL, 680 Broadway Street, Paterson, NJ, Zip 07514–1472; tel. 973/977–6600; Dominick R. Calgi, President and Chief Executive Officer

BAYSHORE COMMUNITY HOSPITAL, 727 North Beers Street, Holmdel, NJ, Zip 07733–1598; tel. 732/739–5900; Thomas Goldman, President and Chief Executive Officer

BETH ISRAEL HOSPITAL, 70 Parker Avenue, Passaic, NJ, Zip 07055–7000; tel. 973/365–5000; Jeffrey S. Moll, President and Chief Executive Officer

BURDETTE TOMLIN MEMORIAL HOSPITAL, 2 Stone Harbor Boulevard, Cape May Court House, NJ, Zip 08210–9990; tel. 609/463–2000; Thomas L. Scott, FACHE, President and Chief Executive Officer

CENTRASTATE HEALTHCARE SYSTEM, 901 West Main Street, Freehold, NJ, Zip 07728–2549; tel. 732/431–2000; Thomas H. Litz, FACHE, President and Chief Executive Officer

CHILTON MEMORIAL HOSPITAL, 97 West Parkway, Pompton Plains, NJ, Zip 07444–1696; tel. 973/831–5000; James J. Doyle, Jr., President and Chief Executive Officer

CHRIST HOSPITAL, 176 Palisade Avenue, Jersey City, NJ, Zip 07306–1196, Mailing Address: P.O. Box J–1, Zip 07306–1196; tel. 201/795–8200; Daniel R. Connell, President

CLARA MAASS HEALTH SYSTEM, 1 Clara Maass Drive, Belleville, NJ, Zip 07109–3557; tel. 973/450–2000; Thomas A. Biga, Executive Director

COMMUNITY MEDICAL CENTER, 99 Route 37 West, Toms River, NJ, Zip 08755–6423; tel. 732/557–8000; Kevin R. Burchill, Executive Director

EAST ORANGE GENERAL HOSPITAL, 300 Central Avenue, East Orange, NJ, Zip 07019–2819; tel. 973/672–8400; Claude D. Watts, Jr., President and Chief Executive Officer

ELIZABETH GENERAL MEDICAL CENTER, 925 East Jersey Street, Elizabeth, NJ, Zip 07201–2728; tel. 908/289–8600; David A. Fletcher, President and Chief Executive Officer

ENGLEWOOD HOSPITAL AND MEDICAL CENTER, 350 Engle Street, Englewood, NJ, Zip 07631–1898; tel. 201/894–3000; Daniel A. Kane, President and Chief Executive Officer

HACKETTSTOWN COMMUNITY HOSPITAL, 651 Willow Grove Street, Hackettstown, NJ, Zip 07840–1798; tel. 908/852–5100; Gene C. Milton, President and Chief Executive Officer

HOLY NAME HOSPITAL, 718 Teaneck Road, Teaneck, NJ, Zip 07666–4281; tel. 201/833–3000; Michael Maron, President and Chief Executive Officer

HUNTERDON MEDICAL CENTER, 2100 Wescott Drive, Flemington, NJ, Zip 08822–4604; tel. 908/788–6100; Robert P. Wise, President and Chief Executive Officer

IRVINGTON GENERAL HOSPITAL, 832 Chancellor Avenue, Irvington, NJ, Zip 07111–0709; tel. 973/399–6000; Paul A. Mertz, Executive Director

JFK MEDICAL CENTER, 65 James Street, Edison, NJ, Zip 08818–3947; tel. 732/321–7000; John P. McGee, President and Chief Executive Officer

KIMBALL MEDICAL CENTER, 600 River Avenue, Lakewood, NJ, Zip 08701–5281; tel. 732/363–1900; Joanne Carrocino, Executive Director

MEDICAL CENTER AT PRINCETON, 253 Witherspoon Street, Princeton, NJ, Zip 08540–3213; tel. 609/497–4000; Dennis W. Doody, President and Chief Executive Officer

MONMOUTH MEDICAL CENTER, 300 Second Avenue, Long Branch, NJ, Zip 07740–6303; tel. 732/222–5200; Frank J. Vozos, M.D., FACS, Executive Director

MUHLENBERG REGIONAL MEDICAL CENTER, 1200 Park Avenue, Plainfield, NJ, Zip 07061; tel. 908/668–2000; John R. Kopicki, President and Chief Executive Officer

NEWARK BETH ISRAEL MEDICAL CENTER, 201 Lyons Avenue, Newark, NJ, Zip 07112–2027; tel. 973/926–7000; Paul A. Mertz, Executive Director

NEWTON MEMORIAL HOSPITAL, 175 High Street, Newton, NJ, Zip 07860–1004; tel. 973/383–2121; Dennis H. Collette, President and Chief Executive Officer

OUR LADY OF LOURDES MEDICAL CENTER, 1600 Haddon Avenue, Camden, NJ, Zip 08103–3117; tel. 609/757–3500; Alexander J. Hatala, President and Chief Executive Officer

PALISADES GENERAL HOSPITAL, 7600 River Road, North Bergen, NJ, Zip 07047–6217; tel. 201/854–5000; Bruce J. Markowitz, President and Chief Executive Officer

PASCACK VALLEY HOSPITAL, 250 Old Hook Road, Westwood, NJ, Zip 07675–3181; tel. 201/358–3000; Louis R. Ycre, Jr., FACHE, President and Chief Executive Officer

ROBERT WOOD JOHNSON UNIVERSITY HOSPITAL, 1 Robert Wood Johnson Place, New Brunswick, NJ, Zip 08903–2601; tel. 732/828–3000; Harvey A. Holzberg, President and Chief Executive Officer

SAINT BARNABAS MEDICAL CENTER, 94 Old Short Hills Road, Livingston, NJ, Zip 07039–5668; tel. 973/322–5000; Vincent D. Joseph, Executive Director

SHORE MEMORIAL HOSPITAL, 1 East New York Avenue, Somers Point, NJ, Zip 08244–2387; tel. 609/653–3500; Richard A. Pitman, President

SOMERSET MEDICAL CENTER, 110 Rehill Avenue, Somerville, NJ, Zip 08876–2598; tel. 908/685–2200; Michael A. Turner, President and Chief Executive Officer

SOUTH JERSEY HOSPITAL, 333 Irving Avenue, Bridgeton, NJ, Zip 08302–2100; tel. 609/451–6600; Chester B. Kaletkowski, President and Chief Executive Officer

SOUTHERN OCEAN COUNTY HOSPITAL, 1140 Route 72 West, Manahawkin, NJ, Zip 08050–2499; tel. 609/978–8900; Joseph P. Coyle, President and Chief Executive Officer

ST. FRANCIS MEDICAL CENTER, 601 Hamilton Avenue, Trenton, NJ, Zip 08629–1986; tel. 609/599–5000; Judith M. Persichilli, President and Chief Executive Officer

ST. JOSEPH'S HOSPITAL AND MEDICAL CENTER, 703 Main Street, Paterson, NJ, Zip 07503–2691; tel. 973/754–2000; Patrick R. Wardell, President and Chief Executive Officer

ST. PETER'S UNIVERSITY HOSPITAL, 254 Easton Avenue, New Brunswick, NJ, Zip 08901–1780, Mailing Address: P.O. Box 591, Zip 08903–0591; tel. 732/745–8600; John E. Matuska, President and Chief Executive Officer

UNDERWOOD–MEMORIAL HOSPITAL, 509 North Broad Street, Woodbury, NJ, Zip 08096–1697, Mailing Address: P.O. Box 359, Zip 08096–7359; tel. 856/845–0100; Steven W. Jackmuff, President and Chief Executive Officer

UNION HOSPITAL, 1000 Galloping Hill Road, Union, NJ, Zip 07083–1652; tel. 908/687–1900; Kathryn W. Coyne, Executive Director and Chief Operating Officer

VALLEY HOSPITAL, 223 North Van Dien Avenue, Ridgewood, NJ, Zip 07450–9982; tel. 201/447–8000; Audrey Meyers, President

VIRTUA–MEMORIAL HOSPITAL BURLINGTON COUNTY, 175 Madison Avenue, Mount Holly, NJ, Zip 08060–2099; tel. 609/267–0700; Donald I. Brunn, President and Chief Executive Officer

WEST HUDSON HOSPITAL, 206 Bergen Avenue, Kearny, NJ, Zip 07032–3399; tel. 201/955–7051; Carmen Bruce Alecci, Executive Director

WEST JERSEY HOSPITAL–BERLIN, 100 Townsend Avenue, Berlin, NJ, Zip 08009–9035; tel. 609/322–3100; Ellen Guarnieri, Executive Director

WEST JERSEY HOSPITAL–CAMDEN, 1000 Atlantic Avenue, Camden, NJ, Zip 08104–1595; tel. 609/246–3000; Carolyn M. Ballard, Executive Director

WEST JERSEY HOSPITAL–MARLTON, 90 Brick Road, Marlton, NJ, Zip 08053–9697; tel. 609/355–6000; Leroy J. Rosenberg, Executive Director

WEST JERSEY HOSPITAL–VOORHEES, 101 Carnie Boulevard, Voorhees, NJ, Zip 08043–1597; tel. 609/325–3000; Joan T. Meyers, R.N., Executive Director

WILLIAM B. KESSLER MEMORIAL HOSPITAL, 600 South White Horse Pike, Hammonton, NJ, Zip 08037–2099; tel. 609/561–6700; Warren E. Gager, Chief Executive Officer

GENERAL HOSPITAL CENTER HEALTH NETWORK
325 Columbia Turnpike, Flortham Park, NJ 07932; tel. 973/660–3100; Richard P. Oths, President & CEO

GENERAL HOSPITAL CENTER AT PASSAIC, 350 Boulevard, Passaic, NJ, Zip 07055–2800; tel. 973/365–4300; Marie Cassese, R.N., President

MORRISTOWN MEMORIAL HOSPITAL, 100 Madison Avenue, Morristown, NJ, Zip 07962–1956; tel. 973/971–5000; Jean M. McMahon, R.N., President

MOUNTAINSIDE HOSPITAL, Bay and Highland Avenues, Montclair, NJ, Zip 07042–4898; tel. 973/429–6000; Robert A. Silver, President

OVERLOOK HOSPITAL, 99 Beauvoir Avenue, Summit, NJ, Zip 07902–0220; tel. 908/522–2000; David H. Freed, President

HEALTHCARE NETWORK OF NEW JERSEY
253 Witherspoon Street, Princeton, NJ 08540–3213; tel. 609/497–4000; Dennis W. Doody, President

QUALCARE INC
242 Old Brunswick Road, Piscataway, NJ 08854; tel. 908/562–2800; Jerry Eisenberg, Network Contact

BAYONNE HOSPITAL, 29 East 29th Street, Bayonne, NJ, Zip 07002–4699; tel. 201/858–5000; Michael R. D'Agnes, President and Chief Executive Officer

BETH ISRAEL HOSPITAL, 70 Parker Avenue, Passaic, NJ, Zip 07055–7000; tel. 973/365–5000; Jeffrey S. Moll, President and Chief Executive Officer

CARRIER FOUNDATION, County Route 601, P.O. Box 147, Belle Mead, NJ, Zip 08502–0147; tel. 908/281–1000; C. Richard Sarle, President and Chief Executive Officer

CENTRASTATE HEALTHCARE SYSTEM, 901 West Main Street, Freehold, NJ, Zip 07728–2549; tel. 732/431–2000; Thomas H. Litz, FACHE, President and Chief Executive Officer

CHILDREN'S SPECIALIZED HOSPITAL, 150 New Providence Road, Mountainside, NJ, Zip 07091–2590; tel. 908/233–3720; Richard B. Ahlfeld, President

COLUMBUS HOSPITAL, 495 North 13th Street, Newark, NJ, Zip 07107–1397; tel. 973/268–1400; John G. Magliaro, President and Chief Executive Officer

COMMUNITY MEDICAL CENTER, 99 Route 37 West, Toms River, NJ, Zip 08755–6423; tel. 732/557–8000; Kevin R. Burchill, Executive Director

ELIZABETH GENERAL MEDICAL CENTER, 925 East Jersey Street, Elizabeth, NJ, Zip 07201–2728; tel. 908/289–8600; David A. Fletcher, President and Chief Executive Officer

HACKENSACK UNIVERSITY MEDICAL CENTER, 30 Prospect Avenue, Hackensack, NJ, Zip 07601–1991; tel. 201/996–2000; John P. Ferguson, FACHE, President and Chief Executive Officer

HOLY NAME HOSPITAL, 718 Teaneck Road, Teaneck, NJ, Zip 07666–4281; tel. 201/833–3000; Michael Maron, President and Chief Executive Officer

HOSPITAL CENTER AT ORANGE, 188 South Essex Avenue, Orange, NJ, Zip 07051; tel. 973/266–2200; James E. Romer, President and Chief Executive Officer

HUNTERDON MEDICAL CENTER, 2100 Wescott Drive, Flemington, NJ, Zip 08822–4604; tel. 908/788–6100; Robert P. Wise, President and Chief Executive Officer

IRVINGTON GENERAL HOSPITAL, 832 Chancellor Avenue, Irvington, NJ, Zip 07111–0709; tel. 973/399–6000; Paul A. Mertz, Executive Director

KESSLER INSTITUTE FOR REHABILITATION, 1199 Pleasant Valley Way, West Orange, NJ, Zip 07052–1419; tel. 973/731–3600; Robert Brehm, President

KIMBALL MEDICAL CENTER, 600 River Avenue, Lakewood, NJ, Zip 08701–5281; tel. 732/363–1900; Joanne Carrocino, Executive Director

MEMORIAL HOSPITAL OF SALEM COUNTY, 310 Woodstown Road, Salem, NJ, Zip 08079–2080; tel. 609/935–1000; Denise R. Williams, President and Chief Executive Officer

MERIDIAN HEALTH SYSTEM, 1945 State Highway 33, Neptune, NJ, Zip 07753; tel. 732/775–5500; John K. Lloyd, Chief Executive Officer

MONMOUTH MEDICAL CENTER, 300 Second Avenue, Long Branch, NJ, Zip 07740–6303; tel. 732/222–5200; Frank J. Vozos, M.D., FACS, Executive Director

NEWARK BETH ISRAEL MEDICAL CENTER, 201 Lyons Avenue, Newark, NJ, Zip 07112–2027; tel. 973/926–7000; Paul A. Mertz, Executive Director

PALISADES GENERAL HOSPITAL, 7600 River Road, North Bergen, NJ, Zip 07047–6217; tel. 201/854–5000; Bruce J. Markowitz, President and Chief Executive Officer

PASCACK VALLEY HOSPITAL, 250 Old Hook Road, Westwood, NJ, Zip 07675–3181; tel. 201/358–3000; Louis R. Ycre, Jr., FACHE, President and Chief Executive Officer

RAHWAY HOSPITAL, 865 Stone Street, Rahway, NJ, Zip 07065–2797; tel. 732/381–4200; Kirk C. Tice, President and Chief Executive Officer

RARITAN BAY MEDICAL CENTER, 530 New Brunswick Avenue, Perth Amboy, NJ, Zip 08861–3685; tel. 732/442–3700; Keith H. McLaughlin, President and Chief Executive Officer

ROBERT WOOD JOHNSON UNIVERSITY HOSPITAL, 1 Robert Wood Johnson Place, New Brunswick, NJ, Zip 08903–2601; tel. 732/828–3000; Harvey A. Holzberg, President and Chief Executive Officer

ROBERT WOOD JOHNSON UNIVERSITY HOSPITAL AT HAMILTON, One Hamilton Health Place, Hamilton, NJ, Zip 08690–3599; tel. 609/586–7900; Christy Stephenson, Chief Administrative Officer

SAINT BARNABAS MEDICAL CENTER, 94 Old Short Hills Road, Livingston, NJ, Zip 07039–5668; tel. 973/322–5000; Vincent D. Joseph, Executive Director

SAINT CLARE'S HEALTH SERVICES, 25 Pocono Road, Denville, NJ, Zip 07834–2995; tel. 973/625–6000; Kathryn J. McDonagh, President and Chief Executive Officer

SHORE MEMORIAL HOSPITAL, 1 East New York Avenue, Somers Point, NJ, Zip 08244–2387; tel. 609/653–3500; Richard A. Pitman, President

SOMERSET MEDICAL CENTER, 110 Rehill Avenue, Somerville, NJ, Zip 08876–2598; tel. 908/685–2200; Michael A. Turner, President and Chief Executive Officer

SOUTH JERSEY HOSPITAL, 333 Irving Avenue, Bridgeton, NJ, Zip 08302–2100; tel. 609/451–6600; Chester B. Kaletkowski, President and Chief Executive Officer

SOUTHERN OCEAN COUNTY HOSPITAL, 1140 Route 72 West, Manahawkin, NJ, Zip 08050–2499; tel. 609/978–8900; Joseph P. Coyle, President and Chief Executive Officer

ST. FRANCIS HOSPITAL, 25 McWilliams Place, Jersey City, NJ, Zip 07302–1698; tel. 201/418–1000; Robert S. Chaloner, President and Chief Executive Officer

ST. JOSEPH'S HOSPITAL AND MEDICAL CENTER, 703 Main Street, Paterson, NJ, Zip 07503–2691; tel. 973/754–2000; Patrick R. Wardell, President and Chief Executive Officer

ST. LAWRENCE REHABILITATION CENTER, 2381 Lawrenceville Road, Lawrenceville, NJ, Zip 08648; tel. 609/896–9500; Charles L. Brennan, Chief Executive Officer

ST. MARY HOSPITAL, 308 Willow Avenue, Hoboken, NJ, Zip 07030–3889; tel. 201/418–1000; Robert S. Chaloner, President and Chief Executive Officer

ST. PETER'S UNIVERSITY HOSPITAL, 254 Easton Avenue, New Brunswick, NJ, Zip 08901–1780, Mailing Address: P.O. Box 591, Zip 08903–0591; tel. 732/745–8600; John E. Matuska, President and Chief Executive Officer

THE COOPER HEALTH SYSTEM, One Cooper Plaza, Camden, NJ, Zip 08103–1489; tel. 609/342–2000; Leslie D. Hirsch, Acting President and Chief Executive Officer

UNDERWOOD–MEMORIAL HOSPITAL, 509 North Broad Street, Woodbury, NJ, Zip 08096–1697, Mailing Address: P.O. Box 359, Zip 08096–7359; tel. 856/845–0100; Steven W. Jackmuff, President and Chief Executive Officer

UNION HOSPITAL, 1000 Galloping Hill Road, Union, NJ, Zip 07083–1652; tel. 908/687–1900; Kathryn W. Coyne, Executive Director and Chief Operating Officer

UNIVERSITY OF MEDICINE AND DENTISTRY OF NEW JERSEY–UNIVERSITY HOSPITAL, 150 Bergen Street, Newark, NJ, Zip 07103–2406; tel. 973/972–4300; Daniel L. Marcantuono, FACHE, Acting Vice President and Chief Executive Officer

VIRTUA–MEMORIAL HOSPITAL BURLINGTON COUNTY, 175 Madison Avenue, Mount Holly, NJ, Zip 08060–2099; tel. 609/267–0700; Donald I. Brunn, President and Chief Executive Officer

WARREN HOSPITAL, 185 Roseberry Street, Phillipsburg, NJ, Zip 08865–9955; tel. 908/859–6700; Jeffrey C. Goodwin, President and Chief Executive Officer

WAYNE GENERAL HOSPITAL, 224 Hamburg Turnpike, Wayne, NJ, Zip 07470–2100; tel. 973/942–6900; Kenneth H. Kozloff, Executive Director

WEST JERSEY HOSPITAL–CAMDEN, 1000 Atlantic Avenue, Camden, NJ, Zip 08104–1595; tel. 609/246–3000; Carolyn M. Ballard, Executive Director

WEST JERSEY HOSPITAL–MARLTON, 90 Brick Road, Marlton, NJ, Zip 08053–9697; tel. 609/355–6000; Leroy J. Rosenberg, Executive Director

WEST JERSEY HOSPITAL–VOORHEES, 101 Carnie Boulevard, Voorhees, NJ, Zip 08043–1597; tel. 609/325–3000; Joan T. Meyers, R.N., Executive Director

SETON HEALTH NETWORK INC
703 Main Street, Paterson, NJ 07503; tel. 201/977–2070; Anthony Losardo, M.D., President

ST. JOSEPH'S HOSPITAL AND MEDICAL CENTER, 703 Main Street, Paterson, NJ, Zip 07503–2691; tel. 973/754–2000; Patrick R. Wardell, President and Chief Executive Officer

SSM HEALTH CARE MINISTRY CORPORATION
22 Bloomfield Avenue, Denville, NJ 07834; tel. 201/625–6505; Joseph Trunfio, Ph.D, President

SAINT CLARE'S HEALTH SERVICES, 25 Pocono Road, Denville, NJ, Zip 07834–2995; tel. 973/625–6000; Kathryn J. McDonagh, President and Chief Executive Officer

ST. JOSEPH'S HOSPITAL AND MEDICAL CENTER, 703 Main Street, Paterson, NJ, Zip 07503–2691; tel. 973/754–2000; Patrick R. Wardell, President and Chief Executive Officer

ST. MARY'S HOSPITAL, 211 Pennington Avenue, Passaic, NJ, Zip 07055–4698; tel. 973/470–3000; Patricia Peterson, President and Chief Executive Officer

NEW MEXICO

LOVELACE
5400 Gibson Boulevard S.E., Albuquerque, NM 87108; tel. 505/262–7000; Martin Hickey, CEO

LOVELACE HEALTH SYSTEM, 5400 Gibson Boulevard S.E., Albuquerque, NM, Zip 87108–4763; tel. 505/262–7000; Martin Hickey, M.D., Chief Executive Officer

MEDICAL NETWORK OF NEW MEXICO
7850 Jefferson, Northeast, Albuquerque, NM 87109; tel. 505/727–8076; Jim Purdy, Executive Director

ST. JOSEPH MEDICAL CENTER, 601 Martin Luther King Jr. Drive N.E., Albuquerque, NM, Zip 87102, Mailing Address: P.O. Box 25555, Zip 87125–0555; tel. 505/727–8000; Steven J. Smith, President

ST. JOSEPH NORTHEAST HEIGHTS HOSPITAL, 4701 Montgomery Boulevard N.E., Albuquerque, NM, Zip 87109–1251, Mailing Address: P.O. Box 25555, Zip 87125–0555; tel. 505/727–7800; C. Vincent Townsend, Jr., Vice President

ST. JOSEPH REHABILITATION HOSPITAL AND OUTPATIENT CENTER, 505 Elm Street N.E., Albuquerque, NM, Zip 87102–2500, Mailing Address: P.O. Box 25555, Zip 87125–5555; tel. 505/727–4700; Mary Lou Coors, Administrator

ST. JOSEPH WEST MESA HOSPITAL, 10501 Golf Course Road N.W., Albuquerque, NM, Zip 87114–5000, Mailing Address: P.O. Box 25555, Zip 87125–0555; tel. 505/727–2000; C. Vincent Townsend, Jr., Vice President

UNIVERSITY HOSPITAL
2211 Lomas Boulevard, N.E., Albuquerque, NM 87106; tel. 505/843–2121; Steve McKernaw, Chief Executive

UNIVERSITY HOSPITAL, 2211 Lomas Boulevard N.E., Albuquerque, NM, Zip 87106–2745; tel. 505/272–2121; Stephen W. McKernan, Chief Executive Officer

UNIVERSITY OF NEW MEXICO MENTAL HEALTH CENTER, 2600 Marble N.E., Albuquerque, NM, Zip 87131–2600; tel. 505/272–2263; Stephen W. McKernan, Chief Executive Officer

NEW YORK

ADIRONDACK RURAL HEALTH NETWORK
100 Park Street, Glens Falls, NY 12801; tel. 518/792–3151; David Kruczlnicki, President

GLENS FALLS HOSPITAL, 100 Park Street, Glens Falls, NY, Zip 12801–9898; tel. 518/792–3151; David G. Kruczlnicki, President and Chief Executive Officer

ALLEGANY RURAL HEALTH NETWORK
191 North Main Street, Wellsville, NY 14895; tel. 716/593–1100; William M. DiBeradino, President & CEO

JONES MEMORIAL HOSPITAL, 191 North Main Street, Wellsville, NY, Zip 14895–1197, Mailing Address: P.O. Box 72, Zip 14895–0072; tel. 716/593–1100; William M. DiBerardino, FACHE, President and Chief Executive Officer

BASSETT HEALTHCARE
1 Atwell Road, Cooperstown, NY 13326; tel. 607/547–3100; William F. Streck, MD, President/CEO

BASSETT HOSPITAL OF SCHOHARIE COUNTY, 41 Grandview Drive, Cobleskill, NY, Zip 12043–1331; tel. 518/234–2511; Donald W. Massey, Administrator

MARY IMOGENE BASSETT HOSPITAL, One Atwell Road, Cooperstown, NY, Zip 13326–1394; tel. 607/547–3100; William F. Streck, M.D., President and Chief Executive Officer

BUFFALO GENERAL HEALTH SYSTEM
100 High Street, Buffalo, NY 14203;
tel. 716/845–2732; John L. Friedlander,
President/CEO

BUFFALO GENERAL HOSPITAL, 100 High Street, Buffalo, NY, Zip 14203–1154; tel. 716/845–5600; John E. Friedlander, President and Chief Executive Officer

DE GRAFF MEMORIAL HOSPITAL, 445 Tremont Street, North Tonawanda, NY, Zip 14120–0750, Mailing Address: P.O. Box 0750, Zip 14120–0750; tel. 716/694–4500; Marcia B. Gutfeld, Vice President and Chief Operating Officer

TRI–COUNTY MEMORIAL HOSPITAL, 100 Memorial Drive, Gowanda, NY, Zip 14070–1194; tel. 716/532–3377; Diane J. Osika, Chief Executive Officer

CHEMUNG COUNTY RURAL HEALTH NETWORK
600 Roe Avenue, Elmira, NY 14905;
tel. 607/737–4100; Anthony J. Cooper,
President & CEO

CHENANGO COUNTY RURAL HEALTH NETWORK
179 North Broad Street, Norwich, NY 13815;
tel. 607/335–4111; Frank W. Mirabito,
President

CHENANGO MEMORIAL HOSPITAL, 179 North Broad Street, Norwich, NY, Zip 13815–1097; tel. 607/337–4111; Frank W. Mirabito, President

COLUMBIA–PRES MED CEN HEALTH ALLIANCE
Columbia–Pres Med Cen, New York, NY
10032; tel. 212/305–2500; William T. Speck,
President & CEO

CORNWALL HOSPITAL, 19 Laurel Avenue, Cornwall, NY, Zip 12518–1499; tel. 914/534–7711; Louis H. Smith, Executive Vice President and Administrator

HELEN HAYES HOSPITAL, Route 9W, West Haverstraw, NY, Zip 10993–1195; tel. 914/786–4000; Magdalena Ramirez, Chief Executive Officer

HOLY NAME HOSPITAL, 718 Teaneck Road, Teaneck, NJ, Zip 07666–4281; tel. 201/833–3000; Michael Maron, President and Chief Executive Officer

HORTON MEDICAL CENTER, 60 Prospect Avenue, Middletown, NY, Zip 10940–4133; tel. 914/343–2424; Jeffrey D. Hirsch, Executive Vice President and Administrator

LAWRENCE HOSPITAL, 55 Palmer Avenue, Bronxville, NY, Zip 10708–3491; tel. 914/787–1000; Roger G. Dvorak, President

NEW MILFORD HOSPITAL, 21 Elm Street, New Milford, CT, Zip 06776–2993; tel. 860/355–2611; Richard E. Pugh, President and Chief Executive Officer

NYACK HOSPITAL, 160 North Midland Avenue, Nyack, NY, Zip 10960–1998; tel. 914/348–2000; Greger C. Anderson, President and Chief Executive Officer

PALISADES GENERAL HOSPITAL, 7600 River Road, North Bergen, NJ, Zip 07047–6217; tel. 201/854–5000; Bruce J. Markowitz, President and Chief Executive Officer

ST. FRANCIS HOSPITAL, 100 Port Washington Boulevard, Roslyn, NY, Zip 11576–1348; tel. 516/562–6000; Alan D. Guerci, M.D., Interim President and Chief Executive Officer

ST. LUKE'S HOSPITAL, 70 Dubois Street, Newburgh, NY, Zip 12550–4898, Mailing Address: P.O. Box 631, Zip 12550–0631; tel. 914/561–4400; Laurence E. Kelly, Executive Vice President and Administrator

VALLEY HOSPITAL, 223 North Van Dien Avenue, Ridgewood, NJ, Zip 07450–9982; tel. 201/447–8000; Audrey Meyers, President

WHITE PLAINS HOSPITAL CENTER, Davis Avenue and Post Road, White Plains, NY, Zip 10601–4699; tel. 914/681–0600; Jon B. Schandler, President and Chief Executive Officer

CONTINUUM HEALTH PARTNERS
555 West 57th Street, New York, NY 10019;
tel. 212/523–8390; Robert Newmas, MD,
President & CEO

BETH ISRAEL MEDICAL CENTER, First Avenue and 16th Street, New York, NY, Zip 10003–3803; tel. 212/420–2000; Matthew E. Fink, M.D., President and Chief Executive Officer

CATHOLIC MEDICAL CENTERS, 88–25 153rd Street, Jamaica, NY, Zip 11432–3731; tel. 718/558–6900; William D. McGuire, President and Chief Executive Officer

PENINSULA HOSPITAL CENTER, 51–15 Beach Channel Drive, Far Rockaway, NY, Zip 11691–1074; tel. 718/945–7100; Robert V. Levine, President and Chief Executive Officer

ST. LUKE'S–ROOSEVELT HOSPITAL CENTER, 1111 Amsterdam Avenue, New York, NY, Zip 10025; tel. 212/523–4300; Sigurd H. Ackerman, M.D., President and Chief Executive Officer

VICTORY MEMORIAL HOSPITAL, 9036 Seventh Avenue, Brooklyn, NY, Zip 11228–3625; tel. 718/630–1234; Krishin L. Bhatia, Administrator

EPISCOPAL HEALTH SERVICES INC
333 Earle Ovington Boulevard, Uniondale, NY
11787; tel. 516/228–6100; Lorna
McBarnette, Executive Director

ST. JOHN'S EPISCOPAL HOSPITAL–SMITHTOWN, 50 Route 25–A, Smithtown, NY, Zip 11787–1398; tel. 516/862–3000; James M. Wilson, Regional Administrator

ST. JOHN'S EPISCOPAL HOSPITAL–SOUTH SHORE, 327 Beach 19th Street, Far Rockaway, NY, Zip 11691–4424; tel. 718/869–7000; Nancy Simmons, Administrator

FIRST CHOICE NETWORK, INC
165 EAB Plaza, West Tower 6, Uniondale, NY
11556–1165; tel. 516/474–6000; Dana
Metzler, Acting Executive Director

EASTERN LONG ISLAND HOSPITAL, 201 Manor Place, Greenport, NY, Zip 11944–1298; tel. 516/477–1000; John M. Gwiazda, President and Chief Executive Officer

SOUTHAMPTON HOSPITAL, 240 Meeting House Lane, Southampton, NY, Zip 11968–5090; tel. 516/726–8555; Thomas B. Doolan, Acting President and Chief Executive Officer

SOUTHSIDE HOSPITAL, 301 East Main Street, Bay Shore, NY, Zip 11706–8458; tel. 516/968–3000; Theodore A. Jospe, President

ST. CHARLES HOSPITAL AND REHABILITATION CENTER, 200 Belle Terre Road, Port Jefferson, NY, Zip 11777; tel. 516/474–6000; Barry T. Zeman, President and Chief Executive Officer

ST. JOHN'S EPISCOPAL HOSPITAL–SMITHTOWN, 50 Route 25–A, Smithtown, NY, Zip 11787–1398; tel. 516/862–3000; James M. Wilson, Regional Administrator

ST. JOHN'S EPISCOPAL HOSPITAL–SOUTH SHORE, 327 Beach 19th Street, Far Rockaway, NY, Zip 11691–4424; tel. 718/869–7000; Nancy Simmons, Administrator

WINTHROP–UNIVERSITY HOSPITAL, 259 First Street, Mineola, NY, Zip 11501; tel. 516/663–2200; Daniel P. Walsh, President and Chief Executive Officer

FOUR LAKES RURAL HEALTH NETWORK
196 North St., Geneva, NY 14456;
tel. 315/787–4000; James J. Dooley,
President & CEO

GENEVA GENERAL HOSPITAL, 196 North Street, Geneva, NY, Zip 14456–1694; tel. 315/787–4000; James J. Dooley, President

SOLDIERS AND SAILORS MEMORIAL HOSPITAL OF YATES COUNTY, 418 North Main Street, Penn Yan, NY, Zip 14527–1085; tel. 315/531–2000; James J. Dooley, President and Chief Executive Officer

GREENE COUNTY RURAL HEALTH NETWORK
71 Prospect Avenue, Catskill, NY 12534;
tel. 518/828–7601; Andrew E. Toga, Acting
CEO

ALBANY MEDICAL CENTER, 43 New Scotland Avenue, Albany, NY, Zip 12208–3478; tel. 518/262–3125; Mary A. Nolan, R.N., MS, Executive Vice President Care Delivery and General Director

COLUMBIA MEMORIAL HOSPITAL, 71 Prospect Avenue, Hudson, NY, Zip 12534–2900; tel. 518/828–8039; Jane Ehrlich, President and Chief Executive Officer

HAMILTON–BASSETT–CROUSE RURAL HEALTH
NETWORK
150 South Broad Street, Hamilton, NY 13346;
tel. 315/598–4735; David Felton,
President/CEO

COMMUNITY MEMORIAL HOSPITAL, 150 Broad Street, Hamilton, NY, Zip 13346–9518; tel. 315/824–1100; David Felton, President and Chief Executive Officer

CROUSE HOSPITAL, 736 Irving Avenue, Syracuse, NY, Zip 13210–1690; tel. 315/470–7111; Kent A. Arnold, President and Chief Executive Officer

HEALTH FIRST
25 Broadway, New York, NY 10019;
tel. 212/801–1500; Paul Dickstein, Network
Contact

NEW YORK UNIVERSITY HOSPITALS CENTER, 550 First Avenue, New York, NY, Zip 10016–4576; tel. 212/263–7300; Theresa A. Bischoff, Deputy Provost and Executive Vice President

BETH ISRAEL MEDICAL CENTER, First Avenue and 16th Street, New York, NY, Zip 10003–3803; tel. 212/420–2000; Matthew E. Fink, M.D., President and Chief Executive Officer

BRONX–LEBANON HOSPITAL CENTER, 1276 Fulton Avenue, Bronx, NY, Zip 10456–3499; tel. 718/590–1800; Miguel A. Fuentes, President and Chief Executive Officer

BROOKLYN HOSPITAL CENTER, 121 DeKalb Avenue, Brooklyn, NY, Zip 11201–5493; tel. 718/250–8005; Frederick D. Alley, President and Chief Executive Officer

BRUNSWICK GENERAL HOSPITAL, 366 Broadway, Amityville, NY, Zip 11701–9820; tel. 516/789–7000; Benjamin M. Stein, M.D., President

INTERFAITH MEDICAL CENTER, 555 Prospect Place, Brooklyn, NY, Zip 11238–4299; tel. 718/935–7000; Corbett A. Price, Chief Executive Officer

JAMAICA HOSPITAL MEDICAL CENTER, 8900 Van Wyck Expressway, Jamaica, NY, Zip 11418–2832; tel. 718/206–6000; David P. Rosen, President

KINGSBROOK JEWISH MEDICAL CENTER, 585 Schenectady Avenue, Brooklyn, NY, Zip 11203–1891; tel. 718/604–5000; Milton M. Gutman, Chief Executive Officer

MAIMONIDES MEDICAL CENTER, 4802 Tenth Avenue, Brooklyn, NY, Zip 11219–2916; tel. 718/283–6000; Stanley Brezenoff, President

MONTEFIORE MEDICAL CENTER, 111 East 210th Street, Bronx, NY, Zip 10467–2490; tel. 718/920–4321; Spencer Foreman, M.D., President

NASSAU COUNTY MEDICAL CENTER, 2201 Hempstead Turnpike, East Meadow, NY, Zip 11554–1854; tel. 516/572–0123; Jerald C. Newman, Chief Executive Officer

STATEN ISLAND UNIVERSITY HOSPITAL, 475 Seaview Avenue, Staten Island, NY, Zip 10305–9998; tel. 718/226–9000; Rick J. Varone, President

UNIVERSITY HOSPITAL, State University of New York, Stony Brook, NY, Zip 11794–8410; tel. 516/689–8333; Michael A. Maffetone, Director and Chief Executive Officer

UNIVERSITY HOSPITAL OF BROOKLYN–STATE UNIVERSITY OF NEW YORK HEALTH SCIENCE CENTER AT BROOKLYN, 445 Lenox Road, Brooklyn, NY, Zip 11203–2098; tel. 718/270–2404; Percy Allen, II, FACHE, Vice President Hospital Affairs and Chief Executive Officer

HEALTH STAR NETWORK
1 North Greenwich Road, Armonk, NY 10504;
tel. 914/273–2850; Kevin G. Murphy, Vice
President & Chief

LAWRENCE HOSPITAL, 55 Palmer Avenue, Bronxville, NY, Zip 10708–3491; tel. 914/787–1000; Roger G. Dvorak, President

NORTHERN WESTCHESTER HOSPITAL CENTER, 400 Main Street, Mount Kisco, NY, Zip 10549–3477; tel. 914/666–1200; Donald W. Davis, President

PHELPS MEMORIAL HOSPITAL CENTER, 701 North Broadway, Sleepy Hollow, NY, Zip 10591–1096; tel. 914/366–3000; Keith F. Safian, President and Chief Executive Officer

WHITE PLAINS HOSPITAL CENTER, Davis Avenue and Post Road, White Plains, NY, Zip 10601–4699; tel. 914/681–0600; Jon B. Schandler, President and Chief Executive Officer

LAKE ONTARIO RURAL HEALTH NETWORK
200 Ohio Street, Medina, NY 14103;
tel. 716/798–2000; Walter S. Becker,
Administrator

MEDINA MEMORIAL HOSPITAL, 200 Ohio Street, Medina, NY, Zip 14103–1095; tel. 716/798–2000; James Sinner, Chief Executive Officer

UNITED MEMORIAL MEDICAL CENTER–BANK STREET, 16 Bank Street, Batavia, NY, Zip 14020–2260; tel. 716/343–3131; Gary DeLisle, Interim Chief Executive Officer

UNITED MEMORIAL MEDICAL CENTER–NORTH STREET, 127 North Street, Batavia, NY, Zip 14020–1697; tel. 716/343–6030; Gary DeLisle, Interim Chief Executive Officer

WYOMING COUNTY COMMUNITY HOSPITAL, 400 North Main Street, Warsaw, NY, Zip 14569–1097; tel. 716/786–2233; Lucille K. Sheedy, Administrator and Chief Executive Officer

MERCYCARE CORPORATION
315 South Manning Boulevard, Albany, NY
12208; tel. 518/454–1550; Steven Boyle,
President

ST. PETER'S HOSPITAL, 315 South Manning Boulevard, Albany, NY, Zip 12208–1789; tel. 518/525–1550; Steven P. Boyle, President and Chief Executive Officer

MOHAWK VALLEY NETWORK, INC
P.O. Box 5068, Utica, NY 13502–5068;
tel. 315/798–6386; Fred Asforth, Network
Vice President

FAXTON HOSPITAL, 1676 Sunset Avenue, Utica, NY, Zip 13502–5475; tel. 315/738–6200; Andrew E. Peterson, President and Chief Executive Officer

LITTLE FALLS HOSPITAL, 140 Burwell Street, Little Falls, NY, Zip 13365–1725; tel. 315/823–1000; David S. Armstrong, Jr., Administrator

ST. LUKE'S MEMORIAL HOSPITAL CENTER, Utica, NY, Mailing Address: P.O. Box 479, Zip 13503–0479; tel. 315/798–6000; Andrew E. Peterson, President and Chief Executive Officer

MOUNT SINAI NYU HEALTH NETWORK
P.O. Box 1068, New York, NY 10029;
tel. 212/241–6500; John W. Rowe, President

ARDEN HILL HOSPITAL, 4 Harriman Drive, Goshen, NY, Zip 10924–2499; tel. 914/294–5441; Wayne Becker, Interim Chief Executive Officer

BROOKDALE HOSPITAL MEDICAL CENTER, Linden Boulevard at Brookdale Plaza, Brooklyn, NY, Zip 11212–3198; tel. 718/240–5000; Frank J. Maddalena, President and Chief Executive Officer

CABRINI MEDICAL CENTER, 227 East 19th Street, New York, NY, Zip 10003–2600; tel. 212/995–6000; Jeffrey Frerichs, President and Chief Executive Officer

ELMHURST HOSPITAL CENTER, 79–01 Broadway, Elmhurst, NY, Zip 11373; tel. 718/334–4000; Pete Velez, Executive Director

ENGLEWOOD HOSPITAL AND MEDICAL CENTER, 350 Engle Street, Englewood, NJ, Zip 07631–1898; tel. 201/894–3000; Daniel A. Kane, President and Chief Executive Officer

GREENVILLE HOSPITAL, 1825 John F. Kennedy Boulevard, Jersey City, NJ, Zip 07305–2198; tel. 201/547–6100; Jonathan M. Metsch, Dr.PH, President and Chief Executive Officer

JERSEY CITY MEDICAL CENTER, 50 Baldwin Avenue, Jersey City, NJ, Zip 07304–3199; tel. 201/915–2000; Jonathan M. Metsch, Dr.PH, President and Chief Executive Officer

LONG BEACH MEDICAL CENTER, 455 East Bay Drive, Long Beach, NY, Zip 11561–2300, Mailing Address: P.O. Box 300, Zip 11561–2300; tel. 516/897–1000; Martin F. Nester, Jr., Chief Executive Officer

LONG ISLAND COLLEGE HOSPITAL, 339 Hicks Street, Brooklyn, NY, Zip 11201–5509; tel. 718/780–1000; Peter A. Kelly, Interim President and Chief Executive Officer

LUTHERAN MEDICAL CENTER, 150 55th Street, Brooklyn, NY, Zip 11220–2570; tel. 718/630–7000; Dominic J. Lodato, Interim President

MAIMONIDES MEDICAL CENTER, 4802 Tenth Avenue, Brooklyn, NY, Zip 11219–2916; tel. 718/283–6000; Stanley Brezenoff, President

MEADOWLANDS HOSPITAL MEDICAL CENTER, 55 Meadowland Parkway, Secaucus, NJ, Zip 07096–1580; tel. 201/392–3100; Paul V. Cavalli, M.D., President

PARKWAY HOSPITAL, 70–35 113th Street, Flushing, NY, Zip 11375; tel. 718/990–4100; Paul E. Svensson, Chief Executive Officer

PHELPS MEMORIAL HOSPITAL CENTER, 701 North Broadway, Sleepy Hollow, NY, Zip 10591–1096; tel. 914/366–3000; Keith F. Safian, President and Chief Executive Officer

QUEENS HOSPITAL CENTER, 82–68 164th Street, Jamaica, NY, Zip 11432–1104; tel. 718/883–3000; Gladiola Sampson, Executive Director

SAINT FRANCIS HOSPITAL, 35 North Road, Poughkeepsie, NY, Zip 12601–1399; tel. 914/471–2000; Sister M. Ann Elizabeth, President

ST. BARNABAS HOSPITAL, 183rd Street and Third Avenue, Bronx, NY, Zip 10457–9998, Mailing Address: 4422 Third Avenue, Zip 10457–9998; tel. 718/960–9000; Ronald Gade, M.D., President

ST. ELIZABETH HOSPITAL, 225 Williamson Street, Elizabeth, NJ, Zip 07202–3600; tel. 908/527–5000; Sister Elizabeth Ann Maloney, President and Chief Executive Officer

ST. JOHN'S EPISCOPAL HOSPITAL–SMITHTOWN, 50 Route 25–A, Smithtown, NY, Zip 11787–1398; tel. 516/862–3000; James M. Wilson, Regional Administrator

ST. JOHN'S EPISCOPAL HOSPITAL–SOUTH SHORE, 327 Beach 19th Street, Far Rockaway, NY, Zip 11691–4424; tel. 718/869–7000; Nancy Simmons, Administrator

ST. JOSEPH'S HOSPITAL AND MEDICAL CENTER, 703 Main Street, Paterson, NJ, Zip 07503–2691; tel. 973/754–2000; Patrick R. Wardell, President and Chief Executive Officer

ST. MARY'S HOSPITAL, 901 45th Street, West Palm Beach, FL, Zip 33407–2495, Mailing Address: P.O. Box 24620, Zip 33416–4620; tel. 561/844–6300; Phillip C. Dutcher, President and Chief Executive Officer

STATEN ISLAND UNIVERSITY HOSPITAL, 475 Seaview Avenue, Staten Island, NY, Zip 10305–9998; tel. 718/226–9000; Rick J. Varone, President

VASSAR BROTHERS HOSPITAL, 45 Reade Place, Poughkeepsie, NY, Zip 12601–3990; tel. 914/454–8500; Ronald T. Mullahey, President

VETERANS AFFAIRS MEDICAL CENTER, 130 West Kingsbridge Road, Bronx, NY, Zip 10468–3992; tel. 718/584–9000; Maryann Musumeci, Director

WESTERN QUEENS COMMUNITY HOSPITAL, 25–10 30th Avenue, Astoria Station, Long Island City, NY, Zip 11102–2495; tel. 718/932–1000; Elliot J. Simon, FACHE, Chief Operating Officer

NEW YORK PRESBYTERIAN HEALTHCARE NETWORK
525 East 68th Street, New York, NY 10021;
tel. 212/746–4036; Dr. Barbara DeBuono,
President

GRACIE SQUARE HOSPITAL, 420 East 76th Street, New York, NY, Zip 10021–3104; tel. 212/988–4400; Frank Bruno, Chief Executive Officer

HOSPITAL FOR SPECIAL SURGERY, 535 East 70th Street, New York, NY, Zip 10021–4898; tel. 212/606–1000; John R. Reynolds, President and Chief Executive Officer

NEW YORK COMMUNITY HOSPITAL, 2525 Kings Highway, Brooklyn, NY, Zip 11229–1798; tel. 718/692–5300; Lin H. Mo, President and Chief Executive Officer

NEW YORK FLUSHING HOSPITAL MEDICAL CENTER, 45th Avenue at Parsons Boulevard, Flushing, NY, Zip 11355–2100; tel. 718/670–5000; Stephen S. Mills, President and Chief Executive Officer

NEW YORK HOSPITAL MEDICAL CENTER OF QUEENS, 56–45 Main Street, Flushing, NY, Zip 11355–5000; tel. 718/670–1231; Stephen S. Mills, President and Chief Executive Officer

NEW YORK METHODIST HOSPITAL, 506 Sixth Street, Brooklyn, NY, Zip 11215–3645; tel. 718/780–3000; Mark J. Mundy, President and Chief Executive Officer

NEW YORK PRESBYTERIAN HOSPITAL, 525 East 68th Street, New York, NY, Zip 10021–4885; tel. 212/746–5454; David B. Skinner, M.D., Vice Chairman and Chief Executive Officer; William T. Speck, President and Chief Operating Officer

UNITED HOSPITAL MEDICAL CENTER, 406 Boston Post Road, Port Chester, NY, Zip 10573–7300; tel. 914/934–3000; Kevin Dahill, President and Chief Executive Officer

WYCKOFF HEIGHTS MEDICAL CENTER, 374 Stockholm Street, Brooklyn, NY, Zip 11237–4099; tel. 718/963–7102; Dominick J. Gio, President and Chief Executive Officer

NORTH SHORE–LIJ HEALTH SYSTEM
150 Community Drive, Great Neck, NY 11021;
tel. 516/465–8000; Jeffrey A. Kraut, Senior
Vice President, Planning

FRANKLIN HOSPITAL MEDICAL CENTER, 900 Franklin Avenue, Valley Stream, NY, Zip 11580–2190; tel. 516/256–6000; William Kowalewski, President and Chief Executive Officer

HUNTINGTON HOSPITAL, 270 Park Avenue, Huntington, NY, Zip 11743–2799; tel. 516/351–2200; J. Ronald Gaudreault, President and Chief Executive Officer

LONG ISLAND JEWISH MEDICAL CENTER, 270–05 76th Avenue, New Hyde Park, NY, Zip 11040–1496; tel. 718/470–7000; David R. Dantzker, M.D., President

MOUNT SINAI–NYU HOSPITALS/HEALTH SYSTEM, One Gustave Levy Place, New York, NY, Zip 10019–6574; tel. 212/241–6500; John W. Rowe, M.D., President

NORTH SHORE UNIVERSITY HOSPITAL, 300 Community Drive, Manhasset, NY, Zip 11030–3876; tel. 516/562–0100; John S. T. Gallagher, Chief Executive Officer

NORTH SHORE UNIVERSITY HOSPITAL AT GLEN COVE, 101 St. Andrews Lane, Glen Cove, NY, Zip 11542; tel. 516/674–7300; Mark R. Stenzler, Vice President Administration

NORTH SHORE UNIVERSITY HOSPITAL AT PLAINVIEW, 888 Old Country Road, Plainview, NY, Zip 11803–4978; tel. 516/719–3000; Deborah Tascone, R.N., MS, Vice President for Administration

NORTH SHORE UNIVERSITY HOSPITAL AT SYOSSET, 221 Jericho Turnpike, Syosset, NY, Zip 11791–4567; tel. 516/496–6400; Deborah Tascone, R.N., MS, Vice President of Administration

SCHNEIDER CHILDREN'S HOSPITAL, 270–05 76th Avenue, New Hyde Park, NY, Zip 11040; tel. 718/470–3000

SOUTHSIDE HOSPITAL, 301 East Main Street, Bay Shore, NY, Zip 11706–8458; tel. 516/968–3000; Theodore A. Jospe, President

STATEN ISLAND UNIVERSITY HOSPITAL, 475 Seaview Avenue, Staten Island, NY, Zip 10305–9998; tel. 718/226–9000; Rick J. Varone, President

NORTHERN NY RURAL HEALTH CARE ALLIANCE
200 Woolworth Building, Watertown, NY
13601; tel. 315/786–0565; Janice Charles,
Chairman

Section B

CARTHAGE AREA HOSPITAL, 1001 West Street, Carthage, NY, Zip 13619–9703; tel. 315/493–1000; Walter S. Becker, Administrator

E. J. NOBLE HOSPITAL SAMARITAN, 19 Fuller Street, Alexandria Bay, NY, Zip 13607; tel. 315/482–2511; Richard A. Brooks, Administrator and Chief Operating Officer

EDWARD JOHN NOBLE HOSPITAL OF GOUVERNEUR, 77 West Barney Street, Gouverneur, NY, Zip 13642–1090; tel. 315/287–1000; Charles P. Conole, FACHE, Administrator

SAMARITAN, 2215 Burdett Avenue, Troy, NY, Zip 12180–2475; tel. 518/271–3300; Paul A. Milton, Chief Operating Officer

NYU MEDICAL CENTER
550 First Avenue, New York, NY 10016; tel. 212/263–5500; John P. Harney, Senior Administrator, Hospital

BROOKLYN HOSPITAL CENTER, 121 DeKalb Avenue, Brooklyn, NY, Zip 11201–5493; tel. 718/250–8005; Frederick D. Alley, President and Chief Executive Officer

HOSPITAL FOR JOINT DISEASES ORTHOPAEDIC INSTITUTE, 301 East 17th Street, New York, NY, Zip 10003–3890; tel. 212/598–6000; John N. Kastanis, FACHE, President and Chief Executive Officer

JAMAICA HOSPITAL MEDICAL CENTER, 8900 Van Wyck Expressway, Jamaica, NY, Zip 11418–2832; tel. 718/206–6000; David P. Rosen, President

LENOX HILL HOSPITAL, 100 East 77th Street, New York, NY, Zip 10021–1883; tel. 212/434–2000; Gladys George, President and Chief Executive Officer

NEW YORK UNIVERSITY DOWNTOWN HOSPITAL, 170 William Street, New York, NY, Zip 10038–2649; tel. 212/312–5000; Leonard A. Aubrey, President and Chief Executive Officer

OSWEGO COUNTY RURAL HEALTH NETWORK
110 West Sixth Avenue, Oswego, NY 13126; tel. 315/349–5511; Corte Spencer, Co–Chairman

ALBERT LINDLEY LEE MEMORIAL HOSPITAL, 510 South Fourth Street, Fulton, NY, Zip 13069–2994; tel. 315/592–2224; Dennis A. Casey, Executive Director

OSWEGO HOSPITAL, 110 West Sixth Street, Oswego, NY, Zip 13126–9985; tel. 315/349–5511; Corte J. Spencer, Chief Executive Officer

PREFERRED HEALTH NETWORK INC
45 Avenue & Parsons Boulevard, Flushing, NY 11355; tel. 718/963–7102; Charles J. Pandola, President

NEW YORK FLUSHING HOSPITAL MEDICAL CENTER, 45th Avenue at Parsons Boulevard, Flushing, NY, Zip 11355–2100; tel. 718/670–5000; Stephen S. Mills, President and Chief Executive Officer

WYCKOFF HEIGHTS MEDICAL CENTER, 374 Stockholm Street, Brooklyn, NY, Zip 11237–4099; tel. 718/963–7102; Dominick J. Gio, President and Chief Executive Officer

QUEENS HOSPITAL CENTER
79–01 Broadway, Elmhurst, NY 11373; tel. 718/334–4000; Peter Velez, Network Senior Vice President

ELMHURST HOSPITAL CENTER, 79–01 Broadway, Elmhurst, NY, Zip 11373; tel. 718/334–4000; Pete Velez, Executive Director

S.U.N.N.Y.
101 Broard Street, Sibley Hall 227, Plattsburg, NY 12901–2681; tel. 800/388–0199; Janice Bonn, PhD, Network Coordinator

CHAMPLAIN VALLEY PHYSICIANS HOSPITAL MEDICAL CENTER, 75 Beekman Street, Plattsburgh, NY, Zip 12901–1493; tel. 518/561–2000; Kevin J. Carroll, President

ELIZABETHTOWN COMMUNITY HOSPITAL, Park Street, Elizabethtown, NY, Zip 12932–0277, Mailing Address: P.O. Box 277, Zip 12932–0277; tel. 518/873–6377; Douglas G. Cushing, Administrator

SETON HEALTH CARE SYSTEM
1300 Massachusetts Avenue, Troy, NY 12180; tel. 518/268–5000; Dr. Mark Donovan, President

SETON HEALTH SYSTEM, 1300 Massachusetts Avenue, Troy, NY, Zip 12180–1695; tel. 518/268–5000; Mark A. Donovan, M.D., President and Chief Executive Officer

SHARED HEALTH NETWORK
125 Wolf Road, Suite 404, Albany, NY 12205; tel. 518/458–8607; Eugene Stearns, Executive Director

ELLIS HOSPITAL, 1101 Nott Street, Schenectady, NY, Zip 12308–2487; tel. 518/243–4000; G. B. Serrill, President and Chief Executive Officer

GLENS FALLS HOSPITAL, 100 Park Street, Glens Falls, NY, Zip 12801–9898; tel. 518/792–3151; David G. Kruczlnicki, President and Chief Executive Officer

MEMORIAL HOSPITAL, 600 Northern Boulevard, Albany, NY, Zip 12204–1083; tel. 518/471–3221; Norman E. Dascher, Jr., Chief Executive Officer

NATHAN LITTAUER HOSPITAL AND NURSING HOME, 99 East State Street, Gloversville, NY, Zip 12078–1293; tel. 518/725–8621; Thomas J. Dowd, President

SAMARITAN HOSPITAL, 2215 Burdett Avenue, Troy, NY, Zip 12180–2475; tel. 518/271–3300; Paul A. Milton, Chief Operating Officer

SARATOGA HOSPITAL, 211 Church Street, Saratoga Springs, NY, Zip 12866–1003; tel. 518/587–3222; David Andersen, President and Chief Executive Officer

SETON HEALTH SYSTEM, 1300 Massachusetts Avenue, Troy, NY, Zip 12180–1695; tel. 518/268–5000; Mark A. Donovan, M.D., President and Chief Executive Officer

ST. CLARE'S HOSPITAL OF SCHENECTADY, 600 McClellan Street, Schenectady, NY, Zip 12304–1090; tel. 518/382–2000; Paul J. Chodkowski, President and Chief Executive Officer

ST. MARY'S HOSPITAL, 427 Guy Park Avenue, Amsterdam, NY, Zip 12010–1095; tel. 518/842–1900; Peter E. Capobianco, President and Chief Executive Officer

ST. PETER'S HOSPITAL, 315 South Manning Boulevard, Albany, NY, Zip 12208–1789; tel. 518/525–1550; Steven P. Boyle, President and Chief Executive Officer

SUNNYVIEW HOSPITAL AND REHABILITATION CENTER, 1270 Belmont Avenue, Schenectady, NY, Zip 12308–2104; tel. 518/382–4500; Bradford M. Goodwin, President and Chief Executive Officer

SISTERS OF CHARITY HEALTHCARE
75 Vanderbilt Ave., Staten Island,, NY 10304; tel. 354/718–5080; John J. DePierro, FACHE, President & CEO

CALVARY HOSPITAL, 1740 Eastchester Road, Bronx, NY, Zip 10461–2392; tel. 718/863–6900; Frank A. Calamari, President and Chief Executive Officer

OUR LADY OF MERCY MEDICAL CENTER, 600 East 233rd Street, Bronx, NY, Zip 10466–2697; tel. 718/920–9000; Gary S. Horan, FACHE, President and Chief Executive Officer

SAINT VINCENTS HOSPITAL AND MEDICAL CENTER, 153 West 11th Street, New York, NY, Zip 10011–8397; tel. 212/604–7000; Karl P. Adler, M.D., President and Chief Executive Officer

SISTERS OF CHARITY MEDICAL CENTER, 355 Bard Avenue, Staten Island, NY, Zip 10310–1699; tel. 718/876–1234; Dominick M. Stanzione, Chief Operating Officer and Executive Vice President

ST. AGNES HOSPITAL, 305 North Street, White Plains, NY, Zip 10605–2299; tel. 914/681–4500; Gary S. Horan, FACHE, President and Chief Executive Officer

ST. CLARE'S HOSPITAL AND HEALTH CENTER, 415 West 51st Street, New York, NY, Zip 10019–6394; tel. 212/586–1500; James A. Rutherford, President and Chief Executive Officer

ST. JOSEPH'S MEDICAL CENTER, 127 South Broadway, Yonkers, NY, Zip 10701–4080; tel. 914/378–7000; Sister Mary Linehan, President

THE BROOKLYN HEALTH NETWORK
121 DeKalb Avenue, Brooklyn, NY 11201; tel. 718/250–8000; Fred Alley, CEO

BROOKLYN HOSPITAL CENTER, 121 DeKalb Avenue, Brooklyn, NY, Zip 11201–5493; tel. 718/250–8005; Frederick D. Alley, President and Chief Executive Officer

INTERFAITH MEDICAL CENTER, 555 Prospect Place, Brooklyn, NY, Zip 11238–4299; tel. 718/935–7000; Corbett A. Price, Chief Executive Officer

KINGSBROOK JEWISH MEDICAL CENTER, 585 Schenectady Avenue, Brooklyn, NY, Zip 11203–1891; tel. 718/604–5000; Milton M. Gutman, Chief Executive Officer

VICTORY MEMORIAL HOSPITAL, 9036 Seventh Avenue, Brooklyn, NY, Zip 11228–3625; tel. 718/630–1234; Krishin L. Bhatia, Administrator

THE EXCELCARE SYSTEM, INC
33 Palmer Avenue, Bronxville, NY 10708; tel. 914/787–3000; Victor C. Botnick, CEO

HUDSON VALLEY HOSPITAL CENTER, 1980 Crompond Road, Cortlandt Manor, NY, Zip 10567; tel. 914/737–9000; John C. Federspiel, President and Chief Executive Officer

LAWRENCE HOSPITAL, 55 Palmer Avenue, Bronxville, NY, Zip 10708–3491; tel. 914/787–1000; Roger G. Dvorak, President

PHELPS MEMORIAL HOSPITAL CENTER, 701 North Broadway, Sleepy Hollow, NY, Zip 10591–1096; tel. 914/366–3000; Keith F. Safian, President and Chief Executive Officer

ST. JOSEPH'S MEDICAL CENTER, 127 South Broadway, Yonkers, NY, Zip 10701–4080; tel. 914/378–7000; Sister Mary Linehan, President

UNITED HOSPITAL MEDICAL CENTER, 406 Boston Post Road, Port Chester, NY, Zip 10573–7300; tel. 914/934–3000; Kevin Dahill, President and Chief Executive Officer

THE NEW YORK HOSPITAL HEALTH PLAN
525 E. 68th Street, New York, NY 10021; tel. 212/297–5510; Robert Chernow, CEO

TRI–STATE HEALTH SYSTEM
255 Lafayette Ave., Suffern, NY 10901; tel. 914/368–5000; James A. Martin, President & CEO

MERCY COMMUNITY HOSPITAL, 160 East Main Street, Port Jervis, NY, Zip 12771–2245, Mailing Address: P.O. Box 1014, Zip 12771–1014; tel. 914/856–5351; Michael Parmer, M.D., Site Administrator

ST. ANTHONY COMMUNITY HOSPITAL, 15 Maple Avenue, Warwick, NY, Zip 10990–5180; tel. 914/986–2276; James A. Martin, President and Chief Executive Officer

UHS HEALTHCARE SYSTEM–BINGHAMTON
P.O. Box 540, Johnson City, NY 13790; tel. 607/763–6000; Matthew Salanger, CEO

UNITY HEALTH SYSTEM
89 Genesee Street, Rochester, NY 14611; tel. 716/464–3203; Timothy R. McCormick, President

PARK RIDGE HOSPITAL, 1555 Long Pond Road, Rochester, NY, Zip 14626–4182; tel. 716/723–7000; Martin E. Carlin, President

ST. MARY'S HOSPITAL, 89 Genesee Street, Rochester, NY, Zip 14611–3285; tel. 716/464–3000; Stewart Putnam, President

VIAHEALTH
150 N. Chestnut St., Rochester, NY 14604; tel. 716/922–3000; John R. Kessler, Jr., Vice President Marketing/PL/PR

GENESEE HOSPITAL, 224 Alexander Street, Rochester, NY, Zip 14607–4055; tel. 716/263–6000; William R. Holman, President

ROCHESTER GENERAL HOSPITAL, 1425 Portland Avenue, Rochester, NY, Zip 14621–3099; tel. 716/338–4000; Richard S. Constantino, M.D., President

NORTH CAROLINA

BLADEN RURAL HEALTH NETWORK
P.O. Box 398, Elizabethtown, NC 28337; tel. 910/862–5178; Leo Petit, CEO

BLADEN COUNTY HOSPITAL, 501 South Poplar Street, Elizabethtown, NC, Zip 28337–0398, Mailing Address: P.O. Box 398, Zip 28337–0398; tel. 910/862–5100; Leo A. Petit, Jr., Chief Executive Officer

CAROLINAS HOSPITAL NETWORK
P.O. Box 32861, Charlotte, NC 28232; tel. 704/355–8625; Austin Letson, President

ANSON COMMUNITY HOSPITAL, 500 Morven Road, Wadesboro, NC, Zip 28170–2745; tel. 704/694–5131; Frederick G. Thompson, Ph.D., Administrator and Chief Executive Officer

CAROLINAS MEDICAL CENTER, 1000 Blythe Boulevard, Charlotte, NC, Zip 28203–5871, Mailing Address: P.O. Box 32861, Zip 28232–2861; tel. 704/355–2000; Paul S. Franz, President

CHARLOTTE INSTITUTE OF REHABILITATION, 1100 Blythe Boulevard, Charlotte, NC, Zip 28203–5864; tel. 704/355–4300; Don Gabriel, Administrator

CLEVELAND REGIONAL MEDICAL CENTER, 201 Grover Street, Shelby, NC, Zip 28150–3940; tel. 704/487–3000; John Young, President and Chief Executive Officer

IREDELL MEMORIAL HOSPITAL, 557 Brookdale Drive, Statesville, NC, Zip 28677–1828, Mailing Address: P.O. Box 1828, Zip 28687–1828; tel. 704/873–5661; S. Arnold Nunnery, President and Chief Executive Officer

MERCY HOSPITAL, 2001 Vail Avenue, Charlotte, NC, Zip 28207–1289; tel. 704/379–5100; C. Curtis Copenhaver, President

RICHMOND MEMORIAL HOSPITAL, 925 Long Drive, Rockingham, NC, Zip 28379–4815; tel. 910/417–3000; David G. Hohl, Chief Executive Officer

UNION REGIONAL MEDICAL CENTER, 600 Hospital Drive, Monroe, NC, Zip 28112–6000, Mailing Address: P.O. Box 5003, Zip 28111–5003; tel. 704/283–3100; John W. Roberts, President and Chief Executive Officer

UNIVERSITY HOSPITAL, 8800 North Tryon Street, Charlotte, NC, Zip 28262–8415, Mailing Address: P.O. Box 560727, Zip 28256–0727; tel. 704/548–6000; W. Spencer Lilly, Administrator

VALDESE GENERAL HOSPITAL, Valdese, NC, Mailing Address: P.O. Box 700, Zip 28690–0700; tel. 828/874–2251; Lloyd E. Wallace, President and Chief Executive Officer

CENTRAL CAROLINA RURAL HOSPITAL ALLIANCE
P.O. Box 938, Albemarle, NC 28002; tel. 704/983–8955; Robert Smith, Executive Director

RICHMOND MEMORIAL HOSPITAL, 925 Long Drive, Rockingham, NC, Zip 28379–4815; tel. 910/417–3000; David G. Hohl, Chief Executive Officer

STANLY MEMORIAL HOSPITAL, 301 Yadkin Street, Albemarle, NC, Zip 28001, Mailing Address: P.O. Box 1489, Zip 28002–1489; tel. 704/984–4000; Roy M. Hinson, CHE, President and Chief Executive Officer

UNION REGIONAL MEDICAL CENTER, 600 Hospital Drive, Monroe, NC, Zip 28112–6000, Mailing Address: P.O. Box 5003, Zip 28111–5003; tel. 704/283–3100; John W. Roberts, President and Chief Executive Officer

DUKE HEALTH NETWORK
3100 Tower Building, Suite 600, Durham, NC 27707; tel. 919/419–5001; Paul Rosenberg, Chief Operating Officer

DUKE UNIVERSITY MEDICAL CENTER, Erwin Road, Durham, NC, Zip 27710, Mailing Address: P.O. Box 3708, Zip 27710–3708; tel. 919/684–8111; Michael D. Israel, Chief Executive Officer and Vice Chancellor

MARIA PARHAM HOSPITAL, 566 Ruin Creek Road, Henderson, NC, Zip 27536–2957; tel. 252/438–4143; Philip S. Lakernick, President and Chief Executive Officer

EASTERN CAROLINA HEALTH NETWORK
P.O. Box 8468, Greenville, NC 27835; tel. 919/816–6750; Randall H.H. Madry, CEO

ALBEMARLE HOSPITAL, 1144 North Road Street, Elizabeth City, NC, Zip 27909, Mailing Address: P.O. Box 1587, Zip 27906–1587; tel. 252/335–0531; Philip D. Bagby, President and Chief Executive Officer

BEAUFORT COUNTY HOSPITAL, 628 East 12th Street, Washington, NC, Zip 27889–3498; tel. 252/975–4100; Kenneth E. Ragland, Administrator

BERTIE MEMORIAL HOSPITAL, 401 Sterlingworth Street, Windsor, NC, Zip 27983–1726, Mailing Address: P.O. Box 40, Zip 27983–1726; tel. 252/794–3141; Anthony F. Mullen, Administrator

CARTERET GENERAL HOSPITAL, 3500 Arendell Street, Morehead City, NC, Zip 28557–2901, Mailing Address: P.O. Box 1619, Zip 28557–1619; tel. 252/247–1616; F. A. Odell, III, FACHE, President

CHOWAN HOSPITAL, 211 Virginia Road, Edenton, NC, Zip 27932–0629, Mailing Address: P.O. Box 629, Zip 27932–0629; tel. 252/482–8451; Barbara R. Cale, Administrator

CRAVEN REGIONAL MEDICAL AUTHORITY, 2000 Neuse Boulevard, New Bern, NC, Zip 28560–3499, Mailing Address: P.O. Box 12157, Zip 28561–2157; tel. 252/633–8111; Raymond Budrys, Chief Executive Officer

DUPLIN GENERAL HOSPITAL, 401 North Main Street, Kenansville, NC, Zip 28349–9989, Mailing Address: P.O. Box 278, Zip 28349–0278; tel. 910/296–0941; Richard E. Harrell, President and Chief Executive Officer

HALIFAX REGIONAL MEDICAL CENTER, 250 Smith Church Road, Roanoke Rapids, NC, Zip 27870–4914, Mailing Address: P.O. Box 1089, Zip 27870–1089; tel. 252/535–8011; M. E. Gilstrap, President and Chief Executive Officer

HERITAGE HOSPITAL, 111 Hospital Drive, Tarboro, NC, Zip 27886–2011; tel. 252/641–7700; Janet Mullaney, President

LENOIR MEMORIAL HOSPITAL, 100 Airport Road, Kinston, NC, Zip 28501, Mailing Address: P.O. Box 1678, Zip 28503–1678; tel. 252/522–7000; Gary E. Black, President and Chief Executive Officer

MARTIN GENERAL HOSPITAL, 310 South McCaskey Road, Williamston, NC, Zip 27892–2150, Mailing Address: P.O. Box 1128, Zip 27892–1128; tel. 252/809–6121; Scott M. Landrum, Chief Executive Officer

NASH HEALTH CARE SYSTEMS, 2460 Curtis Ellis Drive, Rocky Mount, NC, Zip 27804–2297; tel. 252/443–8000; Richard Kirk Toomey, President and Chief Executive Officer

ONSLOW MEMORIAL HOSPITAL, 317 Western Boulevard, Jacksonville, NC, Zip 28540, Mailing Address: P.O. Box 1358, Zip 28540–1358; tel. 910/577–2281; Douglas Kramer, Chief Executive Officer

PITT COUNTY MEMORIAL HOSPITAL–UNIVERSITY HEALTH SYSTEMS OF EASTERN CAROLINA, 2100 Stantonsburg Road, Greenville, NC, Zip 27835–6028, Mailing Address: Box 6028, Zip 27835–6028; tel. 252/816–4451; Dave C. McRae, President and Chief Executive Officer

PUNGO DISTRICT HOSPITAL, 202 East Water Street, Belhaven, NC, Zip 27810–9998; tel. 919/943–2111; Thomas O. Miller, Administrator

ROANOKE–CHOWAN HOSPITAL, 500 South Academy Street, Ahoskie, NC, Zip 27910, Mailing Address: P.O. Box 1385, Zip 27910–1385; tel. 252/209–3000; Susan S. Lassiter, President and Chief Executive Officer

WASHINGTON COUNTY HOSPITAL, 958 U.S. Highway 64 East, Plymouth, NC, Zip 27962–9591; tel. 252/793–4135; Lawrence H. McAvoy, Administrator

WAYNE MEMORIAL HOSPITAL, 2700 Wayne Memorial Drive, Goldsboro, NC, Zip 27534–8001, Mailing Address: P.O. Box 8001, Zip 27533–8001; tel. 919/736–1110; James W. Hubbell, President and Chief Executive Officer

WILSON MEMORIAL HOSPITAL, 1705 South Tarboro Street, Wilson, NC, Zip 27893–3428; tel. 252/399–8040; Christopher T. Durrer, President and Chief Executive Officer

HOSPITAL ALLIANCE FOR COMMUNITY HEALTH
c/o Peter J. Morris, MD MPH, P.O. Box 46833, Raleigh, NC 27620–6833; tel. 919/250–3813; Peter J. Morris MD MPH, Secretary

RALEIGH COMMUNITY HOSPITAL, 3400 Wake Forest Road, Raleigh, NC, Zip 27609–7373, Mailing Address: P.O. Box 28280, Zip 27611–8280; tel. 919/954–3000; James E. Raynor, Chief Executive Officer

REX HEALTHCARE, 4420 Lake Boone Trail, Raleigh, NC, Zip 27607–6599; tel. 919/784–3100; James W. Albright, President and Chief Executive Officer

WAKE MEDICAL CENTER, 3000 New Bern Avenue, Raleigh, NC, Zip 27610–1295; tel. 919/250–8000; Raymond L. Champ, President

MISSION & SAINT JOSEPH
509 Biltmore Avenue, Asheville, NC 28801; tel. 704/255–3100; Robert F. Burgin, President & CEO

MEMORIAL MISSION HOSPITAL, 509 Biltmore Avenue, Asheville, NC, Zip 28801–4690

ST. JOSEPH'S HOSPITAL, 428 Biltmore Avenue, Asheville, NC, Zip 28801–9839; tel. 828/255–3100

NORTH CAROLINA HEALTH
P.O. Box 668800, Charlotte, NC 28266; tel. 704/529–3300; Rose Duncan, Interim Director

MOSES CONE HEALTH SYSTEM, 1200 North Elm Street, Greensboro, NC, Zip 27401–1020; tel. 336/832–1000; Dennis R. Barry, President

UNC HEALTH NETWORK
101 Manning Drive, Chapel Hill, NC 27514; tel. 919/966–3709; Carol Straight, Network Development

ALAMANCE REGIONAL MEDICAL CENTER, 1240 Huffman Mill Road, Burlington, NC, Zip 27216–0202, Mailing Address: P.O. Box 202, Zip 27216–0202; tel. 336/538–7000; Thomas E. Ryan, President

CHATHAM HOSPITAL, West Third Street and Ivy Avenue, Siler City, NC, Zip 27344–2343, Mailing Address: P.O. Box 649, Zip 27344; tel. 919/663–2113; Woodrow W. Hathaway, Jr., Chief Executive Officer

COLUMBUS COUNTY HOSPITAL, 500 Jefferson Street, Whiteville, NC, Zip 28472–9987; tel. 910/642–8011; William S. Clark, Chief Executive Officer

FIRSTHEALTH MOORE REGIONAL HOSPITAL, 155 Memorial Drive, Pinehurst, NC, Zip 28374, Mailing Address: P.O. Box 3000, Zip 28374–3000; tel. 910/215–1000; Charles T. Frock, President and Chief Executive Officer

GOOD HOPE HOSPITAL, 410 Denim Drive, Erwin, NC, Zip 28339–0668, Mailing Address: P.O. Box 668, Zip 28339–0668; tel. 910/897–6151; Donald E. Annis, Chief Executive Officer

GRANVILLE MEDICAL CENTER, 1010 College Street, Oxford, NC, Zip 27565–2507, Mailing Address: Box 947, Zip 27565–0947; tel. 919/690–3000; Joe W. Pollard, Jr., Chief Executive Officer

JOHNSTON MEMORIAL HOSPITAL, 509 North Bright Leaf Boulevard, Smithfield, NC, Zip 27577–1376, Mailing Address: P.O. Box 1376, Zip 27577–1376; tel. 919/934–8171; Leland E. Farnell, President

Section B

MARIA PARHAM HOSPITAL, 566 Ruin Creek Road, Henderson, NC, Zip 27536–2957; tel. 252/438–4143; Philip S. Lakernick, President and Chief Executive Officer

MOREHEAD MEMORIAL HOSPITAL, 117 East King's Highway, Eden, NC, Zip 27288–5299; tel. 336/623–9711; Robert Enders, President

NORTH CAROLINA BAPTIST HOSPITAL, Medical Center Boulevard, Winston–Salem, NC, Zip 27157; tel. 336/716–2011; Len B. Preslar, Jr., President and Chief Executive Officer

SAMPSON REGIONAL MEDICAL CENTER, 607 Beaman Street, Clinton, NC, Zip 28328–2697, Mailing Address: Drawer 258, Zip 28329–0258; tel. 910/592–8511; Lee Pridgen, Jr., Administrator

SCOTLAND MEMORIAL HOSPITAL, 500 Lauchwood Drive, Laurinburg, NC, Zip 28352–5599; tel. 910/291–7000; Gregory C. Wood, Chief Executive Officer

SOUTHEASTERN REGIONAL MEDICAL CENTER, 300 West 27th Street, Lumberton, NC, Zip 28358–3017, Mailing Address: P.O. Box 1408, Zip 28359–1408; tel. 910/671–5000; J. L. Welsh, Jr., President and Chief Executive Officer

UNIVERSITY OF NORTH CAROLINA HOSPITALS, 101 Manning Drive, Chapel Hill, NC, Zip 27514–4220; tel. 919/966–4131; Eric B. Munson, President and Chief Executive Officer

WAKE MEDICAL CENTER, 3000 New Bern Avenue, Raleigh, NC, Zip 27610–1295; tel. 919/250–8000; Raymond L. Champ, President

WAKE FOREST UNIVERSITY BAPTIST MEDICAL CENTER Medical Center Boulevard, Winston–Salem, NC 27157; tel. 336/716–7840; G. Douglas Atkinson, Associate Dean/Vice President of Networks

ALEXANDER COMMUNITY HOSPITAL, 326 Third Street S.W., Taylorsville, NC, Zip 28681–3096; tel. 828/632–4282; Joe W. Pollard, Jr., Chief Executive Officer

ALLEGHANY MEMORIAL HOSPITAL, 233 Doctors Street, Sparta, NC, Zip 28675–0009, Mailing Address: P.O. Box 9, Zip 28675–0009; tel. 336/372–5511; James Yarborough, Chief Executive Officer

ANGEL MEDICAL CENTER, Riverview and White Oak Streets, Franklin, NC, Zip 28734, Mailing Address: P.O. Box 1209, Zip 28744; tel. 828/524–8411; Michael E. Zuliani, Chief Executive Officer

ASHE MEMORIAL HOSPITAL, 200 Hospital Avenue, Jefferson, NC, Zip 28640; tel. 336/246–7101; R. D. Williams, Administrator and Chief Executive Officer

BLOWING ROCK HOSPITAL, Chestnut Street, Blowing Rock, NC, Zip 28605–0148, Mailing Address: Box 148, Zip 28605–0148; tel. 828/295–3136; Patricia Gray, Administrator and Chief Executive Officer

CALDWELL MEMORIAL HOSPITAL, 321 Mulberry Street S.W., Lenoir, NC, Zip 28645–5720, Mailing Address: P.O. Box 1890, Zip 28645–1890; tel. 828/757–5100; Frederick L. Soule, President and Chief Executive Officer

CATAWBA MEMORIAL HOSPITAL, 810 Fairgrove Church Road S.E., Hickory, NC, Zip 28602–9643; tel. 828/326–3000; J. Anthony Rose, President and Chief Executive Officer

HOOTS MEMORIAL HOSPITAL, 624 West Main Street, Yadkinville, NC, Zip 27055–7804, Mailing Address: P.O. Box 68, Zip 27055–0068; tel. 336/679–2041; Lance E. Labine, President

HUGH CHATHAM MEMORIAL HOSPITAL, Parkwood Drive, Elkin, NC, Zip 28621–0560, Mailing Address: P.O. Box 560, Zip 28621–0560; tel. 336/527–7000; Richard D. Osmus, Chief Executive Officer

LEXINGTON MEMORIAL HOSPITAL, 250 Hospital Drive, Lexington, NC, Zip 27292, Mailing Address: P.O. Box 1817, Zip 27293–1817; tel. 336/248–5161; John A. Cashion, FACHE, President

MEMORIAL HOSPITAL OF MARTINSVILLE AND HENRY COUNTY, 320 Hospital Drive, Martinsville, VA, Zip 24112–1981, Mailing Address: Box 4788, Zip 24115–4788; tel. 540/666–7200; Joseph Roach, Chief Executive Officer

MOREHEAD MEMORIAL HOSPITAL, 117 East King's Highway, Eden, NC, Zip 27288–5299; tel. 336/623–9711; Robert Enders, President

NORTH CAROLINA BAPTIST HOSPITAL, Medical Center Boulevard, Winston–Salem, NC, Zip 27157; tel. 336/716–2011; Len B. Preslar, Jr., President and Chief Executive Officer

NORTHERN HOSPITAL OF SURRY COUNTY, 830 Rockford Street, Mount Airy, NC, Zip 27030–5365, Mailing Address: P.O. Box 1101, Zip 27030–1101; tel. 336/719–7000; William B. James, Chief Executive Officer

PATRICK COMMUNITY HOSPITAL, 18688 Jeb Stuart Highway, Stuart, VA, Zip 24171–9512; tel. 540/694–3151; John M. Faulkner, FACHE, President and Chief Executive Officer

ROWAN REGIONAL MEDICAL CENTER, 612 Mocksville Avenue, Salisbury, NC, Zip 28144–2799; tel. 704/638–1000; James M. Freeman, Chief Executive Officer

RUTHERFORD HOSPITAL, 288 South Ridgecrest Avenue, Rutherfordton, NC, Zip 28139–3097; tel. 828/286–5000; Robert D. Jones, President

STOKES–REYNOLDS MEMORIAL HOSPITAL, Danbury, NC, Mailing Address: P.O. Box 10, Zip 27016–0010; tel. 336/593–2831; Sandra D. Priddy, President

TWIN COUNTY REGIONAL HOSPITAL, 200 Hospital Drive, Galax, VA, Zip 24333–2283; tel. 540/236–8181; Marcus G. Kuhn, President and Chief Executive Officer

UNIVERSITY OF NORTH CAROLINA HOSPITALS, 101 Manning Drive, Chapel Hill, NC, Zip 27514–4220; tel. 919/966–4131; Eric B. Munson, President and Chief Executive Officer

WILKES REGIONAL MEDICAL CENTER, 1370 West D Street, North Wilkesboro, NC, Zip 28659–3506, Mailing Address: P.O. Box 609, Zip 28659–0609; tel. 336/651–8100; David L. Henson, Chief Executive Officer

WESTERN NORTH CAROLINA HEALTH NETWORK 509 Biltmore Avenue, Asheville, NC 28801; tel. 704/255–4495; MaryAnn Digman, Administrator Regional Services

HARRIS REGIONAL HOSPITAL, 68 Hospital Road, Sylva, NC, Zip 28779–2795; tel. 828/586–7000; Mark Leonard, Chief Executive Officer

MARGARET R. PARDEE MEMORIAL HOSPITAL, 715 Fleming Street, Hendersonville, NC, Zip 28791–2563; tel. 828/696–1000; Frank J. Aaron, Jr., Chief Executive Officer

MCDOWELL HOSPITAL, 100 Rankin Drive, Marion, NC, Zip 28752–4989, Mailing Address: P.O. Box 730, Zip 28752–0730; tel. 828/659–5000; Jeffrey M. Judd, President and Chief Executive Officer

MEMORIAL MISSION HOSPITAL, 509 Biltmore Avenue, Asheville, NC, Zip 28801–4690

MURPHY MEDICAL CENTER, 4130 U.S. Highway 64 East, Murphy, NC, Zip 28906–7917; tel. 828/837–8161; Mike Stevenson, Administrator

RUTHERFORD HOSPITAL, 288 South Ridgecrest Avenue, Rutherfordton, NC, Zip 28139–3097; tel. 828/286–5000; Robert D. Jones, President

ST. JOSEPH'S HOSPITAL, 428 Biltmore Avenue, Asheville, NC, Zip 28801–9839; tel. 828/255–3100

TRANSYLVANIA COMMUNITY HOSPITAL, Hospital Drive, Brevard, NC, Zip 28712–1116, Mailing Address: Box 1116, Zip 28712–1116; tel. 828/884–9111; Robert J. Bednarek, President and Chief Executive Officer

NORTH DAKOTA

HEARTLAND NETWORK, INC. 510 South 4th Street, Fargo, ND 58103; tel. 701/241–7077; Walter Rogers, President & Chief Executive

DAKOTA HEARTLAND HEALTH SYSTEM, 1720 South University Drive, Fargo, ND, Zip 58103–4994; tel. 701/280–4100; Louis Kauffman, President and Chief Executive Officer

MEDCENTER ONE HEALTH SYSTEMS 300 North 7th St. P.O. Box 5525, Bismarck, ND 58506–5525; tel. 701/323–6000; Terrance G. Brosseau, President/CEO

JACOBSON MEMORIAL HOSPITAL CARE CENTER, 601 East Street North, Elgin, ND, Zip 58533–0376; tel. 701/584–2792; Jacqueline Seibel, Administrator

MEDCENTER ONE, 300 North Seventh Street, Bismarck, ND, Zip 58501–4439, Mailing Address: P.O. Box 5525, Zip 58506–5525; tel. 701/323–6000; Terrance G. Brosseau, President and Chief Executive Officer

MERITCARE HEALTH SYSTEM 720 Fourth St. North, Fargo, ND 58122; tel. 701/234–6000; Roger Gilbertson, MD, President

GRIGGS COUNTY HOSPITAL AND NURSING HOME, 1200 Roberts Avenue, Cooperstown, ND, Zip 58425, Mailing Address: P.O. Box 728, Zip 58425–0728; tel. 701/797–2221; Bruce D. Bowersox, Administrator and Chief Executive Officer

UNITED HOSPITAL 1200 South Columbia Road, Grand Forks, ND 58201; tel. 701/780–5000; Rosemary Jacobson, President & Chief Executive

ALTRU HEALTH SYSTEM, 1000 South Columbia Road, Grand Forks, ND, Zip 58201; tel. 701/780–5000; Gregory Gerloff, Chief Executive Officer

OHIO

BLANCHARD VALLEY HEALTH ASSOCIATION 145 W. Wallace, Findlay, OH 45840; tel. 419/423–5201; William Ruse, President

BLANCHARD VALLEY HEALTH ASSOCIATION SYSTEM, 145 West Wallace Street, Findlay, OH, Zip 45840–1299; tel. 419/423–4500; William E. Ruse, FACHE, President and Chief Executive Officer

CARITAS HEALTHCARE 2322 E. 22nd Street, Suite 302, Cleveland, OH 44115; tel. 216/436–4640; C. Michael Rutherford, CEO

CLEVELAND HEALTH NETWORK 9500 Euclid Avenue H18, Independence, OH 44131; tel. 216/328–7550; Dennis Pijor, Executive Vice–President/COO

ASHTABULA COUNTY MEDICAL CENTER, 2420 Lake Avenue, Ashtabula, OH, Zip 44004–4993; tel. 440/997–2262; R. D. Richardson, President and Chief Executive Officer

BARBERTON CITIZENS HOSPITAL, 155 Fifth Street N.E., Barberton, OH, Zip 44203–3398; tel. 330/745–1611; Ronald J. Elder, President

CHILDREN'S HOSPITAL MEDICAL CENTER OF AKRON, One Perkins Square, Akron, OH, Zip 44308–1062; tel. 330/379–8200; William H. Considine, President

CLEVELAND CLINIC FOUNDATION, 9500 Euclid Avenue, Cleveland, OH, Zip 44195–5108; tel. 216/444–2200; Frank L. Lordeman, Chief Operating Officer

DOCTORS HOSPITAL OF STARK COUNTY, 400 Austin Avenue N.W., Massillon, OH, Zip 44646–3554; tel. 330/837–7200; Thomas E. Cecconi, Chief Executive Officer

EMH AMHERST HOSPITAL, 254 Cleveland Avenue, Amherst, OH, Zip 44001–1699; tel. 440/988–6000; Kevin C. Martin, President and Chief Executive Officer

EMH REGIONAL MEDICAL CENTER, 630 East River Street, Elyria, OH, Zip 44035–5902; tel. 440/329–7500; Kevin C. Martin, President and Chief Executive Officer

EUCLID HOSPITAL, 18901 Lake Shore Boulevard, Euclid, OH, Zip 44119–1090; tel. 216/531–9000; Denise Zeman, Chief Operating Officer

FAIRVIEW HOSPITAL, 18101 Lorain Avenue, Cleveland, OH, Zip 44111–5656; tel. 216/476–7000; Louis P. Caravella, M.D., Chief Executive Officer

FIRELANDS COMMUNITY HOSPITAL, 1101 Decatur Street, Sandusky, OH, Zip 44870–3335; tel. 419/626–7400; Dennis A. Sokol, President and Chief Executive Officer

FISHER–TITUS MEDICAL CENTER, 272 Benedict Avenue, Norwalk, OH, Zip 44857–2374; tel. 419/668–8101; Patrick J. Martin, President and Chief Executive Officer

HAMOT MEDICAL CENTER, 201 State Street, Erie, PA, Zip 16550–0002; tel. 814/877–6000; John T. Malone, President and Chief Executive Officer

LAKEWOOD HOSPITAL, 14519 Detroit Avenue, Lakewood, OH, Zip 44107–4383; tel. 216/521–4200; Revonda L. Shumaker, R.N., President and Chief Executive Officer

LUTHERAN HOSPITAL, 1730 West 25th Street, Cleveland, OH, Zip 44113; tel. 216/696–4300; Jack E. Bell, Chief Operating Officer

MARYMOUNT HOSPITAL, 12300 McCracken Road, Garfield Heights, OH, Zip 44125–2975; tel. 216/581–0500; Thomas J. Trudell, President and Chief Executive Officer

MERIDIA HILLCREST HOSPITAL, 6780 Mayfield Road, Cleveland, OH, Zip 44124–2202; tel. 216/449–4500; Catherine B. Leary, R.N., Chief Operating Officer

MERIDIA HURON HOSPITAL, 13951 Terrace Road, Cleveland, OH, Zip 44112–4399; tel. 216/761–3300; Beverly Lozar, Chief Operating Officer

METROHEALTH MEDICAL CENTER, 2500 MetroHealth Drive, Cleveland, OH, Zip 44109–1998; tel. 216/778–7800; Terry R. White, President and Chief Executive Officer

PARMA COMMUNITY GENERAL HOSPITAL, 7007 Powers Boulevard, Parma, OH, Zip 44129–5495; tel. 440/888–1800; Thomas A. Selden, President and Chief Executive Officer

ST. ELIZABETH HEALTH CENTER, 1044 Belmont Avenue, Youngstown, OH, Zip 44501, Mailing Address: P.O. Box 1790, Zip 44501–1790; tel. 330/746–7211; Robert W. Shroder, Executive Vice President Operations

ST. JOSEPH HEALTH CENTER, 667 Eastland Avenue S.E., Warren, OH, Zip 44484–4531; tel. 330/841–4000; Robert W. Shroder, Vice President Operations

SUMMA HEALTH SYSTEM, Akron, OH, Albert F. Gilbert, Ph.D., President and Chief Executive Officer

WADSWORTH–RITTMAN HOSPITAL, 195 Wadsworth Road, Wadsworth, OH, Zip 44281–9505; tel. 330/334–1504; James W. Brumlow, Jr., President and Chief Executive Officer

COMMUNITY HOSPITALS OF OHIO
1320 West Main Street, Newark, OH 43055–3699; tel. 614/344–0331; William J. Andrews, President

ADENA HEALTH SYSTEM, 272 Hospital Road, Chillicothe, OH, Zip 45601–0708; tel. 740/779–7500; Allen V. Rupiper, President

BERGER HEALTH SYSTEM, 600 North Pickaway Street, Circleville, OH, Zip 43113–1499; tel. 740/474–2126; Brian R. Colfack, CHE, President and Chief Executive Officer

COSHOCTON COUNTY MEMORIAL HOSPITAL, 1460 Orange Street, Coshocton, OH, Zip 43812–6330, Mailing Address: P.O. Box 1330, Zip 43812–6330; tel. 740/622–6411; Gregory M. Nowak, Administrator and Chief Executive Officer

FORT HAMILTON HOSPITAL, 630 Eaton Avenue, Hamilton, OH, Zip 45013–2770; tel. 513/867–2000; James A. Kingsbury, President and Chief Executive Officer

GENESIS HEALTHCARE SYSTEM, 800 Forest Avenue, Zanesville, OH, Zip 43701–2881; tel. 740/454–5000; Thomas L. Sieber, President and Chief Executive Officer

GRADY MEMORIAL HOSPITAL, 561 West Central Avenue, Delaware, OH, Zip 43015–1485; tel. 740/369–8711; Everett P. Weber, Jr., President and Chief Executive Officer

HOCKING VALLEY COMMUNITY HOSPITAL, Route 2, State Route 664, Logan, OH, Zip 43138–0966, Mailing Address: Box 966, Zip 43138–0966; tel. 740/385–5631; Larry Willard, Administrator

HOLZER MEDICAL CENTER, 100 Jackson Pike, Gallipolis, OH, Zip 45631–1563; tel. 740/446–5000; Charles I. Adkins, Jr., President

KNOX COMMUNITY HOSPITAL, 1330 Coshocton Road, Mount Vernon, OH, Zip 43050–1495; tel. 740/393–9000; Robert G. Polahar, Chief Executive Officer

LICKING MEMORIAL HOSPITAL, 1320 West Main Street, Newark, OH, Zip 43055–3699; tel. 740/348–4000; William J. Andrews, President

MARIETTA MEMORIAL HOSPITAL, 401 Matthew Street, Marietta, OH, Zip 45750–1699; tel. 740/374–1400; Larry J. Unroe, President

ST. RITA'S MEDICAL CENTER, 730 West Market Street, Lima, OH, Zip 45801–4670; tel. 419/227–3361; James P. Reber, President

COMPREHENSIVE HEALTHCARE OF OHIO, INC
630 East River Street, Elyria, OH 44035; tel. 440/329–7591; Donald Miller, Vice President–Operations

EMH AMHERST HOSPITAL, 254 Cleveland Avenue, Amherst, OH, Zip 44001–1699; tel. 440/988–6000; Kevin C. Martin, President and Chief Executive Officer

EMH REGIONAL MEDICAL CENTER, 630 East River Street, Elyria, OH, Zip 44035–5902; tel. 440/329–7500; Kevin C. Martin, President and Chief Executive Officer

COUNTY BASED HEALTHCARE NETWORK
2420 Lake Avenue, Ashtabula, OH 44004; tel. 216/997–2262; Doy Gillespie, Vice President of Business Development

FORUM HEALTH
3530 Belmont Avenue, Suite 7, Youngstown, OH 44505; tel. 330/759–4090; Jim Yanci, Planning Research Associate

TRUMBALL MEMORIAL HOSPITAL, 1350 East Market Street, Warren, OH 44482; tel. 330/841–9011; Gary Kaatz, President and Chief Executive Officer

WESTERN RESERVE CARE SYSTEM, P.O. Box 990, Youngstown, OH 44501–0990; tel. 330/747–0777; Gary Kaatz, President and Chief Executive Officer

GOOD SAMARITAN HOSPITAL
375 Dixsmyth, Cincinnati, OH 45220; tel. 513/872–1828; John Prout, President & CEO

BETHESDA NORTH HOSPITAL, 10500 Montgomery Road, Cincinnati, OH, Zip 45242–4415; tel. 513/745–1111; John S. Prout, President and Chief Executive Officer

BETHESDA OAK HOSPITAL, 619 Oak Street, Cincinnati, OH, Zip 45206–1690; tel. 513/569–6111; Linda D. Schaffner, R.N., Vice President and Administrator

GOOD SAMARITAN HOSPITAL, 375 Dixmyth Avenue, Cincinnati, OH, Zip 45220–2489; tel. 513/872–1400; John S. Prout, President and Chief Executive Officer

HEALTH CARE ALLIANCE
6001 East Broad Street, Columbus, OH 43213; tel. 614/868–6000; Dale St. Arnold, President

ADENA HEALTH SYSTEM, 272 Hospital Road, Chillicothe, OH, Zip 45601–0708; tel. 740/779–7500; Allen V. Rupiper, President

BERGER HEALTH SYSTEM, 600 North Pickaway Street, Circleville, OH, Zip 43113–1499; tel. 740/474–2126; Brian R. Colfack, CHE, President and Chief Executive Officer

MOUNT CARMEL HEALTH SYSTEM, Columbus, OH, Mailing Address: 793 West State Street, Zip 43222–1551; tel. 614/234–5423; Joseph Calvaruso, Chief Executive Officer

HEALTH CLEVELAND
18101 Lorain Avenue, Cleveland, OH 44111; tel. 216/476–7020; Kenneth Misener, Executive Vice President

FAIRVIEW HOSPITAL, 18101 Lorain Avenue, Cleveland, OH, Zip 44111–5656; tel. 216/476–7000; Louis P. Caravella, M.D., Chief Executive Officer

LUTHERAN HOSPITAL, 1730 West 25th Street, Cleveland, OH, Zip 44113; tel. 216/696–4300; Jack E. Bell, Chief Operating Officer

HEALTHCARE CONSORTIUM OF OHIO
410 West Tenth Avenue, Columbus, OH 43210; tel. 614/293–8000; R. Reed Fraley, Executive Director

ARTHUR G. JAMES CANCER HOSPITAL AND RICHARD J. SOLOVE RESEARCH INSTITUTE, 300 West Tenth Avenue, Columbus, OH, Zip 43210–1240; tel. 614/293–5485; David E. Schuller, M.D., Chief Executive Officer

BARNESVILLE HOSPITAL ASSOCIATION, 639 West Main Street, Barnesville, OH, Zip 43713–1096, Mailing Address: P.O. Box 309, Zip 43713–0309; tel. 740/425–3941; Richard L. Doan, Chief Executive Officer

MARY RUTAN HOSPITAL, 205 Palmer Avenue, Bellefontaine, OH, Zip 43311–2298; tel. 937/592–4015; Ewing H. Crawfis, President

OHIO STATE UNIVERSITY MEDICAL CENTER, 410 West 10th Avenue, Columbus, OH, Zip 43210–1240; tel. 614/293–8000; R. Reed Fraley, Associate Vice President for Health Sciences and Chief Executive Officer

PIKE COMMUNITY HOSPITAL, 100 Dawn Lane, Waverly, OH, Zip 45690–9664; tel. 740/947–2186; Richard E. Sobota, President and Chief Executive Officer

RIVER VALLEY HEALTH SYSTEM, 2228 South Ninth Street, Ironton, OH, Zip 45638–2526; tel. 614/532–3231; Terry L. Vanderhoof, President and Chief Executive Officer

WYANDOT MEMORIAL HOSPITAL, 885 North Sandusky Avenue, Upper Sandusky, OH, Zip 43351–1098; tel. 419/294–4991; Joseph A. D'Ettorre, Chief Executive Officer

LAKE ERIE HEALTH ALLIANCE
2142 North Cove Boulevard, Toledo, OH 43606; tel. 419/471–5422; John Horn, President & CEO

LAKE HOSPITAL SYSTEM
10 East Washington, Painesville, OH 44077; tel. 216/354–2400; Cynthia Moore–Hardy, President & CEO

LAKE HOSPITAL SYSTEM, 10 East Washington, Painesville, OH, Zip 44077–3402; tel. 216/354–2400; Cynthia Ann Moore–Hardy, President and Chief Executive Officer

MEDCENTRAL HEALTH SYSTEM
335 Glessner Avenue, Mansfield, OH 04490–3222; tel. 419/526–8403; James Meyer, President & CEO

MERCY REGIONAL HEALTH
4340 Glendale–Milliford, Cincinnati, OH 45242; tel. 513/483–5200; Julie Hanser, President & CEO

CLERMONT MERCY HOSPITAL, 3000 Hospital Drive, Batavia, OH, Zip 45103–1998; tel. 513/732–8200; Fred L. Kolb, President

MERCY HOSPITAL, Hamilton, OH, Mailing Address: P.O. Box 418, Zip 45012–0418; tel. 513/867–6400; David A. Ferrell, President

MERCY HOSPITAL ANDERSON, 7500 State Road, Cincinnati, OH, Zip 45255–2492; tel. 513/624–4500; Fred L. Kolb, President

MERIDA HEALTH SYSTEM
6700 Beta Drive Suite 200, Mayfield Village, OH 44143; tel. 216/446–8000; Charles B. Miner, President & CEO

EUCLID HOSPITAL, 18901 Lake Shore Boulevard, Euclid, OH, Zip 44119–1090; tel. 216/531–9000; Denise Zeman, Chief Operating Officer

MERIDIA HILLCREST HOSPITAL, 6780 Mayfield Road, Cleveland, OH, Zip 44124–2202; tel. 216/449–4500; Catherine B. Leary, R.N., Chief Operating Officer

MERIDIA HURON HOSPITAL, 13951 Terrace Road, Cleveland, OH, Zip 44112–4399; tel. 216/761–3300; Beverly Lozar, Chief Operating Officer

MERIDIA SOUTH POINTE HOSPITAL, 4110 Warrensville Center Road, Warrensville Heights, OH, Zip 44122–7099; tel. 216/491–6000; Kathleen A. Rice, Chief Operating Officer

NORTHEAST OHIO HEALTH NETWORK
400 Wabash Avenue, Akron, OH 44307; tel. 216/384–6781; Jeffrey P. Houck, Executive Director

AKRON GENERAL MEDICAL CENTER, 400 Wabash Avenue, Akron, OH, Zip 44307–2433; tel. 330/384–6000; Alan J. Bleyer, President

BARBERTON CITIZENS HOSPITAL, 155 Fifth Street N.E., Barberton, OH, Zip 44203–3398; tel. 330/745–1611; Ronald J. Elder, President

CHILDREN'S HOSPITAL MEDICAL CENTER OF AKRON, One Perkins Square, Akron, OH, Zip 44308–1062; tel. 330/379–8200; William H. Considine, President

CUYAHOGA FALLS GENERAL HOSPITAL, 1900 23rd Street, Cuyahoga Falls, OH, Zip 44223–1499; tel. 330/971–7000; Fred Anthony, President and Chief Executive Officer

MEDINA GENERAL HOSPITAL, 1000 East Washington Street, Medina, OH, Zip 44256–2170; tel. 330/725–1000; Gary D. Hallman, President and Chief Executive Officer

ROBINSON MEMORIAL HOSPITAL, 6847 North Chestnut Street, Ravenna, OH, Zip 44266–1204, Mailing Address: P.O. Box 1204, Zip 44266–1204; tel. 330/297–0811; Stephen Colecchi, President and Chief Executive Officer

PHS MOUNT SINAI MEDICAL CENTER
One Mt Sinai Drive, Cleveland, OH 44106; tel. 216/421–4000; Michael Autrey, President & CEO

PROMEDICA NETWORK
2142 North Cove Boulevard, Toledo, OH 43606; tel. 419/471–4000; Daniel Rissing, CEO

FLOWER HOSPITAL, 5200 Harroun Road, Sylvania, OH, Zip 43560–2196; tel. 419/824–1444; Randall Kelley, President

THE TOLEDO HOSPITAL, 2142 North Cove Boulevard, Toledo, OH, Zip 43606–3896; tel. 419/471–4000; Barbara Steele, President

PROVIDERS SOLUTION
3521 Briarfield Blvd., Maumee, OH 43537; tel. 419/534–2000; Annette Leslie, Director of Marketing

ST. LUKE'S HOSPITAL, 5901 Monclova Road, Maumee, OH, Zip 43537–1899; tel. 419/893–5911; Frank J. Bartell, III, President and Chief Executive Officer

ST LUKES MEDICAL CENTER
11311 Shaker Boulevard, Cleveland, OH 44104; tel. 216/368–7354; James L. Heffernan, Sr Vice President

SAINT LUKE'S MEDICAL CENTER, 11311 Shaker Boulevard, Cleveland, OH, Zip 44104–3805; tel. 216/368–7000; Alan H. Channing, Chief Executive Officer

SUMMA HEALTH SYSTEM
525 East Market Street, Akron, OH 44309; tel. 330/375–3000; Albert Gilbert, Ph.D., President

SUMMA HEALTH SYSTEM, Akron, OH, Albert F. Gilbert, Ph.D., President and Chief Executive Officer

SUMMA HEALTH SYSTEM, Akron, OH, Albert F. Gilbert, Ph.D., President and Chief Executive Officer

THE METROHEALTH SYSTEM
2500 MetroHealth Drive, Cleveland, OH 44109–1998; tel. 216/398–6000; Terry White, President & CEO

METROHEALTH MEDICAL CENTER, 2500 MetroHealth Drive, Cleveland, OH, Zip 44109–1998; tel. 216/778–7800; Terry R. White, President and Chief Executive Officer

UNITED HEALTH PARTNERS
2213 Cherry Street, Toledo, OH 43608; tel. 419/321–3232; David Crane, VP of Marketing

BELLEVUE HOSPITAL, 811 Northwest Street, Bellevue, OH, Zip 44811, Mailing Address: P.O. Box 8004, Zip 44811–8004; tel. 419/483–4040; Michael K. Winthrop, President

DEFIANCE HOSPITAL, 1206 East Second Street, Defiance, OH, Zip 43512–2495; tel. 419/783–6955; Robert J. Coholich, President

FISHER–TITUS MEDICAL CENTER, 272 Benedict Avenue, Norwalk, OH, Zip 44857–2374; tel. 419/668–8101; Patrick J. Martin, President and Chief Executive Officer

FOSTORIA COMMUNITY HOSPITAL, 501 Van Buren Street, Fostoria, OH, Zip 44830–0907, Mailing Address: P.O. Box 907, Zip 44830–0907; tel. 419/435–7734; Brad A. Higgins, President and Chief Executive Officer

FULTON COUNTY HEALTH CENTER, 725 South Shoop Avenue, Wauseon, OH, Zip 43567–1701; tel. 419/335–2015; E. Dean Beck, Administrator

MEMORIAL HOSPITAL, 715 South Taft Avenue, Fremont, OH, Zip 43420–3200; tel. 419/332–7321; John A. Gorman, Chief Executive Officer

MERCY HOSPITAL, 485 West Market Street, Tiffin, OH, Zip 44883–0727, Mailing Address: P.O. Box 727, Zip 44883–0727; tel. 419/447–3130; Mark Shugarman, President

MERCY HOSPITAL–WILLARD, 110 East Howard Street, Willard, OH, Zip 44890–1611; tel. 419/933–2931; Dale E. Thornton, President

PROVIDENCE HOSPITAL, 1912 Hayes Avenue, Sandusky, OH, Zip 44870–4736; tel. 419/621–7000; Sister Nancy Linenkugel, FACHE, President and Chief Executive Officer

ST. VINCENT MERCY MEDICAL CENTER, 2213 Cherry Street, Toledo, OH, Zip 43608–2691; tel. 419/251–3232; Steven L. Mickus, President and Chief Executive Officer

WOOD COUNTY HOSPITAL, 950 West Wooster Street, Bowling Green, OH, Zip 43402–2699; tel. 419/354–8900; Michael A. Miesle, Administrator

UNIVERSITY HOSPITALS OF CLEVELAND
11000 Euclid Avenue, Cleveland, OH 44106; tel. 216/844–1000; James G. Lubetkin, Vice President Corporate

UHHS BEDFORD MEDICAL CENTER, 44 Blaine Avenue, Bedford, OH, Zip 44146–2799; tel. 440/439–2000; Arlene A. Rak, R.N., President

UHHS GEAUGA REGIONAL HOSPITAL, 13207 Ravenna Road, Chardon, OH, Zip 44024–9012; tel. 440/269–6000; Richard J. Frenchie, President and Chief Executive Officer

UHHS–MEMORIAL HOSPITAL OF GENEVA, 870 West Main Street, Geneva, OH, Zip 44041–1295; tel. 440/466–1141; Gerard D. Klein, Chief Executive Officer

UNIVERSITY HOSPITALS OF CLEVELAND, 11100 Euclid Avenue, Cleveland, OH, Zip 44106–2602; tel. 216/844–1000; Farah M. Walters, President and Chief Executive Officer

UPPER VALLEY MEDICAL
3130 North Dixie Highway, Troy, OH 45373; tel. 937/492–3775; Michele Elam, Financial Coordinator

UPPER VALLEY MEDICAL CENTER, 3130 North Dixie Highway, Troy, OH, Zip 45373; tel. 937/440–7500; David J. Meckstroth, President and Chief Executive Officer

WEST CENTRAL OHIO REGIONAL HEALTHCARE ALLIANCE, LTD.
730 West Market Street, Lima, OH 45801; tel. 419/226–9085; P. Anthony Long, Executive Director

JOINT TOWNSHIP DISTRICT MEMORIAL HOSPITAL, 200 St. Clair Street, Saint Marys, OH, Zip 45885–2400; tel. 419/394–3387; James R. Chick, President and Chief Executive Officer

MARY RUTAN HOSPITAL, 205 Palmer Avenue, Bellefontaine, OH, Zip 43311–2298; tel. 937/592–4015; Ewing H. Crawfis, President and Chief Executive Officer

MERCER COUNTY JOINT TOWNSHIP COMMUNITY HOSPITAL, 800 West Main Street, Coldwater, OH, Zip 45828–1698; tel. 419/678–2341; James W. Isaacs, Chief Executive Officer

ST. RITA'S MEDICAL CENTER, 730 West Market Street, Lima, OH, Zip 45801–4670; tel. 419/227–3361; James P. Reber, President and Chief Executive Officer

VAN WERT COUNTY HOSPITAL, 1250 South Washington Street, Van Wert, OH, Zip 45891–2599; tel. 419/238–2390; Mark J. Minick, President and Chief Executive Officer

OKLAHOMA

EASTERN OKLAHOMA HEALTH NETWORK
110 West 7th Street Ste. 2520, Tulsa, OK 74114; tel. 918/579–7856; Dale Harris, Regional Development

DOCTORS HOSPITAL, 2323 South Harvard Avenue, Tulsa, OK, Zip 74114–3370; tel. 918/744–4000; Kenneth Noteboom, Chief Executive Officer

HILLCREST MEDICAL CENTER, 1120 South Utica, Tulsa, OK, Zip 74104–4090; tel. 918/579–1000; Donald A. Lorack, Jr., President and Chief Executive Officer

WAGONER COMMUNITY HOSPITAL, 1200 West Cherokee, Wagoner, OK, Zip 74467–4681, Mailing Address: Box 407, Zip 74477–0407; tel. 918/485–5514; John W. Crawford, Chief Executive Officer

FIRST HEALTH WEST
4411 West Gore Boulevard, Lawton, OK 73505; tel. 405/355–8620; Tanya Case, Director of Network

CARNEGIE TRI–COUNTY MUNICIPAL HOSPITAL, 102 North Broadway, Carnegie, OK, Zip 73015, Mailing Address: P.O. Box 97, Zip 73015–0097; tel. 580/654–1050; Phil Hawkins, Administrator

COMANCHE COUNTY MEMORIAL HOSPITAL, 3401 Gore Boulevard, Lawton, OK, Zip 73505–0129, Mailing Address: Box 129, Zip 73502–0129; tel. 580/355–8620; Randall K. Segler, Chief Executive Officer

CORDELL MEMORIAL HOSPITAL, 1220 North Glenn English Street, Cordell, OK, Zip 73632–2099; tel. 580/832–3339; Charles H. Greene, Jr., Administrator

ELKVIEW GENERAL HOSPITAL, 429 West Elm Street, Hobart, OK, Zip 73651–1699; tel. 580/726–3324; J. W. Finch, Jr., Administrator

HARMON MEMORIAL HOSPITAL, 400 East Chestnut Street, Hollis, OK, Zip 73550–2030, Mailing Address: P.O. Box 791, Zip 73550–0791; tel. 580/688–3363; Al Allee, Administrator

JEFFERSON COUNTY HOSPITAL, Highway 70 and 81, Waurika, OK, Zip 73573, Mailing Address: P.O. Box 90, Zip 73573–0090; tel. 580/228–2344; Richard Tallon, Administrator

SOUTHWESTERN MEMORIAL HOSPITAL, 215 North Kansas Street, Weatherford, OK, Zip 73096–5499; tel. 580/772–5551; Ronnie D. Walker, President

HILLCREST HEALTHCARE SYSTEM
1120 South Utica Avenue, Tulsa, OK 74104; tel. 918/579–1000; Donald A. Lorack, Jr., President & CEO

CHILDREN'S MEDICAL CENTER, 5300 East Skelly Drive, Tulsa, OK, Zip 74135–6599, Mailing Address: P.O. Box 35648, Zip 74153–0648; tel. 918/664–6600; Donald A. Lorack, Jr., President and Chief Executive Officer

CUSHING REGIONAL HOSPITAL, 1027 East Cherry Street, Cushing, OK, Zip 74023–4101, Mailing Address: P.O. Box 1409, Zip 74023–1409; tel. 918/225–2915; Ron Cackler, President and Chief Executive Officer

EASTERN OKLAHOMA MEDICAL CENTER, 105 Wall Street, Poteau, OK, Zip 74953, Mailing Address: P.O. Box 1148, Zip 74953–1148; tel. 918/647–8161; Craig R. Cudworth, Chief Executive Officer

Section B

HILLCREST MEDICAL CENTER, 1120 South Utica, Tulsa, OK, Zip 74104–4090; tel. 918/579–1000; Donald A. Lorack, Jr., President and Chief Executive Officer

INTEGRIS HEALTH
3366 N.W. Expressway, Suite 800, Oklahoma City, OK 73112; tel. 405/949–6066; Trevor D. Shipley, Administrative Resident

BLACKWELL REGIONAL HOSPITAL, 710 South 13th Street, Blackwell, OK, Zip 74631–3700; tel. 580/363–2311; Greg Martin, Administrator and Chief Executive Officer

CHOCTAW MEMORIAL HOSPITAL, 1405 East Kirk Road, Hugo, OK, Zip 74743–3603; tel. 580/326–6414; L. Eugene Matthews, Administrator

DRUMRIGHT MEMORIAL HOSPITAL, 501 South Lou Allard Drive, Drumright, OK, Zip 74030–4899; tel. 918/352–2525; James L. Clough, Administrator

INTEGRIS BAPTIST MEDICAL CENTER, 3300 N.W. Expressway, Oklahoma City, OK, Zip 73112–4481; tel. 405/949–3011; Thomas R. Rice, FACHE, President and Chief Operating Officer

INTEGRIS BAPTIST REGIONAL HEALTH CENTER, 200 Second Street S.W., Miami, OK, Zip 74354–6830, Mailing Address: P.O. Box 1207, Zip 74355–1207; tel. 918/540–7100; Steven G. Kelly, Administrator

INTEGRIS BASS BAPTIST HEALTH CENTER, 600 South Monroe Street, Enid, OK, Zip 73701, Mailing Address: P.O. Box 3168, Zip 73702–3168; tel. 580/233–2300; William E. Mosteller, Jr., Interim Administrator

INTEGRIS GROVE GENERAL HOSPITAL, 1310 South Main Street, Grove, OK, Zip 74344–1310; tel. 918/786–2243; Dee Renshaw, Administrator

INTEGRIS SOUTHWEST MEDICAL CENTER, 4401 South Western, Oklahoma City, OK, Zip 73109–3441; tel. 405/636–7000; Thomas R. Rice, FACHE, President and Chief Operating Officer

INTERGRIS CLINTON REGIONAL HOSPITAL, 100 North 30th Street, Clinton, OK, Zip 73601–3117, Mailing Address: P.O. Box 1569, Zip 73601–1569; tel. 580/323–2363; Jerry Jones, Administrator

MARSHALL MEMORIAL HOSPITAL, 1 Hospital Drive, Madill, OK, Zip 73446, Mailing Address: P.O. Box 827, Zip 73446–0827; tel. 405/795–3384; Norma Howard, Administrator

MAYES COUNTY MEDICAL CENTER, 129 North Kentucky Street, Pryor, OK, Zip 74361–4211, Mailing Address: P.O. Box 278, Zip 74362–0278; tel. 918/825–1600; W. Charles Jordan, Administrator

PAWNEE MUNICIPAL HOSPITAL, 1212 Fourth Street, Pawnee, OK, Zip 74058–4046, Mailing Address: P.O. Box 467, Zip 74058–0467; tel. 918/762–2577; John Ketring, Administrator

MERCY HEALTH SYSTEM
4300 West Memorial Road, Oklahoma City, OK 73120; tel. 405/752–3754; Michael Packnett, President & CEO

MERCY HEALTH CENTER, 4300 West Memorial Road, Oklahoma City, OK, Zip 73120–8362; tel. 405/755–1515; Michael J. Packnett, President and Chief Executive Officer

MERCY MEMORIAL HEALTH CENTER, 1011 14th Street N.W., Ardmore, OK, Zip 73401–1889; tel. 580/223–5400; Bobby G. Thompson, President and Chief Executive Officer

ST. MARY'S MERCY HOSPITAL, 305 South Fifth Street, Enid, OK, Zip 73701–5899, Mailing Address: Box 232, Zip 73702–0232; tel. 580/233–6100; Frank Lopez, FACHE, President and Chief Executive Officer

UNIVERSITY HEALTH PARTNERS
6501 North Broadway, Oklahoma City, OK 73116; tel. 405/879–0999; David Dunlap, CEO

EDMOND MEDICAL CENTER, 1 South Bryant Street, Edmond, OK, Zip 73034–4798; tel. 405/341–6100; Stanley D. Tatum, Chief Executive Officer

PRESBYTERIAN HOSPITAL, 700 N.E. 13th Street, Oklahoma City, OK, Zip 73104–5070; tel. 405/271–5100

SEMINOLE MEDICAL CENTER, 2401 Wrangler Boulevard, Seminole, OK, Zip 74868; tel. 405/303–4000; Stephen R. Schoaps, Chief Executive Officer

SOUTHWESTERN MEDICAL CENTER, 5602 S.W. Lee Boulevard, Lawton, OK, Zip 73505–9635, Mailing Address: P.O. Box 7290, Zip 73506–7290; tel. 580/531–4700; Thomas L. Rine, President and Chief Executive Officer

UNIVERSITY HOSPITALS
P.O. Box 26307, Oklahoma City, OK 73104; tel. 405/271–6165; Gerald Maier, CEO

OREGON

COORDINATED HEALTHCARE NETWORK
3030 S.W. Moody, Suite 230, Portland, OR 97201–4897; tel. 503/222–3100; John Pihas, Network Contact

HEALTH FUTURE, INC
825 East Main Street Suite D., Medford, OR 97504; tel. 541/772–3062; Hans Wiik, Executive Director

ALBANY GENERAL HOSPITAL, 1046 West Sixth Avenue, Albany, OR, Zip 97321–1999; tel. 541/812–4000; Richard J. Delano, President

ASHLAND COMMUNITY HOSPITAL, 280 Maple Street, Ashland, OR, Zip 97520, Mailing Address: P.O. Box 98, Zip 97520; tel. 541/482–2441; James R. Watson, Administrator

BAY AREA HOSPITAL, 1775 Thompson Road, Coos Bay, OR, Zip 97420–2198; tel. 541/269–8111; Dale Jessup, President and Chief Executive Officer

COLUMBIA MEMORIAL HOSPITAL, 2111 Exchange Street, Astoria, OR, Zip 97103; tel. 503/325–4321; Terry O. Finklein, Chief Executive Officer

DOUGLAS COMMUNITY MEDICAL CENTER, 738 West Harvard Avenue, Roseburg, OR, Zip 97470–2996; tel. 541/673–6641; Leslie Paul Luke, Chief Executive Officer

GOOD SAMARITAN HOSPITAL CORVALLIS, 3600 N.W. Samaritan Drive, Corvallis, OR, Zip 97330, Mailing Address: P.O. Box 1068, Zip 97339; tel. 541/757–5111; Larry A. Mullins, President and Chief Executive Officer

GOOD SHEPHERD COMMUNITY HOSPITAL, 610 N.W. 11th Street, Hermiston, OR, Zip 97838–9696; tel. 541/567–6483; Dennis E. Burke, President

GRANDE RONDE HOSPITAL, 900 Sunset Drive, La Grande, OR, Zip 97850, Mailing Address: P.O. Box 3290, Zip 97850; tel. 541/963–8421; James A. Mattes, President

LEBANON COMMUNITY HOSPITAL, 525 North Santiam Highway, Lebanon, OR, Zip 97355, Mailing Address: P.O. Box 739, Zip 97355–0739; tel. 541/258–2101; Steven W. Jasperson, Executive Vice President Operations

MERCY MEDICAL CENTER, 2700 Stewart Parkway, Roseburg, OR, Zip 97470–1297; tel. 541/673–0611; Victor J. Fresolone, FACHE, President and Chief Executive Officer

MERLE WEST MEDICAL CENTER, 2865 Daggett Street, Klamath Falls, OR, Zip 97601–1180; tel. 541/882–6311; Paul R. Stewart, President and Chief Executive Officer

MID–COLUMBIA MEDICAL CENTER, 1700 East 19th Street, The Dalles, OR, Zip 97058–3316; tel. 541/296–1111; Mark D. Scott, President

OHSU HOSPITAL, 3181 S.W. Sam Jackson Park Road, Portland, OR, Zip 97201–3098; tel. 503/494–8311; Roy G. Vinyard, II, President and Chief Executive Offiecer

ROGUE VALLEY MEDICAL CENTER, 2825 East Barnett Road, Medford, OR, Zip 97504–8332; tel. 541/608–4900; Mark W. Folger, FACHE, Senior Vice President

SILVERTON HOSPITAL, 342 Fairview Street, Silverton, OR, Zip 97381; tel. 503/873–1500; William E. Winter, Administrative Director

ST. CHARLES MEDICAL CENTER, 2500 N.E. Neff Road, Bend, OR, Zip 97701–6015; tel. 541/382–4321; James T. Lussier, President and Chief Executive Officer

INTER COMMUNITY HEALTH NETWORK
3600 North Samaritan Drive, Corvallis, OR 97339; tel. 541/757–5377; Larry Mullins, Chairman

ALBANY GENERAL HOSPITAL, 1046 West Sixth Avenue, Albany, OR, Zip 97321–1999; tel. 541/812–4000; Richard J. Delano, President

GOOD SAMARITAN HOSPITAL CORVALLIS, 3600 N.W. Samaritan Drive, Corvallis, OR, Zip 97330, Mailing Address: P.O. Box 1068, Zip 97339; tel. 541/757–5111; Larry A. Mullins, President and Chief Executive Officer

LEBANON COMMUNITY HOSPITAL, 525 North Santiam Highway, Lebanon, OR, Zip 97355, Mailing Address: P.O. Box 739, Zip 97355–0739; tel. 541/258–2101; Steven W. Jasperson, Executive Vice President Operations

LEGACY HEALTH SYSTEM
1919 N.W. Lovejoy Street, Portland, OR 97209; tel. 503/415–5600; Bob Pallari, President/CEO

LEGACY EMANUEL HOSPITAL AND HEALTH CENTER, 2801 North Gantenbein Avenue, Portland, OR, Zip 97227–1674; tel. 503/413–2200; Stephani White, Vice President and Site Administrator

LEGACY GOOD SAMARITAN HOSPITAL AND MEDICAL CENTER, 1015 N.W. 22nd Avenue, Portland, OR, Zip 97210; tel. 503/413–7711

LEGACY MERIDIAN PARK HOSPITAL, 19300 S.W. 65th Avenue, Tualatin, OR, Zip 97062–9741; tel. 503/692–1212; Jeff Cushing, Vice President and Site Administrator

LEGACY MOUNT HOOD MEDICAL CENTER, 24800 S.E. Stark, Gresham, OR, Zip 97030–0154; tel. 503/667–1122; Thomas S. Parker, Site Administrator

PEACE HEALTH
770 E. 11th Avenue, Eugene, OR 97440–1479; tel. 503/686–3660; Sister Monica Heeran, Executive Director

PROVIDENCE HEALTH SYSTEM IN OREGON
1235 N.E. 47fth Ave., Suite 299, Portland, OR 97213; tel. 503/215–4700; Mary Stoneman, Sr. Planning Associate

ALBANY GENERAL HOSPITAL, 1046 West Sixth Avenue, Albany, OR, Zip 97321–1999; tel. 541/812–4000; Richard J. Delano, President

ASHLAND COMMUNITY HOSPITAL, 280 Maple Street, Ashland, OR, Zip 97520, Mailing Address: P.O. Box 98, Zip 97520; tel. 541/482–2441; James R. Watson, Administrator

BLUE MOUNTAIN HOSPITAL, 170 Ford Road, John Day, OR, Zip 97845; tel. 541/575–1311; Robert Houser, Chief Executive Officer

CENTRAL OREGON DISTRICT HOSPITAL, 1253 North Canal Boulevard, Redmond, OR, Zip 97756–1395; tel. 541/548–8131; James A. Diegel, CHE, Executive Director

COLUMBIA MEMORIAL HOSPITAL, 2111 Exchange Street, Astoria, OR, Zip 97103; tel. 503/325–4321; Terry O. Finklein, Chief Executive Officer

GOOD SAMARITAN HOSPITAL CORVALLIS, 3600 N.W. Samaritan Drive, Corvallis, OR, Zip 97330, Mailing Address: P.O. Box 1068, Zip 97339; tel. 541/757–5111; Larry A. Mullins, President and Chief Executive Officer

HARNEY DISTRICT HOSPITAL, 557 West Washington Street, Burns, OR, Zip 97720–1497; tel. 503/573–7281; David L. Harman, Administrator

HOOD RIVER MEMORIAL HOSPITAL, 13th and May Streets, Hood River, OR, Zip 97031, Mailing Address: P.O. Box 149, Zip 97031; tel. 541/386–3911; Larry Bowe, JD, Chief Executive Officer

LAKE DISTRICT HOSPITAL, 700 South J Street, Lakeview, OR, Zip 97630–1679; tel. 503/947–2114; Richard T. Moore, Administrator

Section B

LEBANON COMMUNITY HOSPITAL, 525 North Santiam Highway, Lebanon, OR, Zip 97355, Mailing Address: P.O. Box 739, Zip 97355–0739; tel. 541/258–2101; Steven W. Jasperson, Executive Vice President Operations

MCKENZIE–WILLAMETTE HOSPITAL, 1460 G Street, Springfield, OR, Zip 97477–4197; tel. 541/726–4400; Roy J. Orr, President and Chief Executive Officer

MOUNTAIN VIEW HOSPITAL DISTRICT, 470 N.E. A Street, Madras, OR, Zip 97741; tel. 541/475–3882; Eric Alexander, Interim Administrator

PEACE HARBOR HOSPITAL, 400 Ninth Street, Florence, OR, Zip 97439, Mailing Address: P.O. Box 580, Zip 97439; tel. 541/997–8412; James Barnhart, Administrator

PIONEER MEMORIAL HOSPITAL, 1201 North Elm Street, Prineville, OR, Zip 97754; tel. 541/447–6254; Donald J. Wee, Executive Director

PROVIDENCE MEDFORD MEDICAL CENTER, 1111 Crater Lake Avenue, Medford, OR, Zip 97504–6241; tel. 541/732–5000; Charles T. Wright, Chief Executive, Southern Oregon Service Area

PROVIDENCE MILWAUKIE HOSPITAL, 10150 S.E. 32nd Avenue, Milwaukie, OR, Zip 97222–6593; tel. 503/513–8300; Janice Burger, Operations Administrator

PROVIDENCE NEWBERG HOSPITAL, 501 Villa Road, Newberg, OR, Zip 97132; tel. 503/537–1555; Mark W. Meinert, CHE, Chief Executive, Yamhill Service Area

PROVIDENCE PORTLAND MEDICAL CENTER, 4805 N.E. Glisan Street, Portland, OR, Zip 97213–2967; tel. 503/215–1111; David T. Underriner, Operations Administrator

PROVIDENCE SEASIDE HOSPITAL, 725 South Wahanna Road, Seaside, OR, Zip 97138–7735; tel. 503/717–7000; Ronald Swanson, Chief Executive Officer

PROVIDENCE ST. VINCENT MEDICAL CENTER, 9205 S.W. Barnes Road, Portland, OR, Zip 97225–6661; tel. 503/216–1234; Donald Elsom, Operations Administrator

SALEM HOSPITAL, 665 Winter Street S.E., Salem, OR, Zip 97301–3959, Mailing Address: Box 14001, Zip 97309–5014; tel. 503/370–5200; Dennis Noonan, President and Chief Executive Officer

SANTIAM MEMORIAL HOSPITAL, 1401 North 10th Avenue, Stayton, OR, Zip 97383; tel. 503/769–2175; Terry L. Fletchall, Administrator

SILVERTON HOSPITAL, 342 Fairview Street, Silverton, OR, Zip 97381; tel. 503/873–1500; William E. Winter, Administrative Director

TUALITY HEALTHCARE, 335 S.E. Eighth Avenue, Hillsboro, OR, Zip 97123; tel. 503/681–1111; Richard Stenson, President and Chief Executive Officer

VALLEY COMMUNITY HOSPITAL, 550 S.E. Clay Street, Dallas, OR, Zip 97338, Mailing Address: P.O. Box 378, Zip 97338; tel. 503/623–8301; Stephen A. Bowles, President

WILLAMETTE FALLS HOSPITAL, 1500 Division Street, Oregon City, OR, Zip 97045–1597; tel. 503/656–1631; Robert A. Steed, President

PENNSYLVANIA

ALBERT EINSTEIN HEALTH CARE NETWORK
1200 West Tabor Road, Philadelphia, PA 19141; tel. 215/456–7890; Martin Goldsmith, CEO

ALBERT EINSTEIN MEDICAL CENTER, 5501 Old York Road, Philadelphia, PA, Zip 19141–3098; tel. 215/456–7890; Martin Goldsmith, President

BELMONT CENTER FOR COMPREHENSIVE TREATMENT, 4200 Monument Road, Philadelphia, PA, Zip 19131–1625; tel. 215/877–2000; Jack H. Dembow, General Director and Vice President

COMMUNITY BENEFITS STRATEGY
P.O. Box 447, DuBois, PA 15801; tel. 814/375–3495; Diane Skroba, Public Relations Manager

DUBOIS REGIONAL MEDICAL CENTER, 100 Hospital Avenue, Du Bois, PA, Zip 15801–1440, Mailing Address: P.O. Box 447, Zip 15801–0447; tel. 814/371–2200; Raymond A. Graeca, President and Chief Executive Officer

COMMUNITY HEALTH NET
1202 State Street, Erie, PA 16501; tel. 814/454–4530; Clearence Pierce, CEO

HAMOT MEDICAL CENTER, 201 State Street, Erie, PA, Zip 16550–0002; tel. 814/877–6000; John T. Malone, President and Chief Executive Officer

METRO HEALTH CENTER, 252 West 11th Street, Erie, PA, Zip 16501–9964; tel. 814/870–3400; Debra M. Dragovan, Chief Executive Officer

SAINT VINCENT HEALTH CENTER, 232 West 25th Street, Erie, PA, Zip 16544–0001; tel. 814/452–5000; Sister Catherine Manning, President and Chief Executive Officer

COVENANT HOME HEALTH CARE
Fourth & Chew Streets, Allentown, PA 18102; tel. 610/776–4500; Joseph M. Cimerola, FACHE

SACRED HEART HOSPITAL, 421 Chew Street, Allentown, PA, Zip 18102–3490; tel. 610/776–4500; Joseph M. Cimerola, FACHE, President and Chief Executive Officer

CROZER–KEYSTONE HEALTH SYSTEM
Healthplex Pavilion II, 100 West Sproul Road, Springfield, PA 19064; tel. 610/338–8203; John C. McMeekin, President & CEO

CROZER–CHESTER MEDICAL CENTER, One Medical Center Boulevard, Upland, PA, Zip 19013–3995; tel. 610/447–2000; Joan K. Richards, President

DELAWARE COUNTY MEMORIAL HOSPITAL, 501 North Lansdowne Avenue, Drexel Hill, PA, Zip 19026–1114; tel. 610/284–8100; Joan K. Richards, President

FOX CHASE NETWORK
8 Huntingdon Pike, 3rd, Rockledge, PA 19046; tel. 215/728–4773; Susan Higman, Vice President

DELAWARE COUNTY MEMORIAL HOSPITAL, 501 North Lansdowne Avenue, Drexel Hill, PA, Zip 19026–1114; tel. 610/284–8100; Joan K. Richards, President

FOX CHASE CANCER CENTER–AMERICAN ONCOLOGIC HOSPITAL, 7701 Burholme Avenue, Philadelphia, PA, Zip 19111–2412; tel. 215/728–6900; Robert C. Young, M.D., President

HUNTERDON MEDICAL CENTER, 2100 Wescott Drive, Flemington, NJ, Zip 08822–4604; tel. 908/788–6100; Robert P. Wise, President and Chief Executive Officer

NORTH PENN HOSPITAL, 100 Medical Campus Drive, Lansdale, PA, Zip 19446–1200; tel. 215/368–2100; Robert H. McKay, President

PAOLI MEMORIAL HOSPITAL, 255 West Lancaster Avenue, Paoli, PA, Zip 19301–1792; tel. 610/648–1000; C. Barry Dykes, Senior Vice President

ST. FRANCIS MEDICAL CENTER, 601 Hamilton Avenue, Trenton, NJ, Zip 08629–1986; tel. 609/599–5000; Judith M. Persichilli, President and Chief Executive Officer

ST. MARY MEDICAL CENTER, Langhorne–Newtown Road, Langhorne, PA, Zip 19047–1295; tel. 215/750–2000; Gregory T. Wozniak, President and Chief Executive Officer

GEISINGER HEALTH CARE SYSTEM
100 North Academy Avenue, Danville, PA 17822–3311; tel. 717/271–6467; Frank J. Trembulak, CEO

GEISINGER MEDICAL CENTER, 100 North Academy Avenue, Danville, PA, Zip 17822–0150; tel. 570/271–6211; Nancy L. Rizzo, Senior Vice President, Operations

PENN STATE GEISINGER WYOMING VALLEY MEDICAL CENTER, 1000 East Mountain Drive, Wilkes–Barre, PA, Zip 18711–0027; tel. 570/826–7300; Conrad W. Schintz, Senior Vice–President Operations

GREAT LAKES HEALTH NETWORK
201 State Street, Erie, PA 16550; tel. 814/877–7053; Andrew J. Glass, President

ASHTABULA COUNTY MEDICAL CENTER, 2420 Lake Avenue, Ashtabula, OH, Zip 44004–4993; tel. 440/997–2262; R. D. Richardson, President and Chief Executive Officer

BLANCHARD VALLEY HEALTH ASSOCIATION SYSTEM, 145 West Wallace Street, Findlay, OH, Zip 45840–1299; tel. 419/423–4500; William E. Ruse, FACHE, President and Chief Executive Officer

BRADFORD REGIONAL MEDICAL CENTER, 116 Interstate Parkway, Bradford, PA, Zip 16701–0218; tel. 814/368–4143; George E. Leonhardt, President and Chief Executive Officer

CORRY MEMORIAL HOSPITAL, 612 West Smith Street, Corry, PA, Zip 16407–1152; tel. 814/664–4641; Joseph T. Hodges, President

HAMOT MEDICAL CENTER, 201 State Street, Erie, PA, Zip 16550–0002; tel. 814/877–6000; John T. Malone, President and Chief Executive Officer

ST. MARYS REGIONAL MEDICAL CENTER, 763 Johnsonburg Road, Saint Marys, PA, Zip 15857–3417; tel. 814/781–7500; Paul A. DeSantis, President

UHHS BROWN MEMORIAL HOSPITAL, 158 West Main Road, Conneaut, OH, Zip 44030–2039, Mailing Address: P.O. Box 648, Zip 44030–0648; tel. 440/593–1131; Gerard D. Klein, President

WOMAN'S CHRISTIAN ASSOCIATION HOSPITAL, 207 Foote Avenue, Jamestown, NY, Zip 14702–9975; tel. 716/487–0141; Betsy T. Wright, President and Chief Executive Officer

HEALTH SHARE
111 S. 11th Street, Philadelphia, PA 19107; tel. 215/955–6000; Carmhill Brown, Assoc VP Marketing

THOMAS JEFFERSON UNIVERSITY HOSPITAL, 111 South 11th Street, Philadelphia, PA, Zip 19107–5096; tel. 215/955–7022; Thomas J. Lewis, President and Chief Executive Officer

JEFERSON HEALTH SYSTEM
259 Radnor Chester Road, Radnor, PA 19087; tel. 610/225–6200; Douglas S. Peters, President & Chief Executive Officer

ALBERT EINSTEIN MEDICAL CENTER, 5501 Old York Road, Philadelphia, PA, Zip 19141–3098; tel. 215/456–7890; Martin Goldsmith, President

ALFRED I.DUPONT HOSPITAL FOR CHILDREN, 1600 Rockland Road, Wilmington, DE, Zip 19803–3616, Mailing Address: Box 269, Zip 19899–0269; tel. 302/651–4000; Thomas P. Ferry, Administrator and Chief Executive

BRYN MAWR HOSPITAL, 130 South Bryn Mawr Avenue, Bryn Mawr, PA, Zip 19010–3160; tel. 610/526–3000; Kenneth Hanover, President and Chief Executive Officer

BRYN MAWR REHABILITATION HOSPITAL, 414 Paoli Pike, Malvern, PA, Zip 19355–3300, Mailing Address: P.O. Box 3007, Zip 19355–3300; tel. 610/251–5400

GERMANTOWN HOSPITAL AND COMMUNITY HEALTH SERVICES, One Penn Boulevard, Philadelphia, PA, Zip 19144–1498; tel. 215/951–8000; David A. Ricci, President and Chief Executive Officer

LANKENAU HOSPITAL, 100 Lancaster Avenue West, Wynnewood, PA, Zip 19096–3411; tel. 610/645–2000; William McCune, Senior Vice President, Operations

MERCY HEALTH SYSTEM OF SOUTHEASTERN PENNSYLVANIA, One Bala Plaza, Suite 402, Bala Cynwyd, PA, Zip 19004–1401; tel. 610/660–7440; Plato A. Marinakos, President and Chief Executive Officer

METHODIST HOSPITAL, 2301 South Broad Street, Philadelphia, PA, Zip 19148; tel. 215/952–9000

OUR LADY OF LOURDES MEDICAL CENTER, 1600 Haddon Avenue, Camden, NJ, Zip 08103–3117; tel. 609/757–3500; Alexander J. Hatala, President and Chief Executive Officer

PAOLI MEMORIAL HOSPITAL, 255 West Lancaster Avenue, Paoli, PA, Zip 19301–1792; tel. 610/648–1000; C. Barry Dykes, Senior Vice President

POTTSTOWN MEMORIAL MEDICAL CENTER, 1600 East High Street, Pottstown, PA, Zip 19464–5008; tel. 610/327–7000; John J. Buckley, President and Chief Executive Officer

RIDDLE MEMORIAL HOSPITAL, 1068 West Baltimore Pike, Media, PA, Zip 19063–5177; tel. 610/566–9400; Donald L. Laughlin, President

THOMAS JEFFERSON UNIVERSITY HOSPITAL, 111 South 11th Street, Philadelphia, PA, Zip 19107–5096; tel. 215/955–7022; Thomas J. Lewis, President and Chief Executive Officer

UNDERWOOD–MEMORIAL HOSPITAL, 509 North Broad Street, Woodbury, NJ, Zip 08096–1697, Mailing Address: P.O. Box 359, Zip 08096–7359; tel. 856/845–0100; Steven W. Jackmuff, President and Chief Executive Officer

WILLS EYE HOSPITAL, 900 Walnut Street, Philadelphia, PA, Zip 19107–5598; tel. 215/928–3000; D. McWilliams Kessler, Executive Director

LAUREL HEALTH SYSTEM
15 Meade St., Suite U–6, Wellsboro, PA 16901–1813; tel. 570/723–0500; Ron Butler, President & CEO

SOLDIERS AND SAILORS MEMORIAL HOSPITAL, 32–36 Central Avenue, Wellsboro, PA, Zip 16901–1899; tel. 570/724–1631; Jan E. Fisher, R.N., Executive Director

PARTNERSHIP FOR COMM HEALTH–LEHIGH VALLEY
P.O. Box 689, Allentown, PA 18105; tel. 610/954–8964; Leo Conners, Chairman

SACRED HEART HOSPITAL, 421 Chew Street, Allentown, PA, Zip 18102–3490; tel. 610/776–4500; Joseph M. Cimerola, FACHE, President and Chief Executive Officer

PRIME CARE
2601 North 3rd Street, Harrisburg, PA 17110; tel. 717/230–3434; Alan Davidson, President

PROVIDENCE HEALTH SYSTEM FOUNDATION
1100 Grampian Boulevard, Williamsport, PA 17701; tel. 717/326–8181; Sister Jean Mohl, President

MUNCY VALLEY HOSPITAL, 215 East Water Street, Muncy, PA, Zip 17756–8700; tel. 717/546–8282

QUALMED PLANS FOR HEALTH OF PENNNSYLVANIA
500 North Gulph Road, Ste200, King of Prussia, PA 19406; tel. 610/992–8700; Douglas Gregory, President

SAINT VINCENT HEALTH SYSTEM
232 West 25th Street, Erie, PA 16544; tel. 814/452–5000; Dorothy Law, Program Leader Marketing

SAINT VINCENT HEALTH CENTER, 232 West 25th Street, Erie, PA, Zip 16544–0001; tel. 814/452–5000; Sister Catherine Manning, President and Chief Executive Officer

UNION CITY MEMORIAL HOSPITAL, 130 North Main Street, Union City, PA, Zip 16438–1094, Mailing Address: P.O. Box 111, Zip 16438–0111; tel. 814/438–1000; Thomas McLoughlin, President and Chief Executive Officer

ST FRANCIS HEALTH SYSTEM
4401 Penn Avenue, Pittsburgh, PA 15224; tel. 412/622–4214; Sister M. Rosita Wellinger, President & CEO

ST. FRANCIS CENTRAL HOSPITAL, 1200 Centre Avenue, Pittsburgh, PA, Zip 15219–3507; tel. 412/562–3000; Robin Z. Mohr, Chief Executive Officer

ST. FRANCIS HOSPITAL OF NEW CASTLE, 1000 South Mercer Street, New Castle, PA, Zip 16101–4673; tel. 724/658–3511; Sister Donna Zwigart, FACHE, Chief Executive Officer

TEMPLE UNIVERSITY HEALTH
3401 North Broad Street., 1st, Philadelphia, PA 19140; tel. 215/707–8000; Leon S. Malmud, M.D.

JEANES HOSPITAL, 7600 Central Avenue, Philadelphia, PA, Zip 19111–2499; tel. 215/728–2000; G. Roger Martin, President and Chief Executive Officer

LOWER BUCKS HOSPITAL, 501 Bath Road, Bristol, PA, Zip 19007–3190; tel. 215/785–9200; Nathan Bosk, FACHE, Chief Executive Officer

NORTHEASTERN HOSPITAL OF PHILADELPHIA, 2301 East Allegheny Avenue, Philadelphia, PA, Zip 19134–4497; tel. 215/291–3000; Lynn Holder, Associate Director

TEMPLE EAST, NEUMANN MEDICAL CENTER, 1741 Frankford Avenue, Philadelphia, PA, Zip 19125–2495; tel. 215/291–2000; Lynn Holder, Executive Director

TEMPLE UNIVERSITY HOSPITAL, Broad and Ontario Streets, Philadelphia, PA, Zip 19140–5192; tel. 215/707–2000; Paul Boehringer, Executive Director

UNIVERSITY OF PENNSYLVANIA
21 Penn Tower, 399 S. 34th Street, Philadelphia, PA 19104–4385; tel. 215/898–5181; William N. Kelley, M.D., CEO

HOSPITAL OF THE UNIVERSITY OF PENNSYLVANIA, 3400 Spruce Street, Philadelphia, PA, Zip 19104–4204; tel. 215/662–4000; Thomas E. Beeman, Senior Vice President, Operations

PRESBYTERIAN MEDICAL CENTER OF THE UNIVERSITY OF PENNSYLVANIA HEALTH SYSTEM, 51 North 39th Street, Philadelphia, PA, Zip 19104–2640; tel. 215/662–8000; Michele M. Volpe, Executive Director

UNIVERSITY OF PITTSBURGH MEDICAL CENTER
3811 O'Hara Street, Pittsburgh, PA 15213; tel. 412/647–3000; Jeffrey Romoff, President

CHILDREN'S HOSPITAL OF PITTSBURGH, 3705 Fifth Avenue at De Soto Street, Pittsburgh, PA, Zip 15213–2583; tel. 412/692–5325; Ronald L. Violi, President and Chief Executive Officer

MAGEE–WOMENS HOSPITAL, 300 Halket Street, Pittsburgh, PA, Zip 15213–3180; tel. 412/641–1000; Irma E. Goertzen, President and Chief Executive Officer

UPMC PRESBYTERIAN, Pittsburgh, PA, Henry A. Mordoh, President

UPMC ST. MARGARET, 815 Freeport Road, Pittsburgh, PA, Zip 15215–3301; tel. 412/784–4000; Stanley J. Kevish, President

WASHINGTON HOSPITAL, 155 Wilson Avenue, Washington, PA, Zip 15301–3398; tel. 724/225–7000; Telford W. Thomas, President and Chief Executive Officer

VANTAGE HEALTH CARE
265 Conneaut Lake Road, Meadville, PA 16335; tel. 814/337–0000; Gerald P. Alonge, Executive Director

MEADVILLE MEDICAL CENTER, 751 Liberty Street, Meadville, PA, Zip 16335–2555; tel. 814/333–5000; Anthony J. DeFail, President and Chief Executive Officer

MILLCREEK COMMUNITY HOSPITAL, 5515 Peach Street, Erie, PA, Zip 16509–2695; tel. 814/864–4031; Mary L. Eckert, President and Chief Executive Officer

NORTHWEST MEDICAL CENTERS, 1 Spruce Street, Franklin, PA, Zip 16323–2544; tel. 814/437–7000; Neil E. Todhunter, Chief Executive Officer

SAINT VINCENT HEALTH CENTER, 232 West 25th Street, Erie, PA, Zip 16544–0001; tel. 814/452–5000; Sister Catherine Manning, President and Chief Executive Officer

TITUSVILLE AREA HOSPITAL, 406 West Oak Street, Titusville, PA, Zip 16354–1404; tel. 814/827–1851; Anthony J. Nasralla, FACHE, President and Chief Executive Officer

UPMC HORIZON, Greenville, PA, J. Larry Heinike, President and Chief Executive Officer

WARREN GENERAL HOSPITAL, 2 Crescent Park West, Warren, PA, Zip 16365–2111, Mailing Address: P.O. Box 68, Zip 16365–2111; tel. 814/723–3300; Alton M. Schadt, Executive Director

RHODE ISLAND

CARE NEW ENGLAND HEALTH
45 Willard Avenue, Providence, RI 02905; tel. 401/453–7900; John J. Hynes, Esq., President & Chief Executive

BUTLER HOSPITAL, 345 Blackstone Boulevard, Providence, RI, Zip 02906–4829; tel. 401/455–6200; Patricia R. Recupero, JD, M.D., President and Chief Executive Officer

KENT COUNTY MEMORIAL HOSPITAL, 455 Tollgate Road, Warwick, RI, Zip 02886–2770; tel. 401/737–7000; Robert E. Baute, M.D., President and Chief Executive Officer

WOMEN AND INFANTS HOSPITAL OF RHODE ISLAND, 101 Dudley Street, Providence, RI, Zip 02905–2499; tel. 401/274–1100; Thomas G. Parris, Jr., President

LIFESPAN
167 Point Street, Providence, RI 02903; tel. 401/331–8500; George A. Vecchione, President and Chief Executive Officer

EMMA PENDLETON BRADLEY HOSPITAL, 1011 Veterans Memorial Parkway, East Providence, RI, Zip 02915–5099; tel. 401/432–1000; Daniel J. Wall, President and Chief Executive Officer

MIRIAM HOSPITAL, 164 Summit Avenue, Providence, RI, Zip 02906–2895; tel. 401/793–2500; Edward M. Schottland, Senior Vice President and Chief Operating Officer

NEW ENGLAND MEDICAL CENTER, 750 Washington Street, Boston, MA, Zip 02111–1845; tel. 617/636–5000; Thomas F. O'Donnell, Jr., M.D., FACS, Chief Executive Officer

NEWPORT HOSPITAL, 11 Friendship Street, Newport, RI, Zip 02840–2299; tel. 401/846–6400; Arthur J. Sampson, President and Chief Executive Officer

RHODE ISLAND HOSPITAL, 593 Eddy Street, Providence, RI, Zip 02903–4900; tel. 401/444–4000; Steven D. Baron, President and Chief Executive Officer

SOUTH COUNTY HOSPITAL, 100 Kenyon Avenue, Wakefield, RI, Zip 02879–4299; tel. 401/782–8000; Patrick L. Muldoon, President and Chief Executive Officer

ST JOSEPH HOSPITAL
200 High Service Avenue, Providence, RI 02904; tel. 401/456–4419; Kathy Monteith, Co–ordinator

ST. JOSEPH HEALTH SERVICES OF RHODE ISLAND, 200 High Service Avenue, North Providence, RI, Zip 02904–5199; tel. 401/456–3000; H. John Keimig, President and Chief Executive Officer

SOUTH CAROLINA

CAROLINA HEALTHCHOICE
1718 Saint Julian Place, Columbia, SC 29204; tel. 803/988–8480; Suzanne H. Catalano, Executive Director

CLARENDON MEMORIAL HOSPITAL, 10 Hospital Street, Manning, SC, Zip 29102, Mailing Address: P.O. Box 550, Zip 29102–0550; tel. 803/435–8463; Edward R. Frye, Jr., Administrator

FAIRFIELD MEMORIAL HOSPITAL, 102 U.S. Highway 321 By–Pass North, Winnsboro, SC, Zip 29180, Mailing Address: P.O. Box 620, Zip 29180–0620; tel. 803/635–5548; Brent R. Lammers, Administrator

KERSHAW COUNTY MEDICAL CENTER, Haile and Roberts Streets, Camden, SC, Zip 29020–7003, Mailing Address: P.O. Box 7003, Zip 29020–7003; tel. 803/432–4311; Donnie J. Weeks, President and Chief Executive Officer

NEWBERRY COUNTY MEMORIAL HOSPITAL, 2669 Kinard Street, Newberry, SC, Zip 29108–0497, Mailing Address: P.O. Box 497, Zip 29108–0497; tel. 803/276–7570; Lynn W. Beasley, President and Chief Executive Officer

Section B

REGIONAL MEDICAL CENTER OF ORANGEBURG AND CALHOUN COUNTIES, 3000 St. Matthews Road, Orangeburg, SC, Zip 29118–1470; tel. 803/533–2200; Thomas C. Dandridge, President

TUOMEY HEALTHCARE SYSTEM, 129 North Washington Street, Sumter, SC, Zip 29150–4983; tel. 803/778–9000; Jay Cox, President and Chief Executive Officer

GREENVILLE HOSPITAL SYSTEM
701 Grove Road, Greenville, SC 29605; tel. 864/455–7000; Chris Sullivan, Director of Planning

ALLEN BENNETT HOSPITAL, 313 Memorial Drive, Greer, SC, Zip 29650–1521; tel. 864/848–8130; Michael W. Massey, Administrator

GREENVILLE MEMORIAL HOSPITAL, 701 Grove Road, Greenville, SC, Zip 29605–4295; tel. 864/455–7000; J. Bland Burkhardt, Jr., Senior Vice President and Administrator

HILLCREST HOSPITAL, 729 S.E. Main Street, Simpsonville, SC, Zip 29681–3280; tel. 864/967–6100; Mark Slyter, Administrator

PREMIER HEALTH SYSTEM, INC
Taylor at Marion Streets, Columbia, SC 29220; tel. 803/988–8999; Frank Riley, President/CEO

ABBEVILLE COUNTY MEMORIAL HOSPITAL, 901 West Greenwood Street, Abbeville, SC, Zip 29620–0887, Mailing Address: P.O. Box 887, Zip 29620–0887; tel. 864/459–5011; Bruce P. Bailey, Administrator

ALLEN BENNETT HOSPITAL, 313 Memorial Drive, Greer, SC, Zip 29650–1521; tel. 864/848–8130; Michael W. Massey, Administrator

ALLENDALE COUNTY HOSPITAL, Highway 278 West, Fairfax, SC, Zip 29827–0278, Mailing Address: Box 218, Zip 29827–0218; tel. 803/632–3311; M. K. Hiatt, Administrator

BAMBERG COUNTY MEMORIAL HOSPITAL AND NURSING CENTER, North and McGee Streets, Bamberg, SC, Zip 29003–0507, Mailing Address: P.O. Box 507, Zip 29003–0507; tel. 803/245–4321; Warren E. Hammett, Administrator

BARNWELL COUNTY HOSPITAL, 811 Reynolds Road, Barnwell, SC, Zip 29812; tel. 803/259–1000; J. L. Dozier, Jr., FACHE, Chief Executive Officer

BON SECOURS–ST. FRANCIS XAVIER HOSPITAL, 2095 Henry Tecklenburg Drive, Charleston, SC, Zip 29414–0001, Mailing Address: P.O. Box 160001, Zip 29414–0001; tel. 803/402–1000; Allen P. Carroll, Chief Executive Officer

CANNON MEMORIAL HOSPITAL, 123 West G. Acker Drive, Pickens, SC, Zip 29671, Mailing Address: P.O. Box 188, Zip 29671–0188; tel. 864/878–4791; Norman G. Rentz, President and Chief Executive Officer

CAROLINAS HOSPITAL SYSTEM–LAKE CITY, 258 North Ron McNair Boulevard, Lake City, SC, Zip 29560–1029, Mailing Address: P.O. Box 1029, Zip 29560–1029; tel. 843/394–2036; David T. Boucher, Chief Executive Officer

CHESTER COUNTY HOSPITAL AND NURSING CENTER, 1 Medical Park Drive, Chester, SC, Zip 29706–9799; tel. 803/581–9400; William H. Bundy, Chief Executive Officer

CHESTERFIELD GENERAL HOSPITAL, Highway 9 West, Cheraw, SC, Zip 29520, Mailing Address: P.O. Box 151, Zip 29520–0151; tel. 843/537–7881; Chris Wolf, Chief Executive Officer

CLARENDON MEMORIAL HOSPITAL, 10 Hospital Street, Manning, SC, Zip 29102, Mailing Address: P.O. Box 550, Zip 29102–0550; tel. 803/435–8463; Edward R. Frye, Jr., Administrator

EAST COOPER REGIONAL MEDICAL CENTER, 1200 Johnnie Dodds Boulevard, Mount Pleasant, SC, Zip 29464–3294; tel. 843/881–0100; Jack Dusenbery, President

EDGEFIELD COUNTY HOSPITAL, 300 Ridge Medical Plaza, Edgefield, SC, Zip 29824; tel. 803/637–3174; W. Joseph Seel, Administrator

FAIRFIELD MEMORIAL HOSPITAL, 102 U.S. Highway 321 By–Pass North, Winnsboro, SC, Zip 29180, Mailing Address: P.O. Box 620, Zip 29180–0620; tel. 803/635–5548; Brent R. Lammers, Administrator

GEORGETOWN MEMORIAL HOSPITAL, 606 Black River Road, Georgetown, SC, Zip 29440–3368, Mailing Address: Drawer 1718, Zip 29442–1718; tel. 843/527–7000; Paul D. Gatens, Sr., Administrator

GREENVILLE MEMORIAL HOSPITAL, 701 Grove Road, Greenville, SC, Zip 29605–4295; tel. 864/455–7000; J. Bland Burkhardt, Jr., Senior Vice President and Administrator

HEALTHSOUTH REHABILITATION HOSPITAL, 2935 Colonial Drive, Columbia, SC, Zip 29203–6811; tel. 803/254–7777; Debbie W. Johnston, Director Operations

HILLCREST HOSPITAL, 729 S.E. Main Street, Simpsonville, SC, Zip 29681–3280; tel. 864/967–6100; Mark Slyter, Administrator

HILTON HEAD MEDICAL CENTER AND CLINICS, 25 Hospital Center Boulevard, Hilton Head Island, SC, Zip 29926–2738, Mailing Address: P.O. Box 21117, Zip 29925–1117; tel. 843/681–6122; Dennis Ray Bruns, President and Chief Executive Officer

KERSHAW COUNTY MEDICAL CENTER, Haile and Roberts Streets, Camden, SC, Zip 29020–7003, Mailing Address: P.O. Box 7003, Zip 29020–7003; tel. 803/432–4311; Donnie J. Weeks, President and Chief Executive Officer

LAURENS COUNTY HEALTHCARE SYSTEM, Highway 76 West, Clinton, SC, Zip 29325, Mailing Address: P.O. Box 976, Zip 29325–0976; tel. 864/833–9100; Michael A. Kozar, Chief Executive Officer

LEXINGTON MEDICAL CENTER, 2720 Sunset Boulevard, West Columbia, SC, Zip 29169–4816; tel. 803/791–2000; Michael J. Biediger, President

MARLBORO PARK HOSPITAL, 1138 Cheraw Highway, Bennettsville, SC, Zip 29512–0738, Mailing Address: P.O. Box 738, Zip 29512–0738; tel. 843/479–2881; Stephen Chapman, Chief Executive Officer

MARY BLACK HEALTH SYSTEM, 1700 Skylyn Drive, Spartanburg, SC, Zip 29307–1061, Mailing Address: P.O. Box 3217, Zip 29304–3217; tel. 864/573–3000; William W. Fox, Chief Executive Officer

NEWBERRY COUNTY MEMORIAL HOSPITAL, 2669 Kinard Street, Newberry, SC, Zip 29108–0497, Mailing Address: P.O. Box 497, Zip 29108–0497; tel. 803/276–7570; Lynn W. Beasley, President and Chief Executive Officer

PALMETTO BAPTIST MEDICAL CENTER EASLEY, 200 Fleetwood Drive, Easley, SC, Zip 29640–2076, Mailing Address: P.O. Box 2129, Zip 29641–2129; tel. 864/855–7200; Roddey E. Gettys, III, Executive Vice President

PALMETTO BAPTIST MEDICAL CENTER/COLUMBIA, Taylor at Marion Street, Columbia, SC, Zip 29220; tel. 803/296–5010; James M. Bridges, Executive Vice President and Chief Operating Officer

PROVIDENCE HOSPITAL, 2435 Forest Drive, Columbia, SC, Zip 29204–2098; tel. 803/256–5300; Stephen A. Purves, CHE, President and Chief Executive Officer

ROPER HOSPITAL, 316 Calhoun Street, Charleston, SC, Zip 29401–1125; tel. 843/724–2000; Edward L. Berdick, President and Chief Executive Officer

SELF MEMORIAL HOSPITAL, 1325 Spring Street, Greenwood, SC, Zip 29646–3860; tel. 864/227–4111; M. John Heydel, President and Chief Executive Officer

ST. JOSEPH'S HOSPITAL, 11705 Mercy Boulevard, Savannah, GA, Zip 31419–1791; tel. 912/927–5404; Paul P. Hinchey, President and Chief Executive Officer

UPSTATE CAROLINA MEDICAL CENTER, 1530 North Limestone Street, Gaffney, SC, Zip 29340–4738; tel. 864/487–1500; Nancy C. Fodi, Executive Director

WILLINGWAY HOSPITAL, 311 Jones Mill Road, Statesboro, GA, Zip 30458–4765; tel. 912/764–6236; Jimmy Mooney, Chief Executive Officer

RICHLAND COMMUNITY HEALTH PARTNERS
3 Medical Park, Suite 100, Columbia, SC 29203; tel. 803/434–3100; Tom Brown, Director

PALMETTO RICHLAND MEMORIAL HOSPITAL, Five Richland Medical Park Drive, Columbia, SC, Zip 29203, Mailing Address: P.O. Box 2266, Zip 29203–2266; tel. 803/434–7000; B. Daniel Paysinger, M.D., Chief Operating Officer

ST FRANCIS HEALTH SYSTEM
One St. Francis Drive, Greeneville, SC 29601; tel. 803/255–1015; Kerbi Waterfield, Plan Coordinator

ST. FRANCIS HEALTH SYSTEM, One St. Francis Drive, Greenville, SC, Zip 29601–3207; tel. 864/255–1000; Richard C. Neugent, President and Chief Executive Officer

SOUTH DAKOTA

BLACK HILLS HEALTHCARE
930 10th Street, Spearfish, SD 57783; tel. 605/642–4641; MaLinda Birkeland, Coordinator of Marketing Communications

LOOKOUT MEMORIAL HOSPITAL, 1440 North Main Street, Spearfish, SD, Zip 57783–1504; tel. 605/642–2617; Deb J. Krmpotic, R.N., Administrator

STURGIS COMMUNITY HEALTH CARE CENTER, 949 Harmon Street, Sturgis, SD, Zip 57785–2452; tel. 605/347–2536; Deb J. Krmpotic, R.N., Administrator

MISSOURI VALLEY HEALTH
1017 West 5th Street, Yankton, SD 57078; tel. 605/665–9005; Lanette Hinchly, Office Manager

AVERA QUEEN OF PEACE, 525 North Foster, Mitchell, SD, Zip 57301–2999; tel. 605/995–2000; Ronald L. Jacobson, President and Chief Executive Officer

AVERA SACRED HEART HEALTH SERVICES, 501 Summit Avenue, Yankton, SD, Zip 57078–3899; tel. 605/668–8000; Pamela J. Rezac, President and Chief Executive Officer

AVERA ST. BENEDICT HEALTH CENTER, Glynn Drive, Parkston, SD, Zip 57366, Mailing Address: P.O. Box B, Zip 57366; tel. 605/928–3311; Gale Walker, Administrator

COMMUNITY MEMORIAL HOSPITAL, Eighth and Jackson, Burke, SD, Zip 57523, Mailing Address: P.O. Box 319, Zip 57523–0319; tel. 605/775–2621; Carol A. Varland, Chief Executive Officer

DOUGLAS COUNTY MEMORIAL HOSPITAL, 708 Eighth Street, Armour, SD, Zip 57313–2102; tel. 605/724–2159; Angelia K. Henry, Administrator

FREEMAN COMMUNITY HOSPITAL, 510 East Eighth Street, Freeman, SD, Zip 57029–0370, Mailing Address: P.O. Box 370, Zip 57029–0370; tel. 605/925–4000; James M. Krehbiel, Chief Executive Officer

GREGORY COMMUNITY HOSPITAL, 400 Park Street, Gregory, SD, Zip 57533–0400, Mailing Address: Box 408, Zip 57533–0408; tel. 605/835–8394; Carol A. Varland, Chief Executive Officer

LANDMANN–JUNGMAN MEMORIAL HOSPITAL, 600 Billars Street, Scotland, SD, Zip 57059–2026; tel. 605/583–2226; William H. Koellner, Administrator

PIONEER MEMORIAL HOSPITAL AND HEALTH SERVICES, 315 North Washington Street, Viborg, SD, Zip 57070, Mailing Address: P.O. Box 368, Zip 57070–0368; tel. 605/326–5161; Georgia Pokorney, Chief Executive Officer

PLATTE COMMUNITY MEMORIAL HOSPITAL, 609 East Seventh, Platte, SD, Zip 57369–2123, Mailing Address: P.O. Box 200, Zip 57369–0200; tel. 605/337–3364; Mark Burket, Chief Executive Officer

ST. MICHAEL'S HOSPITAL, Douglas Street and Broadway, Tyndall, SD, Zip 57066, Mailing Address: P.O. Box 27, Zip 57066–0027; tel. 605/589–3341; Carol Deurmier, Chief Executive Officer

WAGNER COMMUNITY MEMORIAL HOSPITAL, Third and Walnut, Wagner, SD, Zip 57380, Mailing Address: P.O. Box 280, Zip 57380–0280; tel. 605/384–3611; Arlene C. Bich, Administrator

WINNER REGIONAL HEALTHCARE CENTER, 745 East Eighth Street, Winner, SD, Zip 57580–2677, Mailing Address: P.O. Box 745, Zip 57580–0745; tel. 605/842–7100; Rebecca L. Cooper, Interim Chief Executive Officer

RAPID CITY REGIONAL HOSPITAL SYSTEM OF CARE
353 Fairmont Boulevard, Rapid City, SD, 57701; tel. 605/341–1000; Carolyn Helfenstein, Director of Marketing & Public Relations

CUSTER COMMUNITY HOSPITAL, 1039 Montgomery Street, Custer, SD, Zip 57730–1397; tel. 605/673–2229; Jason Petik, Administrator

FIVE COUNTIES HOSPITAL, 401 Sixth Avenue West, Lemmon, SD, Zip 57638–1318, Mailing Address: P.O. Box 479, Zip 57638–0479; tel. 605/374–3871; Helen S. Lindquist, Administrator

HANS P. PETERSON MEMORIAL HOSPITAL, 603 West Pine, Philip, SD, Zip 57567, Mailing Address: P.O. Box 790, Zip 57567–0790; tel. 605/859–2511; David Dick, Administrator

NORTHERN HILLS GENERAL HOSPITAL, 61 Charles Street, Deadwood, SD, Zip 57732–1303; tel. 605/578–2313; Richard G. Soukup, Chief Executive Officer

RAPID CITY REGIONAL HOSPITAL SYSTEM OF CARE, 353 Fairmont Boulevard, Rapid City, SD, Zip 57701–7393, Mailing Address: P.O. Box 6000, Zip 57709–6000; tel. 605/341–1000; Adil M. Ameer, President and Chief Executive Officer

WESTON COUNTY HEALTH SERVICES, 1124 Washington Street, Newcastle, WY, Zip 82701–2996; tel. 307/746–4491; Jack Brinkers, CHE, Administrator

TENNESSEE

CHATTANOOGA HEALTHCARE NETWORK
401 Chestnut Street, Suite 222, Chattanooga, TN 37402; tel. 615/266–5174; Judy Clay, Network Contact

ATHENS REGIONAL MEDICAL CENTER, 1114 West Madison Avenue, Athens, TN, Zip 37303–4150, Mailing Address: P.O. Box 250, Zip 37371–0250; tel. 423/745–1411; John R. Workman, Chief Executive Officer

GRANDVIEW MEDICAL CENTER, 1000 Highway 28, Jasper, TN, Zip 37347; tel. 423/837–9500; Phil Rowland, Chief Executive Officer

COLUMBIA HEALTHCARE NETWORK
Two Maryland Farms, Suite 300, Brentwood, TN 37027; tel. 615/661–7200; Luis A. Rosa, Chief Executive Officer

CENTENNIAL MEDICAL CENTER AND PARTHENON PAVILION, 2300 Patterson Street, Nashville, TN, Zip 37203–1528; tel. 615/342–1000; Larry Kloess, President

CHEATHAM MEDICAL CENTER, 313 North Main Street, Ashland City, TN, Zip 37015–1358; tel. 615/792–3030; Rick Wallace, FACHE, Chief Executive Officer and Administrator

HENDERSONVILLE HOSPITAL, 355 New Shackle Island Road, Hendersonville, TN, Zip 37075–2393; tel. 615/264–4000; Robert Klein, Chief Executive Officer

HORIZON MEDICAL CENTER, 111 Highway 70 East, Dickson, TN, Zip 37055–2033; tel. 615/441–2357; Rick Wallace, FACHE, Chief Executive Officer and Administrator

NASHVILLE MEMORIAL HOSPITAL, 612 West Due West Avenue, Madison, TN, Zip 37115–4474; tel. 615/865–3511; Allyn R. Harris, Chief Executive Officer

NORTH CREST MEDICAL CENTER, 100 North Crest Drive, Springfield, TN, Zip 37172–2984; tel. 615/384–2411; William A. Kenley, President and Chief Executive Officer

PSYCHIATRIC HOSPITAL AT VANDERBILT, 1601 23rd Avenue South, Nashville, TN, Zip 37212–3198; tel. 615/320–7770; Richard A. Bangert, Chief Executive Officer and Administrator

RIVER PARK HOSPITAL, 1559 Sparta Road, McMinnville, TN, Zip 37110–1316; tel. 931/815–4000; Terry J. Gunn, Chief Executive Officer

SOUTHERN HILLS MEDICAL CENTER, 391 Wallace Road, Nashville, TN, Zip 37211–4859; tel. 615/781–4000; Jeffrey Whitehorn, Chief Executive Officer

STONES RIVER HOSPITAL, 324 Doolittle Road, Woodbury, TN, Zip 37190–1139; tel. 615/563–4001; Bill Patterson, Interim Administrator

SUMMIT MEDICAL CENTER, 5655 Frist Boulevard, Hermitage, TN, Zip 37076–2053; tel. 615/316–3000; Bryan K. Dearing, Chief Executive Officer

COVENANT HEALTH
100 Fort Sanders West Boulevard, Knoxville, TN 37922–3353; tel. 423/531–5555; Max Shell, Sr. V.P., Marketing & Planning

FORT SANDERS LOUDON MEDICAL CENTER, 1125 Grove Street, Loudon, TN, Zip 37774–1512, Mailing Address: P.O. Box 217, Zip 37774–0217; tel. 423/458–8222; Martha O'Regan Chill, President and Chief Administrative Officer

FORT SANDERS REGIONAL MEDICAL CENTER, 1901 Clinch Avenue S.W., Knoxville, TN, Zip 37916–2394; tel. 423/541–1111; James R. Burkhart, FACHE, Administrator

FORT SANDERS–SEVIER MEDICAL CENTER, 709 Middle Creek Road, Sevierville, TN, Zip 37862–5016, Mailing Address: P.O. Box 8005, Zip 37864–8005; tel. 423/429–6100; Ellen Wilhoit, Administrator

FRANK T. RUTHERFORD MEMORIAL HOSPITAL, 130 Lebanon Highway, Carthage, TN, Zip 37030–2955, Mailing Address: P.O. Box 319, Zip 37030–0319; tel. 615/735–9815; Wayne Winfree, Chief Executive Officer

METHODIST MEDICAL CENTER OF OAK RIDGE, 990 Oak Ridge Turnpike, Oak Ridge, TN, Zip 37830–6976, Mailing Address: P.O. Box 2529, Zip 37831–2529; tel. 423/481–1000; Daniel J. Bonk, President and Chief Administrative Officer

PENINSULA HOSPITAL, 2347 Jones Bend Road, Louisville, TN, Zip 37777–5213, Mailing Address: P.O. Box 2000, Zip 37777–2000; tel. 423/970–9800; David H. McReynolds, Chief Operating Officer and Administrator

HIGHLANDS WELLMONT HEALTH
1 Medical Park Boulevard, Bristol, TN 37621–0989; tel. 423/844–4186; Glynn Hughes, Senior Vice President – Integration Strategies

NORTON COMMUNITY HOSPITAL, 100 15th Street N.W., Norton, VA, Zip 24273–1699; tel. 540/679–9600

WELLMONT BRISTOL REGIONAL MEDICAL CENTER, 1 Medical Park Boulevard, Bristol, TN, Zip 37620–7434; tel. 423/844–4200; Randall M. Olson, Administrator

WELLMONT HOLSTON VALLEY MEDICAL CENTER, West Ravine Street, Kingsport, TN, Zip 37662–0224, Mailing Address: Box 238, Zip 37662–0224; tel. 423/224–4000; Louis H. Bremer, President and Chief Executive Officer

WELLMONT LONESOME PINE HOSPITAL, 1990 Holton Avenue East, Big Stone Gap, VA, Zip 24219–0230; tel. 540/523–3111; Paul A. Bishop, Administrator

METHODIST MEDICAL CENTER
1211 Union Avenue Suite 700, Memphis, TN 38104; tel. 901/726–8273; Maurice Elliott, President

METHODIST HEALTHCARE – FAYETTE HOSPITAL, 214 Lakeview Drive, Somerville, TN, Zip 38068; tel. 901/465–0532; Michael Blome', Administrator

METHODIST HEALTHCARE – MCKENZIE HOSPITAL, 161 Hospital Drive, McKenzie, TN, Zip 38201–1636; tel. 901/352–5344; Richard McCormick, Administrator

METHODIST HEALTHCARE MIDDLE MISSISSIPPI HOSPITAL, 239 Bowling Green Road, Lexington, MS, Zip 39095–9332; tel. 601/834–1321; James K. Greer, Administrator

METHODIST HEALTHCARE– DYERSBURG HOSPITAL, 400 Tickle Street, Dyersburg, TN, Zip 38024–3182; tel. 901/285–2410; Richard McCormick, Administrator

METHODIST HEALTHCARE–LEXINGTON HOSPITAL, 200 West Church Street, Lexington, TN, Zip 38351–2014; tel. 901/968–3646; Eugene Ragghianti, Administrator

METHODIST HEALTHCARE–MEMPHIS HOSPITAL, 1265 Union Avenue, Memphis, TN, Zip 38104–3499; tel. 901/726–7000; David L. Ramsey, President

MIDDLE TENNESSEE HEALTHCARE INC
2000 Church Street, Nashville, TN 37236; tel. 615/329–5555; James E. Ward, President

BAPTIST HOSPITAL, 2000 Church Street, Nashville, TN, Zip 37236–0002; tel. 615/329–5555; Erie Chapman, III, President and Chief Executive Officer

BEDFORD COUNTY MEDICAL CENTER, 845 Union Street, Shelbyville, TN, Zip 37160–9971; tel. 931/685–5433; Richard L. Graham, Administrator

COOKEVILLE REGIONAL MEDICAL CENTER, 142 West Fifth Street, Cookeville, TN, Zip 38501–1760, Mailing Address: P.O. Box 340, Zip 38503–0340; tel. 931/528–2541; Tod N. Lambert, Administrator and Chief Executive Officer

CUMBERLAND MEDICAL CENTER, 421 South Main Street, Crossville, TN, Zip 38555–5031; tel. 931/484–9511; Edwin S. Anderson, President

GATEWAY HEALTH SYSTEM, 1771 Madison Street, Clarksville, TN, Zip 37043–4900, Mailing Address: P.O. Box 3160, Zip 37043–3160; tel. 931/552–6622; James Lee Decker, President and Chief Executive Officer

MAURY REGIONAL HOSPITAL, 1224 Trotwood Avenue, Columbia, TN, Zip 38401–4823; tel. 931/381–1111; William R. Walter, Chief Executive Officer

MIDDLE TENNESSEE MEDICAL CENTER, 400 North Highland Avenue, Murfreesboro, TN, Zip 37130–3854, Mailing Address: P.O. Box 1178, Zip 37133–1178; tel. 615/849–4100; Arthur W. Hastings, President and Chief Executive Officer

ST. THOMAS HEALTH SERVICES, 4220 Harding Road, Nashville, TN, Zip 37205–2095, Mailing Address: P.O. Box 380, Zip 37202–0380; tel. 615/222–2111; John Lucas, M.D., President and Chief Executive Officer

SUMNER REGIONAL MEDICAL CENTER, 555 Hartsville Pike, Gallatin, TN, Zip 37066–2449, Mailing Address: P.O. Box 1558, Zip 37066–1558; tel. 615/452–4210; William T. Sugg, President and Chief Executive Officer

TENNESSEE CHRISTIAN MEDICAL CENTER, 500 Hospital Drive, Madison, TN, Zip 37115–5032; tel. 615/865–2373; Clint Kreitner, President and Chief Executive Officer

VANDERBILT UNIVERSITY HOSPITAL, 1161 21st Avenue South, Nashville, TN, Zip 37232–2102; tel. 615/322–5000; Norman B. Urmy, Executive Vice President Clinical Affairs

WILLIAMSON MEDICAL CENTER, 2021 Carothers Road, Franklin, TN, Zip 37067–5822, Mailing Address: P.O. Box 681600, Zip 37068–1600; tel. 615/791–0500; Ronald G. Joyner, Chief Executive Officer

MOUNTAIN STATES HEALTHCARE NETWORK
400 North State of Franklin Road, Johnson City, TN 37604; tel. 615/461–6810; Richard Kramer, President

Section B

CHARLES A. CANNON JR. MEMORIAL HOSPITAL, 805 Shawneehaw Avenue, Banner Elk, NC, Zip 28604–9724, Mailing Address: P.O. Box 8, Zip 28604–0008; tel. 828/898–5111

CLINCH VALLEY MEDICAL CENTER, 2949 West Front Street, Richlands, VA, Zip 24641–2099; tel. 540/596–6000; James W. Thweatt, Chief Executive Officer

JOHNSON CITY MEDICAL CENTER, 400 North State of Franklin Road, Johnson City, TN, Zip 37604–6094; tel. 423/431–6111; Dennis Vonderfecht, President and Chief Executive Officer

JOHNSTON MEMORIAL HOSPITAL, 351 Court Street N.E., Abingdon, VA, Zip 24210–2921; tel. 540/676–7000; Clark R. Beil, Chief Executive Officer

LAKEWAY REGIONAL HOSPITAL, 726 McFarland Street, Morristown, TN, Zip 37814–3990; tel. 423/586–2302; Robert B. Wampler, CPA, Chief Executive Officer

LEE COUNTY COMMUNITY HOSPITAL, West Morgan Avenue, Pennington Gap, VA, Zip 24277, Mailing Address: P.O. Box 70, Zip 24277–0070; tel. 540/546–1440; James L. Davis, Chief Executive Officer

MORRISTOWN–HAMBLEN HOSPITAL, 908 West Fourth North Street, Morristown, TN, Zip 37816, Mailing Address: P.O. Box 1178, Zip 37816; tel. 423/586–4231; Richard L. Clark, Administrator and Chief Executive Officer

TAKOMA ADVENTIST HOSPITAL, 401 Takoma Avenue, Greeneville, TN, Zip 37743–4668; tel. 423/639–3151; Carlyle L. E. Walton, President

UNICOI COUNTY MEMORIAL HOSPITAL, 100 Greenway Circle, Erwin, TN, Zip 37650–2196, Mailing Address: P.O. Box 802, Zip 37650–0802; tel. 423/743–3141; James L. McMackin, Chief Executive Officer

WOODRIDGE HOSPITAL, 403 State of Franklin Road, Johnson City, TN, Zip 37604–6009; tel. 423/928–7111; Donald Larkin, Ph.D., Administrator

NASHVILLE HEALTHCARE PARTNERSHIP
161 Fourth Avenue North, Nashville, TN 37219; tel. 615/259–4786; Joanne F. Pulles, Executive Director

ST. THOMAS HEALTH SERVICES, 4220 Harding Road, Nashville, TN, Zip 37205–2095, Mailing Address: P.O. Box 380, Zip 37202–0380; tel. 615/222–2111; John Lucas, M.D., President and Chief Executive Officer

TENNESSEE CHRISTIAN MEDICAL CENTER, 500 Hospital Drive, Madison, TN, Zip 37115–5032; tel. 615/865–2373; Clint Kreitner, President and Chief Executive Officer

VANDERBILT UNIVERSITY HOSPITAL, 1161 21st Avenue South, Nashville, TN, Zip 37232–2102; tel. 615/322–5000; Norman B. Urmy, Executive Vice President Clinical Affairs

ST THOMAS HOSPITAL
P.O. Box 380–4220, Nashville, TN 37205; tel. 615/222–6800; Greg Pope, Executive Director

ST. THOMAS HEALTH SERVICES, 4220 Harding Road, Nashville, TN, Zip 37205–2095, Mailing Address: P.O. Box 380, Zip 37202–0380; tel. 615/222–2111; John Lucas, M.D., President and Chief Executive Officer

VANDERBILT UNIVERSITY HOSPITAL, 1161 21st Avenue South, Nashville, TN, Zip 37232–2102; tel. 615/322–5000; Norman B. Urmy, Executive Vice President Clinical Affairs

WELLMONT HEALTH SYSTEM
P.O. Box 689, Kingsport, TN 37662; tel. 423/224–3003; Eddie George, President & CEO

WEST TENNESSEE HEALTHCARE
708 West Forest, Jackson, TN 38301; tel. 901/664–4254; Jim Moss, Chief Executive Officer

BOLIVAR GENERAL HOSPITAL, 650 Nuckolls Road, Bolivar, TN, Zip 38008–1500; tel. 901/658–3100; George L. Austin, Administrator

CAMDEN GENERAL HOSPITAL, 175 Hospital Drive, Camden, TN, Zip 38320–1617; tel. 901/584–6135; John M. Carruth, Administrator

DECATUR COUNTY GENERAL HOSPITAL, 969 Tennessee Avenue South, Parsons, TN, Zip 38363–0250, Mailing Address: Box 250, Zip 38363–0250; tel. 901/847–3031; Larry N. Lindsey, Administrator and Chief Executive Officer

GIBSON GENERAL HOSPITAL, 200 Hospital Drive, Trenton, TN, Zip 38382–3300; tel. 901/855–7900; Kelly R. Yenawine, Administrator

HARDIN COUNTY GENERAL HOSPITAL, 2006 Wayne Road, Savannah, TN, Zip 38372–2294; tel. 901/925–4954; Charlotte Burns, Administrator and Chief Executive Officer

HENRY COUNTY MEDICAL CENTER, 301 Tyson Avenue, Paris, TN, Zip 38242–4544, Mailing Address: Box 1030, Zip 38242–1030; tel. 901/644–8537; Thomas H. Gee, Administrator

HUMBOLDT GENERAL HOSPITAL, 3525 Chere Carol Road, Humboldt, TN, Zip 38343–3699; tel. 901/784–0301; Bill Kail, Administrator

JACKSON–MADISON COUNTY GENERAL HOSPITAL, 708 West Forest Avenue, Jackson, TN, Zip 38301–3855; tel. 901/425–5000; James T. Moss, President and Chief Executive Officer

MILAN GENERAL HOSPITAL, 4039 South Highland, Milan, TN, Zip 38358; tel. 901/686–1591; Alfred P. Taylor, Administrator and Chief Executive Officer

TEXAS

BAY AREA HEALTHCARE GROUP, LTD
5650 South Staples Suite 108, Corpus Christi, TX 78411; tel. 512/881–1600; Don Stewart, President

ALICE REGIONAL HOSPITAL, 300 East Third Street, Alice, TX, Zip 78332–4794; tel. 361/664–4376; Abraham Martinez, Chief Executive Officer

CORPUS CHRISTI MEDICAL CENTER, 3315 South Alameda Street, Corpus Christi, TX, Zip 78411–1883, Mailing Address: P.O. Box 3828, Zip 78463–3828; tel. 361/857–1400; Steven Woerner, Chief Executive Officer

CORPUS CHRISTI MEDICAL CENTER BAY AREA, 7101 South Padre Island Drive, Corpus Christi, TX, Zip 78412–4999; tel. 361/985–1200; Steven Woerner, Chief Executive Officer

CORPUS CHRISTI MEDICAL CENTER–BAYVIEW PSYCHIATRIC CENTER, 6226 Saratoga Boulevard, Corpus Christi, TX, Zip 78414–3421; tel. 361/993–9700; Janie L. Harwood, Administrator

DOCTORS HOSPITAL OF LAREDO, 500 East Mann Road, Laredo, TX, Zip 78041–2699; tel. 956/723–1131; Benjamin Everett, Chief Executive Officer

NORTH BAY HOSPITAL, 1711 West Wheeler Avenue, Aransas Pass, TX, Zip 78336–4536; tel. 361/758–8585; John Krogness, Chief Executive Officer

NORTHWEST REGIONAL HOSPITAL, 13725 Farm to Market Road 624, Corpus Christi, TX, Zip 78410–5199; tel. 512/767–4300; Winston Borland, Chief Executive Officer

REHABILITATION HOSPITAL OF SOUTH TEXAS, 6226 Saratoga Boulevard, Corpus Christi, TX, Zip 78414–3421; tel. 361/991–9690; Kevin N. Fowler, Chief Executive Officer

RIO GRANDE REGIONAL HOSPITAL, 101 East Ridge Road, McAllen, TX, Zip 78503–1299; tel. 956/632–6000; Randall M. Everts, Chief Executive Officer

VALLEY REGIONAL MEDICAL CENTER, 100A Alton Gloor Boulevard, Brownsville, TX, Zip 78526, Mailing Address: P.O. Box 3710, Zip 78521–3710; tel. 956/350–7101; Charles F. Sexton, Chief Executive Officer

BAYLOR HEALTH CARE NETWORK
2625 Elm Street, Suite 204, Dallas, TX 75226; tel. 214/820–3425; Bill Cook, President

BAYLOR CENTER FOR RESTORATIVE CARE, 3504 Swiss Avenue, Dallas, TX, Zip 75204–6224; tel. 214/820–9700; Gerry Brueckner, R.N., Executive Director

BAYLOR MEDICAL CENTER AT GARLAND, 2300 Marie Curie Boulevard, Garland, TX, Zip 75042–5706; tel. 972/487–5000; John B. McWhorter, III, Executive Director

BAYLOR MEDICAL CENTER AT GRAPEVINE, 1650 West College Street, Grapevine, TX, Zip 76051–1650; tel. 817/329–2500; Mark C. Hood, Executive Director

BAYLOR MEDICAL CENTER AT IRVING, 1901 North MacArthur Boulevard, Irving, TX, Zip 75061–2291; tel. 972/579–8100; Michael F. O'Keefe, FACHE, Executive Director

BAYLOR MEDICAL CENTER–ELLIS COUNTY, 1405 West Jefferson Street, Waxahachie, TX, Zip 75165–2275; tel. 972/923–7000; James Michael Lee, Executive Director

BAYLOR UNIVERSITY MEDICAL CENTER, 3500 Gaston Avenue, Dallas, TX, Zip 75246–2088; tel. 214/820–0111; M. Tim Parris, Executive Vice President and Chief Operating Officer

BAYLOR/ RICHARDSON MEDICAL CENTER, 401 West Campbell Road, Richardson, TX, Zip 75080–3499; tel. 972/498–4000; Ronald L. Boring, President and Chief Executive Officer

HOPKINS COUNTY MEMORIAL HOSPITAL, 115 Airport Road, Sulphur Springs, TX, Zip 75482–0115; tel. 903/885–7671; Richard L. Goddard, Chief Executive Officer

BRAZO'S VALLEY HEALTH NETWORK
3115 Pine Avenue, Waco, TX 76708; tel. 817/757–3882; Don Reeves, Executive Director

CENTRAL TEXAS HOSPITAL, 806 North Crockett Avenue, Cameron, TX, Zip 76520–2599; tel. 254/697–6591; Jodi Beauregard, Administrator

GOODALL–WITCHER HEALTHCARE, 101 South Avenue T, Clifton, TX, Zip 76634–1897, Mailing Address: P.O. Box 549, Zip 76634–0549; tel. 254/675–8322; Jim B. Smith, President and Chief Executive Officer

LIMESTONE MEDICAL CENTER, 701 McClintic Street, Groesbeck, TX, Zip 76642–2105; tel. 254/729–3281; Penny Gray, Administrator and Chief Executive Officer

CARE ALLIANCE OF THE SOUTHWEST
14901 Quorum Drive, Suite 200, Dallas, TX 75240; tel. 214/490–0433; Marsha Ballard, Interim CEO

ARLINGTON MEMORIAL HOSPITAL, 800 West Randol Mill Road, Arlington, TX, Zip 76012–2503; tel. 817/548–6100; Wayne N. Clark, President and Chief Executive Officer

ST. JOSEPH'S HOSPITAL AND HEALTH CENTER, 820 Clarksville Street, Paris, TX, Zip 75460–9070, Mailing Address: P.O. Box 9070, Zip 75461–9070; tel. 903/785–4521; Monty E. McLaurin, President

CENTRAL TEXAS RURAL HEALTH NETWORK
503 E. 4th Street, Harrietsville, TX 77964–2824; tel. 512/798–2302; Marcella V. Henke, Executive Director

CENTRAL TEXAS HOSPITAL, 806 North Crockett Avenue, Cameron, TX, Zip 76520–2599; tel. 254/697–6591; Jodi Beauregard, Administrator

FALLS COMMUNITY HOSPITAL AND CLINIC, 322 Coleman Street, Marlin, TX, Zip 76661–2358, Mailing Address: Box 60, Zip 76661–0060; tel. 254/803–3561; Willis L. Reese, Administrator

GOODALL–WITCHER HEALTHCARE, 101 South Avenue T, Clifton, TX, Zip 76634–1897, Mailing Address: P.O. Box 549, Zip 76634–0549; tel. 254/675–8322; Jim B. Smith, President and Chief Executive Officer

HILL REGIONAL HOSPITAL, 101 Circle Drive, Hillsboro, TX, Zip 76645–2670; tel. 254/582–8425; Jan McClure, Chief Executive Officer

LAKE WHITNEY MEDICAL CENTER, 200 North San Jacinto Street, Whitney, TX, Zip 76692–2388, Mailing Address: P.O. Box 458, Zip 76692–0458; tel. 254/694–3165; Ruth Ann Crow, Administrator

LIMESTONE MEDICAL CENTER, 701 McClintic Street, Groesbeck, TX, Zip 76642–2105; tel. 254/729–3281; Penny Gray, Administrator and Chief Executive Officer

PARKVIEW REGIONAL HOSPITAL, 312 East Glendale Street, Mexia, TX, Zip 76667–3608; tel. 254/562–5332; Tim Adams, Administrator and Chief Executive Officer

WEST COMMUNITY HOSPITAL, 501 Meadow Drive, West, TX, Zip 76691–1018, Mailing Address: P.O. Box 478, Zip 76691–0478; tel. 817/826–7000; Betty York, Executive Director

GOOD SHEPARD HEALTH NETWORK
700 East Marshall Avenue, Longview, TX 75601; tel. 903/236–2000; Dr. Rebecca Burrow, Executive Director

GOOD SHEPHERD MEDICAL CENTER, 700 East Marshall Avenue, Longview, TX, Zip 75601–5571; tel. 903/236–2000; Jerry D. Adair, President and Chief Executive Officer

GULF COAST PROVIDER NETWORK
2900 North Loop West Ste1230, Houston, TX 77092; tel. 281/291–9808; Susan D. Cowan, President

BAYSHORE MEDICAL CENTER, 4000 Spencer Highway, Pasadena, TX, Zip 77504–1294; tel. 713/359–2000; Donald L. Stewart, Chief Executive Officer

BELLAIRE MEDICAL CENTER, 5314 Dashwood Street, Houston, TX, Zip 77081–4689; tel. 713/512–1200; Walter Leleux, Chief Executive Officer

CYPRESS FAIRBANKS MEDICAL CENTER, 10655 Steepletop Drive, Houston, TX, Zip 77065–4297; tel. 281/890–4285; Bill Klier, Chief Executive Officer

HERMANN HOSPITAL, 6411 Fannin, Houston, TX, Zip 77030–1501; tel. 713/704–4000; James E. Eastham, Senior Vice President and Chief Executive Officer

HOUSTON NORTHWEST MEDICAL CENTER, 710 FM 1960 West, Houston, TX, Zip 77090–3496; tel. 281/440–1000; James Kelly, Chief Executive Officer

POLLY RYON MEMORIAL HOSPITAL, 1705 Jackson Street, Richmond, TX, Zip 77469–3289; tel. 281/341–3000; Sam L. Steffee, Executive Director and Chief Executive Officer

ROSEWOOD MEDICAL CENTER, 9200 Westheimer Road, Houston, TX, Zip 77063–3599; tel. 713/780–7900; Maura Walsh, Chief Executive Officer

SAN JACINTO METHODIST HOSPITAL, 4401 Garth Road, Baytown, TX, Zip 77521–3160; tel. 281/420–8600; William Simmons, President and Chief Executive Officer

SPRING BRANCH MEDICAL CENTER, 8850 Long Point Road, Houston, TX, Zip 77055–3082; tel. 713/467–6555; Pat Currie, Chief Executive Officer

THE WOMAN'S HOSPITAL OF TEXAS, 7600 Fannin Street, Houston, TX, Zip 77054–1900; tel. 713/790–1234; Linda B. Russell, President

WEST HOUSTON MEDICAL CENTER, 12141 Richmond Avenue, Houston, TX, Zip 77082–2499; tel. 281/558–3444; Jeffrey S. Holland, Chief Executive Officer

HEALTHCARE PARTNERS OF EAST TEXAS, INC
P.O. Box 6340, Tyler, TX 75711; tel. 903/533–0684; Cindy Martinez, Exec Dir / President

CHRISTUS ST. MICHAEL HEALTH SYSTEM, 2600 St. Michael Drive, Texarkana, TX, Zip 75503–2372; tel. 903/614–1000; Don A. Beeler, President and Chief Executive Officer

COZBY–GERMANY HOSPITAL, 707 North Waldrip Street, Grand Saline, TX, Zip 75140–1555; tel. 903/962–4242; William Rowton, Chief Executive Officer

DOCTORS MEMORIAL HOSPITAL, 1400 West Southwest Loop 323, Tyler, TX, Zip 75701; tel. 903/561–3771; Olie E. Clem, Chief Executive Officer

EAST TEXAS MEDICAL CENTER ATHENS, 2000 South Palestine Street, Athens, TX, Zip 75751–5610; tel. 903/675–2216; Patrick L. Wallace, Administrator

EAST TEXAS MEDICAL CENTER CARTHAGE, 409 Cottage Road, Carthage, TX, Zip 75633–1466, Mailing Address: P.O. Box 549, Zip 75633–0549; tel. 903/693–3841; Gary Mikeal Hudson, Administrator

EAST TEXAS MEDICAL CENTER JACKSONVILLE, 501 South Ragsdale Street, Jacksonville, TX, Zip 75766–2413; tel. 903/541–5000; Steve Bowen, President

EAST TEXAS MEDICAL CENTER PITTSBURG, 414 Quitman Street, Pittsburg, TX, Zip 75686–1032; tel. 903/856–6663; W. Perry Henderson, Administrator

EAST TEXAS MEDICAL CENTER RUSK, 500 North Bonner Street, Rusk, TX, Zip 75785, Mailing Address: P.O. Box 317, Zip 75785–0317; tel. 903/683–2273; Brenda Copley, Acting Administrator

EAST TEXAS MEDICAL CENTER–FAIRFIELD, 125 Newman Street, Fairfield, TX, Zip 75840–1499; tel. 903/389–2121; David Kuhn, Administrator

EAST TEXAS MEDICAL CENTER–MOUNT VERNON, Highway 37 South, Mount Vernon, TX, Zip 75457, Mailing Address: P.O. Box 477, Zip 75457–0477; tel. 903/537–4552; Jerry Edwards, CHE, Administrator

EAST TEXAS MEDICAL CENTER–QUITMAN, 117 Winnsboro Street, Quitman, TX, Zip 75783–2144, Mailing Address: P.O. Box 1000, Zip 75783–1000; tel. 903/763–4505; Marion W. Stanberry, Administrator

GOOD SHEPHERD MEDICAL CENTER, 700 East Marshall Avenue, Longview, TX, Zip 75601–5571; tel. 903/236–2000; Jerry D. Adair, President and Chief Executive Officer

HENDERSON MEMORIAL HOSPITAL, 300 Wilson Street, Henderson, TX, Zip 75652–5956; tel. 903/657–7541; George T. Roberts, Jr., Chief Executive Officer

HUNTSVILLE MEMORIAL HOSPITAL, 485 I–45 South, Huntsville, TX, Zip 77340–4362, Mailing Address: P.O. Box 4001, Zip 77342–4001; tel. 409/291–3411; Ralph E. Beaty, Administrator

LINDEN MUNICIPAL HOSPITAL, 404 North Kaufman Street, Linden, TX, Zip 75563–5235; tel. 903/756–5561; Richard D. Arnold, Administrator

MEMORIAL HOSPITAL OF CENTER, 602 Hurst Street, Center, TX, Zip 75935–3414, Mailing Address: P.O. Box 1749, Zip 75935–1749; tel. 409/598–2781; Robert V. Deen, Chief Executive Officer

MEMORIAL MEDICAL CENTER, 602 East Church Street, Livingston, TX, Zip 77351–1257, Mailing Address: P.O. Box 1257, Zip 77351–1257; tel. 409/327–4381; James C. Dickson, Administrator

MEMORIAL MEDICAL CENTER OF EAST TEXAS, 1201 West Frank Avenue, Lufkin, TX, Zip 75904–3357, Mailing Address: P.O. Box 1447, Zip 75902–1447; tel. 409/634–8111; Gary Lex Whatley, President and Chief Executive Officer

NACOGDOCHES MEMORIAL HOSPITAL, 1204 North Mound Street, Nacogdoches, TX, Zip 75961–4061; tel. 409/568–8520; G. W. Jones, Administrator

PINELANDS HOSPITAL, 4632 Northeast Stallings Drive, Nacogdoches, TX, Zip 75961–1617, Mailing Address: P.O. Box 1004, Zip 79563–1004; tel. 409/560–5900; Steve Scott, Chief Executive Officer

PRESBYTERIAN HOSPITAL OF WINNSBORO, 719 West Coke Road, Winnsboro, TX, Zip 75494–3098, Mailing Address: P.O. Box 628, Zip 75494–0628; tel. 903/342–5227; Dan Noteware, Senior Vice President and Executive Director

ROY H. LAIRD MEMORIAL HOSPITAL, 1612 South Henderson Boulevard, Kilgore, TX, Zip 75662–3594; tel. 903/984–3505; Roderick G. La Grone, President

TITUS REGIONAL MEDICAL CENTER, 2001 North Jefferson Avenue, Mount Pleasant, TX, Zip 75455–2398; tel. 903/577–6000; Steven K. Jacobson, Chief Executive Officer

TRINITY VALLEY MEDICAL CENTER, 2900 South Loop 256, Palestine, TX, Zip 75801–6958; tel. 903/731–1000; Larry C. Bozeman, Chief Executive Officer

LUBBOCK METHODIST HOSPITAL SYSTEM
3615 19th Street, Lubbock, TX 79410; tel. 806/793–4217; Charlie Trimble, CEO

ANSON GENERAL HOSPITAL, 101 Avenue J, Anson, TX, Zip 79501–2198; tel. 915/823–3231; Dudley R. White, Administrator

BROWNFIELD REGIONAL MEDICAL CENTER, 705 East Felt, Brownfield, TX, Zip 79316–3439; tel. 806/637–3551; Mike Click, Administrator

CAMPBELL HEALTH SYSTEM, 713 East Anderson Street, Weatherford, TX, Zip 76086–9971; tel. 817/596–8751; John B. Millstead, Chief Executive Officer

COCHRAN MEMORIAL HOSPITAL, 201 East Grant Street, Morton, TX, Zip 79346–3444; tel. 806/266–5565; Paul McKinney, Administrator

COMANCHE COMMUNITY HOSPITAL, 211 South Austin Street, Comanche, TX, Zip 76442–3224; tel. 915/356–5241; W. Evan Moore, Administrator

DE LEON HOSPITAL, 407 South Texas Avenue, De Leon, TX, Zip 76444–1947, Mailing Address: P.O. Box 319, Zip 76444–0319; tel. 254/893–2011; Michael K. Hare, Administrator

FISHER COUNTY HOSPITAL DISTRICT, Roby Highway, Rotan, TX, Zip 79546, Mailing Address: Drawer F, Zip 79546; tel. 915/735–2256; Ella Raye Helms, Administrator

HEREFORD REGIONAL MEDICAL CENTER, 801 East Third Street, Hereford, TX, Zip 79045–5727, Mailing Address: P.O. Box 1858, Zip 79045–1858; tel. 806/364–2141; John S. Studsrud, Administrator

LAMB HEALTHCARE CENTER, 1500 South Sunset, Littlefield, TX, Zip 79339–4899; tel. 806/385–6411; Randall A. Young, Administrator

MEDICAL ARTS HOSPITAL, 1600 North Bryan Avenue, Lamesa, TX, Zip 79331; tel. 806/872–2183; Karl R. Stinson, CHE, Chief Executive Officer

MITCHELL COUNTY HOSPITAL, 1543 Chestnut Street, Colorado City, TX, Zip 79512–3998; tel. 915/728–3431; Roland K. Rickard, Administrator

MOORE COUNTY HOSPITAL DISTRICT, 224 East Second Street, Dumas, TX, Zip 79029–3808; tel. 806/935–7171; Scott R. Brown, Administrator and Chief Executive Officer

MULESHOE AREA MEDICAL CENTER, 708 South First Street, Muleshoe, TX, Zip 79347–3627; tel. 806/272–4524; Jim G. Bone, Interim Administrator

PECOS COUNTY GENERAL HOSPITAL, 305 West Fifth Street, Iraan, TX, Zip 79744, Mailing Address: P.O. Box 665, Zip 79744–2057; tel. 915/639–2871; David B. Shaw, Administrator and Chief Executive Officer

PECOS COUNTY MEMORIAL HOSPITAL, Sanderson Highway, Fort Stockton, TX, Zip 79735, Mailing Address: P.O. Box 1648, Zip 79735–1648; tel. 915/336–2241; David B. Shaw, Administrator and Chief Executive Officer

PERMIAN GENERAL HOSPITAL, Northeast By-Pass, Andrews, TX, Zip 79714, Mailing Address: P.O. Box 2108, Zip 79714–2108; tel. 915/523–2200; Randy R. Richards, Chief Executive Officer

MEMORIAL/SISTERS OF CHARITY HEALTH NETWORK
7737 S.W. Freeway Suite 200, Houston, TX 77074; tel. 713/776–6992; Dan Wilford, President

Section B

ANGLETON–DANBURY GENERAL HOSPITAL, 132 East Hospital Drive, Angleton, TX, Zip 77515–4197; tel. 409/849–7721; David A. Bleakney, Administrator

MEMORIAL HERMAN BEHAVIORAL HEALTH CENTER, 2801 Gessner, Houston, TX, Zip 77080–2599; tel. 713/462–4000; Sue E. Green, Vice President and Chief Executive Officer

MEMORIAL HOSPITAL SOUTHWEST, 7600 Beechnut, Houston, TX, Zip 77074–1850; tel. 713/776–5000; Lynn Schroth, Chief Executive Officer

MEMORIAL HOSPITAL–MEMORIAL CITY, 920 Frostwood Drive, Houston, TX, Zip 77024–9173; tel. 713/932–3000; Jerel T. Humphrey, Vice President, Chief Executive Officer and Administrator

MEMORIAL HOSPITAL–THE WOODLANDS, 9250 Pinecroft Drive, The Woodlands, TX, Zip 77380–3225; tel. 281/364–2300; Steve Sanders, Vice President and Chief Executive Officer

POLLY RYON MEMORIAL HOSPITAL, 1705 Jackson Street, Richmond, TX, Zip 77469–3289; tel. 281/341–3000; Sam L. Steffee, Executive Director and Chief Executive Officer

TOMBALL REGIONAL HOSPITAL, 605 Holderrieth Street, Tomball, TX, Zip 77375–0889, Mailing Address: Box 889, Zip 77377–0889; tel. 281/351–1623; Robert F. Schaper, President and Chief Executive Officer

METHODIST HEALTH CARE SYSTEM
7550 IH 10 West, Suite 1000, San Antonio, TX 78229; tel. 210/377–1647; John Hornbeak, President

METHODIST WOMEN'S AND CHILDREN'S HOSPITAL, 8109 Fredericksburg Road, San Antonio, TX, Zip 78229–3383; tel. 210/692–5000; Arthur E. Marlin, M.D., Chief Executive Officer

METROPOLITAN METHODIST HOSPITAL, 1310 McCullough Avenue, San Antonio, TX, Zip 78212–2617; tel. 210/208–2200; Mark L. Bernard, Chief Executive Officer

NORTHEAST METHODIST HOSPITAL, 12412 Judson Road, San Antonio, TX, Zip 78233–3272, Mailing Address: P.O. Box 659510, Zip 78265–9510; tel. 210/650–4949; Mark L. Bernard, Chief Executive Officer

SAN ANTONIO COMMUNITY HOSPITAL, 8026 Floyd Curl Drive, San Antonio, TX, Zip 78229–3915; tel. 210/692–8110; James C. Scoggin, Jr., Chief Executive Officer

SOUTHWEST TEXAS METHODIST HOSPITAL, 7700 Floyd Curl Drive, San Antonio, TX, Zip 78229–3993; tel. 210/575–4000; James C. Scoggin, Jr., Chief Executive Officer

NORTH TEXAS HEALTH NETWORK
5601 MacArthur Suite 300, Irving, TX 75038; tel. 214/751–0047; Charlie Cod, President

BAYLOR CENTER FOR RESTORATIVE CARE, 3504 Swiss Avenue, Dallas, TX, Zip 75204–6224; tel. 214/820–9700; Gerry Brueckner, R.N., Executive Director

BAYLOR INSTITUTE FOR REHABILITATION, 3505 Gaston Avenue, Dallas, TX, Zip 75246–2018; tel. 214/826–7030; Laura J. Lycan, Executive Director

BAYLOR MEDICAL CENTER AT GARLAND, 2300 Marie Curie Boulevard, Garland, TX, Zip 75042–5706; tel. 972/487–5000; John B. McWhorter, III, Executive Director

BAYLOR MEDICAL CENTER AT GRAPEVINE, 1650 West College Street, Grapevine, TX, Zip 76051–1650; tel. 817/329–2500; Mark C. Hood, Executive Director

BAYLOR UNIVERSITY MEDICAL CENTER, 3500 Gaston Avenue, Dallas, TX, Zip 75246–2088; tel. 214/820–0111; M. Tim Parris, Executive Vice President and Chief Operating Officer

MEDICAL CENTER AT TERRELL, 1551 Highway 34 South, Terrell, TX, Zip 75160–4833; tel. 972/563–7611; Ronald J. Ensor, Chief Executive Officer

OUR CHILDREN'S HOUSE AT BAYLOR, 3301 Swiss Avenue, Dallas, TX, Zip 75204–6219; tel. 214/820–9838; Geraldine Brueckner, Administrator

PRESBYTERIAN HOSPITAL OF PLANO, 6200 West Parker Road, Plano, TX, Zip 75093–7914; tel. 972/608–8000; Philip M. Wentworth, FACHE, Senior Vice President and Executive Director

NORTH TEXAS HEALTHCARE NETWORK
3333 Lee Parkway, Suite 900, Dallas, TX 75919; tel. 214/820–3425; Bob Bracon, President

BAYLOR CENTER FOR RESTORATIVE CARE, 3504 Swiss Avenue, Dallas, TX, Zip 75204–6224; tel. 214/820–9700; Gerry Brueckner, R.N., Executive Director

BAYLOR INSTITUTE FOR REHABILITATION, 3505 Gaston Avenue, Dallas, TX, Zip 75246–2018; tel. 214/826–7030; Laura J. Lycan, Executive Director

BAYLOR MEDICAL CENTER AT GARLAND, 2300 Marie Curie Boulevard, Garland, TX, Zip 75042–5706; tel. 972/487–5000; John B. McWhorter, III, Executive Director

BAYLOR MEDICAL CENTER AT GRAPEVINE, 1650 West College Street, Grapevine, TX, Zip 76051–1650; tel. 817/329–2500; Mark C. Hood, Executive Director

BAYLOR MEDICAL CENTER–ELLIS COUNTY, 1405 West Jefferson Street, Waxahachie, TX, Zip 75165–2275; tel. 972/923–7000; James Michael Lee, Executive Director

BAYLOR UNIVERSITY MEDICAL CENTER, 3500 Gaston Avenue, Dallas, TX, Zip 75246–2088; tel. 214/820–0111; M. Tim Parris, Executive Vice President and Chief Operating Officer

BAYLOR/ RICHARDSON MEDICAL CENTER, 401 West Campbell Road, Richardson, TX, Zip 75080–3499; tel. 972/498–4000; Ronald L. Boring, President and Chief Executive Officer

HARRIS CONTINUED CARE HOSPITAL, 1301 Pennsylvania Avenue, 4th Floor, Fort Worth, TX, Zip 76104–2190, Mailing Address: P.O. Box 3471, Zip 76113–3471; tel. 817/878–5500; Larry Thompson, Senior Vice President and Executive Director

HARRIS METHODIST FORT WORTH, 1301 Pennsylvania Avenue, Fort Worth, TX, Zip 76104–2895; tel. 817/882–2000; Barclay E. Berdan, Chief Executive Officer

HARRIS METHODIST NORTHWEST, 108 Denver Trail, Azle, TX, Zip 76020–3697; tel. 817/444–8600; Larry Thompson, Vice President and Administrator

HARRIS METHODIST SOUTHWEST, 6100 Harris Parkway, Fort Worth, TX, Zip 76132–4199; tel. 817/346–5050; Stansel Harvey, Senior Executive Vice President, Executive Director/Administrator

HARRIS METHODIST–ERATH COUNTY, 411 North Belknap Street, Stephenville, TX, Zip 76401–3415, Mailing Address: P.O. Box 1399, Zip 76401–1399; tel. 254/965–1500; Ronald E. Dorris, Senior Vice President and Executive Director

HARRIS METHODIST–HEB, 1600 Hospital Parkway, Bedford, TX, Zip 76022–6913, Mailing Address: P.O. Box 669, Zip 76095–0669; tel. 817/685–4000; Jack McCabe, Senior Vice President and Administrator

PRESBYTERIAN HOSPITAL OF DALLAS, 8200 Walnut Hill Lane, Dallas, TX, Zip 75231–4402; tel. 214/345–6789; Mark H. Merrill, Executive Director

PRESBYTERIAN HOSPITAL OF KAUFMAN, 850 Highway 243 West, Kaufman, TX, Zip 75142–9998, Mailing Address: P.O. Box 310, Zip 75142–0310; tel. 972/932–7200; Michael J. McBride, CHE, Senior Vice President and Executive Director

PRESBYTERIAN HOSPITAL OF PLANO, 6200 West Parker Road, Plano, TX, Zip 75093–7914; tel. 972/608–8000; Philip M. Wentworth, FACHE, Senior Vice President and Executive Director

PRESBYTERIAN HOSPITAL OF WINNSBORO, 719 West Coke Road, Winnsboro, TX, Zip 75494–3098, Mailing Address: P.O. Box 628, Zip 75494–0628; tel. 903/342–5227; Dan Noteware, Senior Vice President and Executive Director

WALLS REGIONAL HOSPITAL, 201 Walls Drive, Cleburne, TX, Zip 76031–1008; tel. 817/641–2551; Brent D. Magers, FACHE, Executive Director and Senior Vice President

PERMIAN BASIN RURAL HEALTH NETWORK
P.O. Box 1648, Fort Stockton, TX 79735; tel. 915/336–2241; George Miller Jr, President

BIG BEND REGIONAL MEDICAL CENTER, 801 East Brown Street, Alpine, TX, Zip 79830–3209; tel. 915/837–3447; Don Edd Green, Chief Executive Officer

BIG SPRING STATE HOSPITAL, Lamesa Highway, Big Spring, TX, Zip 79720, Mailing Address: P.O. Box 231, Zip 79721–0231; tel. 915/267–8216; Edward Moughon, Superintendent

CRANE MEMORIAL HOSPITAL, 1310 South Alford Street, Crane, TX, Zip 79731–3899; tel. 915/558–3555; Stan Wiley, Administrator

MARTIN COUNTY HOSPITAL DISTRICT, 610 North St. Peter Street, Stanton, TX, Zip 79782, Mailing Address: P.O. Box 640, Zip 79782–0640; tel. 915/756–3345; Rick Jacobus, Administrator

MCCAMEY HOSPITAL, Highway 305 South, McCamey, TX, Zip 79752, Mailing Address: P.O. Box 1200, Zip 79752–1200; tel. 915/652–8626; Bill Boswell, Chief Executive Officer

MEDICAL ARTS HOSPITAL, 1600 North Bryan Avenue, Lamesa, TX, Zip 79331; tel. 806/872–2183; Karl R. Stinson, CHE, Chief Executive Officer

MEDICAL CENTER HOSPITAL, 500 West Fourth Street, Odessa, TX, Zip 79761–5059, Mailing Address: P.O. Drawer 7239, Zip 79760–7239; tel. 915/640–4000; J. Michael Stephans, Administrator

MEMORIAL HOSPITAL, 821 Jeffee Drive, Kermit, TX, Zip 79745–4696, Mailing Address: Drawer H, Zip 79745–6008; tel. 915/586–5864; Judene Willhelm, Administrator

MEMORIAL HOSPITAL, 209 N.W. Eighth Street, Seminole, TX, Zip 79360–3447; tel. 915/758–5811; Steve Beck, Chief Executive Officer and Administrator

MEMORIAL HOSPITAL AND MEDICAL CENTER, 2200 West Illinois Avenue, Midland, TX, Zip 79701–6499; tel. 915/685–1111; Harold Rubin, President and Chief Executive Officer

PECOS COUNTY GENERAL HOSPITAL, 305 West Fifth Street, Iraan, TX, Zip 79744, Mailing Address: P.O. Box 665, Zip 79744–2057; tel. 915/639–2871; David B. Shaw, Administrator and Chief Executive Officer

PECOS COUNTY MEMORIAL HOSPITAL, Sanderson Highway, Fort Stockton, TX, Zip 79735, Mailing Address: P.O. Box 1648, Zip 79735–1648; tel. 915/336–2241; David B. Shaw, Administrator and Chief Executive Officer

PERMIAN GENERAL HOSPITAL, Northeast By–Pass, Andrews, TX, Zip 79714, Mailing Address: P.O. Box 2108, Zip 79714–2108; tel. 915/523–2200; Randy R. Richards, Chief Executive Officer

RANKIN HOSPITAL DISTRICT, 1105 Elizabeth Street, Rankin, TX, Zip 79778, Mailing Address: P.O. Box 327, Zip 79778–0327; tel. 915/693–2443; John Paul Loyless, Administrator

REAGAN MEMORIAL HOSPITAL, 805 North Main Street, Big Lake, TX, Zip 76932–3999; tel. 915/884–2561; Ron Galloway, Administrator

REEVES COUNTY HOSPITAL, 2323 Texas Street, Pecos, TX, Zip 79772–7338; tel. 915/447–3551; Charles N. Butts, Interim Chief Executive Officer

SCENIC MOUNTAIN MEDICAL CENTER, 1601 West 11th Place, Big Spring, TX, Zip 79720–4198; tel. 915/263–1211; Loren F. Chandler, Interim Chief Executive Officer

VETERANS AFFAIRS MEDICAL CENTER, 300 Veterans Boulevard, Big Spring, TX, Zip 79720–5500; tel. 915/263–7361; Cary D. Brown, Director

WARD MEMORIAL HOSPITAL, 406 South Gary Street, Monahans, TX, Zip 79756–4798, Mailing Address: P.O. Box 40, Zip 79756–0040; tel. 915/943–2511; Joe Wright, Administrator

PRESBYTERIAN HEALTHCARE SYSTEM
8200 Walnut Hill Lane, Dallas, TX 75231; tel. 214/345–8486; Charles Spiler, Adm Resident

HUNT MEMORIAL HOSPITAL DISTRICT, 4215 Joe Ramsey Boulevard, Greenville, TX, Zip 75401–7899, Mailing Address: P.O. Drawer 1059, Zip 75403–1059; tel. 903/408–5000; Richard Carter, Chief Executive Officer

MCCUISTION REGIONAL MEDICAL CENTER, 865 Deshong Drive, Paris, TX, Zip 75462–2097, Mailing Address: P.O. Box 160, Zip 75461–0160; tel. 903/737–1111; Michael J. McBride, CHE, Senior Vice President and Executive Director

PRESBYTERIAN HOSPITAL OF DALLAS, 8200 Walnut Hill Lane, Dallas, TX, Zip 75231–4402; tel. 214/345–6789; Mark H. Merrill, Executive Director

PRESBYTERIAN HOSPITAL OF KAUFMAN, 850 Highway 243 West, Kaufman, TX, Zip 75142–9998, Mailing Address: P.O. Box 310, Zip 75142–0310; tel. 972/932–7200; Michael J. McBride, CHE, Senior Vice President and Executive Director

PRESBYTERIAN HOSPITAL OF PLANO, 6200 West Parker Road, Plano, TX, Zip 75093–7914; tel. 972/608–8000; Philip M. Wentworth, FACHE, Senior Vice President and Executive Director

PRESBYTERIAN HOSPITAL OF WINNSBORO, 719 West Coke Road, Winnsboro, TX, Zip 75494–3098, Mailing Address: P.O. Box 628, Zip 75494–0628; tel. 903/342–5227; Dan Noteware, Senior Vice President and Executive Director

PRIMARY CARE NETWORK OF TEXAS
62443 IH 10 W, Suite 1001, San Antonio, TX 78201; tel. 210/704–4800; Susan Ginnity, Network Contact

CHRISTUS SANTA ROSA HEALTH CARE, 519 West Houston Street, San Antonio, TX, Zip 78207–3108; tel. 210/704–2011; William C. Finlayson, President and Chief Execuctive Officer

REGIONAL HEALTHCARE ALLIANCE
800 East Dawson, Tyler, TX 75701; tel. 903/531–4449; John Webb, President

ATLANTA MEMORIAL HOSPITAL, Highway 77 at South Williams, Atlanta, TX, Zip 75551, Mailing Address: P.O. Box 1049, Zip 75551–1049; tel. 903/799–3000; Tom Crow, Administrator

BAYLOR UNIVERSITY MEDICAL CENTER, 3500 Gaston Avenue, Dallas, TX, Zip 75246–2088; tel. 214/820–0111; M. Tim Parris, Executive Vice President and Chief Operating Officer

CHILDREN'S MEDICAL CENTER OF DALLAS, 1935 Motor Street, Dallas, TX, Zip 75235–7794; tel. 214/456–7000; George D. Farr, President and Chief Executive Officer

CHRISTUS SCHUMPERT MEDICAL CENTER, One St. Mary Place, Shreveport, LA, Zip 71101–4399, Mailing Address: P.O. Box 21976, Zip 71120–1076; tel. 318/681–4500; Daniel J. Rissing, Acting Chief Executive Officer

COZBY–GERMANY HOSPITAL, 707 North Waldrip Street, Grand Saline, TX, Zip 75140–1555; tel. 903/962–4242; William Rowton, Chief Executive Officer

EAST TEXAS MEDICAL CENTER CARTHAGE, 409 Cottage Road, Carthage, TX, Zip 75633–1466, Mailing Address: P.O. Box 549, Zip 75633–0549; tel. 903/693–3841; Gary Mikeal Hudson, Administrator

EAST TEXAS MEDICAL CENTER–FAIRFIELD, 125 Newman Street, Fairfield, TX, Zip 75840–1499; tel. 903/389–2121; David Kuhn, Administrator

EAST TEXAS MEDICAL CENTER–QUITMAN, 117 Winnsboro Street, Quitman, TX, Zip 75783–2144, Mailing Address: P.O. Box 1000, Zip 75783–1000; tel. 903/763–4505; Marion W. Stanberry, Administrator

GOOD SHEPHERD MEDICAL CENTER, 700 East Marshall Avenue, Longview, TX, Zip 75601–5571; tel. 903/236–2000; Jerry D. Adair, President and Chief Executive Officer

HEALTHSOUTH REHABILITATION HOSPITAL–TYLER, 3131 Troup Highway, Tyler, TX, Zip 75701–8352; tel. 903/510–7000; Sharla Anderson, Interim Chief Executive Officer

HENDERSON MEMORIAL HOSPITAL, 300 Wilson Street, Henderson, TX, Zip 75652–5956; tel. 903/657–7541; George T. Roberts, Jr., Chief Executive Officer

HOPKINS COUNTY MEMORIAL HOSPITAL, 115 Airport Road, Sulphur Springs, TX, Zip 75482–0115; tel. 903/885–7671; Richard L. Goddard, Chief Executive Officer

LINDEN MUNICIPAL HOSPITAL, 404 North Kaufman Street, Linden, TX, Zip 75563–5235; tel. 903/756–5561; Richard D. Arnold, Administrator

MARSHALL REGIONAL MEDICAL CENTER, 811 South Washington Avenue, Marshall, TX, Zip 75670–5336, Mailing Address: P.O. Box 1599, Zip 75671–1599; tel. 903/927–6000; Thomas N. Cammack, Jr., Chief Executive Officer

NACOGDOCHES MEDICAL CENTER, 4920 N.E. Stallings, Nacogdoches, TX, Zip 75961–1200, Mailing Address: P.O. Box 631604, Zip 75963–1604; tel. 409/568–3380; Glenn A. Robinson, Chief Executive Officer

PINELANDS HOSPITAL, 4632 Northeast Stallings Drive, Nacogdoches, TX, Zip 75961–1617, Mailing Address: P.O. Box 1004, Zip 79563–1004; tel. 409/560–5900; Steve Scott, Chief Executive Officer

PRESBYTERIAN HOSPITAL OF DALLAS, 8200 Walnut Hill Lane, Dallas, TX, Zip 75231–4402; tel. 214/345–6789; Mark H. Merrill, Executive Director

PRESBYTERIAN HOSPITAL OF KAUFMAN, 850 Highway 243 West, Kaufman, TX, Zip 75142–9998, Mailing Address: P.O. Box 310, Zip 75142–0310; tel. 972/932–7200; Michael J. McBride, CHE, Senior Vice President and Executive Director

PRESBYTERIAN HOSPITAL OF WINNSBORO, 719 West Coke Road, Winnsboro, TX, Zip 75494–3098, Mailing Address: P.O. Box 628, Zip 75494–0628; tel. 903/342–5227; Dan Noteware, Senior Vice President and Executive Director

ROY H. LAIRD MEMORIAL HOSPITAL, 1612 South Henderson Boulevard, Kilgore, TX, Zip 75662–3594; tel. 903/984–3505; Roderick G. La Grone, President

TITUS REGIONAL MEDICAL CENTER, 2001 North Jefferson Avenue, Mount Pleasant, TX, Zip 75455–2398; tel. 903/577–6000; Steven K. Jacobson, Chief Executive Officer

TRINITY MOTHER FRANCES HEALTH SYSTEM, 800 East Dawson, Tyler, TX, Zip 75701–2093; tel. 903/593–8441; J. Lindsey Bradley, Jr., FACHE, President and Chief Administrative Officer

UNIVERSITY OF TEXAS HEALTH CENTER AT TYLER, 11937 Highway 271, Tyler, TX, Zip 75708–3154; tel. 903/877–3451; Ronald F. Garvey, M.D., President

WILLIS–KNIGHTON MEDICAL CENTER, 2600 Greenwood Road, Shreveport, LA, Zip 71103–2600, Mailing Address: P.O. Box 32600, Zip 71130–2600; tel. 318/632–4600; James K. Elrod, President and Chief Executive Officer

SE TEXAS HOSPITAL SYSTEM
233 W. 10th Street, Dallas, TX 75208; tel. 214/943–3582; Bob McElearney, Interim President

CITIZENS MEDICAL CENTER, 2701 Hospital Drive, Victoria, TX, Zip 77901–5749; tel. 361/573–9181; David P. Brown, Administrator

CUERO COMMUNITY HOSPITAL, 2550 North Esplanade Street, Cuero, TX, Zip 77954–4716; tel. 512/275–6191; James E. Buckner, Jr., Administrator

DRISCOLL CHILDREN'S HOSPITAL, 3533 South Alameda Street, Corpus Christi, TX, Zip 78411–1785, Mailing Address: P.O. Box 6530, Zip 78466–6530; tel. 512/694–5000; Stephen Hough, Interim President and Chief Executive Officer

EL CAMPO MEMORIAL HOSPITAL, 303 Sandy Corner Road, El Campo, TX, Zip 77437–9535; tel. 409/543–6251; Steve Gularte, Administrator

JACKSON COUNTY HOSPITAL, 1013 South Wells Street, Edna, TX, Zip 77957–4098; tel. 361/782–5241; Marcella V. Henke, Administrator and Chief Executive Officer

LAVACA MEDICAL CENTER, 1400 North Texana Street, Hallettsville, TX, Zip 77964–2099; tel. 512/798–3671; James Vanek, Administrator

MEMORIAL MEDICAL CENTER, 815 North Virginia Street, Port Lavaca, TX, Zip 77979–3025, Mailing Address: P.O. Box 25, Zip 77979–0025; tel. 361/552–6713; Bob L. Bybee, President and Chief Executive Officer

REFUGIO COUNTY MEMORIAL HOSPITAL, 107 Swift Street, Refugio, TX, Zip 78377–2425; tel. 512/526–2321; William G. Jones, Administrator

VICTORIA REGIONAL MEDICAL CENTER, 101 Medical Drive, Victoria, TX, Zip 77904–3198; tel. 512/573–6100; Aston Hecker, Chief Executive Officer

YOAKUM COMMUNITY HOSPITAL, 1200 Carl Ramert Drive, Yoakum, TX, Zip 77995–4198, Mailing Address: P.O. Box 753, Zip 77995–0753; tel. 361/293–2321; Jeff R. Egbert, Chief Executive Officer

SE TEXAS INTEGRATED COMM HEALTH NETWORK
2600 North Loop, Houston, TX 77092; tel. 713/681–8877; Stanley T. Urban, President/CEO

CHRISTUS ST. ELIZABETH HOSPITAL, 2830 Calder Avenue, Beaumont, TX, Zip 77702, Mailing Address: P.O. Box 5405, Zip 77726–5405; tel. 409/892–7171; Edward W. Myers, Chief Executive Officer

CHRISTUS ST. JOSEPH HOSPITAL, 1919 LaBranch Street, Houston, TX, Zip 77002; tel. 713/757–1000; Sally E. Jeffcoat, Chief Executive Officer

CHRISTUS ST. MARY HOSPITAL, 3600 Gates Boulevard, Port Arthur, TX, Zip 77642–3601, Mailing Address: P.O. Box 3696, Zip 77643–3696; tel. 409/985–7431; Jeffrey Webster, Chief Executive Officer

ST. JOHN HOSPITAL, 18300 St. John Drive, Nassau Bay, TX, Zip 77058; tel. 281/333–5503; Thomas Permetti, Chief Executive Officer

SOUTHWEST TEXAS RURAL HEALTH ALLIANCE
143 East Garza, New Braunfels, TX 78130; tel. 210/606–9111; Johnny Johnson, President

CENTRAL TEXAS MEDICAL CENTER, 1301 Wonder World Drive, San Marcos, TX, Zip 78666–7544; tel. 512/353–8979; Ken Bacon, President and Chief Executive Officer

DIMMIT COUNTY MEMORIAL HOSPITAL, 704 Hospital Drive, Carrizo Springs, TX, Zip 78834–3836; tel. 830/876–2424; Ernest Flores, Jr., Administrator

FRIO HOSPITAL, 320 Berry Ranch Road, Pearsall, TX, Zip 78061–3998; tel. 830/334–3617; Alan D. Holmes, Chief Executive Officer

GUADALUPE VALLEY HOSPITAL, 1215 East Court Street, Seguin, TX, Zip 78155–5189; tel. 830/379–2411; Don L. Richey, Administrator

HILL COUNTRY MEMORIAL HOSPITAL, 1020 Kerrville Road, Fredericksburg, TX, Zip 78624, Mailing Address: P.O. Box 835, Zip 78624–0835; tel. 830/997–4353; Jeff A. Bourgeois, Chief Executive Officer

KIMBLE HOSPITAL, 2101 Main Street, Junction, TX, Zip 76849–2101; tel. 915/446–3321; Jamie R. Jacoby, Administrator

MCKENNA MEMORIAL HOSPITAL, 600 North Union Avenue, New Braunfels, TX, Zip 78130; tel. 830/606–9111; Bill Morton, President and Chief Executive Officer

MEDINA COMMUNITY HOSPITAL, 3100 Avenue East, Hondo, TX, Zip 78861–3599; tel. 830/741–4677; Elwood E. Currier, Jr., CHE, Administrator

MEMORIAL HOSPITAL, Highway 90A By-Pass, Gonzales, TX, Zip 78629, Mailing Address: P.O. Box 587, Zip 78629-0587; tel. 830/672-7581; Douglas Langley, Administrator

OTTO KAISER MEMORIAL HOSPITAL, 3349 South Highway 181, Kenedy, TX, Zip 78119-5240; tel. 830/583-3401; Harold L. Boening, Administrator

SETON EDGAR B. DAVIS HOSPITAL, 130 Hays Street, Luling, TX, Zip 78648-3207, Mailing Address: P.O. Box 510, Zip 78648-0510; tel. 830/875-5643; Neal Kelley, Administrator

SID PETERSON MEMORIAL HOSPITAL, 710 Water Street, Kerrville, TX, Zip 78028-5398; tel. 830/896-4200; Frederic W. Hall, Jr., Administrator

TRI-CITY COMMUNITY HOSPITAL, 1604 Highway 97 East, Jourdanton, TX, Zip 78026, Mailing Address: P.O. Box 189, Zip 78026-0189; tel. 830/769-3515; S. Allan Smith, Administrator

UVALDE COUNTY HOSPITAL AUTHORITY, 1025 Garner Field Road, Uvalde, TX, Zip 78801-1025; tel. 830/278-6251; Ben M. Durr, Administrator

VAL VERDE REGIONAL MEDICAL CENTER, 801 Bedell Avenue, Del Rio, TX, Zip 78840-4185, Mailing Address: P.O. Box 1527, Zip 78840-1527; tel. 830/775-8566; Don Griffin, Chief Executive Officer

WARM SPRINGS REHABILITATION HOSPITAL, Gonzales, TX, Mailing Address: P.O. Box 58, Zip 78629-0058; tel. 830/672-6592; John W. Davis, Administrator

WILSON MEMORIAL HOSPITAL, 1301 Hospital Boulevard, Floresville, TX, Zip 78114-2798; tel. 830/393-3122; Robert Duffield, Administrator

ST DAVID'S HEALTH NETWORK
P.O. Box 49192, Austin, TX 78765; tel. 512/.40-8700; Sharon J. Alvis, Executive Director

ROUND ROCK HOSPITAL, 2400 Round Rock Avenue, Round Rock, TX, Zip 78681-4097; tel. 512/341-1000; Deborah L. Ryle, Chief Executive Officer

ST. DAVID'S MEDICAL CENTER, 919 East 32nd Street, Austin, TX, Zip 78705-2709, Mailing Address: P.O. Box 4039, Zip 78765-4039; tel. 512/476-7111; Cole C. Eslyn, Chief Executive Officer

ST. DAVID'S PAVILION, 1025 East 32nd Street, Austin, TX, Zip 78765; tel. 512/867-5800; Cole C. Eslyn, Chief Executive Officer

ST. DAVID'S REHABILITATION CENTER, 1005 East 32nd Street, Austin, TX, Zip 78705-2705, Mailing Address: P.O. Box 4270, Zip 78765-4270; tel. 512/867-5100; Cole C. Eslyn, Chief Executive Officer

ST. DAVID'S SOUTH HOSPITAL, 901 West Ben White Boulevard, Austin, TX, Zip 78704-6903; tel. 512/447-2211; Richard W. Klusmann, Chief Executive Officer

TEXOMA HEALTH NETWORK
1600 11th Street, Wichita Falls, TX 76301; tel. 817/872-1126; David Whitaker, Exec Director

BOWIE MEMORIAL HOSPITAL, 705 East Greenwood Avenue, Bowie, TX, Zip 76230-3199; tel. 940/872-1126; Joyce Crumpler, R.N., Administrator

CHILLICOTHE HOSPITAL DISTRICT, 303 Avenue I, Chillicothe, TX, Zip 79225, Mailing Address: P.O. Box 370, Zip 79225-0370; tel. 817/852-5131; Linda Hall, Administrator

CLAY COUNTY MEMORIAL HOSPITAL, 310 West South Street, Henrietta, TX, Zip 76365-3399; tel. 940/538-5621; Edward E. Browning, Chief Executive Officer and Administrator

ELECTRA MEMORIAL HOSPITAL, 1207 South Bailey Street, Electra, TX, Zip 76360-3221, Mailing Address: P.O. Box 1112, Zip 76360-1112; tel. 940/495-3981; Jan A. Reed, CPA, Administrator and Chief Executive Officer

FAITH COMMUNITY HOSPITAL, 717 Magnolia Street, Jacksboro, TX, Zip 76458-1111; tel. 940/567-6633; Don Hopkins, Administrator

HAMILTON HOSPITAL, 903 West Hamilton Street, Olney, TX, Zip 76374-1725, Mailing Address: P.O. Box 158, Zip 76374-0158; tel. 940/564-5521; William R. Smith, Administrator

HARDEMAN COUNTY MEMORIAL HOSPITAL, 402 Mercer Street, Quanah, TX, Zip 79252-4026, Mailing Address: P.O. Box 90, Zip 79252-0090; tel. 940/663-2795; Charles Hurt, Administrator

NOCONA GENERAL HOSPITAL, 100 Park Street, Nocona, TX, Zip 76255-3616; tel. 940/825-3235; Jamers Brasier, Administrator

SEYMOUR HOSPITAL, 200 Stadium Drive, Seymour, TX, Zip 76380-2344; tel. 940/888-5572; Charles Norris, Administrator

THROCKMORTON COUNTY MEMORIAL HOSPITAL, 802 North Minter Street, Throckmorton, TX, Zip 76483, Mailing Address: P.O. Box 729, Zip 76483-0729; tel. 940/849-2151; Charles Norris, Administrator

THE HEART NETWORK OF TEXAS
101 East Park Boulevard, Plano, TX 75074; tel. 214/516-3817; Bruce Hoffman, Executive Director

BAYLOR UNIVERSITY MEDICAL CENTER, 3500 Gaston Avenue, Dallas, TX, Zip 75246-2088; tel. 214/820-0111; M. Tim Parris, Executive Vice President and Chief Operating Officer

HARRIS CONTINUED CARE HOSPITAL, 1301 Pennsylvania Avenue, 4th Floor, Fort Worth, TX, Zip 76104-2190, Mailing Address: P.O. Box 3471, Zip 76113-3471; tel. 817/878-5500; Larry Thompson, Senior Vice President and Executive Director

HARRIS METHODIST FORT WORTH, 1301 Pennsylvania Avenue, Fort Worth, TX, Zip 76104-2895; tel. 817/882-2000; Barclay E. Berdan, Chief Executive Officer

HARRIS METHODIST NORTHWEST, 108 Denver Trail, Azle, TX, Zip 76020-3697; tel. 817/444-8600; Larry Thompson, Vice President and Administrator

HARRIS METHODIST SOUTHWEST, 6100 Harris Parkway, Fort Worth, TX, Zip 76132-4199; tel. 817/346-5050; Stansel Harvey, Senior Executive Vice President, Executive Director/Administrator

HARRIS METHODIST-ERATH COUNTY, 411 North Belknap Street, Stephenville, TX, Zip 76401-3415, Mailing Address: P.O. Box 1399, Zip 76401-1399; tel. 254/965-1500; Ronald E. Dorris, Senior Vice President and Executive Director

HARRIS METHODIST-HEB, 1600 Hospital Parkway, Bedford, TX, Zip 76022-6913, Mailing Address: P.O. Box 669, Zip 76095-0669; tel. 817/685-4000; Jack McCabe, Senior Vice President and Administrator

HENDRICK HEALTH SYSTEM, 1242 North 19th Street, Abilene, TX, Zip 79601-2316; tel. 915/670-2000; Michael C. Waters, FACHE, President

HILLCREST BAPTIST MEDICAL CENTER, 3000 Herring Avenue, Waco, TX, Zip 76708-3299, Mailing Address: Box 5100, Zip 76708-0100; tel. 254/202-2000; Richard E. Scott, President

TEXOMA HEALTHCARE SYSTEM, 1000 Memorial Drive, Denison, TX, Zip 75020-2035, Mailing Address: P.O. Box 890, Zip 75021-9988; tel. 903/416-4000; Arthur L. Hohenberger, FACHE, President and Chief Executive Officer

TRINITY MOTHER FRANCES HEALTH SYSTEM, 800 East Dawson, Tyler, TX, Zip 75701-2093; tel. 903/593-8441; J. Lindsey Bradley, Jr., FACHE, President and Chief Administrative Officer

WADLEY REGIONAL MEDICAL CENTER, 1000 Pine Street, Texarkana, TX, Zip 75501-5170, Mailing Address: Box 1878, Zip 75504-1878; tel. 903/798-8000; Hugh R. Hallgren, President and Chief Executive Officer

WALLS REGIONAL HOSPITAL, 201 Walls Drive, Cleburne, TX, Zip 76031-1008; tel. 817/641-2551; Brent D. Magers, FACHE, Executive Director and Senior Vice President

UTAH

INTERMOUNTAIN HEALTH CARE
36 South State Street, Suite 2100, Salt Lake City, UT 84102; tel. 801/442-3587; Bill Nelson, President & CEO

ALTA VIEW HOSPITAL, 9660 South 1300 East, Sandy, UT, Zip 84094-3793; tel. 801/501-2600; Wes Thompson, Administrator and Chief Executive Officer

AMERICAN FORK HOSPITAL, 170 North 1100 East, American Fork, UT, Zip 84003-9787; tel. 801/763-3300; Keith N. Alexander, Administrator and Chief Operating Officer

BEAR RIVER VALLEY HOSPITAL, 440 West 600 North, Tremonton, UT, Zip 84337-2497; tel. 435/257-7441; Robert F. Jex, Administrator

CASSIA REGIONAL MEDICAL CENTER, 1501 Hiland Avenue, Burley, ID, Zip 83318-2675; tel. 208/678-4444; Richard Packer, Administrator

COTTONWOOD HOSPITAL MEDICAL CENTER, 5770 South 300 East, Salt Lake City, UT, Zip 84107-6186; tel. 801/262-3461; Douglas R. Fonnesbeck, Administrator and Chief Executive Officer

DELTA COMMUNITY MEDICAL CENTER, 126 South White Sage Avenue, Delta, UT, Zip 84624-8937; tel. 435/864-5591; James E. Beckstrand, Administrator

DIXIE REGIONAL MEDICAL CENTER, 544 South 400 East, Saint George, UT, Zip 84770-3799; tel. 435/688-4000; L. Steven Wilson, Administrator

EVANSTON REGIONAL HOSPITAL, 190 Arrowhead Drive, Evanston, WY, Zip 82930-9266; tel. 307/789-3636; Robert W. Allen, Administrator

FILLMORE COMMUNITY MEDICAL CENTER, 674 South Highway 99, Fillmore, UT, Zip 84631-5013; tel. 435/743-5591; James E. Beckstrand, Administrator

GARFIELD MEMORIAL HOSPITAL AND CLINICS, 200 North 400 East, Panguitch, UT, Zip 84759, Mailing Address: P.O. Box 389, Zip 84759-0389; tel. 435/676-8811; Eric Packer, Administrator

LDS HOSPITAL, Eighth Avenue and C Street, Salt Lake City, UT, Zip 84143-0001; tel. 801/408-1100; Richard M. Cagen, Chief Executive Officer and Administrator

LOGAN REGIONAL HOSPITAL, 1400 North 500 East, Logan, UT, Zip 84341-2455; tel. 435/716-1000; Richard Smith, Administrator

MCKAY-DEE HOSPITAL CENTER, 3939 Harrison Boulevard, Ogden, UT, Zip 84409-2386, Mailing Address: Box 9370, Zip 84409-0370; tel. 801/398-2800; Patricia Harrington, Administrator and Chief Operating Officer

OREM COMMUNITY HOSPITAL, 331 North 400 West, Orem, UT, Zip 84057-1999; tel. 801/224-4080; Kim Nielsen, Administrator and Chief Operating Officer

POCATELLO REGIONAL MEDICAL CENTER, 777 Hospital Way, Pocatello, ID, Zip 83201-2797; tel. 208/234-0777; Earl L. Christison, Administrator

PRIMARY CHILDREN'S MEDICAL CENTER, 100 North Medical Drive, Salt Lake City, UT, Zip 84113-1100; tel. 801/588-2000; Joseph R. Horton, Chief Executive Officer and Administrator

SANPETE VALLEY HOSPITAL, 1100 South Medical Drive, Mount Pleasant, UT, Zip 84647-2222; tel. 435/462-2441; George Winn, Administrator

SEVIER VALLEY HOSPITAL, 1100 North Main Street, Richfield, UT, Zip 84701-1843; tel. 435/896-8271; Gary E. Beck, Administrator

STAR VALLEY HOSPITAL, 110 Hospital Lane, Afton, WY, Zip 83110-0579, Mailing Address: P.O. Box 579, Zip 83110-0579; tel. 307/886-5800; Alberto Vasquez, Administrator

UTAH VALLEY REGIONAL MEDICAL CENTER, 1034 North 500 West, Provo, UT, Zip 84604-3337; tel. 801/373-7850; Mary Ann Young, R.N., Administrator

VALLEY VIEW MEDICAL CENTER, 595 South 75 East, Cedar City, UT, Zip 84720–3462; tel. 435/586–6587; Craig M. Smedley, Administrator

WASATCH COUNTY HOSPITAL, 55 South 500 East, Heber City, UT, Zip 84032–1999; tel. 435/654–2500; Randall K. Probst, Administrator

PARACELSUS HEALTH CARE
2500 South State Street, Salt Lake City, UT 84115; tel. 801/461–6666; David L. Jones, Assistant Vice President

VERMONT

FLETCHER ALLEN HEALTH CARE
111 Colchester Avenue, Burlington, VT 05401; tel. 802/656–2455; William J. Boettcher, CEO

FLETCHER ALLEN HEALTH CARE, 111 Colchester Avenue, Burlington, VT, Zip 05401–1429; tel. 802/656–2345; William V. Boettcher, Chief Executive Officer

VIRGINIA

CARILION HEALTH SYSTEM
1212 Third Street, S.W., Roanoke, VA 24016; tel. 703/981–7900; Randy Edwards, Executive VP

CARILION BEDFORD MEMORIAL HOSPITAL, 1613 Oakwood Street, Bedford, VA, Zip 24523–0688, Mailing Address: P.O. Box 688, Zip 24523–0688; tel. 540/586–2441; Howard Ainsley, Vice President and Hospital Director

CARILION FRANKLIN MEMORIAL HOSPITAL, 180 Floyd Avenue, Rocky Mount, VA, Zip 24151–1389; tel. 540/483–5277; Matthew J. Perry, Director

CARILION GILES MEMORIAL HOSPITAL, 1 Taylor Avenue, Pearisburg, VA, Zip 24134–1932; tel. 540/921–6000; Morris D. Reece, Administrator and Chief Executive Officer

CARILION MEDICAL CENTER, Belleview at Jefferson Street, Roanoke, VA, Zip 24014, Mailing Address: P.O. Box 13367, Zip 24033–3367; tel. 540/981–7000; Lucas A. Snipes, FACHE, Director

CARILION NEW RIVER VALLEY MEDICAL CENTER, 2900 Tyler Road, Radford, VA, Zip 24141–2430, Mailing Address: P.O. Box 5, Zip 24141–0005; tel. 540/731–2000; Virginia Ousley, Director

CARILION SAINT ALBANS HOSPITAL, Route 11, Lee Highway, Radford, VA, Zip 24143, Mailing Address: P.O. Box 3608, Zip 24143–3608; tel. 540/639–2481; Janet McKinney Crawford, Vice President and Administrator

CENTRAL VIRGINIA HEALTH NETWORK
8100 Three Chopt–Ste 209, Richmond, VA 23229; tel. 804/673–2846; Michael Matthews, Network Contact

BON SECOURS ST. MARY'S HOSPITAL, 5801 Bremo Road, Richmond, VA, Zip 23226–1900; tel. 804/285–2011; Ann E. Honeycutt, Executive Vice President and Administrator

BON SECOURS–RICHMOND COMMUNITY HOSPITAL, 1500 North 28th Street, Richmond, VA, Zip 23223–5396, Mailing Address: Box 27184, Zip 23261–7184; tel. 804/225–1700; Samuel F. Lillard, Executive Vice President and Administrator

BON SECOURS–STUART CIRCLE, 413 Stuart Circle, Richmond, VA, Zip 23220–3799; tel. 804/358–7051; Edward Gerardo, Executive Vice President and Administrator

COMMUNITY MEMORIAL HEALTHCENTER, 125 Buena Vista Circle, South Hill, VA, Zip 23970–0090, Mailing Address: P.O. Box 90, Zip 23970–0090; tel. 804/447–3151; W. Scott Burnette, President

MARY IMMACULATE HOSPITAL, 2 Bernardine Drive, Newport News, VA, Zip 23602–4499; tel. 757/886–6000; Cynthia B. Farrand, Executive Vice President and Administrator

MEMORIAL REGIONAL MEDICAL CENTER, 8260 Atlee Road, Mechanicsville, VA, Zip 23116, Mailing Address: P.O. Box 26783, Richmond, Zip 23261–6783; tel. 804/764–6102; Michael Robinson, Executive Vice President and Administrator

RAPPAHANNOCK GENERAL HOSPITAL, 101 Harris Drive, Kilmarnock, VA, Zip 22482, Mailing Address: P.O. Box 1449, Zip 22482–1449; tel. 804/435–8000; James M. Holmes, President and Chief Executive Officer

SHELTERING ARMS REHABILITATION HOSPITAL, 1311 Palmyra Avenue, Richmond, VA, Zip 23227–4418; tel. 804/342–4100; Jack A. Carroll, Ph.D., President

SOUTHSIDE REGIONAL MEDICAL CENTER, 801 South Adams Street, Petersburg, VA, Zip 23803–5133; tel. 804/862–5000; David S. Dunham, President

UNIVERSITY OF VIRGINIA MEDICAL CENTER, Jefferson Park Avenue, Charlottesville, VA, Zip 22908, Mailing Address: P.O. Box 10050, Zip 22906–0050; tel. 804/924–0211; William E. Carter, Jr., Senior Associate Vice President for Operations

DEPAUL MEDICAL CENTER GROUP
150 Kingsley Lane, Norfolk, VA 23505; tel. 757/889–5000; David McCombs, President & CEO

BON SECOURS–DEPAUL MEDICAL CENTER, 150 Kingsley Lane, Norfolk, VA, Zip 23505–4650; tel. 757/889–5000; David J. McCombs, Executive Vice President and Administrator

INOVA HEALTH SYSTEM
8001 Braddock Road, Springfield, VA 22151; tel. 703/321–4213; J. Knox Singleton, President & CEO

INOVA FAIR OAKS HOSPITAL, 3600 Joseph Siewick Drive, Fairfax, VA, Zip 22033–1709; tel. 703/391–3600; William A. Brown, Vice President and Administrator

INOVA FAIRFAX HOSPITAL, 3300 Gallows Road, Falls Church, VA, Zip 22042–3300; tel. 703/698–1110; Steven E. Brown, Administrator

INOVA MOUNT VERNON HOSPITAL, 2501 Parker's Lane, Alexandria, VA, Zip 22306–3209; tel. 703/664–7000; Susan Herbert, Administrator

PREFERRED CARE OF RICHMOND
P.O. Box 13739, Richmond, VA 23225; tel. 804/560–4160; Richard Morrow, Network Coordinator

CHIPPENHAM AND JOHNSTON–WILLIS HOSPITALS, 7101 Jahnke Road, Richmond, VA, Zip 23225–4044; tel. 804/320–3911; Marilyn B. Tavenner, Chief Executive Officer

HENRICO DOCTORS' HOSPITAL, 1602 Skipwith Road, Richmond, VA, Zip 23229–5298; tel. 804/289–4500; Patrick W. Farrell, Chief Executive Officer

JOHN RANDOLPH MEDICAL CENTER, 411 West Randolph Road, Hopewell, VA, Zip 23860, Mailing Address: P.O. Box 971, Zip 23860; tel. 804/541–1600; Daniel J. Wetta, Jr., Chief Executive Officer

RETREAT HOSPITAL, 2621 Grove Avenue, Richmond, VA, Zip 23220–4308; tel. 804/254–5100; Paul L. Baldwin, Chief Executive Officer

SENTARA HEALTH SYSTEM
6015 Poplar Hall Dr–Ste306, Norfolk, VA 23502; tel. 757/455–7170; David Bernd, CEO

SENTARA BAYSIDE HOSPITAL, 800 Independence Boulevard, Virginia Beach, VA, Zip 23455–6076; tel. 757/363–6100; Virginia Bogue, Site Administrator

SENTARA HAMPTON GENERAL HOSPITAL, 3120 Victoria Boulevard, Hampton, VA, Zip 23661–1585, Mailing Address: Drawer 640, Zip 23669–0640; tel. 757/727–7000; Russell Kenwood, Administrator

SENTARA LEIGH HOSPITAL, 830 Kempsville Road, Norfolk, VA, Zip 23502–3981; tel. 757/466–6000; Darleen S. Anderson, R.N., MSN, Site Administrator

SENTARA NORFOLK GENERAL HOSPITAL, 600 Gresham Drive, Norfolk, VA, Zip 23507–1999; tel. 757/668–3000; Mark R. Gavens, President

SENTARA VIRGINIA BEACH GENERAL HOSPITAL, 1060 First Colonial Road, Virginia Beach, VA, Zip 23454–9000; tel. 757/481–8000; Robert L. Graves, Administrator

WILLIAMSBURG COMMUNITY HOSPITAL, 301 Monticello Avenue, Williamsburg, VA, Zip 23187–8700, Mailing Address: Box 8700, Zip 23187–8700; tel. 757/259–6000; Les A. Donahue, President and Chief Executive Officer

TIDEWATER HEALTH CARE
1080 First Colonial Road, Virginia Beach, VA 23454; tel. 757/496–6100; Douglas L. Johnson, Ph. D., President/ CEO

SENTARA VIRGINIA BEACH GENERAL HOSPITAL, 1060 First Colonial Road, Virginia Beach, VA, Zip 23454–9000; tel. 757/481–8000; Robert L. Graves, Administrator

VALLEY HEALTH SYSTEM
P.O. Box 3340, Winchester, VA 22604; tel. 703/722–8024; George Caley, CEO

WARREN MEMORIAL HOSPITAL, 1000 Shenandoah Avenue, Front Royal, VA, Zip 22630–3598; tel. 540/636–0300; Charlie M. Horton, President

WINCHESTER MEDICAL CENTER, 1840 Amherst Street, Winchester, VA, Zip 22601–2540, Mailing Address: P.O. Box 3340, Zip 22604–3340; tel. 540/722–8000; George B. Caley, President

VIRGINIA HEALTH NETWORK
7400 Beaufont Springs Drive, Suite 505, Richmond, VA 23225; tel. 804/320–3837; David Keplinger, Marketing Vice President

BON SECOURS ST. MARY'S HOSPITAL, 5801 Bremo Road, Richmond, VA, Zip 23226–1900; tel. 804/285–2011; Ann E. Honeycutt, Executive Vice President and Administrator

BON SECOURS–DEPAUL MEDICAL CENTER, 150 Kingsley Lane, Norfolk, VA, Zip 23505–4650; tel. 757/889–5000; David J. McCombs, Executive Vice President and Administrator

BON SECOURS–RICHMOND COMMUNITY HOSPITAL, 1500 North 28th Street, Richmond, VA, Zip 23223–5396, Mailing Address: Box 27184, Zip 23261–7184; tel. 804/225–1700; Samuel F. Lillard, Executive Vice President and Administrator

BON SECOURS–STUART CIRCLE, 413 Stuart Circle, Richmond, VA, Zip 23220–3799; tel. 804/358–7051; Edward Gerardo, Executive Vice President and Administrator

CHARTER BEHAVIORAL HEALTH SYSTEM OF CHARLOTTESVILLE, 2101 Arlington Boulevard, Charlottesville, VA, Zip 22903–1593; tel. 804/977–1120; Wayne Adams, Chief Executive Officer

CHARTER WESTBROOK BEHAVIORAL HEALTH SYSTEM, 1500 Westbrook Avenue, Richmond, VA, Zip 23227–3399; tel. 804/266–9671; Stephen P. Fahey, Administrator

CHESAPEAKE GENERAL HOSPITAL, 736 Battlefield Boulevard North, Chesapeake, VA, Zip 23320–4941, Mailing Address: P.O. Box 2028, Zip 23327–2028; tel. 757/312–8121; Donald S. Buckley, FACHE, President

CHILDREN'S HOSPITAL OF THE KING'S DAUGHTERS, 601 Children's Lane, Norfolk, VA, Zip 23507–1971; tel. 757/668–7700; Robert I. Bonar, Jr., President and Chief Executive Officer

COMMUNITY MEMORIAL HEALTHCENTER, 125 Buena Vista Circle, South Hill, VA, Zip 23970–0090, Mailing Address: P.O. Box 90, Zip 23970–0090; tel. 804/447–3151; W. Scott Burnette, President

GREENSVILLE MEMORIAL HOSPITAL, 214 Weaver Avenue, Emporia, VA, Zip 23847–1482; tel. 804/348–2000; Gerald R. Lundberg, Interim Chief Executive Officer

LOUISE OBICI MEMORIAL HOSPITAL, 1900 North Main Street, Suffolk, VA, Zip 23434–4323, Mailing Address: P.O. Box 1100, Zip 23439–1100; tel. 757/934–4000; William C. Giermak, President and Chief Executive Officer

Section B

MARTHA JEFFERSON HOSPITAL, 459 Locust Avenue, Charlottesville, VA, Zip 22902–9940; tel. 804/982–7000; James E. Haden, President and Chief Executive Officer

MARYVIEW HOSPITAL, 3636 High Street, Portsmouth, VA, Zip 23707–3236; tel. 757/398–2200; Wayne Jones, Executive Vice President and Administrator

MEDICAL COLLEGE OF VIRGINIA HOSPITALS, VIRGINIA COMMONWEALTH UNIVERSITY, 401 North 12th Street, Richmond, VA, Zip 23219, Mailing Address: P.O. Box 980510, Zip 23298–0510; tel. 804/828–9000; Carl R. Fischer, Associate Vice President and Chief Executive Officer

MEMORIAL REGIONAL MEDICAL CENTER, 8260 Atlee Road, Mechanicsville, VA, Zip 23116, Mailing Address: P.O. Box 26783, Richmond, Zip 23261–6783; tel. 804/764–6102; Michael Robinson, Executive Vice President and Administrator

RIVERSIDE REGIONAL MEDICAL CENTER, 500 J. Clyde Morris Boulevard, Newport News, VA, Zip 23601–1976; tel. 757/594–2000; Gerald R. Brink, President and Chief Executive Officer

RIVERSIDE TAPPAHANNOCK HOSPITAL, 618 Hospital Road, Tappahannock, VA, Zip 22560; tel. 804/443–3311; Elizabeth J. Martin, Vice President and Administrator

RIVERSIDE WALTER REED HOSPITAL, 7519 Hospital Drive, Gloucester, VA, Zip 23061–4178, Mailing Address: P.O. Box 1130, Zip 23061–1130; tel. 804/693–8800; Grady W. Philips, III, Vice President and Administrator

SENTARA VIRGINIA BEACH GENERAL HOSPITAL, 1060 First Colonial Road, Virginia Beach, VA, Zip 23454–9000; tel. 757/481–8000; Robert L. Graves, Administrator

SHELTERING ARMS REHABILITATION HOSPITAL, 1311 Palmyra Avenue, Richmond, VA, Zip 23227–4418; tel. 804/342–4100; Jack A. Carroll, Ph.D., President

SOUTHAMPTON MEMORIAL HOSPITAL, 100 Fairview Drive, Franklin, VA, Zip 23851–1206, Mailing Address: P.O. Box 817, Zip 23851–0817; tel. 757/569–6100; Edward J. Patnesky, President and Chief Executive Officer

WILLIAMSBURG COMMUNITY HOSPITAL, 301 Monticello Avenue, Williamsburg, VA, Zip 23187–8700, Mailing Address: Box 8700, Zip 23187–8700; tel. 757/259–6000; Les A. Donahue, President and Chief Executive Officer

WASHINGTON

COLUMBIAN BASIN HEALTH NETWORK
P.O. Box 185, Mead, WA 99021; tel. 509/238–2167; Jamie Norr, Network Contact

COLUMBIA BASIN HOSPITAL, 200 Southeast Boulevard, Ephrata, WA, Zip 98823–1997; tel. 509/754–4631; Allen L. Beach, Administrator

COULEE COMMUNITY HOSPITAL, 411 Fortuyn Road, Grand Coulee, WA, Zip 99133–8718; tel. 509/633–1753; Charlotte Lang, Administrator

EAST ADAMS RURAL HOSPITAL, 903 South Adams Street, Ritzville, WA, Zip 99169–2298; tel. 509/659–1200; James G. Parrish, Administrator

LINCOLN HOSPITAL, 10 Nichols Street, Davenport, WA, Zip 99122; tel. 509/725–7101; Kenneth J. Hall, Administrator

MID–VALLEY HOSPITAL, 810 Jasmine, Omak, WA, Zip 98841, Mailing Address: P.O. Box 793, Zip 98841; tel. 509/826–1760; Michael D. Billing, Administrator

OTHELLO COMMUNITY HOSPITAL, 315 North 14th Street, Othello, WA, Zip 99344; tel. 509/488–2636; Jerry Lane, Administrator

QUINCY VALLEY MEDICAL CENTER, 908 Tenth Avenue S.W., Quincy, WA, Zip 98848; tel. 509/787–3531; Alan MacPhee, Administrator

SAMARITAN HEALTHCARE, 801 East Wheeler Road, Moses Lake, WA, Zip 98837–1899; tel. 509/765–5606; Keith J. Baldwin, Administrator

DOMINICAN NETWORK
5633 North Lidgerwood, Spokane, WA 99207; tel. 509/482–2458; Ron Schurra, President

DEER PARK HOSPITAL, East 1015 D Street, Deer Park, WA, Zip 99006, Mailing Address: P.O. Box 742, Zip 99006; tel. 509/276–5061; Garvin Olson, Chief Operating Officer

HOLY FAMILY HOSPITAL, North 5633 Lidgerwood Avenue, Spokane, WA, Zip 99207; tel. 509/482–0111; Cathy J. Simchuk, Interim Chief Executive Officer

MOUNT CARMEL HOSPITAL, 982 East Columbia Street, Colville, WA, Zip 99114–0351, Mailing Address: Box 351, Zip 99114–0351; tel. 509/684–2561; Gloria Cooper, Chief Executive Officer

ST. JOSEPH HOSPITAL, 2901 Squalicum Parkway, Bellingham, WA, Zip 98225–1898; tel. 360/734–5400; Nancy J. Bitting, Chief Executive Officer

GROUP HEALTH COOP OF PUGENT SOUND
521 Wall Street, Seattle, WA 98121; tel. 206/326–3000; Phil Nudelman, PhD, President & CEO

THE EASTSIDE HOSPITAL, 2700 152nd Avenue N.E., Redmond, WA, Zip 98052–5560; tel. 425/883–5151; Patricia Kennedy–Scott, Northern Region Vice President

HEALTH WASHINGTON
700 Fifth Avenue, Ste 4500, Seattle, WA 98104–5044; tel. 206/233–7610; Charlie Beard, Network Coordinator

EVERGREEN COMMUNITY HEALTH CENTER, 12040 N.E. 128th Street, Kirkland, WA, Zip 98034; tel. 425/899–1000; Andrew Fallat, FACHE, Chief Executive Officer

MARY BRIDGE CHILDREN'S HOSPITAL AND HEALTH CENTER, 317 Martin Luther King Jr. Way, Tacoma, WA, Zip 98405–0299, Mailing Address: Box 5299, Zip 98405–0299; tel. 253/403–1400; Diane Cecchettini, Executive Vice President

STEVENS HEALTHCARE, 21601 76th Avenue West, Edmonds, WA, Zip 98026–7506; tel. 425/640–4000; Steve C. McCary, President and Chief Executive Officer

SWEDISH HEALTH SERVICES, 747 Broadway Avenue, Seattle, WA, Zip 98122–4307; tel. 206/386–6000; Richard H. Peterson, President and Chief Executive Officer

TACOMA GENERAL HOSPITAL, 315 Martin Luther King Jr. Way, Tacoma, WA, Zip 98405–0299, Mailing Address: P.O. Box 5299, Zip 98405–0299; tel. 253/403–1000; Diane Cecchettini, Executive Vice President

LINCOLN COUNTY PUBLIC HEALTH
90 Nicholas, Davenport, WA 99122; tel. 509/725–1001; Rand Masteller, Administrator

LINCOLN HOSPITAL, 10 Nichols Street, Davenport, WA, Zip 99122; tel. 509/725–7101; Kenneth J. Hall, Administrator

MULTICARE HEALTH SYSTEM
P.O. Box 5299, Tacoma, WA 98415; tel. 253/552–1419; William B. Connelly, President

ALLENMORE HOSPITAL, South 19th and Union Avenue, Tacoma, WA, Zip 98405, Mailing Address: P.O. Box 11414, Zip 98411–0414; tel. 253/403–2323

MARY BRIDGE CHILDREN'S HOSPITAL AND HEALTH CENTER, 317 Martin Luther King Jr. Way, Tacoma, WA, Zip 98405–0299, Mailing Address: Box 5299, Zip 98405–0299; tel. 253/403–1400; Diane Cecchettini, Executive Vice President

TACOMA GENERAL HOSPITAL, 315 Martin Luther King Jr. Way, Tacoma, WA, Zip 98405–0299, Mailing Address: P.O. Box 5299, Zip 98405–0299; tel. 253/403–1000; Diane Cecchettini, Executive Vice President

PEACEHEALTH
15325 S.E. 30th Pl, #300, Bellevue, WA 98007; tel. 360/636–4122; Mark McGourty, CEO

EVERGREEN COMMUNITY HEALTH CENTER, 12040 N.E. 128th Street, Kirkland, WA, Zip 98034; tel. 425/899–1000; Andrew Fallat, FACHE, Chief Executive Officer

KETCHIKAN GENERAL HOSPITAL, 3100 Tongass Avenue, Ketchikan, AK, Zip 99901–5746; tel. 907/225–5171; Edward F. Mahn, Chief Executive Officer

PEACE HARBOR HOSPITAL, 400 Ninth Street, Florence, OR, Zip 97439, Mailing Address: P.O. Box 580, Zip 97439; tel. 541/997–8412; James Barnhart, Administrator

SACRED HEART MEDICAL CENTER, 1255 Hilyard Street, Eugene, OR, Zip 97401, Mailing Address: P.O. Box 10905, Zip 97440; tel. 541/686–7300; Judy Hodgson, Administrator

ST. JOHN MEDICAL CENTER, 1615 Delaware Street, Longview, WA, Zip 98632, Mailing Address: P.O. Box 3002, Zip 98632–0302; tel. 360/414–2000; Mark E. McGourty, Regional Chief Executive Officer

ST. JOSEPH HOSPITAL, 2901 Squalicum Parkway, Bellingham, WA, Zip 98225–1898; tel. 360/734–5400; Nancy J. Bitting, Chief Executive Officer

PROVIDENCE SERVICES
9 East Ninth Street, Spokane, WA 99202; tel. 509/742–7337; Richard Umdenstock, President & CEO

BENEFIS HEALTH CARE, 500 15th Avenue South, Great Falls, MT, Zip 59403–4389; tel. 406/455–5000; Lloyd V. Smith, President and Chief Executive Officer

HOLY FAMILY HOSPITAL, North 5633 Lidgerwood Avenue, Spokane, WA, Zip 99207; tel. 509/482–0111; Cathy J. Simchuk, Interim Chief Executive Officer

MOUNT CARMEL HOSPITAL, 982 East Columbia Street, Colville, WA, Zip 99114–0351, Mailing Address: Box 351, Zip 99114–0351; tel. 509/684–2561; Gloria Cooper, Chief Executive Officer

SACRED HEART MEDICAL CENTER, West 101 Eighth Avenue, Spokane, WA, Zip 99220, Mailing Address: P.O. Box 2555, Zip 99220; tel. 509/455–3040; Ryland P. Davis, President

ST. JOSEPH HOSPITAL, Skyline Drive and 14th Avenue, Polson, MT, Zip 59860, Mailing Address: P.O. Box 1010, Zip 59860–1010; tel. 406/883–5377; John W. Glueckert, President

ST. JOSEPH'S HOSPITAL, 500 East Webster Street, Chewelah, WA, Zip 99109, Mailing Address: P.O. Box 197, Zip 99109; tel. 509/935–8211; Gary V. Peck, Chief Executive Officer

ST. MARY MEDICAL CENTER, 401 West Poplar Street, Walla Walla, WA, Zip 99362, Mailing Address: Box 1477, Zip 99362–0312; tel. 509/525–3320; John A. Isely, President

ST. PATRICK HOSPITAL, 500 West Broadway, Missoula, MT, Zip 59802–4096, Mailing Address: Box 4587, Zip 59806–4587; tel. 406/543–7271; Lawrence L. White, Jr., President

WEST VIRGINIA

CAMDEN–CLARK MEMORIAL HOSPITAL
P.O. Box 718, Parkersburg, WV 26102; tel. 304/424–2111; Iris McCrady, Network Contact

CAMDEN–CLARK MEMORIAL HOSPITAL, 800 Garfield Avenue, Parkersburg, WV, Zip 26101–5378, Mailing Address: P.O. Box 718, Zip 26102–0718; tel. 304/424–2111; Thomas J. Corder, President and Chief Executive Officer

SISTERSVILLE GENERAL HOSPITAL, 314 South Wells Street, Sistersville, WV, Zip 26175–1098; tel. 304/652–2611; F. David Richardson, Ph.D., Administrator

GRANT MEMORIAL HOSPITAL
P.O. Box 1019, Petersburg, WV 26847; tel. 304/257–1026; Robert L. Harman, Chairman

GRANT MEMORIAL HOSPITAL, Route 55 West, Petersburg, WV, Zip 26847, Mailing Address: P.O. Box 1019, Zip 26847–1019; tel. 304/257–1026; Robert L. Harman, Administrator

HEALTH PARNERS NETWORK, IKNC.
1000 Technology Drive, Suite 2320, Fairmont, WV 26554; tel. 304/368–2740; William G. Maclean, Chief Operating Officer

UNITED HOSPITAL CENTER, Route 19 South, Clarksburg, WV, Zip 26301, Mailing Address: P.O. Box 1680, Zip 26302–1680; tel. 304/624–2121; Bruce C. Carter, President

WEST VIRGINIA UNIVERSITY HOSPITALS, Medical Center Drive, Morgantown, WV, Zip 26506–4749; tel. 304/598–4000; Bruce McClymonds, President

INTEGRATED PROVIDER NETWORK
7000 Hampton Center, Suite F., Morgantown, WV 26505; tel. 304/598–3911; Brad Minton, Network Contact

UNITED HOSPITAL CENTER, Route 19 South, Clarksburg, WV, Zip 26301, Mailing Address: P.O. Box 1680, Zip 26302–1680; tel. 304/624–2121; Bruce C. Carter, President

WEST VIRGINIA UNIVERSITY HOSPITALS, Medical Center Drive, Morgantown, WV, Zip 26506–4749; tel. 304/598–4000; Bruce McClymonds, President

MORGAN CITY PRIMARY CARE NETWORK
1124 Fairfax Street, Berkeley Springs, WV 25411; tel. 304/258–1234; David Sweeney, Administrator

PARTNERS IN HEALTH NETWORK, INC
3411 Virgina Avenue, S.E., Charleston, WV 25304; tel. 304/388–7385; Scot Mitchell, CEO

BECKLEY APPALACHIAN REGIONAL HOSPITAL, 306 Stanaford Road, Beckley, WV, Zip 25801–3142; tel. 304/255–3000; David R. Lyon, Administrator

BOONE MEMORIAL HOSPITAL, 701 Madison Avenue, Madison, WV, Zip 25130–1699; tel. 304/369–1230; Tommy H. Mullins, Administrator

BRAXTON COUNTY MEMORIAL HOSPITAL, 100 Hoylman Drive, Gassaway, WV, Zip 26624–9320; tel. 304/364–5156; Tony E. Atkins, Administrator

CHARLESTON AREA MEDICAL CENTER, 501 Morris Street, Charleston, WV, Zip 25301–1300, Mailing Address: P.O. Box 1547, Zip 25326–1547; tel. 304/348–5432; Robert L. Savage, President and Chief Executive Officer

JACKSON GENERAL HOSPITAL, Pinnell Street, Ripley, WV, Zip 25271, Mailing Address: P.O. Box 720, Zip 25271–0720; tel. 304/372–2731; Richard L. Rohaley, President and Chief Executive Officer

MAN ARH HOSPITAL, 700 East McDonald Avenue, Man, WV, Zip 25635–1011; tel. 304/583–8421; Erica McDonald, Administrator

MINNIE HAMILTON HEALTHCARE CENTER, High Street, Grantsville, WV, Zip 26147, Mailing Address: Route 1, Box 1A, Zip 26147; tel. 304/354–9244; Barbara Lay, Administrator

MONTGOMERY GENERAL HOSPITAL, 401 Sixth Avenue, Montgomery, WV, Zip 25136–0270, Mailing Address: P.O. Box 270, Zip 25136–0270; tel. 304/442–5151; William R. Laird, IV, President and Chief Executive Officer

PLATEAU MEDICAL CENTER, 430 Main Street, Oak Hill, WV, Zip 25901–3455; tel. 304/469–8600; Hank Woodson, Administrator

RICHWOOD AREA COMMUNITY HOSPITAL, Riverside Addition, Richwood, WV, Zip 26261; tel. 304/846–2573; D. Parker Haddix, Chief Executive Officer

ROANE GENERAL HOSPITAL, 200 Hospital Drive, Spencer, WV, Zip 25276–1060; tel. 304/927–4444; Lewis Newberry, Interim Chief Executive Officer

SUMMERS COUNTY APPALACHIAN REGIONAL HOSPITAL, Terrace Street, Hinton, WV, Zip 25951, Mailing Address: Drawer 940, Zip 25951–0940; tel. 304/466–1000; Rocco K. Massey, Administrator

WILLIAMSON ARH HOSPITAL, 260 Hospital Drive, South Williamson, KY, Zip 41503–4072; tel. 606/237–1700; Louis G. Roe, Jr., Administrator

SOUTHERN VIRGINIA RURAL
500 A. Cherry Street, Suite 7, Bluefield, WV 24701; tel. 304/324–7123; Jean Henshaw, Network Coordinator

BLUEFIELD REGIONAL MEDICAL CENTER, 500 Cherry Street, Bluefield, WV, Zip 24701–3390; tel. 304/327–1100; Eugene P. Pawlowski, President

PRINCETON COMMUNITY HOSPITAL, 12th Street, Princeton, WV, Zip 24740–1369, Mailing Address: P.O. Box 1369, Zip 24740–1369; tel. 304/487–7000; Daniel C. Dunmyer, Chief Executive Officer

TRI-STATE COMMUNITY CARE
601 Colliers Way, Weirton, WV 26062; tel. 304/797–6413; Cynthia R. Nixon, Chief Financial Officer

WEIRTON MEDICAL CENTER, 601 Colliers Way, Weirton, WV, Zip 26062–5091; tel. 304/797–6000; Donald Muhlenthaler, FACHE, President and Chief Executive Officer

WEBSTER COUNTY MEMORIAL HOSPITAL
P.O. Box 312, Webster Springs, WV 26288; tel. 304/847–5682; Steve Gavalchik, President

UNITED HOSPITAL CENTER, Route 19 South, Clarksburg, WV, Zip 26301, Mailing Address: P.O. Box 1680, Zip 26302–1680; tel. 304/624–2121; Bruce C. Carter, President

WEBSTER COUNTY MEMORIAL HOSPITAL, 324 Miller Mountain Drive, Webster Springs, WV, Zip 26288–1087; tel. 304/847–5682; Stephen M. Gavalchik, Administrator

WISCONSIN

AFFINITY HEALTH SYSTEM, INC
631 Hazel Street, Oshkosh, WI 54902–5677; tel. 414/236–2010; Otto L. Cox, CEO

MERCY MEDICAL CENTER, 631 Hazel Street, Oshkosh, WI, Zip 54901–4680, Mailing Address: P.O. Box 1100, Zip 54902–1100; tel. 920/236–2000; Otto L. Cox, President

ST. ELIZABETH HOSPITAL, 1506 South Oneida Street, Appleton, WI, Zip 54915–1397; tel. 920/738–2000; Otto L. Cox, President

ALL SAINTS HEALTHCARE SYSTEM
3801 Spring Street, Racine, WI 53405; tel. 414/636–4860; Ed DeMeulenaere, President

SAINT MARY'S MEDICAL CENTER, 3801 Spring Street, Racine, WI, Zip 53405–1690; tel. 414/636–4011; Kenneth R. Buser, President

ST. LUKE'S MEMORIAL HOSPITAL, 1320 Wisconsin Avenue, Racine, WI, Zip 53403–1987; tel. 414/636–2011; Kenneth R. Buser, President

AURORA HEALTH CARE
P.O. Box 343910, Milwaukee, WI 53234–3910; tel. 414/647–3000; G. Edwin Howe, President

HARTFORD MEMORIAL HOSPITAL, 1032 East Sumner Street, Hartford, WI, Zip 53027–1698; tel. 414/673–2300; Mark Schwartz, Administrator

LAKELAND MEDICAL CENTER, West 3985 County Road NN, Elkhorn, WI, Zip 53121, Mailing Address: P.O. Box 1002, Zip 53121–1002; tel. 414/741–2000; Loren J. Anderson, Executive Vice President

MEMORIAL HOSPITAL CORPORATION OF BURLINGTON, 252 McHenry Street, Burlington, WI, Zip 53105–1828; tel. 414/767–6000; Loren J. Anderson, Executive Vice President

MILWAUKEE PSYCHIATRIC HOSPITAL, 1220 Dewey Avenue, Wauwatosa, WI, Zip 53213–2598; tel. 414/454–6600; James A. Moore, Administrator

SHEBOYGAN MEMORIAL MEDICAL CENTER, 2629 North Seventh Street, Sheboygan, WI, Zip 53083–4998; tel. 920/451–5000; T. Gregg Watson, Administrator

SINAI SAMARITAN MEDICAL CENTER, 945 North 12th Street, Milwaukee, WI, Zip 53233–1337, Mailing Address: P.O. Box 342, Zip 53201–0342; tel. 414/219–2000; Leonard E. Wilk, Administrator

ST. LUKE'S MEDICAL CENTER, 2900 West Oklahoma Avenue, Milwaukee, WI, Zip 53215–4330, Mailing Address: P.O. Box 2901, Zip 53201–2901; tel. 414/649–6000; Mark S. Wiener, Administrator

ST. MARY'S KEWAUNEE AREA MEMORIAL HOSPITAL, 810 Lincoln Street, Kewaunee, WI, Zip 54216; tel. 920/388–2210; Cathie A. Kocourek, Acting Administrator

TWO RIVERS COMMUNITY HOSPITAL AND HAMILTON MEMORIAL HOME, 2500 Garfield Street, Two Rivers, WI, Zip 54241–2399; tel. 920/793–1178; Cathie A. Kocourek, Acting Administrator

VALLEY VIEW MEDICAL CENTER, 901 Reed Street, Plymouth, WI, Zip 53073–2409; tel. 920/893–1771; T. Gregg Watson, Administrator

WEST ALLIS MEMORIAL HOSPITAL, 8901 West Lincoln Avenue, West Allis, WI, Zip 53227–0901, Mailing Address: P.O. Box 27901, Zip 53227–0901; tel. 414/328–6000; Richard A. Kellar, Administrator

COLUMBIA– ST. MARY'S, INC.
2025 East Newport Avenue, Milwaukee, WI 53211; tel. 414/961–3638; John Schueler, President & CEO

COLUMBIA HOSPITAL, 2025 East Newport Avenue, Milwaukee, WI, Zip 53211–2990; tel. 414/961–3300; Susan Henckel, Executive Vice President and Chief Executive Officer

SACRED HEART REHABILITATION INSTITUTE, 2350 North Lake Drive, Milwaukee, WI, Zip 53211–4507, Mailing Address: P.O. Box 392, Zip 53201–0392; tel. 414/298–6700; William H. Lange, Administrator and Senior Vice President

ST. MARY'S HOSPITAL, 2323 North Lake Drive, Milwaukee, WI, Zip 53211–9682, Mailing Address: P.O. Box 503, Zip 53201–0503; tel. 414/291–1000; Charles C. Lobeck, Chief Executive Officer

ST. MARY'S HOSPITAL OZAUKEE, 13111 North Port Washington Road, Mequon, WI, Zip 53097–2416; tel. 414/243–7300; Therese B. Pandl, Senior Vice President and Chief Operating Officer

COMMUNITY HEALTH CARE, INC
425 Pine Ridge Boulevard, Wausau, WI 54401; tel. 715/847–2121; L. J. Olkowski, Senior Vice President

MEMORIAL HOSPITAL OF TAYLOR COUNTY, 135 South Gibson Street, Medford, WI, Zip 54451–1696; tel. 715/748–8100; Greg Roraff, President and Chief Executive Officer

WAUSAU HOSPITAL, 333 Pine Ridge Boulevard, Wausau, WI, Zip 54401–4187, Mailing Address: P.O. Box 1847, Zip 54402–1847; tel. 715/847–2121; Paul A. Spaude, President and Chief Executive Officer

COMMUNITY HEALTH NETWORK, INC
225 Memorial Drive, Berlin, WI 54923; tel. 414/361–5580; Craig W. C. Schmidt, President & CEO

BERLIN MEMORIAL HOSPITAL, 225 Memorial Drive, Berlin, WI, Zip 54923–1295; tel. 920/361–1313; Craig W. C. Schmidt, President and Chief Executive Officer

WILD ROSE COMMUNITY MEMORIAL HOSPITAL, 601 Grove Avenue, Wild Rose, WI, Zip 54984, Mailing Address: P.O. Box 243, Zip 54984–0243; tel. 414/622–3257; Donald Caves, President

Section B

COVENANT HEALTHCARE SYSTEM, INC.
1126 South 70th Street, Suite S306,
Milwaukee, WI 53214–0970;
tel. 414/456–2300; E. Thomas Sheahan,
President & CEO

ELMBROOK MEMORIAL HOSPITAL, 19333 West North Avenue, Brookfield, WI, Zip 53045–4198; tel. 414/785–2000; Kimry A. Johnsrud, President

LAKEVIEW HOSPITAL, 10010 West Bluemound Road, Wauwatosa, WI, Zip 53226; tel. 414/259–7200; J. E. Race, Administrator and Chief Executive Officer

MARQUETTE GENERAL HEALTH SYSTEM, 420 West Magnetic Street, Marquette, MI, Zip 49855–2794; tel. 906/228–9440; William Nemacheck, Chief Executive Officer

ST. FRANCIS HOSPITAL, 3237 South 16th Street, Milwaukee, WI, Zip 53215–4592; tel. 414/647–5000; Gregory A. Banaszynski, President

ST. JOSEPH'S HOSPITAL, 5000 West Chambers Street, Milwaukee, WI, Zip 53210–9988; tel. 414/447–2000; Patricia A. Kaldor, R.N., President

ST. MICHAEL HOSPITAL, 2400 West Villard Avenue, Milwaukee, WI, Zip 53209–4999; tel. 414/527–8000; Jeffrey K. Jenkins, President

ST. NICHOLAS HOSPITAL, 1601 North Taylor Drive, Sheboygan, WI, Zip 53081–2496; tel. 920/459–8300; Michael J. Stenger, Executive Vice President and Administrator

FELICIAN HEALTH CARE, INC.
3237 South 16th, Milwaukee, WI 53215;
tel. 414/647–5622; Sister Mary Clarette,
President of Felician Health

ST. FRANCIS HOSPITAL, 3237 South 16th Street, Milwaukee, WI, Zip 53215–4592; tel. 414/647–5000; Gregory A. Banaszynski, President

ST. MARY'S HOSPITAL, 400 North Pleasant Avenue, Centralia, IL, Zip 62801–3091; tel. 618/532–6731; James W. McDowell, President and Chief Executive Officer

FELICIAN HEALTH CARE–MILWAUKEE REGION
3237 S. 16th Street, Milwaukee, WI 53215;
tel. 414/647–5622; Mark V. Knight, CEO

FRANCISCAN HEALTH SYSTEM, INC
615 South Tenth Street, LaCrosse, WI 54601;
tel. 608/.79–9788; Brian C. Campion, MD,
President/CEO

FRANCISCAN SKEMP HEALTHCARE–ARCADIA CAMPUS, 464 South St. Joseph Avenue, Arcadia, WI, Zip 54612–1401; tel. 608/323–3341; Robert M. Tracey, Administrator

FRANCISCAN SKEMP HEALTHCARE–LA CROSSE CAMPUS, 700 West Avenue South, La Crosse, WI, Zip 54601–4783; tel. 608/785–0940; Glenn Forbes, M.D., President and Chief Executive Officer

FRANCISCAN SKEMP HEALTHCARE–SPARTA CAMPUS, 310 West Main Street, Sparta, WI, Zip 54656–2171; tel. 608/269–2132; William P. Sexton, Administrator

HEALTH CARE NETWORK OF WISCONSIN
250 Bishops Way, Suite 300, Brookfield, WI
53005; tel. 414/784–0223; Jim Wrocklage,
President

AGNESIAN HEALTHCARE, 430 East Division Street, Fond Du Lac, WI, Zip 54935–0385; tel. 920/929–2300; Robert A. Fale, President

BURNETT MEDICAL CENTER, 257 West St. George Avenue, Grantsburg, WI, Zip 54840–7827; tel. 715/463–5353; Timothy J. Wick, Chief Executive Officer

CHILDREN'S HOSPITAL OF WISCONSIN, 9000 West Wisconsin Avenue, Milwaukee, WI, Zip 53226–4810, Mailing Address: P.O. Box 1997, Zip 53201–1997; tel. 414/266–2000; Jon E. Vice, President and Chief Executive Officer

COLUMBIA HOSPITAL, 2025 East Newport Avenue, Milwaukee, WI, Zip 53211–2990; tel. 414/961–3300; Susan Henckel, Executive Vice President and Chief Executive Officer

COMMUNITY MEMORIAL HOSPITAL, W180 N8085 Town Hall Road, Menomonee Falls, WI, Zip 53051, Mailing Address: P.O. Box 408, Zip 53052–0408; tel. 414/251–1000; Robert Eugene Drisner, President and Chief Executive Officer

COMMUNITY MEMORIAL HOSPITAL, 855 South Main Street, Oconto Falls, WI, Zip 54154–1296; tel. 920/846–3444; Tom Thompson, Administrator

ELMBROOK MEMORIAL HOSPITAL, 19333 West North Avenue, Brookfield, WI, Zip 53045–4198; tel. 414/785–2000; Kimry A. Johnsrud, President

FROEDTERT MEMORIAL LUTHERAN HOSPITAL, 9200 West Wisconsin Avenue, Milwaukee, WI, Zip 53226–3596, Mailing Address: P.O. Box 26099, Zip 53226–3596; tel. 414/259–3000; William D. Petasnick, President

HARTFORD MEMORIAL HOSPITAL, 1032 East Sumner Street, Hartford, WI, Zip 53027–1698; tel. 414/673–2300; Mark Schwartz, Administrator

HUDSON MEDICAL CENTER, 400 Wisconsin Street, Hudson, WI, Zip 54016–1600; tel. 715/386–9321; Marian M. Furlong, R.N., Chief Executive Officer

MEMORIAL HOSPITAL CORPORATION OF BURLINGTON, 252 McHenry Street, Burlington, WI, Zip 53105–1828; tel. 414/767–6000; Loren J. Anderson, Executive Vice President

OCONOMOWOC MEMORIAL HOSPITAL, 791 Summit Avenue, Oconomowoc, WI, Zip 53066–3896; tel. 414/569–9400; Douglas Guy, President and Chief Executive Officer

SHEBOYGAN MEMORIAL MEDICAL CENTER, 2629 North Seventh Street, Sheboygan, WI, Zip 53083–4998; tel. 920/451–5000; T. Gregg Watson, Administrator

SINAI SAMARITAN MEDICAL CENTER, 945 North 12th Street, Milwaukee, WI, Zip 53233–1337, Mailing Address: P.O. Box 342, Zip 53201–0342; tel. 414/219–2000; Leonard E. Wilk, Administrator

ST. CATHERINE'S HOSPITAL, 3556 Seventh Avenue, Kenosha, WI, Zip 53140–2595; tel. 414/656–2011; Richard O. Schmidt, Jr., President and Chief Executive Officer

ST. CLARE HOSPITAL AND HEALTH SERVICES, 707 14th Street, Baraboo, WI, Zip 53913–1597; tel. 608/356–1400; David B. Jordahl, FACHE, President

ST. CROIX VALLEY MEMORIAL HOSPITAL, 204 South Adams Street, Saint Croix Falls, WI, Zip 54024–9400; tel. 715/483–3261; Steve L. Urosevich, Chief Executive Officer

ST. FRANCIS HOSPITAL, 3237 South 16th Street, Milwaukee, WI, Zip 53215–4592; tel. 414/647–5000; Gregory A. Banaszynski, President

ST. JOSEPH'S COMMUNITY HOSPITAL OF WEST BEND, 551 South Silverbrook Drive, West Bend, WI, Zip 53095–3898; tel. 414/334–5533; Gregory T. Burns, Executive Director

ST. JOSEPH'S HOSPITAL, 5000 West Chambers Street, Milwaukee, WI, Zip 53210–9988; tel. 414/447–2000; Patricia A. Kaldor, R.N., President

ST. LUKE'S MEDICAL CENTER, 2900 West Oklahoma Avenue, Milwaukee, WI, Zip 53215–4330, Mailing Address: P.O. Box 2901, Zip 53201–2901; tel. 414/649–6000; Mark S. Wiener, Administrator

ST. LUKE'S MEMORIAL HOSPITAL, 1320 Wisconsin Avenue, Racine, WI, Zip 53403–1987; tel. 414/636–2011; Kenneth R. Buser, President

ST. MARY'S HOSPITAL, 2323 North Lake Drive, Milwaukee, WI, Zip 53211–9682, Mailing Address: P.O. Box 503, Zip 53201–0503; tel. 414/291–1000; Charles C. Lobeck, Chief Executive Officer

ST. MARY'S HOSPITAL OF SUPERIOR, 3500 Tower Avenue, Superior, WI, Zip 54880–5395; tel. 715/392–8281; Delores E. Schultz, R.N., Administrator

ST. MARYS HOSPITAL MEDICAL CENTER, 707 South Mills Street, Madison, WI, Zip 53715–0450; tel. 608/251–6100; Gerald W. Lefert, President

ST. MICHAEL HOSPITAL, 2400 West Villard Avenue, Milwaukee, WI, Zip 53209–4999; tel. 414/527–8000; Jeffrey K. Jenkins, President

VALLEY VIEW MEDICAL CENTER, 901 Reed Street, Plymouth, WI, Zip 53073–2409; tel. 920/893–1771; T. Gregg Watson, Administrator

WAUKESHA MEMORIAL HOSPITAL, 725 American Avenue, Waukesha, WI, Zip 53188–5099; tel. 414/544–2011; Rexford W. Titus, III, President and Chief Executive Officer

WAUPUN MEMORIAL HOSPITAL, 620 West Brown Street, Waupun, WI, Zip 53963–1799; tel. 920/324–5581; James E. Baer, FACHE, President

WEST ALLIS MEMORIAL HOSPITAL, 8901 West Lincoln Avenue, West Allis, WI, Zip 53227–0901, Mailing Address: P.O. Box 27901, Zip 53227–0901; tel. 414/328–6000; Richard A. Kellar, Administrator

HORIZON HEALTHCARE INC
2300 North Mayfair Road Suite 550,
Milwaukee, WI 53226; tel. 414/257–3888; Sis.
Renee Rose, President & CEO

COLUMBIA HOSPITAL, 2025 East Newport Avenue, Milwaukee, WI, Zip 53211–2990; tel. 414/961–3300; Susan Henckel, Executive Vice President and Chief Executive Officer

COMMUNITY MEMORIAL HOSPITAL, W180 N8085 Town Hall Road, Menomonee Falls, WI, Zip 53051, Mailing Address: P.O. Box 408, Zip 53052–0408; tel. 414/251–1000; Robert Eugene Drisner, President and Chief Executive Officer

FROEDTERT MEMORIAL LUTHERAN HOSPITAL, 9200 West Wisconsin Avenue, Milwaukee, WI, Zip 53226–3596, Mailing Address: P.O. Box 26099, Zip 53226–3596; tel. 414/259–3000; William D. Petasnick, President

KENOSHA HOSPITAL AND MEDICAL CENTER, 6308 Eighth Avenue, Kenosha, WI, Zip 53143–5082; tel. 414/656–2011; Richard O. Schmidt, Jr., President and Chief Executive Officer

ST. MARY'S HOSPITAL, 2323 North Lake Drive, Milwaukee, WI, Zip 53211–9682, Mailing Address: P.O. Box 503, Zip 53201–0503; tel. 414/291–1000; Charles C. Lobeck, Chief Executive Officer

ST. MARY'S HOSPITAL OZAUKEE, 13111 North Port Washington Road, Mequon, WI, Zip 53097–2416; tel. 414/243–7300; Therese B. Pandl, Senior Vice President and Chief Operating Officer

LUTHER/MIDELFORT/MAYO HEALTH SYSTEM
733 West Clairmont, Eau Claire, WI 54701;
tel. 715/838–6732; William C. Rupp,
President & CEO

BARRON MEDICAL CENTER–MAYO HEALTH SYSTEM, 1222 Woodland Avenue, Barron, WI, Zip 54812–1798; tel. 715/537–3186; Mark D. Wilson, Administrator

BLOOMER COMMUNITY MEMORIAL HOSPITAL AND THE MAPLEWOOD, 1501 Thompson Street, Bloomer, WI, Zip 54724–1299; tel. 715/568–2000; John Perushek, Administrator

LUTHER HOSPITAL, 1221 Whipple Street, Eau Claire, WI, Zip 54702–4105; tel. 715/838–3311; William Rupp, M.D., President and Chief Executive Officer

OSSEO AREA HOSPITAL AND NURSING HOME, 13025 Eighth Street, Osseo, WI, Zip 54758, Mailing Address: P.O. Box 70, Zip 54758–0070; tel. 715/597–3121; Bradley D. Groseth, Administrator

LUTHERAN HEALTH SYSTEM
1910 South Avenue, LaCrosse, WI 54601;
tel. 608/785–0530; Phillip Dahlberg, M.D.,
President

LUTHERAN HOSPITAL–LA CROSSE, 1910 South Avenue, La Crosse, WI, Zip 54601–9980; tel. 608/785–0530; Philip J. Dahlberg, M.D., President

TRI–COUNTY MEMORIAL HOSPITAL, 18601 Lincoln Street, Whitehall, WI, Zip 54773–0065, Mailing Address: P.O. Box 65, Zip 54773–0065; tel. 715/538–4361; Ronald B. Fields, President

MARSHFIELD CLINIC'S REGIONAL SYSTEM
1000 North Oak Avenue, Marshfield, WI 54449; tel. 715/389–4884; John Smylie, Director of Regional Operations

FLAMBEAU HOSPITAL, 98 Sherry Avenue, Park Falls, WI, Zip 54552–1467, Mailing Address: P.O. Box 310, Zip 54552–0310; tel. 715/762–2484; Curtis A. Johnson, Administrator

PRAIRIE DU CHIEN PARTNERSHIP
705 East Taylor Street, Prairie du Chien, WI 53821; tel. 608/326–2431; Ellen Nierling, Network Contact

PRAIRIE DU CHIEN MEMORIAL HOSPITAL, 705 East Taylor Street, Prairie Du Chien, WI, Zip 53821–2196; tel. 608/326–2431; Harold W. Brown, Chief Executive Officer

PROHEALTH CARE, INC.
725 American Avenue, Waukesha, WI 53188; tel. 414/544–2011; Donald Fundingsland, President

WAUKESHA MEMORIAL HOSPITAL, 725 American Avenue, Waukesha, WI, Zip 53188–5099; tel. 414/544–2011; Rexford W. Titus, III, President and Chief Executive Officer

SOUTHERN WISCONSIN HEALTH CARE SYSTEM
1000 Mineral Point Avenue, Janesville, WI 53547–5003; tel. 608/756–6000; Joseph D. Nemeth, Vice President & CEO

MERCY HEALTH SYSTEM, 1000 Mineral Point Avenue, Janesville, WI, Zip 53545–5003, Mailing Address: P.O. Box 5003, Zip 53547–5003; tel. 608/756–6000; Javon R. Bea, President and Chief Executive Officer

UNIVERSITY OF WISCONSIN HOSP & CLINICS
600 Highland Avenue, Madison, WI 53792; tel. 608/263–6400; Gordon Derzon, CEO

UNIVERSITY OF WISCONSIN HOSPITAL AND CLINICS, 600 Highland Avenue, Madison, WI, Zip 53792–0002; tel. 608/263–6400; Gordon M. Derzon, Chief Executive Officer

WYOMING

COMMUNITY HEALTH CARE
P.O. Box 428, Jackson, WY 83001; tel. 307/733–3636; Nancy Johnsen, Wellkness Coordinator

ST. JOHN'S HOSPITAL AND LIVING CENTER, 625 East Broadway Street, Jackson, WY, Zip 83001, Mailing Address: P.O. Box 428, Zip 83001–0428; tel. 307/733–3636; John Valiante, Chief Executive Officer

WYOMING INTEGRATED NETWORK
1233 E. 2nd Street, Casper, WY 82601; tel. 307/577–2153; Dan Hampton, Network Contact

IVINSON MEMORIAL HOSPITAL, 255 North 30th Street, Laramie, WY, Zip 82070–5195; tel. 307/742–2141; J. Michael Boyd, Chief Executive Officer

WYOMING MEDICAL CENTER, 1233 East Second Street, Casper, WY, Zip 82601–2988; tel. 307/577–7201; Michael E. Schrader, President and Chief Executive Officer

Statistics for Multihospital Health Care Systems and their Hospitals

The following tables describing multihospital health care systems refer to information in section B of the 1999/2000 *AHA Guide*.

Table 1 shows the number of multihospital health care systems by type of control. Table 2 provides a breakdown of the number of systems that own, lease, sponsor or contract manage hospitals within each control category. Table 3 gives the number of hospitals and beds in each control category as well as total hospitals and beds. Finally, Table 4 shows the percentage of hospitals and beds in each control category.

For more information on multihospital health care systems, please write to the Section for Health Care Systems, One North Franklin, Chicago, Illinois 60606–3401 or call 312/422–3000.

Table 1. Multihospital Health Care Systems, by Type of Organizaton Control

Type of Control	Code	Number of Systems
Catholic (Roman) church–related	CC	48
Other church–related	CO	11
Subtotal, church–related		59
Other not–for–profit	NP	185
Subtotal, not–for–profit		244
Investor Owned	IO	39
Federal Government	FG	5
Total		288

Table 2. Multihospital Health Care Systems, by Type of Ownership and Control

Type of Ownership	Catholic Church–Related (CC)	Other Church–Related (CO)	Total Church–Related (CC + CO)	Other Not–for–Profit (NP)	Total Not–for–Profit (CC, CO, + NP)	Investor–Owned (IO)	Federal Government	All Systems
Systems that only own, lease or sponsor	37	6	43	152	195	32	5	232
Systems that only contract–manage	0	0	0	4	4	2	0	6
Systems that manage, own, lease, or sponsor	11	5	16	29	45	5	0	50
Total	48	11	59	185	244	39	5	288

Table 3. Hospitals and Beds in Multihospital Health Care Systems, by Type of Ownership and Control

Type of Ownership	Catholic Church–Related (CC)		Other Church–Related (CO)		Total Church–Related (CC + CO)		Other Not–for–Profit (NP)		Total Not–for–Profit (CC, CO, + NP)		Investor–Owned (IO)		Federal Government		All Systems	
	H	B	H	B	H	B	H	B	H	B	H	B	H	B	H	B
Owned, leased or sponsored	504	112,219	90	19,335	594	131,888	941	215,646	1,535	347,534	885	121,287	276	59,262	2,696	528,083
Contract–managed	51	3,063	7	643	58	3,706	120	12,393	178	16,099	270	25,359	0	0	448	41,458
Total	555	115,282	97	19,978	652	135,594	1,061	228,039	1,713	363,633	1,155	146,646	276	59,262	3,144	569,541

H = hospitals; **B** = beds.

Table 4. Hospitals and Beds in Multihospital Health Care Systems, by Type of Ownership and Control as a Percentage of All Systems

Type of Ownership	Catholic Church–Related (CC)		Other Church–Related (CO)		Total Church–Related (CC + CO)		Other Not–for–Profit (NP)		Total Not–for–Profit (CC, CO, + NP)		Investor–Owned (IO)		Federal Government		All Systems	
	H	B	H	B	H	B	H	B	H	B	H	B	H	B	H	B
Owned, leased or sponsored	18.7	21.3	3.3	3.7	22.0	25.0	34.9	40.8	56.9	65.8	32.8	23.0	10.2	11.2	100.0	100.0
Contract–managed	11.4	7.4	1.6	1.6	12.9	8.9	26.8	29.9	39.7	38.8	60.3	61.2	0.0	0.0	100.0	100.0
Total	17.7	20.3	3.1	3.5	20.7	23.8	33.7	40.0	54.5	63.8	36.7	25.7	8.8	10.4	100.0	100.0

H = hospitals; **B** = beds.
*Please note that figures may not always equal the provided subtotal or total percentages due to rounding.

Section B

0071: ACCORD HEALTH CARE CORPORATION (IO)
3696 Ulmerton Road, Clearwater, FL Zip 33762;
tel. 727/573–1755; Stephen H. Noble, President

GEORGIA: STEWART–WEBSTER HOSPITAL (O, 25 beds) 300 Alston Street, Richland, GA Zip 31825–1406, Mailing Address: P.O. Box 190, Zip 31825–0190; tel. 912/887–3366; Stephen H. Noble, President

WHEELER COUNTY HOSPITAL (O, 30 beds) 111 Third Street, Glenwood, GA Zip 30428, Mailing Address: P.O. Box 398, Zip 30428–0398; tel. 912/523–5113; Brenda Josey, Administrator

Owned, leased, sponsored:	2 hospitals	55 beds
Contract–managed:	0 hospitals	0 beds
Totals:	2 hospitals	55 beds

★0235: ADVENTIST HEALTH (CO)
2100 Douglas Boulevard, Roseville, CA Zip 95661–3898, Mailing Address: P.O. Box 619002, Zip 95661–9002; tel. 916/781–2000; Donald R. Ammon, President

CALIFORNIA: CENTRAL VALLEY GENERAL HOSPITAL (O, 40 beds) 1025 North Douty Street, Hanford, CA Zip 93230, Mailing Address: Box 480, Zip 93232; tel. 559/583–2100; Kendall R. Fults, Chief Operating Officer
Web address: www.hanfordhealth.com

FEATHER RIVER HOSPITAL (O, 122 beds) 5974 Pentz Road, Paradise, CA Zip 95969–5593; tel. 530/877–9361; Michael Schultz, Chief Executive Officer

FRANK R. HOWARD MEMORIAL HOSPITAL (L, 28 beds) 1 Madrone Street, Willits, CA Zip 95490; tel. 707/459–6801; Kevin R. Erich, President

GLENDALE ADVENTIST MEDICAL CENTER (O, 396 beds) 1509 Wilson Terrace, Glendale, CA Zip 91206–4007; tel. 818/409–8000; Fred Manchur, President and Chief Executive Officer
Web address: www.glendaleadventist.com

HANFORD COMMUNITY MEDICAL CENTER (O, 59 beds) 450 Greenfield Avenue, Hanford, CA Zip 93230–0240, Mailing Address: Box 240, Zip 93232–0240; tel. 209/582–9000; Darwin R. Remboldt, President and Chief Executive Officer
Web address: www.adventisthealth.org

PARADISE VALLEY HOSPITAL (O, 236 beds) 2400 East Fourth Street, National City, CA Zip 91950; tel. 619/470–4321; Eric Martinsen, President

REDBUD COMMUNITY HOSPITAL (O, 34 beds) 18th Avenue and Highway 53, Clearlake, CA Zip 95422, Mailing Address: P.O. Box 6720, Zip 95422; tel. 707/994–6486; Richard D. Hathaway, Chief Operating Officer

SAN JOAQUIN COMMUNITY HOSPITAL (O, 178 beds) 2615 Eye Street, Bakersfield, CA Zip 93301, Mailing Address: Box 2615, Zip 93303–2615; tel. 661/395–3000; Douglas L. Lafferty, President and Chief Executive Officer

SELMA DISTRICT HOSPITAL (C, 47 beds) 1141 Rose Avenue, Selma, CA Zip 93662–3293; tel. 559/891–2201; Edward C. Palacios, R.N., Acting Chief Executive Officer

SIMI VALLEY HOSPITAL AND HEALTH CARE SERVICES (O, 225 beds) 2975 North Sycamore Drive, Simi Valley, CA Zip 93065–1277; tel. 805/527–2462; Alan J. Rice, President

SONORA COMMUNITY HOSPITAL (O, 118 beds) 1 South Forest Road, Sonora, CA Zip 95370; tel. 209/532–3161; Lary Davis, President
Web address: www.sonoracom.com

SOUTH COAST MEDICAL CENTER (O, 155 beds) 31872 Coast Highway, South Laguna, CA Zip 92677; tel. 949/499–1311; T. Michael Murray, President

ST. HELENA HOSPITAL (O, 168 beds) 650 Sanitarium Road, Deer Park, CA Zip 94576, Mailing Address: P.O. Box 250, Zip 94576; tel. 707/963–3611; JoAline Olson, R.N., President and Chief Executive Officer

UKIAH VALLEY MEDICAL CENTER (O, 85 beds) 275 Hospital Drive, Ukiah, CA Zip 95482; tel. 707/462–3111; ValGene Devitt, President and Chief Executive Officer

WHITE MEMORIAL MEDICAL CENTER (O, 344 beds) 1720 Cesar E Chavez Avenue, Los Angeles, CA Zip 90033–2481; tel. 323/268–5000; Fred Manchur, President and Chief Executive Officer

HAWAII: CASTLE MEDICAL CENTER (O, 150 beds) 640 Ulukahiki Street, Kailua, HI Zip 96734–4498; tel. 808/263–5500; Robert J. Walker, President
Web address: www.cmc.ah.org

OREGON: ADVENTIST MEDICAL CENTER (O, 214 beds) 10123 S.E. Market, Portland, OR Zip 97216–2599; tel. 503/257–2500; Deryl L. Jones, President
Web address: www.adventisthealthnw.com

TILLAMOOK COUNTY GENERAL HOSPITAL (L, 30 beds) 1000 Third Street, Tillamook, OR Zip 97141–3430; tel. 503/842–4444; Wendell Hesseltine, President

WASHINGTON: WALLA WALLA GENERAL HOSPITAL (O, 72 beds) 1025 South Second Avenue, Walla Walla, WA Zip 99362, Mailing Address: Box 1398, Zip 99362; tel. 509/525–0480; Morre Dean, President

Owned, leased, sponsored:	18 hospitals	2654 beds
Contract–managed:	1 hospital	47 beds
Totals:	19 hospitals	2701 beds

★4165: ADVENTIST HEALTH SYSTEM SUNBELT HEALTH CARE CORPORATION (CO)
111 North Orlando Avenue, Winter Park, FL Zip 32789–3675; tel. 407/975–1417; Mardian J. Blair, President

FLORIDA: EAST PASCO MEDICAL CENTER (O, 120 beds) 7050 Gall Boulevard, Zephyrhills, FL Zip 33541–1399; tel. 813/788–0411; Paul Michael Norman, President

FLORIDA HOSPITAL (O, 1382 beds) 601 East Rollins Street, Orlando, FL Zip 32803–1489; tel. 407/896–6611; Thomas L. Werner, President
Web address: www.flhosp.org

FLORIDA HOSPITAL HEARTLAND DIVISION (O, 195 beds) 4200 Sun'n Lake Boulevard, Sebring, FL Zip 33872, Mailing Address: P.O. Box 9400, Zip 33872; tel. 941/314–4466; John R. Harding, President and Chief Executive Officer
Web address: www.flhosp–heartland.org

FLORIDA HOSPITAL WATERMAN (O, 181 beds) 201 North Eustis Street, Eustis, FL Zip 32726–3488, Mailing Address: P.O. Box B, Zip 32727–0377; tel. 352/589–3333; Kenneth R. Mattison, President and Chief Executive Officer
Web address: www.fhwat.org

GEORGIA: EMORY–ADVENTIST HOSPITAL (O, 54 beds) 3949 South Cobb Drive S.E., Smyrna, GA Zip 30080–6300; tel. 770/434–0710; Terry Owen, Chief Executive Officer

GORDON HOSPITAL (O, 54 beds) 1035 Red Bud Road, Calhoun, GA Zip 30701–2082, Mailing Address: P.O. Box 12938, Zip 30703–7013; tel. 706/629–2895; Dennis Kiley, President

ILLINOIS: GLENOAKS HOSPITAL (O, 116 beds) 701 Winthrop Avenue, Glendale Heights, IL Zip 60139–1403; tel. 630/545–8000; Brinsley Lewis, Senior Executive Officer
Web address: www.glenoaks.org

HINSDALE HOSPITAL (O, 339 beds) 120 North Oak Street, Hinsdale, IL Zip 60521–3890; tel. 630/856–9000; Ernie W. Sadau, President and Chief Executive Officer
Web address: www.hinsdalehospital.org

LA GRANGE MEMORIAL HOSPITAL (O, 175 beds) 5101 South Willow Spring Road, La Grange, IL Zip 60525–2680; tel. 708/352–1200; Todd S. Werner, Senior Executive Officer

KENTUCKY: MEMORIAL HOSPITAL (O, 61 beds) 401 Memorial Drive, Manchester, KY Zip 40962–9156; tel. 606/598–5104; Jimm Bunch, Chief Executive Officer

For explanation of codes following names, see page B2.
★ Indicates Type III membership in the American Hospital Association.

NORTH CAROLINA: PARK RIDGE HOSPITAL (O, 92 beds) Naples Road, Fletcher, NC Zip 28732, Mailing Address: P.O. Box 1569, Zip 28732–1569; tel. 828/684–8501; Michael V. Gentry, President
Web address: www.ahss.org

PUERTO RICO: BELLA VISTA HOSPITAL (C, 157 beds) State Road 349, Mayaguez, PR Zip 00680, Mailing Address: P.O. Box 1750, Zip 00681; tel. 787/834–6000; Ruth M. Ortiz, Chief Operating Officer

TENNESSEE: JELLICO COMMUNITY HOSPITAL (L, 54 beds) 188 Hospital Lane, Jellico, TN Zip 37762–4400; tel. 423/784–7252; Jimm Bunch, President and Chief Executive Officer
Web address: www.ahss.org

TAKOMA ADVENTIST HOSPITAL (O, 80 beds) 401 Takoma Avenue, Greeneville, TN Zip 37743–4668; tel. 423/639–3151; Carlyle L. E. Walton, President

TENNESSEE CHRISTIAN MEDICAL CENTER (O, 288 beds) 500 Hospital Drive, Madison, TN Zip 37115–5032; tel. 615/865–2373; Clint Kreitner, President and Chief Executive Officer

TEXAS: CENTRAL TEXAS MEDICAL CENTER (O, 113 beds) 1301 Wonder World Drive, San Marcos, TX Zip 78666–7544; tel. 512/353–8979; Ken Bacon, President and Chief Executive Officer

HUGULEY MEMORIAL MEDICAL CENTER (O, 169 beds) 11801 South Freeway, Burleson, TX Zip 76028, Mailing Address: P.O. Box 6337, Fort Worth, Zip 76115–6337; tel. 817/293–9110; Peter M. Weber, President and Chief Executive Officer

METROPLEX ADVENTIST HOSPITAL (O, 213 beds) 2201 South Clear Creek Road, Killeen, TX Zip 76542–9305; tel. 254/526–7523; Kenneth A. Finch, Chief Executive Officer

WISCONSIN: CHIPPEWA VALLEY HOSPITAL AND OAKVIEW CARE CENTER (O, 83 beds) 1220 Third Avenue West, Durand, WI Zip 54736–1600, Mailing Address: P.O. Box 224, Zip 54736–0224; tel. 715/672–4211; Douglas R. Peterson, President and Chief Executive Officer

Owned, leased, sponsored:	18 hospitals	3769 beds
Contract–managed:	1 hospital	157 beds
Totals:	19 hospitals	3926 beds

★0064: ADVOCATE HEALTH CARE (NP)
2025 Windsor Drive, Oak Brook, IL Zip 60523; tel. 630/990–5010; Richard R. Risk, President and Chief Executive Officer

ILLINOIS: BETHANY HOSPITAL (O, 102 beds) 3435 West Van Buren Street, Chicago, IL Zip 60624–3399; tel. 773/265–7700; Lena Dobbs–Johnson, Chief Executive
Web address: www.advocatehealth.com

CHRIST HOSPITAL AND MEDICAL CENTER (O, 607 beds) 4440 West 95th Street, Oak Lawn, IL Zip 60453–2699; tel. 708/425–8000; Carol Schneider, Chief Executive Officer
Web address: www.advocatehealth.com

GOOD SAMARITAN HOSPITAL (O, 267 beds) 3815 Highland Avenue, Downers Grove, IL Zip 60515–1590; tel. 630/275–5900; David M. McConkey, Chief Executive
Web address: www.advocatehealth.com

GOOD SHEPHERD HOSPITAL (O, 154 beds) 450 West Highway 22, Barrington, IL Zip 60010–1901; tel. 847/381–9600; Russell E. Feurer, Chief Executive
Web address: www.advocatehealth.com

LUTHERAN GENERAL HOSPITAL (O, 555 beds) 1775 Dempster Street, Park Ridge, IL Zip 60068–1174; tel. 847/723–2210; Kenneth J. Rojek, Chief Executive
Web address: www.advocatehealth.com

RAVENSWOOD HOSPITAL MEDICAL CENTER (O, 301 beds) 4550 North Winchester Avenue, Chicago, IL Zip 60640–5205; tel. 773/878–4300; John E. Blair, Chief Executive

SOUTH SUBURBAN HOSPITAL (O, 185 beds) 17800 South Kedzie Avenue, Hazel Crest, IL Zip 60429–0989; tel. 708/799–8000; Robert Rutkowski, Chief Executive
Web address: www.advocatehealth.com

TRINITY HOSPITAL (O, 217 beds) 2320 East 93rd Street, Chicago, IL Zip 60617–9984; tel. 773/978–2000; John N. Schwartz, Chief Executive Officer

Owned, leased, sponsored:	8 hospitals	2388 beds
Contract–managed:	0 hospitals	0 beds
Totals:	8 hospitals	2388 beds

0225: ALAMEDA COUNTY HEALTH CARE SERVICES AGENCY (NP)
1850 Fairway Drive, San Leandro, CA Zip 94577; tel. 510/351–1367; David J. Kears, Director

CALIFORNIA: ALAMEDA COUNTY MEDICAL CENTER (O, 193 beds) 15400 Foothill Boulevard, San Leandro, CA Zip 94578–1091; tel. 510/667–7920; Michael G. Smart, Administrator

ALAMEDA COUNTY MEDICAL CENTER–HIGHLAND CAMPUS (O, 247 beds) 1411 East 31st Street, Oakland, CA Zip 94602; tel. 510/437–5081; Michael Smart, Chief Executive Officer

Owned, leased, sponsored:	2 hospitals	440 beds
Contract–managed:	0 hospitals	0 beds
Totals:	2 hospitals	440 beds

1685: ALBERT EINSTEIN HEALTHCARE NETWORK (NP)
5501 Old York Road, Philadelphia, PA Zip 19141–3098; tel. 215/456–7890; Martin Goldsmith, President

PENNSYLVANIA: ALBERT EINSTEIN MEDICAL CENTER (O, 701 beds) 5501 Old York Road, Philadelphia, PA Zip 19141–3098; tel. 215/456–7890; Martin Goldsmith, President

BELMONT CENTER FOR COMPREHENSIVE TREATMENT (O, 146 beds) 4200 Monument Road, Philadelphia, PA Zip 19131–1625; tel. 215/877–2000; Jack H. Dembow, General Director and Vice President

Owned, leased, sponsored:	2 hospitals	847 beds
Contract–managed:	0 hospitals	0 beds
Totals:	2 hospitals	847 beds

0065: ALEXIAN BROTHERS HEALTH SYSTEM, INC. (CC)
600 Alexian Way, Elk Grove Village, IL Zip 60007–3395; tel. 847/640–7550; Brother Thomas Keusenkothen, President and Chief Executive Officer

ILLINOIS: ALEXIAN BROTHERS BEHAVIORAL HEALTH HOSPITAL (O, 94 beds) 1650 Moon Lake Boulevard, Hoffman Estates, IL Zip 60194–5000; tel. 847/882–1600; Mark A. Frey, President and Chief Executive Officer

ALEXIAN BROTHERS MEDICAL CENTER (O, 395 beds) 800 Biesterfield Road, Elk Grove Village, IL Zip 60007–3397; tel. 847/437–5500; Michael J. Schwartz, President and Chief Executive Officer
Web address: www.alexian.org

ST. ALEXIUS MEDICAL CENTER (O, 195 beds) 1555 Barrington Road, Hoffman Estates, IL Zip 60194; tel. 847/843–2000; Edward M. Goldberg, President and Chief Executive Officer

Owned, leased, sponsored:	3 hospitals	684 beds
Contract–managed:	0 hospitals	0 beds
Totals:	3 hospitals	684 beds

★2305: ALLEGHENY UNIVERSITY HOSPITALS–WEST (NP)
320 East North Avenue, Pittsburgh, PA Zip 15221–2173; tel. 412/359–3010; Anthony M. Sanzo, President and Chief Executive Officer

PENNSYLVANIA: ALLEGHENY UNIVERSITY HOSPITALS–FORBES METROPOLITAN (O, 155 beds) 225 Penn Avenue, Pittsburgh, PA Zip 15221–2173; tel. 412/247–2424; April A. Stevens, R.N., Vice President and Administrator

ALLEGHENY UNIVERSITY HOSPITALS, ALLEGHENY GENERAL (O, 552 beds) 320 East North Avenue, Pittsburgh, PA Zip 15212–4756; tel. 412/359–3131; Connie M. Cibrone, President and Chief Executive Officer
Web address: www.allhealth.edu

ALLEGHENY UNIVERSITY HOSPITALS, ALLEGHENY VALLEY (O, 268 beds) 1301 Carlisle Street, Natrona Heights, PA Zip 15065–1192; tel. 724/224–5100; Joseph Calig, President and Chief Executive Officer

For explanation of codes following names, see page B2.
★ Indicates Type III membership in the American Hospital Association.

ALLEGHENY UNIVERSITY HOSPITALS, CANONSBURG (O, 120 beds) 100 Medical Boulevard, Canonsburg, PA Zip 15317–9762; tel. 724/745–6100; Barbara A. Bensaia, Chief Executive Officer

ALLEGHENY UNIVERSITY HOSPITALS, FORBES REGIONAL (O, 342 beds) 2570 Haymaker Road, Monroeville, PA Zip 15146–3592; tel. 412/858–2000; Dana W. Ramish, FACHE, President and Chief Executive Officer

Owned, leased, sponsored:	5 hospitals	1437 beds
Contract–managed:	0 hospitals	0 beds
Totals:	5 hospitals	1437 beds

★0041: ALLINA HEALTH SYSTEM (NP)

5601 Smetana Drive, Minneapolis, MN Zip 55343, Mailing Address: P.O. Box 9310, Zip 55440–9310; tel. 612/992–3992; Gordon M. Sprenger, President

MINNESOTA: ABBOTT NORTHWESTERN HOSPITAL (O, 619 beds) 800 East 28th Street, Minneapolis, MN Zip 55407–3799; tel. 612/863–4201; Mark Dixon, Administrator
Web address: www.allina.com

BUFFALO HOSPITAL (O, 30 beds) 303 Catlin Street, Buffalo, MN Zip 55313–1947; tel. 612/682–7180; Mary Ellen Wells, Administrator
Web address: www.allina.com

CAMBRIDGE MEDICAL CENTER (O, 81 beds) 701 South Dellwood Street, Cambridge, MN Zip 55008–1920; tel. 612/689–7700; Anne Renz, Interim Administrator

COMMUNITY HOSPITAL AND HEALTH CARE CENTER (C, 118 beds) 618 West Broadway, Saint Peter, MN Zip 56082–1327; tel. 507/931–2200; Colleen A. Spike, Administrator

GRANITE FALLS MUNICIPAL HOSPITAL AND MANOR (C, 94 beds) 345 Tenth Avenue, Granite Falls, MN Zip 56241–1499; tel. 320/564–3111; George Gerlach, Administrator

HUTCHINSON AREA HEALTH CARE (C, 193 beds) 1095 Highway 15 South, Hutchinson, MN Zip 55350–3182; tel. 320/234–5000; Philip G. Graves, Administrator

MERCY HOSPITAL (O, 194 beds) 4050 Coon Rapids Boulevard, Coon Rapids, MN Zip 55433–2586; tel. 612/421–8888; Marvin L. Dehne, Lead Administrator
Web address: www.allina.com

MILLE LACS HEALTH SYSTEM (C, 98 beds) 200 North Elm Street, Onamia, MN Zip 56359–7978; tel. 320/532–3154; Randall A. Farrow, Administrator

NEW ULM MEDICAL CENTER (O, 47 beds) 1324 Fifth Street North, New Ulm, MN Zip 56073–1553, Mailing Address: P.O. Box 577, Zip 56073–0577; tel. 507/354–2111; David A. Grundstrom, Administrator

NORTHFIELD HOSPITAL (C, 67 beds) 801 West First Street, Northfield, MN Zip 55057–1697; tel. 507/645–6661; Kendall C. Bank, Administrator

OWATONNA HOSPITAL (O, 66 beds) 903 Oak Street South, Owatonna, MN Zip 55060–3234; tel. 507/451–3850; Daniel J. Werner, Administrator
Web address: www.allina.com

PHILLIPS EYE INSTITUTE (O, 10 beds) 2215 Park Avenue, Minneapolis, MN Zip 55404–3756; tel. 612/336–6000; Shari E. Levy, Administrator
Web address: www.allina.com

ST. FRANCIS REGIONAL MEDICAL CENTER (O, 63 beds) 1455 St. Francis Avenue, Shakopee, MN Zip 55379–3380; tel. 612/403–3000; Venetia Kudrle, Administrator

STEVENS COMMUNITY MEDICAL CENTER (C, 37 beds) 400 East First Street, Morris, MN Zip 56267–1407, Mailing Address: P.O. Box 660, Zip 56267–0660; tel. 320/589–1313; John Rau, Administrator

UNITED HOSPITAL (O, 386 beds) 333 North Smith Street, Saint Paul, MN Zip 55102–2389; tel. 651/220–8000; M. Barbara Balik, MSN, Ed.D., Administrator
Web address: www.allina.com

UNITED HOSPITAL DISTRICT (C, 24 beds) 515 South Moore Street, Blue Earth, MN Zip 56013–2158, Mailing Address: P.O. Box 160, Zip 56013–0160; tel. 507/526–3273; Brian Kief, Administrator

UNITY HOSPITAL (O, 190 beds) 550 Osborne Road N.E., Fridley, MN Zip 55432–2799; tel. 612/421–2222;
Web address: www.allina.com

WISCONSIN: RIVER FALLS AREA HOSPITAL (O, 36 beds) 1629 East Division Street, River Falls, WI Zip 54022–1571; tel. 715/425–6155; Sharon Whelan, Administrator

Owned, leased, sponsored:	11 hospitals	1722 beds
Contract–managed:	7 hospitals	631 beds
Totals:	18 hospitals	2353 beds

★0135: ANCILLA SYSTEMS INC. (CC)

1000 South Lake Park Avenue, Hobart, IN Zip 46342–5970; tel. 219/947–8500; William D. Harkins, President and Chief Executive Officer

ILLINOIS: ST. ELIZABETH'S HOSPITAL (O, 224 beds) 1431 North Claremont Avenue, Chicago, IL Zip 60622–1791; tel. 773/278–2000; JoAnn Birdzell, President and Chief Executive Officer

ST. MARY'S HOSPITAL (O, 119 beds) 129 North Eighth Street, East St. Louis, IL Zip 62201–2999; tel. 618/274–1900; Richard J. Mark, President and Chief Executive Officer

INDIANA: COMMUNITY HOSPITAL OF BREMEN (C, 28 beds) 411 South Whitlock Street, Bremen, IN Zip 46506–1699, Mailing Address: P.O. Box 8, Zip 46506–0008; tel. 219/546–2211; Scott R. Graybill, Chief Executive Officer and Administrator

ST. CATHERINE HOSPITAL (O, 188 beds) 4321 Fir Street, East Chicago, IN Zip 46312–3097; tel. 219/392–7000; JoAnn Birdzell, President and Chief Executive Officer

ST. JOSEPH COMMUNITY HOSPITAL (O, 100 beds) 215 West Fourth Street, Mishawaka, IN Zip 46544–1999; tel. 219/259–2431; Mary Roos, President and Chief Executive Officer
Web address: www.ancillahealthcare.org

ST. MARY MEDICAL CENTER (O, 102 beds) 1500 South Lake Park Avenue, Hobart, IN Zip 46342–6699; tel. 219/942–0551; Milton Triana, President and Chief Executive Officer
Web address: www.stmary–hobart.com

Owned, leased, sponsored:	5 hospitals	733 beds
Contract–managed:	1 hospital	28 beds
Totals:	6 hospitals	761 beds

0145: APPALACHIAN REGIONAL HEALTHCARE (NP)

1220 Harrodsburg Road, Lexington, KY Zip 40504, Mailing Address: P.O. Box 8086, Zip 40533–8086; tel. 606/226–2440; Forrest Calico, M.D., President

KENTUCKY: ARH REGIONAL MEDICAL CENTER (O, 288 beds) 100 Medical Center Drive, Hazard, KY Zip 41701–1000; tel. 606/439–6610; Charles E. Housley, FACHE, Administrator
Web address: www.arh.org

HARLAN ARH HOSPITAL (O, 125 beds) 81 Ball Park Road, Harlan, KY Zip 40831–1792; tel. 606/573–8100; Daniel Fitzpatrick, Chief Executive Officer

MCDOWELL ARH HOSPITAL (O, 74 beds) Route 122, McDowell, KY Zip 41647, Mailing Address: P.O. Box 247, Mc Dowell, Zip 41647–0247; tel. 606/377–3400; Dena C. Sparkman, Administrator

MIDDLESBORO APPALACHIAN REGIONAL HOSPITAL (O, 96 beds) 3600 West Cumberland Avenue, Middlesboro, KY Zip 40965–2614, Mailing Address: P.O. Box 340, Zip 40965–0340; tel. 606/242–1101; Paul V. Miles, Administrator

MORGAN COUNTY APPALACHIAN REGIONAL HOSPITAL (L, 45 beds) 476 Liberty Road, West Liberty, KY Zip 41472–2049, Mailing Address: P.O. Box 579, Zip 41472–0579; tel. 606/743–3186; Dennis R. Chaney, Administrator
Web address: www.2.arh.org

WHITESBURG APPALACHIAN REGIONAL HOSPITAL (O, 71 beds) 240 Hospital Road, Whitesburg, KY Zip 41858–1254; tel. 606/633–3600; Donnie Fields, Administrator

WILLIAMSON ARH HOSPITAL (O, 148 beds) 260 Hospital Drive, South Williamson, KY Zip 41503–4072; tel. 606/237–1700; Louis G. Roe Jr., Administrator
Web address: www.arh.org

For explanation of codes following names, see page B2.
★ Indicates Type III membership in the American Hospital Association.

WEST VIRGINIA: BECKLEY APPALACHIAN REGIONAL HOSPITAL (O, 173 beds) 306 Stanaford Road, Beckley, WV Zip 25801–3142; tel. 304/255–3000; David R. Lyon, Administrator

MAN ARH HOSPITAL (O, 46 beds) 700 East McDonald Avenue, Man, WV Zip 25635–1011; tel. 304/583–8421; Erica McDonald, Administrator

SUMMERS COUNTY APPALACHIAN REGIONAL HOSPITAL (L, 50 beds) Terrace Street, Hinton, WV Zip 25951, Mailing Address: Drawer 940, Zip 25951–0940; tel. 304/466–1000; Rocco K. Massey, Administrator
Web address: www.arh.org

Owned, leased, sponsored:	10 hospitals	1116 beds
Contract–managed:	0 hospitals	0 beds
Totals:	10 hospitals	1116 beds

0104: ARCHBOLD MEDICAL CENTER (NP)
910 South Broad Street, Thomasville, GA Zip 31792–6113; tel. 912/228–2739; Ken B. Beverly, President and Chief Executive Officer

GEORGIA: BROOKS COUNTY HOSPITAL (L, 35 beds) 903 North Court Street, Quitman, GA Zip 31643–1315, Mailing Address: P.O. Box 5000, Zip 31643–5000; tel. 912/263–4171; Andrew J. Finnegan, CHE, Administrator

EARLY MEMORIAL HOSPITAL (L, 164 beds) 630 Columbia Street, Blakely, GA Zip 31723–1798; tel. 912/723–4241; Rodney C. Watford, Administrator

GRADY GENERAL HOSPITAL (L, 45 beds) 1155 Fifth Street S.E., Cairo, GA Zip 31728–3142, Mailing Address: P.O. Box 360, Zip 31728–0360; tel. 912/377–1150; Glen C. Davis, Administrator
Web address: www.archbold.org

JOHN D. ARCHBOLD MEMORIAL HOSPITAL (O, 264 beds) Gordon Avenue at Mimosa Drive, Thomasville, GA Zip 31792–6113, Mailing Address: P.O. Box 1018, Zip 31799–1018; tel. 912/228–2000; Jason H. Moore, President and Chief Executive Officer
Web address: www.archbold.org

MITCHELL COUNTY HOSPITAL (L, 24 beds) 90 Stephens Street, Camilla, GA Zip 31730–1899, Mailing Address: P.O. Box 639, Zip 31730–0639; tel. 912/336–5284; Ronald M. Gilliard, FACHE, Administrator

Owned, leased, sponsored:	5 hospitals	532 beds
Contract–managed:	0 hospitals	0 beds
Totals:	5 hospitals	532 beds

★0094: ASANTE HEALTH SYSTEM (NP)
2650 Siskiyou Boulevard, Suite 200, Medford, OR Zip 97504–8389; tel. 541/608–4100; Roy G. Vinyard II, Chief Administrative Officer

OREGON: ROGUE VALLEY MEDICAL CENTER (O, 249 beds) 2825 East Barnett Road, Medford, OR Zip 97504–8332; tel. 541/608–4900; Mark W. Folger, FACHE, Senior Vice President

THREE RIVERS COMMUNITY HOSPITAL AND HEALTH CENTER (O, 150 beds) 715 N.W. Dimmick Street, Grants Pass, OR Zip 97526–1596; tel. 541/476–6831; Paul Janke, Chief Operating Officer

Owned, leased, sponsored:	2 hospitals	399 beds
Contract–managed:	0 hospitals	0 beds
Totals:	2 hospitals	399 beds

★2215: AURORA HEALTH CARE (NP)
3000 West Montana, Milwaukee, WI Zip 53215–3268, Mailing Address: P.O. Box 343910, Zip 53234–3910; tel. 414/647–3000; G. Edwin Howe, President

WISCONSIN: HARTFORD MEMORIAL HOSPITAL (O, 71 beds) 1032 East Sumner Street, Hartford, WI Zip 53027–1698; tel. 414/673–2300; Mark Schwartz, Administrator

LAKELAND MEDICAL CENTER (O, 78 beds) West 3985 County Road NN, Elkhorn, WI Zip 53121, Mailing Address: P.O. Box 1002, Zip 53121–1002; tel. 414/741–2000; Loren J. Anderson, Executive Vice President

MEMORIAL HOSPITAL CORPORATION OF BURLINGTON (O, 87 beds) 252 McHenry Street, Burlington, WI Zip 53105–1828; tel. 414/767–6000; Loren J. Anderson, Executive Vice President

MILWAUKEE PSYCHIATRIC HOSPITAL (O, 75 beds) 1220 Dewey Avenue, Wauwatosa, WI Zip 53213–2598; tel. 414/454–6600; James A. Moore, Administrator

SHEBOYGAN MEMORIAL MEDICAL CENTER (O, 219 beds) 2629 North Seventh Street, Sheboygan, WI Zip 53083–4998; tel. 920/451–5000; T. Gregg Watson, Administrator

SINAI SAMARITAN MEDICAL CENTER (O, 316 beds) 945 North 12th Street, Milwaukee, WI Zip 53233–1337, Mailing Address: P.O. Box 342, Zip 53201–0342; tel. 414/219–2000; Leonard E. Wilk, Administrator
Web address: www.aurorahealthcare.org

ST. LUKE'S MEDICAL CENTER (O, 765 beds) 2900 West Oklahoma Avenue, Milwaukee, WI Zip 53215–4330, Mailing Address: P.O. Box 2901, Zip 53201–2901; tel. 414/649–6000; Mark S. Wiener, Administrator

ST. MARY'S KEWAUNEE AREA MEMORIAL HOSPITAL (O, 18 beds) 810 Lincoln Street, Kewaunee, WI Zip 54216; tel. 920/388–2210; Cathie A. Kocourek, Acting Administrator

TWO RIVERS COMMUNITY HOSPITAL AND HAMILTON MEMORIAL HOME (O, 138 beds) 2500 Garfield Street, Two Rivers, WI Zip 54241–2399; tel. 920/793–1178; Cathie A. Kocourek, Acting Administrator

VALLEY VIEW MEDICAL CENTER (O, 92 beds) 901 Reed Street, Plymouth, WI Zip 53073–2409; tel. 920/893–1771; T. Gregg Watson, Administrator

WEST ALLIS MEMORIAL HOSPITAL (O, 158 beds) 8901 West Lincoln Avenue, West Allis, WI Zip 53227–0901, Mailing Address: P.O. Box 27901, Zip 53227–0901; tel. 414/328–6000; Richard A. Kellar, Administrator

Owned, leased, sponsored:	11 hospitals	2017 beds
Contract–managed:	0 hospitals	0 beds
Totals:	11 hospitals	2017 beds

★5255: AVERA HEALTH (CC)
610 West 23rd Street, Yankton, SD Zip 57078, Mailing Address: P.O. Box 38, Zip 57078–0038; tel. 605/322–7050; John T. Porter, President and Chief Executive Officer

IOWA: AVERA HOLY FAMILY HEALTH (O, 36 beds) 826 North Eighth Street, Estherville, IA Zip 51334–1598; tel. 712/362–2631; Thomas Nordwick, President and Chief Executive Officer

FLOYD VALLEY HOSPITAL (C, 44 beds) Highway 3 East, Le Mars, IA Zip 51031, Mailing Address: P.O. Box 10, Zip 51031–0010; tel. 712/546–7871; Michael Donlin, Administrator
Web address: www.floydvalleyhospital.org

HEGG MEMORIAL HEALTH CENTER (C, 123 beds) 1202 21st Avenue, Rock Valley, IA Zip 51247–1497; tel. 712/476–5305; Chris Thomas, Administrator and Chief Executive Officer

OSCEOLA COMMUNITY HOSPITAL (C, 32 beds) Ninth Avenue North, Sibley, IA Zip 51249–0258, Mailing Address: P.O. Box 258, Zip 51249–0258; tel. 712/754–2574; Janet Dykstra, Chief Executive Officer

SIOUX CENTER COMMUNITY HOSPITAL AND HEALTH CENTER (C, 90 beds) 605 South Main Avenue, Sioux Center, IA Zip 51250–1398; tel. 712/722–1271; Marla Toering, Administrator

MINNESOTA: DIVINE PROVIDENCE HEALTH CENTER (C, 69 beds) 312 East George Street, Ivanhoe, MN Zip 56142–0136, Mailing Address: P.O. Box G., Zip 56142–0136; tel. 507/694–1414; Patrick Branco, Administrator

PIPESTONE COUNTY MEDICAL CENTER (C, 76 beds) 911 Fifth Avenue S.W., Pipestone, MN Zip 56164; tel. 507/825–6125; Carl P. Vaagenes, Administrator

TYLER HEALTHCARE CENTER (C, 63 beds) 240 Willow Street, Tyler, MN Zip 56178–0280; tel. 507/247–5521; James G. Blum, Administrator

NEBRASKA: AVERA ST. ANTHONY'S HOSPITAL (C, 29 beds) Second and Adams Streets, O'Neill, NE Zip 68763–1597; tel. 402/336–2611; Ronald J. Cork, President and Chief Executive Officer

SOUTH DAKOTA: AVERA MCKENNAN HOSPITAL (O, 521 beds) 800 East 21st Street, Sioux Falls, SD Zip 57105–1096, Mailing Address: P.O. Box 5045, Zip 57117–5045; tel. 605/322–8000; Fredrick Slunecka, President and Chief Executive Officer
Web address: www.mckennan.com

AVERA QUEEN OF PEACE (O, 183 beds) 525 North Foster, Mitchell, SD Zip 57301–2999; tel. 605/995–2000; Ronald L. Jacobson, President and Chief Executive Officer

For explanation of codes following names, see page B2.
★ Indicates Type III membership in the American Hospital Association.

AVERA SACRED HEART HEALTH SERVICES (C, 257 beds) 501 Summit Avenue, Yankton, SD Zip 57078–3899; tel. 605/668–8000; Pamela J. Rezac, President and Chief Executive Officer

AVERA ST. BENEDICT HEALTH CENTER (C, 105 beds) Glynn Drive, Parkston, SD Zip 57366, Mailing Address: P.O. Box B, Zip 57366; tel. 605/928–3311; Gale Walker, Administrator
Web address: www.parkston.com

AVERA ST. LUKE'S (O, 224 beds) 305 South State Street, Aberdeen, SD Zip 57402–4450; tel. 605/622–5000; Dale J. Stein, President and Chief Executive Officer
Web address: www.averastlukes.org

COMMUNITY MEMORIAL HOSPITAL (C, 16 beds) Eighth and Jackson, Burke, SD Zip 57523, Mailing Address: P.O. Box 319, Zip 57523–0319; tel. 605/775–2621; Carol A. Varland, Chief Executive Officer

EUREKA COMMUNITY HEALTH SERVICES (C, 6 beds) 410 Ninth Street, Eureka, SD Zip 57437–0517; tel. 605/284–2661; Robert A. Dockter, Administrator

FLANDREAU MUNICIPAL HOSPITAL (C, 18 beds) 214 North Prairie Avenue, Flandreau, SD Zip 57028–1243; tel. 605/997–2433; Curtis Hohman, Interim Administrator

HAND COUNTY MEMORIAL HOSPITAL (C, 21 beds) 300 West Fifth Street, Miller, SD Zip 57362–1238; tel. 605/853–2421; Clarence A. Lee, Administrator

MARSHALL COUNTY HEALTHCARE CENTER (C, 20 beds) 413 Ninth Street, Britton, SD Zip 57430–0230, Mailing Address: Box 230, Zip 57430–0230; tel. 605/448–2253; Stephanie Lulewicz, Administrator

PLATTE COMMUNITY MEMORIAL HOSPITAL (C, 63 beds) 609 East Seventh, Platte, SD Zip 57369–2123, Mailing Address: P.O. Box 200, Zip 57369–0200; tel. 605/337–3364; Mark Burket, Chief Executive Officer

Owned, leased, sponsored:	4 hospitals	964 beds
Contract–managed:	16 hospitals	1032 beds
Totals:	20 hospitals	1996 beds

0150: BAPTIST HEALTH (NP)
2105 East South Boulevard, Montgomery, AL Zip 36116–2498; tel. 334/286–2970; Michael D. DeBoer, President and Chief Executive Officer

ALABAMA: BAPTIST MEDICAL CENTER (O, 329 beds) 2105 East South Boulevard, Montgomery, AL Zip 36116–2498, Mailing Address: Box 11010, Zip 36111–0010; tel. 334/288–2100; Michael D. DeBoer, President and Chief Executive Officer

BAPTIST MEDICAL CENTER DOWNTOWN (O, 250 beds) 301 South Ripley Street, Montgomery, AL Zip 36104–4495; tel. 334/269–8000; Alfred E. Hargrave, Administrator

BAPTIST MEDICAL CENTER EAST (O, 150 beds) 400 Taylor Road, Montgomery, AL Zip 36117–3512, Mailing Address: P.O. Box 241267, Zip 36124–1267; tel. 334/277–8330; John W. Melton, Administrator

CRENSHAW BAPTIST HOSPITAL (O, 52 beds) 1625 South Forrest Avenue, Luverne, AL Zip 36049; tel. 334/335–3374; L. Wayne Sasser, Vice President and Administrator

PRATTVILLE BAPTIST HOSPITAL (O, 51 beds) 124 South Memorial Drive, Prattville, AL Zip 36067–3619, Mailing Address: P.O. Box 681630, Zip 36067–1638; tel. 334/365–0651; William E. Hines, Administrator

SELMA BAPTIST HOSPITAL (O, 192 beds) 1015 Medical Center Parkway, Selma, AL Zip 36701–6352; tel. 334/418–4100; John Anderson, Administrator

Owned, leased, sponsored:	6 hospitals	1024 beds
Contract–managed:	0 hospitals	0 beds
Totals:	6 hospitals	1024 beds

★0355: BAPTIST HEALTH (NP)
9601 Interstate 630, Exit 7, Little Rock, AR Zip 72205–7299; tel. 501/202–2000; Russell D. Harrington Jr., President

ARKANSAS: BAPTIST MEDICAL CENTER (O, 519 beds) 9601 Interstate 630, Exit 7, Little Rock, AR Zip 72205–7299; tel. 501/202–2000; Steven Douglas Weeks, Senior Vice President and Administrator

BAPTIST MEDICAL CENTER ARKADELPHIA (L, 57 beds) 3050 Twin Rivers Drive, Arkadelphia, AR Zip 71923–4299; tel. 870/245–1100; Dan Gathright, Senior Vice President and Administrator

BAPTIST MEDICAL CENTER HEBER SPRINGS (L, 24 beds) 2319 Highway 110 West, Heber Springs, AR Zip 72543; tel. 501/206–3000; Edward L. Lacy, Administrator

BAPTIST MEMORIAL MEDICAL CENTER (L, 200 beds) One Pershing Circle, North Little Rock, AR Zip 72114–1899; tel. 501/202–3000; Harrison M. Dean, Senior Vice President and Administrator
Web address: www.baptist–health.org

BAPTIST REHABILITATION INSTITUTE (O, 100 beds) 9601 Interstate 630, Exit 7, Little Rock, AR Zip 72205–7249; tel. 501/202–7000; Steven Douglas Weeks, Senior Vice President and Administrator

Owned, leased, sponsored:	5 hospitals	900 beds
Contract–managed:	0 hospitals	0 beds
Totals:	5 hospitals	900 beds

0185: BAPTIST HEALTH CARE CORPORATION (NP)
1717 North E Street, Suite 320, Pensacola, FL Zip 32501–6335; tel. 850/469–2337; Alfred G. Stubblefield, President

ALABAMA: MIZELL MEMORIAL HOSPITAL (O, 57 beds) 702 Main Street, Opp, AL Zip 36467–1626, Mailing Address: P.O. Box 1010, Zip 36467–1010; tel. 334/493–3541; Allen Foster, Administrator

FLORIDA: BAPTIST HOSPITAL (O, 492 beds) 1000 West Moreno, Pensacola, FL Zip 32501–2393, Mailing Address: P.O. Box 17500, Zip 32522–7500; tel. 850/469–2313; Quinton Studer, President
Web address: www.bhcpns.org

GULF BREEZE HOSPITAL (O, 60 beds) 1110 Gulf Breeze Parkway, Gulf Breeze, FL Zip 32561, Mailing Address: P.O. Box 159, Zip 32562; tel. 850/934–2000; Richard C. Fulford, Administrator

JAY HOSPITAL (L, 47 beds) 221 South Alabama Street, Jay, FL Zip 32565–1070, Mailing Address: P.O. Box 397, Zip 32565–0397; tel. 850/675–8000; Robert E. Gowing, Administrator

THE FRIARY OF BAPTIST HEALTH CENTER (O, 30 beds) 4400 Hickory Shores Boulevard, Gulf Breeze, FL Zip 32561–9113; tel. 904/932–9375; Leo J. Donnelly, Executive Director

Owned, leased, sponsored:	5 hospitals	686 beds
Contract–managed:	0 hospitals	0 beds
Totals:	5 hospitals	686 beds

0265: BAPTIST HEALTH SYSTEM (CO)
200 Concord Plaza, Suite 900, San Antonio, TX Zip 78216; tel. 210/297–1000; Fred R. Mills, President and Chief Executive Officer

TEXAS: BAPTIST MEDICAL CENTER (O, 481 beds) 111 Dallas Street, San Antonio, TX Zip 78205–1230; tel. 210/297–7000; Perry Willmore, Vice President Operations
Web address: www.baptisthealthsystem.org

NORTH CENTRAL BAPTIST HOSPITAL (O, 50 beds) 520 Madison Oak Drive, San Antonio, TX Zip 78258–3912; Dan Brown, Administrator

NORTHEAST BAPTIST HOSPITAL (O, 210 beds) 8811 Village Drive, San Antonio, TX Zip 78217–5440; tel. 210/653–2330; Dan Brown, Administrator

SOUTHEAST BAPTIST HOSPITAL (O, 153 beds) 4214 East Southcross Boulevard, San Antonio, TX Zip 78222–3740; tel. 210/297–3000; Kevin Walters, Administrator

ST. LUKE'S BAPTIST HOSPITAL (O, 219 beds) 7930 Floyd Curl Drive, San Antonio, TX Zip 78229–0100; tel. 210/692–8703

Owned, leased, sponsored:	5 hospitals	1113 beds
Contract–managed:	0 hospitals	0 beds
Totals:	5 hospitals	1113 beds

★0345: BAPTIST HEALTH SYSTEM (CO)
Birmingham, AL Mailing Address: P.O. Box 830605, Zip 35283–0605; tel. 205/715–5319; Dennis A. Hall, President

For explanation of codes following names, see page B2.
★ Indicates Type III membership in the American Hospital Association.

Section B

ALABAMA: CHEROKEE BAPTIST MEDICAL CENTER (O, 45 beds) 400 Northwood Drive, Centre, AL Zip 35960–1023; tel. 256/927–5531; Barry S. Cochran, President

CITIZENS BAPTIST MEDICAL CENTER (O, 97 beds) 604 Stone Avenue, Talladega, AL Zip 35160–2217, Mailing Address: P.O. Box 978, Zip 35161–0978; tel. 256/362–8111; Steven M. Johnson, President
Web address: www.bhsala.com

COOSA VALLEY BAPTIST MEDICAL CENTER (O, 176 beds) 315 West Hickory Street, Sylacauga, AL Zip 35150–2996; tel. 256/249–5000; Steven M. Johnson, President

CULLMAN REGIONAL MEDICAL CENTER (O, 115 beds) 1912 Alabama Highway 157, Cullman, AL Zip 35055, Mailing Address: P.O. Box 1108, Zip 35056–1108; tel. 256/737–2000; Jesse O. Weatherly, President

DEKALB BAPTIST MEDICAL CENTER (O, 91 beds) 200 Medical Center Drive, Fort Payne, AL Zip 35968–3415, Mailing Address: P.O. Box 680778, Zip 35968–1608; tel. 256/845–3150; Barry S. Cochran, President
Web address: www.bhsala.com

LAWRENCE BAPTIST MEDICAL CENTER (L, 30 beds) 202 Hospital Street, Moulton, AL Zip 35650–0039, Mailing Address: P.O. Box 39, Zip 35650–0039; tel. 256/974–2200; Cheryl Hays, Administrator

MARION BAPTIST MEDICAL CENTER (L, 112 beds) 1256 Military Street South, Hamilton, AL Zip 35570–5001; tel. 205/921–6200; Evan S. Dillard, President

MONTCLAIR BAPTIST MEDICAL CENTER (O, 1023 beds) 800 Montclair Road, Birmingham, AL Zip 35213–1984; tel. 205/592–1000; John Shelton, President

PRINCETON BAPTIST MEDICAL CENTER (O, 1033 beds) 701 Princeton Avenue S.W., Birmingham, AL Zip 35211–1305; tel. 205/783–3000; Charlie Faulkner, President

RANDOLPH COUNTY HOSPITAL (C, 71 beds) 59928 Highway 22, Roanoke, AL Zip 36274, Mailing Address: P.O. Box 670, Zip 36274–0670; tel. 334/863–4111; Moultrie D. Plowden, CHE, President

SHELBY BAPTIST MEDICAL CENTER (O, 228 beds) 1000 First Street North, Alabaster, AL Zip 35007–0488, Mailing Address: Box 488, Zip 35007–0488; tel. 205/620–8100; Charles C. Colvert, President

WALKER BAPTIST MEDICAL CENTER (O, 245 beds) 3400 Highway 78 East, Jasper, AL Zip 35501–8956, Mailing Address: P.O. Box 3547, Zip 35502–3547; tel. 205/387–4000; Jeff Brewer, President

WEDOWEE HOSPITAL (C, 34 beds) 209 North Main Street, Wedowee, AL Zip 36278–5138, Mailing Address: P.O. Box 307, Zip 36278–0307; tel. 256/357–2111; Moultrie D. Plowden, CHE, President

Owned, leased, sponsored:	11 hospitals	3195 beds
Contract–managed:	2 hospitals	105 beds
Totals:	13 hospitals	3300 beds

0122: BAPTIST HEALTH SYSTEM OF SOUTH FLORIDA (NP)
6855 Red Road, Suite 600, Coral Gables, FL Zip 33143–3632; tel. 305/273–2333; Brian E. Keeley, President and Chief Executive Officer

FLORIDA: BAPTIST HOSPITAL OF MIAMI (O, 457 beds) 8900 North Kendall Drive, Miami, FL Zip 33176–2197; tel. 305/596–1960; Lee S. Huntley, Chief Executive Officer
Web address: www.baptisthealth.net

HOMESTEAD HOSPITAL (O, 100 beds) 160 N.W. 13th Street, Homestead, FL Zip 33030–4299; tel. 305/248–3232; Bo Boulenger, Chief Executive Officer

MARINERS HOSPITAL (S, 31 beds) 91500 Overseas Highway, Tavernier, FL Zip 33070; tel. 305/852–4418; Robert H. Luse, Chief Executive Officer
Web address: www.bhssf.org

SOUTH MIAMI HOSPITAL (O, 397 beds) 6200 S.W. 73rd Street, Miami, FL Zip 33143–9990; tel. 305/661–4611; D. Wayne Brackin, Chief Executive Officer
Web address: www.baptisthealth.net

Owned, leased, sponsored:	4 hospitals	985 beds
Contract–managed:	0 hospitals	0 beds
Totals:	4 hospitals	985 beds

2155: BAPTIST HEALTH SYSTEM OF TENNESSEE (NP)
137 Blount Avenue S.E., Knoxville, TN Zip 37920–1643, Mailing Address: P.O. Box 1788, Zip 37901–1788; tel. 615/632–5099; Dale Collins, President and Chief Executive Officer

TENNESSEE: BAPTIST HOSPITAL OF COCKE COUNTY (O, 109 beds) 435 Second Street, Newport, TN Zip 37821–3799; tel. 423/625–2200; Wayne Buckner, Administrator
Web address: www.baptistoneword.org/

BAPTIST HOSPITAL OF EAST TENNESSEE (O, 299 beds) 137 Blount Avenue S.E., Knoxville, TN Zip 37920–1643, Mailing Address: P.O. Box 1788, Zip 37901–1788; tel. 423/632–5011; Jon Foster, Executive Vice President and Administrator

Owned, leased, sponsored:	2 hospitals	408 beds
Contract–managed:	0 hospitals	0 beds
Totals:	2 hospitals	408 beds

★0315: BAPTIST HEALTHCARE SYSTEM (CO)
4007 Kresge Way, Louisville, KY Zip 40207–4677; tel. 502/896–5000; Tommy J. Smith, President and Chief Executive Officer

KENTUCKY: BAPTIST HOSPITAL EAST (O, 407 beds) 4000 Kresge Way, Louisville, KY Zip 40207–4676; tel. 502/897–8100; Susan Stout Tamme, President
Web address: www.baptisteast.com

BAPTIST REGIONAL MEDICAL CENTER (O, 240 beds) 1 Trillium Way, Corbin, KY Zip 40701–8420; tel. 606/528–1212; John S. Henson, President

CENTRAL BAPTIST HOSPITAL (O, 355 beds) 1740 Nicholasville Road, Lexington, KY Zip 40503; tel. 606/260–6100; William G. Sisson, President
Web address: www.centralbap.com

HARDIN MEMORIAL HOSPITAL (C, 270 beds) 913 North Dixie Avenue, Elizabethtown, KY Zip 42701–2599; tel. 502/737–1212; David L. Gray, President
Web address: www.hmh.net

TRI COUNTY BAPTIST HOSPITAL (O, 105 beds) 1025 New Moody Lane, La Grange, KY Zip 40031–0559; tel. 502/222–5388; Dennis B. Johnson, Administrator

WESTERN BAPTIST HOSPITAL (O, 267 beds) 2501 Kentucky Avenue, Paducah, KY Zip 42003–3200; tel. 502/575–2100; Larry O. Barton, President

Owned, leased, sponsored:	5 hospitals	1374 beds
Contract–managed:	1 hospital	270 beds
Totals:	6 hospitals	1644 beds

★8810: BAPTIST HOSPITALS AND HEALTH SYSTEMS, INC. (NP)
2224 West Northern Avenue, Suite D–300, Phoenix, AZ Zip 85021–4987; tel. 602/864–1184; Gerald L. Wissink, President and Chief Executive Officer

ARIZONA: ARROWHEAD COMMUNITY HOSPITAL AND MEDICAL CENTER (C, 104 beds) 18701 North 67th Avenue, Glendale, AZ Zip 85308–5722; tel. 602/561–1000; Richard S. Alley, Executive Vice President and Chief Executive Officer
Web address: www.baptisthealth.com

LA PAZ REGIONAL HOSPITAL (C, 39 beds) 1200 Mohave Road, Parker, AZ Zip 85344–6349; tel. 520/669–9201; William G. Coe, Executive Vice President and Chief Executive Officer

PHOENIX BAPTIST HOSPITAL AND MEDICAL CENTER (C, 222 beds) 2000 West Bethany Home Road, Phoenix, AZ Zip 85015–2110; tel. 602/249–0212; Michael Purvis, Executive Vice President and Chief Executive Officer
Web address: www.baptisthealth.com

WESTERN ARIZONA REGIONAL MEDICAL CENTER (C, 203 beds) 2735 Silver Creek Road, Bullhead City, AZ Zip 86442–8303; tel. 520/763–2273; James Sato, Senior Vice President and Chief Executive Officer

For explanation of codes following names, see page B2.
★ Indicates Type III membership in the American Hospital Association.

Section B

Owned, leased, sponsored:	0 hospitals	0 beds
Contract–managed:	4 hospitals	568 beds
Totals:	4 hospitals	568 beds

★1625: BAPTIST MEMORIAL HEALTH CARE CORPORATION (NP)

899 Madison Avenue, Memphis, TN Zip 38146–0001; tel. 901/227–5117; Stephen Curtis Reynolds, President and Chief Executive Officer

ARKANSAS: BAPTIST MEMORIAL HOSPITAL–BLYTHEVILLE (L, 195 beds) 1520 North Division Street, Blytheville, AR Zip 72315, Mailing Address: P.O. Box 108, Zip 72316–0108; tel. 870/838–7300; Al Sypniewski, Administrator
Web address: www.bmhcc.org

BAPTIST MEMORIAL HOSPITAL–FORREST CITY (L, 86 beds) 1601 Newcastle Road, Forrest City, AR Zip 72335, Mailing Address: P.O. Box 667, Zip 72336–0667; tel. 870/261–0000; Charles R. Daugherty, Administrator

BAPTIST MEMORIAL HOSPITAL–OSCEOLA (L, 59 beds) 611 West Lee Avenue, Osceola, AR Zip 72370–3001, Mailing Address: P.O. Box 607, Zip 72370–0607; tel. 870/563–7000; Joel E. North, Administrator

MISSISSIPPI: BAPTIST MEMORIAL HOSPITAL–BOONEVILLE (L, 99 beds) 100 Hospital Street, Booneville, MS Zip 38829–3359; tel. 601/720–5000; Pamela W. Roberts, Administrator

BAPTIST MEMORIAL HOSPITAL–DESOTO (O, 260 beds) 7601 Southcrest Parkway, Southaven, MS Zip 38671–4742; tel. 601/349–4000; Melvin E. Walker, Administrator

BAPTIST MEMORIAL HOSPITAL–GOLDEN TRIANGLE (L, 328 beds) 2520 Fifth Street North, Columbus, MS Zip 39703–2095, Mailing Address: P.O. Box 1307, Zip 39701–1307; tel. 601/244–1000; Douglas L. Johnson, Administrator

BAPTIST MEMORIAL HOSPITAL–NORTH MISSISSIPPI (L, 204 beds) 2301 South Lamar Boulevard, Oxford, MS Zip 38655–5338, Mailing Address: P.O. Box 946, Zip 38655–0946; tel. 601/232–8100; James Hahn, Administrator

BAPTIST MEMORIAL HOSPITAL–UNION COUNTY (L, 153 beds) 200 Highway 30 West, New Albany, MS Zip 38652–3197; tel. 601/538–7631; John Tompkins, Administrator

TIPPAH COUNTY HOSPITAL (C, 110 beds) 1005 City Avenue North, Ripley, MS Zip 38663–0499; tel. 601/837–9221; Jerry Green, Administrator

TENNESSEE: BAPTIST MEMORIAL HOSPITAL (O, 1072 beds) 899 Madison Avenue, Memphis, TN Zip 38146–0001; tel. 901/227–2727; Stephen Curtis Reynolds, President and Chief Executive Officer

BAPTIST MEMORIAL HOSPITAL–HUNTINGDON (O, 70 beds) 631 R. B. Wilson Drive, Huntingdon, TN Zip 38344–1675; tel. 901/986–4461; Susan M. Breeden, Administrator

BAPTIST MEMORIAL HOSPITAL–LAUDERDALE (O, 70 beds) 326 Asbury Road, Ripley, TN Zip 38063–9701; tel. 901/221–2200; Joe Hunsucker, Administrator
Web address: www.bmhcc.org

BAPTIST MEMORIAL HOSPITAL–TIPTON (O, 48 beds) 1995 Highway 51 South, Covington, TN Zip 38019–3635; tel. 901/476–2621; Glenn Baker, Administrator

BAPTIST MEMORIAL HOSPITAL–UNION CITY (O, 133 beds) 1201 Bishop Street, Union City, TN Zip 38261–5403, Mailing Address: P.O. Box 310, Zip 38281–0310; tel. 901/884–8601; Mike Perryman, Administrator
Web address: www.columbia.net

BAPTIST REHABILITATION–GERMANTOWN (O, 75 beds) 2100 Exeter Road, Germantown, TN Zip 38138; tel. 901/757–1350; Paula Gisler, Administrator

Owned, leased, sponsored:	14 hospitals	2852 beds
Contract–managed:	1 hospital	110 beds
Totals:	15 hospitals	2962 beds

★0095: BAYLOR HEALTH CARE SYSTEM (CO)

3500 Gaston Avenue, Dallas, TX Zip 75226–2088; tel. 214/820–0111; Boone Powell Jr., President

TEXAS: BAYLOR CENTER FOR RESTORATIVE CARE (O, 72 beds) 3504 Swiss Avenue, Dallas, TX Zip 75204–6224; tel. 214/820–9700; Gerry Brueckner, R.N., Executive Director
Web address: www.baylordallas.edu/

BAYLOR INSTITUTE FOR REHABILITATION (O, 92 beds) 3505 Gaston Avenue, Dallas, TX Zip 75246–2018; tel. 214/826–7030; Laura J. Lycan, Executive Director
Web address: www.bhcs.com

BAYLOR MEDICAL CENTER AT GARLAND (O, 186 beds) 2300 Marie Curie Boulevard, Garland, TX Zip 75042–5706; tel. 972/487–5000; John B. McWhorter III, Executive Director

BAYLOR MEDICAL CENTER AT GRAPEVINE (O, 97 beds) 1650 West College Street, Grapevine, TX Zip 76051–1650; tel. 817/329–2500; Mark C. Hood, Executive Director

BAYLOR MEDICAL CENTER AT IRVING (L, 235 beds) 1901 North MacArthur Boulevard, Irving, TX Zip 75061–2291; tel. 972/579–8100; Michael F. O'Keefe, FACHE, Executive Director
Web address: www.bhcs.com/irving

BAYLOR MEDICAL CENTER–ELLIS COUNTY (O, 83 beds) 1405 West Jefferson Street, Waxahachie, TX Zip 75165–2275; tel. 972/923–7000; James Michael Lee, Executive Director
Web address: www.baylordallas.edu

BAYLOR UNIVERSITY MEDICAL CENTER (O, 891 beds) 3500 Gaston Avenue, Dallas, TX Zip 75246–2088; tel. 214/820–0111; M. Tim Parris, Executive Vice President and Chief Operating Officer
Web address: www.bhcs.com

Owned, leased, sponsored:	7 hospitals	1656 beds
Contract–managed:	0 hospitals	0 beds
Totals:	7 hospitals	1656 beds

★1095: BAYSTATE HEALTH SYSTEM, INC. (NP)

759 Chestnut Street, Springfield, MA Zip 01199–0001; tel. 413/794–0000; Michael J. Daly, President

MASSACHUSETTS: BAYSTATE MEDICAL CENTER (O, 579 beds) 759 Chestnut Street, Springfield, MA Zip 01199–0001; tel. 413/794–0000; Mark R. Tolosky, Chief Executive Officer
Web address: www.baystatehealth.com

FRANKLIN MEDICAL CENTER (O, 85 beds) 164 High Street, Greenfield, MA Zip 01301–2613; tel. 413/773–0211; Harlan J. Smith, President and Chief Executive Officer
Web address: www.baystatehealth.com

MARY LANE HOSPITAL (O, 31 beds) 85 South Street, Ware, MA Zip 01082–1697; tel. 413/967–6211; Christine Shirtcliff, Executive Vice President
Web address: www.baystatehealth.com

Owned, leased, sponsored:	3 hospitals	695 beds
Contract–managed:	0 hospitals	0 beds
Totals:	3 hospitals	695 beds

0069: BEHAVIORAL HEALTHCARE CORPORATION (IO)

102 Woodmont Boulevard, Suite 800, Nashville, TN Zip 37205–2287; tel. 615/269–3492; Edward A. Stack, President and Chief Executive Officer

ARKANSAS: BHC PINNACLE POINTE HOSPITAL (O, 98 beds) 11501 Financial Center Parkway, Little Rock, AR Zip 72211–3715; tel. 501/223–3322; Jerry Hooper, Chief Executive Officer

CALIFORNIA: BHC ALHAMBRA HOSPITAL (O, 98 beds) 4619 North Rosemead Boulevard, Rosemead, CA Zip 91770–1498, Mailing Address: P.O. Box 369, Zip 91770; tel. 626/286–1191; Peggy Minnick, Administrator

BHC CANYON RIDGE HOSPITAL (O, 59 beds) 5353 G Street, Chino, CA Zip 91710; tel. 909/590–3700; Cynthia K. Brown, R.N., Chief Executive Officer

BHC CEDAR VISTA HOSPITAL (O, 61 beds) 7171 North Cedar Avenue, Fresno, CA Zip 93720; tel. 209/449–8000; Richard Adams, Ph.D., Administrator

For explanation of codes following names, see page B2.
★ Indicates Type III membership in the American Hospital Association.

BHC FREMONT HOSPITAL (O, 78 beds) 39001 Sundale Drive, Fremont, CA Zip 94538; tel. 510/796–1100; Ed Owen, Chief Executive Officer
Web address: www.fremonthospital.com

BHC HERITAGE OAKS HOSPITAL (O, 76 beds) 4250 Auburn Boulevard, Sacramento, CA Zip 95841; tel. 916/489–3336; Ingrid L. Whipple, Chief Executive Officer

BHC ROSS HOSPITAL (O, 56 beds) 1111 Sir Francis Drake Boulevard, Kentfield, CA Zip 94904; tel. 415/258–6900; Judy G. House, Chief Executive Officer

BHC SAN LUIS REY HOSPITAL (O, 122 beds) 335 Saxony Road, Encinitas, CA Zip 92024–2723; tel. 619/753–1245; William T. Sparrow, Chief Executive Officer

BHC SIERRA VISTA HOSPITAL (O, 72 beds) 8001 Bruceville Road, Sacramento, CA Zip 95823; tel. 916/423–2000; Ingrid L. Whipple, Chief Executive Officer

BHC VISTA DEL MAR HOSPITAL (O, 89 beds) 801 Seneca Street, Ventura, CA Zip 93001; tel. 805/653–6434; Jerry Conway, Chief Executive Officer

BHC WALNUT CREEK HOSPITAL (O, 108 beds) 175 La Casa Via, Walnut Creek, CA Zip 94598; tel. 925/933–7990; Jay R. Kellison, Chief Executive Officer

FLORIDA: BHC FORT LAUDERDALE HOSPITAL (O, 100 beds) 1601 East Las Olas Boulevard, Fort Lauderdale, FL Zip 33301–2393; tel. 954/463–4321; Andrew Fuhrman, Chief Executive Officer

ST. JOHNS RIVER HOSPITAL (O, 66 beds) 6300 Beach Boulevard, Jacksonville, FL Zip 32216–2782; tel. 904/724–9202; Paul Pruitt, Administrator

IDAHO: BHC INTERMOUNTAIN HOSPITAL (O, 75 beds) 303 North Allumbaugh Street, Boise, ID Zip 83704–9266; tel. 208/377–8400; Vernon G. Garrett, Chief Executive Officer

ILLINOIS: BHC STREAMWOOD HOSPITAL (O, 100 beds) 1400 East Irving Park Road, Streamwood, IL Zip 60107–3203; tel. 630/837–9000; Jeff Bergren, Chief Executive Officer and Administrator

INDIANA: BHC VALLE VISTA HOSPITAL (O, 88 beds) 898 East Main Street, Greenwood, IN Zip 46143–1400; tel. 317/887–1348; Gordon L. Steinhaurer, Chief Executive Officer

BEHAVIORAL HEALTHCARE OF NORTHERN INDIANA (O, 80 beds) 1800 North Oak Road, Plymouth, IN Zip 46563–3492; tel. 219/936–3784; Wayne T. Miller, Administrator

BEHAVIORAL HEALTHCARE–COLUMBUS (O, 60 beds) 2223 Poshard Drive, Columbus, IN Zip 47203–1844, Mailing Address: P.O. Box 1549, Zip 47203–1844; tel. 812/376–1711; John M. Hart, Chief Executive Officer

KANSAS: BHC COLLEGE MEADOWS HOSPITAL (O, 90 beds) 14425 College Boulevard, Lenexa, KS Zip 66215; tel. 913/469–1100; Jerome R. Kearney, Chief Executive Officer

LOUISIANA: BHC EAST LAKE HOSPITAL (O, 52 beds) 5650 Read Boulevard, New Orleans, LA Zip 70127–3145; tel. 504/241–0888; Darlene Brennan, Chief Executive Officer

BHC MEADOW WOOD HOSPITAL (O, 55 beds) 9032 Perkins Road, Baton Rouge, LA Zip 70810–1507; tel. 225/766–8553; Ralph J. Waite III, Chief Executive Officer

MISSISSIPPI: BHC SAND HILL BEHAVIORAL HEALTHCARE (O, 60 beds) 11150 Highway 49 North, Gulfport, MS Zip 39503–4110; tel. 601/831–1700; David C. Bell, Chief Operating Officer

MISSOURI: BHC SPIRIT OF ST. LOUIS HOSPITAL (O, 104 beds) 5931 Highway 94 South, Saint Charles, MO Zip 63304–5601; tel. 314/441–7300; Greg Panter, Interim Chief Executive Officer

NEVADA: BHC MONTEVISTA HOSPITAL (O, 80 beds) 5900 West Rochelle Avenue, Las Vegas, NV Zip 89103–3327; tel. 702/364–1111; Darryl S. Dubroca, Chief Executive Officer and Administrator

BHC WEST HILLS HOSPITAL (O, 95 beds) 1240 East Ninth Street, Reno, NV Zip 89512–2997, Mailing Address: P.O. Box 30012, Zip 89520–0012; tel. 775/323–0478; Pamela McCullough Broughton, Chief Executive Officer

BHC WILLOW SPRINGS RESIDENTIAL TREATMENT CENTER (O, 68 beds) 690 Edison Way, Reno, NV Zip 89502–4135; tel. 775/858–3303; Robert Bartlett, Administrator

NEW MEXICO: BHC MESILLA VALLEY HOSPITAL (O, 84 beds) 3751 Del Rey Boulevard, Las Cruces, NM Zip 88012–8526, Mailing Address: P.O. Box 429, Zip 88004–0429; tel. 505/382–3500; Alison Druck, R.N., Ed.D., Chief Executive Officer

BHC PINON HILLS HOSPITAL (O, 34 beds) 313 Camino Alire, Santa Fe, NM Zip 87501–2319; tel. 505/988–8003; Jerry Smith, Chief Executive Officer

OHIO: BHC BELMONT PINES HOSPITAL (O, 77 beds) 615 Churchill–Hubbard Road, Youngstown, OH Zip 44505–1379; tel. 330/759–2700; Edward Nasca, Chief Executive Officer
Web address: www.belmontpines.com

BHC FOX RUN HOSPITAL (O, 65 beds) 67670 Traco Drive, Saint Clairsville, OH Zip 43950–9375; tel. 740/695–2131; Charles L. Visalli, Chief Executive Officer

BHC WINDSOR HOSPITAL (O, 50 beds) 115 East Summit Street, Chagrin Falls, OH Zip 44022–2750; tel. 440/247–5300; Donald K. Sykes Jr., Chief Executive Officer

OREGON: PACIFIC GATEWAY HOSPITAL AND COUNSELING CENTER (O, 66 beds) 1345 S.E. Harney, Portland, OR Zip 97202; tel. 503/234–5353; Robert Marshall, Chief Executive Officer

PUERTO RICO: BHC HOSPITAL SAN JUAN CAPESTRANO (O, 88 beds) San Juan, PR Mailing Address: Rural Route 2, Box 11, Zip 00926; tel. 787/760–0222; Laura Vargas, Administrator and Chief Executive Officer

TEXAS: BHC MILLWOOD HOSPITAL (O, 82 beds) 1011 North Cooper Street, Arlington, TX Zip 76011–5517; tel. 817/261–3121; Wayne Hallford, Chief Executive Officer

UTAH: BHC OLYMPUS VIEW HOSPITAL (O, 82 beds) 1430 East 4500 South, Salt Lake City, UT Zip 84117–4208; tel. 801/272–8000; Barry W. Woodward, Administrator

WASHINGTON: BHC FAIRFAX HOSPITAL (O, 133 beds) 10200 N.E. 132nd Street, Kirkland, WA Zip 98034; tel. 425/821–2000; Michelle Egerer, Chief Executive Officer

Owned, leased, sponsored:	36 hospitals	2851 beds
Contract–managed:	0 hospitals	0 beds
Totals:	36 hospitals	2851 beds

O515: BENEDICTINE HEALTH SYSTEM (CC)
503 East Third Street, Duluth, MN Zip 55805–1964; tel. 218/720–2370; Barry J. Halm, President and Chief Executive Officer

IDAHO: CLEARWATER VALLEY HOSPITAL AND CLINICS (L, 18 beds) 301 Cedar, Orofino, ID Zip 83544–9029; tel. 208/476–4555; Richard L. Wheat, Chief Financial Officer
Web address: www.cvh–clrwater.com

ST. MARY'S HOSPITAL (O, 28 beds) Lewiston and North Streets, Cottonwood, ID Zip 83522, Mailing Address: P.O. Box 137, Zip 83522–0137; tel. 208/962–3251; Casey Uhling, Chief Executive Officer

MINNESOTA: ITASCA MEDICAL CENTER (C, 84 beds) 126 First Avenue S.E., Grand Rapids, MN Zip 55744–3698; tel. 218/326–3401; Gary Kenner, President and Chief Executive Officer

PINE MEDICAL CENTER (C, 106 beds) 109 Court Avenue South, Sandstone, MN Zip 55072–5120; tel. 320/245–2212; Michael D. Hedrix, Administrator

ST. JOSEPH'S MEDICAL CENTER (O, 153 beds) 523 North Third Street, Brainerd, MN Zip 56401–3098; tel. 218/829–2861; Thomas K. Prusak, President
Web address: www.stjosephsmedicalctr.com

ST. MARY'S MEDICAL CENTER (S, 287 beds) 407 East Third Street, Duluth, MN Zip 55805–1984; tel. 218/726–4000; Sister Kathleen Hofer, President
Web address: www.smdc.org

ST. MARY'S REGIONAL HEALTH CENTER (O, 163 beds) 1027 Washington Avenue, Detroit Lakes, MN Zip 56501–3598; tel. 218/847–5611; John H. Solheim, Chief Executive Officer
Web address: www.stmaryshealthcenter.com

TRINITY HOSPITAL (O, 85 beds) 3410–213th Street West, Farmington, MN Zip 55024–1197; tel. 651/463–7825; Donald J. Leivermann, Chief Executive Officer

WISCONSIN: ST. MARY'S HOSPITAL OF SUPERIOR (S, 42 beds) 3500 Tower Avenue, Superior, WI Zip 54880–5395; tel. 715/392–8281; Delores E. Schultz, R.N., Administrator

For explanation of codes following names, see page B2.
★ Indicates Type III membership in the American Hospital Association.

wned, leased, sponsored:	7 hospitals	776 beds
ontract–managed:	2 hospitals	190 beds
otals:	9 hospitals	966 beds

545: BENEDICTINE SISTERS OF THE ANNUNCIATION (CC)
7520 University Drive, Bismarck, ND Zip 58504–9653;
tel. 701/255–1520; Sister Susan Berger, Prioress

ORTH DAKOTA: GARRISON MEMORIAL HOSPITAL (S, 30 beds) 407 Third
Avenue S.E., Garrison, ND Zip 58540–0039; tel. 701/463–2275; Richard
Spilovoy, Administrator

ST. ALEXIUS MEDICAL CENTER (S, 269 beds) 900 East Broadway, Bismarck,
ND Zip 58501–4586, Mailing Address: P.O. Box 5510, Zip 58506–5510;
tel. 701/224–7000; Richard A. Tschider, FACHE, Administrator and Chief
Executive Officer
Web address: www.st.alexius.org

wned, leased, sponsored:	2 hospitals	299 beds
ontract–managed:	0 hospitals	0 beds
otals:	2 hospitals	299 beds

2435: BERKSHIRE HEALTH SYSTEMS, INC. (NP)
725 North Street, Pittsfield, MA Zip 01201–4124;
tel. 413/447–2743; David E. Phelps, President and Chief Executive
Officer

MASSACHUSETTS: BERKSHIRE MEDICAL CENTER (O, 272 beds) 725 North
Street, Pittsfield, MA Zip 01201–4124; tel. 413/447–2000; Ruth P.
Blodgett, Chief Operating Officer

FAIRVIEW HOSPITAL (O, 35 beds) 29 Lewis Avenue, Great Barrington, MA
Zip 01230–1713; tel. 413/528–0790; Claire L. Bowen, President

wned, leased, sponsored:	2 hospitals	307 beds
ontract–managed:	0 hospitals	0 beds
otals:	2 hospitals	307 beds

415: BETHESDA HOSPITAL, INC. (NP)
619 Oak Street, Cincinnati, OH Zip 45206–1690;
tel. 513/569–6141; John S. Prout, President and Chief Executive
Officer

HIO: BETHESDA NORTH HOSPITAL (O, 245 beds) 10500 Montgomery Road,
Cincinnati, OH Zip 45242–4415; tel. 513/745–1111; John S. Prout,
President and Chief Executive Officer
Web address: www.trihealth.com

BETHESDA OAK HOSPITAL (O, 116 beds) 619 Oak Street, Cincinnati, OH
Zip 45206–1690; tel. 513/569–6111; Linda D. Schaffner, R.N., Vice
President and Administrator
Web address: www.trihealth.com

Owned, leased, sponsored:	2 hospitals	361 beds
Contract–managed:	0 hospitals	0 beds
otals:	2 hospitals	361 beds

0051: BJC HEALTH SYSTEM (NP)
4444 Forest Park Avenue, Saint Louis, MO Zip 63108–2259;
tel. 314/286–2000; Edward B. Case, Executive Vice President and
Chief Operating Officer

LLINOIS: ALTON MEMORIAL HOSPITAL (O, 202 beds) One Memorial Drive,
Alton, IL Zip 62002–6722; tel. 618/463–7311; Ronald B. McMullen,
President
Web address: www.bjc.org

CLAY COUNTY HOSPITAL (C, 31 beds) 700 North Mill Street, Flora, IL
Zip 62839–1823, Mailing Address: P.O. Box 280, Zip 62839–0280;
tel. 618/662–2131; Tony Schwarm, President
Web address: www.wabash.net

FAYETTE COUNTY HOSPITAL (L, 142 beds) Seventh and Taylor Streets,
Vandalia, IL Zip 62471–1296; tel. 618/283–1231; Daniel L. Gantz, President

PUBLIC HOSPITAL OF THE TOWN OF SALEM (C, 31 beds) 1201 Ricker Drive,
Salem, IL Zip 62881–6250, Mailing Address: P.O. Box 1250,
Zip 62881–1250; tel. 618/548–3194; James E. Robertson Jr., President

MISSOURI: BARNES–JEWISH HOSPITAL (O, 927 beds) One Barnes–Jewish
Hospital Plaza, Saint Louis, MO Zip 63110–1094; tel. 314/747–3000;
Peter L. Slavin, M.D., President

BARNES–JEWISH ST. PETERS HOSPITAL (O, 84 beds) 10 Hospital Drive,
Saint Peters, MO Zip 63376–1659; tel. 314/916–9000; Carm Moceri,
President

BARNES–JEWISH WEST COUNTY HOSPITAL (O, 91 beds) 12634 Olive
Boulevard, Saint Louis, MO Zip 63141–6354; tel. 314/996–8000; William
Behrendt, Interim President

BOONE HOSPITAL CENTER (L, 327 beds) 1600 East Broadway, Columbia,
MO Zip 65201–5897; tel. 573/815–8000; Michael Shirk, President and
Senior Executive Officer
Web address: www.boone.org

CHRISTIAN HOSPITAL NORTHEAST–NORTHWEST (O, 563 beds) 11133 Dunn
Road, Saint Louis, MO Zip 63136–6192; tel. 314/653–5000; John
O'Shaughnessy, President and Senior Executive Officer
Web address: www.bjc.org

MISSOURI BAPTIST HOSPITAL OF SULLIVAN (O, 46 beds) 751 Sappington
Bridge Road, Sullivan, MO Zip 63080–2354, Mailing Address: P.O. Box 190,
Zip 63080–0190; tel. 573/468–4186; Davis D. Skinner, President

MISSOURI BAPTIST MEDICAL CENTER (O, 372 beds) 3015 North Ballas Road,
Town and Country, MO Zip 63131–2374; tel. 314/996–5000; Mark A.
Eustis, President

PARKLAND HEALTH CENTER (O, 94 beds) 1101 West Liberty Street,
Farmington, MO Zip 63640–1997; tel. 573/756–6451; Richard L. Conklin,
President

ST. LOUIS CHILDREN'S HOSPITAL (O, 235 beds) One Children's Place, Saint
Louis, MO Zip 63110–1077; tel. 314/454–6000; Ted W. Frey, President
Web address: www.STLOUISCHILDRENS.ORG

Owned, leased, sponsored:	11 hospitals	3083 beds
Contract–managed:	2 hospitals	62 beds
Totals:	13 hospitals	3145 beds

● ★0053: BLUE WATER HEALTH SERVICES CORPORATION (NP)
1221 Pine Grove Avenue, Port Huron, MI Zip 48060–3568;
tel. 810/989–3717; Donald C. Fletcher, President and Chief
Executive Officer

MICHIGAN: PORT HURON HOSPITAL (O, 186 beds) 1221 Pine Grove Avenue,
Port Huron, MI Zip 48061–5011; tel. 810/987–5000; Donald C. Fletcher,
President and Chief Executive Officer

Owned, leased, sponsored:	1 hospital	186 beds
Contract–managed:	0 hospitals	0 beds
Totals:	1 hospital	186 beds

★5085: BON SECOURS HEALTH SYSTEM, INC. (CC)
1505 Marriottsville Road, Marriottsville, MD Zip 21104–1399;
tel. 410/442–5511; Christopher M. Carney, President and Chief
Executive Officer

FLORIDA: BON SECOURS–ST. JOSEPH HEALTHCARE GROUP (O, 313 beds)
2500 Harbor Boulevard, Port Charlotte, FL Zip 33952–5396;
tel. 941/766–4122; Michael L. Harrington, Chief Executive Officer

BON SECOURS–VENICE HOSPITAL (O, 254 beds) 540 The Rialto, Venice, FL
Zip 34285–2900; tel. 941/485–7711; Michael G. Guley, Chief Executive
Officer
Web address: www.bshsi.fl.com

MARYLAND: BON SECOURS BALTIMORE HEALTH SYSTEM (O, 106 beds)
2000 West Baltimore Street, Baltimore, MD Zip 21223–1597;
tel. 410/362–3000; Henry DeVries, Acting Chief Executive Officer
Web address: www.bonsecours.org

LIBERTY MEDICAL CENTER (O, 95 beds) 2600 Liberty Heights Avenue,
Baltimore, MD Zip 21215–7892; tel. 410/383–4000; Henry DeVries, Acting
Chief Executive Officer

For explanation of codes following names, see page B2.
★ Indicates Type III membership in the American Hospital Association.
● Single hospital health care system

MICHIGAN: BON SECOURS HOSPITAL (O, 235 beds) 468 Cadieux Road, Grosse Pointe, MI Zip 48230–1592; tel. 313/343–1000; Richard Van Lith, Chief Executive Officer
Web address: www.bonsecoursmi.com

COTTAGE HOSPITAL (O, 148 beds) 159 Kercheval Avenue, Grosse Pointe Farms, MI Zip 48236–3692; tel. 313/640–1000; Richard Van Lith, Chief Executive Officer

PENNSYLVANIA: BON SECOURS–HOLY FAMILY REGIONAL HEALTH SYSTEM (O, 161 beds) 2500 Seventh Avenue, Altoona, PA Zip 16602–2099; tel. 814/944–1681; Barbara H. Biehner, Chief Executive Officer

SOUTH CAROLINA: BON SECOURS–ST. FRANCIS XAVIER HOSPITAL (O, 147 beds) 2095 Henry Tecklenburg Drive, Charleston, SC Zip 29414–0001, Mailing Address: P.O. Box 160001, Zip 29414–0001; tel. 803/402–1000; Allen P. Carroll, Chief Executive Officer

VIRGINIA: BON SECOURS ST. MARY'S HOSPITAL (O, 391 beds) 5801 Bremo Road, Richmond, VA Zip 23226–1900; tel. 804/285–2011; Ann E. Honeycutt, Executive Vice President and Administrator

BON SECOURS–DEPAUL MEDICAL CENTER (O, 202 beds) 150 Kingsley Lane, Norfolk, VA Zip 23505–4650; tel. 757/889–5000; David J. McCombs, Executive Vice President and Administrator

BON SECOURS–RICHMOND COMMUNITY HOSPITAL (O, 88 beds) 1500 North 28th Street, Richmond, VA Zip 23223–5396, Mailing Address: Box 27184, Zip 23261–7184; tel. 804/225–1700; Samuel F. Lillard, Executive Vice President and Administrator

BON SECOURS–STUART CIRCLE (O, 158 beds) 413 Stuart Circle, Richmond, VA Zip 23220–3799; tel. 804/358–7051; Edward Gerardo, Executive Vice President and Administrator

MARY IMMACULATE HOSPITAL (O, 110 beds) 2 Bernardine Drive, Newport News, VA Zip 23602–4499; tel. 757/886–6000; Cynthia B. Farrand, Executive Vice President and Administrator
Web address: www.mihospital.com

MARYVIEW HOSPITAL (O, 441 beds) 3636 High Street, Portsmouth, VA Zip 23707–3236; tel. 757/398–2200; Wayne Jones, Executive Vice President and Administrator
Web address: www.bonsecours.com

MEMORIAL REGIONAL MEDICAL CENTER (O, 272 beds) 8260 Atlee Road, Mechanicsville, VA Zip 23116, Mailing Address: P.O. Box 26783, Richmond, Zip 23261–6783; tel. 804/764–6102; Michael Robinson, Executive Vice President and Administrator

Owned, leased, sponsored:	15 hospitals	3121 beds
Contract–managed:	0 hospitals	0 beds
Totals:	15 hospitals	3121 beds

0073: BOWDON CORPORATE OFFICES (IO)
4250 Perimeter Park South, Suite 102, Atlanta, GA Zip 30341; tel. 770/452–1221; Bill E. Ehrhardt, Executive Director

GEORGIA: BOWDON AREA HOSPITAL (O, 41 beds) 501 Mitchell Avenue, Bowdon, GA Zip 30108–1499; tel. 770/258–7207; Yvonne Willis, Administrator

NEW MEXICO: ALLIANCE HOSPITAL OF SANTA TERESA (L, 72 beds) 100 Laura Court, Santa Teresa, NM Zip 88008, Mailing Address: P.O. Box 6, Las Cruces, Zip 88008–0006; tel. 505/589–0033; Michele Irwin, Administrator

Owned, leased, sponsored:	2 hospitals	113 beds
Contract–managed:	0 hospitals	0 beds
Totals:	2 hospitals	113 beds

2455: BRADFORD HEALTH SERVICES (IO)
2101 Magnolia Avenue South, Suite 518, Birmingham, AL Zip 35205; tel. 205/251–7753; Jerry W. Crowder, President and Chief Executive Officer

ALABAMA: BRADFORD HEALTH SERVICES AT BIRMINGHAM (O, 90 beds) 1221 Alton Drive, Birmingham, AL Zip 35210–4308, Mailing Address: P.O. Box 129, Warrior, Zip 35180–0129; tel. 205/833–4000; W. Clay Simmons, Executive Vice President

BRADFORD HEALTH SERVICES AT HUNTSVILLE (O, 84 beds) 1600 Browns Ferry Road, Madison, AL Zip 35758–9769, Mailing Address: P.O. Box 176, Zip 35758–0176; tel. 205/461–7272; Bob Hinds, Executive Director

BRADFORD HEALTH SERVICES AT OAK MOUNTAIN (O, 84 beds) 2280 Highway 35, Pelham, AL Zip 35124–6120; tel. 205/664–3460; William Weaver, Administrator

Owned, leased, sponsored:	3 hospitals	258 beds
Contract–managed:	0 hospitals	0 beds
Totals:	3 hospitals	258 beds

★0585: BRIM HEALTHCARE, INC. (IO)
105 Westwood Place, Suite 300, Brentwood, TN Zip 37027; tel. 615/309–6053; Jim McKinney, President

ARIZONA: COBRE VALLEY COMMUNITY HOSPITAL (C, 41 beds) One Hospital Drive, Claypool, AZ Zip 85532, Mailing Address: P.O. Box 3261, Zip 85532–3261; tel. 520/425–3261; Charles E. Bill, CHE, Chief Executive Officer

NAVAPACHE REGIONAL MEDICAL CENTER (C, 54 beds) 2200 Show Low Lake Road, Show Low, AZ Zip 85901–7800; tel. 520/537–4375; Leigh Cox, Chief Executive Officer
Web address: www.nrmc.org

NORTHERN COCHISE COMMUNITY HOSPITAL (C, 48 beds) 901 West Rex Allen Drive, Willcox, AZ Zip 85643–1009; tel. 520/384–3541; Chris Cronberg, Chief Executive Officer

CALIFORNIA: CORCORAN DISTRICT HOSPITAL (C, 32 beds) 1310 Hanna Avenue, Corcoran, CA Zip 93212, Mailing Address: Box 758, Zip 93212; tel. 209/992–5051; David R. Green, Administrator

HAZEL HAWKINS MEMORIAL HOSPITAL (C, 71 beds) 911 Sunset Drive, Hollister, CA Zip 95023–5695; tel. 831/637–5711; Keith Mesmer, Chief Executive Officer

PIONEERS MEMORIAL HEALTHCARE DISTRICT (C, 80 beds) 207 West Legion Road, Brawley, CA Zip 92227–9699; tel. 760/351–3333; Claire Kuczkowski, Administrator

SAN GORGONIO MEMORIAL HOSPITAL (C, 68 beds) 600 North Highland Springs Avenue, Banning, CA Zip 92220; tel. 909/845–1121; Donald N. Larkin, Chief Executive Officer

TEHACHAPI HOSPITAL (C, 28 beds) 115 West E Street, Tehachapi, CA Zip 93561, Mailing Address: P.O. Box 1900, Zip 93581; tel. 661/822–3241; Raymond T. Hino, Chief Executive Officer

ILLINOIS: HAMMOND–HENRY HOSPITAL (C, 105 beds) 210 West Elk Street, Geneseo, IL Zip 61254–1099; tel. 309/944–6431; Nathan C. Olson, President and Chief Executive Officer

HILLSBORO AREA HOSPITAL (C, 95 beds) 1200 East Tremont Street, Hillsboro, IL Zip 62049–1900; tel. 217/532–6111; Rex H. Brown, President

SPARTA COMMUNITY HOSPITAL (C, 35 beds) 818 East Broadway Street, Sparta, IL Zip 62286–0297, Mailing Address: P.O. Box 297, Zip 62286–0297; tel. 618/443–2177; Joann Emge, Chief Executive Officer

WOOD RIVER TOWNSHIP HOSPITAL (C, 55 beds) 101 East Edwardsville Road, Wood River, IL Zip 62095–1332; tel. 618/251–7103; David G. Triebes, Chief Executive Officer

INDIANA: WIRTH REGIONAL HOSPITAL (C, 11 beds) Highway 64 West, Oakland City, IN Zip 47660–9379, Mailing Address: Rural Route 3, Box 14A, Zip 47660–9379; tel. 812/749–6111; Frank G. Fougerousse, President and Chief Executive Officer

LOUISIANA: IBERIA GENERAL HOSPITAL AND MEDICAL CENTER (C, 75 beds) 2315 East Main Street, New Iberia, LA Zip 70560–4031, Mailing Address: P.O. Box 13338, Zip 70562–3338; tel. 318/364–0441; Isaac S. Coe, Interim Administrator

LADY OF THE SEA GENERAL HOSPITAL (C, 55 beds) 200 West 134th Place, Cut Off, LA Zip 70345–4145; tel. 504/632–6401; Lane M. Cheramie, Chief Executive Officer

MINNESOTA: SWIFT COUNTY–BENSON HOSPITAL (C, 31 beds) 1815 Wisconsin Avenue, Benson, MN Zip 56215–1653; tel. 320/843–4232; Frank Lawatsch, Chief Executive Officer

For explanation of codes following names, see page B2.
★ Indicates Type III membership in the American Hospital Association.

© 1999 AHA Guide

MONTANA: BARRETT MEMORIAL HOSPITAL (C, 22 beds) 1260 South Atlantic Street, Dillon, MT Zip 59725–3597; tel. 406/683–3000; John M. Mootry, Chief Executive Officer
Web address: www.barretthospital.org

BIG HORN COUNTY MEMORIAL HOSPITAL (C, 53 beds) 17 North Miles Avenue, Hardin, MT Zip 59034–0430, Mailing Address: P.O. Box 430, Zip 59034–0430; tel. 406/665–2310; Robert G. Notarianni, Chief Executive Officer

MINERAL COMMUNITY HOSPITAL (C, 30 beds) Roosevelt and Brooklyn, Superior, MT Zip 59872, Mailing Address: P.O. Box 66, Zip 59872–0066; tel. 406/822–4841; Steven Smoot, Chief Executive Officer

NORTHERN MONTANA HOSPITAL (C, 259 beds) 30 13th Street, Havre, MT Zip 59501–5222, Mailing Address: P.O. Box 1231, Zip 59501–1231; tel. 406/265–2211; David Henry, Chief Executive Officer

POWELL COUNTY MEMORIAL HOSPITAL (C, 35 beds) 1101 Texas Avenue, Deer Lodge, MT Zip 59722–1828; tel. 406/846–2212; Connie Huber, R.N., Chief Executive Officer

ROSEBUD HEALTH CARE CENTER (C, 75 beds) 383 North 17th Avenue, Forsyth, MT Zip 59327; tel. 406/356–2161; John M. Chioutsis, Chief Executive Officer

ROUNDUP MEMORIAL HOSPITAL (C, 54 beds) 1202 Third Street West, Roundup, MT Zip 59072–1816, Mailing Address: P.O. Box 40, Zip 59072–0040; tel. 406/323–2302; Dave McIvor, Administrator

ST. JOHN'S LUTHERAN HOSPITAL (C, 26 beds) 350 Louisiana Avenue, Libby, MT Zip 59923–2198; tel. 406/293–7761; Richard L. Palagi, Chief Executive Officer
Web address: www.libby.org/sjlh

NEBRASKA: TRI–VALLEY HEALTH SYSTEM (C, 56 beds) West Highway 6 and 34, Cambridge, NE Zip 69022–0488, Mailing Address: P.O. Box 488, Zip 69022–0488; tel. 308/697–3329; Jerry W. Harris, Interim Chief Executive Officer

NEW MEXICO: NORTHEASTERN REGIONAL HOSPITAL (C, 54 beds) 1235 Eighth Street, Las Vegas, NM Zip 87701–4254, Mailing Address: P.O. Box 248, Zip 87701–0238; tel. 505/425–6751; Jerry B. Scott, Chief Executive Officer

UNION COUNTY GENERAL HOSPITAL (C, 28 beds) 301 Harding Street, Clayton, NM Zip 88415–3321, Mailing Address: P.O. Box 489, Zip 88415–0489; tel. 505/374–2585; W. C. McElhannon, Administrator

NEW YORK: ADIRONDACK MEDICAL CENTER (C, 75 beds) Lake Colby Drive, Saranac Lake, NY Zip 12983, Mailing Address: P.O. Box 471, Zip 12983–0471; tel. 518/891–4141; Chandler M. Ralph, Chief Executive Officer
Web address: www.northnet.org/adirondackmedcenter

LEWIS COUNTY GENERAL HOSPITAL (C, 214 beds) 7785 North State Street, Lowville, NY Zip 13367–1297; tel. 315/376–5200; Ernest R. McNeely Jr., Chief Executive Officer and Administrator

THE HOSPITAL (C, 87 beds) 43 Pearl Street West, Sidney, NY Zip 13838–1399; tel. 607/561–2153; Russell A. Test, Administrator and Chief Executive Officer
Web address: www.thehospital.org

OREGON: BLUE MOUNTAIN HOSPITAL (C, 73 beds) 170 Ford Road, John Day, OR Zip 97845; tel. 541/575–1311; Robert Houser, Chief Executive Officer

TEXAS: DE LEON HOSPITAL (C, 14 beds) 407 South Texas Avenue, De Leon, TX Zip 76444–1947, Mailing Address: P.O. Box 319, Zip 76444–0319; tel. 254/893–2011; Michael K. Hare, Administrator

WASHINGTON: COULEE COMMUNITY HOSPITAL (C, 48 beds) 411 Fortuyn Road, Grand Coulee, WA Zip 99133–8718; tel. 509/633–1753; Charlotte Lang, Administrator

SUNNYSIDE COMMUNITY HOSPITAL (C, 34 beds) 10th and Tacoma Avenue, Sunnyside, WA Zip 98944, Mailing Address: P.O. Box 719, Zip 98944–0719; tel. 509/837–1650; Jon D. Smiley, Chief Executive Officer
Web address: www.televar.com/sch

WISCONSIN: BURNETT MEDICAL CENTER (C, 70 beds) 257 West St. George Avenue, Grantsburg, WI Zip 54840–7827; tel. 715/463–5353; Timothy J. Wick, Chief Executive Officer

COMMUNITY MEMORIAL HOSPITAL (C, 26 beds) 855 South Main Street, Oconto Falls, WI Zip 54154–1296; tel. 920/846–3444; Tom Thompson, Administrator

GRANT REGIONAL HEALTH CENTER (C, 28 beds) 507 South Monroe Street, Lancaster, WI Zip 53813–2099; tel. 608/723–2143; Larry D. Rentfro, FACHE, President and Chief Executive Officer

MEMORIAL COMMUNITY HOSPITAL (C, 115 beds) 313 Stoughton Road, Edgerton, WI Zip 53534–1198; tel. 608/884–3441; Charles E. Bruhn, Chief Executive Officer

MEMORIAL HOSPITAL OF IOWA COUNTY (C, 82 beds) 825 South Iowa Street, Dodgeville, WI Zip 53533–1999; tel. 608/935–2711; Ray Marmorstone, Chief Executive Officer

RIPON MEDICAL CENTER (C, 29 beds) 933 Newbury Street, Ripon, WI Zip 54971–1798, Mailing Address: P.O. Box 390, Zip 54971–0390; tel. 920/748–3101; Jon W. Baker, Chief Executive Officer
Web address: www.riponmedicalcenter.com

SHAWANO MEDICAL CENTER (C, 46 beds) 309 North Bartlette Street, Shawano, WI Zip 54166–0477; tel. 715/526–2111; John J. Kestly, Administrator

SOUTHWEST HEALTH CENTER (C, 165 beds) 250 Camp Street, Platteville, WI Zip 53818–1703; tel. 608/348–2331; Anne K. Klawiter, President and Chief Executive Officer
Web address: www.southwesthealth.org

SPOONER HEALTH SYSTEM (C, 136 beds) 819 Ash Street, Spooner, WI Zip 54801–1299; tel. 715/635–2111; Michael Schafer, Chief Executive Officer

ST. JOSEPH'S MEMORIAL HOSPITAL AND NURSING HOME (C, 85 beds) 400 Water Avenue, Hillsboro, WI Zip 54634–0527, Mailing Address: P.O. Box 527, Zip 54634–0527; tel. 608/489–2211; Nancy Bauman, Chief Executive Officer

WYOMING: POWELL HOSPITAL (C, 140 beds) 777 Avenue H, Powell, WY Zip 82435–2296; tel. 307/754–2267; Rod Barton, Chief Executive Officer
Web address: www.wir.net/powell–hospital

Owned, leased, sponsored:	0 hospitals	0 beds
Contract–managed:	45 hospitals	3043 beds
Totals:	45 hospitals	3043 beds

★**0595: BRONSON HEALTHCARE GROUP, INC.** (NP)
One Healthcare Plaza, Kalamazoo, MI Zip 49007–5345; tel. 616/341–6000; Frank J. Sardone, President and Chief Executive Officer

MICHIGAN: BRONSON METHODIST HOSPITAL (O, 307 beds) 252 East Lovell Street, Kalamazoo, MI Zip 49007–5345; tel. 616/341–6000; Frank J. Sardone, President and Chief Executive Officer
Web address: www.bronsonhealth.com

BRONSON VICKSBURG HOSPITAL (O, 41 beds) 13326 North Boulevard, Vicksburg, MI Zip 49097–1099; tel. 616/649–2321; Frank J. Sardone, President
Web address: www.bronsonhealth.com

Owned, leased, sponsored:	2 hospitals	348 beds
Contract–managed:	0 hospitals	0 beds
Totals:	2 hospitals	348 beds

0077: CAMBRIDGE INTERNATIONAL, INC, (IO)
7505 Fannin, Suite 680, Houston, TX Zip 77225; tel. 713/790–1153; Timothy Sharma, M.D., President

TEXAS: FOREST SPRINGS HOSPITAL (O, 48 beds) 1120 Cypress Station, Houston, TX Zip 77090–3031; tel. 281/893–7200; Deo Shanker, CPA, Chief Executive Officer

INTRACARE MEDICAL CENTER HOSPITAL (O, 100 beds) 7601 Fannin Street, Houston, TX Zip 77054–1905; tel. 713/790–0949; Alice Hiniker, Ph.D., Administrator

For explanation of codes following names, see page B2.
★ Indicates Type III membership in the American Hospital Association.

Owned, leased, sponsored:	2 hospitals	148 beds
Contract–managed:	0 hospitals	0 beds
Totals:	2 hospitals	148 beds

★0955: CAMCARE, INC. (NP)
501 Morris Street, Charleston, WV Zip 25301–1300, Mailing Address: P.O. Box 1547, Zip 25326–1547; tel. 304/348–5432; Phillip H. Goodwin, President and Chief Executive Officer

WEST VIRGINIA: BRAXTON COUNTY MEMORIAL HOSPITAL (O, 30 beds) 100 Hoylman Drive, Gassaway, WV Zip 26624–9320; tel. 304/364–5156; Tony E. Atkins, Administrator
Web address: www.pihn.org

CHARLESTON AREA MEDICAL CENTER (O, 784 beds) 501 Morris Street, Charleston, WV Zip 25301–1300, Mailing Address: P.O. Box 1547, Zip 25326–1547; tel. 304/348–5432; Robert L. Savage, President and Chief Executive Officer
Web address: www.camcare.com

PLATEAU MEDICAL CENTER (O, 79 beds) 430 Main Street, Oak Hill, WV Zip 25901–3455; tel. 304/469–8600; Hank Woodson, Administrator

Owned, leased, sponsored:	3 hospitals	893 beds
Contract–managed:	0 hospitals	0 beds
Totals:	3 hospitals	893 beds

0113: CANCER TREATMENT CENTERS OF AMERICA (IO)
3455 West Salt Creek Lane, Arlington Heights, IL Zip 60005–1080; tel. 847/342–7400; William A. Sanger, President and Chief Executive Officer

ILLINOIS: MIDWESTERN REGIONAL MEDICAL CENTER (O, 70 beds) 2520 Elisha Avenue, Zion, IL Zip 60099–2587; tel. 847/872–4561; Roger C. Cary, President and Chief Executive Officer
Web address: www.pulbiconline.com/=mrmc

OKLAHOMA: CANCER TREATMENT CENTERS OF AMERICA–TULSA (O, 72 beds) 2408 East 81st Street, Tulsa, OK Zip 74137–4210; tel. 918/496–5000; Joseph A. Gagliardi, President and Chief Executive Officer

Owned, leased, sponsored:	2 hospitals	142 beds
Contract–managed:	0 hospitals	0 beds
Totals:	2 hospitals	142 beds

0124: CAPE COD HEALTHCARE, INC. (NP)
88 Lewis Bay Road, Hyannis, MA Zip 02601–5210; tel. 508/862–5011; James F. Lyons, President and Chief Executive Officer

MASSACHUSETTS: CAPE COD HOSPITAL (O, 236 beds) 27 Park Street, Hyannis, MA Zip 02601–5203; tel. 508/771–1800; Gail M. Frieswick, Ed.D., President and Chief Executive Officer

FALMOUTH HOSPITAL (O, 84 beds) 100 Ter Heun Drive, Falmouth, MA Zip 02540–2599; tel. 508/457–3500; Gail Frieswick, President

Owned, leased, sponsored:	2 hospitals	320 beds
Contract–managed:	0 hospitals	0 beds
Totals:	2 hospitals	320 beds

★0099: CARE NEW ENGLAND HEALTH SYSTEM (NP)
45 Willard Avenue, Providence, RI Zip 02905–3218; tel. 401/453–7900; John J. Hynes, President and Chief Executive Officer

RHODE ISLAND: BUTLER HOSPITAL (O, 105 beds) 345 Blackstone Boulevard, Providence, RI Zip 02906–4829; tel. 401/455–6200; Patricia R. Recupero, JD, M.D., President and Chief Executive Officer
Web address: www.butler.org

KENT COUNTY MEMORIAL HOSPITAL (O, 326 beds) 455 Tollgate Road, Warwick, RI Zip 02886–2770; tel. 401/737–7000; Robert E. Baute, M.D., President and Chief Executive Officer

WOMEN AND INFANTS HOSPITAL OF RHODE ISLAND (O, 197 beds) 101 Dudley Street, Providence, RI Zip 02905–2499; tel. 401/274–1100; Thomas G. Parris Jr., President
Web address: www.wihri.org

Owned, leased, sponsored:	3 hospitals	628 beds
Contract–managed:	0 hospitals	0 beds
Totals:	3 hospitals	628 beds

★0096: CAREGROUP (NP)
375 Longwood Avenue, Boston, MA Zip 02215–5395; tel. 617/975–6060; James Reinertsen, M.D., Chief Executive Officer

MASSACHUSETTS: BETH ISRAEL DEACONESS MEDICAL CENTER (O, 671 beds) 330 Brookline Avenue, Boston, MA Zip 02215–5491; tel. 617/667–7000; Herbert Yehude Kressel, M.D., President

DEACONESS WALTHAM HOSPITAL (O, 198 beds) Hope Avenue, Waltham, MA Zip 02254–9116; tel. 781/647–6000; Allen Danis, Acting Administrator

DEACONESS–GLOVER HOSPITAL CORPORATION (O, 47 beds) 148 Chestnut Street, Needham, MA Zip 02192–2483; tel. 781/453–3000; John Dalton, President and Chief Executive Officer
Web address: www.caregroup.com

DEACONESS–NASHOBA HOSPITAL (O, 49 beds) 200 Groton Road, Ayer, MA Zip 01432–3300; tel. 978/784–9000; Jeffrey R. Kelly, President and Chief Executive Officer

MOUNT AUBURN HOSPITAL (O, 164 beds) 330 Mount Auburn Street, Cambridge, MA Zip 02138; tel. 617/499–5700; Jeanette G. Clough, President and Chief Executive Officer

NEW ENGLAND BAPTIST HOSPITAL (O, 141 beds) 125 Parker Hill Avenue, Boston, MA Zip 02120–3297; tel. 617/754–5800; Alan H. Robbins, M.D., President
Web address: www.nebh.org

Owned, leased, sponsored:	6 hospitals	1270 beds
Contract–managed:	0 hospitals	0 beds
Totals:	6 hospitals	1270 beds

★0070: CARILION HEALTH SYSTEM (NP)
101 Elm Avenue S.E., Roanoke, VA Zip 24013, Mailing Address: P.O. Box 13727, Zip 24036–3727; tel. 540/981–7347; Thomas L. Robertson, President and Chief Executive Officer

VIRGINIA: CARILION BEDFORD MEMORIAL HOSPITAL (O, 161 beds) 1613 Oakwood Street, Bedford, VA Zip 24523–0688, Mailing Address: P.O. Box 688, Zip 24523–0688; tel. 540/586–2441; Howard Ainsley, Vice President and Hospital Director

CARILION FRANKLIN MEMORIAL HOSPITAL (O, 37 beds) 180 Floyd Avenue, Rocky Mount, VA Zip 24151–1389; tel. 540/483–5277; Matthew J. Perry, Director
Web address: www.carilion.com

CARILION GILES MEMORIAL HOSPITAL (O, 53 beds) 1 Taylor Avenue, Pearisburg, VA Zip 24134–1932; tel. 540/921–6000; Morris D. Reece, Administrator and Chief Executive Officer

CARILION MEDICAL CENTER (O, 677 beds) Belleview at Jefferson Street, Roanoke, VA Zip 24014, Mailing Address: P.O. Box 13367, Zip 24033–3367; tel. 540/981–7000; Lucas A. Snipes, FACHE, Director
Web address: www.carilion.com

CARILION NEW RIVER VALLEY MEDICAL CENTER (O, 158 beds) 2900 Tyler Road, Radford, VA Zip 24141–2430, Mailing Address: P.O. Box 5, Zip 24141–0005; tel. 540/731–2000; Virginia Ousley, Director

CARILION SAINT ALBANS HOSPITAL (O, 68 beds) Route 11, Lee Highway, Radford, VA Zip 24143, Mailing Address: P.O. Box 3608, Zip 24143–3608; tel. 540/639–2481; Janet McKinney Crawford, Vice President and Administrator
Web address: www.carilion.com

SMYTH COUNTY COMMUNITY HOSPITAL (O, 279 beds) 565 Radio Hill Road, Marion, VA Zip 24354–3526, Mailing Address: P.O. Box 880, Zip 24354–0880; tel. 540/782–1234; Roger W. Cooper, President

SOUTHSIDE COMMUNITY HOSPITAL (C, 88 beds) 800 Oak Street, Farmville, VA Zip 23901–1199; tel. 804/392–8811; John H. Greer, President

For explanation of codes following names, see page B2.
★ Indicates Type III membership in the American Hospital Association.

TAZEWELL COMMUNITY HOSPITAL (C, 38 beds) 141 Ben Bolt Avenue, Tazewell, VA Zip 24651–9700; tel. 540/988–2506; Craig B. James, President and Chief Executive Officer

WYTHE COUNTY COMMUNITY HOSPITAL (O, 90 beds) 600 West Ridge Road, Wytheville, VA Zip 24382–1099; tel. 540/228–0200; Larry H. Chewning III, Chief Executive Officer
Web address: www.wcch.org

Owned, leased, sponsored:	8 hospitals	1523 beds
Contract–managed:	2 hospitals	126 beds
Totals:	10 hospitals	1649 beds

★0141: CARITAS CHRISTI HEALTH CARE (NP)
736 Cambridge Street, Boston, MA Zip 02135–2997; tel. 617/789–2500; Michael F. Collins, M.D., President

MASSACHUSETTS: CARITAS NORWOOD HOSPITAL (S, 150 beds) 800 Washington Street, Norwood, MA Zip 02062–3487; tel. 781/278–6001; Delia O'Connor, President

CARNEY HOSPITAL (S, 201 beds) 2100 Dorchester Avenue, Dorchester, MA Zip 02124–5666; tel. 617/296–4000; Joyce A. Murphy, President

GOOD SAMARITAN MEDICAL CENTER (S, 222 beds) 235 North Pearl Street, Brockton, MA Zip 02401–1794; tel. 508/427–3000; Frank J. Larkin, President and Chief Executive Officer

HOLY FAMILY HOSPITAL AND MEDICAL CENTER (S, 243 beds) 70 East Street, Methuen, MA Zip 01844–4597; tel. 978/687–0151; William L. Lane, President
Web address: www.holyfamilyhosp.org

SAINT ANNE'S HOSPITAL (S, 139 beds) 795 Middle Street, Fall River, MA Zip 02721–1798; tel. 508/674–5741; Michael W. Metzler, President

ST. ELIZABETH'S MEDICAL CENTER OF BOSTON (S, 232 beds) 736 Cambridge Street, Brighton, MA Zip 02135–2997; tel. 617/789–3000; Michael F. Collins, M.D., President
Web address: www.semc.org

ST. JOHN OF GOD HOSPITAL (S, 31 beds) 296 Allston Street, Brighton, MA Zip 02146–1659; tel. 617/277–5750; William K. Brinkert, President

Owned, leased, sponsored:	7 hospitals	1218 beds
Contract–managed:	0 hospitals	0 beds
Totals:	7 hospitals	1218 beds

0705: CAROLINAS HEALTHCARE SYSTEM (NP)
1000 Blythe Boulevard, Charlotte, NC Zip 28203–5871, Mailing Address: P.O. Box 32861, Zip 28232–2861; tel. 704/355–2000; Harry A. Nurkin, Ph.D., President and Chief Executive Officer

NORTH CAROLINA: ANNIE PENN HOSPITAL (C, 126 beds) 618 South Main Street, Reidsville, NC Zip 27320–5094; tel. 336/634–1010; Susan H. Fitzgibbon, President and Chief Executive Officer

ANSON COMMUNITY HOSPITAL (O, 125 beds) 500 Morven Road, Wadesboro, NC Zip 28170–2745; tel. 704/694–5131; Frederick G. Thompson, Ph.D., Administrator and Chief Executive Officer

CAROLINAS MEDICAL CENTER (O, 736 beds) 1000 Blythe Boulevard, Charlotte, NC Zip 28203–5871, Mailing Address: P.O. Box 32861, Zip 28232–2861; tel. 704/355–2000; Paul S. Franz, President
Web address: www.carolinas.org

CHARLOTTE INSTITUTE OF REHABILITATION (O, 118 beds) 1100 Blythe Boulevard, Charlotte, NC Zip 28203–5864; tel. 704/355–4300; Don Gabriel, Administrator

CLEVELAND REGIONAL MEDICAL CENTER (L, 308 beds) 201 Grover Street, Shelby, NC Zip 28150–3940; tel. 704/487–3000; John Young, President and Chief Executive Officer

CRAWLEY MEMORIAL HOSPITAL (C, 51 beds) 315 West College Avenue, Boiling Springs, NC Zip 28017, Mailing Address: P.O. Box 996, Zip 28017–0996; tel. 704/434–9466; Gail McKillop, President

KINGS MOUNTAIN HOSPITAL (O, 72 beds) 706 West King Street, Kings Mountain, NC Zip 28086–2708, Mailing Address: P.O. Box 339, Zip 28086–0339; tel. 704/739–3601; Hank Neal, Administrator

MERCY HOSPITAL (O, 224 beds) 2001 Vail Avenue, Charlotte, NC Zip 28207–1289; tel. 704/379–5100; C. Curtis Copenhaver, President

UNION REGIONAL MEDICAL CENTER (L, 223 beds) 600 Hospital Drive, Monroe, NC Zip 28112–6000, Mailing Address: P.O. Box 5003, Zip 28111–5003; tel. 704/283–3100; John W. Roberts, President and Chief Executive Officer
Web address: www.carolinas.org

UNIVERSITY HOSPITAL (O, 122 beds) 8800 North Tryon Street, Charlotte, NC Zip 28262–8415, Mailing Address: P.O. Box 560727, Zip 28256–0727; tel. 704/548–6000; W. Spencer Lilly, Administrator

VALDESE GENERAL HOSPITAL (O, 199 beds) Valdese, NC Mailing Address: P.O. Box 700, Zip 28690–0700; tel. 828/874–2251; Lloyd E. Wallace, President and Chief Executive Officer

SOUTH CAROLINA: ROPER HOSPITAL (C, 398 beds) 316 Calhoun Street, Charleston, SC Zip 29401–1125; tel. 843/724–2000; Edward L. Berdick, President and Chief Executive Officer

ROPER HOSPITAL NORTH (C, 104 beds) 2750 Speissegger Drive, Charleston, SC Zip 29405–8294; tel. 843/745–2800; John C. Hales Jr., FACHE, President and Chief Executive Officer

Owned, leased, sponsored:	9 hospitals	2127 beds
Contract–managed:	4 hospitals	679 beds
Totals:	13 hospitals	2806 beds

★5945: CARONDELET HEALTH SYSTEM (CC)
13801 Riverport Drive, Suite 300, Saint Louis, MO Zip 63043–4810; tel. 314/770–0333; Gary Christiansen, President and Chief Executive Officer

ARIZONA: CARONDELET HOLY CROSS HOSPITAL (O, 80 beds) 1171 West Target Range Road, Nogales, AZ Zip 85621–2496; tel. 520/287–2771; Carol Field, Senior Corporate Director and Administrator

CARONDELET ST. JOSEPH'S HOSPITAL (O, 300 beds) 350 North Wilmot Road, Tucson, AZ Zip 85711–2678; tel. 520/296–3211; Sister St. Joan Willert, President and Chief Executive Officer

CARONDELET ST. MARY'S HOSPITAL (O, 354 beds) 1601 West St. Mary's Road, Tucson, AZ Zip 85745–2682; tel. 520/622–5833; Sister St. Joan Willert, President and Chief Executive Officer

CALIFORNIA: DANIEL FREEMAN MARINA HOSPITAL (O, 179 beds) 4650 Lincoln Boulevard, Venice, CA Zip 90291–6360; tel. 310/823–8911; Joseph W. Dunn, Ph.D., Chief Executive Officer

DANIEL FREEMAN MEMORIAL HOSPITAL (O, 360 beds) 333 North Prairie Avenue, Inglewood, CA Zip 90301–4514; tel. 310/674–7050; Joseph W. Dunn, Ph.D., Chief Executive Officer

SANTA MARTA HOSPITAL (O, 83 beds) 319 North Humphreys Avenue, Los Angeles, CA Zip 90022–1499; tel. 323/266–6500; Harry E. Whitney, President and Chief Executive Officer

GEORGIA: ST. JOSEPH HOSPITAL (O, 149 beds) 2260 Wrightsboro Road, Augusta, GA Zip 30904–4726; tel. 706/481–7000; J. William Paugh, President and Chief Executive Officer
Web address: www.stjoshosp.org

WALTON REHABILITATION HOSPITAL (O, 58 beds) 1355 Independence Drive, Augusta, GA Zip 30901–1037; tel. 706/724–7746; Dennis B. Skelley, President and Chief Executive Officer
Web address: www.wrh.org

IDAHO: ST. JOSEPH REGIONAL MEDICAL CENTER (O, 156 beds) 415 Sixth Street, Lewiston, ID Zip 83501–0816; tel. 208/743–2511; Howard A. Hayes, President and Chief Executive Officer

MISSOURI: SAINT JOSEPH HEALTH CENTER (O, 267 beds) 1000 Carondelet Drive, Kansas City, MO Zip 64114–4673; tel. 816/942–4400; Andrew W. Allen, Interim President and Chief Executive Officer

ST. MARY'S HOSPITAL OF BLUE SPRINGS (O, 112 beds) 201 West R. D. Mize Road, Blue Springs, MO Zip 64014; tel. 816/228–5900; Gordon Docking, Senior Executive Officer

NEW YORK: ST. JOSEPH'S HOSPITAL (O, 224 beds) 555 East Market Street, Elmira, NY Zip 14902–1512; tel. 607/733–6541; Sister Marie Castagnaro, President and Chief Executive Officer
Web address: www.stjosephs.org

Section B

For explanation of codes following names, see page B2.
★ Indicates Type III membership in the American Hospital Association.

ST. MARY'S HOSPITAL (O, 143 beds) 427 Guy Park Avenue, Amsterdam, NY Zip 12010–1095; tel. 518/842–1900; Peter E. Capobianco, President and Chief Executive Officer
Web address: www.smha.org

WASHINGTON: LOURDES COUNSELING CENTER (O, 32 beds) 1175 Carondelet Drive, Richland, WA Zip 99352–1175; tel. 509/943–9104; Thomas Corley, Chief Executive Officer

LOURDES MEDICAL CENTER (O, 132 beds) 520 North Fourth Avenue, Pasco, WA Zip 99301, Mailing Address: P.O. Box 2568, Zip 99302; tel. 509/547–7704; Thomas Corley, Chief Executive Officer
Web address: www.cbvcp.com\healthcenter

Owned, leased, sponsored:	15 hospitals	2629 beds
Contract–managed:	0 hospitals	0 beds
Totals:	15 hospitals	2629 beds

0126: CARRAWAY METHODIST HEALTH SYSTEM (NP)
1600 Carraway Boulevard, Birmingham, AL Zip 35234–1990; tel. 205/502–6000; Robert M. Carraway, M.D., Chairman and Chief Executive Officer

ALABAMA: CARRAWAY BURDICK WEST MEDICAL CENTER (O, 43 beds) Highway 195 East, Haleyville, AL Zip 35565–9536, Mailing Address: P.O. Box 780, Zip 35565–0780; tel. 205/486–5213; Donald J. Jones, Administrator

CARRAWAY METHODIST MEDICAL CENTER (O, 383 beds) 1600 Carraway Boulevard, Birmingham, AL Zip 35234–1990; tel. 205/502–6000; Cindy Williams, FACHE, Administrator
Web address: www.carraway.org

CARRAWAY NORTHWEST MEDICAL CENTER (O, 63 beds) Highway 78 West, Winfield, AL Zip 35594, Mailing Address: P.O. Box 130, Zip 35594–0130; tel. 205/487–7000; Robert E. Henger, Administrator
Web address: www.carraway.org

Owned, leased, sponsored:	3 hospitals	489 beds
Contract–managed:	0 hospitals	0 beds
Totals:	3 hospitals	489 beds

6545: CATHEDRAL HEALTHCARE SYSTEM, INC. (CC)
219 Chestnut Street, Newark, NJ Zip 07105–1558; tel. 201/690–3600; Frank L. Fumai, President and Chief Executive Officer

NEW JERSEY: SAINT JAMES HOSPITAL OF NEWARK (O, 189 beds) 155 Jefferson Street, Newark, NJ Zip 07105; tel. 973/589–1300; Ceu Cirne–Neves, Administrator

SAINT MICHAEL'S MEDICAL CENTER (O, 299 beds) 268 Dr. Martin Luther King Jr. Boulevard, Newark, NJ Zip 07102–2094; tel. 973/877–5000; Barbara Loughney, Administrator
Web address: www.cathedralhealthcare.org

Owned, leased, sponsored:	2 hospitals	488 beds
Contract–managed:	0 hospitals	0 beds
Totals:	2 hospitals	488 beds

0136: CATHOLIC HEALTH EAST (CC)
14 Campus Boulevard, Suite 300, Newtown Square, PA Zip 19073–3277; tel. 610/355–2000; Daniel F. Russell, President and Chief Executive Officer

ALABAMA: MERCY MEDICAL (O, 162 beds) 101 Villa Drive, Daphne, AL Zip 36526–4653, Mailing Address: P.O. Box 1090, Zip 36526–1090; tel. 334/626–2694; Sister Mary Eileen Wilhelm, President and Chief Executive Officer
Web address: www.mercymedical.com

FLORIDA: GOOD SAMARITAN MEDICAL CENTER (S, 341 beds) Flagler Drive at Palm Beach Lakes Boulevard, West Palm Beach, FL Zip 33401–3499; tel. 561/655–5511; Phillip C. Dutcher, President and Chief Executive Officer

HOLY CROSS HOSPITAL (O, 437 beds) 4725 North Federal Highway, Fort Lauderdale, FL Zip 33308–4668, Mailing Address: P.O. Box 23460, Zip 33307–3460; tel. 954/771–8000; John C. Johnson, Chief Executive Officer
Web address: www.holy–cross.com

MERCY HOSPITAL (O, 339 beds) 3663 South Miami Avenue, Miami, FL Zip 33133–4237; tel. 305/854–4400; Edward J. Rosasco Jr., President and Chief Executive Officer

ST. ANTHONY'S HOSPITAL 1200 Seventh Avenue North, Saint Petersburg, FL Zip 33705–1388, Mailing Address: P.O. Box 12588, Zip 33733–2588; tel. 727/825–1100; Sue G. Brody, President and Chief Executive Officer
Web address: www.stanthonys.org

ST. JOSEPH'S HOSPITAL (S, 883 beds) 3001 West Martin Luther King Jr. Boulevard, Tampa, FL Zip 33607–6387, Mailing Address: P.O. Box 4227, Zip 33677–4227; tel. 813/870–4000; Isaac Mallah, President and Chief Executive Officer

ST. MARY'S HOSPITAL (S, 460 beds) 901 45th Street, West Palm Beach, FL Zip 33407–2495, Mailing Address: P.O. Box 24620, Zip 33416–4620; tel. 561/844–6300; Phillip C. Dutcher, President and Chief Executive Officer

GEORGIA: SAINT JOSEPH'S HOSPITAL OF ATLANTA (O, 346 beds) 5665 Peachtree Dunwoody Road N.E., Atlanta, GA Zip 30342–1764; tel. 404/851–7001; Brue Chandler, President and Chief Executive Officer
Web address: www.stjosephsatlanta.org

ST. MARY'S HEALTH CARE SYSTEM (O, 283 beds) 1230 Baxter Street, Athens, GA Zip 30606–3791; tel. 706/548–7581; Edward J. Fechtel Jr., President and Chief Executive Officer
Web address: www.stmarysathens.com

MAINE: MERCY HOSPITAL PORTLAND (O, 159 beds) 144 State Street, Portland, ME Zip 04101–3795; tel. 207/879–3000; Howard R. Buckley, President
Web address: www.mercyhospital.com

MASSACHUSETTS: MERCY HOSPITAL (O, 352 beds) 271 Carew Street, Springfield, MA Zip 01104–2398, Mailing Address: P.O. Box 9012, Zip 01102–9012; tel. 413/748–9000; Vincent J. McCorkle, President

NEW JERSEY: OUR LADY OF LOURDES MEDICAL CENTER (O, 327 beds) 1600 Haddon Avenue, Camden, NJ Zip 08103–3117; tel. 609/757–3500; Alexander J. Hatala, President and Chief Executive Officer
Web address: www.lourdesnet.org

RANCOCAS HOSPITAL (O, 237 beds) 218–A Sunset Road, Willingboro, NJ Zip 08046–1162; tel. 609/835–2900; Joseph Flamini, Chief Executive Officer

NEW YORK: KENMORE MERCY HOSPITAL (S, 184 beds) 2950 Elmwood Avenue, Kenmore, NY Zip 14217–1390; tel. 716/447–6100; Sister Mary Joel Schimscheiner, Chief Executive Officer

MERCY HOSPITAL (S, 457 beds) 565 Abbott Road, Buffalo, NY Zip 14220–2095; tel. 716/826–7000; John P. Davanzo, President and Chief Executive Officer
Web address: www.mercywyn,org

ST. JAMES MERCY HOSPITAL (O, 200 beds) 411 Canisteo Street, Hornell, NY Zip 14843–2197; tel. 607/324–8000; William G. Connors, President and Chief Executive Officer
Web address: www.sjmh.org

ST. JOSEPH HOSPITAL (S, 208 beds) 2605 Harlem Road, Cheektowaga, NY Zip 14225–4097; tel. 716/891–2400; Patrick J. Wiles, President and Chief Executive Officer
Web address: www.sjh.org

ST. PETER'S HOSPITAL (O, 437 beds) 315 South Manning Boulevard, Albany, NY Zip 12208–1789; tel. 518/525–1550; Steven P. Boyle, President and Chief Executive Officer

PENNSYLVANIA: MERCY COMMUNITY HOSPITAL (O, 97 beds) 2000 Old West Chester Pike, Havertown, PA Zip 19083–2712; tel. 610/853–7000; George F. McLaughlin, Chief Executive Officer

MERCY HOSPITAL OF PITTSBURGH (O, 422 beds) 1400 Locust Street, Pittsburgh, PA Zip 15219–5166; tel. 412/232–8111; J. Penn Krause, Executive Vice President Operations

MERCY PROVIDENCE HOSPITAL (O, 120 beds) 1004 Arch Street, Pittsburgh, PA Zip 15212–5235; tel. 412/323–5600; Sister Kathi Sweeney, Administrator

For explanation of codes following names, see page B2.
★ Indicates Type III membership in the American Hospital Association.

NORTH PHILADELPHIA HEALTH SYSTEM (C, 315 beds) 16th Street and Girard Avenue, Philadelphia, PA Zip 19130–1615; tel. 215/787–9000; George J. Walmsley III, President and Chief Executive Officer

SUBURBAN GENERAL HOSPITAL (O, 106 beds) 2701 DeKalb Pike, Norristown, PA Zip 19401–1820; tel. 610/278–2000; Edward R. Solvibile, President

Owned, leased, sponsored:	21 hospitals	6557 beds
Contract–managed:	1 hospital	315 beds
Totals:	22 hospitals	6872 beds

★**0092: CATHOLIC HEALTH INITIATIVES** (CC)
1999 Broadway, Suite 2605, Denver, CO Zip 80202–4004; tel. 303/298–9100; Patricia A. Cahill, President and Chief Executive Officer

ARKANSAS: ST. VINCENT INFIRMARY MEDICAL CENTER (S, 657 beds) Two St. Vincent Circle, Little Rock, AR Zip 72205–5499; tel. 501/660–3000; Diana T. Hueter, President and Chief Executive Officer
Web address: www.stvincenthealth.org

COLORADO: MERCY MEDICAL CENTER (S, 81 beds) 375 East Park Avenue, Durango, CO Zip 81301; tel. 970/247–4311; Kirk Dignum, Administrator
Web address: www.mercydurango.org

PENROSE–ST. FRANCIS HEALTH SERVICES (S, 423 beds) Colorado Springs, CO Donna L. Bertram, R.N., Administrator

ST. ANTHONY CENTRAL HOSPITAL (S, 302 beds) 4231 West 16th Avenue, Denver, CO Zip 80204–4098; tel. 303/629–3511; Matthew S. Fulton, Senior Vice President and Administrator

ST. ANTHONY NORTH HOSPITAL (S, 118 beds) 2551 West 84th Avenue, Westminster, CO Zip 80030–3887; tel. 303/426–2151; Matthew S. Fulton, Chief Executive Officer

ST. MARY–CORWIN MEDICAL CENTER (S, 261 beds) 1008 Minnequa Avenue, Pueblo, CO Zip 81004–3798; tel. 719/560–4000; John D. Julius, Interim Administrator

ST. THOMAS MORE HOSPITAL AND PROGRESSIVE CARE CENTER (S, 218 beds) 1338 Phay Avenue, Canon City, CO Zip 81212–2221; tel. 719/269–2000; C. Ray Honaker, Chief Executive Officer
Web address: www.centura.org

DELAWARE: ST. FRANCIS HOSPITAL (S, 240 beds) Seventh and Clayton Streets, Wilmington, DE Zip 19805–0500, Mailing Address: P.O. Box 2500, Zip 19805–0500; tel. 302/421–4100; Daniel J. Sinnott, President and Chief Executive Officer

IDAHO: MERCY MEDICAL CENTER (S, 149 beds) 1512 12th Avenue Road, Nampa, ID Zip 83686–6008; tel. 208/467–1171; Joseph Messmer, President and Chief Executive Officer

IOWA: ALEGENT HEALTH MERCY HOSPITAL (S, 209 beds) 800 Mercy Drive, Council Bluffs, IA Zip 51503–3128, Mailing Address: P.O. Box 1C, Zip 51502–3001; tel. 712/328–5000; Charles J. Marr, Chief Executive Officer

MERCY HOSPITAL (S, 22 beds) 703 Rosary Drive, Corning, IA Zip 50841, Mailing Address: P.O. Box 368, Zip 50841–0368; tel. 515/322–3121; James C. Ruppert, Administrator

MERCY HOSPITAL MEDICAL CENTER (S, 556 beds) 400 University Avenue, Des Moines, IA Zip 50314–3190; tel. 515/247–3121; David H. Vellinga, President and Chief Executive Officer
Web address: www.mercydesmoines.org

ST. JOSEPH'S MERCY HOSPITAL (S, 54 beds) 1 St. Joseph's Drive, Centerville, IA Zip 52544; tel. 515/437–4111; William C. Assell, President and Chief Executive Officer

KANSAS: CENTRAL KANSAS MEDICAL CENTER (S, 175 beds) 3515 Broadway Street, Great Bend, KS Zip 67530–3691; tel. 316/792–2511; Thomas W. Sommers, President and Chief Executive Officer

ST. CATHERINE HOSPITAL (S, 100 beds) 410 East Walnut, Garden City, KS Zip 67846–5672; tel. 316/272–2222; Mark B. Steadham, President and Chief Executive Officer

KENTUCKY: CARITAS MEDICAL CENTER (S, 213 beds) 1850 Bluegrass Avenue, Louisville, KY Zip 40215–1199; tel. 502/361–6000; Peter J. Bernard, President and Chief Executive Officer

CARITAS PEACE CENTER (S, 156 beds) 2020 Newburg Road, Louisville, KY Zip 40205–1879; tel. 502/451–3330; Peter J. Bernard, President and Chief Executive Officer

FLAGET MEMORIAL HOSPITAL (S, 36 beds) 201 Cathedral Manor, Bardstown, KY Zip 40004–1299; tel. 502/348–3923; Suzanne Reasbeck, President and Chief Executive Officer
Web address: www.flaget.com

MARYMOUNT MEDICAL CENTER (S, 70 beds) 310 East Ninth Street, London, KY Zip 40741–1299; tel. 606/877–3705; Lowell Jones, Chief Executive Officer

OUR LADY OF THE WAY HOSPITAL (S, 39 beds) 11022 Main Street, Martin, KY Zip 41649–0910; tel. 606/285–5181; Lowell Jones, Chief Executive Officer

SAINT JOSEPH HOSPITAL (S, 357 beds) One St. Joseph Drive, Lexington, KY Zip 40504–3754; tel. 606/278–3436; Thomas J. Murray, President
Web address: www.sjhlex.org

MARYLAND: ST. JOSEPH MEDICAL CENTER (S, 414 beds) 7620 York Road, Towson, MD Zip 21204–7582; tel. 410/337–1000; James J. Cullen, President and Chief Executive Officer
Web address: www.sjmcmd.org

MINNESOTA: ALBANY AREA HOSPITAL AND MEDICAL CENTER (S, 15 beds) 300 Third Avenue, Albany, MN Zip 56307–9363; tel. 320/845–2121; Ben Koppelman, Administrator

LAKEWOOD HEALTH CENTER (S, 64 beds) 600 South Main Avenue, Baudette, MN Zip 56623; tel. 218/634–2120; SharRay Palm, President and Chief Executive Officer

ST. FRANCIS MEDICAL CENTER (S, 171 beds) 415 Oak Street, Breckenridge, MN Zip 56520–1298; tel. 218/643–3000; David A. Nelson, President and Chief Executive Officer

ST. GABRIEL'S HOSPITAL (S, 205 beds) 815 Second Street S.E., Little Falls, MN Zip 56345–3596; tel. 320/632–5441; Larry A. Schulz, President and Chief Executive Officer
Web address: www.upstel.net/~falls/unf.html

ST. JOSEPH'S AREA HEALTH SERVICES (S, 40 beds) 600 Pleasant Avenue, Park Rapids, MN Zip 56470–1432; tel. 218/732–3311; David R. Hove, President and Chief Executive Officer

MISSOURI: ST. JOHN'S REGIONAL MEDICAL CENTER (S, 367 beds) 2727 McClelland Boulevard, Joplin, MO Zip 64804–1694; tel. 417/781–2727; Gary L. Rowe, President and Chief Executive Officer
Web address: www.stj.com

NEBRASKA: ALEGENT HEALTH BERGAN MERCY MEDICAL CENTER (S, 549 beds) 7500 Mercy Road, Omaha, NE Zip 68124; tel. 402/343–4410; Charles J. Marr, Chief Executive Officer

GOOD SAMARITAN HEALTH SYSTEMS (S, 267 beds) 10 East 31st Street, Kearney, NE Zip 68847–2926, Mailing Address: P.O. Box 1990, Zip 68848–1990; tel. 308/865–7100; William Wilson Hendrickson, President and Chief Executive Officer

SAINT ELIZABETH REGIONAL MEDICAL CENTER (S, 170 beds) 555 South 70th Street, Lincoln, NE Zip 68510–2494; tel. 402/489–7181; Robert J. Lanik, President
Web address: www.stez.org

ST. FRANCIS MEDICAL CENTER (S, 198 beds) 2620 West Faidley Avenue, Grand Island, NE Zip 68803–4297, Mailing Address: P.O. Box 9804, Zip 68802–9804; tel. 308/384–4600; Michael R. Gloor, FACHE, President and Chief Executive Officer
Web address: www.sfmc–gi.org

ST. MARY'S HOSPITAL (S, 28 beds) 1314 Third Avenue, Nebraska City, NE Zip 68410–1999; tel. 402/873–3321; Daniel J. Kelly, President and Chief Executive Officer

NEW JERSEY: ST. FRANCIS MEDICAL CENTER (S, 214 beds) 601 Hamilton Avenue, Trenton, NJ Zip 08629–1986; tel. 609/599–5000; Judith M. Persichilli, President and Chief Executive Officer

NEW MEXICO: ST. JOSEPH MEDICAL CENTER (S, 218 beds) 601 Martin Luther King Jr. Drive N.E., Albuquerque, NM Zip 87102, Mailing Address: P.O. Box 25555, Zip 87125–0555; tel. 505/727–8000; Steven J. Smith, President

For explanation of codes following names, see page B2.
★ Indicates Type III membership in the American Hospital Association.

Section B

ST. JOSEPH NORTHEAST HEIGHTS HOSPITAL (S, 87 beds) 4701 Montgomery Boulevard N.E., Albuquerque, NM Zip 87109–1251, Mailing Address: P.O. Box 25555, Zip 87125–0555; tel. 505/727–7800; C. Vincent Townsend Jr., Vice President

ST. JOSEPH REHABILITATION HOSPITAL AND OUTPATIENT CENTER (S, 63 beds) 505 Elm Street N.E., Albuquerque, NM Zip 87102–2500, Mailing Address: P.O. Box 25555, Zip 87125–5555; tel. 505/727–4700; Mary Lou Coors, Administrator

ST. JOSEPH WEST MESA HOSPITAL (S, 74 beds) 10501 Golf Course Road N.W., Albuquerque, NM Zip 87114–5000, Mailing Address: P.O. Box 25555, Zip 87125–0555; tel. 505/727–2000; C. Vincent Townsend Jr., Vice President

NORTH DAKOTA: CARRINGTON HEALTH CENTER (S, 70 beds) 800 North Fourth Street, Carrington, ND Zip 58421–1217; tel. 701/652–3141; Brian J. McDermott, President and Chief Executive Officer

MERCY HOSPITAL (S, 35 beds) 1031 Seventh Street, Devils Lake, ND Zip 58301–2798; tel. 701/662–2131; Marlene Krein, President and Chief Executive Officer

MERCY HOSPITAL (S, 50 beds) 570 Chautauqua Boulevard, Valley City, ND Zip 58072–3199; tel. 701/845–6400; Jane Bissel, President and Chief Executive Officer

MERCY MEDICAL CENTER (S, 93 beds) 1301 15th Avenue West, Williston, ND Zip 58801–3896; tel. 701/774–7400; M. Thomas Mitchell, President and Chief Executive Officer
Web address: www.dia.net/mercy

OAKES COMMUNITY HOSPITAL (S, 30 beds) 314 South Eighth Street, Oakes, ND Zip 58474–2099; tel. 701/742–3291; Bradley D. Burris, President and Chief Executive Officer

ST. ANSGAR'S HEALTH CENTER (S, 20 beds) 115 Vivian Street, Park River, ND Zip 58270–0708; tel. 701/284–7500; Michael D. Mahrer, President

ST. JOSEPH'S HOSPITAL AND HEALTH CENTER (S, 90 beds) 30 Seventh Street West, Dickinson, ND Zip 58601–4399; tel. 701/225–7200; Greg Hanson, President and Chief Executive Officer
Web address: www.stjosehospital.org

OHIO: GOOD SAMARITAN HOSPITAL (S, 441 beds) 375 Dixmyth Avenue, Cincinnati, OH Zip 45220–2489; tel. 513/872–1400; John S. Prout, President and Chief Executive Officer
Web address: www.trihealth.com

GOOD SAMARITAN HOSPITAL AND HEALTH CENTER (S, 324 beds) 2222 Philadelphia Drive, Dayton, OH Zip 45406–1813; tel. 937/278–2612; K. Douglas Deck, President and Chief Executive Officer

OREGON: HOLY ROSARY MEDICAL CENTER (S, 74 beds) 351 S.W. Ninth Street, Ontario, OR Zip 97914–2693; tel. 541/881–7000; Bruce Jensen, Chief Executive Officer and Team Leader

MERCY MEDICAL CENTER (S, 103 beds) 2700 Stewart Parkway, Roseburg, OR Zip 97470–1297; tel. 541/673–0611; Victor J. Fresolone, FACHE, President and Chief Executive Officer
Web address: www.mercyrose.org

ST. ANTHONY HOSPITAL (S, 49 beds) 1601 S.E. Court Avenue, Pendleton, OR Zip 97801–3297; tel. 541/276–5121; Jeffrey S. Drop, President and Chief Executive Officer

ST. ELIZABETH HEALTH SERVICES (S, 134 beds) 3325 Pocahontas Road, Baker City, OR Zip 97814; tel. 541/523–6461; Robert T. Mannix Jr., President and Chief Operations Officer

PENNSYLVANIA: NAZARETH HOSPITAL (S, 222 beds) 2601 Holme Avenue, Philadelphia, PA Zip 19152–2007; tel. 215/335–6000; Gregory T. Wozniak, President and Chief Executive Officer

ST. AGNES MEDICAL CENTER (S, 172 beds) 1900 South Broad Street, Philadelphia, PA Zip 19145–2304; tel. 215/339–4100; Sister Margaret T. Sullivan, President, Chief Executive Officer and Chief Operating Officer

ST. JOSEPH HOSPITAL (S, 256 beds) 250 College Avenue, Lancaster, PA Zip 17604, Mailing Address: P.O. Box 3509, Zip 17604–3509; tel. 717/291–8211; John Kerr Tolmie, President and Chief Executive Officer
Web address: www.chieast.org

ST. JOSEPH MEDICAL CENTER (S, 417 beds) Twelth and Walnut Streets, Reading, PA Zip 19603–0316, Mailing Address: P.O. Box 316, Zip 19603–0316; tel. 610/378–2000; Christopher B. Rumpf, M.D., Interim President
Web address: www.chi–east.org/

ST. MARY MEDICAL CENTER (S, 244 beds) Langhorne–Newtown Road, Langhorne, PA Zip 19047–1295; tel. 215/750–2000; Gregory T. Wozniak, President and Chief Executive Officer

SOUTH DAKOTA: GETTYSBURG MEDICAL CENTER (S, 61 beds) 606 East Garfield, Gettysburg, SD Zip 57442–1398; tel. 605/765–2480; Mark Schmidt, Administrator

ST. MARY'S HEALTHCARE CENTER (S, 191 beds) 800 East Dakota Avenue, Pierre, SD Zip 57501–3313; tel. 605/224–3100; James D. M. Russell, Chief Executive Officer
Web address: www.st–marys.com

TENNESSEE: MEMORIAL HOSPITAL (S, 287 beds) 2525 De Sales Avenue, Chattanooga, TN Zip 37404–3322; tel. 423/495–2525; L. Clark Taylor Jr., President and Chief Executive Officer
Web address: www.memorial.org

MEMORIAL NORTH PARK HOSPITAL (S, 83 beds) 2051 Hamill Road, Chattanooga, TN Zip 37343–4096; tel. 423/870–6100; Sean S. McMurray, CHE, Administrator

WASHINGTON: ST. CLARE HOSPITAL (S, 60 beds) 11315 Bridgeport Way S.W., Lakewood, WA Zip 98499–0998, Mailing Address: P.O. Box 99998, Zip 98499–0998; tel. 253/588–1711; Joseph W. Wilczek, President and Chief Executive Officer

ST. FRANCIS HOSPITAL (S, 67 beds) 34515 Ninth Avenue South, Federal Way, WA Zip 98003–9710; tel. 253/927–9700; Joseph W. Wilczek, President and Chief Executive Officer

ST. JOSEPH MEDICAL CENTER (S, 271 beds) 1717 South J Street, Tacoma, WA Zip 98405, Mailing Address: P.O. Box 2197, Zip 98401–2197; tel. 253/627–4101; Joseph W. Wilczek, President and Chief Executive Officer

WISCONSIN: GOOD SAMARITAN HEALTH CENTER OF MERRILL (S, 63 beds) 601 Center Avenue South, Merrill, WI Zip 54452–3404; tel. 715/536–5511; Michael Hammer, President and Chief Executive Officer

Owned, leased, sponsored:	64 hospitals	11487 beds
Contract–managed:	0 hospitals	0 beds
Totals:	64 hospitals	11487 beds

0079: CATHOLIC HEALTH PARTNERS (CC)
2913 North Commonwealth, Chicago, IL Zip 60657–6296; tel. 773/665–3170; Sister Theresa Peck, President and Chief Executive Officer

ILLINOIS: COLUMBUS HOSPITAL (S, 227 beds) 2520 North Lakeview Avenue, Chicago, IL Zip 60614–1895; tel. 773/388–7300; Sister Theresa Peck, President and Chief Executive Officer
Web address: www.cath–health.org

SAINT ANTHONY HOSPITAL (S, 165 beds) 2875 West 19th Street, Chicago, IL Zip 60623–3596; tel. 773/521–1710; Sister Theresa Peck, President and Chief Executive Officer
Web address: www.cath–health.org

ST. JOSEPH HOSPITAL (S, 324 beds) 2900 North Lake Shore Drive, Chicago, IL Zip 60657–6274; tel. 773/665–3000; Sister Theresa Peck, President and Chief Executive Officer

Owned, leased, sponsored:	3 hospitals	716 beds
Contract–managed:	0 hospitals	0 beds
Totals:	3 hospitals	716 beds

5155: CATHOLIC HEALTHCARE PARTNERS (CC)
615 Elsinore Place, Cincinnati, OH Zip 45202; tel. 513/639–2827; Michael D. Connelly, President and Chief Executive Officer

For explanation of codes following names, see page B2.
★ Indicates Type III membership in the American Hospital Association.

KENTUCKY: LOURDES HOSPITAL (S, 389 beds) 1530 Lone Oak Road, Paducah, KY Zip 42003, Mailing Address: P.O. Box 7100, Zip 42002–7100; tel. 502/444–2444; Robert P. Goodwin, President and Chief Executive Officer
Web address: www.lourdes–pad.org

MARCUM AND WALLACE MEMORIAL HOSPITAL (S, 26 beds) 60 Mercy Court, Irvine, KY Zip 40336–1331, Mailing Address: P.O. Box 928, Zip 40336–0928; tel. 606/723–2115; James F. Heitzenrater, Administrator

ST. ELIZABETH MEDICAL CENTER–GRANT COUNTY (O, 20 beds) 238 Barnes Road, Williamstown, KY Zip 41097–9460; tel. 606/824–2400; Chris Carle, Administrator

ST. ELIZABETH MEDICAL CENTER–NORTH (O, 466 beds) 401 East 20th Street, Covington, KY Zip 41014–1585; tel. 606/292–4000; Joseph W. Gross, President and Chief Executive Officer

OHIO: CLERMONT MERCY HOSPITAL (S, 133 beds) 3000 Hospital Drive, Batavia, OH Zip 45103–1998; tel. 513/732–8200; Fred L. Kolb, President
Web address: www.mercy.health–partners.org

FRANCISCAN HOSPITAL–MOUNT AIRY CAMPUS (O, 240 beds) 2446 Kipling Avenue, Cincinnati, OH Zip 45239–6650; tel. 513/853–5000; R. Christopher West, President

FRANCISCAN HOSPITAL–WESTERN HILLS CAMPUS (O, 224 beds) 3131 Queen City Avenue, Cincinnati, OH Zip 45238–2396; tel. 513/389–5000; R. Christopher West, President

LORAIN COMMUNITY/ST. JOSEPH REGIONAL HEALTH CENTER (S, 303 beds) 3700 Kolbe Road, Lorain, OH Zip 44053–1697; tel. 216/960–3000; Brian C. Lockwood, President and Chief Executive Officer

MERCY HOSPITAL (S, 248 beds) Hamilton, OH Mailing Address: P.O. Box 418, Zip 45012–0418; tel. 513/867–6400; David A. Ferrell, President
Web address: www.mercy.health–partners.org

MERCY HOSPITAL (S, 60 beds) 485 West Market Street, Tiffin, OH Zip 44883–0727, Mailing Address: P.O. Box 727, Zip 44883–0727; tel. 419/447–3130; Mark Shugarman, President

MERCY HOSPITAL ANDERSON (S, 156 beds) 7500 State Road, Cincinnati, OH Zip 45255–2492; tel. 513/624–4500; Fred L. Kolb, President

MERCY HOSPITAL–WILLARD (S, 30 beds) 110 East Howard Street, Willard, OH Zip 44890–1611; tel. 419/933–2931; Dale E. Thornton, President

MERCY MEDICAL CENTER (S, 218 beds) 1343 North Fountain Boulevard, Springfield, OH Zip 45501–1380; tel. 937/390–5000; Teresa Richle, Interim Senior Vice President Acute Care Operations

MERCY MEMORIAL HOSPITAL (S, 20 beds) 904 Scioto Street, Urbana, OH Zip 43078–2200; tel. 937/653–5231; Richard Rogers, Senior Vice President

RIVERSIDE MERCY HOSPITAL (S, 162 beds) 1600 North Superior Street, Toledo, OH Zip 43604–2199; tel. 419/729–6000; Scott E. Shook, President

ST. CHARLES MERCY HOSPITAL (S, 309 beds) 2600 Navarre Avenue, Oregon, OH Zip 43616–3297; tel. 419/698–7479; Cathleen K. Nelson, President and Chief Executive Officer

ST. ELIZABETH HEALTH CENTER (S, 339 beds) 1044 Belmont Avenue, Youngstown, OH Zip 44501, Mailing Address: P.O. Box 1790, Zip 44501–1790; tel. 330/746–7211; Robert W. Shroder, Executive Vice President Operations

ST. JOSEPH HEALTH CENTER (S, 136 beds) 667 Eastland Avenue S.E., Warren, OH Zip 44484–4531; tel. 330/841–4000; Robert W. Shroder, Vice President Operations
Web address: www.hmhs.org

ST. RITA'S MEDICAL CENTER (S, 320 beds) 730 West Market Street, Lima, OH Zip 45801–4670; tel. 419/227–3361; James P. Reber, President
Web address: www.mercy.com\srmc

ST. VINCENT MERCY MEDICAL CENTER (S, 483 beds) 2213 Cherry Street, Toledo, OH Zip 43608–2691; tel. 419/251–3232; Steven L. Mickus, President and Chief Executive Officer
Web address: www.mercyweb.org

PENNSYLVANIA: MERCY HOSPITAL OF SCRANTON (S, 265 beds) 746 Jefferson Avenue, Scranton, PA Zip 18501–1624; tel. 717/348–7100; Susan Petula, President

MERCY HOSPITAL OF WILKES–BARRE (S, 173 beds) 25 Church Street, Wilkes–Barre, PA Zip 18765–0999, Mailing Address: P.O. Box 658, Zip 18765–0658; tel. 570/826–3100

MERCY SPECIAL CARE HOSPITAL (S, 38 beds) 128 West Washington Street, Nanticoke, PA Zip 18634–3113; tel. 570/735–5000; Robert D. Williams, Administrator

TENNESSEE: JEFFERSON MEMORIAL HOSPITAL (L, 22 beds) 1800 Bishop Avenue, Jefferson City, TN Zip 37760–1992, Mailing Address: P.O. Box 560, Zip 37760–0560; tel. 423/475–2091; Michael C. Hicks, President and Chief Executive Officer
Web address: www.mercy.com/stmarys

ST. MARY'S HEALTH SYSTEM (S, 300 beds) 900 East Oak Hill Avenue, Knoxville, TN Zip 37917–4556; tel. 423/545–8000; Richard C. Williams, President and Chief Executive Officer

Owned, leased, sponsored:	25 hospitals	5080 beds
Contract–managed:	0 hospitals	0 beds
Totals:	25 hospitals	5080 beds

★5205: CATHOLIC HEALTHCARE WEST (CC)
1700 Montgomery Street, Suite 300, San Francisco, CA Zip 94111–9603; tel. 415/438–5500; Richard J. Kramer, President and Chief Executive Officer

ARIZONA: ST. JOSEPH'S HOSPITAL AND MEDICAL CENTER (S, 514 beds) 350 West Thomas Road, Phoenix, AZ Zip 85013–4496, Mailing Address: P.O. Box 2071, Zip 85001–2071; tel. 602/406–3100; Mary G. Yarbrough, President and Chief Executive Officer
Web address: www.chw.edu

CALIFORNIA: BAKERSFIELD MEMORIAL HOSPITAL (S, 345 beds) 420 34th Street, Bakersfield, CA Zip 93301, Mailing Address: P.O. Box 1888, Zip 93303–1888; tel. 805/327–1792; C. Larry Carr, Regional Executive Vice President and President

CALIFORNIA HOSPITAL MEDICAL CENTER (O, 303 beds) 1401 South Grand Avenue, Los Angeles, CA Zip 90015–3063; tel. 213/748–2411; Melinda D. Beswick, President
Web address: www.chmcla.com

COMMMUNITY HOSPITAL OF SAN BERNARDINO (O, 380 beds) 1805 Medical Center Drive, San Bernardino, CA Zip 92411; tel. 909/887–6333; Bruce G. Satzger, Administrator
Web address: www.chsb.org

DOMINICAN HOSPITAL (S, 275 beds) 1555 Soquel Drive, Santa Cruz, CA Zip 95065; tel. 831/462–7700; Sister Julie Hyer, President and Chief Executive Officer
Web address: www.dominicanhospital.org

GLENDALE MEMORIAL HOSPITAL AND HEALTH CENTER (O, 275 beds) 1420 South Central Avenue, Glendale, CA Zip 91204–2594; tel. 818/502–2201; Arnold R. Schaffer, President and Chief Executive Officer
Web address: www.glandalememorial.com

LA PALMA INTERCOMMUNITY HOSPITAL (O, 139 beds) 7901 Walker Street, La Palma, CA Zip 90623–5850, Mailing Address: P.O. Box 5850, Buena Park, Zip 90622; tel. 714/670–7400; Stephen E. Dixon, President and Chief Executive Officer
Web address: www.unihealth.org

LONG BEACH COMMUNITY MEDICAL CENTER (O, 278 beds) 1720 Termino Avenue, Long Beach, CA Zip 90804; tel. 562/498–1000; Makoto Nakayama, President
Web address: www.lbcommunity,com

MARIAN MEDICAL CENTER (O, 225 beds) 1400 East Church Street, Santa Maria, CA Zip 93454, Mailing Address: Box 1238, Zip 93456; tel. 805/739–3000; Charles J. Cova, Executive Vice President and Chief Operating Officer

MARK TWAIN ST. JOSEPH'S HOSPITAL (S, 30 beds) 768 Mountain Ranch Road, San Andreas, CA Zip 95249–9710; tel. 209/754–2515; Michael P. Lawson, Administrator

MARTIN LUTHER HOSPITAL (O, 205 beds) 1830 West Romneya Drive, Anaheim, CA Zip 92801–1854; tel. 714/491–5200; Stephen E. Dixon, President and Chief Executive Officer
Web address: www.mdselect.com

MERCY AMERICAN RIVER/MERCY SAN JUAN HOSPITAL (S, 352 beds) 6501 Coyle Avenue, Carmichael, CA Zip 95608, Mailing Address: P.O. Box 479, Zip 95608; tel. 916/537–5000; Michael H. Erne, President

MERCY GENERAL HOSPITAL (S, 402 beds) 4001 J Street, Sacramento, CA Zip 95819; tel. 916/453–4950; Thomas A. Petersen, Vice President and Chief Operating Officer

MERCY HOSPITAL (S, 261 beds) 2215 Truxtun Avenue, Bakersfield, CA Zip 93301, Mailing Address: Box 119, Zip 93302; tel. 661/632–5000; Bernard J. Herman, President and Chief Executive Officer
Web address: www.chw.edu

MERCY HOSPITAL AND HEALTH SERVICES (S, 101 beds) 2740 M Street, Merced, CA Zip 95340–2880; tel. 209/384–6444; John Headding, Chief Administrative Officer

MERCY HOSPITAL OF FOLSOM (S, 95 beds) 1650 Creekside Drive, Folsom, CA Zip 95630; tel. 916/983–7400; Donald C. Hudson, Vice President and Chief Operating Officer

MERCY MEDICAL CENTER MOUNT SHASTA (S, 80 beds) 914 Pine Street, Mount Shasta, CA Zip 96067, Mailing Address: P.O. Box 239, Zip 96067–0239; tel. 530/926–6111; Rick J. Barnett, Executive Vice President and Chief Operating Officer
Web address: www.mercy.org

MERCY MEDICAL CENTER REDDING (S, 202 beds) 2175 Rosaline Avenue, Redding, CA Zip 96001, Mailing Address: P.O. Box 496009, Zip 96049–6009; tel. 530/225–6000; John Di Perry Jr., Executive Vice President and Chief Operating Officer
Web address: www.mercy.org

MERCY SOUTHWEST HOSPITAL (O, 67 beds) 400 Old River Road, Bakersfield, CA Zip 93311; tel. 805/663–6000

MERCY WESTSIDE HOSPITAL (S, 73 beds) 110 East North Street, Taft, CA Zip 93268; tel. 661/763–4211; Margo Arnold, Administrator

METHODIST HOSPITAL OF SACRAMENTO (S, 258 beds) 7500 Hospital Drive, Sacramento, CA Zip 95823; tel. 916/423–3000; Stanley C. Oppegard, Vice President and Chief Operating Officer

NORTHRIDGE HOSPITAL MEDICAL CENTER–ROSCOE BOULEVARD CAMPUS (O, 415 beds) 18300 Roscoe Boulevard, Northridge, CA Zip 91328; tel. 818/885–8500; Roger E. Seaver, President and Chief Executive Officer

NORTHRIDGE HOSPITAL AND MEDICAL CENTER, SHERMAN WAY CAMPUS (O, 211 beds) 14500 Sherman Circle, Van Nuys, CA Zip 91405; tel. 818/997–0101; Richard D. Lyons, President and Chief Executive Officer

O'CONNOR HOSPITAL (S, 257 beds) 2105 Forest Avenue, San Jose, CA Zip 95128; tel. 408/947–2500; Joan A. Bero, Regional Vice President and Chief Operating Officer

OAK VALLEY DISTRICT HOSPITAL (O, 141 beds) 350 South Oak Street, Oakdale, CA Zip 95361; tel. 209/847–3011; Norman J. Andrews, Chief Executive Officer

ROBERT F. KENNEDY MEDICAL CENTER (S, 195 beds) 4500 West 116th Street, Hawthorne, CA Zip 90250; tel. 310/973–1711; Peter P. Aprato, Administrator and Chief Operating Officer

SAINT FRANCIS MEMORIAL HOSPITAL (S, 190 beds) 900 Hyde Street, San Francisco, CA Zip 94109, Mailing Address: Box 7726, Zip 94120–7726; tel. 415/353–6000; Cheryl A. Fama, Administrator, Vice President and Chief Operating Officer

SAINT LOUISE HOSPITAL (S, 55 beds) 18500 Saint Louise Drive, Morgan Hill, CA Zip 95037; tel. 408/779–1500; Terrence Curley, Administrator

SAN GABRIEL VALLEY MEDICAL CENTER (O, 274 beds) 438 West Las Tunas Drive, San Gabriel, CA Zip 91776, Mailing Address: P.O. Box 1507, Zip 91778–1507; tel. 626/289–5454; Thomas D. Mone, President and Chief Executive Officer
Web address: www.unihealth.org/sgvmc

SEQUOIA HOSPITAL (S, 231 beds) 170 Alameda De Las Pulgas, Redwood City, CA Zip 94062; tel. 650/369–5811; Glenna L. Vaskelis, Administrator
Web address: www.chwbay.org

SETON MEDICAL CENTER (S, 283 beds) 1900 Sullivan Avenue, Daly City, CA Zip 94015; tel. 650/992–4000; Bernadette Smith, Chief Operating Officer
Web address: www.chwwestbay.org

SETON MEDICAL CENTER COASTSIDE (S, 121 beds) Marine Boulevard and Etheldore Street, Moss Beach, CA Zip 94038; tel. 650/728–5521; Bernadette Smith, Chief Operating Officer

SIERRA NEVADA MEMORIAL HOSPITAL (S, 58 beds) 155 Glasson Way, Grass Valley, CA Zip 95945, Mailing Address: P.O. Box 1029, Zip 95945–1029; tel. 530/274–6000; C. Thomas Collier, President and Chief Executive Officer

ST. BERNARDINE MEDICAL CENTER (S, 268 beds) 2101 North Waterman Avenue, San Bernardino, CA Zip 92404; tel. 909/883–8711; Bruce G. Satzger, Administrator

ST. DOMINIC'S HOSPITAL (S, 65 beds) 1777 West Yosemite Avenue, Manteca, CA Zip 95337; tel. 209/825–3500; Richard Aldred, Chief Administrative Officer

ST. ELIZABETH COMMUNITY HOSPITAL (S, 53 beds) 2550 Sister Mary Columba Drive, Red Bluff, CA Zip 96080–4397; tel. 530/529–8000; Thomas F. Grimes III, Executive Vice President and Chief Operating Officer
Web address: www.mercy.org

ST. FRANCIS MEDICAL CENTER (S, 414 beds) 3630 East Imperial Highway, Lynwood, CA Zip 90262; tel. 310/603–6000; Gerald T. Kozai, President

ST. FRANCIS MEDICAL CENTER OF SANTA BARBARA (O, 20 beds) 601 East Micheltorena Street, Santa Barbara, CA Zip 93103; tel. 805/568–5705; Ron Biscaro, Administrator and Chief Operating Officer

ST. JOHN'S PLEASANT VALLEY HOSPITAL (S, 180 beds) 2309 Antonio Avenue, Camarillo, CA Zip 93010–1459; tel. 805/389–5800; William J. Clearwater, Vice President and Site Administrator

ST. JOHN'S REGIONAL MEDICAL CENTER (S, 230 beds) 1600 North Rose Avenue, Oxnard, CA Zip 93030; tel. 805/988–2500; James R. Hoss, Administrator and Chief Operating Officer

ST. JOSEPH'S BEHAVIORAL HEALTH CENTER (S, 24 beds) 2510 North California Street, Stockton, CA Zip 95204–5568; tel. 209/948–2100; James Sondecker, Director
Web address: www.sjrhs.org

ST. JOSEPH'S MEDICAL CENTER (S, 294 beds) 1800 North California Street, Stockton, CA Zip 95204, Mailing Address: P.O. Box 213008, Zip 95213–3008; tel. 209/943–2000; Donald J. Wiley, Senior Vice President and Chief Operating Officer
Web address: www.sjrhs.org

ST. MARY MEDICAL CENTER (S, 402 beds) 1050 Linden Avenue, Long Beach, CA Zip 90801, Mailing Address: P.O. Box 887, Zip 90813–0887; tel. 562/491–9000; Tammie McMann Brailsford, Administrator and Chief Operating Officer
Web address: www.sc.chw.edu

ST. MARY'S MEDICAL CENTER (S, 256 beds) 450 Stanyan Street, San Francisco, CA Zip 94117–1079; tel. 415/668–1000; Rosemary Fox, Vice President and Chief Operating Officer

ST. VINCENT MEDICAL CENTER (S, 317 beds) 2131 West Third Street, Los Angeles, CA Zip 90057–0992, Mailing Address: P.O. Box 57992, Zip 90057; tel. 213/484–7111; William D. Parente, President
Web address: www.stvincentmedicalcenter.com

WOODLAND HEALTHCARE (S, 103 beds) 1325 Cottonwood Street, Woodland, CA Zip 95695–5199; tel. 530/662–3961; William Hunt, Chief Operating Officer

NEVADA: ST. ROSE DOMINICAN HOSPITAL (S, 143 beds) 102 Lake Mead Drive, Henderson, NV Zip 89015–5524; tel. 702/564–2622; Rod A. Davis, President and Chief Executive Officer

Owned, leased, sponsored:	47 hospitals	10060 beds
Contract–managed:	0 hospitals	0 beds
Totals:	47 hospitals	10060 beds

★**2265:   CENTRA HEALTH, INC.** (NP)
1920 Atherholt Road, Lynchburg, VA Zip 24501–1104; tel. 804/947–4700; George W. Dawson, President

VIRGINIA: LYNCHBURG GENERAL HOSPITAL (O, 350 beds) 1901 Tate Springs Road, Lynchburg, VA Zip 24501–1167; tel. 804/947–3000; L. Darrell Powers, President
Web address: www.centrahealth.com

VIRGINIA BAPTIST HOSPITAL (O, 322 beds) 3300 Rivermont Avenue, Lynchburg, VA Zip 24503–9989; tel. 804/947–4000; Thomas C. Jividen, Senior Vice President
Web address: www.centrahealth.com

Owned, leased, sponsored:	2 hospitals	672 beds
Contract–managed:	0 hospitals	0 beds
Totals:	2 hospitals	672 beds

For explanation of codes following names, see page B2.
★ Indicates Type III membership in the American Hospital Association.

0665: CENTURY HEALTHCARE CORPORATION (IO)
5555 East 71st Street, Suite 9220, Tulsa, OK Zip 74136–6540; tel. 918/491–0780; Jerry D. Dillon, President and Chief Executive Officer

ARIZONA: WESTBRIDGE TREATMENT CENTER (O, 78 beds) 1830 East Roosevelt Street, Phoenix, AZ Zip 85006–3641; tel. 602/254–0884; Mike Perry, Chief Executive Officer

OKLAHOMA: HIGH POINTE (O, 68 beds) 6501 N.E. 50th Street, Oklahoma City, OK Zip 73141–9613; tel. 405/424–3383; Johnny J. Smith, Chief Executive Officer

Owned, leased, sponsored:	2 hospitals	146 beds
Contract–managed:	0 hospitals	0 beds
Totals:	2 hospitals	146 beds

0114: CHILDREN'S COMPREHENSIVE SERVICES, INC. (IO)
3401 West End Avenue, Suite 500, Nashville, TN Zip 37203–0376; tel. 615/383–0376; William J. Ballard, Chief Executive Officer

ARKANSAS: RIVENDELL BEHAVIORAL HEALTH SERVICES (O, 77 beds) 100 Rivendell Drive, Benton, AR Zip 72015–9100; tel. 501/316–1255; Mark E. Schneider, Chief Executive Officer

MICHIGAN: RIVENDELL OF MICHIGAN (O, 63 beds) 101 West Townsend Road, Saint Johns, MI Zip 48879–9200; tel. 517/224–1177; Roger Rohall, Chief Executive Officer

UTAH: COPPER HILLS YOUTH CENTER (O, 80 beds) 5899 West Rivendell Drive, West Jordan, UT Zip 84088–5700, Mailing Address: P.O. Box 459, Zip 84084–0459; tel. 801/561–3377; Sandy Podley, Chief Executive Officer

Owned, leased, sponsored:	3 hospitals	220 beds
Contract–managed:	0 hospitals	0 beds
Totals:	3 hospitals	220 beds

●★0131: CHRISTIANA CARE CORPORATION (NP)
501 West 14th Street, Wilmington, DE Zip 19899, Mailing Address: P.O. Box 1668, Zip 19899; tel. 302/428–2570; Charles M. Smith, M.D., President and Chief Executive Officer

DELAWARE: CHRISTIANA CARE (O, 872 beds) 4755 Ogletown–Stanton Road, Newark, DE Zip 19718; tel. 302/733–1000; Charles M. Smith, M.D., President and Chief Executive Officer
Web address: www.christianacare.org

Owned, leased, sponsored:	1 hospital	872 beds
Contract–managed:	0 hospitals	0 beds
Totals:	1 hospital	872 beds

★0605: CHRISTUS HEALTH (CC)
2600 North Loop West, Houston, TX Zip 77092–8999; tel. 713/681–8877; Sister Christina Murphy, Co–Chief Executive Officer

ARKANSAS: MAGNOLIA HOSPITAL (C, 62 beds) 101 Hospital Drive, Magnolia, AR Zip 71753–2416, Mailing Address: Box 629, Zip 71753–0629; tel. 870/235–3000; Kirk Reamey, Chief Executive Officer

LOUISIANA: CHRISTUS COUSHATTA HEALTH CARE CENTER (O, 74 beds) 1635 Marvel Street, Coushatta, LA Zip 71019–9022, Mailing Address: P.O. Box 589, Zip 71019–0369; tel. 318/932–2000; Sister Laureen Painter, Chief Executive Officer

CHRISTUS SCHUMPERT MEDICAL CENTER (O, 486 beds) One St. Mary Place, Shreveport, LA Zip 71101–4399, Mailing Address: P.O. Box 21976, Zip 71120–1076; tel. 318/681–4500; Daniel J. Rissing, Acting Chief Executive Officer

CHRISTUS ST. FRANCES CABRINI HOSPITAL (O, 227 beds) 3330 Masonic Drive, Alexandria, LA Zip 71301–3899; tel. 318/487–1122; Daniel J. Rissing, Acting Chief Executive Officer

CHRISTUS ST. PATRICK HOSPITAL (O, 298 beds) 524 South Ryan Street, Lake Charles, LA Zip 70601–5799, Mailing Address: P.O. Box 3401, Zip 70602–3401; tel. 318/436–2511; James E. Gardner Jr., Chief Executive Officer

NATCHITOCHES PARISH HOSPITAL (C, 175 beds) 501 Keyser Avenue, Natchitoches, LA Zip 71457–6036, Mailing Address: P.O. Box 2009, Zip 71457–2009; tel. 318/352–1200; Mark E. Marley, Executive Director

TEXAS: CHRISTUS SPOHN HOSPITAL BEEVILLE (O, 69 beds) 1500 East Houston Street, Beeville, TX Zip 78102; tel. 361/354–2125; David S. Wagner, Vice President and Administrator

CHRISTUS ST. ELIZABETH HOSPITAL (O, 468 beds) 2830 Calder Avenue, Beaumont, TX Zip 77702, Mailing Address: P.O. Box 5405, Zip 77726–5405; tel. 409/892–7171; Edward W. Myers, Chief Executive Officer

CHRISTUS ST. JOSEPH HOSPITAL (O, 443 beds) 1919 LaBranch Street, Houston, TX Zip 77002; tel. 713/757–1000; Sally E. Jeffcoat, Chief Executive Officer
Web address: www.stjoe.sch.org

CHRISTUS ST. MARY HOSPITAL (O, 223 beds) 3600 Gates Boulevard, Port Arthur, TX Zip 77642–3601, Mailing Address: P.O. Box 3696, Zip 77643–3696; tel. 409/985–7431; Jeffrey Webster, Chief Executive Officer

CHRISTUS ST. MICHAEL HEALTH SYSTEM (O, 319 beds) 2600 St. Michael Drive, Texarkana, TX Zip 75503–2372; tel. 903/614–1000; Don A. Beeler, President and Chief Executive Officer
Web address: www.smhcc.org

JASPER MEMORIAL HOSPITAL (L, 54 beds) 1275 Marvin Hancock Drive, Jasper, TX Zip 75951–4995; tel. 409/384–5461; George N. Miller Jr., Chief Executive Officer

ST. JOHN HOSPITAL (O, 135 beds) 18300 St. John Drive, Nassau Bay, TX Zip 77058; tel. 281/333–5503; Thomas Permetti, Chief Executive Officer

Owned, leased, sponsored:	11 hospitals	2796 beds
Contract–managed:	2 hospitals	237 beds
Totals:	13 hospitals	3033 beds

★5565: CHRISTUS HEALTH (CC)
9311 San Pedro, Suite 1250, San Antonio, TX Zip 78216–4469; tel. 210/524–4100; Joseph Blasko Jr., President and Chief Executive Officer

CHRISTUS SANTA ROSA HEALTH CARE (O, 609 beds) 519 West Houston Street, San Antonio, TX Zip 78207–3108; tel. 210/704–2011; William C. Finlayson, President and Chief Executive Officer

CHRISTUS SPOHN HEALTH SYSTEM (O, 432 beds) 1702 Santa Fe, Corpus Christi, TX Zip 78404; tel. 512/881–3400; Jake Henry Jr., President

CHRISTUS SPOHN HOSPITAL KLEBERG (O, 100 beds) 1311 General Cavazos Boulevard, Kingsville, TX Zip 78363–1197, Mailing Address: P.O. Box 1197, Zip 78363–1197; tel. 361/595–1661; Ernesto M. Flores Jr., Administrator

CHRISTUS SPOHN HOSPITAL MEMORIAL (O, 273 beds) 2606 Hospital Boulevard, Corpus Christi, TX Zip 78405–1818, Mailing Address: Box 5280, Zip 78465–5280; tel. 361/902–4000; Steven R. Kamber, Vice President and Administrator

ST. JOSEPH'S HOSPITAL AND HEALTH CENTER (O, 175 beds) 820 Clarksville Street, Paris, TX Zip 75460–9070, Mailing Address: P.O. Box 9070, Zip 75461–9070; tel. 903/785–4521; Monty E. McLaurin, President
Web address: www.stjosephhc.com

Owned, leased, sponsored:	5 hospitals	1589 beds
Contract–managed:	0 hospitals	0 beds
Totals:	5 hospitals	1589 beds

0101: CITRUS VALLEY HEALTH PARTNERS (NP)
210 West San Bernardino Road, Covina, CA Zip 91723; tel. 626/938–7577; Peter E. Makowski, President and Chief Executive Officer

CALIFORNIA: CITRUS VALLEY MEDICAL CENTER INTER–COMMUNITY CAMPUS (O, 252 beds) 210 West San Bernardino Road, Covina, CA Zip 91723–1901; tel. 626/331–7331; Peter E. Makowski, President and Chief Executive Officer

CITRUS VALLEY MEDICAL CENTER–QUEEN OF THE VALLEY CAMPUS (O, 263 beds) 1115 South Sunset Avenue, West Covina, CA Zip 91790, Mailing Address: Box 1980, Zip 91793; tel. 626/962–4011; Peter E. Makowski, President and Chief Executive Officer

Section B

For explanation of codes following names, see page B2.
★ Indicates Type III membership in the American Hospital Association.
● Single hospital health care system

FOOTHILL PRESBYTERIAN HOSPITAL–MORRIS L. JOHNSTON MEMORIAL (O, 106 beds) 250 South Grand Avenue, Glendora, CA Zip 91741; tel. 626/963–8411; Larry S. Fetters, Administrator and Chief Operating Officer

Owned, leased, sponsored:	3 hospitals	621 beds
Contract–managed:	0 hospitals	0 beds
Totals:	**3 hospitals**	**621 beds**

★**0152: COFFEE HEALTH GROUP** (NP)
205 Marengo Street, Florence, AL Zip 35630–6033; tel. 256/768–9191; Richard H. Peck, President and Chief Executive Officer

ALABAMA: ELIZA COFFEE MEMORIAL HOSPITAL (O, 455 beds) 205 Marengo Street, Florence, AL Zip 35630–6033, Mailing Address: P.O. Box 818, Zip 35631–0818; tel. 256/768–9191; Richard H. Peck, President and Chief Executive Officer

FLORENCE HOSPITAL (O, 155 beds) 2111 Cloyd Boulevard, Florence, AL Zip 35630–1595, Mailing Address: P.O. Box 2010, Zip 35631–2010; tel. 256/767–8700; Carl W. Bailey, Chief Executive Officer

MEDICAL CENTER SHOALS (O, 128 beds) 201 Avalon Avenue, Muscle Shoals, AL Zip 35661–2805, Mailing Address: P.O. Box 3359, Zip 35662–3359; tel. 256/386–1600; Connie Hawthorne, Chief Executive Officer

RUSSELLVILLE HOSPITAL (O, 100 beds) 15155 Highway 43, Russellville, AL Zip 35653, Mailing Address: P.O. Box 1089, Zip 35653–1089; tel. 256/332–1611; Christine R. Stewart, President and Chief Executive Officer

Owned, leased, sponsored:	4 hospitals	838 beds
Contract–managed:	0 hospitals	0 beds
Totals:	**4 hospitals**	**838 beds**

0076: COLLEGE HEALTH ENTERPRISES (IO)
17100 Pioneer Boulevard, Suite 300, Costa Mesa, CA Zip 92627; tel. 949/642–3734; Dale A. Kirby, President

CALIFORNIA: COLLEGE HOSPITAL (O, 125 beds) 10802 College Place, Cerritos, CA Zip 90703–1579; tel. 562/924–9581; Stephen Witt, Chief Executive Officer

COLLEGE HOSPITAL COSTA MESA (O, 119 beds) 301 Victoria Street, Costa Mesa, CA Zip 92627; tel. 949/574–3322; Dale A. Kirby, Chief Executive Officer

Owned, leased, sponsored:	2 hospitals	244 beds
Contract–managed:	0 hospitals	0 beds
Totals:	**2 hospitals**	**244 beds**

★**0048: COLUMBIA/HCA HEALTHCARE CORPORATION** (IO)
One Park Plaza, Nashville, TN Zip 37203–1548; tel. 615/344–2003; Jack O. Bovender Jr., President and Chief Operating Officer

ALASKA: ALASKA REGIONAL HOSPITAL (O, 189 beds) 2801 Debarr Road, Anchorage, AK Zip 99508, Mailing Address: P.O. Box 143889, Zip 99514–3889; tel. 907/276–1131; Ernie Meier, President and Chief Executive Officer

ARKANSAS: ST. VINCENT DOCTORS HOSPITAL (S, 308 beds) 6101 West Capitol, Little Rock, AR Zip 72205–5331; tel. 501/661–4000

CALIFORNIA: CHINO VALLEY MEDICAL CENTER (O, 114 beds) 5451 Walnut Avenue, Chino, CA Zip 91710; tel. 909/464–8600; Gary Maier, Chief Executive Officer
Web address: www.cvmc.com

GOOD SAMARITAN HOSPITAL (O, 333 beds) 2425 Samaritan Drive, San Jose, CA Zip 95124, Mailing Address: P.O. Box 240002, Zip 95154–2402; tel. 408/559–2011; William K. Piche, Chief Executive Officer

GOOD SAMARITAN HOSPITAL (O, 64 beds) 901 Olive Drive, Bakersfield, CA Zip 93308–4137; tel. 805/399–4461; Robert W. Orr, Administrator

HUNTINGTON BEACH HOSPITAL (O, 114 beds) 17772 Beach Boulevard, Huntington Beach, CA Zip 92647–9932; tel. 714/842–1473; Carol B. Freeman, Chief Executive Officer

LAS ENCINAS HOSPITAL (O, 138 beds) 2900 East Del Mar Boulevard, Pasadena, CA Zip 91107–4375; tel. 626/795–9901; Roland Metivier, Chief Executive Officer

LOS ROBLES REGIONAL MEDICAL CENTER (O, 255 beds) 215 West Janss Road, Thousand Oaks, CA Zip 91360–1899; tel. 805/497–2727; Robert C. Shaw, President and Chief Executive Officer
Web address: www.losrobleshospital.com

SAN JOSE MEDICAL CENTER (O, 327 beds) 675 East Santa Clara Street, San Jose, CA Zip 95112, Mailing Address: P.O. Box 240003, Zip 95154–2403; tel. 408/998–3212; William L. Gilbert, Chief Executive Officer

SOUTH VALLEY HOSPITAL (O, 93 beds) 9400 No Name Uno, Gilroy, CA Zip 95020–2368; tel. 408/848–2000; Beverly Gilmore, Chief Executive Officer

WEST ANAHEIM MEDICAL CENTER (O, 219 beds) 3033 West Orange Avenue, Anaheim, CA Zip 92804–3184; tel. 714/827–3000; David Culberson, Chief Executive Officer

WEST HILLS HOSPITAL AND MEDICAL CENTER (O, 236 beds) 7300 Medical Center Drive, West Hills, CA Zip 91307–9937, Mailing Address: P.O. Box 7937, Zip 91309–9937; tel. 818/676–4000; James F. Sherman, President and Chief Executive Officer
Web address: www.whrmc.com

COLORADO: AURORA REGIONAL MEDICAL CENTER (O, 334 beds) 1501 South Potomac Street, Aurora, CO Zip 80012–5499; tel. 303/695–2600; Louis O. Garcia, President and Chief Executive Officer

NORTH SUBURBAN MEDICAL CENTER (O, 125 beds) 9191 Grant Street, Thornton, CO Zip 80229–4341; tel. 303/451–7800; Margaret C. Cain, Chief Executive Officer

PRESBYTERIAN–ST. LUKE'S MEDICAL CENTER (O, 442 beds) 1719 East 19th Avenue, Denver, CO Zip 80218–1281; tel. 303/839–6000; Kevin Gross, Chief Executive Officer

ROSE MEDICAL CENTER (O, 250 beds) 4567 East Ninth Avenue, Denver, CO Zip 80220–3941; tel. 303/320–2121; Kenneth H. Feiler, President and Chief Executive Officer
Web address: www.rosebabies.com

SPALDING REHABILITATION HOSPITAL (O, 138 beds) 900 Potomac Street, Aurora, CO Zip 80011–6716; tel. 303/367–1166; Lynn Dawson, Chief Executive Officer

SWEDISH MEDICAL CENTER (O, 349 beds) 501 East Hampden Avenue, Englewood, CO Zip 80110–0101; tel. 303/788–5000; Mary M. White, President and Chief Executive Officer
Web address: www.swedishhospital.com

DELAWARE: ROCKFORD CENTER (O, 70 beds) 100 Rockford Drive, Newark, DE Zip 19713–2121; tel. 302/996–5480; Barbara Neuse, Chief Executive Officer

FLORIDA: ATLANTIC MEDICAL CENTER–DAYTONA (O, 214 beds) 400 North Clyde Morris Boulevard, Daytona Beach, FL Zip 32114–2770, Mailing Address: P.O. Box 9000, Zip 32120–9000; tel. 904/239–5000; Pam Corliss, Chief Executive Officer

ATLANTIC MEDICAL CENTER–ORMOND (O, 119 beds) 264 South Atlantic Avenue, Ormond Beach, FL Zip 32176–8192; tel. 904/672–4161; Pam Corliss, Chief Executive Officer

AVENTURA HOSPITAL AND MEDICAL CENTER (O, 316 beds) 20900 Biscayne Boulevard, Miami, FL Zip 33180–1407; tel. 305/682–7100; Davide M. Carbone, Chief Executive Officer
Web address: www.aventurahospital.com

BLAKE MEDICAL CENTER (O, 284 beds) 2020 59th Street West, Bradenton, FL Zip 34209–4669, Mailing Address: P.O. Box 25004, Zip 34206–5004; tel. 941/792–6611; Lindell W. Orr, Chief Executive Officer

BRANDON REGIONAL HOSPITAL (O, 255 beds) 119 Oakfield Drive, Brandon, FL Zip 33511–5799; tel. 813/681–5551; Michael M. Fencel, Chief Executive Officer
Web address: www.brandonhospital.com

CEDARS MEDICAL CENTER (O, 493 beds) 1400 N.W. 12th Avenue, Miami, FL Zip 33136–1003; tel. 305/325–5511; Steven Sonenreich, Chief Executive Officer

CENTRAL FLORIDA REGIONAL HOSPITAL (O, 226 beds) 1401 West Seminole Boulevard, Sanford, FL Zip 32771–6764; tel. 407/321–4500; Doug Sills, President and Chief Executive Officer

For explanation of codes following names, see page B2.
★ Indicates Type III membership in the American Hospital Association.

Section B

COLUMBIA HOSPITAL (O, 250 beds) 2201 45th Street, West Palm Beach, FL Zip 33407–2069; tel. 561/842–6141; Sharon L. Roush, Chief Executive Officer

COMMUNITY HOSPITAL OF NEW PORT RICHEY (O, 414 beds) 5637 Marine Parkway, New Port Richey, FL Zip 34652–4331, Mailing Address: P.O. Box 996, Zip 34656–0996; tel. 727/848–1733; Andrew Oravec Jr., Administrator

DEERING HOSPITAL (O, 233 beds) 9333 S.W. 152nd Street, Miami, FL Zip 33157–1780; tel. 305/256–5100; Jude Torchia, Chief Executive Officer

DOCTORS HOSPITAL OF SARASOTA (O, 168 beds) 5731 Bee Ridge Road, Sarasota, FL Zip 34233–5056; tel. 941/342–1100; William C. Lievense, President and Chief Executive Officer

DORAL PALMS HOSPITAL (O, 88 beds) 11100 N.W. 27th Street, Miami, FL Zip 33172–5000; tel. 305/591–3230; Cheryl Siegwald–Mays, Administrator

EAST POINTE HOSPITAL (O, 88 beds) 1500 Lee Boulevard, Lehigh Acres, FL Zip 33936–4897; tel. 941/369–2101; Valerie A. Jackson, Chief Executive Officer

EDWARD WHITE HOSPITAL (O, 134 beds) 2323 Ninth Avenue North, Saint Petersburg, FL Zip 33713–6898, Mailing Address: P.O. Box 12018, Zip 33733–2018; tel. 727/323–1111; Barry S. Stokes, President and Chief Executive Officer
Web address: www.columbia.net

ENGLEWOOD COMMUNITY HOSPITAL (O, 100 beds) 700 Medical Boulevard, Englewood, FL Zip 34223–3978; tel. 941/475–6571; Robert C. Meade, Chief Executive Officer

FAWCETT MEMORIAL HOSPITAL (O, 249 beds) 21298 Olean Boulevard, Port Charlotte, FL Zip 33952–6765, Mailing Address: P.O. Box 4028, Punta Gorda, Zip 33949–4028; tel. 941/629–1181; Terry Chaffin, President and Chief Executive Officer

FORT WALTON BEACH MEDICAL CENTER (O, 247 beds) 1000 Mar–Walt Drive, Fort Walton Beach, FL Zip 32547–6795; tel. 850/862–1111; Wayne Campbell, Chief Executive Officer

GULF COAST HOSPITAL (O, 120 beds) 13681 Doctors Way, Fort Myers, FL Zip 33912–4309; tel. 941/768–5000; Valerie A. Jackson, Chief Executive Officer

GULF COAST MEDICAL CENTER (O, 176 beds) 449 West 23rd Street, Panama City, FL Zip 32405–4593, Mailing Address: P.O. Box 15309, Zip 32406–5309; tel. 850/769–8341; Brent A. Marsteller, Chief Executive Officer

HAMILTON MEDICAL CENTER (O, 20 beds) 506 N.W. Fourth Street, Jasper, FL Zip 32052; tel. 904/792–7200; Amelia Tompkins, Administrator

J. F. K. MEDICAL CENTER (O, 363 beds) 5301 South Congress Avenue, Atlantis, FL Zip 33462–1197; tel. 561/965–7300; Phillip D. Robinson, Chief Executive Officer

KENDALL MEDICAL CENTER (O, 235 beds) 11750 Bird Road, Miami, FL Zip 33175–3530; tel. 305/223–3000; Victor Maya, Chief Executive Officer

LAKE CITY MEDICAL CENTER (O, 75 beds) 1050 Commerce Boulevard North, Lake City, FL Zip 32055–3718; tel. 904/719–9000; Todd Gallati, Chief Executive Officer

LARGO MEDICAL CENTER (O, 243 beds) 201 14th Street S.W., Largo, FL Zip 33770–3133, Mailing Address: P.O. Box 2905, Zip 33779–2905; tel. 727/588–5200; Thomas L. Herron, FACHE, President and Chief Executive Officer
Web address: www.largomedicalcenter.com

LAWNWOOD REGIONAL MEDICAL CENTER (O, 363 beds) 1700 South 23rd Street, Fort Pierce, FL Zip 34950–0188; tel. 561/461–4000; Thomas R. Pentz, President and Executive Officer

LUCERNE MEDICAL CENTER (O, 267 beds) 818 Main Lane, Orlando, FL Zip 32801; tel. 407/649–6111;
Web address: www.columbia.net

MEMORIAL HOSPITAL OF JACKSONVILLE (O, 310 beds) 3625 University Boulevard South, Jacksonville, FL Zip 32216–4240, Mailing Address: P.O. Box 16325, Zip 32216–6325; tel. 904/399–6111; H. Rex Etheredge, President and Chief Executive Officer

MIAMI HEART INSTITUTE AND MEDICAL CENTER (O, 278 beds) 4701 Meridian Avenue, Miami, FL Zip 33140–2910; tel. 305/674–3114; Ralph A. Aleman, Chief Executive Officer

NORTH FLORIDA REGIONAL MEDICAL CENTER (O, 278 beds) 6500 Newberry Road, Gainesville, FL Zip 32605–4392, Mailing Address: P.O. Box 147006, Zip 32614–7006; tel. 352/333–4000; Brian C. Robinson, Chief Executive Officer

NORTHSIDE HOSPITAL AND HEART INSTITUTE (O, 301 beds) 6000 49th Street North, Saint Petersburg, FL Zip 33709–2145; tel. 727/521–4411; Bradley K. Grover Sr., Ph.D., FACHE, President and Chief Executive Officer
Web address: www.northsidehospital.com

NORTHWEST MEDICAL CENTER (O, 150 beds) 2801 North State Road 7, Pompano Beach, FL Zip 33063–5727, Mailing Address: P.O. Box 639002, Margate, Zip 33063–9002; tel. 954/978–4000; Gina Melby, Chief Executive Officer

OAK HILL HOSPITAL (O, 204 beds) 11375 Cortez Boulevard, Spring Hill, FL Zip 34611, Mailing Address: P.O. Box 5300, Zip 34611–5300; tel. 352/596–6632; Jaime A. Wesolowski, Chief Executive Officer

OCALA REGIONAL MEDICAL CENTER (O, 210 beds) 1431 S.W. First Avenue, Ocala, FL Zip 34474–4058, Mailing Address: P.O. Box 2200, Zip 34478–2200; tel. 352/401–1000; Stephen Mahan, Chief Executive Officer

ORANGE PARK MEDICAL CENTER (O, 196 beds) 2001 Kingsley Avenue, Orange Park, FL Zip 32073–5156; tel. 904/276–8500; Robert M. Krieger, Chief Executive Officer

OSCEOLA REGIONAL MEDICAL CENTER (O, 156 beds) 700 West Oak Street, Kissimmee, FL Zip 34741–4996, Mailing Address: P.O. Box 422589, Zip 34742–2589; tel. 407/846–2266; E. Tim Cook, Chief Executive Officer

PALMS WEST HOSPITAL (O, 117 beds) 13001 Southern Boulevard, Loxahatchee, FL Zip 33470–1150; tel. 561/798–3300; Alex M. Marceline, Chief Executive Officer
Web address: www.web–xpress.com/palmswest

PASCO COMMUNITY HOSPITAL (O, 120 beds) 13100 Fort King Road, Dade City, FL Zip 33525–5294; tel. 352/521–1100; William G. Buck, President and Chief Executive Officer

PLANTATION GENERAL HOSPITAL (O, 264 beds) 401 N.W. 42nd Avenue, Plantation, FL Zip 33317–2882; tel. 954/587–5010; Anthony M. Degina Jr., Chief Executive Officer

PUTNAM COMMUNITY MEDICAL CENTER (O, 141 beds) Highway 20 West, Palatka, FL Zip 32177, Mailing Address: P.O. Box 778, Zip 32178–0778; tel. 904/328–5711; Rodney R. Smith, Chief Executive Officer

RAULERSON HOSPITAL (O, 101 beds) 1796 Highway 441 North, Okeechobee, FL Zip 34972, Mailing Address: P.O. Box 1307, Zip 34973–1307; tel. 941/763–2151; Frank Irby, Chief Executive Officer

REGIONAL MEDICAL CENTER–BAYONET POINT (O, 256 beds) 14000 Fivay Road, Hudson, FL Zip 34667–7199; tel. 727/863–2411; Don Griffin, Ph.D., President and Chief Executive Officer

SOUTH BAY HOSPITAL (O, 112 beds) 4016 State Road 674, Sun City Center, FL Zip 33573–5298; tel. 813/634–3301; Hal Muetzel, Chief Executive Officer

SOUTHWEST FLORIDA REGIONAL MEDICAL CENTER (O, 400 beds) 2727 Winkler Avenue, Fort Myers, FL Zip 33901–9396; tel. 941/939–1147; Stephen L. Royal, President and Chief Executive Officer

SPECIALTY HOSPITAL JACKSONVILLE (O, 61 beds) 4901 Richard Street, Jacksonville, FL Zip 32207; tel. 904/737–3120; W. Raymond C. Ford, Chief Executive Officer
Web address: www.heartofhealthcare.com

ST. LUCIE MEDICAL CENTER (O, 150 beds) 1800 S.E. Tiffany Avenue, Port St. Lucie, FL Zip 34952–7580; tel. 561/335–4000; Gary Cantrell, President and Chief Executive Officer

ST. PETERSBURG GENERAL HOSPITAL (O, 160 beds) 6500 38th Avenue North, Saint Petersburg, FL Zip 33710–1629; tel. 727/384–1414; Daniel J. Friedrich III, President and Chief Executive Officer

TALLAHASSEE COMMUNITY HOSPITAL (O, 180 beds) 2626 Capital Medical Boulevard, Tallahassee, FL Zip 32308–4499; tel. 850/656–5000; Thomas Paul Pemberton, Chief Executive Officer

TWIN CITIES HOSPITAL (O, 75 beds) 2190 Highway 85 North, Niceville, FL Zip 32578–1045; tel. 850/678–4131; David Whalen, Chief Executive Officer

UNIVERSITY HOSPITAL AND MEDICAL CENTER (O, 211 beds) 7201 North University Drive, Tamarac, FL Zip 33321–2996; tel. 954/721–2200; James A. Cruickshank, Chief Executive Officer

For explanation of codes following names, see page B2.
★ Indicates Type III membership in the American Hospital Association.

Section B

WEST FLORIDA REGIONAL MEDICAL CENTER (O, 531 beds) 8383 North Davis Highway, Pensacola, FL Zip 32514–6088, Mailing Address: P.O. Box 18900, Zip 32523–8900; tel. 850/494–4000; Stephen Brandt, President and Chief Executive Officer

WESTSIDE REGIONAL MEDICAL CENTER (O, 204 beds) 8201 West Broward Boulevard, Plantation, FL Zip 33324–9937; tel. 954/473–6600; Michael G. Joseph, Chief Executive Officer

WINTER PARK MEMORIAL HOSPITAL (O, 339 beds) 200 North Lakemont Avenue, Winter Park, FL Zip 32792–3273; tel. 407/646–7000; Douglas P. DeGraaf, Chief Executive Officer

GEORGIA: COLISEUM MEDICAL CENTERS (O, 194 beds) 350 Hospital Drive, Macon, GA Zip 31213; tel. 912/765–7000; Timothy C. Tobin, Chief Executive Officer

COLISEUM PSYCHIATRIC HOSPITAL (O, 92 beds) 340 Hospital Drive, Macon, GA Zip 31217–8002; tel. 912/741–1355; Edward W. Ruffin, Administrator

COLUMBIA CARTERSVILLE MEDICAL CENTER (O, 80 beds) 960 Joe Frank Harris Parkway, Cartersville, GA Zip 30120, Mailing Address: P.O. Box 200008, Zip 30120–9001; tel. 770/382–1530; Keith Sandlin, Chief Executive Officer

COLUMBIA–AUGUSTA MEDICAL CENTER (O, 284 beds) 3651 Wheeler Road, Augusta, GA Zip 30909–6426; tel. 706/651–3232; Michael K. Kerner, President and Chief Executive Officer
Web address: www.columbia.augusta.com

DOCTORS HOSPITAL (O, 171 beds) 616 19th Street, Columbus, GA Zip 31901–1528, Mailing Address: P.O. Box 2188, Zip 31902–2188; tel. 706/571–4262; Hugh D. Wilson, Chief Executive Officer

DUNWOODY MEDICAL CENTER (O, 140 beds) 4575 North Shallowford Road, Atlanta, GA Zip 30338–6499; tel. 770/454–2000; Thomas D. Gilbert, President and Chief Executive Officer
Web address: www.columbia.net

EASTSIDE MEDICAL CENTER (O, 114 beds) 1700 Medical Way, Snellville, GA Zip 30078, Mailing Address: P.O. Box 587, Zip 30078–0587; tel. 770/979–0200; Les Beard, Chief Executive Officer

FAIRVIEW PARK HOSPITAL (O, 190 beds) 200 Industrial Boulevard, Dublin, GA Zip 31021–2997, Mailing Address: P.O. Box 1408, Zip 31040–1408; tel. 912/275–2000; James B. Wood, Chief Executive Officer

HUGHSTON SPORTS MEDICINE HOSPITAL (O, 100 beds) 100 First Court, Columbus, GA Zip 31908–7188, Mailing Address: P.O. Box 7188, Zip 31908–7188; tel. 706/576–2101; Hugh C. Tappan, Chief Executive Officer
Web address: www.hughstonsports.com/hsmh.htm

LANIER PARK HOSPITAL (O, 119 beds) 675 White Sulphur Road, Gainesville, GA Zip 30505, Mailing Address: P.O. Box 1354, Zip 30503–1354; tel. 770/503–3000; Jerry Fulks, Chief Executive Officer
Web address: www.lanierpark.com

MACON NORTHSIDE HOSPITAL (O, 103 beds) 400 Charter Boulevard, Macon, GA Zip 31210–4853, Mailing Address: P.O. Box 4627, Zip 31208–4627; tel. 912/757–8200; Bud Costello, Administrator and Chief Executive Officer

METROPOLITAN HOSPITAL (O, 64 beds) 3223 Howell Mill Road N.W., Atlanta, GA Zip 30327–4135; tel. 404/351–0500; Jean Calhoun, Administrator

MIDDLE GEORGIA HOSPITAL (O, 119 beds) 888 Pine Street, Macon, GA Zip 31201–2186, Mailing Address: P.O. Box 6278, Zip 31208–6278; tel. 912/751–1111; Richard L. McConahy, Chief Executive Officer

NORTHLAKE REGIONAL MEDICAL CENTER (O, 112 beds) 1455 Montreal Road, Tucker, GA Zip 30084; tel. 770/270–3000; Thomas D. Gilbert, Chief Executive Officer

PALMYRA MEDICAL CENTERS (O, 156 beds) 2000 Palmyra Road, Albany, GA Zip 31702–1908, Mailing Address: P.O. Box 1908, Zip 31702–1908; tel. 912/434–2000; Allen Golson, Chief Executive Officer
Web address: www.columbia.net

PARKWAY MEDICAL CENTER (O, 233 beds) 1000 Thornton Road, Lithia Springs, GA Zip 30122, Mailing Address: P.O. Box 570, Zip 30122–0570; tel. 770/732–7777; Deborah S. Guthrie, Chief Executive Officer
Web address: www.columbia–parkway.com

PEACHTREE REGIONAL HOSPITAL (O, 144 beds) 60 Hospital Road, Newnan, GA Zip 30264, Mailing Address: P.O. Box 2228, Zip 30264–2228; tel. 770/253–1912; Linda Jubinsky, Chief Executive Officer

POLK MEDICAL CENTER (O, 35 beds) 424 North Main Street, Cedartown, GA Zip 30125–2698; tel. 770/748–2500; Mark Nichols, Chief Executive Officer

REDMOND REGIONAL MEDICAL CENTER (O, 199 beds) 501 Redmond Road, Rome, GA Zip 30165–7001, Mailing Address: Box 107001, Zip 30164–7001; tel. 706/291–0291; James R. Thomas, Chief Executive Officer
Web address: www.columbia.hca.com

WEST PACES MEDICAL CENTER (O, 294 beds) 3200 Howell Mill Road N.W., Atlanta, GA Zip 30327–4101; tel. 404/350–5600; Thomas D. Gilbert, President and Chief Executive Officer

IDAHO: EASTERN IDAHO REGIONAL MEDICAL CENTER (O, 294 beds) 3100 Channing Way, Idaho Falls, ID Zip 83404–7533, Mailing Address: P.O. Box 2077, Zip 83403–2077; tel. 208/529–6111; Douglas Crabtree, Chief Executive Officer
Web address: www.eirmc.org

WEST VALLEY MEDICAL CENTER (O, 122 beds) 1717 Arlington, Caldwell, ID Zip 83605–4864; tel. 208/459–4641; Mark Adams, Chief Executive Officer
Web address: www.columbia.net

ILLINOIS: CHICAGO LAKESHORE HOSPITAL (O, 102 beds) 4840 North Marine Drive, Chicago, IL Zip 60640–4296; tel. 773/878–9700; Marcia S. Shapiro, Chief Executive Officer

OLYMPIA FIELDS OSTEOPATHIC HOSPITAL AND MEDICAL CENTER (O, 181 beds) 20201 South Crawford Avenue, Olympia Fields, IL Zip 60461–1080; tel. 708/747–4000; David Scott Koenig, Chief Executive Officer

RIVEREDGE HOSPITAL (O, 96 beds) 8311 West Roosevelt Road, Forest Park, IL Zip 60130–2500; tel. 708/771–7000; Thomas J. Dattalo, Chief Executive Officer

INDIANA: TERRE HAUTE REGIONAL HOSPITAL (O, 236 beds) 3901 South Seventh Street, Terre Haute, IN Zip 47802–4299; tel. 812/232–0021; Jerry Dooley, Chief Executive Officer

WOMEN'S HOSPITAL–INDIANAPOLIS (O, 132 beds) 8111 Township Line Road, Indianapolis, IN Zip 46260–8043; tel. 317/875–5994; Steven B. Reed, President and Chief Executive Officer

KANSAS: WESLEY MEDICAL CENTER (O, 506 beds) 550 North Hillside Avenue, Wichita, KS Zip 67214–4976; tel. 316/688–2000; Carl W. Fitch Sr., President and Chief Executive Officer
Web address: www.wesleymc.com

KENTUCKY: FRANKFORT REGIONAL MEDICAL CENTER (O, 147 beds) 299 King's Daughters Drive, Frankfort, KY Zip 40601–4186; tel. 502/875–5240; David P. Steitz, Chief Executive Officer

GREENVIEW REGIONAL HOSPITAL (O, 211 beds) 1801 Ashley Circle, Bowling Green, KY Zip 42104–3384, Mailing Address: P.O. Box 90024, Zip 42102–9024; tel. 502/793–1000; Phillip A. Clendenin, Chief Executive Officer
Web address: www.columbia–hca.com

SAMARITAN HOSPITAL (O, 193 beds) 310 South Limestone Street, Lexington, KY Zip 40508–3008; tel. 606/226–7151; Frank Beirne, Chief Executive Officer

LOUISIANA: AVOYELLES HOSPITAL (O, 55 beds) 4231 Highway 1192, Marksville, LA Zip 71351, Mailing Address: P.O. Box 255, Zip 71351; tel. 318/253–8611; David M. Mitchel, Chief Executive Officer

DAUTERIVE HOSPITAL (O, 92 beds) 600 North Lewis Street, New Iberia, LA Zip 70560, Mailing Address: P.O. Box 11210, Zip 70562–1210; tel. 318/365–7311; Kyle J. Viator, Chief Executive Officer

DOCTORS' HOSPITAL OF OPELOUSAS (O, 105 beds) 5101 Highway 167 South, Opelousas, LA Zip 70570–8975; tel. 318/948–2100; Bethy W. Walker, Administrator

HIGHLAND HOSPITAL (O, 160 beds) 1453 East Bert Kouns Industrial Loop, Shreveport, LA Zip 71105–6050; tel. 318/798–4300; Anthony S. Sala Jr., Chief Executive Officer

LAKELAND MEDICAL CENTER (O, 140 beds) 6000 Bullard Avenue, New Orleans, LA Zip 70128; tel. 504/241–6335; Tracy A. Rogers, Chief Executive Officer
Web address: www.columbia.net

LAKESIDE HOSPITAL (O, 75 beds) 4700 I-10 Service Road, Metairie, LA Zip 70001–1269; tel. 504/885–3342; Gerald A. Fornoff, Chief Executive Officer

For explanation of codes following names, see page B2.
★ Indicates Type III membership in the American Hospital Association.

LAKEVIEW REGIONAL MEDICAL CENTER (O, 163 beds) 95 East Fairway Drive, Covington, LA Zip 70433–7507; tel. 504/867–3800; Darrell Blaylock, Chief Executive Officer

MEDICAL CENTER OF SOUTHWEST LOUISIANA (O, 107 beds) 2810 Ambassador Caffery Parkway, Lafayette, LA Zip 70506–5900; tel. 318/981–2949; Madeleine L. Roberson, Chief Executive Officer
Web address: www.medicalcentersw.com

NORTH MONROE HOSPITAL (O, 186 beds) 3421 Medical Park Drive, Monroe, LA Zip 71203–2399; tel. 318/388–1946; George E. Miller, Chief Executive Officer

OAKDALE COMMUNITY HOSPITAL (O, 54 beds) 130 North Hospital Drive, Oakdale, LA Zip 71463–4004, Mailing Address: P.O. Box 629, Zip 71463–0629; tel. 318/335–3700; LaQuita Johnson, Chief Executive Officer

RAPIDES REGIONAL MEDICAL CENTER (O, 359 beds) 211 Fourth Street, Alexandria, LA Zip 71301–8421, Mailing Address: Box 30101, Zip 71301–8421; tel. 318/473–3000; A. C. Buchanan, President and Chief Executive Officer
Web address: www.rapidesregional.com

SAVOY MEDICAL CENTER (O, 330 beds) 801 Poinciana Avenue, Mamou, LA Zip 70554–2298; tel. 318/468–5261; J. E. Richardson, Chief Executive Officer

TULANE UNIVERSITY HOSPITAL AND CLINIC (O, 326 beds) 1415 Tulane Avenue, New Orleans, LA Zip 70112–2632; tel. 504/588–5263; Shirley A. Stewart, President and Chief Executive Officer
Web address: www.tuhc.com

WINN PARISH MEDICAL CENTER (O, 103 beds) 301 West Boundary Street, Winnfield, LA Zip 71483–3427, Mailing Address: P.O. Box 152, Zip 71483–0152; tel. 318/628–2721; Bobby Jordan, Chief Executive Officer

WOMEN'S AND CHILDREN'S HOSPITAL (O, 96 beds) 4600 Ambassador Caffery Parkway, Lafayette, LA Zip 70508–6923, Mailing Address: P.O. Box 88030, Zip 70598–8030; tel. 318/981–9100; Madeleine L. Roberson, Chief Executive Officer

MISSISSIPPI: GARDEN PARK COMMUNITY HOSPITAL (O, 97 beds) 1520 Broad Avenue, Gulfport, MS Zip 39501, Mailing Address: P.O. Box 1240, Zip 39502–1240; tel. 228/864–4210; William E. Peaks, Chief Executive Officer

VICKSBURG MEDICAL CENTER (O, 154 beds) 1111 North Frontage Road, Vicksburg, MS Zip 39180; tel. 601/619–3800; Rob Followell, Chief Operating Officer and Administrator

MISSOURI: RESEARCH PSYCHIATRIC CENTER (O, 100 beds) 2323 East 63rd Street, Kansas City, MO Zip 64130–3495; tel. 816/444–8161; Todd Krass, Administrator and Chief Executive Officer

NEVADA: MOUNTAINVIEW HOSPITAL (O, 120 beds) 3100 North Tenaya Way, Las Vegas, NV Zip 89128; tel. 702/255–5000; Mark J. Howard, President and Chief Executive Officer
Web address: www.mountainview–hospital.com

SUNRISE HOSPITAL AND MEDICAL CENTER (O, 675 beds) 3186 Maryland Parkway, Las Vegas, NV Zip 89109–2306, Mailing Address: P.O. Box 98530, Zip 89193–8530; tel. 702/731–8000; Jerald F. Mitchell, President and Chief Executive Officer
Web address: www.sunrise.columbia.net

NEW HAMPSHIRE: PARKLAND MEDICAL CENTER (O, 53 beds) One Parkland Drive, Derry, NH Zip 03038–2750; tel. 603/432–1500; Scott W. Goodspeed, President and Chief Executive Officer
Web address: www.parklandmc.com

PORTSMOUTH REGIONAL HOSPITAL AND PAVILION (O, 179 beds) 333 Borthwick Avenue, Portsmouth, NH Zip 03801–7004; tel. 603/436–5110; William J. Schuler, Chief Executive Officer

NORTH CAROLINA: HIGHSMITH–RAINEY MEMORIAL HOSPITAL (O, 133 beds) 150 Robeson Street, Fayetteville, NC Zip 28301–5570; tel. 910/609–1000; Joel F. Engles, Chief Executive Officer

HOLLY HILL/ CHARTER BEHAVIORAL HEALTH SYSTEM (O, 108 beds) 3019 Falstaff Road, Raleigh, NC Zip 27610–1812; tel. 919/250–7000; James B. Brawley, Chief Executive Officer

OHIO: SAINT LUKE'S MEDICAL CENTER (O, 165 beds) 11311 Shaker Boulevard, Cleveland, OH Zip 44104–3805; tel. 216/368–7000; Alan H. Channing, Chief Executive Officer
Web address: www.cn.com/stlukes

OKLAHOMA: EDMOND MEDICAL CENTER (O, 81 beds) 1 South Bryant Street, Edmond, OK Zip 73034–4798; tel. 405/341–6100; Stanley D. Tatum, Chief Executive Officer

SEMINOLE MEDICAL CENTER 2401 Wrangler Boulevard, Seminole, OK Zip 74868; tel. 405/303–4000; Stephen R. Schoaps, Chief Executive Officer

SOUTHWESTERN MEDICAL CENTER (O, 139 beds) 5602 S.W. Lee Boulevard, Lawton, OK Zip 73505–9635, Mailing Address: P.O. Box 7290, Zip 73506–7290; tel. 580/531–4700; Thomas L. Rine, President and Chief Executive Officer
Web address: www.columbia–swmc.com

SOUTH CAROLINA: COLLETON MEDICAL CENTER (O, 131 beds) 501 Robertson Boulevard, Walterboro, SC Zip 29488–5714; tel. 843/549–2000; Rebecca T. Brewer, CHE, Chief Executive Officer

GRAND STRAND REGIONAL MEDICAL CENTER (O, 186 beds) 809 82nd Parkway, Myrtle Beach, SC Zip 29572–1413; tel. 803/692–1100; Doug White, Chief Executive Officer

SUMMERVILLE MEDICAL CENTER (O, 99 beds) 295 Midland Parkway, Summerville, SC Zip 29485–8104; tel. 843/832–5100; Steven M. Anderson, Chief Executive Officer

TRIDENT MEDICAL CENTER (O, 286 beds) 9330 Medical Plaza Drive, Charleston, SC Zip 29406–9195; tel. 843/797–7000; Michael P. Joyce, President and Chief Executive Officer

TENNESSEE: ATHENS REGIONAL MEDICAL CENTER (O, 91 beds) 1114 West Madison Avenue, Athens, TN Zip 37303–4150, Mailing Address: P.O. Box 250, Zip 37371–0250; tel. 423/745–1411; John R. Workman, Chief Executive Officer
Web address: www.columbiachat.com

CENTENNIAL MEDICAL CENTER AND PARTHENON PAVILION (O, 680 beds) 2300 Patterson Street, Nashville, TN Zip 37203–1528; tel. 615/342–1000; Larry Kloess, President

CHEATHAM MEDICAL CENTER (O, 29 beds) 313 North Main Street, Ashland City, TN Zip 37015–1358; tel. 615/792–3030; Rick Wallace, FACHE, Chief Executive Officer and Administrator
Web address: www.columbia.net

GRANDVIEW MEDICAL CENTER (O, 47 beds) 1000 Highway 28, Jasper, TN Zip 37347; tel. 423/837–9500; Phil Rowland, Chief Executive Officer

HENDERSONVILLE HOSPITAL (O, 68 beds) 355 New Shackle Island Road, Hendersonville, TN Zip 37075–2393; tel. 615/264–4000; Robert Klein, Chief Executive Officer

HORIZON MEDICAL CENTER (O, 176 beds) 111 Highway 70 East, Dickson, TN Zip 37055–2033; tel. 615/441–2357; Rick Wallace, FACHE, Chief Executive Officer and Administrator
Web address: www.columbia.net

NASHVILLE MEMORIAL HOSPITAL (O, 250 beds) 612 West Due West Avenue, Madison, TN Zip 37115–4474; tel. 615/865–3511; Allyn R. Harris, Chief Executive Officer

PARKRIDGE MEDICAL CENTER (O, 517 beds) 2333 McCallie Avenue, Chattanooga, TN Zip 37404–3285; tel. 423/493–1486; Niels P. Vernegaard, President
Web address: www.columbia.net

PSYCHIATRIC HOSPITAL AT VANDERBILT (O, 88 beds) 1601 23rd Avenue South, Nashville, TN Zip 37212–3198; tel. 615/320–7770; Richard A. Bangert, Chief Executive Officer and Administrator

RIVER PARK HOSPITAL (O, 90 beds) 1559 Sparta Road, McMinnville, TN Zip 37110–1316; tel. 931/815–4000; Terry J. Gunn, Chief Executive Officer
Web address: www.columbia.net

SOUTHERN HILLS MEDICAL CENTER (O, 140 beds) 391 Wallace Road, Nashville, TN Zip 37211–4859; tel. 615/781–4000; Jeffrey Whitehorn, Chief Executive Officer
Web address: www.columbia.net

STONES RIVER HOSPITAL (O, 55 beds) 324 Doolittle Road, Woodbury, TN Zip 37190–1139; tel. 615/563–4001; Bill Patterson, Interim Administrator
Web address: www.wth.net

For explanation of codes following names, see page B2.
★ Indicates Type III membership in the American Hospital Association.

SUMMIT MEDICAL CENTER (O, 204 beds) 5655 Frist Boulevard, Hermitage, TN Zip 37076–2053; tel. 615/316–3000; Bryan K. Dearing, Chief Executive Officer

TEXAS: BAYSHORE MEDICAL CENTER (O, 296 beds) 4000 Spencer Highway, Pasadena, TX Zip 77504–1294; tel. 713/359–2000; Donald L. Stewart, Chief Executive Officer

BEAUMONT MEDICAL AND SURGICAL HOSPITAL (O, 372 beds) 3080 College, Beaumont, TX Zip 77701–4689, Mailing Address: P.O. Box 5817, Zip 77726–5817; tel. 409/833–1411; Luis G. Silva, Chief Executive Officer and Regional Administrator

BELLAIRE MEDICAL CENTER (O, 202 beds) 5314 Dashwood Street, Houston, TX Zip 77081–4689; tel. 713/512–1200; Walter Leleux, Chief Executive Officer
Web address: www.columbia.net

CLEAR LAKE REGIONAL MEDICAL CENTER (O, 375 beds) 500 Medical Center Boulevard, Webster, TX Zip 77598–4286; tel. 281/338–3110; Donald A. Shaffett, Chief Executive Officer

COLUMBIA BEHAVIORAL CENTER (O, 37 beds) 1155 Idaho Street, El Paso, TX Zip 79902–1699; tel. 915/544–4000; Serena Pickman, Director
Web address: www.columbia–elp.com

COLUMBIA MEDICAL CENTER WEST (O, 221 beds) 1801 North Oregon Street, El Paso, TX Zip 79902–3591; tel. 915/521–1200; Hank Hernandez, Chief Executive Officer
Web address: www.columbia–hca.com

COLUMBIA MEDICAL CENTER–EAST (O, 299 beds) 10301 Gateway West, El Paso, TX Zip 79925–7798; tel. 915/595–9000; Douglas A. Matney, Senior Vice President Operations
Web address: www.columbia wtd.com

COLUMBIA REHABILITATION HOSPITAL (O, 40 beds) 300 Waymore Drive, El Paso, TX Zip 77902–1628; tel. 915/577–2600; Cristina Huerta, Administrative Director

CONROE REGIONAL MEDICAL CENTER (O, 244 beds) 504 Medical Boulevard, Conroe, TX Zip 77304, Mailing Address: P.O. Box 1538, Zip 77305–1538; tel. 409/539–1111; Russell Meyers, Chief Executive Officer
Web address: www.columbia.net

CORPUS CHRISTI MEDICAL CENTER (O, 237 beds) 3315 South Alameda Street, Corpus Christi, TX Zip 78411–1883, Mailing Address: P.O. Box 3828, Zip 78463–3828; tel. 361/857–1400; Steven Woerner, Chief Executive Officer
Web address: www.columbia.net

CORPUS CHRISTI MEDICAL CENTER BAY AREA (O, 534 beds) 7101 South Padre Island Drive, Corpus Christi, TX Zip 78412–4999; tel. 361/985–1200; Steven Woerner, Chief Executive Officer

CORPUS CHRISTI MEDICAL CENTER–BAYVIEW PSYCHIATRIC CENTER (O, 40 beds) 6226 Saratoga Boulevard, Corpus Christi, TX Zip 78414–3421; tel. 361/993–9700; Janie L. Harwood, Administrator
Web address: www.columbia.net

DALLAS SOUTHWEST MEDICAL CENTER (O, 107 beds) 2929 South Hampton Road, Dallas, TX Zip 75224–3026; tel. 214/330–4611; James B. Warren, Chief Executive Officer

DENTON REGIONAL MEDICAL CENTER (O, 271 beds) 4405 North Interstate 35, Denton, TX Zip 76207–3499; tel. 940/566–4000; Bob Haley, Chief Executive Officer

DOCTORS HOSPITAL AIRLINE (O, 114 beds) 5815 Airline Drive, Houston, TX Zip 77076–4996; tel. 281/765–2600; Joe G. Baldwin, Chief Executive Officer

EAST HOUSTON REGIONAL MEDICAL CENTER (O, 121 beds) 13111 East Freeway, Houston, TX Zip 77015; tel. 713/393–2000; Merrily Walters, Administrator

FORT BEND MEDICAL CENTER (O, 65 beds) 3803 FM 1092 at Highway 6, Missouri City, TX Zip 77459; tel. 281/403–4800; Rod Brace, Chief Executive Officer
Web address: www.columbia.net

GREEN OAKS HOSPITAL (O, 106 beds) 7808 Clodus Fields Drive, Dallas, TX Zip 75251–2206; tel. 972/991–9504; Dennis Wade, Administrator
Web address: www.koala.com

KATY MEDICAL CENTER (O, 73 beds) 5602 Medical Center Drive, Katy, TX Zip 77494–6399; tel. 281/392–1111; Brian S. Barbe, Chief Executive Officer

KINGWOOD MEDICAL CENTER (O, 153 beds) 22999 U.S. Highway 59, Kingwood, TX Zip 77339; tel. 281/359–7500; Charles D. Schuetz, Chief Executive Officer

MAINLAND MEDICAL CENTER (O, 182 beds) 6801 E F Lowry Expressway, Texas City, TX Zip 77591; tel. 409/938–5000; Alice G. Adams, Administrator
Web address: www.columbia.net

MEDICAL CENTER AT LANCASTER (O, 79 beds) 2600 West Pleasant Run Road, Lancaster, TX Zip 75146–1199; tel. 972/223–9600; Ernest C. Lynch III, Chief Executive Officer
Web address: www.columbia–hca.com

MEDICAL CENTER OF ARLINGTON (O, 178 beds) 3301 Matlock Road, Arlington, TX Zip 76015–2998; tel. 817/465–3241; Michael R. Burroughs, FACHE, President and Chief Executive Officer
Web address: www.medicalcenterarlington.com

MEDICAL CENTER OF LEWISVILLE (O, 116 beds) 500 West Main, Lewisville, TX Zip 75057–3699; tel. 972/420–1000; Raymond M. Dunning Jr., Chief Executive Officer
Web address: www.lewisvillemedical.com

MEDICAL CENTER OF PLANO (O, 265 beds) 3901 West 15th Street, Plano, TX Zip 75075–7799; tel. 972/596–6800; Harvey L. Fishero, President and Chief Executive Officer

MEDICAL CITY DALLAS HOSPITAL (O, 511 beds) 7777 Forest Lane, Dallas, TX Zip 75230–2598; tel. 972/566–7000; Stephen Corbeil, President and Chief Executive Officer
Web address: www.columbia.net

METHODIST AMBULATORY SURGERY HOSPITAL (O, 37 beds) 9150 Huebner Road, San Antonio, TX Zip 78240–1545; tel. 210/691–0800; Elaine F. Morris, Administrator

METHODIST WOMEN'S AND CHILDREN'S HOSPITAL (O, 150 beds) 8109 Fredericksburg Road, San Antonio, TX Zip 78229–3383; tel. 210/692–5000; Arthur E. Marlin, M.D., Chief Executive Officer
Web address: www.mhshealthcare.com

METROPOLITAN METHODIST HOSPITAL (O, 228 beds) 1310 McCullough Avenue, San Antonio, TX Zip 78212–2617; tel. 210/208–2200; Mark L. Bernard, Chief Executive Officer
Web address: www.mhshealthcare.com

NORTH AUSTIN MEDICAL CENTER (O, 150 beds) 12221 MoPac Expressway North, Austin, TX Zip 78758–2483; tel. 512/901–1000; Donald H. Wilkerson, Chief Executive Officer
Web address: www.columbia.stdavids.com

NORTH BAY HOSPITAL (O, 69 beds) 1711 West Wheeler Avenue, Aransas Pass, TX Zip 78336–4536; tel. 361/758–8585; John Krogness, Chief Executive Officer

NORTH CENTRAL MEDICAL CENTER (O, 215 beds) 4500 Medical Center Drive, McKinney, TX Zip 75069–3499; tel. 972/547–8000; Dale Mulder, Chief Executive Officer
Web address: www.columbia.net

NORTH HILLS HOSPITAL (O, 133 beds) 4401 Booth Calloway Road, North Richland Hills, TX Zip 76180–7399; tel. 817/284–1431; Randy Moresi, Chief Executive Officer
Web address: www.columbia.net

NORTH HOUSTON MEDICAL CENTER (O, 109 beds) 233 West Parker Road, Houston, TX Zip 77076–2999; tel. 281/765–2600; Joe G. Baldwin, Chief Executive Officer

NORTHEAST METHODIST HOSPITAL (O, 99 beds) 12412 Judson Road, San Antonio, TX Zip 78233–3272, Mailing Address: P.O. Box 659510, Zip 78265–9510; tel. 210/650–4949; Mark L. Bernard, Chief Executive Officer
Web address: www.mhshealthcare.com

NORTHWEST REGIONAL HOSPITAL (O, 64 beds) 13725 Farm to Market Road 624, Corpus Christi, TX Zip 78410–5199; tel. 512/767–4300; Winston Borland, Chief Executive Officer

For explanation of codes following names, see page B2.
★ Indicates Type III membership in the American Hospital Association.

PLAZA MEDICAL CENTER OF FORT WORTH (O, 289 beds) 900 Eighth Avenue, Fort Worth, TX Zip 76104–3986; tel. 817/347–5857; Stephen Bernstein, FACHE, Chief Executive Officer
Web address: www.columbia.net

REHABILITATION HOSPITAL OF SOUTH TEXAS (O, 40 beds) 6226 Saratoga Boulevard, Corpus Christi, TX Zip 78414–3421; tel. 361/991–9690; Kevin N. Fowler, Chief Executive Officer

RIO GRANDE REGIONAL HOSPITAL (O, 216 beds) 101 East Ridge Road, McAllen, TX Zip 78503–1299; tel. 956/632–6000; Randall M. Everts, Chief Executive Officer
Web address: www.columbia.net

ROSEWOOD MEDICAL CENTER (O, 184 beds) 9200 Westheimer Road, Houston, TX Zip 77063–3599; tel. 713/780–7900; Maura Walsh, Chief Executive Officer

ROUND ROCK HOSPITAL (O, 64 beds) 2400 Round Rock Avenue, Round Rock, TX Zip 78681–4097; tel. 512/341–1000; Deborah L. Ryle, Chief Executive Officer
Web address: www.columbia–stdavids.com

SAN ANTONIO COMMUNITY HOSPITAL (O, 291 beds) 8026 Floyd Curl Drive, San Antonio, TX Zip 78229–3915; tel. 210/692–8110; James C. Scoggin Jr., Chief Executive Officer
Web address: www.mhshealthcare.com

SOUTHWEST TEXAS METHODIST HOSPITAL (O, 774 beds) 7700 Floyd Curl Drive, San Antonio, TX Zip 78229–3993; tel. 210/575–4000; James C. Scoggin Jr., Chief Executive Officer
Web address: www.mhshealthcare.com

SPRING BRANCH MEDICAL CENTER (O, 318 beds) 8850 Long Point Road, Houston, TX Zip 77055–3082; tel. 713/467–6555; Pat Currie, Chief Executive Officer

ST. DAVID'S MEDICAL CENTER (O, 296 beds) 919 East 32nd Street, Austin, TX Zip 78705–2709, Mailing Address: P.O. Box 4039, Zip 78765–4039; tel. 512/476–7111; Cole C. Eslyn, Chief Executive Officer
Web address: www.columbia.net

ST. DAVID'S PAVILION (O, 38 beds) 1025 East 32nd Street, Austin, TX Zip 78765; tel. 512/867–5800; Cole C. Eslyn, Chief Executive Officer
Web address: www.columbia.net

ST. DAVID'S REHABILITATION CENTER (O, 104 beds) 1005 East 32nd Street, Austin, TX Zip 78705–2705, Mailing Address: P.O. Box 4270, Zip 78765–4270; tel. 512/867–5100; Cole C. Eslyn, Chief Executive Officer
Web address: www.columbia.net

ST. DAVID'S SOUTH HOSPITAL (O, 164 beds) 901 West Ben White Boulevard, Austin, TX Zip 78704–6903; tel. 512/447–2211; Richard W. Klusmann, Chief Executive Officer

TEXAS ORTHOPEDIC HOSPITAL (O, 49 beds) 7401 South Main Street, Houston, TX Zip 77030–4509; tel. 713/799–8600; Beryl Ramsey, Chief Executive Officer
Web address: www.columbia.net

THE WOMAN'S HOSPITAL OF TEXAS (O, 162 beds) 7600 Fannin Street, Houston, TX Zip 77054–1900; tel. 713/790–1234; Linda B. Russell, President
Web address: www.columbia.net

VALLEY REGIONAL MEDICAL CENTER (O, 177 beds) 100A Alton Gloor Boulevard, Brownsville, TX Zip 78526, Mailing Address: P.O. Box 3710, Zip 78521–3710; tel. 956/350–7101; Charles F. Sexton, Chief Executive Officer
Web address: www.columbia.net

WEST HOUSTON MEDICAL CENTER (O, 169 beds) 12141 Richmond Avenue, Houston, TX Zip 77082–2499; tel. 281/558–3444; Jeffrey S. Holland, Chief Executive Officer
Web address: www.columbia.net

UTAH: BRIGHAM CITY COMMUNITY HOSPITAL (O, 49 beds) 950 South Medical Drive, Brigham City, UT Zip 84302–3090; tel. 435/734–9471; Tad A. Morley, Chief Executive Officer
Web address: www.columbia.net

LAKEVIEW HOSPITAL (O, 90 beds) 630 East Medical Drive, Bountiful, UT Zip 84010–4996; tel. 801/292–6231; Craig Preston, Chief Executive Officer
Web address: www.columbia.net

MOUNTAIN VIEW HOSPITAL (O, 126 beds) 1000 East 100 North, Payson, UT Zip 84651–1690; tel. 801/465–9201; Kevin Johnson, Chief Executive Officer

OGDEN REGIONAL MEDICAL CENTER (O, 179 beds) 5475 South 500 East, Ogden, UT Zip 84405–6978; tel. 801/479–2111; Steven B. Bateman, Chief Executive Officer
Web address: www.columbia.net

ST. MARK'S HOSPITAL (O, 229 beds) 1200 East 3900 South, Salt Lake City, UT Zip 84124–1390; tel. 801/268–7111; John Hanshaw, Chief Executive Officer
Web address: www.columbia.net

VIRGINIA: ALLEGHANY REGIONAL HOSPITAL (O, 156 beds) One ARH Lane, Low Moor, VA Zip 24457, Mailing Address: P.O. Box 7, Zip 24457–0007; tel. 540/862–6011; Ward W. Stevens, CHE, Chief Executive Officer
Web address: www.columbia.net

ARLINGTON HOSPITAL 1701 North George Mason Drive, Arlington, VA Zip 22205–3698; tel. 703/558–5000; James B. Cole, President and Chief Executive Officer

CHIPPENHAM AND JOHNSTON–WILLIS HOSPITALS (O, 748 beds) 7101 Jahnke Road, Richmond, VA Zip 23225–4044; tel. 804/320–3911; Marilyn B. Tavenner, Chief Executive Officer

CLINCH VALLEY MEDICAL CENTER (O, 200 beds) 2949 West Front Street, Richlands, VA Zip 24641–2099; tel. 540/596–6000; James W. Thweatt, Chief Executive Officer
Web address: www.ccvmc.com

COLUMBIA PENTAGON CITY HOSPITAL (O, 102 beds) 2455 Army Navy Drive, Arlington, VA Zip 22206–2999; tel. 703/920–6700; Thomas Anderson, Chief Executive Officer
Web address: www.columbia.net

COLUMBIA RESTON HOSPITAL CENTER (O, 121 beds) 1850 Town Center Parkway, Reston, VA Zip 20190–3298; tel. 703/689–9000; William A. Adams, President and Chief Executive Officer
Web address: www.columbia.net

DOMINION HOSPITAL (O, 100 beds) 2960 Sleepy Hollow Road, Falls Church, VA Zip 22044–2001; tel. 703/536–2000; Barbara D. S. Hekimian, Chief Executive Officer

HENRICO DOCTORS' HOSPITAL (O, 340 beds) 1602 Skipwith Road, Richmond, VA Zip 23229–5298; tel. 804/289–4500; Patrick W. Farrell, Chief Executive Officer

JOHN RANDOLPH MEDICAL CENTER (O, 271 beds) 411 West Randolph Road, Hopewell, VA Zip 23860, Mailing Address: P.O. Box 971, Zip 23860; tel. 804/541–1600; Daniel J. Wetta Jr., Chief Executive Officer

LEWIS–GALE MEDICAL CENTER (O, 521 beds) 1900 Electric Road, Salem, VA Zip 24153–7494; tel. 540/776–4000; William B. Downey, Administrator

MONTGOMERY REGIONAL HOSPITAL (O, 115 beds) 3700 South Main Street, Blacksburg, VA Zip 24060–7081, Mailing Address: P.O. Box 90004, Zip 24062–9004; tel. 540/953–5101; David R. Williams, Chief Executive Officer
Web address: www.montreghosp.com

PENINSULA BEHAVIORAL CENTER (O, 60 beds) 2244 Executive Drive, Hampton, VA Zip 23666–2430; tel. 757/827–1001; Steuart A. Kimmeth, Chief Executive Officer

PULASKI COMMUNITY HOSPITAL (O, 62 beds) 2400 Lee Highway, Pulaski, VA Zip 24301–0759, Mailing Address: P.O. Box 759, Zip 24301–0759; tel. 540/994–8100; Jack Nunley, Chief Executive Officer
Web address: www.pch–va.com

RETREAT HOSPITAL (O, 146 beds) 2621 Grove Avenue, Richmond, VA Zip 23220–4308; tel. 804/254–5100; Paul L. Baldwin, Chief Executive Officer

WASHINGTON: CAPITAL MEDICAL CENTER (O, 110 beds) 3900 Capital Mall Drive S.W., Olympia, WA Zip 98502–8654, Mailing Address: P.O. Box 19002, Zip 98507–0013; tel. 360/754–5858; Joseph Sharp, Chief Executive Officer

WEST VIRGINIA: COLUMBIA RIVER PARK HOSPITAL (O, 125 beds) 1230 Sixth Avenue, Huntington, WV Zip 25701–2312, Mailing Address: P.O. Box 1875, Zip 25719–1875; tel. 304/526–9111; Scott C. Stamm, Chief Executive Officer
Web address: www.columbia.net

For explanation of codes following names, see page B2.
★ Indicates Type III membership in the American Hospital Association.

Section B

PUTNAM GENERAL HOSPITAL (O, 64 beds) 1400 Hospital Drive, Hurricane, WV Zip 25526–9210, Mailing Address: P.O. Box 900, Zip 25526–0900; tel. 304/757–1700; Patsy Hardy, Administrator
Web address: www.columbia–hca.com

RALEIGH GENERAL HOSPITAL (O, 303 beds) 1710 Harper Road, Beckley, WV Zip 25801–3397; tel. 304/256–4100; David B. Darden, Chief Executive Officer

SAINT FRANCIS HOSPITAL (O, 155 beds) 333 Laidley Street, Charleston, WV Zip 25301–1628, Mailing Address: P.O. Box 471, Zip 25322–0471; tel. 304/347–6500; Dan Lauffer, Chief Executive Officer

ST. LUKE'S HOSPITAL (O, 79 beds) 1333 Southview Drive, Bluefield, WV Zip 24701–4399, Mailing Address: P.O. Box 1190, Zip 24701–1190; tel. 304/327–2900; Deane E. Beamer, President and Chief Executive Officer
Web address: www.columbiastlukes.com

Owned, leased, sponsored:	222 hospitals	42276 beds
Contract–managed:	0 hospitals	0 beds
Totals:	222 hospitals	42276 beds

★**0161: COLUMBUS REGIONAL HEALTH SYSTEM** (NP)
707 Center Street, Suite 400, Columbus, GA Zip 31902; tel. 706/660–6100; Larry Sanders, FACHE, Chairman and Chief Executive Officer

ALABAMA: PHENIX REGIONAL HOSPITAL (O, 114 beds) 1707 21st Avenue, Phenix City, AL Zip 36867–3753, Mailing Address: P.O. Box 190, Zip 36868–0190; tel. 334/291–8502; Lance B. Duke, FACHE, President and Chief Executive Officer

GEORGIA: THE MEDICAL CENTER (O, 537 beds) 710 Center Street, Columbus, GA Zip 31902, Mailing Address: P.O. Box 951, Zip 31902–0951; tel. 706/571–1000; Lance B. Duke, FACHE, President and Chief Executive Officer

Owned, leased, sponsored:	2 hospitals	651 beds
Contract–managed:	0 hospitals	0 beds
Totals:	2 hospitals	651 beds

0215: COMMUNITY CARE SYSTEMS, INC. (IO)
203 Grove Street, Wellesley, MA Zip 02482–2413; tel. 781/416–5300; Frederick J. Thacher, Chairman

MAINE: SPRING HARBOR HOSPITAL (O, 106 beds) 175 Running Hill Road, South Portland, ME Zip 04106; tel. 207/761–2200; Dennis King, President

MASSACHUSETTS: CHARLES RIVER HOSPITAL (O, 62 beds) 203 Grove Street, Wellesley, MA Zip 02181–7413; tel. 781/304–2800; Juliette Fay, President and Chief Executive Officer

Owned, leased, sponsored:	2 hospitals	168 beds
Contract–managed:	0 hospitals	0 beds
Totals:	2 hospitals	168 beds

★**1085: COMMUNITY HEALTH SYSTEM OF NORTHERN CALIFORNIA** (NP)
Fresno and R Streets, Fresno, CA Zip 93721, Mailing Address: P.O. Box 1232, Zip 93721; tel. 559/459–6000; J. Philip Hinton, M.D., President and Chief Executive Officer

CALIFORNIA: CLOVIS COMMUNITY MEDICAL CENTER (O, 143 beds) 2755 Herndon Avenue, Clovis, CA Zip 93611; tel. 209/323–4000; Mike Barber, Facility Service Integrator

FRESNO COMMUNITY HOSPITAL AND MEDICAL CENTER (O, 375 beds) Fresno and R Streets, Fresno, CA Zip 93721, Mailing Address: Box 1232, Zip 93715; tel. 209/442–6000; J. Philip Hinton, M.D., President and Chief Executive Officer

UNIVERSITY MEDICAL CENTER (O, 334 beds) 445 South Cedar Avenue, Fresno, CA Zip 93702–2907; tel. 209/459–4000; Andres Fernandez, Facility Services Integrator and Administrator

Owned, leased, sponsored:	3 hospitals	852 beds
Contract–managed:	0 hospitals	0 beds
Totals:	3 hospitals	852 beds

★**0080: COMMUNITY HEALTH SYSTEMS, INC.** (IO)
155 Franklin Road, Suite 400, Brentwood, TN Zip 37027–4600, Mailing Address: P.O. Box 217, Zip 37024–0217; tel. 615/373–9600; Wayne T. Smith, President and Chief Executive Officer

ALABAMA: EDGE REGIONAL MEDICAL CENTER (O, 87 beds) 1330 Highway 231 South, Troy, AL Zip 36081–1224; tel. 334/670–5000; David E. Loving, Chief Executive Officer

HARTSELLE MEDICAL CENTER (O, 150 beds) 201 Pine Street N.W., Hartselle, AL Zip 35640–2309, Mailing Address: P.O. Box 969, Zip 35640–0969; tel. 256/773–6511; Mike H. McNair, Chief Executive Officer

L. V. STABLER MEMORIAL HOSPITAL (O, 67 beds) Highway 10 West, Greenville, AL Zip 36037–0915, Mailing Address: Box 1000, Zip 36037–0915; tel. 334/382–2676; Tom R. McDougal Jr., Chief Executive Officer

PARKWAY MEDICAL CENTER HOSPITAL (O, 94 beds) 1874 Beltline Road S.W., Decatur, AL Zip 35601–5509, Mailing Address: P.O. Box 2211, Zip 35609–2211; tel. 256/350–2211; Phillip J. Mazzuca, Chief Executive Officer

WOODLAND MEDICAL CENTER (O, 100 beds) 1910 Cherokee Avenue S.E., Cullman, AL Zip 35055–5599; tel. 256/739–3500; Lowell S. Benton, Executive Director

ARIZONA: PAYSON REGIONAL MEDICAL CENTER (O, 34 beds) 807 South Ponderosa Street, Payson, AZ Zip 85541–5599; tel. 520/474–3222; Russell V. Judd, Chief Executive Officer

ARKANSAS: HARRIS HOSPITAL (O, 88 beds) 1205 McLain Street, Newport, AR Zip 72112–3533; tel. 870/523–8911; Robin E. Lake, Chief Executive Officer

RANDOLPH COUNTY MEDICAL CENTER (L, 50 beds) 2801 Medical Center Drive, Pocahontas, AR Zip 72455–9497; tel. 870/892–6000; Michael G. Layfield, Chief Executive Officer

CALIFORNIA: BARSTOW COMMUNITY HOSPITAL (L, 56 beds) 555 South Seventh Street, Barstow, CA Zip 92311; tel. 760/256–1761; George F. Naylor III, Chief Executive Officer

WATSONVILLE COMMUNITY HOSPITAL (O, 130 beds) 75 Nielson Street, Watsonville, CA Zip 95076; tel. 831/724–4741; Barry S. Schneider, Chief Executive Officer
Web address: www.watsonville.com\hospital

FLORIDA: DOCTORS MEMORIAL HOSPITAL (L, 34 beds) 401 East Byrd Avenue, Bonifay, FL Zip 32425–3007, Mailing Address: P.O. Box 188, Zip 32425–0188; tel. 850/547–1120; Dale Larson, Chief Executive Officer

NORTH OKALOOSA MEDICAL CENTER (O, 83 beds) 151 Redstone Avenue S.E., Crestview, FL Zip 32539–6026; tel. 850/689–8100; Roger L. Hall, Chief Executive Officer

GEORGIA: BERRIEN COUNTY HOSPITAL (O, 155 beds) 1221 East McPherson Street, Nashville, GA Zip 31639–2326, Mailing Address: P.O. Box 665, Zip 31639–0665; tel. 912/686–7471; James L. Jarrett, Chief Executive Officer

FANNIN REGIONAL HOSPITAL (O, 46 beds) 2855 Old Highway 5, Blue Ridge, GA Zip 30513; tel. 706/632–3711; Barry L. Mousa, Chief Executive Officer

ILLINOIS: CROSSROADS COMMUNITY HOSPITAL (O, 37 beds) 8 Doctors Park Road, Mount Vernon, IL Zip 62864–6224; tel. 618/244–5500; Donald J. Frederic, Chief Executive Officer

MARION MEMORIAL HOSPITAL (L, 84 beds) 917 West Main Street, Marion, IL Zip 62959–1836; tel. 618/997–5341; Ronald Seal, President and Chief Executive Officer

KENTUCKY: KENTUCKY RIVER MEDICAL CENTER (L, 55 beds) 540 Jett Drive, Jackson, KY Zip 41339–9620; tel. 606/666–6305; O. David Bevins, Chief Executive Officer

PARKWAY REGIONAL HOSPITAL (O, 70 beds) 2000 Holiday Lane, Fulton, KY Zip 42041; tel. 502/472–2522; Mary Jo Lewis, Chief Executive Officer

For explanation of codes following names, see page B2.
★ Indicates Type III membership in the American Hospital Association.

THREE RIVERS MEDICAL CENTER (O, 90 beds) Highway 644, Louisa, KY Zip 41230, Mailing Address: P.O. Box 769, Zip 41230–0769; tel. 606/638–9451; Greg Kiser, Chief Executive Officer

LOUISIANA: BYRD REGIONAL HOSPITAL (O, 59 beds) 1020 West Fertitta Boulevard, Leesville, LA Zip 71446–4697; tel. 318/239–9041; Donald Henderson, Chief Executive Officer

RIVER WEST MEDICAL CENTER (O, 80 beds) 59355 River West Drive, Plaquemine, LA Zip 70764–9543; tel. 225/687–9222; Mark Nosacka, Chief Executive Officer

SABINE MEDICAL CENTER (O, 48 beds) 240 Highland Drive, Many, LA Zip 71449–3718; tel. 318/256–5691; Patrick W. Gandy, Chief Executive Officer

MISSOURI: MOBERLY REGIONAL MEDICAL CENTER (O, 92 beds) 1515 Union Avenue, Moberly, MO Zip 65270–9449, Mailing Address: P.O. Box 3000, Zip 65270–3000; tel. 660/263–8400; Daniel E. McKay, Chief Executive Officer

NEW MEXICO: EASTERN NEW MEXICO MEDICAL CENTER (O, 168 beds) 405 West Country Club Road, Roswell, NM Zip 88201–9981; tel. 505/622–8170; Ronald J. Shafer, President and Chief Executive Officer
Web address: www.enmmc.com

MIMBRES MEMORIAL HOSPITAL (O, 119 beds) 900 West Ash Street, Deming, NM Zip 88030–4098, Mailing Address: P.O. Box 710, Zip 88031–0710; tel. 505/546–2761; Timothy E. Schmidt, Chief Executive Officer

NORTH CAROLINA: MARTIN GENERAL HOSPITAL (O, 49 beds) 310 South McCaskey Road, Williamston, NC Zip 27892–2150, Mailing Address: P.O. Box 1128, Zip 27892–1128; tel. 252/809–6121; Scott M. Landrum, Chief Executive Officer

PENNSYLVANIA: BERWICK HOSPITAL CENTER (O, 409 beds) 701 East 16th Street, Berwick, PA Zip 18603–2397; tel. 570/759–5000; David R. Sirk, President and Chief Executive Officer

SOUTH CAROLINA: CHESTERFIELD GENERAL HOSPITAL (O, 66 beds) Highway 9 West, Cheraw, SC Zip 29520, Mailing Address: P.O. Box 151, Zip 29520–0151; tel. 843/537–7881; Chris Wolf, Chief Executive Officer

MARLBORO PARK HOSPITAL (O, 105 beds) 1138 Cheraw Highway, Bennettsville, SC Zip 29512–0738, Mailing Address: P.O. Box 738, Zip 29512–0738; tel. 843/479–2881; Stephen Chapman, Chief Executive Officer

SPRINGS MEMORIAL HOSPITAL (O, 169 beds) 800 West Meeting Street, Lancaster, SC Zip 29720–2298; tel. 803/286–1214; Robert M. Luther, Chief Executive Officer

TENNESSEE: CLEVELAND COMMUNITY HOSPITAL (O, 70 beds) 2800 Westside Drive N.W., Cleveland, TN Zip 37312–3599; tel. 423/339–4100; Marty Smith, Chief Executive Officer

LAKEWAY REGIONAL HOSPITAL (O, 135 beds) 726 McFarland Street, Morristown, TN Zip 37814–3990; tel. 423/586–2302; Robert B. Wampler, CPA, Chief Executive Officer

SCOTT COUNTY HOSPITAL (L, 77 beds) 18797 Alberta Avenue, Oneida, TN Zip 37841–4939, Mailing Address: P.O. Box 4939, Zip 37841–4939; tel. 423/569–8521; Peter T. Petruzzi, Chief Executive Officer

WHITE COUNTY COMMUNITY HOSPITAL (O, 60 beds) 401 Sewell Road, Sparta, TN Zip 38583–1299; tel. 931/738–9211; David Conejo, Chief Executive Officer

TEXAS: BIG BEND REGIONAL MEDICAL CENTER (O, 25 beds) 801 East Brown Street, Alpine, TX Zip 79830–3209; tel. 915/837–3447; Don Edd Green, Chief Executive Officer
Web address: www.overland.net/~bbrmc

CLEVELAND REGIONAL MEDICAL CENTER (O, 93 beds) 300 East Crockett Street, Cleveland, TX Zip 77327–4062, Mailing Address: P.O. Box 1688, Zip 77328–1688; tel. 281/593–1811; Deborah Hopps, Interim Chief Executive Officer
Web address: www.crmcr.com

HIGHLAND MEDICAL CENTER (O, 123 beds) 2412 50th Street, Lubbock, TX Zip 79412–2494; tel. 806/788–4060; John D. Brock, Chief Executive Officer

HILL REGIONAL HOSPITAL (O, 80 beds) 101 Circle Drive, Hillsboro, TX Zip 76645–2670; tel. 254/582–8425; Jan McClure, Chief Executive Officer

LAKE GRANBURY MEDICAL CENTER (L, 49 beds) 1310 Paluxy Road, Granbury, TX Zip 76048–5699; tel. 817/573–2683; Mike Pruitt, Chief Executive Officer

NORTHEAST MEDICAL CENTER (O, 46 beds) 504 Lipscomb Boulevard, Bonham, TX Zip 75418–4096, Mailing Address: P.O. Drawer C, Zip 75418–4096; tel. 903/583–8585; Gwen S. Eddleman, R.N., Interim Chief Executive Officer

SCENIC MOUNTAIN MEDICAL CENTER (O, 128 beds) 1601 West 11th Place, Big Spring, TX Zip 79720–4198; tel. 915/263–1211; Loren F. Chandler, Interim Chief Executive Officer
Web address: www.smmccare.com

UTAH: TOOELE VALLEY REGIONAL MEDICAL CENTER (O, 107 beds) 211 South 100 East, Tooele, UT Zip 84074–2794; tel. 435/882–1697; Brent Cope, Chief Executive Officer

VIRGINIA: GREENSVILLE MEMORIAL HOSPITAL (L, 144 beds) 214 Weaver Avenue, Emporia, VA Zip 23847–1482; tel. 804/348–2000; Gerald R. Lundberg, Interim Chief Executive Officer

RUSSELL COUNTY MEDICAL CENTER (O, 78 beds) Carroll and Tate Streets, Lebanon, VA Zip 24266–4510; tel. 540/889–1224; David L. Brash, Chief Executive Officer

Owned, leased, sponsored:	44 hospitals	4089 beds
Contract–managed:	0 hospitals	0 beds
Totals:	44 hospitals	4089 beds

0014: CONNECTICUT DEPARTMENT OF MENTAL HEALTH AND ADDICTION SERVICES (NP)
410 Capitol Avenue, Hartford, CT Zip 06134, Mailing Address: P.O. Box 341431, Zip 06134–1431; tel. 860/418–6969; Albert J. Solnit, M.D., Commissioner

CONNECTICUT: CEDARCREST HOSPITAL (O, 146 beds) 525 Russell Road, Newington, CT Zip 06111–1595; tel. 860/666–4613; John H. Simsarian, Superintendent

CONNECTICUT MENTAL HEALTH CENTER (O, 39 beds) 34 Park Street, New Haven, CT Zip 06519–1187, Mailing Address: P.O. Box 1842, Zip 06508–1842; tel. 203/974–7144; Selby Jacobs, M.D., Director

CONNECTICUT VALLEY HOSPITAL (O, 418 beds) Silver Street, Middletown, CT Zip 06457–7023, Mailing Address: P.O. Box 351, Zip 06457–0351; tel. 860/262–5000; Garrell S. Mullaney, Chief Executive Officer

SOUTHWEST CONNECTICUT MENTAL HEALTH SYSTEM (O, 62 beds) 1635 Central Avenue, Bridgeport, CT Zip 06610–2700, Mailing Address: P.O. Box 5117, Zip 06610–5117; tel. 203/551–7444; James M. Pisciotta, Chief Executive Officer

Owned, leased, sponsored:	4 hospitals	665 beds
Contract–managed:	0 hospitals	0 beds
Totals:	4 hospitals	665 beds

★0127: CONTINUUM HEALTH PARTNERS (NP)
555 West 57th Street, New York, NY Zip 10019; tel. 212/523–8390; Robert G. Newman, M.D., President

NEW YORK: BETH ISRAEL MEDICAL CENTER (O, 1254 beds) First Avenue and 16th Street, New York, NY Zip 10003–3803; tel. 212/420–2000; Matthew E. Fink, M.D., President and Chief Executive Officer
Web address: www.bethisraelny.org

LONG ISLAND COLLEGE HOSPITAL (O, 419 beds) 339 Hicks Street, Brooklyn, NY Zip 11201–5509; tel. 718/780–1000; Peter A. Kelly, Interim President and Chief Executive Officer
Web address: www.lich.org

ST. LUKE'S–ROOSEVELT HOSPITAL CENTER (O, 724 beds) 1111 Amsterdam Avenue, New York, NY Zip 10025; tel. 212/523–4300; Sigurd H. Ackerman, M.D., President and Chief Executive Officer
Web address: www.wehealnewyork.org

Owned, leased, sponsored:	3 hospitals	2397 beds
Contract–managed:	0 hospitals	0 beds
Totals:	3 hospitals	2397 beds

For explanation of codes following names, see page B2.
★ Indicates Type III membership in the American Hospital Association.

0016: COOK COUNTY BUREAU OF HEALTH SERVICES (NP)
1900 West Polk Street, Suite 220, Chicago, IL Zip 60612;
tel. 312/633–6820; Ruth M. Rothstein, Chief

ILLINOIS: COOK COUNTY HOSPITAL (O, 591 beds) 1835 West Harrison, Chicago, IL Zip 60612–3785; tel. 312/633–6000; Lacy Thomas, Director

OAK FOREST HOSPITAL OF COOK COUNTY (O, 687 beds) 15900 South Cicero Avenue, Oak Forest, IL Zip 60452; tel. 708/687–7200; Cynthia T. Henderson, M.D., M.P.H., Director and Chief Operating Officer

PROVIDENT HOSPITAL OF COOK COUNTY (O, 113 beds) 500 East 51st Street, Chicago, IL Zip 60615–2494; tel. 312/572–2000; Stephanie Wright–Griggs, Chief Operating Officer

Owned, leased, sponsored:	3 hospitals	1391 beds
Contract–managed:	0 hospitals	0 beds
Totals:	3 hospitals	1391 beds

0103: COTTAGE HEALTH SYSTEM (NP)
Pueblo at Bath Streets, Santa Barbara, CA Zip 93102, Mailing Address: P.O. Box 689, Zip 93102; tel. 805/682–7111; James L. Ash, President and Chief Executive Officer

CALIFORNIA: GOLETA VALLEY COTTAGE HOSPITAL (O, 79 beds) 351 South Patterson Avenue, Santa Barbara, CA Zip 93111, Mailing Address: Box 6306, Zip 93160; tel. 805/967–3411; Diane Wisby, President and Chief Executive Officer

SANTA BARBARA COTTAGE HOSPITAL (O, 336 beds) Pueblo at Bath Streets, Santa Barbara, CA Zip 93105, Mailing Address: Box 689, Zip 93102; tel. 805/682–7111; James L. Ash, President and Chief Executive Officer

SANTA YNEZ VALLEY COTTAGE HOSPITAL (O, 20 beds) 700 Alamo Pintado Road, Solvang, CA Zip 93463; tel. 805/688–6431; James L. Ash, President and Chief Executive Officer

Owned, leased, sponsored:	3 hospitals	435 beds
Contract–managed:	0 hospitals	0 beds
Totals:	3 hospitals	435 beds

0123: COVENANT HEALTH (NP)
100 Fort Sanders West Boulevard, Knoxville, TN Zip 37922; tel. 423/531–5555; Alan C. Guy, President and Chief Executive Officer

TENNESSEE: FORT SANDERS LOUDON MEDICAL CENTER (O, 50 beds) 1125 Grove Street, Loudon, TN Zip 37774–1512, Mailing Address: P.O. Box 217, Zip 37774–0217; tel. 423/458–8222; Martha O'Regan Chill, President and Chief Administrative Officer

FORT SANDERS REGIONAL MEDICAL CENTER (O, 406 beds) 1901 Clinch Avenue S.W., Knoxville, TN Zip 37916–2394; tel. 423/541–1111; James R. Burkhart, FACHE, Administrator

FORT SANDERS–PARKWEST MEDICAL CENTER (O, 280 beds) 9352 Park West Boulevard, Knoxville, TN Zip 37923–4387, Mailing Address: P.O. Box 22993, Zip 37933–0993; tel. 423/694–5700; James R. Burkhart, FACHE, President and Chief Executive Officer

FORT SANDERS–SEVIER MEDICAL CENTER (O, 100 beds) 709 Middle Creek Road, Sevierville, TN Zip 37862–5016, Mailing Address: P.O. Box 8005, Zip 37864–8005; tel. 423/429–6100; Ellen Wilhoit, Administrator

METHODIST MEDICAL CENTER OF OAK RIDGE (O, 295 beds) 990 Oak Ridge Turnpike, Oak Ridge, TN Zip 37830–6976, Mailing Address: P.O. Box 2529, Zip 37831–2529; tel. 423/481–1000; Daniel J. Bonk, President and Chief Administrative Officer

Owned, leased, sponsored:	5 hospitals	1131 beds
Contract–managed:	0 hospitals	0 beds
Totals:	5 hospitals	1131 beds

★5885: COVENANT HEALTH SYSTEMS, INC. (CC)
420 Bedford Street, Lexington, MA Zip 02420–1502; tel. 781/862–1634; David R. Lincoln, President and Chief Executive Officer

MAINE: ST. MARY'S REGIONAL MEDICAL CENTER (O, 187 beds) 45 Golder Street, Lewiston, ME Zip 04240–6033, Mailing Address: P.O. Box 291, Zip 04243–0291; tel. 207/777–8100; James E. Cassidy, President and Chief Executive Officer
Web address: www.stmarysmaine.com

MASSACHUSETTS: YOUVILLE LIFECARE (O, 286 beds) 1575 Cambridge Street, Cambridge, MA Zip 02138–4398; tel. 617/876–4344; Daniel P. Leahey, President and Chief Executive Officer

NEW HAMPSHIRE: ST. JOSEPH HOSPITAL (O, 135 beds) 172 Kinsley Street, Nashua, NH Zip 03061; tel. 603/882–3000; Peter B. Davis, President and Chief Executive Officer
Web address: www.nh–healthcare.org

Owned, leased, sponsored:	3 hospitals	608 beds
Contract–managed:	0 hospitals	0 beds
Totals:	3 hospitals	608 beds

0179: COX HEALTH SYSTEM (NP)
3800 South National Avenue, Springfield, MO Zip 65807; tel. 417/269–3108; Larry D. Wallis, President and Chief Executive Officer

MISSOURI: COX HOSPITAL SOUTH (O, 140 beds) 1000 East Walnut Lawn, Springfield, MO Zip 65807–7399; tel. 417/882–4700; Michelle Fischer, Administrator

COX MEDICAL CENTER (O, 521 beds) 1423 North Jefferson Street, Springfield, MO Zip 65802–1988; tel. 417/269–3000; Larry D. Wallis, President and Chief Executive Officer

COX MONETT HOSPITAL (O, 53 beds) 801 Lincoln Avenue, Monett, MO Zip 65708–1698; tel. 417/354–1400; Gregory D. Johnson, Administrator

Owned, leased, sponsored:	3 hospitals	714 beds
Contract–managed:	0 hospitals	0 beds
Totals:	3 hospitals	714 beds

★0008: CROZER–KEYSTONE HEALTH SYSTEM (NP)
100 West Sproul Road, Springfield, PA Zip 19064; tel. 610/338–8200; John C. McMeekin, President and Chief Executive Officer

PENNSYLVANIA: CROZER–CHESTER MEDICAL CENTER (O, 589 beds) One Medical Center Boulevard, Upland, PA Zip 19013–3995; tel. 610/447–2000; Joan K. Richards, President

DELAWARE COUNTY MEMORIAL HOSPITAL (O, 231 beds) 501 North Lansdowne Avenue, Drexel Hill, PA Zip 19026–1114; tel. 610/284–8100; Joan K. Richards, President

Owned, leased, sponsored:	2 hospitals	820 beds
Contract–managed:	0 hospitals	0 beds
Totals:	2 hospitals	820 beds

★1855: DAUGHTERS OF CHARITY NATIONAL HEALTH SYSTEM (CC)
4600 Edmundson Road, Saint Louis, MO Zip 63134–3806, Mailing Address: P.O. Box 45998, Zip 63145–5998; tel. 314/253–6700; Donald A. Brennan, President and Chief Executive Officer

ALABAMA: PROVIDENCE HOSPITAL (S, 349 beds) 6801 Airport Boulevard, Mobile, AL Zip 36608–3785, Mailing Address: P.O. Box 850429, Zip 36685–0429; tel. 334/633–1000; John R. Roeder, President and Chief Executive Officer
Web address: www.providencehospital.org

ST. VINCENT'S HOSPITAL (S, 338 beds) 810 St. Vincent's Drive, Birmingham, AL Zip 35205–1695, Mailing Address: P.O. Box 12407, Zip 35202–2407; tel. 205/939–7000; Curtis James, Acting President and Chief Executive Officer
Web address: www.stv.org

CONNECTICUT: ST. VINCENT'S MEDICAL CENTER (S, 259 beds) 2800 Main Street, Bridgeport, CT Zip 06606–4292; tel. 203/576–6000; William J. Riordan, President and Chief Executive Officer
Web address: www.stvincents.org

For explanation of codes following names, see page B2.
★ Indicates Type III membership in the American Hospital Association.

Section B

DISTRICT OF COLUMBIA: PROVIDENCE HOSPITAL (S, 556 beds) 1150 Varnum Street N.E., Washington, DC Zip 20017–2180; tel. 202/269–7000; Sister Carol Keehan, President
Web address: www.provhosp.org

FLORIDA: BAPTIST MEDICAL CENTER (S, 506 beds) 800 Prudential Drive, Jacksonville, FL Zip 32207–8203; tel. 904/202–2000; John F. Wilbanks, Senior Vice President and Administrator

BAPTIST MEDICAL CENTER–BEACHES (S, 82 beds) 1350 13th Avenue South, Jacksonville Beach, FL Zip 32250–3205; tel. 904/247–2900; Joseph Mitrick, Administrator

BAPTIST MEDICAL CENTER–NASSAU (S, 24 beds) 1250 South 18th Street, Fernandina Beach, FL Zip 32034–3098; tel. 904/321–3501; Jim L. Mayo, Administrator
Web address: www.baptist–stvincents.com

SACRED HEART HOSPITAL OF PENSACOLA (S, 520 beds) 5151 North Ninth Avenue, Pensacola, FL Zip 32504–8795, Mailing Address: P.O. Box 2700, Zip 32513–2700; tel. 850/416–7000; Patrick J. Madden, President and Chief Executive Officer
Web address: www.sacred–heart.org

ST. VINCENT'S MEDICAL CENTER (S, 722 beds) 1800 Barrs Street, Jacksonville, FL Zip 32204–2982, Mailing Address: P.O. Box 2982, Zip 32203–2982; tel. 904/308–7300; John W. Logue, Executive Vice President and Chief Operating Officer
Web address: www.baptist–stvincents.com

INDIANA: ST. JOSEPH HOSPITAL & HEALTH CENTER (S, 145 beds) 1907 West Sycamore Street, Kokomo, IN Zip 46904–9010, Mailing Address: P.O. Box 9010, Zip 46904–9010; tel. 765/452–5611; Kathleen M. Korbelak, President and Chief Executive Officer
Web address: www.stjhhc.org

ST. MARY'S HOSPITAL WARRICK (S, 28 beds) 1116 Millis Avenue, Boonville, IN Zip 47601–0629, Mailing Address: Box 629, Zip 47601–0629; tel. 812/897–4800; Jim M. Hayes, Executive Vice President and Aministrator

ST. MARY'S MEDICAL CENTER OF EVANSVILLE (S, 487 beds) 3700 Washington Avenue, Evansville, IN Zip 47750; tel. 812/485–4000; Jay D. Kasey, President

ST. VINCENT HOSPITALS AND HEALTH SERVICES (S, 802 beds) 2001 West 86th Street, Indianapolis, IN Zip 46260–1991, Mailing Address: P.O. Box 40970, Zip 46240–0970; tel. 317/338–2345; Marsha N. Casey, President
Web address: www.stvincent.com

ST. VINCENT MERCY HOSPITAL (S, 32 beds) 1331 South A Street, Elwood, IN Zip 46036–1942; tel. 765/552–4600; David Masterson, Administrator
Web address: www.stvincent.org

ST. VINCENT WILLIAMSPORT HOSPITAL (S, 16 beds) 412 North Monroe Street, Williamsport, IN Zip 47993–0215; tel. 765/762–4000; Jane Craigin, Chief Executive Officer
Web address: www.stvincent.org

MARYLAND: MEMORIAL HOSPITAL AND MEDICAL CENTER OF CUMBERLAND (S, 187 beds) 600 Memorial Avenue, Cumberland, MD Zip 21502–3797; tel. 301/723–4000; Thomas C. Dowdell, Executive Director
Web address: www.wmhs.com

SACRED HEART HOSPITAL (S, 304 beds) 900 Seton Drive, Cumberland, MD Zip 21502–1874; tel. 301/759–4200; William T. Bradel, Executive Director

ST. AGNES HEALTHCARE (S, 565 beds) 900 Caton Avenue, Baltimore, MD Zip 21229–5299; tel. 410/368–6000; Robert W. Adams, President and Chief Executive Officer
Web address: www.stagnes.org

MICHIGAN: PROVIDENCE HOSPITAL AND MEDICAL CENTERS (S, 369 beds) 16001 West Nine Mile Road, Southfield, MI Zip 48075–4854, Mailing Address: Box 2043, Zip 48037–2043; tel. 248/424–3000; Robert F. Casalou, Interim President and Chief Executive Officer

ST. MARY'S MEDICAL CENTER (S, 268 beds) 830 South Jefferson Avenue, Saginaw, MI Zip 48601–2594; tel. 517/776–8000; Frederic L. Fraizer, President and Chief Executive Officer
Web address: www.saintmarys–saginaw.org

NEW YORK: MOUNT ST. MARY'S HOSPITAL OF NIAGARA FALLS (S, 179 beds) 5300 Military Road, Lewiston, NY Zip 14092–1997; tel. 716/297–4800; Angelo G. Calbone, President and Chief Executive Officer

OUR LADY OF LOURDES MEMORIAL HOSPITAL (S, 184 beds) 169 Riverside Drive, Binghamton, NY Zip 13905–4198; tel. 607/798–5111; John D. O'Neil, President and Chief Executive Officer
Web address: www.lourdes.com

PARK RIDGE HOSPITAL (S, 239 beds) 1555 Long Pond Road, Rochester, NY Zip 14626–4182; tel. 716/723–7000; Martin E. Carlin, President
Web address: www.parkridgehs.org

SETON HEALTH SYSTEM (S, 344 beds) 1300 Massachusetts Avenue, Troy, NY Zip 12180–1695; tel. 518/268–5000; Mark A. Donovan, M.D., President and Chief Executive Officer
Web address: www.setonhealth.org

ST. MARY'S HOSPITAL (S, 73 beds) 89 Genesee Street, Rochester, NY Zip 14611–3285; tel. 716/464–3000; Stewart Putnam, President
Web address: www.unityhealth.org

PENNSYLVANIA: GOOD SAMARITAN REGIONAL MEDICAL CENTER (S, 153 beds) 700 East Norwegian Street, Pottsville, PA Zip 17901–2798; tel. 570/621–4000; Gino J. Pazzaglini, President and Chief Executive Officer
Web address: www.goodsamrmc.com

TENNESSEE: ST. THOMAS HEALTH SERVICES (S, 514 beds) 4220 Harding Road, Nashville, TN Zip 37205–2095, Mailing Address: P.O. Box 380, Zip 37202–0380; tel. 615/222–2111; John Lucas, M.D., President and Chief Executive Officer

TEXAS: BRACKENRIDGE HOSPITAL (L, 291 beds) 601 East 15th Street, Austin, TX Zip 78701–1996; tel. 512/324–7000; Susan McClernon, Administrator

PROVIDENCE HEALTH CENTER (S, 427 beds) 6901 Medical Parkway, Waco, TX Zip 76712–7998, Mailing Address: P.O. Box 2589, Zip 76702–2589; tel. 254/751–4000; Kent A. Keahey, President and Chief Executive Officer
Web address: www.providence–waco.org

SETON HIGHLAND LAKES (S, 26 beds) Highway 281 South, Burnet, TX Zip 78611, Mailing Address: P.O. Box 1219, Zip 78611–0840; tel. 512/756–6000; Terry R. Andris, CHE, Administrator

SETON MEDICAL CENTER (S, 490 beds) 1201 West 38th Street, Austin, TX Zip 78705–1056; tel. 512/324–1000; Gregory R. Angle, Administrator
Web address: www.seton.org

SETON SHOAL CREEK HOSPITAL (S, 118 beds) 3501 Mills Avenue, Austin, TX Zip 78731–6391; tel. 512/452–0361; Gail M. Oberta, Administrator and Chief Executive Officer

WISCONSIN: SACRED HEART REHABILITATION INSTITUTE (S, 59 beds) 2350 North Lake Drive, Milwaukee, WI Zip 53211–4507, Mailing Address: P.O. Box 392, Zip 53201–0392; tel. 414/298–6700; William H. Lange, Administrator and Senior Vice President

ST. MARY'S HOSPITAL (S, 257 beds) 2323 North Lake Drive, Milwaukee, WI Zip 53211–9682, Mailing Address: P.O. Box 503, Zip 53201–0503; tel. 414/291–1000; Charles C. Lobeck, Chief Executive Officer
Web address: www.columbia–stmarys.com

ST. MARY'S HOSPITAL OZAUKEE (S, 82 beds) 13111 North Port Washington Road, Mequon, WI Zip 53097–2416; tel. 414/243–7300; Therese B. Pandl, Senior Vice President and Chief Operating Officer
Web address: www.columbia–stmarys.com

Owned, leased, sponsored:	35 hospitals	9995 beds
Contract–managed:	0 hospitals	0 beds
Totals:	35 hospitals	9995 beds

★1825: DCH HEALTH SYSTEM (NP)
809 University Boulevard East, Tuscaloosa, AL Zip 35401; tel. 205/759–7111; Bryan Kindred, President and Chief Executive Officer

ALABAMA: DCH REGIONAL MEDICAL CENTER (O, 485 beds) 809 University Boulevard East, Tuscaloosa, AL Zip 35401–9961; tel. 205/759–7111; William H. Cassels, Administrator
Web address: www.chhealthcare.com

FAYETTE MEDICAL CENTER (L, 183 beds) 1653 Temple Avenue North, Fayette, AL Zip 35555–1314, Mailing Address: P.O. Drawer 878, Zip 35555–0878; tel. 205/932–5966; Harold Reed, Administrator

For explanation of codes following names, see page B2.
★ Indicates Type III membership in the American Hospital Association.

Section B

NORTHPORT MEDICAL CENTER (O, 156 beds) 2700 Hospital Drive, Northport, AL Zip 35476–3380; tel. 205/333–4500; Charles L. Stewart, Administrator

Owned, leased, sponsored:	3 hospitals	824 beds
Contract–managed:	0 hospitals	0 beds
Totals:	3 hospitals	824 beds

9655: DEPARTMENT OF NAVY (FG)
2300 East Street N.W., Washington, DC Zip 20372–5300

CALIFORNIA: NAVAL HOSPITAL (O, 25 beds) 930 Franklin Avenue, Lemoore, CA Zip 93246–5000; tel. 209/998–4201; Captain Steven Hart, Commanding Officer
Web address: www.lenhfsa.med.navy.mil

NAVAL HOSPITAL (O, 209 beds) Camp Pendleton, CA Mailing Address: Box 555191, Zip 92055–5191; tel. 760/725–1288; Captain Thomas Burkhard, Commanding Officer

NAVAL HOSPITAL (O, 30 beds) Twentynine Palms, CA Mailing Address: Box 788250, MCAGCC, Zip 92278–8250; tel. 760/830–2492; Captain R. S. Kayler, MSC, USN, Commanding Officer
Web address: http://nh29palms.med.navy.mil/nhtp/

NAVAL MEDICAL CENTER (O, 288 beds) 34800 Bob Wilson Drive, San Diego, CA Zip 92134–5000; tel. 619/532–6400; Rear Admiral Alberto Diaz Jr., MC, USN, Commander

FLORIDA: NAVAL HOSPITAL (O, 69 beds) 2080 Child Street, Jacksonville, FL Zip 32214–5000; tel. 904/777–7300; Captain M. J. Benson, MSC, USN, Commanding Officer

NAVAL HOSPITAL (O, 113 beds) 6000 West Highway 98, Pensacola, FL Zip 32512–0003; tel. 850/505–6413; Commander Patrick J. Kelly, Director, Administration

GUAM: U. S. NAVAL HOSPITAL (O, 55 beds) Agana, GU Mailing Address: PSC 490, Box 7607, FPO, APZip 96538–1600; tel. 671/344–9340; Captain David Wheeler Sr., Chief Executive Officer

ILLINOIS: NAVAL HOSPITAL (O, 75 beds) 3001A Sixth Street, Great Lakes, IL Zip 60088–5230; tel. 847/688–4560; Captain Elaine C. Holmes, MC, USN, Commanding Officer

MARYLAND: NATIONAL NAVAL MEDICAL CENTER (O, 217 beds) 8901 Wisconsin Avenue, Bethesda, MD Zip 20889–5600; tel. 301/295–5800; Rear Admiral Bonnie B. Potter, Commander

NORTH CAROLINA: NAVAL HOSPITAL (O, 102 beds) Camp Lejeune, NC Mailing Address: P.O. Box 10100, Zip 28547–0100; tel. 910/450–4300; Captain Thomas R. Collison, Commanding Officer

NAVAL HOSPITAL (O, 23 beds) Cherry Point, NC Mailing Address: PSC Box 8023, Zip 28533–0023; tel. 252/466–0266; Captain Jones A. Bold, Commanding Officer

PUERTO RICO: U. S. NAVAL HOSPITAL (O, 35 beds) Roosevelt Roads, PR Mailing Address: P.O. Box 3007, FPO, AAZip 34051–8100; tel. 787/865–5762; Captain G. R. Brown, Commanding Officer

SOUTH CAROLINA: NAVAL HOSPITAL (O, 20 beds) 1 Pinckney Boulevard, Beaufort, SC Zip 29902–6148; tel. 803/525–5301; Captain Clint E. Adams, MC, USN, Commanding Officer

NAVAL HOSPITAL (O, 32 beds) 3600 Rivers Avenue, North Charleston, SC Zip 29405; tel. 803/743–7000; Captain John M. Mateczun, Commanding Officer
Web address: www.nhchasn.med.navy.mil

TEXAS: NAVAL HOSPITAL (O, 25 beds) 10651 E Street, Corpus Christi, TX Zip 78419–5131; tel. 512/961–2688; Captain Elizabeth R. Barker, Commanding Officer
Web address: www.nhcc.med.navy.mil

VIRGINIA: NAVAL MEDICAL CENTER (O, 310 beds) 620 John Paul Jones Circle, Portsmouth, VA Zip 23708–2197; tel. 757/953–7424; Rear Admiral Marion Balsam, MC, USN, Commander
Web address: www.164.167.49.190/

WASHINGTON: NAVAL HOSPITAL (O, 91 beds) Boone Road, Bremerton, WA Zip 98312–1898; tel. 360/475–4000; Captain Gregg S. Parker, Commanding Officer
Web address: www.nh_bremerton.med.navy.mil

NAVAL HOSPITAL (O, 25 beds) 3475 North Saratoga Street, Oak Harbor, WA Zip 98278–8800; tel. 360/257–9500; Captain Michael W. Benway, Commanding Officer

Owned, leased, sponsored:	18 hospitals	1744 beds
Contract–managed:	0 hospitals	0 beds
Totals:	18 hospitals	1744 beds

9495: DEPARTMENT OF THE AIR FORCE (FG)
110 Luke Avenue, Room 400, Bowling AFB, DC Zip 20332–7050; tel. 202/767–5066; Lieutenant General Charles H. Roadman II, Surgeon General

ALASKA: U. S. AIR FORCE REGIONAL HOSPITAL (O, 35 beds) 24800 Hospital Drive, Elmendorf AFB, AK Zip 99506–3700; tel. 907/552–4033; Colonel Larry J. Sutterer, MSC, USAF, Administrator

ARIZONA: U. S. AIR FORCE HOSPITAL (O, 20 beds) 4175 South Alamo Avenue, Davis–Monthan AFB, AZ Zip 85707–4405; tel. 520/228–2930; Lieutenant Colonel Nancy A. Waite, Administrator and Deputy Commander

U. S. AIR FORCE HOSPITAL LUKE (O, 38 beds) Luke AFB, 7219 Litchfield Road, Glendale, AZ Zip 85309–1525; tel. 602/856–7501; Colonel Talbot N. Vivian, MSC, USAF, Administrator

ARKANSAS: U. S. AIR FORCE HOSPITAL LITTLE ROCK (O, 12 beds) Little Rock AFB, Jacksonville, AR Zip 72099–5057; tel. 501/987–7411; Colonel Norman L. Sims, MSC, USAF, Commander

CALIFORNIA: DAVID GRANT MEDICAL CENTER (O, 185 beds) 101 Bodin Circle, Travis AFB, CA Zip 94535–1800; tel. 707/423–7300; Lieutenant Colonel John Hill, MSC, USAF, FACHE, Administrator

U. S. AIR FORCE HOSPITAL (O, 8 beds) 338 South Dakota, Vandenberg AFB, CA Zip 93437–6307; tel. 805/734–8232; Colonel Donald T. Davies, Commander

U. S. AIR FORCE HOSPITAL (O, 6 beds) 15301 Warren Shingle Road, Beale AFB, CA Zip 95903–1907; tel. 530/634–4838; Lieutenant Colonel Robert G. Quinn, MSC, USAF, FACHE, Administrator

U. S. AIR FORCE HOSPITAL (O, 10 beds) 30 Hospital Road, Building 5500, Edwards AFB, CA Zip 93524–1730; tel. 661/277–2010; Lieutenant Colonel Thomas E. Yingst, USAF, MSC, Administrator

COLORADO: U. S. AIR FORCE ACADEMY HOSPITAL (O, 46 beds) 4102 Pinion Drive, USAF Academy, CO Zip 80840–4000; tel. 719/333–5102; Colonel Jay D. Sprenger, MSC, USAF, Commander

DELAWARE: U. S. AIR FORCE HOSPITAL DOVER (O, 16 beds) 260 Chad Street, Dover, DE Zip 19902–7260; tel. 302/677–2525; Lieutenant Colonel Frederick L. Woods, MSC, USAF, Administrator

FLORIDA: U. S. AIR FORCE HOSPITAL (O, 25 beds) Tyndall AFB, Panama City, FL Zip 32403–5300; tel. 850/283–7515; Admiral James H. Foster, Commander

U. S. AIR FORCE HOSPITAL (O, 50 beds) 8415 Bayshore Boulevard, MacDill AFB, FL Zip 33621–1607; tel. 813/828–3258; Colonel Gregory C. Baggerly, MC, USAF, Commander

U. S. AIR FORCE REGIONAL HOSPITAL (O, 85 beds) 307 Boatner Road, Suite 114, Eglin AFB, FL Zip 32542–1282; tel. 850/883–8221; Colonel William C. Head, MSC, USAF, Administrator

GEORGIA: U. S. AIR FORCE HOSPITAL MOODY (O, 16 beds) 3278 Mitchell Boulevard, Moody AFB, GA Zip 31699–1500; tel. 912/257–3772; Colonel Stephan A. Giesecke, USAF, MSC, Commander

U. S. AIR FORCE HOSPITAL ROBINS (O, 32 beds) 655 Seventh Street, Robins AFB, GA Zip 31098–2227; tel. 912/327–7996; Colonel John A. Lee, USAF, MSC, Commander
Web address: www.robins.af.mil/orgs/abw/78MEDGP/INEX/HTM

IDAHO: U. S. AIR FORCE HOSPITAL MOUNTAIN HOME (O, 10 beds) 90 Hope Drive, Mountain Home AFB, ID Zip 83648–5300; tel. 208/828–7600; Colonel Cynthia Terriberry, USAF, Commanding Officer

ILLINOIS: SCOTT MEDICAL CENTER (O, 45 beds) 310 West Losey Street, Scott AFB, IL Zip 62225–5252; tel. 618/256–7456; Colonel Stephen J. Pribyl, MSC, USAF, Administrator

LOUISIANA: U. S. AIR FORCE HOSPITAL (O, 25 beds) Barksdale AFB, Shreveport, LA Zip 71110–5300; tel. 318/456–6004; Colonel Dennis Marquardt, USAF, Commander

For explanation of codes following names, see page B2.
★ Indicates Type III membership in the American Hospital Association.

MARYLAND: MALCOLM GROW MEDICAL CENTER (O, 93 beds) 1050 West Perimeter, Andrews AFB, MD Zip 20762–6600, Mailing Address: 1050 West Perimeter, Suite A1–19, Zip 20762–6600; tel. 240/857–3000; Colonel Jeffrey L. Butler, Administrator

MISSISSIPPI: U. S. AIR FORCE HOSPITAL (O, 7 beds) 201 Independence, Suite 235, Columbus, MS Zip 39701–5300; tel. 601/434–2297; Lieutenant Colonel Mark L. Allen, MSC, USAF, Administrator

U. S. AIR FORCE MEDICAL CENTER KEESLER (O, 185 beds) 301 Fisher Street, Room 1A132, Keesler AFB, MS Zip 39534–2519; tel. 228/377–6510; Colonel Randall W. Hartley, Administrator
Web address: www.81mdg06.keesler.af.mil/index.cgi

NEBRASKA: EHRLING BERGQUIST HOSPITAL (O, 45 beds) 2501 Capehart Road, Offutt AFB, NE Zip 68113–2160; tel. 402/294–7312; Colonel John R. Sheehan, USAF, MSC, Deputy Commander

NEVADA: MIKE O'CALLAGHAN FEDERAL HOSPITAL (O, 94 beds) 4700 Las Vegas Boulevard North, Suite 2419, Las Vegas, NV Zip 89191–6601; tel. 702/653–2000; Colonel Jack A. Gupton, MSC, USAF, Administrator

NEW MEXICO: U. S. AIR FORCE HOSPITAL (O, 7 beds) 280 First Street, Holloman AFB, NM Zip 88330–8273; tel. 505/475–5587; Colonel Marilyn J. Abu–Ghusson, USAF, Commander

U. S. AIR FORCE HOSPITAL (O, 10 beds) 208 West Casablanca Avenue, Cannon AFB, NM Zip 88103–5300; tel. 505/784–6318; Major John Sell, MSC, USAF, Administrator

U. S. AIR FORCE HOSPITAL–KIRTLAND (O, 10 beds) 2050A Second Street S.E., Kirtland AFB, NM Zip 87117–5559; tel. 505/846–3547; Colonel Jimmie M. Smith, USAF, Commander

NORTH CAROLINA: U. S. AIR FORCE HOSPITAL SEYMOUR JOHNSON (O, 41 beds) 1050 Jabara Avenue, Seymour Johnson AFB, NC Zip 27531–5300; tel. 919/722–0001; Colonel Michael Lischak, MC, USAF, Commander

NORTH DAKOTA: U. S. AIR FORCE HOSPITAL (O, 12 beds) Grand Forks SAC, Grand Forks AFB, ND Zip 58205–6332, Mailing Address: Grand Forks SAC, 220 G. Street, Zip 58205–6332; tel. 701/747–5391; Lieutenant Colonel Robert J. Rennie, Administrator

U. S. AIR FORCE REGIONAL HOSPITAL (O, 15 beds) 10 Missile Avenue, Minot, ND Zip 58705–5024; tel. 701/723–5103; Colonel David L. Clark, Commander

OHIO: U. S. AIR FORCE MEDICAL CENTER WRIGHT–PATTERSON (O, 135 beds) 4881 Sugar Maple Drive, Wright–Patterson AFB, OH Zip 45433–5529; tel. 937/257–0940; Brigadier General Joseph Kelley, Commander

OKLAHOMA: U. S. AIR FORCE HOSPITAL ALTUS (O, 15 beds) Altus AFB, Altus, OK Zip 73523–5005; tel. 580/481–7347; Colonel David L. Clark, USAF, Commander

SOUTH CAROLINA: U. S. AIR FORCE HOSPITAL SHAW (O, 16 beds) 431 Meadowlark Street, Shaw AFB, SC Zip 29152–5319; tel. 803/895–6324; Lieutenant Colonel Donald Taylor, Administrator

SOUTH DAKOTA: U. S. AIR FORCE HOSPITAL (O, 31 beds) 2900 Doolittle Drive, Ellsworth AFB, SD Zip 57706; tel. 605/385–3201; Colonel Farley Howell, Commanding Officer
Web address: www.elsworth.af.mil/~medge/index.htm

TEXAS: U. S. AIR FORCE HOSPITAL (O, 20 beds) 7th Medical Group, Dyess AFB, Abilene, TX Zip 79607–1367; tel. 915/696–5429; Major John G. Wiseman, Administrator

U. S. AIR FORCE REGIONAL HOSPITAL–SHEPPARD (O, 65 beds) 149 Hart Street, Suite 1, Sheppard AFB, TX Zip 76311–3478; tel. 940/676–2010; Colonel Richard D. Maddox, Administrator

WILFORD HALL MEDICAL CENTER (O, 715 beds) 2200 Bergquist Drive, Lackland AFB, TX Zip 78236–5300; tel. 210/292–7353; Colonel Arthur E. Aenchbacher Jr., Administrator

UTAH: U. S. AIR FORCE HOSPITAL (O, 15 beds) 7321 11th Street, Hill AFB, UT Zip 84056–5012; tel. 801/777–5457; Colonel John A. Reyburn Jr., Commander
Web address: www.75mdg.hill.af.mil

VIRGINIA: U. S. AIR FORCE HOSPITAL (O, 59 beds) 45 Pine Street, Hampton, VA Zip 23665–2080; tel. 757/764–6969; Colonel Glenn R. Willauer, Administrator

WASHINGTON: U. S. AIR FORCE HOSPITAL (O, 35 beds) 701 Hospital Loop, Fairchild AFB, WA Zip 99011–8701; tel. 509/247–5217; Major Scott F. Wardell, Administrator

WYOMING: U. S. AIR FORCE HOSPITAL (O, 15 beds) 6900 Alden Drive, Cheyenne, WY Zip 82005–3913; tel. 307/773–2045; Major Brenda Bullard, Administrator

Owned, leased, sponsored:	40 hospitals	2304 beds
Contract–managed:	0 hospitals	0 beds
Totals:	40 hospitals	2304 beds

9395: DEPARTMENT OF THE ARMY, OFFICE OF THE SURGEON GENERAL (FG)
5109 Leesburg Pike, Falls Church, VA Zip 22041; tel. 703/681–3114; Major Beverly Pritchett, Executive Officer

ALABAMA: LYSTER U. S. ARMY COMMUNITY HOSPITAL (O, 35 beds) U.S. Army Aeromedical Center, Fort Rucker, AL Zip 36362–5333; tel. 334/255–7360; Lieutenant Colonel Donald Henderson Jr., Deputy Commander for Administration

ALASKA: BASSETT ARMY COMMUNITY HOSPITAL (O, 43 beds) 1060 Gaffney Road, Box 7400, Fort Wainwright, AK Zip 99703–7400; tel. 907/353–5108; Lieutenant Colonel Gordon Lewis, Deputy Commander for Administration

CALIFORNIA: WEED ARMY COMMUNITY HOSPITAL (O, 27 beds) Fort Irwin, CA Zip 92310–5065; tel. 760/380–3108; Colonel Michael McCaffrey, Commander

COLORADO: EVANS U. S. ARMY COMMUNITY HOSPITAL (O, 117 beds) Fort Carson, CO Zip 80913–5101; tel. 719/526–7200; Lieutenant Colonel Michael D. Wheeler, MSC, Deputy Commander, Administration

DISTRICT OF COLUMBIA: WALTER REED ARMY MEDICAL CENTER (O, 439 beds) 6825 16th Street N.W., Washington, DC Zip 20307–5001; tel. 202/782–6393; Colonel Robert James Heckert Jr., MSC, Chief of Staff

GEORGIA: DWIGHT DAVID EISENHOWER ARMY MEDICAL CENTER (O, 313 beds) Hospital Drive, Building 300, Fort Gordon, GA Zip 30905–5650; tel. 706/787–3253; Lieutenant Colonel David A. Rubenstein, Chief Operating Officer
Web address: www.ddeamc.amedd.army.mil

MARTIN ARMY COMMUNITY HOSPITAL (O, 126 beds) Fort Benning, GA Mailing Address: P.O. Box 56100, Building 9200, Zip 31905–6100; tel. 706/544–2516; Lieutenant Colonel Joe W. Butler, Deputy Commander Administration

WINN ARMY COMMUNITY HOSPITAL (O, 83 beds) 1061 Harmon Avenue, Hinesville, GA Zip 31314–5611; tel. 912/370–6965; Colonel Donald J. Kasperik, Commander

HAWAII: TRIPLER ARMY MEDICAL CENTER (O, 254 beds) Honolulu, HI Zip 96859–5000; tel. 808/433–6661; Major Nancy R. Adams, Commander
Web address: www.tamc.amedd.army.mil

KANSAS: IRWIN ARMY COMMUNITY HOSPITAL (O, 44 beds) 600 Caisson Hill Road, Fort Riley, KS Zip 66442; tel. 785/239–7555; Lieutenant Colonel Scott D. Hendrickson, Deputy Commander for Administration

MUNSON ARMY HEALTH CENTER (O, 20 beds) 550 Pope Avenue, Fort Leavenworth, KS Zip 66027–2332; tel. 913/684–6420; Colonel James Dunn, Commander

KENTUCKY: COLONEL FLORENCE A. BLANCHFIELD ARMY COMMUNITY HOSPITAL (O, 81 beds) 650 Joel Drive, Fort Campbell, KY Zip 42223–5349; tel. 502/798–8040; Colonel Lester Martinez–Lopez, Director Health Services

IRELAND ARMY COMMUNITY HOSPITAL (O, 56 beds) 851 Ireland Loop, Fort Knox, KY Zip 40121–5520; tel. 502/624–9020; Lieutenant Colonel Robert T. Foster, Deputy Commander for Administration

LOUISIANA: BAYNE–JONES ARMY COMMUNITY HOSPITAL (O, 52 beds) 1585 Third Street, Fort Polk, LA Zip 71459–5110; tel. 318/531–3928; Lieutenant Colonel Mark D. Moore, Deputy Commander and Administrator

Section B

MARSHALL ISLANDS: KWAJALEIN HOSPITAL (O, 14 beds) U.S. Army Kwajalein Atoll, Kwajalein Island, MH Zip 96960, Mailing Address: Box 1702, APO, APZip 96555–5000; tel. 805/355–2225; Mike Mathews, Administrator

MISSOURI: GENERAL LEONARD WOOD ARMY COMMUNITY HOSPITAL (O, 97 beds) 126 Missouri Avenue, Fort Leonard Wood, MO Zip 65473–8952; tel. 573/596–0414; Lieutenant Colonel Julie Martin, Administrator
Web address: www.webglwach.leonardwood.amedd.army.mil

NEW YORK: KELLER ARMY COMMUNITY HOSPITAL (O, 44 beds) U.S. Military Academy, West Point, NY Zip 10996–1197; tel. 914/938–4837; Lieutenant Colonel Kenneth Franklin, Deputy Commander for Clinical Services
Web address: www.wramc.amedd.army.mil.wp

WILCOX ARMY COMMUNITY HOSPITAL (O, 30 beds) Fort Drum, NY Zip 13602–5004

NORTH CAROLINA: WOMACK ARMY MEDICAL CENTER (O, 173 beds) Normandy Drive, Fort Bragg, NC Zip 28307–5000; tel. 910/432–4802; Colonel Thomas H. Auer, Commander

OKLAHOMA: REYNOLDS ARMY COMMUNITY HOSPITAL (O, 116 beds) 4301 Mow–way Street, Fort Sill, OK Zip 73503–6300; tel. 580/458–3000; Colonel Gary Ripple, Commander

SOUTH CAROLINA: MONCRIEF ARMY COMMUNITY HOSPITAL (O, 91 beds) Fort Jackson, SC Mailing Address: P.O. Box 500, Zip 29207–5720; tel. 803/751–2284; Colonel Dale Carroll, Commander

TEXAS: BROOKE ARMY MEDICAL CENTER (O, 464 beds) Fort Sam Houston, San Antonio, TX Zip 78234–6200; tel. 210/916–4141; Colonel Joseph P. Gonzales, MS, USA, Chief of Staff

DARNALL ARMY COMMUNITY HOSPITAL (O, 169 beds) 36000 Darnall Loop, Fort Hood, TX Zip 76544–4752; tel. 254/288–8000; Colonel Kenneth L. Farmer Jr., Commander

WILLIAM BEAUMONT ARMY MEDICAL CENTER (O, 209 beds) 5005 North Piedras Street, El Paso, TX Zip 79920–5001; tel. 915/569–2121; Colonel Jimmy Sanders, Chief of Staff

VIRGINIA: DEWITT ARMY COMMUNITY HOSPITAL (O, 62 beds) 9501 Farrell Road, Fort Belvoir, VA Zip 22060–5901; tel. 703/805–0510; Colonel James W. Martin, Commander

MCDONALD ARMY COMMUNITY HOSPITAL (O, 30 beds) Jefferson Avenue, Fort Eustis, Newport News, VA Zip 23604–5548; tel. 757/314–7501; Colonel George Weightman, Commander

WASHINGTON: MADIGAN ARMY MEDICAL CENTER (O, 172 beds) Tacoma, WA Zip 98431–5000; tel. 253/968–1110; Brigadier General Mack C. Hill, Commanding General
Web address: www.mamc.amedd.army.mil

Owned, leased, sponsored:	27 hospitals	3361 beds
Contract–managed:	0 hospitals	0 beds
Totals:	27 hospitals	3361 beds

9295: DEPARTMENT OF VETERANS AFFAIRS (FG)
810 Vermont Avenue N.W., Washington, DC Zip 20420; tel. 202/273–5781; Kenneth W. Kizer, M.D., M.P.H., Under Secretary for Health

ALABAMA: CENTRAL ALABAMA VETERAN AFFAIRS HEALTH CARE SYSTEM (O, 443 beds) 215 Perry Hill Road, Montgomery, AL Zip 36109–3798; tel. 334/272–4670; Kenneth Rugle, Interim Director

VETERANS AFFAIRS MEDICAL CENTER (O, 317 beds) 700 South 19th Street, Birmingham, AL Zip 35233–1927; tel. 205/933–8101; Y. C. Parris, Director
Web address: www.va.gov

VETERANS AFFAIRS MEDICAL CENTER (O, 352 beds) 3701 Loop Road, Tuscaloosa, AL Zip 35404–5015; tel. 205/554–2000; W. Kenneth Ruyle, Director

ARIZONA: CARL T. HAYDEN VETERANS AFFAIRS MEDICAL CENTER (O, 331 beds) 650 East Indian School Road, Phoenix, AZ Zip 85012–1892; tel. 602/277–5551; John R. Fears, Director
Web address: www.va.gov

VETERANS AFFAIRS MEDICAL CENTER (O, 268 beds) 3601 South 6th Avenue, Tucson, AZ Zip 85723–0002; tel. 520/792–1450; Jonathan H. Gardner, Chief Executive Officer

VETERANS AFFAIRS MEDICAL CENTER (O, 225 beds) 500 Highway 89 North, Prescott, AZ Zip 86313–5000; tel. 520/445–4860; Patricia A. McKlem, Medical Center Director

ARKANSAS: CENTRAL ARKANSAS VETERANS AFFAIRS HEALTHCARE SYSTEM (O, 502 beds) 4300 West Seventh Street, Little Rock, AR Zip 72205–5484; tel. 501/257–1000; George H. Gray Jr., Director

VETERANS AFFAIRS MEDICAL CENTER (O, 51 beds) 1100 North College Avenue, Fayetteville, AR Zip 72703–6995; tel. 501/443–4301; Richard F. Robinson, Director

CALIFORNIA: JERRY L. PETTIS MEMORIAL VETERANS MEDICAL CENTER (O, 231 beds) 11201 Benton Street, Loma Linda, CA Zip 92357; tel. 909/825–7084; Dean R. Stordahl, Chief Executive Officer
Web address: www.desertpacific.med.va.gov

VETERANS AFFAIRS MEDICAL CENTER (O, 205 beds) 2615 East Clinton Avenue, Fresno, CA Zip 93703; tel. 559/225–6100; Alan S. Perry, Director
Web address: www.fresno.med.va.gov

VETERANS AFFAIRS MEDICAL CENTER (O, 448 beds) 5901 East Seventh Street, Long Beach, CA Zip 90822–5201; tel. 562/494–5400; Lawrence C. Stewart, Director
Web address: www.long–beach.va.gov

VETERANS AFFAIRS MEDICAL CENTER (O, 232 beds) 3350 LaJolla Village Drive, San Diego, CA Zip 92161; tel. 619/552–8585; Gary J. Rossio, Director and Chief Executive Officer

VETERANS AFFAIRS MEDICAL CENTER (O, 244 beds) 4150 Clement Street, San Francisco, CA Zip 94121–1598; tel. 415/221–4810; Sheila M. Cullen, Director

VETERANS AFFAIRS MEDICAL CENTER–WEST LOS ANGELES (O, 1327 beds) 11301 Wilshire Boulevard, Los Angeles, CA Zip 90073–0275; tel. 310/268–3132; Smith Jenkins Jr., Acting Chief Executive Officer

VETERANS AFFAIRS PALO ALTO HEALTH CARE SYSTEM (O, 949 beds) 3801 Miranda Avenue, Palo Alto, CA Zip 94304–1207; tel. 650/493–5000; James A. Goff, FACHE, Director
Web address: www.icon.palo–alto.med.va.gov

COLORADO: VETERANS AFFAIRS MEDICAL CENTER (O, 228 beds) 1055 Clermont Street, Denver, CO Zip 80220–3877; tel. 303/399–8020; Edgar Thorsland Jr., Director

VETERANS AFFAIRS MEDICAL CENTER (O, 53 beds) 2121 North Avenue, Grand Junction, CO Zip 81501–6499; tel. 970/242–0731; Kurt W. Schlegelmilch, M.D., Director

CONNECTICUT: VETERANS AFFAIRS CONNECTICUT HEALTHCARE SYSTEM–WEST HAVEN DIVISION (O, 343 beds) 950 Campbell Avenue, West Haven, CT Zip 06516; tel. 203/932–5711; Paul J. McCool, Acting Director

DELAWARE: VETERANS AFFAIRS MEDICAL CENTER (O, 138 beds) 1601 Kirkwood Highway, Wilmington, DE Zip 19805–4989; tel. 302/633–5201; Dexter D. Dix, Director
Web address: www.va.gov/station

DISTRICT OF COLUMBIA: VETERANS AFFAIRS MEDICAL CENTER (O, 278 beds) 50 Irving Street N.W., Washington, DC Zip 20422–0002; tel. 202/745–8100; Sanford M. Garfunkel, Director
Web address: www.va.gov/station

FLORIDA: JAMES A. HALEY VETERANS HOSPITAL (O, 640 beds) 13000 Bruce B. Downs Boulevard, Tampa, FL Zip 33612–4798; tel. 813/972–2000; Richard A. Silver, Director

MALCOM RANDALL VETERANS AFFAIRS MEDICAL CENTER (O, 256 beds) 1601 S.W. Archer Road, Gainesville, FL Zip 32608–1197; tel. 352/376–1611; Elwood J. Headley, M.D., System Director
Web address: www.va.gov

VETERANS AFFAIRS MEDICAL CENTER (O, 533 beds) Bay Pines & 100 Way, Bay Pines, FL Zip 33744, Mailing Address: P.O. Box 5005, Zip 33744–5005; tel. 727/398–6661; Thomas H. Weaver, FACHE, Director

VETERANS AFFAIRS MEDICAL CENTER (O, 192 beds) 7305 North Military Trail, West Palm Beach, FL Zip 33410–6400; tel. 561/882–8262; Edward H. Seiler, Director
Web address: www.vagov.com

VETERANS AFFAIRS MEDICAL CENTER (O, 504 beds) 1201 N.W. 16th Street, Miami, FL Zip 33125–1624; tel. 305/324–4455; Thomas C. Doherty, Medical Director

For explanation of codes following names, see page B2.
★ Indicates Type III membership in the American Hospital Association.

VETERANS AFFAIRS MEDICAL CENTER (O, 313 beds) 801 South Marion Street, Lake City, FL Zip 32025–5898; tel. 904/755–3016; Marlis Meyer, Division Director

GEORGIA: VETERANS AFFAIRS MEDICAL CENTER (O, 291 beds) 1670 Clairmont Road, Decatur, GA Zip 30033–4004; tel. 404/321–6111; Robert A. Perreault, Director

VETERANS AFFAIRS MEDICAL CENTER (O, 444 beds) 1 Freedom Way, Augusta, GA Zip 30904–6285; tel. 706/733–0188; Ellen DeGeorge–Smith, Director
Web address: www.va.gov

VETERANS AFFAIRS MEDICAL CENTER (O, 253 beds) 1826 Veterans Boulevard, Dublin, GA Zip 31021–3620; tel. 912/272–1210; James F. Trusley III, Director

IDAHO: VETERANS AFFAIRS MEDICAL CENTER (O, 176 beds) 500 West Fort Street, Boise, ID Zip 83702–4598; tel. 208/422–1100; Wayne C. Tippets, Director

ILLINOIS: VETERANS AFFAIRS CHICAGO HEALTH CARE SYSTEM–LAKESIDE DIVISION (O, 252 beds) 333 East Huron Street, Chicago, IL Zip 60611–3004; tel. 312/640–2100; Joseph L. Moore, Director

VETERANS AFFAIRS CHICAGO HEALTH CARE SYSTEM–WEST SIDE DIVISION (O, 323 beds) 820 South Damen Avenue, Chicago, IL Zip 60612–3776, Mailing Address: P.O. Box 8195, Zip 60680–8195; tel. 312/666–6500; Joseph L. Moore, Director

VETERANS AFFAIRS EDWARD HINES, JR. HOSPITAL (O, 957 beds) Fifth Avenue & Roosevelt Road, Hines, IL Zip 60141–5000, Mailing Address: P.O. Box 5000, Zip 60141–5000; tel. 708/202–8387; John J. DeNardo, Director

VETERANS AFFAIRS MEDICAL CENTER (O, 484 beds) 1900 East Main Street, Danville, IL Zip 61832–5198; tel. 217/442–8000; James S. Jones, Director

VETERANS AFFAIRS MEDICAL CENTER (O, 836 beds) 3001 Green Bay Road, North Chicago, IL Zip 60064–3049; tel. 847/688–1900; Alfred S. Pate, Director

VETERANS AFFAIRS MEDICAL CENTER (O, 99 beds) 2401 West Main Street, Marion, IL Zip 62959–1194; tel. 618/997–5311; Earl F. Falast, Medical Center Director
Web address: www.za.va.gov

INDIANA: RICHARD L. ROUDEBUSH VETERANS AFFAIRS MEDICAL CENTER (O, 158 beds) 1481 West Tenth Street, Indianapolis, IN Zip 46202–2884; tel. 317/554–0000; Robert H. Sabin, Acting Director

VETERANS AFFAIRS NORTHERN INDIANA HEALTH CARE SYSTEM (O, 469 beds) 2121 Lake Avenue, Fort Wayne, IN Zip 46805–5347; tel. 219/460–1310; Michael W. Murphy, Ph.D., Director

IOWA: VETERANS AFFAIRS CENTRAL IOWA HEALTH CARE SYSTEM (O, 359 beds) 3600 30th Street, Des Moines, IA Zip 50310–5774; tel. 515/699–5999; Donald C. Cooper, Director

VETERANS AFFAIRS MEDICAL CENTER (O, 113 beds) 601 Highway 6 West, Iowa City, IA Zip 52246–2208; tel. 319/338–0581; Gary L. Wilkinson, Director
Web address: www.icva.gov

KANSAS: VETERANS AFFAIRS EASTERN KANSAS HEALTH CARE SYSTEM (O, 423 beds) 2200 Gage Boulevard, Topeka, KS Zip 66622–0002; tel. 785/350–3111; Edgar L. Tucker, Director

VETERANS AFFAIRS MEDICAL AND REGIONAL OFFICE CENTER (O, 47 beds) 5500 East Kellogg, Wichita, KS Zip 67218; tel. 316/685–2221; Kent D. Hill, Director

KENTUCKY: VETERANS AFFAIRS MEDICAL CENTER–LEXINGTON (O, 407 beds) 2250 Leestown Pike, Lexington, KY Zip 40511–1093; tel. 606/233–4511; Helen K. Cornish, Director

VETERANS AFFAIRS MEDICAL CENTER–LOUISVILLE (O, 104 beds) 800 Zorn Avenue, Louisville, KY Zip 40206–1499; tel. 502/895–3401; Larry J. Sander, FACHE, Director
Web address: www.va.gov/603louisville

LOUISIANA: OVERTON BROOKS VETERANS AFFAIRS MEDICAL CENTER (O, 100 beds) 510 East Stoner Avenue, Shreveport, LA Zip 71101–4295; tel. 318/221–8411; Billy M. Valentine, Director

VETERANS AFFAIRS MEDICAL CENTER (O, 257 beds) Shreveport Highway, Alexandria, LA Zip 71306–6002; tel. 318/473–0010; Allan S. Goss, Director

VETERANS AFFAIRS MEDICAL CENTER (O, 197 beds) 1601 Perdido Street, New Orleans, LA Zip 70112–1262; tel. 504/568–0811; John D. Church Jr., Director

MAINE: VETERANS AFFAIRS MEDICAL CENTER (O, 200 beds) 1 VA Center, Togus, ME Zip 04330; tel. 207/623–8411; John H. Sims Jr., Director
Web address: www.togus,med.va.gov

MARYLAND: VA MARYLAND HEALTH CARE SYSTEM–FORT HOWARD DIVISION (O, 245 beds) 9600 North Point Road, Fort Howard, MD Zip 21052–9989; tel. 410/477–1800; Dennis H. Smith, Director

VETERANS AFFAIRS MARYLAND HEALTH CARE SYSTEM–BALTIMORE DIVISION (O, 897 beds) 10 North Greene Street, Baltimore, MD Zip 21201–1524; tel. 410/605–7001; Dennis H. Smith, Director

VETERANS AFFAIRS MARYLAND HEALTH CARE SYSTEM–PERRY POINT DIVISION (O, 697 beds) Circle Drive, Perry Point, MD Zip 21902; tel. 410/642–2411; Dennis H. Smith, Director

MASSACHUSETTS: BROCKTON VETERANS AFFAIRS MEDICAL CENTER (O, 483 beds) 940 Belmont Street, Brockton, MA Zip 02401–5596; tel. 508/583–4500; Roland E. Moore, Acting Director

EDITH NOURSE ROGERS MEMORIAL VETERANS HOSPITAL (O, 493 beds) 200 Springs Road, Bedford, MA Zip 01730–1198; tel. 781/687–2000; William A. Conte, Director

VETERANS AFFAIRS MEDICAL CENTER (O, 202 beds) Boston, MA Mailing Address: 150 South Huntington Avenue, Jamaica Plain Station, Zip 02130–4820; tel. 617/232–9500; Roland E. Moore, Acting Medical Center Director

VETERANS AFFAIRS MEDICAL CENTER (O, 215 beds) 421 North Main Street, Leeds, MA Zip 01053–9764; tel. 413/584–4040; Robert McNamara, Director

MICHIGAN: ALEDA E. LUTZ VETERANS AFFAIRS MEDICAL CENTER (O, 114 beds) 1500 Weiss Street, Saginaw, MI Zip 48602–5298; tel. 517/793–2340; Robert H. Sabin, Acting Director

JOHN D. DINGELL VETERANS AFFAIRS MEDICAL CENTER (O, 218 beds) 4646 John R Street, Detroit, MI Zip 48201–1932; tel. 313/576–1000; Carlos B. Lott Jr., Director

VETERANS AFFAIRS MEDICAL CENTER (O, 164 beds) 2215 Fuller Road, Ann Arbor, MI Zip 48105–2399; tel. 734/769–7100; James W. Roseborough, CHE, Director
Web address: www.ann–arbor.med.va.gov

VETERANS AFFAIRS MEDICAL CENTER (O, 410 beds) 5500 Armstrong Road, Battle Creek, MI Zip 49016; tel. 616/966–5600; Michael K. Wheeler, Director

VETERANS AFFAIRS MEDICAL CENTER (O, 57 beds) 325 East H Street, Iron Mountain, MI Zip 49801–4792; tel. 906/774–3300; Thomas B. Arnold, Director

MINNESOTA: VETERANS AFFAIRS MEDICAL CENTER (O, 361 beds) One Veterans Drive, Minneapolis, MN Zip 55417–2399; tel. 612/725–2000; Steven Kleingloss, Acting Director

VETERANS AFFAIRS MEDICAL CENTER (O, 411 beds) 4801 Eighth Street North, Saint Cloud, MN Zip 56303–2099; tel. 320/252–1670; Barry I. Bahl, Director

MISSISSIPPI: G.V. MONTGOMERY VETERANS AFFAIRS MEDICAL CENTER (O, 443 beds) 1500 East Woodrow Wilson Drive, Jackson, MS Zip 39216–5199; tel. 601/364–1201; Richard P. Miller, Director
Web address: www.visn16.med.va.gov

VETERANS AFFAIRS MEDICAL CENTER (O, 510 beds) 400 Veterans Avenue, Biloxi, MS Zip 39531–2410; tel. 228/388–5541; Julie A. Catellier, Director

MISSOURI: HARRY S. TRUMAN MEMORIAL VETERANS HOSPITAL (O, 161 beds) 800 Hospital Drive, Columbia, MO Zip 65201–5297; tel. 573/814–6300; Gary L. Campbell, Director

JOHN J. PERSHING VETERANS AFFAIRS MEDICAL CENTER (O, 48 beds) 1500 North Westwood Boulevard, Poplar Bluff, MO Zip 63901–3318; tel. 573/686–4151; Nancy Arnold, Director

VETERANS AFFAIRS MEDICAL CENTER (O, 355 beds) 1 Jefferson Barracks Drive, Saint Louis, MO Zip 63125–4199; tel. 314/652–4100; Linda Kurz, Acting Director

VETERANS AFFAIRS MEDICAL CENTER (O, 165 beds) 4801 Linwood Boulevard, Kansas City, MO Zip 64128–2295; tel. 816/861–4700; Hugh F. Doran, Director

For explanation of codes following names, see page B2.
★ Indicates Type III membership in the American Hospital Association.

MONTANA: VETERANS AFFAIRS MONTANA HEALTHCARE SYSTEM (O, 45 beds) Highway 12 and William Street, Fort Harrison, MT Zip 59636; tel. 406/442–6410; Joseph Underkofler, Director **Web address:** www.ft–harrison.va.gov

NEBRASKA: VETERANS AFFAIRS GREATER NEBRASKA HEALTH CARE SYSTEM (O, 129 beds) 600 South 70th Street, Lincoln, NE Zip 68510–2493; tel. 402/489–3802; David Asper, Director

VETERANS AFFAIRS MEDICAL CENTER (O, 122 beds) 4101 Woolworth Avenue, Omaha, NE Zip 68105–1873; tel. 402/449–0600; John J. Phillips, Director

NEVADA: IOANNIS A. LOUGARIS VETERANS AFFAIRS MEDICAL CENTER (O, 140 beds) 1000 Locust Street, Reno, NV Zip 89520–0111; tel. 702/786–7200; Gary R. Whitfield, Director

VETERANS AFFAIRS SOUTHERN NEVADA HEALTHCARE SYSTEM (O, 100 beds) 1700 Vegas Drive, Las Vegas, NV Zip 89106; tel. 702/636–3000; Ramon J. Reevey, Director

NEW HAMPSHIRE: VETERANS AFFAIRS MEDICAL CENTER (O, 157 beds) 718 Smyth Road, Manchester, NH Zip 03104–4098; tel. 603/624–4366; Paul J. McCool, Director

NEW JERSEY: VETERANS AFFAIRS NEW JERSEY HEALTH CARE SYSTEM (O, 930 beds) 385 Tremont Avenue, East Orange, NJ Zip 07018–1095; tel. 973/676–1000; Kenneth H. Mizrach, Director

NEW MEXICO: VETERANS AFFAIRS MEDICAL CENTER (O, 209 beds) 1501 San Pedro S.E., Albuquerque, NM Zip 87108–5138; tel. 505/265–1711; Norman E. Browne, Director **Web address:** www.va.gov

NEW YORK: VETERANS AFFAIRS HUDSON VALLEY HEALTH CARE SYSTEM–F.D. ROOSEVELT HOSPITAL (O, 651 beds) Montrose, NY Mailing Address: P.O. Box 100, Zip 10548–0110; tel. 914/737–4400; Michael A. Sabo, Director

VETERANS AFFAIRS MEDICAL CENTER (O, 158 beds) 113 Holland Avenue, Albany, NY Zip 12208–3473; tel. 518/462–3311; Clyde Parkis, Director

VETERANS AFFAIRS MEDICAL CENTER (O, 426 beds) 76 Veterans Avenue, Bath, NY Zip 14810–0842; tel. 607/776–2111; John F. Dunn Jr., Acting Director

VETERANS AFFAIRS MEDICAL CENTER (O, 399 beds) 800 Poly Place, Brooklyn, NY Zip 11209–7104; tel. 718/630–3500; John J. Donnellan Jr., Director **Web address:** www.vaww.va.gov/

VETERANS AFFAIRS MEDICAL CENTER (O, 626 beds) 400 Fort Hill Avenue, Canandaigua, NY Zip 14424–1197; tel. 716/394–2000; W. David Smith, Director

VETERANS AFFAIRS MEDICAL CENTER (O, 328 beds) 130 West Kingsbridge Road, Bronx, NY Zip 10468–3992; tel. 718/584–9000; Maryann Musumeci, Director

VETERANS AFFAIRS MEDICAL CENTER (O, 201 beds) 423 East 23rd Street, New York, NY Zip 10010–5050; tel. 212/686–7500; John J. Donnellan Jr., Director

VETERANS AFFAIRS MEDICAL CENTER (O, 659 beds) 79 Middleville Road, Northport, NY Zip 11768–2293; tel. 516/261–4400; Mary A. Dowling, Director

VETERANS AFFAIRS MEDICAL CENTER (O, 129 beds) 800 Irving Avenue, Syracuse, NY Zip 13210–2796; tel. 315/476–7461; Philip P. Thomas, Director

VETERANS AFFAIRS WESTERN NEW YORK HEALTHCARE SYSTEM–BATAVIA DIVISION (O, 158 beds) 222 Richmond Avenue, Batavia, NY Zip 14020–1288; tel. 716/343–7500; Richard S. Droske, Director

VETERANS AFFAIRS WESTERN NEW YORK HEALTHCARE SYSTEM–BUFFALO DIVISION (O, 250 beds) 3495 Bailey Avenue, Buffalo, NY Zip 14215–1129; tel. 716/834–9200; William F. Feeley, Director

NORTH CAROLINA: VETERANS AFFAIRS MEDICAL CENTER (O, 235 beds) 508 Fulton Street, Durham, NC Zip 27705–3897; tel. 919/286–0411; Michael B. Phaup, Director

VETERANS AFFAIRS MEDICAL CENTER (O, 159 beds) 2300 Ramsey Street, Fayetteville, NC Zip 28301–3899; tel. 910/822–7059; Richard J. Baltz, Director

VETERANS AFFAIRS MEDICAL CENTER (O, 389 beds) 1100 Tunnel Road, Asheville, NC Zip 28805–2087; tel. 828/298–7911; James A. Christian, Director **Web address:** www.va.gov

VETERANS AFFAIRS MEDICAL CENTER (O, 551 beds) 1601 Brenner Avenue, Salisbury, NC Zip 28144–2559; tel. 704/638–9000; Timothy May, Director

NORTH DAKOTA: VETERANS AFFAIRS MEDICAL AND REGIONAL OFFICE CENTER (O, 113 beds) 2101 Elm Street, Fargo, ND Zip 58102–2498; tel. 701/232–3241; Douglas M. Kenyon, Director

OHIO: VETERANS AFFAIRS MEDICAL CENTER (O, 817 beds) 10701 East Boulevard, Cleveland, OH Zip 44106–1702; tel. 216/791–3800; Richard S. Citron, Acting Director

VETERANS AFFAIRS MEDICAL CENTER (O, 324 beds) 17273 State Route 104, Chillicothe, OH Zip 45601–0999; tel. 740/773–1141; Michael W. Walton, Director **Web address:** www.bright.net/~vachilli

VETERANS AFFAIRS MEDICAL CENTER (O, 240 beds) 3200 Vine Street, Cincinnati, OH Zip 45220–2288; tel. 513/861–3100; Gary N. Nugent, Medical Director

VETERANS AFFAIRS MEDICAL CENTER (O, 539 beds) 4100 West Third Street, Dayton, OH Zip 45428–1002; tel. 937/268–6511; Steven M. Cohen, M.D., Director

OKLAHOMA: VETERANS AFFAIRS MEDICAL CENTER (O, 50 beds) 1011 Honor Heights Drive, Muskogee, OK Zip 74401–1399; tel. 918/683–3261; Allen J. Colston, Director **Web address:** www.visn16.med.va.gov

VETERANS AFFAIRS MEDICAL CENTER (O, 277 beds) 921 N.E. 13th Street, Oklahoma City, OK Zip 73104–5028; tel. 405/270–0501; Steven J. Gentling, Director

OREGON: VETERANS AFFAIRS MEDICAL CENTER (O, 303 beds) 3710 S.W. U.S. Veterans Hospital Road, Portland, OR Zip 97201; tel. 503/220–8262; James Tuchschmidt, M.D., Chief Executive Officer

VETERANS AFFAIRS ROSEBURG HEALTHCARE SYSTEM (O, 229 beds) 913 N.W. Garden Valley Boulevard, Roseburg, OR Zip 97470–6513; tel. 541/440–1000; George Marnell, Director

PENNSYLVANIA: JAMES E. VAN ZANDT VETERANS AFFAIRS MEDICAL CENTER (O, 78 beds) 2907 Pleasant Valley Boulevard, Altoona, PA Zip 16602–4377; tel. 814/943–8164; Gerald L. Williams, Director and Chief Executive Officer

VETERANS AFFAIRS MEDICAL CENTER (O, 170 beds) 325 New Castle Road, Butler, PA Zip 16001–2480; tel. 724/287–4781; Michael E. Moreland, Director **Web address:** www.va.gov/station/529–butler

VETERANS AFFAIRS MEDICAL CENTER (O, 721 beds) 1400 Black Horse Hill Road, Coatesville, PA Zip 19320–2097; tel. 610/384–7711; Gary W. Devansky, Chief Executive Officer

VETERANS AFFAIRS MEDICAL CENTER (O, 61 beds) 135 East 38th Street, Erie, PA Zip 16504–1559; tel. 814/860–2576; Stephen M. Lucas, Chief Executive Officer **Web address:** www.erie.net/~vamcerie

VETERANS AFFAIRS MEDICAL CENTER (O, 321 beds) 1700 South Lincoln Avenue, Lebanon, PA Zip 17042–7529; tel. 717/272–6621; Charleen R. Szabo, FACHE, Chief Executive Officer **Web address:** www.va.gov

VETERANS AFFAIRS MEDICAL CENTER (O, 656 beds) University and Woodland Avenues, Philadelphia, PA Zip 19104–4594; tel. 215/823–5800; Michael J. Sullivan, Director

VETERANS AFFAIRS MEDICAL CENTER (O, 289 beds) 1111 East End Boulevard, Wilkes–Barre, PA Zip 18711–0026; tel. 570/824–3521; Reedes Hurt, Chief Executive Officer

VETERANS AFFAIRS PITTSBURGH HEALTHCARE SYSTEM (O, 889 beds) Delafield Road, Pittsburgh, PA Zip 15240–1001; tel. 412/784–3900; Thomas A. Cappello, Director **Web address:** www.pitt.edu

PUERTO RICO: VETERANS AFFAIRS MEDICAL CENTER (O, 693 beds) One Veterans Plaza, San Juan, PR Zip 00927–5800; tel. 787/766–5665; James A. Palmer, Director

For explanation of codes following names, see page B2.
★ Indicates Type III membership in the American Hospital Association.

Section B

RHODE ISLAND: VETERANS AFFAIRS MEDICAL CENTER (O, 78 beds) 830 Chalkstone Avenue, Providence, RI Zip 02908–4799; tel. 401/457–3042; James P. Cody, Acting Director

SOUTH CAROLINA: RALPH H. JOHNSON VETERANS AFFAIRS MEDICAL CENTER (O, 161 beds) 109 Bee Street, Charleston, SC Zip 29401–5703; tel. 843/577–5011; R. J. Vogel, Chief Executive Officer

WILLIAM JENNINGS BRYAN DORN VETERANS MEDICAL CENTER (O, 156 beds) 6439 Garners Ferry Road, Columbia, SC Zip 29209–1639; tel. 803/776–4000; Brian Heckert, Medical Center Director

SOUTH DAKOTA: ROYAL C. JOHNSON VETERANS MEMORIAL HOSPITAL (O, 110 beds) 2501 West 22nd Street, Sioux Falls, SD Zip 57105–1394, Mailing Address: P.O. Box 5046, Zip 57117–5046; tel. 605/336–3230; R. Vincent Crawford, Director

VETERANS AFFAIRS BLACK HILLS HEALTH CARE SYSTEM (O, 163 beds) 113 Comanche Road, Fort Meade, SD Zip 57741–1099; tel. 605/347–2511; Peter P. Henry, Director

TENNESSEE: ALVIN C. YORK VETERANS AFFAIRS MEDICAL CENTER (O, 637 beds) 3400 Lebanon Pike, Murfreesboro, TN Zip 37129–1236; tel. 615/867–6100; Richard S. Citron, Acting Director
Web address: www.va.gov/murfreesboro.htm

JAMES H. QUILLEN VETERANS AFFAIRS MEDICAL CENTER (O, 322 beds) Mountain Home, TN Zip 37684–4000; tel. 423/926–1171; Carl J. Gerber, M.D., Ph.D., Director

VETERANS AFFAIRS MEDICAL CENTER (O, 274 beds) 1030 Jefferson Avenue, Memphis, TN Zip 38104–2193; tel. 901/523–8990; K. L. Mulholland Jr., Director

VETERANS AFFAIRS MEDICAL CENTER (O, 161 beds) 1310 24th Avenue South, Nashville, TN Zip 37212–2637; tel. 615/327–5332; William A. Mountcastle, Director
Web address: www.nashville.med.va.gov

TEXAS: CENTRAL TEXAS VETERANS AFFAIRS HEALTHCARE SYSTEM (O, 1852 beds) 1901 South First Street, Temple, TX Zip 76504–7493; tel. 254/778–4811; Dean Billick, Director

SOUTH TEXAS VETERANS HEALTH CARE SYSTEM (O, 1112 beds) 7400 Merton Minter Boulevard, San Antonio, TX Zip 78284–5799; tel. 210/617–5140; Jose R. Coronado, FACHE, Director

VETERANS AFFAIRS MEDICAL CENTER (O, 218 beds) 6010 Amarillo Boulevard West, Amarillo, TX Zip 79106–1992; tel. 806/354–7801; Wallace M. Hopkins, FACHE, Director

VETERANS AFFAIRS MEDICAL CENTER (O, 189 beds) 300 Veterans Boulevard, Big Spring, TX Zip 79720–5500; tel. 915/263–7361; Cary D. Brown, Director

VETERANS AFFAIRS MEDICAL CENTER (O, 859 beds) 2002 Holcombe Boulevard, Houston, TX Zip 77030–4298; tel. 713/791–1414; David Whatley, Director

VETERANS AFFAIRS NORTH TEXAS HEALTH CARE SYSTEM (O, 1031 beds) 4500 South Lancaster Road, Dallas, TX Zip 75216–7167; tel. 214/742–8387; Alan G. Harper, Director

UTAH: VETERANS AFFAIRS MEDICAL CENTER (O, 138 beds) 500 Foothill Drive, Salt Lake City, UT Zip 84148–0002; tel. 801/582–1565; James R. Floyd, Medical Center Director

VERMONT: VETERANS AFFAIRS MEDICAL CENTER (O, 60 beds) North Hartland Road, White River Junction, VT Zip 05009–0001; tel. 802/295–9363; Gary M. De Gasta, Center Director
Web address: www.wrjva1.hitchcock.org

VIRGINIA: HUNTER HOLMES MCGUIRE VETERANS AFFAIRS MEDICAL CENTER (O, 404 beds) 1201 Broad Rock Boulevard, Richmond, VA Zip 23249–0002; tel. 804/675–5000; James W. Dudley, Director

VETERANS AFFAIRS MEDICAL CENTER (O, 670 beds) 100 Emancipation Drive, Hampton, VA Zip 23667–0001; tel. 757/722–9961; Bettye W. Story, Ph.D., Director
Web address: www.152.128.127.205

VETERANS AFFAIRS MEDICAL CENTER (O, 387 beds) 1970 Roanoke Boulevard, Salem, VA Zip 24153; tel. 540/982–2463; Stephen L. Lemons, Ed.D., Director
Web address: www.vaww.salem.med.va.gov

WASHINGTON: JONATHAN M. WAINWRIGHT MEMORIAL VETERANS AFFAIRS MEDICAL CENTER (O, 46 beds) 77 Wainwright Drive, Walla Walla, WA Zip 99362–3994; tel. 509/525–5200

VETERANS AFFAIRS MEDICAL CENTER (O, 192 beds) North 4815 Assembly Street, Spokane, WA Zip 99205–6197; tel. 509/327–0200; Joseph M. Manley, Director

VETERANS AFFAIRS PUGET SOUND HEALTH CARE SYSTEM (O, 557 beds) 1660 South Columbian Way, Seattle, WA Zip 98108–1597; tel. 206/762–1010; Timothy B. Williams, Director

WEST VIRGINIA: LOUIS A. JOHNSON VETERANS AFFAIRS MEDICAL CENTER (O, 160 beds) 1 Medical Center Drive, Clarksburg, WV Zip 26301–4199; tel. 304/623–3461; Michael W. Neusch, FACHE, Director

VETERANS AFFAIRS MEDICAL CENTER (O, 90 beds) 200 Veterans Avenue, Beckley, WV Zip 25801–6499; tel. 304/255–2121; Gerard P. Husson, Director

VETERANS AFFAIRS MEDICAL CENTER (O, 80 beds) 1540 Spring Valley Drive, Huntington, WV Zip 25704–9300; tel. 304/429–6741; David N. Pennington, Chief Executive Officer
Web address: www.va.gov/station

VETERANS AFFAIRS MEDICAL CENTER (O, 566 beds) Charles Town Road, Martinsburg, WV Zip 25401–0205; tel. 304/263–0811; George Moore, Director
Web address: www.va.gov/visn5

WISCONSIN: CLEMENT J. ZABLOCKI VETERANS AFFAIRS MEDICAL CENTER (O, 566 beds) 5000 West National Avenue, Milwaukee, WI Zip 53295; tel. 414/384–2000; Glen W. Grippen, Director

VETERANS AFFAIRS MEDICAL CENTER (O, 569 beds) 500 East Veterans Street, Tomah, WI Zip 54660; tel. 608/372–3971; Stan Johnson, Medical Center Director

WILLIAM S. MIDDLETON MEMORIAL VETERANS HOSPITAL (O, 200 beds) 2500 Overlook Terrace, Madison, WI Zip 53705–2286; tel. 608/256–1901; Nathan L. Geraths, Director

WYOMING: VETERANS AFFAIRS MEDICAL CENTER (O, 71 beds) 2360 East Pershing Boulevard, Cheyenne, WY Zip 82001–5392; tel. 307/778–7550; Richard Fry, Director

VETERANS AFFAIRS MEDICAL CENTER (O, 121 beds) 1898 Fort Road, Sheridan, WY Zip 82801–8320; tel. 307/672–3473; Maureen Humphrys, Director

Owned, leased, sponsored:	141 hospitals	49666 beds
Contract–managed:	0 hospitals	0 beds
Totals:	141 hospitals	49666 beds

★2145: DETROIT MEDICAL CENTER (NP)
3663 Woodward Avenue, Suite 200, Detroit, MI Zip 48201–2403; tel. 313/578–2020; Arthur Porter, M.D., President and Chief Executive Officer

MICHIGAN: CHILDREN'S HOSPITAL OF MICHIGAN (O, 245 beds) 3901 Beaubien Street, Detroit, MI Zip 48201–9985; tel. 313/745–0073; Larry Fleischmann, M.D., Interim Senior Vice President
Web address: www.dmc.org/chm

DETROIT RECEIVING HOSPITAL AND UNIVERSITY HEALTH CENTER (O, 290 beds) 4201 St. Antoine Boulevard, Detroit, MI Zip 48201–2194; tel. 313/745–3603; Leslie C. Bowman, Regional Administrator, Ancillary Services and Site Administrator
Web address: www.dmc.org

GRACE HOSPITAL (O, 352 beds) 6071 West Outer Drive, Detroit, MI Zip 48235–2679; tel. 313/966–3525; Anne M. Regling, Senior Vice President
Web address: www.dmc.org

HARPER HOSPITAL (O, 427 beds) 3990 John R, Detroit, MI Zip 48201–9027; tel. 313/745–8040; John R. Whitcomb, Interim Senior Vice President

HURON VALLEY–SINAI HOSPITAL (O, 139 beds) 1 William Carls Drive, Commerce Township, MI Zip 48382–2201; tel. 248/360–3300; Robert J. Yellan, Senior Vice President

HUTZEL HOSPITAL (O, 243 beds) 4707 St. Antoine Boulevard, Detroit, MI Zip 48201–0154; tel. 313/745–7555; Mark McNash, Operations Officer

For explanation of codes following names, see page B2.
★ Indicates Type III membership in the American Hospital Association.

REHABILITATION INSTITUTE OF MICHIGAN (O, 94 beds) 261 Mack Boulevard, Detroit, MI Zip 48201–2495; tel. 313/745–1203; Bruce M. Gans, M.D., Senior Vice President
Web address: www.dmc.org

SINAI HOSPITAL (O, 469 beds) 6767 West Outer Drive, Detroit, MI Zip 48235–2899; tel. 313/493–6800; Anne M. Regling, Senior Vice President

Owned, leased, sponsored:	8 hospitals	2259 beds
Contract–managed:	0 hospitals	0 beds
Totals:	8 hospitals	2259 beds

0845: DEVEREUX FOUNDATION (NP)
444 Deveraux Drive, Villanova, PA Zip 19085, Mailing Address: P.O. Box 400, Devon, Zip 19333–0400; tel. 610/520–3000; Ronald P. Burd, President and Chief Executive Officer

FLORIDA: DEVEREUX HOSPITAL AND CHILDREN'S CENTER OF FLORIDA (O, 100 beds) 8000 Devereux Drive, Melbourne, FL Zip 32940–7907; tel. 407/242–9100; Michael Becker, Executive Director

GEORGIA: DEVEREUX GEORGIA TREATMENT NETWORK (O, 115 beds) 1291 Stanley Road N.W., Kennesaw, GA Zip 30152–4359; tel. 770/427–0147; Elizabeth M. Chadwick, JD, Executive Director
Web address: www.devereux.org

PENNSYLVANIA: DEVEREUX MAPLETON PSYCHIATRIC INSTITUTE–MAPLETON CENTER (O, 13 beds) 655 Sugartown Road, Malvern, PA Zip 19355–0297, Mailing Address: Box 297, Zip 19355–0297; tel. 610/296–6923; Richard Warden, Executive Director

TEXAS: DEVEREUX TEXAS TREATMENT NETWORK (O, 88 beds) 1150 Devereux Drive, League City, TX Zip 77573–2043; tel. 281/335–1000; L. Gail Atkinson, Executive Director
Web address: www.devereux.org

Owned, leased, sponsored:	4 hospitals	316 beds
Contract–managed:	0 hospitals	0 beds
Totals:	4 hospitals	316 beds

★0029: DIMENSIONS HEALTH CORPORATION (NP)
9200 Basil Court, Largo, MD Zip 20774; tel. 301/925–7000; Winfield M. Kelly Jr., President and Chief Executive Officer

MARYLAND: LAUREL REGIONAL HOSPITAL (O, 185 beds) 7300 Van Dusen Road, Laurel, MD Zip 20707–9266; tel. 301/725–4300; Patrick F. Mutch, President
Web address: www.laurelregionalhospital.org

PRINCE GEORGE'S HOSPITAL CENTER (O, 370 beds) 3001 Hospital Drive, Cheverly, MD Zip 20785–1189; tel. 301/618–2000; Phyllis Wingate–Jones, President
Web address: www.princegeorgeshospital.org

Owned, leased, sponsored:	2 hospitals	555 beds
Contract–managed:	0 hospitals	0 beds
Totals:	2 hospitals	555 beds

0010: DIVISION OF MENTAL HEALTH SERVICES, DEPARTMENT OF HUMAN SERVICES, STATE OF NEW JERSEY (NP)
Capital Center, P.O. Box 727, Trenton, NJ Zip 08625–0727; tel. 609/777–0702; Alan G. Kaufman, Director

NEW JERSEY: ANCORA PSYCHIATRIC HOSPITAL (O, 625 beds) 202 Spring Garden Road, Ancora, NJ Zip 08037–9699; tel. 609/561–1700; Yvonne A. Pressley, Chief Executive Officer

GREYSTONE PARK PSYCHIATRIC HOSPITAL (O, 605 beds) Central Avenue, Greystone Park, NJ Zip 07950, Mailing Address: P.O. Box A, Zip 07950; tel. 973/538–1800; Michael Greenstein, Chief Executive Officer

SENATOR GARRETT T. W. HAGEDORN GERO PSYCHIATRIC HOSPITAL (O, 181 beds) 200 Sanitorium Road, Glen Gardner, NJ Zip 08826–9752; tel. 908/537–2141; Donald A. Bruckman, Acting Chief Executive Officer

TRENTON PSYCHIATRIC HOSPITAL (O, 379 beds) Sullivan Way, Trenton, NJ Zip 08625, Mailing Address: P.O. Box 7500, West Trenton, Zip 08628–7500; tel. 609/633–1500; Joseph Jupin Jr., Chief Executive Officer

Owned, leased, sponsored:	4 hospitals	1790 beds
Contract–managed:	0 hospitals	0 beds
Totals:	4 hospitals	1790 beds

0164: DOCTORS COMMUNITY HEALTHCARE CORPORATION (IO)
6730 North Scottsdale Road, Suite 200, Scottsdale, AZ Zip 85253; tel. 602/348–9800; Melvin Redman, President and Chief Operating Officer

CALIFORNIA: BREA COMMUNITY HOSPITAL (O, 60 beds) 380 West Central Avenue, Brea, CA Zip 92821; tel. 714/529–0211; Gaetano Zanfini, Chief Executive Officer

PACIFICA HOSPITAL OF THE VALLEY (O, 197 beds) 9449 San Fernando Road, Sun Valley, CA Zip 91352; tel. 818/252–2380; Trude Williams, R.N., Administrator

DISTRICT OF COLUMBIA: HADLEY MEMORIAL HOSPITAL (O, 148 beds) 4601 Martin Luther King Jr. Avenue S.W., Washington, DC Zip 20032–1199; tel. 202/574–5700; Ana Raley, Administrator

ILLINOIS: MICHAEL REESE HOSPITAL AND MEDICAL CENTER (O, 523 beds) 2929 South Ellis Avenue, Chicago, IL Zip 60616–3376; tel. 312/791–2000; Ken Bauer, Chief Executive Officer

Owned, leased, sponsored:	4 hospitals	928 beds
Contract–managed:	0 hospitals	0 beds
Totals:	4 hospitals	928 beds

1895: EAST TEXAS MEDICAL CENTER REGIONAL HEALTHCARE SYSTEM (NP)
1000 South Beckham Street, Tyler, TX Zip 75701–1996, Mailing Address: P.O. Box 6400, Zip 75711–6400; tel. 903/535–6211; Elmer G. Ellis, President and Chief Executive Officer

TEXAS: EAST TEXAS MEDICAL CENTER ATHENS (L, 108 beds) 2000 South Palestine Street, Athens, TX Zip 75751–5610; tel. 903/675–2216; Patrick L. Wallace, Administrator

EAST TEXAS MEDICAL CENTER CARTHAGE (L, 30 beds) 409 Cottage Road, Carthage, TX Zip 75633–1466, Mailing Address: P.O. Box 549, Zip 75633–0549; tel. 903/693–3841; Gary Mikeal Hudson, Administrator

EAST TEXAS MEDICAL CENTER CROCKETT (L, 68 beds) 1100 Loop 304 East, Crockett, TX Zip 75835–1810; tel. 409/544–2002; Nelda K. Welch, Administrator

EAST TEXAS MEDICAL CENTER JACKSONVILLE (L, 83 beds) 501 South Ragsdale Street, Jacksonville, TX Zip 75766–2413; tel. 903/541–5000; Steve Bowen, President

EAST TEXAS MEDICAL CENTER PITTSBURG (L, 42 beds) 414 Quitman Street, Pittsburg, TX Zip 75686–1032; tel. 903/856–6663; W. Perry Henderson, Administrator

EAST TEXAS MEDICAL CENTER REHABILITATION CENTER (O, 49 beds) 701 Olympic Plaza Circle, Tyler, TX Zip 75701–1996; tel. 903/596–3000; Eddie L. Howard, Vice President and Chief Operating Officer

EAST TEXAS MEDICAL CENTER RUSK (L, 25 beds) 500 North Bonner Street, Rusk, TX Zip 75785, Mailing Address: P.O. Box 317, Zip 75785–0317; tel. 903/683–2273; Brenda Copley, Acting Administrator

EAST TEXAS MEDICAL CENTER TRINITY (L, 22 beds) 900 Prospect Drive, Trinity, TX Zip 75862–0471, Mailing Address: P.O. Box 471, Zip 75862–0471; tel. 409/594–3541; James C. Whitmire, CHE, Administrator

EAST TEXAS MEDICAL CENTER TYLER (O, 369 beds) 1000 South Beckham Street, Tyler, TX Zip 75701–1996, Mailing Address: Box 6400, Zip 75711–6400; tel. 903/597–0351; Robert B. Evans, Administrator and Chief Executive Officer

EAST TEXAS MEDICAL CENTER–CLARKSVILLE (L, 36 beds) 3000 Highway 82 West, Clarksville, TX Zip 75426, Mailing Address: P.O. Box 1270, Zip 75426–1270; tel. 903/427–3851; Terry Cutler, Administrator and Chief Operating Officer

For explanation of codes following names, see page B2.
★ Indicates Type III membership in the American Hospital Association.

B94 Networks, Health Care Systems and Alliances © 1999 AHA Guide

EAST TEXAS MEDICAL CENTER–FAIRFIELD (L, 19 beds) 125 Newman Street, Fairfield, TX Zip 75840–1499; tel. 903/389–2121; David Kuhn, Administrator

EAST TEXAS MEDICAL CENTER–MOUNT VERNON (L, 30 beds) Highway 37 South, Mount Vernon, TX Zip 75457, Mailing Address: P.O. Box 477, Zip 75457–0477; tel. 903/537–4552; Jerry Edwards, CHE, Administrator

EAST TEXAS MEDICAL CENTER–QUITMAN (L, 17 beds) 117 Winnsboro Street, Quitman, TX Zip 75783–2144, Mailing Address: P.O. Box 1000, Zip 75783–1000; tel. 903/763–4505; Marion W. Stanberry, Administrator

Owned, leased, sponsored:	13 hospitals	898 beds
Contract–managed:	0 hospitals	0 beds
Totals:	13 hospitals	898 beds

★0100: EASTERN HEALTH SYSTEM, INC. (NP)
48 Medical Park East Drive, 450, Birmingham, AL Zip 35235; tel. 205/838–3999; Robert C. Chapman, FACHE, President and Chief Executive Officer

ALABAMA: MEDICAL CENTER BLOUNT (L, 56 beds) 150 Gilbreath, Oneonta, AL Zip 35121–2534, Mailing Address: P.O. Box 1000, Zip 35121–1000; tel. 205/625–3511; George McGowan, FACHE, Chief Executive Officer

MEDICAL CENTER EAST (O, 257 beds) 50 Medical Park East Drive, Birmingham, AL Zip 35235–9987; tel. 205/838–3000; David E. Crawford, FACHE, Executive Vice President and Chief Operating Officer

ST. CLAIR REGIONAL HOSPITAL (C, 51 beds) 2805 Hospital Drive, Pell City, AL Zip 35125–1499; tel. 205/338–3301; Douglas H. Beverly, CHE, Chief Operating Officer

Owned, leased, sponsored:	2 hospitals	313 beds
Contract–managed:	1 hospital	51 beds
Totals:	3 hospitals	364 beds

★0555: EASTERN MAINE HEALTHCARE (NP)
489 State Street, Bangor, ME Zip 04401–6674, Mailing Address: P.O. Box 404, Zip 04402–0404; tel. 207/973–7045; Norman A. Ledwin, President and Chief Executive Officer

MAINE: ACADIA HOSPITAL (O, 72 beds) 268 Stillwater Avenue, Bangor, ME Zip 04401–3945, Mailing Address: P.O. Box 422, Zip 04402–0422; tel. 207/973–6100; Ali A. Elhaj, President and Chief Exective Officer
Web address: www.emh.org

CHARLES A. DEAN MEMORIAL HOSPITAL (O, 50 beds) Pritham Avenue, Greenville, ME Zip 04441–1395, Mailing Address: P.O. Box 1129, Zip 04441–1129; tel. 207/695–2223; Philomena A. Marshall, R.N., President and Chief Executive Officer

EASTERN MAINE MEDICAL CENTER (O, 347 beds) 489 State Street, Bangor, ME Zip 04401–6674, Mailing Address: P.O. Box 404, Zip 04402–0404; tel. 207/973–7000; Norman A. Ledwin, President and Chief Executive Officer

INLAND HOSPITAL (O, 44 beds) 200 Kennedy Memorial Drive, Waterville, ME Zip 04901–4595; tel. 207/861–3000; Wilfred J. Addison, President and Chief Executive Officer

Owned, leased, sponsored:	4 hospitals	513 beds
Contract–managed:	0 hospitals	0 beds
Totals:	4 hospitals	513 beds

0945: EMPIRE HEALTH SERVICES (NP)
West 800 Fifth Avenue, Spokane, WA Zip 99204, Mailing Address: P.O. Box 248, Zip 99210–0248; tel. 509/458–7960; Thomas M. White, President

WASHINGTON: DEACONESS MEDICAL CENTER–SPOKANE (O, 326 beds) 800 West Fifth Avenue, Spokane, WA Zip 99204, Mailing Address: P.O. Box 248, Zip 99210–0248; tel. 509/458–5800

VALLEY HOSPITAL AND MEDICAL CENTER (O, 117 beds) 12606 East Mission Avenue, Spokane, WA Zip 99216–9969; tel. 509/924–6650; Michael T. Liepman, Chief Operating Officer

Owned, leased, sponsored:	2 hospitals	443 beds
Contract–managed:	0 hospitals	0 beds
Totals:	2 hospitals	443 beds

★0735: EPISCOPAL HEALTH SERVICES INC. (CO)
333 Earle Ovington Boulevard, Uniondale, NY Zip 11553–3645; tel. 516/544–5200; Lorna McBarnette, Chief Executive Officer

NEW YORK: ST. JOHN'S EPISCOPAL HOSPITAL–SMITHTOWN (O, 366 beds) 50 Route 25–A, Smithtown, NY Zip 11787–1398; tel. 516/862–3000; James M. Wilson, Regional Administrator

ST. JOHN'S EPISCOPAL HOSPITAL–SOUTH SHORE (O, 314 beds) 327 Beach 19th Street, Far Rockaway, NY Zip 11691–4424; tel. 718/869–7000; Nancy Simmons, Administrator

Owned, leased, sponsored:	2 hospitals	680 beds
Contract–managed:	0 hospitals	0 beds
Totals:	2 hospitals	680 beds

1255: ESCAMBIA COUNTY HEALTH CARE AUTHORITY (NP)
1301 Belleville Avenue, Brewton, AL Zip 36426; tel. 334/368–2500; Phillip L. Parker, Administrator

ALABAMA: ATMORE COMMUNITY HOSPITAL (O, 51 beds) 401 Medical Park Drive, Atmore, AL Zip 36502–3091; tel. 334/368–2500; Robert E. Gowing, Interim Administrator

D. W. MCMILLAN MEMORIAL HOSPITAL (O, 67 beds) 1301 Belleville Avenue, Brewton, AL Zip 36426–1306, Mailing Address: P.O. Box 908, Zip 36427–0908; tel. 334/867–8061; Phillip L. Parker, Administrator
Web address: www.bhcpns.org

Owned, leased, sponsored:	2 hospitals	118 beds
Contract–managed:	0 hospitals	0 beds
Totals:	2 hospitals	118 beds

0148: ESR CHILDREN'S HEALTH CARE SYSTEM, INC. (NP)
2200 Century Parkway, Suite 450, Atlanta, GA Zip 30345; tel. 404/250–2211; James E. Tally, Ph.D., President and Chief Executive Officer

GEORGIA: EGLESTON CHILDREN'S HOSPITAL (O, 202 beds) 1405 Clifton Road N.E., Atlanta, GA Zip 30322–1101; tel. 404/325–6000; James E. Tally, Ph.D., President and Chief Executive Officer

SCOTTISH RITE CHILDREN'S MEDICAL CENTER (O, 165 beds) 1001 Johnson Ferry Road N.E., Atlanta, GA Zip 30342–1600; tel. 404/256–5252; James E. Tally, Ph.D., President and Chief Executive Officer
Web address: www.srcmc.org

Owned, leased, sponsored:	2 hospitals	367 beds
Contract–managed:	0 hospitals	0 beds
Totals:	2 hospitals	367 beds

★0134: EXEMPLA HEALTHCARE, INC. (NP)
600 Grant Street, Suite 700, Denver, CO Zip 80203; tel. 303/813–5000; Jeffrey D. Selberg, President and Chief Executive Officer

COLORADO: EXEMPLA LUTHERAN MEDICAL CENTER (O, 489 beds) 8300 West 38th Avenue, Wheat Ridge, CO Zip 80033–6005; tel. 303/425–4500; Jeffrey D. Selberg, President and Chief Executive Officer

EXEMPLA SAINT JOSEPH HOSPITAL (O, 404 beds) 1835 Franklin Street, Denver, CO Zip 80218–1191; tel. 303/837–7111; Jeffrey D. Selberg, President and Chief Executive Officer

Owned, leased, sponsored:	2 hospitals	893 beds
Contract–managed:	0 hospitals	0 beds
Totals:	2 hospitals	893 beds

Section B

For explanation of codes following names, see page B2.
★ Indicates Type III membership in the American Hospital Association.

★1325:   FAIRVIEW HOSPITAL AND HEALTHCARE SERVICES (NP)

2450 Riverside Avenue, Minneapolis, MN Zip 55454–1400; tel. 612/672–6300; David R. Page, President and Chief Executive Officer

MINNESOTA: FAIRVIEW LAKES REGIONAL MEDICAL CENTER (O, 38 beds) 5200 Fairview Boulevard, Wyoming, MN Zip 55092–8013; tel. 651/982–7000; Daniel K. Anderson, Senior Vice President and Administrator

FAIRVIEW NORTHLAND REGIONAL HEALTH CARE (O, 40 beds) 911 Northland Drive, Princeton, MN Zip 55371–2173; tel. 612/389–6300; Jeanne Lally, Senior Vice President and Administrator

FAIRVIEW RED WING HOSPITAL (O, 68 beds) 1407 West Fourth Street, Red Wing, MN Zip 55066–2198; tel. 651/388–6721; Scott Wordelman, President and Chief Executive Officer
Web address: www.fairview.org

FAIRVIEW RIDGES HOSPITAL (O, 124 beds) 201 East Nicollet Boulevard, Burnsville, MN Zip 55337–5799; tel. 612/892–2000; Mark M. Enger, Senior Vice President and Administrator
Web address: www.fairview.org

FAIRVIEW SOUTHDALE HOSPITAL (O, 355 beds) 6401 France Avenue South, Minneapolis, MN Zip 55435–2199; tel. 612/924–5000; Mark M. Enger, Senior Vice President and Administrator
Web address: www.fairview.org

FAIRVIEW–UNIVERSITY MEDICAL CENTER (O, 1362 beds) 2450 Riverside Avenue, Minneapolis, MN Zip 55454–1400; tel. 612/672–6000; Gordon L. Alexander, M.D., Senior Vice President and Administrator

UNIVERSITY MEDICAL CENTER–MESABI (O, 132 beds) 750 East 34th Street, Hibbing, MN Zip 55746–4600; tel. 218/262–4881; Richard W. Dinter, M.D., Chief Operating Officer

Owned, leased, sponsored:	7 hospitals	2119 beds
Contract–managed:	0 hospitals	0 beds
Totals:	7 hospitals	2119 beds

2515:   FAIRVIEW HOSPITAL SYSTEM (NP)

18101 Lorain Avenue, Cleveland, OH Zip 44111–5656; tel. 216/476–7000; Kenneth T. Misener, Vice President and Chief Operating Officer

OHIO: FAIRVIEW HOSPITAL (O, 437 beds) 18101 Lorain Avenue, Cleveland, OH Zip 44111–5656; tel. 216/476–7000; Louis P. Caravella, M.D., Chief Executive Officer

LUTHERAN HOSPITAL (O, 204 beds) 1730 West 25th Street, Cleveland, OH Zip 44113; tel. 216/696–4300; Jack E. Bell, Chief Operating Officer

Owned, leased, sponsored:	2 hospitals	641 beds
Contract–managed:	0 hospitals	0 beds
Totals:	2 hospitals	641 beds

★0166:   FAY–WEST HEALTH SYSTEM (NP)

508 South Church Street, Mount Pleasant, PA Zip 15666–1790; tel. 724/547–1500; Rodney L. Gunderson, Chief Executive Officer

PENNSYLVANIA: FRICK HOSPITAL (O, 171 beds) 508 South Church Street, Mount Pleasant, PA Zip 15666–1790; tel. 724/547–1500; Rodney L. Gunderson, Chief Executive Officer

HIGHLANDS HOSPITAL (O, 87 beds) 401 East Murphy Avenue, Connellsville, PA Zip 15425–2700; tel. 724/628–1500; Michael J. Evans, Chief Executive Officer

Owned, leased, sponsored:	2 hospitals	258 beds
Contract–managed:	0 hospitals	0 beds
Totals:	2 hospitals	258 beds

2635:   FHC HEALTH SYSTEMS (IO)

240 Corporate Boulevard, Norfolk, VA Zip 23502–4950; tel. 757/459–5100; Ronald I. Dozoretz, M.D., Chairman

SOUTHWOOD PSYCHIATRIC HOSPITAL (O, 50 beds) 2575 Boyce Plaza Road, Pittsburgh, PA Zip 15241–3925; tel. 412/257–2290; Alan A. Axelson, M.D., Chief Executive Officer

PUERTO RICO: FIRST HOSPITAL PANAMERICANO (O, 155 beds) State Road 787 KM 1 5, Cidra, PR Zip 00739, Mailing Address: P.O. Box 1398, Zip 00739; tel. 787/739–5555; Jorge Torres, Executive Director

Owned, leased, sponsored:	2 hospitals	205 beds
Contract–managed:	0 hospitals	0 beds
Totals:	2 hospitals	205 beds

0174:   FORUM HEALTH (NP)

3530 Belmont Avenue, Suite 7, Youngstown, OH Zip 44505; tel. 330/759–4090; Gary E. Kaatz, Executive Vice President and Chief Operating Officer

OHIO: HILLSIDE REHABILITATION HOSPITAL (O, 47 beds) 8747 Squires Lane N.E., Warren, OH Zip 44484–1649; tel. 330/841–3700; Margaret Edwards, Chief Operating Officer

TRUMBULL MEMORIAL HOSPITAL (O, 279 beds) 1350 East Market Street, Warren, OH Zip 44482–6628; tel. 330/841–9011; Gary E. Kaatz, Chief Operating Officer

WESTERN RESERVE CARE SYSTEM (O, 371 beds) 345 Oak Hill Avenue, Youngstown, OH Zip 44501–0990, Mailing Address: P.O. Box 990, Zip 44501–0990; tel. 330/747–0777; Charles A. Johns, President and Chief Executive Officer

Owned, leased, sponsored:	3 hospitals	697 beds
Contract–managed:	0 hospitals	0 beds
Totals:	3 hospitals	697 beds

1485:   FRANCISCAN HEALTH PARTNERSHIP, INC. (CC)

8 Airport Park Boulevard, Latham, NY Zip 12110; tel. 518/783–5257; James H. Flynn Jr., President and Chief Executive Officer

KENTUCKY: OUR LADY OF BELLEFONTE HOSPITAL (S, 194 beds) St. Christopher Drive, Ashland, KY Zip 41101, Mailing Address: P.O. Box 789, Zip 41105–0789; tel. 606/833–3333; Robert J. Maher, President

NEW JERSEY: ST. FRANCIS HOSPITAL (S, 238 beds) 25 McWilliams Place, Jersey City, NJ Zip 07302–1698; tel. 201/418–1000; Robert S. Chaloner, President and Chief Executive Officer

ST. MARY HOSPITAL (S, 328 beds) 308 Willow Avenue, Hoboken, NJ Zip 07030–3889; tel. 201/418–1000; Robert S. Chaloner, President and Chief Executive Officer

NEW YORK: GOOD SAMARITAN HOSPITAL (S, 308 beds) 255 Lafayette Avenue, Suffern, NY Zip 10901–4869; tel. 914/368–5000; James A. Martin, Chief Executive Officer

MERCY COMMUNITY HOSPITAL (O, 187 beds) 160 East Main Street, Port Jervis, NY Zip 12771–2245, Mailing Address: P.O. Box 1014, Zip 12771–1014; tel. 914/856–5351; Michael Parmer, M.D., Site Administrator

ST. ANTHONY COMMUNITY HOSPITAL (S, 73 beds) 15 Maple Avenue, Warwick, NY Zip 10990–5180; tel. 914/986–2276; James A. Martin, President and Chief Executive Officer

OHIO: FRANCISCAN MEDICAL CENTER–DAYTON CAMPUS (S, 321 beds) One Franciscan Way, Dayton, OH Zip 45408–1498; tel. 937/229–6000; Duane L. Erwin, Chief Executive Officer

Owned, leased, sponsored:	7 hospitals	1649 beds
Contract–managed:	0 hospitals	0 beds
Totals:	7 hospitals	1649 beds

★1475:   FRANCISCAN MISSIONARIES OF OUR LADY HEALTH SYSTEM, INC. (CC)

4200 Essen Lane, Baton Rouge, LA Zip 70809; tel. 225/923–2701; John J. Finan Jr., President and Chief Executive Officer

For explanation of codes following names, see page B2.
★ Indicates Type III membership in the American Hospital Association.

LOUISIANA: OUR LADY OF LOURDES REGIONAL MEDICAL CENTER (O, 246 beds) 611 St. Landry Street, Lafayette, LA Zip 70506–4697, Mailing Address: Box 4027, Zip 70502–4027; tel. 318/289–2000; Dudley Romero, President and Chief Executive Officer
Web address: www.lourdes.net

OUR LADY OF THE LAKE REGIONAL MEDICAL CENTER (O, 660 beds) 5000 Hennessy Boulevard, Baton Rouge, LA Zip 70808–4350; tel. 225/765–6565; Robert C. Davidge, Chief Executive Officer

ST. FRANCIS MEDICAL CENTER (O, 257 beds) 309 Jackson Street, Monroe, LA Zip 71201–7498, Mailing Address: P.O. Box 1901, Zip 71210–1901; tel. 318/327–4000; H. Gerald Smith, President and Chief Executive Officer
Web address: www.stfran.com

Owned, leased, sponsored:	3 hospitals	1163 beds
Contract–managed:	0 hospitals	0 beds
Totals:	3 hospitals	1163 beds

★5375: FRANCISCAN SERVICES CORPORATION (CC)
6832 Convent Boulevard, Sylvania, OH Zip 43560–2897; tel. 419/882–8373; John W. O'Connell, President

OHIO: PROVIDENCE HOSPITAL (S, 170 beds) 1912 Hayes Avenue, Sandusky, OH Zip 44870–4736; tel. 419/621–7000; Sister Nancy Linenkugel, FACHE, President and Chief Executive Officer
Web address: www.providencehealth.org

TRINITY HEALTH SYSTEM (S, 533 beds) 380 Summit Avenue, Steubenville, OH Zip 43952–2699; tel. 740/283–7000; Fred B. Brower, President and Chief Executive Officer
Web address: www.trinityhealth.com

TEXAS: BURLESON ST. JOSEPH HEALTH CENTER (S, 30 beds) 1101 Woodson Drive, Caldwell, TX Zip 77836–1052, Mailing Address: P.O. Drawer 360, Zip 77836–0360; tel. 409/567–3245; William H. Craig, President and Chief Executive Officer
Web address: www.st–joseph.org/

MADISON ST. JOSEPH HEALTH CENTER (S, 35 beds) 100 West Cross Street, Madisonville, TX Zip 77864–0698, Mailing Address: Box 698, Zip 77864–0698; tel. 409/348–2631; Reed Edmundson, Interim Administrator

ST. JOSEPH REGIONAL HEALTH CENTER (S, 283 beds) 2801 Franciscan Drive, Bryan, TX Zip 77802–2599; tel. 409/776–3777; Sister Gretchen Kunz, President and Chief Executive Officer

TRINITY COMMUNITY MEDICAL CENTER OF BRENHAM (S, 60 beds) 700 Medical Parkway, Brenham, TX Zip 77833–5498; tel. 409/836–6173; John L. Simms, President and Chief Executive Officer
Web address: www.trinitymed.com

Owned, leased, sponsored:	6 hospitals	1111 beds
Contract–managed:	0 hospitals	0 beds
Totals:	6 hospitals	1111 beds

★1455: FRANCISCAN SISTERS OF CHRISTIAN CHARITY HEALTHCARE MINISTRY, INC (CC)
1415 South Rapids Road, Manitowoc, WI Zip 54220–9302; tel. 920/684–7071; Sister Laura J. Wolf, President

NEBRASKA: ST. FRANCIS MEMORIAL HOSPITAL (O, 102 beds) 430 North Monitor Street, West Point, NE Zip 68788–1595; tel. 402/372–2404; Ronald O. Briggs, President

OHIO: GENESIS HEALTHCARE SYSTEM (O, 467 beds) 800 Forest Avenue, Zanesville, OH Zip 43701–2881; tel. 740/454–5000; Thomas L. Sieber, President and Chief Executive Officer

WISCONSIN: HOLY FAMILY MEMORIAL MEDICAL CENTER (O, 176 beds) 2300 Western Avenue, Manitowoc, WI Zip 54220, Mailing Address: P.O. Box 1450, Zip 54221–1450; tel. 920/684–2011; Daniel B. McGinty, President and Chief Executive Officer
Web address: www.hfmhealth.org

Owned, leased, sponsored:	3 hospitals	745 beds
Contract–managed:	0 hospitals	0 beds
Totals:	3 hospitals	745 beds

★9650: FRANCISCAN SKEMP HEALTHCARE (CC)
700 West Avenue South, La Crosse, WI Zip 54601–4796; tel. 608/791–9710; Glenn Forbes, M.D., President and Chief Executive Officer

FRANCISCAN SKEMP HEALTHCARE–ARCADIA CAMPUS (O, 101 beds) 464 South St. Joseph Avenue, Arcadia, WI Zip 54612–1401; tel. 608/323–3341; Robert M. Tracey, Administrator

FRANCISCAN SKEMP HEALTHCARE–LA CROSSE CAMPUS (O, 213 beds) 700 West Avenue South, La Crosse, WI Zip 54601–4783; tel. 608/785–0940; Glenn Forbes, M.D., President and Chief Executive Officer
Web address: www.mayo.edu/fsh/

FRANCISCAN SKEMP HEALTHCARE–SPARTA CAMPUS (O, 59 beds) 310 West Main Street, Sparta, WI Zip 54656–2171; tel. 608/269–2132; William P. Sexton, Administrator

Owned, leased, sponsored:	3 hospitals	373 beds
Contract–managed:	0 hospitals	0 beds
Totals:	3 hospitals	373 beds

2115: FREMONT–RIDEOUT HEALTH GROUP (NP)
989 Plumas Street, Yuba City, CA Zip 95991; tel. 530/751–4010; Thomas P. Hayes, Chief Executive Officer

CALIFORNIA: FREMONT MEDICAL CENTER (O, 78 beds) 970 Plumas Street, Yuba City, CA Zip 95991; tel. 530/751–4000; Thomas P. Hayes, Chief Executive Officer

RIDEOUT MEMORIAL HOSPITAL (O, 97 beds) 726 Fourth Street, Marysville, CA Zip 95901–2128, Mailing Address: 989 Plumas Street, Yuba City, Zip 95991; tel. 530/749–4300; Thomas P. Hayes, Chief Executive Officer

Owned, leased, sponsored:	2 hospitals	175 beds
Contract–managed:	0 hospitals	0 beds
Totals:	2 hospitals	175 beds

★0775: GENERAL HEALTH SYSTEM (NP)
3600 Florida Boulevard, Baton Rouge, LA Zip 70806–3854; tel. 225/237–1603; Milton R. Siepman, Ph.D., President and Chief Executive Officer

LOUISIANA: BATON ROUGE GENERAL HEALTH CENTER (O, 72 beds) 8585 Picardy Avenue, Baton Rouge, LA Zip 70809–3679, Mailing Address: P.O. Box 84330, Zip 70884–4330; tel. 225/763–4500; Margare Peterson, Ph.D., Administrator
Web address: www.generalhealth.org

BATON ROUGE GENERAL MEDICAL CENTER (O, 371 beds) 3600 Florida Street, Baton Rouge, LA Zip 70806–3889, Mailing Address: P.O. Box 2511, Zip 70821–2511; tel. 225/387–7770; Milton R. Siepman, Ph.D., President and Chief Executive Officer
Web address: www.generalhealth.org

VERMILION HOSPITAL (O, 54 beds) 2520 North University Avenue, Lafayette, LA Zip 70507–5306, Mailing Address: P.O. Box 91526, Zip 70509–1526; tel. 318/234–5614; William A. Ferry, Administrator

Owned, leased, sponsored:	3 hospitals	497 beds
Contract–managed:	0 hospitals	0 beds
Totals:	3 hospitals	497 beds

★0138: GEORGIA BAPTIST HEALTH CARE SYSTEM (NP)
100 10th Street, Atlanta, GA Zip 30365; tel. 404/253–3011; David E. Harrell, Chief Executive Officer

GEORGIA: BAPTIST HOSPITAL, WORTH COUNTY (O, 49 beds) 807 South Isabella Street, Sylvester, GA Zip 31791–0545, Mailing Address: Box 545, Zip 31791–0545; tel. 912/776–6961; Billy Hayes, Administrator

BAPTIST MEDICAL CENTER (O, 30 beds) 1200 Baptist Medical Center Drive, Cumming, GA Zip 30041; tel. 770/887–2355; John M. Herron, Administrator

BAPTIST MERIWETHER HOSPITAL (L, 105 beds) 5995 Spring Street, Warm Springs, GA Zip 31830, Mailing Address: P.O. Box 8, Zip 31830–0008; tel. 706/655–3331; Lynn Jackson, Administrator

Section B

For explanation of codes following names, see page B2.
★ Indicates Type III membership in the American Hospital Association.

DOOLY MEDICAL CENTER (L, 32 beds) 1300 Union Street, Vienna, GA Zip 31092–7541, Mailing Address: P.O. Box 278, Zip 31092–0278; tel. 912/268–4141; Kent W. McMackin, Administrator

Owned, leased, sponsored:	4 hospitals	216 beds
Contract–managed:	0 hospitals	0 beds
Totals:	4 hospitals	216 beds

★1535: **GREAT PLAINS HEALTH ALLIANCE, INC.** (NP)
625 Third Street, Phillipsburg, KS Zip 67661–2138, Mailing Address: P.O. Box 366, Zip 67661–0366; tel. 785/543–2111; Roger S. John, President and Chief Executive Officer

KANSAS: ASHLAND HEALTH CENTER (C, 48 beds) 709 Oak Street, Ashland, KS Zip 67831, Mailing Address: P.O. Box 188, Zip 67831; tel. 316/635–2241; Bryan Stacey, Administrator

CHEYENNE COUNTY HOSPITAL (L, 16 beds) 210 West First Street, Saint Francis, KS Zip 67756, Mailing Address: P.O. Box 547, Zip 67756–0547; tel. 785/332–2104; Leslie Lacy, Administrator

COMANCHE COUNTY HOSPITAL (C, 14 beds) Second and Frisco Streets, Coldwater, KS Zip 67029, Mailing Address: HC 65, Box 8A, Zip 67029; tel. 316/582–2144; Nancy Zimmerman, Administrator

ELLINWOOD DISTRICT HOSPITAL (L, 12 beds) 605 North Main Street, Ellinwood, KS Zip 67526–1440; tel. 316/564–2548; Marge Conell, R.N., Administrator

FREDONIA REGIONAL HOSPITAL (C, 51 beds) 1527 Madison Street, Fredonia, KS Zip 66736–1751, Mailing Address: P.O. Box 579, Zip 66736–0579; tel. 316/378–2121; Terry Deschaine, Chief Executive Officer

GREELEY COUNTY HOSPITAL (L, 48 beds) 506 Third Street, Tribune, KS Zip 67879, Mailing Address: P.O. Box 338, Zip 67879–0338; tel. 316/376–4221; Jerrell J. Horton, Chief Executive Officer

GRISELL MEMORIAL HOSPITAL DISTRICT ONE (C, 46 beds) 210 South Vermont, Ransom, KS Zip 67572–0268, Mailing Address: P.O. Box 268, Zip 67572–0268; tel. 785/731–2231; Kristine Ochs, R.N., Administrator

KIOWA COUNTY MEMORIAL HOSPITAL (L, 46 beds) 501 South Walnut Street, Greensburg, KS Zip 67054–1951; tel. 316/723–3341; CeCe Noll, Administrator

LANE COUNTY HOSPITAL (C, 31 beds) 243 South Second, Dighton, KS Zip 67839, Mailing Address: P.O. Box 969, Zip 67839–0969; tel. 316/397–5321; Donna McGowan, R.N., Administrator

LINCOLN COUNTY HOSPITAL (C, 34 beds) 624 North Second Street, Lincoln, KS Zip 67455–1738, Mailing Address: P.O. Box 406, Zip 67455–0406; tel. 913/524–4403; Jolene Yager, R.N., Administrator

MEDICINE LODGE MEMORIAL HOSPITAL (C, 42 beds) 710 North Walnut Street, Medicine Lodge, KS Zip 67104–1019, Mailing Address: P.O. Drawer C, Zip 67104; tel. 316/886–3771; Kevin A. White, Administrator

MINNEOLA DISTRICT HOSPITAL (C, 15 beds) 212 Main Street, Minneola, KS Zip 67865–8511; tel. 316/885–4264; Blaine K. Miller, Administrator

MITCHELL COUNTY HOSPITAL (L, 89 beds) 400 West Eighth, Beloit, KS Zip 67420–1605, Mailing Address: P.O. Box 399, Zip 67420–0399; tel. 785/738–2266; John M. Osse, Administrator

OSBORNE COUNTY MEMORIAL HOSPITAL (C, 29 beds) 424 West New Hampshire Street, Osborne, KS Zip 67473–0070, Mailing Address: P.O. Box 70, Zip 67473–0070; tel. 785/346–2121; Patricia Bernard, R.N., Administrator

OTTAWA COUNTY HEALTH CENTER (L, 53 beds) 215 East Eighth, Minneapolis, KS Zip 67467–1999, Mailing Address: P.O. Box 209, Zip 67467–0209; tel. 785/392–2122; Joy Reed, R.N., Administrator

PHILLIPS COUNTY HOSPITAL (L, 62 beds) 1150 State Street, Phillipsburg, KS Zip 67661–1799, Mailing Address: P.O. Box 607, Zip 67661–0607; tel. 785/543–5226; James Wahlmeier, Administrator

RAWLINS COUNTY HEALTH CENTER (C, 24 beds) 707 Grant Street, Atwood, KS Zip 67730–4700, Mailing Address: Box 47, Zip 67730–4700; tel. 785/626–3211; Donald J. Kessen, Administrator and Chief Executive Officer

REPUBLIC COUNTY HOSPITAL (L, 86 beds) 2420 G Street, Belleville, KS Zip 66935–2499; tel. 785/527–2255; Charles A. Westin, FACHE, Administrator

SABETHA COMMUNITY HOSPITAL (L, 27 beds) 14th and Oregon Streets, Sabetha, KS Zip 66534, Mailing Address: P.O. Box 229, Zip 66534; tel. 785/284–2121; Rita K. Buurman, Chief Executive Officer

SATANTA DISTRICT HOSPITAL (C, 45 beds) 401 South Cheyenne Street, Satanta, KS Zip 67870, Mailing Address: P.O. Box 159, Zip 67870–0159; tel. 316/649–2761; T. G. Lee, Administrator

SMITH COUNTY MEMORIAL HOSPITAL (L, 54 beds) 614 South Main Street, Smith Center, KS Zip 66967–0349, Mailing Address: P.O. Box 349, Zip 66967–0349; tel. 785/282–6845; John Terrill, Administrator

TREGO COUNTY–LEMKE MEMORIAL HOSPITAL (C, 73 beds) 320 North 13th Street, Wakeeney, KS Zip 67672–2099; tel. 785/743–2182; Lisa J. Freeborn, R.N., Administrator

NEBRASKA: COMMUNITY MEDICAL CENTER (C, 35 beds) 2307 Barada Street, Falls City, NE Zip 68355–1599; tel. 402/245–2428; Victor Lee, Chief Executive Officer and Administrator

HARLAN COUNTY HEALTH SYSTEM (C, 25 beds) 717 North Brown Street, Alma, NE Zip 68920–0836, Mailing Address: P.O. Box 836, Zip 68920–0836; tel. 308/928–2151; Allen Van Driel, Administrator

Owned, leased, sponsored:	10 hospitals	493 beds
Contract–managed:	14 hospitals	512 beds
Totals:	24 hospitals	1005 beds

0144: **GREATER HUDSON VALLEY HEALTH SYSTEM** (NP)
600A Stony Brook Court, Newburgh, NY Zip 12550; tel. 914/568–6050; Paul Dell Uomo, President and Chief Executive Officer

NEW YORK: CORNWALL HOSPITAL (O, 125 beds) 19 Laurel Avenue, Cornwall, NY Zip 12518–1499; tel. 914/534–7711; Louis H. Smith, Executive Vice President and Administrator

HORTON MEDICAL CENTER (O, 168 beds) 60 Prospect Avenue, Middletown, NY Zip 10940–4133; tel. 914/343–2424; Jeffrey D. Hirsch, Executive Vice President and Administrator

ST. LUKE'S HOSPITAL (O, 184 beds) 70 Dubois Street, Newburgh, NY Zip 12550–4898, Mailing Address: P.O. Box 631, Zip 12550–0631; tel. 914/561–4400; Laurence E. Kelly, Executive Vice President and Administrator
Web address: www.stlukeshospital.org

Owned, leased, sponsored:	3 hospitals	477 beds
Contract–managed:	0 hospitals	0 beds
Totals:	3 hospitals	477 beds

★2015: **GREATER SOUTHEAST HEALTHCARE SYSTEM** (NP)
1310 Southern Avenue S.E., Washington, DC Zip 20032–4692; tel. 202/574–6611; George E. Gilbert, M.D., M.P.H., President and Chief Executive Officer

DISTRICT OF COLUMBIA: GREATER SOUTHEAST COMMUNITY HOSPITAL (O, 262 beds) 1310 Southern Avenue S.E., Washington, DC Zip 20032–4699; tel. 202/574–6000; Stephen C. Rupp, Chief Operating Officer

MARYLAND: FORT WASHINGTON HOSPITAL (O, 37 beds) 11711 Livingston Road, Fort Washington, MD Zip 20744–5164; tel. 301/292–7000; Paul Porter, Chief Operating Officer

Owned, leased, sponsored:	2 hospitals	299 beds
Contract–managed:	0 hospitals	0 beds
Totals:	2 hospitals	299 beds

★1555: **GREENVILLE HOSPITAL SYSTEM** (NP)
701 Grove Road, Greenville, SC Zip 29605–4211; tel. 864/455–7000; Frank D. Pinckney, President

SOUTH CAROLINA: ALLEN BENNETT HOSPITAL (O, 146 beds) 313 Memorial Drive, Greer, SC Zip 29650–1521; tel. 864/848–8130; Michael W. Massey, Administrator

GREENVILLE MEMORIAL HOSPITAL (O, 850 beds) 701 Grove Road, Greenville, SC Zip 29605–4295; tel. 864/455–7000; J. Bland Burkhardt Jr., Senior Vice President and Administrator

For explanation of codes following names, see page B2.
★ Indicates Type III membership in the American Hospital Association.

HILLCREST HOSPITAL (O, 46 beds) 729 S.E. Main Street, Simpsonville, SC Zip 29681–3280; tel. 864/967–6100; Mark Slyter, Administrator

Owned, leased, sponsored:	3 hospitals	1042 beds
Contract–managed:	0 hospitals	0 beds
Totals:	3 hospitals	1042 beds

★0675: GUTHRIE HEALTHCARE SYSTEM (NP)
Guthrie Square, Sayre, PA Zip 18840; tel. 570/888–6666; Mark Stensager, President and Chief Executive Officer

PENNSYLVANIA: ROBERT PACKER HOSPITAL (O, 265 beds) 1 Guthrie Square, Sayre, PA Zip 18840–1698; tel. 570/888–6666; William F. Vanaskie, President and Chief Executive Officer
Web address: www.inet.guthrie.org

TROY COMMUNITY HOSPITAL (O, 35 beds) 100 John Street, Troy, PA Zip 16947–0036; tel. 570/297–2121; Mark Webster, President

Owned, leased, sponsored:	2 hospitals	300 beds
Contract–managed:	0 hospitals	0 beds
Totals:	2 hospitals	300 beds

3555: HAWAII HEALTH SYSTEMS CORPORATION (NP)
3675 Kilauea Avenue, Honolulu, HI Zip 96816; tel. 808/586–4416; Thomas M. Driskill Jr., President and Chief Executive Officer

HAWAII: HALE HO'OLA HAMAKUA (O, 50 beds) Honokaa, HI Mailing Address: P.O. Box 237, Zip 96727–0237; tel. 808/775–7211; Romel Dela Cruz, Administrator

HILO MEDICAL CENTER (O, 274 beds) 1190 Waianuenue Avenue, Hilo, HI Zip 96720–2095; tel. 808/974–4743; Robert Morris, M.D., Administrator

KAU HOSPITAL (O, 21 beds) Pahala, HI Mailing Address: P.O. Box 40, Zip 96777–0040; tel. 808/928–8331; Dawn S. Pung, Administrator

KAUAI VETERANS MEMORIAL HOSPITAL (O, 49 beds) Waimea Canyon Road, Waimea, HI Zip 96796, Mailing Address: P.O. Box 337, Zip 96796–0337; tel. 808/338–9431; Orianna A. Skomoroch, Chief Executive Officer

KOHALA HOSPITAL (O, 26 beds) Kohala, HI Mailing Address: P.O. Box 10, Kapaau, Zip 96755–0010; tel. 808/889–6211; Herbert K. Yim, Administrator

KONA COMMUNITY HOSPITAL (O, 75 beds) Kealakekua, HI Mailing Address: P.O. Box 69, Zip 96750–0069; tel. 808/322–4429; Joseph C. Wall, Administrator

KULA HOSPITAL (O, 105 beds) 204 Kula Highway, Kula, HI Zip 96790–9499; tel. 808/878–1221; Alan G. Lee, Administrator

LANAI COMMUNITY HOSPITAL (O, 14 beds) 628 Seventh Street, Lanai City, HI Zip 96763–0797, Mailing Address: P.O. Box 797, Zip 96763–0797; tel. 808/565–6411; John Schaumburg, Administrator

LEAHI HOSPITAL (O, 192 beds) 3675 Kilauea Avenue, Honolulu, HI Zip 96816; tel. 808/733–8000; Jerry Walker, Administrator

MAUI MEDICAL MEMORIAL CENTER (O, 203 beds) 221 Mahalani Street, Wailuku, HI Zip 96793–2581; tel. 808/244–9056; William B. Kleefisch, Chief Executive Officer

SAMUEL MAHELONA MEMORIAL HOSPITAL (O, 82 beds) 4800 Kawaihau Road, Kapaa, HI Zip 96746–1998; tel. 808/822–4961; Neva M. Olson, Chief Executive Officer

Owned, leased, sponsored:	11 hospitals	1091 beds
Contract–managed:	0 hospitals	0 beds
Totals:	11 hospitals	1091 beds

★0082: HEALTH ALLIANCE OF GREATER CINCINNATI (NP)
3200 Burnet Avenue, Cincinnati, OH Zip 45229; tel. 513/585–6000; Jack M. Cook, President and Chief Executive Officer

KENTUCKY: ST. LUKE HOSPITAL EAST (O, 167 beds) 85 North Grand Avenue, Fort Thomas, KY Zip 41075–1796; tel. 606/572–3100; Daniel M. Vinson, CPA, Senior Vice President

ST. LUKE HOSPITAL WEST (O, 136 beds) 7380 Turfway Road, Florence, KY Zip 41042–1337; tel. 606/525–5200; Daniel M. Vinson, CPA, Senior Vice President

OHIO: CHRIST HOSPITAL (O, 483 beds) 2139 Auburn Avenue, Cincinnati, OH Zip 45219–2989; tel. 513/585–2000; Richard L. Seim, Senior Vice President

FORT HAMILTON HOSPITAL (O, 181 beds) 630 Eaton Avenue, Hamilton, OH Zip 45013–2770; tel. 513/867–2000; James A. Kingsbury, President and Chief Executive Officer

JEWISH HOSPITAL KENWOOD (O, 142 beds) 4777 East Galbraith Road, Cincinnati, OH Zip 45236; tel. 513/686–3000; M. Aurora Lambert, Senior Vice President

UNIVERSITY HOSPITAL (O, 411 beds) 234 Goodman Street, Cincinnati, OH Zip 45219–2316; tel. 513/558–1000; Elliot G. Cohen, Senior Vice President

Owned, leased, sponsored:	6 hospitals	1520 beds
Contract–managed:	0 hospitals	0 beds
Totals:	6 hospitals	1520 beds

1775: HEALTH MANAGEMENT ASSOCIATES (IO)
5811 Pelican Bay Boulevard, Suite 500, Naples, FL Zip 34108; tel. 941/598–3175; William J. Schoen, Chairman and Chief Executive Officer

ALABAMA: RIVERVIEW REGIONAL MEDICAL CENTER (O, 281 beds) 600 South Third Street, Gadsden, AL Zip 35901–5399, Mailing Address: P.O. Box 268, Zip 35999–0268; tel. 205/543–5200; J. David McCormack, Executive Director

STRINGFELLOW MEMORIAL HOSPITAL (L, 66 beds) 301 East 18th Street, Anniston, AL Zip 36207–3999; tel. 205/235–8900; Vincent T. Cherry Jr., Administrator

ARKANSAS: CRAWFORD MEMORIAL HOSPITAL (L, 103 beds) East Main & South 20th Streets, Van Buren, AR Zip 72956, Mailing Address: P.O. Box 409, Zip 72957–0409; tel. 501/474–3401; Richard Boone, Executive Director
Web address: www.noonanrusso.com

SOUTHWEST REGIONAL MEDICAL CENTER (O, 125 beds) 11401 Interstate 30, Little Rock, AR Zip 72209–7056; tel. 501/455–7100; R. Mark Cain, Executive Director

FLORIDA: BROOKSVILLE REGIONAL HOSPITAL (L, 91 beds) 55 Ponce De Leon Boulevard, Brooksville, FL Zip 34601–0037, Mailing Address: P.O. Box 37, Zip 34605–0037; tel. 352/796–5111; Robert Foreman, Associate Administrator

CHARLOTTE REGIONAL MEDICAL CENTER (O, 148 beds) 809 East Marion Avenue, Punta Gorda, FL Zip 33950–3898, Mailing Address: P.O. Box 51–1328, Zip 33951–1328; tel. 941/639–3131; Joshua S. Putter, Executive Director

FISHERMEN'S HOSPITAL (L, 58 beds) 3301 Overseas Highway, Marathon, FL Zip 33050–0068; tel. 305/743–5533; Patrice L. Tavernier, Administrator

HEART OF FLORIDA BEHAVIORAL CENTER (O, 40 beds) 2510 North Florida Avenue, Lakeland, FL Zip 33805–2298; tel. 941/682–6105; David M. Polunas, Administrator and Chief Executive Officer

HEART OF FLORIDA REGIONAL MEDICAL CENTER (O, 51 beds) 1615 U.S. Highway 27N, Davenport, FL Zip 33837, Mailing Address: P.O. Box 67, Haines City, Zip 33844–0067; tel. 941/422–4971; Robert Mahaffey, Administrator

HIGHLANDS REGIONAL MEDICAL CENTER (L, 126 beds) 3600 South Highlands Avenue, Sebring, FL Zip 33870–5495, Mailing Address: Drawer 2066, Zip 33871–2066; tel. 941/385–6101; Micheal Terry, Executive Director

LOWER FLORIDA KEYS HEALTH SYSTEM (L, 169 beds) 5900 College Road, Key West, FL Zip 33040–4396, Mailing Address: P.O. Box 9107, Zip 33041–9107; tel. 305/294–5531; Roberto Sanchez, Administrator

SANDYPINES (O, 60 beds) 11301 S.E. Tequesta Terrace, Tequesta, FL Zip 33469–8146; tel. 561/744–0211; Mary S. Bohne', Administrator

SEBASTIAN RIVER MEDICAL CENTER (O, 133 beds) 13695 North U.S. Highway 1, Sebastian, FL Zip 32958–3230, Mailing Address: Box 780838, Zip 32978–0838; tel. 561/589–3186; Diane D. Torres, R.N., Executive Director

SPRING HILL REGIONAL HOSPITAL (L, 75 beds) 10461 Quality Drive, Spring Hill, FL Zip 34609; tel. 352/688–8200; Thomas Bard, Chief Executive Officer

For explanation of codes following names, see page B2.
★ Indicates Type III membership in the American Hospital Association.

Section B

UNIVERSITY BEHAVIORAL CENTER (O, 100 beds) 2500 Discovery Drive, Orlando, FL Zip 32826–3711; tel. 407/281–7000; David L. Beardsley, Administrator

GEORGIA: BULLOCH MEMORIAL HOSPITAL (O, 158 beds) 500 East Grady Street, Statesboro, GA Zip 30458–5105, Mailing Address: P.O. Box 1048, Zip 30459–1048; tel. 912/486–1000; C. Scott Campbell, Executive Director

KENTUCKY: PAUL B. HALL REGIONAL MEDICAL CENTER (O, 72 beds) 625 James S Trimble Boulevard, Paintsville, KY Zip 41240–1055, Mailing Address: P.O. Box 1487, Zip 41240–1487; tel. 606/789–3511; Deborah C. Trimble, Administrator

MISSISSIPPI: BILOXI REGIONAL MEDICAL CENTER (L, 153 beds) 150 Reynoir Street, Biloxi, MS Zip 39530–4199, Mailing Address: P.O. Box 128, Zip 39533–0128; tel. 228/432–1571; Joseph J. Mullany, Chief Executive Officer

CENTRAL MISSISSIPPI MEDICAL CENTER (L, 317 beds) 1850 Chadwick Drive, Jackson, MS Zip 39204–3479, Mailing Address: P.O. Box 59001, Zip 39204–9001; tel. 601/376–1000; Joseph J. Mullany, Chief Executive Officer

NATCHEZ COMMUNITY HOSPITAL (O, 101 beds) 129 Jefferson Davis Boulevard, Natchez, MS Zip 39120–5100, Mailing Address: P.O. Box 1203, Zip 39121–1203; tel. 601/445–6200; Raymond Bane, Executive Director

NORTHWEST MISSISSIPPI REGIONAL MEDICAL CENTER (L, 195 beds) 1970 Hospital Drive, Clarksdale, MS Zip 38614–7204, Mailing Address: P.O. Box 1218, Zip 38614–1218; tel. 601/627–2329; Roger C. LeDoux, Executive Director

RANKIN MEDICAL CENTER (L, 105 beds) 350 Crossgates Boulevard, Brandon, MS Zip 39042–2698; tel. 601/825–2811; Robert L. Hammond Jr., Executive Director

RILEY MEMORIAL HOSPITAL (O, 180 beds) 1102 21st Avenue, Meridian, MS Zip 39301–4096, Mailing Address: P.O. Box 1810, Zip 39302–1810; tel. 601/693–2511; Carl Etter, Chief Executive Officer

RIVER OAKS HOSPITAL (O, 109 beds) 1030 River Oaks Drive, Jackson, MS Zip 39208–9729, Mailing Address: P.O. Box 5100, Zip 39296–5100; tel. 601/932–1030; John J. Cleary, President and Chief Executive Officer

WOMEN'S HOSPITAL AT RIVER OAKS (O, 76 beds) 1026 North Flowood Drive, Jackson, MS Zip 39208–9599, Mailing Address: P.O. Box 4546, Zip 39296–4546; tel. 601/932–1000; Carl Etter, Executive Director

NORTH CAROLINA: FRANKLIN REGIONAL MEDICAL CENTER (O, 85 beds) 100 Hospital Drive, Louisburg, NC Zip 27549–2256, Mailing Address: P.O. Box 609, Zip 27549–0609; tel. 919/496–5131; Ann Barnhart, Executive Director

HAMLET HOSPITAL (O, 64 beds) Rice and Vance Streets, Hamlet, NC Zip 28345, Mailing Address: P.O. Box 1109, Zip 28345–1109; tel. 910/582–3611; Nancy C. Fodi, Executive Director

LAKE NORMAN REGIONAL MEDICAL CENTER (O, 111 beds) 610 East Center Avenue, Mooresville, NC Zip 28115, Mailing Address: P.O. Box 360, Zip 28115–0360; tel. 704/663–1113; P. Paul Smith Jr., Executive Director

OKLAHOMA: MEDICAL CENTER OF SOUTHEASTERN OKLAHOMA (O, 103 beds) 1800 University Boulevard, Durant, OK Zip 74701–3006, Mailing Address: P.O. Box 1207, Zip 74702–1207; tel. 580/924–3080; Jacquelyn Harms, Executive Director

MIDWEST REGIONAL MEDICAL CENTER (L, 214 beds) 2825 Parklawn Drive, Midwest City, OK Zip 73110–4258; tel. 405/610–4411; Peter Lawson, Chief Executive Officer

SOUTH CAROLINA: BYERLY HOSPITAL (L, 100 beds) 413 East Carolina Avenue, Hartsville, SC Zip 29550–4309; tel. 843/339–2100; Page Vaughan, Executive Director

UPSTATE CAROLINA MEDICAL CENTER (O, 125 beds) 1530 North Limestone Street, Gaffney, SC Zip 29340–4738; tel. 864/487–1500; Nancy C. Fodi, Executive Director

WEST VIRGINIA: WILLIAMSON MEMORIAL HOSPITAL (O, 76 beds) 859 Alderson Street, Williamson, WV Zip 25661–3215, Mailing Address: P.O. Box 1980, Zip 25661–1980; tel. 304/235–2500; William Kinzley, Chief Executive Officer

Owned, leased, sponsored:	33 hospitals	3970 beds
Contract–managed:	0 hospitals	0 beds
Totals:	33 hospitals	3970 beds

★**8815: HEALTH MIDWEST** (NP)
2304 East Meyer Boulevard, Suite A–20, Kansas City, MO Zip 64132–4104; tel. 816/276–9181; Richard W. Brown, President and Chief Executive Officer

KANSAS: ALLEN COUNTY HOSPITAL (L, 41 beds) 101 South First Street, Iola, KS Zip 66749–3505, Mailing Address: P.O. Box 540, Zip 66749–0540; tel. 316/365–1000; Bill May, Chief Executive Officer

MENORAH MEDICAL CENTER (O, 129 beds) 5721 West 119th Street, Overland Park, KS Zip 66209; tel. 913/498–6000; Steven D. Wilkinson, President and Chief Executive Officer
Web address: www.healthmidwest.org/hospitals/mmp.shtml

OVERLAND PARK REGIONAL MEDICAL CENTER (L, 269 beds) 10500 Quivira Road, Overland Park, KS Zip 66215–2373, Mailing Address: P.O. Box 15959, Shawnee Mission, Zip 66215–5959; tel. 913/541–5000; Kevin J. Hicks, President and Chief Executive Officer
Web address: www.overlandparkregional.com

MISSOURI: BAPTIST MEDICAL CENTER (O, 265 beds) 6601 Rockhill Road, Kansas City, MO Zip 64131–1197; tel. 816/276–7000; Darrell W. Moore, President and Chief Executive Officer

CASS MEDICAL CENTER (C, 35 beds) 1800 East Mechanic Street, Harrisonville, MO Zip 64701–2099; tel. 816/884–3291; Alan O. Freeman, Chief Executive Officer

HEDRICK MEDICAL CENTER (L, 80 beds) 100 Central Avenue, Chillicothe, MO Zip 64601–1599; tel. 660/646–1480; James K. Johnson, Chief Executive Officer

INDEPENDENCE REGIONAL HEALTH CENTER (L, 329 beds) 1509 West Truman Road, Independence, MO Zip 64050–3498; tel. 816/836–8100; Michael W. Chappelow, President and Chief Executive Officer

LAFAYETTE REGIONAL HEALTH CENTER (L, 37 beds) 1500 State Street, Lexington, MO Zip 64067–1199; tel. 660/259–2203; Jeffrey S. Tarrant, Administrator

LEE'S SUMMIT HOSPITAL (O, 83 beds) 530 North Murray Road, Lees Summit, MO Zip 64081–1497; tel. 816/969–6000; John L. Jacobson, President and Chief Executive Officer

MEDICAL CENTER OF INDEPENDENCE (O, 123 beds) 17203 East 23rd Street, Independence, MO Zip 64057–1899; tel. 816/478–5000; J. Kent Howard, President and Chief Executive Officer

PARK LANE MEDICAL CENTER (O, 83 beds) 5151 Raytown Road, Kansas City, MO Zip 64133–2199; tel. 816/358–8000; Derell Taloney, President and Chief Executive Officer

REHABILITATION INSTITUTE (O, 36 beds) 3011 Baltimore, Kansas City, MO Zip 64108–3465; tel. 816/751–7900; Ronald L. Herrick, President

RESEARCH BELTON HOSPITAL (O, 47 beds) 17065 South 71 Highway, Belton, MO Zip 64012–2165; tel. 816/348–1200; Daniel F. Sheehan, Administrator
Web address: www.healthmidwest.org/hospitals/rbh/shtml

RESEARCH MEDICAL CENTER (O, 491 beds) 2316 East Meyer Boulevard, Kansas City, MO Zip 64132–1199; tel. 816/276–4000; Steven R. Newton, President and Chief Executive Officer
Web address: www.healthmidwest.org

TRINITY LUTHERAN HOSPITAL (O, 334 beds) 3030 Baltimore Avenue, Kansas City, MO Zip 64108–3404; tel. 816/751–4600; Ronald A. Ommen, President and Chief Executive Officer

Owned, leased, sponsored:	14 hospitals	2347 beds
Contract–managed:	1 hospital	35 beds
Totals:	15 hospitals	2382 beds

0395: HEALTHCARE AMERICA, INC. (IO)
1407 West Stassney Lane, Austin, TX Zip 78745–2998, Mailing Address: P.O. Box 4008, Zip 78765–4008; tel. 512/464–0200; John P. Harcourt Jr., President and Chief Executive Officer

For explanation of codes following names, see page B2.
★ Indicates Type III membership in the American Hospital Association.

COLORADO: CEDAR SPRINGS PSYCHIATRIC HOSPITAL (O, 100 beds) 2135 Southgate Road, Colorado Springs, CO Zip 80906–2693; tel. 719/633–4114; Connie Mull, Chief Executive Officer
Web address: www.brownschools.com

OKLAHOMA: THE BROWN SCHOOLS AT SHADOW MOUNTAIN (O, 100 beds) 6262 South Sheridan Road, Tulsa, OK Zip 74133–4099; tel. 918/492–8200; Nancy J. Cranton, Chief Executive Officer

TEXAS: BROWN SCHOOLS REHABILITATION CENTER (O, 60 beds) 1106 West Dittmar, Austin, TX Zip 78745–9990, Mailing Address: P.O. Box 150459, Zip 78715–0459; tel. 512/444–4835; Kay Peck, Chief Executive Officer

CYPRESS CREEK HOSPITAL (O, 80 beds) 17750 Cali Drive, Houston, TX Zip 77090–2700; tel. 713/586–7600; Terry Scovill, Administrator
Web address: www.brownschools.com

WEST OAKS HOSPITAL (O, 144 beds) 6500 Hornwood Drive, Houston, TX Zip 77074–5095; tel. 713/995–0909; Terry Scovill, Chief Executive Officer

VIRGINIA: CUMBERLAND, A BROWN SCHOOLS HOSPITAL FOR CHILDREN AND ADOLESCENTS (O, 84 beds) 9407 Cumberland Road, New Kent, VA Zip 23124–2029; tel. 804/966–2242; Ernest C. Priddy III, Chief Executive Officer

Owned, leased, sponsored:	6 hospitals	568 beds
Contract–managed:	0 hospitals	0 beds
Totals:	6 hospitals	568 beds

2795: HEALTHCORP OF TENNESSEE, INC. (IO)
735 Broad Street, Chattanooga, TN Zip 37402; tel. 615/267–8406; T. Farrell Hayes, President

ALABAMA: LAKESHORE COMMUNITY HOSPITAL (C, 28 beds) 201 Mariarden Road, Dadeville, AL Zip 36853, Mailing Address: P.O. Box 248, Zip 36853–0248; tel. 256/825–7821; Mavis B. Halko, Administrator

LAKEVIEW COMMUNITY HOSPITAL (C, 74 beds) 820 West Washington Street, Eufaula, AL Zip 36027–1899; tel. 205/687–5761; Carl D. Brown, Administrator

ARKANSAS: DALLAS COUNTY HOSPITAL (O, 26 beds) 201 Clifton Street, Fordyce, AR Zip 71742–3099; tel. 501/352–3155; Greg R. McNeil, Administrator

Owned, leased, sponsored:	1 hospital	26 beds
Contract–managed:	2 hospitals	102 beds
Totals:	3 hospitals	128 beds

★2185: HEALTHEAST (NP)
559 Capitol Boulevard, 6–South, Saint Paul, MN Zip 55103–0000; tel. 651/232–2300; Timothy H. Hanson, President and Chief Executive Officer

MINNESOTA: HEALTHEAST BETHESDA REHABILITATION HOSPITAL (O, 129 beds) 559 Capitol Boulevard, Saint Paul, MN Zip 55103–2101; tel. 651/232–2000; Scott Batulis, Vice President and Administrator
Web address: www.healtheast.org

HEALTHEAST ST. JOHN'S HOSPITAL (O, 150 beds) 1575 Beam Avenue, Maplewood, MN Zip 55109; tel. 651/232–7000; Douglas P. Cropper, Vice President and Administrator
Web address: www.healtheast.org

HEALTHEAST ST. JOSEPH'S HOSPITAL (O, 292 beds) 69 West Exchange Street, Saint Paul, MN Zip 55102–1053; tel. 651/232–3000; Douglas P. Cropper, Vice President and Administrator
Web address: www.healtheast.org

Owned, leased, sponsored:	3 hospitals	571 beds
Contract–managed:	0 hospitals	0 beds
Totals:	3 hospitals	571 beds

0023: HEALTHSOUTH CORPORATION (IO)
One Healthsouth Parkway, Birmingham, AL Zip 35243; tel. 205/967–7116; Anthony J. Tanner, Executive Vice President

ALABAMA: HEALTHSOUTH LAKESHORE REHABILITATION HOSPITAL (O, 100 beds) 3800 Ridgeway Drive, Birmingham, AL Zip 35209–5599;

tel. 205/868–2000; Terry Brown, Administrator and Chief Executive Officer

HEALTHSOUTH MEDICAL CENTER (O, 181 beds) 1201 11th Avenue South, Birmingham, AL Zip 35205–5299; tel. 205/930–7000; Luke Standeffer, Chief Operating Officer

HEALTHSOUTH REHABILITATION HOSPITAL OF MONTGOMERY (O, 87 beds) 4465 Narrow Lane Road, Montgomery, AL Zip 36116–2900; tel. 334/284–7700; Linda Wade, Administrator and Director of Operations

HEALTHSOUTH REHABILITATION HOSPITAL OF NORTH ALABAMA (O, 59 beds) 107 Governors Drive S.W., Huntsville, AL Zip 35801–4329; tel. 205/535–2300; Rod Moss, Chief Executive Officer

ARIZONA: HEALTHSOUTH MERIDIAN POINT REHABILITATION HOSPITAL (O, 43 beds) 11250 North 92nd Street, Scottsdale, AZ Zip 85260–6148; tel. 602/860–0671; Denise Kann, Administrator and Chief Operating Officer

HEALTHSOUTH REHABILITATION INSTITUTE OF TUCSON (O, 80 beds) 2650 North Wyatt Drive, Tucson, AZ Zip 85712–6108; tel. 520/325–1300; Jason Roeback, Chief Executive Officer

HEALTHSOUTH VALLEY OF THE SUN REHABILITATION HOSPITAL (O, 42 beds) 13460 North 67th Avenue, Glendale, AZ Zip 85304–1042; tel. 602/878–8800

ARKANSAS: HEALTHSOUTH REHABILITATION HOSPITAL (O, 60 beds) 153 East Monte Painter Drive, Fayetteville, AR Zip 72703–4002; tel. 501/444–2200; Dennis R. Shelby, Chief Executive Officer

HEALTHSOUTH REHABILITATION HOSPITAL OF FORT SMITH (O, 80 beds) 1401 South J Street, Fort Smith, AR Zip 72901–5155; tel. 501/785–3300; Claudia A. Eisenmann, Director Operations

HEALTHSOUTH REHABILITATION HOSPITAL OF JONESBORO (O, 60 beds) 1201 Fleming Avenue, Jonesboro, AR Zip 72401–4311, Mailing Address: P.O. Box 1680, Zip 72403–1680; tel. 870/932–0440; Brenda Antwine, Administrator

ST. VINCENT REHABILITATION HOSPITAL (S, 60 beds) 2201 Wildwood Avenue, Sherwood, AR Zip 72120–5074, Mailing Address: P.O. Box 6930, Zip 72124–6930; tel. 501/834–1800; Ronnie Sairls, Administrator

CALIFORNIA: HEALTHSOUTH BAKERSFIELD REHABILITATION HOSPITAL (O, 60 beds) 5001 Commerce Drive, Bakersfield, CA Zip 93309; tel. 661/323–5500; Robyn Field, Ph.D., Chief Operating Officer

FLORIDA: HEALTHSOUTH DOCTORS' HOSPITAL (O, 157 beds) 5000 University Drive, Coral Gables, FL Zip 33146–2094; tel. 305/666–2111; Lincoln S. Mendez, Chief Executive Officer
Web address: www.healthsouth.com

HEALTHSOUTH REHABILITATION HOSPITAL (O, 60 beds) 901 North Clearwater–Largo Road, Largo, FL Zip 33770; tel. 727/586–2999; Elaine O. Ebaugh, Chief Executive Officer

HEALTHSOUTH REHABILITATION HOSPITAL (O, 45 beds) 20601 Old Cutler Road, Miami, FL Zip 33189–2400; tel. 305/251–3800; Nelson Lazo, Chief Executive Officer

HEALTHSOUTH REHABILITATION HOSPITAL OF SARASOTA (O, 60 beds) 3251 Proctor Road, Sarasota, FL Zip 34231–8538; tel. 941/921–8600; Jeff Garber, Administrator and Chief Executive Officer

HEALTHSOUTH REHABILITATION HOSPITAL OF TALLAHASSEE (O, 70 beds) 1675 Riggins Road, Tallahassee, FL Zip 32308–5315; tel. 850/656–4800; Armando Colombo, Chief Executive Officer

HEALTHSOUTH SEA PINES REHABILITATION HOSPITAL (O, 80 beds) 101 East Florida Avenue, Melbourne, FL Zip 32901–9966; tel. 407/984–4600; Henry J. Cranston, Chief Executive Officer

HEALTHSOUTH SUNRISE REHABILITATION HOSPITAL (O, 108 beds) 4399 Nob Hill Road, Fort Lauderdale, FL Zip 33351–5899; tel. 954/749–0300; Kevin R. Conn, Administrator

HEALTHSOUTH TREASURE COAST REHABILITATION HOSPITAL (O, 70 beds) 1600 37th Street, Vero Beach, FL Zip 32960–6549; tel. 561/778–2100; Denise B. McGrath, Chief Executive Officer

GEORGIA: HEALTHSOUTH CENTRAL GEORGIA REHABILITATION HOSPITAL (O, 50 beds) 3351 Northside Drive, Macon, GA Zip 31210–2591; tel. 912/471–3536; Elbert T. McQueen, Chief Executive Officer

---

For explanation of codes following names, see page B2.
★ Indicates Type III membership in the American Hospital Association.

INDIANA: HEALTHSOUTH TRI–STATE REHABILITATION HOSPITAL (O, 80 beds) 4100 Covert Avenue, Evansville, IN 47714–5567, Mailing Address: P.O. Box 5349, Zip 47716–5349; tel. 812/476–9983; Gerald F. Vozel, Administrator and Chief Executive Officer

HEALTHSOUTH REHABILITATION HOSPITAL OF KOKOMO (O, 60 beds) 829 North Dixon Road, Kokomo, IN Zip 46901–7709; tel. 765/452–6700; David Bailey, Chief Executive Officer

KANSAS: MID–AMERICA REHABILITATION HOSPITAL (O, 80 beds) 5701 West 110th Street, Overland Park, KS Zip 66211; tel. 913/491–2400; Mark J. Stepanik, Interim Chief Executive Officer

WESLEY REHABILITATION HOSPITAL (O, 50 beds) 8338 West 13th Street North, Wichita, KS Zip 67212–2984; tel. 316/729–9999; Lisa James, Chief Operating Officer

KENTUCKY: HEALTHSOUTH NORTHERN KENTUCKY REHABILITATION HOSPITAL (O, 40 beds) 201 Medical Village Drive, Covington, KY Zip 41017–3407; tel. 606/341–2044; Timothy W. Mitchell, Chief Executive Officer

HEALTHSOUTH REHABILITATION HOSPITAL OF CENTRAL KENTUCKY (O, 40 beds) 134 Heartland Drive, Elizabethtown, KY Zip 42701–2778; tel. 502/769–3100; Teresa K. Stranko, Chief Executive Officer

LOUISIANA: HEALTHSOUTH NORTH LOUISIANA REHABILITATION HOSPITAL (O, 90 beds) 1401 Ezell Street, Ruston, LA Zip 71270–7221, Mailing Address: P.O. Box 490, Zip 71273–0490; tel. 318/251–5354; Mark Rice, Chief Executive Officer

HEALTHSOUTH REHABILITATION HOSPITAL OF BATON ROUGE (O, 80 beds) 8595 United Plaza Boulevard, Baton Rouge, LA Zip 70809–2251; tel. 225/927–0567; Michael D. Marshall, Chief Executive Officer

HEALTHSOUTH REHABILITATION HOSPITAL OF SOUTH LOUISIANA (O, 40 beds) 4040 North Boulevard, Baton Rouge, LA Zip 70806–3829; tel. 504/383–5055; Michael D. Marshall, Chief Executive Officer

MAINE: NEW ENGLAND REHABILITATION HOSPITAL OF PORTLAND (O, 76 beds) 335 Brighton Avenue, Portland, ME Zip 04102; tel. 207/775–4000; Amy Morse, Chief Executive Officer

MARYLAND: HEALTHSOUTH CHESAPEAKE REHABILITATION HOSPITAL (O, 42 beds) 220 Tilghman Road, Salisbury, MD Zip 21804–1921; tel. 410/546–4600; William Roth, Chief Executive Officer

MASSACHUSETTS: FAIRLAWN REHABILITATION HOSPITAL (O, 110 beds) 189 May Street, Worcester, MA Zip 01602–4399; tel. 508/791–6351; Peter M. Mantegazza, President and Chief Executive Officer

HEALTHSOUTH BRAINTREE REHABILITATION HOSPITAL (O, 187 beds) 250 Pond Street, Braintree, MA Zip 02185–5391; tel. 781/848–5353; Anne M. MacRitchie, President and Chief Executive Officer

HEALTHSOUTH NEW ENGLAND REHABILITATION HOSPITAL (O, 198 beds) Two Rehabilitation Way, Woburn, MA Zip 01801–6098; tel. 781/935–5050; Mary Moscato, Chief Executive Officer

HEALTHSOUTH REHABILITATION HOSPITAL OF WESTERN MASSACHUSETTS (O, 40 beds) 14 Chestnut Place, Ludlow, MA Zip 01056–3460; tel. 413/589–7581; R. David Richer, Administrator

NEW HAMPSHIRE: HEALTHSOUTH REHABILITATION HOSPITAL (O, 50 beds) 254 Pleasant Street, Concord, NH Zip 03301–2508; tel. 603/226–9800; Lori Manor, Administrator

NEW JERSEY: HEALTHSOUTH REHABILITATION HOSPITAL OF NEW JERSEY (O, 155 beds) 14 Hospital Drive, Toms River, NJ Zip 08755–6470; tel. 732/244–3100; Patricia Ostaszewski, Chief Executive Officer and Administrator

NEW MEXICO: HEALTHSOUTH REHABILITATION CENTER (O, 60 beds) 7000 Jefferson N.E., Albuquerque, NM Zip 87109–4357; tel. 505/344–9478; Darby Brockette, Administrator

OKLAHOMA: HEALTHSOUTH REHABILITATION HOSPITAL (O, 46 beds) 700 N.W. Seventh Street, Oklahoma City, OK Zip 73102–1295; tel. 405/553–1192; Hank Ross, Chief Executive Officer

PENNSYLVANIA: HEALTHSOUTH GREATER PITTSBURGH REHABILITATION HOSPITAL (O, 89 beds) 2380 McGinley Road, Monroeville, PA Zip 15146–4400; tel. 412/856–2400; Faith A. Deigan, Administrator and Chief Executive Officer
Web address: www.healthsouth.com

HEALTHSOUTH HARMARVILLE REHABILITATION HOSPITAL (O, 202 beds) Guys Run Road, Pittsburgh, PA Zip 15238–0460, Mailing Address: Box 11460,

Guys Run Road, Zip 15238–0460; tel. 412/781–5700; Frank G. DeLisi III, CHE, Chief Executive Officer and Director Operations

HEALTHSOUTH LAKE ERIE INSTITUTE OF REHABILITATION (O, 99 beds) 137 West Second Street, Erie, PA Zip 16507–1403; tel. 814/453–5602; Louis M. Condrasky, Chief Executive Officer

HEALTHSOUTH NITTANY VALLEY REHABILITATION HOSPITAL (O, 88 beds) 550 West College Avenue, Pleasant Gap, PA Zip 16823–8808; tel. 814/359–3421; Mary Jane Hawkins, Administrator and Chief Executive Officer

HEALTHSOUTH READING REHABILITATION HOSPITAL (O, 95 beds) 1623 Morgantown Road, Reading, PA Zip 19607–9455; tel. 610/796–6000; Tammy L. Ober, Administrator and Chief Executive Officer
Web address: www.rdgrehab.com

HEALTHSOUTH REHABILITATION HOSPITAL OF ALTOONA (O, 70 beds) 2005 Valley View Boulevard, Altoona, PA Zip 16602–4598; tel. 814/944–3535; Scott Filler, Administrator

HEALTHSOUTH REHABILITATION HOSPITAL OF ERIE (O, 108 beds) 143 East Second Street, Erie, PA Zip 16507–1595; tel. 814/878–1200; Louis M. Condrasky, Chief Executive Officer

HEALTHSOUTH REHABILITATION HOSPITAL OF YORK (O, 88 beds) 1850 Normandie Drive, York, PA Zip 17404–1534; tel. 717/767–6941; Cheryl Fleming, Chief Executive Officer

HEALTHSOUTH REHABILITATION OF MECHANICSBURG (O, 103 beds) 175 Lancaster Boulevard, Mechanicsburg, PA Zip 17055–0736, Mailing Address: P.O. Box 2016, Zip 17055–2016; tel. 717/691–3700; Melissa Kutz, Administrator and Chief Executive Officer

SOUTH CAROLINA: HEALTHSOUTH REHABILITATION HOSPITAL (O, 87 beds) 2935 Colonial Drive, Columbia, SC Zip 29203–6811; tel. 803/254–7777; Debbie W. Johnston, Director Operations

HEALTHSOUTH REHABILITATION HOSPITAL (O, 88 beds) 900 East Cheves Street, Florence, SC Zip 29506–2704; tel. 843/679–9000; Dennis A. Lofe, FACHE, Chief Executive Officer

TENNESSEE: HEALTHSOUTH CHATTANOOGA REHABILITATION HOSPITAL (O, 69 beds) 2412 McCallie Avenue, Chattanooga, TN Zip 37404–3398; tel. 423/698–0221; Susan Heath, Chief Executive Officer
Web address: www.healthsouth.com

HEALTHSOUTH REHABILITATION HOSPITAL (O, 50 beds) 113 Cassel Drive, Kingsport, TN Zip 37660–3775; tel. 423/246–7240; Terry R. Maxhimer, Regional Vice President

HEALTHSOUTH REHABILITATION HOSPITAL (O, 80 beds) 1282 Union Avenue, Memphis, TN Zip 38104–3414; tel. 901/722–2000; Jerry Gray, Administrator

TEXAS: HEALTHSOUTH HOUSTON REHABILITATION INSTITUTE (O, 80 beds) 17506 Red Oak Drive, Houston, TX Zip 77090–7721, Mailing Address: P.O. Box 73684, Zip 77273–3684; tel. 281/580–1212; Anne R. Leon, Chief Executive Officer

HEALTHSOUTH MEDICAL CENTER (O, 106 beds) 2124 Research Row, Dallas, TX Zip 75235–2504; tel. 214/904–6100; Robert M. Smart, Area Manager and Chief Executive Officer

HEALTHSOUTH PLANO REHABILITATION HOSPITAL (O, 62 beds) 2800 West 15th Street, Plano, TX Zip 75075–7526; tel. 972/612–9000; Tracy Nixon, Chief Executive Officer

HEALTHSOUTH REHABILITATION HOSPITAL (O, 60 beds) 19002 McKay Drive, Humble, TX Zip 77338–5701; tel. 281/446–6148; Darrell L. Pile, Administrator

HEALTHSOUTH REHABILITATION HOSPITAL OF ARLINGTON (O, 60 beds) 3200 Matlock Road, Arlington, TX Zip 76015–2911; tel. 817/468–4000; S. Denise Borroni, Administrator and Chief Executive Officer

HEALTHSOUTH REHABILITATION HOSPITAL OF AUSTIN (O, 80 beds) 1215 Red River Street, Austin, TX Zip 78701, Mailing Address: P.O. Box 13366, Zip 78711–3366; tel. 512/474–5700; William O. Mitchell Jr., Chief Executive Officer

HEALTHSOUTH REHABILITATION HOSPITAL OF BEAUMONT (O, 61 beds) 3340 Plaza 10 Boulevard, Beaumont, TX Zip 77707; tel. 409/835–0835; Michael Hagen, Administrator

For explanation of codes following names, see page B2.
★ Indicates Type III membership in the American Hospital Association.

HEALTHSOUTH REHABILITATION HOSPITAL OF FORT WORTH (O, 60 beds) 1212 West Lancaster Avenue, Fort Worth, TX Zip 76102–4510; tel. 817/870–2336; S. Denise Borroni, Administrator and Chief Executive Officer
Web address: www.healthsouth.com

HEALTHSOUTH REHABILITATION HOSPITAL OF TEXARKANA (O, 60 beds) 515 West 12th Street, Texarkana, TX Zip 75501–4416; tel. 903/793–0088; Jeffrey A. Livingston, Chief Executive Officer

HEALTHSOUTH REHABILITATION HOSPITAL–CITYVIEW (O, 62 beds) 6701 Oakmont Boulevard, Fort Worth, TX Zip 76132–2957; tel. 817/370–4700; S. Denise Borroni, Administrator and Chief Executive Officer

HEALTHSOUTH REHABILITATION HOSPITAL–TYLER (O, 63 beds) 3131 Troup Highway, Tyler, TX Zip 75701–8352; tel. 903/510–7000; Sharla Anderson, Interim Chief Executive Officer

HEALTHSOUTH REHABILITATION INSTITUTE OF SAN ANTONIO (O, 108 beds) 9119 Cinnamon Hill, San Antonio, TX Zip 78240–5401; tel. 210/691–0737; Diane B. Lampe, Administrator and Chief Executive Officer

UTAH: HEALTHSOUTH REHABILITATION HOSPITAL OF UTAH (O, 58 beds) 8074 South 1300 East, Sandy, UT Zip 84094–0743; tel. 801/561–3400; Richard M. Richards, Administrator

VIRGINIA: HEALTHSOUTH MEDICAL CENTER (O, 147 beds) 7700 East Parham Road, Richmond, VA Zip 23294–4301; tel. 804/747–5600; Charles A. Stark, CHE, Administrator, Chief Executive Officer and Regional Vice President
Web address: www.healthsouth–richmond.com

HEALTHSOUTH REHABILITATION HOSPITAL OF VIRGINIA (O, 40 beds) 5700 Fitzhugh Avenue, Richmond, VA Zip 23226–1800; tel. 804/288–5700; Jeff Ruskan, Administrator

WEST VIRGINIA: HEALTHSOUTH HUNTINGTON REHABILITATION HOSPITAL (O, 40 beds) 6900 West Country Club Drive, Huntington, WV Zip 25705–2000; tel. 304/733–1060; John Forester, Chief Operating Officer

HEALTHSOUTH SOUTHERN HILLS REHABILITATION HOSPITAL (O, 46 beds) 120 Twelfth Street, Princeton, WV Zip 24740–2312; tel. 304/487–8000; Ken Howell, Administrator
Web address: www.healthsouth.com

HEALTHSOUTH WESTERN HILLS REGIONAL REHABILITATION HOSPITAL (O, 40 beds) 3 Western Hills Drive, Parkersburg, WV Zip 26101–8122, Mailing Address: P.O. Box 1428, Zip 26102–1428; tel. 304/420–1300; Thomas Heller, Administrator

HEALTHSOUTH MOUNTAINVIEW REGIONAL REHABILITATION HOSPITAL (O, 80 beds) 1160 Van Voorhis Road, Morgantown, WV Zip 26505–3435; tel. 304/598–1100; Sharon Noro, Chief Executive Officer
Web address: www.healthsouth.com

Owned, leased, sponsored:	73 hospitals	5765 beds
Contract–managed:	0 hospitals	0 beds
Totals:	73 hospitals	5765 beds

1985: HEALTHSYSTEM MINNESOTA (NP)
6500 Excelsior Boulevard, Saint Louis Park, MN Zip 55426–4702; tel. 612/993–5000; David Wessner, President and Chief Executive Officer

MINNESOTA: GLENCOE AREA HEALTH CENTER (C, 149 beds) 705 East 18th Street, Glencoe, MN Zip 55336–1499; tel. 320/864–3121; Jon D. Braband, Chief Executive Officer

METHODIST HOSPITAL HEALTHSYSTEM MINNESOTA (O, 367 beds) 6500 Excelsior Boulevard, Saint Louis Park, MN Zip 55426–4702, Mailing Address: Box 650, Minneapolis, Zip 55440–0650; tel. 612/993–5000; Mark Skubic, Vice President

Owned, leased, sponsored:	1 hospital	367 beds
Contract–managed:	1 hospital	149 beds
Totals:	2 hospitals	516 beds

★9505: HENRY FORD HEALTH SYSTEM (NP)
One Ford Place, Detroit, MI Zip 48202–3067; tel. 313/876–8715; Gail L. Warden, President and Chief Executive Officer

MICHIGAN: BI–COUNTY COMMUNITY HOSPITAL (O, 149 beds) 13355 East Ten Mile Road, Warren, MI Zip 48089–2065; tel. 810/759–7300; Gary W. Popiel, Executive Vice President and Chief Executive Officer

HENRY FORD HOSPITAL (O, 634 beds) 2799 West Grand Boulevard, Detroit, MI Zip 48202–2689; tel. 313/916–2600; Stephen H. Velick, Chief Executive Officer
Web address: www.henryfordhealth.org

HENRY FORD WYANDOTTE HOSPITAL (O, 355 beds) 2333 Biddle Avenue, Wyandotte, MI Zip 48192–4693; tel. 734/284–2400; William R. Alvin, President
Web address: www.henryfordhealth.org

KINGSWOOD HOSPITAL (O, 64 beds) 10300 West Eight Mile Road, Ferndale, MI Zip 48220–2198; tel. 248/398–3200; Glenn Black, Associate Vice President and Chief Operating Officer

RIVERSIDE OSTEOPATHIC HOSPITAL (O, 148 beds) 150 Truax Street, Trenton, MI Zip 48183–2151; tel. 734/676–4200; Dennis R. Lemanski, D.O., Vice President and Chief Executive Officer

Owned, leased, sponsored:	5 hospitals	1350 beds
Contract–managed:	0 hospitals	0 beds
Totals:	5 hospitals	1350 beds

★0130: HILLCREST HEALTHCARE SYSTEM (NP)
1120 South Utica, Tulsa, OK Zip 74104–4090; tel. 918/579–1000; Donald A. Lorack Jr., President and Chief Executive Officer

OKLAHOMA: BRISTOW MEMORIAL HOSPITAL (O, 16 beds) Seventh and Spruce Streets, Bristow, OK Zip 74010, Mailing Address: P.O. Box 780, Zip 74010–0780; tel. 918/367–2215; William L. Legate, Administrator

CHILDREN'S MEDICAL CENTER (C, 90 beds) 5300 East Skelly Drive, Tulsa, OK Zip 74135–6599, Mailing Address: P.O. Box 35648, Zip 74153–0648; tel. 918/664–6600; Donald A. Lorack Jr., President and Chief Executive Officer

CLEVELAND AREA HOSPITAL (L, 17 beds) 1401 West Pawnee Street, Cleveland, OK Zip 74020–3019; tel. 918/358–2501; Thomas Henton, President and Chief Executive Officer

DOCTORS HOSPITAL (O, 121 beds) 2323 South Harvard Avenue, Tulsa, OK Zip 74114–3370; tel. 918/744–4000; Kenneth Noteboom, Chief Executive Officer
Web address: www.columbia.net

FAIRFAX MEMORIAL HOSPITAL (L, 21 beds) Taft Avenue and Highway 18, Fairfax, OK Zip 74637, Mailing Address: P.O. Box 219, Zip 74637–0219; tel. 918/642–3291; Annabeth Murray, Administrator

HILLCREST MEDICAL CENTER (C, 439 beds) 1120 South Utica, Tulsa, OK Zip 74104–4090; tel. 918/579–1000; Donald A. Lorack Jr., President and Chief Executive Officer
Web address: www.hillcrest.com

HILLCREST SPECIALTY HOSPITAL (O, 45 beds) 2408 East 81st Street, 2500, Tulsa, OK Zip 74137–4210; tel. 918/491–2400; Kenneth Noteboom, Chief Executive Officer
Web address: www.columbia.net

HURLEY HEALTH CENTER (C, 95 beds) 6 North Covington Street, Coalgate, OK Zip 74538–2002, Mailing Address: P.O. Box 326, Zip 74538; tel. 580/927–2327; Dan A. Clements, Chief Executive Officer

PRAGUE MUNICIPAL HOSPITAL (O, 19 beds) 1322 Klabzuba Avenue, Prague, OK Zip 74864, Mailing Address: P.O. Drawer S, Zip 74864; tel. 405/567–4922; Chris Mattingly, Chief Executive Officer

TULSA REGIONAL MEDICAL CENTER (O, 255 beds) 744 West Ninth Street, Tulsa, OK Zip 74127–9990; tel. 918/599–5900; Steve Dobbs, Executive Vice President and Chief Executive Officer

WAGONER COMMUNITY HOSPITAL (O, 100 beds) 1200 West Cherokee, Wagoner, OK Zip 74467–4681, Mailing Address: Box 407, Zip 74477–0407; tel. 918/485–5514; John W. Crawford, Chief Executive Officer

Owned, leased, sponsored:	8 hospitals	594 beds
Contract–managed:	3 hospitals	624 beds
Totals:	11 hospitals	1218 beds

For explanation of codes following names, see page B2.
★ Indicates Type III membership in the American Hospital Association.

★5585: HOLY CROSS HEALTH SYSTEM CORPORATION (CC)
3575 Moreau Court, South Bend, IN Zip 46628–4320;
tel. 219/233–8558; Sister Patricia Vandenberg, President and Chief
Executive Officer

CALIFORNIA: SAINT AGNES MEDICAL CENTER (O, 326 beds) 1303 East
Herndon Avenue, Fresno, CA Zip 93720–3397; tel. 559/449–3000;
Sister Ruth Marie Nickerson, President and Chief Executive Officer
Web address: www.samc.org

IDAHO: CASCADE MEDICAL CENTER (C, 10 beds) 402 Old State Highway,
Cascade, ID Zip 83611, Mailing Address: P.O. Box 151, Zip 83611–0151;
tel. 208/382–4242; Vicki Shelly, R.N., Interim Administrator

ELMORE MEDICAL CENTER (C, 80 beds) 895 North Sixth East Street,
Mountain Home, ID Zip 83647–2207, Mailing Address: P.O. Box 1270,
Zip 83647–1270; tel. 208/587–8401; Gregory L. Maurer, Administrator

MCCALL MEMORIAL HOSPITAL (C, 15 beds) 1000 State Street, McCall, ID
Zip 83638, Mailing Address: P.O. Box 906, Zip 83638–0906;
tel. 208/634–2221; Karen J. Kellie, President

SAINT ALPHONSUS REGIONAL MEDICAL CENTER (O, 287 beds) 1055 North
Curtis Road, Boise, ID Zip 83706–1370; tel. 208/378–2121; Sandra B.
Bruce, President and Chief Executive Officer

ST. BENEDICTS FAMILY MEDICAL CENTER (C, 65 beds) 709 North Lincoln
Avenue, Jerome, ID Zip 83338–1851, Mailing Address: P.O. Box 586,
Zip 83338–0586; tel. 208/324–4301; Lynne M. Mattison, FACHE, Interim
Administrator

INDIANA: SAINT JOHN'S HEALTH SYSTEM (O, 267 beds) 2015 Jackson
Street, Anderson, IN Zip 46016–4339; tel. 765/649–2511; Jerry D.
Brumitt, President and Chief Executive Officer
Web address: www.stjohnshealthsystem.org

SAINT JOSEPH'S REGIONAL MEDICAL CENTER–PLYMOUTH CAMPUS (O, 36
beds) 1915 Lake Avenue, Plymouth, IN Zip 46563–9905, Mailing Address:
P.O. Box 670, Zip 46563–9905; tel. 219/936–3181; Brian E. Dietz, FACHE,
Executive Vice President
Web address: www.sjrmc.com

SAINT JOSEPH'S REGIONAL MEDICAL CENTER–SOUTH BEND CAMPUS (O,
310 beds) 801 East LaSalle, South Bend, IN Zip 46617–2800;
tel. 219/237–7111; Robert L. Beyer, President and Chief Executive Officer
Web address: www.sjmed.com

MARYLAND: HOLY CROSS HOSPITAL OF SILVER SPRING (O, 454 beds) 1500
Forest Glen Road, Silver Spring, MD Zip 20910–1484;
tel. 301/754–7000; Kevin J. Sexton, President and Chief Executive Officer

OHIO: MOUNT CARMEL HEALTH SYSTEM (O, 1036 beds) Columbus, OH
Mailing Address: 793 West State Street, Zip 43222–1551;
tel. 614/234–5423; Joseph Calvaruso, Chief Executive Officer
Web address: www.mchs.com

Owned, leased, sponsored:	7 hospitals	2716 beds
Contract–managed:	4 hospitals	170 beds
Totals:	11 hospitals	2886 beds

★0027: HORIZON HEALTHCARE, INC. (NP)
2300 North Mayfair Road, Suite 550, Milwaukee, WI
Zip 53226–1508; tel. 414/257–3888; Sister Renee Rose, President
and Chief Executive Officer

WISCONSIN: COLUMBIA HOSPITAL (C, 334 beds) 2025 East Newport
Avenue, Milwaukee, WI Zip 53211–2990; tel. 414/961–3300; Susan
Henckel, Executive Vice President and Chief Executive Officer

COMMUNITY MEMORIAL HOSPITAL (C, 153 beds) W180 N8085 Town Hall
Road, Menomonee Falls, WI Zip 53051, Mailing Address: P.O. Box 408,
Zip 53052–0408; tel. 414/251–1000; Robert Eugene Drisner, President and
Chief Executive Officer
Web address: www.communitymemorial.com

FROEDTERT MEMORIAL LUTHERAN HOSPITAL (C, 467 beds) 9200 West
Wisconsin Avenue, Milwaukee, WI Zip 53226–3596, Mailing Address: P.O.
Box 26099, Zip 53226–3596; tel. 414/259–3000; William D. Petasnick,
President

KENOSHA HOSPITAL AND MEDICAL CENTER (C, 116 beds) 6308 Eighth
Avenue, Kenosha, WI Zip 53143–5082; tel. 414/656–2011; Richard O.
Schmidt Jr., President and Chief Executive Officer

Owned, leased, sponsored:	0 hospitals	0 beds
Contract–managed:	4 hospitals	1070 beds
Totals:	4 hospitals	1070 beds

0455: HOSPITAL GROUP OF AMERICA (IO)
1265 Drummers Lane, Suite 107, Wayne, PA Zip 19087;
tel. 610/687–5151; Mark R. Russell, President and Chief Executive
Officer

DELAWARE: MEADOW WOOD BEHAVIORAL HEALTH SYSTEM (O, 50 beds)
575 South Dupont Highway, New Castle, DE Zip 19720–4600;
tel. 302/328–3330; Joseph Pyle, Administrator

ILLINOIS: HARTGROVE HOSPITAL (O, 119 beds) 520 North Ridgeway Avenue,
Chicago, IL Zip 60624–1299; tel. 773/722–3113; Suzanne Barry,
Administrator and Chief Operating Officer

NEW JERSEY: HAMPTON HOSPITAL (O, 83 beds) Rancocas Road,
Westampton Township, NJ Zip 08073, Mailing Address: P.O. Box 7000,
Zip 08073; tel. 609/267–7000; Joanne Wilson, Chief Executive Officer

Owned, leased, sponsored:	3 hospitals	252 beds
Contract–managed:	0 hospitals	0 beds
Totals:	3 hospitals	252 beds

★5355: HOSPITAL SISTERS HEALTH SYSTEM (CC)
Springfield, IL Mailing Address: P.O. Box 19431, Zip 62794–9431;
tel. 217/523–4747; Sister Jomary Trstensky, President

ILLINOIS: ST. ANTHONY'S MEMORIAL HOSPITAL (O, 146 beds) 503 North
Maple Street, Effingham, IL Zip 62401–2099; tel. 217/347–1495;
Anthony D. Pfitzer, Executive Vice President and Administrator
Web address: www.effingham.net

ST. ELIZABETH'S HOSPITAL (O, 319 beds) 211 South Third Street, Belleville,
IL Zip 62222–0694; tel. 618/234–2120; Gerald M. Harman, Executive Vice
President and Administrator
Web address: www.apci.net/~ste

ST. FRANCIS HOSPITAL (O, 97 beds) 1215 Franciscan Drive, Litchfield, IL
Zip 62056, Mailing Address: P.O. Box 1215, Zip 62056–1215;
tel. 217/324–2191; Michael Sipkoski, Executive Vice President and
Administrator

ST. JOHN'S HOSPITAL (O, 579 beds) 800 East Carpenter Street, Springfield,
IL Zip 62769–0002; tel. 217/544–6464; Allison C. Laabs, Executive Vice
President and Administrator

ST. JOSEPH'S HOSPITAL (O, 57 beds) 9515 Holy Cross Lane, Breese, IL
Zip 62230–0099; tel. 618/526–4511; Jacolyn M. Schlautman, Executive
Vice President and Administrator

ST. JOSEPH'S HOSPITAL (O, 76 beds) 1515 Main Street, Highland, IL
Zip 62249–1656; tel. 618/654–7421; Anthony G. Mastrangelo, Executive
Vice President and Administrator
Web address: www.stjosephs–highland.org

ST. MARY'S HOSPITAL (O, 176 beds) 1800 East Lake Shore Drive, Decatur,
IL Zip 62521–3883; tel. 217/464–2966; Keith L. Callahan, Executive
President and Administrator

ST. MARY'S HOSPITAL (O, 170 beds) 111 East Spring Street, Streator, IL
Zip 61364–3399; tel. 815/673–2311; James F. Dover, Executive Vice
President and Administrator
Web address: www.ortelco.com/~stmaryl

WISCONSIN: SACRED HEART HOSPITAL (O, 261 beds) 900 West Clairemont
Avenue, Eau Claire, WI Zip 54701–5105; tel. 715/839–4121; Stephen F.
Ronstrom, Executive Vice President and Administrator
Web address: www.sacredhearthospital–ec.org

ST. JOSEPH'S HOSPITAL (O, 127 beds) 2661 County Highway I, Chippewa
Falls, WI Zip 54729–1498; tel. 715/723–1811; David B. Fish, Executive Vice
President and Administrator

ST. MARY'S HOSPITAL MEDICAL CENTER (O, 119 beds) 1726 Shawano
Avenue, Green Bay, WI Zip 54303–3282; tel. 920/498–4200; James G.
Coller, Executive Vice President and Administrator
Web address: www.stmgb.org

For explanation of codes following names, see page B2.
★ Indicates Type III membership in the American Hospital Association.

ST. NICHOLAS HOSPITAL (O, 185 beds) 1601 North Taylor Drive, Sheboygan, WI Zip 53081–2496; tel. 920/459–8300; Michael J. Stenger, Executive Vice President and Administrator
Web address: www.stnicholashospital.org

ST. VINCENT HOSPITAL (O, 353 beds) 835 South Van Buren Street, Green Bay, WI Zip 54307–3508, Mailing Address: P.O. Box 13508, Zip 54307–3508; tel. 920/433–0111; Joseph J. Neidenbach, Executive Vice President and Administrator
Web address: www.stvgb.org

Owned, leased, sponsored:	13 hospitals	2665 beds
Contract–managed:	0 hospitals	0 beds
Totals:	13 hospitals	2665 beds

2025: INFIRMARY HEALTH SYSTEM, INC. (NP)
3 Mobile Infirmary Circle, Mobile, AL Zip 36607–3520; tel. 334/435–5500; E. Chandler Bramlett Jr., President and Chief Executive Officer

ALABAMA: GROVE HILL MEMORIAL HOSPITAL (C, 41 beds) 295 South Jackson Street, Grove Hill, AL Zip 36451, Mailing Address: P.O. Box 935, Zip 36451; tel. 334/275–3191; Floyd N. Price, Administrator

MOBILE INFIRMARY MEDICAL CENTER (O, 489 beds) 5 Mobile Infirmary Drive North, Mobile, AL Zip 36601, Mailing Address: P.O. Box 2144, Zip 36652–2144; tel. 334/435–2400; E. Chandler Bramlett Jr., President and Chief Executive Officer
Web address: www.mimc.com

THOMASVILLE INFIRMARY (O, 27 beds) 1440 Highway 43 North, Thomasville, AL Zip 36784–3302; tel. 334/636–4431; Albert Ban Jr., Administrator

WASHINGTON COUNTY INFIRMARY AND NURSING HOME (C, 88 beds) St. Stephens Avenue, Chatom, AL Zip 36518, Mailing Address: P.O. Box 597, Zip 36518–0597; tel. 334/847–2223; John S. Eads, Administrator

Owned, leased, sponsored:	2 hospitals	516 beds
Contract–managed:	2 hospitals	129 beds
Totals:	4 hospitals	645 beds

★1305: INOVA HEALTH SYSTEM (NP)
8110 Gatehouse Road, Falls Church, VA Zip 22042; tel. 703/289–2069; J. Knox Singleton, President and Chief Executive Officer

VIRGINIA: INOVA ALEXANDRIA HOSPITAL (O, 316 beds) 4320 Seminary Road, Alexandria, VA Zip 22304–1594; tel. 703/504–3000; H. Patrick Walters, Administrator
Web address: www.inova.com

INOVA FAIR OAKS HOSPITAL (O, 133 beds) 3600 Joseph Siewick Drive, Fairfax, VA Zip 22033–1709; tel. 703/391–3600; William A. Brown, Vice President and Administrator

INOVA FAIRFAX HOSPITAL (O, 656 beds) 3300 Gallows Road, Falls Church, VA Zip 22042–3300; tel. 703/698–1110; Steven E. Brown, Administrator
Web address: www.inova.com

INOVA MOUNT VERNON HOSPITAL (O, 229 beds) 2501 Parker's Lane, Alexandria, VA Zip 22306–3209; tel. 703/664–7000; Susan Herbert, Administrator
Web address: www.inova.com

Owned, leased, sponsored:	4 hospitals	1334 beds
Contract–managed:	0 hospitals	0 beds
Totals:	4 hospitals	1334 beds

★0305: INTEGRIS HEALTH (NP)
3366 N.W. Expressway, Suite 800, Oklahoma City, OK Zip 73112–9756; tel. 405/949–6068; Stanley F. Hupfeld, President and Chief Executive Officer

OKLAHOMA: BLACKWELL REGIONAL HOSPITAL (L, 34 beds) 710 South 13th Street, Blackwell, OK Zip 74631–3700; tel. 580/363–2311; Greg Martin, Administrator and Chief Executive Officer

DRUMRIGHT MEMORIAL HOSPITAL (L, 15 beds) 501 South Lou Allard Drive, Drumright, OK Zip 74030–4899; tel. 918/352–2525; James L. Clough, Administrator

INTEGRIS BAPTIST MEDICAL CENTER (O, 506 beds) 3300 N.W. Expressway, Oklahoma City, OK Zip 73112–4481; tel. 405/949–3011; Thomas R. Rice, FACHE, President and Chief Operating Officer
Web address: www.integris–health.com

INTEGRIS BAPTIST REGIONAL HEALTH CENTER (O, 123 beds) 200 Second Street S.W., Miami, OK Zip 74354–6830, Mailing Address: P.O. Box 1207, Zip 74355–1207; tel. 918/540–7100; Steven G. Kelly, Administrator
Web address: www.integris–health.com

INTEGRIS BASS BAPTIST HEALTH CENTER (O, 207 beds) 600 South Monroe Street, Enid, OK Zip 73701, Mailing Address: P.O. Box 3168, Zip 73702–3168; tel. 580/233–2300; William E. Mosteller Jr., Interim Administrator

INTEGRIS GROVE GENERAL HOSPITAL (O, 72 beds) 1310 South Main Street, Grove, OK Zip 74344–1310; tel. 918/786–2243; Dee Renshaw, Administrator
Web address: www.ohs.com

INTEGRIS MENTAL HEALTH SYSTEM–SPENCER (O, 44 beds) 2601 North Spencer Road, Spencer, OK Zip 73084–3699, Mailing Address: P.O. Box 11137, Oklahoma City, Zip 73136–0137; tel. 405/427–2441; Murali Krishna, M.D., President and Chief Operating Officer

INTEGRIS SOUTHWEST MEDICAL CENTER (O, 302 beds) 4401 South Western, Oklahoma City, OK Zip 73109–3441; tel. 405/636–7000; Thomas R. Rice, FACHE, President and Chief Operating Officer

INTERGRIS CLINTON REGIONAL HOSPITAL (L, 49 beds) 100 North 30th Street, Clinton, OK Zip 73601–3117, Mailing Address: P.O. Box 1569, Zip 73601–1569; tel. 580/323–2363; Jerry Jones, Administrator

MARSHALL MEMORIAL HOSPITAL (C, 25 beds) 1 Hospital Drive, Madill, OK Zip 73446, Mailing Address: P.O. Box 827, Zip 73446–0827; tel. 405/795–3384; Norma Howard, Administrator

MAYES COUNTY MEDICAL CENTER (L, 34 beds) 129 North Kentucky Street, Pryor, OK Zip 74361–4211, Mailing Address: P.O. Box 278, Zip 74362–0278; tel. 918/825–1600; W. Charles Jordan, Administrator

PAWNEE MUNICIPAL HOSPITAL (L, 32 beds) 1212 Fourth Street, Pawnee, OK Zip 74058–4046, Mailing Address: P.O. Box 467, Zip 74058–0467; tel. 918/762–2577; John Ketring, Administrator

Owned, leased, sponsored:	11 hospitals	1418 beds
Contract–managed:	1 hospital	25 beds
Totals:	12 hospitals	1443 beds

★1815: INTERMOUNTAIN HEALTH CARE, INC. (NP)
36 South State Street, 22nd Floor, Salt Lake City, UT Zip 84111–1453; tel. 801/442–2000; William H. Nelson, President and Chief Executive Officer

IDAHO: CASSIA REGIONAL MEDICAL CENTER (O, 87 beds) 1501 Hiland Avenue, Burley, ID Zip 83318–2675; tel. 208/678–4444; Richard Packer, Administrator

POCATELLO REGIONAL MEDICAL CENTER (O, 87 beds) 777 Hospital Way, Pocatello, ID Zip 83201–2797; tel. 208/234–0777; Earl L. Christison, Administrator
Web address: www.ihc.com

UTAH: ALTA VIEW HOSPITAL (O, 72 beds) 9660 South 1300 East, Sandy, UT Zip 84094–3793; tel. 801/501–2600; Wes Thompson, Administrator and Chief Executive Officer
Web address: www.ihc.com

AMERICAN FORK HOSPITAL (O, 72 beds) 170 North 1100 East, American Fork, UT Zip 84003–9787; tel. 801/763–3300; Keith N. Alexander, Administrator and Chief Operating Officer
Web address: www.ihc.com

BEAR RIVER VALLEY HOSPITAL (O, 58 beds) 440 West 600 North, Tremonton, UT Zip 84337–2497; tel. 435/257–7441; Robert F. Jex, Administrator

COTTONWOOD HOSPITAL MEDICAL CENTER (O, 162 beds) 5770 South 300 East, Salt Lake City, UT Zip 84107–6186; tel. 801/262–3461; Douglas R.

Section B

For explanation of codes following names, see page B2.
★ Indicates Type III membership in the American Hospital Association.

Fonnesbeck, Administrator and Chief Executive Officer
Web address: www.ihc.com

DELTA COMMUNITY MEDICAL CENTER (O, 20 beds) 126 South White Sage Avenue, Delta, UT Zip 84624–8937; tel. 435/864–5591; James E. Beckstrand, Administrator

DIXIE REGIONAL MEDICAL CENTER (O, 116 beds) 544 South 400 East, Saint George, UT Zip 84770–3799; tel. 435/688–4000; L. Steven Wilson, Administrator
Web address: www.ihc.com

FILLMORE COMMUNITY MEDICAL CENTER (O, 20 beds) 674 South Highway 99, Fillmore, UT Zip 84631–5013; tel. 435/743–5591; James E. Beckstrand, Administrator
Web address: www.ihc.com

GARFIELD MEMORIAL HOSPITAL AND CLINICS (O, 44 beds) 200 North 400 East, Panguitch, UT Zip 84759, Mailing Address: P.O. Box 389, Zip 84759–0389; tel. 435/676–8811; Eric Packer, Administrator

LDS HOSPITAL (O, 412 beds) Eighth Avenue and C Street, Salt Lake City, UT Zip 84143–0001; tel. 801/408–1100; Richard M. Cagen, Chief Executive Officer and Administrator
Web address: www.ihcweb.co.ihc.com

LOGAN REGIONAL HOSPITAL (O, 112 beds) 1400 North 500 East, Logan, UT Zip 84341–2455; tel. 435/716–1000; Richard Smith, Administrator
Web address: www.ihc.com

MCKAY–DEE HOSPITAL CENTER (O, 293 beds) 3939 Harrison Boulevard, Ogden, UT Zip 84409–2386, Mailing Address: Box 9370, Zip 84409–0370; tel. 801/398–2800; Patricia Harrington, Administrator and Chief Operating Officer
Web address: www.ihc.com

OREM COMMUNITY HOSPITAL (O, 20 beds) 331 North 400 West, Orem, UT Zip 84057–1999; tel. 801/224–4080; Kim Nielsen, Administrator and Chief Operating Officer

PRIMARY CHILDREN'S MEDICAL CENTER (O, 183 beds) 100 North Medical Drive, Salt Lake City, UT Zip 84113–1100; tel. 801/588–2000; Joseph R. Horton, Chief Executive Officer and Administrator

SANPETE VALLEY HOSPITAL (O, 20 beds) 1100 South Medical Drive, Mount Pleasant, UT Zip 84647–2222; tel. 435/462–2441; George Winn, Administrator

SEVIER VALLEY HOSPITAL (O, 27 beds) 1100 North Main Street, Richfield, UT Zip 84701–1843; tel. 435/896–8271; Gary E. Beck, Administrator

UTAH VALLEY REGIONAL MEDICAL CENTER (O, 314 beds) 1034 North 500 West, Provo, UT Zip 84604–3337; tel. 801/373–7850; Mary Ann Young, R.N., Administrator

VALLEY VIEW MEDICAL CENTER (O, 36 beds) 595 South 75 East, Cedar City, UT Zip 84720–3462; tel. 435/586–6587; Craig M. Smedley, Administrator

WASATCH COUNTY HOSPITAL (L, 20 beds) 55 South 500 East, Heber City, UT Zip 84032–1999; tel. 435/654–2500; Randall K. Probst, Administrator

WYOMING: EVANSTON REGIONAL HOSPITAL (O, 38 beds) 190 Arrowhead Drive, Evanston, WY Zip 82930–9266; tel. 307/789–3636; Robert W. Allen, Administrator

STAR VALLEY HOSPITAL (C, 39 beds) 110 Hospital Lane, Afton, WY Zip 83110–0579, Mailing Address: P.O. Box 579, Zip 83110–0579; tel. 307/886–5800; Alberto Vasquez, Administrator
Web address: www.ihc.com

Owned, leased, sponsored:	21 hospitals	2213 beds
Contract–managed:	1 hospital	39 beds
Totals:	22 hospitals	2252 beds

★0061: IOWA HEALTH SYSTEM (NP)
1200 Pleasant Street, Des Moines, IA Zip 50309–1453; tel. 515/241–6161; Samuel T. Wallace, President

IOWA: ALLEN MEMORIAL HOSPITAL (O, 201 beds) 1825 Logan Avenue, Waterloo, IA Zip 50703–1916; tel. 319/235–3987; Richard A. Seidler, FACHE, Chief Executive Officer

ANAMOSA COMMUNITY HOSPITAL (L, 17 beds) 104 Broadway Place, Anamosa, IA Zip 52205–1100; tel. 319/462–6131; Vickie Asbe, Administrator

BUENA VISTA COUNTY HOSPITAL (C, 30 beds) 1525 West Fifth Street, Storm Lake, IA Zip 50588–0309; tel. 712/732–4030; James O. Nelson, Administrator

CLARKE COUNTY HOSPITAL (C, 48 beds) 800 South Fillmore Street, Osceola, IA Zip 50213; tel. 515/342–2184; Jack A. Burrows, Administrator

COMMUNITY MEMORIAL HOSPITAL (C, 33 beds) 1316 South Main Street, Clarion, IA Zip 50525; tel. 515/532–2811; Steve J. Simonin, Chief Executive Officer

DALLAS COUNTY HOSPITAL (C, 49 beds) 610 10th Street, Perry, IA Zip 50220–2221, Mailing Address: P.O. Box 608, Zip 50220–0608; tel. 515/465–3547; Kari L. Engholm, Administrator and Chief Executive Officer

FINLEY HOSPITAL (O, 139 beds) 350 North Grandview Avenue, Dubuque, IA Zip 52001–6392; tel. 319/582–1881; Kevin L. Rogols, President and Chief Executive Officer

GRUNDY COUNTY MEMORIAL HOSPITAL (C, 75 beds) 201 East J Avenue, Grundy Center, IA Zip 50638–2096; tel. 319/824–5421; James A. Faulwell, Administrator

GUTTENBERG MUNICIPAL HOSPITAL (C, 20 beds) Second and Main Street, Guttenberg, IA Zip 52052–0550, Mailing Address: Box 550, Zip 52052–0550; tel. 319/252–1121; Roland D. Gee, Chief Executive Officer

HUMBOLDT COUNTY MEMORIAL HOSPITAL (C, 49 beds) 1000 North 15th Street, Humboldt, IA Zip 50548–1008; tel. 515/332–4200

IOWA LUTHERAN HOSPITAL (O, 222 beds) 700 East University Avenue, Des Moines, IA Zip 50316–2392; tel. 515/263–5612; James H. Skogsbergh, President
Web address: www.ilsdesmoines.org

IOWA METHODIST MEDICAL CENTER (O, 489 beds) 1200 Pleasant Street, Des Moines, IA Zip 50309–9976; tel. 515/241–6212; James H. Skogsbergh, President
Web address: www.ihsdesmoines.org

LORING HOSPITAL (C, 54 beds) 211 Highland Avenue, Sac City, IA Zip 50583–0217, Mailing Address: P.O. Box 217, Zip 50583–0217; tel. 712/662–7105; Greg Miner, Administrator

ST. LUKE'S HOSPITAL (O, 421 beds) 1026 A Avenue N.E., Cedar Rapids, IA Zip 52402–3026, Mailing Address: P.O. Box 3026, Zip 52406–3026; tel. 319/369–7211; Stephen E. Vanourny, M.D., President and Chief Executive Officer

ST. LUKE'S REGIONAL MEDICAL CENTER (O, 196 beds) 2720 Stone Park Boulevard, Sioux City, IA Zip 51104–2000; tel. 712/279–3500; John D. Daniels, President and Chief Executive Officer
Web address: www.siouxlan.com/stlukes

Owned, leased, sponsored:	7 hospitals	1685 beds
Contract–managed:	8 hospitals	358 beds
Totals:	15 hospitals	2043 beds

★7775: JEFFERSON HEALTH SYSTEM (NP)
259 Radnor–Chester Road, Suite 290, Wayne, PA Zip 19087–5288; tel. 610/225–6200; Douglas S. Peters, President and Chief Executive Officer

PENNSYLVANIA: BRYN MAWR HOSPITAL (O, 300 beds) 130 South Bryn Mawr Avenue, Bryn Mawr, PA Zip 19010–3160; tel. 610/526–3000; Kenneth Hanover, President and Chief Executive Officer
Web address: www.jeffersonhealth.org

BRYN MAWR REHABILITATION HOSPITAL (O, 141 beds) 414 Paoli Pike, Malvern, PA Zip 19355–3300, Mailing Address: P.O. Box 3007, Zip 19355–3300; tel. 610/251–5400

FRANKFORD HOSPITAL OF THE CITY OF PHILADELPHIA (O, 490 beds) Knights and Red Lion Roads, Philadelphia, PA Zip 19114–1486; tel. 215/612–4000; Roy A. Powell, President

GERMANTOWN HOSPITAL AND COMMUNITY HEALTH SERVICES (O, 158 beds) One Penn Boulevard, Philadelphia, PA Zip 19144–1498; tel. 215/951–8000; David A. Ricci, President and Chief Executive Officer

LANKENAU HOSPITAL (O, 314 beds) 100 Lancaster Avenue West, Wynnewood, PA Zip 19096–3411; tel. 610/645–2000; William McCune, Senior Vice President, Operations
Web address: www.jeffersonhealth.org

For explanation of codes following names, see page B2.
★ Indicates Type III membership in the American Hospital Association.

MAGEE REHABILITATION HOSPITAL (O, 96 beds) Six Franklin Plaza, Philadelphia, PA Zip 19102–1177; tel. 215/587–3099; William E. Staas Jr., President and Medical Director
Web address: www.mageerehab.org

PAOLI MEMORIAL HOSPITAL (O, 129 beds) 255 West Lancaster Avenue, Paoli, PA Zip 19301–1792; tel. 610/648–1000; C. Barry Dykes, Senior Vice President
Web address: www.mlhs.org

THOMAS JEFFERSON UNIVERSITY HOSPITAL (O, 992 beds) 111 South 11th Street, Philadelphia, PA Zip 19107–5096; tel. 215/955–7022; Thomas J. Lewis, President and Chief Executive Officer
Web address: www.jeffersonhealth.org

Owned, leased, sponsored:	8 hospitals	2620 beds
Contract–managed:	0 hospitals	0 beds
Totals:	8 hospitals	2620 beds

★0052: JEWISH HOSPITAL HEALTHCARE SERVICES (NP)
217 East Chestnut Street, Louisville, KY Zip 40202–1886; tel. 502/587–4011; Henry C. Wagner, President

INDIANA: CLARK MEMORIAL HOSPITAL (C, 243 beds) 1220 Missouri Avenue, Jeffersonville, IN Zip 47130–3743, Mailing Address: Box 69, Zip 47131–0069; tel. 812/282–6631; Merle E. Stepp, President and Chief Executive Officer
Web address: www.cmhl.com

SCOTT MEMORIAL HOSPITAL (C, 45 beds) 1415 North Gardner Street, Scottsburg, IN Zip 47170–0430, Mailing Address: Box 430, Zip 47170–0430; tel. 812/752–8500; Clifford D. Nay, Executive Director
Web address: www.scottcounty.hsonline.com

SOUTHERN INDIANA REHABILITATION HOSPITAL (O, 60 beds) 3104 Blackiston Boulevard, New Albany, IN Zip 47150–9579; tel. 812/941–8300; Randy L. Napier, President and Chief Executive Officer

WASHINGTON COUNTY MEMORIAL HOSPITAL (C, 58 beds) 911 North Shelby Street, Salem, IN Zip 47167; tel. 812/883–5881; Rodney M. Coats, President and Chief Executive Officer

KENTUCKY: FRAZIER REHABILITATION CENTER (O, 95 beds) 220 Abraham Flexner Way, Louisville, KY Zip 40202–1887; tel. 502/582–7400; Barth A. Weinberg, Vice President, Inpatient Rehabilitation

JEWISH HOSPITAL (O, 539 beds) 217 East Chestnut Street, Louisville, KY Zip 40202–1886; tel. 502/587–4011; Douglas E. Shaw, President
Web address: www.jhhs.org

JEWISH HOSPITAL–SHELBYVILLE (O, 58 beds) 727 Hospital Drive, Shelbyville, KY Zip 40065–1699; tel. 502/647–4000; Timothy L. Jarm, President
Web address: www.jhhs.org

PATTIE A. CLAY HOSPITAL (C, 80 beds) EKU By–Pass, Richmond, KY Zip 40475, Mailing Address: P.O. Box 1600, Zip 40476–2603; tel. 606/625–3131; Richard M. Thomas, President

TAYLOR COUNTY HOSPITAL (C, 90 beds) 1700 Old Lebanon Road, Campbellsville, KY Zip 42718–9600; tel. 502/465–3561; David R. Hayes, President

UNIVERSITY OF LOUISVILLE HOSPITAL (C, 272 beds) 530 South Jackson Street, Louisville, KY Zip 40202–3611; tel. 502/562–3000; James H. Taylor, President and Chief Executive Officer
Web address: www.ulh.org

Owned, leased, sponsored:	4 hospitals	752 beds
Contract–managed:	6 hospitals	788 beds
Totals:	10 hospitals	1540 beds

★1015: JOHNS HOPKINS HEALTH SYSTEM (NP)
600 North Wolfe Street, Baltimore, MD Zip 21287–1193; tel. 410/955–5000; Ronald R. Peterson, President

MARYLAND: HOWARD COUNTY GENERAL HOSPITAL (O, 160 beds) 5755 Cedar Lane, Columbia, MD Zip 21044–2912; tel. 410/740–7710; Victor A. Broccolino, President and Chief Executive Officer
Web address: www.hcgh.org

JOHNS HOPKINS BAYVIEW MEDICAL CENTER (O, 655 beds) 4940 Eastern Avenue, Baltimore, MD Zip 21224–2780; tel. 410/550–0100; Gregory F. Schaffer, Senior Vice President Operations
Web address: www.jhbmc.jhu.edu

JOHNS HOPKINS HOSPITAL (O, 840 beds) 600 North Wolfe Street, Baltimore, MD Zip 21287–0002; tel. 410/955–5000; Ronald R. Peterson, President
Web address: www.med.jhu.edu

Owned, leased, sponsored:	3 hospitals	1655 beds
Contract–managed:	0 hospitals	0 beds
Totals:	3 hospitals	1655 beds

★2105: KAISER FOUNDATION HOSPITALS (NP)
One Kaiser Plaza, Oakland, CA Zip 94612–3600; tel. 510/271–5910; David M. Lawrence, M.D., Chairman and Chief Executive Officer

CALIFORNIA: KAISER FOUNDATION HOSPITAL (O, 236 beds) 2425 Geary Boulevard, San Francisco, CA Zip 94115; tel. 415/202–2000; Julie A. Petrini, Senior Vice President and Area Manager

KAISER FOUNDATION HOSPITAL (O, 103 beds) 401 Bicentennial Way, Santa Rosa, CA Zip 95403; tel. 707/571–4000; Susan Janvrin, R.N., Site Leader and Nurse Executive
Web address: www.ca.kaiserpermanente.org

KAISER FOUNDATION HOSPITAL (O, 384 beds) 4747 Sunset Boulevard, Los Angeles, CA Zip 90027–6072; tel. 323/783–4011; Joseph W. Hummel, Senior Vice President
Web address: www.lac.usc.org

KAISER FOUNDATION HOSPITAL (O, 121 beds) 7300 North Fresno Street, Fresno, CA Zip 93720; tel. 559/448–4555; Edward S. Glavis, Administrator

KAISER FOUNDATION HOSPITAL (O, 264 beds) 280 West MacArthur Boulevard, Oakland, CA Zip 94611; tel. 510/987–1000; Bettie L. Coles, R.N., Senior Vice President

KAISER FOUNDATION HOSPITAL (O, 210 beds) 1425 South Main Street, Walnut Creek, CA Zip 94596; tel. 925/295–4000; Sandra Small, Administrator

KAISER FOUNDATION HOSPITAL (O, 150 beds) 441 North Lakeview Avenue, Anaheim, CA Zip 92807; tel. 714/279–4100; Major Janice Head, Vice President and Service Area Manager
Web address: www.kaiserpermanenteca.org

KAISER FOUNDATION HOSPITAL (O, 317 beds) 9961 Sierra Avenue, Fontana, CA Zip 92335–6794; tel. 909/427–5000; Gerald A. McCall, Senior Vice President and Service Area Manager

KAISER FOUNDATION HOSPITAL (O, 189 beds) 25825 South Vermont Avenue, Harbor City, CA Zip 90710; tel. 310/325–5111; Judith Ann North, Administrator

KAISER FOUNDATION HOSPITAL (O, 198 beds) 27400 Hesperian Boulevard, Hayward, CA Zip 94545–4297; tel. 510/784–4313; Richard D. Cordova, Senior Vice President

KAISER FOUNDATION HOSPITAL (O, 343 beds) 4647 Zion Avenue, San Diego, CA Zip 92120; tel. 619/528–5000; Kenneth F. Colling, Senior Vice President and Area Manager

KAISER FOUNDATION HOSPITAL (O, 144 beds) 1150 Veterans Boulevard, Redwood City, CA Zip 94063–2087; tel. 650/299–2000; Helen Wilmot, Administrator

KAISER FOUNDATION HOSPITAL (O, 304 beds) 2025 Morse Avenue, Sacramento, CA Zip 95825–2115; tel. 916/973–5000; Sarah Krevans, Administrator

KAISER FOUNDATION HOSPITAL (O, 221 beds) 6600 Bruceville Road, Sacramento, CA Zip 95823; tel. 916/688–2430; Sarah Krevans, Senior Vice President

KAISER FOUNDATION HOSPITAL (O, 119 beds) 99 Montecillo Road, San Rafael, CA Zip 94903–3397; tel. 415/444–2000; Mary Ann Thode, Administrator

KAISER FOUNDATION HOSPITAL (O, 249 beds) 900 Kiely Boulevard, Santa Clara, CA Zip 95051–5386; tel. 408/236–6400; Helen Wilmot, Administrator

KAISER FOUNDATION HOSPITAL (O, 79 beds) 1200 El Camino Real, South San Francisco, CA Zip 94080–3299; tel. 650/742–2401; Gail Wuotila, Director Hospital Operations

Section B

For explanation of codes following names, see page B2.
★ Indicates Type III membership in the American Hospital Association.

KAISER FOUNDATION HOSPITAL (O, 166 beds) 13652 Cantara Street, Panorama City, CA Zip 91402; tel. 818/375–2000; Dev Mahadevan, Administrator

KAISER FOUNDATION HOSPITAL (O, 188 beds) 5601 DeSoto Avenue, Woodland Hills, CA Zip 91365–4084; tel. 818/719–3808; Deborah M. Lee-Eddie, Senior Vice President and Area Manager

KAISER FOUNDATION HOSPITAL AND REHABILITATION CENTER (O, 287 beds) 975 Sereno Drive, Vallejo, CA Zip 94589; tel. 707/651–1000; Sandra Small, Senior Vice President and Area Manager

KAISER FOUNDATION HOSPITAL–BELLFLOWER (O, 306 beds) 9400 East Rosecrans Avenue, Bellflower, CA Zip 90706–2246; tel. 562/461–3000; Margaret Silebi, Director Operations
Web address: www.ca.kaiserpermanente.org

KAISER FOUNDATION HOSPITAL–RIVERSIDE (O, 166 beds) 10800 Magnolia Avenue, Riverside, CA Zip 92505–3000; tel. 909/353–4600; Robert S. Lund, Administrator

KAISER FOUNDATION HOSPITAL–WEST LOS ANGELES (O, 160 beds) 6041 Cadillac Avenue, Los Angeles, CA Zip 90034; tel. 323/857–2201; Joseph W. Hummel, Administrator

SANTA TERESA COMMUNITY HOSPITAL (O, 218 beds) 250 Hospital Parkway, San Jose, CA Zip 95119; tel. 408/972–7000; Joann Zimmerman, Administrator

HAWAII: KAISER FOUNDATION HOSPITAL (O, 196 beds) 3288 Moanalua Road, Honolulu, HI Zip 96819; tel. 808/834–5333; Bruce Behnke, Administrator
Web address: www.kaiserhawaii.com

OREGON: KAISER SUNNYSIDE MEDICAL CENTER (O, 178 beds) 10180 S.E. Sunnyside Road, Clackamas, OR Zip 97015–9303; tel. 503/652–2880; Kathleen S. Wegener, Chief Executive Officer

Owned, leased, sponsored:	26 hospitals	5496 beds
Contract–managed:	0 hospitals	0 beds
Totals:	26 hospitals	5496 beds

0102: KALEIDA HEALTH (NP)
901 Washington Street, Buffalo, NY Zip 14203; tel. 716/843–7525; John E. Friedlander, President and Chief Executive Officer

NEW YORK: BUFFALO GENERAL HOSPITAL (O, 965 beds) 100 High Street, Buffalo, NY Zip 14203–1154; tel. 716/845–5600; John E. Friedlander, President and Chief Executive Officer

CHILDREN'S HOSPITAL (O, 313 beds) 219 Bryant Street, Buffalo, NY Zip 14222–2099; tel. 716/878–7000; Joseph A. Ruffolo, President and Chief Executive Officer

DE GRAFF MEMORIAL HOSPITAL (O, 210 beds) 445 Tremont Street, North Tonawanda, NY Zip 14120–0750, Mailing Address: P.O. Box 0750, Zip 14120–0750; tel. 716/694–4500; Marcia B. Gutfeld, Vice President and Chief Operating Officer

MILLARD FILLMORE GATES CIRCLE HOSPITAL (O, 588 beds) 3 Gates Circle, Buffalo, NY Zip 14209–9986; tel. 716/887–4600; Joyce Korzen, R.N., Chief Operating Officer
Web address: www.mfhs.edu

TRI–COUNTY MEMORIAL HOSPITAL (O, 65 beds) 100 Memorial Drive, Gowanda, NY Zip 14070–1194; tel. 716/532–3377; Diane J. Osika, Chief Executive Officer

Owned, leased, sponsored:	5 hospitals	2141 beds
Contract–managed:	0 hospitals	0 beds
Totals:	5 hospitals	2141 beds

0149: KISHWAUKEE HEALTH SYSTEM (NP)
626 Bethany Road, De Kalb, IL Zip 60115–4939, Mailing Address: P.O. Box 707, Zip 60115–4939; tel. 815/756–1521; Robert S. Thebeau, President and Chief Executive Officer

ILLINOIS: KISHWAUKEE COMMUNITY HOSPITAL (O, 114 beds) 626 Bethany Road, De Kalb, IL Zip 60115–4939, Mailing Address: P.O. Box 707, Zip 60115–0707; tel. 815/756–1521; Robert S. Thebeau, President and Chief Executive Officer

VALLEY WEST COMMUNITY HOSPITAL (O, 35 beds) 11 East Pleasant Avenue, Sandwich, IL Zip 60548–0901; tel. 815/786–8484; Roland R. Carlson, Chief Executive Officer
Web address: www.snd.softfarm.com/sandhosp

Owned, leased, sponsored:	2 hospitals	149 beds
Contract–managed:	0 hospitals	0 beds
Totals:	2 hospitals	149 beds

★2755: LEGACY HEALTH SYSTEM (NP)
1919 N.W. Lovejoy Street, Portland, OR Zip 97209–1503; tel. 503/415–5600; Robert Pallari, President and Chief Executive Officer

OREGON: LEGACY EMANUEL HOSPITAL AND HEALTH CENTER (O, 359 beds) 2801 North Gantenbein Avenue, Portland, OR Zip 97227–1674; tel. 503/413–2200; Stephani White, Vice President and Site Administrator
Web address: www.legacyhealth.org

LEGACY GOOD SAMARITAN HOSPITAL AND MEDICAL CENTER (O, 294 beds) 1015 N.W. 22nd Avenue, Portland, OR Zip 97210; tel. 503/413–7711;
Web address: www.legacyhealth.org

LEGACY MERIDIAN PARK HOSPITAL (O, 116 beds) 19300 S.W. 65th Avenue, Tualatin, OR Zip 97062–9741; tel. 503/692–1212; Jeff Cushing, Vice President and Site Administrator
Web address: www.legacyhealth.org

LEGACY MOUNT HOOD MEDICAL CENTER (O, 86 beds) 24800 S.E. Stark, Gresham, OR Zip 97030–0154; tel. 503/667–1122; Thomas S. Parker, Site Administrator
Web address: www.legacyhealth.org

Owned, leased, sponsored:	4 hospitals	855 beds
Contract–managed:	0 hospitals	0 beds
Totals:	4 hospitals	855 beds

0172: LENAWEE HEALTH ALLIANCE (NP)
818 Riverside Avenue, Adrian, MI Zip 49221; tel. 517/265–0900; John R. Robertstad, President and Chief Executive Officer

MICHIGAN: BIXBY MEDICAL CENTER, LENAWEE HEALTH ALLIANCE (O, 89 beds) 818 Riverside Avenue, Adrian, MI Zip 49221–1496; tel. 517/265–0900; John R. Robertstad, President and Chief Executive Officer
Web address: www.lhanet.org

HERRICK MEMORIAL HOSPITAL, LENAWEE HEALTH ALLIANCE (O, 88 beds) 500 East Pottawatamie Street, Tecumseh, MI Zip 49286–2097; tel. 517/424–3000; John R. Robertstad, President and Chief Executive Officer
Web address: www.lhanet.org

Owned, leased, sponsored:	2 hospitals	177 beds
Contract–managed:	0 hospitals	0 beds
Totals:	2 hospitals	177 beds

0173: LIBERTY HEALTHCARE SYSTEM (NP)
50 Baldwin Avenue, Jersey City, NJ Zip 07304–3199; tel. 201/915–2000; Jonathan M. Metsch, Dr.PH, President and Chief Executive Officer

NEW JERSEY: GREENVILLE HOSPITAL (O, 86 beds) 1825 John F. Kennedy Boulevard, Jersey City, NJ Zip 07305–2198; tel. 201/547–6100; Jonathan M. Metsch, Dr.PH, President and Chief Executive Officer

JERSEY CITY MEDICAL CENTER (O, 487 beds) 50 Baldwin Avenue, Jersey City, NJ Zip 07304–3199; tel. 201/915–2000; Jonathan M. Metsch, Dr.PH, President and Chief Executive Officer

MEADOWLANDS HOSPITAL MEDICAL CENTER (O, 173 beds) 55 Meadowland Parkway, Secaucus, NJ Zip 07096–1580; tel. 201/392–3100; Paul V. Cavalli, M.D., President

Owned, leased, sponsored:	3 hospitals	746 beds
Contract–managed:	0 hospitals	0 beds
Totals:	3 hospitals	746 beds

For explanation of codes following names, see page B2.
★ Indicates Type III membership in the American Hospital Association.

★0158: LIFEBRIDGE HEALTH (NP)
2401 West Belvedere Avenue, Baltimore, MD Zip 21215;
tel. 410/601–5134; Warren A. Green, President and Chief Executive
Officer

MARYLAND: LEVINDALE HEBREW GERIATRIC CENTER AND HOSPITAL (O,
288 beds) 2434 West Belvedere Avenue, Baltimore, MD Zip 21215–5299;
tel. 410/466–8700; Ronald Rothstein, Chief Executive Officer
Web address: www.sinai–balt.com

NORTHWEST HOSPITAL CENTER (O, 160 beds) 5401 Old Court Road,
Randallstown, MD Zip 21133–5185; tel. 410/521–2200; Robert W. Fischer,
President

SINAI HOSPITAL OF BALTIMORE (O, 436 beds) 2401 West Belvedere Avenue,
Baltimore, MD Zip 21215–5271; tel. 410/601–9000; Neil M. Meltzer,
President and Chief Operating Officer
Web address: www.sinai–balt.com

Owned, leased, sponsored:	3 hospitals	884 beds
Contract–managed:	0 hospitals	0 beds
Totals:	3 hospitals	884 beds

★0180: LIFEPOINT HOSPITALS, INC. (IO)
4525 Harding Road, Suite 300, Nashville, TN Zip 37205;
tel. 615/344–6261; Scott Mercy, Chairman and Chief Executive
Officer

ALABAMA: ANDALUSIA REGIONAL HOSPITAL (O, 87 beds) 849 South Three
Notch Street, Andalusia, AL Zip 36420–5325, Mailing Address: P.O. Box
760, Zip 36420–0760; tel. 334/222–8466; Barry L. Keel, Chief
Executive Officer

FLORIDA: BARTOW MEMORIAL HOSPITAL (O, 56 beds) 1239 East Main
Street, Bartow, FL Zip 33830–5005, Mailing Address: Box 1050,
Zip 33830–1050; tel. 941/533–8111; Brian P. Baumgardner,
Administrator
Web address: www.koala.columbia.net

GEORGIA: BARROW MEDICAL CENTER (O, 60 beds) 316 North Broad Street,
Winder, GA Zip 30680–2150, Mailing Address: P.O. Box 768,
Zip 30680–0768; tel. 770/867–3400; Randy Mills, Chief Executive Officer

KANSAS: HALSTEAD HOSPITAL (O, 137 beds) 328 Poplar Street, Halstead,
KS Zip 67056–2099; tel. 316/835–2651; David Nevill, President and
Chief Executive Officer

WESTERN PLAINS REGIONAL HOSPITAL (O, 101 beds) 3001 Avenue A,
Dodge City, KS Zip 67801–6508, Mailing Address: P.O. Box 1478,
Zip 67801–1478; tel. 316/225–8400; Ken Hutchenrider, President and Chief
Executive Officer

KENTUCKY: BOURBON COMMUNITY HOSPITAL (O, 58 beds) 9 Linville Drive,
Paris, KY Zip 40361–2196; tel. 606/987–1000; Rob Smart, Chief
Executive Officer

GEORGETOWN COMMUNITY HOSPITAL (O, 61 beds) 1140 Lexington Road,
Georgetown, KY Zip 40324–9362; tel. 502/868–1100; Jeffrey G. Seraphine,
President and Chief Executive Officer

LAKE CUMBERLAND REGIONAL HOSPITAL (O, 227 beds) 305 Langdon
Street, Somerset, KY Zip 42501, Mailing Address: P.O. Box 620,
Zip 42502–2750; tel. 606/679–7441; Jon C. O'Shaughnessy, President and
Chief Executive Officer

LOGAN MEMORIAL HOSPITAL (O, 63 beds) 1625 South Nashville Road,
Russellville, KY Zip 42276–8834, Mailing Address: P.O. Box 10,
Zip 42276–0010; tel. 502/726–4011; Michael Clark, Chief Executive Officer

MEADOWVIEW REGIONAL MEDICAL CENTER (O, 65 beds) 989 Medical Park
Drive, Maysville, KY Zip 41056–8750; tel. 606/759–5311; Curtis B.
Courtney, Chief Executive Officer

PINELAKE REGIONAL HOSPITAL (O, 106 beds) 1099 Medical Center Circle,
Mayfield, KY Zip 42066–1179, Mailing Address: P.O. Box 1099,
Zip 42066–1099; tel. 502/251–4100; Mary Jo Lewis, Chief Executive Officer
Web address: www.columbia.net

LOUISIANA: RIVERVIEW MEDICAL CENTER (O, 75 beds) 1125 West Louisiana
Highway 30, Gonzales, LA Zip 70737; tel. 504/647–5000; Kathy Bobbs,
Chief Executive Officer

SPRINGHILL MEDICAL CENTER (O, 63 beds) 2001 Doctors Drive, Springhill,
LA Zip 71075, Mailing Address: P.O. Box 920, Zip 71075–0920;
tel. 318/539–1000

TENNESSEE: CROCKETT HOSPITAL (O, 98 beds) U.S. Highway 43 South,
Lawrenceburg, TN Zip 38464–0847, Mailing Address: P.O. Box 847,
Zip 38464–0847; tel. 931/762–6571; Jack S. Buck, Chief Executive
Officer

HILLSIDE HOSPITAL (O, 85 beds) 1265 East College Street, Pulaski, TN
Zip 38478–4541; tel. 931/363–7531; James H. Edmondson, Chief Executive
Officer and Administrator

LIVINGSTON REGIONAL HOSPITAL (O, 88 beds) 315 Oak Street, Livingston,
TN Zip 38570, Mailing Address: P.O. Box 550, Zip 38570–0550;
tel. 931/823–5611; Timothy W. McGill, Chief Executive Officer

SMITH COUNTY MEMORIAL HOSPITAL (O, 40 beds) 158 Hospital Drive,
Carthage, TN Zip 37030–1096; tel. 615/735–1560; Jerry H. Futrell, Chief
Executive Officer

SOUTHERN TENNESSEE MEDICAL CENTER (O, 211 beds) 185 Hospital Road,
Winchester, TN Zip 37398–2468; tel. 931/967–8200; Kenneth E. Alexander,
Chief Executive Officer

TRINITY HOSPITAL (O, 28 beds) 353 Main Street, Erin, TN Zip 37061–0489,
Mailing Address: P.O. Box 489, Zip 37061–0489; tel. 931/289–4211; Jay
Woodall, Chief Executive Officer

UTAH: ASHLEY VALLEY MEDICAL CENTER (O, 29 beds) 151 West 200 North,
Vernal, UT Zip 84078–1907; tel. 435/789–3342; Ronald J. Perry, Chief
Executive Officer
Web address: www.avmc–hospital.com

CASTLEVIEW HOSPITAL (O, 60 beds) 300 North Hospital Drive, Price, UT
Zip 84501–4200; tel. 435/637–4800; Jeff Frandsen, Chief Executive Officer

WYOMING: RIVERTON MEMORIAL HOSPITAL (O, 59 beds) 2100 West Sunset
Drive, Riverton, WY Zip 82501–2274; tel. 307/856–4161;
Web address: www.riverton–hospital.com

Owned, leased, sponsored:	22 hospitals	1857 beds
Contract–managed:	0 hospitals	0 beds
Totals:	22 hospitals	1857 beds

★0060: LIFESPAN CORPORATION (NP)
167 Point Street, Providence, RI Zip 02903–4771;
tel. 401/444–3500; George A. Vecchione, President

MASSACHUSETTS: NEW ENGLAND MEDICAL CENTER (O, 314 beds) 750
Washington Street, Boston, MA Zip 02111–1845; tel. 617/636–5000;
Thomas F. O'Donnell Jr., M.D., FACS, Chief Executive Officer

RHODE ISLAND: EMMA PENDLETON BRADLEY HOSPITAL (O, 60 beds) 1011
Veterans Memorial Parkway, East Providence, RI Zip 02915–5099;
tel. 401/432–1000; Daniel J. Wall, President and Chief Executive Officer

MIRIAM HOSPITAL (O, 198 beds) 164 Summit Avenue, Providence, RI
Zip 02906–2895; tel. 401/793–2500; Edward M. Schottland, Senior Vice
President and Chief Operating Officer

NEWPORT HOSPITAL (O, 110 beds) 11 Friendship Street, Newport, RI
Zip 02840–2299; tel. 401/846–6400; Arthur J. Sampson, President and
Chief Executive Officer
Web address: www.lifespan.org

RHODE ISLAND HOSPITAL (O, 677 beds) 593 Eddy Street, Providence, RI
Zip 02903–4900; tel. 401/444–4000; Steven D. Baron, President and Chief
Executive Officer

Owned, leased, sponsored:	5 hospitals	1359 beds
Contract–managed:	0 hospitals	0 beds
Totals:	5 hospitals	1359 beds

**2295: LITTLE COMPANY OF MARY SISTERS HEALTHCARE
SYSTEM** (CC)
9350 South California Avenue, Evergreen Park, IL Zip 60805–2595;
tel. 708/229–5491; Sister Carol Pacini, Provincialate Superior

CALIFORNIA: BAY HARBOR HOSPITAL (O, 346 beds) 1437 West Lomita
Boulevard, Harbor City, CA Zip 90710–2097; tel. 310/325–1221; John
M. Wilson, President

Section B

LITTLE COMPANY OF MARY HOSPITAL (O, 348 beds) 4101 Torrance Boulevard, Torrance, CA Zip 90503–4698; tel. 310/540–7676; Mark Costa, President
Web address: www.lcmhs.org

SAN PEDRO PENINSULA HOSPITAL (O, 309 beds) 1300 West Seventh Street, San Pedro, CA Zip 90732; tel. 310/832–3311; John M. Wilson, President and Chief Executive Officer

ILLINOIS: LITTLE COMPANY OF MARY HOSPITAL AND HEALTH CARE CENTERS (O, 323 beds) 2800 West 95th Street, Evergreen Park, IL Zip 60805–2795; tel. 708/422–6200; Sister Kathleen McIntyre, President

INDIANA: MEMORIAL HOSPITAL AND HEALTH CARE CENTER (O, 124 beds) 800 West Ninth Street, Jasper, IN Zip 47546–2516; tel. 812/482–2345; Raymond W. Snowden, President and Chief Executive Officer
Web address: www.mhhcc.org

Owned, leased, sponsored:	5 hospitals	1450 beds
Contract–managed:	0 hospitals	0 beds
Totals:	5 hospitals	1450 beds

2175: LOMA LINDA UNIVERSITY HEALTH SCIENCES CENTER (NP)
11161 Anderson Street, Loma Linda, CA Zip 92350; tel. 909/824–4540; B. Lyn Behrens, President

CALIFORNIA: LOMA LINDA UNIVERSITY BEHAVIORAL MEDICINE CENTER (O, 89 beds) 1710 Barton Road, Redlands, CA Zip 92373; tel. 909/793–9333; Alan Soderblom, Administrator

LOMA LINDA UNIVERSITY MEDICAL CENTER (O, 653 beds) 11234 Anderson Street, Loma Linda, CA Zip 92354–2870, Mailing Address: P.O. Box 2000, Zip 92354–0200; tel. 909/824–0800; B. Lyn Behrens, President
Web address: www.llumc.edu

Owned, leased, sponsored:	2 hospitals	742 beds
Contract–managed:	0 hospitals	0 beds
Totals:	2 hospitals	742 beds

5755: LOS ANGELES COUNTY–DEPARTMENT OF HEALTH SERVICES (NP)
313 North Figueroa Street, Room 912, Los Angeles, CA Zip 90012–2691; tel. 213/240–8101; Mark Finucane, Director Health Services

LAC–HARBOR–UNIVERSITY OF CALIFORNIA AT LOS ANGELES MEDICAL CENTER (O, 336 beds) 1000 West Carson Street, Torrance, CA Zip 90509; tel. 310/222–2101; Tecla A. Mickoseff, Administrator

LAC–HIGH DESERT HOSPITAL (O, 75 beds) 44900 North 60th Street West, Lancaster, CA Zip 93536; tel. 661/945–8461; Mel Grussing, Administrator

LAC–KING–DREW MEDICAL CENTER (O, 249 beds) 12021 South Wilmington Avenue, Los Angeles, CA Zip 90059; tel. 310/668–4321; Randall S. Foster, Administrator and Chief Executive Officer

LAC–OLIVE VIEW–UCLA MEDICAL CENTER (O, 220 beds) 14445 Olive View Drive, Sylmar, CA Zip 91342–1495; tel. 818/364–1555; Melinda Anderson, Administrator

LAC–RANCHO LOS AMIGOS NATIONAL REHABILITATION CENTER (O, 190 beds) 7601 East Imperial Highway, Downey, CA Zip 90242; tel. 562/401–7022; Consuelo C. Diaz, Chief Executive Officer
Web address: www.rancho.org

LAC/UNIVERSITY OF SOUTHERN CALIFORNIA MEDICAL CENTER (O, 1328 beds) 1200 North State Street, Los Angeles, CA Zip 90033–1084; tel. 323/226–2622; Roberto Rodriguez, Executive Director

Owned, leased, sponsored:	6 hospitals	2398 beds
Contract–managed:	0 hospitals	0 beds
Totals:	6 hospitals	2398 beds

0047: LOUISIANA STATE HOSPITALS (NP)
210 State Street, New Orleans, LA Zip 70118–5797; tel. 504/897–3400; M. E. Teague, Chief Executive Officer

LOUISIANA: CENTRAL LOUISIANA STATE HOSPITAL (O, 216 beds) 242 West Shamrock Avenue, Pineville, LA Zip 71361–5031, Mailing Address: P.O.

Box 5031, Zip 71361–5031; tel. 318/484–6200; Gary S. Grand, Chief Executive Officer

EAST LOUISIANA STATE HOSPITAL (O, 452 beds) Jackson, LA Mailing Address: P.O. Box 498, Zip 70748–0498; tel. 504/634–0100; Warren T. Price Jr., Chief Executive Officer

EASTERN LOUISIANA MENTAL HEALTH SYSTEM/GREENWELL SPRING CAMPUS (O, 104 beds) 23260 Greenwell Springs Road, Greenwell Springs, LA Zip 70739–0999, Mailing Address: P.O. Box 549, Zip 70739–0549; tel. 504/261–2730; Warren T. Price Jr., Chief Executive Officer

NEW ORLEANS ADOLESCENT HOSPITAL (O, 95 beds) 210 State Street, New Orleans, LA Zip 70118–5797; tel. 504/897–3400; Walter W. Shervington, M.D., Chief Executive Officer

SOUTHEAST LOUISIANA HOSPITAL (O, 231 beds) Mandeville, LA Mailing Address: P.O. Box 3850, Zip 70470–3850; tel. 504/626–6300; Joseph C. Vinturella, Chief Executive Officer

Owned, leased, sponsored:	5 hospitals	1098 beds
Contract–managed:	0 hospitals	0 beds
Totals:	5 hospitals	1098 beds

★0715: LSU MEDICAL CENTER HEALTH CARE SERVICES DIVISION (NP)
8550 United Plaza Boulevard, 4th Floor, Baton Rouge, LA Zip 70809; tel. 225/922–0490; Cary M. Dougherty Jr., Chief Operating Officer

E. A. CONWAY MEDICAL CENTER (O, 174 beds) 4864 Jackson Street, Monroe, LA Zip 71202–6497, Mailing Address: P.O. Box 1881, Zip 71210–1881; tel. 318/330–7000; Roy D. Bostick, Director

EARL K. LONG MEDICAL CENTER (O, 204 beds) 5825 Airline Highway, Baton Rouge, LA Zip 70805–2498; tel. 225/358–1000; Jonathan Roberts, Dr.PH, Chief Executive Officer

HUEY P. LONG MEDICAL CENTER (O, 123 beds) 352 Hospital Boulevard, Pineville, LA Zip 71360, Mailing Address: P.O. Box 5352, Zip 71361–5352; tel. 318/448–0811; James E. Morgan, Director

LSU MEDICAL CENTER–UNIVERSITY HOSPITAL (O, 414 beds) 1541 Kings Highway, Shreveport, LA Zip 71130–4299, Mailing Address: P.O. Box 33932, Zip 71130–3932; tel. 318/675–5000; Ingo Angermeier, FACHE, Administrator and Chief Executive Officer
Web address: www.shrinershq.org

LALLIE KEMP MEDICAL CENTER (O, 68 beds) 52579 Highway 51 South, Independence, LA Zip 70443–2231; tel. 504/878–9421; LeVern Meades, Administrator

LEONARD J. CHABERT MEDICAL CENTER (O, 123 beds) 1978 Industrial Boulevard, Houma, LA Zip 70363–7094; tel. 504/873–2200; Daniel Trahan, Acting Administrator

MEDICAL CENTER OF LOUISIANA AT NEW ORLEANS (O, 681 beds) 2021 Perdido Street, New Orleans, LA Zip 70112–1396; tel. 504/588–3000; John S. Berault, Chief Executive Officer

UNIVERSITY MEDICAL CENTER (O, 146 beds) 2390 West Congress Street, Lafayette, LA Zip 70506–4298, Mailing Address: P.O. Box 69300, Zip 70596–9300; tel. 318/261–6001; Lawrence T. Dorsey, Administrator

WALTER OLIN MOSS REGIONAL MEDICAL CENTER (O, 74 beds) 1000 Walters Street, Lake Charles, LA Zip 70605; tel. 318/475–8100; Clay Dunaway, Administrator

WASHINGTON–ST. TAMMANY REGIONAL MEDICAL CENTER (O, 55 beds) 400 Memphis Street, Bogalusa, LA Zip 70427–0040, Mailing Address: Box 40, Zip 70429–0040; tel. 504/735–1322; Larry R. King, Administrator

Owned, leased, sponsored:	10 hospitals	2062 beds
Contract–managed:	0 hospitals	0 beds
Totals:	10 hospitals	2062 beds

★0036: LUBBOCK METHODIST HOSPITAL SYSTEM (NP)
3615 19th Street, Lubbock, TX Zip 79410–1201; tel. 806/792–1011; George H. McCleskey, President and Chief Executive Officer

NEW MEXICO: NOR–LEA GENERAL HOSPITAL (C, 28 beds) 1600 North Main Avenue, Lovington, NM Zip 88260–2871; tel. 505/396–6611; David R. Jordan, Ph.D., Administrator and Chief Executive Officer

For explanation of codes following names, see page B2.
★ Indicates Type III membership in the American Hospital Association.

TEXAS: FISHER COUNTY HOSPITAL DISTRICT (C, 23 beds) Roby Highway, Rotan, TX Zip 79546, Mailing Address: Drawer F, Zip 79546; tel. 915/735–2256; Ella Raye Helms, Administrator

LAMB HEALTHCARE CENTER (C, 41 beds) 1500 South Sunset, Littlefield, TX Zip 79339–4899; tel. 806/385–6411; Randall A. Young, Administrator

MITCHELL COUNTY HOSPITAL (C, 25 beds) 1543 Chestnut Street, Colorado City, TX Zip 79512–3998; tel. 915/728–3431; Roland K. Rickard, Administrator

MULESHOE AREA MEDICAL CENTER (C, 25 beds) 708 South First Street, Muleshoe, TX Zip 79347–3627; tel. 806/272–4524; Jim G. Bone, Interim Administrator

REEVES COUNTY HOSPITAL (C, 44 beds) 2323 Texas Street, Pecos, TX Zip 79772–7338; tel. 915/447–3551; Charles N. Butts, Interim Chief Executive Officer
Web address: www.rchd.org

Owned, leased, sponsored:	0 hospitals	0 beds
Contract–managed:	6 hospitals	186 beds
Totals:	6 hospitals	186 beds

★2235: LUTHERAN HEALTH SYSTEMS (NP)
4310 17th Avenue S.W., Fargo, ND Zip 58103–3339, Mailing Address: P.O. Box 6200, Zip 58106–6200; tel. 701/277–7500; Steven R. Orr, Chairman and Chief Executive Officer

ALASKA: FAIRBANKS MEMORIAL HOSPITAL (L, 198 beds) 1650 Cowles Street, Fairbanks, AK Zip 99701; tel. 907/452–8181; Michael K. Powers, Administrator

ARIZONA: MESA LUTHERAN HOSPITAL (O, 272 beds) 525 West Brown Road, Mesa, AZ Zip 85201–3299; tel. 602/834–1211; Robert A. Rundio, Executive Director of Hospital Operations

VALLEY LUTHERAN HOSPITAL (O, 232 beds) 6644 Baywood Avenue, Mesa, AZ Zip 85206–1797; tel. 602/981–2000; Robert A. Rundio, Executive Director of Hospital Operations

WICKENBURG REGIONAL HOSPITAL (L, 73 beds) 520 Rose Lane, Wickenburg, AZ Zip 85390–1447; tel. 520/684–5421; David Garnas, Administrator

CALIFORNIA: LASSEN COMMUNITY HOSPITAL (O, 58 beds) 560 Hospital Lane, Susanville, CA Zip 96130–4809; tel. 530/257–5325; David S. Anderson, FACHE, Administrator

COLORADO: EAST MORGAN COUNTY HOSPITAL (L, 24 beds) 2400 West Edison Street, Brush, CO Zip 80723–1640; tel. 970/842–5151; Anne Platt, Administrator

MCKEE MEDICAL CENTER (O, 108 beds) 2000 Boise Avenue, Loveland, CO Zip 80538–4281; tel. 970/669–4640; Charles F. Harms, Administrator

NORTH COLORADO MEDICAL CENTER (L, 262 beds) 1801 16th Street, Greeley, CO Zip 80631–5199; tel. 970/352–4121; Karl B. Gills, Administrator

STERLING REGIONAL MEDCENTER (O, 36 beds) 615 Fairhurst Street, Sterling, CO Zip 80751–0500, Mailing Address: P.O. Box 3500, Zip 80751–0500; tel. 970/522–0122; Michael J. Gillen, Administrator

KANSAS: DECATUR COUNTY HOSPITAL (L, 74 beds) 810 West Columbia Street, Oberlin, KS Zip 67749–2450, Mailing Address: P.O. Box 268, Zip 67749–0268; tel. 785/475–2208; Lynn Doeden, R.N., Interim Administrator

ST. LUKE HOSPITAL (L, 54 beds) 1014 East Melvin, Marion, KS Zip 66861–1299; tel. 316/382–2179; Craig Hanson, Administrator

NEBRASKA: OGALLALA COMMUNITY HOSPITAL (L, 29 beds) 300 East Tenth Street, Ogallala, NE Zip 69153–1509; tel. 308/284–4011; Linda Morris, Administrator

NEVADA: CHURCHILL COMMUNITY HOSPTIAL (O, 40 beds) 801 East Williams Avenue, Fallon, NV Zip 89406–3052; tel. 702/423–3151; Jeffrey Feike, Administrator

PERSHING GENERAL HOSPITAL (C, 34 beds) 855 Sixth Street, Lovelock, NV Zip 89419, Mailing Address: P.O. Box 661, Zip 89419–0661; tel. 702/273–2621; Jon Smith, Administrator

NEW MEXICO: LOS ALAMOS MEDICAL CENTER (O, 47 beds) 3917 West Road, Los Alamos, NM Zip 87544–2293; tel. 505/662–4201; Paul J. Wilson, Administrator

NORTH DAKOTA: LISBON MEDICAL CENTER (O, 70 beds) 905 Main Street, Lisbon, ND Zip 58054–0353, Mailing Address: P.O. Box 353, Zip 58054–0353; tel. 701/683–5241; Michael Matthews, Administrator
Web address: www.lhsnet.com

PEMBINA COUNTY MEMORIAL HOSPITAL AND WEDGEWOOD MANOR (L, 89 beds) 301 Mountain Street East, Cavalier, ND Zip 58220–4015; tel. 701/265–8461; George A. Rohrich, Administrator

OREGON: CENTRAL OREGON DISTRICT HOSPITAL (C, 48 beds) 1253 North Canal Boulevard, Redmond, OR Zip 97756–1395; tel. 541/548–8131; James A. Diegel, CHE, Executive Director

PIONEER MEMORIAL HOSPITAL (C, 30 beds) 1201 North Elm Street, Prineville, OR Zip 97754; tel. 541/447–6254; Donald J. Wee, Executive Director

SOUTH DAKOTA: GREGORY COMMUNITY HOSPITAL (O, 84 beds) 400 Park Street, Gregory, SD Zip 57533–0400, Mailing Address: Box 408, Zip 57533–0408; tel. 605/835–8394; Carol A. Varland, Chief Executive Officer

LOOKOUT MEMORIAL HOSPITAL (O, 32 beds) 1440 North Main Street, Spearfish, SD Zip 57783–1504; tel. 605/642–2617; Deb J. Krmpotic, R.N., Administrator

STURGIS COMMUNITY HEALTH CARE CENTER (O, 114 beds) 949 Harmon Street, Sturgis, SD Zip 57785–2452; tel. 605/347–2536; Deb J. Krmpotic, R.N., Administrator

WYOMING: COMMUNITY HOSPITAL (O, 36 beds) 2000 Campbell Drive, Torrington, WY Zip 82240–1597; tel. 307/532–4181; Charles Myers, Administrator

PLATTE COUNTY MEMORIAL HOSPITAL (L, 86 beds) 201 14th Street, Wheatland, WY Zip 82201–3201, Mailing Address: P.O. Box 848, Zip 82201–0848; tel. 307/322–3636; Dana K. Barnett, Administrator

WASHAKIE MEMORIAL HOSPITAL (L, 30 beds) 400 South 15th Street, Worland, WY Zip 82401–3531, Mailing Address: P.O. Box 700, Zip 82401–0700; tel. 307/347–3221; James Kiser, Administrator

Owned, leased, sponsored:	22 hospitals	2048 beds
Contract–managed:	3 hospitals	112 beds
Totals:	25 hospitals	2160 beds

0695: MAGELLAN HEALTH SERVICES (IO)
3414 Peachtree Road N.E., Suite 1400, Atlanta, GA Zip 30326; tel. 404/841–9200; Henry Harbin, M.D., President and Chief Executive Officer

ALABAMA: CHARTER BEHAVIORAL HEALTH SYSTEM (O, 94 beds) 5800 Southland Drive, Mobile, AL Zip 36693–3396, Mailing Address: P.O. Box 991800, Zip 36691–1800; tel. 334/661–3001; Keith Cox, CHE, Chief Executive Officer

ALASKA: CHARTER NORTH STAR BEHAVIORAL HEALTH SYSTEM (O, 34 beds) 1650 South Bragaw, Anchorage, AK Zip 99508–3467; tel. 907/258–7575; Kathleen Cronen, Chief Executive Officer

CHARTER NORTH STAR BEHAVIORAL HEALTH SYSTEM (O, 80 beds) 2530 DeBarr Road, Anchorage, AK Zip 99508; tel. 907/258–7575; Kathleen Cronen, Chief Executive Officer

ARIZONA: CHARTER BEHAVIORAL HEALTH SYSTEM OF ARIZONA/DESERT VISTA (O, 119 beds) 570 West Brown Road, Mesa, AZ Zip 85201–3227; tel. 602/962–3900; Kimbrough Hall, Chief Executive Officer

CHARTER BEHAVIORAL HEALTH SYSTEM–EAST VALLEY (O, 80 beds) 2190 North Grace Boulevard, Chandler, AZ Zip 85224–7903; tel. 602/899–8989; Sal A. Edwards, Chief Executive Officer

CHARTER BEHAVIORAL HEALTH SYSTEM–GLENDALE (O, 90 beds) 6015 West Peoria Avenue, Glendale, AZ Zip 85302–1201; tel. 602/878–7878; Marsha Olender, Chief Executive Officer

ARKANSAS: CHARTER BEHAVIORAL HEALTH SYSTEM OF LITTLE ROCK (O, 60 beds) 1601 Murphy Drive, Maumelle, AR Zip 72113; tel. 501/851–8700; Lucinda DeBruce, Chief Executive Officer

CHARTER BEHAVIORAL HEALTH SYSTEM OF NORTHWEST ARKANSAS (O, 49 beds) 4253 North Crossover Road, Fayetteville, AR Zip 72703–4596; tel. 501/521–5731; Patrick Kelly, Chief Executive Officer

Section B

For explanation of codes following names, see page B2.
★ Indicates Type III membership in the American Hospital Association.

CALIFORNIA: CHARTER BEHAVIORAL HEALTH SYSTEM OF SAN DIEGO (O, 80 beds) 11878 Avenue of Industry, San Diego, CA Zip 92128; tel. 619/487–3200; Robert A. Deney, Chief Executive Officer

CHARTER BEHAVIORAL HEALTH SYSTEM OF SOUTHERN CALIFORNIA–CHARTER OAK (O, 95 beds) 1161 East Covina Boulevard, Covina, CA Zip 91724–1161; tel. 626/966–1632; Todd A. Smith, Chief Executive Officer

CHARTER BEHAVIORAL HEALTH SYSTEM OF SOUTHERN CALIFORNIA–CORONA (O, 92 beds) 2055 Kellogg Avenue, Corona, CA Zip 91719; tel. 909/735–2910; Diana C. Hanyak, Chief Executive Officer

CHARTER BEHAVIORAL HEALTH SYSTEM OF SOUTHERN CALIFORNIA/MISSION VIEJO (O, 80 beds) 23228 Madero, Mission Viejo, CA Zip 92691; tel. 714/830–4800; Timothy Allen, Chief Executive Officer

CHARTER BEHAVIORAL HEALTH SYSTEM–PALM SPRINGS (O, 80 beds) 69–696 Ramon Road, Cathedral City, CA Zip 92234; tel. 760/321–2000; Diane W. Sharpe, Chief Executive Officer

COLORADO: CHARTER CENTENNIAL PEAKS BEHAVIORAL HEALTH SYSTEM (O, 72 beds) 2255 South 88th Street, Louisville, CO Zip 80027–9716; tel. 303/673–9990; Sharon Worsham, Administrator

CONNECTICUT: ELMCREST BEHAVIORAL HEALTH NETWORK (O, 92 beds) 25 Marlborough Street, Portland, CT Zip 06480–1829; tel. 860/342–0480; Anthony A. Ferrante, M.D., President and Chief Executive Officer

FLORIDA: CHARTER BEHAVIORAL HEALTH SYSTEM OF TAMPA BAY (O, 146 beds) 4004 North Riverside Drive, Tampa, FL Zip 33603–3212; tel. 813/238–8671; James C. Hill, Chief Executive Officer

CHARTER BEHAVIORAL HEALTH SYSTEM OF TAMPA BAY AT LARGO (O, 64 beds) 12891 Seminole Boulevard, Largo, FL Zip 33778; tel. 727/587–6000; Jim Hill, Chief Executive Officer

CHARTER BEHAVIORAL HEALTH SYSTEM–ORLANDO (O, 60 beds) 206 Park Place Drive, Kissimmee, FL Zip 34741–2356; tel. 407/846–0444; Daniel Kearney, Chief Executive Officer

CHARTER GLADE BEHAVIORAL HEALTH SYSTEM (O, 104 beds) 3550 Colonial Boulevard, Fort Myers, FL Zip 33912–1065; tel. 941/939–0403; Vickie Lewis, Chief Executive Officer
Web address: www.charterbehavioral.com

CHARTER HOSPITAL OF PASCO (O, 72 beds) 21808 State Road 54, Lutz, FL Zip 33549–6938; tel. 813/948–2441; Miriam K. Williams, Administrator

CHARTER SPRINGS HOSPITAL (O, 92 beds) 3130 S.W. 27th Avenue, Ocala, FL Zip 34474–4485, Mailing Address: P.O. Box 3338, Zip 34478–3338; tel. 352/237–7293; David C. Nissen, Chief Executive Officer

GEORGIA: CHARTER ANCHOR HOSPITAL (O, 84 beds) 5454 Yorktowne Drive, Atlanta, GA Zip 30349–5305; tel. 770/991–6044; Matthew Crouch, Chief Executive Officer
Web address: www.talbottcampus.com

CHARTER BEHAVIORAL HEALTH SYSTEM OF ATLANTA (O, 40 beds) 811 Juniper Street N.E., Atlanta, GA Zip 30308–1398; tel. 404/881–5800; Dennis Workman, M.D., Medical Director

CHARTER BEHAVIORAL HEALTH SYSTEM OF ATLANTA AT PEACHFORD (O, 224 beds) 2151 Peachford Road, Atlanta, GA Zip 30338–6599; tel. 770/455–3200; Aleen S. Davis, Chief Executive Officer

CHARTER BEHAVIORAL HEALTH SYSTEM/CENTRAL GEORGIA (O, 118 beds) 3500 Riverside Drive, Macon, GA Zip 31210–2509; tel. 912/474–6200; Blair R. Johanson, Administrator

CHARTER SAVANNAH BEHAVIORAL HEALTH SYSTEM (O, 112 beds) 1150 Cornell Avenue, Savannah, GA Zip 31406–2797; tel. 912/354–3911; Thomas L. Ryba, Chief Executive Officer

CHARTER WINDS HOSPITAL (O, 80 beds) 240 Mitchell Bridge Road, Athens, GA Zip 30606–2043; tel. 706/546–7277; Susan Lister, Chief Executive Officer

CHARTER BY–THE–SEA BEHAVIORAL HEALTH SYSTEM (O, 101 beds) 2927 Demere Road, Saint Simons Island, GA Zip 31522–1620; tel. 912/638–1999; Wes Robbins, Chief Executive Officer

INDIANA: CHARTER BEACON (O, 97 beds) 1720 Beacon Street, Fort Wayne, IN Zip 46805–4700; tel. 219/423–3651; Robert Hails, Chief Executive Officer

CHARTER BEHAVIORAL HEALTH SYSTEM OF INDIANA AT JEFFERSON (O, 100 beds) 2700 Vissing Park Road, Jeffersonville, IN Zip 47130–5943; tel. 812/284–3400; James E. Ledbetter, Ph.D., Chief Executive Officer

CHARTER BEHAVIORAL HEALTH SYSTEM OF NORTHWEST INDIANA (O, 60 beds) 101 West 61st Avenue and State Road 51, Hobart, IN Zip 46342–6489; tel. 219/947–4464; Michael J. Perry, Chief Executive Officer

CHARTER BEHAVIORAL HEALTH SYSTEMS (O, 64 beds) 3700 Rome Drive, Lafayette, IN Zip 47905–4465, Mailing Address: P.O. Box 5969, Zip 47903–5969; tel. 765/448–6999; Sheila Mishler, Chief Executive Officer

CHARTER INDIANAPOLIS BEHAVIORAL HEALTH SYSTEM (O, 80 beds) 5602 Caito Drive, Indianapolis, IN Zip 46226–1356; tel. 317/545–2111; Marina Cecchini, Chief Executive Officer

KENTUCKY: CHARTER BEHAVIORAL HEALTH SYSTEM OF PADUCAH (O, 56 beds) 435 Berger Road, Paducah, KY Zip 42003–4579, Mailing Address: P.O. Box 7609, Zip 42002–7609; tel. 502/444–0444; Pat Harrod, Chief Executive Officer

CHARTER RIDGE BEHAVIORAL HEALTH SYSTEM (O, 110 beds) 3050 Rio Dosa Drive, Lexington, KY Zip 40509–9990; tel. 606/269–2325; Barbara Kitchen, Chief Executive Officer

CHARTER LOUISVILLE BEHAVIORAL HEALTH SYSTEM (O, 66 beds) 1405 Browns Lane, Louisville, KY Zip 40207–4672; tel. 502/896–0495; Charles L. Webb Jr., Administrator

LOUISIANA: BAYOU OAKS BEHAVIORAL HEALTH SYSTEM (O, 70 beds) 8134 Main Street, Houma, LA Zip 70360–3404, Mailing Address: P.O. Box 4374, Zip 70361–4374; tel. 504/876–2020; Alan Hodges, Interim Chief Executive Officer

CHARTER BRENTWOOD BEHAVIORAL HEALTH SYSTEM (O, 200 beds) 1006 Highland Avenue, Shreveport, LA Zip 71101–4103; tel. 318/227–2221; Scott F. Blakley, Chief Executive Officer

CHARTER CYPRESS BEHAVIORAL HEALTH SYSTEM (O, 70 beds) 302 Dulles Drive, Lafayette, LA Zip 70506–3099; tel. 318/233–9024; Brooks Cagle, Chief Executive Officer

MARYLAND: CHARTER BEHAVIORAL HEALTH SYSTEM OF MARYLAND AT POTOMAC RIDGE (O, 140 beds) 14901 Broschart Road, Rockville, MD Zip 20850–3321; tel. 301/251–4500; Craig S. Juengling, Chief Executive Officer

MASSACHUSETTS: PEMBROKE HOSPITAL (O, 115 beds) 199 Oak Street, Pembroke, MA Zip 02359–1953; tel. 781/826–8161; Michael P. Krupa, Ed.D., Chief Executive Officer

WESTWOOD LODGE HOSPITAL (O, 100 beds) 45 Clapboardtree Street, Westwood, MA Zip 02090–2930; tel. 781/762–7764; Michael P. Krupa, Ed.D., Chief Executive Officer

MISSISSIPPI: CHARTER BEHAVIORAL HEALTH SYSTEM (O, 111 beds) 3531 Lakeland Drive, Jackson, MS Zip 39208–9794, Mailing Address: P.O. Box 4297, Zip 39296–4297; tel. 601/939–9030; Rick H. Gray, Ph.D., Chief Executive Officer

CHARTER PARKWOOD BEHAVIORAL HEALTH SYSTEM (O, 66 beds) 8135 Goodman Road, Olive Branch, MS Zip 38654–2199; tel. 601/895–4900; M. Andrew Mayo, Chief Executive Officer

NEVADA: CHARTER BEHAVIORAL HEALTH SYSTEM OF NEVADA (O, 84 beds) 7000 West Spring Mountain Road, Las Vegas, NV Zip 89117–3816; tel. 702/876–4357; Alan G. Chapman, Chief Executive Officer

NEW HAMPSHIRE: CHARTER BROOKSIDE BEHAVIORAL HEALTH SYSTEM OF NEW ENGLAND (O, 100 beds) 29 Northwest Boulevard, Nashua, NH Zip 03063–4005; tel. 603/886–5000; T. Mark Gallagher, Chief Executive Officer

NEW JERSEY: CHARTER BEHAVIORAL HEALTH SYSTEM OF NEW JERSEY–SUMMIT (O, 90 beds) 19 Prospect Street, Summit, NJ Zip 07902–0100; tel. 908/522–7000; James Gallagner, Chief Executive Officer

NEW MEXICO: CHARTER HEIGHTS BEHAVIORAL HEALTH SYSTEM (O, 172 beds) 103 Hospital Loop N.E., Albuquerque, NM Zip 87109–2115; tel. 505/883–8777; Joseph R. Brunson, Chief Executive Officer

NORTH CAROLINA: CHARTER ASHEVILLE BEHAVIORAL HEALTH SYSTEM (O, 139 beds) 60 Caledonia Road, Asheville, NC Zip 28803–2555, Mailing Address: P.O. Box 5534, Zip 28813–5534; tel. 704/253–3681; Tammy B. Wood, Chief Executive Officer

CHARTER BEHAVIORAL HEALTH SYSTEM OF WINSTON–SALEM (O, 111 beds) 3637 Old Vineyard Road, Winston–Salem, NC Zip 27104–4835; tel. 336/768–7710; Michael J. Carney, Chief Executive Officer

For explanation of codes following names, see page B2.
★ Indicates Type III membership in the American Hospital Association.

CHARTER GREENSBORO BEHAVIORAL HEALTH SYSTEM (O, 68 beds) 700 Walter Reed Drive, Greensboro, NC Zip 27403–1129, Mailing Address: P.O. Box 10399, Zip 27404–0399; tel. 336/852–4821; Nancy Reaves, Chief Executive Officer

OHIO: FOCUS HEALTHCARE OF OHIO (O, 38 beds) 1725 Timber Line Road, Maumee, OH Zip 43537–4015; tel. 419/891–9333; Dennis J. Sajdak, Chief Executive Officer

PENNSYLVANIA: CHARTER BEHAVIORAL HEALTH SYSTEM AT COVE FORGE (O, 100 beds) New Beginnings Road, P.O. Box B, Williamsburg, PA Zip 16693; tel. 814/832–2121; Jonathan Wolf, Chief Executive Officer

CHARTER FAIRMOUNT BEHAVIORAL HEALTH SYSTEM (O, 136 beds) 561 Fairthorne Avenue, Philadelphia, PA Zip 19128–2499; tel. 215/487–4000; Diane Kiddy, Chief Executive Officer

SOUTH CAROLINA: CHARTER GREENVILLE BEHAVIORAL HEALTH SYSTEM (O, 66 beds) 2700 East Phillips Road, Greer, SC Zip 29650–4816; tel. 864/968–6300; William L. Callison, Chief Executive Officer

CHARTER HOSPITAL OF CHARLESTON (O, 70 beds) 2777 Speissegger Drive, Charleston, SC Zip 29405–8299; tel. 803/747–5830; Anne Battin, Administrator

CHARTER RIVERS BEHAVIORAL HEALTH SYSTEM (O, 66 beds) 2900 Sunset Boulevard, West Columbia, SC Zip 29169–3422; tel. 803/796–9911; R. Andy Hanner, Chief Executive Officer

CHARTER SANDS BEHAVIORAL HEALTH SYSTEM OF CONWAY (O, 48 beds) 152 Waccamaw Medical Park Drive, Conway, SC Zip 29526–8922; tel. 803/347–7156; Dale Armstrong, Chief Executive Officer

TENNESSEE: CHARTER LAKESIDE BEHAVIORAL HEALTH SYSTEM (O, 174 beds) 2911 Brunswick Road, Memphis, TN Zip 38133–4199, Mailing Address: P.O. Box 341308, Zip 38134–1308; tel. 901/377–4700; Rob S. Waggener, Chief Executive Officer

TEXAS: CHARTER BEHAVIORAL HEALTH SYSTEM OF AUSTIN (O, 29 beds) 8402 Cross Park Drive, Austin, TX Zip 78754–4588, Mailing Address: P.O. Box 140585, Zip 78714–0585; tel. 870/837–1800; Armin Steege, Chief Executive Officer

CHARTER BEHAVIORAL HEALTH SYSTEM OF SOUTHEAST TEXAS–KINGWOOD (O, 80 beds) 2001 Ladbrook Drive, Kingwood, TX Zip 77339–3004; tel. 281/358–4501; Ramona Key, Chief Executive Officer

CHARTER BEHAVIORAL HEALTH SYSTEM–CORPUS CHRISTI (O, 80 beds) 3126 Rodd Field Road, Corpus Christi, TX Zip 78414–3901; tel. 361/993–8893; John S. Lacy, Chief Executive Officer

CHARTER GRAPEVINE BEHAVIORAL HEALTH SYSTEM (O, 80 beds) 2300 William D. Tate Avenue, Grapevine, TX Zip 76051–9964; tel. 817/481–1900; Sandra C. Podley, Chief Executive Officer

CHARTER PALMS BEHAVIORAL HEALTH SYSTEM (O, 40 beds) 1421 East Jackson Avenue, McAllen, TX Zip 78501–1602, Mailing Address: P.O. Box 5239, Zip 78502–5239; tel. 956/631–5421; Leslie Bingham, Chief Executive Officer

CHARTER PLAINS BEHAVIORAL HEALTH SYSTEM (O, 80 beds) 801 North Quaker Avenue, Lubbock, TX Zip 79416–2408, Mailing Address: P.O. Box 10560, Zip 79408–0560; tel. 806/744–5505; Earl W. Balzen, R.N., Chief Executive Officer and Administrator

CHARTER REAL BEHAVIORAL HEALTH SYSTEM (O, 90 beds) 8550 Huebner Road, San Antonio, TX Zip 78240–1897, Mailing Address: P.O. Box 380157, Zip 78280–0157; tel. 210/699–8585; James M. Hunt, Chief Executive Officer

HAVEN HOSPITAL (O, 27 beds) 800 Kirnwood Drive, De Soto, TX Zip 75115–2092; tel. 972/709–3700; Sheila C. Kelly, R.N., MS, Chief Executive Officer

VIRGINIA: CHARTER BEHAVIORAL HEALTH SYSTEM AT SPRINGWOOD (O, 77 beds) 42009 Charter Springwood Lane, Leesburg, VA Zip 20176–6269; tel. 703/777–0800; Craig S. Juengling, Chief Executive Officer

CHARTER BEHAVIORAL HEALTH SYSTEM OF CHARLOTTESVILLE (O, 62 beds) 2101 Arlington Boulevard, Charlottesville, VA Zip 22903–1593; tel. 804/977–1120; Wayne Adams, Chief Executive Officer

CHARTER WESTBROOK BEHAVIORAL HEALTH SYSTEM (O, 210 beds) 1500 Westbrook Avenue, Richmond, VA Zip 23227–3399; tel. 804/266–9671; Stephen P. Fahey, Administrator

NORFOLK PSYCHIATRIC CENTER (O, 77 beds) 860 Kempsville Road, Norfolk, VA Zip 23502–3980; tel. 757/461–4565; J. Frank Gallagher III, Administrator

WISCONSIN: CHARTER HOSPITAL OF MILWAUKEE (O, 80 beds) 11101 West Lincoln Avenue, Milwaukee, WI Zip 53227–1166; tel. 414/327–3000; Robert Kwech, Chief Executive Officer

Owned, leased, sponsored:	72 hospitals	6473 beds
Contract–managed:	0 hospitals	0 beds
Totals:	72 hospitals	6473 beds

★5305: MARIAN HEALTH SYSTEM (CC)
Tulsa, OK Mailing Address: P.O. Box 4753, Zip 74159–0753; tel. 918/742–9988; Sister M. Therese Gottschalk, President

MINNESOTA: ST. ELIZABETH HOSPITAL (O, 175 beds) 1200 Fifth Grand Boulevard West, Wabasha, MN Zip 55981–1098; tel. 651/565–4531; Thomas Crowley, President

NEW JERSEY: SAINT CLARE'S HEALTH SERVICES (O, 657 beds) 25 Pocono Road, Denville, NJ Zip 07834–2995; tel. 973/625–6000; Kathryn J. McDonagh, President and Chief Executive Officer
Web address: www.saintclares.org

OKLAHOMA: BARTLETT MEMORIAL MEDICAL CENTER (O, 113 beds) 519 South Division Street, Sapulpa, OK Zip 74066–4501, Mailing Address: P.O. Box 1368, Zip 74067–1368; tel. 918/224–4280; W. D. Robinson, Chief Executive Officer

ST. JOHN MEDICAL CENTER (O, 552 beds) 1923 South Utica Avenue, Tulsa, OK Zip 74104–5445; tel. 918/744–2345; David Pynn, President and Chief Executive Officer
Web address: www.sjmc.org

WISCONSIN: FLAMBEAU HOSPITAL (O, 42 beds) 98 Sherry Avenue, Park Falls, WI Zip 54552–1467, Mailing Address: P.O. Box 310, Zip 54552–0310; tel. 715/762–2484; Curtis A. Johnson, Administrator

SACRED HEART–ST. MARY'S HOSPITALS (O, 52 beds) 1044 Kabel Avenue, Rhinelander, WI Zip 54501–3998; tel. 715/369–6600; Kevin J. O'Donnell, President and Chief Executive Officer
Web address: www.ministryhealth.org

SAINT JOSEPH'S HOSPITAL (O, 524 beds) 611 St. Joseph Avenue, Marshfield, WI Zip 54449–1898; tel. 715/387–1713; Michael A. Schmidt, President and Chief Executive Officer

SAINT MICHAEL'S HOSPITAL (O, 114 beds) 900 Illinois Avenue, Stevens Point, WI Zip 54481–3196; tel. 715/346–5000; Jeffrey L. Martin, President and Chief Executive Officer
Web address: www.smhosp.org

VICTORY MEDICAL CENTER (O, 127 beds) 230 East Fourth Avenue, Stanley, WI Zip 54768–1298; tel. 715/644–5571; Cynthia Eichman, Chief Executive Officer and Administrator

Owned, leased, sponsored:	9 hospitals	2356 beds
Contract–managed:	0 hospitals	0 beds
Totals:	9 hospitals	2356 beds

1975: MARSHALL COUNTY HEALTH CARE AUTHORITY (NP)
8000 Alabama Highway 69, Guntersville, AL Zip 35976; tel. 205/753–8000; Julian Sparks, Board Chairman

ALABAMA: MARSHALL MEDICAL CENTER NORTH (O, 90 beds) 8000 Alabama Highway 69, Guntersville, AL Zip 35976; tel. 256/753–8000; Gary R. Gore, Chief Executive Officer
Web address: www.mmcnorth.com

MARSHALL MEDICAL CENTER SOUTH (O, 102 beds) U.S. Highway 431 North, Boaz, AL Zip 35957–0999, Mailing Address: P.O. Box 758, Zip 35957–0758; tel. 256/593–8310; J. Marlin Hanson, Administrator

Owned, leased, sponsored:	2 hospitals	192 beds
Contract–managed:	0 hospitals	0 beds
Totals:	2 hospitals	192 beds

0013: MASSACHUSETTS DEPARTMENT OF MENTAL HEALTH (NP)
25 Staniford Street, Boston, MA Zip 02114–2575; tel. 617/727–5600; Marylou Sudders, Commissioner

For explanation of codes following names, see page B2.
★ Indicates Type III membership in the American Hospital Association.

Section B

MASSACHUSETTS: MEDFIELD STATE HOSPITAL (O, 212 beds) 45 Hospital Road, Medfield, MA Zip 02052–1099; tel. 508/359–7312; Theodore E. Kirousis, Area Director

TAUNTON STATE HOSPITAL (O, 185 beds) 60 Hodges Avenue Extension, Taunton, MA Zip 02780–3034, Mailing Address: P.O. Box 4007, Zip 02780–4007; tel. 508/824–7551; Katherine Chmiel, R.N., MSN, Administrator and Chief Operating Officer

WESTBOROUGH STATE HOSPITAL (O, 220 beds) Lyman Street, Westborough, MA Zip 01581–0288, Mailing Address: P.O. Box 288, Zip 01581–0288; tel. 508/366–4401; Theodore E. Kirousis, Area Director

WORCESTER STATE HOSPITAL (O, 176 beds) 305 Belmont Street, Worcester, MA Zip 01604–1695; tel. 508/795–1197; Raymond Robinson, Chief Operating Officer

Owned, leased, sponsored:	4 hospitals	793 beds
Contract–managed:	0 hospitals	0 beds
Totals:	4 hospitals	793 beds

2505: MATAGORDA COUNTY HOSPITAL DISTRICT (NP)
1115 Avenue G, Bay City, TX Zip 77414–3544; tel. 409/245–6383; Wendell H. Baker Jr., District Administrator

TEXAS: MATAGORDA GENERAL HOSPITAL (O, 67 beds) 1115 Avenue G, Bay City, TX Zip 77414–3544; tel. 409/245–6383; Wendell H. Baker Jr., Chief Executive Officer

WAGNER GENERAL HOSPITAL (O, 6 beds) 310 Green Street, Palacios, TX Zip 77465–3214, Mailing Address: P.O. Box 859, Zip 77465–0859; tel. 512/972–2511; Kevin Hecht, Director

Owned, leased, sponsored:	2 hospitals	73 beds
Contract–managed:	0 hospitals	0 beds
Totals:	2 hospitals	73 beds

★1875: MAYO FOUNDATION (NP)
200 S.W. First Street, Rochester, MN Zip 55905–0002; tel. 507/284–2511; Michael B. Wood, M.D., President and Chief Executive Officer

ARIZONA: MAYO CLINIC HOSPITAL (O, 178 beds) 5777 East Mayo Boulevard, Phoenix, AZ 85024; tel. 480/515–6296; Thomas C. Bour, Administrator

FLORIDA: ST. LUKE'S HOSPITAL (O, 239 beds) 4201 Belfort Road, Jacksonville, FL Zip 32216–5898; tel. 904/296–3700; Robert M. Walters, Administrator

IOWA: FLOYD COUNTY MEMORIAL HOSPITAL (C, 31 beds) 800 Eleventh Street, Charles City, IA Zip 50616–3499; tel. 515/228–6830; Bill D. Faust, Administrator

MINNESOTA: ALBERT LEA MEDICAL CENTER (O, 72 beds) 404 West Fountain Street, Albert Lea, MN Zip 56007–2473; tel. 507/373–2384; Ronald A. Harmon, M.D., Chief Executive Officer

IMMANUEL ST. JOSEPH'S–MAYO HEALTH SYSTEM (O, 147 beds) 1025 Marsh Street, Mankato, MN 56001–4700, Mailing Address: P.O. Box 8673, Zip 56002–8673; tel. 507/625–4031; W. Neath Folger, M.D., President and Chief Executive Officer

ROCHESTER METHODIST HOSPITAL (O, 335 beds) 201 West Center Street, Rochester, MN Zip 55902–3084; tel. 507/266–7890; John M. Panicek, Administrator

SAINT MARYS HOSPITAL (O, 797 beds) 1216 Second Street S.W., Rochester, MN Zip 55902–1970; tel. 507/255–5123; John M. Panicek, Administrator

WISCONSIN: BARRON MEDICAL CENTER–MAYO HEALTH SYSTEM (C, 92 beds) 1222 Woodland Avenue, Barron, WI Zip 54812–1798; tel. 715/537–3186; Mark D. Wilson, Administrator

BLOOMER COMMUNITY MEMORIAL HOSPITAL AND THE MAPLEWOOD (C, 101 beds) 1501 Thompson Street, Bloomer, WI Zip 54724–1299; tel. 715/568–2000; John Perushek, Administrator

LUTHER HOSPITAL (O, 179 beds) 1221 Whipple Street, Eau Claire, WI Zip 54702–4105; tel. 715/838–3311; William Rupp, M.D., President and Chief Executive Officer

OSSEO AREA HOSPITAL AND NURSING HOME (C, 76 beds) 13025 Eighth Street, Osseo, WI Zip 54758, Mailing Address: P.O. Box 70, Zip 54758–0070; tel. 715/597–3121; Bradley D. Groseth, Administrator

Owned, leased, sponsored:	7 hospitals	1947 beds
Contract–managed:	4 hospitals	300 beds
Totals:	11 hospitals	2247 beds

★0154: MEDSTAR HEALTH (NP)
5565 Sterrett Place, 5th Floor, Columbia, MD Zip 21044; tel. 410/772–6500; Michael R. Merson, President and Chief Executive Officer

DISTRICT OF COLUMBIA: NATIONAL REHABILITATION HOSPITAL (O, 160 beds) 102 Irving Street N.W., Washington, DC Zip 20010–2949; tel. 202/877–1000; Edward A. Eckenhoff, President and Chief Executive Officer

WASHINGTON HOSPITAL CENTER (O, 714 beds) 110 Irving Street N.W., Washington, DC Zip 20010–2975; tel. 202/877–7000; Kenneth A. Samet, President
Web address: www.whc.mhg.edu

MARYLAND: CHURCH HOSPITAL CORPORATION (O, 167 beds) 100 North Broadway, Baltimore, MD Zip 21231–1593; tel. 410/522–8000; Ann C. Failing, President
Web address: www.helixhealth.org

FRANKLIN SQUARE HOSPITAL CENTER (O, 243 beds) 9000 Franklin Square Drive, Baltimore, MD Zip 21237–3998; tel. 410/682–7000; Charles D. Mross, President
Web address: www.helix.org

GOOD SAMARITAN HOSPITAL OF MARYLAND (O, 272 beds) 5601 Loch Raven Boulevard, Baltimore, MD Zip 21239–2995; tel. 410/532–8000; Lawrence M. Beck, President
Web address: www.helixhealth.com

HARBOR HOSPITAL CENTER (O, 176 beds) 3001 South Hanover Street, Baltimore, MD Zip 21225–1290; tel. 410/347–3200; L. Barney Johnson, President and Chief Executive Officer

UNION MEMORIAL HOSPITAL (O, 378 beds) 201 East University Parkway, Baltimore, MD Zip 21218–2391; tel. 410/554–2000; Harry Ryder, President and Chief Executive Officer
Web address: www.helix.org

Owned, leased, sponsored:	7 hospitals	2110 beds
Contract–managed:	0 hospitals	0 beds
Totals:	7 hospitals	2110 beds

0084: MEMORIAL HEALTH SERVICES (NP)
2801 Atlantic Avenue, Long Beach, CA Zip 90801, Mailing Address: P.O. Box 1428, Zip 90801–1428; tel. 562/933–9700; Thomas J. Collins, President and Chief Executive Officer

CALIFORNIA: ANAHEIM MEMORIAL MEDICAL CENTER (O, 192 beds) 1111 West La Palma Avenue, Anaheim, CA Zip 92801; tel. 714/774–1450; Michael C. Carter, Chief Executive Officer

LONG BEACH MEMORIAL MEDICAL CENTER (O, 726 beds) 2801 Atlantic Avenue, Long Beach, CA Zip 90806, Mailing Address: Box 1428, Zip 90801–1428; tel. 562/933–2000; Chris D. Van Gorder, Chief Executive Officer
Web address: www.memorialcare.org

ORANGE COAST MEMORIAL MEDICAL CENTER (O, 170 beds) 9920 Talbert Avenue, Fountain Valley, CA Zip 92708; tel. 714/378–7000; Barry S. Arbuckle, Ph.D., Chief Executive Officer
Web address: www.memorialcare.org

SADDLEBACK MEMORIAL MEDICAL CENTER (O, 148 beds) 24451 Health Center Drive, Laguna Hills, CA Zip 92653; tel. 949/837–4500; Barry S. Arbuckle, Ph.D., Chief Executive Officer

Owned, leased, sponsored:	4 hospitals	1236 beds
Contract–managed:	0 hospitals	0 beds
Totals:	4 hospitals	1236 beds

For explanation of codes following names, see page B2.
★ Indicates Type III membership in the American Hospital Association.

2335: MEMORIAL HEALTH SERVICES (IO)
706 North Parrish Avenue, Adel, GA Zip 31620–2064, Mailing Address: P.O. Box 677, Zip 31620–0677; tel. 912/896–2251; Wade E. Keck, Chief Executive Officer

GEORGIA: BLECKLEY MEMORIAL HOSPITAL (C, 45 beds) 408 Peacock Street, Cochran, GA Zip 31014–1559, Mailing Address: P.O. Box 536, Zip 31014–0536; tel. 912/934–6211; Scott D. Adkins, Administrator

SMITH HOSPITAL (C, 71 beds) 117 East Main Street, Hahira, GA Zip 31632–1156, Mailing Address: P.O. Box 337, Zip 31632–0337; tel. 912/794–2502; Amanda M. Hall, Administrator

TELFAIR COUNTY HOSPITAL (C, 52 beds) U.S. 341 South, McRae, GA Zip 31055, Mailing Address: P.O. Box 150, Zip 31055–0150; tel. 912/868–5621; Gail B. Norris, Administrator

Owned, leased, sponsored:	0 hospitals	0 beds
Contract–managed:	3 hospitals	168 beds
Totals:	3 hospitals	168 beds

★0086: MEMORIAL HEALTH SYSTEM (NP)
701 North First Street, Springfield, IL Zip 62781–0001; tel. 217/788–3000; Robert T. Clarke, President and Chief Executive Officer

ILLINOIS: ABRAHAM LINCOLN MEMORIAL HOSPITAL (O, 60 beds) 315 8th Street, Lincoln, IL Zip 62656–2698; tel. 217/732–2161; Forrest G. Hester, President and Chief Executive Officer
Web address: www.almh.com

MEMORIAL MEDICAL CENTER (O, 431 beds) 701 North First Street, Springfield, IL Zip 62781–0001; tel. 217/788–3000; Robert T. Clarke, President and Chief Executive Officer
Web address: www.mhsil.com

ST. VINCENT MEMORIAL HOSPITAL (S, 149 beds) 201 East Pleasant Street, Taylorville, IL Zip 62568–1597; tel. 217/824–3331; Daniel J. Raab, President and Chief Executive Officer

Owned, leased, sponsored:	3 hospitals	640 beds
Contract–managed:	0 hospitals	0 beds
Totals:	3 hospitals	640 beds

0176: MEMORIAL HEALTH SYSTEM OF EAST TEXAS (NP)
1201 West Frank Avenue, Lufkin, TX Zip 75904–3357; tel. 409/634–8111; Gary Lex Whatley, President and Chief Executive Officer

TEXAS: MEMORIAL MEDICAL CENTER (O, 28 beds) 602 East Church Street, Livingston, TX Zip 75351–1257, Mailing Address: P.O. Box 1257, Zip 77351–1257; tel. 409/327–4381; James C. Dickson, Administrator

MEMORIAL MEDICAL CENTER OF EAST TEXAS (O, 233 beds) 1201 West Frank Avenue, Lufkin, TX Zip 75904–3357, Mailing Address: P.O. Box 1447, Zip 75902–1447; tel. 409/634–8111; Gary Lex Whatley, President and Chief Executive Officer

MEMORIAL MEDICAL CENTER OF SAN AUGUSTINE (O, 16 beds) 511 East Hospital Street, San Augustine, TX Zip 75972–2121, Mailing Address: P.O. Box 658, Zip 75972–0658; tel. 409/275–3446; Terry Napper, Administrator

Owned, leased, sponsored:	3 hospitals	277 beds
Contract–managed:	0 hospitals	0 beds
Totals:	3 hospitals	277 beds

★2615: MEMORIAL HEALTH SYSTEMS (NP)
770 West Granada Boulevard, Ormond Beach, FL Zip 32174–5197; tel. 904/615–4100; Richard A. Lind, President and Chief Executive Officer

FLORIDA: MEMORIAL HOSPITAL–FLAGLER (O, 81 beds) Moody Boulevard, Bunnell, FL Zip 32110, Mailing Address: HCR1, Box 2, Zip 32110; tel. 904/437–2211; Clark P. Christianson, Senior Vice President and Administrator

MEMORIAL HOSPITAL–ORMOND BEACH (O, 205 beds) 875 Sterthaus Avenue, Ormond Beach, FL Zip 32174–5197; tel. 904/676–6000; Clark P. Christianson, Senior Vice President and Administrator

MEMORIAL HOSPITAL–WEST VOLUSIA (L, 130 beds) 701 West Plymouth Avenue, De Land, FL Zip 32720–3291, Mailing Address: P.O. Box 6509, DeLand, Zip 32721–0509; tel. 904/943–3320; Johnette L. Vodenicker, Administrator

Owned, leased, sponsored:	3 hospitals	416 beds
Contract–managed:	0 hospitals	0 beds
Totals:	3 hospitals	416 beds

★0083: MEMORIAL HEALTHCARE SYSTEM (NP)
3501 Johnson Street, Hollywood, FL Zip 33021–5487; tel. 954/985–5805; Frank V. Sacco, FACHE, Chief Executive Officer

MEMORIAL HOSPITAL PEMBROKE (L, 190 beds) 7800 Sheridan Street, Pembroke Pines, FL Zip 33024; tel. 954/962–9650; J. E. Piriz, Administrator

MEMORIAL HOSPITAL WEST (O, 110 beds) 703 North Flamingo Road, Pembroke Pines, FL Zip 33028; tel. 954/436–5000; Zeff Ross, Administrator

MEMORIAL REGIONAL HOSPITAL (O, 674 beds) 3501 Johnson Street, Hollywood, FL Zip 33021–5421; tel. 954/987–2000; C. Kennon Hetlage, Administrator
Web address: www.mhs–net.com

Owned, leased, sponsored:	3 hospitals	974 beds
Contract–managed:	0 hospitals	0 beds
Totals:	3 hospitals	974 beds

★2645: MEMORIAL HERMANN HEALTHCARE SYSTEM (NP)
7737 S.W. Freeway, Suite 200, Houston, TX Zip 77074–1800; tel. 713/776–6992; Dan S. Wilford, President and Chief Executive Officer

TEXAS: HERMANN HOSPITAL (O, 624 beds) 6411 Fannin, Houston, TX Zip 77030–1501; tel. 713/704–4000; James E. Eastham, Senior Vice President and Chief Executive Officer

MEMORIAL HERMAN BEHAVIORAL HEALTH CENTER (L, 108 beds) 2801 Gessner, Houston, TX Zip 77080–2599; tel. 713/462–4000; Sue E. Green, Vice President and Chief Executive Officer
Web address: www.mhcs.org

MEMORIAL HOSPITAL PASADENA (O, 172 beds) 906 East Southmore Avenue, Pasadena, TX Zip 77502–1124, Mailing Address: P.O. Box 1879, Zip 77502–1879; tel. 713/477–0411; Dennis M. Knox, Vice President and Chief Executive Officer
Web address: www.mhcs.org

MEMORIAL HOSPITAL SOUTHWEST (O, 886 beds) 7600 Beechnut, Houston, TX Zip 77074–1850; tel. 713/776–5000; Lynn Schroth, Chief Executive Officer
Web address: www.mhcs.org

MEMORIAL HOSPITAL–MEMORIAL CITY (L, 340 beds) 920 Frostwood Drive, Houston, TX Zip 77024–9173; tel. 713/932–3000; Jerel T. Humphrey, Vice President, Chief Executive Officer and Administrator
Web address: www.mhcs.org

MEMORIAL HOSPITAL–THE WOODLANDS (O, 73 beds) 9250 Pinecroft Drive, The Woodlands, TX Zip 77380–3225; tel. 281/364–2300; Steve Sanders, Vice President and Chief Executive Officer
Web address: www.mhhs.org

MEMORIAL REHABILITATION HOSPITAL (L, 106 beds) 3043 Gessner Drive, Houston, TX Zip 77080–2597; tel. 713/462–2515; Roger Truskoloski, Vice President and Chief Executive Officer
Web address: www.mhcs.com

Owned, leased, sponsored:	7 hospitals	2309 beds
Contract–managed:	0 hospitals	0 beds
Totals:	7 hospitals	2309 beds

★5165: MERCY HEALTH SERVICES (CC)
34605 Twelve Mile Road, Farmington Hills, MI Zip 48331–3221; tel. 248/489–6000; Judith Pelham, President and Chief Executive Officer

For explanation of codes following names, see page B2.
★ Indicates Type III membership in the American Hospital Association.

Section B

ILLINOIS: MORRISON COMMUNITY HOSPITAL (C, 60 beds) 303 North Jackson Street, Morrison, IL Zip 61270–3042; tel. 815/772–4003; Mark F. Fedyk, Administrator

IOWA: BAUM HARMON MEMORIAL HOSPITAL (C, 16 beds) 255 North Welch Avenue, Primghar, IA Zip 51245–1034, Mailing Address: P.O. Box 528, Zip 51245–0528; tel. 712/757–2300; Trudy Pfeiffer, Interim Administrator

BELMOND COMMUNITY HOSPITAL (C, 22 beds) 403 First Street S.E., Belmond, IA Zip 50421–1201, Mailing Address: P.O. Box 326, Zip 50421–0326; tel. 515/444–3223; Kim Price, Administrator

CENTRAL COMMUNITY HOSPITAL (C, 16 beds) 901 Davidson Street N.W., Elkader, IA Zip 52043–9799; tel. 319/245–2250; Fran Zichal, Chief Executive Officer

ELDORA REGIONAL MEDICAL CENTER (C, 18 beds) 2413 Edgington Avenue, Eldora, IA Zip 50627–1541; tel. 515/939–5416; Richard C. Hamilton, Administrator

ELLSWORTH MUNICIPAL HOSPITAL (C, 40 beds) 110 Rocksylvania Avenue, Iowa Falls, IA Zip 50126–2431; tel. 515/648–4631; John O'Brien, Administrator

FRANKLIN GENERAL HOSPITAL (C, 82 beds) 1720 Central Avenue East, Hampton, IA Zip 50441–1859; tel. 515/456–5000; Scott Wells, Chief Executive Officer

HANCOCK COUNTY MEMORIAL HOSPITAL (C, 26 beds) 532 First Street N.W., Britt, IA Zip 50423–0068, Mailing Address: P.O. Box 68, Zip 50423–0068; tel. 515/843–3801; Harriet Thompson, Administrator

HAWARDEN COMMUNITY HOSPITAL (C, 17 beds) 1111 11th Street, Hawarden, IA Zip 51023–1999; tel. 712/551–3100; Stuart A. Katz, FACHE, Administrator

KOSSUTH REGIONAL HEALTH CENTER (C, 29 beds) 1515 South Phillips Street, Algona, IA Zip 50511–3649; tel. 515/295–2451; James G. Fitzpatrick, Administrator and Chief Executive Officer

MARIAN HEALTH CENTER (O, 284 beds) 801 Fifth Street, Sioux City, IA Zip 51102, Mailing Address: P.O. Box 3168, Zip 51102–3168; tel. 712/279–2010; Deborah VandenBroek, President and Chief Executive Officer
Web address: www.mercyhealth.com/marian

MERCY HEALTH CENTER (O, 385 beds) 250 Mercy Drive, Dubuque, IA Zip 52001–7360; tel. 319/589–8000; Russell M. Knight, President and Chief Executive Officer
Web address: www.mercyhealth.com

MITCHELL COUNTY REGIONAL HEALTH CENTER (C, 28 beds) 616 North Eighth Street, Osage, IA Zip 50461–1498; tel. 515/732–6005; Kimberly J. Miller, CHE, Administrator

NORTH IOWA MERCY HEALTH CENTER (O, 255 beds) 1000 Fourth Street S.W., Mason City, IA Zip 50401–2800; tel. 515/422–7000; James J. Sexton, President and Chief Executive Officer
Web address: www.northiowamercy.com

PALO ALTO HEALTH SYSTEM (C, 54 beds) 3201 First Street, Emmetsburg, IA Zip 50536–2599; tel. 712/852–2434; Darrell E. Vondrak, Administrator
Web address: www.northiowamercy.com

REGIONAL HEALTH SERVICES OF HOWARD COUNTY (C, 32 beds) 235 Eighth Avenue West, Cresco, IA Zip 52136–1098; tel. 319/547–2101; Elizabeth A. Doty, President and Chief Executive Officer
Web address: www.rhshc.com

SAINT JOSEPH COMMUNITY HOSPITAL (O, 55 beds) 308 North Maple Avenue, New Hampton, IA Zip 50659–1142; tel. 515/394–4121; Carolyn Martin-Shaw, President

SAMARITAN HEALTH SYSTEM (O, 375 beds) 1410 North Fourth Street, Clinton, IA Zip 52732–2999; tel. 319/244–5555; Thomas J. Hesselmann, President and Chief Executive Officer
Web address: www.samhealth.com

MICHIGAN: BATTLE CREEK HEALTH SYSTEM (O, 378 beds) 300 North Avenue, Battle Creek, MI Zip 49016–3396; tel. 616/966–8000; Arthur Knueppel, Interim President and Chief Executive Officer

DECKERVILLE COMMUNITY HOSPITAL (C, 17 beds) 3559 Pine Street, Deckerville, MI Zip 48427–0126, Mailing Address: P.O. Box 126, Zip 48427–0126; tel. 810/376–2835; Edward L. Gamache, Administrator

MCPHERSON HOSPITAL (O, 45 beds) 620 Byron Road, Howell, MI Zip 48843–1093; tel. 517/545–6000; Patricia Claffey, Executive Director

MERCY GENERAL HEALTH PARTNERS (O, 189 beds) 1500 East Sherman Boulevard, Muskegon, MI Zip 49443; tel. 616/739–3901; Roger Spoelman, President and Chief Executive Officer

MERCY HEALTH SERVICES NORTH–GRAYLING (O, 98 beds) 1100 Michigan Avenue, Grayling, MI Zip 49738–1398; tel. 517/348–5461; Stephanie J. Riemer–Matuzak, Chief Executive Officer

MERCY HEALTH SERVICES–NORTH (O, 78 beds) 400 Hobart Street, Cadillac, MI Zip 49601–9596; tel. 616/876–7200; John Sewell, Interim Chief Executive Officer
Web address: www.mercyhealth.com

MERCY HOSPITAL (O, 268 beds) 5555 Conner Avenue, Detroit, MI Zip 48213–3499; tel. 313/579–4000; David Spivey, President and Chief Executive Officer
Web address: www.mercyhealth.com/detroit

MERCY HOSPITAL (O, 119 beds) 2601 Electric Avenue, Port Huron, MI Zip 48060; tel. 810/985–1510; Mary R. Trimmer, President and Chief Executive Officer
Web address: www.mercyporthuron.com

SAINT JOSEPH MERCY HEALTH SYSTEM (O, 475 beds) 5301 East Huron River Drive, Ann Arbor, MI Zip 48106, Mailing Address: P.O. Box 995, Zip 48106–0995; tel. 734/712–3456; Garry C. Faja, President and Chief Executive Officer
Web address: www.sjmh.com

SAINT MARY'S HEALTH SERVICES (O, 300 beds) 200 Jefferson Avenue S.E., Grand Rapids, MI Zip 49503–4598; tel. 616/752–6090; David J. Ameen, President and Chief Executive Officer
Web address: www.mercyhealth.com\smhc

SALINE COMMUNITY HOSPITAL (O, 38 beds) 400 West Russell Street, Saline, MI Zip 48176–1101; tel. 734/429–1500; Garry C. Faja, President and Chief Executive Officer

ST. JOSEPH MERCY OAKLAND (O, 409 beds) 900 Woodward Avenue, Pontiac, MI Zip 48341–2985; tel. 248/858–3000; Thomas L. Feurig, President and Chief Executive Officer
Web address: www.mercyhealth.com/oakland

ST. JOSEPH'S MERCY HOSPITALS AND HEALTH SERVICES (O, 346 beds) Clinton Township, MI Jack Weiner, President and Chief Executive Officer

NEBRASKA: PENDER COMMUNITY HOSPITAL (C, 30 beds) 603 Earl Street, Pender, NE Zip 68047–0100, Mailing Address: P.O. Box 100, Zip 68047–0100; tel. 402/385–3083; Roger Mazour, Administrator

Owned, leased, sponsored:	17 hospitals	4097 beds
Contract–managed:	15 hospitals	487 beds
Totals:	32 hospitals	4584 beds

8835: MERIDIA HEALTH SYSTEM (NP)

17325 Euclid Avenue, 4th Floor, Cleveland, OH Zip 44112; tel. 216/430–8000; Charles B. Miner, President and Chief Executive Officer

OHIO: EUCLID HOSPITAL (O, 187 beds) 18901 Lake Shore Boulevard, Euclid, OH Zip 44119–1090; tel. 216/531–9000; Denise Zeman, Chief Operating Officer
Web address: www.meridia.com

MERIDIA HILLCREST HOSPITAL (O, 305 beds) 6780 Mayfield Road, Cleveland, OH Zip 44124–2202; tel. 216/449–4500; Catherine B. Leary, R.N., Chief Operating Officer
Web address: www.meridia.com

MERIDIA HURON HOSPITAL (O, 163 beds) 13951 Terrace Road, Cleveland, OH Zip 44112–4399; tel. 216/761–3300; Beverly Lozar, Chief Operating Officer
Web address: www.meridia.com

MERIDIA SOUTH POINTE HOSPITAL (O, 178 beds) 4110 Warrensville Center Road, Warrensville Heights, OH Zip 44122–7099; tel. 216/491–6000; Kathleen A. Rice, Chief Operating Officer
Web address: www.southpointegme.com

For explanation of codes following names, see page B2.
★ Indicates Type III membership in the American Hospital Association.

Owned, leased, sponsored:	4 hospitals	833 beds
Contract–managed:	0 hospitals	0 beds
Totals:	4 hospitals	833 beds

Owned, leased, sponsored:	10 hospitals	1781 beds
Contract–managed:	0 hospitals	0 beds
Totals:	10 hospitals	1781 beds

★7235: **METHODIST HEALTH CARE SYSTEM** (CO)
6565 Fannin Street, D–200, Houston, TX Zip 77030–2707;
tel. 713/790–2221; Peter W. Butler, President and Chief Executive
Officer

TEXAS: DIAGNOSTIC CENTER HOSPITAL (O, 115 beds) 6447 Main Street,
Houston, TX Zip 77030–1595; tel. 713/790–0790; William A. Gregory,
Chief Executive Officer
Web address: www.tmh.tmc.edi/

METHODIST HEALTH CENTER–SUGAR LAND (O, 22 beds) 16655 S.W.
Freeway, Sugar Land, TX Zip 77479; tel. 281/274–8000; Joan Damon,
Administrator

SAN JACINTO METHODIST HOSPITAL (O, 231 beds) 4401 Garth Road,
Baytown, TX Zip 77521–3160; tel. 281/420–8600; William Simmons,
President and Chief Executive Officer
Web address: www.methodisthealth.com\sanjacinto

THE METHODIST HOSPITAL (O, 879 beds) 6565 Fannin Street, Houston, TX
Zip 77030–2707; tel. 713/790–3311; R. G. Girotto, Executive Vice President
and Chief Operating Officer
Web address: www.methodisthealth.com

Owned, leased, sponsored:	4 hospitals	1247 beds
Contract–managed:	0 hospitals	0 beds
Totals:	4 hospitals	1247 beds

★9345: **METHODIST HEALTHCARE** (CO)
1211 Union Avenue, Suite 700, Memphis, TN 38104–6600;
tel. 901/726–2300; Maurice W. Elliott, Chief Executive Officer

MISSISSIPPI: METHODIST HEALTHCARE MIDDLE MISSISSIPPI HOSPITAL (O,
80 beds) 239 Bowling Green Road, Lexington, MS Zip 39095–9332;
tel. 601/834–1321; James K. Greer, Administrator

TENNESSEE: METHODIST HEALTHCARE – FAYETTE HOSPITAL (O, 38 beds)
214 Lakeview Drive, Somerville, TN Zip 38068; tel. 901/465–0532;
Michael Blome', Administrator
Web address: www.methodisthealth.org

METHODIST HEALTHCARE – MCKENZIE HOSPITAL (O, 27 beds) 161 Hospital
Drive, McKenzie, TN Zip 38201–1636; tel. 901/352–5344; Richard
McCormick, Administrator

METHODIST HEALTHCARE– DYERSBURG HOSPITAL (O, 105 beds) 400 Tickle
Street, Dyersburg, TN Zip 38024–3182; tel. 901/285–2410; Richard
McCormick, Administrator
Web address: www.methodisthealth.org

METHODIST HEALTHCARE–BROWNSVILLE HOSPITAL (O, 44 beds) 2545
North Washington Avenue, Brownsville, TN Zip 38012–1697;
tel. 901/772–4110; Sandra Bailey, Administrator

METHODIST HEALTHCARE–LEXINGTON HOSPITAL (O, 32 beds) 200 West
Church Street, Lexington, TN Zip 38351–2014; tel. 901/968–3646; Eugene
Ragghianti, Administrator

METHODIST HEALTHCARE–MCNAIRY HOSPITAL (O, 86 beds) 705 East Poplar
Avenue, Selmer, TN Zip 38375–1748; tel. 901/645–3221; John R. Borden,
Administrator

METHODIST HEALTHCARE–MEMPHIS HOSPITAL (O, 1201 beds) 1265 Union
Avenue, Memphis, TN Zip 38104–3499; tel. 901/726–7000; David L.
Ramsey, President
Web address: www.methodisthealth.org

METHODIST HEALTHCARE–VOLUNTEER HOSPITAL (L, 65 beds) 161 Mount
Pelia Road, Martin, TN Zip 38237–0967, Mailing Address: P.O. Box 967,
Zip 38237–0967; tel. 901/587–4261; R. Coleman Foss, Chief Executive
Officer

METHODIST LEBONHEUR HEALTHCARE–JACKSON (L, 103 beds) 367
Hospital Boulevard, Jackson, TN Zip 38305–4518, Mailing Address: P.O. Box
3310, Zip 38303–0310; tel. 901/661–2000; Tim Brady, Chief Executive
Officer
Web address: www.regionalhospital.com

★2735: **METHODIST HOSPITALS OF DALLAS** (NP)
1441 North Beckley Avenue, Dallas, TX Zip 75203–1201, Mailing
Address: P.O. Box 655999, Zip 75265–5999; tel. 214/947–8181;
Howard M. Chase, FACHE, President and Chief Executive Officer

TEXAS: CHARLTON METHODIST HOSPITAL (O, 134 beds) 3500 West
Wheatland Road, Dallas, TX Zip 75237, Mailing Address: Box 225357,
Zip 75222–5357; tel. 214/947–7500; David L. Knocke, CHE, Executive
Director
Web address: www.mhd.com

METHODIST MEDICAL CENTER (O, 362 beds) 1441 North Beckley Avenue,
Dallas, TX Zip 75203–1201, Mailing Address: Box 655999,
Zip 75265–5999; tel. 214/947–8181; Kim Hollon, FACHE, Executive Director
Web address: www.mhd.com

Owned, leased, sponsored:	2 hospitals	496 beds
Contract–managed:	0 hospitals	0 beds
Totals:	2 hospitals	496 beds

★0001: **MIDMICHIGAN HEALTH** (NP)
4005 Orchard Drive, Midland, MI Zip 48670–0001;
tel. 517/839–3000; Terence F. Moore, President

MICHIGAN: MIDMICHIGAN MEDICAL CENTER–CLARE (O, 64 beds) 104 West
Sixth Street, Clare, MI Zip 48617–1409; tel. 517/386–9951; Lawrence F.
Barco, President

MIDMICHIGAN MEDICAL CENTER–GLADWIN (O, 42 beds) 515 South Quarter
Street, Gladwin, MI Zip 48624–1918; tel. 517/426–9286; Mark E. Bush,
Executive Vice President

MIDMICHIGAN MEDICAL CENTER–MIDLAND (O, 250 beds) 4005 Orchard
Drive, Midland, MI Zip 48670; tel. 517/839–3000; David A. Reece, President
Web address: www.midmichigan.org

Owned, leased, sponsored:	3 hospitals	356 beds
Contract–managed:	0 hospitals	0 beds
Totals:	3 hospitals	356 beds

2855: **MISSIONARY BENEDICTINE SISTERS AMERICAN
PROVINCE** (CC)
300 North 18th Street, Norfolk, NE Zip 68701–3687;
tel. 402/371–3438; Sister M. Agnes Salber, Prioress

MINNESOTA: GRACEVILLE HEALTH CENTER (O, 92 beds) 115 West Second
Street, Graceville, MN Zip 56240–0157, Mailing Address: P.O. Box 157,
Zip 56240–0157; tel. 320/748–7223; Helen Jorve, Chief Executive
Officer

NEBRASKA: FAITH REGIONAL HEALTH SERVICES (O, 225 beds) 2700 Norfolk
Avenue, Norfolk, NE Zip 68702–0869, Mailing Address: P.O. BOX 869,
Zip 68702–0869; tel. 402/644–7201; Robert L. Driewer, Chief Executive
Officer

PROVIDENCE MEDICAL CENTER (O, 34 beds) 1200 Providence Road, Wayne,
NE Zip 68787–1299; tel. 402/375–3800; Marcile Thomas, Administrator

Owned, leased, sponsored:	3 hospitals	351 beds
Contract–managed:	0 hospitals	0 beds
Totals:	3 hospitals	351 beds

0017: **MISSISSIPPI STATE DEPARTMENT OF MENTAL
HEALTH** (NP)
1101 Robert E Lee Building, Jackson, MS Zip 39201–1101;
tel. 601/359–1288; Roger McMurtry, Chief Mental Health Bureau

MISSISSIPPI: EAST MISSISSIPPI STATE HOSPITAL (O, 633 beds) 4555
Highland Park Drive, Meridian, MS Zip 39307–5498, Mailing Address: Box
4128, West Station, Zip 39304–4128; tel. 601/482–6186; Ramiro J.
Martinez, M.D., Director

For explanation of codes following names, see page B2.
★ Indicates Type III membership in the American Hospital Association.

Section B

MISSISSIPPI STATE HOSPITAL (O, 1299 beds) Whitfield, MS
Zip 39193–0157; tel. 601/351–8000; James G. Chastain, Director

Owned, leased, sponsored:	2 hospitals	1932 beds
Contract–managed:	0 hospitals	0 beds
Totals:	2 hospitals	1932 beds

1335: MORTON PLANT MEASE HEALTH CARE (NP)
601 Main Street, Dunedin, FL Zip 34698, Mailing Address: P.O. Box
760, Zip 34697–0760; tel. 727/733–1111; Philip K. Beauchamp,
FACHE, President and Chief Executive Officer

FLORIDA: MEASE COUNTRYSIDE HOSPITAL (O, 100 beds) 3231
McMullen–Booth Road, Safety Harbor, FL Zip 34695–1098, Mailing
Address: P.O. 1098, Zip 34695–1098; tel. 813/725–6111; James A.
Pfeiffer, Chief Operating Officer

MEASE HOSPITAL DUNEDIN (O, 258 beds) 601 Main Street, Dunedin, FL
Zip 34698–5891, Mailing Address: P.O. Box 760, Zip 34697–0760;
tel. 727/733–1111; James A. Pfeiffer, Chief Operating Officer

MORTON PLANT HOSPITAL (O, 742 beds) 323 Jeffords Street, Clearwater, FL
Zip 33756, Mailing Address: P.O. Box 210, Zip 34657–0210;
tel. 727/462–7000; Philip K. Beauchamp, FACHE, President and Chief
Executive Officer

Owned, leased, sponsored:	3 hospitals	1100 beds
Contract–managed:	0 hospitals	0 beds
Totals:	3 hospitals	1100 beds

0167: MOUNTAIN STATES HEALTH ALLIANCE (NP)
400 North State of Franklin, Johnson City, TN Zip 37604;
tel. 423/431–6111; Dennis Vonderfecht, President and Chief
Executive Officer

TENNESSEE: INDIAN PATH MEDICAL CENTER (O, 196 beds) 2000 Brookside
Drive, Kingsport, TN Zip 37660–4604; tel. 423/392–7000; Randy Cook,
Administrator

JAMES H. AND CECILE C. QUILLEN REHABILITATION HOSPITAL (O, 60 beds)
2511 Wesley Street, Johnson City, TN Zip 37601–1723; tel. 423/283–0700;
John Turner, Chief Executive Officer

JOHNSON CITY MEDICAL CENTER (O, 407 beds) 400 North State of Franklin
Road, Johnson City, TN Zip 37604–6094; tel. 423/431–6111; Dennis
Vonderfecht, President and Chief Executive Officer
Web address: www.jcmc.com

JOHNSON CITY SPECIALTY HOSPITAL (O, 49 beds) 203 East Watauga
Avenue, Johnson City, TN Zip 37601–4651; tel. 423/926–1111; Gary
Varner, Interim Chief Executive Officer
Web address: www.columbia.net

SYCAMORE SHOALS HOSPITAL (O, 112 beds) 1501 West Elk Avenue,
Elizabethton, TN Zip 37643–1368; tel. 423/542–1300; Scott Williams, Chief
Executive Officer

Owned, leased, sponsored:	5 hospitals	824 beds
Contract–managed:	0 hospitals	0 beds
Totals:	5 hospitals	824 beds

6555: MULTICARE HEALTH SYSTEM (NP)
315 Martin Luther King Jr. Way, Tacoma, WA Zip 98405, Mailing
Address: P.O. Box 5299, Zip 98405–0299; tel. 253/403–1000;
Diane Cecchettini, Executive Vice President

WASHINGTON: MARY BRIDGE CHILDREN'S HOSPITAL AND HEALTH CENTER
(O, 72 beds) 317 Martin Luther King Jr. Way, Tacoma, WA
Zip 98405–0299, Mailing Address: Box 5299, Zip 98405–0299;
tel. 253/403–1400; Diane Cecchettini, Executive Vice President
Web address: www.multicare.com

TACOMA GENERAL HOSPITAL (O, 365 beds) 315 Martin Luther King Jr. Way,
Tacoma, WA Zip 98405–0299, Mailing Address: P.O. Box 5299,
Zip 98405–0299; tel. 253/403–1000; Diane Cecchettini, Executive Vice
President
Web address: www.multicare.com

Owned, leased, sponsored:	2 hospitals	437 beds
Contract–managed:	0 hospitals	0 beds
Totals:	2 hospitals	437 beds

★1465: MUNSON HEALTHCARE (NP)
1105 Sixth Street, Traverse City, MI Zip 49684–2386;
tel. 616/935–6502; John M. Rockwood Jr., President

MICHIGAN: KALKASKA MEMORIAL HEALTH CENTER (C, 76 beds) 419 South
Coral Street, Kalkaska, MI Zip 49646; tel. 616/258–7500; James D.
Austin, CHE, Administrator

LEELANAU MEMORIAL HEALTH CENTER (O, 91 beds) 215 South High Street,
Northport, MI Zip 49670, Mailing Address: P.O. Box 217, Zip 49670–0217;
tel. 616/386–0000; Jayne R. Bull, Administrator

MUNSON MEDICAL CENTER (O, 368 beds) 1105 Sixth Street, Traverse City,
MI Zip 49684–2386; tel. 616/935–5000; Ralph J. Cerny, President and Chief
Executive Officer
Web address: www.mhc.net

PAUL OLIVER MEMORIAL HOSPITAL (O, 48 beds) 224 Park Avenue, Frankfort,
MI Zip 49635; tel. 616/352–9621; James D. Austin, CHE, Administrator
Web address: www.benzie.com

Owned, leased, sponsored:	3 hospitals	507 beds
Contract–managed:	1 hospital	76 beds
Totals:	4 hospitals	583 beds

0116: NETCARE HEALTH SYSTEMS, INC. (IO)
424 Church Street, Suite 2100, Nashville, TN Zip 37219;
tel. 615/742–8500; Michael A. Koban Jr., Chief Executive Officer

ALABAMA: CHILTON MEDICAL CENTER (O, 45 beds) 1010 Lay Dam Road,
Clanton, AL Zip 35045; tel. 205/755–2500; Randy Smith, Chief Executive
Officer

CALIFORNIA: SAN CLEMENTE HOSPITAL AND MEDICAL CENTER (O, 71
beds) 654 Camino De Los Mares, San Clemente, CA Zip 92673;
tel. 949/496–1122; Patricia L. Wolfram, R.N., Chief Executive Officer

GEORGIA: CHATUGE REGIONAL HOSPITAL AND NURSING HOME (O, 142
beds) 110 Main Street, Hiawassee, GA Zip 30546, Mailing Address: P.O.
Box 509, Zip 30546–0509; tel. 706/896–2222; Charles T. Adams,
President and Chief Executive Officer

CHESTATEE REGIONAL HOSPITAL (O, 49 beds) 227 Mountain Drive,
Dahlonega, GA Zip 30533; tel. 706/864–6136; Anne Thompson, Chief
Executive Officer

NORTH GEORGIA MEDICAL CENTER (O, 150 beds) 1362 South Main Street,
Ellijay, GA Zip 30540–0346, Mailing Address: P.O. Box 2239,
Zip 30540–0346; tel. 706/276–4741; Randy Carson, Chief Executive Officer

MISSISSIPPI: MARSHALL COUNTY MEDICAL CENTER (O, 40 beds) 1430 East
Salem, Holly Springs, MS Zip 38635, Mailing Address: P.O. Box 6000,
Zip 38634–6000; tel. 601/252–1212; Bill Renick, Administrator

STONE COUNTY HOSPITAL (O, 50 beds) 1434 East Central Avenue, Wiggins,
MS Zip 39577; tel. 601/928–6600; Regina Moore, Interim Chief Executive
Officer

TRACE REGIONAL HOSPITAL (O, 84 beds) Highway 8 East, Houston, MS
Zip 38851, Mailing Address: P.O. Box 626, Zip 38851–0626;
tel. 601/456–3700; Bristol Messer, Chief Executive Officer

MISSOURI: DEXTER MEMORIAL HOSPITAL (O, 48 beds) 1200 North One Mile
Road, Dexter, MO Zip 63841–1099; tel. 573/624–5566; Randal
Tennison, Administrator

NORTH CAROLINA: BRUNSWICK COMMUNITY HOSPITAL (L, 56 beds) 1
Medical Center Drive, Supply, NC Zip 28462–3350, Mailing Address: P.O.
Box 139, Zip 28462–0139; tel. 910/755–8121; C. Mark Gregson, Chief
Executive Officer

DAVIS MEDICAL CENTER (O, 132 beds) 218 Old Mocksville Road, Statesville,
NC Zip 28625, Mailing Address: P.O. Box 1823, Zip 28687–1823;
tel. 704/873–0281; R. Alan Larson, Chief Executive Officer

TEXAS: CENTRAL TEXAS HOSPITAL (O, 44 beds) 806 North Crockett Avenue,
Cameron, TX Zip 76520–2599; tel. 254/697–6591; Jodi Beauregard,
Administrator

For explanation of codes following names, see page B2.
★ Indicates Type III membership in the American Hospital Association.

Section B

DENTON COMMUNITY HOSPITAL (O, 110 beds) 207 North Bonnie Brae Street, Denton, TX Zip 76201–3798; tel. 940/898–7000; Timothy Charles, Chief Executive Officer
Web address: www.dentonhospital.com

WEST VIRGINIA: GREENBRIER VALLEY MEDICAL CENTER (O, 122 beds) 202 Maplewood Avenue, Ronceverte, WV Zip 24970–0497, Mailing Address: P.O. Box 497, Zip 24970–0497; tel. 304/647–4411; Donald D. Sandoval, FACHE, Chief Executive Officer

Owned, leased, sponsored:	14 hospitals	1143 beds
Contract–managed:	0 hospitals	0 beds
Totals:	14 hospitals	1143 beds

0163: NEW AMERICAN HEALTHCARE CORPORATION (IO)
109 Westpark Drive, Suite 440, Brentwood, TN Zip 37027, Mailing Address: P.O. Box 3689, Zip 37024; tel. 615/221–5070; Thomas Singleton, President and Chief Executive Officer

GEORGIA: MEMORIAL HOSPITAL OF ADEL (O, 155 beds) 706 North Parrish Avenue, Adel, GA Zip 31620–0677, Mailing Address: Box 677, Zip 31620–0677; tel. 912/896–2251; Greg Griffith, Chief Executive Officer

IOWA: DAVENPORT MEDICAL CENTER (O, 105 beds) 1111 West Kimberly Road, Davenport, IA Zip 52806–5913; tel. 319/445–4020; James Fraser, Chief Executive Officer

MISSISSIPPI: CROSBY MEMORIAL HOSPITAL (C, 71 beds) 801 Goodyear Boulevard, Picayune, MS Zip 39466–3221, Mailing Address: P.O. Box 909, Zip 39466–0909; tel. 601/798–4711; Fred Woody, Administrator
Web address: www.CROSBYHOSPITAL.COM

MISSOURI: DOCTORS HOSPITAL (O, 90 beds) 500 Medical Drive, Wentzville, MO Zip 63385–0711; tel. 314/327–1000; Barry A. Papania, President and Chief Executive Officer

OREGON: EASTMORELAND HOSPITAL (O, 77 beds) 2900 S.E. Steele Street, Portland, OR Zip 97202; tel. 503/234–0411; J. Phillip Young, Chief Executive Officer

WOODLAND PARK HOSPITAL (O, 123 beds) 10300 N.E. Hancock, Portland, OR Zip 97220; tel. 503/257–5500; J. Phillip Young, Assistant Administrator Operations

TENNESSEE: DELTA MEDICAL CENTER (O, 134 beds) 3000 Getwell Road, Memphis, TN Zip 38118–2299; tel. 901/369–8500; Larry D. Walker, Chief Executive Officer

TEXAS: DOLLY VINSANT MEMORIAL HOSPITAL (O, 49 beds) 400 East U.S. Highway 77, San Benito, TX Zip 78586–5310, Mailing Address: P.O. Box 42, Zip 78586–0042; tel. 956/399–1313; Mark Dooley, Chief Executive Officer

MEMORIAL HOSPITAL OF CENTER (O, 46 beds) 602 Hurst Street, Center, TX Zip 75935–3414, Mailing Address: P.O. Box 1749, Zip 75935–1749; tel. 409/598–2781; Robert V. Deen, Chief Executive Officer

WYOMING: LANDER VALLEY MEDICAL CENTER (O, 102 beds) 1320 Bishop Randall Drive, Lander, WY Zip 82520–3996; tel. 307/332–4420; Andrew Gramlich, Chief Executive Officer
Web address: www.landerhospital.com

Owned, leased, sponsored:	9 hospitals	881 beds
Contract–managed:	1 hospital	71 beds
Totals:	10 hospitals	952 beds

★0142: NEW YORK & PRESBYTERIAN HEALTHCARE (NP)
525 East 68th Street, New York, NY Zip 10021–4885; tel. 212/746–4000; David B. Skinner, M.D., Vice Chairman and Chief Executive Officer

NEW YORK: BROOKLYN HOSPITAL CENTER (O, 653 beds) 121 DeKalb Avenue, Brooklyn, NY Zip 11201–5493; tel. 718/250–8005; Frederick D. Alley, President and Chief Executive Officer

GRACIE SQUARE HOSPITAL (O, 130 beds) 420 East 76th Street, New York, NY Zip 10021–3104; tel. 212/988–4400; Frank Bruno, Chief Executive Officer

HOSPITAL FOR SPECIAL SURGERY (O, 138 beds) 535 East 70th Street, New York, NY Zip 10021–4898; tel. 212/606–1000; John R. Reynolds, President and Chief Executive Officer
Web address: www.hss.edu

NEW YORK COMMUNITY HOSPITAL (O, 134 beds) 2525 Kings Highway, Brooklyn, NY Zip 11229–1798; tel. 718/692–5300; Lin H. Mo, President and Chief Executive Officer

NEW YORK FLUSHING HOSPITAL MEDICAL CENTER (O, 250 beds) 45th Avenue at Parsons Boulevard, Flushing, NY Zip 11355–2100; tel. 718/670–5000; Stephen S. Mills, President and Chief Executive Officer

NEW YORK HOSPITAL MEDICAL CENTER OF QUEENS (O, 457 beds) 56–45 Main Street, Flushing, NY Zip 11355–5000; tel. 718/670–1231; Stephen S. Mills, President and Chief Executive Officer
Web address: www.nyhq.org

NEW YORK METHODIST HOSPITAL (O, 560 beds) 506 Sixth Street, Brooklyn, NY Zip 11215–3645; tel. 718/780–3000; Mark J. Mundy, President and Chief Executive Officer
Web address: www.nym.org

NEW YORK PRESBYTERIAN HOSPITAL (O, 2278 beds) 525 East 68th Street, New York, NY Zip 10021–4885; tel. 212/746–5454; David B. Skinner, M.D., Vice Chairman and Chief Executive Officer

UNITED HOSPITAL MEDICAL CENTER (O, 191 beds) 406 Boston Post Road, Port Chester, NY Zip 10573–7300; tel. 914/934–3000; Kevin Dahill, President and Chief Executive Officer
Web address: www.uhmc.com

WYCKOFF HEIGHTS MEDICAL CENTER (O, 324 beds) 374 Stockholm Street, Brooklyn, NY Zip 11237–4099; tel. 718/963–7102; Dominick J. Gio, President and Chief Executive Officer

Owned, leased, sponsored:	10 hospitals	5115 beds
Contract–managed:	0 hospitals	0 beds
Totals:	10 hospitals	5115 beds

3075: NEW YORK CITY HEALTH AND HOSPITALS CORPORATION (NP)
125 Worth Street, Room 514, New York, NY Zip 10013–4006; tel. 212/788–3321; Luis R. Marcos, M.D., President

BELLEVUE HOSPITAL CENTER (O, 811 beds) 462 First Avenue, New York, NY Zip 10016–9198, Mailing Address: 462 First Avenue, ME–8, Zip 10016–9198; tel. 212/562–4141; Carlos Perez, Executive Director

COLER MEMORIAL HOSPITAL (O, 1025 beds) Roosevelt Island, New York, NY Zip 10044; tel. 212/848–6000; Samuel Lehrfeld, Executive Director

CONEY ISLAND HOSPITAL (O, 409 beds) 2601 Ocean Parkway, Brooklyn, NY Zip 11235–7795; tel. 718/616–3000; William Walsh, Executive Director

ELMHURST HOSPITAL CENTER (O, 525 beds) 79–01 Broadway, Elmhurst, NY Zip 11373; tel. 718/334–4000; Pete Velez, Executive Director

GOLDWATER MEMORIAL HOSPITAL (O, 991 beds) Franklin D. Roosevelt Island, New York, NY Zip 10044; tel. 212/318–8000; Samuel Lehrfeld, Executive Director
Web address: www.coler–goldwater.org

HARLEM HOSPITAL CENTER (O, 414 beds) 506 Lenox Avenue, New York, NY Zip 10037–1894; tel. 212/939–1000; John M. Palmer, Ph.D., Executive Director

JACOBI MEDICAL CENTER (O, 549 beds) Pelham Parkway South and Eastchester Road, Bronx, NY Zip 10461–1197; tel. 718/918–5000; Joseph S. Orlando, Executive Director
Web address: www.nychhc.org

KINGS COUNTY HOSPITAL CENTER (O, 728 beds) 451 Clarkson Avenue, Brooklyn, NY Zip 11203–2097; tel. 718/245–3131; Jean G. Leon, R.N., Senior Vice President

LINCOLN MEDICAL AND MENTAL HEALTH CENTER (O, 330 beds) 234 East 149th Street, Bronx, NY Zip 10451–9998; tel. 718/579–5700; Jose R. Sanchez, Executive Director

METROPOLITAN HOSPITAL CENTER (O, 351 beds) 1901 First Avenue, New York, NY Zip 10029–7496; tel. 212/423–6262; Jose R. Sanchez, Executive Director

For explanation of codes following names, see page B2.
★ Indicates Type III membership in the American Hospital Association.

NORTH CENTRAL BRONX HOSPITAL (O, 255 beds) 3424 Kossuth Avenue, Bronx, NY Zip 10467–2489; tel. 718/519–3500; Arthur Wagner, Chief Operating Officer

QUEENS HOSPITAL CENTER (O, 276 beds) 82–68 164th Street, Jamaica, NY Zip 11432–1104; tel. 718/883–3000; Gladiola Sampson, Executive Director

WOODHULL MEDICAL AND MENTAL HEALTH CENTER (O, 358 beds) 760 Broadway Street, Brooklyn, NY Zip 11206–5383; tel. 718/963–8000; Cynthia Carrington–Murray, R.N., MS, Executive Director

Owned, leased, sponsored:	13 hospitals	7022 beds
Contract–managed:	0 hospitals	0 beds
Totals:	13 hospitals	7022 beds

0009: NEW YORK STATE DEPARTMENT OF MENTAL HEALTH (NP)
44 Holland Avenue, Albany, NY Zip 12229–3411; tel. 518/447–9611; Jesse Nixon Jr., Ph.D., Director

BINGHAMTON PSYCHIATRIC CENTER (O, 216 beds) 425 Robinson Street, Binghamton, NY Zip 13901–4198; tel. 607/724–1391; Margaret R. Dugan, Executive Director

BRONX CHILDREN'S PSYCHIATRIC CENTER (O, 75 beds) 1000 Waters Place, Bronx, NY Zip 10461–2799; tel. 718/892–0808; E. Richard Feinberg, M.D., Executive Director

BRONX PSYCHIATRIC CENTER (O, 658 beds) 1500 Waters Place, Bronx, NY Zip 10461–2796; tel. 718/931–0600; LeRoy Carmichael, Executive Director

BUFFALO PSYCHIATRIC CENTER (O, 260 beds) 400 Forest Avenue, Buffalo, NY Zip 14213–1298; tel. 716/885–2261; George Molnar, M.D., Executive Director
Web address: www.omh.state.ny.us

CAPITAL DISTRICT PSYCHIATRIC CENTER (O, 200 beds) 75 New Scotland Avenue, Albany, NY Zip 12208–3474; tel. 518/447–9611; Jesse Nixon Jr., Ph.D., Director

CREEDMOOR PSYCHIATRIC CENTER (O, 524 beds) Jamaica, NY Mailing Address: 80–45 Winchester Boulevard, Queens Village, Zip 11427–2199; tel. 718/264–3300; Charlotte Seltzer, Chief Executive Officer

ELMIRA PSYCHIATRIC CENTER (O, 103 beds) 100 Washington Street, Elmira, NY Zip 14901–2898; tel. 607/737–4739; George A. Roets, Director

HUDSON RIVER PSYCHIATRIC CENTER (O, 460 beds) 373 North Road, Poughkeepsie, NY Zip 12601–1197; tel. 914/452–8000; James Regan, Ph.D., Chief Executive Officer

KINGSBORO PSYCHIATRIC CENTER (O, 400 beds) 681 Clarkson Avenue, Brooklyn, NY Zip 11203–2199; tel. 718/221–7395; John M. Palmer, Ph.D., Director

MANHATTAN PSYCHIATRIC CENTER–WARD'S ISLAND (O, 745 beds) 600 East 125th Street, New York, NY Zip 10035–9998; tel. 212/369–0500; Eileen Consilvio, R.N., MS, Executive Director

MIDDLETOWN PSYCHIATRIC CENTER (O, 205 beds) 122 Dorothea Dix Drive, Middletown, NY Zip 10940–6198; tel. 914/342–5511; James H. Bopp, Executive Director

MOHAWK VALLEY PSYCHIATRIC CENTER (O, 614 beds) 1400 Noyes, Utica, NY Zip 13502–3803; tel. 315/797–6800; Sarah F. Rudes, Executive Director

NEW YORK STATE PSYCHIATRIC INSTITUTE (O, 58 beds) 1051 Riverside Drive, New York, NY Zip 10032–2695; tel. 212/543–5000; John M. Oldham, M.D., Director

PILGRIM PSYCHIATRIC CENTER (O, 744 beds) 998 Crooked Hill Road, Brentwood, NY Zip 11717–1087; tel. 516/761–3500; Kathleen Kelly, Chief Executive Officer

QUEENS CHILDREN'S PSYCHIATRIC CENTER (O, 106 beds) 74–03 Commonwealth Boulevard, Jamaica, NY Zip 11426–1890; tel. 718/264–4506; Gloria Faretra, M.D., Executive Director

RICHARD H. HUTCHINGS PSYCHIATRIC CENTER (O, 136 beds) 620 Madison Street, Syracuse, NY Zip 13210–2319; tel. 315/473–4980; Bryan F. Rudes, Executive Director

ROCHESTER PSYCHIATRIC CENTER (O, 288 beds) 1111 Elmwood Avenue, Rochester, NY Zip 14620–3005; tel. 716/473–3230; Bryan F. Rudes, Executive Director

ROCKLAND CHILDREN'S PSYCHIATRIC CENTER (O, 54 beds) 599 Convent Road, Orangeburg, NY Zip 10962; tel. 914/359–7400; Marcia Werby, Administrator

ROCKLAND PSYCHIATRIC CENTER (O, 470 beds) 140 Old Orangeburg Road, Orangeburg, NY Zip 10962–0071; tel. 914/359–1000; James H. Bopp, Executive Director

SAGAMORE CHILDREN'S PSYCHIATRIC CENTER (O, 69 beds) 197 Half Hollow Road, Huntington Station, NY Zip 11746; tel. 516/673–7700; Robert Schweitzer, Ed.D., Executive Director

SOUTH BEACH PSYCHIATRIC CENTER (O, 325 beds) 777 Seaview Avenue, Staten Island, NY Zip 10305–3499; tel. 718/667–2300; Lucy Sarkis, M.D., Executive Director

ST. LAWRENCE PSYCHIATRIC CENTER (O, 120 beds) 1 Chimney Point Drive, Ogdensburg, NY Zip 13669–2291; tel. 315/393–3000; John R. Scott, Director

WESTERN NEW YORK CHILDREN'S PSYCHIATRIC CENTER (O, 46 beds) 1010 East and West Road, Buffalo, NY Zip 14224–3698; tel. 716/674–9730; Jed M. Cohen, Acting Executive Director

Owned, leased, sponsored:	23 hospitals	6876 beds
Contract–managed:	0 hospitals	0 beds
Totals:	23 hospitals	6876 beds

★3115: NORTH BROWARD HOSPITAL DISTRICT (NP)
303 S.E. 17th Street, Fort Lauderdale, FL Zip 33316–2510; tel. 954/355–5100; G. Wil Trower, President and Chief Executive Officer

FLORIDA: BROWARD GENERAL MEDICAL CENTER (O, 548 beds) 1600 South Andrews Avenue, Fort Lauderdale, FL Zip 33316–2510; tel. 954/355–4400; Timothy P. Menton, Interim Administrator

CORAL SPRINGS MEDICAL CENTER (O, 167 beds) 3000 Coral Hills Drive, Coral Springs, FL Zip 33065; tel. 954/344–3000; Debbie Mulvihill, Interim Administrator

IMPERIAL POINT MEDICAL CENTER (O, 160 beds) 6401 North Federal Highway, Fort Lauderdale, FL Zip 33308–1495; tel. 954/776–8500; Dorothy J. Mancini, R.N., Regional Vice President Administration

NORTH BROWARD MEDICAL CENTER (O, 334 beds) 201 Sample Road, Pompano Beach, FL Zip 33064–3502; tel. 954/941–8300; James R. Chromik, Regional Vice President, Administration

Owned, leased, sponsored:	4 hospitals	1209 beds
Contract–managed:	0 hospitals	0 beds
Totals:	4 hospitals	1209 beds

0032: NORTH MISSISSIPPI HEALTH SERVICES, INC. (NP)
830 South Gloster Street, Tupelo, MS Zip 38801–4996; tel. 601/841–3136; Jeffrey B. Barber, Dr.PH, President and Chief Executive Officer

MISSISSIPPI: CLAY COUNTY MEDICAL CENTER (O, 60 beds) 835 Medical Center Drive, West Point, MS Zip 39773–9320; tel. 601/495–2300; David M. Reid, Administrator

IUKA HOSPITAL (O, 48 beds) 1777 Curtis Drive, Iuka, MS Zip 38852–1001, Mailing Address: P.O. Box 860, Zip 38852–0860; tel. 601/423–6051; Daniel Perryman, Administrator

NORTH MISSISSIPPI MEDICAL CENTER (O, 724 beds) 830 South Gloster Street, Tupelo, MS Zip 38801–4934; tel. 601/841–3000; Jeffrey B. Barber, Dr.PH, President and Chief Executive Officer

PONTOTOC HOSPITAL AND EXTENDED CARE FACILITY (L, 71 beds) 176 South Main Street, Pontotoc, MS Zip 38863–3311, Mailing Address: P.O. Box 790, Zip 38863–0790; tel. 601/489–5510; Fred B. Hood, Administrator

WEBSTER HEALTH SERVICES (L, 76 beds) 500 Highway 9 South, Eupora, MS Zip 39744; tel. 601/258–6221; Harold H. Whitaker Sr., Administrator

Owned, leased, sponsored:	5 hospitals	979 beds
Contract–managed:	0 hospitals	0 beds
Totals:	5 hospitals	979 beds

For explanation of codes following names, see page B2.
★ Indicates Type III membership in the American Hospital Association.

★0062: NORTH SHORE– LONG ISLAND JEWISH HEALTH SYSTEM (NP)
145 Community Drive, Great Neck, NY Zip 11021; tel. 516/465–8100; John S. T. Gallagher, Chief Executive Officer

NEW YORK: FRANKLIN HOSPITAL MEDICAL CENTER (C, 425 beds) 900 Franklin Avenue, Valley Stream, NY Zip 11580–2190; tel. 516/256–6000; William Kowalewski, President and Chief Executive Officer

HUNTINGTON HOSPITAL (C, 265 beds) 270 Park Avenue, Huntington, NY Zip 11743–2799; tel. 516/351–2200; J. Ronald Gaudreault, President and Chief Executive Officer
Web address: www.hunthosp.org

LONG ISLAND JEWISH MEDICAL CENTER (O, 784 beds) 270–05 76th Avenue, New Hyde Park, NY Zip 11040–1496; tel. 718/470–7000; David R. Dantzker, M.D., President
Web address: www.lij.edu

NORTH SHORE UNIVERSITY HOSPITAL (O, 705 beds) 300 Community Drive, Manhasset, NY Zip 11030–3876; tel. 516/562–0100; John S. T. Gallagher, Chief Executive Officer

NORTH SHORE UNIVERSITY HOSPITAL AT GLEN COVE (O, 265 beds) 101 St. Andrews Lane, Glen Cove, NY Zip 11542; tel. 516/674–7300; Mark R. Stenzler, Vice President Administration

NORTH SHORE UNIVERSITY HOSPITAL AT PLAINVIEW (O, 279 beds) 888 Old Country Road, Plainview, NY Zip 11803–4978; tel. 516/719–3000; Deborah Tascone, R.N., MS, Vice President for Administration

NORTH SHORE UNIVERSITY HOSPITAL AT SYOSSET (O, 186 beds) 221 Jericho Turnpike, Syosset, NY Zip 11791–4567; tel. 516/496–6400; Deborah Tascone, R.N., MS, Vice President of Administration

NORTH SHORE UNIVERSITY HOSPITAL–FOREST HILLS (O, 231 beds) Flushing, NY Mailing Address: 102–01 66th Road, Zip 11375; tel. 718/830–4000; Andrew J. Mitchell, Vice President, Administration

SOUTHSIDE HOSPITAL (C, 356 beds) 301 East Main Street, Bay Shore, NY Zip 11706–8458; tel. 516/968–3000; Theodore A. Jospe, President

STATEN ISLAND UNIVERSITY HOSPITAL (C, 617 beds) 475 Seaview Avenue, Staten Island, NY Zip 10305–9998; tel. 718/226–9000; Rick J. Varone, President

Owned, leased, sponsored:	6 hospitals	2450 beds
Contract–managed:	4 hospitals	1663 beds
Totals:	10 hospitals	4113 beds

★2075: NORTHBAY HEALTHCARE SYSTEM (NP)
1200 B Gale Wilson Boulevard, Fairfield, CA Zip 94533–3587; tel. 707/429–7809; Gary J. Passama, President and Chief Executive Officer

CALIFORNIA: NORTHBAY MEDICAL CENTER (O, 121 beds) 1200 B. Gale Wilson Boulevard, Fairfield, CA Zip 94533–3587; tel. 707/429–3600; Deborah Sugiyama, President
Web address: www.northbay.org

VACAVALLEY HOSPITAL (O, 43 beds) 1000 Nut Tree Road, Vacaville, CA Zip 95687; tel. 707/446–4000; Deborah Sugiyama, President
Web address: www.northbay.org

Owned, leased, sponsored:	2 hospitals	164 beds
Contract–managed:	0 hospitals	0 beds
Totals:	2 hospitals	164 beds

★2285: NORTON HEALTHCARE (NP)
234 East Gray Street, Suite 225, Louisville, KY Zip 40202, Mailing Address: P.O. Box 35070, Zip 40232–5070; tel. 502/629–8000; Stephen A. Williams, President

ILLINOIS: FAIRFIELD MEMORIAL HOSPITAL (C, 185 beds) 303 N.W. 11th Street, Fairfield, IL Zip 62837–1203; tel. 618/842–2611; Terry Thompson, Chief Executive Officer

MASSAC MEMORIAL HOSPITAL (C, 38 beds) 28 Chick Street, Metropolis, IL Zip 62960–2481, Mailing Address: P.O. Box 850, Zip 62960–0850; tel. 618/524–2176; Mark Edwards, Chief Executive Officer

PARIS COMMUNITY HOSPITAL (C, 49 beds) 721 East Court Street, Paris, IL Zip 61944–2420; tel. 217/465–4141; J. Jay Purvis, Interim Administrator

WABASH GENERAL HOSPITAL DISTRICT (C, 56 beds) 1418 College Drive, Mount Carmel, IL Zip 62863–2638; tel. 618/262–8621; James R. Farris, CHE, Chief Executive Officer

INDIANA: BLACKFORD COUNTY HOSPITAL (C, 36 beds) 503 East Van Cleve Street, Hartford City, IN Zip 47348–1897; tel. 765/348–0300; Steven J. West, Chief Executive Officer

DECATUR COUNTY MEMORIAL HOSPITAL (C, 70 beds) 720 North Lincoln Street, Greensburg, IN Zip 47240–1398; tel. 812/663–4331; Charles Duffy, President

GIBSON GENERAL HOSPITAL (C, 109 beds) 1808 Sherman Drive, Princeton, IN Zip 47670–1043; tel. 812/385–3401; Michael J. Budnick, Administrator and Chief Executive Officer

HARRISON COUNTY HOSPITAL (C, 47 beds) 245 Atwood Street, Corydon, IN Zip 47112–1774; tel. 812/738–4251; Steven L. Taylor, Chief Executive Officer

PERRY COUNTY MEMORIAL HOSPITAL (C, 38 beds) 1 Hospital Road, Tell City, IN Zip 47586–0362; tel. 812/547–7011; Bradford W. Dykes, Chief Executive Officer
Web address: www.pchospital.org

RANDOLPH COUNTY HOSPITAL AND HEALTH SERVICES (C, 27 beds) 325 South Oak Street, Winchester, IN Zip 47394–2235, Mailing Address: P.O. Box 407, Zip 47394–0407; tel. 765/584–9001; James M. Full, Chief Executive Officer

RUSH MEMORIAL HOSPITAL (C, 52 beds) 1300 North Main Street, Rushville, IN Zip 46173–1198; tel. 765/932–4111; H. William Hartley, Chief Executive Officer

KENTUCKY: BRECKINRIDGE MEMORIAL HOSPITAL (C, 45 beds) 1011 Old Highway 60, Hardinsburg, KY Zip 40143–2597; tel. 502/756–7000; George Walz, CHE, Chief Executive Officer
Web address: www.multiplan.com

CARROLL COUNTY HOSPITAL (L, 39 beds) 309 11th Street, Carrollton, KY Zip 41008–1400; tel. 502/732–4321; Roger Williams, Chief Executive Officer

CAVERNA MEMORIAL HOSPITAL (C, 28 beds) 1501 South Dixie Street, Horse Cave, KY Zip 42749–1477; tel. 502/786–2191; James J. Kerins Sr., Administrator

NORTON AUDUBON HOSPITAL (O, 420 beds) One Audubon Plaza Drive, Louisville, KY Zip 40217–1397, Mailing Address: P.O. Box 17550, Zip 40217–0550; tel. 502/636–7111; Thomas D. Kmetz, Chief Administrative Officer

NORTON HEALTHCARE (O, 646 beds) 200 East Chestnut Street, Louisville, KY Zip 40202–1800, Mailing Address: P.O. Box 35070, Zip 40232–5070; tel. 502/629–8000; Stephen M. Tullman, Chief Administrative Officer
Web address: www.northonhealthcare.org

NORTON HEALTHCARE PAVILION (O, 178 beds) 315 East Broadway, Louisville, KY Zip 40202; tel. 502/629–2000; Stephen A. Williams, President and Chief Executive Officer

NORTON SOUTHWEST HOSPITAL (O, 108 beds) 9820 Third Street Road, Louisville, KY Zip 40272–9984; tel. 502/933–8100; James W. Pope, Chief Administrative Officer

NORTON SPRING VIEW HOSPITAL (O, 113 beds) 320 Loretto Road, Lebanon, KY Zip 40033–0320; tel. 502/692–3161; Patricia Ekdahl, Chief Executive Officer

NORTON SUBURBAN HOSPITAL (O, 250 beds) 4001 Dutchmans Lane, Louisville, KY Zip 40207–4799; tel. 502/893–1000; John A. Marshall, President and Chief Executive Officer

RUSSELL COUNTY HOSPITAL (C, 45 beds) Dowell Road, Russell Springs, KY Zip 42642, Mailing Address: P.O. Box 1610, Zip 42642–1610; tel. 502/866–4141; Richard Hacker, Interim Administrator

THE JAMES B. HAGGIN MEMORIAL HOSPITAL (C, 64 beds) 464 Linden Avenue, Harrodsburg, KY Zip 40330–1862; tel. 606/734–5441; Earl James Motzer, Ph.D., FACHE, Chief Executive Officer

TWIN LAKES REGIONAL MEDICAL CENTER (C, 75 beds) 910 Wallace Avenue, Leitchfield, KY Zip 42754–1499; tel. 502/259–9400; Stephen L. Meredith, Chief Executive Officer

Section B

For explanation of codes following names, see page B2.
★ Indicates Type III membership in the American Hospital Association.

Owned, leased, sponsored:	7 hospitals	1754 beds
Contract–managed:	16 hospitals	964 beds
Totals:	23 hospitals	2718 beds

★**0139: NOVANT HEALTH** (NP)
3333 Silas Creek Parkway, Winston Salem, NC Zip 27103–3090; tel. 336/718–5000; Paul M. Wiles, President and Chief Executive Officer

NORTH CAROLINA: COMMUNITY GENERAL HOSPITAL OF THOMASVILLE (O, 123 beds) 207 Old Lexington Road, Thomasville, NC Zip 27360, Mailing Address: P.O. Box 789, Zip 27361–0789; tel. 336/472–2000; Lynn Ingram Boggs, President and Chief Executive Officer
Web address: www.cghp.org

DAVIE COUNTY HOSPITAL (L, 32 beds) 223 Hospital Street, Mocksville, NC Zip 27028–2038, Mailing Address: P.O. Box 1209, Zip 27028–1209; tel. 336/751–8100; Mike Kimel, Administrator
Web address: www.novanthealth.org

FORSYTH MEDICAL CENTER (O, 680 beds) 3333 Silas Creek Parkway, Winston–Salem, NC Zip 27103–3090; tel. 336/718–5000; Gregory J. Beier, President
Web address: www.novanthealth.org

MEDICAL PARK HOSPITAL (O, 59 beds) 1950 South Hawthorne Road, Winston–Salem, NC Zip 27103–3993, Mailing Address: P.O. Box 24728, Zip 27114–4728; tel. 336/718–0600; Eduard R. Koehler, Administrator

PRESBYTERIAN HOSPITAL (O, 853 beds) 200 Hawthorne Lane, Charlotte, NC Zip 28204–2528, Mailing Address: P.O. Box 33549, Zip 28233–3549; tel. 704/384–4000; Thomas R. Revels, President and Chief Executive Officer
Web address: www.phsc.com

PRESBYTERIAN HOSPITAL–MATTHEWS (O, 76 beds) 1500 Matthews Township Parkway, Matthews, NC Zip 28105, Mailing Address: P.O. Box 3310, Zip 28106–3310; tel. 704/384–6500; Mark R. Farmer, Vice President and Administrator

PRESBYTERIAN SPECIALTY HOSPITAL (O, 15 beds) 1600 East Third Street, Charlotte, NC Zip 28204–3282, Mailing Address: P.O. Box 34425, Zip 28234–4425; tel. 704/384–6000; Patricia Mabe, Vice President and Chief Nursing Officer

PRESBYTERIAN–ORTHOPAEDIC HOSPITAL (O, 166 beds) 1901 Randolph Road, Charlotte, NC Zip 28207–1195; tel. 704/375–6792; Grayce M. Crockett, Administrator

Owned, leased, sponsored:	8 hospitals	2004 beds
Contract–managed:	0 hospitals	0 beds
Totals:	8 hospitals	2004 beds

★**1165: OAKWOOD HEALTHCARER, INC.** (NP)
One Parklane Boulevard, Suite 1000E, Dearborn, MI Zip 48126; tel. 313/253–6007; Gerald D. Fitzgerald, President and Chief Executive Officer

MICHIGAN: OAKWOOD HOSPITAL ANNAPOLIS CENTER (O, 167 beds) 33155 Annapolis Road, Wayne, MI Zip 48184–2493; tel. 734/467–4000; Thomas Kochis, Administrator

OAKWOOD HOSPITAL BEYER CENTER–YPSILANTI (O, 71 beds) 135 South Prospect Street, Ypsilanti, MI Zip 48198–5693; tel. 734/484–2200; Richard Hillbom, Chief Administrative Officer
Web address: www.oakwood.org

OAKWOOD HOSPITAL SEAWAY CENTER (O, 89 beds) 5450 Fort Street, Trenton, MI Zip 48183–4625; tel. 734/671–3800; Brian Peltz, Administrator
Web address: www.oalwood.org

OAKWOOD HOSPITAL AND MEDICAL CENTER–DEARBORN (O, 565 beds) 18101 Oakwood Boulevard, Dearborn, MI Zip 48124–4093, Mailing Address: P.O. Box 2500, Zip 48123–2500; tel. 313/593–7000; Joseph Tasse, Administrator
Web address: www.oakwood.org

OAKWOOD HOSPITAL–HERITAGE CENTER (O, 243 beds) 10000 Telegraph Road, Taylor, MI Zip 48180–3349; tel. 313/295–5000; Edward E. Freysinger, Administrator

Owned, leased, sponsored:	5 hospitals	1135 beds
Contract–managed:	0 hospitals	0 beds
Totals:	5 hospitals	1135 beds

★**0162: OHIOHEALTH** (NP)
3555 Olentangy River Road, 4000, Columbus, OH Zip 43214–3900; tel. 614/566–5424; William W. Wilkins, President and Chief Executive Officer

OHIO: BUCYRUS COMMUNITY HOSPITAL (C, 47 beds) 629 North Sandusky Avenue, Bucyrus, OH Zip 44820–0627, Mailing Address: Box 627, Zip 44820–0627; tel. 419/562–4677; LaMar L. Wyse, Chief Executive Officer

DOCTORS HOSPITAL (O, 380 beds) 1087 Dennison Avenue, Columbus, OH Zip 43201–3496; tel. 614/297–4000; John A. Bowers, Executive Vice President and Chief Operating Officer
Web address: www.doctorshospital.org

DOCTORS HOSPITAL OF NELSONVILLE (O, 70 beds) 1950 Mount Saint Mary Drive, Nelsonville, OH Zip 45764–1193; tel. 740/753–1931; Mark R. Seckinger, Administrator

GALION COMMUNITY HOSPITAL (C, 109 beds) 269 Portland Way South, Galion, OH Zip 44833–2399; tel. 419/468–4841; Lyndon J. Christman, Administrator and Chief Operating Officer

GRANT/RIVERSIDE METHODIST HOSPITALS–GRANT CAMPUS (O, 459 beds) 111 South Grant Avenue, Columbus, OH Zip 43215–1898; tel. 614/566–9000; David P. Blom, President
Web address: www.ohiohealth.com

GRANT/RIVERSIDE METHODIST HOSPITALS–RIVERSIDE CAMPUS (O, 812 beds) 3535 Olentangy River Road, Columbus, OH Zip 43214–3998; tel. 614/566–5000; David P. Blom, President
Web address: www.ohiohealth.com

HARDIN MEMORIAL HOSPITAL (O, 51 beds) 921 East Franklin Street, Kenton, OH Zip 43326–2099, Mailing Address: P.O. Box 710, Zip 43326–0710; tel. 419/673–0761; Don J. Sabol, Chief Executive Officer

MARION GENERAL HOSPITAL (O, 133 beds) 1000 McKinley Park Drive, Marion, OH Zip 43302–6397; tel. 740/383–8400; Frank V. Swinehart, President and Chief Executive Officer
Web address: www.mariongeneral.org

MORROW COUNTY HOSPITAL (C, 75 beds) 651 West Marion Road, Mount Gilead, OH Zip 43338–1096; tel. 419/946–5015; Alan C. Pauley, Administrator

SOUTHERN OHIO MEDICAL CENTER (O, 281 beds) 1805 27th Street, Portsmouth, OH Zip 45662–2400; tel. 740/354–5000; Randal M. Arnett, President and Chief Executive Officer
Web address: www.somc.org

Owned, leased, sponsored:	7 hospitals	2186 beds
Contract–managed:	3 hospitals	231 beds
Totals:	10 hospitals	2417 beds

0018: OKLAHOMA STATE DEPARTMENT OF MENTAL HEALTH AND SUBSTANCE ABUSE SERVICES (NP)
1200 N.E. 13th Street, Oklahoma City, OK Zip 73152, Mailing Address: P.O. Box 53277, Zip 73152–3277; tel. 405/522–3908; Sharron D. Boehler, Commissioner

OKLAHOMA: EASTERN STATE HOSPITAL (O, 314 beds) Vinita, OK Mailing Address: P.O. Box 69, Zip 74301–0069; tel. 918/256–7841; William T. Burkett, Chief Executive Officer

GRIFFIN MEMORIAL HOSPITAL (O, 182 beds) 900 East Main Street, Norman, OK Zip 73071–5305, Mailing Address: P.O. Box 151, Zip 73070–0151; tel. 405/321–4880; Don Bowen, Superintendent

WESTERN STATE PSYCHIATRIC CENTER (O, 156 beds) 1222 10th Street, Suite 211, Fort Supply, OK Zip 73841–0001; tel. 580/571–3233; Steve Norwood, Executive Director

Owned, leased, sponsored:	3 hospitals	652 beds
Contract–managed:	0 hospitals	0 beds
Totals:	3 hospitals	652 beds

For explanation of codes following names, see page B2.
★ Indicates Type III membership in the American Hospital Association.

3355: ORLANDO REGIONAL HEALTHCARE SYSTEM (NP)
1414 Kuhl Avenue, Orlando, FL Zip 32806–2093;
tel. 407/841–5111; John Hillenmeyer, President and Chief Executive
Officer

FLORIDA: ORLANDO REGIONAL MEDICAL CENTER (O, 1049 beds) 1414 Kuhl
Avenue, Orlando, FL Zip 32806–2093; tel. 407/841–5111; Abe Lopman,
Executive Director
Web address: www.orhs.org

SOUTH LAKE HOSPITAL (O, 64 beds) 847 Eighth Street, Clermont, FL
Zip 34711–2196; tel. 352/394–4071; Leslie Longacre, Executive Director
and Chief Executive Officer

SOUTH SEMINOLE HOSPITAL (O, 206 beds) 555 West State Road 434,
Longwood, FL Zip 32750–4999; tel. 407/767–1200; Sue Whelan–Williams,
Site Administrator

ST. CLOUD HOSPITAL, A DIVISION OF ORLANDO REGIONAL HEALTHCARE
SYSTEM (O, 68 beds) 2906 17th Street, Saint Cloud, FL Zip 34769–6099;
tel. 407/892–2135; Jim Norris, Executive Director

Owned, leased, sponsored:	4 hospitals	1387 beds
Contract–managed:	0 hospitals	0 beds
Totals:	4 hospitals	1387 beds

★5335: OSF HEALTHCARE SYSTEM (CC)
800 N.E. Glen Oak Avenue, Peoria, IL Zip 61603–3200;
tel. 309/655–2852; Sister Frances Marie Masching, President

ILLINOIS: SAINT ANTHONY MEDICAL CENTER (O, 184 beds) 5666 East State
Street, Rockford, IL Zip 61108–2472; tel. 815/226–2000; David A.
Schertz, Administrator
Web address: www.osfhealth.com

SAINT FRANCIS MEDICAL CENTER (O, 536 beds) 530 N.E. Glen Oak Avenue,
Peoria, IL Zip 61637; tel. 309/655–2000; Keith E. Steffen, Administrator

SAINT JAMES HOSPITAL (O, 81 beds) 610 East Water Street, Pontiac, IL
Zip 61764–2194; tel. 815/842–2828; David Ochs, Administrator
Web address: www.osfhealthcare.org

SAINT JOSEPH HOSPITAL (O, 58 beds) 1005 Julien Street, Belvidere, IL
Zip 61008–9932; tel. 815/544–3411; David A. Schertz, Administrator

ST. JOSEPH MEDICAL CENTER (O, 154 beds) 2200 East Washington Street,
Bloomington, IL Zip 61701–4323; tel. 309/662–3311; Kenneth J. Natzke,
Administrator
Web address: www.osfhealthcare.org

ST. MARY MEDICAL CENTER (O, 141 beds) 3333 North Seminary Street,
Galesburg, IL Zip 61401–1299; tel. 309/344–3161; Richard S. Kowalski,
Administrator and Chief Executive Officer

MICHIGAN: ST. FRANCIS HOSPITAL (O, 66 beds) 3401 Ludington Street,
Escanaba, MI Zip 49829–1377; tel. 906/786–3311; Roger M. Burgess,
Administrator
Web address: www.osfhealthcare.com

Owned, leased, sponsored:	7 hospitals	1220 beds
Contract–managed:	0 hospitals	0 beds
Totals:	7 hospitals	1220 beds

0110: OUR LADY OF MERCY HEALTHCARE SYSTEM, INC.
(CC)
600 East 233 Street, New York, NY Zip 10466–2697;
tel. 718/920–9000; Gary S. Horan, FACHE, President and Chief
Executive Officer

NEW YORK: OUR LADY OF MERCY MEDICAL CENTER (O, 478 beds) 600
East 233rd Street, Bronx, NY Zip 10466–2697; tel. 718/920–9000; Gary
S. Horan, FACHE, President and Chief Executive Officer
Web address: www.ourladyofmercy.com

ST. AGNES HOSPITAL (O, 142 beds) 305 North Street, White Plains, NY
Zip 10605–2299; tel. 914/681–4500; Gary S. Horan, FACHE, President and
Chief Executive Officer
Web address: www.saintagneshospital.com

Owned, leased, sponsored:	2 hospitals	620 beds
Contract–managed:	0 hospitals	0 beds
Totals:	2 hospitals	620 beds

0435: PACIFIC HEALTH CORPORATION (IO)
249 East Ocean Boulevard, Long Beach, CA Zip 90802;
tel. 310/435–1300; Jens Mueller, Chairman

CALIFORNIA: BELLFLOWER MEDICAL CENTER (O, 145 beds) 9542 East
Artesia Boulevard, Bellflower, CA Zip 90706; tel. 562/925–8355; Stanley
Otake, Chief Executive Officer

LOS ANGELES METROPOLITAN MEDICAL CENTER (O, 173 beds) 2231 South
Western Avenue, Los Angeles, CA Zip 90018–1399; tel. 323/730–7342;
Marc A. Furstman, Chief Executive Officer

Owned, leased, sponsored:	2 hospitals	318 beds
Contract–managed:	0 hospitals	0 beds
Totals:	2 hospitals	318 beds

★4155: PALMETTO HEALTH ALLIANCE (CO)
Columbia, SC Mailing Address: P.O. Box 2266, Zip 29202–2266;
tel. 803/296–2000; Charles D. Beaman Jr., President

SOUTH CAROLINA: PALMETTO BAPTIST MEDICAL CENTER EASLEY (O, 106
beds) 200 Fleetwood Drive, Easley, SC Zip 29640–2076, Mailing
Address: P.O. Box 2129, Zip 29641–2129; tel. 864/855–7200; Roddey
E. Gettys III, Executive Vice President

PALMETTO BAPTIST MEDICAL CENTER/COLUMBIA (O, 369 beds) Taylor at
Marion Street, Columbia, SC Zip 29220; tel. 803/296–5010; James M.
Bridges, Executive Vice President and Chief Operating Officer
Web address: www.bhsc.hbocvan.com

PALMETTO RICHLAND MEMORIAL HOSPITAL (O, 595 beds) Five Richland
Medical Park Drive, Columbia, SC Zip 29203, Mailing Address: P.O. Box
2266, Zip 29203–2266; tel. 803/434–7000; B. Daniel Paysinger, M.D.,
Chief Operating Officer
Web address: www.rmh.edu

Owned, leased, sponsored:	3 hospitals	1070 beds
Contract–managed:	0 hospitals	0 beds
Totals:	3 hospitals	1070 beds

★7555: PALOMAR POMERADO HEALTH SYSTEM (NP)
15255 Innovation Drive, Suite 204, San Diego, CA Zip 92128–3410;
tel. 619/675–5100; Norman F. Gruber, President and Chief
Executive Officer

CALIFORNIA: PALOMAR MEDICAL CENTER (O, 424 beds) 555 East Valley
Parkway, Escondido, CA Zip 92025–3084; tel. 760/739–3000; Victoria
M. Penland, Administrator and Chief Operating Officer

POMERADO HOSPITAL (O, 238 beds) 15615 Pomerado Road, Poway, CA
Zip 92064; tel. 619/485–6511; Marvin W. Levenson, M.D., Administrator and
Chief Operating Officer
Web address: www.pphs.org

Owned, leased, sponsored:	2 hospitals	662 beds
Contract–managed:	0 hospitals	0 beds
Totals:	2 hospitals	662 beds

5765: PARACELSUS HEALTHCARE CORPORATION (IO)
515 West Greens Road, Suite 800, Houston, TX Zip 77067–4511;
tel. 281/774–5100; Charles R. Miller, President and Chief Operating
Officer

LANCASTER COMMUNITY HOSPITAL (O, 117 beds) 43830 North Tenth Street
West, Lancaster, CA Zip 93534; tel. 661/948–4781; John E. Fidler, FACHE,
Chief Executive Officer

FLORIDA: SANTA ROSA MEDICAL CENTER (O, 96 beds) 1450 Berryhill Road,
Milton, FL Zip 32570–4028, Mailing Address: P.O. Box 648,
Zip 32572–0648; tel. 850/626–7762; M. P. Gandy Jr., Chief Executive
Officer

For explanation of codes following names, see page B2.
★ Indicates Type III membership in the American Hospital Association.

Section B

GEORGIA: FLINT RIVER COMMUNITY HOSPITAL (O, 49 beds) 509 Sumter Street, Montezuma, GA Zip 31063–0770, Mailing Address: P.O. Box 770, Zip 31063–0770; tel. 912/472–3100; James D. Tesar, Chief Executive Officer

MISSISSIPPI: SENATOBIA COMMUNITY HOSPITAL (O, 52 beds) 401 Getwell Drive, Senatobia, MS Zip 38668–2213, Mailing Address: P.O. Box 648, Zip 38668–0648; tel. 601/562–3100; Dan Aranda, Chief Executive Officer

NORTH DAKOTA: DAKOTA HEARTLAND HEALTH SYSTEM (O, 203 beds) 1720 South University Drive, Fargo, ND Zip 58103–4994; tel. 701/280–4100; Louis Kauffman, President and Chief Executive Officer
Web address: www.dakotahealthland.com

TENNESSEE: BLEDSOE COUNTY GENERAL HOSPITAL (O, 26 beds) 128 Wheelertown Road, Pikeville, TN Zip 37367, Mailing Address: P.O. Box 699, Zip 37367–0699; tel. 423/447–2112; Gary Burton, Chief Executive Officer

CUMBERLAND RIVER HOSPITAL NORTH (O, 66 beds) 100 Old Jefferson Street, Celina, TN Zip 38551; tel. 931/243–3581; Patrick J. Gray, Chief Executive Officer

FENTRESS COUNTY GENERAL HOSPITAL (O, 73 beds) Highway 52 West, Jamestown, TN Zip 38556, Mailing Address: P.O. Box 1500, Zip 38556; tel. 931/879–8171; Patrick J. Gray, Chief Executive Officer

TEXAS: BAYCOAST MEDICAL CENTER (O, 191 beds) 1700 James Bowie Drive, Baytown, TX Zip 77520–3386; tel. 281/420–6100; Walter J. Ornsteen, President and Chief Executive Officer

MEDICAL CENTER OF MESQUITE (O, 176 beds) 1011 North Galloway Avenue, Mesquite, TX Zip 75149–2433; tel. 214/320–7000; Terry J. Fontenot, President and Chief Executive Officer

WESTWOOD MEDICAL CENTER (O, 86 beds) 4214 Andrews Highway, Midland, TX Zip 79703–4861; tel. 915/522–2273; Michael S. Potter, President and Chief Executive Officer
Web address: www.westwoodmed.com

UTAH: DAVIS HOSPITAL AND MEDICAL CENTER (O, 126 beds) 1600 West Antelope Drive, Layton, UT Zip 84041–1142; tel. 801/825–9561; Bruce A. Baldwin, Chief Executive Officer

JORDAN VALLEY HOSPITAL (O, 50 beds) 3580 West 9000 South, West Jordan, UT Zip 84088–8811; tel. 801/561–8888; Jeffrey J. Manley, Chief Executive Officer

PIONEER VALLEY HOSPITAL (O, 127 beds) 3460 South Pioneer Parkway, Salt Lake City, UT Zip 84120–2648; tel. 801/964–3100; Keith Tintle, Chief Executive Officer

SALT LAKE REGIONAL MEDICAL CENTER (O, 138 beds) 1050 East South Temple, Salt Lake City, UT Zip 84102–1599; tel. 801/350–4111; Kay Matsumura, Chief Executive Officer

VIRGINIA: CAPITOL MEDICAL CENTER (O, 131 beds) 701 West Grace Street, Richmond, VA Zip 23220–4191; tel. 804/775–4100; Priscilla J. Shuler, Chief Executive Officer

Owned, leased, sponsored:	16 hospitals	1707 beds
Contract–managed:	0 hospitals	0 beds
Totals:	16 hospitals	1707 beds

0159: PARKVIEW HEALTH SYSTEM (NP)
2200 Randallia Drive, Fort Wayne, IN Zip 46805; tel. 219/470–8200; Charles H. Mason Jr., President and Chief Executive Officer

INDIANA: HUNTINGTON MEMORIAL HOSPITAL (O, 37 beds) 1215 Etna Avenue, Huntington, IN Zip 46750–3696; tel. 219/356–3000; L. Kent McCoy, President

PARKVIEW HOSPITAL (O, 509 beds) 2200 Randallia Drive, Fort Wayne, IN Zip 46805–4699; tel. 219/484–6636; Frank D. Byrne, M.D., President

WHITLEY MEMORIAL HOSPITAL (O, 131 beds) 353 North Oak Street, Columbia City, IN Zip 46725–1623; tel. 219/244–6191; John M. Hatcher, President

Owned, leased, sponsored:	3 hospitals	677 beds
Contract–managed:	0 hospitals	0 beds
Totals:	3 hospitals	677 beds

★**1785: PARTNERS HEALTHCARE SYSTEM, INC.** (NP)
800 Boylston Street, Suite 1150, Boston, MA Zip 02199–8001; tel. 617/278–1004; Samuel O. Thier, M.D., President and Chief Executive Officer

MASSACHUSETTS: ATLANTICARE MEDICAL CENTER (O, 189 beds) 500 Lynnfield Street, Lynn, MA Zip 01904–1487; tel. 781/581–9200; Andrew J. Riddell, President

BRIGHAM AND WOMEN'S HOSPITAL (O, 650 beds) 75 Francis Street, Boston, MA Zip 02115–6195; tel. 617/732–5500; Jeffrey Otten, President
Web address: www.partners.org

FAULKNER HOSPITAL (O, 127 beds) Boston, MA Mailing Address: 1153 Centre Sreet, Zip 02130–3400; tel. 617/983–7000; David J. Trull, President and Chief Executive Officer
Web address: www.faulknerhospital.org

MASSACHUSETTS GENERAL HOSPITAL (O, 848 beds) 55 Fruit Street, Boston, MA Zip 02114–2696; tel. 617/726–2000; James J. Mongan, M.D., President

MCLEAN HOSPITAL (O, 135 beds) 115 Mill Street, Belmont, MA Zip 02478–9106; tel. 617/855–2000; Bruce M. Cohen, M.D., President and Psychiatrist–in–Chief
Web address: www.mcleanhospital.org

NEWTON–WELLESLEY HOSPITAL (O, 228 beds) 2014 Washington Street, Newton Lower Falls, MA Zip 02462–1699; tel. 617/243–6000; John P. Bihldorff, President and Chief Executive Officer
Web address: www.nwh.org

SALEM HOSPITAL (O, 228 beds) 81 Highland Avenue, Salem, MA Zip 01970–2768; tel. 978/741–1200; Stanley Reczek, President

SHAUGHNESSY–KAPLAN REHABILITATION HOSPITAL (O, 160 beds) Dove Avenue, Salem, MA Zip 01970–2999; tel. 978/745–9000; Anthony Sciola, President
Web address: www.nsmc.partners.org

SPAULDING REHABILITATION HOSPITAL (O, 296 beds) 125 Nashua Street, Boston, MA Zip 02114–1198; tel. 617/573–7000; John E. Cupples, Chief Executive Officer
Web address: www.spauldingrehab.org

Owned, leased, sponsored:	9 hospitals	2861 beds
Contract–managed:	0 hospitals	0 beds
Totals:	9 hospitals	2861 beds

★**5415: PEACEHEALTH** (CC)
15325 S.E. 30th Place, Suite 300, Bellevue, WA Zip 98007; tel. 425/747–1711; John Hayward, President and Chief Executive Officer

ALASKA: KETCHIKAN GENERAL HOSPITAL (L, 64 beds) 3100 Tongass Avenue, Ketchikan, AK Zip 99901–5746; tel. 907/225–5171; Edward F. Mahn, Chief Executive Officer

OREGON: PEACE HARBOR HOSPITAL (O, 21 beds) 400 Ninth Street, Florence, OR Zip 97439, Mailing Address: P.O. Box 580, Zip 97439; tel. 541/997–8412; James Barnhart, Administrator

SACRED HEART MEDICAL CENTER (O, 395 beds) 1255 Hilyard Street, Eugene, OR Zip 97401, Mailing Address: P.O. Box 10905, Zip 97440; tel. 541/686–7300; Judy Hodgson, Administrator
Web address: www.peacehealth.com

WASHINGTON: ST. JOHN MEDICAL CENTER (O, 178 beds) 1615 Delaware Street, Longview, WA Zip 98632, Mailing Address: P.O. Box 3002, Zip 98632–0302; tel. 360/414–2000; Mark E. McGourty, Regional Chief Executive Officer

ST. JOSEPH HOSPITAL (O, 189 beds) 2901 Squalicum Parkway, Bellingham, WA Zip 98225–1898; tel. 360/734–5400; Nancy J. Bitting, Chief Executive Officer
Web address: www.peacehealth

Owned, leased, sponsored:	5 hospitals	847 beds
Contract–managed:	0 hospitals	0 beds
Totals:	5 hospitals	847 beds

For explanation of codes following names, see page B2.
★ Indicates Type III membership in the American Hospital Association.

★5570: PENN STATE GEISINGER HEALTH SYSTEM (NP)
2601 Market Place, Suite 300, Harrisburg, PA Zip 17110–9360;
tel. 717/214–2254; Stuart Heydt, M.D., Chief Executive Officer

PENNSYLVANIA: GEISINGER MEDICAL CENTER (O, 548 beds) 100 North
Academy Avenue, Danville, PA Zip 17822–0150; tel. 570/271–6211;
Nancy L. Rizzo, Senior Vice President, Operations
Web address: www.psghs.edu

PENN STATE GEISINGER HEALTH SYSTEM–MILTON S. HERSHEY MEDICAL
CENTER (O, 455 beds) 500 University Drive, Hershey, PA Zip 17033–0850,
Mailing Address: P.O. Box 850, Zip 17033–0850; tel. 717/531–8521;
Theodore E. Townsend, Senior Vice President, Operations
Web address: www.collmed.psu.edu/

PENN STATE GEISINGER WYOMING VALLEY MEDICAL CENTER (O, 124 beds)
1000 East Mountain Drive, Wilkes–Barre, PA Zip 18711–0027;
tel. 570/826–7300; Conrad W. Schintz, Senior Vice–President Operations

Owned, leased, sponsored:	3 hospitals	1127 beds
Contract–managed:	0 hospitals	0 beds
Totals:	3 hospitals	1127 beds

0091: PIONEER BEHAVIORAL HEALTH (IO)
200 Lake Street, Suite 102, Peabody, MA Zip 01960–4780;
tel. 978/536–2777; Bruce A. Shear, President and Chief Executive
Officer

MICHIGAN: HARBOR OAKS HOSPITAL (O, 64 beds) 35031 23 Mile Road,
New Baltimore, MI Zip 48047–2097; tel. 810/725–5777; Harry Hunter
Jr., Administrator and Chief Operating Officer

UTAH: HIGHLAND RIDGE HOSPITAL (O, 32 beds) 175 West 7200 South,
Midvale, UT Zip 84047; tel. 801/272–9851

VIRGINIA: MOUNT REGIS CENTER (O, 25 beds) 405 Kimball Avenue, Salem,
VA Zip 24153–6299; tel. 703/389–4761; Gail S. Basham, Chief
Operating Officer

Owned, leased, sponsored:	3 hospitals	121 beds
Contract–managed:	0 hospitals	0 beds
Totals:	3 hospitals	121 beds

● ★0034: PMH HEALTH RESOURCES, INC. (NP)
1201 South Seventh Avenue, Phoenix, AZ Zip 85007–3913, Mailing
Address: P.O. Box 21207, Zip 85036–1207; tel. 602/824–3321;
Reginald M. Ballantyne III, President

ARIZONA: PHOENIX MEMORIAL HEALTH SYSTEM (O, 195 beds) 1201 South
Seventh Avenue, Phoenix, AZ Zip 85007–3995; tel. 602/258–5111;
Jeffrey K. Norman, Chief Executive Officer
Web address: www.phzmemorialhospital.com

Owned, leased, sponsored:	1 hospital	195 beds
Contract–managed:	0 hospitals	0 beds
Totals:	1 hospital	195 beds

★3505: PRESBYTERIAN HEALTHCARE SERVICES (CO)
5901 Harper Drive N.E., Albuquerque, NM Zip 87109–3589, Mailing
Address: P.O. Box 26666, Zip 87125–6666; tel. 505/260–6300;
James H. Hinton, President and Chief Executive Officer

COLORADO: DELTA COUNTY MEMORIAL HOSPITAL (C, 44 beds) 100
Stafford Lane, Delta, CO Zip 81416–2297, Mailing Address: P.O. Box
10100, Zip 81416–5003; tel. 970/874–7681; Jerry Cantwell,
Administrator

NEW MEXICO: ARTESIA GENERAL HOSPITAL (C, 20 beds) 702 North 13th
Street, Artesia, NM Zip 88210–1199; tel. 505/748–3333; Anthony J.
Plantier, Administrator

DR. DAN C. TRIGG MEMORIAL HOSPITAL (L, 37 beds) 301 East Miel De Luna
Avenue, Tucumcari, NM Zip 88401–3810, Mailing Address: P.O. Box 608,
Zip 88401–0608; tel. 505/461–0141; Dell Willis, Administrator

ESPANOLA HOSPITAL (O, 80 beds) 1010 Spruce Street, Espanola, NM
Zip 87532–2746; tel. 505/753–7111; Marcella A. Romero, Administrator

LINCOLN COUNTY MEDICAL CENTER (L, 31 beds) 211 Sudderth Drive,
Ruidoso, NM Zip 88345–6043, Mailing Address: P.O. Box 8000,
Zip 88345–8000; tel. 505/257–7381; James P. Gibson, Administrator

PLAINS REGIONAL MEDICAL CENTER (O, 74 beds) 2100 North Thomas
Street, Clovis, NM Zip 88101–9412, Mailing Address: P.O. Box 1688,
Zip 88101–1688; tel. 505/769–2141; Gordon Aird, Interim Administrator

PRESBYTERIAN HOSPITAL (O, 424 beds) 1100 Central Avenue S.E.,
Albuquerque, NM Zip 87106–4934, Mailing Address: P.O. Box 26666,
Zip 87125–6666; tel. 505/841–1234; James Jeppson, Administrator
Web address: www.phs.org

PRESBYTERIAN KASEMAN HOSPITAL (O, 120 beds) 8300 Constitution Avenue
N.E., Albuquerque, NM Zip 87110–7624, Mailing Address: P.O. Box 26666,
Zip 87125–6666; tel. 505/291–2000; Robert A. Garcia, Administrator

SOCORRO GENERAL HOSPITAL (O, 30 beds) 1202 Highway 60 West,
Socorro, NM Zip 87801, Mailing Address: P.O. Box 1009, Zip 87801–1009;
tel. 505/835–1140; Jeff Dye, Administrator

Owned, leased, sponsored:	7 hospitals	796 beds
Contract–managed:	2 hospitals	64 beds
Totals:	9 hospitals	860 beds

0153: PROHEALTH CARE (NP)
725 American Avenue, Waukesha, WI Zip 53188;
tel. 414/544–2241; Donald W. Fundingsland, Chief Executive Officer

WISCONSIN: OCONOMOWOC MEMORIAL HOSPITAL (O, 73 beds) 791 Summit
Avenue, Oconomowoc, WI Zip 53066–3896; tel. 414/569–9400; Douglas
Guy, President and Chief Executive Officer

WAUKESHA MEMORIAL HOSPITAL (O, 294 beds) 725 American Avenue,
Waukesha, WI Zip 53188–5099; tel. 414/544–2011; Rexford W. Titus III,
President and Chief Executive Officer
Web address: www.phci.org

Owned, leased, sponsored:	2 hospitals	367 beds
Contract–managed:	0 hospitals	0 beds
Totals:	2 hospitals	367 beds

★0147: PROMEDICA HEALTH SYSTEM (NP)
2121 Hughes Drive, 4th Floor, Toledo, OH Zip 43606;
tel. 419/291–7176; Alan W. Brass, FACHE, President and Chief
Executive Officer

OHIO: DEFIANCE HOSPITAL (O, 80 beds) 1206 East Second Street, Defiance,
OH Zip 43512–2495; tel. 419/783–6955; Robert J. Coholich, President
Web address: www.promedica.org

FLOWER HOSPITAL (O, 487 beds) 5200 Harroun Road, Sylvania, OH
Zip 43560–2196; tel. 419/824–1444; Randall Kelley, President
Web address: www.promedica.org

ST. FRANCIS HEALTH CARE CENTRE (C, 186 beds) 401 North Broadway,
Green Springs, OH Zip 44836–9653; tel. 419/639–2626; Dan Schwanke,
Executive Director

THE TOLEDO HOSPITAL (O, 561 beds) 2142 North Cove Boulevard, Toledo,
OH Zip 43606–3896; tel. 419/471–4000; Barbara Steele, President
Web address: www.promedica.org

Owned, leased, sponsored:	3 hospitals	1128 beds
Contract–managed:	1 hospital	186 beds
Totals:	4 hospitals	1314 beds

★0132: PROVENA HEALTH (NP)
9223 West St. Francis Road, Frankfort, IL Zip 60423–8334;
tel. 815/928–6901; Joseph S. Feth, Chief Executive Officer

ILLINOIS: PROVENA COVENANT MEDICAL CENTER (O, 258 beds) 1400 West
Park Street, Urbana, IL Zip 61801–2396; tel. 217/337–2000; Diane
Friedman, R.N., President and Chief Executive Officer
Web address: www.covenant–cu.com

Section B

For explanation of codes following names, see page B2.
★ Indicates Type III membership in the American Hospital Association.
● Single hospital health care system

PROVENA MERCY CENTER (O, 241 beds) 1325 North Highland Avenue, Aurora, IL Zip 60506; tel. 630/859–2222; Mary R. Sheahen, President and Chief Executive Officer
Web address: www.provenamercy.com

PROVENA SAINT JOSEPH HOSPITAL (O, 186 beds) 77 North Airlite Street, Elgin, IL Zip 60123–4912; tel. 847/695–3200; Larry Narum, President

PROVENA SAINT JOSEPH MEDICAL CENTER (O, 412 beds) 333 North Madison Street, Joliet, IL Zip 60435–6595; tel. 815/725–7133

PROVENA SAINT THERESE MEDICAL CENTER (O, 254 beds) 2615 Washington Street, Waukegan, IL Zip 60085–4988; tel. 847/249–3900; Timothy P. Selz, President and Chief Executive Officer

PROVENA ST. MARY'S HOSPITAL (O, 197 beds) 500 West Court Street, Kankakee, IL Zip 60901–3661; tel. 815/937–2400; Paula Jacobi, President and Chief Executive Officer
Web address: www.provena–stmarys.com

PROVENA UNITED SAMARITANS MEDICAL CENTER (O, 308 beds) 812 North Logan, Danville, IL Zip 61832–3788; tel. 217/443–5000; Dennis J. Doran, President and Chief Executive Officer
Web address: www.provenausmc.org

Owned, leased, sponsored:	7 hospitals	1856 beds
Contract–managed:	0 hospitals	0 beds
Totals:	7 hospitals	1856 beds

★**5265: PROVIDENCE SERVICES** (CC)
9 East Ninth Avenue, Spokane, WA Zip 99202; tel. 509/742–7337; Richard J. Umbdenstock, President and Chief Executive Officer

MONTANA: BENEFIS HEALTH CARE (S, 304 beds) 500 15th Avenue South, Great Falls, MT Zip 59403–4389; tel. 406/455–5000; Lloyd V. Smith, President and Chief Executive Officer
Web address: www.benefis.org

ST. JOSEPH HOSPITAL (S, 22 beds) Skyline Drive and 14th Avenue, Polson, MT Zip 59860, Mailing Address: P.O. Box 1010, Zip 59860–1010; tel. 406/883–5377; John W. Glueckert, President

ST. PATRICK HOSPITAL (S, 213 beds) 500 West Broadway, Missoula, MT Zip 59802–4096, Mailing Address: Box 4587, Zip 59806–4587; tel. 406/543–7271; Lawrence L. White Jr., President
Web address: www.saintpatrick.org

WASHINGTON: DEER PARK HOSPITAL (S, 26 beds) East 1015 D Street, Deer Park, WA Zip 99006, Mailing Address: P.O. Box 742, Zip 99006; tel. 509/276–5061; Garvin Olson, Chief Operating Officer

HOLY FAMILY HOSPITAL (S, 190 beds) North 5633 Lidgerwood Avenue, Spokane, WA Zip 99207; tel. 509/482–0111; Cathy J. Simchuk, Interim Chief Executive Officer
Web address: www.holy–family.org

MOUNT CARMEL HOSPITAL (S, 32 beds) 982 East Columbia Street, Colville, WA Zip 99114–0351, Mailing Address: Box 351, Zip 99114–0351; tel. 509/684–2561; Gloria Cooper, Chief Executive Officer

SACRED HEART MEDICAL CENTER (S, 607 beds) West 101 Eighth Avenue, Spokane, WA Zip 99220, Mailing Address: P.O. Box 2555, Zip 99220; tel. 509/455–3040; Ryland P. Davis, President

ST. JOSEPH'S HOSPITAL (S, 65 beds) 500 East Webster Street, Chewelah, WA Zip 99109, Mailing Address: P.O. Box 197, Zip 99109; tel. 509/935–8211; Gary V. Peck, Chief Executive Officer

ST. MARY MEDICAL CENTER (S, 107 beds) 401 West Poplar Street, Walla Walla, WA Zip 99362, Mailing Address: Box 1477, Zip 99362–0312; tel. 509/525–3320; John A. Isely, President

Owned, leased, sponsored:	9 hospitals	1566 beds
Contract–managed:	0 hospitals	0 beds
Totals:	9 hospitals	1566 beds

0108: PROVINCE HEALTHCARE CORPORATION (IO)
105 Westwood Place, Suite 400, Brentwood, TN Zip 37027; tel. 615/370–1377; Marty Rash, President and Chief Executive Officer

ARIZONA: HAVASU REGIONAL MEDICAL CENTER (O, 118 beds) 101 Civic Center Lane, Lake Havasu City, AZ Zip 86403–5683; tel. 520/855–8185; Kevin P. Poorten, Chief Executive Officer

CALIFORNIA: COLORADO RIVER MEDICAL CENTER (O, 49 beds) 1401 Bailey Avenue, Needles, CA Zip 92363; tel. 760/326–4531; James Arp, Chief Executive Officer

GENERAL HOSPITAL (O, 66 beds) 2200 Harrison Avenue, Eureka, CA Zip 95501; tel. 707/445–5111; Martin Love, Chief Executive Officer

OJAI VALLEY COMMUNITY HOSPITAL (O, 116 beds) 1306 Maricopa Highway, Ojai, CA Zip 93023–3180; tel. 805/646–1401; Mark Turner, Chief Executive Officer

PALO VERDE HOSPITAL (O, 35 beds) 250 North First Street, Blythe, CA Zip 92225; tel. 760/922–4115; M. Victoria Clark, Chief Executive Officer

COLORADO: COLORADO PLAINS MEDICAL CENTER (O, 40 beds) 1000 Lincoln Street, Fort Morgan, CO Zip 80701–3298; tel. 970/867–3391; Thomas Thomson, Chief Executive Officer

INDIANA: STARKE MEMORIAL HOSPITAL (O, 35 beds) 102 East Culver Road, Knox, IN Zip 46534–2299; tel. 219/772–6231; Kathryn J. Norem, Executive Director

LOUISIANA: EUNICE COMMUNITY MEDICAL CENTER (O, 67 beds) 400 Moosa Boulevard, Eunice, LA Zip 70535; tel. 318/457–5244; Mark L. Manuel, Administrator

NEVADA: ELKO GENERAL HOSPITAL (O, 50 beds) 1297 College Avenue, Elko, NV Zip 89801–3499; tel. 775/753–1999; Richard L. Kilburn, Chief Executive Officer

TEXAS: MEMORIAL MOTHER FRANCES HOSPITAL (O, 84 beds) 4000 South Loop 256, Palestine, TX Zip 75801–8467, Mailing Address: P.O. Box 4070, Zip 75802–4070; tel. 903/731–5000; Randell G. Stokes, Chief Executive Officer
Web address: www.mmfh.org

PARKVIEW REGIONAL HOSPITAL (O, 44 beds) 312 East Glendale Street, Mexia, TX Zip 76667–3608; tel. 254/562–5332; Tim Adams, Administrator and Chief Executive Officer

Owned, leased, sponsored:	11 hospitals	704 beds
Contract–managed:	0 hospitals	0 beds
Totals:	11 hospitals	704 beds

0011: PUERTO RICO DEPARTMENT OF HEALTH (NP)
Building A – Medical Center, San Juan, PR Zip 00936, Mailing Address: Call Box 70184, Zip 00936; tel. 809/274–7676; Carmen Feliciano De Melecio, M.D., Secretary of Health

PUERTO RICO: AGUADILLA GENERAL HOSPITAL (O, 110 beds) Carr Aguadilla San Juan, Aguadilla, PR Zip 00605, Mailing Address: P.O. Box 4036, Zip 00605; tel. 787/891–3000; William Rodriguez Castro, Executive Director

ARECIBO REGIONAL HOSPITAL (O, 183 beds) 129 San Luis Avenue, Arecibo, PR Zip 00612, Mailing Address: P.O. Box 659, Zip 00613; tel. 787/878–7272; Samuel Monroig, Vice President for Administration

CAGUAS REGIONAL HOSPITAL (O, 256 beds) Carretera Caguas A Cidra, Caguas, PR Zip 00725, Mailing Address: P.O. Box 5729, Zip 00726; tel. 787/744–2500; Noemi Davis Marte, M.D., Medical Director

DR. RAMON E. BETANCES HOSPITAL–MAYAGUEZ MEDICAL CENTER BRANCH (O, 206 beds) 410 Hostos Avenue, Mayaguez, PR Zip 00680; tel. 787/834–8686; Maria Del Pilar Rodriguez, Administrator

HOSPITAL SUB–REGIONAL DR. VICTOR R. NUNEZ (O, 83 beds) Avenida Tejas, Expreso Cruz Ortiz Stella, Humacao, PR Zip 00791; tel. 787/852–2727; Ahmed Alvarez Pabon, Executive Director

HOSPITAL UNIVERSITARIO DR. RAMON RUIZ ARNAU (O, 340 beds) Avenue Laurel, Santa Juanita, Bayamon, PR Zip 00956; tel. 787/787–5151; Nilda E. Diaz, Executive Director

PONCE REGIONAL HOSPITAL (O, 307 beds) 917 Tito Castro Avenue, Ponce, PR Zip 00731; tel. 787/844–2080; Julio Andino Rodriguez, Executive Director

STATE PSYCHIATRIC HOSPITAL (O, 425 beds) Monacillos Avenue, San Juan, PR Zip 00936, Mailing Address: Call Box 2100, Caparra Heights Station, Zip 00922–2100; tel. 787/766–4646; Guadalupe Alvarez, Administrator

For explanation of codes following names, see page B2.
★ Indicates Type III membership in the American Hospital Association.

© 1999 AHA Guide

UNIVERSITY HOSPITAL (O, 297 beds) Puerto Rico Medical Center, Rio Piedras Station, San Juan, PR Zip 00935; tel. 787/754–3633; Betty Ocasio, Executive Director

Owned, leased, sponsored:	9 hospitals	2207 beds
Contract–managed:	0 hospitals	0 beds
Totals:	**9 hospitals**	**2207 beds**

★0040: QUEEN'S HEALTH SYSTEMS (NP)

1099 Alakea Street, Suite 1100, Honolulu, HI Zip 96813; tel. 808/532–6100; Richard L. Griffith, President and Chief Executive Officer

HAWAII: MOLOKAI GENERAL HOSPITAL (O, 30 beds) Kaunakakai, HI Mailing Address: P.O. Box 408, Zip 96748–0408; tel. 808/553–5331; Calvin M. Ichinose, Administrator

QUEEN'S MEDICAL CENTER (O, 430 beds) 1301 Punchbowl Street, Honolulu, HI Zip 96813; tel. 808/538–9011; Arthur A. Ushijima, President and Chief Executive Officer
Web address: www.quens.org

Owned, leased, sponsored:	2 hospitals	460 beds
Contract–managed:	0 hospitals	0 beds
Totals:	**2 hospitals**	**460 beds**

★0002: QUORUM HEALTH GROUP/QUORUM HEALTH RESOURCES, INC. (IO)

103 Continental Place, Brentwood, TN Zip 37027; tel. 615/371–7979; James E. Dalton Jr., President and Chief Executive Officer

ALABAMA: FLOWERS HOSPITAL (O, 215 beds) 4370 West Main Street, Dothan, AL Zip 36305, Mailing Address: P.O. Box 6907, Zip 36302–6907; tel. 334/793–5000; Keith Granger, President and Chief Executive Officer

GADSDEN REGIONAL MEDICAL CENTER (O, 233 beds) 1007 Goodyear Avenue, Gadsden, AL Zip 35903–1195; tel. 256/494–4000; James F. O'Loughlin, Chief Executive Officer

JACKSONVILLE HOSPITAL (O, 56 beds) 1701 Pelham Road South, Jacksonville, AL Zip 36265–3399, Mailing Address: P.O. Box 999, Zip 36265–0999; tel. 256/435–4970; Charles Mitchener Jr., Chief Executive Officer
Web address: www.jaxhosp.com

MEDICAL CENTER ENTERPRISE (O, 117 beds) 400 North Edwards Street, Enterprise, AL Zip 36330–9981; tel. 334/347–0584; Earl S. Whiteley, CHE, Chief Executive Officer

MONROE COUNTY HOSPITAL (C, 59 beds) 1901 South Alabama Avenue, Monroeville, AL Zip 36460, Mailing Address: P.O. Box 886, Zip 36461–0886; tel. 334/575–3111; Joe Zager, Chief Executive Officer

ALASKA: BARTLETT REGIONAL HOSPITAL (C, 64 beds) 3260 Hospital Drive, Juneau, AK Zip 99801; tel. 907/586–2611; Robert F. Valliant, Administrator
Web address: www.bartletthospital.org

CENTRAL PENINSULA GENERAL HOSPITAL (C, 43 beds) 250 Hospital Place, Soldotna, AK Zip 99669; tel. 907/262–4404; Roy C. Vinson, Interim Chief Executive Officer

ARIZONA: CASA GRANDE REGIONAL MEDICAL CENTER (C, 244 beds) 1800 East Florence Boulevard, Casa Grande, AZ Zip 85222–5399; tel. 520/426–6300; J. Marty Dernier, President and Chief Executive Officer

CENTRAL ARIZONA MEDICAL CENTER (O, 77 beds) Adamsville Road, Florence, AZ Zip 85232, Mailing Address: P.O. Box 2080, Zip 85232–2080; tel. 520/868–2003; Carmen G. Perea, R.N., Interim Administrator

MARICOPA MEDICAL CENTER (C, 491 beds) 2601 East Roosevelt Street, Phoenix, AZ Zip 85008–4956; tel. 602/334–5111; Mark Hillard, Chief Executive Officer
Web address: www.maricopa.gov/medcentwer/mmc.htmc

ARKANSAS: CHICOT MEMORIAL HOSPITAL (C, 35 beds) 2729 Highway 65 and 82 South, Lake Village, AR Zip 71653, Mailing Address: P.O. Box 512, Zip 71653–0512; tel. 870/265–5351; Robert R. Reddish, Administrator and Chief Executive Officer

DELTA MEMORIAL HOSPITAL (C, 35 beds) 300 East Pickens Street, Dumas, AR Zip 71639–2710, Mailing Address: P.O. Box 887, Zip 71639–0887; tel. 870/382–4303; Kurt Meyer, Administrator

HELENA REGIONAL MEDICAL CENTER (C, 125 beds) 1801 Martin Luther King Drive, Helena, AR Zip 72342, Mailing Address: P.O. Box 788, Zip 72342–0788; tel. 870/338–5800; Steve Reeder, Chief Executive Officer

HOWARD MEMORIAL HOSPITAL (C, 50 beds) 800 West Leslie Street, Nashville, AR Zip 71852–0381, Mailing Address: Box 381, Zip 71852–0381; tel. 870/845–4400; Rex Jones, Chief Executive Officer

MENA MEDICAL CENTER (C, 42 beds) 311 North Morrow Street, Mena, AR Zip 71953–2516; tel. 501/394–6100; Albert Pilkington III, Administrator and Chief Executive Officer

NORTHWEST MEDICAL CENTER (O, 222 beds) 609 West Maple Avenue, Springdale, AR Zip 72764–5394, Mailing Address: P.O. Box 47, Zip 72765–0047; tel. 501/751–5711; Greg K. Stock, Chief Executive Officer

REBSAMEN MEDICAL CENTER (C, 113 beds) 1400 West Braden Street, Jacksonville, AR Zip 72076–3788; tel. 501/985–7000; Thomas R. Siemers, Chief Executive Officer

SALINE MEMORIAL HOSPITAL (C, 77 beds) 1 Medical Park Drive, Benton, AR Zip 72015–3354; tel. 501/776–6000; Roger D. Feldt, FACHE, President and Chief Executive Officer
Web address: www.scmc.com

SILOAM SPRINGS MEMORIAL HOSPITAL (C, 52 beds) 205 East Jefferson Street, Siloam Springs, AR Zip 72761–3697; tel. 501/524–4141; Donald E. Patterson, Administrator

CALIFORNIA: LOMPOC HEALTHCARE DISTRICT (C, 170 beds) 508 East Hickory Street, Lompoc, CA Zip 93436, Mailing Address: Box 1058, Zip 93438; tel. 805/737–3300; James Raggio, Administrator

SANTA PAULA MEMORIAL HOSPITAL (C, 54 beds) 825 North Tenth Street, Santa Paula, CA Zip 93060–0270, Mailing Address: P.O. Box 270, Zip 93061–0270; tel. 805/525–7171; William M. Greene, FACHE, President

COLORADO: ARKANSAS VALLEY REGIONAL MEDICAL CENTER (C, 182 beds) 1100 Carson Avenue, La Junta, CO Zip 81050–2799; tel. 719/383–6000; Lynn Crowell, Chief Executive Officer

GRAND RIVER HOSPITAL DISTRICT (C, 75 beds) 701 East Fifth Street, Rifle, CO Zip 81650–2970, Mailing Address: P.O. Box 912, Zip 81650–0912; tel. 970/625–1510; Robert Peterson, Interim Administrator

HEART OF THE ROCKIES REGIONAL MEDICAL CENTER (C, 33 beds) 448 East First Street, Salida, CO Zip 81201–0429, Mailing Address: P.O. Box 429, Zip 81201–0429; tel. 719/539–6661; Howard D. Turner, Chief Executive Officer
Web address: www.hrrmc.com

MEMORIAL HOSPITAL (C, 29 beds) 785 Russell Street, Craig, CO Zip 81625–9906; tel. 970/824–9411; M. Randell Phelps, Administrator

MONTROSE MEMORIAL HOSPITAL (C, 63 beds) 800 South Third Street, Montrose, CO Zip 81401–4291; tel. 970/249–2211; Jan V. Carrell, Chief Executive Officer and Administrator

MOUNT SAN RAFAEL HOSPITAL (C, 31 beds) 410 Benedicta Avenue, Trinidad, CO Zip 81082–2093; tel. 719/846–9213; Paul Herman, Chief Executive Officer

PARKVIEW MEDICAL CENTER (C, 260 beds) 400 West 16th Street, Pueblo, CO Zip 81003–2781; tel. 719/584–4000; C. W. Smith, President and Chief Executive Officer
Web address: www.parkviewmc.com

PIONEERS HOSPITAL OF RIO BLANCO COUNTY (C, 46 beds) 345 Cleveland Street, Meeker, CO Zip 81641–0000; tel. 970/878–5047; Thomas E. Lake, Chief Executive Officer

PROWERS MEDICAL CENTER (C, 40 beds) 401 Kendall Drive, Lamar, CO Zip 81052–3993; tel. 719/336–4343; Earl J. Steinhoff, Chief Executive Officer

SOUTHWEST MEMORIAL HOSPITAL (C, 42 beds) 1311 North Mildred Road, Cortez, CO Zip 81321–2299; tel. 970/565–6666; Bob Peterson, Chief Executive Officer

For explanation of codes following names, see page B2.
★ Indicates Type III membership in the American Hospital Association.

Section B

VALLEY VIEW HOSPITAL (C, 54 beds) 1906 Blake Avenue, Glenwood Springs, CO Zip 81601–4259, Mailing Address: P.O. Box 1970, Zip 81602–1970; tel. 970/945–6535; Gary L. Brewer, Chief Executive Officer
Web address: www.vvh.com

FLORIDA: BASCOM PALMER EYE INSTITUTE–ANNE BATES LEACH EYE HOSPITAL (C, 35 beds) 900 N.W. 17th Street, Miami, FL Zip 33136–1199, Mailing Address: Box 016880, Zip 33101–6880; tel. 305/326–6000; Richard C. Thomas, Administrator
Web address: www.bpei.med.miami.edu

BERT FISH MEDICAL CENTER (C, 116 beds) 401 Palmetto Street, New Smyrna Beach, FL Zip 32168–7399; tel. 904/424–5000; Kathy Leonard, Vice President and Administrator
Web address: www.bertfish.com

DESOTO MEMORIAL HOSPITAL (C, 62 beds) 900 North Robert Avenue, Arcadia, FL Zip 34266–8765, Mailing Address: P.O. Box 2180, Zip 34265–2180; tel. 941/494–3535; Vincent B. DiFranco, Interim Chief Executive Officer

H. LEE MOFFITT CANCER CENTER AND RESEARCH INSTITUTE (C, 117 beds) 12902 Magnolia Drive, Tampa, FL Zip 33612–9497; tel. 813/972–4673; John C. Ruckdeschel, M.D., Director and Chief Executive Officer
Web address: www.moffitt.usf.edu

HENDRY REGIONAL MEDICAL CENTER (C, 45 beds) 500 West Sugarland Highway, Clewiston, FL Zip 33440–3094; tel. 941/983–9121; J. Rudy Reinhardt, Administrator

JACKSON HOSPITAL (C, 85 beds) 4250 Hospital Drive, Marianna, FL Zip 32446–1939, Mailing Address: P.O. Box 1608, Zip 32447–1608; tel. 850/526–2200

UNIVERSITY OF MIAMI HOSPITAL AND CLINICS (C, 40 beds) 1475 N.W. 12th Avenue, Miami, FL Zip 33136–1002; tel. 305/243–6418; Admiral John Rossfeld, Administrator

GEORGIA: CAMDEN MEDICAL CENTER (C, 40 beds) 2000 Dan Proctor Drive, Saint Marys, GA Zip 31558; tel. 912/576–4200; Alan E. George, Administrator

ELBERT MEMORIAL HOSPITAL (C, 42 beds) 4 Medical Drive, Elberton, GA Zip 30635–1897; tel. 706/283–3151; Mark LeNeave, Chief Executive Officer

HABERSHAM COUNTY MEDICAL CENTER (C, 159 beds) Highway 441, Demorest, GA Zip 30535, Mailing Address: P.O. Box 37, Zip 30535–0037; tel. 706/754–2161; C. Richard Dwozan, President

HIGGINS GENERAL HOSPITAL (C, 39 beds) 200 Allen Memorial Drive, Bremen, GA Zip 30110–2012, Mailing Address: P.O. Box 655, Zip 30110–0655; tel. 770/537–5851; Robbie Smith, Administrator

MCDUFFIE COUNTY HOSPITAL (C, 33 beds) 521 Hill Street S.W., Thomson, GA Zip 30824–2199; tel. 706/595–1411; Douglas C. Keir, Chief Executive Officer
Web address: www.mch.com

MEMORIAL HEALTH SYSTEM (C, 373 beds) 4700 Waters Avenue, Savannah, GA Zip 31404–6283, Mailing Address: P.O. Box 23089, Zip 31403–3089; tel. 912/350–8000; Robert A. Colvin, President and Chief Executive Officer
Web address: www.memorialmed.com

OCONEE REGIONAL MEDICAL CENTER (C, 143 beds) 821 North Cobb Street, Milledgeville, GA Zip 31061–2351, Mailing Address: P.O. Box 690, Zip 31061–0690; tel. 912/454–3500; Brian L. Riddle, President and Chief Executive Officer

SOUTHEAST GEORGIA REGIONAL MEDICAL CENTER (C, 337 beds) 3100 Kemble Avenue, Brunswick, GA Zip 31520–4252, Mailing Address: P.O. Box 1518, Zip 31521–1518; tel. 912/264–7000; E. Berton Whitaker, President and Chief Executive Officer

TANNER MEDICAL CENTER (C, 176 beds) 705 Dixie Street, Carrollton, GA Zip 30117–3818; tel. 770/836–9666; Loy M. Howard, Chief Executive Officer
Web address: www.tanner.org/

TANNER MEDICAL CENTER–VILLA RICA (C, 45 beds) 601 Dallas Road, Villa Rica, GA Zip 30180–1202, Mailing Address: P.O. Box 638, Zip 30180–0638; tel. 770/456–3100; Larry N. Steed, Administrator
Web address: www.tanner.org

UPSON REGIONAL MEDICAL CENTER (C, 115 beds) 801 West Gordon Street, Thomaston, GA Zip 30286–2831, Mailing Address: P.O. Box 1059, Zip 30286–1059; tel. 706/647–8111; Samuel S. Gregory, Administrator

WALTON MEDICAL CENTER (C, 113 beds) 330 Alcovy Street, Monroe, GA Zip 30655–2140, Mailing Address: P.O. Box 1346, Zip 30655–1346; tel. 770/267–8461; Ronald L. Campbell, Chief Executive Officer

WAYNE MEMORIAL HOSPITAL (C, 110 beds) 865 South First Street, Jesup, GA Zip 31598, Mailing Address: P.O. Box 408, Zip 31598–0408; tel. 912/427–6811; Charles R. Morgan, Administrator

WILLS MEMORIAL HOSPITAL (C, 38 beds) 120 Gordon Street, Washington, GA Zip 30673–1602, Mailing Address: P.O. Box 370, Zip 30673–0370; tel. 706/678–2151; Tim E. Merritt, Chief Executive Officer

HAWAII: WAHIAWA GENERAL HOSPITAL (C, 162 beds) 128 Lehua Street, Wahiawa, HI Zip 96786, Mailing Address: P.O. Box 580, Zip 96786–0580; tel. 808/621–8411; Tyler A. Erickson, Chief Executive Officer

IDAHO: BINGHAM MEMORIAL HOSPITAL (C, 100 beds) 98 Poplar Street, Blackfoot, ID Zip 83221–1799; tel. 208/785–4100; Louis Kraml, Chief Executive Officer

GRITMAN MEDICAL CENTER (C, 35 beds) 700 South Washington Street, Moscow, ID Zip 83843–3047; tel. 208/882–4511; Thomas Stegbauer, Chief Executive Officer

ILLINOIS: COMMUNITY MEMORIAL HOSPITAL (C, 44 beds) 400 Caldwell Street, Staunton, IL Zip 62088–1499; tel. 618/635–2200; Patrick B. Heise, Chief Executive Officer

CRAWFORD MEMORIAL HOSPITAL (C, 93 beds) 1000 North Allen Street, Robinson, IL Zip 62454; tel. 618/546–1234; Wallace R. Simmons, Chief Executive Officer

GIBSON AREA HOSPITAL AND HEALTH SERVICES (C, 82 beds) 1120 North Melvin Street, Gibson City, IL Zip 60936–1066, Mailing Address: P.O. Box 429, Zip 60936–0429; tel. 217/784–4251; Craig A. Jesiolowski, Chief Executive Officer

ILLINI COMMUNITY HOSPITAL (C, 45 beds) 640 West Washington Street, Pittsfield, IL Zip 62363–1397; tel. 217/285–2113; Jete Edmisson, President and Chief Executive Officer

MEMORIAL HOSPITAL (C, 59 beds) South Adams Street, Carthage, IL Zip 62321, Mailing Address: P.O. Box 160, Zip 62321–0160; tel. 217/357–3131; Keith E. Heuser, Chief Executive Officer

MEMORIAL HOSPITAL (C, 40 beds) 1900 State Street, Chester, IL Zip 62233–0609, Mailing Address: P.O. Box 609, Zip 62233–0609; tel. 618/826–4581; Eric Freeburg, Administrator

SACRED HEART HOSPITAL (C, 96 beds) 3240 West Franklin Boulevard, Chicago, IL Zip 60624–1599; tel. 773/722–3020; Edward Novak, President and Chief Executive Officer

THOMAS H. BOYD MEMORIAL HOSPITAL (C, 60 beds) 800 School Street, Carrollton, IL Zip 62016–1498; tel. 217/942–6946; Deborah Campbell, Administrator

INDIANA: CLINTON COUNTY HOSPITAL (O, 53 beds) 1300 South Jackson Street, Frankfort, IN Zip 46041–3394, Mailing Address: P.O. Box 669, Zip 46041–0669; tel. 765/659–4731; Brian R. Zeh, Chief Executive Officer
Web address: www.cchosp/accs.net

DAVIESS COUNTY HOSPITAL (C, 85 beds) 1314 East Walnut Street, Washington, IN Zip 47501–2198, Mailing Address: P.O. Box 760, Zip 47501–0760; tel. 812/254–2760; Marc Chircop, Chief Executive Officer
Web address: www.dchosp.org

KOSCIUSKO COMMUNITY HOSPITAL (O, 161 beds) 2101 East Dubois Drive, Warsaw, IN Zip 46580–3288; tel. 219/267–3200; Wayne Hendrix, President
Web address: www.kch.org

LUTHERAN HOSPITAL OF INDIANA (O, 449 beds) 7950 West Jefferson Boulevard, Fort Wayne, IN Zip 46804–1677; tel. 219/435–7001; Thomas D. Miller, President and Chief Executive Officer

ST. JOSEPH HOSPITAL (O, 191 beds) 700 Broadway, Fort Wayne, IN Zip 46802–1493; tel. 219/425–3000; Michael H. Schatzlein, M.D., President and Chief Executive Officer
Web address: www.stjoehealthguides.com

SULLIVAN COUNTY COMMUNITY HOSPITAL (C, 46 beds) 2200 North Section Street, Sullivan, IN Zip 47882, Mailing Address: P.O. Box 10, Zip 47882–0010; tel. 812/268–4311; Thomas J. Hudgins, Administrator

---

For explanation of codes following names, see page B2.
★ Indicates Type III membership in the American Hospital Association.

IOWA: BOONE COUNTY HOSPITAL (C, 57 beds) 1015 Union Street, Boone, IA Zip 50036–4898; tel. 515/432–3140; Joseph S. Smith, Chief Executive Officer
Web address: www.boonehospital.com

DES MOINES GENERAL HOSPITAL (C, 155 beds) 603 East 12th Street, Des Moines, IA Zip 50309–5515; tel. 515/263–4200; Roy W. Wright, President and Chief Executive Officer

FORT MADISON COMMUNITY HOSPITAL (C, 50 beds) Highway 61 West, Fort Madison, IA Zip 52627–0174, Mailing Address: 5445 Avenue O, Box 174, Zip 52627–0174; tel. 319/372–6530; C. James Platt, Chief Executive Officer
Web address: www.fmchcares.com

KNOXVILLE AREA COMMUNITY HOSPITAL (C, 52 beds) 1002 South Lincoln Street, Knoxville, IA Zip 50138–3121; tel. 515/842–2151; Jim Murphy, Chief Executive Officer

WASHINGTON COUNTY HOSPITAL (C, 83 beds) 400 East Polk Street, Washington, IA Zip 52353, Mailing Address: P.O. Box 909, Zip 52353; tel. 319/653–5481; Ronald D. Davis, Chief Executive Officer

KANSAS: BOB WILSON MEMORIAL GRANT COUNTY HOSPITAL (C, 39 beds) 415 North Main Street, Ulysses, KS Zip 67880–2196; tel. 316/356–1266; Steven G. Daniel, Administrator

COFFEYVILLE REGIONAL MEDICAL CENTER (C, 123 beds) 1400 West Fourth, Coffeyville, KS Zip 67337–3306; tel. 316/251–1200; Gerald Joseph Marquette Jr., Chief Executive Officer

NEOSHO MEMORIAL REGIONAL MEDICAL CENTER (C, 60 beds) 629 South Plummer, Chanute, KS Zip 66720–1928; tel. 316/431–4000; Murray L. Brown, Administrator

NEWMAN MEMORIAL COUNTY HOSPITAL (C, 110 beds) 1201 West 12th Avenue, Emporia, KS Zip 66801–2597; tel. 316/343–6800; Terry R. Lambert, Chief Executive Officer

WILSON COUNTY HOSPITAL (C, 38 beds) 205 Mill Street, Neodesha, KS Zip 66757–1817, Mailing Address: P.O. Box 360, Zip 66757–0360; tel. 316/325–2611; Deanna Pittman, Administrator

KENTUCKY: CALDWELL COUNTY HOSPITAL (C, 15 beds) 101 Hospital Drive, Princeton, KY Zip 42445–0410, Mailing Address: Box 410, Zip 42445–0410; tel. 502/365–0300; Robert R. Stanley, Interim Chief Executive Officer

CRITTENDEN COUNTY HOSPITAL (C, 50 beds) Highway 60 South, Marion, KY Zip 42064, Mailing Address: P.O. Box 386, Zip 42064–0386; tel. 502/965–1018; Rick Napper, Chief Executive Officer

CUMBERLAND COUNTY HOSPITAL (C, 31 beds) Highway 90 West, Burkesville, KY Zip 42717–0280, Mailing Address: P.O. Box 280, Zip 42717–0280; tel. 502/864–2511; Howard C. Andersen, Interim Chief Executive Officer

FLEMING COUNTY HOSPITAL (C, 52 beds) 920 Elizaville Avenue, Flemingsburg, KY Zip 41041, Mailing Address: P.O. Box 388, Zip 41041–0388; tel. 606/849–5000; Luther E. Reeves, Chief Executive Officer

FRANKLIN–SIMPSON MEMORIAL HOSPITAL (C, 28 beds) Brookhaven Road, Franklin, KY Zip 42135–2929, Mailing Address: P.O. Box 2929, Zip 42135–2929; tel. 502/586–3253; William P. Macri, Chief Executive Officer

JENNIE STUART MEDICAL CENTER (C, 139 beds) 320 West 18th Street, Hopkinsville, KY Zip 42241–2400, Mailing Address: P.O. Box 2400, Zip 42241–2400; tel. 502/887–0100; Lewis T. Peeples, Chief Executive Officer
Web address: www.jsmc.org

MARSHALL COUNTY HOSPITAL (C, 80 beds) 503 George McClain Drive, Benton, KY Zip 42025–1399, Mailing Address: P.O. Box 630, Zip 42025–0630; tel. 502/527–4800; David G. Fuqua, R.N., Chief Executive Officer

MONROE COUNTY MEDICAL CENTER (C, 49 beds) 529 Capp Harlan Road, Tompkinsville, KY Zip 42167–1840; tel. 502/487–9231; Mark E. Thompson, Chief Executive Officer

MUHLENBERG COMMUNITY HOSPITAL (C, 135 beds) 440 Hopkinsville Street, Greenville, KY Zip 42345–1172, Mailing Address: P.O. Box 387, Zip 42345–0387; tel. 502/338–8000; Charles D. Lovell Jr., Chief Executive Officer

OHIO COUNTY HOSPITAL (C, 54 beds) 1211 Main Street, Hartford, KY Zip 42347–1619; tel. 502/298–7411; Blaine Pieper, Administrator

LOUISIANA: BOGALUSA COMMUNITY MEDICAL CENTER (C, 101 beds) 433 Plaza Street, Bogalusa, LA Zip 70427–3793; tel. 504/732–7122; Terry G. Whittington, Chief Executive Officer and Administrator

FRANKLIN FOUNDATION HOSPITAL (C, 60 beds) 1501 Hospital Avenue, Franklin, LA Zip 70538–3724; tel. 318/828–0760; Patricia Luker, Chief Executive Officer
Web address: www.franklinfoundation.org

LAKEWOOD MEDICAL CENTER (C, 122 beds) 1125 Marguerite Street, Morgan City, LA Zip 70380–1855, Mailing Address: Drawer 2308, Zip 70381–2308; tel. 504/384–2200; Joyce Grove Hein, Chief Executive Officer

LANE MEMORIAL HOSPITAL (C, 137 beds) 6300 Main Street, Zachary, LA Zip 70791–9990; tel. 225/658–4000; David W. Fuller, Chief Executive Officer
Web address: www.lanehospital.org

NORTH OAKS MEDICAL CENTER (C, 254 beds) 15790 Medical Center Drive, Hammond, LA Zip 70403–1436, Mailing Address: P.O. Box 2668, Zip 70404–2668; tel. 504/345–2700; James E. Cathey Jr., Chief Executive Officer
Web address: www.northoaks.org

OPELOUSAS GENERAL HOSPITAL (C, 140 beds) 520 Prudhomme Lane, Opelousas, LA Zip 70570–6454, Mailing Address: P.O. Box 1208, Zip 70571–1208; tel. 318/948–3011; Daryl J. Doise, Administrator
Web address: www.opelousasgeneral.com

SUMMIT HOSPITAL (O, 143 beds) 17000 Medical Center Drive, Baton Rouge, LA Zip 70816–3224; tel. 225/755–4800; Steve Grimm, CHE, Chief Executive Officer

THIBODAUX REGIONAL MEDICAL CENTER (C, 150 beds) 602 North Acadia Road, Thibodaux, LA Zip 70301–4847, Mailing Address: P.O. Box 1118, Zip 70302–1118; tel. 504/447–5500; David M. Snyder, Chief Executive Officer
Web address: www.thibodaux.com

MAINE: CALAIS REGIONAL HOSPITAL (C, 57 beds) 50 Franklin Street, Calais, ME Zip 04619–1398; tel. 207/454–7521; Ray H. Davis Jr., Chief Executive Officer

CARY MEDICAL CENTER (C, 74 beds) 163 Van Buren Road, Suite 1, Caribou, ME Zip 04736–2599; tel. 207/498–3111; Kris Doody–Chabre, Chief Executive Officer
Web address: www.carymed.org

DOWN EAST COMMUNITY HOSPITAL (C, 38 beds) Upper Court Street, Machias, ME Zip 04654, Mailing Address: Rural Route 1, Box 11, Zip 04654–9702; tel. 207/255–3356; Philo D. Hall, Interim Chief Executive Officer
Web address: www.nemaine.com

HOULTON REGIONAL HOSPITAL (C, 73 beds) 20 Hartford Street, Houlton, ME Zip 04730–9998; tel. 207/532–9471; Thomas J. Moakler, Chief Executive Officer

MAINE COAST MEMORIAL HOSPITAL (C, 48 beds) 50 Union Street, Ellsworth, ME Zip 04605–1599; tel. 207/667–5311

MAYO REGIONAL HOSPITAL (C, 46 beds) 75 West Main Street, Dover–Foxcroft, ME Zip 04426–1099; tel. 207/564–8401; Ralph Gabarro, Chief Executive Officer
Web address: www.mayohospital.com

MILLINOCKET REGIONAL HOSPITAL (C, 16 beds) 200 Somerset Street, Millinocket, ME Zip 04462–1298; tel. 207/723–5161; Marie E. Arant, Interim Chief Executive Officer

PENOBSCOT VALLEY HOSPITAL (C, 41 beds) Transalpine Road, Lincoln, ME Zip 04457–0368, Mailing Address: P.O. Box 368, Zip 04457–0368; tel. 207/794–3321; Ronald D. Victory, Administrator

MASSACHUSETTS: HALE HOSPITAL (C, 108 beds) 140 Lincoln Avenue, Haverhill, MA Zip 01830–6798; tel. 978/374–2000; Robert J. Ingala, Chief Executive Officer

HUBBARD REGIONAL HOSPITAL (C, 26 beds) 340 Thompson Road, Webster, MA Zip 01570–0608; tel. 508/943–2600; Gerald J. Barbini, Administrator and Chief Executive Officer

For explanation of codes following names, see page B2.
★ Indicates Type III membership in the American Hospital Association.

© 1999 AHA Guide   Networks, Health Care Systems and Alliances **B129**

Section B

QUINCY HOSPITAL (C, 146 beds) 114 Whitwell Street, Quincy, MA Zip 02169–1899; tel. 617/773–6100; Jeffrey Doran, Chief Executive Officer

MICHIGAN: ALLEGAN GENERAL HOSPITAL (C, 63 beds) 555 Linn Street, Allegan, MI Zip 49010–1594; tel. 616/673–8424; James A. Klun, President
Web address: www.accn.org/~agh

COMMUNITY HEALTH CENTER OF BRANCH COUNTY (C, 96 beds) 274 East Chicago Street, Coldwater, MI Zip 49036–2088; tel. 517/279–5400; Lieutenant Douglas L. Rahn, Chief Executive Officer
Web address: www.chcbc.com

COMMUNITY HOSPITAL (C, 55 beds) Medical Park Drive, Watervliet, MI Zip 49098–0158, Mailing Address: P.O. Box 158, Zip 49098–0158; tel. 616/463–3111; Dennis Turney, Chief Executive Officer

KELSEY MEMORIAL HOSPITAL (C, 66 beds) 418 Washington Avenue, Lakeview, MI Zip 48850; tel. 517/352–7211; James Cliborne, Chief Operating Officer

LAKEVIEW COMMUNITY HOSPITAL (C, 168 beds) 408 Hazen Street, Paw Paw, MI Zip 49079–1019, Mailing Address: P.O. Box 209, Zip 49079–0209; tel. 616/657–3141; Sue E. Johnson–Phillippe, Chief Executive Officer

MARLETTE COMMUNITY HOSPITAL (C, 91 beds) 2770 Main Street, Marlette, MI Zip 48453–0307, Mailing Address: P.O. Box 307, Zip 48453–0307; tel. 517/635–4000; David S. McEwen, Chief Executive Officer

MECOSTA COUNTY GENERAL HOSPITAL (C, 52 beds) 405 Winter Avenue, Big Rapids, MI Zip 49307–2099; tel. 616/796–8691; Thomas E. Daugherty, Administrator
Web address: www.mecoscountygeneral.com

STURGIS HOSPITAL (C, 67 beds) 916 Myrtle, Sturgis, MI Zip 49091–2001; tel. 616/651–7824; David James, Chief Executive Officer

THREE RIVERS AREA HOSPITAL (C, 60 beds) 1111 West Broadway, Three Rivers, MI Zip 49093–9362; tel. 616/278–1145; Matthew Chambers, Chief Executive Officer
Web address: www.trah.org

MINNESOTA: FALLS MEMORIAL HOSPITAL (C, 35 beds) 1400 Highway 71, International Falls, MN Zip 56649–2189; tel. 218/283–4481; Mary Klimp, Administrator and Chief Executive Officer

VIRGINIA REGIONAL MEDICAL CENTER (C, 199 beds) 901 Ninth Street North, Virginia, MN Zip 55792–2398; tel. 218/741–3340; Kyle Hopstad, Administrator

MISSISSIPPI: BOLIVAR MEDICAL CENTER (C, 144 beds) Highway 8 East, Cleveland, MS Zip 38732–9722, Mailing Address: P.O. Box 1380, Zip 38732–1380; tel. 601/846–0061; Robert L. Hawley Jr., Chief Executive Officer

DELTA REGIONAL MEDICAL CENTER (C, 159 beds) 1400 East Union Street, Greenville, MS Zip 38703–3246, Mailing Address: P.O. Box 5247, Zip 38704–5247; tel. 601/378–3783; Barton A. Hove, Chief Executive Officer

FIELD MEMORIAL COMMUNITY HOSPITAL (C, 66 beds) 270 West Main Street, Centreville, MS Zip 39631, Mailing Address: P.O. Box 639, Zip 39631–0639; tel. 601/645–5221; Brock A. Slabach, Administrator

H. C. WATKINS MEMORIAL HOSPITAL (C, 43 beds) 605 South Archusa Avenue, Quitman, MS Zip 39355–2398; tel. 601/776–6925; Thomas G. Bartlett, President and Chief Executive Officer

HANCOCK MEDICAL CENTER (C, 66 beds) 149 Drinkwater Boulevard, Bay Saint Louis, MS Zip 39521–2790, Mailing Address: P.O. Box 2790, Zip 39521–2790; tel. 228/467–8600; Hal W. Leftwich, FACHE, Administrator
Web address: www.hmc.org

KING'S DAUGHTERS MEDICAL CENTER (C, 109 beds) 427 Highway 51 North, Brookhaven, MS Zip 39601–2600, Mailing Address: P.O. Box 948, Zip 39602–0948; tel. 601/833–6011; Phillip L. Grady, Chief Executive Officer
Web address: www.kdmc.org

MAGNOLIA REGIONAL HEALTH CENTER (C, 163 beds) 611 Alcorn Drive, Corinth, MS Zip 38834–9368; tel. 601/293–1000; Douglas Garner, Chief Executive Officer

NATCHEZ REGIONAL MEDICAL CENTER (C, 121 beds) Seargent S Prentiss Drive, Natchez, MS Zip 39120, Mailing Address: P.O. Box 1488, Zip 39121–1488; tel. 601/443–2100; Karen A. Fiducia, Interim Chief Executive Officer

NESHOBA COUNTY GENERAL HOSPITAL (C, 192 beds) 1001 Holland Avenue, Philadelphia, MS Zip 39350–2161, Mailing Address: P.O. Box 648, Zip 39350–0648; tel. 601/663–1200; Lawrence Graeber, Administrator

PARKVIEW REGIONAL MEDICAL CENTER (O, 197 beds) 100 McAuley Drive, Vicksburg, MS Zip 39180–2897, Mailing Address: P.O. Box 590, Zip 39181–0590; tel. 601/631–2131; Florence Jones, Administrator

UNIVERSITY HOSPITALS AND CLINICS, UNIVERSITY OF MISSISSIPPI MEDICAL CENTER (C, 610 beds) 2500 North State Street, Jackson, MS Zip 39216–4505; tel. 601/984–4100; Frederick Woodrell, Director

WESLEY MEDICAL CENTER (O, 211 beds) 5001 Hardy Street, Hattiesburg, MS Zip 39402, Mailing Address: P.O. Box 16509, Zip 39404–6509; tel. 601/268–8000; William K. Ray, President and Chief Executive Officer

MISSOURI: NEVADA REGIONAL MEDICAL CENTER (C, 85 beds) 800 South Ash Street, Nevada, MO Zip 64772–3223; tel. 417/667–3355; Robert B. Ohlen, President and Chief Executive Officer

MONTANA: CENTRAL MONTANA MEDICAL CENTER (C, 124 beds) 408 Wendell Avenue, Lewistown, MT Zip 59457–2261, Mailing Address: P.O. Box 580, Zip 59457–0580; tel. 406/538–7711; David M. Faulkner, Chief Executive Officer and Administrator

COMMUNITY HOSPITAL OF ANACONDA (C, 92 beds) 401 West Pennsylvania Street, Anaconda, MT Zip 59711–1999; tel. 406/563–8500; Sam J. Allen, Administrator

GLACIER COUNTY MEDICAL CENTER (C, 59 beds) 802 Second Street S.E., Cut Bank, MT Zip 59427–3331; tel. 406/873–2251; Dale E. Polla, Administrator

NORTH VALLEY HOSPITAL (C, 99 beds) 6575 Highway 93 South, Whitefish, MT Zip 59937; tel. 406/863–2501; Kenneth E. S. Platou, Chief Executive Officer
Web address: www.nvhosp.org

WHEATLAND MEMORIAL HOSPITAL (C, 54 beds) 530 Third Street North, Harlowton, MT Zip 59036, Mailing Address: P.O. Box 287, Zip 59036–0287; tel. 406/632–4351; Craig E. Aasved, Administrator

NEBRASKA: GREAT PLAINS REGIONAL MEDICAL CENTER (C, 99 beds) 601 West Leota Street, North Platte, NE Zip 69101–6598, Mailing Address: P.O. Box 1167, Zip 69103–1167; tel. 308/534–9310; Lucinda A. Bradley, President

PHELPS MEMORIAL HEALTH CENTER (C, 28 beds) 1220 Miller Street, Holdrege, NE Zip 68949–0828, Mailing Address: P.O. Box 828, Zip 68949–0828; tel. 308/995–2211; Jerome Seigfreid Jr., Chief Executive Officer

NEW HAMPSHIRE: LITTLETON REGIONAL HOSPITAL (C, 49 beds) 262 Cottage Street, Littleton, NH Zip 03561–4101; tel. 603/444–7731; Robert S. Pearson, Administrator
Web address: www.littletonhospital.org

NEW MEXICO: CIBOLA GENERAL HOSPITAL (C, 22 beds) 1212 Bonita Avenue, Grants, NM Zip 87020–2104; tel. 505/287–4446; Walter Topp III, Administrator

GERALD CHAMPION MEMORIAL HOSPITAL (C, 73 beds) 1209 Ninth Street, Alamogordo, NM Zip 88310; tel. 505/439–2100; Carl W. Mantey, Administrator

GILA REGIONAL MEDICAL CENTER (C, 59 beds) 1313 East 32nd Street, Silver City, NM Zip 88061; tel. 505/538–4000; Polly Pine, Administrator

HOLY CROSS HOSPITAL (C, 34 beds) 1397 Weimer Road, Taos, NM Zip 87571, Mailing Address: P.O. Box DD, Zip 87571; tel. 505/758–8883; Warren K. Spellman, Administrator

NEW YORK: AMSTERDAM MEMORIAL HOSPITAL (C, 242 beds) 4988 State Highway 30, Amsterdam, NY Zip 12010–1699; tel. 518/842–3100; Cornelio R. Catena, President and Chief Executive Officer

AURELIA OSBORN FOX MEMORIAL HOSPITAL (C, 246 beds) 1 Norton Avenue, Oneonta, NY Zip 13820–2697; tel. 607/432–2000; John R. Remillard, President
Web address: www.foxcarenetwork.com

ELLIS HOSPITAL (C, 450 beds) 1101 Nott Street, Schenectady, NY Zip 12308–2487; tel. 518/243–4000; G. B. Serrill, President and Chief Executive Officer
Web address: www.shine.org

MEDINA MEMORIAL HOSPITAL (C, 101 beds) 200 Ohio Street, Medina, NY Zip 14103–1095; tel. 716/798–2000; James Sinner, Chief Executive Officer

For explanation of codes following names, see page B2.
★ Indicates Type III membership in the American Hospital Association.

NORTH CAROLINA: ALLEGHANY MEMORIAL HOSPITAL (C, 46 beds) 233 Doctors Street, Sparta, NC Zip 28675–0009, Mailing Address: P.O. Box 9, Zip 28675–0009; tel. 336/372–5511; James Yarborough, Chief Executive Officer

ANGEL MEDICAL CENTER (C, 59 beds) Riverview and White Oak Streets, Franklin, NC Zip 28734, Mailing Address: P.O. Box 1209, Zip 28744; tel. 828/524–8411; Michael E. Zuliani, Chief Executive Officer

ASHE MEMORIAL HOSPITAL (C, 115 beds) 200 Hospital Avenue, Jefferson, NC Zip 28640; tel. 336/246–7101; R. D. Williams, Administrator and Chief Executive Officer
Web address: www.ashememorial.org

CHATHAM HOSPITAL (C, 35 beds) West Third Street and Ivy Avenue, Siler City, NC Zip 27344–2343, Mailing Address: P.O. Box 649, Zip 27344; tel. 919/663–2113; Woodrow W. Hathaway Jr., Chief Executive Officer

COLUMBUS COUNTY HOSPITAL (C, 117 beds) 500 Jefferson Street, Whiteville, NC Zip 28472–9987; tel. 910/642–8011; William S. Clark, Chief Executive Officer
Web address: www.cchospital.com

GOOD HOPE HOSPITAL (C, 72 beds) 410 Denim Drive, Erwin, NC Zip 28339–0668, Mailing Address: P.O. Box 668, Zip 28339–0668; tel. 910/897–6151; Donald E. Annis, Chief Executive Officer
Web address: www.goodhopehospital.org

GRANVILLE MEDICAL CENTER (C, 128 beds) 1010 College Street, Oxford, NC Zip 27565–2507, Mailing Address: Box 947, Zip 27565–0947; tel. 919/690–3000; Joe W. Pollard Jr., Chief Executive Officer

HUGH CHATHAM MEMORIAL HOSPITAL (C, 201 beds) Parkwood Drive, Elkin, NC Zip 28621–0560, Mailing Address: P.O. Box 560, Zip 28621–0560; tel. 336/527–7000; Richard D. Osmus, Chief Executive Officer

JOHNSTON MEMORIAL HOSPITAL (C, 127 beds) 509 North Bright Leaf Boulevard, Smithfield, NC Zip 27577–1376, Mailing Address: P.O. Box 1376, Zip 27577–1376; tel. 919/934–8171; Leland E. Farnell, President

MOREHEAD MEMORIAL HOSPITAL (C, 236 beds) 117 East King's Highway, Eden, NC Zip 27288–5299; tel. 336/623–9711; Robert Enders, President
Web address: www.morehead.org

NORTHERN HOSPITAL OF SURRY COUNTY (C, 103 beds) 830 Rockford Street, Mount Airy, NC Zip 27030–5365, Mailing Address: P.O. Box 1101, Zip 27030–1101; tel. 336/719–7000; William B. James, Chief Executive Officer

PENDER MEMORIAL HOSPITAL (C, 86 beds) 507 Freemont Street, Burgaw, NC Zip 28425; tel. 910/259–5451; Ronald J. Vigus, Chief Executive Officer

RUTHERFORD HOSPITAL (C, 261 beds) 288 South Ridgecrest Avenue, Rutherfordton, NC Zip 28139–3097; tel. 828/286–5000; Robert D. Jones, President

WASHINGTON COUNTY HOSPITAL (C, 33 beds) 958 U.S. Highway 64 East, Plymouth, NC Zip 27962–9591; tel. 252/793–4135; Lawrence H. McAvoy, Administrator

NORTH DAKOTA: KENMARE COMMUNITY HOSPITAL (O, 42 beds) 317 First Avenue N.W., Kenmare, ND Zip 58746–7104, Mailing Address: P.O. Box 697, Zip 58746–0697; tel. 701/385–4296; Verlin D. Buechler, Administrator and Chief Executive Officer

UNIMED MEDICAL CENTER (O, 160 beds) 407 3rd Street S.E., Minot, ND Zip 58702–5001; tel. 701/857–2000; Michael L. Mullins, Chief Executive Officer

OHIO: BARBERTON CITIZENS HOSPITAL (O, 251 beds) 155 Fifth Street N.E., Barberton, OH Zip 44203–3398; tel. 330/745–1611; Ronald J. Elder, President
Web address: www.barbhosp.com

BROWN COUNTY GENERAL HOSPITAL (C, 53 beds) 425 Home Street, Georgetown, OH Zip 45121–1407; tel. 937/378–6121; David T. Wallace, President and Chief Executive Officer
Web address: www.bcgh.org

DOCTORS HOSPITAL OF STARK COUNTY (O, 110 beds) 400 Austin Avenue N.W., Massillon, OH Zip 44646–3554; tel. 330/837–7200; Thomas E. Cecconi, Chief Executive Officer
Web address: www.drshospital.com

FAYETTE COUNTY MEMORIAL HOSPITAL (C, 35 beds) 1430 Columbus Avenue, Washington Court House, OH Zip 43160–1791; tel. 740/335–1210; Francis G. Albarano, Administrator

GREENFIELD AREA MEDICAL CENTER (C, 36 beds) 545 South Street, Greenfield, OH Zip 45123–1400; tel. 937/981–2116; Mark E. Marchetti, Chief Executive Officer

KNOX COMMUNITY HOSPITAL (C, 75 beds) 1330 Coshocton Road, Mount Vernon, OH Zip 43050–1495; tel. 740/393–9000; Robert G. Polahar, Chief Executive Officer

MEMORIAL HOSPITAL (C, 114 beds) 715 South Taft Avenue, Fremont, OH Zip 43420–3200; tel. 419/332–7321; John A. Gorman, Chief Executive Officer

PAULDING COUNTY HOSPITAL (C, 51 beds) 11558 State Road 111, Paulding, OH Zip 45879–9220; tel. 419/399–4080; Gary W. Adkins, Interim Chief Executive Officer
Web address: www.bright.net/pch

SELBY GENERAL HOSPITAL (C, 52 beds) 1106 Colegate Drive, Marietta, OH Zip 45750–1323; tel. 740/373–0582; Richard C. Sommer, Interim Chief Executive Officer
Web address: www.selby.wscc.edu

WOOSTER COMMUNITY HOSPITAL (C, 90 beds) 1761 Beall Avenue, Wooster, OH Zip 44691–2342; tel. 330/263–8100; William E. Sheron, Chief Executive Officer

OKLAHOMA: ATOKA MEMORIAL HOSPITAL (C, 25 beds) 1501 South Virginia Avenue, Atoka, OK Zip 74525–3298; tel. 580/889–3333; Paul David Moore, Administrator

CUSHING REGIONAL HOSPITAL (L, 75 beds) 1027 East Cherry Street, Cushing, OK Zip 74023–4101, Mailing Address: P.O. Box 1409, Zip 74023–1409; tel. 918/225–2915; Ron Cackler, President and Chief Executive Officer

EASTERN OKLAHOMA MEDICAL CENTER (L, 72 beds) 105 Wall Street, Poteau, OK Zip 74953, Mailing Address: P.O. Box 1148, Zip 74953–1148; tel. 918/647–8161; Craig R. Cudworth, Chief Executive Officer

HENRYETTA MEDICAL CENTER (L, 46 beds) Dewey Bartlett and Main Streets, Henryetta, OK Zip 74437, Mailing Address: P.O. Box 1269, Zip 74437–1269; tel. 918/652–4463; James P. Bailey, President and Chief Executive Officer

HOLDENVILLE GENERAL HOSPITAL (C, 27 beds) 100 Crestview Drive, Holdenville, OK Zip 74848–9700; tel. 405/379–6631; Shawn Morrow, Chief Executive Officer and Administrator

KINGFISHER REGIONAL HOSPITAL (C, 38 beds) 500 South Ninth Street, Kingfisher, OK Zip 73750–3528, Mailing Address: P.O. Box 59, Zip 73750–0059; tel. 405/375–3141; Daryle Voss, Chief Executive Officer

LOGAN HOSPITAL AND MEDICAL CENTER (C, 32 beds) Highway 33 West at Academy Road, Guthrie, OK Zip 73044, Mailing Address: P.O. Box 1017, Zip 73044–1017; tel. 405/282–6700; Judy Feuquay, Chief Executive Officer

MCCURTAIN MEMORIAL HOSPITAL (C, 89 beds) 1301 Lincoln Road, Idabel, OK Zip 74745–7341; tel. 580/286–7623; Claude E. Camp III, Chief Executive Officer

PERRY MEMORIAL HOSPITAL (C, 28 beds) 501 14th Street, Perry, OK Zip 73077–5099; tel. 580/336–3541; Joe Duerr, Chief Executive Officer

PURCELL MUNICIPAL HOSPITAL (C, 20 beds) 1500 North Green Avenue, Purcell, OK Zip 73080–1699, Mailing Address: P.O. Box 511, Zip 73080–0511; tel. 405/527–6524; Curtis R. Pryor, Administrator

SAYRE MEMORIAL HOSPITAL (C, 46 beds) 501 East Washington Street, Sayre, OK Zip 73662, Mailing Address: P.O. Box 680, Zip 73662; tel. 580/928–5541; Larry Anderson, Administrator

SHARE MEDICAL CENTER (C, 117 beds) 800 Share Drive, Alva, OK Zip 73717–3699, Mailing Address: P.O. Box 727, Zip 73717–0727; tel. 580/327–2800; Barbara Oestmann, Chief Executive Officer

WATONGA MUNICIPAL HOSPITAL (C, 23 beds) 500 North Nash Boulevard, Watonga, OK Zip 73772–0370, Mailing Address: Box 370, Zip 73772–0370; tel. 580/623–7211; Terry Buckner, Administrator

WOODWARD HOSPITAL AND HEALTH CENTER (C, 68 beds) 900 17th Street, Woodward, OK Zip 73801–2423; tel. 580/256–5511; Joel A. Hart, Chief Executive Officer

PENNSYLVANIA: BROWNSVILLE GENERAL HOSPITAL (C, 115 beds) 125 Simpson Road, Brownsville, PA Zip 15417–9699; tel. 724/785–7200; Richard D. Constantine, Chief Executive Officer
Web address: www.bghlink.com

For explanation of codes following names, see page B2.
★ Indicates Type III membership in the American Hospital Association.

Section B

CARLISLE HOSPITAL AND HEALTH SERVICES (C, 166 beds) 246 Parker Street, Carlisle, PA Zip 17013–3618; tel. 717/249–1212; Michael J. Halstead, President and Chief Executive Officer
Web address: www.chhs.org

CLARION HOSPITAL (C, 86 beds) One Hospital Drive, Clarion, PA Zip 16214–8599; tel. 814/226–9500; Donald D. Evans, President and Chief Executive Officer
Web address: www.pen.com/clarionhospital

CORRY MEMORIAL HOSPITAL (C, 55 beds) 612 West Smith Street, Corry, PA Zip 16407–1152; tel. 814/664–4641; Joseph T. Hodges, President

GREENE COUNTY MEMORIAL HOSPITAL (C, 60 beds) Seventh Street and Bonar Avenue, Waynesburg, PA Zip 15370–1697; tel. 724/627–3101; Raoul Walsh, Chief Executive Officer

J. C. BLAIR MEMORIAL HOSPITAL (C, 104 beds) 1225 Warm Springs Avenue, Huntingdon, PA Zip 16652–2398; tel. 814/643–2290; Richard E. D'Alberto, Chief Executive Officer
Web address: www.JCBlair.Org

JERSEY SHORE HOSPITAL (C, 49 beds) 1020 Thompson Street, Jersey Shore, PA Zip 17740–1794; tel. 570/398–0100; Louis A. Ditzel Jr., President and Chief Executive Officer

LOCK HAVEN HOSPITAL (C, 195 beds) 24 Cree Drive, Lock Haven, PA Zip 17745–2699; tel. 570/893–5000; Gary R. Rhoads, President and Chief Executive Officer

MEMORIAL HOSPITAL (C, 93 beds) One Hospital Drive, Towanda, PA Zip 18848–9702; tel. 570/265–2191; Gary A. Baker, President

OHIO VALLEY GENERAL HOSPITAL (C, 103 beds) 25 Heckel Road, McKees Rocks, PA Zip 15136–1694; tel. 412/777–6161; William Provenzano, President

POTTSVILLE HOSPITAL AND WARNE CLINIC (C, 196 beds) 420 South Jackson Street, Pottsville, PA Zip 17901–3692; tel. 570/621–5000; Donald R. Gintzig, President and Chief Executive Officer
Web address: www.pottsville.com/hospital

TYRONE HOSPITAL (C, 59 beds) One Hospital Drive, Tyrone, PA Zip 16686–1810; tel. 814/684–1255; Philip J. Stoner, Chief Executive Officer

SOUTH CAROLINA: ABBEVILLE COUNTY MEMORIAL HOSPITAL (C, 42 beds) 901 West Greenwood Street, Abbeville, SC Zip 29620–0887, Mailing Address: P.O. Box 887, Zip 29620–0887; tel. 864/459–5011; Bruce P. Bailey, Administrator

CAROLINAS HOSPITAL SYSTEM (O, 340 beds) 805 Pamplico Highway, Florence, SC Zip 29505, Mailing Address: P.O. Box 100550, Zip 29501–0550; tel. 843/674–5000; David A. McClellan, Chief Executive Officer
Web address: www.carolinashospital.com

CAROLINAS HOSPITAL SYSTEM–KINGSTREE (O, 47 beds) 500 Nelson Boulevard, Kingstree, SC Zip 29556–4027, Mailing Address: P.O. Drawer 568, Zip 29556–0568; tel. 843/354–9661; David T. Boucher, Chief Executive Officer

CAROLINAS HOSPITAL SYSTEM–LAKE CITY (O, 40 beds) 258 North Ron McNair Boulevard, Lake City, SC Zip 29560–1029, Mailing Address: P.O. Box 1029, Zip 29560–1029; tel. 843/394–2036; David T. Boucher, Chief Executive Officer

GEORGETOWN MEMORIAL HOSPITAL (C, 131 beds) 606 Black River Road, Georgetown, SC Zip 29440–3368, Mailing Address: Drawer 1718, Zip 29442–1718; tel. 843/527–7000; Paul D. Gatens Sr., Administrator

LAURENS COUNTY HEALTHCARE SYSTEM (C, 85 beds) Highway 76 West, Clinton, SC Zip 29325, Mailing Address: P.O. Box 976, Zip 29325–0976; tel. 864/833–9100; Michael A. Kozar, Chief Executive Officer
Web address: www.lchcs.org

MARY BLACK HEALTH SYSTEM (O, 210 beds) 1700 Skylyn Drive, Spartanburg, SC Zip 29307–1061, Mailing Address: P.O. Box 3217, Zip 29304–3217; tel. 864/573–3000; William W. Fox, Chief Executive Officer

NEWBERRY COUNTY MEMORIAL HOSPITAL (C, 65 beds) 2669 Kinard Street, Newberry, SC Zip 29108–0497, Mailing Address: P.O. Box 497, Zip 29108–0497; tel. 803/276–7570; Lynn W. Beasley, President and Chief Executive Officer

REGIONAL MEDICAL CENTER OF ORANGEBURG AND CALHOUN COUNTIES (C, 295 beds) 3000 St. Matthews Road, Orangeburg, SC Zip 29118–1470; tel. 803/533–2200; Thomas C. Dandridge, President

TUOMEY HEALTHCARE SYSTEM (C, 239 beds) 129 North Washington Street, Sumter, SC Zip 29150–4983; tel. 803/778–9000; Jay Cox, President and Chief Executive Officer
Web address: www.tuomey.com

WALLACE THOMSON HOSPITAL (C, 220 beds) 322 West South Street, Union, SC Zip 29379–2857, Mailing Address: P.O. Box 789, Zip 29379–0789; tel. 864/429–2600; Harrell L. Connelly, Chief Executive Officer

SOUTH DAKOTA: HURON REGIONAL MEDICAL CENTER (C, 61 beds) 172 Fourth Street S.E., Huron, SD Zip 57350–2590; tel. 605/353–6200; John L. Single, Chief Executive Officer

TENNESSEE: LINCOLN COUNTY HEALTH FACILITIES (C, 51 beds) 700 West Maple Street, Fayetteville, TN Zip 37334–3202; tel. 931/438–1111; Gary G. Kendrick, Chief Executive Officer

MACON COUNTY GENERAL HOSPITAL (C, 43 beds) 204 Medical Drive, Lafayette, TN Zip 37083–1799, Mailing Address: P.O. Box 378, Zip 37083–0378; tel. 615/666–2147; Dennis A. Wolford, FACHE, Administrator

RHEA MEDICAL CENTER (C, 131 beds) 7900 Rhea County Highway, Dayton, TN Zip 37321–5912; tel. 423/775–1121; Kennedy L. Croom Jr., Administrator and Chief Executive Officer

WELLMONT BRISTOL REGIONAL MEDICAL CENTER (C, 275 beds) 1 Medical Park Boulevard, Bristol, TN Zip 37620–7434; tel. 423/844–4200; Randall M. Olson, Administrator
Web address: www.wellmont.org

WELLMONT HOLSTON VALLEY MEDICAL CENTER (C, 380 beds) West Ravine Street, Kingsport, TN Zip 37662–0224, Mailing Address: Box 238, Zip 37662–0224; tel. 423/224–4000; Louis H. Bremer, President and Chief Executive Officer

TEXAS: ABILENE REGIONAL MEDICAL CENTER (O, 157 beds) 6250 Highway 83–84 at Antilley Road, Abilene, TX Zip 79606–5299; tel. 915/695–9900; Woody Gilliland, Chief Executive Officer
Web address: www.abilene.com/armc

BRAZOSPORT MEMORIAL HOSPITAL (C, 156 beds) 100 Medical Drive, Lake Jackson, TX Zip 77566–9983; tel. 409/297–4411; Wesley W. Oswald, Chief Executive Officer
Web address: www.brazosportmemorial.com

CAMPBELL HEALTH SYSTEM (C, 67 beds) 713 East Anderson Street, Weatherford, TX Zip 76086–9971; tel. 817/596–8751; John B. Millstead, Chief Executive Officer

DALLAS–FORT WORTH MEDICAL CENTER (C, 162 beds) 2709 Hospital Boulevard, Grand Prairie, TX Zip 75051–1083; tel. 972/641–5000; Robert A. Ficken, Chief Executive Officer
Web address: www.dfwmedicalcenter.com

FORT DUNCAN MEDICAL CENTER (C, 69 beds) 350 South Adams Street, Eagle Pass, TX Zip 78852; tel. 830/773–5321; Don Spaulding, Administrator and Chief Executive Officer

HENDERSON MEMORIAL HOSPITAL (C, 96 beds) 300 Wilson Street, Henderson, TX Zip 75652–5956; tel. 903/657–7541; George T. Roberts Jr., Chief Executive Officer

HUNTSVILLE MEMORIAL HOSPITAL (C, 130 beds) 485 I–45 South, Huntsville, TX Zip 77340–4362, Mailing Address: P.O. Box 4001, Zip 77342–4001; tel. 409/291–3411; Ralph E. Beaty, Administrator
Web address: www.huntsvillememorial.com

MISSION HOSPITAL (C, 110 beds) 900 South Bryan Road, Mission, TX Zip 78572–6613; tel. 956/580–9000; Paul H. Ballard, Chief Executive Officer
Web address: www.missionhosp.com

TITUS REGIONAL MEDICAL CENTER (C, 92 beds) 2001 North Jefferson Avenue, Mount Pleasant, TX Zip 75455–2398; tel. 903/577–6000; Steven K. Jacobson, Chief Executive Officer

VERMONT: NORTHEASTERN VERMONT REGIONAL HOSPITAL (C, 28 beds) Hospital Drive, Saint Johnsbury, VT Zip 05819–9962, Mailing Address: P.O. Box 905, Zip 05819–9962; tel. 802/748–8141; Paul R. Bengtson, Chief Executive Officer

For explanation of codes following names, see page B2.
★ Indicates Type III membership in the American Hospital Association.

NORTHWESTERN MEDICAL CENTER (C, 70 beds) 131 Fairfield Street, Saint Albans, VT Zip 05478–1734, Mailing Address: P.O. Box 1370, Zip 05478–1370; tel. 802/524–5911; Peter A. Hofstetter, Chief Executive Officer
Web address: www.nmcinc.org

VIRGINIA: BUCHANAN GENERAL HOSPITAL (C, 144 beds) Grundy, VA Mailing Address: Route 5, Box 20, Zip 24614–9611; tel. 540/935–1000; John West, Administrator

HALIFAX REGIONAL HOSPITAL (C, 157 beds) 2204 Wilborn Avenue, South Boston, VA Zip 24592–1638; tel. 804/575–3100; Chris A. Lumsden, Chief Executive Officer

MEMORIAL HOSPITAL OF MARTINSVILLE AND HENRY COUNTY (C, 152 beds) 320 Hospital Drive, Martinsville, VA Zip 24112–1981, Mailing Address: Box 4788, Zip 24115–4788; tel. 540/666–7200; Joseph Roach, Chief Executive Officer
Web address: www.martinsvillehospital.org

RICHMOND EYE AND EAR HOSPITAL (C, 32 beds) 1001 East Marshall Street, Richmond, VA Zip 23219–1993; tel. 804/775–4500; James W. Worrell, Chief Executive Officer

SOUTHSIDE REGIONAL MEDICAL CENTER (C, 268 beds) 801 South Adams Street, Petersburg, VA Zip 23803–5133; tel. 804/862–5000; David S. Dunham, President
Web address: www.srmconline.com

WELLMONT LONESOME PINE HOSPITAL (C, 53 beds) 1990 Holton Avenue East, Big Stone Gap, VA Zip 24219–0230; tel. 540/523–3111; Paul A. Bishop, Administrator

WASHINGTON: KADLEC MEDICAL CENTER (C, 124 beds) 888 Swift Boulevard, Richland, WA Zip 99352–9974; tel. 509/946–4611; Marcel Loh, President and Chief Executive Officer
Web address: www.kadlecmed.com

WEST VIRGINIA: CITY HOSPITAL (C, 143 beds) Dry Run Road, Martinsburg, WV Zip 25401, Mailing Address: P.O. Box 1418, Zip 25402–1418; tel. 304/264–1000; Peter L. Mulford, Administrator

FAIRMONT GENERAL HOSPITAL (C, 211 beds) 1325 Locust Avenue, Fairmont, WV Zip 26554–1435; tel. 304/367–7100; Richard W. Graham, FACHE, President
Web address: www.fghi.com

PRESTON MEMORIAL HOSPITAL (C, 60 beds) 300 South Price Street, Kingwood, WV Zip 26537–1495; tel. 304/329–1400; Charles Lonchar, President and Chief Executive Officer

WISCONSIN: AMERY REGIONAL MEDICAL CENTER (C, 10 beds) 225 Scholl Court, Amery, WI Zip 54001–1292; tel. 715/268–8000; Michael Karuschak Jr., Chief Executive Officer

RIVERSIDE MEDICAL CENTER (C, 40 beds) 800 Riverside Drive, Waupaca, WI Zip 54981–1999; tel. 715/258–1000; Craig A. Kantos, Chief Executive Officer

WYOMING: WEST PARK HOSPITAL (C, 179 beds) 707 Sheridan Avenue, Cody, WY Zip 82414; tel. 307/527–7501; Douglas A. McMillan, Administrator and Chief Executive Officer

Owned, leased, sponsored:	25 hospitals	3875 beds
Contract–managed:	217 hospitals	21787 beds
Totals:	242 hospitals	25662 beds

0405: RAMSAY HEALTH CARE, INC. (IO)
1 Alhambra Plaza, Suite 750, Coral Gables, FL Zip 33134–5217; tel. 305/569–6993; Bert Cibran, President and Chief Operating Officer

ALABAMA: HILL CREST BEHAVIORAL HEALTH SERVICES (O, 119 beds) 6869 Fifth Avenue South, Birmingham, AL Zip 35212–1866; tel. 205/833–9000; Steve McCabe, Chief Executive Officer

FLORIDA: GULF COAST TREATMENT CENTER (O, 79 beds) 1015 Mar–Walt Drive, Fort Walton Beach, FL Zip 32547–6612; tel. 850/863–4160; Raul D. Ruelas, M.D., Administrator

LOUISIANA: GREENBRIER BEHAVIORAL HEALTH SYSTEM (O, 66 beds) 201 Greenbrier Boulevard, Covington, LA Zip 70433–9126; tel. 504/893–2970; Cheryl M. Schleuss, Chief Executive Officer

MICHIGAN: HAVENWYCK HOSPITAL (O, 120 beds) 1525 University Drive, Auburn Hills, MI Zip 48326–2675; tel. 810/373–9200; Robert A. Kercorian, Chief Executive Officer

MISSOURI: HEARTLAND BEHAVIORAL HEALTH SERVICES (O, 30 beds) 1500 West Ashland Street, Nevada, MO Zip 64772–1710; tel. 417/667–2666; Ed Goosman, Chief Executive Officer

NORTH CAROLINA: BRYNN MARR BEHAVIORAL HEALTHCARE SYSTEM (O, 76 beds) 192 Village Drive, Jacksonville, NC Zip 28546–7299; tel. 910/577–1400; Dale Armstrong, Chief Executive Officer

OKLAHOMA: INTEGRIS BASS BEHAVIORAL HEALTH SYSTEM (O, 50 beds) 2216 South Van Buren Street, Enid, OK Zip 73703–8299; tel. 580/234–2220; James Hutchison, Director

TEXAS: MISSION VISTA BEHAVIORAL HEALTH SYSTEM (L, 16 beds) 14747 Jones Maltsberger, San Antonio, TX Zip 78247–3713; tel. 210/490–0000; Holly Minnis, Chief Executive Officer

UTAH: BENCHMARK BEHAVIORAL HEALTH SYSTEMS (O, 68 beds) 592 West 1350 South, Woods Cross, UT Zip 84087–1665; tel. 801/299–5300; Richard O. Hurt, Ph.D., Chief Executive Officer

WEST VIRGINIA: CHESTNUT RIDGE HOSPITAL (O, 70 beds) 930 Chestnut Ridge Road, Morgantown, WV Zip 26505–2854; tel. 304/293–4000; Lawrence J. Drake, Chief Executive Officer

Owned, leased, sponsored:	10 hospitals	694 beds
Contract–managed:	0 hospitals	0 beds
Totals:	10 hospitals	694 beds

0171: RESURRECTION HEALTH CARE CORPORATION (CC)
7435 West Talcott Avenue, Chicago, IL Zip 60631

ILLINOIS: OUR LADY OF THE RESURRECTION MEDICAL CENTER (O, 282 beds) 5645 West Addison Street, Chicago, IL Zip 60634–4455; tel. 773/282–7000; Ronald E. Struxness, Executive Vice President and Chief Executive Officer
Web address: www.reshealthcare.org

RESURRECTION MEDICAL CENTER (O, 667 beds) 7435 West Talcott Avenue, Chicago, IL Zip 60631–3746; tel. 773/774–8000; Sister Donna Marie, Executive Vice President and Chief Executive Officer
Web address: www.reshealthcare.org

ST. FRANCIS HOSPITAL (O, 440 beds) 355 Ridge Avenue, Evanston, IL Zip 60202–3399; tel. 847/316–4000; Kenneth W. Wood, President and Chief Executive Officer

WESTLAKE COMMUNITY HOSPITAL (O, 239 beds) 1225 Lake Street, Melrose Park, IL Zip 60160–4000; tel. 708/681–3000; Kenneth W. Wood, Chief Executive Officer

Owned, leased, sponsored:	4 hospitals	1628 beds
Contract–managed:	0 hospitals	0 beds
Totals:	4 hospitals	1628 beds

4810: RIVERSIDE HEALTH SYSTEM (NP)
606 Denbigh Boulevard, Suite 601, Newport News, VA Zip 23608; tel. 757/875–7500; Nelson L. St. Clair, President

VIRGINIA: LAKE TAYLOR HOSPITAL (C, 330 beds) 1309 Kempsville Road, Norfolk, VA Zip 23502–2286; tel. 757/461–5001; David B. Tate Jr., President and Chief Executive Officer
Web address: www.laketaylor.org

RIVERSIDE REGIONAL MEDICAL CENTER (O, 576 beds) 500 J. Clyde Morris Boulevard, Newport News, VA Zip 23601–1976; tel. 757/594–2000; Gerald R. Brink, President and Chief Executive Officer

RIVERSIDE TAPPAHANNOCK HOSPITAL (O, 100 beds) 618 Hospital Road, Tappahannock, VA Zip 22560; tel. 804/443–3311; Elizabeth J. Martin, Vice President and Administrator

RIVERSIDE WALTER REED HOSPITAL (O, 71 beds) 7519 Hospital Drive, Gloucester, VA Zip 23061–4178, Mailing Address: P.O. Box 1130, Zip 23061–1130; tel. 804/693–8800; Grady W. Philips III, Vice President and Administrator

For explanation of codes following names, see page B2.
★ Indicates Type III membership in the American Hospital Association.

Owned, leased, sponsored:	3 hospitals	747 beds
Contract–managed:	1 hospital	330 beds
Totals:	4 hospitals	1077 beds

★0109: **RURAL HEALTH MANAGEMENT CORPORATION** (NP)
549 North 400 East, Nephi, UT Zip 84648–1226;
tel. 435/623–4924; Mark R. Stoddard, President

UTAH: ALLEN MEMORIAL HOSPITAL (L, 38 beds) 719 West 400 North Street, Moab, UT Zip 84532–2297, Mailing Address: P.O. Box 998, Zip 84532–0998; tel. 435/259–7191; Charles A. Davis, Administrator and Chief Executive Officer

CENTRAL VALLEY MEDICAL CENTER (L, 22 beds) 549 North 400 East, Nephi, UT Zip 84648–1226; tel. 435/623–1242; Mark R. Stoddard, President

GUNNISON VALLEY HOSPITAL (C, 21 beds) 64 East 100 North, Gunnison, UT Zip 84634, Mailing Address: P.O. Box 759, Zip 84634–0759; tel. 435/528–7246; Greg Rosenvall, Administrator

MILFORD VALLEY MEMORIAL HOSPITAL (C, 34 beds) 451 North Main Street, Milford, UT Zip 84751–0640, Mailing Address: P.O. Box 640, Zip 84751–0640; tel. 435/387–2411; John E. Gledhill, Administrator

Owned, leased, sponsored:	2 hospitals	60 beds
Contract–managed:	2 hospitals	55 beds
Totals:	4 hospitals	115 beds

★3855: **RUSH–PRESBYTERIAN–ST. LUKE'S MEDICAL CENTER** (NP)
1653 West Congress Parkway, Chicago, IL Zip 60612–3864; tel. 312/942–5000; Leo M. Henikoff, President

ILLINOIS: RUSH NORTH SHORE MEDICAL CENTER (O, 237 beds) 9600 Gross Point Road, Skokie, IL Zip 60076–1257; tel. 847/677–9600; John S. Frigo, President

RUSH–COPLEY MEDICAL CENTER (O, 140 beds) 2000 Ogden Avenue, Aurora, IL Zip 60504–4206; tel. 630/978–6200; Martin Losoff, President and Chief Operating Officer

RUSH–PRESBYTERIAN–ST. LUKE'S MEDICAL CENTER (O, 719 beds) 1653 West Congress Parkway, Chicago, IL Zip 60612–3833; tel. 312/942–5000; Leo M. Henikoff, President and Chief Executive Officer

Owned, leased, sponsored:	3 hospitals	1096 beds
Contract–managed:	0 hospitals	0 beds
Totals:	3 hospitals	1096 beds

★0118: **SAINT BARNABAS HEALTH CARE SYSTEM** (NP)
95 Old Short Hills Road, West Orange, NJ Zip 07052; tel. 973/322–4001; Ronald Del Mauro, President and Chief Executive Officer

NEW JERSEY: CLARA MAASS HEALTH SYSTEM (O, 644 beds) 1 Clara Maass Drive, Belleville, NJ Zip 07109–3557; tel. 973/450–2000; Thomas A. Biga, Executive Director

COMMUNITY MEDICAL CENTER (O, 435 beds) 99 Route 37 West, Toms River, NJ Zip 08755–6423; tel. 732/557–8000; Kevin R. Burchill, Executive Director
Web address: www.sbhcs.com

IRVINGTON GENERAL HOSPITAL (O, 157 beds) 832 Chancellor Avenue, Irvington, NJ Zip 07111–0709; tel. 973/399–6000; Paul A. Mertz, Executive Director

KIMBALL MEDICAL CENTER (O, 248 beds) 600 River Avenue, Lakewood, NJ Zip 08701–5281; tel. 732/363–1900; Joanne Carrocino, Executive Director
Web address: www.sbhcs.com

MONMOUTH MEDICAL CENTER (O, 435 beds) 300 Second Avenue, Long Branch, NJ Zip 07740–6303; tel. 732/222–5200; Frank J. Vozos, M.D., FACS, Executive Director

NEWARK BETH ISRAEL MEDICAL CENTER (O, 490 beds) 201 Lyons Avenue, Newark, NJ Zip 07112–2027; tel. 973/926–7000; Paul A. Mertz, Executive Director

SAINT BARNABAS MEDICAL CENTER (O, 571 beds) 94 Old Short Hills Road, Livingston, NJ Zip 07039–5668; tel. 973/322–5000; Vincent D. Joseph, Executive Director

UNION HOSPITAL (O, 148 beds) 1000 Galloping Hill Road, Union, NJ Zip 07083–1652; tel. 908/687–1900; Kathryn W. Coyne, Executive Director and Chief Operating Officer
Web address: www.sbhcs.com

WAYNE GENERAL HOSPITAL (O, 170 beds) 224 Hamburg Turnpike, Wayne, NJ Zip 07470–2100; tel. 973/942–6900; Kenneth H. Kozloff, Executive Director

WEST HUDSON HOSPITAL (O, 217 beds) 206 Bergen Avenue, Kearny, NJ Zip 07032–3399; tel. 201/955–7051; Carmen Bruce Alecci, Executive Director

Owned, leased, sponsored:	10 hospitals	3515 beds
Contract–managed:	0 hospitals	0 beds
Totals:	10 hospitals	3515 beds

0120: **SAINT LUKE'S SHAWNEE MISSION HEALTH SYSTEM** (NP)
10920 Elm Avenue, Kansas City, MO Zip 64134–4108; tel. 816/932–3377; G. Richard Hastings, President and Chief Executive Officer

KANSAS: ANDERSON COUNTY HOSPITAL (O, 56 beds) 421 South Maple, Garnett, KS Zip 66032–1334, Mailing Address: P.O. Box 309, Zip 66032–0309; tel. 785/448–3131; Dennis A. Hachenberg, Senior Executive Officer

SAINT LUKE'S SOUTH (O, 75 beds) 12300 Metcalf Avenue, Overland Park, KS Zip 66213; tel. 913/317–7000; George E. Hays, Senior Executive Officer

SHAWNEE MISSION MEDICAL CENTER (O, 341 beds) 9100 West 74th Street, Shawnee Mission, KS Zip 66204–4019, Mailing Address: Box 2923, Zip 66201–1323; tel. 913/676–2000; William G. Robertson, Senior Executive Officer

MISSOURI: CRITTENTON (O, 113 beds) 10918 Elm Avenue, Kansas City, MO Zip 64134–4199; tel. 816/765–6600; Gary L. Watson, FACHE, Senior Executive Officer

SAINT LUKE'S HOSPITAL (O, 510 beds) 4400 Wornall Road, Kansas City, MO Zip 64111–3238; tel. 816/932–2000; G. Richard Hastings, President and Chief Executive Officer
Web address: www.dia.net/mercy

SAINT LUKE'S NORTHLAND HOSPITAL (O, 58 beds) 5830 N.W. Barry Road, Kansas City, MO Zip 64154; tel. 816/891–6000; N. Gary Wages, Senior Executive Officer

SAINT LUKE'S NORTHLAND HOSPITAL–SMITHVILLE CAMPUS (O, 59 beds) 601 South 169 Highway, Smithville, MO Zip 64089–9334; tel. 816/532–3700; Don Sipes, Senior Executive Officer
Web address: www.saint–lukes.org

WRIGHT MEMORIAL HOSPITAL (O, 38 beds) 701 East First Street, Trenton, MO Zip 64683–0648, Mailing Address: P.O. Box 628, Zip 64683–0628; tel. 660/359–5621; Ralph G. Goodrich, Senior Executive Officer

Owned, leased, sponsored:	8 hospitals	1250 beds
Contract–managed:	0 hospitals	0 beds
Totals:	8 hospitals	1250 beds

★2535: **SAMARITAN HEALTH SYSTEM** (NP)
1441 North 12th Street, Phoenix, AZ Zip 85006–2666; tel. 602/495–4000; James C. Crews, President and Chief Executive Officer

ARIZONA: DESERT SAMARITAN MEDICAL CENTER (O, 536 beds) 1400 South Dobson Road, Mesa, AZ Zip 85202–9879; tel. 602/835–3000; Bruce E. Pearson, Senior Vice President and Chief Executive Officer
Web address: www.samariran.edu

GOOD SAMARITAN REGIONAL MEDICAL CENTER (O, 697 beds) 1111 East McDowell Road, Phoenix, AZ Zip 85006–2666, Mailing Address: P.O. Box 2989, Zip 85062–2989; tel. 602/239–2000; Steven L. Seiler, Senior Vice President and Chief Executive Officer
Web address: www.samaritan.edu

For explanation of codes following names, see page B2.
★ Indicates Type III membership in the American Hospital Association.

PAGE HOSPITAL (C, 25 beds) 501 North Navajo Drive, Page, AZ Zip 86040, Mailing Address: P.O. Box 1447, Zip 86040–1447; tel. 520/645–2424; Richard Polheber, Chief Executive Officer

SAMARITAN BEHAVIORAL HEALTH CENTER–SCOTTSDALE (O, 60 beds) 7575 East Earll Drive, Scottsdale, AZ Zip 85251–6998; tel. 602/941–7500; Robert F. Meyer, M.D., Chief Executive Officer

SAMARITAN–WENDY PAINE O'BRIEN TREATMENT CENTER (O, 89 beds) 5055 North 34th Street, Phoenix, AZ Zip 85018–1498; tel. 602/955–6200; Robert F. Meyer, M.D., Chief Executive Officer

THUNDERBIRD SAMARITAN MEDICAL CENTER (O, 266 beds) 5555 West Thunderbird Road, Glendale, AZ Zip 85306–4696; tel. 602/588–5555; Robert H. Curry, Senior Vice President and Chief Executive Officer

Owned, leased, sponsored:	5 hospitals	1648 beds
Contract–managed:	1 hospital	25 beds
Totals:	6 hospitals	1673 beds

★0037: SCOTTSDALE HEALTHCARE (NP)
3621 Wells Fargo Avenue, Scottsdale, AZ Zip 85251–5607; tel. 602/481–4324; Max Poll, President and Chief Executive Officer

SCOTTSDALE HEALTHCARE–OSBORN (O, 258 beds) 7400 East Osborn Road, Scottsdale, AZ Zip 85251–6403; tel. 480/675–4000; Peggy Reiley, Senior Vice President and Chief Clinical Officer
Web address: www.smhsi.com

SCOTTSDALE HEALTHCARE–SHEA (O, 251 beds) 9003 East Shea Boulevard, Scottsdale, AZ Zip 85260–6771; tel. 602/860–3000; Thomas J. Sadvary, FACHE, Senior Vice President and Chief Operating Officer
Web address: www.shc.org

Owned, leased, sponsored:	2 hospitals	509 beds
Contract–managed:	0 hospitals	0 beds
Totals:	2 hospitals	509 beds

★1505: SCRIPPS HEALTH (NP)
4275 Campus Point Court, San Diego, CA Zip 92121, Mailing Address: P.O. Box 28, La Jolla, Zip 92038; tel. 619/678–7472; Sister Mary Jo Anderson, Senior Vice President, Hospital Operations

CALIFORNIA: GREEN HOSPITAL OF SCRIPPS CLINIC (O, 165 beds) 10666 North Torrey Pines Road, La Jolla, CA Zip 92037–1093; tel. 619/455–9100; Thomas C. Gagen, Senior Vice President

SCRIPPS HOSPITAL–CHULA VISTA (O, 159 beds) 435 H Street, Chula Vista, CA Zip 91912–1537, Mailing Address: P.O. Box 1537, Zip 91910–1537; tel. 619/691–7000; John Grah, Administrator

SCRIPPS MEMORIAL HOSPITAL EAST COUNTY (O, 105 beds) 1688 East Main Street, El Cajon, CA Zip 92021; tel. 619/440–1122; Deborah Dunne, Administrator
Web address: www.scrippshealth.org

SCRIPPS MEMORIAL HOSPITAL–ENCINITAS (O, 145 beds) 354 Santa Fe Drive, Encinitas, CA Zip 92024, Mailing Address: P.O. Box 230817, Zip 92023; tel. 760/753–6501; Rebecca Ropchan, Administrator

SCRIPPS MEMORIAL HOSPITAL–LA JOLLA (O, 431 beds) 9888 Genesee Avenue, La Jolla, CA Zip 92037–1276, Mailing Address: P.O. Box 28, Zip 92038–0028; tel. 619/626–4123; Thomas C. Gagen, Senior Vice President and Regional Administrator

SCRIPPS MERCY HOSPITAL (O, 417 beds) 4077 Fifth Avenue, San Diego, CA Zip 92103–2180; tel. 619/294–8111; Thomas A. Gammiere, Senior Vice President and Regional Administrator

Owned, leased, sponsored:	6 hospitals	1422 beds
Contract–managed:	0 hospitals	0 beds
Totals:	6 hospitals	1422 beds

★2565: SENTARA HEALTH SYSTEM (NP)
6015 Poplar Hall Drive, Norfolk, VA Zip 23502–3800; tel. 757/455–7000; David L. Bernd, President and Chief Executive Officer

VIRGINIA: SENTARA BAYSIDE HOSPITAL (O, 116 beds) 800 Independence Boulevard, Virginia Beach, VA Zip 23455–6076; tel. 757/363–6100; Virginia Bogue, Site Administrator
Web address: www.sentara.com

SENTARA HAMPTON GENERAL HOSPITAL (O, 178 beds) 3120 Victoria Boulevard, Hampton, VA Zip 23661–1585, Mailing Address: Drawer 640, Zip 23669–0640; tel. 757/727–7000; Russell Kenwood, Administrator
Web address: www.sentara.com

SENTARA LEIGH HOSPITAL (O, 214 beds) 830 Kempsville Road, Norfolk, VA Zip 23502–3981; tel. 757/466–6000; Darleen S. Anderson, R.N., MSN, Site Administrator
Web address: www.sentara.com

SENTARA NORFOLK GENERAL HOSPITAL (O, 479 beds) 600 Gresham Drive, Norfolk, VA Zip 23507–1999; tel. 757/668–3000; Mark R. Gavens, President
Web address: www.sentara.com

SENTARA VIRGINIA BEACH GENERAL HOSPITAL (O, 274 beds) 1060 First Colonial Road, Virginia Beach, VA Zip 23454–9000; tel. 757/481–8000; Robert L. Graves, Administrator
Web address: www.tidehealth.com

WILLIAMSBURG COMMUNITY HOSPITAL (C, 100 beds) 301 Monticello Avenue, Williamsburg, VA Zip 23187–8700, Mailing Address: Box 8700, Zip 23187–8700; tel. 757/259–6000; Les A. Donahue, President and Chief Executive Officer
Web address: www.sentara.com

Owned, leased, sponsored:	5 hospitals	1261 beds
Contract–managed:	1 hospital	100 beds
Totals:	6 hospitals	1361 beds

★0111: SHANDS HEALTHCARE (NP)
1600 S.W. Archer Road, Gainesville, FL Zip 32610–0326; tel. 352/395–0421; J. Richard Gaintner, M.D., Chief Executive Officer

FLORIDA: SHANDS REHAB HOSPITAL (O, 40 beds) 8900 N.W. 39th Avenue, Gainesville, FL Zip 32606–5625; tel. 352/338–0091; Cynthia M. Toth, Administrator

SHANDS AT AGH (O, 269 beds) 801 S.W. Second Avenue, Gainesville, FL Zip 32601–6289; tel. 352/372–4321; Robert B. Williams, Administrator

SHANDS AT LAKE SHORE (L, 128 beds) 560 East Franklin Street, Lake City, FL Zip 32055–3047, Mailing Address: P.O. Box 1989, Zip 32056–1989; tel. 904/754–8000; Neil Whipkey, Administrator
Web address: www.shands.org

SHANDS AT LIVE OAK (O, 17 beds) 1100 S.W. 11th Street, Live Oak, FL Zip 32060–3608, Mailing Address: P.O. Drawer X, Zip 32060; tel. 904/362–1413; Rhonda Sherrod, Administrator

SHANDS AT STARKE (O, 23 beds) 922 East Call Street, Starke, FL Zip 32091–3699; tel. 904/368–2300; Jeannie Baker, Administrator

SHANDS AT THE UNIVERSITY OF FLORIDA (O, 564 beds) 1600 S.W. Archer Road, Gainesville, FL Zip 32610–0326, Mailing Address: P.O. Box 100326, Zip 32610–0326; tel. 352/395–0111; Jodi J. Mansfield, Executive Vice President and Chief Operating Officer

Owned, leased, sponsored:	6 hospitals	1041 beds
Contract–managed:	0 hospitals	0 beds
Totals:	6 hospitals	1041 beds

★2065: SHARP HEALTHCARE (NP)
3131 Berger Avenue, San Diego, CA Zip 92123; tel. 619/541–4000; Michael Murphy, President and Chief Executive Officer

CALIFORNIA: GROSSMONT HOSPITAL (C, 384 beds) 5555 Grossmont Center Drive, La Mesa, CA Zip 91942, Mailing Address: Box 158, Zip 91944–0158; tel. 619/465–0711; Michele T. Tarbet, R.N., Chief Executive Officer
Web address: www.sharp.com

SHARP CABRILLO HOSPITAL (O, 227 beds) 3475 Kenyon Street, San Diego, CA Zip 92110–5067; tel. 619/221–3400; Randi Larsson, Chief Operating Officer and Administrator

---

For explanation of codes following names, see page B2.
★ Indicates Type III membership in the American Hospital Association.

Section B

SHARP CHULA VISTA MEDICAL CENTER (O, 306 beds) 751 Medical Center Court, Chula Vista, CA Zip 91911, Mailing Address: Box 1297, Zip 91912; tel. 619/482–5800; Britt Berrett, Chief Executive Officer

SHARP CORONADO HOSPITAL (C, 195 beds) 250 Prospect Place, Coronado, CA Zip 92118; tel. 619/522–3600; Marcia K. Hall, Chief Executive Officer

SHARP MEMORIAL HOSPITAL (O, 488 beds) 7901 Frost Street, San Diego, CA Zip 92123–2788; tel. 619/541–3400; Dan Gross, Chief Executive Officer

Owned, leased, sponsored:	3 hospitals	1021 beds
Contract–managed:	2 hospitals	579 beds
Totals:	5 hospitals	1600 beds

★4125: SHRINERS HOSPITALS FOR CHILDREN (NP)
2900 Rocky Point Drive, Tampa, FL Zip 33607–1435, Mailing Address: Box 31356, Zip 33631–3356; tel. 813/281–0300; Joseph E. Melchiorre Jr., CHE, Executive Administrator

SHRINERS HOSPITALS FOR CHILDREN, LOS ANGELES (O, 60 beds) 3160 Geneva Street, Los Angeles, CA Zip 90020–1199; tel. 213/388–3151; Frank LaBonte, FACHE, Administrator

SHRINERS HOSPITALS FOR CHILDREN, NORTHERN CALIFORNIA (O, 48 beds) 2425 Stockton Boulevard, Sacramento, CA Zip 95817–2215; tel. 916/453–2000; Margaret Bryan, Administrator
Web address: www.shrinershq.org

FLORIDA: SHRINERS HOSPITALS FOR CHILDREN, TAMPA (O, 60 beds) 12502 North Pine Drive, Tampa, FL Zip 33612–9499; tel. 813/972–2250; John Holtz, Administrator

HAWAII: SHRINERS HOSPITALS FOR CHILDREN, HONOLULU (O, 40 beds) 1310 Punahou Street, Honolulu, HI Zip 96826–1099; tel. 808/941–4466; Thomas J. Brotherton, Administrator
Web address: www.shrinershq.org

ILLINOIS: SHRINERS HOSPITALS FOR CHILDREN–CHICAGO (O, 60 beds) 2211 North Oak Park Avenue, Chicago, IL Zip 60707; tel. 773/622–5400; A. James Spang, Administrator

KENTUCKY: SHRINERS HOSPITALS FOR CHILDREN–LEXINGTON (O, 50 beds) 1900 Richmond Road, Lexington, KY Zip 40502–1298; tel. 606/266–2101; Tony Lewgood, Administrator

LOUISIANA: SHRINERS HOSPITALS FOR CHILDREN, SHREVEPORT (O, 45 beds) 3100 Samford Avenue, Shreveport, LA Zip 71103–4289; tel. 318/222–5704; Thomas R. Schneider, Administrator

MASSACHUSETTS: SHRINERS HOSPITALS FOR CHILDREN, SHRINERS BURNS HOSPITAL–BOSTON (O, 30 beds) 51 Blossom Street, Boston, MA Zip 02114–2699; tel. 617/722–3000; Robert F. Bories Jr., FACHE, Administrator
Web address: www.shrinershq.org

SHRINERS HOSPITALS FOR CHILDREN, SPRINGFIELD (O, 40 beds) 516 Carew Street, Springfield, MA Zip 01104–2396; tel. 413/787–2000; Mark L. Niederpruem, Administrator
Web address: www.shrinerspfld.org

MINNESOTA: SHRINERS HOSPITALS FOR CHILDREN, TWIN CITIES (O, 40 beds) 2025 East River Parkway, Minneapolis, MN Zip 55414–3696; tel. 612/335–5300; Laurence E. Johnson, Administrator
Web address: www.shrinershq.org

MISSOURI: SHRINERS HOSPITALS FOR CHILDREN, ST. LOUIS (O, 80 beds) 2001 South Lindbergh Boulevard, Saint Louis, MO Zip 63131–3597; tel. 314/432–3600; Carolyn P. Golden, Administrator

OHIO: SHRINERS HOSPITALS FOR CHILDREN, SHRINERS BURNS HOSPITAL, CINCINNATI (O, 30 beds) 3229 Burnet Avenue, Cincinnati, OH Zip 45229–3095; tel. 513/872–6000; Ronald R. Hitzler, Administrator

OREGON: SHRINERS HOSPITALS FOR CHILDREN, PORTLAND (O, 25 beds) 3101 S.W. Sam Jackson Park Road, Portland, OR Zip 97201; tel. 503/241–5090; Nancy Jones, Administrator

PENNSYLVANIA: SHRINERS HOSPITALS FOR CHILDREN, ERIE (O, 30 beds) 1645 West 8th Street, Erie, PA Zip 16505–5007; tel. 814/875–8700; Richard W. Brzuz, Administrator

SHRINERS HOSPITALS FOR CHILDREN, PHILADELPHIA (O, 59 beds) 3551 North Broad Street, Philadelphia, PA Zip 19140–4105; tel. 215/430–4000; Sharon J. Rajnic, Administrator

SOUTH CAROLINA: SHRINERS HOSPITALS FOR CHILDREN, GREENVILLE (O, 50 beds) 950 West Faris Road, Greenville, SC Zip 29605–4277; tel. 864/271–3444; Gary F. Fraley, Administrator

TEXAS: SHRINERS HOSPITALS FOR CHILDREN, GALVESTON BURNS HOSPITAL (O, 30 beds) 815 Market Street, Galveston, TX Zip 77550–2725; tel. 409/770–6600; John A. Swartwout, Administrator
Web address: www.shrinershq.org

SHRINERS HOSPITALS FOR CHILDREN, HOUSTON (O, 40 beds) 6977 Main Street, Houston, TX Zip 77030–3701; tel. 713/797–1616; Steven B. Reiter, Administrator

UTAH: SHRINERS HOSPITALS FOR CHILDREN–INTERMOUNTAIN (O, 40 beds) Fairfax Road and Virginia Street, Salt Lake City, UT Zip 84103–4399; tel. 801/536–3500; J. Craig Patchin, Administrator
Web address: www.shriners.com

WASHINGTON: SHRINERS HOSPITALS FOR CHILDREN–SPOKANE (O, 30 beds) 911 West Fifth Avenue, Spokane, WA Zip 99204–2901, Mailing Address: P.O. Box 2472, Zip 99210–2472; tel. 509/455–7844; Charles R. Young, Administrator

Owned, leased, sponsored:	20 hospitals	887 beds
Contract–managed:	0 hospitals	0 beds
Totals:	20 hospitals	887 beds

0067: SINGING RIVER HOSPITAL SYSTEM (NP)
2101 Highway 90, Gautier, MS Zip 39553; tel. 228/497–7907; Chris Anderson, Chief Executive Officer

MISSISSIPPI: OCEAN SPRINGS HOSPITAL (O, 124 beds) 3109 Bienville Boulevard, Ocean Springs, MS Zip 39564–4361; tel. 228/818–1111; Dwight Rimes, Administrator

SINGING RIVER HOSPITAL (O, 282 beds) 2809 Denny Avenue, Pascagoula, MS Zip 39581–5301; tel. 228/809–5000; Lynn Truelove, Administrator
Web address: www.srhshealth.com

Owned, leased, sponsored:	2 hospitals	406 beds
Contract–managed:	0 hospitals	0 beds
Totals:	2 hospitals	406 beds

★0078: SIOUX VALLEY HOSPITALS AND HEALTH SYSTEM (NP)
1100 South Euclid Avenue, Sioux Falls, SD Zip 57105–0496; tel. 605/333–1000; Kelby K. Krabbenhoft, President

IOWA: MERRILL PIONEER COMMUNITY HOSPITAL (L, 16 beds) 801 South Greene Street, Rock Rapids, IA Zip 51246–1998; tel. 712/472–2591; Gordon Smith, Administrator

NORTHWEST IOWA HEALTH CENTER (L, 139 beds) 118 North Seventh Avenue, Sheldon, IA Zip 51201–1235; tel. 712/324–5041; Charles R. Miller, Chief Executive Officer

ORANGE CITY HOSPITAL AND CLINIC (C, 113 beds) 400 Central Avenue N.W., Orange City, IA Zip 51041–1398; tel. 712/737–4984; Martin W. Guthmiller, Administrator

SPENCER MUNICIPAL HOSPITAL (C, 86 beds) 1200 First Avenue East, Spencer, IA Zip 51301–4321; tel. 712/264–6198; John Allen, President and Chief Executive Officer

MINNESOTA: ARNOLD MEMORIAL HEALTH CARE CENTER (L, 50 beds) 601 Louisiana Avenue, Adrian, MN Zip 56110–0279, Mailing Address: Box 279, Zip 56110–0279; tel. 507/483–2668; Gerald E. Carl, Administrator

JACKSON MEDICAL CENTER (L, 41 beds) 1430 North Highway, Jackson, MN Zip 56143–1098; tel. 507/847–2420; Charlotte Heitkamp, Chief Executive Officer

LUVERNE COMMUNITY HOSPITAL (C, 28 beds) 305 East Luverne Street, Luverne, MN Zip 56156–2519, Mailing Address: P.O. Box 1019, Zip 56156–1019; tel. 507/283–2321; Gerald E. Carl, Administrator

MURRAY COUNTY MEMORIAL HOSPITAL (C, 25 beds) 2042 Juniper Avenue, Slayton, MN Zip 56172–1016; tel. 507/836–6111; Jerry Bobeldyk, Administrator

ORTONVILLE AREA HEALTH SERVICES (C, 105 beds) 750 Eastvold Avenue, Ortonville, MN Zip 56278–1133; tel. 320/839–2502; Paul J. Anderson, Administrator

---

For explanation of codes following names, see page B2.
★ Indicates Type III membership in the American Hospital Association.

SIOUX VALLEY CANBY CAMPUS (L, 94 beds) 112 St. Olaf Avenue South, Canby, MN Zip 56220–1433; tel. 507/223–7277; Robert J. Salmon, Chief Executive Officer
Web address: www.siouxvalley.org

TRACY AREA MEDICAL SERVICES (L, 18 beds) 251 Fifth Street East, Tracy, MN Zip 56175–1536; tel. 507/629–3200; Thomas J. Quinlivan, Administrator

WESTBROOK HEALTH CENTER (L, 8 beds) 920 Bell Avenue, Westbrook, MN Zip 56183–0188, Mailing Address: P.O. Box 188, Zip 56183–0188; tel. 507/274–6121; Thomas J. Quinlivan, Administrator

WINDOM AREA HOSPITAL (C, 35 beds) Highways 60 and 71 North, Windom, MN Zip 56101, Mailing Address: P.O. Box 339, Zip 56101–0339; tel. 507/831–2400; J. Stephen Pautler, CHE, Administrator

WORTHINGTON REGIONAL HOSPITAL (C, 66 beds) 1018 Sixth Avenue, Worthington, MN Zip 56187–2202, Mailing Address: P.O. Box 997, Zip 56187–0997; tel. 507/372–2941; Melvin J. Platt, Administrator

SOUTH DAKOTA: CANTON–INWOOD MEMORIAL HOSPITAL (L, 25 beds) 440 North Hiawatha Drive, Canton, SD Zip 57013–9404; tel. 605/987–2621; John Devick, Chief Executive Officer

DEUEL COUNTY MEMORIAL HOSPITAL (L, 16 beds) 701 Third Avenue South, Clear Lake, SD Zip 57226–1037, Mailing Address: P.O. Box 1037, Zip 57226–1037; tel. 605/874–2141; Robert J. Salmon, Administrator

LAKE AREA HOSPITAL (L, 26 beds) North First Street, Webster, SD Zip 57274, Mailing Address: P.O. Box 489, Zip 57274–0489; tel. 605/345–3336; Donald J. Finn, Administrator

MID DAKOTA HOSPITAL (L, 54 beds) 300 South Byron Boulevard, Chamberlain, SD Zip 57325–9741; tel. 605/734–5511; Earl N. Sheehy, Administrator

PIONEER MEMORIAL HOSPITAL AND HEALTH SERVICES (C, 64 beds) 315 North Washington Street, Viborg, SD Zip 57070, Mailing Address: P.O. Box 368, Zip 57070–0368; tel. 605/326–5161; Georgia Pokorney, Chief Executive Officer

PRAIRIE LAKES HOSPITAL AND CARE CENTER (C, 119 beds) 400 Tenth Avenue N.W., Watertown, SD Zip 57201–6210, Mailing Address: P.O. Box 1210, Zip 57201–1210; tel. 605/882–7000; Edmond L. Weiland, President and Chief Executive Officer
Web address: www.prairielakes.com

SIOUX VALLEY HOSPITAL (O, 503 beds) 1100 South Euclid Avenue, Sioux Falls, SD Zip 57105–0496, Mailing Address: P.O. Box 5039, Zip 57117–5039; tel. 605/333–1000; Becky Nelson, President

SIOUX VALLEY VERMILLION CAMPUS (L, 95 beds) 20 South Plum Street, Vermillion, SD Zip 57069–3346; tel. 605/624–2611; Larry W. Veitz, Chief Executive Officer

WINNER REGIONAL HEALTHCARE CENTER (C, 116 beds) 745 East Eighth Street, Winner, SD Zip 57580–2677, Mailing Address: P.O. Box 745, Zip 57580–0745; tel. 605/842–7100; Rebecca L. Cooper, Interim Chief Executive Officer

Owned, leased, sponsored:	13 hospitals	1085 beds
Contract–managed:	10 hospitals	757 beds
Totals:	23 hospitals	1842 beds

5995: SISTERS OF CHARITY CENTER (CC)

Mount St. Vincent on Hudson, New York, NY Zip 10471–9930; tel. 718/549–9200; Sister Elizabeth A. Vermaelen, President

NEW YORK: SAINT VINCENTS HOSPITAL AND MEDICAL CENTER (S, 580 beds) 153 West 11th Street, New York, NY Zip 10011–8397; tel. 212/604–7000; Karl P. Adler, M.D., President and Chief Executive Officer

ST. JOSEPH'S MEDICAL CENTER (S, 394 beds) 127 South Broadway, Yonkers, NY Zip 10701–4080; tel. 914/378–7000; Sister Mary Linehan, President
Web address: www.stjosephs.org

Owned, leased, sponsored:	2 hospitals	974 beds
Contract–managed:	0 hospitals	0 beds
Totals:	2 hospitals	974 beds

★5095: SISTERS OF CHARITY OF LEAVENWORTH HEALTH SERVICES CORPORATION (CC)

4200 South Fourth Street, Leavenworth, KS Zip 66048–5054; tel. 913/682–1338; Sister Marie Damian Glatt, President

CALIFORNIA: SAINT JOHN'S HOSPITAL AND HEALTH CENTER (O, 271 beds) 1328 22nd Street, Santa Monica, CA Zip 90404–2032; tel. 310/829–5511; Bruce Lamoureux, Chief Executive Officer

COLORADO: ST. MARY'S HOSPITAL AND MEDICAL CENTER (O, 281 beds) 2635 North 7th Street, Grand Junction, CO Zip 81501–8204, Mailing Address: P.O. Box 1628, Zip 81502–1628; tel. 970/244–2273; Kenneth Tomlon, Interim Chief Executive Officer

KANSAS: BETHANY MEDICAL CENTER (O, 251 beds) 51 North 12th Street, Kansas City, KS Zip 66102–9990; tel. 913/281–8400; Keith R. Poisson, President and Chief Executive Officer

PROVIDENCE MEDICAL CENTER (O, 219 beds) 8929 Parallel Parkway, Kansas City, KS Zip 66112–1636; tel. 913/596–4000; Francis V. Creeden Jr., President and Chief Executive Officer
Web address: www.pmc–sjh.org

SAINT JOHN HOSPITAL (O, 36 beds) 3500 South Fourth Street, Leavenworth, KS Zip 66048–5092; tel. 913/680–6000; Mark J. Jaeger, CHE, Administrator

ST. FRANCIS HOSPITAL AND MEDICAL CENTER (O, 266 beds) 1700 West Seventh Street, Topeka, KS Zip 66606–1690; tel. 785/295–8000; Sister Loretto Marie Colwell, President and Chief Executive Officer
Web address: www.stfrancistopeda.org

MONTANA: HOLY ROSARY HEALTH CENTER (O, 151 beds) 2600 Wilson Street, Miles City, MT Zip 59301–5094; tel. 406/233–2600; H. Ray Gibbons, FACHE, Administrator and Senior Executive Officer

SAINT VINCENT HOSPITAL AND HEALTH CENTER (O, 257 beds) 1233 North 30th Street, Billings, MT Zip 59101–0165, Mailing Address: P.O. Box 35200, Zip 59107–5200; tel. 406/657–7000; Patrick M. Hermanson, Senior Executive Officer
Web address: www.svhhc.org

ST. JAMES COMMUNITY HOSPITAL (O, 100 beds) 400 South Clark Street, Butte, MT Zip 59701–2328, Mailing Address: P.O. Box 3300, Zip 59702–3300; tel. 406/723–2500; Robert Rodgers, Administrator and Senior Executive Officer

Owned, leased, sponsored:	9 hospitals	1832 beds
Contract–managed:	0 hospitals	0 beds
Totals:	9 hospitals	1832 beds

5125: SISTERS OF CHARITY OF ST. AUGUSTINE HEALTH SYSTEM (CC)

2351 East 22nd Street, Cleveland, OH Zip 44115–3197; tel. 216/696–5560; Sister Judith Ann Karam, President and Chief Executive Officer

OHIO: MERCY MEDICAL CENTER (S, 374 beds) 1320 Mercy Drive N.W., Canton, OH Zip 44708–2641; tel. 330/489–1000; Norman W. Wengerd, Interim President and Chief Executive Officer

ST. JOHN WEST SHORE HOSPITAL (S, 183 beds) 29000 Center Ridge Road, Cleveland, OH Zip 44145–5219; tel. 440/835–8000; Fred M. DeGrandis, President and Chief Executive Officer

ST. VINCENT CHARITY HOSPITAL (S, 266 beds) 2351 East 22nd Street, Cleveland, OH Zip 44115–3111; tel. 216/861–6200; Alan H. Channing, Chief Executive Officer

SOUTH CAROLINA: PROVIDENCE HOSPITAL (S, 235 beds) 2435 Forest Drive, Columbia, SC Zip 29204–2098; tel. 803/256–5300; Stephen A. Purves, CHE, President and Chief Executive Officer
Web address: www.provhosp.com

Owned, leased, sponsored:	4 hospitals	1058 beds
Contract–managed:	0 hospitals	0 beds
Totals:	4 hospitals	1058 beds

Section B

5805: SISTERS OF MARY OF THE PRESENTATION HEALTH CORPORATION (CC)
1102 Page Drive S.W., Fargo, ND Zip 58106–0007, Mailing Address: P.O. Box 10007, Zip 58106–0007; tel. 701/237–9290; Aaron Alton, President

ILLINOIS: ST. MARGARET'S HOSPITAL (O, 123 beds) 600 East First Street, Spring Valley, IL Zip 61362–2034; tel. 815/664–5311; Timothy Muntz, President
Web address: www.st.margarets.com

IOWA: VAN BUREN COUNTY HOSPITAL (C, 40 beds) Highway 1 North, Keosauqua, IA Zip 52565, Mailing Address: P.O. Box 70, Zip 52565–0070; tel. 319/293–3171; Lisa Schnedler, Administrator
Web address: www.netins.net/showcase/forhealth/

NORTH DAKOTA: PRESENTATION MEDICAL CENTER (O, 102 beds) 213 Second Avenue N.E., Rolla, ND Zip 58367–7153, Mailing Address: P.O. Box 759, Zip 58367–0759; tel. 701/477–3161; Kimber Wraalstad, Chief Executive Officer

ST. ALOISIUS MEDICAL CENTER (O, 165 beds) 325 East Brewster Street, Harvey, ND Zip 58341–1605; tel. 701/324–4651; Ronald J. Volk, President

ST. ANDREW'S HEALTH CENTER (O, 67 beds) 316 Ohmer Street, Bottineau, ND Zip 58318–1018; tel. 701/228–2255; Keith Korman, President

Owned, leased, sponsored:	4 hospitals	457 beds
Contract–managed:	1 hospital	40 beds
Totals:	5 hospitals	497 beds

★5185: SISTERS OF MERCY HEALTH SYSTEM–ST. LOUIS (CC)
2039 North Geyer Road, Saint Louis, MO Zip 63131–0902, Mailing Address: P.O. Box 31902, Zip 63131–0902; tel. 314/965–6100; Ronald B. Ashworth, Chief Executive Officer

ARKANSAS: CARROLL REGIONAL MEDICAL CENTER (O, 39 beds) 214 Carter Street, Berryville, AR Zip 72616–4303; tel. 870/423–3355; Rudy Darling, President and Chief Executive Officer
Web address: www.carrollregional.com

H.S.C. MEDICAL CENTER (O, 77 beds) 1001 Schneider Drive, Malvern, AR Zip 72104–4828; tel. 501/337–4911; Jeff Curtis, President and Chief Executive Officer

HARBOR VIEW MERCY HOSPITAL (O, 80 beds) 10301 Mayo Road, Fort Smith, AR Zip 72903–1631, Mailing Address: P.O. Box 17000, Zip 72917–7000; tel. 501/484–5550; Richard Cameron, M.D., Administrator

MERCY HOSPITAL OF SCOTT COUNTY (O, 129 beds) Highways 71 and 80, Waldron, AR Zip 72958–9984, Mailing Address: Box 2230, Zip 72958–2230; tel. 501/637–4135; Sister Mary Alvera Simon, Administrator

MERCY HOSPITAL–TURNER MEMORIAL (O, 39 beds) 801 West River Street, Ozark, AR Zip 72949–3000; tel. 501/667–4138; John C. Neal, Regional Administrator and Chief Administrative Officer

NORTH LOGAN MERCY HOSPITAL (O, 16 beds) 500 East Academy, Paris, AR Zip 72855–4099; tel. 501/963–6101; Jim L. Maddox, Chief Administrative Officer

ST. EDWARD MERCY MEDICAL CENTER (O, 260 beds) 7301 Rogers Avenue, Fort Smith, AR Zip 72903–4189, Mailing Address: P.O. Box 17000, Zip 72917–7000; tel. 501/484–6000; Michael L. Morgan, President and Chief Executive Officer

ST. JOSEPH'S REGIONAL HEALTH CENTER (O, 266 beds) 300 Werner Street, Hot Springs, AR Zip 71913–6448, Mailing Address: P.O. Box 29001, Zip 71913–9001; tel. 501/622–1000; Randall J. Fale, FACHE, President and Chief Executive Officer
Web address: www.saintjosephs.com

ST. MARY–ROGERS MEMORIAL HOSPITAL (O, 102 beds) 1200 West Walnut Street, Rogers, AR Zip 72756–3599; tel. 501/636–0200; Susan Barrett, President and Chief Executive Officer
Web address: www.mercyhealthnwa.smhs.com

ILLINOIS: ST. CLEMENT HEALTH SERVICES (O, 115 beds) One St. Clement Boulevard, Red Bud, IL Zip 62278–1194; tel. 618/282–3831; Michael Thomas McManus, President

KANSAS: MERCY HOSPITAL (O, 108 beds) 821 Burke Street, Fort Scott, KS Zip 66701–2497; tel. 316/223–2200; Jerry L. Stevenson, President and Chief Executive Officer

MERCY HOSPITAL (O, 58 beds) 800 West Myrtle Street, Independence, KS Zip 67301–3240, Mailing Address: P.O. Box 388, Zip 67301–0388; tel. 316/331–2200; Jerry L. Stevenson, President and Chief Executive Officer

MISSOURI: ALEXIAN BROTHERS HOSPITAL (O, 203 beds) 3933 South Broadway, Saint Louis, MO Zip 63118–9984; tel. 314/865–3333; Glenn Appelbaum, Senior Vice President

BREECH REGIONAL MEDICAL CENTER (O, 35 beds) 100 Hospital Drive, Lebanon, MO Zip 65536–2317, Mailing Address: P.O. Box N, Zip 65536–2317; tel. 417/533–6100; Gary W. Pulsipher, President

ST. ANTHONY'S MEDICAL CENTER (O, 685 beds) 10010 Kennerly Road, Saint Louis, MO Zip 63128–2185; tel. 314/525–1000; David P. Seifert, President

ST. FRANCIS HOSPITAL (O, 20 beds) Highway 60, Mountain View, MO Zip 65548, Mailing Address: P.O. Box 82, Zip 65548–0082; tel. 417/934–2246; Gary W. Jordan, President and Chief Executive Officer

ST. JOHN'S MERCY MEDICAL CENTER (O, 898 beds) 615 South New Ballas Road, Saint Louis, MO Zip 63141–8277; tel. 314/569–6000; Mark Weber, FACHE, President

ST. JOHN'S REGIONAL HEALTH CENTER (O, 734 beds) 1235 East Cherokee Street, Springfield, MO Zip 65804–2263; tel. 417/885–2000; Robert T. Brodhead, Interim Chief Executive Officer

ST. LUKE'S HOSPITAL (O, 495 beds) 232 South Woods Mill Road, Chesterfield, MO Zip 63017–3480; tel. 314/434–1500; Gary R. Olson, President

OKLAHOMA: MERCY HEALTH CENTER (O, 304 beds) 4300 West Memorial Road, Oklahoma City, OK Zip 73120–8362; tel. 405/755–1515; Michael J. Packnett, President and Chief Executive Officer

MERCY MEMORIAL HEALTH CENTER (O, 199 beds) 1011 14th Street N.W., Ardmore, OK Zip 73401–1889; tel. 580/223–5400; Bobby G. Thompson, President and Chief Executive Officer
Web address: www.mercyok.com

ST. MARY'S MERCY HOSPITAL (O, 137 beds) 305 South Fifth Street, Enid, OK Zip 73701–5899, Mailing Address: Box 232, Zip 73702–0232; tel. 580/233–6100; Frank Lopez, FACHE, President and Chief Executive Officer
Web address: www.mercyok.com

TEXAS: MERCY REGIONAL MEDICAL CENTER (O, 320 beds) 1515 Logan Avenue, Laredo, TX Zip 78040–4617, Mailing Address: Drawer 2068, Zip 78044–2068; tel. 956/718–6222; Mark S. Stauder, President and Chief Executive Officer
Web address: www.mhst.smhs.com

Owned, leased, sponsored:	23 hospitals	5319 beds
Contract–managed:	0 hospitals	0 beds
Totals:	23 hospitals	5319 beds

6015: SISTERS OF MERCY OF THE AMERICAS–REGIONAL COMMUNITY OF BALTIMORE (CC)
1300 Northern Parkway, Baltimore, MD Zip 21239, Mailing Address: P.O. Box 11448, Zip 21239; tel. 410/435–4400; Sister Margaret Beatty, President

GEORGIA: ST. JOSEPH'S HOSPITAL (O, 305 beds) 11705 Mercy Boulevard, Savannah, GA Zip 31419–1791; tel. 912/927–5404; Paul P. Hinchey, President and Chief Executive Officer

MARYLAND: MERCY MEDICAL CENTER (O, 246 beds) 301 St. Paul Place, Baltimore, MD Zip 21202–2165; tel. 410/332–9000; Sister Helen Amos, President and Chief Executive Officer
Web address: www.mercymed.com

Owned, leased, sponsored:	2 hospitals	551 beds
Contract–managed:	0 hospitals	0 beds
Totals:	2 hospitals	551 beds

★5275: SISTERS OF PROVIDENCE HEALTH SYSTEM (CC)
520 Pike Street, Seattle, WA Zip 98101, Mailing Address: P.O. Box 11038, Zip 98111–9038; tel. 206/464–3355; Henry G. Walker, President and Chief Executive Officer

For explanation of codes following names, see page B2.
★ Indicates Type III membership in the American Hospital Association.

ALASKA: PROVIDENCE ALASKA MEDICAL CENTER (O, 341 beds) 3200 Providence Drive, Anchorage, AK Zip 99508, Mailing Address: P.O. Box 196604, Zip 99519–6604; tel. 907/562–2211; Gene L. O'Hara, Administrator

PROVIDENCE KODIAK ISLAND MEDICAL CENTER (L, 44 beds) 1915 East Rezanof Drive, Kodiak, AK Zip 99615; tel. 907/486–3281; Phillip E. Cline, Administrator

PROVIDENCE SEWARD MEDICAL CENTER (L, 20 beds) 417 First Avenue, Seward, AK Zip 99664, Mailing Address: P.O. Box 365, Zip 99664–0365; tel. 907/224–5205; J. C. Rathje, Administrator

CALIFORNIA: PROVIDENCE HOLY CROSS MEDICAL CENTER (O, 255 beds) 15031 Rinaldi Street, Mission Hills, CA Zip 91345–1285; tel. 818/365–8051; Michael J. Madden, Chief Executive Officer
Web address: www.providence.org

PROVIDENCE SAINT JOSEPH MEDICAL CENTER (O, 423 beds) 501 South Buena Vista Street, Burbank, CA Zip 91505–4866; tel. 818/843–5111; Michael J. Madden, Chief Executive Officer
Web address: www.providence.org

OREGON: HOOD RIVER MEMORIAL HOSPITAL (O, 31 beds) 13th and May Streets, Hood River, OR Zip 97031, Mailing Address: P.O. Box 149, Zip 97031; tel. 541/386–3911; Larry Bowe, JD, Chief Executive Officer

PROVIDENCE MEDFORD MEDICAL CENTER (O, 117 beds) 1111 Crater Lake Avenue, Medford, OR Zip 97504–6241; tel. 541/732–5000; Charles T. Wright, Chief Executive, Southern Oregon Service Area
Web address: www.providence.org

PROVIDENCE MILWAUKIE HOSPITAL (O, 56 beds) 10150 S.E. 32nd Avenue, Milwaukie, OR Zip 97222–6593; tel. 503/513–8300; Janice Burger, Operations Administrator

PROVIDENCE NEWBERG HOSPITAL (O, 35 beds) 501 Villa Road, Newberg, OR Zip 97132; tel. 503/537–1555; Mark W. Meinert, CHE, Chief Executive, Yamhill Service Area

PROVIDENCE PORTLAND MEDICAL CENTER (O, 380 beds) 4805 N.E. Glisan Street, Portland, OR Zip 97213–2967; tel. 503/215–1111; David T. Underriner, Operations Administrator
Web address: www.providence.org

PROVIDENCE SEASIDE HOSPITAL (L, 50 beds) 725 South Wahanna Road, Seaside, OR Zip 97138–7735; tel. 503/717–7000; Ronald Swanson, Chief Executive Officer
Web address: www.providence.org

PROVIDENCE ST. VINCENT MEDICAL CENTER (O, 442 beds) 9205 S.W. Barnes Road, Portland, OR Zip 97225–6661; tel. 503/216–1234; Donald Elsom, Operations Administrator
Web address: www.phsworld.phsor.org

WASHINGTON: MARK REED HOSPITAL (C, 7 beds) 322 South Birch Street, McCleary, WA Zip 98557; tel. 360/495–3244; Jean E. Roberts, Administrator

MORTON GENERAL HOSPITAL (C, 48 beds) 521 Adams Street, Morton, WA Zip 98356, Mailing Address: Drawer C, Zip 98356–0019; tel. 360/496–5112; Mike Lee, Superintendent

PROVIDENCE CENTRALIA HOSPITAL (O, 142 beds) 914 South Scheuber Road, Centralia, WA Zip 98531; tel. 360/736–2803; Steve Burdick, Administrator

PROVIDENCE GENERAL MEDICAL CENTER (O, 262 beds) 1321 Colby Street, Everett, WA Zip 98206, Mailing Address: P.O. Box 1067, Zip 98206–1067; tel. 425/261–2000; Mel Pyne, Administrator

PROVIDENCE SEATTLE MEDICAL CENTER (O, 310 beds) 500 17th Avenue, Seattle, WA Zip 98122, Mailing Address: P.O. Box 34008, Zip 98124–1008; tel. 206/320–2000; Nancy A. Giunto, FACHE, Operations Administrator

PROVIDENCE ST. PETER HOSPITAL (O, 315 beds) 413 Lilly Road N.E., Olympia, WA Zip 98506–5116; tel. 360/491–9480; C. Scott Bond, Administrator
Web address: www.providence.org

PROVIDENCE TOPPENISH HOSPITAL (O, 48 beds) 502 West Fourth Avenue, Toppenish, WA Zip 98948, Mailing Address: P.O. Box 672, Zip 98948–0672; tel. 509/865–3105; Larry Anthony, Administrator

PROVIDENCE YAKIMA MEDICAL CENTER (O, 169 beds) 110 South Ninth Avenue, Yakima, WA Zip 98902–3397; tel. 509/575–5000; Barbara A. Hood, Chief Executive Officer
Web address: www.providence.org

Owned, leased, sponsored:	18 hospitals	3440 beds
Contract–managed:	2 hospitals	55 beds
Totals:	20 hospitals	3495 beds

★5345: SISTERS OF ST. FRANCIS HEALTH SERVICES, INC. (CC)
1515 Dragoon Trail, Mishawaka, IN Zip 46546–1290, Mailing Address: P.O. Box 1290, Zip 46546–1290; tel. 219/256–3935; Kevin D. Leahy, President and Chief Executive Officer

ILLINOIS: ST. JAMES HOSPITAL AND HEALTH CENTERS (O, 332 beds) 1423 Chicago Road, Chicago Heights, IL Zip 60411–3483; tel. 708/756–1000; Peter J. Murphy, President and Chief Executive Officer
Web address: www.st jameshhc.org

INDIANA: SAINT ANTHONY MEMORIAL HEALTH CENTERS (O, 162 beds) 301 West Homer Street, Michigan City, IN Zip 46360–4358; tel. 219/879–8511; Bruce E. Rampage, President and Chief Executive Officer

SAINT MARGARET MERCY HEALTHCARE CENTERS (O, 624 beds) 5454 Hohman Avenue, Hammond, IN Zip 46320–1999; tel. 219/933–2074; Eugene C. Diamond, President and Chief Executive Officer
Web address: www.clarian.com

ST. ANTHONY MEDICAL CENTER (O, 248 beds) 1201 South Main Street, Crown Point, IN Zip 46307–8483; tel. 219/738–2100; Stephen O. Leurck, President and Chief Executive Officer

ST. FRANCIS HOSPITAL AND HEALTH CENTERS (O, 409 beds) 1600 Albany Street, Beech Grove, IN Zip 46107–1593; tel. 317/787–3311; Robert J. Brody, President and Chief Executive Officer
Web address: www.stfrancis–indy.com

Owned, leased, sponsored:	5 hospitals	1775 beds
Contract–managed:	0 hospitals	0 beds
Totals:	5 hospitals	1775 beds

★0133: SISTERS OF ST. JOSEPH HEALTH SYSTEM (CC)
455 East Eisenhower Parkway, 300, Ann Arbor, MI Zip 48108–3324; tel. 734/741–1160; John S. Lore, President and Chief Executive Officer

MICHIGAN: BORGESS MEDICAL CENTER (O, 405 beds) 1521 Gull Road, Kalamazoo, MI Zip 49001–1640; tel. 616/226–4800; Randall Stasik, President and Chief Executive Officer
Web address: www.borgess.com

GENESYS REGIONAL MEDICAL CENTER (O, 379 beds) One Genesys Parkway, Grand Blanc, MI Zip 48439–8066; tel. 810/606–5000; Elliot T. Joseph, President and Chief Executive Officer
Web address: www.genesys.org

LEE MEMORIAL HOSPITAL (O, 47 beds) 420 West High Street, Dowagiac, MI Zip 49047–1907; tel. 616/782–8681; Fritz Fahrenbacher, President and Chief Executive Officer

ST. JOHN DETROIT RIVERVIEW HOSPITAL (O, 230 beds) 7733 East Jefferson Avenue, Detroit, MI Zip 48214–2598; tel. 313/499–4000; Richard T. Young, President

ST. JOHN HOSPITAL AND MEDICAL CENTER (O, 737 beds) 22101 Moross Road, Detroit, MI Zip 48236–2172; tel. 313/343–4000; Timothy J. Grajewski, President and Chief Executive Officer

ST. JOHN MACOMB HOSPITAL (O, 273 beds) 11800 East Twelve Mile Road, Warren, MI Zip 48093–3494; tel. 810/573–5000; John E. Knox, President
Web address: www.dmhc.com

ST. JOHN NORTHEAST COMMUNITY HOSPITAL (O, 161 beds) 4777 East Outer Drive, Detroit, MI Zip 48234–0401; tel. 313/369–9100; Michael F. Breen, President

ST. JOHN OAKLAND HOSPITAL (O, 196 beds) 27351 Dequindre, Madison Heights, MI Zip 48071–3499; tel. 248/967–7000; Robert Deputat, President

For explanation of codes following names, see page B2.
★ Indicates Type III membership in the American Hospital Association.

ST. JOHN RIVER DISTRICT HOSPITAL (O, 68 beds) 4100 River Road, East China, MI Zip 48054; tel. 810/329-7111; Frank W. Poma, President

ST. JOSEPH HEALTH SYSTEM (O, 49 beds) 200 Hemlock Street, Tawas City, MI Zip 48763, Mailing Address: P.O. Box 659, Zip 48764-0659; tel. 517/362-3411; Paul R. Schmidt, CHE, President and Chief Executive Officer

Owned, leased, sponsored:	10 hospitals	2545 beds
Contract-managed:	0 hospitals	0 beds
Totals:	10 hospitals	2545 beds

5955: SISTERS OF THE 3RD FRANCISCAN ORDER (CC)
2500 Grant Boulevard, Syracuse, NY Zip 13208-1713; tel. 315/425-0115; Sister Grace Anne Dillenschneider, General Superior

HAWAII: ST. FRANCIS MEDICAL CENTER (O, 221 beds) 2230 Liliha Street, Honolulu, HI Zip 96817-9979, Mailing Address: P.O. Box 30100, Zip 96820-0100; tel. 808/547-6484; Cynthia Okinaka, Administrator
Web address: www.sfhs-hi.org

ST. FRANCIS MEDICAL CENTER-WEST (O, 100 beds) 91-2141 Fort Weaver Road, Ewa Beach, HI Zip 96706; tel. 808/678-7000; Sister Gretchen Gilroy, President and Chief Executive Officer

NEW YORK: ST. ELIZABETH MEDICAL CENTER (O, 166 beds) 2209 Genesee Street, Utica, NY Zip 13501-5999; tel. 315/798-8100; Sister Rose Vincent, President and Chief Executive Officer
Web address: www.stemc.org

ST. JOSEPH'S HOSPITAL HEALTH CENTER (O, 431 beds) 301 Prospect Avenue, Syracuse, NY Zip 13203-1895; tel. 315/448-5111; Theodore M. Pasinski, President
Web address: www.SJHSYR.ORG

Owned, leased, sponsored:	4 hospitals	918 beds
Contract-managed:	0 hospitals	0 beds
Totals:	4 hospitals	918 beds

5575: SISTERS OF THE HOLY FAMILY OF NAZARETH-SACRED HEART PROVINCE (CC)
310 North River Road, Des Plaines, IL Zip 60016-1211; tel. 847/298-6760; Sister Marie Kielanowicz, Provincial Superior

ILLINOIS: HOLY FAMILY MEDICAL CENTER (O, 183 beds) 100 North River Road, Des Plaines, IL Zip 60016-1255; tel. 847/297-1800; Sister Patricia Ann Koschalke, President and Chief Executive Officer

SAINT MARY OF NAZARETH HOSPITAL CENTER (O, 325 beds) 2233 West Division Street, Chicago, IL Zip 60622-3086; tel. 312/770-2000; Sister Stella Louise, President and Chief Executive Officer

Owned, leased, sponsored:	2 hospitals	508 beds
Contract-managed:	0 hospitals	0 beds
Totals:	2 hospitals	508 beds

★8855: SOLARIS HEALTH SYSTEM (NP)
80 James Street, 2nd Floor, Edison, NJ Zip 08820-3998; tel. 732/632-1500; John P. McGee, President and Chief Executive Officer

NEW JERSEY: JFK JOHNSON REHABILITATION INSTITUTE (O, 92 beds) 65 James Street, Edison, NJ Zip 08818-3059; tel. 732/321-7050; Scott Gebhard, Senior Vice President Operations

JFK MEDICAL CENTER (O, 380 beds) 65 James Street, Edison, NJ Zip 08818-3947; tel. 732/321-7000; John P. McGee, President and Chief Executive Officer
Web address: www.jfkhs.org

MUHLENBERG REGIONAL MEDICAL CENTER (O, 303 beds) 1200 Park Avenue, Plainfield, NJ Zip 07061; tel. 908/668-2000; John R. Kopicki, President and Chief Executive Officer

Owned, leased, sponsored:	3 hospitals	775 beds
Contract-managed:	0 hospitals	0 beds
Totals:	3 hospitals	775 beds

● ★0068: SOUTH CENTRAL COMMUNITY HEALTH (NP)
1001 South George Street, York, PA Zip 17405-3645; tel. 717/851-2345; Bruce M. Bartels, President

PENNSYLVANIA: YORK HOSPITAL (O, 434 beds) 1001 South George Street, York, PA Zip 17405-3645; tel. 717/851-2345; Brian A. Gragnolati, President
Web address: www.yorkhealth.org

Owned, leased, sponsored:	1 hospital	434 beds
Contract-managed:	0 hospitals	0 beds
Totals:	1 hospital	434 beds

0151: SOUTH JERSEY HEALTH SYSTEM (NP)
333 Irving Avenue, Bridgeton, NJ Zip 08302-2100; tel. 609/451-6600; Paul S. Cooper, Chief Executive Officer

NEW JERSEY: NEWCOMB MEDICAL CENTER (O, 139 beds) 65 South State Street, Vineland, NJ Zip 08360-4893; tel. 609/691-9000; Chester B. Kaletkowski, President and Chief Executive Officer

SOUTH JERSEY HOSPITAL (O, 340 beds) 333 Irving Avenue, Bridgeton, NJ Zip 08302-2100; tel. 609/451-6600; Chester B. Kaletkowski, President and Chief Executive Officer
Web address: www.sjhs.com

Owned, leased, sponsored:	2 hospitals	479 beds
Contract-managed:	0 hospitals	0 beds
Totals:	2 hospitals	479 beds

★0106: SOUTHERN CALIFORNIA HEALTHCARE SYSTEMS (NP)
1300 East Green Street, Pasadena, CA Zip 91106; tel. 626/397-2900; Stephen A. Ralph, President and Chief Executive Officer

CALIFORNIA: HUNTINGTON EAST VALLEY HOSPITAL (O, 128 beds) 150 West Alosta Avenue, Glendora, CA Zip 91740-4398; tel. 626/335-0231; James W. Maki, Chief Executive Officer

HUNTINGTON MEMORIAL HOSPITAL (O, 557 beds) 100 West California Boulevard, Pasadena, CA Zip 91105, Mailing Address: P.O. Box 7013, Zip 91109-7013; tel. 626/397-5000; Stephen A. Ralph, President and Chief Executive Officer

METHODIST HOSPITAL OF SOUTHERN CALIFORNIA (O, 409 beds) 300 West Huntington Drive, Arcadia, CA Zip 91007, Mailing Address: P.O. Box 60016, Zip 91066-6016; tel. 626/445-4441; Dennis M. Lee, President

Owned, leased, sponsored:	3 hospitals	1094 beds
Contract-managed:	0 hospitals	0 beds
Totals:	3 hospitals	1094 beds

★4175: SOUTHERN ILLINOIS HOSPITAL SERVICES (NP)
608 East College Street, Carbondale, IL Zip 62901-3309, Mailing Address: P.O. Box 3988, Zip 62902-3988; tel. 618/457-5200; John J. Buckley Jr., President

ILLINOIS: FERRELL HOSPITAL (O, 51 beds) 1201 Pine Street, Eldorado, IL Zip 62930-1634; tel. 618/273-3361; E. T. Seely, Administrator

FRANKLIN HOSPITAL AND SKILLED NURSING CARE UNIT (L, 117 beds) 201 Bailey Lane, Benton, IL Zip 62812-1999; tel. 618/439-3161; Virgil Hannig, Senior Vice President and Administrator

HERRIN HOSPITAL (O, 92 beds) 201 South 14th Street, Herrin, IL Zip 62948-3631; tel. 618/942-2171; Virgil Hannig, Senior Vice President and Administrator
Web address: www.sih.net

MEMORIAL HOSPITAL OF CARBONDALE (O, 133 beds) 405 West Jackson Street, Carbondale, IL Zip 62901-1467, Mailing Address: P.O. Box 10000, Zip 62902-9000; tel. 618/549-0721; George Maroney, Senior Vice President and Administrator

ST. JOSEPH MEMORIAL HOSPITAL (O, 59 beds) 2 South Hospital Drive, Murphysboro, IL Zip 62966-3333; tel. 618/687-3157; Betty Gaffney, Senior Vice President and Administrator
Web address: www.sih.net

For explanation of codes following names, see page B2.
★ Indicates Type III membership in the American Hospital Association.
● Single hospital health care system

UNITED MINE WORKERS OF AMERICA UNION HOSPITAL (O, 20 beds) 507 West St. Louis Street, West Frankfort, IL Zip 62896–1999; tel. 618/932–2155; Virgil Hannig, Senior Vice President and Administrator

Owned, leased, sponsored:	6 hospitals	472 beds
Contract–managed:	0 hospitals	0 beds
Totals:	6 hospitals	472 beds

★4195: SPARTANBURG REGIONAL HEALTHCARE SYSTEM (NP)

101 East Wood Street, Spartanburg, SC Zip 29303–3016; tel. 864/560–6000; Joseph Michael Oddis, President

SOUTH CAROLINA: B.J. WORKMAN MEMORIAL HOSPITAL (O, 32 beds) 751 East Georgia Street, Woodruff, SC Zip 29388, Mailing Address: P.O. Box 699, Zip 29388–0699; tel. 864/476–8122; G. Curtis Walker, R.N., Administrator

SPARTANBURG HOSPITAL FOR RESTORATIVE CARE (O, 45 beds) 389 Serpentine Drive, Spartanburg, SC Zip 29303; tel. 864/560–3280; Anita M. Butler, Administrator

SPARTANBURG REGIONAL MEDICAL CENTER (O, 471 beds) 101 East Wood Street, Spartanburg, SC Zip 29303–3016; tel. 864/560–6000; Joseph Michael Oddis, President

Owned, leased, sponsored:	3 hospitals	548 beds
Contract–managed:	0 hospitals	0 beds
Totals:	3 hospitals	548 beds

0177: SPECTRUM HEALTH (NP)

100 Michigan Street N.E., Grand Rapids, MI Zip 49503–2551; tel. 616/391–1174; William G. Gonzalez, President and Chief Executive Officer

MICHIGAN: KENT COMMUNITY HOSPITAL (C, 356 beds) 750 Fuller Avenue N.E., Grand Rapids, MI Zip 49503–1995; tel. 616/336–3360; Lori Portfleet, Chief Executive Officer

SPECTRUM HEALTH–DOWNTOWN CAMPUS (O, 529 beds) 100 Michigan Street N.E., Grand Rapids, MI Zip 49503–2551; tel. 616/391–1174; William G. Gonzalez, Pres
Web address: www.spectrum–health.com

SPECTRUM HEALTH–EAST CAMPUS (O, 332 beds) 1840 Wealthy Street S.E., Grand Rapids, MI Zip 49506–2921; tel. 616/774–7444; William G. Gonzalez, President
Web address: www.spectrum–health.org

SPECTRUM HEALTH–REED CITY CAMPUS (O, 83 beds) 7665 Patterson Road, Reed City, MI Zip 49677–1122, Mailing Address: P.O. Box 75, Zip 49677–0075; tel. 616/832–3271; David M. Coates, Ph.D., President and Chief Executive Officer

Owned, leased, sponsored:	3 hospitals	944 beds
Contract–managed:	1 hospital	356 beds
Totals:	4 hospitals	1300 beds

★5455: SSM HEALTH CARE (CC)

477 North Lindbergh Boulevard, Saint Louis, MO Zip 63141–7813; tel. 314/994–7800; Sister Mary Jean Ryan, President and Chief Executive Officer

ILLINOIS: GOOD SAMARITAN REGIONAL HEALTH CENTER (O, 127 beds) 605 North 12th Street, Mount Vernon, IL Zip 62864–2899; tel. 618/242–4600; Leo F. Childers Jr., FACHE, President
Web address: www.stmarys–goodsamaritan.com

SAINT FRANCIS HOSPITAL AND HEALTH CENTER (O, 254 beds) 12935 South Gregory Street, Blue Island, IL Zip 60406–2470; tel. 708/597–2000; Jay E. Kreuzer, FACHE, President

ST. MARY'S HOSPITAL (C, 276 beds) 400 North Pleasant Avenue, Centralia, IL Zip 62801–3091; tel. 618/532–6731; James W. McDowell, President and Chief Executive Officer

WASHINGTON COUNTY HOSPITAL (C, 53 beds) 705 South Grand Street, Nashville, IL Zip 62263; tel. 618/327–8236; Michael P. Ellermann, Administrator

MISSOURI: ARCADIA VALLEY HOSPITAL (O, 50 beds) Highway 21, Pilot Knob, MO Zip 63663, Mailing Address: P.O. Box 548, Zip 63663–0548; tel. 573/546–3924; H. Clark Duncan, Administrator

CARDINAL GLENNON CHILDREN'S HOSPITAL (O, 172 beds) 1465 South Grand Boulevard, Saint Louis, MO Zip 63104–1095; tel. 314/577–5600; Douglas A. Ries, President

DEPAUL HEALTH CENTER (O, 272 beds) 12303 DePaul Drive, Saint Louis, MO Zip 63044–2588; tel. 314/344–6000; Robert G. Porter, President

PIKE COUNTY MEMORIAL HOSPITAL (C, 31 beds) 2305 West Georgia Street, Louisiana, MO Zip 63353–0020; tel. 573/754–5531; Gregory C. Reed, Administrator

SSM REHAB (O, 100 beds) 6420 Clayton Road, Suite 600, Saint Louis, MO Zip 63117–1861; tel. 314/768–5300; Melinda Clark, President

ST. FRANCIS HOSPITAL AND HEALTH SERVICES (O, 54 beds) 2016 South Main Street, Maryville, MO Zip 64468–2693; tel. 660/562–2600; Michael Baumgartner, President

ST. JOSEPH HEALTH CENTER (O, 176 beds) 300 First Capitol Drive, Saint Charles, MO Zip 63301–2835; tel. 314/947–5000; Kevin F. Kast, President

ST. JOSEPH HOSPITAL WEST (O, 59 beds) 100 Medical Plaza, Lake Saint Louis, MO Zip 63367–1395; tel. 314/625–5200; Kevin F. Kast, President

ST. JOSEPH HOSPITAL OF KIRKWOOD (O, 213 beds) 525 Couch Avenue, Saint Louis, MO Zip 63122–5594; tel. 314/966–1500; Carla S. Baum, President

ST. MARY'S HEALTH CENTER (O, 441 beds) 6420 Clayton Road, Saint Louis, MO Zip 63117–1811; tel. 314/768–8000; Michael E. Zilm, President

ST. MARYS HEALTH CENTER (O, 167 beds) 100 St. Marys Medical Plaza, Jefferson City, MO Zip 65101–1601; tel. 573/761–7000; Mark R. Taylor, President

OKLAHOMA: BONE AND JOINT HOSPITAL (O, 89 beds) 1111 North Dewey Avenue, Oklahoma City, OK Zip 73103–2615; tel. 405/552–9100; James A. Hyde, Administrator

HILLCREST HEALTH CENTER (L, 141 beds) 2129 S.W. 59th Street, Oklahoma City, OK Zip 73119–7001; tel. 405/685–6671; Ray Brazier, President

MISSION HILL MEMORIAL HOSPITAL (L, 49 beds) 1900 South Gordon Cooper Drive, Shawnee, OK Zip 74801–8600; tel. 405/273–2240; Thomas G. Honaker III, Administrator

ST. ANTHONY HOSPITAL (O, 408 beds) 1000 North Lee Street, Oklahoma City, OK Zip 73102–1080, Mailing Address: P.O. Box 205, Zip 73101–0205; tel. 405/272–7000; Valinda Rutledge, President

WISCONSIN: ST. CLARE HOSPITAL AND HEALTH SERVICES (O, 76 beds) 707 14th Street, Baraboo, WI Zip 53913–1597; tel. 608/356–1400; David B. Jordahl, FACHE, President
Web address: www.stclare.com

ST. MARYS HOSPITAL MEDICAL CENTER (O, 303 beds) 707 South Mills Street, Madison, WI Zip 53715–0450; tel. 608/251–6100; Gerald W. Lefert, President
Web address: www.ssmhc.com

Owned, leased, sponsored:	18 hospitals	3151 beds
Contract–managed:	3 hospitals	360 beds
Totals:	21 hospitals	3511 beds

★2255: ST. FRANCIS HEALTH SYSTEM (NP)

4401 Penn Avenue, Pittsburgh, PA Zip 15224–1334; tel. 412/622–4214; Sister M. Rosita Wellinger, President and Chief Executive Officer

PENNSYLVANIA: ST. FRANCIS CENTRAL HOSPITAL (O, 136 beds) 1200 Centre Avenue, Pittsburgh, PA Zip 15219–3507; tel. 412/562–3000; Robin Z. Mohr, Chief Executive Officer
Web address: www.sfhs.edu

ST. FRANCIS HOSPITAL OF NEW CASTLE (O, 187 beds) 1000 South Mercer Street, New Castle, PA Zip 16101–4673; tel. 724/658–3511; Sister Donna Zwigart, FACHE, Chief Executive Officer
Web address: www.w.sfhs.edu

For explanation of codes following names, see page B2.
★ Indicates Type III membership in the American Hospital Association.

ST. FRANCIS MEDICAL CENTER (O, 832 beds) 400 45th Street, Pittsburgh, PA Zip 15201–1198; tel. 412/622–4343; Sister Florence Brandt, Chief Executive Officer

Owned, leased, sponsored:	3 hospitals	1155 beds
Contract–managed:	0 hospitals	0 beds
Totals:	3 hospitals	1155 beds

★**5425: ST. JOSEPH HEALTH SYSTEM** (CC)
440 South Batavia Street, Orange, CA Zip 92868–3995, Mailing Address: P.O. Box 14132, Zip 92613–1532; tel. 714/997–7690; Richard Statuto, Chief Executive Officer

CALIFORNIA: MISSION HOSPITAL REGIONAL MEDICAL CENTER (O, 252 beds) 27700 Medical Center Road, Mission Viejo, CA Zip 92691; tel. 949/364–1400; Peter F. Bastone, President and Chief Executive Officer
Web address: www.mhrmc.com

NORTH COAST HEALTH CARE CENTERS (O, 119 beds) 1287 Fulton Road, Santa Rosa, CA Zip 95401; tel. 707/543–2400; Robert H. Fish, President and Chief Executive Officer

PETALUMA VALLEY HOSPITAL (L, 84 beds) 400 North McDowell Boulevard, Petaluma, CA Zip 94954–2339; tel. 707/778–1111; Alanna Brogan, Chief Operating Officer

QUEEN OF THE VALLEY HOSPITAL (O, 163 beds) 1000 Trancas Street, Napa, CA Zip 94558, Mailing Address: Box 2340, Zip 94558; tel. 707/252–4411; Dennis Sisto, President and Chief Executive Officer

REDWOOD MEMORIAL HOSPITAL (O, 35 beds) 3300 Renner Drive, Fortuna, CA Zip 95540; tel. 707/725–3361; Neil Martin, President and Chief Executive Officer

SAINT JOSEPH HOSPITAL (O, 96 beds) 2700 Dolbeer Street, Eureka, CA Zip 95501; tel. 707/445–8121; Gary G. Fybel, President and Chief Executive Officer

SANTA ROSA MEMORIAL HOSPITAL (O, 225 beds) 1165 Montgomery Drive, Santa Rosa, CA Zip 95405, Mailing Address: Box 522, Zip 95402; tel. 707/546–3210; Robert H. Fish, President and Chief Executive Officer

ST. MARY REGIONAL MEDICAL CENTER (O, 195 beds) 18300 Highway 18, Apple Valley, CA Zip 92307–0725, Mailing Address: Box 7025, Zip 92307–0725; tel. 760/242–2311; Catherine M. Pelley, President and Chief Executive Officer

ST. JOSEPH HOSPITAL (O, 395 beds) 1100 West Stewart Drive, Orange, CA Zip 92668, Mailing Address: P.O. Box 5600, Zip 92613–5600; tel. 714/633–9111; Larry K. Ainsworth, President and Chief Executive Officer

ST. JUDE MEDICAL CENTER (O, 347 beds) 101 East Valencia Mesa Drive, Fullerton, CA Zip 92635; tel. 714/992–3000; Robert J. Fraschetti, President and Chief Executive Officer

TEXAS: COVENANT CHILDREN'S HOSPITAL (O, 73 beds) 3610 21st Street, Lubbock, TX Zip 79410–1218; tel. 806/784–5040; George H. McCleskey, President and Chief Executive Officer
Web address: www.methlube.org

COVENANT HOSPITAL PLAINVIEW (O, 34 beds) 2601 Dimmitt Road, Plainview, TX Zip 79072–1833; tel. 806/296–5531; Joe S. Langford, Chief Executive Officer

COVENANT HOSPITAL–LEVELLAND (O, 44 beds) 1900 South College Avenue, Levelland, TX Zip 79336–6508; tel. 806/894–4963; Jerry Osburn, Administrator

COVENANT MEDICAL CENTER (O, 520 beds) 3615 19th Street, Lubbock, TX Zip 79410–1201, Mailing Address: Box 1201, Zip 79408–1201; tel. 806/792–1011; George H. McCleskey, President and Chief Executive Officer
Web address: www.methlub.org

COVENANT MEDICAL CENTER–LAKESIDE (O, 410 beds) 4000 24th Street, Lubbock, TX Zip 79410–1894; tel. 806/796–6000; Charley O. Trimble, President and Chief Executive Officer

CROSBYTON CLINIC HOSPITAL (C, 35 beds) 710 West Main Street, Crosbyton, TX Zip 79322–2143; tel. 806/675–2382; Michael Johnson, Administrator and Chief Executive Officer

D. M. COGDELL MEMORIAL HOSPITAL (C, 64 beds) 1700 Cogdell Boulevard, Snyder, TX Zip 79549–6198; tel. 915/573–6374; Jeff Reecer, Chief Executive Officer

SWISHER MEMORIAL HOSPITAL DISTRICT (C, 26 beds) 539 Southeast Second, Tulia, TX Zip 79088–2403, Mailing Address: P.O. Box 808, Zip 79088–0808; tel. 806/995–3581; Jeffrey Madison, Chief Executive Officer

YOAKUM COUNTY HOSPITAL (C, 24 beds) 412 Mustang Avenue, Denver City, TX Zip 79323–2750, Mailing Address: P.O. Drawer 1130, Zip 79323–1130; tel. 806/592–5484; Edward Rodgers, Chief Executive Officer

Owned, leased, sponsored:	15 hospitals	2992 beds
Contract–managed:	4 hospitals	149 beds
Totals:	19 hospitals	3141 beds

●**0905: SUMMIT HOSPITAL CORPORATION** (IO)
5 Concourse Parkway, Suite 800, Atlanta, GA Zip 30328–6111; tel. 770/392–1454; Ken Couch, President

LOUISIANA: SUMMIT HOSPITAL OF NORTHWEST LOUISIANA (O, 54 beds) 4900 Medical Drive, Bossier City, LA Zip 71112–4596; tel. 318/747–9500; Louise Wiggins, Chief Executive Officer and Administrator

Owned, leased, sponsored:	1 hospital	54 beds
Contract–managed:	0 hospitals	0 beds
Totals:	1 hospital	54 beds

★**0030: SUN HEALTH CORPORATION** (NP)
13180 North 103rd Drive, Sun City, AZ Zip 85351–3038, Mailing Address: P.O. Box 1278, Zip 85372–1278; tel. 623/876–5301; Leland W. Peterson, President and Chief Executive Officer

ARIZONA: DEL E. WEBB MEMORIAL HOSPITAL (O, 170 beds) 14502 West Meeker Boulevard, Sun City West, AZ Zip 85375–5299, Mailing Address: P.O. Box 5169, Sun City, Zip 85375–5169; tel. 623/214–4000; Thomas C. Dickson, Executive Vice President and Chief Operating Officer
Web address: www.sunhealth.org

WALTER O. BOSWELL MEMORIAL HOSPITAL (O, 267 beds) 10401 West Thunderbird Boulevard, Sun City, AZ Zip 85351–3092, Mailing Address: P.O. Box 1690, Zip 85372–1690; tel. 623/977–7211; George Perez, Executive Vice President and Chief Operating Officer

Owned, leased, sponsored:	2 hospitals	437 beds
Contract–managed:	0 hospitals	0 beds
Totals:	2 hospitals	437 beds

★**8795: SUTTER HEALTH** (NP)
One Capitol Mall, Sacramento, CA Zip 95814, Mailing Address: P.O. Box 160727, Zip 95816–0727; tel. 916/733–8800; Van R. Johnson, President and Chief Executive Officer

CALIFORNIA: ALTA BATES MEDICAL CENTER–ASHBY CAMPUS (O, 468 beds) 2450 Ashby Avenue, Berkeley, CA Zip 94705; tel. 510/204–4444; Warren J. Kirk, President and Chief Administrative Officer
Web address: www.ahabates.com

CALIFORNIA PACIFIC MEDICAL CENTER (O, 613 beds) 2333 Buchanan Street, San Francisco, CA Zip 94115, Mailing Address: P.O. Box 7999, Zip 94120; tel. 415/563–4321; Martin Brotman, M.D., President and Chief Executive Officer
Web address: www.cpmc.org

DAMERON HOSPITAL (O, 211 beds) 525 West Acacia Street, Stockton, CA Zip 95203; tel. 209/944–5550; Luis Arismendi, M.D., Administrator

EDEN MEDICAL CENTER (O, 258 beds) 20103 Lake Chabot Road, Castro Valley, CA Zip 94546; tel. 510/537–1234; George Bischalaney, President and Chief Executive Officer
Web address: www.edenmedcenter.org

EL CAMINO HOSPITAL (O, 242 beds) 2500 Grant Road, Mountain View, CA Zip 94040, Mailing Address: P.O. Box 7025, Zip 94039; tel. 650/940–7000; Richard M. Warren, Chief Executive Officer

For explanation of codes following names, see page B2.
★ Indicates Type III membership in the American Hospital Association.
● Single hospital health care system

B142 / Networks, Health Care Systems and Alliances

© 1999 AHA Guide

MARIN GENERAL HOSPITAL (O, 165 beds) 250 Bon Air Road, Greenbrae, CA Zip 94904, Mailing Address: Box 8010, San Rafael, Zip 94912–8010; tel. 415/925–7000; Henry J. Buhrmann, President and Chief Executive Officer

MEMORIAL HOSPITALS ASSOCIATION (O, 273 beds) Modesto, CA Mailing Address: P.O. Box 942, Zip 95353; tel. 209/526–4500; David P. Benn, President and Chief Executive Officer

MILLS–PENINSULA HEALTH SERVICES (O, 395 beds) 1783 El Camino Real, Burlingame, CA Zip 94010–3205; tel. 650/696–5400; Robert W. Merwin, Chief Executive Officer

NOVATO COMMUNITY HOSPITAL (O, 33 beds) 1625 Hill Road, Novato, CA Zip 94947, Mailing Address: P.O. Box 1108, Zip 94948; tel. 415/897–3111; Anne Hosfeld, Chief Administrative Officer

SUTTER AMADOR HOSPITAL (O, 85 beds) 810 Court Street, Jackson, CA Zip 95642–2379; tel. 209/223–7500; Scott Stenberg, Chief Executive Officer

SUTTER AUBURN FAITH COMMUNITY HOSPITAL (O, 105 beds) 11815 Education Street, Auburn, CA Zip 95604, Mailing Address: Box 8992, Zip 95604–8992; tel. 530/888–4518; Joel E. Grey, Administrator

SUTTER CENTER FOR PSYCHIATRY (O, 69 beds) 7700 Folsom Boulevard, Sacramento, CA Zip 95826–2608; tel. 916/386–3000; Diane Gail Stewart, Administrator
Web address: www.sutterhealth.org

SUTTER COAST HOSPITAL (O, 47 beds) 800 East Washington Boulevard, Crescent City, CA Zip 95531; tel. 707/464–8511; John E. Menaugh, Chief Executive Officer

SUTTER DAVIS HOSPITAL (O, 48 beds) 2000 Sutter Place, Davis, CA Zip 95616, Mailing Address: P.O. Box 1617, Zip 95617; tel. 530/756–6440; Lawrence A. Maas, Administrator

SUTTER DELTA MEDICAL CENTER (O, 100 beds) 3901 Lone Tree Way, Antioch, CA Zip 94509; tel. 925/779–7200; Linda Horn, Administrator

SUTTER LAKESIDE HOSPITAL (O, 54 beds) 5176 Hill Road East, Lakeport, CA Zip 95453–6111; tel. 707/262–5001; Gilbert Silbernagel, Chief Executive Officer
Web address: www.sutterlake.org

SUTTER MATERNITY AND SURGERY CENTER OF SANTA CRUZ (O, 30 beds) 2900 Chanticleer Avenue, Santa Cruz, CA Zip 95065–1816; tel. 831/477–2200; Iris C. Frank, Administrator

SUTTER MEDICAL CENTER (O, 497 beds) 5151 F Street, Sacramento, CA Zip 95819–3295; tel. 916/454–3333; Lou Lazatin, Chief Executive Officer
Web address: www.sutterhealth.org

SUTTER MEDICAL CENTER, SANTA ROSA (O, 114 beds) 3325 Chanate Road, Santa Rosa, CA Zip 95404; tel. 707/576–4000; Cliff Coates, Chief Executive Officer

SUTTER MERCED MEDICAL CENTER (O, 158 beds) 301 East 13th Street, Merced, CA Zip 95340–6211; tel. 209/385–7000; Brian S. Bentley, Administrator
Web address: www.sutterhealth.org

SUTTER ROSEVILLE MEDICAL CENTER (O, 183 beds) One Medical Plaza, Roseville, CA Zip 95661–3477; tel. 916/781–1000; Patrick R. Brady, Chief Executive Officer

SUTTER SOLANO MEDICAL CENTER (O, 60 beds) 300 Hospital Drive, Vallejo, CA Zip 94589–2517, Mailing Address: P.O. Box 3189, Zip 94589; tel. 707/554–4444; Polly J. Walker, R.N., Interim Chief Executive Officer
Web address: www.sutterhealth.org

SUTTER TRACY COMMUNITY HOSPITAL (O, 61 beds) 1420 North Tracy Boulevard, Tracy, CA Zip 95376–3497; tel. 209/835–1500; Gary D. Rapaport, Chief Executive Officer
Web address: www.suttertracy.org

HAWAII: KAHI MOHALA (O, 88 beds) 91–2301 Fort Weaver Road, Ewa Beach, HI Zip 96706; tel. 808/671–8511; Margi Drue, Administrator

Owned, leased, sponsored:	24 hospitals	4357 beds
Contract–managed:	0 hospitals	0 beds
Totals:	24 hospitals	4357 beds

0039:   TARRANT COUNTY HOSPITAL DISTRICT (NP)
1500 South Main Street, Fort Worth, TX Zip 76104–4941; tel. 817/927–1230; Anthony J. Alcini, President and Chief Executive Officer

TEXAS: JPS HEALTH NETWORK (O, 293 beds) 1500 South Main Street, Fort Worth, TX Zip 76104–4941; tel. 817/921–3431; Anthony J. Alcini, President and Chief Executive Officer
Web address: www.jpshealthnet.org

TRINITY SPRINGS PAVILION (O, 34 beds) 1500 South Main Street, Fort Worth, TX Zip 76104–4917; tel. 817/927–3636; Robert N. Bourassa, Executive Director

Owned, leased, sponsored:	2 hospitals	327 beds
Contract–managed:	0 hospitals	0 beds
Totals:	2 hospitals	327 beds

0169:   TEMPLE UNIVERSITY HEALTH SYSTEM (NP)
3401 North Broad Street, 1st Floor, Philadelphia, PA Zip 19140; tel. 215/707–8000; Leon S. Malmud, M.D., President

PENNSYLVANIA: JEANES HOSPITAL (O, 206 beds) 7600 Central Avenue, Philadelphia, PA Zip 19111–2499; tel. 215/728–2000; G. Roger Martin, President and Chief Executive Officer
Web address: www.jeanes.com

LOWER BUCKS HOSPITAL (O, 163 beds) 501 Bath Road, Bristol, PA Zip 19007–3190; tel. 215/785–9200; Nathan Bosk, FACHE, Chief Executive Officer

NORTHEASTERN HOSPITAL OF PHILADELPHIA (O, 166 beds) 2301 East Allegheny Avenue, Philadelphia, PA Zip 19134–4497; tel. 215/291–3000; Lynn Holder, Associate Director

TEMPLE EAST, NEUMANN MEDICAL CENTER (O, 166 beds) 1741 Frankford Avenue, Philadelphia, PA Zip 19125–2495; tel. 215/291–2000; Lynn Holder, Executive Director
Web address: www.neumann.org

TEMPLE UNIVERSITY HOSPITAL (O, 398 beds) Broad and Ontario Streets, Philadelphia, PA Zip 19140–5192; tel. 215/707–2000; Paul Boehringer, Executive Director
Web address: www.allcet.com/tuhs/index.htm

Owned, leased, sponsored:	5 hospitals	1099 beds
Contract–managed:	0 hospitals	0 beds
Totals:	5 hospitals	1099 beds

★0063:   TENET HEALTHCARE CORPORATION (IO)
3820 State Street, Santa Barbara, CA Zip 93105, Mailing Address: P.O. Box 31907, Zip 93130; tel. 805/563–7000; Jeffrey Barbakow, Chairman and Chief Executive Officer

ALABAMA: BROOKWOOD MEDICAL CENTER (O, 468 beds) 2010 Brookwood Medical Center Drive, Birmingham, AL Zip 35209; tel. 205/877–1000; Gregory H. Burfitt, President and Chief Executive Officer
Web address: www.brookwood–medical.com

LLOYD NOLAND HOSPITAL AND HEALTH SYSTEM (O, 222 beds) 701 Lloyd Noland Parkway, Fairfield, AL Zip 35064–2699; tel. 205/783–5106; Garry L. Gause, Chief Executive Officer
Web address: www.tenethealth.com

ARIZONA: COMMUNITY HOSPITAL MEDICAL CENTER (O, 59 beds) 6501 North 19th Avenue, Phoenix, AZ Zip 85015–1690; tel. 602/249–3434; Patrick T. Walz, Chief Executive Officer
Web address: www.tenethealth.com/communityhospital

MESA GENERAL HOSPITAL MEDICAL CENTER (L, 143 beds) 515 North Mesa Drive, Mesa, AZ Zip 85201–5989; tel. 602/969–9111; Patrick T. Walz, Chief Executive Officer

ST. LUKE'S BEHAVIORAL HEALTH CENTER (O, 70 beds) 1800 East Van Buren, Phoenix, AZ Zip 85006–3742; tel. 602/251–8484; Patrick D. Waugh, Chief Executive Officer

ST. LUKE'S MEDICAL CENTER (L, 296 beds) 1800 East Van Buren Street, Phoenix, AZ Zip 85006–3742; tel. 602/251–8100; Mary Jo Gregory, Chief Executive Officer

For explanation of codes following names, see page B2.
★ Indicates Type III membership in the American Hospital Association.

Section B

TEMPE ST. LUKE'S HOSPITAL (L, 110 beds) 1500 South Mill Avenue, Tempe, AZ Zip 85281–6699; tel. 602/784–5510; Mary Jo Gregory, Chief Executive Officer

TUCSON GENERAL HOSPITAL (O, 80 beds) 3838 North Campbell Avenue, Tucson, AZ Zip 85719–1497; tel. 520/318–6300; Allan Harrington Jr., Chief Executive Officer

ARKANSAS: CENTRAL ARKANSAS HOSPITAL (O, 120 beds) 1200 South Main Street, Searcy, AR Zip 72143–7397; tel. 501/278–3131; David C. Laffoon, CHE, Chief Executive Officer

NATIONAL PARK MEDICAL CENTER (O, 166 beds) 1910 Malvern Avenue, Hot Springs, AR Zip 71901–7799; tel. 501/321–1000; Jerry D. Mabry, Executive Director

REGIONAL MEDICAL CENTER OF NORTHEAST ARKANSAS (O, 104 beds) 3024 Stadium Boulevard, Jonesboro, AR Zip 72401–7493; tel. 870/972–7000; Philip H. Walkley Jr., Chief Executive Officer
Web address: www.tenethealth.com/jonesboro

SAINT MARY'S REGIONAL MEDICAL CENTER (O, 157 beds) 1808 West Main Street, Russellville, AR Zip 72801–2724; tel. 501/968–2841; Mike McCoy, Chief Executive Officer

CALIFORNIA: ALVARADO HOSPITAL MEDICAL CENTER (O, 199 beds) 6655 Alvarado Road, San Diego, CA Zip 92120–5298; tel. 619/287–3270; Barry G. Weinbaum, Chief Executive Officer

BROTMAN MEDICAL CENTER (O, 240 beds) 3828 Delmas Terrace, Culver City, CA Zip 90231–2459, Mailing Address: Box 2459, Zip 90231–2459; tel. 310/836–7000; Sonja Hagel, Chief Executive Officer

CENTINELA HOSPITAL MEDICAL CENTER (O, 377 beds) 555 East Hardy Street, Inglewood, CA Zip 90301–4073, Mailing Address: Box 720, Zip 90307–0720; tel. 310/673–4660; Michael A. Rembis, FACHE, Chief Executive Officer

CENTURY CITY HOSPITAL (L, 156 beds) 2070 Century Park East, Los Angeles, CA Zip 90067; tel. 310/553–6211; John R. Nickens III, Chief Executive Officer

CHAPMAN MEDICAL CENTER (L, 40 beds) 2601 East Chapman Avenue, Orange, CA Zip 92869; tel. 714/633–0011; Maxine T. Cooper, Chief Executive Officer

COASTAL COMMUNITIES HOSPITAL (O, 177 beds) 2701 South Bristol Street, Santa Ana, CA Zip 92704–9911; tel. 714/754–5454; Kent G. Clayton, Chief Executive Officer

COMMUNITY HOSPITAL OF HUNTINGTON PARK (L, 226 beds) 2623 East Slauson Avenue, Huntington Park, CA Zip 90255; tel. 323/583–1931; Charles Martinez, Ph.D., Chief Executive Officer

COMMUNITY HOSPITAL OF LOS GATOS (L, 153 beds) 815 Pollard Road, Los Gatos, CA Zip 95030; tel. 408/378–6131; Daniel P. Doore, Chief Executive Officer

DESERT REGIONAL MEDICAL CENTER (L, 348 beds) 1150 North Indian Canyon Drive, Palm Springs, CA Zip 92262, Mailing Address: Box 2739, Zip 92263; tel. 760/323–6511; Truman L. Gates, President and Chief Executive Officer

DOCTORS HOSPITAL OF MANTECA (O, 73 beds) 1205 East North Street, Manteca, CA Zip 95336; tel. 209/823–3111; Patrick W. Rafferty, Administrator

DOCTORS MEDICAL CENTER (O, 392 beds) 1441 Florida Avenue, Modesto, CA Zip 95350–4418, Mailing Address: P.O. Box 4138, Zip 95352–4138; tel. 209/578–1211; Tim A. Joslin, Chief Executive Officer

DOCTORS MEDICAL CENTER–PINOLE CAMPUS (L, 137 beds) 2151 Appian Way, Pinole, CA Zip 94564; tel. 510/970–5000; Gary Sloan, Chief Executive Officer
Web address: www.tenethealth.com

DOCTORS MEDICAL CENTER–SAN PABLO CAMPUS (L, 286 beds) 2000 Vale Road, San Pablo, CA Zip 94806; tel. 510/970–5102; Gary Sloan, Chief Executive Officer

ENCINO–TARZANA REGIONAL MEDICAL CENTER ENCINO CAMPUS (L, 138 beds) 16237 Ventura Boulevard, Encino, CA Zip 91436–2201; tel. 818/995–5000

ENCINO–TARZANA REGIONAL MEDICAL CENTER TARZANA CAMPUS (L, 232 beds) 18321 Clark Street, Tarzana, CA Zip 91356; tel. 818/881–0800; Dale Surowitz, President and Chief Executive Officer

FOUNTAIN VALLEY REGIONAL HOSPITAL AND MEDICAL CENTER (O, 384 beds) 17100 Euclid at Warner, Fountain Valley, CA Zip 92708; tel. 714/966–7200; Tim Smith, President and Chief Executive Officer

GARDEN GROVE HOSPITAL AND MEDICAL CENTER (O, 167 beds) 12601 Garden Grove Boulevard, Garden Grove, CA Zip 92843–1959; tel. 714/741–2700; Mark A. Meyers, President and Chief Executive Officer

GARFIELD MEDICAL CENTER (O, 207 beds) 525 North Garfield Avenue, Monterey Park, CA Zip 91754; tel. 626/573–2222; Philip A. Cohen, Chief Executive Officer

GREATER EL MONTE COMMUNITY HOSPITAL (O, 115 beds) 1701 South Santa Anita Avenue, South El Monte, CA Zip 91733–9918; tel. 626/579–7777; Elizabeth A. Primeaux, Chief Executive Officer

IRVINE MEDICAL CENTER (L, 176 beds) 16200 Sand Canyon Avenue, Irvine, CA Zip 92618–3714; tel. 949/753–2000; Dan F. Ausman, Chief Executive Officer

JOHN F. KENNEDY MEMORIAL HOSPITAL (O, 130 beds) 47–111 Monroe Street, Indio, CA Zip 92201, Mailing Address: P.O. Drawer LLLL, Zip 92202–2558; tel. 760/347–6191; Larry W. Payton, Chief Operating Officer

LAKEWOOD REGIONAL MEDICAL CENTER (O, 148 beds) 3700 East South Street, Lakewood, CA Zip 90712; tel. 562/531–2550; Gustavo A. Valdespino, Chief Executive Officer

LOS ALAMITOS MEDICAL CENTER (O, 173 beds) 3751 Katella Avenue, Los Alamitos, CA Zip 90720; tel. 562/598–1311; Gustavo A. Valdespino, Chief Executive Officer

MIDWAY HOSPITAL MEDICAL CENTER (O, 150 beds) 5925 San Vicente Boulevard, Los Angeles, CA Zip 90019–6696; tel. 323/938–3161; John R. Nickens III, Chief Executive Officer

MONTEREY PARK HOSPITAL (O, 95 beds) 900 South Atlantic Boulevard, Monterey Park, CA Zip 91754; tel. 626/570–9000; Philip A. Cohen, Interim Chief Executive Officer

PLACENTIA LINDA HOSPITAL (O, 114 beds) 1301 Rose Drive, Placentia, CA Zip 92870; tel. 714/993–2000; Maxine T. Cooper, Chief Executive Officer
Web address: www.tenethealth.com/placentialinda

QUEEN OF ANGELS–HOLLYWOOD PRESBYTERIAN MEDICAL CENTER (O, 409 beds) 1300 North Vermont Avenue, Los Angeles, CA Zip 90027–0069; tel. 213/413–3000; John V. Fenton, Chief Executive Officer

RANCHO SPRINGS MEDICAL CENTER (O, 91 beds) 25500 Medical Center Drive, Murrieta, CA Zip 92562–5966; tel. 909/696–6000; Juanice Lovett, Chief Executive Officer

REDDING MEDICAL CENTER (O, 162 beds) 1100 Butte Street, Redding, CA Zip 96001–0853, Mailing Address: Box 496072, Zip 96049–6072; tel. 530/244–5454; Steve Schmidt, Chief Executive Officer

SAN DIMAS COMMUNITY HOSPITAL (O, 93 beds) 1350 West Covina Boulevard, San Dimas, CA Zip 91773–0308; tel. 909/599–6811; Patrick A. Petre, Chief Executive Officer
Web address: www.tenethealth.com

SAN RAMON REGIONAL MEDICAL CENTER (O, 95 beds) 6001 Norris Canyon Road, San Ramon, CA Zip 94583; tel. 925/275–9200; Philip P. Gustafson, Administrator
Web address: www.sanramonmedctr.com

SANTA ANA HOSPITAL MEDICAL CENTER (L, 76 beds) 1901 North Fairview Street, Santa Ana, CA Zip 92706; tel. 714/554–1653; Kent G. Clayton, Chief Executive Officer

SIERRA VISTA REGIONAL MEDICAL CENTER (O, 175 beds) 1010 Murray Street, San Luis Obispo, CA Zip 93405, Mailing Address: Box 1367, Zip 93406–1367; tel. 805/546–7600; Sean O'Neal, Administrator

ST. LUKE MEDICAL CENTER (O, 120 beds) 2632 East Washington Boulevard, Pasadena, CA Zip 91107–1994; tel. 626/797–1141; Kenneth I. Rivers, Chief Executive Officer

SUBURBAN MEDICAL CENTER (L, 132 beds) 16453 South Colorado Avenue, Paramount, CA Zip 90723; tel. 562/531–3110; Gustavo Valdespino, Chief Executive Officer
Web address: www.tenethealth.com/suburban

TWIN CITIES COMMUNITY HOSPITAL (O, 84 beds) 1100 Las Tablas Road, Templeton, CA Zip 93465; tel. 805/434–3500; Harold E. Chilton, Chief Executive Officer

For explanation of codes following names, see page B2.
★ Indicates Type III membership in the American Hospital Association.

USC UNIVERSITY HOSPITAL (L, 285 beds) 1500 San Pablo Street, Los Angeles, CA Zip 90033–4585; tel. 323/442–8500; Edward Schreck, Chief Executive Officer
Web address: www.uscuh.com

UNIVERSITY OF SOUTHERN CALIFORNIA–KENNETH NORRIS JR. CANCER HOSPITAL (O, 60 beds) 1441 Eastlake Avenue, Los Angeles, CA Zip 90033–1085, Mailing Address: P.O. Box 33804, Zip 90033–3804; tel. 323/865–3000; Adrianne Black Bass, Administrator
Web address: www.uscnorris.com

WESTERN MEDICAL CENTER HOSPITAL ANAHEIM (O, 171 beds) 1025 South Anaheim Boulevard, Anaheim, CA Zip 92805; tel. 714/533–6220; Mark A. Meyers, President and Chief Executive Officer

WESTERN MEDICAL CENTER–SANTA ANA (O, 288 beds) 1001 North Tustin Avenue, Santa Ana, CA Zip 92705–3502; tel. 714/835–3555; Daniel Brothman, Chief Executive Officer
Web address: www.tenethealth.com/westermedical

WHITTIER HOSPITAL MEDICAL CENTER (O, 172 beds) 9080 Colima Road, Whittier, CA Zip 90605; tel. 562/907–1541; Sandra M. Chester, Chief Executive Officer

FLORIDA: CORAL GABLES HOSPITAL (O, 205 beds) 3100 Douglas Road, Coral Gables, FL Zip 33134–6990; tel. 305/445–8461; Martha Garcia, Chief Executive Officer

DELRAY MEDICAL CENTER (O, 211 beds) 5352 Linton Boulevard, Delray Beach, FL Zip 33484–6580; tel. 561/498–4440; Mitchell S. Feldman, Chief Executive Officer
Web address: www.tenethealth.com

FAIR OAKS HOSPITAL (O, 102 beds) 5440 Linton Boulevard, Delray Beach, FL Zip 33484–6578; tel. 561/495–1000; Bill Russell, Chief Operating Officer and Administrator

FLORIDA MEDICAL CENTER HOSPITAL (O, 459 beds) 5000 West Oakland Park Boulevard, Fort Lauderdale, FL Zip 33313–1585; tel. 954/735–6000; Joel Bergenfeld, Chief Executive Officer

HIALEAH HOSPITAL (O, 411 beds) 651 East 25th Street, Hialeah, FL Zip 33013–3878; tel. 305/693–6100; Clifford J. Bauer, Chief Executive Officer

HOLLYWOOD MEDICAL CENTER (O, 238 beds) 3600 Washington Street, Hollywood, FL Zip 33021–8216; tel. 954/966–4500; Holly Lerner, Chief Executive Officer

MEMORIAL HOSPITAL OF TAMPA (O, 174 beds) 2901 Swann Avenue, Tampa, FL Zip 33609–4057; tel. 813/873–6400; Charles F. Scott, President and Chief Executive Officer
Web address: www.tenethealth.com/tampa

NORTH BAY HOSPITAL (O, 122 beds) 6600 Madison Street, New Port Richey, FL Zip 34652–1900; tel. 727/842–8468; William A. Jennings, Chief Operating Officer and Administrator

NORTH RIDGE MEDICAL CENTER (O, 391 beds) 5757 North Dixie Highway, Fort Lauderdale, FL Zip 33334–4182, Mailing Address: P.O. Box 23160, Zip 33307; tel. 954/776–6000; Emil P. Miller, Chief Executive Officer
Web address: www.tenethealth/northridge.com

NORTH SHORE MEDICAL CENTER (O, 197 beds) 1100 N.W. 95th Street, Miami, FL Zip 33150–2098; tel. 305/835–6000; Steven M. Klein, President and Chief Executive Officer
Web address: www.nsmc.com

PALM BEACH GARDENS MEDICAL CENTER (L, 204 beds) 3360 Burns Road, Palm Beach Gardens, FL Zip 33410–4304; tel. 561/622–1411; Clint Matthews, Chief Executive Officer
Web address: www.TENETHEALTH.COM/PALMBEACHGARDENS

PALMETTO GENERAL HOSPITAL (O, 360 beds) 2001 West 68th Street, Hialeah, FL Zip 33016–1898; tel. 305/823–5000; Ron Stern, Chief Executive Officer

PALMS OF PASADENA HOSPITAL (O, 213 beds) 1501 Pasadena Avenue South, Saint Petersburg, FL Zip 33707–3798; tel. 727/381–1000; John D. Bartlett, Chief Executive Officer

PARKWAY REGIONAL MEDICAL CENTER (O, 392 beds) 160 N.W. 170th Street, North Miami Beach, FL Zip 33169–5576; tel. 305/654–5050; Peter A. Marmerstein, Chief Executive Officer

PINECREST REHABILITATION HOSPITAL (O, 90 beds) 5360 Linton Boulevard, Delray Beach, FL Zip 33484–6538; tel. 561/495–0400; Paul D. Echelard, Administrator

SEVEN RIVERS COMMUNITY HOSPITAL (O, 128 beds) 6201 North Suncoast Boulevard, Crystal River, FL Zip 34428–6712; tel. 352/795–6560; Michael L. Collins, Chief Executive Officer

TOWN AND COUNTRY HOSPITAL (O, 155 beds) 6001 Webb Road, Tampa, FL Zip 33615–3291; tel. 813/885–6666; Charles F. Scott, President and Chief Executive Officer
Web address: www.tenethealth.com/town&country

WEST BOCA MEDICAL CENTER (O, 150 beds) 21644 State Road 7, Boca Raton, FL Zip 33428–1899; tel. 561/488–8000; Richard Gold, Chief Executive Officer

GEORGIA: ATLANTA MEDICAL CENTER (O, 450 beds) 303 Parkway Drive N.E., Atlanta, GA Zip 30312–1239; tel. 404/265–4000; James E. Lathren, President and Chief Executive Officer

NORTH FULTON REGIONAL HOSPITAL (L, 167 beds) 3000 Hospital Boulevard, Roswell, GA Zip 30076–9930; tel. 770/751–2500; John F. Holland, President
Web address: www.tenethealth.com/northfulton

SPALDING REGIONAL HOSPITAL (O, 158 beds) 601 South Eighth Street, Griffin, GA Zip 30224–4294, Mailing Address: P.O. Drawer V, Zip 30224–1168; tel. 770/228–2721; Jim Litchford, Executive Director

SYLVAN GROVE HOSPITAL (L, 28 beds) 1050 McDonough Road, Jackson, GA Zip 30233–1599; tel. 770/775–7861; Mike Patterson, Administrator
Web address: www.tenethealth.com

INDIANA: CULVER UNION HOSPITAL (O, 98 beds) 1710 Lafayette Road, Crawfordsville, IN Zip 47933–1099; tel. 765/362–2800; Gregory D. Starnes, Chief Executive Officer

WINONA MEMORIAL HOSPITAL (O, 169 beds) 3232 North Meridian Street, Indianapolis, IN Zip 46208–4693; tel. 317/924–3392; Clifford A. Yeager, Chief Executive Officer
Web address: www.tenethealth.com

LOUISIANA: DOCTORS HOSPITAL OF JEFFERSON (L, 144 beds) 4320 Houma Boulevard, Metairie, LA Zip 70006–2973; tel. 504/849–4000; L. Rene' Goux, Chief Executive Officer
Web address: www.tenethealth.com

KENNER REGIONAL MEDICAL CENTER (O, 213 beds) 180 West Esplanade Avenue, Kenner, LA Zip 70065–6001; tel. 504/468–8600; Deborah C. Keel, Chief Executive Officer

MEADOWCREST HOSPITAL (O, 187 beds) 2500 Belle Chase Highway, Gretna, LA Zip 70056–7196; tel. 504/392–3131; Gerald L. Parton, Chief Executive Officer
Web address: www.tenethealth.com

MEMORIAL MEDICAL CENTER (O, 717 beds) New Orleans, LA Randall L. Hoover, Chief Executive Officer

MINDEN MEDICAL CENTER (O, 101 beds) 1 Medical Plaza, Minden, LA Zip 71055–3330; tel. 318/377–2321; George E. French III, Chief Executive Officer
Web address: www.tenethealth.com/minden

NORTHSHORE PSYCHIATRIC HOSPITAL (O, 58 beds) 104 Medical Center Drive, Slidell, LA Zip 70461–7838; tel. 504/646–5500; George H. Perry, Ph.D., Chief Executive Officer

NORTHSHORE REGIONAL MEDICAL CENTER (L, 147 beds) 100 Medical Center Drive, Slidell, LA Zip 70461–8572; tel. 504/649–7070; Lynn C. Orfgen, Chief Executive Officer

ST. CHARLES GENERAL HOSPITAL (O, 163 beds) 3700 St. Charles Avenue, New Orleans, LA Zip 70115–4680; tel. 504/899–7441; Rene Goux, Chief Executive Officer
Web address: www.tenethealth.com

MASSACHUSETTS: METROWEST MEDICAL CENTER (O, 357 beds) 115 Lincoln Street, Framingham, MA Zip 01702; tel. 508/383–1000; Thomas G. Hennessy, Chief Executive Officer
Web address: www.mwmc.com

SAINT VINCENT HOSPITAL (O, 369 beds) 25 Winthrop Street, Worcester, MA Zip 01604–4593; tel. 508/798–1234; Robert E. Maher Jr., President and Chief Executive Officer
Web address: www.svh–worc.com

MISSISSIPPI: GULF COAST MEDICAL CENTER (O, 189 beds) 180–A Debuys Road, Biloxi, MS Zip 39531–4405; tel. 228/388–6711; Gary L. Stokes, Chief Executive Officer

MISSOURI: COLUMBIA REGIONAL HOSPITAL (O, 265 beds) 404 Keene Street, Columbia, MO Zip 65201–6698; tel. 573/875–9000; Bruce Eady, Chief Executive Officer

COMPTON HEIGHTS HOSPITAL (O, 214 beds) 3545 Lafayette Avenue, Saint Louis, MO Zip 63104–9984; tel. 314/865–6500; Lee Stoll, Chief Executive Officer

DES PERES HOSPITAL (O, 93 beds) 2345 Dougherty Ferry Road, Saint Louis, MO Zip 63122–3313; tel. 314/768–3000; Michele C. Meyer, Interim Chief Executive Officer

FOREST PARK HOSPITAL (O, 296 beds) 6150 Oakland Avenue, Saint Louis, MO Zip 63139–3297; tel. 314/768–3000; Glennon K. McFadden, Chief Executive Officer

LUCY LEE HOSPITAL (L, 173 beds) 2620 North Westwood Boulevard, Poplar Bluff, MO Zip 63901–2341, Mailing Address: P.O. Box 88, Zip 63901–2341; tel. 573/785–7721; Brian T. Flynn, Chief Executive Officer
Web address: www.tenethealth.com

SAINT LOUIS UNIVERSITY HOSPITAL (O, 303 beds) 3635 Vista at Grand Boulevard, Saint Louis, MO Zip 63110–0250, Mailing Address: P.O. Box 15250, Zip 63110–0250; tel. 314/577–8000; Leona D. Stoll, Chief Executive Officer

SOUTHPOINTE HOSPITAL (O, 243 beds) 2639 Miami Street, Saint Louis, MO Zip 63118–3999; tel. 314/772–1456; Doug Doris, Chief Executive Officer

TWIN RIVERS REGIONAL MEDICAL CENTER (O, 116 beds) 1301 First Street, Kennett, MO Zip 63857–2508; tel. 573/888–4522; John W. Sanders, Chief Executive Officer

NEBRASKA: ST. JOSEPH HOSPITAL (O, 277 beds) 601 North 30th Street, Omaha, NE Zip 68131–2197; tel. 402/449–5021; J. Richard Stanko, President and Chief Executive Officer

NEVADA: LAKE MEAD HOSPITAL MEDICAL CENTER (O, 184 beds) 1409 East Lake Mead Boulevard, North Las Vegas, NV Zip 89030–7197; tel. 702/649–7711; Randall Hempling, Administrator
Web address: www.tenethealth.com

NORTH CAROLINA: CENTRAL CAROLINA HOSPITAL (O, 137 beds) 1135 Carthage Street, Sanford, NC Zip 27330; tel. 919/774–2100; L. Glenn Davis, Executive Director
Web address: www.tenethealth.com/centralcarolina

FRYE REGIONAL MEDICAL CENTER (L, 355 beds) 420 North Center Street, Hickory, NC Zip 28601–5049; tel. 828/322–6070; Dennis Phillips, Chief Executive Officer

PENNSYLVANIA: CITY AVENUE HOSPITAL (O, 195 beds) 4150 City Avenue, Philadelphia, PA Zip 19131–1610; tel. 215/871–1000; Andrea F. Gilbert, Chief Executive Officer

ELKINS PARK HOSPITAL (O, 158 beds) 60 East Township Line Road, Elkins Park, PA Zip 19027–2220; tel. 215/663–6000; Richard Centafont, Interim Chief Executive Officer
Web address: www.auhs.edu

GRADUATE HOSPITAL (O, 198 beds) One Graduate Plaza, Philadelphia, PA Zip 19146–1407; tel. 215/893–2000; Christopher DiCicco, Chief Executive Officer

HAHNEMANN UNIVERSITY HOSPITAL (O, 540 beds) Broad and Vine Streets, Philadelphia, PA Zip 19102–1192; tel. 215/762–7000; Michael P. Halter, Chief Executive Officer
Web address: www.auhs.edu

MEDICAL COLLEGE OF PENNSYLVANIA HOSPITAL (O, 369 beds) 3300 Henry Avenue, Philadelphia, PA Zip 19129–1121; tel. 215/842–6000; Richard S. Freeman, Chief Executive Officer

PARKVIEW HOSPITAL (O, 165 beds) 1331 East Wyoming Avenue, Philadelphia, PA Zip 19124–3808; tel. 215/537–7400; Ernest N. Perilli, Chief Executive Officer

ST. CHRISTOPHER'S HOSPITAL FOR CHILDREN (O, 130 beds) Erie Avenue at Front Street, Philadelphia, PA Zip 19134–1095; tel. 215/427–5000; Calvin Bland, President and Chief Executive Officer
Web address: www.allegheny.edu

WARMINSTER HOSPITAL (O, 132 beds) 225 Newtown Road, Warminster, PA Zip 18974–5221; tel. 215/441–6600; Jeffrey Yarnel, Chief Executive Officer
Web address: www.auhs.edu

SOUTH CAROLINA: EAST COOPER REGIONAL MEDICAL CENTER (O, 112 beds) 1200 Johnnie Dodds Boulevard, Mount Pleasant, SC Zip 29464–3294; tel. 843/881–0100; Jack Dusenbery, President

HILTON HEAD MEDICAL CENTER AND CLINICS (O, 79 beds) 25 Hospital Center Boulevard, Hilton Head Island, SC Zip 29926–2738, Mailing Address: P.O. Box 21117, Zip 29925–1117; tel. 843/681–6122; Dennis Ray Bruns, President and Chief Executive Officer
Web address: www.tenethealth.com

PIEDMONT HEALTHCARE SYSTEM (O, 276 beds) 222 Herlong Avenue, Rock Hill, SC Zip 29732–1952; tel. 803/329–1234; Charles F. Miller, Interim President

TENNESSEE: HARTON REGIONAL MEDICAL CENTER (O, 137 beds) 1801 North Jackson Street, Tullahoma, TN Zip 37388–2201, Mailing Address: P.O. Box 460, Zip 37388–0460; tel. 931/393–3000; David C. Wilson, Chief Executive Officer
Web address: www.tenethealth.com\harton\

MEDICAL CENTER OF MANCHESTER (L, 49 beds) 481 Interstate Drive, Manchester, TN Zip 37355–3108, Mailing Address: P.O. Box 1409, Zip 37355–1409; tel. 931/728–6354; David C. Wilson, Chief Executive Officer

SAINT FRANCIS HOSPITAL (O, 558 beds) 5959 Park Avenue, Memphis, TN Zip 38119–5198, Mailing Address: P.O. Box 171808, Zip 38187–1808; tel. 901/765–1000; David L. Archer, Chief Executive Officer

UNIVERSITY MEDICAL CENTER (O, 225 beds) 1411 Baddour Parkway, Lebanon, TN Zip 37087–2573; tel. 615/444–8262; Larry W. Keller, Chief Executive Officer

TEXAS: BAYOU CITY MEDICAL CENTER (O, 283 beds) 4200 Portsmouth Street, Houston, TX Zip 77027–6899; tel. 713/623–2500; Steve Altmiller, Chief Executive Officer

BROWNSVILLE MEDICAL CENTER (O, 205 beds) 1040 West Jefferson Street, Brownsville, TX Zip 78520–5829, Mailing Address: P.O. Box 3590, Zip 78523–3590; tel. 956/544–1400; John M. Chubb, Chief Executive Officer

CYPRESS FAIRBANKS MEDICAL CENTER (O, 136 beds) 10655 Steepletop Drive, Houston, TX Zip 77065–4297; tel. 281/890–4285; Bill Klier, Chief Executive Officer
Web address: www.tenethealth.com/cypressfairbanks

DOCTORS HOSPITAL OF DALLAS (O, 204 beds) 9440 Poppy Drive, Dallas, TX Zip 75218–3694; tel. 214/324–6100; Robert S. Freymuller, Chief Executive Officer
Web address: www.tenethealth.com/doctorsdallas

GARLAND COMMUNITY HOSPITAL (O, 113 beds) 2696 West Walnut Street, Garland, TX Zip 75042–6499; tel. 972/276–7116; Gene Miller, Chief Executive Officer

HOUSTON NORTHWEST MEDICAL CENTER (O, 408 beds) 710 FM 1960 West, Houston, TX Zip 77090–3496; tel. 281/440–1000; James Kelly, Chief Executive Officer
Web address: www.houstonnorthwestmed.com

LAKE POINTE MEDICAL CENTER (O, 92 beds) 6800 Scenic Drive, Rowlett, TX Zip 75088, Mailing Address: P.O. Box 1550, Zip 75030–1550; tel. 972/412–2273; Kenneth R. Teel, Administrator
Web address: www.tenethealth.com/lakepointe

MID–JEFFERSON HOSPITAL (O, 138 beds) Highway 365 and 27th Street, Nederland, TX Zip 77627–6288, Mailing Address: P.O. Box 1917, Zip 77627–1917; tel. 409/727–2321; Wilson J. Weber, Chief Executive Officer
Web address: www.tenethealth.com/lakepointe

NACOGDOCHES MEDICAL CENTER (O, 150 beds) 4920 N.E. Stallings, Nacogdoches, TX Zip 75961–1200, Mailing Address: P.O. Box 631604, Zip 75963–1604; tel. 409/568–3380; Glenn A. Robinson, Chief Executive Officer
Web address: www.tenethealth.com/nacogdoches

ODESSA REGIONAL HOSPITAL (O, 44 beds) 520 East Sixth Street, Odessa, TX Zip 79761–4565, Mailing Address: P.O. Box 4859, Zip 79760–4859; tel. 915/334–8200; Lex A. Guinn, Chief Executive Officer
Web address: www.orh.net

For explanation of codes following names, see page B2.
★ Indicates Type III membership in the American Hospital Association.

PARK PLACE MEDICAL CENTER (O, 219 beds) 3050 39th Street, Port Arthur, TX Zip 77642–5535, Mailing Address: P.O. Box 1648, Zip 77641–1648; tel. 409/983–4951; Wilson J. Weber, Chief Executive Officer

PARK PLAZA HOSPITAL (O, 370 beds) 1313 Hermann Drive, Houston, TX Zip 77004–7092; tel. 713/527–5000; Robert L. Quist, Chief Executive Officer
Web address: www.tenethealth.com

PROVIDENCE MEMORIAL HOSPITAL (O, 379 beds) 2001 North Oregon Street, El Paso, TX Zip 79902–3368; tel. 915/577–6011; L. Marcus Fry Jr., Chief Executive Officer

RHD MEMORIAL MEDICAL CENTER (L, 150 beds) Seven Medical Parkway, Dallas, TX Zip 75381, Mailing Address: P.O. Box 819094, Zip 75381–9094; tel. 972/247–1000; Craig E. Sims, President and Chief Executive Officer
Web address: www.tenethealth.com

RIO VISTA PHYSICAL REHABILITATION HOSPITAL (O, 100 beds) 1740 Curie Drive, El Paso, TX Zip 79902–2900; tel. 915/544–3399; Patsy A. Parker, Administrator and Chief Executive Officer

SIERRA MEDICAL CENTER (O, 328 beds) 1625 Medical Center Drive, El Paso, TX Zip 79902–5044; tel. 915/747–4000; Thomas E. Casaday, President and Chief Executive Officer

SOUTHWEST GENERAL HOSPITAL (O, 200 beds) 7400 Barlite Boulevard, San Antonio, TX Zip 78224–1399; tel. 210/921–2000; Keith Swinney, Chief Executive Officer
Web address: www.tenethealth.comswgh

TRINITY MEDICAL CENTER (L, 144 beds) 4343 North Josey Lane, Carrollton, TX Zip 75010–4691; tel. 972/492–1010; Craig E. Sims, President
Web address: www.tenethealth.com

TRINITY VALLEY MEDICAL CENTER (O, 150 beds) 2900 South Loop 256, Palestine, TX Zip 75801–6958; tel. 903/731–1000; Larry C. Bozeman, Chief Executive Officer

Owned, leased, sponsored:	134 hospitals	27150 beds
Contract–managed:	0 hospitals	0 beds
Totals:	134 hospitals	27150 beds

0020:   TEXAS DEPARTMENT OF HEALTH (NP)
1100 West 49th Street, Austin, TX Zip 78756–3199; tel. 512/458–7111; William R. Archer III, M.D., Commissioner

SOUTH TEXAS HOSPITAL (O, 60 beds) 1301 Rangerville Road, Harlingen, TX Zip 78552–7609, Mailing Address: P.O. Box 592, Zip 78551–0592; tel. 956/423–3420; Mary Diaz, R.N., Ed.D., Interim Director
Web address: www.tdh.texas.gov

TEXAS CENTER FOR INFECTIOUS DISEASE (O, 109 beds) 2303 S.E. Military Drive, San Antonio, TX Zip 78223–3597; tel. 210/534–8857; James N. Elkins, FACHE, Director

Owned, leased, sponsored:	2 hospitals	169 beds
Contract–managed:	0 hospitals	0 beds
Totals:	2 hospitals	169 beds

★0129:   TEXAS HEALTH RESOURCES (NP)
600 East Las Colinas Boulevard, Suite 1550, Irving, TX Zip 75039, Mailing Address: 600 East Las Colinas Boulevard, 1550, Zip 75039; tel. 214/818–4500; Douglas D. Hawthorne, President and Chief Executive Officer

ARLINGTON MEMORIAL HOSPITAL (O, 338 beds) 800 West Randol Mill Road, Arlington, TX Zip 76012–2503; tel. 817/548–6100; Wayne N. Clark, President and Chief Executive Officer

HARRIS CONTINUED CARE HOSPITAL (O, 10 beds) 1301 Pennsylvania Avenue, 4th Floor, Fort Worth, TX Zip 76104–2190, Mailing Address: P.O. Box 3471, Zip 76113–3471; tel. 817/878–5500; Larry Thompson, Senior Vice President and Executive Director
Web address: www.hmhs.com

HARRIS METHODIST FORT WORTH (O, 502 beds) 1301 Pennsylvania Avenue, Fort Worth, TX Zip 76104–2895; tel. 817/882–2000; Barclay E. Berdan, Chief Executive Officer
Web address: www.hmhs.com

HARRIS METHODIST NORTHWEST (O, 44 beds) 108 Denver Trail, Azle, TX Zip 76020–3697; tel. 817/444–8600; Larry Thompson, Vice President and Administrator
Web address: www.hmhs.com

HARRIS METHODIST SOUTHWEST (O, 85 beds) 6100 Harris Parkway, Fort Worth, TX Zip 76132–4199; tel. 817/346–5050; Stansel Harvey, Senior Executive Vice President, Executive Director/Administrator
Web address: www.hmhs.com

HARRIS METHODIST–ERATH COUNTY (O, 75 beds) 411 North Belknap Street, Stephenville, TX Zip 76401–3415, Mailing Address: P.O. Box 1399, Zip 76401–1399; tel. 254/965–1500; Ronald E. Dorris, Senior Vice President and Executive Director
Web address: www.hmhs.com

HARRIS METHODIST–HEB (O, 184 beds) 1600 Hospital Parkway, Bedford, TX Zip 76022–6913, Mailing Address: P.O. Box 669, Zip 76095–0669; tel. 817/685–4000; Jack McCabe, Senior Vice President and Administrator
Web address: www.hmhs.com

MCCUISTION REGIONAL MEDICAL CENTER (O, 158 beds) 865 Deshong Drive, Paris, TX Zip 75462–2097, Mailing Address: P.O. Box 160, Zip 75461–0160; tel. 903/737–1111; Michael J. McBride, CHE, Senior Vice President and Executive Director

PRESBYTERIAN HOSPITAL OF DALLAS (O, 667 beds) 8200 Walnut Hill Lane, Dallas, TX Zip 75231–4402; tel. 214/345–6789; Mark H. Merrill, Executive Director
Web address: www.texashealth.org

PRESBYTERIAN HOSPITAL OF KAUFMAN (O, 68 beds) 850 Highway 243 West, Kaufman, TX Zip 75142–9998, Mailing Address: P.O. Box 310, Zip 75142–0310; tel. 972/932–7200; Michael J. McBride, CHE, Senior Vice President and Executive Director

PRESBYTERIAN HOSPITAL OF PLANO (O, 91 beds) 6200 West Parker Road, Plano, TX Zip 75093–7914; tel. 972/608–8000; Philip M. Wentworth, FACHE, Senior Vice President and Executive Director
Web address: www.texashealth.org

PRESBYTERIAN HOSPITAL OF WINNSBORO (O, 46 beds) 719 West Coke Road, Winnsboro, TX Zip 75494–3098, Mailing Address: P.O. Box 628, Zip 75494–0628; tel. 903/342–5227; Dan Noteware, Senior Vice President and Executive Director

ST. PAUL MEDICAL CENTER (O, 348 beds) 5909 Harry Hines Boulevard, Dallas, TX Zip 75235–6285; tel. 214/879–1000; Frank Tiedemann, President and Chief Executive Officer

WALLS REGIONAL HOSPITAL (O, 112 beds) 201 Walls Drive, Cleburne, TX Zip 76031–1008; tel. 817/641–2551; Brent D. Magers, FACHE, Executive Director and Senior Vice President
Web address: www.hmhs.com

Owned, leased, sponsored:	14 hospitals	2728 beds
Contract–managed:	0 hospitals	0 beds
Totals:	14 hospitals	2728 beds

★0178:   TRIAD HOSPITALS, INC. (IO)
13455 Noel Road, 20th Floor, Dallas, TX Zip 75240; tel. 972/789–2700; James Shelton, Chairman and Chief Executive Officer

ALABAMA: CRESTWOOD MEDICAL CENTER (O, 92 beds) One Hospital Drive, Huntsville, AL Zip 35801–3403; tel. 256/882–3100; Thomas M. Weiss, Chief Executive Officer

ARIZONA: EL DORADO HOSPITAL (O, 166 beds) 1400 North Wilmot Road, Tucson, AZ Zip 85712–4498, Mailing Address: P.O. Box 13070, Zip 85732–3070; tel. 520/886–6361; Rhonda Dean, Chief Executive Officer
Web address: www.eldoradohospital.com

NORTHWEST MEDICAL CENTER (O, 152 beds) 6200 North La Cholla Boulevard, Tucson, AZ Zip 85741–3599; tel. 520/742–9000; W. Jefferson Comer, FACHE, Chief Executive Officer

PARADISE VALLEY HOSPITAL (O, 140 beds) 3929 East Bell Road, Phoenix, AZ Zip 85032–2196; tel. 602/867–1881; Rebecca C. Kuhn, President and Chief Executive Officer

For explanation of codes following names, see page B2.
★ Indicates Type III membership in the American Hospital Association.

Section B

PHOENIX REGIONAL MEDICAL CENTER (O, 174 beds) 1947 East Thomas Road, Phoenix, AZ Zip 85016–7795; tel. 602/650–7600; Denny W. Powell, Chief Executive Officer

ARKANSAS: DE QUEEN REGIONAL MEDICAL CENTER (O, 75 beds) 1306 Collin Raye Drive, De Queen, AR Zip 71832–2198; tel. 870/584–4111; Charles H. Long, Chief Executive Officer
Web address: www.columbia.net

MEDICAL CENTER OF SOUTH ARKANSAS (O, 167 beds) 700 West Grove Street, El Dorado, AR Zip 71730–4416, Mailing Address: P.O. Box 1998, Zip 71731–1998; tel. 870/864–3200; Luther J. Lewis, Chief Executive Officer
Web address: www.mesaeldo.com

MEDICAL PARK HOSPITAL (O, 79 beds) 2001 South Main Street, Hope, AR Zip 71801–8194; tel. 870/777–2323; Jimmy Leopard, Chief Executive Officer

CALIFORNIA: MISSION BAY HOSPITAL (O, 91 beds) 3030 Bunker Hill Street, San Diego, CA Zip 92109–5780; tel. 619/274–7721; Deborah Brehe, Chief Executive Officer
Web address: www.mbhosp.com

SAN LEANDRO HOSPITAL (O, 136 beds) 13855 East 14th Street, San Leandro, CA Zip 94578–0398; tel. 510/357–6500; Kelly Mather, Chief Executive Officer

LOUISIANA: WOMEN AND CHILDREN'S HOSPITAL–LAKE CHARLES (O, 72 beds) 4200 Nelson Road, Lake Charles, LA Zip 70605–4118; tel. 318/474–6370; Alan E. McMillin, Chief Executive Officer

NEW MEXICO: CARLSBAD MEDICAL CENTER (O, 131 beds) 2430 West Pierce Street, Carlsbad, NM Zip 88220–3597; tel. 505/887–4100; Thomas McClintock, Chief Executive Officer
Web address: www.columbia.com

LEA REGIONAL HOSPITAL (O, 141 beds) 5419 North Lovington Highway, Hobbs, NM Zip 88240–9125, Mailing Address: P.O. Box 3000, Zip 88240–3000; tel. 505/392–6581; Bill Gresco, Administrator

OKLAHOMA: CLAREMORE REGIONAL HOSPITAL (O, 68 beds) 1202 North Muskogee Place, Claremore, OK Zip 74017–3036; tel. 918/341–2556; Ken Seidel, Executive Director

OREGON: DOUGLAS COMMUNITY MEDICAL CENTER (O, 100 beds) 738 West Harvard Avenue, Roseburg, OR Zip 97470–2996; tel. 541/673–6641; Leslie Paul Luke, Chief Executive Officer

WILLIAMETTE VALLEY MEDICAL CENTER (O, 67 beds) 2700 Three Mile Lane, McMinnville, OR Zip 97128–6498; tel. 503/472–6131; Rosemari Davis, Chief Executive Officer
Web address: www.columbia.net

TEXAS: ALICE REGIONAL HOSPITAL (O, 120 beds) 300 East Third Street, Alice, TX Zip 78332–4794; tel. 361/664–4376; Abraham Martinez, Chief Executive Officer

BROWNWOOD REGIONAL MEDICAL CENTER (O, 164 beds) 1501 Burnet Drive, Brownwood, TX Zip 76801–5933, Mailing Address: P.O. Box 760, Zip 76804–0760; tel. 915/646–8541; Tim Lancaster, Chief Executive Officer

COLLEGE STATION MEDICAL CENTER (O, 119 beds) 1604 Rock Prairie Road, College Station, TX Zip 77845–8345, Mailing Address: P.O. Box 10000, Zip 77842–3500; tel. 409/764–5100; Thomas W. Jackson, Chief Executive Officer
Web address: www.columbia.net

COMMUNITY MEDICAL CENTER SHERMAN (O, 160 beds) 1111 Gallagher Road, Sherman, TX Zip 75090–1798; tel. 903/870–7000; John F. Adams, Chief Executive Officer
Web address: www.columbia–hca.com

DETAR HOSPITAL (O, 217 beds) 506 East San Antonio Street, Victoria, TX Zip 77901–6060, Mailing Address: Box 2089, Zip 77902–2089; tel. 512/575–7441; William R. Blanchard, Chief Executive Officer
Web address: www.detar.com

GULF COAST MEDICAL CENTER (O, 161 beds) 1400 Highway 59, Wharton, TX Zip 77488–3004, Mailing Address: P.O. Box 3004, Zip 77488–3004; tel. 409/532–2500; Michael D. Murphy, Chief Executive Officer
Web address: www.gulfcoastmedical.com

LONGVIEW REGIONAL MEDICAL CENTER (O, 164 beds) 2901 North Fourth Street, Longview, TX Zip 75605–5191, Mailing Address: P.O. Box 14000, Zip 75607–4000; tel. 903/758–1818; Vicki L. Romero, Chief Executive Officer
Web address: www.columbia.net/index.html

MEDICAL CENTER AT TERRELL (O, 131 beds) 1551 Highway 34 South, Terrell, TX Zip 75160–4833; tel. 972/563–7611; Ronald J. Ensor, Chief Executive Officer

NAVARRO REGIONAL HOSPITAL (O, 144 beds) 3201 West Highway 22, Corsicana, TX Zip 75110; tel. 903/654–6800; Nancy A. Byrnes, Chief Executive Officer
Web address: www.columbia.net

PAMPA REGIONAL MEDICAL CENTER (O, 107 beds) One Medical Plaza, Pampa, TX Zip 79065; tel. 806/665–3721; Phillip E. Fowler, Interim Chief Executive Officer
Web address: www.cmcp.com

SAN ANGELO COMMUNITY MEDICAL CENTER (O, 135 beds) 3501 Knickerbocker Road, San Angelo, TX Zip 76904–7698; tel. 915/949–9511; Samuel G. Feazell, Chief Executive Officer

VICTORIA REGIONAL MEDICAL CENTER (O, 122 beds) 101 Medical Drive, Victoria, TX Zip 77904–3198; tel. 512/573–6100; Aston Hecker, Chief Executive Officer

WOODLAND HEIGHTS MEDICAL CENTER (O, 110 beds) 505 South John Redditt Drive, Lufkin, TX Zip 75904, Mailing Address: P.O. Box 150610, Zip 75915–0610; tel. 409/634–8311; Don H. McBride, Chief Executive Officer

Owned, leased, sponsored:	29 hospitals	3705 beds
Contract–managed:	0 hospitals	0 beds
Totals:	29 hospitals	3705 beds

★9255: TRUMAN MEDICAL CENTER (NP)
2301 Holmes Street, Kansas City, MO Zip 64108–2677; tel. 816/556–3000; John W. Bluford, Executive Director and Chief Executive Officer

MISSOURI: TRUMAN MEDICAL CENTER–EAST (C, 302 beds) 7900 Lee's Summit Road, Kansas City, MO Zip 64139–1241; tel. 816/373–4415; Donald R. Smithburg, Administrator

TRUMAN MEDICAL CENTER–WEST (C, 215 beds) 2301 Holmes Street, Kansas City, MO Zip 64108–2677; tel. 816/556–3000; Cathy Disch, Director Operations

Owned, leased, sponsored:	0 hospitals	0 beds
Contract–managed:	2 hospitals	517 beds
Totals:	2 hospitals	517 beds

9195: U. S. PUBLIC HEALTH SERVICE INDIAN HEALTH SERVICE (FG)
5600 Fishers Lane, Rockville, MD Zip 20857; tel. 301/443–1083; Michael Trujillo, M.D., M.P.H., Director

ALASKA: ALASKA NATIVE MEDICAL CENTER (O, 140 beds) 4315 Diplomacy Drive, Anchorage, AK Zip 99508; tel. 907/563–2662; Richard Mandsager, M.D., Administrator

KANAKANAK HOSPITAL (O, 16 beds) Dillingham, AK Mailing Address: P.O. Box 130, Zip 99576; tel. 907/842–5201; Darrel C. Richardson, Chief Operating Officer

MANIILAQ HEALTH CENTER (O, 17 beds) Kotzebue, AK Zip 99752–0043; tel. 907/442–3321; Clinton Gray Jr., Administrator

NORTON SOUND REGIONAL HOSPITAL (O, 34 beds) Bering Straits, Nome, AK Zip 99762, Mailing Address: P.O. Box 966, Zip 99762–0966; tel. 907/443–3311; Charles Fagerstrom, Vice President
Web address: www.nshcorp.org

SAMUEL SIMMONDS MEMORIAL HOSPITAL (O, 15 beds) 1296 Agvik Street, Barrow, AK Zip 99723, Mailing Address: P.O. Box 29, Zip 99723; tel. 907/852–4611; Michael S. Herring, Administrator

SEARHC MT. EDGECUMBE HOSPITAL (O, 60 beds) 222 Tongass Drive, Sitka, AK Zip 99835–9416; tel. 907/966–2411; Frank Sutton, Vice President Hospital Services

For explanation of codes following names, see page B2.
★ Indicates Type III membership in the American Hospital Association.

YUKON–KUSKOKWIM DELTA REGIONAL HOSPITAL (O, 50 beds) Bethel, AK Mailing Address: P.O. Box 528, Zip 99559–3000; tel. 907/543–6300; Edwin L. Hansen, Vice President

ARIZONA: CHINLE COMPREHENSIVE HEALTH CARE FACILITY (O, 60 beds) Highway 191, Chinle, AZ Zip 86503, Mailing Address: P.O. Drawer PH, Zip 86503; tel. 520/674–7011; Ronald Tso, Chief Executive Officer

FORT DEFIANCE INDIAN HEALTH SERVICE HOSPITAL (O, 49 beds) Fort Defiance, AZ Mailing Address: P.O. Box 649, Zip 86504–0649; tel. 520/729–5741; Franklin Freeland, Ed.D., Chief Executive Officer

HUHUKAM MEMORIAL HOSPITAL (O, 10 beds) Seed Farm & Skill Center Road, Sacaton, AZ Zip 85247–0038, Mailing Address: P.O. Box 38, Zip 85247–0038; tel. 602/528–1200; Viola L. Johnson, Chief Executive Officer

TUBA CITY INDIAN MEDICAL CENTER (O, 69 beds) Main Street, Tuba City, AZ Zip 86045–6211, Mailing Address: P.O. Box 600, Zip 86045–6211; tel. 520/283–2501; Susie John, M.D., Chief Executive Officer

U. S. PUBLIC HEALTH SERVICE INDIAN HOSPITAL (O, 18 beds) Parker, AZ Mailing Address: Route 1, Box 12, Zip 85344; tel. 520/669–2137; Gary Davis, Service Unit Director

U. S. PUBLIC HEALTH SERVICE INDIAN HOSPITAL (O, 34 beds) Sells, AZ Mailing Address: P.O. Box 548, Zip 85634–0548; tel. 520/383–7251; Darrell Rumley, Service Unit Director and Chief Executive Officer

U. S. PUBLIC HEALTH SERVICE INDIAN HOSPITAL (O, 28 beds) San Carlos, AZ Mailing Address: P.O. Box 208, Zip 85550–0208; tel. 520/475–2371; Nella Ben, Chief Executive Officer

U. S. PUBLIC HEALTH SERVICE INDIAN HOSPITAL (O, 36 beds) State Route 73, Box 860, Whiteriver, AZ Zip 85941–0860; tel. 520/338–4911; Carla Alchesay–Nachu, Service Unit Director

U. S. PUBLIC HEALTH SERVICE PHOENIX INDIAN MEDICAL CENTER (O, 127 beds) 4212 North 16th Street, Phoenix, AZ Zip 85016–5389; tel. 602/263–1200; Anna Albert, Chief Executive Officer

U. S. PUBLIC HEALTH SERVICES INDIAN HOSPITAL (O, 17 beds) Keams Canyon, AZ Mailing Address: P.O. Box 98, Zip 86034–0098; tel. 520/738–2211; Taylor Satala, Service Unit Director

CALIFORNIA: U. S. PUBLIC HEALTH SERVICE INDIAN HOSPITAL (O, 34 beds) Winterhaven, CA Mailing Address: P.O. Box 1368, Yuma, AZZip 85366–1368; tel. 760/572–0217; Hortense Miguel, R.N., Service Unit Director

MARYLAND: WARREN G. MAGNUSON CLINICAL CENTER, NATIONAL INSTITUTES OF HEALTH (O, 314 beds) 9000 Rockville Pike, Bethesda, MD Zip 20892–1504; tel. 301/496–4114; John I. Gallin, M.D., Director
Web address: www.cc.nih.gov

MINNESOTA: U. S. PUBLIC HEALTH SERVICE INDIAN HOSPITAL (O, 13 beds) 7th Street and Grant Utley Avenue N.W., Cass Lake, MN Zip 56633, Mailing Address: Rural Route 3, Box 211, Zip 56633; tel. 218/335–2293; Luella Brown, Service Unit Director

U.S. PUBLIC HEALTH SERVICE INDIAN HOSPITAL (O, 23 beds) Highway 1, Redlake, MN Zip 56671; tel. 218/679–3912; Essimae Stevens, Service Unit Director

MISSISSIPPI: CHOCTAW HEALTH CENTER (O, 35 beds) Highway 16 West, Philadelphia, MS Zip 39350, Mailing Address: Route 7, Box R–50, Zip 39350; tel. 601/656–2211; James D. Wallace, Executive Director

MONTANA: U. S. PUBLIC HEALTH SERVICE BLACKFEET COMMUNITY HOSPITAL (O, 25 beds) Browning, MT Mailing Address: P.O. Box 760, Zip 59417–0760; tel. 406/338–6100; Reis Fisher, Service Unit Director

U. S. PUBLIC HEALTH SERVICE INDIAN HOSPITAL (O, 24 beds) Crow Agency, MT Mailing Address: P.O. Box 9, Zip 59022–0009; tel. 406/638–2626; Tennyson Doney, Service Unit Director

U. S. PUBLIC HEALTH SERVICE INDIAN HOSPITAL (O, 53 beds) Rural Route 1, Box 67, Harlem, MT Zip 59526; tel. 406/353–3100; Charles D. Plumage, Director

NEBRASKA: U. S. PUBLIC HEALTH SERVICE INDIAN HOSPITAL (O, 30 beds) Highway 7577, Winnebago, NE Zip 68071; tel. 402/878–2231; Donald Lee, Service Unit Director

NEVADA: U. S. PUBLIC HEALTH SERVICE OWYHEE COMMUNITY HEALTH FACILITY (O, 15 beds) Owyhee, NV Mailing Address: P.O. Box 130, Zip 89832–0130; tel. 775/757–2415; Walden Townsend, Service Unit Director

NEW MEXICO: ACOMA–CANONCITO–LAGUNA HOSPITAL (O, 15 beds) San Fidel, NM Mailing Address: P.O. Box 130, Zip 87049–0130; tel. 505/552–6634; Richard L. Zephier, Ph.D., Service Unit Director

GALLUP INDIAN MEDICAL CENTER (O, 99 beds) 516 East Nizhoni Boulevard, Gallup, NM Zip 87301–5748, Mailing Address: P.O. Box 1337, Zip 87305–1337; tel. 505/722–1000; Timothy G. Fleming, M.D., Chief Executive Officer

NORTHERN NAVAJO MEDICAL CENTER (O, 59 beds) Shiprock, NM Mailing Address: P.O. Box 160, Zip 87420–0160; tel. 505/368–6001; Dee Hutchison, Chief Executive Officer

PHS SANTA FE INDIAN HOSPITAL (O, 39 beds) 1700 Cerrillos Road, Santa Fe, NM Zip 87505–3554; tel. 505/988–9821; Lawrence A. Jordan, Director

PUBLIC HEALTH SERVICE INDIAN HOSPITAL (O, 28 beds) 801 Vassar Drive N.E., Albuquerque, NM Zip 87106–2799; tel. 505/248–4000; Cheri Lyon, Service Unit Director

U. S. PUBLIC HEALTH SERVICE INDIAN HOSPITAL (O, 32 beds) Crownpoint, NM Mailing Address: P.O. Box 358, Zip 87313–0358; tel. 505/786–5291; Anita Muneta, Chief Executive Officer

U. S. PUBLIC HEALTH SERVICE INDIAN HOSPITAL (O, 13 beds) Mescalero, NM Mailing Address: Box 210, Zip 88340–0210; tel. 505/671–4441; Jo Ann Skaggs, Service Unit Director

U. S. PUBLIC HEALTH SERVICE INDIAN HOSPITAL (O, 24 beds) Zuni, NM Mailing Address: P.O. Box 467, Zip 87327–0467; tel. 505/782–4431; Jean Othole, Service Unit Director

NORTH CAROLINA: U. S. PUBLIC HEALTH SERVICE INDIAN HOSPITAL (O, 30 beds) Hospital Road, Cherokee, NC Zip 28719, Mailing Address: Hospital Road, Caller Box C–26, Zip 28719; tel. 828/497–9163; Edwin McLemore, Administrator

NORTH DAKOTA: U. S. PUBLIC HEALTH SERVICE INDIAN HOSPITAL (O, 42 beds) Belcourt, ND Mailing Address: P.O. Box 160, Zip 58316–0160; tel. 701/477–6111; Ray Grandbois, M.P.H., Service Unit Director

U. S. PUBLIC HEALTH SERVICE INDIAN HOSPITAL (O, 14 beds) N 10 North River Road, Fort Yates, ND Zip 58538, Mailing Address: P.O. Box J, Zip 58538; tel. 701/854–3831; Terry Pourier, Service Unit Director

OKLAHOMA: CARL ALBERT INDIAN HEALTH FACILITY (O, 53 beds) 1001 North Country Club Road, Ada, OK Zip 74820–2847; tel. 580/436–3980; Bruce A. Bennett, Administrator

CHOCTAW NATION INDIAN HOSPITAL (O, 44 beds) Rural Route 2, Box 1725, Talihina, OK Zip 74571–9517; tel. 918/567–2211; Rosemary Hooser, Administrator

CREEK NATION COMMUNITY HOSPITAL (O, 34 beds) 309 North 14th Street, Okemah, OK Zip 74859–2099; tel. 918/623–1424; Frank H. Wahpepah, M.P.H., Administrator

U. S. PUBLIC HEALTH SERVICE COMPREHENSIVE INDIAN HEALTH FACILITY (O, 46 beds) 101 South Moore Avenue, Claremore, OK Zip 74017–5091; tel. 918/342–6434; John Daugherty Jr., Service Unit Director

U. S. PUBLIC HEALTH SERVICE INDIAN HOSPITAL (O, 11 beds) Clinton, OK Mailing Address: Route 1, Box 3060, Zip 73601–9303; tel. 580/323–2884; Thedis V. Mitchell, Director

U. S. PUBLIC HEALTH SERVICE INDIAN HOSPITAL (O, 44 beds) 1515 Lawrie Tatum Road, Lawton, OK Zip 73507–3099; tel. 580/353–0350; George E. Howell, Service Unit Director

WILLIAM W. HASTINGS INDIAN HOSPITAL (O, 60 beds) 100 South Bliss Avenue, Tahlequah, OK Zip 74464–3399; tel. 918/458–3100; Hickory Starr Jr., Administrator

SOUTH DAKOTA: INDIAN HEALTH SERVICE HOSPITAL (O, 32 beds) 3200 Canyon Lake Drive, Rapid City, SD Zip 57702–8197; tel. 605/355–2280; Michelle Leach, Director

U. S. PUBLIC HEALTH SERVICE INDIAN HOSPITAL (O, 23 beds) Eagle Butte, SD Mailing Address: P.O. Box 1012, Zip 57625–1012; tel. 605/964–3001; Donald D. Annis, Service Unit Director

U. S. PUBLIC HEALTH SERVICE INDIAN HOSPITAL (O, 46 beds) Pine Ridge, SD Mailing Address: P.O. Box 1201, Zip 57770–1201; tel. 605/867–5131; Vern F. Donnell, Service Unit Director

U. S. PUBLIC HEALTH SERVICE INDIAN HOSPITAL (O, 35 beds) Highway 18, Soldier Creek Road, Rosebud, SD Zip 57570; tel. 605/747–2231; Gayla J. Twiss, Service Unit Director

Section B

For explanation of codes following names, see page B2.
★ Indicates Type III membership in the American Hospital Association.

U. S. PUBLIC HEALTH SERVICE INDIAN HOSPITAL (O, 18 beds) Chestnut Street, Sisseton, SD Zip 57262, Mailing Address: P.O. Box 189, Zip 57262–0189; tel. 605/698–7606; Richard Huff, Administrator
Web address: www.home.aberdeen.his.gov

Owned, leased, sponsored:	50 hospitals	2187 beds
Contract–managed:	0 hospitals	0 beds
Totals:	50 hospitals	2187 beds

★**0156: UCSF STANFORD HEALTH CARE** (NP)
5 Thomas Mellon Circle, 305, San Francisco, CA Zip 94134; tel. 415/353–4500; Peter Van Etten, President and Chief Executive Officer

CALIFORNIA: LUCILE SALTER PACKARD CHILDREN'S HOSPITAL AT STANFORD (O, 162 beds) 725 Welch Road, Palo Alto, CA Zip 94304; tel. 650/497–8000; Christopher G. Dawes, President

STANFORD HOSPITAL AND CLINICS (O, 440 beds) 300 Pasteur Drive, Stanford, CA Zip 94305–5584; tel. 650/723–4000; William B. Kerr, Executive Vice President and Chief Operating Officer
Web address: www.ucsfstanford.org

UNIVERSITY OF CALIFORNIA SAN FRANCISCO MEDICAL CENTER (O, 663 beds) 500 Parnassus, San Francisco, CA Zip 94143–0296; tel. 415/476–1000; Bruce Schroffel, Chief Operating Officer
Web address: www.ucsfstanford.org

Owned, leased, sponsored:	3 hospitals	1265 beds
Contract–managed:	0 hospitals	0 beds
Totals:	3 hospitals	1265 beds

★**2445: UNITED HEALTH GROUP** (NP)
Five Innovation Court, Appleton, WI Zip 54914–1663, Mailing Address: P.O. Box 8025, Zip 54913–8025; tel. 920/730–0330; James Edward Raney, President and Chief Executive Officer

WISCONSIN: APPLETON MEDICAL CENTER (O, 146 beds) 1818 North Meade Street, Appleton, WI Zip 54911–3496; tel. 920/731–4101; Robert H. Malte, Senior Vice President
Web address: www.unitedhealth.org

THEDA CLARK MEDICAL CENTER (O, 216 beds) 130 Second Street, Neenah, WI Zip 54956–2883, Mailing Address: P.O. Box 2021, Zip 54957–2021; tel. 920/729–3100; Robert H. Malte, Senior Vice President
Web address: www.unitedhealth.org

Owned, leased, sponsored:	2 hospitals	362 beds
Contract–managed:	0 hospitals	0 beds
Totals:	2 hospitals	362 beds

1765: UNITED HOSPITAL CORPORATION (IO)
6189 East Shelby Drive, Memphis, TN Zip 38115; tel. 901/794–8440; James C. Henson, President

ALABAMA: FLORALA MEMORIAL HOSPITAL (O, 23 beds) 515 East Fifth Avenue, Florala, AL Zip 36442–0189, Mailing Address: P.O. Box 189, Zip 36442–0189; tel. 334/858–3287; Blair W. Henson, Administrator

ARKANSAS: OZARK HEALTH MEDICAL CENTER (C, 144 beds) Highway 65 South, Clinton, AR Zip 72031, Mailing Address: P.O. Box 206, Zip 72031–0206; tel. 501/745–2401; Barry Brady, Administrator

Owned, leased, sponsored:	1 hospital	23 beds
Contract–managed:	1 hospital	144 beds
Totals:	2 hospitals	167 beds

9605: UNITED MEDICAL CORPORATION (IO)
603 Main Street, Windermere, FL Zip 34786–3548, Mailing Address: P.O. Box 1100, Zip 34786–1100; tel. 407/876–2200; Donald R. Dizney, Chairman

KENTUCKY: TEN BROECK HOSPITAL (O, 94 beds) 8521 Old LaGrange Road, Louisville, KY Zip 40242–3800; tel. 502/426–6380; Pat Hammer, Chief Executive Officer

LOUISIANA: ST. CLAUDE MEDICAL CENTER (O, 136 beds) 3419 St. Claude Avenue, New Orleans, LA Zip 70117–6198; tel. 504/948–8200; Joseph R. Tucker, President

PUERTO RICO: HOSPITAL DOCTOR GUBERN (O, 51 beds) 110 Antonio R. Barcelo, Fajardo, PR Zip 00738, Mailing Address: P.O. Box 846, Zip 00738–0846; tel. 787/863–0669; Edwin Sueiro, Executive Director

HOSPITAL PAVIA–HATO REY (O, 105 beds) San Juan, PR Mailing Address: 435 Ponce De Leon, Hato Rey, Zip 00917; tel. 787/754–0909; Jorge De Jesus, Executive Director

HOSPITAL PAVIA–SANTURCE (O, 183 beds) 1462 Asia Street, San Juan, PR Zip 00909, Mailing Address: Box 11137, Santurce Station, Zip 00910; tel. 787/727–6060; Jorge De Jesus, Executive Director

HOSPITAL PEREA (O, 82 beds) 15 Basora Street, Mayaguez, PR Zip 00681; Mailing Address: P.O. Box 170, Zip 00681; tel. 787/834–0101; Ramon Lopez, Administrator

SAN JORGE CHILDREN'S HOSPITAL (O, 85 beds) 258 San Jorge Avenue, San Juan, PR Zip 00912; tel. 787/727–1000; Domingo Cruz Vivaldi, Administrator

Owned, leased, sponsored:	7 hospitals	736 beds
Contract–managed:	0 hospitals	0 beds
Totals:	7 hospitals	736 beds

9555: UNIVERSAL HEALTH SERVICES, INC. (IO)
367 South Gulph Road, King of Prussia, PA Zip 19406–0958; tel. 610/768–3300; Alan B. Miller, President and Chief Executive Officer

ARKANSAS: BRIDGEWAY (L, 70 beds) 21 Bridgeway Road, North Little Rock, AR Zip 72113; tel. 501/771–1500; Barry Pipkin, Chief Executive Officer and Managing Director

CALIFORNIA: DEL AMO HOSPITAL (O, 166 beds) 23700 Camino Del Sol, Torrance, CA Zip 90505; tel. 310/530–1151; Lisa K. Montes, Administrator and Chief Executive Officer

INLAND VALLEY REGIONAL MEDICAL CENTER (L, 80 beds) 36485 Inland Valley Drive, Wildomar, CA Zip 92595; tel. 909/677–1111; Christopher L. Boyd, Chief Executive Officer and Managing Director

DISTRICT OF COLUMBIA: GEORGE WASHINGTON UNIVERSITY HOSPITAL (O, 285 beds) 901 23rd Street N.W., Washington, DC Zip 20037–2377; tel. 202/994–1000; Phillip S. Schaengold, JD, Chief Executive Officer
Web address: www.gwumc.edu

FLORIDA: MANATEE MEMORIAL HOSPITAL (O, 512 beds) 206 Second Street East, Bradenton, FL Zip 34208–1000; tel. 941/746–5111; Michael Marquez, Chief Executive Officer

WELLINGTON REGIONAL MEDICAL CENTER (L, 93 beds) 10101 Forest Hill Boulevard, West Palm Beach, FL Zip 33414–6199; tel. 561/798–8500; Gregory E. Boyer, Chief Executive Officer
Web address: www.wellingtonregmedctr.com

GEORGIA: TURNING POINT HOSPITAL (O, 59 beds) 3015 East By–Pass, Moultrie, GA Zip 31776, Mailing Address: P.O. Box 1177, Zip 31768–1177; tel. 912/985–4815; Ben Marion, Chief Executive Officer

ILLINOIS: THE PAVILION (O, 46 beds) 809 West Church Street, Champaign, IL Zip 61820; tel. 217/373–1700; Nina W. Eisner, Chief Executive Officer

LOUISIANA: CHALMETTE MEDICAL CENTER (L, 106 beds) 9001 Patricia Street, Chalmette, LA Zip 70043–1799; tel. 504/277–8011; Larry M. Graham, Chief Executive Officer

DOCTORS' HOSPITAL OF SHREVEPORT (L, 99 beds) 1130 Louisiana Avenue, Shreveport, LA Zip 71101–3998, Mailing Address: P.O. Box 1526, Zip 71165–1526; tel. 318/227–1211; Charles E. Boyd, Administrator

RIVER OAKS HOSPITAL (O, 94 beds) 1525 River Oaks Road West, New Orleans, LA Zip 70123–2199; tel. 504/734–1740; Daryl Sue White, Chief Executive Officer and Managing Director
Web address: www.riveroakshospital.com

RIVER PARISHES HOSPITAL (O, 79 beds) 500 Rue De Sante, La Place, LA Zip 70068–5418; tel. 504/652–7000; B. Ann Kuss, Chief Executive Officer and Managing Director

For explanation of codes following names, see page B2.
★ Indicates Type III membership in the American Hospital Association.

© 1999 AHA Guide

MASSACHUSETTS: ARBOUR H. R. I. HOSPITAL (O, 57 beds) 227 Babcock Street, Brookline, MA Zip 02146; tel. 617/731–3200; Roy A. Ettlinger, Chief Executive Officer
Web address: www.arbourhealth.com

ARBOUR HOSPITAL (O, 118 beds) 49 Robinwood Avenue, Boston, MA Zip 02130–2156, Mailing Address: P.O. Box 9, Zip 02130; tel. 617/522–4400; Roy A. Ettlinger, Chief Executive Officer

FULLER MEMORIAL HOSPITAL (O, 46 beds) 200 May Street, South Attleboro, MA Zip 02703–5599; tel. 508/761–8500; Landon Kite, President

MICHIGAN: FOREST VIEW HOSPITAL (O, 62 beds) 1055 Medical Park Drive S.E., Grand Rapids, MI Zip 49546–3671; tel. 616/942–9610; John F. Kuhn, Chief Executive Officer
Web address: www.forestview.com

MISSOURI: TWO RIVERS PSYCHIATRIC HOSPITAL (O, 80 beds) 5121 Raytown Road, Kansas City, MO Zip 64133–2141; tel. 816/356–5688; Linda Berridge, Chief Executive Officer
Web address: www.torivershospital.com

NEVADA: DESERT SPRINGS HOSPITAL (O, 225 beds) 2075 East Flamingo Road, Las Vegas, NV Zip 89119–5121, Mailing Address: P.O. Box 19204, Zip 89132–9204; tel. 702/733–8800; John Lloyd Hummer, Chief Executive Officer

NORTHERN NEVADA MEDICAL CENTER (O, 100 beds) 2375 East Prater Way, Sparks, NV Zip 89434–9645; tel. 702/331–7000; James R. Pagels, Chief Executive Officer and Managing Director
Web address: www.nnmc.com

VALLEY HOSPITAL MEDICAL CENTER (O, 365 beds) 620 Shadow Lane, Las Vegas, NV Zip 89106–4194; tel. 702/388–4000; Roger Collins, Chief Executive Officer and Managing Director

PENNSYLVANIA: CLARION PSYCHIATRIC CENTER (O, 52 beds) 2 Hospital Drive, Clarion, PA Zip 16214–9424, Mailing Address: Rural Delivery 3, Box 188, Zip 16214–9424; tel. 814/226–9545; Michael R. Keefer, CHE, Administrator and Chief Executive Officer

HORSHAM CLINIC (O, 138 beds) 722 East Butler Pike, Ambler, PA Zip 19002–2398; tel. 215/643–7800; David A. Baron, D.O., Medical Director

KEYSTONE CENTER (O, 76 beds) 2001 Providence Avenue, Chester, PA Zip 19013–5504; tel. 610/876–9000; Jimmy Patton, Chief Executive Officer and Managing Director

MEADOWS PSYCHIATRIC CENTER (O, 101 beds) Centre Hall, PA Mailing Address: Rural Delivery 1, Box 259, Zip 16828–9798; tel. 814/364–2161; Joseph Barszczewski, Chief Executive Officer and Managing Director

PUERTO RICO: DR. JOSE RAMOS LEBRON HOSPITAL (O, 107 beds) General Valero Avenue, #194, Fajardo, PR Zip 00738, Mailing Address: P.O. Box 1028, Zip 00738; tel. 787/863–0505; Maria Elena Rodriguez, Executive Administrator

HOSPITAL SAN FRANCISCO (O, 150 beds) 371 De Diego Avenue, San Juan, PR Zip 00923, Mailing Address: P.O. Box 29025, Zip 00929–0025; tel. 787/767–2528; Domingo Nevarez, Executive Director

HOSPITAL SAN PABLO (O, 364 beds) Calle San Cruz 70, Bayamon, PR Zip 00961, Mailing Address: P.O. Box 236, Zip 00960; tel. 787/740–4747; Jorge De Jesus, Executive Director

SOUTH CAROLINA: AIKEN REGIONAL MEDICAL CENTERS (O, 269 beds) 302 University Parkway, Aiken, SC Zip 29801–2757, Mailing Address: P.O. Box 1117, Zip 29802–1117; tel. 803/641–5000; Richard H. Satcher, Chief Executive Officer

TEXAS: DOCTORS HOSPITAL OF LAREDO (O, 117 beds) 500 East Mann Road, Laredo, TX Zip 78041–2699; tel. 956/723–1131; Benjamin Everett, Chief Executive Officer
Web address: www.columbia.net

EDINBURG REGIONAL MEDICAL CENTER (O, 163 beds) 333 West Freddy Gonzalez Drive, Edinburg, TX Zip 78539–6199; tel. 956/383–6211; Chris Smolik, Chief Executive Officer
Web address: www.uhsermc.com

GLEN OAKS HOSPITAL (O, 54 beds) 301 East Division, Greenville, TX Zip 75402; tel. 903/454–6000; Thomas E. Rourke, Administrator

MCALLEN MEDICAL CENTER (L, 455 beds) 301 West Expressway 83, McAllen, TX Zip 78503; tel. 956/632–4000; Daniel P. McLean, Executive Director
Web address: www.uhsmmc.com

MERIDELL ACHIEVEMENT CENTER (L, 78 beds) 12550 West Highway 29, Liberty Hill, TX Zip 78642, Mailing Address: P.O. Box 87, Zip 78642–0087; tel. 800/366–8656; Trish Mitchell, Chief Executive Officer

NORTHWEST TEXAS HEALTHCARE SYSTEM (O, 345 beds) 1501 South Coulter Avenue, Amarillo, TX Zip 79106–1790, Mailing Address: P.O. Box 1110, Zip 79175–1110; tel. 806/354–1000; Michael A. Callahan, Chief Executive Officer
Web address: www.nwths.com

RIVER CREST HOSPITAL (O, 80 beds) 1636 Hunters Glen Road, San Angelo, TX Zip 76901–5016; tel. 915/949–5722; Larry Grimes, Managing Director

TIMBERLAWN MENTAL HEALTH SYSTEM (O, 124 beds) 4600 Samuell Boulevard, Dallas, TX Zip 75228–6800, Mailing Address: P.O. Box 151489, Zip 75315–1489; tel. 214/381–7181; Debra S. Lowrance, R.N., Chief Executive Officer and Managing Director
Web address: www.timberlawn.com

WASHINGTON: AUBURN REGIONAL MEDICAL CENTER (O, 100 beds) 202 North Division, Plaza One, Auburn, WA Zip 98001–4908; tel. 253/833–7711; Michael M. Gherardini, Chief Executive Officer and Managing Director

Owned, leased, sponsored:	37 hospitals	5515 beds
Contract–managed:	0 hospitals	0 beds
Totals:	37 hospitals	5515 beds

0112: UNIVERSITY HOSPITALS HEALTH SYSTEM (NP)
11100 Euclid Avenue, Cleveland, OH Zip 44106–5000; tel. 216/844–1000; Farah M. Walters, President and Chief Executive Officer

OHIO: UHHS BEDFORD MEDICAL CENTER (O, 110 beds) 44 Blaine Avenue, Bedford, OH Zip 44146–2799; tel. 440/439–2000; Arlene A. Rak, R.N., President

UHHS BROWN MEMORIAL HOSPITAL (O, 51 beds) 158 West Main Road, Conneaut, OH Zip 44030–2039, Mailing Address: P.O. Box 648, Zip 44030–0648; tel. 440/593–1131; Gerard D. Klein, President

UHHS GEAUGA REGIONAL HOSPITAL (O, 126 beds) 13207 Ravenna Road, Chardon, OH Zip 44024–9012; tel. 440/269–6000; Richard J. Frenchie, President and Chief Executive Officer
Web address: www.uhhs.com/geauga/index.html

UHHS LAURELWOOD HOSPITAL (O, 70 beds) 35900 Euclid Avenue, Willoughby, OH Zip 44094–4648; tel. 440/953–3000; Farshid Afsarifard, Ph.D., President

UHHS–MEMORIAL HOSPITAL OF GENEVA (O, 35 beds) 870 West Main Street, Geneva, OH Zip 44041–1295; tel. 440/466–1141; Gerard D. Klein, Chief Executive Officer

UNIVERSITY HOSPITALS OF CLEVELAND (O, 747 beds) 11100 Euclid Avenue, Cleveland, OH Zip 44106–2602; tel. 216/844–1000; Farah M. Walters, President and Chief Executive Officer
Web address: www.uhhs.com/uhhs/eeauga/index.html

Owned, leased, sponsored:	6 hospitals	1139 beds
Contract–managed:	0 hospitals	0 beds
Totals:	6 hospitals	1139 beds

6405: UNIVERSITY OF CALIFORNIA–SYSTEMWIDE ADMINISTRATION (NP)
300 Lakeside Drive, 18th Floor, Oakland, CA Zip 94612–3550; tel. 510/987–9701; Cornelius L. Hopper, M.D., Vice President Health Affairs

CALIFORNIA: SANTA MONICA–UCLA MEDICAL CENTER (O, 221 beds) 1250 16th Street, Santa Monica, CA Zip 90404–1200; tel. 310/319–4000

UNIVERSITY OF CALIFORNIA LOS ANGELES MEDICAL CENTER (L, 650 beds) 10833 Le Conte Avenue, Los Angeles, CA Zip 90095–1730; tel. 310/825–9111; Michael Karpf, M.D., Vice Provost Hospital System and Director Medical Center
Web address: www.medctr.ucla.edu

For explanation of codes following names, see page B2.
★ Indicates Type III membership in the American Hospital Association.

Section B

UNIVERSITY OF CALIFORNIA LOS ANGELES NEUROPSYCHIATRIC HOSPITAL (O, 117 beds) 760 Westwood Plaza, Los Angeles, CA Zip 90095; tel. 310/825–0511; Fawzy I. Fawzy, M.D., Medical Director
Web address: www.npi.ucla.edu

UNIVERSITY OF CALIFORNIA SAN DIEGO MEDICAL CENTER (O, 439 beds) 200 West Arbor Drive, San Diego, CA Zip 92103–8970; tel. 619/543–6222; Sumiyo E. Kastelic, Director

UNIVERSITY OF CALIFORNIA, DAVIS MEDICAL CENTER (O, 448 beds) 2315 Stockton Boulevard, Sacramento, CA Zip 95817–2282; tel. 916/734–2011; Robert E. Chason, Interim Director

UNIVERSITY OF CALIFORNIA, IRVINE MEDICAL CENTER (O, 383 beds) 101 The City Drive, Orange, CA Zip 92668–3298; tel. 714/456–6011; Mark R. Laret, Director
Web address: www.ucihealth.com

Owned, leased, sponsored:	6 hospitals	2258 beds
Contract–managed:	0 hospitals	0 beds
Totals:	6 hospitals	2258 beds

★**0058:   UNIVERSITY OF CHICAGO HEALTH SYSTEM** (NP) 322 South Green Street, Suite 500, Chicago, IL Zip 60607; tel. 312/697–8403; Ralph W. Muller, Chief Executive Officer

ILLINOIS: LOUIS A. WEISS MEMORIAL HOSPITAL (O, 200 beds) 4646 North Marine Drive, Chicago, IL Zip 60640–1501; tel. 773/878–8700; Gregory A. Cierlik, President and Chief Executive Officer
Web address: www.weisshospital.org

UNIVERSITY OF CHICAGO HOSPITALS (O, 517 beds) 5841 South Maryland Avenue, Chicago, IL Zip 60637–1470; tel. 773/702–1000; Steven Lipstein, President and Chief Operating Officer

Owned, leased, sponsored:	2 hospitals	717 beds
Contract–managed:	0 hospitals	0 beds
Totals:	2 hospitals	717 beds

0021:   UNIVERSITY OF NEW MEXICO (NP) 915 Camino De Salud, Albuquerque, NM Zip 87131–0001; tel. 505/272–5849; R. Philip Eaton, M.D., Vice President Health Scences

NEW MEXICO: CARRIE TINGLEY HOSPITAL (O, 20 beds) 1127 University Boulevard N.E., Albuquerque, NM Zip 87102–1715; tel. 505/272–5200; Robert T. Maruca, Administrator

UNIVERSITY HOSPITAL (O, 271 beds) 2211 Lomas Boulevard N.E., Albuquerque, NM Zip 87106–2745; tel. 505/272–2121; Stephen W. McKernan, Chief Executive Officer
Web address: www.unm.edu

UNIVERSITY OF NEW MEXICO CHILDREN'S PSYCHIATRIC HOSPITAL (O, 55 beds) 1001 Yale Boulevard N.E., Albuquerque, NM Zip 87131–3830; tel. 505/272–2945; Christina B. Gunn, Chief Executive Officer
Web address: www.cph.unm.edu

UNIVERSITY OF NEW MEXICO MENTAL HEALTH CENTER (O, 60 beds) 2600 Marble N.E., Albuquerque, NM Zip 87131–2600; tel. 505/272–2263; Stephen W. McKernan, Chief Executive Officer
Web address: www.mhc.unm.edu

Owned, leased, sponsored:	4 hospitals	406 beds
Contract–managed:	0 hospitals	0 beds
Totals:	4 hospitals	406 beds

0168:   UNIVERSITY OF PENNSYLVANIA HEALTH SYSTEM (NP) 399 South 34th Street, 21st Floor, Philadelphia, PA Zip 19104–4385; tel. 215/662–2230; William N. Kelley, M.D., Chief Executive Officer

PENNSYLVANIA: HOSPITAL OF THE UNIVERSITY OF PENNSYLVANIA (O, 659 beds) 3400 Spruce Street, Philadelphia, PA Zip 19104–4204; tel. 215/662–4000; Thomas E. Beeman, Senior Vice President, Operations
Web address: www.upenn.edu

PENNSYLVANIA HOSPITAL (O, 346 beds) 800 Spruce Street, Philadelphia, PA Zip 19107–6192; tel. 215/829–3000; Timothy O. Morgan, Executive Director
Web address: www.pahosp.com

PHOENIXVILLE HOSPITAL OF THE UNIVERSITY OF PENNSYLVANIA HEALTH SYSTEM (O, 127 beds) 140 Nutt Road, Phoenixville, PA Zip 19460–0809, Mailing Address: P.O. Box 809, Zip 19460–0809; tel. 610/983–1000; Richard E. Seagrave, Executive Director and Chief Operating Officer

PRESBYTERIAN MEDICAL CENTER OF THE UNIVERSITY OF PENNSYLVANIA HEALTH SYSTEM (O, 325 beds) 51 North 39th Street, Philadelphia, PA Zip 19104–2640; tel. 215/662–8000; Michele M. Volpe, Executive Director
Web address: www.health.upenn.edu/pmc

Owned, leased, sponsored:	4 hospitals	1457 beds
Contract–managed:	0 hospitals	0 beds
Totals:	4 hospitals	1457 beds

0057:   UNIVERSITY OF SOUTH ALABAMA HOSPITALS (NP) 2451 Fillingim Street, Mobile, AL Zip 36617–2293; tel. 334/471–7000; Stephen H. Simmons, Senior Administrator

ALABAMA: USA CHILDREN'S AND WOMEN'S HOSPITAL (O, 131 beds) 1700 Center Street, Mobile, AL Zip 36604–3391; tel. 334/415–1000; Stanley K. Hammack, Administrator

UNIVERSITY OF SOUTH ALABAMA KNOLLWOOD PARK HOSPITAL (O, 150 beds) 5600 Girby Road, Mobile, AL Zip 36693–3398; tel. 334/660–5120; Thomas J. Gibson, Administrator

UNIVERSITY OF SOUTH ALABAMA MEDICAL CENTER (O, 316 beds) 2451 Fillingim Street, Mobile, AL Zip 36617–2293; tel. 334/471–7000; Stephen H. Simmons, Administrator

Owned, leased, sponsored:	3 hospitals	597 beds
Contract–managed:	0 hospitals	0 beds
Totals:	3 hospitals	597 beds

0033:   UNIVERSITY OF TEXAS SYSTEM (NP) 601 Colorado Street, Austin, TX Zip 78701–2982; tel. 512/499–4224; Charles B. Mullins, Executive Vice Chancellor

TEXAS: HARRIS COUNTY PSYCHIATRIC CENTER (O, 193 beds) 2800 South MacGregor Way, Houston, TX Zip 77021–1000, Mailing Address: P.O. Box 20249, Zip 77225–0249; tel. 713/741–5000; Robert W. Guynn, M.D., Executive Director
Web address: www.uth.tmc.edu

UNIVERSITY OF TEXAS HEALTH CENTER AT TYLER (O, 136 beds) 11937 Highway 271, Tyler, TX Zip 75708–3154; tel. 903/877–3451; Ronald F. Garvey, M.D., President

UNIVERSITY OF TEXAS M. D. ANDERSON CANCER CENTER (O, 437 beds) 1515 Holcombe Boulevard, Box 91, Houston, TX Zip 77030–4095; tel. 713/792–6000; John Mendelsohn, M.D., President and Chief Executive Officer
Web address: www.mdanderson.org

UNIVERSITY OF TEXAS MEDICAL BRANCH HOSPITALS (O, 894 beds) 301 University Boulevard, Galveston, TX Zip 77555–0138; tel. 409/772–1011; David S. Lopez, FACHE, Senior Executive Director
Web address: www.utmb.edu

Owned, leased, sponsored:	4 hospitals	1660 beds
Contract–managed:	0 hospitals	0 beds
Totals:	4 hospitals	1660 beds

0137:   UPMC HEALTH SYSTEM (NP) 200 Lothrop, Pittsburgh, PA Zip 15213; tel. 412/647–2345; Jeffrey A. Romoff, President

PENNSYLVANIA: UPMC BEAVER VALLEY (O, 104 beds) 2500 Hospital Drive, Aliquippa, PA Zip 15001–2123; tel. 724/857–1212; Thomas P. Timcho, President

For explanation of codes following names, see page B2.
★ Indicates Type III membership in the American Hospital Association.

Section B

UPMC BEDFORD MEMORIAL (O, 59 beds) 10455 Lincoln Highway, Everett, PA Zip 15537–7046; tel. 814/623–6161; James C. Vreeland, FACHE, President and Chief Executive Officer
Web address: www.bedford.org

UPMC BRADDOCK (O, 179 beds) 400 Holland Avenue, Braddock, PA Zip 15104–1599; tel. 412/636–5000; Margaret Priselac, R.N., Chief Operating Officer

UPMC HORIZON (O, 286 beds) Greenville, PA J. Larry Heinike, President and Chief Executive Officer
Web address: www.hhs.org

UPMC LEE REGIONAL (O, 224 beds) 320 Main Street, Johnstown, PA Zip 15901–1694; tel. 814/533–0123; David R. Davis, President and Chief Executive Officer
Web address: www.city page.com/lee

UPMC MCKEESPORT (O, 320 beds) 1500 Fifth Avenue, McKeesport, PA Zip 15132–2482; tel. 412/664–2000; Ronald H. Ott, President and Chief Executive Officer

UPMC PASSAVANT (O, 193 beds) 9100 Babcock Boulevard, Pittsburgh, PA Zip 15237–5815; tel. 412/367–6700; Raymond J. Beck, President and Chief Executive Officer

UPMC PRESBYTERIAN (O, 782 beds) Pittsburgh, PA Henry A. Mordoh, President
Web address: www.upmc.edu

UPMC SHADYSIDE (O, 508 beds) 5230 Centre Avenue, Pittsburgh, PA Zip 15232–1304; tel. 412/623–2121; Henry A. Mordoh, President
Web address: www.upmc.edu

UPMC SOUTH SIDE (O, 165 beds) 2000 Mary Street, Pittsburgh, PA Zip 15203–2095; tel. 412/488–5550; Marcie S. Caplan, Acting Chief Executive Officer
Web address: www.upmc.edu

UPMC ST. MARGARET (O, 223 beds) 815 Freeport Road, Pittsburgh, PA Zip 15215–3301; tel. 412/784–4000; Stanley J. Kevish, President

Owned, leased, sponsored:	11 hospitals	3043 beds
Contract–managed:	0 hospitals	0 beds
Totals:	11 hospitals	3043 beds

★0038: UPPER CHESAPEAKE HEALTH SYSTEM (NP)
1916 Belair Road, Fallston, MD Zip 21047–2797; tel. 410/893–0322; Lyle Ernest Sheldon, President and Chief Executive Officer

MARYLAND: FALLSTON GENERAL HOSPITAL (O, 113 beds) 200 Milton Avenue, Fallston, MD Zip 21047–2777; tel. 410/877–3700; Lyle Ernest Sheldon, President and Chief Executive Officer

HARFORD MEMORIAL HOSPITAL (O, 157 beds) 501 South Union Avenue, Havre De Grace, MD Zip 21078–3493; tel. 410/939–2400; Lyle Ernest Sheldon, President and Chief Executive Officer

Owned, leased, sponsored:	2 hospitals	270 beds
Contract–managed:	0 hospitals	0 beds
Totals:	2 hospitals	270 beds

★0043: VALLEY HEALTH SYSTEM (NP)
1117 East Devonshire Avenue, Hemet, CA Zip 92543; tel. 909/652–2811; John P. Lauri, Chief Executive Officer

CALIFORNIA: HEMET VALLEY MEDICAL CENTER (O, 285 beds) 1117 East Devonshire Avenue, Hemet, CA Zip 92543; tel. 909/652–2811; Barbara Taylor, R.N., Interim Administrator

MENIFEE VALLEY MEDICAL CENTER (O, 84 beds) 28400 McCall Boulevard, Sun City, CA Zip 92585–9537; tel. 909/679–8888; Susan Ballard, Administrator

MORENO VALLEY COMMUNITY HOSPITAL (O, 71 beds) 27300 Iris Avenue, Moreno Valley, CA Zip 92555; tel. 909/243–0811; Janice Ziomek, Administrator

Owned, leased, sponsored:	3 hospitals	440 beds
Contract–managed:	0 hospitals	0 beds
Totals:	3 hospitals	440 beds

0128: VALLEY HEALTH SYSTEM (IO)
1840 Amherst Street, Winchester, VA Zip 22604, Mailing Address: P.O. Box 3340, Zip 22604–1334; tel. 540/722–8024; Michael J. Halseth, President and Chief Executive Officer

VIRGINIA: WARREN MEMORIAL HOSPITAL (O, 95 beds) 1000 Shenandoah Avenue, Front Royal, VA Zip 22630–3598; tel. 540/636–0300; Charlie M. Horton, President

WINCHESTER MEDICAL CENTER (O, 376 beds) 1840 Amherst Street, Winchester, VA Zip 22601–2540, Mailing Address: P.O. Box 3340, Zip 22604–3340; tel. 540/722–8000; George B. Caley, President
Web address: www.valleyhealthlink.com

WEST VIRGINIA: MORGAN COUNTY WAR MEMORIAL HOSPITAL (C, 44 beds) 1124 Fairfax Street, Berkeley Springs, WV Zip 25411–1718; tel. 304/258–1234; David A. Sweeney, FACHE, Administrator

Owned, leased, sponsored:	2 hospitals	471 beds
Contract–managed:	1 hospital	44 beds
Totals:	3 hospitals	515 beds

0097: VALLEYCARE HEALTH SYSTEM (NP)
5575 West Las Positas Boulevard, 300, Pleasanton, CA Zip 94588; tel. 925/447–7000; Marcy Feit, Chief Executive Officer

CALIFORNIA: VALLEYCARE MEDICAL CENTER (O, 68 beds) 5555 West Positas Boulevard, Pleasanton, CA Zip 94588, Mailing Address: 555 West Los Positas Boulevard, Zip 94588; tel. 925/847–3000; Marcy Feit, Chief Executive Officer

VALLEYCARE MEMORIAL HOSPITAL (O, 110 beds) 1111 East Stanley Boulevard, Livermore, CA Zip 94550; tel. 925/447–7000; Marcelina Feit, President and Chief Executive Officer

Owned, leased, sponsored:	2 hospitals	178 beds
Contract–managed:	0 hospitals	0 beds
Totals:	2 hospitals	178 beds

0081: VALUEMARK HEALTHCARE SYSTEMS, INC. (IO)
300 Galleria Parkway, Suite 650, Atlanta, GA Zip 30339; tel. 770/933–5500; James T. McAfee Jr., Chairman, President and Chief Executive Officer

PINE GROVE HOSPITAL (O, 62 beds) 7011 Shoup Avenue, Canoga Park, CA Zip 91307; tel. 818/348–0500; Stacey Gentry–Young, Chief Executive Officer

FLORIDA: VALUEMARK BEHAVIORAL HEALTHCARE SYSTEM OF FLORIDA (O, 52 beds) 6601 Central Florida Parkway, Orlando, FL Zip 32821–8091; tel. 407/345–5000; Robert Berteau, Chief Executive Officer

GEORGIA: VALUEMARK–BRAWNER BEHAVIORAL HEALTHACARE SYSTEM–NORTH (O, 108 beds) 3180 Atlanta Street S.E., Smyrna, GA Zip 30080–8256; tel. 404/436–0081; Edward J. Osborne, Chief Executive Officer

MISSOURI: VALUEMARK BEHAVIORAL HEALTHCARE SYSTEM OF KANSAS CITY (O, 72 beds) 4800 N.W. 88th Street, Kansas City, MO Zip 64154–2757; tel. 816/436–3900; John Hunter, Chief Executive Officer

VIRGINIA: VALUEMARK WEST END BEHAVIORAL HEALTHCARE SYSTEM (O, 84 beds) 12800 West Creek Parkway, Richmond, VA Zip 23238–1116; tel. 804/784–2200; James D. McBeath, Chief Executive Officer

Owned, leased, sponsored:	5 hospitals	378 beds
Contract–managed:	0 hospitals	0 beds
Totals:	5 hospitals	378 beds

For explanation of codes following names, see page B2.
★ Indicates Type III membership in the American Hospital Association.

Section B

0026: VENCOR, INCORPORATED (IO)

1 Vernon Place, 680 S. 4th Avenue, Louisville, KY Zip 40202–2412; tel. 502/596–7300; Edward L. Kuntz, Board Chairman, President and Chief Executive Officer

ARIZONA: VENCOR HOSPITAL – TUCSON (O, 51 beds) 355 North Wilmot Road, Tucson, AZ Zip 85711–2635; tel. 520/747–8200; Kevin Christiansen, Administrator

VENCOR HOSPITAL–PHOENIX (O, 58 beds) 40 East Indianola Avenue, Phoenix, AZ Zip 85012–2059; tel. 602/280–7000; John L. Harrington Jr., FACHE, Administrator

CALIFORNIA: RECOVERY INN OF MENLO PARK (O, 16 beds) 570 Willow Road, Menlo Park, CA Zip 94025; tel. 415/324–8500; Carole Wilson, Administrator

VENCOR HOSPITAL–BREA (O, 48 beds) 875 North Brea Boulevard, Brea, CA Zip 92821; tel. 714/529–6842; Mindy S. Moore, Administrator

VENCOR HOSPITAL–LOS ANGELES (O, 81 beds) 5525 West Slauson Avenue, Los Angeles, CA Zip 90056; tel. 310/642–0325; Theresa Hamilton, Chief Executive Officer

VENCOR HOSPITAL–ONTARIO (O, 100 beds) 550 North Monterey, Ontario, CA Zip 91764; tel. 909/391–0333; Virgis Narbutas, Administrator

VENCOR HOSPITAL–SACRAMENTO (O, 32 beds) 223 Fargo Way, Folsom, CA Zip 95630; tel. 916/351–9151; Meredith Taylor, Administrator

VENCOR HOSPITAL–SAN DIEGO (O, 70 beds) 1940 El Cajon Boulevard, San Diego, CA Zip 92104; tel. 619/543–4500; Michael D. Cress, Administrator

VENCOR HOSPITAL–SAN LEANDRO (O, 58 beds) 2800 Benedict Drive, San Leandro, CA Zip 94577; tel. 510/357–8300; Wayne M. Lingenfelter, Ed.D., Administrator and Chief Executive Officer

FLORIDA: VENCOR HOSPITAL – CENTRAL TAMPA (O, 102 beds) 4801 North Howard Avenue, Tampa, FL Zip 33603–1484; tel. 813/874–7575; Ken Stone, Administrator

VENCOR HOSPITAL–CORAL GABLES (O, 53 beds) 5190 S.W. Eighth Street, Coral Gables, FL Zip 33134–2495; tel. 305/445–1364; Theodore Welding, Chief Executive Officer

VENCOR HOSPITAL–FORT LAUDERDALE (O, 64 beds) 1516 East Las Olas Boulevard, Fort Lauderdale, FL Zip 33301–2399; tel. 954/764–8900; Lewis A. Ransdell, Administrator
Web address: www.vencor.com

VENCOR HOSPITAL–ST PETERSBURG (O, 60 beds) 3030 Sixth Street South, Saint Petersburg, FL Zip 33705–3720; tel. 727/894–8719; Pamela M. Riter, R.N., Administrator

VENCOR HOSPITAL–TAMPA (O, 73 beds) 4555 South Manhattan Avenue, Tampa, FL Zip 33611–2397; tel. 813/839–6341; Theresa Hunkins, Administrator

VENCOR–NORTH FLORIDA (O, 60 beds) 801 Oak Street, Green Cove Springs, FL Zip 32043–4317; tel. 904/284–9230; Tim Simpson, Administrator

GEORGIA: VENCOR HOSPITAL–ATLANTA (O, 70 beds) 705 Juniper Street N.E., Atlanta, GA Zip 30365–2500; tel. 404/873–2871; Skip Wright, Administrator

ILLINOIS: VENCOR HOSPITAL–CHICAGO CENTRAL (O, 76 beds) 4058 West Melrose Street, Chicago, IL Zip 60641–4797; tel. 773/736–7000; Richard Cerceo, Administrator
Web address: www.vencor.com

VENCOR HOSPITAL–CHICAGO NORTH (O, 111 beds) 2544 West Montrose Avenue, Chicago, IL Zip 60618–1589; tel. 773/267–2622; Susan Legg, Administrator

VENCOR HOSPITAL–SYCAMORE (O, 50 beds) 225 Edward Street, Sycamore, IL Zip 60178–2197; tel. 815/895–2144; Betty Walker, Administrator

INDIANA: VENCOR HOSPITAL–LAGRANGE (O, 53 beds) 207 North Townline Road, LaGrange, IN Zip 46761–1325; tel. 219/463–2143; Joe Murrell, Administrator

KENTUCKY: VENCOR HOSPITAL–LOUISVILLE (O, 156 beds) 1313 St. Anthony Place, Louisville, KY Zip 40204–1765; tel. 502/587–7001; James H. Wesp, Administrator

LOUISIANA: VENCOR HOSPITAL – NEW ORLEANS (O, 78 beds) 3601 Coliseum Street, New Orleans, LA Zip 70115–3606; tel. 504/899–1555; John R. Watkins, Chief Executive Officer

MASSACHUSETTS: VENCOR HOSPITAL NORTH SHORE (O, 50 beds) 15 King Street, Peabody, MA Zip 01960–4268; tel. 978/531–2900; Steven E. Levitsky, Administrator

VENCOR HOSPITAL–BOSTON (O, 52 beds) 1515 Commonwealth Avenue, Boston, MA Zip 02135–3696; tel. 617/254–1100; Donald E. Schwarz, Administrator

MICHIGAN: VENCOR HOSPITAL–METRO DETROIT (O, 114 beds) 2700 Martin Luther King Boulevard, Detroit, MI Zip 48208; tel. 313/594–6000; Deborah A. Sopo, Administrator
Web address: www.vencor.com

MINNESOTA: VENCOR HOSPITAL–MINNEAPOLIS (O, 111 beds) 4101 Golden Valley Road, Golden Valley, MN Zip 55422; tel. 612/588–2750; Thomas N. Theroult, Administrator

MISSOURI: VENCOR HOSPITAL–KANSAS CITY (O, 110 beds) 8701 Troost Avenue, Kansas City, MO Zip 64131–3495; tel. 816/995–2000; Robert F. Berry, Administrator

NEVADA: VENCOR HOSPITAL–LAS VEGAS (O, 52 beds) 5100 West Sahara Avenue, Las Vegas, NV Zip 89102–3436; tel. 702/871–1418

NEW MEXICO: VENCOR HOSPITAL – ALBUQUERQUE (O, 58 beds) 700 High Street N.E., Albuquerque, NM Zip 87102–2565; tel. 505/242–4444; Jeanne Koester, Chief Executive Officer

NORTH CAROLINA: VENCOR HOSPITAL–GREENSBORO (O, 124 beds) 2401 Southside Boulevard, Greensboro, NC Zip 27406–3311; tel. 336/271–2800; Leanne Fiorentino, Chief Executive Officer

PENNSYLVANIA: VENCOR HOSPITAL–PHILADELPHIA (O, 52 beds) 6129 Palmetto Street, Philadelphia, PA Zip 19111–5729; tel. 215/722–8555; Debra Condon, Administrator

VENCOR HOSPITAL–PITTSBURGH (O, 63 beds) 7777 Steubenville Pike, Oakdale, PA Zip 15071–3409; tel. 412/494–5500; Patricia B. Speak, Administrator

TENNESSEE: VENCOR HOSPITAL–CHATTANOOGA (O, 43 beds) 709 Walnut Street, Chattanooga, TN Zip 37402–1961; tel. 423/266–7721; Steven E. McGraw, Administrator

TEXAS: VENCOR ARLINGTON, TEXAS (O, 80 beds) 1000 North Cooper Street, Arlington, TX Zip 76011–5540; tel. 817/543–0200

VENCOR HOSPITAL – DALLAS (O, 76 beds) 9525 Greenville Avenue, Dallas, TX Zip 75243; tel. 214/355–2600; Dorothy J. Elford, Executive Director and Administrator

VENCOR HOSPITAL–FORT WORTH SOUTHWEST (O, 80 beds) 7800 Oakmont Boulevard, Fort Worth, TX Zip 76132–4299; tel. 817/346–0094; Robert L. McNew, Administrator

VENCOR HOSPITAL–HOUSTON (O, 94 beds) 6441 Main Street, Houston, TX Zip 77030–1596; tel. 713/790–0500; Bob Stein, Executive Director
Web address: www.vencor.com

VENCOR HOSPITAL–MANSFIELD (O, 115 beds) 1802 Highway 157 North, Mansfield, TX Zip 76063–9555; tel. 817/473–6101; Bill Grey, Administrator

VIRGINIA: NORTHERN VIRGINIA COMMUNITY HOSPITAL (O, 175 beds) 601 South Carlin Springs Road, Arlington, VA Zip 22204–1096; tel. 703/671–1200; Mark Aanonson, Administrator
Web address: www.vencorhospital–arlington.com

WASHINGTON: VENCOR HOSPITAL SEATTLE (O, 49 beds) 10560 Fifth Avenue N.E., Seattle, WA Zip 98125–0977; tel. 206/364–2050; Jim Steinruck, CHE, Administrator and Chief Executive Officer
Web address: www.vencor.com

WISCONSIN: VENCOR HOSPITAL–MILWAUKEE (O, 34 beds) 5017 South 110th Street, Greenfield, WI Zip 53228; tel. 414/427–8282; Daniel R. West, Administrator

VENCOR HOSPITAL–MILWAUKEE (O, 60 beds) 5700 West Layton Avenue, Milwaukee, WI Zip 53202; tel. 414/325–5900; E. Kay Gray, Interim Administrator

Owned, leased, sponsored:	42 hospitals	3112 beds
Contract–managed:	0 hospitals	0 beds
Totals:	42 hospitals	3112 beds

For explanation of codes following names, see page B2.
★ Indicates Type III membership in the American Hospital Association.

5435: VIA CHRISTI HEALTH SYSTEM (CC)
818 North Emporia, Wichita, KS Zip 67214–3725;
tel. 316/268–5000; LeRoy E. Rheault, President and Chief Executive
Officer

CALIFORNIA: ST. ROSE HOSPITAL (O, 175 beds) 27200 Calaroga Avenue,
Hayward, CA Zip 94545–4383; tel. 510/264–4000; Michael P. Mahoney,
President and Chief Executive Officer

KANSAS: MERCY HEALTH CENTER OF MANHATTAN (O, 99 beds) 1823
College Avenue, Manhattan, KS Zip 66502–3381; tel. 785/776–3322;
Richard L. Allen, President and Chief Executive Officer

MOUNT CARMEL MEDICAL CENTER (O, 126 beds) 1102 East Centennial,
Pittsburg, KS Zip 66762–6686; tel. 316/231–6100; John Daniel Lingor,
President and Chief Executive Officer

VIA CHRISTI REGIONAL MEDICAL CENTER (O, 913 beds) 929 North St.
Francis Street, Wichita, KS Zip 67214–3882; tel. 316/268–5000; Randall G.
Nyp, President and Chief Executive Officer
Web address: www.via–christi.org

OKLAHOMA: ST. JOSEPH REGIONAL MEDICAL CENTER OF NORTHERN
OKLAHOMA (O, 90 beds) 14th Street and Hartford Avenue, Ponca City, OK
Zip 74601–2035, Mailing Address: Box 1270, Zip 74602–1270;
tel. 580/765–3321; Garry L. England, President and Chief Executive
Officer

Owned, leased, sponsored:	5 hospitals	1403 beds
Contract–managed:	0 hospitals	0 beds
Totals:	5 hospitals	1403 beds

★0046: VIA HEALTH (NP)
150 North Chestnut, Rochester, NY Zip 14604; tel. 716/922–3000;
Roger S. Hunt, President and Chief Executive Officer

NEW YORK: GENESEE HOSPITAL (O, 325 beds) 224 Alexander Street,
Rochester, NY Zip 14607–4055; tel. 716/263–6000; William R. Holman,
President

ROCHESTER GENERAL HOSPITAL (O, 476 beds) 1425 Portland Avenue,
Rochester, NY Zip 14621–3099; tel. 716/338–4000; Richard S. Constantino,
M.D., President
Web address: www.viahealth.org/

VIAHEALTH OF WAYNE (O, 267 beds) Driving Park Avenue, Newark, NY
Zip 14513, Mailing Address: P.O. Box 111, Zip 14513–0111;
tel. 315/332–2022; W. Neil Stroman, President

Owned, leased, sponsored:	3 hospitals	1068 beds
Contract–managed:	0 hospitals	0 beds
Totals:	3 hospitals	1068 beds

0012: VIRGINIA DEPARTMENT OF MENTAL HEALTH (NP)
1220 Bank Street, Richmond, VA Zip 23219–3623, Mailing Address:
P.O. Box 1797, Zip 23218–1797; tel. 804/786–3921; Richard E.
Kellogg, Acting Commissioner

VIRGINIA: CATAWBA HOSPITAL (O, 171 beds) Catawba, VA Mailing Address:
P.O. Box 200, Zip 24070–0200; tel. 540/375–4200; James S. Reinhard,
M.D., Director

CENTRAL STATE HOSPITAL (O, 516 beds) 26317 West Washington Street,
Petersburg, VA Zip 23803, Mailing Address: P.O. Box 4030,
Zip 23803–4030; tel. 804/524–7000; Larry L. Latham, Director

CENTRAL VIRGINIA TRAINING CENTER (O, 1112 beds) 210 East Colony Road,
Madison Heights, VA Zip 24572–2005, Mailing Address: P.O. Box 1098,
Lynchburg, Zip 24505–1098; tel. 804/947–6326; Judy Dudley, Director

DE JARNETTE CENTER (O, 48 beds) 1355 Richmond Road, Staunton, VA
Zip 24401–1091, Mailing Address: Box 2309, Zip 24402–2309;
tel. 540/332–2100; Andrea C. Newsome, FACHE, Director

EASTERN STATE HOSPITAL (O, 581 beds) Williamsburg, VA Mailing Address:
P.O. Box 8791, Zip 23187–8791; tel. 757/253–5161; John M. Favret,
Director

NORTHERN VIRGINIA MENTAL HEALTH INSTITUTE (O, 62 beds) 3302 Gallows
Road, Falls Church, VA Zip 22042–3398; tel. 703/207–7110; John Russotto,
Facility Director

PIEDMONT GERIATRIC HOSPITAL (O, 210 beds) Burkeville, VA Mailing
Address: P.O. Box 427, Zip 23922–0427; tel. 804/767–4401; Willard R.
Pierce Jr., Director

SOUTHERN VIRGINIA MENTAL HEALTH INSTITUTE (O, 96 beds) 382 Taylor
Drive, Danville, VA Zip 24541–4023; tel. 804/799–6220; Constance N.
Fletcher, Ph.D., Director

SOUTHWESTERN VIRGINIA MENTAL HEALTH INSTITUTE (O, 266 beds) 502
East Main Street, Marion, VA Zip 24354–3390; tel. 540/783–1200; Gerald
E. Deans, Director

WESTERN STATE HOSPITAL (O, 369 beds) 1301 Richmond Avenue, Staunton,
VA Zip 24401–9146, Mailing Address: P.O. Box 2500, Zip 24402–2500;
tel. 540/332–8000; Lynwood F. Harding, Director

Owned, leased, sponsored:	10 hospitals	3431 beds
Contract–managed:	0 hospitals	0 beds
Totals:	10 hospitals	3431 beds

★6725: VIRTUA HEALTH (NP)
94 Brick Road, Suite 200, Marlton, NJ Zip 08053;
tel. 609/355–0005; Richard P. Miller, President and Chief Executive
Officer

NEW JERSEY: VIRTUA–MEMORIAL HOSPITAL BURLINGTON COUNTY (O, 348
beds) 175 Madison Avenue, Mount Holly, NJ Zip 08060–2099;
tel. 609/267–0700; Donald I. Brunn, President and Chief Executive Officer
Web address: www.virtua.org

WEST JERSEY HOSPITAL–BERLIN (O, 79 beds) 100 Townsend Avenue, Berlin,
NJ Zip 08009–9035; tel. 609/322–3100; Ellen Guarnieri, Executive Director

WEST JERSEY HOSPITAL–CAMDEN (O, 94 beds) 1000 Atlantic Avenue,
Camden, NJ Zip 08104–1595; tel. 609/246–3000; Carolyn M. Ballard,
Executive Director

WEST JERSEY HOSPITAL–MARLTON (O, 177 beds) 90 Brick Road, Marlton,
NJ Zip 08053–9697; tel. 609/355–6000; Leroy J. Rosenberg, Executive
Director
Web address: www.wjhs.org

WEST JERSEY HOSPITAL–VOORHEES (O, 244 beds) 101 Carnie Boulevard,
Voorhees, NJ Zip 08043–1597; tel. 609/325–3000; Joan T. Meyers, R.N.,
Executive Director
Web address: www.wjhs.org

Owned, leased, sponsored:	5 hospitals	942 beds
Contract–managed:	0 hospitals	0 beds
Totals:	5 hospitals	942 beds

★0995: WELLSTAR HEALTH SYSTEM (NP)
805 Sandy Plains Road, Marietta, GA Zip 30066;
tel. 770/792–5012; Thomas E. Hill, Chief Executive Officer

GEORGIA: WELLSTAR COBB HOSPITAL (O, 311 beds) 3950 Austell Road,
Austell, GA Zip 30106–1121; tel. 770/732–4000; Thomas E. Hill, Chief
Executive Officer
Web address: www.promina.org

WELLSTAR DOUGLAS HOSPITAL (O, 98 beds) 8954 Hospital Drive,
Douglasville, GA Zip 30134–2282; tel. 770/949–1500; Thomas E. Hill, Chief
Executive Officer
Web address: www.promina.org

WELLSTAR KENNESTONE HOSPITAL (O, 439 beds) 677 Church Street,
Marietta, GA Zip 30060–1148; tel. 770/793–5000; Thomas E. Hill, Chief
Executive Officer

WELLSTAR PAULDING HOSPITAL (O, 208 beds) 600 West Memorial Drive,
Dallas, GA Zip 30132–1335; tel. 770/445–4411; Thomas E. Hill, Chief
Executive Officer

WELLSTAR WINDY HILL HOSPITAL (O, 100 beds) 2540 Windy Hill Road,
Marietta, GA Zip 30067–8632; tel. 770/644–1000; Thomas E. Hill, Chief
Executive Officer

Owned, leased, sponsored:	5 hospitals	1156 beds
Contract–managed:	0 hospitals	0 beds
Totals:	5 hospitals	1156 beds

Section B

For explanation of codes following names, see page B2.
★ Indicates Type III membership in the American Hospital Association.

★0004: WEST TENNESSEE HEALTHCARE (NP)
708 West Forest Avenue, Jackson, TN Zip 38301–3901;
tel. 901/425–5000; James T. Moss, President

TENNESSEE: BOLIVAR GENERAL HOSPITAL (O, 47 beds) 650 Nuckolls Road, Bolivar, TN Zip 38008–1500; tel. 901/658–3100; George L. Austin, Administrator

CAMDEN GENERAL HOSPITAL (O, 34 beds) 175 Hospital Drive, Camden, TN Zip 38320–1617; tel. 901/584–6135; John M. Carruth, Administrator

GIBSON GENERAL HOSPITAL (O, 42 beds) 200 Hospital Drive, Trenton, TN Zip 38382–3300; tel. 901/855–7900; Kelly R. Yenawine, Administrator
Web address: www.wth.net

HUMBOLDT GENERAL HOSPITAL (O, 46 beds) 3525 Chere Carol Road, Humboldt, TN Zip 38343–3699; tel. 901/784–0301; Bill Kail, Administrator
Web address: www.wth.net

JACKSON–MADISON COUNTY GENERAL HOSPITAL (O, 567 beds) 708 West Forest Avenue, Jackson, TN Zip 38301–3855; tel. 901/425–5000; James T. Moss, President and Chief Executive Officer

MILAN GENERAL HOSPITAL (O, 62 beds) 4039 South Highland, Milan, TN Zip 38358; tel. 901/686–1591; Alfred P. Taylor, Administrator and Chief Executive Officer

PATHWAYS OF TENNESSEE (O, 57 beds) 238 Summar Drive, Jackson, TN Zip 38301–3982; tel. 901/935–8200; John D. Rudnick Jr., FACHE, Executive Director

Owned, leased, sponsored:	7 hospitals	855 beds
Contract–managed:	0 hospitals	0 beds
Totals:	7 hospitals	855 beds

0119: WEST VIRGINIA UNITED HEALTH SYSTEM (NP)
1000 Technology Drive, Suite 2320, Fairmont, WV Zip 26554; tel. 304/368–2700; Bernard G. Westfall, President and Chief Executive Officer

WEST VIRGINIA: BROADDUS HOSPITAL (O, 72 beds) College Hill, Philippi, WV Zip 26416–1051; tel. 304/457–1760; Susannah Higgins, Chief Executive Officer

DAVIS MEMORIAL HOSPITAL (O, 115 beds) Gorman Avenue and Reed Street, Elkins, WV Zip 26241, Mailing Address: P.O. Box 1484, Zip 26241–1484; tel. 304/636–3300; Robert L. Hammer II, Chief Executive Officer
Web address: www.davishealthcare.com

UNITED HOSPITAL CENTER (O, 360 beds) Route 19 South, Clarksburg, WV Zip 26301, Mailing Address: P.O. Box 1680, Zip 26302–1680; tel. 304/624–2121; Bruce C. Carter, President
Web address: www.uhcwv.org

WEST VIRGINIA UNIVERSITY HOSPITALS (O, 401 beds) Medical Center Drive, Morgantown, WV Zip 26506–4749; tel. 304/598–4000; Bruce McClymonds, President
Web address: www.wvhealth.wvu.edu

Owned, leased, sponsored:	4 hospitals	948 beds
Contract–managed:	0 hospitals	0 beds
Totals:	4 hospitals	948 beds

★6745: WHEATON FRANCISCAN SERVICES, INC. (CC)
26W171 Roosevelt Road, Wheaton, IL Zip 60189–0667, Mailing Address: P.O. Box 667, Zip 60189–0667; tel. 630/462–9271; Wilfred F. Loebig Jr., President and Chief Executive Officer

ILLINOIS: MARIANJOY REHABILITATION HOSPITAL AND CLINICS (O, 110 beds) 26 West 171 Roosevelt Road, Wheaton, IL Zip 60187–0795, Mailing Address: P.O. Box 795, Zip 60189–0795; tel. 630/462–4000; Kathleen C. Yosko, President and Chief Executive Officer

OAK PARK HOSPITAL (O, 176 beds) 520 South Maple Avenue, Oak Park, IL Zip 60304–1097; tel. 708/383–9300; Bruce M. Elegant, President and Chief Executive Officer

IOWA: COVENANT MEDICAL CENTER (O, 293 beds) 3421 West Ninth Street, Waterloo, IA Zip 50702–5499; tel. 319/272–8000; Raymond F. Burfeind, President

MERCY HOSPITAL OF FRANCISCAN SISTERS (O, 64 beds) 201 Eighth Avenue S.E., Oelwein, IA Zip 50662–2447; tel. 319/283–6000; Richard Schrupp, President and Chief Executive Officer

SARTORI MEMORIAL HOSPITAL (O, 87 beds) 515 College Street, Cedar Falls, IA Zip 50613–2599; tel. 319/268–3000; Daniel J. Woods, Chief Executive Officer

WISCONSIN: ELMBROOK MEMORIAL HOSPITAL (O, 136 beds) 19333 West North Avenue, Brookfield, WI Zip 53045–4198; tel. 414/785–2000; Kimry A. Johnsrud, President

SAINT MARY'S MEDICAL CENTER (O, 179 beds) 3801 Spring Street, Racine, WI Zip 53405–1690; tel. 414/636–4011; Kenneth R. Buser, President

ST. CATHERINE'S HOSPITAL (O, 148 beds) 3556 Seventh Avenue, Kenosha, WI Zip 53140–2595; tel. 414/656–2011; Richard O. Schmidt Jr., President and Chief Executive Officer

ST. ELIZABETH HOSPITAL (S, 155 beds) 1506 South Oneida Street, Appleton, WI Zip 54915–1397; tel. 920/738–2000; Otto L. Cox, President

ST. FRANCIS HOSPITAL (S, 260 beds) 3237 South 16th Street, Milwaukee, WI Zip 53215–4592; tel. 414/647–5000; Gregory A. Banaszynski, President

ST. JOSEPH'S HOSPITAL (O, 484 beds) 5000 West Chambers Street, Milwaukee, WI Zip 53210–9988; tel. 414/447–2000; Patricia A. Kaldor, R.N., President
Web address: www.covhealth.org

ST. LUKE'S MEMORIAL HOSPITAL (O, 187 beds) 1320 Wisconsin Avenue, Racine, WI Zip 53403–1987; tel. 414/636–2011; Kenneth R. Buser, President

ST. MICHAEL HOSPITAL (O, 212 beds) 2400 West Villard Avenue, Milwaukee, WI Zip 53209–4999; tel. 414/527–8000; Jeffrey K. Jenkins, President

Owned, leased, sponsored:	13 hospitals	2491 beds
Contract–managed:	0 hospitals	0 beds
Totals:	13 hospitals	2491 beds

★9575: WILLIAM BEAUMONT HOSPITAL CORPORATION (NP)
3601 West Thirteen Mile Road, Royal Oak, MI Zip 48073–6769; tel. 248/551–5000; Ted D. Wasson, President and Chief Executive Officer

MICHIGAN: WILLIAM BEAUMONT HOSPITAL–ROYAL OAK (O, 869 beds) 3601 West Thirteen Mile Road, Royal Oak, MI Zip 48073–6769; tel. 248/551–5000; John D. Labriola, Senior Vice President and Hospital Director
Web address: www.beaumont.edu

WILLIAM BEAUMONT HOSPITAL–TROY (O, 189 beds) 44201 Dequindre Road, Troy, MI Zip 48098–1198; tel. 248/828–5100; Eugene F. Michalski, Vice President and Director
Web address: www.beaumont.edu

Owned, leased, sponsored:	2 hospitals	1058 beds
Contract–managed:	0 hospitals	0 beds
Totals:	2 hospitals	1058 beds

★0157: YALE NEW HAVEN HEALTH SYSTEM (NP)
789 Howard Avenue, New Haven, CT Zip 06519; tel. 203/688–2608; Joseph A. Zaccagnino, President and Chief Executive Officer

For explanation of codes following names, see page B2.
★ Indicates Type III membership in the American Hospital Association.

CONNECTICUT: BRIDGEPORT HOSPITAL (O, 346 beds) 267 Grant Street, Bridgeport, CT Zip 06610–2875, Mailing Address: P.O. Box 5000, Zip 06610–0120; tel. 203/384–3000; Robert J. Trefry, President and Chief Executive Officer

GREENWICH HOSPITAL (O, 160 beds) 5 Perryridge Road, Greenwich, CT Zip 06830–4697; tel. 203/863–3000; Frank A. Corvino, President and Chief Executive Officer
Web address: www.greenhosp.chime.org

YALE–NEW HAVEN HOSPITAL (O, 735 beds) 20 York Street, New Haven, CT Zip 06504–3202; tel. 203/688–4242; Joseph A. Zaccagnino, President and Chief Executive Officer
Web address: www.ynhh.org

Owned, leased, sponsored:	3 hospitals	1241 beds
Contract–managed:	0 hospitals	0 beds
Totals:	3 hospitals	1241 beds

For explanation of codes following names, see page B2.
★ Indicates Type III membership in the American Hospital Association.

Section B

Headquarters of Health Care Systems

ALABAMA

Birmingham: 0345 ★ BAPTIST HEALTH SYSTEM Mailing Address: P.O. Box 830605, Zip 35283–0605; tel. 205/715–5319; Dennis A. Hall, President, p. B63

2455 BRADFORD HEALTH SERVICES 2101 Magnolia Avenue South, Suite 518, Zip 35205; tel. 205/251–7753; Jerry W. Crowder, President and Chief Executive Officer, p. B68

0126 CARRAWAY METHODIST HEALTH SYSTEM 1600 Carraway Boulevard, Zip 35234–1990; tel. 205/502–6000; Robert M. Carraway, M.D., Chairman and Chief Executive Officer, p. B72

0100 ★ EASTERN HEALTH SYSTEM, INC. 48 Medical Park East Drive, 450, Zip 35235; tel. 205/838–3999; Robert C. Chapman, FACHE, President and Chief Executive Officer, p. B95

0023 HEALTHSOUTH CORPORATION One Healthsouth Parkway, Zip 35243; tel. 205/967–7116; Anthony J. Tanner, Executive Vice President, p. B101

Brewton: 1255 ESCAMBIA COUNTY HEALTH CARE AUTHORITY 1301 Belleville Avenue, Zip 36426; tel. 334/368–2500; Phillip L. Parker, Administrator, p. B95

Florence: 0152 ★ COFFEE HEALTH GROUP 205 Marengo Street, Zip 35630–6033; tel. 256/768–9191; Richard H. Peck, President and Chief Executive Officer, p. B78

Guntersville: 1975 MARSHALL COUNTY HEALTH CARE AUTHORITY 8000 Alabama Highway 69, Zip 35976; tel. 205/753–8000; Julian Sparks, Board Chairman, p. B113

Mobile: 2025 INFIRMARY HEALTH SYSTEM, INC. 3 Mobile Infirmary Circle, Zip 36607–3520; tel. 334/435–5500; E. Chandler Bramlett Jr., President and Chief Executive Officer, p. B105

0057 UNIVERSITY OF SOUTH ALABAMA HOSPITALS 2451 Fillingim Street, Zip 36617–2293; tel. 334/471–7000; Stephen H. Simmons, Senior Administrator, p. B152

Montgomery: 0150 BAPTIST HEALTH 2105 East South Boulevard, Zip 36116–2498; tel. 334/286–2970; Michael D. DeBoer, President and Chief Executive Officer, p. B63

Tuscaloosa: 1825 ★ DCH HEALTH SYSTEM 809 University Boulevard East, Zip 35401; tel. 205/759–7111; Bryan Kindred, President and Chief Executive Officer, p. B87

ARIZONA

Phoenix: 8810 ★ BAPTIST HOSPITALS AND HEALTH SYSTEMS, INC. 2224 West Northern Avenue, Suite D–300, Zip 85021–4987; tel. 602/864–1184; Gerald L. Wissink, President and Chief Executive Officer, p. B64

0034 ★ PMH HEALTH RESOURCES, INC. 1201 South Seventh Avenue, Zip 85007–3913, Mailing Address: P.O. Box 21207, Zip 85036–1207; tel. 602/824–3321; Reginald M. Ballantyne III, President, p. B125

2535 ★ SAMARITAN HEALTH SYSTEM 1441 North 12th Street, Zip 85006–2666; tel. 602/495–4000; James C. Crews, President and Chief Executive Officer, p. B134

Scottsdale: 0164 DOCTORS COMMUNITY HEALTHCARE CORPORATION 6730 North Scottsdale Road, Suite 200, Zip 85253; tel. 602/348–9800; Melvin Redman, President and Chief Operating Officer, p. B94

0037 ★ SCOTTSDALE HEALTHCARE 3621 Wells Fargo Avenue, Zip 85251–5607; tel. 602/481–4324; Max Poll, President and Chief Executive Officer, p. B135

Sun City: 0030 ★ SUN HEALTH CORPORATION 13180 North 103rd Drive, Zip 85351–3038, Mailing Address: P.O. Box 1278, Zip 85372–1278; tel. 623/876–5301; Leland W. Peterson, President and Chief Executive Officer, p. B142

ARKANSAS

Little Rock: 0355 ★ BAPTIST HEALTH 9601 Interstate 630, Exit 7, Zip 72205–7299; tel. 501/202–2000; Russell D. Harrington Jr., President, p. B63

CALIFORNIA

Costa Mesa: 0076 COLLEGE HEALTH ENTERPRISES 17100 Pioneer Boulevard, Suite 300, Zip 92627; tel. 949/642–3734; Dale A. Kirby, President, p. B78

Covina: 0101 CITRUS VALLEY HEALTH PARTNERS 210 West San Bernardino Road, Zip 91723; tel. 626/938–7577; Peter E. Makowski, President and Chief Executive Officer, p. B77

Fairfield: 2075 ★ NORTHBAY HEALTHCARE SYSTEM 1200 B Gale Wilson Boulevard, Zip 94533–3587; tel. 707/429–7809; Gary J. Passama, President and Chief Executive Officer, p. B121

Fresno: 1085 ★ COMMUNITY HEALTH SYSTEM OF NORTHERN CALIFORNIA Fresno and R Streets, Zip 93721, Mailing Address: P.O. Box 1232, Zip 93721; tel. 559/459–6000; J. Philip Hinton, M.D., President and Chief Executive Officer, p. B84

Hemet: 0043 ★ VALLEY HEALTH SYSTEM 1117 East Devonshire Avenue, Zip 92543; tel. 909/652–2811; John P. Lauri, Chief Executive Officer, p. B153

Loma Linda: 2175 LOMA LINDA UNIVERSITY HEALTH SCIENCES CENTER 11161 Anderson Street, Zip 92350; tel. 909/824–4540; B. Lyn Behrens, President, p. B110

Long Beach: 0084 MEMORIAL HEALTH SERVICES 2801 Atlantic Avenue, Zip 90801, Mailing Address: P.O. Box 1428, Zip 90801–1428; tel. 562/933–9700; Thomas J. Collins, President and Chief Executive Officer, p. B114

0435 PACIFIC HEALTH CORPORATION 249 East Ocean Boulevard, Zip 90802; tel. 310/435–1300; Jens Mueller, Chairman, p. B123

Los Angeles: 5755 LOS ANGELES COUNTY–DEPARTMENT OF HEALTH SERVICES 313 North Figueroa Street, Room 912, Zip 90012–2691; tel. 213/240–8101; Mark Finucane, Director Health Services, p. B110

Oakland: 2105 ★ KAISER FOUNDATION HOSPITALS One Kaiser Plaza, Zip 94612–3600; tel. 510/271–5910; David M. Lawrence, M.D., Chairman and Chief Executive Officer, p. B107

6405 UNIVERSITY OF CALIFORNIA–SYSTEMWIDE ADMINISTRATION 300 Lakeside Drive, 18th Floor, Zip 94612–3550; tel. 510/987–9701; Cornelius L. Hopper, M.D., Vice President Health Affairs, p. B151

Orange: 5425 ★ ST. JOSEPH HEALTH SYSTEM 440 South Batavia Street, Zip 92868–3995, Mailing Address: P.O. Box 14132, Zip 92613–1532; tel. 714/997–7690; Richard Statuto, Chief Executive Officer, p. B142

Pasadena: 0106 ★ SOUTHERN CALIFORNIA HEALTHCARE SYSTEMS 1300 East Green Street, Zip 91106; tel. 626/397–2900; Stephen A. Ralph, President and Chief Executive Officer, p. B140

Pleasanton: 0097 VALLEYCARE HEALTH SYSTEM 5575 West Las Positas Boulevard, 300, Zip 94588; tel. 925/447–7000; Marcy Feit, Chief Executive Officer, p. B153

Roseville: 0235 ★ ADVENTIST HEALTH 2100 Douglas Boulevard, Zip 95661–3898, Mailing Address: P.O. Box 619002, Zip 95661–9002; tel. 916/781–2000; Donald R. Ammon, President, p. B59

Sacramento: 8795 ★ SUTTER HEALTH One Capitol Mall, Zip 95814, Mailing Address: P.O. Box 160727, Zip 95816–0727; tel. 916/733–8800; Van R. Johnson, President and Chief Executive Officer, p. B142

San Diego: 7555 ★ PALOMAR POMERADO HEALTH SYSTEM 15255 Innovation Drive, Suite 204, Zip 92128–3410; tel. 619/675–5100; Norman F. Gruber, President and Chief Executive Officer, p. B123

1505 ★ SCRIPPS HEALTH 4275 Campus Point Court, Zip 92121, Mailing Address: P.O. Box 28, La Jolla, Zip 92038; tel. 619/678–7472; Sister Mary Jo Anderson, Senior Vice President, Hospital Operations, p. B135

2065 ★ SHARP HEALTHCARE 3131 Berger Avenue, Zip 92123; tel. 619/541–4000; Michael Murphy, President and Chief Executive Officer, p. B135

San Francisco: 5205 ★ CATHOLIC HEALTHCARE WEST 1700 Montgomery Street, Suite 300, Zip 94111–9603; tel. 415/438–5500; Richard J. Kramer, President and Chief Executive Officer, p. B75

0156 ★ UCSF STANFORD HEALTH CARE 5 Thomas Mellon Circle, 305, Zip 94134; tel. 415/353–4500; Peter Van Etten, President and Chief Executive Officer, p. B150

San Leandro: 0225 ALAMEDA COUNTY HEALTH CARE SERVICES AGENCY 1850 Fairway Drive, Zip 94577; tel. 510/351–1367; David J. Kears, Director, p. B60

Santa Barbara: 0103 COTTAGE HEALTH SYSTEM Pueblo at Bath Streets, Zip 93102, Mailing Address: P.O. Box 689, Zip 93102; tel. 805/682–7111; James L. Ash, President and Chief Executive Officer, p. B86

0063 ★ TENET HEALTHCARE CORPORATION 3820 State Street, Zip 93105, Mailing Address: P.O. Box 31907, Zip 93130; tel. 805/563–7000; Jeffrey Barbakow, Chairman and Chief Executive Officer, p. B143

Yuba City: 2115 FREMONT–RIDEOUT HEALTH GROUP 989 Plumas Street, Zip 95991; tel. 530/751–4010; Thomas P. Hayes, Chief Executive Officer, p. B97

COLORADO

Denver: 0092 ★ CATHOLIC HEALTH INITIATIVES 1999 Broadway, Suite 2605, Zip 80202–4004; tel. 303/298–9100; Patricia A. Cahill, President and Chief Executive Officer, p. B73

0134 ★ EXEMPLA HEALTHCARE, INC. 600 Grant Street, Suite 700, Zip 80203; tel. 303/813–5000; Jeffrey D. Selberg, President and Chief Executive Officer, p. B95

CONNECTICUT

Hartford: 0014 CONNECTICUT DEPARTMENT OF MENTAL HEALTH AND ADDICTION SERVICES 410 Capitol Avenue, Zip 06134, Mailing Address: P.O. Box 341431, Zip 06134–1431; tel. 860/418–6969; Albert J. Solnit, M.D., Commissioner, p. B85

New Haven: 0157 ★ YALE NEW HAVEN HEALTH SYSTEM 789 Howard Avenue, Zip 06519; tel. 203/688–2608; Joseph A. Zaccagnino, President and Chief Executive Officer, p. B156

DELAWARE

Wilmington: 0131 ★ CHRISTIANA CARE CORPORATION 501 West 14th Street, Zip 19899, Mailing Address: P.O. Box 1668, Zip 19899; tel. 302/428–2570; Charles M. Smith, M.D., President and Chief Executive Officer, p. B77

DISTRICT OF COLUMBIA

Bowling AFB: 9495 DEPARTMENT OF THE AIR FORCE 110 Luke Avenue, Room 400, Zip 20332–7050; tel. 202/767–5066; Lieutenant General Charles H. Roadman II, Surgeon General, p. B88

Washington: 9655 DEPARTMENT OF NAVY 2300 East Street N.W., Zip 20372–5300, p. B88

9295 DEPARTMENT OF VETERANS AFFAIRS 810 Vermont Avenue N.W., Zip 20420; tel. 202/273–5781; Kenneth W. Kizer, M.D., M.P.H., Under Secretary for Health, p. B90

2015 ★ GREATER SOUTHEAST HEALTHCARE SYSTEM 1310 Southern Avenue S.E., Zip 20032–4692; tel. 202/574–6611; George E. Gilbert, M.D., M.P.H., President and Chief Executive Officer, p. B98

FLORIDA

Clearwater: 0071 ACCORD HEALTH CARE CORPORATION 3696 Ulmerton Road, Zip 33762; tel. 727/573–1755; Stephen H. Noble, President, p. B59

Coral Gables: 0122 BAPTIST HEALTH SYSTEM OF SOUTH FLORIDA 6855 Red Road, Suite 600, Zip 33143–3632; tel. 305/273–2333; Brian E. Keeley, President and Chief Executive Officer, p. B64

0405 RAMSAY HEALTH CARE, INC. 1 Alhambra Plaza, Suite 750, Zip 33134–5217; tel. 305/569–6993; Bert Cibran, President and Chief Operating Officer, p. B133

Dunedin: 1335 MORTON PLANT MEASE HEALTH CARE 601 Main Street, Zip 34698, Mailing Address: P.O. Box 760, Zip 34697–0760; tel. 727/733–1111; Philip K. Beauchamp, FACHE, President and Chief Executive Officer, p. B118

Fort Lauderdale: 3115 ★ NORTH BROWARD HOSPITAL DISTRICT 303 S.E. 17th Street, Zip 33316–2510; tel. 954/355–5100; G. Wil Trower, President and Chief Executive Officer, p. B120

Gainesville: 0111 ★ SHANDS HEALTHCARE 1600 S.W. Archer Road, Zip 32610–0326; tel. 352/395–0421; J. Richard Gaintner, M.D., Chief Executive Officer, p. B135

Hollywood: 0083 ★ MEMORIAL HEALTHCARE SYSTEM 3501 Johnson Street, Zip 33021–5487; tel. 954/985–5805; Frank V. Sacco, FACHE, Chief Executive Officer, p. B115

Naples: 1775 HEALTH MANAGEMENT ASSOCIATES 5811 Pelican Bay Boulevard, Suite 500, Zip 34108; tel. 941/598–3175; William J. Schoen, Chairman and Chief Executive Officer, p. B99

Orlando: 3355 ORLANDO REGIONAL HEALTHCARE SYSTEM 1414 Kuhl Avenue, Zip 32806–2093; tel. 407/841–5111; John Hillenmeyer, President and Chief Executive Officer, p. B123

Ormond Beach: 2615 ★ MEMORIAL HEALTH SYSTEMS 770 West Granada Boulevard, Zip 32174–5197; tel. 904/615–4100; Richard A. Lind, President and Chief Executive Officer, p. B115

Pensacola: 0185 BAPTIST HEALTH CARE CORPORATION 1717 North E Street, Suite 320, Zip 32501–6335; tel. 850/469–2337; Alfred G. Stubblefield, President, p. B63

Tampa: 4125 ★ SHRINERS HOSPITALS FOR CHILDREN 2900 Rocky Point Drive, Zip 33607–1435, Mailing Address: Box 31356, Zip 33631–3356; tel. 813/281–0300; Joseph E. Melchiorre Jr., CHE, Executive Administrator, p. B136

Windermere: 9605 UNITED MEDICAL CORPORATION 603 Main Street, Zip 34786–3548, Mailing Address: P.O. Box 1100, Zip 34786–1100; tel. 407/876–2200; Donald R. Dizney, Chairman, p. B150

Winter Park: 4165 ★ ADVENTIST HEALTH SYSTEM SUNBELT HEALTH CARE CORPORATION 111 North Orlando Avenue, Zip 32789–3675; tel. 407/975–1417; Mardian J. Blair, President, p. B59

GEORGIA

Adel: 2335 MEMORIAL HEALTH SERVICES 706 North Parrish Avenue, Zip 31620–2064, Mailing Address: P.O. Box 677, Zip 31620–0677; tel. 912/896–2251; Wade E. Keck, Chief Executive Officer, p. B115

Atlanta: 0073 BOWDON CORPORATE OFFICES 4250 Perimeter Park South, Suite 102, Zip 30341; tel. 770/452–1221; Bill E. Ehrhardt, Executive Director, p. B68

0148 ESR CHILDREN'S HEALTH CARE SYSTEM, INC. 2200 Century Parkway, Suite 450, Zip 30345; tel. 404/250–2211; James E. Tally, Ph.D., President and Chief Executive Officer, p. B95

0138 ★ GEORGIA BAPTIST HEALTH CARE SYSTEM 100 10th Street, Zip 30365; tel. 404/253–3011; David E. Harrell, Chief Executive Officer, p. B97

0695 MAGELLAN HEALTH SERVICES 3414 Peachtree Road N.E., Suite 1400, Zip 30326; tel. 404/841–9200; Henry Harbin, M.D., President and Chief Executive Officer, p. B111

0905 SUMMIT HOSPITAL CORPORATION 5 Concourse Parkway, Suite 800, Zip 30328–6111; tel. 770/392–1454; Ken Couch, President, p. B142

0081 VALUEMARK HEALTHCARE SYSTEMS, INC. 300 Galleria Parkway, Suite 650, Zip 30339; tel. 770/933–5500; James T. McAfee Jr., Chairman, President and Chief Executive Officer, p. B153

Columbus: 0161 ★ COLUMBUS REGIONAL HEALTH SYSTEM 707 Center Street, Suite 400, Zip 31902; tel. 706/660–6100; Larry Sanders, FACHE, Chairman and Chief Executive Officer, p. B84

Marietta: 0995 ★ WELLSTAR HEALTH SYSTEM 805 Sandy Plains Road, Zip 30066; tel. 770/792–5012; Thomas E. Hill, Chief Executive Officer, p. B155

Thomasville: 0104 ARCHBOLD MEDICAL CENTER 910 South Broad Street, Zip 31792–6113; tel. 912/228–2739; Ken B. Beverly, President and Chief Executive Officer, p. B62

HAWAII

Honolulu: 3555 HAWAII HEALTH SYSTEMS CORPORATION 3675 Kilauea Avenue, Zip 96816; tel. 808/586–4416; Thomas M. Driskill Jr., President and Chief Executive Officer, p. B99

0040 ★ QUEEN'S HEALTH SYSTEMS 1099 Alakea Street, Suite 1100, Zip 96813; tel. 808/532–6100; Richard L. Griffith, President and Chief Executive Officer, p. B127

ILLINOIS

Arlington Heights: 0113 CANCER TREATMENT CENTERS OF AMERICA 3455 West Salt Creek Lane, Zip 60005–1080; tel. 847/342–7400; William A. Sanger, President and Chief Executive Officer, p. B70

Carbondale: 4175 ★ SOUTHERN ILLINOIS HOSPITAL SERVICES 608 East College Street, Zip 62901–3309, Mailing Address: P.O. Box 3988, Zip 62902–3988; tel. 618/457–5200; John J. Buckley Jr., President, p. B140

Chicago: 0079 CATHOLIC HEALTH PARTNERS 2913 North Commonwealth, Zip 60657–6296; tel. 773/665–3170; Sister Theresa Peck, President and Chief Executive Officer, p. B74

0016 COOK COUNTY BUREAU OF HEALTH SERVICES 1900 West Polk Street, Suite 220, Zip 60612; tel. 312/633–6820; Ruth M. Rothstein, Chief, p. B86

0171 RESURRECTION HEALTH CARE CORPORATION 7435 West Talcott Avenue, Zip 60631, p. B133

3855 ★ RUSH–PRESBYTERIAN–ST. LUKE'S MEDICAL CENTER 1653 West Congress Parkway, Zip 60612–3864; tel. 312/942–5000; Leo M. Henikoff, President, p. B134

0058 ★ UNIVERSITY OF CHICAGO HEALTH SYSTEM 322 South Green Street, Suite 500, Zip 60607; tel. 312/697–8403; Ralph W. Muller, Chief Executive Officer, p. B152

De Kalb: 0149 KISHWAUKEE HEALTH SYSTEM 626 Bethany Road, Zip 60115–4939, Mailing Address: P.O. Box 707, Zip 60115–4939; tel. 815/756–1521; Robert S. Thebeau, President and Chief Executive Officer, p. B108

Des Plaines: 5575 SISTERS OF THE HOLY FAMILY OF NAZARETH–SACRED HEART PROVINCE 310 North River Road, Zip 60016–1211; tel. 847/298–6760; Sister Marie Kielanowicz, Provincial Superior, p. B140

Elk Grove Village: 0065 ALEXIAN BROTHERS HEALTH SYSTEM, INC. 600 Alexian Way, Zip 60007–3395; tel. 847/640–7550; Brother Thomas Keusenkothen, President and Chief Executive Officer, p. B60

Evergreen Park: 2295 LITTLE COMPANY OF MARY SISTERS HEALTHCARE SYSTEM 9350 South California Avenue, Zip 60805–2595; tel. 708/229–5491; Sister Carol Pacini, Provincialate Superior, p. B109

Frankfort: 0132 ★ PROVENA HEALTH 9223 West St. Francis Road, Zip 60423–8334; tel. 815/928–6901; Joseph S. Feth, Chief Executive Officer, p. B125

Oak Brook: 0064 ★ ADVOCATE HEALTH CARE 2025 Windsor Drive, Zip 60523; tel. 630/990–5010; Richard R. Risk, President and Chief Executive Officer, p. B60

Peoria: 5335 ★ OSF HEALTHCARE SYSTEM 800 N.E. Glen Oak Avenue, Zip 61603–3200; tel. 309/655–2852; Sister Frances Marie Masching, President, p. B123

Springfield: 5355 ★ HOSPITAL SISTERS HEALTH SYSTEM Mailing Address: P.O. Box 19431, Zip 62794–9431; tel. 217/523–4747; Sister Jomary Trstensky, President, p. B104

0086 ★ MEMORIAL HEALTH SYSTEM 701 North First Street, Zip 62781–0001; tel. 217/788–3000; Robert T. Clarke, President and Chief Executive Officer, p. B115

Wheaton: 6745 ★ WHEATON FRANCISCAN SERVICES, INC. 26W171 Roosevelt Road, Zip 60189–0667, Mailing Address: P.O. Box 667, Zip 60189–0667; tel. 630/462–9271; Wilfred F. Loebig Jr., President and Chief Executive Officer, p. B156

INDIANA

Fort Wayne: 0159 PARKVIEW HEALTH SYSTEM 2200 Randallia Drive, Zip 46805; tel. 219/470–8200; Charles H. Mason Jr., President and Chief Executive Officer, p. B124

Hobart: 0135 ★ ANCILLA SYSTEMS INC. 1000 South Lake Park Avenue, Zip 46342–5970; tel. 219/947–8500; William D. Harkins, President and Chief Executive Officer, p. B61

Mishawaka: 5345 ★ SISTERS OF ST. FRANCIS HEALTH SERVICES, INC. 1515 Dragoon Trail, Zip 46546–1290, Mailing Address: P.O. Box 1290, Zip 46546–1290; tel. 219/256–3935; Kevin D. Leahy, President and Chief Executive Officer, p. B139

South Bend: 5585 ★ HOLY CROSS HEALTH SYSTEM CORPORATION 3575 Moreau Court, Zip 46628–4320; tel. 219/233–8558; Sister Patricia Vandenberg, President and Chief Executive Officer, p. B104

IOWA

Des Moines: 0061 ★ IOWA HEALTH SYSTEM 1200 Pleasant Street, Zip 50309–1453; tel. 515/241–6161; Samuel T. Wallace, President, p. B106

KANSAS

Leavenworth: 5095 ★ SISTERS OF CHARITY OF LEAVENWORTH HEALTH SERVICES CORPORATION 4200 South Fourth Street, Zip 66048–5054; tel. 913/682–1338; Sister Marie Damian Glatt, President, p. B137

Phillipsburg: 1535 ★ GREAT PLAINS HEALTH ALLIANCE, INC. 625 Third Street, Zip 67661–2138, Mailing Address: P.O. Box 366, Zip 67661–0366; tel. 785/543–2111; Roger S. John, President and Chief Executive Officer, p. B98

Wichita: 5435 VIA CHRISTI HEALTH SYSTEM 818 North Emporia, Zip 67214–3725; tel. 316/268–5000; LeRoy E. Rheault, President and Chief Executive Officer, p. B155

KENTUCKY

Lexington: 0145 APPALACHIAN REGIONAL HEALTHCARE 1220 Harrodsburg Road, Zip 40504, Mailing Address: P.O. Box 8086, Zip 40533–8086; tel. 606/226–2440; Forrest Calico, M.D., President, p. B61

Louisville: 0315 ★ BAPTIST HEALTHCARE SYSTEM 4007 Kresge Way, Zip 40207–4677; tel. 502/896–5000; Tommy J. Smith, President and Chief Executive Officer, p. B64

0052 ★ JEWISH HOSPITAL HEALTHCARE SERVICES 217 East Chestnut Street, Zip 40202–1886; tel. 502/587–4011; Henry C. Wagner, President, p. B107

2285 ★ NORTON HEALTHCARE 234 East Gray Street, Suite 225, Zip 40202, Mailing Address: P.O. Box 35070, Zip 40232–5070; tel. 502/629–8000; Stephen A. Williams, President, p. B121

0026 VENCOR, INCORPORATED 1 Vernon Place, 680 S. 4th Avenue, Zip 40202–2412; tel. 502/596–7300; Edward L. Kuntz, Board Chairman, President and Chief Executive Officer, p. B154

LOUISIANA

Baton Rouge: 1475 ★ FRANCISCAN MISSIONARIES OF OUR LADY HEALTH SYSTEM, INC. 4200 Essen Lane, Zip 70809; tel. 225/923–2701; John J. Finan Jr., President and Chief Executive Officer, p. B96

0775 ★ GENERAL HEALTH SYSTEM 3600 Florida Boulevard, Zip 70806–3854; tel. 225/237–1603; Milton R. Siepman, Ph.D., President and Chief Executive Officer, p. B97

0715 ★ LSU MEDICAL CENTER HEALTH CARE SERVICES DIVISION 8550 United Plaza Boulevard, 4th Floor, Zip 70809; tel. 225/922–0490; Cary M. Dougherty Jr., Chief Operating Officer, p. B110

New Orleans: 0047 LOUISIANA STATE HOSPITALS 210 State Street, Zip 70118–5797; tel. 504/897–3400; M. E. Teague, Chief Executive Officer, p. B110

MAINE

Bangor: 0555 ★ EASTERN MAINE HEALTHCARE 489 State Street, Zip 04401–6674, Mailing Address: P.O. Box 404, Zip 04402–0404; tel. 207/973–7045; Norman A. Ledwin, President and Chief Executive Officer, p. B95

MARYLAND

Baltimore: 1015 ★ JOHNS HOPKINS HEALTH SYSTEM 600 North Wolfe Street, Zip 21287–1193; tel. 410/955–5000; Ronald R. Peterson, President, p. B107

0158 ★ LIFEBRIDGE HEALTH 2401 West Belvedere Avenue, Zip 21215; tel. 410/601–5134; Warren A. Green, President and Chief Executive Officer, p. B109

6015 SISTERS OF MERCY OF THE AMERICAS–REGIONAL COMMUNITY OF BALTIMORE 1300 Northern Parkway, Zip 21239, Mailing Address: P.O. Box 11448, Zip 21239; tel. 410/435–4400; Sister Margaret Beatty, President, p. B138

Columbia: 0154 ★ MEDSTAR HEALTH 5565 Sterrett Place, 5th Floor, Zip 21044; tel. 410/772–6500; Michael R. Merson, President and Chief Executive Officer, p. B114

Fallston: 0038 ★ UPPER CHESAPEAKE HEALTH SYSTEM 1916 Belair Road, Zip 21047–2797; tel. 410/893–0322; Lyle Ernest Sheldon, President and Chief Executive Officer, p. B153

Largo: 0029 ★ DIMENSIONS HEALTH CORPORATION 9200 Basil Court, Zip 20774; tel. 301/925–7000; Winfield M. Kelly Jr., President and Chief Executive Officer, p. B94

Marriottsville: 5085 ★ BON SECOURS HEALTH SYSTEM, INC. 1505 Marriottsville Road, Zip 21104–1399; tel. 410/442–5511; Christopher M. Carney, President and Chief Executive Officer, p. B67

Rockville: 9195 U. S. PUBLIC HEALTH SERVICE INDIAN HEALTH SERVICE 5600 Fishers Lane, Zip 20857; tel. 301/443–1083; Michael Trujillo, M.D., M.P.H., Director, p. B148

MASSACHUSETTS

Boston: 0096 ★ CAREGROUP 375 Longwood Avenue, Zip 02215–5395; tel. 617/975–6060; James Reinertsen, M.D., Chief Executive Officer, p. B70

0141 ★ CARITAS CHRISTI HEALTH CARE 736 Cambridge Street, Zip 02135–2997; tel. 617/789–2500; Michael F. Collins, M.D., President, p. B71

0013 MASSACHUSETTS DEPARTMENT OF MENTAL HEALTH 25 Staniford Street, Zip 02114–2575; tel. 617/727–5600; Marylou Sudders, Commissioner, p. B113

1785 ★ PARTNERS HEALTHCARE SYSTEM, INC. 800 Boylston Street, Suite 1150, Zip 02199–8001; tel. 617/278–1004; Samuel O. Thier, M.D., President and Chief Executive Officer, p. B124

Hyannis: 0124 CAPE COD HEALTHCARE, INC. 88 Lewis Bay Road, Zip 02601–5210; tel. 508/862–5011; James F. Lyons, President and Chief Executive Officer, p. B70

Lexington: 5885 ★ COVENANT HEALTH SYSTEMS, INC. 420 Bedford Street, Zip 02420–1502; tel. 781/862–1634; David R. Lincoln, President and Chief Executive Officer, p. B86

Peabody: 0091 PIONEER BEHAVIORAL HEALTH 200 Lake Street, Suite 102, Zip 01960–4780; tel. 978/536–2777; Bruce A. Shear, President and Chief Executive Officer, p. B125

Pittsfield: 2435 ★ BERKSHIRE HEALTH SYSTEMS, INC. 725 North Street, Zip 01201–4124; tel. 413/447–2743; David E. Phelps, President and Chief Executive Officer, p. B67

Springfield: 1095 ★ BAYSTATE HEALTH SYSTEM, INC. 759 Chestnut Street, Zip 01199–0001; tel. 413/794–0000; Michael J. Daly, President, p. B65

Wellesley: 0215 COMMUNITY CARE SYSTEMS, INC. 203 Grove Street, Zip 02482–2413; tel. 781/416–5300; Frederick J. Thacher, Chairman, p. B84

MICHIGAN

Adrian: 0172 LENAWEE HEALTH ALLIANCE 818 Riverside Avenue, Zip 49221; tel. 517/265–0900; John R. Robertstad, President and Chief Executive Officer, p. B108

Ann Arbor: 0133 ★ SISTERS OF ST. JOSEPH HEALTH SYSTEM 455 East Eisenhower Parkway, 300, Zip 48108–3324; tel. 734/741–1160; John S. Lore, President and Chief Executive Officer, p. B139

Dearborn: 1165 ★ OAKWOOD HEALTHCARER, INC. One Parklane Boulevard, Suite 1000E, Zip 48126; tel. 313/253–6007; Gerald D. Fitzgerald, President and Chief Executive Officer, p. B122

Detroit: 2145 ★ DETROIT MEDICAL CENTER 3663 Woodward Avenue, Suite 200, Zip 48201–2403; tel. 313/578–2020; Arthur Porter, M.D., President and Chief Executive Officer, p. B93

9505 ★ HENRY FORD HEALTH SYSTEM One Ford Place, Zip 48202–3067; tel. 313/876–8715; Gail L. Warden, President and Chief Executive Officer, p. B103

Farmington Hills: 5165 ★ MERCY HEALTH SERVICES 34605 Twelve Mile Road, Zip 48331–3221; tel. 248/489–6000; Judith Pelham, President and Chief Executive Officer, p. B115

Grand Rapids: 0177 SPECTRUM HEALTH 100 Michigan Street N.E., Zip 49503–2551; tel. 616/391–1174; William G. Gonzalez, President and Chief Executive Officer, p. B141

Kalamazoo: 0595 ★ BRONSON HEALTHCARE GROUP, INC. One Healthcare Plaza, Zip 49007–5345; tel. 616/341–6000; Frank J. Sardone, President and Chief Executive Officer, p. B69

Midland: 0001 ★ MIDMICHIGAN HEALTH 4005 Orchard Drive, Zip 48670–0001; tel. 517/839–3000; Terence F. Moore, President, p. B117

Port Huron: 0053 ★ BLUE WATER HEALTH SERVICES CORPORATION 1221 Pine Grove Avenue, Zip 48060–3568; tel. 810/989–3717; Donald C. Fletcher, President and Chief Executive Officer, p. B67

Royal Oak: 9575 ★ WILLIAM BEAUMONT HOSPITAL CORPORATION 3601 West Thirteen Mile Road, Zip 48073–6769; tel. 248/551–5000; Ted D. Wasson, President and Chief Executive Officer, p. B156

Traverse City: 1465 ★ MUNSON HEALTHCARE 1105 Sixth Street, Zip 49684–2386; tel. 616/935–6502; John M. Rockwood Jr., President, p. B118

MINNESOTA

Duluth: 0515 BENEDICTINE HEALTH SYSTEM 503 East Third Street, Zip 55805–1964; tel. 218/720–2370; Barry J. Halm, President and Chief Executive Officer, p. B66

Minneapolis: 0041 ★ ALLINA HEALTH SYSTEM 5601 Smetana Drive, Zip 55343, Mailing Address: P.O. Box 9310, Zip 55440–9310; tel. 612/992–3992; Gordon M. Sprenger, President, p. B61

1325 ★ FAIRVIEW HOSPITAL AND HEALTHCARE SERVICES 2450 Riverside Avenue, Zip 55454–1400; tel. 612/672–6300; David R. Page, President and Chief Executive Officer, p. B96

Rochester: 1875 ★ MAYO FOUNDATION 200 S.W. First Street, Zip 55905–0002; tel. 507/284–2511; Michael B. Wood, M.D., President and Chief Executive Officer, p. B114

Saint Louis Park: 1985 HEALTHSYSTEM MINNESOTA 6500 Excelsior Boulevard, Zip 55426–4702; tel. 612/993–5000; David Wessner, President and Chief Executive Officer, p. B103

Saint Paul: 2185 ★ HEALTHEAST 559 Capitol Boulevard, 6–South, Zip 55103–0000; tel. 651/232–2300; Timothy H. Hanson, President and Chief Executive Officer, p. B101

MISSISSIPPI

Gautier: 0067 SINGING RIVER HOSPITAL SYSTEM 2101 Highway 90, Zip 39553; tel. 228/497–7907; Chris Anderson, Chief Executive Officer, p. B136

Jackson: 0017 MISSISSIPPI STATE DEPARTMENT OF MENTAL HEALTH 1101 Robert E Lee Building, Zip 39201–1101; tel. 601/359–1288; Roger McMurtry, Chief Mental Health Bureau, p. B117

Tupelo: 0032 NORTH MISSISSIPPI HEALTH SERVICES, INC. 830 South Gloster Street, Zip 38801–4996; tel. 601/841–3136; Jeffrey B. Barber, Dr.PH, President and Chief Executive Officer, p. B120

MISSOURI

Kansas City: 8815 ★ HEALTH MIDWEST 2304 East Meyer Boulevard, Suite A–20, Zip 64132–4104; tel. 816/276–9181; Richard W. Brown, President and Chief Executive Officer, p. B100

0120 SAINT LUKE'S SHAWNEE MISSION HEALTH SYSTEM 10920 Elm Avenue, Zip 64134–4108; tel. 816/932–3377; G. Richard Hastings, President and Chief Executive Officer, p. B134

9255 ★ TRUMAN MEDICAL CENTER 2301 Holmes Street, Zip 64108–2677; tel. 816/556–3000; John W. Bluford, Executive Director and Chief Executive Officer, p. B148

Saint Louis: 0051 ★ BJC HEALTH SYSTEM 4444 Forest Park Avenue, Zip 63108–2259; tel. 314/286–2000; Edward B. Case, Executive Vice President and Chief Operating Officer, p. B67

5945 ★ CARONDELET HEALTH SYSTEM 13801 Riverport Drive, Suite 300, Zip 63043–4810; tel. 314/770–0333; Gary Christiansen, President and Chief Executive Officer, p. B71

1855 ★ DAUGHTERS OF CHARITY NATIONAL HEALTH SYSTEM 4600 Edmundson Road, Zip 63134–3806, Mailing Address: P.O. Box 45998, Zip 63145–5998; tel. 314/253–6700; Donald A. Brennan, President and Chief Executive Officer, p. B86

5185 ★ SISTERS OF MERCY HEALTH SYSTEM–ST. LOUIS 2039 North Geyer Road, Zip 63131–0902, Mailing Address: P.O. Box 31902, Zip 63131–0902; tel. 314/965–6100; Ronald B. Ashworth, Chief Executive Officer, p. B138

5455 ★ SSM HEALTH CARE 477 North Lindbergh Boulevard, Zip 63141–7813; tel. 314/994–7800; Sister Mary Jean Ryan, President and Chief Executive Officer, p. B141

Springfield: 0179 COX HEALTH SYSTEM 3800 South National Avenue, Zip 65807; tel. 417/269–3108; Larry D. Wallis, President and Chief Executive Officer, p. B86

NEBRASKA

Norfolk: 2855 MISSIONARY BENEDICTINE SISTERS AMERICAN PROVINCE 300 North 18th Street, Zip 68701–3687; tel. 402/371–3438; Sister M. Agnes Salber, Prioress, p. B117

NEW JERSEY

Bridgeton: 0151 SOUTH JERSEY HEALTH SYSTEM 333 Irving Avenue, Zip 08302–2100; tel. 609/451–6600; Paul S. Cooper, Chief Executive Officer, p. B140

Edison: 8855 ★ SOLARIS HEALTH SYSTEM 80 James Street, 2nd Floor, Zip 08820–3998; tel. 732/632–1500; John P. McGee, President and Chief Executive Officer, p. B140

Jersey City: 0173 LIBERTY HEALTHCARE SYSTEM 50 Baldwin Avenue, Zip 07304–3199; tel. 201/915–2000; Jonathan M. Metsch, Dr.PH, President and Chief Executive Officer, p. B108

Marlton: 6725 ★ VIRTUA HEALTH 94 Brick Road, Suite 200, Zip 08053; tel. 609/355–0005; Richard P. Miller, President and Chief Executive Officer, p. B155

Newark: 6545 CATHEDRAL HEALTHCARE SYSTEM, INC. 219 Chestnut Street, Zip 07105–1558; tel. 201/690–3600; Frank L. Fumai, President and Chief Executive Officer, p. B72

Trenton: 0010 DIVISION OF MENTAL HEALTH SERVICES, DEPARTMENT OF HUMAN SERVICES, STATE OF NEW JERSEY Capital Center, P.O. Box 727, Zip 08625–0727; tel. 609/777–0702; Alan G. Kaufman, Director, p. B94

West Orange: 0118 ★ SAINT BARNABAS HEALTH CARE SYSTEM 95 Old Short Hills Road, Zip 07052; tel. 973/322–4001; Ronald Del Mauro, President and Chief Executive Officer, p. B134

NEW MEXICO

Albuquerque: 3505 ★ PRESBYTERIAN HEALTHCARE SERVICES 5901 Harper Drive N.E., Zip 87109–3589, Mailing Address: P.O. Box 26666, Zip 87125–6666; tel. 505/260–6300; James H. Hinton, President and Chief Executive Officer, p. B125

0021 UNIVERSITY OF NEW MEXICO 915 Camino De Salud, Zip 87131–0001; tel. 505/272–5849; R. Philip Eaton, M.D., Vice President Health Scences, p. B152

NEW YORK

Albany: 0009 NEW YORK STATE DEPARTMENT OF MENTAL HEALTH 44 Holland Avenue, Zip 12229–3411; tel. 518/447–9611; Jesse Nixon Jr., Ph.D., Director, p. B120

Buffalo: 0102 KALEIDA HEALTH 901 Washington Street, Zip 14203; tel. 716/843–7525; John E. Friedlander, President and Chief Executive Officer, p. B108

Great Neck: 0062 ★ NORTH SHORE– LONG ISLAND JEWISH HEALTH SYSTEM 145 Community Drive, Zip 11021; tel. 516/465–8100; John S. T. Gallagher, Chief Executive Officer, p. B121

Latham: 1485 FRANCISCAN HEALTH PARTNERSHIP, INC. 8 Airport Park Boulevard, Zip 12110; tel. 518/783–5257; James H. Flynn Jr., President and Chief Executive Officer, p. B96

New York: 0127 ★ CONTINUUM HEALTH PARTNERS 555 West 57th Street, Zip 10019; tel. 212/523–8390; Robert G. Newman, M.D., President, p. B85

0142 ★ NEW YORK & PRESBYTERIAN HEALTHCARE 525 East 68th Street, Zip 10021–4885; tel. 212/746–4000; David B. Skinner, M.D., Vice Chairman and Chief Executive Officer, p. B119

3075 NEW YORK CITY HEALTH AND HOSPITALS CORPORATION 125 Worth Street, Room 514, Zip 10013–4006; tel. 212/788–3321; Luis R. Marcos, M.D., President, p. B119

0110 OUR LADY OF MERCY HEALTHCARE SYSTEM, INC. 600 East 233 Street, Zip 10466–2697; tel. 718/920–9000; Gary S. Horan, FACHE, President and Chief Executive Officer, p. B123

5995 SISTERS OF CHARITY CENTER Mount St. Vincent on Hudson, Zip 10471–9930; tel. 718/549–9200; Sister Elizabeth A. Vermaelen, President, p. B137

Newburgh: 0144 GREATER HUDSON VALLEY HEALTH SYSTEM 600A Stony Brook Court, Zip 12550; tel. 914/568–6050; Paul Dell Uomo, President and Chief Executive Officer, p. B98

Rochester: 0046 ★ VIA HEALTH 150 North Chestnut, Zip 14604; tel. 716/922–3000; Roger S. Hunt, President and Chief Executive Officer, p. B155

Syracuse: 5955 SISTERS OF THE 3RD FRANCISCAN ORDER 2500 Grant Boulevard, Zip 13208–1713; tel. 315/425–0115; Sister Grace Anne Dillenschneider, General Superior, p. B140

Uniondale: 0735 ★ EPISCOPAL HEALTH SERVICES INC. 333 Earle Ovington Boulevard, Zip 11553–3645; tel. 516/544–5200; Lorna McBarnette, Chief Executive Officer, p. B95

NORTH CAROLINA

Charlotte: 0705 CAROLINAS HEALTHCARE SYSTEM 1000 Blythe Boulevard, Zip 28203–5871, Mailing Address: P.O. Box 32861, Zip 28232–2861; tel. 704/355–2000; Harry A. Nurkin, Ph.D., President and Chief Executive Officer, p. B71

Winston Salem: 0139 ★ NOVANT HEALTH 3333 Silas Creek Parkway, Zip 27103–3090; tel. 336/718–5000; Paul M. Wiles, President and Chief Executive Officer, p. B122

NORTH DAKOTA

Bismarck: 0545 BENEDICTINE SISTERS OF THE ANNUNCIATION 7520 University Drive, Zip 58504–9653; tel. 701/255–1520; Sister Susan Berger, Prioress, p. B67

Fargo: 2235 ★ LUTHERAN HEALTH SYSTEMS 4310 17th Avenue S.W., Zip 58103–3339, Mailing Address: P.O. Box 6200, Zip 58106–6200; tel. 701/277–7500; Steven R. Orr, Chairman and Chief Executive Officer, p. B111

5805 SISTERS OF MARY OF THE PRESENTATION HEALTH CORPORATION 1102 Page Drive S.W., Zip 58106–0007, Mailing Address: P.O. Box 10007, Zip 58106–0007; tel. 701/237–9290; Aaron Alton, President, p. B138

OHIO

Cincinnati: 0415 BETHESDA HOSPITAL, INC. 619 Oak Street, Zip 45206–1690; tel. 513/569–6141; John S. Prout, President and Chief Executive Officer, p. B67

5155 CATHOLIC HEALTHCARE PARTNERS 615 Elsinore Place, Zip 45202; tel. 513/639–2827; Michael D. Connelly, President and Chief Executive Officer, p. B74

0082 ★ HEALTH ALLIANCE OF GREATER CINCINNATI 3200 Burnet Avenue, Zip 45229; tel. 513/585–6000; Jack M. Cook, President and Chief Executive Officer, p. B99

Cleveland: 2515 FAIRVIEW HOSPITAL SYSTEM 18101 Lorain Avenue, Zip 44111–5656; tel. 216/476–7000; Kenneth T. Misener, Vice President and Chief Operating Officer, p. B96

8835 MERIDIA HEALTH SYSTEM 17325 Euclid Avenue, 4th Floor, Zip 44112; tel. 216/430–8000; Charles B. Miner, President and Chief Executive Officer, p. B116

5125 SISTERS OF CHARITY OF ST. AUGUSTINE HEALTH SYSTEM 2351 East 22nd Street, Zip 44115–3197; tel. 216/696–5560; Sister Judith Ann Karam, President and Chief Executive Officer, p. B137

0112 UNIVERSITY HOSPITALS HEALTH SYSTEM 11100 Euclid Avenue, Zip 44106–5000; tel. 216/844–1000; Farah M. Walters, President and Chief Executive Officer, p. B151

Columbus: 0162 ★ OHIOHEALTH 3555 Olentangy River Road, 4000, Zip 43214–3900; tel. 614/566–5424; William W. Wilkins, President and Chief Executive Officer, p. B122

Sylvania: 5375 ★ FRANCISCAN SERVICES CORPORATION 6832 Convent Boulevard, Zip 43560–2897; tel. 419/882–8373; John W. O'Connell, President, p. B97

Toledo: 0147 ★ PROMEDICA HEALTH SYSTEM 2121 Hughes Drive, 4th Floor, Zip 43606; tel. 419/291–7176; Alan W. Brass, FACHE, President and Chief Executive Officer, p. B125

Youngstown: 0174 FORUM HEALTH 3530 Belmont Avenue, Suite 7, Zip 44505; tel. 330/759–4090; Gary E. Kaatz, Executive Vice President and Chief Operating Officer, p. B96

OKLAHOMA

Oklahoma City: 0305 ★ INTEGRIS HEALTH 3366 N.W. Expressway, Suite 800, Zip 73112–9756; tel. 405/949–6068; Stanley F. Hupfeld, President and Chief Executive Officer, p. B105

0018 OKLAHOMA STATE DEPARTMENT OF MENTAL HEALTH AND SUBSTANCE ABUSE SERVICES 1200 N.E. 13th Street, Zip 73152, Mailing Address: P.O. Box 53277, Zip 73152–3277; tel. 405/522–3908; Sharron D. Boehler, Commissioner, p. B122

Tulsa: 0665 CENTURY HEALTHCARE CORPORATION 5555 East 71st Street, Suite 9220, Zip 74136–6540; tel. 918/491–0780; Jerry D. Dillon, President and Chief Executive Officer, p. B77

0130 ★ HILLCREST HEALTHCARE SYSTEM 1120 South Utica, Zip 74104–4090; tel. 918/579–1000; Donald A. Lorack Jr., President and Chief Executive Officer, p. B103

5305 ★ MARIAN HEALTH SYSTEM Mailing Address: P.O. Box 4753, Zip 74159–0753; tel. 918/742–9988; Sister M. Therese Gottschalk, President, p. B113

OREGON

Medford: 0094 ★ ASANTE HEALTH SYSTEM 2650 Siskiyou Boulevard, Suite 200, Zip 97504–8389; tel. 541/608–4100; Roy G. Vinyard II, Chief Administrative Officer, p. B62

Portland: 2755 ★ LEGACY HEALTH SYSTEM 1919 N.W. Lovejoy Street, Zip 97209–1503; tel. 503/415–5600; Robert Pallari, President and Chief Executive Officer, p. B108

PENNSYLVANIA

Harrisburg: 5570 ★ PENN STATE GEISINGER HEALTH SYSTEM 2601 Market Place, Suite 300, Zip 17110–9360; tel. 717/214–2254; Stuart Heydt, M.D., Chief Executive Officer, p. B125

King of Prussia: 9555 UNIVERSAL HEALTH SERVICES, INC. 367 South Gulph Road, Zip 19406–0958; tel. 610/768–3300; Alan B. Miller, President and Chief Executive Officer, p. B150

Mount Pleasant: 0166 ★ FAY–WEST HEALTH SYSTEM 508 South Church Street, Zip 15666–1790; tel. 724/547–1500; Rodney L. Gunderson, Chief Executive Officer, p. B96

Newtown Square: 0136 CATHOLIC HEALTH EAST 14 Campus Boulevard, Suite 300, Zip 19073–3277; tel. 610/355–2000; Daniel F. Russell, President and Chief Executive Officer, p. B72

Philadelphia: 1685 ALBERT EINSTEIN HEALTHCARE NETWORK 5501 Old York Road, Zip 19141–3098; tel. 215/456–7890; Martin Goldsmith, President, p. B60

0169 TEMPLE UNIVERSITY HEALTH SYSTEM 3401 North Broad Street, 1st Floor, Zip 19140; tel. 215/707–8000; Leon S. Malmud, M.D., President, p. B143

0168 UNIVERSITY OF PENNSYLVANIA HEALTH SYSTEM 399 South 34th Street, 21st Floor, Zip 19104–4385; tel. 215/662–2230; William N. Kelley, M.D., Chief Executive Officer, p. B152

Pittsburgh: 2305 ★ ALLEGHENY UNIVERSITY HOSPITALS–WEST 320 East North Avenue, Zip 15221–2173; tel. 412/359–3010; Anthony M. Sanzo, President and Chief Executive Officer, p. B60

2255 ★ ST. FRANCIS HEALTH SYSTEM 4401 Penn Avenue, Zip 15224–1334; tel. 412/622–4214; Sister M. Rosita Wellinger, President and Chief Executive Officer, p. B141

0137 UPMC HEALTH SYSTEM 200 Lothrop, Zip 15213; tel. 412/647–2345; Jeffrey A. Romoff, President, p. B152

Sayre: 0675 ★ GUTHRIE HEALTHCARE SYSTEM Guthrie Square, Zip 18840; tel. 570/888–6666; Mark Stensager, President and Chief Executive Officer, p. B99

Springfield: 0008 ★ CROZER–KEYSTONE HEALTH SYSTEM 100 West Sproul Road, Zip 19064; tel. 610/338–8200; John C. McMeekin, President and Chief Executive Officer, p. B86

Villanova: 0845 DEVEREUX FOUNDATION 444 Deveraux Drive, Zip 19085, Mailing Address: P.O. Box 400, Devon, Zip 19333–0400; tel. 610/520–3000; Ronald P. Burd, President and Chief Executive Officer, p. B94

Wayne: 0455 HOSPITAL GROUP OF AMERICA 1265 Drummers Lane, Suite 107, Zip 19087; tel. 610/687–5151; Mark R. Russell, President and Chief Executive Officer, p. B104

Section B Index

7775 ★ JEFFERSON HEALTH SYSTEM 259 Radnor–Chester Road, Suite 290, Zip 19087–5288; tel. 610/225–6200; Douglas S. Peters, President and Chief Executive Officer, p. B106

ork: 0068 ★ SOUTH CENTRAL COMMUNITY HEALTH 1001 South George Street, Zip 17405–3645; tel. 717/851–2345; Bruce M. Bartels, President, p. B140

UERTO RICO

an Juan: 0011 PUERTO RICO DEPARTMENT OF HEALTH Building A – Medical Center, Zip 00936, Mailing Address: Call Box 70184, Zip 00936; tel. 809/274–7676; Carmen Feliciano De Melecio, M.D., Secretary of Health, p. B126

HODE ISLAND

rovidence: 0099 ★ CARE NEW ENGLAND HEALTH SYSTEM 45 Willard Avenue, Zip 02905–3218; tel. 401/453–7900; John J. Hynes, President and Chief Executive Officer, p. B70

0060 ★ LIFESPAN CORPORATION 167 Point Street, Zip 02903–4771; tel. 401/444–3500; George A. Vecchione, President, p. B109

OUTH CAROLINA

olumbia: 4155 ★ PALMETTO HEALTH ALLIANCE Mailing Address: P.O. Box 2266, Zip 29202–2266; tel. 803/296–2000; Charles D. Beaman Jr., President, p. B123

reenville: 1555 ★ GREENVILLE HOSPITAL SYSTEM 701 Grove Road, Zip 29605–4211; tel. 864/455–7000; Frank D. Pinckney, President, p. B98

partanburg: 4195 ★ SPARTANBURG REGIONAL HEALTHCARE SYSTEM 101 East Wood Street, Zip 29303–3016; tel. 864/560–6000; Joseph Michael Oddis, President, p. B141

OUTH DAKOTA

ioux Falls: 0078 ★ SIOUX VALLEY HOSPITALS AND HEALTH SYSTEM 1100 South Euclid Avenue, Zip 57105–0496; tel. 605/333–1000; Kelby K. Krabbenhoft, President, p. B136

ankton: 5255 ★ AVERA HEALTH 610 West 23rd Street, Zip 57078, Mailing Address: P.O. Box 38, Zip 57078–0038; tel. 605/322–7050; John T. Porter, President and Chief Executive Officer, p. B62

ENNESSEE

rentwood: 0585 ★ BRIM HEALTHCARE, INC. 105 Westwood Place, Suite 300, Zip 37027; tel. 615/309–6053; Jim McKinney, President, p. B68

0080 ★ COMMUNITY HEALTH SYSTEMS, INC. 155 Franklin Road, Suite 400, Zip 37027–4600, Mailing Address: P.O. Box 217, Zip 37024–0217; tel. 615/373–9600; Wayne T. Smith, President and Chief Executive Officer, p. B84

0163 NEW AMERICAN HEALTHCARE CORPORATION 109 Westpark Drive, Suite 440, Zip 37027, Mailing Address: P.O. Box 3689, Zip 37024; tel. 615/221–5070; Thomas Singleton, President and Chief Executive Officer, p. B119

0108 PROVINCE HEALTHCARE CORPORATION 105 Westwood Place, Suite 400, Zip 37027; tel. 615/370–1377; Marty Rash, President and Chief Executive Officer, p. B126

0002 ★ QUORUM HEALTH GROUP/QUORUM HEALTH RESOURCES, INC. 103 Continental Place, Zip 37027; tel. 615/371–7979; James E. Dalton Jr., President and Chief Executive Officer, p. B127

Chattanooga: 2795 HEALTHCORP OF TENNESSEE, INC. 735 Broad Street, Zip 37402; tel. 615/267–8406; T. Farrell Hayes, President, p. B101

Jackson: 0004 ★ WEST TENNESSEE HEALTHCARE 708 West Forest Avenue, Zip 38301–3901; tel. 901/425–5000; James T. Moss, President, p. B156

Johnson City: 0167 MOUNTAIN STATES HEALTH ALLIANCE 400 North State of Franklin, Zip 37604; tel. 423/431–6111; Dennis Vonderfecht, President and Chief Executive Officer, p. B118

Knoxville: 2155 BAPTIST HEALTH SYSTEM OF TENNESSEE 137 Blount Avenue S.E., Zip 37920–1643, Mailing Address: P.O. Box 1788, Zip 37901–1788; tel. 615/632–5099; Dale Collins, President and Chief Executive Officer, p. B64

0123 COVENANT HEALTH 100 Fort Sanders West Boulevard, Zip 37922; tel. 423/531–5555; Alan C. Guy, President and Chief Executive Officer, p. B86

Memphis: 1625 ★ BAPTIST MEMORIAL HEALTH CARE CORPORATION 899 Madison Avenue, Zip 38146–0001; tel. 901/227–5117; Stephen Curtis Reynolds, President and Chief Executive Officer, p. B65

9345 ★ METHODIST HEALTHCARE 1211 Union Avenue, Suite 700, Zip 38104–6600; tel. 901/726–2300; Maurice W. Elliott, Chief Executive Officer, p. B117

1765 UNITED HOSPITAL CORPORATION 6189 East Shelby Drive, Zip 38115; tel. 901/794–8440; James C. Henson, President, p. B150

Nashville: 0069 BEHAVIORAL HEALTHCARE CORPORATION 102 Woodmont Boulevard, Suite 800, Zip 37205–2287; tel. 615/269–3492; Edward A. Stack, President and Chief Executive Officer, p. B65

0114 CHILDREN'S COMPREHENSIVE SERVICES, INC. 3401 West End Avenue, Suite 500, Zip 37203–0376; tel. 615/383–0376; William J. Ballard, Chief Executive Officer, p. B77

0048 ★ COLUMBIA/HCA HEALTHCARE CORPORATION One Park Plaza, Zip 37203–1548; tel. 615/344–2003; Jack O. Bovender Jr., President and Chief Operating Officer, p. B78

0180 ★ LIFEPOINT HOSPITALS, INC. 4525 Harding Road, Suite 300, Zip 37205; tel. 615/344–6261; Scott Mercy, Chairman and Chief Executive Officer, p. B109

0116 NETCARE HEALTH SYSTEMS, INC. 424 Church Street, Suite 2100, Zip 37219; tel. 615/742–8500; Michael A. Koban Jr., Chief Executive Officer, p. B118

TEXAS

Austin: 0395 HEALTHCARE AMERICA, INC. 1407 West Stassney Lane, Zip 78745–2998, Mailing Address: P.O. Box 4008, Zip 78765–4008; tel. 512/464–0200; John P. Harcourt Jr., President and Chief Executive Officer, p. B100

0020 TEXAS DEPARTMENT OF HEALTH 1100 West 49th Street, Zip 78756–3199; tel. 512/458–7111; William R. Archer III, M.D., Commissioner, p. B147

0033 UNIVERSITY OF TEXAS SYSTEM 601 Colorado Street, Zip 78701–2982; tel. 512/499–4224; Charles B. Mullins, Executive Vice Chancellor, p. B152

Bay City: 2505 MATAGORDA COUNTY HOSPITAL DISTRICT 1115 Avenue G, Zip 77414–3544; tel. 409/245–6383; Wendell H. Baker Jr., District Administrator, p. B114

Dallas: 0095 ★ BAYLOR HEALTH CARE SYSTEM 3500 Gaston Avenue, Zip 75226–2088; tel. 214/820–0111; Boone Powell Jr., President, p. B65

2735 ★ METHODIST HOSPITALS OF DALLAS 1441 North Beckley Avenue, Zip 75203–1201, Mailing Address: P.O. Box 655999, Zip 75265–5999; tel. 214/947–8181; Howard M. Chase, FACHE, President and Chief Executive Officer, p. B117

0178 ★ TRIAD HOSPITALS, INC. 13455 Noel Road, 20th Floor, Zip 75240; tel. 972/789–2700; James Shelton, Chairman and Chief Executive Officer, p. B147

Fort Worth: 0039 TARRANT COUNTY HOSPITAL DISTRICT 1500 South Main Street, Zip 76104–4941; tel. 817/927–1230; Anthony J. Alcini, President and Chief Executive Officer, p. B143

Houston: 0077 CAMBRIDGE INTERNATIONAL, INC, 7505 Fannin, Suite 680, Zip 77225; tel. 713/790–1153; Timothy Sharma, M.D., President, p. B69

0605 ★ CHRISTUS HEALTH 2600 North Loop West, Zip 77092–8999; tel. 713/681–8877; Sister Christina Murphy, Co–Chief Executive Officer, p. B77

2645 ★ MEMORIAL HERMANN HEALTHCARE SYSTEM 7737 S.W. Freeway, Suite 200, Zip 77074–1800; tel. 713/776–6992; Dan S. Wilford, President and Chief Executive Officer, p. B115

7235 ★ METHODIST HEALTH CARE SYSTEM 6565 Fannin Street, D–200, Zip 77030–2707; tel. 713/790–2221; Peter W. Butler, President and Chief Executive Officer, p. B117

5765 PARACELSUS HEALTHCARE CORPORATION 515 West Greens Road, Suite 800, Zip 77067–4511; tel. 281/774–5100; Charles R. Miller, President and Chief Operating Officer, p. B123

Irving: 0129 ★ TEXAS HEALTH RESOURCES 600 East Las Colinas Boulevard, Suite 1550, Zip 75039, Mailing Address: 600 East Las Colinas Boulevard, 1550, Zip 75039; tel. 214/818–4500; Douglas D. Hawthorne, President and Chief Executive Officer, p. B147

Lubbock: 0036 ★ LUBBOCK METHODIST HOSPITAL SYSTEM 3615 19th Street, Zip 79410–1201; tel. 806/792–1011; George H. McCleskey, President and Chief Executive Officer, p. B110

Lufkin: 0176 MEMORIAL HEALTH SYSTEM OF EAST TEXAS 1201 West Frank Avenue, Zip 75904–3357; tel. 409/634–8111; Gary Lex Whatley, President and Chief Executive Officer, p. B115

San Antonio: 0265 BAPTIST HEALTH SYSTEM 200 Concord Plaza, Suite 900, Zip 78216; tel. 210/297–1000; Fred R. Mills, President and Chief Executive Officer, p. B63

5565 ★ CHRISTUS HEALTH 9311 San Pedro, Suite 1250, Zip 78216–4469; tel. 210/524–4100; Joseph Blasko Jr., President and Chief Executive Officer, p. B77

Tyler: 1895 EAST TEXAS MEDICAL CENTER REGIONAL HEALTHCARE SYSTEM 1000 South Beckham Street, Zip 75701–1996, Mailing Address: P.O. Box 6400, Zip 75711–6400; tel. 903/535–6211; Elmer G. Ellis, President and Chief Executive Officer, p. B94

Section B Index

UTAH

Nephi: 0109 ★ RURAL HEALTH MANAGEMENT CORPORATION 549 North 400 East, Zip 84648–1226; tel. 435/623–4924; Mark R. Stoddard, President, p. B134

Salt Lake City: 1815 ★ INTERMOUNTAIN HEALTH CARE, INC. 36 South State Street, 22nd Floor, Zip 84111–1453; tel. 801/442–2000; William H. Nelson, President and Chief Executive Officer, p. B105

VIRGINIA

Falls Church: 9395 DEPARTMENT OF THE ARMY, OFFICE OF THE SURGEON GENERAL 5109 Leesburg Pike, Zip 22041; tel. 703/681–3114; Major Beverly Pritchett, Executive Officer, p. B89

1305 ★ INOVA HEALTH SYSTEM 8110 Gatehouse Road, Zip 22042; tel. 703/289–2069; J. Knox Singleton, President and Chief Executive Officer, p. B105

Lynchburg: 2265 ★ CENTRA HEALTH, INC. 1920 Atherholt Road, Zip 24501–1104; tel. 804/947–4700; George W. Dawson, President, p. B76

Newport News: 4810 RIVERSIDE HEALTH SYSTEM 606 Denbigh Boulevard, Suite 601, Zip 23608; tel. 757/875–7500; Nelson L. St. Clair, President, p. B133

Norfolk: 2635 FHC HEALTH SYSTEMS 240 Corporate Boulevard, Zip 23502–4950; tel. 757/459–5100; Ronald I. Dozoretz, M.D., Chairman, p. B96

2565 ★ SENTARA HEALTH SYSTEM 6015 Poplar Hall Drive, Zip 23502–3800; tel. 757/455–7000; David L. Bernd, President and Chief Executive Officer, p. B135

Richmond: 0012 VIRGINIA DEPARTMENT OF MENTAL HEALTH 1220 Bank Street, Zip 23219–3623, Mailing Address: P.O. Box 1797, Zip 23218–1797; tel. 804/786–3921; Richard E. Kellogg, Acting Commissioner, p. B155

Roanoke: 0070 ★ CARILION HEALTH SYSTEM 101 Elm Avenue S.E., Zip 24013, Mailing Address: P.O. Box 13727, Zip 24036–3727; tel. 540/981–7347; Thomas L. Robertson, President and Chief Executive Officer, p. B70

Winchester: 0128 VALLEY HEALTH SYSTEM 1840 Amherst Street, Zip 22604, Mailing Address: P.O. Box 3340, Zip 22604–1334; tel. 540/722–8024; Michael J. Halseth, President and Chief Executive Officer, p. B153

WASHINGTON

Bellevue: 5415 ★ PEACEHEALTH 15325 S.E. 30th Place, Suite 300, Zip 98007; tel. 425/747–1711; John Hayward, President and Chief Executive Officer, p. B124

Seattle: 5275 ★ SISTERS OF PROVIDENCE HEALTH SYSTEM 520 Pike Street, Zip 98101, Mailing Address: P.O. Box 11038, Zip 98111–9038; tel. 206/464–3355; Henry G. Walker, President and Chief Executive Officer, p. B138

Spokane: 0945 EMPIRE HEALTH SERVICES West 800 Fifth Avenue, Zip 99204, Mailing Address: P.O. Box 248, Zip 99210–0248; tel. 509/458–7960; Thomas M. White, President, p. B95

5265 ★ PROVIDENCE SERVICES 9 East Ninth Avenue, Zip 99202; tel. 509/742–7337; Richard J. Umbdenstock, President and Chief Executive Officer, p. B126

Tacoma: 6555 MULTICARE HEALTH SYSTEM 315 Martin Luther King Jr. Way, Zip 98405, Mailing Address: P.O. Box 5299, Zip 98405–0299; tel. 253/403–1000; Diane Cecchettini, Executive Vice President, p. B118

WEST VIRGINIA

Charleston: 0955 ★ CAMCARE, INC. 501 Morris Street, Zip 25301–1300, Mailing Address: P.O. Box 1547, Zip 25326–1547; tel. 304/348–5432; Phillip H. Goodwin, President and Chief Executive Officer, p. B70

Fairmont: 0119 WEST VIRGINIA UNITED HEALTH SYSTEM 1000 Technology Drive, Suite 2320, Zip 26554; tel. 304/368–2700; Bernard G. Westfall, President and Chief Executive Officer, p. B156

WISCONSIN

Appleton: 2445 ★ UNITED HEALTH GROUP Five Innovation Court, Zip 54914–1663, Mailing Address: P.O. Box 8025, Zip 54913–8025; tel. 920/730–0330; James Edward Raney, President and Chief Executive Officer, p. B150

La Crosse: 9650 ★ FRANCISCAN SKEMP HEALTHCARE 700 West Avenue South, Zip 54601–4796; tel. 608/791–9710; Glenn Forbes, M.D., President and Chief Executive Officer, p. B97

Manitowoc: 1455 ★ FRANCISCAN SISTERS OF CHRISTIAN CHARITY HEALTHCARE MINISTRY, INC 1415 South Rapids Road, Zip 54220–9302; tel. 920/684–7071; Sister Laura J. Wolf, President, p. B97

Milwaukee: 2215 ★ AURORA HEALTH CARE 3000 West Montana, Zip 53215–3268, Mailing Address: P.O. Box 343910, Zip 53234–3910; tel. 414/647–3000; G. Edwin Howe, President, p. B62

0027 ★ HORIZON HEALTHCARE, INC. 2300 North Mayfair Road, Suite 550, Zip 53226–1508; tel. 414/257–3888; Sister Renee Rose, President and Chief Executive Officer, p. B104

Waukesha: 0153 PROHEALTH CARE 725 American Avenue, Zip 53188; tel. 414/544–2241; Donald W. Fundingsland, Chief Executive Officer, p. B125

Alliances

ALLIANCE OF INDEPENDENT ACADEMIC MEDICAL CENTERS
435 N Michigan Ave, Ste 2700, Chicago, IL Zip 60611; tel. 312/923–9770; Ms Nancie Noie, Managing Director

ARIZONA
Phoenix
Member
Good Samaritan Regional Medical Center
Maricopa Medical Center
St. Joseph's Hospital and Medical Center

CALIFORNIA
Long Beach
Member
Long Beach Memorial Medical Center

Los Angeles
Member
Cedars–Sinai Medical Center

Oakland
Member
Kaiser Foundation Hospital

CONNECTICUT
Hartford
Member
Saint Francis Hospital and Medical Center

DISTRICT OF COLUMBIA
Washington
Member
Washington Hospital Center

FLORIDA
Miami Beach
Member
Mount Sinai Medical Center

Orlando
Member
Orlando Regional Medical Center

ILLINOIS
Berwyn
Member
MacNeal Hospital

Chicago
Shareholder
Illinois Masonic Medical Center

Park Ridge
Member
Lutheran General Hospital

INDIANA
Indianapolis
St. Vincent Hospitals and Health Services

LOUISIANA
New Orleans
Member
Ochsner Foundation Hospital

MAINE
Portland
Member
Maine Medical Center

MASSACHUSETTS
Springfield
Member
Baystate Medical Center

MICHIGAN
Detroit
Member
Henry Ford Health System

Royal Oak
Member
William Beaumont Hospital–Royal Oak

MISSOURI
Kansas City
Member
Saint Luke's Hospital

Saint Louis
St. John's Mercy Medical Center

NEW JERSEY
Livingston
Member
Saint Barnabas Medical Center

Long Branch
Member
Monmouth Medical Center

Paterson
Member
St. Joseph's Hospital and Medical Center

NEW YORK
Bronx
Member
Bronx–Lebanon Hospital Center

Brooklyn
Member
Maimonides Medical Center

Mineola
Member
Winthrop–University Hospital

New Hyde Park
Member
Long Island Jewish Medical Center

NORTH CAROLINA
Charlotte
Member
Carolinas Medical Center

OHIO
Akron
Member
Akron General Medical Center

Columbus
Member
Grant/Riverside Methodist Hospitals–Riverside Campus

PENNSYLVANIA
Allentown
Member
Lehigh Valley Hospital

Philadelphia
Member
Albert Einstein Medical Center

Pittsburgh
Member
Mercy Hospital of Pittsburgh
Western Pennsylvania Hospital

SOUTH CAROLINA
Columbia
Member
Palmetto Richland Memorial Hospital

Greenville
Member
Greenville Hospital System

TEXAS
Dallas
Member
Baylor University Medical Center

APPLING HEALTHCARE SYSTEM
301 East Tollison Street, Baxley, GA Zip 31513–2898; tel. 912/367–9841; Mr Terry Stratton, Chief Executive Officer

CALIFORNIA
San Diego
Premier, Inc.

ASSOCIATION OF INDEPENDENT HOSPITALS
8300 Troost, Kansas City, MO Zip 64131; tel. 816/276–7580; Mr Jeff Tindle, President and Chief Executive Officer

KANSAS
Council Grove
Member
Morris County Hospital

Garnett
Member
Anderson County Hospital

Girard
Member
Crawford County Hospital District One

Holton
Member
Holton Community Hospital

Horton
Member
Horton Health Foundation

Iola
Member
Allen County Hospital

Junction City
Member
Geary Community Hospital

Kansas City
Member
University of Kansas Medical Center

Lawrence
Member
Lawrence Memorial Hospital

Manhattan
Member
Mercy Health Center of Manhattan

Marysville
Member
Community Memorial Healthcare

Onaga
Member
Community Hospital Onaga

Ottawa
Member
Ransom Memorial Hospital

Overland Park
Member
Menorah Medical Center
Overland Park Regional Medical Center

Pittsburg
Member
Mount Carmel Medical Center

Seneca
Member
Nemaha Valley Community Hospital

Topeka
Member
St. Francis Hospital and Medical Center

Wamego
Member
Wamego City Hospital

MISSOURI
Albany
Member
Gentry County Memorial Hospital

Belton
Member
Research Belton Hospital

Bethany
Member
Harrison County Community Hospital

Boonville
Member
Cooper County Memorial Hospital

Brookfield
Member
General John J. Pershing Memorial Hospital

Carrollton
Member
Carroll County Memorial Hospital

Section B

Carthage
Member
McCune–Brooks Hospital

Chillicothe
Member
Hedrick Medical Center

Clinton
Member
Golden Valley Memorial Hospital

Columbia
Member
University Hospitals and Clinics

Excelsior Springs
Member
Excelsior Springs Medical Center

Fairfax
Member
Community Hospital Association

Farmington
Member
Mineral Area Regional Medical Center

Fulton
Affiliate
Callaway Community Hospital

Hannibal
Member
Hannibal Regional Hospital

Harrisonville
Member
Cass Medical Center

Hermann
Member
Hermann Area District Hospital

Independence
Member
Independence Regional Health Center
Medical Center of Independence

Jefferson City
Member
Capital Region Medical Center

Joplin
Member
St. John's Regional Medical Center

Kansas City
Member
Baptist Medical Center
Park Lane Medical Center
Research Medical Center
Trinity Lutheran Hospital

Kirksville
Affiliate
Northeast Regional Medical Center–Jefferson Campus

Lees Summit
Member
Lee's Summit Hospital

Lexington
Member
Lafayette Regional Health Center

Macon
Affiliate
Samaritan Memorial Hospital

Memphis
Affiliate
Scotland County Memorial Hospital

Mexico
Member
Audrain Medical Center

Milan
Affiliate
Sullivan County Memorial Hospital

Nevada
Member
Nevada Regional Medical Center

North Kansas City
Member
North Kansas City Hospital

Osceola
Member
Sac–Osage Hospital

Richmond
Affiliate
Ray County Memorial Hospital

Saint Joseph
Member
Heartland Regional Medical Center

Warrensburg
Member
Western Missouri Medical Center

ATLANTIC HEALTH SYSTEM
325 Columbia Turnpike, Florham Park, NJ Zip 07932–0959; tel. 973/660–3100; Mr Richard P Oths, President and Chief Executive Officer

ILLINOIS
Chicago
Member
Alliance of Independent Academic Medical Centers

AVERA HEALTH
610 West 23rd Street, Yankton, SD Zip 57078; tel. 605/322–7050; Mr John T Porter, President and Chief Executive Officer

ILLINOIS
Oak Brook
Member
Consolidated Catholic Health Care

BATON ROUGE GENERAL MEDICAL CENTER
3600 Florida Street, Baton Rouge, LA Zip 70806–3889; tel. 225/387–7770; Dr Milton R Siepman , Ph.D., President and Chief Executive Officer

ILLINOIS
Chicago
Member
Alliance of Independent Academic Medical Centers

CALIFORNIA PACIFIC MEDICAL CENTER
2333 Buchanan Street, San Francisco, CA Zip 94115; tel. 415/563–4321; Dr Martin Brotman , M.D., President and Chief Executive Officer

ILLINOIS
Chicago
Member
Alliance of Independent Academic Medical Centers

CATHOLIC HEALTHCARE WEST
1700 Montgomery St, Suite 300, San Francisco, CA Zip 94111–9603; tel. 415/438–5500; Mr Richard J Kramer, President and Chief Executive Officer

ILLINOIS
Oak Brook
Member
Consolidated Catholic Health Care

CHILD HEALTH CORPORATION OF AMERICA
6803 West 64th Street, Ste 208, Shawnee Mission, KS Zip 66202; tel. 913/262–1436; Mr Don C Black, President and Chief Executive Officer

ALABAMA
Birmingham
Member
Children's Hospital of Alabama

ARKANSAS
Little Rock
Member
Arkansas Children's Hospital

CALIFORNIA
Los Angeles
Member
Childrens Hospital of Los Angeles

Madera
Member
Valley Children's Hospital

Oakland
Member
Children's Hospital Oakland

Orange
Member
Children's Hospital of Orange County

Palo Alto
Member
Lucile Salter Packard Children's Hospital at Stanford

San Diego
Member
Children's Hospital and Health Center

COLORADO
Denver
Member
Children's Hospital

DISTRICT OF COLUMBIA
Washington
Member
Children's National Medical Center

FLORIDA
Miami
Member
Miami Children's Hospital

Saint Petersburg
Member
All Children's Hospital

GEORGIA
Atlanta
Member
Egleston Children's Hospital

ILLINOIS
Chicago
Member
Children's Memorial Hospital

LOUISIANA
New Orleans
Member
Children's Hospital

MASSACHUSETTS
Boston
Member
Children's Hospital

MICHIGAN
Detroit
Member
Children's Hospital of Michigan

MINNESOTA
Minneapolis
Member
Children's Hospitals and Clinics, Minneapolis

MISSOURI
Kansas City
Member
Children's Mercy Hospital

Saint Louis
Member
St. Louis Children's Hospital

NEBRASKA
Omaha
Member
Children's Hospital

NEW YORK
Buffalo
Member
Children's Hospital

OHIO
Akron
Member
Children's Hospital Medical Center of Akron

Cincinnati
Member
  Children's Hospital Medical Center

Columbus
Member
  Children's Hospital

Dayton
Member
  Children's Medical Center

PENNSYLVANIA
Philadelphia
Member
  Children's Hospital of Philadelphia

Pittsburgh
Member
  Children's Hospital of Pittsburgh

TENNESSEE
Memphis
Member
  Le Bonheur Children's Medical Center

TEXAS
Corpus Christi
Member
  Driscoll Children's Hospital

Dallas
Member
  Children's Medical Center of Dallas

Fort Worth
Member
  Cook Children's Medical Center

Houston
Member
  Texas Children's Hospital

VIRGINIA
Norfolk
Member
  Children's Hospital of The King's Daughters

WASHINGTON
Seattle
Member
  Children's Hospital and Regional Medical Center

WISCONSIN
Milwaukee
Member
  Children's Hospital of Wisconsin

CHILDREN'S MERCY HOSPITAL
2401 Gillham Road, Kansas City, MO
Zip 64108–9898; tel. 816/234–3000; Dr
Randall L O'Donnell , Ph.D., President and
Chief Executive Officer

ILLINOIS
Chicago
Member
  Alliance of Independent Academic Medical Centers

CHRISTIANA CARE CORPORATION
501 West 14th Street, Wilmington, DE
Zip 19899; tel. 302/428–2570; Dr
Charles M Smith , M.D., President and
Chief Executive Officer

ILLINOIS
Chicago
Member
  Alliance of Independent Academic Medical Centers

CHRISTUS HEALTH
9311 San Pedro, Suite 1250, San
Antonio, TX Zip 78216–4469;
tel. 210/524–4100; Mr Joseph Blasko,
Jr., President and Chief Executive Officer

ILLINOIS
Oak Brook
Member
  Consolidated Catholic Health Care

CONSOLIDATED CATHOLIC HEALTH CARE
1301 W 22nd Street, Suite 202, Oak
Brook, IL Zip 60523; tel. 630/990–2242;
Mr Roger N Butler, Executive Director

CALIFORNIA
Orange
Member
  St. Joseph Health System

COLORADO
Denver
Member
  Catholic Health Initiatives

ILLINOIS
Frankfort
Member
  Provena Health

INDIANA
Mishawaka
Member
  Sisters of St. Francis Health Services, Inc.

South Bend
Member
  Holy Cross Health System Corporation

KANSAS
Leavenworth
Member
  Sisters of Charity of Leavenworth Health Services
  Corporation

Wichita
Member
  Via Christi Health System

MARYLAND
Marriottsville
Member
  Bon Secours Health System, Inc.

MICHIGAN
Ann Arbor
Member
  Sisters of St. Joseph Health System

Farmington Hills
Member
  Mercy Health Services

MISSOURI
Saint Louis
Member
  Carondelet Health System
  Daughters of Charity National Health System

NEW YORK
Latham
Member
  Franciscan Health Partnership, Inc.

OHIO
Cincinnati
Member
  Catholic Healthcare Partners

Sylvania
Member
  Franciscan Services Corporation

PENNSYLVANIA
Newtown Square
Member
  Catholic Health East

TEXAS
San Antonio
Member
  Christus Health

WASHINGTON
Seattle
Member
  Sisters of Providence Health System

HOSPITAL NETWORK, INC.
One Healthcare Plaza, Kalamazoo, MI
Zip 49007; tel. 616/341–8888; Mr
George Angelidis, President and Chief
Executive Officer

MICHIGAN
Allegan
Member
  Allegan General Hospital

Hastings
Member
  Pennock Hospital

Kalamazoo
Member
  Bronson Healthcare Group, Inc.
  Bronson Methodist Hospital

Marshall
Member
  Oaklawn Hospital

Sturgis
Member
  Sturgis Hospital

Vicksburg
Member
  Bronson Vicksburg Hospital

ILLINOIS MASONIC MEDICAL CENTER
836 West Wellington Avenue, Chicago, IL
Zip 60657–5193; tel. 773/975–1600; Mr
Bruce C Campbell, President and Chief
Executive Officer

ILLINOIS
Chicago
Member
  Alliance of Independent Academic Medical Centers

INOVA FAIRFAX HOSPITAL
3300 Gallows Road, Falls Church, VA
Zip 22042–3300; tel. 703/698–1110; Mr
Steven E Brown, Administrator

ILLINOIS
Chicago
Member
  Alliance of Independent Academic Medical Centers

INTERHEALTH
2550 University Ave W, Ste 233, Saint
Paul, MN Zip 55114; tel. 612/646–5574;
Mr Benjamin Aune, President and Chief
Executive Officer

ALABAMA
Birmingham
Member
  Baptist Health System

ILLINOIS
Normal
Member
  BroMenn Healthcare

Oak Brook
Member
  Advocate Health Care

Rock Island
Member
  Trinity Medical Center–West Campus

LOUISIANA
New Orleans
Member
  Southern Baptist Health System

MICHIGAN
Bay City
Member
  Bay Health Systems

MINNESOTA
Duluth
Member
  Benedictine Health System

Saint Paul
Member
  HealthEast

MISSOURI
Saint Louis
Member
  Forest Park Hospital

Section B

OHIO
Cleveland
Member
Fairview Hospital System

Kettering
Member
Kettering Medical Center

TEXAS
Houston
Member
Memorial Hermann Healthcare System

JERSEY SHORE HOSPITAL
1020 Thompson Street, Jersey Shore, PA Zip 17740–1794; tel. 570/398–0100; Mr Louis A Ditzel, Jr., President and Chief Executive Officer

ILLINOIS
Chicago
Member
Alliance of Independent Academic Medical Centers

JORDAN HOSPITAL
275 Sandwich Street, Plymouth, MA Zip 02360–2196; tel. 508/746–2001; Mr Alan D Knight, President and Chief Executive Officer

MASSACHUSETTS
Andover
Affiliate
Yankee Alliance

LENOX HILL HOSPITAL
100 East 77th Street, New York, NY Zip 10021–1883; tel. 212/434–2000; Ms Gladys George, President and Chief Executive Officer

ILLINOIS
Chicago
Member
Alliance of Independent Academic Medical Centers

MEDSTAR HEALTH
5565 Sterrett Place, 5th Floor, Columbia, MD Zip 21044; tel. 410/772–6500; Mr Michael R Merson, President and Chief Executive Officer

ILLINOIS
Chicago
Member
Alliance of Independent Academic Medical Centers

PHOENIX CHILDREN'S HOSPITAL
1111 East McDowell Road, Phoenix, AZ Zip 85006–2666; tel. 602/239–5960; Mr Burl E Stamp, Chief Executive Officer

KANSAS
Shawnee Mission
Member
Child Health Corporation of America

PREMIER, INC.
3 Westbrook Corporate Center, 9th Floor, San Diego, CA Zip 92130; tel. 619/481–2727; Mr Richard A Norling, Chief Executive Officer

ALABAMA
Birmingham
Member
Children's Hospital of Alabama
Eye Foundation Hospital

Dadeville
Member
Lakeshore Community Hospital

Daphne
Member
Mercy Medical

Dothan
Member
Flowers Hospital
Southeast Alabama Medical Center

Enterprise
Member
Medical Center Enterprise

Gadsden
Member
Gadsden Regional Medical Center

Geneva
Member
Wiregrass Medical Center

Jacksonville
Member
Jacksonville Hospital

Monroeville
Member
Monroe County Hospital

Opelika
Member
East Alabama Medical Center

Valley
Member
Lanier Health Services

ALASKA
Anchorage
Member
Providence Alaska Medical Center

Cordova
Affiliate
Cordova Community Medical Center

Fairbanks
Member
Fairbanks Memorial Hospital

Homer
Member
South Peninsula Hospital

Juneau
Member
Bartlett Regional Hospital

Ketchikan
Member
Ketchikan General Hospital

Kodiak
Member
Providence Kodiak Island Medical Center

Palmer
Member
Valley Hospital

Seward
Affiliate
Providence Seward Medical Center

Valdez
Member
Valdez Community Hospital

ARIZONA
Bullhead City
Member
Western Arizona Regional Medical Center

Casa Grande
Member
Casa Grande Regional Medical Center

Ganado
Member
Sage Memorial Hospital

Glendale
Member
Arrowhead Community Hospital and Medical Center

Mesa
Member
Mesa Lutheran Hospital
Valley Lutheran Hospital

Phoenix
Member
Baptist Hospitals and Health Systems, Inc.
Maricopa Medical Center
Phoenix Baptist Hospital and Medical Center

Prescott
Member
Yavapai Regional Medical Center

ARKANSAS
Ashdown
Member
Little River Memorial Hospital

Batesville
Shareholder
White River Medical Center

Benton
Member
Saline Memorial Hospital

Camden
Member
Ouachita Medical Center

Crossett
Shareholder
Ashley County Medical Center

Danville
Shareholder
Chambers Memorial Hospital

Dardanelle
Shareholder
Dardanelle Hospital

De Witt
Shareholder
DeWitt City Hospital

Dumas
Member
Delta Memorial Hospital

Gravette
Shareholder
Gravette Medical Center Hospital

Harrison
Shareholder
North Arkansas Regional Medical Center

Hot Springs National Park
Shareholder
Levi Hospital

Jacksonville
Member
Rebsamen Medical Center

Lake Village
Member
Chicot Memorial Hospital

Little Rock
Shareholder
Arkansas Children's Hospital

Magnolia
Shareholder
Magnolia Hospital

McGehee
Shareholder
McGehee–Desha County Hospital

Mena
Member
Mena Medical Center

Monticello
Shareholder
Drew Memorial Hospital

Nashville
Member
Howard Memorial Hospital

Paragould
Shareholder
Arkansas Methodist Hospital

Pine Bluff
Shareholder
Jefferson Regional Medical Center

Siloam Springs
Member
Siloam Springs Memorial Hospital

Springdale
Shareholder
  Northwest Medical Center

Warren
Shareholder
  Bradley County Medical Center

West Memphis
Shareholder
  Crittenden Memorial Hospital

CALIFORNIA
Alhambra
Member
  Alhambra Hospital

Anaheim
Member
  Martin Luther Hospital

Apple Valley
Member
  St. Mary Regional Medical Center

Arroyo Grande
Member
  Arroyo Grande Community Hospital

Bakersfield
Member
  Kern Medical Center
  San Joaquin Community Hospital

Burbank
Member
  Providence Saint Joseph Medical Center

Chula Vista
Member
  Sharp Chula Vista Medical Center

Clearlake
Member
  Redbud Community Hospital

Corona
Member
  Corona Regional Medical Center

Coronado
Member
  Sharp Coronado Hospital

Deer Park
Member
  St. Helena Hospital

Delano
Member
  Delano Regional Medical Center

Escondido
Member
  Palomar Medical Center

Eureka
Member
  Saint Joseph Hospital

Fortuna
Member
  Redwood Memorial Hospital

Fullerton
Member
  St. Jude Medical Center

Glendale
Member
  Glendale Adventist Medical Center
  Glendale Memorial Hospital and Health Center

Hanford
Member
  Hanford Community Medical Center

Harbor City
Member
  Bay Harbor Hospital

La Mesa
Member
  Grossmont Hospital

La Palma
Member
  La Palma Intercommunity Hospital

Lompoc
Member
  Lompoc Healthcare District

Long Beach
Member
  Long Beach Community Medical Center

Los Angeles
Member
  California Hospital Medical Center
  Childrens Hospital of Los Angeles
  White Memorial Medical Center

Madera
Member
  Valley Children's Hospital

Mission Hills
Member
  Providence Holy Cross Medical Center

Mission Viejo
Member
  Mission Hospital Regional Medical Center

Murrieta
Member
  Rancho Springs Medical Center

Napa
Member
  Queen of the Valley Hospital

National City
Member
  Paradise Valley Hospital

Northridge
Member
  Northridge Hospital Medical Center–Roscoe Boulevard
    Campus

Oakland
Member
  Children's Hospital Oakland
  Summit Medical Center

Orange
Affiliate
  Children's Hospital of Orange County
Member
  St. Joseph Health System
  St. Joseph Hospital

Palo Alto
Member
  Lucile Salter Packard Children's Hospital at Stanford

Paradise
Member
  Feather River Hospital

Petaluma
Member
  Petaluma Valley Hospital

Poway
Member
  Pomerado Hospital

Rancho Mirage
Member
  Eisenhower Memorial Hospital and Betty Ford Center
    at Eisenhower

Roseville
Member
  Adventist Health

San Diego
Member
  Children's Hospital and Health Center
  Mesa Vista Hospital
  Palomar Pomerado Health System
  Sharp Cabrillo Hospital
  Sharp Healthcare
  Sharp Memorial Hospital

San Gabriel
Member
  San Gabriel Valley Medical Center

San Luis Obispo
Member
  French Hospital Medical Center

San Pedro
Member
  San Pedro Peninsula Hospital

Santa Paula
Member
  Santa Paula Memorial Hospital

Santa Rosa
Member
  Santa Rosa Memorial Hospital

Selma
Member
  Selma District Hospital

Simi Valley
Member
  Simi Valley Hospital and Health Care Services

Sonora
Member
  Sonora Community Hospital

South Laguna
Member
  South Coast Medical Center

Susanville
Member
  Lassen Community Hospital

Torrance
Affiliate
  Little Company of Mary Hospital

Ukiah
Member
  Ukiah Valley Medical Center

Vallejo
Member
  First Hospital Vallejo

Van Nuys
Member
  Northridge Hospital and Medical Center, Sherman
    Way Campus

Victorville
Member
  Victor Valley Community Hospital

Willits
Member
  Frank R. Howard Memorial Hospital

COLORADO
Brush
Member
  East Morgan County Hospital

Cortez
Member
  Southwest Memorial Hospital

Craig
Member
  Memorial Hospital

Delta
Member
  Delta County Memorial Hospital

Denver
Member
  Children's Hospital

Glenwood Springs
Member
  Valley View Hospital

Greeley
Member
  North Colorado Medical Center

Holyoke
Member
  Melissa Memorial Hospital

Lamar
Member
  Prowers Medical Center

Loveland
Member
  McKee Medical Center

Meeker
Member
  Pioneers Hospital of Rio Blanco County

Montrose
Member
  Montrose Memorial Hospital

Pueblo
Member
  Parkview Medical Center

Rifle
Member
Grand River Hospital District

Salida
Member
Heart of the Rockies Regional Medical Center

Sterling
Member
Sterling Regional Medcenter

Trinidad
Member
Mount San Rafael Hospital

Yuma
Affiliate
Yuma District Hospital

CONNECTICUT
Bristol
Member
Bristol Hospital

Hartford
Member
Saint Francis Hospital and Medical Center

New Haven
Member
Hospital of Saint Raphael

Stafford Springs
Member
Johnson Memorial Hospital

DELAWARE
Dover
Affiliate
Bayhealth Medical Center

Lewes
Member
Beebe Medical Center

Newark
Affiliate
Christiana Hospital

Seaford
Member
Nanticoke Memorial Hospital

Wilmington
Member
Alfred I.duPont Hospital for Children
Christiana Care Corporation
Eugene Dupont Preventive Medicine and Rehabilitation
Institute

DISTRICT OF COLUMBIA
Washington
Member
Children's National Medical Center
Columbia Hospital for Women Medical Center
George Washington University Hospital
Greater Southeast Community Hospital
Sibley Memorial Hospital

FLORIDA
Altamonte Springs
Member
Florida Hospital–Altamonte

Apopka
Member
Florida Hospital–Apopka

Arcadia
Member
DeSoto Memorial Hospital

Belle Glade
Member
Glades General Hospital

Brooksville
Member
Brooksville Regional Hospital

Bunnell
Member
Memorial Hospital–Flagler

Clearwater
Member
Accord Health Care Corporation

Clewiston
Member
Hendry Regional Medical Center

Coral Springs
Member
Coral Springs Medical Center

De Land
Member
Memorial Hospital–West Volusia

Dunedin
Member
Mease Hospital Dunedin
Morton Plant Mease Health Care

Eustis
Member
Florida Hospital Waterman

Fernandina Beach
Member
Baptist Medical Center–Nassau

Fort Lauderdale
Member
Broward General Medical Center
Cleveland Clinic Hospital
Holy Cross Hospital
Imperial Point Medical Center
North Broward Hospital District

Gainesville
Member
AvMed–Santa Fe

Hollywood
Member
Memorial Regional Hospital

Homestead
Member
Homestead Hospital

Jacksonville
Member
St. Vincent's Medical Center

Jacksonville Beach
Member
Baptist Medical Center–Beaches

Jupiter
Member
Jupiter Medical Center

Kissimmee
Member
Florida Hospital Kissimmee

Largo
Member
Sun Coast Hospital

Marianna
Member
Jackson Hospital

Miami
Member
Baptist Hospital of Miami
Bascom Palmer Eye Institute–Anne Bates Leach Eye
Hospital
Miami Children's Hospital
Pan American Hospital
South Miami Hospital

Miami Beach
Member
Mount Sinai Medical Center

Naples
Member
Naples Community Hospital

New Port Richey
Member
North Bay Hospital

New Smyrna Beach
Member
Bert Fish Medical Center

Orange City
Member
Florida Hospital Fish Memorial

Orlando
Member
Florida Hospital

Ormond Beach
Member
Memorial Health Systems
Memorial Hospital–Ormond Beach

Pembroke Pines
Member
Memorial Hospital Pembroke
Memorial Hospital West

Plant City
Member
South Florida Baptist Hospital

Pompano Beach
Member
North Broward Medical Center

Port Charlotte
Member
Bon Secours–St. Joseph Healthcare Group

Rockledge
Member
Wuesthoff Hospital

Safety Harbor
Member
Mease Countryside Hospital

Saint Petersburg
Member
All Children's Hospital
Bayfront Medical Center
St. Anthony's Hospital

Sebring
Member
Florida Hospital Heartland Division

Spring Hill
Member
Spring Hill Regional Hospital

Tampa
Member
H. Lee Moffitt Cancer Center and Research Institute
St. Joseph's Hospital
Tampa Children's Hospital at St. Joseph's, St.
Joseph's Women's Hospital – Tampa

Tarpon Springs
Member
Helen Ellis Memorial Hospital

Tavernier
Member
Mariners Hospital

Titusville
Member
Parrish Medical Center

Venice
Member
Bon Secours–Venice Hospital

Vero Beach
Member
Indian River Memorial Hospital

Winter Haven
Member
Winter Haven Hospital

Winter Park
Member
Adventist Health System Sunbelt Health Care
Corporation

Zephyrhills
Member
East Pasco Medical Center

GEORGIA
Athens
Member
St. Mary's Health Care System

Atlanta
Member
Egleston Children's Hospital
Northside Hospital
Saint Joseph's Hospital of Atlanta

Augusta
Member
University Health Care System
Walton Rehabilitation Hospital

Blairsville
Member
Union General Hospital

Bremen
Member
Higgins General Hospital

Brunswick
Member
  Southeast Georgia Regional Medical Center

Calhoun
Member
  Gordon Hospital

Carrollton
Member
  Tanner Medical Center

Clayton
Member
  Ridgecrest Hospital

Columbus
Member
  St. Francis Hospital

Cumming
Member
  Baptist Medical Center

Demorest
Member
  Habersham County Medical Center

Elberton
Member
  Elbert Memorial Hospital

Fort Oglethorpe
Member
  Hutcheson Medical Center

Glenwood
Member
  Wheeler County Hospital

Greensboro
Member
  Minnie G. Boswell Memorial Hospital

Jesup
Member
  Wayne Memorial Hospital

La Grange
Member
  West Georgia Health System

Macon
Member
  Macon Northside Hospital
  Middle Georgia Hospital

Milledgeville
Member
  Oconee Regional Medical Center

Monroe
Member
  Walton Medical Center

Richland
Member
  Stewart–Webster Hospital

Saint Marys
Member
  Camden Medical Center

Savannah
Member
  Candler Hospital
  Memorial Health System
  St. Joseph's Hospital

Smyrna
Member
  Emory–Adventist Hospital

Sparta
Member
  Hancock Memorial Hospital

Sylvania
Member
  Screven County Hospital

Sylvester
Member
  Baptist Hospital, Worth County

Thomaston
Member
  Upson Regional Medical Center

Thomson
Member
  McDuffie County Hospital

Tifton
Member
  Tift General Hospital

Vienna
Member
  Dooly Medical Center

Villa Rica
Member
  Tanner Medical Center–Villa Rica

Warm Springs
Member
  Baptist Meriwether Hospital

Washington
Member
  Wills Memorial Hospital

IDAHO
Blackfoot
Member
  Bingham Memorial Hospital

Moscow
Member
  Gritman Medical Center

ILLINOIS
Aurora
Member
  Provena Mercy Center

Barrington
Member
  Good Shepherd Hospital

Blue Island
Member
  Saint Francis Hospital and Health Center

Canton
Member
  Graham Hospital

Carmi
Member
  White County Medical Center

Carrollton
Member
  Thomas H. Boyd Memorial Hospital

Carthage
Member
  Memorial Hospital

Centralia
Member
  St. Mary's Hospital

Chicago
Member
  Children's Memorial Hospital
  Mercy Hospital and Medical Center
  Mount Sinai Hospital Medical Center of Chicago
  Our Lady of the Resurrection Medical Center
  Ravenswood Hospital Medical Center
  Resurrection Medical Center
  Thorek Hospital and Medical Center
  Trinity Hospital

Downers Grove
Member
  Good Samaritan Hospital

Elk Grove Village
Member
  Alexian Brothers Medical Center

Galesburg
Member
  Galesburg Cottage Hospital

Geneva
Member
  Delnor–Community Hospital

Gibson City
Member
  Gibson Area Hospital and Health Services

Hazel Crest
Member
  South Suburban Hospital

Hinsdale
Member
  Hinsdale Hospital

Hoopeston
Member
  Hoopeston Community Memorial Hospital

Melrose Park
Member
  Gottlieb Memorial Hospital

Metropolis
Member
  Massac Memorial Hospital

Morrison
Member
  Morrison Community Hospital

Mount Carmel
Member
  Wabash General Hospital District

Mount Vernon
Member
  Good Samaritan Regional Health Center

Nashville
Member
  Washington County Hospital

Oak Brook
Member
  Advocate Health Care

Oak Lawn
Member
  Christ Hospital and Medical Center

Ottawa
Member
  Community Hospital of Ottawa

Paris
Member
  Paris Community Hospital

Park Ridge
Member
  Lutheran General Hospital

Peoria
Member
  Methodist Health Services Corporation
  Methodist Medical Center of Illinois

Pinckneyville
Member
  Pinckneyville Community Hospital

Pittsfield
Member
  Illini Community Hospital

Robinson
Member
  Crawford Memorial Hospital

Staunton
Member
  Community Memorial Hospital

Urbana
Member
  Carle Foundation Hospital

Winfield
Member
  Central DuPage Hospital

INDIANA
Brazil
Member
  Clay County Hospital

Charlestown
Member
  Medical Center of Southern Indiana

Evansville
Member
  Welborn Memorial Baptist Hospital

Frankfort
Member
  Clinton County Hospital

Gary
Member
  Methodist Hospitals

Greensburg
Member
  Decatur County Memorial Hospital

Hartford City
Member
　Blackford County Hospital

Jeffersonville
Member
　Clark Memorial Hospital

North Vernon
Member
　Jennings Community Hospital

Princeton
Member
　Gibson General Hospital

Rushville
Member
　Rush Memorial Hospital

Salem
Member
　Washington County Memorial Hospital

Scottsburg
Member
　Scott Memorial Hospital

Sullivan
Member
　Sullivan County Community Hospital

Tell City
Member
　Perry County Memorial Hospital

Wabash
Member
　Wabash County Hospital

Washington
Member
　Daviess County Hospital

Winchester
Member
　Randolph County Hospital and Health Services

IOWA

Algona
Member
　Kossuth Regional Health Center

Ames
Member
　Mary Greeley Medical Center

Anamosa
Member
　Anamosa Community Hospital

Belmond
Member
　Belmond Community Hospital

Boone
Member
　Boone County Hospital

Britt
Member
　Hancock County Memorial Hospital

Burlington
Member
　Burlington Medical Center

Cedar Rapids
Member
　Mercy Medical Center
　St. Luke's Hospital

Chariton
Member
　Lucas County Health Center

Charles City
Member
　Floyd County Memorial Hospital

Clarion
Member
　Community Memorial Hospital

Clinton
Member
　Samaritan Health System

Corning
Member
　Mercy Hospital

Council Bluffs
Member
　Alegent Health Mercy Hospital

Cresco
Member
　Regional Health Services of Howard County

Davenport
Member
　Genesis Medical Center

De Witt
Member
　DeWitt Community Hospital

Des Moines
Member
　Harrison Treat and Rehabilitation Center
　Iowa Health System
　Iowa Lutheran Hospital
　Iowa Methodist Medical Center

Dubuque
Member
　Finley Hospital
　Mercy Health Center

Dyersville
Member
　Mercy Health Center–St. Mary's Unit

Eldora
Member
　Eldora Regional Medical Center

Elkader
Member
　Central Community Hospital

Emmetsburg
Member
　Palo Alto Health System

Estherville
Member
　Avera Holy Family Health

Fairfield
Member
　Jefferson County Hospital

Fort Dodge
Member
　Trinity Regional Hospital

Fort Madison
Member
　Fort Madison Community Hospital

Grinnell
Member
　Grinnell Regional Medical Center

Hampton
Member
　Franklin General Hospital

Hawarden
Member
　Hawarden Community Hospital

Humboldt
Member
　Humboldt County Memorial Hospital

Iowa City
Member
　Mercy Hospital

Iowa Falls
Member
　Ellsworth Municipal Hospital

Knoxville
Member
　Knoxville Area Community Hospital

Manchester
Member
　Regional Medical Center of Northeast Iowa and
　　Delaware County

Maquoketa
Member
　Jackson County Public Hospital

Marengo
Member
　Marengo Memorial Hospital

Marshalltown
Member
　Marshalltown Medical and Surgical Center

Mason City
Member
　North Iowa Mercy Health Center

Missouri Valley
Member
　Alegent Health Community Memorial Hospital

New Hampton
Member
　Saint Joseph Community Hospital

Newton
Member
　Skiff Medical Center

Osage
Member
　Mitchell County Regional Health Center

Osceola
Member
　Clarke County Hospital

Oskaloosa
Member
　Mahaska County Hospital

Ottumwa
Member
　Ottumwa Regional Health Center

Pella
Member
　Pella Regional Health Center

Pocahontas
Member
　Pocahontas Community Hospital

Primghar
Member
　Baum Harmon Memorial Hospital

Rock Valley
Member
　Hegg Memorial Health Center

Sac City
Member
　Loring Hospital

Shenandoah
Member
　Shenandoah Memorial Hospital

Sibley
Member
　Osceola Community Hospital

Sioux City
Member
　Marian Health Center
　St. Luke's Regional Medical Center

Spencer
Member
　Spencer Municipal Hospital

Storm Lake
Member
　Buena Vista County Hospital

Washington
Member
　Washington County Hospital

Waterloo
Member
　Allen Memorial Hospital

Winterset
Member
　Madison County Memorial Hospital

KANSAS

Chanute
Member
　Neosho Memorial Regional Medical Center

Coffeyville
Member
　Coffeyville Regional Medical Center

Emporia
Member
　Newman Memorial County Hospital

Eureka
Member
　Greenwood County Hospital

Iola
Member
Allen County Hospital

Lawrence
Member
Lawrence Memorial Hospital

Marion
Member
St. Luke Hospital

Neodesha
Member
Wilson County Hospital

Oberlin
Member
Decatur County Hospital

Overland Park
Member
Menorah Medical Center

Ulysses
Member
Bob Wilson Memorial Grant County Hospital

KENTUCKY

Benton
Member
Marshall County Hospital

Berea
Member
Berea Hospital

Bowling Green
Member
The Medical Center at Bowling Green

Burkesville
Member
Cumberland County Hospital

Cadiz
Member
Trigg County Hospital

Campbellsville
Member
Taylor County Hospital

Carrollton
Member
Carroll County Hospital

Corbin
Member
Baptist Regional Medical Center

Elizabethtown
Member
Hardin Memorial Hospital

Flemingsburg
Member
Fleming County Hospital

Franklin
Member
Franklin–Simpson Memorial Hospital

Glasgow
Member
T. J. Samson Community Hospital

Greensburg
Member
Jane Todd Crawford Hospital

Greenville
Member
Muhlenberg Community Hospital

Hardinsburg
Member
Breckinridge Memorial Hospital

Harrodsburg
Member
The James B. Haggin Memorial Hospital

Hartford
Member
Ohio County Hospital

Henderson
Member
Methodist Hospital

Hopkinsville
Member
Jennie Stuart Medical Center

Horse Cave
Member
Caverna Memorial Hospital

Irvine
Member
Marcum and Wallace Memorial Hospital

La Grange
Member
Tri County Baptist Hospital

Lancaster
Member
Garrard County Memorial Hospital

Leitchfield
Member
Twin Lakes Regional Medical Center

Lexington
Member
Central Baptist Hospital
Saint Joseph Hospital East

Louisville
Charter louisville Behavioral Health System
Member
Baptist Healthcare System
Baptist Hospital East
Frazier Rehabilitation Center
Jewish Hospital
Kosair Children's Hospital
Norton Healthcare
Norton Healthcare
University of Louisville Hospital

Manchester
Member
Memorial Hospital

Marion
Member
Crittenden County Hospital

Morganfield
Member
Methodist Hospital Union County

Mount Sterling
Member
Gateway Regional Health System
Mary Chiles Hospital Extended Care Facility

Mount Vernon
Member
Rockcastle Hospital and Respiratory Care Center

Murray
Member
Murray–Calloway County Hospital

Paducah
Member
Lourdes Hospital
Western Baptist Hospital

Pikeville
Member
Pikeville United Methodist Hospital of Kentucky

Pineville
Member
Pineville Community Hospital Association

Princeton
Member
Caldwell County Hospital

Richmond
Member
Pattie A. Clay Hospital

Russell Springs
Member
Russell County Hospital

Salem
Member
Livingston Hospital and Healthcare Services

Shelbyville
Member
Jewish Hospital–Shelbyville

Tompkinsville
Member
Monroe County Medical Center

Versailles
Member
Woodford Hospital

Winchester
Member
Clark Regional Medical Center

LOUISIANA

Alexandria
Member
Christus St. Frances Cabrini Hospital

Baton Rouge
Member
Baton Rouge General Health Center
Baton Rouge General Medical Center
General Health System
Woman's Hospital

Bogalusa
Bogalusa Community Medical Center

Bossier City
Member
Bossier Medical Center

Breaux Bridge
Affiliate
Gary Memorial Hospital

Farmerville
Member
Union General Hospital

Franklin
Member
Franklin Foundation Hospital

Hammond
Member
North Oaks Medical Center

Homer
Member
Homer Memorial Hospital

Houma
Member
Terrebonne General Medical Center

Jena
Member
LaSalle General Hospital

Kaplan
Member
Abrom Kaplan Memorial Hospital

Lafayette
Member
Lafayette General Medical Center

Lake Charles
Member
Christus St. Patrick Hospital
Dubuis Hospital for Continuing Care

Lutcher
Member
St. James Parish Hospital

Marrero
Member
West Jefferson Medical Center

Morgan City
Member
Lakewood Medical Center

Natchitoches
Member
Natchitoches Parish Hospital

New Orleans
Member
Children's Hospital
Touro Infirmary

Opelousas
Member
Opelousas General Hospital

Raceland
Member
St. Anne General Hospital

Shreveport
Member
Christus Schumpert Medical Center

Sterlington
Member
Sterlington Hospital

Tallulah
Member
Madison Parish Hospital

Alliances

Thibodaux
Member
   Thibodaux Regional Medical Center

Ville Platte
Member
   Ville Platte Medical Center

West Monroe
Member
   Glenwood Regional Medical Center

Zachary
   Lane Memorial Hospital

MAINE

Blue Hill
Member
   Blue Hill Memorial Hospital

Brunswick
Member
   Parkview Hospital

Calais
Member
   Calais Regional Hospital

Caribou
Member
   Cary Medical Center

Dover–Foxcroft
Member
   Mayo Regional Hospital

Ellsworth
Member
   Maine Coast Memorial Hospital

Houlton
Member
   Houlton Regional Hospital

Lewiston
Member
   St. Mary's Regional Medical Center

Lincoln
Member
   Penobscot Valley Hospital

Machias
Member
   Down East Community Hospital

Millinocket
Member
   Millinocket Regional Hospital

Portland
Member
   Mercy Hospital Portland

MARYLAND

Annapolis
Member
   Anne Arundel Medical Center

Baltimore
Member
   Bon Secours Baltimore Health System
   Church Hospital Corporation
   Franklin Square Hospital Center
   Good Samaritan Hospital of Maryland
   Harbor Hospital Center
   Liberty Medical Center
   Mercy Medical Center
   Mt. Washington Pediatric Hospital
   Sinai Hospital of Baltimore
   The New Children's Hospital
   Union Memorial Hospital

Berlin
Member
   Atlantic General Hospital

Bethesda
Member
   Suburban Hospital

Cheverly
Member
   Prince George's Hospital Center

Columbia
Member
   Howard County General Hospital
   MedStar Health

Cumberland
Member
   Memorial Hospital and Medical Center of Cumberland
   Sacred Heart Hospital

Elkton
Member
   Union Hospital

Fort Washington
Member
   Fort Washington Hospital

Frederick
Member
   Frederick Memorial Hospital

Glen Burnie
Member
   North Arundel Hospital

Hagerstown
Member
   Washington County Health System

Lanham
Member
   Doctors Community Hospital

Laurel
Member
   Laurel Regional Hospital

Marriottsville
Member
   Bon Secours Health System, Inc.

Olney
Member
   Montgomery General Hospital

Randallstown
Member
   Northwest Hospital Center

Rockville
Member
   Shady Grove Adventist Hospital

Salisbury
Member
   Peninsula Regional Medical Center

Takoma Park
Member
   Washington Adventist Hospital

Westminster
Member
   Carroll County General Hospital

MASSACHUSETTS

Attleboro
Member
   Sturdy Memorial Hospital

Ayer
Member
   Deaconess–Nashoba Hospital

Boston
Member
   Beth Israel Deaconess Medical Center
   Boston Medical Center
   Children's Hospital
   New England Baptist Hospital

Braintree
Member
   Massachusetts Respiratory Hospital

Brockton
Member
   Brockton Hospital
   Good Samaritan Medical Center

Cambridge
Member
   Youville Lifecare

Fall River
Member
   Southcoast Hospitals Group

Great Barrington
Member
   Fairview Hospital

Greenfield
Member
   Franklin Medical Center

Haverhill
Member
   Hale Hospital

Lexington
Member
   Covenant Health Systems, Inc.

Lowell
Member
   Saints Memorial Medical Center

Needham
Member
   Deaconess–Glover Hospital Corporation

Palmer
Member
   Wing Memorial Hospital and Medical Centers

Pittsfield
Member
   Berkshire Medical Center

Plymouth
Member
   Jordan Hospital

Quincy
Member
   Quincy Hospital

Springfield
Member
   Baystate Health System, Inc.
   Baystate Medical Center

Waltham
Member
   Deaconess Waltham Hospital

Ware
Member
   Mary Lane Hospital

Webster
Member
   Hubbard Regional Hospital

Winchester
Member
   Winchester Hospital

Worcester
Member
   UMass Memorial Health Care–Memorial Campus

MICHIGAN

Allegan
Member
   Allegan General Hospital

Alma
Member
   Gratiot Community Hospital

Ann Arbor
Member
   Saint Joseph Mercy Health System

Battle Creek
Member
   Battle Creek Health System

Big Rapids
Member
   Mecosta County General Hospital

Cadillac
Member
   Mercy Health Services–North

Carson City
Member
   Carson City Hospital

Chelsea
Member
   Chelsea Community Hospital

Clinton Township
Member
   St. Joseph's Mercy Hospitals and Health Services

Commerce Township
Member
   Huron Valley–Sinai Hospital

Detroit
Member
Detroit Medical Center
Detroit Receiving Hospital and University Health
Center
Grace Hospital
Harper Hospital
Henry Ford Health System
Henry Ford Hospital
Hutzel Hospital
Mercy Hospital
Sinai Hospital
St. John Detroit Riverview Hospital

Dowagiac
Member
Lee Memorial Hospital

Farmington Hills
Member
Botsford General Hospital
Mercy Health Services

Flint
Member
McLaren Regional Medical Center

Frankfort
Member
Paul Oliver Memorial Hospital

Garden City
Member
Garden City Hospital

Grand Rapids
Spectrum Health–East Campus
Member
Metropolitan Hospital
Saint Mary's Health Services

Grayling
Member
Mercy Health Services North–Grayling

Grosse Pointe
Member
Bon Secours Hospital

Grosse Pointe Farms
Member
Cottage Hospital

Hillsdale
Member
Hillsdale Community Health Center

Jackson
Member
Doctors Hospital of Jackson
W. A. Foote Memorial Hospital

Kalamazoo
Member
Borgess Medical Center

Kalkaska
Member
Kalkaska Memorial Health Center

Lakeview
Member
Kelsey Memorial Hospital

Lansing
Member
Ingham Regional Medical Center
Sparrow Health System

Lapeer
Member
Lapeer Regional Hospital

Madison Heights
Member
Madison Community Hospital
St. John Oakland Hospital

Marlette
Member
Marlette Community Hospital

Mount Clemens
Member
Mount Clemens General Hospital

Mount Pleasant
Member
Central Michigan Community Hospital

Muskegon
Member
Mercy General Health Partners

Northport
Member
Leelanau Memorial Health Center

Paw Paw
Member
LakeView Community Hospital

Pontiac
Member
POH Medical Center
St. Joseph Mercy Oakland

Port Huron
Member
Mercy Hospital

Rochester
Member
Crittenton Hospital

Romeo
Member
St. Joseph's Mercy–North

Saginaw
Member
HealthSource Saginaw

Saint Johns
Member
Clinton Memorial Hospital

Saline
Member
Saline Community Hospital

Southfield
Member
Straith Hospital for Special Surgery

Sturgis
Member
Sturgis Hospital

Tecumseh
Member
Herrick Memorial Hospital, Lenawee Health Alliance

Three Rivers
Member
Three Rivers Area Hospital

Traverse City
Member
Munson Medical Center

Trenton
Member
Riverside Osteopathic Hospital

Warren
Member
Bi–County Community Hospital
St. John Macomb Hospital

Watervliet
Member
Community Hospital

Wyandotte
Member
Henry Ford Wyandotte Hospital

MINNESOTA
Aitkin
Member
Riverwood Health CareCenter

Alexandria
Member
Douglas County Hospital

Austin
Member
Austin Medical Center

Burnsville
Member
Fairview Ridges Hospital

Cloquet
Member
Cloquet Community Memorial Hospital

Cook
Member
Cook Hospital and Convalescent Nursing Care Unit

Crosby
Member
Cuyuna Regional Medical Center

Duluth
Member
Miller Dwan Medical Center

Ely
Member
Ely–Bloomenson Community Hospital

Fairmont
Member
Fairmont Community Hospital

Glencoe
Member
Glencoe Area Health Center

Hibbing
Member
University Medical Center–Mesabi

International Falls
Member
Falls Memorial Hospital

Litchfield
Member
Meeker County Memorial Hospital

Minneapolis
Member
Fairview Hospital and Healthcare Services
Fairview Southdale Hospital
Fairview–University Medical Center

Monticello
Member
Monticello Big Lake Hospital

Moose Lake
Member
Mercy Hospital and Health Care Center

Mora
Member
Kanabec Hospital

New Prague
Member
Queen of Peace Hospital

Northfield
Member
Northfield Hospital

Ortonville
Member
Ortonville Area Health Services

Pipestone
Member
Pipestone County Medical Center

Princeton
Member
Fairview Northland Regional Health Care

Red Wing
Member
Fairview Red Wing Hospital

Robbinsdale
Member
North Memorial Health Care

Rochester
Member
Olmsted Medical Center

Saint Louis Park
Member
HealthSystem Minnesota

Sandstone
Member
Pine Medical Center

Staples
Member
Lakewood Health System

Stillwater
Member
Lakeview Hospital

Tyler
Member
Tyler Healthcare Center

Virginia
Member
Virginia Regional Medical Center

Wadena
Member
  Tri–County Hospital

Winona
Member
  Winona Community Memorial Hospital

Wyoming
Member
  Fairview Lakes Regional Medical Center

MISSISSIPPI

Amory
Member
  Gilmore Memorial Hospital

Bay Saint Louis
Member
  Hancock Medical Center

Bay Springs
Member
  Jasper General Hospital

Brookhaven
Member
  King's Daughters Medical Center

Centreville
Member
  Field Memorial Community Hospital

Cleveland
Member
  Bolivar Medical Center

Columbia
Member
  Marion General Hospital

Corinth
Member
  Magnolia Regional Health Center

Durant
Member
  University Hospital and Clinics–Durant

Greenville
Member
  Delta Regional Medical Center
  King's Daughters Hospital

Grenada
Member
  Grenada Lake Medical Center

Hattiesburg
Member
  Wesley Medical Center

Jackson
Member
  Central Mississippi Medical Center
  Mississippi Baptist Health Systems
  University Hospitals and Clinics, University of
    Mississippi Medical Center

Laurel
Member
  South Central Regional Medical Center

Lexington
Member
  Methodist Healthcare Middle Mississippi Hospital

Louisville
Member
  Winston Medical Center

Magee
Member
  Magee General Hospital

Meridian
Member
  Rush Foundation Hospital

Natchez
Member
  Natchez Regional Medical Center

Philadelphia
Member
  Neshoba County General Hospital

Picayune
Member
  Crosby Memorial Hospital

Prentiss
Member
  Prentiss Regional Hospital and Extended Care
    Facilities

Quitman
Member
  H. C. Watkins Memorial Hospital

Union
Member
  Laird Hospital

Vicksburg
Member
  Parkview Regional Medical Center

Yazoo City
Member
  King's Daughters Hospital

MISSOURI

Albany
Member
  Gentry County Memorial Hospital

Belton
Member
  Research Belton Hospital

Bethany
Member
  Harrison County Community Hospital

Bridgeton
Member
  DePaul Hospital

Carrollton
Member
  Carroll County Memorial Hospital

Fairfax
Member
  Community Hospital Association

Farmington
Member
  Mineral Area Regional Medical Center

Harrisonville
Member
  Cass Medical Center

Independence
Member
  Medical Center of Independence

Jefferson City
Member
  St. Marys Health Center

Kansas City
Member
  Baptist Medical Center
  Children's Mercy Hospital
  Health Midwest
  Park Lane Medical Center
  Research Medical Center
  Trinity Lutheran Hospital

Lake Saint Louis
Member
  St. Joseph Hospital West

Lees Summit
Member
  Lee's Summit Hospital

Lexington
Member
  Lafayette Regional Health Center

Louisiana
Member
  Pike County Memorial Hospital

Maryville
Member
  St. Francis Hospital and Health Services

Mexico
Member
  Audrain Medical Center

Nevada
Member
  Nevada Regional Medical Center

Pilot Knob
Member
  Arcadia Valley Hospital

Rolla
Member
  Phelps County Regional Medical Center

Saint Charles
Member
  St. Joseph Health Center

Saint Joseph
Member
  Heartland Regional Medical Center

Saint Louis
Member
  Cardinal Glennon Children's Hospital
  SSM Health Care
  St. Joseph Hospital of Kirkwood
  St. Mary's Health Center

West Plains
Member
  Ozarks Medical Center

MONTANA

Anaconda
Member
  Community Hospital of Anaconda

Cut Bank
Member
  Glacier County Medical Center

Great Falls
Member
  Benefis Health Care
  Benefis Health Care–West Campus

Harlowton
Member
  Wheatland Memorial Hospital

Lewistown
Member
  Central Montana Medical Center

Missoula
Member
  St. Patrick Hospital

Plains
Member
  Clark Fork Valley Hospital

Polson
Member
  St. Joseph Hospital

Whitefish
Member
  North Valley Hospital

NEBRASKA

Ainsworth
Member
  Brown County Hospital

Albion
Member
  Boone County Health Center

Atkinson
Member
  West Holt Memorial Hospital

Auburn
Member
  Nemaha County Hospital

Aurora
Member
  Memorial Hospital

Bassett
Member
  Rock County Hospital

Central City
Member
  Litzenberg Memorial County Hospital

Chadron
Member
  Chadron Community Hospital and Health Services

Cozad
Member
  Cozad Community Hospital

Creighton
Member
  Creighton Area Health Services

Fairbury
Member
    Jefferson Community Health Center

Fremont
Member
    Fremont Area Medical Center

Geneva
Member
    Fillmore County Hospital

Genoa
Member
    Genoa Community Hospital

Gordon
Member
    Gordon Memorial Hospital District

Gothenburg
Member
    Gothenburg Memorial Hospital

Hebron
Member
    Thayer County Health Services

Henderson
Member
    Henderson Health Care Services

Holdrege
Member
    Phelps Memorial Health Center

Imperial
Member
    Chase County Community Hospital

Lynch
Member
    Niobrara Valley Hospital

North Platte
Member
    Great Plains Regional Medical Center

O'Neill
Member
    Avera St. Anthony's Hospital

Oakland
Member
    Oakland Memorial Hospital

Ogallala
Member
    Ogallala Community Hospital

Omaha
Member
    Alegent Health Bergan Mercy Medical Center
    Alegent Health Immanuel Medical Center
    Boys Town National Research Hospital

Ord
Member
    Valley County Hospital

Osceola
Member
    Annie Jeffrey Memorial County Health Center

Papillion
Member
    Alegent–Health Midlands Community Hospital

Pawnee City
Member
    Pawnee County Memorial Hospital

Pender
Member
    Pender Community Hospital

Red Cloud
Member
    Webster County Community Hospital

Saint Paul
Member
    Howard County Community Hospital

Schuyler
Member
    Alegent Health–Memorial Hospital

Seward
Member
    Memorial Health Care Systems

Superior
Member
    Brodstone Memorial Hospital

Syracuse
Member
    Community Memorial Hospital

Tecumseh
Member
    Johnson County Hospital

Valentine
Member
    Cherry County Hospital

Wahoo
Member
    Saunders County Health Service

Wayne
Member
    Providence Medical Center

West Point
Member
    St. Francis Memorial Hospital

NEVADA
Fallon
Member
    Churchill Community Hosptial

Las Vegas
Member
    Desert Springs Hospital

Lovelock
Member
    Pershing General Hospital

NEW HAMPSHIRE
Exeter
Member
    Exeter Hospital

Littleton
Member
    Littleton Regional Hospital

Manchester
Member
    Catholic Medical Center
    Elliot Hospital

Nashua
Member
    St. Joseph Hospital

NEW JERSEY
Belleville
Member
    Clara Maass Health System

Edison
Member
    JFK Medical Center
    Solaris Health System

Englewood
Member
    Englewood Hospital and Medical Center

Freehold
Member
    CentraState Healthcare System

Hackensack
Member
    Hackensack University Medical Center

Hackettstown
Member
    Hackettstown Community Hospital

Holmdel
Member
    Bayshore Community Hospital

Irvington
Member
    Irvington General Hospital

Jersey City
Member
    Greenville Hospital
    Jersey City Medical Center

Kearny
Member
    West Hudson Hospital

Lakewood
Member
    Kimball Medical Center

Livingston
Member
    Saint Barnabas Medical Center

Long Branch
Member
    Monmouth Medical Center

Manahawkin
Member
    Southern Ocean County Hospital

Newark
Member
    Newark Beth Israel Medical Center

Passaic
Member
    Beth Israel Hospital

Paterson
Member
    Barnert Hospital
    St. Joseph's Hospital and Medical Center

Salem
Member
    Memorial Hospital of Salem County

Secaucus
Member
    Meadowlands Hospital Medical Center

Toms River
Member
    Community Medical Center

Union
Member
    Union Hospital

Wayne
Member
    Wayne General Hospital

West Orange
Member
    Saint Barnabas Health Care System

NEW MEXICO
Alamogordo
Member
    Gerald Champion Memorial Hospital

Albuquerque
Member
    Presbyterian Healthcare Services
    Presbyterian Hospital
    Presbyterian Kaseman Hospital

Artesia
Member
    Artesia General Hospital

Clovis
Member
    Plains Regional Medical Center

Espanola
Member
    Espanola Hospital

Grants
Member
    Cibola General Hospital

Los Alamos
Member
    Los Alamos Medical Center

Ruidoso
Member
    Lincoln County Medical Center

Silver City
Member
    Gila Regional Medical Center

Socorro
Member
    Socorro General Hospital

Taos
Member
    Holy Cross Hospital

Truth or Consequences
Member
    Sierra Vista Hospital

Tucumcari
Member
Dr. Dan C. Trigg Memorial Hospital

NEW YORK
Albany
Member
Albany Medical Center
St. Peter's Hospital

Amityville
Affiliate
South Oaks Hospital

Amsterdam
Member
Amsterdam Memorial Hospital

Batavia
Member
United Memorial Medical Center–Bank Street
United Memorial Medical Center–North Street

Bath
Member
Ira Davenport Memorial Hospital

Bayside
Member
St. Mary's Hospital for Children

Beacon
Member
Saint Francis Hospital–Beacon

Bethpage
Member
New Island Hospital

Brockport
Member
Lakeside Memorial Hospital

Bronx
Member
Bronx–Lebanon Hospital Center
Calvary Hospital
Fulton Division
Jewish Home and Hospital for Aged
Montefiore Medical Center
Our Lady of Mercy Healthcare System, Inc.
Our Lady of Mercy Medical Center
St. Barnabas Hospital
Union Hospital of the Bronx

Brooklyn
Member
Brookdale Hospital Medical Center
Interfaith Medical Center
Kingsbrook Jewish Medical Center
Long Island College Hospital
Lutheran Medical Center
Maimonides Medical Center
New York Methodist Hospital
St. Mary's Hospital of Brooklyn
University Hospital of Brooklyn–State University of
New York Health Science Center at Brooklyn
Victory Memorial Hospital

Buffalo
Member
Brylin Hospitals
Children's Hospital
Mercy Hospital
Millard Fillmore Gates Circle Hospital
Sheehan Memorial Hospital

Canandaigua
Member
F. F. Thompson Health System

Cheektowaga
Member
St. Joseph Hospital

Clifton Springs
Member
Clifton Springs Hospital and Clinic

Corning
Member
Corning Hospital

Cortlandt Manor
Member
Hudson Valley Hospital Center

Dansville
Member
Nicholas H. Noyes Memorial Hospital

Dobbs Ferry
Member
Community Hospital at Dobbs Ferry

Elizabethtown
Member
Elizabethtown Community Hospital

Elmira
Member
Arnot Ogden Medical Center
St. Joseph's Hospital

Far Rockaway
Member
Peninsula Hospital Center
St. John's Episcopal Hospital–South Shore

Flushing
Member
Parkway Hospital
St. John's Queens Hospital
St. Joseph's Hospital

Glen Oaks
Member
Hillside Hospital

Glens Falls
Member
Glens Falls Hospital

Hornell
Member
St. James Mercy Hospital

Irving
Member
Lake Shore Hospital

Jamaica
Member
Catholic Medical Centers
Jamaica Hospital Medical Center

Kenmore
Member
Kenmore Mercy Hospital

Lackawanna
Member
Our Lady of Victory Hospital

Long Beach
Member
Long Beach Medical Center

Long Island City
Member
Western Queens Community Hospital

Medina
Member
Medina Memorial Hospital

Mineola
Member
Winthrop–University Hospital

Montour Falls
Member
Schuyler Hospital

Mount Vernon
Member
Mount Vernon Hospital

New Hyde Park
Member
Long Island Jewish Medical Center
Schneider Children's Hospital

New York
Member
Cabrini Medical Center
Hospital for Special Surgery
Lenox Hill Hospital
Manhattan Eye, Ear and Throat Hospital
Mount Sinai–NYU Hospitals/Health System
New York Eye and Ear Infirmary
North General Hospital
Saint Vincents Hospital and Medical Center
St. Clare's Hospital and Health Center
St. Luke's–Roosevelt Hospital Center

Newfane
Member
Inter–Community Memorial Hospital

Oceanside
Member
South Nassau Communities Hospital

Oneonta
Member
Aurelia Osborn Fox Memorial Hospital

Patchogue
Member
Brookhaven Memorial Hospital Medical Center

Penn Yan
Member
Soldiers and Sailors Memorial Hospital of Yates
County

Plattsburgh
Member
Champlain Valley Physicians Hospital Medical Center

Port Jefferson
Member
John T. Mather Memorial Hospital
St. Charles Hospital and Rehabilitation Center

Poughkeepsie
Member
Saint Francis Hospital
Vassar Brothers Hospital

Rochester
Member
Genesee Hospital
Monroe Community Hospital
Rochester General Hospital

Rockville Centre
Member
Mercy Medical Center

Roslyn
Member
St. Francis Hospital

Schenectady
Member
Ellis Hospital

Seaford
Member
Massapequa General Hospital

Smithtown
Member
St. John's Episcopal Hospital–Smithtown
St. John's Episcopal Medical Healthcare Center

Staten Island
Member
Doctors' Hospital of Staten Island
Sisters of Charity Healthcare
Sisters of Charity Medical Center
Staten Island University Hospital

Syracuse
Member
University Hospital–SUNY Health Science Center at
Syracuse

Troy
Member
Samaritan Hospital

Uniondale
Member
Episcopal Health Services Inc.

Valhalla
Member
Blythedale Children's Hospital
Westchester Medical Center

Warsaw
Member
Wyoming County Community Hospital

West Islip
Member
Good Samaritan Hospital Medical Center

Westfield
Member
Westfield Memorial Hospital

White Plains
Member
St. Agnes Hospital

Williamsville
Member
Millard Fillmore Suburban Hospital

Yonkers
Member
St. John's Riverside Hospital
Yonkers General Hospital

NORTH CAROLINA

Albemarle
Member
  Stanly Memorial Hospital

Andrews
Member
  District Memorial Hospital

Asheboro
Member
  Randolph Hospital

Asheville
Member
  Mission St. Joseph's Health
  Thoms Rehabilitation Hospital

Blowing Rock
Member
  Blowing Rock Hospital

Boiling Springs
Member
  Crawley Memorial Hospital

Boone
Member
  Watauga Medical Center

Brevard
Member
  Transylvania Community Hospital

Bryson City
Member
  Swain County Hospital

Burgaw
Member
  Pender Memorial Hospital

Burlington
Member
  Alamance Regional Medical Center

Charlotte
Member
  Presbyterian Specialty Hospital

Clinton
Member
  Sampson Regional Medical Center

Clyde
Member
  Haywood Regional Medical Center

Columbus
Member
  St. Luke's Hospital

Danbury
Member
  Stokes–Reynolds Memorial Hospital

Durham
Member
  Durham Regional Hospital

Eden
Member
  Morehead Memorial Hospital

Edenton
Member
  Chowan Hospital

Elizabethtown
Member
  Bladen County Hospital

Elkin
Member
  Hugh Chatham Memorial Hospital

Erwin
Member
  Good Hope Hospital

Fayetteville
Member
  Behavioral Health Care of Cape Fear Valley Health
    System
  Cape Fear Valley Health System

Fletcher
Member
  Park Ridge Hospital

Franklin
Member
  Angel Medical Center

Gastonia
Member
  Gaston Memorial Hospital

Goldsboro
Member
  Wayne Memorial Hospital

Henderson
Member
  Maria Parham Hospital

Hendersonville
Member
  Margaret R. Pardee Memorial Hospital

Hickory
Member
  Catawba Memorial Hospital

Jefferson
Member
  Ashe Memorial Hospital

Kenansville
Member
  Duplin General Hospital

Kinston
Member
  Lenoir Memorial Hospital

Laurinburg
Member
  Scotland Memorial Hospital

Lenoir
Member
  Caldwell Memorial Hospital

Lexington
Member
  Lexington Memorial Hospital

Lumberton
Member
  Southeastern Regional Medical Center

Marion
Member
  McDowell Hospital

Matthews
Member
  Presbyterian Hospital–Matthews

Morganton
Member
  Grace Hospital

Mount Airy
Member
  Northern Hospital of Surry County

Murphy
Member
  Murphy Medical Center

North Wilkesboro
Member
  Wilkes Regional Medical Center

Oxford
Member
  Granville Medical Center

Pinehurst
Member
  FirstHealth Moore Regional Hospital

Plymouth
Member
  Washington County Hospital

Raleigh
Member
  Rex Healthcare

Roanoke Rapids
Member
  Halifax Regional Medical Center

Roxboro
Member
  Person Memorial Hospital

Rutherfordton
Member
  Rutherford Hospital

Shelby
Member
  Cleveland Regional Medical Center

Siler City
Member
  Chatham Hospital

Smithfield
Member
  Johnston Memorial Hospital

Sparta
Member
  Alleghany Memorial Hospital

Spruce Pine
Member
  Spruce Pine Community Hospital

Statesville
Member
  Iredell Memorial Hospital

Sylva
Member
  Harris Regional Hospital

Taylorsville
Member
  Alexander Community Hospital

Troy
Member
  FirstHealth Montgomery Memorial Hospital

Whiteville
Member
  Columbus County Hospital

Williamston
Member
  Martin General Hospital

Wilmington
Member
  New Hanover Regional Medical Center

Wilson
Member
  Wilson Memorial Hospital

Winston–Salem
Member
  North Carolina Baptist Hospital

Yadkinville
Member
  Hoots Memorial Hospital

NORTH DAKOTA

Cavalier
Member
  Pembina County Memorial Hospital and Wedgewood
    Manor

Kenmare
Member
  Kenmare Community Hospital

Lisbon
Member
  Lisbon Medical Center

Minot
Member
  UniMed Medical Center

OHIO

Akron
Member
  Akron City Hospital
  Children's Hospital Medical Center of Akron
  Edwin Shaw Hospital for Rehabilitation
  Saint Thomas Hospital
  Summa Health System

Alliance
Member
  Alliance Community Hospital

Amherst
Member
  EMH Amherst Hospital

Ashtabula
Member
  Ashtabula County Medical Center

Barberton
Member
  Barberton Citizens Hospital

Batavia
Member
  Clermont Mercy Hospital

Cincinnati
Member
  Bethesda North Hospital
  Bethesda Oak Hospital
  Catholic Healthcare Partners
  Children's Hospital Medical Center
  Mercy Hospital Anderson

Cleveland
Member
  Cleveland Clinic Foundation
  Fairview Hospital
  Fairview Hospital System
  Grace Hospital
  Health Hill Hospital for Children
  Lutheran Hospital
  Meridia Health System
  Meridia Hillcrest Hospital
  Meridia Huron Hospital
  MetroHealth Medical Center

Columbus
Member
  Children's Hospital
  Ohio State University Hospital East

Dayton
Member
  Children's Medical Center
  Good Samaritan Hospital and Health Center
  Grandview Hospital and Medical Center

Defiance
Member
  Defiance Hospital

Dennison
Member
  Twin City Hospital

East Liverpool
Member
  East Liverpool City Hospital

Elyria
Member
  EMH Regional Medical Center

Euclid
Member
  Euclid Hospital

Fremont
Member
  Memorial Hospital

Garfield Heights
Member
  Marymount Hospital

Georgetown
Member
  Brown County General Hospital

Green Springs
Member
  St. Francis Health Care Centre

Greenfield
Member
  Greenfield Area Medical Center

Hamilton
Member
  Mercy Hospital

Kettering
Member
  Kettering Medical Center

Lakewood
Member
  Lakewood Hospital

Lima
Member
  St. Rita's Medical Center

Lodi
Member
  Lodi Community Hospital

Lorain
Member
  Lorain Community/St. Joseph Regional Health Center

Marietta
Member
  Selby General Hospital

Marysville
Member
  Memorial Hospital

Massillon
Member
  Doctors Hospital of Stark County
  Massillon Community Hospital

Middleburg Heights
Member
  Southwest General Health Center

Mount Vernon
Member
  Knox Community Hospital

Oberlin
Member
  Allen Memorial Hospital

Oregon
Member
  St. Charles Mercy Hospital

Parma
Member
  Parma Community General Hospital

Paulding
Member
  Paulding County Hospital

Sandusky
Member
  Providence Hospital

Springfield
Member
  Mercy Medical Center

Tiffin
Member
  Mercy Hospital

Toledo
Member
  Riverside Mercy Hospital
  St. Vincent Mercy Medical Center

Urbana
Member
  Mercy Memorial Hospital

Van Wert
Member
  Van Wert County Hospital

Wadsworth
Member
  Wadsworth–Rittman Hospital

Warren
Member
  Hillside Rehabilitation Hospital
  St. Joseph Health Center

Warrensville Heights
Member
  Meridia South Pointe Hospital

Washington Court House
Member
  Fayette County Memorial Hospital

Willard
Member
  Mercy Hospital–Willard

Wooster
Member
  Wooster Community Hospital

Youngstown
Member
  St. Elizabeth Health Center
  Youngstown Osteopathic Hospital

OKLAHOMA

Alva
Member
  Share Medical Center

Atoka
Member
  Atoka Memorial Hospital

Cordell
Member
  Cordell Memorial Hospital

Cushing
Member
  Cushing Regional Hospital

Frederick
Member
  Memorial Hospital

Guthrie
Member
  Logan Hospital and Medical Center

Henryetta
Member
  Henryetta Medical Center

Holdenville
Member
  Holdenville General Hospital

Idabel
Member
  McCurtain Memorial Hospital

Kingfisher
Member
  Kingfisher Regional Hospital

Lawton
Member
  Comanche County Memorial Hospital

Mangum
Member
  Mangum City Hospital

Oklahoma City
Member
  Bone and Joint Hospital
  Hillcrest Health Center
  St. Anthony Hospital

Okmulgee
Affiliate
  Okmulgee Memorial Hospital
Member
  Okmulgee Memorial Hospital Authority

Perry
Member
  Perry Memorial Hospital

Purcell
Member
  Purcell Municipal Hospital

Sayre
Member
  Sayre Memorial Hospital

Seiling
Member
  Seiling Hospital

Seminole
Member
  Seminole Medical Center

Tahlequah
Member
  Tahlequah City Hospital

Tulsa
Member
  Laureate Psychiatric Clinic and Hospital
  Saint Francis Hospital

Watonga
Member
  Watonga Municipal Hospital

Woodward
Member
  Woodward Hospital and Health Center

OREGON

Dallas
Member
  Valley Community Hospital

Eugene
Member
  Sacred Heart Medical Center

Florence
Member
  Peace Harbor Hospital

Gold Beach
Member
  Curry General Hospital

Gresham
Member
  Legacy Mount Hood Medical Center

Heppner
Member
  Pioneer Memorial Hospital

Section B

Lakeview
Member
  Lake District Hospital

Lebanon
Member
  Lebanon Community Hospital

Lincoln City
Member
  North Lincoln Hospital

Medford
  Providence Medford Medical Center

Milwaukie
Member
  Providence Milwaukie Hospital

Newberg
Member
  Providence Newberg Hospital

Newport
Member
  Pacific Communities Health District

Portland
Member
  Adventist Medical Center
  Colonial Manor Sanitarium
  Legacy Good Samaritan Hospital and Medical Center
  Legacy Health System
  Providence St. Vincent Medical Center

Prineville
Member
  Pioneer Memorial Hospital

Salem
Member
  Salem Hospital

Seaside
Member
  Providence Seaside Hospital

Springfield
Member
  McKenzie–Willamette Hospital

Stayton
Member
  Santiam Memorial Hospital

Tillamook
Member
  Tillamook County General Hospital

Tualatin
Member
  Legacy Meridian Park Hospital

PENNSYLVANIA

Altoona
Member
  Bon Secours–Holy Family Regional Health System

Berwick
Member
  Berwick Hospital Center

Bethlehem
Member
  St. Luke's Hospital and Health Network

Brownsville
Member
  Brownsville General Hospital

Bryn Mawr
Member
  Bryn Mawr Hospital
  Bryn Mawr Hospital

Carlisle
Member
  Carlisle Hospital and Health Services

Clarion
Member
  Clarion Hospital

Coaldale
Member
  Miner's Memorial Medical Center

Corry
Member
  Corry Memorial Hospital

Danville
Member
  Geisinger Medical Center

Darby
Member
  Mercy Fitzgerald Hospital

East Stroudsburg
Member
  Pocono Medical Center

Easton
Member
  Easton Hospital

Erie
Member
  Millcreek Community Hospital
  Saint Vincent Health Center

Harrisburg
Member
  Penn State Geisinger Health System

Havertown
Member
  Mercy Community Hospital

Hazleton
Member
  Hazleton–St. Joseph Medical Center

Hershey
Member
  Penn State Geisinger Health System–Milton S.
    Hershey Medical Center

Huntingdon
Member
  J. C. Blair Memorial Hospital

Jersey Shore
Member
  Jersey Shore Hospital

Kane
Member
  Kane Community Hospital

Lock Haven
Member
  Lock Haven Hospital

Malvern
Member
  Bryn Mawr Rehabilitation Hospital

McKees Rocks
Member
  Ohio Valley General Hospital

Meadville
Member
  Meadville Medical Center

Media
Member
  Riddle Memorial Hospital

Monroeville
Member
  Allegheny University Hospitals, Forbes Regional

Nanticoke
Member
  Mercy Special Care Hospital

Newtown Square
Member
  Catholic Health East

Palmerton
Member
  Palmerton Hospital

Paoli
Member
  Paoli Memorial Hospital

Philadelphia
Member
  Albert Einstein Healthcare Network
  Albert Einstein Medical Center
  Belmont Center for Comprehensive Treatment
  Children's Hospital of Philadelphia
  Germantown Hospital and Community Health Services
  Mercy Hospital of Philadelphia
  Methodist Hospital
  Thomas Jefferson University Hospital
  Wills Eye Hospital

Pittsburgh
Member
  Allegheny University Hospitals–Forbes Metropolitan
  Children's Hospital of Pittsburgh
  Mercy Hospital of Pittsburgh
  Mercy Providence Hospital
  Suburban General Hospital
  Western Pennsylvania Hospital

Pottsville
Member
  Pottsville Hospital and Warne Clinic

Ridley Park
Member
  Taylor Hospital

Scranton
Member
  Mercy Hospital of Scranton

Spangler
Member
  Miners Hospital Northern Cambria

Titusville
Member
  Titusville Area Hospital

Towanda
Member
  Memorial Hospital

Tyrone
Member
  Tyrone Hospital

Union City
Member
  Union City Memorial Hospital

Warren
Member
  Warren General Hospital

Wayne
Member
  Jefferson Health System

Waynesburg
Member
  Greene County Memorial Hospital

West Grove
Member
  Southern Chester County Medical Center

Wilkes–Barre
Member
  Mercy Hospital of Wilkes–Barre
  Penn State Geisinger Wyoming Valley Medical Center

Wynnewood
Member
  Lankenau Hospital

York
Member
  Memorial Hospital

PUERTO RICO

Mayaguez
Member
  Bella Vista Hospital

Ponce
Member
  Hospital De Damas

RHODE ISLAND

Providence
Member
  Roger Williams Medical Center

SOUTH CAROLINA

Abbeville
Member
  Abbeville County Memorial Hospital

Anderson
Member
  Anderson Area Medical Center

Beaufort
Member
  Beaufort Memorial Hospital

Camden
Member
  Kershaw County Medical Center

Charleston
Member
  Bon Secours–St. Francis Xavier Hospital
  Roper Hospital
  Roper Hospital North

Clinton
Member
  Laurens County Healthcare System

Columbia
Member
  Palmetto Richland Memorial Hospital

Conway
Member
  Conway Hospital

Dillon
Member
  Saint Eugene Medical Center

Edgefield
Member
  Edgefield County Hospital

Florence
Member
  Carolinas Hospital System
  McLeod Regional Medical Center

Greenville
Member
  Greenville Hospital System
  Greenville Memorial Hospital
  Shriners Hospitals for Children, Greenville

Greenwood
Member
  Self Memorial Hospital

Greer
Member
  Allen Bennett Hospital

Kingstree
Member
  Carolinas Hospital System–Kingstree

Lake City
Member
  Carolinas Hospital System–Lake City

Lexington
Member
  Keisler Nursing Home

Loris
Member
  Loris Community Hospital

Newberry
Member
  Newberry County Memorial Hospital

Orangeburg
Member
  Regional Medical Center of Orangeburg and Calhoun
    Counties

Pickens
Member
  Cannon Memorial Hospital

Ridgeland
Member
  Low Country General Hospital

Simpsonville
Member
  Hillcrest Hospital

Spartanburg
Member
  Mary Black Health System
  Spartanburg Regional Medical Center

Sumter
Member
  Tuomey Healthcare System

Union
Member
  Wallace Thomson Hospital

West Columbia
Member
  Lexington Medical Center

Winnsboro
Member
  Fairfield Memorial Hospital

Woodruff
Member
  B.J. Workman Memorial Hospital

SOUTH DAKOTA

Aberdeen
Member
  Avera St. Luke's

Armour
Member
  Douglas County Memorial Hospital

Britton
Member
  Marshall County Healthcare Center

Burke
Member
  Community Memorial Hospital

Custer
Member
  Custer Community Hospital

Deadwood
Member
  Northern Hills General Hospital

Dell Rapids
Member
  Dell Area Health Center

Eureka
Member
  Eureka Community Health Services

Faulkton
Member
  Faulk County Memorial Hospital

Flandreau
Member
  Flandreau Municipal Hospital

Gregory
Member
  Gregory Community Hospital

Hoven
Member
  Holy Infant Hospital

Huron
Member
  Huron Regional Medical Center

Martin
Member
  Bennett County Healthcare Center

Milbank
Member
  St. Bernard's Providence Hospital

Miller
Member
  Hand County Memorial Hospital

Mitchell
Member
  Avera Queen of Peace

Parkston
Member
  Avera St. Benedict Health Center

Platte
Member
  Platte Community Memorial Hospital

Rapid City
Member
  Rapid City Regional Hospital System of Care

Redfield
Member
  Community Memorial Hospital

Scotland
Member
  Landmann–Jungman Memorial Hospital

Sioux Falls
Member
  Avera McKennan Hospital

Spearfish
Member
  Lookout Memorial Hospital

Sturgis
Member
  Sturgis Community Health Care Center

Tyndall
Member
  St. Michael's Hospital

Wagner
Member
  Wagner Community Memorial Hospital

Watertown
Member
  Prairie Lakes Hospital and Care Center

Wessington Springs
Member
  Weskota Memorial Medical Center

Yankton
Member
  Avera Health
  Avera Sacred Heart Health Services

TENNESSEE

Bristol
Member
  Wellmont Bristol Regional Medical Center

Brownsville
Member
  Haywood County Memorial Hospital

Chattanooga
Member
  Siskin Hospital for Physical Rehabilitation

Cleveland
Member
  Bradley Memorial Hospital

Copperhill
Member
  Copper Basin Medical Center

Crossville
Member
  Cumberland Medical Center

Dayton
Member
  Rhea Medical Center

Dyersburg
Member
  Methodist Healthcare– Dyersburg Hospital

Erwin
Member
  Unicoi County Memorial Hospital

Etowah
Member
  Woods Memorial Hospital District

Fayetteville
Member
  Lincoln County Health Facilities

Gallatin
Member
  Sumner Regional Medical Center

Greeneville
Member
  Takoma Adventist Hospital

Jackson
Member
  Jackson–Madison County General Hospital

Jefferson City
Member
  Jefferson Memorial Hospital

Jellico
Member
  Jellico Community Hospital

Johnson City
Member
  Johnson City Medical Center

Kingsport
Member
  Wellmont Holston Valley Medical Center

Knoxville
Member
  Baptist Hospital of East Tennessee
  St. Mary's Health System

La Follette
Member
  La Follette Medical Center

Lafayette
Member
  Macon County General Hospital

Lexington
Member
  Methodist Healthcare–Lexington Hospital

Madison
Member
  Tennessee Christian Medical Center

Maryville
Member
  Blount Memorial Hospital

McKenzie
Member
  Methodist Healthcare – McKenzie Hospital

Memphis
Member
  Extendicare of Memphis
  Methodist Healthcare
  Methodist Healthcare–Memphis Hospital
  Regional Medical Center at Memphis
  St. Jude Children's Research Hospital

Morristown
Member
  Morristown–Hamblen Hospital

Nashville
Member
  Vanderbilt University Hospital

Newport
Member
  Baptist Hospital of Cocke County

Rockwood
Member
  Baptist Urgent Care

Rogersville
Member
  Hawkins County Memorial Hospital

Somerville
Member
  Methodist Healthcare – Fayette Hospital

Sweetwater
Member
  Sweetwater Hospital

Tazewell
Member
  Claiborne County Hospital

TEXAS

Abilene
Member
  Abilene Regional Medical Center
  Hendrick Health System

Anahuac
Member
  Bayside Community Hospital

Anson
Member
  Anson General Hospital

Aspermont
Member
  Stonewall Memorial Hospital

Azle
Member
  Harris Methodist Northwest

Ballinger
Member
  Ballinger Memorial Hospital

Bay City
Member
  Matagorda General Hospital

Beaumont
Member
  Christus St. Elizabeth Hospital

Bedford
Member
  Harris Methodist–HEB

Big Lake
Member
  Reagan Memorial Hospital

Bowie
Member
  Bowie Memorial Hospital

Brady
Member
  Heart of Texas Memorial Hospital

Breckenridge
Member
  Stephens Memorial Hospital

Brenham
Member
  Trinity Community Medical Center of Brenham

Bryan
Member
  St. Joseph Regional Health Center

Burleson
Member
  Huguley Memorial Medical Center

Burnet
Member
  Seton Highland Lakes

Caldwell
Member
  Burleson St. Joseph Health Center

Canadian
Member
  Hemphill County Hospital

Carrizo Springs
Member
  Dimmit County Memorial Hospital

Childress
Member
  Childress Regional Medical Center

Chillicothe
Member
  Chillicothe Hospital District

Cleburne
Member
  Walls Regional Hospital

Clifton
Member
  Goodall–Witcher Healthcare

Coleman
Member
  Coleman County Medical Center

Columbus
Member
  Columbus Community Hospital

Comanche
Member
  Comanche Community Hospital

Commerce
Member
  Presbyterian Hospital of Commerce

Corpus Christi
Member
  Driscoll Children's Hospital

Crane
Member
  Crane Memorial Hospital

Crosbyton
Member
  Crosbyton Clinic Hospital

Dallas
Member
  Charlton Methodist Hospital
  Children's Medical Center of Dallas
  Methodist Hospitals of Dallas
  Methodist Medical Center
  Presbyterian Hospital of Dallas
  St. Paul Medical Center

Decatur
Member
  Decatur Community Hospital

Denison
Member
  Texoma Medical Center Restorative Care Hospital

Denver City
Member
  Yoakum County Hospital

Dimmitt
Member
  Plains Memorial Hospital

Eagle Lake
Member
  Rice Medical Center

Eagle Pass
Member
  Fort Duncan Medical Center

Eastland
Member
  Eastland Memorial Hospital

Eden
Member
  Concho County Hospital

Edna
Member
  Jackson County Hospital

El Campo
Member
  El Campo Memorial Hospital

El Paso
Member
  R. E. Thomason General Hospital

Eldorado
Member
  Schleicher County Medical Center

Fort Stockton
Member
  Pecos County Memorial Hospital

Fort Worth
Member
  Cook Children's Medical Center
  Harris Methodist Fort Worth
  Harris Methodist Health System
  Harris Methodist Southwest
  Osteopathic Medical Center of Texas

Fredericksburg
Member
  Hill Country Memorial Hospital

Friona
Member
  Parmer County Community Hospital

Galveston
Member
  University of Texas Medical Branch Hospitals

Graham
Member
  Graham Regional Medical Center

Grand Prairie
Member
  Dallas–Fort Worth Medical Center

Greenville
Member
  Presbyterian Hospital of Greenville

Groves
Member
  Doctors Hospital

Hale Center
Member
  Hi–Plains Hospital

Hallettsville
Member
  Lavaca Medical Center

Hamilton
Member
  Hamilton General Hospital

Hamlin
Member
  Hamlin Memorial Hospital

Haskell
Member
  Haskell Memorial Hospital

Henderson
Member
  Henderson Memorial Hospital

Hondo
Member
  Medina Community Hospital

Houston
Member
Christus St. Joseph Hospital
Methodist Health Care System
St. Luke's Episcopal Health System
Texas Children's Hospital
The Methodist Hospital
University of Texas M. D. Anderson Cancer Center

Irving
Member
Texas Health Resources

Jasper
Member
Jasper Memorial Hospital

Junction
Member
Kimble Hospital

Kaufman
Member
Presbyterian Hospital of Kaufman

Kenedy
Member
Otto Kaiser Memorial Hospital

Kermit
Member
Memorial Hospital

Killeen
Member
Metroplex Adventist Hospital

Knox City
Member
Knox County Hospital

Lake Jackson
Member
Brazosport Memorial Hospital

Lamesa
Member
Medical Arts Hospital

Livingston
Member
Memorial Medical Center

Lockney
Member
W. J. Mangold Memorial Hospital

Lubbock
Member
Covenant Medical Center–Lakeside
University Medical Center

Lufkin
Member
Memorial Medical Center of East Texas

Luling
Member
Seton Edgar B. Davis Hospital

Madisonville
Member
Madison St. Joseph Health Center

McAllen
Member
McAllen Medical Center

Midland
Member
Westwood Medical Center

Mineral Wells
Member
Palo Pinto General Hospital

Mission
Member
Mission Hospital

Monahans
Member
Ward Memorial Hospital

Morton
Member
Cochran Memorial Hospital

Mount Pleasant
Member
Titus Regional Medical Center

Muleshoe
Member
Muleshoe Area Medical Center

Nacogdoches
Member
Nacogdoches Memorial Hospital

Nassau Bay
Member
St. John Hospital

Navasota
Member
Grimes St. Joseph Health Center

Nocona
Member
Nocona General Hospital

Olney
Member
Hamilton Hospital

Paris
Member
McCuistion Regional Medical Center

Pecos
Member
Reeves County Hospital

Plano
Member
Presbyterian Hospital of Plano

Port Arthur
Member
Christus St. Mary Hospital

Quanah
Member
Hardeman County Memorial Hospital

Rockdale
Member
Richards Memorial Hospital

Rotan
Member
Fisher County Hospital District

San Augustine
Member
Memorial Medical Center of San Augustine

San Marcos
Member
Central Texas Medical Center

Seminole
Member
Memorial Hospital

Seymour
Member
Seymour Hospital

Shamrock
Member
Shamrock General Hospital

Snyder
Member
D. M. Cogdell Memorial Hospital

Sonora
Member
Lillian M. Hudspeth Memorial Hospital

Spearman
Member
Hansford Hospital

Stamford
Member
Stamford Memorial Hospital

Stanton
Member
Martin County Hospital District

Stephenville
Member
Harris Methodist–Erath County

Sweetwater
Member
Rolling Plains Memorial Hospital

Tahoka
Member
Lynn County Hospital District

Texarkana
Member
Christus St. Michael Health System

Throckmorton
Member
Throckmorton County Memorial Hospital

Tulia
Member
Swisher Memorial Hospital District

Van Horn
Member
Culberson Hospital District

Weatherford
Member
Campbell Health System

Wellington
Member
Collingsworth General Hospital

Weslaco
Member
Knapp Medical Center

Whitney
Member
Lake Whitney Medical Center

Winnie
Member
Medical Center of Winnie

Winnsboro
Member
Presbyterian Hospital of Winnsboro

Winters
Member
North Runnels Hospital

UTAH
Monticello
Member
San Juan Hospital

VERMONT
Saint Albans
Member
Northwestern Medical Center

Saint Johnsbury
Member
Northeastern Vermont Regional Hospital

VIRGINIA
Abingdon
Member
Johnston Memorial Hospital

Alexandria
Member
Inova Alexandria Hospital
Inova Mount Vernon Hospital

Bedford
Member
Carilion Bedford Memorial Hospital

Big Stone Gap
Member
Wellmont Lonesome Pine Hospital

Chesapeake
Member
Chesapeake General Hospital

Culpeper
Member
Culpeper Memorial Hospital

Danville
Member
Danville Regional Medical Center

Emporia
Member
Greensville Memorial Hospital

Fairfax
Member
Inova Fair Oaks Hospital

Falls Church
Member
Inova Fairfax Hospital
Inova Health System

Farmville
Member
Southside Community Hospital

Front Royal
Member
Warren Memorial Hospital

Galax
Member
Twin County Regional Hospital

Gloucester
Member
Riverside Walter Reed Hospital

Grundy
Member
Buchanan General Hospital

Kilmarnock
Member
Rappahannock General Hospital

Leesburg
Member
Loudoun Hospital Center

Lexington
Member
Stonewall Jackson Hospital

Luray
Member
Page Memorial Hospital

Manassas
Member
Prince William Hospital

Marion
Member
Smyth County Community Hospital

Martinsville
Member
Memorial Hospital of Martinsville and Henry County

Mechanicsville
Member
Memorial Regional Medical Center

Nassawadox
Member
Shore Memorial Hospital

Newport News
Member
Mary Immaculate Hospital
Riverside Health System
Riverside Regional Medical Center
Riverside Rehabilitation Institute

Norfolk
Member
Bon Secours–DePaul Medical Center
Children's Hospital of The King's Daughters

Norton
Member
Norton Community Hospital

Pearisburg
Member
Carilion Giles Memorial Hospital

Pennington Gap
Member
Lee County Community Hospital

Petersburg
Member
Southside Regional Medical Center

Portsmouth
Member
Maryview Hospital
Portsmouth General Hospital

Radford
Member
Carilion New River Valley Medical Center

Richmond
Member
Bon Secours St. Mary's Hospital
Bon Secours–Richmond Community Hospital
Bon Secours–Stuart Circle
Children's Hospital
Richmond Eye and Ear Hospital

Roanoke
Member
Carilion Health System
Carilion Medical Center

Rocky Mount
Member
Carilion Franklin Memorial Hospital

South Boston
Member
Halifax Regional Hospital

South Hill
Member
Community Memorial Healthcenter

Stuart
Member
Patrick Community Hospital

Suffolk
Member
Louise Obici Memorial Hospital

Tappahannock
Member
Riverside Tappahannock Hospital

Tazewell
Member
Tazewell Community Hospital

Virginia Beach
Member
Sentara Virginia Beach General Hospital
Tidewater Health Care, Inc.

Warrenton
Member
Fauquier Hospital

Winchester
Member
Valley Health System
Winchester Medical Center

Woodbridge
Member
Potomac Hospital

Woodstock
Member
Shenandoah Memorial Hospital

Wytheville
Member
Wythe County Community Hospital

WASHINGTON

Aberdeen
Member
Grays Harbor Community Hospital

Bellevue
Member
Overlake Hospital Medical Center
PeaceHealth

Bellingham
Member
St. Joseph Hospital

Brewster
Member
Okanogan–Douglas County Hospital

Centralia
Member
Providence Centralia Hospital

Chelan
Member
Lake Chelan Community Hospital

Chewelah
Member
St. Joseph's Hospital

Clarkston
Member
Tri–State Memorial Hospital

Colfax
Member
Whitman Hospital and Medical Center

Colville
Member
Mount Carmel Hospital

Coupeville
Member
Whidbey General Hospital

Davenport
Member
Lincoln Hospital

Deer Park
Member
Deer Park Hospital

Edmonds
Member
Stevens Healthcare

Ephrata
Member
Columbia Basin Hospital

Everett
Member
Providence General Medical Center

Grand Coulee
Member
Coulee Community Hospital

Kirkland
Member
Evergreen Community Health Center

Longview
Member
St. John Medical Center

Morton
Member
Morton General Hospital

Moses Lake
Member
Samaritan Healthcare

Newport
Member
Newport Community Hospital

Odessa
Member
Odessa Memorial Hospital

Olympia
Member
Providence St. Peter Hospital

Omak
Member
Mid–Valley Hospital

Othello
Member
Othello Community Hospital

Prosser
Member
Prosser Memorial Hospital

Pullman
Member
Pullman Memorial Hospital

Puyallup
Member
Good Samaritan Community Healthcare

Quincy
Member
Quincy Valley Medical Center

Redmond
Member
The Eastside Hospital

Renton
Member
Valley Medical Center

Republic
Member
Ferry County Memorial Hospital

Richland
Member
Kadlec Medical Center

Ritzville
Member
East Adams Rural Hospital

Seattle
Member
Children's Hospital and Regional Medical Center
Highline Community Hospital
Northwest Hospital
Providence Seattle Medical Center
Regional Hospital for Respiratory and Complex Care
Sisters of Providence Health System

Section B

Shelton
Member
  Mason General Hospital

Spokane
Member
  Deaconess Medical Center–Spokane
  Empire Health Services
  Holy Family Hospital
  Providence Services
  Sacred Heart Medical Center
  Shriners Hospitals for Children–Spokane
  St. Lukes Rehabilitation Institute
  Valley Hospital and Medical Center

Tonasket
Member
  North Valley Hospital

Toppenish
Member
  Providence Toppenish Hospital

Vancouver
Member
  Southwest Washington Medical Center
  Woodside Hospital

Walla Walla
Member
  St. Mary Medical Center
  Walla Walla General Hospital

Wenatchee
Member
  Central Washington Hospital

Yakima
Member
  Providence Yakima Medical Center

WEST VIRGINIA

Berkeley Springs
Member
  Morgan County War Memorial Hospital

Bluefield
Member
  Bluefield Regional Medical Center

Buckhannon
Member
  St. Joseph's Hospital of Buckhannon

Clarksburg
Member
  United Hospital Center

Elkins
Member
  Davis Memorial Hospital

Fairmont
Member
  Fairmont General Hospital

Huntington
Member
  St. Mary's Hospital

Keyser
Member
  Potomac Valley Hospital

Kingwood
Member
  Preston Memorial Hospital

Martinsburg
Member
  City Hospital

Morgantown
Member
  Monongalia General Hospital

Parkersburg
Member
  Camden–Clark Memorial Hospital

Petersburg
Member
  Grant Memorial Hospital

Philippi
Member
  Broaddus Hospital

Point Pleasant
Member
  Pleasant Valley Hospital

Ranson
Member
  Jefferson Memorial Hospital

Romney
Member
  Hampshire Memorial Hospital

Sistersville
Member
  Sistersville General Hospital

South Charleston
Member
  Thomas Memorial Hospital

Summersville
Member
  Summersville Memorial Hospital

Weirton
Member
  Weirton Medical Center

Weston
Member
  Stonewall Jackson Memorial Hospital

WISCONSIN

Amery
Member
  Amery Regional Medical Center

Baldwin
Member
  Baldwin Hospital

Baraboo
Member
  St. Clare Hospital and Health Services

Barron
Member
  Barron Medical Center–Mayo Health System

Berlin
Member
  Berlin Memorial Hospital

Burlington
Member
  Memorial Hospital Corporation of Burlington

Cumberland
Member
  Cumberland Memorial Hospital

Durand
Member
  Chippewa Valley Hospital and Oakview Care Center

Elkhorn
Member
  Lakeland Medical Center

Green Bay
Member
  Bellin Hospital

Hartford
Member
  Hartford Memorial Hospital

Janesville
Member
  Mercy Health System

Kewaunee
Member
  St. Mary's Kewaunee Area Memorial Hospital

Madison
Member
  St. Marys Hospital Medical Center

Marinette
Member
  Bay Area Medical Center

Milwaukee
Member
  Children's Hospital of Wisconsin
  Sinai Samaritan Medical Center
  St. Luke's Medical Center

Monroe
Member
  The Monroe Clinic

Osceola
Member
  Osceola Medical Center

Plymouth
Member
  Valley View Medical Center

Sheboygan
Member
  Sheboygan Memorial Medical Center

Two Rivers
Member
  Two Rivers Community Hospital and Hamilton
    Memorial Home

Viroqua
Member
  Vernon County Hospital

Waupaca
Member
  Riverside Medical Center

West Allis
Member
  West Allis Memorial Hospital

WYOMING

Buffalo
Member
  Johnson County Healthcare Center

Cody
Member
  West Park Hospital

Gillette
Member
  Campbell County Memorial Hospital

Jackson
Member
  St. John's Hospital and Living Center

Lusk
Member
  Niobrara County Hospital District

Newcastle
Member
  Weston County Health Services

Sundance
Member
  Crook County Medical Services District

Torrington
Member
  Community Hospital

Wheatland
Member
  Platte County Memorial Hospital Nursing Home

Worland
Member
  Washakie Memorial Hospital

SYNERNET, INC.
222 St John Street, Portland, ME
Zip 04102; tel. 207/775–6081; Mr Paul I
Davis, III, President

MAINE

Bangor
Member
  St. Joseph Hospital

Bar Harbor
Member
  Mount Desert Island Hospital

Bath
Member
  Mid Coast Hospital

Belfast
Member
  Waldo County General Hospital

Biddeford
Member
  Southern Maine Medical Center

Blue Hill
Member
  Blue Hill Memorial Hospital

Bridgton
Member
  Northern Cumberland Memorial Hospital

Damariscotta
Member
Miles Memorial Hospital

Farmington
Member
Franklin Memorial Hospital

Fort Kent
Member
Northern Maine Medical Center

Lewiston
Member
St. Mary's Regional Medical Center

Norway
Member
Stephens Memorial Hospital

Pittsfield
Member
Sebasticook Valley Hospital

Portland
Member
Mercy Hospital Portland

Rockport
Member
Penobscot Bay Medical Center

Rumford
Member
Rumford Community Hospital

Sanford
Member
Henrietta D. Goodall Hospital

Skowhegan
Member
Redington–Fairview General Hospital

Waterville
Member
Inland Hospital

Westbrook
Member
Westbrook Community Hospital

York
Member
York Hospital

UNIVERSITY HEALTH SYSTEM OF NEW JERSEY

154 West State Street, Trenton, NJ Zip 08608; tel. 609/656–9600; Dr Thomas E Terrill , Ph.D., President

NEW JERSEY

Camden
Member
The Cooper Health System

Flemington
Member
Hunterdon Medical Center

Florham Park
Member
Atlantic Health System

Hackensack
Member
Hackensack University Medical Center

Hamilton
Member
Robert Wood Johnson University Hospital at Hamilton

New Brunswick
Member
Robert Wood Johnson University Hospital

Newark
Member
University of Medicine and Dentistry of New Jersey–University Hospital

Phillipsburg
Member
Warren Hospital

Somerville
Member
Somerset Medical Center

Trenton
Member
Capital Health System at Mercer

West Orange
Member
Kessler Institute for Rehabilitation

UNIVERSITY HEALTHSYSTEM CONSORTIUM, INC.

2001 Spring Road, Suite 700, Oak Brook, IL Zip 60523; tel. 630/954–1700; Mr Robert J Baker, President and Chief Executive Officer

ALABAMA

Birmingham
Member
University of Alabama Hospital

Mobile
Affiliate
University of South Alabama Knollwood Park Hospital
Member
University of South Alabama Medical Center

ARIZONA

Tucson
Member
University Medical Center

ARKANSAS

Little Rock
Member
University Hospital of Arkansas

CALIFORNIA

Downey
Affiliate
LAC–Rancho Los Amigos National Rehabilitation Center

Lancaster
Affiliate
LAC–High Desert Hospital

Los Angeles
Member
LAC–King–Drew Medical Center
LAC/University of Southern California Medical Center
University of California Los Angeles Medical Center

Martinez
Affiliate
Contra Costa Regional Medical Center

Moreno Valley
Affiliate
Riverside County Regional Medical Center

Orange
Member
University of California, Irvine Medical Center

Sacramento
Member
University of California, Davis Medical Center

San Diego
Member
University of California San Diego Medical Center

San Francisco
Affiliate
University of California–San Francisco Mount Zion Medical Center
Member
San Francisco General Hospital Medical Center

San Jose
Affiliate
Santa Clara Valley Health and Hospital System

San Leandro
Affiliate
Alameda County Medical Center

Santa Monica
Affiliate
Santa Monica–UCLA Medical Center

Stanford
Member
Stanford Hospital and Clinics

Sylmar
Affiliate
LAC–Olive View–UCLA Medical Center

Torrance
Member
LAC–Harbor–University of California at Los Angeles Medical Center

Valencia
Affiliate
Henry Mayo Newhall Memorial Hospital

COLORADO

Denver
Affiliate
National Jewish Medical and Research Center
Member
Denver Health Medical Center
University of Colorado Hospital

CONNECTICUT

Farmington
Member
University of Connecticut Health Center, John Dempsey Hospital

New Haven
Member
Yale–New Haven Hospital

DISTRICT OF COLUMBIA

Washington
Member
Georgetown University Hospital
Howard University Hospital

FLORIDA

Gainesville
Affiliate
Shands at AGH
Member
Shands at the University of Florida

Jacksonville
Affiliate
University Medical Center

Lake City
Affiliate
Shands at Lake Shore

Live Oak
Affiliate
Shands at Live Oak

Starke
Affiliate
Shands at Starke

Tampa
Member
Tampa General Healthcare

GEORGIA

Atlanta
Member
Crawford Long Hospital of Emory University
Emory University Hospital

Augusta
Member
Medical College of Georgia Hospital and Clinics

ILLINOIS

Chicago
Affiliate
Cook County Hospital
Louis A. Weiss Memorial Hospital
Member
University of Chicago Hospitals
University of Illinois at Chicago Medical Center

Maywood
Member
Loyola University Medical Center

INDIANA

Indianapolis
Member
Clarian Health Partners
Wishard Health Services

IOWA

Iowa City
Member
University of Iowa Hospitals and Clinics

KANSAS

Kansas City
Member
University of Kansas Medical Center

KENTUCKY

Lexington
Member
University of Kentucky Hospital

LOUISIANA

Shreveport
Member
LSU Medical Center–University Hospital

MARYLAND

Baltimore
Affiliate
James Lawrence Kernan Hospital
Member
University of Maryland Medical System

MASSACHUSETTS

Boston
Member
Brigham and Women's Hospital
Massachusetts General Hospital

Clinton
Affiliate
Clinton Hospital

Marlborough
Affiliate
UMass Marlborough Hospital

MICHIGAN

Ann Arbor
Member
University of Michigan Hospitals and Health Centers

MINNESOTA

Minneapolis
Affiliate
Hennepin County Medical Center

MISSOURI

Columbia
Member
University Hospitals and Clinics

NEBRASKA

Omaha
Member
Nebraska Health System

NEVADA

Las Vegas
Affiliate
University Medical Center

NEW JERSEY

Neptune
Affiliate
Meridian Health System

New Brunswick
Member
Robert Wood Johnson University Hospital

Newark
Member
University of Medicine and Dentistry of New
Jersey–University Hospital

NEW YORK

Albany
Member
Albany Medical Center

Brooklyn
Member
University Hospital of Brooklyn–State University of
New York Health Science Center at Brooklyn

Stony Brook
Member
University Hospital

Syracuse
Member
University Hospital–SUNY Health Science Center at
Syracuse

NORTH CAROLINA

Ahoskie
Affiliate
Roanoke–Chowan Hospital

Chapel Hill
Member
University of North Carolina Hospitals

Greenville
Member
Pitt County Memorial Hospital–University Health
Systems of Eastern Carolina

Windsor
Affiliate
Bertie Memorial Hospital

Winston–Salem
Member
North Carolina Baptist Hospital

OHIO

Bedford
Affiliate
UHHS Bedford Medical Center

Chardon
Affiliate
UHHS Geauga Regional Hospital

Cincinnati
Member
University Hospital

Cleveland
Member
University Hospitals of Cleveland

Columbus
Member
Ohio State University Medical Center

Conneaut
Affiliate
UHHS Brown Memorial Hospital

Geneva
Affiliate
UHHS–Memorial Hospital of Geneva

Ironton
Affiliate
River Valley Health System

Toledo
Member
Medical College of Ohio Hospitals

Waverly
Affiliate
Pike Community Hospital

Willoughby
Affiliate
UHHS Laurelwood Hospital

OREGON

Portland
Member
OHSU Hospital

PENNSYLVANIA

Philadelphia
Affiliate
Friends Hospital
Presbyterian Medical Center of the University of
Pennsylvania Health System
Thomas Jefferson University Hospital
Member
Hospital of the University of Pennsylvania

Phoenixville
Affiliate
Phoenixville Hospital of the University of Pennsylvania
Health System

Pittsburgh
Member
UPMC Presbyterian

SOUTH CAROLINA

Charleston
Affiliate
Charleston Memorial Hospital
Member
MUSC Medical Center of Medical University of South
Carolina

TENNESSEE

Knoxville
Member
University of Tennessee Memorial Hospital

Memphis
Member
University of Tennessee Bowld Hospital

TEXAS

Dallas
Member
Zale Lipshy University Hospital

Galveston
Member
University of Texas Medical Branch Hospitals

Houston
Member
Hermann Hospital

Tyler
Affiliate
University of Texas Health Center. at Tyler

UTAH

Salt Lake City
Member
University of Utah Hospitals and Clinics

VIRGINIA

Charlottesville
Member
University of Virginia Medical Center

Richmond
Member
Medical College of Virginia Hospitals, Virginia
Commonwealth University

WASHINGTON

Seattle
Member
Harborview Medical Center
University of Washington Medical Center

WISCONSIN

Antigo
Affiliate
Langlade Memorial Hospital

Madison
Member
University of Wisconsin Hospital and Clinics

Medford
Affiliate
Memorial Hospital of Taylor County

Merrill
Affiliate
Good Samaritan Health Center of Merrill

Milwaukee
Member
Froedtert Memorial Lutheran Hospital

Wausau
Affiliate
Wausau Hospital

VHA, INC.

220 East Las Colinas Boulevard, Irving,
TX Zip 75039–5500; tel. 972/830–0000;
Mr C Thomas Smith, President and Chief
Executive Officer

ALABAMA

Anniston
Partner
Northeast Alabama Regional Medical Center

Athens
Partner
Athens–Limestone Hospital

Birmingham
Shareholder
Baptist Health System

Cullman
Partner
Cullman Regional Medical Center

Decatur
Partner
Decatur General Hospital

Florence
Partner
Eliza Coffee Memorial Hospital

Guntersville
Partner
Marshall County Health Care Authority

Jackson
Partner
  Jackson Medical Center

Mobile
Shareholder
  Infirmary Health System, Inc.

Montgomery
Shareholder
  Baptist Medical Center

Scottsboro
Partner
  Jackson County Hospital

Tuscaloosa
Partner
  DCH Health System

ARIZONA

Phoenix
Shareholder
  Samaritan Health System

Tucson
Shareholder
  Health Partners of Southern Arizona

ARKANSAS

Fayetteville
Partner
  Washington Regional Medical Center

Fort Smith
Shareholder
  Sparks Regional Medical Center

Jonesboro
Partner
  St. Bernards Regional Medical Center

Little Rock
Shareholder
  Baptist Health

CALIFORNIA

Anaheim
Partner
  Anaheim Memorial Medical Center

Covina
Partner
  Citrus Valley Health Partners

Fresno
Shareholder
  Community Health System of Northern California

La Jolla
Shareholder
  Scripps Memorial Hospital–La Jolla

Lancaster
Partner
  Antelope Valley Hospital

Long Beach
Shareholder
  Memorial Health Services

Los Angeles
Shareholder
  Cedars–Sinai Medical Center

Modesto
Partner
  Memorial Hospitals Association

Newport Beach
Shareholder
  Hoag Memorial Hospital Presbyterian

Pasadena
Partner
  Southern California Healthcare Systems

Pomona
Partner
  Pomona Valley Hospital Medical Center

Riverside
Partner
  Riverside Community Hospital

Sacramento
Shareholder
  Sutter Health

San Francisco
Shareholder
  California Pacific Medical Center

Santa Barbara
Partner
  Santa Barbara Cottage Hospital

Stockton
Partner
  St. Joseph's Regional Health System

Torrance
Partner
  Torrance Memorial Medical Center

Turlock
Partner
  Emanuel Medical Center

Valencia
Partner
  Santa Clarita Health Care Association

Van Nuys
Partner
  Valley Presbyterian Hospital

Whittier
Partner
  Presbyterian Intercommunity Hospital

COLORADO

Alamosa
Partner
  San Luis Valley Regional Medical Center

Aspen
Partner
  Aspen Valley Hospital District

Boulder
Partner
  Boulder Community Hospital

Colorado Springs
Partner
  Memorial Hospital

Englewood
Shareholder
  HealthONE Healthcare System

Grand Junction
Partner
  Community Hospital

La Junta
Partner
  Arkansas Valley Regional Medical Center

Longmont
Partner
  Longmont United Hospital

Steamboat Springs
Partner
  Routt Memorial Hospital

Vail
Shareholder
  Vail Valley Medical Center

Wheat Ridge
Shareholder
  Exempla Lutheran Medical Center

CONNECTICUT

Danbury
Partner
  Danbury Hospital

Greenwich
Partner
  Greenwich Hospital

Hartford
Shareholder
  Hartford Hospital

Meriden
Partner
  MidState Medical Center

Middletown
Partner
  Middlesex Hospital

Stamford
Partner
  Stamford Hospital

Torrington
Partner
  Charlotte Hungerford Hospital

FLORIDA

Boca Raton
Partner
  Boca Raton Community Hospital

Boynton Beach
Partner
  Bethesda Memorial Hospital

Daytona Beach
Shareholder
  Halifax Community Health System

Fort Myers
Partner
  Lee Memorial Health System

Inverness
Partner
  Citrus Memorial Hospital

Jacksonville
Partner
  Methodist Medical Center
  St. Luke's Hospital

Lakeland
Shareholder
  Lakeland Regional Medical Center

Melbourne
Shareholder
  Holmes Regional Medical Center

Miami
Partner
  South Miami Hospital

Ocala
Partner
  Munroe Regional Medical Center

Orlando
Shareholder
  Orlando Regional Healthcare System

Panama City
Partner
  Bay Medical Center

Pensacola
Shareholder
  Baptist Health Care Corporation

Saint Petersburg
Partner
  Bayfront Medical Center

Sarasota
Partner
  Sarasota Memorial Hospital

Stuart
Partner
  Martin Memorial Health Systems

Tallahassee
Shareholder
  Tallahassee Memorial HealthCare

Tampa
Partner
  University Community Hospital

West Palm Beach
Partner
  Good Samaritan Medical Center

GEORGIA

Albany
Partner
  Phoebe Putney Memorial Hospital

Athens
Partner
  Athens Regional Medical Center

Atlanta
Partner
  Northside Hospital
Shareholder
  Piedmont Hospital

Columbus
Partner
  Columbus Regional Health Care System, Inc

Dalton
Partner
  Hamilton Medical Center

Section B

Decatur
Partner
  DeKalb Medical Center

East Point
Partner
  South Fulton Medical Center

Gainesville
Partner
  Northeast Georgia Health Services

Lawrenceville
Partner
  Promina Gwinnett Hospital System

Macon
Partner
  Medical Center of Central Georgia

Marietta
Partner
  WellStar Kennestone Hospital

Riverdale
Partner
  Southern Regional Medical Center

Rome
Partner
  Floyd Medical Center

Royston
Partner
  Cobb Memorial Hospital

Savannah
Partner
  Candler Hospital

Thomasville
Partner
  Archbold Medical Center
  John D. Archbold Memorial Hospital

Valdosta
Partner
  South Georgia Medical Center

HAWAII
Honolulu
Shareholder
  Queen's Medical Center

IDAHO
Boise
Shareholder
  St. Luke's Regional Medical Center

Coeur D'Alene
Partner
  Kootenai Medical Center

Pocatello
Partner
  Bannock Regional Medical Center

Twin Falls
Partner
  Magic Valley Regional Medical Center

ILLINOIS
Arlington Heights
Partner
  Northwest Community Healthcare

Berwyn
Partner
  MacNeal Hospital

Carbondale
Partner
  Southern Illinois Hospital Services

Chicago
Shareholder
  Northwestern Memorial Hospital
  Rush–Presbyterian–St. Luke's Medical Center

De Kalb
Partner
  Kishwaukee Community Hospital

Decatur
Shareholder
  Decatur Memorial Hospital

Dixon
Partner
  Katherine Shaw Bethea Hospital

Elgin
Partner
  Sherman Hospital

Elmhurst
Partner
  Elmhurst Memorial Hospital

Evanston
Shareholder
  Evanston Northwestern Healthcare

Evergreen Park
Partner
  Little Company of Mary Hospital and Health Care
    Centers

Freeport
Partner
  Freeport Memorial Hospital

Harvey
Shareholder
  Ingalls Health System
  Ingalls Hospital

Highland Park
Partner
  Highland Park Hospital

Jacksonville
Partner
  Passavant Area Hospital

Joliet
Partner
  Silver Cross Hospital

Kankakee
Partner
  Riverside Medical Center

Macomb
Partner
  McDonough District Hospital

Maryville
Partner
  Anderson Hospital

Mattoon
Partner
  Sarah Bush Lincoln Health Center

Normal
Partner
  BroMenn Healthcare

Oak Brook
Shareholder
  Advocate Health Care

Quincy
Partner
  Blessing Hospital

Rock Island
Partner
  Trinity Medical Center–West Campus

Rockford
Partner
  Rockford Memorial Hospital

Springfield
Shareholder
  Memorial Medical Center
  Memorial Medical Center System

INDIANA
Bloomington
Partner
  Bloomington Hospital

Columbus
Partner
  Columbus Regional Hospital

Danville
Partner
  Hendricks Community Hospital

Elkhart
Partner
  Elkhart General Hospital

Evansville
Shareholder
  Deaconess Hospital

Fort Wayne
Partner
  Parkview Hospital

Indianapolis
Shareholder
  Clarian Health Partners
  Community Hospitals Indianapolis

La Porte
Partner
  La Porte Regional Health System

Madison
Partner
  King's Daughters' Hospital

Marion
Partner
  Marion General Hospital

Muncie
Shareholder
  Ball Memorial Hospital

New Albany
Partner
  Floyd Memorial Hospital and Health Services

Noblesville
Partner
  Riverview Hospital

Richmond
Partner
  Reid Hospital and Health Care Services

South Bend
Shareholder
  Memorial Health System, Inc.

Terre Haute
Partner
  Union Hospital

Valparaiso
Partner
  Porter Memorial Hospital

Vincennes
Partner
  Good Samaritan Hospital

IOWA
Atlantic
Shareholder
  Cass County Memorial Hospital

Council Bluffs
Shareholder
  Jennie Edmundson Memorial Hospital

Keokuk
Shareholder
  Keokuk Area Hospital

Red Oak
Shareholder
  Montgomery County Memorial Hospital

Sioux City
Shareholder
  St. Luke's Regional Medical Center

KANSAS
Atchison
Shareholder
  Atchison Hospital

Colby
Shareholder
  Citizens Medical Center

Hays
Shareholder
  Hays Medical Center

Hutchinson
Shareholder
  Hutchinson Hospital Corporation

Kansas City
Shareholder
  Bethany Medical Center

Liberal
Shareholder
  Southwest Medical Center

Phillipsburg
Shareholder
  Great Plains Health Alliance, Inc.

Pratt
Shareholder
  Pratt Regional Medical Center

Salina
Partner
  Salina Regional Health Center

Shawnee Mission
Shareholder
  Shawnee Mission Medical Center

Topeka
Partner
  St. Francis Hospital and Medical Center
Shareholder
  Stormont–Vail HealthCare

Wichita
Partner
  Via Christi Health System

KENTUCKY
Fort Thomas
Partner
  St. Luke Hospital East

Madisonville
Partner
  Regional Medical Center of Hopkins County

LOUISIANA
Baton Rouge
Member
  Our Lady of the Lake Regional Medical Center
Partner
  Woman's Hospital

Crowley
Partner
  American Legion Hospital

De Ridder
Partner
  Beauregard Memorial Hospital

Lafayette
Partner
  Our Lady of Lourdes Regional Medical Center

Lake Charles
Partner
  Lake Charles Memorial Hospital

Monroe
Partner
  St. Francis Medical Center

New Orleans
Partner
  Pendleton Memorial Methodist Hospital
Shareholder
  Ochsner Foundation Hospital

Ruston
Partner
  Lincoln General Hospital

Shreveport
Shareholder
  Willis–Knighton Medical Center

MAINE
Bangor
Partner
  Eastern Maine Healthcare

Biddeford
Shareholder
  Southern Maine Medical Center

Lewiston
Shareholder
  Central Maine Medical Center

Portland
Shareholder
  Maine Medical Center

Waterville
Shareholder
  MaineGeneral Medical Center–Waterville Campus

MARYLAND
Easton
Partner
  Memorial Hospital at Easton Maryland

Fallston
Partner
  Upper Chesapeake Health System

MASSACHUSETTS
Beverly
Partner
  Beverly Hospital

Boston
Partner
  Massachusetts Eye and Ear Infirmary
Shareholder
  New England Medical Center
  Partners HealthCare System, Inc.

Cambridge
Partner
  Mount Auburn Hospital

Concord
Partner
  Emerson Hospital

Fall River
Member
  Southcoast Hospitals Group

Hyannis
Partner
  Cape Cod Hospital

Lawrence
Owner
  Lawrence General Hospital

Leominster
Partner
  Health Alliance Hospitals

Lowell
Partner
  Lowell General Hospital

Melrose
Partner
  Melrose–Wakefield Hospital

Newton
Partner
  Newell Home Health Service

South Weymouth
Partner
  South Shore Health & Education Corporation

Southbridge
Partner
  Harrington Memorial Hospital

Worcester
Partner
  Saint Vincent Hospital

MICHIGAN
Bay City
Partner
  Bay Medical Center

Dearborn
Member
  Oakwood Healthcarer, Inc.

Detroit
Partner
  St. John Hospital and Medical Center

Flint
Partner
  Genesys Health System

Grand Rapids
Shareholder
  Spectrum Health–Downtown Campus

Holland
Partner
  Holland Community Hospital

Kalamazoo
Partner
  Bronson Healthcare Group, Inc.

Lansing
Partner
  Michigan Capital Healthcare

Monroe
Partner
  Mercy Memorial Hospital

Petoskey
Partner
  Healthshare Group

Port Huron
Partner
  Blue Water Health Services Corporation

Royal Oak
Shareholder
  William Beaumont Hospital–Royal Oak

MINNESOTA
Bemidji
Partner
  North Country Regional Hospital

Duluth
Partner
  St. Luke's Hospital

Fergus Falls
Partner
  Lake Region Healthcare Corporation

Mankato
Partner
  Immanuel St. Joseph's–Mayo Health System

Minneapolis
Shareholder
  Allina Health System

Saint Cloud
Partner
  St. Cloud Hospital

Saint Paul
Shareholder
  HealthEast

Waconia
Partner
  Ridgeview Medical Center

Willmar
Partner
  Rice Memorial Hospital

MISSISSIPPI
Gautier
Partner
  Singing River Hospital System

Greenwood
Partner
  Greenwood Leflore Hospital

Gulfport
Partner
  Memorial Hospital at Gulfport

Hattiesburg
Partner
  Forrest General Hospital

Jackson
Partner
  St. Dominic–Jackson Memorial Hospital

McComb
Partner
  Southwest Mississippi Regional Medical Center

Meridian
Partner
  Jeff Anderson Regional Medical Center

Tupelo
Shareholder
  North Mississippi Health Services, Inc.

MISSOURI
Bolivar
Partner
  Citizens Memorial Hospital

Branson
Partner
  Skaggs Community Health Center

Cameron
Partner
  Cameron Community Hospital

Cape Girardeau
Partner
  Saint Francis Medical Center
  Southeast Missouri Hospital

Carthage
Partner
  McCune–Brooks Hospital

Joplin
Partner
  Freeman Health System
  Freeman Hospital West

Kansas City
Shareholder
  Saint Luke's Hospital
  Saint Luke's Shawnee Mission Health System

Liberty
Partner
  Liberty Hospital

Saint Louis
Shareholder
  BJC Health System

Springfield
Shareholder
  Cox Health Systems

West Plains
Partner
  Ozarks Medical Center

MONTANA

Billings
Partner
  Deaconess Billings Clinic

Bozeman
Partner
  Bozeman Deaconess Hospital

Great Falls
Partner
  Benefis Health Care–East Campus

Helena
Partner
  St. Peter's Hospital

NEBRASKA

Aurora
Partner
  Memorial Hospital

Beatrice
Partner
  Beatrice Community Hospital and Health Center

Columbus
Partner
  Columbus Community Hospital

Hastings
Partner
  Mary Lanning Memorial Hospital

Norfolk
Partner
  Faith Regional Health Services

Omaha
Partner
  Children's Hospital
Shareholder
  Nebraska Methodist Hospital

Scottsbluff
Partner
  Regional West Medical Center

NEW HAMPSHIRE

Concord
Partner
  Capital Region Family Health Center

Dover
Partner
  Wentworth–Douglass Hospital

Keene
Partner
  Cheshire Medical Center

Nashua
Partner
  Southern New Hampshire Medical Center

Rochester
Partner
  Frisbie Memorial Hospital

NEW JERSEY

Belleville
Shareholder
  Clara Maass Health System

Camden
Partner
  Our Lady of Lourdes Medical Center

Elizabeth
Partner
  Elizabeth General Medical Center

Flemington
Partner
  Hunterdon Medical Center

Florham Park
Shareholder
  Atlantic Health System

Hackettstown
Partner
  Hackettstown Community Hospital

Hammonton
Partner
  William B. Kessler Memorial Hospital

Jersey City
Partner
  Christ Hospital

Mount Holly
Shareholder
  Virtua–Memorial Hospital Burlington County

Newton
Partner
  Newton Memorial Hospital

Phillipsburg
Partner
  Warren Hospital

Plainfield
Partner
  Muhlenberg Regional Medical Center

Pompton Plains
Partner
  Chilton Memorial Hospital

Rahway
Partner
  Rahway Hospital

Somers Point
Partner
  Shore Memorial Hospital

Toms River
Shareholder
  Community Medical Center

Trenton
Partner
  Capital Health System

Woodbury
Partner
  Underwood–Memorial Hospital

NEW MEXICO

Albuquerque
Partner
  University Hospital

Farmington
Partner
  San Juan Regional Medical Center

Gallup
Partner
  Rehoboth McKinley Christian Hospital

Las Cruces
Partner
  Memorial Medical Center

Roswell
Partner
  Eastern New Mexico Medical Center

NEW YORK

Binghamton
Shareholder
  United Health Services Hospitals–Binghamton

Brooklyn
Partner
  Brooklyn Hospital Center

Cobleskill
Partner
  Bassett Hospital of Schoharie County

Geneva
Partner
  Geneva General Hospital

Great Neck
Partner
  North Shore– Long Island Jewish Health System

Ithaca
Partner
  Cayuga Medical Center at Ithaca

Jamestown
Partner
  Woman's Christian Association Hospital

Mount Kisco
Partner
  Northern Westchester Hospital Center

New Rochelle
Partner
  Sound Shore Medical Center of Westchester

New York
Partner
  Lenox Hill Hospital
  St. Luke's–Roosevelt Hospital Center

North Tonawanda
Partner
  De Graff Memorial Hospital

Plattsburgh
Partner
  Champlain Valley Physicians Hospital Medical Center

Rochester
Partner
  Highland Hospital of Rochester
  Park Ridge Health System

Rockville Centre
Partner
  Mercy Medical Center

Southampton
Partner
  Southampton Hospital

Suffern
Partner
  Good Samaritan Hospital

Syracuse
Partner
  Crouse Hospital

Troy
Partner
  Samaritan Hospital

Utica
Partner
  Mohawk Valley Psychiatric Center

White Plains
Partner
  White Plains Hospital Center

Yonkers
Partner
  St. John's Riverside Hospital

NORTH CAROLINA

Charlotte
Shareholder
  Carolinas HealthCare System

Raleigh
Partner
  Wake Medical Center

Rocky Mount
Partner
  Nash Health Care Systems

Thomasville
Partner
  Community General Hospital of Thomasville

Winston–Salem
Shareholder
  Carolina Medicorp, Inc.

NORTH DAKOTA

Bismarck
Partner
  MedCenter One

Fargo
Shareholder
  MeritCare Health System

Grand Forks
Partner
  Altru Health System

Jamestown
Partner
  Jamestown Hospital

Minot
Partner
  Trinity Health

OHIO

Akron
Shareholder
Akron General Medical Center

Ashtabula
Partner
Ashtabula County Medical Center

Cincinnati
Partner
Bethesda Corporate Health Services
Shareholder
Christ Hospital

Columbus
Member
OhioHealth

Dover
Partner
Union Hospital

Elyria
Partner
EMH Regional Medical Center

Fremont
Partner
Memorial Hospital

Garfield Heights
Partner
Marymount Hospital

Hamilton
Partner
Fort Hamilton Hospital

Lima
Partner
Lima Memorial Hospital

Mansfield
Partner
Mansfield Hospital

Maumee
Partner
St. Luke's Hospital

Middletown
Partner
Middletown Regional Hospital

Painesville
Partner
Lake Hospital System

Springfield
Partner
Community Hospital

Steubenville
Partner
Trinity Health System

Toledo
Shareholder
The Toledo Hospital

Troy
Partner
Upper Valley Medical Center

Xenia
Partner
Greene Memorial Hospital

Zanesville
Partner
Genesis HealthCare System

OKLAHOMA

Ada
Partner
Valley View Regional Hospital

Altus
Partner
Jackson County Memorial Hospital

Ardmore
Partner
Mercy Memorial Health Center

Chickasha
Partner
Grady Memorial Hospital

Duncan
Partner
Duncan Regional Hospital

McAlester
Partner
McAlester Regional Health Center

Midwest City
Partner
Midwest Regional Medical Center

Muskogee
Partner
Muskogee Regional Medical Center

Norman
Partner
Norman Regional Hospital

Oklahoma City
Partner
Deaconess Hospital
Shareholder
Oklahoma Health System

Poteau
Partner
Eastern Oklahoma Medical Center

Stillwater
Partner
Stillwater Medical Center

Tulsa
Shareholder
Hillcrest Medical Center

OREGON

Hillsboro
Partner
Tuality Healthcare

PENNSYLVANIA

Allentown
Shareholder
Lehigh Valley Hospital

Altoona
Partner
Altoona Hospital

Bristol
Partner
Lower Bucks Hospital

Butler
Partner
Butler Health System

Erie
Shareholder
Hamot Health Systems

Johnstown
Partner
Conemaugh Valley Memorial Hospital

Kingston
Partner
Wyoming Valley Health Care System

Lancaster
Partner
Lancaster General Hospital

Latrobe
Partner
Latrobe Area Hospital

Natrona Heights
Partner
Allegheny University Hospitals, Allegheny Valley

Norristown
Partner
Montgomery Hospital

Philadelphia
Partner
Chestnut Hill HealthCare
Episcopal Hospital
Frankford Hospital of the City of Philadelphia
Jeanes Health System
Shareholder
Pennsylvania Hospital

Pittsburgh
Partner
St. Clair Memorial Hospital
UPMC Shadyside
UPMC St. Margaret
Shareholder
Allegheny University Hospitals–West

Pottstown
Partner
Pottstown Memorial Medical Center

Reading
Partner
Reading Hospital and Medical Center

Sayre
Shareholder
Guthrie Healthcare System

Scranton
Partner
Community Medical Center

Sellersville
Partner
Grand View Hospital

Sewickley
Partner
Valley Medical Facilities

Springfield
Shareholder
Crozer–Keystone Health System

Uniontown
Partner
Uniontown Hospital

Washington
Partner
Washington Hospital

West Chester
Partner
Chester County Hospital

Williamsport
Partner
Susquehanna Health System

York
Partner
South Central Community Health

RHODE ISLAND

Providence
Shareholder
Lifespan Corporation
Rhode Island Hospital

SOUTH CAROLINA

Columbia
Shareholder
Palmetto Health Alliance

SOUTH DAKOTA

Sioux Falls
Shareholder
Sioux Valley Hospital

TENNESSEE

Jackson
Shareholder
West Tennessee Healthcare

Knoxville
Shareholder
Fort Sanders Alliance

Memphis
Shareholder
Baptist Memorial Hospital

Nashville
Shareholder
Baptist Hospital

Oak Ridge
Partner
Methodist Medical Center of Oak Ridge

TEXAS

Amarillo
Partner
Baptist St. Anthony Health System

Arlington
Partner
Arlington Memorial Hospital

Austin
Partner
St. David's Medical Center

Beaumont
Partner
Baptist Hospital of Southeast Texas

Dallas
Shareholder
Baylor Health Care System

El Paso
Partner
Providence Memorial Hospital

Fort Worth
Shareholder
All Saints Episcopal Hospital of Fort Worth

Grapevine
Partner
Baylor Medical Center at Grapevine

Harlingen
Partner
Valley Baptist Medical Center

Houston
Shareholder
Memorial Hospital Southwest

Irving
Partner
Baylor Medical Center at Irving

Lubbock
Shareholder
Lubbock Methodist Hospital System

Marshall
Partner
Marshall Regional Medical Center

Midland
Partner
Memorial Hospital and Medical Center

San Antonio
Partner
Baptist Health System

Sherman
Partner
Wilson N. Jones Regional Health System

Temple
Partner
King's Daughters Hospital

Texarkana
Partner
Wadley Regional Medical Center

Waco
Partner
Hillcrest Baptist Medical Center

Wichita Falls
Partner
United Regional Health Care System

VERMONT
Barre
Partner
Central Vermont Medical Center

Burlington
Shareholder
Fletcher Allen Health Care

Rutland
Partner
Rutland Regional Medical Center

VIRGINIA
Alexandria
Partner
Inova Alexandria Hospital

Arlington
Partner
Arlington Hospital

Charlottesville
Partner
Martha Jefferson Hospital

Franklin
Partner
Southampton Memorial Hospital

Fredericksburg
Partner
MWH Medicorp

Harrisonburg
Partner
Rockingham Memorial Hospital

Lynchburg
Partner
Centra Health, Inc.

Norfolk
Shareholder
Sentara Health System

Richmond
Partner
Children's Hospital

Warrenton
Partner
Fauquier Hospital

WASHINGTON
Tacoma
Shareholder
MultiCare Health System

WEST VIRGINIA
Charleston
Shareholder
Camcare, Inc.

Glen Dale
Partner
Reynolds Memorial Hospital

Huntington
Partner
Cabell Huntington Hospital

Morgantown
Partner
West Virginia University Hospitals

Parkersburg
Owner
St. Joseph's Hospital

Princeton
Partner
Princeton Community Hospital

Wheeling
Partner
Wheeling Hospital

WISCONSIN
Appleton
Shareholder
United Health Group

Beaver Dam
Partner
Beaver Dam Community Hospitals

Eau Claire
Partner
Luther Hospital

Green Bay
Partner
Bellin Hospital

Kenosha
Partner
Kenosha Hospital and Medical Center

La Crosse
Shareholder
Lutheran Hospital–La Crosse

Madison
Shareholder
Meriter Hospital

Menomonee Falls
Partner
Community Memorial Hospital

Milwaukee
Partner
Columbia Hospital
Froedtert Memorial Lutheran Hospital
Horizon Healthcare, Inc.

Rice Lake
Partner
Lakeview Medical Center

Watertown
Partner
Watertown Memorial Hospital

Waukesha
Partner
Waukesha Health System, Inc.

West Bend
Owner
St. Joseph's Community Hospital of West Bend

WYOMING
Casper
Partner
Wyoming Medical Center

Cheyenne
Partner
United Medical Center

Laramie
Partner
Ivinson Memorial Hospital

Sheridan
Partner
Memorial Hospital of Sheridan County

VANTAGE HEALTH GROUP
265 Conneaut Lake Road, Meadville, PA
Zip 16335; tel. 814/337–0000; Mr David
C Petno, Vice President Business
Development

PENNSYLVANIA
Erie
Member
Millcreek Community Hospital
Saint Vincent Health Center

Franklin
Member
Northwest Medical Centers

Greenville
Member
UPMC Horizon

Meadville
Member
Meadville Medical Center

Titusville
Member
Titusville Area Hospital

Warren
Member
Warren General Hospital

WHEATON FRANCISCAN SERVICES, INC.
26W171 Roosevelt Road, Wheaton, IL
Zip 60189–0667; tel. 630/462–9271; Mr
Wilfred F Loebig, Jr., President and Chief
Executive Officer

ILLINOIS
Oak Brook
Member
Consolidated Catholic Health Care

YANKEE ALLIANCE
300 Brickstone Square, 5th Floor,
Andover, MA Zip 01810–1429;
tel. 978/475–2000; Mr R Paul O'Neill,
President

CONNECTICUT
New Haven
Member
Hospital of Saint Raphael

MAINE
Blue Hill
Affiliate
Blue Hill Memorial Hospital

Lewiston
Member
St. Mary's Regional Medical Center

MASSACHUSETTS
Attleboro
Affiliate
Sturdy Memorial Hospital

Boston
Member
Boston Medical Center

Cambridge
Member
  Youville Lifecare

Fall River
Member
  Southcoast Hospitals Group

Great Barrington
Member
  Fairview Hospital

Lexington
Member
  Covenant Health Systems, Inc.

Lowell
Member
  Saints Memorial Medical Center

North Adams
Affiliate
  North Adams Regional Hospital

Pittsfield
Member
  Berkshire Health Systems, Inc.
  Berkshire Medical Center

Winchester
Member
  Winchester Hospital

NEW HAMPSHIRE
Manchester
Affiliate
  Catholic Medical Center
  Elliot Hospital

Nashua
Member
  St. Joseph Hospital

NEW YORK
Albany
Member
  Albany Medical Center

Elizabethtown
Affiliate
  Elizabethtown Community Hospital

Glens Falls
Member
  Glens Falls Hospital

Plattsburgh
Affiliate
  Champlain Valley Physicians Hospital Medical Center

Troy
Member
  Samaritan Hospital

Section B

†List supplied by the Joint Commission on Accreditation of Healthcare Organizations

Description of Lists

This section was compiled to provide a directory of information useful to the health care field.

National and International Organizations

The national and international lists include many types of voluntary organizations concerned with matters of interest to the health care field. The organizational information includes address, telephone number, FAX number, and the contact person. For organizations that maintain permanent offices, office addresses and telephone numbers are given. For organizations not maintaining offices, the addresses and telephone numbers given are those of their corresponding secretaries. The information was obtained directly from the organizations.

National Organizations are listed alphabetically by their full names. International Organizations are grouped alphabetically by country.

Also included is the Healthfinder listings. The Healthfinder is composed of two listing types: toll–free numbers for health information and federal health information centers and clearinghouses. Organizations are listed alphabetically by topic area.

We present this list simply as a convenient directory. Inclusion or omission of any organization's name indicates neither approval nor disapproval by Health Forum LLC, an affiliate of the American Hospital Association.

United States Government Agencies

National agencies concerned with health–related matters are listed by the major department of government under which the different functions fall.

State and Local Organizations and Agencies

The lists of organizations in states, associated areas, and provinces include Blue Cross and Blue Shield plans, health systems agencies, hospital associations and councils, hospital licensure agencies, medical and nursing licensure agencies, peer review organizations, state health planning and development agencies, and statewide health coordinating councils.

There are many active local organizations that do not fall within these categories. Contact the hospital association of the state or province for information about such additional groups. The hospital association and councils listed have offices with full-time executives.

The selected state and provincial government agencies include those within state departments of health and welfare, and other agencies, such as comprehensive health planning, crippled children's services, maternal and child health, mental health, and vocational rehabilitation.

Health Care Providers

Lists of JCAHO Accredited Freestanding Long–Term Care Organizations, Health Maintenance Organizations, Freestanding Ambulatory Surgery Centers, Freestanding Hospices, JCAHO Accredited Freestanding Substance Abuse Organizations, JCAHO Accredited Freestanding Mental Health Care Organizations are provided in this section. The lists were developed from information supplied by the providers themselves.

As with the lists of National and International Organizations, these lists are provided simply as a convenient directory. Inclusion or omission of any organization's name indicates neither approval nor disapproval by Health Forum LLC.

A

Academy for Implants and Transplants, P.O. Box 223, Springfield, VA 22150; tel. 703/451–0001; FAX. 703/451–0004; Anthony J. Viscido, D.D.S., Secretary–Treasurer

Academy of Dentistry for Persons with Disabilities, 211 East Chicago Avenue, 5th Floor, Chicago, IL 60611; tel. 312/440–2660; FAX. 312/440–2824; John S. Rutkauskas, M.S., D.D.S., Executive Director

Academy of General Dentistry, 211 East Chicago Avenue, Suite 1200, Chicago, IL 60611–2670; tel. 312/440–4300; FAX. 312/440–0559; Harold E. Donnell, Jr., Executive Director

Academy of Oral Dynamics, 1590 West Street Road, Warminster, PA 18974; tel. 215/957–0700; FAX. 215/957–0703; Dr. William J. Crielly, Treasurer

Academy of Oral Dynamics, 8919 Sudley Road, Manassas, VA 20110–5016; tel. 703/365–2616; FAX. 703/331–0356; Dr. E. Paul Byrne, Secretary

Academy of Organizational and Occupational Psychiatry, 6728 Old McLean Village Drive, McLean, VA 22101; tel. 703/556–9222; FAX. 703/556–8729; George K. Degnon, Executive Director

Accreditation Association for Ambulatory Health Care, 9933 Lawler Avenue, Skokie, IL 60077–3708; tel. 847/676–9610; FAX. 847/676–9628; John E. Burke, Ph. D., Executive Director

ADARA: Professionals Networking for Excellence in Service Delivery, Individuals Who are Deaf or Hard of Hearing, P.O. Box 6956, San Mateo, CA 94403–6956; tel. 650/372–0620; FAX. 650/372–0661; Elizabeth Charlson, Ph.D.

Aerospace Medical Association, 320 South Henry Street, Alexandria, VA 22314–3579; tel. 703/739–2240; FAX. 703/739–9652; Russell B. Rayman, M.D., Executive Director

Alexander Graham Bell Association for the Deaf, Inc., 3417 Volta Place, N.W., Washington, DC 20007; tel. 202/337–5220; FAX. 202/337–8314; Elissa M. Brooks, Development/PR

Allergy Associates, 2004 Grand Avenue, Baldwin, NY 11510; tel. 516/223–7656; FAX. 516/223–0583; Joseph d'amour, M.D.

Alliance for Children & Family, Inc., 11700 West Lake Park Drive, Milwaukee, WI 53224; tel. 414/359–1040; FAX. 414/359–1074; Peter B. Goldberg, President and CEO

Alliance of Cardiovascular Professionals, 910 Charles Street, Fredericksburg, VA 22408; tel. 540/370–0102; FAX. 540/370–0015; Peggy McElgunn, Executive Director

Alzheimer's Association, (Alzheimer's Disease and Related Disorders Association, Inc.), 919 North Michigan Avenue, Suite 1000, Chicago, IL 60611; tel. 312/335–8700; FAX. 312/335–1110; Thomas Kirk, Vice President, Patient, Family and Education

Ambulatory Pediatric Association, 6728 Old McLean Village Drive, McLean, VA 22101; tel. 703/556–9222; FAX. 703/556–8729; Marge Degnon, Executive Director

America's Blood Centers, 725 15th Street, N.W., Suite 700, Washington, DC 20005–2109; tel. 202/393–5725; FAX. 202/393–1282; Jim MacPherson, Executive Director

American Academy for Cerebral Palsy and Developmental Medicine, 6300 North River Road, Suite 727, Rosemont, IL 60018–4226; tel. 847/698–1635; FAX. 847/823–0536; Sheril King, Executive Director

American Academy of Allergy, Asthma and Immunology, 611 East Wells Street, Milwaukee, WI 53202; tel. 414/272–6071; FAX. 414/272–6070; Rick Iber, Executive Vice President

American Academy of Child and Adolescent Psychiatry, 3615 Wisconsin Avenue, N.W., Washington, DC 20016; tel. 202/966–7300; FAX. 202/966–2891; Virginia Q. Anthony, Executive Director

American Academy of Dental Electrosurgery, Planetarium Station, P.O. Box 374, New York, NY 10024; tel. 212/595–1925; Maurice J. Oringer, D.D.S., Executive Secretary

American Academy of Dental Practice Administration, 1063 Whippoorwill Lane, Palatine, IL 60067; tel. 847/934–4404; Kathleen Uebel, Executive Director

American Academy of Dermatology, P.O. Box 40141, Schaumburg, IL 60168–4014; tel. 847/330–0230; FAX. 847/330–0050; Bradford W. Claxton, Executive Director

American Academy of Family Physicians, 8880 Ward Parkway, Kansas City, MO 64114; tel. 816/333–9700; FAX. 816/333–2237; Robert Graham, M.D., Executive Vice President

American Academy of Healthcare Attorneys (AHA), One North Franklin, Chicago, IL 60606–3491; tel. 312/422–3700; FAX. 312/422–4574

American Academy of Insurance Medicine, P.O. Box 59811, Potomac, MD 20859–9811; tel. 301/365–3572; FAX. 301/365–7705; Russell E. Barker, C.A.E., Executive Vice President

American Academy of Medical Administrators, 30555 Southfield Road, Suite 150, Southfield, MI 48076–7747; tel. 248/540–4310; FAX. 248/645–0590; Thomas R. O'Donovan, Ph.D., FAAMA, President

American Academy of Neurology, 1080 Montreal Avenue, St. Paul, MN 55116–2325; tel. 612/695–1940; FAX. 612/695–2791; Catherine Rydell, Executive Director

American Academy of Ophthalmology, 655 Beach Street, P.O. Box 7424, San Francisco, CA 94120; tel. 415/561–8500; FAX. 415/561–8533; H. Dunbar Hoskins, Jr., M.D., Executive Vice President

American Academy of Optometry, 6110 Executive Boulevard, Suite 506, Rockville, MD 20852; tel. 301/984–1441; FAX. 301/984–4737; Lois Schoenbrun, CAE, Executive Director

American Academy of Oral Medicine, 2910 Lightfoot Drive, Baltimore, MD 21209–1452; tel. 410/602–8585; Mrs. Joyce Caplan, Executive Secretary

American Academy of Orthopaedic Surgeons, 6300 North River Road, Rosemont, IL 60018–4262; tel. 847/823–7186; FAX. 847/823–8125; William W. Tipton, Jr., M.D., Executive Vice President

American Academy of Otolaryngic Allergy, 8455 Colesville Road, Suite 745, Silver Spring, MD 20910–9998; tel. 301/588–1800; FAX. 301/588–2454; Jami Lucas, Executive Director

American Academy of Otolaryngology–Head and Neck Surgery, Inc., One Prince Street, Alexandria, VA 22314; tel. 703/836–4444; FAX. 703/683–5100; Michael D. Maves, M.D., M.B.A., Executive VP

American Academy of Pain Management, 13947 Mono Way, Suite A, Sonora, CA 95370–2807; tel. 209/533–9744; FAX. 209/533–9750; Richard S. Weiner, Ph.D., Executive Director

American Academy of Pediatric Dentistry, 211 East Chicago Avenue, Suite 700, Chicago, IL 60611; tel. 312/337–2169; FAX. 312/337–6329; Dr. John S. Rutkauskas, Executive Director

American Academy of Pediatrics, 141 Northwest Point Boulevard, P.O. Box 927, Elk Grove Village, IL 60009–0927; tel. 847/228–5005; FAX. 847/228–5027; Joe M. Sanders, Jr., M.D., Executive Director

American Academy of Physical Medicine and Rehabilitation, One IBM Plaza, Suite 2500, Chicago, IL 60611–3604; tel. 312/464–9700; FAX. 312/464–0227; Ronald A. Henrichs, CAE, Executive Director

American Academy of Physician Assistants, 950 North Washington Street, Alexandria, VA 22314; tel. 703/836–2272; FAX. 703/684–1924; Stephen C. Crane, Ph.D., M.P.H., Executive Vice President

American Academy of Psychoanalysis, 47 East 19th Street, Sixth Floor, New York, NY 10003; tel. 212/475–7980; FAX. 212/475–8101; Dianne Gabriele, Executive Director

American Academy of Restorative Dentistry, 1184 College Avenue, Elko, NV 89801; tel. 775/738–7165; FAX. 775/778–0310; John H. Martin, Jr., D.D.S., Secretary–Treasurer

American Aging Association, The Sally Balin Medical Center, 110 Chesley Drive, Media, PA 19063; tel. 610/627–2626; FAX. 610/565–9747; Arthur K. Balin, M.D., Ph.D., Executive Director

American Alliance for Health, Physical Education, Recreation & Dance, 1900 Association Drive, Reston, VA 20191; tel. 703/476–3400; FAX. 703/476–9527; Michael G. Davis, Executive Vice President

American Ambulance Association, 1255 23rd Street, NW, Washington, DC 20037; tel. 202/452–8888; FAX. 202/452–0005; Steve Haracznak, Executive Vice President

American Art Therapy Association, 1202 Allanson Road, Mundelein, IL 60060; tel. 847/949–6064; FAX. 847/566–4580; Edward J. Stygar, Jr., Executive Director

American Assembly for Men in Nursing, % NYSA, 11 Cornel Road, Latham, NY 12110–1499; tel. 904/782–9400; FAX. 904/484–8762; David Sprouse, President

American Association for Adult and Continuing Education, 1200 19th Street, N.W., Suite 300, Washington, DC 20036; tel. 202/429–5131; FAX. 202/223–4579; Anna Darin, Association Manager

American Association for Clinical Chemistry, Inc., 2101 L Street, N.W., Suite 202, Washington, DC 20037; tel. 202/857–0717; FAX. 202/887–5093; Richard Flaherty, Executive Vice President

American Association for Dental Research, 1619 Duke Street, Alexandria, VA 22314–3406; tel. 703/548–0066; FAX. 703/548–1883; John J. Clarkson, BDS, Ph.D., Executive Director

American Association for Laboratory Animal Science, 9190 Crestwyn Hills Drive, Memphis, TN 38125; tel. 901/754–8620; FAX. 901/753–0046; Michael R. Sondag, Executive Director

American Association for Respiratory Care, 11030 Ables Lane, Dallas, TX 75229; tel. 972/243–2272; FAX. 972484–2720; Sam P. Giordano, Executive Director

American Association for the Advancement of Science, 1200 New York Avenue, N.W., Washington, DC 20005; tel. 202/326–6400; FAX. 202/321–5526; Richard S. Nicholson, Executive Officer

American Association for the Study of Headache, 19 Mantua Road, Mt. Royal, NJ 8080; tel. 609/423–0043; FAX. 609/423–0082; Linda McGillicuddy, Executive Director

American Association for the Surgery of Trauma, Department of Surgery, UCLA Medical Center, Room 21–178 CHS, Los Angeles, CA 90024; tel. 310/794–4210; FAX. 310/794–4251; H. Gill Cryer, M.D., Secretary–Treasurer

American Association of Ambulatory Surgery Centers, 401 North Michigan Avenue, Chicago, IL 60611–4267; tel. 800/237–3768; FAX. 312/527–6636; Kari Dabrowski, Account Coordinator

American Association of Anatomists, Department of Anatomy, Tulane Medical School, New Orleans, LA 70112; FAX. 504/584–1687; Robert Yates, Secretary–Treasurer

American Association of Bioanalysts, 917 Locust Street, Suite 1100, St. Louis, MO 63101–1413; tel. 314/241–1445; FAX. 314/241–1449; Mark S. Birenbaum, Ph.D., Administrator

American Association of Certified Orthoptists, 501 Hill Street, Waycross, GA 31501; tel. 912/285–2020; FAX. 912/285–8112; Jill Clark, President

American Association of Colleges of Nursing, One Dupont Circle, N.W., Suite 530, Washington, DC 20036; tel. 202/463–6930; FAX. 202/785–8320; Geraldine Bednash, Ph.D., RN, FAAN, Executive Director

American Association of Colleges of Pharmacy, 1426 Prince Street, Alexandria, VA 22314–2841; tel. 703/739–2330; FAX. 703/836–8982; Richard P. Penna, Pharm.D., Executive Vice President

American Association of Colleges of Podiatric Medicine, 1350 Piccard Drive, Suite 322, Rockville, MD 20850–4307; tel. 301/990–7400; FAX. 301/990–2807; Anthony J. McNevin, CAE, President

American Association of Critical–Care Nurses, 101 Columbia, Suite 200, Aliso Viejo, CA 92656–1491; tel. 949/362–2000; FAX. 949/362–2020; Sarah J. Sanford, RN, M.A., CNAA, FAAN, CEO

American Association of Dental Consultants, Inc., P.O. Box 3345, Lawrence, KS 66046; tel. 785/749–2727; FAX. 785/749–1140; Ed Schooley, D.D.S., Secretary–Treasurer

American Association of Dental Schools, 1625 Massachusetts Avenue, N.W., Suite 600, Washington, DC 20036; tel. 202/667–9433; FAX. 202/667–0642; Richard W. Valachonic, D.M.D., Executive Director

American Association of Endodontists, 211 East Chicago Avenue, Suite 1100, Chicago, IL 60611; tel. 312/266–7255; FAX. 312/266–9867; Irma S. Kudo, Executive Director

American Association of Fund–Raising Counsel, Inc., 37 east 28th Street, Suite 902, New York, NY 10016; tel. 212/354–5799; FAX. 212/768–1795; Ann Kaplan, Research Director

American Association of Health Plans, (AAHP), 1129 20th Street, N.W., Suite 600, Washington, DC 20036–3421; tel. 202/778–3200; FAX. 202/778–8486; Charles W. Stellar, Executive Vice President

American Association of Healthcare Administrative Management, (Formerly The American Guild of Patient Account Management), 1200 19th Street, N.W., Suite 300, Washington, DC 20036; tel. 202/857–1179; FAX. 202/223–4579; Dennis E. Smeage, Executive Director

American Association of Healthcare Consultants, 11208 Waples Mill Road, Suite 109, Fairfax, VA 22030; tel. 800/362–4674; FAX. 703/691–2247; Vaughan A. Smith, President and CEO

American Association of Homes and Services for the Aging, 901 E Street, N.W., Suite 500, Washington, DC 20004–2011; tel. 202/783–2242; FAX. 202/783–2255; Sheldon L. Goldberg, President

American Association of Hospital Dentists, Inc., 211 East Chicago Avenue, Suite 948, 5th Floor, Chicago, IL 60611; tel. 312/440–2661; FAX. 312/440–2824; John S. Rutkauskas, M.S., D.D.S., Executive Director

American Association of Hospital Dentists, Inc., 211 East Chicago Avenue, 5th Floor, Chicago, IL 60611; tel. 312/440–2661; FAX. 312/440–2824; John S. Rutkauskas, M.S., D.D.S., Executive Director

American Association of Kidney Patients, 100 South Ashley Drive, Suite 280, Tampa, FL 33602; tel. 800/749–2257; FAX. 813/223–0001; Kris Robinson, Executive Director

American Association of Medical Assistants, 20 North Wacker Drive, Suite 1575, Chicago, IL 60606–2903; tel. 312/899–1500; FAX. 312/899–1259; Donald A. Balasa, J.D., M.B.A., Executive Director, Le

American Association of Neuroscience Nurses, 224 North DesPlaines, Suite 601, Chicago, IL 60661; tel. 312/993–0043; FAX. 312/993–0362; Shelly A. Johnson, Executive Director

American Association of Nurse Anesthetists, 222 South Prospect Avenue, Park Ridge, IL 60068–4001; tel. 847/692–7050; FAX. 847/692–6968; John F. Garde, CRNA, M.S., FAAN, Executive Director

American Association of Nutritional Consultants, 870 Canarios Court, Chula Vista, CA 91910; tel. 619/482–8533; FAX. 619/482–4485; Lenda Summerfield, Administrator

American Association of Occupational Health Nurses, Inc., 2920 Brandywine Road, Suite 100, Atlanta, GA 30341–4146; tel. 770/455–7757; FAX. 770/455–7271; Ann R. Cox, CAE, Executive Director

American Association of Oral and Maxillofacial Surgeons, 9700 West Bryn Mawr Avenue, Rosemont, IL 60018–5701; tel. 847/678–6200; FAX. 847/678–6286; Robert C. Rinadi, Ph.D., Executive Director

American Association of Orthodontists, 401 North Lindbergh Boulevard, St. Louis, MO 63141–7816; tel. 314/993–1700; FAX. 314/997–1745; Ronald S. Moen, Executive Director

American Association of Pastoral Counselors, 9504A Lee Highway, Fairfax, VA 22031–2303; tel. 703/385–6967; FAX. 703/352–7725; C. Roy Woodruff, Ph.D., Executive Director

American Association of Physicists in Medicine, One Physics Ellipse, College Park, MD 20740–3846; tel. 301/209–3350; FAX. 301/209–0862; Salvatore Trofi, Jr., Executive Director

American Association of Plastic Surgeons, 2317 Seminole Road, Atlantic Beach, FL 32233; tel. 904/359–3759; FAX. 904/359–3789; Francis A. Harris, Executive Secretary

American Association of Poison Control Centers, 3201 New Mexico Avenue, N.W., Suite 310, Washington, DC 20016; tel. 202/362–7217; Rose Ann Soloway, RN, MSED, ABAT

American Association of Psychiatric Technicians, Inc., A.A.P.T., 336 Johnson Road, Suite 2, Michigan, IN 46360; tel. 800/391–7589; George Blake, Ph.D., Director

American Association of Public Health Dentistry, A.A.P.H.D. National Office, 3760 SW Lyle Court, Portland, OR 97221; tel. 503–242–0712; FAX. 503–242–0721; James Toothaker, D.D.S., M.D., Executive Director

American Association of Public Health Physicians, 515 North State Street, 14th Floor, Chicago, IL 60610; tel. 312/464–4299; FAX. 312/464–5993; David Cloud, Executive Manager

American Association on Mental Retardation, 444 North Capitol Street, N.W., Suite 846, Washington, DC 20001–1512; tel. 202/387–1968; FAX. 202/387–2193; M. Doreen Croser, Executive Director

American Baptist Homes and Hospitals Association, P.O. Box 851, Valley Forge, PA 19482–0851; tel. 610/768–2411; FAX. 610/768–2453; Rosalie Norman–McNaney, Director

American Board of Allergy and Immunology, A Conjoint Board of the American Board of Internal Medicine, 510 Walnut Street, Suite 1701, Philadelphia, PA 19106–3699; tel. 215/592–9466; FAX. 215/592–9411; John W. Yunginger, M.D., Executive Secretary

American Board of Anesthesiology, 4101 Lake Boone Trail, Suite 510, Raleigh, NC 27607–7506; tel. 919/881–2570; FAX. 919/881–2575; Francis M. James III, M.D., Secretary – Treasurer

American Board of Cardiovascular Perfusion, 207 North 25th Avenue, Hattiesburg, MS 39401; tel. 601–582–2227; FAX. 601–582–2271; Beth A. Richmond, Ph.D., Mark G. Richmond, Ed.D., Co–E

American Board of Colon and Rectal Surgery, 20600 Eureka Road, Suite 713, Taylor, MI 48180; tel. 734/282–9400; FAX. 734/282–9402; Herand Abcarian, M.D., Executive Director

American Board of Dermatology, Inc., Henry Ford Hospital, One Ford Place, Detroit, MI 48202–3450; tel. 313/874–1088; FAX. 313/872–3221; Harry J. Hurley, M.D., Executive Director

American Board of Emergency Medicine, 3000 Coolidge Road, East Lansing, MI 48823; tel. 517/332–4800; FAX. 517/332–2234; Benson S. Munger, Ph.D., Executive Director

American Board of Family Practice, Inc., 2228 Young Drive, Lexington, KY 40505; tel. 606/269–5626; FAX. 606/335–7501; Robert F. Avant, M.D., Executive Director

American Board of Internal Medicine, 510 Walnut Street, Suite 1700, Philadelphia, PA 19106–3699; tel. 215/446–3500; FAX. 215/446–3473; Harry R. Kimball, M.D., President

American Board of Medical Management, 4890 West Kennedy Boulevard, Suite 200, Tampa, FL 33609–2575; tel. 813/287–2815; FAX. 813/287–8993; Roger S. Schenke, Executive Vice President

American Board of Medical Specialties, 1007 Church Street, Suite 404, Evanston, IL 60201–5913; tel. 847/491–9091; FAX. 847/328–3596; Stephen H. Miller, M.D., MPH, Executive Vice–President

American Board of Neurological Surgery, 6550 Fanning Street, Suite 2139, Houston, TX 77030; tel. 713/790–6015; FAX. 713–794–0207; Mary Louise Sanderson, Administrator

American Board of Nuclear Medicine, 900 Veteran Avenue, Los Angeles, CA 90024; tel. 310/825–6787; FAX. 310/825–9433; Joseph F. Ross, M.D., President

American Board of Ophthalmology, 111 Presidential Boulevard, Suite 241, Bala Cynwyd, PA 19004; tel. 610/664–1175; FAX. 610/664–6503; Denis M. O'Day, M.D., Executive Director

American Board of Oral and Maxillofacial Surgery, 625 North Michigan Avenue, Suite 1820, Chicago, IL 60611; tel. 312/642–0070; FAX. 312/642–8584; Cheryl E. Mounts, Executive Secretary

American Board of Orthopedic Surgery, Inc., 400 Silver Cedar Court, Chapel Hill, NC 27514; tel. 919/929–7103; FAX. 919/942–8988; G. Paul De Rosa, M.D., Executive Director

American Board of Otolaryngology, 2211 Norfolk, Suite 800, Houston, TX 77098; tel. 713/528–6200; FAX. 713/528–1171; Robert W. Cantrell, M.D., Executive Vice President

American Board of Pathology, One Urban Centre, 4830 West Kennedy Boulevard, Tampa, FL 33622–5915; tel. 813/286–2444; FAX. 813/289–5279; William H. Hartmann, M.D., Executive Vice President

American Board of Pediatric Dentistry, 1193 Woodgate Drive, Carmel, IN 46033–9232; tel. 317/573–0877; FAX. 317/846–7235; James R. Roche, D.D.S., Executive Secretary–Treasurer

American Board of Pediatrics, Inc., 111 Silver Cedar Court, Chapel Hill, NC 27514; tel. 919/929–0461; FAX. 919/929–9255; James A. Stockman III, M.D., President

American Board of Physical Medicine and Rehabilitation, Norwest Center, Suite 674, 21 First Street, S.W., Rochester, MN 55902; tel. 507/282–1776; FAX. 507/282–9242; Donna Morgan, Administrator

American Board of Podiatric Surgery, 1601 Dolores Street, San Francisco, CA 94110–4906; tel. 415/826–3200; FAX. 415/826–4640; James A. Lamb, Executive Director

American Board of Preventive Medicine, Inc., 9950 West Lawrence Avenue, Suite 106, Schiller Park, IL 60176; tel. 847/671–1750; FAX. 847/671–1751; James M. Vanderploeg, M.D., MPH

American Board of Prosthodontics, P.O. Box 8437, Atlanta, GA 31106; tel. 404/876–2625; FAX. 404/872–8804; William D. Culpepper, D.D.S., M.S.D., Executive Director

American Board of Psychiatry and Neurology, Inc., 500 Lake Cook Road, Suite 335, Deerfield, IL 60015; tel. 847/945–7900; FAX. 847/945–1146; Stephen C. Scheiber, M.D., Executive Vice President

American Board of Quality Assurance and Utilization Review, 2120 Range Road, Clearwater, FL 33765; tel. 727/298/8777; FAX. 727/449/0555; H.E. Hartsell, Chief Operating Officer

American Board of Radiology, 5255 East Williams Circle, Suite 3200, Tucson, AZ 85711; tel. 520/790–2900; FAX. 520/790–3200; M. Paul Capp, M.D., Executive Director

American Board of Surgery, Inc., 1617 John F. Kennedy Boulevard, Suite 860, Philadelphia, PA 19103; tel. 215/568–4000; FAX. 215/563–5718; Wallace P. Ritchie, Jr., M.D., Executive Director

American Board of Thoracic Surgery, One Rotary Center, Suite 803, Evanston, IL 60201; tel. 847/475–1520; FAX. 847/475–6240; Richard J. Cleveland, M.D., Secretary–Treasurer

American Broncho–Esophagological Association, Vanderbilt University Medical Center, Department of Otolaryngology, S–2100, Nashville, TN 37232–2559; tel. 615/322–7267; FAX. 615/343–7604; James A. Duncavage, M.D., Secretary

American Burn Association, 625 North Michigan Avenue, Suite 1530, Chicago, IL 60611; tel. 312/642–9260; FAX. 312/642–9130; John Krichbaum, J.D., Executive Director

American Cancer Society, 1599 Clifton Road, N.E., Atlanta, GA 30329; tel. 404/320–3333; Gerald P. Murphy, M.D., Senior Vice President

American Center for the Alexander Technique, Inc., 129 West 67th Street, New York, NY 10023; tel. 212/799–0468; Jane Tomkiewiez, Executive Director

American Chiropractic Association, 1701 Clarendon Boulevard, Arlington, VA 22209; tel. 703/276–8800; FAX. 703/243–2593; Garrett F. Cuaco, Executive Vice President

American Cleft Palate–Craniofacial Association, 104 S. Estes Drive, Suite 204, Chapel Hill, NC 27514; tel. 919/933–9044; FAX. 919/933–9604; Nancy C. Smythe, Executive Director

American Clinical Neurophysiology Society, (formerly the American Electroencephalographic Society), One Regency Drive, P.O. Box 30, Bloomfield, CT 06002; tel. 203/243–3977; FAX. 203/286–0787; Jacquelyn T. Coleman, Executive Director

American College Health Association, P.O. Box 28937, Baltimore, MD 21240–8937; tel. 410/859–1500; FAX. 410/859–1510; Doyle E. Randol, MS, Executive Director

American College of Allergy, Asthma and Immunology, 85 West Algonquin Road, Suite 550, Arlington Heights, IL 60005; tel. 847/427–1200; FAX. 847/427–1294; James R. Slawny, Executive Director

American College of Apothecaries, P.O. Box 341266, Bartlett, TN 38184; tel. 901/383–8119; FAX. 901/383–8882; D. C. Huffman, Jr., Ph.D., Executive Vice President

American College of Cardiology, 9111 Old Georgetown Road, Bethesda, MD 20814; tel. 800/253–4636; FAX. 301/897–9745; Christine McEntee, Executive Vice President

American College of Chest Physicians, 3300 Dundee Road, Northbrook, IL 60062–2348; tel. 847/498–1400; FAX. 847/498–5460; Alvin Lever, Executive Vice President and CEO

American College of Dentists, 839 Quince Orchard Boulevard, Suite J, Gaithersburg, MD 20878–1614; tel. 301/977–3223; FAX. 301/977–3330; Stephen A. Ralls, D.D.S.

American College of Emergency Physicians, P.O. Box 619911, Dallas, TX 75261–9911; tel. 972/550–0911; FAX. 972/580–2816; Colin C. Rorrie, Jr., Ph.D., CAE, Executive Director

American College of Foot and Ankle Surgeons, 515 Busse Highway, Park Ridge, IL 60068–3150; tel. 847/292–2237; FAX. 847/292–2022; Thomas R. Schedler, CAE, Executive Director

American College of Health Care Administrators, 325 South Patrick Street, Alexandria, VA 22314; tel. 703/739–7900; FAX. 703/739–7901; Karen S. Tucker, CAE, President and CEO

American College of Healthcare Executives, One North Franklin, Suite 1700, Chicago, IL 60606–3491; tel. 312/424–2800; FAX. 312/424–0023; Thomas C. Dolan, Ph.D., FACHE, CAE, President/Chief Ex

American College of Legal Medicine, 611 East Wells Street, Milwaukee, WI 53202; tel. 800/433–9137; FAX. 414/276–3349; Janet Haynes, Executive Director

American College of Medical Staff Development, 6855 Jimmy Carter Blvd., Suite 2100, Norcross, GA 30071; tel. 770/734–9904; FAX. 770/734–9709; Jan Maixner, Director of Education

American College of MOHS Micrographic Surgery and Cutaneous On, 930 North Meacham, Schaumburg, IL 60173–4965; tel. 847/330–9830; FAX. 847/330–1135; Sherrie Traficano, Executive Director

American College of Nurse–Midwives, 818 Connecticut Avenue, N.W., Suite 900, Washington, DC 20006; tel. 202/728–9860; FAX. 202/728–9897; Deanne Williams, Executive Director

American College of Obstetricians and Gynecologists, 409 12th Street, S.W., Washington, DC 20024–2188; tel. 202/638–5577; FAX. 202/484–5107; Ralph W. Hale, M.D., Executive Vice President

American College of Occupational and Environmental Medicine, (Includes ACOEM Research and Education Fund, and Occupational, 55 West Seegers, Arlington Heights, IL 60005; tel. 847/228–6850; FAX. 847/228–1856; Donald L. Hoops, Ph.D., Executive Vice President

American College of Physician Executives, 4890 West Kennedy Boulevard, Suite 200, Tampa, FL 33609–2575; tel. 813/287–2000; FAX. 813/287–8993; Roger S. Schenke, Executive Vice President

American College of Preventive Medicine, 1660 L Street, N.W., Washington, DC 20036; tel. 202/466–2044; FAX. 202/466–2662; Jordan H. Richland, MPH, Executive Director

American College of Radiology, 1891 Preston White Drive, Reston, VA 20191–4397; tel. 703/648–8900; FAX. 703/648–9176; John J. Curry, Executive Director

American College of Rheumatology, 1800 Century Place, Suite 150, Atlanta, GA 30345; tel. 404/633–3777; FAX. 404/633–1870; Lynn Bonfiglio, Director, Membership

American College of Sports Medicine, P.O. Box 1440, Indianapolis, IN 46206–1440; tel. 317/637–9200; FAX. 317/634–7817; James R. Whitehead, Executive Vice President

American College of Surgeons, 633 N. Saint Clair Street, Chicago, IL 60611; tel. 312/202–5000; FAX. 312/440–7014; Samuel A. Wells, Jr., M.D., Director

American Congress of Rehabilitation Medicine, 4700 West Lake Avenue, Glenview, IL 60025; tel. 847/375–4725; FAX. 847/375–4777; Diane Burgher, Executive Director

American Council on Pharmaceutical Education, Inc., 311 West Superior Street, Suite 512, Chicago, IL 60610; tel. 312/664–3575; FAX. 312/664–4652; Daniel A. Nona, Ph.D., Executive Director

American Dental Assistants Association, 203 North LaSalle, Suite 1320, Chicago, IL 60601; tel. 312/541–1550; FAX. 312/541–1496; Lawrence H. Sepin, Executive Director

American Dental Association, 211 East Chicago Avenue, Chicago, IL 60611; tel. 312/440–2500; FAX. 312/440–7494; John S. Zapp, D.D.S., Executive Director

American Dental Society of Anesthesiology, Inc., 211 East Chicago Avenue, Suite 780, Chicago, IL 60611; tel. 312/664–8270; FAX. 312/642–9713; R. Knight Charlton, Executive Secretary

American Diabetes Association, Inc., 1660 Duke Street, Alexandria, VA 22314; tel. 703/549–1500; FAX. 703/836–7439; John H. Graham IV, Chief Executive Officer

American Dietetic Association, 216 West Jackson Boulevard, Suite 800, Chicago, IL 60606–6995; tel. 312/899–0040; FAX. 312/899–1758; Beverly Bajus, Chief Operating Officer

American Federation for Medical Research, 1200 19th Street, N.W., Suite 300, Washington, DC 20036–2422; tel. 202/429–5161; FAX. 202/223–4579; Antinette Turner, Director of Programs & Services

American Foundation for Aging Research, North Carolina State University, Biochemistry Department, Raleigh, NC 27695–7622; tel. 919/515–5679; FAX. 919/515–2047; Paul F. Agris, President

American Foundation for AIDS Research, 120 Wall Street, 13th Floor, New York, NY 10005; tel. 212/860/1600; Mathilde Krim, Ph.D., Founding Co–Chair and Chairman

American Foundation for the Blind, Inc., 11 Penn Plaza, Suite 300, New York, NY 10001; tel. 212/502–7600; FAX. 212/502–7770; Liz Greco, Vice President, Communications

American Fracture Association, Rural Route 6, Box 8, Bloomington, IL 61704; tel. 309–828–2815; FAX. 309–828–1499; Sarah Olson, Executive Secretary

American Geriatrics Society, 770 Lexington Avenue, Suite 300, New York, NY 10021; tel. 212/308–1414; FAX. 212/832–8646; Linda Hiddemen Barondess, Executive Vice President

American Group Psychotherapy Association, Inc., 25 East 21st Street, Sixth Floor, New York, NY 10010; tel. 212/477–2677; FAX. 212/979–6627; Marsha S. Block, CAE, Chief Executive Officer

American Head and Neck Society, 203 Lothrop Street, Suite 519, Pittsburgh, PA 15213; tel. 414/647–2227; FAX. 412/647–8944; Jonas T. Johnson, M.D., Secretary

American Health Care Association, 1201 L Street, N.W., Washington, DC 20005; tel. 202/842–4444; FAX. 202/842–3860; Paul R. Willging, Ph.D., President

American Health Foundation, One Dana Road, Valhalla, NY 10595; tel. 914/789–7122; FAX. 914/592–6317; Ernst L. Wynder, M.D., President

American Health Information Management Association, 919 North Michigan Avenue, Suite 1400, Chicago, IL 60611; tel. 312/787–2672; FAX. 312/787–9793; Linda Kloss, R.R.A., Executive Vice President/CEO

American Health Lawyers Association, 1120 Connecticut Avenue, N.W., Suite 950, Washington, DC 20036; tel. 202/833–1100; FAX. 202/833–1105; Wayne Miller, CAE, Interim Chief Staff Officer

American Health Planning Association, 7245 Arlington Boulevard, Suite 300, Falls Church, VA 22042; tel. 703/573–3103; FAX. 703/573–1276; Dean Montgomery

American Healthcare Radiology Administrators, P.O. Box 334, Sudbury, MA 01776; tel. 978/443–7591; FAX. 978/443–8046; Mary Reitter, Executive Director

American Heart Association, Inc., Office of Scientific Affairs, 7272 Greenville Avenue, Dallas, TX 75231; tel. 214/706–1446; FAX. 214/373–9818; Rodman D. Starke, M.D., Executive Vice President

American Hospital Association, One North Franklin, Chicago, Chicago, IL 60606–3491; tel. 312–422–3000; Richard J. Davidson, President

American Hospital Association, 325 Seventh Street, N.W., Washington, DC 20004; tel. 202–638–1100; FAX. 202–626–2345; Richard J. Davidson, President

American Hospital Association, 5412 Idylwild Trail, Suite 108, Boulder, CO 80301; tel. 303/516–9709; FAX. 303/516–9710; Marcia Desmond, Regional Executive

American Hospital Association, Washington Office, 325 Seventh Street, N.W., Suite 700, Washington, DC 20004; tel. 202/638–1100; FAX. 202/626–2345; Richard Pollack, Executive Vice President, Government Public Affairs

American Institute of Architects, Academy of Architecture for Health, 1735 New York Avenue, N.W., Washington, DC 20006; tel. 202/626–7429; FAX. 206/626–7518; Gail B. Dym, Director

American Juvenile Arthritis Organization, Council, Arthritis Foundation, 1330 West Peachtree Street, Atlanta, GA 30309; tel. 404/872–7100; FAX. 404/872–9559; Janet S. Austin, Ph.D., Vice President

American Laryngological Association, Department of Otolaryngology, S–2100 Medical Center North, Nashville, TN 37232–6326; tel. 615/322–6326; G. B. Healy, M.D., Secretary

American Library Association, 50 East Huron Street, Chicago, IL 60611; tel. 312/280–5044; FAX. 312/944–3897; Linda Wallace, Executive Director

American Lung Association, 1740 Broadway, New York, NY 10019–4374; tel. 212/315–8700; FAX. 212/765–7876; John R. Garrison, Managing Director

American Lung Association of Ohio, Dayton Office, 7560 McEwen Road, Dayton, OH 45459; tel. 937/291–0451; FAX. 937/291–0453; Roberta M. Taylor, Director

American Medical Association, 515 North State Street, Chicago, IL 60610; tel. 312/464–5000; FAX. 312/464–4184; E. Ratcliffe Anderson, Jr., M.D., Executive V.P. and CEO

American Medical Association Alliance, 515 North State Street, Chicago, IL 60610; tel. 312/464–4470; FAX. 312/464–5020; Hazel J. Lewis, Executive Director

American Medical Group Association, Inc., 1422 Duke Street, Alexandria, VA 22314–3430; tel. 703/838–0033; FAX. 703/548–1890; Donald W. Fisher, Ph.D., Chief Executive Officer

American Medical Student Association/Foundation, 1902 Association Drive, Reston, VA 22091; tel. 703/620–6600; FAX. 703/620–5873; Paul R. Wright, Executive Director

American Medical Technologists, 710 Higgins Road, Park Ridge, IL 60068; tel. 847/823–5169; FAX. 847/823–0458; Gerard P. Boe, Ph.D., Executive Director

American Medical Women's Association, Inc., 800 North Fairfax Street, Suite 400, Alexandria, VA 22314; tel. 703/838–0500; FAX. 703/549–3864; Eileen McGrath, J.D., CAE, Executive Director

American Medical Writers Association, 9650 Rockville Pike, Bethesda, MD 20814–3998; tel. 301/493–0003; FAX. 301/493–6384; Lillian Sablack, Executive Director

American Music Therapy Association, (Formerly The National Association for Music Therapy), 8455 Colesville Road, Suite 1000, Silver Spring, MD 20910; tel. 301/589–3300; FAX. 301/589–5175; Andrea Farbman, Ed.D., Executive Director

American National Standards Institute, 11 West 42nd Street, New York, NY 10036; tel. 212/642–4900; FAX. 212/398–0023; Sergio Mazza, President

American Nephrology Nurses' Association, East Holly Avenue, P.O. Box 56, Pitman, NJ 08071; tel. 609/256–2320; FAX. 609/589–7463; T.B.D., Executive Director

American Neurological Association, 5841 Cedar Lake Road, Suite 108, Minneapolis, MN 55416; tel. 612/545–6284; FAX. 612/545–6073; Linda Wilkerson, Executive Director

American Nurses' Association, 600 Maryland Avenue, S.W., Suite 100 W, Washington, DC 20024–2571; tel. 202/651–7012; FAX. 202/651–7006; David Hennage, Ph.D., M.B.A.

American Occupational Therapy Association, Inc., 4720 Montgomery Lane, P.O. Box 31220, Bethesda, MD 20824–1220; tel. 301/652–2682; FAX. 301/652–7711; Jeanette Bair,M.B.A.,O.T.,F.A.O.T.A., Executive Director

American Ontological Society, Inc., Loyola University Medical Center, 2160 South First Avenue, Building 105, Number 1870, Maywood, IL 60153; tel. 708/216–8526; FAX. 708/216–4834; Gregory J. Matz, M.D., Secretary–Treasurer

American Ophthalmological Society, P.O. Box 193940, San Francisco, CA 94119–3940; tel. 415/561–8578; FAX. 415/561–8575; Charles P. Wilkinson, M.D., Secretary–Treasurer

American Optometric Association, 243 North Lindbergh Boulevard, St. Louis, MO 63141; tel. 314/991–4100; FAX. 314/991–4101; Michael D. Jones, O.D., Executive Director

American Organization of Nurse Executives (AONE), One North Franklin, 34th Floor, Chicago, IL 60606; tel. 312/422–2800; FAX. 312/422–4503; Marjorie Beyers, RN, Ph.D., FAAN

American Orthopsychiatric Association, 330 Seventh Avenue, 18th Floor, New York, NY 10001; tel. 212/564–5930; FAX. 212/564–6180; Gale Siegel, M.S.W., Executive Director

American Orthoptic Council, 3914 Nakoma Road, Madison, WI 53711; tel. 608/233–5383; FAX. 608/263–4247; Leslie France, Administrator

American Osteopathic Association, 142 East Ontario Street, Chicago, IL 60611; tel. 312/202–8000; FAX. 312/202–8212; John B. Crosby, J.D.., Executive Director

American Parkinson Disease Association, Inc., 1250 Hylan Boulevard, Suite 4B, Staten Island, NY 10305; tel. 800/223–2732; FAX. 718/981–4399; G. Maestrone, D.V.M., Scientific and Medical Affairs Director

American Pediatric Society, Inc., 3400 Research Forest Drive, Suite B7, The Woodlands, TX 77381; tel. 281–419–0052; FAX. 281–419–0082; Kathy Cannon, Associate Executive Director

American Pharmaceutical Association, 2215 Constitution Avenue, N.W., Washington, DC 20037; tel. 202/628–4410; FAX. 202/783–2351; John A. Gans, Pharm.D., Executive Vice President

American Physical Therapy Association, 1111 North Fairfax Street, Alexandria, VA 22314; tel. 703/684–2782; FAX. 703/684–7343; Francis J. Mallon, Esq., Chief Executive Officer

American Physiological Society, 9650 Rockville Pike, Bethesda, MD 20814–3991; tel. 301/530–7118; FAX. 301/571–8305; Martin Frank, Ph.D., Executive Director

American Podiatric Medical Association, 9312 Old Georgetown Road, Bethesda, MD 20814–1698; tel. 301/571–9200; FAX. 301/530–2752; Glenn B. Gastwirth, DPM, Executive Director

American Psychiatric Association, 1400 K Street, N.W., Washington, DC 20005; tel. 202/682–6000; FAX. 202/682–6114; Steven M. Mirin, M.D., Medical Director

American Psychoanalytic Association, 309 East 49th Street, New York, NY 10017; tel. 212/752–0450; FAX. 212/593–0571; Ellen B. Fertig, Administrative Director

American Psychological Association, 750 First Street, N.E., Washington, DC 20002–4242; tel. 202/336–5500; FAX. 202/336–6069; Russ Newman, Ph.D., J.D., Executive Director,

American Psychosomatic Society, 6728 Old McLean Village Drive, McLean, VA 22101; tel. 703/556–9222; George K. Degnon, Executive Director

American Public Health Association, 1015 15th Street, N.W., Suite 300, Washington, DC 20005; tel. 202/789–5600; FAX. 202/789–5661; Mohammed N. Akhter, M.D., MPH, Executive Vice President

American Public Welfare Association, 810 First Street, N.E., Suite 500, Washington, DC 20002; tel. 202/682–0100; FAX. 202/289–6555; Sidney Johnson III, Executive Director

American Red Cross, National Headquarters, 8111 Gatehouse Road, Falls Church, VA 22042; tel. 703/206–7764; FAX. 703/206–7765; Susan M. Livingstone, Vice President, Health and Safety

American Registry of Medical Assistants, 69 Southwick Road, Suite A, Westfield, MA 01085–4729; tel. 800/527–2762; Annette H. Heyman, R.M.A., Director

American Registry of Radiologic Technologists, 1255 Northland Drive, St. Paul, MN 55120; tel. 651/687–0048; Jerry B. Reid, Ph.D., Executive Director

American Rhinologic Society, Department of Otolaryngology/Head and Neck Surgery, LSU Medical Center, Shreveport, LA 71130; tel. 888/520–9585; FAX. 318/675–6260; Fred J. Stucker, M.D., Secretary

American Roentgen Ray Society, 1891 Preston White Drive, Reston, VA 22091; tel. 703/648–8992; FAX. 703/264–8863; Paul R. Fullagar, Executive Director

American School Health Association, 7263 S.R. 43, P.O. Box 708, Kent, OH 44240–0708; tel. 330/678–1601; FAX. 330/678–4526; Susan Wooley, Ph.D., CHES

American Society for Adolescent Psychiatry, 4340 East West Highway, Suite 401, Bethesda, MD 20814; tel. 301/718–6502; FAX. 301/656–0989; Ann T. Loew, Ed.M.

American Society for Biochemistry and Molecular Biology, Inc., 9650 Rockville Pike, Bethesda, MD 20814–3996; tel. 301/530–7145; FAX. 301/571–1824; Charles C. Hancock, Executive Officer

American Society for Clinical Laboratory Science, 7910 Woodmont Avenue, Suite 530, Bethesda, MD 20814; tel. 301/657–2768; FAX. 301/657–2909; Elissa Passiment, Executive Director

American Society for Clinical Pharmacology and Therapeutics, 117 West Ridge Pike, Suite 2, Conshonen, PA 19428–1216; tel. 610/825–3838; FAX. 610/834–8652; Denise Garetti, Assistant Executive Director

American Society for Cytotechnology, 4101 Lake Boone Trail, Suite 2A, Raleigh, NC 27607; tel. 919/787–5181; FAX. 919/787–4916; Banner Huggins, Executive Director

American Society for Healthcare Central Service Professionals, One North Franklin, 31st Floor, Chicago, IL 60606; tel. 312/422–3570; FAX. 312/422–4573; Patti Costello, Director of Educational Product Development and Programs

American Society for Healthcare Education and Training (AHA), One North Franklin, Chicago, IL 60606; tel. 312/422–3720; FAX. 312/422–4579; Linda H. Brooks, Executive Director

American Society for Healthcare Engineering (AHA), One North Franklin, Chicago, IL 60606; tel. 312/422–3800; FAX. 312/422–4571; Joseph Martori, Executive Director

American Society for Healthcare Food Service Administrators (AHA), One North Franklin, Chicago, IL 60606; tel. 312/422–3870; FAX. 312/422–4581; Patricia Burton, Executive Director

American Society for Healthcare Human Resources Administration, One North Franklin, 31st Floor, Chicago, IL 60606; tel. 312/422–3720; FAX. 312/422–4579; Linda H. Brooks, Executive Director

American Society for Healthcare Risk Management (AHA), One North Franklin, Chicago, IL 60606; tel. 312/422–3980; FAX. 312/422–4580; Christy Kessler, Executive Director

American Society for Investigative Pathology, 9650 Rockville Pike, Bethesda, MD 20814–3993; tel. 301/530–7130; FAX. 301/571–1879; Frances A. Pitlick, Ph.D., Executive Officer

American Society for Laser Medicine and Surgery, Inc., 2404 Stewart Square, Wausau, WI 54401; tel. 715/845–9283; FAX. 715/848–2493; Richard O. Gregory, M.D., Secretary

American Society for Microbiology, 1325 Massachusetts Avenue, N.W., Washington, DC 20005; tel. 202/924–9265; FAX. 202/942–9333; Michael I. Goldberg, Ph.D., Executive Director

American Society for Pharmacology and Experimental Therapeutic, 9650 Rockville Pike, Bethesda, MD 20814–3995; tel. 301/530–7060; FAX. 301/530–7061; Christine K. Carrico, Ph. D., Executive Officer

American Society for Public Administration, 1120 G Street, N.W., Suite 700, Washington, DC 20005; tel. 202/393–7878; FAX. 202/638–4952; Mary Hamilton, Executive Director

American Society for Reproductive Medicine, (formerly The American Fertility Society), 1209 Montgomery Highway, Birmingham, AL 35216–2809; tel. 205/978–5000; FAX. 205/978–5005; Benjamin Younger, M.D., Executive Director

American Society for the Advancement of Anesthesia in Dentistry, Six East Union Avenue, P.O. Box 551, Bound Brook, NJ 08805; tel. 732/469–9050; FAX. 732/271–1985; David Crystal, D.D.S., Executive Secretary

American Society for Therapeutic Radiology and Oncology, 1891 Preston White Drive, Reston, VA 20191; tel. 703–295–6760; FAX. 703/476–8167; Frank Malouff, Executive Director

American Society of Anesthesiologists, 520 North Northwest Highway, Park Ridge, IL 60068; tel. 847/825–5586; FAX. 847/825–1692; Glenn W. Johnson, Executive Director

American Society of Clinical Oncology, 435 North Michigan Avenue, Suite 1717, Chicago, IL 60611–4067; tel. 312/644–0828; FAX. 312/644–8557; Robert E. Becker, J.D., CAE, Executive Director

American Society of Clinical Pathologists., (Includes Board of Registry), 2100 West Harrison Street, Chicago, IL 60612–3798; tel. 312/738–1336; FAX. 312/738–9798; Robert C. Rock, M.D., Executive Vice President

American Society of Colon and Rectal Surgeons, 85 West Algonquin Road, Suite 550, Arlington Heights, IL 60005; tel. 847/290–9184; FAX. 847/290–9203; James Slawny, Executive Director

American Society of Consultant Pharmacists, 1321 Duke Street, Alexandria, VA 22314–3563; tel. 703/739–1300; FAX. 703/739–1321; R. Timothy Webster, Executive Director

American Society of Contemporary Medicine and Surgery, 4711 Golf Road, Suite 408, Skokie, IL 60076; tel. 800/621–4002; FAX. 847/568–1527; Randall T. Bellows, M.D., Director

American Society of Contemporary Ophthalmology, 4711 Golf Road, Suite 408, Skokie, IL 60076; tel. 800/621–4002; FAX. 847/568–1527; Randall T. Bellows, M.D., Director

American Society of Cytopathology, 400 West Ninth Street, Suite 201, Wilmington, DE 19801; tel. 302/429–8802; FAX. 302/429–8807; Petrina M. Smith, RN, M.B.A., Executive Secretary

Section C

American Society of Dentistry for Children, John Hancock Center, 875 North Michigan Avenue, Suite 4040, Chicago, IL 60611; tel. 312/943–1244; FAX. 312/943–5341; Dr. Peter Fos, Interim Executive Director

American Society of Directors of Volunteer Services (AHA), One North Franklin, Chicago, IL 60606; tel. 312/422–3938; FAX. 312/422–4575; Nancy A. Brown, Executive Director

American Society of Electroneurodiagnostic Technologists, Inc., 204 West Seventh Street, Carroll, IA 51401–2317; tel. 712/792–2978; FAX. 712/792–6962; M. Fran Pedelty, Executive Director

American Society of Extra–Corporeal Technology, Inc., 11480 Sunset Hills Road, Suite 210E, Reston, VA 20190–5208; tel. 703/435–8556; FAX. 703/435–0056; George M. Cate, Executive Director

American Society of Group Psychodrama and Psychotherapy, 6728 Old McLean Village Drive, McLean, VA 22101; tel. 703/556–9222; George K. Degnon, Executive Director

American Society of Health–System Pharmacists, 7272 Wisconsin Avenue, Bethesda, MD 20814; tel. 301/657–3000; FAX. 301/652–8278; Henri R. Manasse, Jr., Executive VP and CEO

American Society of Internal Medicine, 190 N. Independence Mall West, Philadelphia, PA 19106–1572; tel. 215/351–2800; FAX. 215/351–2829; Walter J. McDonald, M.D., FACP, Executive Vice President

American Society of Internal Medicine, 2011 Pennsylvania Avenue, N.W., Suite 800, Washington, DC 20006–1808; tel. 202/835–2746; FAX. 202/835–0443; Alan R. Nelson, M.D., Executive Vice President

American Society of Internal Medicine, 190 North Independence Mall West, Philadelphia, PA 19106–1572; tel. 215–351–2800; FAX. 215–351–2829; Walter J. McDonald, M.D., F.A.C.P., Executive Vice President

American Society of Law, Medicine & Ethics, 765 Commonwealth Avenue, 16th Floor, Boston, MA 02215; tel. 617/262–4990; FAX. 617/437–7596; Michael Vasko, M.A., Associate Director

American Society of Maxillofacial Surgeons, 444 East Algonquin Road, Arlington Heights, IL 60005; tel. 847/228–8375; FAX. 847/228–6509; Gina Cappellania, Administrative Coordinator

American Society of Neuroimaging, 5841 Cedar Lake Road, Suite 204, Minneapolis, MN 55416; tel. 612/545–6291; FAX. 612/545–6073; Linda Wilkerson, Executive Director

American Society of Plastic and Reconstructive Surgeons, 444 East Algonquin Road, Arlington Heights, IL 60005; tel. 847/228–9900; FAX. 847/228–9131; Dave Fellers, CAE, Executive Director

American Society of Radiologic Technologists, 15000 Central Avenue, S.E., Albuquerque, NM 87123–3917; tel. 505/298–4500; FAX. 505/298–5063; Joan L. Parsons, Executive Vice President, Operations

American Speech–Language–Hearing Association, 10801 Rockville Pike, Rockville, MD 20852; tel. 301/897–5700; FAX. 301/571–0457; Frederick T. Spahr, Ph.D., Executive Director

American Surgical Association, 13 Elm Street, Manchester, MA 01944; tel. 978/526–8330; FAX. 978/526–4018; John L. Cameron, M.D., Secretary

American Thoracic Society, 1740 Broadway, New York, NY 10019–4374; tel. 212/315–8700; FAX. 212/315–6498; Carl C. Booberg, Executive Director

American Thyroid Association, Inc., Montefiore Medical Center, 111 East 210th Street, Room 311, Bronx, NY 10467; tel. 718/882–6047; FAX. 718/882–6085; Martin I. Surks, M.D., Secretary

American Trauma Society, 8903 Presidential Parkway, Suite 512, Upper Marlboro, MD 20772–2656; tel. 800/556–7890; FAX. 301/420–0617; Harry Teter, Executive Director

American Urological Association, Inc., 1120 North Charles Street, Baltimore, MD 21201; tel. 410/727–1100; FAX. 410/223–4370; G. James Gallagher, Executive Director

Arthritis Foundation, 1330 West Peachtree Street, Atlanta, GA 30309; tel. 404/872–7100; FAX. 404/872–3458; Don L. Riggin, President and CEO

Association for Applied Psychophysiology and Biofeedback, 10200 West 44th Avenue, Suite 304, Wheat Ridge, CO 80033; tel. 303/422–8436; FAX. 303/422–8894; Francine Butler, Ph.D., Executive Director

Association for Clinical Pastoral Education, Inc., 1549 Clairmont Road, Suite 103, Decatur, GA 30033; tel. 404/320–1472; FAX. 404/320–0849; Stuart A. Plummer, Interim Executive Director

Association for Healthcare Philanthropy, 313 Park Avenue, Suite 400, Falls Church, VA 22046; tel. 703/532–6243; FAX. 703/532–7170; Dr. William C. McGinly, CAE, President and CEO

Association for Healthcare Resource Materials Management (AHA), One North Franklin, Chicago, IL 60606–3491; tel. 312/422–3840; FAX. 312/422–4573; Albert J. Sunseri, Ph.D., Executive Director

Association for Hospital Medical Education, 1200 19th Street, N.W., Suite 300, Washington, DC 20036–2422; tel. 202/857–1196; FAX. 202/223–4579; Dennis Smeage, Executive Director

Association for Professionals in Infection Control and Epidemiology, 1275 K Street. NW, Suite 1000, Washington, DC 20036; tel. 202/789–1890; FAX. 202/789–1899; Christopher E. Laxton, Executive Director

Association for Quality HealthCare, Inc., P.O. Box 670, Columbus, GA 31902; tel. 404/571–2122; FAX. 404/571–2650; L. B. Skip Teaster, Executive Director

Association for the Advancement of Automotive Medicine, 2340 DesPlaines Avenue, Suite 106, Des Plaines, IL 60018; tel. 847/390–8927; FAX. 847/390–9962; Elaine Petrucelli, Executive Director

Association for the Advancement of Medical Instrumentation, 3330 Washington Boulevard, Suite 400, Arlington, VA 22201–4598; tel. 703/525–4890; FAX. 703/276–0793; Michael J. Miller, J.D., President

Association of American Medical Colleges, 2450 N Street, N.W., Washington, DC 20037–1127; tel. 202/828–0400; FAX. 202/828–1125; Jordan J. Cohen, M.D., President

Association of American Physicians, Krannert Institute of Cardiology, Indiana University School of Medicine, Indianapolis, IN 46202–4800; tel. 317/630–7712; FAX. 317/274–9697; David R. Hathaway, M.D., Secretary

Association of American Physicians and Surgeons, Inc., 1601 North Tucson Boulevard, Suite Nine, Tucson, AZ 85716; tel. 520/327–4885; FAX. 520/325–4230; Jane M. Orient, M.D., Executive Director

Association of Birth Defect Children, 930 Woodcock Road, Suite 270, Orlando, FL 32803; tel. 407/245–7035; FAX. 407/245–7087; Betty Mekdeci, Executive Director

Association of Community Cancer Centers, 11600 Nebel Street, Suite 201, Rockville, MD 20852–2587; tel. 301/984–9496; FAX. 301/770–1949; Lee E. Mortenson, DPA, Executive Director

Association of Mental Health Administrators, 60 Revere Drive, Suite 500, Northbrook, IL 60062; tel. 847/480–9626; FAX. 847/480–9282; Alison C. Brown, Executive Director

Association of Military Surgeons of the U.S., 9320 Old Georgetown Road, Bethesda, MD 20814; tel. 301/897–8800; FAX. 301/530–5446; Rear Admiral Frederic G. Sanford, MC, USN Ret.

Association of Operating Room Nurses, Inc., 2170 South Parker Road, Suite 300, Denver, CO 80231–5711; tel. 303/755–6300; FAX. 303/750–2927; Pat Palmer, RN, M.S., CAE, MNM, Executive Director

Association of Professional Chaplains, 1701 East Woodfield Road, Suite 311, Schaumburg, IL 60173–5191; tel. 847/240–1014; FAX. 847/240–1015; Jo Schrader, Administrative Director

Association of Schools of Allied Health Professions, 1730 M Street, N.W., Suite 500, Washington, DC 20036; tel. 202/293–4848; FAX. 202/293–4852; Thomas W. Elwood, Dr. P.H., Executive Director

Association of Schools of Public Health, Inc., 1660 L Street, N.W., Suite 204, Washington, DC 20036; tel. 202/296–1099; FAX. 202/296–1252; Michael K. Gemmell, CAE, Executive Director

Association of Specialized and Cooperative Library Agencies A Division of the American Library Ass., 50 East Huron Street, Chicago, IL 60611; tel. 312/280–4399; FAX. 312/944–8085; Cathleen Bourdon, ASCLA, Executive Director

Association of State and Territorial Health Officials, 1275 K Street, NW, Suite 800, Washington, DC 20005–4006; tel. 202/371–9090; FAX. 202/371–9797; Cheryl A. Beversdorf, RN, M.H.S., CAE, Executive Vice

Association of Surgical Technologists, Inc., 7108–C South Alton Way, Englewood, CO 80112–2106; tel. 303/694–9130; FAX. 303/694–9169; William J. Teutsch, Executive Director

Association of University Anesthesiologists, 2150 N. 107th Street, Suite 205, Seattle, WA 98133–9009; tel. 206/367–8704; FAX. 206/367–8777; Shirley Bishop

Association of University Programs in Health Administration, 1110 Vermont Avenue, NW, Suite 220, Washington, DC 20005–3500; tel. 202/822–8550; FAX. 202/822–8555; Janet Porter, Ph.D., Interim President and CEO

Asthma and Allergy Foundation of America, 1125 15th Street, N.W., Suite 502, Washington, DC 20005; tel. 202/466–7643; FAX. 202/466–8940; Mary E. Worstell, M.P.H., Executive Director

Asthma Foundation of Southern Arizona, P.O. Box 30069, Tucson, AZ 85751–0069; tel. 602/323–6046; FAX. 602/324–1137; Lynn Krust, Executive Director

AVSC International, 79 Madison Avenue, Seventh Floor, New York, NY 10016; tel. 212/561–8065; Bob Geisler, Director, Information Services

B

BCS Financial Corporation, 676 North St. Clair, Chicago, IL 60611; tel. 312/951–7700; FAX. 312/951–7777; Edward J. Baran, Chairman and CEO

Bereavement Services, Gundersen Lutheran Medical Center, 1910 South Avenue, La Crosse, WI 54601; tel. 800/362–9567; FAX. 608/791–5137; Fran Rybarik, Director

Biological Photographic Association, Inc., 1819 Peachtree Road, N.E., Suite 620, Atlanta, GA 30309; tel. 404/351–6300; FAX. 404/351–3348; William Just, Executive Director

Biological Stain Commission, Inc., University of Rochester, Department Pathology, Rochester, NY 14642–0001; tel. 716/275–6335; FAX. 716/442–8993; David P. Penney, Ph.D., Treasurer

Blinded Veterans Association, 477 H Street, N.W., Washington, DC 20001; tel. 800/669–7079; FAX. 202/371–8258; Thomas H. Miller, Executive Director

Blue Cross and Blue Shield Association, 225 N. Michigan Avenue, Chicago, IL 60601; tel. 312/297–6010; FAX. 312/297–6120; Patrick G. Hays, President and CEO

C

Catholic Health Association of the United States, 4455 Woodson Road, St. Louis, MO 63134–3797; tel. 314/427–2500; FAX. 314/427–0029; Rev. Michael D. Place, STD, President and CEO

Catholic Medical Association, 850 Elm Grove Road, Elm Grove, WI 53122; tel. 414/784–3435; FAX. 414/782–8788; Michael J. Herzog, Executive Director

Section C

Center for Health Administration Studies, University of Chicago, 969 East 60th Street, Chicago, IL 60637; tel. 773/702-7104; FAX. 773/702-7222; Kristiana Raube, Ph.D., Acting Director

Central Neuropsychiatric Association, 128 East Milltown Road, Wooster, OH 44691; tel. 330/345-6555; FAX. 330/345-6648; Dennis O. Helmuth, M.D., Secretary-Treasurer

Central Surgical Association, Loyola University Medical Center, Department of Surgery, 2160 South First Avenue, Maywood, IL 60153; tel. 708/327-2685; FAX. 708/327-2810; William H. Baker, M.D., Secretary-CSA

Children's Rights Council (CRC), formerly National Council for Children's Rights, 300 Eye Street, N.E., Suite 401, Washington, DC 20002; tel. 202/547-6227; FAX. 202/546-4272; David E. Levy, Esq., President & Chief Executive Officer

Christian Record Services, Inc., 4444 South 52nd Street, Lincoln, NE 68516; tel. 402/488-0981; FAX. 402/488-7582; Ron Bowes, Public Relations Director

College of American Pathologists, 325 Waukegan Road, Northfield, IL 60093-2750; tel. 847/832-7000; FAX. 847/832-8151; Lee VanBremen, Ph.D., Executive Vice President

Commission on Accreditation of Rehabilitation Facilities, 4891 East Grant Road, Tucson, AZ 85712; tel. 520/325-1044; FAX. 520/318-1129; Donald E. Galvin, Ph.D., President & Chief Executive Officer

Committee of Interns and Residents, 386 Park Avenue, S., New York, NY 10016; tel. 212/725-5500; FAX. 212/779-2413; John Ronches, Executive Director

Cooley's Anemia Foundation, Inc., 129-09 26th Avenue, Suite 203, Flushing, NY 11354; tel. 800/522-7222; FAX. 718/321-3340; Gina Cioffi, Esq. National Executive Director

Corporate Angel Network, Inc., CAN (Arranges Free Air Transportation for Cancer Patients, Westchester County Airport, One Loop Road, White Plains, NY 10604; tel. 914/328-1313; FAX. 914/328-4226; Liz Lockwood, Director of Volunteers

Council of Jewish Federations, Inc., 730 Broadway, New York, NY 10003; tel. 212/475-5000; FAX. 212/529-5842; Martin S. Kraar, Executive Vice President

Council of Medical Specialty Societies, 51 Sherwood Terrace, Suite M, Lake Bluff, IL 60044; tel. 847/295-3456; FAX. 847/295-3759; Rebecca R. Gschwend, M.A., M.B.A., Executive Vice President

Council of State Administrators of Vocational Rehabilitation, P.O. Box 3776, Washington, DC 20007; tel. 202/638-4634; Jack G. Duncan, General Counsel, Rehabilitation Policy

Council on Education for Public Health, 1015 Fifteenth Street, N.W., Washington, DC 20005; tel. 202/789-1050; FAX. 202/789-1895; Patricia P. Evans, Executive Director

Council on Social Work Education, 1600 Duke Street, Alexandria, VA 22314; tel. 703/683-8080; FAX. 703/683-8099; Donald W. Beless, Ph.D., Executive Director

Crohn's and Colitis Foundation of America, Inc., 386 Park Avenue, S., 17th Floor, New York, NY 10016-8804; tel. 800/932-2423; FAX. 212/779-4098; James V. Romano, Ph. D., President and CEO

Cystic Fibrosis Foundation, 6931 Arlington Road, Bethesda, MD 20814; tel. 301/951-4422; FAX. 301/951-6378; Robert J. Beally, Ph.D., President and CEO

D

Damien Dutton Society for Leprosy Aid, Inc., 616 Bedford Avenue, Bellmore, NY 11710; tel. 516/221-5829; FAX. 516/221-5909; Howard E. Crouch, President

Delta Dental Plans Association, 211 East Chicago Avenue, Suite 800, Chicago, IL 60611; tel. 312/337-4707; FAX. 312/337-7991; James Bonk, President

Dermatology Foundation, 1560 Sherman Avenue, Evanston, IL 60201-4802; tel. 847/328-2256; FAX. 847/328-0509; Sandra Rahn Goldman, Executive Director

Dietary Managers Association, 406 Surrey Woods Drive, St. Charles, IL 60174; tel. 630/587-6336; FAX. 630/587-6308; William St. John, President

Dysautonomia Foundation, Inc., 20 East 46th Street, Suite 302, New York, NY 10017; tel. 212/949-6644; FAX. 212/682-7625; Lenore F. Roseman, Executive Director

E

Eastern Orthopaedic Association, Inc., Pier Five North, Suite 5D, Seven North Columbus Boulevard, Philadelphia, PA 19106-1486; tel. 215/351-4110; FAX. 215/351-1825; Elizabeth F. Capella, Executive Director

ECRI, 5200 Butler Pike, Plymouth Meet, PA 19462; tel. 610/825-6000; FAX. 610/834-1275; Joel J. Nobel, M.D., President

Educational Commission for Foreign Medical Graduates, 3624 Market Street, Philadelphia, PA 19104-2685; tel. 215/386-5900; FAX. 215/387-9963; Nancy E. Gary, M.D., President and CEO

Ehlers-Danlos National Foundation, P.O. Box 13157, Richmond, VA 23225; tel. 804/320-8192; FAX. 804/320-8192; Susan L. Stephenson, Vice President, Patient Advocate

Emergency Nurses Association, 216 Higgins Road, Park Ridge, IL 60068-5736; tel. 847/698-9400; FAX. 847/698-9406; Executive Office

Epilepsy Foundation of America, 4351 Garden City Drive, Landover, MD 20785-2267; tel. 301/459-3700; FAX. 301/577-2684; Eric Hargis, Chief Executive Officer

Epilepsy Foundation of Connecticut, 1800 Silas Deane Highway, Suite 168, Rocky Hill, CT 06067; tel. 860/721-9226; Linda Wallace

F

Federation of American Health Systems, 1111 19th Street, N.W., Suite 402, Washington, DC 20036; tel. 202/833-3090; FAX. 202/861-0063; Thomas A. Scully, President & Chief Executive Officer

Federation of State Medical Boards of the United States, Inc., 400 Fuller Wiser Road, Suite 300, Euless, TX 76039-3855; tel. 817/868-4000; FAX. 817/868-4099; James R. Winn, M.D., Executive Vice President

Financial Accounting Standards Board, 401 Merritt 7, P.O. Box 5116, Norwalk, CT 06856-5116; tel. 203/847-0700; FAX. 203/849-9714; Timothy S. Lucas, Director, Research, Technical Activities

Foundation for Chiropractic Education and Research, 1330 Beacon Street, Suite 315, Brookline, MA 02146-3202; tel. 617/734-3397; FAX. 617/734-0989; Anthony L. Rosner, Ph.D., Director of Research and Education

G

Gerontological Society of America, 1030 15 Street, NW, suite 250, Washington, DC 20005-1503; tel. 202/842-1275; FAX. 202/842-1150; Carol A. Schutz, Executive Director

Great Plains Health Alliance, Inc., 625 Third Street, Box 366, Phillipsburg, KS 67661; tel. 785/543-2111; FAX. 785/543-5098; Roger S. John, President and CEO

Guide Dog Users, Inc., 57 Grandview Avenue, Watertown, MA 02472; tel. 617/926-9198; FAX. 617-923-0004; Kim Charlson, Editor

H

Health Industry Distributors Association, 66 Canal Center Plaza, Suite 520, Alexandria, VA 22314-1591; tel. 703/549-4432; FAX. 703/549-6495; S. Wayne Kay, President & Chief Executive Officer

Health Industry Manufacturers Association, 1200 G Street, N.W., Suite 400, Washington, DC 20005; tel. 202/783-8700; FAX. 202/783-8750; Alan H. Magazine, President

Health Research and Educational Trust, One North Franklin, Chicago, IL 60606; tel. 312/422-2624; FAX. 312/422-4568; Deborah Bohr, Vice President

Healthcare Council of MidMichigan, 3927 Beecher Road, Flint, MI 48532; tel. 810/766-8898; FAX. 810/762-4108; Marlene Soderstrom, President

Healthcare Financial Management Association, Two Westbrook Corporate Center, Suite 700, Westchester, IL 60154; tel. 708/531-9600; FAX. 708/531-0032; Richard L. Clarke, F.H.F.M.A., President

Healthcare Information and Management Systems Society (HIMSS), 230 East Ohio Street, Suite 500, Chicago, IL 60611-3201; tel. 312/664-4467; FAX. 312/664-6143; John A. Page, Executive Director

HEAR Center, 301 East Del Mar Boulevard, Pasadena, CA 91101; tel. 626/796-2016; FAX. 626/796-2320; Josephine Wilson, Executive Director

Hispanic American Geriatrics Society, One Cutts Road, Durham, NH 03824-3102; tel. 603/868-5757; Eugene E. Tillock, Ed.D., President

Histochemical Society, Inc., Department of Neurology, University of Washington, Seattle, WA 98195; tel. 206/764-2088; FAX. 206/764-2164

Huntington's Disease Society of America, Inc., 158 West 29th Street, 7th Floor, New York, NY 10001-5300; tel. 800/345-HDSA; FAX. 212/243-2443; Barbara T. Boyle, National Executive Director/CEO

I

Institutes for the Achievement of Human Potential, 8801 Stenton Avenue, Wyndmoor, PA 19038; tel. 215-233-2050; FAX. 215/233-3940; Coralee Thompson, M.D.

InterHealth, P.O. Box 10624, White Bear Lake, MN 55110; tel. 612/407-7075; FAX. 612/407-7077; Thomas LaMotte, Chairman of the Board

International Childbirth Education Association, Inc., P.O. Box 20048, Minneapolis, MN 55420-0048; tel. 612/854-8660; FAX. 612/854-8772; Doris Olson, Administrator

International College of Surgeons/United States Section, 1516 North Lake Shore Drive, Chicago, IL 60610-1694; tel. 312/787-6274; FAX. 312/787-9289; Susan Zelner, Meeting and Convention Manager

International Council for Health, Physical Education, Recreation, Sport and Dance, 1900 Association Drive, Reston, VA 20191; tel. 703/476-3486; FAX. 703/476-9527; Dr. Dong Ja Yang, Secretary General

Intravenous Nurses Society, Inc., Fresh Pond Square, 10 Fawcett Street, Cambridge, MA 02138; tel. 617/441-3008; FAX. 617/576-5452; Mary Alexander, Chief Executive Officer

J

J. S. Anesthesia Consultants, P.O. Box 232, Jersey Shore, PA 17740; tel. 717/769–7735; John A. Hunter, D.D.S., Secretary

John Milton Society for the Blind, 475 Riverside Drive, Suite 455, New York, NY 10115; tel. 212/870–3335; FAX. 212/870–3229; Darcy Quigley, Executive Director

Joint Commission on Accreditation of Healthcare Organizations, One Renaissance Boulevard, Oakbrook Terr, IL 60181; tel. 630/792–5000; FAX. 630/792–5005; Dennis S. O'Leary, M.D., President

L

Lamaze International, Inc., (formerly ASPO/LAMAZE), 1200 19th Street, N.W., Suite 300, Washington, DC 20036; tel. 202/857–1128; FAX. 202/223–4579; Linda L. Harmon, Executive Director

Leukemia Society of America, Inc., 600 Third Avenue, New York, NY 10016; tel. 212/573–8484; FAX. 212/856–9686; Dwayne Howell, President and CEO

LHS, Inc./ Lutheran Health Systems, Box 6200, 4310 17th Avenue, S.W., Fargo, ND 58106–6200; tel. 701–277–7500; FAX. 701/277–7636; Steven R. Orr, Chairman, Chief Executive Officer

Long Term Acute Care Hospital Association of America, 1301 K Street, N.W., Suite 1100 East Tower, Washington, DC 20005–3317; tel. 202/296–4446; FAX. 202/414–9299; James T. Marrinan, Executive Director

Lupus Foundation of America, Inc., 1300 Piccard Drive, Suite 200, Rockville, MD 20850; tel. 301/670–9292; FAX. 301/670–9486; K. Hurley, Director, Information Services

M

March of Dimes Birth Defects Foundation, 1275 Mamaroneck Avenue, White Plains, NY 10605; tel. 914/428–7100; FAX. 914/428–8203; Jennifer L. Howse, Ph.D., President

Medic Alert, 2323 Colorado Avenue, Turlock, CA 95382; tel. 800/825–3785; FAX. 209/668–8752; David Roth, Public Relations

Medical Group Management Association, 104 Inverness Terrace, E., Englewood, CO 80112–5306; tel. 888/608–5601; FAX. 303/643–4427; Thomas L. Adams, CAE, Chief Executive Officer

Medical Library Association, 65 East Wacker Drive, Suite 1900, Chicago, IL 60601–7298; tel. 312/419–9094; FAX. 312/419–8950; Carla J. Funk, Executive Director

Mended Hearts, Inc., 7272 Greenville Avenue, Dallas, TX 75231; tel. 214/706–1442; FAX. 214/706–5231; Darla Bonham, Executive Director

Minnesota Healthcare Conference, 2221 University Avenue, S.E., Suite 425, Minneapolis, MN 55414; tel. 612/331–5571; FAX. 612/331–1001; Peggy Westby, Manager

Muscular Dystrophy Association, 3300 East Sunrise Drive, Tucson, AZ 85718; tel. 520–529–2000; FAX. 520–529–5300; Robert Ross, Senior Vice President and Executive Director

N

National Academy of Sciences, National Research Council/Commission on Life Sciences, 2101 Constitution Avenue, N.W., NAS 343, Washington, DC 20418; tel. 202/334–2500; FAX. 202/334–1639; Paul Gilman, Ph.D., Executive Director

National Accreditation Council for Agencies Serving the Blind , 260 Northland Blvd., Suite 233, Cincinnati, OH 45246; tel. 513/772–8449; FAX. 513/772–8854; Dr. Gerald W. Mundy, Executive Director

National Accrediting Agency for Clinical Laboratory Sciences, 8410 West Bryn Mawr, Suite 670, Chicago, IL 60631–3415; tel. 773/714–8880; FAX. 773/714–8886; Olive M. Kimball, Executive Director

National Alliance for the Mentally Ill, 200 N. Glebe Road, Suite 1015, Arlington, VA 22203–3754; tel. 703/524–7600; FAX. 703/524–9094; Laurie Flynn, Executive Director

National Assembly on School Based Health Care, 1522 K Street NW, Suite 600, Washington, DC 20005; tel. 202/289–5400; FAX. 202/289–0776; John Schlitt, Executive Director

National Association for Home Care, 228 Seventh Street, S.E., Washington, DC 20003; tel. 202/547–7424; FAX. 202/547–3540; Val J. Halamandaris, President

National Association for Medical Equipment Services (NAMES), 625 Slaters Lane, Suite 200, Alexandria, VA 22314–1171; tel. 703/836–6263; FAX. 703/836–6730; William D. Coughlan, CAE, President and CEO

National Association for Practical Nurse Education and Service, 1400 Spring Street, Suite 330, Silver Spring, MD 20910; tel. 301/588–2491; FAX. 301/588–2839; John H. Word, LPN, Executive Director

National Association Medical Staff Services, 631 East Butterfield, Suite 311, Lombard, IL 60148; tel. 630/271–9814; FAX. 630/271–0295; Robert A. Dengler, CAE, CMP, Executive Director

National Association of Boards of Pharmacy, 700 Busse Highway, Park Ridge, IL 60068; tel. 847/698–6227; FAX. 847/698–0124; Carmen A. Catizone, R.Ph., M.S., Executive Director, S

National Association of Children's Hospitals and Related Institutes, 401 Wythe Street, Alexandria, VA 22314; tel. 703/684–1355; FAX. 703/684–1589; Lawrence A. McAndrews, President and CEO

National Association of Dental Assistants, 900 South Washington, Suite G13, Falls Church, VA 22046; tel. 703/237–8616; S. Young, Director

National Association of Dental Laboratories, (Includes National Board for Certification in Dental Laboratory Technology), 8201 Greensboro Drive, Suite 300, McLean, VA 22102; tel. 800/684–5310; FAX. 703/549–4788; Carrie B. Beeton, Director of Member & Component Services

National Association of Health Services Executives, 8630 Fenton Street, Suite 126, Silver Spring, MD 20910; tel. 202/628–3953; FAX. 301/588–0011; Ozzie Jenkins, CMP, Executive Director

National Association of Hospital Hospitality Houses, Inc., 4915 Auburn Avenue, Suite 303, Bethesda, MD 20814; tel. 800/542–9730; FAX. 301/961–3094; Martha J. Lockwood, CAE, APR, Executive Director

National Association of Institutional Laundry Managers, 781 Twin Oaks Avenue, Chula Vista, CA 92010; tel. 619/420–1396; FAX. 619/420–1396; Betty Conard, Executive Secretary

National Association of Psychiatric Health Systems, 1317 F Street, N.W., Suite 301, Washington, DC 20004; tel. 202/393–6700; FAX. 202/783–6041; Mark J. Covall, Executive Director

National Association of Social Workers, Inc., 750 First Street, N.E., Suite 700, Washington, DC 20002; tel. 202/408–8600; FAX. 202/336–8311; Senior Staff Associate, Health, Mental

National Association of State Mental Health Program Directors, 66 Canal Center Plaza, Suite 302, Alexandria, VA 22314; tel. 703/739–9333; FAX. 703/548–9517; Robert W. Glover, Ph.D., Executive Director

National Board for Respiratory Care, 8310 Nieman Road, Lenexa, KS 66214; tel. 913/599–4200; FAX. 913/541–0156; Steven K. Bryant, Executive Director

National Board of Medical Examiners, 3750 Market Street, Philadelphia, PA 19104; tel. 215/590–9500; FAX. 215/590–9755; L. Thompson Bowles, M.D., Ph.D., President

National Children's Eye Care Foundation, P.O. Box 795069, Dallas, TX 75379–5069; tel. 972/407–0404; FAX. 972/407–0616; Suzanne C. Beauchamp, Administrator

National Council on Alcoholism and Drug Dependence, Inc., 12 West 21st Street, New York, NY 10010; tel. 212/206–6770; FAX. 212/645–1690; Jeffrey Hon, Director, Public Information

National Council on Radiation Protection and Measurements, 7910 Woodmont Avenue, Suite 800, Bethesda, MD 20814; tel. 301/657–2652; FAX. 301/907–8768; William M. Beckner, Executive Director

National Council on the Aging, Inc., 409 Third Street, S.W., Suite 200, Washington, DC 20024; tel. 202/479–1200; FAX. 202/479–0735; James Firman, President

National Dental Association, 5506 Connecticut Avenue, N.W., Suite 24–25, Washington, DC 20015; tel. 202/244–7555; FAX. 202/244–5992; Robert S. Johns, Executive Director

National Depressive and Manic–Depressive Association, 730 North Franklin Street, Suite 501, Chicago, IL 60610; tel. 312/642–0049; FAX. 312/642–7243; Lydia Lewis, Executive Director

National Easter Seal Society, 230 West Monroe Street, Suite 1800, Chicago, IL 60606–4802; tel. 312/726–6200; FAX. 312/726–1494; James E. Williams, Jr., President

National Environmental Health Association, 720 South Colorado Boulevard, South Tower, Suite, Denver, CO 80222; tel. 303/756–9090; FAX. 303/691–9490; Nelson Fabian, Executive Director

National Federation of Licensed Practical Nurses, 893 Highway, 70 West, Suite 202, Garner, NC 27529; tel. 919/779–0046; FAX. 919/779–5642; Charlene Barbour, Executive Director

National Fire Protection Association, P.O. Box 9101, One Batterymarck Park, Quincy, MA 02269–9101; tel. 617/770–3000; FAX. 617/770–7110; Burton R. Klein, Health Care Fire Protection Engineer

National Gaucher Foundation, 11140 Rockville Pike, Suite 350, Rockville, MD 20852; tel. 301/816–1515; FAX. 301/816–1516; Rhonda Buyers, Executive Director

National Headache Foundation, 428 West St. James Place, Second Floor, Chicago, IL 60614–2750; tel. 888/NHF–5552; FAX. 773/525–7357; Suzanne Simons, Executive Director

National Health Council, Inc., 1730 M Street, N.W., Suite 500, Washington, DC 20036; tel. 202/785–3910; FAX. 202/785–5923; Myrl Weinberg, CAE, President

National Hemophilia Foundation, 116 West 32nd Street, 11th Floor, New York, NY 10001; tel. 212/328–3700; FAX. 212/328–9247; Stephen E. Bajard, Executive Director

National Institute for Jewish Hospice, Central Telephone Network, P.O. Box 48025, Los Angeles, CA 90048; tel. 800/446–4448; Levana Lev, Executive Director, or Shirley Lam, Exec

National Kidney Foundation, 30 East 33rd Street, New York, NY 10016; tel. 800/622–9010; FAX. 212/779–0068; John Davis, Chief Executive Officer

National League for Nursing, 350 Hudson Street, New York, NY 10014; tel. 212/989–9393; FAX. 212/989–9256; Ruth D. Corcorau, EdD, RN, Chief Executive Officer

National Medical Association, 1012 10th Street, N.W., Washington, DC 20001; tel. 202/347–1895; FAX. 202/842–3293; Lorraine Cole, Ph.D., Executive Director

National Mental Health Association, 1021 Prince Street, Alexandria, VA 22314–2971; tel. 703/684–7722; FAX. 703/684–5968; Michael M. Faenza, President and CEO

National Multiple Sclerosis Society, 733 Third Avenue, New York, NY 10017; tel. 212/986–3240; FAX. 212/986–7981; Dwayne Howell, Executive Vice President

National Parkinson Foundation, Inc., 1501 Northwest Ninth Avenue, Miami, FL 33136–1494; tel. 305/547–6666; FAX. 305/548–4403; Brian Morton, Controller

National Perinatal Association, 3500 East Fletcher Avenue, Suite 209, Tampa, FL 33613–4712; tel. 813/971–1008; FAX. 813/971–9306; Judith Burke, Executive Director

National Recreation and Park Association, 22377 Belmont Ridge Road, Ashburn, VA 20148; tel. 703/858–0784; FAX. 703/858–0794; R. Dean Tice, Executive Director

National Registry in Clinical Chemistry, 815 15th Street, N.W., Suite 630, Washington, DC 20005; tel. 202/393–7140; FAX. 202/393–4059; Gilbert E. Smith, Ph.D., Executive Director

National Registry of Emergency Medical Technicians, 6610 Busch Boulevard, P.O. Box 29233, Columbus, OH 43229; tel. 614/888–4484; William E. Brown, Jr., Executive Director

National Rehabilitation Association, (Includes Nine National Associations and 58 Affiliate Chapters), 633 South Washington Street, Alexandria, VA 22314; tel. 703/836–0850; FAX. 703/836–0848; Michelle A. Vaughan, Executive Director

National Resident Matching Program, 2450 N Street, N.W., Suite 201, Washington, DC 20037–1141; tel. 202/828–0676; FAX. 202/828–1121; Robert L. Beran, Ph. D., Deputy Executive Director

National Rural Health Association, 1320 19th Street, N.W., Suite 350, Washington, DC 20036–1610; tel. 202/232–6200; FAX. 202/232–1133; Darin E. Johnson, Government Affairs Director

National Safety Council, P.O. Box 558, Itasca, IL 60143–0558; tel. 630/285–1121; FAX. 630/285–0797; Kimberly D. Spoolstra, Customer Service

National Spinal Cord Injury Association, 545 Concord Avenue, Suite 29, Cambridge, MA 02138; tel. 617/441–8500; FAX. 617/441–3449; Dianne M. Barry, Executive Director

National Student Nurses' Association, Inc., 555 West 57th Street, Suite 1327, New York, NY 10019; tel. 212/581–2211; FAX. 212/581–2368; Diane J. Mancino, Ed.D., RN, CAE, Executive Director

National Tay–Sachs and Allied Diseases Association, 2001 Beacon Street, Suite 204, Brighton, MA 02135; tel. 800/90–NTSAD; FAX. 617/277–0134; Jayne C. Gershkowitz, Executive Director

Neurotics Anonymous, 11140 Bainbridge Drive, Little Rock, AR 72212; tel. 501/221–2809; FAX. 501/221–2809; Grover Boydston, Chairman

New England Gerontological Association, One Cutts Road, Durham, NH 03824–3102; tel. 603/868–5757; Eugene E. Tillock, Ed.D., Executive Director

NSF International, 3475 Plymouth Road, P.O. Box 130140, Ann Arbor, MI 48113–0140; tel. 313/769–8010; FAX. 313/769–0109; Dennis R. Mangino, Ph. D., President, Chief Executive

O

Osteogenesis Imperfecta Foundation, Inc., 804 West Diamond Avenue, Suite 210, Gaithersburg, MD 20878; tel. 301/947–0083; FAX. 301/947–0456; Heller An Shapiro, Executive Director

Otosclerosis Study Group, 6465 Yale, Tulsa, OK 74136; Roger E. Wehrs, M.D., Secretary–Treasurer

P

Pan American Health Organization, 525 23rd Street, N.W., Washington, DC 20037; tel. 202/974–3000; Daniel Lopez Acuna, Director, HSP

Parkinson's Disease Foundation, Inc, (Formerly United Parkinson Foundation), 833 West Washington Boulevard, Chicago, IL 60607; tel. 312/733–1893; FAX. 312/733–1896; Jeanne Lee, Manager

Physician Executive Management Center, 3403 West Fletcher Avenue, Tampa, FL 33618–2813; tel. 813/963–1800; FAX. 813/264–2207; David R. Kirschman, President

Pilot Dogs, Inc., 625 West Town Street, Columbus, OH 43215; tel. 614/221–6367; FAX. 614/221–1577; J. Jay Gray, Executive Director

Prevent Blindness America, 500 East Remington Road, Schaumburg, IL 60173–4557; tel. 800/331–2020; FAX. 847/843–8458; Richard T. Hellner, President and CEO

Public Relations Society of America, 33 Irving Place, New York, NY 10003–2376; tel. 212/995–2230; FAX. 212/995–0757; Ray Gaulke, President and COO

R

Radiological Society of North America, Inc., 2021 Spring Road, Suite 600, Oak Brook, IL 60523; tel. 630/571–2670; FAX. 630/571–7837; Delmar J. Stauffer, Executive Director

Recording for the Blind and Dyslexic, 20 Roszel Road, Princeton, NJ 08540; tel. 609/452–0606; FAX. 609/520–7990; Richard O. Scribner, President

Renal Physicians Association, 2011 Pennsylvania Avenue, N.W., Suite 800, Washington, DC 20006–1808; tel. 202/835–0436; FAX. 202/835–0443; Dale Singer, MHA, Executive Director

Robert Wood Johnson Foundation, P.O. Box 2316, Route One and College Road East, Princeton, NJ 08543–2316; tel. 609/452–8701; FAX. 609/987–8845; Richard J. Toth, Director, Office of Proposal Management

S

Shriners Hospitals for Children, P.O. Box 31356, Tampa, FL 33631–3356; tel. 813/281–0300; FAX. 813/281–8113; Melody Lewis, Executive Secretary

Sickle Cell Disease Foundation of Greater New York, 127 West 127th Street, Suite 421, New York, NY 10027; tel. 212/865–1500; FAX. 212/865–0917; Beryl Murray, Executive Director

Society for Academic Emergency Medicine, 901 North Washington Avenue, Lansing, MI 48906; tel. 517/485–5484; FAX. 517/485–0801; Mary Ann Schropp, Executive Director

Society for Adolescent Medicine, Inc., 1916 Northwest Copper Oaks Circle, Blue Springs, MO 64015; tel. 816/224–8010; FAX. 816/224–8009; Edie Moore, Administrative Director

Society for Healthcare Consumer Advocacy, One North Franklin, Chicago, IL 60606; tel. 312/422–3774; FAX. 312/422–4580; Bruce Deakin, Administrative Assistant

Society for Healthcare Strategy and Market Development, of the American Hospital Association, One North Franklin, 31st Floor, Chicago, IL 60606; tel. 312/422–3888; FAX. 312/422–4579; Lauren A. Barnett, Executive Director

Society for Occupational and Environmental Health, 6728 Old McLean Village Drive, McLean, VA 22101; tel. 703/556–9222; FAX. 703/556–8729; Robin Turner, Account Manager

Society for Pediatric Pathology, 6728 Old McLean Village Drive, McLean, VA 22101; tel. 703/556–9222; FAX. 703/556–8729; Merrill A. Ferber, Associate Director

Society for Social Work Administrators in Health Care, One North Franklin, Chicago, IL 60606–3401; tel. 312/422–3774; FAX. 312/422–4580; Bruce Deakin, Administrative Assistant

Society of Critical Care Medicine, 8101 East Kaiser Boulevard, Anaheim, CA 92808–2214; tel. 714/282–6000; FAX. 714/282–6050; Steven Seekins, Chief Executive Officer

Society of Neurological Surgeons, New England Medical Center, Department of Neurosurgery, Boston, MA 02111; tel. 617/636–5858; William Shucart, M.D., Secretary

Society of Nuclear Medicine, 1850 Samuel Morse Drive, Reston, VA 22090; tel. 703/708–9000; FAX. 703/708–9777; c/o Administrator

Society of University Otolaryngologists–Head and Neck Surgeons, USC School of Medicine, Department of Otolaryngology, Los Angeles, CA 90083; tel. 323/226–7315; FAX. 323/226–2780; Donna Hoffman, M.A., Executive Director

Southeastern Healthcare Association, 1345 Carmichael Way, P.O. Box 11126, Montgomery, AL 36111–0126; tel. 334/260–8600; FAX. 205/260–0023; Tommy R. McDougal, FACHE, President

T

Technologist Section, Society of Nuclear Medicine, 1850 Samuel Morse Drive, Reston, VA 22090; tel. 703/708–9000; FAX. 703/708–9015; Virginia M. Pappas, Administrator

The Alliance For Healthcare Strategy And Marketing, 11 South LaSalle, Suite 2300, Suite 2300, Chicago, IL 60603; tel. 312/704–9700; FAX. 312/704–9709; Carla Windhorst, President

The American Association of Immunologists, 9650 Rockville Pike, Bethesda, MD 20814; tel. 301/530–7178; FAX. 301/571–1816; M. Michele Hogan, Ph.D., Executive Director

The American Board of Obstetrics and Gynecology, Inc., 2915 Vine Street, Dallas, TX 75204; tel. 214/871–1619; FAX. 214/871–1943; Dr. Norman F. Gant, Executive Director

The American Board of Plastic Surgery, Inc., Seven Penn Center, Suite 400, 1635 Market Street, Philadelphia, PA 75204; tel. 215/587–9322; FAX. 215/587–9622; Terry M. Cullison, RNC, MSN, Administrator

The American Board of Professional Disability Consultants, 1350 Beverly Road, Suite 115–327, McLean, VA 22101; tel. 703/790–8644; Taras J. Cerkevitch, Ph.D., Director, Operations

The American Board of Urology, Inc., 2216 Ivy Road, Suite 210, Charlottesville, VA 22903; tel. 804/979–0059; FAX. 804/979–0266; Stuart S. Howards, M.D., Executive Secretary

The American Orthopaedic Association, 6300 North River Road, Suite 300, Rosemont, IL 60018–4263; tel. 847/318–7330; FAX. 847/318–7339; Hildegard A. Weiler, Executive Director

The Arc of the United States, Formerly Association for Retarded Citizens, 500 East Border Street, Suite 300, Arlington, TX 76011; tel. 817/640–0204; FAX. 817/277–3491; Alan Abeson, Ed.D., Executive Director

The Association for Research in Vision and Ophthalmology, 9650 Rockville Pike, Suite 1500, Bethesda, MD 20814–3998; tel. 301/571–1844; FAX. 301/571–8311; Joanne G. Angle, Executive Director

The Association of Medical Illustrators, 1819 Peachtree Street, N.E., Suite 712, Atlanta, GA 30309; tel. 404/350–7900; FAX. 404/351–3348; William H. Just, Executive Director

The Association of Women's Health, Obstetric, and Neonatal Nurses, 2000 L. Street, NW, Suite 740, Washington, DC 20036; tel. 202/261–2400; FAX. 201/728–0575; Gail G. Kincaide, Executive Director

The Duke Endowment, 100 North Tryon Street, Suite 3500, Charlotte, NC 28202; tel. 704/376–0291; FAX. 704/376–9336; Elizabeth H. Locke, President

The Endocrine Society, 4350 East West Highway, Suite 500, Bethesda, MD 20814–4410; tel. 301/941–0200; FAX. 301/941–0259; David Thomas, Director, Public Affairs

The Foundation Fighting Blindness, Executive Plaza I, Suite 800, 11350 McCormick Road, Hunt Valley, MD 21031–1014; tel. 800/683–5555; FAX. 410/771–9470; Edward J. Crenin, Jr., Chief Operating Officer

The Foundation for Ichthyosis and Related Skin Types, Inc., (F.I.R.S.T.), P.O. Box 669, Ardmore, PA 19003–0669; tel. 601–789–3995; Elena Levitan, Executive Director

The Healthcare Assembly, Inc., 500 Spaulding Turnpike, Suite W–310, Portsmouth, NH 03802–7100; tel. 603/422–6100; FAX. 603/422–6101; Pamela Lawrence, President and CEO

The Institute for Rehabilitation and Research, 1333 Moursound, Houston, TX 77030; tel. 713/799–5000; FAX. 713/799–7095; Louisa Adelung, Chief Executive Officer

The International Dyslexia Association, (Formerly The Orton Dyslexia Society), Chester Building, Suite 382, 8600 LaSalle Road, Baltimore, MD 21286; tel. 410/296–0232; FAX. 410/321–5069; Susan Brickley, Director, Marketing and Public Relations

The Points of Light Foundation, 1737 H Street, N.W., Washington, DC 20006; tel. 202/223–9186; FAX. 202/223–9256; Yael Israel, Customer Information Coordinator

The Salvation Army National Corporation, 615 Slaters Lane, P.O. Box 269, Alexandria, VA 22313; tel. 703/684–5500; FAX. 703/684–3478; Commissioner Robert A. Watson, National Commander

The Seeing Eye, Inc., Washington Valley Road, Box 375, Morristown, NJ 07963–0375; tel. 973/539–4425; FAX. 973/539–0922; Kenneth Rosenthal, President

The Southwestern Surgical Congress, 401 North Michigan Avenue, Chicago, IL 60611–4267; tel. 312/527–6667; FAX. 312/321–6869; Thomas E. Stautzenbach, Executive Director

U

UCLA Medical Surgery./Neurosurgery, Box 957039, Room 18–228 NPI, Los Angeles, CA 90095–7039; tel. 310/825–3998; FAX. 310/794–5836; Donald P. Becker, M.D.

United Cerebral Palsy Associations, Inc., 1660 L Street, N.W., Suite 700, Washington, DC 20036; tel. 800/872–5827; Michael Morris, Executive Director

United Methodist Association of Health and Welfare Ministries, 601 West Riverview Avenue, Dayton, OH 45406–5543; tel. 937/227–9494; FAX. 937/222–7364; Dean W. Pulliam, President and CEO

United Ostomy Association, Inc., 36 Executive Park, Suite 120, Irvine, CA 92714; tel. 800/826–0826; FAX. 714/660–9262; Darlene A. Smith, Executive Director

United Way of America, 701 North Fairfax Street, Alexandria, VA 22314–2045; tel. 703/836–7100; FAX. 703/683–7840; Betty Stanley Beene, President

USP, 12601 Twinbrook Parkway, Rockville, MD 20852; tel. 301/881–0666; FAX. 301/816–8299; Jerome A. Halperin, Executive Vice President, Chief Executive Officer

W

Western Orthopaedic Association, 1834 First Street, Suite 3, Napa, CA 94559–2353; tel. 707/259–9481; FAX. 707/259–9486; Susan Hanf, Executive Director

Western Surgical Association, Mayo Clinic, 200 First Street, S.W., Rochester, MN 55905; Jon A. VanHeerden, M.D., Secretary

Healthfinder

Healthfinder® is composed of two listing types: toll–free numbers for health information and federal health information centers and clearinghouses. Toll–free numbers are listed first, followed by the federal numbers.

This file was released in 1999. This document is revised annually.

This Federal document is in the public domain, but is distributed subject to two conditions: 1) Any person or organization posting and/or distributing this document in electronic or paper form MUST respect the integrity of the document and post or distribute it ONLY in its entirety, including this paragraph, and without any change whatsoever; and 2) Any person or organization either posting or distributing this document MUST agree to post and/or distribute future editions of the document in the same manner as this edition to ensure that the most current information is made available to those parties who received the earlier version.

If you would like more information, contact the U.S. Department of Health and Human Services, or visit the internet site at www.healthfinder.net.

1999 TOLL–FREE NUMBERS FOR HEALTH INFORMATION

This Healthfinder lists selected toll–free numbers for organizations that provide health–related information, education, and support. These organizations do NOT diagnose or recommend treatment for any disease. Some of the organizations use recorded messages; others provide personalized counseling and referrals. Most offer educational materials; some charge handling fees.

Organizations that provide crisis assistance are listed under the heading, *Crisis Intervention*. The *Rare Disorders* category includes diseases and disorders that affect less than 1 percent of the population at any given time. Groups in the *Professional Organizations* section do offer consumer information.

Unless otherwise stated, numbers can be reached within the continental United States 24 hours a day, 7 days a week. Inclusion of an information source in this publication does not imply endorsement by the U.S. Department of Health and Human Services.

This information is in the public domain. Duplication is encouraged.

ADOPTION

Bethany Christian Services
(800)238–4269
8 a.m.–12 midnight daily
National Adoption Center
(800)TO–ADOPT
9 a.m.–5 p.m.

AGING

American Health Assistance Foundation
(800)437–2423

Eldercare Locator
(800)677–1116
9 a.m.–11 p.m.

National Institute on Aging Information Center
(800)222–2225
(800)222–4225 (TTY)
8:30 a.m.–5 p.m.

AIDS/HIV

AIDS Clinical Trials Information Service
(800)874–2572
9 a.m.–7 p.m.
CDC National AIDS Clearinghouse
(800)458–5231 (orders only)
(800)243–7012 (TDD)
(800)458– 5231 (NAC Fax–Back Service)
info@cdcnac.org (E–Mail)
9 a.m.–6 p.m.

CDC National HIV/AIDS Hotline
(800)342–2437 (English)
(800)344–7432 (Spanish)
(800)243–7889 (TTY) 10 a.m.–10 p.m.,
Monday–Friday.

HIV/AIDS Treatment Information Service
(800)HIV–0440
9 a.m.–7 p.m. All calls are confidential.

Project Inform National HIV/AIDS Treatment Hotline
(800)822–7422
(415)558–9051
9 a.m.–5 p.m., Monday–Friday, 10 a.m. – 4:00 p.m. Saturday (Pacific).

ALCOHOL ABUSE

See Alcohol /Drug Abuse

ADCARE Hospital Helpline
(800)ALCOHOL
Operates 24 hours.

Al–Anon Family Group Headquarters
(800)356–9996
9 a.m.–4:30 p.m.

Alcohol and Drug Helpline
(800)821–4357
Operates 24 hours.

American Council on Alcoholism
(800)527–5344
9 a.m.–5 p.m.

Calix Society
(800)398–0524

Children of Alcoholics Foundation
(800)359–COAF

National Clearinghouse for Alcohol and Drug Information
(800)729–6686
(800)487–4889 (TTY/TDD)
8 a.m.–7 p.m.

National Council on Alcoholism and Drug Dependence, Inc.
(800)622–2255
9 a.m.–5 p.m.

National Woman's Christian Temperance Union
(800)755–1321

ALLERGY/ASTHMA

See LUNG DISEASE/ASTHMA/ALLERGY

The Food Allergy Network
(800)929–4040

ALZHEIMER'S DISEASE

See also AGING

Alzheimer's Association
(800)272–3900
The information and referral line is available 24 hours; operators staff the line 8:30 a.m.–5 p.m. Central, M–F. Leave message after hours.

Alzheimer's Disease Education and Referral Center
(800)438–4380
adear@alzheimers.org (E–mail)
8:30 a.m.–5 p.m.

ARTHRITIS

American Juvenile Arthritis Organization
(800)283–7800

Arthritis Foundation Information Line
(800)283–7800
24 hours.

Lyme Disease Foundation, Inc.
(800)886–5963

AUDIOVISUALS

See Library Services

AUTISM

See CHILD DEVELOPMENT

AUTOIMMUNE DISEASES

American Autoimmune Related Diseases Association, Inc.
(800)598–4668

BONE MARROW

See CANCER
BONE DISEASE

Osteoporosis and Related Bone Diseases National Resource Center
(800)624–BONE

BRAIN TUMORS

American Brain Tumor Association
(800)886–2282

The Brain Tumor Society
(800)770–TBTS

National Brain Tumor Foundation
(800)934–CURE

CANCER

ACS, National Cancer Information Center
(800)227–2345 (Voice/TDD/TT)
24 hours

Cancer Information Service
(800)422–6237
9 a.m.–4:30 p.m.

Cancer Hope Network
(877)HOPENET

Candlelighters Childhood Cancer Foundation
(800)366–2223

Komen Breast Cancer Foundation
(800)462–9273

National Alliance of Breast Cancer Organizations
(800)719–9154

National Bone Marrow Transplant Link
(800)546–5268

National Kidney Cancer Association
(800)850–9132

National Marrow Donor Program(R)
(800)627–7692
Professional staff answer questions from 8 a.m.–6 p.m. (Central); recorded message at all other times.

Reach to Recovery Program
(800)227–2345

Us Too International
(800)808–7866

Y–Me National Breast Cancer Organization
(800)221–2141 (English)
(800)986–9505 (Spanish)
9 a.m.–5 p.m. (Central).
Local number operates 24 hours.

CEREBRAL PALSY

See RARE DISORDERS

CHEMICAL PRODUCTS/PESTICIDES

See also HOUSING

Chemtrec Non–Emergency Services Hotline
(800)262–8200
9 a.m.–6 p.m.

National Pesticide Telecommunications Network
(800)858–7378
TDD capability
6:30 a.m.–4:30 p.m. (Pacific) voice mail provided
for off–hours calls.

CHILD ABUSE/MISSING CHILDREN/MENTAL HEALTH

Boys Town National Hotline
(800)448–3000
(800)448–1833 (TDD)
Spanish–speaking operators available
TDD capability
Operates 24 hours.

Child Find of America, Inc.
(800)426–5678 (I–AM–LOST)
Operates 24 hours.

(800)292–9688 (A–WAY–OUT)
Operates 24 hours.

CHILDHELP/IOF Foresters National Child Abuse Hotline
(800)422–4453
(800)222–4453 (TDD)
Operates 24 hours.

Covenant House Nineline
(800)999–9999
Operates 24 hours.

National Center for Missing and Exploited Children
(800)843–5678
(800)826–7653 (TDD)
Ability to serve callers in over 140 languages
Operates 24 hours.

National Child Safety Council Childwatch
(800)222–1464
Operates 24 hours.

National Clearinghouse on Child Abuse and Neglect Information
(800)394–3366
nccanch@calibcom (E–mail)
8:30 a.m.–5:30 p.m.

National Runaway Switchboard
(800)621–4000
(800)621–0394 (TDD)
Has access to AT&T Language Line
Operates 24 hours.

National Youth Crisis Hotline
(800)448–4663
Operates 24 hours.

CHILD DEVELOPMENT/PARENTING

Association for the Care of Children's Health
(800)808–2224 x327
9:00 a.m.–5:00 p.m.

Association of Birth Defect Children
(800)313–2223

Autism Society of America
(800)328–3476

The MAGIC Foundation for Children's Growth
(800)362–4423

National Association for the Education of Young Children
(800)424–2460
9 a.m.–5 p.m.

National Institute of Child Health and Human Development
Public Information and Communications Branch,
(800)505–2742 (SIDS Information Line)

National Lekotek Center
(800)366–7529
(800)573–4446 (Voice and TTY)

National Organization on Fetal Alcohol Syndrome
(800)666–6327

Pediatric Projects, Inc.
(800)947–0947

Starlight Children's Foundation
(800)274–7823
Zero to Three: National Center for Infants, Toddlers and Families
(800)899–4301

CRISIS INTERVENTION

Boys Town National Hotline
(800)448–3000
(800)448–1833 (TDD)
Provides short–term intervention and counseling and refers callers to local community resources. Counsels on parent–child conflicts, family issues, suicide, pregnancy, runaway youth, physical and sexual abuse, and other issues that impact children and families. Spanish–speaking operators are available. TDD capability. Operates 24 hours.

(800)292–9688 (A–WAY–OUT)
Provides unique crisis mediation program for parents contemplating abduction of their children, or who have already abducted their children and want to use Child Find Volunteer Family Mediators to resolve their custody dispute. Operates 24 hours.

CHILDHELP/IOF ForestersNational Child Abuse Hotline
(800)422–4453
(800)222–4453 (TDD)
Provides multilingual crisis intervention and professional counseling on child abuse and domestic violence issues. Gives referrals to local agencies offering counseling and other services related to child abuse, adult survivor issues, and domestic violence. Provides literature on child abuse in English and Spanish.
Operates 24 hours.

Covenant House Nineline
(800)999–9999
Crisis line for youth, teens, and families. Locally based referrals throughout the United States. Help for youth and parents regarding drugs, abuse, homelessness, runaway children, and message relays. Operates 24 hours.

National Center for Missing and Exploited Children
(800)843–5678
(800)826–7653 (TDD)
Operates a hotline for reporting missing children and sightings of missing children. Offers assistance and training to law enforcement agents. Takes reports of sexually exploited children. Serves as the National Child Porn TipLine. Provides books and other publications on prevention and issues related to missing and sexually exploited children. Ability to serve callers in over 140 languages.
Operates 24 hours.

National Runaway Switchboard
(800)621–4000
(800)621–0394 (TDD)
Provides crisis intervention and travel assistance information to runaways. Gives referrals to shelters nationwide. Also relays messages to, or sets up conference calls with, parents at the request of the child. Has access to AT&T Language Line.
Operates 24 hours.

National Youth Crisis Hotline
(800)448–4663
Provides counseling and referrals to local drug treatment centers, shelters, and counseling services. Responds to youth dealing with pregnancy, molestation, suicide, and child abuse. Operates 24 hours.

Rape, Abuse, and Incest National Network
(800)656–4673
Connects caller to the nearest counseling center which provides counseling for rape, abuse, and incest victims.

CYSTIC FIBROSIS

See RARE DISORDERS

DIABETES/DIGESTIVE DISEASES

American Association of Diabetes Educators
(800)832–6874

American Diabetes Association
(800)232–3472
(800)ADA–ORDER (Fax, Order Fulfillment)
8:30 a.m.–5 p.m.

Crohn's and Colitis Foundation of America, Inc.
(800)932–2423
(800)343–3637 (Warehouse)
9 a.m.–5 p.m. Recording after hours. Warehouse is open 8 a.m.–5 p.m.

Juvenile Diabetes Foundation International Hotline
(800)223–1138
9 a.m.–5 p.m.

DISABLING CONDITIONS/DISABILITIES ACCESS

Americans with Disabilities Act Hotline
(800)514–0301
(800)514–0383 (TTY)
ADA Specialists available 10 a.m.–6 p.m. on Monday, Tuesday, Wednesday, and Friday and 1 p.m.–6 p.m. on Thursday.

ADA Technical Assistance Hotline
(800)466–4232

Children's Craniofacial Association
(800)535–3643

FACES: The National Craniofacial Association
(800)332–2373

Families of Spinal Muscular Atrophy
(800)886–1762
7:30 a.m.–1:30 p.m. (Central)

Job Accommodation Network
(800)232–9675 (Voice/TDD)
(800)526–7234 (Voice/TDD)
(800)526–2262 (in Canada)
Services available in English, Spanish, and French. 8 a.m.–8 p.m., Monday–Thursday; 8 a.m.–5 p.m., Friday

National Easter Seal Society
(800)221–6827
8:30 a.m.–5 p.m. (Central)

National Information Center for Children and Youth with Disabilities
(800)695–0285 (Voice/TT)
nichcy@aed.org
9:30 a.m.–6:30 p.m. or leave recorded message after hours.

National Rehabilitation Information Center (NARIC)
(800)346–2742 (Voice/TDD)
Spanish–speaking operators available. 8:30 a.m.–5:30 p.m. Scoliosis Association
(800)800–0669

DOWN SYNDROME

See RARE DISORDERS

DRINKING WATER SAFETY

Safe Drinking Water Hotline
(800)426–4791
sdwa@epamail.epa.gov (E–mail)
Information provided in English, Spanish, French, Lebanese, and Persian. 9 a.m.–5:30 p.m., weekdays, except Federal holidays.

Water Quality Association
(800)749–0234 (Consumer Information)

DRUG ABUSE

See also ALCOHOL ABUSE and SUBSTANCE ABUSE

Drug Help
(800)378–4435
(800)202–2463
Operates 24 hours.

Housing and Urban Development Drug Information and Strategy Clearinghouse
(800)578–3472
8 a.m.–5 p.m.

National Parents Resource Institute for Drug Education
(800)279–6361
(800)677–7433 (Customer Service)
Youth Power
(800)258–2766
7 a.m.–5 p.m. (Pacific).

DWARFISM

Human Growth Foundation
(800)451–6434
8:30 a.m.–5 p.m.

Little People of America
(888)LPA–2001

DYSLEXIA

See LEARNING DISORDERS

ENDOMETRIOSIS

See WOMEN

ENVIRONMENT

Electric and Magnetic Fields (EMF)
Environmental Health Clearinghouse, NIEHS
Information Line
(800)363–2383
9:00 a.m.–6:00 p.m.

Indoor Air Quality Information Clearinghouse
(800)438–4318
9 a.m.–5 p.m.

U.S. Environmental Protection Agency,
Environmental Justice
(800)962–6215
8:30 a.m. to 5:00 p.m., Monday through Friday,
excluding Federal holidays.

EPILEPSY

See RARE DISORDERS

ETHICS

Joseph and Rose Kennedy Institute of Ethics,
National Reference Center for Bioethics
Literature
(800)633–3849
medethx@gunet.georgetown.edu (E–mail)
9 a.m.–5 p.m., Monday, Wednesday, Thursday,
Friday; 9 a.m.–9 p.m., Tuesday; 10 a.m.–3 p.m.,
Saturday, except summers and holidays.

FIRE PREVENTION

National Fire Protection Association
(800)344–3555 (Customer Service)
8:30 a.m.–5 p.m.

FITNESS

Aerobics and Fitness Foundation of America
(800)446–2322 (For Professionals)
(800)968–7263 (Consumer Hotline)
7:00 a.m.–6:00 p.m. (Pacific).

American Running and Fitness Association
(800)776–2732

Consumer Fitness Hotline
(800)529–8227
8 a.m. 5 p.m. (Pacific)
The Weight Control Information Network, NIDDK
(800)WIN–8098

TOPS Club, Inc.
(800)932–8677

YMCA of the USA
(800)872–9622
8 a.m.–5 p.m. (Central).

FOOD SAFETY

Food Labeling Hotline
Meat and Poultry Hotline
(800)535–4555
10 a.m.–4 p.m.

Seafood Hotline
(800)332–4010
12 p.m.–4 p.m. Automated hotline operates 24
hours.

GENERAL HEALTH

Agency for Health Care Policy and Research
Clearinghouse
(800)358–9295
9 a.m.–5 p.m.

Air Lifeline
(800)446–1231
7:30–4:30 (Pacific)

American Chiropractic Association
(800)986–4636

American Podiatric Medical Association, Inc.
(800)366–8227
Operates 24 hours.

American Osteopathic Association
(800)621–1773

MedicAlert Foundation
(800)432–5378
(800)344–3226
Operates 24 hours.

Mercy Medical Airlift
(800)296–1191

National Health Service Corps
(800)221–9393 (Recruitment/Loans)
(800)638–0824 (Medical Scholarship Programs)

National Health Information Center
(800)336–4797
nhicinfo@health.org (E–Mail)

National Center for Complementary and
Alternative Medicine Clearinghouse
(888)644–6226 (Voice and TTY)
(800)531–1794 (Fax–back)
8:30 a.m. to 5:00 p.m., Monday through Friday,
EST.

Office for Civil Rights
(800)368–1019
(800)527–7697 (TDD)

Office of Consumer Affairs, FDA
(800)332–1088 (Medwatch)
(800)532–4440 (Consumer Inquiries)

People's Medical Society
(800)624–8773

Well Spouse Foundation
(800)838–0879

GRIEF

Grief Recovery Helpline
(800)445–4808
9 a.m.–5 p.m., Monday– Friday (Pacific).

HEADACHE/HEAD INJURY

American Council for Headache Education
(800)255–ACHE

Brain Injury Association, Inc.
(800)444–6443 (Family Helpline)
9 a.m.–5 p.m.

National Headache Foundation
(800)843–2256
9 a.m.–5 p.m. (Central) Monday–Friday.

HEARING AND SPEECH

American Society for Deaf Children
(800)942–2732

American Speech–Language–Hearing
Association
(800)638–8255
8:30 a.m.–5 p.m.

DB–Link
(800)438–9376

Deafness Research Foundation
(800)535–3323
9 a.m.–5 p.m.

Dial A Hearing Screening Test
(800)222–3277 (Voice/TDD)
9 a.m.–5 p.m.

The Ear Foundation at Baptist Hospital
(800)545–4327
8:30 a.m.–4:30 p.m. (Central) or leave recorded
message after hours.

Hear Now
(800)648–4327 (Voice/TDD)
8 a.m.–4 p.m. (Mountain)

John Tracy Clinic
(800)522–4582 (Voice/TTY)
8 a.m.–4 p.m. (Pacific). Leave recorded message
after hours.

International Hearing Society
(800)521–5247
10 a.m.–4 p.m.

National Family Association for Deaf–Blind
(800)255–0411, ext. 275

National Institute on Deafness and Other
Communication Disorders Information
Clearinghouse
(800)241–1044
(800)241–1055 (TT)
8:30 a.m.–5 p.m.

LEAD LINE
(800)352–8888 (Voice/TDD in the United States)
(800)287–4763
blincoln@hci.org (E–Mail)
8 a.m.–5 p.m. (Pacific) or leave recorded message
after hours.

Vestibular Disorders Association
(800)837–8428

HEART DISEASE

American Heart Association
(800)242–8721
9 a.m.–5 p.m.

The Coronary Club, Inc.
(800)478–4255

Heart Information Service
(800)292–2221

National Heart, Lung and Blood Institute
Information Center
(800)575–9355L (High Blood Pressure and
Cholesterol Info. Hotline)
24–hour recording of information on high blood
pressure and high blood cholesterol in English and
Spanish.

HISTIOCYTOSIS

See RARE DISORDERS
HOMELESSNESS

National Resource Center on Homelessness and
Mental Illness
(800)444–7415
8 a.m.–5 p.m.

HORMONAL DISORDERS

Thyroid Foundation of America, Inc.
(800)832–8321

The Thyroid Society for Education and Research
(800)849–7643

HOSPITAL/HOSPICE CARE

Children's Hospice International
(800)242–4453
9:00 a.m.–5:00 p.m.

Hill–Burton Hospital Free Care
(800)638–0742
(800)492–0359 (in MD)
9:30 a.m.–5:30 p.m. or leave recorded message
after hours.

Hospice Education Institute "Hospice Link"
(800)331–1620
9 a.m.–4 p.m.

National Association of Hospitality Houses, Inc.
(800)542–9730

National Hospice Organization
(800)658–8898

Shriners Hospital Referral Line
(800)237–5055
8 a.m.–5 p.m.

HOUSING

See also CHEMICAL PRODUCTS/PESTICIDES,
LEAD

Housing and Urban Development User
(800)245–2691
(800)483–2209 (TDD)
8:30 a.m.–5:15 p.m.

HUNTINGTON'S DISEASE

See RARE DISORDERS
IMMUNIZATION

CDC Immunization Hotline
(800)232–7468

IMPOTENCE

Impotence Information Center
(800)843–4315
(800)543–9632
8:30 a.m.–5 p.m. (Central) or leave recorded
message after hours.

INSURANCE/MEDICARE/MEDICAID

DHHS Inspector General's Hotline
(800)447–8477
9 a.m.–8 p.m.

Medicare Issues Hotline
(800)638–6833
(800)820–1202 (TDD/TTY)
8 a.m.–8 p.m.

Health Insurance Association of America Consumer Helpline
(800)942–4242
8 a.m.–8 p.m.

Pension Benefit Guaranty Corporation
(800)400–7242
Social Security Administration
(800)772–1213

JUSTICE

National Criminal Justice Reference Service (NCJRS)
(800)851–3420
8:30 a.m.–7 p.m. Leave recorded message after hours.

KIDNEY DISEASE

See UROLOGICAL DISORDERS

LEAD

See also HOUSING

National Lead Information Center
(800)532–3394(Hotline)
(800)424–5323 (Clearinghouse)
nlic@optimus.corp.com (E–mail)
8:30 a.m.–5 p.m.

LEARNING DISORDERS

Children and Adults with Attention Deficit Disorders (CH.A.D.D.)
(800)233–4050

The Orton Dyslexia Society
(800)222–3123 (Recording and mail box)
Operates 24 hours.

LIBRARY SERVICES

Captioned Films/Videos Programs, The National Association of the Deaf
(800)237–6213 (Voice/TTY)
(800)538–5636 (Fax)
8:30 a.m.–5 p.m.

National Library Service for the Blind and Physically Handicapped
(800)424–8567
8 a.m.–4:30 p.m.

Recording for the Blind and Dyslexic
(800)221–4792

LIVER DISEASES

American Liver Foundation
(800)223–0179
9 a.m.–5 p.m.

Hepatitis Foundation International
(800)891–0707

LUNG DISEASE/ASTHMA/ALLERGY

American Lung Association
(800)586–4872

Asthma and Allergy Foundation of America
(800)7–ASTHMA (727–8462)
Provides 24–hour recording

Asthma Information Line
(800)822–2762
Operates 24 hours.

Lung Line National Jewish Medical and Research Center
(800)222–5864
(800)552–LUNG (LUNG FACTS)
8 a.m.–5 p.m. (Mountain).
LUNG FACTS, a companion to LUNG LINE, is a 24–hour, 7–days–a–week automated information service.

MATERNAL AND INFANT HEALTH

Alliance of Genetic Support Groups
(800)336–4363

La Leche League International
(800)525–3243
9 a.m.–3 p.m. (Central)

National Fragile X Foundation
(800)688–8765

National Life Center
(800)848–5683

Prenatal Care Hotline
(800)311–2229 (English)
(800)504–7081 (Spanish)

MEDICARE/MEDICAID

See INSURANCE/MEDICARE/MEDICAID

MENTAL HEALTH

See also CHILD ABUSE/MISSING CHILDREN/ MENTAL HEALTH

American Academy of Child and Adolescent Psychiatry
(800)333–7636

Anxiety Disorders Information, NIMH
(888)826–9438

Depression Awareness, Recognition, and Treatment (D/ART)
(800)421–4211

National Alliance for the Mentally Ill
(800)950–6264

National Clearinghouse on Family Support and Children's Mental Health
(800)628–1696
Recording operates 24 hours.

National Council on Problem Gambling
(800)522–4700

National Foundation for Depressive Illness
(800)248–4344
NAFDI@pipeline.com (E–mail)
24–hour recorded message

National Gaucher Foundation
(800)925–8885

National Institute for Mental Health Information Line
(800)647–2642
Operates 24 hours.

National Mental Health Association
(800)969–6642

National Mental Health Services, Knowledge Exchange Network
(800)789–2647
(800)790–2647
9 a.m.–5:30 p.m.

The Arc of the United States
(800)433–5255

MINORITY HEALTH

Office of Minority Health Resource Center
(800)444–6472
9 a.m.–5 p.m.

NUTRITION

American Dietetic Association's Consumer Nutrition Hotline
(800)366–1655
9 a.m.–4 p.m. (Central). TDD available.

American Institute for Cancer Research
(800)843–8114
9 a.m.–5 p.m.

National Dairy Council
(800)426–8271
8:30 a.m.–4:30 p.m. (Central)

ORAL HEALTH

American Dental Association
(800)947–4746

ORGAN DONATION

See also VISION and UROLOGICAL DISORDERS

The Living Bank
(800)528–2971
Operates 24 hours.

National Marrow Donor Program(R)
(800)627–7692

United Network for Organ Sharing
(800)243–6667
Operates 24 hours.

PARALYSIS AND SPINAL CORD INJURY

See also STROKE

American Paralysis Association
(800)225–0292
9 a.m.–5 p.m.

National Rehabilitation Information Center
(800)346–2742 (Voice/TDD)
8:30 a.m.–5:30 p.m.

National Spinal Cord Injury Association
(800)962–9629 (Members and individuals with spinal cord injuries; no vendors)
9 a.m.–5 p.m.

National Spinal Cord Injury Hotline
(800)526–3456
24–hour answering service will page for emergency.
9 a.m.–5 p.m.

National Stroke Association
(800)787–6537
7 a.m.–4:30 p.m. (Mountain) Monday–Friday

Paralyzed Veterans of America
(800)424–8200
(800)795–4327 (TDD)

PARKINSON'S DISEASE

American Parkinson's Disease Association
(800)223–2732
9 a.m.–5 p.m. Leave recorded message after hours.

National Parkinson Foundation, Inc.
(800)327–4545
8 a.m.–5 p.m., Monday–Friday; recorded messages at all other times.

Parkinson's Disease Foundation
(800)457–6676

PESTICIDES

See CHEMICAL PRODUCTS/PESTICIDES

PRACTITIONER REPORTING

USP Practitioners Reporting Network
(800)487–7776
(800)233–7767 (Medication error)
Recording operates 24 hours a day; staff available 9 a.m.–4:30 p.m., Monday–Friday. Medication error telephone number records information 24 hours a day.

PREGNANCY/MISCARRIAGE

American Academy of Husband–Coached Childbirth
(800)422–4784
9 a.m.–5 p.m. (Pacific). Leave recorded message after hours.

Bradley Method of Natural Childbirth, Lamaze International
(800)368–4404
lamaze@dc.sba.com (E–mail)
9 a.m.–5 p.m.

DES Action USA
(800)337–9288

International Childbirth Education Association
(800)624–4934 (Book Center orders)
7 a.m.–4:30 p.m. (Central)

Liberty Godparent Home
(800)542–4453
Operates 24 hours.

National Abortion Federation
(800)772–9100

PROFESSIONALS

Alopecia Areata Research Foundation
(800)941–4223

American Academy of Allergy, Asthma and Immunology
(800)822–2762
24 hours

American Academy of Ophthalmology
(800)222–3937
8 a.m.–4 p.m. (Pacific)

American Association for Active Lifestyles and Fitness
(800)213–7193

American Association of Critical Care Nurses
(800)899–2226
7:30 a.m.–5:30 p.m. (Pacific)

American Council for the Blind
(800)424–8666
2:30 a.m.–5:30 p.m.

American Counseling Association (800)347–6647

American Nurses Association
(800)274–4ANA
8:00 a.m.–6:00 p.m.

American Occupational Therapy Association
(800)377–8555

American School Food Service Association
(800)877–8822

American Social Health Association
(800)227–8922
8 a.m.–11 p.m.

Aplastic Anemia Foundation of America
(800)747–2820
9 a.m.–5 p.m.

Arthritis National Research Foundation
(800)588–2873
8:30 a.m.–5 p.m. (Pacific)

Association for Applied Psychophysiology and Biofeedback
(800)477–8892
8 a.m.–5 p.m.

Association of American Physicians and Surgeons
(800)635–1196 8 a.m.–6 p.m.

Association of Operating Room Nurses
(800)755–2676
8 a.m.–4:30 p.m. (Mountain)

Business Responds to AIDS and Labor Responds to AIDS Programs
(800)458–5231 9 a.m.–6 p.m.

Center for Substance Abuse Treatment, SAMHSA
(800)662–4357
24 hours

College of American Pathologists
(800)323–4040
8 a.m.–5 p.m.

Dystonia Medical Research Foundation
(800)377–3978

Family Violence and Sexual Assault Institute
(800)898–4543

Federal Emergency Management Agency
(800)879–6076
8 a.m.–4:30 p.m.

Federal Information Center, GSA
(800)688–9889

Glaucoma Research Foundation
(800)826–6693

Immune Deficiency Foundation
(800)296–4433
9 a.m.–5 p.m.

International Childbirth Education Association
(800)624–4934
8:30 a.m.–4:30 p.m. (Central)

International Chiropractors Association
(800)423–4690
9 a.m.–5:30 p.m.

Leukemia Society Of America
(800)955–4572

Lighthouse National Center for Vision and Aging
(800)829–0500

Medical Institue for Sexual Health
(800)892–9484
8 a.m.–5:00 p.m. (Central)

National Center for Disability Services
(800)949–4232

National Center for Women and Retirement Research
(800)426–7386

National Child Care Information Center, ACF
(800)516–2242
(800)616–2242 (TTY)
8:30 a.m.–5 p.m.

National Clearinghouse of Rehabilitation Training Materials
(800)223–5219 8 a.m.–5 p.m.

National Committee to Prevent Child Abuse
(800)556–2722

National Jewish Medical and Research Association
(800)552–5864
8 a.m.–5 p.m. (Central)

National Pediculosis Association
(800)446–4672
24–hour voice mail

National Resource Center on Domestic Violence
(800)537–2238
(800)553–2508 (TTY)
9 a.m.–5 p.m. (Central), 24–hour voice mail

National Technical Information Service
(800)553–6847
8 a.m.–8 p.m.

NIOSH, CDC
(800)356–4674

Office of the National Drug Control Policy
(800)666–3332
8:30 a.m.–5 :15 p.m.

Research to Prevent Blindness
(800)621–0026 9 a.m.–5 p.m.

The Alliance for Aging Research
(800)639–2421 9 a.m.–5 p.m.
24–hour voice mail

RADIATION

National Association of Radiation Survivors
(800)798–5102

RADON

Radon Hotline
(800)707–7266
(800)526–5456 (TDD)24–hour recording

RARE DISORDERS

A rare disorder is defined as a disorder that affects less than 1 percent of the population at any given time.

American Behcet's Disease Association
(800)723–4238

American Cleft Palate–Craniofacial Association/ Cleft Palate Foundation
(800)242–5338
CLEFTLINE operates 24 hours. Spanish–speaking operators available 8:30 a.m.–4:30 p.m., Monday–Friday.

American Leprosy Missions (Hansen's Disease)
(800)543–3135
8 a.m.–5 p.m.

American SIDS Institute
(800)232–7437
(800)847–7437 (in GA)
8 a.m.–5 p.m. Leave recorded message after hours.

American Syringomyelia Alliance Project
(800)272–7282

Amyotrophic Lateral Sclerosis Association (ALS, Lou Gehrig's Disease)
(800)782–4747
8 a.m.–5 p.m. (Pacific). Leave recorded message after hours.

Batten's Disease Support and Research Association
(800)448–4570
24–hour recording

Beckwith–Wiedemann Support Network
(800)837–2976

The CFIDS Association of America
(800)442–3437

Charcot–Marie–Tooth Association
(800)606–2682

Cooley's Anemia Foundation
(800)522–7222
9 a.m.–5 p.m.

Cornelia de Lange Syndrome Foundation, Inc.
(800)223–8355
(800)753–2357 (U.S. and Canada) 9 a.m.–5:00 p.m. Leave recorded message after hours.

Cystic Fibrosis Foundation
(800)344–4823
8:30 a.m.–5:30 p.m.

Epilepsy Foundation of America
(800)332–1000
(800)213–5821 (Publications)
9 a.m.–5 p.m.

Epilepsy Information Service
(800)642–0500
8:30 a.m.–5 p.m.

Fibromyalgia Network
(800)853–2929
8 a.m.–4 p.m. (Mountain)

Gillis W. Long Hansen's Disease Center
(800)642–2477
8:30 a.m.–4:30 p.m. (Central)

Histiocytosis Association
(800)548–2758
9:00 a.m.–4:30 p.m., Monday–Friday. Voice mail at all other times.

Huntington's Disease Society of America, Inc.
(800)345–4372
9 a.m.–5 p.m.

International Rett Syndrome Association
(800)818–7388
9 a.m.–5 p.m.

Les Turner Amyotrophic Lateral Sclerosis Foundation, Ltd.
(888)ALS–1107
8:30 a.m.–4:30 p.m. (Central)

Multiple Sclerosis Association of America
(800)532–7667
9 a.m.–5 p.m.

Multiple Sclerosis Foundation
(800)441–7055
9 a.m.–5 p.m.

Muscular Dystrophy Association
(800)572–1717
9 a.m.–5 p.m.

Myasthenia Gravis Foundation
(800)541–5454
8:45 a.m.–4:45 p.m. (Central)

National Down Syndrome Congress
(800)232–6372
ndsccenter@aol.com (E–mail)
9 a.m.–5:30 p.m. Recording after hours.

National Down Syndrome Society Hotline
(800)221–4602
9 a.m.–5 p.m.

National Hemophilia Foundation
(888)463–6643
9 a.m.–5 p.m.

National Lymphedema Network
(800)541–3259
9:30 a.m.–5:30 p.m. (Pacific)
Leave recorded message.

National Marfan Foundation
(800)862–7326
8 a.m.–3:30 p.m.

National Multiple Sclerosis Society
(800)344–4867 11 a.m.–5 p.m., Monday–Thursday.

National Neurofibromatosis Foundation
(800)323–7938
9 a.m.–5 p.m.

National Organization for Albinism and Hypopigmentation
(800)473–2310

National Organization for Rare Disorders
(800)999–6673
9 a.m.–5 p.m. Monday–Friday.
Leave recorded message after hours.

National Reye's Syndrome Foundation
(800)233–7393
8 a.m.–5 p.m.
Leave recorded message after hours.

National Sjogren's Syndrome Association
(800)395–6772

National Sarcoidosis Foundation
(800)223–6429
24–hour recording

National Spasmodic Torticollis Association
(800)487–8385

National Tuberous Sclerosis Association
(800)225–6872
8:30 a.m.–5 p.m.

Neurofibromatosis, Inc.
(800)942–6825
24–hour message line

Office of Orphan Products Development, Food and Drug Administration
(800)300–7469
8 a.m.–4:30 p.m.

Osteogenesis Imperfecta Foundation
(800)981–2663
9 a.m.–5 p.m.

The Paget Foundation for Paget's Disease of Bone and Related Disorders
(800)237–2438
9 a.m.–5 p.m.
(800)926–4797
9 a.m.–7 p.m.

Scleroderma Foundation
(800)722–4673
8:30 a.m.–5:00 p.m.

Sickle Cell Disease Association of America, Inc.
(800)421–8453
8:30 a.m.–5 p.m. (Pacific)
Recording after hours and weekends.

SIDS Alliance
(800)221–7437
9 a.m.–5 p.m. Phoneline available 24 hours.

Sjogren's Syndrome Foundation, Inc.
(800)475–6473
9 a.m.–5 p.m.

Spina Bifida Association of America
(800)621–3141
9 a.m.–5 p.m.

Spondylitis Association of America (formerly the Ankylosing Spondylitis Association)
(800)777–8189
9 a.m.–5 p.m. (Pacific). Leave recorded message after hours.

Sturge–Weber Foundation
(800)627–5482
9 a.m.–5:30 p.m., Monday–Wednesday
8:00–2:30 Tuesday and Thursday

Sudden Infant Death Syndrome Network
(800)560–1454

Support Organization for Trisomy 18, 13 and Related Disorders
(800)716–7638

Tourette Syndrome Association, Inc.
(800)237–0717
9 a.m.–5 p.m.

Treacher Collins Foundation
(800)823–2055

Turner's Syndrome Society of the United States
(800)365–9944

United Cerebral Palsy Association
(800)872–5827
8:30 a.m.–5:30 p.m.

United Leukodystrophy Foundation
(800)728–5483
8:30 a.m.–8:30 p.m. (Central)

Wegener's Granulomatosis Support Group, Inc.
(800)277–9474
8:00 a.m.–5:00 p.m. (Central)

Wilson's Disease Association
(800)399–0266

REHABILITATION

See DISABLING CONDITIONS, PARALYSIS AND SPINAL CORD INJURY

ABLEDATA
(800)227–0216
8:00 a.m. to 5:30 p.m., EST, Monday through Friday

National Institute for Rehabilitation Engineering
(800)736–2216
9 a.m.–5 p.m.

National Institute for Rehabilitation Engineering
(800)736–2216

Phoenix Society for Burn Survivors
(800)888–2876
9 a.m.–5 p.m.

United Ostomy Association
(800)826–0826
6:30 a.m.–4:30 p.m., Monday – Thursday
6:30 a.m.–3:30 p.m., Friday (Pacific)

RURAL

Rural Information Center Health Service (RICHS)
(800)633–7701
ric@nalusda.gov (E–mail)
8 a.m.–4:30 p.m.

SAFETY

See also CHEMICAL PRODUCTS/PESTICIDES

Clearinghouse for Occupational Safety and Health Information, National Institute for Occupational Safety and Health
(800)356–4674
9 a.m.–4 p.m.

The Danny Foundation
(800)83–DANNY

National Child Safety Council Childwatch
(800)222–1464
8:30 a.m.–4:45 p.m.

National Highway Traffic Safety Administration Auto Safety Hotline
(800)424–9393
(800)424–9153 (TTY)
8 a.m.–10 p.m.

National Program for Playground Safety
(800)554–7529

National Safety Council
(800)621–7615
(800)767–7236 (National Radon Hotline)

Office of Navigation Safety and Waterway Services U.S. Coast Guard Customer Infoline
(800)368–5647 (800)689–0816 (TDD/TT)
8 a.m.–4 p.m. Safe Sitter
(800)255–4089

U.S. Consumer Product Safety Commission Hotline
(800)638–2772
(800)638–8270 (TDD)
info@cpsc.gov
24–hour messages

SEXUAL EDUCATION

Planned Parenthood Federation of America, Inc.
(800)669–0156 (800)230–7526

SEXUALLY TRANSMITTED DISEASES

Centers for Disease Control and Prevention National STD Hotline
(800)227–8922
8 a.m.–11 p.m.

Herpes Resource Center
(800)230–6039
9 a.m.–7 p.m.

SKIN DISEASE

Foundation for Ichthyosis and Related Skin Types, Inc.
(800)545–3286
9 a.m.–5 p.m. , Monday – Thursday
National Psoriasis Foundation
(800)723–9166
8 a.m.–5 p.m. (Pacific)

SPINAL CORD INJURY

See PARALYSIS AND SPINAL CORD INJURY

SMOKING

Office on Smoking and Health
(800)232–1311

STROKE

See also PARALYSIS AND SPINAL CORD INJURY

American Heart Association Stroke Connection
(800)553–6321
7:30 a.m.–7 p.m. (Central)

National Institute of Neurological Disorders and Stroke
(800)352–9424
8 a.m.–5 p.m.

STUTTERING

National Center for Stuttering
(800)221–2483
10 a.m.–6 p.m. Stuttering Foundation of America
(800)992–9392
9 a.m.–5 p.m.

SUBSTANCE ABUSE

see also ALCOHOL ABUSE and DRUG ABUSE

National Inhalant Prevention Coalition
(800)269–4237
8 a.m.–7 p.m. (Central)

SUDDEN INFANT DEATH SYNDROME

See RARE DISORDERS

SURGERY/FACIAL PLASTIC SURGERY

American Society for Dermatologic Surgery, Inc.
(800)441–2737
8:30 a.m.–5 p.m. (Central)

American Society of Plastic and Reconstructive Surgeons, Inc.
(800)635–0635
8:30 a.m.–4:30 p.m. (Central). Leave recorded message after hours.

Facial Plastic Surgery Information Service
(800)332–3223
24 hours.

TRAUMA

American Trauma Society (ATS)
(800)556–7890
8:30 a.m.–4:30 p.m.

UROLOGICAL DISORDERS

American Association of Kidney Patients
(800)749–2257
8:30 a.m.–5 p.m.

American Foundation for Urologic Disease
(800)242–2383
24–hour recording

American Kidney Fund
(800)638–8299
8 a.m.–5 p.m.

Incontinence Information Center
(800)843–4315
(800)543–9632
8:00 a.m.–5 p.m. (Central) or leave recorded message after hours

National Association for Continence
(800)252–3337
8 a.m.–5 p.m.

National Kidney Foundation
(800)622–9010
8:30 a.m.–5 p.m.

Polycystic Kidney Research Foundation
(800)753–2873
8 a.m.–5 p.m.

The Simon Foundation for Continence
(800)237–4666
24 hours

VENEREAL DISEASES

See SEXUALLY TRANSMITTED DISEASES

Section C

VETERANS

Persian Gulf Veterans Information Helpline
(800)749–8387
Vietnam Veterans Agent Orange Victims
(800)521–0198
9 a.m.–5 p.m.

VISION

See also LIBRARY SERVICES and HEARING AND SPEECH

American Council of the Blind
(800)424–8666
hcraff@ACCESS.DIGEX.NET (E–mail)
3p.m.–5:30 p.m.)

American Foundation for the Blind
232–5163

Better Vision Institute
(800)424–8422
9 a.m.–5 p.m.

Braille Institute
(800)272–4553
8:30 a.m.–5 p.m.

Blind Childrens Center
(800)222–3566 (800)222–3567
ncrabb@acb.org (E–mail)
8 a.m.–4 p.m. (Pacific).

DB–Link
(800)438–9376
9 a.m.–5 p.m.

The Foundation Fighting Blindness
(800)683–5555
(800)683–5551 (TDD)
8:30 a.m.–5 p.m.

Guide Dog Foundation for the Blind, Inc.
(800)548–4337
Operates 24 hours.

Guide Dogs for the Blind
(800)295–4050
8 a.m.–5 p.m. (Pacific)

The Lighthouse National Center for Education
(800)334–5497
9 a.m.–5 p.m. Leave recorded message after hours.

Louisiana Center for the Blind
(800)234–4166
8 a.m.–5 p.m. (Central)

National Alliance of Blind Students
(800)424–8666

National Association for Parents of the Visually Impaired
(800)562–6265
9 a.m.–5 p.m.

National Eye Care Project Helpline
(800)222–EYES (3937)
8 a.m.–4 p.m. (Pacific)

National Eye Research Foundation
(800)621–2258
8:30 a.m.–5 p.m. Leave recorded message after hours.

National Family Association for Deaf–Blind
(800)255–0411, ext. 275

Prevent Blindness Center for Sight
(800)331–2020
8:30 a.m.–5:45 p.m.

VIOLENCE

National Domestic Violence Hotline
(800)787–3224 (TDD)
(800)799–7233
24 hours

National Organization for Victim Assistance
(800)879–6682
Operated 24 hours

Rape, Abuse, and Incest National Network
(800)656–4673
24 hours

WOMEN

Endometriosis Association
(800)992–3636
24–hour recording

National Osteoporosis Foundation
(800)223–9994

National Women's Health Information Center
994–96626
9 a.m.–6 p.m.

PMS Access
(800)222–4767
7:30 a.m.–5:30 p.m. (Central)

Women's Health America Group
(800)558–7046

Women's Sports Foundation
(800)227–3988.

TOLL–FREE NUMBERS FOR HEALTH INFORMATION

DIAL 1–800 (UNLESS 888 IS SPECIFIED)
ABLEDATA, 227–0216
ACS, National Cancer Information Center, 227–2345 (Voice /TDD/TT)
ADA Technical Assistance Hotline, 466–4232
ADCARE Hospital Helpline, 252–6465
Aerobics and Fitness Foundation of America, 968–7263 (Consumers); 446–2322 (Professionals)
Alliance of Genetic Support Groups, 336–4363
Agency for Health Care Policy and Research Clearinghouse, 358–9295
AIDS Clinical Trials Information Service, 874–2572
Al–Anon Family Group Headquarters, 356–9996
Alcohol and Drug Helpline, 821–4357
Alzheimer's Association, 272–3900
Alzheimer's Disease Education and Referral Center, 438–4380
American Academy of Child and Adolescent Psychiatry, 333–7636
American Academy of Husband–Coached Childbirth, 422–4784
American Association of Diabetes Educators, TEAM–UP 4
American Association of Kidney Patients, 749–2257
American Autoimmune Related Diseases Association, Inc., 598–4668
American Behcet's Disease Association, 723–4238
American Brain Tumor Association, 886–2282
American Chiropractic Association, 986–4636
American Cleft Palate–Craniofacial Association/Cleft Palate Foundation, 242–5338
American Council for Headache Education, 255–ACHE
American Council on Alcoholism, 527–5344
American Council of the Blind, 424–8666
American Dental Association, 947–4746
American Diabetes Association, 232–3472, 232–6733 (Fax Order Fulfillment)
American Dietetic Association's Consumer Nutrition Hotline, 366–1655
American Foundation for the Blind, 232–5163
American Foundation for Urologic Disease, 242–2383
American Health Assistance Foundation, 437–2423
American Heart Association, 242–8721
American Heart Association Stroke Connection, 553–6321
American Institute for Cancer Research, 843–8114
American Juvenile Arthritis Organization, 283–7800
American Kidney Fund, 638–8299
American Leprosy Missions (Hansen's Disease), 543–3135
American Liver Foundation, 223–0179
American Lung Association, 586–4872; 528–2971 (Living Bank)
American Osteopathic Association, 621–1773
American Paralysis Association, 225–0292
American Parkinson's Disease Association, 223–2732
American Podiatric Medical Association, Inc., 366–8227
American Running and Fitness Association, 776–2732
American School Food Service Association, 877–8822
American SIDS Institute, 232–7437; 847–7437
American Society for Deaf Children, 942–2732
American Society for Dermatologic Surgery, Inc., 441–2737
American Society of Plastic and Reconstructive Surgeons, Inc. 635–0635
American Speech–Language–Hearing Association, 638–8255
American Syringomyelia Alliance Project, ASAP–282
American Trauma Society, 556–7890

Americans with Disabilities Act Hotline, 514–0301; 514–0383 (TTY)
Amyotrophic Lateral Sclerosis Association, 782–4747
Anxiety Disorders Information, NIMH, (888)8–ANXIETY
Arc of the United States, The, 433–5255
Arthritis Foundation Information Hotline, 283–7800
Association for the Care of Children's Health, 808–2224 x327
Association of Birth Defect Children, 313–ABDC
Association of Operating Room Nurses, 755–2676
Asthma and Allergy Foundation of America, 727–8462
Asthma Information Line, 822–2762
Autism Society of America, 328–8476
A WAY OUT, 292–4688
Batten's Disease Support and Research Association, 448–4570
Beckwith–Wiedemann Support Network, 837–2976
Bethany Christian Services, 238–4269
Better Vision Institute, 424–8422
Blind Children's Center, 222–3566; 222–3567 (California only)
Boys Town National Hotline, 448–3000; 448–1833 (TDD)
Bradley Method of Natural Childbirth, Lamaze International, 368–4404
Braille Institute, 272–4553
Brain Injury Association, 444–6443
Brain Tumor Society, The, 770–TBTS
Calix Society, 398–0524
Captioned Films/Videos Programs, the National Association of the Deaf, 237–6213 (Voice/TTY)
Cancer Hope Network, (877)HOPENET
Cancer Information Service, 422–6237
Candlelighters Childhood Cancer Foundation, 366–2223
CDC Immunization Hotline, 232–7468
CDC National AIDS Clearinghouse, 458–5231; 243–7012 (TDD); 458–5231 (NAC Fax–Back Service)
CDC National HIV/AIDS Hotline, 342–2437 (English); 344–7432(Spanish); 243–7889 (TDD)
Centers for Disease Control National STD Hotline, 227–8922
CFIDS Association of America, The, 442–3437
Charcot–Marie–Tooth Association, 606–2682
Chemtrec Non–Emergency Services Hotline, 262–8200
Child Find of America, Inc., 426–5678; 292–9688
CHILDHELP/IOF Foresters National Child Abuse Hotline, 422–4453; 222–4453 (TDD)
Children and Adults with Attention Deficit Disorder, 233–4050
Children of Alcoholics Foundation, 359–COAF
Children's Craniofacial Association, 535–3643
Children's Hospice International, 242–4453
Clearinghouse for Occupational Safety and Health Information, National Institute for Occupational Safety and Health, 356–4674
Consumer Fitness Hotline, 529–8227
Cooley's Anemia Foundation, 522–7222
Cornelia de Lange Syndrome Foundation, 223–8355; 753–2357
Coronary Club, Inc., The, 478–4255
Covenant House Nineline, 999–9999
Crohn's and Colitis Foundation of America, Inc., 932–2423
Cystic Fibrosis Foundation, 344–4823
Danny Foundation, The, 83–DANNY
DB–Link, 438–9376
Deafness Research Foundation, 535–3323
Depression Awareness, Recognition, and Treatment (D/ART), 421–4211
DES Action USA, DES–9288
DHHS Inspector General's Hotline, 447–8477
Dial A Hearing Screening Test, 222–3277 (Voice/TDD)
Drug Help, DRUG–HELP, COCAINE
Ear Foundation at Baptist Hospital, The, 545–4327
Eldercare Locator, 677–1116
Electric and Magnetic Fields (EMF) Environmental Health Clearinghouse, NIEHS Information Center, 363–2383
Endometriosis Association, 992–3636
Epilepsy Foundation of America, 332–1000; 213–5821 (Publications)
Epilepsy Information Service, 642–0500
FACES: The National Craniofacial Association, 332–2373

Facial Plastic Surgery Information Service, 332–3223

Families of Spinal Muscular Atrophy, 886–1762

Fibromyalgia Network, 853–2929

Food Allergy Network, The, 929–4040

Food Labeling Hotline, Meat and Poultry Hotline, 535–4555

Foundation Fighting Blindness, The, 683–5555; 683–5551 (TDD)

Foundation for Ichthyosis and Related Skin Types, Inc., 545–3286

Gillis W. Long Hansen's Disease Center, 642–2477

Grief Recovery Helpline, 445–4808

Guide Dog Foundation for the Blind, Inc., 548–4337

Guide Dogs for the Blind, 295–4050

Helath Insurance Association of America Consumer Hotline, 942–4242

Hear Now, 648–4327 (Voice/TDD)

Heart Information Service, 292–2221

Hepatitis Foundation International, 891–0707

Herpes Resource Center, 230–6039

Hill–Burton Hospital Free Care, 638–0742; 492–0359 (in MD)

Histiocytosis Association, 548–2758

HIV/AIDS Treatment Information Service, 448–0440

Hospice Education Institute 'Hospice Link,' 331–1620

Housing and Urban Development Drug Information and Strategy Clearinghouse, 578–3472

Housing and Urban Development User, 245–2691; 483–2209 (TDD)

Human Growth Foundation, 451–6434

Huntington's Disease Society of America, 345–4372 Impotence Information Center, 843–4315; 543–9632

Incontinence Information Center, 843–4315; 543–9632

Indoor Air Quality Information Clearinghouse, 438–4318

International Childbirth Education Association, 624–4934 (orders only)

International Hearing Society, 521–5247

International Rett Syndrome Association, 818–7388

Job Accommodation Network, 232–9675 (Voice/TDD); 526–7234 (Voice/TDD); 526–2262 (in Canada)

John Tracy Clinic, 522–4582 (Voice/TTY)

Joseph and Rose Kennedy Institute of Ethics, 633–3849

Juvenile Diabetes Foundation International Hotline, 223–1138

La Leche League International, 525–3243

LEAD LINE, 352–8888 (Voice/TDD); 287–4763 Les Turner Amyotrophic Lateral Sclerosis Foundation, Ltd., (888)ALS–1107

Liberty Godparent Home, 542–4453

Lighthouse National Center for Education, The, 334–5497 Lighthouse National Center for Vision and Aging, 829–0500

Little People of America, (888)LPA–2001

Living Bank, The, 528–2971

Louisiana Center for the Blind, 234–4166

Lung Line National Jewish Medical and Research Center, 222–5864; 552–5864 (LUNG FACTS)

Lupus Foundation of America, 558–0121 (English); 558–0231 (Spanish)

Lyme Disease Foundation, Inc., 886–5963

MAGIC Foundation for Children's Growth, The, 3–MAGIC–3

MedicAlert Foundation, 432–5378; 344–3226

Medical Institute for Sexual Dysfunction, 892–9484

Medicare Issues Hotline, 638–6833; 820–1202 (TDD/TTY)

Mercy Medical Airlift, 296–1191

Multiple Sclerosis Association of America, LEARN–MS

Multiple Sclerosis Foundation, 441–7055

Muscular Dystrophy Association, 572–1717

Myasthenia Gravis Foundation, 541–5454

National Abortion Federation, 772–9100

National Adoption Center, 862–3678

National Alliance for the Mentally Ill, 950–6264

National Alliance of Blind Students, 424–8666

National Alliance of Breast Cancer Organizations, 719–9154

National Association for Continence, 252–3337

National Association for the Education of Young Children, 424–2460

National Association for Parents of the Visually Impaired, 562–6265

National Association of Hospitality Houses, Inc., 542–9730

National Association of Radiation Survivors, 798–5102

National Bone Marrow Transplant Link, LINK–BMT

National Brain Tumor Foundation, 934–CURE

National Center for Complementary and Alternative Medicine Clearinghouse, (888)644–6226 (Voice and TTY); (800)531–1794 (Fax–back)

National Center for Missing and Exploited Children, 843–5678; 826–7653 (TDD)

National Center for Stuttering, 221–2483

National Child Safety Council Childwatch, 222–1464

National Clearinghouse for Alcohol and Drug Information, 729–6686; 487–4889 (TTY/TDD)

National Clearinghouse on Child Abuse and Neglect Information, 394–3366

National Clearinghouse on Family Support and Children's Mental Health, 628–1696

National Council on Problem Gambling, 522–4700

NATIONAL COUNCIL ON ALCOHOLISM AND DRUG DEPENDENCE, INC., 622–2255

National Criminal Justice Reference Service, 851–3420

National Dairy Council, 426–8271; 974–6455 (Fax)

National Down Syndrome Congress, 232–6372

National Domestic Violence Hotline, 787–3224 (TDD); 799–SAFE

National Down Syndrome Society Hotline, 221–4602

National Easter Seal Society, 221–6827

National Eye Care Project Helpline, 222–3937

National Eye Research Foundation, 621–2258

National Eye Research Foundation's Memorial Eye Clinic, The, 621–2258

National Family Association for Deaf–Blind, 255–0411, ext. 275

National Fire Protection Association, 344–3555

National Foundation for Depressive Illness, 248–4344

National Fragile X Foundation, 688–8765

National Gaucher Foundation, 925–8885

National Headache Foundation, 843–2256

National Health Information Center, 336–4797

National Health Service Corps, 221–9393 (Recruitment/Loans); 638–0824 (Medical Scholarship Programs)

National Heart, Lung, and Blood Institute's Information Center, 575–WELL (High Blood Pressure and Cholesterol Information Hotline)

National Hemophilia Foundation, (888)INFO–NHF

National Highway Traffic Safety Administration Auto Safety Hotline, 424–9393; 424–9153 (TTY)

National Hospice Organization, 658–8898

National Information Center for Children and Youth With Disabilities, 695–0285 (Voice/TT)

National Inhalant Prevention Coalition, 269–4237

National Institute for Mental Health Information Line, 647–2642

National Institute for Rehabilitation Engineering, 736–2216

National Institute of Child Health and Human Development, Public Information & Communications Branch, 505–CRIB (SIDS Information Line)

National Institute of Neurological Disorders and Stroke, 352–9424

National Institute on Aging Information Center, 222–2225; 222–4225 (TTY)

National Institute on Deafness and Other Communication Disorders Information Clearinghouse, 241–1044;241–1055 (TT)

National Insurance Consumer Helpline, 942–4242

National Kidney Cancer Association, 850–9132

National Kidney Foundation, 622–9010

National Lead Information Hotline, LEAD–FYI (Hotline); 424–LEAD (Clearinghouse); 526–5456 (TDD)

National Leigh's Disease Foundation, 819–2551

National Lekotek Center, 366–PLAY; 573–4446 (Voice and TTY)

National Library of Medicine, 272–4787

National Library Service for the Blind and Physically Handicapped, 424–8567

National Life Center, 848–5683

National Lymphedema Network, 541–3259

National Marfan Foundation, 8–MARFAN

National Marrow Donor Program(R), MARROW–2

National Mental Health Association, 969–6642

National Mental Health Services, Knowledge Exchange Network, 789–2647; 790–2647

National Multiple Sclerosis Society, 344–4867

National Neurofibromatosis Foundation, 323–7938

National Organization for Albinism and Hypopigmentation; 473–2310

National Organization for Rare Disorders, 999–6673

National Organization for Victim Assistance, TRY–NOVA

National Organization on Fetal Alcohol Syndrome, 66–NOFAS

National Osteoporosis Foundation, 464–6700

National Parents Resource Institute for Drug Education, 279–6361; 677–7433 (Taped Drug Information)

National Parkinson Foundation, Inc., 327–4545

National Pesticide Telecommunications Network, 858–7378

National Program for Playground Safety, 554–PLAY

National Psoriasis Foundation, 723–9166

National Rehabilitation Information Center, 346–2742 (Voice/TDD)

National Resource Center on Homeless–ness and Mental Illness, 444–7415

National Reye's Syndrome Foundation, 233–7393

National Runaway Switchboard, 621–4000; 621–0394 (TDD)

National Safety Council, 621–7615

National Sarcoidosis Foundation, 223–6429

National Sjogren's Syndrome Association, 395–6772

National Spasmodic Torticollis Association, 487–8385

National Spinal Cord Injury Association, 962–9629

National Spinal Cord Injury Hotline, 526–3456

National Stroke Association, STROKES

National Tuberous Sclerosis Association, 225–6872

National Woman's Christian Temperance Union, 755–1321

NATIONAL WOMEN'S HEALTH INFORMATION CENTER, 994–96626

National Youth Crisis Hotline, 448–4663

Neurofibromatosis, Inc., 942–6825

Office for Civil Rights, 368–1019; 527–7697 (TDD)

Office of Consumer Affairs, FDA, 332–1088 (Medwatch); 532–4440 (Consumer Inquiries)

Office of Minority Health Resource Center, 444–6472

Office of Navigation Safety and Waterway Services, U.S. Coast Guard Customer InfoLine, 368–5647, 689–0816 (TDD/TT)

Office of Orphan Products Development, Food and Drug Administration, 300–7469

Office on Smoking and Health, CDC–1311

Orton Dyslexia Society, The, 222–3123

Osteogenesis Imperfecta Foundation, 981–BONE OSTEOPOROSIS AND RELATED BONE DISEASES NATIONAL RESOURCE CENTER, (800)624–BONE

Paget Foundation for Paget's Disease of Bone and Related Disorders, 237–2438

Paralyzed Veterans of America, 424–8200; 416–7622 (TDD)

Parkinson's Disease Foundation, 457–6676

Pediatric Projects, Inc., 947–0947

Pension Benefit Guaranty Corporation, 400–PBGC

People's Medical Society, 624–8773

Persian Gulf Veterans Information Helpline, PGW–VETS

Phoenix Society for Burn Survivors, 888–2876

Planned Parenthood, 230–7526; 669–0156

PMS Access, 222–4767

Polycystic Kidney Research Foundation, 753–2873

Prader–Willi Syndrome Association, 926–4797

Prenatal Care Hotline, 311–BABY (English); 504–7081 (Spanish)

Prevent Blindness Center for Sight, 331–2020

Project Inform HIV/AIDS Treatment Hotline, 822–7422

Radon Hotline, 767–7236; 526–5456 (TDD)

Rape, Abuse, and Incest National Network, 656–4673

Reach to Recovery Program, 227–2345

Recording for the Blind and Dyslexic, 221–4792

Rural Information Center Health Service, 633–7701

Safe Drinking Water Hotline, 426–4791

Safe Sitter, 255–4089

Scleroderma Foundation, 722–4673

Scoliosis Association, 800–0669

Seafood Hotline, 332–4010

Shriners Hospital Referral Line, 237–5055

Sickle Cell Disease Association of America, Inc., 421–8453

SIDS Alliance, 221–7437

Simon Foundation for Continence, The, 237–4666

Sjogren's Syndrome Foundation, Inc., 475–6473

Section C

Social Security Administration, 772–1213
Spina Bifida Association of America, 621–3141
Spondylitis Association of America, 777–8189
Starlight Children's Foundation, 274–7827
Sturge–Weber Foundation, 627–5482
Stuttering Foundation of America, 992–9392
Sudden Infant Death Syndrome Network, 560–1454
Support Organization for Trisomy 18, 13 and
    Related Disorders, 716–SOFT
Susan G. Komen Breast Cancer Foundation,
    462–9273
Thyroid Foundation of America, Inc., 832–8321
Thyroid Society for Education and Research, The,
    THYROID
TOPS Club, Inc., 932–8677
Tourette Syndrome Association, Inc., 237–0717
Treacher Collins Foundation, TCF–2055
TURNER'S SYNDROME SOCIETY OF THE UNITED
    STATES, (800)365–9944
United Cerebral Palsy Association, 872–5827
United Leukodystrophy Foundation, 728–5483
United Network for Organ Sharing, 243–6667
United Ostomy Association, 826–0826
U.S. Consumer Product Safety Commission Hotline,
    638–2772; 638–8270 (TDD)
U.S. Environmental Protection Agency, 962–6215
USP Practitioners Reporting Network, 487–7776;
    233–7767 (Medication Error)
Us Too International, 808–7866
Vestibular Disorders Association, 837–8428
Vietnam Veterans Agent Orange Victims, 521–0198
Water Quality Association, 749–0234 (Consumer
    Information)
Wegener's Granulomatosis Support Group, Inc.,
    277–9474
Weight Control Information Network, NIDDK, The,
    WIN–8098
Well Spouse Foundation, 838–0879
Wilson's Disease Association, 399–0266
Women's Health America Group, 558–7046
Women's Sports Foundation, 227–3988
YMCA of the USA, 872–9622
Y–ME National Organization for Breast Cancer
    Information Support Program, 221–2141
    (English), 986–9505 (Spanish)
Youth Power, 258–2766
Zero to Three: National Center for Infants, Toddlers
    and Families, 899–4301

This healthfinder® is one in a series of publications, on a variety of health topics, prepared by the National Health Information Center (NHIC). NHIC is a service of the Office of Disease Prevention and Health Promotion, Office of Public Health and Science, U.S. Department of Health and Human Services.

This publication is in the public domain. Duplication is encouraged.

For a single copy of this publication, or a full listing of other publications available, please write to NHIC, P.O. Box 1133, Washington, DC 20013–1133.

NHIC also maintains a database of more than 1,100 health information resources and can help you locate information, publications, or programs. Inclusion of an information source in publications or the database does not imply endorsement by the U.S. Department of Health and Human Services.

1999 FEDERAL HEALTH INFORMATION CENTERS AND CLEARINGHOUSES

The Federal Government operates many clearinghouses and information centers that focus on specific topics. Their services include distributing publications, providing referrals, and answering inquiries. Many offer toll–free numbers. Unless otherwise stated, numbers can be reached within the continental United States Monday through Friday, during normal business hours, and hours of operation are eastern time. The clearinghouses are listed below by keyword.

This information is in the public domain. Duplication is encouraged.

National ADOPTION Information Clearinghouse
330 C Street NW.
Washington, DC 20447
(888)251–0075
(703)352–3488
(703)385–3206 (Fax)
naic@calib.com (E–Mail)
http://www.calib.com/naic
Provides professionals and the general public with easily accessible information on all aspects of adoption, including infant and intercountry adoption and the adoption of children with special needs. NAIC maintains an adoption literature database, a database of adoption experts, listings of adoption agencies, crisis pregnancy centers, and other adoption–related services, as well as excerpts of State and Federal laws on adoption. Ultimately, NAIC's goal is to strengthen adoptive family life. NAIC does not place children for adoption or provide counseling. It does however, make referrals for such services. NAIC is funded by the Children's Bureau, Administration for Children and Families, U.S. Department of Health and Human Services.

National ADOPTION Center
1500 Walnut Street, Suite 701
Philadelphia, PA 19102
(800)TO–ADOPT
(215)735–9988
(215)735–9410 (Fax)
nac@adopt.org (E–Mail)
http://www.adopt.org/adopt
Mission is to expand adoption opportunities throughout the United States for children with special needs and those from minority cultures. Offers information and referral services. Provides publications on special needs adoption, single parent adoption, open adoption, and searching for birth parents.

National AGING Information Center
U.S. Administration on Aging
330 Independence Avenue SW.
Room 4656
Washington, DC 20201
(202)619–7501
(202)401–7620 (Fax)
naic@bangate.aoa.dhhs.gov (E–Mail)
http://www.aoa.dhhs.gov/naic/
Central source for a wide variety of program– and policy–related materials, demographic, and other statistical data on health, economic, and social status of older Americans. NAIC develops special reports on key aging issues for publication and dissemination to the aging community; produces statistical reports and data tables; and compiles an annual compendium of Title IV products.

National Institute on AGING Information Center
P.O. Box 8057
Gaithersburg, MD 20898–8057
(800)222–2225 (Voice/TTY)
(301)587–2528
(800)222–4225 (TDD)
(301)589–3014 (Fax)
niainfo@access.digex.net (E–Mail)
http://www.nih.gov/nia/
Provides publications on health topics of interest to older adults, doctors, nurses, social activities directors, health educators and the public.
U.S. Department of AGRICULTURE Extension Service

See the listing in the government section of your telephone book for your local extension office. Provides information on health, nutrition, fitness, and family well–being.

CDC National AIDS Clearinghouse
P.O. Box 6003
Rockville, MD 20849–6003
(800)458–5231
(800)243–7012 (TDD)
(800)874–2572 AIDS Clinical Trials
(800)458–5231 (NAC Fax–Back Service)
(800)448–0440 HIV/AIDS Treatment
(301)519–0459 (Voice, International all services)
(301)738–6616 (Fax)
aidsinfo@cdcnac.aspensys.com (E–Mail)
http://www.cdcnac.org
Sponsored by the Centers for Disease Control and Prevention. A national reference, referral, and distribution service for HIV/AIDS–related information. Answers questions and provides technical assistance; distributes published HIV–related materials including current information on scientific findings, CDC guidelines, and trends in the HIV epidemic; and provides specific information on AIDS–related organizations, educational materials, funding opportunities, and other topics. Services include a 24–hour Fax–back service for HIV/AIDS–related information and the Business and Labor Resource Service for resources, technical assistance, publications, and referrals concerning managing AIDS in the workplace. Provides information and publications in English and Spanish. 9 a.m.–6 p.m.

National Clearinghouse for ALCOHOL and DRUG Information
P.O. Box 2345
Rockville, MD 20847–2345
(800)729–6686
(301)468–2600
(800)487–4889 (TTY/TDD)
(301)230–2867 (TTY/TDD)
(301)468–6433 (Fax)
info@health.org (E–Mail)
http://www.health.org
Sponsored by the Center for Substance Abuse Prevention, Substance Abuse and Mental Health Services Administration. Gathers and disseminates information on alcohol and other drug–related subjects, including tobacco. Distributes publications. Services include subject searches and provision of statistics and other information. Operates the Regional Alcohol and Drug Awareness Resource Network, a nationwide linkage of alcohol and other drug information centers. Maintains a library open to the public. Library open to the public 8:00 a.m – 6:00 p.m., Monday through Friday. 800 number offers 24–hour voice mail service.

National Institute of ALLERGY and INFECTIOUS DISEASES
Office of Communications
Building 31
Room 7A50
9000 Rockville Pike
Bethesda, MD 20892
(301)496–5717
niaidoc@flash.niaid.nih.gov (E–Mail)
http://www.niaid.nih.gov/
Distributes publications to the public and to doctors, nurses, and researchers.

National Center for Complementary and ALTERNATIVE MEDICINE (NCCAM) Clearinghouse
P.O. Box 8218
Silver Spring, Maryland 20907–8218
(888)644–6226 (Voice – Toll–free)
(888)644–6226 (Voice – TTY/TDY)
(301)495–4957 (FAX)
(800)531–1794 (FAXBACK)
http://altmed.od.nih.gov/nccam/clearinghouse/
Develops and disseminates fact sheets, information packages, and publications to enhance public understanding about complementary and alternative medicine research supported by the NIH. NCCAM public information is currently free of charge; however, due to printing and duplication costs, only a limited number of copies can be requested. Information Specialists can answer inquiries in English or Spanish. After normal business hours, callers have the option of receiving fact sheets and other information by Fax.

ALZHEIMER'S DISEASE Education and Referral Center
P.O. Box 8250
Silver Spring, MD 20907–8250
(800)438–4380
(301)495–3311
(301)495–3334 (Fax)
adear@alzheimers.org (E–mail)
http://www.alzheimers.org
Sponsored by the National Institute on Aging. Provides information and publications on Alzheimer's disease to health and service professionals, patients and their families, caregivers, and the public.

National ARTHRITIS and Musculoskeletal and Skin Diseases Information Clearinghouse
1 AMS Circle
Bethesda, MD 20892–3675
(301)495–4484
(301)565–2966 (TTY)
(301)718–6366 (Fax)
(301)881–2731 (Fax–back, 24 hour service)
http://www.nih.gov/niams/
Designed to help patients and health professionals identify educational materials concerning arthritis and musculoskeletal and skin diseases. Distributes publications and maintains a file on the Combined Health Information Database (CHID) that indexes publications and audiovisuals. Personal information requests from patients are referred to appropriate organizations for additional information.

National Library Service for the BLIND and Physically Handicapped
Library of Congress
1291 Taylor Street NW.
Washington, DC 20542
(800)424–8567
(202)707–5100
(202)707–0744 (TDD)
(202)707–0712 (Fax)
nls@loc.gov (E–Mail)
http://lcweb.loc.gov/nls/
A network of 56 regional and 87 local libraries that work in cooperation with the Library of Congress to provide free library service to anyone who is unable to read standard print due to visual or physical disabilities. Delivers recorded and Braille books and magazines to eligible readers. Specially designed phonographs and cassette players also are loaned. A list of participating local and regional libraries is available.

U.S. Coast Guard Office of BOATING SAFETY
2100 Second Street SW.
Washington, DC 20593–0001
(800)368–5647 (Customer InfoLine)
(202)267–1077
(800)689–0816 (TTY)
(703)313–5910 (BBS)
http://www.uscgboating.org/
Provides safety information to recreational boaters; assists the public in finding boating education classes; answers technical questions; and distributes literature on boating safety, Federal laws, and the prevention of recreational boating casualties.

CANCER Information Service
Office of Cancer Communications
National Cancer Institute
31 Center Drive MSC 2580
Building 31, Room 10A07
Bethesda, MD 20892–2580
(800)4–CANCER
(800)332–8615 (TTY)
(301)496–5583
(301)402–2594 (Fax)
cancernet@icicb.nci.nih.gov (E–Mail)
http://cis/nci.nih.goc
Provides information about cancer and cancer–related resources to patients, the public, and health professionals. Inquiries are handled by trained information specialists. Spanish–speaking staff members are available. Distributes free publications from the National Cancer Institute. Operates 9 a.m.–7 p.m.

National Clearinghouse on CHILD ABUSE and Neglect Information
330 C Street SW.
Washington, DC 20447
(800)FYI–3366
(703)385–7565
(703)385–3206 (Fax)
nccanch@calib.com (E–mail)
http://www.calib.com/nccanch
Serves as a national resource for the acquisition and dissemination of child abuse and neglect materials and distributes a free publications catalog upon request. Maintains bibliographic databases of documents, audiovisuals, and national organizations. Services include searches of databases and annotated bibliographies on frequently requested topics.

National CHILD CARE Information Center
243 Church Street NW., 2nd Floor
Vienna, VA 22180
(800)516–2242 (Voice/TTY)
(800)716–2242 (Fax)
agoldstein@nccic.org (E–Mail)
http://nccic.org
Disseminates child care information; reaches out to ACF child care grantees and broader child care community via toll–free 800 number, and by Fax, mail and electronic media; and publication of the Child Care Bulletin; supports the Child Care Bureau in the collection and analysis of child care data; and maintains the database of information reported by State, Tribal and Territorial Grantees. The information Center assists the Child Care Bureau with its analysis of programmatic and expenditure data. Information and resources are available on–line through the Internet.

National Clearinghouse on Family Support and CHILDREN'S MENTAL HEALTH
Portland State University P.O. Box 751
Portland, OR 97207–0751
(800)628–1696
(800)735–2900 (TTY)
(503)725–4040
(503)725–4180 (Fax)
Sponsored by the National Institute on Disability and Rehabilitation Research, U.S. Department of Education, and the Center for Mental Health Services, U.S. Department of Health and Human Services. Provides publications on parent/family support groups, financing, early intervention, various mental disorders, and other topics concerning children's mental health. Also offers a computerized databank and a State–by–State resource file. Recording operates 24 hours a day.

NIH CONSENSUS Program Information Center
Office of Medical Applications of Research
P.O. Box 2577
Kensington, MD 20891
(888)644–2667
(301)593–9485 (Fax)
(301)816–9840 (Electronic Bulletin Board)
http://consensus.nih.gov
A service of the Office of Medical Applications of Research, National Institutes of Health. Provides up–to–date information on biomedical technologies to all health care providers. Offers a 24–hour voice mail service to order consensus statements produced by non–Federal panels of experts that evaluate scientific information on biomedical technologies. Information Specialists available between 8:30 a.m. and 5 p.m. (Eastern). Consensus statements can also be ordered by mail, Fax, and electronic bulletin board.

CONSUMER INFORMATION Center
Pueblo, CO 81009
(719)948–4000
catalog.pueblo@gsa.gov (E–Mail)
http://www.pueblo.gsa.gov/
Distributes Federal agency publications. Publishes quarterly catalog of Federal publications of consumer interest.

National Institute on DEAFNESS and Other Communication Disorders Information Clearinghouse
1 Communication Avenue
Bethesda, MD 20892–3456
(800)241–1044
(800)241–1055 (TT)
(301)907–8830 (Fax)
nidcd@aerie.com (E–Mail)
http://www.nih.gov/nidcd
Collects and disseminates information on hearing, balance, smell, taste, voice, speech, and language for health professionals, patients, people in industry, and the public. Maintains a database of references to brochures, books, articles, fact sheets, organizations, and educational materials, which is a subfile on CHID. Develops publications, including directories, fact sheets, brochures, information packets, and newsletters.

National DIABETES Information Clearinghouse
1 Information Way
Bethesda, MD 20892–3560
(301)654–3327
(301)907–8906 (Fax)
NDIC@info.niddk.nih.gov (E–mail)
http://www.niddk.nih.gov/
The National Diabetes Information Clearinghouse (NDIC) is an information and referral service of the National Institute of Diabetes and Digestive and Kidney Diseases, one of the National Institutes of Health. The clearinghouse responds to written inquiries, develops and distributes publications about diabetes, and provides referrals to diabetes organizations, including support groups. The NDIC maintains a database of patient and professional education materials from which literature searches are generated.

National DIGESTIVE DISEASES Information Clearinghouse
2 Information Way
Bethesda, MD 20892–3570
(301)654–3810
(301)907–8906 (Fax)
NDIC@info.niddk.nih.gov (E–mail)
http://www.niddk.nih.gov/
The National Digestive Diseases Information Clearinghouse (NDDIC) is an information and referral service of the National Institute of Diabetes and Digestive and Kidney Diseases, one of the National Institutes of Health. A central information resource on the prevention and management of digestive diseases, the clearinghouse responds to written inquiries, develops and distributes publications about digestive diseases, and provides referrals to digestive disease organizations, including support groups. The NDDIC maintains a database of patient and professional education materials from which literature searches are generated.

National Information Center for Children and Youth with DISABILITIES
P.O. Box 1492
Washington, DC 20013–1492
(800)695–0285 (Voice/TT)
(202)884–8200 (Voice/TT)
(202)884–8441 (Fax)
nichcy@aed.org (E–mail)
http://www.nichcy.org
Sponsored by the U.S. Department of Education. Assists individuals by providing information on disabilities and disability–related issues, with a special focus on children and youth with disabilities (birth to age 22). Services include responses to questions, referrals, and technical assistance to parents, educators, caregivers, and advocates. Develops and distributes fact sheets on disability and general information on parent support groups and public advocacy. All information and services are provided free of charge.

Section C

OSERS/Communications and Media Support Services (DISABILITIES, REHABILITATION)
Office of Special Education and Rehabilitative Services (OSERS)
U.S. Department of Education
330 C Street SW.
Switzer Building
Room 3132
Washington, DC 20202–2524
(202)205–8241
(202)401–2608 (Fax)
http://www.ed.gov/offices/OSERS/
Responds to inquiries on a wide range of topics, especially in the areas of Federal funding, legislation, and programs benefiting people with disabling conditions.
Provides referrals.

National Center for Chronic DISEASE PREVENTION and Health Promotion (NCCDPHP)
Technical Information and Editorial Services Branch
Centers for Disease Control and Prevention
4770 Buford Highway
MS K13
Atlanta, GA 30341–3724
(770)488–5080
(770)488–5969 (Fax)
http://www.cdc.gov/nccdphp/nccdhome.htm
Provides information and referrals to the public and to professionals. Gathers information on chronic disease prevention and health promotion. Develops the following bibliographic databases focusing on health promotion program information: Health Promotion and Education, Cancer Prevention and Control, Comprehensive School Health with an AIDS school health component, Prenatal Smoking Cessation, and Epilepsy Education and Prevention Activities. Produces bibliographies on topics of interest in chronic disease prevention and health promotion. The NCCDPHP Information Center collections include approximately 400 periodical subscriptions, 4,000 books, and 400 reference books. Visitors may use the collection by appointment. Produces the CDP File CD-ROM, which includes the above databases and the Chronic Disease Prevention Directory, a listing of key contacts in public health.

DRUG POLICY Information Clearinghouse
2277 Research Boulevard
Rockville, MD 20850
(800)666–3332
A service of the Bureau of Justice Statistics (BJS), Office of Justice Programs, U.S. Department of Justice. Responds to policymakers' need for the most current data about illegal drugs, drug law violations, drug–related crime, drug–using offenders in the criminal justice system, and the impact of drugs on criminal justice administration. The data center prepares special reports on drugs and crime; analyzes and evaluates existing drug data; prepares annotated bibliographies of drugs–and–crime reports; and responds to requests for drug and crime information. The clearinghouse disseminates BJS and other Department of Justice publications relating to drugs and crime; distributes information on specific drugs–and–crime topics; maintains a database of reports, books, and articles on crime; and maintains a reading room where visitors can use the clearinghouse collection. Leave recorded message after hours.

ERIC Clearinghouse on Teaching and Teacher EDUCATION
1307 New York Avenue NW, Suite 300
Washington, DC 20005
(202)293–2450
(202)457–8095 (Fax)
query@aacte.org (E–Mail)
http://www.ericsp.org
Sponsored by the U.S. Department of Education. Acquires, evaluates, abstracts, and indexes literature on the preparation and development of education personnel and on selected aspects of health and physical education, recreation, and dance. Publishes monographs, trends and issues papers, ERIC Digests and ERIC Recent Resources (annotated bibliographies from the ERIC database). Performs computer searches of the ERIC database and sponsors workshops on searching the ERIC database.

U.S. ENVIRONMENTAL PROTECTION Agency Public Information Center
401 M Street SW., M2904
Washington, DC 20460
(202)260–5922
(202)260–6257 (Fax)
library–hq@epamail.epa.gov (E–Mail)
http://www.epa.gov
Offers general information about the agency and nontechnical publications on various environmental topics, such as air quality, pesticides, radon, indoor air, drinking water, water quality, and Superfund. Refers inquiries for technical information to the appropriate regional or program office. The public may visit the center between the hours of 8 a.m. and 5 p.m., Monday–Friday, except Federal holidays.

National Clearinghouse on FAMILIES AND YOUTH
P.O. Box 13505
Silver Spring, MD 20911
(301)608–8098
(301)608–8721 (FAX)
info@ncfy.com (E–Mail)
http://www.ncfy.com
Links those interested in youth issues with the resources they need to serve young people, families, and communities better. Offers services that can assist in locating answers to questions or in making valuable contacts with other programs.

FEDERAL INFORMATION Center (FIC) Program
(800)688–9889
(800)326–2996 (TDD/TTY)
http://fic.info.gov
Provides information about the Federal Government's agencies, programs, and services. Information specialists use an automated database, printed reference materials, and other resources to provide answers to inquiries or accurate referrals. Callers who speak Spanish will be assisted. A descriptive brochure on the FIC program is available free from Department 584B at the Consumer Information Center (see listing in this publication). 9 a.m.–5 p.m. Pacific Monday–Friday except Federal holidays.

FOOD AND DRUG Administration
Office of Consumer Affairs
5600 Fishers Lane
HFE–88
Rockville, MD 20857
(301)827–4420
(301)443–9767 (Fax)
http://www.fda.gov/fdahomepage.html
Responds to consumer requests for information and publications on foods, drugs, cosmetics, medical devices, radiation–emitting products, and veterinary products. 10 a.m.–4 p.m.

FOOD AND NUTRITION Information Center
National Agricultural Library/FNIC
U.S. Department of Agriculture, ARS
10301 Baltimore Boulevard
Room 304
Beltsville, MD 20705–2351
(301)504–5719
(301)504–6409 (Fax)
fnic@nalusda.gov (E–Mail)
http://www.nal.usda.gov/fnic/
Provides information on human nutrition, food service management, and food technology. Acquires and lends books and audiovisual materials. Offers database searching and access through electronic mail.

Agency for HEALTH CARE POLICY and Research Clearinghouse
P.O. Box 8547
Silver Spring, MD 20907–8547
(800)358–9295
(301)495–3453
info@ahcpr.gov (E–mail)
http://www.ahcpr.gov
Distributes lay and scientific publications produced by the agency, including clinical practice guidelines on a variety of topics, reports from the National Medical Expenditure Survey, and health care technology assessment reports.

National HEALTH INFORMATION Center
P.O. Box 1133
Washington, DC 20013–1133
(800)336–4797
(301)565–4167
(301)984–4256 (Fax) nhicinfo@health.org (E–Mail)
http://nhic–nt.health.org
Helps the public and health professionals locate health information through identification of health information resources, an information and referral system, and publications. Uses a database containing descriptions of health–related organizations to refer inquirers to the most appropriate resources. Does not diagnose medical conditions or give medical advice. Prepares and distributes publications and directories on health promotion and disease prevention topics.

National Center for HEALTH STATISTICS
Data Dissemination Branch
6525 Belcrest Road
Room 1064
Hyattsville, MD 20782
(301)436–8500
nchsquery@cdc.gov (E–Mail)
http://www.cdc.gov/nchshome.htm
The Data Dissemination Branch of the National Center for Health Statistics answers requests for catalogs of publications and electronic data products; single copies of publications, such as Advance Data reports; ordering information for publications and electronic products sold through the Government Printing Office and National Technical Information Service; adding addresses to the mailing list for new publications; and specific statistical data collected by the National Center for Health Statistics.

National HEART, LUNG, AND BLOOD Institute (NHLBI) Information Center
P.O. Box 30105
Bethesda, MD 20824–0105
(301)251–1222
(301)251–1223 (Fax)
nhlbiic@dgsys.com (E–Mail)
http://www.nhlbi.nih.gov/nhlbi/infcntr/infocent.htm
NHLBI serves as a source of information and materials on risk factors for cardiovascular disease. Services include dissemination of public education materials, programmatic and scientific information for health professionals, and materials on worksite health, as well as responses to information requests. Materials on cardiovascular health are available to consumers and professionals.

National HIGHWAY TRAFFIC SAFETY Administration
U.S. Department of Transportation
400 Seventh Street, SW.
Washington, DC 20590
(800)424–9393 (Hotline)
(202)366–0123 (Hotline)
(800)424–9153 (TTY)
(202)366–5962 (Fax)
http://www.nhtsa.dot.gov/
Provides information and referral on the effectiveness of occupant protection, such as safety belt use, child safety seats, and automobile recalls. Gives referrals to other Government agencies for consumer questions on warranties, service, automobile safety regulations, and reporting safety problems. Works with private organizations to promote safety programs. Provides technical and financial assistance to State and local governments and awards grants for highway safety. 8 a.m.–10 p.m.

The National Resource Center on HOMELESSNESS and Mental Illness
262 Delaware Avenue
Delmar, NY 12054
(800)444–7415
(518)439–7415
(518)439–7612 (Fax)
nrc@prainc.com. (E–Mail)
http://www.samhsa.gov/cmhs/cmhs.htm
Collects, synthesizes, and disseminates information on the services, supports, and housing needs of homeless people with serious mental illnesses. Maintains extensive database of published and unpublished materials, prepares customized database searches, holds workshops and national conferences, provides technical assistance.

HOUSING AND URBAN DEVELOPMENT (HUD)
User
P.O. Box 6091
Rockville, MD 20850
(800)245-2691
(800)483-2209 (TDD)
(301)519-5767 (Fax)
huduser@aspensys.com (E-mail)
http://www.huduser.org
Disseminates publications for U.S. Department of Housing and Urban Development's Office of Policy Development and Research. Offers database searches on housing research. Provides reports on housing safety, housing for elderly and handicapped persons and lead-based paint.

INDOOR AIR Quality Information Clearinghouse
P.O. Box 37133
Washington, DC 20013-7133
(800)438-4318
(703)356-4020
(703)356-5386 (Fax)
iaqinfo@aop.com (E-mail)
http://www.epa.gov/iaq/
Information specialists provide information, referrals, publications, and database searches on indoor air quality. Information is provided about pollutants and sources, health effects, control methods, commercial building operations and maintenance, standards and guidelines, and Federal and State legislation.

National INJURY Information Clearinghouse
U.S. Consumer Product Safety Commission
National Injury Information Clearinghouse
Washington, DC 20207
(301)504-0424
(301)504-0124 (Fax)
info@cpsc.gov (E-Mail)
http://www.cpsc.gov/
Sponsored by the U.S. Consumer Product Safety Commission (CPSC). The clearinghouse collects and disseminates information on the causes and prevention of death, injury, and illness associated with consumer products. Compiles data obtained from accident reports, consumer complaints, death certificates, news clips, and the National Electronic Injury Surveillance System operated by the CPSC. Publications include statistical analyses of data and hazard and accident patterns.

National KIDNEY AND UROLOGIC Diseases Information Clearinghouse
3 Information Way
Bethesda, MD 20892-3580
(301)654-4415
(301)907-8906 (Fax)
NKUDIC@aerie.com
http://www.niddk.nih.gov/Brochures/NKUDIC.htm
The National Kidney and Urologic Diseases Information Clearinghouse (NKUDIC) is an information and referral service of the National Institute of Diabetes and Digestive and Kidney Diseases, one of the National Institutes of Health. The clearinghouse responds to written inquiries, develops and distributes publications about kidney and urologic diseases, and provides referrals to digestive disease organizations, including support groups. The NKUDIC maintains a database of patient and professional education materials, from which literature searches are generated.

National LEAD Information Center
8601 Georgia Avenue, Suite 503
Silver Spring, MD 20910
(800)424-LEAD (Clearinghouse)
(800)LEAD-FYI (Hotline)
(800)526-5456 (TDD)
(202)659-1192 (Fax)
hotline.lead@epamail.epa.gov (E-mail)
http://www.epa.gov/lead/nlic.htm
Sponsored by the Environmental Protection Agency. Responds to inquiries regarding lead and lead poisoning. Provides information on lead poisoning and children, lead-based paint, a list of local and State contacts who can help, and other lead-related questions.

National Center for Education in MATERNAL AND CHILD HEALTH
2000 15th Street, North
Suite 701
Arlington, VA 22201-2617
(703)524-7802
(703)524-9335 (Fax)
ncemch@gumedlib.dml.georgetown.edu (E-mail)
http://www.ncemch.org
Sponsored by the Maternal and Child Health Bureau, Health Resources and Services Administration. Provides information to health professionals and the public, develops educational and reference materials, and provides technical assistance in program development. Subjects covered are women's health including pregnancy and childbirth; infant, child, and adolescent health; nutrition; children with special health needs; injury and violence prevention; health and safety in day care; and maternal and child health programs and services. Types of materials include professional literature, curricula, patient education materials, audiovisuals, and information about organizations and programs.

Appointment preferred for on-site visits. Participates in the following electronic services: the Combined Health Information Database (CHID), National Library of Medicine's DIRLINE, and MCH-NetLink.

National MATERNAL AND CHILD HEALTH Clearinghouse
2070 Chain Bridge Road, Suite 450
Vienna, VA 22182-2536
(703)356-1964
(703)821-2098 (Fax)
nmchc@circsol.com (E-Mail)
http://www.circsol.com/mch/
Sponsored by the Maternal and Child Health Bureau, Health Resources and Services Administration. Centralized source of materials and information in the areas of human genetics and maternal and child health. Distributes publications and provides referrals.

National Institute of MENTAL HEALTH (NIMH)
Information Resources and Inquiries Branch
5600 Fishers Lane
Room 7C-02
Rockville, MD 20857
(301)443-4513
(301)443-4279 (Fax)
(301)443-5158 (MENTAL HEALTH FAX4U-Fax Information System)
(800)64-PANIC (PANIC DISORDER Information)
(800)421-4211 (Depression/Awareness, Recognition, and Treatment Information)
nimhinfo@nih.gov (E-Mail)
http://www.nimh.nih.gov
Responds to information requests from the public, clinicians, and the scientific community with a variety of printed materials on such subjects as children's mental disorders, schizophrenia, depression, bipolar disorder, seasonal affective disorder, anxiety and panic disorders, obsessive-compulsive disorder, eating disorders, learning disabilities, and Alzheimer's disease. Information and publications on the Depression/ Awareness, Recognition, and Treatment Program (D/ART) and on the Panic Disorder Education Program, NIMH-sponsored educational programs on depressive and panic disorders, their symptoms and treatment, are distributed. Single copies of publications are free of charge. A list of NIMH publications, including several in Spanish, is available upon request.

Office of MINORITY HEALTH Resource Center
P.O. Box 37337
Washington, DC 20013-7337
(800)444-6472
(301)589-0951 (TDD)
(301)589-0884 (Fax)
info@omhrc.gov (E-Mail)
http://www.omhrc.gov/
Responds to information requests from health professionals and consumers on minority health issues and locates sources of technical assistance. Provides referrals to relevant organizations and distributes materials. Spanish- and Asian-speaking operators are available.

Clearinghouse for OCCUPATIONAL SAFETY AND HEALTH INFORMATION
4676 Columbia Parkway
Cincinnati, OH 45226-1998
(800)35-NIOSH
(513)533-8326
(513)533-8347 (Fax)
pubstaff@cdc.gov (E-Mail)
http://www.cdc.gov/niosh/homepage.html
Provides technical information support for National Institute for Occupational Safety and Health (NIOSH) research programs and disseminates information to others on request. Services include reference and referral, and information about NIOSH studies. Distributes a publications list of NIOSH materials. Maintains automated database covering the field of occupational safety and health.

OPA (Office of Population Affairs) Clearinghouse
P.O. Box 30686
Bethesda, MD 20824-0686
(301)654-6190
(301)215-7731 (Fax)
opa@osophs.dhhs.gov (E-Mail)
http://www.hhs.gov/progorg/opa/clearing.html
Sponsored by the Office of Population Affairs. Provides information and distributes publications to health professionals and the public in the areas of family planning, adolescent pregnancy, and adoption. Makes referrals to other information centers in related subject areas.

National ORAL HEALTH Information Clearinghouse
1 NOHIC Way
Bethesda, MD 20892-3500
(301)402-7364 (301)907-8830 (Fax)
nidr@aerie.com (E-Mail)
http://www.aerie.com/nohicweb
A service of the National Institute of Dental and Craniofacial Research. Focuses on the oral health concerns of special care patients, including people with genetic disorders or systemic diseases that compromise oral health, people whose medical treatment causes oral problems, and people with mental or physical disabilities that make good oral hygiene practices and dental care difficult. Develops and distributes information and educational materials on special care topics, maintains a bibliographic database on oral health information and materials, and provides information services with trained staff to respond to specific interests and questions.

OSTEOPOROSIS and Related Bone Diseases
1150 17th Street NW., Suite 500
Washington, DC 20036
(800)624-BONE (202)223-0344
(202)466-4315 (TDD)
(202)223-2237 (Fax)
orbdnrc@nof.org (E-Mail)
http://www.osteo.org/
Sponsored by the National Institute of Arthritis and Musculoskeletal and Skin Diseases. Provides patients, health professionals, and the public with resources and information on metabolic bone diseases such as osteoporosis, Paget's disease of the bone, osteogenesis imperfecta, and primary hyperparathyroidism. Specific populations include the elderly, men, women, and adolescents.

President's Council on PHYSICAL FITNESS and Sports
200 Independence Avenue SW.
Hubert H. Humphrey Building, Room 738-H
Washington, DC 20201
(202)690-9000
(202)690-5211 (Fax)
http://www.whitehouse.gov/WH/PCPFS/html/fitnet.html
Conducts a public service advertising program, prepares educational materials, and works to promote the development of physical fitness leadership, facilities, and programs. Helps schools, clubs, recreation agencies, employers, and Federal agencies design and implement programs. Offers a variety of testing, recognition, and incentive programs for individuals, institutions, and organizations. Materials on exercise and physical fitness for all ages are available.

Section C

POLICY Information Center (PIC)
Office of the Assistant Secretary for Planning and
Evaluation
U.S. Department of Health and Human Services
Hubert H. Humphrey Building, Room 438F
200 Independence Avenue SW.
Washington, DC 20201
(202)690–6445
pic@osaspe.dhhs.gov
http://aspe.os.dhhs.gov/PIC/gate2pic.htm
A centralized repository of evaluations, short–term
evaluative research reports and program
inspections/audits relevant to the department's
operations, programs, and policies. It includes
relevant reports from the General Accounting
Office, Congressional Budget Office, and the
Institute of Medicine and the National Research
Council's Committee on National Statistics, both
part of the National Academy of Sciences. Reports
are also available from Departments of Agriculture,
Labor, and Education, as well as the private sector.
Final reports and executive summaries are available
for review at the facility, or final reports may be
purchased from the National Technical Information
Service. In addition, the PIC online database of
evaluation abstracts is accessible through HHS
HomePage, http://www.os.dhhs.gov or gopher.os.
dhhs.gov. The database includes over 6,000
project descriptions of both in–process and
completed studies. *PIC Highlights*, a quarterly
publication, features articles of recently completed
studies.

**National Clearinghouse for PRIMARY CARE
Information**
Ticon Courthouse
2070 Chain Bridge Road, Suite 450
Vienna, VA 22182
(703)821–8955, ext. 248
(703)566–4831 (TTY)
(703)902–0248 (Direct dial without receptionist)
(703)821–2098 (Fax)
http://www.bphc.hrsa.dhhs.gov
Sponsored by the Bureau of Primary Health Care
(BPHC), Health Resources and Services
Administration. Provides information services to
support the planning, development, and delivery of
ambulatory health care to urban and rural areas
that have shortages of medical personnel and
services. A primary role of the clearinghouse is to
identify, obtain, and disseminate information to
community and migrant health centers. Distributes
publications focusing on ambulatory care, financial
management, primary health care, and health
services administration of special interest to
professionals working in primary care centers
funded by BPHC. Materials are available on health
education, governing boards, financial
management, administrative management, and
clinical care. Bilingual medical phrase books, a
directory of federally funded health centers, and an
annotated bibliography are available also.

**U.S. Consumer PRODUCT SAFETY Commission
Hotline**
Washington, DC 20207
(800)638–2772
(800)638–8270 (TT)
(301)504–0580
(301)504–0399 (Fax)
http://www.cpsc.gov
Maintains the National Injury Information
Clearinghouse, conducts investigations of alleged
unsafe/defective products, and establishes product
safety standards. Assists consumers in evaluating
the comparative safety of products and conducts
education programs to increase consumer
awareness. Operates the National Electronic Injury
Surveillance System, which monitors a statistical
sample of hospital emergency rooms for injuries
associated with consumer products. Maintains free
hotline to provide information about recalls and to
receive reports on unsafe products and
product–related injuries. Publications describe
hazards associated with electrical products and
children's toys. Spanish–speaking operator available
through the toll–free number listed above.

National REHABILITATION Information Center
8455 Colesville Road, Suite 935
Silver Spring, MD 20910
(800)346–2742
(301)588–9284
(703)495–5626 (TTY)
(301)587–1967 (Fax)
http://www.naric.com/naric
The National Rehabilitation Center (NARIC) is a
library and information center on disability and
rehabilitation. Funded by the National Institute on
Disability and Rehabilitation Research, NARIC
collects and disseminates the results of federally
funded research projects. The collection, which also
includes books, journal articles, and audiovisuals,
grows at a rate of about 300 documents per
month.

**RURAL Information Center Health Service
(RICHS)**
National Agricultural Library
Room 304 10301 Baltimore Boulevard
Beltsville, MD 20705–2351
(800)633–7701
(301)504–5547
(301)504–6856 (TDD)
(301)504–5181 (Fax)
ric@nalusda.gov (E–mail)
http://www.nal.usda.gov/ric/richs
Disseminates information on a variety of rural health
issues including health professions, health care
financing, special populations and the delivery of
health care services. Provides information,
referrals, publications, brief complimentary
literature searches and access to an electronic
bulletin board to professionals and the public. Posts
rural health information on the Internet. RICHS is
funded by the Federal Office of Rural Health Policy,
DHHS and is part of the USDA Rural Information
Center, which provides information on rural issues
such as economic development, and community
well–being.

National Center on SLEEP DISORDERS Research
2 Rockledge Center
6701 Rockledge Drive
MSC 7920
Bethesda, MD 20892–7920
(301)435–0199
(301)480–3451 (FAX)
http://www.nhlbi.nih.gov/nhlbi/nhlbi.htm
Promotes basic, clinical and applied research on
sleep and sleep disorders by strengthening existing
sleep research programs, training new
investigators, and creating new programs aimed at
addressing important gaps and opportunities in
sleep and sleep disorders.

Office on SMOKING and Health
Centers for Disease Control and Prevention National
Center for Chronic Disease Prevention and Health
Promotion Mailstop K–50
4770 Buford Highway NE. Atlanta, GA
30341–3724
(800)CDC–1311
(770)488–5705, (770)488–5939 (Fax)
ccdinfo@ccdod1.em.cdc.gov (E–Mail)
http://www.cdc.gov/tobacco
Develops and distributes the annual *Surgeon
General's Report on Smoking and Health*,
coordinates a national public information and
education program on tobacco use and health, and
coordinates tobacco education and research efforts
within the Department of Health and Human
Services and throughout both Federal and State
governments. Maintains the Smoking and Health
database, consisting of approximately 60,000
records available on CD–ROM (CDP File) through
the Government Printing Office (Superintendent of
Documents, Government Printing Office,
Washington, DC 20402). Provides information on
smoking cessation, ETS/passive smoking,
pregnancy/infants, professional/technical
information, and a publications list upon request.

**National SUDDEN INFANT DEATH SYNDROME
Resource Center**
2070 Chain Bridge Road
Vienna, VA 22182
(703)821–8955
(703)821–2098 (Fax)
sids@circsol.com (E–Mail)
http://www.circsol.com/SIDS
Sponsored by the Maternal and Child Health
Bureau, Health Resources and Services
Administration. Provides information and
educational materials on sudden infant death
syndrome (SIDS), apnea, and other related issues.
Responds to information requests from
professionals and from the public. Maintains a
library of standard reference materials on topics
related to SIDS. Maintains and updates mailing lists
of State programs, groups, and individuals
concerned with SIDS. Also develops fact sheets,
catalogs, and bibliographies on areas of special
interest to the community. Conducts customized
searches of database on SIDS and SIDS–related
materials.

National TECHNICAL INFORMATION Service
U.S. Department of Commerce
Springfield, VA 22161 (800)553–NTIS
(703)605–6900 (Fax)
http://www.fedworld.gov/ntis/ntishome.html
Sells more than 9,000 federally produced
audiovisual programs. Provides catalogs at no cost.
Several catalogs cover health–related topics,
including alcohol and other drug abuse, emergency
fire services, industrial safety, and occupational
health.

**National Clearinghouse for WORKER SAFETY and
Health Training for Hazardous Materials,
Waste Operations, and Emergency Response**
c/o The George Meany Center for Labor Studies
5107 Benton Avenue
Bethesda, MD 20814
(301)571–4226
(301)897–5848 (Fax)
chouse@dgsys.com (E–mail)
http://www.niehs.nih.gov/wetp/clear.htm
The clearinghouse is supported by the Superfund
Worker Training Program of the National Institute of
Environmental Health Sciences (NIEHS) to provide
information and support services to NIEHS–funded
hazardous materials, waste operations, and
emergency response worker training programs.
Disseminates related information and materials to
the public.

**FEDERAL HEALTH INFORMATION CENTERS AND
CLEARINGHOUSES SUMMARY**

*Agency for Health Care Policy and Research
Clearinghouse*
(800)358–9295, (301)495–3453, info@ahcpr.gov
(E–mail)
http://www.ahcpr.gov

*Alzheimer's Disease Education and Referral
Center*
(800)438–4380, (301)495–3334 (Fax)
adear@alzheimers.org (E–mail)
http://www.alzheimers.org

Cancer Information Service
(800)4–CANCER
(301)496–5583, (800)332–8615 (TTY)
(301)402–2594 (Fax)
cancernet@icicb.nci.nih.gov (E–mail)
http://www.cis.nci.nih.gov

CDC National AIDS Clearinghouse
(800)458–5231, (800)243–7012 (TDD)
(800)874–2572 (AIDS Clinical Trials)
(800)448–0440 (HIV/AIDS Treatment)
(800)458–5231 (NAC Fax–Back Service)
(301)519–0459 (Voice, International all services)
(301)519–0459 (International) (301)519–6616 (Fax)
aidsinfo@cdcnac.org (E–mail)
http://www.cdcnac.org

*Clearinghouse for Occupational Safety and
Health Information*
(800)35–NIOSH (513)533–8326, (513)533–8347
(Fax)
pubstaff@cdc.gov (E–mail)
http://www.cdc.gov/niosh/homepage.html

Consumer Information Center
(719)948–4000
catalog.pueblo@gsa.gov (E–Mail)
http://www.pueblo.gsa.gov/

Drug Policy Information Clearinghouse
(800)666–3332
ondcp@ncjrs.org (E–Mail)
http://www.whitehousedrugpolicy.gov/

ERIC Clearinghouse on Teaching and Teacher Education
(202)293–2450 , (202)457–8095 (Fax)
query@aacte.org (E–Mail)
http://www.ericsp.org

Federal Information Center Program
(800)688–9889, (800)326–2996 (TDD/TTY)
http://fic.info.gov/

Food and Drug Administration
Office of Consumer Affairs
(301)827–4420, (301)443–9767 (Fax)
http://www.fda.gov/fdahomepage.html

Food and Nutrition Information Center
(301)504–5719, (301)504–6409 (Fax)
fnic@nalusda.gov (E–mail)
http://www.nal.usda.gov/fnic/

Housing and Urban Development (HUD) User
(800)245–2691, (800)483–2209 (TDD),
(301)519–5767 (Fax)
huduser@aspensys.com
http://www.hud.gov

Indoor Air Quality Information Clearinghouse
(800)438–4318, (703)356–4020, (703)356–5386
(Fax)
iaqinfo@aop.com
http://www.epa.gov/iaq/

NIH Consensus Program Information Center
(888)644–2667
(301)816–9840 (Electronic Bulletin Board)
(301)593–9485 (Fax)
http://consensus.nih.gov

National Adoption Center
(800)TO–ADOPT, (215)735–9410 (Fax)
naic@adopt.org (E–Mail)
http://www.adopt.org/adopt

National Adoption Information Clearinghouse
(800)To–ADOPT, (703)352–3488, (703)385–3206
(FAX)
naic@calib.com (E–Mail)
http://www.calib.com/naic

National Aging Information Center
(202)619–7501, (202)401–7620 (FAX)
naic@bangate.aca.dhhs.gov (E–Mail)
http://www.aoa.dhhs.gov/naic/

National Arthritis and Musculoskeletal and Skin Diseases Information Clearinghouse
(301)495–4484, (301)718–6366 (Fax),
(301)881–2731 (Faxback 24–hour service)
http://www.nih.gov/niams/

National Center for Chronic Disease Prevention and Health Promotion
(770)488–5080, (770)488–5969 (Fax)
http://www.cdc.gov/nccdphp/nccdhome.htm

National Center for Complementary and Alternative Medicine Clearinghouse
(888)644–6226 (Voice/Toll–free)
(888)644–6226 (Voice/TTY/TDY)
(301)495–4957 (FAX)
(800)531–1794 (FAXBACK)
http://altmed.od.nih.gov/nccam/clearinghouse/

National Center for Education in Maternal and Child Health
(703)524–7802, (703)524–9335 (Fax)
ncemch@gumedlib.dml.georgetown.edu (E–mail)
http://www.ncemch.org

National Center for Health Statistics
(301)436–8500
nchsquery@cdc.gov (E–Mail)
http://www.cdc.gov/nchshome.htm

National Center on Sleep Disorders Research
(301)435–0199, (301)480–3451 (FAX)
http://www.nhlbi.nih.gov/nhlbi/nhlbi.htm

National Child Care Information Center
(800)516–2242 (Voice – TTY)
(800)616–2242 (Voice), (800)716–2242 (Fax)
agoldstein@nccic.org (E–Mail)
http://nccic.org

National Clearinghouse for Alcohol and Drug Information
(800)729–6686, (301)468–2600
(800)487–4889 (TTY/TDD)
(301)230–2867 (TTY/TDD)
(301)468–6433 (Fax) info@health.org (E–Mail)
http://www.health.org

National Clearinghouse for Primary Care Information
(703)821–8955, ext. 248
(703)566–4831 (TTY), (703)821–2098 (Fax)
http://www.bphc.hrsa.dhhs.gov

National Clearinghouse for Worker Safety and Health Training for Hazardous Materials, Waste Operations, and Emergency Response
(301)571–4226, (301)897–5848 (Fax)
chouse@dgsys.com (E–mail) http://
www.niehs.nih.gov/wetp/clear.htm

National Clearinghouse on Child Abuse and Neglect Information
(800)FYI–3366
(703)385–7565, (703)385–3206 (Fax)
nccanch@calib.com (E–mail)
http://www.calib.com/nccanch

National Clearinghouse on Families and Youth
(301)608–8098
(301)608–8721 (FAX)
info@ncfy.com (E–Mail)
http://www.ncfy.com

National Clearinghouse on Family Support and Children's Mental Health
(800)628–1696, (800)735–2900 (TTY)
(503)725–4040, (503)725–4180 (Fax)

National Diabetes Information Clearinghouse
(301)654–3327, (301)907–8906 (Fax)
NDIC@info.niddk.nih.gov (E–mail) http://
www.niddk.nih.gov/Brochures/NDIC.htm

National Digestive Diseases Information Clearinghouse
(301)654–3810,(301)907–8906 (Fax)
NDIC@info.niddk.nih.gov (E–mail) http://
www.niddk.nih.gov/

National Health Information Center
(800)336–4797
(301)565–4167, (301)984–4256 (Fax)
nhicinfo@health.org (E–mail)
http://nhic–nt.health.org

National Heart, Lung, and Blood Institute Information Center
(301)251–1222, (301)251–1223 (Fax)
nhlbiic@dgsys.com (E–Mail)
http://www.nhlbi.nih.gov/nhlbi/infcntr/infocent.htm

National Highway Traffic Safety Administration
(800)424–9393 (Hotline), (800)424–9153 (TTY)
(202)366–0123 (Hotline), (202)366–5962 (Fax)
http://www.nhtsa.dot.gov/

National Information Center for Children and Youth With Disabilities
(800)695–0285 (Voice/TT)
(202)884–8200 (Voice/TT)
(202)884–8441 (Fax)
nichcy@aed.org (E–mail)
http://www.nichcy.org

National Injury Information Clearinghouse
(301)504–0424, (301)504–0124 (Fax)
info@cpsc.gov (E–mail)
http://www.cpsc.gov/

National Institute of Allergy and Infectious Diseases
(301)496–5717
niaidoc@flash.niaid.nih.gov (E–Mail)
http://www.niaid.nih.gov/

National Institute of Mental Health
(301)443–4513,
(800)64–PANIC (Panic Disorder Information)
(800)421–4211 (D/ART Information)
(301)443–5158 (Mental Health FAX4U)
(301)443–4279 (Fax)
nimhpubs@nih.gov (E–Mail)

nimhinfo@nih.gov (E–Mail)
http://www.nimh.nih.gov

National Institute on Aging Information Center
(301)587–2528, (800)222–2225 (Voice/TTY)
(800)222–4225(TDD), (301)589–3014 (Fax)
niainfo@access.digex.net (E–Mail)
http://www.nih.gov/nia/

National Institute on Deafness and Other Communication Disorders Information Clearinghouse
(800)241–1044
(800)241–1055(TT), (301)907–8830 (Fax)
nidcd@aerie.com (E–Mail)
http://www.nih.gov/nidcd

National Kidney and Urologic Diseases Information Clearinghouse
(301)654–4415, (301)907–8906 (Fax)
NKUDIC@aerie.com (E–Mail)
http://www.niddk.nih.gov/Brochures/NKUDIC.htm

National Lead Information Center
(800)424–LEAD (Clearinghouse)
(800)LEAD–FYI (Hotline)
(800)526–5456(TDD), (202)659–1192 (Fax)
lhotline.lead@epamail.epa.gov (E–Mail)
http://www.epa.gov/lead/nlic.htm

National Maternal and Child Health Clearinghouse
(703)356–1964, (703)821–2098 (Fax)
nmchc@circsol.com (E–Mail)
http://www.circsol.com/mch/

National Oral Health Information Clearinghouse
(301)402–7364, (301)907–8830 (Fax),
(301)656–7581 (TTY)
nidr@aerie.com (E–Mail)
http://www.nidr.nih.gov http://www.aerie.com/
nohicweb

National Rehabilitation Information Center
(800)346–2742, (301)588–9284,(301)495–5626
(301)587–1967 (Fax)
http://www.naric.com/naric

National Resource Center on Homelessness and Mental Illness
(800)444–7415
(518)439–7415, (518)439–7612 (Fax)
nrc@prainc.com. (E–Mail)
http://www.samhsa.gov/cmhs/cmhs.htm

National Sudden Infant Death Syndrome Resource Center
(703)821–8955, (703)821–2098 (Fax)
sids@circsol.com (E–Mail)
http://www.circsol.com/SIDS

National Technical Information Service
(800)553–NTIS, (703)605–6900 (Fax)
http://www.fedworld.gov/ntis/ntishome.html

Office of Alternative Medicine Clearinghouse
(888)644–6226 (Voice/TTY), (301)5496–4957
(Fax), (800)531–1794 (Fax–back)
info@omhrc.gov (E–Mail)
http://altmed.od.nih.gov/nccam/clearinghouse/

Office of Minority Health Resource Center
(800)444–6472, (301)589–0951 (TDD),
(301)589–0884 (Fax)
info@omhrc.gov (E–Mail)
http://www.omhrc.gov/

Office of Population Affairs (OPA)Clearinghouse
(301)654–6190 (Voice), (301)215–7731 (Fax)
opa@osophs.dhhs.gov (E–Mail)
http://www.hhs.gov/progorg/opa/clearing.html

Office on Smoking and Health
(800)CDC–1311
(770)488–5705, (770)488–5939 (Fax)
ccdinfo@ccdod1.em.cdc.gov (E–Mail)
http://www.cdc.gov/tobacco/

OSERS/Communications and Media Support Services
(202)205–8241, (202)401–2608 (Fax)
http://www.ed.gov/offices/OSERS/

Osteoporosis and Related Bone Diseases National Resource Center
(800)624–BONE, (202)223–0344 (202)466–4315
(TDD), (202)223–2237 (Fax) orbdnrc@nof.org
(E–mail)
http://www.osteo.org/

Policy Information Center
(202)690–6445
pic@osaspe.dhhs.gov (E–Mail)
http://aspe.os.dhhs.gov/PIC/gate2pic.htm

President's Council on Physical Fitness and Sports
(202)690–9000, (202)690–5211 (Fax)
http://www.whitehouse.gov/WH/PCPFS/html/fitnet.html

Rural Information Center Health Service
(800)633–7701, (301)504–5547
(301)504–6856(TDD), (301)504–5181 (Fax)
http://www.nal.usda.gov/ric/richs ric@nalusda.gov (Email)

U.S. Coast Guard Office of Boating Safety
(800)368–5647 (Customer InfoLine)
(800)689–0816 (TTY), (202)267–1077,
(703)313–5910 (BBS)
http://www.uscgboating.org/

U.S. Consumer Product Safety Commission Hotline
(800)638–2772, (800)638–8270 (TT)
(301)504–0580, (301)504–0399 (Fax)
http://www.cpsc.gov

U.S. Department of Agriculture Extension Service
(see listing in Government section of local telephone directories)

U.S. Environmental Protection Agency Public Information Center
(202)260–5922
(202)260–6257 (Fax)
library–hq@epamail.epa.gov (E–mail)
http://www.epa.gov

ARGENTINA

Argentinan Association of Dermatology, Asociacion Argentina De Dermatolo, Mexico 1720, 1100 Buenos A; tel. 381–2737; FAX. 381–2737; Dra. Lidia Ester Valle, Chairman

AUSTRALIA

Australian Healthcare Association, P.O. Box 54, Deakin West, , 2600; tel. +612 6285148; FAX. +612 6282239; Tracey Turner, Office Manager

BELGIUM

International Federation of Oto–Rhino–Laryngological Societies, IFOS–MISA–NKO Oosterveldlaan 24, 2610 WILRIJK; tel. 3 4433611; Ms. Gadeyne, Administrator, Publication Manager

Verbond der Verzorgingsinstellingen V.Z.W., 1, Guimardstraat, Brussels 1040; tel. 2 5118008; FAX. 2 5135269; Mrs. C. Boonen, M.D., General Director

BRAZIL

Fraternidade Crista De Doentes E Deficientes, Cap. Correa Pacheco 134, Americana, SP, 13470; tel. 0 194 619754; Celso Zoppi

CANADA

Association des Medecins de langue francaise du Canada, 8355 St. Laurent Boulevard, Montreal, PQ H2P 2Z6; tel. 514/388–2228; FAX. 514/388–5335; Andre' de Seve, General Director

Canadian Anesthesiologists' Society, One Eglinton Avenue East, Suite 208, Toronto, ON M4P 3A1; tel. 416/480–0602; FAX. 416/480–0320; Angela Fritsch, Director

Canadian Association of Medical Radiation Technologists, 280 Metcalfe Street, Suite 410, Ottawa, ON K2P 1R7; tel. 613/234–0012; FAX. 613/234–1097; Earl P. Rooney, Executive Director

Canadian Association of Pathologists, Office of the Secretariat, 774 Echo Drive, Ottawa, ON K1S 5N8; tel. 613–730–6230; FAX. 613/730–0260; Dr. Roger Amy, Secretary–Treasurer

Canadian Association of Social Workers, 383 Parkdale Avenue, Suite 402, Ottawa, ON K1Y 4R4; tel. 613/729–6668; FAX. 613/729–9608; Eugenia Repetur Moreno, Executive Director

Canadian Cancer Society, 10 Alcorn Avenue, Suite 200, Toronto, ON M4V 3B1; tel. 416/961–7223; FAX. 416/961–4189; Dorothy Lamont, Chief Executive Officer

Canadian Cardiovascular Society, 222 Queen Street, Suite 1403, Ottawa, On K1P SV9; tel. 613/569–3407; FAX. 613/569–6574; Charles Shields, Jr., Executive Director

Canadian College of Health Record Administrators, Canadian Health Record Association, 1090 Don Mills Road, Suite 501, Don Mills, ON M3C 3G8; tel. 416/447–4900; FAX. 416/447–4598; Deborah Del Duca, Executive Director

Canadian Council of the Blind, 396 Cooper Street, Suite 405, Ottawa, ON K2P 2H7; tel. 613/567–0311; FAX. 613/567–2728; Sharon E. Davis, Executive Assistant – National

Canadian Council on Social Development, 441 Maclaren, Fourth Floor, Ottawa, ON K2P 2H3; tel. 613/236–8977; FAX. 613/236–2750; Nancy Perkins, Communications Coordinator

Canadian Dental Association, 1815 Alta Vista Drive, Ottawa, ON K1G 3Y6; tel. 613/523–1770; FAX. 613/523–7736; Jardine Neilson, Executive Director

Canadian Healthcare Association, Association Canadian des soins de sante, 17 York Street, Suite 100, Ottawa, ON K1N 9J6; tel. 613/241–8005; FAX. 613/241–5055; Sharon Sholzberg–Gray, President

Canadian Medical Engineering Consultants, 594 Bush Street, Belfountain, ON L0N 1B0; tel. 519/927–3286; FAX. 519/927–9440; A. M. Dolan, President

Canadian Mental Health Association, 2160 Yonge Street, Toronto, ON M4S 2Z3; tel. 416/484–7750; FAX. 416/484–4617; Edward J. Pennington, General Director

Canadian National Institute for the Blind, 320 McLeod Street, Ottawa, ON K2P1A3; tel. 613/563–4021; FAX. 416/480–7677; Angelo Nikias, National Director, Gov't Relations and

Canadian Nurses Association, 50 Driveway, Ottawa, ON K2P 1E2; tel. 613/237–2133; FAX. 613/237–3520; Mary Ellen Jeans, RN, Ph.D., Executive Director

Canadian Orthopaedic Association, 1440 Ste. Catherine Street, W., Suite 320, Montreal, PQ H3G 1R8; tel. 514/874–9003; FAX. 514/874–0464; Dr. David Petrie, President

Canadian Pharmacists Association, 1785 Alta Vista Drive, Ottawa, ON K1G 3Y6; tel. 613/523–7877; FAX. 613/523–0445; Leroy C. Fevang, Executive Director

Canadian Physiotherapy Association, National Office, 2345 Yonge Street, Suite 410, Toronto, ON M4P 2E5; tel. 416/932–1888; FAX. 416/932–9708; Dan Stapleton, Chief Executive Officer

Canadian Psychiatric Association, 441 MacLaren Street, Suite 260, Ottawa, ON K2P2H3; tel. 613/234–2815; FAX. 613/234–9857; Alex Saunders, Chief Executive Officer

Canadian Public Health Association, 1565 Carling Avenue, Suite 400, Ottawa, ON K1Z 8R1; tel. 613/725–3769; FAX. 613/725–9826; Gerald H. Dafoe, M.H.A., Chief Executive Officer

Canadian Rehabilitation Council for the Disabled, 45 Sheppard Avenue, E., Suite 801, Toronto, ON M2N 5W9; tel. 416/250–7490; FAX. 416/229–1371; Henry Botchford, National Executive Director

Canadian Society for Medical Laboratory Science, Box 2830, LCD 1, Hamilton, ON L8N 3N8; tel. 905/528–8642; FAX. 905/528–4968; Kurt H. Davis, Executive Director

Canadian Society of Hospital Pharmacists, 1145 Hunt Club Road, Suite 350, Ottawa, ON K1V 0Y3; tel. 613/736–9733; FAX. 613/736–5660; Bill Leslie, Executive Director

Catholic Health Association of Canada, 1247 Kilborn Place, Ottawa, ON K1H 6K9; tel. 613/731–7148; FAX. 613/731–7797; Richard Haughian, President

College des medecins du Quebec, 2170, boul. Rene–Levesque Quest, Montreal, PQ H3H 2T8; tel. 514/933–4441; FAX. 514/993–3112; Joelle Lescop, M.D., Secretary General

College of Family Physicians of Canada, 2630 Skymark Avenue, Mississauga, ON L4W 5A4; tel. 905/629–0900; FAX. 905/629–0893; Dr. Claude A. Renaud, Director, Professional Affairs

College of Physicians and Surgeons of New Brunswick, One Hampton Road, Suite 300, Rothesay, NB E2E 5K8; tel. 506/849–5050; FAX. 506/849–5069; Ed Schollenberg, M.D., Registrar

Dietitians of Canada, 480 University Avenue, Suite 604, Toronto, ON M5G 1V2; tel. 416/596–0857; FAX. 416/596–0603; Marsha Sharp, Chief Executive Officer

National Cancer Institute of Canada, 10 Alcorn Avenue, Suite 200, Toronto, ON M4V 3B1; tel. 416/961–7223; FAX. 416/961–4189; Robert A. Phillips, Ph. D., Executive Director

The Canadian Hearing Society, 271 Spadina Road, Toronto, ON M5R 2V3; tel. 416/964–9595; FAX. 416/928–2506; David Allen, Executive Director

The Canadian Medical Association, Box 8650, Ottawa, ON K1G 0G8; tel. 613/731–9331; FAX. 613/731–7314; Leo–Paul Landry, M.D., Secretary General

The Canadian Red Cross Society, National Office, 1800 Alta Vista Drive, Ottawa, ON K1G 4J5; tel. 613/739–2220; FAX. 613/739–2505; Claude Houde, National Director, Blood Services

The Royal College of Physicians and Surgeons of Canada, 774 Echo Drive, Ottawa, ON K1S 5N8; tel. 613/730–6201; FAX. 613/730–2410; Mrs. Pierrette Leonard, APR, Head Communications Section

World Federation of Hemophilia, 1425 Rene devesque Blvd. West, Suite 1010, Montreal, PQ ; tel. 5148757944; FAX. 514/8758916; Mrs. Line Robillard, Executive Director

DENMARK

Amtsradsforeningen, Dampfaergevej 22, Postboks 2593, DK–2100 Copen; tel. +45 35 29 81; FAX. +45 35 29 83; Ida Sofie Jensen, Assistant Director

Danish Dental Association, Amaliegade 17, Postboks 143, Copenhagen; tel. 45 33157711; FAX. 45 33151637; Karsten Thuen, Chief Executive Director

National Committee for Danish Hospitals, Amtsradsforeningen, Dampfaergevej 22, Postboks 2593, DK–2100 Copenhagen 0; tel. 45 35298196; FAX. 45 35298337; Peder Ring, Assistant Director

ENGLAND

British Medical Association, B.M.A. House Tavistock Square, London, WCH1 9JP; tel. 0171/387–449; FAX. 0171/383–640; Dr. E.M. Armstrong, B. Sc., LFRCP(Glas),FRCGP,LFRCP ED

European Association of Poisons/Centres and Clinical Toxicology, City Hospital, Birmingham, B187QH; tel. (44) 121 507; FAX. (44) 121 507; Dr. Allister Vale, President

Institute of Health Services Management (United Kingdom and In, 7–10 Chandos Street, London,WIM,9D; tel. 0171/460–765; FAX. 0171/460–765; Suzanne Tyler, Deputy Director

International Hospital Federation, Hospital Federation, 46–48 Grosvenor Gardens, London, SW1WOEB; tel. 44/171881922; FAX. 44/171881922; Professor Per–Gunnar Svensson, Director General

King's Fund, 11–13 Cavendish Square, London, W1M 0AN; tel. 0171/307–262; FAX. 0171/307–280; Rabbi Julia Neuberger, Chief Executive Officer

Nuffield Trust, 59 New Cavendish Street, London W1 7RD; tel. 0171/631–845; FAX. 0171/631–845; John Wyn Owen, Secretary

FRANCE

World Medical Association, 28 Avenue des Alpes, B.P. 63, Cedex; tel. 450 407575; FAX. 450 405937; Dr. Delon Human, Secretary General

GERMANY

Deutsche Krankenhausgesellschaft, (German Hospital Association), Tersteegenstrasse 9, D40474, Dusseldorf; tel. 211 454730; FAX. 211 4547361; Jorg Robbers, Director General

International Academy of Cytology, Universitaets–Frauenklinik, Hugstetterstrausse 55, D–79106 Freib; tel. 761 2703012; FAX. 761 2703112; Manuel Hilgarth, M.D., F.I.A.C.

HUNGARY

Magyar Korhazszovetseg, Fogaskereku U–6, 1125 Budapest, Hungary; tel. (36–1) 21451; Dr. I. Uarga, President

KOREA

Korean Hospital Association, (Mapo Hyun Dai Building), Seoul 121–050; tel. 2 7187521; FAX. 2 7187522; Ho Uk Ha, Ph.D., Vice President

MEXICO

Federacion Latinoamericana de Hospitales, Apartado Postal 107–076, C.P. 06741, Mexico D.F.; tel. 5 482650; Dr. Guillermo Fajardo, Representative

NETHERLANDS

Federation of Health Care Organizations in the Netherlands, Postbus 9696, NL–3506 GR Ut; tel. 30 739911; FAX. 30 739438

PERU

Peruvian Hospital Association, Av. Dos De Mayo 8502 Of. 203, San Isidro, L; tel. 14 419546; Arturo Vasi Paez, President

PHILIPPINES

Philippine Hospital Association, 14 Kamias Rd., Quezon City–1; tel. 2 9227674/75; Thelma Navarrete–Clemente, M.D., M.H.A., President

SOUTH AFRICA

Provincial Administration, Health Services Branch, P.O. Box 517, South Africa; tel. 051/4055818; FAX. 051/304958; Dr. J. H. Kotze

SWITZERLAND

H+ Die Spitaler der Schweiz, (Swiss Hospital Association), Rain 32, Aarau; tel. 62 824 1222; FAX. 62 822 33 35; Mr. Christof Haudenschild, Director

World Health Organization, 20 Avenue Appia, CH–1211 Geneva; tel. 22 791 21 11; FAX. 22 791 07 46; Hiroshi Nakajima, M.D., Ph.D., Director–General

UNITED STATES

American College of Gastroenterology, 4900B South 31st Street, Arlington, VA 22206; tel. 703/820–7400; FAX. 703/931–4520; Thomas F. Fise, Executive Director

American Society for Testing and Materials, 100 Barr Harbor Drive, West Conshoho, PA 19428–2959; tel. 610/832–9672; FAX. 610/832–9666; Kenneth C. Pearson, Vice President

Association for Assessment and Accreditation of Laboratory Animals, 11300 Rockville Pike, Suite 1211, Rockville, MD 20852–3035; tel. 301/231–5353; FAX. 301/231–8282; Dr. John G. Miller, Executive Director

Association for Volunteer Administration, P.O. Box 32092, Richmond, VA 23294; tel. 804/346–2266; FAX. 804/346–3318; Katherine H. Campbell, Executive Director

International Academy of Podiatric Medicine (IAPM), 4603 Highway 95 South, P.O. Box 39, Cocolalla, ID 83813–0039; tel. 208/683–3900; FAX. 208/683–3700; Judith A. Baerg, Executive Director

International Aid, Inc., 17011 West Hickory, Spring Lake, MI 49456–9712; tel. 616/846–7490; FAX. 616/846–3842; Warren L. Prelesnik, FACHE, Director of Medical Procurement

International Association for Dental Research, 1619 Duke Street, Alexandria, VA 22314–3406; tel. 703/548–0066; FAX. 703/548–1883; Eli Schwarz, DDS, MPH, Ph.D., Executive Director

International Association of Ocular Surgeons, 4711 Golf Road, Suite 408, Skokie, IL 60076; tel. 847/568–1500; FAX. 847/568–1527; Randall T. Bellows, M.D., Director

International Association of Pediatric Laboratory Medicine, 6728 Old McLean Village Drive, McLean, VA 22101; tel. 703/556–9222; FAX. 703/556–8729; Merrill Ferber, Executive Director

International Council on Social Welfare/U.S. Committee, 750 First Street, N.E., Washington, DC 20002; tel. 202/336–8274; FAX. 202/336–8311; Toshio Tatara, Chair

International Executive Housekeepers Association, Inc., 1001 Eastwind Drive, Suite 301, Westerville, OH 43081–3361; tel. 800/200–6342; FAX. 614/895–1248; Beth Risinger, CEO and Executive Director

International Tremor Foundation, 7046 W. 105th Street, Overland Park, KS 66212–1803; tel. 913/341–3880; FAX. 913/341–1296; Catherine S. Rice, Executive Director

Rehabilitation International, 25 East 21st Street, New York, NY 10010; tel. 212/420–1500; FAX. 212/505–0871; Arthur O'Reilly, President

Sigma Theta Tau International Honor Society of Nursing, 550 West North Street, Indianapolis, IN 46202; tel. 317/634–8171; FAX. 317/634–8188; Nancy A. Dickenson–Hazard, Executive Officer

World Federation of Public Health Associations, c/o APHA, 1015 15th Street, N., Washington, DC 20005; tel. 202/789–5696; FAX. 202/789–5681; Allen K. Jones, Ph.D., Executive Secretary

VENEZUELA

Latin American Association for the Study of the Liver (LAASL), P.O. Box 51890, Sabana Grande, Caracas, 1050; tel. 58–2–9799380; FAX. 58–2–9799380; Dr. Miguel A. Garassini, President

Section C

U. S. GOVERNMENT AGENCIES

*The following information is based on data available as of March 1999.
For more information about U.S. government agencies, consult the U.S. Government Manual, available from the
Office of the Federal Register, National Archives and Records Service, Washington, DC 20408. A telephone
directory of the U.S. Department of Health and Human Services is available from the Superintendent of Documents,
Government Printing Office, Washington, DC 20402. Additional assistance may be obtained by contacting the
American Hospital Association's Washington office, 325 Seventh Street, N.W., Washington, DC 20004.*

Executive Office of the President
tel. 202/456–1414

Counsel to the President: Charles Ruff; 202/456–2632

Chief of Staff: Erskine Bowles; 202/456–6797

Assistant to the President for Economic Policy: Gene B.
Sperling; 202/456–5808

Assistant to the President for Domestic Policy: Bruce
Reed; 202/456–2216

Assistant to the President and Director of Public Liaison:
Minyon Moore; 202/456–2930

COUNCIL OF ECONOMIC ADVISORS
Chairman: Dr. Janet Yellen

OFFICE OF MANAGEMENT AND BUDGET
Director: vacant; 202/395–3080

Department of Agriculture
tel. 202/720–8732

Secretary: Dan Glickman; 202/720–3631

Department of Commerce
tel. 202/482–2000

Secretary: William M. Daley; 202/482–2112
BUREAU OF ECONOMIC ANALYSIS
Director: Steven Landefeld; 202/606–9900
ECONOMIC DEVELOPMENT ADMINISTRATION
Assistant Secretary: Phillip Singerman; 202/482–5112
**NATIONAL INSTITUTE OF STANDARDS AND
TECHNOLOGY**
Director: Raymond Krammer; 301/975–3058

Department of Defense
tel. 703/545–6700

Secretary: William S. Cohen; 703/695–5261

Assistant Secretary of Defense (Health Affairs): VACANT
**CIVILIAN HEALTH AND MEDICAL PROGRAMS OF
THE UNIFORMED SERVICES (OCHAMPUS)
(Denver, CO)**
Director: Seileen Mullen; 303/361–1313
**UNIFORMED SERVICES UNIVERSITY OF THE
HEALTH SCIENCES**
President: James A. Zimble; 301/295–3030
DEPARTMENT OF THE AIR FORCE
Surgeon General: Charles H. Roadman II;
202/767–4343
DEPARTMENT OF THE ARMY
Surgeon General: Lt. Gen. Ronald R. Blanck;
703/681–3000
DEPARTMENT OF THE NAVY
Surgeon General of the Navy: V.A.D.M. Harold M.
Koenig; 202/762–3701

Department of Education
tel. 202/401–2000

Secretary: Richard W. Riley; 202/401–3000

Department of Health and Human Services
tel. 202/619–0257

Secretary: Donna E. Shalala; 202/690–7000
General Counsel: Harriet Rabb; 202/690–7741

MANAGEMENT AND BUDGET
Assistant Secretary: John J. Callahan, Ph.D.;
202/690–6396

HEALTH
Assistant Secretary: James O'Hara; 202/690–7694

ADMINISTRATION FOR CHILDREN AND FAMILIES
Assistant Secretary: Olivia A. Golden; 202/401–2337

LEGISLATION
Assistant Secretary/Designate: Richard J. Tarplin;
202/690–7627

PLANNING AND EVALUATION
Principal deputy Association Secretary: vacant;
202/690–7858

PUBLIC AFFAIRS
Assistant Secretary: Melissa Skolfield; 202/690–7850

PUBLIC HEALTH SERVICE
Surgeon General: David Satcher, M.D.; 301/443–4000

Center for Disease Control, Atlanta 30333
Deputy Director: Dr. Claire V. Broome; 404/639–7000

Food and Drug Administration, Rockville, MD 20857
Commissioner: VACANT

Health Resources and Services Administration,
Hyattsville, MD 20782
Administrator: Ciro Sumaya, M.D.; 301/443–2216

Rockville, MD 20857
Administrator: Claude E. Fox, M.D. (Acting)

National Institutes of Health, Bethesda, MD 20892
Director: Harold Varmus, M.D.; 301/496–2433

**Substance Abuse and Mental Health Services
Administration**, Rockville, MD
Administrator: Nelba Chavez, Ph.D.; 301/443–4795

HEALTH CARE FINANCING ADMINISTRATION
Administrator: Nancy-Ann Min De Parle; 202/690–6726

SOCIAL SECURITY ADMINISTRATION: Baltimore, MD
21235
Commissioner: John W. Callahan; 410/965–7700
Regional Commissioners telephone: 800/772–1213
(1) Boston
Manny Vaz
(2) New York
Beatrice M. Disman
(3) Philadelphia
Larry G. Massanari
(4) Atlanta
Gordon M. Sherman
(5) Chicago
Jeff F. Martin
(6) Dallas
Horace L. Dickerson
(7) Kansas City
Michael Grochowski
(8) Denver
Richard J. Gonzalez
(9) San Francisco
Linda S. McMahon
(10) Seattle
Maria Keller

Department of Housing and Urban Development
tel. 202/708–1112

Secretary: Andrew Cuomo; 202/708–0417

Department of Justice
tel. 202/514–2000

Attorney General: Janet Reno; 202/514–2000

DRUG ENFORCEMENT ADMINISTRATION
Administrator: Thomas A. Constantine; 202/307–8000

Department of Labor
tel. 202/219–5000

Secretary: Alexis M. Herman; 202/219–8271

BUREAU OF LABOR STATISTICS
Commissioner: Katharine G. Abraham; 202/606–7800

EMPLOYMENT AND TRAINING ADMINISTRATION
Acting Assistant Secretary: Ray Uhalde; 202/219–6050

**OCCUPATIONAL SAFETY AND HEALTH
ADMINISTRATION**
Acting Assistant Secretary: Charles Jeffress;
202/219–7162

Department of State
tel. 202/647–4000

Secretary: Madeleine Albright; 202/647–6575

AGENCY FOR INTERNATIONAL DEVELOPMENT
Administrator: J. Brian Atwood; 202/647–9620

Independent Agencies

U.S. COMMISSION ON CIVIL RIGHTS
Chairperson: Mary Frances Berry; 202/376–7572

CONSUMER PRODUCT SAFETY COMMISSION
Chairperson: Ann Brown; 301/504–0213

ENVIRONMENTAL PROTECTION AGENCY
Administrator: Carol M. Browner; 202/260–4700

**EQUAL EMPLOYMENT OPPORTUNITY
COMMISSION**
Chairman: Paul M. Igasaki; 202/663–4001

FEDERAL EMERGENCY MANAGEMENT AGENCY
Director: James Lee Witt; 202/646–3923

Government-Related Groups
*Federally aided corporations and quasi–official agencies,
such as American Red Cross, National Academy
of Sciences and World Health Organization, are
listed with International, National, and Regional
Organizations beginning on page C3.*

Section C

Blue Cross–Blue Shield Plans

The following list of Blue Cross and Blue Shield Plans is based on a directory of Blue Cross and Blue Shield organizations and the agencies themselves. For more information contact: Blue Cross and Blue Shield Association, 225 N. Michigan Ave., Chicago, IL 60601; tel. 312/297–6000. When addressing mail to a plan, use the post office box number.

United States

ALABAMA: Blue Cross and Blue Shield of Alabama, 450 Riverchase Parkway, E., P.O. Box 995, Birmingham, AL 35298; tel. 205/988–2200; FAX. 205/985–5881; H.L. Jones, Chief Executive Officer

ARIZONA: Blue Cross and Blue Shield of Arizona, Inc., 2341 W. Royal Palm Road, P.O. Box 13466, Phoenix, AZ 85002–3466; tel. 602/864–5653; FAX. 602/864–4184; Lynn McKay, Director of Market Management

ARKANSAS: Arkansas Blue Cross and Blue Shield, a Mutual Insurance Company, 601 Gaines Street, P.O. Box 2181, Little Rock, AR 72203; tel. 501/378–2010; FAX. 501/378–2037; Robert L. Shoptaw, President and CEO

CALIFORNIA: Blue Cross of California, CaliforniaCare Health Plans, 21555 Oxnard Street, P.O. Box 70000, Van Nuys, CA 91470; tel. 818/703–2345; FAX. 818/703–2848; Leonard D. Schaeffer, Chairman and CEO

Blue Shield of California, California Physicians' Service Corporation, P.O. Box 7168, San Francisco, CA 94120; tel. 415/229–5000; FAX. 415/229–5056; Wayne R. Moon, Chairman and CEO

COLORADO: Blue Cross and Blue Shield of Colorado, Rocky Mountain Hospital and Medical Service, 700 Broadway, Denver, CO 80273–0002; tel. 303/831–2131; FAX. 303/830–0887; C. David Kikumoto, President and CEO

CONNECTICUT: Anthem Blue Cross and Blue Shield of Connecticut, Inc., 370 Bassett Road, P.O. Box 504, North Haven, CT 06473; tel. 203/239–4911; FAX. 203/239–7742; Majorie W. Dorr, Chief Operating Officer

DELAWARE: Blue Cross and Blue Shield of Delaware, Blue Cross and Blue Shield of Delaware, Inc., One Brandywine Gateway, P.O. Box 1991, Wilmington, DE 19899; tel. 302/429–0260; FAX. 302/421–2089; Robert C. Cole, Jr., President and CEO

DISTRICT OF COLUMBIA: Care First Blue Cross Blue Shield, 550 12th Street, S.W., Washington, DC 20065; tel. 202/479–8000; FAX. 202/479–3520; Larry C. Glasscock, President and CEO

FLORIDA: Blue Cross and Blue Shield of Florida, Inc., 4800 Deerwood Campus Parkway, P.O. Box 1798, Jacksonville, FL 32246; tel. 904/791–6111; FAX. 904/791–8081; Michael Cascone, Jr., President and CEO

GEORGIA: Blue Cross and Blue Shield of Georgia, Inc., Capital City Plaza, P.O. Box 4445, Atlanta, GA 30326; tel. 404/842–8000; FAX. 404/842–8010; Richard D. Shirk, President and CEO

HAWAII: Blue Cross and Blue Shield of Hawaii, Hawaii Medical Service Association, 818 Keeaumoku Street, P.O. Box 860, Honolulu, HI 96808–0860; tel. 808/948–5517; FAX. 808/948–5999; Robert P. Hiam, President

IDAHO: Blue Cross of Idaho Health Service, Inc., 3000 East Pine Avenue, Meridian, ID 83642; tel. 208/345–4550; FAX. 208/331–7311; David L. Barnett, President and CEO

Regence BlueShield of Idaho, 1602 21st Avenue, P.O. Box 1106, Lewiston, ID 83501; tel. 208/798–2102; FAX. 208/798–2085; John Ruch, President and CEO

ILLINOIS: Blue Cross and Blue Shield of Illinois, 300 East Randolph Street, P.O. Box 1364, Chicago, IL 60690; tel. 312/653–7500; FAX. 312/819–1220; Raymond F. McCaskey, President and CEO

INDIANA: Anthem Blue Cross and Blue Shield, Anthem Insurance Companies, Inc., 120 Monument Circle, Indianapolis, IN 46204; tel. 317/488–6057; FAX. 317/488–6477; L. Ben Lyle, Chairman, President and CEO

IOWA: Wellmark Inc., Blue Cross and Blue Shield of Iowa, 636 Grand Avenue, Des Moines, IA 50309; tel. 515/245–4545; FAX. 515/245–5090; John D. Forsyth, President and CEO

KANSAS: Blue Cross and Blue Shield of Kansas, Inc., 1133 Topeka Boulevard, P.O. Box 239, Topeka, KS 66601–0239; tel. 800/432–3990; FAX. 913/291–8997; John W. Knack, President and CEO

KENTUCKY: Anthem Blue Cross and Blue Shield, Anthem Insurance Companies, Inc., 9901 Linn Station Road, Louisville, KY 40223; tel. 502/423–2011; FAX. 502/339–5483; Jim LeMaster, President

LOUISIANA: Blue Cross and Blue Shield of Louisiana, Louisiana Health Service and Indemnity Company, 5525 Reitz Avenue, P.O. Box 98029, Baton Rouge, LA 70898–9029; tel. 504/295–2511; FAX. 504/295–2506; P. J. Mills, President and CEO

MAINE: Blue Cross Blue Shield of Maine, Associated Hospital Service of Maine, Two Gannett Drive, South Portland, ME 04106–6911; tel. 207/822–7000; FAX. 207/822–7350; Andrew W. Greene, President and CEO

MARYLAND: CareFirst Blue Cross Blue Shield, 10455 Mill Run Circle, P.O. Box 1010, Owings Mills, MD 21117; tel. 800/524–4555; FAX. 410/998–5576; William L. Jews, President and CEO

MASSACHUSETTS: Blue Cross and Blue Shield of Massachusetts, Inc., 100 Summer Street, Boston, MA 02110; tel. 617/832–3300; FAX. 617/832–3353; William C. Van Faasen, President and CEO

MICHIGAN: Blue Cross and Blue Shield of Michigan, 600 Lafayette East, Detroit, MI 48226–2998; tel. 313/225–8000; FAX. 313/225–6239; Richard E. Whitmer, President and CEO

MINNESOTA: Blue Cross and Blue Shield of Minnesota, BCBSM, Inc., 3535 Blue Cross Road, P.O. Box 64560, St. Paul, MN 55164; tel. 651/456–8400; FAX. 651/456–1989; Andrew P. Czajkowski, Chief Executive Officer

MISSISSIPPI: Blue Cross & Blue Shield of Mississippi, a Mutual Insurance Company, 3545 Lakeland Drive, P.O. Box 1043, Jackson, MS 39215–1043; tel. 601/932–3704; FAX. 601/939–7035; Richard J. Hale, President and CEO

MISSOURI: Alliance Blue Cross Blue Shield, 1831 Chestnut Street, St. Louis, MO 63103–2275; tel. 314/923–4444; FAX. 314/923–4809; John A. O'Rourke, Chairman, President and CEO

Blue Cross and Blue Shield of Kansas City, 2301 Main, P.O. Box 419169, Kansas City, MO 64141–6169; tel. 816/395–2222; FAX. 816/395–2035; Richard P. Krecker, President and CEO

MONTANA: Blue Cross Blue Shield of Montana, Inc., 560 North Park Avenue, P.O. Box 4309, Helena, MT 59604–4309; tel. 406/444–8200; FAX. 406/442–6946; Alan F. Cain, President and CEO

NEBRASKA: Blue Cross and Blue Shield of Nebraska, 7261 Mercy Road, P.O. Box 3248 Main P.O. Station, Omaha, NE 68180–0001; tel. 402/390–1800; FAX. 402/392–2141; Richard L. Guffey, Chairman of the Board and CEO

NEVADA: Blue Cross and Blue Shield of Nevada, 5250 South Virginia Street, P.O. Box 10330, Reno, NV 89520–0330; tel. 702/829–4040; FAX. 702/829–4101; C. David Kikumoto, President and CEO

NEW HAMPSHIRE: Blue Cross and Blue Shield of New Hampshire, New Hampshire–Vermont Health Service, 3000 Goffs Falls Road, Manchester, NH 03111–0001; tel. 603/695–7064; FAX. 603/695–7304; David Jensen, President and CEO

NEW JERSEY: Horizon Blue Cross and Blue Shield of New Jersey, Inc., Three Penn Plaza East, P.O. Box 420, Newark, NJ 07105–2200; tel. 201/466–4000; FAX. 201/466–8762; William J. Marino, President and CEO

NEW MEXICO: Blue Cross and Blue Shield of New Mexico, New Mexico Blue Cross and Blue Shield, Inc., 12800 Indian School Road, N.E., P.O. Box 27630, Albuquerque, NM 87125–7630; tel. 505/291–3500; FAX. 505/237–5324; Norman P. Becker, President and COO

NEW YORK: Blue Cross and Blue Shield of Central New York,, Excellus Health Plan, Inc., 344 South Warren Street, P.O. Box 4809, Syracuse, NY 13221–4809; tel. 315/448–3700; FAX. 315/448–4922; Howard F. Beacham III, President and COO

Blue Cross and Blue Shield of Western New York, Inc., 1901 Main Street, P.O. Box 80, Buffalo, NY 14240–0080; tel. 716/884–2911; FAX. 716/887–8981; Thomas P. Hartnett, Ph.D., President

Empire Blue Cross and Blue Shield, 622 Third Avenue, P.O. Box 345, New York, NY 10163–0345; tel. 800/261–5962; FAX. 212/983–7615; Michael A. Stocker, M.D., President and CEO

Finger Lakes Blue Cross and Blue Shield, Finger Lakes Medical Insurance Company, Inc., 150 East Main Street, Rochester, NY 14647; tel. 716/454–1700; FAX. 716/238–4400; David Klein, President and COO

Utica–Watertown Health Insurance Company, Inc., d/b/a Blue Cross and Blue Shield of Utica–Watertown an Excellus Company, Utica Business Park, 12 Rhodes Drive, Utica, NY 13502–6398; tel. 315/798–4200; FAX. 315/797–4288; Christopher D. Perna, President and CEO

NORTH CAROLINA: Blue Cross and Blue Shield of North Carolina, 5901 Chapel Hill Road, P.O. Box 2291, Durham, NC 27702; tel. 919/498–7431; FAX. 919/765–7105; Kenneth C. Otis II, President

NORTH DAKOTA: Blue Cross Blue Shield of North Dakota, 4510 13th Avenue, S.W., Fargo, ND 58121–0001; tel. 800/342–4718; FAX. 701/282–1866; Michael B. Unhjem, President and CEO

OHIO: Anthem Blue Cross and Blue Shield, Community Insurance Company, Anthem Insurance Companies, Inc., 1351 William Howard Taft Road, Cincinnati, OH 45206; tel. 513/977–8811; FAX. 513/977–8812; Dwane R. Houser, Chairman of the Board and CEO

Blue Cross and Blue Shield of Ohio, Medical Mutual of Ohio, 2060 East Ninth Street, Cleveland, OH 44115–1355; tel. 216/687–7000; FAX. 216/687–6044; Kent W. Chapp, Chairman, President and CEO

OKLAHOMA: Blue Cross and Blue Shield of Oklahoma, 1215 South Boulder Avenue, P.O. Box 3283, Tulsa, OK 74102–3283; tel. 918/560–3500; FAX. 918/560–2095; Ronald F. King, Chief Executive Officer

OREGON: Blue Cross and Blue Shield of Oregon, 100 Southwest Market Street, P.O. Box 1271, Portland, OR 97207; tel. 800/452–7390; FAX. 503/225–5232; Richard L. Woolworth, President and CEO

PENNSYLVANIA: Blue Cross of Northeastern Pennsylvania, Hospital Service Association of Northeastern Pennsylvania, 70 North Main Street, Wilkes Barre, PA 18711; tel. 717/831–3676; FAX. 717/831–3670; Thomas J. Ward, President and CEO

Capital Blue Cross, 2500 Elmerton Avenue, Harrisburg, PA 17177–1032; tel. 717/541–7000; FAX. 717/541–7405; James M. Mead, President and CEO

Section C

Highmark Blue Cross Blue Shield, 120 Fifth Avenue, Pittsburgh, PA 15222–3099; tel. 412/255–7000; FAX. 412/255–8158; William M. Lowry, President and CEO

Independence Blue Cross, 1901 Market Street, Philadelphia, PA 19103; tel. 800/358–0050; FAX. 215/241–3824; G. Fred DiBona, Jr., President and CEO

RHODE ISLAND: Blue Cross & Blue Shield of Rhode Island, 444 Westminster Street, Providence, RI 02903–3279; tel. 401/459–1200; FAX. 401/459–1290; Douglas J. McIntosh, President

SOUTH CAROLINA: Blue Cross and Blue Shield of South Carolina, I–20 East at Alpine Road, Columbia, SC 29219; tel. 803/788–3860; FAX. 803/736–3420; M. Edward Sellers, President and CEO

SOUTH DAKOTA: Blue Cross and Blue Shield of South Dakota, Wellmark of South Dakota, Inc., 1601 West Madison Street, Sioux Falls, SD 57104; tel. 605/361–5801; FAX. 605/361–5898; Philip M. Davis, Chief Operating Officer

TENNESSEE: Blue Cross Blue Shield of Tennessee, 801 Pine Street, Chattanooga, TN 37402; tel. 423/755–5600; FAX. 423/755–2178; Thomas Kinser, Chief Executive Officer

Blue Cross Blue Shield of Tennessee, Memphis Hospital Service and Surgical Association, Inc., 85 North Danny Thomas Boulevard, P.O. Box 98, Memphis, TN 38101; tel. 901/544–2111; FAX. 901/544–2565; Calvin Anderson, Vice President

TEXAS: Blue Cross and Blue Shield of Texas, 901 South Central Expressway, P.O. Box 655730, Dallas, TX 75265–5730; tel. 972/766–6900; FAX. 972/766–8586; Rogers K. Coleman, M.D., President,

UTAH: Regence Blue Cross Blue Shield of Utah, 2890 East Cottonwood Parkway, Salt Lake City, UT 84121; tel. 801/333–5295; FAX. 301/333–6516; Jed H. Pitcher, Chairman, President and CEO

VERMONT: Blue Cross and Blue Shield of Vermont, One East Road, P.O. Box 186, Montpelier, VT 05601; tel. 802/223–6131; FAX. 802/229–0511; Preston Jordan, President and CEO

VIRGINIA: Trigon Blue Cross Blue Shield, Blue Cross and Blue Shield of Virginia, 2015 Staples Mill Road, P.O. Box 27401, Richmond, VA 23279; tel. 804/354–7173; FAX. 804/354–7044; Norwood H. Davis, Jr., Chairman and CEO

WASHINGTON: Blue Cross Blue Shield of Alaska, Blue Cross of Washington, Blue Shield in North Central Washington, 7001 220th Street, S.W., P.O. Box 327, Seattle, WA 98111–0327; tel. 425/670–5900; FAX. 425/670–4900; Betty Woods, President and CEO

Medical Service Corporation of Eastern Washington, 3900 East Sprague Avenue, P.O. Box 3048, Spokane, WA 99220–3048; tel. 509/536–4500; FAX. 509/536–4770; Henry F. Keaton, President

Northwest Washington Medical Bureau, P.O. Box 699, Mount Vernon, WA 98273; tel. 360/336–9660; FAX. 360/336–2028; Karen Larson, President and CEO

Premera Blue Cross, 7001 220th Street, S.W., P.O. Box 327, Seattle, WA 98043–2124; tel. 425/670–4000; Betty Woods, President and CEO

Regence Blue Shield, 1800 Ninth Avenue, P.O. Box 21267, Seattle, WA 98111–3267; tel. 206/464–3600; FAX. 206/389–6778; Dale M. Francis, President and CEO

Washington Physicians Service Association, 1800 Ninth Avenue, P.O. Box 2010, Seattle, WA 98111; tel. 206/389–7520; FAX. 206/389–7521; William Van Hollebeke, Executive Director

Whatcom Medical Bureau, 3000 Northwest Avenue, P.O. Box 9753, Bellingham, WA 98227–9753; tel. 360/734–8000; FAX. 360/734–6676; Bela M. Biro, Chief Financial Officer

WEST VIRGINIA: Mountain State Blue Cross & Blue Shield, Inc., 700 Market Square, P.O. Box 1948, Parkersburg, WV 26102; tel. 304/424–7732; FAX. 304/424–7789; Gregory K. Smith, President and CEO

WISCONSIN: Blue Cross and Blue Shield United of Wisconsin, 401 West Michigan Street, P.O. Box 2025, Milwaukee, WI 53201; tel. 414/224–6100; FAX. 414/226–5488; Thomas R. Hefty, Chairman and CEO

WYOMING: Blue Cross and Blue Shield of Wyoming, 4000 House Avenue, P.O. Box 2266, Cheyenne, WY 82003–2266; tel. 307/634–1393; FAX. 307/778–8582; C. E. Chapman, President

U.S. Associated Areas

JAMAICA: Blue Cross of Jamaica, 85 Hope Road, Kingston 6, JA 9; tel. 809/927–9821; FAX. 809/927–9817; Henry Lowe, Ph.D., C.D., J.P., President and CEO

PUERTO RICO: La Cruz Azul de Puerto Rico, Blue Cross of Puerto Rico, Carretera Estatal 1, K.M. 17.3–Rio Piedras, PR 0092, P.O. Box 366068, San Juan, PR 00936–6068; tel. 787/272–9898; FAX. 787/272–7867; Jose Julian Alvarez, Executive President

Triple–S, Inc., P.O. Box 363628, San Juan, PR 00936–3628; tel. 809/749–4114; FAX. 809/749–4191; Miguel A. Vazquez–Deynes, President

Canada

ALBERTA: Alberta Blue Cross Plan, 10009–108th Street, Edmonton, AB T5J 3C5; tel. 403/498–8000; FAX. 403/425–4627; V. George Ward, President and CEO

BRITISH COLUMBIA: Pacific Blue Cross, 4250 Canada Way, Burnaby, BC V5G1G8; tel. 604/417–2021; FAX. 604/419–2020; Robert B. Bucher, President and CEO

MANITOBA: Manitoba Blue Cross, United Health Services Corporation, 100A Polo Park Centre, 1485 Portage Avenue, Winnipeg, MB R3G OW, Winnipeg, MB R3C 2X7; tel. 204/775–0161; FAX. 204/774–1761; Kerry V. Bittner, President

NEW BRUNSWICK: Blue Cross in Ontario, (Moncton Office), 644 Main Street, Moncton, NB E1C 1E2, P.O. Box 220, Moncton, NB E1C 8L3; tel. 506/853–1811; FAX. 506/867–4646; Pierre–Yves Julien, President and CEO

Blue Cross of Atlantic Canada, 644 Main Street, Moncton, NB E1C 1E2, P.O. Box 220, Moncton, NB E1C 8L3; tel. 506/853–1811; FAX. 506/853–4651; Leon R. Furlong, President and CEO

Blue Cross of Atlantic Canada, 644 Main Street, Moncton, NB E1C 1E2, P.O. Box 220, Moncton, NB E1C 8L3; tel. 506/853–1811; FAX. 506/867–4651; Leon R. Furlong, President and CEO

ONTARIO: Blue Cross in Ontario, (Ontario Office), 185 The West Mall, Suite 600, Etobicoke, ON M9C 5P1; tel. 416/626–1688; FAX. 416/626–0997; Andrew Yorke, Chief Operating Officer

QUEBEC: Quebec Blue Cross Quebec Hospital Service Association, 550 Sherbrooke Street, W., Suite 160, Montreal, PQ H3A 1B9; tel. 514/286–8482; FAX. 514/286–8475; Claude Bolvin, CA, President and CEO

SASKATCHEWAN: Saskatchewan Blue Cross, 516 Second Avenue, N., Saskatoon, SK S7K 2C5, P.O. Box 4030, Saskatoon, SK S7K 3T2; tel. 306/244–1192; FAX. 306/664–1945; Terry R. Brash, President and CEO

Section C

Health Systems Agencies

The following is a list of federally funded Health Systems Agencies. The information was obtained from the National Directory of Health Planning Policy and Regulatory Agencies, published by the Missouri Department of Health, Certificate of Need Program and the agencies themselves. For information about other local agencies and organizations that fulfill similar functions, contact the state or metropolitan hospital associations; see also the list of State Health Planning and Development Agencies in section C.

United States

FLORIDA: Big Bend Health Council, Inc. (District Two), 2629 West 10th Street, Panama City, FL 32401; tel. 904/872–4128; FAX. 904/872–4131; David W. Carter, Executive Director

Broward Regional Health Planning Council (District 10), 915 Middle River Drive, Suite 521, Fort Lauderdale, FL 33304; tel. 954/561–9681; FAX. 954/561–9685; John H. Werner, Chief Executive Officer

Health Council of South Florida, Inc., 5757 Blue Lagoon Drive, Suite 170, Miami, FL 33126; tel. 305/263–9020; FAX. 305/262–9905; Sonya Albury, Executive Director

Health Council of West Central Florida (District Six), 9721 Executive Center Drive, N., St. Petersburg, FL 33702–2438; tel. 813/576–7772; FAX. 813/570–3033; Elizabeth Rugg, Director

Health Planning Council of Northeast Florida, Inc., 900 University Blvd. N, Suite 202, Jacksonville, FL 32211; tel. 904/745–3050; FAX. 904/745–3054; Lori A. Bilello, Executive Director

Health Planning Council of Southwest Florida, Inc., 9250 College Parkway, Suite Three, Fort Myers, FL 33919; tel. 941/433–4600; FAX. 941/433–6703; Ron Burris, Executive Director

North Central Florida Health Planning Council, 11 West University Avenue, Suite Seven, Gainesville, FL 32601; tel. 904/955–2264; FAX. 904/955–3109; Carol J. Gormley, Executive Director

Northwest Florida Health Council, Inc. (District One), 2629 West 10th Street, Panama City, FL 32401; tel. 904/872–4128; FAX. 904/872–4131; David W. Carter, Executive Director

Suncoast Health Council, Inc. (District Five), 9800 4th Street North, Suite 206, St. Petersburg, FL 33702–2451; tel. 727/217–7070; Elizabeth Rugg, Executive Director

The Local Health Council of East Central Florida Inc., 1155 South Semoran Boulevard, Suite 1, Winter Park, FL 32792–5505; tel. 407/671–2005; Steve Windham, Chief Executive Officer

Treasure Coast Health Council, Inc. (District Nine), 4152 W. Blue Heron Blvd, Suite 229, Riviera Beach, FL 33404; tel. 561/844–4220; FAX. 516/844–3310; Barbara H. Jacobowitz, Executive Director

MARYLAND: Chesapeake Health Planning System, Inc., P.O. Box 773, Cambridge, MD 21613; tel. 410/221–0907; FAX. 410/221–2605; John Bennett, President

MINNESOTA: Region 1 (Northwest MN) and Region II (Northeast MN), Regional Coordinating Boards, Minnesota Department of Health, P.O. Box 64975, St. Paul, MN 55164–0975; tel. 612/282–5644; FAX. 612/282–5628; Michele Holten

Region III (Central MN) and Region IV (Twin City Metro), Minnesota Department of Health, P.O. Box 64975, St. Paul, MN 55164–0975; tel. 612/282–6330; Kristin Pederson

Region V (Southwest MN) and Region VI (Southeast MN), Minnesota Department of Health, CHS Division, Suite 460, St. Paul, MN 55164–0975; tel. 651/282–6328; FAX. 651/282–5628; Kay Markling

NEW JERSEY: Essex and Union Advisory Board for Health Planning, Inc., 14 South Orange Avenue, South Orange, NJ 07079; tel. 201/761–6969; FAX. 201/761–7401; Sharon Postel, Executive Director

Fairleigh Dickinson University, Region Two Health Planning Advisory Board, 1000 River Road, Teaneck, NJ 07666; tel. 201/692–7180; FAX. 201/692–7189; Thomas Pavlak, Ph.D., Executive Director

Health Visions, Inc., 6981 North Park Drive, East Building, Suite 307, Pennsauken, NJ 08109; tel. 609/662–2050; FAX. 609/662–2261; Charles Daly, Vice President, Health Planning

Mid–State Health Advisory Corporation–Rider University, Rider University, 2083 Lawrenceville Road, Lawrenceville, NJ 08648; tel. 609/219–2121; FAX. 609/219–2120; Bernadette West, Executive Director

South Central Health Planning Council, Inc., Local Advisory Board 3, 515 Route 70, Suite 208, Brick, NJ 08723; tel. 732/262–9047; FAX. 732/262–9049; Eleanor Jaeger, Executive Director

NEW YORK: Central New York Health Systems Agency, Inc., 101 Intrepid Lane, Syracuse, NY 13205; tel. 315/492–8557; FAX. 315/492–8563; Timothy J. Bobo, Executive Director

Finger Lakes Health Systems Agency, 1150 University Avenue, Rochester, NY 14607; tel. 716/461–3520; FAX. 716/461–0997; Martha P. Bond, Executive Director

Health Systems Agency of New York City, 450 Seventh Avenue, 13th Floor, New York, NY 10001; tel. 212/244–8100; FAX. 212/244–8120; Robert D. Gumbs, Executive Director

Health Systems Agency of Western New York, 2070 Sheridan Drive, Buffalo, NY 14223; tel. 716/876–7131; FAX. 716/876–4968; Brian G. McBride, Executive Director

Hudson Valley Health Systems Agency, P.O. Box 696, Tuxedo, NY 10987; tel. 914/351–5146; Regina M. Kelly, Executive Director

Nassau–Suffolk Health Systems Agency, 1537 Old Country Road, Plainview, NY 11803; tel. 516/293–5740; FAX. 516/293–6288; Renee Pekmezaris, Ph.D., Executive Director

New York State Public Health Association, Pine West Plaza, One United Way, Albany, NY 12205–5558; tel. 518/452–3300; FAX. 518/452–5943; Bruce R. Stanley, Executive Director

NY Penn Health Systems Agency, 84 Court Street, Suite 300, Binghamton, NY 13901; tel. 607/772–0336; FAX. 607/772–0158; Denise Murray, Executive Director

OHIO: Health Planning and Resource Development Association of Central, Ohio River Valley, 35 East Seventh Street, Suite 311, Cincinnati, OH 45202; tel. 513/621–2434; FAX. 513/621–4307; James F. Sandmann, President

Health Systems Agency, 415 Bulkley Building, 1501 Euclid Avenue, Cleveland, OH 44115–2108; tel. 216/771–6814; FAX. 216/771–2939; Nancy J. Roth, Executive Director

Lake to River Health Care Coalition, 106 Robbins Avenue, Niles, OH 44446–1768; tel. 330/652–8111; FAX. 330/652–0003; Thomas J. Flynn, Executive Director

Miami Valley Health Improvement Council, 7049C Taylorsville Road, Huber Heights, OH 45424–3103; tel. 937/236–5358; FAX. 937/237–9750; Rudolph P. Arnold, M.D., President and CEO

Northwest Ohio Health Planning, Inc., 635 North Erie Street, Toledo, OH 43624; tel. 419/255–1190; FAX. 419/255–2900; David G. Pollick, Executive Director

Scioto Valley Health Systems Agency (SVHSA), 600 West Spring Street, Rear, Columbus, OH 43215–2327; tel. 614/645–7438; FAX. 614/645–5531; Franklin Hirsch, Executive Director

VIRGINIA: Central Virginia Health Planning Agency, Inc., P.O. Box 24287, Richmond, VA 23224; tel. 804/233–6206; FAX. 804/233–8834; Karen L. Cameron, Executive Director

Eastern Virginia Health Systems Agency, Inc., The Koger Center, Suite 232, Norfolk, VA 23502; tel. 757/461–4834; FAX. 757/461–3255; Paul M. Boynton, Executive Director

Health Systems Agency of Northern Virginia, 7245 Arlington Boulevard, Suite 300, Falls Church, VA 22042; tel. 703/573–3100; FAX. 703/573–1276; Dean Montgomery, Executive Director

Northwestern Virginia Health Systems Agency, 1924 Arlington Boulevard, Suite 211, Charlottesville, VA 22903; tel. 804/977–6010; FAX. 804/977–0748; Margaret P. King, Executive Director

Southwest Virginia Health Systems Agency, Inc., 3100–A Peters Creek Road, N.W., Roanoke, VA 24019; tel. 540/362–9528; FAX. 540/362–9676; Pamela P. Clark, MPA, Executive Director

The following list of state and metropolitan hospital associations is derived from the American Hospital Association's Directory of Hospital and Health System Associations.

United States

ALABAMA: Alabama Hospital Association, 500 East Boulevard, P.O. Box 210759, Montgomery, AL 36121–0759; tel. 334/272–8781; FAX. 334/270–9527; J. Michael Horsley, President and Chief Executive Officer

ALASKA: Alaska State Hospital and Nursing Home Association, 426 Main Street, Juneau, AK 99801; tel. 907/586–1790; FAX. 907/463–3573; Laraine Derr, President and Chief Executive Officer

ARIZONA: Arizona Hospital and Healthcare Association, 1501 West Fountainhead Parkway, Suite 650, Tempe, AZ 85282; tel. 602/968–1083; FAX. 602/967–2029; John R. Rivers, President and Chief Executive Officer

ARKANSAS: Arkansas Hospital Association, 419 Natural Resources Drive, Little Rock, AR 72205–1539; tel. 501/224–7878; FAX. 501/224–0519; James R. Teeter, President and Chief Executive Officer

CALIFORNIA: California Healthcare Association, 1201 K. Street, Suite 800, Sacramento, CA 95814–1100; tel. 916/443–7401; FAX. 916/552–7596; C. Duane Duaner, President
Healthcare Association of San Diego and Imperial Counties, 402 West Broadway, 22nd Floor, San Diego, CA 92101–3542; tel. 619/544–0777; FAX. 619/544–0888; Gary R. Stephany, President and Chief Executive Officer
Healthcare Association of Southern California, 515 South Figueroa Street, Suite 1300, Los Angeles, CA 90071–3322; tel. 213/538–0700; FAX. 213/629–4272; James D. Barber, President and Chief Executive Officer
Hospital Council of Northern and Central California, 1201 K. Street, P.O. Box 1100, Sacramento, CA 95812–1100; tel. 916/552–7608; FAX. 916/552–7596; Gregg Schnepple, President and Chief Executive Officer

COLORADO: Colorado Health and Hospital Association, 7335 East Orchard Road, Suite 100, Englewood, CO 80111; tel. 720/489–1630; FAX. 720/489–9400; Larry Wall, President

CONNECTICUT: Connecticut Hospital Association, 110 Barnes Road, P.O. Box 90, Wallingford, CT 06492–0090; tel. 203/265–7611; FAX. 203/284–9318; Dennis P. May, President

DELAWARE: Delaware Healthcare Association, 1280 South Governors Avenue, Dover, DE 19904–4802; tel. 302/674–2853; FAX. 302/734–2731; Joseph M. Letnaunchyn, President

DISTRICT OF COLUMBIA: District of Columbia Hospital Association, 1250 Eye Street, N.W., Suite 700, Washington, DC 20005–3930; tel. 202/682–1581; FAX. 202/371–8151; Robert A. Malson, President

FLORIDA: Florida Hospital Association, 307 Park Lake Circle, P.O. Box 531107, Orlando, FL 32853–1107; tel. 407/841–6230; FAX. 407/422–5948; Charles F. Pierce, Jr., President
South Florida Hospital and Healthcare Association, Inc, 6363 Taft Street, Suite 200, Hollywood, FL 33024; tel. 954/964–1660; FAX. 954/962–1260; Linda S. Quick, President

GEORGIA: GHA: An Association of Hospitals and Health Systems, 1675 Terrell Mill Road, Marietta, GA 30067; tel. 770/955–0324; FAX. 770/955–5801; Joseph A. Parker, President

HAWAII: Healthcare Association of Hawaii, 932 Ward Avenue, Suite 430, Honolulu, HI 96814–2126; tel. 808/521–8961; FAX. 808/599–2879; Richard E. Meiers, President and Chief Executive Officer

IDAHO: Idaho Hospital Association, 802 West Bannock Street, Suite 500, Boise, ID 83702–5842; tel. 208/338–5100; FAX. 208/338–7800; Steven A. Milliard, President

ILLINOIS: Illinois Hospital and HealthSystems Association, 1151 East Warrenville Road, P.O. Box 3015, Naperville, IL 60566–7015; tel. 630/505–7777; FAX. 630/505–9457; Kenneth C. Robbins, President

Metropolitan Chicago Healthcare Council, 222 South Riverside Plaza, 19th Floor, Chicago, IL 60606; tel. 312/906–6000; FAX. 312/993–0779; Earl C. Bird, President

INDIANA: Indiana Hospital & Health Association, One American Square, P.O. Box 82063, Indianapolis, IN 46282; tel. 317/633–4870; FAX. 317/633–4875; Kenneth G. Stella, President

IOWA: The Association of Iowa Hospitals and Health Systems, 100 East Grand Avenue, Suite 100, Des Moines, IA 50309; tel. 515/288–1955; FAX. 515/283–9366; Stephen F. Brenton, President

KANSAS: Kansas Hospital Association, 215 SE 8th Street, Topeka, KS 66601–2308; tel. 785/233–7436; FAX. 785/233–6955; Donald A. Wilson, President

KENTUCKY: KHA: An Association of Kentucky Hospitals and Health Systems, 2501 Nelson Miller Parkway, P.O. Box 436629, Louisville, KY 40253–6629; tel. 502/426–6220; FAX. 502/426–6226; Michael T. Rust, President

LOUISIANA: Louisiana Hospital Association, 9521 Brookline Avenue, Baton Rouge, LA 70809–1431; tel. 225/928–0026; FAX. 225/923–1004; Robert D. Merkel, President
Metropolitan Hospital Council of New Orleans, 2450 Severn Avenue, Suite 210, Metairie, LA 70001; tel. 504/837–1171; FAX. 504/837–1174; John J. Finn, Ph.D., President

MAINE: MHA...An Association of Maine Hospitals and HealthCare Organizations, 150 Capitol Street, Augusta, ME 04330; tel. 207/622–4794; FAX. 207/622–3073; Steven R. Michaud, President

MARYLAND: MHA: The Association of Maryland Hospitals & Health Systems, 6820 Deerpath Road, Elkridge, MD 21075; tel. 410/379–6200; FAX. 410/379–8239; Calvin M. Pierson, President
Healthcare Council of the National Capital Area, 8201 Corporate Drive, Suite 410, Landover, MD 20785–2229; tel. 301/731–4700; FAX. 301/731–8286; Joseph P. Burns, President and Chief Executive Officer

MASSACHUSETTS: Massachusetts Hospital Association, Five New England Executive Park, Burlington, MA 01803; tel. 781/272–8000; FAX. 781/272–0466; Ronald M. Hollander, President

MICHIGAN: Michigan Health and Hospital Association, 6215 West St. Joseph Highway, Lansing, MI 48917; tel. 517/323–3443; FAX. 517/323–0946; Spencer C. Johnson, President
Center for Health Affairs, 3075 Charleviox Drive, SE, Grand Rapids, MI 49546; tel. 616/940–3337; FAX. 616/940–0723; Edward A. Rode, President
Healthcare Council of MidMichigan, 3927 Beecher Road, Flint, MI 48532–3803; tel. 810/766–8898; FAX. 810/762–4108; Marlene Soderstrom, President
Hospital Council of East Central Michigan, 141 Harrow Lane, Suite 11, Saginaw, MI 48603; tel. 517/792–1725; FAX. 517/792–3099; Randolph K. Flechsig, President
North Central Council of MHA, 114 North Court Street, Gaylord, MI 49735; tel. 517/732–7002; FAX. 517/732–3059; Mary E. Fox, Executive Director
Southeast Michigan Health and Hospital Council, 24725 West Twelve Mile Road, Suite 1040, Southfield, MI 48034; tel. 248/358–2950; FAX. 248/358–1098; Donald P. Potter, President
Southwestern Michigan Hospital Council, 6215 West St. Joseph Highway, Lansing, MI 48917; tel. 517/323–3443; FAX. 517/323–0946; Clark R. Ballard, President

MINNESOTA: Minnesota Hospital and Healthcare Partnership, 2550 University Avenue, W., Suite 350S, St. Paul, MN 55114–1900; tel. 651/641–1121; FAX. 651/659–1477; Bruce J. Reuben, President

MISSISSIPPI: Mississippi Hospital Association, 6425 Lakeover Road, P.O. Box 16444, Jackson, MS 39236–6444; tel. 800/289–8884; FAX. 601/368–3200; Sam W. Cameron, President and Chief Executive Officer

MISSOURI: Missouri Hospital Association, P.O. Box 60, Jefferson City, MO 65102–0060; tel. 573/893–3700; FAX. 573/893–2809; Marc D. Smith, President
Greater Kansas City Health Council, 10401 Holmes Road, Suite 280, Kansas City, MO 64131–3368; tel. 816/941–3800; FAX. 816/941–0818; Vickie Cook, Executive Director

MONTANA: MHA... An Association of Health Care Providers, 1720 Ninth Avenue, P.O. Box 5119, Helena, MT 59604; tel. 406/442–1911; FAX. 406/443–3894; James F. Ahrens, President

NEBRASKA: Nebraska Association of Hospitals and Health Systems, 1640 L. Street, Suite D, Lincoln, NE 68508; tel. 402/458–4900; FAX. 402/475–4091; Harlan M. Heald, Ph.D., President

NEVADA: Nevada Association of Hospitals and Health Systems, 4600 Kietzke Lane, Suite A–108, Reno, NV 89502; tel. 775/827–0184; FAX. 775/827–0190; Bill M. Welch, President and Chief Executive Officer

NEW HAMPSHIRE: New Hampshire Hospital Association, 125 Airport Road, Concord, NH 03301–5388; tel. 603/225–0900; FAX. 603/225–4346; Michael J. Hill, President

NEW JERSEY: New Jersey Hospital Association, P.O. Box One, 760 Alexander Road, CN–1, Princeton, NJ 08543–0001; tel. 609/275–4000; FAX. 609/275–4100; Gary S. Carter, FACHE, President and Chief Executive Officer

NEW MEXICO: New Mexico Hospitals and Health Systems Association, 2121 Osuna Road, N.E., Albuquerque, NM 87113; tel. 505/343–0010; FAX. 505/343–0012; Maureen L. Boshier, President and Chief Executive Officer

NEW YORK: Healthcare Association of New York State, 74 North Pearl Street, Albany, NY 12207; tel. 518/431–7600; FAX. 518/431–7915; Daniel Sisto, President
Greater New York Hospital Association, Subsidiaries, and Affiliates, 555 West 57 Street, 15th Floor, New York, NY 10019; tel. 212/246–7100; FAX. 212/262–6350; Kenneth E. Raske, President
Iroquois Healthcare Alliance, 17 Halfmoon Executive Park Drive, Clifton Park, NY 12065; tel. 518/383–5060; FAX. 518/383–2616; Gary J. Fitzgerald, President
Nassau–Suffolk Hospital Council, Inc, 3001 Expressway Drive North, Suite 300, Hauppauge, NY 11788; tel. 516/435–3000; FAX. 516/435–2343; Peter M. Sullivan, Executive President and Chief Executive Officer
Northern Metropolitan Hospital Association, 400 Stony Brook Court, Newburgh, NY 12550; tel. 914/562–7520; FAX. 914/562–0187; Arthur E. Weintraub, President
Rochester Regional Healthcare Association, 3445 Winton Place, Rochester, NY 14623; tel. 716/273–8180; FAX. 716/273–8189; Robert M. Swinnerton, President and Chief Executive Officer
Western New York Healthcare Association, 1876 Niagara Falls Boulevard, Tonawanda, NY 14150–6439; tel. 716/695–0843; FAX. 716/695–0073; William D. Pike, President

NORTH CAROLINA: NCHA, P.O. Box 4449, Cary, NC 27519–4449; tel. 919/677–2400; FAX. 919/677–4200; C. Edward McCauley, President

NORTH DAKOTA: North Dakota Healthcare Association, 1121 N. 13th Street, Suite 1, Bismarck, ND 58501; tel. 701/224–9732; FAX. 701/224–9529; Arnold R. Thomas, President

OHIO: OHA: The Association for Hospitals and Health Systems, 155 East Broad Street, Columbus, OH 43215; tel. 614/221–7614; FAX. 614/221–4771; James R. Castle, President and Chief Executive Officer
Akron Regional Hospital Association, 190 Montrose West Ave., Suite 201, Akron, OH 44321–2786; tel. 330/668–6180; FAX. 330/668–2013; Marianne G. Lorini, President
Greater Cincinnati Health Council, 2100 Sherman Avenue, Suite 100, Cincinnati, OH 45212–2775; tel. 513/531–0200; FAX. 513/531–0278; Lynn R. Olman, President

Greater Dayton Area Hospital Association, 32 North Main Street, Suite 1441, Dayton, OH 45402; tel. 937/228–1000; FAX. 937/228–1035; Joseph M. Krella, President

Hospital Council of Northwest Ohio, 3231 Central Park West Drive, Suite 200, Toledo, OH 43614; tel. 419/842–0800; FAX. 419/843–8889; W. Scott Fry, President and Chief Executive Officer

The Center for Health Affairs, 1226 Huron Road, Cleveland, OH 44115; tel. 216/696–6900; FAX. 216/696–1837; C. Wayne Rice, Ph.D., President and Chief Executive Officer

OKLAHOMA: Oklahoma Hospital Association, 4000 Lincoln Boulevard, Oklahoma City, OK 73105; tel. 405/427–9537; FAX. 405/424–4507; Craig W. Jones, President

Greater Oklahoma City Hospital Council, 4000 Lincoln Boulevard, Oklahoma City, OK 73105; tel. 405/427–9537; FAX. 405/424–4507; Stanley Tatum, Chairman

OREGON: Oregon Association of Hospitals and Health Systems, 4000 Kruse Way Place, Building 2, Suite 100, Lake Oswego, OR 97035–2543; tel. 503/636–2204; FAX. 503/636–8310; Kenneth M. Rutledge, President

PENNSYLVANIA: The Hospital & Healthsystem Association of Pennsylvania, 4750 Lindle Road, P.O. Box 8600, Harrisburg, PA 17105–8600; tel. 717/564–9200; FAX. 717/561–5334; Caroyln F. Scanlan, President and Chief Executive Officer

Hospital Council of Western Pennsylvania, 500 Commonwealth Drive, Warrendale, PA 15086; tel. 724/776–6400; FAX. 724/776–6969; Ian G. Rawson, Ph.D., President

The Delaware Valley Healthcare Council of HAP, 121 South Broad Street, 20th Floor, Philadelphia, PA 19107; tel. 215/735–9695; FAX. 215/790–1267; Andrew B. Wigglesworth, President

RHODE ISLAND: Hospital Association of Rhode Island, 880 Butler Drive, Suite One, Providence, RI 02906; tel. 401/274–4274; FAX. 401/274–1838; Edward Quinlan, President

SOUTH CAROLINA: South Carolina Health Alliance, 101 Medical Circle, P.O. Box 6009, West Columbia, SC 29171–6009; tel. 803/796–3080; FAX. 803/796–2938; Ken A. Shull, FACHE, President

SOUTH DAKOTA: South Dakota Association of Healthcare Organizations, 3708 Brooks Place, Suite 1, Sioux Falls, SD 57106; tel. 605/361–2281; FAX. 605/361–5175; David R. Hewett, President and Chief Executive Officer

TENNESSEE: THA: An Association of Hospitals and Health Systems, 500 Interstate Boulevard, South, Nashville, TN 37210; tel. 615/256–8240; FAX. 615/242–4803; Craig A. Becker, President

TEXAS: THA: The Association of Texas Hospitals and Health Care Organizations, 6225 U.S. Highway 290, E, P.O. Box 15587, Austin, TX 78761–5587; tel. 512/465–1000; FAX. 512/465–1090; Terry Townsend, FACHE, CAE, President and Chief Executive Officer

Dallas–Forth Worth Hospital Council, 250 Decker Court, Irving, TX 75062; tel. 972/719–4900; FAX. 972/719–4009; John C. Gavras, President

Greater San Antonio Hospital Council, 8620 North New Braunfels, Suite 420, San Antonio, TX 78217; tel. 210/820–3500; FAX. 210/820–3888; William Dean Rasco, FACHE, President and Chief Executive Officer

UTAH: UHA: Utah Hospital and Health Systems Association, 2180 South 1300 East, Suite 440, Salt Lake City, UT 84106–2843; tel. 801/486–9915; FAX. 801/486–0882; Richard B. Kinnersley, President

VERMONT: Vermont Association of Hospitals and Health Systems, 148 Main Street, Montpelier, VT 05602; tel. 802/223–3461; FAX. 802/223–0364; Norman E. Wright, President

VIRGINIA: Virginia Hospital & Healthcare Association, 4200 Inslake Drive, P.O. Box 31394, Richmond, VA 23294; tel. 804/747–8600; FAX. 804/965–0475; Laurens Sartoris, President

WASHINGTON: Washington State Hospital Association, 300 Elliott Avenue, W, Suite 300, Seattle, WA 98119–4118; tel. 206/281–7211; FAX. 206/283–6122; Leo F. Greenawalt, President and Chief Executive Officer

WEST VIRGINIA: West Virginia Hospital Association, 100 Association Drive, Charleston, WV 25311; tel. 304/344–9744; FAX. 304/344–9745; Steven J. Summer, President

WISCONSIN: Wisconsin Health and Hospital Association, 5721 Odana Road, Madison, WI 53719–1289; tel. 608–274–1820; FAX. 608–274–8554; Robert C. Taylor, President and Chief Executive Officer

WYOMING: Wyoming Hospital Association, P.O. Box 249, Cheyenne, WY 82003; tel. 307/632–9344; FAX. 307/632–9347; Robert C. Kidd, II, President

U.S. Associated Areas

PUERTO RICO: Puerto Rico Hospital Association, Officina 101–103, Villa Nevarez Professional Center, Centro Commercial Villa Nevarez, San Juan, PR 00927; tel. 787/764–0290; FAX. 787/753–9748; Juan Rivera, Executive Vice President

Canada

ALBERTA: Provincial Health Authorities of Alberta, 200–44 Capital Boulevard, 10044–108 Street, NW, Edmonton, AB AB T5J 3S7; tel. 403/424–4309; FAX. 403/424–4309; E. Michael Higgins, Executive Director

NEW BRUNSWICK: New Brunswick Healthcare Association, 861 Woodstock Road, Fredericton, NB E3B 7R7; tel. 506/451–0750; FAX. 506/451–0760; Michel J. Poirier, Executive Director

NEWFOUNDLAND: Newfoundland Hospital and Nursing Home Association, P.O. Box 8234, St. John's, NF A1B–3N5; tel. 709/364–7701; FAX. 709/364–6460; John F. Peddle, Executive Director

NORTHWEST TERRITORIES: Northwest Territories Health Care Association, 4921 49th Street, Suite 401, P.O. Box 1709, Yellowknife, NT X1A–2P3; tel. 867/873–9253; FAX. 867/873–9254; Dwight Morley, Executive Director

NOVA SCOTIA: Nova Scotia Association of Health Organizations, Bedford Professional Centre, 2 Dartmouth Road, Bedford, NS B4A–2K7; tel. 902/832–8500; FAX. 902/832–8505; Robert A. Cook, President and Chief Executive Officer

ONTARIO: Ontario Hospital Association, 200 Front Street, W, Suite 2000, Toronto, ON M5V–3L1; tel. 416/205–1300; FAX. 416/205–1360; David MacKinnon, President

Catholic Health Association of Canada, 1247 Kilborn Place, Ottawa, On K1H–6K9; tel. 613/731–7148; FAX. 613/731–7797; Richard Haughian, D.Th., President

PRINCE EDWARD ISLAND: Health Association of PEI, Inc., 10 Pownal Street, P.O. Box 490, Charlottetown, PEI C1A–3V6; tel. 902/368–3901; FAX. 902/368–3231; Carol Gabanna, Executive Director

QUEBEC: Quebec Hospital Association, 505 boulevard de Maisonneuve, W, Suite 400, Montreal, PQ H3A–3C2; tel. 514/842–4861; FAX. 514/282–4271; Yvon Marcoux, Executive Vice President

SASKATCHEWAN: Saskatchewan Association of Health Organizations, 1445 Park Street, Regina, SK S4N–4C5; tel. 306/347–5500; FAX. 306/347–5500; Arliss Wright, President and Chief Executive Officer

Hospital Licensure Agencies

Information for the following list of state hospital licensure agencies was obtained directly from the agencies.

United States

ALABAMA: Alabama Department of Public Health, **Division of Health Care Facilities,** The RSA Tower, P.O. Box 303017, Montgomery, AL 36130–3017; tel. 334/206–5075; FAX. 334/206–5088; Elva Goldman, Director

Alabama Department of Public Health, Division of Provider Services, The RSA Tower, P.O. Box 303017, Montgomery, AL 36130–3017; tel. 334/206–5079; FAX. 334/206–5219; Jimmy D. Prince, Associate Director

ALASKA: Health Facilities Licensing and Certification, 4730 Business Park Boulevard, Building H, Anchorage, AK 99503–7137; tel. 907/561–8081; FAX. 907/561–3011; Shelbert Larsen, Administrator

ARIZONA: Arizona Department of Health Services Office of Health Care, Office of Health Care Licensing /Medical Facilities Section, 1647 East Morten Avenue, Suite 160, Phoenix, AZ 85020; tel. 602/674–9750; FAX. 602/395–8913; Mary Madden, Program Manager

ARKANSAS: Division of Health Facility Services, Arkansas Department of Health, 5800 West 10th Street, Suite 4, Little Rock, AR 72204–9916; tel. 501/661–2201; FAX. 501/661–2468; Valetta M. Buck, Director

CALIFORNIA: Licensing and Certification, Department of Health Services, 1800 Third Street, Suite 210,, P.O. Box 942732, Sacramento, CA 94234–7320; tel. 916/445–2070; FAX. 916/445–6979; Brenda Klutz, Deputy Director

COLORADO: Health Facilities Division, Colorado Department of Public Health and Environment, 4300 Cherry Creek Drive, S., Denver, CO 80246–1530; tel. 303/692–2800; FAX. 303/782–4883; Paul Daraghy, Director

CONNECTICUT: Department of Public Health, Division of Health Systems Regulation, 410 Capitol Avenue, Hartford, CT 06134–0308; tel. 860/509–7400; FAX. 860/509–7543; Cynthia Denne, RN, MPA, Director

DELAWARE: Office of Health Facilities Licensing and Certification, Department of Health and Social Services, 2055 Limestone Road, Suite 200, Wilmington, DE 19808; tel. 302/995–8521; FAX. 302/995–8529; Ellen T. Reap, Director

DISTRICT OF COLUMBIA: Licensing Regulation Administration, 614 H Street, N.W., Suite 1003, Washington, DC 20001; tel. 202/727–7190; FAX. 202/727–7780; Geraldine K. Sykes

FLORIDA: Division of Health Quality Assurance, Hospital and Outpatient , Agency for Health Care Administration, 2727 Mahan Drive, Tallahassee, FL 32308; tel. 850/487–2717; FAX. 850/487–6240; Daryl Barowicz, Unit Manager

GEORGIA: Health Care Section, Office of Regulatory Services, Georgia Department of Human Resources, Two Peachtree Street, N.W., Room 33–250, Atlanta, GA 30303–3167; tel. 404/657–5550; FAX. 404/657–8934; Susie M. Woods, Director

HAWAII: Hawaii Department of Health, Hospital and Medical Facilities Branch, P.O. Box 3378, Honolulu, HI 96801; tel. 808/586–4080; FAX. 808/586–4747; Helen K. Yoshimi, B.S.N., M.P.H., Chief, HMFB

IDAHO: Bureau of Facility Standards, Department of Health and Welfare, P.O. Box 83720, Boise, ID 83720–0036; tel. 208/334–6626; FAX. 208/364–1888; Sylvia Creswell, Supervisor, Non–Long Term Care

ILLINOIS: Division of Health Care Facilities and Programs, Illinois Department of Public Health, 525 West Jefferson Street, Springfield, IL 62761; tel. 217/782–7412; FAX. 217/782–0382; Michelle Gentry–Wiseman, Chief

INDIANA: Division of Acute Care, Indiana State Department of Health, Two North Meridian Street, Indianapolis, IN 46204; tel. 317/233–7472; FAX. 317/233–7157; Mary Azbill, Director

IOWA: Division of Health Facilities, Iowa State Department of Inspections and Appeals, Lucas State Office Building, Des Moines, IA 50319; tel. 515/281–4115; FAX. 515/242–5022; David Werning, Media Relations

KANSAS: Kansas Department of Health and Environment, Bureau of Adult and Child Care, 900 Southwest Jackson, Suite 1, Topeka, KS 66612–1290; tel. 785/296–1280; FAX. 785/296–1266; George A. Dugger, Medical Facilities Certification Administrator

KENTUCKY: Division of Licensing and Regulation, Cabinet for Health Services, 275 East Main Street, 4E–A, Frankfort, KY 40621; tel. 502/564–2800; FAX. 502/564–6546; Rebecca J. Cecil, R.Ph., Director

LOUISIANA: Health Standards Section, Louisiana Department of Health and Hospitals, P.O. Box 3767, Baton Rouge, LA 70821; tel. 504/342–0415; FAX. 504/342–5292; Lisa Deaton, RN, Manager

MAINE: Division of Licensing and Certification, Department of Human Services, State House, Station 11, Augusta, ME 04333; tel. 207/624–5443; FAX. 207/624–5378; Louis Dorogi, Director

MARYLAND: Department of Health and Mental Hygiene, Licensing and Certification Administration, 4201 Patterson Avenue, Baltimore, MD 21215; tel. 410/764–4970; FAX. 410/358–0750; James L. Ralls, Assistant Director

MASSACHUSETTS: Massachusetts Department of Public Health, Division of Health Care Quality, 10 West Street, Fifth Floor, Boston, MA 02111; tel. 617/753–8000; FAX. 617/753–8125; Paul I. Dreyer, Ph.D., Director

MICHIGAN: Bureau of Health Systems, Michigan Department of Consumer and Industry Service, 525 West Ottawa, P.O. Box 30664, Lansing, MI 48909; tel. 517/334–8408; FAX. 517/334–8473; David A. Rector, Chief

MINNESOTA: Facility and Provider Compliance Division, Minnesota Department of Health, 85 East Seventh Place, P.O. Box 64900, St. Paul, MN 55164–0900; tel. 651/215–8700; FAX. 651/215–8710; Linda G. Sutherland, Director

MISSISSIPPI: Division of Health Facilities Licensure and Certification, Mississippi State Department of Health, P.O. Box 1700, Jackson, MS 39215; tel. 601/354–7300; FAX. 601/354–7230; Vanessa Phipps, Director

MISSOURI: Bureau of Health Facility Regulation, Missouri Department of Health, P.O. Box 570, Jefferson City, MO 65102; tel. 573/751–6303; FAX. 573/526–3621; Michele Reznicek, RN, Esq., Administrator

MONTANA: Division of Quality Assurance, Department of Public Health and Human Services, Cogswell Building, 1400 Broadway, Helena, MT 59620; tel. 406/444–2037; FAX. 406/444–1742; Denzel Davis, Administrator

NEBRASKA: Nebraska Department of Regulation and Licensure, Credentialing Division, 301 Centennial Mall, S., P.O. Box 95007, Lincoln, NE 68509–5007; tel. 402/471–2946; FAX. 402/471–3577; Helen Meeks, Director

NEVADA: Bureau of Licensure and Certification, Nevada Health Division, 1550 East College Parkway, Suite, Carson City, NV 89706–7921; tel. 775/687–4475; FAX. 775/687–6588; Richard J. Panelli, Chief

NEW HAMPSHIRE: Bureau of Health Facilities Administration, Office of Program Support, Licensure and Regulation, Health and Human Services Building, Six Hazen Drive, Concord, NH 03301; tel. 603/271–4966; FAX. 603/271–4968; Raymond Rusim, Bureau Chief

NEW JERSEY: Certificate of Need and Acute Care Licensing, N.J. Department of Health and Senior Services, P.O. Box 360, Trenton, NJ 08625–0360; tel. 609/292–8773; FAX. 609/292–3780; John Calabria, Director

NEW MEXICO: Department of Health, Health Facility Licensing & Certification Bureau Me, 525 Camino de los Marquez, Suite Two, Santa Fe, NM 87501; tel. 505/827–4200; FAX. 505/827–4203; Matthew Gervase, Bureau Chief

NEW YORK: New York State Department of Health, Bureau of Hospital and Primary Care Services, Hedley Park Place, Suite 303, 433 River Street, Troy, NY 12180–2299; tel. 518/402–1003; FAX. 518/402–1010; Frederick J. Heigel, Director

NORTH CAROLINA: Division of Facility Services, Department of Human Resources, 701 Barbour Drive, P.O. Box 29530, Raleigh, NC 27626–0530; tel. 919/733–1610; FAX. 919/733–3207; Steve White, Chief, Licensure and Certification

NORTH DAKOTA: Health Resources Section, State Department of Health, 600 East Boulevard Avenue, Bismarck, ND 58505–0200; tel. 701/328–2352; FAX. 701/328–1890; Darleen Bartz, Director

OHIO: Bureau of Quality Assessment and Improvement, Department of Health, P.O. Box 118, Columbus, OH 43266–0118; tel. 614/644–7230; FAX. 614/644–8661; Louis Pomerantz, Chief, Bureau of Quality Assessment a

OKLAHOMA: State Department of Health, 1000 Northeast 10th, Oklahoma City, OK 73117; tel. 405/271–4200; FAX. 405/271–3431; Jerry R. Nida, M.D., Commissioner

OREGON: Health Care Licensure and Certification, Oregon Health Division, P.O. Box 14450, Portland, OR 97293–0450; tel. 503/731–4013; FAX. 503/731–4080; Kathleen Smail, Manager

PENNSYLVANIA: Division of Acute and Ambulatory Care Facilities, Bureau of Quality Assurance, Health and Welfare Building, S, Harrisburg, PA 17120; tel. 717/783–8980; FAX. 717/772–2163; Dean F. Glick, Director

RHODE ISLAND: Rhode Island Department of Health, Division of Facilities Regulation, Three Capitol Hill, Providence, RI 02908–5097; tel. 401/222–2566; FAX. 401/222–3999; Wayne I. Farrington, Division Chief, Facilities Regulator

SOUTH CAROLINA: Department of Health and Environmental Control, Division of Health Licensing, 2600 Bull Street, Columbia, SC 29201; tel. 803/737–7370; FAX. 803/737–7212; Jerry Paul, Director

SOUTH DAKOTA: Office of Health Care Facilities Licensure and Certification, State Department of Health, Health Lab, 615 E. 4th Street, Pierre, SD 57501–1700; tel. 605/773–3356; FAX. 605/773–6667; Joan Bachman, Administrator

TENNESSEE: Tennessee Department of Health, Division of Health Care Facilities, 425 5th Avenue North, Cordell Hull, 1st Floor, Nashville, TN 37247–0508; tel. 615/741–7294; FAX. 615/741–7051; Ken Murray, Director

TEXAS: Health Facility Compliance Division, Texas Department of Health, 1100 West 49th Street, Austin, TX 78756–3199; tel. 512/834–6650; FAX. 512/834–6653; Nance Stearman, RN, M.S.N., Director

UTAH: Utah State Department of Health, Bureau of Licensing, Box 142003, Salt Lake City, UT 84114–2003; tel. 801/538–6152; FAX. 801/538–6325; Debra Wynkoop–Green, Director

Section C

VERMONT: Health Improvement, Vermont Department of Health, 108 Cherry Street, P.O. Box 70, Burlington, VT 05402; tel. 802/863–7606; FAX. 802/651–1634; Ellen B. Thompson, Planning Chief

VIRGINIA: Center for Quality Health Care Services and Consumer Protection, Virginia Department of Health, 3600 Centre, Suite 216, Richmond, VA 23230; tel. 804/367–2102; FAX. 804/367–2149; Nancy R. Hofheimer, Director

WASHINGTON: Acute Care and In–Home Services, Washington Department of Health, Target Plaza, Suite 500, 2725 Harrison Avenue,, Olympia, WA 98504–7852; tel. 360/705–6612; FAX. 360/705–6654; Byron Plan, Acute Care Manager

WEST VIRGINIA: Office of Health Facility Licensure and Certification, West Virginia Division of Health, State Capitol Complex, Building Three, Suite, Charleston, WV 25305; tel. 304/558–0050; FAX. 304/558–2515; John Wilkinson, Director

WISCONSIN: Bureau of Quality Assurance, Division of Supportive Living, Department of Health and Family Services, One West Wilson Street, P.O. Box 309, Madison, WI 53701–0309; tel. 608/267–7185; FAX. 608/267–0352; Rita Prigionit, Interim Director

WYOMING: Office of Health Quality, Health Facilities Licensing, 2020 Carey Avenue, Eighth Floor, Cheyenne, WY 82002; tel. 307/777–7123; FAX. 307/777–7127; K. Wagner, Nurse Administrator

Medical and Nursing Licensure Agencies

Information for the following list of state medical licensure agencies was obtained from the Federation of State Medical Board and nursing licensure agencies was obtained from the National League for Nursing.

United States

ALABAMA
Alabama Board of Nursing, RSA Plaza, Suite 250, 770 Washington Avenue, Montgomery, AL 36130–3900; tel. 334/242–4060; FAX. 334/242–4360; Lynn Norman, Interim Executive Officer

Alabama State Board of Medical Examiners, 848 Washington Avenue, Zip 36104, P.O. Box 946, Montgomery, AL 36101–0946; tel. 334/242–4116; FAX. 334/242–4155; Larry D. Dixon, Executive Director

ALASKA
Alaska Board of Nursing, Division of Occupational Licensing, 3601 C Street, Suite 722, Anchorage, AK 99503; tel. 907/269–8161; FAX. 907/269–8156; Dorothy Fulton, Executive Secretary

Alaska State Medical Board, Division of Occupational Licensing, 3601 C Street, Suite 722, Anchorage, AK 99503; tel. 907/269–8163; FAX. 907/269–8196; Leslie G. Abel, Executive Administrator

ARIZONA
Arizona Board of Osteopathic Examiners in Medicine and Surgery, AZ Osteopathic Examiners in Medicine and Surgery, 9535 E. Doubletree Ranch Road, Scottsdale, AZ 85258; tel. 602/657–7703; FAX. 602/657–7715; Ann Marie Berger, Executive Director

Arizona State Board of Medical Examiners, 1651 East Morton, Suite 210, Phoenix, AZ 85020; tel. 602/255–3751; FAX. 602/255–1848; Claudia Fontz, Executive Director

Arizona State Board of Nursing, 1651 East Morten, Suite 150, Phoenix, AZ 85020; tel. 602/331–8111; FAX. 602/906–9365; Joey Ridenour, RN, M.N., Executive Director

ARKANSAS
Arkansas State Board of Nursing, University Tower Building, Suite 800, 1123 South University Avenue, Little Rock, AR 72204; tel. 501/686–2700; FAX. 501/686–2714; Faith A. Fields, M.S.N., RN, Executive Director

Arkansas State Medical Board, 2100 Riverfront Drive, Suite 200, Little Rock, AR 72202; tel. 501/296–1802; FAX. 501/296–1805; Peggy P. Cryer, Executive Secretary

CALIFORNIA
California Board of Registered Nursing, 400 R Street, Suite 4030, Zip 95814, Sacramento, CA 94244–2100; tel. 916/322–3350; FAX. 916/227–4402; Ruth Ann Terry, RN, M.P.H., Executive Officer

Medical Board of California, 1426 Howe Avenue, Suite 54, Sacramento, CA 95825; tel. 916/263–2344; FAX. 916/263–2487; Ron Joseph, Executive Director

Osteopathic Medical Board of California, 444 North Third Street, Suite A–200, Sacramento, CA 95814; tel. 916/322–4306; FAX. 916/327–6119; Linda J. Bergmann, Executive Director

COLORADO
Colorado State Board of Medical Examiners, 1560 Broadway, Suite 1300, Denver, CO 80202–5140; tel. 303/894–7690; FAX. 303/894–7692; Susan Miller, Program Administrator

Colorado State Board of Nursing, 1560 Broadway, Suite 670, Denver, CO 80202; tel. 303/894–2430; FAX. 303/894–2821; Patricia Uris, RN, Ph.D., Program Administrator

CONNECTICUT
Connecticut Board of Examiners for Nursing, Department of Public Health, 410 Capitol Avenue, MS #12 HSR, P.O. Box 340308, Hartford, CT 06134–0308; tel. 860/509–7624; FAX. 860/509–7286; Wendy H. Furniss, RNC., M.S., Public Health Services Manager

Connecticut Department of Public Health, 410 Capitol Avenue, MS #12 APP, P.O. Box 340308, Hartford, CT 06134–0308; tel. 860/509–7563; FAX. 860/509–8457; Debra J. Tomassone, Public Health Service Manager

DELAWARE
Delaware Board of Medical Practice, Cannon Building, 861 Silver Lake Boulevard, Suite 203, Dover, DE 19901; tel. 302/739–4522; FAX. 302/739–2711; Gail Melvin, Interim Executive Director

Delaware Board of Nursing, Cannon Building, Suite 203, 861 Silver Lake Boulevard, Suite 203, Dover, DE 19904; tel. 302/739–4522; FAX. 302/739–2711; Iva J. Boardman, RN, M.S.N., Executive Director

DISTRICT OF COLUMBIA
District of Columbia Board of Medicine, 825 North Capital Street, NE, 2nd Floor, Washington, DC 20002; tel. 202/727–5365; FAX. 202/727–4087; James R. Granger, Jr., Executive Director

District of Columbia Board of Nursing, 614 H Street, N.W., Washington, DC 20001; tel. 202/727–7461; FAX. 202/727–8030; Barbara Hatcher, Chairperson

FLORIDA
Florida Board of Medicine, 2020 Capital Circle S.E., Bin #C03, Tallahassee, FL 32399–3253; tel. 850/488–3622; FAX. 850/922–3040; Tonya Williams, Board Director

Florida Board of Osteopathic Medicine, 2020 Capital Circle, SE, Bin #6, Tallahassee, FL 32399–3256; tel. 850/488–0595; FAX. 904/921–6184; Pamela King

Florida State Board of Nursing, 4080 Woodcock Drive, Suite 202, Jacksonville, FL 32207; tel. 904/858–6940; FAX. 904/858–6964; Marilyn A. Bloss, RNC, M.S.N., Executive Director

GEORGIA
Georgia Board of Nursing, 166 Pryor Street, S.W., Atlanta, GA 30303; tel. 404/656–3943; FAX. 404/657–7489; Shirley A. Camp, RN, J.D., Executive Director

Georgia Composite State Board of Medical Examiners, 166 Pryor Street, S.W., Atlanta, GA 30303; tel. 404/656–3913; FAX. 404/656–9723; Greg W. Schader, Acting Executive Director

HAWAII
Hawaii Board of Medical Examiners, Department of Commerce and Consumer Affairs, 1010 Richards Street, Zip 96813, P.O. Box 3469, Honolulu, HI 96801; tel. 808/586–3000; Constance Cabral–Makanani, Executive Officer

Hawaii Board of Nursing, P.O. Box 3469, Honolulu, HI 96801; tel. 808/586–3000; FAX. 808/586–2689; Kathy Yokouchi, Executive Officer

IDAHO
Idaho State Board of Medicine, 280 North Eighth Street, Suite 202, Boise, ID 83720–0058; tel. 208/334–2822; FAX. 203/334–2801; Darleen Thorsted, Executive Director

Idaho State Board of Nursing, 280 North Eighth Street, Suite 210, P.O. Box 83720, Boise, ID 83720–0061; tel. 208/334–3110; FAX. 208/334–3262; Sandra Evans, Executive Director

ILLINOIS
Illinois Department of Professional Regulation, 320 West Washington Street, Springfield, IL 62786; tel. 217/782–0458; FAX. 217/782–7645; Tony Sanders, Public Information Officer

Illinois Department of Professional Regulation, James R. Thompson Center, 100 West Randolph Street, Suite 9–300, Chicago, IL 60601; tel. 312/814–4500; FAX. 312/814–1837; Leonard A. Sherman, Director

INDIANA
Indiana Health Professions Bureau, Medical Licensing Board of Indiana, 402 West Washington, Suite 041, Indianapolis, IN 46204; tel. 317/233–4401; FAX. 317/233–4236; Laura Langford, Executive Director

Indiana State Board of Nursing, Health Professions Bureau, 402 West Washington, Suite 041, Indianapolis, IN 46204; tel. 317/233–4405; FAX. 317/233–4236; Gina Voorhies, Board Administrator

IOWA
Iowa Board of Nursing, State Capitol Complex, 1223 East Court Avenue, Des Moines, IA 50319; tel. 515/281–3255; FAX. 515/281–4825; Lorinda K. Inman, RN, M.S.N., Executive Director

Iowa State Board of Medical Examiners, Executive Hills West, 1209 East Court Avenue, Des Moines, IA 50319–0180; tel. 515/281–5171; FAX. 515/242–5908; Ann M. Martino, Ph.D., Executive Director

KANSAS
Kansas State Board of Healing Arts, 235 Southwest Topeka Boulevard, Topeka, KS 66603–3068; tel. 913/296–7413; FAX. 913/296–0852; Lawrence T. Buening, Jr., J.D., Executive Director

Kansas State Board of Nursing, Landon State Office Building, 900 Southwest, Topeka, KS 66612–1230; tel. 785/296–4929; FAX. 785/296–3929; Patsy Johnson, RN, M.N., Executive Administrator

KENTUCKY
Kentucky Board of Medical Licensure, The Hurstbourne Office Park, 310 Whittington Parkway, Suite 1B, Louisville, KY 40222; tel. 502/429–8046; FAX. 502/429–9923; C. William Schmidt, Executive Director

Kentucky Board of Nursing, 312 Whittington Parkway, Suite 300, Louisville, KY 40222; tel. 502/329–7000; FAX. 502/329–7011; Sharon M. Weisenbeck, M.S., RN, Executive Director

LOUISIANA
Louisiana State Board of Medical Examiners, P.O. Box 30250, New Orleans, LA 70190–0250; tel. 504/524–6763; FAX. 504/568–8893; Mrs. Delmar Rorison, Executive Director

Louisiana State board of Nursing, 912 Pere Marquette Building, New Orleans, LA 70112; tel. 504/568–5464; FAX. 504/568–5467; Barbara L. Morvant, RN, M.N., Executive Director

MAINE
Maine Board of Licensure in Medicine, Two Bangor Street, 137 State House Station, Augusta, ME 04333–0137; tel. 207/287–3601; FAX. 207/287–6590; Randal C. Manning, Executive Director

Maine Board of Osteopathic Licensure, 142 State House Station, Two Bangor Street, Augusta, ME 04333–0142; tel. 207/287–2480; FAX. 207/287–2480; Susan E. Stout, Executive Secretary

Maine State Board of Nursing, 24 Stone Street, 158 State House Station, Augusta, ME 04333; tel. 207/287–1133; FAX. 207/287–1149; Myra A. Broadway, J.D., MS, RN, Executive Director

MARYLAND
Maryland Board of Nursing, 4140 Patterson Avenue, Baltimore, MD 21215; tel. 410/585–1900; FAX. 410/358–3530; Donna M. Dorsey, RN, M.S., Executive Director

Maryland Board of Physician Quality Assurance, 4201 Patterson Avenue, Third Floor, P.O. Box 2571, Baltimore, MD 21215–0095; tel. 800/492–6836; FAX. 410/358–2252; J. Michael Compton, Executive Director

MASSACHUSETTS
Massachusetts Board of Registration in Medicine, 10 West Street, Third Floor, Boston, MA 02111; tel. 617/727–3086; FAX. 617/451–9568; Alexander F. Fleming, J.D., Executive Director

Massachusetts Board of Registration in Nursing, 100 Cambridge Street, Suite 1519, Boston, MA 02202; tel. 617/727–9961; FAX. 617/727–1630; Theresa M. Bonanno, M.S.N., RN, Executive Director

MICHIGAN
Michigan Board of Medicine, 611 West Ottawa Street, Fourth Floor, Box 30670, Lansing, MI 48909; tel. 517/373–6873; FAX. 517/373–2179; Carole Hakala Engle, Director of Licensing

Michigan Board of Nursing, Department of Consumer and Industry Service, 611 West Ottawa Street, P.O. Box 30670, Lansing, MI 48909; tel. 517/335–0918; FAX. 517/373–2179; Doris Foley, Licensing Administrator

Michigan Board of Osteopathic Medicine and Surgery, 611 West Ottawa Street, Fourth Floor, P.O. Box 30670, Lansing, MI 48909; tel. 517/335–0918; FAX. 517/373–2179; Brenda Rogers, Assistant Administrator

MINNESOTA

Minnesota Board of Medical Practice, 2829 University Avenue, S.E., Suite 400, Minneapolis, MN 55414–3246; tel. 612/617–2130; FAX. 612/617–2166; Robert A. Leach, Executive Director

Minnesota Board of Nursing, 2829 University Avenue, S.E., Suite 500, Minneapolis, MN 55414–3253; tel. 612/617–2270; FAX. 612/617–2190; Joyce M. Schowalter, Executive Director

MISSISSIPPI

Mississippi Board of Nursing, 1935 Lakeland Drive, Suite B, Jackson, MS 39216–5014; tel. 601/987–4188; FAX. 601/364–2352; Marcia M. Rachel, Ph.D., RN, Executive Director

Mississippi State Board of Medical Licensure, 2600 Insurance Center Drive, Suite 200–B, Jackson, MS 39216; tel. 601/987–3079; FAX. 601/987–4159; W. Joseph Burnett, M.D., Executive Director

MISSOURI

Missouri State Board of Nursing, 3605 Missouri Boulevard, P.O. Box 656, Jefferson City, MO 65102; tel. 573/751–0681; FAX. 573/751–0075; JoAnn Hanley, Executive Assistant

Missouri State Board of Registration for the Healing Arts, 3605 Missouri Boulevard, Zip 65109, P.O. Box Four, Jefferson City, MO 65102; tel. 314/751–0098; FAX. 314/751–3166; Tina M. Steinman, Executive Director

MONTANA

Montana Board of Medical Examiners, 111 North Jackson, P.O. Box 200513, Helena, MT 59620–0513; tel. 406/444–4284; FAX. 406/444–9396; Patricia I. England, J.D., Executive Secretary

Montana State Board of Nursing, 111 North Jackson–4C, P.O. Box 200513, Helena, MT 59620–0513; tel. 406/444–2071; FAX. 406/444–7759; Joan Bowers, Administrative Assistant

NEBRASKA

Nebraska State Board of Examiners in Medicine and Surgery, 301 Centennial Mall, S., P.O. Box 94986, Lincoln, NE 68509–4986; tel. 402/471–2118; FAX. 402/471–3577; Katherine A. Brown, Executive Secretary

NEVADA

Nevada State Board of Medical Examiners, 1105 Terminal Way, Suite 301, Zip 89502, P.O. Box 7238, Reno, NV 89510; tel. 702/688–2559; FAX. 702/688–2321; Larry D. Lessly, Executive Director

Nevada State Board of Nursing, 1755 East Plum Lane, Suite 260, Las Vegas, NV 89103; tel. 775/688–2620; FAX. 775/688–2628; Kathy Apple, Executive Director

Nevada State Board of Osteopathic Medicine, 2950 East Flamingo Road, Suite E–3, Las Vegas, NV 89121; tel. 702/732–2147; FAX. 702/732–2079; Larry J. Tarno, D.O., Executive Director

NEW HAMPSHIRE

New Hampshire Board of Medicine, Two Industrial Park Drive, Suite Eight, Concord, NH 03301; tel. 603/271–1203; FAX. 603/271–6702; Allen Hall, Administrator

New Hampshire State Board of Nursing, 78 Regional Drive, P.O. Box 3898, Concord, NH 03302–3898; tel. 603/271–2323; FAX. 603/271–6605; Doris G. Nuttelman, RN, Ed.D., Executive Director

NEW JERSEY

New Jersey Board of Nursing, P.O. Box 3898, Newark, NJ 07101; tel. 973/504–6430; FAX. 973/648–3481; Patricia A. Polansky, Executive Director

New Jersey State Board of Medical Examiners, 140 East Front Street, Second Floor, Trenton, NJ 08608; tel. 609/826–7100; FAX. 609/984–3930; Kevin B. Earle, Executive Director

NEW MEXICO

New Mexico Board of Osteopathic Medical Examiners, 2055 S. Pacheco, P.O. Box 25101, Santa Fe, NM 87504; tel. 505/827–7171; FAX. 505/827–7095; Liz Z. Montoya

New Mexico State Board of Medical Examiners, 491 Old Santa Fe Trail, Lamy Building, Second Floor, Santa Fe, NM 87501; tel. 505/827–5022; FAX. 505/827–7377; Kristen A. Hedrick, Executive Secretary

State of New Mexico, Board of Nursing, 4206 Louisiana, N.E., Suite A, Albuquerque, NM 87109; tel. 505/841–8340; FAX. 505/841–8347; Nancy L. Twigg, Executive Director

NEW YORK

New York Board for Professional Medical Conduct, State Department of Health, 433 River Street, Suite 303, Troy, NY 12180–2299; tel. 518/402–0855; FAX. 518/402–0866; Anne F. Saile, Director

New York State Board for Nursing, State Education Department, The Cultural Center, Suite 3023, Albany, NY 12230; tel. 518/474–3845; FAX. 518/474–3706; Milene A. Sowers, Ph.D., RN, Executive Secretary

New York State Division of Professional Licensing Services, Cultural Education Center, Suite 3000, Empire State Plaza, Albany, NY 12230; tel. 518/474–3817; FAX. 518/473–0578; Robert G. Bentley, Director, Professional Licensing

NORTH CAROLINA

North Carolina Board of Nursing, P.O. Box 2129, Raleigh, NC 27602–2129; tel. 919/782–3211; FAX. 919/781–9461; Mary P. Johnson, RN, MSN, Executive Director

North Carolina Medical Board, P.O. Box 20007, Raleigh, NC 27619; tel. 919/326–1100; FAX. 919/326–1130; Andrew W. Watry, Executive Director

NORTH DAKOTA

North Dakota Board of Nursing, 919 South Seventh Street, Suite 504, Bismarck, ND 58504–5881; tel. 701/328–9777; FAX. 701/328–9785; Constance Kalanek, RN, Executive Director

North Dakota State Board of Medical Examiners, City Center Plaza, Suite 12, 418 East Broadway Avenue, Bismarck, ND 58501; tel. 701/328–6500; FAX. 701/328–6505; Rolf P. Sletten, Executive Secretary–Treasurer

OHIO

Ohio Board of Nursing, 77 South High Street, 17th Floor, Columbus, OH 43266–0316; tel. 614/466–3947; FAX. 614/466–0388; Dorothy Fiorino, RN, Executive Director

State Medical Board of Ohio, 77 South High Street, 17th Floor, Columbus, OH 43266–0315; tel. 614/466–3934; FAX. 614/728–5946; Ray Q. Bumgarner, Executive Director

OKLAHOMA

Oklahoma Board of Nursing, 2915 North Classen Boulevard, Suite 524, Oklahoma City, OK 73106; tel. 405/962–1800; FAX. 405/962–1821; Norma Wallace, Executive Secretary

Oklahoma Board of Osteopathic Examiners, 4848 North Lincoln Boulevard, Suite 100, Oklahoma City, OK 73105–3321; tel. 405/528–8625; FAX. 405/557–0653; Gary R. Clark, Executive Director

Oklahoma State Board of Medical Licensure and Supervision, 5104 North Francis, Suite C, Oklahoma City, OK 73118, Oklahoma City, OK 73154–0256; tel. 405/848–6841; FAX. 405/848–8240; Lyle Kelsey, Executive Director

OREGON

Oregon Board of Medical Examiners, 620 Crown Plaza, Portland, OR 97201–5826; tel. 503/229–5770; FAX. 503/229–6543; Kathleen Haley, J.D., Executive Director

Oregon State Board of Nursing, 800 Northeast Oregon Street, Suite 465, Portland, OR 97232–2162; tel. 503/731–4745; FAX. 503/731–4755; Joan C. Bouchard, Executive Director

PENNSYLVANIA

Pennsylvania State Board of Medicine, P.O. Box 2649, Harrisburg, PA 17105–2649; tel. 717/783–1400; FAX. 717/787–7769; Cindy L. Warner, Administrative Officer

Pennsylvania State Board of Nursing, Department of State, P.O. Box 2649, Harrisburg, PA 17105–2649; tel. 717/783–7142; FAX. 717/783–0822; Miriam H. Limo, Executive Secretary

Pennsylvania State Board of Osteopathic Medicine, P.O. Box 2649, Harrisburg, PA 17105–2649; tel. 717/783–4858; FAX. 717/787–7769; Gina Bittner, Administrative Assistant

RHODE ISLAND

Board of Nursing Education and Nurse Registration, Three Capitol Hill, Room 104, Providence, RI 02908–5097; tel. 401/222–1827; FAX. 401/222–1272; Carol Lietar, RN, M.S.N., Director

Rhode Island Board of Medical Licensure and Discipline, Rhode Island Department of Health, Room 205, 3 Capitol Hill, Providence, RI 02908–5097; tel. 401/222–3855; FAX. 401/222–2158; Milton W. Hamolsky, M.D., Chief Administrative Officer

SOUTH CAROLINA

Department of Labor, Licensing and Regulation, State Board of Nursing for South Carolina, 110 Centerview Drive, Columbia, SC 29211; tel. 803/896–4550; FAX. 803/896–4525; Nancy Carlson, Board of Administrative Assistant

South Carolina Department of Labor, Licensing and Regulation, Board of Medical Examiners, 110 Centerview Drive, Suite 202, Columbia, S.C. 29210, Columbia, SC 29211–1289; tel. 803/896–4500; FAX. 803/896–4545; Aaron Kozloski, J.D., Board Administrator

SOUTH DAKOTA

South Dakota Board of Nursing, 4300 South Louise Avenue, Sioux Falls, SD 57106; tel. 605/362–2760; FAX. 605/362–2768; Diana Vander Woude, Executive Secretary

South Dakota State Board of Medical and Osteopathic Examiners, 1323 South Minnesota Avenue, Sioux Falls, SD 57105; tel. 605/336–1965; FAX. 605/336–0270; Robert D. Johnson, Executive Secretary

TENNESSEE

Tennessee Board of Nursing, Cordell Hull Building, 1st Floor, 425 Fifth avenue, N, Nashville, TN 37247; tel. 888/310–4650; FAX. 615/741–7899; Elizabeth J. Lund, RN, Executive Director

Tennessee State Board of Medical Examiners, Cordell Hull Building, 425 Fifth Avenue, N, First Floor, Nashville, TN 37247–1010; tel. 888/310–4650; FAX. 615/532–5369; Yarnell Beatty, Director

Tennessee State Board of Osteopathic Examination, First Floor, Cordell Hull Building, 425 Fifth Avenue, N., Nashville, TN 37247–1010; tel. 615/532–5080; FAX. 615/532–5369; Vickie Penterart, Administrator

TEXAS

Texas Board of Nurse Examiners, P.O. Box 430, Austin, TX 78767–0430; tel. 512/305–7400; FAX. 512/305–7401; Katherine Thomas, MN, RN, Executive Director

Texas State Board of Medical Examiners, 333 Guadalupe, Tower Three, Suite 610, P.O. Box 2018, Austin, TX 78768–7008; tel. 512/305–7010; FAX. 512/305–7008; Bruce A. Levy, M.D., J.D., Executive Director

UTAH

Utah Physicians Licensing Board, Division of Occupational and Professional Licensure, Heber M. Wells Building, Fourth Floor, 160 East 300 South, Salt Lake City, UT 84114–6741; tel. 801/530–6628; FAX. 801/530–6511; Karen Reimherr, Bureau Manager

Utah State Board of Nursing, 160 East 300 South, Box 146741, Salt Lake City, UT 84114–6741; tel. 801/530–6628; FAX. 801/530–6511; Laura Poe, Executive Administrator

VERMONT

Vermont Board of Medical Practice, 109 State Street, Montpelier, VT 05609–1106; tel. 802/828–2673; FAX. 802/828–5450; Barbara Neuman, J.D., Executive Director

Vermont Board of Nursing Licensure and Regulation Division, 109 State Street, Montpelier, VT 05609–1106; tel. 802/828–2396; FAX. 802/828–2484; Anita Ristau, RN, M.S., Executive Director

Vermont Board of Osteopathic Physicians and Surgeons, 26 Terrace Street, Drawer 09, Montpelier, VT 05609–1106; tel. 802/828–2373; FAX. 802/828–2465; Peggy Atkins, Staff Assistant

VIRGINIA

Virginia Board of Medicine, 6606 West Broad Street, Fourth Floor, Richmond, VA 23230–1717; tel. 804/662–9908; FAX. 804/662–9517; Warren W. Koontz, Jr., M.D., Executive Director

Virginia Board of Nursing, 6606 West Broad Street, Fourth Floor, Richmond, VA 23230; tel. 804/662–9909; FAX. 804/662–7512; Nancy K. Durrett, RN, Executive Director

WASHINGTON

Washington State Board of Osteopathic Medicine and Surgery, Department of Health, 1300 Southeast Quince Street, P.O. Box 47870, Olympia, WA 98504–7870; tel. 360/236–4943; FAX. 360/586–0745; Karen T. Maasjo, Administrative Assistant

Washington State Medical Quality Assurance Commission, 1300 Southeast Quince Street, P.O. Box 47866, Olympia, WA 98504–7866; tel. 360/236–4800; FAX. 360/586–4573; Bonnie L. King, Executive Director

Washington State Nursing Care Quality Assurance Commission, Department of Health, 1300 Southeast Quince Street, P.O. Box 47864, Olympia, WA 98504–7864; tel. 360/236–4713; FAX. 360/586–5935; Patty L. Hayes, RN, M.N., Executive Director

WEST VIRGINIA

West Virginia Board of Examiners for Registered Professional Nurses, 101 Dee Drive, Charleston, WV 25311–1620; tel. 304/558–3596; FAX. 304/558–3666; Laura S. Rhodes, RN, M.S.N., Executive Secretary

West Virginia Board of Medicine, 101 Dee Drive, Charleston, WV 25311; tel. 304/558–2921; FAX. 304/558–2084; Ronald D. Walton, Executive Director

West Virginia Board of Osteopathy, 334 Penco Road, Weirton, WV 26062; tel. 304/723–4638; FAX. 304/723–2877; Cheryl D. Schreiber, Executive Secretary

WISCONSIN

Division of Health Professions and Services Licensing, 1400 East Washington Avenue, Room 178, P.O. Box 8935, Madison, WI 53708–8935; tel. 608/266–2911; FAX. 608/266–0145; Patrick D. Brastr, Division Director

Wisconsin Medical Examining Board, 1400 East Washington Avenue, Zip 53702, P.O. Box 8935, Madison, WI 53708; tel. 608/266–2811; FAX. 608/261–7083; Patrick D. Braatz, Administrator

WYOMING

Wyoming Board of Medicine, The Colony Building, 211 West 19th Street, Cheyenne, WY 82002; tel. 307/778–7053; FAX. 307/778–2069; Carole Shotwell, Executive Secretary

Wyoming State Board of Nursing, 2020 Carey Avenue, Suite 110, Cheyenne, WY 82002; tel. 307/777–7601; FAX. 307/777–3519; Toma A. Nisbet, RN, M.S., Executive Director

U.S. Associated Areas

AMERICAN SAMOA

American Samoa Health Services Regulatory Board, LBJ Tropical Medical Center, Pago Pago, AS 96799; tel. 684/633–5995; FAX. 684/633–1869; Etenauga L. Lutu, RN, Executive Secretary

GUAM

Guam Board of Medical Examiners, 1304 East Sunset Boulevard, Barrigada, GU 96913; tel. 671/475–0251; FAX. 671/477–4733; Teofila P. Cruz, Administrator

Guam Board of Nurse Examiners, Department of Public Health and Social Serv, 1304 East Sunset Boulevard, Barrigada (Tiyan), Guam, P.O. Box 2816, Agana, GU 96910; tel. 671/475–0251; FAX. 671/477–4733; Teofila P. Cruz, RN, M.S., Administrator

PUERTO RICO

Council on Higher Education of Puerto Rico, UPR Station, P.O. Box 23305, San Juan, PR 00931–3305; tel. 809/758–3356; Madeline Quilichini Paz, Director, Office of Licensing

Puerto Rico Board of Medical Examiners, Kennedy Avenue, ILA Building, Hogar del Obrero Portuario, Piso 8, Puerto, San Juan, PR 00908; tel. 787/782–8989; FAX. 787/782–8733; Ivonne M. Fernandez, Executive Director

VIRGIN ISLANDS

Virgin Islands Board of Medical Examiners, Virgin Islands Department of Health, 48 Sugar Estate, St. Thomas, VI 00802; tel. 809/774–0117; FAX. 809/777–4001; Lydia T. Scott, Executive Assistant to the Boards

Virgin Islands Board of Nursing Licensure, P.O. Box 4247, St. Thomas, VI 00803; tel. 809/776–7397; FAX. 809/777–4003; Winifred L. Garfield, CRNA, Executive Secretary

Canada

ALBERTA

College of Physicians and Surgeons of Alberta, 900 Manulife Place, 10180–101 Street, Edmonton, AB T5J 4P8; tel. 780/423–4764; FAX. 780/420–0651; Dr. L.R. Ohlhauser, Registrar

MANITOBA

College of Physicians and Surgeons of Manitoba, 494 St. James Street, Winnipeg, MB R3G 3J4; tel. 204/774–4344; FAX. 204/774–0750; Kenneth R. Brown, M.D., Registrar

NEW BRUNSWICK

College of Physicians and Surgeons of New Brunswick, One Hampton Road, Rothesay, NB E2E 5K8; tel. 506/849–5050; FAX. 506/849–5069; Dr. Ed Schollenberg, Registrar

NOVA SCOTIA

College of Physicians and Surgeons of Nova Scotia, Office of the Registrar, 5248 Morris Street, Halifax, NS B3J 1B4; tel. 902/422–5823; FAX. 902/422–5035; Dr. Cameron Little, Registrar

PRINCE EDWARD ISLAND

College of Physicians and Surgeons of Prince Edward Island, 199 Grafton Street, Charlottetown, PE C1A 1L2; tel. 902/566–3861; FAX. 902/566–3861; H. E. Ross, M.D., Registrar

QUEBEC

College des medecins du Quebec, 2170, boul. Rene–Levesque Quest, Montreal, PQ H3H 2T8; tel. 514/933–4441; FAX. 514/933–3112; Joelle Lescop, M.D., Secretary General

SASKATCHEWAN

College of Physicians and Surgeons of Saskatchewan, 211 Fourth Avenue, S., Saskatoon, SK S7K 1N1; tel. 306/244–7355; FAX. 306/244–0090; D. A. Kendel, M.D., Registrar

Peer Review Organizations

The following list of PROs was obtained from the Office of Medical Review, Division of Program Operation, HCFA. For more information, contact the office at 410/786–8781.

United States

ALABAMA: Alabama Quality Assurance Foundation, One Perimeter Park, S., Suite 200 North, Birmingham, AL 35243–2354; tel. 205/970–1600; FAX. 205/970–1616; H. Terrell Lindsey, President and CEO

ARIZONA: Health Services Advisory Group, Inc., 301 East Bethany Home Road, Suite B–1, Phoenix, AZ 85012; tel. 602/264–6382; FAX. 602/241–0757; Lawrence J. Shapiro, M.D., President and CEO

ARKANSAS: Arkansas Foundation for Medical Care, Inc., 2201 Brooken Hill Drive, P.O. Box 180001, Fort Smith, AR 72918–0001; tel. 501/649–8501; FAX. 501/649–8180; Russell G. Brasher, Ph.D., Chief Executive Officer

CALIFORNIA: California Medical Review, Inc., One Sansome Street, Suite 600, San Francisco, CA 94104; tel. 415/677–2000; FAX. 415/677–2195; Jo Ellen H. Ross, Chief Executive Officer

COLORADO: Colorado Foundation for Medical Care, 2851 South Parker Road, Suite 200, Aurora, CO 80014–2713; tel. 303/695–3300; FAX. 303/695–3350; Arja P. Adair, Jr., Executive Director

CONNECTICUT: Connecticut Peer Review Organization, Inc., 100 Roscommon Drive, Suite 200, Middletown, CT 06457; tel. 860/632–2008; FAX. 860/632–5865; Marcia K. Petrillo, Chief Executive Officer
Rhode Island Quality Partners, Inc. (C/O CT PRO), 100 Roscommon Drive, Suite 200, Middletown, CT 06457; tel. 860/632–2008; FAX. 860/632–5865; Marcia K. Petrillo, Chief Executive Officer

FLORIDA: Florida Medical Quality Assurance, Inc., 4350 West Cypress Street, Suite 900, Tampa, FL 33607; tel. 813/354–9111; FAX. 813/354–0737; Jennifer Barnett, President and CEO

GEORGIA: Georgia Medical Care Foundation, 57 Executive Park, S., Suite 200, Atlanta, GA 30329; tel. 404/982–0411; FAX. 404/982–7584; Tom W. Williams, Chief Executive Officer

HAWAII: Mountain–Pacific Quality Health Foundation, 1360 South Beretania Street, Suite 400, Honolulu, HI 96814; tel. 808/545–2550; FAX. 808/599–2875; Dee Nelson, Director of Hawaii Office

INDIANA: Health Care Excel, Incorporated, 2901 Ohio Boulevard, P.O. Box 3713, Terre Haute, IN 47803; tel. 812/234–1499; FAX. 812/232–6167; Philip L. Morphew, Chief Executive Officer

IOWA: Iowa Foundation for Medical Care/The Sunderbruch Corporation – Nebraska, Illinois Foundation for Quality Health Care, 6000 Westown Parkway, Suite 350E, West Des Moines, IA 50266–7771; tel. 515/223–2900; FAX. 515/222–2407; Rebecca Hemann, VP Government Quality Improvement Program
Iowa Foundation for Medical Care/The Sunderbruch Corporation/, Illinois Foundation for Quality Health, 6000 Westown Parkway, Suite 350E, West Des Moines, IA 50266–7771; tel. 515/223–2900; FAX. 515/222–2407; Fred A. Ferree, Executive Vice President
Iowa Foundation for Medical Care/The Sunderbruch Corporation/, Illinois Foundation for Quality Health, 6000 Westown Parkway, Suite 350E, West Des Moines, IA 50266–7771; tel. 515/223–2900; FAX. 515/222–2407; Fred Ferree, Executive Vice President

KANSAS: The Kansas Foundation for Medical Care, Inc., 2947 Southwest Wanamaker Drive, Topeka, KS 66614; tel. 785/273–2552; FAX. 785/273–5130; Larry Pitman, President and CEO

KENTUCKY: Health Care Excel, Incorporated, 9502 Williamsburg Plaza, Suite 102, P.O. Box 23540, Louisville, KY 40222; tel. 502/339–7442; FAX. 502/339–8641; Philip L. Morphew, Chief Executive Officer

LOUISIANA: Louisiana Health Care Review, Inc., 8591 United Plaza Boulevard, Suite 270, Baton Rouge, LA 70809; tel. 504/926–6353; FAX. 504/923–0957; Leo Stanley, Chief Executive Officer

MARYLAND: Delmarva Foundation for Medical Care, Inc., 9240 Centreville Road, Easton, MD 21601; tel. 410/822–0697; FAX. 410/822–9572; Thomas J. Schaefer, Chief Executive Officer
Delmarva Foundation for Medical Care, Inc., 9240 Centreville Road, Easton, MD 21601; tel. 410/822–0697; FAX. 410/822–7971; Thomas J. Schaefer, Chief Executive Officer

MASSACHUSETTS: Massachusetts Peer Review Organization, Inc., 235 Wyman Street, Waltham, MA 02154–1231; tel. 781/890–0011; FAX. 781/487–0083; Kathleen E. McCarthy, President and CEO

MICHIGAN: Michigan Peer Review Organization, 40600 Ann Arbor Road, Suite 200, Plymouth, MI 48170–4495; tel. 313/459–0900; FAX. 313/454–7301; Sheryl L. Stogis, Chief Executive Officer

MINNESOTA: Stratis Health, 2901 Metro Drive, Suite 400, Bloomington, MN 55425; tel. 612/854–3306; FAX. 612/853–8503; David M. Ziegenhagen, Chief Executive Officer

MISSISSIPPI: I.Q.H., Information & Quality Healthcare, 735 Riverside Drive, P.O. Box 4665, Jackson, MS 39296–4665; tel. 601/948–8894; FAX. 601/948–8917; James McIlwain, M.D.

MISSOURI: Missouri Patient Care Review Foundation, 505 Hobbs Road, Suite 100, Jefferson City, MO 65109; tel. 573/893–7900; FAX. 573/893–5827; Sara A. Grim, MHA, CHE, Chief Executive Officer

MONTANA: Mountain Pacific Quality Health Foundation, 400 North Park Avenue, Second Floor, Helena, MT 59601; tel. 406/443–4020; FAX. 406/443–4585; Steve Wallace, M.D., President
Mountain–Pacific Quality Health Foundation, 400 North Park Avenue, Second Floor, Helena, MT 59601; tel. 406/443–4020; FAX. 406/443–4585; Janice Connors, Executive Director

NEW HAMPSHIRE: Northeast Health Care Quality Foundation, 15 Old Rollinsford Road, Suite 302, Dover, NH 03820–2830; tel. 603/749–1641; FAX. 603/749–1195; Robert A. Aurilio, Chief Executive Officer

NEW JERSEY: The Peer Review Organization of New Jersey, Inc., Central Division, 557 Cranbury Road, Suite 21, East Brunswick, NJ 08816; tel. 732/238–5570; FAX. 732/238–7766; Martin P. Margolies, Chief Executive Officer

NEW MEXICO: NMMRA, (New Mexico Medical Review Association), 2340 Menaul Blvd., NE, Suite 300, P.O. Box 3200, Albuquerque, NM 87190–3200; tel. 505/998–9898; FAX. 505/998–9899; Gary Horvat, Chief Executive Officer

NEW YORK: IPRO, 1979 Marcus Avenue, First Floor, Lake Success, NY 11042–1002; tel. 516/326–7767; FAX. 516/328–2310; Theodore O. Will, Executive Vice President

NORTH CAROLINA: Medical Review of North Carolina, Inc., 5625 Dillard Drive, Suite 203, Cary, NC 27511–9227; tel. 919/851–2955; FAX. 919/851–8457; Charles Riddick, Executive Director

NORTH DAKOTA: North Dakota Health Care Review Inc., 800 31st Avenue S.W., Minot, ND 58701; tel. 701/852–4231; FAX. 701/838–6009; David Remillard, Chief Executive Officer

OHIO: Peer Review Systems, Inc., 757 Brooksedge Plaza Drive, Westerville, OH 43081–4913; tel. 614/895–9900; FAX. 614/895–6784; Gregory J. Dykes, Chief Executive Officer

OKLAHOMA: Oklahoma Foundation for Medical Quality, Inc., The Paragon Building, 5801 Broadway Extension, Suite 400, Oklahoma City, OK 73118–7489; tel. 405/840–2891; FAX. 405/840–1343; Jim L. Williams, President and CEO

OREGON: Oregon Medical Professional Review Organization, 2020 S.W. 4th Avenue, Suite 520, Portland, OR 97201–4960; tel. 503/279–0100; FAX. 503/279–0190; Robert S. Kinoshita, President

PENNSYLVANIA: Keystone Peer Review Organization, Inc., 777 East Park Drive, P.O. Box 8310, Harrisburg, PA 17105–8310; tel. 717/564–8288; FAX. 717/564–4188; John DiNardi III, Executive Director

SOUTH CAROLINA: Carolina Medical Review, 250 Berryhill Road, Suite 101, Columbia, SC 29210; tel. 803/731–8225; FAX. 803/731–8229; Diana M. Zona, Communications Manager

SOUTH DAKOTA: South Dakota Foundation for Medical Care, 1323 South Minnesota Avenue, Sioux Falls, SD 57105; tel. 605/336–3505; FAX. 605/336–0270; Mark Hoven, Chief Executive Officer

TENNESSEE: Mid–South Foundation for Medical Care, Inc., 6401 Poplar Avenue, Suite 400, Memphis, TN 38119; tel. 901/682–0381; FAX. 901/761–3786; Logan Malone, Chief Executive Officer

TEXAS: Texas Medical Foundation, Barton Oaks Plaza Two, Suite 200, 901 Mopac Expressway, S., Austin, TX 78746–5799; tel. 512/329–6610; FAX. 512/327–7159; Phillip K. Dunne, Chief Executive Officer

UTAH: HealthInsight, 675 East 2100 South, Suite 270, Salt Lake City, UT 84106–1864; tel. 801/487–2290; FAX. 801/487–2296; James Q. Cannon, President and CEO
HealthInsight, 675 East 2100 South, Suite 270, Salt Lake City, UT 84106–1864; tel. 801/487–2290; FAX. 801/487–2296; Gary D. Lower, M.D., Chairman of the Board

VIRGINIA: Virginia Health Quality Center, 1604 Santa Rosa Road, Suite 200, Richmond, VA 23288–0070; tel. 804/289–5320; FAX. 804/289–5324; Joy Hogan Rozman, Executive Director

WASHINGTON: PRO–WEST, 10700 Meridian Avenue, N., Suite 100, Seattle, WA 98133–9075; tel. 206/364–9700; FAX. 206/368–2427; John W. Daise, Chief Executive Officer
PRO–WEST, 10700 Meridian Avenue, N., Suite 100, Seattle, WA 98133–9075; tel. 206/364–9700; FAX. 206/368–2760; Christine T. Kelley, Director of Business Development

WEST VIRGINIA: West Virginia Medical Institute, Inc., 3001 Chesterfield Place, Charleston, WV 25304; tel. 304/346–9864; FAX. 304/346–9863; Mabel M. Stevenson, M.D., President

WISCONSIN: Meta Star, 2909 Landmark Place, Madison, WI 53713; tel. 608/274–1940; FAX. 608/274–5008; Greg E. Simmons, President and CEO

U.S. Associated Areas

PUERTO RICO: Quality Improvement Professional Research Organization, Mercantile Plaza Building, Suite 605, Hato Rey, PR 00918; tel. 787/753–6705; FAX. 787/753–6885; Jose Robles, Chief Executive Officer

VIRGIN ISLANDS: Virgin Islands Medical Institute, Inc., 1AD Estate Diamond Ruby, P.O. Box 5989, St. Croix, VI 00823–5989; tel. 340/712–2400; FAX. 340–712–2449; Denise E. Singleton, Chief Executive Officer

State Health Planning and Development Agencies

The following is a list of state health planning and development agencies. The information was obtained from the Missouri Department of Health, Certificate of Need Program and the agencies themselves. For information about other state agencies and organizations that fulfill many of the same functions, contact the state or metropolitan hospital associations.

United States

ALABAMA: State Health Planning and Development Agency, 100 North Union Street, Suite 870, Montgomery, AL 36104; tel. 334/242–4103; FAX. 334/242–4113; Alva Lambert, Executive Director

ALASKA: Facilities and Planning Section, Department of Health and Social Services, P.O. Box 110650, Juneau, AK 99811–0650; tel. 907/465–3015; FAX. 907/465–2499; Larry J. Streuber, Section Chief

ARIZONA: Office of Health Planning, Evaluation and Statistics, 1740 West Adams, Room 301, Phoenix, AZ 85007; tel. 602/542–1216; FAX. 602/542–1244; Merle Lustig, Chief

CALIFORNIA: Office of Statewide Health Planning and Development, 1600 Ninth Street, Suite 440, Sacramento, CA 95814; tel. 916/654–2087; FAX. 916/654–3138; Priscilla Gonzalez–Leiva, RN, Deputy Director

COLORADO: Colorado Department of Public Health and Environment, Rural and Primary Health Program, 4300 Cherry Creek Drive, S., Denver, CO 80246–1530; tel. 303/692–2470; FAX. 303/782–5576; Susan Rehak, Program Director

CONNECTICUT: Connecticut Department of Public Health, Office of Policy, Planning and Evaluation, 410 Capitol Avenue, MS# 13PPE, Hartford, CT 06134–0308; tel. 860/509–7123; FAX. 860/509–7160; Michael Hoffman, Director

DELAWARE: Bureau of Health Planning and Resources Management, Department of Health and Social Services, P.O. Box 637, Dover, DE 19903; tel. 302/739–4776; FAX. 302/739–3008; Robert I. Welch, Director

DISTRICT OF COLUMBIA: Plan Development and Implementation Division, 825 North Capital Street, N.E., Third Floor, Washington, DC 20002; tel. 202/442–5875; Rhoda Knaff, Acting Chief

FLORIDA: Agency for Health Care Administration, Medicaid Program Development, 2727 Mahan Drive, Tallahassee, FL 32308–5403; tel. 904/922–9347; FAX. 904/414–6236; H. Robert Sharpe, Deputy Director of Medicaid

GEORGIA: State Health Planning Agency, Planning and Implementation Division, 2 Peach Tree Street, Room 34.262, Atlanta, GA 30303–3142; tel. 404/656–0654; FAX. 404/656–0655; Karen Butler–Decker, Director, Planning and Data Management

HAWAII: Hawaii State Health Planning and Development Agency, 1177 Alakea Street, Suite 402, Honolulu, HI 96813; tel. 808/587–0788; FAX. 808/587–0783; Marilyn A. Matsunaga, Administrator

IDAHO: Center for Vital Statistics and Health Policy, Division of Health, Idaho Department of Health and Welfare, 450 West State Street, First Floor, P.O. Box 83720, Boise, ID 83720–0036; tel. 208/334–5976; FAX. 208/334–0685; Jane Smith, Chief

ILLINOIS: Illinois Department of Public Health, Division of Health Policy, 525 West Jefferson, Springfield, IL 62761; tel. 217/782–6235; FAX. 217/785–4308; Angela Oldfield, M.S.W., L.S.W., Chief

INDIANA: Indiana State Department of Health, Local Liaison Office, Two North Meridian Street, Suite Eight–B, Indianapolis, IN 46204–3003; tel. 317/233–7846; FAX. 317/233–7761; Randall Ritter, M.P.A.

IOWA: Department of Public Health, Division of Substance Abuse and Health Promotion, Lucas State Office Building, Des Moines, IA 50319; tel. 515/281–5914; FAX. 515/281–4535; Ronald Eckoff, Medical Director

KANSAS: Health Care Commission, 900 Southwest Jackson, Ninth Floor, Landon State Office B, Topeka, KS 66612; tel. 785/296–7488; FAX. 785/368–7180; Steve Ashley

MAINE: Division of Health Planning, Bureau of Health, 35 Anthony Ave., SHS #11, Augusta, ME 04330–0011; tel. 207/624–5424; FAX. 207/624–5431; Helen Zidowecki, Director

MARYLAND: Maryland Health Resources Planning Commission, 4201 Patterson Avenue, Baltimore, MD 21215–2299; tel. 410/764–3255; FAX. 410/358–1311; Pamela Barelay. Acting Executive Director

MINNESOTA: Division of Community Health Services, Health Systems and Special Populations, Metro Square Building, St. Paul, MN 55164–0975; tel. 651/296–9720; FAX. 651/296–9362; Ryan Church, Director

MISSISSIPPI: Mississippi State Department of Health, Health Planning and Resource Development Division, 2423 North State Street, P.O. Box 1700, Jackson, MS 39215–1700; tel. 601/576–7874; FAX. 601/576–7530; Harold B. Armstrong, Chief

MISSOURI: Missouri Department of Health, 920 Wildwood, P.O. Box 570, Jefferson City, MO 65102; tel. 573/751–6001; FAX. 573/751–6041; Maureen Dempsey, Director

MONTANA: Health Policy and Services Division, Department of Public Health and Human Services, Cogswell Building, P.O. Box 202951, Helena, MT 59620–2951; tel. 406/444–4540; FAX. 406/444–1861; Nancy Ellery, Administrator

NEBRASKA: Nebraska Health and Human Services, Regulation and Licensure, Research and Performance Management, Nebraska State Office Building–5th Floor, 301 Centennial Mall South, Lincoln, NE 68509; tel. 402/471–8941; FAX. 402/471–7049; Paula Hartig, Unit Leader

NEVADA: State Health Division, Bureau of Health Planning and Statistics, 505 East King Street, Suite 102, Carson City, NV 89701–4749; tel. 775/684–4218; FAX. 775/684–4156; Emil DeJan, Chief

NEW HAMPSHIRE: Office of Health Services Planning and Review, Six Hazen Drive, Concord, NH 03301–6527; tel. 603/271–4606; FAX. 603/271–4141; William Bolton, Chief

NEW JERSEY: Certificate of Need and Acute Care Licensure Program, New Jersey Department of Health and Senior Services, CN 360, John Fitch Plaza, Trenton, NJ 08625–0360; tel. 609/292–8773; FAX. 609/292–3780; John A. Calabria, Director

NEW MEXICO: New Mexico Health Policy Commission, 2055 S. Pacheco Street, Suite 200, Santa Fe, NM 87505; tel. 505/424–3200; FAX. 505/424–3222; Katherine Ganz, M.D., Director

NEW YORK: New York State Department of Health, Division of Planning, Policy and Resource Development, Corning Tower, Suite 1495, Empire State Plaza, Albany, NY 12237; tel. 518/474–0180; FAX. 518/474–5450; Judith Arnold, Deputy Commissioner

NORTH CAROLINA: Medical Facilities Planning Section, P.O. Box 29530, Raleigh, NC 27626–0530; tel. 919/733–2342; FAX. 919/733–2757; Bonnie M. Cramer, Assistant Director, Division of Facility Services

NORTH DAKOTA: Division of Health Information Systems, Office of Community Assistance, 600 East Boulevard Avenue, Bismarck, ND 58505–0200; tel. 701/328–2894; FAX. 701/328–1890; Gary Garland, Director

OKLAHOMA: Oklahoma State Department of Health, Health Promotion and Policy Analysis, 1000 Northeast 10th Street, Oklahoma City, OK 73117–1299; tel. 405/271–1110; FAX. 405/271–1225; Jerry Pillman, Director Planning

PENNSYLVANIA: Bureau of Health Planning, Pennsylvania Department of Health, Health and Welfare Building, Room 833, P.O. Box 90, Harrisburg, PA 17108; tel. 717/772–5298; FAX. 717/783–3794; Joseph B. May, Director

RHODE ISLAND: Rhode Island Department of Health, Cannon Building, Three Capitol Hill, Suite 401, Providence, RI 02908; tel. 401/277–2231; FAX. 401/277–6548; William J. Waters, Jr., Ph.D., Deputy Director

SOUTH CAROLINA: DHEC, Division of Planning and Certificate of Need, 2600 Bull Street, Columbia, SC 29201; tel. 803/737–7200; FAX. 803/737–7579; Albert Whiteside, Director

SOUTH DAKOTA: South Dakota Department of Health, Division of Administration, 600 East Capitol Avenue, Pierre, SD 57501–3185; tel. 605/773–3361; FAX. 605/773–5683; Joan Adam, Director, Division of Administration

TENNESSEE: Assessment and Planning, Tennessee Department of Health, Cordell Hull Building, Sixth Floor, Nashville, TN 37247–5261; tel. 615/741–0244; FAX. 615/253–1688; Arthur Mader, Health Planner

TEXAS: Bureau of State Health Data and Policy Analysis, Texas Department of Health, 1100 West 49th Street, Austin, TX 78756; tel. 512/458–7261; FAX. 512/458–7344; Rick A. Danko, Planning Director

VERMONT: Division of Health Care Administration, Department of Banking Insurance, Securities, and Health Care Administration, 89 Main Street, Drawer 20, Montpelier, VT 05620–3601; tel. 802/828–2900; FAX. 802/828–2949; Stan Lane, Policy Analyst

VIRGINIA: Virginia Department of Health, Division of Certificate of Public Need, 3600 West Broad Street, Suite 216, Richmond, VA 23220; tel. 804/367–2126; FAX. 804/367–2206; Paul E. Parker, Director

WASHINGTON: Washington State Board of Health, 1102 SE Quince Street, P.O. Box 47990, Olympia, WA 98504–7990; tel. 360/586–0399; FAX. 360/586–6033; Sylvia I. Beck, M.P.A., Executive Director

WEST VIRGINIA: West Virginia Health Care Authority, 100 Dee Drive, Charleston, WV 25311; tel. 304/558–7000; FAX. 304/558–7001; D. Parker Haddix

WYOMING: Department of Health, 117 Hathaway Building, Cheyenne, WY 82002; tel. 307/777–7656; FAX. 307/777–7439; Douglas Thiede, Data and Communications Manager

Section C

State and Provincial Government Agencies

The following list includes state departments of health and welfare, and their subagencies as well as such independent agencies as those for children's services, maternal and child health, mental health, and vocational rehabilitation. The information was obtained directly from the agencies.

United States

ALABAMA
The Honorable Fob James, Jr., Governor, 334/242-7100

Health

Alabama Department of Public Health, Bureau of Family Health Services, The RSA Tower, P.O. Box 303017, Montgomery, AL 36130-3017; tel. 334/206-2940; FAX. 334/206-2950; Thomas M. Miller, M.D., M.P.H., Director

Alabama Department of Public Health, Division of Licensure and Certification, The RSA Tower, P.O. Box 303017, Montgomery, AL 36130-3017; tel. 334/206-2940; FAX. 334/206-2950; Thomas M. Miller, M.D., M.P.H., Director

Department of Public Health, 201 Monroe Street, P.O. Box 303017, Montgomery, AL 36130-3017; tel. 334/206-5200; FAX. 334/206-2008; Donald E. Williamson, M.D., State Health Officer

Insurance

Department of Insurance, 201 Monroe Street, Suite 1700, Montgomery, AL 36130; tel. 334/241-4101; FAX. 334/241-4192; David Parsons, Acting Commissioner

Licensing

Alabama Board of Nursing, RSA Plaza, 770 Washington Avenue, Suite 250, Montgomery, AL 36130; tel. 334/242-4060; FAX. 334/242-4360; Lynn Norman, RN, M.S.N., Interim Executive Officer

Social Services

Alabama Medicaid Agency, 501 Dexter Avenue, P.O. Box 5624, Montgomery, AL 36103-5624; tel. 334/242-5600; FAX. 334/242-5097; W. Dale Walley, Acting Commissioner

Department of Human Resources, Gordon Persons Building, 50 Ripley Street, Montgomery, AL 36130; tel. 334/242-1160; FAX. 334/242-0198; Tony Petelos, Commissioner

Department of Rehabilitation Services, 2129 East South Boulevard, Montgomery, AL 36116; tel. 800/441-7607; FAX. 334/281-1973; Lamona H. Lucas, Commissioner

State Department of Mental Health and Mental Retardation, RSA Union, 100 North Union Street, Montgomery, AL 36130-1410; tel. 334/242-3107; FAX. 334/242-0684; Virginia A. Rogers, Commissioner

Other

State Department of Education, Gordon Persons Building, Suite 5114, P.O. Box 302101, Montgomery, AL 36130-2101; tel. 334/242-9700; FAX. 334/242-9708; Ed Richardson, Superintendent

ALASKA
The Honorable Tony Knowles, Governor, 907/465-3500

Health Facilities Licensing and Certification, 4730 Business Park Boulevard, Suite 18, Anchorage, AK 99503-7137; tel. 907/561-8081; FAX. 907/561-3011; Shelbert Larsen, Administrator

Health

Division of Mental Health and Developmental Disabilities, P.O. Box 110620, Juneau, AK 99811-0620; tel. 907/465-3370; FAX. 907/465-2668; Karl Brimner, Director

Licensing

Alaska Board of Nursing, 3601 C Street, Suite 722, Anchorage, AK 99503; tel. 907/269-8160; FAX. 907/269-8156; Dorothy P. Fulton, RN, M.A., Executive Administrator

Department of Commerce and Economic Development, Division of Occupational Licensing, State Medical Board, 3601 C Street, Suite 722, Anchorage, AK 99503; tel. 907/269-8163; FAX. 907/269-8196; Leslie G. Abel, Executive Administrator

Health Facilities Licensing and Certification, 4730 Business Park Boulevard, Suite 18, Anchorage, AK 99503-7137; tel. 907/561-8081; FAX. 907/561-3011; Shelbert Larsen, Administrator

Social Services

Department of Health and Social Services, 350 Main Street, Room 229, P.O. Box 110601, Juneau, AK 99811-0601; tel. 907/465-3030; FAX. 907/465-3068; Jay A. Livey, Acting Commissioner

Division of Administrative Services, Department of Health and Social Services, P.O. Box 110650, Juneau, AK 99811-0650; tel. 907/465-3082; FAX. 907/465-2499; Janet E. Clarke, Director

Division of Family and Youth Services, P.O. Box 110630, Juneau, AK 99811; tel. 907/465-3191; FAX. 907/465-3397; Theresa Tanoury, Family Services Administrator

Division of Medical Assistance, P.O. Box 110660, Juneau, AK 99811-0660; tel. 907/465-3355; FAX. 907/465-2204; Bob Labbe, Director

Division of Vocational Rehabilitation, 801 West 10th Street, Suite 200, Juneau, AK 99801-1894; tel. 907/465-2814; FAX. 907/465-2856; Duane M. French, Director

Mental Health and Substance Abuse Services, P.O. Box 110607, Juneau, AK 99811-0607; tel. 907/465-2071; FAX. 907/465-2185; Loren A. Jones, Director

State of Alaska, Division of Medical Assistance, P.O. 110660, Juneau, AK 99811-0640; tel. 907/465-3355; FAX. 907/465-2204; Bob Labbe, Director

State of Alaska, Department of Health and Social Services, 350 Main Street, Room 229, P.O. Box 110601, Juneau, AK 99811-0601; tel. 907/465-3030; FAX. 907/465-3068; Jay A. Livey, Deputy Commissioner

Other

Department of Education, 801 West 10th Street, Suite 200, Juneau, AK 99801-1894; tel. 907/465-2887; FAX. 907/465-2713; Beth Shober, Health Promotion Specialist

ARIZONA
The Honorable Jane Dee Hull, Governor, 602/542-4331

Health

Arizona Department of Health Services, 1740 West Adams Street, Suite 407, Phoenix, AZ 85007; tel. 602/542-1025; FAX. 602/542-1062; James R. Allen, M.D., M.P.H.

Arizona Department of Health Services, Division of Health and Child Care Review Services, Office, 1647 East Morten, Phoenix, AZ 85020; tel. 602/255-1197; FAX. 602/255-1135; John Zemaitis, Assistant Director

Arizona Department of Health Services, Division of Public Health, Bureau of Epidemiology and Disease Control Services, 3815 North Black Canyon Highway, Phoenix, AZ 85015; tel. 602/230-5808; FAX. 602/230-5959; Lee A. Bland, Bureau Chief

Insurance

Department of Insurance, 3030 North Third Street, Suite 1100, Phoenix, AZ 85012; tel. 602/255-5400; FAX. 602/255-5316

Licensing

Arizona Board of Medical Examiners, 1651 East Morten, Suite 210, Phoenix, AZ 85020; tel. 602/255-3751; FAX. 602/255-1848; Claudia Fontz, Executive Director

Arizona State Board of Nursing, 1651 East Morten, Suite 150, Phoenix, AZ 85020; tel. 602/331-8111; FAX. 6029069365

Social Services

Community and Family Health Services, 1740 West Adams Street, Suite 307, Phoenix, AZ 85007; tel. 602/542-1223; FAX. 602/542-1265; Elsie E. Eyer, M.S., Bureau Chief

Division of Behavioral Health Services, Arizona Department of Health Services, 2122 East Highland, Suite 100, Phoenix, AZ 85016; tel. 602/381-8999; FAX. 602/553-9140; Ronald Smith, Assistant Director

Office for Children with Special Health Care Needs, Administrative Offices, 1740 West Adams Street, Phoenix, AZ 85007; tel. 602/542-1860; FAX. 602/542-2589; Susan Burke, Chief

Rehabilitation Services Administration (930A), 1789 West Jefferson, Second Floor Northwest, Phoenix, AZ 85007; tel. 602/542-3332; FAX. 602/542-3778; Skip Bingham, Administrator

Other

Arizona Department of Environmental Quality, 3033 North Central Avenue, Phoenix, AZ 85012; tel. 602/207-2300; FAX. 602/207-2218; Russell F. Rhoades, Director

Department of Economic Security, Site Code 010A, P.O. Box 6123, Phoenix, AZ 85005; tel. 602/542-5678; FAX. 602/542-5339; Linda J. Blessing, Director

ARKANSAS
The Honorable Mike Huckabee, Governor, 501/682-2345

Health

Arkansas Department of Health, 4815 West Markham Street, Slot 39, Little Rock, AR 72205-3867; tel. 501/661-2000; FAX. 501/671-1450; Fay W. Boozman, III, M.D.

Arkansas Department of Health, Bureau of Community Health Services, 4815 West Markham Street, Slot 2, Little Rock, AR 72205-3867; tel. 501/661-2167; FAX. 501/661-2601; Jim Mills, Director

Arkansas Department of Health, Planning and Policy Development, 4815 West Markham, Slot 55, Little Rock, AR 72205; tel. 501/661-2238; FAX. 501/661-2414; Gail Gannaway, Acting Deputy Director

Bureau of Administrative Support, State Health Building, Little Rock, AR 72205-3867; tel. 501/661-2252; Tom Butler, Director

Bureau of Health Resources, Arkansas Department of Health, 4815 West Markham Street, Slot 21, Little Rock, AR 72205-3867; tel. 501/661-2831; FAX. 501/661-2544; C. Lewis Leslie, Director

Children's Medical Service, Donaghey Plaza South, Seventh and Main Streets, Little Rock, AR 72203; tel. 501/682-8202; FAX. 501/682-8247; G. A. Buchanan, M.D., Medical Director

Division of Health Facility Services, Department of Health, 5800 West 10th Street, Suite 400, Little Rock, AR 72204; tel. 501/661-2201; FAX. 501/661-2165; Valetta M. Buck, Director

Division of Medical Services, Donaghey Building, Seventh and Main Streets, Little Rock, AR 72203; tel. 501/682-8292; FAX. 501/682-1197; Ray Hanley, Director

Insurance

Arkansas Insurance Department, 1200 W. 3rd Street, Little Rock, AR 72201; tel. 501/371-2600; FAX. 501/371-2626; Mike Pickens, Insurance Commissioner

Licensing

Arkansas State Board of Nursing, University Tower Building, Suite 800, 1123 South University Avenue, Little Rock, AR 72204; tel. 501/686-2700; FAX. 501/686-2714; Faith A. Fields, M.S.N., RN, Executive Director

Social Services

Arkansas Department of Human Services, P.O. Box 1437, Little Rock, AR 72203-1437; tel. 501/682-8650; FAX. 501/682-6836; Kurk Knickrchm

Arkansas Rehabilitation Services, 1616 Brookwood, P.O. Box 3781, Little Rock, AR 72203; tel. 501/296-1616; FAX. 501/296-1675; Bobby C. Simpson, Commissioner

Bureau of Alcohol & Drug Abuse Prevention, Freeway Medical Center, Suite 907, 5800 West 10th Street, Little Rock, AR 72204; tel. 501/280-4501; FAX. 501/280-4532; Joe M. Hill, Director

Bureau of Public Health Programs, Arkansas Department of Health, 4815 West Markham Street, Slot 41, Little Rock, AR 72205-3867; tel. 501/661-2243; FAX. 501/661-2055; Martha Hiett, Director

Division of Aging and Adult Services, P.O. Box 1437, Slot 1412, Little Rock, AR 72203-1437; tel. 501/682-2441; FAX. 501/682-8155; Herb Sanderson, Director

Division of Mental Health Services, Arkansas State Hospital, 4313 West Markham, Little Rock, AR 72205-4096; tel. 501/686-9000; FAX. 501/686-9182; John Selig, Director

Office of Long-Term Care, Lafayette Building, Sixth and Louisiana Streets, Little Rock, AR 72203-8059; tel. 501/682-8487; FAX. 501/682-6955; Shirley Gamble, Director

CALIFORNIA
The Honorable Gray Davis, Governor, 916/445-2841

Health

Department of Developmental Services, 1600 Ninth Street, Suite 240, Sacramento, CA 95814; tel. 916/654-1897; FAX. 916/654-2167; Cliff Allenby, Director

Department of Health Services, 714 P Street, Suite 1253, Sacramento, CA 95814; tel. 916/651-1425; FAX. 916/657-1156; S. Kimberly Belshe, Director

Licensing

Board of Registered Nursing, 400 R Street, Suite 4030, P.O. Box 944210, Sacramento, CA 94244-2100; tel. 916/322-3350; FAX. 916/327-4402; Ruth Ann Terry, M.P.H., RN, Executive Officer

Board of Vocational Nursing and Psychiatric Technicians, 2535 Capitol Oaks Drive, Suite 205, Sacramento, CA 95833; tel. 916/263-7800; FAX. 916/263-7859; Teresa Bello-Jones, J.D., M.S.N., RN, Executive Officer

Medical Board of California, 1426 Howe Avenue, Suite 54, Sacramento, CA 95825-3236; tel. 916/263-2389; FAX. 916/263-2387; Ron Joseph, Executive Director

Social Services

Community Resources Development Section, California Department of Rehabilitation, 2000 Evergreen Street, Sacramento, CA 95815; tel. 916/263-7374; FAX. 916/322-0503; Sig Brivkalns, Chief

Department of Alcohol and Drug Programs, 1700 K Street, Sacramento, CA 95814; tel. 916/445-1943; FAX. 916/323-5873; Position vacation at this time

Department of Mental Health, 1600 Ninth Street, Room 151, Sacramento, CA 95814; tel. 916/654-2309; FAX. 916/654-3198; Stephen W. Mayberg, Ph.D., Director

Department of Rehabilitation, 830 K Street Mall, Sacramento, CA 95814; tel. 916/445-8638

Department of Social Services, 744 P Street, Sacramento, CA 95814; tel. 916/657-3661; FAX. 916/654-2049; Eloise Anderson, Director

Health and Welfare Agency, Office of the Secretary, 1600 Ninth Street, Suite 460, Sacramento, CA 95814; tel. 916/654-3454; FAX. 916/654-3343; Garry Morck, Manager, Administrative Services

Other

Department of Corporations, Health Care Division, 3700 Wilshire Boulevard, Suite 600, Los Angeles, CA 90010-3001; tel. 213/736-2776; Gary G. Hagen, Assistant Commissioner

COLORADO
The Honorable Bill Owens, Governor, 303/866-2471

Health

Colorado Department of Public Health and Environment, 4300 Cherry Creek Drive, S., Denver, CO 80222-1530; tel. 303/692-2000; FAX. 303/782-0095; Jane E. Norton, Executive Director

Colorado Department of Public Health and Environment, Health Facilities Division, 4300 Cherry Creek Drive S., Denver, CO 80246-1530; tel. 303/692-2100; FAX. 303/691-7702; Patti Shwayder, Executive Director

State Department of Health Care Policy and Financing, 1575 Sherman Street, Fourth Floor, Denver, CO 80203; tel. 303/866-2859; FAX. 303/866-2803; Richard Allen, Manager, Medical Assistance

State Department of Health Care Policy and Financing, 1575 Sherman Street, 10th Floor, Denver, CO 80203-1714; tel. 303/866-2993; FAX. 303/866-4411; Barbara McDonnell, Acting Director

Insurance

Division of Insurance, 1560 Broadway, Suite 850, Denver, CO 80202; tel. 303/894-7499; FAX. 303/894-7455; Jack Ehnes, Commissioner

Licensing

Colorado Board of Medical Examiners, 1560 Broadway, Suite 1300, Denver, CO 80202-5140; tel. 303/894-7690; FAX. 303/894-7692; Susan Miller, Program Administrator

Department of Regulatory Agencies, 1560 Broadway, Suite 1550, Denver, CO 80202; tel. 303/894-7855; FAX. 303/894-7885; M. Michael Cooke, Executive Director

Social Services

Alcohol and Drug Abuse Division, Colorado Department of Human Services, 4300 Cherry Creek Drive South, Denver, CO 80222; tel. 303/692-2930; FAX. 303/753-9775; Robert Aukerman, Director

Department of Human Services, 1575 Sherman Street, Eighth Floor, Denver, CO 80203; tel. 303/866-5096; FAX. 303/866-4740; Marva Livingston Hammons, Executive Director

Division of Aging and Adult Services, Colorado Department of Human Services, 110 16th Street, Second Floor, Denver, CO 80202; tel. 303/620-4127; FAX. 303/620-4191; Rita A. Barreras, Director

Family and Community Health Services Division, Colorado Department of Public Health and Environment, 4300 Cherry Creek Drive South, Denver, CO 80246-1530; tel. 303/692-2302; FAX. 303/753-9249; Merrill Stern, Director

Mental Health Services, 3824 West Princeton Circle, Denver, CO 80236; tel. 303/366-7400; FAX. 303/866-7428; Thomas J. Barrett, Ph.D., Director

CONNECTICUT
The Honorable John G. Rowland, Governor, 860/566-4840

Health

, Bureau of Health Promotion, 150 Washington Street, Hartford, CT 06106; tel. 203/566-5475; FAX. 203/566-1400; Peter Galbraith, D.M.D., Bureau Chief

Department of Health Services, 150 Washington Street, Hartford, CT 06106; tel. 203/566-2038; Frederick G. Adams, D.D.S., M.P.H., Commissioner

Department of Public Health, 410 Capitol Avenue, Mail Stop 12APP, Hartford, CT 06134-0308; tel. 860/509-7579; FAX. 860/509-8457; Cynthia Denne, Director

Department of Public Health, 410 Capitol Avenue, P.O. Box 340308, Hartford, CT 06134-0308; tel. 860/509-7101; FAX. 860/509-7111; Stephen A. Harriman, Commissioner

Department of Public Health, Division of Health Systems Regulation, 410 Capitol Avenue, Mail Stop 12 HSR, Hartford, CT 06134-0308; tel. 860/509-7407; FAX. 860/509-7539; Cynthia Denne, RN, M.P.A., Director

Insurance

Department of Insurance, P.O. Box 816, Hartford, CT 06142-0816; tel. 860/297-3862; FAX. 860/297-3941; Mary Ellen Breault, Director, Life and Health Division

Licensing

Connecticut Board of Examiners for Nursing, Department of Public Health – MS#13ADJ, 410 Capital Avenue, P.O. Box 340308, Hartford, CT 06134-0308; tel. 860/509-7624; FAX. 860/509-7286; Wendy H. Furniss, RNC, MS, Public Health Services Manager

Social Services

Department of Social Services, 25 Sigourney Street, Hartford, CT 06106; tel. 203/424-5008; Patricia Giardi, Commissioner

Department of Social Services, Bureau of Rehabilitation Service, Division of Organizational Support, 10 Griffin Road, N., Windsor, CT 06095; tel. 203/298-2032; FAX. 203/298-9590; John J. Galiette, Chief

Elderly Services Division, Department of Social Services, 25 Sigourney Street, Hartford, CT 06106-5033; tel. 203/424-5277; FAX. 203/424-4966; Christine M. Lewis, Director

State Department of Mental Health and Addiction Services, 410 Capitol Avenue, P.O. Box 341431, Hartford, CT 6134; tel. 860/418-7000; FAX. 860/418-6691; Albert J. Solnit, M.D., Commissioner

Other

Department of Education, 165 Capitol Avenue, Hartford, CT 06145; tel. 203/566-5061; FAX. 203/566-8964

DELAWARE
The Honorable Thomas R. Carper, Governor, 302/739-4101

Health

Community Health Care Access, Jesse Cooper Building, Dover, DE 19901; tel. 302/739-4768; FAX. 302/739-6653; Prudence Kobasa, Public Health Nursing Director

Delaware Office of Emergency Medical Services, Blue Hen Corporate Center, 655 South Bay Road, Dover, DE 19901; tel. 302/739-4710; FAX. 302/739-2352; Bill Stevenson, EMS Director

Delaware Public Health Laboratory, 30 Sunnyside Road, P.O. Box 1047, Smyrna, DE 19977-1047; tel. 302/653-2870; FAX. 302/653-2877; Christopher K. Zimmerman, M.A., Acting Director

Division of Public Health, P.O. Box 637, Dover, DE 19903; tel. 302/739-4700; FAX. 302/739-6659; Steven F. Boedigheimer, Deputy Director

Division of Public Health, Community Health Care Access Section, Jesse S. Cooper Building, Federal Street, Dover, DE 19903; tel. 302/739-4785; FAX. 302/739-6617

Licensing

Delaware Board of Medical Practice, Cannon Building, Suite 203, 861 Silver Lake Boulevard, Dover, DE 19901; tel. 302/739-4522; FAX. 302/739-2711; Brenda D. Petty-Ball, Executive Director

Delaware Board of Nursing, Cannon Building, Suite 203, 861 Silver Lake Boulevard, Dover, DE 19904; tel. 302/739-4522; FAX. 302/739-2711; Iva J. Boardman, RN, M.S.N., Executive Director

Office of Health Facilities Licensing and Certification, Department of Health and Social Services, Three Mill Road, Suite 308, Wilmington, DE 19806; tel. 302/577-6666; FAX. 302/577-6672; Ellen Reap, Director

Social Services

Delaware Psychiatric Center, Division of Alcoholism, Drug Abuse and Mental Health, 1901 North DuPont Highway, New Castle, DE 19720; tel. 302/577-4000; FAX. 302/577-4359; Jiro R. Shimond, AGSW, Hospital Director

Department of Health and Social Services, 1901 North DuPont Highway, Main Administration Building, New Castle, DE 19720; tel. 302/577-4500; FAX. 302/577-4510

Department of Labor, Division of Vocational Rehabilitation, 4425 North Market Street, Wilmington, DE 19802; tel. 302/761-8275; FAX. 302/761-6611; Michelle P. Pointer, Director

Division of Services for Aging and Adults with Physical Disabilities, 1901 North DuPont Highway, 2nd Floor Annex, New Castle, DE 19720; tel. 302/577-4791; FAX. 302/577-4793; Eleanor L. Cain, Director

Division of Social Services, P.O. Box 906, New Castle, DE 19720; tel. 302/577-4400; FAX. 302/577-4405; Elaine Archangelo, Director

Family Health Services, Division of Public Health, P.O. Box 637, Dover, DE 19903; tel. 302/739-4785; FAX. 302/739-6653; Joan Powell, MPA, Director

DISTRICT OF COLUMBIA
Governor Swithboard, 202/727-1000

Health

Commission on Mental Health Services, Office of the Receiver, 4301 Conn. Avenue, N.W., Washington, DC 20008; tel. 202/364-3422; FAX. 202/373-6484; Dr. Scott H. Nelson, Receiver

D.C. Department of Public Health, 800 Ninth Street, S.W., Washington, DC 20024; tel. 202/645-5556; FAX. 202/645-0526; Allan S. Noonan, M.D., M.P.H.

Department of Health, 800 9th Street, S.E., 3rd Floor, Washington, DC 20024; tel. 202/645-5556; FAX. 202/645-0627; Allan S. Noonan, M.D., M.P.H.

Department of Health, Preventive Health Services Administration, 800 Ninth Street, S.W., Second Floor, Washington, DC 20024; tel. 202/645-5550; FAX. 202/645-0454; Administrator, PHSA

Licensing

Department of Consumer and Regulatory Affairs, 614 H Street, N.W., Suite 1120, Washington, DC 20001; tel. 202/727-7120; FAX. 202/727-8073; Lloyd J. Jordan, Director

Department of Consumer and Regulatory Affairs, Licensing Regulation Administration, 614 H Street, N.W., Suite 1003, Washington, DC 20001; tel. 202/727-7190; FAX. 202/727-7780; Geraldine K. Sykes, Administrator

Occupational and Professional Licensing Administration, Department of Consumer and Regulatory Affairs, 614 H Street, N.W., Suite 903, Washington, DC 20001; tel. 202/727-7480; FAX. 202/727-7662; Winnie R. Huston, Administrator

Social Services

Alcohol and Drug Abuse Services Administration, 1300 1st Street, N.E., Washington, DC 20002; tel. 202/727-1762; FAX. 202/535-2028

Bureau of Maternal and Child Health Services, Dept. of Health, Office of Maternal and Child Health, 800 Ninth Street, S.W., 3rd Floor, Washington, DC 20024; tel. 202/645-5653; Michelle S. Davis, M.S.P.H., Interim Chief

Commission on Social Services, 609 H Street, N.E., Fifth Floor, Washington, DC 20002; tel. 202/727-5930; FAX. 202/727-6529; A. Sue Brown, Acting Commissioner of Social Services

Long-Term Care Administration, 1660 L Street, N.W., 10th Floor, Washington, DC 20036; tel. 202/673-3597; A. Sue Brown, Administrator

Rehabilitation Services Administration, 800 Ninth Street, S.W., Fourth Floor, Washington, DC 20024; tel. 202/645-5703; FAX. 202/645-0840

FLORIDA

The Honorable Jeb Bush, Governor, 850/488-4441

Health

Children's Medical Services, 2020 Capital Circle, SE, Bin A-06, Tallahassee, FL 32399-1700; tel. 904/487-2690; FAX. 904/488-3813; Eric G. Handler, M.D., M.P.H., Director, CMS

Department of Health, Secretary's Office, 2020 Capital Circle, SE, Bin #A00, Tallahassee, FL 32399-1700; tel. 904/487-2945; FAX. 904/487-3729; Robert G. Brooks, M.D., Secretary

Department of Health, Secretary's Office, 1317 Winewood Boulevard, Building Six, Tallahassee, FL 32399-0700; tel. 904/487-2945; FAX. 904/487-3729; James T. Howell, M.D., M.P.H., Secretary

Insurance

Department of Insurance, Bureau of Specialty Insurers, 200 East Gaines Street, Tallahassee, FL 32399; tel. 904/488-6766; FAX. 904/488-0313; Al Willis, Chief

Licensing

Division of Health Quality Assurance, 2727 Mahan Drive, Tallahassee, FL 32308; tel. 850/487-2528; FAX. 850/487-6240; Pete J. Buigas, Director

Florida Board of Medicine, 2020 capital Circle S.E., Bin # C03, Tallahassee, FL 32399-3253; tel. 850/488-3622; Tonya Williams, Board Director

Social Services

Adult Services, 1317 Winewood Boulevard, Building 8, Room 327, Tallahassee, FL 32399-0700; tel. 904/488-8922; Ms. Nancy Fulton, Director, Adult Services

Certificate of Need/Budget Review Office, Agency for Health Care Administration, 2727 Mahan Drive, Tallahassee, FL 32308; tel. 904/488-8673; FAX. 904/922-6964; Elfie Stamm, Chief

Department of Health and Rehabilitative Services, Alcohol, Drug Abuse and Mental Health Program Office, 1317 Winewood Boulevard, Tallahassee, FL 32399-0700; tel. 904/488-8304; FAX. 904/487-2239

Department of Labor and Employment Security, 2012 Capital Circle, S.E., 303 Hartman Building, Tallahassee, FL 32399-2152; tel. 904/922-7021; FAX. 904/488-8930; Mary B. Hooks, Secretary

Division of Vocational Rehabilitation, 2002 Old St. Augustine Road, Building A, Tallahassee, FL 32399-0696; tel. 850/488-6210; FAX. 850/921-7215; Tamara Allen Bibb, Director

GEORGIA

The Honorable Roy Barnes, Governor, 404/656-1776

Health

Diagnostic Services Unit, 878 Peachtree Street, N.E., Suite 719, Atlanta, GA 30309-3997; tel. 404/894-4747; FAX. 404/894-2185; Betty Logan, Director

Division of Public Health, Two Peachtree Street, S.W., Suite 7-300, Atlanta, GA 30303; tel. 404/657-2700; FAX. 404/657-2715; Kathleen E. Toomay, M.D., M.P.H.

State Health Planning Agency, Four Executive Park Drive, N.E., Suite 2100, Atlanta, GA 30329; tel. 404/679-4821; FAX. 404/679-4914; Pamela S. Stephenson, Esq., Executive Director

Insurance

Office of Commissioner of Insurance, Two Martin Luther King, Jr. Drive, Seventh Floor, West Tower, Floyd Build, Atlanta, GA 30334; tel. 404/656-2056; FAX. 404/656-4030; John W. Oxendine, Commissioner of Insurance

Licensing

Child Care Licensing Section, Two Peachtree Street, N.W., 32-458, Atlanta, GA 30303; tel. 404/657-5562; FAX. 404/657-8936; Jo Cato, Director

Composite State Board of Medical Examiners, 166 Pryor Street, S.W., Atlanta, GA 30303; tel. 404/656-3913; FAX. 404/656-9723; Gregg W. Scheder, Acting Executive Director

Diagnostic Services Unit, Health Care Section, Office of Regulatory Services, Two Peachtree Street, N.W., 33rd Floor, Room 250, Atlanta, GA 30303-3142; tel. 404/657-5447; FAX. 404/657-8934; Betty J. Logan, Regional Director, Diagnostic Services

Georgia Board of Nursing, 166 Pryor Street, S.W., Atlanta, GA 30303; tel. 404/656-3943; FAX. 404/657-7489; Shirley A. Camp, Executive Director

Social Services

Department of Human Resources, Two Peachtree N.W., Suite 29.250, Atlanta, GA 30303-3142; tel. 404/656-5680; FAX. 404/651-8669; Tommy C. Olmstead, Commissioner

Department of Human Resources, Office of Regulatory Services, Health Care Section, Two Peachtree Street, N.W., Suite 33.250, Atlanta, GA 30303-3167; tel. 404/657-5550; FAX. 404/657-8934; Susie M. Woods, Director of the HCS

Division of Mental Health, Mental Retardation and Substance Abuse, Two Peachtree Street, NW., 22-205, Atlanta, GA 30303; tel. 404/657-2252; FAX. 404/657-1137; Carl E. Roland, Jr., Director

Division of Rehabilitation Services, Two Peachtree Street, N.W., 35th Floor, Atlanta, GA 30303-3142; tel. 404/657-3000; FAX. 404/657-3079; Peggy Rosser, Director

Office of Regulatory Services, Georgia Department of Human Resources, Two Peachtree Street, N.W., Room 32-415, Atlanta, GA 30303-3142; tel. 404/657-5700; FAX. 404/657-5708; Martin J. Rotter, Director

Personal Care Home Program, Office of Regulatory Services, Two Peachtree Street, 31st Floor, Atlanta, GA 30303-3167; tel. 404/657-4076; FAX. 404/657-3655; Victoria L. Flynn, Director

HAWAII

The Honorable Benjamin J. Cayetano, Governor, 808/586-0034

Health

Adult Mental Health Division, P.O. Box 3378, Honolulu, HI 96801-3378; tel. 808/586-4677; FAX. 808/586-4745; Linda Fox, Ph.D.

Communicable Disease Division, P.O. Box 3378, Honolulu, HI 96801; tel. 808/586-4580; FAX. 808/586-4595; Richard L. Vogt, M.D., State Epidemiologist

Dental Health Division, 1700 Lanakila Avenue, Suite 203, Honolulu, HI 96817-2199; tel. 808/832-5700; FAX. 808/832-5722; Mark H.K. Greer, D.M.D., M.P.H., Chief

Hawaii Department of Health, P.O. Box 3378, Honolulu, HI 96801; tel. 808/586-4410; FAX. 808/586-4444; Bruce S. Anderson, Ph.D., M.P.H., Director

State Health Planning and Development Agency, 335 Merchant Street, Suite 214 E, Honolulu, HI 96813; tel. 808/587-0788; FAX. 808/587-0783; Patrick J. Boland, Administrator

Licensing

Department of Commerce and Consumer Affairs, Board of Medical Examiners, P.O. Box 3469, Honolulu, HI 96801; tel. 808/586-2708; Constance Cabral-Makanani, Executive Officer

Department of Health/Hospital and Medical Facilities, Licensing and Certification, P.O. Box 3378, Honolulu, HI 96801; tel. 808/586-4080; FAX. 808/586-4444; Helen K. Yoshimi, B.S.N., M.P.H., Chief, H.M.F.B.

Social Services

Alcohol and Drug Abuse Division, Department of Health, State of Hawaii, 601 Kamokila Blvd., Room 360, Kapolei, HI 96707; tel. 808/692-7506; FAX. 808/692-7521; Elaine Wilson, Chief

Department of Human Services, Med-QUEST Division, 601 Kamokila Boulevard, Room 518, Box 339, Honolulu, HI 96809; tel. 808-692-8050; FAX. 808-692-8173; Charles C. Duarte, Med-QUEST Administrator

Department of Labor and Industrial Relations, Disability Compensation Division, P.O. Box 3769, Honolulu, HI 96812; tel. 808/586-9151; FAX. 808/586-9219; Gary S. Hamada, Administrator

Family Health Services Division, Hawaii State Department of Health, 1250 Punchbowl Street, Room 216, Honolulu, HI 96813; tel. 808/586-4122; FAX. 808/586-9303; Nancy L. Kuntz, M.D, Chief, Family Health Services Division

Vocational Rehabilitation, 601 Kamokila Blvd, Room 515, Kapolei, HI 96707; tel. 808/692-7715; FAX. 808/692-7727; Neil Shim, Administrator

Other

Environmental Management Division, 919 Ala Mona Boulevard, Room 300, Honolulu, HI 96814; tel. 808-586-4304; FAX. 808-586-4352; Thomas E. Aritumi, Chief

IDAHO

The Honorable Dirk Kempthorne, Governor, 208/334-2100

Health

Bureau of Emergency Medical Services, P.O. Box 83720, Boise, ID 83720-0036; tel. 208/334-4000; FAX. 208/334-4015; Dia Gainor, Bureau Chief

Center for Vital Statistics and Health Policy, 450 West State, First Floor, P.O. Box 83720, Boise, ID 83720-0036; tel. 208/334-5976; FAX. 208/334-0685; Jane S. Smith, State Registrar, Chief

Insurance

Department of Insurance, 700 West State Street, Third Floor, P.O. Box 83720, Boise, ID 83720-0043; tel. 208/334-4250; FAX. 208/334-4398; James M. Alcorn, Director

Licensing

Bureau of Facility Standards, Department of Health and Welfare, P.O. Box 83720, Boise, ID 83720-0036; tel. 208/334-6626; FAX. 208/332-7204; Sylvia Creswell, Supervisor-Non LTC

Idaho State Board of Medicine, 280 North Eighth Street, Suite 202, P.O. Box 83720, Boise, ID 83720-0058; tel. 208/334-2822; FAX. 208/334-2801; Darlene Thorsted, Executive Director

Idaho State Board of Nursing, 280 North Eighth Street, Suite 210, Boise, ID 83720-0061; tel. 208/334-3110; FAX. 208/334-3262; Sandra Evans, MA., Ed., RN, Executive Director

Social Services

Bureau of Clinical and Preventive Services, P.O. Box 83720, Boise, ID 83720-0036; tel. 208/334-5930; FAX. 208/332-7307; Roger Perotto, Chief

Department of Health and Welfare, Division of Health, 450 West State, Fourth Floor, P.O. Box 83720, Boise, ID 83720-0036; tel. 208/334-5945; FAX. 208/334-6581; Richard H. Schultz, Administrator

Division of Family and Community Services, Bureau of Mental Health and Substance Abuse, P.O. Box 83720, Boise, ID 83720-0036; tel. 208/334-5935; FAX. 208/334-6664; Tina Klamt, Substance Abuse Project Manager

Vocational Rehabilitation, 650 West State, P.O. Box 83720, Boise, ID 83720-0096; tel. 208/334-3390; FAX. 208/334-5305; F. Pat Young, Interim Administrator

Other

Bureau of Laboratories, 2220 Old Penitentiary Road, Boise, ID 83712; tel. 208/334-2235; FAX. 208/334-2382; Richard F. Hudson, Ph.D., Chief

ILLINOIS
The Honorable George Ryan, Governor, 217/782-6830

Health
Illinois Department of Public Health, 535 West Jefferson Street, Springfield, IL 62761; tel. 217/782-4977; FAX. 217/782-3987; John R. Lumpkin, M.D., M.P.H., Director

Illinois Department of Public Health, Office of Epidemiology & Health Systems Development, 525 West Jefferson Street, Springfield, IL 62761; tel. 217/785-2040; FAX. 217/785-4308; Laura B. Landrum, Deputy Director

Illinois Department of Public Health, Office of Health Care Regulation, 525 West Jefferson Street, Springfield, IL 62761; tel. 217/782-2913; FAX. 217/524-6292; William A. Bell, Deputy Director

Illinois Department of Public Health, Office of Health Protection, 525 West Jefferson Street, Springfield, IL 62761; tel. 217/782-3984; FAX. 217/524-0802; Dave King, Deputy Director

Illinois Department of Public Health Laboratories, 825 North Rutledge Street, P.O. Box 19435, Springfield, IL 62794-9435; tel. 217/782-6562; FAX. 217/524-7924; David Carpenter, Ph.D., State Laboratory Director

Illinois Department of Public Health, Office of Health Care Resources, Bureau of Hospitals and Ambulatory Services, 525 West Jefferson Street, Fourth Floor, Springfield, IL 62761; tel. 217/782-7412; FAX. 217/782-0382; Catherine M. Stokes, Assistant Deputy Director

Insurance
Department of Insurance, 320 West Washington Street, Fourth Floor, Springfield, IL 62767; tel. 217/782-4515; FAX. 217/782-5020; Arnold Dutcher, Acting Director

Licensing
Illinois Department of Professional Regulation, James R. Thompson Center, 100 West Randolph, Chicago, IL 60601; tel. 312/814-4500; FAX. 312/814-1837; Leonard A. Sherman, Director

Social Services
Department of Public Aid, 201 South Grand Avenue, E., Springfield, IL 62763; tel. 217/782-1200; FAX. 217/524-7979; Ann Patla, Director

Division of Specialized Care for Children, University of Illinois, (Illinois' Title V Program for Children with Special Care Needs), 2815 West Washington, Suite 300, Springfield, IL 62794-9481; tel. 217/793-2350; FAX. 217/793-0773; Charles N. Onufer, M.D., Director

Illinois Department of Human Services, 100 South Grand Avenue East, Springfield, IL 62762; tel. 217/557-1601; FAX. 217/557-1647; Howard A. Peters III, Secretary

Illinois Department of Human Services, 100 S. Grand Avenue, East, Springfield, IL 62762; tel. 217/557-2109; FAX. 217/557-2112; James R. Nelson, Director, Community Health and Prevention

Illinois Department of Human Services, Division of Disability a, Office of Rehabilitation Services Home Services Program, 623 East Adams Street, P.O. Box 19509, Springfield, IL 62794-9509; tel. 217/782-2722; FAX. 217/557-0142; Rob Kilbury, Assistant Bureau Chief, Home Service Program

Office of Finance and Administration, 535 West Jefferson Street, Springfield, IL 62761; tel. 217/785-2033; FAX. 217/782-3987; Gary Robinson, Deputy Director

INDIANA
The Honorable Frank O'Bannon, Governor, 317/232-4567

Health
Children's Special Health Care Services, Indiana State Department of Health, Two North Meridian Street, Section 7B, Indianapolis, IN 46204; tel. 317/233-5578; FAX. 317/233-5609; Wendy S. Gettelfinger, Director

Indiana State Department of Health, Two North Meridian Street, Indianapolis, IN 46204; tel. 317/233-7400; FAX. 317/233-7387; Richard D. Feldman, M.D., State Health Commissioner

Indiana State Department of Health, Division of Acute Care, Two North Meridian Street, Indianapolis, IN 46204; tel. 317/233-7474; FAX. 317/233-7157; Mary Azbill, Director

Insurance
Department of Insurance, 311 West Washington Street, Suite 300, Indianapolis, IN 46204; tel. 317/232-2387; FAX. 317/232-5251; Liz Carroll, Chief Deputy Commissioner

Licensing
Indiana State Board of Nursing, Health Professions Bureau, 402 West Washington Street, Room 041, Indianapolis, IN 46204; tel. 317/232-1105; FAX. 317/233-4236; Barbara Powers, Director

Medical Licensing Board of Indiana, Health Professions Bureau, 402 West Washington, Suite 041, Indianapolis, IN 46204; tel. 317/232-2960; FAX. 317/233-4236

Social Services
Division of Long Term Care, Two North Meridian Street, Fourth Floor, Indianapolis, IN 46204; tel. 317/233-7442; FAX. 317/233-7322; Suzanne Hornstein, Director

Indiana Family and Social Services Administration, 402 West Washington Street, P.O. Box 7083, Indianapolis, IN 46207-7083; tel. 317/233-4454; FAX. 317/233-4693; Venita J. Moore, Interim Secretary

Indiana Family and Social Services Administration, Division of Mental Health, Indiana Government Center-South, W353, 402 West Washington Street, Indianapolis, IN 46204; tel. 317/232-7800; FAX. 317/233-3472; Patrick Sullivan, Ph.D., Director

Indiana Family and Social Services Administration, Office of Medicaid Policy and Planning, Indiana Government Center-South, 402 West Washington, Room W 382, Indianapolis, IN 46204-2739; tel. 317/233-4455; FAX. 317/232-7382; Kathleen D. Gifford, Assistant Secretary

Maternal and Child Health Services, Indiana State Department of Health, Two North Meridian Street, Suite 700, Indianapolis, IN 46204; tel. 317/233-1262; FAX. 317/233-1299; Judith A. Ganser, M.D., M.P.H., Medical Director

IOWA
The Honorable Thomas Vilsack, Governor, 515/281-5211

Health
Center for Health Policy, Iowa Department of Public Health, Lucas State Office Building, Fourth Floor, Des Moines, IA 50319; tel. 515/281-4346; FAX. 515/281-4958; Gerd Clabaugh, Director

Department of Public Health, Lucas State Office Building, 1st, 3rd and 4th Floors, Des Moines, IA 50319-0075; tel. 515/281-5605; FAX. 515/281-4958; Christopher G. Atchison, Director

Division of Health Protection, Iowa Department of Public Health, Lucas State Office Building, First Floor, Des Moines, IA 50319; tel. 515/281-7785; FAX. 515/281-4529; John R. Kelly, Director

Insurance
Division of Insurance, 330 E. Maple, Des Moines, IA 50319-0065; tel. 515/281-5705; FAX. 515/281-3059; Therese M. Vaughan, Commissioner

Licensing
Department of Inspection and Appeals, Division of Health Facilities, Lucas State Office Building, Des Moines, IA 50319; tel. 515/281-4115; FAX. 515/242-5022; J. B. Bennett, Administrator

Iowa Board of Nursing, State Capitol Complex, Des Moines, IA 50319; tel. 515/281-3255; FAX. 515/281-4825; Lorinda K. Inman, RN, M.S.N., Executive Director

Iowa State Board of Medical Examiners, State Capitol Complex, Executive Hills West, Des Moines, IA 50319; tel. 515/281-5171; FAX. 515/242-5908; Ann M. Martino, Ph.D., Executive Director

Social Services
Child Health Specialty Clinics, 247 Hospital School, Iowa City, IA 52242-1011; tel. 319/356-1469; FAX. 319/356-3715; Jeffrey G. Labas, M.D., Director

Department of Human Services, Hoover State Office Building, Des Moines, IA 50319; tel. 515/281-5452; FAX. 515/281-4597; Charles M. Palmer, Director

Division of Mental Health/Developmental Disabilities, Hoover State Office Building, Des Moines, IA 50319-0114; tel. 515/281-5874; FAX. 515/281-4597; Division Administrator

Division of Substance Abuse and Health Promotion, Iowa Department of Public Health, Lucas State Office Building, 321 East 12th Street, Des Moines, IA 50319-0075; tel. 515/281-3641; FAX. 515/281-4535; Janet Zwick, Director

Governor's Alliance on Substance Abuse, Lucas State Office Building, Des Moines, IA 50319; tel. 515/281-4518; FAX. 515/242-6390; Dale Woolery, Administrator

Iowa Department of Elder Affairs, 200 – 10th, 3rd Floor, Des Moines, IA 50309-3609; tel. 515/281-5187; FAX. 515/281-4036; Betty L. Grandquist, Executive Director

Other
Department of Education, Division of Vocational Rehabilitation Services, 510 East 12th Street, Des Moines, IA 50319; tel. 515/281-4211; FAX. 515/281-4703; Dwight R. Carlson, Acting Administrator

KANSAS
The Honorable Bill Graves, Governor, 785/296-3232

Health
Kansas Department of Health and Environment, Landon State Office Building, 900 Southwest Jackson, Topeka, KS 66612-1290; tel. 913/296-0461; FAX. 913/368-6368; Clyde Graeber, Secretary, Kansas Health and Environment

Insurance
Kansas Insurance Department, 420 Southwest Ninth, Topeka, KS 66612; tel. 913/296-3071; FAX. 913/296-2283; Kathleen Sebelius, Commissioner, Insurance

Kansas Insurance Department, Accident and Health Division, 420 Southwest Ninth, Topeka, KS 66612; tel. 913/296-7850; FAX. 913/296-2283; Richard G. Huncker, Supervisor

Licensing
Kansas State Board of Healing Arts, 235 South Topeka Boulevard, Topeka, KS 66603-3068; tel. 913/296-7413; FAX. 913/296-0852; Lawrence T. Buening, Jr., Executive Director

Kansas State Board of Nursing, Landon State Office Building, Topeka, KS 66612-1230; tel. 785/296-4929; FAX. 785/296-3929; Patsy Johnson, RN, M.N., Executive Administrator

Social Services
Adult and Medical Services, Docking State Office Building, 915 Southwest Harrison, Topeka, KS 66612; tel. 913/296-3981; FAX. 913/296-4813; Ann E. Koci, Commissioner

Field Services, Kansas Department of Health and Bureau of Health Facility Regulation, Bureau of Adult and Child Care Facilities, 900 Southwest Jackson, Suite 1001, Topeka, KS 66612-1290; tel. 913/296-3362; FAX. 913/296-1266; Greg L. Reser, Assistant Director, Field Services

Mental Health and Developmental Disabilities, Docking State Office Building, Fifth Floor–N, Topeka, KS 66612; tel. 913/296-3773; FAX. 913/296-6142; Connie Hubbell, Commissioner

Rehabilitation Services, 3640 SW Topeka Blvd., Suite 150, Topeka, KS 66611-2373; tel. 785/267-5301; Joyce A. Cussimanio, Commissioner

State Department of Social and Rehabilitation Services, Docking State Office Building, Suite 681–W, Topeka, KS 66612; tel. 913/296-6750; FAX. 913/296-6960; Candy Shively, Commissioner

KENTUCKY
The Honorable Paul E. Patton, Governor, 502/564-2611

Health
Commission for Children with Special Health Care Needs, 982 Eastern Parkway, Louisville, KY 40217; tel. 502/595-4459; FAX. 502/595-4673; Beverly Hampton, Executive Staff Advisor

Commission for Health Economics Control, 275 East Main Street, Frankfort, KY 40621; tel. 502/564-6620; W. R. Hourigan, Ph.D., Chairman

Department For Mental Health/Mental Retardation Services, 100 Fair Oaks Lane, Frankfort, KY 40621-0001; tel. 502/564-4527; FAX. 502/564-5478; Elizabeth Rehm Wachtel, Ph.D., Commissioner

Department for Public Health, Cabinet for Health Services, 275 East Main Street, Frankfort, KY 40621; tel. 502/564-3970; FAX. 502/564-6533; Rice C. Leach, M.D., MSHSA, Commissioner

Health Data Branch, 275 East Main Street, HSIE–C, Frankfort, KY 40621; tel. 502/564-2757; FAX. 502/564-6533; George Robertson, Manager

---

Insurance

Department of Insurance, Division of Health Policy and Managed Care, 215 West Main Street, P.O. Box 517, Frankfort, KY 40602; tel. 502/564-6088; FAX. 502/564-2728; Carrie Banahan, Branch Manager

Licensing

Division of Licensing and Regulation, Office of Inspector General, C.H.R. Building, Fourth Floor, E., 275 East Main Street – 4ES, Frankfort, KY 40621; tel. 502/564-2800; FAX. 502/565-6546; Rebecca J. Cecil, R.Ph., Director

Kentucky Board of Nursing, 312 Whittington Parkway, Suite 300, Louisville, KY 40222-5172; tel. 502/329-7000; FAX. 502/329-7011; Sharon M. Weisenbeck, M.S., RN, Executive Director

Social Services

Department for Community Based Services, 3rd Floor West, 275 East Main Street, Frankfort, KY 40621; tel. 502/564-3703; FAX. 502/564-6907; Dietra Paris, Commissioner

Department for Medicaid Services, 275 East Main Street, Frankfort, KY 40621; tel. 502/564-4321; FAX. 502/564-6917; John Morse, Commissioner

Department of Vocational Rehabilitation, 209 St. Clair Street, Frankfort, KY 40601; tel. 502/564-4440; FAX. 502/564-6745; Sam Seraglio, Commissioner

LOUISIANA
The Honorable Mike Foster, Governor, 225/342-7015

Health

Department of Health and Hospitals, Bureau of Health Services , Health Standards Section, Box 3767, Baton Rouge, LA 70821; tel. 504/342-0138; FAX. 504/342-5292; Lily W. McAlister, RN, Manager, Health Standards Section

Louisiana Department of Health and Hospitals, P.O. Box 629 Bin 2, Baton Rouge, LA 70821; tel. 504/342-9509; FAX. 504/342-9508; Rose V. Forrest, Secretary

Louisiana State University Medical Center, Health Care Services Division, 8550 United Plaza Boulevard, Fourth Floor, Baton Rouge, LA 70809; tel. 504/922-0490; FAX. 504/922-2259; Cary M. Dougherty, Jr., Chief Operating Officer

Louisiana State University Medical Center, Health Care Services Division–Medical Center of LA at New Orleans, 2021 Perdido Street, New Orleans, LA 70112-1352; tel. 504/588-3332; FAX. 504/588-3580; John S. Berault, MSPH, Chief Executive Officer

Insurance

Department of Insurance, P.O. Box 94214, Baton Rouge, LA 70804; tel. 504/342-0860; FAX. 504/342-3078; James H. Brown, Commissioner

Licensing

Louisiana State Board of Medical Examiners, 630 Camp Street, Zip 70130, P.O. Box 30250, New Orleans, LA 70190-0250; tel. 504/524-6763; FAX. 504/568-8893; Paula M. Mensen, Administrative Manager II

Louisiana State Board of Nursing, 150 Baronne Street, New Orleans, LA 70112; tel. 504/568-5464; Barbara L. Movant, RN, M.N.

Louisiana State Board of Practical Nurse Examiners, 3421 North Causeway Boulevard, Suite 203, Metairie, LA 70002; tel. 504/838-5791; FAX. 504/838-5279; Dennis S. Mann, Esq., Executive Director

Social Services

Office of Alcohol and Drug Abuse, P.O. Box 2790, Baton Rouge, LA 70821-2790; tel. 504/342-6717; FAX. 504/342-3875; Alton E. Hadley, Assistant Secretary

Office of Community Services, P.O. Box 3318, Baton Rouge, LA 70821; tel. 504/342-2297; FAX. 504/342-2268; Shirley Goodwin, Assistant Secretary

Office of Family Support, P.O. Box 94065, Baton Rouge, LA 70804-9065; tel. 225/342-3950; Vera W. Blakes, Assistant Secretary

Other

Office of The Secretary, P.O. Box 629, Baton Rouge, LA 70821; tel. 504/342-9500; FAX. 504/342-5568; David W. Hood, Secretary

MAINE
The Honorable Angus S. King, Jr., Governor, 297/287-3531

Health

Bureau of Health, Department of Human Services, 11 State House Station, Augusta, ME 04333; tel. 207/287-8016; FAX. 207/287-9058; Dora Anne Mills, M.D., M.P.H., Director

Division of Community and Family Health, 151 Capitol Street, 11 State House Station, Augusta, ME 04333-0011; tel. 207/287-3311; FAX. 207/287-4631; Valerie Ricker, MSN, MS, NP

Insurance

Bureau of Insurance, Department of Professional and Financial Regulation, 34 State House Station, Augusta, ME 04333; tel. 207/624-8475; FAX. 207/624-8599; David Stetson, Supervisor, Life and Health Division

Licensing

Board of Licensure in Medicine, Two Bangor Street, 137 State House Station, Augusta, ME 04333; tel. 207/287-3601; FAX. 207/287-6590; Randal C. Manning, Executive Director

Department of Professional and Financial Regulation, 35 State House Station, Augusta, ME 04333; tel. 207/624-8511; FAX. 207/624-8595; S. Catherine Longley, Commissioner

Division of Licensing and Certification, Department of Human Services, 35 Anthony Avenue, Station 11, Augusta, ME 04333; tel. 207/624-5443; FAX. 207/624-5378; Louis Dorogi, Director

Maine State Board of Nursing, 24 Stone Street, 158 State House Station, Augusta, ME 04333; tel. 207/287-1133; FAX. 207/287-1149; Myra A. Broadway, J.D., RN, Executive Director

Social Services

Bureau of Elder and Adult Services, 35 Anthony Avenue, State House Station, Augusta, ME 04333; tel. 207/624-5335; FAX. 207/624-5361; Christine Gianopoulos, Director

Bureau of Rehabilitation Services, 150 State House Station, Augusta, ME 04333-0150; tel. 207/287-5100; FAX. 207/287-5166; Linda Jariz, Director

Bureau of Rehabilitation Services, Division of Deafness, 35 Anthony Avenue, Augusta, ME 04333-0150; tel. 207/624-5318; FAX. 207/624-5302; Alice C. Johnson, State Coordinator

Department of Human Services, Bureau of Medical Services, State House, Station 11, Augusta, ME 04333; tel. 207/287-2674; FAX. 207/287-2675; Francis T. Finnegan, Jr., Director

Department of Mental Health, Mental Retardation and Substance , State House Station 40, Augusta, ME 04333; tel. 207/287-4220; FAX. 207/287-4268; Andrea Blanch, Associate Commissioner, Programs

Department of Mental Health, Mental Retardation and Substance , Abuse Services, 40 State House Station, Augusta, ME 04333-0040; tel. 207/287-4223; FAX. 207/287-4268; Melodie J. Peet, Commissioner

Division for the Blind and Visually Impaired, 150 State House Station, Augusta, ME 04333-0150; tel. 207/287-5256; FAX. 207/287/5166; Harold Lewis, Director

Maine Department of Human Services, State House, Station 11, Augusta, ME 04333; tel. 207/287-2736; FAX. 207/287-3005; Kevin W. Concannon, Commissioner

MARYLAND
The Honorable Parris N. Glendening, Governor, 410/974-3901

Health

Community and Public Health Administration, 201 West Preston Street, Baltimore, MD 21201; tel. 410/225-5300; FAX. 410/333-7106; Dr. Carlossia Hussein, Director

Department of Health and Mental Hygiene, 201 West Preston Street, Room 500, Baltimore, MD 21201; tel. 410/767-6500; FAX. 410/767-6489; Martin P. Wasserman, M.D., J.D., Secretary

Department of Health and Mental Hygiene, 201 West Preston Street, Baltimore, MD 21201; tel. 410/767-6500; FAX. 410/767-6489; Martin P. Wasserman, M.D., J.D., Secretary

Insurance

Maryland Insurance Administration, 502 St. Paul Place, Baltimore, MD 21202; tel. 410/468-2000; FAX. 410/468-2020; Steven B. Larsen, Insurance Commissioner

Licensing

Board of Physician Quality Assurance, 4201 Patterson Avenue, Baltimore, MD 21215; tel. 800/492-6836; FAX. 410/358-2252; J. Michael Compton, Executive Director

Licensing and Certification Administration, 4201 West Patterson Avenue, Baltimore, MD 21215; tel. 410/764-2750; FAX. 410/358-0750; Carol Benner, Director

Maryland Board of Nursing, 4140 Patterson Avenue, Baltimore, MD 21215-2254; tel. 410/585-1900; FAX. 410/358-3530; Donna M. Dorsey, RN, M.S., Executive Director

Social Services

Alcohol and Drug Abuse Administration, 201 West Preston Street, Baltimore, MD 21201; tel. 410/767-6925; FAX. 410/333-7206; Thomas Davis, Director

Developmental Disabilities Administration, 201 West Preston Street., Baltimore, MD 21201; tel. 410/767-5600; FAX. 410/767-5850; Diane K. Coughlin, Director

Division of Rehabilitation Services, 2301 Argonne Drive, Baltimore, MD 21218-1696; tel. 410/554-9385; FAX. 410/554-9412; Robert A. Burns, Assistant State Superintendent

Local and Family Health Administration, 201 West Preston Street, Baltimore, MD 21201; tel. 410/767-5300; FAX. 410/333-7106; Carlessia A. Hussein, Dr.P.H., Director

Mental Hygiene Administration, 201 West Preston Street, Baltimore, MD 21201; tel. 410/767-6655; FAX. 410/333-5402; Oscar L. Morgan, Director

Social Services Administration, 311 West Saratoga Street, Fifth Floor, Baltimore, MD 21201; tel. 410/767-7216; FAX. 410/333-0127; Linda D. Ellard, Executive Director

Other

Laboratories Administration, 201 West Preston Street, Baltimore, MD 21201; tel. 410/767-6100; FAX. 410/333-5403; J. Mehsen Joseph, Ph.D., Director

Maryland Department of the Environment, Office of Environmental Health Coordination, 2500 Broening Highway, Baltimore, MD 21224; tel. 410/631-3851; FAX. 410/631-4112; Tom Allen, Director

Maryland State Department of Education, 200 West Baltimore Street, Baltimore, MD 21201-1595; tel. 410/767-0100; FAX. 410/333-6033; Nancy S. Grasmick, State Superintendent of Schools

Office of Planning and Capital Financing, 201 West Preston Street, Baltimore, MD 21201; tel. 410/767-6816; FAX. 410/333-7525; Elizabeth G. Barnard, Director

MASSACHUSETTS
The Honorable Argeo Paul Cellucci, Governor, 617/727-9173

Health

Bureau of Environmental Health Assessment, 250 Washington Street, Seventh Floor, Boston, MA 02108; tel. 617/624-5757; FAX. 617/624-5777; Suzanne K. Condon, Director

Bureau of Health Quality Management, Massachusetts Department of Public Health, 250 Washington Street, Boston, MA 02108-4619; tel. 617/624-5280; FAX. 617/624-5046; Nancy Ridley, Assistant Commissioner

Bureau of Health Statistics, Research and Evaluation, Massachusetts Department of Public Health, 250 Washington Street, Sixth Floor, Boston, MA 02108-4619; tel. 617/624-5613; FAX. 617/624-5698; Daniel J. Friedman, Ph.D., Assistant Commissioner

Department of Transitional Assistance, 600 Washington Street, Boston, MA 02111; tel. 617/348-8402; FAX. 617/348-8575; Claire McIntire, Commissioner

Office of Emergency Medical Services, 470 Atlantic Avenue, Second Floor, Boston, MA 02210-2208; tel. 617/753-8300; FAX. 617/753-8350; Louise Goyette, Director

Insurance

Division of Insurance, 470 Atlantic Avenue, Boston, MA 02210-2223; tel. 617/521-7794; FAX. 617/521-7770; Linda Ruthardt, Commissioner

Licensing

Board of Registration in Medicine, Commonwealth of Massachusetts, Boston, MA 02111; tel. 617/727-3086; FAX. 617/451-9568; Alexander F. Fleming, Executive Director

Division of Health Care Quality, 10 West Street, Fifth Floor, Boston, MA 02111; tel. 617/753–8100; FAX. 617/753–8125; Paul I. Dreyer, Ph.D., Director

Massachusetts Board of Registration in Nursing, 100 Cambridge Street, Suite 1519, Boston, MA 02202; tel. 617/727–9961; FAX. 617/727–1630; Theresa M. Bonanno, M.S.N., RN, Executive Director

Social Services

Commission for the Blind, 88 Kingston Street, Boston, MA 02111; tel. 617/727–5550; FAX. 617/727–5960; David Govostes, Commissioner

Massachusetts Department of Mental Health, Central Office, 25 Stanford Street, Boston, MA 02114; tel. 617/727–5500; FAX. 617/727–4350; Marylou Sudders, Commissioner

Massachusetts Department of Public Health, 150 Tremont Street, 10th Floor, Boston, MA 02111; tel. 617/727–2700; FAX. 617/727–2559; David H. Mulligan, Commissioner

Massachusetts Department of Public Health, Bureau of Substance Abuse, 250 Washington Street, Third Floor, Boston, MA 02108–4619; tel. 617/624–5111; FAX. 617/624–5185; Mayra Rodriguez–Howard, Director

Massachusetts Rehabilitation Commission, Fort Point Place, 27–43 Wormwood Street, Boston, MA 02210–1606; tel. 617/204–3600; FAX. 617/727–1354; Elmer C. Bartels, Commissioner

MICHIGAN
The Honorable John Engler, Governor, 517/335-7858

Health

Bureau of Health Systems, Michigan Department of Consumer and Industry Services, 525 West Ottawa, P.O. Box 30664, Lansing, MI 48909; tel. 517/241–2626; FAX. 517/241–2635; Walter S. Wheeler III, Director

Division of Chronic Disease and Injury Control, 3423 North Martin Luther King, Jr. Boulevard, P.O. Box 30195, Lansing, MI 48909; tel. 517/335–8368; FAX. 517/335–8593; Jean Chabut, Director

Medical Services Administration, 400 South Pine, P.O. Box 30037, Lansing, MI 48909; tel. 517/335–5000; FAX. 517/335–5007; Robert M. Smedes, Chief Executive Officer

Licensing

Department of Consumer and Industry Services, Michigan Insurance Bureau, 611 West Ottawa, Second Floor, P.O. Box 30220, Lansing, MI 48909–7720; tel. 517/373–9273; FAX. 517/335–4978; Frank M. Fitzgerald, Commissioner

Division of Licensing and Certification, 3500 North Logan Street, Lansing, MI 48909; tel. 517/335–8505; Nancy Graham, Supervisor

Managed Care Quality Assessment and Improvement Division, Michigan Department of Community Health, P.O. Box 30195, Lansing, MI 48909; tel. 517/335–8551; FAX. 517/335–9239; Julia Harris Griffith, Director

Michigan Board of Medicine, 611 West Ottawa Street, Box 30670, Lansing, MI 48909; tel. 517/373–6873; FAX. 517/373–2179; Carole Hakala Engle, Director, Licensing

Michigan Board of Nursing, 611 West Ottawa Street, Box 30670, Lansing, MI 48909; tel. 517/335–0918; FAX. 517/373–2179; Doris Foley, Licensing Administrator

Social Services

Bureau of Rehabilitation and Disability Determination, Box 30010, Lansing, MI 48909; tel. 517/373–3390; Ivan L. Cotman, Associate Superintendent

Bureau of Substance Abuse Services, Michigan Department of Community Health, 320 S. Walnut Street, Lewis Cass Building, Lansing, MI 48913; tel. 517/335–0278; FAX. 517/241–2611; Deborah J. Hollis, Acting Director

Michigan Department of Community Health, Lewis Cass Building, Lansing, MI 48913; tel. 517/373–3500; FAX. 517/335–3090; James K. Haveman, Jr., Director

Michigan Department of Community Health, Community Public Health Agency, 3423 North Martin Luther King, Jr. Boulevard, Lansing, MI 48909; tel. 517/335–0267; FAX. 517/335–3090; James K. Haveman, Jr., Director, MDCH

Michigan Department of Community Health, Health Legislation and Policy Development, 320 S. Walnut Street, Lewis Cass Building, 6th Floor, Lansing, MI 48913; tel. 517/373–2559; FAX. 517/241–1200; Carol L. Isaacs, Deputy Director

Office of Health and Human Services, Michigan Department of Management and Budget, Lewis Cass Building, Box 30026, Lansing, MI 48909; tel. 517/373–1076; FAX. 517/373–3624; Paul Reinhart, Director

Office of Services to the Aging, P.O. Box 30026, Lansing, MI 48909; tel. 517/373–8230; FAX. 517/373–4092; Carol Parr, Acting Director

Other

Department of Education, Box 30008, Lansing, MI 48909; tel. 517/373–7247; FAX. 517/373–1233; Patricia Nichols, Supervisor, School Health Programs U

Michigan Department of Consumer and Industry Services, Office of Health Services, Box 30670, Lansing, MI 48909; tel. 517/373–8068; FAX. 517/241–3082; Thomas C. Lindsay II, Director

Michigan Department of Consumer and Industry Services, Laboratories, Laboratory Improvement Section, Lansing, MI 48909; tel. 517/241–2640; FAX. 517/241–2635; Richard J. Benson, Chief

Michigan Department of Environmental Quality, Drinking Water and Radiological Protection Division, Medical Waste Regulatory Program, 3423 North Martin Luther King Jr. Boulevard, P.O. Box 30630, Lansing, MI 48909; tel. 517/335–8637; FAX. 517/335–9033; John N. Gohlke, R.S., M.S.A., Program Chief

Michigan Family Independence Agency, 235 South Grand Avenue, P.O. Box 30037, Lansing, MI 48909; tel. 517/373–2035; FAX. 517335–6236; Mark Jasonowicz – Interim Director

Office of Health Services, Department of Consumer and Industry Services, P.O. Box 30670, Lansing, MI 48909; tel. 517/373–8068; FAX. 517/373–2179; Thomas C. Lindsay II, Director

MINNESOTA
The Honorable Jesse Ventura, Governor, 651/296-3391

Health

Division of Environmental Health, 121 East Seventh Place, P.O. Box 64975, St. Paul, MN 55164–0975; tel. 651/215–0700; FAX. 651/215–0979; Patricia A. Bloomgren, Director

Minnesota Department of Health, 85 East 7th Place, Suite 400, St. Paul, MN 55101; tel. 651/215–5813; FAX. 651/215–5801; Jan K. Malcolm, Commissioner

Minnesota Department of Health, Division of Finance and Administration, 121 East 7th Place, P.O. Box 64975, St. Paul, MN 55164–0975; tel. 651–296–4625; FAX. 651–282–3832

Minnesota Department of Health, Office of Regulatory Reform, 121 East Seventh Place, P.O. Box 64975, St. Paul, MN 55164–0975; tel. 612/282–5627; FAX. 612/282–3839; Nanette M. Schroeder, Director

Public Health Laboratory Division, 717 Southeast Delaware Street, P.O. Box 9441, Minneapolis, MN 55440; tel. 612/623–5331; FAX. 612/623–5514; Pauline Bouchard, J.D., Director

Licensing

Facility and Provider Compliance Division, Minnesota Department of Health, 393 North Dunlap Street, P.O. Box 64900, St. Paul, MN 55164–0900; tel. 612/643–2100; FAX. 612/643–2593; Linda G. Sutherland, Director

Licensing and Certification, 393 North Dunlap Street, P.O. Box 64900, St. Paul, MN 55164–0900; tel. 612/643–2130; FAX. 612/643–3534; Carol Hirschfeld, Supervisor, Program Assurance Unit

Minnesota Board of Medical Practice, 2829 University Avenue, S.E., Suite 400, Minneapolis, MN 55414–3246; tel. 612/617–2130; FAX. 612/617–2166; Robert A. Leach, Executive Director

Minnesota Board of Nursing, 2829 University Avenue, S.E., Suite 500, Minneapolis, MN 55414–3253; tel. 612/617–2270; FAX. 612/617–2190; Joyce M. Schowalter, Executive Director

Social Services

Minnesota Department of Health, Division of Community Health Services, Metro Square Building, Suite 460, 121 East Seventh Place, Zip 55101, St. Paul, MN 55164–0975; tel. 651–296–9720; FAX. 651–296–9362; Ryan Church, Director

Minnesota Department of Health, Division of Disease Prevention and Control, 717 Southeast Delaware Street, P.O. Box 9441, Minneapolis, MN 55440–9441; tel. 612/676–5363; FAX. 612/676–5666; Agnes T. Leitheiser, Director

Minnesota Department of Health, Division of Family Health, 717 Southeast Delaware Street, P.O. Box 9441, Minneapolis, MN 55440; tel. 612/623–5167; FAX. 612/623–5442; Norbert Hirschhorn, M.D., Director

Minnesota Department of Human Services, 444 Lafayette Road, N., St. Paul, MN 55155; tel. 651/296–6117; FAX. 651/296–6244; Michael O'Keefe, Commissioner

Rehabilitation Services Branch, 390 North Robert Street, Fifth Floor, St. Paul, MN 55101; tel. 612/296–1822; FAX. 612/296–0994; Michael T. Coleman, Assistant Commissioner

Other

Department of Commerce, 133 East Seventh Street, St. Paul, MN 55101; tel. 612/296–4026; FAX. 612/296–4328; David B. Gruenes

MISSISSIPPI
The Honorable Kirk Fordice, Governor, 601/359-3150

Health

Bureau of Environmental Health, Mississippi State Department of Health, Felix J. Underwood State Board of Health Building, Jackson, MS 32915–1700; tel. 601/960–7680; FAX. 601/354–6794; Ricky Boggan, Director

Bureau of Health Services, Felix J. Underwood State Board of Health Building An, P.O. Box 1700, Jackson, MS 32915; tel. 601/960–7472; FAX. 601/960–7480; Michael J. Gandy, Ed.D., Bureau Director, Deputy

Department of Health, Felix J. Underwood State Board of Health Building, P.O. Box 1700, Jackson, MS 32915–1700; tel. 601–576–7634; FAX. 601–576–7931; F.E. Thompson, Jr., M.D., M.P.H., State Health Officer

Health Planning and Resources Development Division, Mississippi State Department of Health, Felix J. Underwood State Board of Health Building, 2423 North State Street, Jackson, MS 39215–1700; tel. 601/576–7874; FAX. 601/576–7530; Harold B. Armstrong, Chief

Mississippi State Department of Health, Felix J. Underwood State Board of Health Building, P.O. Box 1700, Jackson, MS 32915–1700; tel. 601/960–7634; Betty Jane Phillips, Dr.P.H. Deputy State Health Officer

Public Health Statistics, Mississippi State Department of Health, Bureau of Health Statistics, Box 1700, Jackson, MS 39215–1700; tel. 601/576–7960; FAX. 601/576–7505; Nita C. Gunter, Director

Licensing

Division of Health Facilities Licensure and Certification, P.O. Box 1700, Jackson, MS 39215; tel. 601/354–7300; FAX. 601/354–7230; Vanessa Phipps, Director

Mississippi Board of Nursing, 1935 Lakeland Drive, Suite B, Jackson, MS 39216–5014; tel. 601/987–4188; FAX. 601/364–2352; Marcia M. Rachel, Ph.D., RN, M.S.N., Executive Director

Social Services

Children's Medical Program, 421 Stadium Circle, P.O. Box 1700, Jackson, MS 39215–1700; tel. 601/987–3965; FAX. 601/987–5560; Mike Gallarno, Director

Department of Mental Health, 1101 Robert E. Lee Building, Jackson, MS 39201; tel. 601/359–1288; FAX. 601/359–6295; Randy Hendrix, Ph.D., Director

Mississippi Department of Human Services, P.O. Box 352, Jackson, MS 39205–0352; tel. 601/359–4480; FAX. 601/359–4477; Donald R. Taylor, Executive Director

State Department of Rehabilitation Services, P.O. Box 1698, Jackson, MS 39215–1698; tel. 601/853–5100; FAX. 601/853–5205; Perry Winegarden, Interim Director

Section C

Other

State Epidemiologist, Underwood Annex, P.O Box 1700, Jackson, MS 32915-1700; tel. 601/960-7725; FAX. 601/354-6061; Mary Currier, M.D., M.P.H.

MISSOURI
The Honorable Mel Carnahan, Governor, 573/751-3222

Health

Center for Health Information Management and Epidemiology (CHIME), Box 570, Jefferson City, MO 65102; tel. 573/751-6272; FAX. 573/526-4102; Garland H. Land, Director

Department of Health, Box 570, Jefferson City, MO 65102; tel. 314/751-6001; FAX. 314/751-6041; Maureen E. Dempsey, M.D., Director

Missouri Department of Health – Bureau of Special Health Care Needs, 930 Wildwood Drive, P.O. Box 570, Jefferson City, MO 65109; tel. 314/751-6246; FAX. 314/751-6237; Richard Brown, Chief

Insurance

Department of Insurance, P.O. Box 690, Jefferson City, MO 65102; tel. 314/751-4126; FAX. 314/751-1165; A.W. McPherson, Acting Director

Licensing

Bureau of Hospital Licensing and Certification, Missouri Department of Health, Box 570, Jefferson City, MO 65102; tel. 314/751-6302; FAX. 314/526-3621; Darrell Hendrickson, Administrator

Missouri State Board of Registration for the Healing Arts, 3605 Missouri Boulevard, Zip 65109, P.O. Box 4, Jefferson City, MO 65102; tel. 314/751-0098; FAX. 314/751-3166; Tina Steinman, Executive Director

Social Services

Department of Mental Health, 1706 East Elm Street, P.O. Box 687, Jefferson City, MO 65102; tel. 573/751-4122; FAX. 573/751-8224; Roy C. Wilson, M.D., Director

Life and Health Section, Missouri Department of Insurance, P.O. Box 690, Jefferson City, MO 65102; tel. 573/751-4363; FAX. 573/526-6075; James W. Casey, Supervisor

Missouri Division of Vocational Rehabilitation, 3024 West Truman Boulevard, Jefferson City, MO 65109-0525; tel. 573/751-3251; FAX. 314/751-1441; Ronald W. Vessell, Assistant Commissioner

Other

Department of Elementary and Secondary Education, 205 Jefferson, P.O. Box 480, Jefferson City, MO 65102; tel. 573/751-4446; FAX. 573/751-1179; Dr. Robert E. Bartman, Commissioner of Education

Division of Nutritional Health and Services, 930 Wildwood Drive, P.O. Box 570, Jefferson City, MO 65109; tel. 314/526-5520; FAX. 314/526-5348; Gretchen C. Wartman, Director

MONTANA
The Honorable Marc Racicot, Governor, 406/444-3111

Health

Health Policy and Services Division, Montana Department of Public Health and Human Services, 1400 Broadway, P.O. Box 202951, Helena, MT 59620-2951; tel. 406/444-4540; FAX. 406/444-1861; Nancy Ellery, Administrator

Licensing

Quality Assurance Division, Department of Public Health and Human Services, Certification Bureau, Cogswell Building, 1400 Broadway, Helena, MT 59620-2951; tel. 406/444-2099; FAX. 406/444-3456; Linda Sandman, Chief

Social Services

Aging Services, Senior and Long Term Care Division, Department of Public Health and Human Services, 111 Sanders, P.O. Box 4210, Helena, MT 59604; tel. 406/444-7785; FAX. 406/444-7743; Robert E. Bartholomew, State Long Term Care Ombudsman

Child and Family Services Division, P.O. Box 8005, Helena, MT 59604-8005; tel. 406/444-5902; FAX. 406/444-5956; Hank Hudson, Administrator

Department of Public Health and Human Services, 111 North Sanders Street, Box 4210, Helena, MT 59604-4210; tel. 406/444-5622; FAX. 406/444-1970; Laurie Ekanger, Director

Disability Services Division, P.O. Box 4210, Helena, MT 59604; tel. 406/444-2590; FAX. 406/444-3632; Joe A. Mathews, Administrator

Family/Maternal and Child Health Services Bureau, W. F. Cogswell Building, Helena, MT 59620; tel. 406/444-4740; FAX. 406/444-2606; JoAnn Walsh Dotson, RN MSN, Bureau Chief

Montana Department of Public Health and Human Services, 111 North Sanders, P.O. Box 4210, Helena, MT 59604; tel. 406/444-5622; FAX. 406/444-1970; Laurie Ekanger, Director

Other

Department of Commerce, Montana State Board of Nursing, Arcade Building – 4-C, 111 North Jackson, Helena, MT 59620-0513; tel. 406/444-2071; FAX. 406/444-7759; Joan Bowers, Administrative Assistant

NEBRASKA
The Honorable Mike Johanns, Governor, 402/471-2244

Insurance

Department of Insurance, 941 O Street, Suite 400, Lincoln, NE 68508; tel. 402/471-2201; FAX. 402/471-4610; L. Tim Wagner, Director

Licensing

Division of Health Policy and Planning, 301 Centennial Mall, S., P.O. Box 95007, Lincoln, NE 68509; tel. 402/471-2337; David Palm, Ph.D., Director

HHS R&L Credentialing Division, 301 Centennial Mall, S., Box 94986, Lincoln, NE 68509-4986; tel. 402/471-2115; FAX. 402/471-3577; Helen L. Meeks, Director

Nebraska Department of Regulation and Licensure, Credentialing Division, 301 Centennial Mall, S., P.O. Box 94986, Lincoln, NE 68509-4986; tel. 402/471-2946; FAX. 402/471-0555; Helen Meeks, Director

Social Services

Department of Health and Human Services – Regulation, Certificate of Need Program and Licensure, P.O. Box 95007, Lincoln, NE 68509-5007; tel. 402/471-2105; FAX. 402/471-0555; Don Smith, Fiscal Analyst

Division of Family Health, Nebraska Department of Health and Human Services, 301 Centennial Mall South, P.O. Box 95044, Lincoln, NE 68509-5044; tel. 402/471-3980; FAX. 402/471-7049; Paula Eurek, R.D., Division Administrator

Nebraska Department of Health & Human Services, Regulation & Licensure, 301 Centennial Mall South, P.O. Box 957007, Lincoln, NE 68509-5007; tel. 402/471-2133; FAX. 402/471-9449; Richard P. Nelson, Director

Nebraska Department of Health and Human Services, Services, 301 Centennial Mall, S., P.O. Box 95044, Lincoln, NE 68509; tel. 402/471-0191; FAX. 402/471-8259; Sue Medinger, Nutrition Consultant

Nebraska Department of Health and Human Services, Special Services for Children and Adults, 301 Centennial Mall, S., P.O. Box 95044, Lincoln, NE 68509-5044; tel. 402/471-9345; FAX. 402/471-9455; Mary Jo Iwan, Administrator

Nebraska Health and Human Services, Finance and Support Medicaid Division Medical Services Division, 301 Centennial Mall, S., P.O. Box 95026, Lincoln, NE 68509; tel. 402/471-9147; FAX. 402/471-9092; Cec Brady, Administrator

Nebraska Health and Human Services System, 301 Centennial Mall, S., P.O. Box 95026, Lincoln, NE 68509-5026; tel. 402/471-9105; FAX. 401/471-9449; Chris Peterson, Policy Secretary

Other

Department of Education, Vocational Rehabilitation, 301 Centennial Mall, S., P.O. Box 94987, Lincoln, NE 68509; tel. 402/471-3644; Frank Lloyd, Assistant Commissioner

Nebraska Department of Health, Division of Radiological Health, 301 Centennial Mall, S., P.O. Box 95007, Lincoln, NE 68509; tel. 402/471-2168; FAX. 402/471-0169; Harold Borchert, Director

NEVADA
The Honorable Kenny Guinn, Governor, 775/684-5670

Health

Bureau of Health Planning and Statistics, Nevada State Health Division, 505 East King Street, Room 102, Carson City, NV 89701-4749; tel. 775/684-4218; FAX. 775/684-4156; Emil DeJan, Chief

Children With Special Health Care Needs Program, Nevada State Health Division, Kinkead Building, 505 East King, Suite 205, Carson City, NV 89710; tel. 775-684-4243; FAX. 775-684-4245; Gloria Deyhle, MCH Nurse Consultant

Division of Mental Health and Mental Retardation, Kinkead Building, Suite 602, 505 East King Street, Carson City, NV 89701-3790; tel. 775/684-5943; FAX. 775/684-5966; Carlos Brandenburg, Ph.D., Administrator

Nevada Division of Health, Kinkead Building, 505 East King Street, Room 201, Carson City, NV 89701-4761; tel. 702/687-3786; FAX. 702/687-3859; Yvonne Sylva, Administrator

Nevada State Health Division, Bureau of Community Health Services, 3656 Research Way, Suite 32, Carson City, NV 89706; tel. 775-687-6944; FAX. 775-687-7693; Mary D. Sassi, Bureau Chief

Nevada State Health Laboratory, 1660 North Virginia Street, Reno, NV 89503; tel. 702/688-1335; FAX. 702/688-1460; Arthur F. DiSalvo, M.D., Director

Insurance

Division of Insurance, Capitol Complex, 1665 Hot Springs Road, Suite 152, Carson City, NV 89710; tel. 702/687-4270; FAX. 702/687-3937; Alice A. Molasky-Arman, Commissioner

Licensing

Bureau of Licensure and Certification, Nevada Health Division, 1550 College Parkway, Capitol Complex, Suite 158, Carson City, NV 89706-7921; tel. 775-687-4475; FAX. 775-687-6588; Richard J. Panelli, Chief

Nevada State Board of Medical Examiners, 1105 Terminal Way, Suite 301, Zip 89502, P.O. Box 7238, Reno, NV 89510; tel. 702/688-2559; FAX. 702/688-2321; Larry D. Lessly, Executive Director

Nevada State Board of Nursing, 1755 East Plumb Lane, Suite 260, Reno, NV 89502; tel. 775/688-2620; FAX. 775/688-2628; Kathy Apple, M.S., RN, Executive Director

Social Services

Department of Human Resources, Kinkead Building, Carson City, NV 89710; tel. 775/684-4000; FAX. 775/684-4010; Charlotte Crawford, Director

Division of Health Care Financing & Administration, 1100 East William Street, Carson City, NV 89710; tel. 702/684-4176; FAX. 702/684-8792; Janice Wright, Acting Administrator

Division of Health Care Financing and Policy–Medicaid, 2527 North Carson Street, Carson City, NV 84706-0113; tel. 775/687-4775; FAX. 775/687-8724; April Townley, Deputy Administrator

Rehabilitation Division, Kinkead Building, 505 East King, Room 502, Carson City, NV 89710; tel. 75/684-4040; FAX. 775/684-4184; Maynard R. Yasmer, Administrator

Other

Nevada Department of Business and Industry, Director's Office, 555 East Washington, Suite 4900, Las Vegas, NV 89101; tel. 702/486-2750; FAX. 702/486-2758; Claudia Cormier, Director

NEW HAMPSHIRE
The Honorable Jeanne Shaheen, Governor, 603/271-2121

Health

Department of Health and Human Services, Six Hazen Drive, Concord, NH 03301-6527; tel. 603/271-4372; FAX. 603/271-4827; William J. Kassler, M.D., M.P.H., State Medical Director

Department of Health and Human Services, Office of Health Management, Six Hazen Drive, Concord, NH 03301-6527; tel. 603/271-4726; FAX. 603-271-4827; William J. Kassler, M.D., M.P.H., State Medical Director

Department of Health and Human Services, Office of The Commissioner, 129 Pleasant Street, Brown Building, Concord, NH 03301; tel. 603/271-4602; FAX. 603/271-4912; Kathleen G. Sgambati, Deputy Commissioner

Division of Public Health Services, Office of Family and Community Health, Health and Welfare Building, Six Hazen Drive, Concord, NH 03301; tel. 603/271-4726; FAX. 603/271-4779; Roger Taillefer, Assistant Director

Insurance

Department of Insurance, 169 Manchester Street, Concord, NH 03301; tel. 603/271-2661; FAX. 603/271-1406; Sylvio L. Dupuis, O.D., Commissioner

State of New Hampshire, Insurance Department, Examination Division, 56 Old Suncook Road, Concord, NH 03301–5151; tel. 603/271–2241; FAX. 603/271–1406; Thomas S. Burke, Director

Licensing

New Hampshire Board of Medicine, Board of Medicine, Two Industrial Park Drive, Concord, NH 03301; tel. 603/271–1203; FAX. 603/271–6702; Allen Hall, Administrator

New Hampshire Board of Nursing, 78 Regional Drive, P.O. Box 3898, Concord, NH 03302–3898; tel. 603/271–2323; FAX. 603/271–6605; Doris G. Nuttelman, RN, Ed.D., Executive Director

Office of Program Support, Licensing and Regulation, Health Facilities Administration, Six Hazen Drive, Concord, NH 03301; tel. 603/271–4966; FAX. 603/271–4968; Raymond Rusin, Chief

Social Services

Department of Health and Human Services, Office of Family Services, 129 Pleasant Street, Concord, NH 03301–3857; tel. 603/271–4321; FAX. 603/271–4727; Richard A. Chevrefils, Assistant Commissioner

New Hampshire Department of Health and Human Services, Office of Health Management, Six Hazen Drive, Concord, NH 03301; tel. 603/271–4496; FAX. 603/271–4933; Richard DiPentima, Program Chief

Office of Community Supports and Long Term Care, State Office Park, S., 105 Pleasant Street, Concord, NH 03301; tel. 603/271–5007; FAX. 603/271–5058; Paul G. Gorman, Ed.D., Director

Vocational Rehabilitation Division, 78 Regional Drive, Concord, NH 03301; tel. 603/271–3471; Bruce A. Archambault, Director

Other

Department of Environmental Services, Six Hazen Drive, Concord, NH 03301; tel. 603/271–3503; FAX. 603/271–2867; Robert W. Varney, Commissioner

State Department of Education, 101 Pleasant Street, State Office Park, S., Concord, NH 03301; tel. 603/271–3494; FAX. 603/271–1953; Elizabeth M. Twomey, Commissioner

NEW JERSEY
The Honorable Christine T. Whittman, Governor, 609/292–6000

Health

Division of Health Care Systems Analysis, CN–360, Trenton, NJ 08625; tel. 609/292–8772; FAX. 609/984–3165; Maria Morgan, Assistant Commissioner

New Jersey Department of Health and Senior Services, Certificate of Need and Acute Care Licensing, P.O. Box 360, Trenton, NJ 08625–0360; tel. 609/292–8773; FAX. 609/292–3780; John A. Calabria, Director

Office of Managed Care, New Jersey State Department of Health, P.O. Box 360, Trenton, NJ 08625; tel. 609/633–0660; FAX. 609/633–0807; Edwin V. Kelleher, Chief

Licensing

Division of Consumer Affairs, 124 Halsey Street, P.O. Box 45027, Newark, NJ 07101; tel. 201/504–6534; FAX. 201/648–3538; Mark S. Herr, Director

New Jersey Board of Nursing, P.O. Box 45010, Newark, NJ 07101; tel. 973–504–6430; FAX. 973–648–3481; Patricia Polansky, Executive Director

State Board of Medical Examiners, 140 East Front Street, Second Floor, Trenton, NJ 08608; tel. 609/826–7100; FAX. 609/984–3930; Kevin B. Earle, Executive Director

Social Services

Department of Law and Public Safety, CN080, Trenton, NJ 08625; tel. 609/292–4925; FAX. 609/292–3508; Peter Verniero, Attorney General

Division of Family Development, P.O. Box 716, Trenton, NJ 08625–0716; tel. 609/588–2401; FAX. 609/584–4404; David C. Heins, Director

Division of Family Health Services, 50 East State Street, P.O. Box 364, Trenton, NJ 08625; tel. 609/292–4043; FAX. 609/292–9599; Henry Spring, M.D., Esq.

Maternal, Child and Community Health, New Jersey Department of Health and Senior Services, 50 East State Street, CN 364, P.O. Box 364, Trenton, NJ 08625–0364; tel. 609–984–1384; FAX. 609/292–3580; Celeste A. Wood, Director

N.J. Department of Health and Senior Services, Office of the Commissioner, CN–360, Trenton, NJ 08625; tel. 609/292–7874; FAX. 609/292–5333; Susan C. Reinhard, RN, Ph.D., Deputy Commissioner

New Jersey Department of Health and Senior Services, Office of the Commissioner, P.O. Box 360, Trenton, NJ 08625–0360; tel. 609/292–7837; FAX. 609/984–5474; Len Fishman, State Commissioner of Health and Senior Services

Other

Health Facilities Construction Service, CN–367, 300 Whitehead Road, Trenton, NJ 08625; tel. 609/588–7731; FAX. 609/588–7823; Kenneth A. Hess, Director

NEW MEXICO
The Honorable Gary E. Johnson, Governor, 505/827–3000

Health

Department of Health, P.O. Box 26110, Santa Fe, NM 87502–6110; tel. 505/827–2613; FAX. 505/827–2530; J. Alex Valdez, Secretary

Public Health Division, Department of Health, P.O. Box 26110, Santa Fe, NM 87502–6110; tel. 505/827–2389; FAX. 505/827–2329; William H. Wiese, Director

Insurance

New Mexico Department of Insurance, P.O. Drawer 1269, Santa Fe, NM 87504–1269; tel. 505/827–4601; FAX. 505/827–4734; Helen Hordes, Manager, Life and Health Forms Division

State Corporation Commission, P.O. Drawer 1269, Santa Fe, NM 87504; tel. 505/827–4529; Eric P. Serna, Chairman

Licensing

Health Facility Licensing and Certification Bureau, Long Term Care Program, 525 Camino de los Marquez, Suite Two, Santa Fe, NM 87501; tel. 505/827–4200; FAX. 505/827–4203; Matthew M. Gervase, Bureau Chief

New Mexico Board of Medical Examiners, 491 Old Santa Fe Trail, Lamy Building, Second Floor, Santa Fe, NM 87501; tel. 505/827–5022; FAX. 505/827–7377; Kristen A. Hedrick, Executive Secretary

State of New Mexico, Board of Nursing, 4206 Louisiana, N.E., Suite A, Albuquerque, NM 87109; tel. 505/841–8340; FAX. 505/841–8340; Debra Brady, Executive Director

Social Services

Division of Vocational Rehabilitation, 435 St. Michaels Drive, Building D, Santa Fe, NM 87505; tel. 505/954–8511; FAX. 505/954–8562; Terry Brigance, Director

Human Services Department, P.O. Box 2348, Santa Fe, NM 87504–2348; tel. 505/827–7750; FAX. 505/827–6286; Duke Rodriguez, Secretary

Income Support Division, P.O. Box 2348, Santa Fe, NM 87504–2348; tel. 505/827–7252; FAX. 505/827–7203; Linda Chaug, Administrator

Social Services Division, P.O. Box 2348, Santa Fe, NM 87504–2348; tel. 505/827–4439; Jack Callaghan, Ph.D., Director

Other

State Department of Education, Education Building, 300 Don Gaspar, Santa Fe, NM 87501–2786; tel. 505/827–6516; FAX. 505/827–6696; Michael J. Davis, State Superintendent of Public Instruction

NEW YORK
The Honorable George E. Pataki, Governor, 518/474–7516

Health

Bureau of Home Health Care Services, New York State Department of Health, Freer Building, 2 Third Street, Troy, NY 12180; tel. 518/271–2741; FAX. 518/271–2771; Dr. Nancy Barhydt, Director

New York State Department of Health, Tower Building, Empire State Plaza, Room 1482, Albany, NY 12237; tel. 518/474–6462; FAX. 518/473–3824

New York State Department of Health, Empire State Plaza, Corning Tower, Room 1466, Albany, NY 12237; tel. 518–486–4803; FAX. 518–486–6852; Ann Clemency Kohler, Deputy Commissioner – Office of Medicaid Management

New York State Department of Health, Office of Managed Care, Bureau of Managed Care Certification and Surveillance, 1911 Corning Tower Building, Empire State Plaza, Albany, NY 12237; tel. 518/473–4842; FAX. 518/473–3583; Vallencia Lloyd, Director

State Department of Health, Tower Building, Empire State Plaza, Albany, NY 12237; tel. 518/474–2011; FAX. 518/474–5450; Barbara A. DeBuono, M.D., M.P.H., Commissioner

Licensing

New York State Board for Medicine, Cultural Education Center, Albany, NY 12230; tel. 518/474–3841; FAX. 518/486–4846; Thomas J. Monahan, Executive Secretary

State Board for Nursing, New York State Education Department, Cultural Education Center, Room 3023, Albany, NY 12230; tel. 518/474–3843; FAX. 518/474–3706; Milene A. Sower, Ph.D., RN, Executive Secretary

Social Services

New York State Education Department, Vocational and Educational Services for Individuals with Disabilities, One Commerce Plaza, Suite 1606, Albany, NY 12234; tel. 518/474–2714; Lawrence C. Gloeckler, Deputy Commissioner

New York State Office of Alcoholism and Substance Abuse Services, 1450 Western Avenue, Albany, NY 12203; tel. 518/457–2061; FAX. 518/457–5474; Jean Somers Miller, Commissioner

New York State Office of Mental Health, 44 Holland Avenue, Albany, NY 12229; tel. 518/474–4403; FAX. 518/474–2149; James L. Stone, M.S.W., CSW Commissioner

Office of Mental Retardation and Developmental Disabilities, 44 Holland Avenue, Albany, NY 12229; tel. 518/473–1997; FAX. 518/473–1271; Thomas A. Maul, Commissioner

Other

Bureau of Project Management, New York State Department of Health, 433 River Street, Suite 303, Troy, NY 12180–2299; tel. 518/402–0911; FAX. 518/402–0975; Robert J. Stackrow, Director

New York State Education Department, Main Education Building, Room 111, Albany, NY 12234; tel. 518/474–5844; FAX. 518/473–4909

Office of Health Systems Management, Tower Building, Empire State Plaza, Room 1441, Albany, NY 12237–0701; tel. 518/474–7028; FAX. 518/486–2564

Wadsworth Center for Laboratories and Research, Clinical Lab Evaluation, P.O. Box 509, Empire State Plaza, Albany, NY 12201–0509; tel. 518/474–7592; Dr. Herbert W. Dickerman, M.D., Ph.D., Director

NORTH CAROLINA
The Honorable James B. Hunt Jr., Governor, 919/733–4240

Health

Department of Health and Human Services, P.O. Box 29526, Raleigh, NC 27626–0526; tel. 919/733–4534; FAX. 919/715–4645; Ronald H. Levine, M.D., M.P.H., Deputy Secretary

Department of Health and Human Services, 101 Blair Drive, Raleigh, NC 27626; tel. 919/733–4534; FAX. 919/715–4645; H. David Bruton, M.D., Secretary

Department of Health and Human Services, Division of Facility Services, 701 Barbour Drive, Raleigh, NC 27603; tel. 919/733–2342; FAX. 919/733–2757; Lynda D. McDaniel, Director

Insurance

Department of Insurance, P.O. Box 26387, Raleigh, NC 27611; tel. 919/733–7343; FAX. 919/733–6495; James E. Long, Commissioner

Licensing

North Carolina Board of Nursing, P.O. Box 2129, Raleigh, NC 27602; tel. 919/782–3211; FAX. 919/781–9461; Mary P. Johnson, RN, MSN, Executive Director

North Carolina Medical Board, P.O. Box 20007, Raleigh, NC 27619; tel. 919–326–1100; FAX. 919–326–1130; Andrew W. Watry, Executive Director

Social Services

Division of Medical Assistance, 1985 Umstead Drive, P.O. Box 29529, Raleigh, NC 27626–0529; tel. 919/857–4011; FAX. 919/733–6608; Paul R. Perruzzi, Director

Division of Mental Health, Developmental Disabilities and Substance Abuse Services, 325 North Salisbury Street, Raleigh, NC 27603; tel. 919/733–7011; FAX. 919/733–9455; John F. Baggett, Ph. D.

Division of Vocational Rehabilitation Services, 805 Ruggles Drive, P.O. Box 26053, Raleigh, NC 27611; tel. 919/733–3364; FAX. 919/733–7968; Bob H.. Philbeck, Director

Section C

NORTH DAKOTA

The Honorable Edward T. Schafer, Governor, 701/328-2200

Health

Children's Special Health Services, Department of Human Services, State Capitol, 600 East Boulevard, Dept 325 Avenue, Bismarck, ND 58505-0269; tel. 701/328-2436; FAX. 701/328-2359; Robert W. Nelson, Director

Division of Health Facilities, North Dakota Department of Health, 600 East Boulevard Avenue, Bismarck, ND 58505-0200; tel. 701/328-2352; FAX. 701/328-1890; Darleen Bartz, Director

Health Resources Section, North Dakota Department of Health, 600 East Boulevard Avenue, Bismarck, ND 58505-0200; tel. 701/328-2352; FAX. 701/328-1890; Daeleen Bartz, Director, Division of Health Facilities

Medical Services Division, North Dakota Department of Human Services, 600 East Boulevard Avenue, Dept 325, Bismarck, ND 58505-0261; tel. 701/328-2321; FAX. 701/328-1544; David J. Zentner, Director

State Department of Health, 600 East Boulevard Avenue, Bismarck, ND 58505-0200; tel. 701/328-2372; FAX. 701/328-4727; Londa Rodahl, Administrative Assistant

Insurance

North Dakota Department of Insurance, State Capitol, 600 East Boulevard, 5th Floor, Bismarck, ND 58505-0320; tel. 701/328-2440; FAX. 701/328-4880; Glenn Pomeroy, Commissioner

Licensing

North Dakota Board of Nursing, 919 South Seventh Street, Suite 504, Bismarck, ND 58504-5881; tel. 701/328-9777; FAX. 701/328-9785; Constance Kalanek, RN, Executive Director

North Dakota State Board of Medical Examiners, City Center Plaza, Bismarck, ND 58501; tel. 701/328-6500; FAX. 701/328-6505; Rolf P. Sletten, Executive Secretary, Treasurer

Social Services

Developmental Disabilities Unit, Disability Services Division, Department of Human Services, 600 South Second Street, Suite 1A, Bismarck, ND 58504-5729; tel. 701/328-8930; FAX. 701/328-8969; Gene Hysjulien, Director

Division of Alcoholism and Drug Abuse, 600 South Second Street, Suite 1E, Bismarck, ND 58504-5729; tel. 701/328-8920; FAX. 701/328-8969; Karen Larson, Director

Division of Maternal and Child Health, North Dakota Department of Health, State Capitol, 600 East Boulevard Avenue, Bismarck, ND 58505-0200; tel. 701/328-2493; FAX. 701/328-1412; Sandra Anseth, Director

Division of Mental Health and Substance Abuse Services, 600 S. 2nd Street, Suite 1D, Bismarck, ND 58504-5729; tel. 701/328-8940; FAX. 701/328-8969; Karen Larson, Director

Office of Economic Assistance, North Dakota Department of Human Services, 600 East Boulevard Avenue, Bismarck, ND 58505-0250; tel. 701/328-2332; FAX. 701/328-1545; Carol K. Olson, Executive Director

Office of Vocational Rehabilitation, Department of Human Services, 400 East Broadway Avenue, Suite 303, Bismarck, ND 58501-4038; tel. 701/328-3999; FAX. 701/328-3976; Gene Hysjulien, Director

Other

Facility Management Division, Office of Management and Budget, 600 East Boulevard, Ave, Dept 130, State Capitol, Bismarck, ND 58505-0130; tel. 701/328-2471; FAX. 701/328-3230; Curt Zimmerman, Director, Facility Management

Program and Policy, State Capitol, 600 East Boulevard Avenue, Bismarck, ND 58505-0265; tel. 701/328-2310; FAX. 701/328-2359; Carol K. Olson, Executive Director

OHIO

The Honorable Bob Taft, Governor, 614/466-3555

Health

Managed Care Division, 2100 Stella Court, Columbus, OH 43215-1067; tel. 614/644-2661; FAX. 614/728-5238; Teresa Reedus, Senior Contract Analyst

Ohio Department of Health, 246 North High Street, Columbus, OH 43266-0588; tel. 614/466-2253; FAX. 614/644-0085; LouEllen Fairlessw, Director

Ohio Department of Health, Bureau of Diagnostics safety and Personnel Certification, 246 North High Street, P.O. Box 118, Columbus, OH 43266-0118; tel. 614/644-7230; FAX. 614/728-9169; Christine Kenney, Health Care Specialist

Ohio Department of Health, Bureau of Local Services, 246 North High Street, Columbus, OH 43266-0118; tel. 614/466-0666; FAX. 614/466-4556; John Wanchick, M.P.A., R.S., Chief

Insurance

Department of Insurance, 2100 Stella Court, Columbus, OH 43215-1067; tel. 614/644-2658; FAX. 614/644-3743; Dave Meyer, Interim Director

Licensing

Division of Quality Assurance, Ohio Department of Health, 246 North High Street, Columbus, OH 43266-0588; tel. 614/466-8739; FAX. 614/644-0208; Rebecca S. Maust, Chief

Ohio Board of Nursing, 77 South High Street, 17th Floor, Columbus, OH 43266-0316; tel. 614/466-3947; FAX. 614/466-0388; Dorothy Fiorino, RN, M.S., Executive Director

State Medical Board of Ohio, 77 South High Street, 17th Floor, Columbus, OH 43266-0315; tel. 614/466-3934; FAX. 614/728-5946; Ray Q. Bumgarner, Executive Director

Social Services

Bureau of Disability Determination, P.O. Box 359001, Columbus, OH 43235-9001; tel. 614/438-1500; FAX. 614/438-1504; Linda Krauss, Director

Department of Mental Health, 30 East Broad Street, Eighth Floor, Columbus, OH 43266-0414; tel. 614/466-2596; FAX. 614/752-9453; Michael F. Hogan, Ph.D., Director

Department of Mental Retardation and Developmental Disability, 30 East Broad Street, Columbus, OH 43266-0415; tel. 614/466-5214; FAX. 614/644-5013; Kenneth Ritchey, Director

Division of Family and Community Health Services, 246 North High Street, P.O. Box 118, Columbus, OH 43266-0118; tel. 614/466-3263; FAX. 614/728-3616; Kathryn K. Peppe, RN, M.S., Chief

Ohio Department of Alcohol and Drug Addiction Services, Two Nationwide Plaza, 280 North High Street, 12th Floor, Columbus, OH 43215-2537; tel. 614/466-3445; FAX. 614/752-8645; Luceille Fleming, Director

Ohio Department of Human Services, 30 East Broad Street, 32nd Floor, Columbus, OH 43266-0423; tel. 614/466-6282; FAX. 614/466-2815; Wayne W. Sholes, Director

Ohio Department of Human Services, Office of Medicaid, 30 East Broad Street, 31st Floor, Columbus, OH 43266-0423; tel. 614/644-0140; FAX. 614/752-3986; Barbara Coulter Edwards, Deputy Director

Ohio Rehabilitation Services Commission, Bureau of Services for the Visually Impaired, 400 East Campus View Boulevard, Columbus, OH 43235-4604; tel. 614/438-1255; FAX. 614/438-1257; William A. Casto II, Director

Ohio Rehabilitation Services Commission, Bureau of Vocational Rehabilitation, 400 East Campus View Boulevard (SW3), Columbus, OH 43235-4604; tel. 614/438-1250; FAX. 614/438-1257; June K. Gutterman, Ed.D., Director

Other

Bureau of Plan Operations, 30 East Broad Street, 31st Floor, Columbus, OH 43266-0423; tel. 614/466-2365; FAX. 614/752-7701; John J. Nichols, Chief

OKLAHOMA

The Honorable Frank Keating, Governor, 405/521-2342

Health

Oklahoma Health Care Authority, 4545 North Lincoln, Suite 124, Oklahoma City, OK 73105; tel. 405/530-3439; FAX. 405-530-4787; Garth L. Splinter, M.D., M.B.A., Chief Executive Officer

Oklahoma Health Care Authority, 4545 North Lincoln Boulevard, Suite 124, Oklahoma City, OK 73105; tel. 405/530-3373; FAX. 405/530-3478; Mike Fogarty, State Medicaid Director

Oklahoma Health Care Authority, Medical Authorization Unit, 4545 North Lincoln Boulevard, Suite 124, Oklahoma City, OK 73105; tel. 405/530-3439; FAX. 405/530-3215; Mike Fogarty, Medicaid Operations

Public Health Laboratory Services, 1000 Northeast 10th, Oklahoma City, OK 73117-1299; tel. 405/271-5070; FAX. 405/271-4850; Garry McKee, Ph.D., Chief

Special Health Services, 1000 Northeast 10th, Oklahoma City, OK 73117-1299; tel. 405/271-6576; FAX. 405/271-1308; Gary Glover, Chief, Medical Facilities

State Department of Health, 1000 Northeast 10th, Oklahoma City, OK 73117-1299; tel. 405/271-4200; FAX. 405/271-3431; Jerry R. Nida, M.D., Commissioner of Health

State Department of Health, Dental Services, 1000 Northeast 10th Street, Oklahoma City, OK 73117-1299; tel. 405/271-5502; FAX. 405/271-6199; Michael L. Morgan, D.D.S., Chief

State Department of Health, Nursing Service, 1000 Northeast 10th Street, Oklahoma City, OK 73117-1299; tel. 405/271-5183; FAX. 405/271-1897; Toni Frioux, M.S., RN, C.N.S.

State Department of Health, Special Health Services, 1000 Northeast 10th, Oklahoma City, OK 73117-1299; tel. 405/271-4200; FAX. 405/271-2632; Brent E. VanMeter, Deputy Commissioner

Licensing

Oklahoma Board of Nursing, 2915 North Classen Boulevard, Suite 524, Oklahoma City, OK 73106; tel. 405/962-1800; FAX. 405/962-1821; Sulinda Moffett, RN, Executive Director

Oklahoma State Board of Medical Licensure and Supervision, P.O. Box 18256, Oklahoma City, OK 73154-0256; tel. 405/848-6841; FAX. 405/848-8240; Lyle Kelsey, Executive Director

Social Services

Aging Services Division, Oklahoma Department of Human Services, 312 Northeast 28th, Oklahoma City, OK 73105; tel. 405/521-2327; FAX. 405/521-2086; Roy R. Keen, Division Administrator

Department of Mental Health and Substance Abuse Services, P.O. Box 53277, Oklahoma City, OK 73152; tel. 405/522-3877; FAX. 405/522-0637; Sharron D. Boehler, Commissioner

Maternal and Child Health Service, 1000 Northeast 10th, Oklahoma City, OK 73117-1299; tel. 405/271-4477; FAX. 405/271-1011; Edd D. Rhoades, M.D., M.P.H., Chief

Maternal and Infant Health Service, 1000 Northeast 10th, Oklahoma City, OK 73117-1299; tel. 405/271-4476; FAX. 405/271-6199; Shari Kinney, RN, M.S., Acting Assistant Chief

Rehabilitation Services, 3535 Northwest 58th Street, Suite 500, Oklahoma City, OK 73112-4815; tel. 405/951-3400; FAX. 405/951-3529; Linda Parker, Director

OREGON

The Honorable John A. Kitzhaber, Governor, 503/378-4582

Health

Oregon Health Division, 800 Oregon Street, Suite 925, Portland, OR 97232; tel. 503/731-4000; FAX. 503/731-4078; Elinor Hall, M.P.H., Administrator

Licensing

Department of Consumer and Business Services, 350 Winter Street, N.E., Salem, OR 97310; tel. 503/947-7200; FAX. 503/378-4351; Nancy Ellison

Oregon Health Division, Health Care Licensure and Certification, P.O. Box 14450, Portland, OR 97214-0450; tel. 503/731-4013; FAX. 503/731-4080; Kathleen Smail, Manager

Oregon State Board of Nursing, 800 Northeast Oregon Street, Suite 465, Portland, OR 97232-2162; tel. 503/731-4745; FAX. 503/731-4755; Joan C. Bouchard, RN, M.N., Executive Director

Social Services

Adult and Family Services Division, 500 Summer Street, N.E., Salem, OR 97310-1013; tel. 503/945-5601; Sandie Hoback, Administrator

Child Development and Rehabilitation Center, Oregon Health Sciences University, Box 574, Portland, OR 97207; tel. 503/494-8362; FAX. 503/494-6868; Clifford J. Sells, M.D., Director

Mental Health and Developmental Disability Services Division, 2575 Bittern Street, N.E., Salem, OR 97310; tel. 503/945-9449; FAX. 503/378-3796; Barry S. Kast, M.S.W., Administrator

Office of Alcohol and Drug Abuse Programs, 500 Summer Street, N.E., Salem, OR 97310-1016; tel. 503/945-5763; FAX. 503/378-8467

Vocational Rehabilitation Division, Human Resources Building, 500 Summer Street N.E., Salem, OR 97310-1018; tel. 503/945-5880; FAX. 503/378-3318; Mr. Joil A. Southwell, Administrator

Other

Oregon State Public Health Laboratory, P.O. Box 275, Portland, OR 97207-0275; tel. 503/229-5882; FAX. 503/229-5682; Michael R. Skeels, Ph.D., M.P.H.

PENNSYLVANIA
The Honorable Tom Ridge, Governor, 717/787-2500

Health

Bureau of Health Planning, 709 Health and Welfare Building, Harrisburg, PA 17120; tel. 717/772-5298; Joseph B. May, Director

Department of Health, Bureau of Laboratories, P.O. Box 500, Exton, PA 19341-0500; tel. 610/363-8500; FAX. 610/436-3346; Dr. Bruce Kleger, Director

Division of Acute and Ambulatory Care, Health and Welfare Building, Room 532, Harrisburg, PA 17120; tel. 717/783-8980; FAX. 717/772-2163; Dean F. Glick, FACHE, Acting Director

Pennsylvania Department of Health, Health and Welfare Building, Suite 802, Harrisburg, PA 17120; tel. 717/787-6436; FAX. 717/787-0191; Daniel F. Hoffmann, Secretary

Pennsylvania Department of Health, Health and Welfare Building, Suite 806, Harrisburg, PA 17120; tel. 717/783-8770; FAX. 717/772-6959

Pennsylvania Department of Health, Division Home Health, 132 Kline Plaza, Suite A, Harrisburg, PA 17104; tel. 717/783-1379; FAX. 717/787-3188; Aralene Trostle, Acting Director

Pennsylvania Department of Health, Public Health Programs, 809 Health and Welfare Building, Harrisburg, PA 17120; tel. 717/787-9857; FAX. 717/772-6959; Helen K. Burns, Acting Deputy Secretary

Insurance

Department of Insurance, 1326 Strawberry Square, Harrisburg, PA 17120; tel. 717/783-0442; FAX. 717/772-1969; M. Diane Koken, Insurance Commissioner

Pennsylvania Insurance Department, Office of Rate and Policy Regulation, 1311 Strawberry Square, Harrisburg, PA 17120; tel. 717/783-5079; FAX. 717/787-8555; Gregory Martino, Deputy Insurance Commissioner

Licensing

Bureau of Quality Assurance, Health and Welfare Building, Room 930, Harrisburg, PA 17120; tel. 717/787-8015; FAX. 717/787-1491; John C. Hair, Acting Director

Pennsylvania Department of Health, Quality Assurance, Health and Welfare Building, Room 805, P.O. Box 90, Harrisburg, PA 17108; tel. 717/783-1078; FAX. 717/772-6959; Molly Raphael, Deputy Secretary

Pennsylvania State Board of Nursing, Department of State, P.O. Box 2649, Harrisburg, PA 17105-2649; tel. 717/783-7142; FAX. 717/783-0822; Miriam H. Limo, Executive Secretary

State Board of Medicine, P.O. Box 2649, Harrisburg, PA 17105-2649; tel. 717/783-1400; FAX. 717/787-7769; Cindy L. Warner, Administrative Offices

Social Services

Mental Health and Substance Abuse Services, Health and Welfare Building, Room 502, P.O. Box 2675, Harrisburg, PA 17120; tel. 717/787-6443; FAX. 717/787-5394; Charles G. Curie, Deputy Secretary, Mental Health and

Office of Children, Youth, and Families, Department of Public Welfare, P.O. Box 2675, Harrisburg, PA 17105-2675; tel. 717/787-4756; FAX. 717/787-0414; Jo Ann R. Lawer, Deputy Secretary

Office of Income Maintenance, Health and Welfare Building, Room 432, Harrisburg, P, P.O. Box 2675, Harrisburg, PA 17105; tel. 717/783-3063; FAX. 717/787-6765; Sherri Z. Heller, Deputy Secretary

Office of Vocational Rehabilitation, Labor and Industry Building, Room 1300, Harrisburg, PA 17120; tel. 717/787-5244; FAX. 717/783-5221; Susan L. Aldrete, Executive Director

Pennsylvania Department of Health, Bureau of Drug and Alcohol Programs, 933 Health and Welfare Building, P.O. Box 90, Harrisburg, PA 17108; tel. 717/783-8200; FAX. 717/787-6285; Gene R. Boyle, Director

Pennsylvania Department of Public Welfare, Office of Medical Assistance Programs, Health and Welfare Building, Room 515, Harrisburg, PA 17120; tel. 717/787-1870; FAX. 717/787-4639; Robert S. Zimmerman, Jr., Deputy Secretary

Other

Division of Laboratory Improvement, Bureau of Laboratories, P.O. Box 500, Exton, PA 19341-0500; tel. 610/363-8500; FAX. 610/436-3346; Joseph W. Gasiewski, Director

RHODE ISLAND
The Honorable Lincoln Almond, Governor, 401/277-2080

Health

Department of Health, Three Capitol Hill, Providence, RI 02908-5097; tel. 401/277-2231; FAX. 401/277-6548; Barbara A. DeBuono, M.D., M.P.H., Director, Health

Division of Medical Services, 600 New London Avenue, Cranston, RI 02920; tel. 401/464-5274; John Young, Associate Director

Rhode Island Department of Health, Three Capitol Hill, Room 401, Providence, RI 02908-5097; tel. 401/222-2231; FAX. 401/222-6548; William J. Waters, Jr., Ph.D., Deputy Director

Rhode Island Department of Health, Division of Family Health, Three Capitol Hill, Room 302, Providence, RI 02908-5097; tel. 401/277-1185; FAX. 401/277-1442; William H. Hollinshead, M.D., M.P.H., Medical Director

Rhode Island Department of Health, Office of Health Systems Development, Three Capitol Hill, Providence, RI 02908-5097; tel. 401/222-2788; FAX. 401/273-4350; John X. Donahue, Chief

Insurance

Division of Insurance, 233 Richmond Street, Suite 233, Providence, RI 02903-4233; tel. 401/277-2223; FAX. 401/751-4887; Charles P. Kwolek, Jr., CPA, Associate Director, Supervisor

Licensing

Division of Professional Regulation, Rhode Island Department of Health, Three Capitol Hill, Suite 104, Providence, RI 02908-5097; tel. 401/222-2827; FAX. 401/222-1272; Russell J. Spaight, Administrator

Social Services

Department of Human Services, 600 New London Avenue, Cranston, RI 02920; tel. 401/464-3575; FAX. 401/464-2174; John Young, Associate Director, Division of Medical Se

Office of Rehabilitation Services, 40 Fountain Street, Providence, RI 02903; tel. 401/421-7005; FAX. 401/421-9259; Raymond A. Carroll, Administrator

Rhode Island Department of Health, Division of Facilities Regulation, Three Capitol Hill, Providence, RI 02908-5097; tel. 401/277-2566; FAX. 401/277-3999; Wayne I. Farrington, Chief

Rhode Island Department of Mental Health, Retardation and Hospitalization, Aime J. Forand Building, Cranston, RI 02920; tel. 401/464-3201; FAX. 401/464-3204; A. Kathryn Power, Director

Other

Department of Business Regulation, 233 Richmond Street, Suite 237, Providence, RI 02903-4237; tel. 401/222-2246; FAX. 401/222-6098; Barry G. Hittner, Director

SOUTH CAROLINA
The Honorable Jim Hodges, Governor, 803/734-9400

Health

Bureau of Maternal and Child Health, South Carolina Department of Health and Environmental Con, Robert Mills Complex, P.O. Box 101106, Columbia, SC 29211; tel. 803/737-4190; FAX. 803/734-4442; Marie Meglen, M.S., C.N.M., Bureau Director

Department of Health and Environmental Control, 2600 Bull Street, Columbia, SC 29201; tel. 803/734-4880; FAX. 803/734-4620; Douglas E. Bryant, Commissioner

Department of Health and Human Services, 1801 Main Street, P.O. Box 8206, Columbia, SC 29202-8206; tel. 803/253-6100; FAX. 803/253-4137; Gwen Power, Director

Division of Environmental Health, 2600 Bull Street, Columbia, SC 29201; tel. 803/935-7945; FAX. 803/935-7825; Jack H. Vaughan, Jr., Chief

Division of Preventive and Personal Health, South Carolina Department of Health and Environmental Con, 2600 Bull Street, Columbia, SC 29201; tel. 803/737-4040; FAX. 803/737-4036; Mick Henry, Division Chief

Licensing

Department of Health and Environmental Control, Division of Health Licensing, 2600 Bull Street, Columbia, SC 29201; tel. 803/737-7370; FAX. 803/737-7212; Jerry Paul, Director

South Carolina Department of Labor, Licensing and Regulation, Board of Medical Examiners, 110 Centerview Drive, Suite 202,Columbia,SC,29210, P.O. Box 11289, Columbia, SC 29211-1289; tel. 803/896-4500; FAX. 803/896-4515; Aaron Kozloski, Board Administrator

Social Services

Department of Labor, Licensing and Regulation, Board of Nursing, 110 Centerview Drive, Columbia, SC 29210; tel. 803/896-4550; FAX. 803/896-4525; Nancy Carlon, Board Administrative Assistant

Division of Drug Control, South Carolina Department of Health and Environmental Control, 2600 Bull Street, Columbia, SC 29201; tel. 803/935-7817; FAX. 803/935-7820; Wilbur L. Harling, Director

South Carolina Commission for the Blind, P.O. Box 79, Columbia, SC 29202-0079; tel. 803/898-8822; FAX. 803/898-8824; Joan Barker Miller, Commissioner

South Carolina Department of Alcohol and Other Drug Abuse Services, 3700 Forest Drive, Suite 300, Columbia, SC 29204; tel. 803/734-9520; FAX. 803/734-9663; Rick C. Wade, Director Designate

South Carolina Department of Disabilities and Special Needs, 3440 Harden Street Extension, P.O. Box 4706, Columbia, SC 29240; tel. 803/737-6444; FAX. 803/737-6323; Philip S. Massey, Ph.D, State Director

South Carolina Department of Health and Environmental Control, Bureau of Home Health Services and Long Term Care, 2600 Bull Street, Columbia, SC 29201; tel. 803/898-0559; FAX. 803/898-0350; Michael Byrd, Program Manager

South Carolina Department of Health and Human Services – Office, 1801 Main Street, P.O. Box 8206, Columbia, SC 29202-8206; tel. 803/253-6100; FAX. 803/253-4137; Constance C. Rinehart, M.S.W., Deputy Director – Officer

South Carolina Department of Social Services, P.O. Box 1520, Columbia, SC 29202; tel. 803/898-7360; FAX. 803/898-7277; Elizabeth G. Patterson. J.D., State Director

State Department of Mental Health, 2414 Bull Street, P.O. Box 485, Columbia, SC 29202; tel. 803-898-8319; FAX. 803-898-8586

Vocational Rehabilitation Department, 1410 Boston Avenue, P.O. Box 15, West Columbia, SC 29171-0015; tel. 803/896-6500; P. Charles LaRosa, Jr., Commissioner

Other

Bureau of Laboratories, P.O. Box 2202, Columbia, SC 29202; tel. 803/935-7045; FAX. 803/935-7357; Sarah J. Robinson, Acting Chief

SOUTH DAKOTA
The Honorable William T. Janklow, Governor, 605/773-3212

Health

Division of Developmental Disabilities, Hillsview Plaza, E. Highway 34, c/o 500 East Capitol, Pierre, SD 57501-5070; tel. 605/773-3438; FAX. 605/773-5483; Kim Malsam-Rysdon, Director

Division of Health Systems Development and Regulation, South Dakota Department of Health, Health Building, Pierre, SD 57501; tel. 605/773-3364; FAX. 605/773-5904; Kevin Forsch, Division Director

Division of Health, Medical and Laboratory Services, 615 East Fourth Street, Pierre, SD 57501; tel. 605/773-3737; FAX. 605/773-5509; Rex VanDenBerg, Director

South Dakota Department of Health, 600 East Capitol, Pierre, SD 57501–2536; tel. 605/773–3361; FAX. 605/773–5683; Doneen B. Hollingsworth, Secretary of Health

Licensing

Office of Health Care Facilities Licensure and Certification, State Department of Health, Anderson Building, Pierre, SD 57501; tel. 605/773–3356; FAX. 605/773–6667; Joan Bachman, Administrator

State Board of Medical and Osteopathic Examiners, 1323 South Minnesota Avenue, Sioux Falls, SD 57105; tel. 605/336–1965; FAX. 605/336–0270; Robert D. Johnson, Executive Secretary

Social Services

Department of Human Services, East Highway 34, Hillsview Plaza, c/o 500 East Capitol, Pierre, SD 57501; tel. 605/773–5990; FAX. 605/773–5483; John N. Jones, Secretary

Department of Social Services, 700 Governors Drive, Pierre, SD 57501–2291; tel. 605/773–3165; FAX. 605/773–4855; James W. Ellenbecker, Secretary

Division of Alcohol and Drug Abuse, 3800 East Highway 34, Hillsview Plaza, Pierre, SD 57501; tel. 605/773–3123; FAX. 605/773–7076; Gilbert Sudbeck, Director

Office of Medical Services, 700 Governor's Drive, Pierre, SD 57501–2291; tel. 605/773–3495; FAX. 605/773–5246; David Christensen, Administrator

Other

Division of Administration Services, South Dakota Department of Health, 600 East Capitol Avenue, Pierre, SD 57501–2536; tel. 605/773–3361; FAX. 605/773–5683; Joan Adam, Director

TENNESSEE
The Honorable Don Sundquist, Governor, 615/741-2001

Health

Department of Health, Cordell Hull Building, 425 Fifth Avenue, N., Nashville, TN 37247–0101; tel. 615/741–3111; FAX. 615/741–2491; Fredia Wadley, State Health Officer

Tennessee Department of Health, Commissioner's Office, Cordell Hull Building, 425 Fifth Avenue,N., Nashville, TN 37217–1010; tel. 615/741–5949; FAX. 615/741–0544; Denise Lewis, Executive Secretary

Licensing

Board for Licensing Health Care Facilities, Cordell Hull Building, 425 Fifth Avenue, N., Nashville, TN 37247–0530; tel. 615/741–7221; FAX. 615/741–7051; Katy Gammon, Director

Department of Health, Office of Health Licensure and Regulation, Cordell Hull Building, 425 Fifth Avenue, N., Nashville, TN 37247–0501; tel. 615/741–8402; FAX. 615/741–5542; Judy Eads, Assistant Commissioner

Tennessee Board of Medical Examiners, Cordell Hull Building, 425 Fifth Avenue, North, Nashville, TN 37247–1010; tel. 800/310–4650; FAX. 615/532–5369; Yarnell Beatty, Director

Tennessee Board of Nursing, Cordell Hull Building, 1st Floor, 425 Fifth Avenue, N., Nashville, TN 37247–1010; tel. 888–310–4650; FAX. 615–741–7899; Elizabeth J. Lund, RN, Executive Director

Tennessee Medical Laboratory Board, Cordell Hull Building, 425 Fifth Avenue, N., Nashville, TN 37247–1010; tel. 615–532–5128; FAX. 615–532–5369; Lynda England, BSMT(ASCP), Administrator/Consultant

Social Services

Bureau of Alcohol and Drug Abuse Services – TN Dept. of Health, Cordell Hull Building, 425 Fifth Avenue, Nashville, TN 37247–4401; tel. 615–741–1921; FAX. 615–532–2419; Stephanie W. Perry, M.D., Assistant Commissioner

Department of Children's Services, Program Operations which includes Departmental Services, , Cordell Hull Building, 436 Sixth Avenue, N., Nashville, TN 37243–1290; tel. 615–532–1102; FAX. 615–532–6495; Cathy Rogers Smith, Assistant Commissioner, Department

Division of Health Care Facilities, Cordell Hull Building, 426 Fifth Avenue N., 1st Floor, Nashville, TN 37247–0508; tel. 615/741–7221; FAX. 615/741–7051; Kennard Murray, Director

Division of Rehabilitation Services, Citizens Plaza State Office Building, 15th Floor, Nashville, TN 37248–0060; tel. 615/313–4714; FAX. 615/741–4165; Carl Brown, Assistant Commissioner

Family Assistance, 400 Deaderick Street, Nashville, TN 37248–0070; tel. 615/313–4712; FAX. 615/741–4165; Michael O'Hara, Assistant Commissioner

Medicaid/TennCare, 729 Church Street, Nashville, TN 37247–6501; tel. 615/741–0213; FAX. 615/741–0882; Brian Lapps, Sr., Director of TennCare

Tennessee Commission on Aging, 500 Deaderick Street, Ninth Floor, Nashville, TN 37243–0860; tel. 615/741–2056; FAX. 615/741–3309; James S. Whaley, Executive Director

Tennessee Department of Human Services, 400 Deaderick Street, Nashville, TN 37248; tel. 615/741–3241; FAX. 615/741–4165; Robert A. Grunow, Commissioner

Tennessee Department of Mental Health and Mental Retardation, 710 James Robertson Parkway, 11th Floor, Nashville, TN 37243–0675; tel. 615/532–6500; FAX. 615/532–6514; Ben Dishman, Acting Commissioner

Tennessee Rehabilitation Center, 460 Ninth Avenue, Smyrna, TN 37167; tel. 615/741–4921; FAX. 615/355–1373; H. Key Dillard, Superintendent

Other

Bureau of Environment, L & C Tower–21st Floor, 401 Church Street, Nashville, TN 37243–1530; tel. 615/532–0220; FAX. 615/532–0120; Wayne K. Scharber, Assistant Commissioner

Office of Budget and Finance, Tennessee Department of Health, Andrew Johnson Tower, Tenth Floor, Nashville, TN 37247–0301; tel. 615/741–3824; FAX. 615/253–1998; Donna Dickens, Director

TEXAS
The Honorable George W. Bush, Governor, 512/463-2000

Health

Bureau of Children's Health, (Texas Department of Health), 1100 West 49th Street, Austin, TX 78756; tel. 512/458–7700; FAX. 512/458–7203; Kathleen Hamilton, Chief

Texas Department of Health, 1100 West 49th Street, Austin, TX 78756; tel. 512/458–7111; William R. Archer III, M.D., Commissioner

Texas Department of Health, 1100 West 49th Street, Austin, TX 78756–3167; tel. 512/338–6501; FAX. 512/338–6945; Randy P. Washington, Deputy Commissioner, Health Care

Texas Department of Health, Bureau of State Health Data and Policy Analysis, 1100 West 49th Street, Austin, TX 78756; tel. 512/458–7261; FAX. 512/458–7344; Ann Henry, Data Division Director

Texas Department of Health, Community Health and Prevention, 1100 West 49th Street, Suite M543, Austin, TX 78756; tel. 512/458–7555; FAX. 512/458–7713; John E. Evans, Deputy Commissioner

Texas Department of Health, Health Facility Compliance Division, 1100 West 49th Street, Austin, TX 78756; tel. 512/834–6650; FAX. 512/834–6653; Nancy Stearman, RN, M.S.N., Director

Texas Department of Mental Health and Mental Retardation, 909 West 45th Street, P.O. Box 12668, Capitol Station, Austin, TX 78751; tel. 512/454–3761; FAX. 512/206–4560; Tex Killion, Deputy Medical Director for Administration

Insurance

Texas Department of Insurance, P.O. Box 149104, Mail Code 106–1A, Austin, TX 78714–9104; tel. 512/322–3401; FAX. 512/322–3552; Ana M. Smith-Daley, Deputy Commissioner, Life/Health Division

Licensing

Board of Nurse Examiners for the State of Texas, P.O. Box 430, Austin, TX 78767–0430; tel. 512/305–7400; FAX. 512/305–7401; Katherine A. Thomas, M.N., RN, Executive Director

Board of Vocational Nurse Examiners, William P. Hobby Building, 333 Guadalupe Street, Austin, TX 78701; tel. 512/305–8100; FAX. 512/305–8101; Mary M. Strange, Executive Director

Bureau of Licensing and Certification, Texas Department of Health, 1100 West 49th Street, Austin, TX 78756–3199; tel. 512/834–6645; FAX. 512/834–6653; Maurice B. Shaw, Chief

UTAH
The Honorable Michael O. Leavitt, Governor, 801/538-1000

Health

Utah Department of Health, 288 North 1460 West, Salt Lake City, UT 84116; tel. 801/538–6111; FAX. 801/538–6306; Rod L. Betit, Executive Director

Utah Department of Health, Bureau of Licensing, Box 142003, Salt Lake City, UT 84114–2003; tel. 801/538–6152; FAX. 801/538–6325; Debra Wynkoop–Green, Director

Utah Department of Health, Bureau of Primary Care and Rural Health Systems, Box 142005, Salt Lake City, UT 84114–2005; tel. 801/538–6113; FAX. 801/538–6387; Robert W. Sherwood, Jr., Bureau Director

Utah Department of Health, Community and Family Health Services Division, P.O. Box 142001, Salt Lake City, UT 84114–2001; tel. 801/538–6901; FAX. 801/538–6510; George Delavan, M.D., Director

Utah Department of Health, Division of Epidemiology and Laboratories, 46 North Medical Drive, Salt Lake City, UT 84113; tel. 801/584–8400; FAX. 801/584–8486; Charles D. Brokopp, Dr.P.H., Director

Insurance

Insurance Department, State Office Building, Suite 3110, Salt Lake City, UT 84114; tel. 801/538–3800; FAX. 801/538–3829; Merwin U. Stewart

Licensing

Division of Occupational and Professional Licensing, Heber M. Wells Building, 160 East 300 South, Salt Lake City, UT 84114–6741; tel. 801/530–6628; FAX. 801/530–6511; Carol W. Inglestan, Administrative Assistant

Office of The Medical Examiners, State of Utah, 48 North Medical Drive, Salt Lake City, UT 84113; tel. 801/584–8410; FAX. 801/584–8435; Todd C. Grey, M.D., Director

Social Services

Department of Human Services, 120 North 200 West, P.O. Box 45500, Salt Lake City, UT 84145–0500; tel. 801/538–4001; FAX. 801/538–4016; Robin Arnold–Williams, Executive Director

Division of Aging and Adult Services, 120 North 200 West, Room 401, Salt Lake City, UT 84103; tel. 801/538–3910; FAX. 801/538–4395; Helen Goddard, Director

Division of Child and Family Services, 120 North. 200 W., Suite 225, Salt Lake City, UT 84103; tel. 801/538–4100; FAX. 801/538–3993; Ken Patterson, Director

Division of Health Care Financing (Utah Medicaid), P.O. Box 143101, Salt Lake City, UT 84114–3101; tel. 801/538–6406; FAX. 801/538–6099; Michael J. Deily, Director

Division of Services for People With Disabilities, 120 North 200 West, Suite 411, Salt Lake City, UT 84103; tel. 801/538–4200; FAX. 801/538–4279; Sue Geary, Ph.D., Director

Division of Substance Abuse, 120 North 200 West, Room 201, Salt Lake City, UT 84145; tel. 801/538–3939; FAX. 801/538–4696; F. Leon PoVey, Director

Mental Health, P.O. Box 45500, Salt Lake City, UT 84145–0500; tel. 801/538–4270; Paul Thorpe, Director

Utah State Office of Rehabilitation, 250 East 500 South, Salt Lake City, UT 84111; tel. 801/538–7530; FAX. 801/538–7522; Blaine Petersen, Ed.D., Executive Director

Youth Corrections, P.O. Box 45500, Salt Lake City, UT 84145–0500; tel. 801/538–4330; FAX. 801/538–4334; Gary K. Dalton, Director

Other

Department of Environmental Quality, 168 No 1950 West, Salt Lake City, UT 84116; tel. 801/536–4404; FAX. 801/538–6016; Dianne R. Nielson, Ph.D., Executive Director

State Office of Education, 250 East 500 South, Salt Lake City, UT 84111; tel. 801/538–7500; FAX. 801/538–7521; Steven O. Laing, State Superintendent

VERMONT
The Honorable Howard Dean, M.D., Governor, 802/828-3333

Section C

Health

Department of Developmental and Mental Health Services, Weeks Building, 103 South Main Street, Waterbury, VT 05671–1601; tel. 802/241–2610; FAX. 802/241–1129; Rodney E. Copeland, Ph.D., Commissioner

Environmental Health Division, 108 Cherry Street, P.O. Box 70, Burlington, VT 05402; tel. 802/863–7220; FAX. 802/863–7425; William C. Bress, Ph. D., Director

Vermont Department of Health, 108 Cherry Street, P.O. Box 70, Burlington, VT 05402; tel. 802/863–7280; FAX. 802/863–7425; Jan K. Carney, M.D., M.P.H., Commissioner

Vermont Department of Health, Division of Community Public Health, P.O. Box 70, Burlington, VT 05402–0070; tel. 802/863–7347; FAX. 802/863–7229; Patricia Berry, Director

Vermont Department of Health, Division of Health Surveillance, Public Health Statistics, 108 Cherry Street, P.O. Box 70, Burlington, VT 05402–0070; tel. 802/863–7300; FAX. 802/865–7701; Karen Baron, Statistical Consultant

Vermont Department of Health Infectious Disease Epidemioology, 108 Cherry Street, P.O. Box 70, Burlington, VT 05402; tel. 802/863–7240; FAX. 802/865–7701; Peter Galbraith, State Epidemiologist

Vermont Department of Health Laboratory, 195 Colchester Avenue, P.O. Box 1125, Burlington, VT 05402–1125; tel. 802/863–7335; FAX. 802/863–7632; Burton W. Wilcke, Jr., Ph.D., Director, Division of Health

Insurance

Department of Banking, Insurance, Securities and Health Care A, 89 Main Street, Drawer 20, Montpelier, VT 05620–3101; tel. 802/828–3301; FAX. 802/828–3306; Elizabeth R. Costle, Commissioner

Licensing

Licensing and Protection, Ladd Hall, 103 South Main Street, Waterbury, VT 05671–2306; tel. 802/241–2345; FAX. 802/241–2358; Laine Lucenti, Director

Vermont Department of Aging and Disabilities, Division of Licensing and Protection, Ladd Hall, 103 South Main Street, Waterbury, VT 05671–2306; tel. 802/241–2345; FAX. 802/241–2358; Loune Lucenti, RN, Director

Vermont State Board of Nursing, 109 State Street, Montpelier, VT 05609–1106; tel. 802/828–2396; FAX. 802/828–2484; Anita Ristau, RN, M.S., Executive Director

Social Services

Agency of Human Services, 103 South Main Street, Waterbury, VT 05676; tel. 802/241–2220; FAX. 802/241–2979; Cornelius Hogan, Secretary

Department of Social and Rehabilitation Services, 103 South Main Street, Waterbury, VT 05671–2401; tel. 802/241–2100; FAX. 802/241–2980; William M. Young, Commissioner

Department of Social Welfare, 103 South Main Street, Waterbury, VT 05671–1201; tel. 802/241–2853; FAX. 802/241–2830; M. Jane Kitchel, Commissioner

Office of Alcohol and Drug Abuse Programs, 108 Cherry Street, Burlington, VT 05401; tel. 802/651–1550; FAX. 802/651–1573; Thomas E. Perras, Director

Office of Vermont Health Access/Medicaid, 103 South Main Street, Waterbury, VT 05671–1201; tel. 802/241–1243; FAX. 802/241–2974; Paul Wallace–Brodeur, Director

Vocational Rehabilitation Division, 103 South Main Street, Waterbury, VT 05671–2303; tel. 802/241–2186; FAX. 802/241–3359; Diane P. Dalmasse, Director

VIRGINIA
The Honorable James S. Gillmore III, Governor, 804/786-2211

Health

State Department of Health, Main Street Station, P.O. Box 2448, Richmond, VA 23218; tel. 804/786–3561; FAX. 804/786–4616; E. Anne Peterson, M.D., M.P.H., Acting State Health Commissioner

Insurance

Bureau of Insurance, Virginia State Corporation Commission, P.O. Box 1157, Richmond, VA 23218; tel. 804/371–9691; FAX. 804/371–9944; Life and Health Consumer Services Section

State Corporation Commission Bureau of Insurance, Company Licensing and Regulatory Compliance Section, P.O. Box 1157, Richmond, VA 23209; tel. 904/371–9636; FAX. 904/371–9396; Andy Delbridge, Supervisor

State Corporation Commission–Bureau of Insurance, P.O. Box 1157, Richmond, VA 23218; tel. 804/371–9869; FAX. 804/371–9511; Douglas C. Stolte, Deputy Insurance Commissioner

Licensing

Center for Quality Health Care Services and Consumer Protection, Virginia Department of Health, 3600 Centre, Suite 216, 3600 West Broad Street, Richmond, VA 23230; tel. 804/367–2102; FAX. 804/367–2149; Nancy R. Hofheimer, Director

Virginia State Board of Medicine, 6606 West Board Street, Fourth Floor, Richmond, VA 23230–1717; tel. 804/662–9908; FAX. 804/662–9943; Warren W. Koontz, Jr., M.D., Executive Director

Social Services

Department for the Aging, 1600 Forest Avenue, Suite 102, Richmond, VA 23229; tel. 804/662–9333; FAX. 804/662–9354; Dr. Ann Y McGee, Commissioner

Department of Medical Assistance Services, 600 East Broad Street, Suite 1300, Richmond, VA 23219; tel. 804/786–8099; FAX. 804/371–4981; Dennis G. Smith, Director

Department of Mental Health, Mental Retardation and Substance Abuse Services, P.O. Box 1797, Richmond, VA 23214; tel. 804/786–3921; FAX. 804/371–6638; Richard E. Kellogg, Commissioner

Department of Rehabilitative Services, 8004 Franklin Farms Drive, P.O. Box K–300, Richmond, VA 23288–0300; tel. 804/662–7010; FAX. 804/662–9532; R. David Ross, Acting Commissioner

Division of Children's Specialty Services, Virginia Department of Health, P.O. Box 2448, Room 135, Richmond, VA 23218; tel. 804/786–3691; FAX. 804/225–3307; Nancy R. Bullock, RN, M.P.H., Director

Division of Women's and Infants' Health, 1500 East Main Street, Suite 135, P.O. Box 2448, Richmond, VA 23218–2448; tel. 804/786–5916; FAX. 804/371–6032; Joan Corder–Mabe, RNC, M.S., OGNP, Acting Director

Virginia Department of Social Services, 730 East Broad Street, Richmond, VA 23219–1949; tel. 804/692–1900; FAX. 804/692–1849; Carol A. Brunty, Commissioner

WASHINGTON
The Honorable Gary Locke, Governor, 360/753-6780

Health

Department of Health, Facilities and Services Licensing, P.O. Box 47852, Olympia, WA 98504–7852; tel. 206/705–6652; FAX. 206/705–6654; Kathy Stout, Director

Department of Health, Office of Emergency Medical and Trauma Prevention, P.O. Box 47853, Olympia, WA 98504–7853; tel. 360/705–6700; FAX. 360/705–6706; Janet Griffith, Director

Washington State Department of Health, P.O. Box 47812, Mail Stop 7812, Olympia, WA 98504–7812; tel. 206/705–6060; FAX. 206/705–6043; Dan Rubin, Director, Special Projects Office

Insurance

Office of the Insurance Commissioner, Insurance Building, P.O. Box 40255, Olympia, WA 98504–0255; tel. 206/753–7300; FAX. 206/586–3535; Deborah Senn, Insurance Commissioner

Licensing

Health Systems Quality Assurance, Department of Health, 1112 Quince, Mail Stop 7851, Olympia, WA 98504–7851; tel. 360/236–4600; FAX. 360/236–4626; Ron Weaver, Assistant Secretary

Social Services

Division of Alcohol and Substance Abuse, P.O. Box 45330, Mail Stop 5330, Olympia, WA 98504–5330; tel. 206/438–8200; FAX. 206/438–8078; Ken Stark, Director

Division of Vocational Rehabilitation, P.O. Box 45340, Olympia, WA 98504–5340; tel. 206/438–8000; FAX. 206/438–8007; Jeanne Munro, Director

Medical Assistance Administration, P.O. Box 45080, Olympia, WA 98504–5080; tel. 360/902–7807; FAX. 360/902–7855; Jtom Bedell, Acting Assistant Secretary

Medical Assistance Administration, P.O. Box 45530, Olympia, WA 98504–5530; tel. 360/664–9419; FAX. 360/753–7315; Nancy L. Fisher, RN, M.D., MPH, Medical Director

State Department of Social and Health Services, P.O. Box 45080, Olympia, WA 98504–5080; tel. 360/902–7807; FAX. 360/902–7855; Tom Bedell, Acting Assistant Secretary, Medical Assistance Administration

Other

Washington State Nursing Care Quality Assurance Commission, 1300 Southeast Quince Street, P.O. Box 47864, Olympia, WA 98504–7864; tel. 206/664–4100; FAX. 206/586–5935; Patty L. Hayes, RN, M.N., Interim Executive Director

WEST VIRGINIA
The Honorable Cecil H. Underwood, Governor, 304/558-2000

Health

Bureau for Public Health, Building Three, Room 519, State Capitol Complex, Charleston, WV 25305; tel. 304/558–2971; FAX. 304/558–1035; Henry G. Taylor, M.D., M.P.H., Commissioner

Bureau of Medical Services, 7012 MacCorkle Avenue, S.E., Charleston, WV 25304; tel. 304/926–1700; FAX. 304/926–1818; Elizabeth S. Lawton, Commissioner

Children with Special Health Care Needs, 1116 Quarrier Street, Charleston, WV 25301; tel. 304/558–3071; FAX. 304/558–2866; Patricia Kent, M.S.W., Administrative Director

Department of Health and Human Resources, Capitol Complex, Building Three, Room 206, Charleston, WV 25305; tel. 304/558–0684; FAX. 304/558–1130; Joan E. Ohl, Secretary

Office of Community and Rural Health Services, Bureau for Public Health, 1411 Virginia Street, Charleston, WV 25301–3013; tel. 304/558–0580; FAX. 304/558–1437

Office of Environmental Health Services, Morrison Building, 815 Quarrier Street, Suite 418, Charleston, WV 25301–2616; tel. 304/558–2981; FAX. 304/558–1291; C. Russell Rader, P.E., Director

West Virginia Department of Health and Human Resources, Division of Primary Care, 1411 Virginia Street, E., Charleston, WV 25301; tel. 304/558–4007; FAX. 304/558–1437; Frances L. Jackson, Director

Insurance

Insurance Commissioners Office, P.O. Box 50540, Charleston, WV 25305–0540; tel. 304/558–3354; FAX. 304/558–0412; Hanley C. Clark, Commissioner

Office of the West Virginia Insurance Commissioner, 1124 Smith Street, Charleston, WV 25301; tel. 304/558–2100; FAX. 304/558–1365; Jeffrey W. VanGilder, Director, Chief Examiner

Licensing

Office of Chief Medical Examiner, State of West Virginia, 701 Jefferson Road, South Charles, WV 25309; tel. 304/558–3920; FAX. 304/558–7886; James A. Kaplan, M.D., Chief Medical Examiner

Office of Health Facility Licensure and Certification, West Virginia Division of Health, Capitol Complex, 1900 Kanawha Boulevard., Charleston, WV 25305; tel. 304/558–0050; FAX. 304/558–2515; John Wilkinson, Director

West Virginia Board of Examiners for Registered Professional N, 101 Dee Drive, Charleston, WV 25311–1620; tel. 304/558–3596; FAX. 304/558–3666; Laura S. Rhodes, M.S.N., RN, Executive Secretary

West Virginia Board of Medicine, 101 Dee Drive, Charleston, WV 25311; tel. 304/558–2921; FAX. 304/558–2084; Ronald D. Walton, Executive Director

Social Services

Division of Rehabilitation Services, P.O. Box 50890, State Capitol Complex, Charleston, WV 25305–0890; tel. 304/766–4601; FAX. 304/766–4905; James S. Jeffers, Director

Division on Alcoholism and Drug Abuse, Capitol Complex, Building Six, Room B–738, Charleston, WV 25305; tel. 304/558–2276; FAX. 304/558–1008; DeDe Severino, Acting Director

Other

West Virginia Department of Education, Division of Technical and Adult Education Services, 1900 Kanawha Boulevard, Bldg. 6 Room B221, Charleston, WV 25305–0330; tel. 304/558–2346; FAX. 304/558–3946; Adam Sponaugle, Assistant State Superintendent

WISCONSIN

The Honorable Tommy G. Thompson, Governor, 608-266-1212

Health

Bureau of Health Services, P.O. Box 7925, Madison, WI 53707–7925; tel. 608/267–1720; FAX. 608/261–7103; Sharon Zunker, Director

Bureau of Public Health, P.O. Box 309, Madison, WI 53701; tel. 608/266–1704; FAX. 608/267–4853

Center for Health Statistics, P.O. Box 309, Madison, WI 53701–0309; tel. 608/266–1334; FAX. 608/261–6380; James John Vaura, Director

Division of Public Health, P.O. Box 2659, Madison, WI 53701–2659; tel. 608–266–1251; FAX. 608/267–2832; John Chapin, Administrator and Kenneth Baldwin, Deputy Administrator

Insurance

Office of the Commissioner of Insurance, 121 East Wilson Street, P.O. Box 7873, Madison, WI 53707–7873; tel. 608/266–3585; FAX. 608/266–9935; Public Information Officer

Licensing

Bureau of Quality Assurance, Division of Supportive Living, Department of Health and F, P.O. Box 309, Madison, WI 53701–0309; tel. 608–266–8481; FAX. 608/267–0352; Rita Prigioni, Interim Director – Bureau of Quality Assurance

Department of Regulation and Licensing, 1400 East Washington Avenue, Room 173, P.O. Box 8935, Madison, WI 53708–8935; tel. 608/266–8609; FAX. 608/267–0644; Grace Schwingel, Secretary

State of Wisconsin, Department of Regulation and Licensing, 1400 East Washington Avenue, Suite 173, P.O. Box 8935, Madison, WI 53708–8935; tel. 608/266–8609; FAX. 608/267–0644; Marlene A. Cummings, Secretary

Wisconsin Medical Examining Board, 1400 East Washington Avenue, P.O. Box 8935, Madison, WI 53708; tel. 608/266–2811; FAX. 608/261–7083; Patrick D. Braatz, Administrator

Social Services

Department of Health and Family Services, P.O. Box 7850, Madison, WI 53707–7850; tel. 608/266–9622; FAX. 608/266–7882; Joe Leean, Secretary

Division for Learning Support: Equity and Advocacy, 125 South Webster Street, P.O. Box 7841, Madison, WI 53707–7841; tel. 608/266–8960; FAX. 608/267–3746; Michael J. Thompson, Student Services, Prevention and

Division of Health Care Financing (Wisconsin Medicaid), One West Wilson Street, Suite 250, P.O. Box 309, Madison, WI 53701–0309; tel. 608/266–8922; FAX. 608/266–1096; Peggy L. Bartels, Administrator

Division of Vocational Rehabilitation, P.O. Box 7852, Madison, WI 53707–7852; tel. 608/243–5600; FAX. 608/243–5680; Thomas E. Dixon, Jr., Administrator

Other

State Department of Public Instruction, 125 South Webster Street, P.O. Box 7841, Madison, WI 53707–7841; tel. 608/266–1771; FAX. 608/267–1052; John T. Benson, State Superintendent

WYOMING

The Honorable Jim Geringer, Governor, 307/777-7434

Health

Children's Health Service, Department of Health, Hathaway Building, Fourth Floor, Cheyenne, WY 82002; tel. 307/777–7941; FAX. 307/777–5402; Cathy Parish, Program Manager

Department of Health, 117 Hathaway Building, Cheyenne, WY 82002; tel. 307/777–7656; FAX. 307/777–7439

Division of Behavioral Health, 447 Hathaway Building, Cheyenne, WY 82002–0480; tel. 307/777–7094; FAX. 307/777–5580; Pablo Hernandez, M.D., Administrator

Preventive Medicine, Hathaway Building, Cheyenne, WY 82002; tel. 307/777–6004; FAX. 307/777–3617

Licensing

Health Facilities Licensing, Department of Health, Metropolitan Bank Building, Eighth Floor, Cheyenne, WY 82002; tel. 307/777–7123; FAX. 307/777–5970; Charlie Simineo, Program Manager

Wyoming Board of Medicine, The Colony Building, Second Floor, 211 West 19th Street, Cheyenne, WY 82002; tel. 307/778–7053; FAX. 307/778–2069; Carole Shotwell, Executive Secretary

Wyoming State Board of Nursing, 2020 Carey Avenue, Suite 110, Cheyenne, WY 82002; tel. 307/777–7601; FAX. 307/777–3519; Toma A. Nisbet, RN, M.S., Executive Director

Social Services

Department of Family Services, Hathaway Building, Third Floor, 2300 Capitol Avenue, Cheyenne, WY 82002–0490; tel. 307/777–7561; FAX. 307/777–7747; Shirley R. Carson, Director

Division of Health Care Financing, 6101 Yellowstone Road, Room 259B, Cheyenne, WY 82002; tel. 307/777–7531; FAX. 307/777–6964; James D. Shepard, Administrator

Division of Vocational Rehabilitation, Herschler Building, Room 1128, Cheyenne, WY 82002; tel. 307/777–7385; FAX. 307/777–5939; Gary W. Child, Administrator

Wyoming Department of Health, Division on Aging, 139 Hathaway Building, Cheyenne, WY 82002; tel. 800/442–2766; FAX. 307/777–5340; Wayne A. Milton, Administrator

U.S. Associated Areas

GUAM

Health

Guam Health Planning and Development Agency, P.O. Box 2950, Agana, GU 96910; tel. 671/477–3920; FAX. 671/477–3956; Helen B. Ripple, Director

Social Services

Department of Public Health and Social Services, Box 2816, Agana, GU 96932; tel. 671/735–7102; FAX. 671/734–5910; Dennis G. Rodriguez, Director

Department of Vocational Rehabilitation, Government of Guam, 122 Harmon Plaza, Suite B201, Harmon Industry, GU 96911; tel. 671/646–9468; FAX. 671/649–7672; Albert San Agustin, Acting Director

Division of Public Welfare, Box 2816, Agana, GU 96910; tel. 671/735–7274; FAX. 671/734–7015; Adoracion A. Solidum, Acting Chief Human Services Administration

PUERTO RICO

Health

Administration for Mental Health and Drug Abuse, P.O. Box 21414, San Juan, PR 00928–1414; tel. 787/764–3795; FAX. 787/765–5895; Dr. Jose Acevedo, Administrator

Dental Health, Building A–Medical Center, Call Box 70184, San Juan, PR 00936; tel. 809/751–4750; FAX. 809/765–5675; Wanda Urbiztondo, D.M.D., Oral Health Coordinator

Department of Health, Secretaryship for Preventive Medicine and Family Health, Building E–Medical Center, Call Box 70184, San Juan, PR 00936; tel. 809/765–0482; FAX. 809/765–5675; Dr. Raul G. Castellanos Bran, Director, Division of FAA

Environmental Health, Department of Health, Building A, Psiq Hospital, Box 70184, San Juan, PR 00936–0184; tel. 787/274–7798; FAX. 787/758–6285; Herman Horta, Assistant Secretary, Environmental Health

Government of Puerto Rico, Department of Health, P.O. Box 70184, San Juan, PR 00936–8184; tel. 787/274–7601; FAX. 787/250–6547; Carmen A. Feliciano–De–Melecio, Secretary of Health

Social Services

Department of Family, Call Box 11398, San Juan, PR 00910; tel. 809/721–4624; FAX. 809/723–1223; Carmen L. Rodriguez de Rivera, Secretary

Vocational Rehabilitation Program, Department of Social Services, Apartado 191118, San Juan, PR 00919–1118; tel. 809/725–1792; FAX. 809/721–6286; Sr. Francisco Vallejo, Assistant Secretary

Other

Administration, Building A–Medical Center, Call Box 70184, San Juan, PR 00565–1616; FAX. 809/250–6547; Antonia Pizarrro Lago, Assistant Secretary for Administrator

Legal Services, Building A–Medical Center, Call Box 70184, San Juan, PR 00936; tel. 809/766–1616; FAX. 809/766–2240; J. Gerardo Cruz–Arroyo, Esq. General Counsel

VIRGIN ISLANDS

Health

Department of Health, Division of Financial Services, Knud Hansen Complex, St. Thomas, VI 00802; tel. 809/774–3171; FAX. 809/777–5120; Alphonse J. Stalliard, Deputy Commissioner

Division of Environmental Health, Old Hospital Complex, Charlotte Amalie, St. Thomas, VI 00802; tel. 809/774–9000; FAX. 809/776–7899; Laura A. Hassell, Director

Division of Hospitals and Medical Services, Roy Lester Schneider Hospital, 9048 Sugar Estate, St. Thomas, VI 00802; tel. 809/776–3687; FAX. 809/777–8421; Bruce Goldman, Chief Executive Officer

Prevention, Health, Promotion and Protection, Department of Health, Charles Harwood Hospital, 3500 Richmond Christiansted, St. Croix, VI 00820–4300; tel. 809/773–1311; FAX. 809/772–5895; Olaf G. Hendricks, M.D., Assistant Commissioner

Virgin Islands Department of Health, St. Thomas Hospital, St. Thomas, VI 00802; tel. 809/774–0117; FAX. 809/777–4001; Ralph A. de Chabert, M.D., Acting Commissioner

Social Services

Disabilities and Rehabilitation Services, Department of Human Services, Knud Hansen Complex–Building A, 1303 Hospital Ground, St. Thomas, VI 00802; tel. 809/774–0930; FAX. 809/774–3466; Sedonie Halbert, Administrator

Division of Maternal and Child Health Services, Virgin Islands Department of Health, Nisky Center Suite 210, St. Thomas, VI 00801; tel. 809/776–3580; FAX. 809/774–8633; Dr. Mavis Matthew, Director

Division of Mental Health, Alcoholism, and Drug Dependency Services, Barbel Plaza South, St. Thomas, VI 00802; tel. 340/774–4888; FAX. 340/774–4701; Mr. Carlos Ortiz, Director

Virgin Islands Department of Human Services, Knud Hansen Complex, Building A, St. Thomas, VI 00802; tel. 340/774–1166; FAX. 340/774–3466; Sedonie Halbert, Acting Commissioner

Canada

ALBERTA

Social Services

Department of Family and Social Services, 109 Street and 97 Avenue, Edmonton, AB T5K 2B6; tel. 403/427–2606; FAX. 403/427–0954; Dr. Lyle Oberg, Minister

BRITISH COLUMBIA

Health

Ministry of Health, Parliament Building, Room 306, Victoria, BC V8V 1X4; tel. 604/387–5394; FAX. 604/387–3696; The Honorable Joy K. MacPhail

MANITOBA

Health

Department of Health, 302 Legislative Building, Winnipeg, MB R3C 0V8; tel. 204/945–3731; FAX. 204/945–0441; The Honorable Erie Stefanson, Minister

Social Services

Department of Manitoba Family Services, 450 Broadway, Winnipeg, MB R3C 0V8; tel. 204/945–4173; FAX. 204/945–5149; The Honorable Bonnie Mitchelson, Minister

NEW BRUNSWICK
Health
> **Department of Health and Community Services,** Box 5100, Fredericton, NB E3B 5G8; tel. 506/453–2581; FAX. 506/453–5243; The Honorable Russell H. T. King, M.D.

NEWFOUNDLAND
Health
> **Department of Health and Community Services,** Confederation Building, P.O. Box 8700, St. John's, NF A1B 4J6; tel. 709/729–3124; FAX. 709/729–0121; Joan Marie Aylward, Minister, Health and Community Services

NOVA SCOTIA
Health
> **Department of Health,** P.O. Box 488, Halifax, NS B3J 2R8; tel. 902/424–5818; FAX. 902/424–0559; The Honorable James Smith, M.D.

PRINCE EDWARD ISLAND
Social Services
> **Department of Health and Social Services,** Sullivan Building, Second Floor, P.O. Box 2000, Charlottetown, PE C1A 7N8; tel. 902/368–4930; FAX. 902/368–4969; The Honorable Walter A. McEwen, Q.C./Minister

QUEBEC
Social Services
> **Ministry of Health and Social Services,** Ministere de la Sante et des Services Sociaux, Quebec, PQ G1S 2M1; tel. 418/643–3160; FAX. 418/644–4534; Jean Rochon, Minister

SASKATCHEWAN
Health
> **Department of Health,** 3475 Albert Street, Third Floor, Regina, SK S4S 6X6; tel. 306/787–3168; FAX. 306/787–8677; The Honorable, Clay Serby, Minister

Section C

Health Care Providers

Health Maintenance Organizations

The following is a list of Health Maintenance Organizations developed with the assistance of state government agencies and the individual facilities listed.

We present this list simply as a convenient directory. Inclusion or omission of any organization indicates neither approval nor disapproval by Health Forum LLC.

United States

ALABAMA

Apex Healthcare of Alabama, Inc., 104 Inverness Center Parkway, Suite 230, Birmingham, AL 35243; tel. 334/279-5000; Stan Sherlin, Executive Director

Apex Healthcare, Inc., 104 Inverness Center Parkway, Suite 320, Birmingham, AL 35242; tel. 205/991-3233

CACH HMO, Inc., 1600 7th Avenue South, Birmingham, AL 35233; tel. 205/939-6905; Mike Burgess, CEO

CIGNA Healthcare of Georgia, Inc., 10 Inverness Center Parkway, Suite 230, Birmingham, AL 35242; tel. 205/991-1005; FAX. 205/995-8511

DirectCare, Inc., 629 Interstate Park Drive, Montgomery, AL 36109; tel. 334/277-6670; T. David Lewis, President & CEO

Foundation Health Plan, 1900 International Park Drive, Suite 200, Birmingham, AL 35243; tel. 205/298-0679; Michael Newman, Acting Executive Director

Health Advantage Plans, Inc., 140 Riverchase Parkway, E., Birmingham, AL 35244; tel. 205/982-8400; FAX. 205/982-8411; James Denman, Chief Executive Officer

Health Maintenance Group of Birmingham, 936 19th Street South, Birmingham, AL 35205; tel. 205/988-2537; Joe Bolen, Director

Health Partners of Alabama, Inc., Two Perimeter Park South, Suite 200W, Birmingham, AL 35243; tel. 205/968-1000; Carl Sather, President & CEO

PrimeHealth of Alabama, 1400 South University Boulevard, Mobile, AL 36609; tel. 334/342-0022; FAX. 334/342-6428; Becky S. Tate, Director

Primehealth of Alabama, Inc., 1400 South University Boulevard, Suite M, Mobile, AL 36609; tel. 334/342-0022; FAX. 334/342-1176; Becky S. Holliman, President

PrimeHealth of Alabama, Inc., 1400 University Boulevard, South, Mobile, AL 36609; tel. 334/342-0022

United Healthcare of Alabama, Inc., 3700 Colonnade Parkway, Birmingham, AL 35243; tel. 205/977-6300; Charles Pitts, President & CEO

Viva Health, Inc., 1401 South 21st Street, Birmingham, AL 35205; tel. 205/939-1718; John Davis, Interim President

ARIZONA

Aetna Health Plan of Arizona, Inc., 7878 North 16th Street, Suite 210, Phoenix, AZ 85020; tel. 602/395-8800; FAX. 602/395-8813; James W. Jones, Acting Vice President, Market Manager

CIGNA HealthCare of Arizona, Inc., 11001 North Black Canyon Highway, Suite 400, Phoenix, AZ 85029; tel. 602/942-4462; FAX. 602/371-2625; Clyde Wright, M.D., President, General Manager

FHP, Inc., 410 North 44th Street, P.O. Box 52078, Phoenix, AZ 85072-2078; tel. 602/244-8200; FAX. 602/681-7680; Clifford Klima, President, Arizona Region

First Health of Arizona, Inc., 10448 West Coggins Drive, Sun City, AZ 85351; tel. 602/933-1344; FAX. 602/933-5819; Glenn D. Jones, Administrative Director

Humana Healthcare Plan, Inc., 2710 E. camelback Road, Phoenix, AZ 85016; tel. 602/381-4300; FAX. 602/381-4381; Elizabeth Kelly, Associate Executive Director

Premier Healthcare, Inc., d/b/a Premier Healthcare of Arizona, 100 East Clarendon, Suite 400, Phoenix, AZ 85013; tel. 602/248-0404; FAX. 602/248-7771; David K. Stewart, Vice President, Marketing, Sales

United Healthcare of Arizona, (formerly Health Partners Health Plan Inc.), 3141 N. Third Avenue, Phoenix, AZ 85013; tel. 888/290-4747; Katie Riley, Communications Manager

University Physicians Health Maintenance Organization, Inc., 575 East River Road, Tucson, AZ 85704-5822; tel. 520/795-3500

ARKANSAS

American Dental Providers, Inc., 614 Center Street, P.O. Box 34045, Little Rock, AR 72203-4045; tel. 501/376-0544; FAX. 501/371-3820; Robert E. Iriana

Healthsource Arkansas, Inc., 333 Executive Court, Little Rock, AR 72205-4548; tel. 501/227-7222; Donald T. Jack

QCA Health Plan, Inc., 10800 Financial Centre Parkway, Suite 540, Little Rock, AR 72211; tel. 501/954-9595; FAX. 501/228-0135; James M. Stewart, President and CEO

United HealthCare of Arkansas, Inc., 415 North McKinley Street, Plaza West Building, Suite 820, Little Rock, AR 72205; tel. 501/664-7700; FAX. 501/664-7768; V. Rob Herndon III

CALIFORNIA

Access Dental Plan, Inc., 555 University Avenue, Suite 182, Sacramento, CA 95825; tel. 916/922-5000; FAX. 916/646-9000; Reza Abbaszaden, D.D.S., Chief Executive Officer

Aetna Health Plans of California, Inc., 201 North Civic Drive, Suite 300, Walnut Creek, CA 94596; tel. 909/386-3145; FAX. 909/386-3330; Michael Dobbs, Market Vice President

Aetna US Healthcare Dental Plan of California, Inc., 2303 Camino Ramon, Suite 100, San Ramon, CA 94583; tel. 925/543-9503; FAX. 925/543-9513; Dr. Robert B. Ouelette, President

Almeda Alliance for Health, 1850 Fairway Drive, San Leandro, CA 94577; tel. 510/895-4500; FAX. 510/483-6038; David J. Kears, President and CEO

Alternative Dental Care of California, Inc., 21700 Oxnard Street, Suite 500, Woodland Hill, CA 91367; tel. 818/710-9400; FAX. 818/704-9817; Sargis Khaziran, Chief Finance Officer

American Healthguard Corporation, Centaguard Dental Plan, 485 E. 17th Street, Suite 604, Costa Mesa, CA 92627; tel. 714/574-8874; David Kutner, M.D., President

American Speciality Health Plans, Inc., 8989 Rio San Diego Drive, Suite 250, San Diego, CA 92108; tel. 619/297-8100; FAX. 619/209-6233; Peggy Kilpatrick, Sales Manager

Ameritas Managed Dental Plan, 151 Kalmus Drive, Suite B-250, Costa Mesa, CA 92626; tel. 714/437-5966; FAX. 714/437-5967; Karin Truxillo, President

Baycare Health Plan, 122 Saratoga Avenue, Suite B, Santa Clara, CA 95051; tel. 408/441-9340; Tracy K. Heeter, D.D.S., President

Blue Cross of California/Wellpoint Health Network Inc./, CaliforniaCare Health Plans, 21555 Oxnard Street, Woodland Hill, CA 91367; tel. 818/703-2412; Thomas Geiser, Executive Vice President/Counsel

Brown and Toland Medical Group, 100 Van Ness Avenue, 28th Floor, Suite 2800, San Francisco, CA 94102; tel. 415/553-6567; FAX. 415/553-6791; Michael Abel, M.D., President and CEO

California Benefits Dental Plan, 4911 Warner Avenue, Suite 208, Huntington Be, CA 92649; tel. 714/840-2852; FAX. 714/840-3213; Robert F. Gosin, D.D.S., President

California Dental Health Plan, 14471 Chambers Road, 92680, P.O. Box 899, Tustin, CA 92681-0899; tel. 714/731-4751; FAX. 714/731-2049; James R. Lindsey, President

California Physicians' Service, Blue Shield of California, 50 Beale Street, 22nd Floor, San Francisco, CA 94105; tel. 415/229-5195; FAX. 415/229-5343; Patricia Ernsberger, Associate General Counsel

Care 1st Health Plan, 1000 S. Fremont Avenue, Suite 11100, Alhambra, CA 91803; tel. 626/299-4299; FAX. 626/458-0415; John Edwards, Chief Executive Officer

CareAmerica, 6300 Canoga Avenue, Woodland Hill, CA 91367; tel. 818/228-2207; FAX. 818/228-5117; Robert P. White, President and CEO

Chinese Community Health Plan, 170 Columbus Avenue, Suite 210, San Francisco, CA 94133; tel. 415/397-3190; FAX. 415/397-6140; Kwong (K.C.) Wong, Administrator

Chriosave, Inc., 3833 Atlantic Avenue, Long Beach, CA 90808; tel. 562/595-8164; J. Rodney Shelley, D.C., President and CEO

CIGNA Dental Health of California, Inc., 5990 Sepulveda Boulevard, Suite 500, Van Nuys, CA 91411; tel. 818/756-2900; FAX. 818/756-2997; Claire Marie Burchill, President and CEO

Cigna Dental Health of California, Inc., 5990 Sepulveda Blvd., Suite 500, Van Nuys, CA 91411; tel. 954/423-5674; Ann Fulks, Director of Compliance

Cohen Medical Corporation, d/b/a Tower Health Service, 200 Ocean Gate, Sixth Floor, Long Beach, CA 90802; tel. 562/435-2676; FAX. 562/432-3477; Robert Cohen, M.D., President

Community Dental Services, Smilecare, 3501 West Sunflower Ave, Suite 110, Santa Ana, CA 92715; tel. 714/850-3333; M. E. Hardin, President and CEO

Community Health Group, 740 Bay Boulevard, Chula Vista, CA 91910; tel. 619/422-0422; FAX. 619/422-5930; Gabriel Arce, Chief Executive Officer

Concentrated Care, 450 East Romie Lane, Salinas, CA 92660; tel. 714/752-8522; Dennis Fratt, Acting President

Contra Costa Health Plan, 595 Center Avenue, Suite 100, Martinez, CA 94553; tel. 925/313-6000; FAX. 925/313-6580; Milton Camhi, Chief Executive Officer

County of Los Angeles, Department of Health Services, d/b/a Community Health Plan, 3l3 North Figueroa Street - Room 904, Los Angeles, CA 90012; tel. 213/240-7775; Melinda Anderson, Interim Director

County of Ventura, Ventura County Health Care Plan, 2323 Knoll Drive, Ventura, CA 93003; tel. 805/677-8787; FAX. 805/677-5177; Patricia S. Neumann, Insurance Administrator

Dedicated Dental Systems, Inc., 3990 Ming Avenue, Bakersfield, CA 93309; tel. 805/397-5513; FAX. 805/397-2888; Vicki Garcia, Membership Services Manager

Delta Dental Plan of California, 100 First Street, San Francisco, CA 94105; tel. 415/972-8463; Carl W. Ludwig, Director, Northern California Sales

Dental Benefit Providers of California, Inc., 311 California Street, Suite 550, San Francisco, CA 94104; tel. 415/391-1211; Jill Schultze Evans, Acting COO

Dental Health Services, 3833 Atlantic Avenue, Long Beach, CA 90807-3505; tel. 310/595-6000; FAX. 310/424-0150; Godfrey Pernell, D.D.S., President, Chief Executive Officer

DentiCare of California, Inc., 125 Technology Drive, Suite 100, Irvine, CA 92618; tel. 949/790-3400; FAX. 949/790-3455; Ed Eberhard, President

Dr. Leventhal's Vision Care Centers of America, 3680 Rosecrans Street, Zip 92110, P.O. Box 87808, San Diego, CA 92138; tel. 619/223-5656; FAX. 619/223-2318; Debra Brant, Chief Operating Officer

Eyecare Service Plan, Inc., 9090 Burton Way, Beverly Hills, CA 90211; tel. 310/271-0145; FAX. 310/271-0784; Matthew Rips, Vice President

Eyexam 2000 of California, Inc., 170 Newport Center Drive, Suite 130, Newport Beach, CA 92661; tel. 513/583-6373; Keith Borders, Attorney

For Eyes Vision Plan, Inc., 2104 Shattuck Avenue, Berkeley, CA 94704; tel. 510/843-0787; Robert Schoen, President

Foundation Health Psychcare Services, Inc., d/b/a Occupational Health Services (OHS), 1600 Los Gamos Drive, Suite 300, San Rafael, CA 94903; tel. 415/491–7232; Nancy B. Diamond, Director of Admin, Reg. Compliance.

Foundation Health Vision Services, Vision Plans, 125 Technology, PO Box 57074, Irvine, CA 92619–7074; tel. 800/999–2848; Ed Eberhard, President

Golden West Dental and Vision Plan, 888 West Ventura Boulevard, Camarillo, CA 93010; tel. 805/987–8941; FAX. 805/987–7491; Karl H. Lehmann, President

Great American Health Plan, 2525 Camino Del Rio, S., Suite 350, San Diego, CA 92108; tel. 619/574–6600; Riley McWilliams, Chief Executive Officer

Greater California Dental Plan, Smilesaver, Signature Dental Plan, 22144 Clarendon Street, First Floor, P.O. Box 4281, Woodland Hill, CA 91365–4281; tel. 818/348–1500; FAX. 818/348–2942; Mark Johnson, President

Greater Pacific HMO, Inc., 9267 Haven Avenue, Suite 210, Rancho Cucamo, CA 91730; tel. 909/483–9595; Lee Reynolds, President

Health & Human Resource Center, 9370 Sky Park Court, Suite 140, San Diego, CA 92123; tel. 619/571–1698; FAX. 619/571–1868; Stephen H. Heidel, M.D., President & CEO

Health and Human Resource Center, 7798 Starling Drive, San Diego, CA 92123; tel. 619/571–1698; FAX. 619/571–1868; Stephen H. Heidel, M.D., President and CEO

Health Net, 155 Grand Avenue, Oakland, CA 94612; tel. 510/287–4586; FAX. 510/287–4654; Marshall Bentley, Vice President and Counsel

Health Net, 21600 Oxnard Street, Woodland Hills, CA 91367, P.O. Box 9103, Van Nuys, CA 91409–9103; tel. 818/719–6800; FAX. 818/719–5450; Arthur Southam, M.D., Chief Executive Officer

Health Plan of the Redwoods, 3033 Cleveland Avenue, Santa Rosa, CA 95403; tel. 707/525–4231; FAX. 707/547–4101; John W. Baxter, Chief Executive Officer

Healthdent of California, Inc., 2848 Arden Way, Suite 100, Sacramento, CA 95825; tel. 916/486–0749; FAX. 916/486–3642; Edward L. Cruchley, D.D.S., President

HMO California, 17922 Fitch, Irvine, CA 92614; tel. 949/756–5555; FAX. 949/756–5550; Raja Takhar, Chief Operating Officer

Holman Professional Counseling Centers, 21050 Vanowen Street, Canoga Park, CA 91303; tel. 818/704–1444; FAX. 818/704–9339; Ron Holman, Ph.D., President

Human Affairs International of California, 300 North Continental Boulevard, Suite 200, El Segundo, CA 90245; tel. 310/414–0066; FAX. 310/414–9282; Jonathan Wormhoudt, Ph.D., Chief Executive Officer

Ideal Dental Health Plan, Inc, 18911 Portola Drive, Suite C, Salinas, CA 93908; tel. 831/455–3400; FAX. 831/455–3409; Stanley Watkinson, President

Inland Empire Health Plan, 303 East Vanderbilt Way, Suite 400, San Bernardin, CA 92408; tel. 909/890–2000; FAX. 909/890–2003; Richard Bruno, Chief Executive Officer

Inter Valley Health Plan, 300 South Park Avenue, Suite 300, Pomona, CA 91766; tel. 909/623–6333; FAX. 909/622–2907; Mark C. Covington, President and CEO

Kaiser Foundation Health Plan, Inc., 1800 Harrison Street, 8th Floor, Oakland, CA 94612; tel. 510/987–2146; Renee Kullick, Director, H.P. Licensing

Kern Health Systems, 1600 Norris Road, Bakersfield, CA 93308; tel. 661/391–4000; FAX. 661/391–4097; Carol L. Sorrell, RN, Chief Executive Officer

Key Health Plan, Inc., 5959 South Mooney Boulevard, Visalia, CA 93277–9329; tel. 209/730–4100; Sheri A. Shannon, Chief Executive Officer

Key Health Plan, Inc., 5959 South Mooney Blvd., Visalia, CA 93277–3929; tel. 559/730–4100; FAX. 559/730–4111; Sheri A. Shannon, Acting CEO

Landmark Healthplan of California, Inc., 1750 Howe Avenue, Suite 300, Sacramento, CA 95825–3369; tel. 800/638–4557; Marla Jane Orth, Chief Executive Officer

Laurel Dental Plan, 5451 Laurel Canyon Blvd., Suite 204, No. Hollywood, CA 91607; tel. 818/980–0929; Patrick C. Brooks, President

Laurel Dental Plan, Inc., 5451 Laurel Canyon Boulevard, Suite 209, North Hollywood, CA 91607; tel. 818/980–0929; FAX. 818/980–4668; Dr. Victor Sands, President

Lifeguard, Inc., 2840 Junction Avenue, San Jose, CA 95134; tel. 408/943–9400; FAX. 408/383–4259; Mark G. Hyde, President and CEO

Lifeguard, Inc., 1851 McCarthy Blvd., Milpatis, CA 95035; tel. 408/432–3608; Holly McCann, VP and General Counsel

Local Initiative Health Authority for LA Co., 3530 Wilshire Blvd., Suite 900, Los Angeles, CA 90010; tel. 213/251–8300; FAX. 213/637–3026; Anthony D. Rodgers, CEO

Managed Dental Care, 6200 Canoga Ave., #100, Woodland Hill, CA 91367; tel. 800/273–3330; FAX. 818/347–7302; Michael Gould, President & CEO

Managed Dental Care of California, 6200 Canoga Avenue, Suite 100, Woodland Hill, CA 91367; tel. 800/273–3330; FAX. 818/347–7302; Michael Gould, President and CEO

Managed Health Network, Inc., 5100 West Goldleaf Circle, Suite 300, Los Angeles, CA 90056; tel. 213/299–0999; FAX. 213/298–2765; Alethea Caldwell, President

Managed health Network, Inc., d/b/a California Wellness plan, 5100 W. Goldleaf Circle, Suite 300, Los Angeles, CA 90056; tel. 916/631–6039; Joseph K. Klinger, VP & Counsel

MAXICARE, 1149 South Broadway Street, Los Angeles, CA 90015; tel. 213/765–2000; FAX. 213/765–2694; Peter J. Ratican, Chairman, President, Chief Executive

Maxicare, 1149 South Broadway Street, Suite 819, Los Angeles, CA 90015; tel. 213/365–3451; FAX. 213/365–3499; Warren D. Foon, Vice President, General Manager

MCC Behavioral Care of California, Inc., 801 North Brand Boulevard, Suite 1150, Glendale, CA 91203; tel. 818/551–2200; Bernhild E. Quintero, Vice President

MCC Behavioral Care of California, Inc., 801 North Brand Blvd., #1150, Glendale, CA 91203; tel. 800/433–5768; Susan Speltz Feltus, VP, Counsel

MedPartners Provider Network, 5000 Airport Plaza Drive, Long Beach, CA 90815; tel. 562/497–4076; FAX. 562/497–4060; Brad Karro, President and Chief Operating Officer

Merit Behavioral Care of California, Inc., 400 Oyster Point Boulevard, Suite 306, South San Francisco, CA 94080; tel. 415/742–0980; FAX. 415/742–0988; Douglas Studebaker, President

Molina Medical Centers, One Golden Shore, Long Beach, CA 90802; tel. 562/435–3666; John Molina, J.D., Vice President

Monarch Plan, Inc., 201 North Salsipuedes, Suite 206, Santa Barbara, CA 93103–3256; tel. 805/963–0566; FAX. 805/564–4167; Peter J. Leeson, D.O., Chief Executive Officer

National Health Plans, 1005 West Orangeburg Avenue, Suite B, Modesto, CA 95350–4163; tel. 209/527–3350; FAX. 209/527–6773; Mike Sheley, President & Chief Executive Officer

Newport Dental Plan, 3540 Howard Way, Costa Mesa, CA 92626; tel. 714/668–1300; FAX. 714/668–9015; Dennis Fratt, Chief Operating Officer

Omni Healthcare, 2450 Venture Oaks Way, Suite 300, Sacramento, CA 95833–3292; tel. 916/921–4000; FAX. 916/921–4100; Robert L. Fahlman, Chief Executive Officer

One Health Plan of California, Inc., 1740 Technology Drive, Suite 320, San Jose, CA 95110; tel. 408/437–4100; FAX. 408/437–0253; Jackie L. James, President

Oral Health Services, Inc., Mida Dental Plan, 21700 Oxnard Street, Suite 500, Woodland Hill, CA 91367; tel. 818/710–9400; FAX. 818/710–9400; Sargis Khaziran, Chief Financial Officer

Pacific Dental Benefits, Inc., 1390 Willow Pass Road, Suite 800, Concord, CA 94520; tel. 925/363–6000; FAX. 925/363–6037; Lee Schneider, Vice President, Sales

PacifiCare Behavioral Health of California, 23046 Avenida de la Carlota, Suite 700, Laguna Hills, CA 92653; tel. 714/859–7971; Heidi Prescott, National Sales Manager

PacifiCare of California, Secure Horizons, 5995 Plaza Drive, P.O. Box 6006, Cypress, CA 90630–6006; tel. 714/236–5674; FAX. 714/236–7887; Nancy J. Monk, Regulatory Affairs, VP

Pearle Vision Care, Inc., 6480 Weathers Place, Suite 225, San Diego, CA 92121; tel. 619/625–9173; FAX. 619/625–9781; Debbie Hyde–Duby, President

Preferred Health Plan, Inc., Personal Dental Services, 4002 Park Boulevard, Suite B, San Diego, CA 92103; tel. 619/297–6670; FAX. 619/297–0317; Joan Contratti, Secretary/Treasurer

Preventive Dental Systems, Inc., 801 Broadway, Sacramento, CA 95818; tel. 916/448–2994; FAX. 916/448–2997; Gregory Thomas, Interim CEO

Priority Health Services, Central Valley Health Plan, Inc., P.O. Box 25790, Fresno, CA 93729–5790; tel. 209/446–6810; FAX. 209/435–7693; Vreeland O. Jones, President and CEO

Private Medical–Care, Inc., PMI, 12898 Towne Center Drive, Cerritos, CA 90701; tel. 310/924–8311; FAX. 310/924–8039; Robert B. Elliott, President

Prudential Health Care Plan of California, Inc., 5800 Canoga Avenue, Woodland Hill, CA 91367; tel. 818/712–5002; FAX. 818/992–2474; Susan Hallett, President

Regents of the University of California, d/b/a UCSD Heudin Plan, 1899 McKee Street, San Diego, CA 92101; tel. 619/294–3743; Nancy White, RN, MPH, Director, UCSD Health Plan

Ross–Loos Health Plan of California, Inc., d/b/a CIGNA HealthCare of California, 505 North Brand Boulevard, P.O. Box 2125, Glendale, CA 91203; tel. 818/500–6726; FAX. 818/500–6831; Leslie A. Margolin, Chief Counsel

Safeguard Health Plans, 505 North Euclid Street, P.O. Box 3210, Anaheim, CA 92803–3210; tel. 714/778–1005; FAX. 714/778–4383; Ronald I. Brendzel, Senior Vice President

Safeguard Health Plans, Inc., P.O. Box 3210, Anaheim, CA 92803–3210; tel. 714/778–1005; Steven J. Baileys, D.D.S., President

San Francisco Health Plan, 568 Howard Street, Fifth Floor, San Francisco, CA 94105; tel. 415/547–7800; FAX. 415/547–7824; Shahnaz Nikpay, Ph.D., Chief Executive Officer

San Joaquin County Health Commission, d/b/a The Health Plan of San Joaquin, 1550 West Fremont Street, Suite 200, Stockton, CA 95203–2643; tel. 209/939–3500; FAX. 209/939–3535; Mr. Terry G. Mack, Chief Executive Officer

Santa Clara County Health Authority, d/b/a Santa Clara Family Health Plan, 4050 Moorpark Avenue, San Jose, CA 95117; tel. 408/260–4490; FAX. 408–260–2016; Leona M. Butler, Chief Executive Officer

Santa Clara Valley Medical Center, Valley Health Plan, 750 South Bascom Avenue, San Jose, CA 95128; tel. 408/885–5704; FAX. 408/885–4050; Roger Wells, Executive Director

SCAN, 3780 Kilroy Airport Way, Suite 600, P.O. Box 22616, Zip 90801–5616, Long Beach, CA 90806–2460; tel. 562/989–5100; FAX. 562/989–5200; Sam L. Ervin, President and CEO

Sharp Health Plan, 9325 Sky Park Court, Suite 300, San Diego, CA 92123; tel. 619/637–6530; FAX. 619/637–6504; Kathlyn Mead, President and CEO

U.S. Behavioral Health Plan, California, 425 Market Street, 27th Floor, San Francisco, CA 94105–2426; tel. 415/547–5294; FAX. 415/547–5512; Kathryn Emery Dougherty, Executive Director

UDC Dental California, Inc., (formerly The Dental Advantage/National Dental Health), 3111 Camino Del Rio North, Suite 1000, San Diego, CA 92108; tel. 800/288–9992; FAX. 619/283–9437; Keith C. Macumber, Senior Vice President, Western Region

United Healthcare of California, Inc., 180 E. Ocloa Boulevard, Suite 500, Long Beach, CA 90802–4708; tel. 562/951–6400; FAX. 562/951–6870; C. Emery Dameron, Chief Executive Officer

Universal Care, 1600 East Hill Street, Signal Hill, CA 90806; tel. 562/424–6200; FAX. 562/427–4634; Jay Davis, Vice President

Value Healthplan of California, Inc., 5251 Viewridge Court, San Diego, CA 92123; tel. 619/278–2273; Lory Wallach, Vice President and COO

Value Options of California, Inc, (formerly Value Behavioral Health of California, Inc), 340 Golden Shore, Long Beach, CA 90802; tel. 562/590–9004; FAX. 562/951–6130; Tim Kotas, Acting Executive Director

Vision First Eye care, Inc., 1937–A Tully Road, San Jose, CA 95122; tel. 408/923–0400; James K. Eu, O.D., Ph.D., President

Vision Plan of America, 3255 Wilshire Blvd, suite 1610, Los Angeles, CA 90010; tel. 213/384–2600; FAX. 213/384–0084; Dr. Stuart Needleman

Vision Service Plan, 3333 Quality Drive, Rancho Cordov, CA 95670; tel. 800/852-7600; Al Schubert, Vice President, Managed Care

Visioncare of California, d/b/a Sterling Visioncare, 6540 Lusk Boulevard, Suite 234, San Diego, CA 92121; tel. 619/458-9983; Abb B. Prickett, CFO

Vista Behavioral Health Plans, 2355 Northside Drive, 3rd floor, San Diego, CA 92108; tel. 619/521-4440; FAX. 619/497-5244; Erik Bradbury, Chief Executive Officer

VivaHealth, Inc., d/b/a BPS HMO, 888 South Figueroa Street, Suite 1400, Los Angeles, CA 90017; tel. 213/489-2694; Barbara E. Rodin, Ph.D., President and CEO

Watts Health Foundation, Inc., UHP Healthcare, 3405 W. Imperial Boulevard, Inglewood, CA 90303; tel. 310/412-3569; FAX. 310/412-7782; Alma Graham, VP and General Counsel

Wellpoint Dental Plan, 21555 Oxnard Street, Woodland Hill, CA 91367; tel. 818/703-2412; Thomas C. Geiser, Senior Vice President, General Counsel

Wellpoint Health Networks, Inc., 21555 Oxnard Street, Woodland Hill, CA 91367; tel. 818/703-2412; FAX. 818/703-4406; Thomas Geiser, Executive Vice President, General Counsel

Wellpoint Pharmacy Plan, 27001 Agoura Road, Suite 325, Calabasas Hill, CA 91301-5339; tel. 818/878-2675; FAX. 818/880-4981; Richard C. Bleil, General Manager

Western Dental Services, Inc., Western Dental Plan, 300 Plaza Alicante, Suite 800, Garden Grove, CA 92640; tel. 714/938-1600; FAX. 714/938-1611; Robert C. Schur, President

Western Health Advantage, 1331 Garden Highway, Suite 100, Sacramento, CA 95833; tel. 916-563-3180; FAX. 916-563-3182; Garry Maisel, Chief Executive Officer

COLORADO

Antero Healthplans, 600 Grant Street, Suite 900, Denver, CO 80203; tel. 303/830-3150; FAX. 303/830-2392; Charlie Stark, President and CEO

Blue Cross/ Blue Shield of Colorado, P.O. Box 1668, Fort Collins, CO 80522; tel. 970/482-8403; FAX. 970/482-8911; Karen Morgan, VP, Group and Member Service

CIGNA HealthCare of Colorado, Inc., 3900 East Mexico Avenue, Suite 1100, Denver, CO 80210-3946; tel. 303/782-1500; FAX. 303/782-1577; Dennis Mouras, General Manager

Colorado Access, 501 South Cherry Street, Suite 700, Denver, CO 80222; tel. 303/355-6707; Judith M. Lenhart, Vice President Operations

Community Health Plan of the Rockies, Inc., 400 South Colorado Boulevard, Suite 300, Denver, CO 80246; tel. 303/355-3220; FAX. 305/355-3224; Fawn Anderson, Human Resources

Denver Health Medical Plan, Inc., 777 Bannock Street, Mail Code 0278, Denver, CO 80204-4507; tel. 303/436-7253; FAX. 303/436-5714

FHP of Colorado, Inc., 6455 South Yosemite Street, Englewood, CO 80111; tel. 303/220-5800; FAX. 303/714-3999; James J. Swayze, Vice President, Sales and Marketing

Foundation Health, a Colorado Health Plan, Inc., P.O. Box 958, Pueblo, CO 81002; tel. 719/583-7500

Frontier Community Health Plans, Inc., 6312 South Fiddler's Green Circle, Suite 260-N, Englewood, CO 80111; tel. 303/771-7200; FAX. 303/771-0366; Dr. Thomas J. Hazy

Health Network of Colorado Springs, Inc., 1115 Tejon, Suite 100, Colorado Springs, CO 80903; tel. 719/227-3450; FAX. 719/227-3451; Janet Pogar, Chief Operating Officer

HMO Colorado, Inc., d/b/a HMO Blue, 700 Broadway, Suite 612, Denver, CO 80273; tel. 303/831-2131

HMO Health Plans, Inc., d/b/a San Luis Valley HMO, Inc., 95 West First Avenue, Monte Vista, CO 81144; tel. 719/852-4055; FAX. 719/852-3481; Douglas Johnson, Executive Director, Chief Executive O

Kaiser Foundation Health Plan of Colorado, 2500 S. Havana Street, Aurora, CO 80014-1622; tel. 303/338-3000; Kathryn A. Paul, President

One Health Plan of Colorado, Inc., 8505 East Orchard Road, Englewood, CO 80111; tel. 303/804-6800

Prudential Health Care Plan, Inc., d/b/a Prudential HealthCare HMO, 4643 South Ulster Street, Suite 1000, Denver, CO 80237; tel. 303/796-6161; FAX. 303/796-6183; Denise Saabye, Communication Manager

Qual-Med Plans for Health of Colorado, Inc., P.O. Box 1986, Pueblo, CO 81002-1986; tel. 719/542-0500; FAX. 719/542-4921; Malik Hasan, M.D., Chairman, President

Rocky Mountain Health Maintenance Organization, d/b/a Rocky Mountain HMO, P.O. Box 10600, Grand Junction, CO 81502-5500; tel. 303/244-7760; FAX. 303/244-7880; Michael J. Weber, Executive Director

Sloans Lake Health Plan, Inc., 1355 South Colorado Boulevard, Suite 902, Denver, CO 80222; tel. 303/691-2200

United HealthCare of Colorado, Inc., 6251 Greenwood Plaza Boulevard, Englewood, CO 80111; tel. 303/694-9336; FAX. 303/267-3599

CONNECTICUT

Anthem BCBS of Connecticut, 370 Bassett Road, North Haven, CT 06473; tel. 203/239-8483; FAX. 203/985-4258; Robert Scalettar, M.D., M.P.H., VP Medical Policy CMO

CIGNA HealthCare of Connecticut, Inc., 900 Cottage Grove Road, A-118, Hartford, CT 06152-1118; tel. 860/769-2300; FAX. 860/769-2399; Donald S. Grossman, M.D., Medical Director

ConnectiCare of Massachusetts, Inc., P.O. Box 522, Farmington, CT 06032-0522; tel. 800/474-1466

ConnectiCare, Inc., 30 Batterson Park Road, Farmington, CT 06032; tel. 860/674-5700; FAX. 860/674-5728; Marcel Gamache, President and CEO

Health Choice of Connecticut Preferred One, 23 Maiden Lane, North Haven, CT 06473; tel. 203/239-7444; FAX. 203/239-5308; Sylvia B. Kelly, Vice President and Executive Director Medicaid

Kaiser Foundation Health Plan, 200 Corporate Place, Suite 300, Rocky Hill, CT 06067; tel. 860/513-6300

M.D. Health Plan, Six Devine Street, North Haven, CT 06473; tel. 800/772-5869; FAX. 203/407-2899; Barbara G. Bradow, President

NYLCare Health Plans of Connecticut, Inc., Four Armstrong Road, Shelton, CT 06484; tel. 203/944-1900; Theresa Atwood, Regional Vice President

Oxford Health Plans, 800 Connecticut Avenue, Norwalk, CT 06854; tel. 800/444-6222; Julie Summers, Marketing Associate

Oxford Health Plans, Inc., 800 Connecticut Avenue, Norwalk, CT 06854; tel. 800/889-7546; Norman Payson, Chief Executive Officer

Prudential Health Care of Connecticut, Inc., 101 Merritt Seven, Norwalk, CT 06851; tel. 203/849-1800; FAX. 203/849-8387; Lewis E. Devendorf, Executive Director

Suburban Health Plan, Inc., 680 Bridgeport Avenue, Shelton, CT 06484; tel. 203/926-8882; FAX. 203/925-1202; Tim Pusch, Manager, Sales, Marketing

DELAWARE

Amerihealth HMO, Inc., 919 North Market Street, Suite 1200, Wilmington, DE 19801-3021; Alfred F. Meyer, Executive Director

CareLink Community Health Partners, Georgetown Professional Park, 600 N. Dupont Highway, Georgetown, DE 19947; tel. 302/856-3100; FAX. 302/856-3999; Don Clark, Vice President, Corporate Development

Cigna Health Plan of Pennsylvania, Inc., One Beaver Valley Road, Suite CHP, Wilmington, DE 19803; tel. 302/477-3700

CIGNA Health Plan of Southern New Jersey, CIGNA HealthCare of PA, NJ & DE, One Beaver Valley Road, Suite CHP, Wilmington, DE 19803; tel. 302/477-3700; FAX. 302/477-3707; Norman Scott, M.D.

CIGNA HealthCare of Pennsylvania, New Jersey and Delaware, One Beaver Valley Road, Suite CHP, Wilmington, DE 19803; tel. 302/477-3000; FAX. 302/477-3707; Norman Scott, M.D., Medical Director

Delaware network Health Plan, 121 South Front Street, Seaford, DE 19973; tel. 302/629-6611; Donald Pinner, Vice President

Total Health, Inc., One Brandywine Gateway, P.O. Box 8792, Wilmington, DE 19899; tel. 302/421-3034; FAX. 302/421-2577; Robert C. Cole, Jr., President

DISTRICT OF COLUMBIA

Capital Care, Inc., 550 12th Street, S.W., Washington, DC 20065; tel. 410/528-7024; FAX. 410/528-7013; Eric R. Baugh, M.D., President

CapitalCare, Inc., 550 12th Street, S.W., Washington, DC 20065-0001; tel. 202/479-3678; FAX. 202/479-3660; M. Bruce Edwards, President

D.C. Chartered Health Plan, Inc., 820 First Street, N.E., Suite LL100, Washington, DC 20002-4205; tel. 202/408-4710; FAX. 202/408-4730; Robert L. Bowles, Jr., DBA, Chairman, President and CEO

United Mine Workers of America, 4455 Connecticut Avenue, N.W., Washington, DC 20008; tel. 202/895-3960; Robert Condra

FLORIDA

AHL Select HMO, Inc., 1776 American Heritage Life Drive, Jacksonville, FL 32224; tel. 904/992-2529; FAX. 904/992-2658; James H. Baum, Administrator

American Medical Healthcare, 1900 Summit Tower Boulevard, Suite 700, Orlando, FL 32810; tel. 407/660-1611; FAX. 407/660-0203; Sandra K. Johnson, President and CEO

AmeriHealth of Florida, Inc., 10151 Deerwood Park Blvd., Bldg. 200, Suite 400, Jacksonville, FL 32256; tel. 904/998-6700; FAX. 904/998-5403; Paul G. Jennings, VP & General Manager

AvMed Health Plan, P.O. Box 749, Gainesville, FL 32606-0749; tel. 352/372-8400; FAX. 352/337-8726; Edward C. Peddie, President and CEO

Beacon Health Plans, Inc., 2511 Ponce de Leon Boulevard, Coral Gables, FL 33134; tel. 305/930-8181; FAX. 305/774-2617; Raymond Noonan, Chief Executive Officer

Capital Group Health Services of Florida, Inc., 2140 Centerville Place, P.O. Box 13267, Tallahassee, FL 32317; tel. 904/386-3161; FAX. 904/385-3193; John Hogan, Administrator

Champion Healthcare, 7406 Fullerton Street, Suite 200, Jacksonville, FL 32256; tel. 904/519-0900; FAX. 904/519-0838; Richard C. Powell, President and CEO

CIGNA Dental Health of North Carolina, Inc., P.O. Box 189060, Plantation, FL 33318-9060; tel. 305/423-5800; David O. Cannady, President

CIGNA HealthCare of Florida, Inc., 5404 Cypress Center Drive, P.O. Box 24203, Tampa, FL 33623; tel. 813/281-1000; FAX. 813/282-0356; Joseph C. Gregor, President and General Manager

Community Health Care Systems, Inc., 2301 Lucien Way, Suite 440, Maitland, FL 32751; tel. 800/635-4345; FAX. 407/481-7190; Eric Scott, Director of Sales

DentiCare, Inc., 8130 Baymeadows Way West, Suite 200, Jacksonville, FL 32256; tel. 904/731-1870; Glenn Kollen

Florida Health Care Plan, Inc., 1340 Ridgewood Avenue, Holly Hill, FL 32117; tel. 904/676-7193; FAX. 904/676-7196; Edward F. Simpson, Jr., President, Chief Executive Off

Florida Ist Health Plan, Inc., 3425 Lake Alfred Road, P.O. Box 9126, Winter Haven, FL 33883-9126; tel. 813/293-0785; FAX. 813/297-9095; John J. Tort, President

Foundation Health, a Florida Health Plan, Inc., 1340 Concord Terrace, Sunrise, FL 33323; tel. 954/858-3000; FAX. 954/846-0331; Steven Griffin, Administrator

Foundation Health, a South Florida Health Plan, Inc., 7950 Northwest 53rd Street, Miami, FL 33166; tel. 305/591-3311

Health First Health Plan, Inc., 8247 Devereux Drive, Suite 103, Melbourne, FL 32940-7955; tel. 407/434-5600; FAX. 407/752-1129; Jerry Senne, President and CEO

Health Options, Inc., 532 Riverside Avenue, Jacksonville, FL 32203; tel. 904/791-6086; Harvey Matoren, President

Health Options, Inc., 532 Riverside Avenue, P.O. Box 60729, Jacksonville, FL 32202; tel. 800/457-4713; FAX. 904/791-6054; Robert I. Lufrano, Administrator

Healthcare USA, Inc., 8705 Perimeter Park Boulevard, Suite Three, Jacksonville, FL 32216; tel. 904/565-2950; FAX. 904/646-9238; Christopher Fey, President and CEO

Healthplan Southeast, Inc., 3520 Thomasville Road, Suite 200, Tallahassee, FL 32308; tel. 800/833-2169; FAX. 850/668-3133; Robert A. Wychulis, Chief Operating Officer

Healthplans of America, Inc., 2605 Maitland Center Parkway, Suite 300, Maitland, FL 32751; tel. 800/769-2848; FAX. 407/875-9581; Robert Flanagan, Administrator

Healthy Palm Beaches, Inc., 324 Datura Street, Suite 401, West Palm Beach, FL 33401; tel. 561/659-1270; FAX. 561/833-9786; Dwight Chenette, Administrator

HIP Health Plan of Florida, Inc., 200 South Park Road, Hollywood, FL 333021; tel. 954/962–3008; FAX. 954/985–4379; Steven M. Cohen, President and CEO

HIP Health Plan of Florida, Inc., formerly: HIP Network of Florida, Inc., 300 South Park Road, Hollywood, FL 33021; tel. 954/962–3008; FAX. 954/986–6217; Steven M. Cohen, President and CEO

Humana Medical Plan, Inc., 3400 Lakeside Drive, Miramar, FL 33027; tel. 305/626–5619; FAX. 305/626–5297; Joe Berding, Vice President, South Florida Market Operations

John Alden Nevadaplus Health Plan, 7300 Corporate Center Drive, Miami, FL 33126

Mayo Health Plans, Inc., 4168 Southpoint Parkway, Suite 102, Jacksonville, FL 32216; tel. 888/279–2646; FAX. 904/279–9777; Patrick Healy, Administrator

Neighborhood Health Partnership, Inc., 7600 Corporate Center Drive, Miami, FL 33126; tel. 800/354–0222; FAX. 305/260–4308; William H. Mauk, Jr., President and CEO

PCA Family Health Plan, Inc., d/b/a Century Medical Health Plan, Inc., 5959 Blue Lagoon Drive, Miami, FL 33126; tel. 800/562–9262; FAX. 605/267–6290; Elias Hourani, Administrator

Physicians Healthcare Plans, Inc., One Harbour Place, 777 South Harbor Island Boulevard, Tampa, FL 33602; tel. 813/229–5300; FAX. 813/229–5301; Miguel B. Fernandez, Chief Executive Officer

Preferred Choice, HMO of Florida Health Choice, Inc., 5300 West Atlantic Avenue, Suite 500, Delray Beach, FL 33484–8190; tel. 800/233–0505; FAX. 407/496–0513; Jeff Keiser, Administrator/Compliance Officer

Preferred Medical Plan, Inc., 4950 SW 8th Street, Coral Gables, FL 33134; tel. 305/669–1501; FAX. 305/667–3957; Sylvia Urlich, President

Principal Health Care of Florida, Inc., 1200 Riverplace Boulevard, Suite 500, Jacksonville, FL 32207; tel. 800/358–6205; FAX. 301/231–1033; Kenneth S. Bryant, Administrator

Principal Health Care of Florida, Inc., 7282 Plantation Road, Suite 200, Pensacola, FL 32504; tel. 904/484–4000; Rebecca McQueen, Executive Director

Prudential Health Care Plan, Inc., d/b/a PruCare, 2301 Lucien Way, Suite 230, Maitland, FL 32751–7086; tel. 800/628–3801; FAX. 201/716–2193; Andrew Crooks, Administrator

Riscorp Health Plan, Inc., 1390 Main Street, Zip 34236, P.O. Box 1598, Sarasota, FL 34230–1598; tel. 800/226–9899; FAX. 813/954–4611; Rich Fogle, Administrator

St. Augustine Health Care, Inc., 1511 N. Westshore Blvd., 7th floor, Tampa, FL 33607; tel. 813/288–7600; FAX. 813/288–7664; Dennis Mihale, M.D., Administrator

Tampa General Healthplan, Inc., 100 South Ashley Drive, Suite 300, Tampa, FL 33602; tel. 813/276–5047; FAX. 813/276–5030; Thelma Czeczotca, Plan Administrator

The Public Health Trust of Dade County, 1500 Northwest 12th Avenue, JMT, Suite West 1001, Miami, FL 33136; tel. 305/585–7120; FAX. 305/545–5212; Joseph Rogers, Administrator

Total Health Choice, Inc., formerly: PacifiCare of Florida, Inc., One Alhambra Plaza, Suite 1000, Coral Gables, FL 33134; tel. 800/887–6888; FAX. 305/443–5445; Kenneth G. Rimmer, Administrator

Ultramedix Health Care Systems, Inc., 3450 West Buschwood Park Drive, Suite 245, Tampa, FL 33618; tel. 813/933–6200; FAX. 813/930–2949; John S. Zaleskie, Chief Executive Officer

United Healthcare of Florida, Inc., 800 N. Magnolia Avenue, Orlando, FL 32803; tel. 800/543–3145; FAX. 305/447–3292; Frederick C. Dunlap, Administrator

Vantage Health Plan, Inc., 4250 Lakeside Drive, Suite 210, Jacksonville, FL 32210; tel. 904/387–4451; FAX. 904/387–0338; James Burt, M.D., Administrator

Well Care HMO, Inc., 11016 North Dale Mabry, Suite 301, Tampa, FL 33618; tel. 813/963–6128; FAX. 813/960–1623; Pradip C. Patel, Administrator

GEORGIA

AETNA Health Plans of Georgia, Inc., 11675 Great Oaks Way, Alpharetta, GA 30022; tel. 404/814–4300; FAX. 404/814–4294; Joseph Wild, General Manager

American Dental Plan of North Carolina, Inc., 100 Mansell Court East, Suite 400, Roswell, GA 30076; tel. 770/998–8936; John Gasiorowski

American Medical Plans of Georgia, Inc., 1355 Peachtree Street, N.E., Suite 1500, Atlanta, GA 30309; tel. 404/347–8005; Tom Stockdale, Executive Director

Athens Area Health Plan Select, Inc., 295 West Clayton Street, Athens, GA 30601; tel. 706/549–0549; FAX. 706/549–8004; Richard Tanzella, Executive Director

CIGNA Healthcare of Georgia, Inc., 100 Peachtree Street, N.E., Suite 700, Equitable Building, Atlanta, GA 30301; tel. 404/681–7100; FAX. 404/681–7135; Jack Towsley, President and GM

Complete Health of Georgia, Inc., 2970 Clairmont Road, N.E., Atlanta, GA 30329; tel. 404/698–8600; Gail Smallridge, Executive Director

FamilyPlus Health Plans of Georgia, Inc., Two Decatur Town Center, 125 Clairemont Road, Decatur, GA 30030; tel. 404/235–1010; FAX. 404/248–3858; Michael Brohm, President

Grady Healthcare, Inc., 100 Edgewood Avenue, Suite 1817, Atlanta, GA 30303; tel. 404/616–5829; FAX. 404/616–8408; Alma Roberts, Executive Director

Healthsource Georgia, Inc., 1000 Parkwood Circle, Suite 700, Atlanta, GA 30339–2175; tel. 770/303–1900; Heywood Donigan, Executive Director

HMO Georgia, Inc., 3350 Peachtree Road, N.E., P.O. Box 3417, Atlanta, GA 30326; tel. 404/842–8422; FAX. 404/842–8451; John Harris, President

Humana Employers Health Plan of Georgia, Inc., 115 Perimeter Center Place, N.E., Suite 540, Atlanta, GA 30346; tel. 770/399–5916; Gregory H. Wolf, Executive Director

John Deere Health Plan of Georgia, Inc., Building 200, 2743 Perimeter Parkway, Suite 105, Augusta, GA 30909; tel. 706/860–6776; Dean Anderson, Executive Director

Kaiser Foundation Health Plan of Georgia, Inc., 3495 Piedmont Road, N.E., Building Nine, Atlanta, GA 30305–1736; tel. 404/364–7000; FAX. 404/364–4791; Carolyn Kenny, President

Master Health Plan, Inc., 3652 J. Dewey Gray Circle, Augusta, GA 30909; tel. 706/863–5955; Libby Young, Executive Director

Principal Health Care of Georgia, Inc., 3715 Northside Parkway, 400 Northcreek, Atlanta, GA 30327; tel. 404/231–9911; Kenneth J. Linde, President

Promina Managed Care Organization, 2000 South Park Place, Suite 200, Atlanta, GA 30339–2049; tel. 770/956–6944; FAX. 770/937–4159; Bonnie Phipps, President and CEO

United Healthcare of Georgia, Inc., 2970 Clairmont Road, Atlanta, GA 30329; tel. 404/364–8800; FAX. 404/364–8818; A. Kelly Atkinson, Executive Director

HAWAII

Health Plan Hawaii, 818 Keeaumoku Street, P.O. Box 860, Honolulu, HI 96814; tel. 808/948–5408; FAX. 808/948–5063; Robert C. Nickel, President and CEO

HMO Hawaii (HMSA), 818 Keeaumoko Street, P.O. Box 860, Honolulu, HI 96808; tel. 808/948–5408; FAX. 808/948–5999; Robert C. Nickel, Vice President

Kaiser Foundation Health Plan, Inc., 3283 Moanaleau Road, Honolulu, HI 96819; tel. 808/834–5333; FAX. 808/834–3944; Bruce Behnke, President

Queens Health Care Plan, Two Waterfront Plaza, Suite 200, 500 Ala Moana Boulevard, Honolulu, HI 96813; tel. 808/532–4114; FAX. 808/532–7996; Nate Nygaard, President

Straub Plan, 888 South King Street, Honolulu, HI 96813; tel. 808/522–4540; FAX. 808/522–4544; Karen Lennox, Executive Director

IDAHO

HealthSense, 1602 21st Avenue, Lewiston, ID 83501; tel. 208/746–2671; FAX. 208/746–1030; Carolyn Steinbrecher–Loera, Manager, Managed Care Program

Primary Health Network, Inc., 800 Park Boulevard, Suite 760, Boise, ID 83712; tel. 208/344–1811; FAX. 208/344–4262; Elden Mitchell, President and CEO

ILLINOIS

Access HMO, Inc., d/b/a Unity HMO of Illinois, 150 South Wacker Drive, Suite 2100, Chicago, IL 60606; tel. 312/251–0955; FAX. 312/251–0294; Robert Currie, President & CEO

Aetna Health Plans of Illinois, Inc., d/b/a Aetna Health Plans of the Midwest, 100 North Riverside Plaza, Chicago, IL 60606; tel. 312/441–3000

Aetna U.S. Healthcare of Illinois, Inc., 100 North Riverside Plaza, 20th Floor, Chicago, IL 60606; tel. 312/928–3000; FAX. 312/441–3067; Robert Mendoza, General Manager

American Health Care Providers, Inc., 142 Towncenter Road, Matteson, IL 60443; tel. 708/503–5000; FAX. 708/503–5001; Asif A. Sayeed, President

BCI HMO, Inc., 300 East Randolph Street, 21st floor, Chicago, IL 60601–5090; tel. 312/653–6699; Eileen Holderbaum, Executive Director

BCI HMO, Inc., (formerly HMO Illinois, Inc.), 233 North Michigan Avenue, Chicago, IL 60601; tel. 312/938–6347; FAX. 312/819–1220; Simeon Martin Hickman, President

Benchmark Health Insurance Company, 2550 Charles Street, Rockford, IL 61108; tel. 815/391–7000; FAX. 815/966–2089; Michael J. Gallagher

CIGNA HealthCare of Illinois, Inc., 525 West Monroe, Suite 1800, Chicago, IL 60661; tel. 312/496–5499; Donna DeFrank, President

CIGNA Healthplan of Illinois, Inc., 1700 Higgins, Suite 600, Des Plaines, IL 60018; tel. 708/699–5600; FAX. 708/699–5675; John W. Rohfritch, Senior Vice President

Community Health Choice, 650 South Clark, Suite 400, Chicago, IL 60605; tel. 312/922–4501; FAX. 312/922–6358; Patsy K. Crawford, CEO

Community Health Plan of Sarah Bush Lincoln, 1000 Health Center Drive, P.O. Box 372, Mattoon, IL 61938–0372; tel. 217/258–2572; FAX. 217/258–2111; Gary L. Barnett, President and CEO

Compass Health Care Plans, 310 South Michigan Avenue, Chicago, IL 60604; tel. 312/294–0200; FAX. 312/294–5826; Aldo Giacchino, Chief Executive Officer

Country Medical Plans, Inc., d/b/a Country Care HMO, PO Box 2000, Bloomington, IL 61702–2000; tel. 309/821–2477; FAX. 309/821–5198; Lori Reel, Manager

Dreyer Health Plans, 1877 West Downer Place, Aurora, IL 60506; tel. 630/859–1100; FAX. 630/906–5100; Richard A. Lutz, President

FHP of Illinois, 747 East 22nd Street, Suite 100, Lombard, IL 60148; tel. 708/916–8400

FHP of Illinois, Inc., One Lincoln Centre, Suite 700, Oakbrook Terr, IL 60181–4260; tel. 630/916–8400; FAX. 630/916–4275; Gary M. Cole, President

First Commonwealth, Inc., 444 North Wells, Suite 600, Chicago, IL 60610; tel. 312/644–1800; FAX. 312/644–1822; Mark R. Lundberg, Vice President, Sales

Harmony Health Plan of Illinois, Inc., 125 South Wacker Drive, Suite 2900, Chicago, IL 60606; tel. 312/630–2025; Keri Rosenbloom, Operations

Health Alliance Medical Plans, Inc., d/b/a Health Alliance HMO, 102 East Main, Suite 200, P.O. Box 6003, Urbana, IL 61801; tel. 217/337–8010; FAX. 217/337–8093; Jeffrey Ingram, CEO

Health Alliance Midwest, Inc., P.O. Box 6003, Urbana, IL 61801; tel. 217/337–8000; Jeffrey Ingram, CEO

Health Alliance Midwest, Inc., 102 East Main Street, Suite 200, Urbana, IL 61801; tel. 217/337–8000; Robert C. Parker, M.D., President

Health Direct Insurance, Inc., 1011 East Touhy Avenue, Suite 500, Des Plaines, IL 60018–2808; tel. 847/391–9590; Jennifer L. Cline, CEO

Heritage National Healthplan, 1300 River Drive, Suite 200, Moline, IL 61265; tel. 309/765–1200; G. Michael Hammes, President

Heritage National Healthplan of Tennessee, Inc., 1515 Fifth Avenue, Suite 200, Moline, IL 61265; tel. 309/765–1200; G. Michael Hammes, President

Heritage National Healthplan, Inc., 1300 River Drive0, Moline, IL 61265–1368; tel. 309/765–1200; FAX. 309/765–1322; G. Michael Hammes, President

Heritage National Healthplan, Inc., 1515 Fifth Avenue, Suite 200, Moline, IL 61265–1368; tel. 309/765–1200; G. Michael Hammes, President

Heritage National Healthplan, Inc., 1515 Fifth Avenue, Suite 200, Moline, IL 61265–1358; tel. 309/765–1203

Heritage National Healthplan, Inc., 909 River Drive, Moline, IL 61265; tel. 309/765–7660; Douglas R. Niska, Director

HMO Illinois a product of Health Care Services Corporation, 300 East Randolph Street, Chicago, IL 60601–5099; tel. 312/653–6000; Ray McCaskey, President

Section C

Humana Health Plan, Inc., 30 South Wacker Drive, Suite 3100, Chicago, IL 60606; tel. 312/441–5350; Barry Averill, Vice President

Illinois Healthcare Insurance Co., 303 E. Washington, Bloomington, IL 61701; tel. 309/829–1061; Thomas J. Pliura, M.D., J.D., President

Illinois Masonic Community Health Plan, 836 West Wellington, Room 1707, Chicago, IL 60657; tel. 773/296–7014; Dana Gilbert, Administrative Director

John Deere Family Health Plan, 1300 River Drive, Suite 200, Moline, IL 61265–1368; tel. 309/765–1200; Richard Van Belle, President

John Deere Family Healthplan, Inc., 1300 River Drive, Moline, IL 61265–1368; tel. 309/765–1600; G. Michael Hammes, President

Maxicare Health Plans of the Midwest, Maxicare Illinois, 111 East Wacker Dr., Suite 1500, Chicago, IL 60601; tel. 312/616–4700

Maxicare Health Plans of the Midwest, Inc., 111 East Wacker Drive, Suite 1500, Chicago, IL 60601; tel. 312/616–4700; FAX. 312/616–4998; Mark Hanrahan, Vice President, General Manager

Mercy Care Corporation, 2600 South Michigan Avenue, Chicago, IL 60616–2477; tel. 312/567–5649; FAX. 312/567–2786; Ramesh Joshi, Director

MetraHealth Care Plan of Illinois, Inc., 1900 East Golf Road, Suite 501, Schaumburg, IL 60173; tel. 708/619–2222

NYLCare Health Plans of the Midwest, Inc., 111 West 22nd Street, 8th floor, Oak Brook, IL 60521; tel. 630/368–1800; FAX. 630/368–1802; William P. Donahue, President

One Health Plan of Illinois, Inc., 6250 River Road, Suite 3030, Rosemont, IL 60018; tel. 847/518–0490; Patricia Ann Moldovan, President

OSF Health Plans, Inc., 300 S.W. Jefferson Street, Peoria, IL 61602–1413; tel. 309/677–8207; FAX. 309/677–8330; Richard H. Bohn, President

Oxford Health Plans, Inc., 9801 West Higgins, Suite 720, Rosemont, IL 60018–4701; tel. 847/685–2273; Aldo Giacchio, President

Personal Care Insurance of Illinois, Inc., 2110 Fox Drive, Champaign, IL 61820; tel. 217/366–1226; FAX. 217/366–5571; Randolph C. Hoffman, President and CEO

Principal Health Care of Illinois, Inc., One Lincoln Center, Suite 1040, Oakbrook Terr, IL 60181–4267; tel. 630/916–6622; FAX. 630/916–9595; Lee Green, Executive Director

Rockford Health Plans, 3401 North Perryville Road, Rockford, IL 61114; tel. 815/654–3600; FAX. 815/654–5186; John W. Zilavy, Executive Director

Rush Prudential Health Plans, 233 South Wacker Drive, Suite 3900, Chicago, IL 60605–6309; tel. 312/234–7000; FAX. 312/986–4859; Scott Serota, President/CEO

Rush Prudential HMO, 233 South Wacker Drive, Suite 3900, Chicago, IL 60606; tel. 312/234–7000; FAX. 312/234–8555; Carmeline Esposito, Public Relations Manager

The Dental Concern, Ltd., 222 North LaSalle Street, Suite 2140, Chicago, IL 60601; tel. 312/201–1260; Polly Reese, D.D.S., Dental Director

UIHMO, Inc., 2023 West Ogden Avenue, Suite 205, M/C 692, Chicago, IL 60612–3741; tel. 312/996–3553; FAX. 312/996–0035; Diane S. Eng, VP for University Programs

Union Health Service, 1634 West Polk, Chicago, IL 60612; tel. 312/829–4224; FAX. 312/829–8241; Helen M. Hrynkiw, Executive Director

United HealthCare of Illinois, Inc., d/b/a Chicago HMO, Ltd., One South Wacker Drive, P.O. Box 909714, Chicago, IL 60609–9714; tel. 312/424–4605; FAX. 312/424–4914; Marshall Rozzi, President and CEO

Universal Health Services, Inc., 403 West 14th Street, Chicago Heights, IL 60411–2498; tel. 708/755–2462; Ralph R. Crescenzo, President

Wellmark Health Plan of Northern Illinois, Inc., 1420 Kensington Road, Suite 203, Oak Brook, IL 60521–2106; tel. 800/345–7848

INDIANA

Anthem Health Plan, d/b/a Key Health Plan, 120 Monument Circle, Indianapolis, IN 46204; tel. 317/488–6000; FAX. 317/290–5695; Dijuana Lewis, Vice President, Health Care Management

Arnett HMO, Inc., 3768 Rome Drive, Lafayette, IN 47905; tel. 317/448–8200; FAX. 317/448–8660; James A. Brunnemer, Executive Director

Coordinated Care Corporation Indiana, Inc., d/b/a Managed Health Services, 8688 Broadway, Merrillville, IN 46410; tel. 219/756–7134

Delta Dental Plan of Indiana, Inc., 5875 Castle Creek Parkway, North Drive, Indianapolis, IN 46250; tel. 317/842–4022

Health Resources, Inc., 314 Southeast Riverside Drive, P.O. Box 3607, Evansville, IN 47735–3607; tel. 812/424–I44I; FAX. 812/424–2096; Edward L. Fritz, D.D.S., President

Healthpoint, LLC, 8900 Keystone Crossing, Suite 500, Indianapolis, IN 46240; tel. 317/574–8181; FAX. 317/574–8182; L. Denise Smith, Administrative Assistant

Healthsource Indiana Managed Care Plan, Inc., 225 South East Street, Suite 240, Indianapolis, IN 46206; tel. 800/933–3466; FAX. 317/687–8500; David H. Smith, Chief Executive Officer

Indiana Vision Services, Inc., 115 West Washington Street, Suite 1370, Indianapolis, IN 46204; tel. 317/687–1066

IU Health Plan, Inc., 3901 West 86th Street, Suite 230, Indianapolis, IN 46268; tel. 317/872–2202; FAX. 317/871–8833; Sarah Blackman, Sales Coordinator

M Plan, Inc., 8802 North Meridian Street, Suite 100, Indianapolis, IN 46260; tel. 317/571–5300; FAX. 317/571–5306; Alex Slabosky, President

Maxicare Indiana, Inc., 9480 Priority Way, West Drive, Indianapolis, IN 46240–3899; tel. 317/844–5775; FAX. 317/574–0713; Vicki F. Perry, Vice President, General Manager

Partners National Health Plans of Indiana, Inc., One Michigan Square, 100 East Wayne, Suite 502, South Bend, IN 46601; tel. 219/233–4899; FAX. 219/234–7484; Richard C. Born, Senior Vice President Finance, Operations

Physicians Health Network, Inc., One Riverfront Place, Suite 400, P.O. Box 3357, Evansville, IN 47732; tel. 812/465–6000; FAX. 812/465–6014; Kevin M. Clancy, Chairman, President, Chief Executive

Physicians Health Plan of Northern Indiana, Inc., 8101 West Jefferson Boulevard, Fort Wayne, IN 46804; tel. 219/432–6690; FAX. 219/432–0493; John P. Smith, M.D., President

Physicians Health Plan of Northern Indiana, Inc., 8101 West Jefferson Boulevard, Fort Wayne, IN 46804–4163; tel. 800/982–6257; FAX. 219/432–0493

Principal Health Care of Indiana, Inc., One North Pennsylvania, Suite 1100, Indianapolis, IN 46204; tel. 317/263–0920; FAX. 317/263–9139; Douglas Stratton, Executive Director

Sagamore Health Network, Inc., 11555 North Meridian, Suite 400, Carmel, IN 46032; tel. 317/573–2904; FAX. 317/580–8488; Malinda Hinkle, Vice President, Marketing

Southeastern Indiana Health Organization, Inc. (SIHO), 432 Washington Street, P.O. Box I787, Columbus, IN 47202–1787; tel. 812/378–7000; FAX. 812/378–7048; Roy H. Flaherty, President and CEO

SpecialMed of Indiana, Inc., 120 Monument Circle, Indianapolis, IN 46204–4903; tel. 317/488–6128; Mike Hostetter, M.D., President

United Dental Care of Indiana, Inc., 50 South Meridian, Suite 700, Indianapolis, IN 46204–3542; tel. 800/262–5388

Welborn Clinic/Welborn HMO, Welborn Health Options, 421 Chestnut Street, Evansville, IN 47713; tel. 812/425–3939; James Krueger, M.D., Medical Director

IOWA

Care Choices HMO, 600 Fourth Street, Terra Centre, Suite 401, Sioux City, IA 51101; tel. 712/252–2344; FAX. 712/233–3684; Bill Windsor, Executive Director

Medical Associates Clinic Health Plan of Wisconsin, 700 Locust Street, Suite 230, Dubuque, IA 52001–6800; tel. 319/556–8070; FAX. 319/556–5134; Ross A. Madden, Chairman of the Board, Director

Medical Associates Health Plan, Inc., 700 Locust Street, PO Box 5002, Dubuque, IA 52004–5002; tel. 319/556–8070; FAX. 319/556–5134; Cynthia C. Thumser, Executive Director

Medical Associates Health Plan, Inc., One CyCare Plaza, Suite 230, Dubuque, IA 5200I; tel. 319/556–8070; FAX. 319/556–5134; Lawrence Cremer, Chief Executive Officer

Mercy Health Plans HMO – IA, (d/b/a Care Choices), 522 Fourth Street, Suite 250, Sioux City, IA 51101–1744; tel. 712/252–2344; Marsha Watts, Iowa Site Manager

Nevada Care, d/b/a Iowa Health Solutions, 300 N. W. Bank Tower, Spruce Hills Drive at Middle Road, Bettendorf, IA 52722; tel. 319/359–8999; FAX. 319/359–8999; Paul C. Carter, Vice President

Principal Health Care of Iowa, Inc., 4600 Westown Parkway, Suite 200, West Des Moines, IA 50266–1099; tel. 515/225–1234; FAX. 515/223–0097; Louis Garcia, CEO

Wellmark Health Plan of Iowa, 636 Grand Avenue, Des Moines, IA 50309; tel. 800/355–2031; Thomas E. Press, President

KANSAS

CIGNA HealthCare of Ohio, Inc.,, dba CIGNA HealthCare of Kansas/Missouri, 7400 West 110th Street, Suite 600, Overland Park, KS 66210; tel. 913/339–4700; FAX. 913/451–0974; James A. Young, President, General Manager

Community Health Plans of KS Inc., 900 Mass., Suite 602, Lawrence, KS 66044; tel. 785/832–6850; FAX. 785/832–6876; Michael Herbert, Executive Vice–President and COO

Exclusive Healthcare, Inc., 11301 Nall, Suite 201, Lealand, KS 66211; tel. 913–451–1777; FAX. 913–451–5748; Rick Cochran, Executive Director

Healthcare America Plans, Inc., 453 South Webb Road, Wichita, KS 67207–1309; tel. 316/262–7400; FAX. 316/262–1395; Stan Vaughn

HealthCare American Plans, Inc., P.O. Box 780467, Wichita, KS 67278–0467

HMO Kansas, Inc., 419 West 29th Street, Topeka, KS 66601–0110; tel. 913/291–7000; John W. Knack, Jr., President

Horizon Health Plan, Inc., 623 Southwest 10th Avenue, Suite 300, Topeka, KS 66612–1627; tel. 913/235–0402; Bruce M. Gosser, President

Kaiser Foundation Health Plan of Kansas City, Inc., 10561 Barkley, Suite 200, Overland Park, KS 66212–1886; tel. 913/967–4638; FAX. 913/967–4647; Gerard Grimaldi, Director External Affairs

MetraHealth Care Plan of Kansas City, Inc., (a wholly owned subsidiary of United HealthCare of the Midwest, Inc.), 9300 West 110th Street, Suite 350A, Overland Park, KS 66210; tel. 913/451–5656; FAX. 913/451–0492; Robert S. Bonney, Vice President

Preferred Plus of Kansas, Inc., 8535 E. 21st. N, Wichita, KS 67206; tel. 316/609–2345; FAX. 316/609–2346; Marlon Dauner, President

Premier Health, Inc., d/b/a Premier Blue, 1133 Topeka Avenue, Topeka, KS 66629–0001; tel. 913/291–7000; John W. Knack, Jr., President

KENTUCKY

Advantage Care, Inc., 120 Prosperous Place, Suite 100, Lexington, KY 40509; tel. 606/264–4600; Jeffrey P. Johnson, Chief Executive Officer

Alternative Health Delivery Systems, Inc., 1901 Campus Place, Louisville, KY 40299; tel. 502/261–2176; FAX. 502/261–2255; Carol H. Muldoon, Vice President and COO

American Health Network of Kentucky, Inc., 300 West Main, Suite 100, Louisville, KY 40202; tel. 502/681–0960; Denise Schifano, Regional Director, Operations

Anthem Blue Cross and Blue Shield, 9901 Linn Station Road, Louisville, KY 40223; tel. 502/423–2373; FAX. 502/423–6974; George L. Walker, Chief Operating Officer

Anthem Blue Cross Blue Shield, 9901 Linn Station Road, Louisville, KY 40223; tel. 502/423–2277; FAX. 502/423–2729; Robert McIntire, Vice President

Anthem Health Plans of Ky, Inc., 9901 Linn Station Road, Louisville, KY 40233; tel., 502/423–2308; Mike Lorch, Director

Bluegrass Family Health, Inc., 651 Perimeter Drive, Suite 300, Lexington, KY 40517; tel. 606/269–4475; FAX. 606/269–6447; James s. Fritz, President and CEO

CHA Health, 220 Canary Road (Street Zip Code 40503–3382), P.O. Box 23468, Lexington, KY 40523–3468; tel. 606/271–5055; Mark Birdwhistell, Chief Executive Officer

CompDent Corporation, 1930 Bishop Lane, 16th Floor, Louisville, KY 40218; tel. 800/456–5500; FAX. 502/456–2772; Allan Brockway Morris, President and CEO

Healthsource Kentucky, Inc., 100 Mallard Creek Road, Suite 300, Louisville, KY 40207; tel. 502/899–7500; Paul E. Stamp, Interim Executive Director

Healthwise of Kentucky, Ltd., 2409 Harodsburg Road, Lexington, KY 40504; tel. 606/296–6100; FAX. 606/255–9134; Harold Bischoff, Executive Director

HMO Kentucky, Inc., 9901 Linn Station Road, Louisville, KY 40223; tel. 502/423–2282; FAX. 502/423–6979; G. Douglas Sutherland, President

Section C

HMPK, 500 West Main Street, P.O. Box 1438, Louisville, KY 40201–1438; tel. 502/580–1854; FAX. 502/580–5044; Heidi Margulis, Director, Government Programs

HMPK, Inc., P.O. Box 740036, Louisville, KY 40201–7436; tel. 502/580–5804; Craig Drablos, Executive Director

HPlan, Inc., 101 East Main Street, 12th Floor, Louisville, KY 40204; tel. 800/245–4446; FAX. 502/580–5044

HPLAN, Inc., 500 West Main Street, P.O. Box 1438, Louisville, KY 40201–1438; tel. 502/580–1854; Heidi Margulis, Director, Government Programs

Humana Health Chicago, Inc., P.O. Box 740036, Louisville, KY 40201–7436; tel. 312/441–9111; Barry Averill, Vice President

Humana Health Plan of Louisiana, Inc., 500 West Main Street, P.O. Box 740036, Louisville, KY 40201–7436; tel. 502/580–1000; James E. Murray, Vice President, Finance

Humana Health Plan of Utah, Inc., 500 West Main Street, 20th Floor, Louisville, KY 40201; tel. 502/580–1000

Humana Health Plan of Washington, Inc., P.O. Box 1438, Louisville, KY 40201–1438; tel. 502/580–3620; FAX. 502/580–3942; Sandra Lewis, Director, Government Compliance

Humana Health Plan, Inc., P.O. Box 740036, Louisville, KY 40201–7436; tel. 502/580–5804; Craig Drablos, Executive Director

Humana Health Plan, Inc., 500 West Main Street, Louisville, KY 40202; tel. 502/580–1860; FAX. 502/580–3127; Greg Donaldson, Director, Corporate Communications

Humana Health Plan, Inc., 500 West Main Street, P.O. Box 1438, Louisville, KY 40201–1438; tel. 502/580–1854; FAX. 502/580–5018; Heidi Margulis, Director, Government Programs

Humana Health Plan, Inc., P.O. Box 740036, Louisville, KY 40201–7436; tel. 502/580–5804; Craig Drablos, Executive Director

Humana Health Plan, Inc., 101 East Main Street, Louisville, KY 40202; tel. 502/580–5005

Humana HealthChicago, Inc., 500 West Main Street, P.O. Box 1438, Louisville, KY 40201–1438; tel. 502/580–1000; Norman J. Beles, President

United Health Care of Kentucky, 2409 Harrodsburg Road, Lexington, KY 40504; tel. 606/296–6000; Budd Fisher, Chief Executive Officer

LOUISIANA

Advantage Health Plan, Inc., 829 St. Charles Avenue, New Orleans, LA 70130; tel. 504/568–9009; FAX. 504/568–0301; Jane Cooper, President and CEO

Aetna Health Plans of Louisiana, Inc., 3900 North Causeway Boulevard, Suite 410, Metairie, LA 70002–7283; tel. 504/830–5600; FAX. 504/837–6571; Michael L. Rogers, President

Capitol Health Network, Inc., 4700 Wichers Drive, Suite 300, Marrero, LA 70072; tel. 504/347–4515; John Sudderth, Chief Executive Officer

CIGNA HealthCare of Louisiana, Inc., 4354 South Sherwood Forest Boulevard, Suite 240, Baton Rouge, LA 70816; tel. 504/295–2800; FAX. 504/295–2888; Linda Gage–White, M.D., Executive Director

CIGNA HealthCare of North Louisiana, Inc., 4354 South Sherwood Forest Boulevard, Suite 240, Baton Rouge, LA 70816; tel. 504/295–2800; FAX. 504/295–2888; Nancy T. Horstmann, Executive Director

Community Health Network of Louisiana, 2431 South Acadian Thruway, Suite 350, P.O. Box 80159, Baton Rouge, LA 70898–0159; tel. 504/237–2106; FAX. 504/237–2222; Glen J. Golemi, President and CEO

Foundation Health, Louisiana Health Plan, Inc., 5353 Essen Lane, Suite 450, Baton Rouge, LA 70809; tel. 504/763–5300; Gilbert Dypre, President

Gulf South Health Plans, Inc., 5615 Corporate Boulevard, Suite Three, P.O. Box 80339, Baton Rouge, LA 70898–0339; tel. 504/237–1700; FAX. 504/237–1939; Jack W. Walker, President

Health Plus of Louisiana, Inc., 2600 Greenwood Road, Shreveport, LA 71103; tel. 318/632–4590; FAX. 318/632–4463; Peter J. Babin, President

HMO of Louisiana, Inc., P.O. Box 98029, Baton Rouge, LA 70898–8024; tel. 504/295–2383; FAX. 504/295–2491; Michael A. Hayes, Executive Director

Medfirst Health Plans of Louisiana, Inc., 3500 North Causeway Boulevard, Suite 520, Metairie, LA 70002; tel. 504/837–4000; FAX. 504/831–1107; Carol A. Solomon, President

NYLCare Health Plans of Louisiana, Inc., 2014 West Pinhook Road, Suite 200, Lafayette, LA 70508; tel. 800/825–0568; FAX. 318/237–1703; Burley J. Pellerin II, Director, Operations

Ochsner Health Plan, Inc. (HMO), One Galleria Boulevard, Suite 1224, Metairie, LA 70001; tel. 504/836–6600; FAX. 504/836–6566; R. Lyle Luman, President and CEO

Principal Health Care of Louisiana, Inc, 2424 Edenborn Ave, Suite 600, Metairie, LA 70001; tel. 504/834–0840; FAX. 504/834–2694; Keith G. Benoit, Sr., Chief Executive Officer

SMA Health Plan, 111 Veteran's Memorial Boulevard, Heritage Plaza, Suite 500, Metairie, LA 70005; tel. 504/837–7374; FAX. 504/837–7366; Robert Ritchey

Sunbelt Health Plan of Louisiana, Inc., 3434 South Causeway Boulevard, Suite 901, Metairie, LA 70001; tel. 504/922–9142; John F. Ales

Vantage Health Plan, Inc., 909 North 18th Street, Suite 201, Monroe, LA 71201; tel. 318/323–2269; Angela Olden, Executive Director

MAINE

Blue Cross and Blue Shield of Maine, Two Gannett Drive, South Portland, ME 04106; tel. 207/822–7000; Nancy Hutchings, Director, Customer Service

CIGNA Healthsource Maine, Two Stonewood Drive, P.O. Box 447, Freeport, ME 04032–0447; tel. 207/865–5000; FAX. 207/865–5632; Richard White, Chief Executive Officer

NYLCare of Maine Health Plans, Inc., One Monument Square, Portland, ME 04102; tel. 207/791–7916; Charlotte Pease, Manager

PMC Medical Management, Inc., 202 US Route One, P.O. Box 165, Falmouth, ME 04105; tel. 207/781–9890; FAX. 207/781–6675; Jeffrey W. Kirby, Controller

MARYLAND

CIGNA HealthCare Mid–Atlantic, Inc., 9700 Patuxent Woods Drive, Columbia, MD 21046; tel. 410/720–5800; Linda Hacker

CIGNA Healthplan Mid–Atlantic, Inc., 9700 Patent Woods Drive, Columbia, MD 21046; tel. 301/720–5800; Timothy P. Fitzgerald, President

CIGNA Healthplan of the MidAtlantic, Inc., 9700 Patent Woods Drive, Columbia, MD 21046; tel. 410/720–5800; FAX. 410/720–5860

Columbia Medical Plan, Inc., Two Knoll North Drive, Columbia, MD 21045; tel. 410/997–8500; FAX. 410/964–4563; Marilyn M. Levinson, Director, Patient Services

Delmarva Health Care Plan, 106 Marlboro Road, P.O. Box 2410, Easton, MD 21601; tel. 410/822–7223; FAX. 410/822–8152; Richard Moore, President

Delmarva Health Plan, Inc., 106 Marlboro Road, Easton, MD 21601; tel. 410/822–7223; Richard Moore, Chief Executive Officer

Free State Health Plan, Inc., 100 South Charles Street, Tower II, Baltimore, MD 21201; tel. 410/528–7000

George Washington University Health Plan, Inc., 4550 Montgomery Avenue, Suite 800, Bethesda, MD 20814; tel. 301/941–2000; FAX. 301/941–2005; Dr. John E. Ott, Executive Director, Chief Executive O

George Washington University Health Plan, Inc., 4550 Montgomery Avenue, Suite 800, Bethesda, MD 20814; tel. 301/941–2000; FAX. 301/941–2005; Lawrence E. Berman, Director, Government Relations and Legal Affairs

George Washington University Health Plan, Inc., 4550 Montgomery Avenue, Suite 800, Bethesda, MD 20814; tel. 301/941–2000; FAX. 301/941–2003; Dr. Stanley Aronovitch, Chief Executive Officer

Healthcare Corporation of Mid–Atlantic, 100 South Charles Street, Baltimore, MD 21201; tel. 301/828–7000; David D. Wolf, Chief Executive Officer

Healthcare Corporation of the Potomac, Inc., Care First–Free State Potomac, Equitable Bank Center's Tower–II, 100 South Charles Street, Baltimore, MD 21201; tel. 410/528–7025; FAX. 410/528–7013; David Wolf, President

HealthPlus, Inc., NYLCare Health Plans of the Mid–Atlantic, Inc., 7601 Ora Glen Drive, Suite 200, Greenbelt, MD 20770–3641; tel. 301/441–1600; FAX. 301/489–5282; Jeff D. Emerson, President and CEO

Kaiser Foundation Health Plan of the Mid–Atlantic States, 2101 East Jefferson Street, Box 6611, Rockville, MD 20849–6611; tel. 301/468–6000; FAX. 301/816–7465; Robert A. Essink, Acting President

Kaiser Foundation Health Plan of the Mid–Atlantic States, Inc., 2101 East Jefferson Street, Rockville, MD 20852; tel. 301/816–6420; FAX. 301/816–7478; Cleve Killingsworth, President

Kaiser Foundation Health Plan of the Mid–Atlantic States, Inc., 2101 East Jefferson Street, Rockville, MD 20852; tel. 301/816–2424; FAX. 301/816–7478; Alan J. Silverstone, President

M.D. Individual Practice Association, Inc., Four Taft Court, Rockville, MD 20850; tel. 800/544–2853; Susan Goff, President

MD Individual Practice Association, Inc, MDIPA/Optimum, Four Taft Court, Rockville, MD 20850; tel. 301/762–8205; FAX. 301/738–1230; Mark D. Groban, M.D., President and CEO

MD–Individual Practice Association, Inc., Four Taft Court, Rockville, MD 20850; tel. 301/294–5100; FAX. 301/309–1709; Susan Goff, President

NYL Care Health Plans of the Mid–Atlantic, Inc., 7601 Ora Glen Drive, Suite 200, Greenbelt, MD 20770; tel. 301/982–0098; FAX. 301/489–5282; Jeff D. Emerson, President and CEO

NYLCare Health Plans of Mid–Atlantic, Inc., 7601 Ora Glen Drive, Suite 200, Greenbelt, MD 20770; tel. 301/982–0098; FAX. 301/489–5282; Jeff D. Emerson, President and CEO

Optimum Choice, MAMSI, Four Taft Court, Rockville, MD 20850; tel. 301/294–5100; FAX. 301/309–1709; George Jochum, President

Optimum Choice Inc./MDIPA, Inc./Alliance PPO, Inc., Four Taft Court, Rockville, MD 20850; tel. 301/762–8205; Gloria Stem, Human Resource, Senior Director

Optimum Choice, Inc., Four Taft Court, Rockville, MD 20850; tel. 301/738–7920; FAX. 301/309–3782; George T. Jochum, President and CEO

Optimum Choice, Inc., Four Taft Court, Rockville, MD 20850; tel. 301/762–8205

PrimeHealth Corporation, 9602 C Martin Luther King Jr. Highway, Lanham, MD 20706; Edward L. Mosley, Jr., President

Prudential Health Care Plan, Inc., Seton Court, 2800 North Charles Street, Baltimore, MD 21218; tel. 410/554–7000; FAX. 410/554–7077

Spectera Dental Services, Inc., (formerly United Dental Services), 2811 Lord Baltimore Drive, Baltimore, MD 21244–2644; tel. 410/265–6033; Oscar B. Camp, President

Spectera, Inc., 2811 Lord Baltimore Drive, Baltimore, MD 21244; tel. 410/265–6033; FAX. 410/844–5903; Sue Cox, Vice President, Marketing

Total Health Care, Inc., 2305 North Charles Street, Baltimore, MD 21218; tel. 410/383–8300; FAX. 410/554–9012; Edwin R. Golden, President

MASSACHUSETTS

Central Massachusetts Health Care, Mechanics Tower, 100 Front Street, Suite 300, Worcester, MA 01608; tel. 508/798–8667; FAX. 508/798–4197; Brian D. Wells, Chief Executive Officer

CIGNA HealthCare of Massachusetts, Inc., Three Newton Executive Park, 2223 Washington Street, Newton, MA 02162; tel. 800/345–9458

Fallon Community Health Plan, One Chestnut Place, 10 Chestnut Street, Worcester, MA 01608; tel. 508/799–2100; FAX. 508/831–0921; Gary J. Zelch, Executive Director

Harvard Community Health Plan, 10 Brookline Place West, Brookline, MA 02146; tel. 617/731–8240; FAX. 617/730–4695; Manuel M. Ferris, President and CEO

Harvard Community Health Plan, 10 Brookline Place West, Brookline, MA 02146; tel. 617/731–8240

Harvard Community Health Plan of New England, Inc., 10 Brookline Place, W., Brookline, MA 02146; tel. 617/731–8250

Harvard Community Health Plan, Inc., 10 Brookline Place West, Brookline, MA 02146; tel. 617/421–6400; Laura Peabody, Assistant General Counsel

Harvard Pilgrim Health Care, Inc., 10 Brookline Place West, Brookline, MA 02445; tel. 617/730–4612; FAX. 617/730–4765; Allan Greenberg, President and CEO

Health New England, One Monarch Place, Springfield, MA 01144; tel. 413/787–4000; FAX. 413/734–3356; Phil M. Pin, Interim President

Healthsource Massachusetts, Inc., (d/b/a Healthsource CMHC), 100 Front Street, Worcester, MA 01608–1449; tel. 800/922–8380

HMO Blue, 100 Summer Street, Boston, MA 02110; tel. 617/832–7797; FAX. 617/832–7973; Maureen Coneys, Executive Director

Kaiser Foundation Health Plan, 170 University Drive, P.O. Box 862, Amherst, MA 01002; tel. 413/256–0151; FAX. 413/549–1601; Linda Todaro, Massachusetts Area Administrator

Neighborhood Health Plan, 253 Summer Street, Boston, MA 02210; tel. 617/772–5500; FAX. 617/772–5513; James Hooley, President & CEO

One Health Plan of Massachusetts, Inc., One University Office Park, 29 Sawyer Road, 3rd Floor, Waltham, MA 02453; tel. 800/725–0748; FAX. 781/788–9366; Melinda Caggiano, Administrative Assistant

Pilgrim Health Care Inc., 1200 Crown Colony Drive, Quincy, MA 02169; tel. 800/742–8326

Prudential HealthCare of New England, 10 New England Business Center, Suite 200, P.O. Box 1827, Andover, MA 01810; tel. 508/681–4723; FAX. 508/659–4198; Larry L. Hsu, M.D., Executive Director

Tufts Associated Health Maintenance Organization, Inc., 333 Wyman Street, P.O. Box 9112, Waltham, MA 02254–9112; tel. 617/466–9400

Tufts Health Plan, 333 Wyman Street, P.O. Box 9112, Waltham, MA 02454; tel. 617/466–9400; FAX. 617/466–9430; Harris A. Berman, M.D., CEO

Tufts Health Plan of New England, Inc., 333 Wyman Street, Waltham, MA 02254–9112; tel. 617/466–9055; Theresa Gallinaro, Manager

Tufts Health Plan of New England, Inc., 333 Wyman Street, P.O. Box 9112, Waltham, MA 02254–9112; tel. 800/442–0422

U.S. Healthcare, Inc., Three Burlington Woods Drive, Burlington, MA 01803; tel. 617/273–5600; Robert Roy, M.D., Medical Director

MICHIGAN

Blue Care Network of East Michigan, 4200 Fashion Square Boulevard, Saginaw, MI 48603; tel. 517/249–3200; FAX. 517/249–3730; Arnold C. DuFort, President and CEO

Blue Care Network of Southeast Michigan, 25925 Telegraph, P.O. Box 5043, Southfield, MI 48086–5043; tel. 313/354–7450; FAX. 313/799–6970; David H. Smith, President and CEO

Blue Care Network–Great Lakes, 1769 South Garfield Avenue, Suite B, Traverse City, MI 49684; tel. 616/941–6000; FAX. 616/941–6012; Sharon Carlin, Regional Director

Blue Care Network–Great Lakes, 3624 South Westnedge, Kalamazoo, MI 49008; tel. 616/388–9500; FAX. 616/388–5156; Marcia Lallaman, Regional Manager

Blue Care Network–Great Lakes, 611 Cascade West Parkway, S.E., Grand Rapids, MI 49546; tel. 616/957–5057; FAX. 616/956–5866; Sharon Carlin, President and CEO

Blue Care Network–Great Lakes, 3375 Merriam Avenue, Muskegon Heights, MI 49444–3173; tel. 616/739–6600; FAX. 616/739–6670; Barbara Carlson, Regional Manager

Blue Care Network–Health Central, 1403 South Creyts Road, Lansing, MI 48917; tel. 517/322–8000; FAX. 517/322–8015; Arnold C. DuFort, President and CEO

Care Choices HMO, 34605 Twelve Mile Road, Farmington Hi, MI 48331; tel. 810/489–6200

Care Choices HMO, Mercy Health Plans, 34605 Twelve Mile Road, Farmington Hi, MI 48331; tel. 313/489–6203; FAX. 810/489–6278; Robert J. Flanagan, Ph.D., President, Chief Executive

Care Choices–Grand Rapids, 1500 East Beltline S.E., Suite 300, Grand Rapids, MI 49506; tel. 616/285–3801; FAX. 616/285–3810; Janie Begeman, Site Manager

Care Choices–Lansing, 2111 University Park, Suite 100, Okemos, MI 48864; tel. 517/349–2111; FAX. 517/349–6449; Jeffrey Ash, Executive Director

Care Choices–Muskegon, 950 West Norton Avenue, Suite 500, Muskegon, MI 49441; tel. 616/737–0307; FAX. 616/733–6352; Elyse Winter, Executive Director

Family Health Plan of Michigan, 901 North Macomb, Monroe, MI 48162–3048; tel. 313/457–5370; FAX. 313/457–5506; Robert Campbell, Executive Vice President

Grand Valley Health Plan, 829 Forest Hill Avenue, S.E., Grand Rapids, MI 49546; tel. 616/949–2410; FAX. 616/949–4978; Roland Palmer, President

Great Lakes Health Plan, Inc., 17117 West Nine Mile Road, Suite 1600, Southfield, MI 48075; tel. 810/559–5656; FAX. 810/559–4640; Donald A. Zinner, President

Health Alliance Plan, 2850 West Grand Boulevard, Detroit, MI 48202; tel. 313/664–8354; FAX. 313/664–8433; Joseph E. Schmitt, Chief Financial Officer

HealthPlus of Michigan, 2050 South Linden Road, P.O. Box 1700, Flint, MI 48501–1700; tel. 810/230–2000; FAX. 810/230–2208; Paul A. Fuhs, Ph.D., President and CEO

HealthPlus of Michigan–Saginaw, 5560 Gratiot Avenue, Saginaw, MI 48603; tel. 517/797–4000; FAX. 517/799–6471; Bruce Hill, Regional Vice President

M–Care, 2301 Commonwealth Boulevard, Ann Arbor, MI 48105–1573; tel. 313/747–8700; FAX. 313/747–7152; Peter W. Roberts, President

Mercy Health Plans, 34605 W. 12 Mile Road, Farmington Hills, MI 48311; tel. 313/971–7667; FAX. 313/971–7455; Dennis Angellis, M.D., Chief Medical Director

MIDA Dental Plans, Inc., 2000 Town Center, Suite 2200, Southfield, MI 48075; tel. 810/353–6410; Walter Knysz, Jr., D.D.S., President

NorthMed HMO, 109 East Front Street, Suite 204, Traverse City, MI 49684; tel. 616/935–0500; FAX. 616/935–0505; Walter J. Hooper III, President

OmniCare Health Plan, 1155 Brewery Park Boulevard, Suite 250, Detroit, MI 48207–2602; tel. 313/259–4000; FAX. 313/393–7944; Gregory H. Moses, Jr., President and CEO

Paramount Care of Michigan, Inc., 1339 North Telegraph Road, Monroe, MI 48162; tel. 313/241–5604; FAX. 313/241–5998; Robert J. Kolodgy, Vice President, Finance

PHP–Kalamazoo, 106 Farmers Alley, P.O. Box 50271, Kalamazoo, MI 49005; tel. 616/349–6692; FAX. 616/349–1476; Michael Koehler, Executive Director

Physicians Health Plan, P.O. Box 30377, Lansing, MI 48909–7877; tel. 517/349–2101; FAX. 517/347–9460; John G. Ruther, President and CEO

Physicians Health Plan of South Michigan, One Jackson Square, 8th Floor, Jackson, MI 49201; tel. 517/782–7154; FAX. 517/782–4512; Susan K. Sharkey, Chief Executive Officer

Physicians Health Plan–Muskegon, Terrace Plaza, 250 Morris Avenue, Suite 550, Muskegon, MI 49440–1143; tel. 616/728–3900; FAX. 616/728–5189; Ronald Franzese, Chief Executive Officer

Priority Health, 1231 East Beltline, Suite 300, Grand Rapids, MI 49505; tel. 616/942–0954; FAX. 616/942–0145; Vic Turvey, President and CEO

Priority Health Managed Benefits, Inc., 1231 East Beltline, N.E., Grand Rapids, MI 49503; tel. 800/942–0954; FAX. 616/942–5651; Kimberly K. Horn, President and CEO

SelectCare HMO, Inc., 2401 West Big Beachver Road, Suite 700, Troy, MI 48084; tel. 248/637–5300; FAX. 248/637–6710; Roman T. Kulich, President and CEO

The Wellness Plan, 1060 West Norton Avenue, Suite Four B, Muskegon, MI 49442; tel. 616/780–4722; FAX. 616/780–3557; Evangeline Zimmerman, Health Systems Manager

The Wellness Plan, One East First Street, Genesse Tower, Suite 1620, Flint, MI 48502; tel. 810/767–7400; FAX. 810/767–6338; Sharon P. Matthews, Regional Administrator

The Wellness Plan, 320 North Washington Square, Lansing, MI 48933; tel. 517/484–1400; FAX. 517/484–8801; Mary Anne Sesti, Health Systems Manager

The Wellness Plan, Comprehensive Health Services, Inc., 6500 John C. Lodge, Detroit, MI 48202; tel. 313/875–6960; FAX. 313/875–7416; Sharon P. Matthews, Regional Administrator

Total Health Care, Inc., 1600 Fisher Building, Detroit, MI 48202; tel. 313/871–7800; FAX. 313/871–0196; Kenneth G. Rimmer, Executive Director

MINNESOTA

Allina Health System, 5601 Smetana Drive, Minneapolis, MN 55440–9310; tel. 612/992–3840; FAX. 612/992–3990; James Ehlen, M.D., President

Blue Plus, P.O. Box 64179, St. Paul, MN 55164; tel. 651/683–2795; FAX. 612/456–6768; Colleen Reitan, President

First Plan HMO, 1010 Fourth Street, Two Harbors, MN 55616; tel. 218/834–7210; John Bjorum, Executive Director

HealthPartners, 8100–34th Avenue South, P.O. Box 1309, Minneapolis, MN 55440–1309; tel. 612/883–5382; FAX. 612/883–5120; George Halvorson, President, Chief Executive Director

HealthPartners, 8100–34th Avenue South, P.O. Box 1309, Minneapolis, MN 55440–1309; tel. 612/883–7000; George Halvorson, President and CEO

Mayo Health Plan, 21 First Street S.W., Suite 401, Rochester, MN 55902; tel. 507/284–2919; FAX. 507/284–5811; Paula e. Mankosky, Executive Director

Medica Health Plans of Wisconsin, Inc., 5901 Smetana Drive, P.O. Box 9310, Minneapolis, MN 55440–9310; tel. 612/992–2000

Metropolitan Health Plan, 822 South Third Street, Suite 140, Minneapolis, MN 55415; tel. 612/347–2340; FAX. 612/904–4214; David R. Johnson, Chief Operating Officer

UCARE Minnesota, 2550 University Avenue, W., Suite 201 S, St. Paul, MN 55114; tel. 651/603–5368; Nancy Feldman, Chief Executive Officer

MISSISSIPPI

American Medical Plans of Mississippi, Inc., 633 North State Street, Suite 211, Jackson, MS 39202; tel. 601/968–9000; FAX. 601/968–9800; Rissa P. Richardson, Director, Provider Relations

Canton Management Group, Inc., 3330 South Liberty Street, Suite 300, Canton, MS 39046; tel. 601/859–4450

Health Link, Inc., 830 South Gloster Street, Tupelo, MS 38801; tel. 800/453–7536; FAX. 800/453–0648; Pamela J. Hansen, Director

HMO of Mississippi, Inc., 3545 Lakeland Drive, Jackson, MS 39208; tel. 601/932–3704; Thomas C. Fenter, M.D., Executive Director

Integrity Health Plan of Mississippi, Inc., 6360 I–55 North, Suite 460, Jackson, MS 39211; tel. 601/977–0010; FAX. 601/977–0019; Robert S. Parenteau, Director, Marketing

Mississippi Managed Care Network, Inc., 713 South Pear Orchard Road, Suite B–102, Ridgeland, MS 39157; tel. 601/977–9834; FAX. 601/977–9553; Jesse Buie, President

Phoenix Healthcare of Mississippi, Inc., 795 Woodlands Parkway, Suite 200, Ridgeland, MS 39157; tel. 601/956–2706; FAX. 601/957–0847; Stephen G. Braden, Executive Director

MISSOURI

Family Health Partners, 215 West Pershing, 6th Floor, Kansas City, MO 64141; tel. 800/347–9363; FAX. 816/842–2326; Joseph R. Cecil, Executive Director

Alliance for Community Health, Inc., d/b/a A Healthcare Partnership, 5615 Pershing, Suite 29, St. Louis, MO 63112; tel. 314/454–0055; FAX. 314/454–9595; James D. Sweat, Chief Executive Officer

Blue–Care, Inc., 2301 Main, Zip 64108–2428, P.O. Box 413163, Kansas City, MO 64141–6163; tel. 816/395–2222; Larry K. Chastain, President

BMA SelectCare, Inc., One Penn Valley Park, P.O. Box 419458, Kansas City, MO 64141; tel. 816/751–5336; FAX. 816/751–5571; Sara L. Adams, Vice President

Children's Mercy Family Plan, 2401 Gilham Road, Kansas City, MO 64108

Cigna HealthCare of St. Louis, Inc., 8182 Maryland Avenue, Suite 900, St. Louis, MO 63105; tel. 314/726–7841; FAX. 314/726–7819; James A. Young, General Manager

CIGNA HealthCare of St. Louis, Inc., 8182 Maryland Avenue, Suite 900, St. Louis, MO 63105–3721; tel. 314/726–7860; FAX. 314/726–7819; Jim Young, General Manager, President

Citizens Advantage, P.O. Box 479, 1500 North Oakland, Bolivar, MO 65613; tel. 417/777–6000

Community Health Plan, 801 Faraon, St. Joseph, MO 64501; tel. 816/271–1247; FAX. 816/271–1248; Joan E. Copeland, Executive Vice President and COO

Community Health Plan, 801 Faraon, St. Joseph, MO 64501; tel. 816/271–1247; FAX. 816/271–1248; Randa Anderson–Stice, Plan Administrator

Cox–Freeman Community HealthPlans, Inc., 2202 West 32nd Street, Joplin, MO 64804–3599; tel. 417/269–2900; FAX. 417/269–2925

Cox–Freeman HealthPlans, Inc., 1443 North Robberson, #700, Springfield, MO 65802; tel. 800/800–2901

FirstGuard Health Plan, Inc., 3801 Blue Parkway, Kansas City, MO 64130; tel. 816/922–7250; FAX. 816/922–7205; Joy Wheeler, Executive Director and COO

GenCare Health Systems, Inc., 969 Executive Parkway, Suite 100, P.O. Box 27379, St. Louis, MO 63141–6301; tel. 314/434–6114; FAX. 314/434–6328; Tom Zorumski, President and CEO

Gencare Health Systems, Inc., P.O. Box 419079, St. Louis, MO 63141–9079; tel. 314/434–6114

Gencare Health Systems, Inc., d/b/a Sanus Health Plan, Inc., P.O.B ox 27379, St. Louis, MO 63141–6301; tel. 800/627–0687; FAX. 314/469–9854; Thomas Zorumski, Chief Executive Officer

Good Health HMO, Inc., d/b/a Blue–Care, Inc., One Pershing Square, 2301 Main Street, Kansas City, MO 64108; tel. 816/395–2222; FAX. 816/395–3811; Larry K. Chastain, President and COO

Group Health Plan, 940 Westport Plaza, Suite 300, St. Louis, MO 63146; tel. 314/453–1700; FAX. 314/453–1958; Jerry Hansen, CEO

Group Health Plan, 940 West Port Plaza, Suite 300, St. Louis, MO 63146; tel. 314/453–1700; FAX. 314/453–0375; Richard H. Jones, President and CEO

Health Partners of the Midwest, 120 Central, Suite 900, St. Louis, MO 63105; tel. 314/505–5000; FAX. 314/567–3627; Dennis Mathies, President

Healthcare USA of Missouri LLC, 100 South Fourth Street, Suite 1100, St. Louis, MO 63102; tel. 800/213–7792; FAX. 314/241–8010; Davina Lane, President and CEO

HealthFirst Health Management Organization, 1102 West 32nd Street, Joplin, MO 64804–3599

Healthlink HMO, Inc., 777 Craig Road, PO Box 410289, St. Louis, MO 63141; tel. 314/569–7200; FAX. 314/569–3268; Dennis McCart, Executive Director

HealthLink HMO, Inc., d/b/a HealthLink HMO, 777 Craig Road, Suite 110, Creve Coeur, MO 63141; tel. 314/569–7200; FAX. 314/569–3268; Dennis McCart, Executive Director

HealthNet, Inc., Two Pershing Square, 2300 Main Street, Suite 700, Kansas City, MO 64108; tel. 816/221–8400; FAX. 816/221–7709; Andrew Dahl, Sc.D., Chief Executive Officer

HealthNet, Inc., 2300 Main Street, Suite 700, Kansas City, MO 64108–2415; tel. 816/221–8400; FAX. 816/221–7709; Beth Johnson, Executive Assistant

HMO Missouri (Blue Choice), 1831 Chestnut Street, P.O. Box 66828, St. Louis, MO 63166–6828; tel. 314/923–4444; FAX. 314/923–8958; John O'Rowrke, President

HMO Missouri, Inc., d/b/a BlueChoice, 4444 Forest Park, St. Louis, MO 63108–2292; tel. 314/658–4444; FAX. 314/289–6239; Seymour Kaplan, President and CEO

Humana Health Plan, Inc., 10450 Holmes, Suite 200, Kansas City, MO 64131–3471; tel. 800/715–4862

Humana Health Plan, Inc., 10450 Holmes, Suite 330, Kansas City, MO 64131–1471; tel. 816/941–8900; FAX. 816/941–8630; David Fields, Executive Director

Humana Kansas City, Inc., 10450 Holmes Road, Kansas City, MO 64131–3471; tel. 816/941–8900; FAX. 816/941–3910; David W. Fields, Executive Director

Humana Kansas City, Inc., 10405 Holmes, Second Floor, Kansas City, MO 64131–3471; tel. 816/941–8900; Gregory H. Wolf, President

Medical Center Health Plan, d/b/a Partners HMO, One City Place Drive, Suite 670, St. Louis, MO 63141; tel. 314/567–6660; Delbert E. Snoberger, Chief Executive Officer

Mercy Health Plans of Missouri, Inc., 12935 North Outer 40 Drive, St. Louis, MO 63141–8636; tel. 314/214–8100; FAX. 314/214–8101; Thomas L. Kelly, President

Mercy Health Plans of Missouri, Inc., 12935 North Outer 40 Drive, St. Louis, MO 63141–8636; tel. 314/214–8100; FAX. 314/214–8101; Thomas L. Kelly, President

Missouri Advantage LLC, 428 East Capital Avenue, 3rd Floor, Jefferson City, MO 65101; tel. 573/659–5200; FAX. 573/659–5222; Kevin G. McRoberts, Executive Director

Missouri Care, LC, 2404 Forum Blvd., Columbia, MO 65203; tel. 573/441–2100

Physicians Health Plan of Greater St. Louis, Inc., 77 West Port Plaza, Suite 500, St. Louis, MO 63146; tel. 314/275–7000; FAX. 314/542–1155; Thomas Zorumski, President and CEO

Physicians Health Plan of Midwest, Inc., 77 Westport Plaza, Suite 500, St. Louis, MO 63146; tel. 314/275–7000; FAX. 314/542–1155

Principal Health Care of Kansas City, Inc., 1001 East 101st Terrace, Suite 230, Kansas City, MO 64131; tel. 816/941–3030; FAX. 816/941–8516; Jan Stallmeyer, Executive Director

Principal Health Care of Kansas City, Inc., 1001 East 101st Terrace, Suite 230, Kansas City, MO 64131; tel. 816/941–3030; FAX. 816/941–8516; Kenneth J. Linde, President

Principal Health Care of St. Louis, Inc., 12312 Olive Boulevard, Suite 150, St. Louis, MO 63141; tel. 314/434–6990; FAX. 314/434–7540; Barbara C. Buenemann, Executive Director

Principal Health Care Plan of St. Louis, Inc., 12312 Olive Boulevard, Suite 150, Creve Coeur, MO 63141; tel. 314/434–6990; FAX. 314/434–7540; Barbara C. Buenemann, Executive Director

Prudential Health Care Plan, Inc., 4600 Madison Avenue, Suite 300, Kansas City, MO 64112; tel. 816/756–5588; FAX. 816/756–5667; David W. Dingley, Executive Director

Prudential Health Care Plan, Inc., 12312 Olive Boulevard, Suite 500, St. Louis, MO 63141; tel. 314/567–1100; Gary C. Hawkins, Executive Director

TriSource HealthCare, Inc., d/b/a Blue Advantage, 2301 Main Street, P.O. Box 419130, Kansas City, MO 64141–6130; tel. 816/395–3636; FAX. 816/395–3811; Larry K. Chastain, President and CEO

TriSource HealthCare, Inc., d/b/a Blue Advantage HMO, P.O. Box 419169, 2301 Main St., Kansas City, MO 64141–6169; tel. 816/395–2045; FAX. 816/802–4451; John W. Kennedy, Senior Vice–President

Trucare, Inc., 2301 Holmes, Kansas City, MO 64108; tel. 816/556–3186; Joseph Cecil, President

Truman Medical Center, Inc., 230l Holmes Street, Kansas City, MO 64l08; tel. 816/556–3094; James J. Morgan, M.D., Executive Director

United Health Care of the Midwest, Inc. (FKA Gencare), 76 West Port Plaza, Suite 500, St. Louis, MO 63145; tel. 314/275–6999; Thomas Zorumski, President

United Healthcare of the Midwest, Inc., 77 West Port Plaza, Suite 500, St. Louis, MO 63141; tel. 800/535–9291; FAX. 314/542–1157; Vic Turvey, President & CEO

United Healthcare of the Midwest, Inc., P.O. Box 419079, St. Louis, MO 63141–9079; tel. 800/627–0607

MONTANA

Glacier Community Health Plan, 1297 Burns Way, Suite Three, Kalispell, MT 59901; tel. 406/758–6900; FAX. 406/758–6907; Patsy Stinger, Administrative Assistant

HMO Montana, 560 North Park, Helena, MT 59604; tel. 406/447–8540; Pam Pedersen, Manager

Yellowstone Community Health, 1233 North 30th Street #100, Billings, MT 59101; tel. 406/238–6868; FAX. 406/238–6898; Jennifer A. Parise, Marketing Director

NEBRASKA

Exclusive Healthcare, Mutual of Omaha Plaza, Omaha, NE 68175; tel. 402/978–2700; FAX. 402/978–2999; Dick L. Easley, President

Exclusive Healthcare, Inc., Mutual of Omaha Plaza, 10250 Regency Circle, Omaha, NE 68124–7012; tel. 402–255–1629; FAX. 402–255–1665; Grete Vaught, Chief Operating Officer

Exclusive Healthcare, Inc., Mutual of Omaha Plaza, Omaha, NE 68175; tel. 402/978–2869; FAX. 402/978–2999; Kurt Irlbeck, Administrative Services Coordinator

Exclusive Healthcare, Inc., Mutual of Omaha of South Dakota and Community Health Plus, HMO, Inc., 10250 Regency Circle, Omaha, NE 68124–7012; tel. 402–255–1662; FAX. 402–255–1665; Jacque Alt, Executive Director

Exclusive Healthcare, Inc., Mutual of Omaha Plaza, Omaha, NE 68175; tel. 402–351–8856; FAX. 402–351–3788; Steve Booma, Executive Vice President

HMO Nebraska, Inc., 10040 Regency Circle, Suite 300, Omaha, NE 68114; tel. 402/392–2800; Richard L. Guffey, President

Mutual of Omaha Health Plans of Lincoln, Inc., 220 South 17th Street, Lincoln, NE 68508; tel. 402/475–7000; FAX. 402/475–6005; Steve Burnham, Chief Operating Officer

Principal Health Care of Nebraska, Inc., 330 N. 117th Street, PO Box 541210, Omaha, NE 68154–9210; tel. 800/288–3343; FAX. 402/333–1116; Kenneth Klaasmeyer, Executive Director

Principal Health Care of Nebraska, Inc., 330 North 117th Street, Omaha, NE 68154–2595; tel. 402/333–1720; FAX. 402/333–1116; John Klaasmeyer, Executive Director

United Health Care of Midlands, Inc., d/b/a Share Health Plan of Nebraska, Inc., 2717 North 118 Circle, Omaha, NE 68164; tel. 402/445–5000; Sara Hemenway, Marketing Communications Manager

United Healthcare of Midlands, Inc., 2717 North 118th Circle, Omaha, NE 68164; tel. 402/445–5000; FAX. 402/445–5572; John M. Braasch, President

NEVADA

Amil International of Nevada, 1050 East Flamingo Road, Suite E–120, Las Vegas, NV 89119; tel. 702/693–5250; FAX. 702/693–5399; Jeff Allen, Director, Provider Relations Director

Health Plan of Nevada, Inc., 2720 North Tenaya Way, Mailing Address: P.O. Box 15645, Las Vegas, NV 89114–5645; tel. 702/242–7300; Donald J. Giancursio, VP, Sales and Marketing

HMO Colorado, Inc., d/b/a HMO Nevada, 6900 Westcliff Drive, Suite 600, Las Vegas, NV 89128; tel. 702/228–2583; FAX. 702/228–1259; William S. Jeffries, Regional Vice President

Hometown Health Plan, Inc., 400 South Wells Avenue, Reno, NV 89502; tel. 702/325–3000; FAX. 702/325–3220; Ed Holme, Executive Director

St. Mary's HealthFirst, 5290 Neil Road, Reno, NV 89502; tel. 702/829–6000; FAX. 702/829–6010; Lin Howland, Executive Director

NEW HAMPSHIRE

Healthsource New Hampshire, 54 Regional Drive, P.O. Box 2041, Concord, NH 03302–2041; tel. 603/225–5077; FAX. 603/229–2983; Donna K. Lencki, Chief Executive Officer

Healthsource New Hampshire, Donovan Street Extension, P.O. Box 2041, Concord, NH 03302; tel. 603/225–5077; FAX. 603/225–7621; Susan Berry, Director, Marketing

Healthsource New Hampshire, Inc., Donovan Street Extension, P.O. Box 2041, Concord, NH 03302–2041; tel. 603/225–5077; FAX. 603/225–7621; Sally Crawford, Chief Executive Officer

HMO Blue, c/o Blue Cross Blue Shield of New Hampshire, 3000 Goffs Falls Road, Manchester, NH 03111–0001; tel. 800/621–3724

Matthew Thornton Health Plan, 3000 Goffs Falls Road, Manchester, NH 03111–0001; tel. 603/695–7000; FAX. 603/695–7304; David a Jensen, President and CEO

Matthew Thornton Health Plan, 43 Constitution Drive, Bedford, NH 03110–6020; tel. 603/695–1100; FAX. 603/695–1157; Everett Page, President

Matthew Thorton Health Plan, Inc., 43 Constitution Drive, Bedford, NH 03110; tel. 800/874–7122

Oxford Health Plans, 10 Tara Boulevard, Nashua, NH 03062; tel. 603/891–7000; FAX. 603/891–7015; Craig Tobin, Regional Chief Executive Officer

NEW JERSEY

Aetna Health Plans of New Jersey, 8000 Midlantic Drive, Suite 100 North, Mount Laurel, NJ 08054; tel. 609/866–7880; Dennis Allen, Medical Director

AltantiCare Health Plans, 6727 Delilah Road, Egg Harbor To, NJ 08234; tel. 609/272–6330; FAX. 609/407–7770; Patricia Koelling, Chief Operating Officer

American Preferred Provider Plan, Inc., 810 Broad Street, Newark, NJ 07102; tel. 201/799–0900; FAX. 201/799–0911; Harold E. Smith, President and CEO

Amerihealth HMO, Inc., 8000 Midlantic Drive, Suite 333, Mount Laurel, NJ 08054; tel. 609/778–6500; FAX. 609/778–6550; Leo Carey, Chief Executive Director

Community Healthcare Plan, 309 Market Street, Camden, NJ 08102; tel. 609/541–7526; FAX. 609/635–9328; Mark R. Bryant, President

First Option Health Plan, The Galleria, Two Bridge Avenue, Building Six, Second Floor, Red Bank, NJ 07701–1106; tel. 908/842–5000; Donald Paris, Senior Vice President, Secretary, General

Garden State Health Plan, CN–712, Trenton, NJ 08625–0712; tel. 800/525–0047; FAX. 609/588–4643; Beverly Blacher, EIDG, Chief Executive Officer

HIP Health Plan of New Jersey, One HIP Plaza, North Brunswig, NJ 08902; tel. 908/937–7600; FAX. 908/937–7870; Victoria A. Wicks, President and CEO

HMO New Jersey, U.S. HealthCare, 55 Lane Road, Fairfield, NJ 07004; tel. 201/575–5600; Andrew Schuyler, M.D., Medical Director

Section C

Horizon HMO, Three Penn Plaza East, Newark, NJ 07105–2000; tel. 201/466–5000; FAX. 201/466–6745; Christy W. Bell, President and COO

Liberty Health Plan, 115 Christopher Columbus Drive, Jersey City, NJ 07302; tel. 201/946–6800; FAX. 201/946–1740; Donald L. Picuri, Senior Vice President and COO

Managed Health Care Systems of New Jersey, Inc., Two Gateway Center, Newark, NJ 07102; tel. 973/297–5500; Lamerial Daniels, VP/General Manager

Physician Health Services of New Jersey, Inc., Mack Centre IV, South 61 Paramus Road, Paramus, NJ 07652; tel. 201/291–9300; Ronald L. Helm, Executive Director

Physician Healthcare Plan of New Jersey, 1009 Lenox Drive, Building Four East, Lawrenceville, NJ 08648; tel. 609/896–1233; FAX. 609/896–3041; Joseph D. Billotti, M.D., Chairman

PruCare of New Jersey, (Northern Division), 200 Wood Avenue, S., Iselin, NJ 08830; tel. 908/632–7333; FAX. 908/494–8207; Paul Conlin, Vice President, Group Operations

University Health Plans, Inc., 60 Park Place, 15th Floor, Newark, NJ 07102; tel. 973–623–8700; FAX. 973–623–3635; Alexander H. McLean, Chief Operating Officer

NEW MEXICO

Cimarron Health Plan, 2801 Academy N.E., Albuquerque, NM 87109; tel. 505/798–7633; FAX. 505/798–7380; Garrey Carruthers, President and CEO

FHP of New Mexico, d/b/a FHP of El Paso, 4300 San Mateo Boulevard, N.E., Albuquerque, NM 87110; tel. 505/881–7900; FAX. 505/875–3305; Mark Zobel, Regional Compliance Officer

FHP of New Mexico, Inc., 4300 San Mateo, N.E., Albuquerque, NM 87110; tel. 505/881–7900; FAX. 505/883–0102; John Tallent, President

HMO New Mexico, 12800 Indian School Road, N.E., Zip 87112, P.O. Box 11968, Albuquerque, NM 87192; tel. 505/271–4441; FAX. 505/237–5324; Blair Christensen, President

Lovelace, Inc., P.O. Box 27107, Albuquerque, NM 87125–7107; tel. 505/262–7363; Derick Pasternak, M.D., President

Presbyterian Health Plan, 7500 Jefferson, N.E., Building Two, Albuquerque, NM 87109; tel. 505/823–0700; FAX. 505/823–0718; Robert L. Simmons, President

Qual–Med, Inc.–New Mexico Health Plan, 6100 Uptown Boulevard, N.E., Suite 400, Albuquerque, NM 87110; tel. 505/889–8800; FAX. 505/889–8819; Michael J. Mayer, President

NEW YORK

Aetna Health Plans of New York, Inc., 2700 Westchester Avenue, Purchase, NY 10577; tel. 914/251–0600; FAX. 914/251–0260; Paula Adderson, President

Better Health Plan, Inc., 120 Pineview Drive, Amherst, NY 14228; tel. 518/482–1200; Daniel Tillotson, Chief Executive Officer

Blue Cross and Blue Shield of Western New York, Community Blue, 1901 Main Street, P.O. Box 159, Buffalo, NY 14240–0159; tel. 716/887–8874; FAX. 716/887–7911; Nora K. McGuire, Executive Director

Capital Area Community Health Plan, Inc., 1201 Troy–Schenectady Road, Latham, NY 12110; tel. 518/783–1864; FAX. 518/783–0234; John Baackes, President and CEO

Capital District Physicians Health Plan, 17 Columbia Circle, Albany, NY 12203; tel. 518/862–3923; FAX. 518/452–3767; Ellen M. Pierce, Director, Accounting

Capital District Physicians' Health Plan, 17 Columbia Circle, Albany, NY 12203; tel. 518/862–3700; FAX. 518/452–0003; Diane E. Bergman, President

CenterCare, Inc., 555 West 57th Street, 18th Floor, New York, NY 10019–2925; tel. 212/293–9200; FAX. 212/293–9298; Julio Belber, President and Chief Operating Officer

Chubbhealth, Inc., 380 Madison Avenue, 20th Floor, New York, NY 10017; tel. 212/880–5455; Keith Collins, M.D., President

CIGNA HealthCare of New York, Inc., 195 Broadway, Eighth Floor, New York, NY 10007; tel. 212/618–4200; FAX. 212/618–4258; Tom Garvey, Assistant Vice President, Network Management

Community Choice Health Plan of Westchester, Inc., 35 East Grassy Sprain Road, Suite 300, Yonkers, NY 10710; tel. 914/337–6908; FAX. 914/337–6919; Lynda G. Gray, Chief Executive Officer

Community Health Plan (CHP), 1201 Troy–Schenectady Road, Latham, NY l2110; tel. 518/783–1864; FAX. 518/783–0234; John Baackes, President and CEO

Community Premier Plus, Inc., 534 W. 135th Street, New York, NY 10031; tel. 212/491–2333; FAX. 212/491–2315; Harris Lampert, M.D., President and CEO

Elderplan, Inc., 6323 Seventh Avenue, Brooklyn, NY 11220; tel. 718/921–7990; FAX. 718/921–7962; Eli S. Feldman, President and CEO

Empire Health Choice, Inc., One World Trade Center, New York, NY 10017–0682; tel. 800/453–0113; Michael Stocker, M.D., Chief Executive Officer

Finger Lakes Blue Cross/Blue Shield, Blue Choice, 150 East Main Street, Rochester, NY 14647; tel. 716/454–1700; FAX. 716/238–4526; Richard D. Dent, M.D., Senior Vice President, Managed

GENESIS Healthplan, Inc., One Executive Boulevard, Second Floor, Yonkers, NY 10701; tel. 914/476–6000; Ms. M. A. Chagnon, President

Health Care Plan, Inc., Guaranty Building, 28 Church Street, Room 100, Buffalo, NY 14202; tel. 716/847–1480; FAX. 716/847–1817; Arthur R. Goshin, M.D., Plan President and CEO

Health Insurance Plan of Greater New York (HIP), Seven West 34th Street, New York, NY l000l; tel. 212/630–3440; FAX. 212/630–0110; Daniel T. McGowan, President and CEO

Health Services Medical Corporation of Central New York, Inc., a/k/a Prepaid Health Plan (PHP) in Syracuse, NY, PHP/SDMN, 8278 Willett Parkway, Baldwinsville, NY 13027; tel. 315/638–2133; FAX. 315/638–0985; Frederick F. Yanni, Jr., President and CEO

HealthFirst PHSP, Inc., 25 Broadway, Ninth Floor, New York, NY 10004; tel. 212/801–6000; FAX. 212/801–1799; Paul Dickstein, Chief Executive Officer

HealthPlus, Inc., 5800 Third Avenue, Brooklyn, NY 11220; tel. 718/745–0030; FAX. 718–745–1180; Thomas Early, Chief Executive Officer

Healthsource HMO of New York, Inc., P.O. Box 1498, Syracuse, NY 132011498; tel. 315/449–1100; FAX. 315/449–2200; Ron Harms, Chief Executive Officer

HMO–CNY, Inc., 344 South Warren Street, P.O. Box 4809, Syracuse, NY 13221; tel. 315/448–4931; FAX. 315/448–6802; Ralph Carelli, Jr., Senior Vice President

HUM HealthCare Systems, Inc., d/b/a Partner's Health Plans, 333 Glen Street, P.O. Box 140, Glens Falls, NY 12801; tel. 518/745–0903; FAX. 518/745–1099; Richard Sanford, Chief Executive Officer

Independent Health, 511 Farber Lakes Drive, Buffalo, NY 14221; tel. 716/631–3001; FAX. 716/635–3838; Frank Colantuono, President and CEO

Institute for Urban Family Health, Inc., d/b/a ABC Health Plan, 16 East 16th Street, New York, NY 10003; tel. 212/633–0800; FAX. 212/691–4610; Neil Calman, M.D., Chief Executive Officer

Kaiser Foundation Health Plan of New York, 210 Westchester Avenue, White Plains, NY l0604; tel. 914/682–6401; FAX. 914/682–6403; Maura Carley, New York Area Operations Manager

MagnaHealth, 100 Garden City Plaza, Garden City, NY 11530; tel. 516/294–0700; Anthony Bacchi, Chief Executive Officer

Managed Healthcare Systems of New York, Inc., Seven Hanover Square, Fifth Floor, New York, NY 10004; tel. 212/509–5999; FAX. 2125091929; Karen Clark, Chief Executive Officer

MDNY Healthcare, 1 Huntington Quadrangle, Suite 4C01, Melville, NY 11747; tel. 516/454–1900; FAX. 516/396–8169; Richard Radoccia, Chief Executive Officer

Metrahealth Care Plan of Upstate New York, Two Penn Plaza, Suite 700, New York, NY 10121; tel. 212/216–6591; James T. Kerr, Chief Executive Officer

Metroplus Health Plan, 11 West 42nd Street, Second Floor, New York, NY 10036; tel. 212/597–8600; FAX. 212/597–8666; Denice F. Davis, J.D., Executive Director

Mohawk Valley Physicians Health Plan, 111 Liberty Street, Schenectady, NY 12305; tel. 518/370–4793; David Oliker, Chief Executive Officer

MVP Health Plan, 111 Liberty Street, P.O. Box 2207, Schenectady, NY 12301–2207; tel. 518/370–4793; David W. Oliker, President

MVP Health Plan, Inc., 111 Liberty Street, Schenectady, NY 12305; tel. 518/370–4793; FAX. 518/370–0852; David W. Oliker, President and CEO

Neighborhood Health Providers, 630 Third Avenue, New York, NY 10017; tel. 212/808–4775; FAX. 212–808–4772; Steven Bory, President and CEO

New York Hospital Community Health Plan, 333 East 38th Street, New York, NY 10016; tel. 212/297–5547; FAX. 212/297–5923; Rosaire McDonald, Chief Executive Officer

North American HealthCare, Inc., 300 Corporate Parkway, Amherst, NY 14226; tel. 716/446–5500; Ronald Zoeller, Chief Executive Officer

North Medical Community Health Plan, Inc., 5112 West Taft Road, Suite R, Liverpool, NY 13088; tel. 315/452–2500; James Butler, Chief Executive Officer

NYLCare Health Plans of New York, Inc., 75–20 Astoria Boulevard, Jackson Heights, NY 11370; tel. 718/899–5200; Arthur J. Drechsler, Executive Director

Physicians Health Services of New York, Inc., Crosswest Office Center, 399 Knollwood Road, Suite 212, White Plains, NY 10603; tel. 914/682–8006; FAX. 914/682–5692; Ronald L. Helm, Executive Director

PruCare of New York, Tri-State Health Care Management, The Office Center at Monticello, Suffern, NY 10901; tel. 914/368–4497

Rochester Area HMO, Inc., d/b/a Preferred Care, 259 Monroe Avenue, Suite A, Rochester, NY 14607; tel. 716/325–3920; FAX. 716/325–3122; John Urban, President

SCHC Total Care, Inc., 819 South Salina Street, Syracuse, NY 13202; tel. 315/476–7921; FAX. 315/475–4713; Rueben Cowart, D.D.S., Chief Executive Officer

St. Barnabas Community Health Plan, d/b/a Partners in Health, 4422 Third Avenue, Bronx, NY 10457; tel. 718/960–9454; FAX. 718/960–9027

Suffolk County Department of Health Services, 225 Rabro Drive, E., Happauge, NY 11788–4290; tel. 516/342–0063; Mary Hibberd, M.D., Chief Executive Officer

The Bronx Health Plan, One Fordham Plaza, Bronx, NY 10458; tel. 718/733–4747; FAX. 718–733–4750; Maura Bluestone, Chief Executive Officer

U.S. Healthcare, Inc., Nassau Omni West, 333 Earle Ovington Boulevard, Uniondale, NY 11553; tel. 516/794–6565; Michael A. Stocker, M.D., President

United Healthcare of Upstate NY, 5015 CampusWood Drive, Suite 303, East Syracuse, NY 13057; tel. 315/433–5851; FAX. 315/433–5850; David Barker, Chief Executive Officer

United HealthCare Plan of NY, Inc., United HealthCare Plan of NJ, Two Penn Plaza, Suite 700, New York, NY 10121; tel. 212/216–6401; FAX. 212/216–6595; R. Channing Wheeler, Chief Executive Officer

Utica–Watertown Health Insurance Co., Inc., The Utica Business Park, 12 Rhoads Drive, Utica, NY 13502; tel. 315/798–4358; FAX. 315/797–4298; Thomas Flannery, M.D.

Vytra Health Plans, Corporate Center, 395 North Service Road, Melville, NY 11747–3127; tel. 516/694–4000; FAX. 516/694–5780; David S. Reynolds, Ph.D., President

WellCare of New York, Inc., P.O. Box 4059, Park West/Hurley Avenue Ext., Kingston, NY 12402; tel. 914/334–7185; FAX. 914/338–0566; Robert Goff, Chief Executive Officer

Westchester Prepaid Health Services Plan, Inc., d/b/a HealthSource and Hudson Health Plan, 303 South Broadway, Suite 321, Tarrytown, NY 10591; tel. 914/631–1611; FAX. 914/631–1615; Georganne Chapin, Chief Executive Officer

NORTH CAROLINA

Aetna Health Plans of the Carolinas, Inc., 1010 Charlotte Plaza, Charlotte, NC 28244; tel. 704/353–7799; FAX. 704/353–7180; Patrick W. Dowd

Aetna Health Plans of the Carolinas, Inc., 1010 Charlotte Plaza, Suite 1010, Charlotte, NC 28244; tel. 704/353–7201

Aetna U.S. Healthcare of the Carolinas, Inc., 201 S. College Street, Suite 1010, Charlotte, NC 28244–0002; tel. 704/559–7250; Michael J. Cardillo, President

Association of Eye Care Centers Total Vision Health Plan, Inc., P.O. Box 7185, 110 Zebulon Court, Rocky Mount, NC 27804; tel. 919/937–6650; FAX. 919/451–2182; Samuel B. Petteway, Jr., President

Blue Cross Blue Shield of North Carolina, P.O. Box 2291, Durham, NC 27702; tel. 919/765–2400; Ken Otis II, President

Carolina Summit Healthcare, Inc., 2100 Stantonsburg Rd., Greenville, NC 27835; tel. 919/816–6751; William Bull

CIGNA Health Plan of North Carolina, Inc., P.O. Box 470068, Charlotte, NC 28247; tel. 704/544–4350; FAX. 704/544–4375; Joseph L. Murgo

Community Choice of North Carolina, Inc., 100 North Green Street, Greensboro, NC 27401; tel. 910/691–3001; Randolph Ferguson

Doctors Health Plan of North Carolina, Inc., 2828 Croasdaile Drive, P.O. Box 15309, Durham, NC 27704; tel. 919/383–4175; FAX. 919/383–3286; Bertram E. Walls, M.D., President and CEO

Doctors Health Plan, Inc., 2828 Croasdaile Drive, Durham, NC 27705; tel. 919/383–4173; FAX. 919/383–4175; Richard Allan Felice, President

Generations Family Health Plan, 6330 Quadrangle Dr., Suite 100, Chapel Hill, NC 27514; tel. 919/490–0102; FAX. 919/490–1790; John C. Hays, President and CEO

Healthsource North Carolina, Inc., 701 Corporate Center Drive, Raleigh, NC 27607; tel. 919/854–7000; FAX. 919/854–7102; Steve White, GM and President

Kaiser Foundation Health Plan of North Carolina, 3120 Highwoods Boulevard, Suite 300, Raleigh, NC 27604–1038; tel. 919/981–6000; FAX. 919/878–5835; Ted Carpenter, Vice President, Regional Manager

Kaiser Foundation Health Plan of North Carolina, 909 Aviation Parkway, Suite 600, Morrisville, NC 27560–9153; tel. 919/469–7200; FAX. 919/469–7441; George Stokes

Kanawha HealthCare, Inc., 4609 Old Course Drive, Charlotte, NC 28277; tel. 704/333–8810; James L. Tillotson

Maxicare North Carolina, Inc., 5550 77 Center Drive, Suite 380, Charlotte, NC 28217–0700; tel. 704/525–0880; FAX. 704/529–0382; Peter J. Ratican

Maxicare North Carolina, Inc., 5550 77 Center Drive, Suite 380, Charlotte, NC 28210; tel. 704/525–0880; FAX. 704/529–0382; Richard T. Hedlund, Vice President, General Manager

Optimum Choice of the Carolinas, Inc., Crabtree Center, 4600 Marriott Drive, Raleigh, NC 27612; tel. 919/881–8481; George T. Jochum

Optimum Choice of the Carolinas, Inc., 4600 Marriott Drive, Suite 300, Raleigh, NC 27612; tel. 800/469–8470; FAX. 919/788–1486; Jim Bendel, Regional Vice–President

Partners National Health Plans of NC, Inc., 2085 Frontis Plaza Boulevard, Winston–Salem, NC 27103; tel. 336/760–4822; FAX. 336/760–6218; Cosby M. Davis, III, Chief Financial Officer

PARTNERS National Health Plans of North Carolina, Inc., 2085 Frontis Plaza Boulevard, P.O. Box 24907, Winston–Salem, NC 27114–4907; tel. 336–760–4822; FAX. 336–760–3198; John W. Jones, President

Personal Care Plan of North Carolina, Inc., P.O. Box 2291, Durham, NC 27702; tel. 919/489–7431; Kenneth C. Otis II

Principal Health Care of the Carolinas, Inc., One Coliseum Center, 2300 Yorkmont Road, Suite 710, Charlotte, NC 28217; tel. 704/357–1421; FAX. 704/357–3164; Stephen H. Nolte, CEO

Principal Health Care of the Carolinas, Inc., 2300 Yorkmont Road, Suite 710, Charlotte, NC 28217; tel. 704/357–1421; Kenneth J. Linde, President

Provident Health Care Plan, Inc. of North Carolina, 701 Corporate Center Dr., Raleigh, NC 27604; tel. 919/460–1610; Barry Martins

Prudential Health Care Plan, Inc., 2701 Coltsgate Road, Suite 300, Charlotte, NC 28211; tel. 704/365–6070; FAX. 704/365–9959; Tracey Baker, Executive Director

QualChoice of North Carolina, Inc., P.O. Box 340, Winston–Salem, NC 27104–0340; tel. 919/716–0907; FAX. 910/716–1090; David Patterson, President and CEO

The Wellness Plan of North Carolina, Inc., P.O. Box 12980, Charlotte, NC 28220–2980; tel. 704–944–3700; FAX. 704–944–3900; Timothy O'Brien, Chief Executive Officer

UnitedHealthcare of North Carolina, Northwestern Plaza, 2307 West Cone Boulevard, Greensboro, NC 27408; tel. 336/282–0900; FAX. 336/545–5099; Frank R. Mascia, President and CEO

WellPath Select, Inc., 6330 Quadrangle Drive, Suite 500, Chapel Hill, NC 27514; tel. 919/493–1210; FAX. 919/419–3872; Anna M. Lore, President and CEO

NORTH DAKOTA

Altru Health Plan, 3065 DeMers Avenue, Grand Forks, ND 58201; tel. 800/675–2467; FAX. 701/780–1683; Darren Evavold

Heart of America HMO, 802 South Main, Rugby, ND 58368; tel. 701/776–5848; FAX. 701/776–5425; Mary Ann Jaeger, Executive Director

OHIO

Aetna U.S. Healthcare, Inc., 4059 Kinross Lakes Parkway, Richfield, OH 44286–5009; tel. 800/537–5312; FAX. 216/464–2723; David K. Ellwanger, Executive Director

Aultcare HMO, 2600 Sixth Street, S.W., Canton, OH 44710; tel. 330–438–6360; FAX. 330–438–2911; Rick L. Haines, Vice President, Managed Care

Bethesda Managed Care, Inc., 619 Oak Street, Cincinnati, OH 45206; tel. 513/569–6490; FAX. 513/569–6233; Robert Smith, M.D., Medical Director

ChoiceCare, 655 Eden Park Drive, Cincinnati, OH 45202; tel. 513/784–5200; FAX. 513/784–5300; Robert W. Quirk, Dir. of Legislative & Regulatory Affairs

ChoiceCare, 655 Eden Park Drive, Suite 400, Cincinnati, OH 45202; tel. 513/784–5200; FAX. 513/784–5300; Daniel A. Gregorie, M.D., Chief Executive Officer

ChoiceCare Health Plans, Inc., 655 Eden Park Drive, Cincinnati, OH 45202; tel. 513/784–5200; FAX. 513/784–5300; Daniel A. Gregorie, M.D., Chief Executive Officer

CIGNA HealthCare of Ohio, Inc., 3700 Corporate Drive, Suite 200, Business Campus N.E. # Five, Columbus, OH 43231; tel. 614/823–7500; FAX. 614/823–7519; Elmond A. Kenyon, President

Cigna Healthcare of Ohio, Inc., 3700 Corporate Drive, Suite 200, Columbus, OH 43231–4963; tel. 614/823–7500; FAX. 614/823–7775; James Massie, General Manager

Community Health Plan of Ohio, 1915 Tamarack Road, Newark, OH 43055–3699; tel. 740/348–1400; FAX. 740/348–1500; Robert R. Kamps, M.D., President and CEO

Day–Med Health Maintenance Plan, 9797 Springboro Pike, Suite 200, Miamisburg, OH 45342; tel. 937/847–5646; FAX. 513/847–5620; Jeanette Prear, President and CEO

Dayton Area Health Plan, One Dayton Centre, One South Main Street, Dayton, OH 45402–9794; tel. 937/224–3300; FAX. 937/224–2272; Pamela B. Morris, President and CEO

Dental Care Plus, Inc., 4500 Lake Forest Drive, Suite 512, Cincinnati, OH 45242; tel. 513/554–1100; FAX. 513/554–3187; John W. O'Neil, President and Chief Operating Officer

Emerald HMO, Inc., Diamond Building, 100 Superior Avenue, 16th Floor, Cleveland, OH 44114–2591; tel. 216/902–7592; FAX. 216/349–2059; Susan M. Simpson, President

Family Health Plan, Inc., 2200 Jefferson Ave., 6th Floor, Toledo, OH 43264; tel. 419/241–6501; FAX. 419/241–5441; James D. Massie, President and CEO

FHP of Ohio, Inc., Spectrum Office Tower, 11260 Chester Road, Suite 800, Cincinnati, OH 45246–9928; tel. 513/772–9191; FAX. 513/772–1466; John Davren, M.D., Plan Director

Genesis Health Plan of Ohio, Inc., Two Summit Park Drive, Suite 340, Cleveland, OH 44131; tel. 216/642–3344; FAX. 216/642–3345; Karl Rajani, President

Health Guard, d/b/a Advantage Health Plan, 3000 Guernsey Street, Bellaire, OH 43906–1598; tel. 614/676–4623; Daniel Splain, President

Health Power HMO, Inc., 560 East Town Street, Columbus, OH 43215–0346; tel. 614/461–9900; FAX. 614/461–0960; Thomas Beaty, Jr., President

HealthFirst, 278 Barks Road West, Marion, OH 43301–1820; tel. 740–387–6355; FAX. 740–383–3840; N. Robert Jones, President and CEO

HealthPledge, a product of OhioHealth Group HMO, Inc., 300 East Wilson Bridge Road, Suite 200, Worthington, OH 43085–2339; tel. 614/566–0111; FAX. 614/566–0403; Colleen M. Tincher, Vice President of Operations

Healthsource Ohio, Inc., 580 Lincoln Park Blvd., Suite 100, Kettering, OH 45429; tel. 937/296–7460; David Smith, Chief Executive Officer

HMO Health Ohio, 2060 East Ninth Street, Cleveland, OH 44115–1355; tel. 216/522–8622; Gerry P. Long, Director, ADS Products

HomeTown Hospital Health Plan, 100 Lillian Gish Boulevard, Suite 301, Massillon, OH 44647; tel. 216/837–6880; FAX. 216/837–6869; William C. Epling, Vice President, Chief Operating Officer

John Alden Health Systems, Inc., 5500 Glendon Court, Dublin, OH 43017; tel. 614/798–2930; William F. Sterling, Vice President, Senior Associate

Kaiser Permanente, North Point Tower, 1001 Lakeside Avenue, Suite 1200, Cleveland, OH 44114–1153; tel. 216/621–5600; FAX. 216/623–8776; Jeffrey Werner, Vice President, Marketing

Medical Value Plan, 405 Madison Avenue, P.O. Box 2147, Toledo, OH 43604; tel. 419/245–5165; Hal A. White, M.D., Medical Director

Mount Carmel Health Plan, Inc., 495 Cooper Road, Suite 300, Westerville, OH 43081; tel. 614/898–8750; FAX. 614/898–8587; Marc Richardson, President

Nationwide Health Plans, Inc., 5525 Parkcenter Circle, Dublin, OH 43017–3584; tel. 614/888–2223; FAX. 614/854–3783; John Susie, Sales Manager

OhioHealth Group HMO, Inc., 300 East Wilson Bridge Road, Suite 200, Worthington, OH 43085–2339; tel. 614/566–0111

PacifiCare of Ohio, Inc., 11260 Chester Road, Suite 800, Cincinnati, OH 45246; tel. 513/772–7325; Thomas D. Anthony

PacifiCare of Ohio, Inc., 11260 Chester Road, Suite 800, Cincinnati, OH 45246; tel. 513/772–7325; Brenda A. Pettit, Supervisor, Compliance

PacifiCare/FHP of Ohio, Spectrum Office Tower, 11260 Chester Road, Cincinnati, OH 45246–9928; tel. 513/772–7325

Paramount Health Care, 1715 Indian Wood Circle, Suite 200, P.O. Box 928, Toledo, OH 43697–0928; tel. 419/891–2500; FAX. 419/891–2530; John C. Randolph, President

Personal Physician Care, Inc., Sterling Building, 1255 Euclid Avenue, Suite 500, Cleveland, OH 44115–1807; tel. 216/687–0015; FAX. 216/687–9484; Wilton A. Savage, Executive Director

PrimeTime Health Plan, 6th St. SW, Canton, OH 44710; tel. 330/438–6360

Prudential HealthCare, 312 Elm Street, Suite 1400, Cincinnati, OH 45202; tel. 513/784–7559; FAX. 513/784–7020; Lynn Gross, Manager, Health Care Services

QualChoice Health Plan, 6000 Parkland Boulevard, Cleveland, OH 44124; tel. 216/460–4010; FAX. 216/460–4000; Ray S. Herschman, Chief Financial Officer

Riverside Dental Care of Indiana, Inc., 1100 Dennison Avenue, Columbus, OH 43201; tel. 614/297–4870; Richard A. Mitchell, President

SummaCare, Inc., 400 West Market Street, P.O. Box 3620, Akron, OH 44309–3620; tel. 330/996–8410; FAX. 330/996–8415; Martin P. Hauser, President

SuperMed HMO, 2060 East Ninth Street, Cleveland, OH 44115; tel. 216/687–7636; FAX. 216/687–6585; Michael P. Walker, Director Contracting –Northern Region

The Health Plan, 52160 National Road, East, St. Clarksville, OH 43950–9365; tel. 614/695–3585; Philip D. Wright, President and COO

The Health Plan of the Upper Ohio Valley, 52160 National Road, E., St. Clarksville, OH 43950; tel. 614/695–3585; Philip D. Wright, President

Total Health Care Plan, Inc., 12800 Shaker Boulevard, Cleveland, OH 44120; tel. 216/991–3000; FAX. 216–991–3011; Donald E. Butler, Acting Chief Executive Officer

United Healthcare of Ohio, Inc., 3650 Olentangy River Road, Columbus, OH 43216–1138; tel. 614/442–7160; Linda Cullen, Manager, Product Administration

United HealthCare of Ohio, Inc., 3650 Olentangy River Road, P.O. Box 1138, Columbus, OH 43216–1138; tel. 614/442–7100; Robert J. Sheehy, President

OKLAHOMA

DentiCare of Arkansas, Inc., Regional Administration Office, 7112 South Mingo, Suite 108, Tulsa, OK 74133; tel. 918/254–9055; FAX. 918/254–9076; John K. Wright, Secretary

Section C

Foundation Health, An Oklahoma Health Plan, Inc., 5810 East Skelly Drive, Suite 1100, Tulsa, OK 74135; tel. 918/621–5900; Richard McCutchen, Senior Vice President, Executive Of

GHS Health Maintenance Organization, Inc., d/b/a BlueLincs HMO, 1400 South Boston, Tulsa, OK 74119–3630; tel. 918/592–9414; FAX. 918/592–0611; Lyndle R. Ellis, Group Vice President

HealthCare Oklahoma, Inc., 3030 Northwest Expressway, Suite 140, Oklahoma City, OK 73112–4481; tel. 405/951–4700; FAX. 405/951–4701; Jon H. Friesen, President and CEO

PacifiCare of Oklahoma, 7666 East 61st Street, Tulsa, OK 74133–1112; tel. 918/459–1100; FAX. 918/459–1451; Chris Whitty, Vice President, General Manager

PROklahoma Care, Inc., 5005 North Lincoln, P.O. Box 25127, Oklahoma City, OK 73126; tel. 405/521–8253; Joe Crosthwait, M.D., Vice President, Medical Director

Prudential Health Care Plan, Inc., d/b/a Prudential Health Care HMO, 7912 East 31st Court, Tulsa, OK 74145; tel. 918/624–4600; FAX. 918/627–9759; Ann Paul, Executive Director

Prudential HealthCare Plan, Inc., 4005 Northwest Expressway, Suite 300, Oklahoma City, OK 73116; tel. 405/879–1780; James K. McNaughton, Executive Director

OREGON

Health Maintenance of Oregon, Inc., 1800 First Avenue, Suite 505, Portland, OR 97201; tel. 503/274–0755; FAX. 503/225–5431; Eric Bush

Health Masters of Oregon, Inc., 201 High Street, S.E., Salem, OR 97301; tel. 503/779–9468; FAX. 503/779–3238; Judd Holtey, Chief Operating Officer, Southern Regional

HMO Oregon, Inc., P.O. Box 1271, Portland, OR 97207; tel. 503/364–4868; FAX. 503/588–4350; Donald P. Secco, President and CEO

Kaiser Foundation Health Plan of the Northwest, 500 Northeast Multnomah Street, Suite 100, Portland, OR 97232–2099; tel. 503/813–2800; Michael H. Katcher, President

Kaiser Foundation Health Plan of the Northwest, 500 Northeast Multnomah, Suite 100, Portland, OR 97232–2099; tel. 503/813–2800; FAX. 503/813–2283; Denise L. Honzel, Vice President

PACC, P.O. Box 286, Clackamas, OR 97015–0286; tel. 503/659–4212; FAX. 503/794–3409; Martin A. Preizler, President and CEO

PACC, d/b/a PACC Health Plans of Washington, 12901 Southeast 97th Avenue, P.O. Box 286, Clackamas, OR 97015–0286; tel. 503/659–4212; FAX. 503/786–5319; Ron Morgan

Pacificare of Oregon, Inc., Five Centerpointe Drive, Suite 600, Lake Oswego, OR 97035–8650; tel. 503/620–9324; FAX. 503/603–7377; Mary O. McWilliams, President

Pacificare of Oregon, Inc., Five Centerpointe Drive, Suite 600, Lake Oswego, OR 97035; tel. 503/620–9324; Patrick Feyen, President

Providence Health Plans, 1235 N.E. 47th Ave, P.O. Box 10106, Portland, OR 97440; tel. 541/686–3948; FAX. 541/984–4030; Larry Abramson, President

Providence Health Plans, l235 Northeast 47th Avenue, Suite 220, Portland, OR 97213; tel. 503/215–2981; FAX. 503/215–7655; Jack Friedman, Executive Director

QualMed Oregon Health Plan, Inc., 4800 Southwest Macadam, Suite 400, Portland, OR 97201; tel. 503/222–5217; FAX. 503/796–6366; Chris du Laney, Executive Director

PENNSYLVANIA

Aetna Health Plans of Central and Eastern Pennsylvania, Inc., 955 Chesterbrook Boulevard, Suite 200, Wayne, PA 19087; tel. 610/644–3800; FAX. 610/251–6441; Anthony Buividas, Chief Executive Officer

Alliance Health Network, 1700 Peach Street, Suite 244, Erie, PA 16501; tel. 814/878–1700; FAX. 814/452–4358; Kenneth S. Bryant, President and CEO

Best Health Care of Western Pennsylvania, 112 Washington Place, Pittsburgh, PA 15218–0440; tel. 412/434–1200

Central Medical Health Plan, d/b/a Advantage Health, 121 Seventh Avenue, Suite 500, Pittsburgh, PA 15222–3408; tel. 412/391–9300; FAX. 412/391–0457; Elizabeth Stolkowski, Executive Vice President, Chief

Geisinger Health Plan, Geisinger Office Building, 100 North Academy Avenue, Danville, PA 17822–3020; tel. 717/271–8760; FAX. 717/271–5268; Howard G. Hughes, M.D., Senior Vice President Health Plans

Health Partners of Philadelphia, 841 Chestnute Street, Suite 900, Philadelphia, PA 19107; tel. 215/849–9606; FAX. 215/991–4130; Wanda Whitted–Smith, Vice President, Human Resources

HealthAmerica of Pennsylvania, Five Gateway Center, Pittsburgh, PA 15222; tel. 412/553–7300; FAX. 412/553–7384; Mike Blackwood, Chief Executive Officer

Healthassurance HMO, 2601 Market Place, Harrisburg, PA 17110–9339; tel. 412/577–4340; FAX. 412/497–5880; Deborah Zuroski, Senior Compliance Analyst

Healthcentral, Inc., 2605 Interstate Drive, Suite 140, Harrisburg, PA 17110; tel. 717/540–0033; Martin R. Miracle, President and CEO

HealthGuard of Lancaster, Inc., 280 Granite Run Drive, Suite 105, Lancaster, PA 17601–6810; tel. 717/560–9049; FAX. 717/581–4580; James R. Godfrey, President

HIP of Pennsylvania, d/b/a HIP Health Plan of Pennsylvania, Six Neshaminy Interplex, Suite 600, Trevose, PA 19053; tel. 215/633–7780; FAX. 215/633–8240

HMO of Northeastern Pennsylvania, d/b/a First Priority Health, 70 North Main Street, Wilkes–Barre, PA 18711; tel. 717/829–6044; FAX. 717/830–6319; Denise S. Cesare, Executive Vice President and COO

Horizon Healthcare, 1700 Market Street, Suite 1050, Philadelphia, PA 19103; tel. 215/575–0530; FAX. 215–575–0537

Keystone Health Plan Central, Inc., 300 Corporate Center Drive, P.O. Box 898812, Camp Hill, PA 17089–8812; tel. 717/763–3458; FAX. 717/975–6895; Joseph M. Pfister, President and CEO

Keystone Health Plan East, Inc., 1901 Market Street, Philadelphia, PA l9101–7516; tel. 215/241–2001; John Daddis, Executive Vice President, COO

Keystone Health Plan West, Inc., Fifth Avenue Place, 120 Fifth Avenue, Suite 3116, Pittsburgh, PA 15222; tel. 412/255–7245; FAX. 412/255–7583; Kenneth R. Melani, M.D., President

NYLCare Health Plans of New Jersey, Inc., 530 East Swedesford Road, Suite 201, Wayne, PA 19087; tel. 610/971–0404; FAX. 610/971–0159; Peter Linder, Executive Director

Optimum Choice, Inc. of Pennsylvania, 1755 Oregon Pike, First Floor, Lancaster, PA 17601; tel. 800/474–6647; FAX. 717/581–3525; J. Steven Dufresne, President

Oxford Health Plans, The Curtis Center, 601 Walnut Street, Suite 900E, Philadelphia, PA 19106; tel. 215/625–8800; FAX. 215/625–5601; Michael C. Gaffney, Chief Executive Officer

Philcare Health Systems, Inc., 2005 Market Street, Suite 500, Philadelphia, PA 19103; tel. 800/371–6664; FAX. 215/564–4204; Mr. Gregory Moses, President

Prudential Health Care Plan, Inc., Prudential HealthCare, 220 Gibralter Road, Suite 200, P.O. Box 901, Horsham, PA 19044–0901; tel. 215/672–1944; FAX. 215/442–2946; Brian J. Keane, Senior Director, Network Management, O

QualMed Plans for Health of Pennsylvania, Inc., 1835 Market Street, Ninth Floor, Philadelphia, PA 19103; tel. 215/209–6300; FAX. 215/209–6561; Diane C. Chiponis, Chief Financial Officer

QualMed Plans for Health, Inc., 1835 Market Street, Ninth Floor, Philadelphia, PA 19103; tel. 215/209–6704; FAX. 215/209–6708; Kenneth B. Allen, Director, Legal Services

Qualmed Plans for Health, Inc., (formerly Greater Atlantic Health Service, Inc.), 3550 Market Street, Philadelphia, PA 19104; tel. 215/823–8600; Ernest Monfiletto, President and CEO

Three Rivers Health Plans, Inc., 300 Oxford Drive, Monroeville, PA 15146; tel. 412/858–4000; FAX. 412/858–4060; Warren Carmichael, Chairman, Chief Executive Officer

U. S. Healthcare, Inc., 980 Jolly Road, P.O. Box 1109, Blue Bell, PA 19422; tel. 215/283–6656; Timothy Nolan, President

U. S. Healthcare, Inc., 980 Jolly Road, P.O. Box 1109, Blue Bell, PA 19422; tel. 215/628–4800

U.S. Healthcare, 980 Jolly Road, Blue Bell, PA 19422; tel. 215/628–4800; FAX. 215/283–6858

United States Health Care Systems, Inc., d/b/a The Health Maintenance Organization of Pennsylvania, 980 Jolly Road, P.O. Box 1109, Blue Bell, PA 19422; tel. 215/628–4800; Leonard Abramson, President

RHODE ISLAND

Blue Cross & Blue Shield of Rhode Island, 444 Westminster Street, Providence, RI 02903; tel. 401/459–1000; Ronald A. Battista, President

Coordinated Health Partners, Inc., d/b/a Blue Chip/Coordinated Health Partners, Inc., 15 LaSalle Square, Providence, RI 02903; tel. 800/528–4141; James E. Bobbitt, Chief Operating Officer

Harvard Pilgrim Health Care of New England, One Hoppin Street, Providence, RI 02903–4199; tel. 401/331–3000; FAX. 401/331–0496; Stephen Schoenbaum, M.D., President

Neighborhood Health Plan of Rhode Island, Inc., 32 Branch Avenue, Providence, RI 02904; tel. 401/459–6000; Chris Schneider

United Health Plans of NE, Inc., 475 Kilvert Street, Warwick, RI 02886–1392; tel. 800/447–1245; FAX. 401/732–7208; Robert K. Winston, Director, Corporate Communications

United Health Plans of New England, Inc., 475 Kilvert Street, Suite 310, Warwick, RI 02886–1392; tel. 401/737–6900; FAX. 401/737–6957; Max Powell, Chief Executive Officer

SOUTH CAROLINA

American Medical Plans of South Carolina, Inc., 246 Stoneridge Drive, Suite 101, Columbia, SC 29210; tel. 803/748–7395; FAX. 803/748–9597; George A. Schneider, Chief Executive Officer

Carolina Care Health Plan, Inc., 111 Stonemark Lane, Suite 202, Columbia, SC 29210; tel. 803/551–5585; FAX. 813/265–6213; Laurie Burrell, Chief Operating Officer

Companion HealthCare Corporation, 200 Arbor Lake Drive, Suite 200, Columbia, SC 29223; tel. 803/786–8466; FAX. 803/754–6386; Harvey L. Galloway, Executive VP and CEO

HealthFirst, Inc., Brookfield Corporate Center, 1041 E. Butler Road, Suite 2400, Greenville, SC 29607–5725; tel. 864/289–3080; FAX. 864/289–3100; Steve Meeker, Chief Financial Officer

Physicians Health Plan of South Carolina, Inc., 201 Executive Center Drive, Suite 300, Columbia, SC 29210–8438; tel. 803/750–7400; FAX. 803/750–7476; Ronald H. Haems, Chief Executive Officer

Preferred Health Systems, Inc., I–20 at Alpine Road, Columbus, SC 29219; tel. 803/788–0222; FAX. 803/736–2851; Gail Bragg, Senior Director

Select Health of South Carolina, Inc., 7410 Northside Drive, Suite 208, North Charles, SC 29420; tel. 803/569–1759; FAX. 803/569–0702; Michael Jernigan, President and CEO

SOUTH DAKOTA

Mutual of Omaha of South Dakota and Community Health Plus HMO,, 3904 Technology Circle, Sioux Falls, SD 57106; tel. 605/361–9591; FAX. 605/361–9593; William P. Jetter, Executive Director

Sioux Valley Health Plan, 1200 North West Avenue, Sioux Falls, SD 57104; tel. 605–357–6800; FAX. 605–357–6811; Tony Morrison, Administration Director

South Dakota State Medical Holding Company, Inc., d/b/a Dakota Care, 1323 South Minnesota Avenue, Sioux Falls, SD 57105; tel. 605/334–4000; FAX. 605/336–0270; Robert D. Johnson, Chief Executive Officer

TENNESSEE

Aetna Health Plans of Tennessee, 1801 West End Avenue, Suite 500, Nashville, TN 37203; tel. 615/322–1600; FAX. 615/322–1217; David R. Field, President

American Healthcare Trust, Inc, 22 North Front Street, Suite 960, Memphis, TN 38103; tel. 901/523–2672; FAX. 901/527–2672; Eric B. Taylor, President

Cigna Healthcare of Tennessee, Inc., 6555 Quince Road, Suite 215, Memphis, TN 38119; tel. 901/755–7411; David O. Hollis, M.D., Medical Director

Community Health Plan of Chattanooga, Inc., d/b/a Wellport Health Plan, Franklin Building, Suite 101, Chattanooga, TN 37411; tel. 423/490–1120; Brian E. Dalbey, President

Health 123, Inc., 706 Church Street, Suite 500, Nashville, TN 37203; tel. 615/782–7811; FAX. 615/782–7812; Thomas J. Nagle, President and CEO

HealthNet HMO, Inc., 44 Vantage Way, Suite 300, Nashville, TN 37228; tel. 800/881–9466; John D. Davis, Chief Executive Officer

Healthsource Tennessee, Inc., 5409 Maryland Way, Suite 300, Brentwood, TN 37027; tel. 615/373–6995; FAX. 615/370–9396; Steve White, Chief Executive Officer

Mid–South Health Plan, Inc., 889 Ridge Lake Boulevard, Suite 111, Memphis, TN 38120; tel. 901/766–7500; William C. Stewart, Jr., Chief Executive Director, Medical Director

Phoenix Healthcare of Tennessee, Inc., 3401 West End Avenue, Suite 470, Nashville, TN 37203; tel. 615/298–3666; FAX. 615/297–2036; Samuel H. Howard, Chairman

PHP Health Plans, Inc., 1420 Centerpoint Boulevard, Knoxville, TN 37932; tel. 423/470–7470; Jerry M. Marsh, CPA, Director, Finance

Southern Health Plan, Inc., 600 Jefferson, Memphis, TN 38105; tel. 901/544–2336; FAX. 901/544–2220; Bill Graham, Executive Director

Tennessee Health Care Network, Inc., P.O. Box 1407, Chattanooga, TN 37401–1407; tel. 423/755–2033; FAX. 615/755–5630; Robert M. Fox, President

TriPoint Health Plan, Inc., 706 Church Street, Suite 500, Nashville, TN 37203–3511; tel. 800/557–4874; Barbara Bennett, General Counsel

Vanderbilt Health Plans, Inc., 706 Church Street Building, Suite 500, Nashville, TN 37203; tel. 615/343–2670; FAX. 615/343–2823; Randal B. Farr, Executive Vice President

TEXAS

AECC Total Vision Health Plan of Texas, Inc., 3010 LBJ Freeway, Suite 240, Dallas, TX 75234; tel. 800/268–8847; FAX. 927/620–9484; Bill Henderson, Chief Executive Officer

Aetna Dental Care of Texas, Inc., 2777 Stemmons Freeway, Suite 300, Dallas, TX 75207; tel. 214/470–7990; Jackie Eveslage, Chief Operating Officer

Aetna Health Plans of Texas, Inc., 2900 North Loop West, Suite 200, Houston, TX 77092; tel. 713/683–7500; FAX. 713/683–5819; Joseph T. Blanford III, General Manager

Aetna U.S. Healthcare of North Texas, Inc., P.O. Box 569440, 2777 Stemmons Freeway, Dallas, TX 75356–9440; tel. 214/401–8610; John Coyle, President

Alpha Dental Programs, Inc., d/b/a Delta Care, 1431 Greenway Drive, Suite 520, Irving, TX 75038; tel. 972/580–1616; FAX. 972/580–1333; Robert Budd, Vice President, Marketing, Western Region

Alternative Dental Care of Texas, Inc., 2023 South Gessner K–3, Houston, TX 77063; tel. 713/781–6607; Thomas Anthony Dzuryachko, President

Americaid Texas, Inc., d/b/a Americaid Community Care, 617 Seventh Avenue, Second Floor, Fort Worth, TX 76104; tel. 817/870–1281; James Donovan, Jr., President

AmeriHealth HMO of Texas, Inc., 770 South Post Oak Lane, Houston, TX 77056; tel. 215/241–2432

Anthem Health Plan of Texas, Inc., 5055 Keller Springs Road, Dallas, TX 75243; tel. 972/732–2000; FAX. 972/732–2043; Joseph W. Hrbek, President

Block Vision of Texas, Inc., 14228 Midway Road, Suite 213, Dallas, TX 75244; tel. 800/914–9795; FAX. 972/991–4704; Andrew Alcorn, President

Certus Healthcare, L.L.C., 1300 North 10th Street, Suite 450, McAllen, TX 78501; tel. 210/630–1956; FAX. 210/630–1957; David Rodriguez, President

CIGNA Dental Health of Texas, Inc., d/b/a CIGNA Dental Health, 600 East Las Colinas Boulevard, Suite 1000, Irving, TX 75039; tel. 800/367–1037; Brent Martin, D.D.S., M.B.A., Chief Executive Officer,

CIGNA HealthCare of Texas, Inc., d/b/a CIGNA HealthCare for Seniors, 600 East Las Colinas Boulevard, Suite lI00, Irving, TX 75039; tel. 214/401–5200; FAX. 214/401–5263; Paul Carter, Associate Vice President of Government Programs

Community Health Choice, Inc., 2525 Holly Hall, Houston, TX 77054; tel. 713/746–6999; FAX. 713/746–4365; Wayne Colson, VP of Finance

Comprehensive Health Services of Texas, Inc., 100 Northeast Loop 410, Suite 675, San Antonio, TX 78217; tel. 210/321–4050; Thomas J. Jackson, Chief Executive Officer

Dental Benefits, Inc., d/b/a Bluecare Dental HMO, 12170 Abrams Road, Dallas, TX 75243; tel. 972–766–6129; FAX. 972–766–6129; Richard A. Clissold

DentiCare, Inc., d/b/a CompDent, 2929 Briarpark Drive, Suite 314, Houston, TX 77042–3709; tel. 713/784–7011; Henry New, President

ECCA Managed Vision Care, Inc., 11103 West Avenue, San Antonio, TX 78213–1392; tel. 800/340–0129; FAX. 210/524–6587; Melissa Kazen, Director

First American Dental Benefits, Inc., 14800 Landmark Boulevard, Suite 700, Dallas, TX 75240; tel. 214/661–5848; Jim Davenport, President, Acting Chief Executive Officer

Foundation Health A Texas Plan, 5525 N. Macarthur Blvd #850, Irving, TX 78746; tel. 972/756–5000; Penny Zagroba, Operations Manager

Harris Health Plan, Inc., d/b/a Harris Methodist Health Plan, 611 Ryan Plaza Drive, Suite 900, Arlington, TX 76011–4009; tel. 817/570–8044; Donna A. Goldin, Chief Operating Officer

Harris Methodist Texas Health Plan, Inc., d/b/a Harris Methodist Health Plan, 611 Ryan Plaza Drive, Suite 900, Arlington, TX 76011–4009; tel. 817/462–7000; FAX. 817/462–6903; Patrick Spehrs, President

Healthcare Partner HMO, 821 ESE, Loop 323, Two American Center, Zip 75701, Tyler, TX 75701; tel. 903/581–2600; Tom Slack, Chief Executive Officer

Healthplan of Texas, Inc., 110 North College Ave., Suite 900, Tyler, TX 75702; tel. 903/531–4447; Edwin McClusky, M.D., Chief Executive Officer

Healthsource Texas, Inc., d/b/a Healthsource, 1701 Directors Blvd., Suite 110, Austin, TX 78744; tel. 512/440–5030; Terry Steven Shilling, President and CEO

HMO Texas, L.C., P.O. Box 42416, Houston, TX 77242–2416; tel. 713/952–6868; FAX. 713/974–1650; John Micale, President

Humana Health Plan of Texas, Inc., d/b/a Humana Health Plan of Dallas, 8431 Fredericksburg Road, San Antonio, TX 78229; tel. 512/617–1000; Brenda Luckett, Executive Director

Humana Health Plan of Texas, Inc., d/b/a Humana Health Plan of San Antonio, 8431 Fredericksburg Road, Suite 570, San Antonio, TX 78229; tel. 210/617–1000; FAX. 210/617–1704; Michael A. Seltzer, Director, Texas Operations

Humana Health Plans of Texas, Inc, 8431 Fredericksburg, Suite 570, San Antonio, TX 78229; tel. 210/617–1708; FAX. 210/617–1704; Michael A. Seltzer, Vice President West Region

Kaiser Foundation Health Plan of Texas, 12720 Hillcrest Road, Suite 600, Dallas, TX 75230; tel. 214/479–0332; Sharon Flaherty, President

Memorial Sisters of Charity HMO, LLC, d/b/a MSCH HMO, 9494 Southwest Freeway, Suite 300, Houston, TX 77074; tel. 713/430–1617; FAX. 713/778–2375; Richard Todd, President and CEO

Mercy Health Plans of Missouri, Inc., 5901 McPherson, Suites 1 & 2B, Laredo, TX 78041; tel. 956–723–2144; FAX. 956–723–8246; Ernesto Segura, Executive Director

MethodistCare, Two Greenway Plaza, Suite 500, Houston, TX 77046; tel. 713–479–4100; FAX. 713–479–4263; James Henderson, President and CEO

Metrowest Health Plan, Inc., 1500 South Main Street, 3rd Floor, Fort Worth, TX 76104; tel. 817/927–3999; FAX. 817/927–3996; Robert G. O'Donnell, President

Mid–Con Health Plans, L.C., d/b/a HMO Blue, Southwest Texas, 500 Chestnut Street, Suite 1699, Abilene, TX 79602; tel. 915/738–3518; FAX. 915/738–3519; M. Ted Haynes, President and CEO

NYLCare Dental Plan of the Southwest, Inc., 4500 Fuller Drive, Irving, TX 75038; tel. 972/650–5500; FAX. 972/650–5707; Steve Yerxa, Chief Executive Officer, Executive Direct

NYLCare Health Plan of the Southwest, 4500 Fuller Drive, Irving, TX 75038; tel. 972/650–5500; FAX. 972/650–5703; Steve Yerxa

NYLCare Health Plans of the Gulf Coast, 2425 West Loop South, Suite 1000, Houston, TX 77027; tel. 713/624–5000; FAX. 713/963–9417; Thomas S. Lucksinger, President and CEO

One Health Plan of Texas, Inc., 10000 North Central Expressway, Suite 900, Dallas, TX 75231; tel. 800/866–3136; Jim White, President

Orthopedic Healthcare of Texas, Inc., 729 Bedford–Euless Road, W., Suite 100, Hurst, TX 76053; tel. 817/282–6905; Edward William Smith, D.O., President

PacifiCare of Texas, Inc., San Antonio Region, 8200 I.H. 10 West, San Antonio, TX 78230; tel. 210/524–9800; Patrick Feyen, President

Parkland Community Health Plan, Inc., 7920 Elmbrook, Suite 120, Dallas, TX 75247; tel. 214/590–2800; Ron J. Anderson, President

Parliament Dental Plans, Inc., 2909 Hillcroft, Suite 515, Houston, TX 77057; tel. 713/784–6262; FAX. 713/784–0488; Paul H. Michael, President

Physicians Care HMO, Inc., 2777 Stemmons Freeway, Suite 957B, Stemmons Place, Dallas, TX 75207; tel. 214/631–0221; FAX. 214/688–7044; Amanullah Khan, President

Principal Health Care of Texas, Inc., 555 North Caracahua, Suite 500, Corpus Christ, TX 78478; tel. 512/887–0101; Diana Tchida, Executive Director

Prudential Dental Maintenance Organization, Inc., Stop 206, One Prudential Circle, Sugar Land, TX 77478–3833; tel. 713/494–6000; FAX. 713/276–3752; Royce Rosemond, Executive Director

Prudential Health Care Plan, Inc., Stop 204, One Prudential Circle, Sugar Land, TX 77478; tel. 713/276–3850; FAX. 713/276–8254; Dennis Edmonds, Executive Director

Prudential Health Care Plan, Inc., One Prudential Circle, Sugar Land, TX 77478–3833; tel. 713/276–3940

Prudential Health Care Plan, Inc., PruCare, 24 Greenway Plaza, Suite 500, Houston, TX 77046; tel. 201/716–8174

Rio Grande HMO, Inc., d/b/a HMO Blue, 4150 Pinnacle, Suite 203, El Paso, TX 79902; tel. 800/831–0576; Anne McDow, Vice President, Operations

Safeguard Health Plans, Inc., 14800 Landmark Blvd., 7th Floor, Dallas, TX 75240; tel. 214/265–7041; FAX. 214/265–7702; David Branstetter, Executive Director

Scott & White Health Plan, 2401 South 31st Street, Temple, TX 76508; tel. 817/742–3030; FAX. 817/742–3011; Deny Radefeld, Executive Director

Seton Health Plan, Inc., 1201 West 38th Street, Austin, TX 78705; tel. 800/749–7404; FAX. 512/323–1952; John H. Evler III, President and COO

Sha, L.L.C., d/b/a Firstcare, 12940 Research Boulevard, Austin, TX 78750; tel. 806/356–5151; Dale Bowerman, President and CEO

Spectera Dental, Inc., (formerly United Healthcare Dental, Inc.), 1445 North Loop West, Suite 1000, Houston, TX 77008; tel. 713/861–3231; Arlene Sheldon, Executive Director

Superior Healthplan, L.P., 816 Congress Ave., Suite 1100, Austin, TX 78701; tel. 512/480–2206; Jose Comacho, Executive Director

Texas Children's Health Plan, Inc., 1919 South Braeswood Boulevard, P.O. Box 301011, Houston, TX 77230–1011; tel. 713/770–2600; FAX. 713/770–2686; Christopher Born, President

Texas Universities Health Plan, Inc., d/b/a TUHP, 700 University Blvd., Galveston, TX 77550; tel. 409/747–5430

Unicare of Texas Health Plans, Inc., (formerly Affiliated Health Plans, Inc.), 11200 Westheimer, Suite 700, Houston, TX 77042; tel. 713/782–4555; Sam John Nicholson II, President

United Dental Care of Texas, Inc., 14755 Preston Road, Suite 300, Dallas, TX 75240; tel. 214/458–7474; James B. Kingston, President

United Healthcare of Texas, Inc., (formerly Metrahealth Care Plan of Texas, Inc.), 1250 Capital of Texas, Highway South, Austin, TX 78746; tel. 800/424–6480; FAX. 512/338–6812; Karen England, Director, Network Operations

United Healthcare of Texas, Inc., Dallas/Fort Worth Division, 4835 LBJ Freeway, Suite 1100, Dallas, TX 75244; tel. 214/866–6000; FAX. 214/866–6018; Richard Cook, Chief Executive Officer

Universal HealthPlan, Inc., 2900 Elgin, Houston, TX 77004; tel. 713/526–2441

USABLE HMO, Inc., d/b/a USABLE Health Advantage, 1406 College Drive, Suite A, Texarkana, TX 75503; tel. 800/844–6047

VHP Dental, Inc., P.O. Box 15800, 7801 North IH 35, Austin, TX 78761; tel. 512/433–1000

Vista Health Plan, Inc., (formerly The Wellness Health Plan of Texas, Inc.), 7801 North IH–35, Austin, TX 78753; tel. 512/433–1000; Paul Tovar, President

West Texas Health Plans, d/b/a HMO Blue, West Texas, Sentry Plaza II, 5225 South Loop 289, Lubbock, TX 79424; tel. 806/798–6362; Michael A. Huesman, President

Section C

UTAH

American Family Care of Utah, Inc., 2120 S. 1300 E #303, Suite 303, Salt Lake City, UT 84106; tel. 801/486–1664; Jose Fernandez, President

Benchoice, Inc., 310 East 4500 South, Suite 550, Murray, UT 84157–0906; tel. 801/262–2999; Talmage Pond, President

CIGNA Health Plan of Utah, Inc., 5295 South 320 West, Suite 280, Salt Lake City, UT 84107; tel. 801/265–2777; FAX. 801/261–5349; Robert Immitt, President

Delta Care Dental Plan, Inc., 257 East 200 South, Suite 375, Salt Lake City, UT 84111; tel. 801/575–5168

Educators Health Care, 852 East Arrowhead Lane, Murray, UT 84107–5298; tel. 801/262–7476; FAX. 801/269–9734; Andy I. Galano, Ph.D., President

Employees Choice Health Option, 35 West Broadway, Salt Lake City, UT 84101; tel. 801/355–1234; Larry Bridge, President

FHP of Utah, Inc., 35 West Broadway, Salt Lake City, UT 84101; tel. 801/355–1234; FAX. 801/531–9003; Larry Bridge, President

HealthWise, 2890 East Cottonwood Parkway, P.O. Box 30270, Salt Lake City, UT 84130–0270; tel. 801/333–2320; Jed H. Pitcher, Chairman

IHC Care, Inc., 36 South State Street, 15th Floor, Salt Lake City, UT 84111; tel. 801/442–5000; FAX. 801/538–5003; Sid Paulson, Chief Operating Officer

IHC Group, Inc., 36 South State Street, 15th Floor, Salt Lake City, UT 84111; tel. 801/442–5000; Sid Paulson, Chief Operating Officer

IHC Health Plans, Inc., 36 South State Street, 15th Floor, Salt Lake City, UT 84111; tel. 801/442–5000; Sid Paulson, Chief Operating Officer

IHC Health Plans, Inc., 36 South State Street, Salt Lake City, UT 84111; tel. 801/442–5000; FAX. 801/442–5003; Martin Byrnes, Compliance Supervisor

IHC Health Plans, Inc., 36 South State Street, 15th Floor, Salt Lake City, UT 84111; tel. 801/442–5000; Sid Paulson, Chief Operating Officer

Intergroup Utah, Inc, 127 South 500 East, Suite 510, Salt Lake City, UT 84102; tel. 801/532–7665; FAX. 801/297–4585; Elden Mitchell, President

U. S. Dental Plan, Inc., 4001 South 700 East, Suite 300, Salt Lake City, UT 84107; tel. 801/263–8884; Christopher A. Jehle, President

United HealthCare of Utah, 7910 South 3500 East, Salt Lake City, UT 84121; tel. 801/942–6200; FAX. 801/944–0940; Colin Gardner, Chief Executive Officer

Utah Community Health Plan, 36 South State Street, Suite 1020, Salt Lake City, UT 84111–1418; tel. 801/442–3780; FAX. 801/442–3791; William K. Wilson, Executive Director

VIRGINIA

Aetna Health Plans of the Mid–Atlantic, Inc., 7600 A Leesburg Pike, Falls Church, VA 22043; tel. 703/903–7100; Jon Glaudemans, Vice President, Health Services

Aetna Health Plans of the Mid–Atlantic, Inc., 7799 Leesburgh Pike South, Suite 1100, Falls Church, VA 22045; tel. 703/903–7100; Russ Dickhart, Executive Director

Americaid Community Care, Americaid Illinois, Inc., 4425 Corporation Lane, Suite 100, Virginia Beach, VA 23462; tel. 804/490–6900; FAX. 757/473–2738; Ted M. Willie., JR., Chief Operating Officer

CIGNA HealthCare of Virginia, Inc., 4050 Innslake Drive, Glen Allen, VA 23060; tel. 804/273–1100; John E. Sharp, Vice President and Executive Director

Health First, Inc., 621 Lynnhaven Parkway, Suite 450, Virginia Beach, VA 23452–7330; tel. 804/431–5298; Russell F. Mohawk, President

HealthKeepers, Inc., 2220 Edward Holland Drive, P.O. Box 26623, Richmond, VA 23230; tel. 804/354–7961; FAX. 804/354–3554; Sam Weidman, Vice President, Finance

HMO Virginia, Inc., Health Keepers, 2220 Edward Holland Drive, Richmond, VA 23230; tel. 804/354–7961; FAX. 804/354–3554; Sam Weidman, Vice President, Finance

National Capital Health Plan, Inc., 5850 Versar Center, Suite 420, Springfield, VA 22151; tel. 703/914–5650

Optimum Choice, 3025 Hamaker Court, Suite 301, Fairfax, VA 22031; tel. 703/207–6570; Susan Hrubes, Senior Director

Peninsula Health Care, Inc., 606 Denbigh Boulevard, Suite 500, Newport News, VA 23608; tel. 757/875–5760; FAX. 757/875–5785; C. Burke King, President

Physicians Health Plan, Inc., Health Keepers, 2220 Edward Holland Drive, Richmond, VA 23230; tel. 804/354–7961; FAX. 804/354–3554; Sam Weidman, Vice President, Finance

Priority Health Plan, Inc., 621 Lynnhaven Parkway, Suite 450, Virginia Beach, VA 23452–7330; tel. 804/463–4600; Russell F. Mohawk, President

Prudential Health Care Plan, Inc., d/b/a PruCare and Prudential Health Care Plan of the Mid–, 1000 Boulders Parkway, Richmond, VA 23225; tel. 804/323–0900; William Patrick Link, President

QualChoice of VA Health Plan, Inc., 1807 Seminole Trail, Suite 201, Charlottesville, VA 22901; tel. 804/975–1212; FAX. 804/975–1414; Martha D'Erasmo, President and CEO

Sentara Health Management, 4417 Corporation Lane, Virginia Beach, VA 23462; tel. 804/552–7400; FAX. 804/552–7396; Michael M. Dudley, President

Sentara Health Plans, Inc., d/b/a Sentara Health Plan, 4417 Corporation Lane, Virginia Beach, VA 23462; tel. 804/552–7100; FAX. 804/552–7396; John E. McNamara III, President

Southern Health Services, 9881 Mayland Drive, P.O. Box 85603, Richmond, VA 23285–5603; tel. 804/747–3700; FAX. 804/747–8723; James L. Gore, President

VA Chartered Health Plan, Inc., 4701 Cox Road, Glen Allen, VA 23060; tel. 804/967–0747; Sheila Blackman, Chief Operating Officer

WASHINGTON

Good Health Plan of Washington, Century Square, 1501 Fourth Avenue, Suite 500, Seattle, WA 98101; tel. 206/622–6111; FAX. 206/346–0969; Lee Hooks, Executive Director

Group Health Cooperative of Puget Sound, Administration and Conference Center, 521 Wall Street, Seattle, WA 98121–1535; tel. 206/448–6460; FAX. 206/448–6080; Phil Nudelman, Ph.D., President and CEO

Group Health Northwest, West 5615 Sunset Highway, Spokane, WA 99204; tel. 509/838–9100; FAX. 509/458–0368; Henry S. Berman, M.D., President and CEO

Group Health Northwest, 5615 West Sunset Highway, Spokane, WA 99204; tel. 509/838–9100; FAX. 509/838–3823; Henry S. Berman, M.D., President and CEO

HealthFirst Partners, Inc., 601 Union Street, Suite 700, Seattle, WA 98101; tel. 206/667–8070; FAX. 206/667–8060; Eileen Duncan

HMO Washington, 1800 Ninth Avenue, P.O. Box 2088, Seattle, WA 98111–2088; tel. 206/389–6721; FAX. 206/389–6719; Bryan Heinrich, Executive Director

Pacificare of Washington, 600 University Street, Suite 700, Seattle, WA 98101; tel. 206/326–4645; FAX. 206/442–5399; Brad Bowlus, President and CEO

QualMed Washington Health Plan, Inc, d/b/a Qual–Med Health Plan, 2331 130th Avenue, N.E., Suite 200, Zip 98009, P.O. Box 3387, Bellevue, WA 98009–3387; tel. 206/869–3500; FAX. 206/869–3568; C.F. du Laney, President

QualMed Washington Health Plan, Inc., West 508 Sixth Avenue, Suite 700, P.O. Box 2470, Spokane, WA 99210–2470; tel. 509/459–6690; FAX. 509/458–2705; Nicolette Bryant, Director of Operations

Unified Physicians of Washington, Inc., 33301 Ninth Avenue, S., Suite 200, Federal Way, WA 98003–6394; tel. 206/815–1888; FAX. 206/815–0486; Dodie Wine, Associate Director, Communications

Virginia Mason Health Plan, Inc., Metropolitan Park West, 1100 Olive Way, Suite 1580, Seattle, WA 98101–1828; tel. 206/223–8844; FAX. 206/223–7506; John Clarke, Director, Operations

WEST VIRGINIA

Advantage Health Plan, Adv. Health/QualMed, 137 Waddles Run Road, Wheeling, WV 26003; tel. 304–243–1489

Anthem Health Plan of West Virginia, Inc., d/b/a PrimeONE, 500 Virginia Street East, Suite 400, Charleston, WV 25301; tel. 304/340–6944; FAX. 304/304/6943; A. Paul Holdren, President/CEO

Carelink Health Plans, 141 Summers Square, Charleston, WV 25326–1711; tel. 304/348–2901; FAX. 304/348–2948; Alan L. Mytty, President

Coventry Health Plan of West Virginia, Inc., (Health Assurance HMO), 887 National Road, Wheeling, WV 26003; tel. 304/234–5100; FAX. 304/234–5119; Marilyn White, Manager

WISCONSIN

Atrium Health Plan, Inc., 2215 Vine Street, Suite E, Hudson, WI 54016–5802; tel. 800/535–4041; FAX. 715/386–8326; Michael L. Christensen, Director of Operations

Compcare Health Services Insurance Corp., 401 West Michigan Street, P.O. Box 2947, Milwaukee, WI 53201–2025; tel. 414/226–6171; FAX. 414/226–6229; Jeffrey J. Nohl, President and COO

Dean Health Plan, Inc., P.O. Box 56099, Madison, WI 53705–9399; tel. 608/836–1400; FAX. 608/836–9620; John A. Turcott, President and CEO

Emphesys Wisconsin Insurance Company, 1100 Employers Boulevard, DePere, WI 54115; tel. 800/558–4444; Mark R. Minsloff, Executive Director

Family Health Plan Cooperative, 11524 West Theo Trecker Way, Milwaukee, WI 53214–7260; tel. 414/256–0006; FAX. 414/256–5681; David Bradford, President

Genesis Health Plan Insurance Corporation, P.O. Box 20007, Greenfield, WI 53220–0007; tel. 414/425–3323; FAX. 414/425–3034; Karl Rajani, Chief Executive Officer

Greater La Crosse Health Plans, Inc., 1285 Rudy Street, Onalaska, WI 54650; tel. 608/782–2638; FAX. 608/781–8862; Steven M. Kunes, Plan Administrator

Group Health Cooperative of Eau Claire, P.O. Box 3217, Eau Claire, WI 54702–3217; tel. 715/836–8552; FAX. 715/836–7683; Claire W. Johnson, General Manager

Group Health Cooperative of South Central Wisconsin, 8202 Excelsior Drive, P.O. Box 44971, Madison, WI 53744–4971; tel. 608/251–4156; FAX. 608/257–3842; Lawrence Zanoni, Executive Director

Gundersen Lutheran Health Plan, Inc., 1836 South Avenue, LaCrosse, WI 54601; tel. 608/798–8020; FAX. 608/791–8042; Jeff Treasure, Chief Executive Officer

Humana Wisconsin Health Organization Insurance Corporation, 111 West Pleasant Street, P.O. Box 12359, Milwaukee, WI 53212–0359; tel. 414/223–3300; FAX. 414/223–7777; William L. Carr, Executive Director

Managed Health Services, 2040 W. Wisconsin Ave #452, Milwaukee, WI 53227; tel. 414/345–4600; FAX. 414/321–9724; Michael F. Neidorff, President and CEO

MercyCare Health Plan, Inc., One Parker Place, Suite 750, Janesville, WI 53545; tel. 608/752–3431; FAX. 608/752–3751; Don Schreiner, Senior Vice President

Network Health Plan of Wisconsin, Inc., 1165 Appleton Road, P.O. Box 120, Menasha, WI 54952–0120; tel. 414/727–0100; FAX. 414/727–5634; Michael D. Wolff, President and CEO

North Central Health Protection Plan, 2000 Westwood Drive, Zip 54401, P.O. Box 969, Wausau, WI 54402–0969; tel. 715/847–8866; Larry A. Baker, Administrator

Physicians Plus Insurance Corporation, 340 West Washington Avenue, P.O. Box 2078, Madison, WI 53703; tel. 608/282–8900; FAX. 608/282–8944; Thomas R. Sobocinski, President and CEO

Premier Medical Insurance Group, Inc., 1277 Deming Way, Madison, WI 53717; tel. 608/836–1400; John A. Turcott, President and CEO

PrimeCare Health Plan, Inc., 10701 West Research Drive, Milwaukee, WI 53226–0649; tel. 414/443–4000; FAX. 414/443–4750; James Schultz, Administrator

Security Health Plan of Wisconsin, Inc., 1000 North Oak Avenue, Marshfield, WI 54449; tel. 715/387–5534; FAX. 715/387–5240; William G. Hocking, M.D., President

United Health of Wisconsin Insurance Company, Inc., P.O. Box 507, Appleton, WI 54912–0507; tel. 414/735–6440; FAX. 414/731–7232; Jay Fulkerson, Chief Executive Officer

Unity Health Plans Insurance Corp., 840 Carolina Street, Sauk City, WI 53583; tel. 800/362–3308; FAX. 608/643–2564; Mary Traver, Interim President

Valley Health Plan, 2270 East Ridge Center, P.O. Box 3128, Eau Claire, WI 54702–3128; tel. 715/832–3235; FAX. 715/836–1298; Kathryn R. Teeters, Director

WYOMING

WinHealth Partners, 2600 East 18th Street, Cheyenne, WY 82001; tel. 307–638–7700; FAX. 307–638–7701; Beth Wasson, Executive Director

U.S. Associated Areas

GUAM

F.H.P., Inc., P.O. Box 6578, Tamunig, GU 96911; tel. 671/646–5824; FAX. 671/646–6923; Edward English, Associate Regional Vice President

Guam Memorial Health Plan, 177 Achalan Pasaheru, Tamunig, GU 96911; tel. 671/646–4647; FAX. 671/647–5048; James W. Gillan, Chief Operating Officer

PUERTO RICO

First Medical Comprehensive Health Care, Inc., (Antes Plan Comprehensive de Salud, Inc.), Apartado 40954, Estacion Minillas, Santurce, PR 00940; tel. 809/723–6016; FAX. 809/723–6014; J. A. Soler, President

Golden Cross HMO Health Plan Corporation, Antes HMO Medical System Corporation, Apartado 9021727, Estacion Viejo San Juan, San Juan, PR 00902–1727; tel. 809/721–0427; FAX. 809/721–5464; Lic Luis F. Hernandez Velez

Humana Puerto Rico, Humana Puerto Rico, Box 192059, San Juan, PR 00919–2059; tel. 787/282–7900; FAX. 787–282–6290; Victor S. Gutierrez, M.D., President

Mennonite General Hospital, Inc., Calle Jose C. Vazquez, Apartado 1379, Aibonito, PR 00705; tel. 809/735–8001; FAX. 809/735–8073; Domingo Torres Zayas, Chief Executive Officer

Plan de Salud de la Federacion de Maestros, de Puerto Rico, Inc., P.O. Box 71336, San Juan, PR 00936–8436; tel. 787/758–5610; FAX. 787/281–7392; Eugenio Aponte, Executive Director

Plan de Salud Hospital de la Concepcion, Inc., Calle Dr. Veve #102, Apartado 39, San German, PR 00683; tel. 787/892–1860; FAX. 787/892–2176; Ivonne Montaluo, Executive Director

Plan de Salud U.I.A., Inc., Calle Mayaguez #49, San Juan, PR 00917; tel. 787/763–4004; FAX. 787/763–7095; Jose E. Sanchez, Consultant

Plan Medico U.T.I. de Puerto Rico, Inc., Apartado 23316–Estacion U.P.R., Rio Piedras, PR 00924; tel. 809/758–1500; FAX. 809/758–3210; David Munoz, President

Ryder Health Plan, Inc., Call Box 859, Humacao, PR 00792; tel. 809/852–0846; FAX. 809/850–4863; Juan L. De Le Rosa, Director

Service Medical, Inc., Avenida Munoz Rivera 402, Parada 31, Hato Rey, PR 00917; tel. 809/758–5555; FAX. 809/250–1425; Lexie Gomez

Servicios de Salud Bella Vista, Bella Vista Gardens Numero 43, Carr. 349–Cerro Las Mesas, Mayaguez, PR 00680; tel. 787/833–8070; FAX. 787/832–5400; Victor Prosper–Rios, President

United Healthcare Plans of Puerto Rico, Inc., (Antes Group Sales and Service of Puerto Rico, Inc.), Rexco Office Park, Apartado 364864, San Juan, PR 00936–4864; tel. 809/782–7005; FAX. 809/782–5269; Luis A. Salgado Munoz, Executive Vice President

Section C

State Government Agencies for HMO's

Information for the following list was obtained directly from the agencies.

United States

ALABAMA: Department of Insurance, 201 Monroe Street, Suite 1700, Montgomery, AL 36104; tel. 334/269-3550; FAX. 334/241-4192; Richard H. Cater, Commissioner of Insurance

ALASKA: Alaska Division of Insurance, P.O. Box 110805, Juneau, AK 99811-0805; tel. 907/465-2596; FAX. 907/465-3422; Marianne K. Burke, Director

ARIZONA: Department of Insurance, 2910 North 44th Street, Suite 210, Phoenix, AZ 85018; tel. 602/912-8443; FAX. 602/912-8453; Mary Butterfield, Assistant Director, Life and Health

ARKANSAS: Arkansas Insurance Department, 1200 West Third Street, Little Rock, AR 72201-1904; tel. 501/371-2600; FAX. 501/371-2629; Mike Pickens, Insurance Commissioner

CALIFORNIA: Department of Corporations, Health Care Service Plan Division, 3700 Wilshire Boulevard, Los Angeles, CA 90010; tel. 213/736-2776; Gary G. Hagen, Assistant Commissioner

COLORADO: Department of Regulatory Agencies, Colorado Division of Insurance, 1560 Broadway, Suite 850, Denver, CO 80202; tel. 303/894-7499; FAX. 303/894-7455; Nancy Litwinski, Assistant Commissioner of Financial Regulation

CONNECTICUT: Department of Insurance, P.O. Box 816, Hartford, CT 06142-0816; tel. 860/297-3800; FAX. 860/566-7410; Mary Ellen Breault, Director, Life and Health Division

DELAWARE: Department of Health and Social Services, Office of Health Facilities Licensure and Certification, Three Mill Road, Suite 308, Wilmington, DE 19806; tel. 302/577-6666; FAX. 302/577-6672; Ellen T. Reap, Director

DISTRICT OF COLUMBIA: District of Columbia Department of Insurance and Securities Re, 810 1st Street NE, Room 701, Washington, DC 20002; tel. 202/727-8000; FAX. 202/727-8055; Herman Hunter, Chief Consumer Services Branch

FLORIDA: Florida Department of Insurance, Bureau of Life and Health Insurer Solvency and Market Con, 200 East Gaines, Tallahassee, FL 32399-0327; tel. 850/922-3153; FAX. 904/413-9019; Mark Shealy, Administrator

GEORGIA: Department of Insurance, 9th West Tower, Floyd Building, Two Martin Luther King Jr. Drive, Atlanta, GA 30334; tel. 404/656-2074; FAX. 404/657-7743; John Oxendine, Commissioner

HAWAII: State of Hawaii Department of Labor and Industrial Relations, Disability Compensation Division, P.O. Box 3769, Honolulu, HI 96812; tel. 808/586-9151; Gary S. Hamada, Administrator

IDAHO: Department of Insurance, 700 West State Street, Third Floor, P.O. Box 83720, Boise, ID 83720-0043; tel. 208/334-4250; FAX. 208/334-4398; Joan Krosch, Health Insurance Coordinator

ILLINOIS: Department of Insurance, 320 West Washington Street, Fourth Floor, Springfield, IL 62767-0001; tel. 217/782-6369; FAX. 217/524-2122; David E. Grant, Health Care Coordinator

INDIANA: Department of Insurance, 311 West Washington Street, Suite 300, Indianapolis, IN 46204; tel. 317/232-5695; FAX. 317/232-5251; Jim Fuller, Health Deputy

IOWA: Iowa Department of Commerce, Division of Insurance, 330 Maple, Des Moines, IA 50319-0065; tel. 515/281-5705; FAX. 515/281-3059; Therese M. Vaughan, Commissioner

KANSAS: Kansas Insurance Department, 420 Southwest Ninth Street, Topeka, KS 66612; tel. 785/296-3071; FAX. 785/296-2283; Kathleen Sebelius, Commissioner

KENTUCKY: Department of Insurance, Life and Health Division, 215 West Main Street, P.O. Box 517, Frankfort, KY 40602; tel. 502/564-6088; FAX. 502/564-2728; Gale Pearce, Director

LOUISIANA: Department of Insurance, Attn: Company Licensing Division, P.O. Box 94214, Baton Rouge, LA 70804; tel. 504/342-1216; FAX. 504/342-3078; Mike Boutwell, Assistant Director of Licensing

MAINE: Department of Professional and Financial Regulation, Bureau of Insurance, 34 State House Station, Augusta, ME 04333; tel. 207/624-8416; FAX. 207/624-8599; Michael F. McGonigle, Senior Insurance Analyst

MARYLAND: Department of Health and Mental Hygiene, Insurance Division, 201 West Preston Street, Baltimore, MD 21201-2399; tel. 410/767-6860; FAX. 410/767-6489; Martin P. Wasserman, M.D., J.D., Secretary

MASSACHUSETTS: Division of Insurance, 470 Atlantic Avenue, Boston, MA 02210-2223; tel. 617/521-7794; FAX. 617/521-7770; Robert Dynan, Company Licensing

MICHIGAN: Department of Community Health, Managed Care Quality Assessment and Improvement Division, 3423 North Logan/Martin Luther King Boulevard, P.O. Box 30195, Lansing, MI 48909; tel. 517/335-8515; FAX. 517/335-9239; Janet Olszewski, Director

MINNESOTA: Minnesota Health Technology Advisory Committee (HTAC), 121 East Seventh Place, Suite 400, P.O. Box 64975, St. Paul, MN 55164-0975; tel. 651/282-5600; FAX. 651/282-5628; Brenda Holden, Director

MISSISSIPPI: Mississippi Department of Insurance, P.O. Box 79, Jackson, MS 39205; tel. 601/359-3577; FAX. 601/359-2474; J. Mark Haire, Special Assistant Attorney General

MISSOURI: Department of Insurance, Division of Market Regulation, Managed Care Section, P.O. Box 690, Jefferson City, MO 65102; tel. 573/522-8767; FAX. 573/526-6075; Wendy Taparanskas, Ph.D., Health Economist Supervisor

MONTANA: Montana State Auditor, Insurance Department, Mitchell Building, Room 270, 126 North Sanders, Helena, MT 59604-4009; tel. 406/444-4372; FAX. 406/444-3497; James Borchardt, Chief Examiner

NEBRASKA: Department of Insurance, 941 O Street, Suite 400, Lincoln, NE 68508; tel. 402/471-2201; FAX. 402/471-4610; Timothy J. Hall, Director

NEVADA: Nevada Division of Insurance, Capitol Complex, 1665 Hot Springs Road, Suite 152, Carson City, NV 89710; tel. 702/687-4270; FAX. 702/687-3937; Alice A. Molasky-Arman, Esq., Commissioner

NEW HAMPSHIRE: Department of Health and Human Services, Office of Community and Public Health, Medicaid Administration Bureau, 6 Hazen Drive, Concord, NH 03301-6521; tel. 603/271-4365; FAX. 603/271-4376; Diane Kemp, Administrator

NEW JERSEY: Department of Health, Office of Managed Care, P.O. Box 360, Trenton, NJ 08625; tel. 609/588-2510; FAX. 609/633-0807; Edwin V. Kelleher, Chief

NEW MEXICO: Public Regulation Commission, Insurance Division, P.O. Box 1269, Santa Fe, NM 87504; tel. 505/827-4601; FAX. 505/827-4734; Life and Health Forms Filing Bureau

NEW YORK: The Bureau of Managed Care Certification and Surveillance, Empire State Plaza, Corning Tower, Room 1911, Albany, NY 12237; tel. 518/474-5515; FAX. 518/473-3583; Vallencia Lloyd, Director

NORTH CAROLINA: Department of Insurance, Financial Evaluation Division, P.O. Box 26387, Raleigh, NC 27611; tel. 919/733-5633; Jackie Obusek, Financial Analyst

NORTH DAKOTA: North Dakota Department of Insurance, State Capitol, 600 East Boulevard, 5th Boulevard, Bismarck, ND 58505-0320; tel. 701/328-2440; FAX. 701/328-4880; Glenn Pomeroy, Commissioner

OHIO: Department of Insurance, Managed Care Division, 2100 Stella Court, Columbus, OH 43215-1067; tel. 614/644-3311; FAX. 614/644-3741; Kay L. Thompson, Chief

OKLAHOMA: Oklahoma State Department of Health, 1000 Northeast 10th Street, Oklahoma City, OK 73117-1299; tel. 405/271-6868; FAX. 405/271-3442; Lajuana Wire, Director of Managed Care Systems

OREGON: Department of Consumer and Business Services, Insurance Division, 350 Winter St. NE #440, Salem, OR 97310; tel. 503/947-7980; FAX. 503/378-4351; Michael Greenfield, Insurance Commissioner

PENNSYLVANIA: Pennsylvania Insurance Department, Company Licensing Division, 1345 Strawberry Square, Harrisburg, PA 17120; tel. 717/787-2735; FAX. 717/787-8557; Robert E. Brackbill, Chief

RHODE ISLAND: Department of Business Regulation, Division of Insurance, 233 Richmond Street, Suite 233, Providence, RI 02903-4233; tel. 401/277-2223; FAX. 401/751-4887; Alfonso E. Mastrostefano, Associate Director

SOUTH CAROLINA: Office of Insurer Licensing and Solvency Services, 1612 Marion Street, Columbia, SC 29201; tel. 803/737-6221; FAX. 803/737-6232; Timothy W. Campbell, Chief Financial Analyst

SOUTH DAKOTA: Division of Administration, South Dakota Department of Health, 600 East Capitol Avenue, Pierre, SD 57501-2536; tel. 605/773-3361; FAX. 605/773-5683; Joan Adam, Division Director

TENNESSEE: Department of Commerce and Insurance, 500 James Robertson Parkway, Nashville, TN 37243-1135; tel. 615/741-6796; FAX. 615/532-2788; Don Spann, Chief Financial Executive

TEXAS: Texas Department of Insurance, Mail Code 103-6A, P.O. Box 149104, Austin, TX 78714-9104; tel. 512/322-4266; FAX. 512/322-4260; Leah Rummel, Deputy Commissioner, HMO/URA/QA

UTAH: Utah Insurance Department, State Office Building, Room 3110, Salt Lake City, UT 84114; tel. 801/538-3800; FAX. 801/538-3829; Jilane Whitby, Information Specialist

VERMONT: Department of Banking, Insurance and Securities, Division of Healthcare Administration, 89 Main Street, Drawer 20, Montpelier, VT 05620-2946; tel. 802/828-2900; FAX. 802/828-2949; Theresa Alberghini, Deputy Commissioner

VIRGINIA: State Corporation Commission, Bureau of Insurance, P.O. Box 1157, Richmond, VA 23218; tel. 804/371-9901; FAX. 804/371-9511; Laura Lee Viergever, Senior Financial Analyst

WASHINGTON: Office of the Insurance Commissioner, Insurance Building, P.O. Box 40255, Olympia, WA 98504-0255; tel. 360/664-8002; FAX. 360/586-3535; Donna Dorris, Manager, Health Care

WEST VIRGINIA: Insurance Commissioner's Office, Financial Conditions Division, 1124 Smith Street, Charleston, WV 25301; tel. 304/558-2100; FAX. 304/558-1365; Jeffrey W. Van Gilder, Director, Chief Examiner

WISCONSIN: Office of the Commissioner of Insurance, P.O. Box 7873, Madison, WI 53707-7873; tel. 608/266-3585; FAX. 608/266-9935; Connie L. O'Connell, Commissioner

Section C

WYOMING: **Department of Insurance,** Herschler Building, Third Floor East, Cheyenne, WY 82002; tel. 307/777–6807; FAX. 307/777–5895; Lloyd Wilder, Insurance Standards Consultant

U.S. Associated Areas

GUAM: **Department of Public Health and Social Services, Government of Guam,** P.O. Box 2816, Agana, GU 96932; tel. 671/735–7102; FAX. 671/734–5910; Dennis G. Rodriguez, Director

PUERTO RICO: **Aurea Lopez, Chief Examiner, Office of the Commissioner of Insurance,** P.O. Box 8330, Fernandez Juncos Station, Santurce, PR 00910–8330; tel. 787/722–8686; FAX. 809/722–4400; Aurea Lopez, Chief Examiner

Section C

Freestanding Ambulatory Surgery Centers

The following list of freestanding ambulatory surgery centers was developed with the assistance of state government agencies and the individual facilities listed.

The AHA Guide contains two types of ambulatory surgery center listings; those that are hospital based and those that are freestanding. Hospital based ambulatory surgery centers are listed in section A of the AHA Guide and are identified by Facility Code F44. Please refer to that section for information on the over 5,000 hospital based ambulatory surgery centers.

We present this list simply as a convenient directory. Inclusion or omission of any organization's name indicates neither approval nor disapproval by Health Forum LLC.

United States

ALABAMA

American Surgery Centers of Alabama, d/b/a American Surgery Center, 2802 Ross Clark Circle, S.W., Dothan, AL 36301; tel. 334/793–3411; FAX. 334/712–0227; Carlotta McCallister, Administrator

Baptist Surgery Center, 2035 East South Boulevard, Montgomery, AL 36111–0000; tel. 334/286–3180; FAX. 334/286–3381; Faye Wimberly, RN, Administrator

Birmingham Endoscopy Center, Inc., 2621 19th Street, South, Homewood, AL 35209; tel. 205/271–8200; Leonard Ou–Tim, M.D., Administrator

Birmingham Outpatient Surgery Center, Ltd., d/b/a Columbia Outpatient CareCenter, 2720 University Boulevard, Birmingham, AL 35233; tel. 205/933–0050; FAX. 205/933–8212; Jackie Harrison, RN, Administrator

Columbia Surgicare of Mobile, 2890 Dauphin Street, Mobile, AL 36606; tel. 334/473–2020; FAX. 334/478–6737; Sandy Bunch, Administrator

Dauphin West Surgery Center, 3701 Dauphin Street, Mobile, AL 36608; tel. 334/341–3405; FAX. 334/341–3404; James L. Spires, Executive Director

Decatur Ambulatory Surgery Center, 2828 Highway 31, S., Decatur, AL 35603; tel. 256/340–1212; FAX. 256/340–0252; Andrew Hetrick, Administrator

Dothan Surgery Center, 1450 Ross Clark Circle, S.E., Dothan, AL 36301; tel. 334/793–3442; FAX. 334/793–3318; Denise Harrington, Facility Administrator

Gadsden Surgery Center, 418 South Fifth Street, Gadsden, AL 35901; tel. 205/543–1253; FAX. 205/543–1260; Bobo Martin, RN, Administrator

Healthsouth Florence Surgery Center, 103 Helton Court, Florence, AL 35630; tel. 256/760–0672; FAX. 256/766–4547; Pam Watson, Administrator

Healthsouth Surgical Center of Tuscaloosa, 1400 McFarland Boulevard, N., Tuscaloosa, AL 35406; tel. 205/345–5500; Jeff Hayes, Administrator

Huntsville Endoscopy Center, Inc., 119 Longwood Drive, Huntsville, AL 35801; tel. 205/533–6488; FAX. 205/533–6495; Michael W. Brown, M.D.

Medplex Outpatient Medical Centers, Inc., 4511 Southlake Parkway, Birmingham, AL 35422; tel. 205/985–4398; FAX. 205/985–4486; Dawn Ousley, RN, Administrator

Mobile Surgery Center, 1721 Springhill Avenue, Mobile, AL 36608; tel. 334/438–3614; Julie Saucier, RN, B.S.N., Facility Administrator

Montgomery Eye Surgery Center, 2752 Zelda Road, Montgomery, AL 36106; tel. 334/270–9677; FAX. 334/213–0622; Chris Green, Center Director

Montgomery Surgical Center, 855 East South Boulevard, Montgomery, AL 36116; tel. 334/284–9600; FAX. 334/284–4233; Susan N. Lamar, Administrator

Outpatient Services East, Inc., 52 Medical Park Drive, E., Suite 401, Birmingham, AL 35235; tel. 205/838–3888; FAX. 205/838–6181; James E. Stidham, President and CEO

The Kirklin Clinic Ambulatory Surgical Center, 2000 Sixth Avenue, S., Birmingham, AL 35233; tel. 205/801–8000; Steven C. Schultz, Executive Vice President

The Surgery Center of Huntsville, 721 Madison Street, Huntsville, AL 35801; tel. 205/533–4888; FAX. 205/532–9510; William Sammons, Chief Executive Officer

Tuscaloosa Endoscopy Center, 100 Rice Mine Road, N.E., Suite E, Tuscaloosa, AL 35406; tel. 205/345–0010; FAX. 205/752–1175; A. B. Reddy, M.D., Medical Director

ALASKA

Alaska Surgery Center, 4001 Laurel Street, Anchorage, AK 99508; tel. 907/563–3327; FAX. 907/562–7042; Louise M. Bjornstad, Executive Director

Alaska Women's Health Services, Inc., 4115 Lake Otis Drive, Anchorage, AK 99508; tel. 907/563–7228; FAX. 907/563–6278; Ellen Cowgill, Administrator

Geneva Woods Surgical Center, 3730 Rhone Circle, Suite 100, Anchorage, AK 99508; tel. 907/562–4764; FAX. 907/561–8519; Heidi Muckey, Administrator

Pacific Cataract & Laser Institute, 1600 'A' Street, Suite 200, Anchorage, AK 99501; tel. 907/272–2423; Hans Kell, O.D., Administrator

Susitna Surgery Center, 950 East Bogard Road, Wasilla, AK 99645, Palmer, AK 99645; tel. 907/746–8625; Patsy Crofford, RN, Chief Clinical Officer

ARIZONA

A.I.M.S. Outpatient Surgery, 3636 Stockton Hill Road, Kingman, AZ 86401; tel. 602/757–3636; FAX. 602/757–7224; Bill Margita

Adobe Plastic Surgery, 2585 North Wyatt Drive, Tucson, AZ 85712; tel. 602/322–5295; FAX. 602/325–7763; Lucricia Banks, Administrator

Aesthetic Reconstructive Associates, P.C., 4222 East Camelback, Suite H–150, Phoenix, AZ 85018; tel. 602/952–8100; FAX. 602/952–9519; Martin L. Johnson, M.D.

Ambulatory Surgicenter, Inc., 1940 East Southern Avenue, Tempe, AZ 85282; tel. 602/820–7101; FAX. 602/820–9291; H. William Reese, D.P.M., Medical Director

Arizona Diagnostic and Surgical Center, 545 North Mesa Drive, Mesa, AZ 85201; tel. 602/461–4407; FAX. 602/461–4401; Lynnette King, RN, Administrator

Arizona Foot Institute, P.C., 1901 West Glendale Avenue, Phoenix, AZ 85021; tel. 602/246–0816; FAX. 602/433–2257; Barry Kaplan

Arizona Medical Clinic, Ltd., 13640 North Plaza Del Rio Boulevard, Peoria, AZ 85381; tel. 602/876–3800; Jan Kaplan, Director, Operations

Arizona Surgical Arts, Inc., 1245 North Wilmot Road, Tucson, AZ 85712; tel. 520/296–7550; FAX. 520/298–5415; Keliu M. Gordon, Administrator

Barnet Dulaney Eye Center, 4800 N. 22nd Street, Phoenix, AZ 85018; tel. 602/955–1000; FAX. 602/957–9202; Ronald W. Barnet, M.D.

Barnet Dulaney Eye Center, 825 20th Avenue, Safford, AZ 85546; tel. 602/428–6930; FAX. 602/428–7272; Beth Curtis, RN

Barnet Dulaney Eye Center, 1375 West 16th Street, Yuma, AZ 85364; tel. 602/955–1000; Imelda Kelly, Director of Nursing

Barnet Eye Center–Mesa, 6335 East Main Street, Mesa, AZ 85205; tel. 602/981–1000; FAX. 602/981–0467; Carolyn Miller, Administrator

Boswell Eye Institute, 10541 West Thunderbird Boulevard, Sun City, AZ 85351; tel. 602/933–3402; FAX. 602/972–5014; Jan Zellmann, Administrator

Carriker Eye Center, 6425 North 16th Street, Phoenix, AZ 85016; tel. 602/274–1703; FAX. 602/274–3216; Richard G. Carriker, M.D.

Casa Blanca Medical Group, 4001 East Baseline Road, Gilbert, AZ 85234; tel. 602/926–6200; FAX. 602/926–6202; Cathy Romano, Executive Director

Cataract Surgery Clinic, 215 South Power Road, Suite 112, Mesa, AZ 85206; tel. 602/981–1345; Robert P. Gervais, M.D., President

CIGNA Healthplan of Arizona, Outpatient Surgery, 755 East McDowell Road, Phoenix, AZ 85006; tel. 602/371–2500; Clifton Worsham, M.D., Administrator

Cochise Eye and Laser, PC, 2445 East Wilcox Drive, Sierra Vista, AZ 85635; tel. 520/458–8131; FAX. 520/458–0422; Douglas R. Knolles, Administrator

Cottonwood Day Surgery Center, Inc., 55 South Sixth Street, P.O. Box 400, Cottonwood, AZ 86326; tel. 602/634–2444; Linda Davis, Administrator

Desert Mountain Surgicenter, Ltd., 7776 Pointe Parkway West, Suite 135, Phoenix, AZ 85044; tel. 602/431–8500; FAX. 602/431–1677; David M. Creech, M.D.

Desert Samaritan Surgicenter, 1500 South Dobson Road, Suite 101, Mesa, AZ 85202; tel. 602/835–3590; FAX. 602/890–4675; Brenda Mastopietro, Administrator

Dooley Outpatient Surgery Center, 151 Riviera Drive, Lake Havasu C, AZ 86403; tel. 602/855–9477; FAX. 602/855–2983; William J. Dooley, Jr., M.D., Medical Director

East Valley Surgical Associates, Ltd., 6424 East Broadway Road, Suite 102, Mesa, AZ 85206; tel. 602/833–2216; Manuel J. Chee

FH–Arizona Surgery Centers, Inc., 750 North Alvernon Way, Tucson, AZ 85711; tel. 602/322–8440; FAX. 602/322–2653; Vicki Gagnier, RN, Manager

Fifty–Ninth Avenue Surgical Facility, Ltd., 8608 North 59th Avenue, Glendale, AZ 85302; tel. 602/934–0272; FAX. 602/930–1891; Mark Gorman, Administrator

Fishkind and Bakewell Eye Care and Surgery Center, 5599 North Oracle Road, Tucson, AZ 85704; tel. 602/293–6740; FAX. 602/293–6771; Kathleen A. Brown, Surgery Center Supervisor

Flagstaff Outpatient Surgery Center, 77 West Forest Avenue, Suite 306, Flagstaff, AZ 86001; tel. 520/773–2597; FAX. 520/773–2327; Jackie Mosier, RN, Administrator

Footcare Surgi Center, 10249 West Thunderbird, Suite 100, Sun City, AZ 85351; tel. 602/979–4466; FAX. 602/933–8354; Gary N. Friedlander, D.P.M.

Footcare Surgi Center of Northern Arizona, 10 West Columbus Avenue, Flagstaff, AZ 86001; tel. 520/774–4191; Dr. Edward L. Wiebe

Gary Hall Laser Center, 2501 North 32nd Street, Phoenix, AZ 85008; tel. 602/957–6799; FAX. 602/957–0172; Gary W. Hall, M.D., President

Glendale Surgicenter, 5757 West Thunderbird Road, Suite E–150, Glendale, AZ 85306; tel. 602/843–1900; FAX. 602/843–5607; Douglas G. Merrill, M.D., Medical Director

Good Samaritan Surgicenter, 1111 B East McDowell Road, Phoenix, AZ 85006; tel. 602/239–2776; FAX. 602/239–5352; Brenda Mastopietro, Administrator

Greenbaum Outpatient Surgery and Recovery Care Center, 3624 Wells Fargo Avenue, Scottsdale, AZ 85251; tel. 602/481–4958; Craig Stout, Administrator

Grimm Eye Clinic and Cataract Institute, P.C., 1502 North Tucson Boulevard, Tucson, AZ 85716; tel. 602/326–4321; Stephen F. Grimm, M.D.; Eleanor M. Grimm, M.D.

Havasu Arthritis and Sports Medicine Institute, 1840 Mesquite Avenue, Suite G, Lake Havasu, AZ 86403; tel. 602/453–2663; Marc H. Zimmerman, M.D., Administrator

Havasu Foot and Ankle Surgi–Center, 90 Riviera Drive, Lake Havasu, AZ 86403; tel. 520/855–7800; FAX. 520/855–5392; Robert Novack, D.P.M., Director

HealthSouth Surgery Center of Tucson, 310 North Wilmot Road, Suite 309, Tucson, AZ 85711; tel. 520/296–7080; FAX. 520/886–6518; Aaron Chatterson, Administrator

Kokopelli Eye Care, P.C., 2820 North Glassford Hill Road, Suite 106, Prescott Vall, AZ 86314; tel. 520/775–5606; FAX. 520/772–4999; Linda Talerico, Administrator

Lear Surgery Clinic–Scottsdale, 7351 East Osborn Road, Suite 104, Scottsdale, AZ 85251–6452; tel. 602/990–9400; FAX. 602/990–2664; David E. Marine, Executive Director

Lear Surgery Clinic–Sun City, 10615 West Thunderbird, Suite A–100, Sun City, AZ 85351; tel. 602/974–9375; FAX. 602/977–2598; David E. Marine, Executive Director

Mayo Clinic Scottsdale Ambulatory Surgery Center, 13400 East Shea Boulevard, Scottsdale, AZ 85259; tel. 602/342–2419; FAX. 602/342–2414; Karen A. Biel, Administrator

McCready Eye Surgery Center, 310 North Wilmot Road, Suite 106, Tucson, AZ 85711; tel. 520/885–6783; FAX. 520/885–5366; Joseph L. McCready, M.D., Administrator

Metro Ambulatory Surgery, Inc., a/k/a Metro Recovery Care Center, 3131 West Peoria Avenue, Phoenix, AZ 85029; tel. 602/375–1083; FAX. 602/789–6833; Carole A. Crevier, Administrator

Mohave Surgery Center, Inc., 1919 Florence Avenue, Kingman, AZ 86401; tel. 520/753–5454; FAX. 520/753–7790; Frank Brown, Administrator

Moon Valley Surgery Center, Inc., 14045 North Seventh Street, Suite Two, Phoenix, AZ 85022; tel. 602/942–3966; Andrew E. Lowy

Nogales Medical Clinic Outpatient Surgery, 480 North Morley Avenue, Nogales, AZ 85621; tel. 520/287–2726; Imogene A. Bell, Administrator

Osborn Ambulatory Surgical Center, 3330 North Second Street, Suite 300, Phoenix, AZ 85012; tel. 602/265–0113; FAX. 602/277–8580; Gudran Anderson, RN, Administrator

Outpatient Surgical Care, Ltd., 1530 West Glendale, Suite 105, Phoenix, AZ 85021; tel. 602/995–3395; FAX. 602/995–1853; James Kennedy, M.D., Medical Director

Outpatient Surgical Center, 456 North Mesa Drive, Mesa, AZ 85201; tel. 602/464–8000; FAX. 602/969–7107; Maddie Dauernheim, Administrator

Porter, Michael, D.P.M., 3620 East Campbell, Suite B, Phoenix, AZ 85018; tel. 602/954–6224; Michael Porter

Prescott Outpatient Surgery Center, Inc., 815 Ainsworth Drive, Prescott, AZ 86301; tel. 602/778–9770; Gail Reidhead, Administrative Director

Prescott Urocenter, Ltd., 811 Ainsworth, Suite 101, Prescott, AZ 86301; tel. 520/771–5282; FAX. 520/771–5283; Gregory Oldani

Santa Cruz Ambulatory Surgical Center, 699 West Ajo Way, Tucson, AZ 85713; tel. 602/746–1711; Richard Edward Quint, Administrator

Scottsdale Eye Surgery Center, P.C., 3320 North Miller Road, Scottsdale, AZ 85251; tel. 602/949–1208; FAX. 602/994–3316; Beth Hurley, RN

Southwestern Eye Center, 1055 S. Stapley, Mesa, AZ 85202; tel. 602/839–1717; John M. Lewis, M.D.

Southwestern Eye Center–Casa Grande, 1919 North Trekell Road, Casa Grande, AZ 85222; tel. 520/426–9224; FAX. 520/426–1554; Lothaire Bluth, Administrator

Southwestern Eye Center–Yuma, 2179 West 24th Street, Yuma, AZ 85364; tel. 520/726–4120; FAX. 520/341–0315; Lance K. Wozniak, M.D.

Southwestern Eye Surgi Center–Falcon Field, 4760 Falcon Drive, Mesa, AZ 85205; tel. 602/985–7400; Pat Bray, RN, CRNO, Director

Southwestern Eye Surgicenter–Flagstaff, 1355 North Beaver, Suite 140, Flagstaff, AZ 86001; tel. 520/773–1184; FAX. 520/773–1815; Suzi Jensen, Surgical Services

Southwestern Eye Surgicenter–Nogales, 1815 North Mastick Way, Nogales, AZ 85621; tel. 520/281–0160; Pat Bray, Administrator

Sun City Endoscopy Center, Inc., 13203 North 103rd Avenue, Suite C 3, Sun City, AZ 85351; tel. 602/972–2116; John E. Phelps, M.D., Medical Director

Sun City Surgical Center, 13260 North 94th Drive, Suite 300, Peoria, AZ 85381; tel. 602/277–0619; FAX. 602/933–5787; H. William Reese, D.P.M., Director

Surgi–Care, 5115 North Central Avenue, Suite B, Phoenix, AZ 85012; tel. 602/264–1818; FAX. 602/264–2172; Ellison F. Herro, M.D., Administrator

Surgical Eye Center of Arizona, Inc., 5133 North Central Avenue, Suite 100, Phoenix, AZ 85012; tel. 602/277–7997; Robert Loncon, Administrator

SurgiCenter, 1040 East McDowell Road, Phoenix, AZ 85006; tel. 602/258–1521; FAX. 602/340–0889; Sharon Shafer, RN, Administrator

Surginet of Arizona, Ltd., 7725 North 43rd Avenue, Suite 510, Phoenix, AZ 85051; tel. 602/931–9400; FAX. 602/930–9884; Yvonne M. Winfrey, Administrator

Swagel Wootton Eye Center, 220 South 63rd Street, Mesa, AZ 85206; tel. 602/641–3937; FAX. 602/924–5096; S. Joyce Graham

T.A.S.I. Surgery Center, 5585 North Oracle Road, Suite B, Tucson, AZ 85704; tel. 602/293–4730; John A. Pierce, M.D., Medical Director

Tempe Surgical Center, Inc., 2000 East Southern Avenue, Suite 106, Tempe, AZ 85282; tel. 602/838–9313; Richard F. Pavese, M.D.

Thunderbird Samaritan Surgicenter, 5555 B West Thunderbird Road, Glendale, AZ 85306–4622; tel. 602/588–5475; FAX. 602/588–5472; Diane Elmore, RN, Administrator

Valley Outpatient Surgery Center, 160 West University Drive, Mesa, AZ 85201; tel. 602/835–7373; FAX. 602/969–7981; Craig R. Cassidy, D.O., President

Vital Sight ASC, dba Eye Institute of Southern Arizona, 5632 East Fifth Street, Tucson, AZ 85711; tel. 520/790–8888; FAX. 520/790–1427; Clara Dupnik

Warner Medical Park Outpatient Surgery, Inc., 604 West Warner Road, Building A, Chandler, AZ 85224; tel. 602/899–2571; FAX. 602/899–4263; Robert Thunberg, Managing Director

White Mountain Ambulatory Surgery Center, 2650 East Show Low Lake Road, Suite Two, Show Low, AZ 85901; tel. 602/537–4240; William J. Waldo

Yuma Outpatient Surgery Center, L.P., 2475 Avenue A, Suite B, Yuma, AZ 85364; tel. 520/726–6910; FAX. 520/726–7423; Cairne–Lee Larson, RN, Facility Manager

ARKANSAS

Ambulatory Surgical Center, Inc., d/b/a Fort Smith Surgi–Center, 7306A Rogers Avenue, Fort Smith, AR 72903; tel. 501/452–7333; Reem Zofari, Administrator

Arkansas Endoscopy Center, P.A., 9501 Lile Drive, Suite 100, Little Rock, AR 72205; tel. 501/224–9100; FAX. 501/224–0420; Ronald D. Hardin, M.D.

Arkansas Otolaryngology Ambulatory Surgery Center, 1200 Medical Towers Building, 9601 Lile Drive, Little Rock, AR 72205; tel. 501/227–5050; Joseph R. Phillips, RN, Administrator

Arkansas Surgery and Endoscopy Center, 4800 Hazel Street, Pine Bluff, AR 71603; tel. 870/536–4800; FAX. 870/536–1609; Sied Samad, M.D., FACP, President

Arkansas Surgery Center, 10 Hospital Circle, Batesville, AR 72501; tel. 870/793–4040; FAX. 870/793–5649; Ronald L. Lowery, M.D., Administrator

Arkansas Surgery Center of Fayetteville, 3873 North Parkview Drive, Suite One, Fayetteville, AR 72703; tel. 501/582–3200; FAX. 501/582–1338; Debra Sexton, Administrator

BEC Surgery Center, One Mercy Lane, Suite 201, P.O. Box 6409, Hot Springs, AR 71902; tel. 501/623–0755; Terry D. Brown

Boozman–Hof Eye Surgery and Laser Center, 3737 West Walnut Street, P.O. Box 1353, Rogers, AR 72757–1353; tel. 501/636–7506; Donna R. Acord, Director

Cooper Clinic Ambulatory Surgery Center, 6801 Rogers Avenue, P.O. Box 3528, Fort Smith, AR 72903; tel. 501/452–2077; FAX. 501/484–4611; Jerry Stewart, M.D., Administrator

Dempsey–McKee, Inc., d/b/a McKee Outpatient Surgery Center, 601 East Matthews, Jonesboro, AR 72401; tel. 501/935–6396; FAX. 501/935–4063; Terry V. DePriest, Administrator

Doctors Surgery Center, 303 West Polk Street, Suite B, West Memphis, AR 72301; tel. 501/732–2100; Doris Davis, Administrator

Endoscopy Center of Hot Springs, 151 McGowan Court, Hot Springs, AR 71913; tel. 501/623–4101; FAX. 501/623–0103; Rebecca Bates, Administrator

H. Lewis Pearson Eye Institute, 3211 Surger Hill Road, Texarkana, AR 71854–9265; tel. 501/772–4440; FAX. 501/772–7190; James Loomis, Comptroller

Holt–Krock Clinic, 1500 Dodson Avenue, Fort Smith, AR 72901; tel. 501/788–4000; Harold H. Mings, M.D., Chief Executive Officer

Hot Springs Outpatient Surgery, 100 Ridgeway Boulevard, Suite Seven, Hot Springs, AR 71901; tel. 501/624–4464; FAX. 501/624–4602; Robert V. Borg, M.D., Administrator

James Trice, M.D., P.A., d/b/a Digestive Disease Center, 7005 South Hazel Street, Pine Bluff, AR 71603; tel. 870/536–3070; FAX. 870/536–3171; Louis Trice, Administrator

Little Rock Diagnostic Clinic ASC, 10001 Lile Drive, Little Rock, AR 72205; tel. 501/227–8000; Roger J. St. Onge, Administrator

Little Rock Pain Clinic, Two Lile Court, Suite 100, Little Rock, AR 72205; tel. 501/224–7246; FAX. 501/224–7644; Virginia Johnson, Administrator

Little Rock Surgery Center, 8820 Knoedl Court, Little Rock, AR 72205; tel. 501/224–6767; FAX. 501/224–8203; Jerri Herron, Administrator

Lowery Medical/Surgical Eye Center, P.A., 105 Central Avenue, Searcy, AR 72143; tel. 501/268–7154; FAX. 501/268–9071; Benjamin R. Lowery, M.D., Administrator

North Hills Gastroenterology Endoscopy Center, Inc., 3344 North Futrall Drive, Fayetteville, AR 72703; tel. 501/582–7280; FAX. 510/582–7279; William C. Martin, M.D.

Northeast Arkansas Surgery Center, Inc., 505 East Matthews, Suite 103, Jonesboro, AR 72401; tel. 501/972–1723; FAX. 501/972–5941; Carol D. Crawford, Administrator

Ozark Eye Center, 360 Highway Five North, Mountain Home, AR 72653; tel. 501/425–2277; Rick Galkoski, Administrator

Physicians Day Surgery Center, 3805 West 28th, Pine Bluff, AR 71603; tel. 501/536–4100; FAX. 501/536–3100; Joan Fletcher, Administrator

Russellville Surgery Center, L.L.C., 2205 West Main Street, P.O. Box 2654, Russellville, AR 72801; tel. 501/890–2654; FAX. 501/890–5101; James Kennedy, Administrator

South Arkansas Surgery Center, 4310 South Mulberry, Pine Bluff, AR 71603; tel. 501/535–5719; Tammy L. Studdard, Administrator

The Center for Day Surgery, 4200 Jenny Lind, Suite A, Fort Smith, AR 72901; tel. 501/648–9496; Monte Wilson, Administrator

The Gastro–Intestinal Center, 405 North University, Little Rock, AR 72205; tel. 501/663–1074; James G. Dunlap, Administrator

The Physicians Surgery Center of Arkansas, Inc., d/b/a Physicians Surgery Center, 1024 North University Avenue, Little Rock, AR 72207; tel. 501/663–0158; FAX. 501/663–4652; Martha Plant, Administrator

CALIFORNIA

Advanced Surgery Center, 5771 North Fresno Street, Suite 101, Fresno, CA 93710; tel. 209/448–9900; David B. Singh, Administrator

Aesthetic Facial Surgery Center of Menlo Park, 2200 Sand Hill Road, Suite 130, Menlo Park, CA 94025; tel. 415/854–6444; Dr. Harry Mittelman

Aestheticare Outpatient Surgery Center, 30260 Rancho Viejo Road, San Juan Capital, CA 92675; tel. 949/661–1700; FAX. 949/661–4321; Ronald E. Moser, M.D.

Ambulatory Surgical Center of Chico, 1950 East 20th Street, Suite 102, Chico, CA 95928; tel. 916/343–1674; Robert G. Basinger, D.P.M.

Ambulatory Surgical Center of Southern California, Gastroenterology Diagnostic Center, 880 South Atlantic Boulevard G–10, Monterey Park, CA 91754; tel. 213/483–9080; Zelman Weingaren, M.D.

Ambulatory Surgical Center of the Zeiter Eye, 117 North San Joaquin Street, Stockton, CA 95202; tel. 209/466–5566; FAX. 209/466–0535; Donna M. Tschirky

Ambulatory Surgical Center, Inc., 14400 Bear Valley Road, Suite 201, Victorville, CA 92392; tel. 760/951–5162; FAX. 818/985–0055; Garey L. Weber, D.P.M., Administrator

Ambulatory Surgical Centers, Inc., 18952 Mac Arthur Boulevard, Suite 102, Irvine, CA 92612; tel. 949–833–3406; FAX. 949–985–0055; Garey L. Weber, D.P.M., Administrator

Anaheim Surgical Center, 1324 South Euclid Street, Anaheim, CA 92802; tel. 714/533–9880; FAX. 714/533–1802; Debra Berntsen, RN, Charge Nurse

Antelope Valley Surgery Center, 44301 North Lorimer Avenue, Lancaster, CA 93534; tel. 805/940–1112; FAX. 805/940–6856; Yolanda Gomez

Apple Valley Surgery Center, 18122 Outer Highway 18, Apple Valley, CA 92307; tel. 760/946–1170; FAX. 760/946–2646; Virginia Budington, Administrator

Arlington Podiatry Surgery Center, 7310 Magnolia Avenue, Riverside, CA 92504; tel. 909/354–8787; FAX. 909/354–0350; James A. De Silva, Administrator

Aspen Outpatient Center, 2750 North Sycamore Drive, Simi Valley, CA 93065; tel. 805/583–5923; FAX. 805/583–0952; Jay Evans, Administrator

Associates Outpatient Surgery Center, 2128 Eureka Way, Redding, CA 96001; tel. 916/246–9737; FAX. 916/246–4052; Jesse M. Kramer, M.D., Administrator

Atherton Plastic Surgery Center, 3351 El Camino Real, Suite 201, Atherton, CA 94027; tel. 415/363–0300; FAX. 415/363–0302; David Apfelberg

Auburn Surgery Center, 3123 Professional Drive, Suite 100, Auburn, CA 95603; tel. 916/888–8899; FAX. 916/888–1464; Charles Smith, Administrator

Bakersfield Endoscopy Center, 1902 B Street, Bakersfield, CA 93301; tel. 805/327–4455; Ramesh Gupta, M.D., Medical Director

Bakersfield Surgery Center, 2120 19th Street, Bakersfield, CA 93301; tel. 661/323–2020; FAX. 661/323–6552; Sheryl Wiggins, Administrator

Beverly Hills Ambulatory Surgery Center, Inc., 9201 Sunset Boulevard, Suite 405, Los Angeles, CA 90069; tel. 310/887–1730; Sandra Cericola, Administrator

Beverly Hills Outpatient Surgery Center, 250 North Robertson Boulevard, Suite 104, Los Angeles, CA 90211; tel. 310/273–9255; FAX. 310/273–6167; Peter Golden, M.D., Medical Director

Beverly Surgical Center, 105 West Beverly Boulevard, Montebello, CA 90640–4375; tel. 213/728–5400; FAX. 213/887–0058; James G. Ovieda, Administrator

Blackhawk Surgery Center, Inc., 4165 Blackhawk Plaza Circle, Suite 195, Danville, CA 94506; tel. 510/736–7881; Molly Healy, Administrator

Bolsa Out–Patient Surgery Center, 10362 Bolsa Avenue, Westminster, CA 92683; tel. 714/775–5690; FAX. 714/775–7405; CO D. L. PHAM, FACOG, M.D., Medical Director

Bonaventure Surgery Center, 221 North Jackson Avenue, San Jose, CA 95116; tel. 408/729–2848; FAX. 408/729–2880; Virginia Field, RN, M.B.A., Director

Brawley Endoscopy and Surgery Center, 205 West Legion Road, Brawley, CA 92227; tel. 619/351–3655; FAX. 619/351–3675; Mahomed Suliman, M.D., Administrator

Brockton Surgical Center, 5905 Brockton Avenue, Suite B, Riverside, CA 92506; tel. 909/686–5373; FAX. 909/778–9064; Michael N. Durrant, D.P.M., M.P.H.

Bruce A. Kaplan, M.D., 39000 Bob Hope Drive, Wright Building, Suite 209, Rancho Mirage, CA 92270; tel. 619/346–5603; FAX. 619/346–5604; Jessie Schumaker

California Eye Clinic, 3747 Sunset Lane, Suite A, Antioch, CA 94509; tel. 510/754–2300; Jean Kemp, Administrator

Camden Surgery Center of Beverly Hills, 414 North. Camden Drive, Suite 800, Beverly Hills, CA 90210; tel. 310/859–3991; FAX. 310/859–7126; Yasmin Sibulo, Administrator

Capistrano Surgicenter, Inc., 30280 Rancho Viejo Road, San Juan Capi, CA 92675; tel. 714/248–5757; FAX. 714/248–9339; Jeffrey A. Klein, President

Cardiac Surgery Mercy Medical Center, 2626 Edith Avenue # D, Redding, CA 96001; tel. 530/243–2626; Edward W. Pottmeyer, M.D.

Cedars–Sinai, Saint John's, Daniel Freeman SurgiCenter, 9675 Brighton Way, Suite 100, Beverly Hills, CA 90210; tel. 310/205–6080; FAX. 310/205–6090; Diane Tharp, Program Coordinator

Center for Ambulatory Medicine and Surgery, 111 East Noble Avenue, Visalia, CA 93277; tel. 209/739–8383; FAX. 209/739–7929; James J. Shea, M.D., Administrator

Central Coast Surgery Center, 1941 Johnson Avenue, Suite 103, San Luis Obis, CA 93406; tel. 805/546–9999; FAX. 804/546–8904; Helen Swanagon, Nurse Administrator

Channel Islands Surgicenter, 2300 Wankel Way, Oxnard, CA 93030; tel. 805/485–1908; FAX. 805/485–5767; Mary K. Fish, Administrator

Children's Surgery Center, 744 Fifty–Second Street, Oakland, CA 94609; tel. 510/428–3133; FAX. 510/450–5606; Terry Hawes, Administrator

Columbia Arcadia Outpatient Surgery, Inc., 614 West Duarte Road, Arcadia, CA 91006; tel. 818/445–4714; Sandy Lazare, Administrator

Columbia Los Gatos Surgical Center, 15195 National Avenue, Los Gatos, CA 95032; tel. 408/356–0454; FAX. 408/358–3924; Martha Ponce, Administrator

Columbia North Coast Surgery Center, 3903 Waring Road, Oceanside, CA 92056; tel. 619/940–0997; FAX. 619/940–0407; Donna Danley, Administrator

Columbia Saddleback Valley Outpatient Surgery, 24302 Paseo De Valencia, Laguna Hills, CA 92653; tel. 714/472–0244; FAX. 714/472–0380; Brian FitzGerald, Administrator

Columbia Sereno Surgery Center, 14601 South Bascom Avenue, Suite 100, Los Gatos, CA 95032–2043; tel. 408/358–2727; FAX. 408/358–2950; Martha Ponce, Administrator

Columbia Southwest Surgical Clinic, Inc., 4201 Torrance Boulevard, Suite 240, Torrance, CA 90503; tel. 310/540–7803; FAX. 310/316–3903; Otto Munchow, M.D., Director

Columbia Surgicenter of South Bay, 23500 Madison Street, Torrance, CA 90505; tel. 310/539–5120; Debra Saxton

Columbia West Hills Surgical Center, 7240 Medical Center Drive, West Hills, CA 91307; tel. 818/226–6170; Carol Valeri, RN, Administrator

Columbia/Woodward Park Surgicenter, 7055 North Fresno Street, Suite 100, Fresno, CA 93720; tel. 209/449–9977; FAX. 209/449–9350; Lori Ruffner, RN, Administrator

Community Surgery Centre, 17190 Bernado Center Drive, Suite 100, San Diego, CA 92128; tel. 619/675–3270; FAX. 619/675–3260; Regina S. Boore, B.S.N., M.S.

Corona Del Mar Plastic Surgery, 1101 Bayside Drive, Suite 100, Corona Del Ma, CA 92625; tel. 714/644–5000; W. Graham Wood, M.D.

Crown Valley Surgicenter, 26921 Crown Valley Parkway, Suite 110, Mission Viejo, CA 92691; tel. 714/348–7252; FAX. 714/348–7246; Maurice Chammas, M.D., Administrator

Cypress Outpatient Surgical Center, Inc., 1665 Dominican Way, Suite 120, Santa Cruz, CA 95065; tel. 408/476–6943; FAX. 408/476–1473; Sandra Warren, Administrator

Cypress Surgery Center, 842 South Akers Road, Visalia, CA 93277; tel. 209/740–4094; FAX. 209/740–4100; Jack K. Waller

Del Rey Surgery Center, 4640 Admiralty Way, Suite 1020, Marina Del Re, CA 90292; tel. 310/305–7570; Lee Estes, Administrator

Desert Surgery Center, 1180 North Palm Canyon, Palm Springs, CA 92262; tel. 760/320–7600; FAX. 760/320–1694; Rosemary Combs, Executive Director

Digestive Disease Center, 24411 Health Center Drive, Suite 450, Laguna Hills, CA 92653; tel. 714/586–9386; FAX. 714/586–0864; Crisynda Buss, RN

Doctors Surgery Center of Whittier, 8135 South Painter Avenue, Suite 103, Whittier, CA 90602; tel. 310/945–8961; FAX. 310/698–3578; Veronica Coughenour, RN

Doctors Surgical Center, Inc., 9461 Grindlay Street, Suite 102, Cypress, CA 90630; tel. 714/995–3001; R. Wayne Ives, Administrator

Doctors' Surgery Center, 1441 Liberty Street, Suite 104, Redding, CA 96001; tel. 916/244–6300; FAX. 916/246–2051; Joy Schultz, Director

Downey Surgery Center, 8555 East Florence Avenue, Downey, CA 90240; tel. 310/923–9784; Marisol Magana, Administrator

E. N. T. Facial Surgery Center, 1351 East Spruce, Fresno, CA 93720; tel. 209/432–3724; FAX. 209/432–8579; JoAnn LoForti, RN, Division of Nursing

East Bay Medical Surgical Center, 20998 Redwood Road, Castro Valley, CA 94546; tel. 510/538–2828; FAX. 510/538–2508; Yoshitsugu Teramoto, M.D., Administrator

El Camino Surgery Center, 2480 Grant Road, Mountain View, CA 94040–4300; tel. 650/961–1200; FAX. 650/960–7041; Nancy Kessler

El Mirador Surgical Center, 1180 North Indian Canyon Drive, Palm Springs, CA 92263; tel. 619/416–4600; Marilyn M. Perkins, Nurse Administrator

Endoscopy Center of Chula Vista, 681 Third Avenue, Suite B, Chula Vista, CA 91910; tel. 619/425–2150; Robert Penner, M.D., Administrator

Endoscopy Center of Southern California, 2336 Santa Monica Boulevard, Suite 204, Santa Monica, CA 90404; tel. 310/453–4477; FAX. 310/453–4811; Parviz D. Afshani

Endoscopy Center of the Central Coast, 77 Casa Street, Suite 106, San Luis Obis, CA 93405; tel. 805/541–1021; FAX. 805/541–3142; Penny Chamousis, Administrator

Escondido Surgery Center, 343 East Second Avenue, Escondido, CA 92025; tel. 619/480–6606; FAX. 619/480–6671; Marvin W. Levenson, M.D., Managing Medical Director

Eye Center of Northern California Surgicenter, 6500 Fairmount Avenue, Suite Two, El Cerrito, CA 94530; tel. 510/525–2600; FAX. 510/524–1887; William Ellis

Eye Life Institute, 6283 Clark Road, Suite Seven, Paradise, CA 95969; tel. 916/877–2020; FAX. 916/877–4641; Almary Hivale, RN, Administrator

Eye Surgery Center of Southern California, Inc./Med. Group, 2023 West Vista Way, Suite E, Vista, CA 92083; tel. 619/941–8152; FAX. 619/726–4822; Regg V. Antle, M.D., Medical Director

Eye Surgery Center of the Desert, 39700 Bob Hope Drive, Suite 111, Rancho Mirage, CA 92270; tel. 619/340–3937; FAX. 619/340–1940; Timothy T. Milauskas, Administrator

Feather River Surgery Center, 370 Del Norte Avenue, Yuba City, CA 95991; tel. 916/751–4800; FAX. 916/751–4884; Elizabeth LaBouyer, RN, CNOR, Perioperative Coordinator

Fig Garden Surgi–Med Center, 1332 West Herndon Avenue # 101, Fresno, CA 93711–0431; tel. 559/439–2040

Foothill Ambulatory Surgery Center, 1030 East Foothill Boulevard, Suite 101B, Upland, CA 91786; tel. 909/981–5859; FAX. 909/981–8293; Montra M. Kanok, M.D.

Fort Sutter Surgery Center, 2801 K Street, Suite 525, Sacramento, CA 95816; tel. 916/733–5017; FAX. 916/733–8738; Bill Davis, Administrator

Four Thirty–Six North Bedford Surgicenter, 436 North Bedford, Suite 101, Beverly Hills, CA 90210; tel. 310/860–0645; FAX. 310/278–1791; Kay Zacharski, RN, Director of Nursing

Fritch Eye Care Medical Center, 2525 Eye Street, Suite A and B, Bakersfield, CA 93301; tel. 805/327–8511; FAX. 805/327–9809; Charles D. Fritch, M.D.

Frost Street Outpatient Surgical Center, LP, 8008 Frost Street, Suite 200, San Diego, CA 92123; tel. 619/576–8320; FAX. 619/576–8568; John Cashman, Administrator

GastroDiagnostics, A Medical Group, 1140 West La Veta, Suite 550, Orange, CA 92868; tel. 714/835–5100; FAX. 714/835–5567; Stephanie Quinn, Administrator

Glendale Eye Surgery Center, 607 North Central, Suite 103, Glendale, CA 91203; tel. 818/956–1010; FAX. 818/543–6083; James M. McCaffery, M.D.

Glenwood Surgical Center, L.P., 8945 Magnolia Avenue, Suite 200, Riverside, CA 92503; tel. 909/688–7270; Calvin Nash

Golden Empire Surgical Center, 1519 Graces Highway, Suite 103, Delano, CA 93215; tel. 805/721–7900; Lucy Lara

Golden Triangle Surgicenter, 25405 Hancock Avenue, Suite 103, Murrieta, CA 92562; tel. 909/698–4670; FAX. 909/698–4675; Ella Stockstill, Administrator

Golden West Pain Therapy Center, 25405 Hancock Avenue, Suite 110, Murrieta, CA 92562–5964; tel. 909/698–4710; FAX. 909/698–4715; Richard Harris, Administrator

Greater Long Beach Endoscopy Center, 2880 Atlantic Avenue, Suite 180, Long Beach, CA 90806; tel. 562/426–2606; FAX. 562/426–5866; Andrea Campbell, Business Office Manager

Greater Sacramento Surgery Center, 2288 Auburn Boulevard, Suite 201, Sacramento, CA 95821; tel. 916/929–7229; FAX. 916/929–2590; Susan Brunone, MHS, Administrator

Grossmont Plaza Surgery Center, 5525 Grossmont Center Drive, La Mesa, CA 91942; tel. 619/644–4561; Lois Hoke, Administrator

Grossmont Surgery Center, 8881 Fletcher Parkway, Suite 100, La Mesa, CA 91942; tel. 619/698–0930; FAX. 619/698–3093; Mary Ribulotta, Administrator

Halcyon Laser and Surgery Center, Inc., 303 South Halcyon Road, Arroyo Grande, CA 93420; tel. 805/489–8254; FAX. 805/474–1997; Sara Pazell, Administrator

Harbor–UCLA Medical Foundation, Inc., Ambulatory Surgery Center, 21840 South Normandie Avenue, Suite 700, Torrance, CA 90502; tel. 310/222–5189; Lee Scher, RN, Administrator

HealthSouth Center for Surgery of Encinitas, 477 North El Camino Real, Suite C–100, Encinitas, CA 92024; tel. 619/942–8800; FAX. 619/942–0106; John Cashman, Co–Administrator

HealthSouth Forest Surgery Center, 2110 Forest Avenue, San Jose, CA 95128; tel. 408/297–3432; FAX. 408/298–3338; Helen Maloney, RN, Administrator

HealthSouth South Bay Ambulatory Surgical Center, 251 Landis Street, Chula Vista, CA 91910; tel. 619/585–1020; FAX. 619/585–0247; Arthur E. Casey, Administrator

HealthSouth Surgery Center of San Luis Obispo, 1304–C Ella Street, San Luis Obis, CA 93401; tel. 805/544–7874; FAX. 805/544–6057; Kim Heath, RN, B.S.N., MBA

HealthSouth Surgery Center–J Street, 3810 J Street, Sacramento, CA 95816; tel. 916/929–9431; FAX. 916/929–0132; Charlene Nakayama, Administrator

HealthSouth Surgery Center–Scripps, 75 Scripps Drive, Sacramento, CA 95825; tel. 916/929–9431; FAX. 916/929–0132; Charlene Nakayama, Administrator

HealthSouth Surgery Center–Solano, 991 Nut Tree Road, Suite 100, Vacaville, CA 95687; tel. 707/447–5400; FAX. 707/447–2356; Bill Davis, Administrator

Heart Institute of the Desert, 39–600 Bob Hope Drive, Rancho Mirage, CA 92270; tel. 619/324–3278; Jack J. Sternlieb, Administrator

Hemet Cataract Surgery Clinic, 162 North Santa Fe, Hemet, CA 92343; tel. 909/929–3200; FAX. 909/929–8124; Stephen K. Schaller, M.D., Administrator

Hemet Endoscopy Center, 2390 East Florida Avenue, Suite 101, Hemet, CA 92544; tel. 909/652–2252; FAX. 909/925–9252; Milan S. Chakrabarty, M.D.

Hemet Healthcare Surgicenter, 301 North San Jacinto Avenue, Hemet, CA 92543; tel. 909/765–1717; FAX. 909/765–1716; Kali Chaudhuri, M.D.

Hesperia Podiatry Surgery Center, 14661 Main Street, Hesperia, CA 92345; tel. 619/244–0222; FAX. 619/244–1242; William S. Beal

Hi–Desert Surgery Center, 18002 Outer Highway 18, Apple Valley, CA 92307; tel. 619/242–5505; FAX. 619/242–3502; Venkat R. Vangala, M.D.

High Desert Endoscopy, 18523 Corwin Road, Suite H2, Apple Valley, CA 92307; tel. 619/242–3000; FAX. 619/262–1802; Raman S. Poola, M.D., Administrator

Hospitality Surgery Center, 275 West Hospitality Lane, Suite 106, San Bernardin, CA 92408; tel. 909/885–0180; Milton A. Miller, M.D., Administrator

Huntington Outpatient Surgery Center, 797 South Fair Oaks Avenue, Pasadena, CA 91105; tel. 626/397–3173; FAX. 626/397–8003; Sandra Bidlack, Administrator

Imperial Valley Surgery Center, 608 G Street, Brawley, CA 92227; tel. 619/344–1101; FAX. 619/344–4985; Vida C. Baron, M.D., Administrator

Inland Endoscopy Center, Inc., d/b/a Mountain View Surgery Center, 10408 Industrial Circle, Redlands, CA 92374; tel. 909/796–0363; FAX. 909/796–0614; Khushal Stanisai

Inland Eye Surgicenter, 361 North San Jacinto, Hemet, CA 92543; tel. 909/652–4343; R. Michael Duffin, M.D., Medical Director

Inland Surgery Center, 1620 Laurel Avenue, Redlands, CA 92373; tel. 909/793–4701; FAX. 909/792–6397; Rodger Slininger, Facility Administrator

Irvine Multi–Specialty Surgical Care, 4900 Barranca Parkway, Suite 104, Irvine, CA 92604–8603; tel. 714/726–0677; FAX. 714/726–0678; Carol R. Stevenson, RN, Administrator

John Muir/Mt. Diablo HealthCare System, Inc., d/b/a Diablo Valley Surgery Center, 2222 East Street, Suite 200, Concord, CA 94520; tel. 510/671–2222; FAX. 510/671–2672; Virginia Goodrich, Administrator

Kaiser Ambulatory Surgical Center, 2025 Morse Avenue, Sacramento, CA 95825; tel. 916/973–7675; FAX. 916/973–7786; Richard R. Stading, RN, MSHA., A.S.C. Manager

Kaiser Ambulatory Surgical Center, 10725 International Drive, Rancho Cordov, CA 95670; tel. 916/631–2000; FAX. 916/631–2013; Steven Metzger, RN, Manager

Kaiser Permanente Medical Facility–Stockton, 7373 West Lane, Stockton, CA 95210; tel. 209/476–3300; Jose R. Rivera, Administrator

La Jolla Gastroenterology Medical Group, Inc., Endoscopy Center, 9850 Genesee Avenue, Suite 980, La Jolla, CA 92037; tel. 619/453–5200; FAX. 619/453–5753; Otto T. Nebel, M.D., Medical Director

La Veta Surgical Center, 725 West La Veta, Suite 270, Orange, CA 92868; tel. 714/744–0900; FAX. 714/744–0283; Joyce Hall, Administrator

Laser and Skin Surgery Center of La Jolla, 9850 Genesee Avenue, Suite 480, La Jolla, CA 92037; tel. 619/558–2424; Angela Richberg, RN

Laser Surgery Center, LTD., 2021 Ygnacio Valley Road, Building H–102, Walnut Creek, CA 94598; tel. 510/944–9400; FAX. 510/947–2160; Lori Fried, Administrator

Lassen Surgery Center, 103 Fair Drive, P.O. Box 1150, Susanville, CA 96130; tel. 530/257–7772; FAX. 530/257–2939; Shannon Viersla, Medical Staff Secretary

Lodi Outpatient Surgical Center, 521 South Ham Lane, Suite F, Lodi, CA 95242; tel. 209/333–0905; FAX. 209/333–0219; Marklin E. Brown, Administrator

Loma Linda Foot and Ankle Center, Ambulatory Surgical Center, 11332 Mountain View Avenue, Suite A, Loma Linda, CA 92354; tel. 909/796–3707; FAX. 909/796–3709; Sheldon Collis, D.P.M., Administrator

Los Robles Surgicenter, 2190 Lynn Road, Suite 100, Thousand Oaks, CA 91360; tel. 805/497–3737; FAX. 805/373–8878; Le Anne Schai, Administrative Director

M/S Surgery Center, 3510 Martin Luther King Boulevard, Lynwood, CA 90262; tel. 310/635–7550; FAX. 310/603–8749; John H. Shammas, M.D., Medical Director

Madera Ambulatory Endoscopy Center, 1015 West Yosemite Avenue, Suite 101, Madera, CA 93637; tel. 209/673–4000; FAX. 209/673–1430; Naeem M. Akhtar, M.D.

Madison Park Surgery and Laser Center, 3445 Pacific Coast Highway, Suite 250, Torrance, CA 90505; tel. 310/530–2900; FAX. 310/891–0367; Mark Sandoro

Magnolia Outpatient Surgery Center, 14571 Magnolia Street, Suite 107, Westminster, CA 92683; tel. 714/898–6448; FAX. 714/893–1681; Cynthia Begg, Administrator

Magnolia Plastic Surgery Center, 10694 Magnolia Avenue, Riverside, CA 92505; tel. 909/358–1445; FAX. 909/688–2803; Alexander Carli

Marin Ophthalmic Surgery Center, 901 E Street, Suite 270, San Rafael, CA 94901; tel. 415/454–2112; FAX. 415/454–6542; Audrey M. DeMars, Administrator

Mariners Bay Surgical Medical Center, 318 South Lincoln Boulevard, Suite 100, Venice, CA 90291; tel. 310/314–2191; FAX. 310/392–8020; Gregory Panos II, Administrator

Martel Eye Surgical Center, 11216 Trinity River, Suite G, Rancho Cordov, CA 95670; tel. 916/635–6161; FAX. 916/635–5145; Joseph Martel, M.D.

McHenry Surgery Center, 1524 McHenry Street, Suite 240, Modesto, CA 95350; tel. 209/576–2900; FAX. 209/575–5815; Syd Fuentes, RN, Director

Medical Arts Ambulatory Surgery Center, 205 South West Street, Suite B, Visalia, CA 93291; tel. 209/625–9601; FAX. 209/625–3124; Thomas F. Mitts, M.D., Administrator

Medical Plaza Orthopedic Surgery Center, 1301 20th Street, Suite 140, Santa Monica, CA 90404; tel. 310/315–0333; FAX. 310/315–0341; Carolyn A. Hankinson, RN, Director, Nursing

Merced Ambulatory Endoscopy Center, 750 West Olive Avenue, Suite 107A, Merced, CA 95348; tel. 209/384–3116; FAX. 209–384–0878; Monika Grasley, Administrator

Mercy Surgical and Diagnostic Center, 3303 North M Street, Merced, CA 95348; tel. 209/384–3533; FAX. 209/383–5047; Lynda Pitts, Administrator

Mission Ambulatory Surgicenter, Ltd., 26730 Crown Valley Parkway, First Floor, Mission Viejo, CA 92691; tel. 714/364–2201; FAX. 714/364–5372; Thomas H. Catlett, Administrator

Mission Valley Surgery Center, 39263 Mission Boulevard, Fremont, CA 94539; tel. 510/796–4500; FAX. 510/796–4573; Sarb S. Hundal, M.D.

Mittleman/Moran Reconstructive Surgery, 2200 Sandhill Road, Suite 130, Menlo Park, CA 94025; tel. 415/854–2000; Mary Lynn Moran, M.D., Administrator

Modesto Surgery Center, Inc., 400 East Orangeburg Avenue, Suite One, Modesto, CA 95350; tel. 209/526–3000; Dr. Greg Teslue, Administrator

Monterey Bay Endoscopy Center, 833 Cass Street, Suite B, Monterey, CA 93940; tel. 408/375–3598; FAX. 408/375–1478; James Farrow, Administrator

Monterey Peninsula Surgery Center, Inc., 966 Cass Street, Suite 210, Monterey, CA 93940; tel. 408/372–2169; FAX. 408/372–6323; William McAfee, M.D., Chairman

Moreno Valley Ambulatory Surgery Center, 24384 Sunnymead Boulevard, Moreno Valley, CA 92388; tel. 714/247–8080; FAX. 714/247–9381; John E. Bohn, Administrator

Napa Surgery Center, 3444 Valle Verde Drive, Napa, CA 94558; tel. 707/252–9660; Eric Grigsby, M.D., Medical Director

Newport Beach Orange Coast Endoscopy Center, 1525 Superior Avenue, Suite 114, Newport Beach, CA 92663; tel. 714/646–6999; FAX. 714/646–9699; Donald Abraham

Newport Beach Surgery Center, 361 Hospital Road, Suite 124, Newport Beach, CA 92663; tel. 714/631–0988; FAX. 714/631–2036; Eric Reints, Administrator

Newport Surgery Institute, 360 San Miguel Drive, Suite 406, Newport Beach, CA 92660; tel. 714/759–0995; Linda Shelman, Office Manager

North Anaheim Surgicenter, 1154 North Euclid, Anaheim, CA 92801; tel. 714/635–6272; FAX. 714/635–0943; Monica Briton, Administrator

North County Outpatient Surgery Center, 1101 Las Tablas Road, P.O. Box 147, Templeton, CA 93465; tel. 805/434–1333; FAX. 805/434–3171; Carolyn Lash, RN, Surgery Center Manager

Northern California Kidney Stone Center, 15195 National Avenue, Suite 204, Los Gatos, CA 95032; tel. 408/358–2111; FAX. 408/356–2359; John Kersten Kraft, Medical Director

Northridge maxillofacial Surgery Center, 18546 Roscoe Boulevard, Suite 125, Northridge, CA 91324; tel. 818/349–8890; FAX. 818/349–1532; Robert G. Hale, D.D.S., Administrator

Northridge Surgery Center, 8327 Reseda Boulevard, Northridge, CA 91324; tel. 818/993–3131; FAX. 818/993–3347; Robert Vassey, Administrator

Optima Ophthalmic Medical Associates, Inc., 1237 B Street, Hayward, CA 94541–2977; tel. 510/886–3937; FAX. 510/886–4465; Nora J. McQuinn, Administrative Director

Orange County Institute of Gastroenterology and Endoscopy, 26732 Crown Valley Parkway, Suite 241, Mission Viejo, CA 92691; tel. 949/364–2611; FAX. 949–364–0226; Ahmad M. Shaban, M.D., Medical Director

Orange County Litho Center, Inc., 12555 Garden Grove Boulevard, Suite 200, Garden Grove, CA 92843; tel. 714/530–6000; FAX. 714/534–7061; Guy A. Biagiotti, M.D.

Orange Surgical Services, 302 West La Veta Avenue, Suite 100, Orange, CA 92866; tel. 714/771–3432; FAX. 714/741–7606; Elizabeth E. Grant, M.S.

Out–Patient Surgery Center, 17752 Beach Boulevard, Huntington Beach, CA 92647; tel. 714/842–1426; FAX. 714/847–1503; Madelyn Tinkler, Administrator

Outpatient Care Surgery Center South, 5225 Kearny Villa Way, Suite 110, San Diego, CA 92123; tel. 619/278–1611; FAX. 619/278–5853; Ronald Gertsch, M.D.

Pacific Dental Surgery Center, 820 34th Street, Suite 201, Bakersfield, CA 93301; tel. 805/327–7878; Charles Nicholson III, Administrator

Pacific Eye Institute, 555 North 13th Avenue, Upland, CA 91786; tel. 909/982–8846; FAX. 909/949–3967; Robert Fabricant, M.D., FACS, Medical Director

Pacific Hills Surgery Center, Inc., 24022 Calle De La Plata, Suite 180, Laguna Hills, CA 92653; tel. 714/951–9470; FAX. 714/951–9478; Norman D. Peterson, M.D., Medical Director

Pacific Surgicenter, Inc., 1301 20th Street, Suite 470, Santa Monica, CA 90404; tel. 310/315–0222; FAX. 310/828–8852; Jocelyne Rosenthal, RN, Administrator

Palm Desert Ambulatory Surgery Center, 73–345 Highway 111, Palm Desert, CA 92260; tel. 619/346–4780; FAX. 619/340–4650; S. C. Shah, M.D., Administrator

Paul L. Archambeau, M.D., Inc., Ambulatory Surgery Center, 380 Tesconi Court, Santa Rosa, CA 95401; tel. 707/544–3375; FAX. 707/544–0808; Paul L. Archambeau, M.D., Administrator

Petaluma Surgicenter, 1400 Professional Drive, Suite 102, Petaluma, CA 94954; tel. 707/763–9325; FAX. 707/769–0751; Ronald M. La Vigna, D.P.M.

Section C

PFC Surgicenter, 3445 Pacific Court Highway, Suite 110, Torrance, CA 90505; tel. 213/539–9100; Rifaat Salem, M.D., Ph.D.

Physician's Surgery Center, 901 Campus Drive, Suite 102, Daly City, CA 94015; tel. 415/991–2000; FAX. 415/755–8638; Kathleen O'Riordan

Physicians Plaza Surgical Center, 6000 Physicians Boulevard, Bakersfield, CA 93301; tel. 805/322–4744; FAX. 805/322–2938; Michael G. Clark, Administrator

Physicians Resource Group, d/b/a Barr Eye Surgery Center, 1805 North California Street, Stockton, CA 95204; tel. 209/948–3241; FAX. 209/948–9321; Susan Ford, Administrator

Plastic and Reconstructive Surgery Center, 1387 Santa Rita Road, Pleasanton, CA 94566; tel. 510/462–3700; FAX. 510/462–4681; Ronald Iverson, Administrator

Plastic Surgery Center, 1515 El Camino Real, Palo Alto, CA 94304; tel. 415/322–2723; FAX. 415/322–3260; Julia Solinger, Administrator

Plaza Surgical Center, Inc., 168 North Brent Street, Suite 403B, Ventura, CA 93003; tel. 805/643–5438; FAX. 805/643–1625; Dale P. Armstrong, M.D.

Podiatric Surgery Center, 255 North Gilbert, Suite B, Hemet, CA 92543; tel. 909/925–2186; FAX. 909/925–4947; Robert Drake, D.P.M., Administrator

Point Loma Surgical Center, 3434 Midway Drive, Suite 1006, San Diego, CA 92110; tel. 619/223–0910; David M. Kupfer, M.D., Medical Director

Porterville Surgical Center, 577 West Putnam Avenue, Porterville, CA 93257; tel. 209/788–6400; Lucy Lara, Administrator

Premier Endoscopy Center of the Desert, 1100 North Palm Canyon Drive, Suite 209, Palm Springs, CA 92262; tel. 619/776–7580; Phillip R. Roy, Administrator

Premier Surgery of Palm Desert, 73–180 El Paseo, Palm Desert, CA 92660; tel. 619/776–7580; Phillip R. Roy

Premiere Surgery Center, Inc., 700 West El Norte Parkway, Escondido, CA 92026; tel. 619/738–7830; FAX. 619/738–7841; R. K. Massengill, M.D., Medical Director

Providence Ambulatory Surgical Center, 1310 West Stewart Drive, Suite 310, Orange, CA 92668; tel. 714/771–6363; FAX. 714/771–0754; Harrell E. Robinson, M.D., President

Providence Holy Cross Surgery Center, 11550 Indian Hills Road, Suite 160, Mission Hills, CA 91345; tel. 818/898–1061; FAX. 818/898–3866; Laura Moore, Administrator

Pueblo Nuevo Aesthetic and Reconstructive Surgery, 1334 Nelson Avenue, Modesto, CA 95350; tel. 209/524–9904; FAX. 209/524–4101; Diane Payne, Administrator

Redlands Dental Surgery Center, 1180 Nevada Street, Suite 100, Redlands, CA 92374; tel. 909/335–0474; Russell O. Seheult, D.D.S.

Richurg Valley Eye Institute Ambulatory Surgical Center, 1680 East Herndon Avenue, Fresno, CA 93710–1234; tel. 209/432–4200; FAX. 209/432–0147; Frederick Richburg, M.D., Administrator

Riverside Community Surgi–Center, 3980 14th Street, Riverside, CA 92501; tel. 909/787–0580; FAX. 909/787–8201; Pat Finley, Administrator

Riverside Eye, Ear, Nose and Throat Institute Surgery Center, 4500 Brockton Avenue, Suite 105, Riverside, CA 92501; tel. 714/788–2788; FAX. 909/788–4374; B. G. Smith, M.D., Medical Director

Riverside Medical Clinic Surgery Center, 7160 Brockton Avenue, Riverside, CA 92506; tel. 714/782–3801; FAX. 909/782–3861; Jan Gough, RN, Office Manager

Rose Eye Cataract Surgical Center, 3325 North Broadway, Los Angeles, CA 90031; tel. 213/221–6121; Michael R. Rose, Administrator

Ross Valley Medical Group, 1350 So Eliseo Drive, Greenbrae, CA 94904; tel. 415/461–1350; Edward J. Boland, Administrator

Sacramento Eye Surgicenter, 3150 J Street, Sacramento, CA 95816; tel. 916/446–2020; Jill Quinn, RN

Sacramento Midtown Endoscopy Center, 3941 J Street, Suite 460, Sacramento, CA 95819; tel. 916/733–6940; FAX. 916/733–6934; Tommy Poirier, M.D.

Saddleback Eye Center, 23161 Moulton Parkway, Laguna Hills, CA 92653; tel. 714/951–4641; FAX. 714/951–4601; Linda Riley, Administrator

Salinas Surgery Center, 955–A Blanco Circle, Salinas, CA 93901; tel. 408/753–5800; FAX. 408/753–5808; Christine Gallagher, Administrator

Samaritan Pain Management Center, 2520 Samaritan Drive, San Jose, CA 95124; tel. 408/356–2731; FAX. 408/356–6366; Ilka E. McAlister, Administrator

San Buenaventura Surgery Center, A Partnership, 3525 Loma Vista Road, Ventura, CA 93003; tel. 805/641–6434; FAX. 805/641–6437; M. P. Bacon, Medical Director

San Diego Endoscopy Center, A Partnership, 4033 Third Avenue, Suite 106, San Diego, CA 92103; tel. 619/291–6064; FAX. 619/291–3078; John D. Goodman, M.D.

San Diego Outpatient Surgical Center, 770 Washington Street, Suite 101, San Diego, CA 92103; tel. 619/299–9530; FAX. 619/296–5386; Carla G. Ramirez, Administrator

San Francisco Surgi Center, 1635 Divisidero Street, Suite 200, San Francisco, CA 94115; tel. 415/346–1218; FAX. 415/346–1819; Peggy Wellman, Administrator

San Gabriel Valley Surgical Center, 1250 South Sunset Avenue, Suite 100, West Covina, CA 91790; tel. 818/960–6623; FAX. 818/962–4341; Susan Raub, Administrator

San Jose Eye Ambulatory Surgicenter, Inc., 4585 Stevens Creek Boulevard, Suite 500, Santa Clara, CA 95051; tel. 408/247–2706; FAX. 408/296–2020; Lolita Ancheta, Clinical Coordinator

San Leandro Surgery Center, 15035 East 14th Street, San Leandro, CA 94578; tel. 510/276–2800; FAX. 510/276–2890; Sheila L. Cook, Executive Director

Sani Eye Surgery Center, 1315 Las Tablas Road, Templeton, CA 93465; tel. 805/434–2533; FAX. 805/434–3037; Jamad N. Sami, M.D., Director

Santa Cruz Surgery Center, 3003 Paul Sweet Road, Santa Cruz, CA 95065; tel. 408/462–5512; FAX. 408/462–2451; Mary Ann Dunlap, RN

Santa Monica Surgery and Laser Center, 2001 Santa Monica Boulevard, Suite 1288W, Santa Monica, CA 90404; tel. 310/829–2005; FAX. 310/453–9201; Cindy Schlaak, RN, Administrator

Scoffield Foot Care Center, 3796 North Fresno Street, Suite 103, Fresno, CA 93726; tel. 209/228–1475; Mark H. Scoffield, Administrator

Sebastopol Ambulatory Surgery Center, 6880 Palm Avenue, Sebastopol, CA 95472; tel. 707/823–7628; FAX. 707/823–1521; Edward J. Boland, Administrator

Sequoia Endoscopy Center, 2900 Whipple Avenue, Suite 100, Redwood City, CA 94062; tel. 415/363–5200; FAX. 415/369–4609; Stuart Weisman, Administrator

Shepard Eye Center Medical Group, 1414 East Main Street, Santa Maria, CA 93454–4806; tel. 805/925–2637; FAX. 809/928–2067; Dennis D. Shepard, M.D.

Sierra Plastic Surgery Center, 6153 North Thesta, Fresno, CA 93710; tel. 209/432–5156; FAX. 209/432–2247; Terry A. Gillian, M.D., Medical Director

Sierra Vista Medical Pavilion Ambulatory Surgery, 77 Casa Street, Suite 203, San Luis Obis, CA 93405; tel. 805/544–6471; James W. Thornton, M.D., Administrator

Simi Health Center, 1350 Los Angeles Avenue, Simi Valley, CA 93065; tel. 805/522–3782; FAX. 805/522–1283; Lorna Holland, Administrator

Solis Surgical Arts Center, 4940 Van Nuys Boulevard, Suite 105, Sherman Oaks, CA 91403; tel. 818/787–1144; Dr. H. William Gottschalk, Administrator

Sonora Eye Surgery Center, 940 Sylva Lane, Suite G, Sonora, CA 95370; tel. 209/532–2020; FAX. 209/532–1687; Pamela Donaldson

South Bay Endoscopy Center, 256 Landis Avenue, Suite 100, Chula Vista, CA 91910; tel. 619/420–6864; FAX. 619/420–0477; Janet Lemon, Director

South Coast Eye Institute, A Medical Clinic, 3420 Bristol Street, Suite 701, Costa Mesa, CA 92626; tel. 714/957–0272; FAX. 714/641–2020; Michael R. Rose, M.D., Medical Director

Southern California Surgery Center, 7305 Pacific Boulevard, Huntington Pa, CA 90255; tel. 213/584–8222; Amgad A. Awad, Administrator

Southland Endoscopy Center, 949 East Calhoun Place, Suite B, Hemet, CA 92543; tel. 909/929–1177; FAX. 909/765–9111; Sreenivasa R. Nakka, M.D., F.A.C.P.

Southwest Surgical Center, 201 New Stine Road, Suite 130, Bakersfield, CA 93309; tel. 661/396–8900; FAX. 661/397–2929; Sheryl Wiggins, Administrator

St. Joseph Surgery and Laser Center, Inc., 436 South Glassell Street, Orange, CA 92666; tel. 714/633–9566; FAX. 714/633–5193

Stanislaus Surgery Center, 1421 Oakdale Road, Modesto, CA 95355; tel. 209/572–2700; Michael Lipomi, Chief Executive Officer

Stevenson Surgery Center, 2675 Stevenson Boulevard, Fremont, CA 94538; tel. 510/793–4987; FAX. 510/745–0136; Margaret Holmes, Director, Nursing

Stockton Eye Surgery Center, 36 West Yokuts Avenue, Stockton, CA 95207; tel. 209/473–2940; FAX. 209/474–1181

Surgecenter of Palo Alto, 400 Forest Avenue, Palo Alto, CA 94301; tel. 415/324–1832; FAX. 415/324–2282; Rose Parkes, Chief Executive Officer

Surgery Center, 1111 Sonoma Avenue, Lower Level, Santa Rosa, CA 95405; tel. 707/578–4100; Ken Alban, Administrator

Surgery Center of Corona, 1124 South Main Street, Suite 102, Corona, CA 91720; tel. 909/737–9091; FAX. 909/737–9093; Melanie Dastrup, Executive Director

Surgery Center of Northern California, 950 Butte Street, Redding, CA 96001; tel. 916/241–4044; FAX. 916/241–1408; Sarah E. Galewick, RN, B.S.N., Director

Surgery Center of Santa Monica, 2121 Wilshire Boulevard, Santa Monica, CA 90403; tel. 310/264–7300; Ruth F. Andrews

Surgery Centers of the Desert, 39700 Bob Hope Drive, Suite 301, Rancho Mirage, CA 92270; tel. 619/346–7696; FAX. 619/776–1069; Marilee Kyler, Administrator

Surgical Eye Care Center, 655 Laguna Drive, Carlsbad, CA 92008; tel. 760/729–7101; FAX. 760/729–7106; Lisa Barron, Administrator

Surgitek Outpatient Center, Inc., 460 North Greenfield Avenue, Suite Eight, Hanford, CA 93230; tel. 209/582–0238; Wiley Elick, Owner, Administrator

Sutter Alhambra Surgery Center, 1201 Alhambra Boulevard, Sacramento, CA 95816; tel. 916/733–8222; FAX. 916/733–8224; Bill Davis, Administrator

Sutter North Procedure Center, 550 B Street, Yuba City, CA 95991; tel. 530/749–3650; FAX. 530/749–3651; Deborah Smith, Ancillary Services Director

The Beverly Hills Center for Special Surgery, 1125 South Beverly Drive, Suite 505, Los Angeles, CA 90035; tel. 310/277–6780; Alina Pnini, Administrator

The Center for Endoscopy, 3921 Waring Road, Suite B, Oceanside, CA 92056; tel. 760/940–6300; FAX. 760/940–8074; Barbara Bockover, RN, Administrator

The Centre for Plastic Surgery, 401 East Highland Avenue, suite 352, San Bernardino, CA 92404; tel. 909/883–8686; FAX. 909/881–6537; Dennis K. Anderson, Administrator

The Darr Eye Clinic Surgical Medical Group, Inc., 44139 Monterey Avenue, Suite A, Palm Desert, CA 92260; tel. 619/773–3099; FAX. 619/341–6863; Joseph L. Darr, M.D., Administrator

The Endoscopy Center, 870 Shasta Street, Suite 100, Yuba City, CA 95991; tel. 530–671–3636; FAX. 530–671–4099; Floyd V. Burton, M.D.

The Endoscopy Center of the South Bay, 23560 Madison Street, Suite 109, Torrance, CA 90505; tel. 310/325–6331; FAX. 310/325–6335; Norman M. Panitch, M.D.

The Eye Surgery Center (Colton), 1900 East Washington, Colton, CA 92324; tel. 909/825–8002; FAX. 909/422–8930; Sally Chalk, RN, Operating Room Manager

The Eye Surgery Center of Northern California, 5959 Greenback Lane, Citrus Height, CA 95621; tel. 916/723–7400; FAX. 916/723–4449; Donna Davis, Administrator

The Eye Surgery Center of Riverside, Inc., 8990 Garfield, Suite One, Riverside, CA 92503; tel. 909/785–5421; FAX. 909/785–0130

The Montebello Surgery Center, 229 East Beverly Boulevard, Montebello, CA 90640; tel. 213/728–7998; Clifton M. Baker, Administrator

The Palos Verdes Ambulatory Surgery Medical Center, 3400 West Lomita Boulevard, Suite 307A, Torrance, CA 90505; tel. 310/517–8689; FAX. 310/517–9916; Christine Petti, M.D., Medical Director

The Plastic Surgery Center Medical Group, Inc., 95 Scripps Drive, Sacramento, CA 95825; tel. 916/929–1833; FAX. 916/929–6730; Mark L. Ross, Administrator

The Sinskey Eye Institute, 2232 Santa Monica Boulevard, Santa Monica, CA 90411; tel. 310/453–8911; FAX. 310/453–2519; Sherry Bennett, Administrator

The Specialists Surgery Center, 2450 Martin Road, Fairfield, CA 94533; tel. 707/422–2325; FAX. 707/429–6088; Ronald D. Fike, Jr.

The Surgery Center, 6840 Sepulveda Boulevard, Van Nuys, CA 91405–4401; tel. 818/785–6840; FAX. 818/785–3931; Grace Sussman, RN, Nurse Manager

The Surgery Center, A HealthSouth Surgery Center, 3875 Telegraph Avenue, Oakland, CA 94609; tel. 510/547–2244; FAX. 510/547–6637; Ann Banchero, Administrator

The Valley Endoscopy Center, 18425 Burbank Boulevard, Suite 525, Tarzana, CA 91356; tel. 818/708–6050; FAX. 818/708–6009; Betty Asato, RN, Clinical Director

Third Street Surgery Center, 420 East Third Street, Suite 604, Los Angeles, CA 90013; tel. 213/617–9194; FAX. 213/617–0605; Yukiko Hattori, Director of Nursing

Thousand Oaks Endoscopy Center, 227 West Janss Road, Suite 240, Thousand Oaks, CA 91360; tel. 805/371–0455; FAX. 805/371–0459; Hector Caballero, M.D., Administrator

Time Surgical Facility, 720 North Tustin Avenue, Suite 202, Santa Ana, CA 92705; tel. 714/972–1811; Denise Reale, Administrator

Torrance Surgicenter, 22410 Hawthorne Boulevard, Suite Three, Torrance, CA 90505; tel. 310/373–2238; FAX. 310/373–8238; Lindon KenKawahara, M.D., Medical Director

Tri–Valley Surgery Center, 4487 Stoneridge Drive, Pleasanton, CA 94588; tel. 510/484–3100; FAX. 510/484–3113; Karen Stevens, RN, CNOR, Administrator

Truxtun Surgery Center, Inc., 4260 Truxtun Avenue, Suite 120, Bakersfield, CA 93309; tel. 805/327–3636; Velma Reed, Administrator

Twin Cities Surgicenter, Inc., 812 Fourth Street, Suite A, Marysville, CA 95901; tel. 916/741–3937; FAX. 916/743–0427; Bonnie Archuleta, Administrator

University Surgi–Center Medical Group, 23961 Calle De La Magdalena, Suite 430, Laguna Hills, CA 92653; tel. 714/830–5500; Bernard Berry, M.D., Administrator

Upland Outpatient Surgical Center, Inc., 1330 San Bernardino Road, Upland, CA 91786; tel. 909/981–8755; FAX. 909/981–9462; Roger E. Murken, M.D., President

UTC Surgicenter, 8929 University Center Lane, Suite 103, San Diego, CA 92122; tel. 619/554–0220; FAX. 619/554–0458; Dawn Ainsworth, RN, Administrator

Valencia Outpatient Surgical Center, L.P., d/b/a Valencia Surgical Center, 24355 Lyons Avenue, Suite 120, Santa Clarita, CA 91321; tel. 805/255–6644; FAX. 805/255–6717; Nina Turner, Administrative Director

Valley Surgical Center, 5555 West Las Positas Boulevard, Pleasanton, CA 94566; tel. 510/734–3360; FAX. 510/734–3358; Beth Combs, RN, Director, Nursing

Ventura Out–Patient Surgery, Inc., 3555 Loma Vista Road, Suite 204, Ventura, CA 93003; tel. 805/653–6765; FAX. 805/653–1470; Brian D. Brantner, M.D.

Victorville Ambulatory Surgery Center, 15030 Seventh Street, Victorville, CA 92392; tel. 619/241–2273; FAX. 619/245–6798; John D. Amar, M.D., Medical Director

Vision Care Surgery Center, 1045 S Street, Fresno, CA 93721; tel. 209/486–2000; Lynn Horton, Executive Director

Walnut Creek Ambulatory Surgery Center, 112 La Casa Via, Suite 300, Walnut Creek, CA 94598; tel. 510/933–0290; Catherine Nichol, Administrator

Wardlow Surgery Center, 200 West Wardlow Road, Long Beach, CA 90806; tel. 310/424–3574; FAX. 310/490–0329; Marisol Magana, Administrator

Washington Outpatient Surgery Center, 2299 Mowry Avenue, First Floor, Fremont, CA 94538; tel. 510/791–5374; FAX. 510/790–8916; Gerald G. Pousho, M.D.

West Olympic Surgery Center and Laser Institute, 11570 West Olympic Boulevard, Los Angeles, CA 90064; tel. 310/479–4211; FAX. 310/473–6069; Chris Klimaszewski, Operating Room Supervisor

West Valley Surgery Center, 3803 South Bascom Avenue, Suite 106, Campbell, CA 95008; tel. 408/559–4886; FAX. 408/559–4908; Annette Wunderlich, RN, Administrator

Westlake Eye Surgery Center, 2900 Townsgate Road, Suite 201, Westlake Village, CA 91361; tel. 805/496–6789; FAX. 805/494–8392; John Darin, M.D., Medical Director

Westwood Surgery Center, 11819 Wilshire Boulevard, Suite 214, Los Angeles, CA 90025; tel. 310/575–1616; FAX. 310/575–1622; Thomas Cloud, M.D., Administrator

Women's Health Care and Cosmetic Surgical Center, 15306 Devonshire Street, Mission Hills, CA 91311; tel. 818/892–0274; FAX. 818/895–0663; Martha P. Nazemi, Administrator

Woodland Surgery Center, 1321 Cottonwood Street, Woodland, CA 95695; tel. 916/662–9112; FAX. 916/668–5783; Donna Fields, Manager

COLORADO

Ambulatory Surgery, Ltd., 320 East Fontanero, Colorado Springs, CO 80907; tel. 719/634–8878; Dana Alexander, Vice President, Clinical Operations

Aurora Outpatient Surgery, 2900 South Peoria Street, Suite D, Aurora, CO 80014; tel. 303/752–2496; FAX. 303/752–2577; L. F. Peede, Jr., M.D., Administrator

Aurora Outpatient Surgery, 2900 S. Peoria St., #D, Aurora, CO 80014; tel. 303/752–2496; Randolph Robinson, Administrator

Aurora Surgery Center LTD, 13701 E. Mississippi, #200, Aurora, CO 80012; tel. 303/363–8646; Beverly Kirchner, RN, Administrator

Aurora Surgery Center, Ltd., 13701 Mississippi Avenue, Suite 200, Aurora, CO 80012; tel. 303/363–8646; FAX. 303/363–8689; Beverly Kirchner, RN, Administrator

Avista Surgery Center, 2525 Fourth Street, Lower Level, Boulder, CO 80304; tel. 303/443–3672; John Sackett, Administrator

Avista Surgery Center, 2525 4th Street, Lower Level, Boulder, CO 80304; tel. 303/443–3672; John Sackett, Administrator

Boulder Medical Center, P C, 2750 Broadway, Boulder, CO 80304; tel. 303/440–3000; Mr. Bradford McKane, Administrator

Boulder Medical Center, P.C., 2750 Broadway, Boulder, CO 80304; tel. 303/440–3000; Bradford B. McKane

Centennial Healthcare Plaza, a Division of Healthone/Columbia, 14200 East Arapahoe Road, Englewood, CO 80112; tel. 303/699–3000; FAX. 303/699–3182; Ginger McNally, Administrator

Center for Reproductive Surgery, 799 East Hampden Avenue, Suite 300, Englewood, CO 80110; tel. 303/788–8309; FAX. 303/788–8310; Dr. William Schoolcraft, Administrator

Centura Health–Summit Surgery Center, Highway Nine at School Road, P.O. Box 4460, Frisco, CO 80443; tel. 303/668–1458; FAX. 970/668–1703; Carol Turrin, Administrator

Centura Health–Surgery LTD, 320 E. Fontanero #101, Pavilion Blvd, Colorado Springs, CO 80907; tel. 719/634–8878; Carol Jackson, Administrator

Cherry Creek Eye Surgery Center, (Rose Medical Center), 4999 East Kentucky Avenue, Denver, CO 80222; tel. 303/692–0903; Jeffrey Dorsey, Administrator

Colorado Outpatient Eye Surgical Center, 2480 South Downing, Suite G–20, Denver, CO 80210; tel. 303/777–3882; FAX. 300/778–0738; Thomas P. Larkin, M.D.

Colorado Outpatient Eye Surgical Center, 2480 S. Downing, Denver, CO 80210; tel. 303/777–3852; Thomas Larkin, Administrator

Colorado Springs Eye Surgery Center, 2920 North Cascade Avenue, Colorado Springs, CO 80907; tel. 719/636–5054; FAX. 719/520–3576; Paul Angotti, Administrator

Colorado Springs Health Partners Ambulatory Surgery Unit, 209 South Nevada Avenue, Colorado Springs, CO 80903; tel. 719/475–7700; FAX. 719/475–1241; Ms. Joan Compton, Administrator

Columbia Centrum Surgical Center, 8200 East Belleview, Suite 300, East Tower, Englewood, CO 80111; tel. 303/290–0600; FAX. 303/290–6359; Jane Klinglesmith, Administrator

Denver Eye Surgery Center, Inc., 13772 Denver West Parkway, Building 55, Golden, CO 80401; tel. 303/273–8770; Larry W. Kreider, M.D., Administrator

Denver Midtown Surgery Center, 1919 East 18th Avenue, Denver, CO 80206; tel. 303/322–3993; Connie Holtz, Administrator

Durango Surgicenter, 316 Sawyer Drive, Durango, CO 81301; tel. 970/259–3818; D.J. Winder, M.D., Administrator

ENT Surgicenter, Inc., 1032 Luke, Fort Collins, CO 80524; tel. 970/484–8686; FAX. 970/484–1064; Debbie Brown, Manager

Eye Center of Northern Colorado Surgery Center, 1725 E. Prospect Ave., Fort Collins, CO 80525; tel. 970/484–5322; Carol Wittmer, Administrator

Eye Surgery Center of Colorado, 8403 Bryant Street, Westminster, CO 80030; tel. 303/426–4810; FAX. 303/426–8708; William G. Self, Jr., M.D., Administrator

Foot Surgery Center of Northern Colorado, 1355 Riverside Ave., #B, Fort Collins, CO 80524; tel. 970/484–4620; Adriann Anderson, Administrator

HealthSouth Denver West Surgery Center, 13952 Denver West Parkway, Building 53, Suite 100, Golden, CO 80401; tel. 303/271–1112; FAX. 303/271–1117; Ms. Susan Byers, Administrator

HealthSouth Pueblo Ambulatory Surgery Center, 25 Montebello Road, Pueblo, CO 81001; tel. 719/544–1600; FAX. 719/544–2599; Marlene Keithley, Administrator

HealthSouth Surgery Center of Colorado Springs, 1615 Medical Center Point, Colorado Springs, CO 80907; tel. 719/635–7740; FAX. 719/635–7750; B. J. Schott, Administrator

HealthSouth Surgery Center of Fort Collins, 1100 East Prospect Road, Fort Collins, CO 80525; tel. 970/493–7200; FAX. 970/493–2380; Alice Fischer, Administrator

Kaiser Permanente Ambulatory Surgery Center, 2045 Franklin Street, Denver, CO 80205; tel. 303/764–4444; Rosemarie Polemi, Director

Lakewood Surgical Center, 2201 Wadsworth Boulevard, Lakewood, CO 80215; tel. 303/234–0445; FAX. 303/232–7182; Connie Holtz, Administrator

Laser Institute of the Rockies, 8400 East Prentice Avenue, Suite 1200, Englewood, CO 80111; tel. 303/793–3000; Jon Dishler, M.D., President

Littleton Day Surgery Center, 8381 South Park Lane, Littleton, CO 80120; tel. 303/795–2244; FAX. 303/795–5965; Keith A. Chambers, Administrator

Mountain View Surgery Center, 1850 N. Boise Ave., P.O. Box 887, Loveland, CO 80538; tel. 970/622–1999; Charles Harms, Administrator

North Denver Surgical Center, Ltd., 10001 North Washington, Thornton, CO 80229; tel. 303/252–0083; FAX. 303/252–9095; Charlotte Santoro, Administrator

Orthopaedic Center of the Rockies Ambulatory Surgery Center, 2500 East Prospect Road, Fort Collins, CO 80525; tel. 303/493–4010; FAX. 303/493–0521; Scott M. Thomas, Executive Director

Pain Management Center, 455 E. Pikes Peak Ave., #201, Colorado Spire, CO 80903; tel. 719/442–0777; Sue Hayes Golden, Administrator

Pikes Peak Endoscopy & Surgery Center, 1699 Medical Center Pt., #100, Colorado Spire, CO 80907; tel. 719/632–7101; Karen Parks, Administrator

Rocky Mountain Surgery Center, LTD., 2405 Broadway, Boulder, CO 80304–4108; tel. 303/449–2020; FAX. 303/440–6893; James R. Schubert, Executive Director

South Denver Endoscopy Center, Inc., 499 East Hampden Avenue, Suite 430, Englewood, CO 80110; tel. 303/788–8888; Dr. Pete Baker, Administrator

Southern Colorado Center for Endoscopy and Surgery, 2002 Lake Avenue, Pueblo, CO 81004; tel. 719/560–7111; FAX. 719/564–0122; Dr. Andrew Perry, Administrator

Spring Creek Surgery Center, Spring Creek Medical Park, 2001 South Shields Street, Building H, Su, Fort Collins, CO 80526; tel. 970/221–9363; FAX. 970/221–9636; Natalie Coubrough, Facility Administrator

Springs Pain Research & Surgery Facility, 1625 Medical Center Point, #240, Colorado Spire, CO 80907; tel. 719/577–9063; Charles Ripp, M.D., Administrator

Springs Pain Research and Surgery Facility, 1625 Medical Center Point, Suite 240, Colorado Springs, CO 80907; tel. 719/577–9063; FAX. 719/577–9124; Charles Ripp, Administrator

Sterling Eye Surgery Center, 1410 S. 7th Ave., P.O. Box 951, Sterling, CO 80751; tel. 970/522–1833; Rashell Fritzler, Administrator

Section C

Sterling Eye Surgical Center, 1410 South Seventh Avenue, Sterling, CO 80751; tel. 303/522–1833; FAX. 970/522–3677; Inez C. Plank, General Manager

Surgicenter of the San Luis Valley Medical, P.C., 2115 Stuart, Alamosa, CO 81101; tel. 719/589–8010; FAX. 719/589–8112; Lauriann Blakeman, RN, Supervisor

Western Rockies Surgery Center, Inc., 1000 Wellington Avenue, Grand Junction, CO 81501; tel. 970/243–9000; FAX. 970/245–4936; Marilyn M. Smith, RN, Surgery Center Administrator

Western Rockies Surgery Center, Inc., 1000 Wellington Ave., Grand Junction, CO 81501; tel. 970/243–9000; Marilyn Smith, Administrator

CONNECTICUT

Bridgeport Surgical Center, 4920 Main Street, Bridgeport, CT 06606; tel. 203/374–1515; FAX. 203/374–4702; Anthony German, Administrative Director

Connecticut Foot Surgery Center, 318 New Haven Avenue, Milford, CT 06460; tel. 203/882–0065; Martin Pressman, D.P.M., Administrator

Connecticut Surgical Center, 81 Gillett Street, Hartford, CT 06105; tel. 203/247–5555; FAX. 203/249–5860; Margaret Rubino, President

Danbury Surgical Center, 73 Sandpit Road, Suite 101, Danbury, CT 06810; tel. 203/743–2400; Bernard A. Kershner, President

Hartford Surgical Center, 100 Retreat Avenue, Hartford, CT 06106; tel. 860/549–7970; FAX. 860/247–4121; Christine M. Quallen, Administrative Director

Johnson Surgery Center, 148 Hazard Avenue, P.O. Box 909, Enfield, CT 06083; tel. 860/763–7650; FAX. 860/763–7675; Anthony T. Valente, Vice President, Chief Operating Officer

Middlesex Surgical Center, 530 Saybrook Road, Middletown, CT 06457; tel. 203/343–0400; FAX. 203/343–0396; Louise DeChesser, RN, CNOR, M.S.

Naugatuck Valley Surgical Center, Ltd., 160 Robbins Street, Waterbury, CT 06708; tel. 203/755–6663; FAX. 203/756–9645; Bernard A. Kershner, President

Stamford Surgical Center, 1290 Summer Street, Stamford, CT 06905; tel. 203/961–1345; FAX. 213/324–1470; Charles Tienken, Administrative Director

Waterbury Outpatient Surgical Center, 87 Grandview Avenue, Waterbury, CT 06708; tel. 203/574–2020; Nancy Noll, Administrator

Woman's Surgical Center, 40 Temple Street, New Haven, CT 06510; tel. 203/624–3080; Bruce I. Fisher, Administrator

Yale–New Haven Ambulatory Services Corporation, d/b/a Temple Surgical Center, 60 Temple Street, New Haven, CT 06510; tel. 203/624–6008; Alvin D. Greenberg, M.D., Administrator

DELAWARE

Bayview Endoscopy Center, Inc., 1539 Savannah Road, Lewes, DE 19958; tel. 302/644–0455; FAX. 302/645–9325; Harry J. Anagnostakos, D.O., President

Central Delaware Endoscopy Unit, 644 South Queen Street, Suite 105, Dover, DE 19904; tel. 302/672–1617; William M. Kaplan, M.D., Medical Director

Central Delaware Surgery Center, 100 Scull Terrace, Dover, DE 19901; tel. 302/735–8290; Paul Fransisco, Administrator

Endoscopy Center of Delaware, Inc., 1090 Old Churchman's Road, Newark, DE 19713; tel. 302/892–2710; FAX. 302/892–2715; Jean–Marie M. Taylor, Administrator

Eye Care of Delaware Cataract and Laser Center, 4201 Ogletown Road, Suite 1, Newark, DE 19713; tel. 302/454–8802

Glasgow Medical Center, L.L.C., 2400 Summit Bridge Road, Newark, DE 19702–4777; tel. 302/536–8350; Joseph M. Rule, Ph.D., Administrator

Limestone Medical Center, Inc., 1941 Limestone Road, Suite 113, Wilmington, DE 19808; tel. 302/633–9873; Thomas Mulhern, Chief Financial Officer

DISTRICT OF COLUMBIA

Hillcrest Northwest, 7603 Georgia Avenue, N.W., Washington, DC 20012; tel. 202/829–5620; FAX. 202/882–8387; Alice Harper, Administrator

Hillcrest Women's Surgi–Center, 3233 Pennsylvania Avenue, S.E., Washington, DC 20020; tel. 202/584–6500; Ms. Caridad V. Wright, Administrator

Medlantic Center for Ambulatory Surgery, Inc., 1145 19th Street, N.W., Suite 850, Washington, DC 20036; tel. 202/223–9040; FAX. 202/223–9047; William Heron, M.D., Medical Director

New Summit Medical Center II, Inc., 1630 Euclid Street, N.W., Suite 130, Washington, DC 20037; tel. 202/337–7200; Johnette Anderson, RNC, Administrator

Planned Parenthood of Metropolitan Washington, D.C., Schumacher Center, 1108 16th Street, N.W., Washington, DC 20036; tel. 202/347–8512; FAX. 202/347–0281; Lorraine D. White, Center Manager

Premier Surgery Center of D.C., 6323 Georgia Avenue, N.W., Suite 200, Washington, DC 20011; tel. 202/291–0126; FAX. 202/291–0126; Eunice Davis, Administrative Director

The Endoscopy Center of Washington, DC, L.P., 2021 K Street, N.W., Suite T–115, Washington, DC 20006; tel. 202/775–8692; FAX. 202/463–1165; Phyllis J. Krchma, Administrator

Washington Surgi–Clinic, 1018 22nd Street, N.W., Washington, DC 20037; tel. 202/659–9403; FAX. 202/467–0056; Maria Barrera, Administrator

FLORIDA

Aesthetic Cosmetic Surgery Center, Inc, 598 Sterthaus Avenue, Ormond Beach, FL 32174; tel. 904/673–2262; FAX. 904/677–3808; Bonnie Dantoni, RN, D.D.N.

Aker–Kasten Cataract and Laser Institute, 1445 Northwest Boca Raton Boulevard, Boca Raton, FL 33432; tel. 407/338–7722; FAX. 407/338–7785; Kim Harrington, Administrator

Alpha Ambulatory Surgery, Inc., 2160 Capital Circle, N.E., Tallahassee, FL 32308; tel. 904/385–0033; FAX. 904/422–0201; Gloria Jeter, Office Manager

Ambulatory Ankle and Foot Center of Florida, 1509 South Orange Avenue, P.O. Box 536951, Orlando, FL 32853; tel. 407/895–2432; Gregory J. Renton, Administrator

Ambulatory Surgery Center, 4500 East Fletcher Avenue, Tampa, FL 33613; tel. 813/977–8550; FAX. 813/977–7941; Carole Cornell, Administrator

Ambulatory Surgery Center of Brevard, 719 East New Haven Avenue, Melbourne, FL 32901; tel. 407/726–4106; Dwight Miller, General Manager

Ambulatory Surgery Center of Naples, 1351 Pine Street, Naples, FL 34104; tel. 941/793–0664; FAX. 941/793–4318; Christian Mogelvang, M.D., Medical Director

Ambulatory Surgery Center/Bradenton, 5817 21st Avenue, W., Bradenton, FL 34209; tel. 813/794–0379; J. Leikensohn, M.D., Medical Director

Ambulatory Surgical Care, 1045 North Courtenay Parkway, Merritt Island, FL 32953; tel. 407/452–4448; FAX. 407/452–4533; Rosemarie M. Eaton, RN, DON, Administrative Director

Ambulatory Surgical Center of Central Florida, Inc., 801 North Stone Street, Deland, FL 32720; tel. 904/734–4431; FAX. 904/738–1045; Albert C. Neumann, M.D., Medical Director

Ambulatory Surgical Center of Lake County, Inc., 803 East Dixie Avenue, Leesburg, FL 32748; tel. 904/787–6656; FAX. 904/787–9008; Patricia R. Hux, RN, Business Manager

Ambulatory Surgical Centre, 8700 North Kendall Drive, Suite 100, Miami, FL 33176; tel. 305/595–9511; FAX. 305/271–0383; Gail Tauriello, Administrator

Ambulatory Surgical Facility of South Florida, LTD–East, 4470 Sheridan Street, Hollywood, FL 33021; tel. 305/962–3210; FAX. 305/962–3466; Carl T. Waskiewicz, Executive Director and Administrator

American Surgery Center of Coral Gables, Inc., 10975 W. Le Jeune Road, Miami, FL 33134; tel. 305/461–1300; Laura Lilburn, RN, Nurse Manager

American Surgery Center of Tallahassee, 3411 Capital Medical Boulevard, P.O. Box 13675, Tallahassee, FL 32317–3675; tel. 904/878–4830; FAX. 904/656–1692; Brenda J. Fletcher, Surgical Coordinator

Atlantic Surgery Center, 541 Health Boulevard, Daytona Beach, FL 32114; tel. 904/239–0021

Atlantic Surgery Center, A HealthSouth Facility, 1707 South 25th Street, Fort Pierce, FL 34947; tel. 561/464–8900; FAX. 561/464–1104; Lisa L. Kodya, CMM, Business Office Coordinator

Atlantic Surgical Center, 150 Southwest 12th Avenue, Suite 450, Pompano Beach, FL 33069; tel. 305/941–3369; Ruben Paradela, Chief Executive Officer

Ayers Surgery Center, 720 Southwest Second Avenue, Suite 101, Gainesville, FL 32601; tel. 904/338–7100; FAX. 904/338–7102; Barbara Hyder, RN, Nurse Manager

Barkley Surgicenter, 63 Barkley Circle, Suite 104, Fort Myers, FL 33907; tel. 813/275–8452; Kerri Gantt, Administrative Director

Bay Med Surgery, 1936 Jenks Avenue, Panama City, FL 32405; tel. 904/763–6700; FAX. 904/763–5779; Stan Hicks, CRNA, Manager

Bayfront Medical Plaza Same Day Surgery, 603 Seventh Street South, St. Petersburg, FL 33701; tel. 813/553–7906; FAX. 813/553–7992; Gail A. Cook, RN, Nurse Manager

Beraja Clinics Laser and Surgery Center, 2550 Douglas Road, Suite 301, Coral Gables, FL 33134

Bethesda Health City Same Day Surgery, 10301 Hagen Ranch Road, Boynton Beach, FL 33437; tel. 561/374–5400; FAX. 561/374–5405; Denver Gray, RN, CNOR, Clinical Manager

Boca Raton Outpatient Surgery and Laser Center, 501 Glades Road, Boca Raton, FL 33432; tel. 561/362–4400; FAX. 561/362–4440; Karen Raiano, Administrator

Bon Secours–Venice HealthPark, 1283 Jacaranda Boulevard, Venice, FL 34292; tel. 941/497–5660; FAX. 941/492–3942; Kermit Knight, Administrator

Brevard Surgery Center, 665 Apollo Boulevard, Melbourne, FL 32901; tel. 407/984–0300; FAX. 407/984–0032; Narda Cotman, Surgical Director

Cape Coral Endoscopy and Surgery Center, 1413 Viscaya Parkway, Cape Coral, FL 33990; tel. 941/772–0404; Nancy Rhodes, Administrator

Cape Surgery Center, 1941 Waldemere Street, Sarasota, FL 34239–3555; tel. 941/917–1900; FAX. 941/917–2356; Sharon Tolhurst, RN, M.B.A., Director

Capital Eye Surgery Center, 2535 Capital Medical Boulevard, Tallahassee, FL 32308; tel. 904/942–3937; FAX. 904/942–6279; Renee Harina, Business Manager

Center for Advanced Eye Surgery, L.P., 3920 Bee Ridge Road Building, Suite C, Sarasota, FL 34233; tel. 941/925–0000; FAX. 941/927–2726; E. Helen Smith, RN, LHRM, Nurse Manager

Center for Digestive Health and Pain Management, 12700 Creekside Lane, Suite 202, P.O. Box 60045, Fort Myers, FL 33919; tel. 941/489–4454; FAX. 941/489–2114; Judy Lane, Administrative Assistant

Central Florida Eye Institute, 3133 Southwest 32nd Avenue, Ocala, FL 34474; tel. 904/237–8400; Thomas L. Croley, M.D.

Clearwater Endoscopy Center, 401 Corbett Street, Suite 220, Clearwater, FL 33756; tel. 727/443–0100; FAX. 727/461–4893; Roberta Hayek, RN, Clinical Director

Cleveland Clinic Florida, 3000 West Cypress Creek Road, Fort Lauderdale, FL 33309

Columbia Belleair Surgery Center, 1130 Ponce de Leon Boulevard, Clearwater, FL 34616; tel. 813/581–4800; FAX. 813/585–0319; Margie Maddock, Administrator

Columbia Brandon Surgery Center, 711 South Parsons, Brandon, FL 33511; tel. 813/654–7771; FAX. 813/654–3347; Charlene Harrell, RN, Administrator

Columbia Cape Coral Surgery Center, 2721 Del Prado Boulevard, S., Suite 100, Cape Coral, FL 33904; tel. 941/458–9000; Barry Kandell, Administrator

Columbia Center for Special Surgery, 4650 Fourth Street, N., St. Petersburg, FL 33703; tel. 727/527–1919; FAX. 727/527–0714; Paula Russo, RN, CNOR, Administrator

Columbia Central Florida SurgiCenter, 814 Griffin Road and 900 Griffin Road, Lakeland, FL 33805; tel. 941/686–1010; FAX. 941/686–1711; Jan Townsend, Administrator

Columbia DeLand Surgery Center, 651 West Plymouth Avenue, Deland, FL 32720; tel. 904/738–6811; FAX. 904/822–4316; Jay Hutcherson, Administrator

Columbia Florida Surgery Center, 180 Boston Avenue, Altamonte Springs, FL 32701; tel. 407/830–0573; FAX. 407/830–4373; Paige L. Adams, Administrator

Columbia Kissimmee Surgery Center, 2275 North Central Avenue, Kissimmee, FL 34741; tel. 407/870–0573; FAX. 407/870–1859; Lou Warmijak, Administrator

Columbia New Port Richey Surgery Center, 5415 Gulf Drive, New Port Rich, FL 34652; tel. 813/848–0446; FAX. 813/842–3166; Sandra McFarland, RN, Administrator

Columbia North County Surgicenter, 4000 Burns Road, Palm Beach, FL 33410; tel. 407/626–6446; Jennifer Rime, Business Manager

Columbia Outpatient Surgical Services, Ltd., 301 Northwest 82nd Avenue, Plantation, FL 33324; tel. 954/424–1766; FAX. 954/424–1966; Debbie Haga–Cofer, Administrator

Columbia Parkside Surgery Center, 2731 Park Street, Jacksonville, FL 32205; tel. 904/389–1077; FAX. 904/389–9959; Chris Edmond, Administrator

Columbia Surgery Center, 3901 University Boulevard #111, Jacksonville, FL 32216; tel. 904/448–1948; Debbie Overton–Raines, Administrator

Columbia Surgery Center at Coral Springs, 967 University Drive, Coral Springs, FL 33071; tel. 954/975–4166; FAX. 954/344–7054

Columbia Surgery Center at St. Andrews, Inc., 1350 East Venice Avenue, Venice, FL 34292; tel. 941/488–2030; FAX. 941/484–2010; Lori Chase, Business Office Manager

Columbia Surgery Center Merritt Island, 270 North Sykes Creek Parkway, Merritt Island, FL 32953; tel. 407/459–0015; Cynthia Johnson, Administrator

Coral View Surgery Center, 8390 West Flager, Suite 216, Miami, FL 33144; tel. 305/226–5574; Victor Suarez, M.D., President

Cordova Ambulatory Surgical Center, 545 Brent Lane, Pensacola, FL 32503; tel. 904/477–5437; Cynthia Blake, Assistant Administrator

Cortez Foot Surgery Center, PA, 1800 Cortez Road, W., Suite 8, Bradenton, FL 34207; tel. 941/758–4608; FAX. 941/755–2901; Margaret Provencher, Administrator

Countryside Surgery Center, 3291 North McMullen Booth Road, Clearwater, FL 33761; tel. 727/725–5800; FAX. 727/797–4002; Sandra McFarland, Administrator

Day Surgery, Inc., 1715 Southeast Tiffany Avenue, Port St. Luci, FL 34952; tel. 407/335–7005; Mary Holobaugh, RN, Administrator

Dermatologic and Cosmetic Surgery Center, 2668 Swamp Cabbage Court, Fort Myers, FL 33901; tel. 813/275–7546; FAX. 813/275–5074; Charles Eby, M.D.

Diagnostic Clinic Center for Outpatient Surgery, 1401 West Bay Drive, Largo, FL 34640; tel. 813/581–8767; FAX. 813/584–1938; Robert R. Dippong, Administrator and CEOicer

Doctors Surgery Center, 921 North Main Street, Kissimmee, FL 34744; tel. 407/933–7800

East Lake Outpatient Center, 3890 Tampa Road, Palm Harbor, FL 34684

Endoscopy Associates of Citrus, 6412 West Gulf to Lake Highway, Crystal River, FL 34429

Endoscopy Center of Ocala, Inc., 1160 Southeast 18th Place, Ocala, FL 34471; tel. 352/732–8679; FAX. 352/732–2440; Linda L. Brooks, RN, Nurse Manager

Endoscopy Center of Sarasota, 1435 Osprey Avenue, Suite 100, Sarasota, FL 34239; tel. 941/366–4475; FAX. 941/366–4390; Susan M. Brongel, RN, Administrator

Eye Care and Surgery Center of Ft. Lauderdale, 2540 Northeast Ninth Street, Ft. Lauderdale, FL 33304; tel. 305/561–3533; FAX. 305/565–9706; Michael Goldstone, Administrator

Eye Surgery and Laser Center, 4120 Del Prado Boulevard, Cape Coral, FL 33904; tel. 813/542–2020; FAX. 813/542–0704; Louise Bennett, RN, Administrator

Eye Surgery and Laser Center of Mid–Florida, Inc., 409 Avenue K, S.E., Winter Haven, FL 33880; tel. 941/294–3504; FAX. 941/294–8305; Sue Koha, ASC Supervisor

Eye Surgery Facility, P.A., 2808 West Martin Luther King Boulevard, Tampa, FL 33607; tel. 813/876–1331; FAX. 813/872–0647; Phyllis S. Chisholm, RN, M.A., Executive Director

Eye Surgicenter, 2521 Northwest 41st Street, Gainesville, FL 32606; tel. 904/377–7733; William A. Newsome, M.D.

Faculty Clinic, Inc., 653 West Eighth Street, Jacksonville, FL 32209; tel. 904/350–6708

Family Medical Center, 100 Commercial Drive, Keystone Heights, FL 32656; tel. 352/473–6595; FAX. 352/473–6597; Sue Russell, Office Manager

Florida Eye Clinic Ambulatory Surgical Center, 160 Boston Avenue, Altamonte Springs, FL 32701; tel. 407/834–7776; FAX. 407/831–8607; Genevieve Parm, Chief Executive Officer

Florida Eye Institute Surgicenter, Inc., 2750 Indian River Boulevard, Vero Beach, FL 32960; tel. 407/569–9500; FAX. 407/569–9507; Mary Lynne Schlitt, Administrator

Florida Medical Clinic Special Procedures Center, 38135 Market Square, Zephyrhills, FL 33540

Forest Oaks Ambulatory Surgical Center, Inc., 7320 Forest Oaks Boulevard, Spring Hill, FL 34606; tel. 904/683–5666; Thomas D. Stelnicki, D.P.M.

Foundation for Advanced Eye Care, 3737 Pine Island Road, Sunrise, FL 33351; tel. 305/572–5888; FAX. 305/572–5994; Andrea B. Lettman, Administrator

Gaskins Eye Care and Surgery Center, 2335 Ninth Street, N., Suite 304, Naples, FL 34103; tel. 941/263–7750; FAX. 941/263–1754; Cindy Gaskins, RN, M.S.N., R.M.

Gulf Coast Endoscopy Center, Inc., 665 Del Prado Boulevard, Cape Coral, FL 33990; tel. 813/772–3800; FAX. 813/772–5073; Mrs. Lee Caruso, Administrator

Gulf Coast Surgery Center, 411 Second Street, E., Bradenton, FL 34208; tel. 941/746–1121; FAX. 941/746–7816; Carlene Bailey, RN, Administrator

Gulfcoast Surgery Center, 12132 Cortez Boulevard, Brooksville, FL 34613; tel. 352/596–0744; Fawzi Soliman, M.D.

Gulfshore Endoscopy Center, 1064 Goodletter Road, Naples, FL 33940

Harborside Surgery Center, 610 East Olympia Avenue, Punta Gorda, FL 33950

HealthSouth Central Florida Outpatient Surgery Center, 11140 West Colonial Drive, Suite Three, Ocoee, FL 34761; tel. 407/656–2700; FAX. 407/877–9432; Antonio Caos, M.D., Medical Director

HealthSouth Citrus Surgery Center, 110 North Lecanto Highway, Lecanto, FL 34461; tel. 352/527–1825; FAX. 352/527–1827; Douglas Vybiral, Facility Administrator

HealthSouth Collier Surgery Center, 800 Goodlette Road, N., Suite 120, Naples, FL 34104; tel. 813/262–5757; FAX. 813/262–6073; Barbara L. Messmer

HealthSouth Emerald Coast Surgery Center, 995 Northwest Mar Walt Drive, Fort Walton B, FL 32547; tel. 904/863–7887; FAX. 904/863–4955; Debbie Meier, Facility Administrator

HealthSouth Indian River Surgery Center, 1200 37th Street, Vero Beach, FL 32960; tel. 407/770–5600; FAX. 407/770–1793; Regina Ludicke, Clinical Administrator

HealthSouth Melbourne Surgery Center, 1340 Medical Park Drive, Suite 101, Melbourne, FL 32901; tel. 407/729–9493; FAX. 407/768–6043; Robert C. Miner, Administrator/CEO

HealthSouth Oakwater Surgical Center, 3885 Oakwater Circle, Suite B, Orlando, FL 32806; tel. 407/438–9533; FAX. 407/438–9542; Doug Oakley, Business Office Manager

HealthSouth Orlando Center for Outpatient Surgery, 1405 South Orange Avenue, Suite 400, Orlando, FL 32806; tel. 407/426–8331; FAX. 407/425–9582

Hialeah Ambulatory Care Center, 445 East 25th Street, Hialeah, FL 33176; tel. 305/691–4450; FAX. 305/693–0823; Jose Kone, Administrative Director

Institute for Plastic and Reconstructive Surgery, 820 Arthur Godfrey Road, Third Floor, Miami Beach, FL 33140; tel. 305/673–6164; FAX. 305/534–9759; Lawrence B. Robbins, M.D.

Jacksonville Surgery Center, 4253 Salisbury Road, Jacksonville, FL 32216; tel. 904/281–0021; FAX. 904/281–0988; Katherine Anderson, RN, B.S.N., Center Director

Johnson Eye Institute Surgery Center, Inc., 5923 Seventh Street, Zephyrhills, FL 33539; tel. 813/788–7656; FAX. 813/788–6011; Jane Dempsey, RN, Surgery Services Coordinator

Kimmel Outpatient Surgical Center, 903 45th Street, West Palm Beach, FL 33407; tel. 407/845–8343; FAX. 407/840–8970; Susan Glendon, Administrator

Lake Surgery and Endoscopy Center, 8100 CR 44A, Leesburg, FL 34788; tel. 352/323–1995; Pam Campbell, Assistant Administrator

Lazenby Eye Care Center, 1109 U.S. Highway 19, Suite B, Holiday, FL 34691; tel. 813/934–5705; Laverne Peyton, Administrator

Lee County Center for Foot and Ankle Surgery, Inc., 12734 Kenwood Lane, Suite 44, Fort Myers, FL 33907; tel. 941/936–2454; FAX. 941/936–1974; Steve Ostendorf, D.P.M.

Leesburg Regional Day Surgery Center, 601 East Dixie Avenue, Plaza 501, Leesburg, FL 34748; tel. 904/365–0700; FAX. 904/365–0758; Renae Vaughn, RN, B.S.N., CNOR, Clinical Director

Lowrey Eye Clinic, 1840 North Highland Avenue, Clearwater, FL 34615–1915; tel. 813/442–4147; FAX. 813/446–9297; Miquel E. Mulet, Jr., M.D.

Manatee Endoscopy Center, Inc., 6010 Pointe West Boulevard, Bradenton, FL 34209; tel. 813/792–4239

Martin Memorial SurgiCenter, 509 Riverside Drive, Suite 100, Stuart, FL 34994; tel. 407/223–5920; FAX. 407/288–1821

Martin Memorial Surgicenter at St. Lucie West, 1095 Northwest St. Lucie West Boulevard, Port St. Luci, FL 34986; tel. 561/223–5945; FAX. 561/223–6862; Charles S. Immordino, RN, Director, Clinical Operation

Mayo Clinic Jacksonville Ambulatory Surgery Center for G.I., 4500 San Pablo Road, Jacksonville, FL 32224; tel. 904/223–2000; Evelyn Leddy, ASC for GI Coordinator

Mayo Outpatient Surgery Center, 4500 San Pablo Road, Jacksonville, FL 32224; tel. 904/953–0100; FAX. 904/953–0019; Debbie Overton, Manager

Mease Countryside Ambulatory Care Center, 1880 Mease Drive, Safety Harbor, FL 34695; tel. 813/726–2873; FAX. 813/791–4317; William G. Harger, Administrator

Medical Development Corporation of Pasco County, 7315 Hudson Avenue, Hudson, FL 34667; tel. 813/868–9563; FAX. 813/869–6918; Dawn M. Ernst, Director, Nursing

Medical Partners Surgery Center, 4545 Emerson Expressway, Jacksonville, FL 32207; tel. 904/399–2600; Kim Chitty, Director

Medivision of Northern Palm Beach County, 2889 10th Avenue, N., Suite 201, Lake Worth, FL 33461; tel. 407/969–0139; FAX. 407/642–1167; Denise Brower, Administrator

Miami Eye Center, 619 Northwest 12th Avenue, Miami, FL 33136; tel. 305/326–0260; FAX. 305/326–1907; Edward C. Gelber, M.D., F.A.C.S.

Mid Florida Surgery Center, 17564 West Highway 441, Mt. Dora, FL 32757; tel. 352–735–4100; FAX. 352–735–2444; Patsy Lentz, RN, Administrative Director

Montgomery Eye Center, 700 Neapolitan Way, Naples, FL 33940; tel. 813/261–8383; FAX. 813/261–8443; Mary Lee Montgomery, Administrator

Mullis Eye Institute, Inc., 1600 Jenks Avenue, Panama City, FL 32405; tel. 904/763–6666; FAX. 904/763–6665; O. Lee Mullis, M.D., Administrator

Naples Day Surgery, 790 Fourth Avenue, N., Naples, FL 33940; tel. 813/263–3863; FAX. 813/263–7429; Sara May McCallum, Executive Director

Naples Day Surgery North, 11161 Health Park Boulevard, Naples, FL 34110; tel. 813/598–3111; FAX. 813/598–1707; Sara May McCallum, Executive Director

New Smyrna Beach Ambulatory Care Center, Inc., 612 Palmetto Street, New Smyrna Be, FL 32168; tel. 904/423–5500

Newgate Surgery Center, Inc., 5200 Tamiami Trail, Suite 202, Naples, FL 34103; tel. 941/263–6766; FAX. 941/263–3320; Dr. R. Crane

North Florida Eye Clinic Surgicenter, 590 Dundas Drive, Jacksonville, FL 32218; tel. 904/751–3600; FAX. 904/757–8922; Mary Miller, RN, Director Surgical Services

North Florida Surgery Center, 4600 North Davis, Pensacola, FL 32503; tel. 904/494–0048; FAX. 904/494–0065; D. M. Whitehead, Administrator and CEOicer

North Florida Surgery Center, 2745 South First Street, Lake City, FL 32025; tel. 904/758–8937; Ann Johnston, Administrator

North Florida Surgical Pavilion, 6705 Northwest 10th Place, Gainesville, FL 32605; tel. 352/333–4555; FAX. 352/333–4569; Becky Hite, Administrative Director

North Ridge Surgery Center, 4650 North Dixie Highway, Fort Lauderdale, FL 33334; tel. 305/772–7995

Northwest Florida Gastroenterology Center, Inc., 202 Doctors Drive, Panama City, FL 32405; tel. 904/769–7599; FAX. 904/769–7389

Northwest Florida Surgery Center, 767 Airport Road, Panama City, FL 32405; tel. 904/747–0400; FAX. 904/913–9744; Ron Samuelian, Chief Executive Officer

Oak Hill Ambulatory Surgery, 11377 Cortez Boulevard, Brooksville, FL 32806; tel. 352/597–3060

Oak Hill Ambulatory Surgery and Endoscopy Center, 11377 Cortez Boulevard, Spring Hill, FL 34613; tel. 904/597–3060; FAX. 904/597–3077; Laura Pacheco, Business Office Director

Section C

Orange Park Surgery Center, 2050 Professional Center Drive, Orange Park, FL 32073; tel. 904/272-2550; FAX. 904/272-7911; Michele K. Cook, RN, Administrator, Nursing Director

Orlando Surgery Center, LTD., 2000 North Orange Avenue, Orlando, FL 32804; tel. 407/894-5808; FAX. 407/894-7802; Barbara J. Forgione, Administrator

Ormond Eye Surgi Center, 26 North Beach Street, Suite A, Ormond Beach, FL 32174; tel. 904/673-3344; FAX. 904/672-1854; Karen S. LaMotte, RN, Assistant Administrator

Pal-Med Same Day Surgery, 6950 West 20th Avenue, Hialeah, FL 33016; tel. 305/821-0079; FAX. 305/558-7494; Mario Machado, RN, Director

Palm Beach Endoscopy Center, 2015 North Flagler Drive, West Palm Beach, FL 33407; tel. 407/659-6543; FAX. 407/659-3533

Palm Beach Eye Clinic, 130 Butler Street, West Palm Beach, FL 33407; tel. 561/832-6113; FAX. 561/833-3003; Andre J. Golino, M.D.

Palm Beach Lakes Surgery Center, 2047 Palm Beach Lakes Boulevard, West Palm Beach, FL 33409; tel. 561/684-1375; FAX. 561/683-0332; Marjorie F. Konigsberg, Administrator

Physician's Surgical Care Center, 2056 Aloma Avenue, Winter Park, FL 32792; tel. 407/647-5100; FAX. 407/647-1966

Physicians Ambulatory Surgery Center, 300 Clyde Morris Boulevard, Suite B, Ormond Beach, FL 32174; tel. 904/672-1080; FAX. 904/672-8628; Joel M. Wilder, RN, Administrator

Physicians Surgery Center,, 4035 Evans Avenue, Fort Myers, FL 33901; tel. 941/939-7375; FAX. 941/275-5248; Judi Schroeder, Administrator

Premier Surgery Center of Zephyrhills, 37834 Medical Arts Court, Zephyrhills, FL 33541; tel. 813/782-8778; FAX. 813/782-2811; Debra Fortenberry, RN, Director, Nursing

Presidential Surgicenter, Inc., 1501 Presidential Way, Suite Nine, West Palm Bea, FL 33401; tel. 407/689-7255; FAX. 407/683-7342; Steve S. Spector, M.D.

Rand Surgical Pavilion Corp., Five West Sample Road, Pompano Beach, FL 33064; tel. 800/782-1711; FAX. 954/782-7490; Deborah Rand, Administrator

Reed Centre for Ambulatory Urological Surgery, 1111 Kane Concourse, Suite 311, Bay Harbor, FL 33154; tel. 305/865-2000

Riverside Park Surgicenter, 2001 College Street, Jacksonville, FL 32204; tel. 904/355-9800; Janice Carter, RN, Director, Nursing

Same-Day Surgicenter of Orlando, Ltd., 88 West Kaley Street, Orlando, FL 32806; tel. 407/423-0573; FAX. 407/841-7317; Sandy Moorehead, Administrator

Samuel Wells Surgicenter, Inc., 3599 University Boulevard, S., Suite 604, Jacksonville, FL 32216; tel. 904/399-0905; FAX. 904/346-0757; Faye T. Evans, Administrator

San Pablo Surgery Center, 14444 Beach Boulevard, Suite 50, Jacksonville, FL 32250; tel. 904/223-7800; FAX. 904/223-0081; Mary McElroy, Director

Santa Lucia Surgical Center Inc., 2441 Southwest 37th Avenue, Miami, FL 33145; tel. 305/442-0066; FAX. 305/445-6896

Sarasota Surgery Center, 983 South Beneva Road, Sarasota, FL 34232; tel. 941/365-5355; FAX. 941/953-7080; Administrator

Seven Springs Surgery Center, Inc., 2024 Seven Springs Boulevard, New Port Rich, FL 34655; tel. 813/376-7000; Barbara Perich, Administrator

Southwest Florida Endoscopy Center, 5050 Mason Corbin Court, Ft. Myers, FL 33907; tel. 813/275-6678; FAX. 813/275-1785; Connie Byrd, Administrator

Southwest Florida Institute of Ambulatory Surgery, 3700 Central Avenue, Suite Two, Ft. Myers, FL 33901; tel. 941/275-0665; Susan Hanzevack, Executive Director

St. Augustine Endoscopy Center, 212 South Park Circle, E., St. Augustine, FL 32086; tel. 904/824-6108; Michael D. Schiff, M.D., President

St. John's Surgery Center, Inc., 8901 Conference Drive, Fort Myers, FL 33919; tel. 941/481-8833; FAX. 941/481-7898; Linda Pavletich, RN, Administrator

St. Joseph's Same Day Surgery Center, 3003 West Martin Luther King Boulevard, Tampa, FL 33607; tel. 813/870-4711; FAX. 813/870-4907; Paula McGuiness, Executive Director

St. Lucy's Outpatient Surgery Center, 21275 Olean Boulevard, Port Charlotte, FL 33952; tel. 813/625-1325; FAX. 813/625-6482; Anthony Limoncelli, M.D.

St. Luke's Surgical Center, 43309 U.S. Highway 19, N., P.O. Box 5000, Tarpon Spring, FL 34688-5000; tel. 813/938-2020; FAX. 813/938-5606; Glenn S. Wolfson, M.D., Medical Director

St. Petersburg Medical Group, Ambulatory Surgery and Endoscopy Center, 1099 Fifth Avenue, N., St. Petersburg, FL 33705-1419; tel. 813/821-1221; FAX. 813/892-8770; Iverson Pace, RN, Facility Manager, Director of Nursing

St. Petersburg Surgery Center, 539 Pasadena Avenue, S., St. Petersburg, FL 33707; tel. 813/345-8337; FAX. 813/347-4675; Patty Grover, Administrator

Suburban Medical Ambulatory Surgical Center, 17615 Southwest 97th Avenue, Miami, FL 33157; tel. 305/255-3950; FAX. 305/233-2503; Jules G. Minkes, D.O., Administrator

Suncoast Endoscopy Center, 601 Seventh Street, S., St. Petersburg, FL 33701; tel. 813/824-7116; FAX. 813/824-7177; Denise Epstein, RN, Director, Nursing

Suncoast Eye Center, Eye Surgery Institute, 14003 Lakeshore Boulevard, Hudson, FL 34667; tel. 727/868-9442; FAX. 727/862-6210; Lawrence A. Seigel, M.D., P.A., Medical Director

Suncoast Skin Surgery Clinic, 4519 U.S. Highway 19, New Port Rich, FL 34652; tel. 813/849-8922; FAX. 813/841-7553; Bethany Carvallo, Administrator

Suncoast Surgery Center of Hernando, Inc., 5060 Commercial Way, Spring Hill, FL 34606; tel. 904/596-3696; FAX. 904/596-2707; Bethany Carvallo, Administrator

Sunrise Surgical Center, 110 Yorktowne Drive, Daytona Beach, FL 32119; tel. 904/788-6696; FAX. 904/788-2219; Carolyn Teal

Surgery Center of Jupiter, Inc., 102 Coastal Way, Jupiter, FL 33477; tel. 560/747-1111; FAX. 560/747-4151; Monroe N. Benaim, M.D., Medical Director

Surgery Center of North Florida, Inc., 6520 Northwest Ninth Boulevard, Gainsville, FL 32615; tel. 352/331-7987; FAX. 352/331-2787; Joy Ingram, Administrator

Surgery Center of Ocala, 3241 Southwest 34th Avenue, Ocala, FL 34474; tel. 352/237-5906; FAX. 352/237-5785; Verla Heffrin, Administrator

Surgery Center of Stuart, 2096 Southeast Ocean Boulevard, Stuart, FL 34996; tel. 561/223-0174; FAX. 561/223-0946; Jill Logan, Administrator

Surgical Center of Central Florida, 3601 South Highlands Avenue, Sebring, FL 33870; tel. 813/382-7500; FAX. 813/385-7332; Sharon Keiber, RN, Administrator

Surgical Center of Florida, 1717-1799 Woolbright Road, Boynton Beach, FL 33426; tel. 407/737-5500; FAX. 407/737-7055; Lily Lee, Administrator

Surgical Licensed Ward, 110 West Underwood Street, Suite B, Orlando, FL 32806; tel. 407/648-9151; FAX. 407/426-7017; Cheryl Modica, RN, Administrator

Surgical Park Center, Ltd., 9100 Southwest 87th Avenue, Miami, FL 33176; tel. 305/271-9100; FAX. 305/270-8527; Rena Coady, Administrator

Surgicare Center, 4101 Evans Avenue, Ft. Myers, FL 33901; tel. 813/939-3456; FAX. 813/939-1164; Robin Fox, Director of Reimbursement

Surgicare Center of Venice, 950 Cooper Street, Venice, FL 34285; tel. 813/485-4868; FAX. 813/484-4084; Jean Matz, RN, CNOR, Director of Nursing

Tallahassee Endoscopy Center, 2400 Miccosukee Road, Tallahassee, FL 32308; tel. 904/877-2105; FAX. 904/942-1761; Noel Withers, Administrator

Tallahassee Outpatient Surgery Center, Inc., 3334 Capital Medical Boulevard, Suite 500, Tallahassee, FL 32308; tel. 904/877-4688; FAX. 904/877-0368; Martin Shipman, Administrator

Tallahassee Single Day Surgery, 1661 Phillips Road, Tallahassee, FL 32308; tel. 850/878-5165; FAX. 850/942-5545; Stacey Dye, Director of Administration

Tampa Bay Surgery Center, Inc., 11811 North Dale Mabry, Tampa, FL 33618; tel. 813/961-8500; FAX. 813/968-6818; Jay L. Rosen, M.D., Executive Director

Tampa Eye Surgery Center, 4302 North Gomez, Tampa, FL 33607; tel. 813/870-6330; FAX. 813/871-3956; Beverly Martin, Administrator

Tampa Outpatient Surgical Facility, 5013 North Armenia Avenue, Tampa, FL 33603; tel. 813/875-0562; FAX. 813/875-1983; Dianne Pugh, Facility Administrator

The Aesthetic Plastic Surgery Center, 135 San Marco Drive, Venice, FL 34285; tel. 941/484-6836; Claudell Crowe, Administrative Director

The Endoscopy Center, 4810 North Davis Highway, Pensacola, FL 32503; tel. 850/474-8988; FAX. 850/478-9903; Alice Cartee, Administrator

The Endoscopy Center of Naples, 150 Tamiami Trail, N., Suite One, Naples, FL 34102; tel. 941/262-8306; Marjorie Rogers, Office Manager

The Endoscopy Center, Inc., 5101 Southwest Eighth Street, Miami, FL 33134

The Eye Associates Surgery Center, 6002 Pointe West Boulevard, Bradenton, FL 34209; tel. 941/792-2020; FAX. 941/792-2832; Linda Colson, RN, Director

The Gastrointestinal Center of Hialeah, 135 West 49th Street, Hialeah, FL 33012; tel. 305/825-0500; FAX. 305/826-6910; Annette Decastro, RN

The Ocala Eye Surgery Center, 3330 Southwest 33rd Street, Ocala, FL 34474; Carol Haiti, RN, Nurse Administrator

The Sheridan Surgery Center, 95 Bulldog Boulevard, Melbourne, FL 32901; tel. 407/952-9800; FAX. 407/952-7889; Patrice Curtis, RN, Clinical Director

The Treasure Coast Cosmetic Surgery Center, 1901 Port St. Lucie Boulevard, Port St. Luci, FL 34952; tel. 407/335-3954; Donato A. Viggiano, M.D.

Total Surgery Center, 130 Tamiami Trail, Suite 210, Naples, FL 33940; tel. 941/434-4118; FAX. 941/434-6343; Elizabeth Ross, Administrator

Treasure Coast Center for Surgery, 1411 East Ocean Boulevard, Stuart, FL 34996; tel. 561/286-8028; FAX. 561/283-6628; Andrea Scoville, Business Office Manager

Trinity Outpatient Center, 2101 Trinity Oaks Boulevard, New Port Rich, FL 34655; tel. 813/372-4000; FAX. 813/372-4065; Nancy Burden, Director

University Surgical Center, 7251 University Boulevard, Suite 100, Winter Park, FL 32792; tel. 407/677-0066; FAX. 407/677-4199; Laura Hoffman, RRA, Director, Operations

Urological Ambulatory Surgery Center, Inc., 1812 North Mills Avenue, Orlando, FL 32803; tel. 407/897-5499; FAX. 407/896-9454; Susan A. Wuerz, Administrator

Urology Center of Florida, Inc., 3201 Southwest 34th Street, Ocala, FL 34474; tel. 904/237-8100; FAX. 904/237-5684; Christopher S. Hill, Administrator

Urology Health Center, 5652 Meadow Lane, New Port Rich, FL 34652; tel. 813/842-9561; FAX. 813/848-7270; Greg Toney, Administrator

Venture Ambulatory Surgery Center, 16853 Northeast Second Avenue, Suite 400, North Miami Beach, FL 33162; tel. 305/652-2999; FAX. 305/652-8156; Lali Perez, RN, B.S.N., Center Director

Vero Eye Center, 70 Royal Palm Boulevard, Vero Beach, FL 32960; tel. 407/569-6600

Volusia Endoscopy & Surgery Center, Inc., 550 Memorial Circle, Suite G, Ormond Beach, FL 32174; tel. 904/672-0017; FAX. 904/676-0506

Winter Park Ambulatory Surgical Center, 1000 South Orlando Avenue, Winter Park, FL 32789; tel. 407/629-1500; FAX. 407/629-1741; Linda Dingman, Administrator

GEORGIA

Advanced Aesthetics Plastic Surgery Center, 499 Arrowhead Boulevard, Jonesboro, GA 30236; tel. 770/603-6000; FAX. 770/603-7064; Paul D. Feldman, President

Advanced Surgery Center of Georgia, 220 Hospital Road, Canton, GA 30114; tel. 770/479-2202; FAX. 770/479-6666; Debbie Moore, Administrator

Aesthetic Laser & Surgery Facility, 416 Gordon Ave., Thomasville, GA 31792-6644; tel. 912/228-7200; Judy Warmack, Administrator

Aesthetica Surgicenter, P.C., 975 Johnson Ferry Road, Suite 160, Atlanta, GA 30342; tel. 404/256-1311; FAX. 404/705-2774; G. Marshall Franklin, Jr., Administrator

Affinity Outpatient Services, 2224 US Highway 41 North, Tifton, GA 31794; tel. 912/391-4299; FAX. 912/391-4291; Barry L. Cutts, Administrator

Albany Ambulatory Surgery Center, 531 Seventh Avenue, Albany, GA 31701; tel. 912/883–3535; FAX. 912/888–1079; J. Kenneth Durham, Medical Director

Ambulatory Foot and Leg Surgical Center, 1650 Mulkey Road, Austell, GA 30001; tel. 404/941–3633; Alan Shaw, D.P.M., Chief Executive Officer

Ambulatory Laser and Surgery Center, 425 Forest Parkway, Suite 103, Forest Park, GA 30297–2135; tel. 404/363–1087; FAX. 404/363–9951; Dr. Paul A. Colon, Medical Director

Ambulatory Surgical Facility of Brunswick, Eight Tower Medical Park, 3215 Shrine Road, Brunswick, GA 31520; tel. 912/264–4882; Jimmy L. Dixon, Administrator

Athens Plastic Surgery Center, 2325 Prince Avenue, Athens, GA 30606; tel. 706/546–0280; FAX. 404/548–0258; James C. Moore, M.D., Administrator

Atlanta Aesthetic Surgery Center, Inc., 4200 Northside Parkway, Building Eight, Atlanta, GA 30327; tel. 404/233–3833; Debbie Clotfelter, Administrator

Atlanta Endoscopy Center, LTD, 2665 North Decatur Road, Suite 545, Decatur, GA 30033; tel. 404/297–5000; FAX. 404/296–9890; Jon McMurphy, RN, Clinical Coordinator

Atlanta Eye Surgery Center, P.C., 3200 Downwood Circle, NW, Suite 200, Atlanta, GA 30327; tel. 404/355–8721; Walter G. Elliott, Administrator

Atlanta Outpatient Peachtree Dunwoody Center, 5505 Peachtree–Dunwoody Road, Suite 150, Atlanta, GA 30342; tel. 404/847–0893; FAX. 404/843–8664; Janie Ellison, Administrator

Atlanta Outpatient Surgery Center, 993 Johnson Ferry Road, Suite 300, Atlanta, GA 30342; tel. 404/252–3074; FAX. 404/843–2089; Marjane Ellison, Administrator

Atlanta Surgi–Center, Inc., 1113 Spring Street, Atlanta, GA 30309; tel. 404/892–8608; FAX. 404/892–8143; Elizabeth Petzelt, Administrator

Atlanta Women's Medical Center, Inc., 235 West Wieuca Road, Atlanta, GA 30342; tel. 404/257–0057; FAX. 404/257–1245; Ann Garzia, Administrator

Augusta Plastic Surgery Center, Inc., 811 13th Street, Suite 28, Richmond, GA 30901–2772; tel. 706/724–5611; Dana S. Bailey, Administrator

Augusta Surgical Center, 915 Russell Street, Augusta, GA 30904–4115; tel. 404/738–4925; Beryl Barrett, Administrator

Brunswick Endoscopy Center, 3217 4th Street, Brunswick, GA 31520–3759; tel. 912/267–1802; FAX. 912/267–0061; Rita Warren, Administrator

Center for Plastic Surgery, Inc., 365 East Paces Ferry Road, Atlanta, GA 30305; tel. 404/814–1100; FAX. 404/814–0015; Dr. Vincent Zubowicz, Medical Director

Center for Reconstructive Surgery, 5335 Old National Highway, College Park, GA 30349; tel. 404/768–3668; FAX. 404/763–2929; Gregory Alvarez, D.P.M.

Clayton Outpatient Surgical Center, Inc., 6911 Tara Boulevard, Jonesboro, GA 30236; tel. 770/477–9535; FAX. 770/471–7826; Yvonne Guettler, Operating Room Supervisor

Cobb Foot and Leg Surgery Center, 792 Church Street, Suite Two, Marietta, GA 30060; tel. 404/422–9864; FAX. 404/984–0303; Glyn Lewis, Administrator

Coliseum Same Day Surgery, 310 Hospital Drive, P.O. Box 6154, Macon, GA 31208; tel. 912/742–1403; FAX. 912/742–1671; Tim Tobin, CEO and Executive Director

Columbia Augusta Surgical Center, 915 Russell Street, Augusta, GA 30904; tel. 706/738–4925; FAX. 706/738–7224; Beryl Barrett, RN, Administrator

Columbia County Medical Plaza–Surgery, 635 Washington West, Evans, GA 30809; tel. 706/868–1050; Jeff Simless, Assistant Vice President, Finance

Columbus Ambulatory Surgery Center, 725–22nd Street, Columbus, GA 31904–8845; tel. 706/322–6335; Freda R. Stewart, Administrator

Columbus Women's Health Organization, Inc., 3850 Rosemont Drive, Columbus, GA 31901; tel. 706/323–8363

Decatur Urological Clinic–Ambulatory Surgery Center, Inc., 428 Winn Court, Decatur, GA 30030; tel. 404/298–0217; FAX. 404/298–0218; Denise Ethridge, Office Manager

DeKalb Endoscopy Center, 2675 North Decatur Road, Suite 506, Decatur, GA 30033; tel. 404/299–1679; FAX. 404/501–7558; Peter Leff, M.D.

Dennis Surgery Center, Inc., 3193 Howell Mill Road, Suite 215, Atlanta, GA 30327; tel. 404/355–1312; Valerie Garrett, Administrator

Dunwoody Outpatient Surgicenter, Inc., 4553 North Shallowford Road, Suite 60C, Atlanta, GA 30338; tel. 770/457–6303; FAX. 770/457–2823; Janet Wakefield, Administrator

Endoscopy Center of Columbus, Inc, 1041 Talbotton Road, Columbus, GA 31904–8745; tel. 706/327–0700; Jean Patterson, RN, Administrator

Endoscopy Center of Southeast Georgia, Inc., 200 Maple Drive, P.O. Box 1367, Vidalia, GA 30475; tel. 912/537–9851; Dixie Calhoun, RN, Administrator

Feminist Women's Health Center, 580 14th Street, N.W., Atlanta, GA 30318; tel. 404/874–7551; FAX. 404/875–7644; Jan Lockridge, Administrator

Friedrich Surgical Center, 2916 Glynn Avenue, Brunswick, GA 31530; tel. 912/265–3210; Ann Friedrich, Administrator

G.I. Endoscopy Center, 6555 Professional Place, Suite B, Riverdale, GA 30274; tel. 404/996–8830; FAX. 404/991–1596; Aruna Jaya Prakash, Administrator

Gainesville Surgery Center, 1945 Beverly Road, Gainesville, GA 30501–2034; tel. 770/287–1500; Mary W. Hoffman, Administrator

Gastrointestinal Endoscopy of Gwinnett, 600 Professional Drive, Suite 130, Lawrenceville, GA 30245; tel. 770/995–7989; FAX. 770/339–8646; Donna Ash, Practice Manager

Georgia Lithotripsy Center, 120 Trinity Place, Athens, GA 30607; tel. 404/543–2718; David C. Allen, M.D., Administrator

Georgia Surgical Centers – South, 541 Forest parkway, Suite 14, Forest Park, GA 30297–6110; tel. 404/366–5652; Trudy Hunley, Administrator

Gwinnet Endoscopy Center, 575 Professional Drive, Suite 150, Lawrenceville, GA 30245; tel. 770/822–5560; FAX. 770/822–4989; Kerry H. King, M.D., President

HealthSouth Surgery Center of Atlanta, 1140 Hammond Drive, Building F, Suite 6100, Atlanta, GA 30328; tel. 770/551–9944; FAX. 770/551–8826; Nichole Busch, Administrator

HealthSouth Surgery Center of Gwinnett, 2131 Fountain Drive, Snellville, GA 30278; tel. 770/979–8200; FAX. 770/979–1327; Dianne Barrow, RN, Administrator

Hollis Eye Surgery Center, Inc., 7351 Old Moon Road, Columbus, GA 31909; tel. 706/323–8127; Kenneth Hopkins, Administrator

Marietta Surgical Center, Ambulatory Surgery Division, Columbia Healthcare Corporate, 796 Church Street, Marietta, GA 30060; tel. 770/422–1579; FAX. 770/422–1057; Charlotte Bellantoni, Administrator

Medical Eye Associates, Inc., 1429 Oglethorpe Street, Macon, GA 31201; tel. 912/743–7061; FAX. 912/743–6296; Linda Henderson, Office Manager

Midtown Urology Surgical Center, 128 North Avenue, N.E., Suite 100, Atlanta, GA 30308; tel. 404/881–0966; FAX. 404/874–5902; Jenelle E. Foote, M.D., Administrator

North Atlanta Endoscopy Center, 5555 Peachtree–Dunwoody Road, Suite G70, Atlanta, GA 30342–1703; tel. 404/843–0500; Phyllis Pritchett, Administrator

North Atlanta Endoscopy Center, L.P., 5555 Peachtree–Dunwoody Road, Suite G–70, Atlanta, GA 30342; tel. 404/843–0500; FAX. 404/843–0675; Laura Dixon, Clinical Supervisor

North Atlanta Head and Neck Surgery Center, 980 Johnson Ferry Road, Northside Doctors Building, Atlanta, GA 30342; tel. 404/256–5428; FAX. 404–250–1881; Ramon S. Franco, M.D.

North Fulton Diagnostic Gastrointestinal, 2500 Hospital Boulevard, Suite 480, Roswell, GA 30076; tel. 770/475–3085; David A. Atefi, M.D.

North Georgia Endoscopy Center, Inc., 320 Hospital Road, Canton, GA 30114; tel. 770/479–5535; FAX. 770/479–8821; Kevin W. Kellogg, Administrator

North Georgia Outpatient Surgery Center, 795 Red Bud Road, Calhoun, GA 30701; tel. 706/629–1852; FAX. 706/629–8004; Herbert E. Kosmahl, President

North Oak Ambulatory Surgical Center, 2718 North Oak Street, Valdosta, GA 31602; tel. 912/242–3668; FAX. 912/242–9905; A. R. Pitts, Jr., D.P.M.

Northeast Georgia Plastic Surgery Center, 1296 Sims Street, Gainesville, GA 30501; tel. 404/534–1856; FAX. 404/531–0355; Sam Richwine, Medical Director

Northlake Ambulatory Surgical Center, 2193 Northlake Parkway, Building 12, Suite 114, Tucker, GA 30084–4113; tel. 770/938–4860; Winfield Butlin, Administrator

Northlake Endoscopy Center, 1459 Montreal Road, Suite 204, Tucker, GA 30084; tel. 770/939–4721; FAX. 770/939–1187; Gayle Carter, Administrator

Northside Foot and Ankle Outpatient Surgical Center, 3415 Holcomb Bridge Road, Norcross, GA 30092; tel. 404/449–1122; FAX. 770/242–8709; Steven T. Arminio, DPM, Administrator

Northside Hospital Outpatient Surgical Center, 3400–A State Bridge Road, Suite 240, Alpharetta, GA 30202; tel. 404/667–4060; Sidney Kirscher, Administrator

Northside Surgery Center, Inc., 5505 Peachtree–Dunwoody Road, Suite 115, Atlanta, GA 30358–2091; tel. 404–256–0948; FAX. 404–843–1008; Irving Miller, Administrator

Northside Women's Clinic, Inc., 3543 Chamblee–Dunwoody Road, Atlanta, GA 30341; tel. 404/455–4210; FAX. 404/451–9529; James W. Gay, M.D., Administrator

Outpatient Center for Foot Surgery, 730 South Eighth Street, Griffin, GA 30224; tel. 770/228–6644; FAX. 770/228–5769; Pam Roberts, RN

Paces Plastic Surgery Center, Inc., 3200 Downwood Circle, Suite 640, Atlanta, GA 30327; tel. 404/351–0051; FAX. 404/351–0632; Lynne Powell, Administrator

Parkwood Ambulatory Surgical Center, 2605 Parkwood Drive, Brunswick, GA 31520; tel. 912/265–4766; FAX. 912/267–9857; Betty Bauer, RN

Piedmont Surgery Center, 4660 Riverside Park Boulevard, Macon, GA 31210; tel. 912/471–6300; Mikell Peed, Administrator

Planned Parenthood of Reproductive Health Services, 1289 Broad Street, Augusta, GA 30911; tel. 706/724–5557; FAX. 706/724–5293; Karen Gates–Bonnet

Podiatric Surgi Center, 215 Clairemont Avenue, Decatur, GA 30030; tel. 404/373–2529; FAX. 404/370–1688; Jerald N. Kramer, President

Pulliam Ambulatory Surgical Center, 4167 Hospital Drive, Covington, GA 30209, P.O. Box 469, Covington, GA 30210; tel. 404/786–1234; M.M. Pulliam, P.C., Medical Director

Resurgens Surgical Center, 5671 Peachtree Dunwoody Road, Suite 800, Atlanta, GA 30342; tel. 404/847–9999; Kay F. Elliott, RN

Roswell Ambulatory Surgery Center, 1240 Upper Hembree Road, Roswell, GA 30076; tel. 770/663–8011

Savannah Medical Clinic, 120 East 34th Street, Savannah, GA 31401; tel. 912/236–1603; FAX. 912/236–1605; William Knorr, M.D., Administrator

Savannah Outpatient Foot Surgery Center, 310 Eisenhower Drive, Suite Seven, Savannah, GA 31406; tel. 912/355–6503; Dr. Kalman Baruch, President

Savannah Plastic Surgicenter, 4750 Waters Avenue, Suite 505, Savannah, GA 31404; tel. 912/351–5050; FAX. 912/351–5051; F. Christopher Pettigrew, M.D.

Southeastern Fertility Institute Surgical Associates, 5505 Peachtree Dunwood Road, Suite 400, Atlanta, GA 30342; tel. 404/257–1900; FAX. 404/256–1528; Ron Davidson, Administrator

Southlake Ambulatory Surgery Center, 4000 Corporate Center Drive, Suite 100, Morrow, GA 30260–1407; tel. 770/960–2701; FAX. 770/960–2702; Linda Simmons, Administrator

Statesboro Ambulatory Surgery Center, 95 Bel–Air Drive, Statesboro, GA 30461–6879; tel. 912/489–6519; FAX. 912/764–7882; Dianne Collins, Office Manager

Surgery Center of Rome, 16 John Maddox Drive, Rome, GA 30161; tel. 404/234–0315; Neal Jochimsen, Director

The Cosmetic and Plastic Surgicenter of South Atlanta, 6524 Professional Place, Riverdale, GA 30274; tel. 770/991–1733; FAX. 770/997–7204; Nabil Elsahy, M.D.

The Emory Clinic Ambulatory Surgery Center, 1365 Clifton Road, N.E., Atlanta, GA 30322; tel. 404/778–5000; W. Mike Mason, Administrator

The Foot Surgery Center, 2520 Windy Hill Road, Suite 105, Marietta, GA 30067; tel. 770/952–0868; L. Susan Rothstein, Administrator

Section C

The Rome Endoscopy Center, Inc., 16 John Maddox Drive, Rome, GA 30165; tel. 706/295–3992; FAX. 706/290–5384; Connie Barris, Administrator

Tifton Endoscopy Center, Inc., 1111 E. 20th Street, Tifton, GA 31794–3668; tel. 912/382–9338; FAX. 912/382–4282; Glenda Whittle, Administrator

HAWAII

Aloha Surgical Center, 239 Hoohana Street, Kahului, HI 96732; tel. 808/877–3984; FAX. 808/871–6498; Russell T. Stodd, M.D., Medical Director

Cataract and Retina Center of Hawaii, 1712 Liliha Street, Suite 400, Honolulu, HI 96817; tel. 808/524–1010; FAX. 808/531–1030; Worldster Lee, M.D., Director

Hawaiian Eye Surgicenter, 606 Kilani Avenue, Wahiawa, HI 96786; tel. 808/621–8448; FAX. 808/621–2082; John M. Corboy, M.D., Surgeon, Director

Kaiser Honolulu Clinic, 1010 Pensacola Street, Honolulu, HI 96814; tel. 808/593–2950; Jonathan Gans, Administrator

Kaiser Wailuku Clinic, 80 Mahalani Street, Wailuku, HI 96793; tel. 808/243–6000; FAX. 808/243–6009; Mary Hew, Clinics Manager

Surgical Suites at Thomas Square, 1100 Ward Avenue, Suite 1001, Honolulu, HI 96814; tel. 808/521–2305; FAX. 808/599–4818; Carlos Omphroy, M.D., President

Surgicare of Hawaii, Inc., 550 South Beretania Street, Honolulu, HI 96813; tel. 808/528–2511; FAX. 808/526–0651; Eileen M. Peyton, Facility Manager

The Endoscopy Center, 134 Pu'uhou Way, Hilo, HI 96720; tel. 808/969–3979; FAX. 808/935–7657; Jody Montell, Administrator

IDAHO

Boise Center for Foot Surgery, 1400 West Bannock, Boise, ID 83702; tel. 208/345–1871; FAX. 208/368–9707; Marshall D. Odgen, D.P.M., Administrator

Boise Gastroenterology Associates, P.A., Idaho Endoscopy Center, 5680 West Gage, Boise, ID 83706; tel. 208–367–2894; FAX. 208–375–5286; Ike D. Tanube, M.D., President

Coeur D'Alene Foot and Ankle Surgery Center, 101 Ironwood Drive, Suite 131, Coeur D'Alene, ID 83814; tel. 208/666–0814; Stephen A. Isham, D.P.M., Chairman, Board of Directors

Coeur D'Alene Surgery Center, 2121 Ironwood Center Drive, Coeur D'Alene, ID 83814; tel. 208/765–9059; FAX. 208/664–9998; Peter C. Jones, M.D., President

Emerald Surgical Center, 811 North Liberty, Boise, ID 83704; tel. 208/323–4522; FAX. 208/376–5258; Connie Alexander, Administrator

Idaho Ambucare Center, Inc., 211 West Iowa, Nampa, ID 83686; tel. 208/463–5160; FAX. 208/463–5178; Gary Botimer, Administrator

Idaho Eye Surgicenter, 2025 East 17th Street, Idaho Falls, ID 83404; tel. 208/524–2025; FAX. 208/529–1924; Kenneth W. Turley, M.D., Medical Director

Idaho Falls Surgical Center, 1945 East 17th Street, Idaho Falls, ID 83404; tel. 208/529–1945; James A. Haney, M.D., Medical Director

Idaho Foot Surgery Center, 782 South Woodruff, Idaho Falls, ID 83401; tel. 208/529–8393; FAX. 208/529–8078; Bruce G. Tolman, D.P.M., Facility Director

Jefferson Day Surgery Center, 220 West Jefferson, Boise, ID 83702; tel. 208/343–3802; William Stano, President

North Idaho Cataract and Laser Center, Inc., 1814 Lincoln Way, Coeur D'Alene, ID 83814; tel. 208/667–2531; Paul Wail, Administrator

North Idaho Day Surgery and Laser Center, Inc., 2205 North Ironwood Place, Coeur D'Alene, ID 83814; tel. 208/664–0543; FAX. 208/765–2867; Michael P. Christensen, M.D., President

Pacific Cataract and Laser Institute, 250 Bobwhite Court, Suite 100, Boise, ID 83706–3983; tel. 208/385–7576; FAX. 208/385–0050; Sherri Mellville, Site Coordinator

Rock Creek Endoscopy Center, 284 Martin Street, Suite Two, Twin Falls, ID 83301; tel. 208/734–1266; FAX. 208/736–0390; Arlene Hansen, Administrator

South Idaho Surgery Center, Addison Surgery Center, 191 Addison Avenue, Twin Falls, ID 83301; tel. 208/734–5993; David A. Blackmer, D.P.M., President

Surgicare Center of Idaho, L.C., 360 East Mallard Drive, Suite 125, Boise, ID 83706; tel. 208/336–8700; W. Andrew Lyle, M.D., Medical Director

The Surgery Center, 115 Falls Avenue, W., P.O. Box 1864, Twin Falls, ID 83303–1864; tel. 208/733–1662; FAX. 208/734–3632; Larry Maxwell, M.D., Administrator

ILLINOIS

25 East Same Day Surgery, 25 East Washington, Chicago, IL 60602; tel. 312/726–3329; FAX. 312/726–3823; Pat Wansley, Administrator

A.C.T. Medical Center, 5714 West Division Street, Chicago, IL 60651; tel. 312/921–4300; Anthony Centrachio, Administrator

A.C.U. Health Center, LTD., 736 York Road, Hinsdale, IL 60521; tel. 630/794–0645; FAX. 630/794–0169; Lisa Shyne, Administrator

Able Health Center, Ltd., 1640 Arlington Heights Road, Suite 110, Arlington Heights, IL 60004; tel. 847/255–7400

Access Health Center, Ltd., 1700 75th Street, Downers Grove, IL 60516; tel. 630/964–0000; FAX. 630/964–0047; Diane L. Duddles, RN, Administrator

Advantage Health Care, LTD., 203 E. Irving Park Road, Wood Dale, IL 60191; tel. 630/595–1515; FAX. 630–595–9097; Lynn Pfingsten, Administrator

Albany Medical Surgical Center, 5086 North Elston, Chicago, IL 60630; tel. 312/725–0200; FAX. 312/725–6152; Diana Lammon, Administrator

Ambulatory Surgicenter of Downers Grove, Ltd., 4333 Main Street, Downers Grove, IL 60515; tel. 630/810–0212; Inga Ferdkoff, M.D., Administrator

American Women's Medical Center, 2744 North Western, Chicago, IL 60647; tel. 773/772–7726; FAX. 773/772–3696; Jan Barton, M.D., Administrator

AmSurg/Columbia HCA, 330 North Madison Street, Joliet, IL 60435; tel. 815/744–3000; FAX. 815/744–7916; Anne M. Cole, Administrator

Arlington Health Center, Ltd., 1640 Arlington Heights Road, Suite 210, Arlington Heights, IL 60004; tel. 847/255–7474

Bel–Clair Ambulatory Surgical Treatment Center, 325 West Lincoln, Belleville, IL 62220; tel. 618/235–2299; FAX. 618/235–2556; David Horace, Administrator

Carbondale Clinic Ambulatory Surgical Treatment Center, 2601 West Main Street, Carbondale, IL 62901; tel. 618/549–5361; FAX. 618/549–5128

Carle Surgicenter, 1702 South Mattis Avenue, Champaign, IL 61821; tel. 217/326–2030; Julie Root, RN, Administrator

Center for Reconstructive Surgery, 6311 West 95th Street, Oak Lawn, IL 60453; tel. 708/499–3355; FAX. 708/423–2305; Lori Brown, Administrator

Chang's Medical Arts Surgicenter, Apple Tree Health Care, 2809 North Center Street, Maryville, IL 62062; tel. 618/288–1882; FAX. 618/288–3575; Jackie Nemsky, RN

Children's Outpatient Services at Westchester, 2301 Enterprise Drive, Westchester, IL 60154; tel. 708/947–4000; FAX. 708/947–4044; Jan Jennings, Administrator

CMP Surgicenter, Ltd, 3412 West Fullerton Avenue, Chicago, IL 60647; tel. 773/235–8000; FAX. 773/235–7018; Carlos G. Baldoceda, M.D., Medical Director

Columbia Surgicare–North Michigan Avenue, L.P., 60 East Delaware, 15th Floor, Chicago, IL 60611; tel. 312/440–5100; FAX. 312/440–5114; Barbara Villa, Administrator

Columbia–Northwest Surgicare, 1100 West Central Road, Arlington Heights, IL 60005; tel. 847/259–3080; FAX. 847/259–3190; Barbara Cerwin, RN, Administrator

Community Health and Emergency Services, R.R. 1, Box 11, P.O. Box 233, Cairo, IL 62914; tel. 618/734–4400; FAX. 618/734–2884; Frederick L. Bernstein, Executive Director

Concord Medical Center, 17 West Grand, Chicago, IL 60610; tel. 312/467–6555; FAX. 312/467–9683; Elizabeth Reiker, Administrator

Concord West Medical Center, Ltd., 530 North Cass Avenue, Westmont, IL 60559; tel. 630/963–2500; Faramarz Farahati, Managing Director

Day SurgiCenters, Inc., 18 South Michigan Avenue, Suite 700, Chicago, IL 60603; tel. 312/726–2000; FAX. 312/726–3921; Andy Andrikos, Regional Vice President

Dimensions Medical Center, Ltd., 1455 East Golf Road, Suite 108, Des Plaines, IL 60016; tel. 847/390–9300; FAX. 847/390–0035; Vera Schmidt, Administrator

Doctors Surgicenter, 1045 Martin Luther King Jr. Drive, Centralia, IL 62801; tel. 618/532–3110; FAX. 618/532–7226; Charles K. Fischer, M.D., Medical Director

Dreyer Ambulatory Surgery Center, 1221 North Highland Avenue, Aurora, IL 60506; tel. 630/264–8400; FAX. 630/264–8402; James Kuyper, RN, Administrator

Eastland Medical Plaza SurgiCenter, 1505 Eastland Drive, Bloomington, IL 61701; tel. 309/662–2500; FAX. 309/662–7143; Marsha Reeves, Director

Edwardsville Ambulatory Surgical Center, LLC, 12, Ginger Creek Parkway, Glen Carbon, IL 62034; tel. 618/656–8200; FAX. 618/656–8204; Maxine Johnson, Interim Administrator

Effingham Ambulatory Surgical Treatment Center, LTD., 904 West Temple Street, Effingham, IL 62401; tel. 217/342–1234; FAX. 217/342–1230; Leanne Fish, RN, CNOR, Administrator

Elmwood Park Same Day Surgery Center, 1614 North Harlem Avenue, Elmwood Park, IL 60635; tel. 708/452–6102; FAX. 708/452–1614; Ronald W. Hugar, DPM, Administrator

Foot and Ankle Surgical Center, Ltd., 1455 Golf Road, Suite 134, Des Plaines, IL 60016; tel. 847/390–7666; Lowell S. Weil, DPM, FACFS, Administrator

Golf Surgical Center, 8901 Golf Road, Des Plaines, IL 60016; tel. 847/299–2273; FAX. 847/299–2297; Bernard Abrams, M.D., Administrator

Hauser–Ross Surgicenter, Inc., 2240 Gateway Drive, Sycamore, IL 60178; tel. 815/756–8571; FAX. 815/756–1226; Barbara Lauger, Administrator

Health South Surgery Center of Southern Illinois, 806 North Treasury, P.O. Box 1729, Marion, IL 62959; tel. 618/993–2113; FAX. 618/993–2041; Linda Bickers, RN, Administrator

HealthSouth Surgery Center of Hawthorn, 1900 Hollister Drive, Suite 100, Libertyville, IL 60048; tel. 847/367–8100; FAX. 847/367–8335; Dr. Gary Rippberger, Administrator

Hinsdale Surgical Center, Inc., 908 North Elm Street, Suite 401, Hinsdale, IL 60521; tel. 630/325–5035; FAX. 630/325–5134; Shirley E. Zemansky, RN, Administrator

Hope Clinic for Women, Ltd., 1602 21st Street, Granite City, IL 62040; tel. 800/844–3130; FAX. 615/451–9092; Sally Burgess–Griffin, MBA, Executive Director

Horizons Ambulatory Surgery Center, 630 Locust Street, Carthage, IL 62321; tel. 217/357–2173; James E. Coeur, M.D., Administrator

Illinois Eye Surgeons Cataract Surgery, 3990 North Illinois Street, Belleville, IL 62221; tel. 618/235–3100; Cathy Vieluf, Administrator

Ingalls Same Day Surgery, 6701 West 159th Street, Tinley Park, IL 60477; tel. 708/429–0222; FAX. 708/429–0293; John Czech, Administrator

Lakeshore Physicians and Surgery Center, 7200 North Western Avenue, Chicago, IL 60645; tel. 773/743–6700; FAX. 773/761–9226; Phyllis J. Allen, RN, Administrator

Loyola Ambulatory Surgery Center at Oakbrook, One South 224 Summit Avenue, Suite 201, Oakbrook Terr, IL 60181; tel. 630/916–7008; George Abbott, Administrator

LP Central Community Halth Centre, 355 East Fifth Ave., P.O. Box 68, Clifton, IL 60927; tel. 815/694–2392; Steve Wilder, Administrator

Magna Surgical Center, 9831 South Western Avenue, Chicago, IL 60643; tel. 312/445–9696; FAX. 312/445–9590; Yadira Martell, Administrator

Midwest Ambulatory Surgicenter, 7340 West College Drive, Palos Heights, IL 60463; tel. 708/361–3233; FAX. 708/361–4876; Thomas A. Evans, Administrator

Midwest Center for Day Surgery, 3811 Highland Avenue, Downers Grove, IL 60515; tel. 630/852–9300; FAX. 630/852–7773; Ronald P. Ladniak, Administrator

Midwest Eye Center, S.C., 1700 East West Road, Calumet City, IL 60409; tel. 708/891–3330; FAX. 708/891–0904; Afzal Ahmad, M.D., Administrator

Naperville Surgical Centre, 1263 Rickert Drive, Naperville, IL 60540; tel. 630/305–3300; FAX. 630/305–3301; Ronald P. Ladniak

North Shore Endoscopy Center, 101 South Waukegan Road, Suite 980, Lake Bluff, IL 60044; tel. 847/604–8700; FAX. 847/604–8711; Everett P. Kirch, M.D., Administrator

North Shore Same Day Surgicenter, 815 Howard Street, Evanston, IL 60202; tel. 847/869–8500; FAX. 847/869–0028; Edward Atkins, M.D., Medical Director

Northern Illinois Surgery Center, 1620 Sauk Road, Dixon, IL 61021; tel. 815/288–7722; FAX. 815/288–7720; James R. Zeman, Administrator

Northern Illinois Women's Center, Ltd., 1400 Broadway Street, Suite 201, Rockford, IL 61104; tel. 815/963–4101; FAX. 815/963–6122; Deborah D. Demars, Administrator

Northwest Community Day Surgery Center, 675 West Kirchoff Road, Arlington Heights, IL 60005; tel. 847/506–4361; FAX. 847/577–4001; Meaghan Reshoft, Administrator

Notre Dame Hills Surgical Center, 28 North 64th Street, Belleville, IL 62223; tel. 618/398–5705; FAX. 618/398–5764; Kathleen Claunch, RN, Administrator

Nova Med Eye Surgery Center of Maryville, L.L.C., 12 Maryville Professional Center, Maryville, IL 62062; tel. 618/288–7483; Adrienne Forsythe, Administrator

NovaMed Eye Surgery Center River Forest, 7427 Lake Street, River Forest, IL 60305; tel. 708/771–3334; FAX. 708/771–0841; Karen Hyman, Administrator

NovaMed Eye Surgery Center–Northshore, 3034 West Peterson Avenue, Chicago, IL 60659; tel. 773/973–7432; FAX. 773/973–1119; Dawn Lastery, Administrator

Oak Brook Surgical Centre, Inc., 2425 West 22nd Street, Oak Brook, IL 60521; tel. 630/990–2212; FAX. 630/990–3130; George H. Olsen, Administrator

Oak Park Eye Center, S.C., 7055–61 West North Avenue, Oak Park, IL 60302; tel. 708/848–1182; FAX. 708/848–5033; James L. McCarthy, M.D., Administrator

One Day Surgery Center, 4211 North Cicero Avenue, Chicago, IL 60641–1699; tel. 773/794–1000; FAX. 773/794–9738; Christopher Lloyd, Administrator

Orthopedic and Sports Medicine Clinic, P.C., 4325 Alby, P.O. Box 3195, Alton, IL 62002; tel. 618/474–8052; FAX. 618/474–8054; Bruce T. Vest, Jr., M.D., Director, Surgery

Orthopedic Institute of Illinois Ambulatory Surgery Center, 303 North Kumpf Boulevard, Peoria, IL 61605; tel. 309/676–5559; FAX. 309/676–5045; Donna Adair, Administrator

Paulina Surgi–Center, Inc., 7616 North Paulina, Chicago, IL 60626; tel. 312/761–0500; Sheldon Schecter, Administrator

Peoria Ambulatory Surgery Center, 4909 North Glen Park Place, Peoria, IL 61614; tel. 309/691–9069; FAX. 309/691–9286; Cynthia J. Simpson, MBA, Administrator

Peoria Day Surgery Center, 7309 North Knoxville, Peoria, IL 61614; tel. 309/692–9210; FAX. 309–693–6472; Wanda Spacht, RN, CNOR, Nursing Administrator

Physicians' Surgical Center, Ltd., 311 West Lincoln, Suite 300, Belleville, IL 62220; tel. 618/233–7077; FAX. 618/234–5650; Cynthia Chapman, RN, Administrator

Planned Parenthood of East Central Illinois, 302 East Stoughton Street, Champaign, IL 61820; tel. 217/359–8022; FAX. 217/359–2683; Robin Beach, Director of Client Services

Poplar Creek Surgical Center, 1800 McDonough Road, Hoffman Estates, IL 60192; tel. 847/742–7272; FAX. 847/697–3210; Walter Jimenez, Area Manager

Quad City Ambulatory Surgery Center, 520 Valley View Drive, Moline, IL 61265; tel. 309/762–1952; FAX. 309/762–3642; Vicki Sullivan, RN, CNOR, Director, Surgical Services

Quad City Endoscopy, 2525 24th Street, Rock Island, IL 61201; tel. 309/788–5624; FAX. 309/788–5668; Najwa Bayrakdar, Administrator

Regional Surgicenter, Ltd., 545 Valley View Drive, Moline, IL 61265; tel. 309/762–5560; FAX. 309/762–7351; Patt Hunter, Administrator

Resurrection Health Care Surgery Center, 3101 North Harlem Avenue, Chicago, IL 60634; tel. 773/889–2000; FAX. 773/745–5522; Sandra Ankebrant, Executive Director

River North Same Day Surgery, One East Erie, Suite 115, Chicago, IL 60611; tel. 312/649–3939; FAX. 312/649–5747; Patricia Wamsley, Administrator

Rockford Ambulatory Surgery Center, 1016 Featherstone Drive, Rockford, IL 61107; tel. 815/226–3300; FAX. 815/226–9990; Dr. Steven Gunderson, Administrator

Rockford Endoscopy Center, 401 Roxbury Road, Rockford, IL 61107; tel. 815/397–7340; FAX. 815/397–7388; Nancy Norman, Administrator

South Shore Surgicenter, Inc., 8300 South Brandon Avenue, Chicago, IL 60617; tel. 312/721–6000; FAX. 312/721–9861; Lucy Morales, RN, Administrator

Spiritus Dei Eye Surgery Center, 7600 West College Drive, Palos Heights, IL 60463; tel. 708/361–0010; Audrey Schmidt–Annerino, Administrator

Springfield Clinic Ambulatory Surgical Treatment Center, Inc., 1025 South Seventh Street, Springfield, IL 62794–9248; tel. 217/528–7541; Michael Maynard

Springfield Clinic Ambulatory Surgical Treatment Center, Inc., 1025 S. Seventh Street, Springfield, IL 62794–7541; tel. 217/528–7541; J. Michael Maynard, Administrator

Suburban Otolaryngology SurgiCenter, 3340 South Oak Park Avenue, Berwyn, IL 60402; tel. 708/749–3070; FAX. 708/749–3410; Edward A. Razim, M.D., Administrator

Surgicare Center, Inc., 333 Dixie Highway, Chicago Heights, IL 60411; tel. 708/754–4890; FAX. 708/756–1149; Paul Katz, Administrator

Surgicore, Inc., 10547 South Ewing Avenue, Chicago, IL 60617; tel. 773/221–1690; William Wood, DPM, Medical Director

The Center for Orthopedic Medicine, LLC, 2502–B East Empire, Bloomington, IL 61704; tel. 309/662–6120; FAX. 309/663–8972; Tracy J. Silver, RN, Administrator

The Center for Surgery, 475 East Diehl Road, Naperville, IL 60563–1253; tel. 630/505–7733; FAX. 630/505–0656; Eric Myers, Administrator

Valley Ambulatory Surgery Center, 2210 Dean Street, St. Charles, IL 60175; tel. 630/584–9800; FAX. 630/584–9805; Mark Mayo, Facility Director

Watertower Surgicenter Corp., 845 North Michigan Avenue, Suite 994–W, Chicago, IL 60611; tel. 312/944–2929; FAX. 312/944–7769; John M. Sevcik, President and CEO

Women's Aid Clinic, 4751 West Touhy Avenue, Lincolnwood, IL 60646; tel. 847/676–2428; Iris Schneider

INDIANA

Aesthetic Surgery Center, 13590 N. Meridian, Carmel, IN 46032; tel. 317/846–0846; FAX. 317/846–0722; William H. Beeson, M.D., Medical Director

Akin Medical Center, 2019 State Street, New Albany, IN 47150–4963; tel. 812/945–3557; FAX. 812/949–3469; Karyn Cureton, RN, Director, Surgery

Broadwest Surgical Center, 315 W. 89th Ave., Merrillville, IN 46410–2904; tel. 219/757–5275; FAX. 219/757–5290; Lisa M. Goranovich, Administrator

Calumet Surgery Center, 7847 Calumet Avenue, Munster, IN 46321–1296; tel. 219/836–5102; FAX. 219/836–4493; Gloria J. Portney, RN, Chief Administrative Officer

Central Indiana Surgery Center, 9002 North Meridian, Lower Level, Indianapolis, IN 46260; tel. 317/846–9906; FAX. 317/846–9949; William E. Whitson, M.D., Medical Director

Columbia Physicancare Outpatient Surgery Center, L.L.P., 7460 North Shadeland, Indianapolis, IN 46250; tel. 317/577–7450; FAX. 317/577–7462; Maureen Chernoff, RN, Administrator

Columbus Surgery Center, 940 North Marr Road, Suite B, Columbus, IN 47201; tel. 812/372–1370; Colleen M. North, Executive Director

Digestive Health Center, 1120 AAA Way, Suite A, Carmel, IN 46032–3210; tel. 317/848–5494; FAX. 317/575–0392; Daniel J. Stout, M.D., President

Dupont Ambulatory Surgery Center, 2510 East Dupont Road, Suite 130, Fort Wayne, IN 46825; tel. 219/489–8785; FAX. 219/489–2148; Rick C. Trego, Administrator

Evansville Surgery Center, 1212 Lincoln Ave., Evansville, IN 47714–1076; tel. 812/428–0810; FAX. 812/421–6070; Cathy Head, RN, Facility Manager

Foot and Ankle Surgery Center, Inc., 1950 West 86th Street, Suite 105, Indianapolis, IN 46260; tel. 317/334–0232; FAX. 317/334–0268; Anthony E. Miller, D.P.M., Administrator

Fort Wayne Cardiology Outpatient Catheterization Laboratory, 1819 Carew Street, Fort Wayne, IN 46805; tel. 219/481–4896; FAX. 219/481–4814; Douglas W. Martin, RN, M.B.A., Director of Clinical Operations

Fort Wayne Ophthalmic Surgical Center, 321 East Wayne Street, Ft. Wayne, IN 46802–2713; tel. 219/422–5976; FAX. 219/424–4511; J. Rex Parent, M.D., Chief Executive Officer

Fort Wayne Orthopaedics LLC Surgicenter, 7601 West Jefferson Boulevard, P.O. Box 2526, Fort Wayne, IN 46801–2526; tel. 219/436–8383; FAX. 219/436–8585; Ronald W. Cousino, Jr., Administrator

Gastrointestinal Endoscopy Center, 801 St. Mary's Drive, Suite 110 West, Evansville, IN 47714; tel. 812/477–6103; FAX. 812/477–4897; Christine Wittman, Administrator

Grand Park Surgical Center, 1479 East 84th Place, Merrillville, IN 46410; tel. 219/738–2828; FAX. 219/756–3349; Chris Macarthy, Administrator

Grossnickle Eye Surgery Center, Inc., 2251 DuBois Drive, Warsaw, IN 46580–3292; tel. 219/269–3777; FAX. 219/269–9828; Shirley Rhodes, RN, Administrative Director

Illiana Surgery Center, 701 Superior Avenue, Munster, IN 46321; tel. 219/924–1300; FAX. 219/922–4856; Virgil Villaflor, Executive Director

IMA Endoscopy Surgicenter, P.C., 8895 Broadway, Merrillville, IN 46411; tel. 219/736–4660; FAX. 219/736–4663; Dawn Graham, Administrator

Indiana Eye Clinic, 30 North Emerson Avenue, Greenwood, IN 46143–9760; tel. 317/881–3931; FAX. 317/887–4008; Charles O. McComnick, M.D., Administrator

Indiana Surgery Center, 8040 Clearvista Parkway, Indianapolis, IN 46256–1695; tel. 317/841–2000; FAX. 317/841–2005; Amy Glover, Administrator

Indiana Surgery Center, 1550 East County Line Road, Suite 100, Indianapolis, IN 46227; tel. 317/887–7600; FAX. 317–887–7606; Peggy Davidson, Administrator

Indiana Surgery Center – North Campus, 8040 Clearvista Parkway, Indianapolis, IN 46256; tel. 317/841–2000; FAX. 317/841–2005; Amy D. Glover, RN, B.S.N., Administrator

Indianapolis Endoscopy Center, 7353 East 21st Street, Indianapolis, IN 46219; tel. 317/353–2232; FAX. 317/353–2522; David Hollander, M.D.

Lafayette Ambulatory Surgery Center, 3733 Rome Drive, Box 6477, Lafayette, IN 47903; tel. 765/449–5272; FAX. 765/449–5856; Dale T. Krynak, Executive Director

Medivision, 1305 Wall Street, Suite 101, Jeffersonville, IN 47130–3898; tel. 812/288–9674; FAX. 812/283–6955; Marsha Parker, Administrator

Meridian Endoscopy Center, 1801 North Senate, Suite 400, Indianapolis, IN 46202; tel. 317/929–5660; FAX. 317/929–2346; Robert J. Whitmore, Executive Director

Meridian Plastic Surgery Center, 170 West 106th Street, Indianapolis, IN 46290–1004; tel. 317/575–0110; FAX. 317/571–8667; Melody McDermitt, RN, Director

MHC Surgical Center Associates, Inc., d/b/a Broadwest Surgical Center, 315 West 89th Avenue, Merrillville, IN 46410–2904; tel. 219/757–5275; FAX. 219/757–5290; Melvin Lichtenfeld, P.D., Administrator

Michigan Endoscopy Center, LLC, 53830 Generation Drive, South Bend, IN 46635; tel. 219–271–0893; FAX. 219–271–1285; John G. Mathis, M.D., CEO

Midwest Surgery Centers, Inc., 650 Surgery Center Drive, Terre Haute, IN 47802; tel. 812/232–8325; FAX. 812/234–8385; Terry Havens, RN, Administrator

Muncie Ambulatory Surgicenter, LLC, 200 North Tillotson Avenue, Muncie, IN 47304–3988; tel. 765/286–8888; FAX. 765/747–7962; L. Marshall Roch, M.D., Medical Director

Munster Same Day Surgery Center, 761 Forty Fifth Avenue, Suite 116, Munster, IN 46321; tel. 219/924–3090; FAX. 219/924–2161; Edward Atkins, President

Nasser Smith and Pinkerton Cardiac Cath Lab, 8333 Naab Road, Suite 400, Indianapolis, IN 46260; tel. 317/338–6094; FAX. 317/338–6066; Stephen A. McAdams, M.D., CEO

North Indianapolis Surgery Center, 8651 North Township Line Road, Indianapolis, IN 46260–1578; tel. 317/876–2090; FAX. 317/876–2097; Dean E. Lehmkuhler, Facility Administrator

North Meridian Surgery Center, 10601 North Meridian, Suite 100, Indianapolis, IN 46290; tel. 317/574–5400; FAX. 317–575–0173; Susan Matouk, Director

Northeast Indiana Endoscopy Center, 7900 West Jefferson Boulevard, Fort Wayne, IN 46804; tel. 219/436–6213; FAX. 219/432–6388; Jerry Steele, Administrator

Northside Cardiac Cath Lab, 8333 Naab Road, Suite 180, Indianapolis, IN 46260; tel. 317/338–9001; FAX. 317/338–9045; Beth Higgins, RN, MSN, Clinical Director

NovaMed Eyecare Management, L.L.C., 8514 Broadway, Merrillville, IN 46410; tel. 219/756–5010; FAX. 219/736–2222; Joan Klug, Administrator

NovaMed Eyecare Management, L.L.C., d/b/a NovaMed Eye Surgery Center–Hammond, 6836 Hohman Avenue, Hammond, IN 46324; tel. 219/937–5063; FAX. 219/937–5068; Renee Peters, Administrator

Oakview Surgical Center, Inc., 120 E. 18th St., Rochester, IN 66975; tel. 219/224–7500; FAX. 219/223–3057; Laurence C. Rogers, D.P.M., Administrator

Outpatient Surgery Center of Indiana, LLP, 711 Gardner Drive, Marion, IN 46952; tel. 317/664–2000; FAX. 317/668–6797; Dixie Hewitt, RN, Director

Richmond Surgery Center, 1900 Chester Boulevard, Richmond, IN 47374; tel. 765/966–1776; FAX. 765/962–1191; Lynn Greene, Director

Riverpointe Surgery Center, 500 Arcade Avenue, Suite 100, Elkhart, IN 46514–2459; tel. 219/522–9505; Robert Scheller, Administrator

Sagamore Surgical Services, Inc., 2320 Concord Road, Suite B, Lafayette, IN 47905; tel. 317/474–7838; FAX. 317/474–7853; Carol Blanar, Administrator

South Bend Clinic Surgicenter, 211 North Eddy Street, P.O. Box 4061, South Bend, IN 46634–4061; tel. 219/237–9366; FAX. 219/237–9363; Kevin R. Boyer, Administrator

Southern Indiana Surgery Center, 2800 Rex Grossman Boulevard, Bloomington, IN 47403; tel. 812/333–8969; FAX. 812/335–2309; Miriam Malone, RN, B.S.N., Executive Director

Surgery Center of Eye Specialists, 1901 North Meridian Street, Indianapolis, IN 46202; tel. 317/925–2200; FAX. 317/921–6614; Dan Bradford, Administrator

Surgery Center of Fort Wayne, L. P., d/b/a HealthSouth Premier Surgery Center, 1333 Maycrest Drive, Fort Wayne, IN 46805–5478; tel. 219/423–3339; FAX. 219/423–6344; Mary Schafer, Administrator

Surgery Center of Southeastern Indiana, Inc., 999 N. Michigan Ave., Greensburg, IN 47240; tel. 812/663–3222; FAX. 812/663–3622; Charlotte Boden, B.S.N., RN

Surgery Center Plus, 7430 North Shadeland Avenue, Suite 100, Indianapolis, IN 46250–2025; tel. 317/841–8005; FAX. 317/577–7538; James Hansen, Administrator

Surgery One, 5052 North Clinton, Fort Wayne, IN 46825–5822; tel. 219/482–5194; FAX. 219/482–5686; Julia Ellert, Director

Surgical Care Center, Inc., 8103 Clearvista Parkway, Indianapolis, IN 46256–4600; tel. 317/842–5173; FAX. 317/570–7429; Brian Smith, Executive Director

Surgical Center of New Albany, 2201 Green Valley Road, New Albany, IN 47150–4648; tel. 812/949–1223; FAX. 812/945–4765; Tamara E. Jones, B.S.N., Administrator

Surgicare, 2907 McIntire Drive, Bloomington, IN 47403; tel. 812/339–8000; FAX. 812/339–2524; Sonya M. Zeller, Administrator

The Ambulatory Care Center, 1125 Professional Boulevard, Evansville, IN 47714; tel. 812/475–1000; FAX. 812/475–1001; Diana McDaniel, Clinical Administrator

The Center for Specialty Surgery of Fort Wayne, Inc., 2730 East State Boulevard, Fort Wayne, IN 46805–4731; tel. 219/483–2540; FAX. 219/483–3097; Andrea Kelley, RN, Director, Nursing

The Endoscopy Center, 8051 South Emerson, Suite 150, Indianapolis, IN 46237; tel. 317/865–2950; FAX. 317/865–2952; Robert Intress, Ph.D., Administrator

The Heart Group Outpatient Cath Lab, 415 West Columbia Street, Evansville, IN 47710; tel. 812/464–0545; FAX. 812/464–0560; Sue Krieg, RN, Clinical Manager

The Indiana Hand Surgery Center, 8501 Harcourt Road, P.O. Box 80434, Indianapolis, IN 46260–0434; tel. 317/875–9105; FAX. 317–471–4382; Valeria M. Wareham, Chief Operating Officer

Unity Surgery Center, 1011 West Second Street, Bloomington, IN 47403–2216; tel. 812/334–1213; FAX. 812/333–5039; Michael D. Bishop, M.D., CEO

Valley Cataract and Laser Institute, Inc., 220 East Virginia, Evansville, IN 47711; tel. 812/435–1600; FAX. 812/435–1603; Lisa J. Gossman–Werner, Facility Administrator

Valparaiso Physician and Surgery Center, 1700 Pointe Drive, Valparaiso, IN 46383; tel. 219/531–5000; FAX. 219/531–5010; Lilly Veljovic, RN, Manager

Welborn Clinic Surgery Center, 421 Chestnut Street, Evansville, IN 47713; tel. 812/426–9412; Claudia R. Earnest, Administrator

Zollman Surgery Center, Inc., 7439 Woodland Drive, Indianapolis, IN 46268; tel. 317/328–1100; FAX. 317/328–6948; Julie Berzins, RN, Administrator

IOWA

Ambulatory Surgery Center, 931 13th Avenue, N., P.O. Box 608, Clinton, IA 52733–0608; tel. 319/242–3937; FAX. 319/242–3845; Renelda Ebensberger, Supervisor

Center for Day Surgery, 931 13th Ave., North, Clinton, IA 52733–0608; tel. 319/242–3937; Patricia McCeachron, Administrator

Iowa Endoscopy Center, 2600 Grand Avenue, Suite 418, Des Moines, IA 50312; tel. 515/288–3342; Gloria Dayton, Administrator

Iowa Eye Institute, 1721 West 18th Street, Spencer, IA 51301; tel. 712/262–8878; FAX. 712/262–8807; Dennis D. Gordy, M.D., Administrator

Jones Eye Clinic, 4405 Hamilton Boulevard, Sioux City, IA 51104; tel. 712/239–3937; Charles E. Jones, M.D., Medical Director

Mississippi Valley Surgery Center, L.C., 3400 Dexter Court, Suite 200, Davenport, IA 52807; tel. 319/344–6600; FAX. 319/344–6699; John B. Dooley, Administrator

Spring Park Surgery Center, LLC, 3319 Spring Street, Suite 202–A, Davenport, IA 52807; tel. 319/355–6236; FAX. 319/359–6347; Paul Rohlf, M.D., Administrator

Surgery Center of Des Moines, 1301 Penn Avenue, Suite 100, Des Moines, IA 50312; tel. 515/266–3140; FAX. 515/266–3073; Kathleen Supplee, RN, Administrator

KANSAS

College Park Family Care Center, 11725 West 112th Street, Overland Park, KS 66210–2761; tel. 913/469–5579; Chuck Chambers, Administrator

Columbia Mt. Oread Surgery Centre, 3500 Clinton Parkway Place, Lawrence, KS 66047–1985; tel. 913/843–9300; FAX. 913/843–9301; Nancy Sturgeon, Administrator

Columbia Surgicenter of Johnson County, 8800 Ballentine Street, Overland Park, KS 66214–1985; tel. 913/894–4050; FAX. 913/894–0384; Nancy E. Sturgeon, Administrator

Comprehensive Health for Women, 4401 West 109th Street, Overland Park, KS 66211–1303; tel. 913/345–1400; Sheila Kostas, Director, Human Resources

Cotton–O'Neil Clinic Endoscopy Center, 823 Southwest Mulvane Street, Suite 375, Topeka, KS 66606–1679; tel. 913/354–0538; FAX. 913/368–0735; Irene Hasenbank, RN, Administrator

Emporia Ambulatory Surgery Center, 2528 West 15th Avenue, Emporia, KS 66801–6102; tel. 316/343–2233; J. E. Bosiljevac, M.D., Administrator

Endoscopic Services, P.A., 1431 South Bluffview Street, Suite 215, Wichita, KS 67218–3000; tel. 316/687–0234; FAX. 316/687–0360; Jace Hyder, M.D.

Endoscopy and Surgery Center of Topeka, L.P., 2200 Southwest Sixth Avenue, Suite 103, Topeka, KS 66606–1707; tel. 913/354–1254; FAX. 913/354–1255; Ashraf M. Sufi, M.D., Medical Director

EyeSurg of Kansas City, 5520 College Boulevard, Overland Park, KS 66211–1600; tel. 913/491–3757; FAX. 913/469–6686; Phillip Hoopes, M.D., Medical Administrator

Great Plains Clinic, 201 East Seventh, Hays, KS 67601; tel. 913/628–8251; William Norris, Administrator

Hutchinson Clinic Ambulatory Surgery Center, 2101 North Waldron, Hutchinson, KS 67502; tel. 316/669–2500; Murray Holcomb, Administrator

Kansas Ambulatory Surgery Center, 7015 East Central Street, Wichita, KS 67206–1940; tel. 316/684–9300; FAX. 316/652–7618; Robert G. Clark, M.D., Medical Director

Laser Center, 1518A East Iron Avenue, Salina, KS 67401–3236; tel. 913/825–6016; Brian E. Conner, M.D., Administrator

Laser Center–Russell, 222 South Kansas, Suite A, Russell, KS 67665–3029; tel. 913/825–6016; Brian Conner, Administrator

Microsurgery, Inc., 920 Southwest Washburn Avenue, Topeka, KS 66606–1527; tel. 913/233–3939; Adrienne V. Prokop, Administrator

Newman–Young Clinic–A.S.C., 710 West Eighth Street, Fort Scott, KS 66701–2404; tel. 316/223–3100; FAX. 316/223–5390; Thomas W. Smith, Administrator

Newton Surgery Centre, 215 South Pine Street, Newton, KS 67114–3761; tel. 316/283–4400; Sondra L. Leatherman, Administrator

Ochsner Eye Medical/Associated Eye Surgical Center, 1100 North Topeka Street, Wichita, KS 67214–2810; tel. 316/263–6273; FAX. 316/263–5568; Bruce B. Ochsner, Medical Director

South Pointe Surgery Center, 151 West 151st Street, Suite 200, Olathe, KS 66061–5351; tel. 913/782–3631; FAX. 913/782–2606; Katherine Thon, RN, Administrator

Surgery Center of Kansas, Inc., 1507 West 21st Street, Wichita, KS 67203–2449; tel. 316/838–8388; FAX. 316/838–2999; Karen Gabbert, RN, B.S.N., Administrator

Surgicare of Wichita, Inc., 810 North Lorraine, Wichita, KS 67214–4841; tel. 316/685–2207; FAX. 316/685–2861; Carolyn J. Exley, Administrator

Team Vision Surgery Center East, 6100 East Central Street, Suite Six, Wichita, KS 67208–4237; tel. 316/684–8013; Linda S. Buettner, Vice President

Team Vision Surgery Center West, 834 North Socora, Suite One, Wichita, KS 67212–3238; tel. 316/681–2020; Linda Buettner, Administrator

The Center for Same Day Surgery, 818 North Emporia Street, Suite 108, Wichita, KS 67214–3725; tel. 316/262–7263; FAX. 316/262–6253; Michele LeGate, RN, B.S., Administrator

The Headache and Pain Center, 11111 Nall Avenue, Suite 222, Leawood, KS 66211–1625; tel. 913/491–3999; FAX. 913/491–6453; Steven D. Waldman, Administrator

The Wichita Clinic DaySurgery, 3311 East Murdock Street, Wichita, KS 67208–3054; tel. 316/689–9349; James A. Greer, Jr., Administrator

Topeka Single Day Surgery, 823 Southwest Mulvane Street, Suite 101, Topeka, KS 66606–1679; tel. 913/354–8737; FAX. 913/354–1440; Linda Daniel, Executive Director

KENTUCKY

Ambulatory Surgery Center, 2831 Lone Oak Road, Paducah, KY 42003; tel. 502/554–8373; FAX. 502/554–8987; Laxmaiah Manchikanti, M.D.

Caritas Surgical Center, 4414 Churchman Avenue, Louisville, KY 40215; tel. 502/366–9525; Danny Cain

Center For Surgical Care, 7575 U.S. 42, Florence, KY 41042; tel. 606/283–9100; FAX. 606/283–6046; Thomas Mayer, M.D., Medical Director

Columbia Owensboro Surgery Center, 1100 Walnut Street, Suite 13, Owensboro, KY 42301; tel. 502/683–2751; FAX. 502/926–1618; Donna R. Norton, Administrator

Dupont Surgery Center, 4004 Dupont Circle, Louisville, KY 40207; tel. 502/896–6428; FAX. 502/895–6787; Vicki Lococo, Nurse Manager

E.M.W. Women's Surgical Center, 138 West Market Street, Louisville, KY 40202; tel. 502/589–2124; FAX. 502/589–1588; Dona F. Wells, Administrator

East Bernstadt Outpatient Surgery Center, 2737 North U.S. Highway 25, East Bernstad, KY 40729; tel. 606/843–6100; Darby Radmanesdh, Administrator

HealthSouth Surge Center of Louisville, 4005 DuPont Circle, Louisville, KY 40207; tel. 502/897–7401; FAX. 502/897–5652; Sheila S. Boros, Administrator

Lexington Clinic, 1221 South Broadway, Lexington, KY 40504; tel. 606/258–4000; FAX. 606/258–4795; Thomas Holets, Executive Director

Lexington Surgery Center, 1725 Harrodsburg Road, Lexington, KY 40504; tel. 606/276–2525; FAX. 606/277–6497; Bemedji Asher, Administrator

Louisville Surgery Center, 614 East Chestnut Street, Louisville, KY 40202; tel. 502/589–9488; FAX. 502/589–9928; Jane E. Burbank, Administrator

McPeak Center For Eye Care, 1507 Bravo Boulevard, Glasgow, KY 42141; tel. 502/651–2181; FAX. 502/651–2183; Nancy McPeak, Administrator

Medical Heights Surgery Center, 2374 Nicholasville Road, Lexington, KY 40503; tel. 606/278–1460; FAX. 606/278–0115; John Johnson, Facility Director

Outpatient Care Center at Jewish Hospital, 225 Abraham Flexner Way, Louisville, KY 40202; tel. 502/587–4709; FAX. 502/587–4323; Kim Tharp–Barrie, Administrator

Pikeville United Methodist Hospital of Kentucky, Inc., 911 South By-Pass Road, Pikeville, KY 41501; tel. 606/437–3500; FAX. 606/432–9479; Martha O'Regan Chill, Administrator and CEO

Somerset Surgery Center, 353 Bogle Street, Suite 101, Somerset, KY 42501; tel. 606/679–9322; FAX. 606/678–2666; Kathy Turner, Administrator

Stone Road Surgery Center, 280 Pasadena Drive, Lexington, KY 40503; tel. 606/278–1316; FAX. 606/276–3847; Ballard Wright, President

Surgical Center of Elizabethtown, 708 Westport Road, Elizabethtown, KY 42701; tel. 502/737–5200; FAX. 502/765–5362; Suzanne Broadwater, Administrator

The Eye Surgery Center of Paducah, 100 Medical Center Drive, P.O. Box 8269, Paducah, KY 42002–8269; tel. 502/442–1024; FAX. 502/442–1001; Kelly Harris, RN, Administrator

Tri-State Digestive Disorder Center Ambulatory Surgery Center, 196 Barnwood Drive, Edgewood, KY 41017; tel. 606/341–3575; Stephen W. Hiltz, M.D.

LOUISIANA

Acadiana Endoscopy Center, 113 St. Louis Street, Lafayette, LA 70506; tel. 318/269–1126; FAX. 318/269–0553; Stephen M. Person, M.D., Administrator

Acadiana Surgery Center, Inc., 1100 Andre Street, Suite 300, New Iberia, LA 70560; tel. 318/364–9680; FAX. 318/364–9689

Alexandria Laser and Surgery Center, 4100 Parliament Drive, Alexandria, LA 71303; tel. 318/487–8342; FAX. 318/487–9942; M. L. Revelett, Administrator

Ambulatory Eye Surgery Center of Louisiana, 3900 Veterans Boulevard, Suite 100, Metairie, LA 70002; tel. 504/455–1550; FAX. 504/455–2011; Mark Brown, Administrator

Baton Rouge Ambulatory Surgicare Services, 5328 Didesse Drive, Baton Rouge, LA 70808; tel. 504/766–1718; FAX. 504/767–3034; Laura B. Cronin, Administrator

Broussard Surgery Institute, 1250 Pecanland Road, Suite E–1, Monroe, LA 71203; tel. 318/387–2015; FAX. 318/387–2097; Gerald Broussard, M.D., Administrator

Browne–McHardy Outpatient Surgery Center, 4315 Houma Boulevard, Metairie, LA 70006–2981; tel. 504/889–5218; FAX. 504/889–5224; Robert L. Goldstein, Chief Administrative Officer

Central Louisiana Ambulatory Surgical Center, 720 Madison Street, P.O. Box 8646, Alexandria, LA 71301; tel. 318/443–3511; Louise Barker, RN, Administrator

Colonnade Surgery, 555 South Ryan Street, Lake Charles, LA 70601; tel. 318/439–6226; FAX. 312/436–6223; Pam Ragusa, Administrator

Columbia Greater New Orleans Surgery Center, 3434 Houma Boulevard, Metairie, LA 70006; tel. 504/888–7100; Claire G. Manuel, RN, Administrator

Columbia Surgicare of Lake Charles, 214 South Ryan Street, Lake Charles, LA 70601; tel. 318/436–6941; FAX. 318/439–3384; Debbie Boudreaux, Administrator

Eye Care and Surgery Center, 10423 Old Hammond Highway, Baton Rouge, LA 70816; tel. 504/923–0960; FAX. 504/923–2419; M. Brian Roper

Foot Surgery Center of Shreveport, 9308 Mansfield Road, Suite 300, Shreveport, LA 71118; tel. 318/686–9622; Arnold M. Castellano, Administrator

Gamble Ambulatory Surgery Center, 2601 Line Avenue, Suite B, Shreveport, LA 71104; tel. 318/424–3291; Michael Drews, D.P.M., Administrator

Green Clinic Surgery Center, 1200 South Farmerville Street, Ruston, LA 71270; tel. 318/255–3690; FAX. 318/251–6116; Glenn Scott, Executive Director

HealthSouth Surgi–Center of Baton Rouge, 5222 Brittany Drive, Baton Rouge, LA 70808; tel. 225/767–5636; FAX. 225/769–9107; Celeste M. Wiggins, Administrator

Hedgewood Surgical Center, 2427 St. Charles Avenue, New Orleans, LA 70130; tel. 504/895–7642; FAX. 504/895–0728; Sally Carpenter, RN

Houma Outpatient Surgery Center, Ltd., 3800 Houma Boulevard, Suite 250, Metairie, LA 70006; tel. 504/456–1515; Jay Weil III, President and CEO

Houma Surgi Center, Inc., 1020 School Street, Houma, LA 70360; tel. 504/868–4320; FAX. 504/868–3617; Robert M. Alexander, M.D., Administrator

LaHaye Center for Advanced Care, 201 Rue Iberville, Lafayette, LA 70508; tel. 318/235–2149; Darryl Wagley

LaHaye Eye and Ambulatory Surgical Center, 100 Harry Guilbeau Road, Opelousas, LA 70570; tel. 318/942–2024; FAX. 318/948–8869; Dana Cockran, Administrator

Lake Forest Surgical Center, 10545 Lake Forest Boulevard, New Orleans, LA 70127; tel. 504/244–3000; FAX. 504/246–2600; Nina Ory, RN, Facility Manager

Lakeview Surgery and Diagnostic Center, Inc., 800 Heavens Drive, Mandeville, LA 70471; tel. 504/845–7100; FAX. 504/845–7596; Glenda P. Escudero–Dobson, Administrator

Laser and Surgery Center of Acadiana, 514 St. Landry Street, Lafayette, LA 70506; tel. 318/234–2020; FAX. 318/234–8230; Barbara L. Azar, Administrator

Laser and Surgery Center of the South, 1101 Audubon Avenue, Suite S–Four, Thibodaux, LA 70301; tel. 504/447–7258; FAX. 504/448–1521; M. L. Revelett, Administrator

Louisiana Endoscopy Center, Inc., 8150 Jefferson Highway, Baton Rouge, LA 70809; tel. 504/927–0970; FAX. 504/927–0988; Lorrie Rogerson, Administrator

Louisville Plaza Surgery Center, 3101 Kilpatrick Boulevard, Suite B, Monroe, LA 71201; tel. 318/322–5916; FAX. 318/322–5916; Frank Wilderman, D.P.M., Administrator

LSU Eye Surgery Center, 2020 Gravier Street, Suite B, New Orleans, LA 70112; tel. 504/568–6700; W. L. Blackwell, Chief Executive Officer

Magnolia Surgical Facility, 3939 Houma Boulevard, Suite 216, Metairie, LA 70006; tel. 504/455–7771; FAX. 504/885–5063; Hamid Massiha, M.D., Administrator

Marrero SurgiCenter, Inc., 4511 Westbank Expressway, Suite B, Marrero, LA 70072; tel. 504/340–1993; John Schiro, M.D., Administrator

MGA GI Diagnostic and Therapeutic Center, 1111 Medical Center Boulevard, Suite 310, Marrero, LA 70072; tel. 504/349–6401; FAX. 504/349–6444; Thomas D. McCaffery, Jr., President

MGA GI Diagnostic and Therapeutic Center, 2633 Napolean Avenue, Suite 707, New Orleans, LA 70115; tel. 504/349–6401; FAX. 504/349–6444; Thomas D. McCaffery, Jr., Administrator

Ochsner Clinic–Center for Cosmetic Surgery, 1514 Jefferson Highway, Fifth Floor, New Orleans, LA 70121; tel. 504/842–3950; FAX. 504/842–5003; Rachel Franz, RN, B.S.N., Manager

Omega Ambulatory Surgical Institute, One Galleria Boulevard, Suite 810, Metairie, LA 70001; tel. 504/832–4200; Rene Rosenson, Administrator

Outpatient Eye Surgery Center, 4324 Veterans Boulevard, Metairie, LA 70006; tel. 504/455–4046; FAX. 504/455–9890; Cheryl Crouse, RN, Administrator

Outpatient Surgery Center for Sight, 550 Connell's Park Lane, Baton Rouge, LA 70809; tel. 504/924–2020; Alan DeCorte, Administrator

Physicians Surgery Center, 218 Corporate Drive, Houma, LA 70360; tel. 504/853–1390; FAX. 504/853–1470; Connie K. Martin, Administrator

Prytania Surgery, Inc., 3525 Prytania Street, New Orleans, LA 70115; tel. 504/897–8880; Jay Weil III, Administrator

Saints Streets ASC Endoscopy Center, Inc., 201 St. Patrick Street, Suite 202, Lafayette, LA 70506; tel. 318/232–6697; FAX. 318/233–8065; Stephen G. Abshire, M.D., Administrator

Shreveport Endoscopy Center, A.M.C., 3217 Mabel Street, P.O. Box 37045, Shreveport, LA 71133–7045; tel. 318/631–0072; FAX. 318/631–9688; Linda Ray, Administrator

Shreveport Surgery Center, 745 Olive Street, Suite 100, Shreveport, LA 71104; tel. 318/227–1163; FAX. 318/227–0413; Mary Jones, Administrator

St. Francis P and S Surgery Center, 312 Grammont Street, P.O. Box 3187, Monroe, LA 71201–3187; tel. 318/388–4040; FAX. 318/388–4099; Keith Kelley, Administrator

Surgery Center, Inc., 1101 South College Road, Suite 100, Lafayette, LA 70503; tel. 318/233–8603; FAX. 318/234–0341; Russell J. Arceneaux, Administrator

Surginet Outpatient Surgery, LLC, 101 La Rue France, Suite 400, Lafayette, LA 70508; tel. 318/269–9828; FAX. 318/269–9823; August J. Rantz III, Administrator

Surgiunit, Inc., 4204 Teuton Street, Metairie, LA 70006; tel. 504/888–3836; Gustavo A. Colon, M.D., Administrator

The Endoscopy Center of Monroe, 316 South Sixth Street, Monroe, LA 71201; tel. 318/325–2649; FAX. 318/325–0717; Andy W. Waldo, Administrator

The Endoscopy Clinic of Lake Charles Medical and Surgical Clinic, 501 South Ryan, Lake Charles, LA 70601; tel. 318/433–8400; Robert Oates, Administrator

The Outpatient Surgery Center of Baton Rouge, 505 East Airport Drive, Baton Rouge, LA 70806; tel. 504/925–2031; FAX. 504/924–2809; Lorraine Caraway, Administrator

The Plastic Surgery Center, Inc., 4224 Houma Boulevard, Suite 430, Metairie, LA 70006; tel. 504/456–5150; FAX. 504/456–5055; James B. Johnson, M.D., Administrator

The Surgery Suite, 103 Medical Center Drive, Slidell, LA 70461; tel. 504/646–4466; FAX. 504/646–4485; Allison F. Maestro, RN, Administrator

Urology Specialty and Surgery Center, 234 South Ryan Street, Lake Charles, LA 70601; tel. 318/433–5282; FAX. 318/433–1159; Charles Enright, Administrator

West Monroe Endoscopy Center, 102 Thomas Road, Suite 506, West Monroe, LA 71291; tel. 318/388–8878; Fred W. Ortmann III, Administrator

Westbank Medical Clinic Surgical Facility, Inc., 4700 Wichers Drive, Suite 200, Marrero, LA 70072; Robert L. Sudderth, Administrator

Young Eye Surgery Center, Inc., 204 North Magdalen Square, Abbeville, LA 70510; tel. 318/893–4452; FAX. 318/893–7870; Virginia Y. Hebert, Administrator

MAINE

Acadia Medical Arts Ambulatory Surgical Suite, 404 State Street, Bangor, ME 04401; tel. 207/990–0928; Jordan J. Shubert, M.D., President

Aroostook County Regional Ophthalmology Center, 148 Academy Street, Presque Isle, ME 04769; tel. 207/764–0376; FAX. 207/764–7612; Craig W. Young, M.D., Director

Eye Care and Surgery Center of Maine, P.A., 53 Sewall Street, Portland, ME 04102; tel. 207/773–6336; FAX. 207/773–7034; William S. Holt, M.D., President

Maine Cataract and Eye Center, 386 Bridgton Road, Route 302, Westbrook, ME 04092; tel. 207/797–9214; FAX. 207/797–8236; Elliot Schweid, D.O., Director

Maine Eye Center, P.A., 15 Lowell Street, Portland, ME 04102; tel. 207/774–8277; FAX. 207/871–1415; Frank Read, M.D., Director

Northern Maine Ambulatory Endoscopy Center, 11 Martin Street, P.O. Box 748, Presque Isle, ME 04769–0151; tel. 207/764–2482; FAX. 207/764–1569; Shelley Kenney, RN, Nurse Manager

Orthopedic Surgery Center, 33 Sewall Street, Portland, ME 04102; tel. 207/828–2130; FAX. 207/828–2190; Linda M. Ruterbories, Medical Director

Portland Endoscopy Center, 131 Chadwick Street, Portland, ME 04102–3266; tel. 207/773–7964; FAX. 207/773–9073; Michael Roy, M.D., President

Western Avenue Day Surgery Center, a/k/a Plastic and Hand Surgical Associates, P.A., 244 Western Avenue, South Portland, ME 04106; tel. 207/775–3446; FAX. 207/879–1646; Jean J. Labelle, M.D., President

MARYLAND

Albert Shoumer, D.P.M., Dundalk Professional Center, 40 South Dundalk Avenue, Dundalk, MD 21222; tel. 410/282–6434; FAX. 410/284–4636; Darleen Grupp, Office Manager

Albert Shoumer, D.P.M., 1645 Liberty Road, Eldersburg, MD 21784; tel. 310/795–2889

Amber Meadows Ambulatory Care Center, Inc., 198 Thomas Johnson Drive, Suite Three, Frederick, MD 21702; tel. 301/695–9669; FAX. 301/695–0346

Amber Ridge Operating Room Center, 1475 Taney Avenue, Suite 101, Frederick, MD 21702; tel. 301/694–5656; FAX. 301/846–4117; Lorin F. Busselberg, M.D., Director

Section C

Ambulatory Foot Surgery Center of Burtonsville, Inc., 15300 Spencerville Court, Suite 101, Burtonsville, MD 20866; tel. 301/421–4286; Dr. Kressin, President

Ambulatory Plastic Surgery–Robert Conrad, M.D., 9715 Medical Center Drive, Rockville, MD 20850; tel. 301/948–5670; FAX. 301/948–5598; Linda Quesenberry, Assistant Office Manager

American Podiatric Surgery, 10236 River Road, Potomac, MD 20854; tel. 301/983–9873; FAX. 301/299–3985; Amy Meehan, Administrator

Annapolis Plastic Surgery Center, 1300 Ritchie Highway, Arnold, MD 21012; tel. 410/544–0707; FAX. 410/544–0724; Jack Frost, M.D., President

Anne Arundel Gastroenterology Endoscopy Center, 703 Giddings Avenue, Suite M, Annapolis, MD 21401; tel. 410/224–2116; Cheryl L. Smith, Office Manager

Armiger, William G., M.D., P.A., d/b/a Chesapeake Plastic Surgery Associates, 1421 South Caton Avenue, Suite 203, Baltimore, MD 21227; tel. 410/646–3226; FAX. 410/644–2134; Sandra Pappas, Administrator

Arundel Ambulatory Center for Endoscopy, 621 Ridgley Avenue, Suite 101, Annapolis, MD 21401; tel. 410/224–3636; FAX. 410/224–6971; Jeff Hazel, Practice Administrator

Ashok K. Narang, M.D., P.A., Two North Avenue, Suite 102, Belair, MD 21014; tel. 410/877–7595

Baltimore Ambulatory Center for Endoscopy, 19 Fontana Lane, Suite 104, Baltimore, MD 21237; tel. 410/574–7776; FAX. 410/574–9038; Dr. V. Sivan, Medical Director

Baltimore County Out–Patient Plastic Surgery Center, 1205 York Road, Suite 36, Lutherville, MD 21093; tel. 410/828–9570; FAX. 410/583–9120; Bernard McGibbon, M.D.

Baltimore Podiatry Group, 5205 East Drive, Suite I, Arbutus, MD 21227; tel. 410/247–5333; FAX. 410/242–5449; Neil Scheffler, D.P.M., President

Baltimore Washington Eye Center, 200 Hospital Drive, Suite 600, Glen Burnie, MD 21061; tel. 410/761–1267; FAX. 410/761–4386; Phillip L. Harrington, Administrator

Bayside Foot and Ankle Center, 8023 Ritchie Highway, Pasadena, MD 21122; tel. 410/761–4190; Sheila Freeze, Office Manager

Beitler, Samuel D., D.P.M. Ambulatory Surgery Center, 795 Aquahart Road, Suite 125, Glen Burnie, MD 21061; tel. 410/768–0702; Samuel D. Beitler, D.P.M.

Bel Air Ambulatory Surgical Center, LLC, 2007 Rock Spring Road, Lower Level, Forest Hill, MD 21050; tel. 410/879–2474; FAX. 410/879–8194; Cindy Banaszak, Clinical Manager

Benson Surgery Center, Inc., 3421 Benson Avenue, Baltimore, MD 21227; tel. 410/644–3311; FAX. 410/247–9446; Ann Rogowski, Assistant Administrator

Bethesda Ambulatory Surgical Center, 8000 Old Georgetown Road, Bethesda, MD 20814; tel. 301/652–2248; FAX. 301/654–1150; John Lydon, D.P.M., Administrator

Bowie Health Center, 15001 Health Center Drive, Bowie, MD 20716; tel. 301/262–5511; FAX. 301/464–3572

Breschi, Sclama and Hoofnagle (Drs.), 6830 Hospital Drive, Suite 204, Baltimore, MD 21237; tel. 410/391–6131; FAX. 410/391–6144; Anthony O. Sclama, M.D., President

Carroll Medicine, d/b/a Steven Shaffer, M.D., 211 Hanover Pike, Hampstead, MD 21074; tel. 410/239–7073

Center for Eye Surgery P.C., 5550 Friendship Boulevard, Suite 270, Chevy Chase, MD 20815; tel. 301/215–7347; FAX. 301/215–7345; Leila Cabrera–Reid, RN, Administrator

Center for Plastic Surgery, 5550 Friendship Boulevard, Suite 130, Chevy Chase, MD 20815; tel. 301/652–7700; Jean, Administrator

Chesapeake Ambulatory Surgery Center, 8028 Governor Ritchie Highway, Suite 100, Pasadena, MD 21122; tel. 410/768–5800; FAX. 410/768–5806; Ira J. Gottlieb, D.P.M., Owner, Administrator

Chesapeake Surgery Center, 145 East Carroll Street, Salisbury, MD 21801; tel. 410/548–1108; FAX. 410/548–2607; Joseph G. Walters, PA–C Administrative Director

Clinical Associates, 515 Fairmont Avenue, Suite 500, Towson, MD 21286; tel. 410/494–1335

Columbia Surgery Center, Inc., 1105 Little Patuxent Parkway, Columbia, MD 21044; tel. 410/730–6673; Paul Valvoe, Administrator

De Leonibus and Palmer, L.L.C., A.S.C., MedSurg Foot Center, 2086 Generals Highway, Suite 101, Annapolis, MD 21401; tel. 410/266–7666; FAX. 410/266–7703

Digestive Disease Consultant of Frederick, 915 Toll House Avenue, Suite 201, Frederick, MD 21701; tel. 301/662–7822; James A. Frizzell, M.D.

Dr. Gary Lieberman, P.A., A.S.C., d/b/a Four Corners Ambulatory Surgical Center, 10101 Lorain Avenue, Silver Spring, MD 20901; tel. 301/681–8400

Dr. Michael K. Schwartz, D.D.S., P.A., 723 South Charles Street, Baltimore, MD 21230; tel. 410/727–4886

Dr. W. Alan Hopson, P.A., 560 Riverside Drive, Suite A–101, Salisbury, MD 21801; tel. 410/749–0121; FAX. 410/749–6807; Pat Timmons, Office Manager

Drs. Abelson and Cameron, P.A., ASC, 1212 York Road, Suite A201, Lutherville, MD 21093; tel. 410/337–7755; FAX. 410/337–7922; Laurie Kolmer, Office Manager

Drs. Smith and Schwartz, D.D.S., P.A., 10 Warren Road, Suite 330, Cockeysville, MD 21030; tel. 410/666–5225; FAX. 410/666–7220; Mary Thompson, Office Manager

Dulaney Eye Institute, 901 Dulaney Valley Road, Towson, MD 21204; tel. 410/583–1000; Andrea Hyatt, Administrator

Dundalk Ambulatory Surgery Center, 1123 Merritt Boulevard, Baltimore, MD 21222; tel. 410/282–6666

Easton Foot Center, 8579 Commerce Drive, Suite 100A, Easton, MD 21061; tel. 410/822–0645

Endocenter of Baltimore, 7211 Park Heights Avenue, Baltimore, MD 21208; tel. 410/764–6107; FAX. 410/358–4167

Eye Surgery Center at Greenspring Station of Ophthalmology Ass, 10755 Falls Road, Suite 110B, Lutherville, MD 21093; tel. 410/583–2810; FAX. 410/583–2807; Shalini Pahuja, Operations Manager

Eye Surgical Center Associates of Baltimore, 1122 Kenilworth Drive, Suite 18, Towson, MD 21204; tel. 410/321–4400; FAX. 410/321–4909; Terry Lewis, Administrator

Facial Plastic Surgicenter, Ltd., 21 Crossroads Drive, Suite 310, Owings Mills, MD 21117; tel. 410/356–1100; Ira D. Papel, M.D., President

Family Foot Health Specialists, P.C., 339 East Antietam Street, Hagerstown, MD 21740; tel. 301/797–7272; Judy Cline, Office Manager

Flaum, Martin/Rockville Podiatry Center, 50 West Edmonston Drive, Suite 306, Rockville, MD 20852; tel. 301/340–8666; Martin C. Flaum, Owner

Foot and Ankle Surgical Center, 2415 Musgrove Road, Suite 103, Silver Spring, MD 20904; tel. 301/384–6500

Foot Care Associates Ambulatory Care Center at Hamilton Foot C, 5508 Harford Road, Baltimore, MD 21214; tel. 410/426–5508

Foot Care Associates Ambulatory Care Center at Joppa Foot Care, 2316 East Joppa Road, Baltimore, MD 21234; tel. 410/882–5100

Footer, Ronald, D.P.M., P.A., 16220 Frederick Avenue, Suite 200, Gaithersburg, MD 20877; tel. 301/948–2995; FAX. 301/948–6056; Maryrose Hanks, Office Manager

Frederick Surgical Center, 915 Toll House Avenue, Suite 103, Frederick, MD 21701; tel. 301/694–3400; FAX. 301/694–3620; Barbara Smith, Administrator

Gastrointestinal Diagnostic Center, 4660 Wilkens Avenue, Suite 302, Baltimore, MD 21229; tel. 410/242–3636; FAX. 410/242–4404; Mary c. Harrison, Business Manager

Gaurdino and Glubo, P.A., 4660 Wilkens Avenue, Baltimore, MD 21229; tel. 410/242–7066; FAX. 410/242–4126; Eileen Giardina, RN

Gehris, Heroy and Associates of Lutherville, 1212 York Road, Suite 201B, Lutherville, MD 21093; tel. 410/821–6130; James H. Heroy III, Administrator

Gynemed Surgi–Center, 17 Fontana Lane, Suite 201, Baltimore, MD 21237; tel. 410/686–8220; FAX. 410/391–0943; David O'Neil, M.D.

Hartford County Ambulatory Surgery Center, 1952–A Pulaski Highway, Edgewood, MD 21040; tel. 410/538–7000; FAX. 410/671–7162; Rafiq Patel, M.D.

HealthSouth Central Maryland Surgery, 1500 John Avenue, Baltimore, MD 21227; tel. 410/536–0012; FAX. 410/536–0016; Thelma Hoerl, RN, Facility Manager

HealthSouth St. Agnes Surgery Center of Ellicott City, 2850 North Ridge Road, Ellicott City, MD 21043; tel. 410/461–1600; FAX. 410/750–7615; Donna Broccolino, Faculty Administrator

Johns Hopkins Plastic Surgery Associates, JHOC 8, 601 North Caroline Street, Baltimore, MD 21287; tel. 410/955–6897; FAX. 410/614–1296

Kaiser–Permanente–Kensington, 10810 Connecticut Avenue, Kensington, MD 20895; tel. 301/929–7100; FAX. 301/929–7433; Kathleen Owens, RN, M.S.N., Director, Surgical Service

Kenneth Margolis, M.D., P.A., Ambulatory Endoscopy Surgical Center, 9101 Franklin Square Drive, Suite 213, Baltimore, MD 21237; tel. 410/687–0202; FAX. 410/687–0985; Jo Ann Smith, Office Manager

Klatsky Plastic Surgery Facility, 122 Slade Avenue, Pikesville, MD 21208; tel. 410/484–0400; FAX. 410/484–2993; Stanley A. Klatsky, M.D., Director

Lake Forest Ambulatory Surgical Center, 702 Russell Avenue, Gaithersburg, MD 20877; tel. 301/948–3668; FAX. 301/926–7787

Laser Surgery Center, 484A Ritchie Highway, Severna Park, MD 21146; tel. 410/544–4600; Stan Karloff, Office Manager

Laurel Foot and Ankle Center, 14440 Cherry Lane Court, Suite 104, Laurel, MD 20707; tel. 301/953–3668; Dr. Frank Smith, Administrator

Maclean, Kishel, Applestein, M.D., A.S.C., 11085 Little Patuxent Parkway, Columbia, MD 21044; tel. 410/997–1930

Maple Springs Ambulatory Surgery Center, 10810 Darnstown Road, Suite 101, Gaithersburg, MD 20878; tel. 301/762–3338; FAX. 301/762–1585

Maryland Digestive Disease Center, 7350 Van Ducen Road, Suite 230, Laurel, MD 20707; tel. 301/498–5500

Maryland Ear, Nose and Throat Group, P.A., 2112 Bell Air Road, Suite Three, Fallston, MD 21047; tel. 410/879–7049; Barbara Huckeba, Corporate Secretary

Maryland Endoscopy Center, L.L.C., 100 West Road, Suite 115, Towson, MD 21204; tel. 410/494–0144; FAX. 410/494–0147; Gretchen Caron, RN, Administrator

Maryland Kidney Stone Center, 6115 Falls Road, Baltimore, MD 21209; tel. 410/377–2622; FAX. 410/377–4410; Walter Weinstein, General Manager

Maryland Outpatient Foot Surgery Center, Dennis M. Weber D.P.M., 4701 Randolph Road, Suite 115, Rockville, MD 20852; tel. 301/770–5741; FAX. 301/468–1093; Dennis M. Weber, D.P.M., Director

McCone, Jonathan, Jr., M.D., 6196 Oxon Hill Road, Suite 640, Oxon Hill, MD 20745; tel. 301/567–2400

Metropolitan Ambulatory Urologic Institute Inc., 7753 Belle Point Drive, Greenbelt, MD 20770; tel. 301/474–5583; FAX. 301/513–5087; Amy Boone, Manager

Michetti, Michael, Dr. of District Heights, 6400 Marlboro Pike, District Heights., MD 20747; tel. 301/736–6900

Mid Shore Surgical Eye Center, 8420 Ocean Gateway, Suite One, Easton, MD 21601; tel. 410/822–0424; FAX. 410/822–2283; Adrienne Welch, RN

Mid–Atlantic Surgery Center, 1120 Professional Court, Hagerstown, MD 21740; tel. 301/739–7900

Montgomery Endoscopy Center, Montgomery Gastroenterology P.A., 12012 Veirs Mill Road, Wheaton, MD 20906; tel. 301/942–3550; FAX. 301/933–3621; Howard Goldberg, M.D., A.S.C Director

Montgomery Surgical Center, 46 West Gude Drive, Rockville, MD 20850; tel. 301/424–6901; FAX. 301/294–7847; Jeannie M. Lohmeyer, RN, CNOR, Administrative Director

Moulsdale, Murphy, Siegelbaum and Lerner, 7505 Osler Drive, Suite 508, Towson, MD 21204; tel. 410/296–0166; FAX. 410/828–7275

Neil J. Napora, D.P.M., 7809 Wise Avenue, Baltimore, MD 21222; tel. 410/285–0310; FAX. 410/288–1569; Neil J. Napora, D.P.M.

North Arundel Plastic Surgery Specialists, 203 Hospital Drive, Suite 308, Glen Burnie, MD 21061; tel. 410/841–5355; FAX. 410/766–7145; Ajia S. Layman, Administrator

Parris–Castro Eye Association, Six North Boulton Street, Bel Air, MD 21014; tel. 410/836–7010; Michael Grasham, Administrator

Peninsula Obstetrics and Gynecology, 314 West Carroll Street, Salisbury, MD 21801; tel. 410/546–3125; FAX. 410/546–3128; J. Cutchin, M.D., Director

Plastic and Aesthetic, Surgical Center of Maryland, Orchard Square, 1212 York Road, Suite B101, Lutherville, MD 21093; tel. 410/337–2551; FAX. 410/321–1550; Oscar M. Ramirez, M.D., Medical Director

Plastic Surgery Specialists, 2448 Holly Avenue, Suite 400, Annapolis, MD 21401; tel. 410/841–5355; FAX. 410/841–6589; Ajia S. Layman, Administrator

Plaza Podiatry, 6568 Reisterstown Road, Suite 501, Baltimore, MD 21215; tel. 410/764–7044; Brian Kashan, Administrator

Podiatry Associates of Hagerstown, A.S.C., 12821 Oak Hill Avenue, Hagerstown, MD 21742; tel. 301/739–1575; FAX. 301/739–1578; Crystal Shockey, Office Manager

Podiatry Associates, P.A., 9712 Bel Air Road, Baltimore, MD 21236; tel. 410/574–6060; FAX. 410/256–2727; Stanley Book

Podiatry Associates, P.A., One North Main Street, Bel Air, MD 21014; tel. 410/879–1212; FAX. 410/893–1081

Podiatry Associates, P.A., 10840 Little Patuxent Parkway, Columbia, MD 21044; tel. 410/730–0970; FAX. 410/730–0161; Dr. Cappello, Podiatrist

Podiatry Associates, P.A., 6569 North Charles Street, Suite 702, Towson, MD 21204; tel. 410/828–5420; Nancy L. Patterson, Billing Manager

Podiatry Associates, P.A., 9101 Franklin Square Drive, Baltimore, MD 21237; tel. 410/574–3900; FAX. 410/574–3902; Vincent J. Martorana, D.P.M.

Podiatry Group, P.A. of Annapolis, 139 Old Solomons Island Road, Suite C, Annapolis, MD 21401; tel. 410/224–4448; FAX. 410/841–5200; Kate Pearson, Administrator

Podiatry Group, P.A. of Laurel, Ambulatory Surgery Center, 14333 Laurel–Bowie Road, Suite 205, Laurel, MD 20708; tel. 301/725–5650; FAX. 301–953–0365; Bruce A. Wenzel, Administrator

Prince George's Ambulatory Care Center/Endoscopy Suites, Inc., 6001 Landover Road, Suite One, Cheverly, MD 20785; tel. 301/773–3900; FAX. 301/773/7869; Jeannette Figueroa, Administrator

Prince George's Multi–Specialty Surgery Centre, Inc., 8700 Central Avenue, Suite 106, Landover, MD 20785; tel. 301/808–0992; FAX. 301/499–1266; Douglas Hallgren, Administrator

Professional Village Surgical Center, 356 Mill Street, Hagerstown, MD 21740; tel. 301/791–1800

Queen Anne Plastic, L.L.C., 2110 Red Apple Plaza, Chester, MD 2161; tel. 410/643–7207; FAX. 410/643–6945

Queen Anne Surgery Center, 2108 DiDonato Drive, Chester, MD 21619; tel. 410/643–7207; FAX. 410/643–9274; Lisa Parks, Administrator

River Reach Outpatient Surgery Center, 790 Governor Ritchie Highway, Suite E–35, Severna Park, MD 21146; tel. 410/544–2487; FAX. 410–544–1872

Rivertowne Surgery Center, 6196 Oxon Hill Road, Suite 650, Oxon Hill, MD 20745; tel. 301/839–7499; FAX. 301/839–8726; Tamara Cleveland, Manager

Robinwood Surgery Center, LLC, 11110 Medical Campus Road, suite 200, Hagerstown, MD 21742; tel. 301/714–4300; FAX. 301/714–4324; Sarah Ann DeBaugh, Office Manager

Roger J. Oldham, M.D., Ambulatory Surgery Center, 10215 Fernwood Road, Suite 412, Bethesda, MD 20817; tel. 301/530–6100; Nancy April, RN

Rotunda Ambulatory Surgery Center, 711 West 40th Street, Suite 410, Baltimore, MD 21211; tel. 410/889–4885

Sagoskin and Levy, M.D., 9707 Medical Center Drive, Suite 230, Rockville, MD 20850; tel. 301/340–1188; Arthur Sagoskin, M.D., Administrator

Saint Mary's Multispecialty Surgery Center, Inc., Route 235 and Chancellors Run Road, Suite 15, P.O. Box 1310, California, MD 20619; tel. 301–862–3948; FAX. 301–862–3335; Douglas H. Hallgren, D.P.M., Administrator

Siegel and Langer (Drs.), P.A., Ambulatory Surgery Center, 1001 Pine Heights Avenue, Suite 104, Baltimore, MD 21229; tel. 410/644–0929; Narang Ashok, Administrator

Silver Spring Ambulatory Surgical Center, Inc., 1104 Spring Street, Suite T110, Silver Spring, MD 20910; tel. 301/589–7664; FAX. 301/589–3410; Todd A. Nitkin, D.P.M., President

Silverman, David H., M.D., 6490 Landover Road, Suite D, Cleverly, MD 20785; tel. 301/322–5885

Smith, Schwartz and Hyatt, D.D.S., P.A. of Owings Mills, 25 Crossroads Drive, Owings Mills, MD 21117; tel. 410/363–7780; Michael K. Schwartz, D.D.S., Administrator

Spector, Adam, D.P.M., Ambulatory Surgery Center, 1111 Spring Street, Silver Spring, MD 20910; tel. 301/589–8886; FAX. 301/589–8889; Adam Spector, D.P.M., Administrator

Suburban Endoscopy Center, L.L.C., 10215 Fernwood Road, Suite 206, Bethesda, MD 20817; tel. 301/530–2800

Sugar, Mark, D.P.M., A.S.C., 6505 Belcrest Road, Suite One, Hyattsville, MD 20782; tel. 301/699–5900; FAX. 301/699–9297; Mark H. Sugar, D.P.M., Director

Suhayl Kalash, Ambulatory Surgery Center, 3455 Wilkens Avenue, Suite 203, Baltimore, MD 21229; tel. 410/646–0330; Bridget Vracar, Accounts Coordinator

Surgical Center of Greater Annapolis, Inc., 83 Church Road, Arnold, MD 21012; tel. 410/757–5018; FAX. 410/757–0632; LoRain Potter, RN, Administrator

The Ambulatory Urosurgical Center, 401 East Jefferson Street, Suite 105, Rockville, MD 20850; tel. 301/309–8219; FAX. 301/309–9370; Jacqueline Hillman, RN, B.S.N. M.S., Director of Nursing

The Endoscopy Center, 7402 York Road, Suite 101, Towson, MD 21204; tel. 410/494–0156; FAX. 410/828–1706; Dianne M. Johnson, General Manager

The SurgiCenter of Baltimore, 23 Crossroads Drive, Suite 100, Owings Mills, MD 21117; tel. 410/356–0300; FAX. 410/356–7507; Jerry W. Henderson, Executive Director

Total Foot Care Surgery Center, Inc., 7525 Greenway Center Drive, Suite 112, Greenbelt, MD 20770; tel. 301/345–4087; FAX. 301/345–0482; Dale Scoville, Office Manager

Tri County Endoscopy, Charlotte Hall, Route Five, Charlotte Hal, MD 20622; tel. 301/884–7322; Dr. Shah, M.D.

Tri County Endoscopy, Calvert Medical Office Building, Suite 303, 110 Hospital Road, Prince Freder, MD 20678; tel. 410/535–4333; Dr. A. Shah

United Foot Care Center, 420 South Crain Highway, Glen Burnie, MD 21061; tel. 410/766–7500; Steven Brownstein, Administrator

Vahos Aesthetic Plastic Surgery Institute, 1001 Pine Heights Avenue, Suite 100, Baltimore, MD 21229; tel. 410/644–4877; FAX. 410/525–1346; Mario Vahos, M.D., Director

Waldorf Endoscopy Center Inc., 11340 Pembroke Square, Suite 202, Waldorf, MD 20603; tel. 310/638–5354; FAX. 301/843–5184; Mary Lou Champney, Office Manager

Washington Surgi Center, 6228 Oxon Hill Road, Oxon Hill, MD 20745; tel. 301/839–0770; FAX. 301/839–1350

Western Maryland Eye Surgical Center, 1003 West Seventh Street, Suite 400, Frederick, MD 21701; tel. 301/662–3721; FAX. 301/698–8164

MASSACHUSETTS

Advanced Pain Management Center, Three Woodland Road, Suite 206, Stoneham, MA 02180; tel. 617/662–2243; FAX. 617/662–4878

Andover Surgical Day Care Clinic, 138 Haverhill Street, Andover, MA 01810; tel. 508/475–2880; FAX. 508/475–9562; Edward G. George, Administrator

Boston Center for Ambulatory Surgery, Inc., 170 Commonwealth Avenue, Boston, MA 02116; tel. 617/267–0701; FAX. 617/236–8704

Boston Eye Surgery & Laser Center, P.C., 50 Stanford Street, Boston, MA 02114; tel. 617/723–2015; FAX. 617/723–7787; Sheila M. Harney, Business Manager

Cataract and Laser Center West, P.C., 171 Interstate Drive, West Springfield, MA 01089; tel. 413/732–2333; FAX. 413/732–3514; John Dunne, Administrator

Cataract and Laser Center, Inc., 333 Elm Street, Dedham, MA 02026; tel. 617/326–3800; John Dunne, Administrator

Cosmetic Surgery Center, 68 Camp Street, Hyannis, MA 02601; tel. 508/775–7026; FAX. 508/778–6327; Laura Norkatis, Office Manager

Eye Institute of the Merrimack Valley, 280 Haverhill Street, Lawrence, MA 01840; tel. 508/685–5366

Goddard Medical Association Outpatient Surgery, One Pearl Street, Caputo Building First Floor, Brockton, MA 02401; tel. 508/586–3600

Greater New Bedford Surgicare, Inc., 540 Hawthorne Street, North Dartmouth, MA 02747; tel. 508/997–1271; FAX. 508/992–7701; George A. Picord, Administrator

HealthSouth Maple Surgery Center, 298 Carew Street, Springfield, MA 01104; tel. 413/739–9668; FAX. 413/781–3652; Kathleen S. Loomis, RN, Facility Administrator

McGowan Eye Care Center, 297 Union Avenue, Framingham, MA 01701; tel. 800/873–4590; FAX. 508/872–0038; Bernard L. McGowan, M.D., Director

New England Eye Surgery Center, 696 Main Street, Weymouth, MA 02190; tel. 617/331–3820; FAX. 617/331–1076; Kenneth Camerota

New England Surgicare, One Brookline Place, Suite 201, Brookline, MA 02146; tel. 617/730–9650; Gratia S. Chase, RN, Administrator

Plymouth Laser and Surgical Center, 40 Industrial Park Road, Plymouth, MA 02360; tel. 508/746–8600; FAX. 508/747–0824; Kathleen Murphy, Administrator

Same Day SurgiClinic, 272 Stanley Street, Fall River, MA 02720; tel. 508/672–2290; FAX. 508/679–3766; John Harries, M.D., Chief Executive Officer

Surgery Center of Waltham, 40 Second Avenue, Suite 200, Waltham, MA 02154

The Eye Center, 15 Florence Street, Route 128, Danvers, MA 01923; tel. 508/774–2040; FAX. 508/750–4463

University Eye Associates, Inc., 90 New State Highway, Raynham, MA 02767; tel. 508/822–8839; FAX. 508/880–3616; Judith A. Orsie, RN, Nurse Manager

Worcester Surgical Center, Inc., 300 Grove Street, Worcester, MA 01650; tel. 508/754–0700; FAX. 508/831–9989; Andy H. Poritz, M.D., Professional Services Director

MICHIGAN

Balian Eye Center, 432 West University Drive, Rochester, MI 48307; tel. 313/651–6122; John V. Balian, M.D.

Birth Control Center, Inc., 2783 Fourteen Mile Road, Sterling Heights, MI 48310; tel. 810/939–4000; Armen Vartanian, Administrator

Borgess at Woodbridge Hills Outpatient Surgery, 7901 Angling Road, Portage, MI 49024; tel. 616/324–8406; FAX. 616/324–8476; Renee Langeland, Administrator

Bronson Outpatient Surgery–Crosstown Center, 150 East Crosstown Parkway, Suite One, Kalamazoo, MI 49007; tel. 616/341–6166; Frank Sardone, Administrator

Castleman Surgery Center, 14050 Dix–Toledo Road, Southgate, MI 48195; tel. 313/283–0500; FAX. 313/283–2720

Centre for Plastic Surgery, 426 Michigan Street, N.E., Suite 300, Grand Rapids, MI 49503; tel. 616/454–1256; FAX. 616/454–0308; Daniel Reeder, Administrator

Community Surgical Center, 30671 Stephenson Highway, Madison Height, MI 48071; tel. 810/588–8000; FAX. 810/588–9140; C. J. Yanos, Administrator

Detroit Medical Center Surgery Center, 27207 Lahser Road, Suite 100, Southfield, MI 48034; tel. 810/357–0880; FAX. 810/357–1738; Patrick Voight, Administrative Manager

East Michigan Eye Surgery Center, 701 South Ballenger, Flint, MI 48532; tel. 810/238–3603; FAX. 810/767–5194; Judith A. Kirby, RN, Administrative Director

Eastside Endoscopy Center, 28963 Little Mack, Suite 103, St. Clair Sho, MI 48081; tel. 810/447–5110; FAX. 810/774–6091; Beth Miller, Administrator

Feminine Health Care Clinic of Flint, 2032 South Saginaw Street, Flint, MI 48503; tel. 800/323–6205; FAX. 313/232–8071; Dawn LoRec, Director

Glascco Ambulatory Surgery Center, 1707 West Lake Lansing Road, Lansing, MI 48912; tel. 517/267–0033; FAX. 517/267–0430; Jane Beshore, Administrator

Hemorrhoid Clinics of America, 22000 Greenfield Road, Oak Park, MI 48237; tel. 248–967–4140; FAX. 248–967–0745; Max Ali, M.D., President

Henry Ford Hospital Fairlane Center, 19401 Hubbard Drive, Dearborn, MI 48126; tel. 313/593–8100; Jay Zerwekh, Administrator

Henry Ford Medical Center–Lakeside Ambulatory Surgery, 14500 Hall Road, Sterling Heights, MI 48313; tel. 810/247–2680; FAX. 810/247–2682; Paul Szilagyi, Administrator

Henry Ford Medical Center–West Bloomfield, Ambulatory Surgery Center, 6777 West Maple Road, West Bloomfield, MI 48322; tel. 248/661–4100; Mary Ann Edwards, Manager, Ambulatory Surgery

Section C

Holland Eye Clinic, 999 South Washington, Holland, MI 49423; tel. 616/396–2316; FAX. 616/396–0085; Kristine Curtis, Assistant Administrator

Hutzel Health Center, 4050 East 12 Mile Road, Warren, MI 48092; tel. 810/573–3140

John Michael Garrett, P.C., 1301 Carpenter Avenue, Iron Mountain, MI 49801; tel. 906/774–1404; FAX. 906/774–8132; Cathy Hartwig, RN, Supervisor

M.D. Surgicenter, 375 Barclay Circle, Rochester Hill, MI 48307; tel. 810/852–3636; FAX. 810/852–3631; Robert Swartz, Administrator

Metropolitan Eye Center, 21711 Greater Mack, St. Clair Sho, MI 48080; tel. 313/774–6820; FAX. 313/777–2214; Richard E. Mertz, Jr., M.D., Director

Michigan Center for Outpatient Ocular Surgery, 33080 Utica Road, P.O. Box 26010, Fraser, MI 48026; tel. 810/296–7250; FAX. 810/296–0276; Norbert P. Czajkowski, M.D., Director

Midwest Health Center, 5050 Schaefer Avenue, Dearborn, MI 48126; tel. 313/581–2600; FAX. 313/581–6013; Mark B. Saffer, M.D., President and CEO

Oakland Surgi Center, 2820 Crooks Road, Rochester Hill, MI 48309; tel. 248–852–7484; Beverly Huffman, CMM, Administrator

Oakwood Healthcare Center–Dearborn, 10151 Michigan Avenue, Dearborn, MI 48126; tel. 313–624–0855; FAX. 313–624–0857; Patricia Glosser, Nursing Supervisor

Park Eye and Surgicenter, 5014 Villa Linde Parkway, Flint, MI 48532

Planned Parenthood League, Inc., 25932 Dequindre, Warren, MI 48091; tel. 810/758–2100; FAX. 810/758–2104; Carrie Haneckow, Administrator

Planned Parenthood of Mid–Michigan, 3100 Professional Drive, P.O. Box 3673, Ann Arbor, MI 48106–3673; tel. 313/973–0710; FAX. 313/973–0595; Peg Hill-Callahan

Planned Parenthood of South Central Michigan, 4201 West Michigan Avenue, Kalamazoo, MI 49006–5833; tel. 616/372–1205; FAX. 616/372–1279; Rev. Mark Pawlowski, Executive Director, Chief Operating Officer

Providence Hospital Ambulatory Surgery Center, 47601 Grand River, Novi, MI 48374; tel. 810/380–4170; Brian Connolly, Administrator

Providence Surgical Center, 29877 Telegraph Road, Suite 200, Southfield, MI 48034

Reconstructive Surgery Center, 125 West Walnut, Kalamazoo, MI 49007; tel. 616/343–1381; Frank J. Newman, M.D., Medical Director

Saginaw General North, 5400 Mackinaw, Saginaw, MI 48603; tel. 517/797–5000

Sinai Surgery Center, 28500 Orchard Lake Road, Farmington Hi, MI 48334; tel. 810/851–9215; FAX. 810/851–2077; Michael K. Rosenberg, M.D., Medical Director

Somerset Troy Surgical Center, 1565 West Big Beaver Road, Building F, Troy, MI 48084; tel. 248–649–7343; FAX. 248–643–0999; Frank A. Nesi, M.D., Medical Director

Spectrum Health Surgical Center, Merger of Blodgett & Butterworth, 1000 East Paris S.E., Suite 100, Grand Rapids, MI 49546; tel. 616–285–1822; FAX. 616–285–1820; Deb Williams, Clinical Site Manager

St. John Surgery Center, 21000 12 Mile Road, St. Clair Shore, MI 48081; tel. 810/447–5015; FAX. 810/447–5012; Cheri Dendy, Administrator

St. Mary's Ambulatory Care Center, 4599 Towne Centre, Saginaw, MI 48604; tel. 517/797–3000; FAX. 517/797–3010; Donna Juhala, Director

Superior Endoscopy Center/U P Digestive Disease Associates, P., 1414 West Fair Avenue, Suite 135, Marquette, MI 49855; tel. 906/226–6025; FAX. 906/226–5366; Jeffrey P. Shaffer, Administrator

Surgery Center of Michigan, 44650 Delco Boulevard, Sterling Heights, MI 48313; tel. 810/254–3391; Jay Novetsky, Administrator

Surgical Care Center of Michigan, 750 East Beltline, N.E., Grand Rapids, MI 49525; tel. 616/940–3600; FAX. 616/954–0216; Kris Kilgore, RN, B.S.N., Administrative Director

University of Michigan Surgery Center, 19900 Haggerty Road, Livonia, MI 48152; tel. 313/462–1888; FAX. 313/462–1944; Pamela Cittan, Administrator

Upper Peninsula Surgery Center, 1414 West Fair Avenue, Suite 232, Marquette, MI 49855; tel. 906/225–7547; FAX. 906/225–7548; Sally J. Achatz, RN, Administrator

MINNESOTA

Centennial Lakes Same Day Surgery Center, 7373 France Avenue, S., Suite 404, Edina, MN 55435; tel. 612/921–0100; FAX. 612/921–0999; Kathleen L. Whatley, Administrator

Children's West, 6050 Clearwater Drive, Minnetonka, MN 55343; tel. 612/930–8600; FAX. 612/930–8650; Jane Price, Director

Columbia St. Cloud Surgical Center, 1526 Northway Drive, St. Cloud, MN 56303; tel. 320/251–8385; FAX. 320/251–1267; Jeanette I. Stack, Administrator

Dakota Clinic, Ltd., 125 East Frazee Street, Detroit Lakes, MN 56501; tel. 218/847–3181; FAX. 218/847–2795; Linda L. Walz, Division Manager

First Eye Care Center, Inc., 9117 Lyndale Avenue, S., Bloomington, MN 55420; tel. 612/884–7568; FAX. 612/884–2656; Barbara McGovern, Administrator

Healtheast Maplewood Surgery Center, 1655 Beam Avenue, Maplewood, MN 55109; tel. 612/232–7780; FAX. 612/232–7786; Sandra Todd, Director

Healtheast St. Paul Endoscopy Center, 17 West Exchange Street, Suite 215, St. Paul, MN 55102; tel. 612/224–9677; FAX. 612/223–5683; Glenda Tims, RN, Clinical Manager

Landmark Surgical Center, 17 West Exchange Street, Suite 307, St. Paul, MN 55102; tel. 612/223–7400; FAX. 612/223–5903; Peg Olin, Administrator

Maplewood Surgery Center, 1655 Beam Ave., Maplewood, MN 55109; tel. 612/232–7780; Sandra Todd, Administrator

Midwest Surgicenter, d/b/a Midwest Eye and Ear Institute, 393 North Dunlap Street, Suite 900, St. Paul, MN 55104; tel. 651/642–1106; FAX. 651/645–3346; H. Joseph Drannen, Administrator

Park Nicollet Clinic Health System Minnesota, 3800 Park Nicollet Boulevard, St. Louis Park, MN 55416; tel. 612/993–1953; FAX. 612/993–9250; Kathy Beckman, RN, Manager

WestHealth, Inc., 2855 Campus Drive, Plymouth, MN 55441; tel. 612/577–7120; FAX. 612/577–7130; Paula Green, Administrator

Willmar Surgery Center, 1320 South First Street, Willmar, MN 56201; tel. 320/235–6506; FAX. 320–235–7069; John Seifert, Medical Director

MISSISSIPPI

Ambu–Care Outpatient Surgery Center, 6204 North State Street, Jackson, MS 39213; tel. 601/956–3251; FAX. 601/957–8456; Frank McCune, M.D., Administrator

Better Living Clinic Endoscopy Center, 3000 Halls Ferry Road, Vicksburg, MS 39180; tel. 601/638–9800; FAX. 601–638–9808; Barbara Neal, Office Manager

Biloxi Outpatient Surgery and Endoscopy Center, Inc., 111 Lameuse Street, Suite 104, Biloxi, MS 39530; tel. 228–374–2130; FAX. 228–374–0938; Michael T. Gossman, Administrator

Columbia Mississippi Surgical Center, 1421 North State Street, Jackson, MS 39202; tel. 601/353–8000; Virginia Brown, Administrator

ENT and Facial Plastic Surgery, 107 Millsaps Drive, P.O. Box 17829, Hattiesburg, MS 39402; tel. 601/268–5131; FAX. 601/268–5138; Pam Carter, Office Manager

Gulf South Outpatient Center, 1206 31st Avenue, P.O. Box 1778, Gulfport, MS 39501; tel. 601/864–0008; FAX. 601/863–1747; Jason V. Smith, M.D., President

Gulfport Outpatient Surgical Center, 1240 Broad Avenue, Gulfport, MS 39501; tel. 601/868–1120; William Peaks, Administrator

Lowery A. Woodall Outpatient Surgery Facility, 105 South 28th Avenue, Hattiesburg, MS 39401; tel. 601/288–1072; FAX. 601/288–3132; Marshall H. Tucker, FACHE, Administrator

North Mississippi Surgery Center, 500 West Eason Boulevard, Tupelo, MS 38801; tel. 601/841–4700; FAX. 601/841–3101; Beth Taylor, RN, Director

Southern Eye Center of Excellence, 1420 South 28th Avenue, Hattiesburg, MS 39402; tel. 601/264–3937; Lynn McMahan, M.D., Medical Director

Southwest Mississippi Ambulatory Surgery Center, 215 Marion Avenue, McComb, MS 39648; tel. 601/249–1477; FAX. 601/249–1375; Norman M. Price, Administrator

Surgicare of Jackson, 766 Lakeland Drive, Jackson, MS 39216; tel. 601/362–8700; FAX. 601/362–6439; Sheila Grillis, RN, Administrator

MISSOURI

Arnold Eye Surgery Center, Inc., 1265 East Primrose, Springfield, MO 65804; tel. 417/886–3937; FAX. 417/886–1285; Stephen C. Sheppard, Administrator

Associated Plastic Surgeons Ambulatory Surgical Center, 6420 Prospect, Suite 115, Kansas City, MO 64132; tel. 816/333–5524; Joni Reist, RN

BarnesCare, 401 Pine Street, St. Louis, MO 63102; tel. 314/331–3000; FAX. 314/331–3012; Gary Payne, Vice President, BJC Corporate Health

Cape Girardeau Outpatient Surgery Center, 1429 Mount Auburn Road, Cape Girardea, MO 63701; tel. 573/334–5895; FAX. 573/335–2392; Stephanie J. Husted, RN, CNOR, Administrator

Cataract and Glaucoma Outpatient Surgicenter, 7220 Watson Road, St. Louis, MO 63119; tel. 314/352–5515; Stanley C. Becker, M.D.

Cataract Surgery Center of St. Louis, Inc., 900 North Highway 67 (Lindbergh), Florissant, MO 63031; tel. 314/838–0321; FAX. 314/838–4682; Karen E. Wilson, RN, Nurse Manager

Cataract Surgery Center of Young Eye Clinic, Inc., 3201 Ashland Avenue, St. Joseph, MO 64506; tel. 816/279–0079; FAX. 816/364–1100; Judy Watowa, RN, B.S.N., Administrator

Center for Eye Surgery, 6650 Troost, Suite 305, Kansas City, MO 64131; tel. 816/276–7757; FAX. 816/926–2231; Connie B. Watson, Administrator

CMMP Surgical Center, 1705 Christy Drive, Jefferson City, MO 65101; tel. 573/635–7022; FAX. 573/635–7029; Angela R. Sumner–Hahn, Business Director

Creekwood Surgery Center, 211 Northeast 54th Street, Suite 100, Kansas City, MO 64118; tel. 816/455–4214; FAX. 816/455–4216; Diana Carr, Administrator

• **Creve Coeur Surgery Center,** 633 Emerson, Creve Coeur, MO 63141; tel. 314/872–7100; Marion Axel, Administrator

Doctors' Park Surgery, Inc., 30 Doctors' Park, Cape Girardea, MO 63701; tel. 314/334–9606; FAX. 314/334–9608; Ronald G. Wittmer, President

ENT/Urology Surgical Care, Inc., 5301 Faraon Street, St. Joseph, MO 64506; tel. 816/364–2772; Sidney G. Christiansen, M.D.

Eye Surgery Center–The Cliffs, 4801 Cliff Avenue, Suite 101, Independence, MO 64055; tel. 816/478–4400; FAX. 816/478–8240; Patricia Thomas, RN, Director of Nursing

G.I. Diagnostics, Inc., 4321 Washington, Suite 5700, Kansas City, MO 64111; tel. 816/561–2000; FAX. 816/931–7559; Craig B. Reeves, Administrator

HealthSouth Surgery Center of West County, 1130 Town and Country Commons, Chesterfield, MO 63017; tel. 314/394–0698; FAX. 314/394–7493; Jim Dickens, Administrator

Hunkeler Eye Surgery Center, Inc., 4321 Washington, Suite 6000, Kansas City, MO 64111; tel. 816/753–6511; FAX. 816/931–9498; Deborah M. Highfill, RN

Kansas City Surgicenter, Ltd., 1800 East Meyer Boulevard, Kansas City, MO 64132; tel. 816/523–0100; FAX. 816/523–6241; Barbara Klein, RN, Administrator

Laser Surgery Center North, 7700 South Florissant Road, St. Louis, MO 63122; tel. 314/261–2020; FAX. 314/821–4080; Irvin C. Hoffman, Administrator

Laser Surgery Center West, 1028 South Kirkwood, St. Louis, MO 63122; tel. 314/984–0080; FAX. 314/821–4080; Irvin C. Hoffman, Administrator

Midwest Eye Institute, 5139 Mattis Road, St. Louis, MO 63128; tel. 314/849–8400; Anwar Shah, M.D.

Missouri Surgery Center, Inc., 300 South Mount Auburn Road, Suite 200, Cape Girardea, MO 63701; tel. 314/339–7575; FAX. 314/339–7887; Steve Telford, Administrator

North County Surgery Center, One Village Square, Hazelwood, MO 63042; tel. 314/895–4001; FAX. 314/895–1791; Connie Moore, Administrator

Outpatient Surgery Center, 450 North New Ballas Road, Suite 103, St. Louis, MO 63141; tel. 314/991–0776; FAX. 314/991–3076; Karen Barrow, Administrator

Regional Surgery Center, P.C., 1531 West 32nd Street, Suite 107, Joplin, MO 64804; tel. 417/781–9595; FAX. 417/781–9814; Cynthia Shofner, Administrator

South County Outpatient Surgery Center, 13303 Tesson Ferry Road, St. Louis, MO 63128; tel. 314/842–3200; Stephen L. Partridge, Administrator

St. Charles County Surgery Center, Inc., 4203 South Cloverleaf Drive, St. Peters, MO 63376; tel. 314/928-0087; FAX. 314/928-1242; Sandi Baber, Administrator

Surgery Center of Springfield, L.P., 1350 East Woodhurst Drive, Springfield, MO 65804; tel. 417/887-5243; FAX. 417/887-6507; Celine Snyder, RN, Administrator

Surgi–Care Center of Independence, 2311 Redwood Avenue, Independence, MO 64057; tel. 816/373-7995; FAX. 816/373-8580; Dolores Sabia, Administrator

The Ambulatory Head and Neck Surgical Center, 1965 South Fremont, Suite 1940, Springfield, MO 65804; tel. 417/887-5750; FAX. 417/887-6612; Charles R. Taylor, Administrator

The Endoscopy Center, 3800 South Whitney, Independence, MO 64055; tel. 816/478-6868; John A. Woltjen, M.D.

The Endoscopy Center II, 5330 North Oak Trafficway, Suite 100, Kansas City, MO 64118; tel. 816/836-1616; Jean Thompson, Public Relations, Marketing

The Surgery Center, 802 North Riverside Road, St. Joseph, MO 64507; tel. 816/364-5030; FAX. 816/364-5810; Nancy Moore, RN

The Tobin Eye Institute, 3902 Sherman Avenue, St. Joseph, MO 64506; tel. 816/279-1363; FAX. 816/233-8936; Linda S. Wildhagen, Administrator

Tri County Surgery Center, 1111 East Sixth Street, Washington, MO 63090; tel. 314/239-1766; FAX. 314/239-2964; Sharry Mohr, RN, Administrator

MONTANA

Billings Cataract and Laser Surgicenter, 1221 North 26th Street, Billings, MT 59101; tel. 406/252-5681

Eye Microsurgery Center, Inc., 1232 North 30th Street, Billings, MT 59101; tel. 406/256-9006; Nancy Oliphant, Office Manager

Flathead Outpatient Surgical Center, 66 Claremont Street, Kalispell, MT 59901; tel. 406/752-8484; FAX. 406/756-8008; Victoria L. Johnson, RN, Facility Manager

Montana Surgical Center, Inc., 840 South Montana, Butte, MT 59701; tel. 406/782-2391; Charles Harris, Manager

Northern Rockies Surgicenter, Inc., 940 North 30th Street, Billings, MT 59101; tel. 406/248-7186; FAX. 406/248-6889; Sharon McLeod, RN, OR Supervisor

Rocky Mountain Eye Surgery Center, 700 West Kent, Missoula, MT 59801; tel. 406/543-8179; Darlene Timmerhoff, Administrator

Same Day Surgery Center, Inc., 300 North Wilson, Suite 600F, Bozeman, MT 59715; tel. 406/586-1956; Ann Guenther, Supervisor

The Eye Surgicenter, 2475 Village Lane, Billings, MT 59102; tel. 406/252-6608; FAX. 406/252-6600; Sara Coleman, Supervisor

NEBRASKA

Aesthetic Surgical Images, P.C., 8900 West Dodge Road, Omaha, NE 68114; tel. 402/390-0100; FAX. 402/390-2711; Rita Petersen, Administrator

Anis Eye Institute, P.C., d/b/a The Nebraska Eye Surgical Center, 1500 South 48th Street, Suite 612, Lincoln, NE 68506; tel. 402-483-7991; FAX. 402-483-4750; Dr. Aziz Y. Anis

Bergan Mercy Surgical Center, 11704 West Center Road, Omaha, NE 68124; tel. 402/333-3111; Richard A. Hachten III

Clarkson Hospital Outpatient Surgery, 4353 Dodge Street, Omaha, NE 68131; tel. 402/552-6065; Dr. Louis Burgher, Administrator

Clarkson West Medical Center, 2727 S. 144th Street, Omaha, NE 68144; tel. 402/778-5300; FAX. 402/778-5310; Cindy Alloway, Vice President

Jones Eye Clinic, 825 North 90th Street, Omaha, NE 68114; tel. 402/397-2010; Craig Borsdorf, Administrator

Lincoln Surgery Center, 1710 South 70th, Suite 200, Lincoln, NE 68506; tel. 402/483-1550; FAX. 402/483-0476; Robin Linnafelter, Administrator

Omaha Surgical Center, 8051 West Center Road, Omaha, NE 68124; tel. 402/391-3333; James Quinn, M.D., Administrator

The Nebraska Eye Surgical Center, 1500 S. 48th Street, Suite 612, Lincoln, NE 68506; tel. 402-483-7991; FAX. 402-483-4750; Aziz Anis, M.D., Administrator

The Omaha Eye Institute Surgery Center, 11606 Nicholas Street, Suite 200, Omaha, NE 68154; tel. 402/493-2020; FAX. 402/493-8987; Dr. Robert S. Vandervort, Administrator

The Urology Center, P.C., 111 1/2 South 90th Street, Omaha, NE 68114; tel. 402/397-9800; Laura Forehead, Administrator

Tobin Eye Institute, 4151 E Street, Omaha, NE 68107; tel. 402/731-1363; Patricia Moffatt, RN, Administrator

NEVADA

Aesthetic Associates Day Surgery Center, 1580 East Desert Inn Road, Las Vegas, NV 89109; tel. 702/735-6755; FAX. 702/733-8221; Charles A. Vinnik, M.D., Administrator

Ambulatory Surgery Center of Nevada, 4631 E. Charleston Blvd., Las Vegas, NV 89104; tel. 702/438-8417; Neal A. Marek, Administrator

American Surgery Center of Las Vegas, 2575 Lindell Road, Las Vegas, NV 89102; tel. 702/362-3937; FAX. 702/362-7935; Elizabeth Sayers, Administrator

Carson Ambulatory Surgery Center, Inc., 1299 Mountain Street, Carson City, NV 89703; tel. 775/883-1700; FAX. 775/883-8905; Joan P. Lapham, B.S.N., MHA, Executive Director

Carson Endoscopy Center, 707 North Minnesota, Carson City, NV 89703; tel. 775/884-8818; FAX. 775/884-4569; Jay M. Coller, Executive Director

Carson Valley Ambulatory Surgery Center, 1107 Highway 395, Gardnerville, NV 89410; tel. 775/782-1595; FAX. 775/782-1592; Richard L. Davis, Administrator

Center for Outpatient Surgery, 343 Elm Street, Suite 100, Reno, NV 89503; tel. 702/789-6500; FAX. 702/789-6535; Christine Balascoe, Executive Director

Columbia Reno Medical Plaza, 2005 Silverada Boulevard, Suite 100, Reno, NV 89512; tel. 702/359-0212; FAX. 702/359-0645; Sandra Walker–Wright, Director, Operations

Columbia Sunrise Flamingo Surgery Center, 2565 East Flamingo Road, Las Vegas, NV 89121; tel. 702/697-7900; FAX. 702/697-5383; Carolyn C. Weaver, Administrator

Columbia Sunrise Surgical Center–Sahara, 2401 Paseo Del Prado, Las Vegas, NV 89102; tel. 702/362-7874; FAX. 702/362-3567; Stephanie Finkelstein, Administrator

Desert Surgery Center, 1569 East Flamingo Road, Suite B, Las Vegas, NV 89119; tel. 702/735-5177; FAX. 702/735-3140; Steven C. Wilson, Administrator

Digestive Disease Center, 2136 East Desert Inn Road, Suite B, Las Vegas, NV 89109; tel. 702/734-0075; Osama Haikal, M.D., Administrator

Digestive Health Center, 5250 Kietzke Lane, Reno, NV 89511; tel. 702/829-8855; FAX. 702/829-3757; Jim LaBorde, Administrator

Endoscopic Institute of Nevada, 3777 Pecos–McLeod, Suite 102, Las Vegas, NV 89121; tel. 702/433-5686; Rebecca Duty, Administrator

Endoscopy Center of Nevada, LTD, 700 Shadow Lane, Suite 165B, Las Vegas, NV 89106; tel. 702/382-8101; Dipak K. Desai, Administrator

Eye Surgery Center of Nevada, 3839 North Carson Street, Carson City, NV 89706; tel. 702/882-3950; FAX. 708/882-1726; Michael J. Fischer, M.D., Administrator

Foot Surgery Center of Northern Nevada, 1300 East Plumb Lane, Suite A, Reno, NV 89502; tel. 702/829-8066; FAX. 702/829-8069; Dr. Frank M. Davis, Jr., Administrator

Ford Center for Foot Surgery, 2321 Pyramid Way, Sparks, NV 89431; tel. 702/331-1919; FAX. 702/331-2008; Dr. L. Bruce Ford, Administrator

Gastrointestinal Diagnostic Clinic, 3196 South Maryland Parkway, Suite 207, Las Vegas, NV 89109; tel. 702/369-3400; Nourollah Gharhreman, MD, Administrator

Goldring Surgical Center, 2020 Goldring, Suite 300, Las Vegas, NV 89106; tel. 817/922-9042; Texas Gustavson, Administrator

La Tourette Surgical Center, 2300 South Rancho Drive, Suite 216, Las Vegas, NV 89102; tel. 702/386-6979; FAX. 702/386-8700; Gary J. La Tourette, Administrator

Las Vegas Surgicare, Ltd., 870 South Rancho Drive, Las Vegas, NV 89106; tel. 702/870-2090; FAX. 702/870-5468; Kathy King, Administrator

Nevada Surgery Center, 4187 Pecos Road, Las Vegas, NV 89121; tel. 702/458-2522; Lyndell Kewley, Administrator

Northern Nevada Plastic Surgery Associates, 932 Ryland Street, Reno, NV 89502; tel. 702/322-3446; FAX. 702/322-4529; Averill M. Moser, RN, Administrator

Reno Endoscopy Center, LLC, 753 Ryland Street, Reno, NV 89502; tel. 775/329-1009; FAX. 775/329-4992; Jay M. Collier, Executive Director

Reno Outpatient Surgery Center, LTD., 350 West Sixth Street, Reno, NV 89503; tel. 702/334-4888; Sandra Walker–Wright, Administrator

Shepherd Eye Surgicenter, 3575 Pecos McLeod, Las Vegas, NV 89121; tel. 702/731-2088; FAX. 702/734-7836; Leslie E. Soper, Administrator

Sierra Center for Foot Surgery, 1801 North Carson, Suite B, Carson City, NV 89701; tel. 702/882-1441; FAX. 702/882-6844; H. Kim Bean, M.D., Administrator

SMA Surgery Center, 2450 West Charleston, Las Vegas, NV 89106; tel. 702/877-8660; FAX. 702/877-5180; Steve Evans, M.D., Medical Director

Valley View Surgery Center, 1330 Valley View Boulevard, Las Vegas, NV 89102; tel. 702/870-7101; FAX. 702/870-7118; Steven C. Wilson, Administrator

NEW HAMPSHIRE

Ambulatory Surgery Center, 100 Hitchcock Way, Manchester, NH 03104; tel. 603/695-2500; Deborah A. Andriski, Administrator

Bedford Ambulatory Surgical Center, 11 Washington Place, Bedford, NH 03110; tel. 603/622-3670; FAX. 603/626-9750; Linda Dwyer, RN, B.S.N., Director, Vice President Clinical Services

Clinic Surgery Center (The), 253 Pleasant Street, Concord, NH 03301; tel. 603/226-2200; Kevin Appleton, Administrator

Day Surgery, 590 Court Street, Keene, NH 03431; tel. 603/357-3411; Michael Chelstowski, Director

Dunning Street Ambulatory Care Center, Seven Dunning Street, Claremont, NH 03743; tel. 603/543-3501; July Bradley, Administrator

Elliot One Day Surgery Center, 445 Cypress Street, Manchester, NH 03103; tel. 603/627-4889; FAX. 603/626-4300; Donna Quinn, RN, B.S.N., M.B.A., Director

Nashua Eye Surgery Center, Inc., Five Coliseum Avenue, Nashua, NH 03063; tel. 603/882-9800; FAX. 603/882-0556; Paul O'Leary, Administrator

Northeast Pain Consultation and Management PC, Pinewood Medical Center, 255 State Route 16, Somersworth, NH 03878; tel. 603/692-3166; FAX. 603/692-3168; Michael J. O'Connell, M.D., M.H.A., Director

Nutfield Surgicenter, Inc., 44 Birch Street, Suite 304, Derry, NH 03038; tel. 603/898-3610; Cynthia Fortune, Administrator

Orthopeadic Surgery Center, 264 Pleasant Street, Concord, NH 03301; tel. 603/228-7211; FAX. 603/228-7192; Gail McNulty, Administrator

Salem Surgery Center, 32 Stiles Road, Salem, NH 03079; tel. 603/898-3610; FAX. 603/890-3313; Deborah M. Baker, Administrator

The Clinic Surgery Center, 253 Pleasant Street, Concord, NH 03301; tel. 603/226-2200; Kevin Appleton, Administrator

NEW JERSEY

A Center for Advanced Surgery, Three Winslow Place, Paramus, NJ 07652; tel. 201/843-9390; FAX. 201/843-0591; Marc L. Reichman, Director of Administration

Affiliated Ambulatory Surgery PA, 182 South Street, Suite One, Morristown, NJ 07960; tel. 973/267-0300; FAX. 973/984-2670; Sylvia Wexler, Administrator

Allan H. Schoenfeld, M.D., PA, 501 Lakehurst Road, Toms River, NJ 08753

Arthur W. Perry, M.D., FACS Plastic Surgery Center, 3055 Route 27, Franklin Park, NJ 08823; tel. 908/422-9600; FAX. 908/422-9606; Arthur W. Perry, M.D., Director

Associated Surgeon of Northern New Jersey, 25 Rockwood Place, Englewood, NJ 07631; tel. 201/567-3999; FAX. 201/567-9288

Atlantic Surgery Center, LLC, 279 Third Avenue,, Long Branch, NJ 07740; tel. 908/222-7373; FAX. 908/229-1556; Daniel B. Goldberg, M.D., President

Atrium Surgery Center, Inc., 195 Route 46, Suite 202, Mine Hill, NJ 07803; tel. 201/989-5185; FAX. 201/328-4097; Jennifer Rand, RN, CNOR, President

Bergen Gastroenterology, 466 Old Hook Road, Suite One, Emerson, NJ 07630; tel. 201/967-8221; FAX. 201/967-0340; Robert Ein, M.D., President

Bergen Surgical Center, Outpatient Surgical Services, One West Ridgewood Avenue, Paramus, NJ 07652; tel. 201/444-7666; Ralph Perricelli, Administrator

Burlington County Internal Medicine, 651 John F Kennedy Way, Willingboro, NJ 08046

Campus Eye Group, 1700 Whitehorse Hamilton Square Road, Suite A, Hamilton Squab, NJ 08690

Cataract and Laser Institute, PA, 101 Prospect Street, Suite 102, Lakewood, NJ 08701; tel. 908/367-0699; FAX. 908/367-0937

Cataract Surgery and Laser Center, Inc., 19 21 Fair Lawn Avenue, Fair Lawn, NJ 07410

Center for Special Surgery, 104 Lincoln Avenue, Hawthorne, NJ 07506; tel. 973–427–6800; FAX. 973–427–9602; John Tauber, Business Administrator

Clifton Surgery Center, 1117 Route 46 East Suite 303, Clifton, NJ 07013; tel. 973/779–7210; FAX. 973/779–7387; Ramon Silen, M.D., President and Medical Director

Drs. Scherl Scherl Chessler and Zingler, P.A., 1555 Center Avenue, Fort Lee, NJ 07024; tel. 201/945–6564; FAX. 201/461–9038; Dorothy Hoffman–Freeman, Office Manger

Endo–Surgi Center, 1201 Morris Avenue, Union, NJ 07083; tel. 908/686–0066; Sharon DeMato, Administrator

Endo/Surgical Center of New Jersey, 925 Clifton Avenue, Clifton, NJ 07013; tel. 201/777–3938; FAX. 201/777–6738; Pauline Perrino, RN, CGRN, Director of Nursing

Englewood Endoscopic Associates, 420 Grand Avenue, Englewood, NJ 07631

Enrico Monti and Murphy, PA, 715 Broadway, Second Floor, Paterson, NJ 07514

Essex Eye Surgery and Laser Center, 1460 Broad Street, Bloomfield, NJ 07003; tel. 201/338–5566; FAX. 201/338–0753; Lin Lee, Director Support Services

Eye Institute of Essex Surgeye Center, 50 Newark Avenue, Belleville, NJ 07109; tel. 201/751–6060; FAX. 201/450–1464; Eileen Beltramba, Administrator

Eye Physician of Sussex County Surgical Center, 183 High Street, Newton, NJ 07860; tel. 973/383–6345; FAX. 973/383–0032; Patricia Fowler, RN

Eye Surgery Princeton, 419 North Harrison Street, Princeton, NJ 08540; tel. 609/921–9437; FAX. 609/921–0277; Richard H. Wong, M.D., Medical Director

Freehold Ent, d/b/a Face to Face, Patriots Park, 222 Schanck Road, Freehold, NJ 07728; tel. 908/431–1666; FAX. 908/431–1665

Garden State Ambulatory Surgical Center, One Plaza Drive, Suite 20–21, Toms River, NJ 08757; tel. 908/341–7010; FAX. 908/341–5066; Moshe Rothkopf, M.D., FACS

Gastroenterology Diagnosis Northern New Jersey, 205 Browertown Road, West Paterson, NJ 07424; Barbara Wattenberg, Administrative Director

Hackensack Surgery Center, 321 Essex Street, Hackensack, NJ 07601

Hand Surgery and Rehabilitation Center of New Jersey, P.A., 5000 Sagemore Drive, Suite 103, Marlton, NJ 08053; tel. 609/983–4263; FAX. 609/983–9362

HealthSouth Surgical Center of South Jersey, 130 Gaither Drive, Suite 160, Mount Laurel, NJ 08054; tel. 609/722–7000; FAX. 609/722–8962; Eleanor O. Peschko, Administrator

Horizon Laser and Eye Surgery Center, 9701 Ventnor Avenue, Suite 301, Margate City, NJ 08402; tel. 609/822–7171; FAX. 609/822–3211; Suzanne D. Bruno, Administrator

Hunterdon Center for Surgery, LLC T/A Surgery Today, 121 Highway 31, Suite 1300, Flemington, NJ 08822; tel. 908/806–7017; FAX. 908/806–2838; Saleha Faruqi, M.D., Medical Director

James Street Surgical Suite, 261 James Street, Morristown, NJ 07960

Mediplex Surgery Center, 98 James Street, Suite 108, Edison, NJ 08820–3998; tel. 908/632–1600; FAX. 908/632–1678; Ruth Mosher, Administrator

Metropolitan Surgical Association, 40 Eagle Street, Englewood, NJ 07631

Mid Atlantic Eye Center, 70 East Front Street, Red Bank, NJ 07701; tel. 732–741–0858; FAX. 732–219–0180; Walter J. Kahn, M.D.

Middlesex Same Day Surgical Center, 561 Cranbury Road, East Brunswick, NJ 08816; tel. 908/390–4300; FAX. 908/390–4405; Evelyn Tornquist, Office Manager

Newark Mini–Surgi Site, Inc., 145 Roseville Avenue, Newark, NJ 07107; tel. 201/485–3300; FAX. 201/485–2404; Monica Chomsky

North Jersey Center for Surgery, 39 Newton Sparta Road, Newton, NJ 07860; tel. 973/383–0153; FAX. 973/300–9002; Bruno J. Casatelli, D.P.M., Administrator

North Jersey Women's Medical Center, Inc., 6000 Kennedy Boulevard, West New York, NJ 07093; tel. 201/869–9293; Saul Luchs, M.D.

Northern New Jersey Eye Institute, 71 Second Street, South Orange, NJ 07079; tel. 973–763–2203; FAX. 973–763–5207; Shirley Vitale, Administrative Director

Northwest Jersey Ambulatory Surgery Center, 350 Sparta Avenue, Sparta, NJ 07871; tel. 201/729–8580; FAX. 201/729–8185; Sharon L. Marquardt, RN, Operating Room Coordinator

Ocean County Eye Associates, P.C., 18 Mule Road, Toms River, NJ 08755

Ocean Surgical Pavilion, Inc., 1907 Highway 35, Suite Nine, Oakhurst, NJ 07755; tel. 908/517–8885; FAX. 908/517–8589; Marie T. Scoles, RN, Administrator

Ophthalmic Physicians of Monmouth, 733 North Beers Street, Holmdel, NJ 07733; tel. 908/739–0707; FAX. 908/739–6722; Beverly Savlov, Office Manager

Pavonia Surgery Center, Inc., 600 Pavonia Avenue, Fourth Floor, Jersey City, NJ 07306; tel. 201/216–1700; FAX. 201/216–1800; William H. Constad, M.D., President

Princeton Ambulatory Surgery Center, Inc., 281 Witherspoon Street, Third Floor, Princeton, NJ 08542; tel. 609/497–4380; FAX. 609/497–4986; Dennis Doody, President

Princeton Orthopedic Association, 727 State Road, Princeton, NJ 08540; tel. 609/924–8131; FAX. 609/924–8731; William G. Hyncik, Jr., Executive Director

Retina Consultants Surgery Center, 39 Sycamore Avenue, Little Silver, NJ 07739

Ridgedale Surgery Center, 14 Ridgedale Avenue, Suite 120, Cedar Knolls, NJ 07927; tel. 201/605–5151; FAX. 201/605–1208; Enza Guagenti, Administrator

Ridgewood Ambulatory Surgery Center, 1200 Ridgewood Avenue, Ridgewood, NJ 07450; tel. 201/444–4499; FAX. 201/612–8114

Roseland Surgery Center, 556 Eagle Rock Avenue, Roseland, NJ 07068; tel. 201/226–1717; FAX. 201/403–9034; Joseph Brandspiegel, Executive Director

Saddle Brook Surgicenter, Inc., 289 Market Street, Saddle Brook, NJ 07663; tel. 201/843–4444; FAX. 201/368–2817; Dr. Ronald Sollitto, President and CEO

Seashore Surgery Center, 1907 New Road, Northfield, NJ 08225; tel. 609/646–2323; FAX. 609/645–9780; Carol A. Leszczynski, Administrator

Shore Surgicenter, Inc., 142 Route 35, Eatontown, NJ 07724; tel. 908/542–9666; FAX. 908/542–9393; Simone Bendary, Manager

Somerset Eye Institute, P.C., 562 Easton Avenue, Somerset, NJ 08873

Somerset Surgical Center, P.A., 1081 Route 22 West, Bridgewater, NJ 08807

South Jersey Endoscopy Center, 17 West Red Bank Avenue, Suite 302, Woodbury, NJ 08096; tel. 609/848–4464; FAX. 609/848–8706; Sue Lampman, Billing Manager

South Jersey Surgicenter, 2835 South Delsea Drive, Vineland, NJ 08360; tel. 609/696–0020; FAX. 609/794–9799; James Yondura, RN, Administrator

Springfield Eye Surgery Laser Center, 105 Morris Avenue, Springfield, NJ 07081; tel. 201/376–3113; FAX. 201/376–1378; Dr. Christine Zolli

St. Barnabas Outpatient Centers, Same Day Surgery Center, 101 Old Short Hills Road, West Orange, NJ 07052; tel. 201/325–6565; FAX. 201/325–6551; Veronica Rose, RN, Acting Administrative Director

Summit Eye Group T/A Suburban Eye Institute, 369 Springfield Avenue, Berkeley Heights, NJ 07922; tel. 908/464–4600; FAX. 908/464–4737; Patricia K. Ketcham, RN, Administrator

Summit Surgical and Endoscopy Center, 110 Carnie Boulevard, Voorhees, NJ 08043; tel. 609/770–5813; FAX. 609/751–8960; Maureen Miller, Executive Director

Surgery Center of Cherry Hill, 408 Route 70 East, Cherry Hill, NJ 08034; tel. 609/354–1600; FAX. 609/429–7555; Yvonne M. Bley, Director of Nursing

Surgicare of Central Jersey, Inc., 40 Stirling Road, Watchung, NJ 07060; tel. 908/769–8000; FAX. 908/668–3139; Jacqueline Jerko, Executive Director

Surgicare Surgical Associates, PC, 15 01 Broadway, Route 4 West, Suite One and Three, Fairlawn, NJ 07410; tel. 201/791–6585; John H. Haffar, M.D., Medical Director

Teaneck Gastroenterology and Endoscopy Center, 1086 Teaneck Road, Suite Three B, Teaneck, NJ 07666; tel. 201/837–9636; FAX. 201/837–9544

The Endoscopy Center of Red Bank, 365 Broad Street, Red Bank, NJ 07701; tel. 908/842–4294; FAX. 908/842–3854; Elizabeth Boyle, Provider Relations

The Endoscopy Center of South Jersey, 2791 South Delsea Drive, South Vinelan, NJ 08360; tel. 609/691–1400; FAX. 609/691–7117; Richard Wagar, Assistant Director

The Eye Care Center, 500 West Main Street, Freehold, NJ 07728; tel. 908/462–8707; FAX. 908/462–1296; Dale A. Ingram, Administrator

The Hernia Center, 222 Schanck Road, Suite 100, Freehold, NJ 07728; tel. 908/462–2999; FAX. 908/462–7760; Jackie Porter, RN

The New Jersey Eye Center, 21 West Main Street, Bergenfield, NJ 07621; tel. 201/384–7333; FAX. 201/385–3881; Joyce Katzman, Administrator

The Peck Center Incorporated, 1200 Route 46, Clifton, NJ 07013; tel. 201/471–3906; FAX. 201/471–7048; George C. Peck, Jr., M.D.

The Surgical Center at South Jersey Eye Physicians, P.A., 509 South Lenola Road, Building 11, Moorestown, NJ 08057; tel. 609/727–9333; FAX. 609/727–0064; Janet Daniels, RN, ASC Nurse Manager

Trocki Plastic Surgery Center, PA, 635 Tilton Road, Northfield, NJ 08225

United Hospital Community Health Center, 194 Clinton Avenue, Newark, NJ 07108; tel. 201/242–2300; Delores Henderson

NEW MEXICO

Alamogordo Eye Clinic and Surgical Center, 1124 10th Street, Alamogordo, NM 88310; tel. 505/434–1200; FAX. 505/437–3947; Donald J. Ham, Administrator

Eastern New Mexico Eye Clinic, 1820 West 21st Street, Clovis, NM 88101; tel. 505/762–2207; Dik S. Cheung, M.D.

Eye Care Surgery, 110 North Coronado Avenue, Espanola, NM 87532; tel. 505/753–7391; FAX. 505/753–2749; Dr. Gary Puro

HealthSouth Albuquerque Surgery Center, 1720 Wyoming Boulevard, N.E., Albuquerque, NM 87112; tel. 505/292–9200; FAX. 505/292–1398; Sharon Prudhomme, Administrator

Lazaro Eye Surgical Center, 1131 Mall Drive, Las Cruces, NM 88011; tel. 505/522–7676; Corine B. Lazaro, M.D., Administrator

Northside Presbyterian, P.O. Box 26666, 5901 Harper Drive, NE, Albuquerque, NM 87125; tel. 505/291–2114; FAX. 505/291–2983; Robert Garcia, Administrator

Presbyterian Family Healthcare, 4100 High Resort Boulevard, Rio Rancho, NM 87124; tel. 505/823–8804; Andrew Scianimanico, Administrator

The Endoscopy Center of Santa Fe, 1650 Hospital Drive, Suite 900, Santa Fe, NM 87505; tel. 505/988–3373; FAX. 505/984–1858; Jim Howlett, Administrator

NEW YORK

Ambulatory Surgery Center of Brooklyn, 313 43rd Street, Brooklyn, NY 11232; tel. 718/369–1900; FAX. 718/965–4157; Michael M. Levi, M.D., Ph.D., Governing Authority

Ambulatory Surgery Center of Greater New York, Inc., 1101 Pelham Parkway, N., Bronx, NY 10469; tel. 718/515–3500; FAX. 718/655–1795; Joanne McLaughlin, Administrator

Brook Plaza Ambulatory Surgical Center, 1901 Utica Avenue, Brooklyn, NY 11234; tel. 718/968–8700; Sharron Resnick, Office Manager

Brooklyn Eye Surgery Center, LLC, 1301–1311 Avenue J, Brooklyn, NY 11230; tel. 718/645–0600; FAX. 718/692–4456; Rosalind A. Kochman, Chief Executive Officer

Buffalo Ambulatory Surgery Center, 3095 Harlem Road, Cheektowaga, NY 14225; tel. 716–896–3815; FAX. 716–896–3015

Central New York Eye Center, 22 Green Street, Poughkeepsie, NY 12601; tel. 914/471–3720; Maureen Lashway

Day–Op Center of Long Island, Inc., 110 Willis Avenue, Mineola, NY 11501; tel. 516/294–0030; FAX. 516/294–0228; Robin Fishman, Executive Director

Fifth Avenue Surgery Center, 1049 Fifth Avenue, New York, NY 10028; tel. 212/772–6667; Francois Simon, Vice President

Harrison Center Outpatient Surgery, Inc., 550 Harrison Center Street, Suite 230, Syracuse, NY 13202; tel. 315/472–4424; FAX. 315/475–8056; Margaret M. Alteri, Administrator and CEO

Hurley Avenue Surgical Center, Inc., 40 Hurley Avenue, Kingston, NY 12401; tel. 914/338–4777; FAX. 914/339–7339; Steven L. Kelley, CHE, Administrator

Lattimore Community Surgicenter, 125 Lattimore Road, Rochester, NY 14620; tel. 716/473–9000; FAX. 716/473–9018; John J. Goehle, CPA, Administrator

Long Island Eye Surgery Center, 601 Suffolk Avenue, Brentwood, NY 11717; tel. 516/231–4455

Long Island Surgi–Center, 1895 Walt Whitman Road, Melville, NY 11747; tel. 516/293–9700; FAX. 516/293–1018; Howard Leemon, D.D.S.

Millard Fillmore Ambulatory Surgery Center, 215 Klein Road, Williamsville, NY 14221; tel. 716/568–6100; FAX. 716/568–6166; Joel C. Farwell, Business Manager

Nassau Center for Ambulatory Surgery, Inc., dba Garden City SurgiCenter, 400 Endo Boulevard, Garden City, NY 11530; tel. 516/832–8504; FAX. 516/832–1085; Charles J. Raab, Chief Executive/Financial Officer

New York Institute for Same Day Surgery, Inc., 99 Dutch Hill Plaza, Orangeburg, NY 10962; tel. 914/359–9000; FAX. 914/359–1495; Richard Sherman, CPA, Director of Finance and Business

North Shore Surgi Center, Inc., 989 Jericho Turnpike, Smithtown, NY 11787; tel. 516/864–7100; FAX. 516/864–7129; Gerald Mazzola, Administrator

Our Lady of Victory Surgery Center, 6300 Powers Road, Orchard Park, NY 14127; tel. 716/667–3222; FAX. 716/667–3120; Dana M. Mata, Administrative Director

Queens Surgi–Center, 83–40 Woodhaven Boulevard, Glendale, NY 11385; tel. 718/849–8700; FAX. 718/849–6523; Stanley H. Kornhauser, Ph.D., Chief Operating Officer

Queens Surgical Community Center, 46–04 31st Avenue, Long Island C, NY 11103; tel. 718/545–5050; FAX. 718/721–8709; Mr. Misk, Partner

Same Day Surgery of Latham, Inc., Seven Century Hill Drive, Latham, NY 12110; tel. 518/785–5741; FAX. 518/785–5741; Judith A. Grady, RN, Administrator

The Mackool Eye Institute, 31–27 41st Street, Astoria, NY 11103; tel. 718/728–3400; FAX. 718/721–7562; Jeanne Mackool, Administrator

Westfall Surgery Center, LLP, 919 Westfall Road, Rochester, NY 14618; tel. 716/256–1330; FAX. 716/256–3823; Gary J. Scott, Administrative Director

NORTH CAROLINA

Asheboro Endoscopy Center, 700 Sunset Avenue, P.O. Box 4830, Asheboro, NC 27203; tel. 910/626–4328; FAX. 910/625–9941; Trudy Hogan, RN, Clinical Director

Asheville Hand Ambulatory Surgery Center, 34 Granby Street, P.O. Box 1980, Asheville, NC 28802; tel. 704/258–0847; FAX. 704/258–0374; E. Brown Crosby, M.D., Executive Officer

Blue Ridge Day Surgery Center, 2308 Wesvill Court, Raleigh, NC 27607; tel. 919/781–4311; FAX. 919/781–0625; Susan S. Swift, Facility Manager

Carteret Surgery Center, 3714 Guardian Avenue, Morehead City, NC 28557; tel. 919/247–2101; Frances Meyer, Administrator

Chapel Hill Surgical Center, 109 Conner Drive, Suite 1201, Chapel Hill, NC 27514; tel. 919/968–0611; FAX. 919/967–8637; Gary S. Berger, M.D., President

Charlotte Surgery and Laser Center, 2825 Randolph Road, Charlotte, NC 28211; tel. 704/377–1647; FAX. 704/358–8267; Margaret Slattery, Manager

Christenbury Ambulatory Surgical Center, 449 North Wendover Road Park Place, Charlotte, NC 28211; tel. 704/332–9365; FAX. 704/364–7384; Brenda Haughney, Administrator

Cleveland Ambulatory Services, 1100 North Lafayette Street, Shelby, NC 28150; tel. 704/482–1331; Thomas D. Bailey, M.D., Medical Director

Columbia Medivision Inc., 2200 East Seventh Street, Charlotte, NC 28204; tel. 704/334–4317; FAX. 704/377–1830; Diane H. Matthews, Administrator

Columbia Medivision of Hickory, 27 13th Avenue, N.E., Hickory, NC 28601; tel. 704/328–1493; FAX. 704/322–6097; Marie Hudson, RN, B.S.N., Administrator

Craven Surgery Center, 630 McCarthy Blvd, P.O. Box 12446, New Bern, NC 28561; tel. 252/633–2000; FAX. 252/633–0096; Lila Cotten, Business Manager

Durham Ambulatory Surgical Center, 120 Carver Street, P.O. Box 15727, Durham, NC 27704; tel. 919/477–9677; FAX. 919/479–6755; Joseph T. Jordan, Director

Eye Surgery and Laser Clinic, 500 Lake Concord Road, N.E., Concord, NC 28025; tel. 704/782–1127; FAX. 704/782–1207; Steven Grabb, Administrator

Eye Surgery Center of Shelby, 1622 East Marion Street, Shelby, NC 28150; tel. 704/482–2020; FAX. 704/482–7707; Frank T. Hannah, Administrator

Fayetteville Ambulatory Surgery Center, 1781 Metromedical Drive, Fayetteville, NC 28304; tel. 910/323–1647; FAX. 910/323–4142; John T. Henley, Jr., M.D., Director

FemCare, 62 Orange Street, Asheville, NC 28801; tel. 704/255–8400; Philip J. Kittner, M.D., Executive Director

Gaston Ambulatory Surgery, 2545 Court Drive, Gastonia, NC 28054; tel. 704/834–2086; FAX. 704/834–2085; James R. Parks, II, Administrator

Goldsboro Endoscopy Center, Inc., 2705 Medical Office Place, Goldsboro, NC 27534; tel. 919/580–9111; FAX. 919/580–0988; Venkata C. Motaparthy, M.D., Chief Executive Officer

Greensboro Center for Digestive Diseases, 520 North Elam Avenue, P.O. Box 10829, Greensboro, NC 27403; tel. 910/547–1718; FAX. 910/547–1711; Paul Green, Operations Director

Greensboro Specialty Surgical Center, 522 North Elam Avenue, Greensboro, NC 27403; tel. 910/294–1833; FAX. 910/294–8831; Cathy Bryant, Administrator

Hawthorne Surgical Center, 1999 South Hawthorne Road, Winston–Salem, NC 27103; tel. 910/718–6800; FAX. 910/718–6847; Teresa L. Carter, Facility Director

HealthSouth Blue Ridge Surgery Center, 2308 Wesvill Court, Raleigh, NC 27607; tel. 919/781–4311; Susan Swift, Administrator

HealthSouth Surgecenter of Wilson, 1709 Medical Park Drive, Wilson, NC 27893; tel. 919/237–5649; Phyllis S. Renfrow, Administrator

HealthSouth Surgery Center of Charlotte, 2825 Randolph Rd., Charlotte, NC 28211; tel. 704/377–1647; Margaret L. Slattery, Administrator

High Point Endoscopy Center, Inc., 624 Quaker Lane, Suite C–106, High Point, NC 27262; tel. 910/885–1400; Lester E. Hurrelbrink, Administrator

High Point Surgery Center, 600 Lindsay Street, P.O. Box 2476, High Point, NC 27261; tel. 336–884–6068; FAX. 336–888–6111; Joan D. Gayle, Administrator

Iredell Head, Neck and Ear Ambulatory Surgery Center, Inc., 707 Bryant Street, Statesville, NC 28677; tel. 704/873–5224; FAX. 704/873–5984; Scott Seagle, Administrator

Iredell Surgical Center, 1720 Davie Avenue, Statesville, NC 28677; tel. 704/871–0081; Kimberly J. Ericson, Administrator

Medivision, Inc., 3312 Battleground Avenue, Greensboro, NC 27410; tel. 919/282–8330; Jeanne Whitley, Administrator

Medivision, Inc., 2170 Midland Road, P.O. Box 1938, Southern Pine, NC 28387; tel. 910/295–1221; FAX. 910/295–0512; Kathy Stout, RN, Administrator

Piedmont Gastroenterology Center, Inc., 1901 South Hawthorne Road, Suite 308, Winston–Salem, NC 27103; tel. 910/760–4340; FAX. 919/765–2869; Charles H. Hauser, Administrator

Plastic Surgery Center of North Carolina, Inc., 2901 Maplewood Avenue, Winston–Salem, NC 27103; tel. 336–768–6210; FAX. 336–768–6236; Melba Edwards, Administrator

Quandrangle Endoscopy Center, 620 South Memorial Drive, Greenville, NC 27834; tel. 919/752–6101; Mark Dellasega

Raleigh Endoscopy Center, 3320 Wake Forest Road, Raleigh, NC 27609; tel. 919/878–1151; Robert N. Harper, Jr., Medical Director

Raleigh Plastic Surgery Center, Inc., 1112 Dresser Court, Raleigh, NC 27609; tel. 919/872–2616; FAX. 919/872–2771; Kelly Hodges, Administrator

Raleigh Women's Health Organization, Inc., 3613 Haworth Drive, Raleigh, NC 27609; tel. 919/783–0444; FAX. 919/781–8432; Susan Hill, Vice President

RMS Surgery Center, 5200 North Croatan Highway, Kitty Hawk, NC 27949; tel. 919/261–9009; FAX. 919/261–4329; Trish Blackmon, Executive Director

SameDay Surgery Center at Presbyterian, 1800 East Fourth Street, P.O. Box 34425, Charlotte, NC 28234; tel. 704/384–4200; Chip Day, Administrator

Southern Eye Associates, P.A., Ophthalmic Surgery Center, 2801 Blue Ridge Road, Suite 200, Raleigh, NC 27607; tel. 919/571–0081; Brian Klaasmeyer, Administrator

Surgery Center of Morganton Eye Physicians, P.A., 335 East Parker Road, Morganton, NC 28655; tel. 704/433–6225; L. A. Raynor, M.D., Medical Director

Surgical Center of Greensboro, Inc., 1211 Virginia Street, P.O. Box 29347, Greensboro, NC 27429; tel. 919/272–0012; FAX. 919/272–4063; Ken Overbey, Administrator

SurgiCenter of Wilson, 209 Richards Street, Wilson, NC 27893; tel. 919/237–5649; FAX. 919/237–4977; Phyllis Renfrow, President

Surgicenter Services of Pitt, Inc., 102 Bethesda Drive, Greenville, NC 27834; tel. 919/816–7700; FAX. 919/816–7733; Anna M. Weaver, Administrator

The Endoscopy Center, 191 Biltmore Avenue, Asheville, NC 28801; tel. 704/254–0881; Michael Grier, M.D.

The Surgery Center, 166 Memorial Court, Jacksonville, NC 28546; tel. 910/353–9565; FAX. 919/353–5497; Takey Crist, M.D., President

WHA Medical Clinic, PLLC, 1202 Medical Center Drive, Wilmington, NC 28401; tel. 910/341–3433; Diane A. Atkinson, Executive Director

Wilmington SurgCare, Inc., 1801 South 17th Street, Wilmington, NC 28401; tel. 910/763–4555; FAX. 910/763–9044; Catherine Peterman, President and CEO

Wilson OB–GYN, 2500 Horton Boulevard, Zip 27893, P.O. Box 7639, Wilson, NC 27895; tel. 919/206–1000; FAX. 919/237–0704; Daniel P. Michalak, M.D., Administrator

Woman Care and Carolina Birth Center, 712 North Elm Street, High Point, NC 27262; tel. 910/889–3646; Robert C. Crawford, M.D., Chief Executive Officer

NORTH DAKOTA

Centennial Medical Center, 1500 24th Avenue, S.W., Minot, ND 58702; tel. 701/852–0777; Dr. Manuel Neto, Administrator

Dakota Day Surgery, 1717 South University Drive, P.O. Box 6014, Fargo, ND 58103; tel. 701/280–4700; FAX. 701–280–4747; Debra Bauer, Administrator

Day Surgery–Wahpeton, 275 South 11th Street, Wahpeton, ND 58075; tel. 701/642–2000; FAX. 701/671–4153; Keith Robberstad, Administrator

Grand Forks Clinic Ltd., ASC, 1000 South Columbia Road, Grand Forks, ND 58201; tel. 701/780–6000; Wayne K. Larson, Associate Administrator

Great Plains Clinic Surgery Center, 33 Ninth Street, W., Dickinson, ND 58601; tel. 701/225–6017; FAX. 701/225–5018; Joel Frey, Administrator

Medical Arts, ASC, Inc., 400 East Burdick Expressway, Minot, ND 58702; tel. 701/857–7000; Phil Gorby, Administrator

North Dakota Surgery Center, 3035 Demers Ave., Grand Forks, ND 58201; tel. 701/775–3151; FAX. 701–775–3153; Ross J. Gonitzke, Administrator

Western Dakota Medical Group, 1102 Main, Williston, ND 58801; tel. 701/572–7711; FAX. 701/572–2283; Mary E. Banta, Administrator

OHIO

Advanced Cosmetic and Laser Surgery Center, Inc., 2200 Philadelphia Drive, Suite 651, Dayton, OH 45406; tel. 937/278–0809; FAX. 937/278–3590

Amend Center for Eye Surgery, 5939 Colerain Avenue, Cincinnati, OH 45239; tel. 513/923–3900; FAX. 513/923–3012

Aultman Center for One Day Surgery, 4715 Whipple Avenue, N.W., Canton, OH 44718; tel. 216/492–3050; Eric Draime, Administrator

Austintown Ambulatory Healthcare Center, 45 North Canfield–Niles Road, Youngstown, OH 44515; tel. 216/792–2722; FAX. 216/793–4883; James M. Conti, President and CEO

Big Run Surgery Center, 950 Georgesville Road, Columbus, OH 43228; tel. 614/234–2144

Bloomberg Eye Center, 1651 West Main Street, Newark, OH 43055; tel. 614/522–3937; FAX. 614/522–6766; John E. Reid, Executive Director

Carnegie Surgery Center, 10681 Carnegie Avenue, Cleveland, OH 44106; tel. 216/231–5566; FAX. 216/231–1441; K. L. Rosacco, RN, CNOR, Nurse Administrator

Central Ohio Eye Surgery Center, 210 Sharon Road, Suite B, Circleville, OH 43113; tel. 614/477-7200; FAX. 614/477-8349; Teresa Meadows, OR Coordinator

Cincinnati Eye Institute and Outpatient Eye Surgery Center, 10494 Montgomery Road, Cincinnati, OH 45242; tel. 513/984-5133; FAX. 513/984-4240; Doris Holton, Administrator

Cincinnati Foot Clinic, Inc., 9600 Colerain Avenue, Suite 400, Cincinnati, OH 45239; tel. 513/385-6946; Robert Hayman, M.D., President

Columbia The Surgery Center, 19250 East Bagley Road, Middleburg Heights, OH 44130; tel. 440-826-3240; FAX. 440-826-3250

Columbus Eye Surgery Center, 5965 East Broad Street, Suite 460, Columbus, OH 43213; tel. 614/751-4080; FAX. 614/751-4092; Terri Gatton, RN, CNOR, Director Surgery

Consultants in Gastroenterology, Inc., 29001 Cedar Road, Suite 110, Lyndhurst, OH 44124; tel. 216/461-2550; FAX. 216/461-5319; Gloria Bradshaw, Office Manager

Crystal Clinic Surgery Center, 3975 Embassy Parkway, Akron, OH 44313; tel. 216/668-4085; Katherine L. McNeal, RN, Administrator

Dayton Ear, Nose and Throat Surgeons, Inc., 7076 Corporate Way, Centerville, OH 45459; tel. 937/434-0555; FAX. 937/434-7413; K. Jean Christian, Administrator

Digestivecare Endoscopy Unit, 75 Sylvania Drive, Beavercreek, OH 45440; tel. 513/325-5065; FAX. 513/325-5060; Patty Mannix, RN, CGRN Endoscopy Coordinator

Endoscopy Center of Dayton LTD, 4200 Indian Ripple Road, Beaver Creek, OH 45440; tel. 937/427-1680; FAX. 937/427-9496; Christy L. McBride, Office Manager

Endoscopy Center West, 3654 Werk Road, Cincinnati, OH 45248; tel. 513/451-6001; FAX. 513/451-7310

Eye Care Center of Cincinnati, 5300 Cornell Road, Cincinnati, OH 45242; tel. 513/489-6161; FAX. 513/489-6442; Amy D. Riegler, Coordinator

Eye Institute of Northwestern Ohio, Inc., 5555 Airport Highway, Suite 110, Toledo, OH 43615; tel. 419/865-3866; FAX. 419/865-3451; Carol R. Kollarits, M.D., President

Eye Surgery Center of Wooster, 3519 Friendsville Road, Wooster, OH 44691; tel. 330/345-6371; FAX. 330/345-8029; Michelle Morrison, Director

Facial Surgery Center, 1130 Congress Avenue, Glendale, OH 45246; tel. 513/772-2442; FAX. 513/772-2844; Joseph J. Moravec, M.D., Medical Director

Firas Atassi, M.D. Outpatient Surgery Center, 34500 Center Ridge Road, North Ridgeville, OH 33039; tel. 216/327-2414

Gastroenterology Associates of Cleveland, 6801 Mayfield Road, Suite 142, Mayfield Heights, OH 44124; tel. 216/461-8800; James Andrassy, Administrator

Gastroenterology Associates, Inc., 4665 Belpar Street, NW, P.O. Box 36329, Canton, OH 44735; tel. 216/493-1480; FAX. 216/493-6805

Gastroenterology Specialists, Inc., 2732 Fulton Drive, N.W., Canton, OH 44718; tel. 330/455-5011; FAX. 330/588-7127; Melissa Smith, RN, C.G.C.

Halpin-Poweleit Eye Surgery Center, (Division of Tri-State Eye Care), 8044 Montgomery Road, Suite 155, Cincinnati, OH 45236; tel. 513/791-3937; FAX. 513/791-1473

Heritage Surgical Associates of Cincinnati, d/b/a Healthsouth Surgery Center of Cincinnati, 2925 Vernon Place, Suite 101, Cincinnati, OH 45219; tel. 513/872-4541; FAX. 513/872-4558; Patti Murphy, RN, Director

Innova Surgery Center East, d/b/a Eastside Surgical Center, 3755 Orange Place, Beachwood, OH 44122; tel. 216/464-7300; FAX. 216/467-3050; Nancy Halkerston, RN, Director Clinical Services

Kahn and Diehl Center for Progressive Eye Care, 2740 Navarre Avenue, Oregon, OH 43616; tel. 419/697-3658; FAX. 419/697-2149; Karen R. Hess, RN, C.O.T., O.R. Supervisor

Kunesh Eye Surgery Center, 2601 Far Hills Avenue, Dayton, OH 45419-1665; tel. 937/298-1093; FAX. 937/298-6344; Lucy Helmers, Administrator

Mercy Ambulatory Surgery Center, 2990 Mack Road, Fairfield, OH 45014; tel. 513/874-6440; FAX. 513/874-6005; Patricia Ann Clark, RN, M.S., Administrator

Mid-Ohio Outpatient Surgery Center, 245 Taylor Station Road, Columbus, OH 43213; tel. 614/861-0448; FAX. 614/861-7717; Dr. Grace Z. Kim, Director

MidWest Eye Center, 119 West Kemper Road, Cincinnati, OH 45246; tel. 513/671-6112; FAX. 513/671-6386; Lorrie Walters, Business Office Supervisor

North Coast Endoscopy, Inc., 9500 Mentor Avenue, Suite 380, Mentor, OH 44060; tel. 216/352-9400; FAX. 216/352-9407; Ahmad Ascha, M.D.

Northshore Endoscopy Center, 850 Columbia Road, Suite 201, Westlake, OH 44145; tel. 216/808-1212

Northwest Ohio Urologic, A.S.C., P.O. Box 351837, Toledo, OH 43635-6254; tel. 419/535-1837; FAX. 419/535-6254; Carl V. Dreyer, M.D., President

Ohio Eye Associates Eye Surgery Center, 466 South Trimble Road, Mansfield, OH 44906; tel. 419/756-8000; FAX. 419/756-7100; John L. Marquardt, M.D.

Ohio Gastroenterology Group, Inc., Endoscopy Center, 777 West State Street, Suite 402, Columbus, OH 43222; tel. 614/221-8368; FAX. 614/341-2408; Jean Yarletts, RN, B.S.N.

Parkside Women's Center, Inc., 1011 Boardman-Canfield Road, Boardman, OH 44512; tel. 216/758-0975; FAX. 216/758-8453

Parkway Urology Center, Inc., 3500 Executive Parkway, Toledo, OH 43606; tel. 419/531-8349; FAX. 419/534-5337; Gregor K. Emmert, Sr., M.D., Chief Executive Officer

Ram Bandi M.D. A.S.C., 1037 North Main Street, Suite B, Akron, OH 44310; tel. 330/923-0094; FAX. 330/923-0193; Ann Marie Faber, RN

Restorative Vision Center, 4452 Eastgate Boulevard, Suite 305, Cincinnati, OH 45245; tel. 513/752-5700; FAX. 513/752-5716; Holly Schwab, RN, Surgery Manager

Richfield Surgery Center, Inc., 3030 Streetsboro Road, Richfield, OH 44286; tel. 216/659-4790; FAX. 216/659-3355; Carol A. Westfall, Vice President

Rockside Surgery Center, 6701 Rockside Road, Suite 101, Independence, OH 44131; tel. 216/520-3030; FAX. 216/520-3068; Elizabeth A. Bus, Administrator

Ross Park Surgical Services, One Ross Park, Steubenville, OH 43952; tel. 614/282-4790; Kathy Lemasters, RN, Manager

Sandusky Surgeons, Inc., 1221 Hayes Avenue, Sandusky, OH 44870; tel. 419/625-1374; Donald Lenhart, M.D., President

Sidney Foot and Ankle Surgical Center, 1000 Michigan, Sidney, OH 45365; tel. 513/492-1211; FAX. 513/492-6557; Micki Heater, Administrative Director

South Dayton Urological Associates, Inc., 10 Southmoor Circle, N.W., Kettering, OH 45429; tel. 513/294-1489; FAX. 513/294-7999; Donald Bailey, Practice Administrator

Stoneridge Endoscopy Center, 3900 Stoneridge Lane, Dublin, OH 43017; tel. 614/889-5001; FAX. 614/889-5913; Cheryl Miller, Clinic Manager

Surgery Alliance Ltd., 975 Sawburg Avenue, Alliance, OH 44601; tel. 216/821-7997; Hazel Thomas, Administrator

Surgery Center At Southwoods, 7525 California Avenue, Youngstown, OH 44513; tel. 330/758-1954

Surgery Center West, 850 Columbia Road, Westlake, OH 44145; tel. 216/808-4000; FAX. 216/808-4010; Michelle Padden, RN, Administrator

Surgiplex, 950 Clague Road, Westlake, OH 44145; tel. 216/333-1020; FAX. 216/333-3278

Taylor Station Surgery Center, 275 Taylor Station Road, Columbus, OH 43213; tel. 614/751-4466; FAX. 614/751-4475; Bridget A. Huston, Manager

The Endoscopy Center, 3439 Granite Circle, Toledo, OH 43617; tel. 419/843-7993; FAX. 419/841-7789; Myung S. Lee, RN, Nurse Manager

The LCA Center for Surgery, 7840 Montgomery Road, Cincinnati, OH 45236; tel. 513/792-9099; FAX. 513/792-5634; Rene Fischer, President and CEO

The Surgical Center of East Liverpool, 16480 St. Clair Avenue, P.O. Box 2640, East Liverpool, OH 43920; tel. 216/386-9000; FAX. 216/386-1255; Robin Menchen, Chief Executive Officer

The Zeeba Clinic, A Meridia Outpatient and Laser Surgery Cente, 29017 Cedar Road, Lyndhurst, OH 44124; tel. 216/461-7774; FAX. 216/461-5401; Sharon Luke, RN, B.S.N., Clinical Manager

Tippecanoe Endoscopy, Inc., 1210 Boardman Canfield Road, Youngstown, OH 44512; tel. 330/726-0132; FAX. 330/726-0571; Mary Amorn, RN, Administrator

Toledo Clinic, Inc., 4235 Secor Road, Toledo, OH 43623; tel. 419/473-3561; FAX. 419/472-0838; David J. Sobczak, Senior Vice President, Chief Finance

Toledo Community Lithotripter Center, 3158 West Central Avenue, Toledo, OH 43606; tel. 419/531-3538

Toledo Plastic Surgeons Center, 2865 North Reynolds Road, Toledo, OH 43615; tel. 419/534-3330; FAX. 419/534-5716; Charles E. Jaeger, General Manager, Chief Executive Officer

Wedgewood Surgery Center, 10330 Sawmill Parkway, Powell, OH 43065; tel. 614/234-0500; FAX. 614/234-0540; Kim Heimlich, RN, Nurse Manager

Western Reserve Surgery Center, LP, 1930 State Route 59, Kent, OH 44240; tel. 216/677-3292; FAX. 330/677-3624; Laurie Simon, Office Manager

Wilson Eye Clinic Surgicenter, 300 West National Road, Vandalia, OH 45377; tel. 513/890-8992

Wright Surgery Center, 1611 South Green Road, Suite 124, South Euclid, OH 44121; tel. 216/382-1868; Barbara McCann, Director of Marketing and Communication

OKLAHOMA

A.M. Surgery, Inc., d/b/a Lawton Physician's Surgery Center, 3617 West Gore Boulevard, Suite D, Lawton, OK 73505; tel. 405/357-1900; FAX. 405/357-1775; Roxanne H. Gibson, Administrator

Ambulatory Surgery Associates, 6160 South Yale Avenue, Tulsa, OK 74136; tel. 918/495-2625; FAX. 918/495-2601; Jaquelyn S. Moore, RN, Director

Center for Plastic Surgery, P.C., 1826 East 15th Street, Tulsa, OK 74104; tel. 918/749-7177; Mark L. Mathers, D.O., Administrator

Central Oklahoma Ambulatory Surgical Center, Inc., 3301 Northwest 63rd Street, Oklahoma City, OK 73116; tel. 405/842-9732; FAX. 405/842-9771; Paul Silverstein, M.D., Administrator

Columbia Oklahoma Surgicare, 13313 North Meridian, Suite B, Oklahoma City, OK 73120; tel. 405/755-6240; FAX. 405/752-1819; Lindie Slater, Administrator

Columbia Surgicare of Tulsa, 4415 South Harvard Avenue, Suite 100, Tulsa, OK 74135; tel. 918/742-2502; FAX. 918/745-9750; Dirk Foxworthy, Administrator

Columbia Surgicare-Midtown, 1000 North Lincoln, Suite 150, Oklahoma City, OK 73104; tel. 405/232-8696; FAX. 405/232-6002; Connie M. Belding, RN, Administrator

Digestive Disease Specialists, Inc., 3366 Northwest Expressway, Suite 400, P.O. Box 99521, Oklahoma City, OK 73199; tel. 405/943-2001; FAX. 405/947-1966; Larry A. Bookman, M.D.

Eastern Oklahoma Surgery Center, L. L. C., 5020 East 68th Street, Tulsa, OK 74136; tel. 918/492-1539; FAX. 918/494-8683; Bobbie Huff, RN, Director

Grisham Eye Surgery Center, P.O. Box 1437, Bartlesville, OK 74005; tel. 918/333-1990; Dennis McKinley

Heritage Eye Surgicenter of Oklahoma, Heritage Building, 6922 South Western, Oklahoma City, OK 73139; tel. 405/636-1508; Edward D. Glinski, D.O., Administrator

Medical Plaza Endoscopy Unit, 1125 North Porter, Suite 304, Norman, OK 73071; tel. 405/360-2799; FAX. 405/447-0321; Philip C. Bird, M.D.

Oklahoma Ambulatory Surgery Center, 6908-B East Reno, Midwest City, OK 73110; tel. 405/737-6900; FAX. 405/732-0885; A.C. Vyas, M.D., Administrator

Oklahoma City Clinic, 701 Northwest 10th Street, Oklahoma City, OK 73104; tel. 405/280-5700; FAX. 405/280-5200; Mike Klein, Executive Director

Orthopedic Associates Ambulatory Surgery Center, Inc., 3301 Northwest 50th Street, P.O. Box 57027, Oklahoma City, OK 73157-7027; tel. 405/947-5610; FAX. 405/947-1341; Thomas H. Flesher, President

Outpatient Surgical Center of Ponca City, 400 Fairview, Ponca City, OK 74601; tel. 405/762-0695; FAX. 405/765-9406; Peggy Maples, RN, Executive Director

Physicians Surgical Center, 805 East Robinson, Norman, OK 73071-6610; tel. 405/364-9789; FAX. 405/366-8081; Ruth Beller, RN, Director

Southern Oklahoma Surgical Center, Inc., 2412 North Commerce, Ardmore, OK 73401; tel. 405/226–5000; Ann Willis, RN, Administrator

Southern Plains Ambulatory Surgery Center, 2222 Iowa Avenue, P.O. Box 1069, Chickasha, OK 73023; tel. 405/224–8111; FAX. 405/222–9557; H. Wayne Delony, Executive Director

Southwest Orthopedic Ambulatory Surgery Center, Inc., 8125 South Walker Avenue, Oklahoma City, OK 73139; tel. 405/631–1014; Anthony L. Cruse, D.O., President

Surgery Center of Edmond, 1700 South State Street, Edmon, OK 73013; tel. 405/330–1003; FAX. 405/330–1087; Timothy A. Gee, Administrator

Surgery Center of Enid, Inc., 1133 West Willow Road, Enid, OK 73703, P.O. Box 5069, Enid, OK 73702; tel. 405/233–6680; Tina C. Brooks, Administrator

Surgery Center of Midwest City, 8121 National Avenue, Suite 108, Midwest City, OK 73110; tel. 405/732–7905; FAX. 405/732–3561; Jackie Reed, Administrator

Surgery Center of Oklahoma, 815 Northwest 12th Street, Oklahoma City, OK 73106; tel. 405/235–4525; Olivia Dick, RN, Administrator

Surgery Center of South Oklahoma City, 100 Southeast 59th Street, Oklahoma City, OK 73109; tel. 405/634–9300; FAX. 405/634–8300; Larry Smith, Administrator

The Cataract Center of Lawton, 4214 Southwest Lee Boulevard, Lawton, OK 73505; tel. 405/353–5860; Stephen W. Gilkeson, Executive Administrator

Three Rivers Surgery Center, 3800 West Okmulgee, Muskogee, OK 74401; tel. 918/682–9899; FAX. 918/687–0786; Doug Blessen, Chief Executive Officer

Tower Day Surgery, 1044 Southwest 44th Street, Suite 100, Oklahoma City, OK 73109; tel. 405/636–1701; FAX. 405/636–4314; Marie Smith, RN, Director

Triad Eye Medical Clinic and Cataract Institute, 6140 South Memorial, Tulsa, OK 74133; tel. 918/252–2020; FAX. 918/252–7466; Marc L. Abel, D.O., Medical Director

Wilson Surgery Center, 5404 West Lee Boulevard, Lawton, OK 73505; tel. 405/357–2020; Gary Wilson, M.D., Administrator

OREGON

Aesthetic Breast Care Center, 10201 Southeast Main, Suite 20, Portland, OR 97216; tel. 503/253–3458; FAX. 503/253–0856; Mary K. Barnhart, M.D., Administrator

Center for Cosmetic and Plastic Surgery, 1353 East McAndrews Road, Medford, OR 97504; tel. 503/770–6776; FAX. 503/770–5791; Robert M. Jensen, M.D., Administrator

Eye Surgery Center, 2925 Siskiyou Boulevard, Medford, OR 97504; tel. 541/779–2020; FAX. 541/770–6838; Loren R. Barrus, M.D., Administrator

Eye Surgery Institute, The, 813 S.W. Highland Ave., Redmond, OR 97756; tel. 541/548–7170; FAX. 541/548–3842; Kathleen Peterson, RN, Administrator

Futures Outpatient Surgical Center, Inc., 1849 Northwest Kearney, Suite 302, Portland, OR 97209; tel. 503/224–0723; FAX. 503/224–0722; Bryce E. Potter, M.D.

GI Endoscopy Center, 2560 N.W. Medical Park Drive, Roseburg, OR 97470; tel. 541–673–2046; FAX. 5410673–0454; Ruth E. Harpole, RN, Administrator

Lawrence W. O'Dell, d/b/a Northwest Eye Center, 9975 Southwest Nimbus Avenue, Beaverton, OR 97005; tel. 503/646–7644; Jim Heath, Administrator

Lovejoy Surgicenter, Inc., 933 Northwest 25th Avenue, Portland, OR 97210; tel. 503/221–1870; FAX. 503/221–1488; Allene M. Klass, Administrator

McKenzie Surgery Center, 940 Country Club Road, Eugene, OR 97401; tel. 541/344–2600; FAX. 541/344–3317; Lynn M. Staples, RN, Administrator

Medford Clinic, P.C., 555 Black Oak Drive, Medford, OR 97504; tel. 541/734–3520; FAX. 541/734–3597; Jon D. Ness, Chief Executive Officer

Medford Plastic Surgeons, 1690 East McAndrews Road, Medford, OR 97504; tel. 541/779–5655; FAX. 541/770–6943; R. Kenneth Pons, M.D., Administrator

North Bend Medical Center, Inc., 1900 Woodland Drive, Coos Bay, OR 97420; tel. 503/267–5151; FAX. 503/269–0797; J. Peter Johnson, Administrator

Northbank Surgical Center, 700 Bellevue Street, S., Suite 300, Salem, OR 97301; tel. 503/364–3704; Peggy Seidler, Administrator

Ontario Surgery Center, 251 S.W. 19th Street, Ontario, OR 97914; tel. 541/889–3198; FAX. 541–881–9106; Jeffrey C. Pitts, M.D., Administrator

Oregon Cataract and Laser Institute, 2700 Southeast 14th Avenue, Albany, OR 97321; tel. 503/928–1666; Darrell Genstler, M.D., Administrator

Oregon Eye Surgery Center, Inc., 1550 Oak Street, Eugene, OR 97401; tel. 541/683–8771; FAX. 541/484–4898; Virginia Pecora, RN, Administrator

Roseburg Surgicenter, LTD., 631 West Stanton, Roseburg, OR 97470; tel. 541–440–6311; FAX. 541–440–6394; Dell Gray, Executive Officer

The Gastroenterology Endoscopy Center, Inc., 6464 Southwest Borland Road, Suite D–4, Tualatin, OR 97062; tel. 503/692–4537; FAX. 503/691–2324; Gale R. Dupek, M.B.A., Administrator

The Oregon Clinic Gastroenterology Division Gresham Office, 24900 Southeast Stark, Suite 205, Gresham, OR 97030; tel. 503/661–2000; FAX. 503/661–2001; Jeffrey S. Albaugh, M.D., Administrator

The Portland Clinic Surgical Center, 800 Southwest 13th Avenue, Portland, OR 97205; tel. 503/221–0161; FAX. 503/274–1697; J. Michael Schwab, Administrator

Tigard Surgery Center, 13240 Southwest Pacific Highway, Suite 200, Tigard, OR 97223; tel. 503/639–6571; FAX. 503/624–6037; Ivan L. Bakos, M.D., Administrator

Willamette Valley Eye SurgiCenter, 2001 Commercial Street, S.E., Salem, OR 97302; tel. 503/363–1500; FAX. 503/588–2028; Gordon Miller, M.D., Administrator

PENNSYLVANIA

Abington Surgical Center, 2701 Blair Mill Road, Suite 35, Willow Grove, PA 19090; tel. 215/443–8505; FAX. 215/957–0565; Deborah S. Kitz, Ph.D., Executive Director

Aesthetic and Reconstructive Surgery, 816 Belvedere Street, Carlisle, PA 17013

Aestique Ambulatory Surgical Center, One Aesthetic Way, Greensburg, PA 15601; tel. 412/832–7555; FAX. 412/832–7568; Theordore A. Lazzaro, M.D., Medical Director

Apple Hill Surgical Center, 25 Monument Road, Suite 270, York, PA 17403; tel. 717/741–8250; FAX. 717/741–8254; Gwendolyn J. Grothouse, RN, Administrative Director

Delaware Valley Laser Surgery Institute, Two Bala Plaza, Pl 33, Bala Cynwd, PA 19004; tel. 215/668–2847; FAX. 215/668–1509; Herbert J. Nevyas, M.D., Medical Director

Dermatologic Surgery Center, P.C., 6415 Bustleton Avenue, Philadelphia, PA 19149

Dermatologic SurgiCenter, 1200 Locust Street, Philadelphia, PA 19107; tel. 215/546–3666; FAX. 215/546–6060; Anthony V. Benedetto, D.O., FACP, Medical Director

Dermatologic SurgiCenter, 2221 Garrett Road, Drexel Hill, PA 19026; tel. 610/623–5885; FAX. 610/623–7276; Anthony V. Benedetto, D.O. Medical Director

Digestive Disease Institute, 897 Poplar Church Road, Camp Hill, PA 17011; tel. 717/763–1239; FAX. 717/763–9854; Iris Garman, Administrator

Eye Clinic Ambulatory Surgical Center, Inc., 601 Wyoming Avenue, Kingston, PA 18704; tel. 717/288–7405; Mark Kelly, Administrator

Fairgrounds Surgical Center, 400 North 17th Street, Suite 300, Allentown, PA 18104; tel. 610/821–2020; FAX. 610/821–2016; Darlene G. Hinkle, Administrative Director

Fort Washington Surgery Center, 467 Pennsylvania Avenue, Fort Washington, PA 19034; tel. 215/628–4300; FAX. 215/628–4253; Elizabeth Brennan, Administrator

Grandview Surgery & Laser Center, 205 Grandview Avenue, Camp Hill, PA 17011; tel. 717/731–5444; FAX. 717/731–0415; Sherry L. Rhodes, RN, Administrative Director

Hanover Surgicenter, 3130 Grandview Road, Building B, Hanover, PA 17331; tel. 717/633–1600; FAX. 717/633–6556; Melvin L. Brooks, Jr., CRNA, Administrator

Healthsouth Mt. Pleasant Surgery Center, 200 Bessemer Road, Mt. Pleasant, PA 15666; tel. 412/547–5432; FAX. 412/547–2435; Brian Kowleczny, Administrative Director

HealthSouth Scranton Surgery and Laser Center, 425 Adams Street, Scranton, PA 18510; tel. 717/348–1114; FAX. 717/347–4351; Nancy A. Nealon, RN, B.S.N., Administrative Director

HealthSouth Surgery Center of Lancaster, 217 Harrisburg Avenue, Suite 103, Lancaster, PA 17603; tel. 717/295–2500; FAX. 717/295–4898; Debra K. Sanders, RN, Administrative Director

Jefferson Surgery Center, Coal Valley Road, P.O. Box 18420, Pittsburgh, PA 15236; tel. 412/469–6060; FAX. 412/469–7322; Sheran Sullivan, Manager

John A. Zitelli, M.D., P.C., Ambulatory Surgery Facility, 5200 Centre Avenue, Suite 303, Pittsburgh, PA 15232; tel. 412/681–9400; FAX. 412/681–5240; John A. Zitelli, M.D.

Kremer Laser Eye Center, 200 Mall Boulevard, King of Pruss, PA 19406; tel. 610/337–1580; FAX. 610/337–1815; Tara Hopewell, RN

Lebanon Outpatient Surgical Center, L.P., 830 Tuck Street, Lebanon, PA 17042; tel. 717/228–1620; FAX. 717/228–1642; Anita Gingrich Fuhrman, Manager

Lowry SurgiCenter, 1115 Lowry Avenue, Jeannette, PA 15644; tel. 412/527–2885; FAX. 412/527–6885; K. Diddle, M.D., Medical Director

Mt. Lebanon Surgical Center, Professional Office Building, 1050 Bower Hill Road, Suite 102, Pittsburgh, PA 15243; tel. 412/563–6808; FAX. 412/563–6857; Patricia Strosnider, Director, Nursing

N.E.I. Ambulatory Surgery, Inc., 204 Mifflin Avenue, Scranton, PA 18503; tel. 717/342–3145; FAX. 717/342–3136

North Shore Surgi–Center, Two Allegheny Center, Suite 530, Pittsburgh, PA 15212–5493; tel. 412/231–0200; FAX. 412/231–0613; Jack Demos, M.D., FACS

Northwood Surgery Center, 3729 Easton–Nazareth Highway, Easton, PA 18045; tel. 610/559–7110; FAX. 610/559–7317; Pankesh Kadam, Administrator

Ophthalmology Laser and Surgery Center, Inc., 92 Tuscarora Street, Harrisburg, PA 17104; tel. 717/233–2020; FAX. 717/232–3294; Jeanne Megella, RN, Director, Nursing

Paoli Surgery Center, One Industrial Boulevard, Paoli, PA 19301; tel. 610/408–0822; FAX. 610/408–9933; Marcia L. Collymore, Facility Manager

Pennsylvania Eye Surgery Center, 4100 Linglestown Road, Harrisburg, PA 17112; tel. 717/657–2020; FAX. 717/657–2071; Sandra Benner, RN, Director, Surgical Services

Pocono Ambulatory Surgery Center, One Veterans Place, Stroudsburg, PA 18360; tel. 717/421–4978; Mary P. Hayden RN, B.S., A.S.C. Coordinator

Ridgeway Esper Medical Center Ambulatory Surgical Center, 5050 West Ridge Road, Erie, PA 16506–1298; tel. 814/833–8800; FAX. 814/833–2079; Deborah Hartmann, RN, Director, Nursing

Sewickley Surgical Center at Edgeworth Commons, 301 Ohio River Boulevard, Edgeworth, Suite 100, Sewickley, PA 15143; tel. 412/741–5866; FAX. 412/741–5884; Carol Figas, RN, CNOR, Supervisor

Shadyside Surgi–Center, Inc., 5727 Centre Avenue, Pittsburgh, PA 15206; tel. 412/363–6626; FAX. 412/363–7008; Susan M. Katch, RN, Director

Southwestern Ambulatory Surgery Center, 500 Lewis Run Road, Pittsburgh, PA 15236; tel. 412/469–6964; FAX. 412/469–6948; Pamela Wrobleski, CRNA, M.P.M., Director

Southwestern Pennsylvania Eye Surgery Center, 750 East Beau Street, Washington, PA 15301; tel. 412/228–7477; FAX. 412/228–8117; Karen A. Dynice, Clinical Director

Specialists Health Care Clinic of Monroeville, 125 Daugherty Drive, Monroeville, PA 15146–2749; tel. 412/374–9385; FAX. 412/374–9490; Carol Fiske, CMSC, Administrative Assistant, Medical Staff Manager

St. Francis Surgery Center North, One St. Francis Way, Cranberry Tow, PA 16066; tel. 412/772–5360; FAX. 412/772–4644; Gerry Matt, RN, M.Ed., Director

Surgery Center of Bucks County, 401 North York Road, Warminster, PA 18974; tel. 215/443–3022; FAX. 215/443–5859; JoAnn Quinn, Director, Nursing

Section C

Surgical Center of York, 1750 Fifth Avenue, P.O. Box 290, York, PA 17405; tel. 717/843-7613; Thomas R. Harlow, Administrative Director

Surgical Eye Institute of Western Pennsylvania, 618 Monongahela Avenue, Glassport, PA 15045; tel. 412/664-7874; FAX. 412/673-5720; Shirley A. Smith, RN

The Surgery Center of Chester County, 460 Creamery Way, Oaklands Corporate Center, Exton, PA 19341-2500; tel. 610/594-8900; FAX. 215/594-8907; Stephen P. Barainyak, Executive Director

The SurgiCenter at Ligonier, 221 West Main Street, Ligonier, PA 15658; tel. 412/238-9573; FAX. 412/238-4709; Kim Kenney-Ciarimboli, Supervisor

West Shore Endoscopy Center, 423 North 21st Street, Camp Hill, PA 17011; tel. 717/975-2430; Marilee Ball, RN, Director

Wills Eye Surgery Center of the Northeast, 1815 Cottman Avenue, Philadelphia, PA 19111; tel. 215/722-2505; FAX. 215/742-6386; Lawrence S. Schaffzin, M.D., Medical Director

Wyoming Valley Surgery Center, 1130 Highway 315, Wilkes-Barre, PA 18702; tel. 717/821-2830; FAX. 717/825-7962; David N. Culp, Chief Executive Officer

RHODE ISLAND

Bayside Endoscopy Center, 120 Dudley Street, Suite 103, Providence, RI 02905; tel. 401/274-1810; FAX. 401/273-9689; Nicholas Califano, M.D., Administrator

Blackstone Valley Surgicare, Inc., 333 School Street, Pawtucket, RI 02860; tel. 401/728-3800; FAX. 401/723-2440; Ann Dugan, Administrator

Koch Eye Surgi Center, Inc., 566 Tollgate Road, Warwick, RI 02886; tel. 401/738-4800; FAX. 401/738-8153; Paul S. Koch, M.D., Administrator

Ocean State Endoscopy, 100 Highland Avenue, Providence, RI 02906; tel. 401/421-6306; Joel Spellun, M.D.

Planned Parenthood of Rhode Island, 111 Point Street, Providence, RI 02903; tel. 401/421-9620; FAX. 401/621-6250; Miriam Inocencio, President and CEO

Wayland Square Surgicare, 17 Seekonk Street, Providence, RI 02906; tel. 401/453-3311; FAX. 401/351-1280; Ann Dugan, Administrator

Women's Medical Center, 1725 Broad Street, Cranston, RI 02905; tel. 401/467-9111; FAX. 401/461-1390; Carol Belding, Administrator

SOUTH CAROLINA

Ambulatory Eye Surgery and Laser Center, Inc., 9297 Medical Plaza Drive, Charleston, SC 29406; tel. 803/572-2888; Margaret A. Thompson

Bay Microsurgical Unit, Inc., 400 Marina Drive, P.O. Drawer L, Georgetown, SC 29442; tel. 803/546-8421; FAX. 803/546-1173; Rebecca Lammonds, Administrator and Director of Nursing

Bearwood Ambulatory Surgery Center, 3031 Highway 81, N., Anderson, SC 29621; tel. 864/226-0837; FAX. 864/226-8367; Patricia P. Smith, Administrator

Bishopville Ambulatory Surgical Center, 800 West Church Street, Bishopville, SC 29010; tel. 803/484-6976; Carolyn Sellers, Administrator

Carolina Eye Ambulatory Surgery Center, 210 University Parkway, Suite 1500 B, Aiken, SC 29801; tel. 803/649-3953; FAX. 803/641-3801; Stephen K. Vanderbilt, M.D.

Carolina Regional Surgery Center, Ltd., 900 Medical Circle, Myrtle Beach, SC 29572; tel. 803/449-7885; FAX. 803/497-5137; Mary Garvey, RN, Administrator

Carolina Surgical Center, 198 South Herlong Avenue, Rock Hill, SC 29732; tel. 803/327-4664; Jackie Ridley, Administrator

Charleston Plastic Surgery Center, Inc., 159 Rutledge Avenue, Charleston, SC 29403; tel. 803/722-1985; FAX. 803/722-4840; Anna Lambert, Office Manager

Columbia Ambulatory Plastic Surgery Center, Inc., 338 Harbison Boulevard, Columbia, SC 29212; tel. 803/732-6655; FAX. 803/732-6644; Vickie H. Ott, Administrator

Columbia Eye Surgery Center, Inc., 1920 Pickens Street, P.O. Box 1754, Columbia, SC 29202; tel. 803/254-7732; FAX. 803/748-7199; Kenneth W. Gibbons, Administrator

Columbia Gastrointestinal Endoscopy Center, 2739 Laurel Street, Suite One-B, Columbia, SC 29240; tel. 803/254-9588; FAX. 803/252-0052; Frederick F. DuRant III, Administrator

Cross Creek Surgery Center of Greenville Hospital System, Nine Doctors Drive, Crosscreek Medical Park, Greenville, SC 29605; tel. 803/455-8400; Greg Rusnak, Administrator

Greenville Endoscopy Center, Inc., 317 St. Francis Drive, Suite 150, Greenville, SC 29601; tel. 803/232-7338; Rebecca K. Swoyer, Administrator

HealthSouth Surgery Center of Charleston, 2690 Lake Park Drive, North Charles, SC 29406; tel. 803/764-0992; FAX. 803/764-3187; Donna Padgette, RN, M.S.N., Facility Manager

Healthsouth Surgery Center of Greenville, Five Memorial Medical Court, Greenville, SC 29605; tel. 864/295-3067; FAX. 864/295-3096; Vickie Waters, Facility Manager

Outpatient Surgery Center of Lexington Medical Center in Irmo, 7035 Saint Andrews Road, Columbia, SC 29212; tel. 803/749-0924; Barbara Williams, Administrator

Pee Dee Ambulatory Surgery Center, 602 Cheves, P.O. Box F-17, Florence, SC 29506; tel. 803/669-3822; Joseph J. McEvoy, Administrator

Roper West Ashley Surgery Center, 18 Farmfield Avenue, Charleston, SC 29407; tel. 803/763-3763; FAX. 803/763-3881; Maria I. Sample, Administrator

Same Day Surgery East, 10 Enterprise Boulevard, Suite 104, Charleston, SC 29615; tel. 803/458-7141; FAX. 803/676-9116; Mary Jane Knottek, RN, B.S.N., CNOR, Clinical Nurse

Spartanburg Urology Surgicenter, Inc., 391 Serpentine Drive, Suite 330, Spartanburg, SC 29303; tel. 864/585-2002; FAX. 864/585-3300; Anita Womick, RN, OR Director

The Greenwood Endoscopy Center, 103 Liner Drive, Greenwood, SC 29646; tel. 803/227-3838; FAX. 803/227-6116; A. A. Ramage, M.D., Administrator

The Microsurgery Center, Inc., 1655 East Greenville Street, P.O. Box 1886, Anderson, SC 29622-1886; tel. 864/225-1933; FAX. 864/225-9035; Ann Geier, Director, Clinical Services

Trident Surgery Center, 9313 Medical Plaza Drive, Suite 102, Charleston, SC 29406; tel. 803/797-8992; FAX. 803/797-4094; Leah J. Dawson, Administrator

SOUTH DAKOTA

Aberdeen Surgical Center, 1200 South Main, Box 1150, Aberdeen, SD 57401-1150; tel. 605/225-2466; Scott H. Berry, M.D., Administrator

Black Hills Regional Eye Surgery Center, 2800 Third Street, Rapid City, SD 57701-7394; tel. 605/341-4100; FAX. 605/341-0278; Richard B. Hanafin, Executive Director

Jones Eye Clinic, 3801 South Elmwood Avenue, Sioux Falls, SD 57105-6565; tel. 605/336-3142; FAX. 605/334-0737; Charles E. Jones, M.D.

Mallard Pointe Surgical Center, 1201 Mickelson Drive, Watertown, SD 57201-7100; tel. 605/882-4743; FAX. 605/882-6064; James Arlt, Operations Director

Medical Associates Surgi Center, 772 East Dakota, Pierre, SD 57501-3399; tel. 605/224-5901; Michael Pfeiffer, Administrator

Sioux Falls Surgical Center, 910 East 20th Street, Sioux Falls, SD 57105-1012; tel. 605/334-6730; Donald A. Schellpfeffer, M.D., Ph.D., Medical Director

Spearfish Surgery Center, Inc., 1316 10th Street, Spearfish, SD 57783-1530; tel. 605/642-3113; FAX. 605/642-3117; Linda Redding, Administrator

SurgiClinic, 1010 Ninth Street, Rapid City, SD 57701-3599; tel. 605/348-7607; FAX. 605/342-1359; Ray G. Burnett, M.D., Medical Director

Women's Health Clinic, 909 South Miller, Mitchell, SD 57301; tel. 605/995-5560; Donna Gerlach, RN, Clinic Director

Yankton Medical Clinic P.C., 1104 West Eighth Street, Yankton, SD 57078-3306; tel. 605/665-7841; FAX. 605/665-0546; Don P. Lake, Administrator

TENNESSEE

Appalachian Ambulatory Surgical Center, Medical Arts Building, 106 Rogosin Drive, Elizabethton, TN 37643; tel. 615/543-5888

Arrowsmith Eye Surgery Center, Parkview Tower, Suite 900, 210 25th Avenue, N., Nashville, TN 37203; tel. 615/327-2244; FAX. 615/321-3175; Sharon Reesor, Surgery Center Administrator

Atrium Memorial Surgical Center, 1949 Gunbarrel Road, Suite 290, Chattanooga, TN 37421; tel. 615/495-3550; FAX. 615/495-3580; Sandy Proctor, Administrator

Baptist Physicians Pavilion Surgery Center, 360 Wallace Road, Nashville, TN 37211; tel. 615/781-9020; FAX. 615/781-9944

Bristol Surgery Center, 350 Blountville Highway, Suite 108, Bristol, TN 37620; tel. 423/844-6120; FAX. 423/844-6126; David Paul Gross, Administrator

Cataract Surgery Center, 5406 Knight Arnold Road, Memphis, TN 38115; tel. 901/360-8081; FAX. 901/368-3822

Centennial Surgery Center, 340 23rd Avenue, N., Nashville, TN 37203; tel. 615/327-1123; FAX. 615/327-0261; Cynthia S. Duvall, RN, B.S., Administrator

Chattanooga Surgery Center, 400 North Holtzclaw Avenue, Chattanooga, TN 37404; tel. 615/698-6871; Becky Myers, Administrator

Clarksville Encoscopy Center, 132 Hillcrest Drive, Clarksville, TN 37043; tel. 615/552-0180; FAX. 615/572-0915

Cleveland Surgery Center, L.P., 137 25th Street, N.E., Cleveland, TN 37311; tel. 423/472-7874; R. Scott Peterson, Executive Director

Columbia Endoscopy Center, Inc., 1510 1/2 Hatcher Lane, Columbia, TN 38401; tel. 615/381-7818; FAX. 615/381-5625; Dianne Roberts, RN, Head Nurse

Columbia Outpatient Surgery, Inc., 1405 Hatcher Lane, Columbia, TN 38401; tel. 615/381-3700; Deborah Woodard, Administrator

Columbia Sullins Surgery Center, 2761 Sullins Street, Knoxville, TN 37919; tel. 423/522-2949; FAX. 423/637-3259; Tina Shelby-Kahl, Assistant Administrator

D D C Surgery Center, Nine Physicians Drive, Jackson, TN 38305; tel. 901/661-0086; Regina Phelps, Billing Manager

Digestive Disease Endoscopy Center, 2021 Church Street, Suite 303, Nashville, TN 37203; tel. 615/340-4625; FAX. 615/340-4628

East Memphis Surgery Center, 80 Humphreys Center Drive, Suite 101, Memphis, TN 38120; tel. 901/747-3233; FAX. 901/747-3230

Endoscopy Center of Kingsport, 2204 Pavilion Drive, Kingsport, TN 37660; tel. 423/392-6100; FAX. 423/392-6159; Barbara Light, Office Manager

Endoscopy Center of Northeast Tennessee, 310 State of Franklin Road, Suite 202, Johnson City, TN 37604; tel. 615/929-7111

Eye Surgery Center of East Tennessee, 1124 Weisgarber Road, Suite 110, Knoxville, TN 37909; tel. 423/588-1037; FAX. 423/909-9104; Donna Chambless, RN

Fort Sanders West Outpatient Surgery Center, Ltd., 210 Fort Sanders West Boulevard, Knoxville, TN 37922; tel. 615/531-5222; FAX. 615/531-5043; Leslie Irwin, Administrator

Franklin Surgery Center at MedCore, 2105 Edward Curd Lane, Franklin, TN 37067; tel. 615/794-7320

G. Baker Hubbard Ambulatory Surgery Center, 616 West Forest Avenue, Jackson, TN 38301; tel. 901/422-0330

G. I. Diagnostic and Therapeutic Center, 1068 Cresthaven Road, Suite 300, Memphis, TN 38119; tel. 901/682-6700; FAX. 901/683-3046; Randolph M. McCloy, M.D., Medical Director

Germantown Ambulatory Surgical Center, Inc., 7499 Old Poplar Pike, Germantown, TN 38138; tel. 901/755-6465; FAX. 901/757-5543; Carol Harper, Facility Manager

Health South Surgery Center of Clarksville, 121 Hillcrest Drive, Clarksville, TN 37043; tel. 615/552-9992

HealthSouth Nashville Surgery Center, 1717 Patterson Street, Nashville, TN 37203; tel. 615/329-1888; FAX. 615/329-0179; Patricia Middleton, Facility Manager

HealthSouth Surgery Center of Chattanooga, 924 Spring Creek Road, Chattanooga, TN 37412; tel. 423/899-1600; FAX. 423/899-2171; Melissa Powers, Administrator

Kingsport Bronchoscopy Center, Inc., 135 West Ravine Road, Suite Eight-A, Kingsport, TN 37660; tel. 615/247-5197; FAX. 615/247-5254; Shirley Hawkins, Administrator

Kingsport Endoscopy Corporation, 135 West Ravine Street, Suite 7A, Kingsport, TN 37660; tel. 423/246-6777; Bettye Reed, Administrator

Knoxville Center for Reproductive Health, 1547 West Clinch Avenue, Knoxville, TN 37916; tel. 423/637-3861; Bernadette McNabb, Executive Director

Knoxville Surgery Center, 9300 Park West Boulevard, Knoxville, TN 37923; tel. 615/691-2725; FAX. 615/691-3090; Ranae Thompson, RN, Facility Administrator

Lebanon Surgery Center, Inc., 1414 Baddour Parkway, P.O. Box 549, Lebanon, TN 37088; tel. 615/444-8944; Sheena Sloan, Administrator

LeBonheur East Surgery Center, L.P., 786 Estate Place, Memphis, TN 38120; tel. 901/681–4100; FAX. 901/681–4140; Diane Swain, Director

Maternity Center of East Tennessee, 1925–B Ailor Avenue, Knoxville, TN 37921; tel. 615/524–4422

Medical Center Endoscopy Group, 930 Madison, Suite 870, Memphis, TN 38103; tel. 901/578–2538; FAX. 901/578–2572; John W. Flowers, Business Manager

Memphis Area Medical Center for Women, 29 South Bellevue Boulevard, Memphis, TN 38104; tel. 901/722–8050

Memphis Center for Reproductive Health, 1462 Poplar Avenue, Memphis, TN 38104; tel. 901/274–3550

Memphis Eye and Cataract Ambulatory Surgery Center, 6485 Poplar Avenue, Memphis, TN 38119; tel. 901/767–3937

Memphis Gastroenterology Group, 80 Humphrey's Blvd., Suite 220, Memphis, TN 38120; tel. 901/747–3630; FAX. 901/747–4039; Sylvia Hawkins, RN, Nurse Manager

Memphis Planned Parenthood, Inc., 1407 Union Avenue, Third Floor, Memphis, TN 38104; tel. 901/725–1717

Memphis Regional Gamma Knife Center, 1265 Union Avenue, Memphis, TN 38104; tel. 901/726–6444

Memphis Surgery Center, 1044 Cresthaven Road, Memphis, TN 38119; tel. 901/682–1516; FAX. 901/682–1545; Barbara Hopper, RN, B.S., CNOR, Facility Manager

Mid–State Endoscopy Center, 2010 Church Street, Suite 420, Nashville, TN 37203; tel. 615/329–2141; FAX. 615/321–0522; Allan H. Bailey, M.D., Medical Director

Nashville Endoscopy Center, 300 20th N., Eighth Floor, Nashville, TN 37203; tel. 615/284–1335; FAX. 615/284–1316; Margaret Sullivan, RN

Nashville Gastrointestinal Endoscopy Center, 4230 Harding Road, Suite 309, Nashville, TN 37205; tel. 615/383–0165; FAX. 615/292–4657; Ron E. Pruitt, M.D.

Ophthalmic Ambulatory Surgery Center, P.C., 342 22nd Street, Nashville, TN 37203; tel. 615/327–2001; FAX. 615/327–2069; Alec Dryden, Administrator

Oral Facial Surgery Center, 322 22nd Avenue, N., Nashville, TN 37203; tel. 615/321–6160; FAX. 615/327–9612; Kelly Ingle, Administrator

Physicians Surgery Center, 207 Stonebridge, Jackson, TN 38305; tel. 901/661–6340; FAX. 901/661–6363; Judy Haskins, RN, Manager

Planned Parenthood Association of Nashville, 412 D.B. Todd Boulevard, Nashville, TN 37203; tel. 615/321–7216

PRISM Aesthetic Surgery Center, 80 Humphreys Center, Suite 310, Memphis, TN 38120; tel. 901/747–0446; FAX. 901/747–4406; Judy Sharp, Director, PRISM ASC

Ridge Lake Ambulatory Surgery Center, 825 Ridge Lake Boulevard, Memphis, TN 38119; tel. 901/685–0777

Rivergate Surgery Center, 647 Myatt Drive, Madison, TN 37115; tel. 615/868–8942; FAX. 615/860–3820; Brenda Cruse, Director

Shea Clinic, 6133 Poplar Pike, Memphis, TN 38119; tel. 901/761–9720; FAX. 901/683–8440

Southern Endoscopy Center, 397 Wallace Road, Suite 407, Nashville, TN 37211; tel. 615/832–5530; FAX. 615/832–5713; Robert W. Herring, Jr., M.D., Medical Director

St. Thomas Medical Group Endoscopy Center, 4230 Harding Road, Suite 400, Nashville, TN 37205; tel. 615/297–2700

Surgical Services, P.C., 604 South Main Street, Sweetwater, TN 37874; tel. 423/337–4508; FAX. 423/337–4588

Surgicenter Of Murfreesboro Medical Clinic, P.A., 1004 North Highland Avenue, Murfreesboro, TN 37130; tel. 615/893–4480; FAX. 615/895–6212

Tennessee Endoscopy Center, 1706 East Lamar Alexander Parkway, Maryville, TN 37804; tel. 615/983–0073; FAX. 615/984–1731; Craig Jarvis, M.D., Administrator

The Cookeville Surgery Center, 100 West Fourth Street, Suite 100, Cookeville, TN 38501; tel. 615/528–6115; FAX. 615/526–2962; Diana Welch, RN, Administrator

The Endoscopy Center, 801 Weisgarber Road, Suite 100, Knoxville, TN 37909, Knoxville, TN 37950–9002; tel. 615/588–5121; Gayle Mahan, Office Manager

The Endoscopy Center of Centennial, L.P., 2400 Patterson Street, Suite 515, Nashville, TN 37203; tel. 615/327–2111; FAX. 615/327–9292; Dawn Lynn Gray, RN, B.S., Endoscopy Administrator

The Eye Surgery Center Oak Ridge, 90 Vermont Avenue, Oak Ridge, TN 37830; tel. 423/482–8894; Sally Jones

The Pain Clinic and Rehabilitation Center, 55 Humphreys Center Drive, Suite 200, Memphis, TN 38120; tel. 901/747–0040; FAX. 901/747–3424; Lori Parris, RN, Administrator

Tullahoma Outpatient Surgery Center, 1918 North Jackson, Tullahoma, TN 37388; tel. 615/455–2006

Urology Surgery Center, Inc., 2011 Church Street, Sixth Floor, Nashville, TN 37203; tel. 615/329–7700; Robert B. Barnett, M.D., Medical Director

Van Dyke Ambulatory Surgery Center, 1024 Kelley Drive, Paris, TN 38242; tel. 901/642–5003; FAX. 901/642–8756; John T. VanDyck III, M.D., Owner

Volunteer Medical Clinic, 313 Concord Street, Knoxville, TN 37919; tel. 423/522–5173; FAX. 423/522–9907

Wesberry Surgery Center, 2900 South Perkins Road, Memphis, TN 38118–3237; tel. 901/362–3100; FAX. 901/362–3372; Jesse Wesberry, Jr., M.D., President

Wesley Ophthalmic Plastic Surgery Center, 250 25th Avenue North, Suite 213, Nashville, TN 37203; tel. 615/329–3624

Women's Wellness and Maternity Center, Inc., 3459 Highway 68, Madisonville, TN 37354; tel. 423/442–6624; FAX. 423/442–5746; Betti Wilson, Administrator

TEXAS

Abilene Cataract and Refractive Surgery Center, 2120 Antilley Road, Abilene, TX 79606; tel. 915/695–2020, FAX. 915/695–2326; Robert W. Cameron, M.D., Medical Director

Abilene Endoscopy Center, 1249 Ambler Avenue, Abilene, TX 79601; tel. 915/695–2020; Royce Harrell

AHCA–Mainland Outpatient Surgery Center, 3810 Hughes Court, Dickinson, TX 77539; tel. 713/337–7001; FAX. 713/337–7091; Terry R. Williams, Administrator

Amarillo Cataract and Eye Surgery Center, Inc., 7310 Fleming Avenue, Amarillo, TX 79106; tel. 806/354–8891; FAX. 806/354–2591; Carol A. Pearson, Director

Ambulatory Urological Surgery Center, Inc., 1149 Ambler, Abilene, TX 79601; tel. 915/676–3557; FAX. 915/673–2143; Angela X. Young, RN, Manager

American Surgery Centers of South Texas, LTD, 7810 Louis Pasteur, Suite 101, San Antonio, TX 78229; tel. 210/692–0218; Britt F. Mitchell, C.O.T., Director, Operations

Bailey Square Surgical Center, Ltd., 1111 West 34th Street, Austin, TX 78705; tel. 512/454–6753; FAX. 512/454–4314; Katherine S. Wilson, RN, M.H.A., Administrator

Barbara Jean Bartlett Memorial Surgery Center, 4200 Andrews Highway, Midland, TX 79707; tel. 915/520–5888; Sylvan Bartlett, M.D., Administrator

Bay Area Endoscopy Center, 444 FM 1959, Houston, TX 77034; tel. 281/481–9400; FAX. 281/481–9490; N. S. Bala, Medical Director

Bay Area Surgery, 7101 South Padre Island Drive, Corpus Christ, TX 78412; tel. 512/985–3500; FAX. 512/985–3754; Gene Hybner, Administrator

Bay Area Surgicare Center, Inc., 502 Medical Center Boulevard, P.O. Box 57767, Webster, TX 77598; tel. 713/332–2433; FAX. 713/332–0619; Mary P. Colombo, Administrator

Baylor SurgiCare, 3920 Worth Street, Dallas, TX 75246; tel. 214/820–2581; FAX. 214/820–7484; Patty Crabb, Administrative Director

Bellaire Surgicare, Inc., 6699 Chimney Rock, Suite 200, Houston, TX 77081; tel. 713/665–1406; FAX. 713/665–8262; Sheila M. Liccketto, Administrator

Brazosport Eye Institute, 103 Parking Way, P.O. Box 369, Lake Jackson, TX 77566; tel. 409/297–2961; FAX. 409/297–2395; Frank J. Grady, M.D., Ph.D., FACS, Director

Brownsville Surgicare, 1024 Los Ebanos Boulevard, Brownsville, TX 78520; tel. 210/548–0101; FAX. 210/541–3752; Norberto J. Sanchez, Administrator

Central Texas Day Surgery Center, L.P., 1817 Southwest Dodgen, Loop, Temple, TX 76502; tel. 817/773–7785; FAX. 817/773–9333; Debby Meyer, Director

Coastal Bend Ambulatory Surgical Center, 900 Morgan, Corpus Christ, TX 78404; tel. 512/888–4288; FAX. 512/888–4786; Barbara VandenBout

Columbia Endoscopy Center of Dallas, 6390 LBJ Freeway, Suite 200, Dallas, TX 75240; tel. 972/934–3691; Jeane Suggs, Administrator

Columbia North Texas Surgi–Center, 917 Midwestern Parkway, E., Wichita Falls, TX 76302; tel. 817/767–7273; FAX. 817/723–9059; Barbara Dawson, Administrator

Columbia Physicians DaySurgery Center, 3930 Crutcher Street, Dallas, TX 75246; tel. 214/827–0760; FAX. 214/827–0944; Vickie Roberts, RN, Administrator

Columbia Surgery Center at Park Central, 12200 Park Central Drive, Third Floor, Dallas, TX 75251; tel. 972/661–0505; FAX. 972/661–0505; Molly Paulose, Administrator

Columbia Surgery Center of Las Colinas, 4255 North Macarthur Boulevard, Irving, TX 75038; tel. 214/257–0144; FAX. 214/258–0436; Bill Beaman, Administrator

Columbia Surgery Center of Sherman, 3400 North Calais Drive, Sherman, TX 75090; tel. 903/813–3377; FAX. 903/870–7617; Brian Roland, Business Office Manager

Columbia Surgical Center, 2800 East 29th Street, P.O. Box 2700, Bryan, TX 77805; tel. 409/776–4300; FAX. 409/774–7149; Joan Dougan, Interim Chief Operating Officer

Columbia Surgical Center of Southeast Texas, 3127 College Street, Beaumont, TX 77701; tel. 409/835–2607; Jim Hoeks, Administrator

Columbia Surgicare Outpatient Center of Victoria, 1903 East Sabine, Victoria, TX 77901; tel. 512/576–4105; FAX. 512/576–9830; Margaret Coleman, RN, Administrator

Columbia West Houston Surgicare, 970 Campbell Road, Houston, TX 77024–2804; tel. 713/461–3547; FAX. 713/722–8921; Penny A. Menge, RN, M.S.N., Administrator

Columbia/Waco Medical Group Surgery Center, 2911 Herring, Waco, TX 76708; tel. 817/755–4430; FAX. 817/755–4590; Kay H. O'Leary, RN, Administrator

Crystal Outpatient Surgery Center, Inc., 215 Oak Drive, S., Suite J, Lake Jackson, TX 77566; tel. 409/299–6118; FAX. 409/299–1007; R. Scott Yarish, M.D., Administrator

Cy–Fair Surgery Center, 11250 Fallbrook Drive, Houston, TX 77065; tel. 713/955–7194; FAX. 713/890–0895; Scott Washko, Administrator

Dallas Day Surgery Center, Inc., 411 North Washington, Suite 5400, Dallas, TX 75246; tel. 214/821–8613; Henry S. Byrd, President

Dallas Eye Surgicenter, Inc., 720 South Cedar Ridge Road, Duncanville, TX 75137; tel. 214/296–6634; William Hamilton, Administrator

Dallas Ophthalmology Center, Inc., 2811 Lemmon Avenue E., Suite 102, Dallas, TX 75204; tel. 214/520–7600; FAX. 214/528–6522; Jean Vining, RN, Administrator

Dallas Surgi Center, 8230 Walnut Hill Lane, Suite 808, Dallas, TX 75231; tel. 214/696–8828; FAX. 214/696–1444

DeHaven Surgical Center, Inc., 1424 East Front Street, Tyler, TX 75702; tel. 903/595–4168; FAX. 903/595–6821; Barbara Shamburger, RN, Administrator

Diagnostic Clinic of San Antonio Ambulatory Surgical Center, 4647 Medical Drive, P.O. Box 29249, San Antonio, TX 78224–3100; tel. 210/692–3382; FAX. 512/692–3397; Nancy Nixon, RN, ASC Supervisor

Doctors Surgery Center, Inc., 5300 North Street, Nacogdoches, TX 75961; tel. 409/569–8278; Robert P. Lehmann, M.D., Director

Duncanville Surgery Center, (an affiliate of ASC Network Corporation), 1018 East Wheatland Road, Duncanville, TX 75116; tel. 214/296–6912; Michael Kincaid, Vice President

East El Paso Surgery Center, 7835 Corral Drive, El Paso, TX 79915; tel. 915/595–3353; FAX. 915/595–6796; Ruth Robertson, Administrator

East Side Surgery Center, Inc., 10918 East Freeway, Houston, TX 77029; tel. 713/451–4299; FAX. 713/451–4383; Clifford E. Kirby, Administrator

East Texas Eye Associates Surgery Center, 1306 Frank Avenue, Lufkin, TX 75901; tel. 409/634–8381; Jo Ann O'Neill, C.O.T., Administrator

El Paso Institute of Eye Surgery, Inc., 1717 North Brown Street, Building Three, El Paso, TX 79902; tel. 915/544–0526; FAX. 915/544–2877; Esthern A. Calderon, Administrator

Elm Place Ambulatory Surgical Center, 2217 South Danville Drive, Abilene, TX 79605; tel. 915/695–0600; FAX. 915/695–3908; Susan King, RN, Director

Eye Surgery Center, 2001 Ed Carey Drive, Suite Three, Harlingen, TX 78550; tel. 210/423–2100; Michael Laney, C.O.M.T., Administrator

Facial Plastic and Cosmetic Surgical Center, 6300 Humana Plaza, Suite 475, Abilene, TX 79606; tel. 915/695–3630; FAX. 915/695–3633; Howard A. Tobin, M.D., FACS, Medical Director

Forest Park Surgery Pavilion, 5920 Forest Park Road, Suite 700, Dallas, TX 75235; tel. 214/350–2400; FAX. 214/352–3853; Mark Turner, Administrator

Fort Worth Endoscopy Center, 1201 Summit Avenue, Suite 400, Fort Worth, TX 76102; tel. 817/332–6500; Donna Drerup, RN, M.S.N., Administrator

Garland Surgery Center L.P., 777 Walter Reed Boulevard, Suite 105, Garland, TX 75042; tel. 214/494–2400; FAX. 214/494–3873; Dan Nicholson, President

Gastroenterology Consultants Outpatient Surgical Center, 8214 Wurzbach, San Antonio, TX 78229; tel. 210/614–1234; FAX. 210/614–7749; Bonnie Draude, B.S.N., RN, C.G.RN, Clinical Manager

Gastrointestinal Endoscopy Center Number Two, LTD, 1600 Coit Road, Suite 401A, Plano, TX 75075; tel. 214/867–0019; Brian Cooley, M.D., Administrator

Gonzaba Surgical Center, 720 Pleasanton Road, San Antonio, TX 78214; tel. 210/921–3826; FAX. 210/921–3825; William Gonzaba, M.D., Chief Executive Officer

Gramercy Outpatient Surgery Center, LTD, 2727 Gramercy, Houston, TX 77025; tel. 713/660–6900; FAX. 713/660–0704; Elaine Hand, RN, CNOR, Clinical Director

Healthsouth Arlington Day Surgery, 918 North Davis Street, Arlington, TX 76012; tel. 817/860–9933; FAX. 817/860–2314; Diane Wood, RN, Administrator

Healthsouth Outpatient Surgery Center, 7515 South Main Street, Suite 800, Houston, TX 77030; tel. 713/796–9666; FAX. 713/796–9660; Joan M. Culberson, RN, Administrator

HealthSouth Surgery Center of Beaumont, 3050 Liberty, Beaumont, TX 77702; tel. 409/835–3535; FAX. 409/835–6005; Tammie Clodfelter, Administrator

HealthSouth Surgery Center of Conroe, 233 Interstate 45 N., P.O. Box 3091, Conroe, TX 77304; tel. 409/760–3443; FAX. 409/760–1322; Kathy Schutz, RN, B.S.N., Facility Administrator

HealthSouth Surgery Center of Dallas, 7150 Greenville Avenue, Suite 200, Dallas, TX 75231; tel. 214/891–0466; FAX. 214/739–4702; Vicki V. Schultz, RN, Administrator

HealthSouth Surgery Center of Southwest Houston, 8111 Southwest Freeway, Houston, TX 77074; tel. 713/988–7600; FAX. 713/988–4070; Karen Whigham, Administrator

Heart of Texas Outpatient Cataract Center, 100 South Park Drive, Brownwood, TX 76801; tel. 915/643–3561; FAX. 915/646–0670; Larry Smith, CRNA, Administrator

Heritage Surgery Center, 1501 Redbud, McKinney, TX 75069; tel. 214/548–0771; FAX. 214/562–2300; Rudolf Churner, M.D., Administrator

Howerton Eye and Laser Surgical Center, 2610 I.H. 35 South, Austin, TX 78704–5703; tel. 512/443–9715; FAX. 512/443–9845; Ernest E. Howerton, M.D., Administrator

Key Whitman Surgery Center, 2801 Lemmon Avenue, Suite 400, Dallas, TX 75204; tel. 214/754–0000; FAX. 214/754–0079; Jeffrey Whitman, M.D.

Longview Ambulatory Surgical Center, 703 East Marshall Avenue, Suite 2000, Longview, TX 75601–5563; tel. 903/236–2111; FAX. 903/236–2479; Jerry D. Adair, President and CEO

Lubbock Surgi Center, LLP, 3610 34th Street, Suite D, Lubbock, TX 79410; tel. 806/793–0255; Robert M. Brodkin, D.P.M., Administrator

Lufkin Endoscopy Center, 317 Gaslight Boulevard, Lufkin, TX 75901; tel. 409/634–3713; FAX. 409/634–8136; Bhagvan R. Malladi, M.D., Administrator

Maddox Outpatient Eye Surgery Center, 1755 Curie Drive, El Paso, TX 79902; tel. 915/544–9597; FAX. 915/533–3460; Robert M. Maddox, M.D., Administrator

Mann Berkeley Eye Center, 1200 Binz, Suite 1000, Houston, TX 77004; tel. 713/526–1600; FAX. 713/529–5254; Darcy Falbey, Director of Nursing

Mann Cataract Surgery Center, 18850 South Memorial Boulevard, Humble, TX 77338; tel. 713/446–9164; Elpidio Fahel, Administrator

Medical City Dallas Ambulatory Surgery Center, 7777 Forest Lane, Suite C–150, Dallas, TX 75230; tel. 214/661–7000; FAX. 214/788–6181; Stephen E. Corbeil, President and CEO

Medical Mall Surgery Center, Inc., 1665 Antilley Road, Suite 170, Abilene, TX 79606; tel. 915/692–6694; FAX. 915/691–1568; Melissa Boyd, RN

Methodist Ambulatory Surgery Center–Central San Antonio, 1008 Brooklyn Avenue, San Antonio, TX 78215–1600; tel. 210/225–0496; FAX. 210/225–8462; Carl J. Collazo, Administrator

Methodist Malone and Hogan–Texas Surgery, 1501 West 11th Place, Suite A, Big Spring, TX 79720–4199; tel. 915/267–1623; FAX. 915/267–1137; Penny Phillips, Administrator

Metroplex Ambulatory Surgical Center, 2717 Osler Drive, Suite 102, Grand Prairie, TX 75051; tel. 214/647–6272; FAX. 214/660–1822; Glenda Daniels, RN, Director

Metroplex Surgicare, 1600 Central Drive, Suite 180, Bedford, TX 76022; tel. 817/571–1999; FAX. 817/571–1220; Julie Walker, Administrator

Mid–Cities Surgi–Center, 2012 Plaza Drive, Bedford, TX 76021; tel. 817/283–5994; Melany Pierson

Mid–Town Surgical Center, Inc., 2105 Jackson Street, Suite 200, Houston, TX 77003; tel. 713/659–3050; FAX. 713/659–3037; Glory Gee, Administrator

MSCH Health Center, 1211 Highway Six, Suite One, Sugarland, TX 77478; tel. 713/242–7200; John Araiza, Administrator

North Carrier Surgicenter, 517 North Carrier Parkway, Suite A, Grand Prairie, TX 75050–5494; tel. 214/264–0533; FAX. 214/262–5974; Abraham F. Syrquin, M.D., Medical Director

North Dallas Surgicare, 375 Municipal Drive, Suite 214, Richardson, TX 75080; tel. 214/918–9400; FAX. 214/918–9749; Bill MacKnight, Administrator

Northeast Surgery Center, 18929 Highway 59, Humble, TX 77338; tel. 713/446–4053; Harold Taylor

Northeast Texas Surgical Center, 1801 Galleria Oaks Drive, Texarkana, TX 75503; tel. 903/792–2108; FAX. 903/792–0606; Ruby Bearden, Business Manager

Northwest Ambulatory Surgery Center, 2833 Babcock Road, San Antonio, TX 78229; tel. 210/705–5100; FAX. 210/705–5025; Jim Brown, Administrator

Outpatient Surgical Center, 2507 Medical Row, Suite 101, Grand Prairie, TX 75051; tel. 214/647–8520; Jack Gray, Administrator

Outpatient Surgisite, 401–A East Pinecrest Drive, Marshall, TX 75670; tel. 903/938–3110; Carol C. Hall

Piney Point Ambulatory Surgery Center, 2500 Fondren, Suite 350, Houston, TX 77063; tel. 713/782–8279; FAX. 713/782–3139

Plano Ambulatory Surgery Associates, L.P., d/b/a Columbia Surgery Center of Plano, 1620 Coit Road, Plano, TX 75075–7799; tel. 972/519–1100; Dolores Holland

Plastic and Reconstructive Surgery Centre of the SW, 461 WestPark Way, Euless, TX 76040; tel. 817/540–1755; Catherine Lugger, Director

Plaza Day Surgery, 909 Ninth Avenue, Fort Worth, TX 76104–3986; tel. 817/336–6060; Nancy Kilekas, RN, B.S., CNOR, Administrator

Port Arthur Day Surgery Center, 3449 Gates Boulevard, Port Arthur, TX 77642; tel. 409/983–6144; Vicki Clark, Administrative Director

Premier Ambulatory Surgery of Austin, 4207 James Casey, Suite 203, Austin, TX 78745; tel. 512/440–7894; FAX. 512/440–1932; Patricia Philbin, Executive Director

Regional Eye Surgery Center, 107 West 30th Street, Pampa, TX 79065; tel. 806/665–0051; FAX. 806/665–0640; George R. Walters, M.D., President

Rio Grande Surgery Center, 1809 South Cynthia, McAllen, TX 78503; tel. 512/618–4402; FAX. 210/618–4174; Janet R. West, Director

San Antonio Digestive Disease Endoscopy Center, 1804 Northeast Loop 410, Suite 101, San Antonio, TX 78217; tel. 210/828–8400; FAX. 210/828–8648

San Antonio Eye Surgicenter, 800 McCullough, San Antonio, TX 78215; tel. 210/226–6169; FAX. 210/226–6383; Carol Harris, Administrator

San Antonio Gastroenterology Endoscopy Center, 520 Euclid Avenue, San Antonio, TX 78212; tel. 210/271–0606; FAX. 210/271–0180; Ernesto Guerra, M.D.

San Antonio Surgery Center, Inc., 5290 Medical Drive, San Antonio, TX 78229; tel. 210/614–0187; FAX. 210/692–7757; Ann Mueller, RN, Facility Administrator

Santa Rose Diagnostic and Surgical Center, 315 North San Saba, San Antonio, TX 78207; tel. 210/704–4000; FAX. 210/704–4014; Julie Meador, Clinical Manager

South Plains Endoscopy Center, 3610 24th Street, Lubbock, TX 79410; tel. 806/797–1015; Pat S. Wheeler, Administrator

South Texas Eye Surgicenter, Inc., 4406 North Laurent, Victoria, TX 77901; tel. 800/352–5928; Robert T. McMahon, M.D., Chief Executive Officer

South Texas Outpatient Surgical Center, Inc., 4025 East Southcross Boulevard, Building Three, Suit, San Antonio, TX 78222; tel. 210/333–0633; FAX. 210/333–0671; Michael P. Lewis, Administrator

South West Surgery Center, 1717 Precinct Line Road, Suite 101, Hurst, TX 76054; tel. 817/788–1881; FAX. 817/656–1490; Caressa Walls, Administrator

Southwest Endoscopy Center, 11803 South Freeway, Suite 115, Fort Worth, TX 76115; tel. 817/293–9292; FAX. 817/551–0616; Pamela Payne, RN

St. Mary Surgicenter, Ltd., 2301 Quaker Avenue, Lubbock, TX 79410; tel. 806/793–8801; David S. Weil, Executive Director

Surgery Center of Fort Worth, 2001 West Rosedale, Fort Worth, TX 76104; tel. 817/877–4777; Debra Delain, RN, Administrator

Surgery Center Southwest, 8230 Walnut Hill Lane, Suite 102, Dallas, TX 75231; tel. 214/345–4076; FAX. 214/345–4055; Tom Blair, Director, PHS

SurgEyeCare, Inc., 5421 La Sierra Drive, Dallas, TX 75231; tel. 214/361–1443; FAX. 214/691–3299; Sandra J. Yankee, Administrator

Surgi–Care Center of Midland, Inc., 3001 West Illinois, Suite Five–A, Midland, TX 79701; tel. 915/697–1067; FAX. 915/697–8802; Michelle Edelbrock, RN, B.S.N., Director

Surgical and Diagnostic Center, Inc., 729 Bedford Euless Road West 100, Hurst, TX 76053; tel. 817/282–6905; FAX. 817/285–8114; Edward William Smith, D.O., Medical Director

Surgical Center of El Paso, 1815 North Stanton, El Paso, TX 79902; tel. 915/533–8412; FAX. 915/542–0367; Thomas Reynolds, Managing Director

Surgicare of Travis Centre, Inc., 6655 Travis, Suite 200, Houston, TX 77030; tel. 713/526–5100; Carol Simons, Administrator

Surgicare, Ltd., 3534 Vista, Pasadena, TX 77504; tel. 713/947–0330; Evelyn Grimes, Administrator

Surgicenter of San Antonio, L.P., 7902 Ewing Halsell Drive, San Antonio, TX 78229; tel. 210/614–7372; FAX. 210/614–7362; Russell Furth, Executive Director

SurgiSystems, Inc., 427 West 20th Street, Houston, TX 77008; tel. 713/868–3641; FAX. 713/865–5460; Jo McBeth, RN

Texarkana Surgery Center, 5404 Summerhill Road, Texarkana, TX 75503; tel. 903/792–7151; Karen Stephens, Director

Texas Ambulatory Surgical Center, Inc., 2505 North Shepherd, Houston, TX 77008; tel. 713/880–3940; FAX. 713/880–1923; Kwang S. Park, Administrator

Texas Institute of Surgery, 12700 North Featherwood Drive, Suite 100, Houston, TX 77034; tel. 713/481–9303; FAX. 713/481–4263; Glenn Rodriguez, Administrator

Texoma Outpatient Surgery Center, Inc., 1712 Eleventh Street, Wichita Falls, TX 76301; tel. 817/723–1274; Tracy Youngblood, Administrator

The Birth Center of Southeast Texas, Inc., 2400 Highway 96 S., Lumberton, TX 77656; tel. 409/755–0252; Dennis D. Riston, M.D., Administrator

The Cataract Center of East Texas, P.A., 802 Turtle Creek Drive, Tyler, TX 75701; tel. 903/595–4333; FAX. 903/535–9845; Connie Bryan, RN

The Center for Sight, P.A., Two Medical Center Boulevard, Lufkin, TX 75904–3175; tel. 409/634–8434; FAX. 409/639–2581; Richard J. Ruckman, M.D.

The Endoscopy Center of Southeast Texas, 950 North 11th Street, Beaumont, TX 77702; tel. 409/833–5555; FAX. 409/833–9911; Royce D. Harrell

The Eye Surgery Center of the Rio Grande Valley, 1402 East Sixth Street, Weslaco, TX 78596; tel. 210/968–6155; FAX. 210/968–8291; Linda Funston, Administrator

The Ocular Surgery Center, Inc., 1100 North Main Avenue, San Antonio, TX 78212; tel. 210/222–2154; FAX. 512/222–0706; Jane Wilson, Administrator

The Surgery Center of Mesquite, 2690 North Galloway Avenue, Mesquite, TX 75150; tel. 972/279–8100; FAX. 972/279–3300; Jeffrey S. Houston, Administrator

The Surgery Center of Texas, 155 East Loop 338, Suite 500, Odessa, TX 79762; tel. 915/367–3906; FAX. 915/367–3895; Ann Wilson, Interim Administrator

The Surgery Center of the Woodlands, 1441 Woodstead Court, Suite 100, The Woodlands, TX 77380; tel. 281/363–0058; FAX. 281/363–0450; Kathy Budd, Administrator

Thorstenson Eye Clinic Surgery Center, 3302 Northeast Stallings Drive, Nacogdoches, TX 75963–2020; tel. 409/564–2411; FAX. 409/564–1280; Lyle S. Thorstenson, M.D., FACS, Administrator

University Surgery Center, Inc., 311 University Drive, Fort Worth, TX 76107; tel. 817/877–1002; FAX. 817/877–1006; Lori Schooler, Administrator

Urological Surgery Center of Fort Worth, 418 South Henderson, Fort Worth, TX 76104; tel. 817/338–4637; Charles Bamberger, M.D.

Valley Endoscopy Center, LLP, 3101 South Sunshine Strip, Harlingen, TX 78550; tel. 210/421–2324; FAX. 210/428–2561; Noel B. Searle, M.D.

Valley Eye Surgery Center, 1515 North Ed Carey Drive, Harlingen, TX 78550; tel. 210/423–2773; FAX. 210/423–5618; Michael D. Laney, Administrator

Valley View Surgery Center, 5744 LBJ Freeway, Suite 200, Dallas, TX 75240; tel. 972/490–4333; FAX. 972/490–3408; Ronald W. Disney, Chief Executive Officer

Vista Healthcare, Inc., 4301 Vista, Pasadena, TX 77504; tel. 713/947–0891; FAX. 713/947–1377; Chiu M. Chan, Administrator

WestPark Surgery Center, 130 South Central Expressway, McKinney, TX 75070; tel. 214/542–9382; FAX. 214/548–5303; Debbie Taylor

Westside Surgery Center, Ltd., 16100 Cairnway, Houston, TX 77084; tel. 713/550–5556; FAX. 713/550–7888; Harold F. Taylor, President and CEO

Wilson Surgicenter, 4315 28th Street, Lubbock, TX 79410; tel. 806/792–2104; Bill W. Wilson, M.D., Chief Executive Officer

UTAH

Central Utah Surgical Center, 1067 North 500 West, Provo, UT 84604; tel. 801/374–0354; FAX. 801–374–3210; Jill Andrews, RN, Administrator

Institute of Facial and Cosmetic Surgery, 5929 Fashion Boulevard, Salt Lake City, UT 84107; tel. 801/261–3637; FAX. 801/261–4096; Dr. Brent D. Kennedy, Administrator

Intermountain Surgical Center, 359 Eighth Avenue, Salt Lake City, UT 84103; tel. 801/321–3200; FAX. 801/321–3035; Joan W. Lelis, Administrative Director

McKay–Dee Surgical Center, 3903 Harrison Boulevard, Suite 100, Ogden, UT 84403; tel. 801/398–2809; FAX. 801/398–5938; Suzanne Richins, Administrator

Provo Surgical Center, 585 North 500 West, Provo, UT 84601; tel. 801/375–0983; Brent K. Ashby, Administrator

Salt Lake Endoscopy Center, 24 South 1100 East, Salt Lake City, UT 84102; tel. 801/355–2987; FAX. 801/531–9704; Clifford G. Harmon, M.D., Administrator

Salt Lake Surgical Center, 617 East 3900 South, Salt Lake City, UT 84107; tel. 801/261–3141; FAX. 801/268–2599; Jay T. Lighthall, Administrator

St. George Surgical Center, 676 South Bluff Street, St. George, UT 84770; tel. 801/673–8080; FAX. 801/673–0096; Terrill Dick, Administrator

St. Mark's Outpatient Surgery Center, 1250 East 3900 South, Suite 100, Salt Lake City, UT 84124; tel. 801/262–0358; FAX. 801/262–0901; Marjorie Kimes, Administrator

The SurgiCare Center of Utah, 755 East 3900 South, Salt Lake City, UT 84107; tel. 801/266–2283; FAX. 801/268–6151; Andrew Lyle, M.D., Administrator

Wasatch Endoscopy, 1220 East 3900 South, Suite 1B, Salt Lake City, UT 84124; tel. 801/281–3657; Marjorie Kimes, RN, Administrator

Wasatch Surgery Center, 555 South Foothill Boulevard, Salt Lake City, UT 84112; tel. 801/585–3088; FAX. 801/581–8962; Patricia Carroll, Administrator, Manager

Western Surgery Center, Inc., 850 East 1200 North, Logan, UT 84341; tel. 801/797–3670; FAX. 801/797–3848; Barbara Smehland, Administrator

VERMONT

David S. Chase, M.D., Ambulatory Surgical Center, 183 St. Paul Street, Burlington, VT 05401; tel. 802/864–0381; David S. Chase, M.D., Administrator

VIRGINIA

Ambulatory Surgery Center, 844 Kempsville Road, Norfolk, VA 23502; tel. 757/466–6900; FAX. 757/466–6313; Darleen S. Anderson, Site Administrator

Cataract and Refractive Surgery Center, 2010 Bremo Road, Suite 128, Richmond, VA 23226; tel. 804/285–0680; FAX. 804/282–6365; Jeffry A. Staples, Administrator

Columbia Fairfax Surgical Center, 10730 Main Street, Fairfax, VA 22030; tel. 703/691–0670; Sharon B. Johnson, Chief Executive Officer

CountrySide Ambulatory Surgery Center, Four Pidgeon Hill Drive, Sterling, VA 20165; tel. 703/444–6060; FAX. 703/444–2278; Deborah F. Arminio, RN, Director

Fredericksburg Ambulatory Surgery Center, Inc., 2216 Princess Anne Street, Fredericksburg, VA 22401; tel. 540/899–3403; FAX. 540/899–6893; Jeane Bullock, Administrator

Hanover Outpatient Center, 7016 Lee Park Road, Mechanicsville, VA 23111; tel. 804/730–9000; FAX. 804/730–1460; Valene S. Rice, RN, Director

Kaiser Permanente Falls Church Medical Center Ambulatory Surge, 201 North Washington Street, Falls Church, VA 22046; tel. 703/237–4046; FAX. 703/536–1400; Debbie Bland, Director, Surgical Services

Lakeview Medical Center, Inc., 2000 Meade Parkway, Suffolk, VA 23424; tel. 804/539–0251; FAX. 804/934–2620; Michael B. Stout, Executive Director

Lewis–Gale Clinic, Inc., Same Day Surgery, 1802 Braeburn Drive, Salem, VA 24153; tel. 703/772–3673; FAX. 703/989–0879; Kay Walker, RN, Director

Piedmont Day Surgery Center, Inc., 1040 Main Street, P.O. Box 1360, Danville, VA 24543–1360; tel. 804/792–1433; FAX. 804/797–1398; Aaron Lieberman, Chief Operating Officer

Riverside Surgery Center–Warwick, 12420 Warwick Boulevard, Building Three, Newport News, VA 23606; tel. 804/594–2796; FAX. 804/594–3911; M. Caroline Martin, Executive Vice President

Sentara Care Plex, 3000 Coliseum Drive, Hampton, VA 23666; tel. 804/827–2000; FAX. 804/827–6748; Jeri Eastridge, Director

Surgi Center of Central Virginia, Inc., 12 White Oak Road, Fredericksburg, VA 22405; tel. 703/371–5349; FAX. 703/373–1745; Janet P. O'Keefe, Facility Administrator

Surgi–Center of Winchester, Inc., 1860 Amherst Street, P.O. Box 2660, Winchester, VA 22604; tel. 540/722–8934; FAX. 540/722–8936; Nelson N. Isenhower, M.D., Administrator

Tuckahoe Surgery Center, Inc., 8919 Three Chopt Road, Richmond, VA 23229; tel. 804/285–4763; FAX. 804/288–2850; Charles A. Stark, CHE, Administrator

Urosurgical Center of Richmond, 5224 Monument Avenue, Richmond, VA 23226; tel. 804/288–4137; FAX. 804/288–3529; Terry W. Coffey, Administrator

Urosurgical Center of Richmond–North, 8228 Meadowbridge Road, Mechanicsville, VA 23111; tel. 804/730–5023; FAX. 804/746–4015; Terry W. Coffey, Administrator

Urosurgical Center of Richmond–South, 7001 Jahnke Road, Richmond, VA 23225; tel. 804/560–4483; FAX. 804/272–1178; Terry W. Coffey, Administrator

Virginia Ambulatory Surgery Center, 337–15th Street, S.W., Charlottesville, VA 22903; tel. 804/295–4800; FAX. 804/977–0544; Gerry Dobrasz, Administrator

Virginia Beach Ambulatory Surgery Center, 1700 Will–o–Wisp Drive, Virginia Beach, VA 23454; tel. 804/496–6400; FAX. 804/496–3137; Brian Murray, M.D., Medical Director

Virginia Eye Institute/Eye Surgeons of Richmond, Inc., 400 Westhampton Station, Richmond, VA 23226; tel. 804/282–3931; FAX. 804/287–4256; Catherine L. Cawley, Administrator

Virginia Heart Institute, LTD., 205 North Hamilton Street, Richmond, VA 23221; tel. 804/359–9265; Charles L. Baird, Jr., M.D., Director

Woodburn Surgery Center, 3289 Woodburn Road, Suite 100, Annandale, VA 22003; tel. 703/207–7520; Jolene Tornabeni, Senior Vice President, Administrator

WASHINGTON

Aesthetic Eye Associates, P.S., 1810 116th Avenue, N.E., Suite B, Bellevue, WA 98004; tel. 206/462–0400; FAX. 206/454–1085; Janet Jordan, Business Manager

Bel–Red Ambulatory Surgical Facility, 1370 116th Avenue, N.E., Suite 209, Bellevue, WA 98004–3825; tel. 625/455–7225; FAX. 425/455–0045

Bellingham Surgery Center, 2980 Squalicum Parkway, Bellingham, WA 98225; tel. 206/671–6933; Richard Brumenschenkel, Managing Agent

Cascade Ambulatory Surgery Center, 407 Northeast 87th Street, Vancouver, WA 98664; tel. 360/253–9201; Joseph R. McFarland, M.D.

Central Washington Cataract Surgery, 1450 North 16th Avenue, Building J, Yakima, WA 98902; tel. 509/457–5000; FAX. 509/457–6498; Paul Almeida, CRNA

Central Washington Surgicare, 307 South 12th Avenue, Suite Nine, Yakima, WA 98902; tel. 509/248–4900; FAX. 509/248–0609

Covington Day Surgery Center, 17700 Southeast 272nd Street, Kent, WA 98042; tel. 206/639–8302; FAX. 206/639–8301; Victoria Fitzpatrick, B.S.N., Director

Ear, Nose, Throat and Plastic Surgery Center, 101 Second Street, N.E., Auburn, WA 98002; tel. 253–833–6241; FAX. 253–833–4113; William Portuese, M.D., Medical Director

Eastside Podiatry Ambulatory Surgery Center, 15617 Bel–Red Road, Bellevue, WA 98008; tel. 206/881–5592; G. Curda, D.P.M.

Edmonds Surgery Center, 21229 84th Avenue W., Edmonds, WA 98026; tel. 206/775–1505; FAX. 206/775–9078; Mark A. Kuzel, D.P.M., F.A.C.F.S

Esteem Outpatient Surgery Center, 1200 North Northgate Way, Seattle, WA 98133–8916; tel. 206/522–0200; FAX. 206/522–7019; Peter R. N. Chatard, Jr., M.D., Medical Director

Everett Surgical Center, Inc., 3025 Rucker Avenue, Everett, WA 98201; tel. 425–339–2464; FAX. 425–252–4700; Rita Sweeney, RNFA, CNOR, Administrator

Evergreen Endoscopy Center, 13030 121st Way, N.E., Suite 101, Kirkland, WA 98034; tel. 206/899–4500; Lynn Bookkeeper

Evergreen Eye Surgery Center, 34719 Sixth Avenue South, Federal Way, WA 98003; tel. 253/874–3969; FAX. 253/661–7383; Richard A. Boudreau, Administrator

Evergreen Surgical Center, 12034 Northeast 130th Lane, Kirkland, WA 98034; tel. 206/821–3131; Ronald E. Abrams, M.D.

Good Samaritan Surgery Center, 1322 Third Street S.E., Suite 100, Puyallup, WA 98372; tel. 206/840–2200; FAX. 206/840–2352; Roger D. Robinett, M.D., Medical Director

Health South, Green River Surgical Center, 126 Auburn Avenue, Suite 200, Auburn, WA 98002; tel. 206/735–0500; FAX. 206/939–8526; Gail A. Okon, Facility Manager

Hernia Treatment Center, NW, 205 Lilly Road, NE, Suite D, Olympia, WA 98506; tel. 360/491–8667; Robert Kugel, M.D., Director

Inland Empire Endoscopy Center, South 820 McClellan, Suite 314, Spokane, WA 99204; tel. 509/747–0143; J. D. Fitterer, M.D.

Inland Eye Center, South 842 Cowley, Spokane, WA 99202; tel. 509/624–5300; FAX. 509/747–1348; Michael H. Cunningham, M.D., President

Kruger Clinic Day Surgery, 21600 Highway 99, Suite 150, Edmonds, WA 98026; tel. 425/774–2636; FAX. 425/774–2688

Lomas Surgery Center, 17800 Talbot Road, S., Renton, WA 98055; tel. 425/255–0986; FAX. 425/271–5703; Inese A. Lomas, Administrator

Madrona Medical Group, ASC, 4370 Cordata Parkway, Bellingham, WA 98226; tel. 360/676–1712

McIntyre Eye Clinic & Surgical Center, 1920 116th Avenue, N.E., Bellevue, WA 98004; tel. 405/454–3937; FAX. 405/646–5914; David McIntyre, M.D., FACS

Mid–Columbia Surgical Suite, Inc., 471 Williams Boulevard, Suite Four, Richland, WA 99352; tel. 509/943–1134; Robert C. Luckey, M.D., Medical Director

Minor & James Medical, PLLC, 515 Minor Avenue, Suite 200, Seattle, WA 98104; tel. 206/386–9500; FAX. 206/386–9605; Sylvia Croy, RN, ASC Coordinator

Monroe Foot Care Associates Ambulatory Surgery Center, 14692 179th Avenue, S.E., Suite 300, Monroe, WA 98272; tel. 206/794–1266; Dr. Brunsman, Medical Director

Moses Lake Surgery Center, 840 East Hill Avenue, Moses Lake, WA 98837; tel. 509/765–0216; John Rodriguez, ASC Manager

North Cascade ENT and Facial Plastic Surgery, 111 South 13th Street, Mount Vernon, WA 98273; tel. 206/336–2178

North Cascade ENT Facial Plastic Surgery, 20302 77th Avenue, N.E., Arlington, WA 98223; tel. 360/435–6300; FAX. 360/435–8381; Alex O'Dell

North Kitsap Ambulatory Surgical Center, 20696 Bond Road, N.E., Poulsbo, WA 98370; tel. 360/779–6527; FAX. 360/697–2743; Susan Chu, RN

Northwest Center for Plastic and Reconstructive Surgery, 16259 Sylvester Road, S.W., Suite 302, Seattle, WA 98166; tel. 206/241–5400; FAX. 206/241–8591; Sindi Miller, Office Manager

Northwest Eye Surgery, P.C., 1120 N. Pines Road, Spokane, WA 99206; tel. 509/927–0700

Northwest Gastroenterology, d/b/a Northwest Endoscopy, 3149 Ellis, Suite 301, Bellingham, WA 98225; tel. 360/734–1420; FAX. 360/734–8748; Kathy Burns, Manager

Northwest Nasal Sinus Center, 10330 Meridan Avenue, N., Suite 240, Seattle, WA 98133; tel. 206/525–2525; FAX. 206/525–0346

Northwest Surgery Center, 1920 100th Street, S.E., Everett, WA 98208; tel. 425/316–3700; FAX. 425/316–6881; Chris Vance, President

Northwest Surgery Center, Inc., West 123 Francis, Spokane, WA 99205; tel. 509/483–9363; FAX. 509/483–0355; Douglas P. Romney

Northwest Surgical Center, 3120 Squalicum Parkway, Bellingham, WA 98225; tel. 360/647–0557; FAX. 360/733–2892; Marianne Karuza, A.R.T.

NW Aesthetic Surgery Center, 550 16th Avenue, Suite 404, Seattle, WA 98122; tel. 206/328–2250; Mary Ann Beberman, Administrator

NW Center for Corrective Jaw Surgery, 550 16th Avenue, Suite 303, Seattle, WA 98122; tel. 206/324–6570; FAX. 206/324–9936; Dohi Miller, Practice Manager

Olympic Ambulatory Surgery Center, Inc., 2601 Cherry Avenue, Suite 115, Bremerton, WA 98310; tel. 206/479–5990; FAX. 360/377–5731; Audrey E. Harris, RN

Olympic Plastic Surgery Suite, 2600 Cherry Avenue, Suite 201, Bremerton, WA 98310; tel. 360/415–0762; Suzanne Fletcher, Administrator

Pacific Cataract and Laser Institute, 2517 Northeast Kresky, Chehalis, WA 98532; tel. 206/748–8632; Debbie Eldredge, Vice President and COO

Pacific Cataract and Laser Institute, 10500 Northeast Eighth Street, Suite 1650, Bellevue, WA 98004–4332; tel. 206/462–7664; FAX. 206/462–6429; Maynard Pohl, O.D., Clinical Director

Pacific Cataract and Laser Institute, 8200 West Grandridge, Kennewick, WA 99336

Pacific Medical Center, 1200 12th Avenue, S., Seventh Floor, Seattle, WA 98144; tel. 206/326–4000; Carolyn Bodeen, RN, Clinic Director

Pacific NW Facial Plastic Ambulatory Surgery Center, 600 Broadway, Suite 280, Seattle, WA 98122; tel. 206/386–3550; FAX. 206/386–3553

Parkway Surgical Center, 2940 Squalicum Parkway, Suite 204, Bellingham, WA 98225; tel. 206/676–8350; FAX. 206/676–8351; Orville Vandergriend, M.D., Administrator

Physicians Eye Surgical Center, 3930 Hoyt Avenue, Everett, WA 98201; tel. 206/259–2020; Carol Schoenfelder, Administrator

Plastic and Reconstructive Surgeons, 17930 Talbot Road, S., Renton, WA 98055; tel. 206/228–3187; Mack D. Richey, M.D.

Plastic Surgery Center, 1017 South 40th Avenue, Yakima, WA 98904; tel. 509/966–6000; FAX. 509/966–6565; Julie Marquis, RN, Quality Assurance Manager

Plastic Surgicenter of Olympia, 400 Lilly Road, N.E., Building Four, Olympia, WA 98506; tel. 360/456–4400; FAX. 360/491–7619; Wayne L. Dickason, M.D.

Professional Surgical Specialists, 1609 Meridian South, Puyallup, WA 98371; tel. 253/841–1222; FAX. 253/770–0360; Doreen Healy, Office Manager

Redmond Foot Care Associates, ASC, 16146 Cleveland Street, Redmond, WA 98052; tel. 206/885–7004

Rockwood Clinic, d/b/a Gastrointestinal Endoscopy Unit, Sacred Heart Building, West 105 Eighth Avenue, Spokane, WA 99204; tel. 509/838–2531; FAX. 509/455–8828; Stephen Burgert, M.D., Administrator

Rockwood Clinic, PS, East 400 Fifth Avenue, Spokane, WA 99202; tel. 509/838–2531; FAX. 509/455–5315; William R. Poppy, Chief Executive Officer

Seattle Endoscopy Center, 11027 Meridian Avenue, N., Suite 100, Seattle, WA 98133; tel. 206/365–4492; FAX. 206/365–3456; Patty Carroll, CGRN, Manager

Seattle Eye Plastic Surgery Center, 1229 Madison Street, Suite 1190, Seattle, WA 98104; tel. 206/621–0800; FAX. 206/621–7023; R. Toby Sutcliffe, M.D.

Seattle Hand Surgery Group, P.C., 600 Broadway, Suite 440, Seattle, WA 98122; tel. 206/292–6252; FAX. 206/292–7893; Suzann H. Demianew, Administrator

Seattle Head and Neck Office Surgery, 515 Minor Avenue, Suite 130, Seattle, WA 98104; tel. 206/682–6103; FAX. 206/682–3012; Debbie Perdue, Director

Seattle Microsurgical Eyecare Center, 5300 17th Avenue, N.W., Seattle, WA 98107; tel. 206/783–3929; Jack C. Bunn, M.D., Medical Director

Seattle Plastic Surgery Center, 600 Broadway, Suite 320, Seattle, WA 98122; tel. 206/324–1120; FAX. 206/720–0800; Wendy Discher, Manager

Seattle Surgery Center, Columbus Pavilion, 900 Terry Avenue, Fourth Floor, Seattle, WA 98104–1240; tel. 206/382–1021; FAX. 206/382–1026; Naya Kehayes, M.P.H., Administrator

Sequim Same Day Surgery, 777 North Fifth Avenue, Sequim, WA 98382; tel. 360/681–0358; FAX. 360/683–0170; Tammy Paolini, Surgical Technician

South Hill Ambulatory Surgical Center, South 3028 Grand Boulevard, Spokane, WA 99203; tel. 509/747–0279; FAX. 509/747–3220

Southwest Washington Ambulatory Surgery Center, Inc., 416 Northeast 87th Avenue, Vancouver, WA 98664; tel. 206/696–4000; FAX. 206/696–4287

Southwest Washington Ambulatory Surgery Center, Inc., 102 West Fourth Plain Boulevard, Vancouver, WA 98666; tel. 206/696–4400; Kim Fehly

Spokane Digestive Disease Center, 105 West Eighth Avenue, Suite 6010, Spokane, WA 99204–2318; tel. 509/838–5950; FAX. 509/838–5961; Margie Troske–Johnson, RN, B.S.N., Director

Spokane Eye Surgery Center, West 208 Fifth Street, Spokane, WA 99204; tel. 509/456–8150; FAX. 509/455–9887; Donald Ellingsen, M.D.

Spokane Foot and Ankle Surgery Center, 9405 East Sprague Avenue, Spokane, WA 99206; tel. 509/922–3199; Rita Kinney, RN

Spokane Surgery Center, North 1120 Pines Road, Spokane, WA 99206; tel. 509/924–3235; FAX. 509/928–1990; Stewart P. Brim, D.P.M.

St. Mark's Micro Surgical Center, Inc., 502 South M Street, Tacoma, WA 98405; tel. 206/627–8266; Roy Baker, Chief Executive Officer

Stanley M. Jackson, M.D., Plastic and Reconstructive Surgery, 105 27th Avenue, S.E., Puyallup, WA 98374; tel. 206/848–8110; FAX. 206/845–3561; Karen Smith, RN

Tacoma Ambulatory Surgery Center, 1112 Sixth Avenue, Suite 100, Tacoma, WA 98405; tel. 206/272–3916; FAX. 206/627–1713; Joan Hoover, Administrator

Tacoma Endoscopy Center, 1112 Sixth Avenue, Suite 200, Tacoma, WA 98405; tel. 206/272–8664; FAX. 206/627–7880; Richard Baerg, M.D., Medical Director

Tacoma Speciality ASU, 209 Martin Luther King Jr. Way, Tacoma, WA 98405; tel. 206/596–3590; Linda Bradley, Manager

The Eastside Endoscopy Center, P.L.L.C., 1700 116th Avenue, N.E., Suite 100, Bellevue, WA 98004–3049; tel. 206/451–7335; FAX. 206/451–7335; Michelle Steele, CGRN, Clerical Manager

The Plastic SurgiCentre, Inc., 535 South Pine Street, Spokane, WA 99202; tel. 509/623–2160; FAX. 509/623–1135; Pamala Silvers, RN, Manager

The Polyclinic, Inc., 1145 Broadway, Seattle, WA 98122; tel. 206/329–1760; Lloyd David, Chief Executive Officer

TLC Northwest Eye, Inc., 10330 Meridian Avenue N., Suite 370, Seattle, WA 98133–9451; tel. 206/528–6000; FAX. 206/528–0014; Wendy R. Williams, Marketing Director

Trenton J. Spolar, 505 Northeast 87th Avenue, Suite 203, Vancouver, WA 98664; tel. 206/254–8596

Valley Outpatient Surgery Center, North 1414 Houk Road, Suite 204, Spokane, WA 99216; tel. 509/922–0362; FAX. 509/927–8316; Dr. Douglas Norquist, President

Valley Surgi Centre, Five South 14th Avenue, Yakima, WA 98902; tel. 509/248–6813; FAX. 509/457–9691

Virginia Mason Federal Way, 33501 First Way South, Federal Way, WA 98003; tel. 253/874–1635; FAX. 253/874–1732; Steven Alley

Virginia Mason–Issaquah, 100 Northeast Gilman Boulevard, Issaquah, WA 98027; tel. 206/557–8000; Bobbie Eatmon, Manager

Washington Centre for Reproductive Medicine, 1370 116th Avenue, N.E., Suite 100, Bellevue, WA 98004; tel. 206/462–6100

Washington Orthopaedic Center, Inc., PS, 1900 Cooks Hill Road, Centralia, WA 98531; tel. 360/736–2889; JoAnn Wilkey, Director

Wenatchee Surgical Center, 600 Orondo Avenue, Wenatchee, WA 98807; tel. 509/662–8956; Shirley DeWitz, RN, Manager

Wenatchee Valley Clinic/Cascade Surgery Center, 820 North Chelan, Wenatchee, WA 98801; tel. 509/663–8711; FAX. 509/665–2309; Dr. Don Paugh, Chief, Cascade Surgery Center

Westlake Surgical Center, 509 Olive Way, Third Floor, Seattle, WA 98101; tel. 206/623–4755; Maria T. Burrows, Administrative Assistant

Whidbey SurgiCare, 31775–SR 20, Suite A Two, Oak Harbor, WA 98277–2334; tel. 360/679–3117; FAX. 360/679–3118; Stephen T. Miller, DPM, Medical Director

Whitehorse Surgical Center, 875 Wesley Street, Suite 160, Arlington, WA 98223; tel. 360/435–6969; FAX. 360/435–1068

WEST VIRGINIA

Anwar Eye Center, 1500 Lafayette Avenue, Moundsville, WV 26041; tel. 304/845–0908; M. F. Anwar, M.D.

Cabell Huntington Surgery Center, 1201 Hal Greer Boulevard, Huntington, WV 25701; tel. 304/523–1885; FAX. 304/523–8942; John Stone, Facility Administrator

Cook Eye Surgery Center, 1300 Third Avenue, Huntington, WV 25701; tel. 304/522–1802; FAX. 304/529–6752; David W. Cook, M.D., President

Jerry N. Black, M.D., Surgical Suite, 10 Amalia Drive, Buckhannon, WV 26201; tel. 304/472–2100; Jerry N. Black, M.D., Medical Director

Kanawha Valley Surgi–Center, 4803 MacCorkle Avenue, S.E., Charleston, WV 25304; tel. 304/925–6390; Gorli Harish, M.D., Medical Director

Lee's Surgi–Center, 415 Morris Street, Suite 200, Charleston, WV 25301; tel. 304/342–1113; FAX. 304/346–2271; Hans Lee, M.D., President

SurgiCare, 3200 MacCorkle Avenue, S.E., Charleston, WV 25304; tel. 304/348–9556; Robert L. Savage, President

West Virginia Surgery Center, Inc., 425 Greenway Avenue, South Charles, WV 25309; tel. 304/768–7310; FAX. 304/768–8211; Nancy Jo Vinson, Administrator

WISCONSIN

Aurora Health Center, 10400 75th Street, Kenosha, WI 53142; tel. 414–697–6907; FAX. 414/697–3022; Thomas M. Warsocki, Administrator

Section C

Bay Lake Surgery Outpatient Surgery Center, Inc., 1843 Michigan Street, P.O. Box 678, Sturgeon Bay, WI 54235; tel. 414/746–1070; FAX. 414/746–1072; Michael Herlache, Administrator

Baycare Surgery Center, 2253 West Mason, P.O. Box 33227, Green Bay, WI 54303–0102; tel. 414/592–9100; FAX. 414/497–6830; Jeff Mason, Administrator

Center for Digestive Health, 2801 West Kinnickinnic River Parkway, Suite 560, Milwaukee, WI 53215; tel. 414/649–3522; FAX. 414/649–5454; Robert Chang, Administrator

Davis Duehr Day Surgery, 1025 Regent Street, Madison, WI 53715; tel. 608/282–2050; Rodney Sturm, M.D., President

Dean St. Mary's Surgery Center, 800 South Brooks Street, Madison, WI 53715; tel. 608/259–3510; FAX. 608/255–1272; Patricia Klitzman, Director

Eau Claire Surgery Center, 950 West Clairemont Avenue, Eau Claire, WI 54701; tel. 715/839–9339; FAX. 715/839–9033; Kathryn Hentz, RN, Facility Manager

Green Bay Surgical Center, Ltd., 704 South Webster Avenue, Green Bay, WI 54301; tel. 920–432–7433; FAX. 920–432–6003; Herbert F. Sandmire, M.D., Medical Director, Administrator

HealthSouth Surgery Center of Wausau, 2809 Westhill Drive, Wausau, WI 54401; tel. 715/842–4490; FAX. 715/842–4645; Kathy Eisenschink, RN, Facility Administrator

Kenosha Surgical Center, Inc., 3505 30th Avenue, Kenosha, WI 53142; tel. 414/656–8638; FAX. 414/656–8631; David Bittner, Business Manager

LaSalle Surgery Center, 1550 Midway Place, Menasha, WI 54952; tel. 414/727–8200; FAX. 414/727–8203; Laura Ruys, Manager

Marshfield Clinic Ambulatory Surgery Center, 1000 North Oak Avenue, Marshfield, WI 54449; tel. 715/387–5315; FAX. 715/387–5240; Robert J. DeVita, Executive Director

Menomonee Falls Ambulatory Surgery Center, W180 N8045 Town Hall Road, Menomonee Falls, WI 53051; tel. 414/250–0950; FAX. 414/250–0955; Robert W. Scheller Jr., CPA, Business Director

Mercy Walworth, ASC, N2950 State Road 67, Lake Geneva, WI 53147; tel. 414/245–0535; Deb Saylor, RN, Team Leader

North Shore Surgical Center, 7007 North Range Line Road, Milwaukee, WI 53209; tel. 414/352–3341; FAX. 414/352–3218; Robert Lonergan, Executive Director

Northlake Surgery Center, 2110 Medical Drive, Box 636, Menomonee, WI 54751; tel. 715/235–8884; Douglas Carson

Northwest Surgery Center, 2300 North Mayfair Road, Wauwatosa, WI 53226; tel. 414/257–3322; Nancy Jones, Administrator

Oshkosh Surgery Center, 1925 Surgery Center Drive, Oshkosh, WI 54901; tel. 920/233–1233; FAX. 920/233–2101; Jean Cox, Administrator

Riverview Surgery Center, 616 North Washington Street, Janesville, WI 53545; tel. 608/758–7300; FAX. 608/758–1050; Cheryl A. Wilson, Director

Surgery Center of Wisconsin, 10401 West Lincoln Avenue, Suite 201, West Allis, WI 53227; tel. 414/321–7850; FAX. 414–328–5899; Daniel R. Hellman, M.D., Facility Administrator

Surgicenter of Greater Milwaukee, 3223 South 103rd Street, Milwaukee, WI 53227; tel. 414/328–5800; Raymond E. Grundman, General Manager

Surgicenter of Racine, Ltd., 5802 Washington Avenue, Racine, WI 53406; tel. 414/886–9100; FAX. 414/886–9130; Dennis J. Kontra, Administrator

Wauwatosa Surgery Center, d/b/a HealthSouth Surgery Center of Wauwatosa, 10900 West Potter Road, Wauwatosa, WI 53226–3424; tel. 414/774–9227; FAX. 414/774–0957; Carol Leitinger, RN, B.S.N., CNOR, Administrator

WYOMING

Casper Endoscopy Center, 167 South Conwell, Suite Seven, Casper, WY 82601; tel. 307/262–3896; Robert A. Schlidt, M.D., Administrator

Gem City Bone and Joint Surgery Center, 1909 Vista Drive, Laramie, WY 82070; tel. 307/745–8851; FAX. 307/742–8851; Trent Kaufman, Admin. Director

Wyoming Endoscopy Center, 1200 East 20th Street, Cheyenne, WY 82001; tel. 307/635–5439; Tracie Brandt, MBA, Administrator

Wyoming Outpatient Services, 5050 Powderhouse Road, Cheyenne, WY 82009; tel. 307/634–1311; FAX. 307/638–6820; Robin Brown, Director

Yellowstone Surgery Center, Ltd., 5201 Yellowstone Road, Cheyenne, WY 82009; tel. 307/635–7070; FAX. 307/632–9920; Linnea McNair, RN, B.S.N., Director

U.S. Associated Areas

PUERTO RICO

Arecibo Medical Center, Carr. 2 Km 80.1, Call Box AMC, Arecibo, PR 00613; tel. 809/878–3185

ASC Espanola Clinic, Box 490, La Quinta, Mayaguez, PR 00681; tel. 787/832–2094

ASC Hato Rey Comm., 435 Ponce de Leon Avenue, Hato Rey, PR 00919; tel. 787/754–0909; FAX. 787/753–1625

ASC Mimiya, P.O. Box 41245, 303 De Diego Avenue, Santurce, PR 00940; tel. 809/721–2590

Cirugia Ambulatoria y Centro de Diagnostico y Tratamiento de S, Box 486, San Sebastian, PR 00755; tel. 809/896–1850

Clinica de Cirugia Ambulatoria de Puerto Rico, Box 3748, Marina Station, Mayaguez, PR 00681; tel. 787/833–4400; Roberto Ruiz, Asencio, Administrator

Clinica del Turabo, P.O. Box 1900, Caguas, PR 00726; tel. 787/746–8899; FAX. 787/258–1776; Jamie L. Olivera, BSIE, MBA, MHSA

Instituto Cirugia, Plastica Del Oeste, 165 Este Mendez Virgo Street, Mayaguez, PR 00680; tel. 787/833–3248; FAX. 787/831–4400; Oscar Vargas, M.D., Medical Director

Instituto de Ojos y Piel, Carr Three, KM 12.3, Carolina, PR 00985; tel. 809/769–2477

Instituto Quirurgico De Un Dia – Dr. Pila, P.O. Box 1910, Ponce, PR 00733; tel. 809/844–5600

OJOS, Inc., Calle Hipodromo, Esquina Las Palmas, Santurce, PR 00908; tel. 787/721–8330; FAX. 787/722–3222; Maria Delos A. Tirado, Administrator

Southern SurgiCenter, Edificio Parra Office 201, Ponce, PR 00731; tel. 787/841–0303; FAX. 787/841–0387; Mr. Roberto Rentas, MHSA

The New San Juan Health Centre, 150 De Diego Avenue, Esquina Baldorioty, San Juan, PR 00911; tel. 809/725–0202; FAX. 809/725–3060

Section C

State Government Agencies for FASC's

United States

ALABAMA
Alabama Department of Public Health, Division of Licensure and Certification, 434 Monroe Street, Montgomery, AL 36130–1701; tel. 334/240–3503; FAX. 334/240–3147; L. O'Neal Green, Director

ARIZONA
Arizona Department of Health Services, Health and Child Care Review Services, 1647 East Morten, Suite 220, Phoenix, AZ 85020; tel. 602/255–1221; FAX. 602/861–0645; Mary Wiley, Assistant Director

ARKANSAS
Department of Health, Division of Health Facility Services, 5800 West 10th Street, Suite 400, Little Rock, AR 72204–9916; tel. 501/661–2201; FAX. 501/661–2165; Valetta Buck, Director

CALIFORNIA
Department of Health Services, Licensing and Certification Program, 1800 Third Street, Suite 210, P.O. Box 942732, Sacramento, CA 94234–7320; tel. 916/445–2070; FAX. 916/327–4355; Diane L. Ford, Branch Chief

COLORADO
Department of Health, Division of Health Facilities, 4300 Cherry Creek Drive South, Denver, CO 80220; tel. 303/692–2800; FAX. 303/782–4883; Diane Carter, Deputy, Director

CONNECTICUT
Public Health Division of Health Systems Regulation, 410 Capital Avenue, Hartford, CT 06134–0308; tel. 860/509–7400; FAX. 860/509–7543; Cynthia Denne, RN, MPA., Director

DELAWARE
Department of Health and Social Services, Licensing and Certification, Office of Health Facilities, 2055 Limestone Road, Suite 200, Wilmington, DE 19808; tel. 302/995–8521; FAX. 302/995–8332; Ellen T. Reap, Director

DISTRICT OF COLUMBIA
Department of Health, Licensing Regulation Administration, 614 H Street, N.W., Suite 1003, Washington, DC 20001; tel. 202/727–7190; FAX. 202/727–7780; Geraldine K. Sykes

FLORIDA
Division of Health Quality Assurance, Agency for Health Care Administration, Fort Knox Executive Office Center, 2727 Mahan Drive, Suite 214, Tallahassee, FL 32308–5407; tel. 850/487–2527; Peter J. Buigas, Director

GEORGIA
Health Care Section – Georgia Dept. of Human Resources, Office of Regulatory Services, Two Peachtree Street, N.W., Room 33–250, Atlanta, GA 30303–3142; tel. 404/657–5550; FAX. 404/657–8934; Susie M. Woods, Director

HAWAII
Hawaii Department of Health, Hospital and Medical Facilities Branch, P.O. Box 3378, Honolulu, HI 96801; tel. 808/586–4080; FAX. 808/586–4747; Helen K. Yoshimi, B.S.N., M.P.H., Chief, HMFB

IDAHO
Bureau of Facility Standards, Department of Health and Welfare, P.O. Box 83720, Boise, ID 83720–0036; tel. 208/334–6626; FAX. 208/364–1888; Sylvia Creswell, Supervisor–Non Long Term Care

ILLINOIS
Department of Public Health, Division of Health Care Facilities and Programs, 525 West Jefferson Street, Springfield, IL 62761; tel. 217/782–7412; FAX. 217/782–0382; Michelle Gentry–Wiseman, Chief

INDIANA
Indiana State Department of Health, Division of Acute Care, Two North Meridian Street, 4/A, Indianapolis, IN 46204; tel. 317/233–7474; FAX. 317/233–7157; Mary Azbill, MT (ASCP)

IOWA
Department of Inspection and Appeals, Division of Health Facilities, Lucas State Office Building, Des Moines, IA 50319; tel. 515/281–4115; FAX. 515/242–5022; Nancy M. Ruzicka, Administrator

KANSAS
Kansas Department of Health and Environment, Bureau of Adult and Child Care, 900 Southwest Jackson, Suite 1001, Topeka, KS 66612–1290; tel. 785/296–1280; FAX. 785/296–1266; George A. Dugger, Medical Facilities Certification Administrator

KENTUCKY
Cabinet for Health Services, Division of Licensing and Regulation, Frankfort, KY 40621; tel. 502/564–2800; FAX. 502/564–6546; Rebecca J. Cecil, R.Ph., Director

LOUISIANA
Department of Health and Hospitals, Bureau of Health Services Financing–Health Standards Section, P.O. Box 3767, Baton Rouge, LA 70821; tel. 504/342–0415; FAX. 504/342–5292; Lisa Deaton, RN, Manager

MAINE
Division of Licensing and Certification, Department of Human Services, 35 Anthony Avenue, Station 11, Augusta, ME 04333; tel. 207/624–5443; FAX. 207/624–5378; Louis Dorogi, Director

MARYLAND
Department of Health and Mental Hygiene, Licensing and Certification, 4201 Patterson Avenue, Baltimore, MD 21215; tel. 410/764–4980; FAX. 410/358–0750; James Ralls, Assistant Director

MASSACHUSETTS
Department of Public Health, Division of Health Care Quality, 80 Boylston Street, Suite 1100, Boston, MA 02116; tel. 617/727–5860; Irene McManus, Director

MICHIGAN
Department of Consumer and Industry Services, Division of Licensing and Certification, P.O. Box 30664, Lansing, MI 48909; tel. 517/241–2626; FAX. 517/241–2635; Pauline DeRose

MINNESOTA
Department of Health, Facility and Provider Compliance Division, Licensing and Certification Program, 85 East Seventh Place, Suite 300, St. Paul, MN 55164–0900; tel. 651/215–8719; FAX. 651/215–8709; Carol Hirschfeld, Supervisor, Records and Information

MISSISSIPPI
Department of Health, Division of Health Facilities Licensure and Certification, P.O. Box 1700, Jackson, MS 39215; tel. 601/354–7300; FAX. 601/354–7230; Vanessa Phipps, Director

MISSOURI
Missouri Department of Health, Bureau of Hospital Licensing and Certification, 920 Wildwood Drive, P.O. Box 570, Jefferson City, MO 65102; tel. 573/751–6302; FAX. 573/526–3621; Michele Reznicek, Administrator

MONTANA
Quality Assurance Division, Department of Public health and Human Services, Steamboat Building, 616 Helena Avenue, Helena, MT 59620; tel. 406/444–2099; FAX. 406/444–3456; Laura Sandman, Division Administrator

NEBRASKA
Credentialing Division, Nebraska Department of Health and Human Services Regulation & Licensure, 301 Centennial Mall, S., P.O. Box 94986, Lincoln, NE 68509–4986; tel. 402/471–2116; FAX. 402/471–3577; Helen L. Meeks, Director

NEVADA
Bureau of Licensure & Certification, Nevada Health Division, 1550 E. College Parkway, Suite 158, Carson City, NV 89706–7921; tel. 775/687–4475; FAX. 775/687–6588; Richard J. Panelli, Chief

NEW HAMPSHIRE
Office of Program Support, Licensing and Regulation – Health Facilities, 129 Pleasant Street, Concord, NH 03301; tel. 603/271–4592; FAX. 603/271–4968; Raymond Rusin, Chief

NEW JERSEY
Division of Health Systems Analysis, Certificate of Need and Acute Care Licensing, P.O. Box 360, Trenton, NJ 08625–0360; tel. 609/292–5960; FAX. 609/292–3780; John A. Calabria., Director

NEW MEXICO
Department of Health and Environment, Health Facility Licensing and Certification Bureau, 525 Camino de los Marquez, Suite Two, Santa Fe, NM 87501; tel. 505/827–4200; FAX. 505/827–4203; Matthew M. Gervase, Chief, Licensing and Certification

NEW YORK
Health Education Services, P.O. Box 7126, Albany, NY 12224; tel. 518/439–7286; FAX. 518/439–7286

NORTH CAROLINA
Department of Human Resources, Division of Facility Services, 701 Barbour Drive, P.O. Box 29530, Raleigh, NC 27626–0530; tel. 919/733–7461; FAX. 919/733–8274; Steve White, Chief, Licensure and Certification

NORTH DAKOTA
North Dakota Department of Health, Health Resources Section, 600 East Boulevard Avenue, Bismarck, ND 58505–0200; tel. 701/328–2352; FAX. 701/328–1890; Darleen Bartz, Director

OHIO
Division of Quality Assurance, Ohio Department of Health, 246 North High Street, Columbus, OH 43266–0588; tel. 614/466–7857; FAX. 614/644–0208; Rebecca Maust, Chief

OKLAHOMA
Department of Health, Special Health Services, 1000 Northeast 10th Street, P.O. Box 53551, Oklahoma City, OK 73152; tel. 405/271–6576; FAX. 405/271–3442; Gary Glover, Chief, Medical Facilities

OREGON
Health Care Licensure and Certification, Oregon Health Division, 800 Northeast Oregon Street, Suite 640, # 21, Portland, OR 97232; tel. 503/731–4013; FAX. 503/731–4080; Kathleen Smail, Manager

PENNSYLVANIA
Bureau of Quality Assurance, Division of Acute and Ambulatory Care Facilities, Health and Welfare Building, Room 532, Harrisburg, PA 17120; tel. 717/783–8980; FAX. 717/772–2163; Jack W. Means, Jr., Director

RHODE ISLAND
Rhode Island Department of Health, Division of Facilities Regulation, Three Capitol Hill, Providence, RI 02908–5097; tel. 401/222–2566; FAX. 401/222–3999; Wayne I. Farrington, Chief

SOUTH CAROLINA
Department of Health and Environmental Control, Division of Health Licensing, 2600 Bull Street, Columbia, SC 29201; tel. 803/737–7202; FAX. 803/737–7212; Alan Samuels, Director

SOUTH DAKOTA
Department of Health, Office of Health Care Facilities Licensure and Certification, 615 East 4th Street, Pierre, SD 57501; tel. 605/773–3356; FAX. 605/773–6667; Joan Bachman, Administrator

TENNESSEE
Department of Health, Division of Health Care Facilities, Cordell Hull Building, First Floor, 425 Fifth Avenue, N., Nashville, TN 37247–0508; tel. 615/741–7221; FAX. 615/741–7051; Marie Fitzgerald, Director

TEXAS
Texas Department of Health, Health Facility Compliance Division, 1100 West 49th Street, Austin, TX 78756; tel. 512/834–6650; FAX. 512/834–6653; Nance Stearman, RN, M.S.N., Director

UTAH
Utah Department of Health, Bureau of Licensing, P.O. Box 142003, Salt Lake City, UT 84114–2003; tel. 801/538–6152; FAX. 801/538–6325; Debra Wynkoop–Green, Director

VERMONT
Department of Aging and Disabilities, 103 South Main Street, Waterbury, VT 05671; tel. 802/241–2400; FAX. 802/241–2325; Dave Yacovone, Commissioner

VIRGINIA
Virginia Department of Health, Center for Quality Health Care Services and Consumer Protection, 3600 Centre, Suite 216, 3600 West Broad Street, Richmond, VA 23230; tel. 804/367–2102; FAX. 804/367–2149; Nancy R. Hofheimer, Director

WASHINGTON
Washington Department of Health, Facilities and Services Licensing, Target Plaza, Suite 500, 2725 Harrison Avenue N.W., Olympia, WA 98504–7852; tel. 360/705–6652; FAX. 360/705–6654; Byron R. Plan, Manager

WEST VIRGINIA
Office of Health Facility Licensure and Certification, West Virginia Division of Health, 1900 Kanawha Boulevard, E., Charleston, WV 25305; tel. 304/558–0050; FAX. 304/588–2515; Bonnie Brauner, Program Manager

WISCONSIN
Bureau of Quality Assurance, Division of Supportive Living, Department of Health and Family Services, P.O. Box 309, Madison, WI 53701–0309; tel. 608/267–7185; FAX. 608/267–0352; Judy Fryback, Director, Bureau of Quality Assurance

WYOMING
Wyoming Department of Health, Health Facilities Licensing, U.S. Bank Building, Eighth Floor, Cheyenne, WY 82001; tel. 307/777–7123; FAX. 307/777–5970; Jane Taylor, Program Manager

U.S. Associated Areas

PUERTO RICO
Department of Health, P. O. Box 70184, San Juan, PR 00936; tel. 809/766–1616; FAX. 809/766–2240; Carmen Feliciano de Melecio, M.D., Secretary of Health

Freestanding Hospices

The following list of freestanding hospices was developed with the assistance of state government agencies and the individual facilities listed. For a complete list of hospital based hospice programs please refer to Section A. In Section A, hospice programs are identified by Facility Code F33.

We present this list simply as a convenient directory. Inclusion or omission of any organization's name indicates neither approval nor disapproval by Health Forum LLC.

United States

ALABAMA

Baptist Hospice Walker County, 302 Blackwall Diary Road, Jasper, AL 35504; tel. 205/387-9339; FAX. 205/387-8226; Roy Whittaker, RN, LBSW, Patient Care Coordinator

Birmingham Area Hospice, 1400 Sixth Avenue, S., P.O. Box 2648, Birmingham, AL 35233; tel. 205/930-1330; FAX. 205/930-1390; Flora Y. Blackledge, Director

Brookwood Hospice, 2010 Brookwood Medical Center Drive, Birmingham, AL 35209; tel. 205/877-2140; FAX. 205/823-0364; Barbara Ballard, Administrator

Caring Hands Hospice, Inc., 225 University Blvd., E., Suite 203, Tuscaloosa, AL 35401; tel. 205/349-3065; FAX. 205/349-3295; Toni D. Welbourne, Administrator

Chattahoochee Hospice, Inc., #6 Medical Park, North, Valley, AL 36854; tel. 334/756-8043; FAX. 334/756-8059; Judy Guin, RN, Administrator

Columbia Community Hospice, 209 Dunson Street, Andalusia, AL 36420; tel. 334/222-7048; Charlotte Parker

Community Hospice of Baldwin County, 1113B North McKenzie Street, Foley, AL 36535; tel. 334/943-5015; FAX. 334/943-3986; Diana L. Cline, RN, Administrator

Community Hospice of Escambia County, 1023 Douglas Avenue, Suite 106, Brewton, AL 36426; tel. 334/867-6993; FAX. 334/867-7271; Daniel M. Scarbrough, M.D., Administrator

Health Services East, Inc., Hospice Care, 7916 Second Avenue, S., Birmingham, AL 35206; tel. 205/838-5745; FAX. 205/838-5778; Elizabeth B. Harvey, RNC, Administrator

Hospice Family Care, 2225 Drake Avenue, S.W., Suite 8, Huntsville, AL 35805; tel. 256/650-1212; FAX. 256/880-2929; Sue Morgan, Executive Director

Hospice of Blount County, Inc., 204 Washington Avenue, E., Oneonta, AL 35121; tel. 205/274-0549; FAX. 205/274-0550; Debbie Hyde

Hospice of Cullman County, Inc., 402 Fourth Avenue, N.E., P.O. Box 1227, Cullman, AL 35055; tel. 205/739-5185; Roger Hood, Administrator

Hospice of EAMC, 665 Opelika Road, Auburn, AL 36830; tel. 334/826-1899; FAX. 334-826-1899; Nancy A. Penaskovic

Hospice of Limestone County, 405 South Marion Street, P.O. Box 626, Athens, AL 35612; tel. 205/232-5017; FAX. 205/230-0085; Patricia P. Jackson, Administrator

Hospice of Marshall County, 8787 U.S. Highway 431, Albertville, AL 35950; tel. 205/891-7724; FAX. 205/891-7754; Rhonda Osborne, RN, B.S.N., CRNH, Executive Director

Hospice of Montgomery, 1111 Holloway Park, Montgomery, AL 36117; tel. 334/279-6677; FAX. 334/277-2223; Clare W. Lacey, Executive Director

Hospice of Northeast Alabama, a Member of the Baptist Health System, 112 College Street, P.O. Box 981, Scottsboro, AL 35768; tel. 205/574-4622; FAX. 205/259-3772; Virginia Stone, Director

Hospice of Northwest Alabama, 170 Bankhead Highway, Suite A, P.O. Box 1216, Winfield, AL 35594; tel. 205/487-8140; FAX. 205/487-8740; Linda Martin Sewell, Executive Director

Hospice of the Shoals, Inc., 1108 Bradshaw Drive, P.O. Box 307, Florence, AL 35630-0000; tel. 256/767-6699; FAX. 256/767-3116; Blake Edwards, Executive Director

Hospice of the Valley, Inc., 216 Johnston Street, S.E., P.O. Box 2745, Decatur, AL 35602; tel. 256/350-5585; FAX. 256/350-5567; Carolyn Dobson, Executive Director

Hospice of West Alabama, 1800 McFarland Boulevard, N., Suite 310, Tuscaloosa, AL 35406; tel. 205/345-0067; FAX. 205/345-9806; Julie Sittason, Executive Director

Hospice South, Inc., 1448 22nd Avenue, Tuscaloosa, AL 35401; tel. 205/366-9681; Dr. Bobby T. Williams, Chief Executive Officer

Hospice South, Inc., Of Livingston, 112 Lafayette Street, Livingston, AL 35470; tel. 205/652-2451; David Looney, Administrator

Infirmary Hospice Care, Inc., 28260 Highway 98, Suite 2, Daphne, AL 36526; tel. 334/625-3333; Andrew McDonald, Administrator

Lakeside Hospice, Inc., 17 Lake Plaza, P.O. Box 544, Pell City, AL 35125; tel. 205/884-1111; FAX. 205/884-1114; Nancy Odom, Director

Lakeview Hospice, 820 West Washington Street, Eufaula, AL 36027; tel. 334/687-1073; Rhonda Cotton, RN, Assistant Administrator

Mercy Medical, 101 Villa Drive, P.O. Box 1090, Daphne, AL 36526; tel. 334/626-2694; FAX. 334/626-0315; Sister Mary Eileen Wilhelm

Providence Hospice, 1141 Montlimar Drive, Mobile, AL 36609; tel. 334/344-2234; FAX. 334/344-4642; Frances Glenn, Administrator

Saad's Hospice Services, Inc., 3725 Airport Boulevard, Suite 180, Mobile, AL 36608; tel. 334/343-9600; FAX. 334/380-3328; Barbara S. Fulgham

Unity Hospice Biham Montclair, Princeton & St. Vincent's Hospice, 2145 Highland Ave., Suite 110, Birmingham, AL 35205; tel. 205/939-8797; FAX. 205/939-1682; Debbie Cox, CRNH, Patient Care Manager

Wiregrass Hospice, Inc., 1211 West Main Street, Dothan, AL 36301; tel. 334/792-1101; FAX. 334/792-0009; Ray L. Shrout, Administrator

Wiregrass Hospice, Inc., 557 Colony Square, Suite Seven and Eight, Glover Avenue, Enterprise, AL 36330; tel. 205/347-3353; Ray Shrout, Administrator

Wiregrass Hospice, Inc., 1211 W. Main Street, Dothan, AL 36301; tel. 334/792-1101; FAX. 334/794-0009; Ray L. Shrout, Administrator

ALASKA

Alaska Home Health Care Agency, Inc., 1200 Airport Heights, Suite 170, Anchorage, AK 99508; tel. 907/272-0018; FAX. 907/272-0014; Lawrence Smith, Title Company President

Hospice of Anchorage, 3305 Arctic Road, Suite 105, Anchorage, AK 99503; tel. 907/561-5322; FAX. 907/561-0334; Paula McCarron

Hospice of Mat-Su, 3051 E. Palmer Wasilla Hwy, Wasilla, AK 99654; tel. 907/352-4800; FAX. 907/352-4801; Kimm Gibson, RN, Director

ARIZONA

Community Hospice, 4330 North Campbell Avenue, Suite 256, Tucson, AZ 85718; tel. 520/544-2273; FAX. 520/577-8862; Bonnie Lindstrom

Dignita Hospice Care, 202 East Earl Drive, Suite 320, Phoenix, AZ 85012; tel. 602/279-0677; FAX. 602/279-1085; Gary Polsky

Hospice Family Care, 3443 East Fort Lowell Road, Tucson, AZ 85716; tel. 520/323-3288; FAX. 520/323-6557; Dan Johnson

Hospice Family Care Inpatient Unit, 5037 East Broadway Road, Mesa, AZ 85206; tel. 602/807-2655; FAX. 602/807-2660; Donna Jazz

Hospice Family Care Inpatient Unit-Santa Rita, 150 North La Canada Drive, Green Valley, AZ 85614; tel. 520/648-3099; Nancy Smith

Hospice Family Care, Inc., 1125 East Southern Avenue, Suite 202, Mesa, AZ 85204; tel. 602/926-6089; Don Johnson

Hospice Family Care, Inc. Green Valley Program, 210 West Continental Road, Suite 134, Green Valley, AZ 85614; tel. 520/648-6166; FAX. 520/648-6165; Karen Hoefle

Hospice of Arizona, 7600 North 15th Street, Suite 165, Phoenix, AZ 85020; tel. 602/678-1313; FAX. 602/678-5220; Jerene Maierle, Administrator

Hospice of Havasu, Inc., 2277 Swanson Ave, Suite A, Lake Havasu C, AZ 86403; tel. 520/453-2111; FAX. 520/453-3003; Nancy Iannone, Administrator

Hospice of the Valley, 1510 East Flower Street, Phoenix, AZ 85014; tel. 602/530-6900; FAX. 602/530-6901; Susan Goldwater, Executive Director

Hospice of the Valley, 2222 South Dobson Road, Suite 401, Mesa, AZ 85202; tel. 602/835-0711; FAX. 602/730-6078; Donna O'Brien

Hospice of the Valley Gardiner Hospice Home, 1522 West Myrtle Avenue, Phoenix, AZ 85021; tel. 602/995-9323; Susan Goldwater, Executive Director

Hospice of Yuma, 1824 South Eighth Avenue, Yuma, AZ 85364; tel. 602/343-2222; FAX. 602/343-0688; Phyllis K. Swanson, Executive Director

Jacob C. Fruchthendler Jewish Community Hospice, 5100 East Grant Road, P.O. Box 13090, Tucson, AZ 85732-3090; tel. 520/881-5300; FAX. 520/322-3620; Jo Turnbull, RN, B.S.

Mt. Graham Community Hospital–Hospice Services, 1600 20th Avenue, Building E, Safford, AZ 85546; tel. 520/348-4045; FAX. 520/428-3868; Lana Sanderson, Clinical Coordinator

Northland Hospice, 1609 S. Plaza Way, P.O. Box 997, Flagstaff, AZ 86002; tel. 520/779-1227; FAX. 520/779-5884; Marilyn J. Pate, Executive Director

RTA Hospice, 107 East Frontier, Payson, AZ 85541; tel. 602/472-6340; FAX. 602/472-6464; Vicki Dietz, RN, B.S.N., Executive Director

RTA Hospice, Inc., 177 West Cottonwood Lane, Suite 10, Casa Grande, AZ 85222; tel. 520/421-7143; FAX. 520/421-7315; Cindy McCarville, Patient Care Administrator

Special Care Hospice, 1514 C Gold Rush Road, Suite 236, Bullhead City, AZ 86442; tel. 602/758-3800; FAX. 602/758-4403; Jayne Knox, Director

Special Care Hospice, 1514 C Gold Rush Road, Suite 236, Bullhead City, AZ 86442; tel. 520/758-3800; Dianne H. Butler, B.S.N., RNC, Administrator

Sun Health Hospice Care Services & Residence, 12740 N. Plaza del rio blvd, Peoria, AZ 85381; tel. 800/858-9428; FAX. 602/974-7894; Marlene Stolz, Acting Director

Vista Hospice Care, Inc., 6991 East Camelback Road, Suite C-250, Scottsdale, AZ 85251; tel. 602/945-2200; Roseanne Berry

ARKANSAS

Area Agency on Aging Hospice of Western Arkansas, 524 Garrison Avenue, P.O. Box 1724, Fort Smith, AR 72902; tel. 501/783-4500; FAX. 501/783-0029; Jim Medley, Executive Director, CEO

Area Agency on Aging of Southeast Arkansas Hospice Two, 529 West Trotter, P.O. Box 722, Monticello, AR 71655; tel. 501/367-9873; Betty Bradshaw, Administrator

Area Agency on Aging of Southeast Arkansas, Inc. Hospice, 709 East Eighth Avenue, P.O. Box 8569, Pine Bluff, AR 71611; tel. 501/534-3268; Betty Bradshaw, President and CEO

Area Agency on Aging of Western Arkansas, Inc., d/b/a Visiting Nurses Agency of Western Arkansas, Inc., 398 School Street, Winslow, AR 72959; tel. 501/634-3812; FAX. 501/634-3912; Jim Medley, Executive Director

Area Agency on Aging of Western Arkansas, Inc., Mena Hospice, 600 Seventh Street, Mena, AR 71953; tel. 501/394-5458; FAX. 501/394-7675; Mary Keith, RNC, Vice President

Area Agency or Aging Hospice of West Central Arkansas, 103 West Parkway Drive, Suite Two A, Russellville, AR 72801; tel. 501/967-9300; Oren Yates, Program Administrator

Area Three Hospice, Faulkner County Health Unit, 811 North Creek Drive, Conway, AR 72033; tel. 501/450-4941; FAX. 501/450-4946; Elese Brown, Administrator

Ark La Tex Visiting Nurses, Inc., d/b/a Ark La Tex Home Health and Hospice Care, 421 Hickory Street, Texarkana, AR 71854; tel. 501/772–0958; Debbie Turner, Director of Nursing

Arkansas Department of Health Hospice 10, 40 Allen Chapel Road, P.O. Box 4267, Batesville, AR 72503; tel. 870/251–2848; FAX. 870/251–3449; Susan Coleman, Hospice Specialist

Arkansas Department of Health Hospice Five, Miller County Health Unit, 503 Walnut, Texarkana, AR 71852; tel. 870/773–2108; Mary Johnson, Administrator

Arkansas Department of Health Hospice Nine West, Monroe County Health Unit, 306 West King Drive, Brinkley, AR 72021; tel. 501/734–1461; FAX. 501/734–1024; John Selig, Administrator

Arkansas Department of Health Hospice Six, Area Six Office, Highway 167 South, Hampton, AR 71744; tel. 870/798–3113; Nealia Neal, Administrator

Arkansas Department of Health–Hospice Area Nine, Crittenden County Health Unit, 901 North Seventh, West Memphis, AR 72301; tel. 501/735–4334; FAX. 501/735–1393; John Selig, Administrator

Baptist Health, d/b/a Baptist Hospice, 11900 Colonel Glenn Road, Suite 2300, Little Rock, AR 72210; tel. 800/900–7474; FAX. 501/202–7793; Becky Pryor, Administrator

Baptist Memorial Regional Home Health Care, d/b/a Arkansas Home Health and Hospice, 824 North Washington, P.O. Box 90, Forrest City, AR 72335; tel. 501/633–6184; Gary Hughes, Administrator

Baptist Memorial Regional Home Health Care, Inc., d/b/a Arkansas Home Health and Hospice–West Memphis, 310 Mid–Continent Building, Suite 400, P.O. Box 2013, West Memphis, AR 72303; tel. 870/735–0363; FAX. 870/735–7156; Gary Hughes, Administrator

CareNetwork, Inc., d/b/a CareNetwork Hospice of Fort Smith, Central Mall, Suite 600, Fort Smith, AR 72903; tel. 501/484–7273; Barny Solomon, Administrator

CareNetwork, Inc., d/b/a CareNetwork of Hot Springs Hospice, 2212 Malvern, Suite 3, Hot Springs, AR 71901; tel. 501/623–5656; Cheryl Drake, Director, Hospice Services

Central Arkansas Area Agency on Aging, d/b/a Hospice of Central Arkansas, 706 West Fourth Street, P.O. Box 5988, North Little , AR 72119; tel. 501/372–5300; FAX. 501/688–7443; Elaine Eubank, Director

County Medical Services of Arkansas, Inc., d/b/a Eastern Ozarks Home Health and Hospice, 2852 C Hwy 62/412, Hardy, AR 72542; tel. 501/856–3241; Debra Windham, RN, Director

Hospice Care for Southeast Arkansas, Inc., d/b/a Hospice Care Services, 2214 South Blake, Pine Bluff, AR 71603; tel. 501/534–4847; Bud Millenbaugh

Hospice Care Foundation, P.O. Box 410, McGeHee, AR 71654; tel. 870/222–5989; FAX. 870/222–5990; Sherri Elam, RN, Patient Care Coordinator

Hospice Home Care, Inc., Prospect Building, 1501 North University Avenue, Little Rock, AR 72207; tel. 501/666–9697; FAX. 501/666–4616; Cecilia Troppoli, Administrator

Hospice of St. Michael Health Care Center, 300 East Fifth Street, Texarkana, AR 75502; tel. 501/779–2720; Steven F. Wright, Administrator

Leo N. Levi National Arthritis Hospital Hospice, 300 Prospect Avenue, Hot Springs AR 71901, P.O. Box 850, Hot Springs, AR 71902; tel. 501/624–1281; FAX. 501/622–3500; Patrick G. McCabe, Jr., Administrator

Share Foundation, d/b/a Community Hospice, 516 West Faulkner, El Dorado, AR 71730; tel. 501/862–0337; FAX. 501/862–0727; Linda D. Swart, Director

Texarkana Memorial Hospital, Inc., d/b/a Wadley Care Source Hospice, 718 East Fifth Street, Texarkana, AR 71854; tel. 903/798–7660; FAX. 903/798–7667; Hugh R. Hallgren, President and CEO

Visiting Nurses Agency of Western Arkansas, Inc., 207 College Avenue, Clarksville, AR 72830; tel. 501/754–8280; Lois Phillips, RNC, Regional Nursing Supervisor

Washington Regional Medical Center Hospice, 4209 Frontage Road, Fayetteville, AR 72703; tel. 501/442–1000; Patrick D. Flynn, Administrator

CALIFORNIA

AIDS Hospice Foundation, 1300 Scott Boulevard, Los Angeles, CA 90026; tel. 213/482–2500; FAX. 213/962–8513; Tay Aston, Cesar Mier, Admissions Officers

All Nations Hospice, Inc., 3325 Wilshire Boulevard, Los Angeles, CA 90010; tel. 213/738–9741; Ugochi Obuge, Chief Executive Officer

American Home Health Hospice, 1950 E. 17th Street, Second Floor, Santa Ana, CA 92705; tel. 714/550–0800; FAX. 714/550–0521; Marylyn A. Hagerty, Ph.D., Chief Executive Officer

Assisted Home Hospice, 16909 Parthenia Street, Suite 201, North Hills, CA 91343; tel. 818/894–8117; FAX. 818/894–8707; Sherry Netherland, M.A., Executive Director, Hospice

Care One Health Center, 1252 Turley Street, Riverside, CA 92501; tel. 909/780–5455; Viola Delphine Donton

Carl Bean House, 2146 West Adams Boulevard, Los Angeles, CA 90018; tel. 213/766–2326; FAX. 213/730–8244; Roland Palencia, Executive Director

Casa Encino, 4600 Woodley Avenue, Encino, CA 91316; tel. 818/905–8625; Ronald Morgan

Children's Homecare, 3020 Children's Way, Mail Code 5059, San Diego, CA 92123; tel. 619/495–4941; FAX. 619/495–4956; Michelle Deitz, Director

Community Home Care Services/Hospice, 1925 East Dakota, Suite 208, Fresno, CA 93726; tel. 559/221–5615; FAX. 559/221–5798; Jami L. de Santigo, Service Integrator

Community Hospice Care–Orange County, 333 South Anita Drive, Suite 950, Orange, CA 92668; tel. 714/921–2273

Community Hospice of the Bay Area, d/b/a Hospice by the Bay, 1540 Market Street, Suite 350, San Francisco, CA 94102–6035; tel. 415/626–5900; FAX. 415/626–7800; Constance L. Borden, Executive Director

Community Hospice, Inc., 601 McHenry Avenue, Modesto, CA 95350; tel. 209/577–0615; FAX. 209/577–0738; Harold A. Peterson III, Chief Executive Officer

Companion Hospice, 12072 Trask Avenue, Suite 100, Garden Grove, CA 92643; tel. 714/741–0953; FAX. 714/534–0998; Michael Uranga, Administrator

Compassionate Care Hospice of San Francisco, L.P., 785 Market Street, Suite 850, San Francisco, CA 94103; tel. 415/979–0925; Victoria A. Condon

Coordinated Hospice, 13800 Arizona Street, Suite 202, Westminster, CA 92683; tel. 714/898–7106; FAX. 714/898–0407; Kay Donald, Hospice Manager

Covina Health Care Center, 5109 North Greer, Covina, CA 91724; tel. 626/339–9460; FAX. 626/331–9560; Rajinder Kutty

Crossroads Home Health Care and Hospice, Inc., 320 Judah Street, Suite Seven, San Francisco, CA 94122; tel. 415/682–2111; Virginia A. Kahn

Elizabeth Hospice, 150 W. Crest Street, Escondido, CA 92025; tel. 760/737–2050; FAX. 760/796–3875; Laura Miller, Executive Director

Fremont–Rideout Home Health Valley Hospice, 16911 Willow Glen Road, Brownsville, CA 95919; tel. 916/692–1410; Cindy White, RN, Supervisor, Patient Care Coordinator

Garden Grove Hospice, 12882 Shackelford Lane, Garden Grove, CA 92841; tel. 714/638–9470; Rosa Valdivia

Gran Care Hospice, 19682 Hesperian Boulevard, Suite 200, Hayward, CA 94541; tel. 510/887–1622; Virginia Bartow

Harmony Hospice, 888 Prospect Street, Suite 201, LaJolla, CA 92037; tel. 619/456–9703; Robert Cohn, Administrator

Hinds Hospice, 1450 E. 27th Street, P.O. Box 763, Merced, CA 95341; tel. 209/383–3123; FAX. 209/383–5308; Nancy Hinds, RN, Administrator

Hinds Hospice Services, 1616 West Shaw Avenue, Suite B–Six, Fresno, CA 93711; tel. 209/226–5683; FAX. 209/226–1028; Nancy Hinds, Administrator, Director of Nursing

Home Health Plus, 2005 De La Cruz Boulevard, Suite 221, Santa Clara, CA 95050; tel. 408/986–1801; Mike Geraughty, Regional Hospice Director

Home Health Plus, 2511 Garden Road, Suite B–200, Monterey, CA 93940; tel. 408/373–8442; Anne Mason

Home Health Plus, 1200 Concord Avenue, Suite 150, Concord, CA 94520; tel. 800/828–0698; FAX. 925/825–6010; Valerie Rodriguez, Hospice Director

Home Health Plus, 2334 Merced Street, San Leandro, CA 94577; tel. 510/357–5852; Anne Mason

Home Health Plus, 411 Borel Avenue, San Mateo, CA 94402; tel. 510/357–5852; Michelle V. Gillmore

Home Health Plus–Hospice, 3558 Round Barn Boulevard, Suite 212, Santa Rosa, CA 95403; tel. 707/523–0111; FAX. 707/623–1034; Penelope J. Hunt

Home Health Plus/Hospice, 1770 Iowa Avenue, Suite 500, Riverside, CA 92507; tel. 909/369–8054; Judith K. Kafantaris

Home Health/Hospice of San Luis Obispo, 285 South Street, Suite J, San Luis Obis, CA 93406; tel. 805/781–4141; FAX. 805/781–1236; Michele S. Groff, Administrator

Hope Hospice, 6500 Dublin Boulevard, Suite 100, Dublin, CA 94568–3151; tel. 925/829–8770; FAX. 925/829–0868; Teresa Drake, Executive Director

Horizon Hospice, 12709 Poway Road, Suite E–Two, Poway, CA 92064; tel. 619/748–3030; Thomas Dusmu–Johnson

Hospice and Palliative Care of Contra Costa, 2051 Harrison Street, Concord, CA 94520; tel. 925/609–1830; FAX. 925/609–1841; Cindy Siljestrom, Executive Director

Hospice by the Sea, 312 South Cedros Street, Suite 250, Solana Beach, CA 92075; tel. 619/794–0195; FAX. 619/794–0147; Kathie Jackson, Administrator

Hospice Care of California, 377 East Chapman Avenue, Suite 280, Placentia, CA 92670; tel. 714/577–9656; FAX. 714/577–9679; Ann Hablitzel, Executive Director

Hospice Care of California, 14241 E. Firestone Blvd, Suite 109, La Mirada, CA 90638; tel. 562/802–6155; FAX. 562/802–6156; Ann Hablitzel, CEO

Hospice Cheer, 4032 Wilshire Boulevard, Suite 305, Los Angeles, CA 90010; tel. 213/383–9905; FAX. 213/383–9908; Bonnie Farwell, RN, B.S.N.

Hospice Family Care, Inc., 17291 Irvine Boulevard, Suite 412, Tustin, CA 92680; tel. 714/730–1114; FAX. 714/730–9236; Sandy Dunn, General Manager

Hospice of Amador, 839 North Highway 49/88, Suite F, Jackson, CA 95642; tel. 209/223–5500; FAX. 209/223–4964; Hazel Joyce, Executive Director

Hospice of Humboldt, Inc., 2010 Myrtle Avenue, Eureka, CA 95501; tel. 707/445–8443; FAX. 707/445–2209; Paul Mueller, Executive Director

Hospice of Madera County, 115 North P Street, P.O. Box 1325, Madera, CA 93639; tel. 209/674–0407; Nancy Hinds, Administrator

Hospice of Marin, 150 Nellen Avenue, P.O. Box 763, Corte Madera, CA 94925; tel. 415/927–2273; FAX. 415/927–2284; Mary Tavema, President

Hospice of Napa Valley, 3299 Claremont Way, Napa, CA 94558; tel. 707/258–9080; FAX. 707/258–9088; Sarah Gorodezby, Executive Director

Hospice of San Joaquin, 2609 East Hammer Lane, Stockton, CA 95210; tel. 209/957–3888; FAX. 209/957–3986; Barbara Tognoli, Administrator

Hospice of the Central Coast/Adobe Home Health, 100 Barnet Segal Lane, Monterey, CA 93940; tel. 408/648–7744; FAX. 408/648–7746; Patricia Cincone

Hospice of the East San Gabriel Valley, d/b/a Home Care Advantage, 820 North Phillips Avenue, West Covina, CA 91791; tel. 818/859–2263; FAX. 818/859–2272

Hospice of the Sierra, 20100 Cedar Road North, Sonora, CA 95370; tel. 209/533–6800; FAX. 209/532–6982; Judy Villalobos, Executive Director

Hospice of the Valley, 1150 South Bascom Avenue, Suite Seven A, San Jose, CA 95128; tel. 408/947–1233; FAX. 408/288–4172; Barbara Noggle, Executive Director

Hospice of Tulare County, Inc., 332 North Johnson, Visalia, CA 93291; tel. 209/733–0642; FAX. 209/733–0658; Debbie Westfall

Hospice Preferred Choice, Inc., d/b/a HPC–Concord, 1470 Enea Circle, Suite 1710, Concord, CA 94520; tel. 510/798–1014; Victoria Condon, Executive Director

Hospice Services of Lake County, 1717 South Main Street, Lakeport, CA 95453; tel. 707/263–6222; FAX. 707/263–4045; Michael Brooks

Hospice Services of Santa Barbara, a Division of the Santa Barbara Visiting Nurse Association, 222 East Canon Perdido, Santa Barbara, CA 93101; tel. 805/963–6794; James S. Rivera, President and CEO

Hospital Home Health Care–Hospice, 2601 Airport Drive, Suite 110, Torrance, CA 90505; tel. 310/530–3800; FAX. 310/534–1754; Kaye Daniels, President

Inland Valley Hospice, 3770 Myers Street, Riverside, CA 92503; tel. 909/360–5848; FAX. 909/360–0811; Katherine L. Allen, Administrator

Kern Hospice, 4300 Stine Road, Suite 720, Bakersfield, CA 93313; tel. 805/327–1012; David Christen, Vice President, General Manager

Livingston Memorial VNA and Hospice, 1996 Eastman Avenue, Suite 101, Ventura, CA 93003; tel. 805/642–0239; FAX. 805/642–2320; Deborah Roberts, RN, B.S.N., President

Madrone Hospice, Inc., P.O. Box 1193, Yreka, CA 96097; tel. 916/842–3160; FAX. 916/842–6412; Audrey Flower, Executive Director

Marian Hospital Homecare and Hospice, 1300 East Cypress, Suite G, Santa Maria, CA 93454; tel. 805/922–9609; FAX. 805/349–9229; Marie Whitford, Vice President, Alternate Care Service

Medshares Home Care and Hospice of Coastal California, 2421 Mendocino Avenue, Suite 150, Santa Rosa, CA 95403; tel. 707/528–4663; FAX. 707/528–2301; Karen Emge, RN, Clinical Manager

Metropolitan Hospice, 4904 Crenshaw Boulevard, Los Angeles, CA 90043; tel. 213/293–6163; FAX. 213/296–3913; Kathleen I. Jones, RN, B.S., Director

Midpeninsula HomeCare and Hospice, 201 San Antonio Circle, Suite 135, Mountain View, CA 94040; tel. 650/949–3029; FAX. 650/949–4317; John D. Hart, Executive Director

Mission Hospice, Inc. of San Mateo County, 151 West 20th Avenue, San Mateo, CA 94403; tel. 650/554–1000; FAX. 650/554–1001; Carol L. Gray, RN, Administrator

Mountain Home Health Services, Inc., 35680 Wish–i–ah Road, Auberry, CA 93602; tel. 209/855–2200; FAX. 209/855–2284; Lori M. Harshman

Nations Healthcare, Inc.–Hospice, 9823 Pacific Heights Boulevard, Suite N, San Diego, CA 92121; tel. 619/546–3834; FAX. 619/546–0701; David Golman, Administrator

Orangegrove Hospice, 12332 Garden Grove Boulevard, Garden Grove, CA 92843; tel. 714/534–1041; FAX. 714/534–7921; Maria Aguilar, Director, Hospice Services

Pacific Home Health and Hospice, 1168 Park Avenue, San Jose, CA 95126–2913; tel. 408/971–4151; Lemuel F. Ignacio, M.S.W., Administrator

Pathways to Care, Hospice, 1650 Iowa Avenue, Suite 220, Riverside, CA 92507; tel. 909/320–7070; FAX. 909/320–7060; Ed Gardner, President

Providence St. Joseph Medical Center Home Hospice, 501 South Buena Vista Street, Burbank, CA 91505; tel. 818/843–5111; Michael Madden, Head of Hospital

Quality Continuum Hospice, 5505 Garden Grove Boulevard, Westminster, CA 92683; tel. 800/797–2686; FAX. 714/379–7910; Sandra Young, Administrator

Ramona Care Center Hospice, 11900 Ramona Boulevard, El Monte, CA 91732; tel. 626/442–5721; FAX. 626/444–9884

San Diego Hospice Corporation, 4311 Third Avenue, San Diego, CA 92103; tel. 619/688–1600; FAX. 619/688–9665; Jan Cetti, President and CEO

Self–Help HomeCare and Hospice, 407 Sansome Street, Suite 300, San Francisco, CA 94111; tel. 415/982–9171; FAX. 415/398–5903; Intake RN

St. Ambrose Hospice Care, 15022 Pacific Street, Suite #A, Midway City, CA 92655; tel. 714/379–6738; FAX. 714/379–6740; Mike Peiton, Director, Operations

St. Joseph Health System Home Care Services–Hospice, 1845 West Orangewood Avenue, Suite 100 A, Orange, CA 92868; tel. 714/712–9559; FAX. 714/712–9529; Junith Coyle, Hospice Director

The Miller Project, 970 North Van Ness, Fresno, CA 93728; tel. 209/264–0061

Tri–City Hospice, 4002 Vista Way, Oceanside, CA 92056; tel. 619/724–8411; Arthur A. Gonzalez, President and CEO

Tri–Med Hospice, 534 West Manchester Boulevard, Inglewood, CA 90301; tel. 310/419–4836; Margaret R. Lanam

Visiting Nurse Association and Hospice of Northern California, 1900 Powell Street, Suite 300, Emeryville, CA 94608; tel. 510/450–8596; FAX. 510/450–8532; Pat Sussman, Director

Visiting Nurse Association and Hospice of Pomona/San Bernardin, 150 West First Street, P.O. Box 908, Claremont, CA 91711; tel. 714/624–3574; FAX. 714/624–8904; Karen H. Green, President

Visiting Nurse Service Hospice, Serving Santa Barbara County and San Luis Obispo County, 521 East Chapel Street, P.O. Box 1029, Santa Maria, CA 93454; tel. 805/925–8694; FAX. 805/925–1387; John W. Puryear, Executive Director

Vitas Healthcare Corporation, 8880 Rio San Diego Drive,, Suite 950, San Diego, CA 92108; tel. 619/280–2273; Judy Piazza, RN, Director of Admissions

VNA and Home Hospice, 1110 North Dutton Avenue, Santa Rosa, CA 95401–4606; tel. 707/542–5045; FAX. 707/542–6731; Rebecca LaLonde, Regional Director

VNA Foundation, 101 S. First Street, Suite 407, Burbank, CA 91502; tel. 818/526–1780; FAX. 818/526–1788; June Simmons, Chief Executive Officer

West Healthcare Hospice Services, 180 Otay Lakes Road, Suite 100, Bonita, CA 91902; tel. 619/472–7500; FAX. 619/472–1534; Suzanne L. Purdy

COLORADO

Angel of Shavano Hospice, 543 East First Street, Salida, CO 81201; tel. 719/539–7638; FAX. 719/539–3699; Diane Rogers, RN

Arkansas Valley Hospice, 118 West Fourth Street, Box 1067, LaJunta, CO 81050; tel. 719/384–8827; FAX. 719/384–2045; Erma J. Isaac, Executive Director

Baca County Hospice, 204 East 10th Avenue, Springfield, CO 81073; tel. 719/523–4851; FAX. 719/523–4763; Annie Dukes, Administrator

Boulder County Hospice, Inc., 2825 Marine Street, Boulder, CO 80303; tel. 303/449–7740; FAX. 303/449–6961; Constance Holden, Director

Bristlecone Home Care and Hospice, Inc., 615 Walsen Avenue, Walsenburg, CO 81089; tel. 970/668–5604; FAX. 970/668–3189; Ms. Grace Rome–Kuhn, Administrator

Caring Unlimited Hospice Services, Inc., 615 Walsen Avenue, Walsenburg, CO 81019; tel. 719/738–1929; FAX. 719/738–2113; Karen Clouse, RN

Exempla Homecare and Hospice, 3964 Youngfield, Wheat Ridge, CO 80033; tel. 303/467–4700; FAX. 303/424–5260; Ms. Kim Hegemann, Administrator

Grand Valley Hospice, d/b/a Hospice of the Grand Valley, 2754 Compass Drive, Suite 577, Grand Junction, CO 81506; tel. 970/241–2212; FAX. 970/257–2400; Christy Whitney, President and CEO

Hospice Associates of America, 2223 S. Monaco, #A–Z, Denver, CO 80222; tel. 303/753–0421; Mr. Edward Lowe, Administrator

Hospice Del Valle, Inc., 617 6th Street, P.O. Box 1554, Alamosa, CO 81101; tel. 719/589–9019; FAX. 719/589–5094; Ms. Mindy Montague, Administrator

Hospice of Custer County, 5th & Rosita, P.O. Box 120, Westcliffe, CO 81252; tel. 719/783–2380; Dr. Robert Bliss, Administrator

Hospice of Estes Valley, 555 Prospect, P.O. Box 2740, Estes Park, CO 80517–2740; tel. 970/586–2273; FAX. 970/586–3895; Susan J. Mock, Director

Hospice of Larimer County, 7604 Colland Drive, Fort Collins, CO 80525; tel. 970/663–3500; FAX. 970/663–1180; Brian Hoag, Executive Director

Hospice of Mercy, 3801 N. Main Street, Durango, CO 81301; tel. 970/382–2000; Ms. Michelle Appenzeller, Administrator

Hospice of Metro Denver, Inc., 425 South Cherry Street, Suite 700, Denver, CO 80246–1234; tel. 303/321–2828; FAX. 303/321–7171; Jacob S. Blass, President and CEO

Hospice of Northern Colorado, 2726 11th Street Road, Greeley, CO 80631; tel. 970/352–8487; FAX. 970/352–6685; Jane M. Schnell, RN, Executive Director

Hospice of Peace, 1601 A Lowell Boulevard, Denver, CO 80204–1545; tel. 303/575–8393; FAX. 303/575–8390; Ann Luke, Executive Director

Hospice of St. John, 1320 Everett Court, Lakewood, CO 80215; tel. 303/232–7900; FAX. 303/232–3614; Ms. Cindy Morrison, Administrator

Hospice of the Comforter of Colorado, 2790 N. Academy Blvd., Suite 100, Colorado Springs, CO 80917; tel. 719/573–4166; FAX. 719/573–4164; Mary McGreevy, RN, Executive Director

Hospice of the Gunnison Valley, 1500 West Tomichi Avenue, Gunnison, CO 81230; tel. 970/641–0704; FAX. 970/641–5593; Robert Patterson, Administrator

Hospice of the Plains, Inc., 125 W. 5th Street, P.O. Box 365, Wray, CO 80758; tel. 970/332–4116; FAX. 970/332–4102; Donna Roberts, Administrator

Hospice Services of Northwest Colorado, 135 Sixth Street, P.O. Box 775816, Steamboat Spree, CO 80477; tel. 970/879–9218; FAX. 970/870–1326; Janet Fritz, Executive Director

Lamar Area Hospice Association, Inc., 1001 South Main, P.O. Box 843, Lamar, CO 81052; tel. 719/336–2100; Linda Earl, Executive Director

LHS Home & Community Care Hospice, 615 Fairhurst Street, P.O. Box 3500, Sterling, CO 80751; tel. 970/521–3126; Mike Gillen, Administrator

Life Source Services, Inc., 245 S. Benton Street, Suite 205, Lakewood, CO 80226; tel. 303/237–4673; FAX. 303/237–2773; Cantee Wells, Executive Director

Mount Evans Hospice, 3721 Evergreen Parkway, P.O. Box 2770, Evergreen, CO 80439; tel. 303/674–6400; Louisa B. Walthers, Executive Director

Pikes Peak Hospice, Inc., 3630 Sinton Road, Suite 302, Colorado Springs, CO 80907; tel. 719/633–3400; FAX. 719/633–1150; Martha Barton, RN, President and CEO

Porter Hospice, 2420 W. 26th Ave, Suite 200D, Denver, CO 80211; tel. 303/561–5100; FAX. 303/561–5199; Terri Walter, Director

Prospect Home Care Hospice, Inc., 321 West Henrietta Avenue, Suite E, P.O. Box 6278, Woodland Park, CO 80866; tel. 719/687–0549; FAX. 719/687–8558; Joleen Bailey, Executive Director

Roaring Fork Hospice, 410 20th Street, #203, Glenwood Springs, CO 81601; tel. 970/928–0601; FAX. 970/945–5123; Susan Jones, Director

Sangre de Cristo Hospice, 704 Elmhurst Place, Pueblo, CO 81004; tel. 719/542–0032; FAX. 719/542–1413; Joni Fair, President and CEO

Trinity Hospice, LLC, 6795 East Tennessee, Suite 250, Denver, CO 80224; tel. 303/355–5890; FAX. 303/355–5976; Kevin Webb, Administrator

CONNECTICUT

Bristol Hospital Home Care Agency, Seven North Washington Street, Plainville, CT 06062; tel. 860/585–4752; FAX. 860/747–6719; Linda St. Pierre, RN, Director

East Hartford Visiting Nurse Association, Inc., 111 Founders Plaza, Suite 200, East Hartford, CT 06108–3213; tel. 860/528–2273; FAX. 860/290–6777; Louise Leita, Hospice Director

Foothills Visiting Nurse & Home Care, Inc., 32 Union Street, Winsted, CT 06098; tel. 860/379–8561; FAX. 860/738–7479; Jeannette Jakubiak, RN, Executive Director

Home and Community Health Services, Inc., The Nirenberg Medical Center, 140 Hazard Avenue, P.O. Box 1199, Enfield, CT 06083; tel. 860/763–7600; FAX. 860/763–7613; Kathryn D. Roby, RN, B.S.N., Administrator

Hospice at Home, A program of Visiting Nurse Services of Connecticut, Inc., 765 Fairfield Avenue, Bridgeport, CT 06606; tel. 203/366–3821; FAX. 203/334–0543; Lois Ravage – Mass, RN, M.S.N, Hospice Director

Hospice of Eastern Connecticut, a Program at VNA East, Inc, 34 Ledgebrook Drive, P.O. Box 716, Mansfield Center, CT 06250; tel. 860/456–7288; FAX. 860/456–4267; Susan Lund, Hospice Director

Hospice of Northeastern Connecticut, 13 Railroad Street, P.O. Box 203, Pomfret Cente, CT 06259; tel. 860/928–0422; FAX. 860/928–4545

Hospice of Southeastern Connecticut, Inc., 179 Gallivan Lane, P.O. Box 902, Uncasville, CT 06382–0902; tel. 860/848–5699; FAX. 860/848–6898; Carol Shaber, Executive Director

McLean Visiting Nursing and Community Services, 75 Great Pond Road, Simsbury, CT 06070; tel. 860/658–3950; FAX. 860/408–1319; Nancy E. Ryan, RN, Administrator

Middlesex Visiting Nurse and Home Health Services, Inc., 51 Broad Street, Middletown, CT 06457; tel. 860/704–5600; Janine Fay, Administrator

New Milford Visiting Nurse Association, Inc., 68 Park Lane Road, New Milford, CT 06776; tel. 860/354–2216; FAX. 860/350–2852; Andrea Wilson, B.S., M.P.A., Executive Director

Project Care, Inc., Home and Hospice Services, 51 Depot Street, Suite 203, Watertown, CT 06795; tel. 860/274–9239; FAX. 860/945–3625; Joel Schlank, Administrator

Regional Hospice of Western Connecticut, Inc., 30 West Street, Danbury, CT 06810; tel. 203/797–1685; Patricia Coyle, RN, Administrator, Supervisor

Salisbury Public Health Nursing Association, Inc., 30 Salmon Kill Road, Salisbury, CT 06068; tel. 203/435–0816; Marilyn Joseph, RN, Administrator, Supervisor

Southington Visiting Nurse Association, Inc., 80 Meriden Avenue, Southington, CT 06489; tel. 203/621–0157; Mary Jane Corn, RN, Administrator

The Connecticut Hospice, Inc., 61 Burban Drive, Branford, CT 06405; tel. 203/481–6231; FAX. 203/483–9539; Rosemary J. Hurzeler, President and CEO

The Greater Bristol VNA, Inc., 10 Maltby Street, P.O. Box 2826, Bristol, CT 06011–2826; tel. 860/583–1644; FAX. 860/584–2100; Anita Baldwin, Hospice Coordinator

Visiting Nurse and Community Care, Inc., Eight Keynote Drive, Vernon, CT 06066; tel. 860/872–9163; FAX. 860/872–3030; Rafael Sciullo, Administrator

Visiting Nurse and Home Care of Manchester, Inc., 545 North Main Street, Manchester, CT 06040; tel. 860/647–1481; FAX. 860/643–4942; Mary Lavery, Hospice Supervisor

Visiting Nurse Association and Hospice, of Pioneer Valley, Inc., 701 Enfield Street, Enfield, CT 06082; tel. 203/253–5316; Kimberly A. Barbaro, RN, M.B.A., Administrator

Visiting Nurse Association of Central Connecticut, Inc., 205 West Main Street, P.O. Box 1327, New Britain, CT 06050; tel. 860/224–7131; FAX. 860/224–8303; Mary Jane Corn, B.S.N., RN, President and CEO

VNA Health at Home, Inc., 27 Princeton Road, Watertown, CT 06795; tel. 860/274–7531; FAX. 860/274–8492; W. Rennard Wieland, President

VNA Hospice, Inc., 103 Woodland Street, Hartford, CT 06105; tel. 860/525–7001; FAX. 860/278–0581; Judith Milewsky Bigler, Executive Director

VNA Valley Care, Inc., Eight Old Mill Lane, Simsbury, CT 06070–1932; tel. 860/651–3539; FAX. 860/651–5082; Incy Severance, RN, M.P.A., Executive Director

DELAWARE

Compassionate Care Hospice of Delaware, 256 Chapman Road, Suite 201–A, Newark, DE 19702; tel. 302/454–7002; FAX. 302/454–7003; Cathy Stauffer Kimble, M.P.H., Regional Director

Delaware Hospice – Northern Division, 100 Clayton Building, 3515 Silverside Road, Wilmington, DE 19810; tel. 302/478–5707; FAX. 302/479–2586; Susan D. Lloyd, RN, M.S.N., Executive Director

Delaware Hospice, Inc.-Southern Division, 600 DuPont Highway, Suite 107, Georgetown Professional Park, Georgetown, DE 19947; tel. 302/856–7717; Susan D. Lloyd, RN, M.S.N., Executive Director

Delaware Hospice–Central Division, Lotus Plaza, 911 South DuPont Highway, Dover, DE 19901; tel. 302/734–4700; FAX. 302/678–4451; Susan D. Lloyd, RN, M.S.N., Executive Director

First State Hospice, 5193 West Woodmill Drive, Suite 28, Wilmington, DE 19808; tel. 302/995–2273; FAX. 302/995–2280; Terry L. Hastings, RN, Executive Director

DISTRICT OF COLUMBIA

Children's Hospice Services, 111 Michigan Avenue, N.W., Washington, DC 20010; tel. 202/884–4663; FAX. 202/884–6950

Home Care Partners, 1234 Massachusetts Avenue, N.W., Washington, DC 20005; tel. 202/638–2382; FAX. 202/638–3169; Phillippa Johnston, CEO

Hospice Care of the District of Columbia, 1331 H. Street, NW, Suite 600, Washington, DC 20005; tel. 202/347–1700; FAX. 202/347–3505; Ann Burden, Executive Director

Hospice of Washington, 3720 Upton Street, N.W., Washington, DC 20016; tel. 202/966–3720; FAX. 202/895–0177; Mary Ann Griffin, Vice President Hospice

Housecall Hospice, 801 Pennsylvania Avenue, S.E., Washington, DC 20003; tel. 202/546–6764; Karlene Conrad, Regional Manager

Inova Health Care–District of Columbia Branch, 1331 Pennsylvania Avenue, N.W., S–500, Washington, DC 20005; tel. 202/638–5828; Regina Silver

Urgent Home Health Care, 1535 P Street, N.W., Washington, DC 20005; tel. 202/483–3355; Pauline NGO Bapack

Visiting Nurses Association of DC, MD and VA, Hospice Services, 6000 New Hampshire Ave, NE, Washington, DC 20011; tel. 202/538–8600; FAX. 202/853–8681; Susan Walker, Hospice Director

FLORIDA

Big Bend Hospice, Inc., 1723 Mahan Center Boulevard, Tallahassee, FL 32308–5428; tel. 904/878–5310; FAX. 904/309–1638; Elaine C. Bartlett, M.S., President and CEO

Bon Secours Hospice, 21234 Olean Boulevard, Suite Four, Port Charlotte, FL 33952; tel. 813/764–8204; FAX. 813/764–6494; Jackie Homes, Team Manager

Catholic Hospice, Inc., 14100 Palmetto Frontage Road, Suite 370, Miami, FL 33016; tel. 305/822–2380; FAX. 305/824–0665; Janet L. Jones, President and CEO

Good Shepherd Hospice of Mid–Florida, 105 Arneson Avenue, Auburndale, FL 33823; tel. 813/297–1880; FAX. 813/965–5601; Mary Ellen Poe, Administrator

Good Shepherd Hospice of Mid–Florida, Inc., 247 South Commerce Avenue, Sebring, FL 33870; tel. 941/471–3700; FAX. 941/471–9452; Ruth Angus, RN, Director Highlands/Hardee

Hernando–Pasco Hospice, Inc., 12107 Majestic Boulevard, Hudson, FL 34667; tel. 813/863–7971; FAX. 813/868–9261; Rodney Taylor, Executive Director

Hope Hospice of Lee County, Inc., 9470 Health Park Circle, Ft. Myers, FL 33908; tel. 941/482–4673; FAX. 941/482–2488; Samira K. Beckwith, President and CEO

Hospice Care of Broward County, Inc., 309 Southeast 18th Street, Ft. Lauderdale, FL 33316; tel. 954/467–7423; FAX. 954/524–6067; Susan G. Telli, Executive Director

Hospice Care of South Florida, 7270 Northwest 12th Street, Penthouse Six, Miami, FL 33126; tel. 305/591–1606; FAX. 305/591–1618; Rose Marie R. Marty, Executive Director

Hospice of Citrus County, Inc., 3350 West Audubon Park Path, Lecanto, FL 34461–8450; tel. 352/527–2020; FAX. 352/527–0386; Marjorie Budd, RN, Executive Director

Hospice of Health First, Inc, 1900 Dairy Road, West Melbourne, FL 32904; tel. 407/952–0494; FAX. 407/952–0382; Roberta Van Dusen, Director

Hospice of Lake and Sumter, Inc., 12300 Lane Park Road, Taveres, FL 32778–9660; tel. 352/343–1341; FAX. 352/343–6115; Patricia Lehorsky, Chief Executive Officer

Hospice of Naples, Inc., 1095 Whippoorwill Lane, Naples, FL 34105; tel. 941/261–4404; FAX. 941/261–3278; Diane S. Cox, President and CEO

Hospice of Northeast Florida, Inc., 4266 Sunbeam Road, The Earl Hadlow Center for Caring, Jacksonville, FL 32257; tel. 904/268–5200; FAX. 904/596–6036; Susan Ponder-Stansel, President and CEO

Hospice of Northwest Florida, Inc., 2001 North Palafox Street, Pensacola, FL 32501; tel. 904/433–2155; FAX. 904/433–7212; Dale O. Knee, President and CEO

Hospice of Okeechobee, Inc., 411 Southeast Fourth Street, Okeechobee, FL 34973; tel. 813/467–2321; FAX. 813/467–8330; Richard S. Green, Executive Director

Hospice of Palm Beach County, Inc., 5300 East Avenue, West Palm Bea, FL 33407; tel. 561/848–5200; FAX. 561/863–2955; David Fielding, President and CEO

Hospice of Pasco, Inc., 6224–6230 Lafayette Street, New Port Rich, FL 34652–2626; tel. 813/845–5707; FAX. 813/846–8661; Katherine Hirst, Executive Director

Hospice of St. Francis, Inc., 2395 South U.S. Highway 1, P.O. Box 5563, Titusville, FL 32783–5563; tel. 407/269–4240; FAX. 407/269–5428; Bruce Walters, Executive Director

Hospice of the Comforter, 595 Montgomery Road, Altamonte Springs, FL 32714; tel. 407/682–0808; FAX. 407/682–5787; Robert G. Wilson, President and Director

Hospice of the Florida Keys, 1319 William Street, Key West, FL 33040; tel. 305/294–8812; FAX. 305/292–9466; Liz Kern, President and CEO

Hospice of the Florida Suncoast, Inc., 300 East Bay Drive, Largo, FL 33770; tel. 813/586–4432; FAX. 813/581–5846; Mary Labyak, M.S.S.W., L.C.S.W., President

Hospice of the Gold Coast H.H.S., 911 East Atlantic Boulevard, Suite 200, Pompano Beach, FL 33060; tel. 305/785–2990; FAX. 305/785–2993; Lynda Friedman, Administrator

Hospice of Treasure Coast, Inc., 805 Virginia Avenue, Suite 15, Ft. Pierce, FL 34982; tel. 561–465–0504; FAX. 561–465–6309; Sharon A. Rivers, President and CEO

Hospice of Volusia and Flagler, 3800 Woodbriar Trail, Port Orange, FL 32119; tel. 904/322–4701; FAX. 904/322–4702; Debbie Harley, Director

Life Path Hospice, Inc, 3010 West Azeele Street, Tampa, FL 33609–3139; tel. 813/877–2200; FAX. 813/872–7037; Susan E. Lang, Director of Marketing

The Hospice of Martin & St. Lucie, Inc., 2030 Southeast Ocean Boulevard, Stuart, FL 34996; tel. 561/287–7860; FAX. 561/287–7982; Mary C. Knox, Executive Director

The Hospice of North Central Florida, 4200 Northwest 90th Blvd., Gainesville, FL 32606; tel. 352/378–2121; FAX. 352/378–4111; Patrice Moore, Administrator

VITAS Healthcare Corporation of Central Florida, Inc., 2500 Maitland Center Parkway, Suite 300, Maitland, FL 32751; tel. 407/875–0028; FAX. 407/875–2074; Brenda K. Horne, General Manager

Vitas Healthcare Corporation of Florida, 3323 West Commercial Boulevard, Suite 200, Ft. Lauderdale, FL 33309; tel. 305/486–4085; FAX. 305/777–5328; Deirdre Lawe, Regional Vice President

VNA Hospice of Indian River County, 1111 36th Street, Vero Beach, FL 32960; tel. 407/567–5551; FAX. 407/567–9308; Sharon L. Kennedy, President and CEO

GEORGIA

Albany Community Hospice, 2332 Lake Park Drive, P.O. Box 1828, Albany, GA 31707; tel. 912/889–7050; FAX. 912/889–7447; Patty Woodall, Executive Director

American HospiceCare, 340 Eisenhower Drive, Building 1400, Suite A, Savannah, GA 31406; tel. 912/356–9090; FAX. 912/356–1155; Mr. Neil Bennett, Administrator

Avondale Hospice Services, Inc., 3500 Kensington Road, Decatus, GA 30032–1328; tel. 404/299–6111; Rachel Waldemar, Administrator

Blue–Gray Community Hospice, Perry House Road, P.O. Box 1349, Fitzgerald, GA 31750–1447; tel. 912/424–7152; Lenora Kirby, RN, Executive Director

Columbus Hospice, Inc., 1315 Delauney Ave., Suite 104, Columbus, GA 31901; tel. 706/327–5153; Mike Smajd, Executive Director

Georgia Mountain Hospice, Inc., 1476 East Church Street, P.O. Box 881, Jasper, GA 30143; tel. 706/692–3491; FAX. 706/692–4300; Lynn Corliss, Executive Director

Hamilton Medical Center–Hospice, P.O. Box 1168, 1200 Memorial Drive, Dalton, GA 30720–1168; tel. 706/278–2848; FAX. 706/272–6417; Judy Hannah, Administrator

Hand In Hand Hospice, 2150 Limestone Parkway, Gainesville, GA 30501; tel. 404/536–0497; FAX. 404/536–0157; Gregory N. Robinson, Administrator

Haven House at Midtown, Inc., 244 14th Street, NE, Atlanta, GA 30309; tel. 404/874–8313; FAX. 404/875–4363; Clyde W. Johnson, Jr., President and CEO

Healthfield Hospice Services, Inc., 2045 Peachtree Road, N.E., Suite 210, Atlanta, GA 30309–1414; tel. 404/355–3134; Richard Stroder, RN Director

Hospice Atlanta, 1244 Park Vista Drive, Atlanta, GA 30319; tel. 404/869–3000; FAX. 404/869–3099; Pamela Melbourne, Administrator

Hospice Care of Carroll County, Inc., 906 South Park Street, Carrolton, GA 30117; tel. 770/214–2355; FAX. 770/214–8301; Pat Alfrey, Administrator

Hospice Care, Inc., 1310 13th Avenue, Suite 200, Columbus, GA 31901; tel. 706/660–8899; FAX. 706/660–8899; Mr. Adeleye Tokes, Ph.D., Administrator

Hospice of Americus and Sumter County, 119 Brannan Street, P.O. Box 1434, Americus, GA 31709; tel. 912/928–4000; FAX. 912/928–1322; Anne F. Speer, Executive Director

Hospice of Baldwin, Inc., 811 North Cobb Street, Milledgeville, GA 31061; tel. 912/453–8432; FAX. 912/453–8432; Jeannie Sweeney, Administrator

Hospice of Central Georgia, 3920 Arkwright Rd., Macon, GA 31210; tel. 912/477–0335; FAX. 912/477–0690; Connie McCracken, Director

Hospice of Georgia, Inc., 3450 New High Shoals Road, P.O. Box 10, High Shoals, GA 30645; tel. 706/769-8835; FAX. 706/769-5944; Fran Keisel, Administrator

Hospice of Houston Co., Inc., The Heart of Georgia Hospice, 2066 Watson Boulevard, Warner Robins, GA 31093; tel. 912/922-1777; FAX. 912/922-9433; Art Holtz, Executive Director

Hospice of Laurens County, 1103 Bellevue Avenue, P.O. Box 1344, Dublin, GA 31021; tel. 912/272-8333; Kaye Bracewell, Executive Director

Hospice of Northeast Georgia, Inc., Highway 76 West, Clayton, GA 30525; tel. 706/782-7505; FAX. 404/782-3343; Julie Ferguson, RN, Patient Care Coordinator

Hospice of Southeast Georgia, Inc., 333 South Ashley Street, P.O. Box 1077, Kingsland, GA 31548; tel. 912/673-7000; Chuck Chapman, President

Hospice of Southwest Georgia, 818 Gordon Avenue, Thomasville, GA 31792; tel. 912/227-5520; FAX. 912/227-5526; Patricia Whetsell, Administrator

Hospice of the Golden Isles, Inc., 1692 Glynco Parkway, Brunswick, GA 31525; tel. 912/265-4735; Cheryl Johns, RN, Executive Director

Hospice of Tift Area, 802 East 20th Street, P.O. Drawer 747, Tifton, GA 31793; tel. 912/382-5030; FAX. 912/388-5633; Kerry Leepor Brock, Director

Hospice of Wilkinson County, Inc., 1046 Mission Farm Road, P.O. Box 920, Gordon, GA 31031; tel. 912/628-5655; Edwin Lavender, Administrator

Hospice Savannah, Inc., 1352 Eisenhower Drive, P.O. Box 13190, Savannah, GA 31406; tel. 912/355-2289; FAX. 912/355-2376; Judith B. Brunger, Executive Director

Northside Hospice, 5825 Glenridge Drive, Building Four, Atlanta, GA 30328-5544; tel. 404/851-6300; FAX. 404/252-7708; Christ Campbell, RN, CCM, Hospice Manager

Ogeechee Area Hospice, 5 West Altman Street, P.O. Box 531, Statesboro, GA 30458; tel. 912/764-8441; FAX. 912/489-8247; Nancy Bryant, RN

Olsten Kimberly Quality Care Hospice, 1395 South Marietta Parkway, Suite 222, Marietta, GA 30061; tel. 770/422-5741; FAX. 770/425-3516; Joan Richters, RN, M.N.

Peachtree Hospice, 3600 DeKalb Technology Parkway, P.O. 942029, Atlanta, GA 30340; tel. 404/451-1903; Curtis Stubblefield, Executive Director

Portsbridge, Inc., 4598 Barclay Drive, Dunwoody, GA 30338-5883; tel. 404/936-9546; FAX. 770/936-9547; T.M. Mahone, Administrator

Samaritan Care Hospice of Georgia, 705 Red Bud Rd., Suite B, Calhoun, GA 30701-1966; tel. 706/629-2722; Cynthia Brown, Administrator

Shepherd's Gate Hospice, Inc., 2149 Pace Street, Covington, GA 30014-6652; tel. 770/784-9200; FAX. 770/784-7650; John J. McBride, Executive Director

Southwest Christian Hospice, 7225 Lester Road, Union City, GA 30291; tel. 404/969-8354; FAX. 404/969-1940; Mike Sorrow, Executive Director

United Hospice of Calhoun, 1195 Curtis Parkway, Calhoun, GA 30701; tel. 706/602-9546; William Wells, Administrator

United Hospice of Macon, Inc., 2484 Ingleside Avenue, Building B, Macon, GA 31204; tel. 912/477-9713; FAX. 912/745-9321; Scott Schull

United Hospice, Inc., 3945 Lawrenceville Highway, Lilburn, GA 30047; tel. 800/544-4788; FAX. 770/925-4619; Matt Annis, Executive Director

Vencare Hospice–Atlanta, 1190 Winchester Parkway, Suite 200, Smyrna, GA 30080-6544; tel. 770/803-0881; Douglas J. Thompson, Administrator

Vencare Hospice–Columbus, 3646 Edgewood Road, Columbus, GA 31907; tel. 706/569-0200; Margarita Jara, Administrator

VistaCare Hospice–Macon, 750 Baconsfield Drive, Suite 115, Macon, GA 31211; tel. 912/750-9777; Lynda Geddis, Administrator

WellStar Community Hospice, 4040 Hospital West Drive, Suite 340, Austell, GA 30106-8117; tel. 770/732-6710; FAX. 770/732-6732; Cam Drinkwater, Admissions Coordinator

West Georgia Hospice, 1510 Vernon Road, Lagrange, GA 30240-4130; tel. 706/845-3905; FAX. 706/812-2650; Charles Foster, President and CEO

Willow Way Hospice, 6000 Lake Forrest Drive, Suite 400, Atlanta, GA 30328; tel. 404/255-4015; FAX. 404/255-8340; Maxine McCullar

Wiregrass Hospice, Inc., 430 E. Shotwell Street, Bainbridge, GA 31717-4058; tel. 912/246-6330; Ray L. Shrout, Administrator

HAWAII

Hospice Hawaii, Inc, 860 Iwilei Road, Honolulu, HI 96817; tel. 808/924-9255; FAX. 808/922-9161; Stephen A. Kula, Ph.D., President, Chief Professional Officer

Hospice Maui, 400 Mahalani Street, Wailuku, HI 96793; tel. 808/244-5555; FAX. 808/244-5557; Dr. Gregory LaGoy, Executive Director

Hospice of Hilo, 1011 Waianuenue Avenue, Hilo, HI 96720; tel. 808/969-1733; FAX. 808/969-4863; Brenda Ho, Executive Director

Hospice of Kona, Inc., 74-5094 Palani Road, Kailua-Kona, HI 96740; tel. 808/334-0334; FAX. 808/334-0365; David Kula, Administrator

Kauai Hospice, 3175 Elua Street, P.O. Box 3286, Lihue, HI 96766; tel. 808/245-7277; FAX. 808/245-5006; Kathleen Boyle

North Hawaii Hospice, Inc., P.O. Box 1236, Kamuela, HI 96743; tel. 808/885-7547; FAX. 808/885-5592; Nancy Bouvet, Executive Director

St. Francis Hospice, 24 Puiwa Road, Honolulu, HI 96817; tel. 808/595-7566; FAX. 808/595-6996; Sister Francine Gries, Administrator

IDAHO

Blackfoot Medical Clinic, Home Care & Hospice, Inc., 625 West Pacific, Blackfoot, ID 83221; tel. 208/785-2600; James Marriott, Administrator

Good Samaritan Community Hospice, 840 East Elva, Idaho Falls, ID 83401; tel. 208/529-8326; FAX. 208/524-1518; H. Ray Belk, RNC, Director

Hospice of Idaho, 812 East Clark, Pocatello, ID 83201; tel. 208/232-0088; FAX. 208/232-7941; Debbie Osborn, Administrator

Hospice of North Idaho, West 280 Prairie Avenue, Coeur D'Alene, ID 83815; tel. 208/772-7994; Dan Kuetemeyer, Director of Finance

Hospice of the Palouse, P.O. Box 9461, Moscow, ID 83843; tel. 208/882-1228; FAX. 208/883-6519; Leslie Park, RN, Director

Hospice of the Palouse, 700 South Main Street, P.O. Box 9461, Moscow, ID 83843-0119; tel. 208/882-1228; FAX. 208/883-2239; Norman Bowers, Administrator

Hospice Visions, Inc., 1300 Kimberly Road, Suite 11, Twin Falls, ID 83301; tel. 208/735-0121; Tamala Slatter, Director

Latah Health Home Care & Hospice, 510 West Palouse River Drive, Moscow, ID 83843; tel. 208/882-4802; FAX. 208/882-1819; Irma Laskowski, RNC, Hospice Director

Life's Doors Hospice, Inc., 1111 South Orchard, Suite 400, P.O. Box 5754, Boise, ID 83705; tel. 208/344-6500; FAX. 208/344-6590; Mary L. Langenfeld, Chief Executive Officer

Magic Valley Staffing Service, Inc., 200 Second Avenue, N., Twin Falls, ID 83301; tel. 208/734-0600; FAX. 208/733-5980; Debbie Osborn, Administrator

MSTI – Hospice of Boise, 151 East Bannock, Boise, ID 83712; tel. 208/386-2711; Nan Hart, Administrator

Southeastern District Hospice, 465 Memorial Drive, Pocatello, ID 83201; tel. 208/239-5240; FAX. 208/234-7169; Judy Moyer, Administrator

XL Hospice, Inc., 1401 North Whitley Drive, Suite 16, Fruitland, ID 83619; tel. 208/452-5911; FAX. 208/452-4090; Leon C. Felder, President

ILLINOIS

Advocate Hospice, 1441 Branding Avenue, Suite 240, Downers Grove, IL 60515; tel. 630/963-6800; FAX. 630/963-6877; Nancy Kitts-Woodworth, Director

All Care, Inc., 900 Jorie Blvd., Suite 220, Oak Brook, IL 60523; tel. 630/346-2575; Robert M. Wesolowski

Ariston Hospice Service, 3051 Oak Grove Road, Downers Grove, IL 60515; tel. 630/435-2111; Lynn MacMillan, Administrator

Beacon of Hope Hospice, Inc., 615 35th Ave., Moline, IL 61265; tel. 309/757-0579; Diane Lang

Beloit Regional Hospice, Inc., 5512 Elevator Road, Roscoe, IL 61073; tel. 608/365-7421; FAX. 608/363-7426; Virginia Burton, Administrator

Bro-Menn Hospice, 1322 S. Main Street, Normal, IL 61761; tel. 309/838-0930; Mary Nugent, Administrator

Bureau Valley Area Hospice, 526 Bureau Valley Parkway, Suite B, Princeton, IL 61356; tel. 815/875-7723; FAX. 815/875-4112; Geraldine Devert, RN, MS, Administrator

Carle Hospice, 2011 Round Barn Road, Champagne, IL 61821; tel. 217/383-3151; Sheryl Imlay, Administrator

Cass–Schuyler Area Hospice, 331 South Main Street, Virginia, IL 62691; tel. 217/452-3057; FAX. 217/452-7245; Linda Upchurch, Administrator

Community Hospices of America Northwest Illinois, 256 South Soangetaha Road, Suite 103, Galesburg, IL 61401-5586; tel. 309/342-3007; FAX. 309/342-6973; Sue Myer, Program Director

Covenant Hospice Care Program, 1400 West Park, Urbana, IL 61801; tel. 217/337-2470; Ruth Madawick

DeKalb County Hospice, 213 E. Locust Street, DeKalb, IL 60115; tel. 815/756-3000; Karen Hagen, RN, M.S., Executive Director

ENH Hospice, 5215 Old Orchard, Suite200, Skokie, IL 60077; tel. 847/581-1717; FAX. 847/581-1919; Janet Sullivan, Executive Director

Family Hospice of Belleville Area, 11B Park Place, Professional Center, Swansea, IL 62221; tel. 618/277-1800; FAX. 618/277-1074; Diane Smith, Administrator

Fox Valley Hospice, 200 Whitfield Drive, P.O. Box 707, Geneva, IL 60134; tel. 630/232-2233; FAX. 630/232-0023; Wilma Drummer, Executive Director

Franciscan Hospice of Central Illinois, 301 W. Washington Street, Pontiac, IL 61764; tel. 815/844-6982; Donna O'Shaughnessy, Administrator

Grundy Community Hospice, 1802 North Division Street, Suite 307, Morris, IL 60450; tel. 815/942-8525; FAX. 815/942-4934; Joan Sereno, Executive Director

Harbor Light Hospice, 800 Roosevelt Road, Building C, Glen Ellyn, IL 60137; tel. 800/419-0542; FAX. 630/942-0118; Dorothy M. Stahl, Administrator

Home Health Plus Hospice Program, 2215 Enterprise Drive, Suite 1512, Westchester, IL 60154; tel. 708/531-9339; FAX. 708/531-9680; Peggy Janka, Administrator

Home Health Plus Hospice Program, 333 Salem Place, Suite 165, Fairview Heights, IL 62208; tel. 618/632-0304; Robin Carnett, Administrator

Horizon Hospice, Inc., 833 West Chicago Avenue, Chicago, IL 60622; tel. 312/733-2233; FAX. 312/733-8931; Michael Preodor, M.D., President

Hospice Alliance, Inc., 3452 North Sheridan Road, Zion, IL 60099; tel. 847/263-1180; Connie Matter, Administrator

Hospice Care, 319 East Madison, Suite Three J, Springfield, IL 62701; tel. 217/789-6506; FAX. 217/789-6113; Kathleen Sgro

Hospice Care of Illinois, Visiting Nurse Association of Central Illinois, 720 North Bond Street, Springfield, IL 62702; tel. 217/757-7322; FAX. 217/757-7322; Sue Ellen Billington, Manager

Hospice of Bond County, 305 West Franklin, Greenville, IL 62246; tel. 618/664-9701; Elnora Hamel, Administrator

Hospice of Dubuque, 50 Sinsinawa, P.O. Box 236, East Dubuque, IL 61025; tel. 815/747-3622; Barbara Zoeller, Administrator

Hospice of Dupage, Inc., 690 East North Avenue, Carol Stream, IL 60188; tel. 630/690-9000; Kimberly Jensen, Administrator

Hospice of Kankakee Valley, Inc., 1015 North Fifth Avenue, Suite Five, Kankakee, IL 60901; tel. 815/939-4141; FAX. 815/939-1501; Dorothea MacDonald-Lagesse, Executive Director

Hospice of Madison County, 2100 Madison Avenue, Granite City, IL 62040; tel. 618/798-3399; FAX. 618/451-4288; Denise Saksa, Administrator

Hospice of Northeastern Illinois, Inc., 410 South Hager Avenue, Barrington, IL 60010; tel. 847/381-5599; FAX. 847/381-5713; Jane Bilyeu, Executive Director

Hospice of Northwest Illinois, Inc., 155 West Front Street, P.O. Box 185, Stockton, IL 61085-0185; tel. 815/947-3260; FAX. 815/947-3257; Deann Anderson, Administrator

Hospice of Southern Illinois, Inc., 305 South Illinois Street, Belleville, IL 62220; tel. 618/235-1703; FAX. 618/235-2828; Rebecca J. Wilson, President and CEO

Hospice of the Calumet Area, Inc., 3224 Ridge Road, Suite 202 and 203, Lansing, IL 60438; tel. 708/895-8332; FAX. 219/922-1947; Adrianne May, Administrator

Hospice of the Good Samaritan, 605 N. 12th Street, Mt. Vernon, IL 62864; tel. 618/242-4600; Christina Adams, Administrator

Hospice of the Great Lakes, 3130 Commercial Avenue, Northbrook, IL 60062; tel. 847/559–8999; FAX. 847/559–9005; Mary Jo Fox, Administrator

Hospice of the North Shore, A Division of Palliative CareCenter of the North Shore, 2821 Central Street, Evanston, IL 60201; tel. 847/467–7423; FAX. 847/866–6023; Dorothy L. Pitner, RN, B.S.N., MM, President

Hospice of the Rock River Valley, 264 Illinois, Route 2, Dixon, IL 61021; tel. 815/288–3673; FAX. 815/288–1181; Cheryl Price, Administrator

Hospice Suburban South, 78 Cherry Street, Park Forest, IL 60466; tel. 708/481–2104; Kaie Romani, Executive Director

Ingalls Home Hospice, One Ingalls Drive, Harvey, IL 60426; tel. 708/331–1360; FAX. 708/915–2749; Jean Laroche, Administrator

Joliet Area Community Hospice, Inc., 335 West Jefferson Street, Joliet, IL 60435; tel. 815/740–4104; FAX. 815/740–4107; Duane A. Krieger, Executive Director

Lourdes Hospice, 600 Market Street, Metropolis, IL 62960; tel. 618/524–3647; FAX. 618/524–3920; Donna Stewart, Director

Monroe Clinic Hospice, 1301 South Kiwanis Drive, Freeport, IL 61032; tel. 800/367–8406; FAX. 608/324–1302; Carla Stadel, Administrator

Northern Illinois Hospice Association, 4215 Newburg Road, Rockford, IL 61108; tel. 815/398–0500; FAX. 815/398–0588; Judith A. Engblom, Executive Director

Ogle County Hospice Association, 421 Pines Road, P.O. Box 462, Oregon, IL 61061; tel. 815/732–2499; Lorrie Barrows, RN, Executive Director

Provena Hospice – Waukegan, 2615 Washington Street, Waukegan, IL 60085; tel. 847/360–2220; Nancy Delaney, Administrator

QLS Community Home Health Based Hospice, 353 South Lewis Lane, Carbondale, IL 62901; tel. 618/529–2262; FAX. 618/457–8599; Monica J. Brahler, Administrator

QV, Inc., d/b/a CareMed Chicago, 322 South Green Street, Suite 300, Chicago, IL 60607–3599; tel. 312/736–8622; FAX. 312/738–1238; Dan Woods, President

Rainbow Hospice, Inc., 444 North Northwest Highway, Suite 145, Park Ridge, IL 60068–1427; tel. 847/699–2000; FAX. 847/685–6390; Patricia Aheen, President

Rockford VNA, 4223 East State Street, Rockford, IL 61108; tel. 815/971–3550; FAX. 815/971–3500; Susan Schreier, Administrator

Rush Hospice Partners, 1035 Madison Street, Oak Park, IL 60302; tel. 708/386–9191; FAX. 708/386–9933; Kathleen Nash

Saint Francis Hospice, 355 Ridge Ave., Evanston, IL 60202; tel. 847/316–7114; Virginia G. Niemann, Administrator

Seasons Hospice, 1600 W. Dempster, Park Ridge, IL 60068; tel. 847/759–9449; FAX. 847/759–9448; Marcia Norman, Executive Director

St. Margaret's Hospice, 600 East First Street, Spring Valley, IL 61362; tel. 815/664–1132; Carol Stevenson, Administrator

St. Thomas Hospice, Inc., Seven Salt Creek Lane, Suite 101, Hinsdale, IL 60521; tel. 630/850–3990; FAX. 630/850–3969; Marilyn Retter, Administrator

Tip Hospice Program, Four Executive Woods Court, Belleville, IL 62226; tel. 618/257–2184; FAX. 618/997–0922; Becky Ashton, Administrator

Vitas Corporation, 100 West 22nd Street, Suite 101, Lombard, IL 60148; tel. 630/495–8484; David Fielding, Administrator

Vitas Corporation, 1055 West 175th Street, Suite One, Homewood, IL 60430; tel. 708/957–8777; Jay Koeper, Administrator

VNA Hospice Care of Central Illinois, 720 North Bond Street, Springfield, IL 62702; tel. 217/523–4113; Barbara Sullivan, Administrator

VNA Lincolnland, Inc., 100 Professional Plaza, Mattoon, IL 61938; tel. 217/234–4044; Connie R. Oetinger, Administrator

VNA of Fox Valley Hospice, 1245 Corporate Boulevard, Aurora, IL 60504; tel. 630/978–2532; FAX. 630/978–1129; Janet S. Craft, President and CEO

VNA of Illinois Hospice, 1809 West McCord, Centralia, IL 62801; tel. 618/533–2781; FAX. 618/533–3265; Celeste Krahl, Administrator

Woodhaven Hospice and Special Support Services, 800 Hoagland Boulevard, Jacksonville, IL 62650; tel. 217/245–0838; Bette Jackson, Administrator

INDIANA

A Priority Hospice, 761 – 45th Street, Munster, IN 46321; tel. 219/922–8695; Barbara Hoyer, Administrator

Americare Home Health and Hospice Services, 49 East Monroe, Franklin, IN 46131; tel. 317/736–6005; Kim Weddle, Administrator

Cameron Home Health Care & Hospice, 416 East Maumee Street, Angola, IN 46703; tel. 219/665–2141; Pat Grosenbacher, Administrator

Care at Home Hospice Services, 1721 South Main Street, Goshen, IN 46527; tel. 219/535–2700; Nancy Buss

Clarian Hospice, Clarian Health Partners, Inc., 2039 North Capitol Avenue, Indianapolis, IN 46202; tel. 317/929–4663; FAX. 317/929–3815; William Loveday, Administrator

Comprecare Home Health and Hospice, 1607 East Dowling Street, P.O. Box 517, Kendallville, IN 46755–0517; tel. 800/824–5860; Marilyn Alligood, Administrator

Deaconess Ohio Valley Hospice, 600 Mary Street, Evansville, IN 47747; tel. 812/426–3169; Rosemary Knight, Administrator

DeKalb Memorial Hospice, 221 N. Main Street, Auburn, IN 46706; tel. 219/927–1640; Annette Vincent, Administrator

Elkhart Community Hospice, Inc., 2020 Indus Trail Parkway, Elkhart, IN 46516; tel. 219/523–3135; FAX. 219/294–3866; Janice M. Yoder, Administrator

Family Hospice of Indiana, LLC, 1710 East 10th L–185, Jeffersonville, IN 47130; tel. 812/284–0455

Family Hospice of Northeast Indiana, 1521 W. Main Street, Berne, IN 46711; tel. 219/589–8598; Bernhard P. Wiebe, Medical Director

Good Samaritan Lincoln Trail, 520 South Seventh Street, Vincennes, IN 47591; tel. 812/885–8035; FAX. 812/885–8048; Vonetta Vories, Administrator

Grancare Hospice Services, 1521 E. Tipton Street, Suite 386, Seymour, IN 47274; tel. 812/523–8200; FAX. 812/522–8200; Kathy Dougald, Administrator

Hancock Memorial Hospice, 801 North State Street, Greenfield, IN 46140; tel. 317/462–0559; FAX. 317/462–0217; Robert Keen, President and CEO

Harbor Light Hospice, 500 West Lincoln Highway, Suite F, Merrillville, IN 46410; tel. 219/793–1200; FAX. 219/793–9292; Stephanie Mayercik, Director

Heartland Hospice, 1315 Directors Row, Suite 206, Fort Wayne, IN 46808; tel. 219/484–7622; FAX. 219/484–5662; Tim Booth, Administrator

Home Hospital Home Health Care, 2500 Ferry Street, Lafayette, IN 47904; tel. 765/449–5046; Cheryl Ransom, Administrator

Hoosier Uplands Hospice, 1500 West Main Street, P.O. Box Nine, Mitchell, IN 47446; tel. 812/849–4447; FAX. 812/849–3068; Edna Jackson, B.S.N., RN, Director

Hope Hospice of Fulton County, 100 West 9th Street, Suite 306, P.O. Box 306, Rochester, IN 46975–0621; tel. 219/224–4673; FAX. 219/224–4444; Rev. Ronald C. Purkey, Executive Director

Hospice of Bloomington, 619 W. First Street, Bloomington, IN 47402; tel. 812/353–9818; FAX. 812/353–9477; Ellen Surburg, CRNH

Hospice of Margaret Mary Community, 321 Mitchell Avenue, Batesville, IN 47006; tel. 812/934–6624; Diane C. Helcher, Director

Hospice of South Central Indiana, Inc., 2400 East 17th Street, Columbus, IN 47201–5351; tel. 812/376–5813; FAX. 812/376–5929; Sandra Carmichael, Executive Director

Hospice of Southern Indiana, 624 East Market Street, P.O. Box 17, New Albany, IN 47150–4621; tel. 812/945–4596; FAX. 812/945–4733; Mary Lang, Director

Hospice of St. Joseph County, Inc., 111 Sunnybrook Court, South Bend, IN 46637; tel. 219/243–3100; FAX. 219/243–3134; Mark Murray, President

Hospice of the Calumet Area, Inc., 600 Superior Avenue, Munster, IN 46321–4032; tel. 219/922–2732; FAX. 219/922–1947; Adrianne May, Executive Director

Hospice of Wabash Valley, 600 South 1st Street, Terre Haute, IN 47807; tel. 812/234–2515; FAX. 812/232–2047; Jacquelyn Fox, Administrator

Hospice Preferred Choice, 8777 Purdue Road, Suite 231, Indianapolis, IN 46238; tel. 317/871–8500; FAX. 317/871–8510; Ferne Squierj, Executive Director

HospiceCare, Inc., 11555 North Meridian, Suite 190, Carmel, IN 46032; tel. 317/580–9336; FAX. 317/580–9346; Jill Ashcraft, Vice President of Hospice Operations

Koseivsko Home Care and Hospice, 902 Provident Drive, Warsaw, IN 46580; tel. 219/372–7810; FAX. 219/372–7811; Julie Bowers, Executive Director

Oakwood Hospice, 1000 N. 16th Street, New Castle, IN 47362; tel. 765/521–1420; Colleen Fedders, Administrator

Odyssey HealthCare of Central Indiana, Inc., 8765 Guion Road, Indianapolis, IN 46268; tel. 317/334–9302; Joseph D. Lingengelter

Parkview Home Health and Hospice, 105 N. Madison, Columbia City, IN 46725; tel. 219/244–6191; Bridget Dolohanty–Johns

Parkview Home Health and Hospice, 2270 Lake Ave., Suite 200, Fort Wayne, IN 46805; tel. 219/484–6636; Sally Boak, Executive Director

Parkview Home Heath & Hospice, 240 South Jefferson Street, Huntington, IN 46750; tel. 219/356–3000; L.K. McCoy, Administrator

Premier Hospice, Inc., 5490 Broadway, Merrillville, IN 46410; tel. 219/985–0160; Donna S. Huddleston, Administrator

Saint Joseph at Home Hospice Services, 400 North Main, Kokomo, IN 46903; tel. 317/452–6066; FAX. 317/457–4817; Darcy Herr, RN, Director

St. Francis Hospice, 438 South Emerson, Greenwood, IN 46143; tel. 317/865–2095; FAX. 317/865–2090; Carla Smith, Hospice Manager

The Community VNA Hospice, 1354 South B Street, Elwood, IN 46036; tel. 317/552–3393; FAX. 317/552–3994; Jessie A. Westlund

Vencare Hospice of Indiana, 2601 Fortune Circle East Drive, Suite 105B, Indianapolis, IN 46241; tel. 317/484–9400; FAX. 317/484–9500; Marita Barthuly, Administrator

Visiting Nurse Association Hospice, 610 East Walnut Street, P.O. Box 3487, Evansville, IN 47734–3487; tel. 800/326–4862; FAX. 812/463–4300; Intake and Referral Department

Visiting Nurse Association of Northwest Indiana, Inc., 201 West 89th Avenue, Merrillville, IN 46410–6283; tel. 219/769–3644; FAX. 219/756–7372; Susan Rehrer, Executive Director

Visiting Nurse Service and Hospice, Inc., 3015 South Wayne Avenue, Fort Wayne, IN 46807; tel. 219/456–9888; FAX. 219/456–8883; Sharon Staller, RN, Hospital Phone Nurse

Visiting Nurse Service Hospice of Central Indiana, 4701 North Keystone Avenue, Indianapolis, IN 46205; tel. 317/722–8200; FAX. 317/722–8223; Scott A. Himelstein, Administrator

Vitas Healthcare Corporation, 5240 Fountain Drive, Suite E, Crown Point, IN 46307; tel. 219/736–8921; FAX. 219/736–0972; Jay Koeper, General Manager

VNA Home Care Services Hospice, Inc., 901 South Woodland Avenue, Michigan City, IN 46360–5672; tel. 219/877–2070; FAX. 219/877–2089; Mary Craymer, Chief Executive Officer

VNA Homecare, Hospice and Family Support Services, 901 South Woodland Avenue, Michigan City, IN 46360–5672; tel. 219/877–2070; FAX. 219/877–2089; Mary Craymer, Chief Executive Officer

VNA Hospice Home Care and Mary E. Bartz Hospice Center, 501 Marquette Street, Valparaiso, IN 46383–2058; tel. 219/462–5195; FAX. 219/462–6020; Laura Harting, Executive Director

VNA Hospice of Southeastern Indiana, 1806 East 10th Street, Jeffersonville, IN 47130; tel. 812/288–2700; FAX. 812/285–8111; Nanci Brill, Hospice Director

IOWA

Beacon of Hope Hospice Inc., 3906 Lillie, Suite Six, Davenport, IA 52806; tel. 319/391–6933; FAX. 319/391–5104; Diane Land, Executive Director

Bremer–Butler Hospice, 406 West Bremer Avenue, Suites C and D, Waverly, IA 50677; tel. 319/352–1274; FAX. 319/352–9001; Rod Meyer, Administrator

Calhoun County HHA/Hospice, 515 Court Street, P.O. Box 71, Rockwell City, IA 50579; tel. 712/297–8323; FAX. 712/297–5309; Jane E. Condon, Administrator

Cedar Valley Hospice, 2101 Kimball Avenue, Suite 401, Waterloo, IA 50702; tel. 319/272–2002; FAX. 319/272–2071; Cheryl A. Hoerner, Executive Director

Grinnell Regional Hospice, 106 Fourth Avenue, Grinnell, IA 50112; tel. 515/236–2418; FAX. 515/236–2956; Sandra Bond, Director

Section C

Hamilton County PHNS–Hospice Division, 821 Seneca Street, Webster City, IA 50595; tel. 515/832-9565; FAX. 515/832-9554; Jacqueline Butler, Administrator

Hope Care Select, 160 South Hayes Avenue, Primghar, IA 51245; tel. 712/757-0060; FAX. 712/757-0060; Sharen Blacken, Executive Director

Hospice of Cass County, 1501 East Tenth Street, Atlantic, IA 50022; tel. 712/243-3250; Patricia A. Markham, Administrator

Hospice of Central Iowa, 401 Railroad Place, West Des Moines, IA 50265; tel. 515/274-3400; FAX. 515/274-1137; William P. Havekost, President and CEO

Hospice of Comfort, 709 West Main Street, P.O. Box 359, Manchester, IA 52057; tel. 319/927-7303; FAX. 319/927-7444; John Kerns, Operations Manager

Hospice of Compassion, 406 Court, P.O. Box 1034, Williamsburg, IA 52361-1034; tel. 319/668-2262; FAX. 319/668-1656; Carole Moore, Executive Director

Hospice of Dubuque, 2255 John F. Kennedy Road, Asbury Square, Dubuque, IA 52002; tel. 319/582-1220; FAX. 319/582-8089; Barbara Zoeller, Director

Hospice of Lee County, Lee County Health Department–Community Nursing, 2218 Avenue H – Suite A, Fort Madison, IA 52627; tel. 319/372-5225; FAX. 319/372-4374; M. Therese O'Brien, Administrator

Hospice of Mahaska County, 1229 C Avenue E., Oskaloosa, IA 52577; tel. 515/672-3100; FAX. 515/672-3266; David E. Rutter, Administrator

Hospice of North Iowa, 232 Second Street, S.E., Mason City, IA 50401; tel. 515/423-3508; FAX. 515/423-5250; Ann MacGregor, Administrator

Hospice of Northwest Iowa, 1200 First Avenue East, Spencer, IA 51301; tel. 712/264-6380; FAX. 712/264-6470; Sheryl Thu, Director

Hospice of Pella, 414 Jefferson Street, Pella, IA 50219; tel. 515/628-6644; Louan Hietbrink, Hospice Manager

Hospice of Siouxland, 224 Fourth Street, Sioux City, IA 51101; tel. 712/233-1298; FAX. 712/233-1123; Linda Todd, Hospice Director

Hospice of the Midlands, 800 Mercy Drive, Council Bluff, IA 51502; tel. 515/328-5106; Denise McNitt, Administrator

Hospice of VNA, 242 North Bluff Boulevard, Clinton, IA 52732; tel. 319/242-7165; FAX. 319/242-7197; Denise Schrader, Administrator

Hospice of Wapello County, 312 East Alta Vista, Ottumwa, IA 52501; tel. 515/682-0684; FAX. 515/684-9209; Cindy Donohue, RN, B.S.N., Director

Hospice Preferred Choice, 508 East Broadway, Council Bluff, IA 51503; tel. 800/591-2273; FAX. 712/325-1895; Lillian Jeppesen, Administrator

Iowa City Hospice, Inc., 613 Bloomington Street, Iowa City, IA 52245; tel. 319/351-5665; FAX. 319/351-5729; Maggie Elliott, Executive Director

Iowa River Hospice, Inc., 206 West Church Street, Marshalltown, IA 50158; tel. 515/753-7704; FAX. 515/753-0379; Brent D. Blackwell, Executive Director

Lyon County Hospice, 803 South Greene Street, Rock Rapids, IA 51246; tel. 712/472-3618; FAX. 712/472-3616; Marge Smith, RN

KANSAS

Central Homecare and Hospice, Inc., 427 S.E. Second, P.O. Box 645, Newton, KS 67114; tel. 316/283-8220; FAX. 316/283-8576; Robert E. Carlton, Executive Director

Community Hospice of Kansas, 1650 South Georgetown, Suite 160, Wichita, KS 67218; tel. 316/686-5999; FAX. 316/686-5634; Karen Everhart, M.Ed., Director

Homecare and Hospice, Inc., 323 Poyntz Avenue, Suite A, Manhattan, KS 66502; tel. 913/537-0688; FAX. 913/537-1309; Pam Oehme, Director, Health Services

Hospice Care in Douglas County, 200 Maine, Lawrence, KS 66044; tel. 913/749-5006; FAX. 913/843-0757; Stephanie A. Stewart, Director

Hospice Inc., 313 South Market, P.O. Box 3267, Wichita, KS 67202-3267; tel. 316/265-9441; FAX. 316/265-6066; John G. Carney, President

Hospice of Jefferson County, 1212 Walnut, Highway 59, P.O. Box 324, Oskaloosa, KS 66066-0275; tel. 913/863-2447; FAX. 913/863-2652; Marilyn Zieg, RN, Hospice Coordinator

Hospice of NE Kansas Multi–County, 326 East Ninth Street, Holton, KS 66436; tel. 913/364-4921; FAX. 913/364-3001; Patricia Scott, RN

Hospice of Reno County, Inc., Three Compound Drive, Hutchinson, KS 67502; tel. 316/665-2473; FAX. 316/669-5959; Carolyn Carter, RN, M.N., Executive Director

Hospice of Salina, Inc., 333 South Santa Fe, P.O. Box 2238, Salina, KS 67402-2238; tel. 785/825-1717; FAX. 785/825-4949; Kim Fair, Executive Director

Hospice of the Prairie, Inc., 2010 First Avenue, P.O. Box 1294, Dodge City, KS 67801-2623; tel. 316/227-7209; FAX. 316/227-7429; Stan Brown, Executive Director

Hospice Services, Inc., 424 Eighth Street, P.O. Box 116, Phillipsburg, KS 67661; tel. 7855432900; FAX. 785/543-5688; Sandy Kuhlman

Leavenworth County Hospice, 920 Sixth Avenue, Leavenworth, KS 66048; tel. 913/684-1305; Charles L. Rogers

Midland Hospice Care, Inc., 200 Southwest Frazier Circle, Topeka, KS 66606-2800; tel. 913/232-2044; FAX. 913/232-5567; Karren Weichert, Executive Director

Ottawa County Home Health/Hospice Agency, 307 North Concord, Suite 200, Minneapolis, KS 67467; tel. 913/392-2822; June Clark, RN

SCCS Home Health and Hospice, P.A., 1410 North Woodlawn, Suite D, Derby, KS 67037; tel. 316/788-7626; FAX. 316/788-7072; Cheryl Pelaccio, RN, Administrator

South Wind Hospice, Inc., 337 North Pine, P.O. Box 862, Pratt, KS 67124; tel. 316/672-7553; FAX. 316/672-7554; Diane L. Johnson, Director

Southwest Homecare and Hospice, 103 East 11th Street, Liberal, KS 67901; tel. 316/629-2456; FAX. 316/629-2453; Ida Rodkey, Administrator

KENTUCKY

Community Hospice, 1538 Carter Avenue, Ashland, KY 41101; tel. 606/329-1890; FAX. 606/329-0018; Susan Hunt, Administrator

Cumberland Valley District Health Department Hospice, P.O. Box 890, Hwy# 421S, Manchester, KY 40962; tel. 606/287-8437; Dottie Dunsil, RN, Nursing Supervisor

Heritage Hospice, 337 West Broadway, P.O. Box 1213, Danville, KY 40422; tel. 606/236-2425; FAX. 606/236-6152; Janelle Lane, Executive Director

Hospice Care Plus, 210 St. George Street, Richmond, KY 40475-2376; tel. 606/624-8820; FAX. 606/624-9230; Gail McGillis, M.S.N., Chief Executive Officer

Hospice East, 24 West Lexington Avenue, P.O. Box 115, Winchester, KY 40392; tel. 606/744-9866; FAX. 606/744-1971; Carol Richardson, Director

Hospice of Central Kentucky, 105 Diecks Drive, P.O. Box 2149, Elizabethtown, KY 42701-2444; tel. 502/737-6300; FAX. 502/737-4053; Gary Bohannon, Director

Hospice of Hope, One West McDonald Parkway, Maysville, KY 41056; tel. 606/564-4848; FAX. 606/564-7615; Kavin Cartmell, Executive Director

Hospice of Lake Cumberland, 108 College Street, P.O. Box 651, Somerset, KY 42502; tel. 606/679-4389; FAX. 606/678-0191; Jeanne Travis, Executive Director

Hospice of Louisville, 3532 Ephraim McDowell Drive, Louisville, KY 40205-3224; tel. 502/456-6200; FAX. 502/456-6655; Helen Donaldson, President and CEO

Hospice of Nelson County, 111 N. Third, Bardstown, KY 40004; tel. 502/348-3660; FAX. 502/349-1292; Sharon Bade, Administrator

Hospice of Pike County, 229 College Street, Pikeville, KY 41501; tel. 606/432-2112; FAX. 606/432-4631; Sharon Branham, President and CEO

Hospice of Southern Kentucky, Inc., 1027 Broadway, Bowling Green, KY 42104; tel. 502/782-3402; FAX. 502/782-3496; Betty Preece – Biggerstaff, Executive Director

Hospice of the Bluegrass, 2312 Alexandria Drive, Lexington, KY 40504; tel. 606/276-5344; FAX. 606/223-0490; Gretchen M. Brown, President and CEO

Jessamine County Hospice, 109 Shannon Parkway, P.O. Box 873, Nicholasville, KY 40356; tel. 606/887-2696; FAX. 606/885-1474; Susan G. Swinford, M.S.W., Executive Director

Lourdes Hospice, 2855 Jackson Street, Paducah, KY 42001; tel. 502/444-2262; FAX. 502/444-2380; Donna Stewart, Administrator

Mountain Community Hospice, P.O. Box 1234, Hazard, KY 41702; tel. 606/439-2111; FAX. 606/439-4198; Gene Rice, M.S.W., Director

Mountain Heritage Hospice, Inc., 163 Belkway, Village Center, Building Two, P.O. Box 189, Harlan, KY 40831-0189; tel. 606/573-6111; FAX. 606/573-7964; Bernice Reynolds, Administrator

Pennyroyal Hospice, Inc., 1821 East Ninth Street, Suite A, Hopkinsville, KY 42240; tel. 502/885-6428; FAX. 502/889-5005; Hanna Sabel, Executive Director

St. Anthony's Hospice, Inc., 2410 South Green Street, P.O. Box 351, Henderson, KY 42420; tel. 502/826-2326; FAX. 502/831-2169; Rebecca S. Curry, Administrator

Tri County Hospice, P.O. Box 395, London, KY 40741; tel. 606/877-3950; Ed Valentine

LOUISIANA

Golden Age Hospice, 5627 South Sherwood Forest Boulevard, Baton Rouge, LA 70816; tel. 504/292-2000; Martha C. Sewell

Good Shepherd in Hospice, Inc., 327 North Canal Boulevard, P.O. Box 1223, Thibodaux, LA 70302-1223; tel. 504/448-2200; Barbara Lofton

Hancock Hospice, P.O. Box 329, Tallulah, LA 71282-0329; tel. 318/574-2240; Ronald Hancock

Hospice Care Foundation, P.O. Box 278, Rayville, LA 71269; tel. 318/728-3060; FAX. 318/728-3080; Ann House, RN, Patient Care Coordinator

Hospice Care Foundation, P.O. Box 2449, Jena, LA 71342; tel. 318/992-2900; FAX. 318/992-2967; Amy Franklin, RN, Patient Care Coordinator

Hospice of Acadiana, Inc., 125 South Buchanan, P.O. Box 3467, Lafayette, LA 70501; tel. 318/232-1234; FAX. 318/232-1297; Nelson Waguespack, Jr., Executive Director

Hospice of Greater Baton Rouge, 8322 One Calais Avenue, Suite A, Baton Rouge, LA 70809-3412; tel. 225/767-4673; FAX. 225/769-8113; Kathryn Grigsby, Executive Director

Hospice of Greater New Orleans, 3616 South I–10 Service Road, Suite 109, New Orleans, LA 70001; tel. 504/838-8944; FAX. 504/838-9034; Jo-Ann Mueller, Chief Executive Officer

Hospice of Jefferson, 3715 Williams Blvd., Suite 240, Kenner, LA 70062; tel. 504/464-7357; FAX. 504/466-9482; Tracy McCann, Administrator

Hospice of South Louisiana, 210 Mystic Boulevard, Houma, LA 70360; tel. 504/851-4273; FAX. 504/872-6543; Dottie Landry, RN, Administration

Hospice of St. Jude, 615 Baronne Street, Suite 300 A, New Orleans, LA 70113; tel. 504/522-7108; Charles C. Harding

Hospice of St. Luke, 237 North Second Street, Eunice, LA 70535; tel. 800/869-2067; Willadean McWhorter, Administrator

Hospice of the Delta, 104 Smart Place, Slidell, LA 70458; tel. 504/641-7373; FAX. 504/641-7374; Juan Camero, Executive Director

Odyssey Healthcare, Inc, 3340 Severn Avenue, Suite 215, Metairie, LA 70002; tel. 504/887-8128; FAX. 504/887-8206; Kathleen Schellhaas, General Manager

Peoples Hospice, 1743 Stump Boulevard, Gretna, LA 70056; tel. 504/364-1494; FAX. 504/362-1056; Maggie Faucheux, RN, Administrator

Red River Hospice, Inc., 5501 John Eskew Drive, Alexandria, LA 71303; tel. 318/443-5694; E. W. Parker, Administrator

Samaritan Care Hospice of Louisiana, 3000 Knight Street, Suite 3000, Shreveport, LA 71105; tel. 318/869-2722; FAX. 318/869-2744; Toni Camp, Administrator

Trinity Hospice of Louisiana, LLC, 5647 Superior Drive, Baton Rouge, LA 70816; tel. 225/293-1948; FAX. 225/292-1502; Linda Leach, Program Director

MAINE

Androscoggin Home Health Services, 15 Strawberry Avenue, P.O. Box 819, Lewiston, ME 04243-0819; tel. 207/777-7740; Richard C. Stephenson, M.D., Medical Director

Community Health And Nursing Services, d/b/a CHANS Hospice Care, 50 Baribeau Drive, Brunswick, ME 04011; tel. 207/729-6782; FAX. 207/725-5640; Juliana L'Heureux, Executive Director

Community Health Services, Inc., 901 Washington Avenue, Suite 104, Portland, ME 04103; tel. 207/775-7231; FAX. 207/775-5520; Robert P. Liversidge, Jr., President, and CEO

HealthReach Hospice, Eight Highwood Street, P.O. Box 1568, Waterville, ME 04903-1568; tel. 207/873-1127; FAX. 207/873-2059; Rebecca K. Colwell, Vice President, Home Care

Hospice of Aroostook, 14 Carroll Street, P.O. Box 688, Caribou, ME 04736; tel. 207/498-2578; FAX. 207/493-3111; Saundra Scott–Adams, Executive Director

Section C

Hospice of Hancock County, 29 Union Street, P.O. Box 224, Ellsworth, ME 04605; tel. 207/667–2531; FAX. 207/667–9406; Vesta Kowalski, Administrative Director

Hospice of Maine, 693 Rear Congress Street, Portland, ME 04102–3303; tel. 207/774–4417; Martha Wooten, Acting Executive Director

Hospice of Mid Coast Maine, P.O. Box 741, 331 Maine Street, Suite 14, Brunswick, ME 04011–0741; tel. 207/729–3602; FAX. 207/729–2721; Gary Araujo, Executive Director

Hospice Volunteers of Kennebec Valley, Maine General Medical Center, 150 Dresden Avenue, Gardiner, ME 04345; tel. 207/626–1779; FAX. 207/582–6819; Barbara Bell, Director

Hospice Volunteers of Waldo County, 118 Northport Avenue, P.O. Box 772, Belfast, ME 04915; tel. 207/338–2268; Michael L. Weaver, RN, Volunteer Coordinator

Hospice Volunteers of Waterville Area, 76 Silver Street, Waterville, ME 04901; tel. 207/873–3615; Susan Hermann–McMorrow, Program Coordinator

Kno–Wal–Lin Coastal Family Hospice, 170 Pleasant Street, Rockland, ME 04841; tel. 207/594–9561; FAX. 207/594–2527; Dolly Wilbur, RNC, Clinical Manager Hospice

Miles Home Health Hospice Division, R.R. Two, P.O. Box 4500, Damariscotta, ME 04543–8903; tel. 207/563–4592; FAX. 207/563–8652; Carol Knipping, Executive Director

New Hope Hospice, Inc., Jarvis Gore Drive, Eddington, ME 04429; tel. 207/843–7521; FAX. 207/843–6645; Nancy S. Burgess, Director

Pine Tree Hospice, 65 West Main Street, Dover–Foxcroft, ME 04426; tel. 207/564–4346; Theresa Boettner, Program Coordinator

Southern Maine Health and Homecare Services, Route One South, P.O. Box 739, Kennebunk, ME 04043; tel. 207/985–4767; FAX. 207/985–6715; Elaine Brady, Executive Director

Visiting Nurse Service, 15 Industrial Park Road, Saco, ME 04072; tel. 207/284–4566; FAX. 207/282–4148; Maryanna Arsenault, Chief Executive Officer

MARYLAND

Calvert Hospice, 238 Merrimac Court, P.O. Box 838, Prince Freder, MD 20678; tel. 410/535–0892; FAX. 301/855–1226; Lynn Bonde, Executive Director

Caroline County Home Health/Hospice, 601 North Sixth Street, P.O. Box 10, Denton, MD 21629; tel. 410/479–3500; FAX. 410/479–3425; L. Carol Smith, Administrator

Carroll Hospice, 95 Carroll Street, Westminster, MD 21157; tel. 410/857–1838; Marie Bossie, Executive Director

Coastal Hospice, Inc., 2604 Old Ocean City Road, P.O. Box 1733, Salisbury, MD 21802–1733; tel. 410/742–6044; FAX. 410/548–5669; Marion F. Keenan, President

Dorchester County Home Health Hospice, 751 Woods Road, Cambridge, MD 21613; tel. 410/228–5860; FAX. 410/228–4475; Joyce T. Hyde, RN, M.S., Director

Holy Cross Home Care and Hospice, 9805 Dameron Drive, Silver Spring, MD 20902; tel. 301/754–7740; FAX. 301/754–7743; Margaret Hadley, Director

Hospice Caring, Inc., Volunteer Hospice, 707 Conservation Lane, Suite 100, Gaithersburg, MD 20878; tel. 301/869–4673; FAX. 301/869–2924; Lisa McKillop, Executive Director

Hospice of Baltimore, Gilchrist Center for Hospice Care, 6601 North Charles Street, Baltimore, MD 21204; tel. 410/512–8200; FAX. 410/512–8284; Regina Bodnar, Director, Clinical Services

Hospice of Charles County, 105 La Grange Avenue, P.O. Box 1703, LaPlata, MD 20646; tel. 888/934–1268; FAX. 301/934–6437; Geri Firosz, President

Hospice of Frederick County, 1730 North Market Street, P.O. Box 1799, Frederick, MD 21702; tel. 301/694–6444; FAX. 301/694–9012; Laurel A. Cucchi, Executive Director

Hospice of Garrett County, 69 Wolf Acres Drive, P.O. Box 271, Oakland, MD 21550; tel. 301/334–5151; FAX. 301/334–5800; Brenda Butcher, Executive Director

Hospice of Prince George's County, 96 Harry Truman Drive, Largo, MD 20774; tel. 301/499–0550; FAX. 301/350–7844; Lois Kimber, Director, Nursing Services

Hospice of Queen Anne's, Inc., 300 Del Rhodes Avenue, Queenstown, MD 21658; tel. 410/827–0426; FAX. 410/827–4678; Mildred H. Barrette, Executive Director

Hospice of the Chesapeake, Inc., 8424 Veterans Highway, Millersville, MD 21108; tel. 410/987–2003; FAX. 410/729–5263; Erwin E. Abrams, President

Hospice of Washington County, 101 East Baltimore Street, Hagerstown, MD 21740; tel. 301/791–6360; FAX. 301/791–6579; Robert Rauch, Executive Director

Jewish Social Service Agency, 6123 Montrose Road, Rockville, MD 20852; tel. 301/881–3700; Ronnie Tobin, Division Director

Joseph Richey Hospice, 828 North Eutaw Street, Baltimore, MD 21201; tel. 410/523–2150; FAX. 410/523–1146; Catherine Hawtin, Coordinator, Admissions

Kent Hospice Foundation, 118 South Lynchburg Street, Chestertown, MD 21620; tel. 410/778–7058; FAX. 410/778–7902; Nancy R. Morris, Executive Director

Mid–Atlantic Hospice Care, 4805 Benson Avenue, Baltimore, MD 21227; tel. 410/247–2900; FAX. 410/247–2581; Darlene Tamburri

Montgomery Hospice, 1450 Research Boulevard, Suite 310, Rockville, MD 20850; tel. 301/279–2566; FAX. 301/309–8791; Ann Mitchell, Executive Director

Potomac Home Health Care, 6001 Montrose Road, Suite 307, Rockville, MD 20852; tel. 301/896–6999; Lauren Simpson, Executive Director and CEO

Stella Maris Hospice Care Program, 2300 Dulaney Valley Road, Towson, MD 21204; tel. 410/252–4500; FAX. 410/560–9675; Sister Karen McNally, R.S.M., Chief Administrative Officer

Talbot Hospice Foundation, 586 Cynwood Drive, Easton, MD 21601; tel. 410/822–6681; FAX. 410/822–5576; Liz Freedlander, Executive Director

VNA Hospice of Maryland L.L.C., 7008 Security Blvd, Baltimore, MD 21244–2504; tel. 410/594–9100; FAX. 410/277–4257; Cindi Corbie, RN, Clinical Manager

MASSACHUSETTS

Athol Memorial Home Health & Hospice, 423 Main Street, Athol, MA 01331; tel. 978/249–5366; FAX. 978/249–8993; Cynthia M. Rode, Director

Cranberry Area Hospice, Inc., 161 Summer Street, Kingston, MA 02364–1224; tel. 617/585–1881; FAX. 617/585–1898; John A. Brennan, Executive Director

Diversified VNA Hospice, 316 Nichols Road, Fitchburg, MA 01420; tel. 978/342–6013; FAX. 978/343–5629; Noreen Basque, Administrator

Good Samaritan Hospice, Inc., 310 Allston Street, Brighton, MA 02146; tel. 617/566–6242; FAX. 617/566–3055; Leo P. Smith, Executive Director

Hampshire County Hospice, Inc., Seven Denniston Place, P.O. Box 1087, Northampton, MA 01061; tel. 413/586–8288; FAX. 413/584–9615; Joan Keochakian, Executive Director

HealthCare Dimensions, 254 South Street, Waltham, MA 02154–2707; tel. 617/894–1100; FAX. 617/736–0908; Patricia A. Field, Executive Director

Hospice Care of Greater Taunton, One Taunton Green, Taunton, MA 02780; tel. 508/822–1447; Joanne Smith, Vice President, Clinical Services

Hospice Care, Inc., 41 Montvale Avenue, Stoneham, MA 02180; tel. 781/279–4100; FAX. 781/279–4677; Kathleen Colburn, Executive Director

Hospice Community Care, 495 Pleasant Street, Winthrop, MA 02152

Hospice of Boston and Hospice of Greater Brockton, 500 Belmont Street, Suite 215, Brockton, MA 02401; tel. 508/583–0383; FAX. 508/583–1193; Ruth Capernaros, Executive Director

Hospice of Cape Cod, Inc., 923 Route 6A, Yarmouthport, MA 02675; tel. 508/362–1103; FAX. 508/362–6885; Marilyn Hannus, RN, Director

Hospice of Central Massachusetts, Inc., 120 Thomas Street, Worcester, MA 01608; tel. 508/756–7176

Hospice of Community Nurse Association, 40 Centre Street, P.O. Box 831, Fairhaven, MA 02719; tel. 508/999–3400; FAX. 508/999–6401; Brenda M. Van Laarhoven, RN, Coordinator

Hospice of Community Visiting Nurse Agency, 141 Park Street, Attleboro, MA 02703; tel. 508/222–0118; FAX. 508/226–8939; Kathleen M. Trier, Executive Director

Hospice of Greater Milford, 12 Hastings Street, P.O. Box 328, Mendon, MA 01756; tel. 508/634–8382; FAX. 508/634–8738; Renee Merolli, RN, M.A., Director

Hospice of the Good Shepherd, 2042 Beacon Street, Newton, MA 02468; tel. 617/969–6130; FAX. 617/928–1450; Ellen Rudikoff, Ph.D., Psy. D., Executive Director

Hospice of the North Shore, Inc., 10 Elm Street, Danvers, MA 01923; tel. 508/774–7566; FAX. 508/774–4389; Diane Stringer, Executive Director

Hospice of the South Shore, P.O. Box 334, 100 Bay State Drive, Braintree, MA 02184; tel. 781/843–0947; Elaine Coughlan, RN, Program Manager

HospiceCare in the Berkshires, Inc., 369 South Street, Pittsfield, MA 01201; tel. 413/443–2994; FAX. 413/433–7814; Anne Kissel, Executive Director

Merrimack Valley Hospice, Inc., One Water Street, Haverhill, MA 01830; tel. 508/470–1615; FAX. 508/470–4690; Raymond Brockill, Director

Merrimack Valley Hospice, Inc., 360 Merrimack Street, Lawrence, MA 01843; tel. 978/470–1615; FAX. 978/470–4690; Diane Bergeron, Administrator

Neponset Valley Hospice, Inc., Three Edgewater Drive, Norwood, MA 02062; tel. 617/769–8282; FAX. 617/762–0718; Susan DiBona, Hospice Manager

Old Colony Hospice, Inc., 14 Page Terrace, Stoughton, MA 02072; tel. 751/341–4145; FAX. 751/297–7345; Analee Wulfhuhle, Executive Director

Staff Builders Hospice Program, 529 Main Street, Suite 1M07, Boston, MA 02129; tel. 617/242–4872; FAX. 617/241–2880; Victoria Gunfolino, Director

Trinity Hospice of Greater Boston, Inc., 111 Cypress Street, Brookline, MA 02146

Visiting Nurse Association and Hospice of Western New England, Inc, 50 Maple Street, P.O. Box 9058, Springfield, MA 01102–9058; tel. 413/781–5070; FAX. 413/739–1423; Maureen Skipper, President

Visiting Nurse Association of Greater Lowell Hospice, 336 Central Street, P.O. Box 1965, Lowell, MA 01853–1965; tel. 978/459–9343; FAX. 978/459–0981; Nancy L. Pettinelli, Executive Director

Visiting Nurse Association of Middlesex–East and Visiting Nurse Hospices, 12 Beacon Street, Stoneham, MA 02180; tel. 617/438–3770; FAX. 617/438–7994; Jacquelyn Galluzzi, Chief Executive Officer

VNA Care Choices, Inc., a VNA care Network, Inc, 186 Alewife Brook Parkway, Suite 206, Cambridge, MA 02138; tel. 800/728–1862; FAX. 617/890–8444; Denise King, Clinical Services Manager

VNA of Greater Gardner Hospice, 34 Pearly Lane, Gardner, MA 01440; tel. 508/632–1230; FAX. 508/632–4513; Elaine Fluet, Director

Wayside Hospice/Parmenter Health Services, 266 Cochituate Road, Wayland, MA 01778; tel. 508/358–3000; FAX. 508/358–3005; Edith L. Murray, Director

Westhills Home Health and Hospice, Inc., 77 Mill Street, Suite 207, Westfield, MA 01085; tel. 413/562–7049; FAX. 413/568–9434; Jacqueline Schmitz, RNC, Hospice Director

MICHIGAN

Andy Scholett Memorial, 12426 State Street, P.O. Box 587, Atlanta, MI 49709–0587; tel. 517/785–3134; FAX. 517/785–2834; Shirley Burnham, Executive Director

Angela Hospice Home Care, Inc. and Care Center, 14100 Newburgh Road, Livonia, MI 48154–5010; tel. 313/464–7810; FAX. 313/464–6930; Mary Giovanni, Administrator

Arbor Hospice, 7445 Allen Road, Allen, MI 41801; tel. 313/383–8800; FAX. 313/383–0115; Bev Spicknall

Arbor Hospice, 2366 Oak Valley Drive, Ann Arbor, MI 48103; tel. 734/662–5999; FAX. 734/662–2330; Bev Spicknall

Arbor Hospice, Home Care and Care–ousel, 7445 Allen Road, Suite 230, Allen Park, MI 48101; tel. 313/383–8800; FAX. 313/383–0115

Arcadia Hospice, Inc., 340 East Big Beaver, Suite 250, Troy, MI 48083; tel. 810/740–1400; FAX. 810/740–8726; Kristen Olson, Administrator

Baraga County Hospice, Inc., 913 Meador Street, L'Anse, MI 49946; tel. 906/524–5168

Barry Community Hospice, A Division of Good Samaritan Hospice Care, Inc., 450 Meadow Run Drive, Suite 200, P.O. Box 308, Hastings, MI 49058; tel. 616/948–8452; FAX. 616/948–9545; Kay Rowley, Patient Care Coordinator

Barry–Eaton District Health Department – Hospice Program, 528 Beech Street, Charlotte, MI 48813; tel. 517/543–2430; FAX. 517/541–2612; Penny Pierce, RN, Director

Blue Water Hospices, Inc., 1422 Lyon Street, Port Huron, MI 48060; tel. 313/982–8809; FAX. 313/984–1612; Brenda K. Clark, Vice President, Operations

Branch–Hillside–St. Joseph DHD, 600 South Lakeview, Sturgis, MI 49091; tel. 616/659–4013; Duke Anderson

Cass Branch Hospice Program, 201 M–62 North, Cassopolis, MI 49031; tel. 616/445–2296; Jill Eldred

Charlevoix County Hospice, 601 Bridge Street, East Jordan, MI 49727; tel. 616/536–2842; FAX. 616/536–7150; Margaret Lasater, Executive Director

Community Home Health & Hospice, G–5095 West Bristol Road, Flint, MI 48507; tel. 810/733–7250; FAX. 810/733–8424; Donna Lloyd, Executive Director

Community Hospice Services, Inc., 32932 Warren Road, Suite 100, Westland, MI 48185; tel. 313/522–4244; FAX. 313/522–2099; Maureen Butrico, Executive Director

Cranbrook Hospice Care, 281 Enterprise Court, Suite 300, Bloomfield, MI 48302–0313; tel. 810/334–6700; FAX. 810/334–7064; Brian Hansen, Director

Dickinson–Iron DHD, 601 Washington Avenue, P.O. Box 516, Stambaugh, MI 49604; tel. 906/774–9910; FAX. 906/265–9913; Linda Piper, RNC, M.P.H.

District Health Department, #3, 220 West Garfield Street, Charleviox, MI 49720; tel. 616/547–6523; FAX. 616/547–1164; Gerald Chase, Administrator

Downriver Hospice, Inc., 1545 Kingsway Court, Trenton, MI 48183; tel. 313/671–6343

Genesys Hospice, 7280 South State Road, Goodrich, MI 48438; tel. 810/636–5000; FAX. 810/636–5019; LaVeme A. McCombs, Administrator

Good Samaritan Hospice Care, Inc., 166 East Goodale Avenue, Battle Creek, MI 49017–2728; tel. 561/666–0360; Mary Cunningham, Executive Director

Grancare Hospice Services, 38935 Ann Arbor Road, Livonia, MI 48150; tel. 313/467–8209; FAX. 313/467–7244; Michelle Strait, Administrator

Grand Traverse Area Hospice, 1105 Sixth Street, Traverse City, MI 49684; tel. 616/935–6520; FAX. 616/935–7270; Kay Benisek, Manager

Gratiot Area Hospice, 302 1/2 East Main, Stanton, MI 48888; tel. 517/831–5045; Carol Goffnett

Heartland Hospice, 814 Adams, Suite 109, Bay City, MI 48708; tel. 517/892–0355; FAX. 517/892–0896; Christine Satkowiak, RN, Administrator

Heartland Hospice, 700 West Ash Street, Suite Three–A, Mason, MI 48854; Lynn Howes

Heartland Hospice, 6504 28th Street, S.E., Suite T, Grand Rapids, MI 49546; tel. 616/942–7733

Helping Hands Hospice, 545 Apple Tree Drive, Ionia, MI 48846; tel. 616/527–5550; FAX. 616/527–5683; Becky Mason, RN, Administrator

Henry Ford Hospice–West Bloomfield, 6020 West Maple Road, Suite 500, West Bloomfield, MI 48322; tel. 810/539–0660; FAX. 810/539–8868; Laura Zeile, RN, B.S.N., Manager

Home Health Plus (Homecare & Hospice), 26211 Central Park Boulevard, Suite 110, Southfield, MI 48076; tel. 248/357–3650; FAX. 248/357–1486; Marilyn M. Chirilut, RN, BSN., Director, Operations

Hospice at Home, Inc., 2618 West John Beers Road, Stevensville, MI 49127; tel. 616/429–7100; FAX. 616/428–3499; Helen Parrott, Administrator

Hospice Care of Southwest Michigan, 301 West Cedar Street, Kalamazoo, MI 49007–5106; tel. 616/345–0273; FAX. 616/345–8522; Jean Maile, Administrator

Hospice of Bay Area, 1460 West Center Avenue, Essexville, MI 48732; tel. 517/895–4750; FAX. 517/895–4701; Christine Chesny

Hospice of Chippewa County/Chippewa County Health Department, 508 Ashmun Street, Suite 120, Salute Ste. Marie, MI 49783; tel. 906/635–1568; FAX. 906/635–1701; Rosemary Blashill, Administrator

Hospice of Clinton Memorial and Sparrow, 304 Brush Street, St. Johns, MI 48879; tel. 517/224–5650; FAX. 517/224–1501; Michelle Wiseman, Director

Hospice of Gladwin Area, Inc., 1312 N. State Street, P.O. Box 557, Gladwin, MI 48624; tel. 517/426–4464; FAX. 517/426–3057; Georgann Schuster, Executive Director

Hospice of Greater Grand Rapids, 1260 Ekhart, N.E., Grand Rapids, MI 49503; tel. 616/454–1426; David G. Zwicky, Program Director

Hospice of Helping Hands, Inc., 801 East Houghton Avenue, P.O. Box 71, West Branch, MI 48661; tel. 517/345–4700; FAX. 517/345–2991; Christopher Lauckner, Director

Hospice of Hillsdale County, 111 South Howell Street, Suite B, Hillsdale, MI 49242; tel. 517/437–5252; FAX. 517/437–5253; Kathryn Aemisegger

Hospice of Holland Home, 2100 Raybrook, S.E., Grand Rapids, MI 49546; tel. 616/235–5100; FAX. 616/235–5111; Karen Bacon Washburn, Director

Hospice of Holland, Inc., 270 Hoover Boulevard, Holland, MI 49423; tel. 616/396–2972; FAX. 616/396–2808; Judith A. Zylman, RN, Executive Director

Hospice of Integrated Health Services, 24445 Northwestern Highway, Suite 105, Southfield, MI 48075; tel. 800/397–9360; FAX. 248/355–5705; Susan Gadlage, Area Administration

Hospice of Ionia, 117 North Depot Street, Ionia, MI 48846; tel. 616/527–0681; Bernice Falsetta

Hospice of Jackson, 915 Airport Road, Jackson, MI 49202; tel. 517/783–2648; FAX. 517/783–2674; Michael L. Freytag, M.A., L.P.C., Executive Director

Hospice of Lake County, 4967 Michigan Ave., Baldwin, MI 49304; tel. 616/745–6161; FAX. 616/745–7676; Thomas Nobel, Administrator

Hospice of Lansing, Inc., 6035 Executive Drive, Suite 103, Lansing, MI 48911; tel. 517/882–4500; FAX. 517/882–3010; Barbara A. Kowalski, M.P.A., Executive Director

Hospice of Lenawee, 415 Mill Road, Adrian, MI 49221; tel. 517/263–2323; FAX. 517/263–1279; Ann Gehoski, Administrator

Hospice of Little Traverse Bay, 416 Connubial Avenue, Petoskey, MI 49770; tel. 616/347–9700; FAX. 616/348–4228; Barbara Terry, Administrator

Hospice of Michigan, Crossroads Building, 16250 Northland Drive, Suite 21, Southfield, MI 48075–5200; tel. 810/559–9209; FAX. 810/559–6489; Carolyn Fitzpatrick, Administrator

Hospice of Michigan, 10 Atkinson Drive, Suite Three, Ludington, MI 49431; tel. 616/845–0321; FAX. 616/845–1802; Jean Taylor, Operations Director

Hospice of Michigan–Roscommon, 107 South Main, P.O. Box 532, Roscommon, MI 48653; tel. 517/275–8967; FAX. 517/275–6130; Sheila Simpson, Program Director

Hospice of Monroe, 502 West Elm Street, Monroe, MI 48161; tel. 313/457–3220; FAX. 313/457–5060; Paul Doerfler, Administrator

Hospice of Muskegon–Oceana, 1095 Third Street, Suite 209, Muskegon, MI 49441; tel. 616/728–3442; FAX. 616/722–0708; Mary Anne Gorman, Executive Director

Hospice of Muskegon–Oceana, 339B Dewey, Shelby, MI 49455; tel. 616/861–4761; FAX. 616/722–0708

Hospice of Newaygo County, A division of Hospice of Michigan, Inc., 819 West Main Street, Fremont, MI 49412; tel. 616/924–6123; FAX. 616/924–8028; Marie Malone, RN, B.S.N., Hospice Director

Hospice of North Ottawa Community, Inc., 1515 South Despelder, Grand Haven, MI 49417; tel. 616/846–2015; FAX. 616/846–7227; Carolyn K. Howes, Executive Director

Hospice of Northeastern Michigan, Inc., 112 West Chisholm, Alpena, MI 49707; tel. 517/354–5258; Jeraldyne Habermehl, Executive Director

Hospice of Southeast Michigan/Detroit, 2990 West Grand Boulevard, Suite 402, Detroit, MI 48202; tel. 313/874–2000; June William

Hospice of Southeast Michigan/Franklin, 12900 West Chicago Boulevard, Detroit, MI 48228; tel. 313/491–0022; Carolyn Fitzgerald

Hospice of Southeastern Michigan – North Oakland, 530 West Huron, Pontiac, MI 48341; tel. 810/253–2580; FAX. 810/253–2599; Rita Ann Mahon, RN, Director

Hospice of Southeastern Michigan–St. Clair Shores, 22811 Greater Mack Avenue, St. Clair Sho, MI 48080; tel. 313/559–9209; Carolyn Fitzgerald

Hospice of Sturgis, 600 South Lakeview Avenue, Sturgis, MI 49091; Pamela Pope

Hospice of the Straits/Vital Care, 761 Lafayette, Cheboygan, MI 49721; tel. 616/627–4774; FAX. 616/627–4416; Fran Hill, Manager

Hospice of Washtenaw, 806 Airport Boulevard, Ann Arbor, MI 48108; tel. 734/327–3400; FAX. 734/327–3273; Teri Turner, Administrator

Hospice of Wexford–Missaukee, A Program of Hospice of Michigan, 932 North Mitchell Street, Cadillac, MI 49601; tel. 616/779–9570; FAX. 616/779–0717; Roberta Schutte, Patient Care Coordinator

Hospice's of Henry Ford Health System, 23000 Mack Avenue, Suite 500, St. Clair Shore, MI 48080; tel. 810/774–4141; FAX. 810/774–0515; Sondra Seely, Administrator

Hospice–Partners in Caring, Division of VNA of Saginaw, 500 South Hamilton, Saginaw, MI 48602; tel. 517/799–6020; FAX. 517/799–6062; S. J. Schultz, B.S.N., M.S., President and CEO

Individualized Hospice, 3003 Washtenaw Avenue, Suite Two, Ann Arbor, MI 48104; tel. 313/971–0444; FAX. 313/971–1980; Patricia Love, Director of Regulatory Affairs

International Pediatric Hospice, 2300 Bull Building, Detroit, MI 48226; tel. 313/965–6100; Paul Manion

Kaleidoscope Kids, 1 Ford Place, 2–A, Detroit, MI 48202; tel. 313/972–1980; Sondra Seely

Karmanos Cancer Institute–Hospice Program, 24601 Northwestern Highway, Southfield, MI 48075; tel. 810/827–1592; FAX. 810/827–0972; Shelia A. Sperti, M.S.N., RN, Administrator

Keweenaw Home Nursing and Hospice, 311 Sixth Street, Calumet, MI 49913; tel. 906/337–5700; FAX. 906/337–9929; Wanda Kolb, Administrator

Lake Superior Hospice Association, 148 West Washington, Marquette, MI 49855; tel. 906/226–2646; FAX. 906/226–7735; Jill Baker, Executive Director

LMAS DHD Hospice, 200 Hamilton Lake Road, Newberry, MI 49868; tel. 906/293–5107; FAX. 906/293–5453; Rosemary Blashill, Administrator

LMAS DHD Hospice/St. Ignace, 749 Hombach Street, St. Ignace, MI 49781; tel. 906/643–7700; FAX. 906/643–7719; Judy Misner, Home Health Nursing Supervisor

Manistee Area Volunteer Hospice, Inc., P.O. Box 293, Manistee, MI 49660; tel. 616/723–6064; Diane Cameron, President

Marquette General Home Health and Hospice, Doctors Park, Suite 105, Escanaba, MI 49829; tel. 906/789–1305; FAX. 906/789–9144; Linda S. Lewandowski, Director, Hospice

McLaren Hospice Service, Inc., 237 Davis Lake Road, Lapeer, MI 48446; tel. 810/667–0042; Terry Morgan, President

Memorial Hospice, 1320 South Carpenter Street, Iron Mountain, MI 48901; tel. 906/774–5589

MI Home Health Care/Terminal Care, 955 East Commerce Drive, Traverse City, MI 49684; tel. 616/943–8451; FAX. 616/943–4515; Lilo Hoelzel–Seipp

Mid Michigan VNA Hospice/Clare, 1438 North McEwan, Clare, MI 48617; tel. 517/539–5320; FAX. 517/839–1773; Sandra Simmons, Administrator

MidMichigan Visiting Nurses Association and Hospice, 3007 North Saginaw Road, Midland, MI 48640; tel. 517/839–1770; FAX. 517/839–1749; Sherry Hockstra, Hospice Manager

North County Hospice, Inc., 301 South Cedar, Kalkaska, MI 49646; tel. 616/258–5286; Eleen R. Bubble, Co–Volunteer Director

North Woods Home Nursing and Hospice, 226 South Cedar, P.O. Box 307, Manistique, MI 49854; tel. 906/341–6963; FAX. 906/341–2490; Susan Bjorne, Administrator

Otsego Area Hospice, a program of Hospice of Michigan, 810 South Otsego, Suite 111, Gaylord, MI 49735; tel. 517/732–2151; FAX. 517/731–2897; Sheila Simpson, Area Director

South Haven Area Hospice, 05055 Blue Star Highway, P.O. Box 990, South Haven, MI 49090–0990; tel. 616/637–3825; FAX. 616/637–6777; Barbara Reicherts, Executive Director

St. Joseph Huron Home Health and Hospice, Inc., 516 Oak Street, Tawas City, MI 48763; tel. 517/362–4611; FAX. 517/362–8771; Ann Balfour, Administrator

St. Joseph's Hospice/Affiliate of Henry Ford Cottage Hospice, 43411 Garfield Boulevard, Building Two, Clinton Towns, MI 48038; tel. 810/263–2840; FAX. 810/263–2895; Patti Ciechanovski, CRNH, Manager

United Home Hospice, Inc., 2401 20th Street, Detroit, MI 48216; tel. 313/964–1133; Alice Okwu, Director, Nursing

Section C

United Hospice Service, Six Eastgate Plaza, Sandusky, MI 48471; tel. 800/635–7490

Upper Peninsula Home Health and Hospice, 1414 West Fair, Suite 44, Marquette, MI 49855; tel. 906/225–4545; FAX. 906/225–7543; Cynthia A. Nyquist, RN, B.S.N., Administrator

Visiting Nurse Hospice, 4801 Willoughby, Suite Seven, Holt, MI 48842; tel. 517/694–8300; FAX. 517/694–4968; Jeanne Zabihaylo, Admissions Coordinator

Visiting Nurse Hospice Services, 348 North Burdick Street, Kalamazoo, MI 49007–3843; tel. 616/343–1396; FAX. 616/382–8686; Jill Eldred

Visiting Nurse Service of Western Michigan Hospice Program, 1401 Cedar, N.E., Grand Rapids, MI 49503; tel. 616/774–2702; FAX. 616/774–7017; Laurie Sefton, RN, M.S.N., Hospice Program Director

VNA of Southwest Michigan Hospice, County Road #681, Suite D, Hartford, MI 49057; tel. 616/621–3154; Jill Eldred

West Bloomfield Hospice, 6020 West Maple Road, Suite 500, West Bloomfield, MI 48322; tel. 810/884–8600; Sondra Seely

Wings of Hope Hospice, Inc. of Allegan County, 663 North 10th Street, Plainwell, MI 49080; tel. 616/685–1645; FAX. 616/685–2105; Nancy Whitley, Executive Director

MINNESOTA

Community Hospice, 323 South Minnesota, Crookston, MN 56716; tel. 218/281–9478; Thomas C. Lenertz, Administrator

Coram Hospice, 1355 Mendota Heights Road, Suite 240, Mendota Heights, MN 55120; tel. 612/452–5600; Deborah Meyer, Administrator

Crossroads Community Hospice, 404 Fountain Street, Albert Lea, MN 56007; tel. 507/377–6385; Shelley Doran, Administrator

Douglas County PHNS Hospice, 725 Elm Street, Suite 1200, Alexandria, MN 56308; tel. 320/763–6018; FAX. 320/763–4127; Mark Lundin, RN

Faibault Area Hospice, 631 Southeast First Street, Faribault, MN 55021; tel. 507/334–6451; James N. Wolf, Administrator

Fairview Hospice, 2450 26th Avenue South, Minneapolis, MN 55406; tel. 612/728–2380; Mark Enger

Faribault County Area Hospice, 519 S. Galbraith St., Box 160, Blue Earth, MN 56013; tel. 507/526–3273; FAX. 507/526–3621; Janet Johansen, Administrator

First Care Hospice, 900 Hilligoss Blvd, Southeast, Fosston, MN 56542; tel. 218/435–1133; David S. Hubbard, Administrator

Healtheast Hospice, 69 West Exchange Street, St. Paul, MN 55102; tel. 612/232–3312; Kathleen M. Lucas, Administrator

HealthSpan Home Care and Hospice, 2750 Arthur Street, Roseville, MN 55113; tel. 612/628–4200; FAX. 612/628–9074; Cletis Hoffer, Acting Administrator

HomeCaring and Hospice, 11685 Lake Boulevard, N., Chicago City, MN 55013; tel. 612/257–8850; FAX. 612/257–8852; Karen Brohaugh, Manager

Homecaring Hospice, 11685 Lake Boulevard North, Chicago City, MN 55013; tel. 612/257–8402; Scott Wordelman, Administrator

HomeHealth Partnership, 320 E. Main Street, Crosby, MN 56441; tel. 218/546–2311; Thomas F. Reek, Administrator

Hospice of Luverne Community Hospital, 305 East Luverne Street, P.O. Box 1019, Luverne, MN 56156; tel. 507/283–2321; Gerald E. Curl, Administrator

Hospice of Murray County, 2129 Broadway, Slayton, MN 56172; tel. 507/836–8114; Holly Miller, Administrator

Hospice of the Lakes, 8100 34th Avenue, S., P.O. Box 1309, Minneapolis, MN 55440–1309; tel. 612/883–6877; FAX. 612/883–6883; Paul Brat, Administrator

Hospice of the Twin Cities Inc., 7100 Northland Circle, Suite 205, Brooklyn Park, MN 55428; tel. 612/531–2424; FAX. 612/531–2422; Lisa Abicht–Swensen, Administrator

Hospice of the Twin Cities, Inc., d/b/a Hospice of the Valley, 7100 Northland Circle, Suite 205, Minneapolis, MN 55428; tel. 800/364–2478; FAX. 612/531–2422; Lisa Abicht Swensen, Administrator

Hospice Partners, Inc., 6750 France Ave. South, Suite 290, Edina, MN 55435; tel. 612/920–0035; Roberta S. Cline, President and CEO

Immanuel St. Joseph's Hospice, 501 Holly Lane, Suite 10, Mankato, MN 56601; tel. 507/345–2618; Jerome Crest, Administrator

Lake City Area Hospice, 904 South Lakeshore Drive, Lake City, MN 55041; tel. 612/345–3321; Mark Rinehardt, Administrator

Lakeland Hospice, Inc., 715 S. Pebble Lake Road, P.O. Box 824, Fergus Falls, MN 56538; tel. 218/736–7885; FAX. 218/736–2231; Delores Peterson, Director

Lakeview Hospice, 927 West Churchill Street, Stillwater, MN 55082; tel. 612/430–3320; Geri Wagner

Litchfield Area Hospice, 218 N. Holcombe, Litchfield, MN 55355; tel. 320/693–7367; Michael P. Boyle, Administrator

Long Prairie Memorial Hospice, 20 Ninth Street Southeast, Long Prairie, MN 56347; tel. 320/732–7287; Rona Bless, Administrator

Mayo Hospice Program, 200 First Street, S.W., Rochester, MN 55905; tel. 507/284–4002; FAX. 507/284–0161; Margaret Gillard, RN, Program Coordinator

Mayo Hospice Program, 200 First Street, S.W., Rochester, MN 55905; tel. 507/284–4002; FAX. 507/284–0161; Ann Bartlett, RN, Coordinator

North Country Hospice, 3525 Pine Ridge Avenue, NW, Bemidji, MN 56601; tel. 218/759–5665; Jessica Conrad, Administrator

North Memorial Medical Center Hospice, 3500 France Avenue North, Suite 101, Robbinsdale, MN 55422; tel. 612/520–3900; FAX. 612/520–3920; Rosemary Moneta, Administrator

Northern Communities Hospice, 715 Delmore Drive, Roseau, MN 56751; tel. 218/463–3211; David Hagen, Administrator

Northfield Hospice, 801 W. First Street, Northfield, MN 55057; tel. 507/645–3386; Kendall C. Bank, Administrator

Owatonna Area Hospice, 903 South Oak Ave., Owatonna, MN 55060; tel. 507/455–7628; Marlene H. Breckner, Administrator

Pine to Prairie Hospice Inc., 201 Hillestad Avenue North, Fosston, MN 56542; tel. 218/435–2017; FAX. 218/435–6909; Bev Leier, Administrator

Pope County Hospice, 10 Fourth Avenue, Southeast, Glenwood, MN 56334; tel. 320/634–4521; Douglas Reker, Administrator

Prairie Home Hospice, 300 South Bruce, Marshall, MN 56258; tel. 507/537–9247; Lynn Yueill, Administrator

Prairie Home Hospice, Inc., 300 South Bruce, Marshall, MN 56258; tel. 507/537–9247; FAX. 507/537–9258; Lynn Yueill, Administrative Director

Red Wing Hospice, 434 West Fourth, Suite 200, Red Wing, MN 55066; tel. 612/385–3410; FAX. 612/385–3414; Beth Krehbiel, Director

Red Wing Hospice, 434 West Fourth Street, Suite 200, Red Wing, MN 55066; tel. 612/385–3410; FAX. 612/385–3414; Beth Krehbiel, Director

Renville County Hospice, 611 East Fairview Ave., Olivia, MN 56277; tel. 320/523–3427; Dean Slagter, Administrator

Rice Hospice Program, 301 Becker Ave., SW, Willmar, MN 56201; tel. 320/231–4450; Margaret Sietsema, Administrator

Ridgeview Hospice, 240 Willow Street, Tyler, MN 56178; tel. 507/247–5521; James A. Rotert, Administrator

Seasons Hospice, 5650 Weatherhill Rd, SW, Rochester, MN 55902; tel. 507/281–3029; Doris Oehlke, Administrator

Shamrock Seasons Hospice, 1242 Whitewater Avenue, St. Charles, MN 55972; tel. 507/932–3949; FAX. 507/932–5125; Doris Oehlke, Administrator

St. Cloud Hospital Hospice, 48 North 29 Avenue, Suite 15, St. Cloud, MN 56303; tel. 320/259–9375; FAX. 320/240–3266; Kathleen Murphy, Care Center Director

St. Joseph's Home Care and Hospice, 303 Kingwood Street, Brainerd, MN 56401; tel. 218/828–7444; FAX. 218/828–7579; Jani Wiebolt, Administrator

St. Luke's Hospice Duluth, 915 East First Street, Duluth, MN 55805; tel. 218/722–6220; Lynette Rauscher, Administrator

St. Mary's Medical Center Hospice, 404 East Fourth Street, Duluth, MN 55805; tel. 218/726–4020; FAX. 218/725–7249; Bonnie King, Hospice Nurse Manager

St. Mary's Medical Center Hospice, 404 East Fourth Street, Duluth, MN 55805; tel. 218/726–4020; Joanne Hagen, Administrator

St. Michael's Hospice, 425 North Elm Street, Sauk Centre, MN 56378; tel. 320/352–2221; Karen Rau, Administrator

The Hospice of Morrison County, 815 Southeast Second Street, Little Falls, MN 56345; tel. 320/632–1144; Dianne Jackson, Administrator

Waseca Area Hospice, Inc., 204 Second Street, N.W., P.O. Box 94, Waseca, MN 56093; tel. 507/835–8983; FAX. 507/835–8737; Linda Grant, Director

Winona Area Hospice Services, 825 Mankato Avenue, Suite 111, Winona, MN 55987; tel. 507/457–4468; Charles R. Haugh, Administrator

Zumbrota Area Hospice Program, 383 West Fifth Street, Zumbrota, MN 55992; tel. 507/732–5131; Daniel E. Will, Administrator

MISSISSIPPI

Appletree Hospice, Inc., 521 Main Street, Suite U–Four, Natchez, MS 39121; tel. 601/446–8000; Linda L. Carlton, Administrator

Baptist Home Care and Hospice, 703A North Lamar, Oxford, MS 38655; tel. 601/234–8553; FAX. 601/236–1459; Sharon Johnson, RN, Director

Baptist Memorial Regional Home Health Care, Inc., Magnolia Health Services and Hospice North, 396 Southcrest Court Five, Southhaven, MS 38671; tel. 601/349–1394; Bill Caldwell, Administrator

Community Hospice of Mississippi, Inc., d/b/a Gulf Coast, 154 Porter Avenue, Biloxi, MS 39530; tel. 601/435–1948; L. Jim Anthis, Ph.D., Administrator

Delta Area Hospice Care, Ltd., 522 Arnold Avenue, P.O. Box 5915, Greenville, MS 38704–5915; tel. 601/335–7040; FAX. 601/335–7048; Gloria Blakely, Administrator

Friendship Hospice of Natchez, Inc., 133 Jeff Davis Boulevard, Natchez, MS 39120; tel. 601/445–0307; Cynthia Paul, Administrator

Hospice Care, 202 South Washington Avenue, Greenville, MS 38701; tel. 601/335–4298; FAX. 601/335–4292; Emry Oxford, Administrator

Hospice Care Foundation, P.O. Box 351, Crystal Springs, MS 39059; tel. 601/892–3324; FAX. 601/892–3350; Kathy Welch, RN, Patient Care Coordinator

Hospice Care Foundation, P.O. Box 378, Edwards, MS 39066; tel. 601/852–4818; FAX. 601/852–4899; Dora Harris, RN, Patient Care Coordinator

Hospice Care Foundation, # 7 Lakeland Circle, Jackson, MS 39216; tel. 601/713–3077; FAX. 601/713–3075; Suzanne Houck, RN, Patient Care Coordinator

Hospice Care Foundation, P.O. Box 727, Magee, MS 39111; tel. 601/849–3025; FAX. 601/713–3074; Karen Walker, RN, Patient Care Coordinator

Hospice Care Foundation, P.O. Box 128, Marks, MS 38646; tel. 601/326–8181; FAX. 601/326–8180; Carol Gurley, RN, Patient Care Coordinator

Hospice Care Foundation, P.O. Box 18427, Natchez, MS 39120; tel. 601/442–3070; FAX. 601/442–3074; Kathy Renfrow, RN, Patient Care Coordinator

Hospice Care Foundation, P.O. Box 119, Philadelphia, MS 39350; tel. 601/389–2006; FAX. 601/389–2202; Marcie Crapps, RN, Patient Care Coordinator

Hospice Care Foundation, P.O. Box 2056, Vicksburg, MS 39180; tel. 601/638–3070; FAX. 601/634–6010; Tiffany Walker, RN, Patient Care Coordinator

Hospice Care Foundation, P.O. Box 667, Winona, MS ; tel. 601/283–4911; FAX. 601/283–4992; Shirley Sullivan, RN, Patient Care Coordinator

Hospice Care Foundation, P.O. Box 1152, Yazoo City, MS ; tel. 601/746–8481; FAX. 601/746–8497; Helen Hanna, RN, Patient Care Coordinator

Hospice Care Foundation, Inc., P.O. Box 2056, Vicksburg, MS 39181; tel. 601/638–3070; FAX. 601/634–6010; Tiffany Walker, RN, Coordinator

Hospice Care Foundation, Inc., 317–B Highland Avenue, Natchez, MS 39120; tel. 601/442–3070; Janie Calloway, Office Manager

Hospice Ministries, 450 Towne Center Blvd., Ridgeland, MS 39157; tel. 601/898–1053; FAX. 601/898–4320; John Fletcher, Executive Director

Hospice Ministries, 450 Towne Center Boulevard, Ridgeland, MS 39157; tel. 601/898–1053; FAX. 601/898–4320; Ronda Marks, Market – Development Director

Hospice of Central Mississippi, Inc., 224 South First Street, Brookhaven, MS 39601; tel. 601/835–1020; FAX. 601/835–1063; Jean Berch, Branch Director

Section C

Hospice of Light, 4341 Gautier & Vancleave Road, Suite Four, Gautier, MS 39553; tel. 228/497-2400; FAX. 228/497-9035; Laurie H. Grady, Nurse Coordinator

Hospice of North Mississippi, 103 South Main, Sardis, MS 38666; tel. 601/487-1827; FAX. 601/487-1060; Kim Hadskey, RN, Patient Care Coordinator

Hospice of North Mississippi Clarksdale, 130 Desota Avenue, P.O. Box 1490, Clarksdale, MS 38614; tel. 601/624-8144; Jessie Rudd, RN, Patient Care Coordinator

Hospice of North Mississippi, Inc., 619 East Lee Street, Sardis, MS 38666; tel. 601/487-1827; FAX. 601/487-1060; Renee Wright, Administrator

Hospice-North Mississippi Medical Center, 600 West Main, Tupelo, MS 38801; tel. 601/841-3612; Laura Kelley, Administrator

HospiceCare, 187 Stateline Road, Suite 10, P.O. Box 744, Southaven, MS 38671; tel. 601/280-8200; FAX. 601/280-8202; Linda Crum, Administrator

Quality Hospice of Gulf Coast, Inc., P.O. Box 549, Biloxi, MS 39533; tel. 228/374-4434; FAX. 228/436-3679; Patricia Hiers, Administrator

Rush Hospital Hospice, Highway 15, Route Nine, Box 28, Philadelphia, MS 39350; tel. 601/656-8388; Ken Boyette, Patient Care Coordinator, Supervisor

Sta-Home Hospice, 105 North Van Buren, Carthage, MS 39051; tel. 800/898-1159; Claudette Hathcock, Administrator

Sta-Home Hospice, 1620 24th Avenue, Meridan, MS 39305; tel. 601/485-8489; FAX. 601/693-7457; Debbie Emerson, RN, Patient Care Coordinator

MISSOURI

American Heartland Hospice, 7555 South Lindbergh Boulevard, St. Louis, MO 63125; tel. 314/894-8189; FAX. 314/894-7334; Susan O'Kane, Administrator

Barr Hospice and Palliative Care, 2701 Rockcreek Parkway, Suite 200, Kansas City, MO 64117; tel. 816/471-2218; FAX. 816/471-2434; Linda Ault, Administrator

Bates County Hospice, 501 North Orange, Butler, MO 64730; tel. 816/679-6108; George Taylor, Administrator

Beacon of Hope Hospice, Inc., 4191 Crescent Drive, Suite A, St. Louis, MO 63129; tel. 314/894-1000; FAX. 314/894-8389; Dawn Counts, Executive Director

BLC Home Care Services, Inc, 9890 Clayton Road, St. Louis, MO 63124; tel. 314/953-1840; FAX. 314/953-1812; Ruth N. Castellano, Director Operations Administration

Community Hospice of America-Central, 3600 I-70 Drive, S.E., Suite H, Columbia, MO 65201; tel. 573/443-8360; FAX. 573/499-4601; Jean Yokley, RN, Patient Care Supervisor

Community Hospice of America-South Central, 101 East Second Street, Mountain Grove, MO 65711; tel. 417/926-4146; FAX. 417/926-6123; Jo Moody, Administrator

Community Hospice of America-Tri Lakes, 1756 Bee Creek Road, Suite G, Branson, MO 65616; tel. 417/335-2004; FAX. 417/335-2012; Janet Gard, Program Director

Comprehealth, Inc., Hospice Services Division, 2001 South Hanley Road, Suite 450, St. Louis, MO 63144; tel. 314/781-2800; FAX. 314/781-4844; Carolynn Ingerson-Hoffman, Interim Administrator

Hands of Hope Hospice, 801 Faraon Street, St. Joseph, MO 64501; tel. 816/271-7190; FAX. 816/271-7672; Jim Pierce, Resource Specialist

Harrison County Hospice, Highway 136 West, P.O. Box 425, Bethany, MO 64424; tel. 816/425-6324; FAX. 816/425-7642; Nola Martz, RN, B.S.N., Administrator

HealthCare, Inc., 3215 LeMone Industrial Boulevard, Suite 100, Columbia, MO 65201-8245; tel. 314/449-0206; Rebecca Rastkar, RN, Administrator

Heart of America Hospice, L.C., 9229 Ward Parkway, Suite 350, Kansas City, MO 64114; tel. 816/333-1980; FAX. 816/333-2421; Jacquelyn Tuohig, Executive Director

HomeCare of Mid-Missouri Hospice, 102 West Reed Street, Moberly, MO 65270; tel. 660/263-1517; FAX. 660/263-8033; Cherie Aird, LCW, Hospice Director

Hospice Care of Mid-America, 3100 Broadway, Suite 300, Kansas City, MO 64111-2415; tel. 816/931-4276; FAX. 816/931-9147; Patricia Walters, Interim Director

Hospice of Integrated Health Services, 10910 Kennerly Road, St. Louis, MO 63128; tel. 314/849-3324; FAX. 314/842-9077; Gay Carlstrom, Administrator

Hospice of Southwest Missouri, 1465 E. Primrose, Suite A, Springfield, MO 65804; tel. 417/882-0453; FAX. 417/882-1245; Richard Williams, President and CEO

HospiceCare of Visiting Nurse Association, 531 B South Union, Springfield, MO 65802; tel. 417/866-4374; FAX. 417/866-0233; Suzanne Dollar, Administrator

HospiceCare, Inc., P.O Box 1000, Mineral Area College, Park Hills, MO 63601; tel. 573/431-0162; Fred McDaniel, Administrator

Howard County Home Health and Hospice, 600 W. Morrison, Suite 10, Fayette, MO 65248; tel. 660/248-1780; FAX. 660/248-3347; Serese M. Wiehardt, Administrator

Kansas City Hospice, 1625 West 92nd Street, Kansas City, MO 64114; tel. 816/363-2600; FAX. 816/523-0068; Elaine McIntosh, President

Lake Ozark Area Home Health and Hospice, A Department of Pulaski County Health Department, 602 Commercial Street, P.O. Box 498, Crocker, MO 65452; tel. 314/736-2219; FAX. 314/736-5847; Beth Hutton, Administrator

Meramec Hospice, 200 North Main, Rolla, MO 65401; tel. 314/364-2425; FAX. 314/364-1575; Shirley Rutz, Administrator

Missouri River Hospice, 1440 Aaron Court, Jefferson City, MO 65101; tel. 314/635-5643; FAX. 314/635-6552; Jackie Adkinson, Director

Pershing Hospice, 225 West Hayden, Marceline, MO 64658; tel. 816/376-2222; FAX. 816/376-2432; Rose Ayers, Director

Pike County Home Health Agency and Hospice, 19 North Main Cross, Bowling Green, MO 63334; tel. 573/324-2111; FAX. 573/324-5517; Lisa Pitzer, RN, Patient Care Coordinator

St. Clair County Hospice, 101 Hospital Drive, Osceola, MO 64776; tel. 417/646-8157; FAX. 417/646-8159; Candice J. Baker, Administrator

Twin Lakes Hospice, Inc., 304 Main, P.O. Box 211, Warsaw, MO 65355; tel. 816/438-9700; FAX. 816/438-6404; Sandra Spooner, Administrator

Visiting Nurse Association Hospice Care, 9450 Manchester Road, Suite 206, St. Louis, MO 63119; tel. 314/918-7171; Susan Pettit, Administrator

VNA of Southeast Missouri Hospice, 100 East Harrison, Kennett, MO 63857; tel. 573/888-5892; FAX. 573/888-0538; Teresa McCulloch, Administrator

MONTANA

Anaconda Pintler Hospice of Community Hospital of Anaconda, 200 Main Street, P.O. Box 596, Anaconda, MT 59711; tel. 406/563-5422; FAX. 406/563-4245; Alice Cortright, Director

Big Sky Hospice, 3021 Sixth Avenue, N., Suite 205, Billings, MT 59103-1049; tel. 406/248-7442; FAX. 406/248-2572; Bernice Bjertness, RN, M.N., Director

Highlands Hospice, 507 Centennial Avenue, Butte, MT 59701; tel. 406/723-5780; FAX. 406/723-9595; Virginia Mick, Director

Hospice of Powell County, 310 Milwaukee Avenue, P.O. Box 808, Deer Lodge, MT 59722; tel. 406/846-3975; Nora E. Meier, Office Manager

Kootenai Volunteer Hospice, P.O. Box 781, Libby, MT 59923; tel. 406/293-3923; Theresa Schneider, Director

Lake County Home Health Hospice, 107 6th Ave SW, Ronan, MT 59864

Partners in Home Care Home Health & Hospice, Inc., 500 North Higgins, Suite 201, Missoula, MT 59801; tel. 406/728-8848; Kate Bratches, RN, Hospice Manager

Partners in Home Care, Inc. (Residential Hospice), 10450 West Mullan Road, Missoula, MT 59802; tel. 406/728-8848; FAX. 406/721-0256; Kate Bratches, Hospice Patient Care Coordinator

Pondera Hospice, 300 North Virginia, Suite 305, Conrad, MT 59425; tel. 406/278-5566; FAX. 406/278-5569

Stillwater Big Sky Hospice Team, 350 West Pike Avenue, P.O. Box 1109, Columbus, MT 59019; tel. 406/322-5100; FAX. 406/322-5737; Sharon Marten, Chairperson

Westmont Home Health Services Inc Hospice, 2525 Colonial Drive, Helena, MT 59601; tel. 406/443-4140; Lynn Zavalney, RN, M.A., Hospice Coordinator

NEBRASKA

Alegent Health Home Care & Hospice, 10802 Farnam Dr., Suite 150, Omaha, NE 68154; tel. 402/898-8000; Denise McNitt, Operations Director

Central Plains Hospice, 300 E. 12th Street, P.O. Box 108, Cozad, NE 69130; tel. 308/784-4630; FAX. 308/784-4691; Rita Johnson, RN, Administrator

Chadron Community Hospital Hospice, 821 Morehead Street, Chadron, NE 69337; tel. 308/432-5586; Harold Krueger, Jr., Administrator

Custer County Hospice, 145 Memorial Dr., P.O. Box 250, Broken Bow, NE 68822-0250; tel. 308/872-6891; FAX. 308/872-6116; Michael Steckler, Administrator

Fremont Area Medical Center Hospice, 450 East 23rd, Fremont, NE 68025; tel. 402/727-3373; Vincent O'Connor, Jr., Administrator

Hospice Care of Nebraska LLC, 1600 South 70th Street, Suite 201, Lincoln, NE 68506; tel. 402/488-1363; FAX. 402/488-5976; Marcia Cederdahl, RN, CRNH, B.S. Ed.

Hospice of Tabitha, 4720 Randolph Street, Lincoln, NE 68510; tel. 402/483-7671; Roberta Daughterty, RN, Administrator

Hospice Preferred Choice, 407 South 27th Ave., Suite 200, Omaha, NE 68131; tel. 402/346-2273; Barbara Coppa, Administrator

Mary Lanning Memorial Hospital Hospice, 715 North St. Joseph Ave., Hastings, NE 68901; tel. 402/461-5161; FAX. 402/461-5091; Marcia Donley, Hospice Coordinator

Memorial Health Center Hospice, 1103 Illinois, Sidney, NE 69162; tel. 308/256-5825; Susan Peters, Administrator

St. Francis Hospice, 430 N. Monitor Street, West Point, NE 68788-1595; tel. 402/372-2404; FAX. 402/372-2360; Ronald Briggs, Administrator

St. Joe Ville Homecare and Hospice, 2305 South Tenth Street, Omaha, NE 68108-1154; tel. 402/345-3333; FAX. 402/345-3826; Carolyn Geiger, Director

Syracuse Hospice, 1527 Midland Street, Syracuse, NE 68446; tel. 402/269-2011; Ron Anderson, Administrator

Visiting Nurse Association of the Midlands, 8710 F Street, Omaha, NE 68127; tel. 402/342-5566; FAX. 402/342-5587; Janice Treml, Administrator

NEVADA

Family Home Hospice, 1701 West Charleston, Suite 150, P.O. Box 15645, Las Vegas, NV 89114-5645; tel. 702/383-0887; FAX. 702/383-9826; Nan Johnson, Clinical Manager

Hospice of Integrated Health Service, 5670 West Flamingo, Suite D, Las Vegas, NV 89103; tel. 702/361-6801; Karen Maxfield, Administrator

Hospice of Northern Nevada, 1155 West Fourth Street, Suite 122, Reno, NV 89503; tel. 702/789-3081; FAX. 702/789-3909; Marva Slight, Director

Hospice of Northern Nevada-Carson City, 809 North Plaza, Carson City, NV 89701; tel. 702/884-8900; FAX. 702/884-8909; Tawny Liddell, Administrator

Nathan Adelson Hospice, 4141 South Swenson Street, Las Vegas, NV 89119; tel. 702/733-0320; FAX. 702/796-3195; Betsy Peirson-Gornet, Chief Executive Officer

Safe Harbor Hospice, Inc., 3910 Pecos McLeod Building, Las Vegas, NV 89121; tel. 702/435-7660; Kristy Thompson, Executive Director

Vista Care, Inc., 1830 East Sahara Avenue, Suite 102, Las Vegas, NV 89104; tel. 702/734-0307; FAX. 702/734-0310; Diana Hopkins-Weiss, Administrator

Washoe Home Care Connection, 780 Kuenzli, Suite 200, Reno, NV 89502; tel. 775/982-5860; FAX. 775/982-5795; Michael Girard, Administrator

NEW HAMPSHIRE

Community Health and Hospice, Inc., 780 North Main Street, P.O. Box 578, Laconia, NH 03247-0578; tel. 603/524-8444; FAX. 603/524-8217; Polly Clough, Administrator

Concord Regional VNA-Hospice, 250 Pleasant Street, P.O. Box 1797, Concord, NH 03302; tel. 603/224-4093; FAX. 603/228-7359; Mary B. DeVeau, President and CEO

Connecticut Valley Home Care Inc., 958 John Stark Highway, Newport, NH 03773; tel. 603/543-0164; Lynn Holland, RN

Elliot Home Care and Hospice, 25 South Maple Street, Manchester, NH 03103; tel. 603/628-4430; FAX. 603/622-4800; Diane LaBossiere, M.S.W.

HCS – Home Healthcare, Hospice and Community Services, Inc., 69L Island Street, P.O. Box 564, Keene, NH 03431; tel. 603/352-2253; FAX. 603/358-3904; Lois Hopkins, Hospice Program Coordinator

Home Health and Hospice Care, 22 Prospect Street, Nashua, NH 03060; tel. 603/882-2941; FAX. 603/883-1515; Gail Spera, Administrator

Hospice America of New Hampshire, 169 Daniel Webster Highway, Suite 14, Meredith, NH 03253; tel. 603/279-4700; FAX. 603/279-1370; Linda Roberts, Administrator

Hospice America of New Hampshire, Inc., 169 D W Highway, Suite 14, Meredith, NH 03253; tel. 603/279-4700; FAX. 603/279-1370; Linda Roberts, Administrator

Hospice at HCS, 69L Island Street, P.O. Box 564, Keene, NH 03431; tel. 603/352-2253; Lois Hopkins, Administrator

Lake Sunapee Home Care and Hospice, 290 County Road, P.O. Box 2209, New London, NH 03257; tel. 603/526-4077; FAX. 603/526-4272; Barbara Boulton, RN, Hospice Patient Care Coordinator

North Country Home Health Agency, 536 Cottage Street, Littleton, NH 03561; tel. 603/444-5317; FAX. 603/444-0980; Cheryl Guinan, Administrator

Optima Health Visiting Nurse Services, VNA Hospice, 1850 Elm Street, Manchester, NH 03104; tel. 603/622-3781; FAX. 603/641-4074; Jane Clough, Director, Hospice

Pemi-Baker Home Health Agency, 258 Highland Street, Plymouth, NH 03264; tel. 603/536-2232; Elaine Vieira, Administrator

Portsmouth Regional Visiting Nurses Association and Hospice, 127 Parrott Avenue, Portsmouth, NH 03801; tel. 603/436-0815; FAX. 603/431-5457; Joan P. Nickell, President

Rochester Visiting Nurse Association, Inc., 89 Charles Street, Rochester, NH 03867; tel. 603/332-1133; FAX. 603/332-9223; Marianne Gagne, Hospice Coordinator

Rockingham VNA and Hospice, 137 Epping Road, Exeter, NH 03833; tel. 603/772-2981; FAX. 603/772-0931; Ann Blair, , RN, Hospice Director

Rural District VNA Inc., 36 Charles Street, Farmington, NH 03835; tel. 603/755-2202; FAX. 603/755-3760; Sue Nash, Director

Seacoast Hospice, 10 Hampton Road, Exeter, NH 03833; tel. 603/778-7391; FAX. 603/772-7692; Susan Cole, Administrator

Souhegan Nursing Association Inc., 24 North River Road, Milford, NH 03055; tel. 603/673-3460; FAX. 603/673-0159; Liane Schubring, Executive Director

Squamscott Visiting Nurse and Hospice Care, 113 New Rochester Rd., Suite 4, Dover, NH 03820; tel. 603/742-7921; FAX. 603/742-3835; Mary Jo Sceggell, Administrator

Tri-Area Visiting Nurse Association, Inc., 301 High Street, Somersworth, NH 03878-1800; tel. 603/692-2112; FAX. 603/692-9940; Susan Karmeris, President and CEO

Tri-Area VNA Hospice, 301 High Street, Somersworth, NH 03878; tel. 603/692-2112; FAX. 603/692-9940; Maxine Lacy, Clinical Services Coordinator

Visiting Nurse and Hospice Care of Northern Carroll County, Route 16, P.O. Box 432, North Conway, NH 03818; tel. 603/447-6766; FAX. 603/447-6370; Kathleen T. Sheehan, Administrator

VNA - Hospice of Southern Carroll County and Vicinity, South Main Street, Wolfeboro, NH 03894; tel. 603/569-2729; FAX. 603/569-2409; Carol C. Tubman, RN, CRNH

NEW JERSEY

Atlantic City Medical Center Hospice, 1406 Doughty Road, Pleasantville, NJ 08232; tel. 609/272-2424; FAX. 609/272-2414; Diana Ciurczak, Director

Atlantic Home Care and Hospice, 33 Bleeker Street, Millburn, NJ 07041

Center for Hope Hospice, Inc., 176 Hussar Street, Linden, NJ 07036; tel. 908/486-0700; FAX. 908/486-2450; Margaret J. Coloney, President

Compassionate Care Hospice, 1373 Broad Street, Suite 304, Clifton, NJ 07013; tel. 201/916-1400; FAX. 201/916-0066; Judith Grey, M.P.H., RNC, Regional Director of New Jersey

Garden State Hospice, 27 Daniel Road West, Fairfield, NJ 07932; tel. 973/882-6100; FAX. 973/882-5599; Nora Nicolosi, RN, Administrator

Holy Redeemer Hospice, 1801 Route Nine North, P.O. Box 280A, Swainton, NJ 08210; tel. 609/465-2082; FAX. 609/465-6185; Arleen Moffitt, ACSW

Hospice at Bergen Community Health Care, 400 Old Hook Road, Westwood, NJ 07675-3131; tel. 201/358-2900; FAX. 201/358-0836; Patricia Hutzelman, RN, Hospice Coordinator

Hospice of New Jersey, 400 Broadacres Drive, Fourth Floor, Bloomfield, NJ 07003; tel. 973/893-0818; FAX. 973/893-0828; Michelle Steganelli, Administrator

Hospice of VNA of Northern New Jersey, 38 Elm Street, Morristown, NJ 07960; tel. 973/539-1216; FAX. 973/539-3352; Marcia Lutschewitz, Hospice Patient Care Manager

Hospice Program of Bayonne VNA, 325 Broadway, Bayonne, NJ 07002; tel. 201/339-2500; FAX. 201/339-1255; Barbara Halosz, RN, B.S.N., Coordinator

HospiceCare of South Jersey, Inc., 2848 South Delsea Drive, Vineland, NJ 08360; tel. 609/794-1515; FAX. 609/691-7660; Yvonne Crouch, Executive Director

Jerseycare Hospice, 50 Newark Avenue, Suite 101, Belleville, NJ 07109

Karen Ann Quinlan Center of Hope Hospice, 99 Sparta Avenue, Newton, NJ 07860; tel. 973/383-0115; FAX. 973/383-6889; Mary Guler, Executive Director

Lighthouse Hospice, A Division of Alternative Healthcare System, 4 Executive Campus, 771 Cuthbert Blvd, Cherry Hill, NJ 08002; tel. 609/661-5600; FAX. 609/661-5650; Susan Curry, Director

Meridian Hospice, 615 Hope Road, Building Four, 2nd Floor, Eatontown, NJ 07724; tel. 908/741-1797; Kerri A. Johnston, Hospice Administrator

Passaic Valley Hospice, VHS of New Jersey, Inc., 783 Riverview Drive, Totowa, NJ 07511; tel. 973/256-4636; FAX. 973/256-6778; Elizabeth Geoghegan

Somerset Valley Visiting Nurse Association Hospice, 586 East Main Street, Bridgewater, NJ 08807; tel. 908/725-9355; FAX. 908/725-1033; Anita G. Busch, B.S.N., CRNH, Hospice Manager

The Center for Hospice Care, Inc., An affiliate of the Saint Barnabas Health Care System, Three High Street, Glen Ridge, NJ 07028-2306; tel. 973/429-0300; FAX. 973/429-9274; Lorraine M. Sciara, Executive Director

Trinity Hospice, 150 Ninth Street, Runnemede, NJ 08078; tel. 609/939-9000; FAX. 609/939-9010; Barbara Billington, Director

Trinity Hospice, Formerly Greater Monmouth VNA Hospice, 111 Union Avenue, Long Branch, NJ 07740; tel. 908/229-0816; FAX. 908/229-0561; Debra Cox, RN, CRNH, Hospice Supervisor

Unity Hospice, 17 Academy Street, Newark, NJ 07102; tel. 201/596-9661; FAX. 201/596-9664; Terry M. Copeland, Administrator

Visiting Nurse and Health Services Hospice, 354 Union Avenue, P.O. Box 170, Elizabeth, NJ 07208; tel. 908/352-5694; FAX. 908/352-9216; Shirley Altman, Hospice Administrator

Visiting Nurse Association Somerset Hills Hospice, 12 Olcott Avenue, Bernardsville, NJ 07924; tel. 908/766-0180; FAX. 908/766-2268; Barbara Fox, Hospice Coordinator

VNA of Central Jersey Hospice, 35 Broad Street, Keyport, NJ 07735; tel. 732/888-4100; Barbara Buczny, Director of Hospice

West Essex Hospice, 799 Bloomfield Avenue, Verona, NJ 07044; tel. 973/857-7300; FAX. 973/857-3433; Thomas Koester, President and CEO

NEW MEXICO

Alamogordo Home Care-Hospice, 505 11th Street, Alamogordo, NM 88310; tel. 800/617-3555; FAX. 505/437-2399; Pat Raub, Administrator

Alternative Home Health Care Service, 1118 National Avenue, Las Vegas, NM 87701; tel. 800/296-1538; FAX. 505/425-7682; Maxine E. Gonzales, Administrator

Caring Unlimited Hospice Services, 200 South Third, Raton, NM 87740; tel. 505/445-5113; Jo Ellen Ferguson, Administrator

Carlsbad Hospice, Inc., 1003 West Riverside Drive, P.O. Drawer PP, Carlsbad, NM 88220; tel. 505/885-8257; Nancy Flanagan, Administrator

Esperanza Home Health Care Hospice, Inc., Highway 518 Buena Vista, P.O. Box 270, Mora, NM 87732; tel. 505/387-2215; Josephine P. Garcia

Helping Hand Hospice, 615 South Second, Tucumcari, NM 88401; tel. 505/461-0099; Diana Beck, Administrator

Hospice of Artesia, 702 North 13th, Artesia, NM 88210; tel. 505/748-3333; FAX. 505/746-8918; Beverly Morehead, RN, Director

Hospice Services, Inc., 90l East Bender, P.O. Box 249, Hobbs, NM 88241; tel. 800/658-6844; FAX. 505/393-3985; Brenda Chambers

Los Alamos Visiting Nurse Service Hospice, 901 18th Street, Suite 203, Los Alamos, NM 87544; tel. 505/662-2525; FAX. 505/662-7093; Deborah Simon, Director

Mesilla Valley Hospice, Inc., 299 East Montana Avenue, Las Cruces, NM 88005; tel. 505/523-4700; FAX. 505/527-2204; Margaret Connealy, Executive Director

Mountain Home Health Hospice, 630 Paseo del Pueblo Sur, Suite 180, Taos, NM 87571; tel. 505/758-4786; Patricia Heinen, Administrator

Northwest New Mexico Hospice, 608 Reilly Avenue, P.O. Box 3336, Farmington, NM 87499; tel. 505/327-0301; FAX. 505/325-2477; Debra Lowe, Administrator

Presbyterian Hospice, P.O. Box 26666, Albuquerque, NM 87125; tel. 505/291-5656; FAX. 505/291-2055; Jane Bergquist, RN

Quality Continuum Hospice, 2625 Pennsylvania NE, Suite 225, Albuquerque, NM 87110; tel. 505/881-3737; FAX. 505/881-4319; Sheila D. Hipper, Administrator

Roswell Hospice Home Care, 600 North Richardson, Roswell, NM 88201; tel. 505/623-5887; FAX. 505/624-8566; Nancy Smith, Program Director

Sandia Hospice, 5740 Osuna, N.E., Albuquerque, NM 87109; tel. 505/888-0095; FAX. 505/888-2025; Catherine A. Esterheld, Executive Director

St. Anthony's Hospice, 1008 Douglas Avenue, P.O. Box 1170, Las Vegas, NM 87701; tel. 505/425-3353; Beatrice R. Velasquez, Administrator

Staff Builders Services, Inc., 826 Camino De Monte Rey, P.O. Box 23448, Santa Fe, NM 87502; tel. 505/983-5408; Pamela Brunsell, RN, Administrator

The Hospice Center, 1422 Paseo De Peralta, Santa Fe, NM 87501; tel. 505/988-2211; FAX. 505/986-1833; Barbara Elder Owas, RN, Executive Director

Victory Home Health Hospice, 624 University, P.O. Box 670, Las Vegas, NM 87701; tel. 505/454-0499; FAX. 505/425-9105; Maria Luisa Padilla, Administrator

VistaCare Family Hospice, 8804 Washington NE, Suite C, Albuquerque, NM 87113; tel. 505/792-4430; FAX. 505/821-5449; Ronald Sanders, Administrator

VNS Health Services, Inc., 706 La Joya, N.E., Espanola, NM 87532; tel. 505/753-2284; FAX. 505/756-2179; Beatrice Sceery, Manager, Home Health, Hospice

NEW YORK

Caring Community Hospice of Cortland, 4281 North Homer Avenue, Cortland, NY 13045; tel. 607/753-9105; FAX. 607/758-7668; Mary Beach, Director

Catskill Area Hospice Palliative Care, Inc., 542 Main Street, Oneonta, NY 13820; tel. 607/432-6773; FAX. 607/432-7741; Lesley Deleski, Executive Director

Christian Nursing Hospice, Inc., d/b/a Little House Residence, 110 Lake Avenue South, Suite 33, Nesconset, NY 11767; tel. 516/265-5300; FAX. 516/265-5789; Camille Harlow, Executive Director

Comstock Hospice Care Network, 1225 West State Street, Olean, NY 14760; tel. 716/372-2106; FAX. 716/372-4635; Kathleen Mack, Hospice Director

East End Hospice, Inc., 1111 Riverhead Road, P.O. Box 1048, Westhampton B, NY 11978; tel. 516/288-8400; FAX. 512/288-8492; Priscilla Ruffin, Executive Director

Herkimer County Hospice, 301 N. Washington Street, Herkimer, NY 13350; tel. 315/867-1317; FAX. 315/867-1371; Sue Campagna, Administrator

High Peaks Hospice, Inc., P.O. Box 840, Trudeau Road, Saranac Lake, NY 12983; tel. 518/891-0606; FAX. 518/891-0657; Maureen Sayles, Executive Director

Hospice Buffalo, Inc., 225 Como Park Boulevard, Cheektowaga, NY 14227-1480; tel. 716/686-1900; FAX. 716/686-8181; J. Donald Schumacher, Psy.D., President and CEO

Hospice Care in Westchester and Putnam, an Affiliate of VNA of Hudson Valley, 100 South Bedford Road, Mount Kisco, NY 10549; tel. 914/666-4228; FAX. 914/666-0378; Cornelia Schimert, Director

Hospice Care Network, Merchants Concourse, Westbury, NY 11590; tel. 516/832-7100; FAX. 516/832-7160; Maureen Hinkleman, Chief Executive Officer

Hospice Care, Inc., 4277 Middlesettlement Road, New Hartford, NY 13413; tel. 315/735-6484; FAX. 315/735-8545; Wes Case, Executive Director

Section C

Hospice Family Care, 550 East Main Street, Batavia, NY 14020; tel. 716/343–7596; FAX. 716/343–7629; Deborah Schafer, Operating Director

Hospice of Central New York, 990 7th North Street, Liverpool, NY 13088; tel. 315/634–1100; FAX. 315/634–1122; Peter Moberg–Sarver, President and CEO

Hospice of Chenango County, Inc., 21 Hayes Street, Norwich, NY 13815; tel. 607/334–3556; FAX. 607/334–3688; Laurie Vogel, Executive Director

Hospice of Greater New York, 6323 Seventh Avenue, Brooklyn, NY 11220; tel. 718/921–7900; FAX. 718/921–0752; Abby Gordon, Administrator

Hospice of Jefferson County, Inc., 425 Washington Street, Watertown, NY 13601; tel. 315/788–7323; FAX. 315/785–9932; Frances Calabrese, Executive Director

Hospice of North Country, 386 Rugar Street, Plattsburgh, NY 12901–2306; tel. 518/561–8465; FAX. 518/561–3182; Sarah Anderson, Executive Director

Hospice of Orleans County, 13996 Route 31 West, Albion, NY 14411; tel. 716/589–0809; Mary Ann Fisher, Executive Director

Hospice of Rochester and Hospice of Wayne and Seneca Counties, 49 Stone Street, Rochester, NY 14604; tel. 716/325–1880; FAX. 716/325–7678; Barbara Quinlan, RN, BSN, Director of Palliative Care Services

Hospice of St. Lawrence Valley, Inc., 6439 State Highway 56, Potsdam, NY 13676; tel. 315/265–3105; FAX. 315/265–0323; Brian Gardam, Executive Director

Hospice of the Finger Lakes, 25 William Street, Auburn, NY 13021; tel. 315/255–2733; FAX. 315/252–9080; Theresa Kenny Kline, Executive Director

Hospice Serving Dutchess and Ulster Counties Inc., 70 South Hamilton Street, Poughkeepsie, NY 12601; tel. 914/485–2273; Benjamin Wallace, Jr., Chief Executive Officer

Hospice VNSW/WPHC, Inc., d/b/a Hospice of Westchester, 95 South Broadway, 4th Floor, The Esplanade, White Plains, NY 10601; tel. 914/682–1484; FAX. 914/682–9425; George Battern, Executive Director

HospiceCare of Tompkins County, Inc., 172 East King Road, Ithaca, NY 14850; tel. 607/272–0212; FAX. 607/272–0237; Nina K. Miller, Executive Director

Jansen Memorial Hospice/Home Nursing Association of Westchester, 69 Main Street, Tuckahoe, NY 10707; tel. 914/961–2818; FAX. 914/961–8654; Lucille D. Winton, Director

Livingston County Hospice, 2 Livingston County Campus, Mount Morris, NY 14510; tel. 716/243–7290; FAX. 716/243–7287; Cheryl Pletcher, Administrator

Mercy Hospice, St. Pius X Service Center, 1220 Front Street, Uniondale, NY 11553; tel. 516/485–3060; FAX. 516/485–1007; Edith Miozzi, Executive Director

Mountain Valley Hospice, 73 North Main Street, Gloversville, NY 12078; tel. 518/725–4545; FAX. 518/725–8066; Nancy Dowd, Executive Director

Niagara Hospice, Inc., 4675 Sunset Drive, Lockport, NY 14094; tel. 716/439–4417; FAX. 716/439–6035; Carol E. Gettings, M.S., Executive Director

Ontario–Yates Hospice, A Program of Finger Lakes VNS, 756 Pre–Emption Road, Geneva, NY 14456; tel. 315/781–0071; FAX. 315/789–7042; Bonnie Hollenbeck, Administrator

Oswego County Hospice, Oswego County Health Department, 70 Bunner Street, Oswego, NY 13126; tel. 315/349–8259; FAX. 315/349–8269; Steven D. Rose, Administrator

Pax Christi Hospice, 355 Bard Avenue, Staten Island, NY 10310; tel. 718/876–1022; Patricia Farrington, Executive Director

Southern Tier Hospice, Inc., 244 West Water Street, Elmira, NY 14901; tel. 607/734–1570; FAX. 607/734–1902; Mary Ann Starbuck, Executive Director

The Community Hospice, Inc, 315 S. Manning Boulevard, Albany, NY 12208; tel. 518/525–1686; FAX. 515/525–1562; Philip G. Di Sorbo, Executive Director

United Hospice of Rockland, 18 Thiells–Mount Ivy Road, Pomona, NY 10970; tel. 914/354–5100; FAX. 914/354–2128; Amy Stern, Executive Director

Visiting Nurse Hospice, 2180 Empire Boulevard, Webster, NY 14580; tel. 716/787–8315; FAX. 716/787–9726; Dorothy Chilton, Administrator

VNS Hospice of Suffolk, 505 Main Street, Northport, NY 11768; tel. 516/261–7200; FAX. 516/261–1985; Joyce Palmier, RN, BSN, Director, Patient Services

VNSNY Hospice Care, 1250 Broadway, New York, NY 10001; tel. 212/290–3888; FAX. 212/290–3933; Eileen Hanley, RN, M.B.A., Administrator

NORTH CAROLINA

3HC Home Health and Hospice Care, Inc, 1614 Harbour Drive, Wilmington, NC 28401; tel. 919/799–0018; FAX. 910/452–3198

3HC Home Health and Hospice Care, Inc, 1023 Beaman Street, Clinton, NC 28323–2343; tel. 910/592–1421; FAX. 910/592–7392

3HC Home Health and Hospice Care, Inc, 100 Westlake Road, Fayetteville, NC 28302; tel. 910/860–7858; FAX. 910/860–8279

3HC Home Health and Hospice Care, Inc, 2402 Wayne Memorial Drive, P.O. Box 88, Goldsboro, NC 27533; tel. 919/753–1386; FAX. 919/731–4985

3HC Home Health and Hospice Care, Inc, 503 Bowman Gary Drive Suite C, P.O. Box 795, Greensville, NC 27858; tel. 252/758–8212; FAX. 252/758–1384

3HC Home Health and Hospice Care, Inc, 744 Airport Road, P.O. Box 1396, Kinston, NC 28503; tel. 252/527–9561; FAX. 252/527–6617

3HC Home Health and Hospice Care, Inc, 1004 Jenkins Avenue, P.O. Box 190, Maysville, NC 28555–0190; tel. 910/743–2800; FAX. 910/743–2321

3HC Home Health and Hospice Care, Inc, 8208 Brownleigh Drive, P.O. Box 31804, Raleigh, NC 27622–1804; tel. 919/789–4241; FAX. 919/789–4245

3HC Home Health and Hospice Care, Inc, 15 Noble Street, P.O. Box 1524, Smithfield, NC 27577–9300; tel. 919/934–0664; FAX. 919/934–9046

Albemarle Home Care, 103 Charles Street, P.O. Box 189, Hertford, NC 27907; tel. 919/426–5488; Paula Vanhorn, Administrator

Albemarle Home Care, Highway 168, P.O. Box 189, Currituck, NC 27907; tel. 919/232–2026; Victoria Rentrop, Administrator

Albemarle Hospice, 400 S. Road Street, P.O. Box 189, Elizabeth City, NC 27907–0189; tel. 800/478–0477; FAX. 919/338–4364; Ronda Wentz, Director

Angel Home Health and Hospice, 170 Church Street, Franklin, NC 28713; tel. 828/369–4206; FAX. 828/369–4400; Sandy Smith, RN, MPH, Director

Caldwell County Hospice, Inc., 902 Kirkwood Street, N.W., Lenoir, NC 28645; tel. 828/754–0101; FAX. 828/757–3335; Cathy S. Simmons, Executive Director

Cape Fear Valley Home Health and Hospice, 3418 Village Drive, Fayetteville, NC 28304; tel. 910/609–6740; FAX. 919/609–6573; Pat Pruitt, M.S.N., Director

Cashiers Home Health, Highway 107 South, 59 Hospital Road, Sylva, NC 28779; tel. 704/586–7410

Center of Living Home Health and Hospice, d/b/a Center of Living Homecare, 416 Vision Drive, P.O. Box 9, Asheboro, NC 27204–0009; tel. 336/672–9300; FAX. 336/672–0868; Billie Vuncannon, President and CEO

Community Home Care and Hospice, 1643 Owen Drive, Fayetteville, NC 28304; tel. 910/323–9816; FAX. 910/484–6724; Robert Reed, Chief Executive Officer

Comprehensive Home Health Care, 3840 Henderson Drive, Jacksonville, NC 28456; tel. 910/346–4800; Linda Powers, Patient Care Manager

Comprehensive Home Health Care, 819 Jefferson Street, P.O. Box 366, Whiteville, NC 28472; tel. 910/642–5808; FAX. 910/640–1374; Sheila Faulk, Director

Comprehensive Home Health Care, 1120 Ocean Highway W, P.O. Box 200, Supply, NC 28462; tel. 910/754–8133; FAX. 910/754–2096; Crystal Floyd, RN, Director

Comprehensive Home Health Care and Comprehensive Hospice, Inc., 101 South Craig Street, P.O. Drawer 2540, Elizabethtown, NC 28337; tel. 910/862–8538; Sherry Hester, Director, Office Operations

Comprehensive Home Health Care–Hospice, 3311 Burnt Mill Drive, Wilmington, NC 28403; tel. 910/251–8111; FAX. 910/343–1218; Debra Nixion Jones, Patient Case Manager

Comprehensive Home Health Care/Comprehensive Hospice, 1800 Skibo Road, Suite 228, Fayetteville, NC 28303; tel. 910/864–8411; Gwendolyn Harrell, Regional Director

Craven County Home Health–Hospice Agency, 2818 Neuse Boulevard, P.O. Drawer 12610, New Bern, NC 28561; tel. 919/636–4930; FAX. 919/636–5301

Davie County Health Department and Home Health Agency, Hospice of Davie, 210 Hospital Street, P.O. Box 848, Mocksville, NC 27028; tel. 336/751–8770; FAX. 336/751–0335; Joseph B. Bass, Jr., M.S.W., Health Director

Duplin Home Care and Hospice Inc., 234 Smith Chapel Road, Mt. Olive, NC 28365; tel. 910/296–0819; FAX. 910/296–0482; Rhonda Lucus, RN, Hospice Coordinator

Duplin Home Care and Hospice, Inc., 101 East Main Street, Wallace, NC 28466; tel. 919/285–1100; FAX. 910/285–1172; Glenda Kenan, RN, Home Health Coordinator

Duplin Home Care and Hospice, Inc., 238 Smith Chapel Road, Mount Olive, NC 28365

Edgecombe County HomeCare and Hospice, 2909 North Main Street, Tarboro, NC 27886; tel. 919/641–7558; FAX. 919/641–7004; Jessie Worthington, Hospice Program Director

FirstHealth Hospice, Five Aviemore Drive, Pinehurst, NC 28374; tel. 910/215–6000; FAX. 910/215–6032; Carole White, Director

Four Seasons Hospice, 802 Old Spartanburg Highway, P.O. Box 2395, Hendersonville, NC 28739; tel. 704/692–6178; FAX. 704/692–2365; Barbara W. Stewart, Executive Director

Good Shepherd Home Health and Hospice Agency, Inc., P.O. Box 465, Hayesville, NC 28904; tel. 704/389–6311; Ruth Kraushaar, RN, Hospice Coordinator

Good Shepherd Home Health and Hospice Agency, Inc., P.O. Box 465, Hayesville, NC 28904; tel. 704/389–6311; FAX. 704/389–9584; Ruth Onsum, Hospice Coordinator

Home Health and Hospice Care, Inc., 1004 Jenkins Avenue, P.O. Box 190, Maysville, NC 28555; tel. 919/743–2800; Janet Haddow–Green, Administrator

Home Health and Hospice Care, Inc., 1023 Beaman Street, P.O. Box 852, Clinton, NC 28328; tel. 800/695–4442; FAX. 910/592–7392; Richard Stone, Administrator

Home Health and Hospice Care, Inc., 2305 Wellington Drive, Suite G, P.O. Box 3673, Wilson, NC 27895–3673; tel. 252/291–4400; FAX. 252/237–4396; Carolyn Yowell, Marketing Director

Home Health and Hospice Care, Inc., 15 Noble Street, P.O. Box 1524, Smithfield, NC 27577–9300; tel. 919/934–0664; FAX. 919/934–9046; Phil Adams Administrator

Home Health and Hospice Care, Inc., 2419 East Ash Street, Suite Four and Five, Goldsboro, NC 27532; tel. 919/735–1386; FAX. 919/731–4985; Jim Wall, Administrator

Home Health and Hospice Care, Inc., 907A Southeast Second Street, Snow Hill, NC 28580

Home Health and Hospice Care, Inc., d/b/a Kitty Askins Hospice Center, 107 Handley Park Court, Goldsboro, NC 27534; tel. 919/735–5887; FAX. 919/735–5948; Marie K. Abrams, RN

Home Health and Hospice of Halifax, 1229 Julian R. Allsbrook Road, Roanoke Rapids, NC 27870; tel. 252/308–0700; FAX. 252/537–1872; Sheila Alford, RN, Home Care Director

Home Health and Hospice of Person County, 325 South Morgan Street, Roxboro, NC 27573; tel. 910/597–2542; FAX. 910/597–3367; Joyce Franke, Administrator

Home Health of NC, Inc., 120 Providence Road, Suite 200, Chapel Hill, NC 27514; tel. 919/401–3000; FAX. 919/402–1952; Linda Sutherin, Executive Director

Home Technology Health Care–Hospice of Tar Heel, U.S. Highway 11 South and Chapman Road, P.O. Box 1645, Greenville, NC 27835; tel. 919/758–4622; FAX. 919/758–7006; Patti Lotts, Executive Director

HomeHealth and Hospice Care Inc., 744 Airport Road, P.O. Box 1396, Kinston, NC 28503; tel. 919/527–9561; Ann Harrison, Clinical Director

Hospice at Charlotte, Inc., 1420 East Seventh Street, Charlotte, NC 28204; tel. 704/375–0100; FAX. 704/375–8623; Janet Fortner, President

Hospice at Greensboro–Beacon Place, 2502 Summit Avenue, Greensboro, NC 27405; tel. 336/621–5301; FAX. 336/375–2348; Pat Gibbons, BSN, Nurse Manager

Hospice Home, 918 Chapel Hill Road, Burlington, NC 27215; tel. 336/513–4460; FAX. 336/513–4471; Judy Bowman, Manager
Hospice of Alamance–Caswell, 730 Hermitage Road, P.O. Box 2122, Burlington, NC 27216; tel. 336/538–8040; FAX. 336/538–8049; Jim Higgins, Executive Director
Hospice of Alexander County, Inc., 50 Lucy Echerd Lane, Taylorsville, NC 28681; tel. 704/632–5026; FAX. 704/632–3707; Ruth Jarrell, Executive Director
Hospice of Alleghany, P.O. Box 1278, Sparta, NC 28675; tel. 910/373–8018; Wanda Branch, Administrator
Hospice of Ashe, 392 Highway 16–88 South, Jefferson, NC 28640; tel. 336/246–6443; FAX. 336/246–8504; Trinja Merit, Administrator
Hospice of Avery County, Inc., 351 West Mitchell Street, P.O. Box 1357, Newland, NC 28657; tel. 704/733–0663; FAX. 704/733–0375; Sharon Cole, RN, Patient Care Coordinator
Hospice of Burke County, Inc., 1721 Eron Road, Valdese, NC 28690; tel. 704/879–1601; FAX. 704/879–3500; Marlene Jernigan, Business Manager
Hospice of Cabarrus County, Inc., 1060 Diploma Place, S.W., P.O. Box 1235, Concord, NC 28026–1235; tel. 704/788–9434; FAX. 704/788–6013; Shirley McDowell, Executive Director
Hospice of Carteret County, Inc., P.O. Box 1818, Morehead City, NC 28557; tel. 919/247–2808; Ruth Yearick–Jones, Administrator
Hospice of Catawba Valley, Inc., 263 Third Avenue, N.W., Hickory, NC 28601; tel. 828/328–4200; FAX. 828/328–3031; David B. Clarke, Executive Director
Hospice of Chatham County, Inc., 200 East Street, P.O. Box 1077, Pittsboro, NC 27312; tel. 919/542–5545; FAX. 919/542–6232; Susan H. Balfour, RN, Executive Director
Hospice of Cleveland County, Inc., 951 Wendover Heights Drive, Shelby, NC 28150; tel. 704/487–4677; FAX. 704/481–8050; Myra McGinnis Hamrick, Executive Director
Hospice of Cumberland County, 235 N. McPherson Church Road, Suite 210, Fayetteville, NC 28303–4403; tel. 910/860–7178; FAX. 910/860–1660; Stacy Pendarvis, M.S.W., Hospice Coordinator
Hospice of Davidson County, Inc., 524 South State Street, P.O. Box 1941, Lexington, NC 27293–1941; tel. 336/248–6185; FAX. 336/248–4574; Gary Drake, Executive Director
Hospice of Gaston County, Inc., d/b/a Gaston Hospice, 258 East Garrison Boulevard, P.O. Box 3984, Gastonia, NC 28054; tel. 704/861–8405; FAX. 704/865–0590; Lee Bucci, Executive Director
Hospice of Harnett County, Inc., 111A North Ellis Avenue, Dunn, NC 28339; tel. 910/892–1213; FAX. 910/892–1229; Grace E. Tart, Administrator
Hospice of Iredell County, Inc., 153 North Main Street, Suite One, Mooresville, NC 28115; tel. 704/663–0051; FAX. 704/872–1810; Judy Snowden, Executive Director
Hospice of Lee County, Inc., P.O. Box 1181, Sanford, NC 27331–1181; tel. 919/774–4169; FAX. 919/774–6348; Janet MacLaren Scovil, Executive Director
Hospice of Lincoln County, Inc., 107 North Cedar Street, Lincolnton, NC 28093–1526; tel. 704/732–6146; FAX. 704/736–0264; Leslie Barlowe, RN, Assistant Director of Patient Services
Hospice of Macon County, Inc., 208 Roller Mill Road, P.O. Box 1594, Franklin, NC 28734; tel. 828/369–6641; FAX. 828/349–4161; Sandra L. Deke, Executive Director
Hospice of McDowell County, Inc., 116 North Logan Street, Marion, NC 28752; tel. 828/652–1318; FAX. 828/659–1631; Cinda Laws, Patient Care Coordinator
Hospice of Mitchell County, P.O. Box 38, Hospital Drive, Spruce Pine, NC 28777; tel. 828/765–5677; FAX. 828/765–5680; Clarice Turner, Executive Director
Hospice of Pamlico County, Inc., 13628 North Carolina Highway 55, Alliance, NC 28509; tel. 919/745–5171; Diane McDaniel, Executive Director
Hospice of Polk County, Inc., 421 North Trade Street, Tryon, NC 28782; tel. 828/859–2270; FAX. 828/859–2731; Jean H. Eckert, Administrator
Hospice of Rockingham County, Inc., 2150 North Carolina 65, P.O. Box 281, Wentworth, NC 27375; tel. 336/427–9022; FAX. 336/427–9030; Rowera P. Sewell, Director

Hospice of Rutherford County, Inc., 374 Hudlow Road, P.O. Box 336, Forest City, NC 28043; tel. 704/245–0095; FAX. 704/248–1035; Rita Burch, Executive Director
Hospice of Scotland County, 600 South Main Street, Suite F, P.O. Box 1033, Laurinburg, NC 28353; tel. 910/276–7176; FAX. 910/277–1941; Linda McQueen, RN, Executive Director
Hospice of Stanly County, Inc., 960 North First Street, Albemarle, NC 28001–3350; tel. 704/983–4216; FAX. 704/983–6662; Elvin T. Henry, Executive Director
Hospice of Stokes County, Highway 8 and 89, P.O. Box 10, Danbury, NC 27016; tel. 336/593–5309; FAX. 336/593–5354; Margaret Arey, Executive Director
Hospice of Surry County, Inc., 688 N. North Bridge Street, Elkin, NC 28621; tel. 910/526–2650; FAX. 910/526–2383; Laney Johnson, Executive Director
Hospice of the Carolina Foothills, Inc., 421 North Tryon Street, Tryon, NC 28782; tel. 704/859–2270; FAX. 704/859–2731; Jean H. Eckert, Executive Director
Hospice of the Piedmont/Care Connection, 1801 Westchester Drive, High Point, NC 27262; tel. 910/889–8446; FAX. 910/889–3450; Leslie Kalinowski, President
Hospice of Union County, Inc., 700 West Roosevelt Boulevard, Monroe, NC 28110; tel. 704/292–2100; FAX. 704/292–2190; Charlene C. Broome, Executive Director
Hospice of Wake County, Inc., 130 St. Mary's Street, 4th Floor, Raleigh, NC 27612; tel. 919/828–1998; Karolyn H. Kaye, Executive Director
Hospice of Watauga, 136 Furman Road, Suite #4, Boone, NC 28607; tel. 828/265–3926; FAX. 828/264–2125; Trinja Merit, Administrator
Hospice of Winston–Salem/Forsyth County, Inc., 1100 –C South Stratford Road, Winston–Salem, NC 27103–3212; tel. 910/768–3972; FAX. 910/659–0461; Jo Ann Davis, Chief Executive Officer
Hospice of Yancey County, Inc, 314 West Main Street, P.O. Box 471, Burnsville, NC 28714; tel. 828/682–9675; FAX. 828/682–4713; Donna Messenger, Executive Director
Lower Cape Fear Hospice, Inc., 725 – A Wellington Avenue, Wilmington, NC 28401; tel. 910/772–5444; FAX. 910/762–9146; Eloise Thomas, Executive Director
Lower Cape Fear Hospice, Inc., 121 West Main Street, P.O. Box 636, Whiteville, NC 28472; tel. 919/642–9051; Barbara Godwin, RN, BSN, Patient Care Coordinator
Lower Cape Fear Hospice, Inc., 2507–B North Marine Boulevard, Jacksonville, NC 28540; tel. 919/347–6266; FAX. 910/347–9279; Lori Griffin, Patient Care Coordinator
Lower Cape Fear Hospice, Inc., 112 Pine Street, P.O. Box 1926, Shallotte, NC 28459; tel. 910/754–5356; FAX. 910/754–5351; Jeff Hickey, Director, Operations
Lower Cape Fear Hospice, Inc., 103 North Morehead Street, Elizabethtown, NC 28337; tel. 910/862–3111; FAX. 910/862–3129; Anita Graber, Community Relations Specialist
Madison Home Care and Hospice, P.O. Box 909, 170 Carl Eller Road, Mars Hill, NC 28754; tel. 704/689–3491; FAX. 704/689–3496; John H. Estes, Executive Director
Mountain Area Hospice, Inc., 85 Zillicoa Street, P.O. Box 16, Asheville, NC 28802; tel. 704/255–0231; FAX. 704/255–2880; Kit Cosgrove, Associate Director
Northern Hospital Home Care and Hospice, 933 Old Rockford Street, P.O. Box 1605, Mount Airy, NC 27030; tel. 336/719–7434; FAX. 336/719–7435; Kitty Horton, Executive Director
Onslow Home Health and Hospice, 612 College Street, Jacksonville, NC 28540; tel. 910/577–6660; FAX. 910/577–6636; Shirley P. Moore, RN, Director
Pemberton Hospice, 106 North Main Street, P.O. Box 3069, Pembroke, NC 28372; tel. 910/521–5550; FAX. 910/521–3335; RD Locklear II, Administrator
Richmond County Hospice, Inc., 230 South Lawrence Street, P.O. Box 2136, Rockingham, NC 28380; tel. 910/997–4464; FAX. 910/997–4484; Lydia P. Talbert, CRNH, Patient Care Coordinator
Roanoke Home Care, 210 West Liberty Street, Williamston, NC 27892; tel. 919/792–5899; Barbara Owens, Nursing Director

Roanoke Home Care–Hospice, 408 Bridge Street, P.O. Box 238, Columbia, NC 27925; tel. 919/796–2681; FAX. 919/796–0818; Barbara Owens, RN, Director, Nursing
Roanoke Home Care–Hospice, 198 North Carolina Highway 45 North, Plymouth, NC 27962; tel. 800/842–8275; FAX. 252/791–3158; Phyllis McCombs, Referrals and Intake
Roanoke–Chowan Hospice, Inc., 521 Myers Street, P.O. Box 272, Ahoskie, NC 27910; tel. 919/332–3392; FAX. 919/332–5705; Brenda Hoggard, Director
St. Joseph of the Pines Home Health Agency, 117 Wortham Street, P.O. Box 974, Wadesboro, NC 28170; tel. 704/694–5992; Kathy Appenzeller, Director, Daily Operations
St. Joseph of the Pines Home Health Agency, 404 North Main Street, Troy, NC 27371; tel. 910/572–4962; FAX. 910/572–5010; Barbara Smith, CRNH Coordinator
St. Joseph of the Pines Home Health Agency, 336 South Main Street, P.O. Box 879, Raeford, NC 28376; tel. 910/875–8198; FAX. 910/875–8862; Ronda Pickler, Administrator
Staff Builders, 112 Broad Street, Oxford, NC 27565
Staff Builders/MedVisit Home Health and Hospice, 1937NC Highway 39, Louisburg, NC 27549; tel. 800/377–5827; FAX. 919/496–7052; Sherry Watson, Administrator
Triangle Hospice, 1804 Martin Luther King, Jr. Parkway, Suite 112, Durham, NC 27707; tel. 919/490–8480; FAX. 919/493–0242; Lucy Worth, Executive Director
Triangle Hospice at the Meadowlands, 1001 Corporate Drive, Hillsborough, NC 27278; tel. 919/644–0764; FAX. 919/644–0932; Jerome Schiro, RN, M.N., Director
Wenover, 953 Wendover Heights Drive, Shelby, NC 28150; tel. 704/487–7018; FAX. 704/487–7028; Myra McGinnis Hamrick, Executive Director
Wilson Home Care, Inc., d/b/a Hometown Hospice, 1705 South Tarboro Street, Wilson, NC 27893; tel. 252/237–4333; FAX. 252/237–1125; Gail Brewer, RN, M.P.H., Home Care Manager
Yadkin County Home Health/Hospice Agency, 217 East Willow Street, P.O. Box 457, Yadkinville, NC 27055; tel. 910/679–4207; FAX. 910/679–6358; Jackie Harrell, Nursing Supervisor

NORTH DAKOTA
Heart of America Hospice, 800 S. Main, Rugby, ND 58368; tel. 701/776–5261; FAX. 701/776–5448; Duane Jerde, Administrator
Heartland Hospice, 30 W. 7th Street, Dickinson, ND 58601; tel. 701/264–4251; FAX. 701/264–4809; Greg Hanson, President and CEO
Hospice of the Red River Valley, 702 28th Avenue, N., Fargo, ND 58102; tel. 701/237–4629; FAX. 701/280–9069; Susan J. Fuglie, Executive Director
Mercy Hospice, 1031 7th Street, Devils Lake, ND 58301; tel. 701/662–2131; FAX. 701/662–4862; Marlene Krein, Administrator
Riveredge Hospice of St. Francis, 415 Oak Street, Breckenridge, ND 56520; tel. 218/643–7594; FAX. 218/643–7502; Cindy Splichal, Director
St. Alexius Hospice, 1120 E. Main Street, Bismarck, ND 58501; tel. 701/224–7888; FAX. 701/224–7811; Barbara Schweitzer, Administrator
Trinity Hospice, 1015 South Broadway, Minot, ND 58701; tel. 701/857–5083; FAX. 701/857–5079; Marilyn Bader, Administrator
United Community Hospice, 407 3rd Street NE, Minot, ND 58701; tel. 701/857–2499; FAX. 701/857–2565; Mary O'Clair, Hospice Care Nurse

OHIO
Allen Hospice, 5700 Southwyck Boulevard, Suite 111, Toledo, OH 43614; tel. 419/867–4655; FAX. 419/865–1601; Jane Wilcox, RN, Executive Director
Aultman Hospice Program, 4510 Dressler Road, N.W., Canton, OH 44718; tel. 216/493–3344; FAX. 330/493–8637; Kathy Cummings, RN, Program Coordinator
Bridge Home Health and Hospice, 1900 South Main Street, Findlay, OH 45840; tel. 419/423–5351; FAX. 419/423–8967; Karen Mallett, Vice President, Home Care Services
Columbia Mercy Medical Center Hospice, 1445 Harrison Avenue, N.W., Suite 201, Canton, OH 44708; tel. 330/489–6855; FAX. 330/489–6868; Ken Wasiniak, L.I.S.W., Hospice Manager
Community Hospice, 2609 Franklin Boulevard, Cleveland, OH 44113; tel. 216/363–2397; FAX. 216/363–2284; Cheryl Carrino, Patient Care Coordinator

Section C

Community Hospice Care, 182 St. Francis Avenue, Rear Suite, Tiffin, OH 44883; tel. 419/447-4040; FAX. 419/447-4657; Rebecca S. Shank, Executive Director

Geauga County Visiting Nurse Service and Hospice, 13221 Ravenna Road, Chardon, OH 44024; tel. 216/286-9461; Patricia Huels, RN, Director, Patient Services

Holmes County Hospice, 931 Wooster Road, Millersburg, OH 44654; tel. 330/674-5035; FAX. 330/674-2528; Rita Miller, RN, B.S.N., Director

HomeCare Matters Home Health & Hospice, 629 N. Sandusky Street, Third Floor, Bucyrus, OH 44820; tel. 419/562-2001; FAX. 419/562-2803; Bert Maglott, RN, Executive Director

Hospice and Health Services of Fairfield County, 1111 East Main Street, Lancaster, OH 43130; tel. 740/654-7077; FAX. 740/654-6321; Paul D. Longenecker, RN, MBA, Executive Director

Hospice Homecare, 92 Northwoods Boulevard, #A, Columbus, OH 43235; tel. 614/781-1444; FAX. 614/781-1450; Belinda R. Shaw, RN, Clinical Manager

Hospice of Alliance VNA, 2367 West State Street, Alliance, OH 44601; tel. 330/821-7055; Lin Severs, M.S.N., Executive Director

Hospice of Appalachia, 282 East State Street, P.O. Box 768, Athens, OH 45701; tel. 614/592-3493; FAX. 614/594-5591; Carol May, Director

Hospice of Care Corporation, 831 South Street, Chardon, OH 44024; tel. 216/338-6628; FAX. 216/286-7662; Elizabeth A. Petersen, RN, Vice President, Operations

Hospice of Cincinnati, Inc., 4310 Cooper Road, Cincinnati, OH 45242; tel. 513/891-7700; FAX. 513/792-6980; Leigh Gerdsen, RN, Director

Hospice of Columbus, 181 South Washington Boulevard, Columbus, OH 43215; tel. 614/645-6471; FAX. 614/645-5895; Larry L. Miracle, Director

Hospice of Coshocton County, Inc., 230 South Fourth, P.O. Box 1284, Coshocton, OH 43812; tel. 740/622-7311; FAX. 740/622-7310; Barbara Brooks-Emmons, Director

Hospice of Darke County, Inc., 122 West Martz Street, Greenville, OH 45331; tel. 937/548-2999; FAX. 937/548-7144; Katie Wehri, Executive Director

Hospice of Dayton, Inc., 324 Wilmington Avenue, Dayton, OH 45420; tel. 513/256-4490; Linda Koeppen, President and CEO

Hospice of Guernsey, Inc., 1401 Campbell Avenue, P.O. Box 1165, Cambridge, OH 43725; tel. 740/432-7440; FAX. 740/432-7424; Patricia Howell-Vaughn, RN, Administrator

Hospice of Henry County, 104 East Washington, Suite 302, Napoleon, OH 43545; tel. 419/599-5545; FAX. 419/599-1714

Hospice of Knox County, 302 East High Street, Mount Vernon, OH 43050; tel. 740/397-5188; FAX. 740/397-5189; Melanie Richardson, Executive Director

Hospice of Medina County, 797 North Court Street, Medina, OH 44256; tel. 330/722-4771; FAX. 330/722-5266; Patricia M. Stropko-O'Leary, Executive Director

Hospice of Miami County, Inc., P.O. Box 502, Troy, OH 45373; tel. 937/335-5191; FAX. 937/335-8841; Sidney J. Pinkus, Chief Executive Officer

Hospice of Morrow County, P.O. Box 86, 851 West Marion Road, Mount Gilead, OH 43338; tel. 419/946-9822; FAX. 419/946-9971; Frances Turner, RN, Executive Director

Hospice of North Central Ohio, Inc., 1605 County Road 1095, Ashland, OH 44805; tel. 419/281-7107; FAX. 419/281-8427; Ruth A. Lindsey, Executive Director

Hospice of Northwest Ohio, 30000 East River Road, Perrysburg, OH 43551; tel. 419/661-4001; FAX. 419/661-4015; Virginia Clifford, Executive Director

Hospice of Pickaway County, 702 Pickaway Street, Circleville, OH 43113; tel. 740/474-3525; FAX. 740/474-1832; Franklin Christmas, Business Manager

Hospice of the Valley, Inc., 5190 Market Street, Youngstown, OH 44512; tel. 330/788-1992; FAX. 330/788-1998; Kenneth O. Drees, Executive Director

Hospice of the Western Reserve, Hospice House, 300 East 185th Street, Cleveland, OH 44119; tel. 216/383-2222; FAX. 216/383-3750; David A. Simpson, Executive Director

Hospice of Tuscarawas County, Inc., 201 West Third Street, Dover, OH 44622; tel. 330/343-7605; FAX. 330/343-3542; Janie Jones, Administrator

Hospice of V.N.A., 1195-C Professional Drive, Van Wert, OH 45891; tel. 419/238-9223; FAX. 419/238-9391; Donna Grimm, President and CEO

Hospice of Visiting Nurse Service, 3358 Ridgewood Road, Akron, OH 44333; tel. 800/335-1455; FAX. 216/668-4680; Patricia Waickman, M.S.N., RN, Vice President, Hospice

Hospice of Wyandot County, 320 West Maple Street, Suite C, Upper Sandusky, OH 43351; tel. 419/294-5787; FAX. 419/294-4721; Susan Barth, RN, Executive Director

Hospice Service of Licking County, Inc., d/b/a Hospice of Central Ohio, Homecare of Central Ohio, 1435 B West Main Street, Newark, OH 43055; tel. 740/344-0311; FAX. 740/344-6577; Michele McMahon, Chief Executive Officer

Hospice, The Caring Way of Defiance County, 197-C Island Park Avenue, Defiance, OH 43512; tel. 419/784-3818; FAX. 419/782-4979; Ruthann Czartoski, Hospice Coordinator

Loving Care Hospice, Inc., 25 W. 5th Street, P.O. Box 445, London, OH 43140; tel. 740/852-7755; FAX. 740/852-7762; Richard Ford, Executive Director

M J Nursing Registry, 2534 Victory Parkway, Cincinnati, OH 45206; tel. 513/961-1000; FAX. 513/872-7550; Sharon Rachford, RN, Hospice Patient Care Coordinator

Madison County Home Health Hospice Inc., 212 North Main Street, London, OH 43140; tel. 614/852-3915; FAX. 614/852-5125; Barbara C. Anderson, Executive Director

Mercy Hospice, 7010 Rowan Hill Drive, Cincinnati, OH 45227; tel. 513/271-1440; FAX. 513/271-2405

Mount Carmel Hospice, 1144 Dublin Road, Columbus, OH 43215; tel. 614/234-0200; FAX. 614/234-0201; Mary Ann Gill, Director

New Life-Choices in LifeCare, 5255 North Abbe Road, Elyria, OH 44035; tel. 216/934-1458; FAX. 216/934-1567; Micki M. Tubbs, President and CEO

Stein Hospice Services, Inc., 1200 Sycamore Line, Sandusky, OH 44870; tel. 800/625-5269; FAX. 419/625-5761; Jan Bucholz, Executive Director

The Hospice of Staff Builders, 6100 Rockside Woods Boulevard, Suite 100, Independence, OH 44131; tel. 216/642-0202; FAX. 216/642-3273; Marion Keathley, Intake Coordinator

Tri County Hospice, Inc., One Park Centre, Suite 209, Wadsworth, OH 44281; tel. 210/336-6595; FAX. 330/334-2102; Kris Lawson, Director

Tricare Hospice, 701 Park Road, Bellefontaine, OH 43311; tel. 800/886-5936; FAX. 513/593-6355; Mary L. Mayer, Director

Valley Hospice, 380 Summit Avenue, Steubenville, OH 43952; tel. 614/264-7161; Karen Nichols, Executive Director

Valley Hospice, Inc., 380 Summit Avenue, Steubenville, OH 43952; tel. 614/283-7487; FAX. 614/283-7507; Karen Nichols, RN, B.S.N., Executive Director

Visiting Nurse Hospice and Health Care, 383 West Dussel Drive, Maumee, OH 43537; tel. 419/897-2803; FAX. 419/897-2810; Nancy Host, Executive Director

VistaCare Hospice, 2055 Reading Road, Suite 240, Cincinnati, OH 45202; tel. 513/241-9209; FAX. 513/241-4012; Beth VanNess, RN, Administrator

VNA of Cleveland Hospice, 2500 East 22nd Street, Cleveland, OH 44115; tel. 216/931-1450; FAX. 216/694-6355; Roberta Laurie, Executive Director, Hospice

OKLAHOMA

Blaine County Hospice, 401 North Clarence Nash, P.O. Box 567, Watonga, OK 73772; tel. 405/623-7414; FAX. 405/623-7412; Lisa Watson, RN

Carter Healthcare & Hospice, 4301 Will Rogers Parkway, Suite 900, Oklahoma City, OK 73108; tel. 888/951-1112; FAX. 405/947-7300; Kathi Egan, Director of Hospice

Carter Hospice Care, 828 North Porter, Norman, OK 73069; tel. 888/951-1112; Stanley F. Carter, Administrator

Carter Hospice Care, Inc., 9916A East 43rd Street, S., Tulsa, OK 74146; tel. 888/951-1112; FAX. 405/947-2718; Stanley F. Carter, Administrator

Columbia Hospice Oklahoma, 7508 North Broadway Extension, Suite 110, Oklahoma City, OK 73112; tel. 800/243-7776; FAX. 405/848-5135; Sharon Collins, RN, CRNH, Hospice Director

Community Hospice, Inc., 1400 South Broadway, Edmond, OK 73034; tel. 405/359-1948; FAX. 405/359-4913; L. Jim Anthis, Ph.D., President and CEO

Crossroads Hospice of Oklahoma, L.L.C., 10810 East 45th Street, Suite 310, Tulsa, OK 74146; tel. 918/663-3234; FAX. 918/663-3334; G. Perry Farmer, Jr., Executive Director

Eastern Oklahoma Hospice, 1301 Reynolds, Poteau, OK 74953; tel. 918/647-8235; Jody L. Shepherd, RN, Agency Director

Four Square Hospice, 223 Plaza, P.O. Box 827, Madill, OK 73446; tel. 405/795-3384; Norma Howard

Good Shepherd Hospice, 1300 Sovereign Row, Oklahoma City, OK 73108; tel. 405/943-0903; FAX. 405/943-0950; Don Greiner, Executive Director

Hospice Circle of Love, 529 N. Grand, Enid, OK 73701; tel. 405/234-2273; FAX. 405/234-1990; Cathy Graber, Director

Hospice of Central Oklahoma, 4549 Northwest 36th Street, Oklahoma City, OK 73122; tel. 405/491-0828; Aaron Barnes, President and CEO

Hospice of Green Country, Inc., 3010 South Harvard, Suite 110, Tulsa, OK 74114-6136; tel. 918/747-2273; FAX. 918/747-2573; Sue Mosher, M.S., Executive Director

Hospice of Lawton Area, Inc., 1930 Northwest Ferris Avenue, Suite 10, Lawton, OK 73505; tel. 405/248-5885; FAX. 405/355-2446; Jeff Henderson, Executive Director

Hospice of McAlester, First National Center, Suite 112, McAlester, OK 74501; tel. 918/423-3911; FAX. 918/426-6335; Vicki Schaff, Executive Director

Hospice of Oklahoma County, Inc., 4334 Northwest Expressway, Suite 106, Oklahoma City, OK 73116-1515; tel. 405/848-8884; FAX. 405/841-4899; Terry Gonsoulin, RN, Executive Director

Hospice of Ponca City, 1904 North Union, Suite 103, Ponca City, OK 74601; tel. 580/762-9102; FAX. 580/762-9111; Melody Lahann, Director

Hospice of the Heartland, 1002 South College, Tahlequah, OK 74464; tel. 918/458-3011; FAX. 918/458-3067; Deborah Huggins, Administrator

Judith Karman Hospice, Inc., 824 South Main Street, P.O. Box 818, Stillwater, OK 74076; tel. 405/377-8012; FAX. 405/624-9007; Mary Lee Warren, Executive Director

Mid-Lakes Hospice Care, 500 East Main Street, P.O. Box 728, Stigler, OK 74462; tel. 918/967-8499; FAX. 918/967-2584; John C. Neal, Administrator

Mission Hospice, Inc., 7301 North Broadway, Suite 225, Oklahoma City, OK 73116; tel. 405/848-3779; FAX. 405/848-8481; Susan Osborne, RN, Administrator

Preferred Hospice, 1200 North Walker, Suite 200, Oklahoma City, OK 73103; tel. 405/235-7674; FAX. 405/235-5478; Dean A. Deason, M.D., Director, Operations

Russell-Murray Hospice, Inc., 221 South Bickford, P.O. Box 1423, El Reno, OK 73036; tel. 405/262-3088; FAX. 405/262-3082; Cathie Sales, Administrator

The Hospice, 1303 West Broadway, Muskogee, OK 74401; tel. 918/683-1192; FAX. 918/687-0750; Jamie Bridgewater, Executive Director

Trinity Hospice LLC, Lawton, 4645 West Gore Boulevard, Lawton, OK 73505; tel. 800/422-8015; FAX. 405/250-0489; Jerry Darnell, Program Director

Trinity Hospice, LLC, 2327 E. 13th Street, Tulsa, OK 74104; tel. 918/582-8163; FAX. 918/582-8310; Ken Ellis, Administrator

Visiting Nurses Agency of Eastern Oklahoma Hospice, 220 South Main Street, Spiro, OK 74959; tel. 918/962-9491; Jim Medley, Chief Executive Officer

Visiting Nurses Agency of Eastern Oklahoma, Inc., Four Eastern Heights Shopping Center, P.O. Box 1647, Muldrow, OK 74948; tel. 918/427-1010; FAX. 918/427-7805; Janice Myers, RN, Vice-President

VistaCare Family Hospice, 4900 Richmond Square, Suite 203, Oklahoma City, OK 73118; tel. 405/843-4097; FAX. 405/843-5629; Steven L. Edwards, Executive Director

VistaCare Family Hospice, 4325 E. 51st Street, Suite 103, Tulsa, OK 74135; tel. 918/488-9477; FAX. 918/488-9506; Jo Brewer, Professional Relation Director

OREGON

Benton Hospice Service, Inc., 917 Northwest Grant Street, P.O. Box 100, Corvallis, OR 97333; tel. 541/757-9616; FAX. 541/757-1760; Judy List, Executive Director

Curry County Home/Health Hospice, 29984 Ellensburg, P.O. Box 746, Gold Beach, OR 97444; tel. 541/247-7084; FAX. 541/247-2117; Lori Kent, RN

Harney County Home Health/Hospice, 420 North Fairview, Burns, OR 97720; tel. 541/573-8360; FAX. 541/573-8389; Cheryl Keniston, Director

Hospice of Bend, 1303 Northwest Galveston, Bend, OR 97701; tel. 541/383-3910; FAX. 541/388-4221

Hospice of Redmond and Sisters, P.O. Box 1092, Redmond, OR 97756; tel. 541/548-7483; FAX. 541/548-1507; Ellen Garcia, Executive Director

Hospice of the Gorge, Inc., 13th and May Street, P.O. Box 36, Hood River, OR 97031; tel. 503/387-6449; FAX. 503/386-6700; Ina Holman, Executive Director

Kaiser Permanente, Home Health/Hospice, 2701 Northwest Vaughn Street, Suite 140, Portland, OR 97210; tel. 503/499-5200; FAX. 503/499-5200; Linda Van Buren, RN, Administrator

Klamath Hospice, Inc., 437 Main Street, Klamath Falls, OR 97601; tel. 541/882-2902; FAX. 541/883-1992; Teresa C. Pastorius

Legacy VNA Hospice, 2701 Northwest Vaughn, Suite 720, P.O. Box 3426, Portland, OR 97208; tel. 503/225-6370; FAX. 503/225-6398; Patti Berrier, Director

Lower Umpqua Hospice, 600 Ranch Road, Reedsport, OR 97467; tel. 541/271-2171; FAX. 541/271-1108; Geraldine Simms, RN, Manager

Mt. Hood Hospice, 17270 Southeast Bluff Road, P.O. Box 835, Sandy, OR 97055; tel. 503/668-5545; FAX. 503/668-7951; Lindy Blaesing, Executive Director

Pathway Hospice, Inc., 323 West Idaho Avenue, Ontario, OR 97914; tel. 541/889-0847; FAX. 541/889-0849; Betty Cooper, RN

Providence Home Services Hospice, 1235 Northeast 47th, Suite 215, 4805 Northeast Glisan (Mailing Address), Portland, OR 97213; tel. 503/331-4601; FAX. 503/215-4624; Karen Bell, Director

South Coast Hospice, 1620 Thompson Road, Coos Bay, OR 97420; tel. 541/269-2986; FAX. 541/267-0458; Linda J. Furman-Grile, Administrator

Washington County Hospice, Inc., 427 Southeast Eighth Avenue, Hillsboro, OR 97123-4519; tel. 503/648-9565; FAX. 503/648-1282; Christine Larch, Administrator

PENNSYLVANIA

Abington Memorial Hospital Home Care Hospice Program, 2510 Maryland Road, Suite 250, Willow Grove, PA 19090-0520; tel. 215/481-5800; FAX. 215/481-5850; Marilyn D. Harris, Administrator

Albert Gallatin Hospice Program, 20 Highland Park Drive, Suite 203, Uniontown, PA 15401; tel. 412/438-6660; FAX. 412/438-4468; Chris Constantine, RN, Administrator

All Care Hospice, 472 1/2 South Poplar Street, Hazelton, PA 18201; tel. 717/459-2004; Mary Ann Barletta, RN, Administrator

Berks Visiting Nurse Association, Inc., 1170 Berkshire Boulevard, Wyoming, PA 19610; tel. 610/378-0481; FAX. 610/378-9762; Lucille D. Gough, RN, President and CEO

Brookline Home Care & Hospice, 3901 South Atherton Street, State College, PA 16801; tel. 814/238-2121; FAX. 814/466-4806; Diane Good, Administrator

Centre Hospice, A Program of Centre HomeCare, Inc., 221 West High Street, Bellefonte, PA 16823-1385; tel. 814/355-2273; FAX. 814/353-9292; Molly Schwantz, Executive Director

Chandler Hall Hospice, 99 Barclay Street, Newtown, PA 18940; tel. 215/860-4000; FAX. 215/860-3458; Jane W. Fox, Executive Director

Clarion Forest VNA Hospice, P.O. Box 668, Knox, PA 16232; tel. 814/797-1492; FAX. 814/797-2698; Deborah J. Kelly, Director of Hospice

Columbia-Montour Home Hospice, Locust Court, 599 East Seventh Street, Bloomsburg, PA 17815; tel. 717/784-1723; FAX. 717/784-8512; Jane Gittler, Chief Executive Officer

Comfort Care Hospice, 205 Grandview Corporate Place, Camp Hill, PA 17011; tel. 800/255-3300; FAX. 717/766-5037; Linda L. Smith, RN, Director

Community Nurses Professional Health Services/Hospice, 99 Erie Avenue, St. Mary's, PA 15857; tel. 814/781-1415; FAX. 814/781-6987; Elizabeth A. Roberts, RN, Executive Director

Ephrata Community Home Care's Hospice Program, 169 Martin Avenue, Box 1002, Ephrata, PA 17522-1002; tel. 717/738-6599; FAX. 717/738-6343; Susan Auxier, RN, Clinical Supervisor

Family Home Hospice of the VNA of Greater Philadelphia and the VNS of New Jersey, One Winding Way, Monroe Office Center, Philadelphia, PA 19131; tel. 215/581-2046; FAX. 215/473-5047; Joanne Reifsnyder, Administrator

Family Hospice of Indiana County, a division of the V.N.A. of Indiana County, 119 Professional Center, 1265 Wayne Avenue, Indiana, PA 15701; tel. 724/463-8711; FAX. 724/463-8907; Linda E. Lutz, B.S.N., RN, Director, Hospice and Special Care Service

Family Hospice, Inc., 250 Mount Lebanon Blvd., Suite 203, Pittsburgh, PA 15234; tel. 412/572-8800; FAX. 412/572-8827; Judy Talbert, Executive Director

Forbes Hospice-Allegheny VNI Hospitals, 6655 Frankstown Avenue, Pittsburgh, PA 15206; tel. 412/665-3301; FAX. 412/665-3238; Maryanne Fello, RN, Manager

General Care Services, d/b/a Hospice of Warren County, Two Crescent Park, W., P.O. Box 68, Warren, PA 16365; tel. 814/723-2455; FAX. 814/723-1177; Elsa L. Redding, Director

Great Lakes Hospice, 300 State Street, Suite 301-H, Erie, PA 16507; tel. 814/877-6120; Debbie Burbules, Director

Guthrie Hospice, R.R. One, P.O. Box 154, Towanda, PA 18848; tel. 800/598-6155; FAX. 717/265-3570; Stacie Covey, Administrator

HealthReach Home Care and Hospice, 409 South Second Street, Harrisburg, PA 17104; tel. 717/231-6363; Janet T. Foreman, RN

Holy Family Home Health and Hospice Care, 900 West Market Street, Owigsburg, PA 17961; tel. 717/366-0990; FAX. 717/366-3735; Arlene L. Mongrain, RN, B.S., Executive Director

Holy Redeemer, Nazarath and St. Home Health Services, 12265 Townsend Road, Philadelphia, PA 19154; tel. 215/671-9200; FAX. 215/671-1950; Jerold S. Cohen, President

Home Hospice Agency of St. Francis, 131 Columbus Innerbelt, New Castle, PA 16101; tel. 412/652-8847; FAX. 412/656-0876; Susan N. Ludu, Executive Director

Home Nursing Agency/VNA Hospice Program, 201 Chestnut Avenue, P.O. Box 352, Altoona, PA 16603-0352; tel. 814/946-5411; FAX. 814/941-2482; Robert R. Packer, Chief Executive Officer

Hospice Community Care, Inc., 385 Wyoming Avenue, Kingston, PA 18704; tel. 717/288-2288; FAX. 717/288-7424; Philip Decker, President

Hospice of Central Pennsylvania, 98 South Enola Drive, P.O. Box 266, Enola, PA 17025-0266; tel. 717/732-1000; FAX. 717/732-5348; Karen M. Paris, Chief Executive Officer

Hospice of Crawford County, Inc., 448 Pine Street, Meadville, PA 16335; tel. 814/333-5403; FAX. 814/333-5407; Sister Mary Ellen Dwyer, Director

Hospice of Lancaster County, 685 Good Drive, P.O. Box 4125, Lancaster, PA 17604-4125; tel. 717/295-3900; FAX. 717/391-9582; Mary Graner, President, Executive Director

Hospice of North Penn Visiting Nurse Association, 51 Medical Campus Drive, Lansdale, PA 19446; tel. 215/855-8297; FAX. 215/855-1305; Jane Spizzirri, Hospice Coordinator

Hospice of the Delaware Valley, 527 Plymouth Road, Suite 417, Plymouth Meet, PA 19462; tel. 610/941-6700; FAX. 610/941-6440; Marcia M. Cook, Administrator

Hospice of the Visiting Nurse Association of Eastern Pennsylvania, 1510 Valley Center Parkway, Suite 200, Bethlehem, PA 18017; tel. 610/691-1100; FAX. 610/691-2271; Halyna Stigura, RN, M.S.N., Chief Executive Officer

Hospice Preferred Choice, Inc., 2400 Ardmore Boulevard, Suite 302, Pittsburgh, PA 15221; tel. 412/271-2273; FAX. 412/271-3361; Christean Dugan, Administrator

Hospice Program/VNA of Hanover and Spring Grove, 440 North Madison Street, Hanover, PA 17331; tel. 717/637-1227; FAX. 717/637-9772; Sandra L. Wojtkowiak, RN, M.S.N., Administrator

Hospice Saint John, 665 Carey Avenue, Wilkes-Barre, PA 18702; tel. 717/823-2114; FAX. 717/823-6438; W. David Keating, Administrator

Hospice Services of the VNA of York County, 218 East Market Street, York, PA 17403; tel. 717/846-9900; FAX. 717/846-1933; Marie V. Fraser, President and CEO

Hospice-The Bridge, Lewistown Hospital, 1126 West Fourth Street, Lewistown, PA 17044-1909; tel. 717/242-5000; FAX. 717/242-5009; Ruth Anne Sieber, RN, CRNH, Interim Clinical Supervisor

HospiceCare of Pittsburgh, 11 Parkway Center, Suite 275, Pittsburgh, PA 15220; tel. 412/937-8088; FAX. 412/922-9609; Fran Romito, RN, Administrator

In Home Health, Inc., 750 Holiday Drive, Foster Plaza Nine, Pittsburgh, PA 15220; tel. 412/928-2126; FAX. 412/928-2127; Margaret Timm, Director, Operations

Jefferson Hospice-Main Line, Gerhard Building, 130 South Bryn Mawr Avenue, Bryn Mawr, PA 19018; tel. 610/526-3265; Timothy P. Cousounis, Executive Director

Lee Regional Hospice, 1425 Scalp Avenue, Johnstown, PA 15904; tel. 814/262-0246; FAX. 814/262-9616; Donna L. Russian, Executive Director

Lehigh Valley Hospice, 2166 South 12th Street, Allentown, PA 18103; tel. 610/402-7400; FAX. 610/402-7382; Bonnie Kosman, M.S.N., RN, CS, Administrator

Lutheran Home Health Care Services, Hospice of the Good Shepherd, 2700 Luther Drive, Chambersburg, PA 17201; tel. 717/264-8178; FAX. 717/264-6347; Diane M. Howell, Executive Director

McKean County VNA Hospice, 20 School Street, P.O. Box 465, Bradford, PA 16701-0465; tel. 814/362-7466; FAX. 814/362-2916; Elizabeth M. Costello, Administrator

Mercy Health Hospice Program, 1500 Lansdowne Avenue, Darby, PA 19023; tel. 610/237-5010; FAX. 610/237-5625; Cathy Franklin

Montgomery Hospital Hospice Program, 25 West Fornance Street, Norristown, PA 19401; tel. 610/272-1080; Elise N. Lamarra, B.S.N.

Neighborhood Visiting Nurse Association, 795 East Marshall Street, West Chester, PA 19380; tel. 610/696-6511; FAX. 610/344-7064; Andrea Devoti, Vice President and Chief Operating Officer

North Penn HH Agency/Hospice Program, 520 Ruah Street, P.O. Box Eight, Blossburg, PA 16912; tel. 717/638-2141; FAX. 717/638-2163; Wilma Hall, Program Director

Northeast Health and Hospice Care, Inc., 38 North Main Street, Pittston, PA 18640; tel. 717/654-0220; FAX. 717/654-0360; Stephan Hannon, Administrator

Odyssey Health Care of Pennsylvania, Park West One, Suite 500, Pittsburgh, PA 15275; tel. 412/494-0870; FAX. 412/494-0879; Robert S. Holder, General Manager

Olsten Kimberly QualityCare Hospice, 749 Northern Boulevard, Clarks Summit, PA 18411; tel. 800/870-0085; Peggy Durkin, Administrator

Penn Care at Home, 51 North 39th Street, Philadelphia, PA 19104; tel. 215/662-8996; Rita P. Rebman, RN, M.S.N.

Pinnacle Health Hospice, 3705 Elmwood Drive, Harrisburg, PA 17110; tel. 717/671-3700; FAX. 717/671-3713; Denise K. Harris, M.S.W., Director

Ridgway Community Nurse Service, Inc., Hospice, 20 North Broad Street, Ridgway, PA 15853; tel. 814/773-5705; FAX. 814/776-6246; Catherine M. Grove, RN, Executive Director

Samaritan Care Hospice of Pennsylvania, 6198 Butler Pike, Suite 275, Blue Bell, PA 19422; tel. 215/653-7310; FAX. 215/653-7340; Peggy Bertels

Sivitz Jewish Hospice, 901 West Street, Pittsburgh, PA 15221; tel. 412/422-5700; FAX. 412/247-5626; Deborah Shtulman, Executive Director

SUN Home Health Services, Inc., 61 Duke Street, Northumberland, PA 17857; tel. 888/478-6227; FAX. 570/473-3070; Karen Adams, Hospice Coordinator

Susquehanna Regional Home Health Services and Hospice, 1101 Grampian Boulevard, 4th Floor, Williamsport, PA 17701-1967; tel. 570/320-7690; FAX. 570/323-0716; Patricia L. Smith, RN, Director of Hospice

Three Rivers Family Hospice, Inc., 3025 Jacks Run Road, White Oak, PA 15131; tel. 412/672-6737; FAX. 412/672-5823; Jan Diehl, RN, M.S.N., Executive Director

Ultimate Home Health and Hospice Care, 212 North Second Street, Girardville, PA 17935; tel. 717/276-1148; Barbara McDonald, Administrator

Section C

Upper Bucks Hospice, a Division of Life Quest Home Care, 2075 Quaker Pointe Drive, Quakertown, PA 18951; tel. 215/529–6100; FAX. 215/529–6253; Beth Gotwals, RN, M.S.N., Hospice Manager

Visiting Nurse Association of Health System, 201 West Independence Street, Shamokin, PA 17872; tel. 800/732–2486; FAX. 717/648–9590; Joseph L. Scopelliti, Jr., Chief Executive Officer

Visiting Nurses Association of the Lehigh Valley, Inc., 1710 Union Boulevard, Allentown, PA 18103; tel. 610/434–6134; FAX. 610/821–1982; Patricia Frenduto, President and CEO

Vitas Health Care Corporation, 805 East Germantown Pike, Suite 805, Norristown, PA 19401; tel. 215/275–2370; Emily B. Fedullo, RN, Director, Development

VNA Health Care Services, 1789 South Braddock Avenue, Pittsburgh, PA 15218; tel. 412/256–6800; Andrew R. Peacock

VNA Hospice, 334 Jefferson Avenue, Scranton, PA 18501; tel. 717/341–6840; Nancy S. Menapace, RN, M.A., Administrator

VNA Hospice Services of Erie County, 1305 Peach Street, Erie, PA 16501; tel. 814/454–2831; FAX. 814/453–5357; James J. Jarvszwicz, Administrator

VNA Hospice, Western Pennsylvania, 154 Hindman Road, Butler, PA 16001; tel. 724/282–6806; FAX. 724/282–7517; Liz Powell, RN, M.N., CRNP, Vice President

VNA of Easton Hospice, 3421 Nightingale Drive, Easton, PA 18045; tel. 215/258–7189; Theresa P. Onorata

VNA of Harrisburg, Inc. Hospice, 118 Washington Street, Harrisburg, PA 17104; tel. 717/233–1035; FAX. 717/233–2759; Thomas Tarasewich, Chief Executive Officer

VNA of Pottstown and Vicinity Comprehensive Hospice Program, 1963 East High Street, Pottstown, PA 19464; tel. 610/327–5700; FAX. 610/327–5701; Sandra Levengood, Executive Director

VNA/Hospice of Monroe County, Inc., R.R. Two, P.O. Box 2159A, East Strouds, PA I8360; tel. 7l7/421–5390; FAX. 717/421–7423; Mark Hodgson, Administrator

White Rose Hospice, 2870 Eastern Boulevard, York, PA 17402; tel. 717/849–5642; FAX. 717/849–5630; Karen Hook, B.S., Manager

Wissahickon Hospice, 8835 Germantown Avenue, Philadelphia, PA 19118; tel. 215/247–0277; FAX. 215/248–3253; Priscilla D. Kissick, RN, M.N., Executive Director

RHODE ISLAND
Hospice Care of Rhode Island, 169 George Street, Pawtucket, RI 02860–3868; tel. 401/727–7070; FAX. 401/727–7080; David Rehm, Executive Director

Hospice of Nursing Placement, 339 Angel Street, P.O. Box 603337, Providence, RI 02906; tel. 401/453–4544; Marcia Bigney, Administrator

Kent County Visiting Nurse Association Hospice, 51 Health Lane, Warwick, RI 02886; tel. 401/737–6050; FAX. 401/738–0247; Nancy Roberts, RN, M.S.N., Chief Executive Officer

Northwest Home Care (Hospice), 185 Putnam Pike, P.O. Box 423, Harmony, RI 02829; tel. 401/949–2600; FAX. 401/949–5115; Beverly McGuire, President

Valley Hospice–VNS of Pawtucket, Central Falls, Lincoln and Cu, 172 Armistice Boulevard, Pawtucket, RI 02860; tel. 401/725–3414; FAX. 401/728–4999; Christopher L. Boys, Chief Executive Officer

Visiting Nurse Health Services Hospice, 1184 East Main Road, P.O. Box 690, Portsmouth, RI 02871; tel. 401/682–2100; FAX. 401/682–2112; Jean Anderson, RN, M.S., Chief Executive Officer

VNA of Rhode Island, 157 Waterman Avenue, Providence, RI 02906; tel. 401/444–9400; FAX. 401/444–9430; Sandra L. Hooper, RN, M.B.A., CNAA, Director, Adult Services

SOUTH CAROLINA
Hitchcock Rehabilitation Center Home Health and Hospice, 690 Medical Park Drive, Aiken, SC 29801; tel. 803/643–0001; FAX. 803/649–0490; Gayle Jones, Director, Home Health Hospice

Hospice Care of the Low Country, Hospice Care of the Low Country Home Health, 20 Palmetto Parkway, Suite 104, Hilton Head, SC 29926; tel. 803/681–7814; FAX. 803/681–7821; Laura Frieden, Executive Director

Hospice Care of the Piedmont, 303 West Alexander Street, Greenwood, SC 29646; tel. 864/227–9393; FAX. 864/227–9377; Nancy B. Corley, Director

Hospice Care of Tri–County, 111 Executive Pointe Boulevard, Columbia, SC 29212; tel. 803/750–8697; FAX. 803/750–8695; Edna McClain, RN, M.N., Administrator

Hospice Community Care, (Serving York, Chester, Lancaster, Cherokee and Union), 325 South Oakland Avenue, Rock Hill, SC 29730; tel. 803/329–4663; FAX. 803/329–5935; Jane Armstrong, Executive Director

Hospice Health Services, One Carriage Lane, Suite F1, Charleston, SC 29407; tel. 803/852–2177; FAX. 803/769–0148; Sylvia Barnes Gaillored, RN, Executive Director

Hospice of Charleston, Inc., 3896 Leeds Avenue, Charleston, SC 29405; tel. 803/529–3100; FAX. 803/529–3111; Carol Younker, Executive Director

Hospice of Chesterfield County, Inc., 140 South Page Street, P.O. Box 293, Chesterfield, SC 29709; tel. 800/623–9155; FAX. 804/623–3833; Monnie W. Bittle, Executive Director

Hospice of Colleton County, Inc., 214 Wichman Street, Walterboro, SC 29488; tel. 803/549–5948; FAX. 803/549–1451; Alfred S. Givens, Administrator

Hospice of Georgetown County, Inc., 2591 North Fraser Street, P.O. Box 1436, Georgetown, SC 29440; tel. 843/546–3410; FAX. 843/527–6964; Brenda Stroup, RN, Executive Director

Hospice of Laurens County, Inc., 16 Peachtree Street, P.O. Box 178, Clinton, SC 29325; tel. 803/833–6287; FAX. 803/833–0556; Judy Calvert, RN, Executive Director

Hospice of Marlboro County, Inc., P.O. Box 474, Bennettsville, SC 29512; tel. 843/479–5979; FAX. 843/479–3711; Kevin Long, Executive Director

Hospice of the Upstate, Inc., Callie & John Rainey Hospice House, 1835 Rogers Road, Anderson, SC 29621; tel. 864/224–3358; FAX. 864/224–9971; Nancy Garrett–Boyle, Administrator

Interim HealthCare Hospice, 775 Spartan Boulevard, Spartanburg, SC 29301; tel. 864/587–9798; FAX. 864/587–2855; Nancy A. Dereng, Director

Island Hospice, 94–C Main Street, Hilton Head I, SC 29926; tel. 803/681–7035; FAX. 803/681–8506; Pamela D. Walker, Administrator

Lutheran Hospice Ministry, Lowman Home–Bolick Building, P.O. Box 444, White Rock, SC 29177; tel. 803/732–8756; Jean Tilley, Administrator

Mercy Hospice of Horry County, Columbus Plaza, 131 Wesley Street, Myrtle Beach, SC 29578; tel. 803/347–2282; FAX. 803/236–4306; Connie Fahey, FSM, Executive Director

Saint Francis Hospital Home Care–Hospice Services, 414 Pettigru Street, P.O. Box 9312, Greenville, SC 29601; tel. 864/233–5300; FAX. 864/233–4873; James A. Rogers

United Hospice, Inc., 6300 St. Andrews Road, Columbia, SC 29212; tel. 803/798–6605; FAX. 803/798–3001; Debbie Graham

SOUTH DAKOTA
Ellen Stephen Hospice, P.O. Box 1805, Pine Ridge, SD 57770; tel. 605/455–1217; FAX. 605/455–1218; Linda Howell, RN

Hospice of the Hills, 1011 11th Street, Rapid City, SD 57701; tel. 605/341–7118; FAX. 605/399–7820; Dorothy Brown, Administrator

Tekawitha Nursing Home, 9, Sisseton, SD 57262; tel. 605/886–8491; Charleen Thompson, RN

TENNESSEE
A Plus Hospice, Inc., 116 Wilson Pike Circle, Suite 103, Brentwood, TN 37027; tel. 615/377–6276; FAX. 615/377–6287; Barbara Brown, Director

Advanced Home Care and Hospice, Inc., 117 Edenway Drive, P.O. Box 1099, White House, TN 37188; tel. 615/384–0962; FAX. 615/672–7398; Gloria Keen, Administrator

Alive Hospice, Inc., 1718 Patterson Street, Nashville, TN 37203; tel. 615/327–1085; FAX. 615/321–8902; Janet L. Jones, President and CEO

Amedisys Home Health, 446 Highway 46 South, Dickson, TN 37055; tel. 615/441–1365; FAX. 615/446–8109; Glenda Pace, Acting Administrator

Baptist Community Home Care and Hospice, 139 East Swan Street, Centerville, TN 37033; tel. 615/729–4500; FAX. 615/729–9000

Buckeye Quality HHA, Inc. Hospice, Highway 52W, P.O. Box 697, Jamestown, TN 38556; tel. 615/879–9928; Sandra Hall, RN, Director, Patient Services

Comprehensive HHC Hospice Services, Inc., P.O. Box 574, Patterson Crossroads, Harrogate, TN 37752; tel. 426/869–5111; FAX. 423/869–5916; Sherri Rowe, Coordinator

Country Hospice, Highway 45 South, Route Two Box 23A, Selmer, TN 38375; tel. 901/645–6475; Andy Gardner, RN, CRNH, Regional Hospice Director

Elk Valley Hospice Services, 1237 Huntsville Highway, Fayetteville, TN 37334; tel. 615/433–7026

Friendship Hospice of Nashville, Inc., 1326 Eighth Avenue, N., Nashville, TN 37203; tel. 615/327–3950; Andre L. Lee, DPA, Chairman of the Board

Home Health Care of East Tennessee, Inc., 1796 Mount Vernon Drive, N.W., Cleveland, TN 37311; tel. 423/479–4581; FAX. 423/479–5422; Annette Green, DOPC

Home–Bound Medical Care, 4355 Highway 58, Suite 101, Chattanooga, TN 37416; tel. 423/855–9128

Home–Bound Medical Care, Inc., 2165 Spicer Cove, Suite One, Memphis, TN 38134; tel. 901/386–5061

Homecare Hospice Services, 115 Vicksburg Avenue, Camden, TN 38320; tel. 901/584–1927; FAX. 901/584–0401

Hospice of Chattanooga, Inc., 165 Hamm Road, Chattanooga, TN 37405; tel. 423/267–6828; FAX. 423/756–4765; Viston Taylor III, Executive Director

Hospice of Chattanooga, Inc., 165 Hamm Road, Chattanooga, TN 37405; tel. 615/267–6828; Ben Johnston, Executive Director

Hospice of Cumberland County, Inc., 140 North Main, Suite 2, Crossville, TN 38555; tel. 931/484–4748; FAX. 931/456–5096; Ann Marie McFarland, Executive Director

Hospice of East Tennessee, 433 Sevier Avenue, Knoxville, TN 37920; tel. 423/632–5711; FAX. 423/549–2065; Debbie Watson, Office Manager

Hospice of Murfreesboro, 417 North University Street, Murfreesboro, TN 37130; tel. 615/896–4663

Hospice of Tennessee, Inc., 112 Louise Avenue, Nashville, TN 37203; tel. 800/252–7442; FAX. 615/773–3033; Debbie Baumgart, RN, Regional Director

Hospice of Tennessee, Inc.–Franklin, 415 Williamson Square, Franklin, TN 37064

Hospice of West Tennessee, 1804 Highway 45 Bypass, West Tennessee Healthcare, Jackson, TN 38305; tel. 901/664–4220; FAX. 901/664–4231; Donna Walter, RN, Director

House Call Hospice, Inc., Executive Business Park, 6025 Lee Highway, Chattanooga, TN 37421; tel. 615/892–2561; Caroline McBrayer

Housecall Hospice, 100 Rogosin Drive, Suite B, Elizabethton, TN 37643; tel. 615/547–0852; FAX. 615/543–6449; Rachel Vollman, Hospice Administrator

Housecall Hospice, 6025 Lee Highway, Executive Business Park, Chattanooga, TN 37421; tel. 615/892–2561; Caroline McBrayer

Housecall Hospice, 5350 Poplar Avenue, Suite 118A, Memphis, TN 38119; tel. 901/685–5300; FAX. 901/761–4321; Lynn Thomasson, Hospice Administrator

Housecall Hospice, 3343 Perimeter Hill Drive, Suite 102, Nashville, TN 37211; tel. 615/333–3995; FAX. 615/333–7953; Andy Baker, Administrator

JEM Health Care Inc., 315 10th Avenue, N., Suite 109, Nashville, TN 37207; tel. 615/726–8668; FAX. 615/726–8665; Marilyn McClain, Administrator

Lazarus House Hospice, Inc., 260 West Fifth Street, Cookeville, TN 38501; tel. 615/528–5133; J. Steve Mathias, Executive Director

Methodist Home Care Services, 1716 Parr Avenue, Dyersburg, TN 38024; tel. 901/287–2307; FAX. 901/287–2174

Procare Support Services, Inc., 1210 Stonebridge Square, Jackson, TN 38305; tel. 800/982–2273; FAX. 901/668–9498; Betty Peeryhouse, Administrator

Smoky Mountain Home Health & Hospice, Inc, 222 Heritage Boulevard, Newport, TN 37821; tel. 423/623–0233; FAX. 423/623–8311; Catherine Kucera, M.S.W., Hospice Administrator

Sumner Hospice, 316 East Main Street, Gallatin, TN 37066; tel. 615/451–6690; FAX. 615/230–6889; Kathy Farley, Manager

Tennessee Nursing Services of Morristown, Coldwell Bank Building, 415 North Fairmont, Morristown, TN 37816; tel. 423/581–7690; FAX. 423/581–8164; Glena Duffield, Director, Hospice

TLC Hospice, 1200 Mountain Creek Road, Suite 440, Chattanooga, TN 37405; tel. 423/877–0983; FAX. 423/877–4944; Gloria J. Dodds, RN, B.S.N., Administrator

Tri County Quality Homecare and Hospice, 20 Lee Avenue, Box 308, McKenzie, TN 38201; tel. 901/352–2240; FAX. 901/352–0320; Kay Taylor, RN, Patient Care Coordinator

Section C

Trinity Hospice, 1049 Cresthaven Road, Memphis, TN 38119; tel. 901/767–6767; FAX. 901/767–4627; Bradford A. Austin, RN, Hospice Director

University Home Health and Hospice, Inc., 135 Kennedy Drive, Martin, TN 38237; tel. 901/587–2996; FAX. 800/627–3228; Kellie Sims, B.S.W., Hospice Director

Willowbrook Hospice, Inc., 145 Southesast Parkway, Suite 100, Franklin, TN 37064; tel. 800/790–8499; June Baldini, RN, Director

TEXAS

Abacus Home Health Care, Inc., 8035 E.R.L. Thornton, Suite 322, Dallas, TX 75228; tel. 214/319–7480; FAX. 214/319–2453; Kathy Russell, M.S.W., Administrator

AIM Hospice, 703 East Concho, P.O. Box 2300, Rockport, TX 78381–2300; tel. 512/729–0507; FAX. 512/790–0243; Judith Johnson, RN, Ph.D., Administrator

American Home Health and Hospice, 315 South Oak, Pecos, TX 79772

American Hospice, Inc., 1349 Empire Central, Suite 707, Dallas, TX 75247; tel. 214/689–1010; FAX. 214/631–4100; Danny Walker, Administrator

Ann's Haven/VNA, 216 West Mulberry Street, Denton, TX 76201; tel. 817/566–6550; FAX. 817/383–4000; Karen Pemberton, RN, B.S.N.

Burton Hospice Care, Inc., 6640 Eastex Freeway, Suite 140, Beaumont, TX 77708; tel. 409/892–7476; FAX. 409/892–7740; Vergie A. Burton, Administrator

Care United Hospice, 801 West Freeway, Suite 500, Grand Prairie, TX 75051

Center for Hospice Care, 1101 Decker Drive, Baytown, TX 77520

Central Texas Medical Center Hospice, 1345 S Thorpe Lane, San Marcos, TX 78666; tel. 512/753–3584; FAX. 512/353–6573; Dawn O'Donnell, RNC, M.A., Administrator

Circle of Hope Hospice of VNA, 2211 East Missouri, Suite 220, El Paso, TX 79923; tel. 915/543–6201; Tom Meagher, Vice President, Hospice

Community Care Services, Inc., 403 East Blackjack, Dublin, TX 76446; tel. 817/445–4675; Bobbie Nichols, Administrator

Community Hospice of St. Joseph, 1000 Summit, Fort Worth, TX 76102

Community Hospice of Waco, 3215 Pine Avenue, Waco, TX 76708; tel. 254/202–5150; FAX. 254/752–3072; Richard E. Scott, President

Comprehensive Home Health Services, 901 North Galloway Avenue, Suite 101, Mesquite, TX 75149; tel. 972/285–3713; FAX. 972/285–3699; Julie Francis, Director

Crawford Hospice Services, Inc., 709 West 34th Street, Suite B, Austin, TX 78705; tel. 800/909–5543; FAX. 512/450–1281; Barbara Powell, Administrator

Crown of Texas Hospice, 1000 South Jefferson, Amarillo, TX 79101; tel. 806/372–7696; FAX. 806/372–2825; Sharla Valdez, B.S.N., CRNH, RN, President

Crown of Texas Hospice, 100 I-45 North, Suite 240, Box 103, Conroe, TX 77301; tel. 409/788–7707; FAX. 409/788–7708; Marsha J. Irwin, RN, Ph.D., Director

Cypress Basin Hospice, Inc., 1805 North Jefferson, P.O. Box 544, Mount Pleasant, TX 75455; tel. 903/577–1510; FAX. 903/577–9377; Edd C. Hess, Executive Director

Denson Community Hospice, 1100 Gulf Freeway, N., Suite 122, League City, TX 77573; tel. 713/332–4970; FAX. 713/338–1766; Suzanne Denson, Administrator

DNS Hospice, 2101 Kemp Boulevard, Wichita Falls, TX 76309; tel. 817/723–2771; FAX. 817/322–1754; Helen Dipprey, Chief Operating Officer

East Harris County Hospice Services, Inc., Holland Avenue Medical Center, 1313 Holland Avenue, Houston, TX 77029; tel. 713/450–4500; FAX. 281/450–4006; Ipe Mathai, Executive Director

Family Hospice of Dallas, 1140 Empire Central, Suite 235, Dallas, TX 75247; tel. 214/631–7273; FAX. 214/630–4032; Jim Grant, RN, B.S.N., M.S., Executive Director

Family Hospice of Fort Worth, 4040 Fossil Creek Boulevard, Suite 204, Fort Worth, TX 76137; tel. 817/232–3492; FAX. 817/232–3499; Sally Day, RN, B.S.N., Executive Director

Family Hospice, Inc., 819 South Fifth Street, Temple, TX 76504; tel. 800/643–3139; FAX. 817/742–2023; Carrie Carson, Administrator

First Community Homecare, 9323 Garland Road, Suite 308, Dallas, TX 75218

Golden Acres Hospice, 2525 Centerville Road, Dallas, TX 75228–2693; tel. 214/327–4503; FAX. 214/319–5974; Robert J. Watson, Executive Director

Harris Hospice, 6000 Western Place, Suite 118, Fort Worth, TX 76107; tel. 817/570–8200; Barbara Hunt, Director

Heart of the Valley Hospice, 320 North Williams Road, San Benito, TX 78586; tel. 800/333–6131; FAX. 210/399–3553; Rebecca Hernandez, RN, Administrator

Heart of West Texas Hospice, 1927 Hickory, Colorado City, TX 79512

Heritage Health Care, 606 Avenue K, Cisco, TX 76437

Home Health Services of Dallas, Inc., 2929 Carlisle Street, Suite 375, Dallas, TX 75204–1050

Home Health Specialists, Inc., 813 South Palestine, Athens, TX 75751; tel. 800/801–8126; FAX. 903/657–9513; Linda Johnson, RN, Administrator

Home Hospice, 516 N. Texas, Odessa, TX 79761; tel. 915/580–9990; FAX. 915/580–9989; Hilton Chancellor, Director

Home Hospice, Grayson County Office, 505 West Center Street, P.O. Box 2306, Sherman, TX 75091; tel. 903/868–9315; FAX. 903/893–2772; Marty Barr, Executive Director

Hospice Care of Tennessee, Inc, 1708 Auburn Road, Suite C, Texas City, TX 77591; tel. 409/938–0070; FAX. 409/938–1509; Sue Mistretta, Executive Director

Hospice Home Care, 10221 Desert Sands, Suite 301, San Antonio, TX 78216; tel. 210/377–1033; FAX. 210/377–2560; Al Hafer, Business Administrator

Hospice in the Pines, 116 South Raguet, Lufkin, TX 75904; tel. 800/324–8557; FAX. 409/632–1352; Sherri D. Flynt, L.S.W., Social Services

Hospice in the Pines, 1300 South Frazier, Suite 315, Conroe, TX 77301; tel. 888/539–5252; FAX. 409/539–5272; Sheryl Wallace, Executive Director

Hospice New Braunfels, 613 North Walnut, New Braunfels, TX 78130; tel. 830/625–7500; FAX. 830/606–1388; Joyce Fox, Administrator

Hospice of Abilene, Inc., 1682 Hickory, Abilene, TX 79602; tel. 915/677–8516; FAX. 915/675–5031; Lana Cunningham, RN, M.S.N., Clinical Director

Hospice of Cedar Lake, 101 E. Market Street, Mabank, TX 75147–8614; tel. 903/887–3772; FAX. 903/887–3700; Lila Shumante, RN

Hospice of East Texas, 3800 Paluxy, Suite 560, Tyler, TX 75703; tel. 903/581–5585; FAX. 903/581–5293; Michael C. Couch, Executive Director

Hospice of El Paso, Inc., 3901 North Mesa, Suite 400, El Paso, TX 79902; tel. 915/532–5699; FAX. 915/532–7822; Charles E. Roark, Ed.D. FACHE

Hospice of HIS, 9535 Forest Lane, Suite 126, Dallas, TX 75243; tel. 972/690–6632; FAX. 972/690–0834; Tim Gellegos, National Director, Hospice Operation

Hospice of Lubbock, Inc., 1102 Slide Road, Suite 3, P.O. Box 53276, Lubbock, TX 79453; tel. 806/795–2751; FAX. 806/795–8464; Linda McMurry, RN, B.S.N.

Hospice of Midland, Inc., 911 West Texas, Midland, TX 79701; tel. 915/682–2855; FAX. 915/682–2989; Carol Armstrong, Executive Director

Hospice of Northeast Texas, 51 North Side Square, Cooper, TX 75432; tel. 903/395–2811; FAX. 903/395–2766; Nicki J. Beeler, Administrator

Hospice of San Angelo, Inc., 36 East Beauregard, Suite 1100, San Angelo, TX 76902; tel. 915/658–6524; David McBride, Executive Director

Hospice of South Texas, 2004 Fagan Circle, Victoria, TX 77901; tel. 512/572–4300; FAX. 512/572–4532; Doug Eaves, Executive Director

Hospice of St. Michael Hospital of Texarkana, 1400 College Drive, Texarkana, TX 75501; tel. 903/794–1206; FAX. 903/735–5390; Tommy McGee, Administrator

Hospice of Texarkana, Inc., 803 Spruce Street, Texarkana, TX 75501; tel. 903/794–4263; FAX. 501/744–1108; Cynthia L. Marsh, Administrator

Hospice of the Big Country, Inc., 3113 Oldham Lane, Abilene, TX 79602; tel. 915/677–1191; FAX. 915/677–1808; Danna L. Clouse, Administrator

Hospice of the Heart, 218 S. San Jacinto, Whitney, TX 76962; tel. 817/694–6009; FAX. 817/694–9926; Mary Flauinsy

Hospice of the Panhandle, 800 North Sumner, P.O. Box 2795, 79066–2795, Pampa, TX 79065; tel. 806/665–6677; Sherry McCavit, Executive Director

Hospice of the Plains, Inc., 7109 Olton Road, Plainview, TX 79072; tel. 806/293–5127; FAX. 806/293–5902; Roxey Williams, Executive Director

Hospice of the Three Rivers, 51 North 11th Street, Beaumont, TX 77702–2224; tel. 800/946–7742; Andi Whitmer, Administrator

Hospice of V.N.A., 2905 Sackett, Houston, TX 77098; tel. 713/630–5521; FAX. 713/630–5529; Paula Wehrman, RN, MHA, Chief Executive Officer

Hospice of Wichita Falls, 4909 Johnson Road, Wichita Falls, TX 76310; tel. 940/691–0982; FAX. 940/691–1608; Jan Banta, Executive Director

Hospice Preferred Choice, 8203 Willow Place South, Suite 530, Houston, TX 77070; tel. 713/469–7990; FAX. 713/894–1294; Diane A. Incognito, Executive Director

Hospice Preferred Choice, 427 West 20th, Suite 603, Houston, TX 77008; tel. 713/864–2626; FAX. 713/864–9476; Linda Dumoir, Administrator

Hospice Uvalde Area, (a program of Hospice San Antonio), P.O. Box 5280, Uvalde, TX 78802–5280; tel. 210/278–6691; FAX. 210/278–8925; Edwin Sasek, Bereavement Coordinator

Houston Hospice, 8811 Gaylord, Suite 100, Houston, TX 77024; tel. 713/468–2441; FAX. 713/468–0879; Margaret Caddy, RN, Executive Director

Huguley Hospice Care, 11801 South Freeway, Ft. Worth, TX 76115; tel. 817/551–2545; FAX. 817/568–3294; Donna Reddell, RN, Director

La Mariposa Hospice, 2001 North Oregon, El Paso, TX 79902; tel. 915/452–6802; Frances Witt, Director

Lakes Area Hospice, 254 Ethel Street, Jasper, TX 75951; tel. 409/384–5995; FAX. 409/384–9655; Jeanette Coffield, Executive Director

Lone Star Hospice, 1212 Palm Valley Boulevard, Round Rock, TX 78664; tel. 512/467–7423; FAX. 512/218–9288; Edward Lower, Executive Director

Managed Home Health Care, 2211 Calder Avenue, Beaumont, TX 77707; tel. 409/832–4164; FAX. 409/832–4182; Charles Bray, CEO

Medshares Hospice of Coastal Texas, Inc, 1102 North Mechanic, El Campo, TX 77437; tel. 409/543–9487; FAX. 409/543–9426; Ruth Kainer, RN, Administrator

Nurses In Touch Community Hospice, 7410 Blanco Road, Suite 100, San Antonio, TX 78216; tel. 210/979–9771; FAX. 210/979–6644; Mary Helen Tieken, RN, B.S.N., Administrator

Odyssey HealthCare, 5440 Harvert Hill Road, Dallas, TX 75230; tel. 888/285–8081; FAX. 972/720–0115; Ron Plute, General Manager

Pacesetter Hospice, Inc., 6800 Manhattan, Suite 401, Fort Worth, TX 76120

Personal Touch Hospice of Texas, Inc., 8200 Brookriver Drive, Suite N109, Dallas, TX 75247; tel. 214/638–0357; FAX. 214/905–8687; Roy W. Terry, RN, Director

Robinson Creek Home Care, Inc., 1000 Westbank Drive, Suite 6B201, Austin, TX 78746; tel. 512/328–7606; Vanessa Nunnelly, Administrator

Rural Hospice, Inc., 501 South Alford, Crane, TX 79731; tel. 888/558–2300; FAX. 915/558–2335; Pam Ross, RN, Director

Samaritan Care Hospice of Texas, 17103 Preston Road, Suite 200, Dallas, TX 75248; tel. 800/669–3695; FAX. 972/407–5021; Martha Schueler, M.S., CRNH, Director Clinical Service

San Juan Home Health and Hospice, 300 North Nebraska Avenue, San Juan, TX 78589; tel. 210/782–0333; FAX. 210/782–0335; Tony Cortez, Director

Spohn Hospice, 600 Elizabeth Street, Corpus Christ, TX 78404; tel. 512/881–3159; FAX. 512/888–7405; Rita Mueller, RN, Director

St. Anthony's Hospice and Life Enrichment Program, 600 North Tyler, P.O. Box 950, Amarillo, TX 79176–0001; tel. 806/378–6777; FAX. 806/378–5031; Sharon Hutchinson, RN, Director

St. Joseph Hospice Houston, 1404 Calhoun Cullen Family Building, Houston, TX 77002; tel. 713/757–7488; FAX. 713/756–5127; Maresa Henry, Associate Director

St. Paul Hospice, 7920 Elmbrook Drive, Suite 112, Dallas, TX 75247; tel. 214/637–7474; Debbie Weir, Director

Stephen's Hospice, 925 A North Graham, Stephenville, TX 76401–4216; tel. 817/965–7119; FAX. 817/965–3228; Kim Davis, Administrator

Taras Prime Home Health Care, Inc., 2765 East Trinity Mills, Carrollton, TX 75006

Tender Loving Care Home Health Hospice Agency, 5787 South Hampton Road, Suite 295, Dallas, TX 75232

Section C

Texas Health Staffing Services, Inc., 1115 Chihuahua Street, Suite B, Laredo, TX 78040; tel. 210/791-3012; Maria Elena Montemayor, Administrator

Texoma Community Hospice, 3821 Wilbarger Street, Vernon, TX 76384; tel. 800/658-6330; FAX. 817/552-2305; Jean Tucker, Administrator

The Hospice at the Texas Medical Center, 1905 Holcombe Boulevard, Houston, TX 77030; tel. 713/467-7423; FAX. 713/677-7177; Brandy R. Hicok, RN, BSN, Director of Clinical Services

The Southeast Texas Hospice, Inc., 912 West Cherry, P.O. Box 2385, Orange, TX 77630; tel. 409/886-0622; FAX. 409/886-0623; Mary McKenna, Administrator

Thee Hospice, POB 6548, Huntsville, TX 77342-6548; tel. 409/291-8439; FAX. 409/295-8582; Patricia Lee, RN, Patient Care Coordinator

Tomlinson Health Services, Hospice Program, 1300 West Mockingbird, Suite 160, Dallas, TX 75247; tel. 214/630-8847; FAX. 817/573-3160; Reba Tomlinson, Chief Executive Officer

Tyler Hospice, 423 South Beckham Avenue, Tyler, TX 75701; tel. 903/592-9703; FAX. 903/593-0639; Sandra L. Bunch, Administrator

Ultimate Hospice Care, 2300 Highway 365, Suite 440, Nederland, TX 77627; tel. 409/722-4993; FAX. 409/721-4930; Lewanna D. Jones, Administrator

Ultra Home Health Care, Inc., 8303 Southwest Freeway, Suite 410, Houston, TX 77074; tel. 713/988-5872; FAX. 713/271-1002; Mr. Tracy Potts, General Manager

Visiting Nurse Association Hospice, 212 Brown Street, Brownwood, TX 76801-2915; tel. 915/646-6500; FAX. 915/646-6412; Mary Suther, President and CEO

Visiting Nurse Association of Texas Hospice, 1440 West Mockingbird Lane, Suite 500, Dallas, TX 75247-4929; tel. 214/689-0000; FAX. 214/689-0010; Judith Bigler

Vista Care Family Hospice, 8701 Shoal Creek Boulevard, Suite 104, Austin, TX 78757; tel. 800/444-2405; FAX. 512/453-4165; Susan Smith – Willeh, Program Director

VistaCare Family Hospice of San Antonio, 6800 Park Ten Boulevard, Suite 110 North, San Antonio, TX 78213-4201; tel. 210/738-4141; FAX. 210/738-3507; Charlene Ross, Interim Program Director

Vitas Healthcare Corporation, 5001 LBJ Freeway, Suite 1050, Dallas, TX 75244; tel. 214/661-2004; FAX. 214/661-3474; David C. Gasmire, General Manager

Vitas Healthcare Corporation, 4828 Loop Central Drive, Suite 890, Houston, TX 77081; tel. 713/663-7777; FAX. 713/663-4990; Diane Incognito, General Manager

Vitas Healthcare Corporation, 211 East Parkwood, Suite 211, Friendswood, TX 77546; tel. 713/996-4400; Ruth Castillo, General Manager

VNA and Hospice of South Texas, 8207 Callaghan, Suite 355, San Antonio, TX 78230; tel. 2108045200; FAX. 2108265987; Mike Mazzocco, Executive Director

VNA and Hospice of the Texas Gulf Coast, P.O. Box 1777, Angleton, TX 77516-1777; tel. 409/849-6476; FAX. 409/849-0343; Jenny Carswell, Administrator

UTAH

Castle Country Hospice, 11 West Main Street, Suite 100, Price, UT 84501; tel. 801/637-8070; Lavina Kirkwood, Administrator

CNS Community Hospice, 2970 South Main, Suite 300, Salt Lake City, UT 84115; tel. 801/461-9500; FAX. 801/486-2193; Grant C. Howarth, President and CEO

Creative Health Services, Inc. Hospice Care, 6777 South 1560 East, Salt Lake City, UT 84121; tel. 801/943-8374; FAX. 801/942-2949; Joyce L. Smith, Administrator

Creekside Hospice Care, 1935 East Vine Street, Suite 350, Salt Lake City, UT 84121; tel. 801/272-8617; FAX. 801/277-3790; Maryann Pales, Administrator

Dixie Regional Home Health Hospice, 354 East 600 South, Suite 304, St. George, UT 84770; tel. 801/634-4567; FAX. 801/634-4564; Kathy Andrus, RN, Administrator

East Lake Home Health Hospice/Family Hospice Care, 668 West 980 North, Provo, UT 84601; tel. 801/374-9986; Kory Coleman, Director

Family Hospice Care, 404 East 5600 South, Murray, UT 84107; tel. 801/268-8083; FAX. 801/268-8096; Pat Burns, Director, Home Care Services

Hospice of Cache Valley, 1400 North 500 East, Logan, UT 84341; tel. 801/750-5477; FAX. 801/750-5361; Neil C. Perkes, RN, M.B.A., Administrator

IHC Home Health Agency–Hospice of IHC, 2250 South 1300 West, Suite A, Salt Lake City, UT 84119; tel. 801/977-9900; FAX. 801/977-9956; Shauna Einerson, Administrator

Premier Hospice Care, 4885 South 900 East, Suite 207, Salt Lake City, UT 84117; tel. 801/288-1619; David West, RN, Administrator

Rocky Mountain Hospice, 315 East 400 South, Bountiful, UT 84010; tel. 801/397-4900; Patricia Kruger, Administrator

Uintah Basin Hospice, 26 West 200 North 78-15, Roosevelt, UT 84066; tel. 435/722-2418; FAX. 435/722-6187; Lloyd Nielsen, RNC, BSN, Director

Vista Care, 1093 South Orem Boulevard, Orem, UT 84058; tel. 801/224-2999; Alan Green, Administrator

VERMONT

Brattleboro Area Hospice, 31 South Main Street, P.O. Box 1053, Brattleboro, VT 05302-1053; tel. 802/257-0775; Susan Parris, Administrator

Caledonia Home Health Care–Hospice, Sherman Drive, P.O. Box 383, St. Johnsbury, VT 05819; tel. 802/748-8116; FAX. 802/748-4628; Brenda B. Smith, Hospice Care Director

Central Vermont Home Health and Hospice, Inc., R.R. 3, Barre, VT 05641; tel. 802/223-1878; FAX. 802/223-6835; Diana Peirce, RN, CRNH, Director, Hospice Services

Franklin County Home Health and Hospice, Three Home Health Circle, St. Albans, VT 05478; tel. 802/527-7531; FAX. 802/527-7533; Janet McCarthy, Executive Director

Hospice of Bennington County, Inc., P.O. Box 1231, Bennington, VT 05201; tel. 802/447-0307; Amy Barber-Thomas, Executive Director

Hospice of Champlain Valley, 1110 Prim Road, Suite 1, Colchester, VT 05446; tel. 802/860-4410; FAX. 802/860-6149; Annette Blanchard, RN, Program Director

Hospice of VNH, 20 South Main Street, White River J, VT 05001; tel. 802/295-2604; FAX. 802/295-3163; Marie Kirn, Executive Director

Hospice Volunteer Sucs, P.O. Box 772, Middlebury, VT 05753; tel. 802/388-4111; Catherine Studley, Executive Director

Lamoille Home Health and Hospice, 54 Farr Avenue, Morrisville, VT 05661; tel. 802/888-4651; FAX. 802/888-7822; Carol McKern, Director

Orleans Essex VNA and Hospice, Inc., Three Lakemont Road, Newport, VT 05855-1550; tel. 802/334-5213; FAX. 802/334-8822; Diana Hamilton, RN, Director, Hospice

Randolph Area Hospice, 36 South Main Street, Randolph, VT 05060; tel. 802/728-6100

Rutland Area Visiting Nurse Association, Seven Albert Cree Drive, Rutland, VT 05701; tel. 802/775-0568; FAX. 802/775-2304; Sally Tobin, Associate Director, Community Health Program

Southern Vermont Home Health Agency, Three Holstein Place, Brattleboro, VT 05301; tel. 802/257-4390; FAX. 802/257-2188; Ellen Bristol, M.S.N., CRNH

Springfield Area Hospice, Inc., 366 River Street, Springfield, VT 05156; tel. 802/886-2525; Marisa Bolognese, Volunteer Coordinator

Visiting Nurse Alliance of Vermont and New Hampshire, Hospice of Vermont and New Hampshire, 46 South Main Street, Old Court House, White River J, VT 05001; tel. 802/295-2604; FAX. 802/295-3163; Marie Kirn, Executive Director

VIRGINIA

Americare InHome Nursing, 5203 Leesburg Pike, Suite 705, Falls Church, VA 22041; tel. 703/931-9002; FAX. 703/826-0076; Mary L. Tatum

Blue Ridge Hospice, Inc., 333 West Cork Street, Winchester, VA 22601; tel. 540/665-5210; FAX. 540/678-0584; Terrie Stevens, Executive Director

Community Hospices of America, Inc., 540 West Main Street, Wytheville, VA 24382; tel. 703/228-5424; FAX. 703/228-9225; Rita C. Cobbs, Program Director

Crater Community Hospice, Inc., 840 W. Roslyn Road, Suite E, Colonial Heights, VA 23834; tel. 804/526-4300; FAX. 804/526-4237; Brenda D. Mitchell, RN

First Choice Home Services, Inc., 915 Central Avenue, P.O. Box 1146, Harrisonburg, VA 22801; tel. 703/434-3916; Diana Berkshire, Administrator

Gentle Shepherd Hospice, Inc., 4040 Franklin Road, S.W., Roanoke, VA 24014; tel. 540/989-6265; FAX. 540/989-1547; Donald A. Eckenroth III, Administrator

Good Samaritan Hospice, Inc., 3528 Electric Road, Suite A, Roanoke, VA 24018; tel. 540/776-0198; FAX. 540/776-0841; Sue Moore, President

Hospice of Central Virginia, 5540 Falmouth Street, Suite 307, Richmond, VA 23230; tel. 804/281-0541; FAX. 804/281-0954; Jane Ishell, Administrator

Hospice of Northern Virginia, 13168 Centerpointe Way, Suite 201-202, Woodbridge, VA 22193; tel. 703/670-5080; FAX. 703/670-3910; Pat Knaus, Manager of Clinical Services

Hospice of Northern Virginia, Inc., 6400 Arlington Boulevard, Suite 1000, Falls Church, VA 22042; tel. 703/534-7070; FAX. 703/538-2163; David J. English, President and CEO

Hospice of Northern Virginia, Inc., 11166 Main Street, Suite 405, Fairfax, VA 22030; tel. 703/352-7115; FAX. 703/591-2376; Jacqueline Wright, Regional Vice President

Hospice of Northern Virginia, Inc., 885 Harrison Street, S.E., Leesburg, VA 21075; tel. 703/777-7866; FAX. 703/771-8904; Jackie Wright, Regional Vice President

Hospice of the Piedmont, Inc., 1290 Seminole Trail, Charlottesville, VA 22901; tel. 804/975-5500; FAX. 804/975-4040; Victoria Todd, Executive Director

Hospice of the Rapidan, Inc., 1200 Sunset Lane, Suite 2320, Culpeper, VA 22701; tel. 703/825-4840; FAX. 703/825-7752; Patricia Tuffy, Executive Director

Housecall Hospice, Two Main Street, P.O. Box 850, Jonesville, VA 24263; tel. 703/346-1095; Ethel Combs, Administrator

Housecall Hospice, 2167 Apperson Drive, Salem, VA 24153; tel. 540/776-3207; FAX. 540/776-3215; Peggy Mental, RN, Administrator

Housecall Hospice, Route 8, Box 335, Martinsville, VA 24112; tel. 540/632-9611; Ellen Boone, Administrator

In Home Health, 5040 Corporate Woods Drive, Virginia Beach, VA 23462; tel. 757/490-9323; FAX. 757/490-8711; Phyllis Muran, Director of Operations

In Home Health and Hospice, 408 W. Washington, Suffolk, VA 23434; tel. 757/934-7935; FAX. 757/934-7940; Phyllis J. Moran, Director of Operations

Jewish Family Service, 7300 Newport Avenue, P.O. Box 9503, Norfolk, VA 23505; tel. 757/489-3111; FAX. 757/451-1796; Harry Graber, Executive Director

Medshares Hospice of Middle Virginia, 9200 Arboretum Parkway, Suite 120, Richmond, VA 23236; tel. 804/327-4445; FAX. 804/327-4467; Michelle G. Nichols, RN, Director

Mountain Regional Hospice, 1533 Ingalls Street, P.O. Box 53, Clifton Forge, VA 24422; tel. 540/863-3333; FAX. 540/863-5353; Glenn Perry, Executive Director

New River Valley Hospice, Inc., 111 West Main Street, Christiansburg, VA 24073; tel. 703/381-5001; FAX. 703/381-5008; Bhanu Iyengar, Executive Director

Rockbridge Area Hospice, Inc., 129 South Randolph Street, P.O. Box 948, Lexington, VA 24450; tel. 540/463-1848; FAX. 540/463-5219; Susan Hogg, Executive Director

Sentara Hospice, Eight Koger Executive Building, Suite 210, Norfolk, VA 23502; tel. 804/628-3602; Dorothy Weeks, Manager

Twin County Hospice, 605 Glendale Road, Galaxy, VA 24333; tel. 540/236-7935; Patty S. Cooke, Administrator

WASHINGTON

Associated Health Services, P.O. Box 5200, Tacoma, WA 98415-0200; tel. 206/552-1825; FAX. 206/552-1838; Beverly Hatter, Director Grief, Loss and Transitional

Assured Home Health and Hospice, 576-B Main Street, Chehalis, WA 98532; tel. 360/748-0151; FAX. 360/748-0518; Wilma Wayson, RN, B.S.N., Director

Central Basin Home Health and Hospice, 410 West Third Avenue, Moses Lake, WA 98837; tel. 509/765-1856; FAX. 509/765-3323; Patti A. Weaver, Administrator

Community Home Health and Hospice, 1035 11th Avenue, P.O. Box 2067, Longview, WA 98632–8189; tel. 360/425–8510; FAX. 360/425–4667; Angie Armstrong, Executive Director

Evergreen Community Hospice, 12822 – 124th Lane, N.E., Kirkland, WA 98034; tel. 206/899–1040; FAX. 206/899–1099; Mary Vanltoomissioin, RN, Director

Group Health Cooperative Hospice Program, 83 South King Street, Suite 515, Seattle, WA 98104–2848; tel. 425/882–2022; FAX. 425/881–7147; Barbara Boyd, Administrator, Home and Community Service

Harbors Home Health and Hospice, 201 Seventh Street, Hoquiam, WA 98550; tel. 360/532–5454; FAX. 360/533–0999; DeLila Thorp, Administrator

Highline Home Care Services, 2801 South 128th, Tukwila, WA 98168; tel. 206/439–9095; FAX. 206/433–1031

Hospice of Snohomish County, 2731 Wetmore Avenue, Suite 520, Everett, WA 98201–3581; tel. 425/261–4800; FAX. 425/258–1097; Mary L. Brueggeman, Executive Director

Hospice of Spokane, West 1325 First Avenue, Suite 200, P.O. Box 2215, Spokane, WA 99210; tel. 888/459–0438; FAX. 509/458–0359; Anne Koepsell, Executive Director

Lower Valley Hospice, 3920 Outlook Road, Sunnyside, WA 98944; tel. 509/837–1676; FAX. 509/837–2878; Vicki Meyer, Executive Director

Okanogan Regional Home Health Care Agency, 217 Second Avenue, S., P.O. Box 1248, Okanogan, WA 98840; tel. 509/422–6721; FAX. 509/422–1835; Jeanette Weyrich, Executive Director

Swedish Home Health and Hospice and Infusion, 5701 Sixth Avenue, S., Suite 504, Seattle, WA 98108–2522; tel. 206/386–6602; FAX. 206/386–6613; Betty Jorgensen, Hospice Director

Tri-Cities Chaplaincy/Hospice and Counseling, 2108 West Entail Avenue, Kennewick, WA 99336; tel. 509/783–7416; FAX. 509/735–7850; Thomas H. Halazon, Executive Director

VNS Hospice, 400 North 34th Street, Suite 202, Seattle, WA 98103–8600; tel. 206/548–2344; FAX. 206/547–6182; Don W. Tarbutton, MHA, Hospice Program Administrator

Walla Community Hospice, P.O. Box 2026, 37 Jade Ave – Suite B, Walla, WA 99362; tel. 509/525–5561; FAX. 509/525–3517; Karyl Ball, Administrative Manager

Whatcom Hospice, 600 Birchwood Avenue, Bellingham, WA 98225; tel. 360/733–5877; FAX. 360/734–9621; Marsha J. Johnson

WEST VIRGINIA

Albert Gallatin Hospice, 3280 University Avenue, Morgantown, WV 25605; tel. 304/598–0226; Christine Constantine, Administrator

Community Home Care and Hospice, 1209 Warwood Avenue, Wheeling, WV 26003; tel. 304/277–1500; FAX. 304/277–1507; Ruth Prosser, M.S.N., RN, Administrator

Community Hospices of America – The Virginias, RR 2 Box 380, Bluefield, WV 24701; tel. 304/325–7220; FAX. 304/325–9384; Rich Bezjak, Program Director

Dignity Hospice of Southern West Virginia, Inc, P.O. Box 200, Chapmanville, WV 25508; tel. 304/855–1132; FAX. 304/855–1129; Sabrina C. Conley, Director

Hospice Care Corporation, P.O. Box 229, Kingwood, WV 26537; tel. 304/329–1161; FAX. 304/329–3285; Malene J. Davis, RN, Executive Director

Hospice of Huntington, 1101 Sixth Avenue, P.O. Box 464, Huntington, WV 25709; tel. 304/529–4217; FAX. 304/523–6051; Charlene Farrell, Executive Director

Hospice of Marion County, P.O. Box 1112, Fairmont, WV 26555–1112; tel. 304/366–0700; FAX. 304/366–9529; Irv Miller, Administrative Hospice Director

Hospice of South West Virginia, 105 South Eisenhower Drive, P.O. Box 1472, Beckley, WV 25802; tel. 304/255–6404; FAX. 304/255–6494; Thomas A. Williams, Executive Director

Hospice of the Panhandle, Inc., 2015 Boyd Orchard Court, Martinsburg, WV 25401; tel. 304/264–0406; FAX. 304/264–0409; Margaret Cogswell, RN, Executive Director

Journey Hospice, 314 South Wells Street, Sisterville, WV 26175; tel. 304/652–2611; FAX. 304/652–3190; Kathy J. Powell, RN, Program Director

Kanawha Hospice Care, Inc., 1143 Dunbar Avenue, Dunbar, WV 25064; tel. 304/768–8523; FAX. 304/768–8627; Shirley Hyatt, Director of Patient Services

Lewis County Home Health and Hospice Care, P.O. Box 1750, Weston, WV 26452; tel. 304/269–6432; FAX. 304/269–8220; Nancy Hosey, RN, Patient Care Coordinator

Monongalia County Health Department Hospice, 453 Van Voorhis Road, Morgantown, WV 26505–3408; tel. 304/598–5500; FAX. 304/598–5167; Vicky Kennedy, Hospice Supervisor, Patient Care Coordinator

Morgantown Hospice, 989 Maple Drive, P.O. Box 4222, Morgantown, WV 26505; tel. 304/285–2777; FAX. 304/285–1456; Margaret M. Kearney, Executive Director

Mountain Hospice, Inc., P.O. Box 173, Philippi, WV 26416; tel. 304/823–3922; FAX. 304/823–3926; Patricia Arnett, Director

People's Hospice, United Hospital Center, P.O. Box 1680, Clarksburg, WV 26302–1680; tel. 304/623–0524; FAX. 304/623–3399; Janice Chapman, Director

St. Joseph's Hospice, 92 West Main Street, Buckannon, WV 26201; tel. 304/472–6846; Sandra Knotts, Director

WISCONSIN

Beloit Regional Hospice, Inc., 2958 Prairie Avenue, Beloit, WI 53511; tel. 608/363–7421; FAX. 608/363–7426; Virginia Young, Administrator

Community Home Hospice, 3149 Saemann Avenue, Sheboygan, WI 53081; tel. 414/457–5770; Bobbi Illig

Community Hospice–VNA, 811 Monitor Street, Suite 101, LaCrosse, WI 54603; tel. 608/796–1666; Margaret Mossholder

Covenant Home Health and Hospice, 4000 Spring Street, P.O. Box 4045, Racine, WI 53404; tel. 414/635–7580; FAX. 414/633–7332; Denise Augustin, Administrator

Crossroads Hospice, 125 Fowler Street, Oconomowoc, WI 53066; tel. 414/569–8711; FAX. 414/569–8744; Barb Lemke, Intake

Dr. Kate–Lakeland Hospice, P.O. Box 770, Woodruff, WI 54568; tel. 715/356–8805; FAX. 715/358–7299; Helen Mozuch, RN, Director, Operations

Franciscan Skemp Healthcare Hospice, 212 South 11th Street, LaCrosse, WI 54601; tel. 608/791–9790; FAX. 608/791–9548; Marilyn Viehl, Administrator

Grant County Hospice, 125 S. Monroe Street, Lancaster, WI 53813; tel. 608/723–6416; FAX. 608/723–6501; Linda S. Adrian, Director, Health Officer

Heartland Hospice, 455 Davis Street, P.O. Box 487, Hammond, WI 54015; tel. 715/796–2223; Mary Troftgruben, Administrator

Hillside Homecare/Hospice, 709 South University Avenue, Beaver Dam, WI 53916; tel. 414/887–4050; FAX. 414/887–6815; Marla Noordhof, Director

Home Health United Hospice, 520 South Boulevard, P.O. Box 527, Baraboo, WI 53913; tel. 608/356–2288; FAX. 608/356–2290; Thomas H. Brown, President

Hope Hospice, Inc., 709 McComb Avenue, P.O. Box 237, Rib Lake, WI 54470; tel. 715/427–3532; FAX. 715/427–3537; Barbara Meyer, Director

Horizon Home Care and Hospice, Inc., 8949 Deebrook Trail, Brown Deer, WI 53223; tel. 414/365–8300; FAX. 414/365–8334; Mary Reynolds, Hospice Executive Director

Hospice Alliance, Inc., 600 – 52nd Street, Kenosha, WI 53140; tel. 414/942–1630; Connie Matler, Director, Clinical Services

Hospice Preferred Choice, 3118 South 27th Street, Milwaukee, WI 53215; tel. 414/649–8302; FAX. 414/649–8441; Linda Gruenewald – Schmitz, Executive Director

Hospice Program of Waupaca County, 811 Harding Street, Waupaca, WI 54981; tel. 715/258–6323; Barbara J. Black

HospiceCare, Inc., 2802 Coho Street, Suite 100, Madison, WI 53713–4521; tel. 608/276–4660; FAX. 608/276–4672; Susan Phillips, Executive Director

Jefferson Home Health and Hospice, 1007 Washington Street, P.O. Box 117, Baraboo, WI 53913; tel. 608/356–7570; FAX. 608/356–2629; William J. Hamilton, Jr., Managing Director

Manitowoc County Community Hospice, 1004 Washington Street, Manitowoc, WI 54220; tel. 414/684–7155; FAX. 414/684–8653; Lynn Seidl–Babcock, RN, B.S.N., Administrator

Marinette–Menominee County Hospice, 3133 Carney Avenue, Marinette, WI 54143; tel. 906/863–6331

Mercy Assisted Care, Home Health, Hospice, DME, 901 Mineral Point Avenue, Janesville, WI 53545; tel. 608/754–2201; FAX. 608/754–1147; Caryn Oleston, Executive Director

Milwaukee Hospice Home Care and Residence, 4067 North 92nd Street, Wauwatosa, WI 53222; tel. 414/438–8000; FAX. 414/438–8010; James Ewens, Mary New, Co–Directors

Northwest Wisconsin HomeCare/Hospice, 2321 East Clairemont Parkway, P.O. Box 2060, Eau Claire, WI 54702–2060; tel. 715/831–0100; FAX. 715/831–0108; Jill Hurlburt, RN, B.S.N., Director, Clinical Services

Rainbow Hospice Care, LLC, 147 West Rockwell Street, Jefferson, WI 53549; tel. 920/674–6255; FAX. 920/674–5288; Keni Christiansen, Director of Clinical Services

Regional Hospice, 2101 Beaser Avenue, Ashland, WI 54806; tel. 715/682–8677; FAX. 715/682–6404; Dianne Zaiser, Director of Clinical Services

Rolland Nelson Memorial Home Hospice, 419 Frederick Street, Waukesha, WI 53186; tel. 414/542–0724; FAX. 414/542–0608; Jacalyn Burdick, Program Manager

United Health Visiting Nurses Hospice, 820 Association Drive, Appleton, WI 54914; tel. 414/733–8562; Susan Kostka, Homecare/Hospice Supervisor

Unity Hospice, P.O. Box 22395, Green Bay, WI 54305–2395; tel. 414/433–7470; FAX. 414/437–1934; Donald W. Seibel, Director

UPC Health Network–Hospice Services, 3724 West Wisconsin Avenue, Milwaukee, WI 53208; tel. 414/342–9292; FAX. 414/342–8721; Walter Orzechowski, National Director, Hospice Service

V.N.A. Home Care and Hospice, 201 East Bell Street, Neenah, WI 54956; tel. 414/727–5555; FAX. 414/727–5552; Judith Eberhardy, President and CEO

Visiting Nurse Association Comforter Hospice, 1539 North 33rd Place, Sheboygan, WI 53081; tel. 920/458–4314; Robert Walters, VP of Regional Operations

Vitas Healthcare, 450 North Sunny Slope Road, Suite 60, Brookfield, WI 53005; tel. 414/821–6500; FAX. 414/821–6533; Suzanne Weltzien, General Manager

VNA Community Hospice, 11333 West National Avenue, Milwaukee, WI 53227; tel. 414/327–2295; FAX. 414/328–4499; Mary Runge, Chief Operating Officer

WYOMING

Central Wyoming Hospice Program, 319 South Wilson Street, Casper, WY 82601; tel. 307/577–4832; FAX. 307/577–4841; Janace Chapman, RN, Director

Hospice of Laramie, 1262 N. 22nd Street, Unit A, Laramie, WY 82072; tel. 307/745–9254; FAX. 307/742–5967; Connie M. Coca, M.S.W., Director

Hospice of Sweetwater County, 809 Thompson, Suite D, Rock Springs, WY 82901; tel. 307/362–1990; FAX. 307/352–6769; Pamela L. Jelaca, Executive Director

Hospice of the Big Horns, 1401 West 5th Street, Sheridan, WY 82801; tel. 307/672–1083; FAX. 307/672–2585; T. Marvin Goldman, Administrator

Hospice of the Tetons, 555 East Broadway, P.O. Box 428, Jackson, WY 83001; tel. 307/739–7465; FAX. 307/739–7645; Catherine Hadden, Director

Northeast Wyoming Hospice, 400 S. Kendrick, #301, P.O. Box 3259, Gillette, WY 82717–3259; tel. 307/682–6570; FAX. 307/682–2781; Ann M. Herman, RN, Administrator

Spirit Mountain Hospice, 707 Sheridan Ave., Cody, WY 82414; tel. 307/578–2413; FAX. 307/578–2294; Fred Whitmore, Administrator

Susie Bowling Lawrence Hospice, 497 West Lott, Buffalo, WY 82834; tel. 307/684–5521; FAX. 307/684–5385; Kent Ward, Administrator

U.S. Associated Areas

PUERTO RICO

Caribbean Hospice, 153 Winston Churchill Avenue, Rio Piedras, PR 00926; tel. 809/764–6565; Adalberto Sandoval

Condado Hospice, P.O. Box 5417, Station Hato , PR 00919–5417; tel. 809/758–2325; Manuel de Leon

Condado Hospice, Avenue Laurel Z–U–6, Bayamon, PR 00956; tel. 809/269–0175; Carmen L. Rosa

Guaynabo Hospice, Nine Jose Julian Acosta Street, Guaynabo, PR 00969; tel. 809/789–7878; Ricardo Larin, President

Hospicio Atencion Medica en el Hogar, Cipres K 1A Turabo, Caguas, PR 9; tel. 809/743–1121; Sandra Torres

Hospicio de Esperanza, Avenue General Valero 267, Fajardo, PR 00738; tel. 809/863–0924; Luis Vazquez

Hospicio El Nuevo Amanecer, Calle Garcia De La, Noceda 38, Rio Grande, PR 00745; tel. 809/888–8885; Melvin Acosta Roman

Hospicio Fe y Esperanza, P.O. Box 1834, Manati, PR 00674–1834; tel. 787/854–4971; FAX. 787/884–3757; Eduardo Alvarez, Administrator

Hospicio La Caridad, Calle Cipres, Villa Turabo, Caguas, PR 00725; tel. 787/286–8745; FAX. 787/746–5750; Glorivette Seneriz

Hospicio La Montana, Road 152 Km 12.4, Cedro Arriba P.O. Box 515, Naranjito, PR 00719; tel. 787/869–5500; FAX. 787/869–4483; Antonia Fortis Santiago

Hospicio La Paz, Calle Jose Rodriguez, Irizarry 152, Arecibo, PR 00612; tel. 809/879–4733; Luis Monrouzeau

Hospicio Luzamor, P.O. Box 1312, Calle Patron, #11, Morovis, PR 00687; tel. 809/862–0608; Ms. Brunilda Otero Declet, Executive Director

Hospicio Nuestra Sra. de la Guadalupe, P.O. Box 7699, Ponce, PR 00732; tel. 787/259–8210; FAX. 787/259–0206; Lucy Gonzalez, Administrator

Hospicio Santa Rita, La Paz Street, Box 1143, Aguada, PR 00602; tel. 787/868–2945; FAX. 787/868–0010; Licedia Rosado

Hospital Sin Paredes, P.O. Box 2015, Hato Rey, PR 00919; tel. 809/767–8959; Luis Serrano

La Piedad Hospice, 626 Escorial Hospice, San Juan, PR 00920; tel. 787/792–2411; FAX. 787/781–1643; Antonio Bisono

La Providencia Hospice, 36 Munoz Street, P.O. Box 10447, Ponce, PR 00731; tel. 787/843–2364; FAX. 787/841–2940; Eyleen Rodriguez Lugo, Executive Director

Monserrate Hospice Care, Inc., P.O. Box 366148, San Juan, PR 00936–6148; tel. 809/754–0449; Luis Class

Programa de Servicios de Adjuntas, Inc., Rodulfo Gonzalez #46, P.O. Box 993, Adjuntas, PR 00601; tel. 787/829–2953; FAX. 787/829–4453; Abraham Gonzalez, Executive Director

San Francisco Asis Hospice, P.O. Box 877, Aguada, PR 00602; tel. 787/868–2920; FAX. 787/252–0211; Dilia Dajer, Executive Director

Santa Rita Hospice, Inc., Condominio Medical Center Plaza, Box 1143, Aguada, PR 00602; tel. 787/831–7225; Licedia Rosado

Sendero de Luz, Inc., 11 Georgetti Street, P.O. Box 875, Comerio, PR 00782; tel. 787/875–5701; FAX. 787/875–0887; Juan C. Santiago, Executive Director

St. Lukes Home Care and Hospice Program, Urb. Industrial, Calle A Edificio A–B, Ponce, PR 00732; tel. 787/843–4185; FAX. 787/843–4076; Luz N. Rodriguez, Executive Director

Un Toque de Amor Hospice, Marginal A–2 Urb, San Salvador, Manati, PR 00674; tel. 809/884–3326; Jenny Olivo

State Government Agencies for Freestanding Hospices

United States

ALABAMA
Alabama Department of Public Health, Division of Licensure and Certification, 434 Monroe Street, Montgomery, AL 36130–1701; tel. 334/240–3503; FAX. 334/240–3147; Rick Harris, Director

ALASKA
Division of Medical Assistance, Health Facilities Licensing and Certification Section, 4730 Business Park Blvd., Suite 18, Anchorage, AK 99503; tel. 907/561–8081; FAX. 907/561–3011; Shelbert Larsen, Administrator

ARIZONA
Arizona Department of Health Services, Health Care Facilities, 1647 East Morten, Phoenix, AZ 85020; tel. 602/674–4200; FAX. 602/861–0645; Mary Wiley, Assistant Director

ARKANSAS
Department of Health, Division of Health Facility Services, 5800 West 10th, Suite 400, Little Rock, AR 72204–9916; tel. 501/661–2201; FAX. 501/661–2165; Valetta M. Buck, Director

CALIFORNIA
Department of Health Services, Licensing and Certification Program, 1800 Third Street, Suite 210, P.O. Box 942732, Sacramento, CA 94234–7320; tel. 916/324–8628; FAX. 916/445–6979; Marilyn Pearman, Chief, Policy Section

COLORADO
Colorado Department of Public Health and Environment, Health Facilities Division A–Two, 4300 Cherry Creek Drive., Denver, CO 80222–1530; tel. 303/692–2800; FAX. 303/782–4883; Priscilla Ezell, RN, Program Administrator

CONNECTICUT
Department of Public Health Division of Health Systems Regulation, 410 Capital Avenue, Hartford, CT 06134–0308; tel. 860/509–7400; FAX. 860/509–7543; Cynthia Denne, RN, MPA., Director

DELAWARE
Department of Health and Social Services, Office of Health Facilities Licensing and Certification, 2055 Limestone Road, Suite 200, Wilmington, DE 19808; tel. 302/995–8521; FAX. 302/577–6672; Ellen T. Reap, Director

DISTRICT OF COLUMBIA
Department of Health Licensing and Regulation, 825 North Capital, NE, Washington, DC 20001; tel. 202/442–5888; FAX. 202/727–7780; Geraldine Sykes, Administrator

FLORIDA
Agency for HealthCare Administration, Division of Health Quality Assurance, Long Term Care Unit, Fort Knox Executive Center, 2727 Mahan Drive, Tallahassee, FL 32308–5407; tel. 850/922–8540; FAX. 850/487–6240; Patricia Hall, Unit Manager

GEORGIA
Health Care Section – Georgia Dept. of Human Resources, Office of Regulatory Services, Two Peachtree Street, N.W., Room 33–250, Atlanta, GA 30303–3142; tel. 404/657–5550; FAX. 404/657–8934; Susie M. Woods, Director

HAWAII
Department of Health, Licensing and Certification, Hospital and Medical Facilities Branch, P.O. Box 3378, Honolulu, HI 96801; tel. 808/586–4080; FAX. 808/586–4444; Helen K. Yoshimi, B.S.N., M.P.H., HMF, Branch Chief

IDAHO
Bureau of Facility Standards, Department of Health and Welfare, P.O. Box 83720, Boise, ID 83720–0036; tel. 208/334–6626; FAX. 208/364–1888; Silva Cresell, Supervisor

ILLINOIS
Department of Public Health, Office of Health Care Regulation, Bureau of Hospitals and Ambulatory Services, 525 West Jefferson Street, Fourth Floor, Springfield, IL 62761; tel. 217/782–7412; FAX. 217/782–0382; Catherine M. Stokes, Assistant Deputy Director

INDIANA
Indiana State Department of Health, Division of Acute Care, Two North Meridian Street, Indianapolis, IN 46204; tel. 317/233–7474; FAX. 317/233–7157; Mary Azbill, MT (ASCP)

IOWA
Department of Inspection and Appeals, Division of Health Facilities, Lucas State Office Building, Des Moines, IA 50319; tel. 515/281–3765; FAX. 515/242–5022; Nancy M. Ruzicka

KANSAS
Department of Health and Environment, Bureau of Health Facility Regulation, 900 Southwest Jackson, Suite 1001, Topeka, KS 66612–0001; tel. 785/296–1280; FAX. 785/296–1266; George A. Dugger, Medical Facilities Certification Administrator

KENTUCKY
Cabinet for Human Resources, Division of Licensing and Regulation, C.H.R. Building, 275 East Main Street, Fourth Floor, East, Frankfort, KY 40621; tel. 502/564–2800; FAX. 502/564–6546; Rebecca J. Cecil, Director

LOUISIANA
Department of Health and Hospitals, Bureau of Health Services , Health Standards Section Licensing Unit, P.O. Box 3767, Baton Rouge, LA 70821; tel. 504/342–0138; FAX. 504/342–5292; Lisa Deaton, RN, Manager

MAINE
Division of Licensing and Certification, Department of Human Services, State House, Station 11, Augusta, ME 04333; tel. 207/624–5443; FAX. 207/624–5378; Louis Dorogi, Director

MARYLAND
Department of Health and Mental Hygiene, Licensing and Certification Administration, 4201 Patterson Avenue, Baltimore, MD 21215; tel. 410/764–4980; FAX. 410/358–0750; James Ralls, Assistant Director

MASSACHUSETTS
Massachusetts Department of Public Health, Division of Health Care Quality, 10 West Street, 5th Floor, Boston, MA 02111; tel. 617/727–5860; Dr. Howard Kyongju Koh New, Commissioner

MICHIGAN
Department of Consumer and Industry Services, Division of Licensing and Certification, G. Mennen Williams Building, 525 W. Ottawa, Lansing, MI 48909; tel. 517/241–2626; Dr. Gladys Thomas, Director

MINNESOTA
Department of Health, Facility and Provider Compliance Division, Licensing and Certification, 85 East Seventh Place, Suite 300, St. Paul, MN 55164–0900; tel. 651/215–8719; FAX. 651/215–8709; Carol Hirschfeld, Supervisor, Program Assurance Unit

MISSISSIPPI
Department of Health, Division of Health Facilities, Licensure and Certification, P.O. Box 1700, Jackson, MS 39215; tel. 601/354–7300; FAX. 601/354–7230; Vanessa Phipps, Director

MISSOURI
Department of Health, Bureau of Home Health Licensing and Certification, P.O. Box 570, Jefferson City, MO 65102; tel. 573/751–6336; FAX. 573/751–6315; Carol Gourd, RN, Administrator

MONTANA
Department of Public Health and Human Services, Quality Assurance Division, Licensure Bureau, Cogswell Building, 1400 Broadway, Helena, MT 59620–2951; tel. 406/444–2676; FAX. 406/444–1742; Roy P. Kemp, Chief

NEBRASKA
Nebraska Department of Health, Health Facility Licensure and Inspection Section, 301 Centennial Mall, South, 3rd Floor., P.O. Box 94986, Lincoln, NE 68509–4980; tel. 402/471–2946; FAX. 402/471–0555; Helen Meeks, Section Administrator

NEVADA
Nevada State Health Division, Bureau of Licensure and Certification, 1550 East College Parkway, Suite 158, Carson City, NV 89706–7921; tel. 775/687–4475; FAX. 775/687–6588; Richard J. Panelli, Chief

NEW HAMPSHIRE
Department of Health and Human Services, Licensing and Regulation, Six Hazen Drive, 2nd Floor, West Wing, Concord, NH 03301; tel. 603/271–4592; FAX. 603/271–4968; Raymond Rusin, Bureau Chief

NEW JERSEY
New Jersey Department of Health and Senior Services, Division , Certificate of Need and Acute Care Licensure, Inspections, John Fitchway, Market and Warren Streets, Trenton, NJ 08625–0360; tel. 609/292–8773; FAX. 609/984–3165; John Caiabira, Director of Certificate of NAAC Lice

NEW MEXICO
Department of Health, Health Facility Licensing and Certification Bureau, 525 Camino de los Marquez, Suite Two, Santa Fe, NM 87501; tel. 505/827–4200; FAX. 505/827–4222; Mathew Gervase, Bureau Chief

NEW YORK
Bureau of Surveillance and Quality Assurance, 161 Delaware Avenue, Delmar, NY 12054; tel. 518/478–1133; FAX. 518/478–1134; Anna D. Colello, Director

NORTH CAROLINA
Department of Human Resources, Division of Facility Services, 701 Barbour Drive, Raleigh, NC 27626–0530; tel. 919/733–7461; FAX. 919/733–8274; Steve White, Chief, Licensure and Certification

NORTH DAKOTA
Department of Health, Health Resources Section, 600 East Boulevard Avenue, Bismarck, ND 58505; tel. 701/328–2352; FAX. 701/328–4727; Darleen Bartz, Director of Health Facilities

OHIO
Division of Quality Assurance, Ohio Department of Health, 246 North High Street, Columbus, OH 43266–0588; tel. 614/466–7857; FAX. 614/644–0208; Rebecca Maust, Chief

OKLAHOMA
Department of Health, Special Health Services, 1000 Northeast 10th Street, Oklahoma City, OK 73117; tel. 405/271–6576; FAX. 405/271–1308; Gary Glover, Chief, Medical Facilities

OREGON
Health Care Licensing and Certification, Oregon Health Division, 800 Northeast Oregon Street, # 21, Suite 640, Portland, OR 97232; tel. 503/731–4013; FAX. 503/731–4080; Kathleen Smail, Manager

Section C

PENNSYLVANIA
Department of Health, Division of Primary Care and Home Health, 132 Kline Plaza, Suite A, Harrisburg, PA 17104; tel. 717/783–1379; FAX. 717/787–3188; Aralene Trostle, Acting Director

RHODE ISLAND
Rhode Island Department of Health, Division of Facilities Regulation, Three Capitol Hill, Providence, RI 02908–5097; tel. 401/222–2566; FAX. 401/222–3999; Wayne I. Farrington, Chief

SOUTH CAROLINA
Department of Health and Environmental Control, Division of Certification, 2600 Bull Street, Columbia, SC 29201; tel. 803/737–7205; FAX. 803/737–7292; Arthur I. Starnes, Division Director

SOUTH DAKOTA
Department of Health, Office of Health Care Facilities Licensure and Certification, 615 East 4th Street, Pierre, SD 57501–1700; tel. 605/773–3356; FAX. 605/773–6667; Joan Bachman, Administrator

TENNESSEE
Department of Health, Division of Health Care Facilities, Cordell Hull Building, 425 5th Ave. North, 1st Floor, Nashville, TN 37247–0508; tel. 615/741–7603; FAX. 615/367–6397; Carol Brown

TEXAS
Texas Department of Health, Health Facility Compliance Division, 1100 West 49th Street, Austin, TX 78756; tel. 512/834–6650; FAX. 512/834–6653; Nance Stearman, RN, M.S.N., Director

UTAH
Utah Department of Health, Bureau of Health Facility Licensure, Box 142003, Salt Lake City, UT 84114–2003; tel. 801/538–6152; FAX. 801/538–6325; Debra Wynkoop–Green, Director

VERMONT
Hospice Council of Vermont, 10 Maine Street, Montpelier, VT 05602; tel. 802/229–0579; FAX. 802/232–6218; Virginia L. Fry, Director

VIRGINIA
Virginia Department of Health, Center for Quality Health Care Services and Consumer Protection, 3600 Centre, Suite 216, Richmond, VA 23230; tel. 804/367–2102; FAX. 804/367–2149; Nancy R. Hofheimer, Director

WASHINGTON
Washington Department of Health, Facilities and Services Licensing, Target Plaza, Suite 500, 2725 Harrison Avenue, N.W., Olympia, WA 98504–7852; tel. 360/705–6611; FAX. 360/705–6654; Byron Plan, Manager

WEST VIRGINIA
Office of Health Facility Licensure and Certification, West Virginia Division of Health, 1900 Kanawha Boulevard, E., Building Three, Suite 550, Charleston, WV 25305; tel. 304/558–0050; FAX. 304/558–2515; Bonnie K. Brauner, RN, BSN, Program Manager

WISCONSIN
Bureau of Quality Assurance, Division of Supportive Living, P.O. Box 309, Madison, WI 53701–0309; tel. 608/267–7185; FAX. 608/267–0352; Judy Fryback, Director, Bureau of Quality Assurance

WYOMING
Department of Health, Office of Health Quality, 2020 Carey Avenue, 8th Floor, Cheyenne, WY 82002; tel. 307/777–7123; FAX. 307/777–7127; Gerald E. Bronnenberg, Administrator

U.S. Associated Areas

PUERTO RICO
Puerto Rico Department of Health, PO Box 70184, San Juan, PR 00936–8184; tel. 787/274–7601; FAX. 787/250–6547; Carmen Feliciano de Melecio, M.D., Secretary of Health

JCAHO Accredited Freestanding Long-Term Care Organizations

The accredited freestanding long–term care organizations listed have been accredited as of April, 1999 by the Joint Commission on Accreditation of Healthcare Organizations by decision of the Accreditation Committee of the Board of Commissioners.

The organizations listed here have been found to be in compliance with the Joint Commission standards for long–term care organizations, as found in the Comprehensive Accreditation Manual for the Long–Term Care Organizations.

Please refer to section A of the AHA Guide for information on hospitals with Long–Term Care services. These hospitals are identified by Facility Code 64. In section A, those hospitals identified by Approval Code 1 are JCAHO accredited.

We present this list simply as a convenient directory. Inclusion or omission of any organization's name indicates neither approval nor disapproval by Health Forum LLC, an affiliate of the American Hospital Association.

United States

ALABAMA
Cedar Crest, 4490 Virginia Loop Road, Montgomery, AL 36116
Integrated Health Services at Hanover, 39 Hanover Circle, Birmingham, AL 35205
Warren Manor Living Center, Number 11 Bell Road, Selma, AL 36701

ARIZONA
Citadel Care Center, 5121 East Broadway Road, Mesa, AZ 85206
Desert Cove Nursing Center, 1750 West Frye Road, Chandler, AZ 85224
Desert Sky Health and Rehabilitation Center, 5125 North 58th Avenue, Glendale, AZ 85301
East Valley Health Care Center, 420 West 10th Place, Mesa, AZ 85201
Glendale Care Center, 4704 West Diana Avenue, Glendale, AZ 85302
GranCare Health Care Center, 16640 North 38th Street, Phoenix, AZ 85032
Hacienda Rehabilitation and Care Center, 660 Coronado Drive, Sierra Vista, AZ 85635
Hearthstone of Sun City, 13818 N Thunderbird Boulevard, Sun City, AZ 85351
Heritage Health Care Center, PO Box 391, Globe, AZ 85502
Kachina Point Health Care and Rehabilitation Center, 505 Jacks Canyon Road, Sedona, AZ 86351
La Canada Care Center, 7970 North La Canada Drive, Tucson, AZ 85704
La Mesa Rehabilitation and Care Center, 2470 South Arizona Avenue, Yuma, AZ 85364
Life Care Center at South Mountain, 8008 South Jesse Owens Parkway, Phoenix, AZ 85040
Life Care Center of North Glendale, 13620 North 55th Avenue, Glendale, AZ 85304
Life Care Center of Paradise Valley, 4065 East Bell Road, Phoenix, AZ 85032
Life Care Center of Scottsdale, 9494 East Becker Lane, Scottsdale, AZ 85260
Life Care Center of Sierra Vista, 2305 East Wilcox, Sierra Vista, AZ 85635
Life Care Center of Tucson, 6211 West LaCholla Boulevard, Tucson, AZ 85741
Life Care Center of Yuma, 2450 South 19th Avenue, Yuma, AZ 85364
ManorCare Health Services, 3705 North Swan Road, Tucson, AZ 85718
Mi Casa Nursing Center, 330 South Pinnule Circle, Mesa, AZ 85206
Payson Care Center, 107 East Lone Pine Drive, Payson, AZ 85541
Pecos Nursing and Rehabilitation Center, 1980 West Pecos Road, Chandler, AZ 85224
Phoenix Living Center, 1314 East McDowell Road, Phoenix, AZ 85006
Scottsdale Heritage Court, 3339 N Civic Center Boulevard, Scottsdale, AZ 85251
Scottsdale Village Square, 2620 North 68th Street, Scottsdale, AZ 85257
Sonoran Rehabilitation and Care Center, 4202 North 20th Avenue, Phoenix, AZ 85015
Sun Health Care Center, 10601 West Santa Fe Drive, Sun City, AZ 85351
Village Green HealthCare Center, 2932 North 14th Street, Phoenix, AZ 85014

CALIFORNIA
Akin's Post Acute Rehabilitation Hospital, 2750 Atlantic Avenue, Long Beach, CA 90806
Alamitos Belmont Rehabilitation Hospital, 3901 East Fourth Street, Long Beach, CA 90814
Almaden Health and Rehab Center, 2065 Los Gatos Almaden Road, San Jose, CA 95124
Anaheim Terrace Care Center, 141 South Knott Avenue, Anaheim, CA 92804
Autumn Hills Health Care Center, 430 North Glendale Avenue, Glendale, CA 91206
Bay Crest Care Center, 3750 Garnet Street, Torrance, CA 90503
Beverly Healthcare, 6700 Sepulveda Boulevard, Van Nuys, CA 91411
Beverly Manor Nursing and Rehabilitation Center, 1041 South Main Street, Burbank, CA 91506
Bixby Knolls Towers Health Care and Rehabilitation Center, 3747 Atlantic Avenue, Long Beach, CA 90807
Brier Oak Terrace Care Center, 5154 Sunset Boulevard, Los Angeles, CA 90027
Brookside Skilled Nursing Hospital, 2620 Flores Street, San Mateo, CA 94403
California Nursing and Rehabilitation Center, 2299 North Indian Canyon, Palm Springs, CA 92262
California Special Care Center, Inc., 8787 Center Drive, La Mesa, CA 91942
Calistoga Care – Nursing and Rehab Center, 1715 Washington Street, Calistoga, CA 94515
Carehouse, 1800 Old Tustin Road, Santa Ana, CA 92705
Casa Colina Peninsula Rehabilitation Center, 26303 Western Avenue, Lomita, CA 90717
Casa Palmera Care Center, Inc., 14750 El Camino Real, Del Mar, CA 92014
Chapman Harbor Skilled Nursing Facility, 12232 West Chapman Avenue, Garden Grove, CA 92840
Clear View Sanitarium and Convalescent Center, 15823 South Western Avenue, Gardena, CA 90247
Colonial Care Center, 1913 East 5th Street, Long Beach, CA 90802
Colony Park Nursing and Rehabilitation Center, 159 East Orangeburg Avenue, Modesto, CA 95350
Country Villa Nursing and Rehabilitation Center, 340 South Alvarado Street, Los Angeles, CA 90057
Country Villa Sheraton Nursing and Rehabilitation Center, 9655 Sepulveda Boulevard, North Hills, CA 91343
Country Villa South, 3515 Overland Avenue, Los Angeles, CA 90034
Country Villa Westwood Nursing Center, 12121 Santa Monica Boulevard, Los Angeles, CA 90025
Covina Rehabilitation Center, 261 West Badillo Street, Covina, CA 91723
Creekside HealthCare Center, 1900 Church Lane, San Pablo, CA 94806
Delta Nursing and Rehabilitation Hospital, 514 North Bridge Street, Visalia, CA 93291
Devonshire Care Center, 1350 East Devonshire Avenue, Hemet, CA 92544
Diamond Ridge HealthCare Center, 2351 Loveridge Road, Pittsburg, CA 94565
Driftwood Health Care Center, 19700 Hesperian Boulevard, Hayward, CA 94541
Driftwood Health Care Center, 4109 Emerald Street, Torrance, CA 90503
Driftwood Healthcare Center, 675 24th Avenue, Santa Cruz, CA 95062
Earlwood Care Center, 20820 Earl Street, Torrance, CA 90503
Eastwood Convalescent Hospital, 4029 East Anaheim Street, Long Beach, CA 90804
Edgewater Convalescent Hospital, 2625 East 4th Street, Long Beach, CA 90814
El Encanto Healthcare & Habilitation Center, 555 South El Encanto Road, Hacienda Heights, CA 91745
El Rancho Vista Healthcare Center, 8925 Mines Avenue, Pico Rivera, CA 90660
Elmcrest Convalescent Hospital, 3111 Santa Anita Avenue, El Monte, CA 91733
Empress Rehabilitation Center, 1020 Termino Avenue, Long Beach, CA 90804
English Oaks Convalescent and Rehabilitation Hospital, 2633 West Rumble Road, Modesto, CA 95350
Eskaton Manzanita Manor, 5318 Manzanita Avenue, Carmichael, CA 95608
Eskaton Village, 3939 Walnut Avenue, Carmichael, CA 95608
Evergreen Rehabilitation Care Center, 2030 Evergreen Avenue, Modesto, CA 95350
Fairfield Heatlh Care Center, 1255 Travis Boulevard, Fairfield, CA 94533
Flagship Healthcare Center, 466 Flagship Road, Newport Beach, CA 92663
Florin Health Care Center, 7400 24th Street, Sacramento, CA 95822
Fountain Care Center, 1835 West LaVeta Avenue, Orange, CA 92868
Fountain View Convalescent Hospital, 5310 Fountain Avenue, Los Angeles, CA 90029
Fremont Health Center, 39022 Presidio Way, Fremont, CA 94538
Fruitvale Health Care Center, 3020 East 15th Street, Oakland, CA 94601
Grand Terrace Convalescent Hospital, 12000 Mt. Vernon Avenue, Grand Terrace, CA 92313
Greenhaven Country Place, 455 Florin Road, Sacramento, CA 95831
Guardian Ygnacio, 1449 Ygnacio Valley Road, Walnut Creek, CA 94598
Hancock Park Convalescent Rehabilitation Center, 505 North LaBrea Avenue, Los Angeles, CA 90036
Hanford Nursing and Rehabilitation Hospital, 1007 West Lacey Boulevard, Hanford, CA 93230–0911
Hayward Hills Health Care Center, 1768 B Street, Hayward, CA 94541
Heritage of Stockton, A Convalescent and Rehab Center, 9107 North Davis Road, Stockton, CA 95209
Huntington Beach Convalescent Hospital, 18811 Florida Street, Huntington Beach, CA 92648
Huntington Drive Health and Rehabilitation Center, 400 West Huntington Drive, Arcadia, CA 91007
Huntington Valley Nursing Center, 8382 Newman Avenue, Huntington Beach, CA 92648
Imperial Convalescent Center, 11926 S La Mirada Boulevard, La Mirada, CA 90638
Inglewood Healthcare Center, 100 South Hillcrest Boulevard, Inglewood, CA 90301
Integrated Health Services at Orange Hills, 5017 East Chapman Avenue, Orange, CA 92669
John Douglas French Center for Alzheimer's Disease, 3951 Katella Avenue, Los Alamitos, CA 90720
Julia Healthcare Center, 276 Sierra Vista Avenue, Mountain View, CA 94043
La Mariposa Nursing and Rehabilitation Center, 1244 Travis Boulevard, Fairfield, CA 94533
La Salette Health and Rehabilitation Center, 538 East Fulton Street, Stockton, CA 95204
Lancaster Health Care Center, 1642 West Avenue J, Lancaster, CA 93534
Laurelwood Health Care Center, 13000 Victory Boulevard, North Hollywood, CA 91606
Leisure Court Nursing Center, 1135 North Leisure Court, Anaheim, CA 92801
Live Oak Rehabilitation Center, 537 West Live Oak, San Gabriel, CA 91776
Lytton Gardens, 437 Webster Street, Palo Alto, CA 94301

Magnolia Gardens Care Center, 1609 Trousdale Drive, Burlingame, CA 94010

Magnolia Special Care Center, 635 South Magnolia, El Cajon, CA 92020

ManorCare Health Services, 1150 Tilton Drive, Sunnyvale, CA 94087

ManorCare Health Services, Inc, 11680 Warner Avenue, Fountain Valley, CA 92708

Marlora Post Acute Rehabilitation Hospital, 3801 East Anaheim Street, Long Beach, CA 90804

Mission Terrace Convalescent Hospital, 623 West Junipero Street, Santa Barbara, CA 93105

Nob Hill Healthcare Center, 1359 Pine Street, San Francisco, CA 94109

Orinda Rehabilitation and Convalescent Hospital, 11 Altarinda Road, Orinda, CA 94563

Pacific Coast Manor, 1935 Wharf Road, Capitola, CA 95010

Pacific Hills Manor, 370 Noble Court, Morgan Hill, CA 95037

Pacific Regency / Bakersfield, 6212 Tudor Way, Bakersfield, CA 93306

Pacifica Nursing and Rehabilitation Center, 385 Esplanade Avenue, Pacifica, CA 94044

Palm Grove Care Center, 13075 Blackbird Street, Garden Grove, CA 92843

Park Anaheim Healthcare Center, 3435 West Ball Road, Anaheim, CA 92804

Park Tustin Rehabilitation and Healthcare Center, 2210 East First Street, Santa Ana, CA 92705

Parkmont Rehabilitation and Nursing Care Center, 2400 Parkside Drive, Fremont, CA 94536

Parkview Health Care Center, 27350 Tampa Avenue, Hayward, CA 94544–4429

Petaluma Care and Rehabilitation, 1115 B Street, Petaluma, CA 94952

Reche Canyon Rehabilitation and Health Care Center, 1350 Reche Canyon Road, Colton, CA 92324

Scripps Memorial, 900 Santa Fe Drive, Encinitas, CA 92024

Scripps Memorial Torrey Pines Convalescent Hospital, 2552 Torrey Pines Road, La Jolla, CA 92037

Sharon Heights Care and Rehab, 1185 Monte Rosa Drive, Menlo Park, CA 94025–6795

Skyline Convalescent Hospital, 2065 Forest Avenue, San Jose, CA 95128

Studio City Convalescent, 11429 Ventura Boulevard, Studio City, CA 91604

Subacute Saratoga Hospital, 13425 Sousa Lane, Saratoga, CA 95070

Sun Rise Care and Rehabilitation – Southbay, 21414 South Vermont Avenue, Torrance, CA 90502

Sun Rise Care Center – Park Central, 2100 Parkside Drive, Fremont, CA 94536

Sunrise Brittany Care Center, 3900 Garfield Avenue, Carmichael, CA 95608

Sunrise Care & Rehabilitation for Glendora, 435 East Gladstone Street, Glendora, CA 91740

SunRise Care & Rehabilitation for Hayward, 26660 Patrick Avenue, Hayward, CA 94544

SunRise Care and Rehabilitation for Burlingame, 1100 Trousdale Drive, Burlingame, CA 94010

Sunrise Care and Rehab Center for Kentfield, 1251 South Eliseo Drive, Kentfield, CA 94904

Sunrise Care and Rehab Center for Monteca, 410 Eastwood Avenue, Manteca, CA 95336

SunRise Care Center for San Dimas, 1033 East Arrow Highway, Glendora, CA 91740

Sunrise Care Center for Santa Monica – 17th Street, 1330 17th Street, Santa Monica, CA 90404

SunRise Care Center for Escondido–West, 201 North Fig Street, Escondido, CA 92025

Sunrise Care Center for Santa Monica – Franklin St, 1321 Franklin Street, Santa Monica, CA 90404

Tarzana Health and Rehabilitation Center, 5650 Reseda Boulevard, Tarzana, CA 91356

The Cloisters of La Jolla, 7160 Fay Avenue, La Jolla, CA 92037

The Cloisters of Mission Hills, 3680 Reynard Way, San Diego, CA 92103

The Homestead of Fair Oaks, 11300 Fair Oaks Boulevard, Fair Oaks, CA 95628–5172

Thousand Oaks Health Care Center, 93 West Avenida de Los Arboles, Thousand Oaks, CA 91360

Totally Kids Specialty Healthcare, 1720 Mountain View Avenue, Loma Linda, CA 92354

Tulare Nursing and Rehabilitation Hospital, 680 East Merritt Street, Tulare, CA 93274

Vacaville Convalescent and Rehabilitation Center, 585 Nut Tree Court, Vacaville, CA 95687

Vale Care Center, 13484 San Pablo Avenue, San Pablo, CA 94806

Valley Manor Rehabilitation Center, 3806 Clayton Road, Concord, CA 94521

Villa Maria Care Center, 425 East Barcellus Avenue, Santa Maria, CA 93454

Village Square Nursing and Rehabilitation Center, 1586 West San Marcos Boulevard, San Marcos, CA 92069

Vista Knoll, 2000 Westwood Road, Vista, CA 92083

Woodland Care Center, 7120 Corbin Avenue, Reseda, CA 91335

COLORADO

Alpine Living Center, 501 East Thornton Parkway, Thornton, CO 80229

Applewood Living Center, 1800 Stroh Place, Longmont, CO 80501

Arvada Health Center, 6121 West 60th Avenue, Arvada, CO 80003

Bethany Healthplex, 5301 W. First Avenue, Lakewood, CO 80226

Bonell Good Samaritan Center, PO Box 1508, Greeley, CO 80632–1508

Boulder Manor Living Center, 4685 East Baseline Road, Boulder, CO 80303

Camellia Health Care Center, 500 Geneva Street, Aurora, CO 80010–4305

Castle Garden Care Center, 401 Malley Drive, Northglenn, CO 80233

Cedars Health Care Center, 1599 Ingalls Street, Lakewood, CO 80214

Cherrelyn Health Care Center, 5555 South Elati Street, Littleton, CO 80120

Cherry Hills Health Care Center, 3575 South Washington Street, Englewood, CO 80110

Garden Terrace Alzheimer's Center of Excellence, 1600 South Potomac Street, Aurora, CO 80012

Hallmark Nursing Center, 3701 West Radcliff Avenue, Denver, CO 80236

IHS of Colorado at Cherry Creek, 14699 East Hampden Avenue, Aurora, CO 80014

Integrated Health Services of Canon City, 515 Fairview, Canon City, CO 81212

Integrated Health Services of Colorado Springs, 3625 Parkmoor Village Drive, Colorado Springs, CO 80917

Julia Temple Center, 3401 South Lafayette Street, Englewood, CO 80110

Kenton Manor, 850 27th Avenue, Greeley, CO 80631

Life Care Center of Aurora, 14101 East Evans Avenue, Aurora, CO 80014

Life Care Center of Evergreen, 2987 Evergreen Parkway, Evergreen, CO 80439

Life Care Center of Pueblo, 2118 Chatalet Lane, Pueblo, CO 81005

Manor Care Nursing and Rehabilitation Center, 2800 Palo Parkway, Boulder, CO 80301

Mariner Health of Denver, 895 South Monaco Parkway, Denver, CO 80224

Mariner Health of Greenwood Village, 6005 South Holly Street, Littleton, CO 80121

Red Rocks HealthCare Center, 4450 East Jewell, Denver, CO 80222

San Juan Living Center, 1043 Ridge, Montrose, CO 81401

Spring Creek HealthCare Center, 1000 East Stuart Street, Fort Collins, CO 80525

Sunrise Bear Creek Care and Rehabilitation of Morrison, PO Box 117, Morrison, CO 80465

Terrace Gardens Health Care Center, 2438 East Fountain Boulevard, Colorado Springs, CO 80910

Vista Grande Rehabilitation and Care Center, PO Box 1718, Cortez, CO 81321

CONNECTICUT

3030 Park Fairfield Health Center, Inc., 118 Jefferson Street, Fairfield, CT 06432

Aaron Manor Nursing and Rehabilitation Center, PO Box 336, Chester, CT 06412

Abbott Terrace Health Center, 44 Abbott Terrace, Waterbury, CT 06702

Adams House Healthcare, 80 Fern Drive, Torrington, CT 06790

Alexandria Manor, 55 Tunxis Avenue, Bloomfield, CT 06002

Ashlar of Newtown, PO Box 5505..., Newtown, CT 06470

Astoria Park, 725 Park Avenue, Bridgeport, CT 06604

Avery Heights, 705 New Britain Avenue, Hartford, CT 06106

Avon Health Center, 652 West Avon Road, Avon, CT 06001–2999

Bayview Health Care Center, 301 Rope Ferry Road, Waterford, CT 06385

Beacon Brook Health Center, 89 Weid Drive, Naugatuck, CT 06770

Beechwood Rehabilitation and Nursing Center, 31 Vauxhall Street, New London, CT 06320

Bel–Air Manor Nursing and Rehabilitation Center, 256 New Britain Avenue, Newington, CT 06111

Bentley Gardens Health Care Center, 310 Terrace Avenue, West Haven, CT 06516–2698

Bethel Health and Rehabilitation Center, LLC, 13 Parklawn Drive, Bethel, CT 06801

Bickford Health Care Center, Fourteen Main Street, Windsor Locks, CT 06096

Bishop Wicke Health and Rehabilitation Center, Inc, 584 Long Hill Avenue, Shelton, CT 06484

Blair Manor, 612 Hazard Avenue, Enfield, CT 06082

Bloomfield Health Care Center, 355 Park Avenue, Bloomfield, CT 06002

Branford Hills Health Care Center, 189 Alps Road, Branford, CT 06405

Bridgeport Health Care Center, 600 Bond Street, Bridgeport, CT 06610

Bridgeport Manor, 540 Bond Street, Bridgeport, CT 06610

Brightview of Avon, 220 Scoville Road, Avon, CT 06001

Brittany Farms Health Center, 400 Brittany Farms Road, New Britain, CT 06053

Brook Hollow Health Care Center, 55 Kondracki Lane, Wallingford, CT 06492

Brookview Health Care Facility, 130 Loomis Drive, West Hartford, CT 06107

Caleb Hitchcock Health Center, 40 Loeffler Road, Bloomfield, CT 06002

Cambridge Manor, 2428 Easton Turnpike, Fairfield, CT 06432

Canterbury Center, Genesis ElderCare Network, 240 Church Street, Newington, CT 06111

Care Manor of Farmington, 20 Scott Swamp Road, Farmington, CT 06032

Carolton Chronic and Convalescent Hospital, Inc, 400 Mill Plain Road, Fairfield, CT 06430

Cedar Lane Rehabilitation and Health Care Center, 128 Cedar Avenue, Waterbury, CT 06705

Center for Optimum Care – Summit, 97 Preston Road, Griswold, CT 06351–2516

Cherry Brook Health Care Center, 102 Dyer Avenue, Collinsville, CT 06022

Cheshire Convalescent Center, 745 Highland Avenue, Cheshire, CT 06410

Cheshire House Health Care and Rehabilitation Center, 3396 East Main Street, Waterbury, CT 06705

Chestelm Health & Rehabilitation Center, PO Box 719, Moodus, CT 06469

Chesterfields Health Care Center, 132 Main Street, Chester, CT 06412

Clifton House Rehabilitation Center, 181 Clifton Street, New Haven, CT 06513

Coccomo Memorial Health Care Center, 33 Cone Avenue, Meriden, CT 06450

Colchester Nursing and Rehab Center, 59 Harrington Court, Colchester, CT 06415

Cook Willow Health Center, 81 Hillside Avenue, Plymouth, CT 06782

Country Manor Health Care Center, PO Box 7060, Prospect, CT 06712

Crescent Manor, 1243 West Main Street, Waterbury, CT 06708–3101

Crestfield Rehabilitation Center and Fenwood Manor, 565 Vernon Street, Manchester, CT 06040

Cromwell Crest Convalescent Home, PO Box 208, Cromwell, CT 06416

Elm Hill Nursing Center, 45 Elm Street, Rocky Hill, CT 06067

Essex Meadows, 30 Bokum Road, Essex, CT 06426

Evergreen Health Care Center, 205 Chestnut Hill Care Center P.O. Box 549, Stafford Springs, CT 06076

Fairview, PO Box 7218, Groton, CT 06340

Filosa Convalescent Home, Inc., 13 Hakim Street, Danbury, CT 06810

Fowler Nursing Center, Inc., 10 Boston Post Road, Guilford, CT 06437

Gardner Heights, 172 Rocky Rest Road, Shelton, CT 06484

Geer Nursing and Rehabilitation Center, PO Box 819, Canaan, CT 06018–0819

Gladeview Health Care Center, 60 Boston Post Road, Old Saybrook, CT 06475

Glastonbury Health Care Center, 1175 Hebron Avenue, Glastonbury, CT 06033

Glen Hill Convalescent Center, One Glen Hill Road, Danbury, CT 06811

Golden Heights Health Center, 62 Coleman Street, Bridgeport, CT 06604

Grant Street Health and Rehabilitation Center, 425 Grant Street, Bridgeport, CT 06610

Greenery Extended Care Center at Cheshire, 50 Hazel Drive, Cheshire, CT 06410

Greenery Rehabilitation Center at Waterbury, 177 Whitewood Road, Waterbury, CT 06708

Greentree Healthcare and Rehabilitation Center, 4 Greentree Drive, Waterford, CT 06385

Groton Regency Nursing and Rehabilitation Center, 1145 Poquonnock Road, Groton, CT 06340

Grove Manor Nursing Home, Inc., 145 Grove Street, Waterbury, CT 06710

Hamilton Rehabilitation and Healthcare Center, 50 Palmer Street, Norwich, CT 06360

Harbor Hill Care Center, Inc., 111 Church Street, Middletown, CT 06457

Harbor View Manor, 308 Savin Avenue, West Haven, CT 06516

Harborside Healthcare – Willows, 225 Amity Road, Woodbridge, CT 06525

Harborside Healthcare – The Reservoir, One Emily Way, West Hartford, CT 06107

Harborside Healthcare Arden House, 850 Mix Avenue, Hamden, CT 06514

Harborside Healthcare Madison House, 34 Wildwood Avenue, Madison, CT 06443

Hebrew Home and Hospital, One Abrahms Boulevard, West Hartford, CT 06117–1525

Heritage Heights Care Center, 22 Hospital Avenue, Danbury, CT 06810

High View Health Care Center, 600 Highland Avenue, Middletown, CT 06457

HillCrest Health Care Center, 5 Richard Brown Drive, Uncasville, CT 06382

Honey Hill Care Center, 34 Midrocks Drive, Norwalk, CT 06851

Ingraham Manor, 400 North Main Street, Bristol, CT 06010

Jerome Home, 975 Corbin Avenue, New Britain, CT 06052

Jewish Home for the Aged, Inc., 169 Davenport Avenue, New Haven, CT 06519

Jewish Home for the Elderly of Fairfield County, Inc., 175 Jefferson Street, Fairfield, CT 06432

Kettle Brook Nonprofit Healthcare Center, 96 Prospect Hill Road, East Windsor, CT 06088

Kimberly Hall South, One Emerson Drive, Windsor, CT 06095

Laurel Woods, Inc., 451 North High Street, East Haven, CT 06512

Laurelwood Rehabilitation and Skilled Nursing Center, 642 Danbury Road, Ridgefield, CT 06877

Ledgecrest Health Care Center, Inc., PO Box 453, Kensington, CT 06037

Liberty Specialty Care Center, Inc., 36 Broadway, Colchester, CT 06415

Litchfield Woods Health Care Center, 255 Roberts Street, Torrington, CT 06790

Lord Chamberlain Nursing Facility/Rehabilitation Center, 7003 Main Street, Stratford, CT 06497

Maefair Health Care Center, 21 Maefair Court, Trumbull, CT 06611

Manchester Manor, 385 West Center Street, Manchester, CT 06040

Mansfield Center for Nursing and Rehabilitation, 100 Warren Circle, Mansfield, CT 06268

Maple View Manor, Inc., 856 Maple Street, Rocky Hill, CT 06067

Mariner Health at Pendleton, 44 Maritime Drive, Mystic, CT 06355

Mariner Health Care at Bride Brook, 23 Liberty Way, Niantic, CT 06357

Mariner Health of Southern Connecticut, 126 Ford Street, Ansonia, CT 06401

Marlborough Health Care Center, Inc., 85 Stage Harbor Road, Marlborough, CT 06447

Mary Elizabeth Nursing Center, PO Box 98, Mystic, CT 06355

McLean Home, 75 Great Pond Road, Simsbury, CT 06070

MeadowBrook of Granby, 350 Salmon Brook Street, Granby, CT 06035

Mediplex of Danbury, 107 Osborne Street, Danbury, CT 06810

Mediplex of Darien, 599 Boston Post Road, Darien, CT 06820

Mediplex of Greater Hartford, 160 Coventry Street, Bloomfield, CT 06002

Mediplex of Milford, 245 Orange Avenue, Milford, CT 06460

Mediplex of Southbury, 162 South Britain Road, Southbury, CT 06488

Mediplex of Stamford, 710 Long Ridge Road, Stamford, CT 06902

Mediplex of Westport, One Burr Road, Westport, CT 06880

Mediplex of Wethersfield, 341 Jordan Lane, Wethersfield, CT 06109

Mediplex Rehab and Skilled Nursing Center of Central CT, 261 Summit Street, Plantsville, CT 06479

Mediplex Rehabilitation and Skilled Nursg Ctr of Sthn CT, PO Box 109, Milford, CT 06460

MercyKnoll, Inc., 243 Steele Road, W Hartford, CT 06117

Meriden Nursing and Rehabilitation Center, 845 Paddock Avenue, Meriden, CT 06450

Meridian Manor Corporation, 1132 Meriden Road, Waterbury, CT 06705

Middlesex Convalescent Center, Inc., 100 Randolph Road, Middletown, CT 06457

Milford Health Care Center, Inc., 195 Platt Street, Milford, CT 06460

Miller Memorial Community, 360 Broad Street, Meriden, CT 06450

Monsignor Bojnowski Manor, 50 Pulaski Street, New Britain, CT 06053

Montowese Health and Rehabilitation Center, Inc., 163 Quinnipiac Avenue, North Haven, CT 06473

New London Rehabilitation and Care Center, 88 Clark Lane, Waterford, CT 06385

Noble Horizons, 17 Cobble Road, Salisbury, CT 06068

Northbridge Health Care Center, 2875 Main Street, Bridgeport, CT 06606

Norwichtown Rehabilitation and Care Center, 93 West Town Street, Norwichtown, CT 06360

Notre Dame Convalescent Home, Inc., 76 West Rocks Road, Norwalk, CT 06851

Parkway Pavilion Healthcare, 1157 Enfield Street, Enfield, CT 06082

Pierce Memorial Baptist Home, Inc., PO Box 326, Brooklyn, CT 06234

Plainville Health Care Center, Inc., 269 Farmington Avenue, Plainville, CT 06062

Pope John Paul II Center for Health Care, 33 Lincoln Avenue, Danbury, CT 06810

Portland Care and Rehabilitation Centre, Inc, 333 Main Street, Portland, CT 06480

Regency House of Wallingford, 181 East Main Street, Wallingford, CT 06492

Rehabilitation and Healthcare Center of Litchfield Hills, 225 Wyoming Avenue, Torrington, CT 06790

Ridgeview Health Care Center, 156 Berlin Road, Cromwell, CT 06416

Ridgewood Health Care Facility, Inc., 582 Meriden Avenue, Southington, CT 06489

Riverside Health and Rehabilitation Center, Inc, 745 Main Street, East Hartford, CT 06108

Rose Haven, Ltd., PO Box 157, Litchfield, CT 06759

Saint Mary Home, Incorporated, 2021 Albany Avenue, W Hartford, CT 06117–2701

Saint Regis Health Center, 1354 Chapel Street, New Haven, CT 06511

Salmon Brook Nursing and Rehabilitation Center, 72 Salmon Brook Drive, Glastonbury, CT 06033

Seabury Retirement Community, 200 Seabury Drive, Bloomfield, CT 06002

Shady Knoll Health Center, 41 Skokorat Street, Seymour, CT 06483

Sharon Health Care Center, PO Box 1268, Sharon, CT 06069

Shelton Lakes Residence and Health Care Center, Inc., 5 Lake Road, Shelton, CT 06484

Sheriden Woods Health Care Center, 321 Stonecrest Drive, Bristol, CT 06010

Skyview Center Rehabilitation Center, Inc., 35 Marc Drive, Wallingford, CT 06492

Southington Care Center, 45 Meriden Avenue, Southington, CT 06489

Southport Manor Convalescent Center, Inc., 930 Mill Hill Terrace, Southport, CT 06490

St. Elizabeth Health Center, 51 Applegate Lane, East Hartford, CT 06118

St. Joseph Living Center, Inc., 14 Club Road, Windham, CT 06280

St. Joseph's Manor, 6448 Main Street, Trumbull, CT 06611–2078

Sterling Manor, Inc., 870 Burnside Avenue, East Hartford, CT 06108

Subacute Center of Bristol, 23 Fair Street, Forestville, CT 06010

Sylvan Manor Healthcare Center, 1037 Sylvan Avenue, Bridgeport, CT 06606

Talmadge Park Health Care, 38 Talmadge Avenue, East Haven, CT 06512

The Center for Optimum Care – Elm City, 50 Mead Street, New Haven, CT 06511

The Center for Optimum Care – New Haven, 915 Ella T Grasso Boulevard, New Haven, CT 06519

The Center for Optimum Care – Sound View, One Care Lane, West Haven, CT 06516

The Center for Optimum Care – Windham, 595 Valley Street, Willimantic, CT 06226

The Center for Optimum Care of Danielson, 111 Westcott Road, Danielson, CT 06239

The Center for Optimum Care Waterford, 171 Rope Ferry Road, Waterford, CT 06385

The Curtis Home, 380 Crown Street, Meriden, CT 06450

The Elim Park Health Care Center, 140 Cook Hill Road, Cheshire, CT 06410

The Flora and Mary Hewitt Memorial Hospital, Inc., 45 Maltby Street, Shelton, CT 06484

The Glendale Center, 4 Hazel Avenue, Naugatuck, CT 06770

The Health Center at Evergreen Woods, 88 Notch Hill Road, North Branford, CT 06471

The Kent, PO Box 340, Kent, CT 06757

The Mary Wade Home, Incorporated, 118 Clinton Avenue, New Haven, CT 06513

The Suffield House, One Canal Road, Suffield, CT 06078

The William and Sally Tandet Center for Continuing Care, 146 West Broad Street, Stamford, CT 06902

Valerie Manor, 1360 Torringford Street, Torrington, CT 06790

Vernon Manor Health Care Center, 180 Regan Rd, Vernon, CT 06066–2818

Victorian Heights Health Care Center, 341 Bidwell Street, Manchester, CT 06040

Village Manor Health Care, 16 Windsor Avenue, Plainfield, CT 06374

Wadsworth Glen Health Care and Rehabilitation Center, 30 Boston Road, Middletown, CT 06457

Walnut Hill Care Center, 55 Grand Street, New Britain, CT 06052

Waterbury Extended Care Facility, 35 Bunker Hill Road, Watertown, CT 06795

Watrous Nursing Center, 9 Neck Road, Madison, CT 06443

Waveny Care Center, 3 Farm Road, New Canaan, CT 06840

Westfield Care and Rehabilitation Center, 65 Westfield Road, Meriden, CT 06450

Westview Nursing Care and Rehabilitation Center, Inc, PO Box 428, Dayville, CT 06241

Wintonbury Healthcare Center, 140 Park Avenue, Bloomfield, CT 06002

Wolcott Hall Nursing Center, 215 Forest Street, Torrington, CT 06790

Wolcott View Manor, Inc., PO Box 6192, Wolcott, CT 06716

Woodlake at Tolland, 26 Shenipsit Lake Road, Tolland, CT 06084

DELAWARE

Arbors at New Castle Subacute and Rehabilitation Center, 32 Buena Vista Drive, New Castle, DE 19720

Harbor Healthcare and Rehabilitation Center, 301 Oceanview Boulevard, Lewes, DE 19958

Lewes Convalescent Center, 440 Market Street, Lewes, DE 19958

Manor Care Health Services, 5651 Limestone Road, Wilmington, DE 19808

Methodist Country House, 4830 Kennett Pike, Wilmington, DE 19807

Parkview Nursing and Rehabilitation Center, 2801 West 6th Street, Wilmington, DE 19805

Seaford Center Genesis Eldercare Network, 1100 Norman Eskridge Highway, Seaford, DE 19973

Silver Lake Center – Genesis Health Care Network, 1080 Silver Lake Boulevard, Dover, DE 19904

St. Franciscan Care Center at Brackenville, 100 St. Claire Drive, Hockessin, DE 19707

DISTRICT OF COLUMBIA

Benjamin King Health Center US Soldiers' and Airmen's Home, 3700 North Capitol Street, NW, Washington, DC 20317–9998

Center For Aging's Health Care Institute, 1380 Southern Avenue Southeast, Washington, DC 20032

Grant Park Care Center, 5000 Nannie Helen Burroughs Avenue, Northeast, Washington, DC 20019

The Washington Home and Hospice, 3720 Upton Street, Northwest, Washington, DC 20016–2299

Washington Nursing Facility, 2425 25th Street Southeast, Washington, DC 20020

FLORIDA

Arbor at Jacksonville, 4101 Southpoint Drive East, Jacksonville, FL 32216

Arbors at Baynnet Point, 105 W. Michigan St., Hudson, FL 34667

Arbors at Brandon, 701 Victoria Street, Brandon, FL 33510

Arbors at Lakeland, 2020 West Lake Parker Drive, Lakeland, FL 33805

Section C

Arbors at Melbourne, 3033 Serno Road, Melbourne, FL 32934

Arbors at Orange Park, 1215 Kingsley Avenue, Orange Park, FL 32073

Arbors at Orlando Subacute and Rehabilitation Center, 1099 West Town Parkway, Altamonte Springs, FL 32714

Arbors at Pensacola, 235 West Airport Boulevard, Pensacola, FL 32505

Arbors at Safety Harbor, 1410 4th Street North, Safety Harbor, FL 34695

Arbors at St. Petersburg, 9393 Park Boulevard, Seminole, FL 34642

Arbors at Tallahassee, 1650 Phillips Road, Tallahassee, FL 32308

Arbors at Tampa, 2811 Campus Hill Drive, Tampa, FL 33612

Atlantis Center, 6026 Old Congress Road, Lantana, FL 33462

Baptist Manor, Inc., 10095 Hillview Road, Pensacola, FL 32514

Bay Pointe Nursing Pavillion, 4201 31st Street South, Saint Petersburg, FL 33712–4051

BayShore Convalescent Center, 16650 West Dixie Highway, North Miami Beach, FL 33160

Beverly Health and Rehab Center – Port St. Lucie, 1655 Southeast Walton Road, Port Saint Lucie, FL 34952

Beverly Health and Rehab Center of Brandon, 1465 Oakfield Drive, Brandon, FL 33511

Beverly Health and Rehab Services – Tarpon Springs, 501 South Walton Avenue, Tarpon Springs, FL 34689

Beverly Health/Rehabilitation Center – Englewood, 1111 Drury Lane, Englewood, FL 34224

Boca Raton Rehabilitation Center, 755 Meadows Road, Boca Raton, FL 33486

Bon Secours Maria Manor Nursing Care Center, Inc., 10300 4th Street North, Saint Petersburg, FL 33716

Boulevard Manor, 2839 South Seacrest Boulevard, Boynton Beach, FL 33435

Brandywyne Lakeside Center, 1801 North Lake Mariam Drive, Winter Haven, FL 33884

Carrollwood Care Center, 15002 Hutchinson Road, Tampa, FL 33625

Central Park Village, 9311 S Orange Blossom Trail, Orlando, FL 32837

Clyatt's Quality Care, 1001 South Beach Street, Daytona Beach, FL 32114

Colonial Care Center, 6300 46th Avenue North, Saint Petersburg, FL 33709

Coquina Center, 170 North Center Street, Ormond Beach, FL 32174

Countryside Health Care Center, 3825 Countryside Boulevard, Palm Harbor, FL 34684

Cross Creek Health Care Center, 10040 Hillview Road, Pensacola, FL 32514

Darcy Hall of Life Care, 2170 Palm Beach Lakes Blvd, West Palm Beach, FL 33409

Deltona Healthcare Rehabilitation Center, 1851 Elkcam Boulevard, Deltona, FL 32725

Desoto Manor Nursing Home, 1002 North Brevard Avenue, Arcadia, FL 33821

Drew Village Rehabilitation and Nursing Center, 401 Fairwood Avenue, Clearwater, FL 34619

Edgewater of Waterman Village, 300 Brookfield Avenue, Mount Dora, FL 32757

Fairway Oaks Center – Genesis ElderCare, 13806 North 46th Street, Tampa, FL 33613

First Coast Health and Rehabilitation Center, 7723 Jasper Avenue, Jacksonville, FL 32211

Florida Club Care Center, 220 Sierra Drive, North Miami Beach, FL 33179

Florida Living Nursing Center, 3355 E. Semoran Blvd., Apopka, FL 32703

Franco Nursing & Rehab Center, 800 NW 95th Street, Miami, FL 33150

Franco Nursing and Rehabilitation Center, 800 Northwest 95th Street, Miami, FL 33150

Gramercy Park Nursing Center, 17475 South Dixie Highway, Miami, FL 33157

Greenbriar Rehabilitation and Nursing Center, 210 21st Avenue West, Bradenton, FL 34205

Greenbrook Nursing and Rehabilitation Center, 1000 24th Street North, Saint Petersburg, FL 33713

Greynolds Park Manor Rehabilitation Center, 17400 West Dixie Highway, North Miami Beach, FL 33160

Hallandale Rehabilitation Center, 2400 E Hallandale Beach Blvd, Hallandale, FL 33009

Harborside – Pinebrook, 1240 Pinebrook Road, Venice, FL 34292

Harborside Healthcare – Brevard, 1775 Huntington Lane, Rockledge, FL 32955

Harborside Healthcare – Clearwater, 1980 Sunset Point Road, Clearwater, FL 34625

Harborside Healthcare – Gulf Coast, 4927 Voorhees Road, New Port Richey, FL 34653

Harborside Healthcare – Naples, 2900 12th Street, North, Naples, FL 34103

Harborside Healthcare – Ocala, 1501 Southeast 24th Road, Ocala, FL 34471

Harborside Healthcare – Palm Harbor, 2600 Highlands Boulevard, N, Palm Harbor, FL 34684

Harborside Healthcare – Sarasota, 4602 Northgate Court, Sarasota, FL 34234

Harborside Healthcare – Tampa Bay, 3865 Tampa Road, Oldsmar, FL 34677

Hardee Manor Care Center, 401 Orange Place, Wauchula, FL 33873

HCR/ManorCare, 375 Northwest 51st Street, Boca Raton, FL 33431

Heartland Health Care and Rehabilitation Center, 7225 Boca Del Mar Drive, Boca Raton, FL 33433–5517

Heartland Health Care and Rehabilitation Center, 5401 Sawyer Drive, Sarasota, FL 34233

Heartland Health Care Center – Fort Myers, 1600 Matthew Drive, Fort Myers, FL 33907

Heartland Health Care Center – Jacksonville, 8495 Normandy Boulevard, Jacksonville, FL 32221

Heartland Health Care Center – Kendall, 9400 Southwest 137th Avenue, Kendall, FL 33186

Heartland Health Care Center – Lauderhill, 2599 Northwest 55th Avenue, Lauderhill, FL 33313

Heartland Health Care Center – Sunrise, 9711 W Oakland Park Boulevard, Sunrise, FL 33351

Heartland Health Care Center Miami Lakes, 5725 Northwest 186th Street, Hialeah, FL 33015

Heartland Healthcare Center – Boynton Beach, 3600 Old Boynton Road, Boynton Beach, FL 33436

Heartland Healthcare Center – Prosperity Oaks, 11375 Prosperity Farms Road, Palm Beach Gardens, FL 33410

Heartland of Brooksville, 575 Lamar Avenue, Brooksville, FL 34601

Heartland of Tamarac, 5901 Northwest 79th Avenue, Tamarac, FL 33321

Heartland of Zephyrhills, 38220 Henry Drive, Zephyrhills, FL 33540

Heritage Health Care Center, 1815 Ginger Drive, Tallahassee, FL 32308

Heritage Park, 37135 Coleman Avenue, Dade City, FL 33525

Highlands Lake Center, 4240 Lakeland Highlands Road, Lakeland, FL 33813

Hollywood Hills Nursing Home, 1200 N. 35th Avenue, Hollywood, FL 33021

Holmes Regional Nursing Center, 606 East Sheridan Road, Melbourne, FL 32901

Horizon Specialty and Rehabilitation Center, 221 Park Place Boulevard, Kissimmee, FL 34741

Human Resources Health Center, 2500 Northwest 22nd Avenue, Miami, FL 33142

IHS at Avenel, 7751 West Broward Boulevard, Plantation, FL 33324

IHS at Greenbriar, 9820 North Kendall Drive, Miami, FL 33176

IHS of Bradenton, 2302 59th Street West, Bradenton, FL 34209

IHS of Florida at Sarasota Pavilion, 2600 Courtland Street, Sarasota, FL 34237

IHS of Orange Park, 2029 Professional Center Drive, Orange Park, FL 32073

IHS of Port Charlotte, 4033 Beaver Lane, Port Charlotte, FL 33952

IHS of Venice North, 437 South Nokomis Avenue, Venice, FL 34285

Indian River Center – Genesis ElderCare, 7201 Greenboro Drive, West Melbourne, FL 32904

Indigo Manor, 595 Williamson Blvd., Daytona Beach, FL 32114

Integrated Health Services at Brandon, 702 South Kings Avenue, Brandon, FL 33511

Integrated Health Services at Ft. Pierce, 703 South 29th Street, Fort Pierce, FL 34947–3699

Integrated Health Services at Gainesville, 4000 Southwest 20th Avenue, Gainesville, FL 32607

Integrated Health Services of Central Florida at Orlando, 1900 Mercy Drive, Orlando, FL 32808

Integrated Health Services of Florida at Clearwater, 2055 Palmetto Street, Clearwater, FL 34625

Integrated Health Services of Florida at Lake Worth, 1201 12th Avenue South, Lake Worth, FL 33460

Integrated Health Services of Florida at West Palm Beach, 2939 South Haverhill Road, West Palm Beach, FL 33415

Integrated Health Services of Fort Myers, 13755 Golf Club Parkway, Fort Myers, FL 33919

Integrated Health Services of Jacksonville, 1650 Fouraker Road, Jacksonville, FL 32221

Integrated Health Services of Lakeland at Oakbridge, 3110 Oakbridge Boulevard, East, Lakeland, FL 33803

Integrated Health Services of Palm Bay, 1515 Port Malabar Boulevard, Palm Bay, FL 32905

Integrated Health Services of Pinellas Park, 8701 49th Street North, Pinellas Park, FL 33782

Integrated Health Services of Sarasota at Beneva, 741 South Beneva Road, Sarasota, FL 34232

Integrated Health Services of Sebring, 3011 Kenilworth Boulevard, Sebring, FL 33870

Integrated Health Services of St. Petersburg, 811 Jackson Street North, St Petersburg, FL 33705

Integrated Health Services of Tarpon Springs, 900 Beckett Way, Tarpon Springs, FL 34689

Integrated Health Services of Vero Beach, 3663 15th Avenue, Vero Beach, FL 32960

Integrated Health Services of Winter Park, 2970 Scarlet Road, Winter Park, FL 32792

Integrated Health Services, Inc., 919 Old Winter Haven Road, Auburndale, FL 33823

John Knox Village, 101 Northlake Drive, Orange City, FL 32763

Laurels Nursing & Rehabilitation Center, 550 9th Avenue South, Saint Petersburg, FL 33701

Longwood Health Care Center, 1520 South Grant Street, Longwood, FL 32750

Manor Care Nursing Center, 3001 South Congress Avenue, Boynton Beach, FL 33426

ManorCare Health Services, 870 Patricia Avenue, Dunedin, FL 34698

ManorCare Health Services, 6931 West Sunrise Boulevard, Plantation, FL 33313

ManorCare Health Services, 3030 West Bearss Avenue, Tampa, FL 33618

Margate Health Care Center, 5951 Colonial Drive, Margate, FL 33063

Mariner Health Care of Orange City, 2810 Enterprise Road, Debary, FL 32713

Mariner Health of Atlantic Shores, 4251 Stack Boulevard, Melbourne, FL 32901

Mariner Health of Belleair, 1150 Ponce de Leon Boulevard, Clearwater, FL 34616

Mariner Health of Clearwater, 4470 East Bay Drive, Clearwater, FL 33764

Mariner Health of Deland, 1200 North Stone Street, Deland, FL 32720

Mariner Health of Palm City, 2505 Southwest Martin Highway, Palm City, FL 34990

Mariner Health of Palmetto, 926 Haben Boulevard, Palmetto, FL 34221

Mariner Health of Port Orange, 5600 Victoria Gardens Blvd, Port Orange, FL 32127

Mariner Health of Port St. Lucie, 1800 Hillmore Drive, Port Saint Lucie, FL 34952

Mariner Health of St. Augustine, 200 Mariner Health Way, Saint Augustine, FL 32086

Mariner Health of Titusville, 2225 Knox McRae Drive, Titusville, FL 32780

Mariner Health of Tuskawilla, 1024 Willa Springs Drive, Winter Springs, FL 32708

Marion House Health Care Center, 3930 E Silver Springs Blvd, Ocala, FL 34470

Medicana Nursing Center, 1710 Lake Worth Road, Lake Worth, FL 33460

Mediplex Rehab – Bradenton, 5627 Ninth Street East, Bradenton, FL 34203

Menorah Manor, Inc., 255 59th Street North, Saint Petersburg, FL 33710

Miami Jewish Home & Hospital for the Aged, 5200 Northeast 2nd Avenue, Miami, FL 33137

Moody Manor, Inc., 7150 Holatee Trail, Fort Lauderdale, FL 33330

Mount Sinai St. Francis Nursing/Rehabilitation Center, 201 NE 112th Street, Miami, FL 33161

New Horizon Rehabilitation Center, 635 Southeast 17th Street, Ocala, FL 34471

NHC HealthCare – Hudson, 7210 Beacon Woods Drive, Hudson, FL 34667

North Florida Rehabilitation and Specialty Care Center, 6700 Northwest 10th Place, Gainesville, FL 32605

Oak Manor Nursing Center, 3500 Oak Manor Lane, Largo, FL 33774

Oakwood Center, 301 South Bay Street, Eustis, FL 32726

Oakwood Terrace Skilled Nursing & Rehabilitation Cntr, 18905 Northeast 25th Avenue, Aventura, FL 33180

Ormond in the Pines, 103 N Clyde Morris Boulevard, Ormond Beach, FL 32174

Section C

Palm Garden – Jacksonville, 5725 Spring Park Road, Jacksonville, FL 32216

Palm Garden – Orlando, 654 Econlockhatchee Trail, Orlando, FL 32825

Palm Garden of Clearwater, 3480 McMullen Booth Road, Clearwater, FL 34621

Palm Garden of Gainesville, 227 Southwest 62nd Boulevard, Gainesville, FL 32607

Palm Garden of Lake City, 920 McFarlane Avenue, Lake City, FL 32025

Palm Garden of Largo, 10500 Starkey Road, Largo, FL 33777

Palm Garden of Ocala, 3400 Southwest 27th Avenue, Ocala, FL 34474

Palm Garden of Pinellas, 200 16th Avenue Southeast, Largo, FL 34641

Palm Garden of Tampa, 3612 East 138th Avenue, Tampa, FL 33613

Palm Garden of West Palm Beach, 300 Executive Center Drive, West Palm Beach, FL 33401

Palmetto Health Center, 6750 West 22nd Court, Hialeah, FL 33016–3918

Perdue Medical Center, 19590 Old Cutler Road, Miami, FL 33157

Plantation Bay Rehabilitation Center, 401 Kissimmee Park Road, Saint Cloud, FL 34769

Regents Park of Boca Raton, 6363 Verde Trail, Boca Raton, FL 33433

Regents Park of Jacksonville, 7130 Southside Boulevard, Jacksonville, FL 32256

Regents Park of Winter Park, 558 North Semoran Boulevard, Winter Park, FL 32792

Renova Health Care Center, 750 Bayberry Drive, Lake Park, FL 33403

River Garden Hebrew Home for the Aged, 11401 Old Saint Augustine Road, Jacksonville, FL 32258

Royal Manor, 600 Business Parkway, Royal Palm Beach, FL 33411

Sabal Palms Health Care Center, 499 Alternate Keene Road, Largo, FL 33771

Shore Acres Rehabilitation and Nursing Center, 4500 Indianapolis Street NE, Saint Petersburg, FL 33703

Southern Pines Nursing Center, 6140 Congress Street, New Port Richey, FL 34653

Spanish Gardens Nursing Center, 1061 Virginia Street, Dunedin, FL 34698

St. Anne's Nursing Center, 11855 Quail Roost Drive, Miami, FL 33177

St. Augustine Health Care & Rehab, 5056 NW 74th Avenue, St. Augustine, FL 32086

St. Catherine Laboure' Manor, 1750 Stockton Street, Jacksonville, FL 32204

Sun Health of the Palm Beaches, 6414 13th Road South, West Palm Beach, FL 33415

Sunbelt East Orlando, 250 S. Chicksaw Trail, Orlando, FL 32828

Sunrise Health and Rehabilitation Center, 4800 Nob Hill Road, Sunrise, FL 33351

Sutton Place Center, 4405 Lakewood Road, Lake Worth, FL 33461

Swanholm Nursing and Rehabilitation Center, 6200 Central Avenue, Saint Petersburg, FL 33707

The Fountains Nursing Home, 3800 North Federal Highway, Boca Raton, FL 33431

The Riverwood Center – Genesis ElderCare Network, 2802 Parental Home Road, Jacksonville, FL 32216

Tierra Pines Center, 7380 Ulmerton Road, Largo, FL 33771

TimberRidge Nursing and Rehabilitation Center, 9848 Southwest 110th Street, Ocala, FL 34481

University Village Health Center, 12250 North 22nd Street, Tampa, FL 33612

Washington Manor Nursing and Rehabilitation Center, 4200 Washington Street, Hollywood, FL 33021

Water's Edge Extended Care, 1500 Southwest Capri Street, Palm City, FL 34990

Whitehall Boca Raton, 7300 Del Prado South, Boca Raton, FL 33433

Windsor Manor, 602 E. Laura Street, Starke, FL 32091

GEORGIA

American Transitional Care – Northside, 5470 Meridian Mark Road, Atlanta, GA 30342

Ashton Woods Rehabilitation Center, 3535 Ashton Woods Drive NE, Atlanta, GA 30319

Azalea Trace Nursing Center, 910 Talbotton Road, Columbus, GA 31904

Beverly Health and Rehabilitation Center, 2650 Highway 138 SE, Jonesboro, GA 30236

Brian Center Nursing Care – Austell, 2130 Anderson Mill Road, Austell, GA 30106

Brian Center Nursing Center / Powder Springs, 3460 Powder Springs Road, Powder Springs, GA 30073

Budd Terrace, 1833 Clifton Road Northeast, Atlanta, GA 30329

Dogwood Health and Rehabilitation, 7560 Butner Road, Fairburn, GA 30213

Dublinair Health Care and Rehabilitation Center, PO Box 1243, Dublin, GA 31040

Family Life Enrichment Centers, Inc., PO Box 10, High Shoals, GA 30645

Georgia War Veterans Nursing Home, 1101 15th Street, Augusta, GA 30910

Green Acres Nursing Home, 313 Allen Memorial Drive SW, Milledgeville, GA 31061

Harvest Heights Nursing Home, 3200 Panthersville Road, Decatur, GA 30034

IHS of Atlanta at Shoreham, 811 Kennesaw Avenue, Marietta, GA 30060

Integrated Health Services of Atlanta at Briarcliff Haven, 1000 Briarcliff Road Northeast, Atlanta, GA 30306

Integrated Health Services of Atlanta at Buckhead, 54 Peachtree Park Drive NE, Atlanta, GA 30309

Life Care Center of Gwinnett, 3850 Safehaven Drive, Lawrenceville, GA 30244

Lilburn Geriatric Center, 788 Indian Trail Road, Lilburn, GA 30047

Magnolia Manor Nursing Center, 2001 South Lee Street, Americus, GA 31709

Mariner Health of Northeast Atlanta, 1500 South Johnson Ferry Road, Atlanta, GA 30319

Marion Memorial Nursing Home, PO Box 197, Buena Vista, GA 31803

Montezuma Health Care Center, PO Box 639, Montezuma, GA 31063

Oak Manor Nursing Home, Inc. / Pine Manor Nursing Home, Inc., PO Box 8828, Columbus, GA 31908–8828

Quinton Memorial Health Care Center, 1114 Burleyson Road, Dalton, GA 30720

Riverside Nursing Center / Thomaston, 101 Old Talbotton Road, Thomaston, GA 30286

Southland Nursing Home, Inc., PO Box 2747, Peachtree City, GA 30269

Starcrest of Lithonia, PO Box 855, Lithonia, GA 30058

Windermere, 3618 J Dewey Gray Circle, Augusta, GA 30909

Winthrop Manor Nursing Center, 12 Chateau Drive, Rome, GA 30161

HAWAII

Life Care Center of Hilo, 944 West Kawailani Street, Hilo, HI 96720

IDAHO

Life Care Center of Boise, 808 North Curtis Road, Boise, ID 83706

Rexburg Nursing Center, 660 South 200 West, Rexburg, ID 83440

ILLINOIS

Advocate Transitional Care Center, 10124 South Kedzie Avenue, Evergreen Park, IL 60642

Alden Estates of Evanston, 2520 Gross Point Road, Evanston, IL 60201

Alden Poplar Creek – Rehabilitation & Hlth Care Ctr, 1545 Barrington Road, Hoffman Estates, IL 60194

Alden Rehabilitation and Health Care Center – Heather, 15600 South Honore, Harvey, IL 60426

Alden Rehabilitation and Health Care Center – Lakeland, 820 West Lawrence Avenue, Chicago, IL 60640

Alden Rehabilitation and Health Care Center – Morrow, 5001 South Michigan, Chicago, IL 60615

Alden Rehabilitation and Health Care Center – Northmoor, 5831 North Northwest Highway, Chicago, IL 60631

Alden Rehabilitation and Health Care Center – Princeton, 255 West 69th Street, Chicago, IL 60621

Alden Rehabilitation and Health Care Center – Wentworth, 201 West 69th Street, Chicago, IL 60621

Alden Rehabilitation and Health Care Center–Lincoln Pk, 504 West Wellington Avenue, Chicago, IL 60657

Alden Rehabilitation and Health Care Center/Long Grove, Box 2308 RFD, Hickes Road, Long Grove, IL 60047

Alden Rehabilitation and Health Care Center/Naperville, 1525 Oxford Lane, Naperville, IL 60565

Alden Rehabilitation and Health Care Center/Orland Park, 16450 South 97th Avenue, Orland Park, IL 60462

Alden Rehabilitation and Health Care Center/Town Manor, 6120 West Ogden Avenue, Cicero, IL 60804

Alden Rehabilitation and Health Care Cnter–Valley Ridge, 275 Army Trail Road, Bloomingdale, IL 60108

Alden Terrace of McHenry, 803 Royal Drive, Mc Henry, IL 60050

Alma Nelson Manor, Inc., 550 South Mulford Road, Rockford, IL 61108

Anchorage of Beecher, 1201 Dixie Highway, Beecher, IL 60401

Applewood Nursing and Rehabilitation Center, 21020 Kostner Avenue, Matteson, IL 60443

ASTA Care Center of Bloomington, 1509 North Calhoun Street, Bloomington, IL 61701

ASTA Care Center of Elgin, 134 North McLean Boulevard, Elgin, IL 60123

ASTA Care Center of Rockford, 707 West Riverside Boulevard, Rockford, IL 61103

ASTA Care Center of Toluca, Rural Route 1, Box 205, Toluca, IL 61369

Barton W. Stone Christian Home, 873 Grove Street, Jacksonville, IL 62650

Bethany Terrace Nursing Centre, 8425 North Waukegan Road, Morton Grove, IL 60053

Bethesda Home and Retirement Center, 2833 North Nordica Avenue, Chicago, IL 60634

Brentwood North, 3705 Deerfield Road, Riverwoods, IL 60015

California Gardens Nursing and Rehabilitation Center, 2829 S California Boulevard, Chicago, IL 60608

Care Centre of Champaign, 1915 South Mattis, Champaign, IL 61821

Care Centre of Urbana, 907 North Lincoln Avenue, Urbana, IL 61801

Care Centre of Wauconda, 176 Thomas Court, Wauconda, IL 60084

Carlton at the Lake, Inc., 725 West Montrose Avenue, Chicago, IL 60613

Carrington Care Center, 759 Kane Street, South Elgin, IL 60177

Chateau Village Nursing and Rehabilitation Center, 7050 Madison Street, Willowbrook, IL 60521

Chevy Chase Nursing and Rehabilitation Center, 3400 South Indiana Avenue, Chicago, IL 60616

Clark Manor Convalescent Center, 7433 North Clark, Chicago, IL 60626

Colonial Hall Center, 515 Bureau Valley Pkwy, Princeton, IL 61356

Community HealthCare Center, 1136 North Mill Street, Naperville, IL 60563–2580

Council for Jewish Ederly – Lieberman Geriatric Health Ctr, 9700 Gross Point Road, Skokie, IL 60076

Countryside Care Centre, 2330 West Galena Boulevard, Aurora, IL 60506

Crestwood Care Centre, 14255 South Cicero Avenue, Crestwood, IL 60445

Danville Care Center, 1701 North Bowman Avenue, Danville, IL 61832

Deerbrook Care Centre, 306 North Larkin Avenue, Joliet, IL 60435

Douglas Healthcare Center, PO Box 978, Mattoon, IL 61938

Elmhurst Extended Care Center, Inc., 200 East Lake Street, Elmhurst, IL 60126

Fairmont Care Centre, 5061 North Pulaski Road, Chicago, IL 60630

Flora HealthCare Center, 120 Frontage Road, Flora, IL 62839

Flora Pavilion Nursing Home Center, Inc., 701 Shadwell Avenue, Flora, IL 62839–0309

Forest Villa, Ltd., 6840 West Touhy, Niles, IL 60714

Galena Park Home, 5533 N Galena Rd, Peoria Heights, IL 61614

Garden View Nursing and Rehabilitation Center, 6450 North Ridge Avenue, Chicago, IL 60626

Geneseo Good Samaritan Village, 704 South Illinois Street, Geneseo, IL 61254

Genesis Lemont Center, 12450 Walker Road, Lemont, IL 60439

Glen Elston Nursing and Rehabilitation Centre, Ltd, 4340 North Keystone Avenue, Chicago, IL 60641

Glen Oaks Nursing and Rehabilitation Centre, Ltd, 270 Skokie Boulevard, Northbrook, IL 60062

GlenBridge Nursing and Rehabilitation Centre, Ltd, 8333 West Golf Road, Niles, IL 60714

Glencrest Nursing and Rehabilitation Centre, 2451 West Touhy Avenue, Chicago, IL 60645

GlenShire Nursing and Rehabilitation Centre, Ltd., 22660 South Cicero Avenue, Richton Park, IL 60471

Glenview Terrace Nursing Center, 1511 Greenwood Road, Glenview, IL 60025

Glenwood Terrace, 19330 Cottage Grove, Glenwood, IL 60425

Halsted Terrace Nursing Center, 10935 South Halsted, Chicago, IL 60628

Hampton Plaza Health Care Center, 9777 Greenwood, Niles, IL 60714

Harmony Nursing and Rehabilitation Center, 3919 West Foster Avenue, Chicago, IL 60625

HCR ManorCare, 600 West Ogden Avenue, Hinsdale, IL 60521

HCR–ManorCare Health Services, 2145 East 170th Street, South Holland, IL 60473

Heartland Health Care Center, 833 16th Avenue, Moline, IL 61265

Heartland Health Care Center – Galesburg, 280 East Losey Street, Galesburg, IL 61401

Heartland Health Care Center – Henry, PO Box 215, Henry, IL 61537

Heartland Health Care Center – Homewood, 940 Maple Avenue, Homewood, IL 60430

Heartland Health Care Center – Macomb, 8 Doctors Lane, Macomb, IL 61455

Heartland Health Care Center – Paxton, 1001 East Pells Street, Paxton, IL 60957

Heartland Health Care Center of Canton, 2081 North Main Street, Canton, IL 61520

Holy Family Health Center, 2380 East Dempster Street, Des Plaines, IL 60016–4898

IHS Chicago at Governors Park, 1420 South Barrington Road, Barrington, IL 60010

Illini Restorative Care Center, 1455 Hospital Road, Silvis, IL 61282

Integrated Health Services at Brentwood, 5400 West 87th Street, Burbank, IL 60459

Jackson Square Nursing and Rehabilitation Center, 5130 West Jackson Boulevard, Chicago, IL 60644

Lake Shore HealthCare and Rehabilitation Centre, 7200 North Sheridan Road, Chicago, IL 60626

Lakewood Nursing and Rehabilitation Center, 1112 North Eastern Avenue, Plainfield, IL 60544

Lutheran Home and Services, 800 West Oakton Street, Arlington Heights, IL 60004

Manor Care Health Services, 6300 West 95th Street, Oak Lawn, IL 60453

Manor HealthCare Corp., 200 West Martin Avenue, Naperville, IL 60540

ManorCare Health Services, 9401 South Kostner Avenue, Oak Lawn, IL 60453

ManorCare Health Services, 600 North Coler Avenue, Urbana, IL 61801

ManorCare Health Services, 512 East Ogden Avenue, Westmont, IL 60559

ManorCare Health Services – Skokie, 4660 Old Orchard Road, Skokie, IL 60076

ManorCare Health Services of Arlington Heights, 715 West Central Road, Arlington Heights, IL 60005

Mariner Health of Westchester, 2901 South Wolf Road, Westchester, IL 60154

Maryhaven, 1700 East Lake Avenue, Glenview, IL 60025

Mid–America Care Center, 4920 North Kenmore Avenue, Chicago, IL 60640

Monroe Pavilion Health and Treatment Center, 1400 West Monroe, Chicago, IL 60607

Morton Terrace, Ltd., 191 East Queenwood, Morton, IL 61550

Norridge Healthcare and Rehabilitation Centre, 7001 West Cullom Avenue, Norridge, IL 60634

Northwoods Care Centre, 2250 Pearl Street, Belvidere, IL 61008

Oak Brook Healthcare Centre, 2013 Midwest Road, Oak Brook, IL 60521

Oakton Pavilion, Inc., 1660 Oakton Place, Des Plaines, IL 60018

Odd Fellow–Rebekah Home, 201 Lafayette Avenue East, Mattoon, IL 61938

Odin Healthcare Center, 300 Green Street, Odin, IL 62870

P. A. Peterson Center for Health, 1311 Parkview Avenue, Rockford, IL 61107

Pavilion of Waukegan II, Inc., 2217 Washington Street, Waukegan, IL 60085

Piatt County Nursing Home, 1111 North State Street, Monticello, IL 61856

Pine Acres Care Center, 1212 South Second Street, De Kalb, IL 60115

Prairie Manor Health Care Center, 345 Dixie Highway, Chicago Heights, IL 60411

Prairie View Care Center of Lewistown, 175 Sycamore Drive, Lewistown, IL 61542

Red Oaks of Highland Park, 2773 Skokie Valley Road, Highland Park, IL 60035

Regency Nursing Centre, 6631 North Milwaukee Avenue, Niles, IL 60714

Renaissance at Hillside, 4600 North Frontage Road, Hillside, IL 60162

Renaissance Care Center, 1675 East Ash, Canton, IL 61520

Rest Haven Illiana Christian Convalescent Home, 13259 South Central Avenue, Palos Heights, IL 60463

Rest Haven South Nursing Home, 16300 South Wausau Avenue, South Holland, IL 60473

Rest Haven West, 3450 Saratoga Avenue, Downers Grove, IL 60515

Resurrection Nursing and Rehabilitation Center, 1001 North Greenwood Avenue, Park Ridge, IL 60068

Ridgeland Nursing and Rehabilitation Center, 12550 South Ridgeland Avenue, Palos Heights, IL 60463

Rivershores Nursing and Rehabilitation Center, 573 West Commercial Street, Marseilles, IL 61341

Rosewood Care Center of Alton, Inc., 3490 Humbert Road, Alton, IL 62002

Sheridan Health Care Center, 2534 Elim Avenue, Zion, IL 60099

Sherman West Court, 1950 Larkin Avenue, Elgin, IL 60123

Skokie Meadows Nursing Center – No. 1, 9615 North Knox Avenue, Skokie, IL 60076

Snow Valley Nursing and Rehabilitation Center, 5000 Lincoln Avenue, Lisle, IL 60532

St. Andrew Home, 7000 North Newark Avenue, Niles, IL 60714

St. Pauls House and Health Care Center, 3800 North California Avenue, Chicago, IL 60618

SunRise Hillside Care & Rehabilitation, 1308 Game Farm Road, Yorkville, IL 60560

The Abington of Glenview, 3901 Glenview Road, Glenview, IL 60025

The Claremont Rehab and Living Center, 150 North Weiland Road, Buffalo Grove, IL 60089

The Imperial Convalescent and Geriatric Center, 1366 West Fullerton Avenue, Chicago, IL 60614

The Neighbors, Inc., 811 West Second Street, Byron, IL 61010

The Willow of Carbondale, Inc., 120 North Tower Road, Carbondale, IL 62901

Villa Scalabrini, 480 North Wolf Road, Northlake, IL 60164

Wagner Health Center, 820 Foster Avenue, Evanston, IL 60201

Walnut Ridge Rehabilitation and Healthcare Center, 555 West Carpenter, Springfield, IL 62702

Westmont Convalescent Center, 6501 South Cass Avenue, Westmont, IL 60559

Whitehall North, 300 Waukegan Road, Deerfield, IL 60015–4988

York Convalescent Center, Ltd., 127 West Diversey, Elmhurst, IL 60126

INDIANA

American Transitional Care – Brookview, 7145 East 21st Street, Indianapolis, IN 46219

Arbors at Fort Wayne, 2827 Northgate Blvd., Fort Wayne, IN 46835

Covington Manor Health Care Center, 1600 East Liberty Street, Covington, IN 47932

Danville Regional Rehabilitation Center, 255 Meadow Drive, Danville, IN 46122

Harborside Healthcare – Decatur, 4851 Tincher Road, Indianapolis, IN 46221

Harborside Healthcare – Indianapolis, 8201 West Washington Street, Indianapolis, IN 46231

Harborside Healthcare – New Haven, 1201 Daly Drive, New Haven, IN 46774

Harborside Healthcare – Terre Haute, 1001 East Springhill Drive, Terre Haute, IN 47802

Harrison Healthcare Corporation, 2026 East 54th Street, Indianapolis, IN 46220

Healthwin Specialized Care Facility, 20531 Darden Road, South Bend, IN 46637

Heartland Health Care Center – Prestwick, 445 South County Road 525E, Plainfield, IN 46168

Heritage Healthcare, 3401 Soldiers Home Road, West Lafayette, IN 47906

Heritage House Rehabilitation and HealthCare Center, 281 S County Road, 200 East, Connersville, IN 47331

Holiday Care Center, 1201 West Buena Vista Road, Evansville, IN 47710

Holy Cross Care and Rehabilitation Center, 17475 Dugdale Drive, South Bend, IN 46635

Integrated Health Services of Indianapolis at Cambridge, 8530 Township Line Road, Indianapolis, IN 46260

Ironwood Health and Rehabilitation Center, 1950 Ridgedale Avenue, South Bend, IN 46614

Lifelines Children's Hospital, PO Box 40407, Indianapolis, IN 46240–0407

ManorCare Health Services – Indianapolis, 8350 Naab Road, Indianapolis, IN 46260

ManorCare Health Services – Indianapolis South, 8549 South Madison Avenue, Indianapolis, IN 46227

Miller's Merry Manor, PO Box 480, Logansport, IN 46947

Munster Med–Inn, 7935 Calumet Avenue, Munster, IN 46321

Northwest Manor Health Care Center, 6440 West 34th Street, Indianapolis, IN 46224

Rensselaer Care Center, 1309 East Grace Street, Rensselaer, IN 47978

Robin Run Village, 6370 Robin Run West Drive, Indianapolis, IN 46268

Southlake Nursing and Rehabilitation Center, 8800 Virginia Place, Merrillville, IN 46410

The Altenheim Community, 3525 East Hanna Avenue, Indianapolis, IN 46237

Transitional Health Services of Clark County, 203 Sparks Avenue, Jeffersonville, IN 47130

Vermillion Convalescent and Rehabilitation Center, 1705 South Main Street, Clinton, IN 47842

Woodlands Convalescent Center, PO Box 400, Newburgh, IN 47630

IOWA

Anamosa Care Center, PO Box 229, Anamosa, IA 52205

Cedar Falls Lutheran Home, 7511 University Avenue, Cedar Falls, IA 50613

Danville Care Center, PO Box 248, Danville, IA 52623

Edgewood Convalescent Home, PO Box 39, Edgewood, IA 52042

Elkader Care Center, BOX 519, Elkader, IA 52043

Great River Care Center, PO Box 370, McGregor, IA 52157

Iowa Veterans Home, 1301 Summit, Marshalltown, IA 50158

Lone Tree Health Care Center, Inc., 501 East Pioneer Road, Lone Tree, IA 52755

Manor Care Nursing and Rehabilitation Center, 815 East Locust, Davenport, IA 52803

Mill Valley Care Center, 1201 Park Avenue, Bellevue, IA 52031

Montezuma Nursing and Rehabilitation Center, PO Box 790, Montezuma, IA 50171

New Hampton Nursing and Rehabilitation Center, PO Box 428, New Hampton, IA 50659

Ramsey Home, 1611 27th Street, Des Moines, IA 50310

St. Luke's Living Center West, 1050 Fourth Avenue Southeast, Cedar Rapids, IA 52403

St. Lukes Living Center East, 1220 Fifth Avenue Southeast, Cedar Rapids, IA 52403–4073

State Center Manor, 702 Third Street, State Center, IA 50247

The Monticello Nursing and Rehabilitation Center, 500 Pinehaven Drive, Monticello, IA 52310

Wheatland Manor, PO Box 368, Wheatland, IA 52777–0368

KANSAS

ManorCare Health Services, 5211 West 103rd Street, Overland Park, KS 66207

Wilson Nursing Center, PO Box 160, Wilson, KS 67490

KENTUCKY

Christopher East Health Care Center, 4200 Brown's Lane, Louisville, KY 40220

Florence Park Care Center, 6975 Burlington Pike, Florence, KY 41042

Harrodsburg Health Care Center, 853 Lexington Road, Harrodsburg, KY 40330

Hermitage Nursing and Rehabilitation Center, 1614 West Parrish Avenue, Owensboro, KY 42301

Highlands of Ft. Thomas Health Care Center and Rehabilitation, 960 Highland Avenue, Fort Thomas, KY 41075

Hillcreek Manor Rehabilitation and Nursing Center, 3116 Breckenridge Lane, Louisville, KY 40220

Hurstbourne Care Centre, 2200 Stony Brook Drive, Louisville, KY 40220

Rosewood Health Care Center, 550 High Street, Bowling Green, KY 42101

Salyersville Health Care Center, PO Box 819, Salyersville, KY 41465

Winchester Centre for Health and Rehabilitation, 200 Glenway Road, Winchester, KY 40391

LOUISIANA

Chateau Living Center, 716 Village Road, Kenner, LA 70065

Gillis W. Long Hansen's Disease Center, 5445 Point Clair Road, Carville, LA 70721–9607

Greenery Neurologic Rehabilitation Center, 1400 Lindberg Drive, Slidell, LA 70458

Lafon Nursing Facility of the Holy Family, 6900 Chef Menteur Highway, New Orleans, LA 70126
Martin de Porres Nursing Home, Inc., PO Box 1294, Lake Charles, LA 70602
Meadowcrest Living Center, 535 Commerce Street, Gretna, LA 70056
Metairie Healthcare Center, 6401 Riverside Drive, Metairie, LA 70003

MAINE
Brewer Rehabilitation and Living Center, 74 Parkway South, Brewer, ME 04412
Cedar Ridge Center for Health Care and Rehabilitation, Rural Route 1, Box 1283, Skowhegan, ME 04976
Courtland Living Center, 38 Court Street, Ellsworth, ME 04605
Eastside Rehabilitation and Living Center, 516 Mt. Hope Avenue, Bangor, ME 04401
Maplecrest Rehabilitation and Living Center, 174 Main Street, Madison, ME 04950
Marshwood Center for Healthcare and Rehabilitation, 33 Roger Street, Lewiston, ME 04240
Oak Grove Rehabilitation and Living Center, 27 Cool Street, Waterville, ME 04901
Pine Point Center for Health Care and Rehabilitation, 67 Pine Point Road, Scarborough, ME 04074
RiverRidge, 79 Cat Mousam Road, Kennebunk, ME 04043
Sandy River Center for Nursing and Rehabilitation, RFD 4, Box 5121, Farmington, ME 04938
Seaside Nursing and Retirement Center, 850 Baxter Boulevard, Portland, ME 04103
Springbrook Center for Healthcare and Rehabilitation, 300 Spring Street, Westbrook, ME 04092
St. Marguerite d'Youville Pavilion, 102 Campus Avenue, Lewiston, ME 04240
Westgate Manor, 750 Union Street, Bangor, ME 04401
Windward Gardens, 105 Mechanic Street, Camden, ME 04843

MARYLAND
Bradford Oaks Nursing and Rehabilitation Center, 7520 Surratts Road, Clinton, MD 20735
Canton Harbor Healthcare Center, Inc., 1300 South Elwood Avenue, Baltimore, MD 21224
Care Matrix of Silver Spring, 2700 Barker Street, Silver Spring, MD 20910
Carriage Hill Bethesda, Inc., 5215 West Cedar Lane, Bethesda, MD 20814
College View Center, 700 Toll House Avenue, Frederick, MD 21701
Cromwell Center – Genesis ElderCare, 8710 Emge Road, Baltimore, MD 21234
Cumberland Villa Nursing Center, PO Box 869, Cumberland, MD 21501–0869
Fairland Adventist Nursing and Rehabilitation Center, 2101 Fairland Road, Silver Spring, MD 20904
Fox Chase Rehabilitation and Nursing Center, 2015 East West Highway, Silver Spring, MD 20910
Franklin Woods Center – Genesis Eldercare Network, 9200 Franklin Square Drive, Baltimore, MD 21237
Frostburg Village of Allegany County, One Kaylor Circle, Frostburg, MD 21532–2099
Future Care – Pineview, 9106 Pineview Lane, Clinton, MD 20735
FutureCare Sandtown – Winchester, 1000 North Gilmor Street, Baltimore, MD 21217
FutureCare Homewood, 2700 North Charles Street, Baltimore, MD 21218
FutureCare Old Court, 5412 Old Court Road, Randallstown, MD 21133–5196
FutureCare–CherryWood, 12020 Reisterstown Road, Reisterstown, MD 21136
FutureCare–Chesapeake, 305 College Parkway, Arnold, MD 21012
Genesis ElderCare – Randallstown Center, 9109 Liberty Road, Randallstown, MD 21133
Genesis ElderCare – Severna Park Center, 24 Truckhouse Road, Severna Park, MD 21146
Glen Meadows Retirement Community, 11630 Glen Arm Road, Glen Arm, MD 21057
Heartland Health Care Center – Adelphi, 1801 Metzerott Road, Adelphi, MD 20783
Heartland Health Care Center – Hyattsville, 6500 Riggs Road, Hyattsville, MD 20783
Herman Wilson Health Care Center Asbury Methodist Village, Inc, 301 Russell Avenue, Gaithersburg, MD 20877
Irvington Knolls Care Center II, Inc., 30 South Athol Avenue, Baltimore, MD 21229

Irvington Knolls Care Center, Inc., 22 South Athol Avenue, Baltimore, MD 21229
Keswick Milti–Care Center, 700 West 40th Street, Baltimore, MD 21211
La Plata Center, 1 Magnolia Drive, La Plata, MD 20646
Larkin Chase Nursing and Restorative Center, 15005 Health Center Drive, Bowie, MD 20716
Layhill Center – Genesis ElderCare Network, 3227 Bel Pre Road, Silver Spring, MD 20906
Levindale Hebrew Geriatric Center and Hospital, Inc., 2434 West Belvedere Avenue, Baltimore, MD 21215
Magnolia Center, 8200 Good Luck Road, Lanham, MD 20706
Manor Care Towson Nursing and Rehabilitation Center, 509 East Joppa Road, Towson, MD 21285
ManorCare Health Services, 6600 Ridge Road, Baltimore, MD 21237
ManorCare Health Services – Ruxton, 7001 North Charles Street, Towson, MD 21204
ManorCare Health Services – Wheaton, 11901 Georgia Avenue, Wheaton, MD 20902
ManorCare Health Services of Potomac, 10714 Potomac Tennis Lane, Potomac, MD 20854
Mariner Health at Circle Manor, 10231 Carroll Place, Kensington, MD 20895
Mariner Health of Bethesda, 5721 Grosvenor Lane, Bethesda, MD 20814
Mariner Health of Greater Laurel, 14200 Laurel Park Drive, Laurel, MD 20707
Mariner Health of Silver Spring, 901 Arcola Avenue, Silver Spring, MD 20902
Mariner Health of Southern Maryland, 9211 Stuart Lane, Clinton, MD 20735
Mariner Post Acute Network of Kensington, 3000 McComas Avenue, Kensington, MD 20895
Multi–Medical Center – Genesis ElderCare Network, 7700 York Road, Towson, MD 21204
Ravenwood Lutheran Village, 1183 Luther Drive, Hagerstown, MD 21740
Salisbury Center: Genesis Eldercare Network, 200 Civic Avenue, Salisbury, MD 21804
Shady Grove Adventist Nursing and Rehabilitation Center, 9701 Medical Center Drive, Rockville, MD 20850
Sligo Creek Nursing and Rehabilitation Center, 7525 Carroll Avenue, Takoma Park, MD 20912
Spa Creek Center Genesis ElderCare, 35 Milkshake Lane, Annapolis, MD 21403
Springbrook Adventist Nursing and Rehabilitation Center, 12325 New Hampshire Avenue, Silver Spring, MD 20904
St. Agnes Nursing and Rehabilitation Center, 3000 North Ridge Road, Ellicott City, MD 21043
Stella Maris, Inc., 2300 Dulaney Valley Road, Timonium, MD 21093
SunriseCare and Rehabilitation for Elkton, One Price Drive, Elkton, MD 21921
Woodside Center – Genesis Eldercare Network, 9101 Second Avenue, Silver Spring, MD 20910

MASSACHUSETTS
Abbott House, 28 Essex Street, Lynn, MA 01902
Aberjona Nursing Center, Inc., PO Box 490, Winchester, MA 01890
Alden Court Nursing Care and Rehabilitation Center, 389 Alden Road, Fairhaven, MA 02719
Anchorage Nursing Home, 904 Mohawk Trail, Shelburne, MA 01370
Apple Valley Nursing and Rehabilitation Center, 400 Groton Road, Ayer, MA 01432
Avery Manor, 100 West Street, Needham, MA 02194
Baldwinville Nursing Home, PO Box 24, Baldwinville, MA 01436
Bay Path at Duxbury Rehabilitation and Nursing Ctr, 308 Kingstown Way, Duxbury, MA 02332
Baypointe Rehabilitation and Skilled Care Center, 50 Christy Place, Brockton, MA 02401
Bear Hill Nursing Center, 11 North Street, Stoneham, MA 02180
Beaumont Rehabilitation and Skilled Nursing Center, 3 Vision Drive, Route 9 West, Natick, MA 01760
Beaumont Rehabilitation and Skilled Nursing Center, PO Box 517, Northbridge, MA 01534
Beaumont Rehabilitation and Skilled Nursing Center, 1 Lyman Street, Westborough, MA 01581
Belmont Manor Nursing Home, Inc., 34 Agassiz Avenue, Belmont, MA 02178
Berkshire Hills North Nursing Home, 170 Prospect Street, Lee, MA 01238
Beverly Health Care East Village, 840 Emerson Gardens Road, Lexington, MA 02173
Beverly Healthcare–Melrose, 40 Martin Street, Melrose, MA 02176

Beverly Manor of Plymouth Nursing Home, 19 Obery Street, Plymouth, MA 02360
Birchwood Care Center, 1199 John Fitch Highway, Fitchburg, MA 01420
Blaire House Long Term Care Facility of New Bedford, 397 County Street, New Bedford, MA 02740
Blaire House of Tewksbury, 10 Erlin Terrace, Tewksbury, MA 01876
Blue Hills Alzheimer's Care Center, 1044 Park Street, Stoughton, MA 02072
Blueberry Hill Healthcare, 75 Brimbal Avenue, Beverly, MA 01915
Bolton Manor, 400 Bolton Street, Marlborough, MA 01752
Bostonian Nursing Care and Rehabilitation Center, 337 Neponset Avenue, Dorchester, MA 02122
Bourne Manor Extended Care Facility, 146 MacArthur Boulevard, Bourne, MA 02532
Braemoor Rehabilitation and Nursing Center, Inc., 34 North Pearl Street, Brockton, MA 02401
Brandon Woods of Dartmouth, 567 Dartmouth Street, South Dartmouth, MA 02748
Brewster Manor Nursing and Rehabilitation Center, Inc, PO Box 1770, Brewster, MA 02631
Briarwood Continuing Care Retirement Community, 70 Briarwood Circle, Worcester, MA 01606
Briarwood Healthcare, 150 Lincoln Street, Needham, MA 02192
Brook Farm Rehabilitation and Nursing Centre, 1190 VFW Parkway, West Roxbury, MA 02132
Cape Cod Nursing and Rehabilitation Center, 8 Lewis Point, Buzzards Bay, MA 02532
Cape Heritage Rehabilitation and Nursing Center, 37 Route 6A, Sandwich, MA 02563
Cape Regency Nursing and Rehabilitation Center, 120 South Main Street, Centerville, MA 02632
CareMatrix of Dedham, 10 CareMatrix Drive, Dedham, MA 02026
Carlyle Nursing Home, Inc., PO Box 2495, Framingham, MA 01701
Catholic Memorial Home, Inc., 2446 Highland Avenue, Fall River, MA 02720–4599
Center for Optimum Care Berkshire, 360 West Housatonic Street, Pittsfield, MA 01201
Chamberlain Nursing Home, 123 Gardner Road, Brookline, MA 02146
Charlene Manor Extended Care Facility, 130 Colrain Road, Greenfield, MA 01301
Charlwell House/A Flatley Rehab and Nursing Center, 305 Walpole Street, Norwood, MA 02062
Chestnut Hill Rehabilitation and Nursing Center, 32 Chestnut Street, East Longmeadow, MA 01028
Chetwynde Health and Rehabilitation Center, 1650 Washington Street, West Newton, MA 02165
Christopher House of Worcester, Inc., 10 Mary Scano Drive, Worcester, MA 01605
Clark House Nursing Center at Fox Hill Village, 30 Longwood Drive, Westwood, MA 02090
Clifton Rehabilitative Nursing Center, 500 Wilbur Avenue, Somerset, MA 02725–2051
Cohasset Knoll Skilled Nursing and Rehabilitation Facility, 1 Chief Justice Cushing Hwy, Cohasset, MA 02025
Colonial Rehabililation & Nursing Center, 125 Broad Street, Weymouth, MA 02188
Colony House Nursing and Rehabilitation Center, 277 Washington Street, Abington, MA 02351–0556
Coolidge House Nursing Care Center, 30 Webster Street, Brookline, MA 02146
Copley at Stoughton Nursing Care Center, 380 Sumner Street, Stoughton, MA 02072
Country Estates Nursing and Rehabilitation Center, 1200 Suffield Street, Agawam, MA 01001
Country Gardens Skilled Nursing and Rehabilitation Ctr, 2045 Grand Army Highway, Swansea, MA 02777
Country Haven, Inc., 184 Mansfield Avenue, Norton, MA 02766
Country Manor Rehabilitation and Nursing Center, 180 Low Street, Newburyport, MA 01950
Courtyard Nursing Care Center, 200 Governors Avenue, Medford, MA 02155
Coyne Healthcare Center, 56 Webster Street, Rockland, MA 02370
Cranberry Pointe Rehab and Skilled Care Center, 111 Headwaters Drive, Harwich, MA 02645–1726
Crawford Skilled Nursing and Rehabilitation Center, 273 Oak Grove Avenue, Fall River, MA 02723
Crestview Healthcare Facility, Inc., 86 Greenleaf Street, Quincy, MA 02169
D'Youville Senior Care, Inc., 981 Varnum Avenue, Lowell, MA 01854
Den–Mar Rehabilitation and Nursing Center, 44 South Street, Rockport, MA 01966

Section C

Deutsches Altenheim, Inc., 2222 Centre Street, West Roxbury, MA 02132

Devereux House Nursing Home, 39 Lafayette Street, Marblehead, MA 01945–1997

Dexter House, 120 Main Street, Malden, MA 02148

Don Orione Nursing Home, 111 Orient Avenue, East Boston, MA 02128

Eagle Pond Rehabilitation and Living Center, PO Box 208, South Dennis, MA 02660

East Longmeadow Skilled Nursing Center, 305 Maple Street, East Longmeadow, MA 01028

Easton Lincoln Rehabilitation and Nursing Center, 184 Lincoln Street, North Easton, MA 02356

Eastpointe Rehabilitation and Skilled Care Center, 255 Central Avenue, Chelsea, MA 02150

Eastwood Care Center, 1007 East Street, Dedham, MA 02026

Edgar P. Benjamin Healthcare Center, 120 Fisher Avenue, Boston, MA 02120

Elihu White Nursing and Rehabilitation Center, 95 Commercial Street, Braintree, MA 02184

Elizabeth Seton Residence, Inc, 125 Oakland Street, Wellesley Hills, MA 02181

Elmhurst Nursing Home, 743 Main Street, Melrose, MA 02176

Embassy House Skilled Nursing and Rehabilitation Center, 2 Beaumont Avenue, Brockton, MA 02402

Emerald Court Health and Rehabilitation Center, 460 Washington Street, Norwood, MA 02062

Emerson Convalescent Home, 59 Coolidge Hill Road, Watertown, MA 02172–2884

Evanswood Center for Older Adults/Bethesda at Evanswood, 17 Chipman Way, Kingston, MA 02364

Fairhaven Nursing Home, Inc., 476 Varnum Avenue, Lowell, MA 01854

Fairlawn Nursing Home, Inc., 370 West Street, Leominster, MA 01453

Fall River Jewish Home, Inc., 538 Robeson Street, Fall River, MA 02720

Forestview Nursing Home of Wareham, Inc., 50 Indian Neck Road, Wareham, MA 02571

Franklin Skilled Nursing and Rehabilitation Center, 130 Chestnut Street, Franklin, MA 02038

Franvale Nursing and Rehabilitation Center, 20 Pond Street, Braintree, MA 02184

Geriatric Authority of Holyoke, 45 Lower Westfield Road, Holyoke, MA 01040

Glen Ridge Nursing Care Center, Hospital Road, Malden, MA 02148

Goddard House, 201 South Huntington Avenue, Jamaica Plain, MA 02130

Governor's Center, 66 Broad Street, Westfield, MA 01085

Great Barrington Rehabilitation and Nursing Center, 148 Maple Avenue, Great Barrington, MA 01230–1998

Greenery Extended Care Center at Danvers, 56 Liberty Street, Danvers, MA 01923–3398

Greenery Extended Care Center at North Andover, 75 Park Street, North Andover, MA 01845

Greenery Extended Care Center of Beverly, 40 Heather Street, Beverly, MA 01915

Greenery Rehabilitation and Skilled Nursing Center, 89 Lewis Bay Road, Hyannis, MA 02601

Greenery Rehabilitation and Skilled Nursing Center, PO Box 1330, Middleboro, MA 02346

Greenery Rehabilitation Center, 99 Chestnut Hill Avenue, Boston, MA 02135

Greycliff at Cape Ann, 272 Washington Street, Gloucester, MA 01930

Grosvenor Park Nursing Center, Inc., 7 Loring Hills Avenue, Salem, MA 01970

Hallmark Nursing and Rehabilitation Center, 1123 Rockdale Avenue, New Bedford, MA 02740–2998

Hammersmith House Nursing Center, 73 Chestnut Street, Saugus, MA 01906

Hancock Park Rehabilitation and Nursing Center, 164 Parkingway, Quincy, MA 02169

Hannah Duston Healthcare Center, 126 Monument Street, Haverhill, MA 01832

Harbor House Rehabilitation and Nursing Center, 11 Condito Road, Hingham, MA 02043

Harborside Healthcare Danvers Twin Oaks Rehab/Nursing Center, 63 Locust Street, Danvers, MA 01923

Harborside Healthcare Northshore, 266 Lincoln Avenue, Saugus, MA 01906

Harrington House Nursing and Rehabilitation Center, 160 Main Street, Walpole, MA 02081

Hathaway Manor, ECF, 863 Hathaway Road, New Bedford, MA 02740

Heathwood Nursing and Rehabilitation Center, 188 Florence Street, Chestnut Hill, MA 02167

Henry C. Nevins Home, Inc., Ten Ingalls Court, Methuen, MA 01844

Heritage Hall East Nursing and Rehabilitation Center, 464 Main Street, Agawam, MA 01001–2588

Heritage Hall West Genesis Eldercare Network, 61 Cooper Street, Agawam, MA 01001

Heritage Nursing Care Center, 841 Merrimack Street, Lowell, MA 01854

Hermitage Health and Rehabilitation Center, 383 Mill Street, Worcester, MA 01602

Hollywell/A Flatley Rehab and Nursing Center, 975 North Main Street, Randolph, MA 02368

Holy Trinity Nursing and Rehabilitation Center, 300 Barber Avenue, Worcester, MA 01606–2476

Integrated Health Services of Greater Boston at Medord, 300 Winthrop Street, Medford, MA 02155

Integrated Health Services of Greater Worcester, 215 Mill Street, Worcester, MA 01602

Jesmond Nursing Home, 271 Nahant Road, Nahant, MA 01908

Jewish Healthcare Center, Inc., 629 Salisbury Street, Worcester, MA 01609

Jewish Nursing Home of Western Massachusetts, Inc., 770 Converse Street, Longmeadow, MA 01106

JML Care Center, Inc., 184 Ter Heun Drive, Falmouth, MA 02540–2503

John Scott House Nursing and Rehabilitation Center, 233 Middle Street, Braintree, MA 02184

Kathleen Daniel, 485 Franklin Street, Framingham, MA 01702

Keystone Center – Genesis ElderCare, 44 Keystone Drive, Leominster, MA 01453

Kimwell/A Flatley Rehab and Nursing Center, 495 New Boston Road, Fall River, MA 02720

Lakeview House Nursing Home, PO Box 1598, Haverhill, MA 01831–1598

Laurel Ridge Rehabilitation and Nursing Center, 174 Forest Hills Street, Jamaica Plain, MA 02130

Ledgewood Rehabilitation and Skilled Nursing Center, 87 Herrick Street, Beverly, MA 01915

Leo P. LaChance Center for Rehabilitation and Nursing, 59 Eastwood Circle, Gardner, MA 01440

Liberty Commons of Chatham, 390 Orleans Road, North Chatham, MA 02650

Life Care Center of Attleboro, 969 Park Street, Attleboro, MA 02703

Life Care Center of Auburn, 14 Masonic Circle, Auburn, MA 01501

Life Care Center of Merrimack Valley, 80 Boston Road, North Billerica, MA 01862

Life Care Center of Plymouth, 94 Obery Street, Plymouth, MA 02360

Life Care Center of Raynham, 546 South Street East, Raynham, MA 02767

Life Care Center of Stoneham, 25 Woodland Road, Stoneham, MA 02180

Life Care Center of the North Shore, 111 Birch Street, Lynn, MA 01902

Life Care Center of the South Shore, PO Box 830 309 Driftway, Scituate, MA 02066

Life Care Center of West Bridgewater, 765 West Center Street, West Bridgewater, MA 02379

Life Care Center of Wilbraham, 2399 Boston Road, Wilbraham, MA 01095

Lighthouse Nursing Care Center, 204 Proctor Avenue, Revere, MA 02151

Lincoln Center, 299 Lincoln Street, Worcester, MA 01605

Linda Manor Extended Care Facility, 349 Haydenville Road, Leeds, MA 01053

Littleton House Nursing Home, 191 Foster Street, Littleton, MA 01460

Logan Healthcare Facility, 861 Main Street, South Weymouth, MA 02190

Loomis Nursing Center, 298 Jarvis Avenue, Holyoke, MA 01040

Lutheran Home of Worcester, 26 Harvard Street, Worcester, MA 01609

Madonna Manor, Inc., 85 North Washington Street, North Attleboro, MA 02760

Marian Manor, Inc., 33 Summer Street, Taunton, MA 02780

Mariner Health at Longwood, 53 Parker Hill Avenue, Boston, MA 02120

Mariner Health Care of Southeastern Massachusetts, 4586 Acushnet Avenue, New Bedford, MA 02745

Mariner Health of Methuen, 480 Jackson Street, Methuen, MA 01844

Maristhill Nursing Home & Rehabilitation Center, 66 Newton Street, Waltham, MA 02154

Mary Ann Morse Nursing and Rehabilitation Center, 45 Union Street, Natick, MA 01760

Mary Lyon Nursing Home, 34 Main Street, Hampden, MA 01036

Masonic Home, Inc., PO Box 1000, Charlton, MA 01507–1000

Mayflower Nursing and Rehabilitation Center, 123 South Street, Plymouth, MA 02360

Mayflower Place Nursing and Rehabilitation Center, 579 Buck Island Road, W Yarmouth, MA 02673

Meadow Green Nursing and Rehabilitation Center, 45 Woburn Street, Waltham, MA 02452

Meadowbrook Nursing, One Meadowbrook Way, Canton, MA 02021

Mediplex Rehabilitation and Skilled Nursing of Northampton, 548 Elm Street, Northampton, MA 01060

Mediplex of Beverly, 265 Essex Street, Beverly, MA 01915

Mediplex of Holyoke, 260 EastHampton Road, Holyoke, MA 01040

Mediplex of Lexington, 178 Lowell Street, Lexington, MA 02173

Mediplex of Lowell Skilled Nursing and Rehab Center, 19 Varnum Street, Lowell, MA 01850

Mediplex of Millbury, 312 Millbury Avenue, Millbury, MA 01527

Mediplex of Newton, 2101 Washington Street, Newton, MA 02162

Mediplex Rehabilitation and Skilled Nursing Center, 70 Granite Street, Lynn, MA 01904

Medway Country Manor Skilled Nursing and Rehabilitation, PO Box 106, Medway, MA 02053

MI Nursing/Restorative Center, Inc., 172 Lawrence Street, Lawrence, MA 01841

Milton Health Care, 1200 Brush Hill Road, Milton, MA 02186

Mont Marie Health Care Center, Inc., 34 Lower Westfield Road, Holyoke, MA 01040–2739

Mount St. Vincent Nursing Home, 35 Holy Family Road, Holyoke, MA 01040–2758

Mt. Greylock Extended Care Facility, 1000 North Street, Pittsfield, MA 01201

New Boston Nursing Center, PO Box 216, Sandisfield, MA 01255

New England Pediatric Care, Inc., 78 Boston Road, North Billerica, MA 01862

Newton & Wellesley Alzheimer Center, 694 Worcester Street, Wellesley, MA 02181

Normandy House Nursing Home, 15 Green Street, Melrose, MA 02176

North End Community Nursing Home, 70 Fulton Street, Boston, MA 02109

Northbridge Nursing and Rehabilitation Center, 2356 Providence Road, Northbridge, MA 01534

Northwood Rehabilitation and Nursing Center, 1010 Varnum Avenue, Lowell, MA 01854

Norwell Knoll Nursing Home, 329 Washington Street, Norwell, MA 02061

Norwood Health and Rehabilitation Center, 767 Washington Street, Norwood, MA 02062

Notre Dame Long Term Care Center, 559 Plantation Street, Worcester, MA 01605

Nursing Care Center at Kimball Farms, 235 Walker Street, Lenox, MA 01240

Oak Hill Nursing and Rehabilitation Center, 76 North Street, Middleboro, MA 02346

Oak Island Skilled Nursing Facility Limited Partnership, 400 Revere Beach Boulevard, Revere, MA 02151

Oak Knoll Health Care Center, 9 Arbetter Drive, Framingham, MA 01701

Oakdale Rehabilitation and Skilled Nursing Center, 76 North Main Street, West Boylston, MA 01583

Oakwood Rehabilitation and Nursing Center, 11 Pontiac Avenue, Webster, MA 01570

Odd Fellows Home of Massachusetts, 104 Randolph Road, Worcester, MA 01606

Olympus Healthcare Center–Lanessa, 751 School Street, Webster, MA 01570

Olympus Healthcare and Nursing Center – Braintree, 1102 Washington Street, Braintree, MA 02184

Olympus Healthcare Center – Webster, 745 School Street, Webster, MA 01570

Olympus Healthcare Center– Hollingsworth, 1120 Washington Street, Braintree, MA 02184

On Broadway Nursing and Rehabilitation Center, 932–934 Broadway, Chelsea, MA 02150

Our Lady's Haven of Fairhaven, Inc., 71 Center Street, Fairhaven, MA 02719

Palm Manor Nursing Home, 40 Parkhurst Road, Chelmsford, MA 01824

Park Avenue Nursing, & Rehabilitation Center, 146 Park Avenue, Arlington, MA 02174

Parkwell Rehabilitation and Nursing Center, 745 Truman Highway, Hyde Park, MA 02136

Peabody Glen Nursing Center, 199 Andover Street, Peabody, MA 01960

Penacook Place, 150 Water Street, Haverhill, MA 01830

Pilgrim Manor Skilled Nursing and Rehabilitation Center, 60 Stafford Street, Plymouth, MA 02360

Pilgrim Rehabilitation and Skilled Nursing Center, 96 Forest Street, Peabody, MA 01960–3907

Pleasant Bay Nursing and Rehabilitation Center, 383 South Orleans Road, Rte 39, Brewster, MA 02631

Pleasant Manor Nursing Home, 193–195 Pleasant Street, Attleboro, MA 02703

Pond Meadow Nursing and Rehabilitation Center, 188 Summer Street, Weymouth, MA 02188

Port Healthcare Center, 113 Low Street, Newburyport, MA 01950

Prescott House Nursing Home, 140 Prescott Street, North Andover, MA 01845

Presentation Nursing and Rehabilitation Center, Ten Bellamy Street, Brighton, MA 02135

Presidential Rehabilitation and Nursing Center, 43 Old Colony Avenue, Quincy, MA 02170

Quabbin Valley Healthcare, 821 Daniel Shays Highway, Athol, MA 01331

Quaboag on the Common, PO Box 386, West Brookfield, MA 01585

Queen Anne Nursing Home, Inc., 50 Recreation Park Drive, Hingham, MA 02043

Quincy Rehabilitation and Nursing Center, 11 McGrath Highway, Quincy, MA 02169–5311

Reservoir Nursing Home, 1841 Trapelo Road, Waltham, MA 02154

Ring Health Care Centers/East, PO Box 478, Springfield, MA 01118

River Terrace, 1675 Main Street, Lancaster, MA 01523

Rivercrest Long Term Care Facility, 80 Deaconess Road, Concord, MA 01742

Riverdale Gardens Rehabilitation and Nursing Center, 42 Prospect Avenue, West Springfield, MA 01089

Rosewood Nursing and Rehabilitation Center, 22 Johnson Street, Peabody, MA 01960

Sachem Skilled Nursing and Rehabilitation Center, 66 Central Street, East Bridgewater, MA 02333

Sacred Heart Nursing Home, 359 Summer Street, New Bedford, MA 02740–5599

Saint Francis Home, 101 Plantation Street, Worcester, MA 01604–3025

Sancta Maria Nursing Facility, 799 Concord Avenue, Cambridge, MA 02138–1077

Sandalwood Nursing and Rehabilitation Center, 3 Pine Street, Oxford, MA 01540

Sarah S. Brayton Nursing Care Center, 4901 North Main Street, Fall River, MA 02720

Seacoast Nursing and Retirement Center, 292 Washington Street, Gloucester, MA 01930

Sharon Senior Care Center, 259 Norwood Street, Sharon, MA 02067

Sherrill House, Inc., 135 South Huntington Avenue, Boston, MA 02130

Sippican Healthcare Center, 15 Mill Street, Marion, MA 02738

Southpointe Rehabilitation and Skilled Care Center, 100 Amity Street, Fall River, MA 02721

Southwood at Norwell Nursing Center, 501 Cordwainer Drive, Norwell, MA 02061

St. Joseph Manor Health Care, Inc., 215 Thatcher Street, Brockton, MA 02402

Stephen Caldwell Memorial Convalescent Home, Inc., 16 Green Street, Ipswich, MA 01938

Suburban Manor Rehabilitation Nursing Center, One Great Road, Acton, MA 01720

Sunny Acres Nursing Home, Inc., 254 Billerica Road, Chelmsford, MA 01824–4184

SunRise Care & Rehabilitation for East Longmeadow, 135 Benton Drive, East Longmeadow, MA 01028

SunRise Care and Rehabilitation for Brookline, 99 Park Street, Brookline, MA 02446

SunRise Care and Rehabilitation for Milford, 10 Veterans Memorial Drive, Milford, MA 01757

SunRise Care and Rehabilitation for New Bedford, 221 Fitzgerald Drive, New Bedford, MA 02745

Sunrise Care and Rehabilitation for Weymouth, 64 Performance Drive, Weymouth, MA 02189

Sunrise Care and Rehabilitation for Wilmington, 750 Woburn Street, Wilmington, MA 01887

Sunrise/Mediplex of Boston, 910 Saratoga Street, East Boston, MA 02128

SunriseCare and Rehabilitation for Hadley @ Elaine Manor, Box 720, Hadley, MA 01035

Sutton Hill Nursing and Retirement Center, 1801 Turnpike Street, North Andover, MA 01845

Sweet Brook Care Centers, Inc., 1561 Cold Spring Road, Williamstown, MA 01267

Taber Street Nursing Home, 19 Taber Street, New Bedford, MA 02740

The Boston Center For Rehabilitative & Subacute Care, 1245 Centre Street, Roslindale, MA 02131

The Center for Optimum Care – Bayview, 26 Sturgis Street, Winthrop, MA 02152

The Center for Optimum Care – Falmouth, 359 Jones Road, Falmouth, MA 02540

The Center for Optimum Care – Mashpee, 161 Falmouth Road – Route 28, Mashpee, MA 02649

The Center for Optimum Care – Wakefield, Bathol Street, Wakefield, MA 01880

The Center for Optimum Care – Westfield, 60 East Silver Street, Westfield, MA 01085

The Center for Optimum Care – Winthrop, 170 Cliff Avenue, Winthrop, MA 02152

The Ellis Nursing and Rehabilitation Center, 135 Ellis Avenue, Norwood, MA 02062

The Goddard Center, 909 Sumner Street, Stoughton, MA 02072

The Greenery Extended Care Center, 59 Acton Street, Worcester, MA 01604

The Guardian Center, 888 North Main Street, Brockton, MA 02401

The Hellenic Nursing Home for the Aged, 601 Sherman Street, Canton, MA 02021–2025

The Highlands, 335 Nichols Road, Fitchburg, MA 01420

The Lafayette Convalescent Home, 25 Lafayette Street, Marblehead, MA 01945

The Meadows Skilled Nursing and Rehabilitation Center, 111 Huntoon Memorial Highway, Rochdale, MA 01542

The Oaks, 4525 Acushnet Avenue, New Bedford, MA 02745

The Oxford, 689 Main Street, Haverhill, MA 01830

Town & Country Nursing Home, 259 Baldwin Street, Lowell, MA 01851

University Commons, 378 Plantation Street, Worcester, MA 01605

Wachusett Extended Care Facility, 56 Boyden Road, Holden, MA 01520–2593

Walden Rehabilitation and Nursing Center, 785 Main Street, Concord, MA 01742

Wedgemere Convalescent Home, 146 Dean Street, Taunton, MA 02780

Wellesley Health and Rehabilitation Center, 878 Worcester Road, Wellesley, MA 02181

West Acres Nursing Home, 804 Pleasant Street, Brockton, MA 02401–3099

Westborough Nursing Center, 5 Colonial Drive, Westborough, MA 01581

Westford Nursing and Rehabilitation Center, 3 Park Drive, Westford, MA 01886

Weston Manor Nursing and Rehabilitation Center, 75 Norumbega Road, Weston, MA 02193

Willow Manor, 30 Princeton Boulevard, Lowell, MA 01851

Willowood Health Care Center of North Adams, 175 Franklin Street, North Adams, MA 01247

Willowood Nursing and Retirement Facility, 151 Christian Hill Road, Great Barrington, MA 01230

Willowood of Pittsfield Health Care Center, 169 Valentine Road, Pittsfield, MA 01201

Willowood of Williamstown, 25 Adams Road, Williamstown, MA 01267

Winchester Nursing Center, Inc, PO Box 490, Winchester, MA 01890

Windsor Skilled Nursing and Rehabilitation Center, 265 North Main Street, South Yarmouth, MA 02664

Wingate at Andover, 80 Andover Street, Andover, MA 01810

Wingate at Brighton Rehabilitative/Skilled Nursing, 100 North Beacon Street, Boston, MA 02134

Wingate at Needham, 589 Highland Avenue, Needham, MA 02194

Wingate at Reading, 1364 Main Street, Reading, MA 01867

Wingate at Sudbury, Inc., 136 Boston Post Road, Sudbury, MA 01776

Wingate at Wilbraham, 9 Maple Street, Wilbraham, MA 01095

Woburn Nursing Center, 18 Frances Street, Woburn, MA 01801

Woodbriar of Wilmington Rehab and Skilled Nursing Center, 90 West Street, Wilmington, MA 01887

Woodford of Ayer, 15 Winthrop Avenue, Ayer, MA 01432

MICHIGAN

Bay County Medical Care Facility, 564 West Hampton Road, Essexville, MI 48732

Boulder Park Terrace, 14676 West Upright, Charlevoix, MI 49720

Brookcrest Christian Nursing Home, 3400 Wilson Avenue, Grandville, MI 49418

Charter House of Farmington Hills, 21017 Middlebelt Road, Farmington Hills, MI 48336

Christian Rest Home Association, 1000 Edison Northwest, Grand Rapids, MI 49504–3999

Crestmont HealthCare Center, 111 Trealout Drive, Fenton, MI 48430

Evangelical Home – Port Huron, 5635 Lakeshore Road, Fort Gratiot, MI 48059

Farmington Health Care, 34225 Grand River Avenue, Farmington, MI 48335

Fraser Villa – A Mercy Living Center, 33300 Utica Road, Fraser, MI 48026

Greenery Health Care Center, 3003 West Grand River, Howell, MI 48843

Haven Park Christian Nursing Home, 285 North State Street, Zeeland, MI 49464

Heartland Health Care Center – Allen Park, 9150 Allen Road, Allen Park, MI 48101

Heartland Health Care Center – Briarwood, 3011 North Center Road, Flint, MI 48506

Heartland Health Care Center – Dearborn Heights, 26001 Ford Road, Dearborn Heights, MI 48127

Heartland Health Care Center – Dorvin, 29270 Morlock Street, Livonia, MI 48152

Heartland Health Care Center – Georgian Bloomfield, 2975 North Adams Road, Bloomfield Hills, MI 48304

Heartland Health Care Center – Georgian East, 21401 Mack Avenue, Grosse Pointe, MI 48236

Heartland Health Care Center – Grand Rapids, 2320 East Beltline Southeast, Grand Rapids, MI 49546

Heartland Health Care Center – Kalamazoo, 3625 West Michigan Avenue, Kalamazoo, MI 49006

Heartland Health Care Center – Knollview, 1061 West Hackley Avenue, Muskegon, MI 49441

Heartland Health Care Center – Plymouth Court, 105 Haggerty Road, Plymouth, MI 48170

Heartland Health Care Center – University, 28550 Five Mile Road, Livonia, MI 48154

Heartland Healthcare Center – Ann Arbor, 4701 East Huron River Drive, Ann Arbor, MI 48105

Holland Health Care Center, 493 West 32nd Street, Holland, MI 49423

Holland Home – Breton Manor, 2589 44th Street Southeast, Kentwood, MI 49512

Holland Home – Fulton Manor, 1450 East Fulton Avenue, Grand Rapids, MI 49503

Holland Home – Raybrook Manor, 2121 Raybrook, Southeast, Grand Rapids, MI 49546

IHS of Michigan @ Clarkston, 4800 Clintonville Road, Clarkston, MI 48346

Integrated Health Services of Michigan at Riverbend, 11941 Belsay Road, Grand Blanc, MI 48439

Isabella County Medical Care Facility, 1222 North Drive, Mount Pleasant, MI 48858

Martha T. Berry Memorial Medical Care Facility, 43533 Elizabeth Road, Mount Clemens, MI 48043

Mercy Pavilion, 80 North 20th Street, Battle Creek, MI 49015

Mercy Services for Aging, 875 Avon Road, Rochester Hills, MI 48307

Metron of Greenville, 828 East Washington Street, Greenville, MI 48838

North Ottawa Care Center, 1615 South Despelder, Grand Haven, MI 49417–2633

Oakland County Medical Care Facility, 1200 North Telegraph Road, Pontiac, MI 48341–0469

Orchard Hills, A Mercy Living Center, 532 Orchard Lake Road, Pontiac, MI 48341

Porter Hills Presbyterian Village, Inc., 3600 East Fulton Street, Grand Rapids, MI 49546–1395

Rivergate Terrace, 14141 Pennsylvania Road, Riverview, MI 48192

Shore Haven, A Mercy Living Center, 900 South Beacon Boulevard, Grand Haven, MI 49417

The Laurels of Hudsonville, 3650 Van Buren Street, Hudsonville, MI 49426

The Marvin and Betty Danto Health Care Center, 6800 West Maple, West Bloomfield, MI 48322

University Park A Mercy Living Center, 570 South Harvey Street, Muskegon, MI 49442

MINNESOTA

Bloomington Health Care & Rehabilitation, 9200 Nicollet Avenue South, Bloomington, MN 55420

Chateau Healthcare Center, 2106 2nd Avenue South, Minneapolis, MN 55404

Greeley Healthcare Center, 313 South Greeley Street, Stillwater, MN 55082

Hillcrest Health Care and Retirement Center, 15409 Wayzata Boulevard, Wayzata, MN 55391

La Crescent Healthcare Center, 701 Main Street, La Crescent, MN 55947

Lake Ridge Health Care Center, 2727 North Victoria, Roseville, MN 55113

Lexington Health and Rehabilitation Center, 375 North Lexington Parkway, Saint Paul, MN 55104

Moorhead Healthcare Center, 2810 2nd Avenue North, Moorhead, MN 56560

Olivia Healthcare Center, PO Box 229, Olivia, MN 56277

Park Health and Rehabilitation Center, 4415 West 36 1/2 Street, Saint Louis Park, MN 55416

St. Louis Park Plaza Health Care Center, 3201 Virginia Avenue South, Saint Louis Park, MN 55426

Trevilla of Golden Valley, 7505 Country Club Drive, Golden Valley, MN 55427

Trevilla of New Brighton, 825 First Avenue Northwest, New Brighton, MN 55112

Twin Rivers Care Center, 305 Fremont Street, Anoka, MN 55303

University Good Samaritan Center, 22 – 27th Avenue Southeast, Minneapolis, MN 55414

Whitewater Healthcare Center, PO Box 8, St Charles, MN 55972

MISSISSIPPI

Beverly Healthcare – Eupora, PO Box 918, Eupora, MS 39744–2029

Countrybrook Living Center, P.O. Box 3369, Brookhaven, MS 39603–7369

Lakeland Health Care Center, 3680 Lakeland Lane, Jackson, MS 39216

United States Naval Home, 1800 Beach Drive, Gulfport, MS 39507–1597

MISSOURI

Alexian Brothers Lansdowne Village, 4624 Lansdowne, Saint Louis, MO 63116

Balanced Care Hermitage, PO Box 325, Hermitage, MO 65668

Balanced Care Lebanon North, PO Box K, Lebanon, MO 65536

Balanced Care Lebanon South, 514 West Fremont Road, Lebanon, MO 65536

BCC at Republic Park Care Center, Inc., PO Box 755, Republic, MO 65738

Harry S. Truman Restorative Center, 5700 Arsenal Street, St. Louis, MO 63139

Integrated Health Services of Kansas City at Alpine North, 4700 Cliff View Drive, Kansas City, MO 64150

Integrated Health Services of St. Louis at Gravois, 10954 Kennerly Road, St. Louis, MO 63128

John Knox Village Care Center, 600 NW Pryor Road, Lees Summit, MO 64081

Life Care Center of Saint Louis, 3520 Chouteau Avenue, Saint Louis, MO 63103

ManorCare Health Services, 1200 Graham Road, Florissant, MO 63034

Village North Health Center, Village North Retirement Community, St. Louis, MO 63136

Village North Manor, 6768 North Highway 67, Florissant, MO 63034

Woodbine Healthcare and Rehabilitation Centre, 2900 Kendallwood Parkway, Gladstone, MO 64118

NEBRASKA

Beverly HealthCare at Lakeview, 1405 West Highway 34, Grand Island, NE 68801

Columbus Manor, PO Box 625, Columbus, NE 68601

Fullerton Manor, PO Box 648, Fullerton, NE 68638

Good Samaritan Village, PO Box 2149, Hastings, NE 68902–2149

Hallmark Care Center, 5505 Grover Street, Omaha, NE 68106

Hartington Nursing Center, PO Box 107, Hartington, NE 68739

Norfolk Nursing Center, 1900 Vicki Lane, Norfolk, NE 68701

Park Place Health Care and Rehabilitation Center, 610 North Darr, Grand Island, NE 68803

Plattsmouth Manor and Rehabilitation Center, 602 South 18th Street, Plattsmouth, NE 68048

Scottsbluff Nursing Center, 111 West 36th Street, Scottsbluff, NE 69361

The Ambassador Lincoln, 4405 Normal Boulevard, Lincoln, NE 68506

The Ambassador of Nebraska City, Box 547, Nebraska City, NE 68410

Valhaven Nursing Center, PO Box 357, Valley, NE 68064

NEW HAMPSHIRE

Dover Rehabilitation and Living Center, 307 Plaza Drive, Dover, NH 03820

Genesis ElderCare Network – Keene Center, 677 Court Street, Keene, NH 03431

Golden View Health Care Center, 19 New Hampshire Route 104, Meredith, NH 03253

Good Shepherd Nursing Home, 20 Plantation Drive, Jaffrey, NH 03452

Greenbriar Terrace Healthcare, 55 Harris Road, Nashua, NH 03062

Hanover Hill Health Care Center, 700 Hanover Street, Manchester, NH 03104

Hanover Terrace Healthcare, 53 Lyme Road, Hanover, NH 03755

Harborside Healthcare – Applewood, 8 Snow Road, Winchester, NH 03470

Harborside Healthcare – Crestwood Rehab and Nursing, 40 Crosby Street, Milford, NH 03055

Harborside Healthcare – Northwood Rehab and Nursing, 30 Colby Court, Bedford, NH 03110

Harborside Healthcare – Pheasant Wood, 100 Pheasant Road, Peterborough, NH 03458

Integrated Health Services of New Hampshire at Claremont, RFD 3, Box 47, Hanover Street Extension, Claremont, NH 03743

Integrated Health Services of Derry, 8 Peabody Road, Derry, NH 03038

Integrated Health Services of New Hampshire at Manchester, 191 Hackett Hill Road, Manchester, NH 03102

Maple Leaf Health Care Center, 198 Pearl Street, Manchester, NH 03104

Mount Carmel Nursing Home, 235 Myrtle Street, Manchester, NH 03104

Ridgewood Center, 25 Ridgewood Road, Bedford, NH 03110

Rochester Manor, 40 Whitehall Road, Rochester, NH 03867

Saint Ann Home, 195 Dover Point Road, Dover, NH 03820

Saint Vincent de Paul Nursing Home, 29 Providence Avenue, Berlin, NH 03570

Seacoast Health Center, 22 Tuck Road, Hampton, NH 03842

St. Francis Home, 406 Court Street, Laconia, NH 03246

St. Teresa's Manor, 519 Bridge Street, Manchester, NH 03104

The Edgewood Centre, 928 South Street, Portsmouth, NH 03801

Villa Crest Nursing and Retirement Center, 1276 Hanover Street, Manchester, NH 03104

NEW JERSEY

Absecon Manor Nursing and Rehabilitation Center, 1020 Pitney Road, Absecon, NJ 08201

Arbor Glen Nursing and Rehabilitation Center, Pompton Avenue/E Lindsley Road, Cedar Grove, NJ 07009

Ashbrook Nursing and Rehabilitation Center, 1610 Raritan Road, Scotch Plains, NJ 07076

Atlantic Coast Rehabilitation and Health Care Center, 485 River Avenue, Lakewood, NJ 08701

Barn Hill Care Center, 249 High Street, Newton, NJ 07860

Barnegat Nursing Center, 859 West Bay Avenue, Barnegat, NJ 08005

Bartley Healthcare Nursing and Rehabilitation, 175 Bartley Road, Jackson, NJ 08527

Berkeley Heights Convalescent Center, 35 Cottage Street, Berkeley Heights, NJ 07922

Bey Lea Village, 1351 Old Freehold Road, Toms River, NJ 08753

Chestnut Hill Convalescent and Rehabilitation Center, 360 Chestnut Street, Passaic, NJ 07055

Cinniminson Nursing and Rehabilitation Center, 1700 Wynwood Drive, Cinnaminson, NJ 08077

Clark Nursing and Rehabilitation Center, 1213 Westfield Avenue, Clark, NJ 07066

Cornell Hall, 234 Chestnut Street, Union, NJ 07083

Courthouse Convalescent Center, 144 Magnolia Drive, Cape May Court House, NJ 08210

Cranbury Nursing and Rehabilitation Center, 292 Applegarth Road, Cranbury, NJ 08512

Crestwood Nursing and Rehabilitation Center, 101 Whippany Road, Whippany, NJ 07981

Daughters of Israel Geriatric Center, 1155 Pleasant Valley Way, West Orange, NJ 07052

Daughters of Miriam Center for the Aged, 155 Hazel Street, Clifton, NJ 07015

Delaire Nursing and Convalescent Center, 400 West Stimpson Avenue, Linden, NJ 07036

Dunroven Health Care Center, 221 County Road, Cresskill, NJ 07626

Eastern Shore Nursing and Rehabilitation Center, 1419 Route 9 North, Cape May Court House, NJ 08210

Forrestal Nursing and Rehabilitation Center, 5000 Windrow Drive, Princeton, NJ 08540

Franklin Convalescent Center, 3371 Route 27, Franklin Park, NJ 08823

Glenside Nursing Center, 144 Gales Drive, New Providence, NJ 07974

Green Acres Manor, 1931 Lakewood Road, Route 9, Toms River, NJ 08755

Greenbrook Manor, 303 Rock Avenue, Green Brook, NJ 08812

Hamilton Park Health Care Center, Ltd., 525–535 Monmouth Street, Jersey City, NJ 07302

Harborside Healthcare Rehab and Nursing Center/Woods Edge, 875 Route 202/206 North, Bridgewater, NJ 08807

Harrogate,Inc., 400 Locust Street, Lakewood, NJ 08701

Inglemoor Care Center, 311 South Livingston Avenue, Livingston, NJ 07039

Integrated Health Services of New Jersey at Somerset Valley, 1621 Route 22 West, Bound Brook, NJ 08805

Jackson Center – Genesis ElderCare, 11 History Lane, Jackson, NJ 08527

JFK Hartwyck at Cedar Brook, 1340 Park Avenue, Plainfield, NJ 07060

JFK Hartwyck at Edison Estates, 465 Plainfield Avenue, Edison, NJ 08817

JFK Hartwyck at Oak Tree Nursing, Convalescent, & Rehabilitation Center, 2048 Oak Tree Road, Edison, NJ 08820

Lakeview Subacute Care Center, 130 Terhune Drive, Wayne, NJ 07470

Lakewood of Voorhees Associates, 1302 Laurel Oak Road, Voorhees, NJ 08043

Laurelton Village, 475 Jack Martin Boulevard, Brick, NJ 08724

Lincoln Park Nursing and Convalescent Home, 521 Pine Brook Road, Lincoln Park, NJ 07035

Linwood Convalescent Center, Route 9 and Central Avenue, Linwood, NJ 08221

Llanfair House, 1140 Black Oak Ridge Road, Wayne, NJ 07470

Mainland Manor Nursing and Rehabilitation Center, PO Box 1309, Pleasantville, NJ 08232

Manchester Manor Associates, 101 State Highway 70, Lakehurst, NJ 08733

ManorCare Health Services, 1412 Marlton Pike, Cherry Hill, NJ 08034

ManorCare Health Services, 1180 Route 22 West, Mountainside, NJ 07092

ManorCare Health Services, 550 Jessup Road, West Deptford, NJ 08066

Marcella Center–Genesis Eldercare, 2305 Rancocas Road, Burlington Township, NJ 08016

Margaret McLaughlin McCarrick Care Center, 15 Dellwood Lane, Somerset, NJ 08873

Meadow View Nursing and Respiratory Care Center, 1328 South Black Horse Pike, Williamstown, NJ 08094

Medford Convalescent and Nursing Center, 185 Tuckerton Road, Medford, NJ 08055

Mediplex of Oradell, 600 Kinderkamack Road, Oradell, NJ 07649

Millhouse, 325 Jersey Street, Trenton, NJ 08611

Morris Hills Genesis Eldercare Center, 77 Madison Avenue, Morristown, NJ 07960–6089

Morris View Nursing Home, PO Box 437, Morris Plains, NJ 07950

Mt. Laurel Nursing and Rehabilitation Center, 3706 Church Road, Mount Laurel, NJ 08054

Neptune ConvaCenter, 101 Walnut Street, Neptune, NJ 07753

Oak Ridge Rehabilitation and Nursing Center, 261 Terhune Drive, Wayne, NJ 07470

Old Bridge Manor, 6989 Route 18 South, Old Bridge, NJ 08857

Parkway Manor Health Center, 480 North Walnut Street/ Parkway Drive, East Orange, NJ 07017

Regent Care Center, 50 Polifly Road, Hackensack, NJ 07601

Riverview Extended Care Residence, 55 West Front Street, Red Bank, NJ 07701

Seacrest Village Nursing and Rehabilitation Center, PO Box 1480, Little Egg Harbor Twp, NJ 08087

Silver Care Center, 1423 Brace Road, Cherry Hill, NJ 08034

South Mountain Healthcare and Rehabilitation Center, 2385 Springfield Avenue, Vauxhall, NJ 07088–1046

Southern Ocean Nursing and Rehabilitation Center, 1361 Route 72 West, Manahawkin, NJ 08050

SunRise Care and Rehabilitation for Southern NJ, 2 Cooper Plaza, Camden, NJ 08103

The Health Center at Bloomingdale, 255 Union Avenue, Bloomingdale, NJ 07403

The Manor, 689 West Main Street, Freehold, NJ 07728–2511

The Pope John Paul II Pavilion at Saint Mary's Life Center, 135 South Center Street, Orange, NJ 07050

Troy Hills Center, 200 Reynolds Avenue, Parsippany, NJ 07054

Valley Health Care Center, 300 Old Hook Road, Westwood, NJ 07675

Voorhees Center – Genesis ElderCare Network, 3001 Evesham Road, Voorhees, NJ 08043

Voorhees Pediatric Facility, 1304 Laurel Oak Road, Voorhees, NJ 08043–4392

Wanaque Operating Company, LP, 1433 Ringwood Avenue, Haskell, NJ 07420

Wayne View Convalescent Center, 2020 Route 23 North, Wayne, NJ 07470

Wellington Hall Care Center, 301 Union Street, Hackensack, NJ 07601

West Caldwell Care Center, 165 Fairfield Avenue, West Caldwell, NJ 07006

Westfield Center – Genesis ElderCare Network, 1515 Lamberts Mill Road, Westfield, NJ 07090

Whiting Healthcare Center, 3000 Hilltop Road, Whiting, NJ 08759

Willow Creek Rehabilitation and Care Center, 1165 Easton Avenue, Somerset, NJ 08873

Woodcrest Center, 800 River Road, New Milford, NJ 07646

NEW MEXICO

Casa Arena Blanca Nursing Center, 205 Moonglow, Alamogordo, NM 88310

Casa Maria Health Care Center, 1601 South Main Street, Roswell, NM 88201

Las Palomas Nursing and Rehabilitation Center, 8100 Palomas, NE, Albuquerque, NM 87109

NEW YORK

Arbor Hill Living Center, 1175 Monroe Avenue, Rochester, NY 14620–1697

Arbor Park Health Care Center, Inc., 2806 George Street, Eden, NY 14057

Aurora Park Health Care Center, Inc., 292 Main Street, East Aurora, NY 14052

Bainbridge Nursing Home, 3518 Bainbridge Avenue, Bronx, NY 10467

Beechwood Residence / Beechwood Nursing Home, 2235 Millersport Highway, Getzville, NY 14068

Beth Abraham Health Services, 612 Allerton Avenue, Bronx, NY 10467

Birchwood Health Care Center, Inc., 4800 Bear Road, Liverpool, NY 13088

Birchwood Nursing Home, 78 Birchwood Drive, Huntington Station, NY 11746

Brandywine Nursing Home, 620 Sleepy Hollow Road, Briarcliff Manor, NY 10510

Briody Health Care Facility, 909 Lincoln Avenue, Lockport, NY 14094

Center for Nursing and Rehabilitation, 520 Prospect Place, Brooklyn, NY 11238

Central Island Healthcare, 825 Old Country Road, Plainview, NY 11803

Clearview Nursing Home, 157–15 19th Avenue, Whitestone, NY 11357

Clove Lakes Health Care and Rehabilitation Center, Inc, 25 Fanning Street, Staten Island, NY 10314

Cobble Hill Health Center, Inc, 380 Henry Street, Brooklyn, NY 11201

College Park Health Care Center, Inc., 9876 Luckey Drive, Houghton, NY 14744

Concourse Rehabilitation and Nursing Center, Inc., 1072 Grand Concourse, Bronx, NY 10456

Cortland Care Center, 193 Clinton Avenue, Cortland, NY 13045

Crown Nursing & Rehabilitation Center, 3457 Nostrand Avenue, Brooklyn, NY 11229

Dr. Susan Smith McKinney Nursing/Rehabilitation Center, 594 Albany Avenue, Brooklyn, NY 11203

Dumont Masonic Home, 676 Pelham Road, New Rochelle, NY 10805

East Haven Nursing Home, 2323 Eastchester Road, Bronx, NY 10469

Eger Health Care and Rehabilitation Center, 140 Meisner Avenue, Staten Island, NY 10306–1200

Father Baker Manor, 6400 Powers Road, Orchard Park, NY 14127

Franklin Center for Rehabilitation and Nursing, 142–27 Franklin Avenue, Flushing, NY 11355

Glengariff Health Care Center, PO Box 71, Glen Cove, NY 11542

Golden Gate Health Care Center, Inc., 191 Bradley Avenue, Staten Island, NY 10314

Gouverneur Nursing Facility, 227 Madison Street, New York, NY 10002

Grace Plaza of Great Neck, Inc, 15 St. Paul's Place, Great Neck, NY 11021

Greater Harlem Nursing Home, 30 West 138th Street, New York, NY 10037

Haven Manor Health Care Center, 1441 Gateway Boulevard, Far Rockaway, NY 11691

Highgate Manor of Cortland, Inc., PO Box 5510, Cortland, NY 13045–5510

Highgate Manor of Rensselaer, Inc., 100 New Turnpike Road, Troy, NY 12182

Highland Healthcare Center, 160 Seneca Street, Wellsville, NY 14895

Hillcrest Nursing and Rehabilitation Center, 661 North Main Street, Spring Valley, NY 10977

Hillside Manor Rehabilitation and Extended Care Center, 182–15 Hillside Avenue, Jamaica Est, NY 11432

Hilltop Manor of Niskayuna, 1805 Providence Avenue, Niskayuna, NY 12309

Horizon Care Center, 64–11 Beach Channel Drive, Arverne, NY 11692

Hudson Valley Rehabilitative and Extended Care Center, 260 Vineyard Avenue, Highland, NY 12528

Indian River Nursing Home, Inc, 17 Madison Street, Granville, NY 12832

Isabella Geriatric Center, 515 Audubon Avenue, New York, NY 10040

Kings Harbor Multicare Center, 2000 East Gun Hill Road, Bronx, NY 10469

Lakewood Health Care Center, Inc., 5775 Maelou Drive, Hamburg, NY 14075

Lawrence Nursing Care Center, Inc., 350 Beach 54th Street, Arverne, NY 11692

Long Beach Grandell Corporation, 645 West Broadway, Long Beach, NY 11561–2902

Long Island Care Center, 144–61 38th Avenue, Flushing, NY 11354

M.J.G. Nursing Home Company, Inc., 4915 Tenth Avenue, Brooklyn, NY 11219

Manhattanville Nursing Care Center, 311 West 231st Street, Bronx, NY 10463

Maplewood Nursing Home, Inc., 100 Daniel Drive, Webster, NY 14580–2983

Margaret Tietz Center for Nursing Care, 164–11 Chapin Parkway, Jamaica, NY 11432

Meadowbrook Healthcare, 154 Prospect Avenue, Plattsburgh, NY 12901

Morris Park Nursing Home, 1235 Pelham Parkway North, Bronx, NY 10469

Mosholu Parkway Nursing Home, 3356 Perry Avenue, Bronx, NY 10467

Nassau Extended Care Center, One Greenwich Street, Hempstead, NY 11550

Niagara Lutheran Home and Rehabilitation Center, 64 Hager Street, Buffalo, NY 14208

North Shore University Hospital Center for Extended Care & Rehabilitation, 330 Community Drive, Manhasset, NY 11030

Northern Manhattan Nursing Home, Inc., 116 East 125th Street, New York, NY 10035

Oakwood Health Care Center, Inc., 200 Bassett Road, Williamsville, NY 14221

Oceanview Nursing Home, PO Box 628, Far Rockaway, NY 11691

Oneonta Nursing and Rehabilitation Center, 330 Chestnut Street, Oneonta, NY 13820

Orchard Park Health Care Center, Inc., 6060 Armor Road, Orchard Park, NY 14127

Palm Gardens Nursing Home, 615 Avenue C, Brooklyn, NY 11218

Park Shore Health Care Center, Inc., 447 Lake Shore Drive West, Dunkirk, NY 14048

Parker Jewish Institute for Health Care and Rehabilitation, 271–11 76th Avenue, New Hyde Park, NY 11040–1433

Promenade Rehabilitation and Health Care Center, 140 Beach 114th Street, Rockaway Park, NY 11694

Prospect Park Nursing Home, Inc., 1455 Coney Island Avenue, Brooklyn, NY 11230

Providence Rest, 3304 Waterbury Avenue, Bronx, NY 10465

Regency Extended Care Center, 65 Ashburton Avenue, Yonkers, NY 10701

Resort Nursing Home, 430 Beach 68th Street, Arverne, NY 11692

River Park Health Care Center, Inc., 5th and Maple Avenue, Allegany, NY 14706

Rivington House – The Nicholas A. Rango Health Care Facility, 45 Rivington Street, New York, NY 10002

Rome Nursing Home, 950 Floyd Avenue, Rome, NY 13440

Rosewood Gardens Convalescent Home, Inc., 284 Troy Road, Rensselaer, NY 12144–9474

Saint Cabrini Nursing Home, Inc., 115 Broadway, Dobbs Ferry, NY 10522

Sands Point Nursing Home, 1440 Port Washington Boulevard, Port Washington, NY 11050

Sarah R. Newman Nursing Home, 845 Palmer Avenue, Mamaroneck, NY 10543

Sea Crest Health Care Center, 3035 West 24th Street, Brooklyn, NY 11224

Sea View Hospital Rehabilitation Center and Home, 460 Brielle Avenue, Staten Island, NY 10314

Shore View Nursing Home, 2865 Brighton 3rd Street, Brooklyn, NY 11235

Shorefront Jewish Geriatric Center, 3015 West 29th Street, Brooklyn, NY 11224

South Shore Healthcare, 275 West Merrick Road, Freeport, NY 11520

St. Elizabeth Ann's Health Care and Rehabilitation Center, 91 Tompkins Avenue, Staten Island, NY 10304

St. Mary's Hospital for Children, 29–01 216th Street, Bayside, NY 11360

Sullivan Park Health Care Center, Inc., 301 Nantucket Drive, Endicott, NY 13760

The Jewish Home and Hospital – Manhattan Division, 120 West 106th Street, New York, NY 10025

The Nathan Miller Center for Nursing Care, Inc., 220 West Post Road, White Plains, NY 10606

The Port Jefferson Health Care Facility, Dark Hollow Road, Port Jefferson, NY 11777

The Rosalind and Joseph Gurwin Jewish Geriatric Center of LI, 68 Hauppauge Road, Commack, NY 11725

The Wartburg, Wartburg Place, Mt Vernon, NY 10552

The Wesley Group, 630 East Avenue, Rochester, NY 14607–2194

Three Rivers Health Care Center, Inc., 101 Creekside Drive, Painted Post, NY 14870

Throgs Neck Extended Care Facility, 707 Throgs Neck Expressway, Bronx, NY 10465

TownHouse Extended Care Center, 755 Hempstead Turnpike, Uniondale, NY 11553

Vestal Nursing Center, 860 Old Vestal Road, Vestal, NY 13850

Victory Lake Nursing Center, PO Box 2008, Hyde Park, NY 12538

Village Park Health Care Center, Inc., 4540 Lincoln Drive, Gasport, NY 14067

Waterfront Health Care Center, Inc., 200 Seventh Street, Buffalo, NY 14201

Waterview Nursing Care Center, 119–15 27th Avenue, Flushing, NY 11354

Wayne Nursing Home, 3530 Wayne Avenue, Bronx, NY 10467

Wedgewood Care Center, 199 Community Drive, Great Neck, NY 11021

Westfield Health Care Center, Inc., 26 Cass Street, Westfield, NY 14787

Wingate at Dutchess Rehabilitative/Skilled Nursing, 3 Summit Court, Fishkill, NY 12524

Wingate at Ulster, One Wingate Way, Highland, NY 12528

Woodbury Center for HealthCare, 8533 Jericho Turnpike, Woodbury, NY 11797

NORTH CAROLINA

Alamance Health Care Center, 1987 Hilton Road, Burlington, NC 27217

Asheboro Health and Rehabilitation Center, PO Box 4218, Asheboro, NC 27203

Asheville Health Care Center, 1270 Highway 70, Swannanoa, NC 28778

Aston Park Health Care Center, Inc., 380 Brevard Road, Asheville, NC 28806

Belaire Health Care Center, 2065 Lyon Street, Gastonia, NC 28052

Beverly Health Care Center, 1000 Western Boulevard, Tarboro, NC 27886–7008

Brian Center – Shamrock, 2727 Shamrock Drive, Charlotte, NC 28205

Brian Center Cabarrus, 250 Bishop Lane, Concord, NC 28025

Brian Center Health and Rehabilitation – Brevard, PO Box 1096, Brevard, NC 28712

Brian Center Health and Rehabilitation – Eden, 226 North Oakland Avenue, Eden, NC 27288

Brian Center Health and Rehabilitation – Gastonia, 969 Cox Road, Gastonia, NC 28054

Brian Center Health and Rehabilitation – Hertford, 200 River Drive, Hertford, NC 27944

Brian Center Health and Rehabilitation – Hickory East, 3031 Tate Boulevard Southeast, Hickory, NC 28602

Brian Center Health and Rehabilitation – Salisbury, 635 Statesville Boulevard, Salisbury, NC 28144

Brian Center Health and Rehabilitation – Spruce Pine, 218 Laurel Creek Court, Spruce Pine, NC 28777

Brian Center Health and Rehabilitation – Wallace, PO Box 966, Wallace, NC 28466

Brian Center Health and Rehabilitation – Windsor, 1306 South King Street, Windsor, NC 27983

Brian Center Health and Rehabilitation / Goldsboro, 1700 Wayne Memorial Drive, Goldsboro, NC 27534

Brian Center Health and Rehabilitation/Durham, 6000 Fayetteville Road, Durham, NC 27713

Brian Center Health and Rehabilitation/Hendersonville, 1870 Pisgah Drive, Hendersonville, NC 28739

Brian Center Health and Rehabilitation/Raleigh, 3000 Holston Lane, Raleigh, NC 27610

Brian Center Health and Rehabilitation/Weaverville, 78 Weaver Boulevard, Weaverville, NC 28787

Brian Center Health and Rehabilitation/Wilson, PO Box 3566, Wilson, NC 27895–3566

Brian Center Health and Retirement, 5939 Reddman Road, Charlotte, NC 28212

Brian Center Health and Retirement, 4911 Brian Center Lane, Winston Salem, NC 27106–6423

Brian Center Health and Retirement – Clayton, 204 Dairy Road, Clayton, NC 27520

Brian Center Health and Retirement – Monroe, 204 Old Highway 74 East, Monroe, NC 28112

Brian Center Health and Retirement – Mooresville, 752 East Center Avenue, Mooresville, NC 28115

Brian Center Hickory/Viewmont, 220 13th Ave Place Northwest, Hickory, NC 28601

Cary Health and Rehabilitation Center, 6590 Tryon Road, Cary, NC 27511

Charlotte Health Care Center, 1735 Toddville Road, Charlotte, NC 28214

Courtland Terrace Nursing Center, 2300 Aberdeen Boulevard, Gastonia, NC 28054

Cypress Pointe Rehabilitation and Health Care Centre, 2006 South 16th Street, Wilmington, NC 28401

Genesis ElderCare – Mooresville Center, 550 Glenwood Drive, Mooresville, NC 28115

Greensboro Health and Rehabilitation Center, 1201 Carolina Street, Greensboro, NC 27401

GreenTree Ridge + The Summit, PO Box 5621, Asheville, NC 28813–5621

Guilford Health Care Center, 2041 Willow Road, Greensboro, NC 27406

Horizon Rehabilitation Center, 3100 Erwin Road, Durham, NC 27705

Hunter Woods Nursing and Rehabilitation Center, 620 Tom Hunter Road, Charlotte, NC 28213

Integrated Health Services at Raleigh at Crabtree Valley, 3830 Blue Ridge Road, Raleigh, NC 27612

Integrated Health Services of Charlotte at Hawthorne, 333 Hawthorne Lane, Charlotte, NC 28204

Lexington Health Care Center, 17 Cornelia Drive, Lexington, NC 27292

Lutheran Nursing Home, Inc. – Hickory Unit, 1265 21st Street Northeast, Hickory, NC 28601

Mariner Health of Wilmington, 820 Wellington Avenue, Wilmington, NC 28401

Meadowbrook Manor of Siler City, 900 West Dolphin Street, Siler City, NC 27344

North Carolina Special Care Center, 4761 Ward Boulevard, Wilson, NC 27893

St. Joseph of the Pines, Inc., 590 Central Drive, Southern Pines, NC 28387–2899

The Nursing Center at Oak Summit, 5680 Windy Hill Drive, Winston Salem, NC 27105

Wilora Lake Healthcare Center, 6001 Wilora Lake Road, Charlotte, NC 28212

OHIO

Americare Marion Nursing and Rehabilitation Center, 524 James Way, Marion, OH 43302–5890

Anna Maria of Aurora, Inc., 889 North Aurora Road, Aurora, OH 44202

Arbors at Canton, 2714 13th Street Northwest, Canton, OH 44708–9970

Arbors at Delaware, 2270 Warrensburg Road, Delaware, OH 43015

Arbors at Fairlawn, 575 S. Cleveland Massillon Rd., Fairlawn, OH 44333

Arbors at Milford, 5900 Meadowcreek Drive, Milford, OH 45150

Arbors at Sylvania, 7120 Post Sylvania Drive, Toledo, OH 43617

Arbors at Toledo, 2920 Cherry Street, Toledo, OH 43608

Arbors East Skilled and Rehabilitation Center, 5500 East Broad Street, Columbus, OH 43213

Arbors West, 375 West Main Street, West Jefferson, OH 43162

Aristocrat Berea Healthcare Center, 255 Front Street, Berea, OH 44017

Arlington Court Nursing and Rehabilitation Center, 1605 NW Professional Plaza, Columbus, OH 43220

Aurora Manor Special Care Centre, 101 Bissell Road, Aurora, OH 44202

Batavia Nursing and Convalescent Inn, 4000 Golden Age Drive, Batavia, OH 45103

Bethany Lutheran Village, 6451 Far Hills Avenue, Centerville, OH 45459

BridgePark Centre for Rehabilitation & Nursing Services, 145 Olive Street, Akron, OH 44310

Broadview Health Care Center, Inc., 5151 North Hamilton Road, Columbus, OH 43230

Broadview Multi–Care Center, 5520 Broadview Road, Parma, OH 44134

Cambridge Health and Rehabilitation Center, 1471 Wills Creek Valley Drive, Cambridge, OH 43725

Carriage Inn of Steubenville, 3102 St. Charles Drive, Steubenville, OH 43952

Chapel Hill Community, 12200 Strausser Road, Canal Fulton, OH 44614

Clermont Nursing and Convalescent Center, 934 State Route 28, Milford, OH 45150

College Park Nursing and Rehabilitation Center, 3201 CR 16, Coshocton, OH 43812

Columbus Alzheimer Care Center, 700 Jasonway Avenue, Columbus, OH 43214

Columbus Center, 4301 Clime Road North, Columbus, OH 43228

Columbus Rehabilitation and Subacute Institute, 44 Souder Avenue, Columbus, OH 43222

CommuniCare of Clifton, 625 Probasco Street, Cincinnati, OH 45220

Community Care Center, 145 East College Street, Alliance, OH 44601

Community Healthcare Center, 175 Community Drive, Marion, OH 43302

Community Multicare Center, PO Box 18669, Fairfield, OH 45018–0669

Cortland Center, 369 North High Street, Cortland, OH 44410

Crestview Manor, 4381 Tonawanda Trail, Dayton, OH 45430

Cuyahoga Falls Country Place, 2728 Bailey Road, Cuyahoga Falls, OH 44221

DaySpring Health Care Center and Rehabilitation, 8001 Dayton–Springfield Road, Fairborn, OH 45324

East Galbraith Health Care Community, 3889 East Galbraith Road, Cincinnati, OH 45236

Eastgate Health Care Center and Rehabilitation, 4400 Glen Este–Withamsville Rd, Cincinnati, OH 45245

Evergreen Rehabilitation and Specialty Care Center, 555 Springbrook Drive, Medina, OH 44256

Fairhaven Community, 850 Marseilles Avenue, Upper Sandusky, OH 433511

Franklin Plaza Extended Care, 3600 Franklin Boulevard, Cleveland, OH 44113

Gables Care Center, 350 Lahm Drive, Hopedale, OH 43976

Gateway Health Care Center, Three Gateway Drive, Euclid, OH 44119

Gibsonburg Health Care Center, 355 Windsor Lane, Gibsonburg, OH 43431

Good Shepherd Community Care Center, 2120 East Fifth Avenue, Columbus, OH 43219

Grande Pointe Healthcare Community, 3 Merit Drive, Richmond Heights, OH 44143

Greenbriar Quality Care of Boardman, 8064 South Avenue, Boardman, OH 44512

Harborside Healthcare – Perrysburg, 28546 Starbright Boulevard, Perrysburg, OH 43551

Harborside Healthcare – Beachwood, 3800 Park East Drive, Beachwood, OH 44122

Harborside Healthcare – Broadview Heights, 2801 East Royalton Road, Broadview Heights, OH 44147

Harborside Healthcare – Defiance, 395 Harding Street, Defiance, OH 43512

Harborside Healthcare – Northwestern Ohio, 1104 Wesley Avenue, Bryan, OH 43506

Harborside Healthcare – Swanton, 401 West Airport Highway, Swanton, OH 43558

Harborside Healthcare – Troy, 512 Crescent Drive, Troy, OH 45373

Harborside Healthcare – Westlake I, 27601 Westchester Parkway, Westlake, OH 44145

Heartland of Beavercreek, 1974 North Fairfield Road, Dayton, OH 45432

Heartland of Browning, 8885 Browning Drive, Waterville, OH 43566

Heartland of Centerburg, PO Box 720, Centerburg, OH 43011

Heartland of Holly Glen, 4293 Monroe Street, Toledo, OH 43606

Heartland of Kettering, 3313 Wilmington Pike, Kettering, OH 45429

Heartland of Marysville, 755 South Plum Street, Marysville, OH 43040

Heartland of Mentor, 8200 Mentor Hills Drive, Mentor, OH 44060

Heartland of Oak Ridge, 450 Oak Ridge Boulevard, Miamisburg, OH 45342

Heartland of Perrysburg, 10540 Fremont Pike, Perrysburg, OH 43551

Heartland of Springfield, 2615 Derr Road, Springfield, OH 45503

Heather Hill Hospital, Health and Care Center, 12340 Bass Lake Road, Chardon, OH 44024

Heatherdowns Convalescent Center, 2401 Cass Road, Toledo, OH 43614

Heritage Care, 24579 Broadway Avenue, Oakwood Village, OH 44146

Hickory Creek Nursing Center, 3421 Pinnacle Road, Dayton, OH 45418

Hickory Creek of Athens, PO Box 98, The Plains, OH 45780

Hillebrand Nursing Center, 4320 Bridgetown Road, Cincinnati, OH 45211

Horizon Village Nursing and Rehabilitation Center, 2473 North Road, Northeast, Warren, OH 44483

Hospitality Homes, 1301 North Monroe Drive, Xenia, OH 45385

IHS at Carriage–by–the–Lake, 1957 North Lakeman Drive, Bellbrook, OH 45305

IHS of New London at Firelands, 204 West Main Street, New London, OH 44851

Integrated Health Services at Waterford Commons, 955 Garden Lake Parkway, Toledo, OH 43614

Integrated Health Services of Huber Heights at Spring Creek, 5440 Charlesgate Road, Huber Heights, OH 45424

Ivy Woods Health Care and Rehabilitation Center, 2025 Wyoming Avenue, Cincinnati, OH 45214

Kettering Convalescent Center, 1150 West Dorothy Lane, Kettering, OH 45409

Laurie Ann Nursing Home and Laurie Ann Home Health Care, 2200 Milton Boulevard, Newton Falls, OH 44444

Lebanon Country Manor, 700 Monroe Road, Lebanon, OH 45036

Lebanon Health Care Center, PO Box 376, Lebanon, OH 45036–0376

Leisure Oaks Convalescent Center, 214 Harding Street, Defiance, OH 43512

Life Care Center of Medina, 2400 Columbia Road, Medina, OH 44256

Llanfair Retirement Community, 1701 Llanfair Avenue, Cincinnati, OH 45224

Magnolia Care and Rehabilitation Center, 365 Johnson Road, Wadsworth, OH 44281

Manor Care at Sycamore Glen, 2175 Leiter Road, Miamisburg, OH 45342

Manor Care Health Services, 23225 Lorain Road, North Olmsted, OH 44070

Manor Care Health Services – Willoughby, 37603 Euclid Avenue, Willoughby, OH 44094

Manor Care Nursing and Rehabilitation Center, 2250 Banning Road, Cincinnati, OH 45239

ManorCare Health Services, 4102 Rocky River Drive, Cleveland, OH 44135

ManorCare Health Services, 3801 Woodridge Boulevard, Fairfield, OH 45014

ManorCare Health Services, 5970 Kenwood Road, Madeira, OH 45243

ManorCare Health Services – Mayfield Heights, 6757 Mayfield Road, Mayfield Heights, OH 44124

ManorCare Health Services of Akron, 1211 West Market Street, Akron, OH 44313

Maple Knoll Village, 11100 Springfield Pike, Cincinnati, OH 45246

Mayfair Village Nursing Care Center, 3000 Bethel Road, Columbus, OH 43220

McCrea Manor Nursing and Rehabilitation, 2040 McCrea Street, Alliance, OH 44601

Menorah Park Center for the Aging, 27100 Cedar Road, Beachwood, OH 44122–1156

Monterey Care Center, 3929 Hoover Road, Grove City, OH 43123

Newark Healthcare Centre, 75 McMillen Drive, Newark, OH 43055

Northland Terrace Medical Center, 5700 Karl Road, Columbus, OH 43229

Oak Grove Manor, 1670 Crider Road, Mansfield, OH 44903

Oak Grove Quality Care, 620 East Water Street, Deshler, OH 43516

Ohio Extended Care Center, 3364 Kolbe Road, Lorain, OH 44053

Ohio Valley Manor, 5280 Routes 62 and 68, Ripley, OH 45167–9774

Orchard Villa, 2841 Munding Drive, Oregon, OH 43616

Oregon Nursing and Rehabilitation Center, 904 Isaac Streets Drive, Oregon, OH 43616

Pataskala Oaks Care Center, 144 East Broad Street, Pataskala, OH 43062

Pebble Creek Convalescent Center, 670 Jarvis Road, Akron, OH 44319

Pine Valley Care Center, 4360 Brecksville Road, Richfield, OH 44286

Pleasant Lake Villa, 7260 Ridge Road, Parma, OH 44129

Rae–Ann Center, 4650 Rocky River Drive, Cleveland, OH 44135

Rittman Nursing and Rehabilitation Center, 275 East Sunset Drive, Rittman, OH 44270

Rockmill Rehabilitation Centre, 3680 Dolson Court Northwest, Carroll, OH 43112

S.E.M. Haven Health Care Center, 225 Cleveland Avenue, Milford, OH 45150

Scenic Hills, 311 Buckridge Road, Bidwell, OH 45614

Somerset Quality Care Nursing and Rehabilitation Center, 411 South Columbus Street, Somerset, OH 43783

Southern Hills Health and Rehabilitation Center, 19530 Bagley Road, Middleburg Heights, OH 44130

St. Augustine Manor, Inc., 7801 Detroit Avenue, Cleveland, OH 44102–2895

Sunset View/Castle Nursing Homes, Inc., PO Box 5001, Millersburg, OH 44654

The Arbors at Marietta, 400 Seventh Street, Marietta, OH 45750

The Convalarium at Indian Run, 6430 Post Road, Dublin, OH 43016

The Corinthian Skilled Nursing and Rehab Center, 320 North Wayne Street, Kenton, OH 43326

The Corinthian, Inc., 4000 Crocker Road, Westlake, OH 44145

The Franciscan at Schroder, 1300 Millville Avenue, Hamilton, OH 45013

The Franciscan at St. Clare, 100 Compton Avenue, Cincinnati, OH 45215

The Franciscan at St. Leonard, 8100 Clyo Road, Dayton, OH 45458

The Franciscan at West Park, 2950 West Park Drive, Cincinnati, OH 45238

The LakeMed Nursing and Rehabilitation Center, 70 Normandy Drive, Painesville, OH 44077

The Maria–Joseph Center, 4830 Salem Avenue, Dayton, OH 45416–

The Northwestern Quality Care Skilled Nursing/Rehab Center, 570 North Rocky River Drive, Berea, OH 44017

The Oakridge Home, 26520 Center Ridge Road, Westlake, OH 44145

The Patrician Skilled Nursing Center, 9001 West 130th Street, North Royalton, OH 44133

The Village at St. Edward Nursing Care, 3131 Smith Road, Fairlawn, OH 44333–2697

The Village of Westerville Nursing Center, 1060 Eastwind Drive, Westerville, OH 43081

The Whetstone Gardens and Care Center, 3710 Olentangy River Road, Columbus, OH 43214

Trinity Community of Beavercreek, 3218 Indian Ripple Road, Dayton, OH 45440

Walnut Creek Nursing Center, 5070 Lamme Road, Kettering, OH 45439

Walton Manor Health Care Centre, 19859 Alexander Road, Walton Hills, OH 44146

West Chester Health Care, 9117 Cincinnati–Columbus Road, West Chester, OH 45069

Western Hills Retirement Village, 6210 Cleves Warsaw Pike, Cincinnati, OH 45233

Wickliffe Country Place, 1919 Bishop Road, Wickliffe, OH 44092

Willard Quality Care Nursing and Rehabilitation Center, 725 Wessor Avenue, Willard, OH 44890

Woodsfield Nursing and Rehabilitation Center, 37930 Airport Road, Woodsfield, OH 43793

OKLAHOMA

ManorCare Health Services – Midwest City, 2900 Parklawn Drive, Midwest City, OK 73110

Saint Simeon's Episcopal Home, Inc., 3701 North Cincinnati Ave., Tulsa, OK 74106

OREGON

Cascade Terrace Nursing Center, 5601 Southeast 122nd Avenue, Portland, OR 97236

Meadow Park Health and Specialty Care Center, 75 Shore Drive, St Helens, OR 97051

PENNSYLVANIA

Abington Manor, 100 Edella Road, Clarks Summit, PA 18411

Adams Manor, 824 Adams Avenue, Scranton, PA 18510

Altoona Hospital Center for Nursing Care, 1020 Green Avenue, Altoona, PA 16601

Attleboro Nursing and Rehabilitation Center, 300 East Winchester Avenue, Langhorne, PA 19047

Baldock Health Care Centre, 8850 Barnes Lake Road, North Huntingdon, PA 15642

Baldwin Health Center, 1717 Skyline Drive, Pittsburgh, PA 15227

Baptist Home of Philadelphia, 8301 Roosevelt Boulevard, Philadelphia, PA 19152

Beacon Manor, Senior Choice,Inc., 1515 Wayne Avenue, Indiana, PA 15701

Berkshire Manor Nursing and Rehabilitation Center, 5501 Perkiomen Avenue, Reading, PA 19606

Bethany Village Retirement Center, 325 Wesley Drive, Mechanicsburg, PA 17055

Beverly Health Care – Murrysville, 3300 Logans Ferry Road, Murrysville, PA 15668

Beverly Healthcare – Oakmont, 26 Ann Street, Oakmont, PA 15139

Beverly Healthcare – Shippenville, 512 South Paint Boulevard, Shippenville, PA 16254

Beverly Healthcare – South Hills, 201 Village Drive, Canonsburg, PA 15317

Beverly Healthcare–Meyersdale, 201 Hospital Drive, Meyersdale, PA 15552

Beverly Healthcare–Richland, 349 Vo–Tech Drive, Johnstown, PA 15904

Beverly Healthcare–Titusville, 81 Dillon Drive, Titusville, PA 16354

Beverly Rehabilitation, 4142 Monroeville Boulevard, Monroeville, PA 15146

Blue Ridge Haven Convalescent Center – East, 3625 North Progress Avenue, Harrisburg, PA 17110

Brethren Village, PO Box 5093, Lancaster, PA 17606–5093

Brinton Manor Genesis Eldercare, 549 Baltimore Park, Glen Mills, PA 19342

Buckingham Valley Rehabilitation and Nursing Center, PO Box 447, Buckingham, PA 18912

Buffalo Valley Lutheran Village, 211 Fairground Road, Lewisburg, PA 17837

Caledonia Manor, 3301 Lincoln Way East, Fayetteville, PA 17222

Camp Hill Care Center, 46 Erford Road, Camp Hill, PA 17011

Carpenter Care Center, 30 Virginia Drive, Tunkhannock, PA 18657

Cathedral Village, 600 East Cathedral Road, Philadelphia, PA 19128

Central Care Center, 121 Central Avenue, Warren, PA 16365

Centre Crest, 502 East Howard Street, Bellefonte, PA 16823–2199

Chandler Hall Friends Nursing Home/Hospice Home Health, 99 Barclay Street, Newtown, PA 18940

Chester Care Center, 15th Street and Shaw Terrace, Chester, PA 19013

Concordia Lutheran Ministries, 615 North Pike Road, Cabot, PA 16023–2299

Conestoga View Nursing Home, 900 East King Street, Lancaster, PA 17602

Dowden Nursing and Rehabilitation Center, 3503 Rhoads Avenue, Newtown Square, PA 19073

Dresher Hill Health and Rehabilitation Center, 1390 Camphill Road, Dresher, PA 19025

East Mountain Manor, 101 East Mountain Boulevard, Wilkes Barre, PA 18702

Ephrata Manor, 99 Bethany Road, Ephrata, PA 17522

Epworth Manor, 951 Washington Avenue, Tyrone, PA 16686

Erie Rehabilitation and Nursing Center, 2686 Peach Street, Erie, PA 16504

Fellowship Manor, 3000 Fellowship Drive, Whitehall, PA 18052

Forest Park Health Center, 700 Walnut Bottom Road, Carlisle, PA 17013

Fox Subacute Center, 2644 Bristol Road, Warrington, PA 18976

Frederick Mennonite Community, Box 498, Frederick, PA 19435–0498

Frey Village Retirement Center, 1020 North Union Street, Middletown, PA 17057

Gettysburg Lutheran Home, 1075 Old Harrisburg Road, Gettysburg, PA 17325

Golden Slipper Club Uptown Home for the Aged, 7800 Bustleton Avenue, Philadelphia, PA 19152

Good Samaritan Nursing Care Center, 1017 Franklin Street, Johnstown, PA 15905

Green Acres Rehabilitation and Nursing Center, 1401 Ivy Hill Road, Philadelphia, PA 19150

Greenery Rehabilitation and Skilled Nursing Center, 2200 Hill Church – Houston Rd., Canonsburg, PA 15317

Gwynedd Square Center for Nursing and Convalescent Care, 773 Sumneytown Pike, Lansdale, PA 19446

HAIDA Manor, PO Box 603, Hastings, PA 16646

Hanover Hall, 267 Frederick Street, Hanover, PA 17331

Harlee Manor Nursing and Rehabilitation Center, 463 West Sproul Road, Springfield, PA 19064

Harmon House Convalescent Center, 601 South Church Street, Mount Pleasant, PA 15666

Haverford Nursing and Rehabilitation Center, 2050 Old West Chester Pike, Havertown, PA 19083

Heartland Health Care Center – Pittsburgh, 550 South Negley Avenue, Pittsburgh, PA 15232

Heritage Towers, 200 Veterans Lane, Doylestown, PA 18901

Hickory House Nursing Home, 3120 Horseshoe Pike, Honey Brook, PA 19344

Highland Manor Nursing Home, 750 Schooley Avenue, Exeter, PA 18643

Hillview Health and Rehabilitation Center, 700 South Cayuga Avenue, Altoona, PA 16602

Homestead Center, 1113 North Easton Road, Willow Grove, PA 19090

IHS at Mt. View, RD #7 Box 249, Sandy Hill Road, Greensburg, PA 15601

IHS at the Clara Burke Community, 251 Stenton Avenue, Plymouth Meeting, PA 19462

IHS of Erie at Bayside, 4114 Schaper Avenue, Erie, PA 16508

IHS of Greater Pittsburgh, 890 Mount Pleasant Road, Greensburg, PA 15601

Indian Creek Nursing Center, 222 West Edison Avenue, New Castle, PA 16101

Inglis House, 2600 Belmont Avenue, Philadelphia, PA 19131–2799

Integrated Health Services of Chestnut Hill, 8833 Stenton Avenue, Wyndmoor, PA 19038

Integrated Health Services of Pennsylvania at Broomall, 50 North Malin Road, Broomall, PA 19008

Integrated Health Services of Pennsylvania at Plymouth, 900 East Germantown Pike, Norristown, PA 19401

Jefferson Manor Health Centers, RR 5, Box 42, Brookville, PA 15825

Kinzua Valley Health Care, 205 Water Street, Warren, PA 16365

Kittanning Care Center, RD 1, Box 27C, Kittanning, PA 16201

Lancashire Hall Nursing and Rehabilitation Center, 2829 Lititz Pike, Lancaster, PA 17601

Langhorne Gardens Rehabilitation & Nursing Ctr, 350 Manor Avenue, Langhorne, PA 19047

LAS/St. John Lutheran Care Center, PO Box 928, Mars, PA 16046

Laurel Nursing and Rehabilitation Center, 125 Holly Road, Hamburg, PA 19526

Laurel Wood Convalescent Center, 100 Woodmont Road, Johnstown, PA 15905

LGAR Health and Rehabilitation Center, 800 Elsie Street, Turtle Creek, PA 15145

Liberty Nursing and Rehab Center, 17th and Allen Streets, Allentown, PA 18104

LifeQuest Nursing Center, 2450 John Fries Highway, Quakertown, PA 18951

Locust Grove Retirement Village, HCR 67, Box 7, Mifflin, PA 17058

Luther Crest Nursing Facility, 800 Hausman Road, Allentown, PA 18104

Luther Woods Convalescent Center, 313 West County Line Road, Hatboro, PA 19040

Main Line Nursing and Rehabilitation Center, 283 East Lancaster Avenue, Malvern, PA 19355

Majestic Oaks, 333 Newtown Road, Warminster, PA 18974

Manchester House Nursing and Convalescent Center, 411 Manchester Avenue, Media, PA 19063

Manor Care Health Services – Lansdale, 640 Bethlehem Pike, Montgomeryville, PA 18936

ManorCare Health Services, 1070 Stouffer Avenue, Chambersburg, PA 17201

ManorCare Health Services, 800 King Russ Road, Harrisburg, PA 17109

ManorCare Health Services, 113 West McMurray Road, Mc Murray, PA 15317–2427

ManorCare Health Services, 1848 Greentree Road, Pittsburgh, PA 15220

ManorCare Health Services, 1105 Perry Highway, Pittsburgh, PA 15237

ManorCare Health Services, 1480 Oxford Valley Road, Yardley, PA 19067

ManorCare Health Services – Laureldale, 2125 Elizabeth Avenue, Laureldale, PA 19605

ManorCare Health Services – Allentown, 1265 S Cedar Crest Boulevard, Allentown, PA 18103

ManorCare Health Services – Bethel Park, 60 Highland Road, Bethel Park, PA 15102

ManorCare Health Services – Bethlehem, 2029 Westgate Drive, Bethlehem, PA 18017

ManorCare Health Services – Carlisle, 940 Walnut Bottom Road, Carlisle, PA 17013

ManorCare Health Services – Kingston, 200 Second Avenue, Kingston, PA 18704

ManorCare Health Services – Lancaster, 100 Abbeyville Road, Lancaster, PA 17603

ManorCare Health Services – Pottstown, 724 North Charlotte Street, Pottstown, PA 19464

ManorCare Health Services – Pottsville, Leader and Pulaski Drives, Pottsville, PA 17901

ManorCare Health Services – West Reading, 425 Buttonwood Street, West Reading, PA 19611

ManorCare Health Services – Williamsport North, 300 Leader Drive, Williamsport, PA 17701

ManorCare Health Services – York, 1770 Barley Road, York, PA 17404

ManorCare Health Services at Fitzgerald Mercy, 600 South Wycombe Avenue, Yeadon, PA 19050

Mansion Nursing Home, 1040 Market Street, Sunbury, PA 17801

Mariner Health of North Hills, 194 Swinderman Road, Wexford, PA 15090

Mariner Health of West Hills, 951 Brodhead Road, Coraopolis, PA 15108

Masonic Homes, One Masonic Drive, Elizabethtown, PA 17022–2199

Mountain Laurel Nursing and Rehabilitation Center, 700 Leonard Street, Clearfield, PA 16830

Mt. Lebanon Manor, 350 Old Gilkeson Road, Pittsburgh, PA 15228

Normandie Ridge, 1700 Normandie Drive, York, PA 17404

North Penn Convalescent Center, 25 West 5th Street, Lansdale, PA 19446

Ohesson Manor, 276 Green Avenue Extended, Lewistown, PA 17044

Penn Lutheran Village, 800 Broad Street, Selinsgrove, PA 17870

Pennknoll Village, PO Box 420, Everett, PA 15537

Pennsylvania Memorial Home, 51 Euclid Avenue, Brookville, PA 15825

Perry Village, Inc., 213 East Main Street, New Bloomfield, PA 17068

Pickering Manor Home, 226 North Lincoln Avenue, Newtown, PA 18940

Presbyterian Medical Center of Oakmont, Inc., 1215 Hulton Road, Oakmont, PA 15139

Prospect Park Health and Rehabilitation Residence, 815 Chester Pike, Prospect Park, PA 19076

Providence Health Care Center, PO Box 140, Beaver Falls, PA 15010

Quakertown Center, 1020 South Main Street, Quakertown, PA 18951–1592

Redstone Highlands Health Care Center, 6 Garden Center Drive, Greensburg, PA 15601–1397

Rest Haven–York, 1050 South George Street, York, PA 17403

Richboro Care Center, 253 Twining Ford Road, Richboro, PA 18954

Ridge Crest Nursing and Rehabilitation Center, 1730 Buck Road, North, Feasterville, PA 19053

River's Edge Nursing and Rehabilitation Center, 9501 State Road, Philadelphia, PA 19114

Riverside Nursing Center, Inc., 100 Eighth Avenue, Mc Keesport, PA 15132

Riverstreet Manor, 440 North River Street, Wilkes Barre, PA 18702

RiverWoods, One River Road, Lewisburg, PA 17837

Rochester Manor, 174 Virginia Avenue, Rochester, PA 15074

Rosemont Manor, 35 Rosemont Avenue, Rosemont, PA 19010

RoseView Center, 1201 Rural Avenue, Williamsport, PA 17701

Roslyn Nursing and Rehabilitation Center, 2630 Woodland Road, Roslyn, PA 19001

Saint John Neumann Nursing Home, 10400 Roosevelt Boulevard, Philadelphia, PA 19116

Saint Joseph Villa, 110 West Wissahickon Avenue, Flourtown, PA 19031–1898

Saint Luke Pavilion, 1000 Stacie Drive, Hazleton, PA 18201

Sanatoga Center, 225 Evergreen Road, Pottstown, PA 19464

Saunders House, 100 Lancaster Avenue, Wynnewood, PA 19096–3494

Sherwood Oaks, 100 Norman Drive, Cranberry Twp, PA 16066

Shrewsbury Lutheran Retirement Village, 200 Luther Road, Shrewsbury, PA 17361

Sidney Square Convalescent Center, 2112 Sidney Street, Pittsburgh, PA 15203

Simpson House, Inc., 2101 Belmont Avenue, Philadelphia, PA 19131–1628

Somerset Patriot Manor, 495 West Patriot Street, Somerset, PA 15501

South Mountain Restoration Center, 10058 South Mountain Road, South Mountain, PA 17261

St. Andrew's Village/Julia Wilson Pounds Health Care Ctr., 1155 Indian Springs Road, Indiana, PA 15701

Statesman Health and Rehabilitation Center, 2629 Trenton Road, Levittown, PA 19056

Stroud Manor, 221 East Brown Street, East Stroudsburg, PA 18301

Suburban General Extended Care Center, Inc., 2751 DeKalb Pike, Norristown, PA 19401

Susque–View Home, Inc., 22 Cree Drive, Lock Haven, PA 17745

Susquehanna Lutheran Village, 990 Medical Road, Millersburg, PA 17061–1235

Swaim Health Center at Green Ridge Village, 210 Big Spring Road, Newville, PA 17241

Sycamore Manor Health Center, 1445 Sycamore Road, Montoursville, PA 17754

The Belvedere Nursing and Rehabilitation Center, 2507 Chestnut Street, Chester, PA 19013

The Bishop Nursing Home, 318 South Orange Street, Media, PA 19063

The Brethren Home Community, PO Box 128, New Oxford, PA 17350–0128

The Fairways at Brookline Village, 1950 Cliffside Drive, State College, PA 16801

The Healthcare Campus at Colonial Manor, 970 Colonial Avenue, York, PA 17403

The Lebanon Valley Home, 550 East Main Street, Annville, PA 17003

The Lutheran Home at Hollidaysburg, 916 Hickory Street, Hollidaysburg, PA 16648

The Lutheran Home at Johnstown, 807 Goucher Street, Johnstown, PA 15905

The Lutheran Home at Topton (Henry Health Care Center), One South Home Avenue, Topton, PA 19562

The Masonic Home of Pennsylvania, 801 Ridge Pike, Lafayette Hill, PA 19444

The Presbyterian Medical Center of Washington, PA Inc., 835 South Main Street, Washington, PA 15301

Thornwald Home, 442 Walnut Bottom Road, Carlisle, PA 17013

Township Manor Health and Rehabilitation Center, 265 East Township Line Road, Elkins Park, PA 19027

Twinbrook Medical Center, 3805 Field St Lawrence Park, Erie, PA 16511

Valley Manor Nursing and Rehabilitation Center, 7650 Route 309, Coopersburg, PA 18036

Wallingford Nursing and Rehabilitation Center, 115 South Providence Road, Wallingford, PA 19086

Warren Manor, 682 Pleasant Drive, Warren, PA 16365

Wayne Center, 30 West Avenue, Wayne, PA 19087

West Shore Health and Rehabilitation Center, 770 Poplar Church Road, Camp Hill, PA 17011

Western Reserve Health and Rehabilitation Center, 1521 West 54th Street, Erie, PA 16509

White Billet Nursing and Rehabilitation Center, 412 South York Road, Hatboro, PA 19040

Wightman Health Center, 2025 Wightman Street, Pittsburgh, PA 15217

William Penn Nursing Facility, 163 Summit Drive, Lewistown, PA 17044

Willow Ridge Center, 3485 Davisville Road, Hatboro, PA 19040

Woodhaven Care Center, 2400 McGinley Road, Monroeville, PA 15146

York Lutheran Home, 1801 Folkemer Circle, York, PA 17404–1771

York Terrace, 2401 West Market Street, Pottsville, PA 17901–1833

Zohlman Nursing Home, PO Box 39, Richlandtown, PA 18955–0039

RHODE ISLAND

Cedar Crest Nursing Centre, 125 Scituate Avenue, Cranston, RI 02921

Cherry Hill Manor, 2 Cherry Hill Road, Johnston, RI 02919

Elmhurst Extended Care Facility, 50 Maude Street, Providence, RI 02908

Evergreen House Health Center, One Evergreen Drive, East Providence, RI 02914

Golden Crest Nursing Centre, 100 Smithfield Road, North Providence, RI 02904

Heatherwood Nursing and Subacute Center, Inc, 398 Bellevue Avenue, Newport, RI 02840

Kent Nursing and Rehabilitation Center, Inc, 660 Commonwealth Avenue, Warwick, RI 02886

Metacom Manor Health Center, One Dawn Hill Road, Bristol, RI 02809

Morgan Health Center, 80 Morgan Avenue, Johnston, RI 02919

Oak Hill Nursing and Rehabilitation Center, 544 Pleasant Street, Pawtucket, RI 02860

Oakland Grove Health Care Center, 560 Cumberland Hill Road, Woonsocket, RI 02895

Saint Elizabeth Home, 109 Melrose Street, Providence, RI 02907–1898

Slater Health Center, Inc., 70 Gill Avenue, Pawtucket, RI 02861

South County Nursing and Subacute Center, 740 Oak Hill Road, North Kingstown, RI 02852

St. Antoine Residence, 400 Mendon Road, North Smithfield, RI 02896–6999

Steere House Inc., 100 Borden Street, Providence, RI 02903

The Clipper Home, Inc., 161 Post Road, Westerly, RI 02891

Watch Hill Manor, Ltd., 79 Watch Hill Road, Westerly, RI 02891

Westerly Health Center, 280 High Street, Westerly, RI 02891

SOUTH CAROLINA

C. M. Tucker, Jr. / Dowdy Gardner Nursing Care Center, 2200 Harden Street, Columbia, SC 29203

Heartland Health Care Center – Charleston, 1800 Eagle Landing Boulevard, Hanahan, SC 29406

IHS Charleston at Driftwood, 2375 Baker Hospital Boulevard, Charleston, SC 29405

Life Care Center of Charleston, 2600 Elms Plantation Boulevard, Charleston, SC 29406

Life Care Center of Columbia, 2514 Faraway Drive, Columbia, SC 29223

Manor Care – Columbia, 2601 Forest Drive, Columbia, SC 29204

National HealthCare Center Greenville, 1305 Boiling Springs Road, Greer, SC 29650

Oakmont East, 601 Sulphur Springs Road, Greenville, SC 29611

Prince George HealthCare Center, 901 Maple Street, Georgetown, SC 29440

Roper Nursing Center, 2230 Ashley Crossing Drive, Charleston, SC 29417

Springdale HealthCare Center, 146 Battleship Road, Camden, SC 29020

SOUTH DAKOTA

Colonial Manor Health and Rehabilitation, PO Box 620, Salem, SD 57058

Covington Heights Health and Rehabilitation Center, 3900 South Cathy Avenue, Sioux Falls, SD 57106

Rapid City Care Center, 916 Mountain View, Rapid City, SD 57702

Whetstone Valley Care Center, 1103 South 2nd Street, Milbank, SD 57252

TENNESSEE

Allen Morgan Health Center, 177 North Highland, Memphis, TN 38111

American Transitional Rehab and Specialty Care, 6733 Quince Road, Memphis, TN 38119

Brandywood Rehabilitation Center, 555 East Bledsoe Street, Gallatin, TN 37066

Fairpark Healthcare Center, PO Box 5477, Maryville, TN 37802

Farragut Health Care Center, 12823 Kingston Pike, Knoxville, TN 37922

Greystone Health Care Center, PO Box 1133, TCAS, Blountville, TN 37617

Life Care Center of Athens, PO Box 786, Athens, TN 37371–0786

Life Care Center of Collegedale, PO Box 658, Collegedale, TN 37315

Life Care Center of East Ridge, 1500 Fincher Avenue, East Ridge, TN 37412

Life Care Center of Jefferson City, 336 West Old A.J. Highway, Jefferson City, TN 37760

Life Care Center of Morristown, PO Box 1899, Morristown, TN 37814

Life Care Center of Tullahoma, 1715 North Jackson Street, Tullahoma, TN 37388

Mariner Health of Nashville, 3939 Hillsboro Circle, Nashville, TN 37215

Maryville Healthcare and Rehabilitation Center, 1012 Jamestown Way, Maryville, TN 37803

McKendree Village, Inc., 4343–47 Lebanon Road, Hermitage, TN 37076

Mountainview Rehabilitation and Nursing Center, 1360 Bypass Road, Winchester, TN 37398

National HealthCare – Murfreesboro, 100 Vine Street, Murfreesboro, TN 37130

NHC HealthCare, 2120 Highland Ave, Knoxville, TN 37916

Ridgeview Terrace of Life Care, PO Box 26, Rutledge, TN 37861

TEXAS
Alameda Oaks Nursing Center, 1101 South Alameda, Corpus Christi, TX 78404
Alamo Heights Health and Rehabilitation Center, 8223 Broadway, San Antonio, TX 782089
Allenbrook Health Care Center, 4109 Allenbrook Drive, Baytown, TX 77521
Autumn Years Lodge, 424 South Adams, Fort Worth, TX 76104
Bay Villa Health Care Center, 1800 – 13th Street, Bay City, TX 77414
Beacon Health, Ltd., 9182 Six Pines Drive, The Woodlands, TX 77380
Brazos Valley Geriatric Center, 1115 Anderson Street, College Station, TX 77840
Brookhaven Nursing Center, 1855 Cheyenne Dr., Carrollton, TX 75008
CASA, A Special Hospital, 1803 Old Spanish Trail, Houston, TX 77054
Colonial Manor – Tyler, 930 South Baxter, Tyler, TX 75701
Coronado Nursing Center, 1751 North 15th Street, Abilene, TX 79603
East Texas Specialty Hospital, PO Box 7018, Tyler, TX 75711–7018
Fort Worth Nursing and Rehabilitation Center, 1000 6th Avenue, Fort Worth, TX 76104
Green Acres Convalescent Center, 93 Isaacks Road, Humble, TX 77338
Green Acres Parkdale, 11025 Old Voth Road, Beaumont, TX 77713
Heart of Texas Health Care & Rehabilitation Center–Changing Seasons, 545 Denver Street, Vidor, TX 77662
Heart of Texas Health Care & Rehabilitation Center– Colonial Park, 104 Enterprise, Devine, TX 78016
Hearthstone Nursing and Rehabilitation Center, 401 Oakwood Boulevard, Round Rock, TX 78681
Heartland Health Care Center, 2939 Woodland Park Drive, Houston, TX 77082
Heartland Health Care Center – Austin, 11406 Rustic Rock Drive, Austin, TX 78750
Heartland Health Care Center – Bedford, 2001 Forest Ridge Drive, Bedford, TX 76021
Heartland Health Care Center at Willowbrook, 13631 Ardfield Drive, Houston, TX 77070
Heartland of Corpus Christi, 202 Fortune Drive, Corpus Christi, TX 78405
Heartland of San Antonio, One Heartland Drive, San Antonio, TX 78247
Heritage Manor, 1621 Coit Road, Plano, TX 75075
IHS of Dallas at Treemont, 5550 Harvest Hill Road, Dallas, TX 75230
Integrated Health Services at Woodridge, 1500 Autumn Drive, Grapevine, TX 76051
Integrated Health Services of Texoma, 1000 Highway 82 East, Sherman, TX 75090
Lake Shore Village Health Care Center, 2320 Lake Shore Drive, Waco, TX 76708
Lexington Place Health Care Center, 1737 North Loop West, Houston, TX 77008
ManorCare Health Services, 3326 Burgoyne Street, Dallas, TX 75233
ManorCare Health Services, 7625 Glenview Drive, Fort Worth, TX 76180
ManorCare Health Services, 8800 Fourwinds, San Antonio, TX 78239
ManorCare Health Services – San Antonio (Babcock), 1975 Babcock Road, San Antonio, TX 78229
ManorCare Health Services – Webster, 750 West Texas Avenue, Webster, TX 77598
ManorCare Health Services Nursing & Rehabilitation Center, 7505 Bellerive, Houston, TX 77036
Mariner Health of Arlington, 2645 West Randol Mill Road, Arlington, TX 76012
Mariner Health of Fort Worth, 4825 Wellesley Avenue, Fort Worth, TX 76107
Mariner Health of Northwest Houston, 17600 Cali Drive, Houston, TX 77090
Marshall Manor Healthcare and Rehab, PO Box 1629, Marshall, TX 75670
Memorial Medical, 307 W. Cypress, San Antonio, TX 78212
Retama Manor Laredo South, 1100 Galveston Street, Laredo, TX 78040
Retama Manor Nursing Center, 1505 South Closner, Edinburg, TX 78539
Seven Acres Jewish Senior Care Services, 6200 North Braeswood, Houston, TX 77074
Silver Leaves Nursing Center, 505 West Centerville Road, Garland, TX 75041

Southfield Health Care Center, 802 Fresa Street, Pasadena, TX 77502
Southwood Care Center, 3759 Valley View, Austin, TX 78704
The Clairmont – Longview, 3201 North Fourth Street, Longview, TX 75605
The Village Healthcare Center, 1341 Blalock Road, Houston, TX 77055
Victoria Nursing Home, 114 Medical Drive, Victoria, TX 77904
Ware Memorial Care Center, 1300 South Harrison, Amarillo, TX 79101
Weatherford Health Care Center, 521 West 7th, Weatherford, TX 76086
West Oaks Geriatric Center, 3625 Greencrest Drive, Houston, TX 77082

UTAH
Rocky Mountain Care – Clearfield, 1450 South 1500 East, Clearfield, UT 84015
South Davis Community Hospital, 401 South, 400 East, Bountiful, UT 84010
Sunshine Terrace Foundation, Inc., 225 North 200 West, Logan, UT 84321–3805
Washington Terrace Nursing Center, 400 East 5350 South, Ogden, UT 84405

VERMONT
Bennington Health and Rehabilitation Center, 360 Dewey St., Bennington, VT 05201
Berlin Health and Rehab Center, RR 3, Box 6684, Barre, VT 05641
Birchwood Terrace Healthcare, 43 Starr Farm Road, Burlington, VT 05401
Burlington Health and Rehabilitation Center, 300 Pearl Street, Burlington, VT 05401
Rowan Court Health and Rehabilitation Center, 378 Prospect Street, Barre, VT 05641
Springfield Health and Rehabilitation Center, 105 Chester Road, Springfield, VT 05156
St. Johnsbury Health and Rehabilitation Center, Hospital Drive, Saint Johnsbury, VT 05819
Starr Farm Nursing Center, 98 Starr Farm Road, Burlington, VT 05401
Verdelle Village Extended Care Facility, Box 80 Sheldon Road, St Albans, VT 05478

VIRGINIA
Annaburg Manor Nursing Home, PO Box 3057, Manassas, VA 22110
Appomattox Healthcare Center, Route 5, Box 800, Appomattox, VA 24522
Autumn Care of Norfolk, PO Box 12569, Norfolk, VA 23502
Bay Pointe Medical and Rehabilitation Centre, 1148 First Colonial Road, Virginia Beach, VA 23454–2499
Bayside Healthcare Center, PO Box 68039, Virginia Beach, VA 23471
Beaufont Healthcare Center, 200 Hioaks Road, Richmond, VA 23225–4048
Beth Sholom Home of Central Virginia, 12000 Gayton Road, Richmond, VA 23233
Bon Secours – Maryview Nursing Care Center, 4775 Bridge Road, Suffolk, VA 23435
Bowling Green Healthcare Center, PO Box 967, Bowling Green, VA 22427
Brian Center Health and Rehabilitation – Alleghany, PO Box 200, Low Moor, VA 24457
Brian Center Health and Rehabilitation – Scott County, 105 Clonce Street, Weber City, VA 24290
Burke Healthcare Center, 9640 Burke Lake Road, Burke, VA 22015–3022
Camelot Hall of Lynchburg, 5615 Seminole Avenue, Lynchburg, VA 24502–2201
Camelot Health and Rehabilitation Center, 1225 South Reservoir Street, Harrisonburg, VA 22801–4499
Cameron Glen Care Center, 1800 Cameron Glen Drive, Reston, VA 22090
Cherrydale Healthcare Center, 3710 Lee Highway, Arlington, VA 22207–3796
Chesapeake Healthcare Center, 688 Kingsborough Square, Chesapeake, VA 23320–4908
Courtland Healthcare Center, 23020 Main Street, Courtland, VA 23837–1207
Culpeper Healthcare Center, 602 Madison Road, Culpeper, VA 22701–3324
Fairfax Nursing Center, Inc., 10701 Main Street, Fairfax, VA 22030
Franklin Healthcare Center, PO Box 555, Rocky Mount, VA 24151
Friendship Manor, Inc., 327 Hershberger Road, NW, Roanoke, VA 24012
Goodwin House West, 3440 South Jefferson Street, Falls Church, VA 22041
Gretna Healthcare Center, PO Box 577, Gretna, VA 24557–0577

Hanover Healthcare Center, 8139 Lee Davis Road, Mechanicsville, VA 23111
Harbour Pointe Medical and Rehabilitation Centre, 1005 Hampton Boulevard, Norfolk, VA 23507
Health of Virginia, 2420 Pemberton Road, Richmond, VA 23233–2099
Henrico Healthcare Center, PO Box 319, Highland Springs, VA 23075–2100
Iliff Nursing and Rehabilitation Center, 8000 Iliff Drive, Dunn Loring, VA 22027
Inova Commonwealth Care Center, 4315 Chain Bridge Road, Fairfax, VA 22030
Integrated Health Services of Northern Virginia, 900 Virginia Avenue, Alexandria, VA 22302
James River Convalescent Center, 540 Aberthaw Avenue, Newport News, VA 23601
Jefferson Park Center Genesis ElderCare Network, P O Box 3815, Charlottesville, VA 22903
Louisa Healthcare Center, PO Box 1310, Louisa, VA 23093
Lovingston Healthcare Center, PO Box 398, Lovingston, VA 22949
Lucy Corr Nursing Home, PO Drawer 170, Chesterfield, VA 23832
Manor Care Skilled Nursing & Rehabilitation, 550 South Carlin Springs Road, Arlington, VA 22204
ManorCare Health Services, 12475 Lee Jackson Memorial Hwy, Fairfax, VA 22033
Nansemond Pointe Rehabilitation & Healthcare Centre, 200 West Constance Road, Suffolk, VA 23434
Norfolk Healthcare Center, 901 East Princess Anne Road, Norfolk, VA 23504–2732
Oak Hill Center, PO Box 2565, Staunton, VA 24402–2565
Oakwood Nursing and Rehabilitation Center, 5520 Indian River Road, Virginia Beach, VA 23464
Parham Nursing and Rehabilitation Center, 2400 East Parham Road, Richmond, VA 23228–3100
Piney Forest Healthcare Center, 450 Piney Forest Road, Danville, VA 24540
Potomac Center – Genesis ElderCare Network, 1785 South Hayes Street, Arlington, VA 22202
Pulaski Healthcare Center, 2401 Lee Highway, Pulaski, VA 24301–2329
Raleigh Court Healthcare Center, 1527 Grandin Road Southwest, Roanoke, VA 24015–2305
Regency Healthcare Center, 112 North Constitution Drive, Yorktown, VA 23692–2792
Ridgecrest Manor Nursing Home, PO Box 280, Duffield, VA 24244
Riverside Healthcare Center, 2344 Riverside Drive, Danville, VA 24540–4212
Riverside Regional Convalescent Center, 1000 Old Denbigh Boulevard, Newport News, VA 23602
Salem Health and Rehabilitation Center, 1945 Roanoke Boulevard, Salem, VA 24153–6487
Shenandoah Valley Health Care Center, PO Box 711, Buena Vista, VA 24416
Stanleytown Healthcare Center, PO Box 538, Stanleytown, VA 24168
The Berkshire Health Care Center, 705 Clearview Drive, Vinton, VA 24179
Virginia Beach Healthcare and Rehabilitation Center, 1801 Camelot Drive, Virginia Beach, VA 23454
Virginia Veterans Care Center, 4550 Shenandoah Avenue, Northwest, Roanoke, VA 24017
Warrenton Overlook Health and Rehabilitation Center, 360 Hospital Drive, Warrenton, VA 20186
Warsaw Healthcare Center, 5373 Richmond Road, Warsaw, VA 22572
Waverly Healthcare Center, PO Box 641, Waverly, VA 23890–0641
Williamsburg Center Genesis ElderCare, 1235 Mt. Vernon Avenue, Williamsburg, VA 23185
Woodbine Rehabilitation and Healthcare Center, 2729 King Street, Alexandria, VA 22302
Woodmont Center, PO Box 419, Fredericksburg, VA 22404–0419

WASHINGTON
Bessie Burton Sullivan, 1020 East Jefferson, Seattle, WA 98122
Cascade Vista Convalescent Center, Inc., 7900 Willows Road Northeast, Redmond, WA 98052
Evergreen Vista Convalescent Center, Inc., 11800 Northeast 128th Street, Kirkland, WA 98034–7201
Harmony Gardens Care Center, 10010 Des Moines Way South, Seattle, WA 98168
Mercer Island Care and Rehabilitation, 7445 Southeast 24th Street, Mercer Island, WA 98040
Meydenbauer Medical and Rehabilitation Center, 150 102nd Avenue Southeast, Bellevue, WA 98004
Oyster Bay Care Center, 3517 11th Street, Bremerton, WA 98312

Section C

Seattle Medical and Rehabilitation Center, 555 16th Avenue, Seattle, WA 98122

SunRise Care & Rehabilitation for Vancouver, 5220 NE Hazel Dell Avenue, Vancouver, WA 98663

SunRise Care & Rehabilitation for Walla Walla Valley, 1200 Southeast 12th Street, College Place, WA 99324

Sunrise Care and Rehabiliation for Richmond Beach, 19235 15th Avenue Northwest, Shoreline, WA 98177

The Care Center at Kelsey Creek, 2210 132nd Avenue Southeast, Bellevue, WA 98005

Wedgwood Care and Rehabilitation, 9132 Ravenna Avenue Northeast, Seattle, WA 98115

WEST VIRGINIA

Bishop Joseph H. Hodges Continuous Care Center, 600 Medical Park, Wheeling, WV 26003

Brightwood Nursing and Rehabilitation Center, 840 Lee Road, Follansbee, WV 26037

Canterbury of Shepherdstown, Route 2, Box 5, Shepherdstown, WV 25443

Care Haven Center, Route 5, Box A167, Martinsburg, WV 25401

Dawnview Center, PO Box 686, Fort Ashby, WV 26719

GlenWood Park Retirement Village, 1924 Glenwood Park Road, Princeton, WV 24740–9244

Heartland of Charleston, 3819 Chesterfield Avenue, Charleston, WV 25304

Rosewood Nursing and Rehabilitation Center, 8 Rose Street, Grafton, WV 26354

Shenandoah Nursing and Rehabilitation Center, 219 Prospect Avenue, Charles Town, WV 25414

Sistersville Nursing and Rehabilitation Center, 201 Wood Street, Sistersville, WV 26175

SunRise Care & Rehabilitation for Putnam, 300 Seville Road, Hurricane, WV 25526

SunRise Pine Lodge Care and Rehabilitation, 405 Stanaford Road, Beckley, WV 25801

The Madison Rehabilitation and Nursing Center, 161 Bakers Ridge Road, Morgantown, WV 26505

The Willows Nursing and Rehabilitation Center, 723 Summers Street, Parkersburg, WV 26101

WISCONSIN

Ashland Health and Rehabilitation Center, 1319 Beaser Avenue, Ashland, WI 54806

Beaver Dam Care Center, PO Box 617, Beaver Dam, WI 53916

Bel Air Health Care Center/ Alzheimers Center, 9350 West Fond Du Lac Avenue, Milwaukee, WI 53225

Bethel Center, 8014 Bethel Road, Arpin, WI 54410

Beverly Health and Rehabilitation, 6735 West Bradley Road, Milwaukee, WI 53223

Beverly Health and Rehabilitation Center/Superior, 1612 North 37th Street, Superior, WI 54880

Beverly Healthcare, Sherwood Heights, 3710 North Oakland Avenue, Shorewood, WI 53211

Clement Manor Health Center, 3939 South 92nd Street, Greenfield, WI 53228

Colonial Center, 702 West Dolf Street, Colby, WI 54421

Colonial Manor Medical and Rehabilitation Center, 1010 East Wausau Avenue, Wausau, WI 54403

Columbus Center, 825 Western Avenue, Columbus, WI 53925

Continental Manor Health and Rehabilitation Center, 502 South High Street, Randolph, WI 53956

Eastview Medical and Rehab Center, 729 Park Street, Antigo, WI 54409–2798

Franciscan Villa, 3601 South Chicago Avenue, South Milwaukee, WI 53172

Franciscan Woods, 19525 West North Avenue, Brookfield, WI 53045

Greendale Health and Rehabilitation Center, 3129 Michigan Avenue, Sheboygan, WI 53081

Heartland Health Care Center – Pewaukee, N26W23977 Watertown Road, Waukesha, WI 53188

Heartland Health Care Center – Washington Manor, 3100 Washington Road, Kenosha, WI 53144

Heritage Square Health Care Centre, 5404 W. Loomis Road, Greendale, WI 53129

Highland Healthcare, 2997 St. Anthony Drive, Green Bay, WI 54311

Karmenta Center, 4502 Milwaukee Street, Madison, WI 53714

ManorCare Health Services, 1335 South Oneida Street, Appleton, WI 54915

ManorCare Health Services, 265 South National Avenue, Fond Du Lac, WI 54935

ManorCare Health Services – Green Bay, 600 South Webster Avenue, Green Bay, WI 54301

ManorCare Health Services – Madison, 801 Braxton Place, Madison, WI 53715

Marian Catholic Center, 3333 West Highland Boulevard, Milwaukee, WI 53208

Marian Franciscan Center, 9632 West Appleton Avenue, Milwaukee, WI 53225

Middleton Village Nursing and Rehabilitation Center, 6201 Elmwood Avenue, Middleton, WI 53562

Mount Carmel Health and Rehabilitation Center, 5700 West Layton Avenue, Milwaukee, WI 53220

Northwest Health Care Center, 7800 West Fond Du Lac Avenue, Milwaukee, WI 53218–2603

Outagamie County Health Center, 3400 West Brewster Street, Appleton, WI 54914–1699

Parkview Manor Health and Rehabilitation Center, 2961 St. Anthony Drive, Green Bay, WI 54311

River Hills South Health Care Center, 2730 West Ramsey Avenue, Milwaukee, WI 53221

River Pines Nursing and Rehabilitation, 1800 Sherman Avenue, Stevens Point, WI 54481

Riverside Health and Rehabilitation, 101 First Street, Oconto, WI 54153

Shady Lane, 1235 South 24th Street, Manitowoc, WI 54220

Silver Spring Health and Rehabilitation Center, 1300 West Silver Spring Drive, Glendale, WI 53209

South Shore Manor, 1915 East Tripoli Avenue, Saint Francis, WI 53235

The Terrace at St. Francis, 3200 South 20th Street, Milwaukee, WI 53215

The Village at Manor Park, Inc, 3023 South 84th Street, West Allis, WI 53227–3798

Western Village Health and Rehabilitation, 1640 Shawano Avenue, Green Bay, WI 54303

Woodland Health Center, 18740 West Bluemound Road, Brookfield, WI 53045

WYOMING

Cheyenne Health Care Center, 2700 East 12th Street, Cheyenne, WY 82001

Poplar Living Center, 4305 Poplar Avenue, Casper, WY 82601

JCAHO Accredited Freestanding Mental Health Care Organizations

The accredited freestanding mental health care organizations listed have been accredited as of April, 1999 by the Joint Commission on Accreditation of Healthcare Organizations by decision of the Accreditation Committee of the Board of Commissioners.

The organizations listed here have been found to be in compliance with the Joint Commissions standards for Accreditation Manual for Mental Health, Chemical Dependency, and Mental Retardation/Development Disabilities Services.

Please refer to section A of the AHA Guide for information on hospitals with inpatient and/or outpatient services. These hospitals are identified by Facility Codes F52, F53, F54, F55, F56, F57, F58 and F59. In section A, those hospitals identified by Approval Code 1 are JCAHO accredited.

We present this list simply as a convenient directory. Inclusion or omission of any organization's name indicates neither approval nor disapproval by Health Forum LLC, an affiliate of the American Hospital Association.

United States

ALABAMA
Alabama Clinical Schools, 1221 Alton Drive, Birmingham, AL 35210
Behavioral Healthcare Center, 306 Paul W Bryant Drive East, Tuscaloosa, AL 35401
Bradford Health Services – Huntsville, 1600 Browns Ferry Road, Madison, AL 35758
Bradford Health Services – Huntsville, 1600 Browns Ferry Road, Madison, AL 35758
Bradford Health Services, Birmingham Lodge, PO Box 129, Warrior, AL 35180
New Perspectives, 1000 Fairfax Park, Tuscaloosa, AL 35406
Pathway, Inc., PO Box 311206, Enterprise, AL 36331
The Catalyst Center, 517 Energy Center Blvd. Suite 1304, Northport, AL 35473
The Quality Life Center of Quality HealthCare, Inc., 2801 West Mall Drive, Florence, AL 35630
Thomasville Mental Health Rehabilitation Center, PO Box 309, Thomasville, AL 36784

ALASKA
Akeela Treatment Services, Inc, 2805 Bering Street, Suite 4, Anchorage, AK 99503
Alaska Children's Services Inc., 4600 Abbott Road, Anchorage, AK 99507
Alaska North Addictions Recovery Center, 4330 Bragaw Street, Anchorage, AK 99508
Anchorage Charter North Counseling Center, 1650 South Bragaw, Anchorage, AK 99508
Charter North Residential Treatment Center, 1650 South Bragaw, Anchorage, AK 99508
Juneau Youth Services, Inc., PO Box 32839, Juneau, AK 99803

ARIZONA
Arizona Baptist Children's Services, P O Box 39239, Phoenix, AZ 85069–9239
Arizona's Children Association, PO Box 7277, Tucson, AZ 85725–7277
Calvary Rehabilitation Center, 720 East Montebello Avenue, Phoenix, AZ 85014
Chandler Valley Hope, PO Box 1839, Chandler, AZ 85244–1839
Cottonwood de Tucson, 4110 West Sweetwater Drive, Tucson, AZ 85745
Desert Hills Center for Youth and Families, 2797 North Introspect Drive, Tucson, AZ 85745
Devereux/Arizona – Richard L. Raskin Treatment Network, 6436 East Sweetwater Avenue, Scottsdale, AZ 85254
La Paloma Family Services, Inc, PO Box 41565, Tucson, AZ 85717–1565
META Services, Inc., 2701 N. 16th St., Suite 106, Phoenix, AZ 85006
Mingus Mountain Estate Residential Center, Inc., 10451 Palmeras Drive, Ste 105N, Sun City, AZ 85373–2052
Parc Place, 5116 East Thomas Road, Phoenix, AZ 85018
PREHAB of Arizona, Inc., PO Drawer 5860, Mesa, AZ 85211–5860
Remuda Ranch Center for Anorexia and Bulimia, One East Apache Street, Wickenburg, AZ 85390
Rosewood Ranch L.P., 36075 South Rincon Road, Wickenburg, AZ 85390
Salvation Army Recovery Center, PO Box 52177, Phoenix, AZ 85072
Sierra Tucson,LLC, 39580 S. Lago del Oro Parkway, Tucson, AZ 85739

Southeastern Arizona Psychiatric Health Facility, PO Box 1296, Benson, AZ 85602
Superstition Mountain Mental Health Center, Inc., PO Box 3160, Apache Junction, AZ 85217
the EXCEL Group, 106 East First Street, Yuma, AZ 85364
The Meadows, 1655 North Tegner, Wickenburg, AZ 85390
The New Foundation, P O Box 3828, Scottsdale, AZ 85257
Touchstone Community, Inc., 6153 West Olive Avenue Suite 1, Glendale, AZ 85302
Vista Care Facility, 4120 East Ramsey Road, Hereford, AZ 85615
Westcenter, 2105 East Allen Road, Tucson, AZ 85719
Youth Development Institute, 1830 East Roosevelt Street, Phoenix, AZ 85006

ARKANSAS
Behavioral Health Services, Inc. of Arkansas, 604 Cherry Street, Helena, AR 72342
Birch Tree Communities, Inc., P.O. Box 1589, Benton, AR 72018–1589
Centers for Youth and Families, PO Box 251970, Little Rock, AR 72225–1970
Community Counseling Services, Inc., PO Box 6399, Hot Springs National Park, AR 71902
Delta Counseling Associates, Inc., PO Box 820, Monticello, AR 71657
Habilitation Center, Inc., PO Box 727, Fordyce, AR 71742
Ozark Counseling Services, Inc, PO Box 1776, Mountain Home, AR 72654
Ozark Guidance Center, Inc., PO Box 6430, Springdale, AR 72762–6430
Timber Ridge Ranch NeuroRehabilitation Center, PO Box 90, Benton, AR 72015–0090
United Methodist Children's Home Inc., PO Box 4848, Little Rock, AR 72214–4848
University of Arkansas for Medical Sciences, 4301 West Markham Street, Mail Slot 554, Little Rock, AR 72205
Youth Home, Inc., 20400 Colonel Glenn Road, Little Rock, AR 72210–5323

CALIFORNIA
A Touch of Care, Inc., 2231 South Carmelina Avenue, Los Angeles, CA 90064
Betty Ford Center, 39000 Bob Hope Drive, Rancho Mirage, CA 92270
Broad Horizons, PO Box 1920, Ramona, CA 92065
Cornerstone Residential Center for Addictions, 13682 Yorba Street, Tustin, CA 92680
Creative Care, Inc., 18850 Devonshire Street, Northridge, CA 91324
Family Recovery Foundation, Inc., 12822 Hewes Avenue, Santa Ana, CA 92705
Impact Drug and Alcohol Treatment Center, 1680 North Fair Oaks Avenue, Pasadena, CA 91103
Kings View Center, 42675 Road 44, Reedley, CA 93654
Learning Services – Northern California, 10855 DeBruin Way, Gilroy, CA 95020
Monterey Psychiatric Health Facility, Inc., 5 Via Joaquin, Monterey, CA 93940
Oak Grove Institute, 24275 Jefferson Avenue, Murrieta, CA 92562
R House, Inc., PO Box 2587, Santa Rosa, CA 95405
S T E P S, 224 East Clara Street, Port Hueneme, CA 93041
San Diego Center for Children, 3002 Armstrong Street, San Diego, CA 92111
SeaBridge, Inc., PO Box 6296, Malibu, CA 90264

Sharp Vista Pacifica, 7989 Linda Vista Road, San Diego, CA 92111
Solano Psychiatric Health Facility, PO Box 2866, Fairfield, CA 94533–0286
Spencer Recovery Centers, Inc., 343 West Foothill Boulevard, Monrovia, CA 91016
Tarzana Treatment Center, 18646 Oxnard Street, Tarzana, CA 91356
The Discovery Adolescent Program, 4136 Ann Arbor Road, Lakewood, CA 90712
The Linden Center, 5750 Wilshire Blvd, Ste 535, Los Angeles, CA 90036
Twin Town Treatment Center, 10741 Los Alamitos Boulevard, Los Alamitos, CA 90720
Vista Del Mar Child and Family Services, 3200 Motor Avenue, Los Angeles, CA 90034
Vista San Diego Center, 3003 Armstrong Street, San Diego, CA 92111
Watts Health Foundation, Inc., 10300 South Compton Avenue, Los Angeles, CA 90002

COLORADO
Adolescent and Family Institute of Colorado, Inc., 10001 West 32nd Avenue, Wheat Ridge, CO 80033
Aurora Behavioral Health Hospital, 1290 South Potomac Street, Aurora, CO 80012
Colorado Boys Ranch, PO Box 681, La Junta, CO 81050
Forest Heights Lodge, PO Box 789, Evergreen, CO 80437–0789
Harmony Foundation, Inc., PO Box 1989, Estes Park, CO 80517
Learning Services – Rocky Mountain Region, 7201 West Hampden Avenue, Lakewood, CO 80227
Managed Adolescent Care, PC, 1025 Pennock, Suite 111, Fort Collins, CO 80524
Parker Valley Hope, PO Box 670, Parker, CO 80134
Pikes Peak Mental Health Center Systems, Inc., 220 Ruskin Drive, Colorado Springs, CO 80910
Southern Colorado Healthcare System, Bldg 5, Room 139, 'C' Street, Fort Lyon, CO 81038

CONNECTICUT
Capitol Region Mental Health Center, 500 Vine Street, Hartford, CT 06112
Community Prevention and Addiction Services, Inc., 1491 West Main Street, Willimantic, CT 06226
Cornerstone of Eagle Hill, Inc., 32 Alberts Hill Road, Sandy Hook, CT 06482
Datahr Rehabilitation Institute, 135 Old State Road, Brookfield, CT 06804
Greater Bridgeport Community Mental Health Center, PO Box 5117, Bridgeport, CT 06610
Guenster Rehabilitation Services, 276 Union Avenue, Bridgeport, CT 06607
Klingberg Family Centers, Inc. Klingberg Comp. Family Servic, 370 Linwood Street, New Britain, CT 06052
Perception Programs, Inc., PO Box 407, Willimantic, CT 06226
Reid Treatment Center, Inc., PO Box 1357, Avon, CT 06001–1357
Riverview Hospital for Children and Youth, PO Box 2797, Middletown, CT 06457
Rushford Center Inc., 1250 Silver Street, Middletown, CT 06457
Southern Connecticut Mental Health & Substance Abuse Treatment Center, 4083 Main Street, Bridgeport, CT 06606
Stonington Institute, 75 Swantown Hill Road, North Stonington, CT 06359
The BlueRidge Center, 1095 Blue Hills Avenue, Bloomfield, CT 06002

The Children's Center, Inc., 1400 Whitney Avenue, Hamden, CT 06517

The Wellspring Foundation, Inc., PO Box 370, Bethlehem, CT 06751

The Wheeler Clinic, 91 Northwest Drive, Plainville, CT 06062

United Services, Inc., PO Box 839, Dayville, CT 06241

Vitam Center, Inc., 57 W Rocks Road, Norwalk, CT 06851–0730

DELAWARE

Brandywine Counseling, Inc., 2713 Lancaster Avenue, Wilmington, DE 19805

Delaware Guidance Services for Children and Youth, Inc., 1213 Delaware Avenue, Wilmington, DE 19806

Open Door, Incorporated, 3301 Green Street, Claymont, DE 19703

Silver Lake Treatment Consortium, 493 East Main Street, Middletown, DE 19709

SODAT – Delaware, Inc., 625 North Orange Street, Wilmington, DE 19801

Terry Children's Psychiatric Center, 10 Central Avenue, New Castle, DE 19720

DISTRICT OF COLUMBIA

Buena Vista Terrace, 4425 Lee Street Northeast, Washington, DC 20019

Devereux Children's Center of Washington, D.C., 3050 R Street, Northwest, Washington, DC 20007

New York Avenue Presbyterian Church/McClendon Center, 1313 New York Avenue, NW, Washington, DC 20005

Riverside, 4460 MacArthur Boulevard, NW, Washington, DC 20007

FLORIDA

45th Street Mental Health Center, Inc., 1041 45th Street, West Palm Beach, FL 33407

Act Corporation, 1220 Willis Avenue, Daytona Beach, FL 32114

Alternatives In Treatment, Inc., 7601 North Federal Highway, Suite 100B, Boca Raton, FL 33487

Apalachee Center for Human Services, Inc., PO Box 1782, Tallahassee, FL 32302

Bayview Center for Mental Health, Inc., 12550 Biscayne Blvd, Suite 919, North Miami, FL 33181

Beachcomber Rehab, Inc., 4493 North Ocean Boulevard, Delray Beach, FL 33483

Behavioral Health Network of West Dade, 11924–32 SW 8th Street, Miami, FL 33184

Camelot Care Centers, Inc., 9160 Oakhurst Road Building One, Seminole, FL 33776

Charlotte Community Mental Health Services, Inc., 1700 Education Avenue, Punta Gorda, FL 33950

Charter Behavioral Health System at Manatee Palms, 4480 51st Street, West, Bradenton, FL 34210

Citrus Health Network, Inc, 4175 West 20th Avenue, Hialeah, FL 33012

Coastal Recovery Centers, Inc., 3830 Bee Ridge Road, Sarasota, FL 34233

Daniel Memorial Hospital, Inc., 4203 Southpoint Blvd, Jacksonville, FL 32216

David Lawrence Center, 6075 Golden Gate Parkway, Naples, FL 34116

Devereux Florida Treatment Network, 5850 T. G. Lee Boulevard, Suite 400, Orlando, FL 32822

Eckerd Alternative Treatment Program at E–How–Kee, 397 Culbreath Road, Brooksville, FL 34602

Fairwinds Treatment Center, 1569 S Fort Harrison Avenue, Clearwater, FL 34616

Florida Institute for Neurologic Rehabilitation, Inc, PO Box 1348, Wauchula, FL 33873–1348

Focus Healthcare of Florida, 5960 Southwest 106th Avenue, Cooper City, FL 33328

Green Cross, Inc., 2645 Douglas Road, Suite 601, Miami, FL 33133

Gulf Coast Treatment Center, 1015 Mar Walt Drive, Fort Walton Beach, FL 32547

Hanley–Hazelden Center at St. Mary's, 5200 East Avenue, West Palm Beach, FL 33407

Hope Horizon Center, Inc., 7821 SW 24th Street, Suite 100, Miami, FL 33155

Jacksonville Therapy Center, 6428 Beach Boulevard, Jacksonville, FL 32216

Kendall Behavioral Healthcare Center, Inc., 13500 SW 88th Street, Ste 265, Miami, FL 33186

La Amistad Behavioral Health Services, 1650 Park Avenue North, Maitland, FL 32751

Lakeside Alternatives, Inc., 434 West Kennedy Boulevard, Orlando, FL 32810

Lakeview Center, Inc., 1221 West Lakeview Avenue, Pensacola, FL 32501

Lifeskills of Boca Raton, Inc., 7301 W Palmetto Park Road, Suite 108B, Boca Raton, FL 33433

LifeStream Behavioral Center, PO Box 491000, Leesburg, FL 34749–1000

Manatee Glens Corporation, PO Box 9478, Bradenton, FL 34206–9478

Marion Citrus Mental Health Centers, Inc., P.O. Box 771929, Ocala, FL 34474

Mental Health Care, Inc. Main Center, 5707 North 22nd Street, Tampa, FL 33610

Mental Health Resource Center, Inc., PO Box 19249, Jacksonville, FL 32245–9249

Meridian Behavioral Healthcare, Inc., PO Box 141750, Gainesville, FL 32614

Northside Mental Health Center, 12512 Bruce B. Downs Boulevard, Tampa, FL 33612–9209

Oak Center, 8889 Corporate Square Court, Jacksonville, FL 32216

Operation PAR, Inc., 6655 66th Street North, Pinellas Park, FL 33781

Pathways to Recovery, Inc., 13132 Barwick Road, Delray Beach, FL 33445

Peace River Center for Personal Development, Inc., 1745 Highway 17 South, Bartow, FL 33830

Personal Enrichment through Mental Health Services, Inc., 11254 58th Street North, Pinellas Park, FL 33782

Recovery Corner, 400 Executive Center Drive Suite 102, West Palm Beach, FL 33401

Renaissance Institute of Palm Beach, Inc., 7000 N Federal Hwy, 2nd Floor, Boca Raton, FL 33487

Ruth Cooper Center for Behavioral Health Care, Inc., 2789 Ortiz Avenue, Fort Myers, FL 33905

Safe Passage CMHC, 5046 Biscayne Boulevard, Miami, FL 33137

SandyPines Hospital, 11301 SE Tequesta Terrace, Tequesta, FL 33469

South County Mental Health Center, Inc., 16158 South Military Trail, Delray Beach, FL 33484

Spectrum Programs, Inc., 11031 Northeast 6th Avenue, Miami, FL 33161

Stewart–Marchman Center for Chemical Dependency, 3875 Tiger Bay Road, Daytona Beach, FL 32124

Tampa Bay Academy, 12012 Boyette Road, Riverview, FL 33569

The Center for Alcohol and Drug Studies, Inc., 321 Northlake Blvd, Suite 214, North Palm Beach, FL 33408

The Inn at Bowling Green, 101 North Oak Streeet, Bowling Green, FL 33834

The Renfrew Center of Florida, Inc., 7700 Renfrew Lane, Coconut Creek, FL 33073

The Village South, Inc., 3180 Biscayne Boulevard, Miami, FL 33137

The Watershed, 3350 NW Boca Raton Boulevard, Suite A–28, Boca Raton, FL 33431

The Willough at Naples, 9001 Tamiami Trail East, Naples, FL 34113

Transitions Recovery Program, 1928 Northeast 154th Street, North Miami Beach, FL 33162

Treatment Resources, Inc., 25 Northeast 167th Street, North Miami Beach, FL 33162

Turning Point of Tampa, 5439 Beaumont Center Blvd, Suite 1010, Tampa, FL 33634

Twelve Oaks, 2068 Healthcare Avenue, Navarre, FL 32566

University Behavioral Health Center, 2500 Discovery Drive, Orlando, FL 32826

Wellness Resource Center, Inc., 660 Linton Boulevard, Ste 112, Delray Beach, FL 33444

Wynwood Community Mental Health, Inc., 3550 Biscayne Blvd, Suite 510, Miami, FL 33137

GEORGIA

Albany Area Community Service Board, PO Box 1988, Albany, GA 31701

Albany Association for Retarded Citizens, PO Box 71026, Albany, GA 31708–1026

Anxiety Disorders Institute of Atlanta, One Dunwoody Park, Suite 112, Atlanta, GA 30338

Behavioral Health Services of South Georgia, PO Box 3409 206 S. Patterson Street, Valdosta, GA 31604–3409

Bridges Outpatient Center, Inc., 1209 Columbia Drive, Milledgeville, GA 31061

Brightmore Day Hospital, 115 Davis Road, Martinez, GA 30907

Charter Behavioral Health System of Atlanta at Laurel Heights, LL, 934 Briarcliff Road, Northeast, Atlanta, GA 30030

Cobb/Douglas Community Service Board, 361 North Marietta Parkway, Marietta, GA 30060

Community Mental Health Center of East Central Georgia, 3421 Mike Padgett Highway, Augusta, GA 30906

Community Service Board of Middle Georgia, 2121A Bellevue Road, Dublin, GA 31021–2998

Decatur Seminole Service Center, 333 Airport Road, Bainbridge, GA 31717

DeKalb Community Service Board, PO Box 1648, Decatur, GA 30031

Devereux Georgia Treatment Network, P.O. Box 1688, Kennesaw, GA 30144–8688

Gateway Community Service Board, 1609 Newcastle Street, Brunswick, GA 31520

Georgia Pines Community Service Board, PO Box 1659, Thomasville, GA 31799

Gracewood State School and Hospital, PO Box 1299, Gracewood, GA 30812-1299

Green Oaks M. R. Service Center, PO Box 2677, Moultrie, GA 31776

Greenleaf Center, Inc., PO Box 3516, Valdosta, GA 31602

Inner Harbour Hospitals, Ltd., 4685 Dorsett Shoals Road, Douglasville, GA 30135

LARC, Inc., 1646 East Park Avenue, Valdosta, GA 31602

Learning Services Southeastern Region, 2400 Highway 29 South, Lawrenceville, GA 30245

McIntosh Trail MH/MR/SA Community Service Board, PO Box 1320, Griffin, GA 30224

Metro Atlanta Recovery Residences, Inc., 2801 Clearview Place, Doraville, GA 30340

Mitchell–Baker Mental Retardation Service Center, 65 Industrial Boulevard, Camilla, GA 31730

Murphy – Harpst – Vashti, Inc., 740 Fletcher Street, Cedartown, GA 30125

New Horizons Community Service Board, PO Box 5328, Columbus, GA 31906–0328

Ogeechee Behavioral Health Services, PO Box 1259, Swainsboro, GA 30401

River Edge Behavioral Health Center, 175 Emery Highway, Macon, GA 31217

Safe Recovery Systems, Inc., 2300 Peachford Rd, Ste 2000, Atlanta, GA 30338

Schizophrenia Treatment and Rehabilitation, LLC, 208 Church Street, Decatur, GA 30030

Skyland Trail, 2573 Skyland Trail, Northeast, Atlanta, GA 30319

Talbott Recovery Campus, 5448 Yorktowne Drive, Atlanta, GA 30349

Thomas Grady Service Center, PO Box 2507, Thomasville, GA 31799

Turning Point Hospital, PO Box 1177, Moultrie, GA 31768

Willingway Hospital, 311 Jones Mill Road, Statesboro, GA 30458

IDAHO

Northview Hospital, 8050 Northview Street, Boise, ID 83704

Walker Center, 1120A Montana Street, Gooding, ID 83330

ILLINOIS

Alexian Brothers Behavioral Health Resources, 901 Biesterfield Road Suite 400, Elk Grove Village, IL 60007

Allendale Association, PO Box 1088, Lake Villa, IL 60046

Allendale Association, PO Box 1088, Lake Villa, IL 60046

American Day Treatment Centers of the Midwest, 1111 Pasquinelli Drive, Ste 50, Westmont, IL 60559

Association House of Chicago, 1116 North Kedzie Ave, Chicago, IL 60651

Aunt Martha's Youth Service Center, Inc., 4343 Lincoln Highway, Ste 340, Matteson, IL 60443

Beacon Therapeutic Diagnostic and Treatment Center, 10650 South Longwood Drive, Chicago, IL 60643

Ben Gordon Center, 12 Health Services Drive, De Kalb, IL 60115

Camelot Care Center, Inc., 1502 N Northwest Highway, Palatine, IL 60067

Center on Deafness, 3444 Dundee Road, Northbrook, IL 60062

Champaign County Association for the Mentally Retarded, PO Box 92, Champaign, IL 61824

Chestnut Health Systems, 1003 Martin Luther King Drive, Bloomington, IL 61701

Circle Family Care, 5002 West Madison, Chicago, IL 60644–4127

Coles County Mental Health Association, Inc., PO Box 1307, Mattoon, IL 61938

Community Counseling Center, 2615 Edwards Street, Alton, IL 62002

Community Counseling Center of the Fox Valley, Inc., 400 Mercy Lane, Aurora, IL 60506

Community Counseling Centers of Chicago, 4740 North Clark Street, Chicago, IL 60640–4633

Community Mental Health Center of Fulton & McDonough Counties, 229 Martin Avenue, Canton, IL 61520

Comprehensive Mental Health Center of St. Clair County, 3911 State Street, East Saint Louis, IL 62205

Counseling Center of Lake View, 3225 North Sheffield Avenue, Chicago, IL 60657

DuPage County Health Dept./ Behavioral & Mental Health Service, 111 North County Farm Road, Wheaton, IL 60187

Family Service and Community Mental Health Center/McHenry, 5320 West Elm Street, Mc Henry, IL 60050

Gateway Youth Care Foundation, 819 South Wabash, Suite 300, Chicago, IL 60605

Heartland Human Services, PO Box 1047, Effingham, IL 62401

Heritage Behavioral Health Center, Inc., P.O. Box 710, Decatur, IL 62524–2820

Horizons Wellness Center, 970 South McHenry Avenue, Crystal Lake, IL 60014

Inter Agency, Inc., 1610 West 89th Street, Chicago, IL 60620

Interventions – Du Page Adolescent Center, 11 S 250 Route 83, Hinsdale, IL 60521

Interventions – Southwood, 5701 South Wood, Chicago, IL 60636

Interventions – Woodridge, 2221 64th Street, Woodridge, IL 60517

Interventions City Girls, 140 North Ashland Avenue, Chicago, IL 60607

Jane Addams, Inc., 1133 W Stephenson Street, Ste 401, Freeport, IL 61032

Janet Wattles Center, Inc., 526 West State Street, Rockford, IL 61101

Josselyn Center for Mental Health, 405 Central Avenue, Northfield, IL 60093–3097

Lake County Health Department / Behavioral Health Services, 3012 Grand Avenue, Waukegan, IL 60085

Leyden Family Service and Mental Health Center, 10001 West Grand Avenue, Franklin Park, IL 60131

McHenry County Youth Service Bureau, 101 South Jefferson Street, Woodstock, IL 60098

McLean County Center for Human Services, Inc., 108 West Market Street, Bloomington, IL 61701

Mental Health and Deafness Resources, Inc., 3444 Dundee Road, Northbrook, IL 60062

Mental Health Center of Champaign County, 1801 Fox Drive, Champaign, IL 61820

New Life Clinic, 2100 Manchester Road, Suite 1410 and 1510, Wheaton, IL 60187

North Central Behavioral Health Systems, Inc., PO Box 1488, La Salle, IL 61301

Northwest Mental Health Center, 1606 Colonial Parkway, Inverness, IL 60067

Perry County Counseling Center, Inc., PO Box 189, Du Quoin, IL 62832

ProCare Centers, 1820 South 25th Avenue, Broadview, IL 60153

RocVale Children's Home, 4450 North Rockton Avenue, Rockford, IL 61103

Rosecrance on Alpine, 1505 North Alpine Road, Rockford, IL 61107

Rosecrance on Harrison, 3815 Harrison Avenue, Rockford, IL 61108

Sinnissippi Centers, Inc., 325 Illinois Route 2, Dixon, IL 61021

Sojourn House, Inc., 565 North Turner Avenue, Freeport, IL 61032

Southeastern Illinois Counseling Centers, Inc., Drawer M, Olney, IL 62450

Southern Illinois Regional Social Services, 604 East College, Suite 101, Carbondale, IL 62901

Stepping Stones of Rockford, Inc., 706 North Main Street, Rockford, IL 61103

Tazwood Center for Human Services, Inc., 1421 Valle Vista Boulevard, Pekin, IL 61554

The Ecker Center for Mental Health, 1845 Granstand Place, Elgin, IL 60123

The Kenneth W. Young Centers, 1001 Rohlwing Road, Elk Grove Village, IL 60007

The Women's Treatment Center, 140 North Ashland Avenue, Chicago, IL 60607

Triangle Center, 120 North Eleventh Street, Springfield, IL 62703–1002

White Oaks Companies of Illinois, 3400 New Leaf Lane, Peoria, IL 61614

INDIANA

Adult and Child Mental Health Center, Inc., 8320 Madison Avenue, Indianapolis, IN 46227

BehaviorCorp, 697 Pro–Med Lane, Carmel, IN 46032–5323

Community Mental Health Center, Inc., 285 Bielby Road, Lawrenceburg, IN 47025

Comprehensive Mental Health Services, Inc., 240 North Tillotson Avenue, Muncie, IN 47304

Evansville Psychiatric Children's Center, 3300 East Morgan Avenue, Evansville, IN 47715

Fairbanks Hospital, Inc., 8102 Clearvista Parkway, Indianapolis, IN 46256–4698

Four County Counseling Center, 1015 Michigan Avenue, Logansport, IN 46947

Grant–Blackford Mental Health, Inc., 505 Wabash Avenue, Marion, IN 46952

Hamilton Center, Inc, PO Box 4323, Terre Haute, IN 47804–0323

LaVerna Lodge, Inc., 13875 Magic Stallion Drive, Carmel, IN 46032

Life Spring Mental Health Center, 207 West 13th Street, Jeffersonville, IN 47130

Madison Center, Inc., PO Box 80, South Bend, IN 46624

Oaklawn, PO Box 809, Goshen, IN 46527–0809

Park Center, Inc., 909 East State Boulevard, Fort Wayne, IN 46805

Porter–Starke Services, Inc., 601 Wall Street, Valparaiso, IN 46383

Quinco Behavioral Health Systems, PO Box 628, Columbus, IN 47202–0628

Sharing and Caring Community Mental Health Center, Inc., 2511 East 46th Street, Ste 0–1, Indianapolis, IN 46205

South Central Community Mental Health Centers, Inc., 645 South Rogers Street, Bloomington, IN 47403

Southlake Community Mental Health Center, Inc., 8555 Taft Street, Merrillville, IN 46410–6199

Southwestern Indiana Mental Health Center, Inc., 415 Mulberry Street, Evansville, IN 47713–1298

Swanson Center, 450 St. John Road, Suite 501, Michigan City, IN 46360–7350

Tara Treatment Center, Inc., 6231 South US 31, Franklin, IN 46131

The Center for Mental Health, Inc., PO Box 1258, Anderson, IN 46015

The Children's Campus, 1411 Lincoln Way West, Mishawaka, IN 46544–1690

The Midwest Center for Youth and Families, PO Box 669, Kouts, IN 46347

The Otis R. Bowen Center for Human Services, Inc., PO Box 497, Warsaw, IN 46581–0497

Tri–City Comprehensive Comm Mental Health Center Inc., 3903 Indianapolis Boulevard, East Chicago, IN 46312

Universal Behavioral Services Community Mental Health Center, 820 Fort Wayne Avenue, Indianapolis, IN 46204

Wabash Valley Hospital, Inc., 2900 North River Road, West Lafayette, IN 47906

IOWA

Beloit Lutheran Children's Home – Lutheran Social Service, 1323 Northwestern Avenue, Ames, IA 50010

Boys and Girls Home and Family Services, Inc., PO Box 1197, Sioux City, IA 51102

Children and Families of Iowa, 1111 University Avenue, Des Moines, IA 50314

Christian Home Association – Children's Square U.S.A., PO Box 8–C, Council Bluffs, IA 51502–3008

Four Oaks, Inc. of Iowa, Psych Medical Instit. for Children, 5400 Kirkwood Boulevard, Southwest, Cedar Rapids, IA 52404

Gerard Treatment Programs, PO Box 1353, Mason City, IA 50402

Gordon Recovery Centers, Inc., PO Box 4519, Sioux City, IA 51104

Hillcrest Family Services, PO Box 1160, Dubuque, IA 52001

Orchard Place – Child Guidance Center, PO Box 35425, Des Moines, IA 50315–0304

Tanager Place, 2309 C Street Southwest, Cedar Rapids, IA 52404–3707

KANSAS

Atchison Valley Hope, PO Box 312, Atchison, KS 66002

Catholic Community Services, Inc., 2220 Central Avenue, Kansas City, KS 66102–4797

Columbia Health Systems, 10114 West 105th Street, Suite 100, Overland Park, KS 66212

Jewish Family and Children Services, 5801 West 115th, Suite 103, Overland Park, KS 66211

Kaw Valley Center, Inc., 4300 Brenner Drive, Kansas City, KS 66104

Norton Valley Hope, PO Box 510, Norton, KS 67654

Parkview Hospital of Topeka, 3707 Southwest 6th Avenue, Topeka, KS 66606–2085

The Saint Francis Academy, Incorporated, 509 East Elm Street, Salina, KS 67401

The Wichita Children's Home, 810 North Holyoke, Wichita, KS 67208

United Methodist Youthville, Inc., PO Box 210, Newton, KS 67114

KENTUCKY

Adanta Behavioral Health Services, 259 Parkers Mill Road, Somerset, KY 42501

Bluegrass Regional Mental Health – Mental Retardation Bd, PO Box 11428, Lexington, KY 40575

Brooklawn, Inc., 2125 Goldsmith Lane, Louisville, KY 40218–1206

Central State ICF/MR, 10510 LaGrange Road, Louisville, KY 40223

Christian Church Homes Children's and Family Services, PO Box 45, Danville, KY 40423–0045

Cumberland River Regional MH/MR Board, Inc., PO Box 568, Corbin, KY 40702

Kentucky Baptist Homes for Children, Inc., 10801 Shelbyville Road, Louisville, KY 40243

NorthKey Community Care, PO Box 2680, Covington, KY 41012

Presbyterian Child Welfare Agency, 116 Buckhorn Lane, Buckhorn, KY 41721

RiverValley Behavioral Health, PO Box 1637, Owensboro, KY 42302–1637

Seven Counties Services, Inc., 101 West Muhammad Ali Bolevad, Louisville, KY 40202

Spectrum Care Academy, Inc., PO Box 911, Columbia, KY 42728

The Home of the Innocents, Inc, 485 East Gray Street, Louisville, KY 40202

The Kentucky United Methodist Homes for Children and Youth, PO Box 749, Versailles, KY 40383

LOUISIANA

Addiction Recovery Resources of New Orleans, 4836 Wabash Street, Suite 202, Metairie, LA 70001

CHARIS Community Mental Health Center, Inc., 8264 One Calais Avenue, Baton Rouge, LA 70809

Crescent Community Care, Inc., 1175 Old Spanish Trail, Slidell, LA 70458

Hope Haven Center, 1101 Barataria Boulevard, Marrero, LA 70072

LA United Methodist Children and Family Services, Inc., PO Box 929, Ruston, LA 71273–0929

New Beginnings Of Opelousas Inc., 1692 Linwood Loop, Opelousas, LA 70570

St. Patrick's Psychiatric Hospital, PO Box 1901, Monroe, LA 71210–1901

Vermilion Hospital for Psychiatric and Addictive Med, PO Box 91526, Lafayette, LA 70509

MAINE

Community Health and Counseling Services, PO Box 425, Bangor, ME 04402–0425

KidsPeace National Ctrs for Kids in Crisis New England,Inc, PO Box 787, Ellsworth, ME 04605

MARYLAND

Allegany County Health Department Addictions Program, PO Box 1745, Cumberland, MD 21501–1745

Ashley, Inc., PO Box 240, Havre de Grace, MD 21078

Baltimore Behavioral Health, Inc., 200 South Arlington Avenue, Baltimore, MD 21223

Charter Behavioral Health Systems at Warwick Manor, 3680 Warwick Road, East New Market, MD 21631

Chesapeake Youth Center, Inc., PO Box 1238, Cambridge, MD 21613

Crossroads Centers, Inc., 2 West Madison Street, Baltimore, MD 21201

Edgemeade, 13400 Edgemeade Road, Upper Marlboro, MD 20772

Glass Substance Abuse Program, Inc., 821 N Eutaw Street, Suite 201, Baltimore, MD 21201

Good Shepherd Center, 4100 Maple Avenue, Baltimore, MD 21227–4099

Hope House, PO Box 546, Crownsville, MD 21032

Hudson Health Services, Inc., PO Box 1096, Salisbury, MD 21802–1096

Maryland Treatment Centers, Inc., PO Box E, Emmitsburg, MD 21727

New Life Addiction Counseling Services, Inc., 2528 Mountain Road, Suite 204, Pasadena, MD 21122

Oakview Treatment Center, 3100 North Ridge Road, Ellicott City, MD 21043–3348

Partners in Recovery, 6509 North Charles Street, Baltimore, MD 21204

Pathways, 2620 Riva Road, Annapolis, MD 21401

Quarterway Houses, Inc., PO Box 31419, Baltimore, MD 21216–6119

Regional Institute for Children and Adolescents, 15000 Broschart Road, Rockville, MD 20850

Regional Institute for Children and Adolescents, 605 South Chapel Gate Lane, Baltimore, MD 21229

Section C

RICA – Southern Maryland, 9400 Surratts Road, Cheltenham, MD 20623

Saint Luke Institute, Inc., 8901 New Hampshire Avenue, Silver Spring, MD 20903

Villa Maria, 2300 Dulaney Valley Road, Timonium, MD 21093–2799

Woodbourne Center, Inc., 1301 Woodbourne Avenue, Baltimore, MD 21239

Worcester County Health Department, PO Box 249, Snow Hill, MD 21863

MASSACHUSETTS

AdCare Hospital of Worcester, Inc., 107 Lincoln Street, Worcester, MA 01605–2499

Baldpate Hospital, Baldpate Road, Georgetown, MA 01833

Brighton Center for Children and Families, 77 Warren Street, Building 4, Brighton, MA 02135

Brockton Multi Service Center, 165 Quincy Street, Brockton, MA 02402

Cape Cod Alcoholism Intervention & Rehabilitation, PO Box 929, Falmouth, MA 02540

Cape Cod and the Islands Community Mental Health Center, 830 County Road, Pocasset, MA 02559

Center for Health and Human Services, Inc., PO Box 2097, New Bedford, MA 02741

Centerpoint, PO Box 374, Tewksbury, MA 01876

Charles River Intensive Treatment Program, 60 Hodges Avenue – Goss 3, Taunton, MA 02780–0997

Chauncy Hall Academy, PO Box 732, Westborough, MA 01581

Choate Health System, Inc., 23 Warren Avenue, Woburn, MA 01801

Doctor Franklin Perkins School, 971 Main Street, Lancaster, MA 01523

Dr. John C. Corrigan Mental Health Center, 49 Hillside Street, Fall River, MA 02720

Dr. Solomon Carter Fuller Mental Health Center, 85 East Newton Street, Boston, MA 02118–2337

Erich Lindemann Mental Health Center, 25 Staniford Street, Boston, MA 02114

Fuller Intensive Residential Treatment Program, 85 E Newton Street, 6th Flr E, Boston, MA 02118

High Point Treatment Center, Inc., 1233 State Road, Plymouth, MA 02360

Intensive Treatment Unit at Hillcrest Educational Centers, PO Box 4699, Pittsfield, MA 01202–4699

Lake Grove at Maple Valley, Inc., PO Box 767, Wendell, MA 01379

Meadowridge Behavioral Health Center, 664 Stevens Road, Swansea, MA 02777

Quincy Mental Health Center, 460 Quincy Avenue, Quincy, MA 02169

The Grove Adolescent Treatment Center, 320 Riverside Drive, Northampton, MA 01060

The Kolburne School, Inc., Southfield Road, New Marlborough, MA 01230

The May Institute, Inc., PO Box 899, South Harwich, MA 02661

The Three Rivers Treatment Program, 26 Ridgewood Terrace, Springfield, MA 01105

The Whitney Academy, Inc., PO Box 619, East Freetown, MA 02717

University of Massachusetts I.R.T.P., 305 Belmont Street, 7th Floor, Worcester, MA 01604

Wild Acre Inns, Inc., 108 Pleasant Street, Arlington, MA 02174–8138

MICHIGAN

ACAC, Inc., 3949 Sparks Drive SE, Ste 103, Grand Rapids, MI 49546

Advanced Counseling Services, P.C., 30700 Telegraph Rd. Ste 2560, Bingham Farms, MI 48025

Alcohol Information and Counseling Center, Home Health, 1575 Suncrest Drive, Lapeer, MI 48446

Alger–Marquette Community Mental Health Center, 200 West Spring Street, Marquette, MI 49855

Antrim Kalkaska Community Mental Health, PO Box 220, Bellaire, MI 49615–0220

AOS of Arbor Circle Group, 1331 Lake Drive Southeast, Grand Rapids, MI 49506

Auro Medical Center, 1711 South Woodward, Suite 102, Bloomfield Hills, MI 48302

Battle Creek Child Guidance Center, Inc., 155 Garfield Avenue, Battle Creek, MI 49017

Bay–Arenac Community Mental Health, 201 Mulholland, Bay City, MI 48708

Berrien Mental Health Authority, 185 East Main, Suite 803, Benton Harbor, MI 49022

Boniface Human Services, 25050 W Outer Drive, Suite 201, Lincoln Park, MI 48146

Brighton Hospital, 12851 East Grand River, Brighton, MI 48116

Catholic Services of Macomb, Inc., 235 South Gratiot Avenue, Mount Clemens, MI 48043

Center For Behavior and Medicine, 2004 Hogback Road, Suite 16, Ann Arbor, MI 48105

Center for Personal Growth, PC, 817 Tenth Avenue, Port Huron, MI 48060

Center of Behavioral Therapy, PC, 24453 Grand River Avenue, Detroit, MI 48219

Central Michigan Community Mental Health Services, 301 South Crapo, Suite 100, Mount Pleasant, MI 48858

Central Therapeutic Services, Inc., 17600 W Eight Mile Road, Ste 7, Southfield, MI 48075

Children's Home of Detroit, 900 Cook Road, Grosse Pointe Woods, MI 48236

CHIP Counseling Center, 6777 U.S. 31 South, Charlevoix, MI 49720

City of Detroit Dept of Human Services/Drug Treatment Div, 5031 Grandy, Detroit, MI 48211

Clinton – Eaton – Ingham Community Mental Health Board, 808 Southland, Suite B, Lansing, MI 48910

Community Care Services, 26184 West Outer Drive, Lincoln Park, MI 48146

Community Mental Health Services for Ionia County, 5827 North Orleans Road, Orleans, MI 48865–0155

Community Mental Health Services of Muskegon County, 376 Apple Avenue, Muskegon, MI 49442

Community Mental Health Services of St. Joseph County, 210 South Main Street, Three Rivers, MI 49093

Comprehensive Psychiatric Services, PC, 28800 Orchard Lake Rd, Ste 250, Farmington Hills, MI 48334

Comprehensive Services, Inc., 4630 Oakman Boulevard, Detroit, MI 48204

Cruz Clinic, 17177 North Laurel Park Drive, Suite 131, Livonia, MI 48152

DBA Spectrum Prevention & Treatment Services, 2301 Platt Road, Ann Arbor, MI 48104

Delta Family Clinic, 2303 East Amelith Road, Bay City, MI 48706

Desgranges Psychiatric Center, PC, G 8145 South Saginaw Street, Grand Blanc, MI 48439

Detroit Central City Community Mental Health, Inc., 10 Peterboro, Suite 208, Detroit, MI 48201

Dimensions of Life, 510 West Willow, Lansing, MI 48906

DOT Caring Centers, Inc., 3190 Hallmark Court, Saginaw, MI 48603–2107

Downriver Guidance Clinic, 13101 Allen Road, Southgate, MI 48195

Empowered Living Human Services, Inc., 18820 Woodward Avenue, Detroit, MI 48203

Evergreen Counseling Centers, 6902 Chicago Road, Warren, MI 48092

Fairlane Behavioral Services, 23400 Michigan Avenue, Ste P24, Dearborn, MI 48124

Gateway Services, 1910 Shaffer Road, Kalamazoo, MI 49001

Gerontology Network, 4695 Danvers Southeast, Ste B, Grand Rapids, MI 49512

Growth Works Incorporated, PO Box 6115, Plymouth, MI 48170–0115

Guest House for Women Religious, PO Box 420, Lake Orion, MI 48361

Hegira Programs, Inc., 8623 N Wayne Road, Suite 200, Westland, MI 48185

Holly Gardens, PO Box 66, Holly, MI 48442

Huron Valley Consultation Center, 955 West Eisenhower Circle Suite B, Ann Arbor, MI 48103

Jensen Counseling Centers, PC, 26105 Orchard Lake Rd, Ste 301, Farmington Hills, MI 48334

Kairos Healthcare, Inc., 4364 State Street, Saginaw, MI 48603

Lapeer County Community Mental Health Center, 1570 Suncrest Drive, Lapeer, MI 48446–1154

Latino Family Services, Inc., 3815 West Fort Street, Detroit, MI 48216

LondonBrook Associates, 26677 West Twelve Mile Road, Suite 124, Southfield, MI 48034

Macomb Child Guidance Clinic, Inc., 40600 Van Dyke, Suite 9, Sterling Heights, MI 48313

Meridian Professional Psychological Consultants, PC, 5031 Park Lake Road, East Lansing, MI 48823

Metro East Substance Abuse Treatment Corporation, PO Box 13408, Detroit, MI 48213

Michiana Addictions and Prevention Services, 1020 Millard Street, Three Rivers, MI 49093–1658

Michigan Counseling Services, 1400 East 12 Mile Road, Madison Heights, MI 48071

Nardin Park Recovery Center, Inc., PO Box 04506, Detroit, MI 48204

National Council on Alcoholism / Lansing Regional Area, Inc., 3400 S Cedar Street, Suite 200, Lansing, MI 48910

National Council on Alcoholism and Addictions, 202 E Boulevard Drive, Ste 310, Flint, MI 48503

National Council on Alcoholism and Drug Dependence / Vantage, 16647 Wyoming, Detroit, MI 48221

Neighborhood Service Organization, 220 Bagley, Suite 1200, Detroit, MI 48226

New Center Community Mental Health Services, 2051 West Grand Boulevard, Detroit, MI 48208

New Era Alternative Treatment Center, Inc., 211 Glendale, Suite S–B, Highland Park, MI 48203

New Light Recovery Center, Inc, 300 West McNichols, Detroit, MI 48203

New Perspectives Center, Inc., 1321 South Fayette Street, Saginaw, MI 48602

Newaygo County Mental Health Center, PO Box 8367, White Cloud, MI 49349

Northeast Guidance Center, 13340 East Warren, Detroit, MI 48215

Northeast Health Services, 3800 Woodward Avenue Suite 1002, Detroit, MI 48234–1263

Northeast Michigan Community Mental Health Services, 400 Johnson Street, Alpena, MI 49707

Northpointe Behavioral Healthcare Systems, 715 Pyle Drive, Kingsford, MI 49802

Oakland Psychological Clinic, PC, PO Box 888, Bloomfield Hills, MI 48303–0888

Orchard Hills Psychiatric Center, 40000 Grand River Ave, Ste 306, Novi, MI 48375–2112

Orchards Children's Services, Inc., 30215 Southfield Road, Southfield, MI 48076

Ottawa County Community Mental Health, 12251 James Street, Suite 100, Holland, MI 49424

Parkside Mental Health and Clinical Services, 18820 Woodward, Highland Park, MI 48203

Parkview Company, dba Parkview Counseling Centers, 18609 West Seven Mile Road, Detroit, MI 48219

Perspectives of Troy, PC, 2690 Crooks Road, Suite 300, Troy, MI 48084

Program for Alcohol and Substance Treatment, 110 Sanborn Avenue, Big Rapids, MI 49307

Psychological Consultants of Michigan, PC, 2518 Capital Avenue SW, Ste 2, Battle Creek, MI 49015

Psychotherapy and Counseling Services, P.C., 670 Griswold, Suite 4, Northville, MI 48167

Quality Behavioral Health, Inc, 3455 Woodward Avenue, Ste 101, Detroit, MI 48201

Redford Counseling Center, 25945 West Seven Mile Road, Redford Township, MI 48240

Renaissance Education and Training Center, 18240 West McNichols, Detroit, MI 48219

Rivendell Center for Behavioral Health, 101 West Townsend Road, St. Johns, MI 48879

River's Bend, P.C., 33975 Dequindre, Troy, MI 48083

Rose Hill Center, Inc., 5130 Rose Hill Boulevard, Holly, MI 48442

Sacred Heart Rehabilitation Center, Inc., 400 Stoddard Road P.O. Box 41038, Memphis, MI 48041

Saginaw County Community Mental Health Authority, 500 Hancock Street, Saginaw, MI 48602

Self Help Addiction Rehabilitation, 1852 West Grand Boulevard, Detroit, MI 48208

Star Center, Inc., 13575 Lesure, Detroit, MI 48227

STM Clinic – Mental Health and Substance Abuse Services, One Tuscola Street, Suite 302, Saginaw, MI 48607–1287

Suburban West Community Center, 11677 Beech Daly Road, Redford Twp, MI 48239

Summit Pointe, 140 West Michigan Avenue, Battle Creek, MI 49017

Taylor Psychological Clinic, PC, 1172 Robert T Longway Blvd, Flint, MI 48503

The Center for Human Resources, 1001 Military Street, Port Huron, MI 48060

The Kalamazoo Child Guidance Clinic, 2615 Stadium Drive, Kalamazoo, MI 49008

The Montcalm Center for Behavioral Health, 611 North State Street, Stanton, MI 48888

Turning Point Programs, 1931 Boston, Southeast, Grand Rapids, MI 49506

Tuscola Behavioral Health Systems, PO Box 239, Caro, MI 48723

W. D. Lee Center for Life Management, Inc., 11000 West McNichols, Ste 222, Detroit, MI 48221

West Michigan Community Mental Health System, 920 Diana Street, Ludington, MI 49431

MINNESOTA

Anthony Louis Center, 1000 Paul Parkway, Blaine, MN 55434

Charter Behavioral Health System of Waverly, 109 North Shore Drive, Waverly, MN 55390–9743

Fountain Lake Treatment Center, Inc., 408 Fountain Street, Albert Lea, MN 56007

Guest House, PO Box 954, Rochester, MN 55903

Hazelden Recovery Services, PO Box 11, Center City, MN 55012

Omegon, Inc., 2000 Hopkins Crossroads, Minnetonka, MN 55343

Pride Institute, 14400 Martin Drive, Eden Prairie, MN 55344

St. Joseph's Home for Children, 1121 East 46th Street, Minneapolis, MN 55407

MISSISSIPPI

CARES Center, Inc., 402 Wesley Avenue, Jackson, MS 39202

COPAC, Inc., 3949 Highway 43 North, Brandon, MS 39047

Diamond Grove Center for Children and Adolescents, PO Box 848, Louisville, MS 39339

Male/Female Receiving Med Psych Services, PO Box 157–A, Whitfield, MS 39193

Millcreek, PO Box 1160, Magee, MS 39111

MISSOURI

Boonville Valley Hope, PO Box 376, Boonville, MO 65233

Boys Town of Missouri, Inc., PO Box 189, St. James, MO 65559

Centrec Care, Inc., 11720 Borman Drive, Suite 103, Saint Louis, MO 63146

Child Advocacy Services Ctr, Inc./The Children's Place, 2 East 59th Street, Kansas City, MO 64113–2116

Child Center of Our Lady, 7900 Natural Bridge, St. Louis, MO 63121

Comprehensive Mental Health Services, Inc., 10901 Winner Road, Independence, MO 64052

Edgewood Children's Center, 330 North Gore Avenue, Webster Groves, MO 63119

Epworth Children and Family Services, 110 North Elm Avenue, Saint Louis, MO 63119

Industrial Rehabilitation Center, 429 Northeast 69 Highway, Kansas City, MO 64119

Marillac Center, 2826 Main Street, Kansas City, MO 64108

Piney Ridge Center, Inc., PO Box 4067, Waynesville, MO 65583

Provident Counseling, Inc., 2650 Olive Street, Saint Louis, MO 63103–1489

Research Mental Health Services, 901 NE Independence Avenue, Lees Summit, MO 64086

Swope Parkway Health Center, 3801 Blue Parkway, Kansas City, MO 64130

MONTANA

Intermountain Children's Home, 500 South Lamborn, Helena, MT 59601

Rocky Mountain Treatment Center, 920 Fourth Avenue North, Great Falls, MT 59401

Yellowstone Boys and Girls Ranch, 1732 South 72nd Street West, Billings, MT 59106

NEBRASKA

Alpha School, 1615 South 6th Street, Omaha, NE 68108

Behavioral Health Specialists, Inc., 600 South 13th Street, Norfolk, NE 68701

Blue Valley Mental Health Clinic, 1121 N. 10th Street, Beatrice, NE 68310

Camelot Care Centers, Inc., 7501 'O' Street, Suite 104, Lincoln, NE 68510

Cedars Youth Services, 770 North Cotner Boulevard Suite 410, Lincoln, NE 68505

Community Mental Health Center of Lancaster County, 2200 St. Mary's Avenue, Lincoln, NE 68502

Epworth Village, Inc., P O Box 503, York, NE 68467–0503

Father Flanagan's Boys' Home, 13603 Flanagan Boulevard, Boys Town, NE 68010

Father Flanagan's Boys' Home, 13603 Flanagan Boulevard, Boys Town, NE 68010

Lincoln Lancaster County Child Guidance Center, 215 Centennial Mall South, Suite 312, Lincoln, NE 68508

Mid–East Nebraska Behavioral Healthcare Services, Inc., PO Box 682, Columbus, NE 68602–0682

O'Neill Valley Hope, PO Box 918, O' Neill, NE 68763–0918

OMNI Behavioral Health, 4150 S 87th Street, Suite 100, Omaha, NE 68127

Uta Halee Girls Village, 10625 Calhoun Road, Omaha, NE 68112

NEVADA

Desert Willow Treatment Center, 6171 W Charleston Boulevard, Building 17, Las Vegas, NV 89102

NEW HAMPSHIRE

Beech Hill Hospital, LLC, PO Box 254, Dublin, NH 03444

Community Council of Nashua, NH, Inc., 7 Prospect Street, Nashua, NH 03060–3990

Lakeview Neurorehabilitation Center, Inc., 101 Highwatch Road, Effingham, NH 03814

Seaborne Hospital, PO Box 518, Dover, NH 03820

Seacoast Mental Health Center, Inc., 1145 Sagamore Avenue, Portsmouth, NH 03801

The Mental Health Center of Greater Manchester, 401 Cypress Street, Manchester, NH 03103

NEW JERSEY

Aaries, Inc., 690 Broadway, Bayonne, NJ 07002

Arthur Brisbane Child Treatment Center, PO Box 625, Farmingdale, NJ 07727

AtlantiCare Behavioral Health, 201 Tilton Road, Unit 13–A, Northfield, NJ 08225

Bancroft Rehabilitation Services, PO Box 20, Haddonfield, NJ 08033

Bonnie Brae, PO Box 825, Liberty Corner, NJ 07938–0825

Cape Counseling Services, 128 Crest Haven Road, Cape May Court House, NJ 08210

Catholic Charities – Diocese of Metuchen, 288 Rues Lane, East Brunswick, NJ 08816

Community Centers for Mental Health, Inc., 2 Park Avenue, Dumont, NJ 07628

Comprehensive Behavioral Healthcare, Inc., PO Box 750, Lyndhurst, NJ 07071

CPC Behavioral Healthcare, Inc, One High Point Center Way, Morganville, NJ 07751

Daytop, New Jersey, 80 West Main Street, Mendham, NJ 07945

Discovery Institute for Addictive Disorders, Inc., PO Box 177, Marlboro, NJ 07746

Drenk Mental Health Center, Inc., 795 Woodland Road, Suite 300, Mount Holly, NJ 08060

Ewing Residential Treatment Center, 1610 Stuyvesant Avenue, Trenton, NJ 08618

Family and Children's Services, 1900 Route 35 South, Oakhurst, NJ 07755

Family Service of Burlington County, 770 Woodlane Road, Mount Holly, NJ 08060

High Focus Centers, 299 Market Street, Suite 110, Saddle Brook, NJ 07663

Honesty House, 1272 Long Hill Road, Stirling, NJ 07980

Lighthouse at Mays Landing, PO Box 899, Mays Landing, NJ 08330

Mid–Bergen Center, Inc., 610 Industrial Avenue, Paramus, NJ 07652

New Hope Foundation, Inc, PO Box 66, Marlboro, NJ 07746

NewBridge Services, Inc., PO Box 336, Pompton Plains, NJ 07444

Ocean Mental Health Services, Inc., 160 Route 9, Bayville, NJ 08721

Preferred Behavioral Health of New Jersey, PO Box 2036, Lakewood, NJ 08701

Seabrook House, Inc., PO Box 5055, Seabrook, NJ 08302–0655

SERV Centers of New Jersey, Inc., 380 Scotch Road, West Trenton, NJ 08628

Sunrise House Foundation, PO Box 600, Lafayette, NJ 07848

UCPC Behavioral Health Care, 117–119 Roosevelt Avenue, Plainfield, NJ 07060

UMDNJ – University Behavioral HealthCare, PO Box 1392, Piscataway, NJ 08854–1392

Vineland Children's Residential Treatment Center, 2000 Maple Avenue, Vineland, NJ 08360

West Bergen Mental Healthcare, Inc., 120 Chestnut Street, Ridgewood, NJ 07450

Willowglen Academy – New Jersey, Inc., PO Box A–1, Newton, NJ 07860

Woodbridge Child Diagnostic and Treatment Center, 15 Paddock Street, Avenel, NJ 07001

Youth Consultation Service, 260 Union Street, Hackensack, NJ 07601

NEW MEXICO

BHC Pinon Hills Residential Treatment Center, Inc., PO Box 428, Velarde, NM 87582

Desert Hills of New Mexico, 5310 Sequoia Northwest, Albuquerque, NM 87120

Family Opportunity Resources, 851 Magee Lane, Santa Fe, NM 87501

Four Corners Regional Adolescent Treatment Center, PO Box 567, Shiprock, NM 87420

Namaste Child and Family Development Center, PO Box 270, Peralta, NM 87042

Sequoyah Adolescent Treatment Center, 3405 W Pan American Freeway NE, Albuquerque, NM 87107

The Adolescent Pointe, PO Box 6, Santa Teresa, NM 88008

The Pointe, PO Box 6, Santa Teresa, NM 88008

NEW YORK

A.R.E.B.A.– Casriel, Inc., 500 West 57th Street, New York, NY 10019

Arms Acres, 75 Seminary Hill Road, Carmel, NY 10512

August Aichhorn R.F.T., 23 West 106th Street, New York, NY 10025

Baker Victory Services, Inc., 780 Ridge Road, Lackawanna, NY 14218

Bronx Addiction Treatment Center, 1500 Waters Place, Building 13, Bronx, NY 10461

Charles K. Post Addiction Treatment Center, Building 1, PPC Campus, West Brentwood, NY 11717

Children's Home RTF, Inc., 638 Squirrel Hill Road, Chenango Forks, NY 13746

Conifer Park, Inc., 79 Glenridge Road, Schenectady, NY 12302

Conners Residential Treatment Facility, Inc., 824 Delaware Avenue, Buffalo, NY 14209

Cornerstone of Medical Arts Center Hospital, 57 West 57th Street, New York, NY 10019

Cornerstone of Rhinebeck, NY, 500 Milan Hollow Road, Rhinebeck, NY 12572

Creedmoor Addiction Treatment Center, 80–45 Winchester Boulevard, Queens Village, NY 11427

Crestwood Children's Center, 2075 Scottsville Road, Rochester, NY 14623–2098

Dick Van Dyke Addiction Treatment Center, 1330 County Route 132, Ovid, NY 14521

Green Chimneys Children's Services, Caller Box 719, Brewster, NY 10509

Harmony Heights Residence, PO Box 569, Oyster Bay, NY 11771

Hillside Children's Center Main Campus, 1183 Monroe Avenue, Rochester, NY 14620

Hope House, Inc., 517 Western Avenue, Albany, NY 12203

Hopevale, Inc., 3780 Howard Road, Hamburg, NY 14075

Jewish Board of Family and Children's Services, 120 West 57th Street, New York, NY 10019

John L. Norris Addiction Treatment Center, 1111 Elmwood Avenue, Rochester, NY 14620

Julia Dyckman Andrus Memorial, 1156 North Broadway, Yonkers, NY 10701

Kingsboro Addiction Treatment Center, 754 Lexington Avenue, Brooklyn, NY 11221

Madonna Heights Services, P. O. Box 8020, Dix Hills, NY 11746–9020

Manhattan Addiction Treatment Center, 600 East 125th Street, M 11 Ward's Island, New York, NY 10035

McPike Addiction Treatment Center, 1213 Court Street, Utica, NY 13502

National Expert Care Consultants, Inc., 455 West 50th Street, New York, NY 10019–6504

Parsons Child and Family Center, 60 Academy Road, Albany, NY 12208

Passages Counseling Center, 3680 Route 112, Coram, NY 11727

Psych Systems of Long Island, 1600 Stewart Avenue, Suite 202, Westbury, NY 11590

Psych Systems of Westchester, 33 West Main Street, Suite 307, Elmsford, NY 10523

Restorative Management Corporation, 15 King Street, Middletown, NY 10940

Richard C. Ward Addiction Treatment Center, 141 Monhagen Avenue, Middletown, NY 10940

Rochester Mental Health Center, 490 East Ridge Road, Rochester, NY 14621

Russell E. Blaisdell Addiction Treatment Center, PO Box 140, Orangeburg, NY 10962

Saint Peter's Addiction Recovery Center, Inc., 3 Mercycare Lane, Guilderland, NY 12084

Salamanca Hospital District Authority, 150 Parkway Drive, Salamanca, NY 14779

Seafield Center, Inc., 7 Seafield Lane, Westhampton Beach, NY 11978

South Beach Addiction Treatment Center, 777 Seaview Avenue, Building 1, Staten Island, NY 10305

St. Christopher–Ottilie, 101 Downing Avenue, Sea Cliff, NY 11579

St. Joseph's Rehabilitation Center, Inc., PO Box 470, Saranac Lake, NY 12983–0470

St. Joseph's Villa of Rochester, 3300 Dewey Avenue, Rochester, NY 14616

St. Lawrence Addiction Treatment Center, 1 Chimney Point Drive, Hamilton Hall, Ogdensburg, NY 13669

St. Mary's Children and Family Services, 525 Convent Road, Syosset, NY 11791–3864

Stutzman Addiction Treatment Center, 360 Forest Avenue, Buffalo, NY 14213

Support Center, Inc., 181 Route 209, Port Jervis, NY 12771

The Astor Home for Children, PO Box 5005, Rhinebeck, NY 12572–5005

The Children's Village, Wetmore Hall, Dobbs Ferry, NY 10522

The Health Association – MAIN QUEST Treatment Center, 774 West Main Street, Rochester, NY 14611

The House of the Good Shepherd, 1550 Champlin Avenue, Utica, NY 13502

The Long Island Center for Recovery, PO Box 774, Hampton Bays, NY 11946

The Saint Francis Academy, Incorporated, Lake Placid, 50 Riverside Drive, Lake Placid, NY 12946

The Villa Outpatient Center, 290 Madison Avenue, 6th Floor, New York, NY 10017

Tully Hill Corporation, PO Box 920, Tully, NY 13159–0920

Veritas Villa, Inc., PO Box 610, Kerhonkson, NY 12446–0610

Westchester Jewish Community Services, Inc., 845 North Broadway, Suite 2, White Plains, NY 10603–2427

NORTH CAROLINA

Alexander Children's Center, Inc., PO Box 220632, Charlotte, NC 28222–9979

American Day Treatment Centers Charlotte, 201 Providence Road Suite 101, Charlotte, NC 28207

Amethyst, PO Box 32861, Charlotte, NC 28232–2861

CenterPoint Human Services, 725 North Highland Avenue, Winston–Salem, NC 27101

Fellowship Hall, Inc., PO Box 13890, Greensboro, NC 27415

Grandfather Home for Children, PO Box 98, Banner Elk, NC 28604

Julian F. Keith Alcohol and Drug Abuse Treatment Center, 301 Tabernacle Road, Black Mountain, NC 28711

PSI Solutions Center, 801 Jones Franklin Rd, Ste 210, Raleigh, NC 27606

The Wilmington Treatment Center, 2520 Troy Drive, Wilmington, NC 28401

Three Springs of North Carolina, PO Box 1370, Pittsboro, NC 27312

Timber Ridge Treatment Center, 14225 Stokes Ferry Road, Gold Hill, NC 28071

Unity Regional Youth Treatment Center, PO Box C–201, Cherokee, NC 28719

NORTH DAKOTA

The Dakota Boys Ranch, PO Box 5007, Minot, ND 58703

OHIO

2 North Park, Inc., 720 Pine Avenue Southeast, Warren, OH 44483

Akron Child Guidance Center Central Office, 312 Locust Street, Akron, OH 44302–1878

Beech Brook, 3737 Lander Road, Pepper Pike, OH 44124

Behavioral Connections of Wood County, Inc., 320 West Gypsy Lane Road, Bowling Green, OH 43402

Bellefaire Jewish Children's Bureau, 22001 Fairmount Boulevard, Shaker Heights, OH 44118

Blick Clinic, Inc., 640 West Market Street, Akron, OH 44303

Center for Chemical Addictions Treatment, 830 Ezzard Charles Drive, Cincinnati, OH 45214

Charles B. Mills Center, Inc., 715 South Plum Street, Marysville, OH 43040

Children's Aid Society, 10427 Detroit Avenue, Cleveland, OH 44102–1694

Children's Resource Center, PO Box 738, Bowling Green, OH 43402

Community Drug Board, 725 East Market Street, Akron, OH 44305

Community Support Services, Inc., 150 Cross Street, Akron, OH 44311

Comprehensive Psychiatry Specialists, 955 Windham Court, Suite 2, Boardman, OH 44512

Counseling Centers of Ohio, 5800 Monroe Street, Building A, Sylvania, OH 43560

Crisis Intervention Center of Stark County, Inc., 2421 13th Street Northwest, Canton, OH 44708

D & E Counseling Center, 142 Javit Court, Youngstown, OH 44515

Family Recovery Center, PO Box 464, Lisbon, OH 44432

Focus Health Care, 5701 North High Street, Suite 8, Worthington, OH 43085

Glenbeigh Health Sources, PO Box 298, Rock Creek, OH 44084–0298

Harbor Behavioral Healthcare, 4334 Secor Road, Toledo, OH 43623–4234

Health Recovery Services, Inc., PO Box 724, Athens, OH 45701

Interval Brotherhood Home Inc., 3445 South Main Street, Akron, OH 44319

Lake Area Recovery Center, 2801 'C' Court, Ashtabula, OH 44004

Lincoln Center for Prevention & Treatment of Chem Dependency, 1918 North Main Street, Findlay, OH 45840

Mahoning County Chemical Dependency Programs, Inc., 527 North Meridan Road, Youngstown, OH 44509

McKinley Hall, Inc., 1101 East High Street, Springfield, OH 45505

Mental Health Services for Clark County, Inc., 1345 Fountain Boulevard, Springfield, OH 45504

Miami Valley Labor Management Healthcare Delivery Systems, 136 Heid Avenue, Dayton, OH 45404

Mount Carmel Behavioral Healthcare, 1808 East Broad Street, Columbus, OH 43203

Neil Kennedy Recovery Clinic, 2151 Rush Boulevard, Youngstown, OH 44507

NEO Psych Consultants, 831 Southwestern Run, Suite 2, Youngstown, OH 44514

New Directions, Inc., 30800 Chagrin Boulevard, Pepper Pike, OH 44124

Nova Behavioral Health, Inc., 832 McKinley Avenue Northwest, Canton, OH 44703

Parkside Behavioral Healthcare, Inc., 349 Olde Ridenour Road, Columbus, OH 43230

Parmadale, Inc., 1111 Superior Avenue, Cleveland, OH 44114

Portage Path Behavioral Health, 340 South Broadway, Akron, OH 44308

PsyCare, Inc., 2980 Belmont Avenue, Youngstown, OH 44505

Psych Systems of Cincinnati, 11223 Cornell Park Dr, Ste 301, Cincinnati, OH 45242

Quest Recovery Services, 1341 Market Avenue, North, Canton, OH 44714–2675

Ravenwood Mental Health Center, 12557 Ravenwood Drive, Chardon, OH 44024

Rescue Mental Health Services, 3350 Collingwood Boulevard, Toledo, OH 43610

Serenity Living, Inc., PO Box 217, Vandalia, OH 45377

Specialty Care Psychiatric Services, Inc, 2657 Niles Courtland Road, SE, Warren, OH 44484

Springview Developmental Center, 3130 East Main Street, Springfield, OH 45505

St. Joseph Children's Treatment Center, 650 St. Paul Avenue, Dayton, OH 45410

Substance Abuse Services, Inc., 1832 Adams Street, Toledo, OH 43624

The Buckeye Ranch, Inc., 5665 Hoover Road, Grove City, OH 43123

The Campus Hospital of Cleveland, 18120 Puritas Road, Cleveland, OH 44135

The Crossroads Center, 311 Martin Luther King Drive, Cincinnati, OH 45219–3116

Transitional Living, Inc. and Affiliates, 2052 Princeton Road, Hamilton, OH 45011

Unison Behavioral Health Group, PO Box 10015, Toledo, OH 43699–0015

Wellspring Retreat & Resource Center, PO Box 67, Albany, OH 45710

Zepf Community Mental Health Center, Inc., 6605 West Central Avenue, Toledo, OH 43617

OKLAHOMA

Brookhaven Hospital, 201 South Garnett, Tulsa, OK 74128–1800

Carl Albert Community Mental Health Center, PO Box 579, Mcalester, OK 74502

Christopher Youth Center, Inc., 2741 East 7th Street, Tulsa, OK 74104

Cushing Valley Hope, PO Box 472, Cushing, OK 74023–0472

High Pointe, 6501 Northeast 50th Street, Oklahoma City, OK 73141

Jim Taliaferro Community Mental Health Center, 602 Southwest 38th Street, Lawton, OK 73505–6999

Oklahoma Youth Center, 320 12th Avenue Northeast, Norman, OK 73071

Parkside, Inc., 1620 East 12th Street, Tulsa, OK 74120

Western State Psychiatric Center, PO Box 1, Fort Supply, OK 73841

Willow Crest Hospital, 130 'A' Street Southwest, Miami, OK 74354

OREGON

BHC Pacific View RTC, 4101 Northeast Division Street, Gresham, OR 97030

Eastern Oregon Adolescent Multi–Treatment Center, Inc., 622 Airport Road, Pendleton, OR 97801

Edgefield Children's Center, 2408 Southwest Halsey Street, Troutdale, OR 97060

Kerr Youth and Family Center, 722 Northeast 162nd Avenue, Portland, OR 97230

RiverBend Youth Center, Inc., 15544 S Clackamas River Drive, Oregon City, OR 97045

Rosemont Treatment Center and School, 9911 SE Mt. Scott Boulevard, Portland, OR 97266

Ryles Center, 3339 Southeast Division Street, Portland, OR 97202

Serenity Lane, Inc., 616 East Sixteenth Avenue, Eugene, OR 97401

Southern Oregon Adolescent Study and Treatment Center, 210 Tacoma Street, Grants Pass, OR 97526

Springbrook Northwest, Inc., 2001 Crestview Drive, Newberg, OR 97132

The Christie School, PO Box 368, Marylhurst, OR 97036

Trillium Family Services, 3550 Southeast Woodward Street, Portland, OR 97202

PENNSYLVANIA

Abraxas I, PO Box 59, Marienville, PA 16239

Adelphoi Village, Inc., 1003 Village Way, Latrobe, PA 15650

American Day Treatment Centers, 468 Thomas Jones Way Suite 150, Exton, PA 19341

American Day Treatment Centers, 468 Thomas Jones Way Suite 150, Exton, PA 19341

Bowling Green of Brandywine, Inc., 1375 Newark Road, Kennett Square, PA 19348

Charter Behavioral Health System at Cove Forge, New Beginnings Road, Williamsburg, PA 16693

Child Guidance Resource Centers, 600 North Olive Street, Media, PA 19063–2418

Children's Aid Home Programs of Somerset County, Inc., PO Box 1195, Somerset, PA 15501

Children's Home of Bradford, 800 East Main Street, Bradford, PA 16701

Children's Home of Bradford, 800 East Main Street, Bradford, PA 16701

Clear Brook, Inc., 1003 Wyoming Avenue, Forty Fort, PA 18704

Conewago Place, 424 Nye Road, Hummelstown, PA 17036–0406

Diversified Family Services, 3679 East State Street, Hermitage, PA 16148

Eagleville Hospital, PO Box 45, Eagleville, PA 19408–0045

Friendship House, PO Box 3778, Scranton, PA 18505

Gateway Rehabilitation Center, Moffett Run Road, Aliquippa, PA 15001

Gaudenzia, Inc. – Common Ground, 2835 North Front Street, Harrisburg, PA 17110

Greenbriar Treatment Center, 800 Manor Drive, Washington, PA 15301

Greenway Center, P.O. Box 188, Henryville, PA 18332

Hoffman Homes, Inc., PO Box 4777, Gettysburg, PA 17325–4777

KidsPeace Corporation, 5300 KidsPeace Drive, Orefield, PA 18069–9101

Lehigh Valley Community Mental Health Centers, Inc., PO Box 5349, Bethlehem, PA 18015–5349

Livengrin Foundation, Inc., 4833 Hulmeville Road, Bensalem, PA 19020–3099

Lutheran Youth and Family Services, PO Box 70, Zelienople, PA 16063–0070

Malvern Institute, 940 King Road, Malvern, PA 19355

Marworth, PO Box 36, Waverly, PA 18471

Milestones Community Healthcare, Inc., 614 North Easton Road, Glenside, PA 19038

Mirmont Treatment Center, 100 Yearsley Mill Road, Glen Riddle Lima, PA 19063–5593

New Vitae Partial Hospitalization Program, PO Box 181, Limeport, PA 18060–0181

Northeast Treatment Centers (NET), 499 North Fifth Street Suite A, Philadelphia, PA 19123

Northern Tier Children's Home Residential Services, Inc., PO Box 94, Harrison Valley, PA 16927

PAMM Human Resources Center, Inc., 2400–10 N Front Street, Philadelphia, PA 19133

Penn Foundation, Inc., 807 Lawn Avenue, P.O. Box 32, Sellersville, PA 18960

Presbyterian Children's Village in Pennsylvania, 452 South Roberts Road, Rosemont, PA 19010

Renewal Centers, PO Box 597, Quakertown, PA 18951

Richard J. Caron Foundation, PO Box A, Wernersville, PA 19565–0501

Roxbury, PO Box L, Shippensburg, PA 17257
Salisbury House of Northeast Pennsylvania, Inc., 60 North 4th Street, Easton, PA 18042
Sarah A. Reed Children's Center, 2445 West 34th Street, Erie, PA 16506
Serenity Hall, Inc., 414 West Fifth Street, Erie, PA 16507
Silver Springs – Martin Luther School, 512 West Township Line Road, Plymouth Meeting, PA 19462–1099
St. John Vianney Hospital, 151 Woodbine Road, Downingtown, PA 19335–3057
The Bradley Center, Inc., 522 Saxonburg Boulevard, Pittsburgh, PA 15238
The Bridge, 8400 Pine Road, Philadelphia, PA 19111
The Mitchell Clinic, 1259 S Cedar Crest Boulevard, Suite 317, Allentown, PA 18103
The Renfrew Center, Inc., 475 Spring Lane, Philadelphia, PA 19128
The Renfrew Center, Inc., 475 Spring Lane, Philadelphia, PA 19128
The Terraces, PO Box 729, Ephrata, PA 17522
TODAY, Inc., PO Box 908, New Town, PA 18940
Twin Lakes Center for Drug and Alcohol Rehabilitation, PO Box 909, Somerset, PA 15501–0909
UHS Recovery Foundation, Inc., 2001 Providence Avenue, Chester, PA 19013–5504
Westmeade Center Warwick, 940 W Valley Road–Ste. 2102, Wayne, PA 19087
White Deer Run, Inc., Devitt Camp Road, Box 97, Allenwood, PA 17810–0097
Wordsworth Academy and Human Services, Pennsylvania Avenue and Camp Hill Road, Fort Washington, PA 19034

RHODE ISLAND
Alternatives, 350 Duncan Drive, Providence, RI 02906
CODAC, Inc., 1052 Park Avenue, Cranston, RI 02910
Community Counseling Center, 101 Bacon Street, Pawtucket, RI 02860
East Bay Mental Health Center, Inc., 2 Old County Road, Barrington, RI 02806
Fellowship Health Resources, Inc., 25 Blackstone Valley Place, Lincoln, RI 02865
Mental Health Services of Cranston, Johnston, 1443 Hartford Avenue, Johnston, RI 02919–3236
Newport County Community Mental Health Center, Inc., 127 Johnnycake Hill Road, Middletown, RI 02842
Riverwood Rehabilitation Services, Inc., PO Box 897, Bristol, RI 02809
South Shore Mental Health Center, Inc., PO Box 899, Charlestown, RI 02813
The Providence Center for Counseling & Psychiatric Svcs, 520 Hope Street, Providence, RI 02906
Tri–Hab, Inc., 58 Hamlet Avenue, Woonsocket, RI 02895

SOUTH CAROLINA
Lexington County Community Mental Health Center, 301 Palmetto Park Blvd, Lexington, SC 29072
New Hope Treatment Centers, Inc., 225 Midland Parkway, Summerville, SC 29485
Southbridge Center, 7901 Farrow Road, Bldg1, Columbia, SC 29202–0041
York Place Episcopal Church Home for Children, 234 Kings Mountain Street, York, SC 29745

SOUTH DAKOTA
Black Hills Children's Home, 24100 South Rockerville Road, Rapid City, SD 57701–9277
Keystone Treatment Center, PO Box 159, Canton, SD 57013
Sioux Falls Children's Home, PO Box 1749, Sioux Falls, SD 57101–1749

TENNESSEE
Academy for Academic Excellence, PO Box 3906, Clarksville, TN 37043
Agency for Youth and Family Development, 5050 Poplar Avenue, Suite 525, Memphis, TN 38137
Buffalo Valley, Inc., PO Box 879, Hohenwald, TN 38462
Camelot Care Center, Inc., 667 – B Emory Valley Road, Oak Ridge, TN 37830
Child and Family Services of Knox County, Inc., 901 East Summit Hill Drive, Knoxville, TN 37915
Compass Intervention Center, LLC, 7900 Lowrance Road, Memphis, TN 38183–0242
Cornerstone of Recovery, 1120 Topside Road, Louisville, TN 37777

Council for Alcohol and Drug Abuse Services, Inc., PO Box 4797, Chattanooga, TN 37405
Cumberland Heights Foundation, PO Box 90727, Nashville, TN 37209
Daybreak Treatment Center, 2262 Germantown Road South, Germantown, TN 38138
FHC – Cumberland Hall of Chattanooga, 7351 Standifer Gap Road, Chattanooga, TN 37421
Greene Valley Developmental Center, PO Box 910, Greeneville, TN 37744–0910
Jackson Academy, LLC, 222 Church Street, Dickson, TN 37055
New Life Lodge, PO Box 430, Burns, TN 37029
Ridgeview Psychiatric Hospital and Center, Inc., 240 West Tyrone Road, Oak Ridge, TN 37830
The Chad Youth Enhancement Center, 1751 Oak Plains Road, Ashland City, TN 37015
Three Springs Outdoor Therapeutic Program, PO Box 297, Centerville, TN 37033
Youth Villages, 2890 Bekemeyer Drive, Arlington, TN 38002

TEXAS
Alternatives Centre for Behavioral Health, 5001 Alabama Street, El Paso, TX 79930
Austin Child Guidance Center, 810 West 45th Street, Austin, TX 78751
BHC Cedar Crest RTC, Inc., 3500 South IH–35, Belton, TX 76513
Burke Center, 4101 South Medford Drive, Lufkin, TX 75901–5699
Camelot Care Centers, Inc., 7400 Blanco Road, Suite 123, San Antonio, TX 78216
Canyon Lakes Residential Treatment Center, 2402 Canyon Lake Drive, Lubbock, TX 79415
Champions, PO Box 2268, Bellaire, TX 77402
Child Study Center, 1300 West Lancaster, Fort Worth, TX 76102
Community Residential Centers of San Antonio, 17720 Corporate Woods Drive, San Antonio, TX 78259–3509
DePelchin Children's Center, 100 Sandman, Houston, TX 77007
Family Service Center, 2707 North Loop West, Ste 520, Houston, TX 77008
La Hacienda Treatment Center, PO Box 1, Hunt, TX 78024
Life Resource, 2750 South 8th Street, Beaumont, TX 77701
Meridell Achievement Center, PO Box 87, Liberty Hill, TX 78642
New Dimensions, 18333 Egret Bay Blvd, Ste 560, Houston, TX 77058
New View Partial Hospitalization Centre, Inc., 4310 Dowlen Road – Suite 13, Beaumont, TX 77706
Paul Meier New Life Day Hospital and Outpatient Clinic, 2071 North Collins Boulevard, Richardson, TX 75080
River Oaks Day Hospital, 8120 Westglen, Houston, TX 77063
San Marcos Treatment Center, PO Box 768, San Marcos, TX 78666
Shiloh Treatment Center, Inc., 4227 County Road 89, Manvel, TX 77578
Shoreline, Inc., PO Box 68, Taft, TX 78390
Summer Sky, Inc., 1100 McCart Street, Stephenville, TX 76401
Sundown Ranch, Inc., Route 4, Box 182, Canton, TX 75103
Synergy Partial Hospital, 5631 Dolores Street, Houston, TX 77057
The Oaks Treatment Center, Inc, 1407 West Stassney Lane, Austin, TX 78745
The Patrician Movement, 222 East Mitchell Street, San Antonio, TX 78210
Upward Reach Residential Treatment Center, 1120 Cypress Station Drive, Houston, TX 77090
Waco Center for Youth, 3501 North 19th Street, Waco, TX 76708

UTAH
Brightway at St. George, 115 West, 1470 South, St. George, UT 84770
Center for Change, Inc., 1790 North State Street, Orem, UT 84057
Copper Hills Youth Center, 5899 West Rivendell Drive, West Jordan, UT 84088
Heritage School, PO Box 105, Provo, UT 84603
Highland Ridge Hospital, 175 West 7200 South, Midvale, UT 84047
Island View Residential Treatment Center, 2650 West 2700 South, Syracuse, UT 84075
New Haven, PO Box 50238, Provo, UT 84605–0238
Provo Canyon School, 1350 E. 750 N, Orem, UT 84057
Sorenson's Ranch School, Inc., Box 440219, Koosharem, UT 84744

Vista Adolescent Treatment Center, PO Box 69, Magna, UT 84044
Youth Care, Inc., PO Box 909, Draper, UT 84020

VIRGINIA
DeJarnette Center, PO Box 2309, Staunton, VA 24402–2309
Graydon Manor, 801 Children's Center Road, S.W., Leesburg, VA 20175–2598
Inova Comprehensive Addiction Treatment Services, 3300 Gallows Road, Falls Church, VA 22042–3300
Inova Kellar Center, 10396 Democracy Lane, Fairfax, VA 22030
Learning Services, 9524 Fairview Avenue, Manassas, VA 22110
Marion Correctional Treatment Center, PO Box 1027, Marion, VA 24354–1027
Mount Regis Center, 405 Kimball Avenue, Salem, VA 24153
Shalom et Benedictus, Inc., PO Box 309, Stephenson, VA 22656
The Barry Robinson Center, 443 Kempsville Road, Norfolk, VA 23502
The Life Center of Galax, PO Box 27, Galax, VA 24333
The Pines Residential Treatment Facility/Crawford, 825 Crawford Parkway, Portsmouth, VA 23704
Williamsburg Place, 5477 Mooretown Road, Williamsburg, VA 23188

WASHINGTON
Martin Center, 2806 Douglas Avenue, Bellingham, WA 98227
Pearl Street Center / Comprehensive Mental Health, 815 South Pearl Street, Tacoma, WA 98465
Seattle Children's Home, 2142 Tenth Avenue West, Seattle, WA 98119
Spokane Mental Health, 107 South Division, Spokane, WA 99202
Sun Health Youth Treatment Center, 6911 226th Place Southwest, Mountlake Terrace, WA 98043
Tamarack Center, 2901 W Ft. George Wright Drive, Spokane, WA 99204
Valley Cities Counseling and Consultation, 2704 'I' Street Northeast, Auburn, WA 98002

WEST VIRGINIA
Elkins Mountain School, 100 Bell Street, Elkins, WV 26241
Olympic Center – Preston, Inc., PO Box 158, Kingwood, WV 26537
Shawnee Hills, Inc., PO Box 3698, Charleston, WV 25336–3698
Worthington Center, Inc., 3199 Core Road, Parkersburg, WV 26104

WISCONSIN
Eau Claire Academy Division of Clinicare Corp, PO Box 1168, Eau Claire, WI 54702–1168
Family Services Lakeshore, Inc, 333 Reed Avenue, Manitowoc, WI 54220
Libertas Treatment Center, 1701 Dousman Street, Green Bay, WI 54303
St. Rose Residence Incorporated, 3801 North 88th Street, Milwaukee, WI 53222

WYOMING
Cathedral Home for Children, PO Box 520, Laramie, WY 82073
Normative Services, Inc., PO Box 3075, Sheridan, WY 82801
St. Joseph's Children's Home, PO Box 1117, Torrington, WY 82240

U.S. Associated Areas

APO/AE
Wellness Branch, ODCSPER, USAREUR 7 Army 1 (Belgium), Hammonds Barracks, Bldg 968 Room 213 – Badenerplatz 1, APO, AE 09014
Wellness Branch, ODCSPER, USAREUR and Army 1 (Germany), Hammonds Barracks, Bldg 968 Room 213, Badenerplatz 1, APO, AE 09014

PUERTO RICO
Instituto Psicoterapeutico de Puerto Rico, Ave Hostos 431, 433, 435, Hato Rey, PR 00919

Section C

The accredited freestanding substance abuse programs listed have been accredited as of April, 1999 by the Joint Commission on Accreditation of Healthcare Organizations by decision of the Accreditation Committee of the Board of Commissioners.

The organizations listed here have been found to be in compliance with the Joint Commission standards for subtance abuse organizations, as found in the Accreditation Manual for Mental Health, Chemical Dependency, and Mental Retardation/Developmental Disabilities Services.

Please refer to section A of the AHA Guide for information on hospitals with inpatient and/or outpatient alcohol and chemical dependency services. These hospitals are identified by Facility Codes F2 and F3. In section A, those hospitals identified by Approval Code 1 are JCAHO accredited.

We present this list simply as a convenient directory. Inclusion or omission of any organization's name indicates neither approval nor disapproval by Health Forum LLC, an affiliate of the American Hospital Association.

United States

ALABAMA
Behavioral Healthcare Center, 306 Paul W Bryant Drive East, Tuscaloosa, AL 35401
Bradford Health Services – Huntsville, 1600 Browns Ferry Road, Madison, AL 35758
Bradford Health Services, Birmingham Lodge, PO Box 129, Warrior, AL 35180
The Catalyst Center, 517 Energy Center Blvd. Suite 1304, Northport, AL 35473
The Quality Life Center of Quality HealthCare, Inc., 2801 West Mall Drive, Florence, AL 35630

ALASKA
Akeela Treatment Services, Inc, 2805 Bering Street, Suite 4, Anchorage, AK 99503
Alaska North Addictions Recovery Center, 4330 Bragaw Street, Anchorage, AK 99508
Anchorage Charter North Counseling Center, 1650 South Bragaw, Anchorage, AK 99508

ARIZONA
Calvary Rehabilitation Center, 720 East Montebello Avenue, Phoenix, AZ 85014
Chandler Valley Hope, PO Box 1839, Chandler, AZ 85244–1839
Cottonwood de Tucson, 4110 West Sweetwater Drive, Tucson, AZ 85745
Desert Hills Center for Youth and Families, 2797 North Introspect Drive, Tucson, AZ 85745
META Services, Inc., 2701 N. 16th St., Suite 106, Phoenix, AZ 85006
Parc Place, 5116 East Thomas Road, Phoenix, AZ 85018
PREHAB of Arizona, Inc., PO Drawer 5860, Mesa, AZ 85211–5860
Rosewood Ranch L.P., 36075 South Rincon Road, Wickenburg, AZ 85390
Salvation Army Recovery Center, PO Box 52177, Phoenix, AZ 85072
Sierra Tucson,LLC, 39580 S. Lago del Oro Parkway, Tucson, AZ 85739
Superstition Mountain Mental Health Center, Inc., PO Box 3160, Apache Junction, AZ 85217
the EXCEL Group, 106 East First Street, Yuma, AZ 85364
The Meadows, 1655 North Tegner, Wickenburg, AZ 85390
The New Foundation, P O Box 3828, Scottsdale, AZ 85257
Vista Care Facility, 4120 East Ramsey Road, Hereford, AZ 85615
Westcenter, 2105 East Allen Road, Tucson, AZ 85719

ARKANSAS
Behavioral Health Services, Inc. of Arkansas, 604 Cherry Street, Helena, AR 72342
Ozark Guidance Center, Inc., PO Box 6430, Springdale, AR 72762–6430
University of Arkansas for Medical Sciences, 4301 West Markham Street, Mail Slot 554, Little Rock, AR 72205

CALIFORNIA
Betty Ford Center, 39000 Bob Hope Drive, Rancho Mirage, CA 92270
Cornerstone Residential Center for Addictions, 13682 Yorba Street, Tustin, CA 92680
Family Recovery Foundation, Inc., 12822 Hewes Avenue, Santa Ana, CA 92705

Impact Drug and Alcohol Treatment Center, 1680 North Fair Oaks Avenue, Pasadena, CA 91103
Kings View Center, 42675 Road 44, Reedley, CA 93654
R House, Inc., PO Box 2587, Santa Rosa, CA 95405
S T E P S, 224 East Clara Street, Port Hueneme, CA 93041
SeaBridge, Inc., PO Box 6296, Malibu, CA 90264
Sharp Vista Pacifica, 7989 Linda Vista Road, San Diego, CA 92111
Spencer Recovery Centers, Inc., 343 West Foothill Boulevard, Monrovia, CA 91016
Tarzana Treatment Center, 18646 Oxnard Street, Tarzana, CA 91356
The Discovery Adolescent Program, 4136 Ann Arbor Road, Lakewood, CA 90712
Twin Town Treatment Center, 10741 Los Alamitos Boulevard, Los Alamitos, CA 90720
Vista San Diego Center, 3003 Armstrong Street, San Diego, CA 92111
Watts Health Foundation, Inc., 10300 South Compton Avenue, Los Angeles, CA 90002

COLORADO
Adolescent and Family Institute of Colorado, Inc., 10001 West 32nd Avenue, Wheat Ridge, CO 80033
Aurora Behavioral Health Hospital, 1290 South Potomac Street, Aurora, CO 80012
Harmony Foundation, Inc., PO Box 1989, Estes Park, CO 80517
Managed Adolescent Care, PC, 1025 Pennock, Suite 111, Fort Collins, CO 80524
Parker Valley Hope, PO Box 670, Parker, CO 80134
Pikes Peak Mental Health Center Systems, Inc., 220 Ruskin Drive, Colorado Springs, CO 80910

CONNECTICUT
Community Prevention and Addiction Services, Inc., 1491 West Main Street, Willimantic, CT 06226
Cornerstone of Eagle Hill, Inc., 32 Alberts Hill Road, Sandy Hook, CT 06482
Greater Bridgeport Community Mental Health Center, PO Box 5117, Bridgeport, CT 06610
Guenster Rehabilitation Services, 276 Union Avenue, Bridgeport, CT 06607
Perception Programs, Inc., PO Box 407, Willimantic, CT 06226
Reid Treatment Center, Inc., PO Box 1357, Avon, CT 06001–1357
Rushford Center Inc., 1250 Silver Street, Middletown, CT 06457
Southern Connecticut Mental Health & Substance Abuse Treatment Center, 4083 Main Street, Bridgeport, CT 06606
Stonington Institute, 75 Swantown Hill Road, North Stonington, CT 06359
The BlueRidge Center, 1095 Blue Hills Avenue, Bloomfield, CT 06002
The Children's Center, Inc., 1400 Whitney Avenue, Hamden, CT 06517
The Wheeler Clinic, 91 Northwest Drive, Plainville, CT 06062
United Services, Inc., PO Box 839, Dayville, CT 06241
Vitam Center, Inc., 57 W Rocks Road, Norwalk, CT 06851–0730

DELAWARE
Brandywine Counseling, Inc., 2713 Lancaster Avenue, Wilmington, DE 19805
Open Door, Incorporated, 3301 Green Street, Claymont, DE 19703
SODAT – Delaware, Inc., 625 North Orange Street, Wilmington, DE 19801

FLORIDA
Act Corporation, 1220 Willis Avenue, Daytona Beach, FL 32114
Alternatives In Treatment, Inc., 7601 North Federal Highway, Suite 100B, Boca Raton, FL 33487
Apalachee Center for Human Services, Inc., PO Box 1782, Tallahassee, FL 32302
Bayview Center for Mental Health, Inc., 12550 Biscayne Blvd, Suite 919, North Miami, FL 33181
Beachcomber Rehab, Inc., 4493 North Ocean Boulevard, Delray Beach, FL 33483
Camelot Care Centers, Inc., 9160 Oakhurst Road Building One, Seminole, FL 33776
Charlotte Community Mental Health Services, Inc., 1700 Education Avenue, Punta Gorda, FL 33950
Coastal Recovery Centers, Inc., 3830 Bee Ridge Road, Sarasota, FL 34233
David Lawrence Center, 6075 Golden Gate Parkway, Naples, FL 34116
Fairwinds Treatment Center, 1569 S Fort Harrison Avenue, Clearwater, FL 34616
Focus Healthcare of Florida, 5960 Southwest 106th Avenue, Cooper City, FL 33328
Hanley–Hazelden Center at St. Mary's, 5200 East Avenue, West Palm Beach, FL 33407
Jacksonville Therapy Center, 6428 Beach Boulevard, Jacksonville, FL 32216
Lakeside Alternatives, Inc., 434 West Kennedy Boulevard, Orlando, FL 32810
Lakeview Center, Inc., 1221 West Lakeview Avenue, Pensacola, FL 32501
Lifeskills of Boca Raton, Inc., 7301 W Palmetto Park Road, Suite 108B, Boca Raton, FL 33433
LifeStream Behavioral Center, PO Box 491000, Leesburg, FL 34749–1000
Manatee Glens Corporation, PO Box 9478, Bradenton, FL 34206–9478
Marion Citrus Mental Health Centers, Inc., P.O. Box 771929, Ocala, FL 34474
Meridian Behavioral Healthcare, Inc., PO Box 141750, Gainesville, FL 32614
Oak Center, 8889 Corporate Square Court, Jacksonville, FL 32216
Operation PAR, Inc., 6655 66th Street North, Pinellas Park, FL 33781
Pathways to Recovery, Inc., 13132 Barwick Road, Delray Beach, FL 33445
Recovery Corner, 400 Executive Center Drive Suite 102, West Palm Beach, FL 33401
Renaissance Institute of Palm Beach, Inc., 7000 N Federal Hwy, 2nd Floor, Boca Raton, FL 33487
Ruth Cooper Center for Behavioral Health Care, Inc., 2789 Ortiz Avenue, Fort Myers, FL 33905
South County Mental Health Center, Inc., 16158 South Military Trail, Delray Beach, FL 33484
Spectrum Programs, Inc., 11031 Northeast 6th Avenue, Miami, FL 33161
Stewart–Marchman Center for Chemical Dependency, 3875 Tiger Bay Road, Daytona Beach, FL 32124
Tampa Bay Academy, 12012 Boyette Road, Riverview, FL 33569
The Center for Alcohol and Drug Studies, Inc., 321 Northlake Blvd, Suite 214, North Palm Beach, FL 33408
The Inn at Bowling Green, 101 North Oak Streeet, Bowling Green, FL 33834
The Village South, Inc., 3180 Biscayne Boulevard, Miami, FL 33137
The Watershed, 3350 NW Boca Raton Boulevard, Suite A–28, Boca Raton, FL 33431
The Willough at Naples, 9001 Tamiami Trail East, Naples, FL 34113

Section C

Transitions Recovery Program, 1928 Northeast 154th Street, North Miami Beach, FL 33162

Turning Point of Tampa, 5439 Beaumont Center Blvd, Suite 1010, Tampa, FL 33634

Twelve Oaks, 2068 Healthcare Avenue, Navarre, FL 32566

Wellness Resource Center, Inc., 660 Linton Boulevard, Ste 112, Delray Beach, FL 33444

GEORGIA

Albany Area Community Service Board, PO Box 1988, Albany, GA 31701

Behavioral Health Services of South Georgia, PO Box 3409 206 S. Patterson Street, Valdosta, GA 31604–3409

Bridges Outpatient Center, Inc., 1209 Columbia Drive, Milledgeville, GA 31061

Brightmore Day Hospital, 115 Davis Road, Martinez, GA 30907

Charter Behavioral Hlth System of Atlanta at Laurel Hgts, LL, 934 Briarcliff Road, Northeast, Atlanta, GA 30306

Cobb/Douglas Community Service Board, 361 North Marietta Parkway, Marietta, GA 30060

Community Mental Health Center of East Central Georgia, 3421 Mike Padgett Highway, Augusta, GA 30906

Community Service Board of Middle Georgia, 2121A Bellevue Road, Dublin, GA 31021–2998

DeKalb Community Service Board, PO Box 1648, Decatur, GA 30031

Gateway Community Service Board, 1609 Newcastle Street, Brunswick, GA 31520

Georgia Pines Community Service Board, PO Box 1659, Thomasville, GA 31799

Greenleaf Center, Inc., PO Box 3516, Valdosta, GA 31602

McIntosh Trail MH/MR/SA Community Service Board, PO Box 1320, Griffin, GA 30224

Metro Atlanta Recovery Residences, Inc., 2801 Clearview Place, Doraville, GA 30340

New Horizons Community Service Board, PO Box 5328, Columbus, GA 31906–0328

Ogeechee Behavioral Health Services, PO Box 1259, Swainsboro, GA 30401

River Edge Behavioral Health Center, 175 Emery Highway, Macon, GA 31217

Safe Recovery Systems, Inc., 2300 Peachford Rd, Ste 2000, Atlanta, GA 30338

Talbott Recovery Campus, 5448 Yorktowne Drive, Atlanta, GA 30349

Turning Point Hospital, PO Box 1177, Moultrie, GA 31768

Willingway Hospital, 311 Jones Mill Road, Statesboro, GA 30458

IDAHO

Northview Hospital, 8050 Northview Street, Boise, ID 83704

Walker Center, 1120A Montana Street, Gooding, ID 83330

ILLINOIS

Alexian Brothers Behavioral Health Resources, 901 Biesterfield Road Suite 400, Elk Grove Village, IL 60007

Association House of Chicago, 1116 North Kedzie Ave, Chicago, IL 60651

Aunt Martha's Youth Service Center, Inc., 4343 Lincoln Highway, Ste 340, Matteson, IL 60443

Ben Gordon Center, 12 Health Services Drive, De Kalb, IL 60115

Camelot Care Center, Inc., 1502 N Northwest Highway, Palatine, IL 60067

Chestnut Health Systems, 1003 Martin Luther King Drive, Bloomington, IL 61701

Community Counseling Center of the Fox Valley, Inc., 400 Mercy Lane, Aurora, IL 60506

Community Counseling Centers of Chicago, 4740 North Clark Street, Chicago, IL 60640–4633

Community Mental Health Center of Fulton & McDonough Countie, 229 Martin Avenue, Canton, IL 61520

Comprehensive Mental Health Center of St. Clair County, 3911 State Street, East Saint Louis, IL 62205

Counseling Center of Lake View, 3225 North Sheffield Avenue, Chicago, IL 60657

Family Service and Community Mental Health Center/McHenry, 5320 West Elm Street, Mc Henry, IL 60050

Gateway Youth Care Foundation, 819 South Wabash, Suite 300, Chicago, IL 60605

Heartland Human Services, PO Box 1047, Effingham, IL 62401

Heritage Behavioral Health Center, Inc., P.O. Box 710, Decatur, IL 62524–2820

Interventions – Du Page Adolescent Center, 11 S 250 Route 83, Hinsdale, IL 60521

Interventions – Southwood, 5701 South Wood, Chicago, IL 60636

Interventions – Woodridge, 2221 64th Street, Woodridge, IL 60517

Interventions City Girls, 140 North Ashland Avenue, Chicago, IL 60607

Josselyn Center for Mental Health, 405 Central Avenue, Northfield, IL 60093–3097

Lake County Health Department / Behavioral Health Services, 3012 Grand Avenue, Waukegan, IL 60085

Leyden Family Service and Mental Health Center, 10001 West Grand Avenue, Franklin Park, IL 60131

McHenry County Youth Service Bureau, 101 South Jefferson Street, Woodstock, IL 60098

New Life Clinic, 2100 Manchester Road, Suite 1410 and 1510, Wheaton, IL 60187

North Central Behavioral Health Systems, Inc., PO Box 1488, La Salle, IL 61301

Perry County Counseling Center, Inc., PO Box 189, Du Quoin, IL 62832

ProCare Centers, 1820 South 25th Avenue, Broadview, IL 60153

Rosecrance on Alpine, 1505 North Alpine Road, Rockford, IL 61107

Rosecrance on Harrison, 3815 Harrison Avenue, Rockford, IL 61108

Sinnissippi Centers, Inc., 325 Illinois Route 2, Dixon, IL 61021

Sojourn House, Inc., 565 North Turner Avenue, Freeport, IL 61032

Southeastern Illinois Counseling Centers, Inc., Drawer M, Olney, IL 62450

Southern Illinois Regional Social Services, 604 East College, Suite 101, Carbondale, IL 62901

Tazwood Center for Human Services, Inc., 1421 Valle Vista Boulevard, Pekin, IL 61554

The Women's Treatment Center, 140 North Ashland Avenue, Chicago, IL 60607

Triangle Center, 120 North Eleventh Street, Springfield, IL 62703–1002

White Oaks Companies of Illinois, 3400 New Leaf Lane, Peoria, IL 61614

INDIANA

Adult and Child Mental Health Center, Inc., 8320 Madison Avenue, Indianapolis, IN 46227

BehaviorCorp, 697 Pro–Med Lane, Carmel, IN 46032–5323

Community Mental Health Center, Inc., 285 Bielby Road, Lawrenceburg, IN 47025

Comprehensive Mental Health Services, Inc., 240 North Tillotson Avenue, Muncie, IN 47304

Fairbanks Hospital, Inc., 8102 Clearvista Parkway, Indianapolis, IN 46256–4698

Four County Counseling Center, 1015 Michigan Avenue, Logansport, IN 46947

Grant–Blackford Mental Health, Inc., 505 Wabash Avenue, Marion, IN 46952

Hamilton Center, Inc, PO Box 4323, Terre Haute, IN 47804–0323

LaVerna Lodge, Inc., 13875 Magic Stallion Drive, Carmel, IN 46032

Life Spring Mental Health Center, 207 West 13th Street, Jeffersonville, IN 47130

Madison Center, Inc., PO Box 80, South Bend, IN 46624

Oaklawn, PO Box 809, Goshen, IN 46527–0809

Park Center, Inc., 909 East State Boulevard, Fort Wayne, IN 46805

Porter–Starke Services, Inc., 601 Wall Street, Valparaiso, IN 46383

Quinco Behavioral Health Systems, PO Box 628, Columbus, IN 47202–0628

Sharing and Caring Community Mental Health Center, Inc., 2511 East 46th Street, Ste 0–1, Indianapolis, IN 46205

South Central Community Mental Health Centers, Inc., 645 South Rogers Street, Bloomington, IN 47403

Southlake Community Mental Health Center, Inc., 8555 Taft Street, Merrillville, IN 46410–6199

Southwestern Indiana Mental Health Center, Inc., 415 Mulberry Street, Evansville, IN 47713–1298

Swanson Center, 450 St. John Road, Suite 501, Michigan City, IN 46360–7350

Tara Treatment Center, Inc., 6231 South US 31, Franklin, IN 46131

The Center for Mental Health, Inc., PO Box 1258, Anderson, IN 46015

The Children's Campus, 1411 Lincoln Way West, Mishawaka, IN 46544–1690

The Otis R. Bowen Center for Human Services, Inc., PO Box 497, Warsaw, IN 46581–0497

Tri–City Comprehensive Comm Mental Health Center Inc., 3903 Indianapolis Boulevard, East Chicago, IN 46312

Wabash Valley Hospital, Inc., 2900 North River Road, West Lafayette, IN 47906

IOWA

Children and Families of Iowa, 1111 University Avenue, Des Moines, IA 50314

Gordon Recovery Centers, Inc., PO Box 4519, Sioux City, IA 51104

Hillcrest Family Services, PO Box 1160, Dubuque, IA 52001

KANSAS

Atchison Valley Hope, PO Box 312, Atchison, KS 66002

Columbia Health Systems, Inc., 10114 West 105th Street, Suite 100, Overland Park, KS 66212

Norton Valley Hope, PO Box 510, Norton, KS 67654

KENTUCKY

Adanta Behavioral Health Services, 259 Parkers Mill Road, Somerset, KY 42501

Bluegrass Regional Mental Health – Mental Retardation Bd, PO Box 11428, Lexington, KY 40575

Cumberland River Regional MH/MR Board, Inc., PO Box 568, Corbin, KY 40702

NorthKey Community Care, PO Box 2680, Covington, KY 41012

RiverValley Behavioral Health, PO Box 1637, Owensboro, KY 42302–1637

Seven Counties Services, Inc., 101 West Muhammad Ali Boulevard, Louisville, KY 40202

LOUISIANA

Addiction Recovery Resources of New Orleans, 4836 Wabash Street, Suite 202, Metairie, LA 70001

CHARIS Community Mental Health Center, Inc., 8264 One Calais Avenue, Baton Rouge, LA 70809

Crescent Community Care, Inc., 1175 Old Spanish Trail, Slidell, LA 70458

New Beginnings Of Opelousas Inc., 1692 Linwood Loop, Opelousas, LA 70570

Vermilion Hospital for Psychiatric and Addictive Med, PO Box 91526, Lafayette, LA 70509

MAINE

Community Health and Counseling Services, PO Box 425, Bangor, ME 04402–0425

MARYLAND

Allegany County Health Department Addictions Program, PO Box 1745, Cumberland, MD 21501–1745

Ashley, Inc., PO Box 240, Havre de Grace, MD 21078

Baltimore Behavioral Health, Inc., 200 South Arlington Avenue, Baltimore, MD 21223

Charter Behavioral Health Systems at Warwick Manor, 3680 Warwick Road, East New Market, MD 21631

Crossroads Centers, Inc., 2 West Madison Street, Baltimore, MD 21201

Glass Substance Abuse Program, Inc., 821 N Eutaw Street, Suite 201, Baltimore, MD 21201

Hope House, PO Box 546, Crownsville, MD 21032

Hudson Health Services, Inc., PO Box 1096, Salisbury, MD 21802–1096

Maryland Treatment Centers, Inc., PO Box E, Emmitsburg, MD 21727

New Life Addiction Counseling Services, Inc., 2528 Mountain Road, Suite 204, Pasadena, MD 21122

Oakview Treatment Center, 3100 North Ridge Road, Ellicott City, MD 21043–3348

Partners in Recovery, 6509 North Charles Street, Baltimore, MD 21204

Pathways, 2620 Riva Road, Annapolis, MD 21401

Quarterway Houses, Inc., PO Box 31419, Baltimore, MD 21216–6119

Saint Luke Institute, Inc., 8901 New Hampshire Avenue, Silver Spring, MD 20903

Worcester County Health Department, PO Box 249, Snow Hill, MD 21863

MASSACHUSETTS

AdCare Hospital of Worcester, Inc., 107 Lincoln Street, Worcester, MA 01605–2499

Baldpate Hospital, Baldpate Road, Georgetown, MA 01833

Cape Cod Alcoholism Intervention & Rehabilitation, PO Box 929, Falmouth, MA 02540

Cape Cod and the Islands Community Mental Health Center, 830 County Road, Pocasset, MA 02559

Center for Health and Human Services, Inc., PO Box 2097, New Bedford, MA 02741

Section C

Choate Health System, Inc., 23 Warren Avenue, Woburn, MA 01801

High Point Treatment Center, Inc., 1233 State Road, Plymouth, MA 02360

MICHIGAN

ACAC, Inc., 3949 Sparks Drive SE, Ste 103, Grand Rapids, MI 49546

Advanced Counseling Services, P.C., 30700 Telegraph Rd. Ste 2560, Bingham Farms, MI 48025

Alcohol Information and Counseling Center, Home Health, 1575 Suncrest Drive, Lapeer, MI 48446

AOS of Arbor Circle Group, 1331 Lake Drive Southeast, Grand Rapids, MI 49506

Auro Medical Center, 1711 South Woodward, Suite 102, Bloomfield Hills, MI 48302

Boniface Human Services, 25050 W Outer Drive, Suite 201, Lincoln Park, MI 48146

Brighton Hospital, 12851 East Grand River, Brighton, MI 48116

Catholic Services of Macomb, Inc., 235 South Gratiot Avenue, Mount Clemens, MI 48043

Center For Behavior and Medicine, 2004 Hogback Road, Suite 16, Ann Arbor, MI 48105

Center for Personal Growth, PC, 817 Tenth Avenue, Port Huron, MI 48060

Center of Behavioral Therapy, PC, 24453 Grand River Avenue, Detroit, MI 48219

Central Therapeutic Services, Inc., 17600 W Eight Mile Road, Ste 7, Southfield, MI 48075

CHIP Counseling Center, 6777 U.S. 31 South, Charlevoix, MI 49720

City of Detroit Dept of Human Services/Drug Treatment Div, 5031 Grandy, Detroit, MI 48211

Clinton – Eaton – Ingham Community Mental Health Board, 808 Southland, Suite B, Lansing, MI 48910

Community Care Services, 26184 West Outer Drive, Lincoln Park, MI 48146

Comprehensive Services, Inc., 4630 Oakman Boulevard, Detroit, MI 48204

DBA Spectrum Prevention & Treatment Services, 2301 Platt Road, Ann Arbor, MI 48104

Delta Family Clinic, 2303 East Amelith Road, Bay City, MI 48706

Detroit Central City Community Mental Health, Inc., 10 Peterboro, Suite 208, Detroit, MI 48201

Dimensions of Life, 510 West Willow, Lansing, MI 48906

DOT Caring Centers, Inc., 3190 Hallmark Court, Saginaw, MI 48603–2107

Downriver Guidance Clinic, 13101 Allen Road, Southgate, MI 48195

Empowered Living Human Services, Inc., 18820 Woodward Avenue, Detroit, MI 48203

Evergreen Counseling Centers, 6902 Chicago Road, Warren, MI 48092

Fairlane Behavioral Services, 23400 Michigan Avenue, Ste P24, Dearborn, MI 48124

Gateway Services, 1910 Shaffer Road, Kalamazoo, MI 49001

Growth Works Incorporated, PO Box 6115, Plymouth, MI 48170–0115

Guest House for Women Religious, PO Box 420, Lake Orion, MI 48361

Hegira Programs, Inc., 8623 N Wayne Road, Suite 200, Westland, MI 48185

Holly Gardens, PO Box 66, Holly, MI 48442

Huron Valley Consultation Center, 955 West Eisenhower Circle Suite B, Ann Arbor, MI 48103

Kairos Healthcare, Inc., 4364 State Street, Saginaw, MI 48603

Latino Family Services, Inc., 3815 West Fort Street, Detroit, MI 48216

Meridian Professional Psychological Consultants, PC, 5031 Park Lake Road, East Lansing, MI 48823

Metro East Substance Abuse Treatment Corporation, PO Box 13408, Detroit, MI 48213

Michiana Addictions and Prevention Services, 1020 Millard Street, Three Rivers, MI 49093–1658

Michigan Counseling Services, 1400 East 12 Mile Road, Madison Heights, MI 48071

Nardin Park Recovery Center, Inc., PO Box 04506, Detroit, MI 48204

National Council on Alcoholism / Lansing Regional Area, Inc., 3400 S Cedar Street, Suite 200, Lansing, MI 48910

National Council on Alcoholism and Addictions, 202 E Boulevard Drive, Ste 310, Flint, MI 48503

National Council on Alcoholism and Drug Dependence / Vantage, 16647 wyoming, Detroit, MI 48221

Neighborhood Service Organization, 220 Bagley, Suite 1200, Detroit, MI 48226

New Center Community Mental Health Services, 2051 West Grand Boulevard, Detroit, MI 48208

New Era Alternative Treatment Center, Inc., 211 Glendale, Suite S–B, Highland Park, MI 48203

New Light Recovery Center, Inc, 300 West McNichols, Detroit, MI 48203

New Perspectives Center, Inc., 1321 South Fayette Street, Saginaw, MI 48602

Northeast Guidance Center, 13340 East Warren, Detroit, MI 48215

Northeast Health Services, 3800 Woodward Avenue Suite 1002, Detroit, MI 48234–1263

Oakland Psychological Clinic, PC, PO Box 888, Bloomfield Hills, MI 48303–0888

Orchard Hills Psychiatric Center, 40000 Grand River Ave, Ste 306, Novi, MI 48375–2112

Parkside Mental Health and Clinical Services, 18820 Woodward, Highland Park, MI 48203

Parkview Company, dba Parkview Counseling Centers, 18609 West Seven Mile Road, Detroit, MI 48219

Perspectives of Troy, PC, 2690 Crooks Road, Suite 300, Troy, MI 48084

Program for Alcohol and Substance Treatment, 110 Sanborn Avenue, Big Rapids, MI 49307

Psychological Consultants of Michigan, PC, 2518 Capital Avenue SW, Ste 2, Battle Creek, MI 49015

Psychotherapy and Counseling Services, P.C., 670 Griswold, Suite 4, Northville, MI 48167

Quality Behavioral Health, Inc, 3455 Woodward Avenue, Ste 101, Detroit, MI 48201

Redford Counseling Center, 25945 West Seven Mile Road, Redford Township, MI 48240

Renaissance Education and Training Center, 18240 West McNichols, Detroit, MI 48219

River's Bend, P.C., 33975 Dequindre, Troy, MI 48083

Sacred Heart Rehabilitation Center, Inc., 400 Stoddard Road P.O. Box 41038, Memphis, MI 48041

Self Help Addiction Rehabilitation, 1852 West Grand Boulevard, Detroit, MI 48208

Star Center, Inc., 13575 Lesure, Detroit, MI 48227

STM Clinic – Mental Health and Substance Abuse Services, One Tuscola Street, Suite 302, Saginaw, MI 48607–1287

Taylor Psychological Clinic, PC, 1172 Robert T Longway Blvd, Flint, MI 48503

The Center for Human Resources, 1001 Military Street, Port Huron, MI 48060

The Kalamazoo Child Guidance Clinic, 2615 Stadium Drive, Kalamazoo, MI 49008

Turning Point Programs, 1931 Boston, Southeast, Grand Rapids, MI 49506

Tuscola Behavioral Health Systems, PO Box 239, Caro, MI 48723

W. D. Lee Center for Life Management, Inc., 11000 West McNichols, Ste 222, Detroit, MI 48221

MINNESOTA

Anthony Louis Center, 1000 Paul Parkway, Blaine, MN 55434

Charter Behavioral Health System of Waverly, 109 North Shore Drive, Waverly, MN 55390–9743

Fountain Lake Treatment Center, Inc., 408 Fountain Street, Albert Lea, MN 56007

Guest House, PO Box 954, Rochester, MN 55903

Hazelden Recovery Services, PO Box 11, Center City, MN 55012

Omegon, Inc., 2000 Hopkins Crossroads, Minnetonka, MN 55343

Pride Institute, 14400 Martin Drive, Eden Prairie, MN 55344

MISSISSIPPI

COPAC, Inc., 3949 Highway 43 North, Brandon, MS 39047

MISSOURI

Boonville Valley Hope, PO Box 376, Boonville, MO 65233

Boys Town of Missouri, Inc., PO Box 189, St. James, MO 65559

Centrec Care, Inc., 11720 Borman Drive, Suite 103, Saint Louis, MO 63146

Comprehensive Mental Health Services, Inc., 10901 Winner Road, Independence, MO 64052

Industrial Rehabilitation Center, 429 Northeast 69 Highway, Kansas City, MO 64119

Marillac Center, 2826 Main Street, Kansas City, MO 64108

Piney Ridge Center, Inc., PO Box 4067, Waynesville, MO 65583

Provident Counseling, Inc., 2650 Olive Street, Saint Louis, MO 63103–1489

Research Mental Health Services, 901 NE Independence Avenue, Lees Summit, MO 64086

Swope Parkway Health Center, 3801 Blue Parkway, Kansas City, MO 64130

MONTANA

Rocky Mountain Treatment Center, 920 Fourth Avenue North, Great Falls, MT 59401

NEBRASKA

Behavioral Health Specialists, Inc., 600 South 13th Street, Norfolk, NE 68701

Blue Valley Mental Health Clinic, 1121 N. 10th Street, Beatrice, NE 68310

Mid–East Nebraska Behavioral Healthcare Services, Inc., PO Box 682, Columbus, NE 68602–0682

O'Neill Valley Hope, PO Box 918, O' Neill, NE 68763–0918

Uta Halee Girls Village, 10625 Calhoun Road, Omaha, NE 68112

NEW HAMPSHIRE

Beech Hill Hospital, LLC, PO Box 254, Dublin, NH 03444

Seaborne Hospital, PO Box 518, Dover, NH 03820

Seacoast Mental Health Center, Inc., 1145 Sagamore Avenue, Portsmouth, NH 03801

The Mental Health Center of Greater Manchester, 401 Cypress Street, Manchester, NH 03103

NEW JERSEY

Aaries, Inc., 690 Broadway, Bayonne, NJ 07002

AtlantiCare Behavioral Health, 201 Tilton Road, Unit 13–A, Northfield, NJ 08225

Bonnie Brae, PO Box 825, Liberty Corner, NJ 07938–0825

Cape Counseling Services, 128 Crest Haven Road, Cape May Court House, NJ 08210

Catholic Charities – Diocese of Metuchen, 288 Rues Lane, East Brunswick, NJ 08816

Community Centers for Mental Health, Inc., 2 Park Avenue, Dumont, NJ 07628

CPC Behavioral Healthcare, Inc, One High Point Center Way, Morganville, NJ 07751

Daytop, New Jersey, 80 West Main Street, Mendham, NJ 07945

Discovery Institute for Addictive Disorders, Inc., PO Box 177, Marlboro, NJ 07746

Family Service of Burlington County, 770 Woodlane Road, Mount Holly, NJ 08060

High Focus Centers, 299 Market Street, Suite 110, Saddle Brook, NJ 07663

Honesty House, 1272 Long Hill Road, Stirling, NJ 07980

Lighthouse at Mays Landing, PO Box 899, Mays Landing, NJ 08330

Mid–Bergen Center, Inc., 610 Industrial Avenue, Paramus, NJ 07652

New Hope Foundation, Inc, PO Box 66, Marlboro, NJ 07746

NewBridge Services, Inc., PO Box 336, Pompton Plains, NJ 07444

Preferred Behavioral Health of New Jersey, PO Box 2036, Lakewood, NJ 08701

Seabrook House, Inc., PO Box 5055, Seabrook, NJ 08302–0655

SERV Centers of New Jersey, Inc., 380 Scotch Road, West Trenton, NJ 08628

Sunrise House Foundation, PO Box 600, Lafayette, NJ 07848

UCPC Behavioral Health Care, 117–119 Roosevelt Avenue, Plainfield, NJ 07060

UMDNJ – University Behavioral HealthCare, PO Box 1392, Piscataway, NJ 08854–1392

West Bergen Mental Healthcare, Inc., 120 Chestnut Street, Ridgewood, NJ 07450

NEW MEXICO

Desert Hills of New Mexico, 5310 Sequoia Northwest, Albuquerque, NM 87120

Family Opportunity Resources, 851 Magee Lane, Santa Fe, NM 87501

Four Corners Regional Adolescent Treatment Center, PO Box 567, Shiprock, NM 87420

The Pointe, PO Box 6, Santa Teresa, NM 88008

NEW YORK

A.R.E.B.A.– Casriel, Inc., 500 West 57th Street, New York, NY 10019

Arms Acres, 75 Seminary Hill Road, Carmel, NY 10512

Bronx Addiction Treatment Center, 1500 Waters Place, Building 13, Bronx, NY 10461

Charles K. Post Addiction Treatment Center, Building 1, PPC Campus, West Brentwood, NY 11717

Conifer Park, Inc., 79 Glenridge Road, Schenectady, NY 12302

Cornerstone of Medical Arts Center Hospital, 57 West 57th Street, New York, NY 10019

Cornerstone of Rhinebeck, NY, 500 Milan Hollow Road, Rhinebeck, NY 12572

Creedmoor Addiction Treatment Center, 80–45 Winchester Boulevard, Queens Village, NY 11427

Dick Van Dyke Addiction Treatment Center, 1330 County Road 132, Ovid, NY 14521

Hope House, Inc., 517 Western Avenue, Albany, NY 12203

Jewish Board of Family and Children's Services, 120 West 57th Street, New York, NY 10019

John L. Norris Addiction Treatment Center, 1111 Elmwood Avenue, Rochester, NY 14620

Kingsboro Addiction Treatment Center, 754 Lexington Avenue, Brooklyn, NY 11221

Manhattan Addiction Treatment Center, 600 East 125th Street, M 11 Ward's Island, New York, NY 10035

McPike Addiction Treatment Center, 1213 Court Street, Utica, NY 13502

National Expert Care Consultants, Inc., 455 West 50th Street, New York, NY 10019–6504

Passages Counseling Center, 3680 Route 112, Coram, NY 11727

Restorative Management Corporation, 15 King Street, Middletown, NY 10940

Richard C. Ward Addiction Treatment Center, 141 Monhagen Avenue, Middletown, NY 10940

Rochester Mental Health Center, 490 East Ridge Road, Rochester, NY 14621

Russell E. Blaisdell Addiction Treatment Center, PO Box 140, Orangeburg, NY 10962

Saint Peter's Addiction Recovery Center, Inc., 3 Mercycare Lane, Guilderland, NY 12084

Salamanca Hospital District Authority, 150 Parkway Drive, Salamanca, NY 14779

Seafield Center, Inc., 7 Seafield Lane, Westhampton Beach, NY 11978

South Beach Addiction Treatment Center, 777 Seaview Avenue, Building 1, Staten Island, NY 10305

St. Joseph's Rehabilitation Center, Inc., PO Box 470, Saranac Lake, NY 12983–0470

St. Joseph's Villa of Rochester, 3300 Dewey Avenue, Rochester, NY 14616

St. Lawrence Addiction Treatment Center, 1 Chimney Point Drive, Hamilton Hall, Ogdensburg, NY 13669

Stutzman Addiction Treatment Center, 360 Forest Avenue, Buffalo, NY 14213

Support Center, Inc., 181 Route 209, Port Jervis, NY 12771

The Astor Home for Children, PO Box 5005, Rhinebeck, NY 12572–5005

The Health Association – MAIN QUEST Treatment Center, 774 West Main Street, Rochester, NY 14611

The Long Island Center for Recovery, PO Box 774, Hampton Bays, NY 11946

The Villa Outpatient Center, 290 Madison Avenue, 6th Floor, New York, NY 10017

Tully Hill Corporation, PO Box 920, Tully, NY 13159–0920

Veritas Villa, Inc., PO Box 610, Kerhonkson, NY 12446–0610

NORTH CAROLINA

Amethyst, PO Box 32861, Charlotte, NC 28232–2861

CenterPoint Human Services, 725 North Highland Avenue, Winston–Salem, NC 27101

Fellowship Hall, Inc., PO Box 13890, Greensboro, NC 27415

Julian F. Keith Alcohol and Drug Abuse Treatment Center, 301 Tabernacle Road, Black Mountain, NC 28711

PSI Solutions Center, 801 Jones Franklin Rd, Ste 210, Raleigh, NC 27606

The Wilmington Treatment Center, 2520 Troy Drive, Wilmington, NC 28401

Unity Regional Youth Treatment Center, PO Box C–201, Cherokee, NC 28719

NORTH DAKOTA

The Dakota Boys Ranch, PO Box 5007, Minot, ND 58703

OHIO

2 North Park, Inc., 720 Pine Avenue Southeast, Warren, OH 44483

Behavioral Connections of Wood County, Inc., 320 West Gypsy Lane Road, Bowling Green, OH 43402

Bellefaire Jewish Children's Bureau, 22001 Fairmount Boulevard, Shaker Heights, OH 44118

Center for Chemical Addictions Treatment, 830 Ezzard Charles Drive, Cincinnati, OH 45214

Charles B. Mills Center, Inc., 715 South Plum Street, Marysville, OH 43040

Community Drug Board, 725 East Market Street, Akron, OH 44305

Community Support Services, Inc., 150 Cross Street, Akron, OH 44311

Comprehensive Psychiatry Specialists, 955 Windham Court, Suite 2, Boardman, OH 44512

Counseling Centers of Ohio, 5800 Monroe Street, Building A, Sylvania, OH 43560

Crisis Intervention Center of Stark County, Inc., 2421 13th Street Northwest, Canton, OH 44708

Family Recovery Center, PO Box 464, Lisbon, OH 44432

Focus Health Care, 5701 North High Street, Suite 8, Worthington, OH 43085

Glenbeigh Health Sources, PO Box 298, Rock Creek, OH 44084–0298

Health Recovery Services, Inc., PO Box 724, Athens, OH 45701

Interval Brotherhood Home Inc., 3445 South Main Street, Akron, OH 44319

Lake Area Recovery Center, 2801 'C' Court, Ashtabula, OH 44004

Lincoln Center for Prevention & Treatment of Chem Dependency, 1918 North Main Street, Findlay, OH 45840

Mahoning County Chemical Dependency Programs, Inc., 527 North Meridan Road, Youngstown, OH 44509

McKinley Hall, Inc., 1101 East High Street, Springfield, OH 45505

Mental Health Services for Clark County, Inc., 1345 Fountain Boulevard, Springfield, OH 45504

Miami Valley Labor Management Healthcare Delivery Systems, 136 Heid Avenue, Dayton, OH 45404

Mount Carmel Behavioral Healthcare, 1808 East Broad Street, Columbus, OH 43203

Neil Kennedy Recovery Clinic, 2151 Rush Boulevard, Youngstown, OH 44507

New Directions, Inc., 30800 Chagrin Boulevard, Pepper Pike, OH 44124

Nova Behavioral Health, Inc., 832 McKinley Avenue Northwest, Canton, OH 44703

Parkside Behavioral Healthcare, Inc., 349 Olde Ridenour Road, Columbus, OH 43230

Parmadale, Inc., 1111 Superior Avenue, Cleveland, OH 44114

PsyCare, Inc., 2980 Belmont Avenue, Youngstown, OH 44505

Psych Systems of Cincinnati, 11223 Cornell Park Dr, Ste 301, Cincinnati, OH 45242

Quest Recovery Services, 1341 Market Avenue, North, Canton, OH 44714–2675

Ravenwood Mental Health Center, 12557 Ravenwood Drive, Chardon, OH 44024

Serenity Living, Inc., PO Box 217, Vandalia, OH 45377

Specialty Care Psychiatric Services, Inc, 2657 Niles Courtland Road, SE, Warren, OH 44484

Substance Abuse Services, Inc., 1832 Adams Street, Toledo, OH 43624

The Buckeye Ranch, Inc., 5665 Hoover Road, Grove City, OH 43123

The Campus Hospital of Cleveland, 18120 Puritas Road, Cleveland, OH 44135

The Crossroads Center, 311 Martin Luther King Drive, Cincinnati, OH 45219–3116

Transitional Living, Inc. and Affiliates, 2052 Princeton Road, Hamilton, OH 45011

OKLAHOMA

Brookhaven Hospital, 201 South Garnett, Tulsa, OK 74128–1800

Cushing Valley Hope, PO Box 472, Cushing, OK 74023–0472

Jim Taliaferro Community Mental Health Center, 602 Southwest 38th Street, Lawton, OK 73505–6999

Western State Psychiatric Center, PO Box 1, Fort Supply, OK 73841

OREGON

BHC Pacific View RTC, 4101 Northeast Division Street, Gresham, OR 97030

Serenity Lane, Inc., 616 East Sixteenth Avenue, Eugene, OR 97401

Springbrook Northwest, Inc., 2001 Crestview Drive, Newberg, OR 97132

PENNSYLVANIA

Abraxas I, PO Box 59, Marienville, PA 16239

Adelphoi Village, Inc., 1003 Village Way, Latrobe, PA 15650

Bowling Green of Brandywine, Inc., 1375 Newark Road, Kennett Square, PA 19348

Charter Behavioral Health System at Cove Forge, New Beginnings Road, Williamsburg, PA 16693

Child Guidance Resource Centers, 600 North Olive Street, Media, PA 19063–2418

Clear Brook, Inc., 1003 Wyoming Avenue, Forty Fort, PA 18704

Conewago Place, 424 Nye Road, Hummelstown, PA 17036–0406

Eagleville Hospital, PO Box 45, Eagleville, PA 19408–0045

Gateway Rehabilitation Center, Moffett Run Road, Aliquippa, PA 15001

Gaudenzia, Inc. – Common Ground, 2835 North Front Street, Harrisburg, PA 17110

Greenbriar Treatment Center, 800 Manor Drive, Washington, PA 15301

Greenway Center, P.O. Box 188, Henryville, PA 18332

Livengrin Foundation, Inc., 4833 Hulmeville Road, Bensalem, PA 19020–3099

Malvern Institute, 940 King Road, Malvern, PA 19355

Marworth, PO Box 36, Waverly, PA 18471

Milestones Community Healthcare, Inc., 614 North Easton Road, Glenside, PA 19038

Mirmont Treatment Center, 100 Yearsley Mill Road, Glen Riddle Lima, PA 19063–5593

Northeast Treatment Centers (NET), 499 North Fifth Street Suite A, Philadelphia, PA 19123

Penn Foundation, Inc., 807 Lawn Avenue, P.O. Box 32, Sellersville, PA 18960

Renewal Centers, PO Box 597, Quakertown, PA 18951

Richard J. Caron Foundation, PO Box A, Wernersville, PA 19565–0501

Roxbury, PO Box L, Shippensburg, PA 17257

Sarah A. Reed Children's Center, 2445 West 34th Street, Erie, PA 16506

Serenity Hall, Inc., 414 West Fifth Street, Erie, PA 16507

The Bridge, 8400 Pine Road, Philadelphia, PA 19111

The Terraces, PO Box 729, Ephrata, PA 17522

TODAY, Inc., PO Box 908, New Town, PA 18940

Twin Lakes Center for Drug and Alcohol Rehabilitation, PO Box 909, Somerset, PA 15501–0909

UHS Recovery Foundation, Inc., 2001 Providence Avenue, Chester, PA 19013–0564

White Deer Run, Inc., Devitt Camp Road, Box 97, Allenwood, PA 17810–0097

RHODE ISLAND

CODAC, Inc., 1052 Park Avenue, Cranston, RI 02910

Community Counseling Center, 101 Bacon Street, Pawtucket, RI 02860

East Bay Mental Health Center, Inc., 2 Old County Road, Barrington, RI 02806

Mental Health Services of Cranston, Johnston, 1443 Hartford Avenue, Johnston, RI 02919–3236

South Shore Mental Health Center, Inc., PO Box 899, Charlestown, RI 02813

The Providence Center for Counseling & Psychiatric Svcs, 520 Hope Street, Providence, RI 02906

Tri–Hab, Inc., 58 Hamlet Avenue, Woonsocket, RI 02895

SOUTH DAKOTA

Keystone Treatment Center, PO Box 159, Canton, SD 57013

TENNESSEE

Academy for Academic Excellence, PO Box 3906, Clarksville, TN 37043

Buffalo Valley, Inc., PO Box 879, Hohenwald, TN 38462

Camelot Care Center, Inc., 667 – B Emory Valley Road, Oak Ridge, TN 37830

Child and Family Services of Knox County, Inc., 901 East Summit Hill Drive, Knoxville, TN 37915

Compass Intervention Center, LLC, 7900 Lowrance Road, Memphis, TN 38183–0242

Cornerstone of Recovery, 1120 Topside Road, Louisville, TN 37777

Council for Alcohol and Drug Abuse Services, Inc., PO Box 4797, Chattanooga, TN 37405

Cumberland Heights Foundation, PO Box 90727, Nashville, TN 37209

Jackson Academy, LLC, 222 Church Street, Dickson, TN 37055

New Life Lodge, PO Box 430, Burns, TN 37029

Ridgeview Psychiatric Hospital and Center, Inc., 240 West Tyrone Road, Oak Ridge, TN 37830

TEXAS

Alternatives Centre for Behavioral Health, 5001 Alabama Street, El Paso, TX 79930

BHC Cedar Crest RTC, Inc., 3500 South IH–35, Belton, TX 76513

Burke Center, 4101 South Medford Drive, Lufkin, TX 75901–5699

Champions, PO Box 2268, Bellaire, TX 77402

Section C

Community Residential Centers of San Antonio, 17720 Corporate Woods Drive, San Antonio, TX 78259–3509

Family Service Center, 2707 North Loop West, Ste 520, Houston, TX 77008

La Hacienda Treatment Center, PO Box 1, Hunt, TX 78024

Life Resource, 2750 South 8th Street, Beaumont, TX 77701

New Dimensions, 18333 Egret Bay Blvd, Ste 560, Houston, TX 77058

New View Partial Hospitalization Centre, Inc., 4310 Dowlen Road – Suite 13, Beaumont, TX 77706

Paul Meier New Life Day Hospital and Outpatient Clinic, 2071 North Collins Boulevard, Richardson, TX 75080

River Oaks Day Hospital, 8120 Westglen, Houston, TX 77063

San Marcos Treatment Center, PO Box 768, San Marcos, TX 78666

Shoreline, Inc., PO Box 68, Taft, TX 78390

Summer Sky, Inc., 1100 McCart Street, Stephenville, TX 76401

Sundown Ranch, Inc., Route 4, Box 182, Canton, TX 75103

Synergy Partial Hospital, 5631 Dolores Street, Houston, TX 77057

The Patrician Movement, 222 East Mitchell Street, San Antonio, TX 78210

Upward Reach Residential Treatment Center, 1120 Cypress Station Drive, Houston, TX 77090

UTAH

Brightway at St. George, 115 West, 1470 South, St. George, UT 84770

Highland Ridge Hospital, 175 West 7200 South, Midvale, UT 84047

New Haven, PO Box 50238, Provo, UT 84605–0238

Vista Adolescent Treatment Center, PO Box 69, Magna, UT 84044

Youth Care, Inc., PO Box 909, Draper, UT 84020

VIRGINIA

Inova Comprehensive Addiction Treatment Services, 3300 Gallows Road, Falls Church, VA 22042–3300

Inova Kellar Center, 10396 Democracy Lane, Fairfax, VA 22030

Mount Regis Center, 405 Kimball Avenue, Salem, VA 24153

Shalom et Benedictus, Inc., PO Box 309, Stephenson, VA 22656

The Life Center of Galax, PO Box 27, Galax, VA 24333

Williamsburg Place, 5477 Mooretown Road, Williamsburg, VA 23188

WASHINGTON

Valley Cities Counseling and Consultation, 2704 'I' Street Northeast, Auburn, WA 98002

WEST VIRGINIA

Olympic Center – Preston, Inc., PO Box 158, Kingwood, WV 26537

Shawnee Hills, Inc., PO Box 3698, Charleston, WV 25336–3698

Worthington Center, Inc., 3199 Core Road, Parkersburg, WV 26104

WISCONSIN

Eau Claire Academy Division of Clinicare Corp, PO Box 1168, Eau Claire, WI 54702–1168

Family Services Lakeshore, Inc, 333 Reed Avenue, Manitowoc, WI 54220

Libertas Treatment Center, 1701 Dousman Street, Green Bay, WI 54303

U.S. Associated Areas

APO/AE

Wellness Branch, ODCSPER, USAREUR 7 Army 1 (Belgium), Hammonds Barracks, Bldg 968 Room 213 – Badenerplatz 1, APO, AE 09014

Wellness Branch, ODCSPER, USAREUR and Army 1 (Germany), Hammonds Barracks, Bldg 968 Room 213, Badenerplatz 1, APO, AE 09014

Abbreviations Used in the AHA Guide

AB, Army Base
ACSW, Academy of Certified Social Workers
AEC, Atomic Energy Commission
AFB, Air Force Base
AHA, American Hospital Association
AK, Alaska
AL, Alabama
AODA, Alcohol and Other Drug Abuse
APO, Army Post Office
AR, Arkansas
A.R.T., Accredited Record Technician
A.S.C., Ambulatory Surgical Center
A.T.C., Alcoholism Treatment Center
Ave., Avenue
AZ, Arizona

B.A., Bachelor of Arts
B.B.A., Bachelor of Business Administration
B.C., British Columbia
Blvd., Boulevard
B.S., Bachelor of Science
B.S.Ed., Bachelor of Science in Education
B.S.H.S., Bachelor of Science in Health Studies
B.S.N., Bachelor of Science in Nursing
B.S.W., Bachelor of Science and Social Worker
CA, California; Controller of Accounts

C.A.A.D.A.C., Certified Alcohol and Drug Abuse Counselor
CAC, Certified Alcoholism Counselor
CAE, Certified Association Executive
CAP, College of American Pathologists
CAPA, Certified Ambulatory Post Anesthesia
C.A.S., Certificate of Advanced Study
CCDC, Certified Chemical Dependency Counselor
C.D., Commander of the Order of Distinction
CDR, Commander
CDS, Chemical Dependency Specialist
CFACHE, Certified Fellow American College of Healthcare Executives
CFRE, Certified Fund Raising Executive
C.G., Certified Gastroenterology
CHC, Certified Health Consultant
C.L.D., Clinical Laboratory Director
CLU, Certified Life Underwriter, Chartered Life Underwriter
CMA, Certified Medical Assistant
C.M.H.A., Certified Mental Health Administrator
CNHA, Certified Nursing Home Administrator
CNM, Certified Nurse Midwife
CNOR, Certified Operating Room Nurse
C.N.S., Clinical Nurse Specialist
CO, Colorado; Commanding Officer
COA, Certified Ophthalmic Assistant
COMT, Commandant
C.O.M.T., Certified Ophthalmic Medical Technician
Conv., Conventions
Corp., Corporation; Corporate
C.O.T., Certified Ophthalmic Technician
CPA, Certified Public Accountant
C.P.H.Q., Certified Professional in Health Care Quality
CPM, Certified Public Manager
CRNA, Certified Registered Nurse Anesthetist
CRNH, Certified Registered Nurse Hospice
C.S.J.B, Catholic Saint John the Baptist
CSW, Certified Social Worker
CT, Connecticut
CWO, Chief Warrant Officer

D.B.A., Doctor of Business Administration

DC, District of Columbia
D.D., Doctor of Divinity
D.D.S., Doctor of Dental Surgery
DE, Delaware
Diet, Dietitian; Dietary; Dietetics
D.M.D., Doctor of Dental Medicine
D.MIN., Doctor of Ministry
D.O., Doctor of Osteopathic Medicine and Surgery, Doctor of Osteopathy
DPA, Doctorate Public Administration
D.P.M., Doctor of Podiatric Medicine
Dr., Drive
Dr.P.h., Doctor of Public Health
D.Sc., Doctor of Science
D.S.W., Doctor of Social Welfare
D.V.M., Doctor of Veterinary Medicine

E., East
Ed.D., Doctor of Education
Ed.S., Specialist in Education
ENS, Ensign
Esq., Esquire
Expwy., Expressway
ext., extension

FAAN, Fellow of the American Academy of Nursing
FACATA, Fellow of the American College of Addiction Treatment Administrators
FACHE, Fellow of the American College of Healthcare Executives
FACMGA, Fellow of the American College of Medical Group Administrators
FACP, Fellow of the American College of Physicians
FACS, Fellow of the American College of Surgeons
FAX, Facsimile
FL, Florida
FPO, Fleet Post Office
FRCPSC, Fellow of the Royal College of Physicians and Surgeons of Canada
FT, Full-time

GA, Georgia
Govt., Government; Governmental

HHS, Department of Health and Human Services
HI, Hawaii
HM, Helmsman
HMO, Health Maintenance Organization
Hon., Honorable; Honorary
H.S.A., Health System Administrator
Hts., Heights
Hwy., Highway

IA, Iowa
ID, Idaho
IL, Illinois
IN, Indiana
Inc., Incorporated

J.D., Doctor of Law
J.P., Justice of the Peace
Jr., Junior

KS, Kansas
KY, Kentucky

LA, Louisiana
LCDR, Lieutenant Commander
LCSW, Licensed Certified Social Worker
L.H.D., Doctor of Humanities

L.I.S.W., Licensed Independent Social Worker
LL.D., Doctor of Laws
L.L.P., Limited Licensed Practitioner
L.M.H.C., Licensed Master of Health Care
L.M.S.W., Licensed Master of Social Work
L.N.H.A., Licensed Nursing Home Administrator
L.P.C., Licensed Professional Counselor
LPN, Licensed Practical Nurse
L.P.N., Licensed Practical Nurse
L.S.W., Licensed Social Worker
Lt., Lieutenant
LTC, Lieutenant Colonel
Ltd., Limited
LT.GEN., Lieutenant General
LTJG, Lieutenant (junior grade)

MA, Massachusetts
M.A., Master of Arts
Maj., Major
M.B., Bachelor of Medicine
M.B.A., Masters of Business Administration
MC, Medical Corps; Marine Corps
M.C., Member of Congress
MD, Maryland
M.D., Doctor of Medicine
ME, Maine
M.Ed., Master of Education
MFCC, Marriage/Family/Child Counselor
MHA, Mental Health Association
M.H.S., Masters in Health Science; Masters in Human Service
MI, Michigan
MM, Masters of Management
MN, Minnesota
M.N., Master of Nursing
MO, Missouri
M.P.A., Master of Public Administration; Master Public Affairs
M.P.H., Master of Public Health
M.P.S., Master of Professional Studies; Master of Public Science
MS, Mississippi
M.S., Master of Science
MSC, Medical Service Corps
M.S.D., Doctor of Medical Science
MSHSA, Master of Science Health Service Administration
M.S.N., Master of Science in Nursing
M.S.P.H., Master of Science in Public Health
M.S.S.W., Master of Science in Social Work
M.S.W., Master of Social Work
MT, Montana
Mt., Mount

N., North
NC, North Carolina
N.C.A.D.C., National Certification of Alcohol and Drug Counselors
ND, North Dakota
NE, Nebraska
NH, New Hampshire
NHA, National Hearing Association; Nursing Home Administrator
NJ, New Jersey
NM, New Mexico
NPA, National Perinatal Association
NV, Nevada
NY, New York

OCN, Oncology Certified Nurse
O.D., Doctor of Optometry
O.F.M., Order Franciscan Monks, Order of Friars Minor
OH, Ohio
OK, Oklahoma
OR, Oregon
O.R., Operating Room
O.R.S., Operating Room Supervisor

OSF, Order of St. Francis

PA, Pennsylvania
P.A., Professional Association
P.C., Professional Corporation
Pharm.D., Doctor of Pharmacy
Ph.B., Bachelor of Philosophy
Ph.D., Doctor of Philosophy
PHS, Public Health Service
Pkwy., Parkway
Pl., Place
PR, Puerto Rico
PS, Professional Services
PSRO, Professional Standards Review Organization

RADM, Rear Admiral
RD, Rural Delivery
Rd., Road
R.F.D., Rural Free Delivery
RI, Rhode Island
R.M., Risk Manager
RN, Registered Nurse
RNC, Republican National Committee; Registered Nurse or Board Certified
R.Ph., Registered Pharmacist
RRA, Registered Record Administrator
R.S.M., Religious Sisters of Mercy
Rte., Route

S., South
SC, South Carolina
S.C., Surgery Center
SCAC, Senior Certified Addiction Counselor
Sc.D., Doctor of Science
Sci., Science, Scientific
SD, South Dakota
SHCC, Statewide Health Coordinating Council
Sgt., Sergeant
SNA, Surgical Nursing Assistant
SNF, Skilled Nursing Facility
Sq., Square
Sr., Senior, Sister
St., Saint, Street
Sta., Station
Ste., Saint; Suite

Tel., Telephone
Terr., Terrace
TN, Tennessee
Tpke, Turnpike
Twp., Township
TX, Texas

USA, United States Army
USAF, United States Air Force
USMC, United States Marine Corps
USN, United States Navy
USPHS, United States Public Health Service
UT, Utah

VA, Virginia
VADM, Vice Admiral
VI, Virgin Islands
Vlg., Village
VT, Vermont

W., West
WA, Washington
WI, Wisconsin
WV, West Virginia
WY, Wyoming

Abbreviations

Terms and Conditions

1. LICENSOR is the owner of the property (hereinafter "DATA") that is the subject of this Agreement, which shall be Health Forum, L.L.C., an American Hospital Association Company. LICENSEE shall be the organization identified on the Data Order Agreement, or if no organization is identified, the individual identified on the Data Order Agreement. LICENSEE is granted a perpetual license to use the DATA at the site to which the DATA were shipped, in accordance with the Terms and Conditions of this Agreement.

2. LICENSEE acknowledges that the DATA are proprietary and confidential property of LICENSOR and constitute valuable trade secret information and that LICENSEE acquires no right in the DATA except to use the DATA solely within its own organization and for its own business purposes, in accordance with this Agreement. Unless otherwise agreed upon in writing by LICENSOR, LICENSEE agrees to hold the DATA in strict confidence and agrees not to provide, disclose, or otherwise make available any DATA to any third party, including but not limited to subsidiary and parent corporations, and that in no event shall LICENSEE release data which might reasonably be used to identify any particular institution without the prior express written permission of LICENSOR and of such institution. Notwithstanding the foregoing, LICENSOR agrees that LICENSEE shall be permitted to disclose and extend use of such DATA to its employees, agents, and consultants whose assigned duties reasonably require such disclosure and use, and only to the extent necessary to enable such persons to reasonably perform their assigned duties. LICENSEE will take appropriate measures, by instruction, agreement, or otherwise, to ensure compliance with this and the other provisions of this Agreement by LICENSEE, its employees, agents, and consultants. This provision shall survive the termination of this Agreement.

3. LICENSEE agrees that if the DATA are supplied on magnetic tape, disk, CD-ROM, or hard copy, no copies of the tape, disk, CD-ROM, or hard copy report shall be made except that one copy may be made solely for back-up purposes. LICENSEE agrees that the DATA will only be used with a single stand-alone computer, integral with a CD-ROM drive containing the DATA, which can only be accessed by a single user. LICENSEE agrees not to use, read, or transfer any part of the DATA by means of a network or modem or by any remote means of accessing the single stand-alone computer or the CD-ROM drive containing the DATA. No restrictions in this Agreement preclude the AFair Use@ printing of relatively small portions of the DATA by either a dedicated printer or through a network connection.

4. LICENSOR acknowledges that LICENSEE may have contact with individual health care institutions that contribute to the DATA in the course of its normal business operation; however, LICENSEE agrees that it will not refer to the DATA during any such contact and will not contact such institutions regarding the DATA or information contained in the DATA. However, at LICENSEE's request and expense, LICENSOR will use its best efforts to clarify any questions LICENSEE may have with reference to the DATA.

5. LICENSEE recognizes that the DATA are collected b LICENSOR and while LICENSOR believes the DAT. be accurate, LICENSOR MAKES NO WARRANTIE OR REPRESENTATIONS, EXPRESS OR IMPLIED, INCLUDING, BUT NOT LIMITED TO, THE IMPLI WARRANTIES OF MERCHANTABILITY AND FITNESS FOR A PARTICULAR PURPOSE. In no event shall LICENSOR's liability for any damages, regardless of the form of action, exceed the fee paid by LICENSEE for use of the DATA. Under no circumstances shall LICENSOR be liable for incident: consequential, special, or exemplary damages of any k or for lost profits.

6. This Agreement also applies to all "Updates" or othe versions of the DATA subsequently supplied to LICENSEE. Thus, LICENSEE may use such updated DATA only in accordance with this Agreement. Suc updated DATA may be used and transferred only as p the single product package which includes the original DATA, and may not be separated for use on more th one computer.

   of

7. Whenever LICENSOR has knowledge or reason to bel that LICENSEE has failed to observe the terms and conditions of this Agreement, LICENSOR will notify LICENSEE of the suspected breach. If, within 30 days such notice, LICENSEE fails to make available for inspection by LICENSOR all records and documents c LICENSEE necessary to verify compliance, LICENSO may terminate the license granted herein and prevent LICENSEE from obtaining future licenses from LICENSOR. Upon termination, LICENSEE shall immediately return all DATA to LICENSOR. This re for breach shall in no way limit LICENSOR from purs whatever other relief it deems appropriate and LICENSEE specifically agrees that in the event of a breach or threatened breach by LICENSEE, LICENSO shall be entitled to an injunction restraining LICENSE from further breaching action.

8. No waiver by LICENSOR of any breach on the part of LICENSEE or of any right or remedy incident thereto shall constitute a continuing waiver or a waiver of any breach or right or remedy incident thereto.

9. This Agreement supersedes all prior agreements and understandings of any nature whatsoever, oral or writ and constitutes the entire understanding between the parties hereto.

10. Each paragraph and provision of this Agreement is severable from the entire Agreement, and if one provi shall be declared invalid, the other provisions shall re in full force and effect without regard to the invalidity said provision.

11. This Agreement may be modified only by a written instrument executed by both parties.

12. This Agreement shall be governed by the laws of the S of Illinois.

The undersigned understands the conditions of the data agreement, as stated on this form, and agrees to abide by same All orders must contain a signature that acknowledges accept of these conditions.

8831R

Signature

Order Agreement

Health Forum, L.L.C.
An American Hospital Association Company

Ordered by: Please print or type - Check if primary user ☐

Name

Title

Organization

Address (UPS WILL NOT DELIVER TO P.O. BOXES)

City   State   ZIP Code

Telephone

Ship to: Complete only if different from ordered by - Check if primary user ☐

Name

Title

Organization

Address (UPS WILL NOT DELIVER TO P.O. BOXES)

City   State   ZIP Code

E-mail Address

Billing Information

Purchase order number required for billed orders

Type of business

Please charge my ☐ VISA ☐ MasterCard ☐ American Express

Credit card number

Cardholder's signature   Expiration date

Name of member

Catalog number	Title	Quantity	Member* price	Nonmember price	Extended price
010099	**1999/2000 AHA Guide to the Health Care Field**		$175.00	$315.00	
011499	**1999/2000 AHA Guide - CD-ROM Version** *(Print and Read Only)*		$175.00	$315.00	
011601	**StreetFinder Deluxe - AHA Guide 1999/2000 Edition**		$ 60.00	$ 60.00	
	*(note: Item numbers 010099, and 011499 **include** one copy of StreetFinder Deluxe - AHA Guide 1999/2000 Edition)*				

Subtotal	
Shipping & Handling	
Express Delivery	
Sales Tax	
U.S. Funds Only **Total**	

This order form can be used for obtaining Health Forum, L.L.C. data products. Licensing terms and conditions on reverse.

The undersigned understands the conditions of the data agreement, as stated on the reverse side of this form, and agrees to abide by same. All orders must contain a signature that acknowledges acceptance of these conditions.

Signature

To order by phone call toll free:
800-AHA-2626 or FAX: 312-422-4505
MasterCard, VISA, American Express, or institutional/company purchase order number accepted. Telephone orders will usually be shipped within 72 hours. Please allow 1 to 2 weeks for delivery.

Mail orders
Mail orders to:
American Hospital Association
P.O. Box 92683
Chicago, IL 60675-2683

Orders from individuals must be prepaid or charged to a credit card. Make checks or money orders payable to American Hospital Association. **Billed orders must be accompanied by a purchase order number.**

Foreign orders
All foreign orders must be prepaid in U.S. funds only. Add 20% of merchandise price for shipping and handling. Allow 3 to 4 weeks for delivery.

Sales Tax
Sales tax must be paid on orders shipped to CA, CO, GA, IL, KS, MA, MO, NJ, NY, OH, PA, and TX unless you provide us with a copy of your tax-exempt certificate.

Prices
Two prices are listed for most items. The member price refers to AHA institutional. The nonmember price refers to all others. Some products may have a single price for both members and nonmembers.

Prices are subject to change without notice.

Shipping and handling charges apply to ALL domestic and Canadian orders

$1.00 to $19.99 ...... add $4.95	$100.00 to $199.99 ...... add $14.95
$20.00 to $34.99 ...... add $6.95	$200.00 to $299.99 ...... add $17.95
$35.00 to $49.99 ...... add $8.95	$300.00 to $399.99 ...... add $20.95
$50.00 to $74.99 ...... add $10.95	$400.00 to $499.99 ...... add $27.95
$75.00 to $99.99 ...... add $12.95	$500.00 and above .... add $34.95

Express delivery available for additional charge.
Next-day delivery - $10.00; two-day delivery - $5.00
We reserve the right to charge actual shipping charges on orders 60 lbs. or more.

Due to the nature of the product, magnetic media data or diskette products are not returnable.

Please photocopy this page if you need additional Order Forms.